Webster's All-In-One Dictionary & Thesaurus

SECOND EDITION

Webster's All-In-One Dictionary & Thesaurus

SECOND EDITION

Created in Cooperation with the Editors of MERRIAM-WEBSTER

FEDERAL STREET PRESS

A Division of Merriam-Webster, Incorporated
Springfield, Massachusetts

This 2013 edition published by
Federal Street Press
A Division of Merriam-Webster, Incorporated
P.O. Box 281
Springfield, MA 01102

Federal Street Press books are available for bulk purchase for sales promotion and premium use. For details write the manager of special sales, Federal Street Press, P.O. Box 281, Springfield, MA 01102

ISBN 13 978-1-59695-147-1

8th printing LSC Communications, Harrisonburg, VA 03/2019 Jouve

Printed in the United States of America

CONTENTS

PREFACE to the SECOND EDITION

This new edition is the result of a reexamination of existing entries and synonym lists with an eye to improved clarity and precision. We have added many new entries and more than 2000 synonyms, including numerous Canadian and British spelling variants, such as **colour, flavour, honour**, and their derived forms, such as **colourless, flavourful, honourable**.

The Canadian and British spellings (shown as *or Can and Brit*) appear at main entries for single words (**color** . . . *or Can and Brit* **colour**) and hyphenated compounds (**color-blind** . . . *or Can and Brit* **colour-blind**) and for inflected forms. The user can assume the spelling variations carry through to open compounds with the same initial word and to undefined run-on entires, such as **color blindness** and **colorfastness**. Additionally, there are a number of British spelling variants (not so common in Canada) entered separately, such as **idealise** *chiefly Brit var of* IDEALIZE.

The work on this new edition was done by Amy K. Harris Van Vranken, one of the editors of the original edition, with assistance by Danial J. Hopkins. We are happy to be able to offer this enhancement in the confidence that it will serve the reader well for many years. We encourage a reading of the original Preface as well as a thorough reading of the section Using the Dictionary to enable you to derive maximum benefit from this volume.

PREFACE

This book combines the features of a dictionary, with its meanings, pronunciations, and usage guidance with the synonym and antonym features of a thesaurus. In this volume they are not just combined but integrated into a unified whole, to give the user the best of both volumes. The work is produced in cooperation with the editors of Merriam-Webster, and as such draws on the experience of a company that has been producing dictionaries for more than 150 years.

The dictionary entries themselves are based on the newest edition of the highly popular *The Merriam-Webster Dictionary* and on *Merriam-Webster's Collegiate Dictionary, Eleventh Edition.* The thesaurus entries are based on Merriam-Webster's newest and most up-to-date thesaurus. The dictionary entries and thesaurus entries have been edited side by side to ensure a precise relationship between dictionary meaning and the choice of similar and contrasting words offered in the thesaurus lists.

The more than 57,000 boldface dictionary entries give coverage to the most frequently used words in the language, and the definitions have been based on examples of actual use. The thesaurus lists offer a total of more than 122,000 alternative words for the writer interested in finding a more precise or more colorful word choice. Thesaurus entries follow their dictionary entries set off in colored type. Every dictionary sense that is followed by a synonym list is marked with a black diamond, and the thesaurus list is likewise marked. When there are multiple dictionary senses highlighted, the thesaurus elements are marked with the related dictionary sense or senses in square brackets to make it easy for the user to choose the right list of alternate words.

> **abide** \ə-ˈbīd\ *vb* **abode** \-ˈbōd\ *or* **abid•ed; abid•ing** **1** ♦ **:** to bear patiently **:** ENDURE **2 a** ♦ **:** to continue in a state or place **b** ♦ **:** to have one's abode — **abide by :** to conform or acquiesce to ⟨*abide by* the law⟩
>
> ♦ [1] bear, brook, countenance, endure, meet, stand, stick out, stomach, support, sustain, take, tolerate ♦ [2a] continue, endure, hold, keep up, last, persist, run on ♦ [2b] dwell, live, reside

Thesaurus entries all show synonyms, and some lists also have common contrasting words (antonyms), which are introduced by a bold italic ***Ant***.

> **fer•tile** \ˈfərt-ᵊl\ *adj* **1** ♦ **:** producing plentifully **:** PRODUCTIVE ⟨~ soils⟩ ⟨a ~ mind⟩ **2 :** capable of developing or reproducing ⟨~ seed⟩ ⟨a ~ bull⟩ — **fer•til•i•ty** \(ˌ)fər-ˈti-lə-tē\ *n*
>
> ♦ fecund, fruitful, luxuriant, productive, prolific, rich ***Ant*** barren, infertile, sterile, unfruitful, unproductive

Because the thesaurus information is relatively self-explanatory and there are numerous distinctive, and sometimes subtle, features of the dictionary, the focus of the following section, Using the Dictionary, is on the dictionary entry.

While this work draws on the work and experience of the Merriam-Webster staff of professional lexicographers, special mention should go to those who have produced this volume. Primary editing was done by Mary Wood Cornog, Amy K. Harris Van Vranken, and Amy West. Additional editing was done by Jocelyn W. Franklin with Cynthia S. Ashby and James G. Lowe. Daniel B. Brandon, Jennifer N. Cislo, Ilya A. Davidovich, Mary M. Dunn, and E. Louise Langford provided further editorial contributions.

USING THE DICTIONARY

The dictionary contains so much information that it is necessary to condense much of it to accommodate the limitations of the printed page. This section provides information on the conventions used throughout the dictionary, from the styling of entries and pronunciation to how we present information on usage and meaning. An understanding of the information contained in these notes will make the dictionary both easier and more rewarding to use.

ENTRIES

A boldface letter or a combination of such letters, including punctuation marks and diacritics where needed, that is set flush with the left-hand margin of each column of type is a main entry. The main entry may consist of letters set solid, of letters joined by a hyphen or a diagonal, or of letters separated by spaces:

alone . . . *adj*
avant-garde . . . *n*
and/or . . . *conj*
assembly language . . . *n*

The material in lightface type that follows each main entry on the same line and on succeeding indented lines presents information about the main entry.

The main entries follow one another in alphabetical order letter by letter: *bird of prey* follows *birdlime*; *Day of Atonement* follows *daylight saving time*. Main entries containing an Arabic numeral are alphabetized as if the numeral were spelled out: *4-H* comes between *fourfold* and *Four Hundred; 3-D* comes between *three* and *three-dimensional*. Those that often begin with the abbreviation *St.* in common usage have the abbreviation spelled out: *Saint Valentine's Day.* Main entries that begin with *Mc* are alphabetized just as they are spelled.

* * *

A pair of guide words is printed at the top of each page. These guide words indicate the range of entries that fall alphabetically on those pages.

The guide words are the alphabetically first and the alphabetically last main entries on the pages:

horseshoe • house

* * *

When one main entry has exactly the same written form as another, the two are distinguished by superscript numerals preceding each word:

[1]melt . . . *vb*
[2]melt *n*
[1]pine . . . *n*
[2]pine *vb*

Full words come before parts of words made up of the same letters; solid compounds come before hyphenated compounds; hyphenated compounds come before open compounds; and lowercase entries come before those with an initial capital:

[1]su·per . . . *n*
[2]super *adj*
super- . . . *prefix*

run·down . . . *n*
run-down . . . *adj*
run down *vb*

dutch . . . *adv*
Dutch . . . *n*

The centered dots within entry words indicate division points at which a hyphen may be put at the end of a line of print or writing. Thus the noun *cap·puc·ci·no* may be ended on one line and continued on the next in this manner:

cap-
puccino
cappuc-
cino
cappucci-
no

Centered dots are not shown after a single initial letter or before a single terminal letter because typesetters seldom cut off a single letter:

abyss . . . *n*
flighty . . . *adj*
idea . . . *n*

Centered dots are not usually shown at the second and succeeding homographs unless they differ among themselves:

[1]sig·nal . . . *n*
[2]signal *vb*
[3]signal *adj*
but
[1]min·ute . . . *n*
[2]mi·nute . . . *adj*

There are acceptable alternative end-of-line divisions just as there are acceptable variant spellings and pronunciations, but no more than one pattern is shown for any entry in this dictionary.

A double hyphen (⸗) at the end of a line in this dictionary (as in the definition at **Bantustan**) stands for a hyphen that is retained when the word is written as a unit on one line. This kind of fixed hyphen is always represented in boldface words in this dictionary with an en dash, longer than an ordinary hyphen.

* * *

When a main entry is followed by the word *or* and another spelling, the two spellings are equal variants. Both are standard, and either one may be used according to personal inclination:

ocher *or* **ochre**

If two variants joined by *or* are out of alphabetical order, they remain equal variants. The one printed first is, however, slightly more common than the second:

¹plow *or* **plough**

When another spelling is joined to the main entry by the word *also*, the spelling after *also* is a secondary variant and occurs less frequently than the first:

ab•sinthe *also* **ab•sinth**

Secondary variants belong to standard usage and may be used according to personal inclination. Once the word *also* is used to signal a secondary variant, all following secondary variants are joined by *or*:

²wool•ly *also* **wool•ie** *or* **wooly**

Variants whose spelling puts them alphabetically more than a column away from the main entry are entered at their own alphabetical places as well as at the main entry:

²gage *var of* GAUGE

. . .

¹gauge *also* **gage**

To show all the stylings that are found for English compounds would require space that can be better used for other information. So this dictionary limits itself to a single styling for a compound:

peace•mak•er
pell–mell
boom box

When a compound is widely used and one styling predominates, that styling is shown. When a compound is uncommon or when the evidence indicates that two or three stylings are approximately equal in frequency, the styling shown is based on the comparison of other similar compounds.

* * *

A main entry may be followed by one or more derivatives or by a homograph with a different functional label. These are run-on entries. Each is introduced by a long dash, and each has a functional label. They are not defined, however, since their meanings are readily understood from the meaning of the root word:

ab•do•men . . . *n* . . . — **ab•dom•i•nal** . . . *adj* — **ab•dom•i•nal•ly** . . . *adv*
seis•mo•graph . . . *n* . . .— **seis•mo•graph•ic** . . . *adj* — **seis•mog•ra•phy** . . . *n*

A main entry may be followed by one or more phrases containing the entry word or an inflected form of it. These are also run-on entries. Each is introduced by a long dash but there is no functional label. They are, however, defined since their meanings are more than the sum of the meanings of their elements:

¹set . . . *vb* . . . — **set sail** : to begin a voyage
¹hand . . . *n* . . . — **at hand** : near in time . . .

Defined phrases of this sort are run on at the entry defining the first major word in the phrase. When there are variants, however, the run-on appears at the entry defining the first major invariable word in the phrase:

¹seed . . . *n* . . . **1 :** the grains of plants used for sowing . . . — **go to seed** *or* **run to seed** **1 :** to develop seed **2 :** DECAY

PRONUNCIATION

The matter between a pair of reversed slashes \ \ following the entry word indicates the pronunciation. The symbols used are explained in the chart at the end of this section.

A hyphen is used in the pronunciation to show syllabic division. These hyphens sometimes coincide with the centered dots in the entry word that indicate end-of-line division, and sometimes they do not:

ab•sen•tee \ˌab-sən-ˈtē\
met•ric \ˈme-trik\

A high-set mark ˈ indicates major (primary) stress or accent; a low-set mark ˌ indicates minor (secondary) stress or accent:

heart•beat \ˈhärt-ˌbēt\

The stress mark stands at the beginning of the syllable that receives the stress.

A syllable with neither a high-set mark nor a low-set mark is unstressed:

¹struc•ture \ˈstrək-chər\

The presence of variant pronunciations indicates that not all educated speakers pronounce words the same way. A second-place variant is not to be regarded as less acceptable than the pronunciation that is given first. It may, in fact, be used by as many educated speakers as the first variant, but the requirements of the printed page are such that one must precede the other:

apri•cot \ˈa-prə-ˌkät, ˈā-\
fore•head \ˈfȯr-əd, ˈfȯr-ˌhed\

Symbols enclosed by parentheses represent elements that are present in the pronunciation of some speakers but are absent from the pronunciation of other speakers, or elements that are present in some but absent from other utterances of the same speaker:

[1]**om·ni·bus** \ˈäm-ni-(ˌ)bəs\
ad·di·tion·al \ə-ˈdi-sh(ə-)nəl\

Thus, the above parentheses indicate that some people say \ˈäm-ni-ˌbəs\ and others say \ˈäm-ni-bəs\; some \ə-ˈdi-shə-nəl\, others \ə-ˈdi-shnəl\.

When a main entry has less than a full pronunciation, the missing part is to be supplied from a pronunciation in a preceding entry or within the same pair of reversed slashes:

cham·pi·on·ship \-ˌship\
pa·la·ver \pə-ˈla-vər, -ˈlä-\

The pronunciation of the first three syllables of *championship* is found at the main entry *champion*. The hyphens before and after \ˈlä\ in the pronunciation of *palaver* indicate that both the first and the last parts of the pronunciation are to be taken from the immediately preceding pronunciation.

In general, no pronunciation is indicated for open compounds consisting of two or more English words that have own-place entry:

witch doctor *n*

Only the first entry in a sequence of numbered homographs is given a pronunciation if their pronunciations are the same:

[1]**re·ward** \ri-ˈwȯrd\ *vb*
[2]**reward** *n*

The absent but implied pronunciation of derivatives and compounds run on after a main entry is a combination of the pronunciation at the main entry and the pronunciation of the other element as given at its alphabetical place in the vocabulary:

— **ab·ject·ness** *n*
— **bungee jumper** *n*

Thus, the pronunciation of *abjectness* is the sum of the pronunciations given at *abject* and *-ness*; that of *bungee jumper*, the sum of the pronunciations of the two elements that make up the phrase.

FUNCTIONAL LABELS

An italic label indicating a part of speech or another functional classification follows the pronunciation or, if no pronunciation is given, the main entry.

The eight traditional parts of speech are indicated as follows:

bold . . . *adj*
forth·with . . . *adv*
[1]**but** . . . *conj*
ge·sund·heit . . . *interj*
bo·le·ro . . . *n*
[2]**un·der** . . . *prep*
[1]**it** . . . *pron*
[1]**slap** . . . *vb*

Other italicized labels used to indicate functional classifications that are not traditional parts of speech include:

AT *abbr*
self- *comb form*
un- . . . *prefix*
-ial *adj suffix*
[2]**-ly** *adv suffix*
[2]**-er** . . . *n suffix*
-ize . . . *vb suffix*
Fe *symbol*
may . . . *verbal auxiliary*

Functional labels are sometimes combined:

afloat . . . *adj or adv*

INFLECTED FORMS

NOUNS

The plurals of nouns are shown in this dictionary when suffixation brings about a change of final *-y* to *-i-*, when the noun ends in a consonant plus *-o* or in *-ey*, when the noun ends in *-oo*, when the noun has an irregular plural or an uninflected plural or a foreign plural, when the noun is a compound that pluralizes any element but the last, when a final consonant is doubled, when the noun has variant plurals, and when it is believed that the dictionary user might have reasonable doubts about the spelling of the plural or when the plural is spelled in a way contrary to what is expected:

[2]**spy** *n, pl* **spies**
si·lo . . . *n, pl* **silos**
val·ley . . . *n, pl* **valleys**
[2]**shampoo** *n, pl* **shampoos**
mouse . . . *n, pl* **mice**
moose . . . *n, pl* **moose**
cri·te·ri·on . . . *n, pl* **-ria**
son-in-law . . . *n, pl* **sons-in-law**
[1]**quiz** . . . *n, pl* **quiz·zes**
[1]**fish** . . . *n, pl* **fish** *or* **fish·es**

pi . . . *n, pl* **pis**
[3]dry *n, pl* **drys**

Cutback inflected forms are used when the noun has three or more syllables:

ame•ni•ty . . . *n, pl* **-ties**

The plurals of nouns are usually not shown when the base word is unchanged by suffixation, when the noun is a compound whose second element is readily recognizable as a regular free form entered at its own place, or when the noun is unlikely to occur in the plural:

night . . . *n*
fore•foot . . . *n*
mo•nog•a•my . . . *n*

Nouns that are plural in form and that are regularly construed as plural are labeled *n pl*:

munch•ies . . . *n pl*

Nouns that are plural in form but that are not always construed as plurals are appropriately labeled:

lo•gis•tics . . . *n sing or pl* : . . .
me•dia . . . *n, pl* **me•di•as** . . . **2** *sing or pl in constr* : MASS MEDIA

VERBS

The principal parts of verbs are shown in this dictionary when suffixation brings about a doubling of a final consonant or an elision of a final *-e* or a change of final *-y* to *-i-*, when final *-c* changes to *-ck* in suffixation, when the verb ends in *-ey*, when the inflection is irregular, when there are variant inflected forms, and when it is believed that the dictionary user might have reasonable doubts about the spelling of an inflected form or when the inflected form is spelled in a way contrary to what is expected:

[2]snag *vb* **snagged; snag•ging**
[1]move . . . *vb* **moved; mov•ing**
[1]cry . . . *vb* **cried; cry•ing**
[1]frol•ic . . . *vb* **frol•icked; frol•ick•ing**
[1]sur•vey . . . *vb* **sur•veyed; sur•vey•ing**
[1]drive . . . *vb* **drove** . . . **driv•en** . . . **driv•ing**
[2]bus *vb* **bused** *or* **bussed; bus•ing** *or* **bus-sing**
[2]visa *vb* **vi•saed** . . . **vi•sa•ing**
[2]chagrin *vb* **cha•grined** . . . **cha•grin•ing**

The principal parts of a regularly inflected verb are shown when it is desirable to indicate the pronunciation of one of the inflected forms:

learn . . . *vb* **learned** \ˈlərnd, ˈlərnt\; **learn•ing**
[1]al•ter \ˈȯl-tər\ *vb* **al•tered; al•ter•ing** \-t(ə-)riŋ\

Cutback inflected forms are usually used when the verb has three or more syllables, when it is a two-syllable word that ends in *-l* and has variant spellings, and when it is a compound whose second element is readily recognized as an irregular verb:

elim•i•nate . . . *vb* **-nat•ed; -nat•ing**
[2]quarrel *vb* **-reled** *or* **-relled; -rel•ing** *or* **-relling**
[1]re•take . . . *vb* **-took** . . . **-tak•en** . . . **-tak•ing**

The principal parts of verbs are usually not shown when the base word is unchanged by suffixation or when the verb is a compound whose second element is readily recognizable as a regular free form entered at its own place:

[1]jump . . . *vb*
pre•judge . . . *vb*

Another inflected form of English verbs is the third person singular of the present tense, which is regularly formed by the addition of *-s* or *-es* to the base form of the verb. This inflected form is not shown except at a handful of entries (as *have* and *do*) for which it is in some way unusual.

ADJECTIVES & ADVERBS

The comparative and superlative forms of adjectives and adverbs are shown in this dictionary when suffixation brings about a doubling of a final consonant or an elision of a final *-e* or a change of final *-y* to *-i-*, when the word ends in *-ey*, when the inflection is irregular, and when there are variant inflected forms:

[1]red . . . *adj* **red•der; red•dest**
[1]tame . . . *adj* **tam•er; tam•est**
[1]kind•ly . . . *adj* **kind•li•er; -est**
hors•ey *also* **horsy** . . . *adj* **hors•i•er; -est**
[1]good . . . *adj* **bet•ter** . . . **best**
[1]far . . . *adv* **far•ther** . . . *or* **fur•ther** . . . **far•thest** *or* **fur•thest**

The superlative forms of adjectives and adverbs of two or more syllables are usually cut back:

[3]fancy *adj* **fan•ci•er; -est**
[1]ear•ly . . . *adv* **ear•li•er; -est**

The comparative and superlative forms of regularly inflected adjectives and adverbs are shown when it is desirable to indicate the pronunciation of the inflected forms:

[1]young \ˈyəŋ\ *adj* **youn•ger** \ˈyəŋ-gər\; **youn•gest** \ˈyəŋ-gəst\

The inclusion of inflected forms in *-er* and *-est* at adjective and adverb entries means nothing more about the use of *more* and *most* with these adjectives and adverbs than that their comparative and superlative degrees may be expressed in either way: *lazier* or *more lazy*; *laziest* or *most lazy*.

At a few adjective entries only the superlative form is shown:

²mere *adj, superlative* **mer·est**

The absence of the comparative form indicates that there is no evidence of its use.

The comparative and superlative forms of adjectives and adverbs are usually not shown when the base word is unchanged by suffixation, when the inflected forms of the word are identical with those of a preceding homograph, or when the word is a compound whose second element is readily recognizable as a regular free form entered at its own place:

¹near . . . *adv*
³good *adv*
un·wor·thy . . . *adj*

Inflected forms are not shown at run-in and undefined run-on entries.

CAPITALIZATION

Most entries in this dictionary begin with a lowercase letter. A few of these have an italicized label *often cap*, which indicates that the word is as likely to be capitalized as not and that it is as acceptable with an uppercase initial as it is with one in lowercase. Some entries begin with an uppercase letter, which indicates that the word is usually capitalized. The absence of an initial capital or of an *often cap* label indicates that the word is not ordinarily capitalized:

salm·on . . . *n*
gar·gan·tuan . . . *adj, often cap*
Mo·hawk . . . *n*

The capitalization of entries that are open or hyphenated compounds is similarly indicated by the form of the entry or by an italicized label:

dry goods . . . *n pl*
french fry *n, often cap 1st F*
un-Amer·i·can . . . *adj*
Par·kin·son's disease . . . *n*
lazy Su·san . . . *n*
Jack Frost *n*

A word that is capitalized in some senses and lowercase in others shows variations from the form of the main entry by the use of italicized labels at the appropriate senses:

Trin·i·ty . . . *n* . . . **2** *not cap*
To·ry . . . *n* . . . **3** *often not cap*
ti·tan . . . *n* **1** *cap*
re·nais·sance . . . *n* **1** *cap* . . . **2** *often cap*

USAGE

Three types of status labels are used in this dictionary—temporal, regional, and stylistic—to signal that a word or a sense of a word is not part of the standard vocabulary of English.

The temporal label *obs* for "obsolete" means that there is no evidence of use since 1755:

³post *n* **1** *obs* **:** COURIER

The label *obs* is a comment on the word being defined. When a thing, as distinguished from the word used to designate it, is obsolete, appropriate orientation is usually given in the definition:

cat·a·pult . . . *n* **1** : an ancient military machine for hurling missiles

The temporal label *archaic* means that a word or sense once in common use is found today only sporadically or in special contexts:

¹mete . . . *vb* . . . **1** *archaic*
¹thou . . . *pron, archaic*

A word or sense limited in use to a specific region of the U.S. has an appropriate label. The adverb *chiefly* precedes a label when the word has some currency outside the specified region, and a double label is used to indicate considerable currency in each of two specific regions:

²wash *n* . . . **5** *West*
do·gie . . . *n, chiefly West*
crul·ler . . . *n* . . . **2** *Northern & Midland*

Words current in all regions of the U.S. have no label.

A word or sense limited in use to one of the other countries of the English-speaking world has an appropriate regional label:

chem·ist . . . *n* . . . **2** *Brit*
loch . . . *n, Scot*
²wireless *n* . . . **2** *chiefly Brit*

The label *dial* for "dialect" indicates that the pattern of use of a word or sense is too complex for summary labeling: it usually includes several regional varieties of American English or of American and British English:

²mind *vb* **1** *chiefly dial*

The stylistic label *slang* is used with words or senses that are especially appropriate in contexts of extreme informality:

³can . . . *vb* . . . **2** *slang*
²grand *n* . . . *slang*

There is no satisfactory objective test for slang, especially with reference to a word out of context. No word, in fact, is invariably slang, and many standard words can be given slang applications.

The stylistic labels *offensive* and *disparaging* are used for those words or senses that in common use are intended to hurt or that are likely to give offense even when they are used without such an intent:

dumb . . . *adj* **1** *often offensive*
half-breed . . . *n, often disparaging*

Definitions are sometimes followed by verbal illustrations that show a typical use of the word in context. These illustrations are enclosed in angle brackets, and the word being illustrated is usually replaced by a lightface swung dash. The swung dash stands for the boldface entry word, and it may be followed by an italicized suffix:

[1]jump . . . *vb* . . . **5** . . . ⟨∼ the gun⟩
all–around . . . *adj* **1** . . . ⟨best ∼ performance⟩
[1]can•on . . . *n* . . . **3** . . . ⟨the ∼*s* of good taste⟩
en•joy . . . *vb* . . . **2** . . . ⟨∼*ed* the concert⟩

The swung dash is not used when the form of the boldface entry word is changed in suffixation, and it is not used for compounds:

[2]deal *vb* . . . **2** . . . ⟨*dealt* him a blow⟩
drum up *vb* **1** . . . ⟨*drum up* business⟩

Definitions are sometimes followed by usage notes that give supplementary information about such matters as idiom, syntax, and semantic relationship. A usage note is introduced by a lightface dash:

[2]cry *n* . . . **5** . . . — usually used in the phrase *a far cry*
[2]drum *vb* . . . **4** . . . — usually used with *out*
[1]jaw . . . *n* . . . **2** . . . — usually used in plural
[1]ada•gio . . . *adv or adj* . . . — used as a direction in music
hajji . . . *n* . . . — often used as a title

Sometimes a usage note is used in place of a definition. Some function words (as conjunctions and prepositions) have chiefly grammatical meaning and little or no lexical meaning; most interjections express feelings but are otherwise untranslatable into lexical meaning; and some other words (as honorific titles) are more amenable to comment than to definition:

or . . . *conj* — used as a function word to indicate an alternative
at . . . *prep* **1** — used to indicate a point in time or space
auf Wie•der•seh•en . . . *interj* . . . — used to express farewell
sir . . . *n* . . . **2** — used as a usually respectful form of address

SENSE DIVISION

A boldface colon is used in this dictionary to introduce a definition:

[1]equine . . . *adj* . . . **:** of or relating to the horse

It is also used to separate two or more definitions of a single sense:

no•ti•fy . . . *vb* . . . **1 :** to give notice of **:** report the occurrence of

Boldface Arabic numerals separate the senses of a word that has more than one sense:

ad•judge . . . *vb* . . . **1 :** to decide or rule upon as a judge **:** JUDGE, ADJUDICATE **2 :** to hold or pronounce to be **:** DEEM **3 :** . . .

A particular semantic relationship between senses is sometimes suggested by the use of an italic sense divider (as *esp* or *also*).

The sense divider *esp* (for *especially*) is used to introduce the most common meaning included in the more general preceding definition:

crys•tal . . . *n* . . . **2 :** something resembling crystal (as in transparency); *esp* **:** a clear glass used for table articles

The sense divider *also* is used to introduce a meaning related to the preceding sense by an easily understood extension of that sense:

chi•na . . . *n* **:** porcelain ware; *also* **:** domestic pottery in general

The order of senses is historical: the sense known to have been first used in English is entered first. This is not to be taken to mean, however, that each sense of a multisense word developed from the immediately preceding sense. It is altogether possible that sense 1 of a word has given rise to sense 2 and sense 2 to sense 3, but frequently sense 2 and sense 3 may have developed independently of one another from sense 1.

When an italicized label follows a boldface numeral, the label applies only to that specific numbered sense. It does not apply to any other boldface numbered senses:

craft . . . *n* . . . **3** *pl usu* **craft**
[1]fa•ther . . . *n* . . . **2** *cap* . . . **5** *often cap*
dul•ci•mer . . . *n* . . . **2** *or* **dul•ci•more** \-ˌmōr\
[2]lift *n* . . . **5** *chiefly Brit*

At *craft* the *pl* label applies to sense 3 but to none of the other numbered senses. At *father* the *cap* label applies only to sense 2 and the *often cap* label only to sense 5. At *dulcimer* the variant spelling and pronunciation apply only to sense 2, and the *chiefly Brit* label at *lift* applies only to sense 5.

CROSS-REFERENCE

Four different kinds of cross-references are used in this dictionary: directional, synonymous, cognate, and inflectional. In each instance the cross-reference is readily recognized by the lightface small capitals in which it is printed.

A cross-reference following a lightface dash and beginning with *compare* is a directional cross-reference. It directs the dictionary user to look elsewhere for further information:

ordinal number . . . *n* . . . — compare CARDINAL NUMBER

A cross-reference following a boldface colon is a synonymous cross-reference. It may stand alone as the only definition for an entry or for a sense of an entry; it may follow an analytical definition; it may be one of two or more synonymous cross-references separated by commas:

fact . . . *n* . . . **1** : DEED . . .
²pa·per *adj* . . . **3** : existing only in theory : NOMINAL

A synonymous cross-reference indicates that an entry, a definition at the entry, or a specific sense at the entry cross-referred to can be substituted as a definition for the entry or the sense in which the cross-reference appears.

A cross-reference following an italic *var of* ("variant of") is a cognate cross-reference:

pick·a·back . . . *var of* PIGGYBACK

Occasionally a cognate cross-reference has a limiting label preceding *var of* as an indication that the variant is not standard American English:

cosy *chiefly Brit var of* COZY

A cross-reference following an italic label that identifies an entry as an inflected form (as of a noun or verb) is an inflectional cross-reference:

calves *pl of* CALF
woven *past part of* WEAVE

Inflectional cross-references appear only when the inflected form falls at least a column away from the entry cross-referred to.

COMBINING FORMS, PREFIXES, & SUFFIXES

An entry that begins or ends with a hyphen is an element that forms part of a compound:

-wise . . . *adv comb form* . . . ⟨slant*wise*⟩
ex- . . . *prefix* . . . **2** . . . ⟨*ex*-president⟩
-let . . . *n suffix* **1** . . . ⟨book*let*⟩

Combining forms, prefixes, and suffixes are entered in this dictionary for two reasons: to make understandable the meaning of many undefined run-ons and to make recognizable the meaningful elements of words that are not entered in the dictionary.

LISTS OF UNDEFINED WORDS

Many words that begin with the prefixes or combining forms *anti-*, *in-*, *non-*, *over-*, *re-*, *self-*, *semi-*, *sub-*, *super-*, and *un-* are self-explanatory combinations of the prefix or combining form and a word entered elsewhere in the dictionary, and these words are listed undefined immediately following the entry for the prefix.

ABBREVIATIONS & SYMBOLS

Abbreviations and symbols for chemical elements are included as main entries in the vocabulary:

RSVP *abbr* . . . please reply
Ca *symbol* calcium

Abbreviations have been normalized to one form. However, there is considerable variation in the use of periods and capitalization (as *vhf*, *v.h.f.*, *VHF*, and *V.H.F.*), and stylings other than those in this dictionary are often acceptable.

BASIC ENGLISH PUNCTUATION

The English writing system uses punctuation marks to separate groups of words for meaning and emphasis; to convey an idea of the variations of pitch, volume, pauses, and intonations of speech; and to help avoid ambiguity. English punctuation marks, together with general rules and bracketed examples of their use, follow.

APOSTROPHE ’

1. indicates the possessive case of nouns and indefinite pronouns

⟨the boy’s mother⟩ ⟨the boys’ mothers⟩

2. marks omissions in contracted words

⟨didn’t⟩ ⟨o’clock⟩

3. often forms plurals of letters, figures, and words referred to as words

⟨You should dot your *i*’s and cross your *t*’s.⟩

⟨several *8*’s⟩

BRACKETS [ ]

1. set off extraneous data such as editorial additions especially within quoted material

⟨wrote that the author was “trying to dazzle his readers with phrases like *jeu de mots* [play on words]”⟩

2. function as parentheses within parentheses

⟨Bowman Act (22 Stat., ch. 4, § [or sec.] 4, p. 50)⟩

COLON :

1. introduces a word, clause, or phrase that explains, illustrates, amplifies, or restates what has gone before

⟨The sentence was poorly constructed: it lacked both unity and coherence.⟩

2. introduces a series

⟨Three countries were represented: England, France, and Belgium.⟩

3. introduces lengthy quoted material set off from the rest of a text by indentation but not by quotation marks

⟨I quote from the text of Chapter One:⟩

4. separates data in time-telling and data in bibliographic and biblical references

⟨8:30 a.m.⟩

⟨New York: Smith Publishing Co.⟩

⟨John 4:10⟩

5. follows the salutation in formal correspondence

⟨Dear Sir:⟩

⟨Gentlemen:⟩

COMMA ,

1. separates main clauses joined by a coordinating conjunction (as *and*, *but*, *or*, *nor*, or *for*) and very short clauses not so joined

⟨She knew very little about him, and he volunteered nothing.⟩

⟨I came, I saw, I conquered.⟩

2. sets off an adverbial clause (or a long phrase) that precedes the main clause

⟨When she found that her friends had deserted her, she sat down and cried.⟩

3. sets off from the rest of the sentence transitional words and expressions (as *on the contrary*, *on the other hand*), conjunctive adverbs (as *consequently*, *furthermore*, *however*), and expressions that introduce an illustration or example (as *namely*, *for example*)

⟨Your second question, on the other hand, remains open.⟩

⟨She expects to travel through two countries, namely, France and England.⟩

4. separates words, phrases, or clauses in series and coordinate adjectives modifying a noun

⟨Men, women, and children crowded into the square.⟩

⟨The harsh, cold wind was strong.⟩

5. sets off from the rest of the sentence parenthetic elements (as nonrestrictive modifiers)

⟨Our guide, who wore a blue beret, was an experienced traveler.⟩

⟨We visited Gettysburg, the site of a famous battle.⟩

6. introduces a direct quotation, terminates a direct quotation that is neither a question nor an exclamation, and encloses split quotations

⟨John said, "I am leaving."⟩

⟨"I am leaving," John said.⟩

⟨"I am leaving," John said with determination, "even if you want me to stay."⟩

7. sets off words in direct address, absolute phrases, and mild interjections

⟨You may go, Mary, if you wish.⟩

⟨I fear the encounter, his temper being what it is.⟩

⟨Ah, that's my idea of an excellent dinner.⟩

8. separates a question from the rest of the sentence which it ends

⟨It's a fine day, isn't it?⟩

9. indicates the omission of a word or words, and especially a word or words used earlier in the sentence

⟨Common stocks are preferred by some investors; bonds, by others.⟩

10. is used to avoid ambiguity

⟨To Mary, Jane was someone special.⟩

11. is used to group numbers into units of three in separating thousands, millions, etc.; however, it is generally not used in numbers of four figures, in page numbers, in dates, or in street numbers

⟨Smithville, pop. 100,000⟩

but

⟨3600 rpm⟩

⟨the year 1973⟩

⟨page 1411⟩

⟨4507 Smith Street⟩

12. punctuates an inverted name

⟨Smith, John W., Jr.⟩

13. separates a proper name from a following academic, honorary, governmental, or military title

⟨John Smith, M.D.⟩

14. sets off geographical names (as state or country from city), items in dates, and addresses from the rest of a text

⟨Shreveport, Louisiana, is the site of a large air base.⟩

⟨On Sunday, June 23, 1940, he was wounded.⟩

⟨Number 10 Downing Street, London, is a famous address.⟩

but when only the year or the month and year are given, the comma is usually omitted

⟨October 1929 brought an end to all that.⟩

15. follows the salutation in informal correspondence and follows the closing line of a formal or informal letter

⟨Dear Mary,⟩

⟨Affectionately,⟩

⟨Very truly yours,⟩

DASH —

1. usu. marks an abrupt change or break in the continuity of a sentence

⟨When in 1960 the stockpile was sold off—indeed, dumped as surplus—natural-rubber sales were hard hit.—Barry Commoner⟩

2. introduces a summary statement after a series

⟨Oil, steel, and wheat—these are the sinews of industrialization.⟩

3. often precedes the attribution of a quotation

⟨My foot is on my native heath. . . . —Sir Walter Scott⟩

ELLIPSES . . . .

1. indicates the omission of one or more words within a quoted passage

⟨The head is not more native to the heart . . . than is the throne of Denmark to thy father. —Shakespeare⟩

2. indicates halting speech or an unfinished sentence in dialogue

⟨"I'd like to . . . that is . . . if you don't mind. . . ." He faltered and then stopped speaking.⟩

3. indicates the omission of one or more sentences within a quoted passage or the omission of words at the end of a sentence by using four spaced dots, the last of which represents the period

⟨That recovering the manuscripts would be worth almost any effort is without question. . . . The monetary value of a body of Shakespeare's manuscripts would be almost incalculable—Charlton Ogburn⟩

4. usu. indicates omission of one or more lines of poetry when ellipsis is extended the length of the line

⟨Thus driven
By the bright shadow of that lovely dream,
. . . .
He fled.
—P. B. Shelley⟩

EXCLAMATION POINT !

1. terminates an emphatic phrase or sentence

⟨Get out of here!⟩

2. terminates an emphatic interjection

⟨Encore!⟩

HYPHEN -

1. marks separation or division of a word at the end of a line

⟨mill-[end of line]stone⟩

⟨pas-[end of line]sion⟩

2. is used between some prefix and word combinations, as prefix + proper name

⟨pre-Renaissance⟩;

prefix ending with a vowel + word beginning often with the same vowel

⟨co-opted⟩

⟨re-ink⟩;

stressed prefix + word, especially when this combination is similar to a different one

⟨re-cover a sofa⟩

but

⟨recover from an illness⟩

3. is used in some compounds, especially those containing prepositions

⟨president-elect⟩

⟨sister-in-law⟩

4. is often used between elements of a unit modifier in attributive position in order to avoid ambiguity

⟨He is a small-business man.⟩

⟨She has gray-green eyes.⟩

5. suspends the first part of a hyphened compound when used with another hyphened compound

⟨a six- or eight-cylinder engine⟩

6. is used in writing out compound numbers between 21 and 99

⟨thirty-four⟩

⟨one hundred twenty-eight⟩

7. is used between the numerator and the denominator in writing out fractions especially when they are used as modifiers

⟨a two-thirds majority of the vote⟩

8. serves instead of the phrase "(up) to and including" between numbers and dates

⟨pages 40-98⟩

⟨the decade 1960-69⟩

PARENTHESES ( )

1. set off supplementary, parenthetic, or explanatory material when the interruption is more marked than that usually indicated by commas

⟨Three old destroyers (all now out of commission) will be scrapped.⟩

⟨He is hoping (as we all are) that this time he will succeed.⟩

2. enclose numerals which confirm a written number in a text

⟨Delivery will be made in thirty (30) days.⟩

3. enclose numbers or letters in a series

⟨We must set forth (1) our long-term goals, (2) our immediate objectives, and (3) the means at our disposal.⟩

PERIOD .

1. terminates sentences or sentence fragments that are neither interrogatory nor exclamatory

⟨Obey the law.⟩

⟨He obeyed the law.⟩

2. follows some abbreviations and contractions

⟨Dr.⟩ ⟨Jr.⟩

⟨etc.⟩ ⟨cont.⟩

QUESTION MARK ?

1. terminates a direct question

⟨Who threw the bomb?⟩

⟨"Who threw the bomb?" he asked.⟩

2. indicates the writer's ignorance or uncertainty

⟨Omar Khayyám, Persian poet (?-?1123)⟩

QUOTATION MARKS, DOUBLE " "

1. enclose direct quotations in conventional usage

⟨He said, "I am leaving."⟩

2. enclose words or phrases borrowed from others, words used in a special way, and often slang when it is introduced into formal writing

⟨He called himself "emperor," but he was really just a dictator.⟩

⟨He was arrested for smuggling "smack."⟩

3. enclose titles of short poems, short stories, articles, lectures, chapters of books, songs, short musical compositions, and radio and TV programs

⟨Robert Frost's "Dust of Snow"⟩

⟨Pushkin's "Queen of Spades"⟩

⟨The third chapter of *Treasure Island* is entitled "The Black Spot."⟩

⟨"America the Beautiful"⟩

⟨Ravel's "Bolero"⟩

⟨NBC's "Today Show"⟩

4. are used with other punctuation marks in the following ways:

the period and the comma fall within the quotation marks

⟨"I am leaving," he said.⟩

⟨His camera was described as "waterproof," but "moisture-resistant" would have been a better description.⟩;

the semicolon falls outside the quotation marks

⟨He spoke of his "little cottage in the country"; he might have called it a mansion.⟩;

the dash, question mark, and exclamation point fall within the quotation marks when they refer to the quoted matter; they fall outside when they refer to the whole sentence

⟨He asked, "When did you leave?"⟩

⟨What is the meaning of "the open door"?⟩

⟨The sergeant shouted, "Halt!"⟩

⟨Save us from his "mercy"!⟩

QUOTATION MARKS, SINGLE ‘ ’

enclose a quotation within a quotation in conventional usage

⟨The witness said, “I distinctly heard him say, ‘Don’t be late,’ and then I heard the door close.”⟩

SEMICOLON ;

1. links main clauses not joined by coordinating conjunctions

⟨Some people have the ability to write well; others do not.⟩

2. links main clauses joined by conjunctive adverbs (as *consequently*, *furthermore*, *however*)

⟨Speeding is illegal; furthermore, it is very dangerous.⟩

3. links clauses which themselves contain commas even when such clauses are joined by coordinating conjunctions

⟨Mr. King, whom you met yesterday, will be our representative on the committee; but you should follow the proceedings carefully yourself, because they are vitally important to us.⟩

SLASH /

1. separates alternatives

⟨. . . intended for high-heat and/or high-speed applications—F. S. Badger, Jr.⟩

2. separates successive divisions (as months or years) of an extended period of time

⟨the fiscal year 1972/73⟩

3. serves as a dividing line between run-in lines of poetry

⟨Say, sages, what’s the charm on earth/Can turn death’s dart aside?—Robert Burns⟩

4. often represents *per* in abbreviations

⟨9 ft/sec⟩

⟨20 km/hr⟩

ABBREVIATIONS IN THIS WORK

ab	about
abbr	abbreviation
abl	ablative
acc	accusative
A.D.	anno Domini
adj	adjective
adv	adverb
alter	alteration
Am, Amer	American
AmerF	American French
AmerInd	American Indian
AmerSp	American Spanish
Ant	Antonym(s)
Ar	Arabic
Aram	Aramaic
B.C.	before Christ
Brit	British
C	Celsius
ca	circa
Calif	California
Canad	Canadian
CanF	Canadian French
cap	capital, capitalized
Celt	Celtic
cen	central
cent	century
Chin	Chinese
comb	combining
compar	comparative
conj	conjunction
D	Dutch
Dan	Danish
dat	dative
deriv	derivative
dial	dialect
dim	diminutive
E	English
Egypt	Egyptian
Eng	English
esp	especially
est	estimated
F	Fahrenheit, French
fem	feminine
fl	flourished
fr	from
ft	feet
G, Ger	German
Gk	Greek
Gmc	Germanic
Heb	Hebrew
Hung	Hungarian
Icel	Icelandic
imit	imitative
imper	imperative
interj	interjection
Ir	Irish
irreg	irregular
It, Ital	Italian
Jp	Japanese
K	Kelvin
km	kilometers
L	Latin
LaF	Louisiana French
LG	Low German
LGk	Late Greek
LHeb	Late Hebrew
lit	literally
LL	Late Latin
m	meters
masc	masculine
MD	Middle Dutch
ME	Middle English
MexSp	Mexican Spanish
MF	Middle French
MGk	Middle Greek
mi	miles
ML	Medieval Latin
modif	modification
MS	manuscript
Mt	Mount
n	noun
neut	neuter
NewEng	New England
NGk	New Greek
NHeb	New Hebrew
NL	New Latin
No	North
Norw	Norwegian
n pl	noun plural
obs	obsolete
OE	Old English
OF	Old French
OIt	Old Italian
ON	Old Norse
OPer	Old Persian
orig	originally
part	participle
Per	Persian
perh	perhaps
Pg	Portuguese
pl	plural
Pol	Polish
pp	past participle
prep	preposition
pres	present, president
prob	probably
pron	pronoun, pronunciation
prp	present participle
pseud	pseudonym
r	reigned
Russ	Russian
Sc	Scotch, Scots
Scand	Scandinavian
ScGael	Scottish Gaelic
Scot	Scottish
sing	singular
Skt	Sanskrit
Slav	Slavic
So	South
Sp, Span	Spanish
St	Saint
superl	superlative
Sw	Swedish
syn	synonym, synonymy
trans	translation
Turk	Turkish
US	United States
USSR	Union of Soviet Socialist Republics
usu	usually
var	variant
vb	verb
vi	verb intransitive
VL	Vulgar Latin
vt	verb transitive
W	Welsh

PRONUNCIATION SYMBOLS

ə	**a**but, c**o**llect, supp**o**se
ˈə, ˌə	h**u**mdr**u**m
^{ə}	(in ^{ə}l, ^{ə}n) batt**le**, cott**on**; (in l^{ə}, m^{ə}, r^{ə}) French tab**le**, pris**me**, tit**re**
ər	op**er**ation, f**ur**th**er**
a	m**a**p, p**a**tch
ā	d**ay**, f**a**te
ä	b**o**ther, c**o**t, f**a**ther
är	c**ar**, h**ear**t
au̇	n**ow**, **ou**t
b	**b**a**b**y, ri**b**
ch	**ch**in, ca**tch**
d	**d**i**d**, a**dd**er
e	s**e**t, r**e**d
er	b**are**, f**air**
ē	b**ea**t, **ea**s**y**
f	**f**i**f**ty, cu**ff**
g	**g**o, bi**g**
h	**h**at, a**h**ead
hw	**wh**ale
i	t**i**p, ban**i**sh
ir	n**ear**, d**eer**
ī	s**i**te, b**uy**
j	**j**ob, e**dge**
k	**k**in, **c**oo**k**
k̲	German Ba**ch**, Scots lo**ch**
l	**l**i**l**y, coo**l**
m	**m**ur**m**ur, di**m**
n	**n**i**n**e, ow**n**
^{n}	indicates that a preceding vowel is pronounced through both nose and mouth, as in French bon \bō^{n}\
ŋ	si**ng**, si**ng**er, fi**ng**er, i**n**k
ō	b**o**ne, holl**ow**
ȯ	s**aw**
ȯr	b**oar**, p**or**t
œ	French b**œu**f, f**eu**, German H**ö**lle, H**ö**hle
ȯi	t**oy**
p	**p**e**pp**er, li**p**
r	**r**a**r**ity
s	**s**our**c**e, le**ss**
sh	**sh**y, mi**ss**ion
t	**t**ie, a**tt**ack
th	**th**in, e**th**er
th̲	**th**en, ei**th**er
ü	b**oo**t, few \ˈfyü\
u̇	p**u**t, pure \ˈpyu̇r\
u̇r	b**oor**, t**our**
ue	French r**ue**, German f**ü**llen, f**üh**len
v	**v**i**v**id, gi**v**e
w	**w**e, a**w**ay
y	**y**ard, cue \ˈkyü\
^{y}	indicates that a preceding \l\, \n\, or \w\ is modified by having the tongue approximate the position for \y\, as in French di**gne** \dēn^{y}\
z	**z**one, rai**se**
zh	vi**s**ion, plea**s**ure
\	slant line used in pairs to mark the beginning and end of a transcription: \ˈpen\
ˈ	mark at the beginning of a syllable that has primary (strongest) stress: \ˈshə-fəl-ˌbȯrd\
ˌ	mark at the beginning of a syllable that has secondary (next-strongest) stress: \ˈshə-fəl-ˌbȯrd\
-	mark of a syllable division in pronunciations (the mark of end-of-line division in boldface entries is a centered dot •)
( )	indicates that what is symbolized between sometimes occurs and sometimes does not occur in the pronunciation of the word: **bakery** \ˈbā-k(ə-)rē\ = \ˈbā-kə-rē, ˈbā-krē\

A

¹a \ˈā\ *n, pl* **a's** *or* **as** \ˈāz\ *often cap* **1 :** the 1st letter of the English alphabet **2 :** a grade rating a student's work as superior
²a \ə, (ˈ)ā\ *indefinite article* **:** ONE, SOME — used to indicate an unspecified or unidentified individual ⟨there's ~ man outside⟩
³a *abbr, often cap* **1** absent **2** acre **3** alto **4** answer **5** are **6** area
AA *abbr* **1** Alcoholics Anonymous **2** antiaircraft **3** associate in arts
AAA *abbr* American Automobile Association
A and M *abbr* agricultural and mechanical
A and R *abbr* artists and repertory
aard•vark \ˈärd-ˌvärk\ *n* **:** a large burrowing African mammal that feeds on ants and termites with its long sticky tongue
¹ab \ˈab\ *n* **:** an abdominal muscle
²ab *abbr* about
AB *abbr* **1** able-bodied seaman **2** airman basic **3** bachelor of arts
ABA *abbr* American Bar Association
aback \ə-ˈbak\ *adv* ♦ **:** by surprise ⟨taken ~⟩

♦ suddenly, unaware, unawares

aba•cus \ˈa-bə-kəs\ *n, pl* **aba•ci** \-ˌsī, -ˌkē\ *or* **aba•cus•es :** an instrument for making calculations by sliding counters along rods or grooves
¹abaft \ə-ˈbaft\ *prep* **:** to the rear of
²abaft *adv* **:** toward or at the stern **:** AFT
ab•a•lo•ne \ˌa-bə-ˈlō-nē, ˈa-bə-ˌ\ *n* **:** any of a genus of large edible sea mollusks with a flattened slightly spiral shell with holes along the edge
¹aban•don \ə-ˈban-dən\ *vb* ♦ **:** to give up completely **:** FORSAKE, DESERT

♦ desert, forsake, maroon, quit

²abandon *n* ♦ **:** a thorough yielding to natural impulses

♦ abandonment, ease, lightheartedness, naturalness, spontaneity, unrestraint *Ant* constraint, restraint

aban•doned \ə-ˈban-dənd\ *adj* **1 :** morally unrestrained **2** ♦ **:** given up **:** FORSAKEN

♦ derelict, deserted, forsaken

aban•don•ment \ə-ˈban-dən-mənt\ *n* **1** ♦ **:** the act of abandoning **2** ♦ **:** freedom from restraint

♦ [1] dereliction, desertion ♦ [2] abandon, ease, lightheartedness, naturalness, spontaneity, unrestraint

abase \ə-ˈbās\ *vb* **abased; abas•ing** ♦ **:** to lower in rank, office, prestige, or esteem **:** HUMBLE, DEGRADE — **abase•ment** *n*

♦ debase, degrade, demean, demoralize, humble, subvert, warp

abash \ə-ˈbash\ *vb* ♦ **:** to destroy the composure of **:** EMBARRASS

♦ confound, confuse, discomfit, disconcert, discountenance, embarrass, faze, fluster, mortify, rattle

abash•ment \ə-ˈbash-mənt\ *n* ♦ **:** the quality or state of being abashed

♦ confusion, discomfiture, embarrassment, fluster, mortification

abate \ə-ˈbāt\ *vb* **abat•ed; abat•ing 1 :** to put an end to ⟨~ a nuisance⟩ **2** ♦ **:** to decrease in amount, number, or degree

♦ decline, decrease, diminish, dwindle, ebb, fall, lessen, recede, subside, taper, wane

abate•ment \ə-ˈbāt-mənt\ *n* **1** ♦ **:** an amount of taking away; *esp* **:** a deduction from a tax **2** ♦ **:** an amount abated or lessened

♦ [1] deduction, discount, reduction ♦ [1, 2] decline, decrease, decrement, diminution, drop, fall, loss, reduction, shrinkage

ab•at•toir \ˈa-bə-ˌtwär\ *n* **:** SLAUGHTERHOUSE
ab•ba•cy \ˈa-bə-sē\ *n, pl* **-cies :** the office or term of office of an abbot or abbess
ab•bé \a-ˈbā, ˈa-ˌ\ *n* **:** a member of the French secular clergy — used as a title
ab•bess \ˈa-bəs\ *n* **:** the superior of a convent for nuns
ab•bey \ˈa-bē\ *n, pl* **abbeys 1** ♦ **:** a house for persons and especially monks under religious vows **:** MONASTERY **2 :** CONVENT **3 :** an abbey church

♦ cloister, friary, monastery, priory

ab•bot \ˈa-bət\ *n* **:** the superior of a monastery for men
abbr *abbr* abbreviation
ab•bre•vi•ate \ə-ˈbrē-vē-ˌāt\ *vb* **-at•ed; -at•ing** ♦ **:** to make briefer **:** SHORTEN, CURTAIL; *esp* **:** to reduce to an abbreviation

♦ abridge, curtail, cut back, shorten

ab•bre•vi•a•tion \ə-ˌbrē-vē-ˈā-shən\ *n* **1** ♦ **:** the act or result of abbreviating **:** ABRIDGMENT **2 :** a shortened form of a word or phrase used for brevity especially in writing

♦ abridgment, condensation, digest

¹ABC \ˌā-(ˌ)bē-ˈsē\ *n, pl* **ABC's** *or* **ABCs** \-ˈsēz\ **1 :** ALPHABET — usually used in plural **2 :** RUDIMENTS — usually used in plural
²ABC *abbr* American Broadcasting Company
Ab•di•as \ab-ˈdī-əs\ *n* **:** OBADIAH
ab•di•cate \ˈab-di-ˌkāt\ *vb* **-cat•ed; -cat•ing** ♦ **:** to give up (as a throne) formally — **ab•di•ca•tion** \ˌab-di-ˈkā-shən\ *n*

♦ abnegate, cede, relinquish, renounce, resign, step down, surrender

ab•do•men \ˈab-də-mən, ab-ˈdō-\ *n* **1** ♦ **:** the cavity in or area of the body between the chest and the pelvis **2 :** the part of the body posterior to the thorax in an arthropod — **ab•dom•i•nal** \ab-ˈdä-mən-ᵊl\ *adj* — **ab•dom•i•nal•ly** *adv*

♦ belly, gut, solar plexus, stomach, tummy

ab•duct \ab-ˈdəkt\ *vb* **:** to take away (a person) by force **:** KIDNAP — **ab•duc•tion** \-ˈdək-shən\ *n* — **ab•duc•tor** \-tər\ *n*
abeam \ə-ˈbēm\ *adv or adj* **:** on a line at right angles to a ship's keel
abed \ə-ˈbed\ *adv or adj* **:** in bed
Abe•na•ki \ˌa-bə-ˈnä-kē\ *n, pl* **Abenaki** *or* **Abenakis :** a member of a group of American Indian peoples of northern New England and southern Quebec
ab•er•rant \a-ˈber-ənt\ *adj* **1** ♦ **:** departing from the right or normal way **2** ♦ **:** departing from the usual or natural type **:** ATYPICAL

♦ [1] abnormal, anomalous, deviant, irregular, unnatural ♦ [2] abnormal, atypical, exceptional, extraordinary, freak, odd, peculiar, uncommon, uncustomary, unique, unusual, unwonted

ab•er•ra•tion \ˌa-bə-ˈrā-shən\ *n* **1 :** deviation especially from a moral standard or normal state **2 :** failure of a mirror or lens to produce exact point-to-point correspondence between an object and its image **3** ♦ **:** unsoundness of mind **:** DERANGEMENT

♦ dementia, derangement, insanity, lunacy, madness, mania

abet \ə-ˈbet\ *vb* **abet•ted; abet•ting 1** ♦ **:** to actively second and encourage (as in wrongdoing) **:** INCITE **2** ♦ **:** to assist or support in the achievement of a purpose

♦ [1, 2] ferment, foment, incite, instigate, provoke, raise, stir, whip ♦ [2] aid, assist, back, help, prop, support

abet•tor *also* **abet•ter** \-ˈbe-tər\ *n* ♦ **:** one that abets

♦ accessory, accomplice, cohort, confederate ♦ ally, backer, confederate, supporter, sympathizer

abey•ance \ə-ˈbā-əns\ *n* ♦ **:** a condition of suspended activity

♦ doldrums, dormancy, latency, quiescence, suspension *Ant* continuance, continuation

ab•hor \əb-ˈhȯr, ab-\ *vb* **ab•horred; ab•hor•ring** ♦ **:** to regard with extreme dislike **:** LOATHE, DETEST

♦ abominate, despise, detest, execrate, hate, loathe

ab•hor•rence \-əns\ *n* **1** ♦ **:** the feeling of one who abhors **2** ♦ **:** one that is abhorred

♦ [1] abomination, execration, hate, hatred, loathing ♦ [2] abomination, anathema, antipathy, aversion, bête noire, hate

ab•hor•rent \-ənt\ *adj* ♦ **:** causing or deserving strong dislike **:** LOATHSOME

♦ abominable, appalling, hideous, horrible, horrid, offensive, repellent, repugnant, repulsive, revolting, shocking

abid•ance \ə-ˈbī-dən(t)s\ *n* ♦ **:** an act or state of abiding

♦ ceaselessness, continuance, continuation, duration, endurance, persistence, subsistence

abide \ə-ˈbīd\ *vb* **abode** \-ˈbōd\ *or* **abid•ed; abid•ing 1** ♦ **:** to bear patiently **:** ENDURE **2 a** ♦ **:** to continue in a state or place **b** ♦ **:** to have one's abode — **abide by** to conform or acquiesce to ⟨*abide by* the law⟩

♦ [1] bear, brook, countenance, endure, meet, stand, stick out, stomach, support, sustain, take, tolerate ♦ [2a] continue, endure, hold, keep up, last, persist, run on ♦ [2b] dwell, live, reside

abid•ing \ə-ˈbī-diŋ\ *adj* ♦ **:** lasting and unchanging **:** ENDURING, CONTINUING ⟨an ~ interest in nature⟩

♦ ageless, continuing, dateless, enduring, eternal, everlasting, immortal, imperishable, lasting, perennial, perpetual, timeless, undying

abil•i•ty \ə-ˈbi-lə-tē\ *n, pl* **-ties** ♦ **:** the quality of being able

♦ capability, capacity, competence, faculty ***Ant*** inability, incapability, incapacity, incompetence, ineptitude

-ability *also* **-ibility** *n suffix* **:** capacity, fitness, or tendency to act or be acted on in a (specified) way ⟨flamm*ability*⟩

ab•ject \ˈab-ˌjekt, ab-ˈjekt\ *adj* **:** low in spirit or hope **:** CRINGING — **ab•jec•tion** \ab-ˈjek-shən\ *n* — **ab•ject•ly** *adv* — **ab•ject•ness** *n*

ab•jure \ab-ˈju̇r\ *vb* **ab•jured; ab•jur•ing 1** ♦ **:** to renounce solemnly **:** RECANT **2 :** to abstain from — **ab•ju•ra•tion** \ˌab-jə-ˈrā-shən\ *n*

♦ recant, renounce, retract, take back, unsay, withdraw ***Ant*** adhere (to)

abl *abbr* ablative

ab•late \a-ˈblāt\ *vb* **ab•lat•ed; ab•lat•ing :** to remove or become removed especially by cutting, abrading, or vaporizing

ab•la•tion \a-ˈblā-shən\ *n* **1 :** surgical cutting and removal **2 :** loss of a part (as the outside of a nose cone) by melting or vaporization

ab•la•tive \ˈab-lə-tiv\ *adj* **:** of, relating to, or constituting a grammatical case (as in Latin) expressing typically the relation of separation and source — **ablative** *n*

ablaze \ə-ˈblāz\ *adj or adv* **1** ♦ **:** being on fire **:** BLAZING **2** ♦ **:** radiant with light

♦ [1] afire, burning, fiery ♦ [2] alight, bright, light

able \ˈā-bəl\ *adj* **abler** \-b(ə-)lər\; **ablest** \-b(ə-)ləst\ **1** ♦ **:** having sufficient power, skill, or resources to accomplish an object **2** ♦ **:** marked by skill or efficiency

♦ [1, 2] capable, competent, fit, good, qualified, suitable

-able *also* **-ible** *adj suffix* **1 :** capable of, fit for, or worthy of (being so acted upon or toward) ⟨break*able*⟩ ⟨collect*ible*⟩ **2 :** tending, given, or liable to ⟨knowledge*able*⟩ ⟨perish*able*⟩

able–bod•ied \ˌā-bəl-ˈbä-dēd\ *adj* ♦ **:** having a sound strong body

♦ chipper, fit, hale, healthy, hearty, robust, sound, well, whole, wholesome

abloom \ə-ˈblüm\ *adj* **:** BLOOMING

ab•lu•tion \ə-ˈblü-shən, a-\ *n* **:** the washing of one's body or part of it

ably \ˈā-blē\ *adv* ♦ **:** in an able manner

♦ adeptly, capably, expertly, masterfully, proficiently, skillfully, well

ABM \ˌā-(ˌ)bē-ˈem\ *n, pl* **ABM's** *or* **ABMs :** ANTIBALLISTIC MISSILE

ab•ne•gate \ˈab-ni-ˌgāt\ *vb* **-gat•ed; -gat•ing 1 :** DENY, RENOUNCE **2** ♦ **:** to give up (as a right or privilege) **:** SURRENDER, RELINQUISH

♦ abdicate, cede, relinquish, renounce, resign, step down, surrender

ab•ne•ga•tion \ˌab-ni-ˈgā-shən\ *n* ♦ **:** restraint or denial of desire or self-interest

♦ renouncement, renunciation, repudiation, self-denial

ab•nor•mal \ab-ˈnȯr-məl\ *adj* ♦ **:** deviating from the normal or average — **ab•nor•mal•ly** *adv*

♦ aberrant, exceptional, extraordinary, rare, singular, uncommon, uncustomary, unique, unusual ♦ aberrant, anomalous, atypical, deviant, irregular, unnatural

ab•nor•mal•i•ty \ˌab-nȯr-ˈma-lə-tē\ *n* ♦ **:** something abnormal

♦ freak, monster, monstrosity

¹aboard \ə-ˈbōrd\ *adv* **1 :** ALONGSIDE **2 :** on, onto, or within a car, ship, or aircraft **3 :** in or into a group or association ⟨welcome new workers ~⟩

²aboard *prep* **:** ON, ONTO, WITHIN

abode \ə-ˈbōd\ *n* **1 :** STAY, SOJOURN **2** ♦ **:** the place where one abides **:** HOME, RESIDENCE

♦ domicile, dwelling, home, house, lodging, quarters, residence

abol•ish \ə-ˈbä-lish\ *vb* ♦ **:** to do away with **:** ANNUL — **ab•o•li•tion** \ˌa-bə-ˈli-shən\ *n*

♦ abrogate, annul, cancel, dissolve, invalidate, negate, nullify, quash, repeal, rescind, void

ab•o•li•tion•ism \ˌa-bə-ˈli-shə-ˌni-zəm\ *n* **:** advocacy of the abolition of slavery — **ab•o•li•tion•ist** \-ˈli-sh(ə-)nist\ *n or adj*

A–bomb \ˈā-ˌbäm\ *n* **:** ATOMIC BOMB — **A–bomb** *vb*

abom•i•na•ble \ə-ˈbä-mə-nə-bəl\ *adj* ♦ **:** worthy of or causing disgust or hatred **:** ODIOUS

♦ abhorrent, appalling, awful, horrible, horrid, odious, offensive, repellent, repugnant, repulsive, revolting

abominable snow•man \-ˈsnō-mən, -ˌman\ *n, often cap A&S* **:** a mysterious creature with human or apelike characteristics reported to exist in the high Himalayas

abom•i•nate \ə-ˈbä-mə-ˌnāt\ *vb* **-nat•ed; -nat•ing** ♦ **:** to hate or loathe intensely **:** LOATHE, DETEST

♦ abhor, despise, detest, execrate, hate, loathe

abom•i•na•tion \ə-ˌbä-mə-ˈnā-shən\ *n* **1** ♦ **:** something abominable **2** ♦ **:** extreme disgust and hatred **:** LOATHING

♦ [1] abhorrence, anathema, antipathy, aversion, bête noire, hate ♦ [2] abhorrence, execration, hate, hatred, loathing

ab•orig•i•nal \ˌa-bə-ˈri-jə-nəl\ *adj* ♦ **:** being the first or earliest known of its kind present in a region **:** INDIGENOUS

♦ born, endemic, indigenous, native

ab•orig•i•ne \ˌa-bə-ˈri-jə-nē\ *n* **:** a member of the original race of inhabitants of a region **:** NATIVE

aborn•ing \ə-ˈbȯr-niŋ\ *adv* **:** while being born or produced

¹abort \ə-ˈbȯrt\ *vb* **1 :** to cause or undergo abortion **2** ♦ **:** to terminate prematurely ⟨~ a spaceflight⟩

♦ call, call off, cancel, drop, recall, repeal, rescind, revoke

²abort *n* **:** the premature termination of a mission of or a procedure relating to an aircraft or spacecraft

abor•tion \ə-ˈbȯr-shən\ *n* **1 :** the spontaneous or induced termination of a pregnancy after, accompanied by, resulting in, or closely followed by the death of the embryo or fetus **2** ♦ **:** arrest of development (as of a part or process); *also* **:** a result of such arrest

♦ calling, cancellation, recall, repeal, rescission, revocation

abor•tion•ist \-sh(ə-)nist\ *n* **:** one who induces abortions

abor•tive \ə-ˈbȯr-tiv\ *adj* ♦ **:** not successful

♦ fruitless, futile, ineffective, unproductive, unsuccessful

abound \ə-ˈbau̇nd\ *vb* **1** ♦ **:** to be plentiful **:** TEEM **2 :** to be fully supplied

♦ brim, bulge, burst, crawl, swarm, teem

¹about \ə-ˈbau̇t\ *adv* **1** ♦ **:** reasonably close to; *also* **:** on the verge of ⟨~ to join the army⟩ **2 :** on all sides **3 :** in the vicinity **:** NEARBY **4** ♦ **:** in the opposite direction

♦ [1] almost, most, much, near, nearly, next to, nigh, practically, some, virtually, well-nigh ♦ [4] around, back, round

²about *prep* **1 :** on every side of **2** ♦ **:** near to **3** ♦ **:** relating to **:** CONCERNING **4** ♦ **:** over or in different parts of

♦ [2] around, by, near, next to ♦ [3] apropos of, concerning, of, on, regarding, respecting, toward ♦ [4] around, over, round, through, throughout

about–face \-ˈfās\ *n* **:** a reversal of direction or attitude — **about–face** *vb*

¹above \ə-ˈbəv\ *adv* **1 :** in the sky; *also* **:** in or to heaven **2** ♦ **:** in or to a higher place; *also* **:** higher on the same page or on a preceding page

♦ aloft, over, overhead, skyward ***Ant*** below, beneath, under

²above *prep* **1 :** in or to a higher place than **:** OVER ⟨storm clouds

~ the bay⟩ **2 :** superior to ⟨he thought her far ~ him⟩ **3 :** more than : EXCEEDING **4 :** as distinct from ⟨~ the noise⟩

above•board \-ˌbōrd\ *adv or adj* **:** without concealment or deception : OPENLY

abp *abbr* archbishop

abr *abbr* abridged; abridgment

ab•ra•ca•dab•ra \ˌa-brə-kə-ˈda-brə\ *n* **1** ♦ **:** a magical charm or incantation against calamity **2** ♦ **:** unintelligible or meaningless language : GIBBERISH

♦ [1, 2] abracadabra, bewitchment, charm, conjuration, enchantment, incantation, spell

abrade \ə-ˈbrād\ *vb* **abrad•ed; abrad•ing** **1 a** ♦ **:** to wear away by friction **b** ♦ **:** to irritate or roughen by rubbing **2 :** to wear down in spirit : IRRITATE

♦ [1a] chafe, erode, fray, fret, gall, rub, wear ♦ [1b] graze, scrape, scratch, scuff

abra•sion \ə-ˈbrā-zhən\ *n* **:** an abraded area of the skin or mucous membrane

1**abra•sive** \ə-ˈbrā-siv\ *n* **:** a substance (as pumice) for abrading, smoothing, or polishing

2**abrasive** *adj* **:** tending to abrade : causing irritation ⟨~ relationships⟩ — **abra•sive•ly** *adv* — **abra•sive•ness** *n*

abreast \ə-ˈbrest\ *adv or adj* **1 :** side by side **2** ♦ **:** up to a standard or level especially of knowledge

♦ conversant, familiar, informed, knowledgeable, up, up-to-date, versed

abridge \ə-ˈbrij\ *vb* **abridged; abridg•ing** ♦ **:** to lessen in length or extent : SHORTEN

♦ abbreviate, curtail, cut back, shorten

abridg•ment *or* **abridge•ment** \ə-ˈbrij-ment\ *n* ♦ **:** a shortened form of a work

♦ abbreviation, condensation, digest

abroad \ə-ˈbrȯd\ *adv or adj* **1 :** over a wide area **2 :** away from one's home **3 :** outside one's country

ab•ro•gate \ˈa-brə-ˌgāt\ *vb* **-gat•ed; -gat•ing** ♦ **:** to abolish by authoritative action : ANNUL — **ab•ro•ga•tion** \ˌa-brə-ˈgā-shən\ *n*

♦ abolish, annul, cancel, dissolve, invalidate, negate, nullify, quash, repeal, rescind, void

abrupt \ə-ˈbrəpt\ *adj* **1 :** broken or as if broken off **2 :** SUDDEN, HASTY **3** ♦ **:** so quick as to seem rude **4 :** DISCONNECTED **5 :** STEEP

♦ bluff, blunt, brusque, curt, snippy

abrupt•ly \-lē\ *adv* **:** in an abrupt manner

abs *abbr* absolute

ab•scess \ˈab-ˌses\ *n, pl* **ab•scess•es** **:** a localized collection of pus surrounded by inflamed tissue — **ab•scessed** \-ˌsest\ *adj*

ab•scis•sa \ab-ˈsi-sə\ *n, pl* **abscissas** *also* **ab•scis•sae** \-ˈsi-(ˌ)sē\ **:** the horizontal coordinate of a point in a plane coordinate system obtained by measuring parallel to the x-axis

ab•scis•sion \ab-ˈsi-zhən\ *n* **1 :** the act or process of cutting off **2 :** the natural separation of flowers, fruits, or leaves from plants — **ab•scise** \ab-ˈsīz\ *vb*

ab•scond \ab-ˈskänd\ *vb* ♦ **:** to depart secretly and hide oneself

♦ clear out, escape, flee, fly, get out, lam, run away, run off

ab•sence \ˈab-səns\ *n* **1 :** the state or time of being absent **2** ♦ **:** failure to be present where needed, wanted, or normally expected : WANT, LACK **3 :** INATTENTION

♦ lack, need, want

1**ab•sent** \ˈab-sənt\ *adj* **1** ♦ **:** not present **2** ♦ **:** to be deficient or missing : LACKING **3 :** not paying attention : INATTENTIVE

♦ [1] away, missing, out *Ant* here, present ♦ [2] missing, nonexistent, wanting *Ant* existent, present

2**ab•sent** \ab-ˈsent\ *vb* **:** to keep (oneself) away

3**ab•sent** \ˈab-sənt\ *prep* **:** in the absence of : WITHOUT

ab•sen•tee \ˌab-sən-ˈtē\ *n* **:** one that is absent or keeps away

absentee ballot *n* **:** a ballot submitted (as by mail) in advance of an election by a voter who is unable to be present at the polls

ab•sen•tee•ism \ˌab-sən-ˈtē-ˌi-zəm\ *n* **:** chronic absence (as from work or school)

ab•sent•mind•ed \ˌab-sənt-ˈmīn-dəd\ *adj* ♦ **:** unaware of one's surroundings or actions : INATTENTIVE — **ab•sent•mind•ed•ly** *adv* — **ab•sent•mind•ed•ness** *n*

♦ abstracted, preoccupied *Ant* alert

ab•sinthe *also* **ab•sinth** \ˈab-ˌsinth\ *n* **:** a liqueur flavored especially with wormwood and anise

ab•so•lute \ˈab-sə-ˌlüt, ˌab-sə-ˈlüt\ *adj* **1** ♦ **:** free from imperfection or mixture **2** ♦ **:** free from control, restriction, or qualification **3 :** lacking grammatical connection with any other word in a sentence ⟨~ construction⟩ **4** ♦ **:** not disputable : POSITIVE ⟨~ proof⟩ **5 :** relating to the fundamental units of length, mass, and time **6 :** FUNDAMENTAL, ULTIMATE

♦ [1] faultless, flawless, ideal, impeccable, letter-perfect, perfect, unblemished ♦ [1] fine, neat, plain, pure, refined, straight, unadulterated, undiluted, unmixed ♦ [2] autocratic, despotic, dictatorial, tyrannical, tyrannous *Ant* limited ♦ [2] complete, consummate, perfect, total, unequivocal, unqualified, utter ♦ [4] clear, conclusive, decisive, definitive, positive

ab•so•lute•ly \-lē\ *adv* ♦ **:** in an absolute manner or condition

♦ all, altogether, clean, completely, entirely, fully, quite, totally, utterly, wholly

absolute pitch *n* **1 :** the position of a tone in a standard scale independently determined by its rate of vibration **2 :** the ability to sing a note asked for or to name a note heard

absolute value *n* **:** a nonnegative number equal to a given real number with any negative sign removed

absolute zero *n* **:** a theoretical temperature marked by a complete absence of heat and motion and equivalent to exactly -273.15°C or -459.67°F

ab•so•lu•tion \ˌab-sə-ˈlü-shən\ *n* ♦ **:** the act of absolving; *esp* **:** a remission of sins pronounced by a priest in the sacrament of reconciliation

♦ amnesty, forgiveness, pardon, remission

ab•so•lut•ism \ˈab-sə-ˌlü-ˌti-zəm\ *n* **1 :** the theory that a ruler or government should have unlimited power **2 :** government by an absolute ruler or authority

ab•solve \əb-ˈzälv, -ˈsälv\ *vb* **ab•solved; ab•solv•ing** ♦ **:** to set free from an obligation or the consequences of guilt

♦ acquit, clear, exculpate, exonerate, vindicate

ab•sorb \əb-ˈsȯrb, -ˈzȯrb\ *vb* **1 :** to take in and make part of an existent whole **2** ♦ **:** to suck up or take in in the manner of a sponge **3** ♦ **:** to engage (one's attention) : ENGROSS **4 :** to receive without recoil or echo ⟨a ceiling that ~*s* sound⟩ **5 :** ASSUME, BEAR ⟨~ all costs⟩ **6 :** to transform (radiant energy) into a different form usually with a resulting rise in temperature

♦ [2] drink, imbibe, soak, sponge, suck ♦ [3] busy, engage, engross, enthrall, fascinate, grip, immerse, interest, intrigue, involve, occupy

ab•sorbed \əb-ˈsȯrbd, -ˈzȯrbd\ *adj* ♦ **:** obliviously engaged or occupied

♦ attentive, engrossed, intent, observant, rapt

ab•sor•bent *also* **ab•sor•bant** \əb-ˈsȯr-bənt, ˈ-zȯr-\ *adj* **:** able to absorb ⟨~ cotton⟩ — **ab•sor•ben•cy** \-bən-sē\ *n* — **absorbent** *also* **absorbant** *n*

ab•sorb•ing \əb-ˈsȯrb-iŋ, -ˈzȯrb-iŋ\ *adj* ♦ **:** fully taking attention : ENGROSSING — **ab•sorb•ing•ly** *adv*

♦ engaging, engrossing, enthralling, fascinating, interesting, intriguing

ab•sorp•tion \əb-ˈsȯrp-shən, -ˈzȯrp-\ *n* **1 :** a process of absorbing or being absorbed **2** ♦ **:** concentration of attention — **absorp•tive** \-tiv\ *adj*

♦ attention, concentration

ab•stain \əb-ˈstān\ *vb* ♦ **:** to refrain from an action or practice — **ab•stain•er** *n* — **ab•sten•tion** \-ˈsten-chən\ *n*

♦ forbear, forgo, keep, refrain

ab•ste•mi•ous \ab-ˈstē-mē-əs\ *adj* ♦ **:** sparing in use of food or drink : TEMPERATE — **ab•ste•mi•ous•ly** *adv* — **ab•ste•mi•ous•ness** *n*

♦ abstinent, sober, temperate *Ant* self-indulgent

ab•sti•nence \ˈab-stə-nəns\ *n* **:** voluntary refraining especially from eating certain foods, drinking liquor, or engaging in sexual intercourse

ab•sti•nent \ˈab-stə-nənt\ *adj* ♦ **:** practicing abstience

♦ abstemious, sober, temperate

abstr *abbr* abstract

1**ab•stract** \ab-ˈstrakt, ˈab-ˌstrakt\ *adj* **1 :** considered apart from a particular instance **2 :** expressing a quality apart from an object ⟨*whiteness* is an ~ word⟩ **3 :** having only intrinsic form with little or no pictorial representation ⟨~ painting⟩ — **ab·stract·ly** *adv* — **ab·stract·ness** *n*

[2]**ab·stract** \ˈab-ˌstrakt; *2 also* ab-ˈstrakt\ *n* **1** ♦ **:** a summary of points (as of a writing) **:** SUMMARY, EPITOME **2 :** an abstract thing or state

♦ digest, encapsulation, epitome, outline, précis, recapitulation, résumé (*or* resume), roundup, sum, summary, synopsis, wrap-up

[3]**ab·stract** \ab-ˈstrakt, ˈab-ˌstrakt; *2 usu* ˈab-ˌstrakt\ *vb* **1 :** REMOVE, SEPARATE **2** ♦ **:** to make an abstract of **:** SUMMARIZE **3 :** to draw away the attention of **4 :** STEAL — **ab·stract·ed·ly** \ab-ˈstrak-təd-lē, ˈab-ˌstrak-\ *adv*

♦ digest, encapsulate, epitomize, outline, recapitulate, sum up, summarize, wrap up

ab·stract·ed \ab-ˈstrak-təd, ˈab-ˌstrak-\ *adj* ♦ **:** lost in thought and unaware of one's surroundings or actions

♦ absentminded, preoccupied

abstract expressionism *n* **:** art that expresses the artist's attitudes and emotions through abstract forms — **abstract expressionist** *n*

ab·strac·tion \ab-ˈstrak-shən\ *n* **1 :** the act of abstracting **:** the state of being abstracted **2 :** an abstract idea **3 :** an abstract work of art

ab·struse \ab-ˈstrüs\ *adj* ♦ **:** hard to understand **:** RECONDITE — **ab·struse·ly** *adv* — **ab·struse·ness** *n*

♦ deep, esoteric, profound

ab·surd \əb-ˈsərd, -ˈzərd\ *adj* ♦ **:** ridiculously unreasonable, unsound, or incongruous — **ab·surd·ly** *adv*

♦ bizarre, crazy, fanciful, fantastic, foolish, insane, nonsensical, preposterous, unreal, wild ♦ comical, derisive, farcical, laughable, ludicrous, preposterous, ridiculous, risible, silly

ab·sur·di·ty \-ˈsər-də-tē, -ˈzər-\ *n* **1** ♦ **:** the quality or state of being absurd **2** ♦ **:** something that is absurd

♦ [1] craziness, daftness, fatuity, folly, foolishness, inanity, insanity, silliness, zaniness ♦ [2] fatuity, folly, foolery, foolishness, idiocy, inanity, madness, stupidity

abun·dance \ə-ˈbən-dəns\ *n* ♦ **:** an ample quantity

♦ deal, gobs, heap, loads, lot, pile, plenty, quantity, scads ♦ plenty, superabundance, wealth

abun·dant \ə-ˈbən-dənt\ *adj* ♦ **:** more than enough **:** amply sufficient — **abun·dance** \-dəns\ *n* — **abun·dant·ly** *adv*

♦ ample, bountiful, comfortable, generous, liberal, plentiful

[1]**abuse** \ə-ˈbyüs\ *n* **1 :** a corrupt practice **2** ♦ **:** incorrect or improper use **:** MISUSE ⟨drug ~⟩ **3** ♦ **:** coarse and insulting speech **4 :** MISTREATMENT ⟨child ~⟩

♦ [2] misuse, perversion ♦ [3] fulmination, invective, vitriol, vituperation

[2]**abuse** \ə-ˈbyüz\ *vb* **abused; abus·ing 1** ♦ **:** to put to a wrong use **:** MISUSE **2** ♦ **:** to use so as to injure or damage **:** MISTREAT **3** ♦ **:** to attack in words **4** to use to excess ⟨~ alcohol⟩ — **abus·er** *n* — **abu·sive·ness** *n*

♦ [1] misapply, misuse, pervert, profane, prostitute ♦ [1] capitalize, cash in, exploit, impose, play, use ♦ [2] ill-treat, maltreat, manhandle, mishandle, mistreat, misuse ♦ [3] assail, attack, belabor, blast, castigate, excoriate, jump, lambaste, slam, vituperate

abu·sive \ə-ˈbyü-siv\ *adj* ♦ **:** characterized by or serving for abuse — **abu·sive·ly** *adv*

♦ opprobrious, scurrilous

abut \ə-ˈbət\ *vb* **abut·ted; abut·ting** ♦ **:** to touch along a border **:** border on

♦ adjoin, border (on), flank, fringe, join, skirt, touch, verge (on)

abut·ment \ə-ˈbət-mənt\ *n* **:** the part of a structure (as a bridge) that supports weight or withstands lateral pressure

abut·ter \ə-ˈbə-tər\ *n* **:** one that abuts; *esp* **:** the owner of a contiguous property

abys·mal \ə-ˈbiz-məl\ *adj* **1 :** immeasurably deep **:** BOTTOMLESS **2 :** absolutely wretched ⟨~ living conditions of the poor⟩ — **abys·mal·ly** *adv*

abyss \ə-ˈbis\ *n* **1 :** the bottomless pit in old accounts of the universe **2 :** an immeasurable depth

abys·sal \ə-ˈbi-səl\ *adj* **:** of or relating to the bottom waters of the ocean depths

ac *abbr* account

-ac *n suffix* **:** one affected with ⟨hypochondri*ac*⟩

Ac *symbol* actinium

AC *abbr* **1** air-conditioning **2** alternating current **3** before Christ **4** before meals **5** area code

aca·cia \ə-ˈkā-shə\ *n* **:** any of numerous leguminous trees or shrubs with round white or yellow flower clusters and often fernlike leaves

acad *abbr* academic; academy

ac·a·deme \ˈa-kə-ˌdēm, ˌa-kə-ˈ\ *n* **:** SCHOOL; *also* **:** academic environment

[1]**ac·a·dem·ic** \ˌa-kə-ˈde-mik\ *n* **:** a person who is academic in background, outlook, or methods

[2]**academic** *adj* **1** ♦ **:** of, relating to, or associated with schools or colleges **2 :** literary or general rather than technical **3 :** theoretical rather than practical — **ac·a·dem·i·cal·ly** \-mi-k(ə-)lē\ *adv*

♦ educational, scholarly, scholastic *Ant* nonacademic, unacademic

ac·a·de·mi·cian \ˌa-kə-də-ˈmi-shən, ə-ˌka-də-\ *n* **1 :** a member of a society of scholars or artists **2 :** ACADEMIC

ac·a·dem·i·cism \ˌa-kə-ˈde-mə-ˌsi-zəm\ *also* **acad·e·mism** \ə-ˈka-də-ˌmi-zəm\ *n* **1 :** a formal academic quality **2 :** purely speculative thinking

acad·e·my \ə-ˈka-də-mē\ *n, pl* **-mies 1 :** a school usually above the elementary level; *esp* **:** a private high school **2 :** a society of scholars or artists

acan·thus \ə-ˈkan-thəs\ *n, pl* **acanthus 1 :** any of a genus of prickly herbs of the Mediterranean region **2 :** an ornamentation (as on a column) representing the leaves of the acanthus

a cap·pel·la *also* **a ca·pel·la** \ˌä-kə-ˈpe-lə\ *adv or adj* **:** without instrumental accompaniment

acc *abbr* accusative

ac·cede \ak-ˈsēd\ *vb* **ac·ced·ed; ac·ced·ing 1 :** to become a party to an agreement **2** ♦ **:** to express approval **3 :** to enter upon an office

♦ acquiesce, agree, assent, come round, consent, subscribe (to) *Ant* dissent

ac·cel·er·ate \ik-ˈse-lə-ˌrāt, ak-\ *vb* **-at·ed; -at·ing 1 :** to bring about earlier **2** ♦ **:** to speed up **:** QUICKEN — **ac·cel·er·a·tion** \-ˌse-lə-ˈrā-shən\ *n*

♦ hasten, hurry, quicken, rush, speed (up), step up, whisk

ac·cel·er·a·tor \ik-ˈse-lə-ˌrā-tər, ak-\ *n* **1 :** one that accelerates **2 :** a pedal for controlling the speed of a motor-vehicle engine **3 :** an apparatus for imparting high velocities to charged particles

ac·cel·er·om·e·ter \ik-ˌse-lə-ˈrä-mə-tər, ak-\ *n* **:** an instrument for measuring acceleration or vibrations

[1]**ac·cent** \ˈak-ˌsent, ak-ˈsent\ *vb* ♦ **:** to give prominence to **:** STRESS, EMPHASIZE

♦ accentuate, emphasize, feature, highlight, play, point, stress, underline, underscore

[2]**ac·cent** \ˈak-ˌsent\ *n* **1 :** a distinctive manner of pronunciation ⟨a foreign ~⟩ **2 :** prominence given to one syllable of a word especially by stress **3 :** a mark (as ´, ` , ˆ) over a vowel used usually to indicate a difference in pronunciation from a vowel not so marked **4** ♦ **:** special concern or attention **:** EMPHASIS — **ac·cen·tu·al** \ak-ˈsen-chə-wəl\ *adj*

♦ accentuation, emphasis, stress, weight

ac·cen·tu·ate \ak-ˈsen-chə-ˌwāt\ *vb* **-at·ed; -at·ing** ♦ **:** to give prominence to **:** ACCENT

♦ accent, emphasize, feature, highlight, play, point, stress, underline, underscore

ac·cen·tu·a·tion \-ˌsen-chə-ˈwā-shən\ *n* ♦ **:** the act or the result of accentuating

♦ accent, emphasis, stress, weight

ac·cept \ik-ˈsept, ak-\ *vb* **1 :** to receive with consent **2** ♦ **:** to make a favorable response to **3** ♦ **:** to recognize as true **4** ♦ **:** to assume an obligation

♦ [2] approve, care, countenance, favor (*or* favour), OK, subscribe ♦ [3] believe, credit, swallow, trust ♦ [4] assume, bear, shoulder, take over, undertake

ac·cept·able \ik-ˈsep-tə-bəl, ak-\ *adj* ♦ **:** capable or worthy of being accepted — **ac·cept·abil·i·ty** \-ˈbi-lə-tē, ak-\ *n*

♦ adequate, all right, decent, fine, OK, passable, respectable, satisfactory, tolerable

ac·cep·tance \ik-ˈsep-təns, ak-\ *n* **1 :** the act of accepting **2 :** the state of being accepted or acceptable **3 :** an accepted bill of exchange

ac·cep·ta·tion \ˌak-ˌsep-ˈtā-shən\ *n* **:** the generally understood meaning of a word

1ac·cess \ˈak-ˌses\ *n* **1** ♦ **:** capacity to enter or approach **2** ♦ **:** a way of approach **:** ENTRANCE

♦ admission, doorway, entrance, entrée, entry, gateway

2access *vb* ♦ **:** to get at **:** gain access to

♦ enter, penetrate, pierce, probe

ac·ces·si·ble \ik-ˈse-sə-bəl, ak-, ek-\ *adj* **1** ♦ **:** capable of being reached ⟨~ by train⟩ **2** ♦ **:** capable of being used, seen, or known **:** OBTAINABLE ⟨~ information⟩ — **ac·ces·si·bil·i·ty** \-ˌse-sə-ˈbi-lə-tē\ *n*

♦ [1] convenient, handy, reachable ♦ [2] acquirable, attainable, available, obtainable, procurable

ac·ces·sion \ik-ˈse-shən, ak-\ *n* **1 :** increase by something added **2 :** something added **3 :** the act of coming to a high office or position

1ac·ces·so·ry *also* **ac·ces·sa·ry** \ik-ˈse-sə-rē, ak-\ *n, pl* **-ries** **1** ♦ **:** a person who though not present abets or assists in the commission of an offense **2** ♦ **:** something helpful but not essential

♦ [1] abettor, accomplice, cohort, confederate ♦ [2] accoutrement (*or* accouterment), adjunct, appendage, attachment

2accessory *adj* ♦ **:** aiding or contributing in a secondary way

♦ auxiliary, peripheral, supplementary

ac·ci·dent \ˈak-sə-dənt\ *n* **1** ♦ **:** an especially unfortunate event occurring by chance or unintentionally **2** ♦ **:** lack of intention or necessity **:** CHANCE ⟨met by ~⟩ **3 :** a nonessential property

♦ [1] casualty, mishap ♦ [2] chance, circumstance, hazard, luck

1ac·ci·den·tal \ˌak-sə-ˈdent-ᵊl\ *adj* **1** ♦ **:** happening unexpectedly or by chance **2 :** happening without intent or through carelessness — **ac·ci·den·tal·ly** \-ˈden-tə-lē\ *also* **ac·ci·dent·ly** \-ˈdent-lē\ *adv*

♦ casual, chance, fluky, fortuitous, incidental, unintended, unintentional, unplanned, unpremeditated, unwitting *Ant* deliberate, intended, intentional, planned, premeditated

2accidental *n* **:** a musical note foreign to a key indicated by a signature

1ac·claim \ə-ˈklām\ *vb* **1** ♦ **:** to express a favorable judgment of **:** APPLAUD, PRAISE **2 :** to declare by acclamation

♦ applaud, cheer, crack up, hail, laud, praise, salute, tout *Ant* knock, pan, slam

2acclaim *n* ♦ **:** the act of acclaiming

♦ accolade, credit, distinction, glory, homage, honor (*or* honour), laurels

ac·cla·ma·tion \ˌa-klə-ˈmā-shən\ *n* **1** ♦ **:** loud eager expression of approval, praise, or assent **2 :** an overwhelming affirmative vote by shouting or applause rather than by ballot

♦ applause, ovation

ac·cli·mate \ˈa-klə-ˌmāt, ə-ˈklī-mət\ *vb* **-mat·ed; -mat·ing** ♦ **:** to accustom or become accustomed to a new environment or situation — **ac·cli·ma·tion** \ˌa-klə-ˈmā-shən, -ˌklī-\ *n*

♦ accommodate, adapt, adjust, condition, conform, fit, shape

ac·cli·ma·tize \ə-ˈklī-mə-ˌtīz\ *vb* **-tized; -tiz·ing :** ACCLIMATE — **ac·cli·ma·ti·za·tion** \-ˌklī-mə-tə-ˈzā-shən\ *n*

ac·cliv·i·ty \ə-ˈkli-və-tē\ *n, pl* **-ties :** an ascending slope

ac·co·lade \ˈa-kə-ˌlād\ *n* ♦ **:** an expression of praise

♦ citation, commendation, encomium, eulogy, homage, paean, panegyric, salutation, tribute ♦ acclaim, credit, distinction, glory, homage, honor (*or* honour), laurels

ac·com·mo·date \ə-ˈkä-mə-ˌdāt\ *vb* **-dat·ed; -dat·ing** **1** ♦ **:** to make fit or suitable **:** ADAPT, ADJUST **2** ♦ **:** to bring into agreement or concord **:** HARMONIZE, RECONCILE **3 :** to provide with something needed **4** ♦ **:** to hold without crowding **5 :** to undergo visual accommodation

♦ [1] acclimate, adapt, adjust, condition, conform, fit, shape ♦ [2] conciliate, conform, coordinate, harmonize, key, reconcile ♦ [4] fit, hold, take

accommodating *adj* ♦ **:** willing to please **:** OBLIGING

♦ friendly, indulgent, obliging

ac·com·mo·da·tion \ə-ˌkä-mə-ˈdā-shən\ *n* **1 :** something supplied to satisfy a need; *esp* **:** LODGINGS — usually used in plural **2** ♦ **:** the act of accommodating **3 :** the automatic adjustment of the eye for seeing at different distances

♦ compromise, concession, give-and-take, negotiation

ac·com·pa·ni·ment \ə-ˈkəm-pə-nē-mənt, -ˈkəmp-nē-\ *n* **:** something that accompanies another; *esp* **:** subordinate music to support a principal voice or instrument

ac·com·pa·ny \-nē\ *vb* **-nied; -ny·ing** **1** ♦ **:** to go or occur with **:** ATTEND **2 :** to play an accompaniment for — **ac·com·pa·nist** \-nist\ *n*

♦ attend, convoy, escort, squire

ac·com·plice \ə-ˈkäm-pləs, -ˈkəm-\ *n* ♦ **:** an associate in crime

♦ abettor, accessory, cohort, confederate

ac·com·plish \ə-ˈkäm-plish, -ˈkəm-\ *vb* ♦ **:** to bring to completion — **ac·com·plish·er** *n*

♦ achieve, carry out, commit, compass, do, execute, follow through, fulfill, make, perform

ac·com·plished *adj* **1** ♦ **:** marked by proficiency **:** EXPERT, SKILLED **2 :** established beyond doubt

♦ ace, adept, crack, experienced, expert, master, masterful, masterly, practiced, proficient, seasoned, skilled, skillful

ac·com·plish·ment \ə-ˈkäm-plish-mənt, -ˈkəm-\ *n* **1** ♦ **:** the act of accomplishing **:** COMPLETION **2** ♦ **:** something completed or effected **:** ACHIEVEMENT **3 :** an acquired excellence or skill

♦ [1] achievement, actuality, attainment, consummation, fruition, fulfillment, realization ♦ [2] achievement, attainment, coup, success, triumph

1ac·cord \ə-ˈkȯrd\ *vb* **1** ♦ **:** to grant or give especially as appropriate, due, or earned **:** GRANT **2** ♦ **:** to be consistent or in harmony **:** AGREE, HARMONIZE — **ac·cor·dant** \-ˈkȯrd-ᵊnt\ *adj*

♦ [1] award, confer, grant ♦ [2] agree, coincide, comport, conform, correspond, fit, go, harmonize

2accord *n* **1** ♦ **:** the act or fact of agreeing or being in harmony **:** AGREEMENT, HARMONY **2** ♦ **:** willingness to act ⟨gave of their own ~⟩

♦ [1] agreement, conformity, consonance, harmony, tune ♦ [1] agreement, concurrence, consensus, unanimity ♦ [2] agreement, bargain, compact, contract, convention, covenant, deal, pact, settlement, understanding ♦ [2] choice, free will, option, self-determination, volition, will

ac·cor·dance \ə-ˈkȯrd-ᵊns\ *n* **1 :** the act or fact of agreeing or being in harmony **:** ACCORD **2 :** the act of granting

ac·cord·ing·ly \ə-ˈkȯr-diŋ-lē\ *adv* **1 :** in accordance **2** ♦ **:** as a result **:** CONSEQUENTLY, SO

♦ consequently, ergo, hence, so, therefore, thus, wherefore

according to *prep* **1 :** in conformity with ⟨paid *according to* ability⟩ **2 :** as stated or attested by ⟨*according to* you⟩

1ac·cor·di·on \ə-ˈkȯr-dē-ən\ *n* **:** a portable keyboard instrument with a bellows and reeds — **ac·cor·di·on·ist** \-ə-nist\ *n*

2accordion *adj* **:** folding like the bellows of an accordion ⟨~ pleats⟩

ac·cost \ə-ˈkȯst\ *vb* **:** to approach and speak to especially aggressively

1ac·count \ə-ˈkau̇nt\ *n* **1** ♦ **:** a statement of business transactions **2 :** a formal business arrangement for regular dealings or services **3 :** a statement of reasons, causes, or motives **4 :** value or importance especially as attributed by others **5** ♦ **:** a sum of money deposited in a bank and subject to withdrawal by the depositor **6** ♦ **:** a description of facts, conditions, or events — **on account of :** BECAUSE OF — **on no account :** under no circumstances — **on one's own account :** on one's own behalf

♦ [1] bill, check, invoice, statement, tab ♦ [5] budget, deposit, fund, kitty, nest egg, pool ♦ [6] chronicle, history, narrative, record, report, story

2account *vb* **1** ♦ **:** to think of as **:** CONSIDER ⟨I ~ him lucky⟩ **2** ♦ **:** to give an explanation — used with *for*

♦ [1] call, consider, count, esteem, hold, rate, reckon, regard, take ♦ *usu* **account for** [2] explain, rationalize

ac·count·able \ə-ˈkau̇n-tə-bəl\ *adj* **1** ♦ **:** subject to giving an account **:** ANSWERABLE, RESPONSIBLE **2 :** EXPLICABLE — **ac·count·abil·i·ty** \-ˌkau̇n-tə-ˈbi-lə-tē\ *n*

♦ answerable, liable, responsible

ac·coun·tant \ə-ˈkau̇nt-ᵊnt\ *n* **:** a person skilled in accounting — **ac·coun·tan·cy** \-ᵊn-sē\ *n*

account executive *n* : a business executive in charge of a client's account
ac•count•ing \ə-ˈkau̇n-tiŋ\ *n* : the art or system of keeping and analyzing financial records
ac•cou•tre *or* **ac•cou•ter** \ə-ˈkü-tər\ *vb* **-cou•tred** *or* **-cou•tered; -cou•tring** *or* **-cou•ter•ing** \-ˈkü-t(ə-)riŋ\ ♦ : to provide with equipment or furnishings : EQUIP, OUTFIT

♦ equip, fit, furnish, outfit, rig, supply

ac•cou•tre•ment *or* **ac•cou•ter•ment** \ə-ˈkü-trə-mənt, -ˈkü-tər-\ *n* **1** ♦ : an accessory item — usually used in plural **2** : an identifying characteristic

♦ accessory, adjunct, appendage, attachment ♦ *usu* **accoutrements** apparatus, equipment, gear, matériel, outfit, paraphernalia, tackle

ac•cred•it \ə-ˈkre-dət\ *vb* **1** ♦ : to endorse or approve officially **2** ♦ : to explain by indicating a cause : CREDIT — **ac•cred•i•ta•tion** \-ˌkre-də-ˈtā-shən\ *n*

♦ [1] authorize, certify, commission, empower, enable, invest, license, qualify ♦ [2] ascribe, attribute, credit, impute

ac•cre•tion \ə-ˈkrē-shən\ *n* **1** : growth or enlargement especially by addition from without **2** ♦ : a product of accretion

♦ addition, augmentation, boost, expansion, gain, increase, increment, plus, proliferation, raise, rise, supplement

ac•cru•al \ə-ˈkrü-əl\ *n* : something that accrues or has accrued
ac•crue \ə-ˈkrü\ *vb* **ac•crued; ac•cru•ing** **1** : to come by way of increase **2** : to be added by periodic growth
acct *abbr* account; accountant
ac•cul•tur•a•tion \ə-ˌkəl-chə-ˈrā-shən\ *n* : cultural modification of an individual or group by borrowing and adapting traits from another culture
ac•cu•mu•late \ə-ˈkyü-myə-ˌlāt\ *vb* **-lat•ed; -lat•ing** ♦ : to gather or pile up — **ac•cu•mu•la•tive** \-ˈkyü-myə-lə-tiv\ *adj* — **ac•cu•mu•la•tor** \-ˈkyü-myə-ˌlā-tər\ *n*

♦ appreciate, build, increase, mount, multiply, proliferate, rise ♦ amass, assemble, collect, gather, group, lump, pile, round up

ac•cu•mu•la•tion \-ˌkyü-myə-ˈlā-shən\ *n* **1** ♦ : something that has accumulated or has been accumulated **2** : the action or process of accumulating

♦ assemblage, collection, gathering

ac•cu•ra•cy \-rə-sē\ *n* ♦ : the quality, state, or degree of being accurate

♦ closeness, delicacy, exactness, fineness, precision, veracity

ac•cu•rate \ˈa-kyə-rət\ *adj* **1** ♦ : free from error : EXACT, PRECISE **2** ♦ : conforming exactly to truth or to a standard — **ac•cu•rate•ness** *n*

♦ [1] close, delicate, exact, fine, mathematical, pinpoint, precise, rigorous ♦ [2] correct, exact, precise, proper, right, so, true

ac•cu•rate•ly \ˈa-kyə-rət-lē\ *adv* ♦ : in an accurate manner

♦ exactly, just, precisely, right, sharp, squarely

ac•cursed \ə-ˈkərst, -ˈkər-səd\ *or* **ac•curst** \ə-ˈkərst\ *adj* **1** : being under a curse **2** : DAMNABLE, EXECRABLE
ac•cus•al \ə-ˈkyü-zəl\ *n* : ACCUSATION
ac•cu•sa•tive \ə-ˈkyü-zə-tiv\ *adj* : of, relating to, or being a grammatical case marking the direct object of a verb or the object of a preposition — **accusative** *n*
ac•cu•sa•to•ry \ə-ˈkyü-zə-ˌtȯr-ē\ *adj* : expressing accusation ⟨an ~ tone⟩
ac•cuse \ə-ˈkyüz\ *vb* **ac•cused; ac•cus•ing** ♦ : to charge with an offense : BLAME — **ac•cu•sa•tion** \ˌa-kyə-ˈzā-shən\ *n* — **ac•cus•er** *n*

♦ charge, incriminate, indict *Ant* absolve, acquit, clear, exculpate, exonerate, vindicate

ac•cused \ə-ˈkyüzd\ *n, pl* **accused** : the defendant in a criminal case
ac•cus•tom \ə-ˈkəs-təm\ *vb* ♦ : to make familiar with through use or experience

♦ acquaint, familiarize, initiate, introduce, orient

ac•cus•tomed \ə-ˈkəs-təmd\ *adj* **1** : USUAL, CUSTOMARY **2** ♦ : being in the habit or custom

♦ given, used, wont *Ant* unaccustomed, unused

¹ace \ˈās\ *n* **1** : a playing card bearing a single large pip in its center **2** : a very small amount or degree **3** : a point (as in tennis) won on a serve that goes untouched **4** : a golf score of one stroke on a hole **5** : a combat pilot who has downed five or more enemy planes **6** ♦ : one that excels in knowledge or skill

♦ authority, crackerjack, expert, maestro, master, virtuoso, whiz, wizard

²ace *vb* **aced; ac•ing** **1** : to score an ace against (an opponent) or on (a golf hole) **2** : to defeat decisively
³ace *adj* ♦ : of first or high rank or quality ⟨an ~ mechanic⟩

♦ accomplished, adept, crack, experienced, expert, master, skilled, skillful

ACE in•hib•i•tor \ˌā-ˌsē-ˈē-in-ˈhi-bə-tər, ˈās-\ *n* : any of a group of drugs that lower blood pressure by relaxing the arteries
acer•bic \ə-ˈsər-bik, a-\ *adj* : acid in temper, mood, or tone
acer•bi•ty \ə-ˈsər-bə-tē\ *n, pl* **-ties** : SOURNESS, BITTERNESS
acet•amin•o•phen \ə-ˌsē-tə-ˈmi-nə-fən\ *n* : a crystalline compound used in chemical synthesis and in medicine to relieve pain and fever
ac•e•tate \ˈa-sə-ˌtāt\ *n* **1** : a salt or ester of acetic acid **2** : a textile fiber made from cellulose and acetic acid; *also* : a fabric or plastic made of this fiber
ace•tic acid \ə-ˈsē-tik-\ *n* : a colorless pungent liquid acid that is the chief acid of vinegar and is used especially in making chemical compounds
ac•e•tone \ˈa-sə-ˌtōn\ *n* : a volatile flammable fragrant liquid compound used in making other chemical compounds and as a solvent
ace•tyl•cho•line \ə-ˌsēt-ᵊl-ˈkō-ˌlēn\ *n* : a compound that is released at nerve endings of the autonomic nervous system and is active in the transmission of nerve impulses
acet•y•lene \ə-ˈset-ᵊl-ən, -ᵊl-ˌēn\ *n* : a colorless flammable gas used as a fuel (as in welding and soldering)
ace•tyl•sal•i•cyl•ic acid \ə-ˈsēt-ᵊl-ˌsa-lə-ˌsi-lik-\ *n* : ASPIRIN 1
¹ache \ˈāk\ *vb* **ached; ach•ing** **1** ♦ : to suffer a usually dull persistent pain **2** ♦ : to experience a painful eagerness or yearning : LONG, YEARN ⟨he *ached* for that new car⟩ — **ache** *n*

♦ [1] hurt, pain, smart ♦ [2] die, hanker, hunger, itch, long, pant, pine, sigh, thirst, yearn ♦ *usu* **ache for** [2] crave, desire, die for, hanker for, hunger for, long for, lust (for *or* after), pine for, repine for, thirst for, want, wish for, yearn for

²ache *n* ♦ : a usually dull persistent pain

♦ pain, pang, prick, smart, sting, stitch, tingle, twinge

achiev•able \-ˈchē-və-bəl\ *adj* ♦ : capable of being achieved

♦ attainable, doable, feasible, possible, practicable, realizable, viable, workable

achieve \ə-ˈchēv\ *vb* **achieved; achiev•ing** **1** ♦ : to carry out successfully : ACCOMPLISH **2** ♦ : to gain by work or effort — **achiev•er** *n*

♦ [1] accomplish, carry out, commit, compass, do, execute, follow through, fulfill, make, perform ♦ [2] attain, hit, make, score, win

achieve•ment \ə-ˈchēv-mənt\ *n* **1** ♦ : the act of achieving **2** ♦ : a result gained by effort

♦ [1] accomplishment, attainment, success ♦ [2] accomplishment, attainment, coup, success, triumph

Achil•les' heel \ə-ˌki-lēz-\ *n* : a vulnerable point
Achil•les tendon \ə-ˌki-lēz-\ *n* : the tendon joining the muscles in the calf of the leg to the bone of the heel
ach•ing *adj* ♦ : afflicted with aches

♦ achy, nasty, painful, sore

ach•ro•mat•ic \ˌa-krə-ˈma-tik\ *adj* : giving an image almost free from extraneous colors ⟨~ lens⟩
achy \ˈā-kē\ *adj* **ach•i•er; ach•i•est** ♦ : afflicted with aches — **ach•i•ness** *n*

♦ aching, nasty, painful, sore

¹ac•id \ˈa-səd\ *adj* **1** ♦ : sour or biting to the taste **2** : of or relating to an acid **3** ♦ : sharp, biting, or sour in manner, disposition, or nature — **acid•ly** *adv*

♦ [1, 3] acidic, sour, tart, vinegary

²acid *n* **1** : a sour substance **2** : a usually water-soluble chemical compound that has a sour taste, reacts with a base to form a salt, and reddens litmus **3** : LSD
acid•ic \ə-ˈsi-dik\ *adj* ♦ : sour or biting to the taste; *also* : sharp or sour in manner

♦ acid, sour, tart, vinegary

acid•i•fy \ə-ˈsi-də-ˌfī\ *vb* **-fied; -fy•ing** **1 :** to make or become acid **2 :** to change into an acid — **acid•i•fi•ca•tion** \-ˌsi-də-fə-ˈkā-shən\ *n*

acid•i•ty \ə-ˈsi-də-tē\ *n* ♦ **:** the quality, state, or degree of being acid

♦ acrimony, asperity, bitterness, cattiness, tartness, virulence, vitriol

ac•i•do•sis \ˌa-sə-ˈdō-səs\ *n, pl* **-do•ses** \-ˌsēz\ **:** an abnormal state of reduced alkalinity of the blood and body tissues

acid precipitation *n* **:** precipitation with above normal acidity that is caused especially by atmospheric pollutants

acid rain *n* **:** acid precipitation in the form of rain

acid test *n* **:** a severe or crucial test

acid•u•lous \ə-ˈsi-jə-ləs\ *adj* **:** somewhat acid or harsh in taste or manner

ack *abbr* acknowledge; acknowledgment

ac•knowl•edge \ik-ˈnä-lij, ak-\ *vb* **-edged; -edg•ing** **1 :** to recognize the rights or authority of **2 :** to admit as true **3 :** to express thanks for; *also* **:** to report receipt of **4** ♦ **:** to recognize as genuine or valid

♦ admit, agree, allow, concede, confess, grant, own

ac•knowl•edg•ment *or* **ac•knowl•edge•ment** \-mənt\ *n* **1** ♦ **:** the act of acknowledging **2 :** recognition or favorable notice of an act or achievement

♦ admission, avowal, concession, confession

ACL \ˌā-ˌsē-ˈel\ *n* **:** ANTERIOR CRUCIATE LIGAMENT

ACLU *abbr* American Civil Liberties Union

ac•me \ˈak-mē\ *n* ♦ **:** the highest point

♦ apex, climax, crown, culmination, head, height, meridian, peak, pinnacle, summit, tip-top, top, zenith

ac•ne \ˈak-nē\ *n* **:** a skin disorder marked by inflammation of skin glands and hair follicles and by pimple formation especially on the face

ac•o•lyte \ˈa-kə-ˌlīt\ *n* **1 :** one who assists a member of the clergy in a liturgical service **2 :** FOLLOWER

ac•o•nite \ˈa-kə-ˌnīt\ *n* **1 :** MONKSHOOD **2 :** a drug obtained from a common Old World monkshood

acorn \ˈā-ˌkȯrn, -kərn\ *n* **:** the nut of the oak

acorn squash *n* **:** an acorn-shaped dark green winter squash with a ridged surface

acous•tic \ə-ˈkü-stik\ *or* **acous•ti•cal** \-sti-kəl\ *adj* **1** ♦ **:** of or relating to the sense or organs of hearing, to sound, or to the science of sounds **2 :** deadening sound ⟨~ tile⟩ **3 :** operated by or utilizing sound waves — **acous•ti•cal•ly** \-k(ə-)lē\ *adv*

♦ auditory, aural, auricular

acous•tics \ə-ˈkü-stiks\ *n sing or pl* **1 :** the science of sound **2 :** the qualities in a room that make it easy or hard for a person in it to hear distinctly

ac•quaint \ə-ˈkwānt\ *vb* **1** ♦ **:** to cause to know personally **2** ♦ **:** to make familiar **:** to cause to know firsthand

♦ [1, 2] accustom, apprise, brief, clue, familiarize, fill in, inform, initiate, introduce, orient

ac•quain•tance \ə-ˈkwān-tᵊns\ *n* **1** ♦ **:** personal knowledge **2 :** a person with whom one is acquainted — **ac•quain•tance•ship** *n*

♦ cognizance, familiarity *Ant* unfamiliarity

ac•qui•esce \ˌa-kwē-ˈes\ *vb* **-esced; -esc•ing** ♦ **:** to accept, comply, or submit without open opposition — **ac•qui•es•cence** \-ˈes-ᵊns\ *n* — **ac•qui•es•cent•ly** *adv*

♦ accede, agree, assent, come round, consent, subscribe (to)

ac•qui•es•cent \-ᵊnt\ *adj* ♦ **:** inclined to acquiesce

♦ passive, resigned, tolerant, unresistant, unresisting, yielding

ac•quir•able \-ˈkwī-rə-bəl\ *adj* ♦ **:** capable of being acquired

♦ accessible, attainable, available, obtainable, procurable

ac•quire \ə-ˈkwīr\ *vb* **ac•quired; ac•quir•ing** ♦ **:** to gain possession of

♦ cultivate, develop, form ♦ attain, capture, carry, draw, earn, gain, garner, get, land, make, obtain, procure, realize, secure, win

ac•quired \ə-ˈkwīrd\ *adj* **1 :** gained by or as a result of effort or experience **2 :** caused by environmental forces and not passed from parent to offspring in the genes ⟨~ characteristics⟩

acquired immune deficiency syndrome *n* **:** AIDS

acquired immunodeficiency syndrome *n* **:** AIDS

ac•quire•ment \ə-ˈkwī(-ə)r-mənt\ *n* **1** ♦ **:** something that has been accomplished **:** ACHIEVEMENT, ACCOMPLISHMENT **2 :** the act of acquiring

♦ accomplishment, achievement, attainment, coup, success, triumph

ac•qui•si•tion \ˌa-kwə-ˈzi-shən\ *n* **1 :** ACQUIREMENT **2 :** something acquired

ac•quis•i•tive \ə-ˈkwi-zə-tiv\ *adj* ♦ **:** eager to acquire **:** GREEDY — **ac•quis•i•tive•ly** *adv*

♦ avaricious, avid, covetous, grasping, greedy, mercenary, rapacious

ac•quis•i•tive•ness \-nəs\ *n* ♦ **:** the quality or state of being acquisitive

♦ avarice, avidity, covetousness, cupidity, greed, rapaciousness

ac•quit \ə-ˈkwit\ *vb* **ac•quit•ted; ac•quit•ting** **1** ♦ **:** to pronounce not guilty **2** ♦ **:** to conduct (oneself) usually satisfactorily

♦ [1] absolve, clear, exculpate, exonerate, vindicate
♦ [2] bear, behave, comport, conduct, demean, deport, quit

ac•quit•tal \ə-ˈkwit-ᵊl\ *n* ♦ **:** a setting free from the charge of an offense by verdict, sentence, or other legal process

♦ exculpation, exoneration, vindication *Ant* conviction

acre \ˈā-kər\ *n* **1** *pl* **:** an area of land under individual ownership **:** ESTATE **2 :** a unit of land measure equal to 43,560 square feet

acre•age \ˈā-k(ə-)rij\ *n* **:** area in acres

ac•rid \ˈa-krəd\ *adj* **1 :** sharp and biting in taste or odor **2** ♦ **:** deeply bitter **:** marked by incisive sarcasm **:** CAUSTIC — **acrid•i•ty** \a-ˈkri-də-tē\ *n* — **ac•rid•ly** *adv*

♦ acrimonious, bitter, hard, rancorous, resentful, sore ♦ biting, caustic, cutting, mordant, sarcastic, satiric, scathing, sharp

ac•rid•ness \-nəs\ *n* **:** the quality or state of being acrid

ac•ri•mo•ni•ous \ˌa-krə-ˈmō-nē-əs\ *adj* ♦ **:** caustic, biting, or rancorous especially in feeling, language, or manner

♦ acrid, bitter, hard, rancorous, resentful, sore

ac•ri•mo•ni•ous•ness \-nəs\ *n* **:** the quality or state of being acrimonious

ac•ri•mo•ny \ˈa-krə-ˌmō-nē\ *n, pl* **-nies** ♦ **:** harsh or biting sharpness especially of words, manner, or disposition — **ac•ri•mo•ni•ous•ly** *adv*

♦ acidity, asperity, bitterness, cattiness, tartness, virulence, vitriol

ac•ro•bat \ˈa-krə-ˌbat\ *n* **:** a performer of gymnastic feats — **ac•ro•bat•ic** \ˌa-krə-ˈba-tik\ *adj* — **ac•ro•bat•i•cal•ly** \-ti-k(ə-)lē\ *adv*

ac•ro•bat•ics \ˌa-krə-ˈba-tiks\ *n sing or pl* **:** the performance of an acrobat

ac•ro•nym \ˈa-krə-ˌnim\ *n* **:** a word (as *radar*) formed from the initial letter or letters of each of the successive parts or major parts of a compound term

ac•ro•pho•bia \ˌa-krə-ˈfō-bē-ə\ *n* **:** abnormal dread of being at a great height

acrop•o•lis \ə-ˈkrä-pə-ləs\ *n* **:** the upper fortified part of an ancient Greek city

¹across \ə-ˈkrȯs\ *adv* **1** ♦ **:** to or on the opposite side **2 :** so as to be understandable ⟨get the point ~⟩

♦ over, through

²across *prep* **1** ♦ **:** to or on the opposite side of ⟨ran ~ the street⟩ **2 :** on so as to cross or pass at an angle ⟨a log ~ the road⟩

♦ athwart, over, through

across–the–board *adj* **1 :** placed to win if a competitor wins, places, or shows ⟨an ~ bet⟩ **2 :** including all classes or categories ⟨an ~ wage increase⟩

acros•tic \ə-ˈkrȯs-tik\ *n* **:** a composition usually in verse in which the initial or final letters of the lines taken in order form a word or phrase — **acrostic** *adj*

acryl•ic \ə-ˈkri-lik\ *n* **1 :** ACRYLIC RESIN **2 :** a paint in which the vehicle is acrylic resin **3 :** a quick-drying synthetic textile fiber

acrylic resin *n* **:** a glassy thermoplastic used for cast and molded parts or as coatings and adhesives

¹act \ˈakt\ *n* **1** ♦ **:** a thing done **:** DEED **2** ♦ **:** the formal product of a legislative body **:** STATUTE; *also* **:** a decision or determination of a sovereign, a legislative council, or a court of justice **3 :** a main division of a play; *also* **:** an item on a variety program **4** ♦ **:** an instance of insincere behavior **:** PRETENSE

♦ [1] action, deed, doing, exploit, feat, thing ♦ [2] enactment, law, ordinance, statute ♦ [4] airs, facade, front, guise, masquerade, pose, pretense, put-on, semblance, show

²**act** *vb* **1** ♦ **:** to perform by action especially on the stage; *also* **:** to make a pretense of **:** FEIGN, SIMULATE, PRETEND **2 :** to take action **3** ♦ **:** to conduct oneself or behave in a certain manner ⟨how did she ~ toward you⟩ **4** ♦ **:** to perform a specified function **5** ♦ **:** to produce an effect

♦ [1] impersonate, perform, play, portray ♦ *usu* **act toward** [3] be, deal, handle, serve, treat, use ♦ [4] function, perform, serve, work ♦ [5] appear, look, make, seem, sound ♦ [5] function, operate, perform, take, work

³**act** *abbr* **1** active **2** actual
ACT *abbr* Australian Capital Territory
actg *abbr* acting
ACTH \ˌā-(ˌ)sē-(ˌ)tē-ˈāch\ *n* **:** a protein hormone of the pituitary gland that stimulates the adrenal cortex
act•ing \ˈak-tiŋ\ *adj* ♦ **:** doing duty temporarily or for another ⟨~ president⟩

♦ interim, provisional, temporary *Ant* long-term, permanent

ac•tin•i•um \ak-ˈti-nē-əm\ *n* **:** a radioactive metallic chemical element
ac•tion \ˈak-shən\ *n* **1** ♦ **:** a legal proceeding **2 :** the manner or method of performing **3 :** ACTIVITY **4** ♦ **:** a thing done **:** ACT, DEED **5 :** the accomplishment of a thing usually over a period of time, in stages, or with the possibility of repetition **6** *pl* ♦ **:** the deportment and expression of one that acts or speaks **:** CONDUCT **7 :** combat in war **:** BATTLE **8 :** the events of a literary plot **9 :** an operating mechanism ⟨the ~ of a gun⟩; *also* **:** the way it operates ⟨stiff ~⟩

♦ [1] lawsuit, proceeding, suit ♦ [4] act, deed, doing, exploit, feat, thing ♦ *usu* **actions** [6] bearing, behavior (*or* behaviour), comportment, conduct, demeanor (*or* demeanour), deportment

ac•tion•able \ˈak-sh(ə-)nə-bəl\ *adj* **:** affording ground for an action or suit at law — **ac•tion•ably** \-blē\ *adv*
action figure *n* **:** a small-scale figure (as of a superhero) used especially as a toy
ac•ti•vate \ˈak-tə-ˌvāt\ *vb* **-vat•ed; -vat•ing** **1** ♦ **:** to spur into action; *also* **:** to make active, reactive, or radioactive **2 :** to treat (as carbon) so as to improve adsorptive properties **3 :** to set up (a military unit) formally; *also* **:** to call to active duty — **ac•ti•va•tion** \ˌak-tə-ˈvā-shən\ *n* — **ac•ti•va•tor** \ˈak-tə-ˌvā-tər\ *n*

♦ actuate, crank, drive, move, propel, run, set off, spark, start, touch off, trigger, turn on *Ant* cut, deactivate, kill, shut off, turn off

ac•tive \ˈak-tiv\ *adj* **1 :** causing or involving action or change **2 :** asserting that the grammatical subject performs the action represented by the verb ⟨~ voice⟩ **3** ♦ **:** briskly alert and energetic **:** BRISK, LIVELY **4** ♦ **:** marked by vigorous activity **:** BUSY **5 :** erupting or likely to erupt ⟨~ volcano⟩ **6** ♦ **:** presently in operation or use **7 :** tending to progress or to cause degeneration ⟨~ tuberculosis⟩ — **active** *n* — **ac•tive•ly** *adv* — **ac•tive•ness** *n*

♦ [3] animate, animated, brisk, energetic, lively, spirited, sprightly, springy ♦ [4] assiduous, busy, diligent, engaged, laborious, occupied, sedulous, working ♦ [6] alive, functional, living, on, operational, operative, running, working *Ant* broken, dead, inactive, inoperative, nonfunctional

ac•tiv•ism \ˈak-ti-ˌvi-zəm\ *n* **:** a doctrine or practice that emphasizes vigorous action for political ends — **ac•tiv•ist** \-vist\ *n or adj*
ac•tiv•i•ty \ak-ˈti-və-tē\ *n, pl* **-ties** **1 :** the quality or state of being active **2** ♦ **:** forceful or energetic action **3 :** an occupation in which one is engaged

♦ exercise, exertion

ac•tor \ˈak-tər\ *n* ♦ **:** a person who acts (as in a play, movie, or television show)

♦ impersonator, mummer, player, trouper

act out *vb* ♦ **:** to behave badly or in a socially unacceptable often self-defeating manner especially as a means of venting painful emotions (as fear or frustration)

♦ act up, carry on, misbehave

ac•tress \ˈak-trəs\ *n* **:** a woman who is an actor
Acts \ˈakts\ *or* **Acts of the Apostles** *n* **:** a book of the New Testament of the Christian Scripture
ac•tu•al \ˈak-chə-wəl, -shə-\ *adj* ♦ **:** really existing **:** REAL

♦ concrete, existent, factual, real, true, very *Ant* hypothetical, ideal, nonexistent, theoretical

ac•tu•al•i•ty \ˌak-chə-ˈwa-lə-tē, -shə-\ *n* ♦ **:** the quality or state of being actual

♦ existence, reality, subsistence ♦ accomplishment, achievement, attainment, consummation, fruition, fulfillment, realization

ac•tu•al•ize \ˈak-chə-wə-ˌlīz, -shə-\ *vb* ♦ **:** to become actual — **ac•tu•al•iza•tion** \ˌak-chə-wə-lə-ˈzā-shən, -shə-\ *n*

♦ begin, commence, get off, launch, open, start

ac•tu•al•ly \ˈak-chə-wə-lē, -shə-\ *adv* **1** ♦ **:** in fact or in truth **:** REALLY **2** ♦ **:** in point of fact — used to suggest something unexpected

♦ [1] admittedly, frankly, honestly, really, truly, truthfully, verily ♦ [2] authentically, genuinely, really, veritably, very

ac•tu•ary \ˈak-chə-ˌwer-ē, -shə-\ *n, pl* **-ar•ies** **:** a person who calculates insurance risks and premiums — **ac•tu•ar•i•al** \ˌak-chə-ˈwer-ē-əl, -shə-\ *adj*
ac•tu•ate \ˈak-chə-ˌwāt\ *vb* **-at•ed; -at•ing** **1** ♦ **:** to put into mechanical action **2** ♦ **:** to move to action — **ac•tu•a•tion** \ˌak-chə-ˈwā-shən, -shə-\ *n* — **ac•tu•a•tor** \ˈak-chə-ˌwā-tər, -shə-\ *n*

♦ [1] activate, crank, drive, move, propel, run, set off, spark, start, touch off, trigger, turn on ♦ [2] drive, impel, move, propel, work

act up *vb* **1 a** ♦ **:** to behave in an unruly, recalcitrant, or capricious manner **:** MISBEHAVE **b** ♦ **:** to seek to attract attention by conspicuous behavior **2 :** to function improperly

♦ [1a] act out, carry on, misbehave ♦ [1b] clown (around), cut up, fool around, monkey, show off, skylark

acu•ity \ə-ˈkyü-ə-tē\ *n, pl* **-ities** ♦ **:** keenness of perception

♦ acuteness, delicacy, keenness, sensitiveness, sensitivity

acu•men \ə-ˈkyü-mən\ *n* ♦ **:** mental keenness and penetration

♦ astuteness, caginess, canniness, hardheadedness, intelligence, keenness, sharpness, shrewdness, wit

acu•pres•sure \ˈa-kyu̇-ˌpre-shər\ *n* **:** the application of pressure (as with the thumbs or fingertips) to the same discrete points on the body stimulated in acupuncture that is used for its therapeutic effects (as the relief of tension or pain)
acu•punc•ture \-ˌpəŋk-chər\ *n* **:** an orig. Chinese practice of puncturing the body (as with needles) at specific points to cure disease or relieve pain — **acu•punc•tur•ist** \ˌa-kyu̇-ˈpəŋk-chə-rist\ *n*
acute \ə-ˈkyüt\ *adj* **acut•er; acut•est** **1 :** SHARP, POINTED **2 :** containing less than 90 degrees ⟨an ~ angle⟩ **3** ♦ **:** sharply perceptive; *esp* **:** mentally keen **4 a** ♦ **:** characterized by sharpness or severity **:** SEVERE ⟨~ distress⟩ **b** ♦ **:** having a sudden onset, sharp rise, and short duration ⟨~ inflammation⟩ **5** ♦ **:** high in pitch **6 :** of, marked by, or being an accent mark having the form ´ — **acute•ly** *adv* — *n*

♦ [3] delicate, keen, perceptive, sensitive, sharp ♦ [4a] agonizing, biting, excruciating, severe, sharp ♦ [4b] critical, dire, imperative, imperious, instant, pressing, urgent *Ant* noncritical ♦ [5] sharp, shrill, squeaky, treble

acute•ness \-nəs\ *n* ♦ **:** the quality or state of being acute

♦ acuity, delicacy, keenness, sensitiveness, sensitivity

acy•clo•vir \(ˌ)ā-ˈsī-klō-ˌvir\ *n* **:** a drug used especially to treat the genital form of herpes simplex
ad \ˈad\ *n* **:** a public notice **:** ADVERTISEMENT
AD *abbr* **1** after date **2** in the year of our Lord — often printed in small capitals and often punctuated **3** assistant director **4** athletic director
ad•age \ˈa-dij\ *n* ♦ **:** an old familiar saying **:** PROVERB, MAXIM

♦ aphorism, byword, epigram, maxim, proverb, saying

¹**ada•gio** \ə-ˈdä-j(ē-ˌ)ō, -zh(ē-ˌ)ō\ *adv or adj* **:** at a slow tempo — used as a direction in music
²**adagio** *n, pl* **-gios** **1 :** an adagio movement **2 :** a ballet duet or trio displaying feats of lifting and balancing
¹**ad•a•mant** \ˈa-də-mənt, -ˌmant\ *n* **:** a stone believed to be impenetrably hard
²**adamant** *adj* ♦ **:** unshakable or insistent especially in maintaining a position or opinion **:** INFLEXIBLE, UNYIELDING — **ad•a•mant•ly** *adv*

♦ hard, immovable, implacable, inflexible, pat, rigid, unbending, uncompromising, unrelenting, unyielding

ad•a•man•tine \ˌa-də-ˈman-ˌtēn, -ˌtīn\ *adj* : rigidly firm : UNYIELDING
Ad•am's apple \ˈa-dəmz-\ *n* : the projection in front of the neck formed by the largest cartilage of the larynx
adapt \ə-ˈdapt\ *vb* ♦ : to make suitable or fit (as for a new use or for different conditions) — **ad•ap•ta•tion** \ˌa-ˌdap-ˈtā-shən\ *n* — **ad•ap•ta•tion•al** \-sh(ə-)nəl\ *adj* — **adap•tive** \ə-ˈdap-tiv\ *adj* — **ad•ap•tiv•i•ty** \ˌa-ˌdap-ˈti-və-tē\ *n*

♦ acclimate, accommodate, adjust, condition, conform, fit, shape

adapt•able \ə-ˈdap-tə-bəl\ *adj* ♦ : capable of being or becoming adapted — **adapt•abil•i•ty** \ə-ˌdap-tə-ˈbi-lə-tē\ *n*

♦ protean, universal, versatile ♦ adjustable, changeable, elastic, flexible, fluid, malleable, variable

adapt•er *also* **adap•tor** \ə-ˈdap-tər\ *n* **1** : one that adapts **2** : a device for connecting two dissimilar parts of an apparatus **3** ♦ : an attachment for adapting an apparatus for uses not orig. intended

♦ *also* **adaptor** ♦ accessory, accoutrement (*or* accouterment), adjunct, appendage, attachment, option

ADC *abbr* **1** aide-de-camp **2** Aid to Dependent Children
add \ˈad\ *vb* **1** ♦ : to join to something else so as to increase in number or amount **2** : to say further ⟨let me ~ this⟩ **3** ♦ : to combine (numbers) into one sum **4** ♦ : to serve as or make an addition ⟨the TV appearance *added* to his fame⟩ ⟨*added* to her savings⟩

♦ [1] adjoin, annex, append, tack ***Ant*** deduct, remove, subtract, take ♦ [3] foot, sum, total ♦ *usu* **add to** [4] aggrandize, amplify, augment, boost, compound, enlarge, escalate, expand, extend, increase, multiply, raise, swell, up

ADD *abbr* attention deficit disorder
ad•dend \ˈa-ˌdend\ *n* : a number to be added to another
ad•den•dum \ə-ˈden-dəm\ *n, pl* **-da** \-də\ : something added; *esp* : a supplement to a book
¹ad•der \ˈa-dər\ *n* **1** : a poisonous European viper or a related snake **2** : any of various harmless No. American snakes (as the hognose snake)
²add•er \ˈa-dər\ *n* : one that adds; *esp* : a device that performs addition
¹ad•dict \ə-ˈdikt\ *vb* **1** : to devote or surrender (oneself) to something habitually or excessively **2** : to cause addiction to a substance in (as a person) — **ad•dic•tive** \-ˈdik-tiv\ *adj*
²ad•dict \ˈa-(ˌ)dikt\ *n* **1** ♦ : one who is addicted especially to a substance **2** ♦ : an ardent follower, supporter, or enthusiast

♦ [1] doper, fiend, user ♦ [2] aficionado, buff, bug, devotee, enthusiast, fan, fanatic, fancier, fiend, freak, lover, maniac, nut

ad•dic•tion \ə-ˈdik-shən\ *n* **1** : the quality or state of being addicted **2** : compulsive need for and use of a habit-forming substance (as heroin, nicotine, or alcohol) characterized by well-defined physiological symptoms upon withdrawal; *also* : persistent compulsive use of a substance known by the user to be harmful
ad•di•tion \ə-ˈdi-shən\ *n* **1** ♦ : the act or process of adding; *also* : something added **2** : the operation of combining numbers to obtain their sum

♦ annex, extension, penthouse ♦ accretion, augmentation, boost, expansion, gain, increase, increment, plus, proliferation, raise, rise, supplement

ad•di•tion•al \ə-ˈdi-sh(ə-)nəl\ *adj* ♦ : coming by way of addition : ADDED

♦ another, else, farther, further, more, other

ad•di•tion•al•ly \ə-ˈdi-sh(ə-)nə-lē\ *adv* ♦ : in or by way of addition : FURTHERMORE

♦ again, also, besides, further, furthermore, likewise, more, moreover, then, too, withal, yet

¹ad•di•tive \ˈa-də-tiv\ *adj* **1** : of, relating to, or characterized by addition **2** : produced by addition — **ad•di•tiv•i•ty** \ˌa-də-ˈti-və-tē\ *n*
²additive *n* : a substance added to another in small quantities to effect a desired change in properties ⟨food ~*s*⟩
ad•dle \ˈad-ᵊl\ *vb* **ad•dled; ad•dling** **1** ♦ : to throw into confusion : MUDDLE **2** : to become rotten ⟨*addled* eggs⟩

♦ baffle, befog, befuddle, bemuse, bewilder, confound, confuse, disorient, muddle, muddy, mystify, perplex, puzzle

addn *abbr* addition
addnl *abbr* additional

add–on \ˈad-ˌȯn, -ˌän\ *n* : something (as a feature or accessory) added especially as an enhancement
¹ad•dress \ə-ˈdres\ *vb* **1** ♦ : to direct the attention of (oneself) **2** : to direct one's remarks to : deliver an address to **3** : to mark directions for delivery on **4** : to identify (as a memory location) by an address

♦ apply, bend, buckle, devote, give

²ad•dress \ə-ˈdres, ˈa-ˌdres\ *n* **1** : skillful management **2** ♦ : a formal speech **3** : the place where a person or organization may be communicated with **4** : the directions for delivery placed on mail; *also* : the designation of a computer account for sending and receiving e-mail **5** : a location (as in a computer's memory) where particular data is stored

♦ declamation, harangue, oration, speech, talk

ad•dress•ee \ˌa-ˌdre-ˈsē, ə-ˌdre-ˈsē\ *n* : one to whom something is addressed
ad•duce \ə-ˈdüs, -ˈdyüs\ *vb* **ad•duced; ad•duc•ing** ♦ : to offer as example, reason, or proof — **ad•duc•er** *n*

♦ cite, instance, mention, quote

add up *vb* **1** ♦ : to come to the expected total **2** ♦ : to reach in kind or quality — used with *to*

♦ *usu* **add up to** [1] amount (to), come, number, sum, total
♦ *usu* **add up to** [2] amount, come, correspond, equal

-ade *n suffix* **1** : act : action ⟨block*ade*⟩ **2** : product; *esp* : sweet drink ⟨lime*ade*⟩
ad•e•nine \ˈad-ᵊn-ˌēn\ *n* : one of the purine bases that make up the genetic code of DNA and RNA
ad•e•noid \ˈad-ˌnȯid, -ᵊn-ˌȯid\ *n* : an enlarged mass of tissue near the opening of the nose into the throat — usually used in plural — **adenoid** *or* **ad•e•noi•dal** \ˌad-ˈnȯi-dəl, -ᵊn-ˈȯi-\ *adj*
aden•o•sine tri•phos•phate \ə-ˈde-nə-ˌsēn-trī-ˈfäs-ˌfāt\ *n* : ATP
¹ad•ept \ˈa-ˌdept\ *n* ♦ : a highly skilled or well-trained individual : EXPERT

♦ artist, authority, expert, master, virtuoso, whiz, wizard

²adept \ə-ˈdept\ *adj* ♦ : highly skilled : EXPERT

♦ accomplished, ace, crack, experienced, expert, master, masterful, masterly, practiced, proficient, seasoned, skilled, skillful, versed

adept•ly \ə-ˈdep(t)-lē\ *adv* ♦ : in an adept manner

♦ ably, capably, expertly, masterfully, proficiently, skillfully, well

adept•ness \-ˈdep(t)-nəs\ *n* ♦ : the quality or state of being adept

♦ adroitness, art, artfulness, artifice, artistry, cleverness, craft, cunning, deftness, masterfulness, skill

ad•e•qua•cy \ˈa-di-kwə-sē\ *n* : the quality or state of being adequate
ad•e•quate \ˈa-di-kwət\ *adj* ♦ : equal to or sufficient for a specific requirement — **ad•e•quate•ness** *n*

♦ acceptable, all right, decent, fine, OK, passable, respectable, satisfactory, tolerable ***Ant*** deficient, inadequate, lacking, unacceptable, unsatisfactory, wanting

ad•e•quate•ly \-lē\ *adv* ♦ : in an adequate manner

♦ enough, satisfactorily

ad•here \ad-ˈhir\ *vb* **ad•hered; ad•her•ing** **1** ♦ : to give support : maintain loyalty **2** ♦ : to stick fast : CLING

♦ *usu* **adhere to** [1] cling, hew, keep, stick ***Ant*** defect (from)
♦ [2] cling, hew, stick

ad•her•ence \-ˈhir-əns\ *n* ♦ : the act, action, or quality of adhering

♦ adhesion, cohesion

¹ad•her•ent \-ənt\ *adj* : able or tending to adhere
²ad•her•ent *n* ♦ : one that adheres: as **a** : a follower of a leader, party, or profession **b** : a believer in or advocate especially of a particular idea or church

♦ convert, disciple, follower, partisan, pupil, votary

ad•he•sion \ad-ˈhē-zhən\ *n* **1** ♦ : the act or state of adhering **2** : the union of bodily tissues abnormally grown together after inflammation; *also* : the newly formed uniting tissue **3** : the molecular attraction between the surfaces of bodies in contact

♦ adherence, cohesion

¹ad•he•sive \-ˈhē-siv, -ziv\ *adj* **1** ♦ : tending to adhere : STICKY **2** : prepared for adhering

♦ gelatinous, gluey, glutinous, gooey, gummy, sticky, viscid, viscous

²adhesive *n* ♦ : an adhesive substance

♦ cement, glue, size

adhesive tape *n* : tape coated on one side with an adhesive mixture; *esp* : one used for covering wounds
¹ad hoc \ˈad-ˈhäk, -ˈhōk\ *adv* : for the case at hand apart from other applications
²ad hoc *adj* : concerned with or formed for a particular purpose ⟨an *ad hoc* committee⟩ ⟨*ad hoc* solutions⟩
adi•a•bat•ic \ˌa-dē-ə-ˈba-tik\ *adj* : occurring without loss or gain of heat — **adi•a•bat•i•cal•ly** \-ti-k(ə-)lē\ *adv*
adieu \ə-ˈdü, -ˈdyü\ *n, pl* **adieus** *or* **adieux** \ə-ˈdüz, -ˈdyüz\ ♦ : a wish of well-being at parting : FAREWELL — often used interjectionally

♦ au revoir, bon voyage, farewell, good-bye

ad in•fi•ni•tum \ˌad-ˌin-fə-ˈnī-təm\ *adv or adj* : without end or limit
ad in•ter•im \ad-ˈin-tə-rəm, -ˌrim\ *adv* : for the intervening time — **ad interim** *adj*
adi•os \ˌa-dē-ˈōs, ˌä-\ *interj* — used to express farewell
ad•i•pose \ˈa-də-ˌpōs\ *adj* : of or relating to animal fat : FATTY
adj *abbr* **1** adjective **2** adjutant
ad•ja•cent \ə-ˈjās-ᵊnt\ *adj* ♦ : situated near or next — **ad•ja•cent•ly** *adv*

♦ adjoining, contiguous, touching *Ant* nonadjacent

ad•jec•tive \ˈa-jik-tiv\ *n* : a word that typically serves as a modifier of a noun — **ad•jec•ti•val** \ˌa-jik-ˈtī-vəl\ *adj* — **ad•jec•ti•val•ly** *adv*
ad•join \ə-ˈjȯin\ *vb* **1** ♦ : to add or attach by joining **2** ♦ : to be situated next to

♦ [1] add, annex, append, tack ♦ [2] abut, border (on), flank, fringe, join, skirt, touch, verge (on)

ad•join•ing *adj* ♦ : touching or bounding at a point or line

♦ adjacent, contiguous, touching

ad•journ \ə-ˈjərn\ *vb* **1** ♦ : to suspend indefinitely or until a stated time **2** : to transfer to another place — **ad•journ•ment** *n*

♦ break off, discontinue, interrupt, recess, suspend

ad•judge \ə-ˈjəj\ *vb* **ad•judged; ad•judg•ing 1** : to decide or rule upon as a judge : JUDGE, ADJUDICATE **2** : to hold or pronounce to be : DEEM **3** : to award by judicial decision
ad•ju•di•cate \ə-ˈjü-di-ˌkāt\ *vb* **-cat•ed; -cat•ing** ♦ : to pass judgment on : to settle judicially — **ad•ju•di•ca•tion** \ə-ˌjü-di-ˈkā-shən\ *n*

♦ arbitrate, decide, determine, judge, referee, rule, settle, umpire

ad•junct \ˈa-ˌjəŋkt\ *n* ♦ : something joined or added to another but not essentially a part of it

♦ accessory, accoutrement (*or* accoutermant), adapter, appendage, attachment

ad•jure \ə-ˈju̇r\ *vb* **ad•jured; ad•jur•ing** : to command solemnly : urge earnestly — **ad•ju•ra•tion** \ˌa-jə-ˈrā-shən\ *n*
ad•just \ə-ˈjəst\ *vb* **1** : to bring to agreement : SETTLE **2** ♦ : to cause to conform : ADAPT, FIT **3** : REGULATE ⟨~ a watch⟩ — **ad•just•er** *also* **ad•jus•tor** \ə-ˈjəs-tər\ *n* — **ad•just•ment** \ə-ˈjəst-mənt\ *n*

♦ acclimate, accommodate, adapt, condition, conform, fit, shape

ad•just•able \-ˈjəs-tə-bəl\ *adj* ♦ : capable of being adjusted

♦ adaptable, changeable, elastic, flexible, fluid, malleable, variable

ad•ju•tant \ˈa-jə-tənt\ *n* : one who assists; *esp* : an officer who assists a commanding officer by handling correspondence and keeping records
ad•ju•vant \ˈa-jə-vənt\ *n* : one that helps or facilitates; *esp* : something that enhances the effectiveness of medical treatment — **adjuvant** *adj*
¹ad–lib \ˈad-ˈlib\ *vb* **ad–libbed; ad–lib•bing** : to improvise (especially lines or a speech) — **ad–lib** *n*
²ad–lib *adj* ♦ : spoken, composed, or performed without preparation

♦ extemporaneous, impromptu, offhand, snap, unplanned, unpremeditated, unprepared, unrehearsed

ad lib \ˈad-ˈlib\ *adv* **1** : at one's pleasure **2** : without limit
adm *abbr* administration; administrative

ADM *abbr* admiral
ad•man \ˈad-ˌman\ *n* : one who writes, solicits, or places advertisements
admin *abbr* administration; administrative
ad•min•is•ter \əd-ˈmi-nə-stər\ *vb* **1** ♦ : to manage or supervise the execution, use, or conduct of **2** ♦ : to mete out : DISPENSE **3** : to give ritually or remedially ⟨~ quinine for malaria⟩ **4** : to perform the office of administrator — **ad•min•is•tra•ble** \-strə-bəl\ *adj* — **ad•min•is•trant** \-strənt\ *n*

♦ [1] apply, enforce, execute, implement ♦ [1] carry on, conduct, control, direct, govern, guide, handle, manage, operate, oversee, regulate, run, superintend, supervise ♦ [2] allocate, apportion, deal, dispense, distribute, mete, parcel, portion, prorate

ad•min•is•tra•tion \ad-ˌmi-nə-ˈstrā- shən\ *n* **1** : the act or process of administering **2** ♦ : performance of executive duties **3** : the officials directing the government of a country **4** : the term of office of an administrative officer or body — **ad•min•is•tra•tive•ly** *adv*

♦ authority, government, jurisdiction, regime, rule ♦ conduct, control, direction, guidance, management, operation, oversight, regulation, running, superintendence, supervision

ad•min•is•tra•tive \ad-ˈmi-nə-ˌstrā-tiv\ *adj* : of or relating to administration
ad•min•is•tra•tor \ad-ˈmi-nə-ˌstrā-tər\ *n* ♦ : one that administers; *esp* : one who settles an intestate estate

♦ director, executive, manager, superintendent, supervisor

ad•mi•ra•ble \ˈad-m(ə-)rə-bəl\ *adj* ♦ : worthy of admiration : EXCELLENT — **ad•mi•ra•bil•i•ty** \ˌad-m(ə-)rə-ˈbi-lə-tē\ *n* — **ad•mi•ra•ble•ness** *n* — **ad•mi•ra•bly** \-blē\ *adv*

♦ applaudable, commendable, creditable, excellent, laudable, meritorious, praiseworthy *Ant* censurable, discreditable, reprehensible

ad•mi•ral \ˈad-m(ə-)rəl\ *n* : a commissioned officer in the navy ranking next below a fleet admiral
ad•mi•ral•ty \ˈad-m(ə-)rəl-tē\ *n* **1** *cap* : a British government department formerly having authority over naval affairs **2** : the court having jurisdiction over questions of maritime law
ad•mi•ra•tion \ˌad-mə-ˈrā-shən\ *n* ♦ : delighted or astonished approval

♦ appreciation, esteem, estimation, favor (*or* favour), regard, respect *Ant* disfavor

ad•mire \əd-ˈmīr\ *vb* **ad•mired; ad•mir•ing** ♦ : to regard with high esteem — **ad•mir•er** *n* — **ad•mir•ing•ly** \-ˈmī-riŋ-lē\ *adv*

♦ appreciate, esteem, regard, respect

ad•mis•si•ble \əd-ˈmi-sə-bəl\ *adj* ♦ : that can be or is worthy to be admitted or allowed : ALLOWABLE ⟨~ evidence⟩ — **ad•mis•si•bil•i•ty** \-ˌmi-sə-ˈbi-lə-tē\ *n*

♦ allowable, permissible, sufferable

ad•mis•sion \əd-ˈmi-shən\ *n* **1** ♦ : the act of admitting **2** ♦ : the privilege of being admitted **3** : a fee paid for admission **4** : the granting of an argument **5** : the acknowledgment of a fact

♦ [1] acknowledgment, avowal, concession, confession ♦ [2] access, doorway, entrance, entrée, entry, gateway

ad•mit \əd-ˈmit\ *vb* **ad•mit•ted; ad•mit•ting 1** : PERMIT, ALLOW **2** ♦ : to recognize as genuine or valid **3** : to allow to enter

♦ acknowledge, agree, allow, concede, confess, grant, own *Ant* deny

ad•mit•tance \əd-ˈmit-ᵊns\ *n* : permission to enter
ad•mit•ted•ly \əd-ˈmi-təd-lē\ *adv* **1** : as has been or must be admitted **2** ♦ : it must be admitted

♦ actually, frankly, honestly, indeed, really, truly, truthfully, verily

ad•mix \ad-ˈmiks\ *vb* : to mix in
ad•mix•ture \ad-ˈmiks-chər\ *n* **1** : something added in mixing **2** ♦ : a product of mixing : MIXTURE

♦ amalgam, blend, combination, composite, compound, fusion, intermixture, mix, mixture

ad•mon•ish \ad-ˈmä-nish\ *vb* ♦ : to express warning or disapproval to especially in a gentle manner — **ad•mon•ish•er** *n* — **ad•mon•ish•ment** *n*

♦ chide, rebuke, reprimand, reproach, reprove

ad•mon•ish•ing \-iŋ\ *adj* ♦ : expressing admonition

♦ admonitory, cautionary, warning

ad•mo•ni•tion \ˌad-mə-ˈni-shən\ *n* ♦ **:** counsel or warning against fault or oversight

♦ alarm, alert, caution, notice, warning

ad•mon•i•to•ry \ad-ˈmä-nə-ˌtōr-ē\ *adj* ♦ **:** expressing admonition

♦ admonishing, cautionary, warning

ad nau•se•am \ad-ˈnȯ-zē-əm\ *adv* **:** to a sickening or excessive degree

ado \ə-ˈdü\ *n* **1** ♦ **:** bustling excitement **:** FUSS **2 :** TROUBLE

♦ commotion, disturbance, furor, fuss, hubbub, hullabaloo, pandemonium, tumult, turmoil, uproar

ado•be \ə-ˈdō-bē\ *n* **1 :** sun-dried brick; *also* **:** clay for making such bricks **2 :** a structure made of adobe bricks

ad•o•les•cence \ˌad-ᵊl-ˈes-ᵊns\ *n* **:** the process or period of growth between childhood and maturity

[1]**ad•o•les•cent** \-ᵊnt\ *n* **:** one that is in the state of adolescence

[2]**adolescent** *adj* **1** ♦ **:** of, relating to, or being in adolescence **2** ♦ **:** emotionally or intellectually immature

♦ [1] immature, juvenile, young, youthful ♦ [2] callow, green, immature, inexperienced, juvenile, raw

adopt \ə-ˈdäpt\ *vb* **1 :** to take (a child of other parents) as one's own child **2** ♦ **:** to take up and practice or use as one's own **3 :** to accept formally and put into effect — **adopt•able** \-ˈdäp-tə-bəl\ *adj* — **adopt•er** *n* — **adop•tion** \-ˈdäp-shən\ *n*

♦ borrow, embrace, take up

adop•tive \ə-ˈdäp-tiv\ *adj* **:** made or acquired by adoption ⟨~ father⟩ — **adop•tive•ly** *adv*

ador•able \ə-ˈdōr-ə-bəl\ *adj* **1** ♦ **:** worthy of adoration **2 :** extremely charming — **ador•able•ness** *n* — **ador•ably** \-blē\ *adv*

♦ darling, dear, endearing, lovable, precious, sweet, winning

adore \ə-ˈdōr\ *vb* **adored; ador•ing 1** ♦ **:** to worship or honor as a deity or as divine **:** WORSHIP **2** ♦ **:** to regard with loving admiration **3** ♦ **:** to be extremely fond of often to the point of excess — **ad•o•ra•tion** \ˌa-də-ˈrā-shən\ *n*

♦ [1] deify, glorify, revere, venerate, worship ♦ [2] cherish, love, worship ♦ [2] delight, enjoy, fancy, like, love, relish, revel ♦ [3] canonize, deify, dote on, idolize, worship

adorn \ə-ˈdȯrn\ *vb* ♦ **:** to enhance the appearance of especially with ornaments

♦ array, beautify, deck, decorate, do, dress, embellish, enrich, garnish, grace, ornament, trim

adorn•ment \-mənt\ *n* ♦ **:** something that adorns

♦ caparison, decoration, embellishment, frill, garnish, ornament, trim

ad•re•nal \ə-ˈdrēn-ᵊl\ *adj* **:** of, relating to, or being a pair of endocrine organs (**adrenal glands**) that are located near the kidneys and produce several hormones and especially epinephrine

adren•a•line \ə-ˈdren-ᵊl-ən\ *n* **:** EPINEPHRINE

adrift \ə-ˈdrift\ *adv or adj* **1 :** afloat without motive power or moorings **2 :** without guidance or purpose

adroit \ə-ˈdrȯit\ *adj* ♦ **:** having or showing skill, cleverness, or resourcefulness in handling situations — **adroit•ly** *adv*

♦ artful, dexterous, masterful, practiced, skillful, virtuoso

adroit•ness \-nəs\ *n* ♦ **:** the quality or state of being adroit

♦ cleverness, craft, dexterity, finesse, sleight ♦ adeptness, art, artfulness, artifice, artistry, cleverness, craft, cunning, deftness, masterfulness, skill

ad•sorb \ad-ˈsȯrb, -ˈzȯrb\ *vb* **:** to take up (as molecules of gases) and hold on the surface of a solid or liquid — **ad•sorp•tion** \-ˈsȯrp-shən, -ˈzȯrp-\ *n*

ad•u•late \ˈa-jə-ˌlāt\ *vb* **-lat•ed; -lat•ing :** to flatter or admire excessively — **ad•u•la•tor** \ˈa-jə-ˌlā-tər\ *n*

ad•u•la•tion \ˌa-jə-ˈlā-shən\ *n* ♦ **:** excessive or slavish admiration or flattery

♦ deification, idolatry, worship ♦ blarney, flattery, overpraise

ad•u•la•to•ry \-lə-ˌtōr-ē\ *adj* ♦ **:** characterized by or given to adulation

♦ fulsome, unctuous

[1]**adult** \ə-ˈdəlt, ˈa-ˌ\ *adj* ♦ **:** fully developed and mature

♦ full-blown, full-fledged, mature, ripe

[2]**adult** *n* **:** one that is adult; *esp* **:** a human being after an age (as 18) specified by law

adul•ter•ant \ə-ˈdəl-tə-rənt\ *n* ♦ **:** something used to adulterate another

♦ contaminant, defilement, impurity, pollutant

adul•ter•ate \ə-ˈdəl-tə-ˌrāt\ *vb* **-at•ed; -at•ing** ♦ **:** to make impure by mixing in a foreign or inferior substance — **adul•ter•a•tion** \-ˌdəl-tə-ˈrā-shən\ *n*

♦ dilute, thin, water, weaken *Ant* enrich, fortify, strengthen

adul•tery \ə-ˈdəl-t(ə-)rē\ *n, pl* **-ter•ies :** sexual unfaithfulness of a married person — **adul•ter•er** \-tər-ər\ *n* — **adul•ter•ess** \-t(ə-)rəs\ *n* — **adul•ter•ous** \-t(ə-)rəs\ *adj*

adult•hood \ə-ˈdəlt-ˌhu̇d\ *n* **:** the state or time of being an adult

ad•um•brate \ˈa-dəm-ˌbrāt\ *vb* **-brat•ed; -brat•ing 1 :** to foreshadow vaguely **:** INTIMATE **2 :** to suggest or disclose partially **3 :** SHADE, OBSCURE — **ad•um•bra•tion** \ˌa-dəm-ˈbrā-shən\ *n*

adv *abbr* **1** adverb **2** advertisement

ad va•lor•em \ˌad-və-ˈlōr-əm\ *adj* **:** imposed at a percentage of the value ⟨an *ad valorem* tax⟩

[1]**ad•vance** \əd-ˈvans\ *vb* **ad•vanced; ad•vanc•ing 1** ♦ **:** to assist the progress of **2** ♦ **:** to bring or move forward **3** ♦ **:** to promote in rank **4 :** to make earlier in time **5** ♦ **:** to bring forward for notice, consideration, or acceptance **:** PROPOSE **6 :** to supply or furnish in expectation of repayment **:** LEND **7 :** to raise in rate **:** INCREASE

♦ [1] cultivate, encourage, forward, foster, further, nourish, nurture, promote ♦ [2] fare, forge, get along, go, march, proceed, progress ♦ [3] elevate, promote, raise, upgrade ♦ [5] offer, pose, proffer, propose, propound, suggest, vote

[2]**advance** *n* **1** ♦ **:** a forward movement **2** ♦ **:** a progressive step **:** IMPROVEMENT **3 :** a rise especially in price or value **4 :** OFFER — **in advance :** BEFOREHAND

♦ [1] advancement, furtherance, headway, march, onrush, passage, process, procession, progress, progression *Ant* recession, regression, retrogression ♦ [2] advancement, breakthrough, enhancement, improvement, refinement *Ant* setback

[3]**advance** *adj* **:** made, sent, or furnished ahead of time ⟨~ sales⟩

ad•vanced \əd-ˈvanst\ *adj* **1** ♦ **:** far on in time or course ⟨a man ~ in years⟩ **2** ♦ **:** being beyond others in progress ⟨a student with ~ abilities⟩

♦ high, progressive, refined *Ant* backward, low, lower, primitive, retarded, rudimentary, undeveloped

ad•vance•ment \-mənt\ *n* ♦ **:** the action of advancing **:** the state of being advanced

♦ ascent, elevation, promotion, rise, upgrade *Ant* abasement, demotion, downgrade, reduction ♦ advancement, breakthrough, enhancement, improvement, refinement *Ant* setback

ad•van•tage \əd-ˈvan-tij\ *n* **1** ♦ **:** superiority of position **2** ♦ **:** something that promotes well-being **:** BENEFIT **3 :** the 1st point won in tennis after deuce — **ad•van•ta•geous•ly** *adv*

♦ [1] better, drop, edge, jump, upper hand, vantage *Ant* disadvantage, handicap, liability ♦ [2] aid, benefit, boon, help

ad•van•ta•geous \ˌad-van-ˈtā-jəs\ *adj* ♦ **:** giving an advantage

♦ beneficial, favorable (*or* favourable), helpful, profitable, salutary

ad•vent \ˈad-ˌvent\ *n* **1** *cap* **:** a penitential period beginning four Sundays before Christmas **2** *cap* **:** the coming of Christ **3 :** a coming into being or use

ad•ven•ti•tious \ˌad-vən-ˈti-shəs\ *adj* **1** ♦ **:** coming from another source and not inherent or innate **2 :** arising or occurring sporadically or in other than the usual location ⟨~ buds⟩ — **ad•ven•ti•tious•ly** *adv*

♦ alien, extraneous, extrinsic, foreign

[1]**ad•ven•ture** \əd-ˈven-chər\ *n* **1 :** a risky undertaking **2** ♦ **:** a remarkable and exciting experience

♦ experience, happening, time

[2]**adventure** *vb* **-ven•tured; -ven•tur•ing** \-ˈven-ch(ə-)riŋ\ ♦ **:** to expose to danger or loss **:** RISK, HAZARD

♦ compromise, gamble with, hazard, imperil, jeopardize, menace, risk, venture

ad•ven•tur•er \əd-ˈven-ch(ə-)rər\ *n* **1 :** a person who engages in new and risky undertakings **2 :** a person who follows a military career for adventure or profit **3 :** a person who tries to gain wealth by questionable means

ad•ven•ture•some \əd-ˈven-chər-səm\ *adj* : inclined to take risks
ad•ven•tur•ess \əd-ˈven-ch(ə-)rəs\ *n* : a female adventurer
ad•ven•tur•ous \-ch(ə-)rəs\ *adj* ♦ : disposed to seek adventure or to cope with the new and unknown

♦ audacious, bold, daring, enterprising, nervy, venturesome

ad•verb \ˈad-ˌvərb\ *n* : a word that typically serves as a modifier of a verb, an adjective, or another adverb — **ad•ver•bi•al** \ad-ˈvər-bē-əl\ *adj* — **ad•ver•bi•al•ly** *adv*
[1]**ad•ver•sary** \ˈad-vər-ˌser-ē\ *n, pl* **-sar•ies** ♦ : one that contends with, opposes, or resists

♦ antagonist, enemy, foe, opponent

[2]**adversary** *adj* : involving antagonistic parties or interests
ad•verse \ad-ˈvərs, ˈad-ˌvərs\ *adj* **1** : acting against or in a contrary direction **2** ♦ : opposed to one's interests : UNFAVORABLE — **ad•verse•ly** *adv*

♦ counter, disadvantageous, hostile, inimical, negative, prejudicial, unfavorable (*or* unfavourable), unfriendly, unsympathetic *Ant* advantageous, favorable, friendly, positive, sympathetic, well-disposed

ad•ver•si•ty \ad-ˈvər-sə-tē\ *n, pl* **-ties** ♦ : hard times : occurrences of misfortune

♦ knock, misadventure, mischance, misfortune, mishap ♦ asperity, difficulty, hardness, hardship, rigor

ad•vert \ad-ˈvərt\ *vb* ♦ : to call attention in the course of speaking or writing : REFER

♦ cite, instance, mention, name, note, notice, quote, refer (to), specify, touch (*on* or *upon*)

ad•ver•tise \ˈad-vər-ˌtīz\ *vb* **-tised; -tis•ing** **1** : INFORM, NOTIFY **2** ♦ : to call public attention to especially in order to sell — **ad•ver•tis•er** *n*

♦ announce, blaze, broadcast, declare, enunciate, placard, post, proclaim, promulgate, publicize, publish, sound

ad•ver•tise•ment \ˌad-vər-ˈtīz-mənt; əd-ˈvər-təs-mənt\ *n* **1** : the act of advertising **2** ♦ : a public notice intended to advertise something

♦ announcement, bulletin, notice, notification, release

ad•ver•tis•ing \ˈad-vər-ˌtī-ziŋ\ *n* : the business of preparing advertisements
ad•vice \əd-ˈvīs\ *n* **1** : recommendation with regard to a course of action : COUNSEL **2** : INFORMATION, REPORT

♦ counsel, guidance, input

ad•vis•able \əd-ˈvī-zə-bəl\ *adj* ♦ : proper to be done : EXPEDIENT — **ad•vis•abil•i•ty** \-ˌvī-zə-ˈbi-lə-tē\ *n*

♦ desirable, expedient, judicious, politic, prudent, tactical, wise

ad•vise \əd-ˈvīz\ *vb* **ad•vised; ad•vis•ing** **1 a** : to give advice to : COUNSEL **b** ♦ : to recommend especially as the best or most expedient act, course, or policy **2** ♦ : to give information or notice to : INFORM **3** ♦ : to take counsel : CONSULT, CONFER

♦ [1b] counsel, suggest ♦ [2] acquaint, apprise, brief, clue, enlighten, familiarize, fill in, inform, instruct, tell, wise ♦ [3] confer, consult, counsel, parley, powwow

ad•vised \əd-ˈvīzd\ *adj* ♦ : thought out : CONSIDERED ⟨well-*advised*⟩

♦ calculated, deliberate, measured, reasoned, studied, thoughtful, thought-out

ad•vis•ed•ly \əd-ˈvī-zəd-lē\ *adv* ♦ : with or after forethought or consideration
ad•vise•ment \əd-ˈvīz-mənt\ *n* **1** ♦ : careful consideration **2** : the act of advising

♦ consideration, debate, deliberation, study, thought

ad•vis•er *also* **ad•vi•sor** \-ˈvī-zər\ *n* : one that gives advice
ad•vi•so•ry \əd-ˈvi-zə-rē\ *adj* **1** : having or exercising power to advise **2** : containing advice
[1]**ad•vo•cate** \ˈad-və-kət, -ˌkāt\ *n* **1** ♦ : one who pleads another's cause **2** ♦ : one who argues or pleads for a cause or proposal — **ad•vo•ca•cy** \-və-kə-sē\ *n*

♦ [1] attorney, counsel, lawyer ♦ [2] apostle, backer, booster, champion, exponent, friend, promoter, proponent, supporter

[2]**ad•vo•cate** \-ˌkāt\ *vb* **-cat•ed; -cat•ing** ♦ : to plead in favor of — **ad•vo•ca•tion** \ˌad-və-ˈkā-shən\ *n*

♦ back, champion, endorse, patronize, support

advt *abbr* advertisement
adze *also* **adz** \ˈadz\ *n* : a tool with a curved blade set at right angles to the handle that is used in shaping wood
AEC *abbr* Atomic Energy Commission
ae•gis \ˈē-jəs\ *n* **1** ♦ : one that protects : SHIELD **2** : PATRONAGE, SPONSORSHIP

♦ armor (*or* armour), cover, defense (*or* defence), guard, protection, safeguard, screen, security, shield, wall, ward

ae•o•li•an harp \ē-ˈō-lē-ən-\ *n* : a box with strings that produce musical sounds when the wind blows on them
ae•on *or* **eon** \ˈē-ən, -ˌän\ *n* ♦ : an indefinitely long time : AGE

♦ age, cycle, eternity

aer•ate \ˈa(-ə)r-ˌāt\ *vb* **aer•at•ed; aer•at•ing** **1** : to supply (blood) with oxygen by respiration **2** : to supply, impregnate, or combine with a gas and especially air — **aer•a•tion** \ˌa(-ə)r-ˈā-shən\ *n* — **aer•a•tor** \ˈa(-ə)r-ˌā-tər\ *n*
[1]**ae•ri•al** \ˈar-ē-əl\ *adj* **1** : inhabiting, occurring in, or done in the air **2** : AIRY **3** : of or relating to aircraft
[2]**aer•i•al** \ˈar-ē-əl\ *n* : ANTENNA 2
ae•ri•al•ist \ˈar-ē-ə-list\ *n* : a performer of feats above the ground especially on a trapeze
ae•rie \ˈar-ē, ˈir-ē\ *n* : a highly placed nest (as of an eagle)
aer•o•bat•ics \ˌar-ə-ˈba-tiks\ *n sing or pl* : spectacular flying feats and maneuvers
aer•o•bic \ˌa(-ə)r-ˈrō-bik\ *adj* **1** : living or active only in the presence of oxygen ⟨∼ bacteria⟩ **2** involving or increasing oxygen consumption ⟨∼ activity⟩; *also* : of or relating to aerobics — **aer•o•bi•cal•ly** \-bi-k(ə-)lē\ *adv*
aer•o•bics \-biks\ *n sing or pl* : strenuous exercises that produce a marked temporary increase in respiration and heart rate; *also* : a system of physical conditioning involving these
aero•drome \ˈar-ə-ˌdrōm\ *n, chiefly Brit* : AIRPORT
aero•dy•nam•ics \ˌar-ō-dī-ˈna-miks\ *n* : the science dealing with the forces acting on bodies in motion in a gas (as air) — **aero•dy•nam•ic** \-mik\ *also* **aero•dy•nam•i•cal** \-mi-kəl\ *adj* — **aero•dy•nam•i•cal•ly** \-mi-k(ə-)lē\ *adv*
aero•naut \ˈar-ə-ˌnȯt\ *n* : one who operates or travels in an airship or balloon
aero•nau•tics \ˌar-ə-ˈnȯ-tiks\ *n* : the science of aircraft operation — **aero•nau•ti•cal** \-ti-kəl\ *also* **aero•nau•tic** \-tik\ *adj*
aero•sol \ˈar-ə-ˌsäl, -ˌsȯl\ *n* **1** : a suspension of fine solid or liquid particles in a gas **2** : a substance (as an insecticide) dispensed from a pressurized container as an aerosol
aero•space \ˈar-ō-ˌspās\ *n* : the earth's atmosphere and the space beyond — **aerospace** *adj*
aery \ˈar-ē\ *adj* **aer•i•er; -est** : having an aerial quality : ETHEREAL
aes•thete \ˈes-ˌthēt\ *n* : a person having or affecting sensitivity to beauty especially in art
aes•thet•ic \es-ˈthe-tik\ *adj* **1** : of or relating to aesthetics : ARTISTIC **2** : appreciative of the beautiful **3** ♦ : pleasing in appearance : ATTRACTIVE — **aes•thet•i•cal•ly** \-ti-k(ə-)lē\ *adv*

♦ attractive, beautiful, cute, fair, gorgeous, handsome, knockout, lovely, pretty, ravishing, stunning

aes•thet•ics \-tiks\ *n* : a branch of philosophy dealing with the nature, creation, and appreciation of beauty
AF *abbr* **1** air force **2** audio frequency
[1]**afar** \ə-ˈfär\ *adv* : from, at, or to a great distance
[2]**afar** *n* : a great distance
AFB *abbr* air force base
AFC *abbr* **1** American Football Conference **2** automatic frequency control
AFDC *abbr* Aid to Families with Dependent Children
af•fa•bil•i•ty \ˌa-fə-ˈbi-lə-tē\ *n* : the quality or state of being affable
af•fa•ble \ˈa-fə-bəl\ *adj* ♦ : courteous and agreeable especially in conversation — **af•fa•bly** \ˈa-fə-blē\ *adv*

♦ agreeable, amiable, genial, good-natured, gracious, nice, sweet, well-disposed ♦ cordial, genial, gracious, hospitable, sociable

af•fair \ə-ˈfar\ *n* **1** : something that relates to or involves one : MATTER **2 a** ♦ : a procedure, action, or occasion only vaguely specified ⟨the most important social ∼ of the year⟩ **b** : an object or collection of objects only vaguely specified ⟨their house was a 2-story ∼⟩ **3** ♦ : a romantic or sexual attachment of limited duration

♦ [2a] blowout, event, fete, function, get-together, party ♦ [2a] circumstance, episode, event, happening, incident, occasion, occurrence, thing ♦ [3] amour, love affair, romance

¹af•fect \ə-ˈfekt, a-\ *vb* **1 :** to be fond of using or wearing **2** ♦ **:** to put on a pretense of **:** SIMULATE, ASSUME, PRETEND

♦ assume, counterfeit, fake, feign, pretend, profess, put on, sham, simulate

²affect *vb* ♦ **:** to produce an effect on **:** INFLUENCE

♦ impact, impress, influence, move, strike, sway, tell, touch

af•fec•ta•tion \ˌa-ˌfek-ˈta-shən\ *n* ♦ **:** an attitude or behavior that is assumed by a person but not genuinely felt

♦ pretense, pretension, pretentiousness

af•fect•ed \a-ˈfek-təd\ *adj* **1** ♦ **:** given to affectation **2** ♦ **:** artificially assumed to impress others — **af•fect•ed•ly** *adv*

♦ [1] grandiose, highfalutin, ostentatious, pompous, pretentious ♦ [2] artificial, assumed, fake, false, feigned, phony, put-on, sham, unnatural

af•fect•ing \a-ˈfek-tiŋ\ *adj* ♦ **:** evoking a strong emotional response ⟨an ~ story⟩ — **af•fect•ing•ly** *adv*

♦ emotional, impressive, moving, poignant, stirring, touching

af•fec•tion \ə-ˈfek-shən\ *n* **1** ♦ **:** tender attachment **2 :** a condition of the living animal or plant body or of one of its parts that impairs normal function **:** DISEASE — **af•fec•tion•ate•ly** *adv*

♦ attachment, devotion, fondness, love, passion

af•fec•tion•ate \-sh(ə-)nət\ *adj* **1** ♦ **:** having affection or warm regard **:** LOVING **2** ♦ **:** motivated by affection **:** TENDER

♦ [1, 2] devoted, fond, loving, tender, tenderhearted

af•fer•ent \ˈa-fə-rənt, -ˌfer-ənt\ *adj* **:** bearing or conducting inward toward a more central part and especially a nerve center (as the brain or spinal cord)

af•fi•ance \ə-ˈfī-əns\ *vb* **-anced; -anc•ing :** BETROTH, ENGAGE

af•fi•da•vit \ˌa-fə-ˈdā-vət\ *n* **:** a sworn statement in writing

¹af•fil•i•ate \ə-ˈfi-lē-ˌāt\ *vb* **-at•ed; -at•ing :** to associate as a member or branch

²af•fil•i•ate \ə-ˈfi-lē-ət\ *n* ♦ **:** an affiliated person or organization

♦ branch, chapter, local

af•fil•i•a•tion \-ˌfi-lē-ˈā-shən\ *n* ♦ **:** the act of affiliating **:** the state or relation of being affiliated

♦ alliance, association, collaboration, confederation, connection, cooperation, hookup, liaison, partnership, relation, relationship, union

af•fin•i•ty \ə-ˈfi-nə-tē\ *n, pl* **-ties 1 :** KINSHIP, RELATIONSHIP **2** ♦ **:** an attraction to or liking for something

♦ bent, devices, disposition, genius, inclination, leaning, partiality, penchant, predilection, predisposition, proclivity, propensity, talent, tendency, turn

af•firm \ə-ˈfərm\ *vb* **1 :** CONFIRM **2** ♦ **:** to assert positively **3 :** to make a solemn and formal declaration or assertion in place of an oath

♦ allege, assert, aver, avouch, avow, claim, contend, declare, insist, maintain, profess, protest, warrant

af•fir•ma•tion \ˌa-fər-ˈmā-shən\ *n* ♦ **:** something affirmed **:** a positive assertion

♦ assertion, avowal, claim, declaration, profession, protestation

¹af•fir•ma•tive \ə-ˈfər-mə-tiv\ *adj* **:** asserting that the fact is so **:** POSITIVE

²affirmative *n* **1 :** an expression of affirmation or assent **2 :** the side that upholds the proposition stated in a debate

affirmative action *n* **:** an active effort to improve the employment or educational opportunities of members of minority groups and women

¹af•fix \ə-ˈfiks\ *vb* **1** ♦ **:** to attach physically ⟨~ a stamp to a letter⟩ **2 :** to attach in any way **:** ADD ⟨~a signature to the document⟩

♦ attach, fasten, fix

²af•fix \ˈa-ˌfiks\ *n* **:** one or more sounds or letters attached to the beginning or end of a word that produce a derivative word or an inflectional form

af•fla•tus \ə-ˈflā-təs\ *n* **:** divine inspiration

af•flict \ə-ˈflikt\ *vb* ♦ **:** to cause pain and distress to

♦ agonize, bedevil, curse, harrow, martyr, persecute, plague, rack, torment, torture

af•flic•tion \-ˈflik-shən\ *n* ♦ **:** great suffering

♦ agony, anguish, distress, misery, pain, torment, torture, tribulation, woe

af•flic•tive \ə-ˈflik-tiv\ *adj* **:** causing affliction **:** DISTRESSING — **af•flic•tive•ly** *adv*

af•flu•ence \ˈa-ˌflü-ən(t)s, a-ˈflü-\ *n* **:** abundant supply; *also* **:** WEALTH, RICHES

af•flu•ent \-ənt\ *adj* ♦ **:** having a generously sufficient and typically increasing supply of material possessions

♦ flush, loaded, moneyed, opulent, rich, wealthy, well-fixed, well-heeled, well-off, well-to-do

af•ford \ə-ˈfōrd\ *vb* **1 :** to manage to bear or bear the cost of without serious harm or loss **2 :** PROVIDE, FURNISH

af•ford•able \ə-ˈfōr-də-bəl\ *adj* ♦ **:** that can be afforded **:** of a cost that can be borne without serious harm or loss

♦ affordable, cheap, cut-rate, inexpensive, low, popular, reasonable

af•for•es•ta•tion \a-ˌfȯr-ə-ˈstā-shən\ *n* **:** the act or process of establishing a forest — **af•for•est** \a-ˈfȯr-əst, -ˈfär-\ *vb*

af•fray \ə-ˈfrā\ *n, chiefly Brit* **:** a fight between two or more people in a public place that disturbs the peace **:** FRAY

af•fright \ə-ˈfrīt\ *vb, archaic* **:** to make afraid **:** FRIGHTEN, ALARM — **affright** *n*

¹af•front \ə-ˈfrənt\ *vb* **1** ♦ **:** to insult especially to the face **2 :** CONFRONT

♦ insult, offend, outrage, slight, wound

²affront *n* ♦ **:** a deliberate offense

♦ barb, dart, dig, indignity, insult, name, offense, outrage, put-down, sarcasm, slight, slur, wound

af•ghan \ˈaf-ˌgan\ *n* **1** *cap* **:** a native or inhabitant of Afghanistan **2 :** a blanket or shawl of colored wool knitted or crocheted in sections — **Afghan** *adj*

Afghan hound *n* **:** any of a breed of tall slim swift hunting dogs with a coat of silky thick hair and a long silky topknot

afi•cio•na•do \ə-ˌfi-sh(ē-)ə-ˈnä-dō, -sē-ə-\ *n, pl* **-dos** ♦ **:** a person who likes, knows about, and appreciates a usually fervently pursued interest or activity **:** DEVOTEE, FAN

♦ addict, buff, bug, devotee, enthusiast, fan, fanatic, fancier, fiend, freak, lover, maniac, nut

afield \ə-ˈfēld\ *adv* **1 :** to, in, or on the field **2 :** away from home **3** ♦ **:** out of the way **:** ASTRAY — **afield** *adj*

♦ amiss, astray, awry, wrong

afire \ə-ˈfīr\ *adj* ♦ **:** being on fire **:** BURNING — **afire** *adv*

♦ ablaze, burning, fiery

AFL *abbr* American Football League

aflame \ə-ˈflām\ *adj* **:** being on fire — **aflame** *adv*

AFL–CIO *abbr* American Federation of Labor and Congress of Industrial Organizations

afloat \ə-ˈflōt\ *adj or adv* **1 :** borne on or as if on the water **2 :** CIRCULATING ⟨rumors were ~⟩ **3 :** ADRIFT

aflut•ter \ə-ˈflə-tər\ *adj* **1 :** FLUTTERING **2** ♦ **:** nervously excited

♦ anxious, edgy, jittery, jumpy, nervous, perturbed, tense, uneasy

afoot \ə-ˈfu̇t\ *adv or adj* **1 :** on foot **2** ♦ **:** in action **:** in progress

♦ ongoing, proceeding

afore•men•tioned \ə-ˈfōr-ˈmen-chənd\ *adj* **:** mentioned previously

afore•said \-ˌsed\ *adj* **:** said or named before

afore•thought \-ˌthȯt\ *adj* **:** PREMEDITATED ⟨with malice ~⟩

a for•ti•o•ri \ˌä-ˌfȯr-tē-ˈōr-ē\ *adv* **:** with even greater reason

afoul of \ə-ˈfau̇l-əv\ *prep* **1 :** in or into conflict with **2 :** in or into collision or entanglement with

Afr *abbr* Africa; African

afraid \ə-ˈfrād\ *adj* ♦ **:** filled with fear or apprehension **:** FRIGHTENED, FEARFUL

♦ aghast, fearful, scared, terrified *Ant* fearless, unafraid

A–frame \ˈā-ˌfrām\ *n* **:** a building having triangular front and rear walls with the roof reaching to the ground

afresh \ə-ˈfresh\ *adv* **:** from a fresh beginning **:** ANEW, AGAIN

Af•ri•can \ˈa-fri-kən\ *n* **1 :** a native or inhabitant of Africa **2 :** a person of African ancestry — **African** *adj*

Af•ri•can–Amer•i•can \-ə-ˈmer-ə-kən\ *n* **:** an American of African and especially of black African descent — **African–American** *adj*

Af•ri•can•ized bee \ˈa-frə-kə-ˌnīzd-\ *n* **:** a highly aggressive hybrid honeybee accidentally produced from Brazilian and African

stocks that has spread from So. America into Mexico and the southern U.S.
Africanized honeybee *n* : AFRICANIZED BEE
African violet *n* : a tropical African plant widely grown indoors for its velvety fleshy leaves and showy purple, pink, or white flowers
Af•ri•kaans \ˌa-fri-ˈkäns\ *n* : a language developed from 17th century Dutch that is one of the official languages of the Republic of So. Africa
Afro \ˈa-frō\ *n, pl* **Afros** : a hairstyle of tight curls in a full evenly rounded shape
Af•ro–Amer•i•can \ˌa-frō-ə-ˈmer-ə-kən\ *n* : an American of African and especially of black African descent — **Afro–American** *adj*
aft \ˈaft\ *adv* : near, toward, or in the stern of a ship or the tail of an aircraft
AFT *abbr* American Federation of Teachers
1af•ter \ˈaf-tər\ *adv* ♦ : following in time or place : AFTERWARD, SUBSEQUENTLY

♦ afterward, later, subsequently, thereafter ***Ant*** before, beforehand, earlier, previously

2after *prep* **1** : behind in place **2** : later than **3** : in pursuit or search of ⟨he's ~ your job⟩
3after *conj* : following the time when
4after *adj* **1** ♦ : later in time **2** : located toward the rear

♦ later, posterior, subsequent

af•ter•birth \ˈaf-tər-ˌbərth\ *n* : the placenta and membranes of the fetus that are expelled after childbirth
af•ter•burn•er \-ˌbər-nər\ *n* : a device incorporated in the tail pipe of a turbojet engine for injecting fuel into the hot exhaust gases and burning it to provide extra thrust
af•ter•care \-ˌker\ *n* : the care, nursing, or treatment of a convalescent patient
af•ter•deck \-ˌdek\ *n* : the rear half of the deck of a ship
af•ter•ef•fect \-ə-ˌfekt\ *n* : an effect that follows its cause after an interval
af•ter•glow \-ˌglō\ *n* : a glow remaining where a light has disappeared
af•ter•im•age \-ˌim-ij\ *n* : a usually visual sensation continuing after the stimulus causing it has ended
af•ter•life \-ˌlīf\ *n* ♦ : an existence after death

♦ eternity, hereafter, immortality

af•ter•math \-ˌmath\ *n* **1** : a second-growth crop especially of hay **2** ♦ : something produced by a cause or necessarily following from a set of conditions : CONSEQUENCE, EFFECT

♦ consequence, effect, outcome, outgrowth, product, result, resultant, sequence, upshot

af•ter•noon \ˌaf-tər-ˈnün\ *n* : the time between noon and evening
af•ter•shave \ˈaf-tər-ˌshāv\ *n* : a usually scented lotion for the face after shaving
af•ter•taste \-ˌtāst\ *n* : a sensation (as of flavor) continuing after the stimulus causing it has ended
af•ter–tax \ˈaf-tər-ˈtaks\ *adj* : remaining after payment of taxes and especially of income tax ⟨an ~ profit⟩
af•ter•thought \-ˌthȯt\ *n* : a later thought; *also* : something thought of later
af•ter•ward \-wərd\ *or* **af•ter•wards** \-wərdz\ *adv* ♦ : at a later time

♦ after, later, subsequently, thereafter

Ag *symbol* silver
AG *abbr* **1** adjutant general **2** attorney general
again \ə-ˈgen, -ˈgin\ *adv* **1** ♦ : once more : ANEW **2** : on the other hand **3** ♦ : in addition : BESIDES

♦ [1] anew, over ***Ant*** nevermore ♦ [3] additionally, also, besides, further, furthermore, likewise, more, moreover, then, too, withal, yet

against \ə-ˈgenst\ *prep* **1** : in opposition to **2** : directly opposite to : FACING **3** : as defense from **4 a** : in the direction of and into contact with ⟨threw him ~ the ropes⟩ **b** : in contact with ⟨leaning ~ the wall⟩
1aga•pe \ä-ˈgä-pā, ˈä-gə-ˌpā\ *n* : unselfish unconditional love for another
2agape \ə-ˈgāp\ *adj or adv* ♦ : being in a state of wonder or expectation

♦ agog, anticipatory, expectant

agar \ˈä-ˌgär\ *n* **1** : a jellylike substance extracted from a red alga and used especially as a gelling and stabilizing agent in foods **2** : a culture medium containing agar
agar–agar \ˌä-ˌgär-ˈä-ˌgär\ *n* : AGAR
ag•ate \ˈa-gət\ *n* **1** : a striped or clouded quartz **2** : a playing marble of agate or of glass
aga•ve \ə-ˈgä-vē\ *n* : any of a genus of spiny-leaved plants (as a century plant) related to the amaryllis
agcy *abbr* agency
1age \ˈāj\ *n* **1** ♦ : the length of time during which a being or thing has lived or existed **2** : the time of life at which some particular qualification is achieved; *esp* : MAJORITY **3** : the latter part of life **4** ♦ : a long time **5** : a period in history

♦ [1] epoch, era, period, time ♦ [4] aeon (*or* eon), cycle, eternity

2age *vb* **aged; ag•ing** *or* **age•ing** **1** : to grow old or cause to grow old **2** ♦ : to become or cause to become mature or mellow

♦ develop, grow, grow up, mature, progress, ripen

-age *n suffix* **1** : aggregate : collection ⟨track*age*⟩ **2** : action : process ⟨haul*age*⟩ **3** : cumulative result of ⟨break*age*⟩ **4** : rate of ⟨dos*age*⟩ **5** : house or place of ⟨orphan*age*⟩ **6** : state : rank ⟨vassal*age*⟩ **7** : fee : charge ⟨post*age*⟩
aged \ˈā-jəd *for 1*; ˈājd *for 2*\ *adj* **1** : of advanced age **2** : having attained a specified age ⟨a man ~ 40 years⟩
age•ism \ˈā-ˌji-zəm\ *n* : discrimination against persons of a particular age and especially the elderly
age•less \ˈāj-ləs\ *adj* **1** : not growing old or showing the effects of age **2** ♦ : not affected by time : having infinite duration : TIMELESS ⟨~ truths⟩

♦ abiding, continuing, dateless, enduring, eternal, everlasting, immortal, imperishable, lasting, perennial, perpetual, timeless, undying

agen•cy \ˈā-jən-sē\ *n, pl* **-cies** **1** ♦ : one through which something is accomplished : INSTRUMENTALITY **2** : the office or function of an agent **3** : an establishment doing business for another **4** : an administrative division (as of a government)

♦ agent, instrument, instrumentality, machinery, means, medium, organ, vehicle

agen•da \ə-ˈjen-də\ *n* ♦ : a list of things to be done : PROGRAM

♦ calendar, docket, program, schedule, timetable

agent \ˈā-jənt\ *n* **1** : one that acts **2** ♦ : something that produces or is capable of producing an effect : MEANS, INSTRUMENT **3** ♦ : a person acting or doing business for another

♦ [2] agency, instrument, instrumentality, machinery, means, medium, organ, vehicle ♦ [3] attorney, commissary, delegate, deputy, envoy, factor, proxy, representative

Agent Orange *n* : an herbicide widely used in the Vietnam War that is composed of 2,4-D and 2,4,5-T and contains a toxic contaminant
agent pro•vo•ca•teur \ˈä-ˌzhä^{n}-prō-ˌvä-kə-ˈtər, ˈā-jənt-\ *n, pl* **agents provocateurs** \ˈä-ˌzhä^{n}-prō-ˌväk-ə-ˈtər, ˈā-jənts-prō-\ : a person hired to infiltrate a group and incite its members to illegal action
age–old \ˈāj-ˈōld\ *adj* ♦ : having existed for ages : ANCIENT

♦ ancient, antediluvian, antique, dateless, old, venerable

ag•er•a•tum \ˌa-jə-ˈrā-təm\ *n, pl* **-tum** *also* **-tums** : any of a large genus of tropical American plants that are related to the daisies and have small showy heads of blue or white flowers
Ag•ge•us \a-ˈgē-əs\ *n* : HAGGAI
1ag•glom•er•ate \ə-ˈglä-mə-ˌrāt\ *vb* **-at•ed; -at•ing** ♦ : to gather into a mass : CLUSTER

♦ ball, cluster, conglomerate, roll, round, wad

2ag•glom•er•ate \-rət\ *n* : rock composed of volcanic fragments
ag•glom•er•a•tion \ə-ˌglä-mə-ˈrā-shən\ *n* ♦ : a cluster of disparate elements

♦ assortment, clutter, jumble, medley, mélange, miscellany, motley, muddle, variety, welter

ag•glu•ti•nate \ə-ˈglüt-ᵊn-ˌāt\ *vb* **-nat•ed; -nat•ing** **1** : to cause to adhere : gather into a group or mass **2** : to cause (as red blood cells or bacteria) to collect into clumps — **ag•glu•ti•na•tion** \-ˌglüt-ᵊn-ˈā-shən\ *n*
ag•gran•dise *Brit var of* AGGRANDIZE
ag•gran•dize \ə-ˈgran-ˌdīz, ˈa-grən-\ *vb* **-dized; -diz•ing** **1** ♦ : to make great or greater **2** ♦ : to enhance the power, wealth, position, or reputation of — **ag•gran•dize•ment** \ə-ˈgran-dəz-mənt, -ˌdīz-; ˌa-grən-ˈdīz-\ *n*

♦ [1] add, amplify, augment, boost, compound, enlarge, escalate, expand, extend, increase, multiply, raise, swell, up ♦ [2] dignify, ennoble, exalt, glorify, magnify

ag•gra•vate \ˈa-grə-ˌvāt\ *vb* **-vat•ed; -vat•ing** **1 :** to make more severe : INTENSIFY **2** ♦ **:** to rouse to displeasure or anger by usually persistent and often petty goading : IRRITATE

♦ annoy, bother, bug, grate, irk, irritate, nettle, peeve, persecute, pique, put out, rile, vex

aggravating *adj* ♦ **:** arousing displeasure, impatience, or anger

♦ annoying, bothersome, frustrating, galling, irksome, irritating, pesty, vexatious

ag•gra•va•tion \ˌa-grə-ˈvā-shən\ *n* ♦ **:** the act, action, or result of aggravating

♦ annoyance, bother, harassment, vexation

¹ag•gre•gate \ˈa-gri-gət\ *adj* **:** formed by the gathering of units into one mass

²ag•gre•gate \-ˌgāt\ *vb* **-gat•ed; -gat•ing :** to collect into one mass

³ag•gre•gate \-gət\ *n* **1 :** a mass or body of units or parts somewhat loosely associated with one another **2** ♦ **:** the whole amount

♦ full, sum, total, totality, whole

ag•gre•ga•tion \ˌa-gri-ˈgā-shən\ *n* **1 :** a group, body, or mass composed of many distinct parts **2 :** the collecting of units or parts into a mass or whole

ag•gres•sion \ə-ˈgre-shən\ *n* **1** ♦ **:** an unprovoked attack **2 :** the practice of making attacks **3** ♦ **:** hostile, injurious, or destructive behavior or outlook especially when caused by frustration

♦ [1] assault, attack, charge, offense (*or* offence), offensive, onset, onslaught, raid, rush, strike ♦ [3] aggressiveness, belligerence, fight, militancy, pugnacity, truculence

ag•gres•sive \ə-ˈgre-siv\ *adj* **1** ♦ **:** tending toward or exhibiting aggression; *esp* **:** marked by combative readiness **2** ♦ **:** marked by driving energy or initiative : ENTERPRISING **3 :** more intensive or comprehensive especially in dosage or extent — **ag•gres•sive•ly** *adv*

♦ [1] argumentative, bellicose, belligerent, combative, contentious, militant, pugnacious, quarrelsome, scrappy, truculent, warlike ♦ [2] ambitious, assertive, enterprising, fierce, go-getting, high pressure, militant, self-assertive *Ant* unaggressive, unambitious, unassertive, unenterprising

ag•gres•sive•ness *n* ♦ **:** the quality or state of being aggressive

♦ aggression, belligerence, fight, militancy, pugnacity, truculence ♦ ambition, drive, enterprise, go, hustle, initiative

ag•gres•sor \-ˈgre-sər\ *n* **:** one that commits or practices aggression

ag•grieve \ə-ˈgrēv\ *vb* **ag•grieved; ag•griev•ing** **1 :** to cause grief to **2 :** to inflict injury on : WRONG

aggrieved *adj* ♦ **:** troubled or distressed in spirit

♦ discontent, discontented, dissatisfied, malcontent

aghast \ə-ˈgast\ *adj* ♦ **:** struck with amazement or horror

♦ afraid, terrified

ag•ile \ˈa-jəl\ *adj* ♦ **:** able to move quickly and easily

♦ graceful, light, lissome, lithe, nimble, spry

agil•i•ty \ə-ˈji-lə-tē\ *n* ♦ **:** the quality or state of being agile

♦ deftness, dexterity, nimbleness, sleight

ag•i•tate \ˈa-jə-ˌtāt\ *vb* **-tat•ed; -tat•ing** **1** ♦ **:** to move or cause to move with an irregular rapid motion **2** ♦ **:** to excite and often trouble the mind or feelings of : DISTURB **3 :** to discuss earnestly **4 :** to attempt to arouse public feeling

♦ [1] convulse, jolt, jounce, quake, quiver, shake, shudder, vibrate, wobble ♦ [2] bother, concern, discompose, disquiet, distress, disturb, perturb, unsettle, upset, worry

agitated *adj* ♦ **:** troubled in mind

♦ feverish, frenzied, heated, hectic, overactive, overwrought

ag•i•ta•tion \ˌa-jə-ˈtā-shən\ *n* ♦ **:** the act or state of agitating or being agitated

♦ anxiety, apprehension, care, concern, disquiet, nervousness, perturbation, uneasiness, worry

ag•i•ta•tor \ˈa-jə-ˌtā-tər\ *n* ♦ **:** one that agitates

♦ demagogue, firebrand, incendiary, inciter, rabble-rouser

ag•it•prop \ˈa-jət-ˌpräp\ *n* **:** political propaganda promulgated especially through the arts

agleam \ə-ˈglēm\ *adj* **:** GLEAMING

aglit•ter \ə-ˈgli-tər\ *adj* **:** GLITTERING

aglow \ə-ˈglō\ *adj* ♦ **:** glowing especially with warmth or excitement : GLOWING

♦ beaming, glowing, radiant, sunny

ag•nos•tic \ag-ˈnäs-tik\ *adj* **:** of or relating to the belief that the existence of any ultimate reality (as God) is unknown and prob. unknowable — **agnostic** *n* — **ag•nos•ti•cism** \-ˈnäs-tə-ˌsi-zəm\ *n*

ago \ə-ˈgō\ *adj or adv* **:** earlier than the present time

agog \ə-ˈgäg\ *adj* ♦ **:** full of intense interest or excitement

♦ agape, anticipatory, expectant ♦ anxious, ardent, athirst, avid, eager, enthusiastic, keen

a–go–go \ä-ˈgō-ˌgō\ *adj* **:** GO-GO

ag•o•nise *Brit var of* AGONIZE

ag•o•nize \ˈa-gə-ˌnīz\ *vb* **-nized; -niz•ing** ♦ **:** to suffer or cause to suffer agony

♦ afflict, bedevil, curse, harrow, martyr, persecute, plague, rack, torment, torture ♦ bleed, feel, grieve, hurt, mourn, sorrow, suffer

agonizing *adj* ♦ **:** causing agony

♦ bitter, cruel, excruciating, galling, grievous, harrowing, harsh, hurtful, painful, tortuous

ag•o•niz•ing•ly \-lē\ *adv* ♦ **:** in a manner that is agonizing

♦ bitterly, grievously, hard, sorrowfully, unhappily, wretchedly

ag•o•ny \ˈa-gə-nē\ *n, pl* **-nies** **1** ♦ **:** extreme pain of mind or body **2 :** a strong sudden display (as of joy or delight) : OUTBURST

♦ affliction, anguish, distress, misery, pain, torment, torture, tribulation, woe

ag•o•ra•pho•bia \ˌa-gə-rə-ˈfō-bē-ə\ *n* **:** abnormal fear of being in a helpless, embarrassing, or inescapable situation characterized especially by avoidance of open or public places — **ag•o•ra•pho•bic** \-ˈfō-bik, -ˈfä-\ *adj or n*

agr *abbr* agricultural; agriculture

agrar•i•an \ə-ˈgrer-ē-ən\ *adj* **1 :** of or relating to land or its ownership ⟨~ reforms⟩ **2 :** of or relating to farmers or farming interests — **agrarian** *n* — **agrar•i•an•ism** *n*

agree \ə-ˈgrē\ *vb* **agreed; agree•ing** **1** ♦ **:** to concur in (as an opinion) : ADMIT, CONCEDE **2** ♦ **:** to be similar : CORRESPOND **3** ♦ **:** to express agreement or approval **4** ♦ **:** to be in harmony **5 :** to settle by common consent **6 :** to be fitting or healthful : SUIT

♦ [1, 3] acknowledge, admit, allow, concede, confess, grant, own ♦ [2] accord, check, coincide, comport, conform, correspond, dovetail, fit, go, harmonize, jibe, square, tally ♦ [3] accede, acquiesce, assent, consent, subscribe (to) ♦ [4] blend, conform, coordinate, harmonize

agree•able \ə-ˈgrē-ə-bəl\ *adj* **1** ♦ **:** pleasing to the mind or senses especially as according well with one's tastes or needs **2 :** ready to consent **3** ♦ **:** being in harmony

♦ [1] all right, alright, fine, good, OK, palatable, satisfactory ♦ [1] congenial, delightful, enjoyable, felicitous, good, pleasant, pleasurable, satisfying ♦ [1] affable, amiable, genial, good-natured, gracious, nice, sweet, well-disposed ♦ [3] amicable, compatible, congenial, harmonious, kindred, unanimous, united

agree•able•ness \-nəs\ *n* ♦ **:** the quality or state of being agreeable

♦ amenity, amiability, geniality, graciousness, niceness, pleasantness, sweetness

agree•ably \-blē\ *adv* ♦ **:** in an agreeable manner

♦ delightfully, favorably (*or* favourably), felicitously, gloriously, nicely, pleasantly, pleasingly, satisfyingly, splendidly, well

agree•ment \ə-ˈgrē-mənt\ *n* **1** ♦ **:** harmony of opinion or action **2** ♦ **:** mutual understanding or arrangement; *also* **:** a document containing such an arrangement

♦ [1] accord, conformity, consonance, harmony, tune ♦ [1] accord, concurrence, consensus, unanimity *Ant* disagreement, dissent ♦ [2] accord, bargain, compact, contract, convention, covenant, deal, pact, settlement, understanding

ag•ri•busi•ness \ˈa-grə-ˌbiz-nəs, -nəz\ *n* **:** an industry engaged in the manufacture and sale of farm equipment and supplies and in the production, processing, storage, and sale of farm commodities

agric *abbr* agricultural; agriculture

ag•ri•cul•tur•al \ˌa-gri-ˈkəl-ch(ə-)rəl\ *adj* **:** of, relating to, used in, or concerned with agriculture

ag•ri•cul•ture \ˈa-gri-ˌkəl-chər\ *n* **:** the science, art, or practice of cultivating the soil, producing crops, and raising livestock and in varying degrees the preparation and marketing of the resulting products : FARMING, HUSBANDRY

ag•ri•cul•tur•ist \-ch(ə-)rist\ *or* **ag•ri•cul•tur•al•ist** \-ch(ə-)rə-list\ *n* ♦ : one that is trained in or practices agriculture

♦ cultivator, farmer, grower, planter, tiller

agron•o•mist \ə-ˈgrä-nə-mist\ *n* : one that is trained in or practices agronomy

agron•o•my \ə-ˈgrä-nə-mē\ *n* : a branch of agriculture that deals with the raising of crops and the care of the soil — **ag•ro•nom•ic** \ˌa-grə-ˈnä-mik\ *adj*

aground \ə-ˈgraünd\ *adv or adj* : on or onto the bottom or shore ⟨ran ~⟩

agt *abbr* agent

ague \ˈā-gyü\ *n* : a fever (as malaria) with recurrent chills and sweating

ahead \ə-ˈhed\ *adv or adj* **1** ♦ : in or toward the front **2** ♦ : into or for the future ⟨plan ~⟩ **3** : in or toward a more advantageous position **4** ♦ : at or to an earlier time

♦ [1, 2] along, forth, forward, on, onward ♦ [4] before, beforehand, previously *Ant* after, afterward, later

ahead of *prep* **1** ♦ : in front or advance of **2** : in excess of : ABOVE

♦ before, ere, of, previous to, prior to, to

AHL *abbr* American Hockey League

ahoy \ə-ˈhȯi\ *interj* — used in hailing ⟨ship ~⟩

AI *abbr* artificial intelligence

1**aid** \ˈād\ *vb* ♦ : to provide with what is useful in achieving an end : ASSIST

♦ abet, assist, back, help, prop, support

2**aid** *n* **1** ♦ : an act or instance of help given : ASSISTANCE **2** ♦ : an assisting person, group, or device : ASSISTANT

♦ [1] assist, assistance, backing, boost, help, lift, support ♦ [2] apprentice, assistant, deputy, helper, helpmate, mate, sidekick ♦ [2] advantage, benefit, boon, help

AID *abbr* Agency for International Development

aide \ˈād\ *n* : a person who acts as an assistant; *esp* : a military officer assisting a superior

aide–de–camp \ˌād-di-ˈkamp, -ˈkä^n\ *n, pl* **aides–de–camp** \ˌādz-di-\ : AIDE

AIDS \ˈādz\ *n* : a serious disease of the human immune system that is characterized by severe reduction in the numbers of helper T cells and increased vulnerability to life-threatening illnesses and that is caused by infection with HIV commonly transmitted in infected blood and in bodily secretions

AIDS–related complex *n* : a group of symptoms (as fever, weight loss, and lymphadenopathy) that is associated with the presence of antibodies to HIV and is followed by the development of AIDS in a certain proportion of cases

AIDS virus *n* : HIV

ai•grette \ā-ˈgret, ˈā-ˌ\ *n* : a plume or decorative tuft for the head

ail \ˈāl\ *vb* **1** ♦ : to be the matter with : be trouble to **2** : to be unwell

♦ agitate, bother, concern, discompose, disquiet, distress, disturb, exercise, freak out, perturb, undo, unhinge, unsettle, upset, worry

ai•lan•thus \ā-ˈlan-thəs\ *n* : any of a genus of Asian trees or shrubs with pinnate leaves and ill-scented greenish flowers

ai•le•ron \ˈā-lə-ˌrän\ *n* : a movable part of an airplane wing used in banking

ail•ment \ˈāl-mənt\ *n* ♦ : a bodily disorder

♦ bug, complaint, complication, condition, disease, disorder, fever, ill, illness, infirmity, malady, sickness, trouble

1**aim** \ˈām\ *vb* **1** : to point a weapon at an object **2** ♦ : to direct one's efforts : ASPIRE **3** ♦ : to direct to or toward a specified object or goal

♦ [2] aspire, contemplate, design, intend, mean, meditate, plan, propose ♦ [3] bend, cast, direct, head, level, set, train

2**aim** *n* **1** : the pointing of a weapon at an object **2** : the ability to hit a target **3** ♦ : a clearly directed intent or purpose : OBJECT, PURPOSE — **aim•less•ly** *adv* — **aim•less•ness** *n*

♦ ambition, aspiration, design, end, goal, intent, object, objective, plan, purpose

aim•less \-ləs\ *adj* ♦ : without aim or purpose

♦ arbitrary, desultory, erratic, haphazard, random, scattered, stray

AIM *abbr* American Indian Movement

ain't \ˈānt\ **1** are not **2** is not **3** am not — though disapproved by many and more common in less educated speech, used in both speech and writing to catch attention and to gain emphasis

Ai•nu \ˈī-nü\ *n, pl* **Ainu** *or* **Ainus** **1** : a member of an indigenous people of northern Japan **2** : the language of the Ainu people

1**air** \ˈar\ *n* **1** : the gaseous mixture surrounding the earth **2** ♦ : a light breeze **3** ♦ : a sweet or agreeable succession or arrangement of sounds : MELODY, TUNE **4** ♦ : the outward appearance of a person or thing : apparent character **5** *usu* **airs** ♦ : an artificial manner **6** : COMPRESSED AIR ⟨~ sprayer⟩ **7** : AIRCRAFT ⟨~ patrol⟩ **8** : AVIATION ⟨~ safety⟩ **9** : the medium of transmission of radio waves; *also* : RADIO, TELEVISION

♦ [2] breath, breeze, puff, waft, zephyr ♦ [3] lay, melody, song, strain, tune, warble ♦ [4] atmosphere, aura, climate, flavor (*or* flavour), mood, note, temper ♦ **airs** [5] act, facade, front, guise, masquerade, pose, pretense, put-on, semblance, show

2**air** *vb* **1** : to expose to the air **2** ♦ : to expose to public view or bring to public notice

♦ express, give, look, sound, state, vent, voice

air bag *n* : a bag designed to inflate automatically to protect automobile occupants in case of collision

air•boat \ˈar-ˌbōt\ *n* : a shallow-draft boat driven by an airplane propeller

air•borne \-ˌbōrn\ *adj* : done or being in the air

air brake *n* **1** : a brake operated by a piston driven by compressed air **2** : a surface projected into the airflow to lower an airplane's speed

air•brush \ˈar-ˌbrəsh\ *n* : a device for applying a fine spray (as of paint) by compressed air — **airbrush** *vb*

air–con•di•tion \ˌar-kən-ˈdi-shən\ *vb* : to equip with an apparatus for filtering air and controlling its humidity and temperature — **air con•di•tion•er** \-ˈdi-sh(ə-)nər\ *n*

air•craft \ˈar-ˌkraft\ *n, pl* **aircraft** : a vehicle for traveling through the air

aircraft carrier *n* : a warship with a deck on which airplanes can be launched and landed

air•drop \ˈar-ˌdräp\ *n* : delivery of cargo or personnel by parachute from an airplane in flight — **air–drop** *vb*

Aire•dale terrier \ˈar-ˌdāl-\ *n* : any of a breed of large terriers with a hard wiry coat

air•fare \ˈar-ˌfar\ *n* : fare for travel by airplane

air•field \-ˌfēld\ *n* : an area of land from which aircraft operate : AIRPORT

air•flow \-ˌflō\ *n* : the motion of air relative to a body in it

air•foil \-ˌfȯil\ *n* : an airplane surface designed to produce reaction forces from the air through which it moves

air force *n* : the military organization of a nation for air warfare

air•frame \ˈar-ˌfrām\ *n* : the structure of an aircraft, rocket, or missile without the power plant

air•freight \-ˈfrāt\ *n* : freight transport by aircraft in volume; *also* : the charge for this service

air gun *n* **1** : a gun operated by compressed air **2** : a hand tool that works by compressed air; *esp* : AIRBRUSH

air•head \ˈar-ˌhed\ *n* : a mindless or stupid person

air lane *n* : AIRWAY 1

air•lift \ˈar-ˌlift\ *n* : transportation (as of supplies or passengers) by aircraft — **airlift** *vb*

air•line \-ˌlīn\ *n* : a transportation system using airplanes

air•lin•er \-ˌlī-nər\ *n* : a large passenger airplane operated by an airline

air lock *n* : an airtight chamber separating areas of different pressure

air•mail \ˈar-ˌmāl\ *n* : the system of transporting mail by aircraft; *also* : mail so transported — **airmail** *vb*

air•man \-mən\ *n* **1** ♦ : a civilian or military pilot, aviator, or aviation technician : AVIATOR, PILOT **2** : an enlisted man in the air force in one of the three ranks below sergeant

♦ aviator, flier, pilot

airman basic *n* : an enlisted man of the lowest rank in the air force

airman first class *n* : an enlisted man in the air force with a rank just below that of sergeant

air mass *n* : a large horizontally homogeneous body of air

air•mo•bile \ˈar-ˌmō-bəl, -ˌbēl\ *adj* : of, relating to, or being a military unit whose members are transported to combat areas usually by helicopter

air•plane \-ˌplān\ *n* : a powered heavier-than-air aircraft that has fixed wings from which it derives lift

air•play \-ˌplā\ *n* : the playing of a musical recording on the air by a radio station

air pocket *n* **:** a condition of the atmosphere that causes an airplane to drop suddenly
air police *n* **:** the military police of an air force
air•port \ˈar-ˌpōrt\ *n* **:** a place from which aircraft operate that usually has paved runways and a terminal
air raid *n* **:** an attack by armed airplanes on a surface target
air•ship \ˈar-ˌship\ *n* **:** a lighter-than-air aircraft having propulsion and steering systems
air•sick \-ˌsik\ *adj* **:** affected with motion sickness associated with flying — **air•sick•ness** *n*
air•space \-ˌspās\ *n* **:** the space above a nation and under its jurisdiction
air•speed \-ˌspēd\ *n* **:** the speed of an object (as an airplane) with relation to the surrounding air
air•strip \-ˌstrip\ *n* **:** a runway without normal airport facilities
air•tight \ˈar-ˈtīt\ *adj* **1 :** so tightly sealed that no air can enter or escape **2 :** leaving no opening for attack
air–to–air *adj* **:** launched from one airplane in flight at another; *also* **:** involving aircraft in flight
air•waves \ˈar-ˌwāvz\ *n pl* **:** AIR 9
air•way \-ˌwā\ *n* **1 :** a regular route for airplanes **2 :** AIRLINE
air•wor•thy \-ˌwər-thē\ *adj* **:** fit for operation in the air ⟨an ~ plane⟩ — **air•wor•thi•ness** *n*
airy \ˈar-ē\ *adj* **air•i•er; -est 1 :** high in the air **:** LOFTY **2 :** lacking in reality **:** EMPTY **3 ♦ :** exceptionally light, delicate, or refined **4 :** BREEZY

♦ ethereal, fluffy, light *Ant* heavy, leaden

aisle \ˈīl\ *n* **1 :** the side of a church nave separated by piers from the nave proper **2 :** a passage between sections of seats
ajar \ə-ˈjär\ *adj or adv* **:** partly open
AK *abbr* Alaska
aka *abbr* also known as
AKC *abbr* American Kennel Club
akim•bo \ə-ˈkim-bō\ *adj or adv* **:** having the hand on the hip and the elbow turned outward
akin \ə-ˈkin\ *adj* **1 ♦ :** related by blood **2 ♦ :** essentially similar or related

♦ [1] kindred, related ♦ [2] alike, analogous, comparable, correspondent, like, parallel, similar

Al *symbol* aluminum
AL *abbr* **1** Alabama **2** American League **3** American Legion
1-al *adj suffix* **:** of, relating to, or characterized by ⟨direction*al*⟩
2-al *n suffix* **:** action **:** process ⟨rehears*al*⟩
Ala *abbr* Alabama
al•a•bas•ter \ˈa-lə-ˌbas-tər\ *n* **1 :** a compact fine-textured usually white and translucent gypsum often carved into objects (as vases) **2 :** a hard translucent calcite
à la carte \ˌa-lə-ˈkärt, ˌä-\ *adv or adj* **:** with a separate price for each item on the menu
alac•ri•ty \ə-ˈla-krə-tē\ *n* **♦ :** cheerful readiness

♦ gameness, goodwill, willingness

à la mode \ˌa-lə-ˈmōd, ˌä-\ *adj* **1 ♦ :** conforming to the custom, fashion, or established mode **:** STYLISH **2 :** topped with ice cream

♦ chic, fashionable, in, modish, sharp, smart, snappy, stylish

1alarm \ə-ˈlärm\ *also* **ala•rum** \ə-ˈlär-əm, -ˈlar-\ *n* **1 ♦ :** a warning signal or device **2 ♦ :** the terror caused by sudden danger

♦ [1] admonition, alert, caution, notice, warning ♦ [2] anxiety, apprehension, dread, fear, fright, horror, panic, terror, trepidation

2alarm *also* **alarum** *vb* **1 :** to warn of danger **2 ♦ :** to strike with fear **:** FRIGHTEN

♦ frighten, horrify, panic, scare, shock, spook, startle, terrify, terrorize

alarm•ist \ə-ˈlär-mist\ *n* **:** a person who alarms others especially needlessly
alas \ə-ˈlas\ *interj* — used to express unhappiness, pity, or concern
al•ba•core \ˈal-bə-ˌkōr\ *n, pl* **-core** *or* **-cores :** a large tuna that is a source of canned tuna
Al•ba•nian \al-ˈbā-nē-ən\ *n* **:** a native or inhabitant of Albania
al•ba•tross \ˈal-bə-ˌtrȯs, -ˌträs\ *n, pl* **-tross** *or* **-tross•es :** any of a family of large web-footed seabirds
al•be•do \al-ˈbē-(ˌ)dō\ *n, pl* **-dos :** the fraction of incident radiation that is reflected by a body or surface
al•be•it \ȯl-ˈbē-ət, al-\ *conj* **♦ :** even though **:** ALTHOUGH

♦ although, howbeit, though, when, while

al•bi•no \al-ˈbī-nō\ *n, pl* **-nos :** a person or nonhuman mammal lacking coloring matter in the skin, hair, and eyes — **al•bi•nism** \ˈal-bə-ˌni-zəm\ *n*
al•bum \ˈal-bəm\ *n* **1 :** a book with blank pages used for making a collection (as of stamps) **2 :** one or more recordings (as on tape or disk) produced as a single unit **3 ♦ :** a collection usually in book form of literary selections, musical compositions, or pictures **:** ANTHOLOGY

♦ anthology, compilation, miscellany

al•bu•men \al-ˈbyü-mən\ *n* **1 :** the white of an egg **2 :** ALBUMIN
al•bu•min \al-ˈbyü-mən\ *n* **:** any of numerous water-soluble proteins of blood, milk, egg white, and plant and animal tissues
al•bu•min•ous \al-ˈbyü-mə-nəs\ *adj* **:** containing or resembling albumen or albumin
alc *abbr* alcohol
al•cal•de \al-ˈkäl-dē\ *n* **:** the chief administrative and judicial officer of a Spanish or Spanish-American town
al•ca•zar \al-ˈkä-zər, -ˈka-\ *n* **:** a Spanish fortress or palace
al•che•my \ˈal-kə-mē\ *n* **:** medieval chemistry chiefly concerned with efforts to turn base metals into gold — **al•che•mist** \ˈal-kə-mist\ *n*
al•co•hol \ˈal-kə-ˌhȯl\ *n* **1 :** a colorless flammable liquid that is the intoxicating agent in fermented and distilled liquors **2 :** any of various carbon compounds similar to alcohol **3 ♦ :** beverages containing alcohol

♦ booze, drink, intoxicant, liquor, moonshine, spirits

1al•co•hol•ic \ˌal-kə-ˈhȯ-lik, -ˈhä-\ *adj* **1 :** of, relating to, caused by, or containing alcohol **2 :** affected with alcoholism — **al•co•hol•i•cal•ly** \-li-k(ə-)lē\ *adv*
2alcoholic *n* **♦ :** a person affected with alcoholism

♦ drunk, drunkard, inebriate, soak, sot, souse, tippler

al•co•hol•ism \ˈal-kə-ˌhȯ-ˌli-zəm\ *n* **:** continued excessive and usually uncontrollable use of alcoholic drinks; *also* **:** a complex chronic psychological and nutritional disorder associated with such use
al•cove \ˈal-ˌkōv\ *n* **1 :** a nook or small recess opening off a larger room **2 ♦ :** a niche or arched opening (as in a wall)

♦ niche, nook, recess

ald *abbr* alderman
al•der \ˈȯl-dər\ *n* **:** a tree or shrub related to the birches and growing in wet areas
al•der•man \ˈȯl-dər-mən\ *n* **:** a member of a city legislative body
ale \ˈāl\ *n* **:** an alcoholic beverage brewed from malt and hops that is usually more bitter than beer
ale•a•tor•ic \ˌā-lē-ə-ˈtȯr-ik\ *adj* **:** characterized by chance or random elements ⟨~ music⟩
ale•a•to•ry \ˈā-lē-ə-ˌtōr-ē\ *adj* **:** ALEATORIC
alee \ə-ˈlē\ *adv* **:** on or toward the lee
ale•house \ˈāl-ˌhau̇s\ *n* **:** a place where ale is sold to be drunk on the premises
1alert \ə-ˈlərt\ *adj* **1 ♦ :** watchful against danger **2 ♦ :** quick to perceive and act — **alert•ly** *adv*

♦ [1] attentive, awake, vigilant, watchful, wide-awake ♦ [2] brainy, bright, brilliant, clever, intelligent, keen, nimble, quick, quick-witted, sharp, smart ♦ [2] expeditious, prompt, quick, ready, willing

2alert *n* **1 ♦ :** a warning signal or device **:** ALARM **2 :** the period during which an alert is in effect

♦ admonition, alarm, caution, notice, warning

3alert *vb* **1 ♦ :** to call to a state of readiness **:** WARN **2 :** to make aware of

♦ caution, forewarn, warn

alert•ness \-nəs\ *n* **♦ :** the quality or state of being alert

♦ attentiveness, lookout, vigilance, watch

Aleut \ˌa-lē-ˈüt, ə-ˈlüt\ *n* **1 :** a member of a people of the Aleutian and Shumagin islands and the western part of Alaska Peninsula **2 :** the language of the Aleuts
ale•wife \ˈāl-ˌwīf\ *n, pl* **ale•wives** \-ˌwīvz\ **:** a food fish of the herring family abundant especially on the Atlantic coast
Al•ex•an•dri•an \ˌa-lig-ˈzan-drē-ən\ *adj* **1 :** of or relating to Alexander the Great **2 :** HELLENISTIC
al•ex•an•drine \-ˈzan-drən\ *n, often cap* **:** a line of six iambic feet
al•fal•fa \al-ˈfal-fə\ *n* **:** a leguminous plant widely grown for hay and forage
al•fres•co \al-ˈfres-kō\ *adj or adv* **:** taking place in the open air
alg *abbr* algebra
al•ga \ˈal-gə\ *n, pl* **al•gae** \ˈal-(ˌ)jē\ **:** any of a group of lower plants having chlorophyll but no vascular system and including seaweeds and related freshwater plants — **al•gal** \-gəl\ *adj*

al•ge•bra \ˈal-jə-brə\ *n* : a branch of mathematics using symbols (as letters) to explore the relationships between numbers and the operations used to work with them — **al•ge•bra•ic** \ˌal-jə-ˈbrā-ik\ *adj* — **al•ge•bra•i•cal•ly** \-ˈbrā-ə-k(ə-)lē\ *adv*

Al•ge•ri•an \al-ˈjir-ē-ən\ *n* : a native or inhabitant of Algeria — **Algerian** *adj*

Al•gon•quin \al-ˈgän-kwən, -ˈgäŋ-\ *n* : a member of an American Indian people of the Ottawa River valley

al•go•rithm \ˈal-gə-ˌri-t͟həm\ *n* : a procedure for solving a problem especially in mathematics or computing — **al•go•rith•mic** \ˌal-gə-ˈrit͟h-mik\ *adj* — **al•go•rith•mi•cal•ly** \-mi-k(ə-)lē\ *adv*

¹alias \ˈā-lē-əs, ˈāl-yəs\ *adv* : otherwise called

²alias *n* ♦ : an assumed or additional name

♦ cognomen, nickname

¹al•i•bi \ˈa-lə-ˌbī\ *n* **1** : a plea offered by an accused person of not having been at the scene of an offense **2** ♦ : an excuse (as for failure)

♦ defense (*or* defence), excuse, justification, plea, reason

²alibi *vb* **-bied; -bi•ing** **1** : to furnish an excuse for **2** : to offer an excuse

¹alien \ˈā-lē-ən, ˈāl-yən\ *adj* ♦ : belonging or relating to another person, place, or thing : FOREIGN

♦ adventitious, extraneous, extrinsic, foreign

²alien *n* **1** : a foreign-born resident who has not been naturalized **2** : EXTRATERRESTRIAL

alien•able \ˈāl-yə-nə-bəl, ˈā-lē-ə-nə-\ *adj* : transferable to the ownership of another ⟨~ property⟩

alien•ate \ˈā-lē-ə-ˌnāt, ˈāl-yə-\ *vb* **-at•ed; -at•ing** **1** ♦ : to make hostile : ESTRANGE **2** : to transfer (property) to another

♦ disaffect, disgruntle, estrange, sour

alien•ation \ˌā-lē-ə-ˈnā-shən, ˌāl-yə-\ *n* ♦ : a withdrawing or separation of a person or a person's affections from an object or position of former attachment

♦ disaffection, estrangement

alien•ist \ˈā-lē-ə-nist, ˈāl-yə-\ *n* : PSYCHIATRIST

¹alight \ə-ˈlīt\ *vb* **alight•ed** *also* **alit** \ə-ˈlit\; **alight•ing** **1** : to get down (as from a vehicle) **2** ♦ : to come to rest from the air

♦ land, light, perch, roost, settle

²alight *adj* ♦ : lighted up

♦ ablaze, bright, light

align *also* **aline** \ə-ˈlīn\ *vb* **1** : to bring into line **2** : to array on the side of or against a cause — **align•er** *n* — **align•ment** *also* **aline•ment** *n*

¹alike \ə-ˈlīk\ *adv* ♦ : in the same manner, form, or degree

♦ also, correspondingly, likewise, similarly, so

²alike *adj* ♦ : exhibiting close resemblance without being identical : LIKE

♦ akin, analogous, comparable, correspondent, like, parallel, similar, such *Ant* different, dissimilar, diverse, unlike

al•i•ment \ˈa-lə-mənt\ *n* : NOURISHMENT 1 — **aliment** *vb*

al•i•men•ta•ry \ˌa-lə-ˈmen-t(ə-)rē\ *adj* : of, relating to, or functioning in nourishment or nutrition

alimentary canal *n* : the tube that extends from the mouth to the anus and functions in the digestion and absorption of food and the elimination of residues

al•i•mo•ny \ˈa-lə-ˌmō-nē\ *n, pl* **-nies** : an allowance made to one spouse by the other for support pending or after legal separation or divorce

A–line \ˈā-ˌlīn\ *adj* : having a flared bottom and a close-fitting top ⟨an ~ skirt⟩

alive \ə-ˈlīv\ *adj* **1** ♦ : having life **2** ♦ : being in force or operation **3** ♦ : knowing or realizing the existence of ⟨~ to the danger⟩ **4** : ALERT, BRISK **5** ♦ : marked by much life, animation, or activity : ANIMATED ⟨streets ~ with traffic⟩ — **alive•ness** *n*

♦ [1] existent, extant, living ♦ [1] animate, live, living *Ant* dead, deceased, defunct, lifeless, nonliving ♦ [2] active, functional, living, on, operational, operative, running, working ♦ [3] aware, cognizant, conscious, mindful, sensible, sentient, witting ♦ [5] animated, astir, busy, lively, vibrant *Ant* asleep, dead, inactive, lifeless, sleepy

alk *abbr* alkaline

al•ka•li \ˈal-kə-ˌlī\ *n, pl* **-lies** *or* **-lis** **1** : a substance (as a hydroxide) that has a bitter taste and neutralizes acids **2** : a mixture of salts in the soil of some dry regions in such amount as to make ordinary farming impossible — **al•ka•line** \-kə-lən, -ˌlīn\ *adj* — **al•ka•lin•i•ty** \ˌal-kə-ˈli-nə-tē\ *n*

al•ka•loid \ˈal-kə-ˌlȯid\ *n* : any of various usually basic and bitter organic compounds found especially in seed plants

al•kane \ˈal-ˌkān\ *n* : a hydrocarbon in which each carbon atom is bonded to 4 other atoms

al•kyd \ˈal-kəd\ *n* : any of numerous synthetic resins used especially for protective coatings and in paint

¹all \ˈȯl\ *adj* **1** ♦ : the whole of **2** : every member of **3** : EVERY ⟨~ manner of problems⟩ **4** : any whatever ⟨beyond ~ doubt⟩ **5** : nothing but ⟨~ ears⟩ **6** : being more than one person or thing ⟨who ~ is coming⟩

♦ concentrated, entire, undivided, whole

²all *adv* **1** ♦ : to the full or entire extent : WHOLLY **2** : selected as the best — used in combination ⟨*all*-state champs⟩ **3** : so much ⟨~ the better for it⟩ **4** : for each side ⟨the score is two ~⟩

♦ absolutely, clean, completely, entirely, fully, quite, totally, utterly, wholly

³all *pron* **1** : the whole number, quantity, or amount ⟨~ of it is gone⟩ **2** : every person or thing ⟨that is ~⟩

⁴all *n* : the whole of one's resources ⟨gave his ~⟩

Al•lah \ˈä-lä, ˈa-; ä-ˈlä\ *n* : the Being perfect in power, wisdom, and goodness who is worshipped as creator and ruler of the universe — used in Islam

all along *adv* : all the time ⟨knew it *all along*⟩

all–Amer•i•can \ˌȯl-ə-ˈmer-ə-kən\ *adj* **1** : selected as the best in the U.S. **2** : composed wholly of American elements **3** : typical of the U.S. — **all–American** *n*

all–around \ˌȯl-ə-ˈrau̇nd\ *adj* **1** ♦ : considered in or encompassing all aspects ⟨best ~ performance⟩ **2** : competent in many fields : VERSATILE ⟨an ~ athlete⟩

♦ general, unlimited, unqualified, unrestricted

all around \ˌȯl-ə-ˈrau̇nd\ *adv* ♦ : without concentration on one area or aspect

♦ altogether, collectively, overall, together

al•lay \ə-ˈlā\ *vb* **1** ♦ : to subdue or reduce in intensity or severity : ALLEVIATE **2** ♦ : to make quiet : CALM

♦ [1] alleviate, assuage, ease, help, mitigate, mollify, palliate, relieve, soothe ♦ [2] calm, compose, quiet, settle, soothe, still, tranquilize

all clear *n* : a signal that a danger has passed

al•lege \ə-ˈlej\ *vb* **al•leged; al•leg•ing** **1** ♦ : to assert without proof **2** : to offer as a reason — **al•le•ga•tion** \ˌa-li-ˈgā-shən\ *n* — **al•leg•ed•ly** \ə-ˈle-jəd-lē\ *adv*

♦ affirm, assert, aver, avouch, avow, claim, contend, declare, insist, maintain, profess, protest, warrant

al•le•giance \ə-ˈlē-jəns\ *n* **1** : loyalty owed by a citizen to a government **2** ♦ : loyalty to a person or cause

♦ constancy, dedication, devotion, faith, faithfulness, fastness, fealty, fidelity, loyalty, steadfastness

al•le•go•ry \ˈa-lə-ˌgōr-ē\ *n, pl* **-ries** : the expression through symbolism of truths or generalizations about human experience; *also* : an instance (as in a story or painting) of such expression — **al•le•gor•i•cal** \ˌa-lə-ˈgȯr-i-kəl\ *adj* — **al•le•gor•i•cal•ly** \-k(ə-)lē\ *adv*

¹al•le•gro \ə-ˈle-grō, -ˈlā-\ *n, pl* **-gros** : an allegro movement

²allegro *adv or adj* : at a brisk lively tempo — used as a direction in music

al•le•lu•ia \ˌa-lə-ˈlü-yə\ *interj* : HALLELUJAH

Al•len wrench \ˈa-lən-\ *n* : an L-shaped hexagonal metal bar of which either end fits the socket of a screw or bolt

al•ler•gen \ˈa-lər-jən\ *n* : something that causes allergy — **al•ler•gen•ic** \ˌa-lər-ˈje-nik\ *adj*

al•ler•gic \ə-ˈlər-jik\ *adj* : of, relating to, affected with, or caused by allergy

al•ler•gist \ˈa-lər-jist\ *n* : a specialist in allergies

al•ler•gy \ˈa-lər-jē\ *n, pl* **-gies** **1** : exaggerated or abnormal reaction (as by sneezing) to substances or situations harmless to most people **2** ♦ : a feeling of antipathy or aversion

♦ aversion, disfavor (*or* disfavour), disinclination, dislike

al•le•vi•ate \ə-ˈlē-vē-ˌāt\ *vb* **-at•ed; -at•ing** ♦ : to remove or lessen (as suffering) : RELIEVE

♦ allay, assuage, ease, help, mitigate, mollify, palliate, relieve, soothe

al•le•vi•a•tion \ə-ˌlē-vē-ˈā-shən\ *n* ♦ **:** the action of alleviating or of being alleviated

♦ comfort, ease, relief

al•ley \ˈa-lē\ *n, pl* **alleys 1 :** a garden or park walk **2 :** a place for bowling **3 :** a narrow passageway especially between buildings
al•ley–oop \ˌa-lē-ˈyüp\ *n* **:** a basketball play in which a player catches a pass above the basket and immediately dunks the ball
al•ley•way \ˈa-le-ˌwā\ *n* **:** ALLEY 3
All•hal•lows \ȯl-ˈha-lōz\ *n, pl* **Allhallows :** ALL SAINTS' DAY
al•li•ance \ə-ˈlī-əns\ *n* **1** ♦ **:** a union to promote common interests **2** ♦ **:** union by relationship in qualities **3 :** a treaty of alliance

♦ [1] bloc, coalition, combination, combine, confederacy, confederation, federation, league, union ♦ [2] affiliation, association, collaboration, confederation, connection, cooperation, hookup, liaison, partnership, relation, relationship, union

al•li•ga•tor \ˈa-lə-ˌgā-tər\ *n* **:** either of two large short-legged reptiles resembling crocodiles but having a shorter and broader snout
alligator pear *n* **:** AVOCADO
al•lit•er•ate \ə-ˈli-tə-ˌrāt\ *vb* **-at•ed; -at•ing 1 :** to form an alliteration **2 :** to arrange so as to make alliteration
al•lit•er•a•tion \ə-ˌli-tə-ˈrā-shən\ *n* **:** the repetition of initial sounds in adjacent words or syllables — **al•lit•er•a•tive** \-ˈli-tə-ˌrā-tiv\ *adj*
al•lo•cate \ˈa-lə-ˌkāt\ *vb* **-cat•ed; -cat•ing** ♦ **:** to apportion for a specific purpose or to particular persons or things

♦ administer, apportion, deal, dispense, distribute, mete, parcel, portion, prorate ♦ allot, allow, apportion, ration

al•lo•ca•tion \ˌa-lə-ˈkā-shən\ *n* **1** ♦ **:** the act or action of allocating **2** ♦ **:** the amount allocated to one sharer

♦ [1] dispensation, distribution, division, issuance ♦ [2] allotment, appropriation, grant, subsidy

al•lot \ə-ˈlät\ *vb* **al•lot•ted; al•lot•ting** ♦ **:** to distribute as a share

♦ allocate, allow, apportion, ration

al•lot•ment \-mənt\ *n* **1 :** the act of allotting **2** ♦ **:** something that is allotted

♦ allocation, appropriation, grant, subsidy ♦ allowance, cut, part, portion, proportion, quota, share

all–out \ˈȯl-ˈau̇t\ *adj* ♦ **:** marked by thoroughness or zeal **:** THOROUGHGOING

♦ clean, complete, comprehensive, exhaustive, full-scale, out-and-out, thorough, thoroughgoing, total

all out *adv* ♦ **:** with maximum effort

♦ full tilt

all over *adv* **:** in every place or part **:** EVERYWHERE
al•low \ə-ˈlau̇\ *vb* **1** ♦ **:** to assign as a share ⟨~ time for rest⟩ **2 :** to count as a deduction **3 :** to make allowance ⟨~ for expansion⟩ **4** ♦ **:** to accept as true, valid, or accurate usually reluctantly **:** ADMIT, CONCEDE **5 a :** to give leave for or make possible **:** PERMIT ⟨~*s* the dog to roam⟩ **b** ♦ **:** to give leave to

♦ [1] allocate, allot, apportion, ration ♦ [4] acknowledge, admit, agree, concede, confess, grant, own *Ant* ban, enjoin, forbid, prohibit, proscribe, veto ♦ [5b] let, permit, suffer *Ant* enjoin, forbid, prohibit

al•low•able \ə-ˈlau̇-ə-bəl\ *adj* ♦ **:** that may be permitted

♦ admissible, permissible, sufferable

al•low•ance \-əns\ *n* **1** ♦ **:** an allotted share **2 :** money given regularly for expenses **3** ♦ **:** the act of allowing **:** PERMISSION **4 :** a taking into account of extenuating circumstances

♦ [1] allotment, cut, part, portion, proportion, quota, share ♦ [3] authorization, clearance, concurrence, consent, leave, license (*or* licence), permission, sanction, sufferance

al•loy \ˈa-ˌlȯi, ə-ˈlȯi\ *n* **1 :** a substance composed of metals melted together **2 :** an admixture that lessens value — **al•loy** \ə-ˈlȯi, ˈa-ˌlȯi\ *vb*
[1]**all right** *adj* **1** ♦ **:** giving satisfaction **:** SATISFACTORY **2** ♦ **:** free from harm or risk **3 :** having qualities that tend to give pleasure — often used as a generalized term of approval

♦ [1] acceptable, adequate, decent, fine, OK, passable, respectable, satisfactory, tolerable ♦ [2] alright, safe, secure

[2]**all right** *adv* **1** ♦ — used interjectionally to express agreement or resignation or to indicate the resumption of a discussion ⟨*all right*, let's go⟩ **2 :** beyond doubt **3** ♦ **:** well enough **:** SATISFACTORILY

♦ [1] alright, OK, yea, yes ♦ [3] adequately, fine, good, nicely, OK, passably, satisfactorily, so-so, tolerably, well

All Saints' Day *n* **:** a Christian feast on November 1 in honor of all the saints
All Souls' Day *n* **:** a day of prayer observed by some Christian churches on November 2 for the souls of the faithful departed
all•spice \ˈȯl-ˌspīs\ *n* **:** the berry of a West Indian tree related to the European myrtle; *also* **:** the mildly pungent and aromatic spice made from it
all–star \ˈȯl-ˌstär\ *n* **:** a member of a team of star performers — **all–star** *adj*
all–ter•rain vehicle *n* **:** a small motor vehicle for use on a wide range of terrain
all told *adv* **:** with everything counted
al•lude \ə-ˈlüd\ *vb* **al•lud•ed; al•lud•ing** ♦ **:** to refer indirectly — **al•lu•sion** \-ˈlü-zhən\ *n* — **al•lu•sive** \-ˈlü-siv\ *adj* — **al•lu•sive•ly** *adv* — **al•lu•sive•ness** *n*

♦ hint, imply, indicate, infer, insinuate, intimate, suggest

[1]**al•lure** \ə-ˈlu̇r\ *vb* **al•lured; al•lur•ing** ♦ **:** to entice by charm or attraction — **allure** *n* — **al•lur•ing•ly** *adv*

♦ beguile, bewitch, captivate, charm, enchant, fascinate, wile ♦ beguile, decoy, entice, lead on, lure, seduce, tempt

[2]**allure** *n* ♦ **:** power of attraction or fascination

♦ appeal, attractiveness, captivation, charisma, charm, enchantment, fascination, glamour, magic, magnetism

alluring *adj* ♦ **:** marked by allure

♦ attractive, captivating, charming, elfin, engaging, fascinating, fetching, glamorous, magnetic, seductive

al•lu•vi•um \ə-ˈlü-vē-əm\ *n, pl* **-vi•ums** *or* **-via** \-vē-ə\ **:** soil material (as clay) deposited by running water — **al•lu•vi•al** \-vē-əl\ *adj or n*
[1]**al•ly** \ə-ˈlī, ˈa-ˌlī\ *vb* **al•lied; al•ly•ing** ♦ **:** to enter into an alliance

♦ associate, band, club, confederate, conjoin, cooperate, federate, league, unite *Ant* break up, disband

[2]**al•ly** \ˈa-ˌlī, ə-ˈlī\ *n* ♦ **:** one that is associated with another as a helper

♦ abettor, backer, confederate, supporter, sympathizer

-ally *adv suffix* **:** [2]-LY ⟨specific*ally*⟩
al•ma ma•ter \ˌal-mə-ˈmä-tər\ *n* **1 :** an educational institute that one has attended **2 :** the song or hymn of an alma mater
al•ma•nac \ˈȯl-mə-ˌnak, ˈal-\ *n* **1 :** a publication especially of astronomical and meteorological data **2 :** a usually annual publication of miscellaneous information
al•man•dite \ˈal-mən-ˌdīt\ *n* **:** a deep red garnet
al•mighty \ȯl-ˈmī-tē\ *adj* **1** *often cap* **:** having absolute power over all ⟨*Almighty* God⟩ **2 :** relatively unlimited in power — **al•might•i•ness** *n*
Almighty *n* ♦ **:** the Being worshipped as the creator and ruler of the universe

♦ deity, Jehovah, Supreme Being

al•mond \ˈä-mənd, ˈa-; ˈal-\ *n* **:** a small tree related to the peach; *also* **:** the edible nutlike kernel of its fruit
al•mo•ner \ˈal-mə-nər, ˈä-mə-\ *n* **:** a person who distributes alms
al•most \ˈȯl-ˌmōst, ȯl-ˈmōst\ *adv* ♦ **:** very nearly but not exactly

♦ about, most, much, near, nearly, next to, nigh, practically, some, virtually, well-nigh

alms \ˈämz, ˈälmz\ *n, pl* **alms** ♦ **:** something given freely to relieve the poor

♦ benefaction, beneficence, charity, contribution, donation, philanthropy

alms•house \-ˌhau̇s\ *n* **:** POORHOUSE
al•oe \ˈa-lō\ *n* **1 :** any of a large genus of succulent chiefly southern African plants related to the lilies **2** *pl* **:** the dried juice of the leaves of an aloe used especially formerly as a laxative
aloft \ə-ˈlȯft\ *adv* **1** ♦ **:** high in the air **2 :** in flight

♦ above, over, overhead, skyward

alo•ha \ə-ˈlō-ə, ä-ˈlō-hä\ *interj* — used to greet or bid farewell
[1]**alone** \ə-ˈlōn\ *adj* **1** ♦ **:** separated from others **2** ♦ **:** not including anyone or anything else **:** ONLY — **alone** *adv*

♦ [1] lone, lonely, lonesome, solitary, unaccompanied *Ant* accompanied ♦ [2] lone, only, singular, sole, solitary, special, unique

²alone *adv* **1** ♦ : to the exclusion of all else : SOLELY **2** ♦ : without aid or support

♦ [1] exclusively, just, only, simply, solely ♦ [2] independently, singly, solely, unaided, unassisted

¹along \ə-ˈlȯŋ\ *prep* **1** : in line with the direction of ⟨sail ~ the coast⟩ **2** : at a point on or during ⟨stopped ~ the way⟩
²along *adv* **1** : FORWARD, ON **2** : as a companion ⟨bring her ~⟩ **3** ♦ : at an advanced point ⟨plans are far ~⟩

♦ ahead, forth, forward, on, onward

along•shore \ə-ˈlȯŋ-ˈshōr\ *adv or adj* : along the shore or coast
¹along•side \-ˌsīd\ *adv* : along or by the side
²alongside *prep* **1** : along or by the side of **2** : in association with
alongside of *prep* : ALONGSIDE
aloof \ə-ˈlüf\ *adj* ♦ : removed or distant physically or emotionally — **aloof•ness** *n*

♦ antisocial, cold, cool, detached, distant, frosty, remote, standoffish, unsociable

al•o•pe•cia \ˌa-lə-ˈpē-sh(ē-)ə\ *n* : BALDNESS
aloud \ə-ˈlau̇d\ *adv* : with the speaking voice
alp \ˈalp\ *n* : a high rugged mountain
al•paca \al-ˈpa-kə\ *n* : a domesticated mammal especially of Peru that is related to the llama; *also* : its woolly hair or cloth made from this
al•pha \ˈal-fə\ *n* **1** : the 1st letter of the Greek alphabet — A or α **2** : something first : BEGINNING
al•pha•bet \ˈal-fə-ˌbet\ *n* : the set of letters or characters used in writing a language
al•pha•bet•i•cal \ˌal-fə-ˈbe-ti-kəl\ *or* **al•pha•bet•ic** \-ˈbe-tik\ *adj* **1** : arranged in the order of the letters of the alphabet **2** : of or employing an alphabet — **al•pha•bet•i•cal•ly** \-ti-k(ə-)lē\ *adv*
al•pha•bet•ize \ˈal-fə-bə-ˌtīz\ *vb* **-ized; -iz•ing** : to arrange in alphabetical order — **al•pha•bet•iz•er** *n*
al•pha•nu•mer•ic \ˌal-fə-nu̇-ˈmer-ik, -nyu̇-\ *adj* : consisting of letters and numbers and often other symbols ⟨an ~ code⟩; *also* : being a character in an alphanumeric system
alpha particle *n* : a positively charged particle identical with the nucleus of a helium atom that is ejected at high speed in certain radioactive transformations
alpha rhythm *n* : ALPHA WAVE
alpha wave *n* : an electrical rhythm of the brain often associated with a state of wakeful relaxation
Al•pine \ˈal-ˌpīn\ *adj* **1** : relating to, located in, or resembling the Alps mountains **2** *often not cap* : of, relating to, or growing on upland slopes above timberline **3** : of or relating to competitive ski events consisting of slalom and downhill racing
al•ready \ȯl-ˈre-dē\ *adv* : by this time : PREVIOUSLY
¹al•right \ȯl-ˈrīt\ *adv* : very well : ALL RIGHT — used interjectionally to express agreement or resignation or to indicate the resumption of a discussion ⟨*alright*, let's go⟩
²alright *adj* **1** ♦ : giving satisfaction : SATISFACTORY **2** ♦ : free from harm or risk **3** ♦ : having qualities that tend to give pleasure — often used as a generalized term of approval

♦ [1] agreeable, all right, fine, good, OK, palatable, satisfactory ♦ [2] all right, safe, secure ♦ [3] OK, yea, yes

al•so \ˈȯl-sō\ *adv* **1** ♦ : in like manner : LIKEWISE **2** ♦ : in addition : TOO

♦ [1] alike, correspondingly, likewise, similarly, so ***Ant*** differently, otherwise ♦ [2] additionally, again, besides, further, furthermore, likewise, more, moreover, then, too, withal, yet

al•so–ran \-ˌran\ *n* **1** : a horse or dog that finishes out of the money in a race **2** : a contestant that does not win
alt *abbr* **1** alternate **2** altitude
Alta *abbr* Alberta
al•tar \ˈȯl-tər\ *n* **1** : a structure on which sacrifices are offered or incense is burned **2** : a table used as a center of ritual or worship
altar boy *n* : a boy who assists the celebrant at a church service
¹al•ter \ˈȯl-tər\ *vb* **al•tered; al•ter•ing** \-t(ə-)riŋ\ **1** ♦ : to make or become different **2** : to remove the sex organs of

♦ change, make over, modify, recast, redo, refashion, remake, remodel, revamp, revise, rework, vary

²alter *abbr* alteration
al•ter•a•tion \ˌȯl-tə-ˈrā-shən\ *n* ♦ : the act, process, or result of altering

♦ change, difference, modification, revise, revision, variation

al•ter•ca•tion \ˌȯl-tər-ˈkā-shən\ *n* ♦ : a noisy or angry dispute

♦ argument, disagreement, dispute, fight, hassle, misunderstanding, quarrel, row, scrap, spat, squabble, wrangle

al•ter ego \ˌȯl-tər-ˈē-gō\ *n* : a second self; *esp* : a trusted friend
¹al•ter•nate \ˈȯl-tər-nət, ˈal-\ *adj* **1** : arranged or succeeding by turns **2** : every other **3** : being an alternative ⟨an ~ route⟩ — **al•ter•nate•ly** *adv*
²al•ter•nate \-ˌnāt\ *vb* **-nat•ed; -nat•ing** : to occur or cause to occur by turns — **al•ter•na•tion** \ˌȯl-tər-ˈnā-shən, ˌal-\ *n*
³alternate *n* : SUBSTITUTE
alternating current *n* : an electric current that reverses its direction at regular intervals
¹al•ter•na•tive \ȯl-ˈtər-nə-tiv, al-\ *adj* : offering a choice
²alternative *n* ♦ : an opportunity for deciding between two or more courses or propositions

♦ choice, discretion, option, pick, preference, way

alternative medicine *n* : any of various systems of healing (as homeopathy) not typically practiced in conventional Western medicine
al•ter•na•tor \ˈȯl-tər-ˌnā-tər, ˈal-\ *n* : an electric generator for producing alternating current
al•though *also* **al•tho** \ȯl-ˈt͟hō\ *conj* ♦ : in spite of the fact that : even though

♦ albeit, howbeit, though, when, while

al•tim•e•ter \al-ˈti-mə-tər, ˈal-tə-ˌmē-tər\ *n* : an instrument for measuring altitude
al•ti•tude \ˈal-tə-ˌtüd, -ˌtyüd\ *n* **1** : angular distance above the horizon **2** ♦ : vertical distance : HEIGHT **3** : the perpendicular distance in a geometric figure from the vertex to the base, from the vertex of an angle to the side opposite, or from the base to a parallel side or face

♦ elevation, height

al•to \ˈal-tō\ *n, pl* **altos** : the lower female voice part in a 4-part chorus; *also* : a singer having this voice or part
¹al•to•geth•er \ˌȯl-tə-ˈge-t͟hər\ *adv* **1** ♦ : to the full or entire extent : WHOLLY **2** ♦ : in all **3** ♦ : on the whole

♦ [1] absolutely, all, clean, completely, dead, entirely, fast, flat, full, fully, perfectly, quite, thoroughly, well, wholly ♦ [2] all around, collectively, overall, together ♦ [3] chiefly, generally, largely, mainly, mostly, overall, predominantly, primarily, principally

²altogether *n* : NUDE ⟨posed in the ~⟩
al•tru•ism \ˈal-tru̇-ˌi-zəm\ *n* : unselfish interest in the welfare of others — **al•tru•ist** \-ist\ *n* — **al•tru•is•ti•cal•ly** \-ti-k(ə-)lē\ *adv*
al•tru•is•tic \ˌal-tru̇-ˈis-tik\ *adj* ♦ : relating to or given to altruism

♦ beneficent, benevolent, charitable, humanitarian, philanthropic

al•um \ˈa-ləm\ *n* : either of two colorless crystalline aluminum-containing compounds used especially as an emetic or as an astringent and styptic
alu•mi•na \ə-ˈlü-mə-nə\ *n* : the oxide of aluminum occurring in nature as corundum and in bauxite
al•u•min•i•um \ˌal-yə-ˈmi-nē-əm\ *n, chiefly Brit* : ALUMINUM
alu•mi•nize \ə-ˈlü-mə-ˌnīz\ *vb* **-nized; -niz•ing** : to treat with aluminum
alu•mi•num \ə-ˈlü-mə-nəm\ *n* : a silver-white malleable ductile light metallic element that is the most abundant metal in the earth's crust
alum•na \ə-ˈləm-nə\ *n, pl* **-nae** \-(ˌ)nē\ : a woman graduate or former student of a college or school
alum•nus \ə-ˈləm-nəs\ *n, pl* **-ni** \-ˌnī\ : a graduate or former student of a college or school
al•ways \ˈȯl-wēz, -wəz, -(ˌ)wāz\ *adv* **1** ♦ : at all times : INVARIABLY **2** ♦ : for a limitless time : FOREVER

♦ [1] constantly, continually, ever, forever, incessantly, invariably, perpetually, unfailingly ***Ant*** ne'er, never ♦ [2] eternally, ever, everlastingly, forever, permanently, perpetually

Alz•hei•mer's disease \ˈälts-ˌhī-mərz-, ˈalts-\ *n* : a degenerative brain disease characterized especially by progressive mental deterioration and memory loss
am *pres 1st sing of* BE
¹Am *abbr* America; American
²Am *symbol* americium
¹AM \ˈā-ˌem\ *n* : a broadcasting system using amplitude modulation; *also* : a radio receiver for broadcasts made by such a system
²AM *abbr* **1** ante meridiem — often not cap. and often punctuated **2** master of arts
AMA *abbr* American Medical Association

amah \ˈä-(ˌ)mä\ *n* : a female servant in eastern Asia; *esp* : a Chinese nurse

amal•gam \ə-ˈmal-gəm\ *n* **1** : an alloy of mercury with another metal used in making dental cements **2** ♦ : a mixture of different elements

♦ admixture, blend, combination, composite, compound, fusion, intermixture, mix, mixture

amal•gam•ate \ə-ˈmal-gə-ˌmāt\ *vb* **-at•ed; -at•ing** ♦ : to unite or merge into one body

♦ blend, combine, commingle, fuse, incorporate, integrate, intermingle, merge, mingle, mix

amal•ga•ma•tion \-ˌmal-gə-ˈmā-shən\ *n* : the result of amalgamating

aman•u•en•sis \ə-ˌman-yə-ˈwen-səs\ *n, pl* **-en•ses** \-ˌsēz\ : one employed to write from dictation or to copy what another has written : SECRETARY

am•a•ranth \ˈa-mə-ˌranth\ *n* **1** : any of a large genus of coarse herbs sometimes grown for their showy flowers **2** : a flower that never fades

am•a•ran•thine \ˌa-mə-ˈran-thən, -ˌthīn\ *adj* **1** : relating to or resembling an amaranth **2** : UNDYING

am•a•ryl•lis \ˌa-mə-ˈri-ləs\ *n* : any of various plants related to the lilies; *esp* : any of several African herbs having bulbs and grown for their clusters of large showy flowers

amass \ə-ˈmas\ *vb* ♦ : to collect into a mass : ACCUMULATE

♦ accumulate, assemble, collect, concentrate, garner, gather, group, lump, pick up, round up, scrape

[1]**am•a•teur** \ˈa-mə-(ˌ)tər, -ˌtu̇r, -ˌtyu̇r, -ˌchu̇r, -chər\ *n* **1** : a person who engages in a pursuit for pleasure and not as a profession **2** : a person who is not expert — **am•a•teur•ism** \ˈa-mə-(ˌ)tər-i-zəm, -ˌtu̇r-, -ˌtyu̇r-, -ˌchu̇r-, -ˌchər-\ *n*

[2]**amateur** *adj* ♦ : engaged in or performed by or as if by an amateur

♦ amateurish, inexperienced, inexpert, nonprofessional, unprofessional, unskilled, unskillful

am•a•teur•ish \ˌa-mə-ˈtər-ish, -ˈtu̇r-, -ˈtyu̇r-, -ˈchu̇r-, -ˈchər-\ *adj* ♦ : having the characteristics of an amateur : lacking professional finish

♦ amateur, inexperienced, inexpert, nonprofessional, unprofessional, unskilled, unskillful *Ant* ace, expert, masterful, professional

am•a•tive \ˈa-mə-tiv\ *adj* : indicative of love : AMOROUS — **am•a•tive•ly** *adv* — **am•a•tive•ness** *n*

am•a•to•ry \ˈa-mə-ˌtōr-ē\ *adj* ♦ : of or expressing sexual love

♦ amorous, erotic, sexy

amaze \ə-ˈmāz\ *vb* **amazed; amaz•ing** ♦ : to fill with wonder : ASTOUND — **amaz•ing•ly** *adv*

♦ astonish, astound, bowl, dumbfound, flabbergast, floor, shock, startle, stun, stupefy, surprise

amazed *adj* ♦ : filled with wonder or astonishment

♦ awestruck, stunned, thunderstruck

amaze•ment \-mənt\ *n* ♦ : the quality or state of being amazed

♦ admiration, astonishment, awe, wonder, wonderment

amazing *adj* ♦ : causing amazement, great wonder, or surprise

♦ astonishing, astounding, eye-opening, shocking, startling, stunning, surprising ♦ astonishing, astounding, awesome, fabulous, marvelous (*or* marvellous), miraculous, surprising, wonderful

am•a•zon \ˈa-mə-ˌzän, -zən\ *n* **1** *cap* : a member of a race of female warriors of Greek mythology **2** : a tall strong often masculine woman — **am•a•zo•ni•an** \ˌa-mə-ˈzō-nē-ən\ *adj, often cap*

amb *abbr* ambassador

am•bas•sa•dor \am-ˈba-sə-dər\ *n* ♦ : a representative especially of a government — **am•bas•sa•do•ri•al** \-ˌba-sə-ˈdōr-ē-əl\ *adj* — **am•bas•sa•dor•ship** *n*

♦ delegate, emissary, envoy, legate, minister, representative

am•ber \ˈam-bər\ *n* : a yellowish or brownish fossil resin used especially for ornamental objects; *also* : the color of this resin

am•ber•gris \ˈam-bər-ˌgris, -ˌgrēs\ *n* : a waxy substance from the sperm whale used in making perfumes

am•bi•dex•trous \ˌam-bi-ˈdek-strəs\ *adj* : using both hands with equal ease — **am•bi•dex•trous•ly** *adv*

am•bi•ence *or* **am•bi•ance** \ˈam-bē-əns, äⁿ-ˈbyäⁿs\ *n* : a pervading atmosphere

am•bi•ent \ˈam-bē-ənt\ *adj* : existing on all sides

am•bi•gu•i•ty \ˌam-bə-ˈgyü-ə-tē\ *n* ♦ : the quality or state of being ambiguous

♦ darkness, murkiness, obscurity, opacity

am•big•u•ous \am-ˈbi-gyə-wəs\ *adj* ♦ : capable of being understood in more than one way — **am•big•u•ous•ly** *adv*

♦ cryptic, enigmatic, equivocal, mysterious, nebulous, obscure

am•bi•tion \am-ˈbi-shən\ *n* **1** ♦ : eager desire for success or power **2** ♦ : the object of ambition

♦ [1] aspiration, go-getting ♦ [2] aim, aspiration, goal, mark, meaning, object, objective, plan, purpose

am•bi•tious \-shəs\ *adj* ♦ : characterized by ambition — **am•bi•tious•ly** *adv*

♦ go-getting, self-seeking

am•biv•a•lence \am-ˈbi-və-ləns\ *n* : simultaneous attraction toward and repulsion from a person, object, or action — **am•biv•a•lent** \-lənt\ *adj*

[1]**am•ble** \ˈam-bəl\ *vb* **am•bled; am•bling** \-b(ə-)liŋ\ : to go at an amble

[2]**amble** *n* : an easy gait especially of a horse

am•bro•sia \am-ˈbrō-zh(ē-)ə\ *n* : the food of the Greek and Roman gods

am•bro•sial \-zh(ē-)əl\ *adj* ♦ : pleasing to the senses especially of taste or smell

♦ aromatic, fragrant, redolent, savory, scented, sweet ♦ appetizing, delectable, delicious, flavorful (*or* flavourful), luscious, palatable, savory, scrumptious, tasty, toothsome, yummy

am•bu•lance \ˈam-byə-ləns\ *n* : a vehicle equipped for carrying the injured or sick

am•bu•lant \ˈam-byə-lənt\ *adj* : AMBULATORY

[1]**am•bu•la•to•ry** \ˈam-byə-lə-ˌtōr-ē\ *adj* **1** : of, relating to, or adapted to walking **2** : able to walk or move about

[2]**ambulatory** *n, pl* **-ries** : a sheltered place (as in a cloister) for walking

am•bus•cade \ˈam-bə-ˌskād\ *n* AMBUSH

[1]**am•bush** \ˈam-ˌbu̇sh\ *n* ♦ : a trap in which concealed persons wait to attack by surprise

♦ net, snare, trap, web ♦ surprise, trap

[2]**ambush** *vb* ♦ : to attack from an ambush

♦ surprise, waylay

amdt *abbr* amendment

ameba, ameboid *var of* AMOEBA, AMOEBOID

ame•lio•rate \ə-ˈmēl-yə-ˌrāt\ *vb* **-rat•ed; -rat•ing** ♦ : to make or grow better : IMPROVE — **ame•lio•ra•tion** \-ˌmēl-yə-ˈrā-shən\ *n*

♦ amend, better, enhance, enrich, improve, perfect, refine

amen \(ˌ)ā-ˈmen, (ˌ)ä-\ *interj* — used especially at the end of prayers to affirm or express approval

ame•na•ble \ə-ˈmē-nə-bəl, -ˈme-\ *adj* **1** : ANSWERABLE **2 a** ♦ : readily brought to yield, submit, or cooperate : COMPLIANT **b** ♦ : inclined or favorably disposed in mind : WILLING

♦ [2a] compliant, conformable, docile, obedient, submissive, tractable ♦ [2b] disposed, game, glad, inclined, ready, willing

amend \ə-ˈmend\ *vb* **1** ♦ : to change for the better : IMPROVE **2** : to alter formally in phraseology — **amend•able** \-ˈmen-də-bəl\ *adj*

♦ ameliorate, better, enhance, enrich, improve, perfect, refine ♦ correct, debug, emend, rectify, reform, remedy

amend•ment \ə-ˈmend-mənt\ *n* **1** : the act of amending **2** : the process of amending a parliamentary motion or a constitution; *also* : the alteration so proposed or made

amends \ə-ˈmendz\ *n sing or pl* : compensation for injury or loss

ame•ni•ty \ə-ˈme-nə-tē, -ˈmē-\ *n, pl* **-ties** **1** ♦ : the quality of being pleasant or agreeable : AGREEABLENESS **2** ♦ : a gesture observed in social relationships **3** ♦ : something that serves as a comfort or convenience

♦ [1] agreeableness, amiability, geniality, graciousness, niceness, pleasantness, sweetness ♦ [2] civility, courtesy, formality, gesture ♦ [3] comfort, extra, frill, indulgence, luxury, superfluity

Amer *abbr* America; American

amerce \ə-ˈmərs\ *vb* **amerced; amerc•ing** **1** : to penalize by a fine determined by the court **2** : PUNISH — **amerce•ment** *n*

Amer•i•can \ə-ˈmer-ə-kən\ *n* **1** : a native or inhabitant of No. or So. America **2** : a citizen of the U.S. — **American** *adj* — **Amer•i•can•ism** \-ə-kə-ˌni-zəm\ *n* — **Amer•i•can•iza•tion** \ə-ˌmer-ə-kə-nə-ˈzā-shən\ *n* — **Amer•i•can•ize** \ə-ˈmer-ə-kə-ˌnīz\ *vb* — **Amer•i•can•ness** *n*

Amer•i•ca•na \ə-ˌmer-ə-ˈka-nə, -ˈkä-\ *n pl* **:** materials concerning or characteristic of America, its civilization, or its culture

American Indian *n* **:** a member of any of the aboriginal peoples of No. and So. America except the Eskimos

American plan *n* **:** a hotel plan whereby the daily rates cover the cost of room and three meals

American Sign Language *n* **:** a sign language for the deaf in which meaning is conveyed by a system of hand gestures and placement

am•er•i•ci•um \ˌam-ə-ˈrish-ē-əm, -ˈris-\ *n* **:** a radioactive metallic chemical element produced artificially from plutonium

Amerind *abbr* American Indian

Am•er•in•di•an \ˌa-mə-ˈrin-dē-ən\ *n* **:** AMERICAN INDIAN — **Amerindian** *adj*

am•e•thyst \ˈa-mə-thəst\ *n* **:** a gemstone consisting of clear purple or bluish violet quartz

ami•a•bil•i•ty \ˌā-mē-ə-ˈbi-lə-tē\ *n* ♦ **:** the quality of being amiable

♦ agreeableness, amenity, geniality, graciousness, niceness, pleasantness, sweetness ***Ant*** disagreeableness, unpleasantness

ami•a•ble \ˈā-mē-ə-bəl\ *adj* **1 :** pleasing to one's mind or senses **:** AGREEABLE **2** ♦ **:** having a friendly and sociable disposition — **ami•a•bly** \ˈā-mē-ə-blē\ *adv*

♦ affable, agreeable, genial, good-natured, gracious, nice, sweet, well-disposed ***Ant*** disagreeable, ill-natured, ill-tempered, ungracious, unpleasant

ami•a•ble•ness \-nəs\ *n* **:** the quality of being amiable

am•i•ca•ble \ˈa-mi-kə-bəl\ *adj* ♦ **:** characterized by friendly goodwill — **am•i•ca•bil•i•ty** \ˌa-mi-kə-ˈbi-lə-tē\ *n* — **am•i•ca•bly** \ˈa-mi-kə-blē\ *adv*

♦ agreeable, compatible, congenial, harmonious, kindred, unanimous, united ♦ companionable, comradely, cordial, friendly, genial, hearty, neighborly, warm, warmhearted

amid \ə-ˈmid\ *or* **amidst** \-ˈmidst\ *prep* ♦ **:** in or into the middle of **:** AMONG

♦ among, midst, through

amid•ships \ə-ˈmid-ˌships\ *adv* **:** in or near the middle of a ship

ami•no acid \ə-ˈmē-nō-\ *n* **:** any of numerous nitrogen-containing acids that include some which are used by cells to build proteins

amir *var of* EMIR

¹amiss \ə-ˈmis\ *adv* **1** ♦ **:** in a mistaken way **:** WRONGLY **2** ♦ **:** off the right path or route **:** ASTRAY **3 :** IMPERFECTLY

♦ [1] erroneously, faultily, improperly, inaptly, incorrectly, mistakenly, wrongly ♦ [2] afield, astray, awry, wrong

²amiss *adj* **1 :** WRONG **2** ♦ **:** out of place under the circumstances **3** ♦ **:** marked by fault or defect **:** FAULTY, IMPERFECT

♦ [2] improper, inappropriate, inapt, infelicitous, unbecoming, unfit, unseemly, unsuitable, wrong ♦ [3] bad, defective, faulty, imperfect

am•i•ty \ˈa-mə-tē\ *n, pl* **-ties :** ♦ **:** the quality or state of being friendly; *esp* **:** friendly relations between nations

♦ benevolence, cordiality, fellowship, friendliness, friendship, goodwill, kindliness

am•me•ter \ˈa-ˌmē-tər\ *n* **:** an instrument for measuring electric current in amperes

am•mo \ˈa-mō\ *n* **:** AMMUNITION

am•mo•nia \ə-ˈmō-nyə\ *n* **1 :** a colorless gaseous compound of nitrogen and hydrogen used in refrigeration and in the making of fertilizers and explosives **2 :** a solution (**ammonia water**) of ammonia in water

am•mo•ni•um \ə-ˈmō-nē-əm\ *n* **:** an ion or chemical group derived from ammonia by combination with hydrogen

ammonium chloride *n* **:** a white crystalline volatile salt used in batteries and as an expectorant

am•mu•ni•tion \ˌam-yə-ˈni-shən\ *n* **1 :** projectiles fired from guns **2 :** explosive items used in war **3 :** material for use in attack or defense

Amn *abbr* airman

am•ne•sia \am-ˈnē-zhə\ *n* **1 :** abnormal loss of memory **2 :** the selective overlooking of events or acts not favorable to one's purpose — **am•ne•si•ac** \-zhē-ˌak, -zē-\ *or* **am•ne•sic** \-zik, -sik\ *adj or n*

am•nes•ty \ˈam-nə-stē\ *n, pl* **-ties** ♦ **:** an act granting a pardon to a group of individuals — **amnesty** *vb*

♦ absolution, forgiveness, pardon, remission

am•nio•cen•te•sis \ˌam-nē-ō-ˌsen-ˈtē-səs\ *n, pl* **-te•ses** \-ˌsēz\ **:** the surgical insertion of a hollow needle through the abdominal wall and uterus of a pregnant female especially to obtain fluid used to check the fetus for chromosomal abnormality and to determine sex

amoe•ba \ə-ˈmē-bə\ *n, pl* **-bas** *or* **-bae** \-(ˌ)bē\ **:** any of various tiny one-celled protozoans that lack permanent cell organs and occur especially in water and soil — **amoe•bic** \-bik\ *adj*

amoe•boid \-ˌbȯid\ *adj* **:** resembling an amoeba especially in moving or readily changing shape

amok \ə-ˈmək, -ˈmäk\ *or* **amuck** \-ˈmək\ *adv* ♦ **:** in a violent, frenzied, or uncontrolled manner ⟨run ~⟩

♦ berserk, frantically, harum-scarum, hectically, helter-skelter, madly, pell-mell, wild, wildly

among \ə-ˈməŋ\ *also* **amongst** \-ˈməŋst\ *prep* **1** ♦ **:** in or through the midst of **2 :** in the number, class, or company of **3 :** in shares to each of **4 :** by common action of

♦ amid, midst, through

amon•til•la•do \ə-ˌmän-tə-ˈlä-dō\ *n, pl* **-dos :** a medium dry sherry

amor•al \ā-ˈmȯr-əl\ *adj* **1 :** neither moral nor immoral; *esp* **:** being outside the sphere to which moral judgments apply **2 :** lacking moral sensibility — **amor•al•ly** *adv*

am•o•rous \ˈa-mə-rəs\ *adj* **1** ♦ **:** strongly moved by love and especially sexual love **2 :** being in love **3** ♦ **:** of or indicative of love and especially sexual love — **am•o•rous•ly** *adv* — **am•o•rous•ness** *n*

♦ [1, 3] amatory, erotic, sexy

amor•phous \ə-ˈmȯr-fəs\ *adj* **1** ♦ **:** having no definite form **:** FORMLESS **2 :** not crystallized

♦ formless, shapeless, unformed, unshaped, unstructured

am•or•tize \ˈa-mər-ˌtīz, ə-ˈmȯr-\ *vb* **-tized; -tiz•ing :** to extinguish (as a mortgage) usually by payment on the principal at the time of each periodic interest payment — **amor•ti•za•tion** \ˌa-mər-tə-ˈzā-shən, ə-ˌmȯr-\ *n*

¹amount \ə-ˈmau̇nt\ *vb* **1** ♦ **:** to be equivalent — usually used with *to* **2** ♦ **:** to reach a total **:** add up — usually used with *to*

♦ *usu* **amount to** [1] add up, come, correspond, equal ♦ *usu* **amount to** [2] add up, come, number, sum, total

²amount *n* **1** ♦ **:** the total number or quantity **2 :** a principal sum plus the interest on it

♦ measure, quantity

amour \ə-ˈmu̇r, ä-, a-\ *n* **1** ♦ **:** a love affair especially when illicit **2 :** LOVER

♦ affair, love affair, romance

amour pro•pre \ˌa-ˌmu̇r-ˈprōprᵊ, ˌä-, -ˈprȯprᵊ\ *n* **:** SELF-ESTEEM

¹amp \ˈamp\ *n* **:** AMPLIFIER; *also* **:** a unit consisting of an electronic amplifier and a loudspeaker

²amp *abbr* ampere

am•per•age \ˈam-p(ə-)rij\ *n* **:** the strength of a current of electricity expressed in amperes

am•pere \ˈam-ˌpir\ *n* **:** a unit of electric current equivalent to a steady current produced by one volt applied across a resistance of one ohm

am•per•sand \ˈam-pər-ˌsand\ *n* **:** a character & used for the word *and*

am•phet•amine \am-ˈfe-tə-ˌmēn, -mən\ *n* **:** a compound or one of its derivatives that stimulates the central nervous system and is used especially to treat hyperactive children and to suppress appetite

am•phib•i•an \am-ˈfi-bē-ən\ *n* **1 :** an amphibious organism; *esp* **:** any of a class of vertebrate animals (as frogs and salamanders) intermediate between fishes and reptiles **2 :** an airplane that can land on and take off from either land or water

am•phib•i•ous \am-ˈfi-bē-əs\ *adj* **1 :** able to live both on land and in water **2 :** adapted for both land and water **3 :** made by joint action of land, sea, and air forces invading from the sea; *also* **:** trained for such action

am•phi•bole \ˈam-fə-ˌbōl\ *n* **:** any of a group of rock-forming minerals of similar crystal structure

am•phi•the•ater \ˈam-fə-ˌthē-ə-tər\ *n* **1 :** an oval or circular structure with rising tiers of seats around an arena **2 :** a very large auditorium

am•pho•ra \ˈam-fə-rə\ *n, pl* **-rae** \-ˌrē\ *or* **-ras :** an ancient Greek jar or vase with two handles that rise almost to the level of the mouth

am•ple \ˈam-pəl\ *adj* **am•pler** \-plər\; **am•plest** \-pləst\ **1** ♦ **:** generous or more than adequate in size, scope, or capacity **:** CAPACIOUS **2** ♦ **:** enough to satisfy **:** ABUNDANT

♦ [1] capacious, commodious, roomy, spacious ♦ [2] abundant, bountiful, comfortable, generous, liberal, plentiful

am•pli•fy \ˈam-plə-ˌfī\ *vb* **-fied; -fy•ing** **1** ♦ **:** to expand by extended treatment **2** ♦ **:** to increase in magnitude or strength; *esp* **:** to make louder — **am•pli•fi•ca•tion** \ˌam-plə-fə-ˈkā-shən\ *n* — **am•pli•fi•er** \ˈam-plə-ˌfī(-ə)r\ *n*

♦ [1] develop, elaborate (on), enlarge (on), expand ♦ [2] add, aggrandize, augment, boost, compound, enlarge, escalate, expand, extend, increase, multiply, raise, swell, up ♦ [2] beef, boost, consolidate, deepen, enhance, heighten, intensify, magnify, redouble, step up, strengthen

am•pli•tude \-ˌtüd, -ˌtyüd\ *n* **1 :** ample extent **:** FULLNESS **2** ♦ **:** the extent or range of a quality, property, process, or phenomenon: as **:** the extent of a vibratory movement (as of a pendulum) or of an oscillation (as of an alternating current or a radio wave)

♦ breadth, compass, extent, range, reach, realm, scope, sweep, width

amplitude modulation *n* **:** modulation of the amplitude of a radio carrier wave in accordance with the strength of the signal; *also* **:** a broadcasting system using such modulation

am•ply \ˈam-plē\ *adv* ♦ **:** in an ample manner

♦ bountifully, generously, handsomely, liberally, unstintingly, well

am•poule *or* **am•pule** *also* **am•pul** \ˈam-ˌpyül, -ˌpül\ *n* **:** a small sealed bulbous glass vessel used to hold a solution for hypodermic injection

am•pu•tate \ˈam-pyə-ˌtāt\ *vb* **-tat•ed; -tat•ing :** to cut off ⟨~ a leg⟩ — **am•pu•ta•tion** \ˌam-pyə-ˈtā-shən\ *n*

am•pu•tee \ˌam-pyə-ˈtē\ *n* **:** one who has had a limb amputated

AMSLAN *abbr* American Sign Language

amt *abbr* amount

amuck *var of* AMOK

am•u•let \ˈam-yə-lət\ *n* ♦ **:** an ornament worn as a charm against evil

♦ charm, fetish, mascot, talisman

amuse \ə-ˈmyüz\ *vb* **amused; amus•ing** ♦ **:** to entertain in a light or playful manner **:** DIVERT

♦ disport, divert, entertain, regale

amuse•ment \-mənt\ *n* ♦ **:** pleasurable diversion

♦ distraction, diversion, entertainment

amus•ing \ə-ˈmyü-ziŋ\ *adj* ♦ **:** giving amusement

♦ delightful, diverting, enjoyable, entertaining, fun, pleasurable

AM•VETS \ˈam-ˌvets\ *abbr* American Veterans (of World War II)

am•y•lase \ˈa-mə-ˌlās, -ˌlaz\ *n* **:** any of several enzymes that accelerate the breakdown of starch and glycogen

an \ən, (ˈ)an\ *indefinite article* **:** A — used before words beginning with a vowel sound

¹-an *or* **-ian** *also* **-ean** *n suffix* **1 :** one that belongs to ⟨Americ*an*⟩ ⟨crustac*ean*⟩ **2 :** one skilled in or specializing in ⟨phoneti*cian*⟩

²-an *or* **-ian** *also* **-ean** *adj suffix* **1 :** of or belonging to ⟨Americ*an*⟩ **2 :** characteristic of **:** resembling ⟨Mozart*ean*⟩

AN *abbr* airman (Navy)

an•a•bol•ic steroid \ˌa-nə-ˈbä-lik-\ *n* **:** any of a group of synthetic steroid hormones sometimes abused by athletes in training to increase temporarily the size of their muscles

anach•ro•nism \ə-ˈna-krə-ˌni-zəm\ *n* **1 :** the error of placing a person or thing in the wrong period **2 :** one that is chronologically out of place — **anach•ro•nis•tic** \ə-ˌna-krə-ˈnis-tik\ *adj* — **anach•ro•nous** \-ˈna-krə-nəs\ *adj*

an•a•con•da \ˌa-nə-ˈkän-də\ *n* **:** a large So. American snake that suffocates and kills its prey by constriction

anad•ro•mous \ə-ˈna-drə-məs\ *adj* **:** ascending rivers from the sea for breeding ⟨~ fish⟩

an•aer•obe \ˈa-nə-ˌrōb\ *n* **:** an anaerobic organism

an•aer•o•bic \ˌa-nə-ˈrō-bik\ *adj* **:** living, active, occurring, or existing in the absence of free oxygen

ana•gram \ˈa-nə-ˌgram\ *n* **:** a word or phrase made by transposing the letters of another word or phrase

¹anal \ˈān-ᵊl\ *adj* **1 :** of, relating to, or situated near the anus **2 :** of, relating to, or characterized by the stage of psychosexual development in psychoanalytic theory during which one is concerned especially with feces **3 :** of, relating to, or characterized by personality traits (as parsimony and ill humor) considered typical of fixation at the anal stage of development — **anal•ly** *adv*

²anal *abbr* **1** analogy **2** analysis; analytic

an•al•ge•sia \ˌan-ᵊl-ˈjē-zhə\ *n* **:** insensibility to pain — **an•al•ge•sic** \-ˈjē-zik, -sik\ *adj*

an•al•ge•sic \-ˈjē-zik, -sik\ *n* **:** an agent for producing analgesia

analog computer \ˈan-ᵊl-ˌȯg-, -ˌäg-\ *n* **:** a computer that operates with numbers represented by directly measurable quantities (as voltages)

anal•o•gous \ə-ˈna-lə-gəs\ *adj* ♦ **:** similar in one or more respects

♦ akin, alike, comparable, correspondent, like, parallel, similar, such

an•a•logue *or* **an•a•log** \ˈan-ᵊl-ˌȯg, -ˌag\ *n* **1 :** something that is analogous to something else **2 :** an organ similar in function to one of another animal or plant but different in structure or origin

anal•o•gy \ə-ˈna-lə-jē\ *n, pl* **-gies** **1 :** inference that if two or more things agree in some respects they will probably agree in others **2 :** a likeness in one or more ways between things otherwise unlike — **an•a•log•i•cal** \ˌan-ᵊl-ˈä-ji-kəl\ *adj* — **an•a•log•i•cal•ly** \-k(ə-)lē\ *adv*

anal•y•sis \ə-ˈna-lə-səs\ *n, pl* **-y•ses** \-ˌsēz\ **1** ♦ **:** separation of a thing into the parts or elements of which it is composed **2 a :** an examination of a thing to determine its parts or elements **b** ♦ **:** a statement showing the results of a critical examination **3 :** PSYCHOANALYSIS — **an•a•lyst** \ˈan-ᵊl-ist\ *n* — **an•a•lyt•i•cal•ly** *adv*

♦ [1] assay, breakdown, breakup, dissection ♦ [2b] comment, commentary, exposition

an•a•lyt•ic \ˌan-ᵊl-ˈi-tik\ *or* **an•a•lyt•i•cal** \-ti-kəl\ *adj* ♦ **:** of or relating to analysis; *esp* **:** separating something into component parts or constituent elements

♦ coherent, good, logical, rational, reasonable, sensible, sober, sound, valid

an•a•lyze \ˈan-ᵊl-ˌīz\ *vb* **-lyzed; -lyz•ing** ♦ **:** to make an analysis of

♦ anatomize, assay, break down, break up, dissect

an•a•pest \ˈa-nə-ˌpest\ *n* **:** a metrical foot of two unaccented syllables followed by one accented syllable — **an•a•pes•tic** \ˌa-nə-ˈpes-tik\ *adj or n*

an•ar•chic \a-ˈnär-kik\ *adj* ♦ **:** of, relating to, or advocating anarchy

♦ disorderly, lawless, unruly

an•ar•chism \ˈa-nər-ˌki-zəm\ *n* **:** the theory that all government is undesirable — **an•ar•chist** \-kist\ *n or adj* — **an•ar•chis•tic** \ˌa-nər-ˈkis-tik\ *adj*

an•ar•chy \ˈan-ər-kē\ *n* **1 a :** a social structure without government or law and order **b :** a state of lawlessness or political disorder due to the absence of governmental authority **2 :** utter confusion — **an•ar•chi•cal•ly** \-ki-k(ə-)lē\ *adv*

anas•to•mo•sis \ə-ˌnas-tə-ˈmō-səs\ *n, pl* **-mo•ses** \-ˌsēz\ **1 :** the union of parts or branches (as of blood vessels) **2 :** NETWORK

anat *abbr* anatomical; anatomy

anath•e•ma \ə-ˈna-thə-mə\ *n* **1 a :** a person or thing accursed **b** ♦ **:** one intensely disliked **2** ♦ **:** a solemn curse

♦ [1b] abhorrence, abomination, antipathy, aversion, bête noire, hate ♦ [2] curse, execration, imprecation, malediction

anath•e•ma•tize \-ˌtīz\ *vb* **-tized; -tiz•ing :** to pronounce an anathema against **:** CURSE

anat•o•mise *Brit var of* ANATOMIZE

anat•o•mize \ə-ˈna-tə-ˌmīz\ *vb* **-mized; -miz•ing** **1 :** to dissect so as to examine the structure and parts **2** ♦ **:** to study or determine the nature and relationship of the parts of by analysis **:** ANALYZE

♦ analyze, assay, break down, break up, dissect

anat•o•my \ə-ˈna-tə-mē\ *n, pl* **-mies** **1 :** a branch of science dealing with the structure of organisms **2 :** structural makeup especially of an organism or any of its parts **3 :** a separating into parts for detailed study **:** ANALYSIS — **an•a•tom•ic** \ˌa-nə-ˈtä-mik\ *or* **an•a•tom•i•cal** \-mi-kəl\ *adj* — **an•a•tom•i•cal•ly** \-mi-k(ə-)lē\ *adv* — **anat•o•mist** \ə-ˈna-tə-mist\ *n*

anc *abbr* ancient

-ance *n suffix* **1 :** action or process ⟨further*ance*⟩ **:** instance of an action or process ⟨perform*ance*⟩ **2 :** quality or state **:** instance of a quality or state ⟨protuber*ance*⟩ **3 :** amount or degree ⟨conduct*ance*⟩

an•ces•tor \ˈan-ˌses-tər\ *n* **1** ♦ **:** one from whom an individual is descended **2** ♦ **:** an individual that exhibits the essential features of a later type

♦ [1] father, forebear, forefather, grandfather ***Ant*** descendant
♦ [2] antecedent, forerunner, precursor ***Ant*** descendant

an•ces•tress \ˈan-ˌses-trəs\ *n* : a female ancestor
an•ces•try \ˈan-ˌses-trē\ *n* **1** ♦ : line of descent : LINEAGE **2** : ANCESTORS — **an•ces•tral** \an-ˈses-trəl\ *adj*

♦ birth, blood, bloodline, breeding, descent, extraction, family tree, genealogy, line, lineage, origin, parentage, pedigree, stock, strain *Ant* issue, posterity, progeny, seed

[1]**an•chor** \ˈaŋ-kər\ *n* **1** : a heavy metal device attached to a ship that catches hold of the bottom and holds the ship in place **2** : a broadcaster who reads the news and introduces the reports of other broadcasters : ANCHORPERSON
[2]**anchor** *vb* ♦ : to hold or become held in place by or as if by an anchor

♦ catch, clamp, fasten, fix, hitch, moor, secure, set

an•chor•age \ˈaŋ-k(ə-)rij\ *n* ♦ : a place suitable for ships to anchor

♦ harbor (*or* harbour), haven, port

an•cho•rite \ˈaŋ-kə-ˌrīt\ *n* ♦ : one that retires from society and lives in solitude : HERMIT

♦ hermit, recluse, solitary

an•chor•man \ˈaŋ-kər-ˌman\ *n* **1** : the member of a team who competes last **2** : an anchorperson who is a man
an•chor•per•son \-ˌpər-sən\ *n* : a broadcaster who reads the news and introduces the reports of other broadcasters
an•chor•wom•an \-ˌwu̇-mən\ *n* **1** : a woman who competes last **2** : an anchorperson who is a woman
an•cho•vy \ˈan-ˌchō-vē, an-ˈchō-\ *n, pl* **-vies** *or* **-vy** : a small herringlike fish used especially for sauces and relishes
an•cien ré•gime \äⁿs-yaⁿ-rā-ˈzhēm\ *n* **1** : the political and social system of France before the Revolution of 1789 **2** : a system no longer prevailing
[1]**an•cient** \ˈān-shənt\ *adj* **1** ♦ : having existed for many years **2** ♦ : belonging to times long past; *esp* : belonging to the period before the Middle Ages

♦ [1] elderly, geriatric, old, senior ♦ [2] age-old, antediluvian, antique, dateless, hoary, old, venerable *Ant* modern, new, recent ♦ [2] early, primal, primeval, primitive

[2]**ancient** *n* **1** : an aged person **2** *pl* : the peoples of ancient Greece and Rome; *esp* : the classical authors of Greece and Rome
an•cil•lary \ˈan-sə-ˌler-ē\ *adj* **1** : SUBORDINATE, SUBSIDIARY **2** : AUXILIARY, SUPPLEMENTARY — **ancillary** *n*
-ancy *n suffix* : quality or state ⟨flamboy*ancy*⟩
and \ənd, (ˈ)and\ *conj* **1** — used to indicate connection or addition especially of items within the same class or type or to join words or phrases of the same grammatical rank or function **2** — used to join one finite verb to another so that together they are equivalent to an infinitive of purpose ⟨come ~ see me⟩
[1]**an•dan•te** \än-ˈdän-ˌtā, -tē\ *adv or adj* : moderately slow — used as a direction in music
[2]**andante** *n* : an andante movement
and•iron \ˈan-ˌdī(-ə)rn\ *n* : one of a pair of metal supports for firewood in a fireplace
and/or \ˈand-ˈȯr\ *conj* — used to indicate that either *and* or *or* may apply ⟨men ~ women means men *and* women or men *or* women⟩
An•dor•ran \an-ˈdȯr-ən\ *n* : a native or inhabitant of Andorra
an•dro•gen \ˈan-drə-jən\ *n* : a male sex hormone
an•drog•y•nous \an-ˈdrä-jə-nəs\ *adj* **1** : having the characteristics of both male and female **2** : suitable for either sex ⟨~ clothing⟩
an•droid \ˈan-ˌdrȯid\ *n* : a mobile robot usually with a human form
an•ec•dot•al \ˌa-nik-ˈdōt-ᵊl\ *adj* **1** : relating to or consisting of anecdotes **2** : based on reports of an unscientific nature — **an•ec•dot•al•ly** *adv*
an•ec•dote \ˈan-ik-ˌdōt\ *n, pl* **-dotes** *also* **-dota** \ˌa-nik-ˈdō-tə\ ♦ : a brief story of an interesting, amusing, or biographical incident

♦ story, tale

ane•mia \ə-ˈnē-mē-ə\ *n* **1** : a condition in which blood is deficient in quantity, in red blood cells, or in hemoglobin and which is marked by pallor, weakness, and irregular heart action **2** : lack of vitality — **ane•mic** \ə-ˈnē-mik\ *adj*
an•e•mom•e•ter \ˌa-nə-ˈmä-mə-tər\ *n* : an instrument for measuring the force or speed of the wind
anem•o•ne \ə-ˈne-mə-nē\ *n* : any of a large genus of herbs related to the buttercups that have showy flowers without petals but with conspicuous often colored sepals
anent \ə-ˈnent\ *prep* : CONCERNING
an•es•the•sia *or Can and Brit* **an•aes•the•sia** \ˌa-nəs-ˈthē-zhə\ *n* : loss of bodily sensation
an•es•the•si•ol•o•gy *or chiefly Brit* **an•aes•the•si•o•lo•gy** \-ˌthē-zē-ˈä-lə-jē\ *n* : a branch of medical science dealing with anesthesia and anesthetics — **an•es•the•si•ol•o•gist** \-jist\ *n*
[1]**an•es•thet•ic** *or Can and Brit* **an•aes•thet•ic** \ˌa-nəs-ˈthe-tik\ *adj* : of, relating to, or capable of producing anesthesia
[2]**anesthetic** *or Can and Brit* **anaesthetic** *n* : an agent that produces anesthesia — **anes•the•tist** \ə-ˈnes-thə-tist\ *n* — **anes•the•tize** \-thə-ˌtīz\ *vb*
an•eu•rysm \ˈan-yə-ˌri-zəm\ *n* an abnormal blood-filled bulge of a blood vessel
anew \ə-ˈnü, -ˈnyü\ *adv* **1** ♦ : over again **2** : in a new form

♦ again, over

an•gel \ˈān-jəl\ *n* **1** : a spiritual being superior to man **2** : an attendant spirit **3** : a winged figure of human form in art **4** ♦ : one that precedes and indicates the approach of another : HARBINGER **5** : a person held to resemble an angel (as in looks or behavior) **6** : a financial backer — **an•gel•ic** \an-ˈje-lik\ *or* **an•gel•i•cal** \-li-kəl\ *adj* — **an•gel•i•cal•ly** \-k(ə-)lē\ *adv*

♦ forerunner, harbinger, herald, precursor

an•gel•fish \ˈān-jəl-ˌfish\ *n* : any of several bright-colored tropical fishes that are flattened from side to side
an•gel•i•ca \an-ˈje-li-kə\ *n* : a biennial herb related to the carrot whose roots and fruit furnish a flavoring oil
[1]**an•ger** \ˈaŋ-gər\ *vb* ♦ : to make angry

♦ antagonize, enrage, incense, inflame, infuriate, madden, outrage, rankle, rile, roil *Ant* delight, gratify, please

[2]**anger** *n* ♦ : a strong feeling of displeasure

♦ furor, fury, indignation, ire, outrage, rage, spleen, wrath, wrathfulness *Ant* delight, pleasure

an•gi•na \an-ˈjī-nə\ *n* : a disorder (as of the heart) marked by attacks of intense pain; *esp* : ANGINA PECTORIS — **an•gi•nal** \an-ˈjīn-ᵊl\ *adj*
angina pec•to•ris \-ˈpek-t(ə-)rəs\ *n* : a heart disease marked by brief attacks of sharp chest pain caused by deficient oxygenation of heart muscles
an•gio•gram \ˈan-jē-ə-ˌgram\ *n* : an X-ray photograph made by angiography
an•gi•og•ra•phy \ˌan-jē-ˈä-grə-fē\ *n* : the use of X-rays to make blood vessels visible (as by photography) after injection of a substance opaque to radiation
an•gio•plas•ty \ˈan-jē-ə-ˌplas-tē\ *n* : surgical repair of a blood vessel especially by using an inflatable catheter to unblock arteries clogged by atherosclerotic deposits
an•gio•sperm \-ˌspərm\ *n* : FLOWERING PLANT
[1]**an•gle** \ˈaŋ-gəl\ *n* **1** : a sharp projecting corner **2** : the figure formed by the meeting of two lines in a point **3 a** ♦ : a point of view **b** ♦ : the aspect seen from such an angle **4** : a special technique or plan : GIMMICK — **an•gled** *adj*

♦ [3a] outlook, perspective, point of view, slant, standpoint, viewpoint ♦ [3b] aspect, facet, hand, phase, side

[2]**angle** *vb* **an•gled; an•gling** \-g(ə-)liŋ\ ♦ : to turn, move, or direct at an angle

♦ cant, cock, heel, incline, lean, list, slant, slope, tilt, tip

[3]**angle** *vb* **an•gled; an•gling** \-g(ə-)liŋ\ : to fish with a hook and line — **an•gler** \-glər\ *n*
an•gle•worm \ˈaŋ-gəl-ˌwərm\ *n* : EARTHWORM
An•gli•can \ˈaŋ-gli-kən\ *adj* **1** : of or relating to the established episcopal Church of England **2** : of or relating to England or the English nation — **Anglican** *n* — **An•gli•can•ism** \-kə-ˌni-zəm\ *n*
an•gli•cize \ˈaŋ-glə-ˌsīz\ *vb* **-cized; -ciz•ing** *often cap* **1** : to make English (as in habits, speech, character, or outlook) **2** : to borrow (a foreign word or phrase) into English without changing form or spelling and sometimes without changing pronunciation — **an•gli•ci•za•tion** \ˌaŋ-glə-sə-ˈzā-shən\ *n, often cap*
an•gling \-gliŋ\ *n* : the action of one who angles; *esp* : the action or sport of fishing with hook and line
An•glo \ˈaŋ-glō\ *n, pl* **Anglos** : a non-Hispanic white inhabitant of the U.S.; *esp* : one of English origin and descent
An•glo–French \ˌaŋ-glō-ˈfrench\ *n* : the French language used in medieval England
An•glo•phile \ˈaŋ-glə-ˌfīl\ *also* **An•glo•phil** \-ˌfil\ *n* : one who greatly admires England and things English
An•glo•phobe \ˈaŋ-glə-ˌfōb\ *n* : one who is averse to England and things English
An•glo–Sax•on \ˌaŋ-glō-ˈsak-sən\ *n* **1** : a member of any of the Germanic peoples who invaded England in the 5th century A.D.

2 : a member of the English people **3 :** the language of the English people before about 1100 — **Anglo–Saxon** *adj*
an•go•ra \aŋ-ˈgōr-ə, an-\ *n* **1 :** yarn or cloth made from the hair of an Angora goat or rabbit **2** *cap* **:** any of a breed of cats, goats, or rabbits with a long silky coat
an•gry \ˈaŋ-grē\ *adj* **an•gri•er; -est ♦ :** feeling or showing anger — **an•gri•ly** \-grə-lē\ *adv*

♦ enraged, furious, irate, sore, wrathful *Ant* delighted, pleased

angst \ˈäŋst\ *n* **:** a feeling of anxiety
ang•strom \ˈaŋ-strəm\ *n* **:** a unit of length equal to one ten-billionth of a meter
an•guish \ˈaŋ-gwish\ *n* **♦ :** extreme pain or distress especially of mind

♦ affliction, agony, distress, misery, pain, torment, torture, tribulation, woe ♦ affliction, dolor, grief, heartache, sorrow, woe

an•guished \-gwisht\ *adj* **1 :** suffering anguish ⟨the ~ martyrs⟩ **2 ♦ :** expressing anguish ⟨~ cries⟩

♦ dolorous, lamentable, mournful, plaintive, sorrowful, sorry, woeful

an•gu•lar \ˈaŋ-gyə-lər\ *adj* **1 :** sharp-cornered **2 :** having one or more angles **3 :** being thin and bony — **an•gu•lar•i•ty** \ˌaŋ-gyə-ˈlar-ə-tē\ *n*
An•gus \ˈaŋ-gəs\ *n* **:** any of a breed of usually black hornless beef cattle originating in Scotland
an•hy•drous \an-ˈhī-drəs\ *adj* **:** free from water
an•i•line \ˈan-ᵊl-ən\ *n* **:** an oily poisonous liquid used in making dyes, medicines, and explosives
an•i•mad•vert \ˌa-nə-ˌmad-ˈvərt\ *vb* **:** to remark critically **:** express censure — **an•i•mad•ver•sion** \-ˈvər-zhən\ *n*
¹**an•i•mal** \ˈa-nə-məl\ *n* **1 :** any of a kingdom of living things typically differing from plants in capacity for active movement, in rapid response to stimulation, and in lack of cellulose cell walls **2 ♦ :** a lower animal as distinguished from human beings; *also* **:** MAMMAL

♦ beast, brute, creature, critter

²**animal** *adj* **1 :** of, relating to, or derived from animals **2 ♦ :** of or relating to the physical as distinguished from the mental or spiritual

♦ bodily, carnal, corporal, fleshly, material, physical, somatic

an•i•mal•cule \ˌa-nə-ˈmal-kyül\ *n* **:** a tiny animal usually invisible to the naked eye
¹**an•i•mate** \ˈa-nə-mət\ *adj* **1 ♦ :** having life **:** ALIVE **2 ♦ :** full of vigor and spirit **:** LIVELY

♦ [1] alive, live, living ♦ [2] active, animated, energetic, lively, peppy, perky, spirited, sprightly, springy, vital, vivacious

²**an•i•mate** \-ˌmāt\ *vb* **-mat•ed; -mat•ing 1 :** to impart life to **2 ♦ :** to give spirit and vigor to **3 :** to make appear to move ⟨~ a cartoon for motion pictures⟩

♦ brace, energize, enliven, fire, invigorate, jazz up, liven up, pep up, quicken, stimulate, vitalize, vivify, zip (up) *Ant* damp, dampen, deaden, dull

an•i•mat•ed \-ˌmā-təd\ *adj* **1 ♦ :** endowed with life or the qualities of life **:** ALIVE **2 ♦ :** full of movement and activity ⟨an ~ crowd⟩ **3 ♦ :** full of vigor and spirit **:** LIVELY

♦ [1, 2] alive, astir, busy, lively, vibrant ♦ [3] active, animate, energetic, lively, peppy, perky, spirited, sprightly, springy, vital, vivacious

an•i•ma•tion \ˌa-nə-ˈmā-shən\ *n* **1 ♦ :** the state of being animate or animated **:** LIVELINESS **2 :** a motion picture made from a series of drawings simulating motions by means of slight progressive changes

♦ briskness, exuberance, liveliness, lustiness, robustness, sprightliness, vibrancy, vitality

an•i•mism \ˈa-nə-ˌmi-zəm\ *n* **:** attribution of conscious life to objects in and phenomena of nature or to inanimate objects — **an•i•mist** \-mist\ *n* — **an•i•mis•tic** \ˌa-nə-ˈmis-tik\ *adj*
an•i•mos•i•ty \ˌa-nə-ˈmä-sə-tē\ *n, pl* **-ties ♦ :** ill will or resentment tending toward active hostility

♦ antagonism, antipathy, bitterness, enmity, gall, grudge, hostility, rancor

an•i•mus \ˈa-nə-məs\ *n* **:** deep-seated resentment and hostility
an•ion \ˈa-ˌnī-ən, -ˌnī-ˌän\ *n* **:** a negatively charged ion
an•ise \ˈa-nəs\ *n* **:** an herb related to the carrot with aromatic seeds (**aniseed** \-sēd\) used in flavoring
an•is•ette \ˌa-nə-ˈset, -ˈzet\ *n* **:** a usually colorless sweet liqueur flavored with aniseed
ankh \ˈäŋk\ *n* **:** a cross having a loop for its upper vertical arm and serving especially in ancient Egypt as an emblem of life
an•kle \ˈaŋ-kəl\ *n* **:** the joint or region between the foot and the leg
an•kle•bone \ˈaŋ-kəl-ˌbōn\ *n* **:** the bone that in human beings bears the weight of the body and with the tibia and fibula forms the ankle joint
an•klet \ˈaŋ-klət\ *n* **1 :** something (as an ornament) worn around the ankle **2 :** a short sock reaching slightly above the ankle
ann *abbr* **1** annals **2** annual
an•nal•ist \ˈan-ᵊl-ist\ *n* **:** a writer of annals
an•nals \ˈan-ᵊlz\ *n pl* **1 ♦ :** a record of events in chronological order **2 :** historical records

♦ chronicle, history, record

an•neal \ə-ˈnēl\ *vb* **1 :** to make (as glass or steel) less brittle by heating and then cooling **2 :** STRENGTHEN, TOUGHEN
¹**an•nex** \ə-ˈneks, ˈa-ˌneks\ *vb* **1 ♦ :** to attach as an addition **2 :** to incorporate (as a territory) within a political domain — **an•nex•a•tion** \ˌa-ˌnek-ˈsā-shən\ *n*

♦ add, adjoin, append, tack

²**an•nex** \ˈa-ˌneks, -niks\ *n* **♦ :** a subsidiary or supplementary structure

♦ addition, extension, penthouse

an•ni•hi•late \ə-ˈnī-ə-ˌlāt\ *vb* **-lat•ed; -lat•ing ♦ :** to destroy completely

♦ blot out, demolish, eradicate, exterminate, liquidate, obliterate, root, rub out, snuff, stamp, wipe out

an•ni•hi•la•tion \-ˌnī-ə-ˈlā-shən\ *n* **♦ :** the act of annihilating or state of being annihilated

♦ demolition, desolation, destruction, devastation, havoc, loss, obliteration, ruin, wastage, wreckage

an•ni•ver•sa•ry \ˌa-nə-ˈvər-sə-rē\ *n, pl* **-ries :** the annual return of the date of a notable event and especially a wedding
an•no Do•mi•ni \ˌa-nō-ˈdä-mə-nē, -ˈdō-, -ˌnī\ *adv, often cap A* — used to indicate that a time division falls within the Christian era
an•no•tate \ˈa-nə-ˌtāt\ *vb* **-tat•ed; -tat•ing :** to furnish with notes — **an•no•ta•tion** \ˌa-nə-ˈtā-shən\ *n* — **an•no•ta•tor** \ˈa-nə-ˌtā-tər\ *n*
an•nounce \ə-ˈnau̇ns\ *vb* **an•nounced; an•nounc•ing 1 ♦ :** to make known publicly **2 :** to give notice of the arrival or presence of

♦ advertise, blaze, broadcast, declare, enunciate, placard, post, proclaim, promulgate, publicize, publish, sound

an•nounce•ment \-mənt\ *n* **♦ :** a public notification or declaration

♦ advertisement, bulletin, notice, notification, release

an•nounc•er \ə-ˈnau̇n-sər\ *n* **:** a person who introduces radio or television programs, makes commercial announcements, or gives station identification
an•noy \ə-ˈnȯi\ *vb* **♦ :** to disturb or irritate especially by repeated acts **:** VEX — **an•noy•ing•ly** *adv*

♦ aggravate, bother, bug, chafe, exasperate, gall, get, grate, irk, irritate, nettle, peeve, rile, vex

an•noy•ance \ə-ˈnȯi-əns\ *n* **1 ♦ :** the act of annoying **2 ♦ :** the state of being annoyed **3 ♦ :** one that is annoying, unpleasant, or obnoxious **:** NUISANCE

♦ [1] aggravation, disturbance, harassment, vexation ♦ [2] aggravation, bother, exasperation, frustration, vexation ♦ [3] bother, exasperation, frustration, hassle, headache, inconvenience, irritant, nuisance, peeve, pest, problem, thorn

an•noy•ing \-iŋ\ *adj* **♦ :** causing vexation

♦ aggravating, bothersome, frustrating, galling, irksome, irritating, pesty, vexatious

¹**an•nu•al** \ˈan-yə-wəl\ *adj* **1 :** covering the period of a year **2 :** occurring once a year **:** YEARLY **3 :** completing the life cycle in one growing season ⟨~ plants⟩ — **an•nu•al•ly** *adv*
²**annual** *n* **1 :** a publication appearing once a year **2 :** an annual plant
annual ring *n* **:** the layer of wood produced by a single year's growth of a woody plant
an•nu•i•tant \ə-ˈnü-ə-tənt, -ˈnyü-\ *n* **:** a beneficiary of an annuity
an•nu•i•ty \ə-ˈnü-ə-tē, -ˈnyü-\ *n, pl* **-i•ties 1 :** an amount payable annually **2 :** the right to receive a annual payment

an•nul \ə-ˈnəl\ *vb* **an•nulled; an•nul•ling** **1** ♦ **:** to make ineffective or inoperative **2** ♦ **:** to make legally void — **an•nul•ment** *n*

♦ abolish, abrogate, cancel, dissolve, invalidate, negate, nullify, quash, repeal, rescind, void

an•nu•lar \ˈan-yə-lər\ *adj* **:** ring-shaped
an•nun•ci•ate \ə-ˈnən-sē-ˌāt\ *vb* **-at•ed; -at•ing :** ANNOUNCE
an•nun•ci•a•tion \ə-ˌnən-sē-ˈā-shən\ *n* **1 :** ANNOUNCEMENT **2** *cap* **:** March 25 observed as a church festival commemorating the announcement of the Incarnation
an•nun•ci•a•tor \ə-ˈnən-sē-ˌā-tər\ *n* **:** one that annunciates; *specif* **:** a usually electrically controlled signal board or indicator
an•ode \ˈa-ˌnōd\ *n* **1 :** the positive electrode of an electrolytic cell **2 :** the negative terminal of a battery **3 :** the electron-collecting electrode of an electron tube — **an•od•ic** \a-ˈnä-dik\ *also* **an•od•al** \-ˈnōd-ᵊl\ *adj*
an•od•ize \ˈa-nə-ˌdīz\ *vb* **-ized; -iz•ing :** to subject (a metal) to electrolytic action as the anode of a cell in order to coat with a protective or decorative film
an•o•dyne \ˈa-nə-ˌdīn\ *n* **:** something that relieves pain **:** a soothing agent
anoint \ə-ˈnȯint\ *vb* **1 :** to apply oil to especially as a sacred rite **2 :** CONSECRATE — **anoint•ment** *n*
anom•a•lous \ə-ˈnä-mə-ləs\ *adj* ♦ **:** deviating from a general rule **:** ABNORMAL

♦ aberrant, abnormal, atypical, deviant, irregular, unnatural

anom•a•ly \ə-ˈnä-mə-lē\ *n, pl* **-lies :** something anomalous
¹anon \ə-ˈnän\ *adv* ♦ **:** in the near future

♦ momentarily, presently, shortly, soon

²anon *abbr* anonymous; anonymously
an•o•nym•i•ty \ˌa-nə-ˈni-mə-tē\ *n* **:** the quality or state of being anonymous
anon•y•mous \ə-ˈnä-nə-məs\ *adj* ♦ **:** of unknown or undeclared origin or authorship — **anon•y•mous•ly** *adv*

♦ nameless, unbaptized, unchristened, unidentified, unnamed, untitled

anoph•e•les \ə-ˈnä-fə-ˌlēz\ *n* **:** any of a genus of mosquitoes that includes all mosquitoes which transmit malaria to human beings
an•o•rec•tic \ˌa-nə-ˈrek-tik\ *adj* **:** ANOREXIC — **anorectic** *n*
an•orex•ia \ˌa-nə-ˈrek-sē-ə\ *n* **1 :** loss of appetite especially when prolonged **2 :** ANOREXIA NERVOSA
anorexia ner•vo•sa \-nər-ˈvō-sə\ *n* **:** a serious disorder in eating behavior marked especially by a pathological fear of weight gain leading to faulty eating patterns, malnutrition, and usually excessive weight loss
an•orex•ic \ˌa-nə-ˈrek-sik\ *adj* **1 :** lacking or causing loss of appetite **2 :** affected with or as if with anorexia nervosa — **anorexic** *n*
¹an•oth•er \ə-ˈnə-t͟hər\ *adj* **1 :** some other **2** ♦ **:** being one in addition **:** one more

♦ additional, else, farther, further, more, other

²another *pron* **1 :** an additional one **:** one more **2 :** one that is different from the first or present one
ans *abbr* answer
¹an•swer \ˈan-sər\ *n* **1** ♦ **:** something spoken or written in reply to a question **2 :** a solution of a problem

♦ comeback, reply, response, retort, return ***Ant*** inquiry, query, question

²answer *vb* **1** ♦ **:** to speak or write in reply to **2** ♦ **:** to be or make oneself responsible or accountable ⟨~ for a debt⟩ **3** ♦ **:** to be in conformity or correspondence ⟨~*ed* to the description⟩ **4 :** to be adequate **5** ♦ **:** to offer a solution for — **an•swer•er** *n*

♦ [1] rejoin, reply, respond, retort, return ***Ant*** inquire, question ♦ [2] comply, fill, fulfill, keep, meet, redeem, satisfy ♦ [3] check, coincide, comport, conform, correspond, dovetail, fit, go, harmonize, jibe, square, tally ♦ [5] break, crack, dope, figure out, puzzle, resolve, riddle, solve, unravel, work, work out

an•swer•able \ˈan-sə-rə-bəl\ *adj* **1** ♦ **:** subject to taking blame or responsibility **2 :** capable of being refuted

♦ accountable, liable, responsible

answering machine *n* **:** a machine that receives telephone calls by playing a recorded message and usually by recording messages from callers
answering service *n* **:** a commercial service that answers telephone calls for its clients
¹ant \ˈant\ *n* **:** any of a family of small social insects related to the bees and living in communities usually in earth or wood
²ant *abbr* antonym
Ant *abbr* Antarctica
¹-ant *n suffix* **1 :** one that performs or promotes (a specified action) ⟨cool*ant*⟩ **2 :** thing that is acted upon (in a specified manner) ⟨inhal*ant*⟩
²-ant *adj suffix* **1 :** performing (a specified action) or being (in a specified condition) ⟨propell*ant*⟩ **2 :** promoting (a specified action or process) ⟨expector*ant*⟩
ant•ac•id \ant-ˈa-səd\ *n* **:** an agent that counteracts acidity — **antacid** *adj*
an•tag•o•nism \an-ˈta-gə-ˌni-zəm\ *n* **1** ♦ **:** active opposition or hostility **2 :** opposition in physiological action

♦ animosity, antipathy, bitterness, enmity, gall, grudge, hostility, rancor

an•tag•o•nist \-nist\ *n* ♦ **:** one that contends with or opposes another **:** ADVERSARY, OPPONENT

♦ adversary, enemy, foe, opponent

an•tag•o•nis•tic \-ˌta-gə-ˈnis-tik\ *adj* ♦ **:** marked by or resulting from antagonism

♦ hostile, inhospitable, inimical, jaundiced, negative, unfriendly, unsympathetic

an•tag•o•nize \an-ˈta-gə-ˌnīz\ *vb* **-nized; -niz•ing** ♦ **:** to provoke the hostility of

♦ anger, enrage, incense, inflame, infuriate, madden, outrage, rankle, rile, roil

ant•arc•tic \ant-ˈärk-tik, -ˈär-tik\ *adj, often cap* **:** of or relating to the south pole or the region near it
antarctic circle *n, often cap A&C* **:** the parallel of latitude that is approximately 66½ degrees south of the equator
¹an•te \ˈan-tē\ *n* **:** a poker stake put up before the deal to build the pot; *also* **:** an amount paid **:** PRICE
²ante *vb* **an•ted; an•te•ing** **1 :** to put up (an ante) **2 :** PAY
ant•eat•er \ˈant-ˌē-tər\ *n* **:** any of several mammals (as an aardvark) that feed mostly on ants or termites
an•te•bel•lum \ˌan-ti-ˈbe-ləm\ *adj* **:** existing before a war; *esp* **:** existing before the U.S. Civil War of 1861-65
an•te•ced•ent \ˌan-tə-ˈsēd-ᵊnt\ *n* **1 :** a noun, pronoun, phrase, or clause referred to by a personal or relative pronoun **2** ♦ **:** a preceding event or cause **3** *pl* **:** the significant conditions of one's earlier life **4 a** ♦ **:** one that precedes **:** PREDECESSOR; *esp* **:** a model or stimulus for later developments **b** *pl* **:** ANCESTORS

♦ [2] cause, occasion, reason ♦ [4a] ancestor, forerunner, precursor

antecedent *adj* ♦ **:** earlier in time or order

♦ anterior, foregoing, preceding, previous, prior

an•te•cham•ber \ˈan-ti-ˌchām-bər\ *n* **:** ANTEROOM
an•te•date \ˈan-ti-ˌdāt\ *vb* **1 :** to date (a paper) as of an earlier day than that on which the actual writing or signing is done **2** ♦ **:** to precede in time

♦ forego, precede

an•te•di•lu•vi•an \ˌan-ti-də-ˈlü-vē-ən, -dī-\ *adj* **1 :** of the period before the biblical flood **2** ♦ **:** made, evolved, or developed a long time ago

♦ age-old, ancient, antique, dateless, hoary, old, venerable

an•te•lope \ˈant-ᵊl-ˌōp\ *n, pl* **-lope** *or* **-lopes** **1 :** any of various deerlike ruminant mammals that chiefly inhabit Africa an have a slender build and horns extending upward and backward **2 :** PRONGHORN
an•te me•ri•di•em \ˈan-ti-mə-ˈri-dē-əm\ *adj* **:** being before noon
an•ten•na \an-ˈte-nə\ *n, pl* **-nae** \-(ˌ)nē\ *or* **-nas** **1 :** one of the long slender paired segmented sensory organs on the head of an arthropod (as an insect or crab) **2** *pl usu -nas* **:** a metallic device (as a rod or wire) for sending out or receiving radio waves
an•te•pe•nult \ˌan-ti-ˈpē-ˌnəlt\ *also* **an•te•pen•ul•ti•ma** \-pi-ˈnəl-tə-mə\ *n* **:** the 3d syllable of a word counting from the end — **an•te•pen•ul•ti•mate** \-pi-ˈnəl-tə-mət\ *adj or n*
an•te•ri•or \an-ˈtir-ē-ər\ *adj* **1 :** situated before or toward the front **2 :** situated near or nearer to the head **3** ♦ **:** coming before in time

♦ antecedent, foregoing, preceding, previous, prior

anterior cruciate ligament *n* **:** a cross-shaped ligament of the knee that connects the tibia and femur
an•te•room \ˈan-ti-ˌrüm, -ˌru̇m\ *n* **:** a room forming the entrance to another and often used as a waiting room

an•them \ˈan-thəm\ *n* **1** ♦ **:** a sacred vocal composition **2** ♦ **:** a song or hymn of praise or gladness

♦ [1, 2] canticle, carol, chorale, hymn, psalm, spiritual

an•ther \ˈan-thər\ *n* **:** the part of a stamen of a seed plant that produces and contains pollen

ant•hill \ˈant-ˌhil\ *n* **:** a mound thrown up by ants or termites in digging their nest

an•thol•o•gy \an-ˈthä-lə-jē\ *n, pl* **-gies** ♦ **:** a collection of literary selections — **an•thol•o•gist** \-jist\ *n* — **an•thol•o•gize** \-ˌjīz\ *vb*

♦ album, compilation, miscellany

an•thra•cite \ˈan-thrə-ˌsīt\ *n* **:** a hard glossy coal that burns without much smoke

an•thrax \ˈan-ˌthraks\ *n* **:** an infectious and usually fatal bacterial disease of warm-blooded animals (as cattle and sheep) that is transmissible to humans; *also* **:** a bacterium causing anthrax

an•thro•po•cen•tric \ˌan-thrə-pə-ˈsen- trik\ *adj* **:** interpreting or regarding the world in terms of human values and experiences

an•thro•poid \ˈan-thrə-ˌpȯid\ *n* **1 :** any of several large tailless apes (as a gorilla) **2 :** a person resembling an ape — **anthropoid** *adj*

an•thro•pol•o•gy \ˌan-thrə-ˈpä-lə-jē\ *n* **:** the science of human beings and especially of their physical characteristics, their origin and the distribution of races, their environment and social relations, and their culture — **an•thro•po•log•i•cal** \-pə-ˈlä-ji-kəl\ *adj* — **an•thro•pol•o•gist** \-ˈpä-lə-jist\ *n*

an•thro•po•mor•phism \ˌan-thrə-pə-ˈmȯr-ˌfi-zəm\ *n* **:** an interpretation of what is not human or personal in terms of human or personal characteristics **:** HUMANIZATION — **an•thro•po•mor•phic** \-fik\ *adj*

an•ti \ˈan-ˌtī, -tē\ *n, pl* **antis :** one who is opposed

anti- \ˌan-ti, -tē, -ˌtī\ *or* **ant-** *or* **anth-** *prefix* **1 :** opposite in kind, position, or action **2 :** opposing **:** hostile toward **3 :** counteractive **4 :** preventive of **:** curative of

antiaging
anti–AIDS
antiaircraft
antialcohol
anti–American
antiapartheid
antibacterial
anticapitalist
anti–Catholic
anticholesterol
anticlerical
anticolonial
anticommunism
anticommunist
antidemocratic
antiestablishment
antifascist
antigovernment
anti–imperialism
anti–imperialist
antiknock
antilabor
antimalarial
antimicrobial
antinausea
antipoverty
antislavery
antispasmodic
antistatic
antisubmarine
antitank
antitumor
antiviral
antiwar

an•ti•abor•tion \ˌan-tē-ə-ˈbȯr-shən, ˌan-ˌtī-\ *adj* **:** opposed to abortion

an•ti•bal•lis•tic missile \ˌan-ti-bə-ˈlis-tik-, ˌan-ˌtī-\ *n* **:** a missile for intercepting and destroying ballistic missiles

an•ti•bi•ot•ic \-bī-ˈä-tik, -bē-\ *n* **:** a substance produced by or derived by chemical alteration of a substance produced by a microorganism (as a fungus or bacterium) that in dilute solution inhibits or kills another microorganism — **antibiotic** *adj*

an•ti•body \ˈan-ti-ˌbä-dē\ *n* **:** any of a large number of proteins of high molecular weight produced normally by specialized B cells after stimulation by an antigen and acting specifically against the antigen in an immune response

[1]**an•tic** \ˈan-tik\ *n* ♦ **:** an often wildly playful or funny act or action

♦ caper, escapade, frolic, monkeyshine, practical joke, prank, trick

[2]**antic** *adj* **1** *archaic* **:** GROTESQUE **2 a** ♦ **:** characterized by clownish extravagance or absurdity **b** ♦ **:** whimsically gay **:** PLAYFUL

♦ [2a] comic, comical, droll, farcical, funny, hilarious, humorous, hysterical, laughable, ludicrous, ridiculous, riotous ♦ [2b] coltish, elfish, fay, frisky, frolicsome, playful, sportive

an•ti•can•cer \ˌan-ti-ˈkan-sər, ˌan-ˌtī-\ *adj* **:** used against or tending to arrest cancer ⟨~ drugs⟩

An•ti•christ \ˈan-ti-ˌkrīst\ *n* **1 :** one who denies or opposes Christ **2 :** a false Christ

an•tic•i•pate \an-ˈti-sə-ˌpāt\ *vb* **-pat•ed; -pat•ing 1** ♦ **:** to foresee and provide for beforehand **2** ♦ **:** to look forward to — **an•tic•i•pa•tion** \-ˌti-sə-ˈpā-shən\ *n*

♦ [1] divine, foreknow, foresee ♦ [2] await, expect, hope, watch

an•tic•i•pa•to•ry \-ˈti-sə-pə-ˌtōr-ē\ *adj* ♦ **:** characterized by anticipation

♦ agape, agog, expectant

an•ti•cli•max \ˌan-ti-ˈklī-ˌmaks\ *n* **:** something closing a series that is strikingly less important than what has preceded it — **an•ti•cli•mac•tic** \-klī-ˈmak-tik\ *adj*

an•ti•cline \ˈan-ti-ˌklīn\ *n* **:** an arch of layers of rock in the earth's crust

an•ti•co•ag•u•lant \ˌan-ti-kō-ˈa-gyə-lənt\ *n* **:** a substance that hinders the clotting of blood — **anticoagulant** *adj*

an•ti•cy•clone \ˌan-ti-ˈsī-ˌklōn\ *n* **:** a system of winds that rotates about a center of high atmospheric pressure — **an•ti•cy•clon•ic** \-sī-ˈklä-nik\ *adj*

[1]**an•ti•de•pres•sant** \ˌan-ti-di-ˈpres-ᵊnt, ˌan-ˌtī-\ *n* **:** a drug used to relieve psychic depression

[2]**antidepressant** *n* **:** an antidepressant drug

an•ti•dote \ˈan-ti-ˌdōt\ *n* **:** a remedy to counteract the effects of poison

an•ti•drug \ˈan-ˌtī-ˌdrəg\ *adj* **:** acting against or opposing illicit drugs

an•ti•fer•til•i•ty \ˌan-ti-fər-ˈti-lə-tē\ *adj* **:** tending to reduce or destroy fertility **:** CONTRACEPTIVE ⟨~ agents⟩

an•ti•freeze \ˈan-ti-ˌfrēz\ *n* **:** a substance added to a liquid to lower its freezing temperature

an•ti•gen \ˈan-ti-jən\ *n* **:** any substance (as a toxin or an enzyme) foreign to the body that induces an immune response — **an•ti•gen•ic** \ˌan-ti-ˈje-nik\ *adj* — **an•ti•ge•nic•i•ty** \-jə-ˈni-sə-tē\ *n*

an•ti•grav•i•ty \ˌan-ti-ˈgra-və-tē, ˌan-ˌtī-\ *adj* **:** reducing or canceling the effect of gravity

an•ti•he•ro \ˈan-ti-ˌhē-rō, ˈan-ˌtī-\ *n* **:** a protagonist who is notably lacking in heroic qualities (as courage)

an•ti•his•ta•mine \ˌan-ti-ˈhis-tə-ˌmēn, ˌan-ˌtī-, -mən\ *n* **:** any of various drugs used in treating allergies and colds

an•ti•hy•per•ten•sive \-ˌhī-pər-ˈten-siv\ *n* **:** a substance that is effective against high blood pressure — **antihypertensive** *adj*

an•ti–in•flam•ma•to•ry \-in-ˈfla-mə-ˌtōr-ē\ *adj* **:** counteracting inflammation — **anti–inflammatory** *n*

an•ti–in•tel•lec•tu•al \-ˌint-ᵊl-ˈek-chə-wəl\ *adj* **:** opposing or hostile to intellectuals or to an intellectual view or approach

an•ti•lock \ˈan-ti-ˌläk, ˈan-ˌtī-\ *adj* **:** being a braking system designed to prevent the wheels from locking

an•ti•log•a•rithm \ˌan-ti-ˈlȯ-gə-ˌri-t͟həm, ˌan-ˌtī-, -ˈlä-\ *n* **:** the number corresponding to a given logarithm

an•ti•ma•cas•sar \ˌan-ti-mə-ˈka-sər\ *n* **:** a cover to protect the back or arms of furniture

an•ti•mat•ter \ˈan-ti-ˌma-tər, ˈan-ˌtī-\ *n* **:** matter composed of antiparticles

an•ti•mo•ny \ˈan-tə-ˌmō-nē\ *n* **:** a brittle silvery white metallic chemical element used especially in alloys

an•ti•neu•tron \ˌan-ti-ˈnü-ˌträn, ˌan-ˌtī-, -ˈnyü-\ *n* **:** the antiparticle of the neutron

an•ti•no•mi•an \ˌan-ti-ˈnō-mē-ən\ *n* **:** one who denies the validity of moral laws

an•tin•o•my \an-ˈti-nə-mē\ *n, pl* **-mies :** a contradiction between two seemingly true statements

an•ti•nov•el \ˈan-ti-ˌnä-vəl, ˈan-ˌtī-\ *n* **:** a work of fiction that lacks all or most of the traditional features of the novel

an•ti•nu•cle•ar \ˌan-ti-ˈnü-klē-ər, -ˈnyü-\ *adj* **:** opposing the use or production of nuclear power plants

an•ti•ox•i•dant \ˌan-tē-ˈäk-sə-dənt, ˌan-ˌtī-\ *n* **:** a substance that inhibits oxidation — **antioxidant** *adj*

an•ti•par•ti•cle \ˈan-ti-ˌpär-ti-kəl, ˈan-ˌtī-\ *n* **:** a subatomic particle identical to another subatomic particle in mass but opposite to it in electric and magnetic properties

an•ti•pas•to \ˌan-ti-ˈpas-tō, ˌän-ti-ˈpäs-\ *n, pl* **-ti** \-(ˌ)tē\ **:** any of various typically Italian hors d'oeuvres

an•ti•pa•thet•ic \ˌan-ti-pə-ˈthe-tik\ *adj* **:** having an aversion to or dislike of

an•tip•a•thy \an-ˈti-pə-thē\ *n, pl* **-thies 1** ♦ **:** settled aversion or dislike **2** ♦ **:** an object of aversion

♦ [1] animosity, antagonism, bitterness, enmity, gall, grudge, hostility, rancor ♦ [2] abhorrence, abomination, anathema, aversion, bête noire, hate

an•ti•per•son•nel \ˌan-ti-ˌpərs-ᵊn-ˈel, ˌan-ˌtī-\ *adj* **:** designed for use against military personnel ⟨~ mine⟩

an•ti•per•spi•rant \-ˈpər-spə-rənt\ *n* **:** a preparation used to check perspiration

an•tiph•o•nal \an-ˈti-fən-ᵊl\ *adj* : performed by two alternating groups — **an•tiph•o•nal•ly** *adv*
an•tip•o•dal \an-ˈti-pəd-ᵊl\ *adj* ♦ : diametrically opposite or opposed to

♦ antithetical, contradictory, contrary, diametric, opposite, polar

an•ti•pode \ˈan-tə-ˌpōd\ *n, pl* **an•tip•o•des** \an-ˈti-pə-ˌdēz\ **1** : the parts of the earth diametrically opposite — usually used in plural **2** ♦ : the exact opposite or contrary

♦ antithesis, contrary, negative, opposite, reverse

an•tip•o•de•an \(ˌ)an-ˌti-pə-ˈdē-ən\ *adj* : diametrically opposite or opposed to
an•ti•pol•lu•tion \ˌan-ti-pə-ˈlü-shən\ *adj* : designed to prevent, reduce, or eliminate pollution ⟨∼ laws⟩
an•ti•pope \ˈan-ti-ˌpōp\ *n* : one elected or claiming to be pope in opposition to the pope canonically chosen
an•ti•pro•ton \ˌan-ti-ˈprō-ˌtän\ *n* : the antiparticle of the proton
an•ti•quar•i•an \ˌan-tə-ˈkwer-ē-ən\ *adj* **1** : of or relating to antiquities **2** : dealing in old books — **antiquarian** *n* — **an•ti•quar•i•an•ism** *n*
an•ti•quary \ˈan-tə-ˌkwer-ē\ *n, pl* **-quar•ies** : a person who collects or studies antiquities
an•ti•quat•ed \ˈan-tə-ˌkwā-təd\ *adj* ♦ : outmoded or discredited by reason of age : OUT-OF-DATE

♦ archaic, dated, obsolete, outdated, outmoded, outworn, passé

[1]**an•tique** \an-ˈtēk\ *n* : an object made in a bygone period
[2]**antique** *adj* **1** ♦ : belonging to antiquity **2** ♦ : being in the style or fashion of former times : OLD-FASHIONED **3** : of a bygone style or period

♦ [1] age-old, ancient, antediluvian, dateless, hoary, old, venerable ♦ [2] old-fashioned, old-time, quaint

[3]**antique** *vb* **-tiqued; -tiqu•ing** **1** : to finish or refinish in antique style : give an appearance of age to **2** : to shop around for antiques — **an•tiqu•er** *n*
an•tiq•ui•ty \an-ˈti-kwə-tē\ *n, pl* **-ties** **1** : ancient times **2** : great age **3** *pl* : relics of ancient times **4** *pl* : matters relating to ancient culture
antis *pl of* ANTI
an•ti–Sem•i•tism \ˌan-ti-ˈse-mə-ˌti-zəm, ˌan-ˌtī-\ *n* : hostility toward Jews as a religious or social minority — **an•ti–Se•mit•ic** \-sə-ˈmi-tik\ *adj*
an•ti•sep•tic \ˌan-tə-ˈsep-tik\ *adj* **1** : killing or checking the growth of germs that cause decay or infection **2** : scrupulously clean : ASEPTIC — **antiseptic** *n* — **an•ti•sep•ti•cal•ly** *adv*
an•ti•se•rum \ˈan-ti-ˌsir-əm, ˈan-ˌtī-\ *n* : a serum containing antibodies
an•ti•so•cial \ˌan-ti-ˈsō-shəl\ *adj* **1** ♦ : disliking the society of others **2** : contrary or hostile to the well-being of society ⟨crime is ∼⟩ — **an•ti•so•cial•ly** *adv*

♦ aloof, cold, cool, detached, distant, frosty, remote, standoffish, unsociable

an•tith•e•sis \an-ˈti-thə-səs\ *n, pl* **-e•ses** \-ˌsēz\ **1** : the opposition or contrast of ideas **2** ♦ : the direct opposite

♦ antipode, contrary, negative, opposite, reverse

an•ti•thet•i•cal \ˌan-tə-ˈthe-ti-kəl\ *also* **an•ti•thet•ic** \-tik\ *adj* ♦ : constituting or marked by antithesis — **an•ti•thet•i•cal•ly** \-ti-k(ə-)lē\ *adv*

♦ antipodal, contradictory, contrary, diametric, opposite, polar

an•ti•tox•in \ˌan-ti-ˈtäk-sən\ *n* : an antibody that is able to neutralize a particular toxin or disease-causing agent; *also* : an antiserum containing an antitoxin
an•ti•trust \ˌan-ti-ˈtrəst\ *adj* : of or relating to legislation against trusts; *also* : consisting of laws to protect trade and commerce from unlawful restraints and monopolies or unfair business practices
an•ti•ven•in \-ˈve-nən\ *n* : an antitoxin to a venom; *also* : a serum containing such antitoxin
ant•ler \ˈant-lər\ *n* : one of the paired deciduous solid bone processes on the head of a deer; *also* : a branch of this — **ant•lered** \-lərd\ *adj*
ant lion *n* : any of various insects having a long-jawed larva that digs a conical pit in which it lies in wait for insects (as ants) on which it feeds
an•to•nym \ˈan-tə-ˌnim\ *n* : a word of opposite meaning
anus \ˈā-nəs\ *n* : the lower or posterior opening of the alimentary canal
an•vil \ˈan-vəl\ *n* **1** : a heavy iron block on which metal is shaped **2** : INCUS

anx•i•ety \aŋ-ˈzī-ə-tē\ *n, pl* **-et•ies** **1** ♦ : painful uneasiness of mind usually over an anticipated ill **2** : abnormal apprehension and fear often accompanied by physiological signs (as sweating and increased pulse), by doubt about the nature and reality of the threat itself, and by self-doubt

♦ agitation, apprehension, care, concern, disquiet, nervousness, perturbation, uneasiness, worry

anx•ious \ˈaŋk-shəs\ *adj* **1** ♦ : uneasy in mind : WORRIED ⟨∼ parents⟩ **2** ♦ : characterized by, resulting from, or causing anxiety ⟨an ∼ night⟩ **3** : earnestly wishing : EAGER — **anx•ious•ly** *adv*

♦ [1, 2] distressful, nervous, restless, tense, unsettling, upsetting, worrisome

[1]**any** \ˈe-nē\ *adj* **1** : one chosen at random **2** : of whatever number or quantity
[2]**any** *pron* **1** : any one or ones ⟨take ∼ of the books you like⟩ **2** : any amount ⟨∼ of the money not used is to be returned⟩
[3]**any** *adv* : to any extent or degree : AT ALL ⟨could not walk ∼ farther⟩
any•body \-ˌbä-dē, -bə-\ *pron* : ANYONE
any•how \-ˌhau̇\ *adv* **1** : in any way **2** : in spite of that; *also* : in any case
any•more \ˌe-nē-ˈmōr\ *adv* **1** : any longer **2** ♦ : at the present time

♦ now, nowadays, presently, right now, today

any•one \ˈe-nē-(ˌ)wən\ *pron* : any person
any•place \-ˌplās\ *adv* : ANYWHERE
any•thing \-ˌthiŋ\ *pron* : any thing whatever
any•time \ˈe-nē-ˌtīm\ *adv* : at any time whatever
any•way \-ˌwā\ *adv* : in spite of that : ANYHOW
any•where \-ˌhwer\ *adv* : in or to any place
any•wise \-ˌwīz\ *adv* : in any way whatever
A–OK \ˌā-ō-ˈkā\ *adv or adj* : very definitely OK
A1 \ˈā-ˈwən\ *adj* ♦ : of the finest quality

♦ excellent, fabulous, fine, grand, great, prime, sensational, splendid, superb, superior, unsurpassed, wonderful

aor•ta \ā-ˈȯr-tə\ *n, pl* **-tas** *or* **-tae** \-tē\ : the main artery that carries blood from the heart — **aor•tic** \-tik\ *adj*
ap *abbr* **1** apostle **2** apothecaries'
AP *abbr* **1** American plan **2** Associated Press
apace \ə-ˈpās\ *adv* ♦ : at a quick pace : SWIFTLY

♦ briskly, fast, hastily, pronto, quick, quickly, rapidly, speedily, swift, swiftly

Apache \ə-ˈpa-chē\ *n, pl* **Apache** *or* **Apach•es** \-ˈpa-chēz, -ˈpa-shəz\ : a member of an American Indian people of the southwestern U.S.; *also* : any of the languages of the Apache people — **Apach•e•an** \ə-ˈpa-chē-ən\ *adj or n*
apart \ə-ˈpärt\ *adv* **1** : separately in place or time **2** : ASIDE **3** : in two or more parts : to pieces
apart•heid \ə-ˈpär-ˌtāt, -ˌtīt\ *n* : a policy of racial segregation practiced in the Republic of So. Africa
apart•ment \ə-ˈpärt-mənt\ *n* : a room or set of rooms occupied as a dwelling; *also* : a building divided into individual dwelling units
ap•a•thet•ic \ˌa-pə-ˈthe-tik\ *adj* ♦ : having or showing apathy

♦ casual, disinterested, indifferent, insouciant, nonchalant, perfunctory, unconcerned, uncurious, uninterested

ap•a•thy \ˈa-pə-thē\ *n* **1** ♦ : lack of emotion **2** ♦ : lack of interest : INDIFFERENCE — **ap•a•thet•i•cal•ly** \-ti-k(ə-)lē\ *adv*

♦ [1] impassivity, numbness, phlegm, stupor *Ant* emotion, feeling, sensibility ♦ [2] disinterestedness, disregard, indifference, insouciance, nonchalance

ap•a•tite \ˈa-pə-ˌtīt\ *n* : any of a group of minerals that are phosphates of calcium and occur especially in phosphate rock and in bones and teeth
APB *abbr* all points bulletin
[1]**ape** \ˈāp\ *n* **1** : any of the larger tailless primates (as a baboon or gorilla); *also* : MONKEY **2** : MIMIC, IMITATOR; *also* : a large uncouth person
[2]**ape** *vb* **aped; ap•ing** ♦ : to copy closely but often clumsily and ineptly : IMITATE, MIMIC

♦ copy, emulate, imitate, mime, mimic

ape–man \ˈāp-ˌman\ *n* : a primate intermediate in character between Homo sapiens and the higher apes
aper•çu \ȧ-per-sü̅e̅, ˌa-pər-ˈsü\ *n, pl* **aperçus** \-sü̅e̅(z), -ˈsüz\ : an immediate impression; *esp* : INSIGHT
aper•i•tif \ˌä-ˌper-ə-ˈtēf\ *n* : an alcoholic drink taken as an appetizer

ap•er•ture \ˈa-pər-ˌchu̇r, -chər\ *n* ♦ : an opening or open space : OPENING, HOLE

♦ hole, opening, orifice, perforation

apex \ˈā-ˌpeks\ *n, pl* **apex•es** *or* **api•ces** \ˈā-pə-ˌsēz, ˈa-\ **1** ♦ : the highest point : PEAK **2** ♦ : the narrowed or pointed end

♦ [1] acme, climax, crown, culmination, head, height, meridian, peak, pinnacle, summit, tip-top, top, zenith ♦ [2] cusp, end, pike, point, tip

apha•sia \ə-ˈfā-zh(ē-)ə\ *n* : loss or impairment of the power to use or comprehend words — **apha•sic** \-zik\ *adj or n*

aph•elion \a-ˈfēl-yən\ *n, pl* **-elia** \-yə\ : the point in an object's orbit most distant from the sun

aphid \ˈā-fəd\ *n* : any of numerous small insects that suck the juices of plants

aphis \ˈā-fəs, ˈa-\ *n, pl* **aphi•des** \-fə-ˌdēz\ : APHID

aph•o•rism \ˈa-fə-ˌri-zəm\ *n* ♦ : a short saying stating a general truth or sentiment : MAXIM

♦ adage, byword, epigram, maxim, proverb, saying

aph•o•ris•tic \ˌa-fə-ˈris-tik\ *adj* : of, resembling, or characterized by aphorisms

aph•ro•di•si•ac \ˌa-frə-ˈdi-zē-ˌak, -ˈdē-zē-\ *n* : an agent that excites sexual desire — **aphrodisiac** *adj*

api•ary \ˈā-pē-ˌer-ē\ *n, pl* **-ar•ies** : a place where bees are kept — **api•a•rist** \-pē-ə-rist\ *n*

api•cal \ˈā-pi-kəl, ˈa-\ *adj* : of, relating to, or situated at an apex — **api•cal•ly** \-k(ə-)lē\ *adv*

apiece \ə-ˈpēs\ *adv* : for each one

aplen•ty \ə-ˈplen-tē\ *adj* : being in plenty or abundance

aplomb \ə-ˈpläm, -ˈpləm\ *n* ♦ : complete composure or self-assurance

♦ calmness, composure, coolness, equanimity, placidity, self-possession, serenity, tranquillity ♦ aplomb, confidence, self-assurance, self-confidence, self-esteem

APO *abbr* army post office

Apoc *abbr* **1** Apocalypse **2** Apocrypha

apoc•a•lypse \ə-ˈpä-kə-ˌlips\ *n* **1** : a writing prophesying a cataclysm in which evil forces are destroyed **2** *cap* : a book of the New Testament of the Christian Scripture — **apoc•a•lyp•tic** \-ˌpä-kə-ˈlip-tik\ *also* **apoc•a•lyp•ti•cal** \-ti-kəl\ *adj*

Apoc•ry•pha \ə-ˈpä-krə-fə\ *n* **1** *not cap* : writings of dubious authenticity **2** : books included in the Septuagint and Vulgate but excluded from the Jewish and Protestant canons of the Old Testament **3** : early Christian writings not included in the New Testament

apoc•ry•phal \-fəl\ *adj* **1** : not canonical : SPURIOUS **2** *often cap* : of or resembling the Apocrypha — **apoc•ry•phal•ly** *adv* — **apoc•ry•phal•ness** *n*

apo•gee \ˈa-pə-(ˌ)jē\ *n* : the point at which an orbiting object is farthest from the body being orbited

apo•lit•i•cal \ˌā-pə-ˈli-ti-kəl\ *adj* **1** : having an aversion for or no interest in political affairs **2** : having no political significance — **apo•lit•i•cal•ly** \-k(ə-)lē\ *adv*

apol•o•get•ic \ə-ˌpä-lə-ˈje-tik\ *adj* ♦ : expressing apology — **apol•o•get•i•cal•ly** \-ti-k(ə-)lē\ *adv*

♦ contrite, penitent, regretful, remorseful, repentant, rueful, sorry

ap•o•lo•gia \ˌa-pə-ˈlō-j(ē-)ə\ *n* : APOLOGY; *esp* : an argument in support or justification

apol•o•gise *Brit var of* APOLOGIZE

apol•o•gize \ə-ˈpä-lə-ˌjīz\ *vb* **-gized; -giz•ing** : to make an apology : express regret — **apol•o•gist** \-jist\ *n*

apol•o•gy \ə-ˈpä-lə-jē\ *n, pl* **-gies** **1** : a formal justification : DEFENSE **2** : an expression of regret for a wrong

ap•o•plexy \ˈa-pə-ˌplek-sē\ *n* : STROKE 3 — **ap•o•plec•tic** \ˌa-pə-ˈplek-tik\ *adj*

aport \ə-ˈpōrt\ *adv* : on or toward the left side of a ship

apos•ta•sy \ə-ˈpäs-tə-sē\ *n, pl* **-sies** : a renunciation or abandonment of a former loyalty (as to a religion)

apos•tate \ə-ˈpäs-ˌtāt, -tət\ *n* ♦ : one who commits apostasy — **apostate** *adj*

♦ betrayer, double-crosser, quisling, recreant, traitor, turncoat

a pos•te•ri•o•ri \ˌä-pō-ˌstir-ē-ˈōr-ē\ *adj* : relating to or derived by reasoning from observed facts — **a posteriori** *adv*

apos•tle \ə-ˈpä-səl\ *n* **1** : one of the group composed of Jesus' 12 original disciples and Paul **2** : the first prominent missionary to a region or group **3 a** : a person who initiates or first advocates a great reform **b** ♦ : an ardent supporter — **apos•tle•ship** *n*

♦ advocate, backer, booster, champion, exponent, friend, promoter, proponent, supporter

ap•os•tol•ic \ˌa-pə-ˈstä-lik\ *adj* **1** : of or relating to an apostle or to the New Testament apostles **2** : of or relating to a succession of spiritual authority from the apostles **3** : PAPAL

[1]**apos•tro•phe** \ə-ˈpäs-trə-(ˌ)fē\ *n* : the rhetorical addressing of a usually absent person or a usually personified thing (as in "O grave, where is thy victory?")

[2]**apostrophe** *n* : a punctuation mark ' used especially to indicate the possessive case or the omission of a letter or figure

apos•tro•phise *Brit var of* APOSTROPHIZE

apos•tro•phize \ə-ˈpäs-trə-ˌfīz\ *vb* **-phized; -phiz•ing** : to address as if present or capable of understanding

apothecaries' weight *n* : a system of weights based on the troy pound and ounce and used chiefly by pharmacists

apoth•e•cary \ə-ˈpä-thə-ˌker-ē\ *n, pl* **-car•ies** : one who prepares and sells drugs or compounds for medicinal purposes : DRUGGIST

ap•o•thegm \ˈa-pə-ˌthem\ *or Can and Brit* **ap•o•phthegm** *n* : APHORISM

apo•the•o•sis \ə-ˌpä-thē-ˈō-səs, ˌa-pə-ˈthē-ə-səs\ *n, pl* **-o•ses** \-ˌsēz\ **1** : DEIFICATION **2** : the perfect example

app *abbr* **1** apparatus **2** appendix

ap•pall *also* **ap•pal** \ə-ˈpȯl\ *vb* **ap•palled; ap•pall•ing** ♦ : to overcome with consternation, shock, or dismay

♦ bowl, floor, jolt, shake up, shock

ap•pall•ing *adj* ♦ : inspiring horror, dismay, or disgust

♦ abhorrent, abominable, awful, distasteful, horrible, horrid, nauseating, noisome, obnoxious, odious, offensive, repellent, revolting ♦ astonishing, awful, dreadful, frightful, ghastly, hideous, horrible, horrid, shocking, terrible

Ap•pa•loo•sa \ˌa-pə-ˈlü-sə\ *n* : any of a breed of saddle horses developed in western No. America and usually having a white or solid-colored coat with small spots

ap•pa•nage \ˈa-pə-nij\ *n* **1** : provision (as a grant of land) made by a sovereign or legislative body for dependent members of the royal family **2** : something that is attached or associated in a natural or necessary way : a natural adjunct

ap•pa•ra•tus \ˌa-pə-ˈra-təs, -ˈrā-\ *n, pl* **-tus•es** *or* **-tus** **1** ♦ : a set of materials or equipment for a particular use **2** : a complex machine or device : MECHANISM **3** : the organization of a political party or underground movement

♦ accoutrements (*or* accouterments), equipment, gear, matériel, outfit, paraphernalia, tackle

[1]**ap•par•el** \ə-ˈpar-əl\ *vb* **-eled** *or* **-elled; -el•ing** *or* **-el•ling** **1** : to put clothes on : CLOTHE **2** : ADORN

[2]**apparel** *n* ♦ : personal attire : CLOTHING, DRESS

♦ attire, clothing, dress, duds, raiment, wear

ap•par•ent \ə-ˈpar-ənt\ *adj* **1** ♦ : open to view : VISIBLE **2** ♦ : clear or manifest to the understanding : EVIDENT, OBVIOUS **3** ♦ : appearing as real or true : SEEMING

♦ [1] observable, visible, visual ♦ [2] clear, distinct, evident, manifest, obvious, plain, transparent, unambiguous, unequivocal, unmistakable ♦ [3] assumed, evident, ostensible, reputed, seeming, supposed

ap•par•ent•ly \-lē\ *adv* ♦ : it seems apparent

♦ evidently, ostensibly, presumably, seemingly, supposedly

ap•pa•ri•tion \ˌa-pə-ˈri-shən\ *n* ♦ : a supernatural appearance : GHOST

♦ bogey, ghost, phantasm, phantom, poltergeist, shade, shadow, specter, spirit, spook, vision, wraith

[1]**ap•peal** \ə-ˈpēl\ *n* **1** ♦ : an earnest plea **2** ♦ : the power of arousing a sympathetic response

♦ [1] cry, entreaty, petition, plea, prayer, solicitation, suit, supplication ♦ [2] allure, attractiveness, captivation, charisma, charm, enchantment, fascination, glamour, magic, magnetism

[2]**appeal** *vb* **1** : to take steps to have (a case) reheard in a higher court **2** ♦ : to plead for help, corroboration, or decision **3** : to arouse a sympathetic response

♦ *usu* **appeal to** beg, beseech, entreat, implore, importune, petition, plead, pray, solicit, supplicate

ap•pear \ə-ˈpir\ *vb* **1** ♦ : to become visible **2** : to come formally before an authority **3** ♦ : to have an outward aspect : SEEM **4** : to become evident **5** : to come before the public

♦ [1] come out, materialize, show up, turn up ***Ant*** disappear, clear, dissolve, evaporate, fade, go (away), melt (away), vanish ♦ [3] act, look, make, seem, sound

ap•pear•ance \ə-ˈpir-əns\ *n* **1** ♦ **:** outward aspect **:** LOOK **2 :** the act of appearing **3 :** PHENOMENON

♦ aspect, look, mien, presence ♦ face, guise, name, semblance, show

ap•pease \ə-ˈpēz\ *vb* **ap•peased; ap•peas•ing 1 :** to cause to subside **:** ALLAY **2** ♦ **:** to bring to a state of peace or quiet **:** PACIFY, CONCILIATE; *esp* **:** to buy off by concessions — **ap•pease•ment** *n* — **ap•peas•able** \-ˈpē-zə-bəl\ *adj*

♦ conciliate, disarm, mollify, pacify, placate, propitiate

ap•pel•lant \ə-ˈpe-lənt\ *n* **:** one who appeals especially from a judicial decision

ap•pel•late \ə-ˈpe-lət\ *adj* **:** having power to review decisions of a lower court

ap•pel•la•tion \ˌa-pə-ˈlā-shən\ *n* ♦ **:** an identifying name or title **:** NAME, DESIGNATION

♦ cognomen, denotation, designation, handle, name, title

ap•pel•lee \ˌa-pə-ˈlē\ *n* **:** one against whom an appeal is taken

ap•pend \ə-ˈpend\ *vb* ♦ **:** to attach especially as something additional

♦ add, adjoin, annex, tack

ap•pend•age \ə-ˈpen-dij\ *n* **1** ♦ **:** something appended to a principal or greater thing **2 :** a projecting part of the body (as an antenna) especially when paired with one on each side

♦ accessory, accoutrement (*or* accoutermant), adjunct, attachment

ap•pen•dec•to•my \ˌa-pən-ˈdek-tə-mē\ *n, pl* **-mies :** surgical removal of the intestinal appendix

ap•pen•di•ci•tis \ə-ˌpen-də-ˈsī-təs\ *n* **:** inflammation of the intestinal appendix

ap•pen•dix \ə-ˈpen-diks\ *n, pl* **-dix•es** *or* **-di•ces** \-də-ˌsēz\ **1 :** supplementary matter added at the end of a book **2 :** a narrow blind tube usually about three or four inches long that extends from the cecum in the lower right-hand part of the abdomen

ap•per•tain \ˌa-pər-ˈtān\ *vb* ♦ **:** to belong or be connected as a rightful part or privilege

♦ apply, bear, pertain, refer, relate

ap•pe•tite \ˈa-pə-ˌtīt\ *n* **1** ♦ **:** natural desire for satisfying some want or need especially for food **2** ♦ **:** individual preference **:** TASTE

♦ [1] craving, desire, drive, hankering, hunger, itch, thirst, urge, yen ♦ [2] fancy, favor (*or* favour), fondness, like, liking, love, partiality, preference, relish, shine, taste, use

ap•pe•tiz•er \ˈa-pə-ˌtī-zər\ *n* **:** a food or drink taken just before a meal to stimulate the appetite

ap•pe•tiz•ing \-ziŋ\ *adj* ♦ **:** tempting to the appetite — **ap•pe•tiz•ing•ly** *adv*

♦ delectable, delicious, flavorful (*or* flavourful), palatable, tasty, toothsome

appl *abbr* applied

ap•plaud \ə-ˈplȯd\ *vb* ♦ **:** to show approval especially by clapping

♦ acclaim, cheer, hail, laud, praise, salute, tout

ap•plaud•able \ə-ˈplȯ-də-bəl\ *adj* ♦ **:** worthy of being applauded

♦ admirable, commendable, creditable, laudable, meritorious, praiseworthy

ap•plause \ə-ˈplȯz\ *n* ♦ **:** approval publicly expressed (as by clapping)

♦ acclamation, ovation ***Ant*** hissing

ap•ple \ˈa-pəl\ *n* **:** a rounded fruit with firm white flesh and a seedy core; *also* **:** a tree that bears this fruit

ap•ple•jack \-ˌjak\ *n* **:** a liquor distilled from fermented cider

app•let \ˈa-ˌplət\ *n* **:** a short computer program especially for perforning a simple specific task

ap•pli•ance \ə-ˈplī-əns\ *n* **1 :** an instrument or device designed for a particular use or function **2 :** a piece of household equipment (as a stove or toaster) operated by gas or electricity

ap•pli•ca•bil•i•ty \ˌa-pli-kə-ˈbi-lə-tē, ə-ˌpli-kə-\ *n* ♦ **:** the quality or state of being applicable

♦ bearing, connection, pertinence, relevance

ap•pli•ca•ble \ˈa-pli-kə-bəl, ə-ˈpli-kə-\ *adj* ♦ **:** capable of being applied

♦ functional, practicable, practical, serviceable, usable, useful, workable, working ♦ appropriate, apt, felicitous, fit, fitting, good, happy, meet, proper, right, suitable ♦ apposite, apropos, germane, material, pertinent, pointed, relative, relevant

ap•pli•cant \ˈa-pli-kənt\ *n* ♦ **:** one who applies

♦ aspirant, campaigner, candidate, contender, hopeful, prospect, seeker

ap•pli•ca•tion \ˌa-plə-ˈkā-shən\ *n* **1** ♦ **:** the act of applying **2 :** assiduous attention **3 :** REQUEST; *also* **:** a form used in making a request **4 :** something placed or spread on a surface **5 :** capacity for use **6 :** a program (as a word processor) that performs one of a computer's major tasks

♦ employment, exercise, operation, play, use

ap•pli•ca•tor \ˈa-plə-ˌkā-tər\ *n* **:** a device for applying a substance (as medicine or polish)

ap•plied \ə-ˈplīd\ *adj* **:** put to practical use ⟨~ art⟩

ap•pli•qué \ˌa-plə-ˈkā\ *n* **:** a fabric decoration cut out and fastened to a larger piece of material — **appliqué** *vb*

ap•ply \ə-ˈplī\ *vb* **ap•plied; ap•ply•ing 1 a** ♦ **:** to put to practical use **b** ♦ **:** to bring into action **c :** to lay or spread on **d** ♦ **:** to put into operation or effect **2 :** to place in contact **:** put or spread on a surface **3** ♦ **:** to employ with close attention **4** ♦ **:** to have reference or connection **5 :** to submit a request

♦ [1a, 1b] employ, exercise, exploit, harness, operate, use, utilize ♦ [1d] administer, enforce, execute, implement ♦ [3] address, bend, buckle, devote, give ♦ [4] appertain, bear, pertain, refer, relate

ap•point \ə-ˈpȯint\ *vb* **1** ♦ **:** to fix or set officially ⟨~ a day for trial⟩ **2** ♦ **:** to name officially **3 :** to fit out **:** EQUIP

♦ [1] designate, fix, name, set ♦ [2] assign, attach, commission, constitute, designate, detail, name

ap•poin•tee \ə-ˌpȯin-ˈtē, ˌa-\ *n* **:** a person appointed

ap•point•ive \ə-ˈpȯin-tiv\ *adj* **:** subject to appointment

ap•point•ment \ə-ˈpȯint-mənt\ *n* **1 :** the act of appointing **2** ♦ **:** an arrangement for a meeting **3** *pl* **:** articles of furniture for the interior of a building **:** FURNISHINGS **4** ♦ **:** a nonelective office or position

♦ [2] date, engagement, rendezvous, tryst ♦ *usu* **appointments** [4] billet, capacity, function, job, place, position, post, situation ♦ [4] assignment, commission, designation ***Ant*** discharge, dismissal, expulsion, firing

ap•por•tion \ə-ˈpōr-shən\ *vb* ♦ **:** to distribute proportionately

♦ allocate, allot, allow, ration ♦ administer, allocate, deal, dispense, distribute, mete, parcel, portion, prorate

ap•por•tion•ment \-mənt\ *n* **:** an act or result of apportioning

ap•po•site \ˈa-pə-zət\ *adj* ♦ **:** highly pertinent or appropriate **:** RELEVANT — **ap•po•site•ly** *adv* — **ap•po•site•ness** *n*

♦ applicable, apropos, germane, material, pertinent, pointed, relative, relevant

ap•po•si•tion \ˌa-pə-ˈzi-shən\ *n* **:** a grammatical construction in which a noun or pronoun is followed by another that has the same referent (as *the poet* and *Burns* in "a biography of the poet Burns")

ap•pos•i•tive \ə-ˈpä-zə-tiv, a-\ *adj* **:** of, relating to, or standing in grammatical apposition — **appositive** *n*

ap•prais•al \ə-ˈprā-zəl\ *n* ♦ **:** an act or instance of appraising

♦ assessment, estimate, estimation, evaluation, judgment (*or* judgement)

ap•praise \ə-ˈprāz\ *vb* **ap•praised; ap•prais•ing 1 :** to set a value on **2** ♦ **:** to evaluate the worth, significance, or status of — **ap•prais•er** *n*

♦ assess, estimate, evaluate, rate, set, value

ap•pre•cia•ble \ə-ˈprē-shə-bəl\ *adj* ♦ **:** large enough to be recognized and measured — **ap•pre•cia•bly** *adv*

♦ detectable, discernible, distinguishable, palpable, perceptible, sensible

ap•pre•ci•ate \ə-ˈprē-shē-ˌāt\ *vb* **-at•ed; -at•ing 1** ♦ **:** to value justly **2** ♦ **:** to judge with understanding **:** be fully aware of **3 :** to be grateful for **4** ♦ **:** to increase in value

♦ [1] cherish, prize, treasure, value ♦ [1] admire, esteem, regard, respect ♦ [2] apprehend, catch, catch on (to), comprehend, get, grasp, make, make out, perceive, see, seize, understand ♦ [4] accumulate, build, expand, increase, mount, multiply, proliferate, rise

ap•pre•ci•a•tion \ə-ˌprē-shē-ˈā-shən\ *n* **1 a** ♦ **:** an opinion or estimate formed by discerning and comparing; *esp* **:** a favorable critical estimate **b :** sensitive awareness **2** ♦ **:** an expression of admiration, approval, or gratitude

♦ [1a] admiration, esteem, estimation, favor (*or* favour), regard, respect ♦ [1a] apprehension, comprehension, grasp, grip, perception, understanding ♦ [2] gratefulness, gratitude, thanks

ap•pre•cia•tive \ə-ˈprē-shə-tiv, -shē-ˌāt-\ *adj* ♦ **:** having or showing appreciation — **ap•pre•cia•tive•ly** *adv*

♦ complimentary, favorable (*or* favourable), friendly, good, positive ♦ grateful, obliged, thankful

ap•pre•hend \ˌa-pri-ˈhend\ *vb* **1** ♦ **:** to take or keep in custody by authority of law **:** ARREST **2 :** to become aware of **3 :** to look forward to with dread **4** ♦ **:** to grasp with the understanding **:** UNDERSTAND

♦ [1] arrest, nab, pick up, restrain, seize ♦ [4] appreciate, catch, catch on (to), comprehend, get, grasp, make, make out, perceive, see, seize, understand

ap•pre•hen•sion \ˌa-pri-ˈhen-chən\ *n* **1 a :** the act or power of perceiving or comprehending **b** ♦ **:** the result of apprehending mentally **2 :** seizure by legal process **3** ♦ **:** suspicion or fear especially of future evil

♦ [1b] appreciation, comprehension, grasp, grip, perception, understanding ♦ [3] agitation, anxiety, care, concern, disquiet, nervousness, perturbation, uneasiness, worry

ap•pre•hen•sive \-ˈhen-siv\ *adj* **:** viewing the future with anxiety — **ap•pre•hen•sive•ly** *adv* — *n*

ap•pre•hen•sive•ness \-nəs\ *n* **:** the quality or state of being apprehensive

¹ap•pren•tice \ə-ˈpren-təs\ *n* **1** ♦ **:** a person learning a craft under a skilled worker **2 :** BEGINNER — **ap•pren•tice•ship** *n*

♦ aid, assistant, helper

²apprentice *vb* **-ticed; -tic•ing :** to bind or set at work as an apprentice

ap•prise \ə-ˈprīz\ *vb* **ap•prised; ap•pris•ing** ♦ **:** to give notice to **:** INFORM

♦ acquaint, advise, brief, clue, enlighten, familiarize, fill in, inform, instruct, tell, wise

¹ap•proach \ə-ˈprōch\ *vb* **1** ♦ **:** to move nearer to **2** ♦ **:** to be almost the same as **3 :** to make advances to especially for the purpose of creating a desired result **4 :** to take preliminary steps toward — **ap•proach•able** *adj*

♦ [1] advance, close, come, near ***Ant*** back (up *or* away), recede, retire, retreat, withdraw ♦ [2] approximate, compare, measure up, stack up

²approach *n* **1** ♦ **:** a means of access **:** AVENUE **2 a :** the taking of preliminary steps toward a particular purpose **b** ♦ **:** a particular manner of taking steps toward an end

♦ [1] avenue, passage, path, route, way ♦ [2b] fashion, form, manner, method, strategy, style, system, tack, tactics, technique, way

ap•pro•ba•tion \ˌa-prə-ˈbā-shən\ *n* ♦ **:** an act of commending **:** APPROVAL

♦ approval, blessing, favor (*or* favour), imprimatur, OK

¹ap•pro•pri•ate \ə-ˈprō-prē-ˌāt\ *vb* **-at•ed; -at•ing 1** ♦ **:** to take possession of **2 :** to set apart for a particular use

♦ arrogate, commandeer, preempt, usurp

²ap•pro•pri•ate \ə-ˈprō-prē-ət\ *adj* ♦ **:** fitted to a purpose or use

♦ applicable, apt, felicitous, fit, fitting, good, happy, meet, proper, right, suitable

ap•pro•pri•ate•ly \-lē\ *adv* ♦ **:** in an appropriate manner

♦ correctly, fittingly, happily, properly, rightly, suitably

ap•pro•pri•ate•ness \-nəs\ *n* ♦ **:** the quality or state of being appropriate

♦ aptness, fitness, rightness, suitability ***Ant*** inaptness, infelicity, unfitness

ap•pro•pri•a•tion \ə-ˌprō-prē-ˈā-shən\ *n* ♦ **:** something (as money) set aside by formal action for a specific use

♦ allocation, allotment, grant, subsidy

ap•prov•al \ə-ˈprü-vəl\ *n* ♦ **:** an act of approving — **on approval :** subject to a prospective buyer's acceptance or refusal

♦ approbation, blessing, favor (*or* favour), imprimatur, OK ***Ant*** disapprobation, disapproval, disfavor

ap•prove \ə-ˈprüv\ *vb* **ap•proved; ap•prov•ing 1** ♦ **:** to have or express a favorable opinion of **2** ♦ **:** to accept as satisfactory **:** RATIFY

♦ [1] authorize, clear, OK, ratify, sanction, warrant ***Ant*** decline, deny, disallow, disapprove, negative, reject, turn down ♦ *usu* **approve of** [2] accept, care, countenance, favor (*or* favour), OK, subscribe ***Ant*** disapprove (of), discountenance, disfavor, frown (on *or* upon)

approx *abbr* approximate; approximately

¹ap•prox•i•mate \ə-ˈpräk-sə-mət\ *adj* ♦ **:** nearly correct or exact — **ap•prox•i•mate•ly** *adv*

♦ comparative, near, relative

²ap•prox•i•mate \-ˌmāt\ *vb* **-mat•ed; -mat•ing** ♦ **:** to come near **:** APPROACH — **ap•prox•i•ma•tion** \ə-ˌpräk-sə-ˈmā-shən\ *n*

♦ approach, compare, measure up, stack up

appt *abbr* appoint; appointed; appointment

ap•pur•te•nance \ə-ˈpərt-nəns, -ᵊn-əns\ *n* **:** something that belongs to or goes with another thing — **ap•pur•te•nant** \ə-ˈpərt-nənt, -ᵊn-ənt\ *adj*

Apr *abbr* April

APR *abbr* annual percentage rate

apri•cot \ˈa-prə-ˌkät, ˈā-\ *n* **:** an oval orange-colored fruit resembling the related peach and plum in flavor; *also* **:** a tree bearing apricots

April \ˈā-prəl\ *n* **:** the 4th month of the year

a pri•o•ri \ˌä-prē-ˈōr-ē\ *adj* **1 :** characterized by or derived by reasoning from self-evident propositions **2 :** independent of experience — **a priori** *adv*

apron \ˈā-prən\ *n* **1 :** a garment tied over the front of the body to protect the clothes **2 :** a paved area for parking or handling airplanes — **aproned** *adj*

¹ap•ro•pos \ˌa-prə-ˈpō, ˈa-prə-ˌpō\ *adv* **1 :** OPPORTUNELY **2 :** in passing **:** INCIDENTALLY

²apropos *adj* ♦ **:** being to the point

♦ applicable, apposite, germane, material, pertinent, pointed, relative, relevant

apropos of *prep* ♦ **:** with regard to

♦ about, concerning, of, on, regarding, respecting, toward

apse \ˈaps\ *n* **:** a projecting usually semicircular and vaulted part of a building (as a church)

¹apt \ˈapt\ *adj* **1** ♦ **:** well adapted **:** SUITABLE **2** ♦ **:** having an habitual tendency **3 :** quick to learn — **apt•ly** *adv*

♦ [1] applicable, appropriate, felicitous, fit, fitting, good, happy, meet, proper, right, suitable ♦ [2] given, inclined, prone

²apt *abbr* **1** apartment **2** aptitude

ap•ti•tude \ˈap-tə-ˌtüd, -ˌtyüd\ *n* **1** ♦ **:** natural ability **:** TALENT **2 :** capacity for learning **3 :** APPROPRIATENESS

♦ endowment, faculty, flair, genius, gift, knack, talent

apt•ness \ˈapt-nəs\ *n* ♦ **:** the quality or state of being apt

♦ proneness, propensity, tendency, way ♦ appropriateness, fitness, rightness, suitability

aqua \ˈa-kwə, ˈä-\ *n* **:** a light greenish blue color

aqua•cul•ture *also* **aqui•cul•ture** \ˈa-kwə-ˌkəl-chər, ˈä-\ *n* **:** the cultivation of aquatic plants or animals (as fish or shellfish) for human use

aqua•ma•rine \ˌa-kwə-mə-ˈrēn, ˌä-\ *n* **1 :** a bluish green gem **2 :** a pale blue to light greenish blue

aqua•naut \ˈa-kwə-ˌnot, ˈä-\ *n* **:** a person who lives in an underwater shelter for an extended period

aqua•plane \-ˌplān\ *n* **:** a board towed behind a motorboat and ridden by a person standing on it — **aquaplane** *vb*

aqua re•gia \ˌa-kwə-ˈrē-j(ē-)ə\ *n* **:** a mixture of nitric and hydrochloric acids that dissolves gold or platinum

aquar•i•um \ə-ˈkwar-ē-əm\ *n, pl* **-i•ums** *or* **-ia** \-ē-ə\ **1 :** a container (as a glass tank) in which living aquatic animals or plants are kept **2 :** a place where aquatic animals and plants are kept and shown

Aquar•i•us \ə-ˈkwar-ē-əs\ *n* **1 :** a zodiacal constellation between Capricorn and Pisces usually pictured as a man pouring water **2 :** the 11th sign of the zodiac in astrology; *also* **:** one born under this sign

¹aquat•ic \ə-ˈkwä-tik, -ˈkwa-\ *adj* **1 :** growing or living in or frequenting water **2 :** performed in or on water

²aquatic *n* **:** an aquatic animal or plant

aqua•vit \ˈä-kwə-ˌvēt\ *n* **:** a clear liquor flavored with caraway seeds
aqua vi•tae \ˌa-kwə-ˈvī-tē, ˌä-\ *n* **:** a strong alcoholic liquor (as brandy)
aq•ue•duct \ˈa-kwə-ˌdəkt\ *n* **1** ♦ **:** a conduit for carrying running water **2 :** a structure carrying a canal over a river or hollow **3 :** a passage in a bodily part

♦ canal, channel, conduit, flume, raceway, watercourse

aque•ous \ˈā-kwē-əs, ˈa-\ *adj* **1 :** WATERY **2 :** made of, by, or with water
aqueous humor *n* **:** a clear fluid occupying the space between the lens and the cornea of the eye
aqui•fer \ˈa-kwə-fər, ˈä-\ *n* **:** a water-bearing stratum of permeable rock, sand, or gravel
aq•ui•line \ˈa-kwə-ˌlīn, -lən\ *adj* **1 :** of or resembling an eagle **2 :** hooked like an eagle's beak ⟨an ~ nose⟩
ar *abbr* arrival; arrive
Ar *symbol* argon
AR *abbr* Arkansas
-ar *adj suffix* **1 :** of or relating to ⟨molecul*ar*⟩ **:** being ⟨spectacul*ar*⟩ **2 :** resembling ⟨oracul*ar*⟩
Ar•ab \ˈar-əb\ *n* **1 :** a member of a Semitic people of the Arabian peninsula in southwestern Asia **2 :** a member of an Arabic-speaking people — **Arab** *adj* — **Ara•bi•an** \ə-ˈrā-bē-ən\ *adj or n*
ar•a•besque \ˌar-ə-ˈbesk\ *n* **:** a design of interlacing lines forming figures of flowers, foliage, and sometimes animals — **arabesque** *adj*
[1]**Ar•a•bic** \ˈar-ə-bik\ *n* **:** a Semitic language of southwestern Asia and northern Africa
[2]**Arabic** *adj* **1 :** of or relating to the Arabs, Arabic, or the Arabian peninsula in southwestern Asia **2 :** expressed in or making use of Arabic numerals
Arabic numeral *n* **:** any of the number symbols 0, 1, 2, 3, 4, 5, 6, 7, 8, 9
ar•a•ble \ˈar-ə-bəl\ *adj* **:** fit for or used for the growing of crops
arach•nid \ə-ˈrak-nəd\ *n* **:** any of a class of usually 8-legged arthropods comprising the spiders, scorpions, mites, and ticks — **arachnid** *adj*
Ar•a•ma•ic \ˌar-ə-ˈmā-ik\ *n* **:** an ancient Semitic language
ar•a•mid \ˈar-ə-məd, -ˌmid\ *n* **:** any of several light but very strong heat-resistant synthetic materials used especially in textiles and plastics
Arap•a•ho *or* **Arap•a•hoe** \ə-ˈra-pə-ˌhō\ *n, pl* **-ho** *or* **-hos** *or* **-hoe** *or* **-hoes :** a member of an American Indian people of the western U.S.
ar•bi•ter \ˈär-bə-tər\ *n* ♦ **:** one having power to decide a dispute

♦ arbitrator, judge, referee, umpire ♦ arbitrator, broker, go-between, intercessor, intermediary, mediator, middleman, peacemaker

ar•bi•trage \ˈär-bə-ˌträzh\ *n* **:** the purchase and sale of the same or equivalent securities in different markets in order to profit from price discrepancies
ar•bi•tra•geur \ˌär-bə-(ˌ)trä-ˈzhər\ *or* **ar•bi•trag•er** \ˈär-bə-ˌträ-zhər\ *n* **:** one who practices arbitrage
ar•bit•ra•ment \är-ˈbi-trə-mənt\ *n* **1 :** the act of deciding a dispute **2 :** the judgment given by an arbitrator
ar•bi•trary \ˈär-bə-ˌtrer-ē\ *adj* **1** ♦ **:** marked by or resulting from the unrestrained and often tyrannical exercise of power **2** ♦ **:** determined by will or caprice **:** selected at random — **ar•bi•trari•ly** \ˌär-bə-ˈtrer-ə-lē\ *adv* — **ar•bi•trari•ness** \ˈär-bə-ˌtrer-ē-nəs\ *n*

♦ [1] dictatorial, high-handed, imperious, peremptory, willful ♦ [2] aimless, desultory, erratic, haphazard, random, scattered, stray

ar•bi•trate \ˈär-bə-ˌtrāt\ *vb* **-trat•ed; -trat•ing 1 :** to act as arbitrator **2** ♦ **:** to act on as arbitrator **3 :** to submit for decision to an arbitrator — **ar•bi•tra•tion** \ˌär-bə-ˈtrā-shən\ *n*

♦ adjudicate, decide, determine, judge, referee, rule, settle, umpire

ar•bi•tra•tor \ˈär-bə-ˌtrā-tər\ *n* ♦ **:** one chosen to settle differences between two parties in a controversy

♦ arbiter, judge, referee, umpire ♦ arbiter, broker, go-between, intercessor, intermediary, mediator, middleman, peacemaker

ar•bor *or Can and Brit* **ar•bour** \ˈär-bər\ *n* **:** a shelter formed of or covered with vines or branches
ar•bo•re•al \är-ˈbōr-ē-əl\ *adj* **1 :** of, relating to, or resembling a tree **2 :** living in trees ⟨~ monkeys⟩
ar•bo•re•tum \ˌär-bə-ˈrē-təm\ *n, pl* **-retums** *or* **-re•ta** \-tə\ **:** a place where trees and plants are grown for scientific and educational purposes
ar•bor•vi•tae \ˌär-bər-ˈvī-tē\ *n* **:** any of various evergreen trees and shrubs with scalelike leaves that are related to the cypresses
ar•bu•tus \är-ˈbyü-təs\ *n* **:** TRAILING ARBUTUS
[1]**arc** \ˈärk\ *n* **1 :** a sustained luminous discharge of electricity (as between two electrodes) **2** ♦ **:** a continuous portion of a curved line (as part of the circumference of a circle)

♦ arch, bend, bow, crook, curve

[2]**arc** *vb* **arced** \ˈärkt\; **arc•ing** \ˈär-kiŋ\ **1 :** to form an electric arc **2** ♦ **:** to follow an arc-shaped course

♦ bend, bow, crook, curve, hook, round, sweep, swerve, wheel

ARC *abbr* **1** AIDS-related complex **2** American Red Cross
ar•cade \är-ˈkād\ *n* **1 :** an arched or covered passageway; *esp* **:** one lined with shops **2 :** a row of arches with their supporting columns **3 :** an amusement center having coin-operated games
ar•cane \är-ˈkān\ *adj* **:** SECRET, MYSTERIOUS
[1]**arch** \ˈärch\ *n* **1 :** a curved structure spanning an opening (as a door) **2** ♦ **:** something resembling an arch **3 :** ARCHWAY

♦ arc, bend, bow, crook, curve

[2]**arch** *vb* **1 :** to cover with an arch **2 :** to form or bend into an arch
[3]**arch** *adj* **1** ♦ **:** most important **:** CHIEF **2** ♦ **:** impertinently bold and impudent — **arch•ly** *adv* — **arch•ness** *n*

♦ [1] chief, dominant, foremost, key, main, predominant, primary, principal ♦ [2] bold, brash, cheeky, cocky, fresh, impertinent, impudent, insolent, nervy, sassy, saucy

[4]**arch** *abbr* architect; architectural; architecture
ar•chae•ol•o•gy *or* **ar•che•ol•o•gy** \ˌär-kē-ˈä-lə-jē\ *n* **:** the study of past human life as revealed by relics left by ancient peoples — **ar•chae•o•log•i•cal** \-ə-ˈlä-ji-kəl\ *adj* — **ar•chae•ol•o•gist** \-ˈä-lə-jist\ *n*
ar•cha•ic \är-ˈkā-ik\ *adj* **1 :** having the characteristics of the language of the past and surviving chiefly in specialized uses ⟨~ words⟩ **2** ♦ **:** belonging to an earlier time **:** ANTIQUATED — **ar•cha•i•cal•ly** \-i-k(ə-)lē\ *adv*

♦ antiquated, dated, obsolete, outdated, outmoded, outworn, passé

arch•an•gel \ˈär-ˌkān-jəl\ *n* **:** a chief angel
arch•bish•op \ärch-ˈbi-shəp\ *n* **:** a bishop of high rank
arch•bish•op•ric \-shə-(ˌ)prik\ *n* **:** the jurisdiction or office of an archbishop
arch•con•ser•va•tive \(ˌ)ärch-kən-ˈsər-və-tiv\ *n* **:** an extreme conservative — **archconservative** *adj*
arch•dea•con \-ˈdē-kən\ *n* **:** a church official who assists a diocesan bishop in ceremonial or administrative functions
arch•di•o•cese \-ˈdī-ə-səs, -ˌsēz\ *n* **:** the diocese of an archbishop
arch•duke \-ˈdük, -ˈdyük\ *n* **1 :** a sovereign prince **2 :** a prince of the imperial family of Austria
Ar•che•an \är-ˈkē-ən\ *adj* **:** of, relating to, or being the earliest eon of geologic history — **Archean** *n*
arch•en•e•my \ˌärch-ˈe-nə-mē\ *n, pl* **-mies :** a principal enemy
Ar•cheo•zo•ic \ˌär-kē-ə-ˈzō-ik\ *adj* **:** ARCHEAN — **Archeozoic** *n*
ar•chery \ˈär-chə-rē\ *n* **:** the art or practice of shooting with bow and arrows — **ar•cher** \ˈär-chər\ *n*
ar•che•type \ˈär-ki-ˌtīp\ *n* **:** the original pattern or model of all things of the same type
arch•fiend \ˌärch-ˈfēnd\ *n* **:** a chief fiend; *esp* **:** SATAN
ar•chi•epis•co•pal \ˌär-kē-ə-ˈpis-kə-pəl\ *adj* **:** of or relating to an archbishop
ar•chi•man•drite \ˌär-kə-ˈman-ˌdrīt\ *n* **:** a dignitary in an Eastern church ranking below a bishop
ar•chi•pel•a•go \ˌär-kə-ˈpe-lə-ˌgō, ˌär-chə-\ *n, pl* **-goes** *or* **-gos :** a group of islands
ar•chi•tect \ˈär-kə-ˌtekt\ *n* **1 :** a person who plans buildings and oversees their construction **2 :** a person who designs and guides a plan or undertaking
ar•chi•tec•ture \ˈär-kə-ˌtek-chər\ *n* **1 :** the art or science of planning and building structures **2 :** a method or style of building **3 :** the manner in which the elements (as of a design) are arranged or organized — **ar•chi•tec•tur•al** \ˌar-kə-ˈtek-chə-rəl, -ˈtek-shrəl\ *adj* — **ar•chi•tec•tur•al•ly** *adv*
ar•chi•trave \ˈär-kə-ˌtrāv\ *n* **:** the supporting horizontal member just above the columns in a building in the classical style of architecture
ar•chive \ˈär-ˌkīv\ *n* **:** a place for keeping public records; *also* **:** public records — often used in plural
ar•chi•vist \ˈär-kə-vist, -ˌkī-\ *n* **:** a person in charge of archives
ar•chon \ˈär-ˌkän, -kən\ *n* **:** a chief magistrate of ancient Athens

arch•way \ˈärch-ˌwā\ *n* **:** a passageway under an arch; *also* **:** an arch over a passage
arc lamp *n* **:** a gas-filled electric lamp that produces light when a current arcs between incandescent electrodes
¹arc•tic \ˈärk-tik, ˈär-tik\ *adj* **1** *often cap* **:** of or relating to the north pole or the region near it **2** ♦ **:** bitter cold **:** FRIGID

♦ bitter, cold, freezing, frigid, frosty, glacial, icy, polar

²arc•tic \ˈär-tik, ˈärk-tik\ *n* **:** a rubber overshoe that reaches to the ankle or above
arctic circle *n, often cap A&C* **:** the parallel of latitude that is approximately 66½ degrees north of the equator
-ard *also* **-art** *n suffix* **:** one that is characterized by performing some action, possessing some quality, or being associated with some thing especially conspicuously or excessively ⟨bragg*art*⟩ ⟨dull*ard*⟩
ar•dent \ˈär-dᵊnt\ *adj* **1** ♦ **:** characterized by warmth of feeling typically expressed in eager zealous support or activity **2 :** FIERY, HOT **3 :** GLOWING — **ar•dent•ly** *adv*

♦ burning, charged, emotional, fervent, fiery, impassioned, passionate, vehement ♦ avid, eager, enthusiastic, gung ho, hot, hungry, keen

ar•dor *or Can and Brit* **ar•dour** \ˈär-dər\ *n* **1 a** ♦ **:** warmth of feeling **b** ♦ **:** eagerness and ardent interest in pursuit of something **2 :** sexual excitement

♦ [1a] emotion, fervency, fervor, heat, intensity, passion, vehemence, warmth *Ant* impassivity ♦ [1b] avidity, eagerness, enthusiasm, excitement, hunger, impatience, keenness, thirst

ar•du•ous \ˈär-jə-wəs, -dyü-wəs\ *adj* **1** ♦ **:** hard to accomplish or achieve **:** DIFFICULT **2** ♦ **:** marked by great labor or effort — **ar•du•ous•ness** *n*

♦ [1, 2] demanding, difficult, exacting, formidable, grueling, hard, laborious, strenuous, toilsome, tough

ar•du•ous•ly \-lē\ *adv* **:** in an arduous manner
¹are *pres 2d sing or pres pl of* BE
²are \ˈar\ *n* **:** a metric measure equal to 100 square meters
ar•ea \ˈar-ē-ə\ *n* **1 :** a flat surface or space **2 :** the amount of surface included (as within the lines of a geometric figure) **3** ♦ **:** range or extent of some thing or concept **:** FIELD **4** ♦ **:** any particular extent of space or surface **:** REGION

♦ [3] arena, demesne, department, discipline, domain, field, line, province, realm, specialty, sphere ♦ [4] demesne, field, region, zone

area code *n* **:** a 3-digit number that identifies each telephone service area in a country (as the U.S. or Canada)
are•na \ə-ˈrē-nə\ *n* **1** ♦ **:** an enclosed area used for public entertainment **2** ♦ **:** a sphere of activity or competition

♦ [1] hall, theater ♦ [2] area, demesne, department, discipline, domain, field, line, province, realm, specialty, sphere

Ar•gen•tine \ˈär-jən-ˌtēn, -ˌtīn\ *or* **Ar•gen•tin•ean** *or* **Ar•gen•tin•i•an** \ˌär-jən-ˈti-nē-ən\ *n* **:** a native or inhabitant of Argentina — **Argentine** *or* **Argentinean** *or* **Argentinian** *adj*
ar•gen•tite \ˈär-jən-ˌtīt\ *n* **:** a dark gray mineral that is an important ore of silver
ar•gon \ˈär-ˌgän\ *n* **:** a colorless odorless gaseous chemical element found in the air and used for filling electric lamps
ar•go•sy \ˈär-gə-sē\ *n, pl* **-sies 1 :** a large merchant ship **2 :** FLEET
ar•got \ˈär-gət, -ˌgō\ *n* ♦ **:** the language of a particular group or class

♦ cant, jargon, language, lingo, slang, terminology, vocabulary

argu•able \ˈär-gyü-ə-bəl\ *adj* ♦ **:** open to argument, dispute, or question

♦ debatable, disputable, doubtful, moot, questionable

ar•gu•ably \ˈär-gyü-(ə-)blē\ *adv* **:** it can be argued
ar•gue \ˈär-gyü\ *vb* **ar•gued; ar•gu•ing 1** ♦ **:** to give reasons for or against something **2** ♦ **:** to contend in words **:** DISPUTE **3** ♦ **:** to consider the pros and cons of **4** ♦ **:** to persuade by giving reasons

♦ [1] assert, contend, maintain, plead, reason ♦ [2] bicker, brawl, dispute, fall out, fight, hassle, quarrel, row, scrap, spat, squabble, wrangle ♦ [3] chew over, debate, discuss, dispute, hash, moot, talk over ♦ [4] convince, get, induce, move, persuade, prevail, satisfy, talk, win

ar•gu•er \ˈär-gyə-wər\ *n* ♦ **:** one who argues

♦ debater, disputant, disputer

ar•gu•ment \ˈär-gyə-mənt\ *n* **1** ♦ **:** a reason offered in proof **2** ♦ **:** discourse intended to persuade **3** ♦ **:** a usually verbal conflict **:** QUARREL

♦ [1] assertion, contention, thesis ♦ [1] case, defense (*or* defence), explanation, rationale, reason ♦ [2] colloquy, conference, deliberation, discourse, discussion, give-and-take, parley, talk ♦ [3] altercation, bicker, brawl, disagreement, dispute, fight, hassle, misunderstanding, quarrel, row, scrap, spat, squabble, wrangle

ar•gu•men•ta•tion \ˌär-gyə-mən-ˈtā- shən\ *n* **:** the art of formal discussion
ar•gu•men•ta•tive \ˌär-gyə-ˈmen-tə-tiv\ *adj* ♦ **:** inclined to argue

♦ contentious, disputatious, quarrelsome, scrappy

ar•gyle *also* **ar•gyll** \ˈär-ˌgīl\ *n, often cap* **:** a geometric knitting pattern of varicolored diamonds on a single background color; *also* **:** a sock knit in this pattern
aria \ˈär-ē-ə\ *n* **:** an accompanied elaborate vocal solo forming part of a larger work
ar•id \ˈar-əd\ *adj* **:** very dry; *esp* ♦ **:** having insufficient rainfall to support agriculture — **arid•i•ty** \ə-ˈri-də-tē\ *n*

♦ dry, sere, thirsty

Ar•i•es \ˈar-ˌēz, -ē-ˌēz\ *n* **1 :** a zodiacal constellation between Pisces and Taurus pictured as a ram **2 :** the 1st sign of the zodiac in astrology; *also* **:** one born under this sign
aright \ə-ˈrīt\ *adv* **:** RIGHT, CORRECTLY
arise \ə-ˈrīz\ *vb* **arose** \-ˈrōz\; **aris•en** \-ˈriz-ᵊn\; **aris•ing** \-ˈrī-ziŋ\ **1 :** to get up **2 a** ♦ **:** to originate from a source **b** ♦ **:** to come into being or to attention **3** ♦ **:** to move upward **:** ASCEND

♦ [2a] begin, commence, dawn, form, materialize, originate, spring, start ♦ [2b] crop, emerge, materialize, spring, surface ♦ [3] ascend, climb, lift, mount, rise, soar, up

ar•is•toc•ra•cy \ˌar-ə-ˈstä-krə-sē\ *n, pl* **-cies 1 :** government by a noble or privileged class; *also* **:** a state so governed **2 :** the governing class of an aristocracy **3 :** UPPER CLASS
aris•to•crat \ə-ˈris-tə-ˌkrat\ *n* ♦ **:** a member of an aristocracy

♦ gentleman, grandee, noble, patrician

aris•to•crat•ic \ə-ˌris-tə-ˈkra-tik\ *adj* ♦ **:** belonging to, having the qualities of, or favoring aristocracy

♦ genteel, gentle, grand, highborn, noble, patrician, wellborn

arith *abbr* arithmetic; arithmetical
arith•me•tic \ə-ˈrith-mə-ˌtik\ *n* **1 :** a branch of mathematics that deals with computations usually with nonnegative real numbers **2** ♦ **:** the process or an act of computing or calculating **:** COMPUTATION, CALCULATION — **ar•ith•met•ic** \ˌar-ith-ˈme-tik\ *or* **ar•ith•met•i•cal** \-ti-kəl\ *adj* — **ar•ith•met•i•cal•ly** \-ti-k(ə-)lē\ *adv* — **arith•me•ti•cian** \ə-ˌrith-mə-ˈti-shən\ *n*

♦ calculation, computation, reckoning

arithmetic mean *n* **:** the sum of a set of numbers divided by the number of numbers in the set
Ariz *abbr* Arizona
ark \ˈärk\ *n* **1 :** a boat held to resemble that of Noah's at the time of the Flood **2 :** the sacred chest in a synagogue representing to Hebrews the presence of God; *also* **:** the repository for the scrolls of the Torah
Ark *abbr* Arkansas
¹arm \ˈärm\ *n* **1 :** a human upper limb and especially the part between the shoulder and wrist; *also* **:** a corresponding limb of a 2-footed vertebrate **2 :** something resembling an arm in shape or position ⟨an ~ of land⟩ ⟨an ~ of a chair⟩ **3** ♦ **:** the power, authority, or resources wielded (as by an individual or group) ⟨the ~ of the law⟩ — **armed** \ˈärmd\ *adj* — **arm•less** *adj*

♦ authority, clutch, command, control, dominion, grip, hold, mastery, power, sway

²arm *vb* **:** to furnish with weapons
³arm *n* **1** ♦ **:** a means (as a weapon) of offense or defense; *esp* **:** FIREARM **2 :** a branch of the military forces **3** *pl* **:** the hereditary heraldic devices of a family

♦ firearm, gun, piece

ar•ma•da \är-ˈmä-də, -ˈmā-\ *n* **1 :** a fleet of warships **2** ♦ **:** a large force or group usually of moving things ⟨an ~ of trailers⟩

♦ caravan, cavalcade, fleet, motorcade, train

ar•ma•dil•lo \ˌär-mə-ˈdi-lō\ *n, pl* **-los :** any of several small burrowing mammals with the head and body protected by an armor of bony plates

Ar•ma•ged•don \ˌär-mə-ˈged-ᵊn\ *n* : a final conclusive battle between the forces of good and evil; *also* : the site or time of this

ar•ma•ment \ˈär-mə-mənt\ *n* **1** : military strength **2** : arms and equipment (as of a tank or combat unit) **3** : the process of preparing for war

ar•ma•ture \ˈär-mə-ˌchu̇r, -chər\ *n* **1** : a protective covering or structure (as the spines of a cactus) **2** : the rotating part of an electric generator or motor; *also* : the movable part in an electromagnetic device (as a loudspeaker)

arm•chair \ˈärm-ˌcher\ *n* : a chair with armrests

armed forces *n pl* ♦ : the combined military, naval, and air forces of a nation

♦ military, services, troops

Ar•me•nian \är-ˈmē-nē-ən\ *n* : a native or inhabitant of Armenia

arm•ful \ˈärm-ˌfu̇l\ *n, pl* **armfuls** *or* **arms•ful** \ˈärmz-ˌfu̇l\ : as much as the arm or arms can hold

arm•hole \ˈärm-ˌhōl\ *n* : an opening for the arm in a garment

ar•mi•stice \ˈär-mə-stəs\ *n* : temporary suspension of hostilities by mutual agreement : TRUCE

arm•let \ˈärm-lət\ *n* : a band worn around the upper arm

ar•mor *or Can and Brit* **ar•mour** \ˈär-mər\ *n* **1** ♦ : protective covering **2** ♦ : a quality or circumstance that affords protection **3** : armored forces and vehicles — **ar•mored** \-mərd\ *adj*

♦ [1] capsule, case, casing, cocoon, cover, housing, husk, jacket, pod, sheath, shell ♦ [2] aegis, cover, defense (*or* defence), guard, protection, safeguard, screen, security, shield, wall, ward

ar•mor•er \ˈär-mər-ər\ *or Can and Brit* **ar•mour•er** *n* **1** : a person who makes arms and armor **2** : a person who services firearms

ar•mo•ri•al \är-ˈmōr-ē-əl\ *or Can and Brit* **ar•mou•ri•al** *adj* : of or bearing heraldic arms

ar•mory \ˈär-mə-rē\ *or Can and Brit* **ar•moury** *n, pl* **ar•mor•ies** *or* **ar•mour•ies** **1** ♦ : a place where arms are stored **2** : a factory where arms are made

♦ arsenal, depot, dump, magazine

arm•pit \ˈärm-ˌpit\ *n* : the hollow under the junction of the arm and shoulder

arm•rest \-ˌrest\ *n* : a support for the arm

ar•my \ˈär-mē\ *n, pl* **armies** **1** ♦ : a body of armed personnel organized for war **2** *often cap* : the complete military organization of a country for land warfare **3** ♦ : a great number ⟨an ~ of birds⟩ **4** : a body of persons organized to advance a cause

♦ [1] battalion, host, legion ♦ [3] crowd, crush, drove, flock, horde, host, legion, mob, multitude, press, swarm, throng

army ant *n* : any of various nomadic social ants

ar•my•worm \ˈär-mē-ˌwərm\ *n* : any of numerous moths whose larvae move about destroying crops

aro•ma \ə-ˈrō-mə\ *n* ♦ : a usually pleasing odor : FRAGRANCE

♦ bouquet, fragrance, incense, perfume, redolence, scent, spice

aro•ma•ther•a•py \ə-ˌrō-mə-ˈther-ə-pē\ *n* : massage with a preparation of fragrant oils extracted from herbs, flowers, and fruits

ar•o•mat•ic \ˌar-ə-ˈma-tik\ *adj* ♦ : of, relating to, or having aroma

♦ ambrosial, fragrant, redolent, savory, scented, sweet

arose *past of* ARISE

¹around \ə-ˈrau̇nd\ *adv* **1** : in a circle or in circumference ⟨a tree five feet ~⟩ **2** : in or along a circuit ⟨the road goes ~ by the lake⟩ **3 a** : on all sides ⟨nothing for miles ~⟩ **b** ♦ : at all times : throughout the extent ⟨mild weather the year ~⟩ **4** ♦ : in or near one's present place or situation : NEARBY ⟨wait ~ awhile⟩ **5** : from one place to another ⟨travels ~ on business⟩ **6** ♦ : in an opposite direction ⟨turn ~⟩

♦ [3b] over, round, through, throughout ♦ [4] by, close, hard, in, near, nearby, nigh ♦ [6] about, back, round

²around *prep* **1 a** : on all sides of : SURROUNDING ⟨trees ~ the house⟩ **b** : so as to encircle or enclose ⟨go ~ the world⟩ **2** : to or on another side of ⟨~ the corner⟩ **3** ♦ : at, within, or to a short distance or time : NEAR ⟨stayed right ~ home⟩ **4** ♦ : here and there in or throughout ⟨barnstorming ~ the country⟩

♦ [3] about, by, near, next to ♦ [4] about, over, round, through, throughout

arouse \ə-ˈrau̇z\ *vb* **aroused; arous•ing** **1** ♦ : to awaken from sleep **2** ♦ : to stir up — **arous•al** \-ˈrau̇-zəl\ *n*

♦ [1] awake, rouse, wake ♦ [2] encourage, excite, fire, incite, instigate, move, pique, provoke, stimulate, stir

ar•peg•gio \är-ˈpe-jē-ˌō, -ˈpe-jō\ *n, pl* **-gios** : a chord whose notes are performed in succession and not simultaneously

arr *abbr* **1** arranged **2** arrival; arrive

ar•raign \ə-ˈrān\ *vb* **1** : to call before a court to answer to an indictment **2** : to accuse of wrong or imperfection — **ar•raign•ment** *n*

ar•range \ə-ˈrānj\ *vb* **ar•ranged; ar•rang•ing** **1** ♦ : to put in order **2** : to make preparations for **3** : to adapt (a musical composition) to voices or instruments other than those for which it was orig. written **4** ♦ : to come to an agreement about : SETTLE — **ar•rang•er** *n*

♦ [1] array, classify, codify, dispose, draw up, marshal, order, organize, range, systematize ♦ [4] decide, fix, set, settle

ar•range•ment \-mənt\ *n* **1 a** ♦ : the state of being arranged **b** : the act of arranging **2** : something arranged: as **a** ♦ : a preparatory act or measure **b** : an adaptation of a musical composition **c** : an informal agreement or settlement **3** : something made by arranging parts or things together ⟨a floral ~⟩

♦ [1a] composition, configuration, design, form, format, layout, makeup, pattern ♦ [1a] array, disposal, disposition, distribution, order, sequence, setup ♦ [2a] blueprint, design, game, plan, project, system

ar•rant \ˈar-ənt\ *adj* : being notoriously without moderation : EXTREME

ar•ras \ˈar-əs\ *n, pl* **arras** **1** : TAPESTRY **2** : a wall hanging or screen of tapestry

¹ar•ray \ə-ˈrā\ *vb* **1** ♦ : to dress or decorate especially splendidly **2** ♦ : to arrange in order

♦ [1] adorn, beautify, clothe, deck, decorate, do, dress, embellish, enrich, garnish, ornament, trim ♦ [2] arrange, classify, codify, dispose, draw up, marshal, order, organize, range, systematize

²array *n* **1** ♦ : a regular arrangement **2** ♦ : rich apparel **3** ♦ : an imposing group

♦ [1] arrangement, disposal, disposition, distribution, order, sequence, setup ♦ [2] attire, best, bravery, caparison, feather, finery, frippery, full dress, gaiety, regalia ♦ [3] assemblage, block, collection, group, lot

ar•rears \ə-ˈrirz\ *n pl* **1** : a state of being behind in the discharge of obligations ⟨in ~ with the rent⟩ **2** : overdue debts

¹ar•rest \ə-ˈrest\ *vb* **1** ♦ : to bring to a stop **2** ♦ : to take into legal custody **3** ♦ : to catch suddenly and engagingly ⟨~ attention⟩

♦ [1] catch, check, draw up, fetch up, halt, hold up, stall, stay, still, stop ♦ [2] apprehend, nab, pick up, restrain, seize ***Ant*** discharge ♦ [3] enchant, enthrall, fascinate, grip, hypnotize, mesmerize

²arrest *n* **1** : the act of stopping; *also* : the state of being stopped **2** : the taking into custody by legal authority

ar•riv•al \ə-ˈrī-vəl\ *n* **1** : the act of arriving **2** : one that arrives

ar•rive \ə-ˈrīv\ *vb* **ar•rived; ar•riv•ing** **1** ♦ : to reach a destination **2** : to make an appearance ⟨the guests have *arrived*⟩ **3** : to attain success — **arrive at** : to reach by effort or thought ⟨*arrived at* a decision⟩

♦ come, land, show up, turn up

ar•ro•gance \ˈar-ə-gəns\ *n* ♦ : an attitude of superiority that shows itself in an overbearing manner or in presumptuous claims or assumptions

♦ haughtiness, loftiness, pretense, pretension, pretentiousness, self-importance, superiority ***Ant*** humility, modesty

ar•ro•gant \ˈar-ə-gənt\ *adj* ♦ : offensively exaggerating one's own importance — **ar•ro•gant•ly** *adv*

♦ cavalier, haughty, high-handed, high-hat, highfalutin, imperious, important, lofty, overweening, peremptory, pompous, presumptuous, pretentious, supercilious ***Ant*** humble, modest

ar•ro•gate \-ˌgāt\ *vb* **-gat•ed; -gat•ing** ♦ : to claim or seize without justification as one's right — **ar•ro•ga•tion** \ˌar-ə-ˈgā-shən\ *n*

♦ appropriate, commandeer, preempt, usurp

ar•row \ˈar-ō\ *n* **1** : a missile shot from a bow and usually having a slender shaft, a pointed head, and feathers at the butt **2** : a pointed mark used to indicate direction

ar•row•head \ˈar-ō-ˌhed\ *n* : the pointed end of an arrow

ar•row•root \-ˌrüt, -ˌru̇t\ *n* : an edible starch from the roots of any of several tropical American plants; *also* : a plant yielding arrowroot

ar•royo \ə-ˈrȯi-ə, -ō\ *n, pl* **-royos** **1 :** a watercourse in a dry region **2 :** a water-carved gully or channel
ar•se•nal \ˈärs-nəl, ˈärs-ᵊn-əl\ *n* **1** ♦ **:** a place for making and storing arms and military equipment **2 :** STORE, REPERTORY

♦ armory, depot, dump, magazine

ar•se•nic \ˈärs-nik, ˈärs-ᵊn-ik\ *n* **1 :** a solid brittle poisonous chemical element of grayish metallic luster **2 :** a very poisonous oxygen compound of arsenic used in making insecticides
ar•son \ˈärs-ᵊn\ *n* **:** the willful or malicious burning of property — **ar•son•ist** \-ist\ *n*
¹**art** \ˈärt\ *n* **1 :** skill acquired by experience or study **2 :** a branch of learning; *esp* **:** one of the humanities **3 :** an occupation requiring knowledge or skill **4** ♦ **:** the use of skill and imagination in the production of things of beauty; *also* **:** works so produced **5 :** ARTFULNESS

♦ adeptness, adroitness, artfulness, artifice, artistry, cleverness, craft, cunning, deftness, masterfulness, skill

²**art** *abbr* **1** article **2** artificial **3** artillery
ar•te•ri•al \är-ˈtir-ē-əl\ *adj* **1 :** of or relating to an artery; *also* **:** relating to or being the oxygenated blood found in most arteries **2 :** of, relating to, or being a route for through traffic
ar•te•ri•ole \är-ˈtir-ē-ˌōl\ *n* **:** one of the small terminal branches of an artery that ends in capillaries — **ar•te•ri•o•lar** \-ˌtir-ē-ˈō-lər\ *adj*
ar•te•rio•scle•ro•sis \är-ˌtir-ē-ō-sklə-ˈrō-səs\ *n* **:** a chronic disease in which arterial walls are abnormally thickened and hardened — **ar•te•rio•scle•rot•ic** \-ˈrä-tik\ *adj or n*
ar•tery \ˈär-tə-rē\ *n, pl* **-ter•ies** **1 :** one of the tubular vessels that carry blood from the heart **2** ♦ **:** a main channel of transportation or communication

♦ avenue, highway, road, route, thoroughfare, turnpike, way

ar•te•sian well \är-ˈtē-zhən-\ *n* **:** a well from which the water flows to the surface by natural pressure; *also* **:** a deep well
art•ful \ˈärt-fəl\ *adj* **1** ♦ **:** performed with or showing art or skill ⟨an ~ performance on the violin⟩ **2 a** ♦ **:** using or characterized by art and skill ⟨an ~ writer⟩ **b** ♦ **:** adroit in attaining an end usually by deceptive or indirect means **:** CRAFTY — **art•ful•ly** *adv*

♦ [1] adroit, dexterous, masterful, practiced, skillful, virtuoso ♦ [2a] clever, creative, imaginative, ingenious ♦ [2b] cagey, crafty, cunning, devious, foxy, guileful, slick, sly, subtle, wily *Ant* artless, ingenuous

art•ful•ness \-nəs\ *n* ♦ **:** the quality or state of being artful

♦ artifice, caginess, canniness, craft, craftiness, cunning, guile, slyness, wiliness ♦ adeptness, adroitness, art, artifice, artistry, cleverness, craft, cunning, deftness, masterfulness, skill

ar•thri•tis \är-ˈthrī-təs\ *n, pl* **-thri•ti•des** \-ˈthri-tə-ˌdēz\ **:** inflammation of the joints — **ar•thrit•ic** \-ˈthri-tik\ *adj or n*
ar•thro•pod \ˈär-thrə-ˌpäd\ *n* **:** any of a phylum of invertebrate animals comprising those (as insects, spiders, or crabs) with segmented bodies and jointed limbs — **arthropod** *adj*
ar•thros•co•py \är-ˈthräs-kə-pē\ *n, pl* **-pies :** visual examination of the interior of a joint (as the knee) with a special surgical instrument; *also* **:** joint surgery using arthroscopy — **ar•thro•scope** \ˈär-thrə-ˌskōp\ *n* — **ar•thro•scop•ic** \ˌär-thrə-ˈskä-pik\ *adj*
ar•ti•choke \ˈär-tə-ˌchōk\ *n* **:** a tall herb related to the daisies; *also* **:** its edible flower head
ar•ti•cle \ˈär-ti-kəl\ *n* **1 :** a distinct part of a written document **2** ♦ **:** a nonfictional prose composition forming an independent part of a publication **3 :** a word (as *an, the*) used with a noun to limit or give definiteness to its application **4 :** a member of a class of things; *esp* **:** COMMODITY

♦ composition, essay, paper, theme

ar•tic•u•lar \är-ˈti-kyə-lər\ *adj* **:** of or relating to a joint
¹**ar•tic•u•late** \är-ˈti-kyə-lət\ *adj* **1 :** divided into meaningful parts **:** INTELLIGIBLE **2** ♦ **:** able to speak; *also* **:** expressing oneself readily and effectively **3 :** JOINTED — **ar•tic•u•late•ly** *adv* — *n*

♦ eloquent, fluent, well-spoken *Ant* inarticulate

²**ar•tic•u•late** \-ˌlāt\ *vb* **-lat•ed; -lat•ing** **1 a** ♦ **:** to give clear and effective utterance to ⟨~ their grievances⟩ **b :** to utter distinctly ⟨~ each note in the musical phrase⟩ **2 :** to unite by or as if by joints

♦ clothe, couch, express, formulate, phrase, put, say, state, word

ar•tic•u•late•ness \-nəs\ *n* ♦ **:** the quality or state of being articulate

♦ eloquence, poetry, rhetoric

ar•tic•u•la•tion \-ˌti-kyə-ˈlā-shən\ *n* **1** ♦ **:** the act of giving utterance or expression **2 :** the act or manner of articulating sounds

♦ expression, formulation, statement, utterance, voice

ar•ti•fact \ˈär-tə-ˌfakt\ *n* **:** something made or modified by humans usually for a purpose; *esp* **:** an object remaining from another time or culture ⟨prehistoric ~*s*⟩
ar•ti•fice \ˈär-tə-fəs\ *n* **1 a** ♦ **:** clever or artful skill **b :** an ingenious device **2 a** ♦ **:** an artful stratagem **:** TRICK **b** ♦ **:** false or insincere behavior

♦ [1a] adeptness, adroitness, art, artfulness, artistry, cleverness, craft, cunning, deftness, masterfulness, skill ♦ [2a] device, dodge, gimmick, jig, ploy, scheme, sleight, stratagem, trick, wile ♦ [2b] craft, craftiness, crookedness, cunning, deceit, deceitfulness, dishonesty, dissimulation, double-dealing, duplicity, guile, wiliness

ar•ti•fi•cer \är-ˈti-fə-sər, ˈär-tə-fə-sər\ *n* ♦ **:** a skilled worker

♦ artisan, craftsman, handicrafter

ar•ti•fi•cial \ˌär-tə-ˈfi-shəl\ *adj* **1** ♦ **:** produced by art rather than nature; *also* **:** made by humans to imitate nature **2** ♦ **:** not genuine **:** FEIGNED — **ar•ti•fi•ci•al•i•ty** \-ˌfi-shē-ˈa-lə-tē\ *n* — **ar•ti•fi•cial•ly** *adv* — **ar•ti•fi•cial•ness** *n*

♦ [1] fake, faux, imitation, mock, sham, synthetic ♦ [2] affected, assumed, bogus, contrived, false, feigned, insincere, mechanical, phony, put-on, spurious, unnatural *Ant* genuine, natural, spontaneous, unfeigned, unforced

artificial insemination *n* **:** introduction of semen into the uterus or oviduct by other than natural means
artificial intelligence *n* **:** the capability of a machine and especially a computer to imitate intelligent human behavior
artificial respiration *n* **:** the rhythmic forcing of air into and out of the lungs of a person whose breathing has stopped
ar•til•lery \är-ˈti-lə-rē\ *n, pl* **-ler•ies** **1 :** crew-served mounted firearms (as guns) **2 :** a branch of the army armed with artillery — **ar•til•ler•ist** \-rist\ *n*
ar•ti•san \ˈär-tə-zən, -sən\ *n* ♦ **:** a skilled manual worker

♦ artificer, craftsman, handicrafter

art•ist \ˈär-tist\ *n* **1 :** one who practices an imaginative art; *esp* **:** one who creates objects of beauty **2 :** ARTISTE **3** ♦ **:** one who is adept at something

♦ adept, authority, expert, master, virtuoso, whiz, wizard

ar•tiste \är-ˈtēst\ *n* **:** a skilled public performer
ar•tis•tic \är-ˈtis-tik\ *adj* **1 :** of, relating to, or characteristic of art or artists **2 :** showing taste and skill — **ar•tis•ti•cal•ly** \-ti-k(ə-)lē\ *adv*
art•ist•ry \ˈär-tə-strē\ *n* ♦ **:** artistic quality or ability

♦ adeptness, adroitness, art, artfulness, artifice, cleverness, craft, cunning, deftness, masterfulness, skill

art•less \ˈärt-ləs\ *adj* **1 :** lacking art or skill **2 a** ♦ **:** made without skill **:** CRUDE **b :** free from artificiality **:** NATURAL **3** ♦ **:** free from guile **:** SINCERE

♦ [2a] clumsy, crude, rough, rude, unrefined ♦ [3] genuine, honest, ingenuous, innocent, naive, natural, real, simple, sincere, true, unaffected, unpretentious

art•less•ly \-lē\ *adv* ♦ **:** in an artless manner

♦ ingenuously, naively, naturally, unaffectedly

art•less•ness \-nəs\ *n* ♦ **:** the quality or state of being artless

♦ greenness, ingenuousness, innocence, naïveté, naturalness, simplicity, unworldliness

art nou•veau \ˌär-nü-ˈvō, ˌärt-\ *n, often cap A&N* **:** a late 19th century design style characterized by sinuous lines and leaf-shaped forms
arty \ˈär-tē\ *adj* **art•i•er; -est :** showily or pretentiously artistic — **art•i•ly** \ˈärt-ᵊl-ē\ *adv* — **art•i•ness** *n*
ar•um \ˈar-əm\ *n* **:** any of a family of plants (as the jack-in-the-pulpit or a skunk cabbage) with flowers in a fleshy enclosed spike
ARV *abbr* American Revised Version
¹**-ary** *n suffix* **:** thing or person belonging to or connected with ⟨function*ary*⟩
²**-ary** *adj suffix* **:** of, relating to, or connected with ⟨budget*ary*⟩
Ary•an \ˈar-ē-ən, ˈer-; ˈär-yən\ *adj* **1 :** INDO-EUROPEAN **2 :** NORDIC — **Aryan** *n*
¹**as** \əz, (ˌ)az\ *adv* **1 :** to the same degree or amount **:** EQUALLY ⟨~ green as grass⟩ **2 :** for instance ⟨various trees, ~ oak or pine⟩

3 : when considered in a specified relation ⟨my opinion ~ distinguished from his⟩

[2]**as** *conj* **1 :** in the same amount or degree in which ⟨green ~ grass⟩ **2 :** in the same way that ⟨farmed ~ his father before him had farmed⟩ **3 :** WHILE, WHEN ⟨spoke to me ~ I was leaving⟩ **4 :** THOUGH ⟨improbable ~ it seems⟩ **5 :** SINCE, BECAUSE ⟨~ I'm not wanted, I'll go⟩ **6 :** that the result is ⟨so guilty ~ to leave no doubt⟩

[3]**as** *pron* **1 :** THAT — used after *same* or *such* ⟨it's the same price ~ before⟩ **2 :** a fact that ⟨he's rich, ~ you know⟩

[4]**as** *prep* **:** in the capacity or character of ⟨this will serve ~ a substitute⟩

As *symbol* arsenic

AS *abbr* **1** American Samoa **2** Anglo-Saxon **3** associate in science

asa•fet•i•da *or* **asa•foe•ti•da** \ˌa-sə-ˈfi-tə-dē, -ˈfe-tə-də\ *n* **:** an ill-smelling plant gum formerly used in medicine

ASAP *abbr* as soon as possible

as•bes•tos \as-ˈbes-təs, az-\ *n* **:** a noncombustible grayish mineral that occurs in fibrous form and has been used as a fireproof material

as•cend \ə-ˈsend\ *vb* **1** ♦ **:** to move upward **:** MOUNT, CLIMB **2 :** to succeed to **:** OCCUPY ⟨he ~*ed* the throne⟩

♦ arise, climb, lift, mount, rise, soar, up *Ant* decline, descend, dip, drop, fall (off)

as•cen•dan•cy *also* **as•cen•den•cy** \ə-ˈsen-dən-sē\ *n* ♦ **:** controlling influence

♦ dominance, dominion, predominance, preeminence, supremacy

[1]**as•cen•dant** *also* **as•cen•dent** \ə-ˈsen-dənt\ *n* **:** a dominant position

[2]**ascendant** *also* **ascendent** *adj* **1 :** moving upward **2 :** DOMINANT

as•cen•sion \ə-ˈsen-chən\ *n* **:** the act or process of ascending

Ascension Day *n* **:** the Thursday 40 days after Easter observed in commemoration of Christ's ascension into heaven

as•cent \ə-ˈsent\ *n* **1 a** ♦ **:** the act of mounting upward **:** CLIMB **b :** an upward slope or rising grade **2** ♦ **:** an advance in social status or reputation

♦ [1a] climb, rise, soar *Ant* descent, dip, drop, fall ♦ [2] advancement, elevation, promotion, rise, upgrade

as•cer•tain \ˌas-ər-ˈtān\ *vb* ♦ **:** to learn with certainty — **as•cer•tain•able** *adj*

♦ catch on, discover, find out, hear, learn, realize, see ♦ detect, determine, discover, ferret out, find, hit on, locate, track down

as•cet•ic \ə-ˈse-tik\ *adj* **:** practicing self-denial especially for spiritual reasons **:** AUSTERE — **ascetic** *n* — **as•cet•i•cism** \-ˈse-tə-ˌsi-zəm\ *n*

ASCII \ˈas-kē\ *n* **:** a computer code for representing alphanumeric information

ascor•bic acid \ə-ˈskȯr-bik-\ *n* **:** VITAMIN C

as•cot \ˈas-kət, -ˌkät\ *n* **:** a broad neck scarf that is looped under the chin

as•cribe \ə-ˈskrīb\ *vb* **as•cribed; as•crib•ing** ♦ **:** to refer to a supposed cause, source, or author **:** ATTRIBUTE — **as•crib•able** *adj* — **as•crip•tion** \-ˈskrip-shən\ *n*

♦ accredit, attribute, credit, impute

asep•tic \ā-ˈsep-tik\ *adj* ♦ **:** free or freed from disease-causing germs

♦ hygienic, sanitary, sterile

asex•u•al \ā-ˈsek-shə-wəl\ *adj* **1 :** lacking sex or functional sex organs **2 :** occurring or formed without the production and union of two kinds of germ cells ⟨~ reproduction⟩ — **asex•u•al•ly** *adv*

as for *prep* **:** with regard to **:** CONCERNING ⟨*as for* the others, they were late⟩

[1]**ash** \ˈash\ *n* **1 :** any of a genus of trees related to the olive and having winged seeds and bark with grooves and ridges **2 :** the tough elastic wood of an ash

[2]**ash** *n* **1 :** the solid matter left when material is burned **2 :** fine mineral particles from a volcano **3** *pl* **:** the remains of the dead human body after cremation or disintegration

ashamed \ə-ˈshāmd\ *adj* **1** ♦ **:** feeling shame **2 :** restrained by anticipation of shame ⟨~ to say anything⟩ — **asham•ed•ly** \-ˈshā-məd-lē\ *adv*

♦ contrite, guilty, hangdog, penitent, remorseful, repentant, shamefaced

ash•en \ˈa-shən\ *adj* ♦ **:** resembling ashes (as in color); *esp* **:** deadly pale

♦ cadaverous, livid, lurid, pale, pasty, peaked

ash•lar \ˈash-lər\ *n* **:** hewn or squared stone; *also* **:** masonry of such stone

ashore \ə-ˈshōr\ *adv* **:** on or to the shore

as how *conj* **:** THAT ⟨allowed *as how* she was glad to be here⟩

ash•ram \ˈäsh-rəm\ *n* **:** a religious retreat especially of a Hindu sage

ash•tray \ˈash-ˌtrā\ *n* **:** a receptacle for tobacco ashes

Ash Wednesday *n* **:** the 1st day of Lent

ashy \ˈa-shē\ *adj* **ash•i•er; -est :** resembling ashes (as in color); *esp* **:** deadly pale **:** ASHEN

Asian \ˈā-zhən\ *adj* **:** of, relating to, or characteristic of the continent of Asia or its people — **Asian** *n*

[1]**aside** \ə-ˈsīd\ *adv* **1 :** to or toward the side ⟨stepped ~⟩ **2 :** out of the way **:** AWAY ⟨put ~ some savings⟩

[2]**aside** *n* **:** an actor's words heard by the audience but supposedly not by other characters on stage

aside from *prep* **1 :** BESIDES ⟨*aside from* being pretty, she's intelligent⟩ **2** ♦ **:** with the exception of ⟨*aside from* one D his grades are excellent⟩

♦ bar, barring, besides, but, except, outside (of), save

as if *conj* **1 :** as it would be if ⟨it's *as if* nothing had changed⟩ **2 :** as one would if ⟨he acts *as if* he'd never been away⟩ **3 :** THAT ⟨it seems *as if* nothing ever happens around here⟩

as•i•nine \ˈas-ᵊn-ˌīn\ *adj* ♦ **:** extremely or utterly foolish

♦ absurd, crazy, cuckoo, fatuous, foolish, mad, nonsensical, nutty, senseless, silly, stupid

as•i•nin•i•ty \ˌa-sə-ˈni-nə-tē\ *n* **1** ♦ **:** the quality or state of being asinine **2 :** something that is asinine

♦ craziness, daftness, folly, foolishness, inanity, insanity, lunacy, madness, silliness

ask \ˈask\ *vb* **asked** \ˈaskt\; **ask•ing 1** ♦ **:** to call on for an answer **2 :** UTTER ⟨~ a question⟩ **3 :** to make a request of ⟨~ him for help⟩ **4** ♦ **:** to make a request for ⟨~ help of her⟩ **5** ♦ **:** to set as a price ⟨~*ed* $800 for the car⟩ **6 :** to increase the likelihood of **:** INVITE

♦ [1] inquire of, interrogate, query, question, quiz *Ant* answer, reply, respond ♦ *usu* **ask for** [4] call, plead, quest, request, seek, solicit, sue ♦ [5] charge, command, demand

askance \ə-ˈskans\ *adv* **1 :** with a side glance **2** ♦ **:** with distrust

♦ distrustfully, dubiously, mistrustfully, suspiciously *Ant* trustfully

askew \ə-ˈskyü\ *adj* ♦ **:** being out of line **:** AWRY — **askew** *adv*

♦ awry, cockeyed, crooked, listing, lopsided, slantwise, uneven

ASL *abbr* American Sign Language

[1]**aslant** \ə-ˈslant\ *adv or adj* **:** in a slanting direction

[2]**aslant** *prep* **:** over or across in a slanting direction

asleep \ə-ˈslēp\ *adv or adj* **1** ♦ **:** in or into a state of sleep **2 :** DEAD **3** ♦ **:** lacking sensation **:** NUMB **4 :** INACTIVE

♦ [1] dormant *Ant* awake, wakeful, wide-awake ♦ [3] dead, numb, unfeeling

as long as *conj* **1 :** provided that ⟨do as you like *as long as* you get home on time⟩ **2 :** INASMUCH AS, SINCE ⟨*as long as* you're up, turn on the light⟩

aso•cial \(ˌ)ā-ˈsō-shəl\ *adj* **:** ANTISOCIAL

as of *prep* **:** AT, DURING, FROM, ON ⟨takes effect *as of* July 1⟩

asp \ˈasp\ *n* **:** a small poisonous African snake

as•par•a•gus \ə-ˈspar-ə-gəs\ *n* **:** a tall branching perennial herb related to the lilies; *also* **:** its edible young stalks

as•par•tame \as-ˈpär-ˌtām\ *n* **:** a crystalline low-calorie sweetener

ASPCA *abbr* American Society for the Prevention of Cruelty to Animals

as•pect \ˈas-ˌpekt\ *n* **1 :** a position facing a particular direction **2** ♦ **:** a particular appearance or countenance **:** APPEARANCE, LOOK **3** ♦ **:** a particular status or phase in which something appears or may be regarded

♦ [2] appearance, look, mien, presence ♦ [3] angle, facet, hand, phase, side

as•pen \ˈas-pən\ *n* **:** any of several poplars with leaves that flutter in the slightest breeze

as per \ˈaz-ˌpər\ *prep* **:** in accordance with ⟨*as per* instructions⟩

as•per•i•ty \a-ˈsper-ə-tē\ *n, pl* **-ties 1** ♦ **:** a characteristic making for hardship : RIGOR **2 :** ROUGHNESS **3 ♦ :** harshness of manner or temper

♦ [1] adversity, difficulty, hardness, hardship, rigor ♦ [3] acidity, acrimony, bitterness, cattiness, tartness, virulence, vitriol

as·per·sion \ə-ˈspər-zhən\ *n* **:** a slanderous or defamatory remark
as·phalt \ˈas-ˌfȯlt\ *also* **as·phal·tum** \as-ˈfȯl-təm\ *n* **:** a dark substance found in natural beds or obtained as a residue in petroleum refining and used especially in paving streets
asphalt jungle *n* **:** a big city or a specified part of a big city
as·pho·del \ˈas-fə-ˌdel\ *n* **:** any of several Old World herbs related to the lilies and bearing flowers in long erect spikes
as·phyx·ia \as-ˈfik-sē-ə\ *n* **:** a lack of oxygen or excess of carbon dioxide in the body usually caused by interruption of breathing and causing unconsciousness
as·phyx·i·ate \-sē-ˌāt\ *vb* **-at·ed; -at·ing :** SUFFOCATE — **as·phyx·i·a·tion** \-ˌfik-sē-ˈā-shən\ *n*
as·pic \ˈas-pik\ *n* **:** a savory meat jelly
as·pi·rant \ˈas-pə-rənt, ə-ˈspī-rənt\ *n* **♦ :** one who aspires

♦ applicant, campaigner, candidate, contender, hopeful, prospect, seeker

1as·pi·rate \ˈas-pə-rət\ *n* **1 :** an independent sound \h\ or a character (as the letter *h*) representing it **2 :** a consonant having aspiration as its final component
2as·pi·rate \ˈas-pə-ˌrāt\ *vb* **-rat·ed; -rat·ing :** to draw, remove, or take up or into by suction
as·pi·ra·tion \ˌas-pə-ˈrā-shən\ *n* **1 :** the pronunciation or addition of an aspirate; *also* **:** the aspirate or its symbol **2 :** a drawing of something in, out, up, or through by or as if by suction **3 a :** a strong desire to achieve something noble **b ♦ :** an object of strong desire

♦ aim, ambition, design, dream, end, goal, intent, object, objective, purpose

as·pire \ə-ˈspīr\ *vb* **as·pired; as·pir·ing 1 ♦ :** to seek to attain or accomplish a particular goal **2 :** to rise aloft

♦ aim, contemplate, design, intend, plan, propose

as·pi·rin \ˈas-pə-rən\ *n, pl* **aspirin** *or* **aspirins 1 :** a white crystalline drug used to relieve pain and fever **2 :** a tablet of aspirin
as regards *also* **as respects** *prep* **:** in regard to **:** with respect to
ass \ˈas\ *n* **1 ♦ :** any of several long-eared mammals smaller than the related horses; *esp* **:** one of Africa ancestral to the donkey **2 :** a stupid person

♦ donkey, jackass

as·sail \ə-ˈsāl\ *vb* **♦ :** to attack violently with blows or words — **as·sail·able** *adj* — **as·sail·ant** *n*

♦ abuse, attack, belabor, blast, castigate, excoriate, jump, lambaste, slam, vituperate ♦ assault, attack, beset, charge, descend, jump, pounce (on *or* upon), raid, rush, storm, strike

as·sas·sin \ə-ˈsas-ᵊn\ *n* **:** a murderer especially for hire or fanatical reasons
as·sas·si·nate \ə-ˈsas-ᵊn-ˌāt\ *vb* **-nat·ed; -nat·ing :** to murder by sudden or secret attack — **as·sas·si·na·tion** \-ˌsas-ᵊn-ˈā-shən\ *n*
1as·sault \ə-ˈsȯlt\ *n* **1 ♦ :** a violent attack **2 :** an unlawful attempt or threat to do harm to another

♦ aggression, attack, charge, descent, offense (*or* offence), offensive, onset, onslaught, raid, rush, strike

2assault *vb* **♦ :** to make an assault on

♦ assail, attack, beset, charge, descend, jump, pounce (on *or* upon), raid, rush, storm, strike

assault rifle *n* **:** a military automatic rifle with a large-capacity magazine
1as·say \ˈa-ˌsā, a-ˈsā\ *n* **♦ :** analysis to determine the quantity of one or more components present in a sample (as of an ore or drug)

♦ analysis, breakdown, breakup, dissection

2as·say \a-ˈsā, ˈa-ˌsā\ *vb* **1 ♦ :** to make an attempt at **:** TRY **2 ♦ :** to subject (as an ore or drug) to an assay **3 :** JUDGE 3

♦ [1] attempt, endeavor (*or* endeavour), essay, seek, strive, try ♦ [2] analyze, anatomize, break down, break up, dissect

as·sem·blage \ə-ˈsem-blij, *3 & 4 also* ˌas-ˌäm-ˈbläzh\ *n* **1 ♦ :** a collection of persons or things **2 :** the act of assembling **3 :** an artistic composition made from scraps, junk, and odds and ends **4 :** the art of making assemblages

♦ assembly, conference, congregation, convocation, gathering, meeting, muster ♦ accumulation, array, bunch, collection, group, lot, package, parcel

as·sem·ble \ə-ˈsem-bəl\ *vb* **-bled; -bling 1 ♦ :** to collect into one place **2 ♦ :** to fit together the parts of **3 ♦ :** to meet together **:** CONVENE

♦ [1] accumulate, amass, collect, concentrate, garner, gather, group, lump, pick up, round up, scrape ♦ [2] build, construct, erect, fabricate, make, make up, piece, put up, raise, rear, set up ♦ [3] cluster, collect, concentrate, conglomerate, congregate, convene, forgather, gather, meet, rendezvous ***Ant*** break up, disband, disperse, split up

as·sem·bly \ə-ˈsem-blē\ *n, pl* **-blies 1 ♦ :** a gathering of persons **:** MEETING **2** *cap* **:** a legislative body; *esp* **:** the lower house of a legislature **3 :** a signal for troops to assemble **4 :** the fitting together of parts (as of a machine)

♦ assemblage, conference, congregation, convocation, gathering, meeting, muster

assembly language *n* **:** a computer language consisting of mnemonic codes corresponding to machine-language instructions
assembly line *n* **:** an arrangement of machines, equipment, and workers in which work passes from operation to operation in a direct line
as·sem·bly·man \ə-ˈsem-blē-mən\ *n* **:** a member of a legislative assembly
as·sem·bly·wom·an \-ˌwu̇-mən\ *n* **:** a woman who is a member of an assembly
as·sent \ə-ˈsent\ *vb* **♦ :** to join with others in agreement **:** AGREE — **assent** *n*

♦ accede, acquiesce, agree, come round, consent, subscribe (to)

as·sert \ə-ˈsərt\ *vb* **1 ♦ :** to state positively **2 :** to demonstrate the existence of

♦ affirm, aver, avouch, avow, declare, lay down, profess ♦ argue, contend, maintain, plead, reason ♦ allege, aver, avouch, avow, claim, contend, declare, insist, maintain, profess, protest, warrant

as·ser·tion \ə-ˈsər-shən\ *n* **♦ :** a positive statement

♦ argument, contention, thesis ♦ affirmation, avowal, claim, declaration, profession, protestation

as·ser·tive \ə-ˈsər-tiv\ *adj* **♦ :** disposed to or characterized by bold or confident assertion

♦ aggressive, dynamic, emphatic, energetic, forceful, resounding, strenuous, vehement, vigorous

as·ser·tive·ness \-nəs\ *n* **♦ :** the quality or state of being assertive

♦ emphasis, fierceness, intensity, vehemence

as·sess \ə-ˈses\ *vb* **1 ♦ :** to fix the rate or amount of **2 ♦ :** to impose (as a tax) at a specified rate **3 :** to evaluate for taxation **4 ♦ :** to determine the importance, size, or value of ⟨~ the problem⟩ — **as·ses·sor** \-ˈse-sər\ *n*

♦ [1, 2] charge, exact, fine, impose, lay, levy, put ♦ [4] appraise, estimate, evaluate, rate, set, value

as·sess·ment \-mənt\ *n* **1 ♦ :** the action or an instance of assessing **:** APPRAISAL **2 ♦ :** the amount assessed

♦ [1] appraisal, estimate, estimation, evaluation, reckoning, valuation ♦ [2] duty, impost, levy, tax

as·set \ˈa-ˌset\ *n* **1** *pl* **♦ :** the entire property of a person or company that may be used to pay debts **2 :** ADVANTAGE, RESOURCE

♦ capital, fortune, means, opulence, riches, substance, wealth, wherewithal

as·sev·er·ate \ə-ˈse-və-ˌrāt\ *vb* **-at·ed; -at·ing :** to assert earnestly — **as·sev·er·a·tion** \-ˌse-və-ˈrā-shən\ *n*
as·si·du·i·ty \ˌa-sə-ˈdü-ə-tē, -ˈdyü-\ *n* **♦ :** the quality or state of being assiduous

♦ diligence, industry

as·sid·u·ous \ə-ˈsi-jə-wəs\ *adj* **♦ :** marked by careful unremitting attention or persistent application **:** DILIGENT

♦ active, busy, diligent, engaged, laborious, occupied, sedulous, working

as·sid·u·ous·ly \ə-ˈsi-jə-wəs-lē\ *adv* **:** in an assiduous manner
as·sid·u·ous·ness \-nəs\ *n* **:** the quality or state of being assiduous
as·sign \ə-ˈsīn\ *vb* **1 ♦ :** to transfer (property) to another **2 ♦ :** to appoint to or as a duty ⟨~ a lesson⟩ **3 :** FIX, SPECIFY ⟨~ a limit⟩ **4 :** ASCRIBE ⟨~ a reason⟩ — **as·sign·able** *adj*

♦ [1] cede, deed, make over, transfer ♦ [2] appoint, attach, commission, constitute, designate, detail, name

as•sig•na•tion \ˌa-sig-ˈnā-shən\ *n* **:** an appointment for a meeting; *esp* **:** TRYST

assigned risk *n* **:** a poor risk (as an accident-prone motorist) that an insurance company is forced to insure by state law

as•sign•ment \ə-ˈsīn-mənt\ *n* **1 :** the act of assigning **2** ♦ **:** something assigned

♦ chore, duty, job, stint, task ♦ charge, job, mission, operation, post

as•sim•i•late \ə-ˈsi-mə-ˌlāt\ *vb* **-lat•ed; -lat•ing 1** ♦ **:** to take up and absorb as nourishment; *also* **:** to absorb into a cultural tradition **2 :** COMPREHEND **3 :** to make or become similar — **as•sim•i•la•tion** \-ˌsi-mə-ˈlā-shən\ *n*

♦ embody, incorporate, integrate

[1]**as•sist** \ə-ˈsist\ *vb* ♦ **:** to give support or aid **:** HELP

♦ abet, aid, back, help, prop, support

[2]**assist** *n* **1** ♦ **:** an act of assistance **2 :** the action of a player who enables a teammate to make a putout (as in baseball) or score a goal (as in hockey)

♦ aid, assistance, backing, boost, help, lift, support

as•sis•tance \-ˈsis-təns\ *n* ♦ **:** the act of assisting or the help supplied

♦ aid, assist, backing, boost, help, lift, support

as•sis•tant \ə-ˈsis-tənt\ *n* ♦ **:** a person who assists **:** HELPER

♦ aid, apprentice, deputy, helper, helpmate, mate, sidekick

as•sist•ed living \ə-ˈsis-təd-\ *n* **:** a system of housing and limited care for senior citizens who need assistance with daily activities but do not require care in a nursing home

as•size \ə-ˈsīz\ *n* **1 :** a judicial inquest **2** *pl* **:** the former regular sessions of superior courts in English counties

assn *abbr* association

assoc *abbr* associate; associated; association

[1]**as•so•ci•ate** \ə-ˈsō-shē-ˌāt, -sē-\ *vb* **-at•ed; -at•ing 1** ♦ **:** to join in companionship or partnership **2** ♦ **:** to connect in thought

♦ [1] ally, band, club, confederate, conjoin, cooperate, federate, league, unite ♦ [1] chum, consort, fraternize, hang around, hobnob, pal ♦ [2] connect, correlate, identify, link, relate

[2]**as•so•ciate** \-shē-ət, -sē-; -shət\ *n* **1 :** a fellow worker **:** PARTNER **2** ♦ **:** one that accompanies another **:** COMPANION **3** *often cap* **:** a degree conferred especially by a junior college ⟨∼ in arts⟩ — **associate** *adj*

♦ cohort, companion, comrade, crony, fellow, mate

as•so•ci•a•tion \ə-ˌsō-shē-ˈā-shən, -sē-\ *n* **1 a :** the act of associating **b** ♦ **:** the state of being associated **2** ♦ **:** an organization of persons **:** SOCIETY

♦ [1b] affiliation, alliance, collaboration, confederation, connection, cooperation, hookup, liaison, partnership, relation, relationship, union *Ant* dissociation ♦ [2] brotherhood, club, college, congress, council, fellowship, fraternity, guild, institute, institution, league, order, organization, society

as•so•cia•tive \ə-ˈsō-shē-ˌā-tiv, -sē-; -shə-tiv\ *adj* **:** of, relating to, or involved in association especially of ideas or images

as•so•nance \ˈa-sə-nəns\ *n* **:** repetition of vowels especially as an alternative to rhyme in verse — **as•so•nant** \-nənt\ *adj or n*

as soon as *conj* **:** immediately at or shortly after the time that ⟨we'll start *as soon as* they arrive⟩

as•sort \ə-ˈsȯrt\ *vb* **1** ♦ **:** to distribute into like groups **:** CLASSIFY **2 :** HARMONIZE

♦ break down, categorize, class, classify, grade, group, peg, place, range, rank, separate, sort

as•sort•ed \-ˈsȯr-təd\ *adj* ♦ **:** consisting of various kinds

♦ heterogeneous, miscellaneous, mixed, motley, varied

as•sort•ment \-ˈsȯrt-mənt\ *n* **1 a :** the act of assorting **b** ♦ **:** the state of being assorted **2** ♦ **:** a collection of assorted things or persons

♦ [1b] diversity, miscellaneous, variety ♦ [2] clutter, jumble, medley, mélange, miscellany, motley, muddle, variety, welter

asst *abbr* assistant

as•suage \ə-ˈswāj\ *vb* **as•suaged; as•suag•ing 1** ♦ **:** to make (as pain or grief) less **:** EASE **2** ♦ **:** to put an end to by satisfying

♦ [1] allay, alleviate, ease, help, mitigate, mollify, palliate, relieve, soothe ♦ [2] quench, sate, satiate, satisfy

as•sume \ə-ˈsüm\ *vb* **as•sumed; as•sum•ing 1** ♦ **:** to take upon oneself **2** ♦ **:** to pretend to have or be **3** ♦ **:** to take as granted or true though not proved

♦ [1] accept, bear, shoulder, take over, undertake *Ant* disavow, disclaim, disown, repudiate ♦ [2] affect, counterfeit, fake, feign, pretend, profess, put on, sham, simulate ♦ [3] postulate, premise, presume, presuppose, suppose

as•sumed \ə-ˈsümd\ *adj* **1** ♦ **:** not real or genuine ⟨an ∼ cheerfulness⟩ ⟨a ∼ name⟩ **2** ♦ **:** taken for granted **:** SUPPOSED

♦ [1] affected, artificial, bogus, contrived, fake, false, feigned, phony, put-on, sham ♦ [2] apparent, evident, ostensible, reputed, seeming, supposed

as•sump•tion \ə-ˈsəmp-shən\ *n* **1 :** the taking up of a person into heaven **2** *cap* **:** August 15 observed in commemoration of the Assumption of the Virgin Mary **3 :** a taking upon oneself **4 :** PRETENSION **5 a :** an assuming that something is true **b** ♦ **:** a fact or statement taken for granted **:** SUPPOSITION

♦ postulate, premise, presumption, supposition

as•sur•ance \ə-ˈshu̇r-əns\ *n* **1 :** PLEDGE **2** *chiefly Brit* **:** INSURANCE **3 :** the state of being assured: as **a :** SECURITY **b** ♦ **:** a being certain in the mind **c** ♦ **:** confidence of mind or manner; *also* **:** excessive self-confidence

♦ [3b] certainty, certitude, confidence, conviction, positiveness, sureness ♦ [3c] aplomb, confidence, self-assurance, self-confidence, self-esteem

as•sure \ə-ˈshu̇r\ *vb* **as•sured; as•sur•ing 1** ♦ **:** to make safe **2 :** to give confidence to **3 :** to state confidently to **4 :** to make certain the coming or attainment of

♦ cinch, ensure, guarantee, guaranty, insure, secure

[1]**as•sured** \ə-ˈshu̇rd\ *adj* **1** ♦ **:** sure of oneself **2** ♦ **:** satisfied as to the certainty or truth of a matter

♦ [1] confident, secure, self-assured, self-confident ♦ [2] certain, clear, cocksure, confident, doubtless, positive, sanguine, sure

[2]**assured** *n, pl* **assured** *or* **assureds :** INSURED

as•ta•tine \ˈas-tə-ˌtēn\ *n* **:** an unstable radioactive chemical element

as•ter \ˈas-tər\ *n* **:** any of various mostly fall-blooming leafy-stemmed composite herbs with daisylike purple, white, pink, or yellow flower heads

as•ter•isk \ˈas-tə-ˌrisk\ *n* **:** a character * used as a reference mark or as an indication of the omission of letters or words

astern \ə-ˈstərn\ *adv or adj* **1 :** in, at, or toward the stern **2 :** BACKWARD

as•ter•oid \ˈas-tə-ˌrȯid\ *n* **:** any of the numerous small celestial bodies found especially between Mars and Jupiter

asth•ma \ˈaz-mə\ *n* **:** a chronic lung disorder marked by recurrent episodes of labored breathing, a feeling of tightness in the chest, and coughing — **asth•mat•ic** \az-ˈma-tik\ *adj or n*

as though *conj* **:** as it would be or as one would do if **:** AS IF

astig•ma•tism \ə-ˈstig-mə-ˌti-zəm\ *n* **:** a defect in a lens or an eye causing improper focusing — **as•tig•mat•ic** \ˌas-tig-ˈma-tik\ *adj*

astir \ə-ˈstər\ *adj* **1** ♦ **:** exhibiting activity **2 :** being out of bed

♦ alive, animated, busy, lively, vibrant

as to *prep* **1 :** ABOUT, CONCERNING ⟨uncertain *as to* what went on⟩ **2 :** ACCORDING TO ⟨graded *as to* size⟩

as•ton•ish \ə-ˈstä-nish\ *vb* ♦ **:** to strike with sudden and usually great wonder **:** AMAZE

♦ amaze, astound, bowl, dumbfound, flabbergast, floor, shock, startle, stun, stupefy, surprise

as•ton•ish•ing \-iŋ\ *adj* ♦ **:** causing astonishment **:** SURPRISING — **as•ton•ish•ing•ly** *adv*

♦ amazing, astounding, eye-opening, shocking, startling, stunning, surprising

as•ton•ish•ment \-mənt\ *n* ♦ **:** the state of being astonished

♦ amazement, awe, wonder, wonderment

as•tound \ə-ˈstau̇nd\ *vb* ♦ **:** to fill with bewilderment or wonder — **as•tound•ing•ly** *adv*

♦ amaze, astonish, bowl, dumbfound, flabbergast, floor, shock, startle, stun, stupefy, surprise

as•tound•ing \-iŋ\ *adj* ♦ : causing astonishment or amazement

♦ amazing, astonishing, awesome, fabulous, marvelous (*or* marvellous), prodigious, stunning, stupendous, surprising, wonderful

[1]**astrad•dle** \ə-ˈstrad-ᵊl\ *adv* : on or above and extending onto both sides

[2]**astraddle** *prep* : ASTRIDE

as•tra•khan \ˈas-trə-kən, -ˌkan\ *n, often cap* **1** : karakul of Russian origin **2** : a cloth with a usually wool, curled, and looped pile resembling karakul

as•tral \ˈas-trəl\ *adj* ♦ : of, relating to, or coming from the stars

♦ star, starry, stellar

astray \ə-ˈstrā\ *adv or adj* **1** ♦ : off the right path or route **2** : into error

♦ afield, amiss, awry, wrong

[1]**astride** \ə-ˈstrīd\ *adv* **1** : with one leg on each side **2** : with legs apart

[2]**astride** *prep* : with one leg on each side of

[1]**as•trin•gent** \ə-ˈstrin-jənt\ *adj* : able or tending to shrink body tissues — **as•trin•gen•cy** \-jən-sē\ *n*

[2]**astringent** *n* : an astringent agent or substance

astrol *abbr* astrologer; astrology

as•tro•labe \ˈas-trə-ˌlāb\ *n* : an instrument formerly used for observing the positions of celestial bodies

as•trol•o•gy \ə-ˈsträ-lə-jē\ *n* : divination based on the supposed influence of the stars upon human events — **as•trol•o•ger** \-jər\ *n* — **as•tro•log•i•cal** \ˌas-trə-ˈlä-ji-kəl\ *adj*

astron *abbr* astronomer; astronomy

as•tro•naut \ˈas-trə-ˌnȯt\ *n* : a traveler in a spacecraft

as•tro•nau•tics \as-trə-ˈnȯ-tiks\ *n* : the science of the construction and operation of spacecraft — **as•tro•nau•tic** \-tik\ *or* **as•tro•nau•ti•cal** \-ti-kəl\ *adj*

as•tro•nom•i•cal \ˌas-trə-ˈnä-mi-kəl\ *also* **as•tro•nom•ic** \-mik\ *adj* **1** : of or relating to astronomy **2** ♦ : extremely large ⟨an ~ amount of money⟩

♦ colossal, enormous, giant, gigantic, ginormous, huge, prodigious, titanic, tremendous, whopping

astronomical unit *n* : a unit of length used in astronomy equal to the mean distance of the earth from the sun or about 93 million miles (150 million kilometers)

as•tron•o•my \ə-ˈsträ-nə-mē\ *n, pl* **-mies** : the science of objects and matter beyond the earth's atmosphere — **as•tron•o•mer** \-mər\ *n*

as•tro•phys•ics \ˌas-trə-ˈfi-ziks\ *n* : astronomy dealing especially with the physical properties and dynamic processes of celestial objects — **as•tro•phys•i•cal** \-zi-kəl\ *adj* — **as•tro•phys•i•cist** \-ˈfi-zə-sist\ *n*

as•tute \ə-ˈstüt, -ˈstyüt, a-\ *adj* ♦ : shrewdly discerning; *also* : WILY — **as•tute•ly** *adv*

♦ canny, hardheaded, knowing, sharp, shrewd, smart, wily

as•tute•ness *n* ♦ : the quality or state of being astute

♦ acumen, caginess, canniness, hardheadedness, intelligence, keenness, sharpness, shrewdness, wit

asun•der \ə-ˈsən-dər\ *adv or adj* **1** : into separate pieces ⟨torn ~⟩ **2** : separated in position from each other

ASV *abbr* American Standard Version

[1]**as well as** *conj* : and in addition : and moreover ⟨brave *as well as* loyal⟩

[2]**as well as** *prep* : in addition to : BESIDES ⟨the coach, *as well as* the team, is ready⟩

asy•lum \ə-ˈsī-ləm\ *n* **1** ♦ : a place of refuge **2** : protection given to especially political fugitives **3** : an institution for the care of the needy or sick and especially of the insane

♦ haven, refuge, retreat, sanctuary, shelter

asym•met•ri•cal \ˌā-sə-ˈme-tri-kəl\ *or* **asym•met•ric** \-trik\ *adj* : not symmetrical — **asym•me•try** \(ˌ)ā-ˈsi-mə-trē\ *n*

as•ymp•tote \ˈa-səmp-ˌtōt\ *n* : a straight line that is associated with a curve and tends to approximate it along an infinite branch — **as•ymp•tot•ic** \ˌa-səmp-ˈtä-tik\ *adj* — **as•ymp•tot•i•cal•ly** \-ti-k(ə-)lē\ *adv*

at \ət, (ˈ)at\ *prep* **1** — used to indicate a point in time or space ⟨be here ~ 3 o'clock⟩ **2** — used to indicate a goal ⟨swung ~ the ball⟩ **3** — used to indicate position or condition ⟨~ rest⟩ **4** — used to indicate means, cause, or manner ⟨sold ~ auction⟩

At *symbol* astatine

AT *abbr* automatic transmission

at all *adv* : in any way : in any circumstances ⟨not *at all* likely⟩

at•a•vism \ˈa-tə-ˌvi-zəm\ *n* : appearance in an individual of a character typical of an ancestral form; *also* : such an individual or character — **at•a•vis•tic** \ˌa-tə-ˈvis-tik\ *adj*

atax•ia \ə-ˈtak-sē-ə\ *n* : an inability to coordinate muscular movements

ate *past of* EAT

[1]**-ate** *n suffix* **1** : one acted upon (in a specified way) ⟨distill*ate*⟩ **2** : chemical compound or complex derived from a (specified) compound or element ⟨acet*ate*⟩

[2]**-ate** *n suffix* **1** : office : function : rank : group of persons holding a (specified) office or rank ⟨episcop*ate*⟩ **2** : state : dominion : jurisdiction ⟨emir*ate*⟩

[3]**-ate** *adj suffix* **1** : acted on (in a specified way) : being in a (specified) state ⟨temper*ate*⟩ ⟨degener*ate*⟩ **2** : marked by having ⟨vertebr*ate*⟩

[4]**-ate** *vb suffix* **1** : cause to be modified or affected by ⟨pollin*ate*⟩ : cause to become ⟨activ*ate*⟩ **2** : furnish with ⟨aer*ate*⟩

ate•lier \ˌat-ᵊl-ˈyā\ *n* **1** : an artist's or designer's studio **2** : WORKSHOP

athe•ist \ˈā-thē-ist\ *n* : one who denies the existence of God — **athe•ism** \-ˌi-zəm\ *n* — **athe•is•tic** \ˌā-thē-ˈis-tik\ *adj*

ath•e•nae•um *or* **ath•e•ne•um** \ˌa-thə-ˈnē-əm\ *n* : LIBRARY 1

ath•ero•scle•ro•sis \ˌa-thə-rō-sklə-ˈrō-səs\ *n* : arteriosclerosis characterized by the deposition of fatty substances in and the hardening of the inner layer of the arteries — **ath•ero•scle•rot•ic** \-ˈrä-tik\ *adj*

athirst \ə-ˈthərst\ *adj* **1** *archaic* : THIRSTY **2** ♦ : having a strong eager desire

♦ eager, enthusiastic, gung ho, keen, raring

ath•lete \ˈath-ˌlēt\ *n* : a person who is trained to compete in athletics

athlete's foot *n* : ringworm of the feet

ath•let•ic \ath-ˈle-tik\ *adj* **1** : of or relating to athletes or athletics **2** : VIGOROUS, ACTIVE **3** : STURDY, MUSCULAR

ath•let•ics \ath-ˈle-tiks\ *n sing or pl* : exercises and games requiring physical skill, strength, and endurance

athletic supporter *n* : an elastic pouch used to support the male genitals and worn especially during athletic activity

[1]**athwart** \ə-ˈthwȯrt\ *prep* **1** ♦ : to or on the opposite side of : ACROSS **2** : in opposition to

♦ across, over, through

[2]**athwart** *adv* ♦ : obliquely across

♦ crosswise, obliquely, transversely

atilt \ə-ˈtilt\ *adv or adj* **1** : in a tilted position **2** : with lance in hand

-ation *n suffix* : action or process ⟨flirt*ation*⟩ : something connected with an action or process ⟨discolor*ation*⟩

Atl *abbr* Atlantic

at•las \ˈat-ləs\ *n* : a book of maps

atm *abbr* atmosphere; atmospheric

ATM *n* : a computerized electronic machine that performs basic banking functions

at•mo•sphere \ˈat-mə-ˌsfir\ *n* **1** : the gaseous envelope of a celestial body; *esp* : the mass of air surrounding the earth **2** ♦ : a surrounding influence or environment **3** : a unit of pressure equal to the pressure of air at sea level or about 14.7 pounds per square inch (10 newtons per square centimeter) **4** : a dominant effect — **at•mo•spher•ic** \ˌat-mə-ˈsfir-ik, -ˈsfer-\ *adj* — **at•mo•spher•i•cal•ly** \-i-k(ə-)lē\ *adv*

♦ air, aura, climate, flavor (*or* flavour), mood, note, temper
♦ climate, environment, environs, medium, milieu, setting, surroundings

at•mo•sphe•rics \ˌat-mə-ˈsfir-iks, -ˈsfer-\ *n pl* : radio noise from atmospheric electrical phenomena

atoll \ˈa-ˌtȯl, -ˌtäl, ˈā-\ *n* : a coral island consisting of a reef surrounding a lagoon

at•om \ˈa-təm\ *n* **1** ♦ : a tiny particle : BIT **2** : the smallest particle of a chemical element that can exist alone or in combination

♦ bit, grain, granule, molecule, particle

atom•ic \ə-ˈtä-mik\ *adj* **1** : of or relating to atoms; *also* : NUCLEAR 2 ⟨~ energy⟩ **2** ♦ : extremely small

♦ infinitesimal, microscopic, miniature, minute, tiny

atomic bomb *n* : a very destructive bomb utilizing the energy released by splitting the atom

atomic clock *n* : a very precise clock regulated by the natural vibration of atoms or molecules (as of cesium)

atomic number *n* : the number of protons in the nucleus of an element

atomic weight *n* : the mass of one atom of an element

at•om•ise, at•om•is•er *Brit var of* ATOMIZE, ATOMIZER

at•om•ize \ˈa-tə-ˌmīz\ *vb* **-ized; -iz•ing** ♦ : to reduce to minute particles

♦ crush, grind, powder, pulverize

at•om•iz•er \ˈa-tə-ˌmī-zər\ *n* : a device for dispensing a liquid (as perfume) as a mist

atom smasher *n* : ACCELERATOR 3

aton•al \ā-ˈtōn-ᵊl\ *adj* : marked by avoidance of traditional musical tonality — **ato•nal•i•ty** \ˌā-tō-ˈna-lə-tē\ *n* — **aton•al•ly** \ā-ˈtōn-ᵊl-ē\ *adv*

atone \ə-ˈtōn\ *vb* **atoned; aton•ing** **1** : to make amends **2** : EXPIATE

atone•ment \ə-ˈtōn-mənt\ *n* **1** : the reconciliation of God and man through the death of Jesus Christ **2** : reparation for an offense : SATISFACTION

[1]**atop** \ə-ˈtäp\ *prep* : on top of

[2]**atop** *adv or adj* : on, to, or at the top

ATP \ˌā-ˌtē-ˈpē\ *n* : a compound that occurs widely in living tissue and supplies energy for many cellular processes by undergoing enzymatic hydrolysis

atri•um \ˈā-trē-əm\ *n, pl* **atria** \-trē-ə\ *also* **atri•ums** **1** : the central room of a Roman house; *also* : an open patio or court in the center of a building (as a hotel) **2** : an anatomical cavity or passage; *esp* : one of the chambers of the heart that receives blood from the veins — **atri•al** \-əl\ *adj*

atro•cious \ə-ˈtrō-shəs\ *adj* **1** : savagely brutal, cruel, or wicked **2** ♦ : inspiring horror, dismay, or disgust : APPALLING **3** ♦ : utterly revolting **4** ♦ : of very poor quality — **atro•cious•ly** *adv*

♦ [2, 3] appalling, awful, dreadful, frightful, ghastly, hideous, horrible, horrid, shocking, terrible ♦ [4] awful, execrable, lousy, punk, rotten, terrible, wretched

atro•cious•ness \-nəs\ *n* ♦ : the quality or state of being atrocious

♦ atrocity, frightfulness, hideousness, horror, monstrosity, repulsiveness

atroc•i•ty \ə-ˈträ-sə-tē\ *n, pl* **-ties** **1** ♦ : the quality or state of being atrocious : ATROCIOUSNESS **2** : an atrocious act or object ⟨the *atrocities* of war⟩

♦ atrociousness, depravity, enormity, heinousness, monstrosity, vileness, wickedness

at•ro•phy \ˈa-trə-fē\ *n, pl* **-phies** : decrease in size or wasting away of a bodily part or tissue — **atrophy** *vb*

at•ro•pine \ˈa-trə-ˌpēn\ *n* : a drug from belladonna and related plants used especially to relieve spasms and to dilate the pupil of the eye

att *abbr* **1** attached **2** attention **3** attorney

at•tach \ə-ˈtach\ *vb* **1** : to seize legally in order to force payment of a debt **2** ♦ : to assign (an individual or unit in the military) temporarily **3** : to bind by personal ties **4** ♦ : to make fast (as by tying or gluing) : FASTEN **5** : to be fastened or connected

♦ [2] appoint, assign, commission, constitute, designate, detail, name ♦ [4] affix, fasten, fix

at•ta•ché \ˌa-tə-ˈshā, ˌa-ˌta-, ə-ˌta-\ *n* : a technical expert on the diplomatic staff of an ambassador

at•ta•ché case \ə-ˈta-shā-, ˌa-tə-ˈshā-\ *n* : a small thin suitcase used especially for carrying business papers; *also* : BRIEFCASE

at•tach•ment \ə-ˈtach-mənt\ *n* **1** : legal seizure of property **2** ♦ : connection by ties of affection and regard **3** : a device attached to a machine or implement **4** : a connection by which one thing is attached to another

♦ affection, devotion, fondness, love, passion

[1]**at•tack** \ə-ˈtak\ *vb* **1** ♦ : to set upon with force or words : ASSAIL **2** : to set to work on

♦ assail, assault, beset, charge, descend, jump, pounce (on *or* upon), raid, rush, storm, strike ♦ abuse, assail, belabor, blast, castigate, excoriate, jump, lambaste, slam, vituperate

[2]**attack** *n* **1** ♦ : the act or action of attacking with physical force or unfriendly words **2** ♦ : a fit of sickness

♦ [1] aggression, assault, charge, descent, offense (*or* offence), offensive, onset, onslaught, raid, rush, strike ♦ [2] bout, case, fit, seizure, siege, spell

at•tain \ə-ˈtān\ *vb* **1** ♦ : to reach as an end : ACHIEVE ⟨∼ a goal⟩ **2** : to come to as the end of a progression or course of movement ⟨∼ the top of the hill⟩ ⟨∼ a ripe old age⟩ — **at•tain•abil•i•ty** \-ˌtā-nə-ˈbi-lə-tē\ *n*

♦ achieve, hit, make, score, win

at•tain•able \ə-ˈtā-nə-bəl\ *adj* ♦ : capable of being attained

♦ achievable, doable, feasible, possible, practicable, realizable, viable, workable ♦ accessible, acquirable, available, obtainable, procurable

at•tain•der \ə-ˈtān-dər\ *n* : extinction of the civil rights of a person upon sentence of death or outlawry

at•tain•ment \ə-ˈtān-mənt\ *n* **1** ♦ : the act of attaining : the condition of being attained **2** ♦ : something that has been accomplished : ACCOMPLISHMENT

♦ [1] accomplishment, actuality, consummation, fruition, fulfillment, realization ♦ [2] accomplishment, achievement, coup, success, triumph

at•taint \ə-ˈtānt\ *vb* : to condemn to loss of civil rights

at•tar \ˈa-tər\ *n* : a fragrant floral oil

[1]**at•tempt** \ə-ˈtempt\ *vb* ♦ : to make an effort toward

♦ assay, endeavor (*or* endeavour), essay, seek, strive, try

[2]**attempt** *n* ♦ : the act or an instance of attempting

♦ bid, crack, endeavor (*or* endeavour), essay, fling, go, pass, shot, stab, trial, try, whack, whirl

at•tend \ə-ˈtend\ *vb* **1** ♦ : to look after : TEND **2** ♦ : to go or stay with as a companion, nurse, or servant **3** : to be present at **4** : to apply oneself **5** ♦ : to pay attention **6** : to direct one's attention

♦ [1] care, mind, oversee, superintend, supervise, tend ♦ [2] accompany, convoy, escort, squire ♦ [5] hark, hear, heed, listen, mind

at•ten•dance \ə-ˈten-dəns\ *n* **1** : the act or fact of attending **2** : the number of persons present; *also* : the number of times a person attends

[1]**at•ten•dant** \ə-ˈten-dənt\ *n* ♦ : one that attends another to render a service

♦ companion, escort, guard, guide

[2]**attendant** *adj* ♦ : accompanying or following as a consequence or result ⟨∼ circumstances⟩

♦ consequent, consequential, due, resultant ♦ coincident, concomitant, concurrent

at•ten•tion \ə-ˈten-chən\ *n* **1** ♦ : the act or state of attending especially through applying the mind to an object of sense or thought **2** : CONSIDERATION **3** : an act of courtesy **4** : a position of readiness assumed on command by a soldier

♦ absorption, concentration *Ant* inattention ♦ awareness, cognizance, ear, eye, heed, notice, observance, observation

attention deficit disorder *n* : a behavioral syndrome especially of children that is marked by hyperactivity, impulsive behavior, and inattention

attention–deficit/hyperactivity disorder *n* : ATTENTION DEFICIT DISORDER

at•ten•tive \ə-ˈten-tiv\ *adj* **1** ♦ : regarding with care or attention : OBSERVANT **2** ♦ : heedful of the comfort of others — **at•ten•tive•ly** *adv*

♦ [1] absorbed, engrossed, intent, observant, rapt *Ant* distracted, inattentive, unfocused, unobservant ♦ [1] alert, awake, vigilant, watchful, wide-awake ♦ [2] considerate, kind, solicitous, thoughtful

at•ten•tive•ness \-nəs\ *n* ♦ : the quality or state of being attentive

♦ alertness, lookout, vigilance, watch

at•ten•u•ate \ə-ˈten-yə-ˌwāt\ *vb* **-at•ed; -at•ing** **1** : to make or become thin **2** : WEAKEN — **attenuate** \-wət\ *adj* — **at•ten•u•a•tion** \-ˌten-yə-ˈwā-shən\ *n*

at•test \ə-ˈtest\ *vb* **1** ♦ : to certify as genuine by signing as a witness **2** : MANIFEST **3** ♦ : to bear witness : TESTIFY

♦ [1] authenticate, avouch, certify, testify, vouch, witness ♦ [3] depose, swear, testify, witness

at•tes•ta•tion \ˌa-ˌtes-ˈtā-shən\ *n* **1** : the act of attesting **2** ♦ : the proof or evidence by which something is attested

♦ confirmation, corroboration, documentation, evidence, proof, substantiation, testament, testimony, validation, witness

at•tic \ˈa-tik\ *n* : the space or room in a building immediately below the roof

[1]**at•tire** \ə-ˈtīr\ *vb* **at•tired; at•tir•ing** ♦ : to put garments on : DRESS, ARRAY

♦ apparel, array, clothe, deck, dress, garb, rig, suit

[2]**attire** *n* ♦ : garments in general : DRESS, CLOTHES

♦ apparel, clothing, dress, duds, raiment, wear

at·ti·tude \'a-tə-ˌtüd, -ˌtyüd\ *n* **1 :** POSTURE **2 :** a mental position or feeling with regard to a fact or state **3 :** the position of something in relation to something else **4 :** a cocky, arrogant, or hostile manner

at·ti·tu·di·nise *Brit var of* ATTITUDINIZE

at·ti·tu·di·nize \ˌa-tə-'tüd-ᵊn-ˌiz, -'tyüd-\ *vb* **-nized; -niz·ing :** to assume an affected mental attitude **:** POSE

attn *abbr* attention

at·tor·ney \ə-'tər-nē\ *n, pl* **-neys ♦ :** one who is legally appointed to transact business on another's behalf; *esp* **:** one whose profession is to conduct lawsuits for clients or to advise as to legal rights and obligations in other matters **:** LAWYER

♦ commissary, delegate, deputy, envoy, factor, proxy, representative ♦ advocate, counsel, lawyer

attorney general *n, pl* **attorneys general** *or* **attorney generals :** the chief legal representative and adviser of a nation or state

at·tract \ə-'trakt\ *vb* **1 :** to draw to or toward oneself **:** cause to approach **2 :** to draw by emotional or aesthetic appeal

at·trac·tant \ə-'trak-tənt\ *n* **:** a substance (as a pheromone) used to attract insects or other animals

at·trac·tion \ə-'trak-shən\ *n* **1 :** the act or power of attracting; *esp* **:** personal charm **2 ♦ :** an attractive quality, object, or feature **3 :** a force tending to draw particles together

♦ draw, lodestone, magnet

at·trac·tive \ə-'trak-tiv\ *adj* **1 ♦ :** having or relating to the power to attract **2 ♦ :** arousing interest or pleasure — **at·trac·tive·ly** *adv*

♦ [1] alluring, captivating, charming, elfin, engaging, fascinating, fetching, glamorous, magnetic, seductive ♦ [2] beautiful, cute, handsome, lovely, pretty

at·trac·tive·ness \-nəs\ *n* **♦ :** the state or quality of being attractive

♦ allure, appeal, captivation, charisma, charm, enchantment, fascination, glamour, magic, magnetism ♦ beauty, comeliness, handsomeness, looks, loveliness, prettiness

attrib *abbr* attributive

[1]**at·tri·bute** \'a-trə-ˌbyüt\ *n* **1 ♦ :** an inherent characteristic **2 :** a word ascribing a quality; *esp* **:** ADJECTIVE

♦ character, characteristic, feature, mark, peculiarity, point, property, quality, trait

[2]**at·trib·ute** \ə-'tri-ˌbyüt, -byət\ *vb* **-ut·ed; -ut·ing 1 ♦ :** to explain as to cause or origin ⟨~ the illness to fatigue⟩ **2 :** to regard as a characteristic — **at·trib·ut·able** *adj* — **at·tri·bu·tion** \ˌa-trə-'byü-shən\ *n*

♦ accredit, ascribe, credit, impute

at·trib·u·tive \ə-'trib-yə-tiv\ *adj* **:** joined directly to a modified noun without a linking verb ⟨*red* in *red hair* is an ~ adjective⟩ — **attributive** *n*

at·tri·tion \ə-'tri-shən\ *n* **1 :** the act of wearing away by or as if by rubbing **2 :** the act of weakening or exhausting by constant harassment, abuse, or attack **3 :** a reduction in numbers as a result of resignation, retirement, or death

at·tune \ə-'tün, -'tyün\ *vb* **:** to bring into harmony **:** TUNE — **at·tune·ment** *n*

atty *abbr* attorney

ATV *abbr* all-terrain vehicle

atyp·i·cal \ā-'ti-pi-kəl\ *adj* **♦ :** not typical — **atyp·i·cal·ly** \-k(ə-)lē\ *adv*

♦ aberrant, abnormal, exceptional, extraordinary, irregular, odd, peculiar, uncommon, uncustomary, unique, unusual, unwonted

Au *symbol* gold

au·burn \'ȯ-bərn\ *adj* **:** reddish brown — **auburn** *n*

au cou·rant \ˌō-kü-'rän\ *adj* **:** UP-TO-DATE, STYLISH

[1]**auc·tion** \'ȯk-shən\ *n* **:** public sale of property to the highest bidder

[2]**auction** *vb* **auc·tioned; auc·tion·ing** \-shə-niŋ\ **:** to sell at auction

auc·tion·eer \ˌȯk-shə-'nir\ *n* **:** an agent who conducts an auction

aud *abbr* audit; auditor

au·da·cious \ȯ-'dā-shəs\ *adj* **1 ♦ :** intrepidly daring **2 :** contemptuous of law, religion, or decorum **:** INSOLENT — **au·da·cious·ly** *adv* — **au·da·cious·ness** *n*

♦ adventurous, bold, daring, enterprising, gutsy, hardy, nervy, venturesome

au·dac·i·ty \ȯ-'da-sə-tē\ *n* **♦ :** the quality or state of being audacious; *also* **:** the quality of being bold to the point of rudeness

♦ brass, brazenness, cheek, chutzpah, effrontery, gall, nerve, presumption, sauce, sauciness, temerity

[1]**au·di·ble** \'ȯ-də-bəl\ *adj* **:** capable of being heard — **au·di·bil·i·ty** \ˌȯ-də-'bi-lə-tē\ *n* — **au·di·bly** \'ȯ-də-blē\ *adv*

[2]**audible** *n* **:** a play called at the line of scrimmage

au·di·ence \'ȯ-dē-əns\ *n* **1 :** a formal interview **2 :** an opportunity of being heard **3 :** an assembly of listeners or spectators

[1]**au·dio** \'ȯ-dē-ˌō\ *adj* **1 :** of or relating to frequencies (as of radio waves) corresponding to those of audible sound waves **2 :** of or relating to sound or its reproduction and especially high-fidelity reproduction **3 :** relating to or used in the transmission or reception of sound

[2]**audio** *n* **1 :** the transmission, reception, or reproduction of sound **2 :** the section of television or motion-picture equipment that deals with sound

au·di·ol·o·gy \ˌȯ-dē-'ä-lə-jē\ *n* **:** a branch of science dealing with hearing and especially with the treatment of individuals having trouble with hearing — **au·di·o·log·i·cal** \-ə-'lä-ji-kəl\ *adj* — **au·di·ol·o·gist** \-'ä-lə-jist\ *n*

au·dio·phile \'ȯ-dē-ō-ˌfīl\ *n* **:** one who is enthusiastic about high-fidelity sound reproduction

au·dio·tape \'ȯ-dē-ō-ˌtāp\ *n* **:** a tape recording of sound

au·dio·vi·su·al \ˌȯ-dē-ō-'vi-zhə-wəl\ *adj* **:** of, relating to, or making use of both hearing and sight

au·dio·vi·su·als \-wəlz\ *n pl* **:** audiovisual teaching materials (as videotapes)

[1]**au·dit** \'ȯ-dət\ *n* **1 :** a formal examination and verification of financial accounts **2 ♦ :** a methodical examination and review

♦ check, checkup, examination, inspection, review, scan, scrutiny, survey

[2]**audit** *vb* **1 ♦ :** to perform an audit on or for **2 :** to attend (a course) without expecting formal credit

♦ check, examine, inspect, review, scan, scrutinize, survey

[1]**au·di·tion** \ȯ-'di-shən\ *n* **:** HEARING; *esp* **:** a trial performance to appraise an entertainer's merits

[2]**audition** *vb* **-tioned; -tion·ing** \-'di-shə-niŋ\ **:** to give an audition to; *also* **:** to give a trial performance

au·di·tor \'ȯ-də-tər\ *n* **1 :** LISTENER **2 :** a person who audits

au·di·to·ri·um \ˌȯ-də-'tōr-ē-əm\ *n, pl* **-riums** *or* **-ria** \-rē-ə\ **1 :** the part of a public building where an audience sits **2 :** a hall or building used for public gatherings

au·di·to·ry \'ȯ-də-ˌtōr-ē\ *adj* **♦ :** of or relating to hearing or to the sense or organs of hearing

♦ acoustic, aural, auricular

auditory tube *n* **:** EUSTACHIAN TUBE

auf Wie·der·seh·en \au̇f-'vē-dər-ˌzān\ *interj* — used to express farewell

Aug *abbr* August

au·ger \'ȯ-gər\ *n* **:** a tool for boring

aught \'ȯt, 'ät\ *n* **♦ :** the arithmetical symbol 0 denoting the absence of all magnitude or quantity **:** ZERO, CIPHER

♦ cipher, naught, nil, nothing, zero, zip

aug·ment \ȯg-'ment\ *vb* **♦ :** to make greater, more numerous, larger, or more intense **:** ENLARGE, INCREASE

♦ add, aggrandize, amplify, boost, compound, enlarge, escalate, expand, extend, increase, multiply, raise, swell, up

aug·men·ta·tion \ˌȯg-mən-'tā-shən\ *n* **1 a :** the act or process of augmenting **b :** the state of being augmented **2 ♦ :** something that augments **:** ADDITION

♦ accretion, addition, boost, expansion, gain, increase, increment, plus, proliferation, raise, rise, supplement

au gra·tin \ō-'grat-ᵊn, ȯ-, -'grät-\ *adj* **:** covered with bread crumbs or grated cheese and browned

[1]**au·gur** \'ȯ-gər\ *n* **♦ :** one held to foretell events by omens **:** DIVINER, SOOTHSAYER

♦ diviner, forecaster, fortune-teller, futurist, prognosticator, prophet, seer, soothsayer

[2]**augur** *vb* **1 ♦ :** to foretell especially from omens **2 ♦ :** to give promise of **:** show potential for a good outcome

♦ [1] forecast, foretell, predict, presage, prognosticate, prophesy ♦ [2] bode, promise

au·gu·ry \'ȯ-gyə-rē, -gə-\ *n, pl* **-ries 1 :** divination from omens **2 ♦ :** an occurrence or phenomenon believed to portend a future event **:** OMEN, PORTENT

♦ auspice, foreboding, omen, portent, presage

au•gust \ȯ-ˈgəst\ *adj* ♦ : marked by majestic dignity or grandeur — **au•gust•ly** *adv*

♦ dignified, grand, imposing, magnificent, majestic, regal, royal, splendid, stately

Au•gust \ˈȯ-gəst\ *n* : the 8th month of the year
au•gust•ness \-nəs\ *n* ♦ : the quality or state of being august

♦ grandeur, grandness, magnificence, majesty, nobility, nobleness, stateliness

au jus \ō-ˈzhü, -ˈzhüs, -ˈjüs; ō-zhü̅e̅\ *adj* : served in the juice obtained from roasting
auk \ˈȯk\ *n* : any of several stocky black-and-white diving seabirds that breed in colder parts of the northern hemisphere
auld \ˈȯl, ˈōld, ˈäl, ˈäld\ *adj, chiefly Scot* : OLD
aunt \ˈant, ˈȧnt\ *n* **1** : the sister of one's father or mother **2** : the wife of one's uncle
au pair \ˈō-ˈpar\ *n* : a usually young foreign person who does domestic work for a family in return for room and board and to learn the family's language
au•ra \ˈȯr-ə\ *n* **1** ♦ : a distinctive atmosphere surrounding a given source **2** : a luminous radiation

♦ air, atmosphere, climate, flavor (*or* flavour), mood, note, temper

au•ral \ˈȯr-əl\ *adj* ♦ : of or relating to the ear or to the sense of hearing

♦ acoustic, auditory, auricular

au•re•ole \ˈȯr-ē-ˌōl\ *or* **au•re•o•la** \ȯ-ˈrē-ə-lə\ *n* : HALO, NIMBUS
au re•voir \ˌō-rə-ˈvwär\ *n* ♦ : a concluding remark or gesture at parting : GOOD-BYE

♦ adieu, bon voyage, farewell, good-bye

au•ri•cle \ˈȯr-i-kəl\ *n* : an atrium of the heart
au•ric•u•lar \ȯ-ˈri-kyə-lər\ *adj* **1** : told privately ⟨~ confession⟩ **2** ♦ : known or recognized by the sense of hearing

♦ acoustic, auditory, aural

au•ro•ra \ə-ˈrōr-ə\ *n, pl* **auroras** *or* **au•ro•rae** \-(ˌ)ē\ **1** ♦ : the first appearance of light in the morning followed by sunrise **2** : a luminous phenomenon of streamers or arches of light appearing in the upper atmosphere especially of a planet's polar regions — **au•ro•ral** \-əl\ *adj*

♦ cockcrow, dawn, morning, sunrise

aurora aus•tra•lis \-ȯ-ˈstrā-ləs\ *n* : an aurora that occurs in earth's southern hemisphere
aurora bo•re•al•is \-ˌbōr-ē-ˈa-ləs\ *n* : an aurora that occurs in earth's northern hemisphere
AUS *abbr* Army of the United States
aus•pice \ˈȯ-spəs\ *n, pl* **aus•pic•es** \-spə-səz, -ˌsēz\ **1** : observation of birds by an augur **2** *pl* : kindly patronage and protection **3** ♦ : a prophetic sign or omen

♦ augury, foreboding, omen, portent, presage

aus•pi•cious \ȯ-ˈspi-shəs\ *adj* **1** ♦ : promising success : PROPITIOUS **2** : FORTUNATE, PROSPEROUS — **aus•pi•cious•ly** *adv* — **aus•pi•cious•ness** *n*

♦ bright, encouraging, heartening, hopeful, likely, promising, propitious, rosy, upbeat

aus•tere \ȯ-ˈstir\ *adj* **1** ♦ : stern and cold in appearance or manner : STERN, SEVERE **2** : ABSTEMIOUS **3** : UNADORNED ⟨~ style⟩ — **aus•tere•ly** *adv* — **aus•ter•i•ty** \-ˈster-ə-tē\ *n*

♦ authoritarian, flinty, hard, harsh, heavy-handed, ramrod, rigid, rigorous, severe, stern, strict

aus•tral \ˈȯs-trəl\ *adj* : SOUTHERN
Aus•tra•lian \ȯ-ˈstrāl-yən\ *n* : a native or inhabitant of Australia — **Australian** *adj*
Aus•tri•an \ˈȯ-strē-ən\ *n* : a native or inhabitant of Austria — **Austrian** *adj*
Aus•tro•ne•sian \ˌȯs-trə-ˈnē-zhən\ *adj* : of, relating to, or constituting a family of languages spoken in the area extending from Madagascar eastward through the Malay Peninsula to Hawaii and Easter Island
auth *abbr* **1** authentic **2** author **3** authorized
au•then•tic \ə-ˈthen-tik, ȯ-\ *adj* ♦ : not false or imitation — **au•then•tic•i•ty** \ˌȯ-ˌthen-ˈti-sə-tē\ *n*

♦ bona fide, genuine, real, right, true ***Ant*** bogus, counterfeit, fake, false, mock, phony, pseudo, sham, spurious, unauthentic, unreal ♦ accurate, exact, faithful, precise, right, strict, true, veracious

au•then•ti•cal•ly \-ti-k(ə-)lē\ *adv* ♦ : in actual fact

♦ actually, genuinely, really, veritably, very

au•then•ti•cate \ə-ˈthen-ti-ˌkāt, ȯ-\ *vb* **-cat•ed; -cat•ing** ♦ : to prove genuine — **au•then•ti•ca•tion** \-ˌthen-ti-ˈkā-shən\ *n*

♦ attest, avouch, certify, testify, vouch, witness

au•thor \ˈȯ-thər\ *n* **1** ♦ : one that originates or creates **2** : one that writes or composes a literary work

♦ creator, father, founder, originator

au•thor•ess \ˈȯ-thə-rəs\ *n* : a woman author
au•tho•ri•sa•tion, au•tho•rise *Brit var of* AUTHORIZATION, AUTHORIZE
au•thor•i•tar•i•an \ȯ-ˌthär-ə-ˈter-ē-ən, ə-, -ˌthȯr-\ *adj* **1** ♦ : characterized by or favoring the principle of blind obedience to authority **2** : characterized by or favoring concentration of political power in an authority not responsible to the people — **authoritarian** *n*

♦ autocratic, bossy, despotic, dictatorial, domineering, imperious, masterful, overbearing, peremptory, tyrannical, tyrannous ♦ austere, flinty, hard, harsh, heavy-handed, ramrod, rigid, rigorous, severe, stern, strict

au•thor•i•ta•tive \ə-ˈthär-ə-ˌtā-tiv, ȯ-, -ˈthȯr-\ *adj* ♦ : supported by, proceeding from, or being an authority — **au•thor•i•ta•tive•ly** *adv* — **au•thor•i•ta•tive•ness** *n*

♦ forceful, influential, weighty

au•thor•i•ty \ə-ˈthär-ə-tē, ȯ-, -ˈthȯr-\ *n, pl* **-ties** **1** : a citation used in support of a statement or in defense of an action; *also* : the source of such a citation **2** ♦ : one appealed to as an expert **3** ♦ : power to influence thought or behavior **4** : freedom granted : RIGHT **5 a** : persons in command **b** ♦ : the office, authority, or function of governing : GOVERNMENT **6** ♦ : convincing force

♦ [2] ace, adept, expert, master, scholar, virtuoso, whiz, wizard ♦ [3] clout, influence, pull, sway, weight ♦ [5b] administration, government, jurisdiction, regime, rule ♦ [6] arm, clutch, command, control, dominion, grip, hold, mastery, power, sway

au•tho•ri•za•tion \ˌȯ-thə-rə-ˈzā-shən\ *n* ♦ : the act of authorizing

♦ allowance, clearance, concurrence, consent, leave, license (*or* licence), permission, sanction, sufferance ♦ commission, delegation, license (*or* licence), mandate

au•tho•rize \ˈȯ-thə-ˌrīz\ *vb* **-rized; -riz•ing** **1** ♦ : to establish by or as if by authority : SANCTION **2** ♦ : to invest especially with legal authority

♦ [1] approve, clear, OK, ratify, sanction, warrant ♦ [2] accredit, certify, commission, empower, enable, invest, license, qualify

au•tho•rized \ˈȯ-thə-ˌrīzd\ *adj* : sanctioned by authority
au•thor•ship \ˈȯ-thər-ˌship\ *n* **1** : the state of being an author **2** : the source of a piece of writing, music, or art
au•tism \ˈȯ-ˌti-zəm\ *n* : a disorder that appears by age three and is characterized especially by impaired ability to communicate with others and form normal social relationships and by repetitive patterns of behavior — **au•tis•tic** \ȯ-ˈtis-tik\ *adj*
[1]**au•to** \ˈȯ-tō\ *n, pl* **autos** : a usually 4-wheeled automotive vehicle designed for passenger transportation : AUTOMOBILE
[2]**auto** *abbr* automatic
au•to•bahn \ˈȯ-tō-ˌbän, ˈau̇-\ *n* : a German, Swiss, or Austrian expressway
au•to•bi•og•ra•phy \ˌȯ-tə-bī-ˈä-grə-fē\ *n* : the biography of a person narrated by that person — **au•to•bi•og•ra•pher** \-fər\ *n* — **au•to•bi•o•graph•i•cal** \-ˌbī-ə-ˈgra-fi-kəl\ *adj* — **au•to•bi•o•graph•i•cal•ly** \-k(ə-)lē\ *adv*
au•toch•tho•nous \ȯ-ˈtäk-thə-nəs\ *adj* : INDIGENOUS, NATIVE
au•to•clave \ˈȯ-tō-ˌklāv\ *n* : an apparatus (as for sterilizing) using superheated high-pressure steam
au•toc•ra•cy \ȯ-ˈtä-krə-sē\ *n, pl* **-cies** ♦ : government by one person having unlimited power

♦ despotism, dictatorship, totalitarianism, tyranny

au•to•crat \ˈȯ-tə-ˌkrat\ *n* **1** ♦ : a person (as a monarch) ruling with unlimited authority **2** ♦ : one who has undisputed influence or power

♦ [1] monarch, ruler, sovereign ♦ [2] despot, dictator, oppressor, tyrant

au•to•crat•ic \ˌȯ-tə-ˈkra-tik\ *adj* **1** : of, relating to, or being an autocracy **2** ♦ : characteristic of or resembling an autocrat : DESPOTIC — **au•to•crat•i•cal•ly** \-ti-k(ə-)lē\ *adv*

◆ absolute, despotic, dictatorial, tyrannical, tyrannous ◆ authoritarian, bossy, domineering, imperious, masterful, overbearing, peremptory

1au·to·graph \ˈȯ-tə-ˌgraf\ *n* **1 :** an original manuscript **2 :** a person's signature written by hand
2autograph *vb* **:** to write one's signature on
au·to·im·mune \ˌȯ-tō-i-ˈmyün\ *adj* **:** of, relating to, or caused by antibodies or lymphocytes that attack molecules, cells, or tissues of the organism producing them ⟨∼ diseases⟩ — **au·to·im·mu·ni·ty** \-i-ˈmyu-nə-te\ *n*
au·to·mate \ˈȯ-tə-ˌmāt\ *vb* **-mat·ed; -mat·ing 1 :** to operate automatically using mechanical or electronic devices **2 :** to convert to automatic operation — **au·to·ma·tion** \ˌȯ-tə-ˈmā-shən\ *n*
automated teller machine *n* **:** a computer terminal allowing access to one's own bank accounts
1au·to·mat·ic \ˌȯ-tə-ˈma-tik\ *adj* **1** ◆ **:** largely or wholly involuntary **2** ◆ **:** made so that certain parts act in a desired manner at the proper time **:** SELF-ACTING — **au·to·mat·i·cal·ly** \-ti-k(ə-)lē\ *adv*

◆ [1] involuntary, mechanical, spontaneous ◆ [2] laborsaving (*or* laboursaving), robotic, self-acting

2automatic *n* **:** an automatic device; *esp* **:** an automatic firearm
au·tom·a·ton \ȯ-ˈtä-mə-tən, -ˌtän\ *n, pl* **-atons** *or* **-a·ta** \-ə-tə, -ə-ˌtä\ **1 :** an automatic machine; *esp* **:** ROBOT **2 :** an individual who acts mechanically
au·to·mo·bile \ˈȯ-tə-mō-ˌbēl, ˌȯ-tə-mə-ˈbēl\ *n* ◆ **:** a usually 4-wheeled automotive vehicle for passenger transportation

◆ car, machine, motor vehicle

au·to·mo·tive \ˌȯ-tə-ˈmō-tiv\ *adj* **1 :** of or relating to automobiles, trucks, or buses **2 :** SELF-PROPELLED
au·to·nom·ic nervous system \ˌȯ-tə-ˈnä-mik-\ *n* **:** a part of the vertebrate nervous system that governs involuntary actions and that consists of the sympathetic nervous system and the parasympathetic nervous system
au·ton·o·mous \ȯ-ˈtä-nə-məs\ *adj* ◆ **:** having the right or power of self-government — **au·ton·o·mous·ly** *adv*

◆ free, independent, self-governing, separate, sovereign

au·ton·o·my \-mē\ *n* ◆ **:** the quality or state of being independent, free, and self-directing

◆ freedom, independence, liberty, self-government, sovereignty

au·top·sy \ˈȯ-ˌtäp-sē, ˈȯ-təp-\ *n, pl* **-sies :** examination of a dead body usually with dissection sufficient to determine the cause of death or extent of change produced by disease — **autopsy** *vb*
au·tumn \ˈȯ-təm\ *n* **:** the season between summer and winter — **au·tum·nal** \ȯ-ˈtəm-nəl\ *adj*
aux *abbr* auxiliary
1aux·il·ia·ry \ȯg-ˈzil-yə-rē, -ˈzi-lə-rē\ *adj* **1** ◆ **:** providing help **2 :** functioning in a subsidiary capacity **3 :** accompanying a verb form to express person, number, mood, or tense ⟨∼ verbs⟩

◆ accessory, peripheral, supplementary *Ant* chief, main, principal

2auxiliary *n, pl* **-ries 1 :** an auxiliary person, group, or device **2 :** an auxiliary verb
aux·in \ˈȯk-sən\ *n* **:** a plant hormone that stimulates growth in length
av *abbr* **1** avenue **2** average **3** avoirdupois
AV *abbr* **1** ad valorem **2** audiovisual **3** Authorized Version
1avail \ə-ˈvāl\ *vb* ◆ **:** to produce or result in as a benefit or advantage

◆ benefit, profit, serve

2avail *n* ◆ **:** advantage toward attainment of a goal or purpose **:** USE ⟨effort was of no ∼⟩

◆ account, service, use, utility

avail·able \ə-ˈvā-lə-bəl\ *adj* **1** ◆ **:** present or ready for immediate use **:** USABLE **2** ◆ **:** capable of being reached **:** ACCESSIBLE — **avail·abil·i·ty** \-ˌvā-lə-ˈbi-lə-tē\ *n*

◆ [1] fit, functional, operable, practicable, serviceable, usable, useful ◆ [2] accessible, acquirable, attainable, obtainable, procurable *Ant* inaccessible, unattainable, unavailable, unobtainable

av·a·lanche \ˈa-və-ˌlanch\ *n* **:** a mass of snow, ice, earth, or rock sliding down a mountainside
avant–garde \ˌä-ˌvän-ˈgärd, -ˌvänt-\ *n* **:** those especially in the arts who create or apply new or experimental ideas and techniques — **avant–garde** *adj*
av·a·rice \ˈa-və-rəs\ *n* ◆ **:** excessive desire for wealth **:** GREED

◆ acquisitiveness, avidity, covetousness, cupidity, greed, rapaciousness

av·a·ri·cious \ˌa-və-ˈri-shəs\ *adj* ◆ **:** excessively acquisitive

◆ acquisitive, avid, covetous, grasping, greedy, mercenary, rapacious

avast \ə-ˈvast\ *vb imper* — a nautical command to stop or cease
av·a·tar \ˈa-və-ˌtär\ *n* **:** INCARNATION
avaunt \ə-ˈvȯnt\ *adv* **:** AWAY, HENCE
avdp *abbr* avoirdupois
ave *abbr* avenue
Ave Ma·ria \ˌä-ˌvā-mə-ˈrē-ə\ *n* **:** HAIL MARY
avenge *vb* **avenged; aveng·ing** ◆ **:** to take vengeance for

◆ requite, retaliate, revenge

aveng·er \ə-ˈven-jər\ *n* ◆ **:** one that avenges

◆ castigator, nemesis, scourge

av·e·nue \ˈa-və-ˌnü, -ˌnyü\ *n* **1** ◆ **:** a way or route to a place or goal **:** PATH **2** ◆ **:** a broad street

◆ [1, 2] approach, passage, path, route, way ◆ [2] artery, road, route, street, way

aver \ə-ˈvər\ *vb* **averred; aver·ring 1 a :** to verify or prove to be true in pleading a cause **b** ◆ **:** to allege or assert in pleading **2** ◆ **:** to declare positively

◆ [1b, 2] affirm, allege, assert, avouch, avow, claim, contend, declare, insist, maintain, profess, protest, warrant

1av·er·age \ˈa-və-rij, ˈa-vrij\ *n* **1 :** ARITHMETIC MEAN **2 a :** an estimation of or approximation to an arithmetic mean **b** ◆ **:** a level (as of intelligence) typical of a group, class, or series **3 :** a ratio of successful tries to total tries especially in athletics ⟨batting ∼ of .303⟩

◆ norm, normal, par, standard

2average *adj* **1 :** equaling or approximating an arithmetic mean **2** ◆ **:** being about midway between extremes **3** ◆ **:** not out of the ordinary

◆ [2] intermediate, median, medium, middle, moderate, modest ◆ [3] common, commonplace, everyday, normal, ordinary, routine, run-of-the-mill, standard, typical, usual

3average *vb* **av·er·aged; av·er·ag·ing 1 :** to be at or come to an average **2 :** to be, do, or get usually **3 :** to find the average of
averse \ə-ˈvərs\ *adj* **:** having an active feeling of dislike or reluctance ⟨∼ to exercise⟩
aver·sion \ə-ˈvər-zhən\ *n* **1** ◆ **:** a feeling of repugnance for something with a desire to avoid it **2 :** something decidedly disliked

◆ disgust, distaste, loathing, nausea, repugnance, repulsion, revulsion ◆ allergy, disfavor (*or* disfavour), disinclination, dislike

avert \ə-ˈvərt\ *vb* **1 :** to turn aside or away ⟨∼ the eyes⟩ **2** ◆ **:** to ward off

◆ forestall, help, obviate, preclude, prevent

avg *abbr* average
avi·an \ˈā-vē-ən\ *adj* **:** of, relating to, or derived from birds
avi·ary \ˈā-vē-ˌer-ē\ *n, pl* **-ar·ies :** a place for keeping birds confined
avi·a·tion \ˌā-vē-ˈā-shən, ˌa-\ *n* **1 :** the operation of heavier-than-air aircraft **2 :** aircraft manufacture, development, and design
avi·a·tor \ˈā-vē-ˌā-tər, ˈa-\ *n* ◆ **:** an airplane pilot

◆ airman, flier, pilot

avi·a·trix \ˌā-vē-ˈā-triks, ˌa-\ *n, pl* **-trix·es** \-trik-səz\ *or* **-tri·ces** \-trə-ˌsēz\ **:** a woman airplane pilot
av·id \ˈa-vəd\ *adj* **1** ◆ **:** desirous to the point of greed **:** GREEDY **2** ◆ **:** enthusiastic in pursuit of an interest — **av·id·ly** *adv* — **av·id·ness** *n*

◆ [1] acquisitive, avaricious, covetous, grasping, greedy, mercenary, rapacious ◆ [2] ardent, eager, enthusiastic, keen, nuts, raring

avid·i·ty \ə-ˈvi-də-tē, a-\ *n* ◆ **:** the quality or state of being avid

◆ acquisitiveness, avarice, covetousness, cupidity, greed, rapaciousness ◆ eagerness, enthusiasm, excitement, keenness, thirst

avi·on·ics \ˌā-vē-ˈä-niks, ˌa-\ *n pl* **:** electronics designed for use in aerospace vehicles — **avi·on·ic** \-nik\ *adj*
av·o·ca·do \ˌa-və-ˈkä-dō, ˌä-\ *n, pl* **-dos** *also* **-does :** a pulpy green to purple nutty-flavored edible fruit of a tropical American tree; *also* **:** this tree

av•o•ca•tion \ˌa-və-ˈkā-shən\ *n* : HOBBY
av•o•cet \ˈa-və-ˌset\ *n* : any of several long-legged shorebirds with webbed feet and slender upward-curving bills
avoid \ə-ˈvȯid\ *vb* **1** ♦ : to keep away from : SHUN **2** : to prevent the occurrence of **3** : to refrain from — **avoid•able** *adj* — **avoid•ably** *adv*

♦ dodge, duck, elude, escape, eschew, evade, shake, shirk, shun

avoid•ance \-ᵊns\ *n* ♦ : an act or practice of avoiding or withdrawing from something

♦ cop-out, escape, evasion, out

av•oir•du•pois \ˌa-vər-də-ˈpȯiz\ *n* **1** : AVOIRDUPOIS WEIGHT **2** : WEIGHT, HEAVINESS; *esp* : personal weight
avoirdupois weight *n* : a system of weights based on a pound of 16 ounces and an ounce of 16 drams (28 grams)
avouch \ə-ˈvau̇ch\ *vb* **1** ♦ : to declare positively : AVER **2** ♦ : to maintain as just or true : vouch for

♦ [1] affirm, allege, assert, aver, avow, claim, contend, declare, insist, maintain, profess, protest, warrant ♦ [2] attest, authenticate, certify, testify, vouch, witness

avow \ə-ˈvau̇\ *vb* ♦ : to declare openly

♦ affirm, allege, assert, aver, avouch, claim, contend, declare, insist, maintain, profess, protest, warrant

avow•al \-ˈvau̇(-ə)l\ *n* ♦ : an open declaration or acknowledgment

♦ acknowledgment, admission, concession, confession ♦ affirmation, assertion, claim, declaration, profession, protestation

avun•cu•lar \ə-ˈvəŋ-kyə-lər\ *adj* : of, relating to, or resembling an uncle
await \ə-ˈwāt\ *vb* ♦ : to wait for : EXPECT

♦ anticipate, expect, hope, watch ♦ bide, hold on, stay, wait

¹awake \ə-ˈwāk\ *vb* **awoke** \-ˈwōk\ *also* **awaked** \-ˈwākt\; **awo•ken** \-ˈwō-kən\ *or* **awaked** *also* **awoke; awak•ing** ♦ : to bring back to consciousness : wake up

♦ arouse, rouse, wake

²awake *adj* ♦ : fully conscious, alert, and aware

♦ sleepless, wakeful, wide-awake ♦ alert, attentive, vigilant, watchful, wide-awake

awak•en \ə-ˈwā-kən\ *vb* **awak•ened; awak•en•ing** \-ˈwā-kə-niŋ\ : to bring back to consciousness : wake up
¹award \ə-ˈwȯrd\ *vb* **1** : to give by judicial decision ⟨∼ damages⟩ **2** ♦ : to confer or bestow as being deserved, earned, or needed

♦ accord, confer, grant

²award *n* **1** : a final decision : JUDGMENT **2** ♦ : something awarded : PRIZE

♦ decoration, distinction, honor (*or* honour), plume, prize

aware \ə-ˈwar\ *adj* ♦ : having perception or knowledge : CONSCIOUS

♦ alive, cognizant, conscious, mindful, sensible, sentient, witting

aware•ness \-nəs\ *n* ♦ : the quality or state of being aware

♦ attention, cognizance, ear, eye, heed, notice, observance, observation

awash \ə-ˈwȯsh, -ˈwäsh\ *adj* **1** : washed by waves or tide **2** : AFLOAT **3** : covered with water : FLOODED
¹away \ə-ˈwā\ *adv* **1** : from this or that place ⟨go ∼⟩ **2** : out of the way **3** : in another direction ⟨turn ∼⟩ **4** : out of existence ⟨fade ∼⟩ **5** : from one's possession ⟨give ∼⟩ **6** : without interruption ⟨chatter ∼⟩ **7** : at a distance in space or time ⟨far ∼⟩ ⟨∼ back in 1910⟩
²away *adj* **1** ♦ : absent from a place : ABSENT **2** ♦ : distant in space or time ⟨a lake 10 miles ∼⟩

♦ [1] absent, missing, out ♦ [2] distant, far, far-off, remote

¹awe \ˈȯ\ *n* **1** ♦ : an emotion variously combining dread, veneration, and wonder that is inspired by authority or by the sacred or sublime **2** : respectful fear inspired by authority

♦ admiration, amazement, astonishment, wonder, wonderment

²awe *vb* **awed; aw•ing** : to inspire with awe
aweigh \ə-ˈwā\ *adj* : just clear of the bottom ⟨anchors ∼⟩
awe•some \ˈȯ-səm\ *adj* **1** : expressive of awe **2** ♦ : inspiring awe

♦ amazing, astonishing, astounding, marvelous (*or* marvellous), stunning, surprising, wonderful

awe•struck \-ˌstrək\ *also* **awe•strick•en** \-ˌstri-kən\ *adj* ♦ : filled with awe

♦ amazed, stunned, thunderstruck

aw•ful \ˈȯ-fəl\ *adj* **1** : inspiring awe **2** ♦ : extremely disagreeable, unpleasant, or shoddy **3** : very great ⟨an ∼ lot of money⟩

♦ appalling, dreadful, frightful, ghastly, grisly, gruesome, hideous, horrible, horrid, repellent, repugnant, repulsive, revolting, shocking, terrible ♦ atrocious, execrable, lousy, punk, rotten, wretched

aw•ful•ly \ˈȯ-fə-lē\ *adv* : to a great degree : VERY
awhile \ə-ˈhwīl\ *adv* : for a while
awhirl \ə-ˈhwərl\ *adj* : being in a whirl
awk•ward \ˈȯ-kwərd\ *adj* **1** ♦ : lacking dexterity or skill (as in the use of hands) **2** ♦ : lacking ease or grace (as of movement or expression) **3** ♦ : difficult to explain : EMBARRASSING **4** ♦ : difficult to deal with — **awk•ward•ly** *adv* — **awk•ward•ness** *n*

♦ [1, 2] clumsy, gauche, gawky, graceless, inelegant, stiff, stilted, uncomfortable, uneasy, ungainly, ungraceful, wooden *Ant* graceful, suave, urbane ♦ [3] disconcerting, embarrassing, uncomfortable ♦ [4] clumsy, cranky, cumbersome, ungainly, unhandy, unwieldy

awl \ˈȯl\ *n* : a pointed instrument for making small holes
aw•ning \ˈȯ-niŋ\ *n* : a rooflike cover (as of canvas) extended over or in front of a place as a shelter
AWOL \ˈā-ˌwȯl, ˌā-ˌdə-bəl-yü-ˌō-ˈel\ *n* : a person who is absent without leave — **AWOL** *adj or adv*
awry \ə-ˈrī\ *adv or adj* **1** ♦ : in a turned or twisted position or direction : ASKEW **2** ♦ : off the correct or expected course : AMISS

♦ [1] askew, cockeyed, crooked, listing, lopsided, slantwise, uneven *Ant* even, level, straight ♦ [2] afield, amiss, astray, wrong

ax *or* **axe** \ˈaks\ *n* : a chopping or cutting tool with an edged head fitted parallel to a handle
ax•i•al \ˈak-sē-əl\ *adj* **1** : of, relating to, or functioning as an axis **2** : situated around, in the direction of, on, or along an axis — **ax•i•al•ly** *adv*
ax•i•om \ˈak-sē-əm\ *n* **1** : a statement generally accepted as true : MAXIM **2** : a proposition regarded as a self-evident truth — **ax•i•om•at•ic** \ˌak-sē-ə-ˈma-tik\ *adj* — **ax•i•om•at•i•cal•ly** \-ti-k(ə-)lē\ *adv*
ax•is \ˈak-səs\ *n, pl* **ax•es** \-ˌsēz\ **1** : a straight line around which a body rotates **2** : a straight line or structure with respect to which a body or figure is symmetrical **3** : one of the reference lines of a system of coordinates **4** : an alliance between major powers
ax•le \ˈak-səl\ *n* : a shaft on which a wheel revolves
ayah \ˈī-ə\ *n* : a nurse or maid native to India
aya•tol•lah \ˌī-ə-ˈtō-lə\ *n* : an Islamic religious leader — used as a title of respect
¹aye *also* **ay** \ˈā\ *adv* : for a limitless time : ALWAYS, EVER
²aye *also* **ay** \ˈī\ *adv* : YES — used as a function word to express assent or agreement
³aye *also* **ay** \ˈī\ *n, pl* **ayes** : an affirmative vote
AZ *abbr* Arizona
aza•lea \ə-ˈzāl-yə\ *n* : any of numerous rhododendrons with funnel-shaped blossoms and usually deciduous leaves
az•i•do•thy•mi•dine \ə-ˌzi-dō-ˈthī-mə-ˌdēn\ *n* : AZT
az•i•muth \ˈa-zə-məth\ *n* : horizontal direction expressed as an angular distance from a fixed point
AZT \ˌā-(ˌ)zē-ˈtē\ *n* : an antiviral drug used to treat AIDS
Az•tec \ˈaz-ˌtek\ *n* : a member of a Nahuatl-speaking people that founded the Mexican empire and were conquered by Hernan Cortes in 1519 — **Az•tec•an** *adj*
azure \ˈa-zhər\ *n* : the blue of the clear sky — **azure** *adj*

B

[1]b \ˈbē\ *n, pl* **b's** *or* **bs** \ˈbēz\ *often cap* **1 :** the 2d letter of the English alphabet **2 :** a grade rating a student's work as good
[2]b *abbr, often cap* **1** bachelor **2** bass **3** bishop **4** book **5** born
B *symbol* boron
Ba *symbol* barium
BA *abbr* **1** bachelor of arts **2** batting average
bab•bitt \ˈba-bət\ *n* **:** an alloy used for lining bearings; *esp* **:** one containing tin, copper, and antimony
[1]bab•ble \ˈba-bəl\ *vb* **bab•bled; bab•bling 1 ♦ :** to talk enthusiastically or excessively **2 ♦ :** to utter meaningless sounds

♦ chatter, drivel, gabble, gibber, jabber, prattle, sputter

[2]babble *n* **1 :** foolish or idle talk **2 ♦ :** continuous meaningless vocal sounds **:** a murmur or a continuity of confused sounds

♦ gabble, gibberish, gobbledygook, hogwash, nonsense, piffle, prattle

bab•bler \-b(ə-)lər\ *n* **:** one that babbles
babe \ˈbāb\ *n* **1 :** an extremely young child **:** BABY **2** *slang* **:** GIRL, WOMAN
ba•bel \ˈbā-bəl, ˈba-\ *n, often cap* **:** a place or scene of noise and confusion; *also* **:** a confused sound
ba•boon \ba-ˈbün\ *n* **:** any of several large apes of Asia and Africa with doglike muzzles
ba•bush•ka \bə-ˈbüsh-kə, -ˈbu̇sh-\ *n* **♦ :** a kerchief for the head

♦ bandanna, do-rag, kerchief, mantilla

[1]ba•by \ˈbā-bē\ *n, pl* **babies 1 ♦ :** a very young child **:** INFANT **2 :** the youngest or smallest of a group **3 :** a childish person — **baby** *adj* — **ba•by•hood** *n*

♦ child, infant, newborn

[2]baby *vb* **ba•bied; ba•by•ing ♦ :** to tend or treat often with excessive care

♦ coddle, mollycoddle, nurse, pamper, spoil *Ant* abuse, ill-treat, ill-use, maltreat, mishandle, mistreat, misuse

baby boom *n* **:** a marked rise in birthrate — **baby boom•er** \-ˈbü-mər\ *n*
ba•by•ish *adj* **♦ :** resembling a baby **:** CHILDISH, INFANTILE

♦ childish, immature, infantile, juvenile, kiddish

baby's breath *n* **:** any of a genus of herbs that are related to the pinks and have small delicate flowers
ba•by•sit \ˈbā-bē-ˌsit\ *vb* **-sat** \-ˌsat\; **-sit•ting :** to care for children usually during a short absence of the parents
ba•by•sit•ter *n* **:** a person usually hired for relatively short periods of time to take care of a child or children while the parents are away from the home
bac•ca•lau•re•ate \ˌba-kə-ˈlȯr-ē-ət\ *n* **1 :** the degree of bachelor conferred by colleges and universities **2 :** a sermon delivered to a graduating class
bac•ca•rat \ˌbä-kə-ˈrä, ˌba-\ *n* **:** a card game in which three hands are dealt and players may bet either or both hands against the dealer's
bac•cha•nal \ˈba-kən-ᵊl, ˌba-kə-ˈnal, ˌbä-kə-ˈnäl\ *n* **1 :** ORGY **2 :** REVELER
bac•cha•na•lia \ˌba-kə-ˈnāl-yə\ *n, pl* **bacchanalia :** a drunken orgy — **bac•cha•na•lian** \-ˈnāl-yən\ *adj or n*
bach•e•lor \ˈba-chə-lər\ *n* **1 :** a person who has received the usually lowest degree conferred by a 4-year college **2 :** an unmarried man — **bach•e•lor•hood** *n*
bach•e•lor•ette \ˌba-chə-lə-ˈret\ *n* **:** a young unmarried woman
bachelor's button *n* **:** a European plant related to the daisies and having blue, pink, or white flower heads
ba•cil•lus \bə-ˈsi-ləs\ *n, pl* **-li** \-ˌlī\ **:** any of numerous rod-shaped bacteria; *also* **:** a disease-producing bacterium — **bac•il•lary** \ˈba-sə-ˌler-ē\ *adj*
[1]back \ˈbak\ *n* **1 :** the rear or dorsal part of the human body; *also* **:** the corresponding part of a lower animal **2 :** the part or surface opposite the front **3 :** a player in the backfield in football — **back•less** \-ləs\ *adj*
[2]back *adv* **1 ♦ :** to, toward, or at the rear **2 :** AGO **3 :** so as to be restrained or retarded **4 ♦ :** to, toward, or in a former place or state **5 :** in return or reply

♦ [1, 4] about, around, round

[3]back *adj* **1 ♦ :** located at or in the back **2 :** OVERDUE **3 :** moving or operating backward **4 :** not current

♦ hind, hindmost, posterior, rear *Ant* anterior, fore, forward, front

[4]back *vb* **1 ♦ :** to assist by material, moral, or financial assistance **:** SUPPORT **2 :** to go or cause to go backward or in reverse **3 :** to furnish with a back **:** form the back of

♦ advocate, champion, endorse, patronize, support ♦ abet, aid, assist, help, prop, support

back•ache \ˈba-ˌkāk\ *n* **:** a pain in the lower back
back away *vb* **♦ :** to move away (as from a stand on an issue or from a commitment)

♦ fall back, recede, retire, retreat, withdraw

back–bench•er \-ˈben-chər\ *n* **:** a rank-and-file member of a British legislature
back•bite \-ˌbīt\ *vb* **-bit** \-ˌbit\; **-bit•ten** \-ˌbit-ᵊn\; **-bit•ing** \-ˌbī-tiŋ\ **:** to say mean or spiteful things about someone who is absent — **back•bit•er** *n*
back•board \-ˌbōrd\ *n* **:** a board placed at or serving as the back of something
back•bone \-ˌbōn\ *n* **1 ♦ :** the bony column in the back of a vertebrate that is the chief support of the trunk and consists of a jointed series of vertebrae enclosing and protecting the spinal cord **2 ♦ :** firm resolute character

♦ [1] spine, vertebral column ♦ [2] fiber (*or* fibre), fortitude, grit, guts, pluck, spunk

back down *vb* **♦ :** to withdraw from a commitment or position

♦ cop out, renege

back•drop \ˈbak-ˌdräp\ *n* **1 :** a painted cloth hung across the rear of a stage **2 :** the scenery or ground behind something **:** BACKGROUND
back•er \ˈba-kər\ *n* **♦ :** one that supports

♦ advocate, apostle, booster, champion, exponent, friend, promoter, proponent, supporter ♦ guarantor, patron, sponsor, surety

back•field \-ˌfēld\ *n* **:** the football players whose positions are behind the line
[1]back•fire \-ˌfīr\ *n* **:** a loud noise caused by the improperly timed explosion of fuel in the cylinder of an internal combustion engine
[2]backfire *vb* **1 :** to make or undergo a backfire **2 :** to have a result opposite to what was intended
back•gam•mon \ˈbak-ˌga-mən\ *n* **:** a game played with pieces on a double board in which the moves are determined by throwing dice
back•ground \ˈbak-ˌgrau̇nd\ *n* **1 :** the scenery behind something **2 :** the setting within which something takes place; *also* **:** the sum of a person's experience, training, and understanding
back•hand \ˈbak-ˌhand\ *n* **:** a stroke (as in tennis) made with the back of the hand turned in the direction of movement; *also* **:** the side on which such a stroke is made — **back•hand** *vb*
back•hand•ed \ˈbak-ˈhan-dəd\ *adj* **1 :** not straightforward and open **:** characterized by wiliness and trickery; *esp* **:** SARCASTIC ⟨a ~ compliment⟩ **2 :** using or made with a backhand
back•hoe \ˈbak-ˌhō\ *n* **:** an excavating machine having a bucket that is drawn toward the machine
back•ing \ˈba-kiŋ\ *n* **1 :** something forming a back **2 ♦ :** the act or process of supporting **:** AID; *also* **:** a body of supporters

♦ aid, assist, assistance, boost, help, lift, support

back•lash \ˈbak-ˌlash\ *n* **1 :** a sudden violent backward movement or reaction **2 :** a strong adverse reaction
[1]back•log \-ˌlȯg, -ˌläg\ *n* **1 :** a large log at the back of a hearth fire **2 :** an accumulation of tasks unperformed or materials not processed
[2]backlog *vb* **:** to accumulate in reserve
back of *prep* **:** in or to a place or situation to the rear of **:** BEHIND
back off *vb* **:** to withdraw from a commitment or position **:** BACK DOWN

back out *vb* **:** to withdraw especially from a commitment or contest

[1]**back•pack** \ˈbak-ˌpak\ *n* **:** a camping pack supported by a frame and carried on the back

[2]**backpack** *vb* **:** to hike with a backpack — **back•pack•er** *n*

back•ped•al \ˈbak-ˌped-ᵊl\ *vb* **:** RETREAT

back•rest \-ˌrest\ *n* **:** a rest for the back

back•side \-ˌsīd\ *n* ♦ **:** the seat of the body **:** BUTTOCKS

♦ bottom, butt, buttocks, posterior, rear, rump, seat

back•slap \-ˌslap\ *vb* **:** to display excessive cordiality — **back•slap•per** *n*

back•slide \-ˌslīd\ *vb* **-slid** \-ˌslid\; **-slid** *or* **-slid•den** \-ˌslid-ᵊn\; **-slid•ing** \-ˌslī-diŋ\ **:** to lapse morally or in religious practice

back•slid•er *n* **:** one that backslides ⟨a ~ who pleads his former righteousness⟩

back•spin \-ˌspin\ *n* **:** a backward rotary motion of a ball

[1]**back•stage** \ˈbak-ˌstāj\ *adj* **1 :** relating to or occurring in the area behind a stage **2 :** of or relating to the private lives of theater people **3 :** of or relating to the inner working or operation

[2]**back•stage** \ˈbak-ˈstāj\ *adv* **1 :** in or to a backstage area **2 :** SECRETLY

back•stairs \-ˌstarz\ *adj* **:** SECRET, FURTIVE; *also* **:** SORDID, SCANDALOUS

[1]**back•stop** \-ˌstäp\ *n* **:** something serving as a stop behind something else; *esp* **:** a screen or fence to keep a ball from leaving the field of play

[2]**backstop** *vb* **1 :** SUPPORT **2 :** to serve as a backstop to

back•stretch \ˈbak-ˈstrech\ *n* **:** the side opposite the homestretch on a racecourse

back•stroke \-ˌstrōk\ *n* **:** a swimming stroke executed on the back

back talk *n* ♦ **:** impudent, insolent, or argumentative replies

♦ cheek, impertinence, impudence, insolence, sauce

back•track \ˈbak-ˌtrak\ *vb* **1 :** to retrace one's course **2 :** to reverse a position or stand

back•up \-ˌəp\ *n* **1** ♦ **:** one that serves as a substitute or alternative **2** ♦ **:** an accumulation caused by a stoppage in the flow ⟨traffic backup⟩

♦ [1] pinch hitter, relief, replacement, reserve, stand-in, sub, substitute

♦ bottleneck, jam, snarl

[1]**back•ward** \ˈbak-wərd\ *or* **back•wards** \-wərdz\ *adv* **1 :** toward the back **2 :** with the back foremost **3 :** in a reverse or contrary direction or way **4 :** toward the past; *also* **:** toward a worse state

[2]**backward** *adj* **1 :** directed, turned, or done backward **2 :** DIFFIDENT, SHY **3 :** retarded in development — **back•ward•ly** *adv* — **back•ward•ness** *n*

back•wash \ˈbak-ˌwȯsh, -ˌwäsh\ *n* **:** a backward flow or movement (as of water or air) produced by a propelling force (as the motion of oars)

back•wa•ter \-ˌwȯ-tər, -ˌwä-\ *n* **1 :** water held or turned back in its course **2 :** an isolated or backward place or condition

back•woods \-ˈwu̇dz\ *n pl* **1** ♦ **:** wooded or partly cleared areas far from cities **2** ♦ **:** a remote or isolated place

♦ [1, 2] bush, frontier, hinterland, sticks, up-country

ba•con \ˈbā-kən\ *n* **:** salted and smoked meat from the sides or back of a pig

bac•te•ri•cid•al \bak-ˌtir-ə-ˈsīd-ᵊl\ *adj* **:** destroying bacteria — **bac•te•ri•cide** \-ˈtir-ə-ˌsīd\ *n*

bac•te•ri•ol•o•gy \bak-ˌtir-ē-ˈä-lə-jē\ *n* **1 :** a science dealing with bacteria **2 :** bacterial life and phenomena — **bac•te•ri•o•log•ic** \-ə-ˈlä-jik\ *or* **bac•te•ri•o•log•i•cal** \-ə-ˈlä-ji-kəl\ *adj* — **bac•te•ri•ol•o•gist** \-ˈä-lə-jist\ *n*

bac•te•rio•phage \bak-ˈtir-ē-ə-ˌfāj\ *n* **:** any of various viruses that attack specific bacteria

bac•te•ri•um \bak-ˈtir-ē-əm\ *n, pl* **-ria** \-ē-ə\ **:** any of a group of single-celled microorganisms including some that are disease producers and others that are valued especially for their chemical effects (as fermentation) — **bac•te•ri•al** \-ē-əl\ *adj*

bad \ˈbad\ *adj* **worse** \ˈwərs\; **worst** \ˈwərst\ **1** ♦ **:** below standard **:** POOR; *also* **:** UNFAVORABLE ⟨a ~ report⟩ **2** ♦ **:** having deteriorated because of spoiling **3 a** ♦ **:** morally unacceptable or reprehensible **:** EVIL **b :** not well-behaved **:** NAUGHTY **4 a** ♦ **:** causing discomfort **:** DISAGREEABLE ⟨a ~ taste⟩ **b** ♦ **:** causing harm **:** HARMFUL **5 :** having a defect **:** FAULTY ⟨~ wiring⟩; *also* **:** not valid ⟨a ~ check⟩ **6 :** being in poor health **:** UNWELL, ILL **7 :** full of regret **:** SORRY

♦ [1] deficient, inferior, lousy, off, poor, substandard, unacceptable, unsatisfactory, wanting, wretched, wrong ***Ant*** acceptable, satisfactory ♦ [2] putrid, rotten ♦ [3a] black, evil, immoral, iniquitous, nefarious, sinful, unethical, unsavory, vile, villainous, wicked ***Ant*** ethical, good, moral, right, righteous, virtuous ♦ [4a] disagreeable, distasteful, nasty, rotten, sour, unpleasant ♦ [4b] adverse, baleful, baneful, damaging, deleterious, detrimental, evil, harmful, hurtful, ill, injurious, mischievous, noxious, pernicious, prejudicial

bade *past and past part of* BID

badge \ˈbaj\ *n* **:** a device or token usually worn as a sign of status

[1]**bad•ger** \ˈba-jər\ *n* **:** any of several sturdy burrowing mammals with long claws on their forefeet

[2]**badger** *vb* **:** to harass or annoy persistently

ba•di•nage \ˌbad-ᵊn-ˈäzh\ *n* **:** playful talk back and forth **:** BANTER

bad•land \ˈbad-ˌland\ *n* **:** a region marked by intricate erosional sculpturing and scanty vegetation — usually used in plural

bad•ly *adv* **:** in a bad manner ⟨played ~⟩

bad•min•ton \ˈbad-ˌmint-ᵊn\ *n* **:** a court game played with light rackets and a shuttlecock volleyed over a net

bad–mouth \ˈbad-ˌmau̇th\ *vb* **:** to criticize severely

bad•ness *n* **:** the quality or state of being bad

Bae•de•ker \ˈbā-di-kər, ˈbe-\ *n* **:** GUIDEBOOK

[1]**baf•fle** \ˈba-fəl\ *vb* **baf•fled; baf•fling** \-fə-liŋ\ **1** ♦ **:** to interfere with or slow the progress of **:** FRUSTRATE, THWART **2** ♦ **:** to cause to be mentally confused **:** PERPLEX

♦ [1] balk, checkmate, foil, frustrate, thwart ♦ [2] addle, befog, befuddle, bemuse, bewilder, confound, confuse, disorient, muddle, muddy, mystify, perplex, puzzle

[2]**baffle** *n* **:** a device (as a wall or screen) to deflect, check, or regulate flow (as of liquid or sound) — **baf•fled** \ˈba-fəld\ *adj*

baf•fle•ment *n* ♦ **:** the state of being baffled

♦ bewilderment, confusion, distraction, muddle, mystification, perplexity, puzzlement, whirl

[1]**bag** \ˈbag\ *n* ♦ **:** a flexible usually closable container (as for storing or carrying)

♦ handbag, pocketbook, purse

[2]**bag** *vb* **bagged; bag•ging** **1 :** to expand from internal pressure **:** BULGE **2 :** to put in a bag **3** ♦ **:** to get possession of; *esp* **:** to take in hunting

♦ capture, catch, get, grab, nab, seize, snare, trap

ba•gasse \bə-ˈgas\ *n* **:** plant residue (as of sugarcane) left after a product (as juice) has been extracted

bag•a•telle \ˌba-gə-ˈtel\ *n* **:** TRIFLE

ba•gel \ˈbā-gəl\ *n* **:** a hard glazed doughnut-shaped roll

bag•gage \ˈba-gij\ *n* **1 :** the traveling bags and personal belongings of a traveler **:** LUGGAGE **2 :** things that get in the way

baggies \ˈba-gēz\ *n pl* **:** baggy pants or shorts

bag•gy \ˈba-gē\ *adj* **bag•gi•er; -est :** puffed out or hanging like a bag — **bag•gi•ly** \-gə-lē\ *adv* — **bag•gi•ness** \-gē-nəs\ *n*

bag•man \ˈbag-mən\ *n* **:** a person who collects or distributes illicitly gained money on behalf of another

ba•gnio \ˈban-yō\ *n, pl* **bagnios :** BROTHEL

bag•pipe \ˈbag-ˌpīp\ *n* **:** a musical wind instrument consisting of a bag, a tube with valves, and sounding pipes — often used in plural

ba•guette \ba-ˈget\ *n* **1 :** a gem having the shape of a narrow rectangle; *also* **:** the shape itself **2 :** a long thin loaf of French bread

Ba•ha•mi•an \bə-ˈhā-mē-ən, -ˈhä-\ *n* **:** a native or inhabitant of the Bahama Islands

[1]**bail** \ˈbāl\ *n* **:** a container for ladling water out of a boat

[2]**bail** *vb* **:** to dip and throw out water from a boat — **bail•er** *n*

[3]**bail** *n* **:** security given to guarantee a prisoner's appearance when legally required; *also* **:** one giving such security or the release secured

[4]**bail** *vb* **:** to release under bail; *also* **:** to procure the release of by giving bail — **bail•able** \ˈbā-lə-bəl\ *adj*

[5]**bail** *n* **:** the arched handle (as of a pail or kettle)

bai•liff \ˈbā-ləf\ *n* **1 :** an aide of a British sheriff who serves writs and makes arrests; *also* **:** a minor officer of a U.S. court **2 :** an estate or farm manager especially in Britain **:** STEWARD

bai•li•wick \ˈbā-li-ˌwik\ *n* **:** one's special province or domain

bail•out \ˈbā-ˌlau̇t\ *n* **:** a rescue from financial distress

bairn \ˈbarn\ *n, chiefly Scot* **:** CHILD

[1]**bait** \ˈbāt\ *vb* **1** ♦ **:** to persecute by continued attacks **2 :** to harass with dogs usually for sport ⟨~ a bear⟩ **3 :** to furnish (as a hook) with bait **4 :** ALLURE, ENTICE **5 :** to give food and drink to (as an animal)

♦ bug, hassle, heckle, needle, ride, taunt, tease

[2]**bait** *n* **1 :** a lure for catching animals (as fish) **2 :** an inducement to pleasure or gain **:** LURE, TEMPTATION

baize \ˈbāz\ *n* **:** a coarse feltlike fabric

[1]**bake** \ˈbāk\ *vb* **baked; bak•ing 1 :** to cook or become cooked in dry heat especially in an oven **2 :** to dry and harden by heat ⟨~ bricks⟩ — **bak•er** *n*

[2]**bake** *n* **:** a social gathering featuring baked food

baker's dozen *n* **:** THIRTEEN

bak•ery \ˈbā-k(ə-)rē\ *n, pl* **-er•ies :** a place for baking or selling baked goods

bake sale *n* **:** a fund-raising event at which usually homemade foods are sold

bake•shop \ˈbāk-ˌshäp\ *n* **:** BAKERY

baking powder *n* **:** a powder that consists of a carbonate, an acid, and a starch and that makes the dough rise in baking cakes and biscuits

baking soda *n* **:** SODIUM BICARBONATE

bak•sheesh \ˈbak-ˌshēsh\ *n* **:** payment (as a tip or bribe) to expedite service

bal *abbr* balance

bal•a•lai•ka \ˌba-lə-ˈlī-kə\ *n* **:** a triangular 3-stringed instrument of Russian origin played by plucking or strumming

[1]**bal•ance** \ˈba-ləns\ *n* **1 :** a weighing device **:** SCALE **2** ♦ **:** a weight, force, or influence counteracting the effect of another **3 :** an oscillating wheel used to regulate a timepiece **4** ♦ **:** a state of equilibrium **5** ♦ **:** a remaining group, part, or trace **:** REST; *esp* **:** an amount in excess especially on the credit side of an account **6 :** mental and emotional steadiness **7** ♦ **:** an aesthetically pleasing integration of elements

♦ [2] canceler, counterbalance, counterweight, offset ♦ [4] equilibrium, equipoise, poise ***Ant*** imbalance ♦ [5] leavings, leftovers, odds and ends, remainder, remains, remnant, residue, rest ♦ [7] coherence, consonance, harmony, proportion, symmetry, symphony, unity

[2]**balance** *vb* **bal•anced; bal•anc•ing 1 :** to compute the balance of an account **2** ♦ **:** to arrange so that one set of elements equals another; *also* **:** to equal or equalize in weight, number, or proportions **3 :** WEIGH **4 :** to bring or come to a state or position of balance; *also* **:** to bring into harmony or proportion

♦ equalize, equate, even, level

bal•anced \-lənst\ *adj* ♦ **:** being in a state of balance (as physically, emotionally, or aesthetically)

♦ clearheaded, lucid, normal, right, sane, stable ♦ congruous, consonant, harmonious

bal•brig•gan \bal-ˈbri-gən\ *n* **:** a knitted cotton fabric used especially for underwear

bal•co•ny \ˈbal-kə-nē\ *n, pl* **-nies 1 :** a platform projecting from the side of a building and enclosed by a railing **2 :** a gallery inside a building

bald \ˈbȯld\ *adj* **1** ♦ **:** lacking a natural or usual covering (as of hair) **2** ♦ **:** lacking embellishment or decoration **:** PLAIN — **bald•ly** *adv* — **bald•ness** *n*

♦ [1] bare, exposed, naked, open, uncovered ♦ [2] plain, simple, unadorned, undecorated, unvarnished

bal•da•chin \ˈbȯl-də-kən, ˈbal-\ *or* **bal•da•chi•no** \ˌbal-də-ˈkē-nō\ *n, pl* **-chins** *or* **-chinos :** a canopylike structure over an altar

bald cypress *n* **:** either of two large swamp trees of the southern U.S. with hard red wood

bald eagle *n* **:** an eagle of No. America that when mature has white head and neck feathers and a white tail

bal•der•dash \ˈbȯl-dər-ˌdash\ *n* **:** NONSENSE

bald•ing \ˈbȯl-diŋ\ *adj* **:** getting bald

bal•dric \ˈbȯl-drik\ *n* **:** a belt worn over the shoulder to carry a sword or bugle

[1]**bale** \ˈbāl\ *n* **:** a large or closely packed bundle

[2]**bale** *vb* **baled; bal•ing :** to pack in a bale — **bal•er** *n*

ba•leen \bə-ˈlēn\ *n* **:** a horny substance attached in plates to the upper jaw of some large whales (**baleen whales**)

bale•ful \ˈbāl-fəl\ *adj* **1** ♦ **:** likely to cause or capable of producing harm or death **2** ♦ **:** foreboding or foreshadowing evil **:** OMINOUS

♦ [1] adverse, bad, baneful, damaging, deleterious, detrimental, evil, harmful, hurtful, pernicious ♦ [2] dire, foreboding, menacing, ominous, portentous, sinister

[1]**balk** \ˈbȯk\ *n* **1** ♦ **:** something that makes movement or progress more difficult **:** HINDRANCE **2 :** an illegal motion of the pitcher in baseball while in position

[2]**balk** *vb* **1** ♦ **:** to hinder the passage, progress, or accomplishment of **:** THWART **2 :** to stop short and refuse to go on **3 :** to commit a balk in sports

♦ baffle, beat, checkmate, foil, frustrate, thwart

balky \ˈbȯ-kē\ *adj* **:** refusing or likely to refuse to proceed, act, or function as directed or expected ⟨a ~ mule⟩

[1]**ball** \ˈbȯl\ *n* **1** ♦ **:** a rounded body or mass (as at the base of the thumb or for use as a missile or in a game) **2 :** a game played with a ball **3 :** a pitched baseball that misses the strike zone and is not swung at by the batter **4 :** a hit or thrown ball in various games ⟨foul ~⟩ — **on the ball :** COMPETENT, KNOWLEDGEABLE, ALERT

♦ orb, sphere

[2]**ball** *vb* ♦ **:** to form into a ball

♦ agglomerate, conglomerate, roll, round, wad

[3]**ball** *n* ♦ **:** a large formal dance

♦ dance, formal, prom

bal•lad \ˈba-ləd\ *n* **1 :** a narrative poem of strongly marked rhythm suitable for singing **2 :** a simple song **:** AIR **3 :** a slow romantic song

bal•lad•eer \ˌba-lə-ˈdir\ *n* **:** a singer of ballads

[1]**bal•last** \ˈba-ləst\ *n* **1 :** heavy material used to stabilize a ship or control a balloon's ascent **2 :** crushed stone laid in a railroad bed or used in making concrete

[2]**ballast** *vb* **:** to provide with ballast

ball bearing *n* **:** a bearing in which the revolving part turns upon steel balls that roll easily in a groove; *also* **:** one of the balls in such a bearing

ball•car•ri•er \ˈbȯl-ˌkar-ē-ər\ *n* **:** the football player carrying the ball in an offensive play

bal•le•ri•na \ˌba-lə-ˈrē-nə\ *n* **:** a female ballet dancer

bal•let \ˈba-ˌlā, ba-ˈlā\ *n* **1 :** dancing in which fixed poses and steps are combined with light flowing movements often to convey a story; *also* **:** a theatrical art form using ballet dancing **2 :** a company of ballet dancers

bal•let•o•mane \ba-ˈle-tə-ˌmān\ *n* **:** a devotee of ballet

bal•lis•tic missile \bə-ˈlis-tik-\ *n* **:** a missile that is guided during ascent and that falls freely during descent

bal•lis•tics \-tiks\ *n sing or pl* **1 :** the science of the motion of projectiles (as bullets) in flight **2 :** the flight characteristics of a projectile — **ballistic** *adj*

[1]**bal•loon** \bə-ˈlün\ *n* **1 :** a bag filled with gas or heated air so as to rise and float in the atmosphere **2 :** a toy consisting of an inflatable bag — **bal•loon•ist** *n*

[2]**balloon** *vb* **1** ♦ **:** to swell or puff out **2 :** to travel in a balloon **3** ♦ **:** to increase rapidly

♦ [1, 3] appreciate, build, burgeon, enlarge, escalate, expand, increase, mushroom, rise, swell, wax ♦ [1] belly, bulge, overhang, poke, project, protrude, start, stick out

[1]**bal•lot** \ˈba-lət\ *n* **1 :** a piece of paper used to cast a vote **2 :** the action or a system of voting; *also* **:** the right to vote

[2]**ballot** *vb* **:** to decide by ballot **:** VOTE

[1]**ball•park** \ˈbȯl-ˌpark\ *n* **:** a park in which ball games are played

[2]**ballpark** *adj* **:** approximately correct ⟨~ estimate⟩

ball•point \ˈbȯl-ˌpȯint\ *n* **:** a pen whose writing point is a small rotating metal ball that inks itself from an inner container

ball•room \ˈbȯl ˌrüm, ˌrum\ *n* **:** a large room for dances

[1]**bal•ly•hoo** \ˈba-lē-ˌhü\ *n, pl* **-hoos :** extravagant statements and claims made for publicity

[2]**ballyhoo** *vb* **bal•ly•hoo•ed; bal•ly•hoo•ing; bal•ly•hoos** ♦ **:** to drum up interest in by means of ballyhoo **:** PUBLICIZE

♦ boast, plug, promote, publicize, tout

balm \ˈbäm, ˈbälm\ *n* **1 :** a fragrant healing or soothing lotion or ointment **2 :** any of several spicy fragrant herbs of the mint family **3 :** something that comforts or soothes

balm•i•ness \ˈbä-mē-nəs, ˈbäl-\ *n* ♦ **:** the quality or state of being balmy

♦ absurdity, asininity, craziness, daftness, fatuity, folly, foolishness, inanity, insanity, lunacy, madness, silliness, simplicity, zaniness

balmy \ˈbä-mē, ˈbäl-\ *adj* **balm•i•er; -est 1 a** ♦ **:** gently soothing **:** MILD **b** ♦ **:** being pleasant and not too cool or too hot **2 a** ♦ **:** disordered in mind **b** ♦ **:** lacking in judgment **:** FOOLISH

♦ [1a] benign, bland, delicate, gentle, light, mellow, mild, soft, soothing, tender ♦ [1b] clement, equable, gentle, mild, moderate, temperate ♦ [2a, 2b] absurd, crazy, cuckoo, fatuous, foolish, mad, nonsensical, nutty, senseless, silly, stupid

ba•lo•ney \bə-ˈlō-nē\ *n* **:** NONSENSE

bal•sa \ˈbȯl-sə\ *n* **:** the extremely light strong wood of a tropical American tree; *also* **:** the tree
bal•sam \ˈbȯl-səm\ *n* **1 :** a fragrant aromatic and usually resinous substance oozing from various plants; *also* **:** a preparation containing or smelling like balsam **2 :** a balsam-yielding tree (as balsam fir) **3 :** a common garden ornamental plant — **bal•sam•ic** \bȯl-ˈsa-mik\ *adj*
balsam fir *n* **:** a resinous American evergreen tree that is widely used for pulpwood and as a Christmas tree
balsamic vinegar *n* **:** an aged Italian vinegar made from white grapes
Bal•ti•more oriole \ˈbȯl-tə-ˌmōr-\ *n* **:** a common American oriole in which the male is brightly colored with orange, black, and white
bal•us•ter \ˈba-lə-stər\ *n* **:** an upright support for a rail (as of a staircase)
bal•us•trade \ˈba-lə-ˌstrād\ *n* **:** a row of balusters topped by a rail
bam•boo \bam-ˈbü\ *n, pl* **bamboos :** any of various woody mostly tall tropical grasses including some with strong hollow stems used for building, furniture, or utensils
bamboo curtain *n, often cap B&C* **:** a political, military, and ideological barrier in eastern Asia
bam•boo•zle \bam-ˈbü-zəl\ *vb* **-boo•zled; -boo•zling :** TRICK, HOODWINK
¹ban \ˈban\ *vb* **banned; ban•ning** ♦ **:** to hinder or prevent by authority

♦ bar, enjoin, forbid, interdict, outlaw, prohibit, proscribe

²ban *n* **1 :** CURSE **2** ♦ **:** a legal or formal prohibition

♦ embargo, interdict, interdiction, prohibition, proscription, veto

ba•nal \bə-ˈnäl, -ˈnal; ˈbān-ᵊl\ *adj* ♦ **:** lacking originality, freshness, or novelty **:** COMMONPLACE, TRITE

♦ commonplace, hackneyed, musty, stale, stereotyped, threadbare, tired, trite

ba•nal•i•ty \bā-ˈna-lə-tē\ *n* ♦ **:** something banal **:** COMMONPLACE

♦ cliché, commonplace, platitude, shibboleth

ba•nana \bə-ˈna-nə\ *n* **:** a treelike tropical plant bearing thick clusters of yellow or reddish finger-shaped fruit; *also* **:** this fruit
¹band \ˈband\ *n* **1** ♦ **:** something that binds, ties, or goes around **2** ♦ **:** a strip or stripe that can be distinguished (as by color or texture) from nearby matter **3 :** a range of wavelengths (as in radio)

♦ [1] bond, chain, fetter, irons, ligature, manacle, shackle ♦ [2] circle, hoop, ring, round ♦ [2] bar, streak, stripe

²band *vb* **1** ♦ **:** to tie up, finish, or enclose with a band **2** ♦ **:** to gather together or unite especially for some common end — often used with *together* **3 :** to furnish or decorate with a band — **band•er** *n*

♦ [1] belt, gird, girdle, wrap ♦ [1] bind, gird, tie, truss ♦ *often* **band together** [2] ally, associate, club, confederate, conjoin, cooperate, federate, league, unite

³band *n* ♦ **:** a group of persons, animals, or things; *esp* **:** a group of musicians organized for playing together

♦ company, crew, gang, outfit, party, squad, team

¹ban•dage \ˈban-dij\ *n* **:** a strip of material used especially in dressing wounds
²bandage *vb* **ban•daged; ban•dag•ing :** to dress or cover with a bandage
ban•dan•na *or* **ban•dana** \ban-ˈda-nə\ *n* ♦ **:** a large colored figured handkerchief

♦ babushka, do-rag, kerchief, mantilla

B and B *abbr* bed-and-breakfast
band•box \ˈband-ˌbäks\ *n* **:** a usually cylindrical box for carrying clothing
band•ed \ˈban-dəd\ *adj* **:** having or marked with bands
ban•de•role *or* **ban•de•rol** \ˈban-də-ˌrōl\ *n* **:** a long narrow forked flag or streamer
ban•dit \ˈban-dət\ *n* **1** *pl also* **ban•dit•ti** \ban-ˈdi-tē\ **:** an outlaw who lives by plunder; *esp* **:** a member of a band of marauders **2 :** ROBBER — **ban•dit•ry** \ˈban-də-trē\ *n*
ban•do•lier *or* **ban•do•leer** \ˌban-də-ˈlir\ *n* **:** a belt slung over the shoulder especially to carry ammunition
band saw *n* **:** a saw in the form of an endless steel belt running over pulleys
band•stand \ˈband-ˌstand\ *n* **:** a usually roofed platform on which a band or orchestra performs outdoors
b and w *abbr* black and white
band•wag•on \ˈband-ˌwa-gən\ *n* **1 :** a wagon carrying musicians in a parade **2** ♦ **:** a movement that attracts growing support

♦ campaign, cause, crusade, drive, movement

¹ban•dy \ˈban-dē\ *vb* **ban•died; ban•dy•ing 1 :** to exchange (as blows or quips) especially in rapid succession **2 :** to use in a glib or offhand way
²bandy *adj* **:** curved outward ⟨∼ legs⟩
bane \ˈbān\ *n* **1** ♦ **:** a substance that through its chemical action usually kills, injures, or impairs an organism **:** POISON **2 :** WOE, HARM; *also* **:** a source of this

♦ poison, toxin, venom

bane•ful \ˈbān-fəl\ *adj* ♦ **:** productive of destruction or woe **:** seriously harmful

♦ bad, baleful, damaging, deleterious, harmful, hurtful, injurious, noxious, pernicious

¹bang \ˈbaŋ\ *vb* **1** ♦ **:** to knock against something with a forceful jolt **:** BUMP ⟨fell and ∼*ed* his knee⟩ **2** ♦ **:** to strike, thrust, or move vigorously and often with a loud noise

♦ [1, 2] bash, bump, collide, crash, hit, impact, knock, smash, strike

²bang *n* **1 :** a resounding blow **2** ♦ **:** a sudden loud noise **3** ♦ **:** a sudden wave of emotion ⟨I get a ∼ out of all this⟩

♦ [2] blast, boom, clap, crack, crash, pop, report, slam, smash ♦ [3] exhilaration, kick, thrill, titillation

³bang *adv* **:** DIRECTLY, RIGHT
⁴bang *n* **:** a fringe of hair cut short (as across the forehead) — usually used in plural
⁵bang *vb* **:** to cut a bang in
Ban•gla•deshi \ˌbäŋ-glə-ˈde-shē\ *n* **:** a native or inhabitant of Bangladesh — **Bangladeshi** *adj*
ban•gle \ˈbaŋ-gəl\ *n* **:** an ornamental band or chain worn around the wrist; *also* **:** a loose-hanging ornament
bang–up \ˈbaŋ-ˌəp\ *adj* ♦ **:** being of the very best kind **:** FIRST-RATE, EXCELLENT ⟨a ∼ job⟩

♦ A1, banner, excellent, fabulous, fine, grand, great, prime, sensational, splendid, superb, superior, unsurpassed, wonderful

ban•ish \ˈba-nish\ *vb* **1** ♦ **:** to require by authority to leave a country **2** ♦ **:** to drive out **:** EXPEL

♦ [1] deport, displace, exile, expatriate, transport ♦ [2] boot (out), bounce, cast, drum, eject, expel, oust, rout, run off, throw out

ban•ish•ment *n* ♦ **:** a legal expulsion from a country

♦ deportation, displacement, exile, expulsion

ban•is•ter \ˈba-nə-stər\ *n* **1 :** an upright often vase-shaped support for a rail **2 :** a handrail with its supporting posts **3 :** HANDRAIL
ban•jo \ˈban-ˌjō\ *n, pl* **banjos** *also* **banjoes :** a musical instrument with a long neck, a drumlike body, and usually five strings — **ban•jo•ist** \-ist\ *n*
¹bank \ˈbaŋk\ *n* **1** ♦ **:** a piled-up mass (as of cloud or earth) **2 :** an undersea elevation **3 :** rising ground bordering a lake, river, or sea **4 :** the sideways slope of a surface along a curve or of a vehicle as it rounds a curve

♦ bar, drift, mound

²bank *vb* **1 :** to form a bank about **2 :** to cover (as a fire) with fuel to keep inactive **3 :** to build (a curve) with the roadbed or track inclined laterally upward from the inside edge **4 :** to pile or heap in a bank; *also* **:** to arrange in a tier **5 :** to incline (an airplane) laterally
³bank *n* **1 :** an establishment concerned especially with the custody, loan, exchange, or issue of money, the extension of credit, and the transmission of funds **2 :** a stock of or a place for holding something in reserve ⟨a blood ∼⟩
⁴bank *vb* **1 :** to conduct the business of a bank **2 :** to deposit money or have an account in a bank — **bank•er** *n* — **bank•ing** *n*
⁵bank *n* **:** a group of objects arranged close together (as in a row or tier) ⟨a ∼ of file drawers⟩
bank•book \ˈbaŋk-ˌbu̇k\ *n* **:** the depositor's book in which a bank records deposits and withdrawals
bank•card \-ˌkärd\ *n* **:** a credit card issued by a bank
bank•note \-ˌnōt\ *n* **:** a promissory note issued by a bank and circulating as money
bank•roll \-ˌrōl\ *n* **:** supply of money **:** FUNDS
¹bank•rupt \ˈbaŋ-(ˌ)krəpt\ *n* **:** an insolvent person; *esp* **:** one whose property is turned over by court action to a trustee to be handled for the benefit of his creditors

[2]**bankrupt** *adj* **1 :** reduced to financial ruin; *esp* **:** legally declared a bankrupt **2 :** wholly lacking in or deprived of some essential ⟨morally ~⟩ — **bank•rupt•cy** \ˈbaŋ-(ˌ)krəpt-sē\ *n*

[3]**bankrupt** *vb* **:** to reduce to bankruptcy

[1]**ban•ner** \ˈba-nər\ *n* **1** ♦ **:** a piece of cloth attached to a staff and used by a leader as his standard **2** ♦ **:** a usually rectangular piece of fabric of distinctive design that is used as a symbol (as of a nation), as a signaling device, or as a decoration **:** FLAG **3 :** an advertisement that runs usually across the top of a Web page

♦ [1, 2] colors (*or* colours), ensign, flag, jack, pennant, standard, streamer

[2]**banner** *adj* ♦ **:** distinguished from all others especially in excellence ⟨a ~ year⟩

♦ A1, boss, excellent, grand, great, stellar, superior, unsurpassed

ban•nock \ˈba-nək\ *n* **:** a flat oatmeal or barley cake usually cooked on a griddle

banns \ˈbanz\ *n pl* **:** public announcement especially in church of a proposed marriage

[1]**ban•quet** \ˈbaŋ-kwət\ *n* ♦ **:** a ceremonial dinner

♦ dinner, feast, feed, spread

[2]**banquet** *vb* **:** to partake of or treat with a banquet

ban•quette \baŋ-ˈket\ *n* **:** a long upholstered bench especially along a wall

ban•shee \ˈban-shē\ *n* **:** a female spirit in Gaelic folklore whose wailing warns a family that one of them will soon die

ban•tam \ˈban-təm\ *n* **1 :** any of numerous small domestic fowls that are often miniatures of standard breeds **2 :** a small but pugnacious person

[1]**ban•ter** \ˈban-tər\ *vb* **:** to speak to in a witty and teasing manner

[2]**banter** *n* ♦ **:** good-natured witty joking

♦ chaff, persiflage, raillery, repartee

Ban•tu \ˈban-ˌtü\ *n, pl* **Bantu** *or* **Bantus** **1 :** a member of a group of African peoples of central and southern Africa **2 :** a group of African languages spoken by the Bantu

Ban•tu•stan \ˌban-tü-ˈstan, ˌbän-tü-ˈstän\ *n* **:** an all-black enclave in the Republic of So. Africa with a limited degree of self-government

ban•yan \ˈban-yən\ *n* **:** a large tropical Asian tree whose aerial roots grow downward to the ground and form new trunks

ban•zai \bän-ˈzī\ *n* **:** a Japanese cheer or cry of triumph

bao•bab \ˈbaù-ˌbab, ˈbā-ə-\ *n* **:** a tropical African tree with a short swollen trunk and sour edible gourdlike fruits

bap•tism \ˈbap-ˌti-zəm\ *n* **1 :** a Christian sacrament signifying spiritual rebirth and symbolized by the ritual use of water **2 :** an act, experience, or ordeal by which one is purified, sanctified, initiated, or named — **bap•tis•mal** \bap-ˈtiz-məl\ *adj*

baptismal name *n* **:** GIVEN NAME

Bap•tist \ˈbap-tist\ *n* **:** a member of any of several Protestant denominations emphasizing baptism by immersion of believers only

bap•tis•tery *or* **bap•tis•try** \ˈbap-tə-strē\ *n, pl* **-ter•ies** *or* **-tries** **:** a place especially in a church used for baptism

bap•tize \bap-ˈtīz, ˈbap-ˌtīz\ *vb* **bap•tized; bap•tiz•ing** **1 a :** to administer baptism to **b :** to give a name to **:** CHRISTEN **2 a :** to purify especially by an ordeal **b** ♦ **:** to induct into membership by or as if by special rites **:** INITIATE

♦ inaugurate, induct, initiate, install, invest

[1]**bar** \ˈbär\ *n* **1 :** a long narrow piece of material (as wood or metal) used especially for a lever, fastening, or support **2 a** ♦ **:** something that blocks or is intended to block passage **:** OBSTACLE **b :** a submerged or partly submerged bank (as of sand) along a shore or in a river often obstructing navigation **3 a :** the railing in a law court at which prisoners are stationed **b :** the legal profession or the whole body of lawyers **4** ♦ **:** a stripe, band, or line much longer than wide **5** ♦ **:** a counter at which food or especially drink is served; *also* **:** BARROOM **6 :** a vertical line across the musical staff

♦ [2a] block, encumbrance, hindrance, inhibition, obstacle ♦ [4] band, streak, stripe ♦ [5] barroom, café, pub, public house, saloon, tavern

[2]**bar** *vb* **barred; bar•ring** **1 :** to fasten, confine, or obstruct with or as if with a bar or bars **2 :** to mark with bars **:** STRIPE **3** ♦ **:** to shut or keep out **:** EXCLUDE **4** ♦ **:** to command against **:** FORBID

♦ [3] ban, count out, debar, eliminate, except, exclude, rule out ♦ [4] ban, enjoin, forbid, interdict, outlaw, prohibit, proscribe

[3]**bar** *prep* ♦ **:** with the exclusion or exception of **:** EXCEPT

♦ aside from, barring, besides, but, except, outside (of), save

[4]**bar** *abbr* barometer; barometric

Bar *abbr* Baruch

barb \ˈbärb\ *n* **1 :** a sharp projection extending backward (as from the point of an arrow) **2** ♦ **:** a biting critical remark — **barbed** \ˈbärbd\ *adj*

♦ affront, dart, dig, indignity, insult, name, offense, outrage, put-down, sarcasm, slight, slur, wound

[1]**bar•bar•ian** \bär-ˈber-ē-ən\ *adj* **1 :** of, relating to, or being a land, culture, or people alien to and usually believed to be inferior to another's **2 :** lacking refinement, learning, or artistic or literary culture

[2]**barbarian** *n* **:** one that is barbarian

bar•bar•ic \bär-ˈbar-ik\ *adj* **1 :** BARBARIAN **2 :** marked by a lack of restraint **:** WILD **3 :** mercilessly harsh or cruel **:** BARBAROUS

bar•ba•rism \ˈbär-bə-ˌri-zəm\ *n* **1 :** the social condition of barbarians; *also* **:** the use or display of barbarian or barbarous acts, attitudes, or ideas **2 :** a word or expression that offends standards of correctness or purity

bar•bar•i•ty \bär-ˈbar-ə-tē\ *n* ♦ **:** barbarous cruelty

♦ brutality, cruelty, inhumanity, sadism, savagery, viciousness, wantonness

bar•ba•rous \ˈbär-bə-rəs\ *adj* **1** ♦ **:** lacking culture or refinement **2 :** using linguistic barbarisms **3** ♦ **:** mercilessly harsh or cruel — **bar•ba•rous•ly** *adv*

♦ [1] heathen, heathenish, Neanderthal, rude, savage, uncivil, uncivilized, uncultivated, wild ♦ [3] brutal, cruel, heartless, inhumane, sadistic, savage, vicious

[1]**bar•be•cue** \ˈbär-bi-ˌkyü\ *n* **:** a social gathering at which barbecued food is served

[2]**barbecue** *vb* **-cued; -cu•ing** **1 :** to cook over hot coals or on a revolving spit **2 :** to cook in a highly seasoned vinegar sauce

bar•bell \ˈbär-ˌbel\ *n* **:** a bar with adjustable weights attached to each end used for exercise and in weight-lifting competition

bar•ber \ˈbär-bər\ *n* **:** one whose business is cutting and dressing hair and shaving and trimming beards

bar•ber•ry \ˈbär-ˌber-ē\ *n* **:** any of a genus of spiny shrubs bearing yellow flowers and oblong red berries

bar•bi•tu•rate \bär-ˈbi-chə-rət\ *n* **:** any of various compounds (as a salt or ester) formed from an organic acid (**bar•bi•tu•ric acid** \ˌbär-bə-ˈtùr-ik-, -ˈtyùr-\); *esp* **:** one used as a sedative or hypnotic

bar•ca•role *or* **bar•ca•rolle** \ˈbär-kə-ˌrōl\ *n* **:** a Venetian boat song characterized by a beat suggesting a rowing rhythm; *also* **:** a piece of music imitating this

bar chart *n* **:** BAR GRAPH

bar code *n* **:** a set of printed and variously spaced bars and sometimes numerals that is designed to be scanned to identify the object it labels — **bar–cod•ed** \ˈbär-ˌkō-dəd\ *adj*

bard \ˈbärd\ *n* ♦ **:** one who writes poetry **:** a maker of verses **:** POET

♦ minstrel, poet, versifier

bard•ic \ˈbär-dik\ *adj* ♦ **:** being, belonging, or relating to a bard or his poetry

♦ lyric, lyrical, poetic

[1]**bare** \ˈbar\ *adj* **bar•er; bar•est** **1** ♦ **:** devoid of customary or natural covering **:** NAKED **2 :** open to view **:** UNCONCEALED, EXPOSED **3** ♦ **:** containing nothing **:** EMPTY **4 :** leaving nothing to spare **:** MERE **5** ♦ **:** lacking ornament **:** PLAIN, UNADORNED

♦ [1] bald, exposed, naked, nude, open, uncovered ♦ [3] blank, devoid, empty, stark, vacant, void ♦ [5] bald, naked, plain, simple, unadorned, undecorated, unvarnished

[2]**bare** *vb* **bared; bar•ing** ♦ **:** to make or lay bare **:** UNCOVER

♦ disclose, discover, divulge, expose, reveal, spill, tell, uncover, unmask, unveil

bare•back \-ˌbak\ *or* **bare•backed** \-ˈbakt\ *adv or adj* **:** without a saddle

bare•faced \-ˈfāst\ *adj* **1 :** having the face uncovered; *esp* **:** BEARDLESS **2 :** not concealed **:** OPEN — **bare•faced•ly** \-ˈfā-səd-lē, -ˈfāst-lē\ *adv*

bare•foot \-ˌfùt\ *or* **bare•foot•ed** \-ˈfù-təd\ *adv or adj* **:** with bare feet

bare–hand•ed \-ˈhan-dəd\ *adv or adj* **1 :** without gloves **2 :** without tools or weapons

bare•head•ed \-ˈhe-dəd\ *adv or adj* **:** without a hat

bare•ly \ˈbar-lē\ *adv* **1 :** PLAINLY, MEAGERLY **2** ♦ **:** by a narrow margin **:** only just ⟨~ enough money⟩

♦ hardly, just, marginally, scarcely, slightly

bare•ness *n* **:** the quality or state of being bare
barf \ˈbärf\ ♦ **:** to discharge the contents of the stomach through the mouth **:** VOMIT

♦ gag, heave, hurl, puke, retch, spit up, throw up, vomit

bar•fly \ˈbär-ˌflī\ *n* **:** a drinker who frequents bars
[1]**bar•gain** \ˈbär-gən\ *n* **1** ♦ **:** an agreement between parties settling a transaction **2** ♦ **:** an advantageous purchase **3 :** a transaction, situation, or event regarded in the light of its results

♦ [1] accord, agreement, compact, contract, convention, covenant, deal, pact, settlement, understanding ♦ [2] buy, deal, steal

[2]**bargain** *vb* **1** ♦ **:** to negotiate over the terms of an agreement; *also* **:** to come to terms **2 :** BARTER

♦ chaffer, deal, dicker, haggle, negotiate, palter

bar•gain–base•ment \ˈbär-gən-ˈbās-mənt\ *adj* **:** markedly inexpensive
[1]**barge** \ˈbärj\ *n* **1 :** a broad flat-bottomed boat usually moved by towing **2 :** a motorboat supplied to a flagship (as for an admiral) **3 :** a ceremonial boat elegantly furnished — **barge•man** \-mən\ *n*
[2]**barge** *vb* **barged; barg•ing 1 :** to carry by barge **2 :** to move or thrust oneself clumsily or rudely
bar graph *n* **:** a graphic technique for comparing amounts by rectangles whose lengths are proportional to the amounts they represent
ba•ris•ta \bə-ˈrēs-tə\ *n* **:** a person who makes and serves coffee to the public
bari•tone \ˈbar-ə-ˌtōn\ *n* **:** a male voice between bass and tenor; *also* **:** a man with such a voice
bar•i•um \ˈbar-ē-əm\ *n* **:** a silver-white metallic chemical element that occurs only in combination
[1]**bark** \ˈbärk\ *vb* **1 :** to make the short loud cry of a dog **2 :** to speak or utter in a curt loud tone **:** SNAP
[2]**bark** *n* **:** the sound made by a barking dog
[3]**bark** *n* **:** the tough corky outer covering of a woody stem or root
[4]**bark** *vb* **1** ♦ **:** to strip the bark from **2** ♦ **:** to rub the skin from

♦ [1, 2] flay, hull, husk, peel, shell, skin

[5]**bark** *n* **:** a ship of three or more masts with the aft mast fore-and-aft rigged and the others square-rigged
bar•keep \ˈbär-ˌkēp\ *also* **bar•keep•er** \-ˌkē-pər\ *n* **:** BARTENDER
bark•er \ˈbär-kər\ *n* **:** a person who stands at the entrance especially to a show and tries to attract customers to it
bar•ley \ˈbär-lē\ *n* **:** a cereal grass with seeds used as food and in making malt liquors; *also* **:** its seed
bar mitz•vah \bär-ˈmits-və\ *n, often cap B&M* **1 :** a Jewish boy who at about 13 years of age assumes religious responsibilities **2 :** the ceremony recognizing a boy as a bar mitzvah
barn \ˈbärn\ *n* **:** a building used especially for storing hay and grain and for housing livestock or farm equipment
bar•na•cle \ˈbär-ni-kəl\ *n* **:** any of numerous small marine crustaceans free-swimming when young but permanently fixed (as to rocks, whales, or ships) when adult
barn•storm \ˈbärn-ˌstȯrm\ *vb* **:** to travel through the country making brief stops to entertain (as with shows or flying stunts) or to campaign for political office
barn•yard \-ˌyärd\ *n* **:** a usually fenced area adjoining a barn
baro•graph \ˈbar-ə-ˌgraf\ *n* **:** a recording barometer
ba•rom•e•ter \bə-ˈräm-ə-tər\ *n* **:** an instrument for measuring atmospheric pressure — **baro•met•ric** \ˌbar-ə-ˈme-trik\ *adj*
bar•on \ˈbar-ən\ *n* **1 :** a member of the lowest grade of the British peerage **2** ♦ **:** a man who possesses great power or influence in some field of activity — **bar•ony** \ˈbar-ə-nē\ *n*

♦ czar, king, magnate, mogul, prince, tycoon

bar•on•age \ˈbar-ə-nij\ *n* **:** PEERAGE
bar•on•ess \ˈbar-ə-nəs\ *n* **1 :** the wife or widow of a baron **2 :** a woman holding a baronial title in her own right
bar•on•et \ˈbar-ə-nət\ *n* **:** a man holding a rank of honor below a baron but above a knight — **bar•on•et•cy** \-sē\ *n*
ba•ro•ni•al \bə-ˈrō-nē-əl\ *adj* **1 :** of or relating to a baron or the baronage **2** ♦ **:** generous or more than adequate in size, scope, or capacity **:** STATELY

♦ grand, grandiose, imposing, magnificent, majestic, monumental, stately

ba•roque \bə-ˈrōk, -ˈräk\ *adj* **:** marked by the use of complex forms, bold ornamentation, and the juxtapositioning of contrasting elements
ba•rouche \bə-ˈrüsh\ *n* **:** a 4-wheeled carriage with a high driver's seat in front and a folding top

bar•racks \ˈbar-əks\ *n sing or pl* **:** a building or group of buildings for lodging soldiers
bar•ra•cu•da \ˌbar-ə-ˈkü-də\ *n, pl* **-da** *or* **-das :** any of several large slender predaceous sea fishes including some used for food
bar•rage \bə-ˈräzh, -ˈräj\ *n* **1 :** a heavy concentration of fire (as of artillery) **2** ♦ **:** vigorous or rapid outpouring of many things at once

♦ bombardment, cannonade, fusillade, hail, salvo, shower, storm, volley

barred \ˈbärd\ *adj* **:** marked by or divided off by bars **:** STRIPED
[1]**bar•rel** \ˈbar-əl\ *n* **1** ♦ **:** a round bulging cask with flat ends of equal diameter **2 a :** the amount contained in a barrel **b** ♦ **:** a great quantity **3 :** a drum or cylindrical part ⟨gun ∼⟩ — **barreled** \-əld\ *adj*

♦ [1] cask, hogshead, keg, pipe, puncheon ♦ [2b] abundance, deal, gobs, heap, loads, lot, pile, plenty, quantity, scads

[2]**barrel** *vb* **-reled** *or* **-relled; -rel•ing** *or* **-rel•ling 1 :** to pack in a barrel **2** ♦ **:** to travel at high speed

♦ dash, fly, hurry, hurtle, rush, speed, tear, zip, zoom

bar•rel•head \-ˌhed\ *n* **:** the flat end of a barrel — **on the barrelhead :** asking for or granting no credit ⟨paid cash *on the barrelhead*⟩
barrel roll *n* **:** an airplane maneuver in which a complete revolution about the longitudinal axis is made
[1]**bar•ren** \ˈbar-ən\ *adj* **1** ♦ **:** not producing fruit, spores, or offspring **:** STERILE **2 a :** not productive ⟨a ∼ scheme⟩ **b** ♦ **:** producing little or no vegetation **:** DESOLATE **3 :** lacking interest or charm **4 :** DULL, STUPID — **bar•ren•ness** \-nəs\ *n*

♦ [1] impotent, infertile, sterile ♦ [2b] infertile, poor, stark, unproductive, waste ***Ant*** fertile, fruitful, lush, luxuriant, productive, rich

[2]**barren** *n* ♦ **:** a tract of barren land

♦ desert, desolation, waste, wasteland

bar•rette \bä-ˈret, bə-\ *n* **:** a clasp or bar for holding the hair in place
[1]**bar•ri•cade** \ˈbar-ə-ˌkād, ˌbar-ə-ˈkād\ *vb* **-cad•ed; -cad•ing 1 :** to block, obstruct, or fortify with a barricade **2** ♦ **:** to prevent access to by means of a barricade

♦ besiege, block, cut off, dam, encircle, surround

[2]**barricade** *n* **1 :** a hastily thrown-up obstruction or fortification **2 :** something that impedes progress or achievement **:** BARRIER
bar•ri•er \ˈbar-ē-ər\ *n* ♦ **:** something that separates, demarcates, or serves as a barricade ⟨racial ∼*s*⟩ ⟨traffic ∼*s*⟩

♦ fence, hedge, wall

barrier island *n* **:** a long broad sandy island lying parallel to a shore
barrier reef *n* **:** a coral reef roughly parallel to a shore and separated from it by a lagoon
bar•ring \ˈbär-iŋ\ *prep* ♦ **:** excluding by exception

♦ aside from, bar, besides, but, except, outside (of), save

bar•rio \ˈbär-ē-ˌō, ˈbar-\ *n, pl* **-ri•os 1 :** a district of a city or town in a Spanish-speaking country **2 :** a Spanish-speaking quarter in a U.S. city
bar•ris•ter \ˈbar-ə-stər\ *n* **:** a British counselor admitted to plead in the higher courts
bar•room \ˈbär-ˌrüm, -ˌru̇m\ *n* ♦ **:** a room or establishment whose main feature is a bar for the sale of liquor

♦ bar, café, pub, public house, saloon, tavern

[1]**bar•row** \ˈbar-ō\ *n* **:** a large burial mound of earth and stones
[2]**barrow** *n* **1 :** WHEELBARROW **2 :** a cart with a boxlike body and two shafts for pushing it
Bart *abbr* baronet
bar•tend•er \ˈbär-ˌten-dər\ *n* **:** a person who serves liquor at a bar
[1]**bar•ter** \ˈbär-tər\ *vb* **:** to trade by exchange of goods — **bar•ter•er** *n*
[2]**barter** *n* **1** ♦ **:** the act or practice of carrying on trade by bartering **2 :** the thing given in exchange in bartering

♦ commutation, exchange, swap, trade, truck

Ba•ruch \ˈbär-ˌu̇k, bə-ˈrük\ *n* **:** homiletic book included in the Roman Catholic canon of the Old Testament and in the Protestant Apocrypha
bas•al \ˈbā-səl\ *adj* **1 :** situated at or forming the base **2 :** BASIC
basal metabolism *n* **:** the turnover of energy in a fasting and resting organism using energy solely to maintain vital cellular activ-

ity, respiration, and circulation as measured by the rate at which heat is given off

ba•salt \bə-ˈsȯlt, ˈbā-ˌsȯlt\ *n* **:** a dark fine-grained igneous rock — **ba•sal•tic** \bə-ˈsȯl-tik\ *adj*

¹base \ˈbās\ *n, pl* **bas•es** \ˈbā-səz\ **1 a ♦ :** the lowest part or place **:** BOTTOM **b ♦ :** the physical or philosophical foundation upon which something is based **2 :** a side or face on which a geometrical figure stands; *also* **:** the length of a base **3 ♦ :** a main ingredient or fundamental part **4 :** the point of beginning an act or operation **5 :** a place on which a force depends for supplies **6 :** a number (as 5 in 5^7) that is raised to a power; *esp* **:** a number that when raised to a power equal to the logarithm of a number yields the number itself ⟨the logarithm of 100 to ∼ 10 is 2 since $10^2 = 100$⟩ **7 :** the number of units in a given digit's place of a number system that is required to give the numeral 1 in the next higher place ⟨the decimal system uses a ∼ of 10⟩; *also* **:** such a system using an indicated base ⟨convert from ∼ 10 to ∼ 2⟩ **8 :** any of the four stations at the corners of a baseball diamond **9 :** a chemical compound (as lime or ammonia) that reacts with an acid to form a salt, has a bitter taste, and turns litmus blue — **base•man** \ˈbās-mən\ *n*

♦ [1a] bottom, foot ♦ [1b] basis, bedrock, cornerstone, footing, foundation, ground, groundwork, keystone, underpinning ♦ [3] center (*or* centre), core, cynosure, eye, focus, heart, hub, mecca, nucleus, seat

²base *vb* **based; bas•ing 1 ♦ :** to form or serve as a base for **2 :** ESTABLISH

♦ ground, rest

³base *adj* **1 :** of inferior quality **:** DEBASED, ALLOYED **2 ♦ :** characterized by baseness, lowness, or meanness **:** CONTEMPTIBLE, IGNOBLE **3 :** MENIAL, DEGRADING **4 :** of little value — **base•ly** *adv* — **base•ness** *n*

♦ contemptible, despicable, detestable, dirty, dishonorable (*or* dishonourable), ignoble, low, mean, snide, sordid, vile, wretched

base•ball \ˈbās-ˌbȯl\ *n* **:** a game played with a bat and ball by two teams on a field with four bases arranged in a diamond; *also* **:** the ball used in this game

base•board \-ˌbōrd\ *n* **:** a line of boards or molding covering the joint of a wall and the adjoining floor

base•born \-ˈbȯrn\ *adj* **1 :** MEAN, IGNOBLE **2 :** of humble birth **3 :** of illegitimate birth

base exchange *n* **:** a post exchange at a naval or air force base

base hit *n* **:** a hit in baseball that enables the batter to reach base safely with no error made and no base runner forced out

BASE jumping \ˈbās-\ *n* **:** the activity of parachuting from a high structure or cliff

base•less \-ləs\ *adj* **♦ :** having no base or basis **:** GROUNDLESS

♦ groundless, invalid, unfounded, unreasonable, unsubstantiated, unsupported, unwarranted *Ant* reasonable, reasoned, substantiated, valid, well-founded

base•line \ˈbās-ˌlīn\ *n* **1 :** a line serving as a basis especially to calculate or locate something **2 :** the area within which a baseball player must keep when running between bases

base•ment \-mənt\ *n* **1 :** the part of a building that is wholly or partly below ground level **2 :** the lowest or fundamental part of something

base on balls : an advance to first base awarded a baseball player who during a turn at bat takes four pitches that are balls

base runner *n* **:** a baseball player who is on base or is attempting to reach a base

¹bash \ˈbash\ *vb* **1 ♦ :** to strike violently **:** HIT **2 :** to smash by a blow **3 ♦ :** to attack physically or verbally

♦ [1] bang, collide, crash, hit, ram, slam, smash, strike ♦ [3] bat, batter, beat, hammer, lambaste, pelt, pound, thrash

²bash *n* **1 :** a heavy blow **2 :** a festive social gathering **:** PARTY

bash•ful \ˈbash-fəl\ *adj* **♦ :** inclined to shrink from public attention — **bash•ful•ness** *n*

♦ coy, demure, diffident, introverted, modest, retiring, sheepish, shy

ba•sic \ˈbā-sik\ *adj* **1 ♦ :** of, relating to, or forming the base or essence **:** FUNDAMENTAL **2 :** of, relating to, or having the character of a chemical base — **ba•sic•i•ty** \bā-ˈsi-sə-tē\ *n*

♦ elemental, elementary, essential, fundamental, rudimentary, underlying

BA•SIC \ˈbā-sik\ *n* **:** a simplified language for programming a computer

ba•si•cal•ly \ˈbā-si-k(ə-)lē\ *adv* **1 :** at a basic level **2 ♦ :** for the most part **3 :** in a basic manner

♦ altogether, chiefly, generally, largely, mainly, mostly, overall, predominantly, primarily, principally

ba•sil \ˈbā-zəl, ˈba-, -səl\ *n* **:** any of several mints with fragrant leaves used in cooking

ba•sil•i•ca \bə-ˈsi-li-kə, -ˈzi-\ *n* **1 :** an early Christian church building consisting of nave and aisles with clerestory and apse **2 :** a Roman Catholic church given ceremonial privileges

bas•i•lisk \ˈba-sə-ˌlisk, ˈba-zə-\ *n* **:** a legendary reptile with fatal breath and glance

ba•sin \ˈbās-ᵊn\ *n* **1 :** an open usually circular vessel with sloping sides for holding liquid (as water) **2 :** a hollow or enclosed place containing water; *also* **:** the region drained by a river

ba•sis \ˈbā-səs\ *n, pl* **ba•ses** \-ˌsēz\ **1 :** the lowest part or place **:** FOUNDATION **2 ♦ :** a fundamental principle

♦ base, bedrock, cornerstone, footing, foundation, ground, groundwork, keystone, underpinning

bask \ˈbask\ *vb* **1 ♦ :** to lie or relax in comfortable warmth **2 :** to enjoy something warmly comforting ⟨∼*ing* in his friends' admiration⟩

♦ loll, lounge, relax, repose, rest

bas•ket \ˈbas-kət\ *n* **:** a container made of woven material (as twigs or grasses); *also* **:** any of various lightweight usually wood containers — **bas•ket•ful** *n*

bas•ket•ball \-ˌbȯl\ *n* **:** a game played on a court by two teams who try to throw an inflated ball through a raised goal; *also* **:** the ball used in this game

basket case *n* **1 :** a person who has all four limbs amputated **2 :** a person who is mentally incapacitated or worn out (as from nervous tension)

basket weave *n* **:** a textile weave resembling the checkered pattern of a plaited basket

basmati rice \ˌbäz-ˈmä-tē-\ *n* **:** an aromatic long-grain rice originating in southern Asia

bas mitzvah *var of* BAT MITZVAH

Basque \ˈbask\ *n* **1 :** a member of a people inhabiting a region bordering on the Bay of Biscay in northern Spain and southwestern France **2 :** the language of the Basque people — **Basque** *adj*

bas–re•lief \ˌbä-ri-ˈlēf\ *n* **:** a sculpture in relief with the design raised very slightly from the background

¹bass \ˈbas\ *n, pl* **bass** *or* **bass•es :** any of numerous sport and food bony fishes (as a striped bass)

²bass \ˈbās\ *adj* **♦ :** of low pitch

♦ deep, low, throaty

³bass \ˈbās\ *n* **1 :** a deep sound or tone **2 :** the lower half of the musical pitch range **3 :** the lowest part in a 4-part chorus; *also* **:** a singer having this voice or part

bas•set hound \ˈba-sət-\ *n* **:** any of an old breed of short-legged hunting dogs of French origin having long ears and a short smooth coat

bas•si•net \ˌba-sə-ˈnet\ *n* **:** a baby's bed that resembles a basket and often has a hood over one end

bas•so \ˈba-sō, ˈbä-\ *n, pl* **bassos** *or* **bas•si** \ˈbä-ˌsē\ **:** a bass singer

bas•soon \bə-ˈsün\ *n* **:** a musical wind instrument lower in pitch than the oboe

bass•wood \ˈbas-ˌwu̇d\ *n* **:** any of several New World lindens or their wood

bast \ˈbast\ *n* **:** BAST FIBER

¹bas•tard \ˈbas-tərd\ *n* **1 :** an illegitimate child **2 :** an offensive or disagreeable person

²bastard *adj* **1 :** not recognized as lawful offspring **:** ILLEGITIMATE **2 :** of an inferior or nontypical kind, size, or form; *also* **:** SPURIOUS — **bas•tardy** *n*

bas•tard•ise *Brit var of* BASTARDIZE

bas•tard•ize \ˈbas-tər-ˌdīz\ *vb* **-ized; -iz•ing :** to reduce from a higher to a lower state **:** DEBASE

¹baste \ˈbāst\ *vb* **bast•ed; bast•ing :** to sew with long stitches so as to keep temporarily in place

²baste *vb* **bast•ed; bast•ing :** to moisten (as meat) at intervals with liquid while cooking

bast fiber *n* **:** a strong woody plant fiber obtained chiefly from phloem and used especially in making ropes

bas•ti•na•do \ˌbas-tə-ˈnā-dō, -ˈnä-\ *or* **bas•ti•nade** \ˌbas-tə-ˈnād, -ˈnäd\ *n, pl* **-na•does** *or* **-nades 1 :** a blow or beating especially with a stick **2 :** a punishment consisting of beating the soles of the feet

bas•tion \ˈbas-chən\ *n* **1 :** a projecting part of a fortification **2** ♦ **:** a fortified position

♦ citadel, fastness, fort, fortification, fortress, hold, stronghold

¹bat \ˈbat\ *n* **1** ♦ **:** a stout stick **:** CLUB **2** ♦ **:** a sharp blow **3 :** an implement (as of wood) used to hit a ball (as in baseball) **4 :** a turn at batting — usually used with *at*

♦ [1] billy club, bludgeon, club, cudgel, staff, truncheon ♦ [2] belt, blow, box, clout, hit, punch, slug, wallop, whack

²bat *vb* **bat•ted; bat•ting :** to hit with or as if with a bat
³bat *n* **:** any of an order of night-flying mammals with forelimbs modified to form wings
⁴bat *vb* **bat•ted; bat•ting :** WINK, BLINK
batch \ˈbach\ *n* **1 :** a quantity (as of bread) baked at one time **2 :** a quantity of material for use at one time or produced at one operation **3** ♦ **:** a quantity (as of persons or things) considered as a group

♦ array, assemblage, block, bunch, collection, group, set

bate \ˈbāt\ *vb* **bat•ed; bat•ing :** MODERATE, REDUCE
bath \ˈbath, ˈbȧth\ *n, pl* **baths** \ˈbat͟hz, ˈbaths, ˈbȧt͟hz, ˈbȧths\ **1 :** a washing of the body **2 :** water for washing the body **3 :** a liquid in which objects are immersed so that it can act on them **4 :** a room containing a bathtub or shower and usually a sink and toilet **:** BATHROOM **5 :** a financial loss ⟨took a ∼ in the market⟩
bathe \ˈbāt͟h\ *vb* **bathed; bath•ing 1** ♦ **:** to wash in liquid and especially water; *also* **:** to apply water or a medicated liquid to ⟨*bathed* her eyes⟩ **2 :** to take a bath; *also* **:** to take a swim **3** ♦ **:** to wash along, over, or against so as to wet **4 :** to suffuse with or as if with light — **bath•er** *n*

♦ [1, 3] douse, drench, soak, sop, souse, wash, water, wet

bath•house \ˈbath-ˌhau̇s, ˈbȧth-\ *n* **1 :** a building equipped for bathing **2 :** a building containing dressing rooms for bathers
bathing suit *n* **:** SWIMSUIT
ba•thos \ˈbā-ˌthäs\ *n* **1 :** the sudden appearance of the commonplace in otherwise elevated matter or style **2 :** insincere or overdone pathos — **ba•thet•ic** \bə-ˈthe-tik\ *adj*
bath•robe \ˈbath-ˌrōb, ˈbȧth-\ *n* **:** a loose often absorbent robe worn before and after bathing or as a dressing gown
bath•room \-ˌrüm, -ˌru̇m\ *n* ♦ **:** a room containing a bathtub or shower and usually a sink and toilet

♦ lavatory, toilet

bath•tub \-ˌtəb\ *n* **:** a usually fixed tub for bathing
ba•tik \bə-ˈtēk, ˈba-tik\ *n* **1 :** an Indonesian method of hand-printing textiles by coating with wax the parts not to be dyed; *also* **:** a design so executed **2 :** a fabric printed by batik
ba•tiste \bə-ˈtēst\ *n* **:** a fine sheer fabric of plain weave
bat•man \ˈbat-mən\ *n* **:** an orderly of a British military officer
bat mitz•vah \bät-ˈmits-və\ *also* **bas mitzvah** \bäs-\ *n, often cap B&M* **1 :** a Jewish girl who at about 13 years of age assumes religious responsibilities **2 :** the ceremony recognizing a girl as a bat mitzvah
ba•ton \bə-ˈtän\ *n* **:** STAFF, ROD; *esp* **:** a stick with which the leader directs an orchestra or band
bats•man \ˈbats-mən\ *n* **:** a batter especially in cricket
bat•tal•ion \bə-ˈtal-yən\ *n* **1** ♦ **:** a large body of troops organized to act together **:** ARMY **2 :** a military unit composed of a headquarters and two or more units (as companies)

♦ army, host, legion

¹bat•ten \ˈbat-ᵊn\ *vb* **1 :** to grow or make fat **2 :** THRIVE
²batten *n* **:** a strip of wood used especially to seal or strengthen a joint
³batten *vb* **:** to fasten with battens
¹bat•ter \ˈba-tər\ *vb* ♦ **:** to beat or damage with repeated blows

♦ bash, beat, bludgeon, club, pound, thrash, thump, wallop

²batter *n* **:** a soft mixture (as for cake) basically of flour and liquid
³batter *n* **:** one that bats; *esp* **:** the player whose turn it is to bat
battering ram *n* **1 :** an ancient military machine for battering down walls **2 :** a heavy metal bar with handles used to batter down doors
bat•tery \ˈba-tə-rē\ *n, pl* **-ter•ies 1 :** BEATING; *esp* **:** unlawful beating or use of force on a person **2 :** a grouping of artillery pieces for tactical purposes; *also* **:** the guns of a warship **3 :** a group of electric cells for furnishing electric current; *also* **:** a single electric cell ⟨a flashlight ∼⟩ **4 :** a number of similar items grouped or used as a unit ⟨a ∼ of tests⟩ **5 :** the pitcher and catcher of a baseball team
bat•ting \ˈba-tiŋ\ *n* **:** layers or sheets of cotton or wool (as for lining quilts)

¹bat•tle \ˈbat-ᵊl\ *n* **1 :** a general military engagement **2** ♦ **:** an extended contest, struggle, or controversy

♦ fight, fray, scrabble, struggle ♦ combat, conflict, confrontation, contest, duel, rivalry, struggle, tug-of-war, warfare

²battle *vb* **bat•tled; bat•tling 1** ♦ **:** to engage in battle **:** FIGHT **2** ♦ **:** to contend with full strength, vigor, skill, or resources

♦ [1] clash, combat, fight, scrimmage, skirmish, war ♦ [2] combat, contend, counter, fight, oppose

bat•tle–ax \ˈbat-ᵊl-ˌaks\ *n* **1 :** a long-handled ax formerly used as a weapon **2 :** a quarrelsome domineering woman
battle fatigue *n* **:** COMBAT FATIGUE
bat•tle•field \ˈbat-ᵊl-ˌfēld\ *n* **:** a place where a battle is fought
bat•tle•ment \-mənt\ *n* **:** a decorative or defensive parapet on top of a wall
bat•tle•ship \-ˌship\ *n* **:** a warship of the most heavily armed and armored class
bat•tle•wag•on \-ˌwa-gən\ *n* **:** BATTLESHIP
bat•ty \ˈba-tē\ *adj* **bat•ti•er; -est :** disordered in mind **:** CRAZY
bau•ble \ˈbȯ-bəl\ *n* ♦ **:** a small ornament (as a jewel or ring) **:** TRINKET

♦ curiosity, gewgaw, knickknack, novelty, trinket

baud \ˈbȯd, *Brit* ˈbōd\ *n, pl* **baud** *also* **bauds :** a unit of data transmission speed
baux•ite \ˈbȯk-ˌsīt\ *n* **:** a clayey mixture that is the chief ore of aluminum
bawd \ˈbȯd\ *n* **1 :** MADAM 2 **2 :** PROSTITUTE
bawd•i•ness \-dē-nəs\ *n* ♦ **:** the quality or state of being bawdy ⟨his ribaldry and ∼⟩

♦ coarseness, indecency, lewdness, nastiness, obscenity, ribaldry, smut, vulgarity

bawdy \ˈbȯ-dē\ *adj* **bawd•i•er; -est** ♦ **:** offensive to morality or virtue **:** LEWD — **bawd•i•ly** \ˈbȯd-ᵊl-ē\ *adv*

♦ coarse, crude, indecent, obscene, smutty, unprintable, vulgar ♦ lewd, racy, ribald, risqué, spicy, suggestive

¹bawl \ˈbȯl\ *vb* ♦ **:** to cry or cry out loudly; *also* **:** to scold harshly

♦ blubber, cry, sob, weep ♦ call, cry, holler, shout, vociferate, yell

²bawl *n* **:** a long loud cry **:** BELLOW
bawl out *vb* ♦ **:** to reprimand loudly or severely

♦ admonish, chide, lecture, rail (at *or* against), rate, rebuke, reprimand, scold

¹bay \ˈbā\ *adj* **:** reddish brown
²bay *n* **1 :** a bay-colored animal **2 :** a reddish brown color
³bay *n* **1 :** a section or compartment of a building or vehicle **2 :** a compartment projecting outward from the wall of a building and containing a window (**bay window**)
⁴bay *vb* ♦ **:** to bark with deep long tones

♦ howl, keen, wail, yowl

⁵bay *n* **1 :** the position of one unable to escape and forced to face danger **2 :** a baying of dogs
⁶bay *n* ♦ **:** an inlet of a body of water (as the sea) usually smaller than a gulf

♦ bight, cove, estuary, firth, fjord, gulf, inlet

⁷bay *n* **:** the European laurel; *also* **:** a shrub or tree resembling this
bay•ber•ry \ˈbā-ˌber-ē\ *n* **:** a hardy deciduous shrub of coastal eastern No. America bearing small hard berries coated with a white wax used for candles; *also* **:** its fruit
bay leaf *n* **:** the dried leaf of the European laurel used in cooking
¹bay•o•net \ˈbā-ə-nət, ˌbā-ə-ˈnet\ *n* **:** a daggerlike weapon made to fit on the muzzle end of a rifle
²bayonet *vb* **-net•ed** *also* **-net•ted; -net•ing** *also* **-net•ting :** to use or stab with a bayonet
bay•ou \ˈbī-yü, -ō\ *n* **:** a marshy or sluggish body of water
bay rum *n* **:** a fragrant liquid used especially as a cologne or after-shave lotion
ba•zaar \bə-ˈzär\ *n* **1 :** a group of shops **:** MARKETPLACE **2 :** a fair for the sale of articles usually for charity
ba•zoo•ka \bə-ˈzü-kə\ *n* **:** a weapon consisting of a tube and launching an explosive rocket able to pierce armor
¹BB \ˈbē-(ˌ)bē\ *n* **:** a small round shot pellet
²BB *abbr* base on balls
BBB *abbr* Better Business Bureau
BBC *abbr* British Broadcasting Corporation
bbl *abbr* barrel; barrels

BC *abbr* **1** before Christ — often printed in small capitals and often punctuated **2** British Columbia
B cell *n* **:** any of the lymphocytes that secrete antibodies when mature
B complex *n* **:** VITAMIN B COMPLEX
bd *abbr* **1** board **2** bound
bdl *or* **bdle** *abbr* bundle
bdrm *abbr* bedroom
be \ˈbē\ *vb, past 1st & 3d sing* **was** \ˈwəz, ˈwäz\; *2d sing* **were** \ˈwər\; *pl* **were;** *past subjunctive* **were;** *past part* **been** \ˈbin\; *pres part* **be•ing** \ˈbe-iŋ\; *pres 1st sing* **am** \əm, ˈam\; *2d sing* **are** \ər, ˈär\; *3d sing* **is** \ˈiz, əz\; *pl* **are;** *pres subjunctive* **be** **1 :** to equal in meaning or symbolically ⟨God *is* love⟩; *also* **:** to have a specified qualification or relationship ⟨leaves *are* green⟩ ⟨this fish *is* a trout⟩ **2 a** ♦ **:** to have objective existence ⟨I think, therefore I *am*⟩ **b** ♦ **:** to have or occupy a particular place ⟨here *is* your pen⟩ **3 :** to take place **:** OCCUR ⟨the meeting *is* tonight⟩ **4** — used with the past participle of transitive verbs as a passive voice auxiliary ⟨the door *was* opened⟩ **5** — used as the auxiliary of the present participle in expressing continuous action ⟨he *is* sleeping⟩ **6** — used as an auxiliary with the past participle of some intransitive verbs to form archaic perfect tenses **7** — used as an auxiliary with *to* and the infinitive to express futurity, prearrangement, or obligation ⟨you *are* to come when called⟩

♦ [2a] breathe, exist, live, subsist ***Ant*** depart, die, expire, pass away, perish, succumb ♦ [2b] lie, sit, stand

Be *symbol* beryllium
¹beach \ˈbēch\ *n* **:** a sandy or gravelly part of the shore of an ocean or lake
²beach *vb* **:** to run or drive ashore
beach buggy *n* **:** DUNE BUGGY
beach•comb•er \ˈbēch-ˌkō-mər\ *n* **:** a person who searches along a shore for something of use or value
beach•head \ˈbēch-ˌhed\ *n* **:** a small area on an enemy-held shore occupied in the initial stages of an invasion
bea•con \ˈbē-kən\ *n* **1 :** a signal fire **2 :** a guiding or warning signal (as a lighthouse) **3 :** a radio transmitter emitting signals for guidance of aircraft
¹bead \ˈbēd\ *n* **1** *pl* **:** a series of prayers and meditations made with a rosary **2 :** a small piece of material pierced for threading on a line (as in a rosary) **3 :** a small globular body **4 :** a narrow projecting rim or band — **bead•ing** *n* — **beady** *adj*
²bead *vb* **:** to form into a bead
bea•dle \ˈbēd-ᵊl\ *n* **:** a usually English parish officer whose duties include keeping order in church
bea•gle \ˈbē-gəl\ *n* **:** a small short-legged smooth-coated hound
beak \ˈbēk\ *n* **:** the bill of a bird and especially of a bird of prey; *also* **:** a pointed projecting part — **beaked** \ˈbēkt\ *adj*
bea•ker \ˈbē-kər\ *n* **1 :** a large widemouthed drinking cup **2 :** a widemouthed thin-walled laboratory vessel
¹beam \ˈbēm\ *n* **1 :** a large long piece of timber or metal **2 :** the bar of a balance from which the scales hang **3 :** the breadth of a ship at its widest part **4 :** a ray or shaft of light **5 :** a collection of nearly parallel rays (as X-rays) or particles (as electrons) **6 :** a constant radio signal transmitted for the guidance of pilots; *also* **:** the course indicated by this signal
²beam *vb* **1 :** to send out light **2 :** to aim (a broadcast) by directional antennas **3 :** to smile with joy
beam•ing *adj* **1** ♦ **:** marked by, emitting, or reflecting strong or clear rays of light **2** ♦ **:** marked by or expressive of extreme and unreserved joy, happiness, or satisfaction

♦ [1] bright, brilliant, incandescent, luminous, shiny ♦ [2] aglow, glowing, radiant, sunny

¹bean \ˈbēn\ *n* **:** the edible seed borne in pods by some leguminous plants; *also* **:** a plant or a pod bearing these
²bean *vb* **:** to strike on the head with an object
bean•bag \ˈbēn-ˌbag\ *n* **:** a cloth bag partially filled typically with dried beans and used as a toy
bean•ball \ˈbēn-ˌbȯl\ *n* **:** a pitch thrown at a batter's head
bean curd *n* **:** TOFU
bean•ie \ˈbē-nē\ *n* **:** a small round tight-fitting skullcap
beano \ˈbē-nō\ *n, pl* **beanos :** BINGO
¹bear \ˈbar\ *n, pl* **bears** **1** *or pl* **bear :** any of a family of large heavy mammals with shaggy hair and small tails **2** ♦ **:** a gruff or sullen person **3 :** one who sells (as securities) in expectation of a price decline

♦ complainer, crab, crank, curmudgeon, grouch, grumbler, whiner

²bear *vb* **bore** \ˈbōr\; **borne** \ˈbōrn\ *also* **born** \ˈbȯrn\; **bear•ing** **1** ♦ **:** to move while supporting **:** CARRY **2 :** to be equipped with **3 :** to give as testimony ⟨∼ witness to the facts of the case⟩ **4 :** to give birth to; *also* **:** PRODUCE, YIELD ⟨a tree that ∼*s* regularly⟩ **5 a** ♦ **:** to support (as a weight or structure) ⟨*bore* the weight on piles⟩ **b** ♦ **:** to accept or allow oneself to be subject to **:** take on or endure ⟨∼ pain⟩ **6 :** to go in an indicated direction ⟨∼ to the right⟩ **7 :** to manage the actions of (oneself) in a particular way **:** CONDUCT **8** ♦ **:** to hold in the mind or emotions **9 :** to exert pressure or influence **10** ♦ **:** to have relevance or a valid connection **:** PERTAIN — often used with *on* or *upon* ⟨facts ∼*ing* on the question⟩ — **bear•er** *n*

♦ [1] carry, cart, convey, ferry, haul, lug, pack, tote, transport ♦ [5a] bolster, brace, buttress, carry, prop, shore, stay, support, uphold ♦ [5b] accept, assume, shoulder, take over, undertake ♦ [5b] abide, brook, countenance, endure, meet, stand, stick out, stomach, support, sustain, take, tolerate ♦ [8] cherish, entertain, harbor (*or* harbour), have, hold, nurse ♦ *usu* **bear on** [10] appertain, apply, pertain, refer, relate

bear•able *adj* ♦ **:** capable of being borne

♦ endurable, sufferable, supportable, sustainable, tolerable ***Ant*** insufferable, insupportable, intolerable, unbearable, unendurable, unsupportable

¹beard \ˈbird\ *n* **1 :** the hair that grows on the face of a man **2 :** a growth of bristly hairs (as on a goat's chin) — **beard•ed** \ˈbir-dəd\ *adj* — **beard•less** *adj*
²beard *vb* ♦ **:** to confront boldly

♦ brave, brazen, confront, dare, defy, face

bear down *vb* **:** to exert full strength and concentrated attention — **bear down on** ♦ **:** to weigh heavily on

♦ *usu* **bear down on** depress, press, shove, weigh

bear•ing \ˈbar-iŋ\ *n* **1** ♦ **:** manner of carrying oneself **:** COMPORTMENT **2 :** a supporting object, purpose, or point **3 :** a machine part in which another part (as an axle or pin) turns **4 :** an emblem in a coat of arms **5 :** the position or direction of one point with respect to another or to the compass; *also* **:** a determination of position **6** *pl* **:** comprehension of one's situation **7** ♦ **:** connection with or influence on something; *also* **:** SIGNIFICANCE

♦ [1] actions, behavior (*or* behaviour), comportment, conduct, demeanor (*or* demeanour), deportment ♦ [7] applicability, pertinence, relevance, significance ♦ [7] association, connection, linkage, relation, relationship

bear•ish *adj* **1** ♦ **:** resembling a bear in build or in roughness, gruffness, or surliness ⟨a ∼ man⟩ **2 :** marked by, tending to cause, or fearful of falling prices (as in a stock market)

♦ bilious, cantankerous, disagreeable, dyspeptic, ill-humored, ill-tempered, ornery, splenetic, surly

bear market *n* **:** a market in which securities or commodities are persistently falling in value
bear out *vb* ♦ **:** to give new assurance of the validity of **:** CONFIRM, SUBSTANTIATE ⟨a theory *borne out* by data⟩

♦ confirm, corroborate, substantiate, support, validate, verify, vindicate

bear•skin \ˈbar-ˌskin\ *n* **:** an article made of the skin of a bear
beast \ˈbēst\ *n* **1** ♦ **:** any of a kingdom of living things typically differing from plants in capacity for active movement, in rapid response to stimulation, and in lack of cellulose cell walls **:** ANIMAL; *esp* **:** a 4-footed mammal **2** ♦ **:** a contemptible person

♦ [1] animal, creature, critter ♦ [2] brute, devil, fiend, monster, savage, villain

¹beast•ly \ˈbēst-lē\ *adj* **beast•li•er; -est** **1 :** BESTIAL **2 :** ABOMINABLE, DISAGREEABLE — **beast•li•ness** \-nəs\ *n*
²beastly *adv* **:** to a high degree **:** VERY, EXCEEDINGLY
¹beat \ˈbēt\ *vb* **beat; beat•en** \ˈbēt-ᵊn\ *or* **beat; beat•ing** **1** ♦ **:** to strike repeatedly **2 :** TREAD **3** ♦ **:** to affect or alter by beating ⟨∼ metal into sheets⟩ **4 :** to sound (as an alarm) on a drum **5 a** ♦ **:** to get the better of **:** OVERCOME **b** ♦ **:** to become better, greater, or stronger than **:** SURPASS **6 :** to act or arrive before ⟨∼ his brother home⟩ **7 :** to beat or vibrate rhythmically **:** THROB **8 :** to flap or thrash at vigorously **9 :** to glare or strike with oppressive intensity ⟨the sun ∼ down on the caravan⟩

♦ [1] bash, bat, batter, club, drub, pound, thrash, thump, wallop, whale, whip ♦ [3] forge, hammer, pound ♦ [5a] best, conquer, crush, defeat, lick, overcome, prevail, rout, skunk, subdue, thrash, triumph, trounce, wallop, whip ***Ant*** lose (to) ♦ [5b] better, eclipse, excel, outdistance, outdo, outshine, outstrip, surpass, top, transcend

²beat *n* **1 a :** a single stroke or blow especially of a series **b** ♦ **:** a rhythmic throbbing, contraction and expansion, or vibration

: PULSATION **2** ♦ **:** a rhythmic stress in poetry or music or the rhythmic effect of these **3 :** a regularly traversed course

♦ [1b] palpitation, pulsation, pulse, throb ♦ [2] cadence, measure, meter (*or* metre), rhythm

³beat *adj* **1** ♦ **:** consumed entirely **:** EXHAUSTED **2 :** of or relating to beatniks

♦ bushed, dead, drained, exhausted, prostrate, spent, weary, worn-out

⁴beat *n* **:** BEATNIK
beat•er *n* **:** one that beats
be•atif•ic \ˌbē-ə-ˈti-fik\ *adj* **:** giving or indicative of great joy or bliss
be•at•i•fy \bē-ˈa-tə-ˌfī\ *vb* **-fied; -fy•ing** **1 :** to make supremely happy **2 :** to declare to have attained the blessedness of heaven and authorize the title "Blessed" for — **be•at•i•fi•ca•tion** \-ˌa-tə-fə-ˈkā-shən\ *n*
be•at•i•tude \bē-ˈa-tə-ˌtüd, -ˌtyüd\ *n* **1 :** a state of utmost bliss **2 :** any of the declarations made in the Sermon on the Mount (Mt 5:3–12) beginning "Blessed are"
beat•nik \ˈbēt-nik\ *n* **:** a person who rejects the mores of established society and indulges in exotic philosophizing and self-expression
beau \ˈbō\ *n, pl* **beaux** \ˈbōz\ *or* **beaus** **1 :** a man of fashion **:** DANDY **2** ♦ **:** one who courts a woman or seeks to marry her

♦ boyfriend, fellow, man, swain

beau geste \bō-ˈzhest\ *n, pl* **beaux gestes** *or* **beau gestes** \bō-ˈzhest\ **:** a graceful or magnanimous gesture
beau ide•al \ˌbō-ī-ˈdē(-ə)l\ *n, pl* **beau ideals** ♦ **:** the perfect type or model

♦ classic, epitome, exemplar, ideal, model, nonpareil, paragon, perfection, quintessence

Beau•jo•lais \ˌbō-zhō-ˈlā\ *n* **:** a French red table wine
beau monde \bō-ˈmänd, -ˈmōⁿd\ *n, pl* **beau mondes** \-ˈmänz, -ˈmändz\ *or* **beaux mondes** \bō-ˈmōⁿd\ **:** the world of high society and fashion
beau•te•ous \ˈbyü-tē-əs\ *adj* **:** having beauty **:** BEAUTIFUL — **beau•te•ous•ly** *adv*
beau•ti•cian \byü-ˈti-shən\ *n* **:** COSMETOLOGIST
beau•ti•ful \ˈbyü-ti-fəl\ *adj* ♦ **:** characterized by beauty **:** LOVELY — **beau•ti•ful•ly** \-f(ə-)lē\ *adv*

♦ attractive, cute, fair, gorgeous, handsome, knockout, lovely, pretty, ravishing, stunning ***Ant*** homely, plain, ugly, unattractive, unhandsome, unlovely

beau•ti•ful•ness \ˈbyü-ti-fəl-nəs\ *n* ♦ **:** the quality or state of being beautiful
beautiful people *n pl, often cap B&P* **:** wealthy or famous people whose lifestyle is usually expensive and well-publicized
beau•ti•fy \ˈbyü-tə-ˌfī\ *vb* **-fied; -fy•ing** ♦ **:** to make more beautiful — **beau•ti•fi•ca•tion** \ˌbyü-tə-fə-ˈkā-shən\ *n* — **beau•ti•fi•er** *n*

♦ adorn, bedeck, deck, decorate, embellish, enrich, garnish, grace, ornament, trim

beau•ty \ˈbyü-tē\ *n, pl* **beauties** **1** ♦ **:** qualities that give pleasure to the senses or exalt the mind **:** LOVELINESS **2** ♦ **:** a beautiful person or thing; *esp* **:** a beautiful woman **3** ♦ **:** an extreme or egregious example or instance

♦ [1] attractiveness, comeliness, handsomeness, looks, loveliness, prettiness ***Ant*** homeliness, plainness, ugliness ♦ [2] enchantress, fox, goddess, knockout, queen ♦ [3] crackerjack, dandy, jim-dandy, knockout, pip

beauty shop *n* **:** an establishment where hairdressing, facials, and manicures are done
beaux arts \bō-ˈzär\ *n pl* **:** FINE ARTS
bea•ver \ˈbē-vər\ *n, pl* **beavers** **:** a large fur-bearing herbivorous rodent that builds dams and underwater houses of mud and sticks; *also* **:** its fur
be•calm \bi-ˈkäm, -ˈkälm\ *vb* **:** to keep (as a ship) motionless by lack of wind
be•cause \bi-ˈkȯz, -ˈkəz\ *conj* ♦ **:** for the reason that

♦ for, now, since, whereas

because of *prep* ♦ **:** by reason of

♦ due to, owing to, through, with

beck \ˈbek\ *n* **:** a beckoning gesture; *also* **:** SUMMONS
beck•on \ˈbe-kən\ *vb* **:** to summon or signal especially by a nod or gesture; *also* **:** ATTRACT
be•cloud \bi-ˈklau̇d\ *vb* ♦ **:** to prevent clear perception or realization of

♦ befog, blur, cloud, darken, dim, fog, haze, mist, obscure, overcast, overshadow, shroud

be•come \bi-ˈkəm\ *vb* **-came** \-ˈkām\; **-come; -com•ing** **1** ♦ **:** to come to be ⟨~ tired⟩ **2 :** to suit or be suitable to ⟨her dress ~*s* her⟩

♦ come, get, go, grow, run, turn, wax

be•com•ing *adj* **:** adapted to a use or purpose **:** SUITABLE, FIT; *also* **:** ATTRACTIVE — **be•com•ing•ly** *adv*
¹bed \ˈbed\ *n* **1** ♦ **:** an article of furniture to sleep on **2 :** a plot of ground prepared for plants **3 :** an underlying base or support **:** BOTTOM **4 :** LAYER, STRATUM

♦ bunk, pad, sack

²bed *vb* **bed•ded; bed•ding** **1 :** to put or go to bed **2 :** to fix in a foundation **:** EMBED **3 :** to plant in beds **4 :** to lay or lie flat or in layers
bed–and–breakfast *n* **:** an establishment offering lodging and breakfast
be•daub \bi-ˈdȯb\ *vb* **:** to spread or daub over a surface **:** SMEAR
be•daz•zle \bi-ˈda-zəl\ *vb* **:** to confuse by or as if by a strong light; *also* **:** FASCINATE — **be•daz•zle•ment** *n*
bed•bug \ˈbed-ˌbəg\ *n* **:** a wingless bloodsucking bug infesting houses and especially beds
bed•clothes \ˈbed-ˌklōthz\ *n pl* **:** BEDDING 1
bed•ding \ˈbe-diŋ\ *n* **1 :** materials for making up a bed **2 :** FOUNDATION
be•deck \bi-ˈdek\ *vb* ♦ **:** to furnish with something ornamental **:** ADORN

♦ adorn, array, beautify, deck, decorate, do, dress, embellish, enrich, garnish, grace, ornament, trim

be•dev•il \bi-ˈde-vəl\ *vb* **1** ♦ **:** to cause distress **:** TORMENT **2 :** CONFUSE, MUDDLE

♦ afflict, agonize, curse, harrow, martyr, persecute, plague, rack, torment, torture

be•dew \bi-ˈdü, -ˈdyü\ *vb* **:** to wet with or as if with dew
bed•fast \ˈbed-ˌfast\ *adj* **:** BEDRIDDEN
bed•fel•low \-ˌfe-lō\ *n* **1 :** one sharing the bed of another **2 :** a close associate **:** ALLY
be•di•zen \bi-ˈdīz-ᵊn, -ˈdiz-\ *vb* **:** to dress or adorn with showy or vulgar finery
bed•lam \ˈbed-ləm\ *n* **1** *often cap* **:** an insane asylum **2** ♦ **:** a scene of uproar and confusion

♦ circus, hell, madhouse

bed•ou•in *or* **bed•u•in** \ˈbe-də-wən\ *n, pl* **bedouin** *or* **bedouins** *or* **beduin** *or* **beduins** *often cap* **:** a nomadic Arab of the Arabian, Syrian, or No. African deserts
bed•pan \ˈbed-ˌpan\ *n* **:** a shallow vessel used by a bedridden person for urination or defecation
bed•post \-ˌpōst\ *n* **:** the post of a bed
be•drag•gled \bi-ˈdra-gəld\ *adj* **:** soiled and disordered as if by being drenched
bed•rid•den \ˈbed-ˌrid-ᵊn\ *adj* **:** kept in bed by illness or weakness
¹bed•rock \-ˈräk\ *n* **1 :** the solid rock underlying surface materials (as soil) **2** ♦ **:** the bottom of something considered as its foundation

♦ base, basis, cornerstone, footing, foundation, ground, groundwork, keystone, underpinning

²bedrock *adj* **:** solidly fundamental, basic, or reliable ⟨traditional ~ values⟩
bed•roll \ˈbed-ˌrōl\ *n* **:** bedding rolled up for carrying
bed•room \-ˌrüm, -ˌru̇m\ *n* **:** a room containing a bed and used especially for sleeping
bed•side \-ˌsīd\ *n* **:** the place beside a bed especially of a sick or dying person
bed•sore \-ˌsōr\ *n* **:** an ulceration of tissue deprived of adequate blood supply by prolonged pressure
bed•spread \-ˌspred\ *n* ♦ **:** a usually ornamental cloth cover for a bed

♦ counterpane, spread

bed•stead \-ˌsted\ *n* **:** the framework of a bed
bed•time \-ˌtīm\ *n* **:** time for going to bed
bed–wet•ting \-ˌwe-tiŋ\ *n* **:** involuntary discharge of urine especially in bed during sleep — **bed–wet•ter** *n*
¹bee \ˈbē\ *n* **:** any of numerous 4-winged insects (as honeybees or

bumblebees) that feed on nectar and pollen and that sometimes produce honey or have a painful sting

²**bee** *n* : a gathering of people for a specific purpose ⟨quilting ~⟩

beech \ˈbēch\ *n, pl* **beech•es** *or* **beech** : any of a genus of deciduous hardwood trees with smooth gray bark and small sweet triangular nuts; *also* : the wood of a beech — **beech•en** \ˈbē-chən\ *adj*

beech•nut \ˈbēch-ˌnət\ *n* : the nut of a beech

¹**beef** \ˈbēf\ *n, pl* **beefs** \ˈbēfs\ *or* **beeves** \ˈbēvz\ **1** : the flesh of a steer, cow, or bull; *also* : the dressed carcass of a beef animal **2** : a steer, cow, or bull especially when fattened for food **3** : MUSCLE, BRAWN **4** *pl beefs* ♦ : expression of grief, pain, or dissatisfaction : COMPLAINT

♦ complaint, fuss, grievance, gripe, grumble, murmur, plaint, squawk

²**beef** *vb* **1** ♦ : to increase or add substance, strength, or power to : STRENGTHEN — usually used with *up* **2** ♦ : to express grief, pain, or discontent : COMPLAIN

♦ *usu* **beef up** [1] fortify, harden, strengthen, toughen ♦ *usu* **beef up** [1] amplify, boost, consolidate, deepen, enhance, heighten, intensify, magnify, redouble, step up ♦ [2] bellyache, carp, complain, crab, gripe, grouse, growl, grumble, kick, moan, squawk, wail, whine

beef•eat•er \ˈbē-ˌfē-tər\ *n* : a yeoman of the guard of an English monarch

beef•steak \-ˌstāk\ *n* : a slice of beef suitable for broiling or frying

beefy \ˈbē-fē\ *adj* **beef•i•er; -est** ♦ : heavily and powerfully built : BRAWNY

♦ brawny, burly, husky

bee•hive \ˈbē-ˌhīv\ *n* : HIVE 1, 3

bee•keep•er \-ˌkē-pər\ *n* : a person who raises bees — **bee•keep•ing** *n*

bee•line \-ˌlīn\ *n* : a straight direct course

been *past part of* BE

beep•er \ˈbē-pər\ *n* : a small radio receiver that beeps when signaled to alert the person carrying it

beer \ˈbir\ *n* : an alcoholic beverage brewed from malt and hops — **beery** *adj*

bees•wax \ˈbēz-ˌwaks\ *n* : WAX 1

beet \ˈbēt\ *n* : a garden plant with edible leaves and a thick sweet root used as a vegetable, as a source of sugar, or as forage; *also* : its root

¹**bee•tle** \ˈbēt-ᵊl\ *n* : any of an order of insects having four wings of which the stiff outer pair covers the membranous inner pair when not in flight

²**beetle** *vb* **bee•tled; bee•tling** ♦ : to jut out : PROJECT

♦ bulge, overhang, poke, project, protrude, stick out

be•fall \bi-ˈfȯl\ *vb* **-fell** \-ˈfel\; **-fall•en** \-ˈfȯ-lən\ ♦ : to happen to : OCCUR

♦ be, betide, chance, come, go, happen, occur, pass, transpire

be•fit \bi-ˈfit\ *vb* ♦ : to be suitable to

♦ do, fit, go, serve, suit

be•fog \bi-ˈfȯg, -ˈfäg\ *vb* **1** ♦ : to make dark, dim, or indistinct : OBSCURE **2** ♦ : to make mentally unclear or uncertain : CONFUSE

♦ [1] becloud, blur, cloud, darken, dim, fog, haze, mist, obscure, overcast, overshadow, shroud ♦ [2] addle, baffle, befuddle, bemuse, bewilder, confound, confuse, disorient, muddle, muddy, mystify, perplex, puzzle

¹**be•fore** \bi-ˈfōr\ *adv or adj* **1** : in front **2** ♦ : at an earlier time : PREVIOUSLY

♦ ahead, beforehand, previously

²**before** *prep* **1** : in front of ⟨stood ~ him⟩ **2** ♦ : earlier than ⟨got there ~ me⟩ **3** : in a more important category than ⟨put quality ~ quantity⟩

♦ ahead of, ere, of, previous to, prior to, to *Ant* after, following

³**before** *conj* **1** : earlier than the time that ⟨he got here ~ I did⟩ **2** : more willingly than ⟨she'd starve ~ she'd steal⟩

be•fore•hand \bi-ˈfōr-ˌhand\ *adv or adj* ♦ : in advance

♦ ahead, before, early, previously

be•foul \bi-ˈfau̇l\ *vb* ♦ : to make foul (as with dirt or waste)

♦ begrime, besmirch, blacken, dirty, muddy, smirch, soil, stain ♦ contaminate, defile, foul, poison, pollute, taint

be•friend \bi-ˈfrend\ *vb* : to act as friend to

be•fud•dle \bi-ˈfəd-ᵊl\ *vb* ♦ : to muddle or stupefy with or as if with drink : CONFUSE

♦ addle, baffle, befog, bemuse, bewilder, confound, confuse, disorient, muddle, muddy, mystify, perplex, puzzle

beg \ˈbeg\ *vb* **begged; beg•ging** **1** ♦ : to ask as a charity; *also* : ENTREAT **2** : EVADE; *also* : assume as established, settled, or proved ⟨~ the question⟩

♦ appeal, beseech, entreat, implore, importune, petition, plead, pray, solicit, supplicate

be•get \bi-ˈget\ *vb* **-got** \-ˈgät\; **-got•ten** \-ˈgät-ᵊn\ *or* **-got; -get•ting** ♦ : to become the father of : SIRE

♦ father, get, produce, sire

¹**beg•gar** \ˈbe-gər\ *n* : one that begs; *esp* : a person who begs as a way of life

²**beggar** *vb* : IMPOVERISH

beg•gar•ly \ˈbe-gər-lē\ *adj* **1** : contemptibly mean or inadequate **2** : marked by unrelieved poverty ⟨a ~ life⟩

beg•gary \ˈbe-gə-rē\ *n* ♦ : extreme poverty

♦ destitution, impecuniousness, impoverishment, indigence, need, pauperism, penury, poverty, want

be•gin \bi-ˈgin\ *vb* **be•gan** \-ˈgan\; **be•gun** \-ˈgən\; **be•gin•ning** **1** ♦ : to do the first part of an action : COMMENCE **2** ♦ : to come into being : ARISE; *also* : FOUND **3** : ORIGINATE, INVENT

♦ [1] commence, embark (on *or* upon), enter, get off, launch, open, start, strike *Ant* conclude, end, finish, terminate ♦ [2] arise, commence, dawn, form, found, materialize, originate, spring, start *Ant* cease, end, stop

be•gin•ner *n* ♦ : one that begins something; *esp* : an inexperienced person

♦ fledgling, freshman, greenhorn, neophyte, newcomer, novice, recruit, rookie, tenderfoot, tyro *Ant* old-timer, vet, veteran

be•gin•ning \bi-ˈgi-niŋ, bē-\ *n* ♦ : the point at which something starts : START

♦ birth, commencement, dawn, genesis, launch, morning, onset, outset, start, threshold *Ant* close, conclusion, end, ending

beg off *vb* : to ask to be excused from something

be•gone \bi-ˈgȯn\ *vb* : to go away : DEPART — used especially in the imperative

be•go•nia \bi-ˈgōn-yə\ *n* : any of a genus of tropical herbs widely grown for their showy leaves and waxy flowers

be•grime \bi-ˈgrīm\ *vb* **be•grimed; be•grim•ing** ♦ : to make dirty

♦ befoul, besmirch, blacken, dirty, foul, grime, mire, muddy, smirch, soil, stain

be•grudge \bi-ˈgrəj\ *vb* **1** : to give or concede reluctantly **2** : to be reluctant to grant or allow

be•guile \-ˈgīl\ *vb* **be•guiled; be•guil•ing** **1** ♦ : to lead by deception **2** : to while away **3** ♦ : to engage the interest of by guile

♦ [1] deceive, dupe, fool, hoax, misinform, mislead, take in, trick ♦ [1] decoy, entice, lead on, lure, seduce, tempt ♦ [3] bewitch, captivate, charm, enchant, fascinate, wile

be•guine \bi-ˈgēn\ *n* : a vigorous popular dance of the islands of Saint Lucia and Martinique

be•gum \ˈbā-gəm, ˈbē-\ *n* : a Muslim woman of high rank

be•half \bi-ˈhaf, -ˈhȧf\ *n* : BENEFIT, SUPPORT, DEFENSE

be•have \bi-ˈhāv\ *vb* **be•haved; be•hav•ing** **1** ♦ : to bear, comport, or conduct oneself in a particular and especially a proper way **2** : to act, function, or react in a particular way

♦ acquit, bear, comport, conduct, demean, deport, quit

be•hav•ior \bi-ˈhā-vyər\ *or Can and Brit* **be•hav•iour** *n* ♦ : way of behaving; *esp* : personal conduct — **be•hav•ior•al** \-vyə-rəl\ *adj*

♦ actions, bearing, comportment, conduct, demeanor (*or* demeanour), deportment

be•hav•ior•ism *or Can and Brit* **be•hav•iour•ism** \bi-ˈhā-vyə-ˌri-zəm\ *n* : a school of psychology concerned with the objective evidence of behavior without reference to conscious experience

be•head \bi-ˈhed\ *vb* : to remove the head from

be•he•moth \bi-ˈhē-məth, ˈbē-ə-ˌmäth\ *n* **1** : a huge powerful animal described in Job 40:15–24 **2** ♦ : something of monstrous size or power

♦ blockbuster, colossus, giant, jumbo, leviathan, mammoth, monster, titan, whale, whopper

be•hest \bi-ˈhest\ *n* **1** ♦ **:** an authoritative order **:** COMMAND **2 :** an urgent prompting

♦ charge, command, commandment, decree, dictate, direction, directive, edict, instruction, order, word

¹be•hind \bi-ˈhīnd\ *adv or adj* **1 :** BACK, BACKWARD ⟨look ~⟩ **2** ♦ **:** later in time **:** LATE

♦ belated, delinquent, late, overdue, tardy

²behind *prep* **1 :** in or to a place or situation in back of or to the rear of ⟨look ~ you⟩ ⟨the staff stayed ~ the troops⟩ **2 :** inferior to (as in rank) **:** BELOW ⟨three games ~ the first-place team⟩ **3 :** in support of **:** SUPPORTING ⟨we're ~ you all the way⟩ **4** — used as a function word to indicate backwardness, delay, or deficiency ⟨~ the times⟩
be•hind•hand \bi-ˈhīnd-ˌhand\ *adj* **:** being in arrears
be•hold \bi-ˈhōld\ *vb* **-held** \-ˈheld\; **-hold•ing** **1** ♦ **:** to have in sight **:** SEE **2** — used imperatively to direct the attention — **be•hold•er** *n*

♦ descry, discern, distinguish, espy, eye, look, note, notice, observe, perceive, regard, remark, see, sight, spy, view, witness

be•hold•en \bi-ˈhōl-dən\ *adj* ♦ **:** owing gratitude or recognition to another **:** OBLIGATED, INDEBTED

♦ indebted, obligated, obliged

be•hoof \bi-ˈhüf\ *n* **:** ADVANTAGE, PROFIT
be•hoove \bi-ˈhüv\ *vb* **be•hooved; be•hoov•ing :** to be necessary, proper, or advantageous for
beige \ˈbāzh\ *n* **:** a pale dull yellowish brown — **beige** *adj*
be•ing \ˈbē-iŋ\ *n* **1 a :** EXISTENCE **b** ♦ **:** something that actually exists **2 :** the qualities or constitution of an existent thing **3** ♦ **:** a living thing; *esp* **:** PERSON

♦ [1b] entity, individual, object, substance, thing ♦ [3] body, creature, human, individual, man, mortal, person

be•la•bor *of Can and Brit* **be•la•bour** \bi-ˈlā-bər\ *vb* ♦ **:** to assail (as with words) tiresomely or at length

♦ abuse, assail, attack, blast, castigate, excoriate, jump, lambaste, slam, vituperate

be•lat•ed \bi-ˈlā-təd\ *adj* ♦ **:** delayed beyond the usual time **:** LATE

♦ behind, delinquent, late, overdue, tardy

be•lay \bi-ˈlā\ *vb* **1 :** to wind (a rope) around a pin or cleat in order to hold secure **2 :** QUIT, STOP — used in the imperative
belch \ˈbelch\ *vb* **1 :** to expel (gas) from the stomach through the mouth **2** ♦ **:** to gush forth ⟨a volcano ~*ing* lava⟩ — **belch** *n*

♦ disgorge, eject, erupt, expel, jet, spew, spout, spurt

bel•dam *or* **bel•dame** \ˈbel-dəm\ *n* **:** an old woman
be•lea•guer \bi-ˈlē-gər\ *vb* **1 :** to surround with armed forces **:** BESIEGE **2 :** HARASS ⟨~*ed* parents⟩
bel•fry \ˈbel-frē\ *n, pl* **belfries :** a tower for a bell (as on a church); *also* **:** the part of the tower in which the bell hangs
Belg *abbr* Belgian; Belgium
Bel•gian \ˈbel-jən\ *n* **:** a native or inhabitant of Belgium — **Belgian** *adj*
Belgian waffle *n* **:** a waffle with large depressions and often served with fruit topping
be•lie \bi-ˈlī\ *vb* **-lied; -ly•ing** **1 :** to give a false impression of **:** MISREPRESENT **2** ♦ **:** to show (something) to be false **3 :** to run counter to

♦ confute, disprove, rebut, refute

be•lief \bə-ˈlēf\ *n* **1 :** CONFIDENCE, TRUST **2** ♦ **:** something (as a tenet or creed) believed

♦ conviction, eye, feeling, judgment (*or* judgement), mind, notion, opinion, persuasion, sentiment, verdict, view ♦ credence, credit, faith ***Ant*** disbelief, discredit, doubt, unbelief

be•liev•able \-ˈlē-və-bəl\ *adj* ♦ **:** capable of being believed especially as within the range of known possibility or probability

♦ credible, likely, plausible, probable ***Ant*** implausible, improbable, incredible, unbelievable, unlikely

be•lieve \bə-ˈlēv\ *vb* **be•lieved; be•liev•ing** **1 :** to have religious convictions **2** ♦ **:** to have a firm conviction about something **:** accept as true **3** ♦ **:** to hold as an opinion **:** SUPPOSE — **be•liev•er** *n*

♦ [2] accept, credit, swallow, trust ***Ant*** disbelieve, discredit, reject ♦ [3] consider, deem, feel, figure, guess, hold, imagine, suppose, think

be•like \bi-ˈlīk\ *adv, archaic* **:** PROBABLY

be•lit•tle \bi-ˈlit-ᵊl\ *vb* **-lit•tled; -lit•tling** **1 :** to make seem little or less **2** ♦ **:** to speak slightingly about **:** DISPARAGE

♦ cry down, decry, deprecate, depreciate, diminish, discount, disparage, minimize, put down, write off

¹bell \ˈbel\ *n* **1 :** a hollow metallic device that makes a ringing sound when struck **2 :** the sounding or stroke of a bell (as on shipboard to tell the time); *also* **:** time so indicated **3 :** something with the flared form of a typical bell
²bell *vb* **:** to provide with a bell
bel•la•don•na \ˌbe-lə-ˈdä-nə\ *n* **:** a medicinal extract (as atropine) from a poisonous European herb related to the potato; *also* **:** this herb
bell–bot•toms \ˈbel-ˈbä-təmz\ *n pl* **:** pants with wide flaring bottoms — **bell–bottom** *adj*
bell•boy \ˈbel-ˌbȯi\ *n* **:** BELLHOP
belle \ˈbel\ *n* **:** an attractive and popular girl or woman
belles let•tres \bel-ˈletrᵊ\ *n pl* **:** literature that is an end in itself and not practical or purely informative — **bel•le•tris•tic** \ˌbe-lə-ˈtris-tik\ *adj*
bell•hop \ˈbel-ˌhäp\ *n* **:** a hotel or club employee who takes guests to rooms, carries luggage, and runs errands
bel•li•cose \ˈbe-li-ˌkōs\ *adj* ♦ **:** favoring or inclined to start quarrels or wars **:** WARLIKE, PUGNACIOUS

♦ aggressive, argumentative, belligerent, combative, contentious, discordant, disputatious, militant, pugnacious, quarrelsome, scrappy, truculent, warlike

bel•li•cos•i•ty \ˌbe-li-ˈkä-sə-tē\ *n* **:** showy or extreme combativeness or aggressiveness
bel•lig•er•ence \-rəns\ *n* ♦ **:** an aggressive or truculent attitude, atmosphere, or disposition

♦ aggression, aggressiveness, fight, militancy, pugnacity, truculence ***Ant*** pacifism

bel•lig•er•en•cy \bə-ˈli-jə-rən-sē\ *n* **1 :** the status of a nation engaged in war **2 :** BELLIGERENCE, TRUCULENCE
bel•lig•er•ent \-rənt\ *adj* **1 :** waging war **2** ♦ **:** inclined to or exhibiting assertiveness, hostility, or combativeness **:** TRUCULENT — **belligerent** *n*

♦ aggressive, argumentative, bellicose, combative, contentious, discordant, disputatious, militant, pugnacious, quarrelsome, scrappy, truculent, warlike ***Ant*** nonbelligerent, pacific, peaceable, peaceful

bel•low \ˈbe-lō\ *vb* **1 :** to make the deep hollow sound characteristic of a bull **2** ♦ **:** to shout in a deep voice — **bellow** *n*

♦ boom, growl, roar, thunder

bel•lows \-lōz, -ləz\ *n sing or pl* **:** a closed device with sides that can be spread apart and then pressed together to draw in air and expel it through a tube
bell•weth•er \ˈbel-ˈwe-t͟hər, -ˌwe-\ *n* **:** one that takes the lead or initiative
¹bel•ly \ˈbe-lē\ *n, pl* **bellies** **1** ♦ **:** the part of the body between the thorax and the pelvis **:** ABDOMEN **2 :** the underpart of an animal's body

♦ abdomen, gut, solar plexus, stomach, tummy

²belly *vb* **bel•lied; bel•ly•ing** ♦ **:** to swell or fill beyond a point **:** BULGE

♦ billow, bulge, overhang, protrude, start, stick out

¹bel•ly•ache \ˈbe-lē-ˌāk\ *n* **:** pain in the abdomen
²bellyache *vb* ♦ **:** to find fault **:** COMPLAIN

♦ beef, carp, complain, crab, croak, fuss, gripe, grouse, growl, grumble, kick, moan, murmur, mutter, repine, squawk, wail, whine

bel•ly•ach•er \ˈbe-lē-ˌā-kər\ *n* ♦ **:** one who bellyaches

♦ bear, complainer, crab, crank, curmudgeon, grouch, grumbler, whiner

belly button *n* **:** the human navel
belly dance *n* **:** a usually solo dance emphasizing movement of the belly — **belly dance** *vb* — **belly dancer** *n*
belly laugh *n* **:** a deep hearty laugh
be•long \bi-ˈlȯŋ\ *vb* **1 :** to be suitable or appropriate; *also* **:** to be properly situated ⟨shoes ~ in the closet⟩ **2 :** to be the property ⟨this ~*s* to me⟩; *also* **:** to be attached (as through birth or membership) ⟨~ to a club⟩ **3 :** to form an attribute or part ⟨this wheel ~*s* to the cart⟩ **4 :** to be classified ⟨whales ~ among the mammals⟩

be•long•ings \-ˈlȯŋ-iŋz\ *n pl* ♦ : moveable property : EFFECTS, POSSESSIONS

♦ chattels, effects, holdings, paraphernalia, possessions, things

¹be•loved \bi-ˈləvd, -ˈlə-vəd\ *adj* ♦ : dearly loved

♦ darling, dear, favorite (*or* favourite), loved, pet, precious, special, sweet

²beloved *n* : one who is loved; *esp* : SWEETHEART

¹be•low \bi-ˈlō\ *adv* **1** ♦ : in or to a lower place or rank **2** : on earth **3** : in hell

♦ down, downward, over ♦ beneath, under *Ant* up

²below *prep* **1** : lower than **2** : inferior to (as in rank)

be•low•decks \bi-ˌlō-ˈdeks, -ˈlō-ˌdeks\ *adv* : inside the superstructure of a boat or down to a lower deck

¹belt \ˈbelt\ *n* **1** ♦ : a strip (as of leather) worn about the waist **2** : a flexible continuous band to communicate motion or convey material **3** ♦ : a region marked by some distinctive feature; *esp* : one suited to a particular crop

♦ [1] cincture, cummerbund, girdle, sash ♦ [3] land, region, tract, zone

²belt *vb* **1** ♦ : to encircle or secure with a belt **2** : to beat with or as if with a belt **3** : to mark with an encircling band **4** : to sing loudly

♦ band, gird, girdle, wrap

³belt *n* **1** ♦ : a jarring blow : WHACK **2** : DRINK ⟨a ~ of whiskey⟩

♦ bat, blow, box, clout, hit, punch, slug, thump, wallop, whack

belt–tightening *n* : a reduction in spending

belt•way \ˈbelt-ˌwā\ *n* : a highway around a city

be•lu•ga \bə-ˈlü-gə\ *n* **1** : a large white sturgeon of the Black Sea, Caspian Sea, and their tributaries that is a source of caviar; *also* : caviar from beluga roe **2** : a whale of arctic and subarctic waters that is white when mature

bel•ve•dere \ˈbel-və-ˌdir\ *n* : a structure (as a summerhouse) designed to command a view

be•mire \bi-ˈmīr\ *vb* : to cover or soil with or sink in mire

be•moan \bi-ˈmōn\ *vb* ♦ : to express deep grief or distress over : LAMENT, DEPLORE

♦ bewail, deplore, grieve, lament, mourn, wail

be•muse \bi-ˈmyüz\ *vb* ♦ : to make confused : BEWILDER

♦ addle, baffle, befog, befuddle, bewilder, confound, confuse, disorient, muddle, muddy, mystify, perplex, puzzle

¹bench \ˈbench\ *n* **1** : a long seat for two or more persons **2** : the seat of a judge in court; *also* : the office or dignity of a judge **3 a** : COURT **b** ♦ : the persons who sit as judges **4** : a table for holding work and tools ⟨a carpenter's ~⟩

♦ court, judge, justice, magistrate

²bench \ˈbench\ *vb* **1** : to furnish with benches **2** : to seat on a bench **3** : to remove from or keep out of a game

bench mark *n* **1** : a mark on a permanent object serving as an elevation reference in topographical surveys **2** *usu* **bench•mark** : a point of reference for measurement; *also* : STANDARD

bench press *n* : a press in weight lifting performed by a lifter lying on a bench — **bench–press** *vb*

bench warrant *n* : a warrant issued by a presiding judge or by a court against a person guilty of contempt or indicted for a crime

¹bend \ˈbend\ *vb* **bent** \ˈbent\; **bend•ing** **1** : to draw (as a bow) taut **2** ♦ : to curve or cause a change of shape in ⟨~ a bar⟩ **3** : to make fast : SECURE **4** : DEFLECT **5** ♦ : to turn in a certain direction ⟨*bent* his steps toward town⟩ **6** ♦ : to direct strenuously or with interest : APPLY ⟨*bent* themselves to the task⟩ **7** : SUBDUE **8** : to curve downward **9** : YIELD, SUBMIT

♦ [2] arc, arch, bow, crook, curve, hook, round, sweep, swerve, wheel ♦ [5] aim, cast, direct, head, level, set, train ♦ [6] address, apply, buckle, devote, give

²bend *n* **1** : an act or process of bending **2** ♦ : something bent; *esp* : CURVE **3** *pl* : a painful and sometimes fatal disorder caused by release of gas bubbles in the tissues upon too rapid decrease in air pressure after a stay in a compressed atmosphere

♦ angle, arc, arch, bow, crook, curve, turn, wind *Ant* straight line

³bend *n* : a knot by which a rope is fastened (as to another rope)

bend•er \ˈben-dər\ *n* : SPREE

¹be•neath \bi-ˈnēth\ *adv* ♦ : in or to a lower position : BELOW

♦ below, under

²beneath *prep* **1** : in or to a lower position than : BELOW, UNDER ⟨stood ~ a tree⟩ **2** : unworthy of ⟨considered such behavior ~ her⟩ **3** : concealed by

bene•dic•tion \ˌbe-nə-ˈdik-shən\ *n* : the invocation of a blessing especially at the close of a public worship service

ben•e•fac•tion \-ˈfak-shən\ *n* ♦ : a charitable donation

♦ alms, beneficence, charity, contribution, donation, philanthropy

ben•e•fac•tor \ˈben-ə-ˌfak-tər\ *n* : one that confers a benefit and especially a benefaction

ben•e•fac•tress \-ˌfak-trəs\ *n* : a woman who is a benefactor

ben•e•fice \ˈbe-nə-fəs\ *n* : an ecclesiastical office to which the revenue from an endowment is attached

be•nef•i•cence \bə-ˈne-fə-səns\ *n* **1** : beneficent quality **2** ♦ : a benefit conferred : BENEFACTION

♦ alms, benefaction, charity, contribution, donation, philanthropy

be•nef•i•cent \-sənt\ *adj* **1** ♦ : doing or producing good (as by acts of kindness or charity) **2** : BENEFICIAL

♦ benevolent, compassionate, good-hearted, humane, kind, kindly, sympathetic, tender, tenderhearted, warmhearted ♦ altruistic, benevolent, charitable, humanitarian, philanthropic

ben•e•fi•cial \ˌbe-nə-ˈfi-shəl\ *adj* ♦ : being of benefit or help : HELPFUL — **ben•e•fi•cial•ly** *adv*

♦ advantageous, favorable (*or* favourable), helpful, profitable, salutary *Ant* disadvantageous, unfavorable, unhelpful

ben•e•fi•cia•ry \ˌbe-nə-ˈfi-shē-ˌer-ē, -ˈfi-shə-rē\ *n, pl* **-ries** : one that receives a benefit (as the income of a trust or the proceeds of an insurance)

¹ben•e•fit \ˈbe-nə-ˌfit\ *n* **1** ♦ : something that promotes well-being : ADVANTAGE ⟨the ~*s* of exercise⟩ **2 a** ♦ : a useful aid **b** : material aid provided or due (as in sickness or unemployment) as a right **3** : a performance or event to raise funds

♦ advantage, aid, boon, help

²benefit *vb* **-fit•ed** \-ˌfi-təd\ *also* **-fit•ted; -fit•ing** *also* **-fit•ting** **1** ♦ : to be useful or profitable to **2** : to receive benefit

♦ avail, profit, serve

be•nev•o•lence \bə-ˈne-və-ləns\ *n* **1** ♦ : charitable nature **2** : an act of kindness : CHARITY — **be•nev•o•lent•ly** *adv*

♦ amity, cordiality, fellowship, friendliness, friendship, goodwill, kindliness

be•nev•o•lent \-lənt\ *adj* ♦ : marked by or disposed to doing good

♦ beneficent, compassionate, good-hearted, humane, kind, kindly, sympathetic, tender, tenderhearted, warmhearted ♦ altruistic, beneficent, charitable, humanitarian, philanthropic

be•night•ed \bi-ˈnī-təd\ *adj* **1** : overtaken by darkness or night **2** : living in ignorance

be•nign \bi-ˈnīn\ *adj* **1** ♦ : of a gentle disposition; *also* : showing kindness **2** : of a mild kind; *esp* : not malignant ⟨~ tumors⟩ — **be•nig•ni•ty** \-ˈnig-nə-tē\ *n*

♦ balmy, bland, delicate, gentle, light, mellow, mild, soft, soothing, tender

be•nig•nant \-ˈnig-nənt\ *adj* : having a kind and gentle nature

ben•i•son \ˈbe-nə-sən, -zən\ *n* : a prayer that blesses : BLESSING, BENEDICTION

bent \ˈbent\ *n* **1** ♦ : strong inclination or interest **2** : power of endurance

♦ affinity, devices, disposition, genius, inclination, leaning, partiality, penchant, predilection, predisposition, proclivity, propensity, talent, tendency, turn

ben•thic \ˈben-thik\ *adj* : of, relating to, or occurring at the bottom of a body of water

ben•ton•ite \ˈbent-ᵊn-ˌīt\ *n* : an absorptive clay used especially as a filler (as in paper)

bent•wood \ˈbent-ˌwu̇d\ *adj* : made of wood bent into shape ⟨a ~ rocker⟩

be•numb \bi-ˈnəm\ *vb* **1** : to make inactive : DULL, DEADEN **2** : to make numb especially by cold

ben•zene \ˈben-ˌzēn\ *n* : a colorless volatile flammable liquid hydrocarbon used in organic synthesis and as a solvent

ben•zine \ˈben-ˌzēn\ *n* : any of various flammable petroleum distillates used as solvents or as motor fuels

ben•zo•ate \ˈben-zə-ˌwāt\ *n* : a salt or ester of benzoic acid

ben•zo•ic acid \ben-ˈzō-ik-\ *n* **:** a white crystalline acid used as a preservative and antiseptic and in synthesizing chemicals
ben•zo•in \ˈben-zə-wən, -ˌzȯin\ *n* **:** a balsamlike resin from trees of southern Asia used especially in medicine and perfumes
be•queath \bi-ˈkwēth, -ˈkwēth\ *vb* **1 :** to leave by will **2 :** to hand down
be•quest \bi-ˈkwest\ *n* **1 :** the action of bequeathing **2** ♦ **:** something bequeathed **:** LEGACY

♦ birthright, heritage, inheritance, legacy

be•rate \-ˈrāt\ *vb* ♦ **:** to scold harshly

♦ admonish, chide, lecture, rail (at *or* against), rate, rebuke, reprimand, scold

Ber•ber \ˈbər-bər\ *n* **:** a member of any of various peoples living in northern Africa west of Tripoli
ber•ceuse \ber-ˈsœz, -ˈsüz\ *n, pl* **berceuses** *same or* -ˈsü-zəz\ **1 :** LULLABY **2 :** a musical composition that resembles a lullaby
[1]**be•reaved** \bi-ˈrēvd\ *adj* **:** grieving the death of a loved one — **be•reave•ment** *n*
[2]**bereaved** *n, pl* **bereaved :** one who is bereaved
be•reft \-ˈreft\ *adj* **1** ♦ **:** deprived of or lacking something — usually used with *of* **2 :** grieving the death of a loved one **:** BEREAVED

♦ destitute, devoid, void

be•ret \bə-ˈrā\ *n* **:** a round soft cap with no visor
berg \ˈbərg\ *n* **:** ICEBERG
beri•beri \ˌber-ē-ˈber-ē\ *n* **:** a deficiency disease marked by weakness, wasting, and nerve damage and caused by lack of thiamine
berke•li•um \ˈbər-klē-əm\ *n* **:** an artificially prepared radioactive chemical element
berm \ˈbərm\ *n* **:** a narrow shelf or path at the top or bottom of a slope; *also* **:** a mound or bank of earth
Ber•mu•das \bər-ˈmyü-dəz\ *n pl* **:** BERMUDA SHORTS
Bermuda shorts *n pl* **:** knee-length walking shorts
ber•ry \ˈber-ē\ *n, pl* **berries 1 :** a small pulpy fruit (as a strawberry) **2 :** a simple fruit (as a grape, tomato, or banana) with the wall of the ripened ovary thick and pulpy **3 :** the dry seed of some plants (as coffee)
[1]**ber•serk** \bər-ˈsərk, -ˈzərk\ *adj* **:** FRENZIED, CRAZED
[2]**berserk** *adv* ♦ **:** in a berserk manner

♦ amok, frantically, harum-scarum, hectically, helter-skelter, madly, pell-mell, wild, wildly

[1]**berth** \ˈbərth\ *n* **1 :** adequate distance especially for a ship to maneuver **2 :** the place where a ship is anchored or a vehicle rests **3 :** ACCOMMODATIONS **4 :** an employment for which one has been hired **:** JOB, POSITION
[2]**berth** *vb* **1 :** to bring or come into a berth **2 :** to allot a berth to
ber•yl \ˈber-əl\ *n* **:** a hard silicate mineral occurring as green, yellow, pink, or white crystals
be•ryl•li•um \bə-ˈri-lē-əm\ *n* **:** a light strong metallic chemical element used as a hardener in alloys
be•seech \bi-ˈsēch\ *vb* **-sought** \-ˈsȯt\ *or* **-seeched; -seech•ing** ♦ **:** to beg earnestly or urgently **:** ENTREAT

♦ appeal, beg, entreat, implore, importune, petition, plead, pray, solicit, supplicate

be•seem \bi-ˈsēm\ *vb, archaic* **:** BEFIT
be•set \-ˈset\ *vb* **1 :** TROUBLE, HARASS **2 a** ♦ **:** to set upon **:** ASSAIL **b :** SURROUND

♦ assail, assault, attack, charge, descend, jump, pounce (on *or* upon), raid, rush, storm, strike

be•set•ting *adj* **:** persistently present
[1]**be•side** \bi-ˈsīd\ *prep* **1 :** by the side of ⟨sit ~ me⟩ **2 :** BESIDES: as **a :** other than **b :** together with **3 :** not relevant to
[2]**beside** *adv, archaic* **:** BESIDES
[1]**be•sides** \bi-ˈsīdz\ *prep* **1** ♦ **:** other than **2 :** together with

♦ aside from, bar, barring, but, except, outside (of), save

[2]**besides** *adv* **1 :** as well **:** ALSO **2** ♦ **:** in addition to what precedes **:** MOREOVER

♦ additionally, again, also, further, furthermore, likewise, more, moreover, then, too, withal, yet

be•siege \bi-ˈsēj\ *vb* **1** ♦ **:** to lay siege to **2 :** to press with requests — **be•sieg•er** *n*

♦ barricade, block, cut off, dam, encircle, surround

be•smear \-ˈsmir\ *vb* **:** to spread with something oily, thick, or sticky **:** SMEAR
be•smirch \-ˈsmərch\ *vb* ♦ **:** to make soiled or tarnished **:** SMIRCH, SOIL

♦ befoul, begrime, blacken, dirty, foul, grime, mire, muddy, smirch, soil, stain

be•som \ˈbē-zəm\ *n* **:** BROOM
be•sot \bi-ˈsät\ *vb* **be•sot•ted; be•sot•ting 1 :** INFATUATE **2 :** to make dull especially by drinking
be•spat•ter \-ˈspa-tər\ *vb* **:** to splash with or as if with a liquid **:** SPATTER
be•speak \bi-ˈspēk\ *vb* **-spoke** \-ˈspōk\; **-spo•ken** \-ˈspō-kən\; **-speak•ing 1 :** to hire, engage, or claim beforehand **:** PREARRANGE **2 :** ADDRESS **3 :** REQUEST **4** ♦ **:** to be a sign or indication of ⟨~*s* considerable practice⟩ **5 :** FORETELL

♦ betray, demonstrate, display, evince, expose, give away, manifest, reveal, show

be•sprin•kle \-ˈspriŋ-kəl\ *vb* **:** SPRINKLE
[1]**best** \ˈbest\ *adj, superlative of* GOOD **1 :** excelling all others **2 :** most productive (as of good or satisfaction) **3 :** LARGEST, MOST
[2]**best** *adv, superlative of* WELL **1 :** in the best way **2 :** MOST
[3]**best** *n* **1** ♦ **:** something that is best **2** ♦ **:** best clothes ⟨Sunday ~⟩

♦ [1] choice, cream, elect, elite, fat, flower, pick, prime ♦ [2] array, bravery, caparison, feather, finery, frippery, full dress, gaiety, regalia

[4]**best** *vb* ♦ **:** to get the better of

♦ beat, defeat, master, overcome, prevail, triumph, trounce, wallop, whip, win

bes•tial \ˈbes-chəl\ *adj* **1 :** of or relating to beasts **2 :** resembling a beast especially in brutality or lack of intelligence
bes•ti•al•i•ty \ˌbes-chē-ˈa-lə-tē, ˌbēs-\ *n, pl* **-ties 1 :** the condition or status of a lower animal **2 :** display or gratification of bestial traits or impulses
bes•ti•ary \ˈbes-chē-ˌer-ē\ *n, pl* **-ar•ies :** a medieval allegorical or moralizing work on the appearance and habits of animals
be•stir \bi-ˈstər\ *vb* **:** to rouse to action
best man *n* **:** the principal groomsman at a wedding
be•stow \bi-ˈstō\ *vb* **1 :** PUT, PLACE, STOW **2** ♦ **:** to present as a gift

♦ contribute, donate, give, present

be•stow•al *n* ♦ **:** something bestowed or given

♦ donation, freebie, gift, lagniappe, present

be•stride \bi-ˈstrīd\ *vb* **-strode** \-ˈstrōd\; **-strid•den** \-ˈstrid-ᵊn\; **-strid•ing :** to ride, sit, or stand astride
[1]**bet** \ˈbet\ *n* **1 a :** something that is wagered, risked, or pledged usually between two parties on the outcome of a contest **b :** the making of such a bet **2 :** OPTION ⟨the back road is your best ~⟩
[2]**bet** *vb* **bet** *also* **bet•ted; bet•ting 1** ♦ **:** to stake on the outcome of an issue or a contest ⟨~ $2 on the race⟩ **2 :** to make a bet with **3 :** to lay a bet

♦ gamble, go, lay, stake, wager

[3]**bet** *abbr* between
be•ta \ˈbā-tə\ *n* **1 :** the 2d letter of the Greek alphabet — Β or β **2 :** a nearly complete version of a new product (as computer software)
beta–block•er \-ˌblä-kər\ *n* **:** any of a group of drugs that decrease the rate and force of heart contractions and lower high blood pressure
be•ta–car•o•tene \-ˈkar-ə-ˌtēn\ *n* **:** an isomer of carotene found in dark green and dark yellow vegetables and fruits
be•take \bi-ˈtāk\ *vb* **-took** \-ˈtu̇k\; **-tak•en** \-ˈtā-kən\; **-tak•ing :** to cause (oneself) to go
beta particle *n* **:** a high-speed electron; *esp* **:** one emitted by a radioactive nucleus
beta ray *n* **1 :** BETA PARTICLE **2 :** a stream of beta particles
beta test *n* **:** a field test of the beta version of a product prior to commercial release
be•tel \ˈbē-tᵊl\ *n* **:** a climbing pepper whose leaves are chewed together with lime and betel nut as a stimulant especially by southern Asians
betel nut *n* **:** the astringent seed of an Asian palm that is chewed with betel leaves
bête noire \ˌbet-ˈnwär, ˌbāt-\ *n, pl* **bêtes noires** *same or* -ˈnwärz\ ♦ **:** a person or thing strongly disliked, avoided, or feared

♦ bogey, bugbear, hobgoblin, ogre ♦ abhorrence, abomination, anathema, antipathy, aversion, hate

beth·el \ˈbe-thəl\ *n* : a place of worship especially for seamen
be·think \bi-ˈthiŋk\ *vb* **-thought** \-ˈthȯt\; **-think·ing** **1** : to bring to mind or think of again : REMEMBER **2** : PONDER
be·tide \bi-ˈtīd\ *vb* ♦ : to happen to

♦ be, befall, chance, come, go, happen, occur, pass, transpire

be·times \bi-ˈtīmz\ *adv* : in good time : EARLY
be·to·ken \bi-ˈtō-kən\ *vb* **1** : PRESAGE **2** ♦ : to give evidence of

♦ display, disport, exhibit, expose, flash, flaunt, parade, show, show off, sport, strut, unveil

be·tray \bi-ˈtrā\ *vb* **1** : to lead astray; *esp* : SEDUCE **2** : to deliver to an enemy **3** : ABANDON **4** : to prove unfaithful to **5** ♦ : to reveal unintentionally; *also* : SHOW

♦ bespeak, demonstrate, display, evince, expose, give away, manifest, reveal, show

be·tray·al *n* ♦ : the act of betraying or fact of being betrayed

♦ disloyalty, double cross, faithlessness, falseness, falsity, infidelity, perfidy, treachery, treason, unfaithfulness

be·tray·er *n* ♦ : one who betrays (something or someone)

♦ blabbermouth, informer, rat, snitch, stool pigeon, tattler, tattletale ♦ apostate, double-crosser, quisling, recreant, traitor, turncoat

be·troth \bi-ˈtrōth, -ˈtrȯth\ *vb* : to promise to marry
be·troth·al *n* ♦ : the act of betrothing or fact of being betrothed; *also* : a mutual promise or contract for a future marriage

♦ engagement, espousal, troth

be·trothed *n* ♦ : the person to whom one is betrothed

♦ intended

1bet·ter \ˈbe-tər\ *adj, comparative of* GOOD **1** : greater than half **2** : improved in health **3** : more attractive, favorable, or commendable **4** : more advantageous or effective **5** : improved in accuracy or performance
2better *vb* **1** ♦ : to make or become better **2** ♦ : to surpass in excellence : EXCEL

♦ [1] ameliorate, amend, enhance, enrich, improve, perfect, refine ♦ [2] beat, eclipse, excel, outdistance, outdo, outshine, outstrip, surpass, top, transcend

3better *adv, comparative of* WELL **1** : in a superior manner **2** : to a higher or greater degree; *also* : MORE
4better *n* **1** : something better; *also* : a superior especially in merit or rank **2** : superiority of position or condition : ADVANTAGE
5better *verbal auxiliary* : had better ⟨you ~ hurry⟩
better half *n* ♦ : the person to whom another is married : SPOUSE

♦ consort, mate, partner, spouse

bet·ter·ment \ˈbe-tər-mənt\ *n* : IMPROVEMENT
bet·tor *or* **bet·ter** \ˈbe-tər\ *n* : one that bets
1be·tween \bi-ˈtwēn\ *prep* **1** : by the common action of ⟨earned $10,000 ~ the two of them⟩ **2** : in the interval separating ⟨an alley ~ two buildings⟩; *also* : in intermediate relation to **3** : in point of comparison of ⟨choose ~ two cars⟩
2between *adv* : in an intervening space or interval
be·twixt \bi-ˈtwikst\ *adv or prep* : BETWEEN
1bev·el \ˈbe-vəl\ *n* **1** : a device for adjusting the slant of the surfaces of a piece of work **2** : the angle or slant that one surface or line makes with another when not at right angles
2bevel *vb* **-eled** *or* **-elled; -el·ing** *or* **-el·ling** **1** : to cut or shape to a bevel **2** : INCLINE, SLANT
bev·er·age \ˈbev-rij\ *n* ♦ : a drinkable liquid

♦ drink, libation, quencher

bevy \ˈbe-vē\ *n, pl* **bev·ies** **1** : a large group or collection **2** : a group of animals and especially quail together
be·wail \bi-ˈwāl\ *vb* ♦ : to express deep sorrow for usually by wailing and lamentation

♦ bemoan, deplore, grieve, lament, mourn, wail

be·ware \-ˈwar\ *vb* ♦ : to be on one's guard : be wary of

♦ *usu* **beware of** guard (against), mind, watch out (for)

be·wil·der \bi-ˈwil-dər\ *vb* ♦ : to perplex or confuse especially by complexity or variety

♦ addle, baffle, befog, befuddle, bemuse, confound, confuse, disorient, muddle, muddy, mystify, perplex, puzzle

be·wil·der·ment *n* **1** ♦ : the quality or state of being bewildered **2** : a bewildering tangle or confusion

♦ bafflement, confusion, distraction, muddle, mystification, perplexity, puzzlement, whirl

be·witch \-ˈwich\ *vb* **1** ♦ : to affect by witchcraft **2** ♦ : to attract as if by the power of witchcraft : CHARM, FASCINATE

♦ [1] charm, enchant, hex, spell ♦ [2] allure, beguile, captivate, charm, enchant, fascinate, wile

be·witch·ment *n* **1** ♦ : the act or power of bewitching; *also* : a spell that bewitches **2** : the state of being bewitched

♦ charm, conjuration, enchantment, incantation, spell ♦ enchantment, magic, necromancy, sorcery, witchcraft, wizardry

bey \ˈbā\ *n* **1** : a former Turkish provincial governor **2** : the former native ruler of Tunis or Tunisia
1be·yond \bē-ˈänd\ *adv* **1** ♦ : on or to the farther side **2** : BESIDES

♦ farther, further, yonder

2beyond *prep* **1** : at a greater distance than **2** ♦ : past the reach or sphere of **3** : BESIDES

♦ outside, without *Ant* within

be·zel \ˈbē-zəl, ˈbe-\ *n* **1** : a rim that holds a transparent covering (as on a watch) **2** : the faceted part of a cut gem that rises above the setting
bf *abbr* boldface
BG *or* **B Gen** *abbr* brigadier general
bhang \ˈbaŋ\ *n* : a mildly intoxicating preparation of the leaves and flowering tops of uncultivated hemp
Bi *symbol* bismuth
BIA *abbr* Bureau of Indian Affairs
bi·an·nu·al \(ˌ)bī-ˈan-yə-wəl\ *adj* : occurring twice a year — **bi·an·nu·al·ly** *adv*
1bi·as \ˈbī-əs\ *n* **1** : a line diagonal to the grain of a fabric **2** ♦ : a personal and sometimes unreasoned judgment : PREJUDICE

♦ favor (*or* favour), partiality, partisanship, prejudice *Ant* impartiality, neutrality, objectivity

2bias *adv* : on the bias : DIAGONALLY
3bias *vb* **bi·ased** *or* **bi·assed; bi·as·ing** *or* **bi·as·sing** : to give a settled and often prejudiced outlook to : PREJUDICE
bi·ased *adj* ♦ : exhibiting or characterized by bias

♦ one-sided, partial, partisan, prejudiced

bi·ath·lon \bī-ˈath-lən, -ˌlän\ *n* : a composite athletic contest consisting of cross-country skiing and target shooting with a rifle
1bib \ˈbib\ *n* : a cloth or plastic shield tied under the chin to protect the clothes while eating
2bib *abbr* Bible; biblical
bi·be·lot \ˈbē-bə-ˌlō\ *n, pl* **bibelots** *same or* -ˌlōz\ : a small household ornament or decorative object
bi·ble \ˈbī-bəl\ *n* **1** *cap* : the sacred scriptures of Christians comprising the Old and New Testaments **2** *cap* : the sacred scriptures of Judaism; *also* : those of some other religion **3** : a publication that is considered authoritative for its subject — **bib·li·cal** \ˈbi-bli-kəl\ *adj*
bib·li·og·ra·phy \ˌbi-blē-ˈä-grə-fē\ *n, pl* **-phies** **1** : the history or description of writings or publications **2** : a list of writings (as on a subject or of an author) — **bib·li·og·ra·pher** \-fər\ *n* — **bib·li·o·graph·ic** \-ə-ˈgra-fik\ *also* **bib·li·o·graph·i·cal** \-fi-kəl\ *adj*
bib·lio·phile \ˈbi-blē-ə-ˌfīl\ *n* : a lover of books
bib·u·lous \ˈbi-byə-ləs\ *adj* **1** : highly absorbent **2** : fond of alcoholic beverages
bi·cam·er·al \ˈbī-ˈka-mə-rəl\ *adj* : having or consisting of two legislative branches
bicarb \(ˌ)bī-ˈkärb, ˈbī-ˌ\ *n* : SODIUM BICARBONATE
bi·car·bon·ate \(ˌ)bī-ˈkär-bə-ˌnāt, -nət\ *n* : an acid carbonate
bi·cen·te·na·ry \ˌbī-sen-ˈte-nə-rē, bī-ˈsent-ᵊn-ˌer-ē\ *n* : BICENTENNIAL — **bicentenary** *adj*
bi·cen·ten·ni·al \ˌbī-sen-ˈte-nē-əl\ *n* : a 200th anniversary or its celebration — **bicentennial** *adj*
bi·ceps \ˈbī-ˌseps\ *n, pl* **biceps** *also* **bicepses** : a muscle (as in the front of the upper arm) having two points of origin
1bick·er \ˈbi-kər\ *n* : petulant quarreling : ALTERCATION
2bicker *vb* ♦ : to engage in a petty quarrel

♦ argue, brawl, dispute, fall out, fight, hassle, quarrel, row, scrap, spat, squabble, wrangle

bick·er·er \ˈbi-kə-rər\ *n* : one who bickers
bi·coast·al \bī-ˈkōst-ᵊl\ *adj* : living or working on both the East and West coasts of the U.S.
bi·con·cave \ˌbī-(ˌ)kän-ˈkāv, (ˌ)bī-ˈkän-ˌkāv\ *adj* : concave on both sides

bi•con•vex \ˌbī-(ˌ)kän-ˈveks, (ˌ)bī-ˈkän-ˌveks\ *adj* **:** convex on both sides
bi•cus•pid \bī-ˈkəs-pəd\ *n* **:** PREMOLAR
¹bi•cy•cle \ˈbī-ˌsi-kəl\ *n* **:** a light 2-wheeled vehicle with a steering handle, saddle, and pedals
²bicycle *vb* **-cy•cled; -cy•cling** \-ˌsi-k(ə-)liŋ, -ˌsī-\ **:** to ride a bicycle — **bi•cy•cler** \-k(ə-)lər\ *n* — **bi•cy•clist** \-k(ə-)list\ *n*
¹bid \ˈbid\ *vb* **bade** \ˈbad, ˈbād\ *or* **bid; bid•den** \ˈbid-ᵊn\ *or* **bid** *also* **bade; bid•ding 1 ♦ :** to issue an order to **:** COMMAND, ORDER **2 :** INVITE **3 :** to give expression to **4 :** to make a bid **:** OFFER — **bid•der** *n*

♦ boss, charge, command, direct, enjoin, instruct, order, tell

²bid *n* **1 :** the act of one who bids; *also* **:** an offer for something **2 :** INVITATION **3 :** an announcement in a card game of what a player proposes to accomplish **4 ♦ :** an attempt to win or gain ⟨a ~ for mayor⟩

♦ attempt, crack, endeavor (*or* endeavour), essay, fling, go, pass, shot, stab, trial, try, whack, whirl

bid•da•ble \ˈbi-də-bəl\ *adj* **1 :** OBEDIENT, DOCILE **2 :** capable of being bid
bid•dy \ˈbi-dē\ *n, pl* **biddies :** HEN; *also* **:** a young chicken
bide \ˈbīd\ *vb* **bode** \ˈbōd\ *or* **bid•ed; bided; bid•ing 1 :** to wait for **2 ♦ :** to wait awhile **:** TARRY **3 :** DWELL

♦ await, hold on, stay, tarry, wait

bi•det \bi-ˈdā\ *n* **:** a bathroom fixture used especially for bathing the external genitals and the posterior parts of the body
bi•di•rec•tion•al \ˌbī-də-ˈrek-sh(ə-)nəl\ *adj* **:** involving, moving, or taking place in two usually opposite directions — **bi•di•rec•tion•al•ly** *adv*
bi•en•ni•al \bī-ˈe-nē-əl\ *adj* **1 :** taking place once in two years **2 :** lasting two years **3 :** producing leaves the first year and fruiting and dying the second year — **biennial** *n* — **bi•en•ni•al•ly** *adv*
bi•en•ni•um \bī-ˈe-nē-əm\ *n, pl* **-niums** *or* **-nia** \-ə\ **:** a period of two years
bier \ˈbir\ *n* **:** a stand bearing a coffin or corpse
bi•fo•cal \ˈbī-ˌfō-kəl\ *adj* **:** having two focal lengths
bifocals \-kəlz\ *n pl* **:** eyeglasses with lenses that have one part that corrects for near vision and one for distant vision
bi•fur•cate \ˈbī-fər-ˌkāt, bī-ˈfər-\ *vb* **-cat•ed; -cat•ing :** to divide into two branches or parts — **bi•fur•ca•tion** \ˌbī-fər-ˈkā-shən\ *n*
big \ˈbig\ *adj* **big•ger; big•gest 1 ♦ :** large in size, amount, or scope **2 :** PREGNANT; *also* **:** SWELLING **3 ♦ :** of great importance or significance **:** IMPORTANT **4 :** POPULAR

♦ [1] bumper, considerable, goodly, grand, great, large, sizable, substantial, voluminous ♦ [3] consequential, eventful, important, major, material, meaningful, momentous, significant, substantial, weighty

big•a•my \ˈbi-gə-mē\ *n* **:** the act of marrying one person while still legally married to another — **big•a•mist** \-mist\ *n* — **big•a•mous** \-məs\ *adj*
big bang theory *n* **:** a theory in astronomy: the universe originated in an explosion (**big bang**) from a single point of nearly infinite energy density
big brother *n* **1 :** an older brother **2 :** a man who serves as a friend, father figure, or role model for a boy **3** *cap both Bs* **:** the leader of an authoritarian state or movement
Big Dipper *n* **:** the seven principal stars of Ursa Major in a form resembling a dipper
big•foot \ˈbig-ˌfu̇t\ *n* **:** SASQUATCH
big•horn \ˈbig-ˌhȯrn\ *n, pl* **bighorn** *or* **bighorns :** a wild sheep of mountainous western No. America
bight \ˈbīt\ *n* **1 ♦ :** a curve in a coast; *also* **:** the bay formed by such a curve **2 :** a slack part in a rope

♦ bay, cove, estuary, fjord, gulf, inlet

big leaguer *n* **♦ :** one who operates at the top rank of an activity or enterprise

♦ big shot, bigwig, kingpin, nabob, nawab, wheel

big–name \ˈbig-ˈnām\ *adj* **:** widely popular ⟨a ~ performer⟩ — **big name** *n*
big•ness *n* **♦ :** quality or state of being big

♦ grandness, greatness, largeness

big•ot \ˈbi-gət\ *n* **:** one intolerantly devoted to his or her own prejudices or opinions — **big•ot•ry** \-trē\ *n*
big•ot•ed \-gə-təd\ *adj* **♦ :** obstinately and blindly attached to some creed, opinion, or practice

♦ intolerant, narrow, narrow-minded, prejudiced

big shot \ˈbig-ˌshät\ *n* **♦ :** an important person

♦ big leaguer, bigwig, kingpin, nabob, nawab, wheel *Ant* lightweight, nobody, nonentity, nothing, shrimp, twerp, whippersnapper, zero, zilch

big time \-ˌtīm\ *n* **1 :** a high-paying vaudeville circuit requiring only two performances a day **2 :** the top rank of an activity or enterprise — **big–tim•er** *n*
big top *n* **1 :** the main tent of a circus **2 :** CIRCUS
big•wig \ˈbig-ˌwig\ *n* **♦ :** an important person

♦ big shot, big leaguer, kingpin, nabob, nawab, wheel

bike \ˈbīk\ *n* **1 :** BICYCLE **2 :** MOTORCYCLE
bik•er *n* **:** MOTORCYCLIST; *esp* **:** one who is a member of an organized gang
bike•way \ˈbīk-ˌwā\ *n* **:** a thoroughfare for bicycles
bi•ki•ni \bə-ˈkē-nē\ *n* **:** a woman's brief 2-piece bathing suit
bi•lat•er•al \bī-ˈla-tə-rəl\ *adj* **1 :** having or involving two sides **2 :** affecting reciprocally two sides or parties — **bi•lat•er•al•ly** *adv*
bile \ˈbīl\ *n* **1 :** a bitter greenish fluid secreted by the liver that aids in the digestion of fats **2 ♦ :** an ill-humored mood

♦ acidity, acrimony, asperity, bitterness, cattiness, tartness, virulence, vitriol

bilge \ˈbilj\ *n* **1 :** the part of a ship that lies between the bottom and the point where the sides go straight up **2 :** stale or worthless remarks or ideas
bi•lin•gual \bī-ˈliŋ-gwəl\ *adj* **:** expressed in, knowing, or using two languages
bil•ious \ˈbil-yəs\ *adj* **1 :** marked by or suffering from disordered liver function **2 ♦ :** of or indicative of a peevish ill-natured disposition **:** ILL-TEMPERED

♦ bearish, cantankerous, disagreeable, dyspeptic, ill-humored, ill-tempered, ornery, splenetic, surly

bil•ious•ness *n* **♦ :** an ill-natured disposition

♦ grumpiness, irritability, peevishness, perverseness, perversity

bilk \ˈbilk\ *vb* **:** CHEAT, SWINDLE
¹bill \ˈbil\ *n* **1 :** the jaws of a bird together with their horny covering; *also* **:** a mouth structure (as of a turtle) resembling these **2 :** the visor of a cap or hood — **billed** \ˈbild\ *adj*
²bill *vb* **:** to caress fondly
³bill *n* **1 ♦ :** an itemized statement of particulars; *also* **:** INVOICE **2 :** a written document or note **3 ♦ :** a printed advertisement (as a poster) announcing an event **4 :** a draft of a law presented to a legislature for enactment **5 :** a written statement of a legal wrong suffered or of some breach of law **6 :** a piece of paper money

♦ [1] account, check, invoice, statement, tab ♦ [3] placard, poster

⁴bill *vb* **1 :** to enter in or prepare a bill; *also* **:** to submit a bill or account to **2 :** to advertise by bills or posters
bill•board \-ˌbōrd\ *n* **:** a flat surface on which advertising bills are posted
¹bil•let \ˈbi-lət\ *n* **1 :** an order requiring a person to provide lodging for a soldier; *also* **:** quarters assigned by or as if by such an order **2 ♦ :** a regular paying position **:** APPOINTMENT

♦ appointment, capacity, function, job, place, position, post, situation

²billet *vb* **♦ :** to assign lodging to by billet

♦ accommodate, chamber, domicile, harbor (*or* harbour), house, lodge, put up, quarter, roof, shelter, take in

bil•let–doux \ˌbi-lā-ˈdü\ *n, pl* **billets–doux** *same or* -ˈdüz\ **:** a love letter
bill•fold \ˈbil-ˌfōld\ *n* **:** WALLET
bil•liards \ˈbil-yərdz\ *n* **:** any of several games played on an oblong table by driving balls against each other or into pockets with a cue
bil•lings•gate \ˈbi-liŋz-ˌgāt, *Brit usu* -git\ *n* **:** coarsely abusive language
bil•lion \ˈbil-yən\ *n* **1 :** a thousand millions **2** *Brit* **:** a million millions — **billion** *adj* — **bil•lionth** \-yənth\ *adj or n*
¹bil•low \ˈbi-lō\ *n* **1 ♦ :** a moving ridge or swell on the surface of a liquid **:** WAVE; *esp* **:** a great wave **2 :** a rolling mass (as of fog or flame) like a great wave — **bil•lowy** \ˈbi-lə-wē\ *adj*

♦ surge, swell, wave

²billow *vb* **1 :** to rise and roll in waves **2 ♦ :** to swell out ⟨~*ing* sails⟩

♦ balloon, beetle, belly, bulge, overhang, poke, project, protrude, start, stick out

bil·ly \ˈbi-lē\ *n, pl* **billies :** a heavy usually wooden club : BILLY CLUB

billy club *n* ♦ **:** a heavy usually wooden club; *esp* **:** a police officer's club

♦ bat, bludgeon, club, cudgel, nightstick, staff, truncheon

bil·ly goat \ˈbi-lē-\ *n* **:** a male goat

bi·met·al \ˈbī-ˌmet-ᵊl\ *adj* **:** BIMETALLIC — **bimetal** *n*

bi·me·tal·lic \ˌbī-mə-ˈta-lik\ *adj* **:** made of two different metals — often used of devices having a bonded expansive part — **bimetallic** *n*

bi·met·al·lism \bī-ˈmet-ᵊl-ˌi-zəm\ *n* **:** the use of two metals at fixed ratios to form a standard of value for a monetary system

1**bi·month·ly** \bī-ˈmənth-lē\ *adj* **1 :** occurring every two months **2 :** occurring twice a month **:** SEMIMONTHLY — **bimonthly** *adv*

2**bimonthly** *n* **:** a bimonthly publication

bin \ˈbin\ *n* ♦ **:** a box, crib, or enclosure used for storage

♦ bin, box, caddy, case, casket, chest, locker, trunk

bi·na·ry \ˈbī-nə-rē, -ˌner-ē\ *adj* **1** ♦ **:** consisting of two things or parts **2 :** relating to, being, or belonging to a system of numbers having 2 as its base ⟨the ~ digits 0 and 1⟩ **3 :** involving a choice between or condition of two alternatives only (as on-off, yes-no) — **binary** *n*

♦ bipartite, double, dual, duplex, twin

binary star *n* **:** a system of two stars revolving around each other

bin·au·ral \bī-ˈnȯr-əl\ *adj* **:** of or relating to sound reproduction involving the use of two separated microphones and two transmission channels to achieve a stereophonic effect

bind \ˈbīnd\ *vb* **bound** \ˈbau̇nd\; **bind·ing** **1 a :** to make secure by tying **b :** to restrain as if by tying **2 :** to put under an obligation; *also* **:** to constrain with legal authority **3 :** to dress or cover with a bandage **4** ♦ **:** to unite into a mass **5 :** to compel as if by a pledge ⟨a handshake ~*s* the deal⟩ **6 :** to strengthen or decorate with a band **7 :** to fasten together and enclose in a cover ⟨~ books⟩ **8 :** to exert a tying, restraining, or compelling effect — **bind·er** *n*

♦ band, gird, tie, truss

bind·ing \ˈbīn-diŋ\ *n* **:** something (as a ski fastening, a cover, or an edging fabric) used to bind

1**binge** \ˈbinj\ *n* ♦ **:** an unrestrained and often excessive indulgence **:** SPREE

♦ fling, frolic, gambol, lark, revel, rollick, romp

2**binge** *vb* **binged; binge·ing** *or* **bing·ing :** to go on a binge and especially an eating binge — **bing·er** *n*

bin·go \ˈbiŋ-gō\ *n, pl* **bingos :** a game of chance played with cards having numbered squares corresponding to numbered balls drawn at random and won by covering five squares in a row

bin·na·cle \ˈbi-ni-kəl\ *n* **:** a container holding a ship's compass

1**bin·oc·u·lar** \bī-ˈnä-kyə-lər, bə-\ *adj* **:** of, relating to, or adapted to the use of both eyes — **bin·oc·u·lar·ly** *adv*

2**bin·oc·u·lar** \bə-ˈnä-kyə-lər, bī-\ *n* **1 :** a binocular optical instrument (as a microscope) **2 :** a hand-held optical instrument composed of two telescopes and a focusing device — usually used in plural

bi·no·mi·al \bī-ˈnō-mē-əl\ *n* **1 :** a mathematical expression consisting of two terms connected by the sign plus (+) or minus (–) **2 :** a biological species name consisting of two terms — **binomial** *adj*

bio·chem·is·try \ˌbī-ō-ˈke-mə-strē\ *n* **:** chemistry that deals with the chemical compounds and processes occurring in living things — **bio·chem·i·cal** \-mi-kəl\ *adj or n* — **bio·chem·ist** \-mist\ *n*

bio·de·grad·able \-di-ˈgrā-də-bəl\ *adj* **:** capable of being broken down especially into innocuous products by the actions of living things (as microorganisms) ⟨a ~ detergent⟩ — **bio·de·grad·abil·i·ty** \-ˌgrā-də-ˈbi-lə-tē\ *n* — **bio·deg·ra·da·tion** \-ˌde-grə-ˈdā-shən\ *n* — **bio·de·grade** \-di-ˈgrād\ *vb*

bio·di·ver·si·ty \-də-ˈvər-sə-tē, -dī-\ *n* **:** biological diversity in an environment as indicated by numbers of different species of plants and animals

bio·en·gi·neer·ing *n* **1 :** the application of engineering principles to medicine and biology **2 :** GENETIC ENGINEERING

bio·eth·ics \-ˈe-thiks\ *n* **:** the ethics of biological research and its applications especially in medicine — **bio·eth·i·cal** \-ˈe-thi-kəl\ *adj* — **bio·eth·i·cist** \-ˈe-thə-sist\ *n*

bio·feed·back \-ˈfēd-ˌbak\ *n* **:** the technique of making unconscious or involuntary bodily processes (as heartbeats or brain waves) objectively perceptible to the senses (as by use of an oscilloscope) in order to manipulate them by conscious mental control

biog *abbr* biographer; biographical; biography

bio·ge·og·ra·phy \ˌbī-ō-jē-ˈä-grə-fē\ *n* **:** a science that deals with the geographical distribution of plants and animals — **bio·ge·og·ra·pher** *n*

bi·og·ra·phy \bī-ˈä-grə-fē, bē-\ *n, pl* **-phies :** a written history of a person's life; *also* **:** such writings in general — **bi·og·ra·pher** *n* — **bi·o·graph·i·cal** \ˌbī-ə-ˈgra-fi-kəl\ *also* **bi·o·graph·ic** \-fik\ *adj*

biol *abbr* biologic; biological; biologist; biology

bi·o·log·i·cal \ˌbī-ə-ˈlä-ji-kəl\ *also* **bi·o·log·ic** \-jik\ *adj* **1 :** of, relating to, or produced by biology or life and living processes **2 :** related by direct genetic relationship rather than by adoption or marriage ⟨~ parents⟩ — **bi·o·log·i·cal·ly** \-ji-k(ə-)lē\ *adv*

biological clock *n* **:** an inherent timing mechanism in a living system that is inferred to exist in order to explain the timing of various physiological and behavioral states and processes

biological warfare *n* **:** warfare in which harmful living organisms (**biological weapons**) are used against an enemy especially to cause large-scale death and disease

bi·ol·o·gy \bī-ˈä-lə-jē\ *n* **1 :** a science that deals with living beings and life processes **2 :** the life processes of an organism or group — **bi·ol·o·gist** \bī-ˈä-lə-jist\ *n*

bio·mass \ˈbī-ō-ˌmas\ *n* **1 :** the amount of living matter (as in a unit area) **2 :** plant materials and animal waste used especially as fuel

bio·med·i·cal \ˌbī-ō-ˈme-di-kəl\ *adj* **:** of, relating to, or involving biological, medical, and physical science

bi·on·ic \bī-ˈä-nik\ *adj* **:** having normal biological capability or performance enhanced by or as if by electronic or mechanical devices

bio·phys·ics \ˌbī-ō-ˈfi-ziks\ *n* **:** a branch of science concerned with the application of physical principles and methods to biological problems — **bio·phys·i·cal** \-zi-kəl\ *adj* — **bio·phys·i·cist** \-ˈfi-zə-sist\ *n*

bi·op·sy \ˈbī-ˌäp-sē\ *n, pl* **-sies :** the removal of tissue, cells, or fluids from the living body for examination

bio·rhythm \ˈbī-ō-ˌri-t͟həm\ *n* **:** an innately determined rhythmic biological process (as sleep); *also* **:** the internal mechanism controlling such a process

bio·sphere \ˈbī-ə-ˌsfir\ *n* **1 :** the part of the world in which life can exist **2 :** living beings together with their environment

bio·tech \ˈbī-ō-ˌtek\ *n* **:** BIOTECHNOLOGY

bio·tech·nol·ogy \ˌbī-ō-tek-ˈnä-lə-jē\ *n* **:** biological science when applied especially in genetic engineering and recombinant DNA technology

bio·ter·ror·ism \-ˈter-ər-ˌi-zəm\ *n* **:** terrorism involving the use of biological weapons

bi·ot·ic \bī-ˈä-tik\ *adj* **:** of or relating to life; *esp* **:** caused by living beings

bi·o·tin \ˈbī-ə-tən\ *n* **:** a vitamin of the vitamin B complex found especially in yeast, liver, and egg yolk and active in growth promotion

bi·o·tite \ˈbī-ə-ˌtīt\ *n* **:** a dark mica containing iron, magnesium, potassium, and aluminum

bi·par·ti·san \bī-ˈpär-tə-zən\ *adj* **:** marked by or involving cooperation, agreement, and compromise between two major political parties — **bi·par·ti·san·ship** \-ˌship\ *n*

bi·par·tite \-ˈpär-ˌtīt\ *adj* **1** ♦ **:** being in two parts **2 :** shared by two ⟨~ treaty⟩

♦ binary, double, dual, duplex, twin

bi·ped \ˈbī-ˌped\ *n* **:** a 2-footed animal — **bi·ped·al** \(ˌ)bī-ˈped-ᵊl\ *adj*

bi·plane \ˈbī-ˌplān\ *n* **:** an aircraft with two wings placed one above the other

bi·po·lar \bī-ˈpō-lər\ *adj* **:** having or involving the use of two poles — **bi·po·lar·i·ty** \ˌbī-pō-ˈlar-ə-tē\ *n*

bipolar disorder *n* **:** any of several psychological disorders of mood characterized by usually alternating episodes of depression and mania

bi·ra·cial \bī-ˈrā-shəl\ *adj* **:** of, relating to, or involving members of two races

1**birch** \ˈbərch\ *n* **1 :** any of a genus of mostly short-lived deciduous shrubs and trees with membranous outer bark and pale close-grained wood; *also* **:** this wood **2 :** a birch rod or bundle of twigs for flogging — **birch** *or* **birch·en** \ˈbər-chən\ *adj*

2**birch** *vb* **:** to beat with or as if with a birch **:** WHIP

1**bird** \ˈbərd\ *n* **:** any of a class of warm-blooded egg-laying vertebrates having the body feathered and the forelimbs modified to form wings

²bird *vb* **:** to observe or identify wild birds in their native habitat — **bird•er** *n*
bird•bath \'bərd-ˌbath, -ˌbȧth\ *n* **:** a usually ornamental basin set up for birds to bathe in
bird•house \-ˌhau̇s\ *n* **:** an artificial nesting place for birds; *also* **:** AVIARY
bird•ie \'bər-dē\ *n* **:** a score of one under par on a hole in golf
bird•lime \-ˌlīm\ *n* **:** a sticky substance smeared on twigs to snare small birds
bird of prey : a carnivorous bird (as a hawk, falcon, or vulture) that feeds wholly or chiefly on meat taken by hunting or on carrion
bird•seed \'bərd-ˌsēd\ *n* **:** a mixture of small seeds (as of hemp or millet) used for feeding birds
bird's–eye \'bərdz-ˌī\ *adj* **1 :** marked with spots resembling birds' eyes ⟨~ maple⟩ **2 a :** seen from above as if by a flying bird ⟨~ view⟩ **b** ♦ **:** having or involving a bird's-eye view **:** CURSORY

♦ broad, cursory, general, nonspecific, overall

bi•ret•ta \bə-'re-tə\ *n* **:** a square cap with three ridges on top worn especially by Roman Catholic clergymen
birth \'bərth\ *n* **1 :** the act or fact of being born or of bringing forth young **2** ♦ **:** descent in a line from a common progenitor **:** LINEAGE **3** ♦ **:** rise, beginning, or derivation from a source

♦ [2] ancestry, blood, bloodline, breeding, descent, extraction, family tree, genealogy, line, lineage, origin, parentage, pedigree, stock, strain ♦ [3] beginning, commencement, dawn, genesis, launch, morning, onset, outset, start, threshold

birth canal *n* **:** the channel formed by the cervix, vagina, and vulva through which the fetus passes during birth
birth control *n* **:** control of the number of children born especially by preventing or lessening the frequency of conception
birth•day \'bərth-ˌdā\ *n* **:** the day or anniversary of one's birth
birth defect *n* **:** a physical or biochemical defect present at birth and inherited or environmentally induced
birth•mark \'bərth-ˌmärk\ *n* **:** an unusual mark or blemish on the skin at birth
birth•place \-ˌplās\ *n* ♦ **:** place of birth or origin

♦ cradle, home

birth•rate \-ˌrāt\ *n* **:** the number of births per number of individuals in a given area or group during a given time
birth•right \-ˌrīt\ *n* ♦ **:** a right, privilege, or possession to which one is entitled by birth

♦ prerogative, right

birth•stone \-ˌstōn\ *n* **:** a gemstone associated symbolically with the month of one's birth
bis•cuit \'bis-kət\ *n* **1 :** a crisp flat cake; *esp, Brit* **:** CRACKER 2 **2 :** a small quick bread made from dough that has been rolled and cut or dropped from a spoon
bi•sect \'bī-ˌsekt\ *vb* **:** to divide into two usually equal parts; *also* **:** CROSS, INTERSECT — **bi•sec•tion** \'bī-ˌsek-shən\ *n* — **bi•sec•tor** \-tər\ *n*
bi•sex•u•al \bī-'sek-shə-wəl\ *adj* **1 :** possessing characters of or having sexual desire for both sexes **2 :** of, relating to, or involving both sexes — **bisexual** *n* — **bi•sex•u•al•i•ty** \ˌbī-ˌsek-shə-'wal-ə-tē\ *n*
bish•op \'bi-shəp\ *n* **1 :** a member of the clergy ranking above a priest and typically governing a diocese **2 :** any of various Protestant church officials who superintend other clergy **3 :** a chess piece that can move diagonally across any number of adjoining unoccupied squares
bish•op•ric \'bi-shə-prik\ *n* **1 :** DIOCESE **2 :** the office of bishop
bis•muth \'biz-məth\ *n* **:** a heavy brittle grayish white metallic chemical element used in alloys and medicine
bi•son \'bīs-ᵊn, 'bīz-\ *n, pl* **bison :** BUFFALO 2
bisque \'bisk\ *n* **:** a thick cream soup
bis•tro \'bēs-trō, 'bis-\ *n, pl* **bistros 1 :** a small or unpretentious restaurant **2 :** BAR; *also* **:** NIGHTCLUB
¹bit \'bit\ *n* **1 :** the biting or cutting edge or part of a tool **2 :** the part of a bridle that is placed in a horse's mouth
²bit *n* **1 a :** a morsel of food **b** ♦ **:** a small piece or quantity of something **2 :** a small coin; *also* **:** a unit of value equal to 12½ cents **3 :** something small or trivial **4** ♦ **:** an indefinite usually small degree or extent ⟨a ~ tired⟩

♦ [1b] ace, crumb, dab, hint, lick, little, mite, nip, particle, shred, speck, spot, touch, trace ♦ [4] space, spell, stretch, while

³bit *n* **:** a unit of computer information equivalent to the result of a choice between two alternatives; *also* **:** its physical representation

¹bitch \'bich\ *n* **1 :** a female canine; *esp* **:** a female dog **2 :** a malicious, spiteful, and domineering woman
²bitch *vb* **:** COMPLAIN
¹bite \'bīt\ *vb* **bit** \'bit\; **bit•ten** \'bit-ᵊn\ *also* **bit; bit•ing** \'bī-tiŋ\ **1** ♦ **:** to grip with teeth or jaws; *also* **:** to wound or sting with or as if with fangs **2 :** to cut or pierce with or as if with an edged instrument **3 :** to cause to smart or sting **4** ♦ **:** to eat away by degrees as if by gnawing **:** CORRODE **5 :** to take bait

♦ *usu* **bite on** [1] champ, chew, chomp, crunch, gnaw, nibble ♦ *usu* **bite at** [4] corrode, eat, erode, fret

²bite *n* **1 :** the act or manner of biting **2** ♦ **:** a small amount of food **3 a :** a wound made by biting **b** ♦ **:** a penetrating effect or sensation

♦ [2] morsel, mouthful, nibble, taste, tidbit ♦ [3b] bitterness, harshness, pungency, sharpness, tartness

bit•ing \'bī-tiŋ\ *adj* ♦ **:** having the power to bite so as to cause physical or mental discomfort ⟨a ~ wind⟩; *esp* **:** able to grip and impress deeply ⟨a ~ wit⟩

♦ bitter, cutting, keen, penetrating, piercing, raw, sharp ♦ acute, agonizing, excruciating, sharp, smart ♦ acrid, caustic, cutting, mordant, pungent, sarcastic, satiric, scathing, sharp, tart

bit•mapped \'bit-ˌmapt\ *adj* **:** of, relating to, or being a digital image or display for which an array of binary data specifies the value of each pixel — **bit•map** \-ˌmap\ *n*
bit•ter \'bi-tər\ *adj* **1 :** being or inducing the one of the basic taste sensations that is acrid, astringent, or disagreeable and is suggestive of hops **2** ♦ **:** marked by intensity or severity (as of distress or hatred) **3** ♦ **:** extremely harsh or cruel **4** ♦ **:** intensely unpleasant especially in coldness or rawness

♦ [2] acrid, acrimonious, hard, rancorous, resentful, sore ♦ [3] agonizing, galling, harrowing, harsh, hurtful, painful, tortuous *Ant* gratifying, pleasing, sweet ♦ [3] brutal, burdensome, grim, hard, harsh, heavy, onerous, oppressive, severe, stiff, tough, trying ♦ [4] arctic, cold, freezing, frigid, frosty, glacial, icy, polar, raw, wintry

bit•ter•ly *adv* ♦ **:** in a bitter manner

♦ hard, sadly, sorrowfully, unhappily, wretchedly

bit•tern \'bi-tərn\ *n* **:** any of various small or medium-sized herons
bit•ter•ness *n* ♦ **:** the quality or state of being bitter; *also* **:** something bitter

♦ animosity, antagonism, antipathy, enmity, gall, grudge, hostility, rancor ♦ bite, harshness, pungency, sharpness, tartness

bit•ters \'bi-tərz\ *n sing or pl* **:** a usually alcoholic solution of bitter and often aromatic plant products used in mixing drinks and as a mild tonic
¹bit•ter•sweet \'bi-tər-ˌswēt\ *n* **1 :** a poisonous nightshade with purple flowers and orange-red berries **2 :** a woody vine with yellow capsules that open when ripe and disclose scarlet seed coverings
²bittersweet *adj* **:** being at once both bitter and sweet
bi•tu•mi•nous coal \bə-'tü-mə-nəs-, bī-, -'tyü-\ *n* **:** a coal that when heated yields considerable volatile waste matter
bi•valve \'bī-ˌvalv\ *n* **:** any of a class of mollusks (as clams or scallops) with a shell composed of two separate parts that open and shut — **bivalve** *adj*
¹biv•ouac \'bi-və-ˌwak\ *n* ♦ **:** a temporary encampment or shelter

♦ camp, encampment

²bivouac *vb* **-ouacked; -ouack•ing :** to form a bivouac **:** CAMP
¹bi•week•ly \ˌbī-'wē-klē\ *adj* **1 :** occurring twice a week **2 :** occurring every two weeks **:** FORTNIGHTLY — **biweekly** *adv*
²biweekly *n* **:** a biweekly publication
bi•year•ly \-'yir-lē\ *adj* **1 :** BIANNUAL **2 :** BIENNIAL
bi•zarre \bə-'zär\ *adj* **:** strikingly out of the ordinary: as **a** ♦ **:** odd, extravagant, or eccentric in style or mode **b** ♦ **:** involving sensational contrasts or incongruities **:** FANTASTIC — **bizarre•ly** *adv*

♦ [a] curious, far-out, funny, odd, outlandish, peculiar, quaint, queer, quirky, screwy, strange, weird ♦ [b] absurd, crazy, fanciful, fantastic, foolish, insane, nonsensical, preposterous, unreal, wild

bk *abbr* **1** bank **2** book
Bk *symbol* berkelium
bkg *abbr* banking
bkgd *abbr* background
bks *abbr* barracks

bkt *abbr* **1** basket **2** bracket

bl *abbr* **1** bale **2** barrel **3** blue

blab \ˈblab\ *vb* **blabbed; blab•bing 1 ♦ :** to talk idly or thoughtlessly **2 :** to reveal a secret especially by indiscreet chatter **:** TATTLE, GOSSIP

♦ chat, converse, gab, jaw, palaver, patter, prattle, rattle, talk, visit

blab•ber•mouth \ˈbla-bər-ˌmau̇th\ *n* **♦ :** a person who talks too much; *esp* **:** TATTLETALE

♦ betrayer, informer, rat, snitch, stool pigeon, tattler, tattletale

blab•by \ˈbla-bē\ *adj* **:** given to talking

[1]**black** \ˈblak\ *adj* **1 ♦ :** of the color black; *also* **:** very dark **2 :** SWARTHY **3 :** of or relating to various groups of dark-skinned people **4 :** of or relating to the African-American people or their culture **5 :** SOILED, DIRTY **6 :** lacking light ⟨a ~ night⟩ **7 ♦ :** thoroughly sinister or evil **:** WICKED ⟨~ magic⟩ **8 ♦ :** very sad, gloomy, or calamitous **:** DISMAL ⟨a ~ outlook⟩ **9 :** SULLEN ⟨a ~ mood⟩ — **black•ish** *adj* — **black•ly** *adv*

♦ [1] ebony, raven ***Ant*** white ♦ [7] bad, evil, immoral, iniquitous, nefarious, rotten, sinful, unethical, unsavory, vicious, vile, villainous, wicked, wrong ♦ [8] bleak, dark, dismal, dreary, gloomy, gray (*or* grey), somber (*or* sombre), wretched

[2]**black** *n* **1 :** a black pigment or dye; *also* **:** something (as clothing) that is black **2 :** the characteristic color of soot or coal **3 :** a person of a dark-skinned race **4 :** AFRICAN-AMERICAN

[3]**black** *vb* **:** BLACKEN

[4]**black** *n* **♦ :** total or nearly total absence of light

♦ dark, darkness, dusk, gloaming, gloom, murk, night, semidarkness, shade, shadows, twilight

black•a•moor \ˈbla-kə-ˌmu̇r\ *n* **:** a dark-skinned person

black–and–blue \ˌbla-kən-ˈblü\ *adj* **:** darkly discolored from blood effused by bruising

black•ball \ˈblak-ˌbȯl\ *vb* **1 ♦ :** to vote against; *esp* **:** to exclude from membership by casting a negative vote **2 :** OSTRACIZE — **black•ball** *n*

♦ kill, negative, veto

black bass *n* **:** any of several freshwater sunfishes native to eastern and central No. America

black bear *n* **:** a usually black-furred bear of the North American forests

[1]**black belt** \ˈblak-ˌbelt\ *n, often cap both Bs* **:** an area densely populated by blacks

[2]**black belt** \-ˈbelt\ *n* **:** one who holds the rating of expert (as in judo or karate); *also* **:** the rating itself

black•ber•ry \-ˌber-ē\ *n* **:** the usually black or purple juicy but seedy edible fruit of various brambles; *also* **:** a plant bearing this fruit

black•bird \-ˌbərd\ *n* **:** any of various birds (as the red-winged blackbird) of which the male is largely or wholly black

black•board \-ˌbōrd\ *n* **:** a smooth usually dark surface used for writing or drawing on with chalk

black•body \-ˈbä-dē\ *n* **:** a body or surface that completely absorbs incident radiation with no reflection

black box *n* **1 :** a usually complicated electronic device whose components and workings are unknown or mysterious to the user **2 :** a device used in aircraft to record cockpit conversations and flight data

black death *n* **:** an epidemic of bacterial plague and especially bubonic plague that spread rapidly in Europe and Asia in the 14th century

black•en \ˈbla-kən\ *vb* **black•ened; black•en•ing 1 ♦ :** to make or become black or dark **2 ♦ :** to speak evil of **:** DEFAME

♦ [1] becloud, cloud, darken, dim, obscure, overcast, overshadow, shadow ♦ [1] befoul, begrime, besmirch, blacken, dirty, muddy, smirch, soil, stain ♦ [2] defame, libel, malign, slander, smear, traduce, vilify

black•ened *adj* **:** coated with spices and quickly seared in a very hot skillet ⟨~ swordfish⟩

black eye *n* **:** a discoloration of the skin around the eye from bruising

black–eyed Su•san \ˌblak-ˌīd-ˈsüz-ᵊn\ *n* **:** a coarse No. American plant that is related to the daisies and has deep yellow to orange flower heads with dark conical centers

Black•foot \ˈblak-ˌfu̇t\ *n, pl* **Black•feet** *or* **Blackfoot :** a member of an American Indian people of Montana, Alberta, and Saskatchewan

black•guard \ˈbla-gərd, -ˌgärd\ *n* **:** SCOUNDREL, RASCAL

black•head \ˈblak-ˌhed\ *n* **:** a small usually dark oily mass plugging the outlet of a skin gland

black hole *n* **:** a hypothetical celestial object with a gravitational field so strong that light cannot escape from it

black•ing \ˈbla-kiŋ\ *n* **:** a substance applied to something to make it black

[1]**black•jack** \ˈblak-ˌjak\ *n* **1 :** a leather-covered club with a flexible handle **2 :** a card game in which the object is to be dealt cards having a higher count than the dealer but not exceeding 21

[2]**blackjack** *vb* **:** to hit with or as if with a blackjack

black light *n* **:** invisible ultraviolet light

black•list \ˈblak-ˌlist\ *n* **:** a list of persons who are disapproved of and are to be punished or boycotted — **blacklist** *vb*

black•mail \ˈblak-ˌmāl\ *n* **:** extortion by threats especially of public exposure; *also* **:** something so extorted — **blackmail** *vb*

black•mail•er *n* **:** one who blackmails another

black market *n* **:** illicit trade in goods; *also* **:** a place where such trade is carried on

Black Mass *n* **:** a travesty of the Christian mass ascribed to worshipers of Satan

Black Muslim *n* **:** a member of a chiefly black group that professes Islamic religious belief

black nationalist *n, often cap B&N* **:** a member of a group of militant blacks who advocate separatism from whites and the formation of self-governing black communities — **black nationalism** *n, often cap B&N*

black•ness *n* **:** the quality or state of being black

black•out \ˈbla-ˌkau̇t\ *n* **1 :** a period of darkness due to electrical power failure **2 ♦ :** a transitory loss or dulling of vision or consciousness **3 :** the prohibition or restriction of the telecasting of a sports event

♦ faint, knockout, swoon

black out *vb* **♦ :** to temporarily lose vision, consciousness, or memory

♦ faint, pass out, swoon

black pepper *n* **:** a spice that consists of the dried berry of a pepper plant that is ground with the black husk still on

black power *n* **:** the mobilization of the political and economic power of black Americans especially to compel respect for their rights and improve their condition

black sheep *n* **:** a member of a group who is disreputable or who is not regarded favorably

black•smith \ˈblak-ˌsmith\ *n* **:** a smith who forges iron — **black•smith•ing** *n*

black•thorn \-ˌthȯrn\ *n* **:** a European thorny plum

black–tie \ˈblak-ˈtī\ *adj* **:** characterized by or requiring semiformal evening clothes consisting of a usually black tie and tuxedo for men and a formal dress for women

black•top \ˈblak-ˌtäp\ *n* **:** a dark tarry material (as asphalt) used especially for surfacing roads — **blacktop** *vb*

black widow *n* **:** a venomous New World spider having the female black with an hourglass-shaped red mark on the underside of the abdomen

blad•der \ˈbla-dər\ *n* **:** a sac in which liquid or gas is stored; *esp* **:** one in a vertebrate into which urine passes from the kidneys

blade \ˈblād\ *n* **1 :** a leaf of a plant and especially of a grass; *also* **:** the flat part of a leaf as distinguished from its stalk **2 :** something (as the flat part of an oar or an arm of a propeller) resembling the blade of a leaf **3 :** the cutting part of an instrument or tool **4 :** a weapon (as a cutlass or rapier) with a long blade for cutting or thrusting that is often used as a symbol of honor or authority **:** SWORD; *also* **:** SWORDSMAN **5 :** a dashing fellow ⟨a gay ~⟩ **6 :** the runner of an ice skate — **blad•ed** \ˈblā-dəd\ *adj*

blain \ˈblān\ *n* **:** an inflammatory swelling or sore

blam•able *adj* **♦ :** deserving blame

♦ blameworthy, censurable, culpable, reprehensible

[1]**blame** \ˈblām\ *vb* **blamed; blam•ing 1 ♦ :** to find fault with **2 :** to hold responsible or responsible for

♦ censure, condemn, criticize, denounce, fault, knock, pan, reprehend

[2]**blame** *n* **1 :** CENSURE, REPROOF **2 ♦ :** responsibility for fault or error

♦ culpability, fault, guilt, rap ***Ant*** blamelessness

blame•less *adj* **♦ :** free from blame or fault — **blame•less•ly** *adv* — **blame•less•ness** *n*

♦ clear, faultless, guiltless, impeccable, innocent, irreproachable

blame•wor•thy \-ˌwər-<u>th</u>ē\ *adj* ◆ : deserving blame — **blame•wor•thi•ness** *n*

◆ blamable, censurable, culpable, reprehensible *Ant* blameless, faultless, impeccable, irreproachable

blanch \ˈblanch\ *vb* ◆ : to make or become white or pale : BLEACH

◆ bleach, blench, dull, fade, pale, wash out, whiten

blanc•mange \blə-ˈmänj, -ˈmä^{n}zh\ *n* : a dessert made from gelatin or a starchy substance and milk usually sweetened and flavored

bland \ˈbland\ *adj* **1** : smooth in manner : SUAVE **2** ◆ : gently soothing ⟨a ~ diet⟩; *also* : INSIPID — **bland•ly** *adv* — **bland•ness** *n*

◆ balmy, benign, delicate, gentle, insipid, light, mellow, mild, soft, soothing, tender

blan•dish•ment \ˈblan-dish-mənt\ *n* : flattering or coaxing speech or action : CAJOLERY

[1]**blank** \ˈblaŋk\ *adj* **1 a** : showing or causing an appearance of dazed dismay **b** ◆ : lacking expression **2** ◆ : free from writing or marks; *also* : having spaces to be filled in **3** : DULL, EMPTY ⟨~ moments⟩ **4** : ABSOLUTE, DOWNRIGHT ⟨a ~ refusal⟩ **5** : not shaped in final form — **blank•ly** *adv*

◆ [1b] deadpan, expressionless, impassive, inexpressive, stolid, vacant *Ant* demonstrative, expressive ◆ [2] bare, devoid, empty, stark, vacant, void

[2]**blank** *n* **1** ◆ : an empty space **2** ◆ : a form with spaces for the entry of data **3** : an unfinished form (as of a key) **4** : a cartridge with propellant and a seal but no projectile

◆ [1] blankness, emptiness, vacancy, vacuity, void ◆ [2] document, form, paper

[3]**blank** *vb* **1** : to cover or close up : OBSCURE **2** : to keep from scoring

blank check *n* **1** : a signed check with the amount unspecified **2** : complete freedom of action

[1]**blan•ket** \ˈblaŋ-kət\ *n* **1** : a heavy woven often woolen covering **2** ◆ : a covering layer ⟨a ~ of snow⟩

◆ cloak, curtain, hood, mantle, mask, shroud, veil

[2]**blanket** *vb* **1** ◆ : to cover with or as if with a blanket **2** ◆ : to cover so as to obscure, interrupt, suppress, or extinguish

◆ [1] carpet, coat, cover, overlay, overlie, overspread ◆ [2] blot out, cloak, conceal, cover, curtain, enshroud, hide, mask, obscure, occlude, occult, screen, shroud, veil

[3]**blanket** *adj* ◆ : covering a group or class ⟨~ insurance⟩; *also* : applicable in all instances ⟨~ rules⟩

◆ common, general, generic, global, overall, universal

blank•ness *n* ◆ : the quality or state of being blank

◆ blank, emptiness, vacancy, vacuity, void

blank verse *n* : unrhymed iambic pentameter

blare \ˈblar\ *vb* **blared; blar•ing** : to sound loud and harsh; *also* : to proclaim loudly — **blare** *n*

blar•ney \ˈblär-nē\ *n* ◆ : skillful flattery : BLANDISHMENT

◆ adulation, flattery, overpraise

bla•sé \blä-ˈzā\ *adj* : apathetic to pleasure or excitement as a result of excessive indulgence; *also* : SOPHISTICATED

blas•pheme \blas-ˈfēm, ˈblas-ˌ\ *vb* **blas•phemed; blas•phem•ing** **1** : to speak of or address with irreverence **2** : to utter blasphemy — **blas•phem•er** *n*

blas•phe•mous \-məs\ *adj* ◆ : impiously irreverent

◆ irreverent, profane, sacrilegious

blas•phe•my \ˈblas-fə-mē\ *n, pl* **-mies** **1** ◆ : the act of expressing lack of reverence for God **2** ◆ : irreverence toward something considered sacred

◆ [1, 2] defilement, desecration, impiety, irreverence, sacrilege *Ant* adoration, glorification, worship

[1]**blast** \ˈblast\ *n* **1** ◆ : a violent gust of wind; *also* : its effect **2** : sound made by a wind instrument **3** : a current of air forced at high pressure through a hole in a furnace (**blast furnace**) **4** : a sudden withering especially of plants : BLIGHT **5** ◆ : an explosion or violent detonation; *also* : the often destructive shock wave of an explosion

◆ [1] blow, flurry, gust, williwaw ◆ [5] detonation, eruption, explosion

[2]**blast** *vb* **1** ◆ : to make a vigorous attack **2 a** : to use an explosive **b** ◆ : to discharge or propel something by means of an explosive : SHOOT **3** ◆ : to shatter by or as if by an explosive

◆ [1] abuse, assail, attack, belabor, castigate, excoriate, jump, lambaste, slam, vituperate ◆ [2b] discharge, fire, loose, shoot ◆ [3] blow up, burst, demolish, explode, pop, shatter, smash

blast off *vb* : TAKE OFF 4 — used especially of rocket-propelled vehicles — **blast•off** \ˈblast-ˌȯf\ *n*

bla•tant \ˈblāt-^{ə}nt\ *adj* ◆ : offensively obtrusive : vulgarly showy — **bla•tan•cy** \-^{ə}n-sē\ *n* — **bla•tant•ly** *adv*

◆ conspicuous, egregious, flagrant, glaring, gross, obvious, patent, prominent, pronounced, rank, striking

blath•er \ˈbla-<u>th</u>ər\ *vb* : to talk foolishly at length — **blather** *n*

blath•er•skite \ˈbla-<u>th</u>ər-ˌskīt\ *n* : a person who blathers

[1]**blaze** \ˈblāz\ *n* **1** : FIRE **2** ◆ : intense direct light often accompanied by heat ⟨the ~ of TV lights⟩ **3** : something (as a dazzling display or sudden outburst) suggesting fire ⟨a ~ of autumn leaves⟩

◆ flare, fluorescence, glare, gleam, glow, illumination, incandescence, light, luminescence, radiance, shine

[2]**blaze** *vb* **blazed; blaz•ing** **1** ◆ : to burn brightly; *also* : to flare up **2** ◆ : to be conspicuously bright

◆ [1] burn, flame, flare, glow ◆ [1, 2] beat, burn, flame, flare, glare

[3]**blaze** *vb* **blazed; blaz•ing** ◆ : to make public or conspicuous

◆ advertise, announce, broadcast, declare, enunciate, flash, herald, placard, post, proclaim, promulgate, publicize, publish, sound

[4]**blaze** *n* **1** : a usually white stripe on the face of an animal **2** : a trail marker; *esp* : one made on a tree

[5]**blaze** *vb* **blazed; blaz•ing** : to mark (as a tree or trail) with blazes

blaz•er \ˈblā-zər\ *n* : a sports jacket often with notched collar and pockets that are stitched on

[1]**bla•zon** \ˈblāz-^{ə}n\ *n* **1** : COAT OF ARMS **2** : ostentatious display

[2]**blazon** *vb* **1** : to publish widely : PROCLAIM **2** : DECK, ADORN

bldg *abbr* building

bldr *abbr* builder

[1]**bleach** \ˈblēch\ *vb* ◆ : to make or become white : BLANCH

◆ blanch, blench, dull, fade, pale, wash out, whiten

[2]**bleach** *n* : a preparation used in bleaching

bleach•ers \ˈblē-chərz\ *n sing or pl* : a usually uncovered stand of tiered seats for spectators

bleak \ˈblēk\ *adj* **1** ◆ : desolately barren and often windswept **2** ◆ : lacking warm or cheering qualities — **bleak•ish** *adj* — **bleak•ly** *adv*

◆ [1] dirty, foul, inclement, nasty, raw, rough, squally, stormy, tempestuous, turbulent ◆ [2] dark, dismal, dreary, gloomy, gray (*or* grey), somber (*or* sombre), wretched

bleak•ness *n* ◆ : the quality or state of being bleak

◆ bite, bitterness, chill, nip, rawness, sharpness

blear \ˈblir\ *adj* : dim with water or tears ⟨~ eyes⟩

bleary \ˈblir-ē\ *adj* **1** : dull or dimmed especially from fatigue or sleep **2** ◆ : poorly outlined or defined

◆ dim, faint, foggy, fuzzy, hazy, indefinite, indistinct, unclear, undefined, undetermined

bleat \ˈblēt\ *n* : the cry of a sheep or goat or a sound like it — **bleat** *vb*

bleed \ˈblēd\ *vb* **bled** \ˈbled\; **bleed•ing** **1** : to lose or shed blood **2 a** : to be wounded **b** ◆ : to feel pain or distress **3 a** ◆ : to flow or ooze from a wounded surface **b** ◆ : to draw fluid from especially in a controlled manner ⟨~ steam from the pipes⟩ ⟨~ a tire⟩ **4** : to extort money from

◆ [2b] agonize, feel, grieve, hurt, mourn, sorrow, suffer ◆ [3a] exude, ooze, percolate, seep, strain, sweat, weep ◆ [3b] drain, draw, pump, siphon, tap

bleed•er \ˈblē-dər\ *n* : one that bleeds; *esp* : HEMOPHILIAC

bleeding heart *n* **1** : a garden plant related to the poppies that has usually deep pink drooping heart-shaped flowers **2** : a person who shows extreme sympathy especially for an object of alleged persecution

[1]**blem•ish** \ˈble-mish\ *vb* ◆ : to spoil by a flaw : MAR

◆ mar, poison, spoil, stain, taint, tarnish, touch, vitiate

[2]**blemish** *n* ◆ : a noticeable flaw

♦ defect, deformity, disfigurement, fault, flaw, imperfection, mark, pockmark, scar

¹blench \ˈblench\ *vb* ♦ **:** to draw back or turn aside from lack of courage **:** FLINCH, QUAIL

♦ flinch, quail, recoil, shrink, wince

²blench *vb* ♦ **:** to grow or make pale

♦ blanch, bleach, dull, fade, pale, wash out, whiten

¹blend \ˈblend\ *vb* **blend•ed; blend•ing 1** ♦ **:** to mix thoroughly **2 :** to prepare (as coffee) by mixing different varieties **3** ♦ **:** to combine into an integrated whole **4 :** to produce a harmonious effect **:** HARMONIZE — **blend•er** *n*

♦ amalgamate, commingle, fuse, incorporate, intermingle, merge, mingle, mix *Ant* break down, break up, separate

²blend *n* ♦ **:** a product of blending

♦ admixture, amalgam, combination, composite, compound, fusion, intermixture, mix, mixture

bless \ˈbles\ *vb* **blessed** \ˈblest\ *also* **blest** \ˈblest\; **bless•ing 1** ♦ **:** to consecrate by religious rite or word **2 :** to sanctify with the sign of the cross **3 :** to invoke divine care for **4** ♦ **:** to give glory to **:** PRAISE, GLORIFY **5 :** to confer happiness upon

♦ [1] consecrate, hallow, sanctify ♦ [4] extol, glorify, laud, magnify, praise

bless•ed \ˈble-səd\ *also* **blest** \ˈblest\ *adj* **1 a** ♦ **:** held in reverence **b** ♦ **:** venerated as or as if sacred **:** HOLY **2 :** BEATIFIED **3 :** DELIGHTFUL — **bless•ed•ly** *adv*

♦ [1a] hallowed, holy, sacred, sacrosanct, sanctified ♦ [1b] divine, godlike, heavenly, holy

bless•ed•ness *n* ♦ **:** the quality or state of being blessed

♦ bliss, felicity, gladness, happiness, joy ♦ devoutness, godliness, holiness, piety, sainthood, sanctity

bless•ing \ˈble-siŋ\ *n* **1 a** ♦ **:** the act or words of one who blesses **b** ♦ **:** acknowledgment and acceptance or support of something **:** APPROVAL ⟨gave their ~ to the proposal⟩ **2** ♦ **:** a thing conducive to happiness **3 :** grace said at a meal

♦ [1a] consecration, sanctification ♦ [1b] approbation, approval, favor (*or* favour), imprimatur, OK ♦ [2] benefit, boon, felicity, godsend, good, manna, windfall *Ant* affliction, bane, curse, evil, plague, scourge

blew *past of* BLOW

¹blight \ˈblīt\ *n* **1 :** a plant disease or injury marked by withering; *also* **:** an organism causing a blight **2 :** an impairing or frustrating influence; *also* **:** a deteriorated condition ⟨urban ~⟩

²blight *vb* **:** to affect with or suffer from blight

blimp \ˈblimp\ *n* **:** a nonrigid airship

¹blind \ˈblīnd\ *adj* **1 :** lacking or grossly deficient in ability to see; *also* **:** intended for blind persons **2 :** not based on reason, evidence, or knowledge ⟨~ faith⟩ **3 :** not intelligently controlled or directed ⟨~ chance⟩ **4 :** performed solely by using aircraft instruments ⟨a ~ landing⟩ **5 :** hard to discern or make out **:** HIDDEN ⟨a ~ seam⟩ **6 :** lacking an opening or outlet ⟨a ~ alley⟩ — **blind•ly** *adv* — **blind•ness** \ˈblīnd-nəs\ *n*

²blind *vb* **1 :** to make blind **2 :** to overpower with brightness **:** DAZZLE **3 :** DARKEN; *also* **:** HIDE

³blind *n* **1 :** something (as a shutter) to hinder vision or keep out light **2 :** a place of concealment **3 :** SUBTERFUGE

blind date *n* **:** a date between persons who have not previously met; *also* **:** either of these persons

blind•er \ˈblīn-dər\ *n* **:** either of two flaps on a horse's bridle to prevent it from seeing to the side

blind•fold \ˈblīnd-ˌfōld\ *vb* **:** to cover the eyes of with or as if with a bandage — **blindfold** *n*

¹blink \ˈbliŋk\ *vb* **1 :** to close and open the eyes involuntarily **:** WINK **2** ♦ **:** to shine dimly or intermittently **:** TWINKLE **3 :** EVADE, IGNORE — often used with *at*

♦ flash, twinkle, wink

²blink *n* **1 :** GLIMMER, SPARKLE **2 :** a usually involuntary shutting and opening of the eye

blink•er \ˈbliŋ-kər\ *n* **:** a blinking light used as a signal

blin•tze \ˈblint-sə\ *or* **blintz** \ˈblints\ *n* **:** a thin rolled pancake with a filling usually of cream cheese

blip \ˈblip\ *n* **1 :** a spot on a radar screen **2 :** ABERRATION 1

bliss \ˈblis\ *n* ♦ **:** complete happiness **:** JOY

♦ blessedness, felicity, gladness, happiness, joy

bliss•ful \-fəl\ *adj* ♦ **:** full of, marked by, or causing bliss — **bliss•ful•ly** *adv*

♦ delighted, glad, happy, joyful, pleased

¹blis•ter \ˈblis-tər\ *n* **1 :** a raised area of skin containing watery fluid; *also* **:** an agent that causes blisters **2 :** something (as a raised spot in paint) suggesting a blister **3 :** a disease of plants marked by large swollen patches on the leaves

²blister *vb* **:** to develop a blister; *also* **:** to cause blisters

blithe \ˈblīth, ˈblīth\ *adj* **blith•er; blith•est** ♦ **:** happily lighthearted — **blithe•ly** *adv*

♦ bright, buoyant, cheerful, cheery, chipper, gay, lightsome, sunny, upbeat ♦ boon, festive, gay, gleeful, jocund, jolly, jovial, merry, mirthful, sunny

blithe•some \-səm\ *adj* **:** full of gaiety or high spirits

¹blitz \ˈblits\ *n* **1 :** an intensive series of air raids **2 :** a fast intensive campaign **3 :** a rush of the passer by the defensive linebackers in football

²blitz *vb* ♦ **:** to subject to a blitz; *esp* **:** to damage by a blitz

♦ bombard, shell

blitz•krieg \-ˌkrēg\ *n* ♦ **:** a sudden violent enemy attack

♦ aggression, assault, attack, charge, descent, offense (*or* offence), offensive, onset, onslaught, raid, rush, strike

bliz•zard \ˈbli-zərd\ *n* **:** a long severe snowstorm

blk *abbr* **1** black **2** block

bloat \ˈblōt\ *vb* **:** to swell by or as if by filling with water or air

blob \ˈbläb\ *n* ♦ **:** a small lump or drop of a thick consistency

♦ chunk, clod, clump, glob, gob, hunk, lump, nub, wad

bloc \ˈbläk\ *n* ♦ **:** a combination of individuals or groups (as nations) working for a common purpose

♦ body, coalition, combination, combine, faction, party, sect, set, side, wing ♦ alliance, coalition, combination, combine, confederacy, confederation, federation, league, union

¹block \ˈbläk\ *n* **1 :** a solid piece of substantial material (as wood or stone) **2** ♦ **:** something that impedes progress or achievement **:** HINDRANCE, OBSTRUCTION; *also* **:** interruption of normal function of body or mind ⟨heart ~⟩ **3 :** a frame enclosing one or more pulleys and having a hook or strap by which it may be attached **4 :** a piece of material with a hand-cut design on its surface from which copies are to be made **5 :** a large building divided into separate units (as apartments or offices) **6 :** a row of houses or shops **7 :** a city square; *also* **:** the distance along one of the sides of such a square **8** ♦ **:** a quantity of things considered as a unit ⟨a ~ of seats⟩

♦ [2] bar, clog, crimp, drag, embarrassment, hindrance, let, obstacle, stop, stumbling block ♦ [8] array, assemblage, batch, bunch, cluster, collection, group, package, set, suite

²block *vb* **1** ♦ **:** to make unsuitable for passage or progress by obstruction **:** OBSTRUCT **2 :** to outline roughly ⟨~ out a design⟩ **3 :** to provide or support with a block ⟨~ up a wheel⟩

♦ dam, fill, pack, plug, stop, stuff ♦ choke, clog, close (off), congest, dam, jam, obstruct, plug (up), stop (up), stuff

¹block•ade \blä-ˈkād\ *n* **:** the isolation of a place usually by troops or ships

²blockade *vb* **:** to subject to or isolate with a blockade — **block•ad•er** *n*

block•age \ˈblä-kij\ *n* **:** an act or instance of obstructing **:** the state of being blocked

block•bust•er \ˈbläk-ˌbəs-tər\ *n* ♦ **:** one that is very large, successful, or violent ⟨a ~ of a movie⟩

♦ hit, smash, success, winner ♦ behemoth, colossus, giant, jumbo, leviathan, mammoth, monster, titan, whale, whopper

block•head \ˈbläk-ˌhed\ *n* ♦ **:** a slow-witted or stupid person **:** DOLT, DUNCE

♦ dope, dummy, idiot, imbecile, jackass, moron, numskull

block•house \-ˌhau̇s\ *n* **:** a small strong building used as a shelter (as from enemy fire) or observation post

¹blond *or* **blonde** \ˈbländ\ *adj* **1 :** fair in complexion **2** ♦ **:** of a light or bleached color ⟨~ mahogany⟩ — **blond•ish** \ˈblän-dish\ *adj*

♦ fair, flaxen, golden, sandy, straw *Ant* dark

²blond *or* **blonde** *n* **:** a person having blond hair

blood \ˈbləd\ *n* **1 :** a usually red liquid that circulates in the heart, arteries, and veins of animals **2 :** LIFEBLOOD; *also* **:** LIFE **3** ♦ **:** human stock or lineage **4 a :** relationship by descent from a common ancestor **b** ♦ **:** persons related by means of a common ancestor **:** KINDRED **5 :** the taking of life **6 :** TEMPER, PASSION **7 :** DANDY 1 — **blood·less** *adj*

♦ [3] ancestry, birth, bloodline, breeding, descent, extraction, family tree, genealogy, line, lineage, origin, parentage, pedigree, stock, strain ♦ [4b] clan, family, folks, house, kin, kindred, kinfolk, line, lineage, people, race, stock, tribe

blood bank *n* **:** a place where blood or plasma is stored
blood·bath \ˈbləd-ˌbath, -ˌbäth\ *n* **:** MASSACRE
blood count *n* **:** the determination of the number of blood cells in a specific volume of blood; *also* **:** the number of cells so determined
blood·cur·dling \ˈbləd-kərd-liŋ, -ˌkər-dᵊl-iŋ\ *adj* **:** arousing fright or horror
blood·ed \ˈblə-dəd\ *adj* **1 :** having blood of a specified kind ⟨warm-*blooded* animals⟩ **2 :** entirely or largely purebred ⟨~ horses⟩
blood group *n* **:** one of the classes into which human beings can be separated by the presence or absence in their blood of specific antigens
blood·hound \ˈbləd-ˌhau̇nd\ *n* **:** any of a breed of large powerful hounds with long drooping ears, a wrinkled face, and keen sense of smell
blood·let·ting \-ˌle-tiŋ\ *n* **1 :** PHLEBOTOMY **2 :** BLOODSHED
blood·line \-ˌlīn\ *n* ♦ **:** a sequence of direct ancestors especially in a pedigree

♦ ancestry, birth, blood, breeding, descent, extraction, family tree, genealogy, line, lineage, origin, parentage, pedigree, stock, strain

blood·mo·bile \-mō-ˌbēl\ *n* **:** a motor vehicle equipped for collecting blood from donors
blood poisoning *n* **:** invasion of the bloodstream by virulent microorganisms from a focus of infection accompanied especially by chills, fever, and prostration
blood pressure *n* **:** pressure of the blood on the walls of blood vessels and especially arteries
blood·root \ˈbləd-ˌrüt, -ˌru̇t\ *n* **:** a plant related to the poppy that has a red root and sap, a solitary leaf, and a white flower in early spring
blood·shed \-ˌshed\ *n* **:** wounding or taking of life **:** CARNAGE, SLAUGHTER
blood·shot \-ˌshät\ *adj* **:** inflamed to redness ⟨~ eyes⟩
blood·stain \-ˌstān\ *n* **:** a discoloration caused by blood
blood·stained \-ˌstānd\ *adj* **:** stained with blood; *also* **:** involved with slaughter
blood·stone \-ˌstōn\ *n* **:** a green quartz sprinkled with red spots
blood·stream \-ˌstrēm\ *n* **:** the flowing blood in a circulatory system
blood·suck·er \-ˌsə-kər\ *n* **:** an animal that sucks blood; *esp* **:** LEECH — **blood·suck·ing** *adj*
blood test *n* **:** a test of the blood; *esp* **:** one for syphilis
blood·thirsty \ˈbləd-ˌthər-stē\ *adj* ♦ **:** eager to shed blood — **blood·thirst·i·ly** \-ˌthər-stə-lē\ *adv* — **blood·thirst·i·ness** \-stē-nəs\ *n*

♦ bloody, homicidal, murderous, sanguinary, sanguine

blood type *n* **:** BLOOD GROUP — **blood–typ·ing** *n*
blood vessel *n* **:** a vessel (as a vein or artery) in which blood circulates in the body
bloody *adj* **1 :** containing or made up of blood; *also* **:** smeared or stained with blood **2** ♦ **:** accompanied by or involving bloodshed

♦ bloodthirsty, homicidal, murderous, sanguinary, sanguine

Bloody Mary \-ˈmer-ē\ *n, pl* **Bloody Marys :** a drink made essentially of vodka and tomato juice
¹bloom \ˈblüm\ *n* **1 :** the part of a seed plant that normally bears reproductive organs **:** FLOWER 1; *also* **:** flowers or amount of flowers (as of a plant) **2 :** the period or state of flowering **3** ♦ **:** a state or time of beauty and vigor **4 :** a powdery coating especially on fruits and leaves **5 :** rosy color; *also* **:** an appearance of freshness or health — **bloomy** *adj*

♦ blossom, flower, flush, heyday, prime

²bloom *vb* **1** ♦ **:** to produce or yield flowers **2 :** MATURE **3 :** to glow especially with healthy color

♦ blossom, blow, burgeon, flower, unfold

bloo·mers \ˈblü-mərz\ *n pl* **:** a woman's garment of short loose trousers gathered at the knee
bloop·er \ˈblü-pər\ *n* **1 :** a fly ball hit barely beyond a baseball infield **2 :** an embarrassing public blunder

¹blos·som \ˈblä-səm\ *n* **1 :** the flower of a plant **2** ♦ **:** the period or state of flowering **3 :** a peak period or stage of development

♦ bloom, flower, flush, heyday, prime

²blossom *vb* ♦ **:** to produce or yield flowers **:** BLOOM, FLOWER

♦ bloom, blow, burgeon, flower, unfold

¹blot \ˈblät\ *n* **1 :** SPOT, STAIN ⟨ink ~*s*⟩ **2** ♦ **:** a mark of reproach **:** moral flaw or blemish ⟨a ~ on her record⟩

♦ brand, smirch, spot, stain, stigma, taint

²blot *vb* **blot·ted; blot·ting 1 :** SPOT, STAIN **2 :** OBSCURE, ECLIPSE **3** *obs* **:** MAR; *esp* **:** DISGRACE **4 :** to dry or remove with or as if with an absorbing material **5 :** to make a blot
blotch \ˈbläch\ *n* **:** a usually large and irregular spot or mark (as of ink or color) — **blotchy** *adj*
blotch *vb* ♦ **:** to mark or mar with blotches

♦ mottle, spot

blot out *vb* **1** ♦ **:** to make obscure, insignificant, or inconsequential ⟨~ out the sun⟩ **2** ♦ **:** to destroy completely

♦ [1] blanket, cloak, conceal, cover, curtain, enshroud, hide, mask, obscure, occlude, occult, screen, shroud, veil ♦ [2] annihilate, demolish, destroy, exterminate, extinguish, obliterate, pulverize, ruin, smash, waste, wipe out, wreck

blot·ter \ˈblä-tər\ *n* **1 :** a piece of blotting paper **2 :** a book for preliminary records (as of sales or arrests)
blot·ting paper *n* **:** a spongy paper used to absorb ink
blouse \ˈblau̇s, ˈblau̇z\ *n* **1 :** a loose outer garment like a smock **2 :** a usually loose garment reaching from the neck to about the waist
¹blow \ˈblō\ *vb* **blew** \ˈblü\; **blown** \ˈblōn\; **blow·ing 1 :** to move forcibly ⟨the wind *blew*⟩ **2 :** to send forth a current of gas (as air) **3 :** to act on with a current of gas or vapor; *esp* **:** to drive with such a current **4 :** to sound or cause to sound ⟨~ a horn⟩ **5** ♦ **:** to breathe quickly or in a labored manner **:** PANT, GASP; *also* **:** to expel moist air in breathing ⟨the whale *blew*⟩ **6 :** BOAST; *also* **:** BLUSTER **7 :** MELT — used of an electrical fuse **8 :** to shape or form by blown or injected air ⟨~ glass⟩ **9 :** to shatter or destroy by or as if by explosion **10 :** to make breathless by exertion **11** ♦ **:** to spend recklessly **12 :** to foul up hopelessly ⟨*blew* her lines⟩ — **blow·er** *n*

♦ [5] gasp, pant, puff, wheeze ♦ [11] dissipate, fritter, lavish, misspend, run through, spend, squander, throw away, waste

²blow *n* **1 :** a usually strong blowing of air **:** GALE **2 :** BOASTING, BRAG **3 :** an act or instance of blowing
³blow *vb* **blew** \ˈblü\; **blown** \ˈblōn\; **blow·ing :** to produce or yield flowers **:** FLOWER, BLOOM
⁴blow *n* **1** ♦ **:** a forcible stroke **2 :** COMBAT ⟨come to ~*s*⟩ **3 :** a severe and usually unexpected calamity

♦ bat, belt, box, clout, hit, punch, slug, thump, wallop, whack

blow–by–blow *adj* **:** minutely detailed ⟨~ account⟩
blow–dry \-ˌdrī\ *vb* **:** to dry and usually style hair with a blow-dryer
blow–dry·er \-ˌdrī(-ə)r\ *n* **:** a hand-held hair dryer
blow·fly \ˈblō-ˌflī\ *n* **:** any of a family of dipteran flies (as a bluebottle) that deposit their eggs or maggots on meat or in wounds
blow·gun \-ˌgən\ *n* **:** a tube from which an arrow or a dart may be shot by the force of the breath
blow·out \ˈblō-ˌau̇t\ *n* **1** ♦ **:** a festive social affair **2 :** a bursting of something (as a tire) because of pressure of the contents (as air)

♦ affair, event, fete, function, get-together, party

blow·sy *also* **blow·zy** \ˈblau̇-zē\ *adj* **:** DISHEVELED, SLOVENLY
blow·torch \ˈblō-ˌtȯrch\ *n* **:** a small portable burner whose flame is made hotter by a blast of air or oxygen
blow·up \ˈblō-ˌəp\ *n* **1 :** EXPLOSION **2** ♦ **:** an outburst of temper **3 :** a photographic enlargement

♦ dudgeon, explosion, fireworks, fit, huff, scene, tantrum

blow up *vb* **1** ♦ **:** to rend apart, shatter, or destroy by or as if by explosion **2** ♦ **:** to lose self-control; *esp* **:** to become violently angry **3** ♦ **:** to undergo or be destroyed by an explosion

♦ [1, 3] blast, burst, demolish, detonate, explode, pop, shatter, smash ♦ [2] flare, flip, fulminate, rant, vituperate ***Ant*** calm (down)

blowy \ˈblō-ē\ *adj* ♦ **:** marked by strong wind **:** WINDY

♦ blustery, breezy, gusty, windy

BLT \ˌbē-ˌel-ˈtē\ *n* **:** a bacon, lettuce, and tomato sandwich

[1]**blub•ber** \ˈblə-bər\ *vb* ◆ **:** to cry noisily

◆ bawl, cry, sob, weep

[2]**blubber** *n* **1 :** the fat of large sea mammals (as whales) **2 :** a noisy crying
[1]**blud•geon** \ˈblə-jən\ *n* ◆ **:** a short often loaded club

◆ bat, billy club, club, cudgel, staff, truncheon

[2]**bludgeon** *vb* ◆ **:** to strike with or as if with a bludgeon

◆ bash, bat, batter, beat, club, pound

[1]**blue** \ˈblü\ *adj* **blu•er; blu•est 1 :** of the color blue; *also* **:** BLUISH **2** ◆ **:** low in spirits **:** MELANCHOLY; *also* **:** DEPRESSING **3 :** PURITANICAL **4 :** INDECENT — **blue•ness** *n*

◆ depressed, down, downcast, glum, low, melancholy, miserable, sad, unhappy

[2]**blue** *n* **1 :** a color between green and violet in the spectrum **:** the color of the clear daytime sky **2** ◆ **:** something (as clothing or the sky or ocean) that is blue

◆ high, sky ◆ brine, deep, ocean, sea

blue baby *n* **:** a baby with bluish skin due to faulty circulation caused by a heart defect
blue•bell \-ˌbel\ *n* **:** any of various plants with blue bell-shaped flowers
blue•ber•ry \ˈblü-ˌber-ē, -bə-rē\ *n* **:** the edible blue or blackish berry of various shrubs of the heath family; *also* **:** one of these shrubs
blue•bird \-ˌbərd\ *n* **:** any of several small No. American thrushes that are blue above and reddish-brown or pale blue below
blue•bon•net \ˈblü-ˌbä-nət\ *n* **:** either of two low-growing annual lupines of Texas with silky foliage and blue flowers
blue•bot•tle \ˈblü-ˌbät-ᵊl\ *n* **:** any of several blowflies with iridescent blue bodies or abdomens
blue cheese *n* **:** cheese having veins of greenish blue mold
blue–col•lar \ˈblü-ˈkä-lər\ *adj* **:** of, relating to, or being the class of workers whose duties call for work clothes
blue•fish \-ˌfish\ *n* **:** a marine sport and food fish bluish above and silvery below
blue•grass \-ˌgras\ *n* **1 :** KENTUCKY BLUEGRASS **2 :** country music played on stringed instruments having free improvisation and close harmonies
blue jay \-ˌjā\ *n* **:** a crested bright blue No. American jay
blue jeans *n pl* **:** pants usually made of blue denim
blue•nose \ˈblü-ˌnōz\ *n* **:** a person who advocates a rigorous moral code
blue•point \-ˌpȯint\ *n* **:** a small oyster typically from the south shore of Long Island, New York
blue•print \-ˌprint\ *n* **1 :** a photographic print in white on a blue ground used especially for copying mechanical drawings and architects' plans **2** ◆ **:** a detailed plan of action

◆ arrangement, design, game, plan, project, scheme, strategy, system

blueprint *vb* **1 :** to make a blueprint of **2** ◆ **:** to work out (as a program or plan) in detail

◆ arrange, calculate, chart, design, frame, lay out, map, plan, project, scheme

blues \ˈblüz\ *n pl* **1** ◆ **:** low spirits **:** MELANCHOLY **2 :** music in a style marked by recurrent minor intervals and melancholy lyrics

◆ dejection, depression, doldrums, dumps, melancholy, sadness

blue screen *n* **:** a cinematic technique in which a subject is filmed in front of a blue background so as to allow the creation of a composite with other footage
blue•stock•ing \ˈblü-ˌstä-kiŋ\ *n* **:** a woman having intellectual interests
blu•et \ˈblü-ət\ *n* **:** a low No. American herb with dainty bluish flowers
blue whale *n* **:** a very large baleen whale that may reach a weight of 150 tons (135 metric tons) and a length of 100 feet (30 meters)
[1]**bluff** \ˈbləf\ *adj* **1 :** having a broad flattened front **2 :** rising steeply with a broad flat front **3 :** good-naturedly frank and outspoken
[2]**bluff** *n* ◆ **:** a high steep bank **:** CLIFF

◆ cliff, crag, escarpment, palisade, precipice, scarp

[3]**bluff** *vb* ◆ **:** to frighten or deceive by pretense or a mere show of strength

◆ deceive, dupe, fool, gull, misinform, mislead, trick

[4]**bluff** *n* **:** an act or instance of bluffing; *also* **:** one who bluffs
blu•ing *or* **blue•ing** \ˈblü-iŋ\ *n* **:** a preparation used in laundering to counteract yellowing of white fabrics
blu•ish \ˈblü-ish\ *adj* **:** somewhat blue
[1]**blun•der** \ˈblən-dər\ *vb* **1** ◆ **:** to move clumsily or unsteadily **2 :** to make a stupid or needless mistake

◆ flounder, limp, lumber, plod, stumble

[2]**blunder** *n* ◆ **:** an avoidable and usually serious mistake

◆ error, fault, flub, fumble, goof, lapse, miscue, misstep, mistake, oversight, slip, stumble

blun•der•buss \ˈblən-dər-ˌbəs\ *n* **:** an obsolete short-barreled firearm with a flaring muzzle
[1]**blunt** \ˈblənt\ *adj* **1** ◆ **:** not sharp **:** DULL **2** ◆ **:** lacking in tact **:** BLUFF — **blunt•ly** *adv* — **blunt•ness** *n*

◆ [1] dull, obtuse ◆ [2] abrupt, brusque, curt, snippy *Ant* circuitous, mealymouthed

[2]**blunt** *vb* ◆ **:** to make or become less sharp, definite, or forceful

◆ dampen, deaden, dull, numb

[1]**blur** \ˈblər\ *n* **1 :** a smear or stain that obscures **2 :** something vaguely perceived; *esp* **:** something moving too quickly to be clearly perceived
[2]**blur** *vb* **blurred; blur•ring** ◆ **:** to make dim, imperfect, or confused **:** CLOUD, OBSCURE

◆ becloud, befog, cloud, confuse, dim, fog, haze, mist, obscure, shroud

blurb \ˈblərb\ *n* **:** a short publicity notice (as on a book jacket)
blur•ry \ˈblər-ē\ *adj* ◆ **:** lacking definition or focus

◆ bleary, dim, faint, foggy, fuzzy, hazy, indefinite, indistinct, indistinguishable, misty, murky, nebulous, obscure, opaque, shadowy, unclear, undefined, undetermined, vague

blurt \ˈblərt\ *vb* ◆ **:** to utter suddenly and impulsively

◆ *usu* **blurt out** bolt, cry, ejaculate, spout

[1]**blush** \ˈbləsh\ *n* **1 :** a reddening of the face (as from modesty or confusion) **:** FLUSH **2 :** a cosmetic used to tint the face pink — **blush•ful** *adj*
[2]**blush** *vb* ◆ **:** to become red in the face especially from shame, modesty, or confusion

◆ bloom, color (*or* colour), crimson, flush, glow, redden

[1]**blus•ter** \ˈbləs-tər\ *vb* **1 :** to blow in stormy noisy gusts **2** ◆ **:** to talk or act with noisy swaggering threats

◆ fulminate, rant, rave, spout

[2]**bluster** *n* **1 :** a violent boisterous blowing **2** ◆ **:** violent commotion **3** ◆ **:** loudly boastful or threatening speech

◆ [2] cacophony, clamor (*or* clamour), din, noise, racket, roar ◆ [3] bombast, brag, gas, grandiloquence, rant

blus•tery \-tə-rē\ *adj* ◆ **:** blowing boisterously ⟨a ~ day⟩

◆ blowy, breezy, gusty, windy

blvd *abbr* boulevard
B lymphocyte *n* **:** B CELL
BM *abbr* bowel movement
B movie *n* **:** a cheaply produced motion picture
BO *abbr* **1** best offer **2** body odor **3** box office **4** branch office
boa \ˈbō-ə\ *n* **1 :** a large snake (as the **boa con•stric•tor** \-kən-ˈstrik-tər\ or the related anaconda) that suffocates and kills its prey by constriction **2 :** a fluffy scarf usually of fur or feathers
boar \ˈbōr\ *n* **:** a male swine; *also* **:** WILD BOAR
[1]**board** \ˈbōrd\ *n* **1 :** the side of a ship **2 :** a thin flat length of sawed lumber; *also* **:** material (as cardboard) or a piece of material formed as a thin flat firm sheet **3** *pl* **:** a theater stage as representing the acting profession **4 a :** a table spread with a meal **b :** daily meals especially when furnished for pay **5 :** a table at which a council or magistrates sit **6 :** a group or association of persons organized for a special responsibility (as the management of a business or institution); *also* **:** an organized commercial exchange **7 :** a sheet of insulating material carrying circuit elements and inserted in an electronic device
[2]**board** *vb* **1 :** to go or put aboard ⟨~ a boat⟩ **2 :** to cover with boards **3** ◆ **:** to provide or be provided with meals and often lodging

◆ accommodate, billet, bunk, domicile, house, lodge, put up, quarter

board•er *n* ♦ : one that boards; *esp* : one that is provided with regular meals or regular meals and lodging

♦ lodger, renter, roomer, tenant

board•ing•house \ˈbōr-diŋ-ˌhau̇s\ *n* : a house at which persons are boarded
board•walk \ˈbōrd-ˌwȯk\ *n* : a promenade (as of planking) along a beach
¹boast \ˈbōst\ *vb* **1** ♦ : to praise oneself **2** ♦ : to mention or assert with excessive pride **3** : to prize as a possession; *also* : HAVE ⟨the house ~*s* a fireplace⟩ — **boast•ful** \-fəl\ *adj* — **boast•ful•ly** *adv*

♦ [1, 2] brag, crow, plume, swagger

²boast *n* **1** : the act or an instance of boasting **2** ♦ : a cause for pride

♦ credit, glory, honor (*or* honour), jewel, pride, treasure

boast•er \ˈbō-stər\ *n* ♦ : one who boasts

♦ brag, braggadocio, braggart, bragger

¹boat \ˈbōt\ *n* ♦ : a small vessel for travel on water; *also* : SHIP

♦ bottom, craft, ship, vessel

²boat *vb* : to go by boat
boat•er \ˈbō-tər\ *n* **1** : one that travels in a boat **2** : a stiff straw hat
boat•load \ˈbōt-ˌlōd\ *n* ♦ : an indefinitely large number

♦ abundance, deal, gobs, heap, loads, lot, pile, plenty, quantity, scads

boat•man \ˈbōt-mən\ *n* : a man who operates, works on, or deals in boats
boat people *n pl* : refugees fleeing by boat
boat•swain \ˈbōs-ᵊn\ *n* : a subordinate officer of a ship in charge of the hull and related equipment
¹bob \ˈbäb\ *vb* **bobbed; bob•bing** **1** ♦ : to move up and down jerkily or repeatedly **2** : to emerge, arise, or appear suddenly or unexpectedly

♦ bobble, jog, jounce, nod, pump, seesaw

²bob *n* : a bobbing movement
³bob *n* **1** : a knob, knot, twist, or curl especially of ribbons, yarn, or hair **2** : a short haircut of a woman or child **3** : FLOAT 2 **4** : a weight hanging from a line
⁴bob *vb* **bobbed; bob•bing** : to cut hair in a bob
⁵bob *n, pl* **bob** *slang Brit* : SHILLING
bob•bin \ˈbä-bən\ *n* : a cylinder or spindle for holding or dispensing thread (as in a sewing machine)
bob•ble \ˈbä-bəl\ *vb* **bob•bled; bob•bling** **1** ♦ : to move up and down in a short quick movement **2** ♦ : to make awkward attempts to do or find something; *also* : FUMBLE — **bobble** *n*

♦ [1] bob, jog, jounce, nod, pump, seesaw ♦ [2] botch, bungle, butcher, flub, foul up, fumble, mangle, mess up, screw up

bob•by \ˈbä-bē\ *n, pl* **bobbies** *Brit* : a police officer
bobby pin *n* : a flat wire hairpin with prongs that press close together
bob•cat \ˈbäb-ˌkat\ *n* : a small usually rusty-colored No. American lynx
bob•o•link \ˈbä-bə-ˌliŋk\ *n* : an American migratory songbird related to the meadowlarks
bob•sled \ˈbäb-ˌsled\ *n* **1** : a short sled usually used as one of a joined pair **2** : a racing sled with two pairs of runners, a steering wheel, and a hand brake — **bobsled** *vb*
bob•white \(ˌ)bäb-ˈhwīt\ *n* : any of a genus of quail; *esp* : a popular game bird of eastern and central No. America
boc•cie *or* **boc•ci** *or* **boc•ce** \ˈbä-chē\ *n* : Italian lawn bowling played on a long narrow court
bock \ˈbäk\ *n* : a strong dark beer usually sold in early spring
bod \ˈbäd\ *n* : BODY
¹bode \ˈbōd\ *vb* **bod•ed; bod•ing** ♦ : to indicate by signs : PRESAGE

♦ augur, promise

²bode *past of* BIDE
bo•de•ga \bō-ˈdā-gə\ *n* : a store specializing in Hispanic groceries
bod•ice \ˈbä-dəs\ *n* : the usually close-fitting part of a dress above the waist
bodi•less \ˈbä-di-ləs\ *adj* ♦ : lacking a body or material form

♦ immaterial, incorporeal, insubstantial, nonmaterial, nonphysical, spiritual, unsubstantial

¹bodi•ly \ˈbäd-ᵊl-ē\ *adj* ♦ : of or relating to the body ⟨~ contact⟩

♦ animal, carnal, corporal, fleshly, material, physical, somatic

²bodily *adv* **1** : in the flesh **2** : as a whole ⟨lifted the crate up ~⟩
bod•kin \ˈbäd-kən\ *n* **1** : DAGGER **2** : a pointed implement for punching holes in cloth **3** : a blunt needle for drawing tape or ribbon through a loop or hem
body \ˈbä-dē\ *n, pl* **bod•ies** **1** : the physical whole of a living or dead organism; *also* : the trunk or main mass of an organism as distinguished from its appendages **2** ♦ : a human being : PERSON **3** ♦ : the main part of something **4** : a mass of matter distinct from other masses **5** ♦ : a group of persons or things **6** : VISCOSITY, FIRMNESS **7** : richness of flavor — used especially of wines — **bod•ied** \ˈbä-dēd\ *adj*

♦ [2] being, creature, human, individual, man, mortal, person ♦ [3] bulk, core, generality, main, mass, staple, weight ♦ [5] array, batch, bunch, cluster, crop, group, huddle, knot, lot, parcel, party

body•build•ing \ˈbä-dē-ˌbil-diŋ\ *n* : a developing of the body through exercise and diet — **body•build•er** \-dər\ *n*
body English *n* : bodily motions made in a usually unconscious effort to influence the movement of a propelled object (as a ball)
body•guard \ˈbä-dē-ˌgärd\ *n* : a personal guard; *also* : RETINUE
body language *n* : body movements or postures interpreted as a means of communication
body stocking *n* : a sheer close-fitting one-piece garment for the torso that often has sleeves and legs
body•work \ˈbä-dē-ˌwərk\ *n* : the making or repairing of vehicle bodies
Boer \ˈbōr, ˈbu̇r\ *n* : a South African of Dutch or Huguenot descent
¹bog \ˈbäg, ˈbȯg\ *n* ♦ : wet, spongy, poorly drained, and usually acid ground — **bog•gy** *adj*

♦ fen, marsh, mire, morass, slough, swamp

²bog *vb* **bogged; bog•ging** : to sink into or as if into a bog
bo•gey *also* **bo•gie** *or* **bo•gy** \ˈbu̇-gē, ˈbō- *for 1*; ˈbō- *for 2*\ *n, pl* **bogeys** *also* **bogies** **1 a** ♦ : a visible disembodied spirit : SPECTER **b** ♦ : a source of fear or annoyance **2** : a score of one over par on a hole in golf

♦ [1a] apparition, ghost, phantasm, phantom, poltergeist, shade, shadow, specter, spirit, spook, vision, wraith ♦ [1b] bête noire, bugbear, hobgoblin, ogre

bo•gey•man \ˈbu̇-gē-ˌman, ˈbō-, ˈbü-\ *n* : an imaginary monster used in threatening children
bog•gle \ˈbä-gəl\ *vb* **bog•gled; bog•gling** : to overwhelm or be overwhelmed with fright or amazement
bo•gus \ˈbō-gəs\ *adj* ♦ : not genuine : SHAM

♦ counterfeit, fake, false, inauthentic, phony, sham, spurious, unauthentic ♦ artificial, fake, faux, imitation, mock, sham, synthetic

Bo•he•mi•an \bō-ˈhē-mē-ən\ *n* **1** : a native or inhabitant of Bohemia **2** *often not cap* : VAGABOND, WANDERER **3** *often not cap* ♦ : a person (as a writer or artist) living an unconventional life — **bohemian** *adj, often cap*

♦ deviant, individualist, loner, maverick, nonconformist

¹boil \ˈbȯil\ *n* : an inflamed swelling on the skin containing pus
²boil *vb* **1 a** : to heat or become heated to a temperature (**boil•ing point**) at which vapor is formed and rises in bubbles ⟨water ~*s* and changes to steam⟩ **b** ♦ : to act on or be acted on by a boiling liquid ⟨~ eggs⟩ **2** ♦ : to be in a state of seething agitation **3** ♦ : to churn violently as if boiling

♦ [1b] coddle, stew ♦ [2, 3] burn, churn, fume, rage, seethe, steam

³boil *n* : the act or state of boiling
boil•er \ˈbȯi-lər\ *n* **1** : a container in which something is boiled **2** : a strong vessel used in making steam **3** : a tank holding hot water
boil•er•mak•er \ˈbȯi-lər-ˌmā-kər\ *n* : whiskey with a beer chaser
boil•ing *adj* ♦ : intensely agitated ⟨~ with anger⟩

♦ angry, furious, irate, mad, rabid, sore

bois•ter•ous \ˈbȯi-st(ə-)rəs\ *adj* ♦ : noisily turbulent or exuberant — **bois•ter•ous•ly** *adv*

♦ rambunctious, raucous, rowdy *Ant* orderly

bok choy \ˈbäk-ˈchȯi\ *n* : a Chinese vegetable related to the mustards that forms a loose head of green leaves with long thick white stalks

bo•la \ˈbō-lə\ *or* **bo•las** \-ləs\ *n, pl* **bolas** \-ləz\ *also* **bo•las•es** : a cord with weights attached to the ends
bold \ˈbōld\ *adj* **1** ♦ : fearless before danger **2** ♦ : overstepping due bounds : IMPUDENT **3** : marked by great and continuous steepness : STEEP **4** : ADVENTUROUS, FREE ⟨a ~ thinker⟩ **5** ♦ : standing out prominently — **bold•ly** *adv* — **bold•ness** \ˈbōld-nəs\ *n*

♦ [1] adventurous, audacious, daring, enterprising, gutsy, hardy, nervy, venturesome ***Ant*** unadventurous, unenterprising ♦ [2] arch, brash, brazen, cheeky, cocky, fresh, impertinent, impudent, insolent, nervy, sassy, saucy ♦ [2] familiar, forward, free, immodest, presumptuous ♦ [5] catchy, conspicuous, emphatic, marked, noticeable, prominent, pronounced, remarkable, striking

bold•face \ˈbōld-ˌfās\ *n* : a heavy-faced type; *also* : printing in boldface — **bold–faced** \-ˈfāst\ *adj*
bole \ˈbōl\ *n* : the trunk of a tree
bo•le•ro \bə-ˈler-ō\ *n, pl* **-ros** **1** : a Spanish dance or its music **2** : a short loose jacket open at the front
Bo•liv•i•an \bə-ˈli-vē-ən\ *n* : a native or inhabitant of Bolivia — **Bolivian** *adj*
boll \ˈbōl\ *n* : a seed pod (as of cotton)
boll weevil *n* : a small grayish weevil that infests the cotton plant both as a larva and as an adult
boll•worm \ˈbōl-ˌwərm\ *n* : any of several moths and especially the corn earworm whose larvae feed on cotton bolls
bo•lo•gna \bə-ˈlō-nē\ *n* : a large smoked sausage of beef, veal, and pork
Bol•she•vik \ˈbōl-shə-ˌvik\ *n, pl* **Bolsheviks** *also* **Bol•she•vi•ki** \ˌbōl-shə-ˈvi-kē\ **1** : a member of the party that seized power in Russia in the revolution of November 1917 **2** : COMMUNIST — **Bolshevik** *adj*
bol•she•vism \ˈbōl-shə-ˌvi-zəm\ *n, often cap* : the doctrine or program of the Bolsheviks advocating violent overthrow of capitalism
¹bol•ster \ˈbōl-stər\ *n* : a long pillow or cushion
²bolster *vb* ♦ : to support with or as if with a bolster; *also* : REINFORCE

♦ bear, brace, buttress, carry, prop, shore, stay, support, uphold

¹bolt \ˈbōlt\ *n* **1** : a missile (as an arrow) for a crossbow or catapult **2** : a flash of lightning : THUNDERBOLT **3** : a sliding bar used to fasten a door **4** : a roll of cloth or wallpaper of specified length **5** : a rod with a head at one end and a screw thread at the other used with a nut to fasten objects together **6** : a metal cylinder that drives the cartridge into the chamber of a firearm
²bolt *vb* **1 a** ♦ : to move suddenly (as in fright or hurry) : START **b** ♦ : to rush off or away (as in fleeing) ⟨he ~*ed* out of the room⟩ **2** : to break away (as from association) ⟨~ from a political platform⟩ **3** : to produce seed prematurely **4** : to secure or fasten with a bolt **5** : to swallow hastily or without chewing **6** ♦ : to say impulsively

♦ [1a] jump, start, startle ♦ [1b] break, flee, fly, retreat, run, run away, run off ♦ [6] blurt, cry, ejaculate, spout

³bolt *n* : an act of bolting
bo•lus \ˈbō-ləs\ *n* **1** : a large pill **2** : a soft mass of chewed food
¹bomb \ˈbäm\ *n* **1** : a fused explosive device designed to detonate under specified conditions (as impact) **2** : an aerosol or foam dispenser (as of insecticide or hair spray) : SPRAY CAN **3** : a long pass in football **4** ♦ : one that has failed : FAILURE, FLOP

♦ bummer, bust, catastrophe, debacle, dud, failure, fiasco, fizzle, flop, lemon, loser, miss, turkey, washout

²bomb *vb* **1** : to attack with bombs **2** : to fail utterly
bom•bard \bäm-ˈbärd\ *vb* **1** ♦ : to attack especially with artillery or bombers **2** : to assail persistently **3** : to subject to the impact of rapidly moving particles (as electrons)

♦ blitz, shell

bom•bar•dier \ˌbäm-bər-ˈdir\ *n* : a bomber-crew member who releases the bombs
bom•bard•ment *n* ♦ : the act or an instance of bombarding or the state of being bombarded

♦ barrage, cannonade, fusillade, hail, salvo, shower, storm, volley

bom•bast \ˈbäm-ˌbast\ *n* ♦ : pretentious wordy speech or writing — **bom•bas•ti•cal•ly** \-ti-k(ə-)lē\ *adv*

♦ bluster, brag, gas, grandiloquence, rant, rhetoric

bom•bas•tic \bäm-ˈbas-tik\ *adj* ♦ : marked by or given to bombast

♦ gaseous, grandiloquent, oratorical, rhetorical, windy

bom•ba•zine \ˌbäm-bə-ˈzēn\ *n* **1** : a twilled fabric with silk warp and worsted filling **2** : a silk fabric in twill weave dyed black
bomb•er \ˈbä-mər\ *n* : one that bombs; *esp* : an airplane for dropping bombs
bomb•proof \ˈbäm-ˌprüf\ *adj* : safe against the explosive force of bombs
bomb•shell \ˈbäm-ˌshel\ *n* **1** : BOMB 1 **2** ♦ : one that stuns, amazes, or completely upsets

♦ bolt, jar, jolt, surprise

bona fide \ˈbō-nə-ˌfīd, ˈbä-; ˌbō-nə-ˈfī-dē, -də\ *adj* **1** : made in good faith ⟨a *bona fide* agreement⟩ **2** ♦ : neither specious nor counterfeit : GENUINE, REAL ⟨a *bona fide* bargain⟩

♦ authentic, genuine, real, right, true

bo•nan•za \bə-ˈnan-zə\ *n* : something yielding a rich return
bon•bon \ˈbän-ˌbän\ *n* : a candy with a creamy center and a soft covering (as of chocolate)
¹bond \ˈbänd\ *n* **1** ♦ : something that binds or restrains : FETTER **2** ♦ : a binding or uniting force or tie ⟨~*s* of friendship⟩ **3** ♦ : an agreement or obligation often made binding by a pledge of money or goods **4** : a person who acts as surety for another **5** : an interest-bearing certificate of public or private indebtedness **6** : the state of goods subject to supervision pending payment of taxes or duties due

♦ [1] band, chain, fetter, irons, ligature, manacle, shackle ♦ [2] cement, knot, ligature, link, tie ♦ [3] contract, covenant, guarantee, guaranty, surety, warranty

²bond *vb* **1** : to assure payment of duties or taxes on (goods) by giving a bond **2** : to insure against losses caused by the acts of ⟨~ a bank teller⟩ **3** : to make or become firmly united as if by bonds ⟨~ iron to copper⟩ **4** : to form a close relationship ⟨gave them a chance to ~ with their father⟩
bond•age \ˈbän-dij\ *n* ♦ : a state of being bound usually by compulsion : SLAVERY, SERVITUDE

♦ enslavement, servitude, slavery, thrall, yoke

bond•hold•er \ˈbänd-ˌhōl-dər\ *n* : one that owns a government or corporation bond
bond•ing *n* **1** : the formation of a close personal relationship especially through frequent or constant association **2** : the attaching of a material (as porcelain) to a tooth surface especially for cosmetic purposes
bond•man \ˈbänd-mən\ *n* ♦ : a person held in servitude as the chattel of another : SLAVE

♦ chattel, slave, thrall

¹bonds•man \ˈbändz-mən\ *n* : SURETY 3
²bondsman *n* ♦ : one who is bound to another as a servant or slave

♦ bondman, chattel, slave, thrall

bond•wom•an \ˈbänd-ˌwu̇-mən\ *n* : a female slave or serf
¹bone \ˈbōn\ *n* **1** : a hard largely calcareous tissue forming most of the skeleton of a vertebrate animal; *also* : one of the pieces of bone making up a vertebrate skeleton **2** : a hard animal substance (as ivory or baleen) similar to true bone **3** : something made of bone — **bone•less** *adj* — **bony** *also* **bon•ey** \ˈbō-nē\ *adj*
²bone *vb* **boned; bon•ing** : to free from bones ⟨~ a chicken⟩
bone black *n* : the black carbon residue from calcined bones used especially as a pigment
bone meal *n* : crushed or ground bone used especially as fertilizer or feed
bon•er \ˈbō-nər\ *n* : a stupid and ridiculous blunder
bone up *vb* **1** : to try to master necessary information quickly **2** : to refresh one's memory ⟨*boned up* on the speech before giving it⟩
bon•fire \ˈbän-ˌfīr\ *n* : a large fire built in the open air
bon•go \ˈbäŋ-gō\ *n, pl* **bongos** *also* **bongoes** : one of a pair of small tuned drums played with the hands
bon•ho•mie \ˌbä-nə-ˈmē\ *n* : good-natured easy friendliness
bo•ni•to \bə-ˈnē-tō\ *n, pl* **-tos** *or* **-to** : any of several medium-sized tunas
bon mot \bōⁿ-ˈmō\ *n, pl* **bons mots** *same*\ *or* **bon mots** *same or* -ˈmōz\ : a clever remark
bon•net \ˈbä-nət\ *n* : a covering (as a cap) for the head; *esp* : a hat for a woman or infant tied under the chin
bon•ny \ˈbä-nē\ *adj* **bon•ni•er; -est** *chiefly Brit* ♦ : ATTRACTIVE, FAIR; *also* : FINE, EXCELLENT

♦ attractive, beautiful, cute, fair, gorgeous, handsome, knockout, lovely, pretty, ravishing, stunning

bon•sai \bōn-ˈsī\ *n, pl* **bonsai :** a potted plant (as a tree) dwarfed by special methods of culture; *also* **:** the art of growing such a plant

bo•nus \ˈbō-nəs\ *n* ♦ **:** something in addition to what is expected

♦ dividend, extra, lagniappe, perquisite, tip

bon vi•vant \ˌbän-vē-ˈvänt, ˌbōⁿ-vē-ˈväⁿ\ *n, pl* **bons vivants** \ˌbän-vē-ˈvänts, ˌbōⁿ-vē-ˈväⁿ\ *or* **bon vivants** *same*\ **:** a person having cultivated, refined, and sociable tastes especially in food and drink

bon voy•age \ˌbōⁿ-ˌvȯi-ˈäzh, ˌbän-; ˌbōⁿ-ˌvwä-ˈyäzh\ *n* ♦ **:** a wish of well-being at parting **:** FAREWELL — often used as an interjection

♦ adieu, au revoir, farewell, good-bye

bony fish *n* **:** any of a very large group of fishes (as a salmon or marlin) with a bony rather than a cartilaginous skeleton

bonze \ˈbänz\ *n* **:** a Buddhist monk

boo \ˈbü\ *n, pl* **boos** ♦ **:** a shout of disapproval or contempt — **boo** *vb*

♦ catcall, hiss, hoot, jeer, raspberry, snort

boo•by \ˈbü-bē\ *n, pl* **boobies** ♦ **:** an awkward foolish person **:** DOPE

♦ dope, fool, goose, jackass, nitwit, nut, simpleton, turkey

booby hatch *n* **:** an insane asylum

booby prize *n* **:** an award for the poorest performance in a contest

booby trap *n* ♦ **:** a trap for the unwary; *esp* **:** a concealed explosive device set to go off when some harmless-looking object is touched — **booby–trap** *vb*

♦ catch, pitfall, snag ♦ explosive

boo•dle \ˈbüd-ᵊl\ *n* **1 :** bribe money **2 :** a large amount of money

¹book \ˈbu̇k\ *n* **1 :** a set of sheets bound into a volume **2 :** a long written or printed narrative or record **3 :** a major division of a long literary work **4** *cap* **:** BIBLE — **in one's book :** in one's opinion

²book *vb* **1 :** to engage, reserve, or schedule by or as if by writing in a book ⟨~ seats on a plane⟩ **2 :** to enter charges against in a police register

book•case \-ˌkās\ *n* **:** a piece of furniture consisting of shelves to hold books

book•end \-ˌend\ *n* **:** a support to hold up a row of books

book•ie \ˈbu̇-kē\ *n* **:** BOOKMAKER

book•ish \ˈbu̇-kish\ *adj* **1 :** fond of books and reading **2 a :** inclined to rely unduly on book knowledge **b** *of words* ♦ **:** literary and formal as opposed to colloquial and informal

♦ erudite, learned, literary ***Ant*** colloquial, nonliterary

book•keep•er \ˈbu̇k-ˌkē-pər\ *n* **:** one who records the accounts or transactions of a business — **book•keep•ing** *n*

book•let \ˈbu̇k-lət\ *n* ♦ **:** a little book; *esp* **:** PAMPHLET

♦ brochure, circular, folder, leaflet, pamphlet

book•mak•er \ˈbu̇k-ˌmā-kər\ *n* **:** one who determines odds and receives and pays off bets — **book•mak•ing** *n*

book•mark \-ˌmärk\ *or* **book•mark•er** \-ˌmär-kər\ *n* **:** a marker for finding a place in a book

book•mo•bile \ˈbu̇k-mō-ˌbēl\ *n* **:** a truck that serves as a traveling library

book off *vi, chiefly Can* **:** to notify an employer that one is not reporting for work (as because of sickness)

book•plate \ˈbu̇k-ˌplāt\ *n* **:** a label pasted in a book to show who owns it

book•sell•er \ˈbu̇k-ˌse-lər\ *n* **:** one who sells books; *esp* **:** the proprietor of a bookstore

book•shelf \-ˌshelf\ *n* **:** a shelf for books

book•worm \ˈbu̇k-ˌwərm\ *n* **:** a person unusually devoted to reading and study

¹boom \ˈbüm\ *vb* **1 :** to make a deep hollow sound **2 :** to grow or cause to grow rapidly especially in value, esteem, or importance

²boom *n* **1** ♦ **:** a booming sound or cry **2 :** a rapid expansion or increase especially of economic activity

♦ bang, blast, clap, crack, crash, pop, report, slam, smash, snap, thwack, whack

³boom *n* **1 :** a long spar used to extend the bottom of a sail **2 :** a line of floating timbers used to obstruct passage or catch floating objects **3 :** a beam projecting from the upright pole of a derrick to support or guide the object lifted **4 :** a long supporting pole or arm (as for a microphone)

boom box *n* **:** a large portable radio and often CD or tape player

boo•mer•ang \ˈbü-mə-ˌraŋ\ *n* **:** a bent or angular club that can be so thrown as to return near the starting point

boom•ing *adj* **1** ♦ **:** making a loud deep sound ⟨his ~ voice⟩ **2 :** forcefully or powerfully executed ⟨hit a ~ serve⟩

♦ clamorous (*or* clamourous), loud, resounding, roaring, sonorous, stentorian, thunderous

¹boon \ˈbün\ *n* **1** ♦ **:** something that promotes well-being; *also* **:** useful aid **2** ♦ **:** something given or granted as a favor

♦ [1] advantage, aid, benefit, help ♦ [1] benefit, blessing, felicity, godsend, good, manna, windfall ♦ [2] courtesy, favor (*or* favour), grace, indulgence, kindness, mercy, service, turn

²boon *adj* ♦ **:** enjoying companionship and the pleasures of feasting and drinking ⟨a ~ companion⟩

♦ companionable, convivial, extroverted, gregarious, outgoing, sociable, social

boon•docks \ˈbün-ˌdäks\ *n pl* **1 :** rough country filled with dense brush **2 :** a rural area

boon•dog•gle \ˈbün-ˌdä-gəl, -ˌdȯ-\ *n* **:** a useless or wasteful project or activity

boor \ˈbu̇r\ *n* **1 :** YOKEL **2** ♦ **:** a rude or insensitive person

♦ beast, churl, clown, creep, cretin, cur, heel, jerk, joker, louse, lout, skunk, slob, snake

boor•ish *adj* ♦ **:** having the qualities or behavior of a boor

♦ churlish, clownish, loutish, uncouth

¹boost \ˈbüst\ *vb* **1** ♦ **:** to push up from below **2** ♦ **:** to make or become greater **:** INCREASE, RAISE ⟨~ prices⟩ **3 :** to enthusiastically promote or support (a cause) ⟨voted a bonus to ~ morale⟩

♦ [1] crane, elevate, heave, heft, heighten, hike, hoist, jack, lift, pick up, raise, up, uphold ♦ [2] add, aggrandize, amplify, augment, compound, enlarge, escalate, expand, extend, increase, multiply, raise, swell, up ♦ [2] amplify, beef, consolidate, deepen, enhance, heighten, intensify, magnify, redouble, step up, strengthen

²boost *n* **1 :** a push upward **2** ♦ **:** an act that brings help or encouragement **3** ♦ **:** an increase in amount

♦ [2] aid, assist, assistance, backing, help, lift, support ♦ [3] accretion, addition, augmentation, expansion, gain, increase, increment, plus, proliferation, raise, rise, supplement

boost•er *n* ♦ **:** one that boosts; *esp* **:** an enthusiastic supporter

♦ advocate, apostle, backer, champion, exponent, friend, promoter, proponent, supporter

¹boot \ˈbüt\ *n, chiefly dial* **:** something to equalize a trade — **to boot :** BESIDES

²boot *vb, archaic* **:** AVAIL, PROFIT

³boot *n* **1 :** a covering for the foot and leg **2 :** a protective sheath (as of a flower) **3** *Brit* **:** an automobile trunk **4 :** KICK; *also* **:** a discharge from employment **5 :** a navy or marine corps trainee

⁴boot *vb* **1 :** KICK **2** ♦ **:** to eject or discharge summarily — often used with *out* **3** *of a computer* **:** to start or make ready for operation

♦ *usu* **boot out** banish, bounce, cast, chase, dismiss, drum, eject, expel, oust, rout, run off, throw out

boot•black \ˈbüt-ˌblak\ *n* **:** a person who shines shoes

boot camp *n* **1 :** a navy or marine corps training camp **2 :** a facility with a rigorous disciplinary program for young offenders

boo•tee *or* **boo•tie** \ˈbü-tē\ *n* **:** an infant's knitted or crocheted sock

booth \ˈbüth\ *n, pl* **booths** \ˈbü*th*z, ˈbüths\ **1 :** a small enclosed stall (as at a fair) **2 :** a small enclosure giving privacy for a person ⟨voting ~⟩ ⟨telephone ~⟩ **3 :** a restaurant accommodation having a table between backed benches

boot•leg \ˈbüt-ˌleg\ *vb* **:** to make, transport, or sell (as liquor) illegally — **boot•leg** *adj or n* — **boot•leg•ger** *n*

boot•less \ˈbüt-ləs\ *adj* ♦ **:** producing no gain, good, or result **:** USELESS — **boot•less•ly** *adv* — **boot•less•ness** *n*

♦ fruitless, futile, ineffective, unproductive, unsuccessful

¹boo•ty \ˈbü-tē\ *n, pl* **booties** ♦ **:** plunder taken (as in war) **:** SPOIL

♦ loot, plunder, spoil, swag

²booty \ˈbü-tē\ *n, pl* **booties** *slang* **:** BUTTOCK 2

¹booze \ˈbüz\ *vb* **boozed; booz•ing :** to drink liquor to excess — **booz•er** *n*

²booze *n* ♦ **:** intoxicating liquor — **boozy** *adj*

♦ alcohol, drink, intoxicant, liquor, moonshine, spirits

[1]**bop** \ˈbäp\ *vb* **bopped; bop•ping :** to reach with a blow **:** HIT, SOCK
[2]**bop** *n* **:** a blow especially with the fist or a club
BOQ *abbr* bachelor officers' quarters
bor *abbr* borough
bo•rate \ˈbōr-ˌāt\ *n* **:** a salt or ester of boric acid
bo•rax \ˈbōr-ˌaks\ *n* **:** a crystalline borate of sodium that occurs as a mineral and is used as a flux and cleanser
bor•del•lo \bȯr-ˈde-lō\ *n, pl* **-los :** BROTHEL
[1]**bor•der** \ˈbȯr-dər\ *n* **1** ♦ **:** an outer part or edge **2** ♦ **:** something that marks or fixes a limit **:** BOUNDARY

♦ [1] borderland, frontier, march ♦ [2] bound, boundary, circumference, compass, confines, edge, end, fringe, margin, perimeter, periphery, rim, skirt, verge

[2]**border** *vb* **bor•dered; bor•der•ing 1** ♦ **:** to put a border on **2** ♦ **:** to touch at the edge or boundary **:** ADJOIN **3 :** to approach the nature of a specified thing **:** VERGE ⟨∼s on the ridiculous⟩

♦ *usu* **border on** [1] bound, fringe, margin, rim, skirt ♦ *usu* **border on** [2] abut, adjoin, flank, fringe, join, skirt, touch, verge (on)

border collie *n, often cap B* **:** any of a British breed of medium-sized long-haired sheepdogs
bor•der•land \ˈbȯr-dər-ˌland\ *n* **1** ♦ **:** territory at or near a border **2 :** an outlying or intermediate region often not clearly defined

♦ border, frontier, march

bor•der•line \-ˌlīn\ *adj* **:** being in an intermediate position or state; *esp* **:** not quite up to what is standard or expected ⟨∼ intelligence⟩
[1]**bore** \ˈbōr\ *vb* **bored; bor•ing 1** ♦ **:** to make a hole in with or as if with a drill **2 :** to make (as a well) by boring or digging away material — **bor•er** *n*

♦ drill, hole, perforate, pierce, punch, puncture

[2]**bore** *n* **1 :** a hole made by or as if by boring **2 :** a cylindrical cavity **3 :** the diameter of a hole or tube; *esp* **:** the interior diameter of a gun barrel or engine cylinder
[3]**bore** *past of* BEAR
[4]**bore** *n* **:** a tidal flood with a high abrupt front
[5]**bore** *n* **:** one that causes boredom
[6]**bore** *vb* **bored; bor•ing** ♦ **:** to weary with tedious dullness

♦ jade, tire, weary *Ant* absorb, engage, engross, grip, interest, intrigue

bo•re•al \ˈbōr-ē-əl\ *adj* **:** of, relating to, or located in northern regions
bore•dom \ˈbōr-dəm\ *n* ♦ **:** the condition of being weary and restless because of dullness

♦ doldrums, ennui, listlessness, restlessness, tedium, tiredness, weariness

bo•ric acid \ˈbōr-ik-\ *n* **:** a white crystalline weak acid that contains boron and is used especially as an antiseptic
born \ˈbȯrn\ *adj* **1 :** brought into life by birth **2** ♦ **:** belonging by birth **:** NATIVE ⟨American-*born*⟩ **3 :** having special natural abilities or character from birth ⟨a ∼ leader⟩

♦ aboriginal, endemic, indigenous, native

born–again *adj* **:** having experienced a revival of a personal faith or conviction ⟨∼ believer⟩ ⟨∼ liberal⟩
borne *past part of* BEAR
bo•ron \ˈbōr-ˌän\ *n* **:** a chemical element that occurs in nature only in combination (as in borax)
bor•ough \ˈbər-ō\ *n* **1 :** a British town that sends one or more members to Parliament; *also* **:** an incorporated British urban area **2 :** an incorporated town or village in some U.S. states; *also* **:** any of the five political divisions of New York City **3 :** a civil division of the state of Alaska corresponding to a county in most other states
bor•row \ˈbär-ō\ *vb* **1 :** to take or receive (something) temporarily and with intent to return **2** ♦ **:** to take into possession or use from another source ⟨∼ a metaphor⟩

♦ adopt, embrace, take up

borscht \ˈbȯrsht\ *or* **borsch** \ˈbȯrsh\ *n* **:** a soup made mainly from beets
bosh \ˈbäsh\ *n* **:** foolish talk or action **:** NONSENSE
bosky \ˈbäs-kē\ *adj* **:** covered with trees or shrubs
[1]**bos•om** \ˈbu̇-zəm, ˈbü-\ *n* **1 :** the front of the human chest; *esp* **:** the female breasts **2 :** the seat of secret thoughts and feelings **3 :** the part of a garment covering the breast — **bos•omed** \-zəmd\ *adj*
[2]**bosom** *adj* ♦ **:** closely acquainted **:** INTIMATE

♦ chummy, close, familiar, friendly, intimate, thick

[1]**boss** \ˈbäs, ˈbȯs\ *n* **:** a knoblike ornament **:** STUD
[2]**boss** *vb* **:** to ornament with bosses
[3]**boss** \ˈbȯs\ *n* **1** ♦ **:** one (as a foreman or manager) exercising control or supervision **2 :** a politician who controls votes or dictates policies

♦ captain, chief, foreman, head, headman, helmsman, kingpin, leader, master, taskmaster

[4]**boss** \ˈbȯs\ *vb* **1** ♦ **:** to act as a boss **:** SUPERVISE **2** ♦ **:** to give usually arbitrary orders to — usually used with *around*

♦ [1] captain, head, oversee, superintend, supervise ♦ *usu* **boss around** [2] bid, charge, command, direct, enjoin, instruct, order, tell

[4]**boss** *adj, slang* ♦ **:** very good of its kind **:** EXCELLENT, FIRST-RATE

♦ A1, bang-up, banner, excellent, fabulous, fine, grand, great, prime, sensational, splendid, superb, superior, unsurpassed, wonderful

bossy *adj* ♦ **:** inclined to issue orders

♦ authoritarian, autocratic, despotic, dictatorial, domineering, imperious, masterful, overbearing, peremptory, tyrannical, tyrannous

bosun *var of* BOATSWAIN
bot *abbr* botanical; botanist; botany
bot•a•ny \ˈbät-ᵊn-ē, ˈbät-nē\ *n, pl* **-nies 1 :** a branch of biology dealing with plants and plant life **2 :** plant life (as of a given region); *also* **:** the biology of a plant or plant group — **bo•tan•i•cal** \bə-ˈta-ni-kəl\ *adj* — **bot•a•nist** \ˈbät-ᵊn-ist, ˈbät-nist\ *n* — **bot•a•nize** \-ᵊn-ˌīz\ *vb*
botch \ˈbäch\ *vb* ♦ **:** to foul up hopelessly **:** BUNGLE — **botch** *n*

♦ bobble, bungle, butcher, flub, foul up, fumble, mangle, mess up, screw up

[1]**both** \ˈbōth\ *pron* **:** both ones **:** the one as well as the other
[2]**both** *conj* — used as a function word to indicate and stress the inclusion of each of two or more things specified by coordinated words, phrases, or clauses ⟨∼ New York and London⟩
[3]**both** *adj* **:** being the two **:** affecting the one and the other
[1]**both•er** \ˈbä-t͟hər\ *vb* **1 a** ♦ **:** to annoy especially by petty provocation **b** ♦ **:** to intrude upon **:** PESTER **2 a** ♦ **:** to become concerned **:** become mentally troubled **b** ♦ **:** to cause to be anxious or concerned

♦ [1a] aggravate, annoy, bug, chafe, exasperate, gall, get, grate, irk, irritate, nettle, peeve, persecute, pique, put out, rasp, rile, vex ♦ [1b] bug, disturb, intrude, pester ♦ [2a] fear, fret, stew, sweat, trouble, worry ♦ [2b] concern, discompose, disquiet, distress, disturb, perturb, unsettle, upset, worry

[2]**bother** *n* **1 a :** a state of petty discomfort, annoyance, or worry **b** ♦ **:** something that causes petty annoyance or worry **2** ♦ **:** needless bustle or excitement

♦ [1b] aggravation, annoyance, exasperation, frustration, hassle, headache, inconvenience, irritant, nuisance, peeve, pest, problem, thorn, vexation ♦ [2] bustle, commotion, disturbance, furor, fuss, pother, stew, stir

both•er•some \-səm\ *adj* ♦ **:** causing bother

♦ aggravating, annoying, frustrating, galling, irksome, irritating, pesty, vexatious

[1]**bot•tle** \ˈbät-ᵊl\ *n* **1 :** a container (as of glass) with a narrow neck and usually no handles **2 :** the quantity held by a bottle **3 :** intoxicating liquor
[2]**bottle** *vb* **bot•tled; bot•tling 1 :** to confine as if in a bottle **:** RESTRAIN **2 :** to put into a bottle
bot•tle•neck \ˈbät-ᵊl-ˌnek\ *n* **1 :** a narrow passage or point of congestion **2** ♦ **:** something that obstructs or impedes

♦ backup, jam, snarl

[1]**bot•tom** \ˈbä-təm\ *n* **1 a** ♦ **:** an under or supporting surface **b** ♦ **:** the seat of the body **:** BUTTOCKS **2 :** the surface on which a body of water lies **3** ♦ **:** the lowest part or place; *also* **:** an inferior position ⟨start at the ∼⟩ **4 :** BOTTOMLAND **5 a :** the part of a ship's hull lying below the water **b** ♦ **:** a craft for traveling on water **:** BOAT — **bottom** *adj* — **bot•tom•less** *adj*

♦ [1a] underbelly, underside *Ant* face, top ♦ [1b] backside, butt, buttocks, posterior, rear, rump, seat ♦ [3] base, foot *Ant* head, top ♦ [5b] boat, craft, ship, vessel

2bottom *vb* **1 :** to furnish with a bottom **2 :** to reach the bottom **3 :** to reach a low point before rebounding — usually used with *out*

bot•tom•land \ˈbä-təm-ˌland\ *n* **:** low land along a river

bottom line *n* **1 :** the essential point **:** CRUX **2 :** the final result **:** OUTCOME

bot•u•lism \ˈbä-chə-ˌli-zəm\ *n* **:** an acute paralytic disease caused by a bacterial toxin (**bot•u•li•num toxin** \ˌbä-chə-ˌlī-nəm-\) especially in tainted food

bou•doir \ˈbü-ˌdwär, ˈbu̇-, ˌbü-ˈ, ˌbu̇-ˈ\ *n* **:** a woman's dressing room or bedroom

bouf•fant \bü-ˈfänt, ˈbü-ˌfänt\ *adj* **:** puffed out ⟨∼ hairdos⟩

bough \ˈbau̇\ *n* **:** a usually large or main branch of a tree

bought *past and past part of* BUY

bouil•la•baisse \ˌbü-yə-ˈbās\ *n* **:** a highly seasoned fish stew made with at least two kinds of fish

bouil•lon \ˈbü-ˌyän; ˈbu̇l-ˌyän, -yən\ *n* **:** a clear soup made usually from beef

boul•der \ˈbōl-dər\ *n* **:** a large detached rounded or worn mass of rock — **boul•dered** \-dərd\ *adj*

bou•le•vard \ˈbu̇-lə-ˌvärd, ˈbü-\ *n* **:** a broad often landscaped thoroughfare

1bounce \ˈbau̇ns\ *vb* **bounced; bounc•ing 1 :** to cause to rebound ⟨∼ a ball⟩ **2** ♦ **:** to rebound after striking **3** ♦ **:** to expel hastily from a place **4 :** to issue (a check) on an account having insufficient funds **5** ♦ **:** to recover quickly from a blow or defeat — usually used with *back*

♦ [2] carom, glance, rebound, ricochet, skim, skip ♦ [3] banish, boot (out), cast, chase, dismiss, drum, eject, expel, oust, rout, run off, throw out ♦ *usu* **bounce back** [5] rally, rebound, recover, snap back

2bounce *n* ♦ **:** the quality or state of being lively — **bouncy** \ˈbau̇n-sē\ *adj*

♦ dash, drive, esprit, pep, punch, snap, spirit, verve, vim, zing, zip

bounc•er \ˈbau̇n-sər\ *n* **:** a person employed in a public place to remove disorderly persons

1bound \ˈbau̇nd\ *adj* ♦ **:** intending to go

♦ decisive, determined, firm, intent, purposeful, resolute, set, single-minded

2bound *n* **:** something that limits or restrains **:** LIMIT, BOUNDARY

3bound *vb* **1** ♦ **:** to set limits to **2** ♦ **:** to form the boundary of **3 :** to name the boundaries of

♦ [1] circumscribe, define, delimit, demarcate, limit, mark, terminate ♦ [2] border, fringe, margin, rim, skirt

4bound *past and past part of* BIND

5bound *adj* **1 :** constrained by or as if by bonds **:** CONFINED, OBLIGED **2 :** enclosed in a binding or cover **3** ♦ **:** firmly decided **:** RESOLVED, DETERMINED; *also* **:** SURE

♦ decisive, determined, firm, intent, purposeful, resolute, set, single-minded

6bound *n* **1** ♦ **:** the act or an instance of leaping into the air **:** JUMP **2 :** REBOUND, BOUNCE

♦ hop, jump, leap, spring, vault

7bound *vb* **:** to move by leaping **:** SPRING, BOUNCE

bound•ary \ˈbau̇n-drē\ *n, pl* **-aries** ♦ **:** something that marks or fixes a limit (as of territory)

♦ bound, ceiling, confines, end, extent, limit, limitation, line, termination ♦ border, bound, circumference, compass, confines, edge, end, fringe, margin, perimeter, periphery, rim, skirt, verge

bound•en \ˈbau̇n-dən\ *adj* **:** BINDING

bound•less *adj* ♦ **:** having no boundaries — **bound•less•ness** *n*

♦ endless, illimitable, immeasurable, indefinite, infinite, limitless, measureless, unbounded, unfathomable, unlimited

boun•te•ous \ˈbau̇n-tē-əs\ *adj* **1 :** bestowing gifts or favors freely **:** GENEROUS **2 :** more than enough **:** ABUNDANT — **boun•te•ous•ly** *adv* — **boun•te•ous•ness** *n*

boun•ti•ful \ˈbau̇n-ti-fəl\ *adj* **1** ♦ **:** giving freely **2** ♦ **:** given or provided abundantly **:** PLENTIFUL

♦ [1] charitable, free, generous, liberal, munificent, openhanded, unselfish, unsparing ♦ [2] abundant, ample, comfortable, generous, liberal, plentiful

boun•ti•ful•ly *adv* ♦ **:** in a bountiful degree

♦ generously, handsomely, liberally, well

boun•ti•ful•ness *n* **:** the quality or state of being bountiful

boun•ty \ˈbau̇n-tē\ *n, pl* **bounties 1** ♦ **:** liberality in giving **:** GENEROSITY **2 :** something given liberally **3 :** a reward, premium, or subsidy given usually for doing something

♦ generosity, liberality, philanthropy, unselfishness

bou•quet \bō-ˈkā, bü-\ *n* **1 :** flowers picked and fastened together in a bunch **2** ♦ **:** a distinctive aroma (as of wine)

♦ aroma, fragrance, incense, perfume, redolence, scent, spice

bour•bon \ˈbər-bən\ *n* **:** a whiskey distilled from a corn mash

bour•geois \ˈbu̇rzh-ˌwä, bu̇rzh-ˈwä\ *n, pl* **bourgeois** *same or* -ˌwäz, -ˈwäz\ **:** a middle-class person — **bourgeois** *adj*

bour•geoi•sie \ˌbu̇rzh-ˌwä-ˈzē\ *n* **:** a social order dominated by bourgeois

bourne *also* **bourn** \ˈbōrn, ˈbu̇rn\ *n* **:** BOUNDARY; *also* **:** DESTINATION

bourse \ˈbu̇rs\ *n* **:** a European stock exchange

bout \ˈbau̇t\ *n* **1** ♦ **:** an athletic match **:** CONTEST **2 a** ♦ **:** a fit of sickness **:** ATTACK ⟨a ∼ of measles⟩ **b :** OUTBREAK **3 :** SESSION

♦ [1] competition, contest, event, game, match, meet, tournament ♦ [2a] attack, case, fit, seizure, siege, spell

bou•tique \bü-ˈtēk\ *n* **:** a small fashionable specialty shop

bou•ton•niere \ˌbüt-ᵊn-ˈiər\ *n* **:** a flower or bouquet worn in a buttonhole

1bo•vine \ˈbō-ˌvīn, -ˌvēn\ *adj* **1 :** of or relating to bovines **2 :** having qualities (as placidity or dullness) characteristic of oxen or cows

2bovine *n* **:** any of a group of mammals including oxen, buffalo, and their close relatives

bovine spon•gi•form encephalopathy \-ˈspən-ji-ˌfȯrm-\ *n* **:** MAD COW DISEASE

1bow \ˈbau̇\ *vb* **1** ♦ **:** to give oneself over to the will or authority of another **:** YIELD **2 :** to bend the head or body (as in submission, courtesy, or assent)

♦ budge, capitulate, concede, give in, knuckle under, quit, submit, succumb, surrender, yield

2bow *n* **:** an act or posture of bowing

3bow \ˈbō\ *n* **1 a** ♦ **:** something bent into a simple curve **:** BEND, ARCH **b :** RAINBOW **2 :** a weapon for shooting arrows; *also* **:** ARCHER **3 :** a knot formed by doubling a line into two or more loops **4 :** a wooden rod strung with horsehairs for playing an instrument of the violin family

♦ angle, arc, arch, bend, crook, curve, turn, wind

4bow \ˈbō\ *vb* **1 :** to bend into a curve **2 :** to play (an instrument) with a bow

5bow \ˈbau̇\ *n* **:** the forward part of a ship — **bow** *adj*

bowd•ler•ise *Brit var of* BOWDLERIZE

bowd•ler•ize \ˈbōd-lə-ˌrīz, ˈbau̇d-\ *vb* **-ized; -iz•ing :** to expurgate by omitting parts considered vulgar

bow•el \ˈbau̇(-ə)l\ *n* **1 :** INTESTINE; *also* **:** one of the divisions of the intestine — usually used in plural **2** *pl* **:** the inmost parts ⟨the ∼*s* of the earth⟩

bow•er \ˈbau̇(-ə)r\ *n* **:** a shelter of boughs or vines **:** ARBOR

1bowl \ˈbōl\ *n* **1 :** a concave vessel used to hold liquids **2 :** a drinking vessel **3** ♦ **:** a bowl-shaped part or structure; *esp* **:** an athletic stadium — **bowl•ful** \-ˌfu̇l\ *n*

♦ circus, coliseum, stadium

2bowl *n* **1 :** a ball for rolling on a level surface in bowling **2 :** a cast of the ball in bowling

3bowl *vb* **1 :** to play a game of bowling; *also* **:** to roll a ball in bowling **2** ♦ **:** to travel (as in a vehicle) rapidly and smoothly **3** ♦ **:** to strike or knock down with a moving object

♦ [2] breeze, coast, drift, flow, glide, roll, sail, skim, slide, slip, stream, sweep, whisk ♦ *usu* **bowl down** [3] down, drop, fell, floor, knock, level

bow•legged \ˈbō-ˌle-gəd\ *adj* **:** having legs that bow outward at or below the knee — **bow•leg** \ˈbō-ˌleg\ *n*

1bowl•er \ˈbō-lər\ *n* **:** a person who bowls

2bow•ler \ˈbō-lər\ *n* **:** DERBY 3

bow•line \ˈbō-lən, -ˌlīn\ *n* **:** a knot used to form a loop that neither slips nor jams

bowl•ing \ˈbō-liŋ\ *n* **:** any of various games in which balls are rolled on a green or alley at an object or a group of objects; *esp* **:** TENPINS

bowl over *vb* ♦ **:** to overwhelm with surprise; *also* **:** to make a vivid impression on

♦ amaze, astonish, astound, dumbfound, flabbergast, floor, shock, startle, stun, stupefy, surprise

bow•man \ˈbō-mən\ *n* **:** ARCHER

bow•sprit \ˈbau̇-ˌsprit\ *n* **:** a spar projecting forward from the prow of a ship
bow•string \ˈbō-ˌstriŋ\ *n* **:** the cord connecting the two ends of a shooting bow
¹box \ˈbäks\ *n, pl* **box** *or* **box•es :** an evergreen shrub or small tree used especially for hedges
²box *n* **1** ♦ **:** a rigid typically rectangular receptacle often with a cover; *also* **:** the quantity held by a box **2 :** a small compartment (as for a group of theater patrons); *also* **:** a boxlike receptacle or division **3 :** any of six spaces on a baseball diamond where the batter, pitcher, coaches, and catcher stand **4 :** PREDICAMENT

♦ caddy, case, casket, chest, locker, trunk

³box *vb* **:** to enclose in or as if in a box
⁴box *n* ♦ **:** a punch or slap especially on the ear

♦ belt, blow, buffet, hit, punch, slug

⁵box *vb* **1 :** to strike with the hand **2 :** to engage in boxing with
box•car \ˈbäks-ˌkär\ *n* **:** a roofed freight car usually with sliding doors in the sides
box cutter *n* **:** a small cutting tool with a retractable razor blade
¹box•er \ˈbäk-sər\ *n* **1** ♦ **:** a person who engages in boxing **2 :** BOXER SHORTS

♦ fighter, prizefighter, pugilist

²boxer *n* **:** any of a German breed of compact medium-sized dogs with a short usually fawn or brindled coat
boxer shorts *n pl* **:** men's loose-fitting shorts worn as underwear
box•ing \ˈbäk-siŋ\ *n* **:** the sport of fighting with the fists
box office *n* **:** an office (as in a theater) where admission tickets are sold
box turtle *n* **:** any of several No. American land turtles able to withdraw completely into their shell
box•wood \ˈbäks-ˌwu̇d\ *n* **:** the tough hard wood of the box; *also* **:** a box tree or shrub
boy \ˈbȯi\ *n* **1** ♦ **:** a male child **:** YOUTH **2 :** SON — **boy•hood** \-ˌhu̇d\ *n* — **boy•ish** *adj* — **boy•ish•ly** *adv* — **boy•ish•ness** *n*

♦ lad, nipper, shaver, stripling, youth

boy•cott \ˈbȯi-ˌkät\ *vb* **:** to refrain from having any dealings with — **boycott** *n*
boy•friend \ˈbȯi-ˌfrend\ *n* **1 :** a male friend **2** ♦ **:** a frequent or regular male companion of a girl or woman

♦ beau, fellow, man, swain

Boy Scout *n* **:** a member of any of various national scouting programs (as the Boy Scouts of America)
boy•sen•ber•ry \ˈbȯiz-ᵊn-ˌber-ē, ˈbȯis-\ *n* **:** a large bramble fruit with a raspberry flavor; *also* **:** the hybrid plant bearing it developed by crossing blackberries and raspberries
bo•zo \ˈbō-ˌzō\ *n, pl* **bozos :** a foolish or incompetent person
bp *abbr* **1** bishop **2** birthplace
BP *abbr* **1** batting practice **2** blood pressure **3** boiling point
bpl *abbr* birthplace
BPOE *abbr* Benevolent and Protective Order of Elks
br *abbr* **1** branch **2** brass **3** brown
¹Br *abbr* Britain; British
²Br *symbol* bromine
BR *abbr* bedroom
bra \ˈbrä\ *n* **:** BRASSIERE
¹brace \ˈbrās\ *vb* **braced; brac•ing 1** *archaic* **:** to make fast **:** BIND **2 :** to tighten preparatory to use; *also* **:** to get ready for **:** prepare oneself **3** ♦ **:** to restore strength and activity to **:** INVIGORATE **4** ♦ **:** to furnish or support with a brace; *also* **:** STRENGTHEN **5 :** to set firmly **6** ♦ **:** to gain courage or confidence

♦ [3] animate, energize, enliven, fire, invigorate, jazz up, liven up, pep up, quicken, stimulate, vitalize, vivify, zip (up) ♦ [4] bear, bolster, buttress, carry, prop, shore, stay, strengthen, support, uphold ♦ [6] forearm, fortify, nerve, psych (up), ready, steel

²brace *n, pl* **brac•es 1** *or pl* **brace** ♦ **:** two of a kind 〈a ~ of dogs〉 **2 :** a crank-shaped device for turning a bit **3** ♦ **:** something (as a tie, prop, or clamp) that distributes, directs, or resists pressure or weight **4** *pl* **:** SUSPENDERS **5 :** an appliance for supporting a body part (as the shoulders) **6** *pl* **:** a dental appliance used to exert pressure to straighten misaligned teeth **7 :** one of two marks { } used to connect words or items to be considered together

♦ [1] couple, duo, pair, twain, twosome ♦ [3] bulwark, buttress, mount, shore, stay, support, underpinning

brace•let \ˈbrā-slət\ *n* **1 :** an ornamental band or chain worn around the wrist **2 :** something (as handcuffs) resembling a bracelet

bra•ce•ro \brä-ˈser-ō\ *n, pl* **-ros :** a Mexican laborer admitted to the U.S. especially for seasonal farm work
brac•ing *adj* ♦ **:** giving strength, vigor, or freshness

♦ invigorating, refreshing, restorative, stimulative, tonic

brack•en \ˈbra-kən\ *n* **:** a large coarse fern; *also* **:** a growth of such ferns
¹brack•et \ˈbra-kət\ *n* **1 :** a projecting framework or arm designed to support weight; *also* **:** a shelf on such framework **2 :** one of a pair of punctuation marks [ ] used especially to enclose interpolated matter **3** ♦ **:** a continuous section of a series; *esp* **:** one of a graded series of income groups

♦ category, class, division, family, grade, group, kind, order, set, species, type

²bracket *vb* **1 :** to furnish or fasten with brackets **2 a :** to place within brackets **b :** to separate or group with or as if with brackets
brack•ish \ˈbra-kish\ *adj* **:** somewhat salty — **brack•ish•ness** *n*
bract \ˈbrakt\ *n* **:** an often modified leaf on or at the base of a flower stalk
brad \ˈbrad\ *n* **:** a slender nail with a small head
brae \ˈbrā\ *n, chiefly Scot* **:** a hillside especially along a river
¹brag \ˈbrag\ *vb* **bragged; brag•ging** ♦ **:** to talk or assert boastfully — **brag•ger** *n*

♦ boast, crow, plume, swagger

²brag *n* **1** ♦ **:** arrogant talk or manner **2 :** one who brags **:** BRAGGART

♦ bluster, bombast, braggadocio, gas, grandiloquence, hot air, rant

brag•ga•do•cio \ˌbra-gə-ˈdō-shē-ˌō, -sē-, -chē-\ *n, pl* **-cios 1** ♦ **:** one who brags **:** BRAGGART **2** ♦ **:** empty boasting **3 :** arrogant pretension **:** COCKINESS

♦ [1] braggart, boaster, bragger ♦ [2] bluster, bombast, brag, gas, grandiloquence, hot air, rant

brag•gart \ˈbra-gərt\ *n* ♦ **:** one who brags

♦ boaster, braggadocio, bragger

brag•ger \ˈbra-gər\ *n* ♦ **:** one who brags

♦ braggart, boaster, braggadocio

Brah•man *or* **Brah•min** \ˈbrä-mən *for 1*; ˈbrā-, ˈbrä-, ˈbra- *for 2*\ *n* **1 :** a Hindu of the highest caste traditionally assigned to the priesthood **2 :** any of a breed of large vigorous humped cattle developed in the southern U.S. from Indian stock **3** *usu Brahmin* **:** a person of high social standing and cultivated intellect and taste
Brah•man•ism \ˈbrä-mə-ˌni-zəm\ *n* **:** orthodox Hinduism
¹braid \ˈbrād\ *vb* **1 :** to form (strands) into a braid **:** PLAIT; *also* **:** to make from braids **2 :** to ornament with braid
²braid *n* **1** ♦ **:** a length of braided hair **2** ♦ **:** a cord or ribbon of three or more interwoven strands

♦ [1, 2] lace, plait

braille \ˈbrāl\ *n, often cap* **:** a system of writing for the blind that uses characters made up of raised dots
¹brain \ˈbrān\ *n* **1 :** the part of the vertebrate central nervous system enclosed in the skull and continuous with the spinal cord that is composed of neurons and supporting structures and is the center of thought and nervous system control; *also* **:** a centralized mass of nerve tissue in an invertebrate **2 a** ♦ **:** INTELLECT, INTELLIGENCE — often used in plural **b** ♦ **:** a very intelligent or intellectual person — **brained** \ˈbrānd\ *adj*

♦ *often* **brains** [2a] gray matter (*or* grey matter), intellect, intelligence, reason, sense ♦ [2b] genius, intellect, thinker, whiz, wizard

²brain *vb* **1 :** to kill by smashing the skull **2 :** to hit on the head
brain•child \ˈbrān-ˌchīld\ *n* **:** a product of one's creative imagination
brain death *n* **:** final cessation of activity in the central nervous system especially as indicated by a flat electroencephalogram — **brain–dead** \-ˌded\ *adj*
brain drain *n* **:** the departure of educated or professional people from one country, sector, or field to another usually for better pay or living conditions
brain•less *adj* **:** lacking intelligence
brain•storm \-ˌstȯrm\ *n* **:** a sudden inspiration or idea — **brainstorm** *vb*
brain•teas•er \-ˌtē-zər\ *n* **:** a challenging puzzle
brain•wash•ing \ˈbrān-ˌwȯ-shiŋ, -ˌwä-\ *n* **1 :** a forcible indoctrination to induce someone to give up basic political, social, or

religious beliefs and attitudes and to accept contrasting regimented ideas **2 :** persuasion by propaganda or salesmanship — **brain•wash** *vb*

brain wave *n* **1 :** BRAINSTORM **2 :** rhythmic fluctuations of voltage between parts of the brain; *also* **:** a current produced by brain waves

brainy *adj* ♦ **:** having or showing a well-developed intellect

♦ alert, bright, brilliant, clever, intelligent, keen, nimble, quick, quick-witted, sharp, smart

braise \ˈbrāz\ *vb* **braised; brais•ing :** to cook (meat) slowly in fat and little moisture in a closed pot

¹brake \ˈbrāk\ *n* **:** a common bracken fern

²brake *n* ♦ **:** rough or wet land heavily overgrown (as with thickets or reeds)

♦ brushwood, chaparral, coppice, covert, thicket

³brake *n* **:** a device for slowing or stopping motion especially by friction — **brake•less** *adj*

⁴brake *vb* **braked; brak•ing 1** ♦ **:** to slow or stop by or as if by a brake **2 :** to apply a brake

♦ decelerate, retard, slow

brake•man \ˈbrāk-mən\ *n* **:** a train crew member who inspects the train and assists the conductor

bram•ble \ˈbram-bəl\ *n* **:** any of a large genus of prickly shrubs (as a blackberry) related to the roses; *also* **:** any rough prickly shrub or vine

bram•bly \-b(ə-)lē\ *adj* ♦ **:** like or full of brambles

♦ prickly, scratchy, thorny

bran \ˈbran\ *n* **:** the edible broken husks of cereal grain sifted from flour or meal

¹branch \ˈbranch\ *n* **1 :** a natural subdivision (as a bough or twig) of a plant stem **2 :** a division (as of an antler or a river) related to a whole like a plant branch to its stem **3 :** a discrete element of a complex system: as **a** ♦ **:** a separate but dependent part of a central organization ⟨the executive ~⟩ **b :** a division of a family descended from one ancestor — **branched** \ˈbrancht\ *adj*

♦ affiliate, chapter, local

²branch *vb* **1 :** to develop branches **2** ♦ **:** to spring out (as from a main stem) **:** DIVERGE **3 :** to extend activities ⟨the business is ~*ing* out⟩

♦ diverge, fan, radiate ♦ *usu* **branch out** diverge, divide, fork, separate

¹brand \ˈbrand\ *n* **1 :** a piece of charred or burning wood **2 a :** a mark made (as by burning) usually to identify **b** ♦ **:** a mark of disgrace **:** STIGMA **3 :** a class of goods identified as the product of a particular firm or producer **4 :** a distinctive kind ⟨my own ~ of humor⟩

♦ blot, smirch, spot, stain, stigma, taint

²brand *vb* **1 :** to mark with a brand **2 :** STIGMATIZE

bran•dish \ˈbran-dish\ *vb* **:** to shake or wave menacingly

brand–new \ˈbran-ˈnü, -ˈnyü\ *adj* ♦ **:** conspicuously new and unused

♦ fresh, pristine, virgin ♦ new, spick-and-span, unused

bran•dy \ˈbran-dē\ *n, pl* **brandies :** a liquor distilled from wine or fermented fruit juice — **brandy** *vb*

brash \ˈbrash\ *adj* **1** ♦ **:** prone to act in a rash, impetuous manner **2** ♦ **:** aggressively self-assertive — **brash•ly** *adv* — **brash-ness** *n*

♦ [1] foolhardy, madcap, overbold, overconfident, reckless ♦ [2] arch, bold, brazen, cheeky, cocky, fresh, impertinent, impudent, insolent, nervy, sassy, saucy

brass \ˈbras\ *n* **1 :** an alloy of copper and zinc; *also* **:** an object of brass **2** ♦ **:** brazen self-assurance **3 :** persons of high rank (as in the military)

♦ audacity, brazenness, cheek, chutzpah, effrontery, gall, nerve, presumption, sauce, sauciness, temerity

bras•siere \brə-ˈzir\ *n* **:** a woman's close-fitting undergarment designed to support the breasts

brassy *adj* **:** shamelessly bold

brat \ˈbrat\ *n* **:** an ill-behaved child — **brat•ti•ness** *n* — **brat•ty** *adj*

bra•va•do \brə-ˈvä-dō\ *n, pl* **-does** *or* **-dos 1 :** blustering swaggering conduct **2 :** a show of bravery

¹brave \ˈbrāv\ *adj* **brav•er; brav•est 1** ♦ **:** showing courage **2 :** EXCELLENT, SPLENDID — **brave•ly** *adv*

♦ courageous, dauntless, doughty, fearless, gallant, greathearted, heroic, intrepid, lionhearted, manful, stalwart, stout, undaunted, valiant, valorous *Ant* cowardly, craven, fainthearted, fearful, pusillanimous, timorous

²brave *vb* **braved; brav•ing** ♦ **:** to face or endure bravely

♦ beard, brazen, confront, dare, defy, face

³brave *n* **:** an American Indian warrior

brav•ery \ˈbrā-və-rē\ *n, pl* **-er•ies 1** ♦ **:** the quality or state of being brave **:** COURAGE **2 :** fine clothes; *also* **:** showy display

♦ courage, daring, fearlessness, gallantry, guts, hardihood, heart, heroism, nerve, stoutness, valor

bra•vo \ˈbrä-vō\ *n, pl* **bravos :** a shout of approval — often used as an interjection in applauding

bra•vu•ra \brə-ˈvyu̇r-ə, -ˈvu̇r-\ *n* **1 :** a florid brilliant musical style **2 :** self-assured brilliant performance — **bravura** *adj*

¹brawl \ˈbrȯl\ *n* ♦ **:** a noisy quarrel — **brawl•er** *n*

♦ altercation, argument, disagreement, dispute, fight, quarrel, row, wrangle ♦ fracas, fray, free-for-all, melee, row

²brawl *vb* ♦ **:** to quarrel or fight noisily

♦ argue, bicker, dispute, fall out, fight, hassle, quarrel, row, scrap, spat, squabble, wrangle

brawn \ˈbrȯn\ *n* **:** strong muscles; *also* **:** muscular strength — **brawn•i•ness** *n*

brawny *adj* ♦ **:** having well-developed muscles

♦ muscular, rugged, sinewy, stalwart, stout, strong

bray \ˈbrā\ *n* **:** the characteristic harsh cry of a donkey — **bray** *vb*

braze \ˈbrāz\ *vb* **brazed; braz•ing :** to solder with an alloy (as brass) that melts at a lower temperature than the metals being joined — **braz•er** *n*

¹bra•zen \ˈbrāz-ᵊn\ *adj* **1 :** made of brass **2 :** sounding harsh and loud **3 :** of the color of brass **4** ♦ **:** marked by contemptuous boldness — **bra•zen•ly** *adv*

♦ arch, bold, brash, cheeky, cocky, fresh, impertinent, impudent, insolent, nervy, sassy, saucy

²brazen *vb* ♦ **:** to face boldly or defiantly

♦ beard, brave, confront, dare, defy, face

bra•zen•ness *n* ♦ **:** the quality or state of being brazen

♦ discourtesy, disrespect, impertinence, impudence, incivility, insolence, rudeness ♦ audacity, brass, cheek, chutzpah, effrontery, gall, nerve, presumption, sauce, sauciness, temerity

¹bra•zier \ˈbrā-zhər\ *n* **:** a worker in brass

²brazier *n* **1 :** a vessel holding burning coals (as for heating) **2 :** a device on which food is grilled

Bra•zil•ian \brə-ˈzil-yən\ *n* **:** a native or inhabitant of Brazil — **Brazilian** *adj*

Bra•zil nut \brə-ˈzil-\ *n* **:** a triangular oily edible nut borne in large capsules by a tall So. American tree; *also* **:** the tree

¹breach \ˈbrēch\ *n* **1** ♦ **:** a breaking of a law, obligation, tie (as of friendship), or standard (as of conduct) **2** ♦ **:** an interruption or opening made by or as if by breaking through

♦ [1] infraction, infringement, offense, transgression, trespass, violation *Ant* observance ♦ [2] break, discontinuity, gap, gulf, hole, interval, opening, rent, rift, separation

²breach *vb* **1 :** to make a breach in **2 :** to leap out of water ⟨whales ~*ing*⟩ **3** ♦ **:** to fail to keep or honor **:** violate a trust

♦ break, transgress, violate

¹bread \ˈbred\ *n* **1 :** baked food made basically of flour or meal **2 :** a substance with food value **:** FOOD

²bread *vb* **:** to cover with bread crumbs before cooking

bread•bas•ket \ˈbred-ˌbas-kət\ *n* **:** a major cereal-producing region

bread•fruit \-ˌfrüt\ *n* **:** a round usually seedless fruit resembling bread in color and texture when baked; *also* **:** a tall tropical tree related to the mulberry and bearing breadfruit

bread•stuff \-ˌstəf\ *n* **:** GRAIN, FLOUR

breadth \ˈbredth, ˈbretth\ *n* **1 a :** distance from side to side **:** WIDTH **b** ♦ **:** a wide expanse **2** ♦ **:** comprehensive quality **:** SCOPE ⟨~ of knowledge⟩

♦ [1b] expanse, extent, reach, spread, stretch ♦ [2] amplitude, compass, extent, range, reach, realm, scope, sweep, width

bread•win•ner \ˈbred-ˌwi-nər\ *n* **:** a member of a family whose wages supply its livelihood

¹break \ˈbrāk\ *vb* **broke** \ˈbrōk\; **bro•ken** \ˈbrō-kən\; **break•ing**

1 ♦ **:** to separate into parts usually suddenly or violently **:** come or force apart **2** ♦ **:** to violate a command or law **:** TRANSGRESS ⟨∼ a law⟩ **3 :** to force a way into, out of, or through **4 a :** to disrupt the order or unity of ⟨∼ ranks⟩ ⟨∼ up a gang⟩ **b :** to cause the destruction or loss of effectiveness of; *also* **:** to bring to submission or helplessness **5 :** EXCEED, SURPASS ⟨∼ a record⟩ **6 a :** to cause to suffer financial ruin **b** ♦ **:** to reduce in rank ⟨*broken* from sargeant to private⟩ **7 a :** to make known **b** ♦ **:** to find an explanation or solution for; *also* **:** to discover the essentials of (a code or cipher system) **8 a** ♦ **:** to stop or bring to an end suddenly **:** HALT **b :** to act or change abruptly (as a course or activity) **9 :** to come especially suddenly into being or notice ⟨as day ∼*s*⟩ **10** ♦ **:** to fail under stress **11 :** HAPPEN, DEVELOP **12** ♦ **:** to escape with sudden forceful effort

♦ [1] bust, fracture, fragment ♦ [2] breach, transgress, violate ♦ [6b] bust, degrade, demote, downgrade, reduce ♦ [7b] answer, crack, decode, dope, figure out, puzzle, resolve, riddle, solve, unravel, work, work out ♦ [8a] break off, cease, cut, desist, discontinue, drop, end, halt, knock off, lay off, leave off, quit, shut off, stop ♦ [10] break down, conk, crash, cut out, die, fail, stall ♦ [12] bolt, flee, fly, retreat, run, run away, run off

2break *n* **1 :** an act of breaking **2** ♦ **:** a result of breaking; *esp* **:** an interruption of strength or continuity ⟨coffee ∼⟩ ⟨a ∼ in the wall⟩ **3 :** a stroke of good luck

♦ breach, discontinuity, gap, gulf, hole, interval, opening, rent, rift, separation ♦ breath, breather, recess, respite

break·able *adj* ♦ **:** capable of being broken — **breakable** *n*

♦ delicate, fragile, frail

break·age \ˈbrā-kij\ *n* **1 :** the action of breaking **2 :** articles or amount broken **3 :** loss due to things broken

break·down \ˈbrāk-ˌdau̇n\ *n* **1 :** functional failure; *esp* **:** a physical, mental, or nervous collapse **2 :** DISINTEGRATION **3** ♦ **:** the process of decomposing **:** DECOMPOSITION **4** ♦ **:** division into categories **:** ANALYSIS

♦ [3] corruption, decay, decomposition, putrefaction, rot, spoilage ♦ [4] analysis, assay, dissection

break down *vb* **1** ♦ **:** to stop functioning because of breakage or wear **2** ♦ **:** to divide into parts or categories **3** ♦ **:** to undergo decomposition **4** ♦ **:** to succumb to mental or emotional stress

♦ [1] break, conk, crash, cut out, die, fail, stall ♦ [2] assort, categorize, class, classify, grade, group, peg, place, range, rank, separate, sort ♦ [3] corrupt, decay, decompose, disintegrate, molder, putrefy, rot, spoil ♦ [4] crack, flip, freak

break·er \ˈbrā-kər\ *n* **1 :** one that breaks **2 :** a wave that breaks into foam (as against the shore)

break·fast \ˈbrek-fəst\ *n* **:** the first meal of the day — **breakfast** *vb*

break in *vb* **1 :** to enter a building by force **2** ♦ **:** to hinder by speaking when another is speaking **:** INTERRUPT; *also* **:** INTRUDE **3 :** TRAIN — **break–in** \ˈbrāk-ˌin\ *n*

♦ chime in, cut in, interpose, interrupt, intrude

break·neck \ˈbrāk-ˈnek\ *adj* ♦ **:** very fast or dangerous ⟨∼ speed⟩

♦ breathless, dizzy, fast, fleet, lightning, rapid, rattling, speedy, swift

break off *vb* ♦ **:** to stop abruptly **:** bring or come to an end

♦ break, cease, cut, desist, discontinue, drop, end, halt, knock off, lay off, leave off, quit, shut off, stop

break out *vb* **1** ♦ **:** to develop or erupt suddenly or with force **2 :** to develop a skin rash

♦ burst, erupt, explode, flame, flare, go off

break·through \ˈbrāk-ˌthrü\ *n* **1 :** an act or instance of breaking through an obstruction or defensive line **2** ♦ **:** a sudden advance in knowledge or technique

♦ advance, advancement, enhancement, improvement, refinement

break·up \-ˌəp\ *n* **1** ♦ **:** the act or process of dissolving **:** DISSOLUTION **2 :** a division into smaller units

♦ dissolution, division, partition, schism, separation, split

break up *vb* **1** ♦ **:** to cease to exist as a unified whole **2** ♦ **:** to break into pieces

♦ [1] disband, disperse, dissolve ♦ [2] disconnect, disjoint, dissever, dissociate, disunite, divide, divorce, part, resolve, separate, sever, split, sunder, unyoke

break·wa·ter \ˈbrāk-ˌwȯ-tər, -ˌwä-\ *n* **:** a structure protecting a harbor or beach from the force of waves

bream \ˈbrim, ˈbrēm\ *n, pl* **bream** *or* **breams :** any of various small freshwater sunfishes

breast \ˈbrest\ *n* **1 :** either of the pair of mammary glands extending from the front of the chest especially in pubescent and adult human females **2 :** the front part of the body between the neck and the abdomen **3 :** the seat of emotion and thought

breast·bone \ˈbrest-ˌbōn\ *n* **:** STERNUM

breast–feed \-ˌfēd\ *vb* **:** to feed (a baby) from a mother's breast rather than from a bottle

breast·plate \-ˌplāt\ *n* **:** a metal plate of armor for the breast

breast·stroke \-ˌstrōk\ *n* **:** a swimming stroke executed by extending both arms forward and then sweeping them back with palms out while kicking backward and outward with both legs

breast·work \-ˌwərk\ *n* **:** a temporary fortification

breath \ˈbreth\ *n* **1 a :** the act or power of breathing **b** ♦ **:** opportunity or time to breathe; *esp* **:** a pause in an activity **2** ♦ **:** a slight breeze **3 :** air inhaled or exhaled in breathing **4 :** spoken sound **5 :** SPIRIT — **breath·less·ly** *adv* — **breath·less·ness** *n* — **breathy** \ˈbre-thē\ *adj*

♦ [1b] break, breather, pause, recess, respite ♦ [2] air, breeze, puff, waft, zephyr

breathe \ˈbrēth\ *vb* **breathed; breath·ing 1 :** to inhale and exhale **2** ♦ **:** to be alive **:** LIVE **3 :** to halt for rest **4 :** to utter softly or secretly — **breath·able** *adj*

♦ be, exist, live, subsist

breath·er \ˈbrē-thər\ *n* **1 :** one that breathes **2** ♦ **:** a short rest

♦ break, breath, recess, respite

breath·less *adj* **1 a :** panting or gasping for breath **b** ♦ **:** not breathing **:** not alive **2** ♦ **:** very rapid or strenuous **3** ♦ **:** oppressive because of no fresh air or breeze

♦ [1b] dead, deceased, defunct, gone, late, lifeless ♦ [2] breakneck, brisk, dizzy, fast, fleet, hasty, lightning, nippy, quick, rapid, rattling, snappy, speedy, swift ♦ [3] close, stuffy

breath·tak·ing \ˈbreth-ˌtā-kiŋ\ *adj* **1 :** making one out of breath **2** ♦ **:** producing excitement **:** EXCITING, THRILLING ⟨∼ beauty⟩ — **breath·tak·ing·ly** *adv*

♦ electric, exciting, exhilarating, rousing, stirring, thrilling

brec·cia \ˈbre-chē-ə, -chə\ *n* **:** a rock consisting of sharp fragments held in fine-grained material

breech \ˈbrēch\ *n* **1** *usu* **breech·es** *usu* ˈbri-chəz\ ♦ **:** trousers ending near the knee; *also* **:** PANTS **2 :** the hind end of the body **:** BUTTOCKS, RUMP **3 :** the part of a firearm at the rear of the barrel

♦ britches, pantaloons, pants, slacks, trousers

1breed \ˈbrēd\ *vb* **bred** \ˈbred\; **breed·ing 1 :** BEGET; *also* **:** ORIGINATE **2** ♦ **:** to propagate sexually; *also* **:** MATE **3** ♦ **:** to bring (a person) to maturity through nurturing care and education **:** BRING UP **4 :** to produce (fissionable material) from material that is not fissionable — **breed·er** *n*

♦ [2] mate, multiply, procreate, propagate, reproduce ♦ [3] bring up, foster, raise, rear

2breed *n* **1 :** a strain of similar and presumably related plants or animals usually developed in domestication **2** ♦ **:** a group, set, or kind sharing common attributes **:** SORT, CLASS

♦ class, description, feather, ilk, kind, like, manner, nature, order, sort, species, type

breed·ing *n* **1** ♦ **:** line of descent **:** ANCESTRY **2 :** training in polite social interaction **3 :** sexual propagation of plants or animals

♦ ancestry, birth, blood, bloodline, descent, extraction, family tree, genealogy, line, lineage, origin, parentage, pedigree, stock, strain

1breeze \ˈbrēz\ *n* **1** ♦ **:** a light wind **2** ♦ **:** something easily done **:** CINCH, SNAP — **breeze·less** *adj*

♦ [1] air, breath, puff, waft, zephyr ♦ [2] child's play, cinch, picnic, pushover, snap

2breeze *vb* **breezed; breez·ing** ♦ **:** to progress quickly and easily; *also* **:** to move swiftly and airily

♦ bowl, coast, drift, flow, glide, roll, sail, skim, slide, slip, stream, sweep, whisk ♦ dash, fly, hasten, hurry, run, rush, speed, whirl, zip, zoom

breeze·way \ˈbrēz-ˌwā\ *n* **:** a roofed open passage connecting two buildings (as a house and garage)

breezy \ˈbrē-zē\ *adj* **1** ♦ **:** swept by breezes **2** ♦ **:** briskly informal — **breez•i•ly** \ˈbrē-zə-lē\ *adv* — **breez•i•ness** \-zē-nəs\ *n*

♦ [1] blowy, blustery, gusty, windy ♦ [2] affable, easygoing, happy-go-lucky, laid-back

breth•ren \ˈbreth-rən, ˈbre-thə-; ˈbre-thərn\ *pl of* BROTHER — used especially in formal or solemn address
Brethren *n pl* **:** members of one of several Protestant denominations originating chiefly in a German religious movement and stressing personal religious experience
bre•via•ry \ˈbrē-vyə-rē, -vē-ˌer-ē\ *n, pl* **-ries** *often cap* **:** a book of prayers, hymns, psalms, and readings used by Roman Catholic priests
brev•i•ty \ˈbre-və-tē\ *n, pl* **-ties 1** ♦ **:** shortness or conciseness of expression **2** ♦ **:** shortness of duration

♦ [1, 2] briefness, conciseness, shortness

brew \ˈbrü\ *vb* **1 :** to prepare (as beer) by steeping, boiling, and fermenting **2 :** to prepare (as tea) by steeping in hot water — **brew** *n* — **brew•er** *n* — **brew•ery** \ˈbrü-ə-rē, ˈbrů(-ə)r-ē\ *n*
¹briar *also* **brier** \ˈbrī-ər\ *n* **:** a plant (as a bramble or rose) with a thorny or prickly usually woody stem
²briar *n* **:** a tobacco pipe made from the root or stem of a European heath
brib•able *adj* ♦ **:** capable of being bribed

♦ corruptible, purchasable, venal

¹bribe \ˈbrīb\ *n* **:** something (as money or a favor) given or promised to a person to influence conduct
²bribe *vb* **bribed; brib•ing :** to influence by offering a bribe — **brib•er** *n* — **brib•ery** \ˈbrī-bə-rē\ *n*
bric–a–brac \ˈbri-kə-ˌbrak\ *n pl* **:** small ornamental articles
¹brick \ˈbrik\ *n* **:** a block molded from moist clay and hardened by heat used especially for building
²brick *vb* **:** to close, cover, or pave with bricks
brick•bat \ˈbrik-ˌbat\ *n* **1 :** a piece of a hard material (as a brick) especially when thrown as a missile **2 :** an uncomplimentary remark
brick•lay•er \ˈbrik-ˌlā-ər\ *n* **:** a person who builds or paves with bricks — **brick•lay•ing** *n*
¹brid•al \ˈbrīd-ᵊl\ *n* **:** a marriage festival or ceremony **:** WEDDING
²bridal *adj* **:** of or relating to a bride or a wedding
bride \ˈbrīd\ *n* **:** a woman just married or about to be married
bride•groom \ˈbrīd-ˌgrüm, -ˌgrům\ *n* **:** a man just married or about to be married
brides•maid \ˈbrīdz-ˌmād\ *n* **:** a woman who attends a bride at her wedding
¹bridge \ˈbrij\ *n* **1 :** a structure built over a depression or obstacle for use as a passageway **2 :** something (as the upper part of the nose) resembling a bridge in form or function **3 :** a curved piece raising the strings of a musical instrument **4 :** the forward part of a ship's superstructure from which it is navigated **5 :** an artificial replacement for missing teeth
²bridge *vb* **bridged; bridg•ing :** to build a bridge over — **bridge•able** *adj*
³bridge *n* **:** a card game for four players developed from whist
bridge•head \-ˌhed\ *n* **:** an advanced position seized in enemy territory
bridge•work \-ˌwərk\ *n* **:** dental bridges
¹bri•dle \ˈbrīd-ᵊl\ *n* **1 :** headgear with which a horse is controlled **2 :** CURB, RESTRAINT
²bridle *vb* **bri•dled; bri•dling 1 a :** to put a bridle on **b** ♦ **:** to restrain with or as if with a bridle **2 :** to show hostility or scorn usually by tossing the head

♦ check, constrain, contain, control, curb, govern, inhibit, regulate, rein, restrain, tame

Brie \ˈbrē\ *n* **:** a soft cheese with a whitish rind and a pale yellow interior
¹brief \ˈbrēf\ *adj* **1** ♦ **:** short in duration or extent **2** ♦ **:** marked by brevity of expression or statement **:** CONCISE; *also* **:** CURT — **brief•ly** *adv*

♦ [1] little, short, short-lived ♦ [2] compact, compendious, concise, crisp, curt, epigrammatic, laconic, pithy, succinct, summary, terse

²brief *n* **1 :** a concise statement or document; *esp* **:** one summarizing a law client's case or a legal argument **2** *pl* **:** short snug underpants
³brief *vb* ♦ **:** to give final instructions or essential information to

♦ acquaint, advise, apprise, clue, enlighten, familiarize, fill in, inform, instruct, tell, wise

brief•case \ˈbrēf-ˌkās\ *n* **:** a flat flexible case for carrying papers
brief•ness *n* ♦ **:** the quality or state of being brief

♦ brevity, conciseness, shortness ♦ brevity, compactness, conciseness, crispness, succinctness, terseness

bri•er *var of* BRIAR
¹brig \ˈbrig\ *n* **:** a 2-masted square-rigged sailing ship
²brig *n* ♦ **:** the place of confinement for offenders on a naval ship

♦ hoosegow, jail, jug, lockup, pen, penitentiary, prison, stockade

³brig *abbr* brigade
bri•gade \bri-ˈgād\ *n* **1 :** a military unit composed of a headquarters, one or more units of infantry or armored forces, and supporting units **2 :** a group organized for a particular purpose (as fire fighting)
brig•a•dier general \ˌbri-gə-ˌdir-\ *n* **:** a commissioned officer (as in the army) ranking next below a major general
brig•and \ˈbri-gənd\ *n* **:** BANDIT — **brig•and•age** \-gən-dij\ *n*
brig•an•tine \ˈbri-gən-ˌtēn\ *n* **:** a 2-masted square-rigged ship with a fore-and-aft mainsail
Brig Gen *abbr* brigadier general
bright \ˈbrīt\ *adj* **1** ♦ **:** radiating or reflecting light **2 :** ILLUSTRIOUS, GLORIOUS **3 a** ♦ **:** having a cheerful nature **b** ♦ **:** mentally quick and resourceful **:** INTELLIGENT, CLEVER **4** ♦ **:** conducive to cheer — **bright** *adv* — **bright•ly** *adv*

♦ [1] beaming, brilliant, effulgent, glowing, incandescent, lambent, lucent, lucid, luminous, lustrous, radiant, refulgent, shiny ***Ant*** dim, dull, lackluster ♦ [1] ablaze, alight, light ***Ant*** blackened, dark, darkened, darkling, dimmed, dusky ♦ [3a] blithe, buoyant, cheerful, cheery, chipper, gay, lightsome, sunny, upbeat ♦ [3b] alert, brainy, brilliant, clever, intelligent, keen, nimble, quick, quick-witted, sharp, smart ♦ [4] auspicious, encouraging, fair, golden, heartening, hopeful, likely, promising, propitious, rosy, upbeat

bright•en \ˈbrīt-ᵊn\ *vb* **:** to make or become bright or brighter — **bright•en•er** *n*
bright•ness *n* **:** the state or quality of being bright
bril•liance \-yəns\ *n* ♦ **:** the quality or state of being brilliant

♦ augustness, glory, grandeur, grandness, magnificence, majesty, nobility, nobleness, resplendence, splendor, stateliness ♦ dazzle, effulgence, illumination, lightness, lucidity, luminosity, radiance, refulgence, splendor ***Ant*** blackness, dark, darkness, duskiness

bril•lian•cy \-yən-sē\ *n* **:** the quality or state of being brilliant
¹bril•liant \ˈbril-yənt\ *adj* **1** ♦ **:** very bright **2 :** STRIKING, DISTINCTIVE **3** ♦ **:** very intelligent — **bril•liant•ly** *adv*

♦ [1] beaming, bright, effulgent, glowing, incandescent, lambent, lucent, lucid, luminous, lustrous, radiant, refulgent, shiny ♦ [3] alert, brainy, bright, clever, intelligent, keen, nimble, quick, quick-witted, sharp, smart

²brilliant *n* **:** a gem cut in a particular form with many facets
¹brim \ˈbrim\ *n* **1 :** an upper or outer margin **:** EDGE, RIM **2 :** the projecting rim of a hat — **brim•less** *adj*
²brim *vb* **brimmed; brim•ming** ♦ **:** to be or become full often to overflowing

♦ abound, bulge, burst, crawl, swarm, teem

brim•ful \-ˈfůl\ *adj* ♦ **:** full to the brim

♦ chock-full, crowded, fat, fraught, full, loaded, packed, replete

brim•stone \ˈbrim-ˌstōn\ *n* **:** SULFUR
brin•dled \ˈbrin-dᵊld\ *adj* **:** having dark streaks or flecks on a gray or tawny ground ⟨a ~ Great Dane⟩
brine \ˈbrīn\ *n* **1 :** water saturated with salt **2** ♦ **:** the water of a sea or salt lake **:** OCEAN

♦ blue, deep, ocean, sea

bring \ˈbriŋ\ *vb* **brought** \ˈbrȯt\; **bring•ing** \ˈbriŋ-iŋ\ **1 :** to cause to come with one **2 :** INDUCE, PERSUADE, LEAD **3 :** PRODUCE, EFFECT **4** ♦ **:** to sell for ⟨~ a good price⟩ — **bring•er** *n*

♦ cost, fetch, go, sell

bring about *vb* ♦ **:** to cause to take place

♦ cause, create, effect, effectuate, generate, induce, make, produce, prompt, result, work, yield

bring up *vb* **1** ♦ **:** to give a parent's fostering care to **2 :** to come or bring to a sudden halt **3** ♦ **:** to call to notice

♦ [1] breed, foster, raise, rear ♦ [3] broach, introduce, moot, raise

brink \ˈbriŋk\ *n* **1 :** an edge at the top of a steep place **2 :** the point of onset

briny \ˈbrī-nē\ *adj* ◆ **:** of, relating to, or resembling brine or the sea — **brin•i•ness** *n*

◆ saline, salty

brio \ˈbrē-ō\ *n* **:** VIVACITY, SPIRIT

bri•quette *or* **bri•quet** \bri-ˈket\ *n* **:** a compacted often brick-shaped mass of fine material ⟨a charcoal ~⟩

bris *also* **briss** \ˈbris\ *n* **:** the Jewish rite of circumcision

brisk \ˈbrisk\ *adj* **1** ◆ **:** keenly alert **:** LIVELY **2 :** INVIGORATING **3 :** acting or capable of acting with speed

◆ active, animate, animated, energetic, jaunty, lively, peppy, perky, pert, spirited, sprightly, springy, vital, vivacious

bris•ket \ˈbris-kət\ *n* **:** the breast or lower chest of a quadruped; *also* **:** a cut of beef from the brisket

brisk•ly *adv* ◆ **:** in a brisk manner

◆ apace, fast, hastily, pronto, quick, quickly, rapidly, speedily, swift, swiftly

brisk•ness *n* ◆ **:** the quality or state of being brisk

◆ animation, exuberance, liveliness, lustiness, robustness, sprightliness, vibrancy, vitality

bris•ling \ˈbriz-liŋ, ˈbris-\ *n* **:** SPRAT

[1]**bris•tle** \ˈbri-səl\ *n* **:** a short stiff coarse hair — **bris•tle•like** \ˈbri-səl-ˌlīk\ *adj*

[2]**bristle** *vb* **bris•tled; bris•tling** **1 :** to stand stiffly erect **2 :** to show angry defiance **3 :** to appear as if covered with bristles

bris•tly *adj* **:** consisting of or like bristles

Brit *abbr* Britain; British

Bri•tan•nic \bri-ˈta-nik\ *adj* **:** BRITISH

britch•es \ˈbri-chəz\ *n pl* ◆ **:** an outer garment covering each leg separately from waist to ankle **:** BREECHES, TROUSERS

◆ breeches, pantaloons, pants, slacks, trousers

Brit•ish \ˈbri-tish\ *n pl* **:** the people of Great Britain or the Commonwealth — **British** *adj* — **Brit•ish•ness** *n*

British thermal unit *n* **:** the quantity of heat needed to raise the temperature of one pound of water one degree Fahrenheit

Brit•on \ˈbrit-ᵊn\ *n* **1 :** a member of a people inhabiting Britain before the Anglo-Saxon invasion **2 :** a native or inhabitant of Great Britain

brit•tle \ˈbrit-ᵊl\ *adj* **brit•tler; brit•tlest** ◆ **:** easily broken — **brit•tle•ness** *n*

◆ crisp, crumbly, flaky, friable, short

bro \ˈbrō\ *n, pl* **bros** **1 :** BROTHER 1 **2 :** SOUL BROTHER

[1]**broach** \ˈbrōch\ *n* **:** a pointed tool

[2]**broach** *vb* **1 :** to pierce (as a cask) in order to draw the contents **2** ◆ **:** to introduce as a topic of conversation

◆ bring up, introduce, moot, raise

[1]**broad** \ˈbrȯd\ *adj* **1 :** having a specified extension from side to side **:** WIDE **2** ◆ **:** extending far and wide **3 :** CLEAR, OPEN **4** ◆ **:** easily understood **:** OBVIOUS ⟨a ~ hint⟩ **5 :** COARSE, CRUDE ⟨~ stories⟩ **6 :** tolerant in outlook **7 :** GENERAL **8** ◆ **:** dealing with main or essential points — **broad•ness** *n*

◆ [2] expansive, extended, extensive, far-flung, far-reaching, wide, widespread ◆ [4] apparent, clear, clear-cut, distinct, evident, lucid, manifest, obvious, palpable, patent, perspicuous, plain, transparent, unambiguous, unequivocal, unmistakable ◆ [8] bird's-eye, general, nonspecific, overall

[2]**broad** *n, slang* **:** WOMAN

broad•band \ˈbrȯd-ˌband\ *n* **:** a system of high-speed telecommunications in which a frequency range is divided into multiple independent channels for simultaneous transmission of signals

[1]**broad•cast** \ˈbrȯd-ˌkast\ *vb* **broadcast** *also* **broad•cast•ed; broad•cast•ing** **1 :** to scatter or sow broadcast **2** ◆ **:** to make widely known **3 :** to transmit a broadcast — **broad•cast•er** *n*

◆ circulate, disseminate, propagate, spread, strew ◆ advertise, announce, blaze, declare, enunciate, placard, post, proclaim, promulgate, publicize, publish, sound

[2]**broadcast** *adv* **:** to or over a wide area

[3]**broadcast** *n* **1 :** the transmission of sound or images by radio or television **2 :** a single radio or television program

broad•cloth \-ˌklȯth\ *n* **1 :** a smooth dense woolen cloth **2 :** a fine soft cloth of cotton, silk, or synthetic fiber

broad•en \ˈbrȯd-ᵊn\ *vb* **:** WIDEN

broad•loom \-ˌlüm\ *adj* **:** woven on a wide loom especially in a solid color

broad•ly *adv* ◆ **:** in a broad manner; *esp* **:** to a great extent

◆ considerably, greatly, largely, much, sizably

broad–mind•ed \-ˈmīn-dəd\ *adj* ◆ **:** tolerant of varied opinions — **broad–mind•ed•ly** *adv* — **broad–mind•ed•ness** *n*

◆ liberal, nonorthodox, nontraditional, open-minded, progressive, radical, unconventional, unorthodox

[1]**broad•side** \-ˌsīd\ *n* **1 :** a sheet of paper printed usually on one side (as an advertisement) **2 :** all of the guns on one side of a ship; *also* **:** their simultaneous firing **3 :** a volley of abuse or denunciation

[2]**broadside** *adv* **1 :** with one side forward **:** SIDEWAYS **2 :** from the side ⟨the car was hit ~⟩

broad–spectrum *adj* **:** effective against a wide range of organisms ⟨~ antibiotics⟩

broad•sword \ˈbrȯd-ˌsōrd\ *n* **:** a broad-bladed sword

broad•tail \-ˌtāl\ *n* **:** a karakul especially with flat and wavy fur

bro•cade \brō-ˈkād\ *n* **:** a usually silk fabric with a raised design

broc•co•li \ˈbrä-kə-lē\ *n* **:** the stems and immature usually green or purple flower heads of either of two garden vegetable plants closely related to the cabbage; *also* **:** either of the plants

bro•chette \brō-ˈshet\ *n* **:** SKEWER

bro•chure \brō-ˈshu̇r\ *n* ◆ **:** an unbound printed publication with no cover or with a paper cover **:** PAMPHLET, BOOKLET

◆ booklet, circular, folder, leaflet, pamphlet

bro•gan \ˈbrō-gən, brō-ˈgan\ *n* **:** a heavy shoe

brogue \ˈbrōg\ *n* **:** a dialect or regional pronunciation; *esp* **:** an Irish accent

broil \ˈbrȯil\ *vb* **:** to cook by exposure to radiant heat **:** GRILL — **broil** *n*

broil•er \ˈbrȯi-lər\ *n* **1 :** a utensil for broiling **2 :** a young chicken fit for broiling

broil•ing *adj* ◆ **:** extremely hot

◆ burning, fiery, hot, red-hot, scorching, sultry, torrid

[1]**broke** \ˈbrōk\ *past of* BREAK

[2]**broke** *adj* ◆ **:** having no money or assets **:** PENNILESS

◆ destitute, impecunious, indigent, needy, penniless, penurious, poor, poverty-stricken

[1]**bro•ken** \ˈbrō-kən\ *past part of* BREAK

[2]**broken** *adj* **1 :** SHATTERED **2 a :** having gaps or breaks **:** INTERRUPTED, DISRUPTED **b** ◆ **:** being irregular, interrupted, or full of obstacles **3 :** SUBDUED, CRUSHED **4 :** BANKRUPT **5 :** imperfectly spoken ⟨~ English⟩ — **bro•ken•ly** *adv*

◆ bumpy, coarse, irregular, jagged, lumpy, pebbly, ragged, rough, rugged, uneven

bro•ken•heart•ed \ˌbrō-kən-ˈhär-təd\ *adj* ◆ **:** overcome by grief or despair

◆ depressed, despondent, disconsolate, heartsick, miserable, mournful, sad, sorrowful, unhappy, wretched

bro•ker \ˈbrō-kər\ *n* ◆ **:** an agent who negotiates contracts of purchase and sale — **broker** *vb*

◆ arbiter, arbitrator, go-between, intercessor, intermediary, mediator, middleman, peacemaker

bro•ker•age \ˈbrō-kə-rij\ *n* **1 :** the business of a broker **2 :** the fee or commission charged by a broker

bro•mide \ˈbrō-ˌmīd\ *n* **:** a compound of bromine and another element or chemical group including some (as potassium bromide) used as sedatives

bro•mid•ic \brō-ˈmi-dik\ *adj* **:** TRITE, UNORIGINAL

bro•mine \ˈbrō-ˌmēn\ *n* **:** a deep red liquid corrosive chemical element that gives off an irritating vapor

bronc \ˈbräŋk\ *n* **:** an unbroken or partly broken range horse of western No. America; *also* **:** MUSTANG

bron•chi•al \ˈbräŋ-kē-əl\ *adj* **:** of, relating to, or affecting the bronchi or their branches

bron•chi•tis \brän-ˈkī-təs, bräŋ-\ *n* **:** inflammation of the bronchi and their branches — **bron•chit•ic** \-ˈki-tik\ *adj*

bron•chus \ˈbräŋ-kəs\ *n, pl* **bron•chi** \ˈbräŋ-ˌkī, -ˌkē\ **:** either of the main divisions of the windpipe each leading to a lung

bron•co \ˈbräŋ-kō\ *n, pl* **broncos** **:** BRONC

bron•to•sau•rus \ˌbrän-tə-ˈsȯr-əs\ *also* **bron•to•saur** \ˈbrän-tə-ˌsȯr\ *n* **:** any of a genus of large 4-footed and probably herbivorous sauropod dinosaurs of the Jurassic

Bronx cheer \ˈbräŋks-\ *n* **:** RASPBERRY 2

[1]**bronze** \ˈbränz\ *vb* **bronzed; bronz•ing** **:** to give the appearance of bronze to

[2]**bronze** *n* **1 :** an alloy of copper and tin and sometimes other elements; *also* **:** something made of bronze **2 :** a yellowish brown color — **bronzy** \ˈbrän-zē\ *adj*

brooch \ˈbrōch, ˈbrüch\ *n* **:** an ornamental clasp or pin

[1]**brood** \ˈbrüd\ *n* **:** a family of young animals or children and especially of birds
[2]**brood** *adj* **:** kept for breeding ⟨a ~ mare⟩
[3]**brood** *vb* **1** ♦ **:** to sit on eggs to hatch them; *also* **:** to shelter (hatched young) with the wings **2 :** to think anxiously or gloomily about something — **brood•ing•ly** *adv*

♦ hatch, incubate, set, sit

brood•er \ˈbrü-dər\ *n* **1 :** one that broods **2 :** a heated structure for raising young birds
[1]**brook** \ˈbru̇k\ *n* ♦ **:** a small natural stream

♦ creek, rill, rivulet, streamlet

[2]**brook** *vb* ♦ **:** to stand for **:** TOLERATE, BEAR

♦ abide, bear, countenance, endure, meet, stand, stick out, stomach, support, sustain, take, tolerate

brook•let \ˈbru̇-klət\ *n* **:** a small brook
brook trout *n* **:** a common speckled cold-water char of No. America
broom \ˈbrüm, ˈbru̇m\ *n* **1 :** any of several shrubs of the legume family with long slender branches and usually yellow flowers **2 :** an implement with a long handle (**broom•stick** \-ˌstik\) used for sweeping
bros *pl of* BRO
broth \ˈbrȯth\ *n, pl* **broths** \ˈbrȯths, ˈbrȯt͟hz\ **1 :** liquid in which meat or sometimes vegetable food has been cooked **2 :** a fluid culture medium
broth•el \ˈbrä-thəl, ˈbrȯ-\ *n* **:** a house of prostitution
broth•er \ˈbrə-t͟hər\ *n, pl* **brothers** *also* **breth•ren** \ˈbret͟h-rən, ˈbre-t͟hə-; ˈbre-t͟hərn\ **1 :** a male having one or both parents in common with another individual **2 :** a man who is a religious but not a priest **3 :** KINSMAN; *also* **:** SOUL BROTHER — **broth•er•li•ness** \-lē-nəs\ *n* — **broth•er•ly** *adj*
broth•er•hood \ˈbrə-t͟hər-ˌhu̇d\ *n* **1 :** the state of being brothers or a brother **2** ♦ **:** an association (as a labor union or monastic society) for a particular purpose **:** FRATERNITY **3 :** the whole body of persons in a business or profession

♦ association, club, college, congress, council, fellowship, fraternity, guild, institute, institution, league, order, organization, society

broth•er–in–law \ˈbrə-t͟hə-rən-ˌlȯ, ˈbrə-t͟hərn-ˌlȯ\ *n, pl* **broth•ers–in–law** \ˈbrə-t͟hər-zən-\ **:** the brother of one's spouse; *also* **:** the husband of one's sister or of one's spouse's sister
brougham \ˈbrü(-ə)m, ˈbrō(-ə)m\ *n* **:** a light closed horse-drawn carriage with the driver outside in front
brought *past and past part of* BRING
brou•ha•ha \ˈbrü-ˌhä-ˌhä\ *n* **:** HUBBUB, UPROAR
brow \ˈbrau̇\ *n* **1 :** the eyebrow or the ridge on which it grows; *also* **:** FOREHEAD **2 :** the projecting upper part of a steep place
brow•beat \ˈbrau̇-ˌbēt\ *vb* **-beat; -beat•en** \-ˈbē-tᵊn\ *or* **-beat; -beat•ing** ♦ **:** to intimidate by sternness or arrogance

♦ bully, cow, hector, intimidate

[1]**brown** \ˈbrau̇n\ *adj* **:** of the color brown; *also* **:** of dark or tanned complexion
[2]**brown** *n* **:** a color like that of coffee or chocolate that is a blend of red and yellow darkened by black — **brown•ish** *adj*
[3]**brown** *vb* **:** to make or become brown
brown bag•ging \-ˈba-giŋ\ *n* **:** the practice of carrying one's lunch usually in a brown bag — **brown bag•ger** *n*
brown bear *n* **:** any of various large typically brown-furred bears including the grizzly bear
brown•ie \ˈbrau̇-nē\ *n* **1** ♦ **:** a legendary cheerful elf who performs good deeds at night **2** *cap* **:** a member of a program of the Girl Scouts for girls in the first through third grades **3 :** a small square or rectangle of chocolate cake

♦ dwarf, elf, fairy, fay, gnome, hobgoblin, leprechaun, pixie, puck, troll

brown•nose \ˈbrau̇n-ˌnōz\ *vb* **:** to ingratiate oneself with — **brownnose** *n*
brown•out \ˈbrau̇-ˌnau̇t\ *n* **:** a period of reduced voltage of electricity caused especially by high demand and resulting in reduced illumination
brown rice *n* **:** hulled but unpolished rice that retains most of the bran layers
brown•stone \ˈbrau̇n-ˌstōn\ *n* **:** a dwelling faced with reddish brown sandstone
[1]**browse** \ˈbrau̇z\ *vb* **browsed; brows•ing** **1** ♦ **:** to feed on browse; *also* **:** GRAZE **2** ♦ **:** to read or look over something in a casual way **3 :** to access (as the World Wide Web) with a browser

♦ [1] forage, graze, pasture ♦ [2] dip, glance, glimpse, peek, skim

[2]**browse** *n* **:** tender shoots, twigs, and leaves fit for food for cattle
brows•er \ˈbrau̇-zər\ *n* **:** a computer program for accessing sites or information on a network (as the World Wide Web)
bru•in \ˈbrü-ən\ *n* **:** BEAR
[1]**bruise** \ˈbrüz\ *vb* **bruised; bruis•ing** **1 :** to inflict a bruise on; *also* **:** to become bruised **2 :** to break down (as leaves or berries) by pounding
[2]**bruise** *n* **:** a surface injury to flesh **:** CONTUSION
bruis•er \ˈbrü-zər\ *n* **:** a big husky man
bruit \ˈbrüt\ *vb* **:** to make widely known by common report
brunch \ˈbrənch\ *n* **:** a meal that combines a late breakfast and an early lunch
bru•net *or* **bru•nette** \brü-ˈnet\ *adj* **:** having brown or black hair and usually a relatively dark complexion — **brunet** *or* **brunette** *n*
brunt \ˈbrənt\ *n* **:** the main shock, force, or stress especially of an attack; *also* **:** the greater burden
bru•schet•ta \brü-ˈshe-tə, -ˈske-\ *n* **:** an appetizer of grilled bread with toppings
[1]**brush** \ˈbrəsh\ *n* **1 :** BRUSHWOOD **2 :** scrub vegetation or land covered with it
[2]**brush** *n* **1 :** a device composed of bristles set in a handle and used especially for cleaning or painting **2 :** a bushy tail (as of a fox) **3 :** an electrical conductor that makes contact between a stationary and a moving part (as of a motor) **4 :** a quick light touch in passing
[3]**brush** *vb* **1 :** to treat (as in cleaning or painting) with a brush **2 a :** to remove with or as if with a brush **b** ♦ **:** to dismiss in an offhand manner — usually used with *aside* or *off* **3** ♦ **:** to touch gently in passing

♦ *usu* **brush aside** *or* **brush off** [2b] condone, disregard, excuse, gloss over, ignore, pardon, pass over, shrug off, wink at ♦ [3] graze, kiss, nick, shave, skim

[4]**brush** *n* ♦ **:** a brief encounter or skirmish **:** SKIRMISH

♦ encounter, run-in, scrape, skirmish

brush–off \ˈbrəsh-ˌȯf\ *n* ♦ **:** a curt offhand dismissal

♦ cold shoulder, rebuff, repulse, snub

brush up *vb* **:** to renew one's skill
brush•wood \ˈbrəsh-ˌwu̇d\ *n* **1 :** small branches of wood especially when cut **2** ♦ **:** a thicket of shrubs and small trees

♦ brake, chaparral, coppice, covert, thicket

brusque \ˈbrəsk\ *adj* ♦ **:** blunt in manner or speech often to the point of ungracious harshness **:** CURT, BLUNT, ABRUPT — **brusque•ly** *adv*

♦ abrupt, blunt, curt, snippy

brus•sels sprout \ˈbrəs-əlz-\ *n, often cap B* **:** one of the edible small heads borne on the stalk of a plant closely related to the cabbage; *also, pl* **:** this plant
bru•tal \ˈbrü-tᵊl\ *adj* **1** ♦ **:** befitting a brute **:** CRUEL **2** ♦ **:** physically discomforting **:** HARSH, SEVERE ⟨~ weather⟩ **3 :** unpleasantly accurate — **bru•tal•ly** *adv*

♦ [1] barbarous, cruel, heartless, inhumane, sadistic, savage, vicious, wanton ♦ [2] bitter, burdensome, cruel, excruciating, grievous, grim, hard, harsh, heavy, inhuman, murderous, onerous, oppressive, rough, rugged, severe, stiff, tough, trying

bru•tal•ise *Brit var of* BRUTALIZE
bru•tal•i•ty \brü-ˈta-lə-tē\ *n* ♦ **:** the quality or state of being brutal

♦ barbarity, cruelty, inhumanity, sadism, savagery, viciousness, wantonness

bru•tal•ize \ˈbrü-tᵊl-ˌīz\ *vb* **-ized; -iz•ing** **1 :** to make brutal **2 :** to treat brutally
[1]**brute** \ˈbrüt\ *adj* **1 :** of or relating to beasts **2 :** BRUTAL **3 :** UNREASONING; *also* **:** purely physical ⟨~ strength⟩
[2]**brute** *n* **1** ♦ **:** a 4-footed animal **:** BEAST **2** ♦ **:** a brutal person

♦ [1] animal, beast, creature, critter ♦ [2] beast, devil, fiend, monster, savage, villain

brut•ish \ˈbrü-tish\ *adj* **1 :** BRUTE 1 **2 :** strongly sensual; *also* **:** showing little intelligence
BS *abbr* bachelor of science
BSA *abbr* Boy Scouts of America
bskt *abbr* basket
Bt *abbr* baronet
btry *abbr* battery

Btu *abbr* British thermal unit
bu *abbr* bushel
[1]**bub•ble** \ˈbə-bəl\ *n* **1 :** a globule of gas in a liquid **2 :** a thin film of liquid filled with gas **3 :** something lacking firmness or solidity
[2]**bubble** *vb* **bub•bled; bub•bling :** to form, rise in, or give off bubbles
bub•bly *adj* ♦ **:** full of or showing good spirits

♦ buoyant, effervescent, exuberant, frolicsome, high-spirited, vivacious

bub•kes \ˈbəp-kəs, ˈbu̇p-\ *n pl* **:** the least amount ⟨didn't win ~⟩
bu•bo \ˈbü-bō, ˈbyü-\ *n, pl* **buboes :** an inflammatory swelling of a lymph gland
bu•bon•ic plague \bü-ˈbä-nik-, byü-\ *n* **:** plague caused by a bacterium transmitted to human beings by flea bites and marked especially by chills and fever and by buboes usually in the groin
buc•ca•neer \ˌbə-kə-ˈnir\ *n* ♦ **:** any of the freebooters preying on Spanish ships and settlements especially in 17th century West Indies; *broadly* **:** PIRATE

♦ corsair, freebooter, pirate, rover

[1]**buck** \ˈbək\ *n, pl* **bucks 1** *or pl* **buck :** a male animal (as a deer or antelope) **2 a** ♦ **:** a male human being **b** ♦ **:** a man with unusual consideration for personal appearance **:** DANDY **3 :** DOLLAR

♦ [2a] chap, dude, fellow, gent, gentleman, guy, hombre, jack, joker, lad, male, man ♦ [2b] dandy, dude, fop, gallant

[2]**buck** *vb* **1** ♦ **:** to spring with an arching leap ⟨a ~*ing* horse⟩ **2 :** to charge against something; *also* **:** to strive for advancement sometimes without regard to ethical behavior **3** ♦ **:** to offer resistance to

♦ [1] hitch, jerk, jolt, twitch ♦ [3] defy, fight, oppose, repel, resist, withstand

buck•board \-ˌbōrd\ *n* **:** a 4-wheeled horse-drawn wagon with a floor of long springy boards
buck•et \ˈbə-kət\ *n* **1 :** a cylindrical open-top container with a handle **:** PAIL **2 a :** an object resembling a bucket in collecting, scooping, or carrying something **b :** as much as a bucket will hold; *broadly* ♦ **:** a large quantity — usually used in plural ⟨has *buckets* or money⟩ — **buck•et•ful** *n*

♦ *usu* **buckets** abundance, deal, gobs, heap, loads, lot, pile, plenty, quantity, scads

bucket seat *n* **:** a low separate seat for one person (as in an automobile)
buck•eye \ˈbə-ˌkī\ *n* **:** any of various trees or shrubs related to the horse chestnut; *also* **:** the large nutlike seed of such a shrub or tree
buck fever *n* **:** nervous excitement of an inexperienced hunter at the sight of game
[1]**buck•le** \ˈbə-kəl\ *n* **:** a clasp (as on a belt) for two loose ends
[2]**buckle** *vb* **buck•led; buck•ling 1 :** to fasten with a buckle **2** ♦ **:** to apply oneself with vigor **3 :** to crumple up **:** BEND, COLLAPSE

♦ address, apply, bend, devote, give

[3]**buckle** *n* **:** BEND, FOLD, KINK
buck•ler \ˈbə-klər\ *n* **:** SHIELD
buck•ram \ˈbə-krəm\ *n* **:** a coarse stiff cloth used especially for binding books
buck•saw \ˈbək-ˌsȯ\ *n* **:** a saw set in a usually H-shaped frame for sawing wood
buck•shot \ˈbək-ˌshät\ *n* **:** lead shot that is from .24 to .33 inch (about 6.1 to 8.4 millimeters) in diameter
buck•skin \-ˌskin\ *n* **1 :** the skin of a buck **2 :** a soft usually suede-finished leather — **buckskin** *adj*
buck•tooth \-ˈtüth\ *n* **:** a large projecting front tooth — **buck•toothed** \-ˈtütht\ *adj*
buck•wheat \-ˌhwēt\ *n* **:** either of two plants grown for their triangular seeds which are used as a cereal grain; *also* **:** these seeds
bu•col•ic \byü-ˈkä-lik\ *adj* ♦ **:** relating to or typical of rural life and especially shepherds or herdsmen **:** PASTORAL

♦ country, pastoral, rural, rustic

[1]**bud** \ˈbəd\ *n* **1 :** an undeveloped plant shoot (as of a leaf or a flower); *also* **:** a partly opened flower **2 :** an asexual reproductive structure that detaches from the parent and forms a new individual **3 :** something not yet fully developed ⟨nipped in the ~⟩
[2]**bud** *vb* **bud•ded; bud•ding 1 :** to form or put forth buds; *also* **:** to reproduce by asexual buds **2 :** to be or develop like a bud **3 :** to reproduce a desired variety (as of peach) by inserting a bud in a plant of a different variety
Bud•dhism \ˈbü-ˌdi-zəm, ˈbu̇-\ *n* **:** a religion of eastern and central Asia growing out of the teachings of Gautama Buddha — **Bud•dhist** \ˈbü-dist, ˈbu̇-\ *n or adj*
bud•dy \ˈbə-dē\ *n, pl* **buddies 1** ♦ **:** one associated with another especially in an action; *also* **:** FRIEND **2 :** FELLOW

♦ chum, comrade, crony, familiar, friend, intimate, pal

budge \ˈbəj\ *vb* **budged; budg•ing 1** ♦ **:** to change the place, position, or direction of **:** MOVE, SHIFT **2** ♦ **:** to give up resistance **:** YIELD

♦ [1] dislocate, displace, disturb, move, remove, shift, transfer ♦ [2] bow, capitulate, concede, give in, knuckle under, quit, submit, succumb, surrender, yield

bud•ger•i•gar \ˈbə-jə-rē-ˌgar\ *n* **:** a small brightly colored Australian parrot often kept as a pet
[1]**bud•get** \ˈbə-jət\ *n* **1** ♦ **:** a store or supply accumulated or available **2 :** a financial report containing estimates of income and expenses; *also* **:** a plan for coordinating income and expenses **3** ♦ **:** the amount of money available for a particular use — **bud•get•ary** \ˈbə-jə-ˌter-ē\ *adj*

♦ [1, 3] account, deposit, fund, kitty, nest egg, pool, supply

[2]**budget** *vb* **1 :** to allow for in a budget **2 :** to draw up a budget
[3]**budget** *adj* **:** INEXPENSIVE
bud•gie \ˈbə-jē\ *n* **:** BUDGERIGAR
[1]**buff** \ˈbəf\ *n* **1 :** a yellow to orange yellow color **2** ♦ **:** one who is ardently attached to a cause, object, or pursuit **:** FAN, ENTHUSIAST

♦ addict, aficionado, bug, devotee, enthusiast, fan, fanatic, fancier, fiend, freak, lover, maniac, nut

[2]**buff** *adj* **:** of the color buff
[3]**buff** *vb* ♦ **:** to make smooth and glossy usually by friction

♦ burnish, dress, gloss, grind, polish, rub, shine, smooth

buf•fa•lo \ˈbə-fə-ˌlō\ *n, pl* **-lo** *or* **-loes** *also* **-los 1 :** WATER BUFFALO **2 :** a large shaggy-maned No. American wild bovine mammal that has short horns and heavy forequarters with a large muscular hump
[1]**buf•fer** \ˈbə-fər\ *n* ♦ **:** something or someone that protects or shields (as from physical damage or a financial blow)

♦ bumper, cushion, fender, pad

[2]**buffer** *n* **:** one that buffs
[1]**buf•fet** \ˈbə-fət\ *n* **:** a blow especially with the hand **:** SLAP
[2]**buffet** *vb* **1 a :** to strike with the hand **b** ♦ **:** to pound repeatedly **2 :** to struggle against or on

♦ bash, bat, batter, beat, hammer, pound, thump

[3]**buf•fet** \(ˌ)bə-ˈfā, bü-\ *n* **1 :** piece of dining-room furniture having compartments and shelves for holding articles of table service **:** SIDEBOARD **2 :** a counter for refreshments; *also* **:** a meal at which people serve themselves informally
buff leather *n* **:** a strong supple oil-tanned leather
buf•foon \(ˌ)bə-ˈfün\ *n* ♦ **:** a ludicrous figure **:** CLOWN — **buf•foon•ery** \-ˈfü-nə-rē\ *n*

♦ clown, harlequin, zany

[1]**bug** \ˈbəg\ *n* **1 :** an insect or other creeping or crawling invertebrate animal; *esp* **:** an insect pest (as a bedbug) **2 :** any of an order of insects with sucking mouthparts and incomplete metamorphosis that includes many plant pests **3 :** an unexpected flaw or imperfection ⟨a ~ in a computer program⟩ **4 a :** a disease-producing germ **b** ♦ **:** a disease caused by a germ **5 :** a concealed listening device **6** ♦ **:** one who is ardently attached to a cause, object, or pursuit — **bug•gy** \ˈbə-gē\ *adj*

♦ [4b] ailment, complaint, complication, condition, disease, disorder, fever, ill, illness, infirmity, malady, sickness, trouble ♦ [6] addict, aficionado, buff, devotee, enthusiast, fan, fanatic, fancier, fiend, freak, lover, maniac, nut

[2]**bug** *vb* **bugged; bug•ging 1** ♦ **:** to annoy especially by petty provocation **2 :** to plant a concealed microphone in

♦ bait, hassle, heckle, needle, ride, taunt, tease ♦ aggravate, annoy, bother, chafe, exasperate, gall, get, grate, irk, irritate, nettle, peeve, persecute, pique, put out, rasp, rile, vex

[3]**bug** *vb* **bugged; bug•ging** *of the eyes* **:** PROTRUDE, BULGE
bug•a•boo \ˈbə-gə-ˌbü\ *n, pl* **-boos :** an imaginary object of fear **:** BOGEY
bug•bear \ˈbəg-ˌbar\ *n* ♦ **:** an imaginary object of fear **:** BOGEY; *also* **:** a source of dread

♦ bête noire, bogey, hobgoblin, ogre

bug•gy \ˈbə-gē\ *n, pl* **buggies** **1 :** a light horse-drawn carriage **2 :** a carriage for a baby
bu•gle \ˈbyü-gəl\ *n* **:** a valveless brass instrument resembling a trumpet and used especially for military calls — **bu•gler** *n*
bug out *vb* **:** to depart in a hurry; *also* **:** to flee in panic
¹**build** \ˈbild\ *vb* **built** \ˈbilt\; **build•ing** **1 a** ♦ **:** to form or have formed by ordering and uniting materials ⟨~ a house⟩ **b** ♦ **:** to develop or bring into being especially according to a set plan **2** ♦ **:** to produce or create gradually ⟨~ an argument on facts⟩ **3** ♦ **:** to become progressively greater **:** INCREASE, ENLARGE; *also* **:** ENHANCE **4 :** to engage in building — **build•er** *n*

♦ [1a, 1b] assemble, construct, erect, fabricate, make, make up, piece, put up, raise, rear, set up ***Ant*** disassemble, dismantle, take down ♦ *usu* **build up** [2] carve, forge, grind, hammer, work out ♦ *usu* **build up** [3] accumulate, appreciate, balloon, burgeon, enhance, enlarge, escalate, expand, increase, mount, multiply, mushroom, proliferate, rise, snowball, swell, wax

²**build** *n* ♦ **:** form or mode of structure; *esp* **:** PHYSIQUE

♦ constitution, figure, form, frame, physique, shape

build•ing \ˈbil-diŋ\ *n* **1 :** a usually roofed and walled structure (as a house) for permanent use **2 :** the art or business of constructing buildings
building block *n* ♦ **:** a unit of construction or composition

♦ component, constituent, element, factor, ingredient, member

build•up \ˈbil-ˌdəp\ *n* **:** the act or process of building up; *also* **:** something produced by this
built–in \ˈbil-ˈtin\ *adj* **1 :** forming an integral part of a structure **2 :** INHERENT
bulb \ˈbəlb\ *n* **1 :** an underground resting stage of a plant (as a lily or an onion) consisting of a short stem base bearing one or more buds enclosed in overlapping leaves; *also* **:** a fleshy plant structure (as a tuber) resembling a bulb **2 :** a plant having or growing from a bulb **3 :** a rounded more or less bulb-shaped object or part (as for an electric lamp) — **bul•bous** \ˈbəl-bəs\ *adj*
Bul•gar•i•an \ˌbəl-ˈgar-ē-ən, bu̇l-\ *n* **:** a native or inhabitant of Bulgaria — **Bulgarian** *adj*
¹**bulge** \ˈbəlj\ *vb* **bulged; bulg•ing** ♦ **:** to become or cause to become protuberant

♦ balloon, beetle, belly, billow, overhang, poke, project, protrude, start, stick out

²**bulge** *n* ♦ **:** a swelling projecting part

♦ overhang, projection, protrusion ***Ant*** concavity, dent, depression, hollow, indentation, pit

bu•li•mia \bü-ˈlē-mē-ə, byü-, -ˈli-\ *n* **1 :** an abnormal and constant craving for food **2 :** a serious eating disorder chiefly of females that is characterized by compulsive overeating usually followed by self-induced vomiting or laxative or diuretic abuse — **bu•lim•ic** \-ˈlē-mik, -ˈli-\ *adj or n*
¹**bulk** \ˈbəlk\ *n* **1 :** MAGNITUDE, VOLUME **2 :** material that forms a mass in the intestine; *esp* **:** FIBER 2 **3 :** a large mass **4** ♦ **:** the major portion

♦ body, core, generality, main, mass, staple, weight

²**bulk** *vb* **1 :** to cause to swell or bulge **2 :** to appear as a factor **:** LOOM
bulk•head \ˈbəlk-ˌhed\ *n* **1 :** a partition separating compartments **2 :** a structure built to cover a shaft or a cellar stairway
bulky \ˈbəl-kē\ *adj* **bulk•i•er; -est :** having bulk; *esp* **:** being large and unwieldy
¹**bull** \ˈbu̇l\ *n* **1 :** a male bovine animal; *also* **:** a usually adult male of various large animals (as the moose, elephant, or whale) **2 :** one who buys securities or commodities in expectation of a price increase — **bull•ish** *adj*
²**bull** *adj* **1 :** of, relating to, or suggestive of a bull **:** MALE **2 :** large of its kind
³**bull** *n* **1 :** a papal letter **2 :** DECREE
⁴**bull** *n, slang* **:** NONSENSE
⁵**bull** *abbr* bulletin
¹**bull•dog** \ˈbu̇l-ˌdȯg\ *n* **:** any of a breed of compact muscular short-haired dogs of English origin
²**bulldog** *vb* **:** to throw (a steer) by seizing the horns and twisting the neck
bull•doze \-ˌdōz\ *vb* **1 :** to move, clear, or level with a tractor-driven machine (**bull•doz•er**) having a broad blade for pushing **2** ♦ **:** to force as if by using a bulldozer

♦ elbow, muscle, press, push

bul•let \ˈbu̇-lət\ *n* **:** a missile to be shot from a firearm
bul•le•tin \ˈbu̇-lət-ᵊn\ *n* **1** ♦ **:** a brief public report intended for immediate release on a matter of public interest **2 :** a periodical publication (as of a college) — **bulletin** *vb*

♦ advertisement, announcement, notice, notification, release

bulletin board *n* **1** a board (as of cork) for posting notices **2 :** a public forum on a computer network in which users write or read messages or download files
bul•let•proof \ˈbu̇-lət-ˌprüf\ *adj* **1 :** impenetrable to bullets; *also* **:** INVINCIBLE **2 :** not subject to corrections, alteration, or modification
bull•fight \ˈbu̇l-ˌfīt\ *n* **:** a spectacle in which people ceremonially fight with and usually kill bulls in an arena — **bull•fight•er** *n*
bull•frog \-ˌfrȯg, -ˌfräg\ *n* **:** a large deep-voiced frog
bull•head \-ˌhed\ *n* **:** any of several common freshwater catfishes of the U.S.
bull•head•ed \-ˈhe-dəd\ *adj* **:** stupidly stubborn **:** HEADSTRONG
bull•head•ed•ness \-ˈhe-dəd-nəs\ *n* ♦ **:** the quality or state of being bullheaded

♦ hardheadedness, mulishness, obduracy, obstinacy, peevishness, persistence, pertinacity, self-will, stubbornness, tenacity

bul•lion \ˈbu̇l-yən\ *n* **:** gold or silver especially in bars or ingots
bull market *n* **:** a market in which securities or commodities are persistently rising in value
bull•ock \ˈbu̇-lək\ *n* **:** a young bull; *also* **:** STEER
bull pen *n* **:** a place on a baseball field where pitchers warm up; *also* **:** the relief pitchers of a baseball team
bull session *n* **:** an informal discussion
bull's–eye \ˈbu̇l-ˌzī\ *n, pl* **bull's–eyes :** the center of a target; *also* **:** a shot that hits the bull's-eye
¹**bul•ly** \ˈbu̇-lē\ *n, pl* **bullies** ♦ **:** a person habitually cruel to others who are weaker

♦ gangster, goon, hood, hoodlum, mobster, mug, punk, rowdy, ruffian, thug, tough

²**bully** *adj* **:** EXCELLENT, FIRST-RATE — often used interjectionally
³**bully** *vb* **bul•lied; bul•ly•ing** ♦ **:** to behave as a bully toward

♦ browbeat, cow, hector, intimidate

bul•rush \ˈbu̇l-ˌrəsh\ *n* **:** any of several large rushes or sedges of wetlands
bul•wark \ˈbu̇l-(ˌ)wərk, -ˌwȯrk; ˈbəl-(ˌ)wərk\ *n* **1 :** a wall-like defensive structure **2** ♦ **:** a strong support or protection

♦ brace, buttress, mount, shore, stay, support, underpinning

¹**bum** \ˈbəm\ *adj* **1 :** of poor quality ⟨~ advice⟩ **2 :** DISABLED ⟨a ~ knee⟩
²**bum** *vb* **bummed; bum•ming 1 :** to spend time unemployed and wandering; *also* **:** LOAF **2 :** to obtain by begging
³**bum** *n* **1 :** LOAFER **2 :** a person who is devoted to a recreational activity ⟨a ski ~⟩ **3** ♦ **:** a person who has no job and wanders from place to place **:** VAGRANT, TRAMP

♦ hobo, tramp, vagabond, vagrant

bum•ble•bee \ˈbəm-bəl-ˌbē\ *n* **:** any of numerous large hairy social bees
bum•mer \ˈbə-mər\ *n* **1 :** an unpleasant experience **2** ♦ **:** something that fails or disappoints **:** FAILURE

♦ bust, catastrophe, debacle, dud, failure, fiasco, fizzle, flop, lemon, loser, turkey, washout

¹**bump** \ˈbəmp\ *n* **1** ♦ **:** a local bulge; *esp* **:** a swelling of tissue **2** ♦ **:** a sudden forceful blow or impact

♦ [1] knot, lump, nodule, swelling ♦ [2] collision, concussion, crash, impact, jar, jolt, shock, smash, strike, wallop

²**bump** *vb* **1 :** to strike or knock forcibly; *also* **:** to move by or as if by bumping **2** ♦ **:** to collide with

♦ bang, bash, collide, crash, hit, impact, knock, ram, slam, smash, strike, swipe, thud

¹**bum•per** \ˈbəm-pər\ *n* **1 :** a cup or glass filled to the brim **2 :** something unusually large
²**bumper** *adj* ♦ **:** unusually large

♦ big, grand, great, large, outsize, oversize, whopping

³**bump•er** \ˈbəm-pər\ *n* ♦ **:** a device for absorbing shock or preventing damage; *esp* **:** a usually metal bar at either end of an automobile

♦ buffer, cushion, fender, pad

bump•kin \ˈbəmp-kən\ *n* ♦ **:** an awkward and unsophisticated country person

♦ clodhopper, hick, hillbilly, provincial, rustic, yokel

bump•tious \ˈbəmp-shəs\ *adj* **:** obtusely and often noisily self-assertive

bumpy *adj* ♦ **:** having or covered with bumps; *also* **:** marked by bumps or jolts

♦ broken, coarse, irregular, jagged, lumpy, pebbly, ragged, rough, rugged, uneven

bun \ˈbən\ *n* **:** a sweet biscuit or roll

¹bunch \ˈbənch\ *n* **1 :** SWELLING **2** ♦ **:** a number of things of the same kind — **bunchy** *adj*

♦ array, assemblage, batch, block, clump, cluster, collection, group, huddle, knot, lot, package, parcel, set, suite

²bunch *vb* ♦ **:** to form into a group or bunch

♦ cluster, crowd, huddle, press

bun•co *or* **bun•ko** \ˈbəŋ-kō\ *n, pl* **buncos** *or* **bunkos :** a swindling scheme — **bunco** *vb*

¹bun•dle \ˈbən-dᵊl\ *n* **1** ♦ **:** several items bunched and fastened together; *also* **:** something wrapped for carrying **2 :** a considerable amount **:** LOT **3 :** a small band of mostly parallel nerve or muscle fibers

♦ pack, package, parcel

²bundle *vb* **bun•dled; bun•dling :** to gather or tie in a bundle

bun•dling \ˈbənd-(ᵊ-)liŋ\ *n* **:** a former custom of a courting couple's occupying the same bed without undressing

bung \ˈbəŋ\ *n* **:** the stopper in the bunghole of a cask

bun•ga•low \ˈbəŋ-gə-ˌlō\ *n* **:** a one-storied house with a low-pitched roof

bun•gee cord \ˈbən-jē-\ *n* **:** a long elastic cord used especially as a fastening or shock-absorbing device

bungee jump *vb* **:** to jump for sport from a height (as from a bridge) while attached to a sturdy bungee cord — **bungee jumper** *n*

bung•hole \ˈbəŋ-ˌhōl\ *n* **:** a hole for emptying or filling a cask

bun•gle \ˈbəŋ-gəl\ *vb* **bun•gled; bun•gling** ♦ **:** to do badly **:** BOTCH — **bungle** *n* — **bun•gler** *n*

♦ bobble, botch, butcher, flub, foul up, fumble, mangle, mess up, screw up

bun•ion \ˈbən-yən\ *n* **:** an inflamed swelling of the first joint of the big toe

¹bunk \ˈbəŋk\ *n* ♦ **:** an article of furniture to sleep on **:** BED; *esp* **:** a built-in bed that is often one of a tier

♦ bed, pad, sack

²bunk *n* ♦ **:** insincere or foolish talk **:** BUNKUM, NONSENSE

♦ claptrap, drivel, folly, foolishness, fudge, hogwash, humbug, nonsense, piffle, rot, silliness, slush, stupidity, trash

bunk bed *n* **:** one of two single beds usually placed one above the other

bun•ker \ˈbəŋ-kər\ *n* **1 :** a bin or compartment for storage (as for coal on a ship) **2 :** a protective embankment or dugout **3 :** a sand trap or embankment constituting a hazard on a golf course

bun•kum *or* **bun•combe** \ˈbəŋ-kəm\ *n* **:** insincere or foolish talk

bun•ny \ˈbə-nē\ *n, pl* **-nies :** RABBIT

Bun•sen burner \ˈbən-sən-\ *n* **:** a gas burner usually consisting of a straight tube with air holes at the bottom

¹bunt \ˈbənt\ *vb* **1 :** ¹BUTT **2 :** to push or tap a baseball lightly without swinging the bat

²bunt *n* **:** an act or instance of bunting; *also* **:** a bunted ball

¹bun•ting \ˈbən-tiŋ\ *n* **:** any of numerous small stout-billed finches

²bunting *n* **:** a thin fabric used especially for flags; *also* **:** FLAGS

¹buoy \ˈbü-ē, ˈbȯi\ *n* **1 :** a floating object anchored in water to mark something (as a channel) **2 :** a float consisting of a ring of buoyant material to support a person who has fallen into the water

²buoy *vb* **1 :** to mark by a buoy **2 :** to keep afloat **3** ♦ **:** to raise the spirits of — usually used with *up*

♦ *usu* **buoy up** cheer, comfort, embolden, encourage, hearten, inspire, steel

buoy•an•cy \ˈbȯi-ən-sē, ˈbü-yən-\ *n* **1 :** the tendency of a body to float or rise when submerged in a fluid **2 :** the power of a fluid to exert an upward force on a body placed in it **3 :** resilience of spirit

buoy•ant \-ənt, -yənt\ *adj* **:** having buoyancy: as **a :** capable of floating **b** ♦ **:** having or inducing high spirits

♦ blithe, bright, cheerful, cheery, chipper, gay, lightsome, sunny, upbeat ♦ bubbly, effervescent, exuberant, frolicsome, high-spirited, vivacious

¹bur \ˈbər\ *var of* BURR

²bur *abbr* bureau

¹bur•den \ˈbərd-ᵊn\ *n* **1 a** ♦ **:** something that is carried **:** LOAD **b** ♦ **:** a duty or obligation one must take care of **:** RESPONSIBILITY **2 :** something oppressive **:** ENCUMBRANCE **3** ♦ **:** goods or merchandise loaded to be conveyed **:** CARGO; *also* **:** capacity for cargo

♦ [1a, 3] cargo, freight, haul, lading, load, payload, weight ♦ [1b] charge, commitment, duty, need, obligation, responsibility

²burden *vb* ♦ **:** to encumber or oppress with something heavy, laborious, or disheartening

♦ depress, oppress, sadden ♦ encumber, load, lumber, saddle, weight

³burden *n* **1** ♦ **:** a phrase or verse recurring regularly in a poem or song **:** REFRAIN, CHORUS **2 :** a main theme or idea **:** GIST

♦ chorus, refrain

bur•den•some \-səm\ *adj* ♦ **:** imposing or constituting a burden

♦ grim, hard, harsh, heavy, oppressive, rough, rugged, severe, stiff, tough, trying ♦ arduous, challenging, demanding, exacting, grueling, laborious, onerous, taxing, toilsome

bur•dock \ˈbər-ˌdäk\ *n* **:** any of a genus of coarse composite herbs with globe-shaped flower heads surrounded by prickly bracts

bu•reau \ˈbyu̇r-ō\ *n, pl* **bureaus** *also* **bu•reaux** \-ōz\ **1 :** a chest of drawers **2** ♦ **:** an administrative unit (as of a government department) **3 :** a branch of a publication or wire service in an important news center

♦ department, desk, division, office

bu•reau•cra•cy \byu̇-ˈrä-krə-sē\ *n, pl* **-cies 1 :** a body of appointive government officials **2 :** government marked by specialization of functions under fixed rules and a hierarchy of authority; *also* **:** an unwieldy administrative system burdened with excessive complexity and lack of flexibility

bu•reau•crat \ˈbyu̇r-ə-ˌkrat\ *n* **:** a member of a bureaucracy — **bu•reau•crat•ic** \ˌbyu̇r-ə-ˈkra-tik\ *adj*

bur•geon \ˈbər-jən\ *vb* **1** ♦ **:** to put forth fresh growth (as from buds) **2** ♦ **:** to grow and expand rapidly

♦ [1] bloom, blossom, blow, flower, unfold ♦ [2] accumulate, appreciate, balloon, build, enlarge, escalate, expand, increase, mount, multiply, mushroom, proliferate, rise, snowball, swell, wax ♦ [2] flourish, prosper, thrive

burgh \ˈbər-ō\ *n* **:** a Scottish town

bur•gher \ˈbər-gər\ *n* **1** ♦ **:** an inhabitant of a borough or a town **2 :** a prosperous solid citizen

♦ townie

bur•glar•ize \ˈbər-glə-ˌrīz\ *vb* ♦ **:** to break into and steal from; *also* **:** to commit burglary

♦ rip off, rob, steal

bur•glary \ˈbər-glə-rē\ *n, pl* **-glar•ies :** forcible entry into a building especially at night with the intent to commit a crime (as theft) — **bur•glar** \-glər\ *n*

bur•gle \ˈbər-gəl\ *vb* **bur•gled; bur•gling :** to commit burglary on

bur•go•mas•ter \ˈbər-gə-ˌmas-tər\ *n* **:** the chief magistrate of a town in some European countries

bur•gun•dy \ˈbər-gən-dē\ *n, pl* **-dies** *often cap* **1 :** a red or white table wine from the Burgundy region of France **2 :** an American red table wine

buri•al \ˈber-ē-əl\ *n* ♦ **:** the act or process of burying

♦ entombment, interment, sepulture ***Ant*** exhumation, unearthing

bur•ka *or* **bur•qa** \ˈbu̇r-kə\ *n* **:** a loose garment that covers the face and body and is worn in public by certain Muslim women

burl \ˈbərl\ *n* **:** a hard woody often flattened hemispherical outgrowth on a tree

bur•lap \ˈbər-ˌlap\ *n* **:** a coarse fabric usually of jute or hemp used especially for bags

¹bur•lesque \(ˌ)bər-ˈlesk\ *n* **1** ♦ **:** a witty or derisive literary or dramatic imitative work **2 :** broadly humorous theatrical entertainment consisting of several items (as songs, skits, or dances)

♦ caricature, parody, spoof, takeoff

²burlesque *vb* **bur•lesqued; bur•lesqu•ing** ♦ **:** to make ludicrous by burlesque

♦ caricature, imitate, mimic, mock, parody, take off, travesty

bur·ly \ˈbər-lē\ *adj* **bur·li·er; -est** ♦ : strongly and heavily built : HUSKY

♦ beefy, brawny, husky

Bur·mese \ˌbər-ˈmēz, -ˈmēs\ *n, pl* **Burmese** : a native or inhabitant of Burma (Myanmar) — **Burmese** *adj*

1**burn** \ˈbərn\ *vb* **burned** \ˈbərnd, ˈbərnt\ *or* **burnt** \ˈbərnt\; **burn·ing** **1** ♦ : to be on fire **2** ♦ : to feel or look as if on fire **3** : to alter or become altered by or as if by the action of fire or heat **4** ♦ : to use as fuel ⟨~ coal⟩; *also* : to destroy by fire ⟨~ trash⟩ **5** : to cause or make by fire ⟨~ a hole⟩; *also* : to affect as if by heat **6** ♦ : to become emotionally excited or agitated **7** : to record (as music or data) on by means of a laser ⟨~ a CD⟩

♦ [1, 2] blaze, flame, flare, glow ♦ [4] fire, ignite, inflame, kindle, light ***Ant*** douse, extinguish, put out, quench, snuff (out) ♦ [6] boil, fume, rage, seethe, steam

2**burn** *n* : an injury or effect produced by or as if by burning

burn·er \ˈbər-nər\ *n* : the part of a fuel-burning or heat-producing device where the flame or heat is produced

burn·ing \ˈbər-niŋ\ *adj* **1 a** ♦ : being on fire **b** ♦ : affecting with or as if with heat **2** ♦ : existing in an extreme degree ⟨a ~ desire⟩

♦ [1a] ablaze, afire, fiery ♦ [1b] broiling, fiery, hot, red-hot, scorching, sultry, torrid ♦ [2] ardent, charged, emotional, fervent, hot-blooded, impassioned, passionate, red-hot, vehement

bur·nish \ˈbər-nish\ *vb* ♦ : to make shiny especially by rubbing : POLISH — **bur·nish·er** *n* — **bur·nish·ing** *adj or n*

♦ buff, dress, gloss, grind, polish, rub, shine, smooth

bur·noose *or* **bur·nous** \(ˌ)bər-ˈnüs\ *n* : a hooded cloak worn especially by Arabs

burn·out \ˈbər-ˌnau̇t\ *n* **1** : the cessation of operation of a jet or rocket engine **2** ♦ : exhaustion of one's physical or emotional strength; *also* : a person suffering from burnout

♦ collapse, exhaustion, fatigue, lassitude, prostration, tiredness, weariness

burn out *vb* **1** : to drive out or destroy the property of by fire **2** ♦ : to cause to fail, wear out, or become exhausted especially from overwork or overuse; *also* : to suffer burnout

♦ do in, drain, exhaust, fag, fatigue, tire, tucker, wash out, wear, wear out, weary

burp \ˈbərp\ *n* : an act of belching — **burp** *vb*

burp gun *n* : a small submachine gun

burr \ˈbər\ *n* **1** *usu* **bur** : a rough or prickly envelope of a fruit; *also* : a plant that bears burs **2** : roughness left in cutting or shaping metal **3** : WHIR — **bur·ry** *adj*

bur·ri·to \bə-ˈrē-tō\ *n* : a flour tortilla rolled around a filling and baked

bur·ro \ˈbər-ō, ˈbu̇r-\ *n, pl* **burros** : a usually small donkey

1**bur·row** \ˈbər-ō\ *n* ♦ : a hole in the ground made by an animal (as a rabbit)

♦ den, hole, lair, lodge

2**burrow** *vb* **1** : to form by tunneling; *also* : to make a burrow **2** : to progress by or as if by digging — **bur·row·er** *n*

bur·sar \ˈbər-sər\ *n* : a treasurer especially of a college

bur·si·tis \(ˌ)bər-ˈsī-təs\ *n* : inflammation of the serous sac (**bursa** \ˈbər-sə\) of a joint (as the elbow or shoulder)

1**burst** \ˈbərst\ *vb* **burst** *or* **burst·ed; burst·ing** **1** ♦ : to fly apart or into pieces : to cause to burst **2** : to show one's feelings suddenly; *also* : PLUNGE ⟨~ into song⟩ **3** ♦ : to enter or emerge suddenly **4** : to be filled to the breaking point

♦ [1] blast, blow up, demolish, explode, pop, shatter, smash ♦ *usu* **burst forth** [3] break out, erupt, explode, flame, flare, go off

2**burst** *n* **1 a** ♦ : a sudden outbreak : SPURT **b** ♦ : a vehement outburst (as of emotion) **2** : EXPLOSION **3** : result of bursting

♦ [1a] flare, flare-up, flash, flurry, flutter, outbreak, outburst, spurt ♦ [1b] agony, eruption, explosion, fit, flare, flare-up, flash, flush, gale, gush, gust, outburst, paroxysm, spasm, storm

Bu·run·di·an \bu̇-ˈrün-dē-ən\ *n* : a native or inhabitant of Burundi

bury \ˈber-ē\ *vb* **bur·ied; bury·ing** **1** : to deposit in the earth; *also* : to inter with funeral ceremonies **2** ♦ : to conceal from view or in obscurity : HIDE **3** : SUBMERGE, ENGROSS — usually used with *in*

♦ cache, conceal, ensconce, hide, secrete

1**bus** \ˈbəs\ *n, pl* **bus·es** *or* **bus·ses** : a large motor vehicle for carrying passengers

2**bus** *vb* **bused** *or* **bussed; bus·ing** *or* **bus·sing** **1** : to travel or transport by bus **2** : to work as a busboy

3**bus** *abbr* business

bus·boy \ˈbəs-ˌbȯi\ *n* : a waiter's helper

bus·by \ˈbəz-bē\ *n, pl* **busbies** : a military full-dress fur hat

bush \ˈbu̇sh\ *n* **1** : SHRUB **2** ♦ : rough uncleared country **3** : a thick tuft ⟨a ~ of hair⟩ — **bushy** *adj*

♦ backwoods, frontier, hinterland, sticks, up-country

bushed \ˈbu̇sht\ *adj* ♦ : drained of strength and energy : TIRED, EXHAUSTED

♦ beat, dead, drained, effete, jaded, limp, prostrate, spent, tired, weary, worn-out

bush·el \ˈbu̇-shəl\ *n* **1** : a measure of dry capacity equal to 4 pecks **2** ♦ : a large quantity

♦ abundance, deal, gobs, heap, loads, lot, pile, plenty, quantity, scads

bush·ing \ˈbu̇-shiŋ\ *n* : a usually removable cylindrical lining for an opening of a mechanical part to limit the size of the opening, resist wear, or serve as a guide

bush·mas·ter \ˈbu̇sh-ˌmas-tər\ *n* : a large venomous tropical American pit viper

bush·whack \-ˌhwak\ *vb* **1** : AMBUSH **2** : to clear a path through especially by chopping down bushes and branches — **bush·whack·er** *n*

busi·ly \ˈbi-zə-lē\ *adv* : in a busy manner

busi·ness \ˈbiz-nəs, -nəz\ *n* **1** : OCCUPATION; *also* : TASK, MISSION **2 a** ♦ : a commercial or industrial enterprise **b** ♦ : the dealings and transactions involved in buying and selling : TRADE ⟨~ is good⟩ **3** : a subject under consideration : AFFAIR, MATTER **4** : personal concern

♦ [2a] company, concern, enterprise, establishment, firm, house, outfit ♦ [2b] commerce, marketplace, trade, traffic

busi·ness·man \-ˌman\ *n* : a man engaged in business especially as an executive

busi·ness·per·son \-ˌpərs-ᵊn\ *n* : a businessman or businesswoman

busi·ness·wom·an \-ˌwu̇-mən\ *n* : a woman engaged in business especially as an executive

bus·kin \ˈbəs-kən\ *n* **1** : a laced boot reaching halfway to the knee **2** : tragic drama

buss \ˈbəs\ *n* : KISS — **buss** *vb*

1**bust** \ˈbəst\ *n* **1** : sculpture representing the upper part of the human figure **2** : the part of the human torso between the neck and the waist; *esp* : the breasts of a woman

2**bust** *vb* **bust·ed** *also* **bust; bust·ing** **1** ♦ : to break or smash especially with force; *also* : BURST **2** ♦ : to ruin financially **3** : TAME **4** ♦ : to reduce to a lower grade or rank : DEMOTE **5** *slang* : ARREST; *also* : RAID **6** ♦ : to strike heavily with or as if with the fist or a bat

♦ [1] break, burst, fracture, fragment ♦ [2] ruin ♦ [4] break, degrade, demote, downgrade, reduce ♦ [6] bash, bat, clobber, clout, hammer, hit, pound, punch, slug, strike, thump

3**bust** *n* **1** : a drinking session **2** ♦ : a complete failure : FLOP **3** : a business depression **4** : a quick blow with or as if with the fist : PUNCH, SOCK **5** *slang* : a police raid; *also* : ARREST

♦ bummer, catastrophe, debacle, dud, failure, fiasco, fizzle, flop, lemon, loser, turkey, washout

1**bus·tle** \ˈbə-səl\ *vb* **bus·tled; bus·tling** : to move or work in a brisk busy manner

2**bustle** *n* ♦ : briskly energetic activity

♦ commotion, disturbance, furor, hubbub, hullabaloo, pandemonium, tumult, turmoil

3**bustle** *n* : a pad or frame worn to support the fullness at the back of a woman's skirt

1**busy** \ˈbi-zē\ *adj* **busi·er; -est** **1** ♦ : engaged in action : not idle **2** : being in use ⟨~ telephones⟩ **3** ♦ : full of activity ⟨~ streets⟩ **4** : MEDDLING

♦ [1] active, assiduous, diligent, engaged, laborious, occupied, sedulous, working ♦ [3] alive, animated, astir, lively, vibrant

2**busy** *vb* **bus·ied; busy·ing** ♦ : to make or keep busy : OCCUPY

♦ absorb, engage, engross, enthrall, fascinate, grip, immerse, interest, intrigue, involve, occupy

busy•body \ˈbi-zē-ˌbä-dē\ *n* ♦ **:** an officious or inquisitive person **:** MEDDLER

♦ interloper, intruder, kibitzer, meddler

busy•work \-ˌwərk\ *n* **:** work that appears productive but only keeps one occupied

[1]but \ˈbət\ *conj* **1** ♦ **:** except for the fact ⟨would have protested ~ that he was afraid⟩ **2 :** THAT ⟨there's no doubt ~ he won⟩ **3 :** without the certainty that ⟨never rains ~ it pours⟩ **4 :** on the contrary ⟨not one, ~ two job offers⟩ **5 :** YET ⟨poor ~ proud⟩ **6 :** with the exception of ⟨none ~ the strongest attempt it⟩

♦ except, only, yet

[2]but *prep* ♦ **:** other than **:** EXCEPT ⟨this letter is nothing ~ an insult⟩; *also* **:** with the exception of ⟨no one here ~ me⟩

♦ aside from, bar, barring, besides, except, outside (of), save

[3]but *adv* **1** ♦ **:** being nothing more than **2** ♦ **:** to the contrary

♦ [1] just, merely, only, simply ♦ [2] howbeit, however, nevertheless, nonetheless, notwithstanding, still, though, withal, yet

bu•tane \ˈbyü-ˌtān\ *n* **:** either of two gaseous hydrocarbons used as a fuel

butch \ˈbu̇ch\ *adj* **:** notably masculine in appearance or manner

[1]butch•er \ˈbu̇-chər\ *n* **1 :** one who slaughters animals or dresses their flesh; *also* **:** a dealer in meat **2 :** one that kills brutally or needlessly **3 :** one that botches

[2]butcher *vb* **1 :** to slaughter and dress for meat ⟨~ hogs⟩ **2** ♦ **:** to kill barbarously **3** ♦ **:** to foul up hopelessly **:** BOTCH

♦ [2] massacre, slaughter ♦ [3] bobble, botch, bungle, flub, foul up, fumble, mangle, mess up, screw up

butch•ery \-chə-rē\ *n* **1 :** the preparation of meat for sale **2** ♦ **:** cruel and ruthless slaughter of human beings

♦ carnage, massacre, slaughter

but•ler \ˈbət-lər\ *n* **:** the chief male servant of a household

[1]butt \ˈbət\ *vb* **:** to strike with the head or horns

[2]butt *n* **:** a blow or thrust with the head or horns

[3]butt *n* **:** a large cask

[4]butt *n* **1 :** TARGET **2** ♦ **:** an object of abuse or ridicule **3** ♦ **:** the seat of the body **:** BUTTOCKS

♦ [2] laughingstock, mark, mock, mockery, target ♦ [3] backside, bottom, buttocks, posterior, rear, rump, seat

[5]butt *n* **1 :** a large, thicker, or bottom end of something **2 :** BUTTOCKS

[6]butt *vb* **1 :** ABUT **2 :** to place or join edge to edge without overlapping

butte \ˈbyüt\ *n* **:** an isolated steep hill

[1]but•ter \ˈbə-tər\ *n* **1 :** a solid edible emulsion of fat obtained from cream by churning **2 :** a substance resembling butter — **but•tery** *adj*

[2]butter *vb* **:** to spread with or as if with butter

but•ter–and–eggs \ˌbə-tə-rə-ˈnegz\ *n sing or pl* **:** a common perennial herb related to the snapdragon that has showy yellow and orange flowers

butter bean *n* **1 :** LIMA BEAN **2 :** WAX BEAN **3 :** a green shell bean

butter cream *n* **:** a sweet butter-based mixture used especially as a filling or frosting

but•ter•cup \ˈbə-tər-ˌkəp\ *n* **:** any of a genus of herbs having usually yellow flowers with five petals and sepals

but•ter•fat \-ˌfat\ *n* **:** the natural fat of milk and chief constituent of butter

but•ter•fin•gered \-ˌfiŋ-gərd\ *adj* **:** likely to let things fall or slip through the fingers — **but•ter•fin•gers** \-gərz\ *n sing or pl*

but•ter•fly \-ˌflī\ *n* **:** any of a group of slender day-flying insects with broad often brightly-colored wings

but•ter•milk \-ˌmilk\ *n* **:** the liquid remaining after butter is churned

but•ter•nut \-ˌnət\ *n* **:** the sweet egg-shaped nut of an American tree related to the walnut; *also* **:** this tree

butternut squash *n* **:** a smooth buff-colored cylindrical winter squash

but•ter•scotch \-ˌskäch\ *n* **:** a candy made from brown sugar, corn syrup, and water; *also* **:** the flavor of such candy

butt in *vb* ♦ **:** to meddle in the affairs of others

♦ interfere, intrude, meddle, mess, nose, obtrude, poke, pry, snoop

but•tock \ˈbə-tək\ *n* **1 :** the back of a hip that forms one of the fleshy parts on which a person sits **2** *usu* **but•tocks** ♦ **:** the seat of the body **:** RUMP

♦ **buttocks** backside, bottom, butt, posterior, rear, rump, seat

[1]but•ton \ˈbət-ᵊn\ *n* **1 :** a small knob secured to an article (as of clothing) and used as a fastener by passing it through a buttonhole or loop **2 :** something that resembles a button **3 :** PUSH BUTTON **4 :** a hidden sensitivity that can be manipulated to produce a desired response ⟨he is constantly pushing my ~*s*⟩ **5 :** a usually box-shaped computer icon that when clicked initiates a software function

[2]button *vb* **:** to close or fasten with or as if with buttons

[1]but•ton•hole \ˈbət-ᵊn-ˌhōl\ *n* **:** a slit or loop for a button to pass through

[2]buttonhole *vb* **:** to detain in conversation by or as if by holding on to the outer garments of

[1]but•tress \ˈbə-trəs\ *n* **1 :** a projecting structure to support a wall **2** ♦ **:** something that supports or strengthens **:** SUPPORT

♦ dependence, mainstay, pillar, reliance, standby, support ♦ brace, bulwark, mount, shore, stay, support, underpinning

[2]buttress *vb* ♦ **:** to furnish or shore up with a buttress **:** SUPPORT

♦ bear, bolster, brace, carry, prop, shore, stay, support, uphold

bux•om \ˈbək-səm\ *adj* **:** healthily plump; *esp* **:** full-bosomed

[1]buy \ˈbī\ *vb* **bought** \ˈbȯt\; **buy•ing** **1** ♦ **:** to obtain for a price **:** PURCHASE; *also* **:** BRIBE **2 :** to accept as true — **buy•er** *n*

♦ acquire, get, obtain, pick up, procure, purchase, secure, take

[2]buy *n* **1 :** PURCHASE 1, 2 **2** ♦ **:** an exceptional value **:** BARGAIN

♦ bargain, deal, steal

[1]buzz \ˈbəz\ *vb* **1 :** to make a buzz **2** ♦ **:** to fly fast and close to

♦ drone, hum, whir, whish, whiz, zip, zoom

[2]buzz *n* **1** ♦ **:** a low humming sound **2 :** RUMOR, GOSSIP

♦ drone, hum, purr, whir, whiz, zoom

buz•zard \ˈbə-zərd\ *n* **:** any of various usually large birds of prey and especially the turkey vulture

buzz•er \ˈbə-zər\ *n* **:** a device that signals with a buzzing sound

buzz saw *n* **:** CIRCULAR SAW

buzz•word \ˈbəz-ˌwərd\ *n* **:** a voguish word or phrase often from technical jargon

BV *abbr* Blessed Virgin

BVM *abbr* Blessed Virgin Mary

BWI *abbr* British West Indies

bx *abbr* box

BX *abbr* base exchange

[1]by \ˈbī, bə\ *prep* **1** ♦ **:** in proximity to **:** NEAR ⟨stood ~ the window⟩ **2 :** through or through the medium of ⟨left ~ the door⟩ **3 :** into the vicinity of and beyond **:** PAST ⟨drove ~ the house⟩ **4 :** DURING, AT ⟨studied ~ night⟩ **5 :** no later than ⟨get here ~ 3 p.m.⟩ **6** ♦ **:** through the means or direct agency of ⟨~ force⟩ **7 :** in conformity with; *also* **:** ACCORDING TO ⟨did it ~ the book⟩ **8 :** with respect to ⟨a vet ~ profession⟩ **9 :** to the amount or extent of ⟨won ~ a nose⟩ **10** — used to express relationship in multiplication, in division, and in measurements ⟨divide *a* ~ *b*⟩ ⟨multiply ~ 6⟩ ⟨15 feet ~ 20 feet⟩

♦ [1] about, around, near, next to ♦ [6] per, through, with

[2]by \ˈbī\ *adv* **1 a** ♦ **:** near at hand **b :** at or to another's house **:** IN ⟨stop ~⟩ **2 :** PAST **3 :** ASIDE, APART

♦ around, close, hard, in, near, nearby, nigh

bye \ˈbī\ *n* **:** a position of a participant in a tournament who advances to the next round without playing

by–elec•tion *also* **bye–elec•tion** \ˈbī-ə-ˌlek-shən\ *n* **:** a special election held between regular elections in order to fill a vacancy

by•gone \ˈbī-ˌgȯn\ *adj* ♦ **:** gone by — **bygone** *n*

♦ dead, defunct, extinct, gone

by•law *or* **bye•law** \ˈbī-ˌlȯ\ *n* **:** a rule adopted by an organization for managing its internal affairs

by–line \ˈbī-ˌlīn\ *n* **:** a line at the beginning of a news story or magazine article giving the writer's name

BYO *abbr* bring your own

BYOB *abbr* bring your own beer; bring your own booze; bring your own bottle

[1]by•pass \ˈbī-ˌpas\ *n* **:** a passage to one side or around a blocked or congested area; *also* **:** a surgical procedure establishing this ⟨a coronary ~⟩

[2]bypass *vb* ♦ **:** to avoid by means of a bypass

♦ circumvent, detour, skirt

by•path \-ˌpath, -ˌpȧth\ *n* **:** BYWAY

by•play \ˈbī-ˌplā\ *n* **:** action engaged in on the side (as of a stage) while the main action proceeds
by–prod•uct \-ˌprä-(ˌ)dəkt\ *n* **:** a sometimes unexpected product or result produced in addition to the main product or result
by•stand•er \-ˌstan-dər\ *n* **:** one present but not participating
byte \ˈbīt\ *n* **:** a group of 8 bits that a computer processes as a unit
by•way \ˈbī-ˌwā\ *n* **1 :** a little-traveled side road **2 :** a secondary aspect
by•word \-ˌwərd\ *n* **1 ♦ :** a proverbial saying **:** PROVERB **2 :** one that is noteworthy or notorious

♦ adage, aphorism, epigram, maxim, proverb, saying

Byz•an•tine \ˈbiz-ᵊn-ˌtēn, ˈbī-, -ˌtīn; bə-ˈzan-, bī-\ *adj* **1 :** of, relating to, or characteristic of the ancient city of Byzantium or the Byzantine Empire **2** *often not cap* **:** intricately involved and often devious

C

[1]c \ˈsē\ *n, pl* **c's** *or* **cs** \ˈsēz\ *often cap* **1 :** the 3d letter of the English alphabet **2** *slang* **:** a sum of $100 **3 :** a grade rating a student's work as fair
[2]c *abbr, often cap* **1** calorie **2** carat **3** Celsius **4** cent **5** centigrade **6** centimeter **7** century **8** chapter **9** circa **10** cocaine **11** copyright
C *symbol* carbon
ca *abbr* circa
Ca *symbol* calcium
CA *abbr* **1** California **2** chartered accountant **3** chief accountant **4** chronological age
cab \ˈkab\ *n* **1 :** a light closed horse-drawn carriage **2 :** an automobile available on call to carry a passenger for a fare determined by a running meter or a flat rate **:** TAXICAB **3 :** the covered compartment for the engineer and controls of a locomotive; *also* **:** a similar compartment (as on a truck)
CAB *abbr* Civil Aeronautics Board
ca•bal \kə-ˈbäl, -ˈbal\ *n* **♦ :** a secret group of plotters or political conspirators

♦ conspiracy, gang, mob, ring, syndicate

cabala *var of* KABBALAH
ca•bana \kə-ˈban-yə, -ˈba-nə\ *n* **:** a shelter at a beach or swimming pool
cab•a•ret \ˌka-bə-ˈrā\ *n* **:** a place of entertainment open at night usually serving food and liquor and often having a floor show **:** NIGHTCLUB
cab•bage \ˈka-bij\ *n* **:** a vegetable related to the mustard with a dense head of leaves
cab•bie *or* **cab•by** \ˈka-bē\ *n, pl* **cabbies :** a driver of a cab
cab•er•net sau•vi•gnon \ˌka-bər-ˈnā-sō-vē-ˈnyōⁿ\ *n* **:** a dry red wine made from a single variety of black grape
cab•in \ˈka-bən\ *n* **1 :** a private room on a ship; *also* **:** a compartment below deck on a boat for passengers or crew **2 :** the passenger or cargo compartment of a vehicle (as an airplane or automobile) **3 ♦ :** a small simple one-story house

♦ camp, cottage, hut, hutch, shack, shanty

cabin boy *n* **:** a boy working as servant on a ship
cabin class *n* **:** a class of accommodations on a passenger ship superior to tourist class and inferior to first class
cabin cruiser *n* **:** CRUISER 3
cab•i•net \ˈkab-nit\ *n* **1 ♦ :** a case or cupboard for holding or displaying articles **2 :** the advisory council of a head of state (as a president or sovereign)

♦ buffet, closet, cupboard, hutch, locker, sideboard

cab•i•net•mak•er \-ˌmā-kər\ *n* **:** a woodworker who makes fine furniture — **cab•i•net•mak•ing** *n*
cab•i•net•work \-ˌwərk\ *n* **:** the finished work of a cabinetmaker
[1]ca•ble \ˈkā-bəl\ *n* **1 ♦ :** a very strong rope, wire, or chain **2 :** a bundle of insulated wires usually twisted around a central core **3 :** CABLEGRAM **4 :** CABLE TELEVISION

♦ cord, lace, line, rope, string, wire

[2]cable *vb* **ca•bled; ca•bling :** to telegraph by cable
cable car *n* **:** a vehicle moved by an endless cable
ca•ble•cast \ˈkā-bəl-ˌkast\ *n* **:** a cable television transmission — **cablecast** *vb*
ca•ble•gram \ˈkā-bəl-ˌgram\ *n* **:** a message sent by a submarine telegraph cable
cable modem *n* **:** a modem for connecting a computer to a network over a cable television line
cable television *n* **:** a system of television reception in which signals from distant stations are sent by cable to the receivers of paying subscribers
cab•o•chon \ˈka-bə-ˌshän\ *n* **:** a gem or bead cut in convex form and highly polished but not given facets; *also* **:** this style of cutting — **cabochon** *adv*
ca•boose \kə-ˈbüs\ *n* **:** a car usually at the rear of a freight train for the use of the train crew and railroad workers
cab•ri•o•let \ˌka-brē-ə-ˈlā\ *n* **1 :** a light 2-wheeled one-horse carriage **2 :** a convertible coupe
cab•stand \ˈkab-ˌstand\ *n* **:** a place where cabs wait for passengers
ca•cao \kə-ˈkau̇, -ˈkā-ō\ *n, pl* **cacaos :** a So. American tree whose seeds (**cacao beans**) are the source of cocoa and chocolate; *also* **:** its dried fatty seeds
cac•cia•to•re \ˌkä-chə-ˈtōr-ē\ *adj* **:** cooked with tomatoes and herbs ⟨chicken ~⟩
[1]cache \ˈkash\ *n* **1 :** a hiding place especially for preserving provisions **2 ♦ :** something hidden or stored in a cache

♦ deposit, hoard, reserve, stash, stockpile, store

[2]cache *vb* **♦ :** to place, hide, or store in a cache

♦ bury, conceal, ensconce, hide, secrete

ca•chet \ka-ˈshā\ *n* **1 :** a seal used especially as a mark of official approval **2 :** a feature or quality conferring prestige; *also* **:** PRESTIGE **3 :** a design, inscription, or advertisement printed or stamped on mail
[1]cack•le \ˈka-kəl\ *vb* **cack•led; cack•ling 1 :** to make the sharp broken cry characteristic of a hen **2 :** to laugh or chatter noisily
[2]cackle *n* **♦ :** the action or noise of cackling

♦ chortle, laugh, laughter, snicker, titter

cack•ler *n* **:** one that cackles
ca•coph•o•nous \ka-ˈkä-fə-nəs\ *adj* **♦ :** marked by cacophony

♦ discordant, dissonant, inharmonious, unmelodious, unmusical

ca•coph•o•ny \ka-ˈkä-fə-nē\ *n, pl* **-nies ♦ :** harsh or discordant sound

♦ bluster, clamor (*or* clamour), din, noise, racket, roar

cac•tus \ˈkak-təs\ *n, pl* **cac•ti** \-ˌtī\ *or* **cac•tus•es** *also* **cactus :** any of a large family of drought-resistant flowering plants with succulent stems and with leaves replaced by scales or prickles
cad \ˈkad\ *n* **:** a man who deliberately disregards another's feelings — **cad•dish** \ˈka-dish\ *adj* — **cad•dish•ly** *adv* — **cad•dish•ness** *n*
ca•dav•er \kə-ˈda-vər\ *n* **:** a dead body especially of a human being
ca•dav•er•ous \kə-ˈda-və-rəs\ *adj* **♦ :** suggesting a corpse especially in gauntness or pallor — **ca•dav•er•ous•ly** *adv*

♦ ashen, livid, lurid, pale, pasty, peaked ♦ gaunt, haggard, skeletal, wasted

cad•die *or* **cad•dy** \ˈka-dē\ *n, pl* **caddies :** a person who assists a golfer especially by carrying the clubs — **caddie** *or* **caddy** *vb*
cad•dy \ˈka-dē\ *n, pl* **caddies ♦ :** a small box, can, or chest; *esp* **:** one to keep tea in

♦ box, case, casket, chest, locker, trunk

ca•dence \ˈkād-ᵊns\ *n* **♦ :** the measure or beat of a rhythmical flow **:** RHYTHM

♦ beat, measure, meter (*or* metre), rhythm

ca•denced \-ᵊnst\ *adj* **♦ :** marked by cadence

♦ measured, metrical, rhythmic

ca•den•za \kə-ˈden-zə\ *n* **:** a brilliant sometimes improvised passage usually toward the close of a musical composition
ca•det \kə-ˈdet\ *n* **1 :** a younger son or brother **2 :** a student in a service academy
Ca•dette \kə-ˈdet\ *n* **:** a member of a Girl Scout program for girls in sixth through ninth grades
cadge \ˈkaj\ *vb* **cadged; cadg•ing :** SPONGE, BEG ⟨~ a free meal⟩ — **cadg•er** *n*
cad•mi•um \ˈkad-mē-əm\ *n* **:** a bluish-white metallic chemical element used especially in protective platings
cad•re \ˈka-ˌdrā, ˈkä-, -drē\ *n* **1 :** FRAMEWORK **2 :** a central unit especially of trained personnel able to assume control and train others **3 :** a group of indoctrinated leaders active in promoting the interests of a revolutionary party
ca•du•ceus \kə-ˈdü-sē-əs, -ˈdyü-, -shəs\ *n, pl* **-cei** \-sē-ˌī\ **1 :** the staff of a herald; *esp* **:** a representation of a staff with two entwined snakes and two wings at the top **2 :** an insignia bearing a caduceus and symbolizing a physician
cae•cum *var of* CECUM
Cae•sar \ˈsē-zər\ *n* **1 :** any of the Roman emperors succeeding Augustus Caesar — used as a title **2** *often not cap* **:** a powerful ruler **:** AUTOCRAT, DICTATOR; *also* **:** the civil or temporal power
caesarean *var of* CESAREAN
cae•sura \si-ˈzhu̇r-ə\ *n, pl* **-suras** *or* **-su•rae** \-ˈzhu̇r-(ˌ)ē\ **:** a break in the flow of sound usually in the middle of a line of verse
ca•fé \ka-ˈfā\ *n* **1 :** a usually small and informal establishment serving various refreshments (as coffee) **:** RESTAURANT **2** ◆ **:** a room or establishment whose main feature is a bar for the sale of liquor **:** BARROOM **3** ◆ **:** a place of entertainment open at night usually serving food and liquor and providing music and space for dancing and often having a floor show **:** NIGHTCLUB

◆ [2] bar, barroom, pub, public house, saloon, tavern ◆ [3] disco, discotheque, nightclub

ca•fé au lait \(ˌ)ka-ˌfā-ō-ˈlā\ *n* **:** coffee with hot milk in about equal parts
caf•e•te•ria \ˌka-fə-ˈtir-ē-ə\ *n* **:** a restaurant in which the customers serve themselves or are served at a counter
caf•fein•at•ed \ˈka-fə-ˌnā-təd\ *adj* **1 :** stimulated by or as if by caffeine **2 :** containing caffeine
caf•feine \ka-ˈfēn, ˈka-ˌfēn\ *n* **:** a stimulating alkaloid found especially in coffee and tea
caf•fe lat•te \ˈkä-fā-ˈlä-tā\ *n* **:** espresso mixed with hot or steamed milk
caf•tan \kaf-ˈtan, ˈkaf-ˌtan\ *n* **:** an ankle-length garment with long sleeves worn in countries of the eastern Mediterranean
[1]**cage** \ˈkāj\ *n* **1** ◆ **:** an openwork enclosure for confining an animal **2 :** something resembling a cage

◆ coop, corral, pen, pound

[2]**cage** *vb* **caged; cag•ing :** to put or keep in or as if in a cage
ca•gey *also* **ca•gy** \ˈkā-jē\ *adj* **ca•gi•er; -est 1 :** wary of being trapped or deceived **:** SHREWD **2** ◆ **:** marked by cleverness — **ca•gi•ly** \-jə-lē\ *adv*

◆ artful, crafty, cunning, devious, foxy, guileful, slick, sly, subtle, wily

ca•gi•ness \-jē-nəs\ *n* ◆ **:** skill in devising or using indirect or subtle methods

◆ artfulness, artifice, canniness, craft, craftiness, cunning, guile, slyness, wiliness

CAGS *abbr* Certificate of Advanced Graduate Study
ca•hoot \kə-ˈhüt\ *n* **:** PARTNERSHIP, LEAGUE — usually used in plural ⟨officials in ~*s* with the underworld⟩
cai•man \ˈkā-mən; kā-ˈman, kī-\ *n* **:** any of several Central and So. American reptiles closely related to alligators and crocodiles
cairn \ˈkarn\ *n* **:** a heap of stones serving as a memorial or a landmark
cais•son \ˈkā-ˌsän, ˈkās-ᵊn\ *n* **1 :** a usually 2-wheeled vehicle for artillery ammunition **2 :** a watertight chamber used in underwater construction work or as a foundation
caisson disease *n* **:** [2]BEND 3
cai•tiff \ˈkā-təf\ *adj* **:** being base, cowardly, or despicable — **caitiff** *n*
ca•jole \kə-ˈjōl\ *vb* **ca•joled; ca•jol•ing** ◆ **:** to persuade or coax especially with flattery or false promises — **ca•jole•ment** *n* — **ca•jol•ery** \-ˈjō-lə-rē\ *n*

◆ coax, wheedle

Ca•jun \ˈkā-jən\ *n* **:** a Louisianian descended from French-speaking immigrants from Acadia (Nova Scotia) — **Cajun** *adj*
[1]**cake** \ˈkāk\ *n* **1 :** a baked or fried breadlike food usually in a small flat shape **2 :** a sweet baked food made from batter or dough usually containing flour, sugar, or shortening, and a leaven (as baking powder) **3 :** a hardened or compacted substance ⟨a ~ of soap⟩ **4 :** something easily done ⟨the quiz was ~⟩
[2]**cake** *vb* **caked; cak•ing 1 :** to cover or overlay with or as if with a crust **:** ENCRUST **2 :** to form or harden into a cake
cake•walk \ˈkāk-ˌwȯk\ *n* **1 :** a stage dance typically involving a high prance with backward tilt **2 :** a one-sided contest or an easy task
cal *abbr* **1** calendar **2** caliber
Cal *abbr* **1** California **2** calorie
cal•a•bash \ˈka-lə-ˌbash\ *n* **:** the fruit of a gourd; *also* **:** a utensil made from its hard shell
cal•a•boose \ˈka-lə-ˌbüs\ *n* **:** JAIL
ca•la•di•um \kə-ˈlā-dē-əm\ *n* **:** any of a genus of tropical American ornamental plants related to the arums
cal•a•mari \ˌkä-lə-ˈmär-ē\ *n* **:** squid used as food
cal•a•mine \ˈka-lə-ˌmīn\ *n* **:** a lotion of oxides of zinc and iron
ca•lam•i•tous \-təs\ *adj* ◆ **:** being, causing, or accompanied by calamity — **ca•lam•i•tous•ly** *adv* — **ca•lam•i•tous•ness** *n*

◆ cataclysmic, catastrophic, destructive, disastrous, fatal, fateful, ruinous, unfortunate

ca•lam•i•ty \kə-ˈla-mə-tē\ *n, pl* **-ties 1 :** great distress or misfortune **2** ◆ **:** an event causing great harm or loss and affliction **:** DISASTER

◆ cataclysm, catastrophe, debacle, disaster, tragedy

calc *abbr* calculate; calculated
cal•car•e•ous \kal-ˈkar-ē-əs\ *adj* **:** resembling calcium carbonate in hardness; *also* **:** containing calcium or calcium carbonate
cal•cif•er•ous \kal-ˈsi-fə-rəs\ *adj* **:** producing or containing calcium carbonate
cal•ci•fy \ˈkal-sə-ˌfī\ *vb* **-fied; -fy•ing :** to make or become calcareous — **cal•ci•fi•ca•tion** \ˌkal-sə-fə-ˈkā-shən\ *n*
cal•ci•mine \ˈkal-sə-ˌmīn\ *n* **:** a thin water paint used especially on plastered surfaces — **calcimine** *vb*
cal•cine \kal-ˈsīn\ *vb* **cal•cined; cal•cin•ing :** to heat to a high temperature but without fusing to drive off volatile matter and often to reduce to powder — **cal•ci•na•tion** \ˌkal-sə-ˈnā-shən\ *n*
cal•cite \ˈkal-ˌsīt\ *n* **:** a crystalline mineral consisting of calcium carbonate — **cal•cit•ic** \kal-ˈsi-tik\ *adj*
cal•ci•um \ˈkal-sē-əm\ *n* **:** a silver-white soft metallic chemical element occurring only in combination
calcium carbonate *n* **:** a substance found in nature as limestone and marble and in plant ashes, bones, and shells
cal•cu•late \ˈkal-kyə-ˌlāt\ *vb* **-lat•ed; -lat•ing 1** ◆ **:** to determine by mathematical processes **:** COMPUTE **2** ◆ **:** to reckon by exercise of practical judgment **:** ESTIMATE **3** ◆ **:** to design or adapt for a purpose by forethought or careful plan **4 :** COUNT, RELY — **cal•cu•la•ble** \-lə-bəl\ *adj* — **cal•cu•la•tor** \-ˌlā-tər\ *n*

◆ [1] compute, figure, reckon, work out ◆ [2] call, conjecture, estimate, figure, gauge, guess, judge, make, place, put, reckon, suppose ◆ [3] arrange, blueprint, chart, design, frame, lay out, map, plan, project, scheme

cal•cu•lat•ed \-ˌlā-təd\ *adj* **1** ◆ **:** undertaken after estimating the probability of success or failure ⟨a ~ risk⟩ **2** ◆ **:** planned purposefully **:** DELIBERATE

◆ [1, 2] advised, deliberate, measured, reasoned, studied, thoughtful, thought-out

cal•cu•lat•ing \-ˌlā-tiŋ\ *adj* **:** marked by shrewd consideration especially of self-interest — **cal•cu•lat•ing•ly** *adv*
cal•cu•la•tion \ˌkal-kyə-ˈlā-shən\ *n* **1** ◆ **:** the process or an act of calculating **2 :** the result of an act of calculating **3 :** studied care; *also* **:** cold heartless planning to promote self-interest

◆ arithmetic, computation, reckoning

cal•cu•lus \ˈkal-kyə-ləs\ *n, pl* **-li** \-ˌlī\ *also* **-lus•es 1 :** a method of computation or calculation in a special notation (as of logic) **2 :** a branch of mathematics concerned with the rate of change of functions and with methods of finding lengths, areas, and volumes **3 :** a concretion usually of mineral salts especially in hollow organs or ducts
cal•de•ra \kal-ˈder-ə, kȯl-, -ˈdir-\ *n* **:** a large crater usually formed by the collapse of a volcanic cone
cal•dron *var of* CAULDRON
[1]**cal•en•dar** \ˈka-lən-dər\ *n* **1 :** an arrangement of time into days, weeks, months, and years; *also* **:** a sheet or folder containing such an arrangement for a period **2** ◆ **:** an orderly list

◆ agenda, docket, program, schedule, timetable

[2]**calendar** *vb* **:** to enter in a calendar

[1]**cal•en•der** \ˈka-lən-dər\ *vb* : to press (as cloth or paper) between rollers or plates so as to make smooth or glossy or to thin into sheets
[2]**calender** *n* : a machine for calendering
ca•lends \ˈka-ləndz, ˈkā-\ *n sing or pl* : the first day of the ancient Roman month
ca•len•du•la \kə-ˈlen-jə-lə\ *n* : any of a genus of yellow-flowered herbs related to the daisies
[1]**calf** \ˈkaf, ˈkäf\ *n, pl* **calves** \ˈkavz, ˈkävz\ **1** : the young of the domestic cow; *also* : the young of various large mammals (as the elephant or whale) **2** : CALFSKIN
[2]**calf** *n, pl* **calves** \ˈkavz, ˈkävz\ : the fleshy back of the leg below the knee
calf•skin \ˈkaf-ˌskin, ˈkäf-\ *n* : leather made of the skin of a calf
cal•i•ber *or Can and Brit* **cal•i•bre** \ˈka-lə-bər\ *n* **1** ♦ : degree of mental capacity, excellence, or importance **2** : the diameter of a projectile **3** : the diameter of the bore of a gun

♦ grade, quality, rate

cal•i•brate \ˈka-lə-ˌbrāt\ *vb* **-brat•ed; -brat•ing** : to adjust precisely
cal•i•bra•tion \ˌka-lə-ˈbrā-shən\ *n* : a set of graduated marks indicating values or positions — usually used in plural
cal•i•co \ˈka-li-ˌkō\ *n, pl* **-coes** *or* **-cos** **1** : printed cotton fabric **2** : a mottled or spotted animal — **calico** *adj*
Calif *abbr* California
Cal•i•for•nia poppy \ˌka-lə-ˈfȯr-nyə-\ *n* : a widely cultivated herb with usually yellow or orange flowers that is related to the poppies
cal•i•for•ni•um \ˌka-lə-ˈfȯr-nē-əm\ *n* : an artificially prepared radioactive chemical element
cal•i•per \ˈka-lə-pər\ *n* **1** : any of various instruments having two arms, legs, or jaws used especially to measure diameter or thickness — usually used in plural **2** : a device for pressing a frictional material against the sides of a rotating wheel or disk
ca•liph \ˈkā-ləf, ˈka-\ *n* : a successor of Muhammad as head of Islam — used as a title — **ca•liph•ate** \-lə-ˌfāt, -fət\ *n*
cal•is•then•ics \ˌka-ləs-ˈthe-niks\ *n sing or pl* : bodily exercises usually done without apparatus — **cal•is•then•ic** *adj*
calk \ˈkȯk\ *var of* CAULK
[1]**call** \ˈkȯl\ *vb* **1 a** ♦ : to speak in a loud distinct voice so as to be heard at a distance especially in order to attract the attention of, summon, or make a request of another : SHOUT, CRY **b** : to utter a characteristic note or cry **2** : to utter in a loud clear voice **3** : to announce authoritatively **4** ♦ : to invite or command (a group) to meet : SUMMON **5** ♦ : to make a request or demand ⟨∼ for an investigation⟩ **6** : to halt (a baseball game or other public event) because of unsuitable conditions (as rain or darkness) **7** : to demand payment of (a loan); *also* : to demand surrender of (as a bond) for redemption **8** ♦ : to get or try to get in communication by telephone **9** ♦ : to make a brief stop or visit at a place ⟨*called* on a friend⟩ **10 a** ♦ : to speak of or address by name : give a name to **b** : regard as or characterize as of a certain kind : describe as **11** ♦ : to estimate or consider for practical purposes ⟨∼ it ten miles⟩ **12** : to temporarily transfer control of computer processing to (as a subroutine or procedure)

♦ [1a] bawl, cry, holler, shout, vociferate, yell ♦ [4] assemble, convene, convoke, muster, summon ♦ [5] ask, insist, plead, press, quest, request, seek, solicit, sue ♦ [5] claim, clamor (*or* clamour), command, demand, enjoin, exact, insist, press, quest, stipulate (for) ♦ [8] dial, telephone ♦ [9] drop (by *or* in), pop (in), stop (by *or* in), visit ♦ [10a] baptize, christen, denominate, designate, dub, entitle, label, name, style, term, title ♦ [11] calculate, conjecture, estimate, figure, gauge, guess, judge, make, place, put, reckon, suppose

[2]**call** *n* **1** : SHOUT **2** : the cry of an animal (as a bird) **3** : a request or a command to come or assemble : INVITATION, SUMMONS **4 a** ♦ : a calling on another for something due or supposed to be due : CLAIM **b** : an instance of asking for something : REQUEST **5** : a brief usually formal visit **6** : an act of calling on the telephone **7** : DECISION ⟨a tough ∼⟩ **8** : a temporary transfer of control of computer processing to a particular set of instructions

♦ claim, pretense, pretension, right

cal•la lily \ˈka-lə-\ *n* : a plant related to the arums and grown for its large white lilylike bract that surrounds a fleshy spike of small yellow flowers
call•back \ˈkȯl-ˌbak\ *n* a calling back; *esp* : RECALL 5
call–board \-ˌbōrd\ *n* : a board for posting notices (as of rehearsal calls)
call down *vb* : REPRIMAND
call•er *n* ♦ : one that calls : a person who makes a brief visit

♦ guest, visitor

call girl *n* : a prostitute with whom appointments are made by phone
cal•lig•ra•phy \kə-ˈli-grə-fē\ *n* : artistic or elegant handwriting; *also* : the art of producing such writing — **cal•lig•ra•pher** \-fər\ *n*
call–in \ˈkȯl-ˌin\ *adj* : allowing listeners to engage in broadcast telephone conversations ⟨a ∼ show⟩
call in *vb* **1** : to order to return or be returned **2** : to summon to one's aid **3** : to report by telephone
call•ing \ˈkȯ-liŋ\ *n* **1** : a strong inner impulse toward a particular course of action **2** ♦ : the activity in which one customarily engages as an occupation

♦ employment, line, occupation, profession, trade, vocation, work

cal•li•ope \kə-ˈlī-ə-(ˌ)pē, ˈka-lē-ˌōp\ *n* : a keyboard musical instrument similar to an organ and made up of a series of whistles
call number *n* : a combination of characters assigned to a library book to indicate its place on a shelf
call off *vb* ♦ : to give up (an undertaking or planned activity) : CANCEL

♦ abort, cancel, drop, recall, repeal, rescind, revoke

cal•los•i•ty \ka-ˈlä-sə-tē\ *n, pl* **-ties** **1** : the quality or state of being callous **2** : CALLUS 1
[1]**cal•lous** \ˈka-ləs\ *adj* **1** : being thickened and hardened ⟨∼ skin⟩ **2** ♦ : feeling no emotion or sympathy — **cal•lous•ly** *adv* — **cal•lous•ness** *n*

♦ hard, heartless, inhuman, inhumane, pitiless, soulless, unfeeling, unsympathetic

[2]**callous** *vb* : to make callous
cal•low \ˈka-lō\ *adj* ♦ : lacking adult sophistication ⟨a ∼ youth⟩ — **cal•low•ness** *n*

♦ adolescent, green, immature, inexperienced, juvenile, raw ***Ant*** adult, experienced, grown-up, mature, ripe

call–up \ˈkȯl-ˌəp\ *n* : an order to report for active military service
call up *vb* : to summon for active military duty
cal•lus \ˈka-ləs\ *n* **1** : a callous area on skin or bark **2** : tissue that is converted into bone in the healing of a bone fracture — **callus** *vb*
call–waiting *n* : a telephone service by which during a call in progress an incoming call is signaled (as by a click)
[1]**calm** \ˈkäm, ˈkälm\ *n* **1** ♦ : a period or a condition free from storms, high winds, or rough water **2** : complete or almost complete absence of wind **3** ♦ : a state of tranquillity

♦ [1, 3] calmness, hush, peace, placidity, quiet, quietness, repose, serenity, still, stillness, tranquillity ***Ant*** bustle, commotion, hubbub, hurly-burly, pandemonium, tumult, turmoil, uproar

[2]**calm** *vb* **1** ♦ : to make or become calm **2** ♦ : to make peaceful : induce quietude and repose in instead of agitation, passion, or excitement — often used with *down*

♦ [1, 2] allay, compose, quiet, settle, soothe, still, tranquilize ***Ant*** agitate, discompose, disquiet, disturb, perturb, upset ♦ [2] collect, compose, control, settle ♦ *usu* **calm down** [2] cool (off *or* down), hush, quiet, settle (down)

[3]**calm** *adj* **1** ♦ : marked by calm : STILL **2** ♦ : free from agitation, excitement, or disturbance ⟨a ∼ manner⟩

♦ [1, 2] collected, composed, cool, placid, self-possessed, serene, still, tranquil, undisturbed, unperturbed, unruffled, unshaken, untroubled, unworried ***Ant*** agitated, discomposed, disturbed, perturbed, upset ♦ [1, 2] halcyon, hushed, peaceful, placid, quiet, serene, still, tranquil, untroubled ***Ant*** agitated, angry, stormy, turbulent

calm•ly *adv* ♦ : in a calm manner : with calm

♦ quiet, quietly, still

calm•ness *n* ♦ : the quality or state of being calm

♦ aplomb, composure, coolness, equanimity, placidity, self-possession, serenity, tranquillity

cal•o•mel \ˈka-lə-məl, -ˌmel\ *n* : a chloride of mercury used especially as a fungicide
ca•lor•ic \kə-ˈlȯ-rik\ *adj* **1** : of or relating to heat **2** : of, relating to, or containing calories
cal•o•rie *also* **cal•o•ry** \ˈka-lə-rē\ *n, pl* **-ries** : a unit for measuring heat; *esp* : one for measuring the value of foods for producing heat and energy in the human body equivalent to the amount of heat required to raise the temperature of one kilogram of water one degree Celsius

cal•o•rim•e•ter \ˌka-lə-ˈri-mə-tər\ *n* **:** an apparatus for measuring quantities of heat — **cal•o•rim•e•try** \-trē\ *n*

cal•u•met \ˈkal-yə-ˌmet, -mət\ *n* **:** an American Indian ceremonial pipe

ca•lum•ni•ate \kə-ˈləm-nē-ˌāt\ *vb* **-at•ed; -at•ing :** to make false and malicious statements about — **ca•lum•ni•a•tion** \-ˌləm-nē-ˈā-shən\ *n* — **ca•lum•ni•a•tor** \-ˈləm-nē-ˌā-tər\ *n*

cal•um•ny \ˈka-ləm-nē\ *n, pl* **-nies :** false and malicious accusation — **ca•lum•ni•ous** \kə-ˈləm-nē-əs\ *adj*

calve \ˈkav, ˈkȧv\ *vb* **calved; calv•ing :** to give birth to a calf

calves *pl of* CALF

Cal•vin•ism \ˈkal-və-ˌni-zəm\ *n* **:** the theological system of John Calvin and his followers — **Cal•vin•ist** \-nist\ *n or adj* — **Cal•vin•is•tic** \ˌkal-və-ˈnis-tik\ *adj*

ca•lyp•so \kə-ˈlip-sō\ *n, pl* **-sos :** a style of music originating in the British West Indies and having lyrics that usually satirize local personalities and events

ca•lyx \ˈkā-liks, ˈka-\ *n, pl* **ca•lyx•es** *or* **ca•ly•ces** \ˈkā-lə-ˌsēz, ˈka-\ **:** the usually green or leaflike outer part of a flower consisting of sepals

cal•zo•ne \kal-ˈzōn, -ˈzō-nē\ *n* **:** a baked or fried turnover of pizza dough stuffed with cheese and various fillings

[1]**cam** \ˈkam\ *n* **:** a rotating or sliding piece in a mechanical linkage by which rotary motion is transformed into linear motion or vice versa

[2]**cam** *n* **:** CAMERA

ca•ma•ra•de•rie \ˌkäm-ˈrä-də-rē, ˌkam-, -ˈra-\ *n* ♦ **:** friendly feeling and goodwill among comrades

♦ companionship, company, comradeship, fellowship, society

cam•bi•um \ˈkam-bē-əm\ *n, pl* **-bi•ums** *or* **-bia** \-bē-ə\ **:** a thin cellular layer between xylem and phloem of most higher plants from which new tissues develop — **cam•bi•al** \-əl\ *adj*

Cam•bo•di•an \kam-ˈbō-dē-ən\ *n* **:** a native or inhabitant of Cambodia — **Cambodian** *adj*

Cam•bri•an \ˈkam-brē-ən, ˈkām-\ *adj* **:** of, relating to, or being the earliest period of the Paleozoic era — **Cambrian** *n*

cam•bric \ˈkām-brik\ *n* **:** a fine thin white linen or cotton fabric

cam•cord•er \ˈkam-ˌkȯr-dər\ *n* **:** a small portable video camera and recorder

came *past of* COME

cam•el \ˈka-məl\ *n* **:** either of two large hoofed cud-chewing mammals used especially in desert regions of Asia and Africa for carrying and riding

camel hair *also* **camel's hair** *n* **1 :** the hair of a camel or a substitute for it **2 :** cloth made of camel hair or of camel hair and wool

ca•mel•lia \kə-ˈmēl-yə\ *n* **:** any of a genus of shrubs and trees related to the tea plant and grown in warm regions and greenhouses for their showy roselike flowers

Cam•em•bert \ˈka-məm-ˌber\ *n* **:** a soft cheese with a grayish rind and yellow interior

cam•eo \ˈka-mē-ˌō\ *n, pl* **-eos 1 :** a gem carved in relief; *also* **:** a small medallion with a profiled head in relief **2 :** a brief appearance especially by a well-known actor in a play or movie

cam•era \ˈkam-rə, ˈka-mər-ə\ *n* **:** a device with a lightproof chamber fitted with a lens through which the image of an object is projected onto a surface for recording (as on film) or for conversion into electrical signals (as for television broadcast) — **cam•era•man** \-ˌman, -mən\ *n* — **cam•era•wom•an** *n*

Cam•er•oon•i•an \ˌka-mə-ˈrü-nē-ən\ *n* **:** a native or inhabitant of the Republic of Cameroon or the Cameroons region — **Cameroonian** *adj*

cam•i•sole \ˈka-mə-ˌsōl\ *n* **:** a short sleeveless garment for women

camomile *var of* CHAMOMILE

[1]**cam•ou•flage** \ˈka-mə-ˌfläzh, -ˌfläj\ *n* **1 :** the disguising of military equipment with paint, nets, or foliage; *also* **:** the disguise itself **2** ♦ **:** concealment by means of disguise **3 :** deceptive behavior

♦ disguise, guise

[2]**camouflage** *vb* ♦ **:** to conceal or disguise by camouflage

♦ cloak, disguise, dress up, mask

[1]**camp** \ˈkamp\ *n* **1** ♦ **:** a place where tents or buildings are erected for usually temporary shelter; *also* **:** a building in such a place for occasional use **2 :** a collection of tents or other shelters **3 :** a program offering recreational activities (as boating and hiking) for a limited time ⟨summer ~⟩ **4 :** a body of persons encamped **5 :** a training session for athletes outside of the regular season

♦ cabin, chalet, cottage, lodge ♦ bivouac, encampment

[2]**camp** *vb* **1 :** to make or occupy a camp **2 :** to live in a camp or outdoors

[3]**camp** *n* **1 :** exaggerated effeminate mannerisms **2 :** something so outrageous, inappropriate, or theatrical as to be considered amusing — **camp** *adj* — **camp•i•ly** \ˈkam-pə-lē\ *adv* — **camp•i•ness** \-pē-nəs\ *n* — **campy** \-pē\ *adj*

[4]**camp** *vb* **:** to engage in camp **:** exhibit the qualities of camp

cam•paign \kam-ˈpān\ *n* **1 :** a series of military operations forming one distinct stage in a war **2** ♦ **:** a series of activities designed to bring about a particular result ⟨advertising ~⟩ — **campaign** *vb*

♦ bandwagon, cause, crusade, drive, movement

cam•paign•er *n* ♦ **:** one that goes on, engages in, or conducts a campaign

♦ applicant, aspirant, candidate, contender, hopeful, prospect, seeker

cam•pa•ni•le \ˌkam-pə-ˈnē-lē\ *n, pl* **-ni•les** *or* **-ni•li** \-ˈnē-lē\ **:** a usually freestanding bell tower

cam•pa•nol•o•gy \ˌkam-pə-ˈnä-lə-jē\ *n* **:** the art of bell ringing — **cam•pa•nol•o•gist** \-jist\ *n*

camp•er \ˈkam-pər\ *n* **1 :** one who camps **2** ♦ **:** a portable dwelling (as a specially equipped vehicle) for use during casual travel and camping

♦ caravan, motor home, trailer

Camp Fire Girl *n* **:** a member of a national organization of girls from ages 5 to 18

camp follower *n* **1 :** a civilian (as a prostitute) who follows a military unit to attend or exploit its personnel **2 :** a follower of a group who is not an adherent; *esp* **:** a politician who joins a movement solely for personal gain

camp•ground \-ˌgraủnd\ *n* **:** the area or place used for a camp, for camping, or for a camp meeting

cam•phor \ˈkam-fər\ *n* **:** a gummy volatile aromatic compound obtained from an evergreen Asian tree (**camphor tree**) and used especially in medicine

camp meeting *n* **:** a series of evangelistic meetings usually held outdoors

camp•o•ree \ˌkam-pə-ˈrē\ *n* **:** a gathering of Boy Scouts or Girl Scouts from a given geographic area

camp•site \-ˌsīt\ *n* **:** a place suitable for or used as the site of a camp

cam•pus \ˈkam-pəs\ *n* **:** the grounds and buildings of a college or school; *also* **:** grounds resembling a campus ⟨hospital ~⟩

cam•shaft \ˈkam-ˌshaft\ *n* **:** a shaft to which a cam is fastened

[1]**can** \kən, ˈkan\ *vb, past* **could** \kəd, ˈkủd\ *pres sing & pl* **can 1 :** be able to **2 :** may perhaps ⟨~ he still be alive⟩ **3 :** be permitted by conscience or feeling to ⟨you ~ hardly blame her⟩ **4 :** have permission to ⟨you ~ go now⟩

[2]**can** \ˈkan\ *n* **1** ♦ **:** a usually cylindrical container or receptacle ⟨garbage ~⟩ ⟨coffee ~⟩ **2 :** JAIL **3 :** TOILET

♦ canister, drum, tin

[3]**can** \ˈkan\ *vb* **canned; can•ning 1 :** to put in a can **:** preserve by sealing in airtight cans or jars **2** *slang* **:** to discharge from employment **3** *slang* **:** to put a stop or an end to — **can•ner** *n*

Can *or* **Canad** *abbr* Canada; Canadian

Canada Day *n* **:** July 1 observed as a legal holiday in commemoration of the proclamation of dominion status in 1867

Can•a•da goose \ˈka-nə-də-\ *n* **:** a common wild goose of No. America

Ca•na•di•an \kə-ˈnā-dē-ən\ *n* **:** a native or inhabitant of Canada — **Canadian** *adj*

Canadian football *n* **:** a game resembling American football that is played on a turfed field between two teams of 12 players each

ca•naille \kə-ˈnī, -ˈnāl\ *n* **:** RABBLE, RIFFRAFF

ca•nal \kə-ˈnal\ *n* **1 :** a tubular passage in the body **:** DUCT **2** ♦ **:** an artificial waterway (as for boats or irrigation)

♦ aqueduct, channel, conduit, flume, raceway, watercourse

can•a•lize \ˈkan-ᵊl-ˌīz\ *vb* **-lized; -liz•ing 1 :** to provide with a canal or make into or like a channel **2 :** to provide with an outlet; *esp* **:** to direct into preferred channels — **ca•nal•i•za•tion** \ˌkan-ᵊl-ə-ˈzā-shən\ *n*

can•a•pé \ˈka-nə-pē, -ˌpā\ *n* **:** a piece of bread or toast or a cracker topped with a savory food

ca•nard \kə-ˈnärd\ *n* **:** a false or unfounded report or story

ca•nary \kə-ˈner-ē\ *n, pl* **ca•nar•ies 1 :** a usually sweet wine similar to Madeira **2 :** a usually yellow or greenish finch often kept in a cage as a pet

ca•nas•ta \kə-ˈnas-tə\ *n* **:** rummy played with two full decks of cards plus four jokers
canc *abbr* canceled
can•can \ˈkan-ˌkan\ *n* **:** a woman's dance of French origin characterized by high kicking
¹**can•cel** \ˈkan-səl\ *vb* **-celed** *or* **-celled; -cel•ing** *or* **-cel•ling** **1** ♦ **:** to destroy the force or validity of ⟨~ a magazine subscription⟩ **2** ♦ **:** to match in force or effect **:** OFFSET — often used with *out* **3 :** to cross out **:** DELETE **4 :** to remove (a common divisor) from a numerator and denominator; *also* **:** to remove (equivalents) on opposite sides of an equation or account **5 :** to mark (a postage stamp or check) so that it cannot be reused **6 :** to neutralize each other's strength or effect

♦ [1] abort, call off, drop, recall, repeal, rescind, revoke *Ant* continue, keep ♦ *often* **cancel out** [2] annul, compensate, correct, counteract, counterbalance, make up, neutralize, offset

²**cancel** *n* **1 :** CANCELLATION **2 :** a deleted part
can•cel•er *or* **can•cel•ler** *n* ♦ **:** a force or influence that cancels out or offsets an opposing force

♦ balance, counterbalance, counterweight, equipoise, offset

can•cel•la•tion \ˌkan-sə-ˈlā-shən\ *n* ♦ **:** the act or an instance of canceling **:** the calling off of an arrangement

♦ abortion, calling, recall, repeal, rescission, revocation *Ant* continuation

can•cer \ˈkan-sər\ *n* **1** *cap* **:** a zodiacal constellation between Gemini and Leo usually pictured as a crab **2** *cap* **:** the 4th sign of the zodiac in astrology; *also* **:** one born under this sign **3 :** a malignant tumor that tends to spread in the body; *also* **:** an abnormal state marked by such tumors **4 :** a malignant evil that spreads destructively — **can•cer•ous** \-sə-rəs\ *adj* — **can•cer•ous•ly** *adv*
can•de•la•bra \ˌkan-də-ˈlä-brə, -ˈla-\ *n* **:** an ornamental branched candlestick or lamp with several lights
can•de•la•brum \-brəm\ *n, pl* **-bra** *also* **-brums :** CANDELABRA
can•did \ˈkan-dəd\ *adj* **1** ♦ **:** marked by honest sincere expression **:** FRANK, STRAIGHTFORWARD **2 :** relating to photography of subjects acting naturally or spontaneously without being posed — **can•did•ly** *adv*

♦ direct, forthright, foursquare, frank, honest, open, outspoken, plain, straight, straightforward, unguarded, unreserved

can•di•da•cy \ˈkan-də-də-sē\ *n, pl* **-cies :** the state of being a candidate
can•di•date \ˈkan-də-ˌdāt, ˈka-nə-, -dət\ *n* ♦ **:** one who seeks or is proposed for an office, honor, or membership

♦ applicant, aspirant, campaigner, contender, hopeful, prospect, seeker

can•di•da•ture \ˈkan-də-də-ˌchu̇r, ˈka-nə-\ *n, chiefly Brit* **:** CANDIDACY
can•did•ness \ˈkan-dəd-nəs\ *n* ♦ **:** the quality or state of being candid

♦ candor (*or* candour), directness, forthrightness, frankness, openness, outspokenness, plainness

can•died \ˈkan-dēd\ *adj* **:** preserved in or encrusted with sugar
¹**can•dle** \ˈkan-dᵊl\ *n* **:** a usually slender mass of tallow or wax molded around a wick that is burned to give light
²**candle** *vb* **can•dled; can•dling :** to examine (as eggs) by holding between the eye and a light — **can•dler** *n*
can•dle•light \ˈkan-dᵊl-ˌlīt\ *n* **1 :** the light of a candle; *also* **:** any soft artificial light **2 :** the time when candles are lit **:** TWILIGHT
can•dle•lit \-ˌlit\ *adj* **:** illuminated by candlelight ⟨a ~ dinner⟩
Can•dle•mas \ˈkan-dᵊl-məs\ *n* **:** February 2 observed as a church festival in commemoration of the presentation of Christ in the temple
can•dle•stick \-ˌstik\ *n* **:** a holder with a socket for a candle
can•dle•wick \-ˌwik\ *n* **:** a soft cotton yarn; *also* **:** embroidery made with this yarn usually in tufts
can•dor \ˈkan-dər\ *or Can and Brit* **can•dour** *n* ♦ **:** unreserved, honest, or sincere expression **:** FRANKNESS

♦ candidness, directness, forthrightness, frankness, openness, plainness *Ant* dissembling, pretense

C and W *abbr* country and western
¹**can•dy** \ˈkan-dē\ *n, pl* **candies 1 :** a confection made from sugar often with flavoring and filling **2 :** something that appeals in a light or frivolous way
²**candy** *vb* **can•died; can•dy•ing :** to encrust in sugar often by cooking in a syrup
candy floss *n, Can and Brit* **:** COTTON CANDY
candy strip•er \-ˈstrī-pər\ *n* **:** a teenage volunteer worker at a hospital
¹**cane** \ˈkān\ *n* **1 :** a slender hollow or pithy stem (as of a reed or bramble) **2 :** a tall woody grass or reed (as sugarcane) **3 a :** a walking stick **b :** a rod for flogging
²**cane** *vb* **caned; can•ing 1 :** to beat with a cane **2 :** to weave or make with cane — **can•er** *n*
cane•brake \ˈkān-ˌbrāk\ *n* **:** a thicket of cane
¹**ca•nine** \ˈkā-ˌnīn\ *n* **1 :** a pointed tooth between the outer incisor and the first premolar **2 :** a canine mammal (as a domestic dog)
²**canine** *adj* **:** of or relating to dogs or to the family to which they belong
can•is•ter \ˈka-nə-stər\ *n* ♦ **:** an often cylindrical container

♦ can, drum, tin

can•ker \ˈkaŋ-kər\ *n* **:** a spreading sore that eats into tissue — **can•ker•ous** \-kə-rəs\ *adj*
can•ker•worm \-ˌwərm\ *n* **:** either of two moths and especially their larvae that are pests of fruit and shade trees
can•na \ˈka-nə\ *n* **:** any of a genus of tropical herbs with large leaves and racemes of bright-colored flowers
can•na•bis \ˈka-nə-bəs\ *n* **:** any of the psychoactive preparations (as marijuana) or chemicals (as THC) derived from hemp; *also* **:** HEMP
canned \ˈkand\ *adj* ♦ **:** prepared in standardized form for general use or wide distribution
can•nery \ˈka-nə-rē\ *n, pl* **-ner•ies :** a factory for the canning of foods
can•ni•bal \ˈka-nə-bəl\ *n* **:** one that eats the flesh of its own kind — **can•ni•bal•ism** \-bə-ˌli-zəm\ *n* — **can•ni•bal•is•tic** \-bə-ˈlis-tik\ *adj*
can•ni•bal•ise *Brit var of* CANNIBALIZE
can•ni•bal•ize \ˈka-nə-bə-ˌlīz\ *vb* **-ized; -iz•ing 1 :** to take usable parts from (as an inoperative machine) to construct or repair another machine **2 :** to practice cannibalism
can•ni•ness \ˈka-nē-nəs\ *n* ♦ **:** skill in devising or using indirect or subtle methods

♦ artfulness, artifice, caginess, craft, craftiness, cunning, guile, slyness, wiliness ♦ acumen, astuteness, caginess, hardheadedness, intelligence, keenness, sharpness, shrewdness, wit

can•non \ˈka-nən\ *n, pl* **cannons** *or* **cannon :** a large heavy gun; *esp* **:** one mounted on a carriage
can•non•ade \ˌka-nə-ˈnād\ *n* **1 :** a heavy fire of artillery **2** ♦ **:** an attack (as with words) likened to artillery fire **:** BOMBARDMENT — **cannonade** *vb*

♦ barrage, bombardment, fusillade, hail, salvo, shower, storm, volley

can•non•ball \ˈka-nən-ˌbȯl\ *n* **:** a usually round solid missile for a cannon
can•non•eer \ˌka-nə-ˈnir\ *n* **:** an artillery gunner
can•not \ˈka-ˌnät, kə-ˈnät\ **:** can not — **cannot but :** to be unable to do otherwise than ⟨we *cannot but* wonder why⟩
can•nu•la \ˈkan-yə-lə\ *n, pl* **-las** *or* **-lae** \-ˌlē\ **:** a small tube for insertion into a body cavity or into a duct or vessel
can•ny \ˈka-nē\ *adj* **can•ni•er; -est** ♦ **:** marked by clever discerning awareness **:** SHREWD ⟨a *canny* lawyer⟩ — **can•ni•ly** \ˈkan-ᵊl-ē\ *adv*

♦ astute, hardheaded, knowing, sharp, shrewd, smart

ca•noe \kə-ˈnü\ *n* **:** a light narrow boat with sharp ends and curved sides that is usually propelled by paddles — **canoe** *vb* — **ca•noe•ist** *n*
ca•no•la \kə-ˈnō-lə\ *n* **:** a rape plant producing seeds that are low in a toxic acid and yield an edible oil (**canola oil**) high in monounsaturated fatty acids; *also* **:** this oil
¹**can•on** \ˈka-nən\ *n* **1 :** a regulation decreed by a church council; *also* **:** a provision of canon law **2 :** an official or authoritative list (as of works of literature) **3 :** an accepted principle ⟨the ~*s* of good taste⟩
²**canon** *n* **:** a member of the clergy on the staff of a cathedral
ca•non•i•cal \kə-ˈnä-ni-kəl\ *adj* **1 :** of, relating to, or forming a canon **2 :** conforming to a general rule or acceptable procedure **:** ORTHODOX **3 :** of or relating to a canon of a cathedral — **ca•non•i•cal•ly** \-k(ə-)lē\ *adv*
can•on•ize \ˈka-nə-ˌnīz\ *vb* **can•on•ized** \-ˌnīzd\; **can•on•iz•ing** **1 :** to declare (a deceased person) an officially recognized saint **2** ♦ **:** to treat as illustrious, preeminent, or sacred — **can•on•i•za•tion** \ˌka-nə-nə-ˈzā-shən\ *n*

♦ adore, deify, dote on, idolize, worship

canon law *n* **:** the law governing a church

can•o•py \ˈka-nə-pē\ *n, pl* **-pies** **1** ♦ **:** an overhanging cover, shelter, or shade **2 :** the uppermost spreading layer of a forest **3 :** a transparent cover for an airplane cockpit **4 :** the fabric part of a parachute — **canopy** *vb*

♦ ceiling, roof, tent

[1]**cant** \ˈkant\ *vb* ♦ **:** to give a slant to

♦ angle, cock, heel, incline, lean, list, slant, slope, tilt, tip

[2]**cant** *n* **1 :** an oblique or slanting surface **2** ♦ **:** upward or downward slant or inclination or degree of slope **:** TILT, SLANT

♦ diagonal, grade, inclination, incline, lean, pitch, slant, slope, tilt, upgrade

[3]**cant** *vb* **1 :** to beg in a whining manner **2 :** to talk hypocritically
[4]**cant** *n* **1** ♦ **:** the special idiom of a profession or trade **:** JARGON **2** ♦ **:** insincere speech; *esp* **:** insincerely pious words or statements

♦ [1] argot, jargon, language, lingo, slang, terminology, vocabulary ♦ [2] dissimulation, hypocrisy, insincerity, piety

Cant *abbr* Canticle of Canticles
can•ta•bi•le \kän-ˈtä-bə-ˌlā\ *adv or adj* **:** in a singing manner — used as a direction in music
can•ta•loupe *also* **can•ta•loup** \ˈkant-ᵊl-ˌōp\ *n* **:** MUSKMELON; *esp* **:** one with orange flesh and rough skin
can•tan•ker•ous \kan-ˈtaŋ-kə-rəs\ *adj* ♦ **:** marked by ill humor, irritability, and determination to disagree **:** ILL-NATURED — **can•tan•ker•ous•ly** *adv* — **can•tan•ker•ous•ness** *n*

♦ bearish, bilious, disagreeable, dyspeptic, ill-humored, ill-tempered, ornery, splenetic, surly

can•ta•ta \kən-ˈtä-tə\ *n* **:** a choral composition usually sung to instrumental accompaniment
canted *adj* ♦ **:** placed at an incline or given a degree of cant **:** SLANTED

♦ diagonal, inclined, listing, oblique, slantwise

can•teen \kan-ˈtēn\ *n* **1 :** a flask for carrying liquids **2 :** a place of recreation and entertainment for military personnel **3 :** a small cafeteria or counter at which snacks are served
can•ter \ˈkan-tər\ *n* **:** a horse's 3-beat gait resembling but smoother and slower than a gallop — **canter** *vb*
Can•ter•bury bell \ˈkant-ər-ˌber-ē-\ *n* **:** any of several plants related to the bluebell that are cultivated for their showy flowers
can•ti•cle \ˈkan-ti-kəl\ *n* **1 :** SONG **2** ♦ **:** any of several liturgical songs taken from the Bible

♦ anthem, carol, chorale, hymn, psalm, spiritual

Canticle of Canticles *n* **:** SONG OF SONGS
[1]**can•ti•le•ver** \ˈkant-ᵊl-ˌē-vər\ *n* **:** a projecting beam or structure supported only at one end; *also* **:** either of a pair of such structures projecting toward each other so that when joined they form a bridge
[2]**cantilever** *vb* **1 :** to support by a cantilever ⟨a ∼*ed* shelf⟩ **2 :** to build as a cantilever **3 :** to project as a cantilever
can•tle \ˈkant-ᵊl\ *n* **:** the upwardly projecting rear part of a saddle
can•to \ˈkan-ˌtō\ *n, pl* **cantos :** one of the major divisions of a long poem
can•ton \ˈkant-ᵊn, ˈkan-ˌtän\ *n* **:** a small territorial division of a country; *esp* **:** one of the political divisions of Switzerland — **can•ton•al** \ˈkant-ᵊn-əl, kan-ˈtän-ᵊl\ *adj*
can•ton•ment \kan-ˈtōn-mənt, -ˈtän-\ *n* **:** usually temporary quarters for troops
can•tor \ˈkan-tər\ *n* **1 :** a choir leader **2 :** a synagogue official who sings liturgical music and leads the congregation in prayer
Ca•nuck \kə-ˈnək *sometimes* -ˈnu̇k\ *n* **:** a Canadian and especially a French Canadian
can•vas *also* **can•vass** \ˈkan-vəs\ *n* **1 :** a strong cloth formerly much used for making tents and sails **2 :** a set of sails **3 :** a group of tents **4 :** a piece of cloth prepared as a surface for painting; *also* **:** a painting on this surface **5 :** the canvas-covered floor of a boxing or wrestling ring
can•vas•back \ˈkan-vəs-ˌbak\ *n* **:** a No. American wild duck with red head and gray back
[1]**can•vass** *also* **can•vas** \ˈkan-vəs\ *vb* **can•vassed; can•vass•ing** ♦ **:** to go through (a district) or to (persons) to solicit votes or orders for goods or to determine public opinion or sentiment — **can•vass•er** *n*

♦ poll, solicit, survey

[2]**canvass** *n* **:** an act or instance of canvassing
can•yon \ˈkan-yən\ *n* ♦ **:** a deep narrow valley with high steep sides

♦ defile, flume, gap, gorge, gulch, notch, pass, ravine

[1]**cap** \ˈkap\ *n* **1** ♦ **:** a covering for the head especially with a visor and no brim **2** ♦ **:** something that serves as a cover or protection especially for a tip, knob, or end ⟨a bottle ∼⟩ **3 :** a container holding an explosive charge **4 :** an upper limit (as on expenditures)

♦ [1] hat, headgear ♦ [2] cover, lid, top

[2]**cap** *vb* **capped; cap•ping** **1 :** to provide or protect with a cap **2 :** to form a cap over **:** CROWN **3 :** OUTDO, SURPASS **4** ♦ **:** to provide a culminating event for **:** CLIMAX — often used with *off*

♦ *often* **cap off** climax, crown

[3]**cap** *abbr* **1** capacity **2** capital **3** capitalize; capitalized
CAP *abbr* Civil Air Patrol
ca•pa•bil•i•ty \ˌkā-pə-ˈbi-lə-tē\ *n* **1** ♦ **:** the quality or state of being capable physically, intellectually, morally, or legally **2** ♦ **:** natural talent or acquired proficiency especially in a particular work or activity

♦ [1] ability, capacity, competence, faculty ♦ [2] credentials, qualification, stuff

ca•pa•ble \ˈkā-pə-bəl\ *adj* ♦ **:** having ability, capacity, or power to do something **:** ABLE, COMPETENT

♦ able, competent, fit, good, qualified, suitable

ca•pa•bly *adv* ♦ **:** in a capable manner

♦ ably, adeptly, expertly, masterfully, proficiently, skillfully, well

ca•pa•cious \kə-ˈpā-shəs\ *adj* ♦ **:** able to contain much — **ca•pa•cious•ly** *adv* — **ca•pa•cious•ness** *n*

♦ ample, commodious, roomy, spacious

ca•pac•i•tance \kə-ˈpa-sə-təns\ *n* **:** the property of an electric nonconductor that permits the storage of energy
ca•pac•i•tor \kə-ˈpa-sə-tər\ *n* **:** an electronic circuit device for temporary storage of electrical energy
[1]**ca•pac•i•ty** \kə-ˈpa-sə-tē\ *n, pl* **-ties** **1 :** legal qualification or fitness **2 :** the ability to contain, receive, or accommodate **3 :** the maximum amount or number that can be contained **4** ♦ **:** an individual's mental or physical ability and skill in doing something **:** ABILITY **5** ♦ **:** position or character assigned or assumed ⟨will be happy to serve in any ∼⟩

♦ [4] ability, capability, competence, faculty ♦ [5] appointment, billet, function, job, place, position, post, situation ♦ [5] function, job, part, place, position, purpose, role, task, work

[2]**capacity** *adj* **:** equaling maximum capacity ⟨a ∼ crowd⟩
cap–a–pie *or* **cap–à–pie** \ˌka-pə-ˈpē\ *adv* **:** from head to foot **:** at all points
[1]**ca•par•i•son** \kə-ˈpar-ə-sən\ *n* **1 :** an ornamental covering for a horse **2** ♦ **:** rich clothing

♦ array, best, bravery, feather, finery, frippery, full dress, gaiety, regalia

[2]**caparison** *vb* **:** to dress richly
[1]**cape** \ˈkāp\ *n* **1** ♦ **:** a point of land jutting out into water **2** *often cap* **:** CAPE COD COTTAGE

♦ headland, peninsula, point, promontory, spit

[2]**cape** *n* **:** a sleeveless garment hanging from the neck over the shoulders
Cape Cod cottage \ˈkāp-ˈkäd-\ *n* **:** a compact rectangular dwelling of one or one-and-a-half stories usually with a steep gable roof
[1]**ca•per** \ˈkā-pər\ *n* **:** the flower bud or young berry of a Mediterranean shrub pickled for use as a relish; *also* **:** this shrub
[2]**caper** *vb* **ca•pered; ca•per•ing** ♦ **:** to leap about in a playful manner

♦ cavort, disport, frisk, frolic, gambol, lark, rollick, romp, sport

[3]**caper** *n* **1 :** a frolicsome leap **2** ♦ **:** a capricious escapade **3 :** an illegal or questionable act

♦ antic, escapade, frolic, monkeyshine, practical joke, prank, trick

cape•skin \ˈkāp-ˌskin\ *n* **:** a light flexible leather made from sheepskins
Cape Verd•ean \-ˈvər-dē-ən\ *n* **:** a native or inhabitant of the Republic of Cape Verde
cap•ful \ˈkap-ˌfu̇l\ *n, pl* **cap•fuls** *also* **caps•ful** \ˈkaps-\ **:** as much as a cap will hold

cap•il•lar•i•ty \ˌka-pə-ˈlar-ə-tē\ *n, pl* **-ties** : the action by which the surface of a liquid where it is in contact with a solid (as in a slender tube) is raised or lowered depending on the relative attraction of the molecules of the liquid for each other and for those of the solid

1**cap•il•lary** \ˈka-pə-ˌler-ē\ *adj* **1** : resembling a hair **2** : having a very small bore ⟨~ tube⟩ **3** : of or relating to capillaries or to capillarity

2**capillary** *n, pl* **-lar•ies** : any of the tiny thin-walled blood vessels that carry blood between the smallest arteries and their corresponding veins

1**cap•i•tal** \ˈka-pət-ᵊl\ *n* : the top part or piece of an architectural column

2**capital** *adj* **1** : conforming to the series A, B, C rather than a, b, c ⟨~ letters⟩ ⟨~ G⟩ **2** : punishable by death ⟨a ~ crime⟩ **3** : most serious ⟨a ~ error⟩ **4** : first in importance or position : CHIEF; *also* : being the seat of government ⟨the ~ city⟩ **5** : of or relating to capital ⟨~ expenditures⟩; *esp* : relating to or being assets that add to the long-term net worth of a corporation **6** : of the first order of size, importance, or quality : FIRST-RATE, EXCELLENT

3**capital** *n* **1** ♦ : accumulated wealth especially as used to produce more wealth **2** : the total face value of shares of stock issued by a company **3** : persons holding capital **4** : ADVANTAGE, GAIN **5** : a letter larger than the ordinary small letter and often different in form **6 a** : the capital city of a state, province, or country **b** : a city preeminent in some activity ⟨the fashion ~⟩

♦ assets, fortune, means, opulence, riches, substance, wealth, wherewithal

capital gain *n* : the increase in value of an asset (as stock or real estate) between the time it is bought and the time it is sold

capital goods *n pl* : machinery, tools, factories, and commodities used in the production of goods

cap•i•tal•ise *Brit var of* CAPITALIZE

cap•i•tal•ism \ˈka-pət-ᵊl-ˌi-zəm\ *n* : an economic system characterized by private or corporate ownership of capital goods and by prices, production, and distribution of goods that are determined mainly by competition in a free market

1**cap•i•tal•ist** \-ist\ *n* **1** : a person who has capital especially invested in business **2** : a person of great wealth : PLUTOCRAT **3** : a believer in capitalism

2**capitalist** *or* **cap•i•tal•is•tic** \ˌka-pət-ᵊl-ˈis-tik\ *adj* **1** : owning capital **2** : practicing or advocating capitalism **3** : marked by capitalism — **cap•i•tal•is•ti•cal•ly** \-ti-k(ə-)lē\ *adv*

cap•i•tal•iza•tion \ˌka-pət-ᵊl-ə-ˈzā-shən\ *n* **1** : the act or process of capitalizing **2** : the total amount of money used as capital in a business

cap•i•tal•ize *or Brit* **cap•i•tal•ise** \ˈka-pət-ᵊl-ˌīz\ *vb* **-ized; -iz•ing** **1** : to write or print with an initial capital or in capitals **2** : to convert into or use as capital **3** ♦ : to supply capital for **4** ♦ : to gain by turning something to advantage ⟨~ on an opponent's mistake⟩

♦ [3] endow, finance, fund, stake, subsidize, underwrite ♦ *usu* **capitalize on** [4] abuse, cash in, exploit, impose, play, use

cap•i•tal•ly \ˈka-pət-ᵊl-ē\ *adv* : ADMIRABLY, EXCELLENTLY

cap•i•ta•tion \ˌka-pə-ˈtā-shən\ *n* : a direct uniform tax levied on each person

cap•i•tol \ˈka-pət-ᵊl\ *n* : the building in which a legislature holds its sessions

ca•pit•u•late \kə-ˈpi-chə-ˌlāt\ *vb* **-lat•ed; -lat•ing** **1** ♦ : to surrender especially on conditions agreed upon **2** ♦ : to cease resisting

♦ bow, budge, concede, give in, give up, knuckle under, quit, submit, succumb, surrender, yield

ca•pit•u•la•tion \-ˌpi-chə-ˈlā-shən\ *n* **1** ♦ : the act of surrendering or yielding **2** : the terms of surrender

♦ relinquishment, submission, surrender

ca•pon \ˈkā-ˌpän, -pən\ *n* : a castrated male chicken

cap•puc•ci•no \ˌka-pə-ˈchē-nō, ˌkä-\ *n* : espresso mixed with foamy hot milk or cream and often flavored with cinnamon

ca•pric•cio \kə-ˈprē-chē-ˌō, -chō\ *n, pl* **-cios** : an instrumental piece in free form usually lively in tempo and brilliant in style

ca•price \kə-ˈprēs\ *n* **1** ♦ : a sudden whim or fancy **2** : an inclination to do things impulsively **3** : CAPRICCIO

♦ fancy, freak, notion, vagary, whim

ca•pri•cious \-ˈpri-shəs\ *adj* **1** ♦ : marked or guided by a sudden whim or fancy **2** ♦ : not guided by steady judgment or purpose — **ca•pri•cious•ly** *adv* — **ca•pri•cious•ness** *n*

♦ [1] impulsive, whimsical ♦ [2] changeable, fickle, fluid, inconstant, mercurial, mutable, temperamental, uncertain, unpredictable, unsettled, unstable, unsteady, variable, volatile

Cap•ri•corn \ˈka-pri-ˌkȯrn\ *n* **1** : a zodiacal constellation between Sagittarius and Aquarius usually pictured as a goat **2** : the 10th sign of the zodiac in astrology; *also* : one born under this sign

cap•ri•ole \ˈka-prē-ˌōl\ *n* : 3CAPER 1; *also* : an upward leap of a horse with a backward kick at the height of the leap — **capriole** *vb*

caps *abbr* **1** capitals **2** capsule

cap•sa•i•cin \kap-ˈsā-ə-sən\ *n* : a colorless compound found in various capsicums that gives hot peppers their hotness

cap•si•cum \ˈkap-si-kəm\ *n* : PEPPER 2

cap•size \ˈkap-ˌsīz, kap-ˈsīz\ *vb* **cap•sized; cap•siz•ing** : to turn over : UPSET, OVERTURN

cap•stan \ˈkap-stən, -ˌstan\ *n* **1** : a machine for moving or raising heavy weights that consists of a vertical drum which can be rotated and around which cable is turned **2** : a rotating shaft that drives recorder tape

cap•su•lar \ˈkap-sə-lər\ *adj* : of, relating to, or resembling a capsule

cap•su•lat•ed \-ˌlā-təd\ *adj* : enclosed in a capsule

1**cap•sule** \ˈkap-səl, -sül\ *n* **1 a** : a membrane or sac enclosing a body part (as of a joint) **b** ♦ : a surrounding saclike structure that protects something held inside **2** : a case bearing spores or seeds **3** ♦ : a gelatin shell for packaging something (as a drug or vitamins) **4** : a small pressurized compartment or vehicle (as for space flight)

♦ [1b] armor, case, casing, cocoon, cover, housing, husk, jacket, pod, sheath, shell ♦ [3] pill, tablet

2**capsule** *adj* **1** ♦ : very brief **2** : very compact

♦ brief, compact, compendious, concise, crisp, epigrammatic, laconic, pithy, succinct, summary, terse

Capt *abbr* captain

1**cap•tain** \ˈkap-tən\ *n* **1** ♦ : a commander of a body of troops **2** : a commissioned officer in the army, air force, or marine corps ranking next below a major **3** : an officer in charge of a ship **4** : a commissioned officer in the navy ranking next below a rear admiral or a commodore **5** ♦ : one who leads or supervises (as a sports team or work crew) **6** : a dominant figure — **cap•tain•cy** *n*

♦ [1] commander ♦ [5] boss, chief, foreman, head, headman, helmsman, kingpin, leader, master, taskmaster

2**captain** *vb* ♦ : to be or fill the role of captain ⟨~*ed* the football team⟩

♦ boss, head, oversee, superintend, supervise ♦ boss, command, control, govern, preside, rule ♦ boss, command, dominate, head, lead, spearhead

cap•tion \ˈkap-shən\ *n* **1** : a heading especially of an article or document : TITLE **2** : the explanatory matter accompanying an illustration **3** : a motion-picture subtitle — **cap•tion** *vb*

cap•tious \ˈkap-shəs\ *adj* ♦ : marked by an inclination to find fault — **cap•tious•ly** *adv* — **cap•tious•ness** *n*

♦ carping, critical, hypercritical, overcritical

cap•ti•vate \ˈkap-tə-ˌvāt\ *vb* **-vat•ed; -vat•ing** ♦ : to attract and hold irresistibly by some special charm or art — **cap•ti•va•tor** \ˈkap-tə-ˌvā-tər\ *n*

♦ allure, beguile, bewitch, charm, enchant, fascinate, wile

cap•ti•vat•ing *adj* ♦ : having the ability to captivate : CHARMING

♦ alluring, attractive, charming, elfin, engaging, fascinating, fetching, glamorous, magnetic, seductive

cap•ti•va•tion \ˌkap-tə-ˈvā-shən\ *n* ♦ : the action or power of influencing and dominating by some special charm or irresistible appeal

♦ allure, appeal, attractiveness, charisma, charm, enchantment, fascination, glamour, magic, magnetism

1**cap•tive** \ˈkap-tiv\ *adj* **1** : made prisoner especially in war **2** : kept within bounds : CONFINED **3** : held under control

2**captive** *n* ♦ : one captured and held prisoner

♦ capture, internee, prisoner ***Ant*** captor

cap•tiv•i•ty \kap-ˈti-və-tē\ *n* ♦ : state or condition of being held captive especially in war

♦ confinement, imprisonment, incarceration, internment

cap•tor \ˈkap-tər\ *n* : one that captures

[1]**cap•ture** \ˈkap-chər\ *n* **1** : the act of capturing **2** : one that has been captured

[2]**capture** *vb* **cap•tured; cap•tur•ing** **1 a** ♦ : to take, seize, or catch especially as captive or prize by effort or skill **b** : to take control of especially by force ⟨~ the city⟩ **c** ♦ : to gain or win especially through effort **2** : to preserve in a relatively permanent form

♦ [1a] bag, catch, collar, corral, get, grab, grapple, hook, land, nab, seize, snare, trap ♦ [1c] acquire, attain, carry, draw, earn, gain, garner, get, land, make, obtain, procure, realize, secure, win

Ca•pu•chin \ˈka-pyə-shən\ *n* : a member of an austere branch of the order of St. Francis of Assisi engaged in missionary work and preaching

car \ˈkär\ *n* **1** ♦ : a vehicle moving on wheels **2** : the compartment of an elevator **3** : the part of a balloon or airship that carries passengers or equipment

♦ automobile, machine, motor vehicle

car•a•cole \ˈkar-ə-ˌkōl\ *n* : a half turn to right or left executed by a mounted horse — **caracole** *vb*

car•a•cul \ˈkar-ə-ˌkəl\ *n* : the pelt of a karakul lamb after the curl begins to loosen

ca•rafe \kə-ˈraf, -ˈräf\ *n* **1** : a bottle with a flaring lip used especially to hold wine **2** : a usually glass pitcher for pouring coffee

car•am•bo•la \ˌkar-əm-ˈbō-lə\ *n* **1** : a five-angled green to yellow edible tropical fruit of star-shaped cross section **2** : a tropical Asian tree widely cultivated for carambolas

car•a•mel \ˈkar-ə-məl, ˈkär-məl\ *n* **1** : an amorphous substance obtained by heating sugar and used for flavoring and coloring **2** : a firm chewy candy

car•a•pace \ˈkar-ə-ˌpās\ *n* : a protective case or shell on the back of some animals (as turtles or crabs)

[1]**carat** *var of* KARAT

[2]**car•at** \ˈkar-ət\ *n* : a unit of weight for precious stones equal to 200 milligrams

car•a•van \ˈkar-ə-ˌvan\ *n* **1** : a group of travelers journeying together through desert or hostile regions **2** ♦ : a group of vehicles traveling in a file **3** ♦ : a covered wagon or motortruck equipped as traveling living quarters

♦ [2] armada, cavalcade, fleet, motorcade, train ♦ [3] camper, motor home, trailer

car•a•van•sa•ry \ˌkar-ə-ˈvan-sə-rē\ *or* **car•a•van•se•rai** \-sə-ˌrī\ *n, pl* **-ries** *or* **-rais** *or* **-rai** **1** : an inn in eastern countries where caravans rest at night **2** : an establishment that provides lodging and usually meals for the public : HOTEL, INN

car•a•vel \ˈkar-ə-ˌvel\ *n* : a small 15th and 16th century ship with a broad bow, high narrow poop, and usually three masts

car•a•way \ˈkar-ə-ˌwā\ *n* : an aromatic herb related to the carrot with fruits (**caraway seed**) used in seasoning and medicine; *also* : its fruit

car•bide \ˈkär-ˌbīd\ *n* : a compound of carbon with another element

car•bine \ˈkär-ˌbēn, -ˌbīn\ *n* : a short-barreled lightweight rifle

car•bo•hy•drate \ˌkär-bō-ˈhī-ˌdrāt, -drət\ *n* : any of various compounds composed of carbon, hydrogen, and oxygen (as sugars and starches)

car•bol•ic acid \ˌkär-ˈbä-lik-\ *n* : PHENOL

car•bon \ˈkär-bən\ *n* **1** : a nonmetallic chemical element occurring in nature especially as diamond and graphite and as a constituent of coal, petroleum, and limestone **2** : a sheet of carbon paper; *also* : CARBON COPY 1 — **car•bon•less** \-ləs\ *adj*

car•bo•na•ceous \ˌkär-bə-ˈnā-shəs\ *adj* : relating to, containing, or composed of carbon

[1]**car•bon•ate** \ˈkär-bə-ˌnāt, -nət\ *n* : a salt or ester of carbonic acid

[2]**car•bon•ate** \-ˌnāt\ *vb* **-at•ed; -at•ing** : to combine or infuse with carbon dioxide ⟨*carbonated* beverages⟩ — **car•bon•ation** \ˌkär-bə-ˈnā-shən\ *n*

carbon black *n* : any of various black substances consisting chiefly of carbon and used especially as pigments

carbon copy *n* **1** : a copy made by carbon paper **2** ♦ : one that strongly resembles or closely corresponds to another : DUPLICATE

♦ counterpart, double, duplicate, duplication, facsimile, image, likeness, match, picture, replica, ringer, spit

carbon dating *n* : the determination of the age of old material (as an archaeological specimen) by its content of carbon 14

carbon dioxide *n* : a heavy colorless gas that does not support combustion and is formed in animal respiration and in the combustion and decomposition of organic substances

carbon 14 *n* : a heavy radioactive form of carbon used especially in dating archaeological materials

car•bon•ic acid \kär-ˈbä-nik-\ *n* : a weak acid that decomposes readily into water and carbon dioxide

car•bon•if•er•ous \ˌkär-bə-ˈni-fə-rəs\ *adj* **1** : producing or containing carbon or coal **2** *cap* : of, relating to, or being the period of the Paleozoic era between the Devonian and the Permian — **Carboniferous** *n*

carbon monoxide *n* : a colorless odorless very poisonous gas formed by the incomplete burning of carbon

carbon paper *n* : a thin paper coated with a pigment and used for making copies

carbon tet•ra•chlo•ride \-ˌte-trə-ˈklōr-ˌīd\ *n* : a colorless nonflammable toxic liquid used especially as a solvent

carbon 12 *n* : the most abundant isotope of carbon having a nucleus of 6 protons and 6 neutrons and used as a standard for measurements of atomic weight

car•boy \ˈkär-ˌbȯi\ *n* : a large container for liquids

car•bun•cle \ˈkär-ˌbəŋ-kəl\ *n* : a painful inflammation of the skin and underlying tissue that discharges pus from several openings

car•bu•re•tor \ˈkär-bə-ˌrā-tər, -byə-\ *n* : an apparatus for premixing vaporized fuel and air and supplying the mixture to an internal combustion engine

car•cass \ˈkär-kəs\ *n* : a dead body; *esp* : one of an animal dressed for food

car•cin•o•gen \kär-ˈsi-nə-jən\ *n* : an agent causing or inciting cancer — **car•ci•no•gen•ic** \ˌkärs-ᵊn-ō-ˈje-nik\ *adj* — **car•ci•no•ge•nic•i•ty** \-jə-ˈni-sə-tē\ *n*

car•ci•no•ma \ˌkärs-ᵊn-ˈō-mə\ *n, pl* **-mas** *also* **-ma•ta** \-tə\ : a malignant tumor of epithelial origin — **car•ci•no•ma•tous** \-təs\ *adj*

[1]**card** \ˈkärd\ *vb* : to comb with a card : cleanse and untangle before spinning — **card•er** *n*

[2]**card** *n* : an instrument for combing fibers (as wool or cotton)

[3]**card** *n* **1** : PLAYING CARD **2** *pl* : a game played with playing cards; *also* : card playing **3** : an emotional issue used to one's advantage (as in a political campaign) **4** ♦ : a usually clownishly amusing person : WAG **5** : a flat stiff usually small piece of paper, cardboard, or plastic often bearing pictures or information **6** : PROGRAM; *esp* : a sports program

♦ comedian, comic, humorist, jester, joker, wag, wit

[4]**card** *vb* **1** : to list or schedule on a card **2** : SCORE **3** : to ask for identification (as at a bar)

[5]**card** *abbr* cardinal

car•da•mom \ˈkär-də-məm\ *n* : the aromatic capsular fruit of an East Indian herb related to the ginger whose seeds are used as a spice or condiment and in medicine; *also* : this plant

card•board \ˈkärd-ˌbōrd\ *n* : a material thicker than paper and made from cellulose fiber

card–car•ry•ing \ˈkärd-ˌkar-ē-iŋ\ *adj* : being a regularly enrolled member of an organization (as a political party)

card catalog *n* : a catalog (as of books) in which the entries are arranged systematically on cards

car•di•ac \ˈkär-dē-ˌak\ *adj* **1** : of, relating to, or located near the heart **2** : of, relating to, or affected with heart disease

car•di•gan \ˈkär-di-gən\ *n* : a sweater or jacket usually without a collar and with a full-length opening in the front

[1]**car•di•nal** \ˈkärd-nəl, ˈkär-dᵊn-əl\ *n* **1** : an ecclesiastical official of the Roman Catholic Church ranking next below the pope **2** : a crested No. American finch that is nearly completely red in the male

[2]**cardinal** *adj* **1** ♦ : of basic importance : CHIEF, MAIN, PRIMARY **2** : very serious ⟨a ~ sin⟩ — **car•di•nal•ly** *adv*

♦ arch, central, chief, dominant, first, foremost, grand, key, main, paramount, predominant, preeminent, premier, primary, principal, sovereign, supreme

car•di•nal•ate \ˈkärd-nə-lət, ˈkär-dᵊn-ə-let, -ˌlāt\ *n* : the office, rank, or dignity of a cardinal

cardinal flower *n* : a No. American plant that bears a spike of brilliant red flowers

cardinal number *n* : a number (as 1, 5, 82, 357) that is used in simple counting and answers the question "how many?"

cardinal point *n* : one of the four principal compass points north, south, east, and west

car•dio \ˈkär-dē-ō\ *adj* : CARDIOVASCULAR 2

car•di•ol•o•gy \ˌkär-dē-ˈä-lə-jē\ *n* : the study of the heart and its action and diseases — **car•di•ol•o•gist** \-jist\ *n*

car•dio•pul•mo•nary resuscitation \ˌkär-dē-ō-ˈpu̇l-mə-ˌner-ē-\ *n* : a procedure to restore normal breathing after cardiac arrest that includes the clearance of air passages to the lungs, mouth-to-mouth method of artificial respiration, and heart massage by the exertion of pressure on the chest

car•dio•vas•cu•lar \-ˈvas-kyə-lər\ *adj* **1 :** of or relating to the heart and blood vessels **2 :** causing a temporary increase in heart rate ⟨a ~ workout⟩

card•sharp•er \ˈkärd-ˌshär-pər\ *or* **card•sharp** \-ˌshärp\ *n* **:** a cheater at cards

¹care \ˈker\ *n* **1 :** a disquieted state of uncertainty and responsibility **:** ANXIETY **2** ♦ **:** painstaking or watchful attention **3** ♦ **:** responsibility for the care of another ⟨under a doctor's ~⟩ **4 :** a person or thing that is an object of attention, anxiety, or solicitude

♦ [2] alertness, carefulness, caution, circumspection, heedfulness ♦ [2] carefulness, heed, heedfulness, pains, scrupulousness *Ant* carelessness, heedlessness ♦ [3] custody, guardianship, keeping, safekeeping, trust, ward ♦ [3] charge, guidance, headship, oversight, regulation, superintendence, supervision

²care *vb* **cared; car•ing 1 :** to feel trouble or anxiety **2 :** to feel interest or concern ⟨~ about freedom⟩ **3** ♦ **:** to give care — usually used with *for* ⟨~ for the sick⟩ **4 a** ♦ **:** to have a liking, fondness, taste, or inclination **b :** have regard or respect **5 :** to be concerned about ⟨nobody ~*s* what I do⟩ **6 :** to have or express a wish for — usually used with *for*

♦ *usu* **care for** [3] aid, minister, mother, nurse ♦ *usu* **care for** [3] attend, mind, oversee, superintend, supervise, tend ♦ *usu* **care for** [4a] accept, approve, countenance, favor (*or* favour), OK, subscribe

CARE *abbr* Cooperative for American Relief to Everywhere

ca•reen \kə-ˈrēn\ *vb* **1 :** to put (a ship or boat) on a beach especially in order to clean or repair its hull **2** ♦ **:** to sway from side to side **3 :** CAREER

♦ lurch, pitch, rock, roll, seesaw, sway, toss, wobble

¹ca•reer \kə-ˈrir\ *n* **1 :** COURSE, PASSAGE; *also* **:** speed in a course ⟨ran at full ~⟩ **2 :** an occupation or profession followed as a life's work

²career *vb* ♦ **:** to go at top speed especially in a headlong manner

♦ barrel, bowl, fly, hurry, hurtle, pelt, race, rocket, rush, shoot, speed, tear, zip, zoom

care•free \ˈker-ˌfrē\ *adj* ♦ **:** free from care or worry

♦ careless, cavalier, easygoing, gay, happy-go-lucky, insouciant, lighthearted, unconcerned *Ant* careworn

care•ful \-fəl\ *adj* **care•ful•ler; care•ful•lest 1** ♦ **:** using or taking care **2** ♦ **:** marked by solicitude, caution, or prudence — **care•ful•ly** *adv*

♦ [1] conscientious, fussy, meticulous, painstaking ♦ [2] alert, cautious, circumspect, considerate, gingerly, guarded, heedful, safe, wary *Ant* careless, heedless, incautious, unguarded, unsafe, unwary

care•ful•ness *n* ♦ **:** the quality of being careful **:** close or steady attention (as to a task)

♦ alertness, care, caution, circumspection, heedfulness

care•giv•er \-ˌgi-vər\ *n* **:** a person who provides direct care (as for children, the disabled, or the chronically ill)

care•less \-ləs\ *adj* **1 :** free from care **:** UNTROUBLED **2** ♦ **:** having no concern or interest ⟨~ of the consequences⟩ **3** ♦ **:** not taking care especially to avoid danger or harm **4 a** ♦ **:** not taking ordinary or proper care **b :** not showing or receiving care — **care•less•ly** *adv*

♦ [2, 3] heedless, mindless, unguarded, unsafe, unwary *Ant* alert, cautious, circumspect, gingerly, guarded, heedful, safe, wary ♦ [4a] derelict, lax, negligent, remiss, slack

care•less•ness *n* ♦ **:** failure to exercise the care that a reasonably prudent person would in like circumstances

♦ dereliction, heedlessness, laxness, negligence, remissness, slackness

¹ca•ress \kə-ˈres\ *n* **:** a tender or loving touch or embrace

²caress *vb* ♦ **:** to touch or stroke tenderly or lovingly — **ca•ress•er** *n*

♦ fondle, love, pat, pet, stroke

car•et \ˈkar-ət\ *n* **:** a mark ^ used to indicate the place where something is to be inserted

care•tak•er \ˈker-ˌtā-kər\ *n* **1** ♦ **:** one in charge usually as occupant in place of an absent owner **2 :** one temporarily fulfilling the functions of an office

♦ custodian, guardian, janitor, keeper, warden, watchman

care•worn \-ˌwōrn\ *adj* **:** showing the effects of grief or anxiety

car•fare \ˈkär-ˌfar\ *n* **:** passenger fare (as on a streetcar or bus)

car•go \ˈkär-gō\ *n, pl* **cargoes** *or* **cargos** ♦ **:** the goods carried in a ship, airplane, or vehicle **:** FREIGHT

♦ freight, load, payload, shipment ♦ burden, freight, haul, lading, load, payload, weight

Ca•rib•be•an \ˌkar-ə-ˈbē-ən, kə-ˈri-bē-ən\ *adj* **:** of or relating to the eastern and southern West Indies or the Caribbean Sea

car•i•bou \ˈkar-ə-ˌbü\ *n, pl* **caribou** *or* **caribous :** a large circumpolar gregarious deer of northern taiga and tundra that usually has palmate antlers in both sexes — used especially for one of the New World

¹car•i•ca•ture \ˈkar-i-kə-ˌchür\ *n* **1** ♦ **:** distorted representation to produce a ridiculous effect **2** ♦ **:** a representation especially in literature or art having the qualities of caricature — **car•i•ca•tur•ist** \-ist\ *n*

♦ [1] farce, joke, mockery, parody, sham, travesty ♦ [2] burlesque, parody, spoof, takeoff

²caricature *vb* ♦ **:** to make or draw a caricature of **:** represent in caricature

♦ burlesque, imitate, mimic, mock, parody, take off, travesty

car•ies \ˈkar-ēz\ *n, pl* **caries :** tooth decay

car•il•lon \ˈkar-ə-ˌlän\ *n* **:** a set of tuned bells sounded by hammers controlled from a keyboard

car•i•ous \ˈkar-ē-əs\ *adj* **:** affected with caries

car•jack•ing \ˈkär-ˌja-kiŋ\ *n* **:** the theft of an automobile by force or intimidation — **car•jack•er** *n*

car•load \ˈkär-ˌlōd\ *n* **:** a load that fills a car

car•mi•na•tive \kär-ˈmi-nə-tiv\ *adj* **:** expelling gas from the alimentary canal — **carminative** *n*

car•mine \ˈkär-mən, -ˌmīn\ *n* **:** a vivid red

car•nage \ˈkär-nij\ *n* ♦ **:** great destruction of life **:** SLAUGHTER

♦ butchery, massacre, slaughter

car•nal \ˈkärn-ᵊl\ *adj* **1** ♦ **:** of or relating to the body **2** ♦ **:** relating to or given to sensual pleasures and appetites **3** ♦ **:** of or relating to this world **:** earthly rather than heavenly or spiritual — **car•nal•i•ty** \kär-ˈna-lə-tē\ *n* — **car•nal•ly** *adv*

♦ [1] animal, bodily, corporal, fleshly, material, physical, somatic ♦ [2] fleshly, luscious, sensual, sensuous, voluptuous ♦ [3] earthly, fleshly, material, mundane, temporal, terrestrial, worldly

car•na•tion \kär-ˈnā-shən\ *n* **:** a cultivated pink of any of numerous usually double-flowered varieties derived from an Old World species

car•nau•ba wax \kär-ˈnȯ-bə-, -ˈnau̇-; ˌkär-nə-ˈü-bə-\ *n* **:** a brittle yellowish wax from a Brazilian palm that is used especially in polishes

car•ne•lian \kär-ˈnēl-yən\ *n* **:** a hard tough reddish quartz used as a gem

car•ni•val \ˈkär-nə-vəl\ *n* **1 :** a season of merrymaking just before Lent **2 :** a boisterous merrymaking **3 :** a traveling enterprise offering amusements **4** ♦ **:** an organized program of entertainment

♦ celebration, festival, festivity, fete, fiesta, gala, jubilee

car•niv•o•ra \kär-ˈni-və-rə\ *n pl* **:** carnivorous mammals

car•ni•vore \ˈkär-nə-ˌvōr\ *n* **:** a flesh-eating animal; *esp* **:** any of an order of mammals (as dogs, cats, bears, minks, and seals) feeding mostly on animal flesh

car•niv•o•rous \kär-ˈni-və-rəs\ *adj* **1 :** feeding on animal tissues **2 :** of or relating to the carnivores — **car•niv•o•rous•ly** *adv* — **car•niv•o•rous•ness** *n*

car•ny *or* **car•ney** *or* **car•nie** \ˈkär-nē\ *n, pl* **carnies** *or* **carneys 1 :** CARNIVAL 3 **2 :** one who works with a carnival

¹car•ol \ˈkar-əl\ *n* ♦ **:** a song of joy or devotion

♦ anthem, canticle, chorale, hymn, psalm, spiritual

²carol *vb* **:** to sing especially in a cheerful manner

car•ol•er *or* **car•ol•ler** *n* ♦ **:** one that carols

♦ singer, songster, vocalist, voice

¹car•om \ˈkar-əm\ *n* **1 :** a shot in billiards in which the cue ball strikes two other balls **2 :** a rebounding especially at an angle

²carom *vb* ♦ **:** to strike and rebound

♦ bounce, glance, rebound, ricochet, skim, skip

car·o·tene \ˈkar-ə-ˌtēn\ *n* **:** any of several orange to red pigments (as beta-carotene) formed especially in plants and used as a source of vitamin A

ca·rot·en·oid \kə-ˈrä-tə-ˌnȯid\ *n* **:** any of various usually yellow to red pigments (as carotenes) found widely in plants and animals

ca·rot·id \kə-ˈrä-təd\ *adj* **:** of, relating to, or being the chief artery or pair of arteries that pass up the neck and supply the head — **carotid** *n*

ca·rous·al \kə-ˈrau̇-zəl\ *n* **:** a period of heavy drinking **:** CAROUSE

ca·rouse \kə-ˈrauz\ *n* **:** a drunken revel — **carouse** *vb* — **ca·rous·er** *n*

car·ou·sel \ˌkar-ə-ˈsel, ˈkar-ə-ˌsel\ *n* **1 :** MERRY-GO-ROUND **2 :** a circular conveyor

[1]**carp** \ˈkärp\ *vb* ♦ **:** to find fault — **carp** *n*

♦ beef, bellyache, cavil, complain, crab, croak, fuss, gripe, grouse, growl, grumble, kick, moan, squawk, wail, whine

[2]**carp** *n, pl* **carp** *or* **carps :** a large variable Asian freshwater fish of sluggish waters often raised for food

[1]**car·pal** \ˈkär-pəl\ *adj* **:** relating to the wrist or the bones of the wrist

[2]**carpal** *n* **:** a carpal element or bone

carpal tunnel syndrome *n* **:** a condition characterized especially by weakness, pain, and disturbances of sensation (as numbness) in the hand and fingers and caused by compression of a nerve in the wrist

car park *n, chiefly Can and Brit* **:** a lot or garage for parking

car·pe di·em \ˈkär-pe-ˈdē-ˌem, -ˈdī-\ *n* **:** enjoyment of the present without concern for the future

car·pel \ˈkär-pəl\ *n* **:** one of the highly modified leaves that together form the ovary of a flower of a seed plant

car·pen·ter \ˈkär-pən-tər\ *n* **:** one who builds or repairs wooden structures — **carpenter** *vb* — **car·pen·try** \-trē\ *n*

carp·er *n* ♦ **:** an excessive faultfinder

♦ castigator, caviler, censurer, critic, faultfinder, nitpicker, railer, scold

[1]**car·pet** \ˈkär-pət\ *n* **:** a heavy fabric used as a floor covering

[2]**carpet** *vb* ♦ **:** to cover with or as if with a carpet

♦ blanket, coat, cover, overlay, overlie, overspread

car·pet·bag \-ˌbag\ *n* **:** a traveling bag common in the 19th century

car·pet·bag·ger \-ˌba-gər\ *n* **:** a Northerner in the South after the American Civil War usually seeking private gain under the reconstruction governments

car·pet·ing \ˈkär-pə-tiŋ\ *n* **:** material for carpets; *also* **:** CARPETS

carping *adj* ♦ **:** marked by or inclined to querulous and often perverse criticism

♦ captious, critical, hypercritical, overcritical

car pool *n* **:** an arrangement in which a group of people commute together by car; *also* **:** a group having this arrangement — **car-pool** \-ˌpül\ *vb*

car·port \ˈkär-ˌpōrt\ *n* **:** an open-sided automobile shelter

car·pus \ˈkär-pəs\ *n* **:** the wrist or its bones

car·ra·geen·an *or* **car·ra·geen·in** \ˌkar-ə-ˈgē-nən\ *n* **:** a colloid extracted especially from a dark purple branching seaweed and used in foods especially to stabilize and thicken them

car·rel \ˈkar-əl\ *n* **:** a table often partitioned or enclosed for individual study in a library

car·riage \ˈkar-ij\ *n* **1 :** the act of carrying **2 :** manner of holding the body **3 :** a wheeled vehicle **4** *Brit* **:** a railway passenger coach **5 :** a movable part of a machine for supporting some other moving part ⟨a typewriter ∼⟩

carriage trade *n* **:** trade from well-to-do or upper-class people

car·ri·er \ˈkar-ē-ər\ *n* **1 :** one that carries **2 :** a person or organization in the transportation business **3 :** AIRCRAFT CARRIER **4 :** one whose system carries the causative agents of a disease but who is immune to the disease **5 :** an individual having a gene for a trait or condition that is not expressed outwardly **6 :** an electromagnetic wave whose amplitude or frequency is varied in order to convey a radio or television signal

carrier pigeon *n* **:** a pigeon used especially to carry messages

car·ri·on \ˈker-ē-ən\ *n* **:** dead and decaying flesh

car·rot \ˈker-ət\ *n* **:** the elongated usually orange root of a common garden plant that is eaten as a vegetable; *also* **:** this plant

carrousel *var of* CAROUSEL

[1]**car·ry** \ˈka-rē, ˈker-ē\ *vb* **car·ried; car·ry·ing 1** ♦ **:** to move while supporting **:** TRANSPORT, CONVEY **2 :** to influence by mental or emotional appeal **3 :** to get possession or control of **:** CAPTURE, WIN **4 :** to transfer from one place (as a column) to another ⟨∼ a number in adding⟩ **5 :** to have or wear on one's person; *also* **:** to bear within one **6** ♦ **:** to have within or as part of itself **:** INVOLVE, INCLUDE **7 :** to hold or bear (oneself) in a specified way **8 :** to keep in stock for sale **9** ♦ **:** to sustain the weight or burden of **:** SUPPORT **10 :** to prolong in space, time, or degree **11 :** to keep on one's books as a debtor **12 :** to succeed in (an election) **13 :** to win adoption (as in a legislature) **14 a :** to present to the public for use or as entertainment **b :** PUBLISH, PRINT **15 :** to reach or penetrate to a distance

♦ [1] bear, cart, convey, ferry, haul, lug, pack, tote, transport ♦ [6] comprehend, contain, embrace, encompass, entail, include, involve, number, take in ♦ [9] bear, bolster, brace, buttress, prop, shore, stay, support, uphold

[2]**carry** *n* **1 :** the range of a gun or projectile or of a struck or thrown ball **2 :** PORTAGE **3 :** an act or method of carrying ⟨fireman's ∼⟩

car·ry·all \ˈkar-ē-ˌȯl\ *n* ♦ **:** a large bag or carrying case

♦ grip, handbag, portmanteau, suitcase, traveling bag

carry away *vb* ♦ **:** to arouse to a high and often excessive degree of emotion

♦ enrapture, enthrall, entrance, ravish, transport

carrying charge *n* **:** a charge added to the price of merchandise sold on the installment plan

car·ry–on *n* **:** a piece of luggage suitable for being carried aboard an airplane by a passenger — **carry–on** *adj*

carry on *vb* **1** ♦ **:** to have the direction of **:** CONDUCT, MANAGE **2** ♦ **:** to behave in a foolish, excited, or improper manner **3 :** to continue in spite of hindrance or discouragement

♦ [1] administer, conduct, control, direct, govern, guide, handle, manage, operate, oversee, regulate, run, superintend, supervise ♦ [2] act out, act up, misbehave

carry out *vb* **1** ♦ **:** to bring to a successful conclusion **2 :** to put into execution

♦ accomplish, achieve, commit, compass, do, execute, follow through, fulfill, make, perform

car·sick \ˈkär-ˌsik\ *adj* **:** affected with motion sickness especially in an automobile — **car sickness** *n*

[1]**cart** \ˈkärt\ *n* **1 :** a heavy 2-wheeled wagon **2 :** a small wheeled vehicle

[2]**cart** *vb* ♦ **:** to convey in or as if in a cart — **cart·er** *n*

♦ bear, carry, convey, ferry, haul, lug, pack, tote, transport

cart·age \ˈkär-tij\ *n* **:** the act of or rate charged for carting

carte blanche \ˈkärt-ˈblä^{n}sh\ *n, pl* **cartes blanches** *same or* -ˈblä^{n}-shəz\ **:** full discretionary power

car·tel \kär-ˈtel\ *n* ♦ **:** a combination of independent business enterprises designed to limit competition

♦ combination, combine, syndicate, trust

car·ti·lage \ˈkär-tə-lij\ *n* **:** a usually translucent somewhat elastic tissue that composes most of the skeleton of young vertebrate embryos and later is mostly converted to bone in higher vertebrates — **car·ti·lag·i·nous** \ˌkärt-^{ə}l-ˈa-jə-nəs\ *adj*

cartilaginous fish *n* **:** any of a class of fishes (as a shark or ray) having the skeleton wholly or largely composed of cartilage

car·tog·ra·phy \kär-ˈtä-grə-fē\ *n* **:** the making of maps — **car·tog·ra·pher** *n* — **car·to·graph·ic** \ˌkär-tə-ˈgra-fik\ *adj*

car·ton \ˈkärt-^{ə}n\ *n* **:** a cardboard box or container

car·toon \kär-ˈtün\ *n* **1** ♦ **:** a preparatory sketch (as for a painting) **2 :** a drawing intended as humor, caricature, or satire **3** ♦ **:** a group of cartoons or drawings arranged in a narrative sequence **:** COMIC STRIP — **cartoon** *vb* — **car·toon·ist** *n*

♦ [1] delineation, drawing, sketch ♦ [3] comic strip

car·tridge \ˈkär-trij\ *n* **1 :** a tube containing a complete charge for a firearm **2 :** a container of material for insertion into an apparatus **3 :** a small case containing a phonograph needle and transducer that is attached to a tonearm **4 :** a case containing a magnetic tape or disk **5 :** a case for holding integrated circuits containing a computer program

cart·wheel \ˈkärt-ˌhwēl\ *n* **1 :** a large coin (as a silver dollar) **2 :** a lateral handspring with arms and legs extended

carve \ˈkärv\ *vb* **carved; carv·ing 1 :** to cut with care or precision **:** shape by cutting **2** ♦ **:** to cut or hew out especially with some effort **:** make or get by or as if by cutting — often used with *out* ⟨∼ out a fortune⟩ **3 :** to slice and serve meat at table — **carv·er** *n*

♦ *usu* **carve out** build, forge, grind, hammer, work out

cary·at·id \ˌkar-ē-ˈa-təd\ *n, pl* **-ids** *or* **-i·des** \-ˈa-tə-ˌdēz\ **:** a sculptured draped female figure used as an architectural column

CAS *abbr* certificate of advanced study
ca•sa•ba \kə-ˈsä-bə\ *n* **:** any of several muskmelons with a yellow rind and sweet flesh
[1]**cas•cade** \ˌkas-ˈkād\ *n* **1 :** a steep usually small waterfall **2 :** something arranged in a series or succession of stages so that each stage derives from or acts upon the product of the preceding
[2]**cas•cade** *vb* **cas•cad•ed; cas•cad•ing :** to fall, pass, or connect in or as if in a cascade
cas•cara \kas-ˈkar-ə\ *n* **:** the dried bark of a small Pacific coastal tree of the U.S. and southern Canada used as a laxative; *also* **:** this tree
[1]**case** \ˈkās\ *n* **1 a ♦ :** a set of circumstances or conditions **b ♦ :** a set of circumstances constituting a problem **:** a matter for consideration or decision **2 :** an inflectional form of a noun, pronoun, or adjective indicating its grammatical relation to other words; *also* **:** such a relation whether indicated by inflection or not **3 :** what actually exists or happens **:** FACT **4 :** a suit or action in law **:** CAUSE **5 ♦ :** a convincing argument **6 a :** an instance of disease or injury **b :** a sick individual especially when awaiting medical care or treatment **:** PATIENT **7 ♦ :** an instance or example of a particular type **:** INSTANCE, EXAMPLE — **in case :** as a precaution — **in case of :** in the event of

♦ [1a] contingency, event, eventuality, possibility ♦ [1b] knot, matter, problem, trouble ♦ [5] argument, defense (*or* defence), explanation, rationale, reason ♦ [7] example, exemplar, illustration, instance, representative, sample, specimen

[2]**case** *n* **1 ♦ :** a box or container for holding something; *also* **:** a box with its contents **2 ♦ :** an outer covering **3 :** a divided tray for holding printing type **4 :** CASING 2

♦ [1] box, caddy, casket, chest, locker, trunk ♦ [2] armor, capsule, casing, cocoon, cover, housing, husk, jacket, pod, sheath, shell

[3]**case** *vb* **cased; cas•ing 1 :** to enclose in or cover with a case **2 :** to inspect especially with intent to rob
ca•sein \ˈkā-ˌsēn, kā-ˈ\ *n* **:** any of several phosphorus-containing proteins occurring in or produced from milk
case•ment \ˈkās-mənt\ *n* **:** a window that opens like a door
case•work \-ˌwərk\ *n* **:** social work that involves the individual person or family — **case•work•er** *n*
[1]**cash** \ˈkash\ *n* **1 :** ready money **2 ♦ :** money or its equivalent paid at the time of purchase or delivery

♦ currency, dough, lucre, money, pelf, tender

[2]**cash** *vb* **:** to pay or obtain cash for
ca•shew \ˈka-shü, kə-ˈshü\ *n* **:** an edible kidney-shaped nut of a tropical American tree related to the sumacs; *also* **:** the tree
[1]**ca•shier** \ka-ˈshir\ *vb* **♦ :** to dismiss from service; *esp* **:** to dismiss in disgrace

♦ dismiss, fire, remove, retire, sack

[2]**cash•ier** \ka-ˈshir\ *n* **1 :** a bank official responsible for moneys received and paid out **2 :** a person who receives and records payments
cashier's check *n* **:** a check drawn by a bank upon its own funds and signed by its cashier
cash in *vb* **1 :** to convert into cash ⟨*cash in* bonds⟩ **2 :** to settle accounts and withdraw from a gambling game or business deal **3 ♦ :** to obtain advantage or financial profit — often used with *on* ⟨*cash in* on a best seller⟩

♦ *usu* **cash in on** abuse, capitalize, exploit, impose, play, use

cash•less \ˈkash-ləs\ *adj* **:** relying on monetary transactions that use electronic means rather than cash
cash•mere \ˈkazh-ˌmir, ˈkash-\ *n* **:** fine wool from the undercoat of an Indian goat (**cashmere goat**) or a yarn spun of this; *also* **:** a soft twilled fabric orig. woven from this yarn
cash out *vb* **:** to convert noncash assets into cash
cash register *n* **:** a business machine that usually has a money drawer, indicates each sale, and records the money received
cash–strapped \ˈkash-ˌstrapt\ *adj* **:** lacking sufficient money
cas•ing \ˈkā-siŋ\ *n* **1 ♦ :** something that encases **2 :** the frame of a door or window

♦ armor, capsule, case, cocoon, cover, housing, husk, jacket, pod, sheath, shell

ca•si•no \kə-ˈsē-nō\ *n, pl* **-nos 1 :** a building or room for social amusements; *esp* **:** one used for gambling **2** *also* **cas•si•no :** a card game in which players win cards by matching those on the table
cask \ˈkask\ *n* **♦ :** a barrel-shaped container usually for liquids; *also* **:** the quantity held by such a container

♦ barrel, hogshead, keg, pipe, puncheon

cas•ket \ˈkas-kət\ *n* **1 ♦ :** a small chest or box (as for jewels) **2 :** a usually fancy coffin for burying a corpse **:** COFFIN

♦ box, caddy, case, chest, locker, trunk

casque \ˈkask\ *n* **:** HELMET
cas•sa•va \kə-ˈsä-və\ *n* **:** any of several tropical spurges with rootstocks yielding a nutritious starch from which tapioca is prepared; *also* **:** the rootstock or its starch
cas•se•role \ˈka-sə-ˌrōl\ *n* **1 :** a dish in which food may be baked and served **2 :** food cooked and served in a casserole
cas•sette *also* **ca•sette** \kə-ˈset\ *n* **1 :** a lightproof container for photographic plates or film **2 :** a plastic case containing magnetic tape
cas•sia \ˈka-shə\ *n* **1 :** a coarse cinnamon bark **2 :** any of a genus of leguminous herbs, shrubs, and trees of warm regions including several which yield senna
cas•sit•er•ite \kə-ˈsi-tə-ˌrīt\ *n* **:** a dark mineral that is the chief tin ore
cas•sock \ˈka-sək\ *n* **:** an ankle-length garment worn especially by Roman Catholic and Anglican clergy
cas•so•wary \ˈka-sə-ˌwer-ē\ *n, pl* **-war•ies :** any of a genus of large flightless birds closely related to the emu
[1]**cast** \ˈkast\ *vb* **cast; cast•ing 1 ♦ :** to cause to move or send forth by throwing **:** THROW, FLING **2 ♦ :** to point, extend, or project in a specified line or course **:** DIRECT ⟨~ a glance⟩ **3 :** to deposit (a ballot) formally **4 ♦ :** to throw off, out, or away **:** DISCARD, SHED **5 :** COMPUTE; *esp* **:** to add up **6 :** to assign the parts of (a play) to actors; *also* **:** to assign to a role or part **7 a :** to shape (a substance) by pouring it in liquid or plastic form into a mold and letting it harden without pressure **b ♦ :** to give form to **:** establish or create in a particular form ⟨the book is ~ in the form of an autobiography⟩ **8 :** to make (as a knot or stitch) by looping or catching up

♦ [1] catapult, chuck, dash, fire, fling, heave, hurl, hurtle, launch, peg, pelt, pitch, sling, throw, toss ♦ [2] aim, bend, direct, head, level, set, train ♦ [4] discard, ditch, dump, fling, jettison, junk, lose, reject, scrap, shed, shuck, slough, throw away, throw out, unload ♦ [7b] compose, craft, draft, draw, formulate, frame, prepare

[2]**cast** *n* **1 :** THROW, FLING **2 :** a throw of dice **3 :** the set of actors in a dramatic production **4 :** something formed in or as if in a mold; *also* **:** a rigid surgical dressing (as for protecting and supporting a fractured bone) **5 ♦ :** a slight change in the appearance of a substance by a trace of some added hue **:** a trace of a particular quality **:** TINGE, HUE **6 a :** a turning of the eye in a particular direction **b ♦ :** a physical form or character **:** SHAPE **c ♦ :** facial aspect or vocal intonation as indicative of feeling **:** LOOK **7 :** something thrown out or off, shed, or expelled ⟨worm ~*s*⟩ **8 :** a forecast or conjecture concerning future events or conditions

♦ [5] color (*or* colour), hue, shade, tinge, tint, tone ♦ [6b] configuration, conformation, figure, form, geometry, shape ♦ [6c] countenance, expression, face, look, visage

cast about *vb* **♦ :** to seek here and there **:** look around

♦ cast around, forage, hunt, pursue, quest, search (for *or* out), seek

cas•ta•net \ˌkas-tə-ˈnet\ *n* **:** a rhythm instrument consisting of two small wooden, ivory, or plastic shells held in the hand and clicked together
cast around *vb* **♦ :** to look around **:** SEEK

♦ cast about, forage, hunt, pursue, quest, search (for *or* out), seek

[1]**cast•away** \ˈkas-tə-ˌwā\ *adj* **1 :** thrown away **:** REJECTED **2 :** cast adrift or ashore as a survivor of a shipwreck
[2]**castaway** *n* **♦ :** one who has been cast away, cast off, or rejected

♦ outcast, reject

caste \ˈkast\ *n* **1 :** one of the hereditary social classes in Hinduism **2 ♦ :** a division of a society based on wealth, inherited rank, or occupation **3 :** social position **:** PRESTIGE **4 :** a system of rigid social stratification

♦ class, estate, folk, order, stratum

cas•tel•lat•ed \ˈkas-tə-ˌlā-təd\ *adj* **:** having battlements like a castle
cast•er \ˈkas-tər\ *n* **1** *or* **cas•tor :** a small container to hold salt or pepper at the table **2 :** a small wheel that turns freely and is used to support and move furniture, trucks, and equipment
cas•ti•gate \ˈkas-tə-ˌgāt\ *vb* **-gat•ed; -gat•ing ♦ :** to punish or criticize severely

♦ admonish, chide, lecture, rail (at *or* against), rate, rebuke, reprimand, scold ♦ chasten, chastise, correct, discipline, penalize, punish

cas·ti·ga·tion \ˌkas-tə-ˈgā-shən\ *n* ♦ : severe punishment or criticism

♦ chastisement, correction, desert, discipline, nemesis, penalty, punishment, wrath

cas·ti·ga·tor \ˈkas-tə-ˌgā-tər\ *n* ♦ : one that castigates

♦ carper, caviler, censurer, critic, faultfinder, nitpicker, railer, scold

cast·ing \ˈkas-tiŋ\ *n* **1 :** CAST 7 **2 :** something cast in a mold
casting vote *n* **:** a deciding vote cast by a presiding officer to break a tie
cast iron *n* **:** a hard brittle alloy of iron, carbon, and silicon cast in a mold
cas·tle \ˈka-səl\ *n* **1 :** a large fortified building or set of buildings **2** ♦ **:** a large or imposing house **3 :** [3]ROOK

♦ estate, hall, manor, mansion, palace, villa

cast–off \ˈkas-ˌtȯf\ *adj* **:** thrown away or aside — **cast·off** *n*
cas·tor oil \ˈkas-tər-\ *n* **:** a thick yellowish oil extracted from the poisonous seeds of an herb (**castor–oil plant**) and used as a lubricant and purgative
cast out *vb* ♦ **:** to banish, expel, or drive away (as from a former home or country)

♦ banish, boot (out), bounce, chase, dismiss, drum, eject, expel, oust, rout, run off, throw out

cas·trate \ˈkas-ˌtrāt\ *vb* **cas·trat·ed; cas·trat·ing :** to deprive of sex glands and especially testes — **cas·tra·tion** \kas-ˈtrā-shən\ *n* — **cas·tra·tor** \-ər\ *n*
ca·su·al \ˈka-zhə-wəl\ *adj* **1** ♦ **:** resulting from or occurring by chance **2** ♦ **:** occurring without regularity **:** OCCASIONAL **3** ♦ **:** feeling or showing little concern **:** NONCHALANT **4** ♦ **:** designed for informal use ⟨~ clothing⟩ — **ca·su·al·ly** *adv*

♦ [1] accidental, chance, fluky, fortuitous, incidental, unintended, unintentional, unplanned, unpremeditated, unwitting ♦ [2] choppy, discontinuous, erratic, fitful, intermittent, irregular, occasional, spasmodic, sporadic, spotty, unsteady ♦ [3] apathetic, disinterested, indifferent, insouciant, nonchalant, perfunctory, unconcerned, uncurious, uninterested ♦ [4] everyday, informal, workaday *Ant* dressy, formal

ca·su·al·ness *n* **:** the quality, state, or fact of being casual or disinterested
ca·su·al·ty \ˈka-zhəl-tē, ˈka-zhə-wəl-\ *n, pl* **-ties 1** ♦ **:** a serious or fatal accident **2 :** a military person lost through death, injury, sickness, or capture or through being missing in action **3** ♦ **:** a person or thing injured, lost, or destroyed

♦ [1] accident, mishap ♦ [3] fatality, loss, victim

ca·su·ist·ry \ˈka-zhə-wə-strē\ *n, pl* **-ries :** specious argument **:** RATIONALIZATION — **ca·su·ist** \-wist\ *n* — **ca·su·is·tic** \ˌka-zhə-ˈwis-tik\ *or* **ca·su·is·ti·cal** \-ti-kəl\ *adj*
ca·sus bel·li \ˌkä-səs-ˈbe-ˌlē, ˌkā-səs-ˈbe-ˌlī\ *n, pl* **ca·sus belli** \ˌkä-ˌsüs-, ˌkā-\ **:** a cause or pretext for a declaration of war
[1]cat \ˈkat\ *n* **1** ♦ **:** a carnivorous mammal long domesticated as a pet and for catching rats and mice **2 :** any of a family of animals (as the lion, lynx, or leopard) including the domestic cat **3 :** a spiteful woman **4 :** GUY

♦ feline, kitty, puss

[2]cat *abbr* catalog
ca·tab·o·lism \kə-ˈta-bə-ˌli-zəm\ *n* **:** destructive metabolism involving the release of energy and resulting in the breakdown of complex materials — **cat·a·bol·ic** \ˌka-tə-ˈbä-lik\ *adj*
cat·a·clysm \ˈka-tə-ˌkli-zəm\ *n* **1** ♦ **:** a surging flood of water **:** DELUGE **2** ♦ **:** a violent change or upheaval

♦ [1] cataract, deluge, flood, inundation, overflow, spate, torrent ♦ [2] calamity, catastrophe, debacle, disaster, tragedy ♦ [2] convulsion, paroxysm, storm, tempest, tumult, upheaval, uproar

cat·a·clys·mic \ˌka-tə-ˈkliz-mik\ *or* **cat·a·clys·mal** \-ˈkliz-məl\ *adj* ♦ **:** of, relating to, or having the characteristics of a cataclysm ⟨a ~ nuclear war⟩

♦ calamitous, catastrophic, destructive, devastating, disastrous, fatal, fateful, ruinous, unfortunate

cat·a·comb \ˈka-tə-ˌkōm\ *n* **:** an underground burial place with galleries and recesses for tombs
cat·a·falque \ˈka-tə-ˌfalk, -ˌfȯlk, -ˌfȯk\ *n* **:** an ornamental structure sometimes used in solemn funerals to hold the body
cat·a·lep·sy \ˈka-tə-ˌlep-sē\ *n, pl* **-sies :** a trancelike nervous condition characterized especially by loss of voluntary motion — **cat·a·lep·tic** \ˌka-tə-ˈlep-tik\ *adj or n*
[1]cat·a·log *or* **cat·a·logue** \ˈkat-ᵊl-ˌȯg\ *n* **1** ♦ **:** a simple series of items (as the names of persons or objects) **:** LIST, REGISTER **2 :** a systematic list of items with descriptive details; *also* **:** a book containing such a list

♦ checklist, list, listing, menu, register, registry, roll, roster, schedule, table

[2]catalog *or* **catalogue** *vb* **-loged** *or* **-logued; -log·ing** *or* **-logu·ing 1 :** to make a catalog of **2** ♦ **:** to enter in a catalog — **cat·a·log·er** *or* **cat·a·logu·er** *n*

♦ enroll, enter, index, inscribe, list, put down, record, register, schedule, slate

ca·tal·pa \kə-ˈtal-pə\ *n* **:** any of a genus of broad-leaved trees with showy flowers and long slim pods
ca·tal·y·sis \kə-ˈta-lə-səs\ *n, pl* **-y·ses** \-ˌsēz\ **:** a change and especially increase in the rate of a chemical reaction brought about by a substance (**cat·a·lyst** \ˈkat-ᵊl-ist\) that is itself unchanged at the end of the reaction — **cat·a·lyt·ic** \ˌkat-ᵊl-ˈi-tik\ *adj* — **cat·a·lyt·i·cal·ly** \-ti-k(ə-)lē\ *adv*
catalytic converter *n* **:** an automobile exhaust-system component in which a catalyst changes harmful gases into mostly harmless products
cat·a·lyze \ˈkat-ᵊl-ˌīz\ *vb* **-lyzed; -lyz·ing :** to bring about the catalysis of (a chemical reaction)
cat·a·ma·ran \ˌka-tə-mə-ˈran\ *n* **:** a boat with twin hulls
cat·a·mount \ˈka-tə-ˌmau̇nt\ *n* **:** a large powerful tawny-brown cat **:** COUGAR; *also* **:** LYNX
[1]cat·a·pult \ˈka-tə-ˌpəlt, -ˌpu̇lt\ *n* **1 :** an ancient military machine for hurling missiles **2 :** a device for launching an airplane (as from an aircraft carrier)
[2]catapult *vb* ♦ **:** to throw or launch by or as if by a catapult

♦ cast, chuck, dash, fire, fling, heave, hurl, hurtle, launch, peg, pelt, pitch, sling, throw, toss

cat·a·ract \ˈka-tə-ˌrakt\ *n* **1 :** a cloudiness of the lens of the eye obstructing vision **2 a :** a large waterfall; *also* **:** steep rapids in a river **b** ♦ **:** an overwhelming downpour or rush

♦ cataclysm, deluge, flood, inundation, overflow, spate, torrent

ca·tarrh \kə-ˈtär\ *n* **:** inflammation of a mucous membrane especially of the nose and throat — **ca·tarrh·al** \-əl\ *adj*
ca·tas·tro·phe \kə-ˈtas-trə-(ˌ)fē\ *n* **1** ♦ **:** a great disaster or misfortune **2 :** utter failure

♦ calamity, cataclysm, debacle, disaster, tragedy

cat·a·stroph·ic \ˌka-tə-ˈsträ-fik\ *adj* ♦ **:** of, relating to, resembling, or resulting in catastrophe — **cat·a·stroph·i·cal·ly** \-fi-k(ə-)lē\ *adv*

♦ calamitous, cataclysmic, destructive, disastrous, fatal, fateful, ruinous, unfortunate

cat·a·ton·ic \ˌka-tə-ˈtä-nik\ *adj* **:** of, relating to, or marked by schizophrenia characterized especially by stupor, negativism, rigidity, purposeless excitement, and bizarre posturing — **catatonic** *n*
cat·bird \ˈkat-ˌbərd\ *n* **:** an American songbird with a catlike mewing call
cat·boat \ˈkat-ˌbōt\ *n* **:** a single-masted sailboat with a single large sail extended by a long boom
cat·call \-ˌkȯl\ *n* ♦ **:** a loud cry made especially to express disapproval — **catcall** *vb*

♦ boo, hiss, hoot, jeer, raspberry *Ant* cheer

[1]catch \ˈkach, ˈkech\ *vb* **caught** \ˈkȯt\; **catch·ing 1 :** to capture especially after pursuit **2** ♦ **:** to capture, take, or entangle in or as if in a snare **:** TRAP **3 :** to discover unexpectedly ⟨*caught* in the act⟩ **4 :** to become suddenly aware of **5 :** to take hold of **:** SNATCH ⟨~ at a straw⟩ **6** ♦ **:** stop or interrupt the progress or course of **7 :** to get entangled **8** ♦ **:** to become affected with or by ⟨~ fire⟩ ⟨~ cold⟩ **9 a** ♦ **:** to seize and hold firmly **b :** to cause to be seized and held **10 :** OVERTAKE **11 :** to be in time for ⟨~ a train⟩ **12 :** to take in and retain ⟨didn't ~ your name⟩ **13 :** to look at or listen to

♦ [2, 9a] bag, capture, collar, corral, get, grab, grapple, hook, land, nab, seize, snare, trap *Ant* miss ♦ [6] arrest, check, draw up, fetch up, halt, hold up, stall, stay, still, stop ♦ [8] come down, contract, get, sicken, take

2catch *n* **1 a :** something caught **b ♦ :** the total quantity caught at one time ⟨a good ~ of fish⟩ **2 :** the act of catching; *also* **:** a game consisting of throwing and catching a ball **3 :** something that catches or checks or holds immovable ⟨a door ~⟩ **4 ♦ :** one that is worth catching or acquiring especially as a mate **5 :** FRAGMENT, SNATCH **6 ♦ :** a concealed difficulty or complication

♦ [1b] haul, take, yield ♦ [4] gem, jewel, pearl, plum, prize, treasure ♦ [6] booby trap, pitfall, snag

catch•all \ˈka-ˌchȯl, ˈke-\ *n* **:** something to hold a variety of odds and ends
catch–as–catch–can *adj* **:** using any means available
catch•er \ˈka-chər, ˈke-\ *n* **:** one that catches; *esp* **:** a player positioned behind home plate in baseball
catch•ing *adj* **1 ♦ :** communicable by infection **:** CONTAGIOUS ⟨the flu is ~⟩ **2 ♦ :** spreading or capable of spreading rapidly to others ⟨their enthusiasm was ~⟩

♦ [1, 2] communicable, contagious, transmittable ♦ [2] contagious, infectious

catch•ment \ˈkach-mənt, ˈkech-\ *n* **1 :** something that catches water **2 :** the action of catching water
catch on *vb* **1 a ♦ :** to become aware **:** LEARN **b ♦ :** to grasp the meaning of **:** UNDERSTAND **2 :** to become popular

♦ [1a] ascertain, discover, find out, hear, learn, realize, see ♦ *usu* **catch on to** [1b] appreciate, apprehend, catch, comprehend, get, grasp, make, make out, perceive, see, seize, understand

catch•pen•ny \ˈkach-ˌpe-nē, ˈkech-\ *adj* **:** using sensationalism or cheapness for appeal ⟨a ~ newspaper⟩
catch•phrase \-ˌfrāz\ *n* **:** a word or expression frequently used to represent or characterize a person, group, idea, or point of view
catch–22 \-ˌtwen-tē-ˈtü\ *n, pl* **catch–22's** *or* **catch–22s** *often cap C* **:** a problematic situation for which the only solution is denied by a circumstance inherent in the problem or by a rule; *also* **:** the circumstance or rule that denies a solution
catchup *var of* KETCHUP
catch up *vb* **:** to travel or work fast enough to overtake or complete
catch•word \ˈkach-ˌwərd, ˈkech-\ *n* **1 :** GUIDE WORD **2 :** CATCHPHRASE
catchy \ˈka-chē, ˈke-\ *adj* **catch•i•er; -est 1 ♦ :** likely to catch the interest or attention **2 ♦ :** requiring skill or caution (as in doing or handling) **:** TRICKY

♦ [1] bold, conspicuous, emphatic, marked, noticeable, prominent, pronounced, remarkable, striking ♦ [2] delicate, difficult, knotty, problematic, spiny, thorny, ticklish, touchy, tough, tricky

cat•e•chism \ˈka-tə-ˌki-zəm\ *n* **:** a summary or test (as of religious doctrine) usually in the form of questions and answers — **cat•e•chist** \-ˌkist\ *n* — **cat•e•chize** \-ˌkīz\ *vb*
cat•e•chu•men \ˌka-tə-ˈkyü-mən\ *n* **:** a religious convert receiving training before baptism
cat•e•gor•i•cal \ˌka-tə-ˈgȯr-i-kəl\ *adj* **1 :** not modified or restricted **:** ABSOLUTE, UNQUALIFIED ⟨a ~ denial⟩ **2 :** of, relating to, or constituting a category — **cat•e•gor•i•cal•ly** \-i-k(ə-)lē\ *adv*
cat•e•go•rise *Brit var of* CATEGORIZE
cat•e•go•rize \ˈka-ti-gə-ˌrīz\ *vb* **-rized; -riz•ing ♦ :** to put into a category **:** CLASSIFY — **cat•e•go•ri•za•tion** \ˌka-ti-gə-rə-ˈzā-shən\ *n*

♦ assort, break down, class, classify, grade, group, peg, place, range, rank, separate, sort

cat•e•go•ry \ˈka-tə-ˌgȯr-ē\ *n, pl* **-ries ♦ :** a division within a system of classification; *esp* **:** CLASS, GROUP, KIND

♦ bracket, class, division, family, grade, group, kind, order, set, species, type

ca•ter \ˈkā-tər\ *vb* **1 ♦ :** to provide a supply of food **2 ♦ :** to supply what is wanted — **ca•ter•er** *n*

♦ [1] board, feed, provision ♦ *usu* **cater to** [2] gratify, humor (*or* humour), indulge

catercorner *or* **cater–cornered** *var of* KITTY-CORNER
cat•er•pil•lar \ˈka-tər-ˌpi-lər\ *n* **:** a wormlike often hairy insect larva especially of a butterfly or moth
cat•er•waul \ˈka-tər-ˌwȯl\ *vb* **:** to make a harsh cry — **caterwaul** *n*
cat•fish \ˈkat-ˌfish\ *n* **:** any of an order of chiefly freshwater stout-bodied fishes with slender tactile processes around the mouth
cat•gut \-ˌgət\ *n* **:** a tough cord made usually from sheep intestines
ca•thar•sis \kə-ˈthär-səs\ *n, pl* **ca•thar•ses** \-ˌsēz\ **1 :** an act of purging or purification **2 :** elimination of a complex by bringing it to consciousness and affording it expression
1ca•thar•tic \kə-ˈthär-tik\ *adj* **:** of, relating to, or producing catharsis
2cathartic *n* **:** PURGATIVE
ca•the•dral \kə-ˈthē-drəl\ *n* **:** the principal church of a diocese
cath•e•ter \ˈka-thə-tər\ *n* **:** a tube for insertion into a bodily passage or cavity usually for injecting or drawing off material or for keeping a passage open
cath•e•ter•i•za•tion \ˌka-thə-tə-rə-ˈzā-shən\ *n* **:** the use of or introduction of a catheter — **cath•e•ter•ize** \ˈka-thə-tə-ˌrīz\ *vb*
cath•ode \ˈka-ˌthōd\ *n* **1 :** the negative electrode of an electrolytic cell **2 :** the positive terminal of a battery **3 :** the electron-emitting electrode of an electron tube — **cath•od•al** \ˈka-ˌthō-dᵊl\ *adj* — **ca•thod•ic** \ka-ˈthä-dik\ *adj*
cathode–ray tube *n* **:** a vacuum tube in which a beam of electrons is projected on a fluorescent screen to produce a luminous spot
cath•o•lic \ˈkath-lik, ˈka-thə-\ *adj* **1** *cap* **:** of or relating to Catholics and especially Roman Catholics **2 :** GENERAL, UNIVERSAL
Cath•o•lic \ˈkath-lik, ˈka-thə-\ *n* **:** a member of a church claiming historical continuity from the ancient undivided Christian church; *esp* **:** a member of the Roman Catholic Church — **Ca•thol•i•cism** \kə-ˈthä-lə-ˌsi-zəm\ *n*
cath•o•lic•i•ty \ˌka-thə-ˈli-sə-tē\ *n, pl* **-ties 1** *cap* **:** the character of being in conformity with a Catholic church **2 :** liberality of sentiments or views **3 :** comprehensive range
cat•ion \ˈkat-ˌī-ən\ *n* **:** the ion in an electrolyte that migrates to the cathode; *also* **:** a positively charged ion
cat•kin \ˈkat-kən\ *n* **:** a long flower cluster (as of a willow) bearing crowded flowers and prominent bracts
cat•like \-ˌlīk\ *adj* **:** resembling a cat or its behavior; *esp* **:** STEALTHY
1cat•nap \-ˌnap\ *n* **♦ :** a very short light nap

♦ doze, drowse, forty winks, nap, siesta, snooze, wink

2catnap *vb* **:** to sleep for a short period of time
cat•nip \-ˌnip\ *n* **:** an aromatic mint that is especially attractive to cats
cat–o'–nine–tails \ˌka-tə-ˈnīn-ˌtālz\ *n, pl* **cat–o'–nine–tails :** a whip made of usually nine knotted cords fastened to a handle
CAT scan \ˈkat-\ *n* **:** an image made by computed tomography
CAT scanner *n* **:** a medical instrument consisting of integrated X-ray and computing equipment that is used to make CAT scans
cat's cradle *n* **:** a game played with a string looped on the fingers in such a way as to resemble a small cradle
cat's–eye \ˈkats-ˌī\ *n, pl* **cat's–eyes :** any of various iridescent gems
cat's–paw \-ˌpȯ\ *n, pl* **cat's–paws :** a person used by another as a tool
cat•tail \ˈkat-ˌtāl\ *n* **:** any of a genus of tall reedlike marsh plants with furry brown spikes of tiny flowers
cat•ti•ly \ˈka-tᵊl-ē\ *adv* **:** in a catty manner
cat•ti•ness *n* **♦ :** the quality or state of being catty

♦ acidity, acrimony, asperity, bitterness, tartness, virulence, vitriol ♦ despite, hatefulness, malice, malignity, meanness, nastiness, spite, spleen, venom, viciousness

cat•tle \ˈkat-ᵊl\ *n pl* **:** LIVESTOCK; *esp* **:** domestic bovines (as cows, bulls, or calves) — **cat•tle•man** \-mən, -ˌman\ *n*
cat•ty \ˈka-tē\ *adj* **cat•ti•er; -est ♦ :** slyly spiteful

♦ cruel, hateful, malevolent, malicious, malign, malignant, mean, nasty, spiteful, virulent

catty–corner *or* **catty–cornered** *var of* KITTY-CORNER
CATV *abbr* community antenna television
cat•walk \ˈkat-ˌwȯk\ *n* **:** a narrow walk (as along a bridge)
Cau•ca•sian \kȯ-ˈkā-zhən\ *adj* **:** of or relating to the white race of mankind — **Caucasian** *n* — **Cau•ca•soid** \ˈkȯ-kə-ˌsȯid\ *adj or n*
cau•cus \ˈkȯ-kəs\ *n* **:** a meeting of a group of persons belonging to the same political party or faction usually to decide upon policies and candidates — **caucus** *vb*
cau•dal \ˈkȯ-dᵊl\ *adj* **:** of, relating to, or located near the tail or the hind end of the body — **cau•dal•ly** *adv*
cau•di•llo \kau̇-ˈthē-(ˌ)yō, -ˈthēl-\ *n, pl* **-llos :** a Spanish or Latin-American military dictator
caught \ˈkȯt\ *past and past part of* CATCH
caul \ˈkȯl\ *n* **:** the inner fetal membrane of higher vertebrates especially when covering the head at birth
caul•dron \ˈkȯl-drən\ *n* **:** a large kettle
cau•li•flow•er \ˈkȯ-li-ˌflau̇(-ə)r\ *n* **:** a garden plant closely related to cabbage and grown for its compact edible head of undeveloped flowers; *also* **:** this head used as a vegetable

cauliflower ear *n* : an ear deformed from injury and excessive growth of scar tissue

[1]**caulk** \ˈkȯk\ *vb* : to stop up and make tight against leakage (as a boat or its seams) — **caulk•er** *n*

[2]**caulk** *also* **caulk•ing** *n* : material used to caulk

caus•al \ˈkȯ-zəl\ *adj* **1** : expressing or indicating cause **2** : relating to or acting as a cause — **cau•sal•i•ty** \kȯ-ˈza-lə-tē\ *n* — **caus•al•ly** *adv*

cau•sa•tion \kȯ-ˈzā-shən\ *n* **1** : the act or process of causing **2** : the means by which an effect is produced

[1]**cause** \ˈkȯz\ *n* **1** : REASON, MOTIVE **2 a** ♦ : something that brings about a result **b** ♦ : a person or thing that is the agent of bringing something about **3** : a suit or action in court : CASE **4** : a question or matter to be decided **5** : a principle or movement earnestly supported — **cause•less** *adj*

♦ [2a] bandwagon, campaign, crusade, drive, movement ♦ [2a, 2b] antecedent, occasion, reason ***Ant*** aftereffect, aftermath, consequence, corollary, development, effect, fate, fruit, issue, outcome, outgrowth, product, result, resultant, sequel, sequence, upshot

[2]**cause** *vb* **caused; caus•ing** ♦ : to be the cause or occasion of — **caus•a•tive** \ˈkȯ-zə-tiv\ *adj* — **caus•er** *n*

♦ bring about, create, effect, effectuate, generate, induce, make, produce, prompt, result, work, yield

cause cé•lè•bre \ˌkōz-sā-ˈlebrᵊ, ˌkȯz-\ *n, pl* **causes célèbres** *same*\ **1** : a legal case that excites widespread interest **2** : a notorious person, thing, incident, or episode

cau•se•rie \ˌkōz-ˈrē, ˌkō-zə-\ *n* **1** : an informal conversation : CHAT **2** : a short informal essay

cause•way \ˈkȯz-ˌwā\ *n* : a raised way or road across wet ground or water

[1]**caus•tic** \ˈkȯ-stik\ *adj* **1** : CORROSIVE **2** ♦ : marked by incisive sarcasm : SHARP 〈∼ wit〉

♦ acrid, biting, cutting, mordant, pungent, sarcastic, satiric, scathing, sharp, tart

[2]**caustic** *n* **1** : a substance that burns or destroys organic tissue by chemical action **2** : SODIUM HYDROXIDE

cau•ter•ize \ˈkȯ-tə-ˌrīz\ *vb* **-ized; -iz•ing** : to burn or sear usually to prevent infection or bleeding — **cau•ter•i•za•tion** \ˌkȯ-tə-rə-ˈzā-shən\ *n*

[1]**cau•tion** \ˈkȯ-shən\ *n* **1** ♦ : a warning or reminder of possible danger or risk : ADMONITION, WARNING **2** ♦ : prudent forethought to minimize risk **3** ♦ : one that astonishes

♦ [1] admonition, alarm, alert, notice, warning ♦ [2] alertness, care, carefulness, circumspection, heedfulness ***Ant*** carelessness, heedlessness, recklessness ♦ [3] flash, marvel, miracle, phenomenon, portent, prodigy, sensation, wonder

[2]**caution** *vb* ♦ : to advise caution to

♦ alert, forewarn, warn

cau•tion•ary \-shə-ˌner-ē\ *adj* ♦ : having the characteristics of or serving as a caution

♦ admonishing, admonitory, warning

cau•tious \ˈkȯ-shəs\ *adj* ♦ : marked by or given to caution : CAREFUL — **cau•tious•ly** *adv*

♦ alert, careful, circumspect, considerate, gingerly, guarded, heedful, safe, wary

cau•tious•ness *n* : the quality or state of being cautious

cav *abbr* **1** cavalry **2** cavity

cav•al•cade \ˌka-vəl-ˈkād\ *n* **1 a** : a procession of riders or carriages **b** ♦ : a procession of vehicles **2** : a dramatic sequence or procession

♦ armada, caravan, fleet, motorcade, train

[1]**cav•a•lier** \ˌka-və-ˈlir\ *n* **1** : a mounted soldier : KNIGHT **2** *cap* : an adherent of Charles I of England **3** : a man who is especially attentive to women : GALLANT

[2]**cavalier** *adj* **1** : DEBONAIR **2** ♦ : marked by or given to offhand dismissal of important matters **3** ♦ : marked by lofty disregard of others' interests or feelings : HAUGHTY — **cav•a•lier•ly** *adv*

♦ [2, 3] arrogant, haughty, high-handed, high-hat, highfalutin, imperious, important, lofty, lordly, masterful, overweening, peremptory, pompous, presumptuous, pretentious, supercilious, superior, uppity

cav•al•ry \ˈka-vəl-rē\ *n, pl* **-ries** : troops mounted on horseback or moving in motor vehicles — **cav•al•ry•man** \-mən, -ˌman\ *n*

[1]**cave** \ˈkāv\ *n* : a natural underground chamber open to the surface

[2]**cave** *vb* **caved; cav•ing** **1** ♦ : to collapse or cause to collapse — usually used with *in* **2** : to cease to resist : SUBMIT — usually used with *in*

♦ *usu* **cave in** collapse, crumple, give, go, yield

ca•ve•at \ˈka-vē-ˌät, -ˌat; ˈkä-vē-ˌät\ *n* : WARNING

caveat emp•tor \-ˈemp-tər, -ˌtȯr\ *n* : a principle in commerce: without a warranty the buyer takes a risk

cave–in \ˈkā-ˌvin\ *n* **1** : the action of caving in **2** : a place where earth has caved in

cave•man \ˈkāv-ˌman\ *n* **1** : a cave dweller especially of the Stone Age **2** : a man who acts in a rough or crude manner

cav•ern \ˈka-vərn\ *n* : a natural underground chamber or series of chambers open to the surface : CAVE; *esp* : one of large or unknown size — **cav•ern•ous** *adj* — **cav•ern•ous•ly** *adv*

cav•i•ar *also* **cav•i•are** \ˈka-vē-ˌär, ˈkä-\ *n* : the salted roe of a large fish (as sturgeon) used as an appetizer

cav•il \ˈka-vəl\ *vb* **-iled** *or* **-illed; -il•ing** *or* **-il•ling** ♦ : to make frivolous objections or raise trivial objections to — **cavil** *n*

♦ carp, fuss, quibble

cav•il•er *or* **cav•il•ler** *n* ♦ : a person who complains and criticizes for trivial reasons

♦ carper, castigator, censurer, critic, faultfinder, nitpicker, railer, scold

cav•ing \ˈkā-viŋ\ *n* : the sport of exploring caves : SPELUNKING

cav•i•ta•tion \ˌka-və-ˈtā-shən\ *n* : the formation of partial vacuums in a liquid by a swiftly moving solid body (as a propeller) or by high-intensity sound waves

cav•i•ty \ˈka-və-tē\ *n, pl* **-ties** **1** ♦ : an unfilled space within a mass : a hollow place **2** : an area of decay in a tooth

♦ concavity, dent, depression, hole, hollow, indentation, pit, recess

ca•vort \kə-ˈvȯrt\ *vb* ♦ : to bound, prance, or frisk about : CAPER

♦ caper, disport, frisk, frolic, gambol, lark, rollick, romp, sport

ca•vy \ˈkā-vē\ *n, pl* **cavies** : GUINEA PIG 1

caw \ˈkȯ\ *vb* : to utter the harsh call of the crow or a similar cry — **caw** *n*

cay \ˈkē, ˈkā\ *n* ♦ : a small area of land surrounded by water : KEY

♦ island, isle, key

cay•enne pepper \ˌkī-ˈen-, ˌkā-\ *n* : a condiment consisting of ground dried fruits or seeds of a hot pepper

cayman *var of* CAIMAN

Ca•yu•ga \kā-ˈü-gə, kī-\ *n, pl* **Cayuga** *or* **Cayugas** : a member of an American Indian people of New York

Cay•use \ˈkī-ˌyüs, kī-ˈ\ *n* **1** *pl* **Cayuse** *or* **Cayuses** : a member of an American Indian people of Oregon and Washington **2** *pl cayuses, not cap, West* : a native range horse

Cb *symbol* columbium

CB \ˈsē-ˈbē\ *n* : CITIZENS BAND; *also* : the radio set used for citizens-band communications

CBC *abbr* Canadian Broadcasting Corporation

CBD *abbr* cash before delivery

CBS *abbr* Columbia Broadcasting System

CBW *abbr* chemical and biological warfare

cc *abbr* cubic centimeter

CC *abbr* **1** carbon copy **2** community college **3** country club

CCD \ˌsē-ˌsē-ˈdē\ *n* : CHARGE-COUPLED DEVICE

CCTV *abbr* closed-circuit television

CCU *abbr* **1** cardiac care unit **2** coronary care unit **3** critical care unit

ccw *abbr* counterclockwise

cd *abbr* cord

Cd *symbol* cadmium

[1]**CD** \ˌsē-ˈdē\ *n* : CERTIFICATE OF DEPOSIT

[2]**CD** *n* : a small optical disk usually containing recorded music or computer data; *also* : the content of a CD

[3]**CD** *abbr* Civil Defense

CDR *abbr* commander

CD–ROM \ˌsē-ˌdē-ˈräm\ *n* : a CD containing computer data that cannot be altered

CDT *abbr* central daylight (saving) time

Ce *symbol* cerium

CE *abbr* **1** chemical engineer **2** civil engineer **3** Corps of Engineers

cease \ˈsēs\ *vb* **ceased; ceas•ing** ♦ : to come or bring to an end : STOP

♦ break off, break up, close, conclude, desist, die, discontinue, end, expire, finish, halt, quit, stop, terminate ***Ant*** continue, hang on, persist

cease–fire \ˈsēs-ˈfī(-ə)r\ *n* : a suspension of active hostilities

cease•less \ˈsēs-ləs\ *adj* ♦ : being without pause or stop : continuing without interruption — **cease•less•ly** *adv*

♦ continual, continuous, incessant, unbroken, unceasing, uninterrupted ♦ dateless, deathless, endless, eternal, everlasting, immortal, permanent, perpetual, undying, unending

cease•less•ness *n* ♦ : the quality or state of being ceaseless

♦ abidance, continuance, duration, endurance, persistence, subsistence

ce•cum *also* **cae•cum** \ˈsē-kəm\ *n, pl* **ce•ca** \-kə\ : the blind pouch at the beginning of the large intestine into which the small intestine opens — **ce•cal** *also* **cae•cal** \-kəl\ *adj*

ce•dar \ˈsē-dər\ *n* : any of numerous coniferous trees (as a juniper) noted for their fragrant durable wood; *also* : this wood

cede \ˈsēd\ *vb* **ced•ed; ced•ing** **1** ♦ : to yield or give up **2** ♦ : to transfer (as property) to another : ASSIGN, TRANSFER — **ced•er** *n*

♦ [1] deliver, give up, hand over, leave, relinquish, render, surrender, turn over, yield ♦ [2] alienate, assign, deed, make over, transfer

ce•dil•la \si-ˈdi-lə\ *n* : a mark placed under the letter *c* (as ç) to show that the *c* is to be pronounced like *s*

ceil•ing \ˈsē-liŋ\ *n* **1** : the overhead inside lining of a room **2** ♦ : something thought of as an overhanging shelter or canopy **3** : the height above the ground of the base of the lowest layer of clouds when over half of the sky is obscured **4** : the greatest height at which an airplane can operate efficiently **5** ♦ : a prescribed upper limit ⟨price ~⟩

♦ [2] canopy, roof, tent ♦ [5] bound, boundary, confines, end, extent, limit, limitation, line, termination

cel•an•dine \ˈse-lən-ˌdīn, -ˌdēn\ *n* : a yellow-flowered herb related to the poppies

cel•e•brant \-brənt\ *n* ♦ : one who celebrates

♦ merrymaker, reveler, roisterer ***Ant*** killjoy, party pooper

cel•e•brate \ˈse-lə-ˌbrāt\ *vb* **-brat•ed; -brat•ing** **1** ♦ : to perform (as a sacrament) with appropriate rites **2** ♦ : to honor (as a holiday) by solemn ceremonies or by refraining from ordinary business **3** : to observe a notable occasion with festivities **4** : EXTOL — **cel•e•bra•to•ry** \-brə-ˌtōr-ē, -ˌtȯr-; ˌse-lə-ˈbrā-tə-rē\ *adj*

♦ [1, 2] commemorate, keep, observe

cel•e•brat•ed *adj* ♦ : widely known and often referred to

♦ famed, famous, noted, notorious, prominent, renowned, star, well-known

cel•e•bra•tion \ˌse-lə-ˈbrā-shən\ *n* ♦ : the act or process of celebrating

♦ carnival, festival, festivity, fete, fiesta, gala, jubilee

cel•e•bra•tor \ˈse-lə-brā-tər\ *n* : one that celebrates

ce•leb•ri•ty \sə-ˈle-brə-tē\ *n, pl* **-ties** **1** ♦ : the state of being celebrated **2** ♦ : a celebrated person

♦ [1] fame, notoriety, renown ♦ [2] figure, light, luminary, notable, personage, personality, somebody, standout, star, superstar, VIP ***Ant*** nobody

ce•ler•i•ty \sə-ˈler-ə-tē\ *n* ♦ : rapidity of motion or action : SPEED, RAPIDITY

♦ fastness, fleetness, haste, hurry, quickness, rapidity, speed, swiftness, velocity

cel•ery \ˈse-lə-rē\ *n, pl* **-er•ies** : a European herb related to the carrot and widely grown for the crisp edible stems of its leaves

celery cabbage *n* : CHINESE CABBAGE 2

ce•les•ta \sə-ˈles-tə\ *or* **ce•leste** \sə-ˈlest\ *n* : a keyboard instrument with hammers that strike steel plates

ce•les•tial \sə-ˈles-chəl\ *adj* **1** ♦ : of, relating to, or suggesting heaven or divinity : HEAVENLY **2** : of or relating to the sky — **ce•les•tial•ly** *adv*

♦ Elysian, empyrean, heavenly, supernal ***Ant*** hellish, infernal

celestial navigation *n* : navigation by observation of the positions of stars

celestial sphere *n* : an imaginary sphere of infinite radius against which the celestial bodies appear to be projected

cel•i•ba•cy \ˈse-lə-bə-sē\ *n* **1** : the state of being unmarried; *esp* : abstention by vow from marriage **2** : abstention from sexual intercourse

cel•i•bate \ˈse-lə-bət\ *n* : one who lives in celibacy — **celibate** *adj*

cell \ˈsel\ *n* **1 a** ♦ : a small room (as in a convent or prison) usually for one person **b** ♦ : a small compartment, cavity, or bounded space **2** : a tiny mass of protoplasm that usually contains a nucleus, is enclosed by a membrane, and forms the smallest structural unit of living matter capable of functioning independently **3** : a container holding an electrolyte either for generating electricity or for use in electrolysis **4** : a single unit in a device for converting radiant energy into electrical energy — **celled** \ˈseld\ *adj*

♦ [1a] chamber, closet, room ♦ [1a, 1b] bay, chamber, compartment, cubicle, room

cel•lar \ˈse-lər\ *n* **1** : the part of a building that is wholly or partly below ground level : BASEMENT **2** : the lowest position (as in an athletic league) **3** : a stock of wines

cel•lar•ette *or* **cel•lar•et** \ˌse-lə-ˈret\ *n* : a case or cabinet for a few bottles of wine or liquor

cell body : the nucleus-containing central part of a neuron

cel•lo \ˈche-lō\ *n, pl* **cellos** : a bass member of the violin family tuned an octave below the viola — **cel•list** \-list\ *n*

cel•lo•phane \ˈse-lə-ˌfān\ *n* : a thin transparent material made from cellulose and used as a wrapping

cell phone *n* : a portable cordless telephone for use in a cellular system

cel•lu•lar \ˈsel-yə-lər\ *adj* **1** : of, relating to, or consisting of cells **2** : of, relating to, or being a radiotelephone system in which a geographical area is divided into small sections each served by a transmitter of limited range

cel•lu•lite \ˈsel-yə-ˌlīt\ *n* : deposits of lumpy fat within connective tissue (as in the thighs, hips, and buttocks)

cel•lu•lose \ˈsel-yə-ˌlōs\ *n* : a complex carbohydrate of the cell walls of plants used especially in making paper or rayon — **cel•lu•los•ic** \ˌsel-yə-ˈlō-sik\ *adj or n*

Cel•si•us \ˈsel-sē-əs\ *adj* : relating to or having a scale for measuring temperature on which the interval between the triple point and the boiling point of water is divided into 99.99 degrees with 0.01° being the triple point and 100.00° the boiling point

Celt \ˈkelt, ˈselt\ *n* : a member of any of a group of peoples (as the Irish or Welsh) of western Europe — **Celt•ic** *adj*

cem•ba•lo \ˈchem-bə-ˌlō\ *n, pl* **-ba•li** \-ˌlē\ *or* **-balos** : HARPSICHORD

[1]**ce•ment** \si-ˈment\ *n* **1** : a powder that is produced from a burned mixture chiefly of clay and limestone and that is used in mortar and concrete; *also* : CONCRETE **2 a** ♦ : a binding element or substance (as glue, paste, or plaster) **b** ♦ : something serving to unite firmly **3** : CEMENTUM; *also* : a substance for filling cavities in teeth

♦ [2a] adhesive, glue, size ♦ [2b] bond, knot, ligature, link, tie

[2]**cement** *vb* **1** : to unite by or as if by cement **2** : to cover with concrete — **ce•ment•er** *n*

ce•men•tum \si-ˈmen-təm\ *n* : a specialized external bony layer covering the dentin of the part of a tooth normally within the gum

cem•e•tery \ˈse-mə-ˌter-ē\ *n, pl* **-ter•ies** : a burial ground : GRAVEYARD

cen•o•bite \ˈse-nə-ˌbīt\ *n* : a member of a religious group living together in a monastic community — **cen•o•bit•ic** \ˌse-nə-ˈbi-tik\ *adj*

ceno•taph \ˈse-nə-ˌtaf\ *n* : a tomb or a monument erected in honor of a person whose body is elsewhere

Ce•no•zo•ic \ˌsē-nə-ˈzō-ik, ˌse-\ *adj* : of, relating to, or being the era of geologic history that extends from about 65 million years ago to the present — **Cenozoic** *n*

cen•ser \ˈsen-sər\ *n* : a vessel for burning incense (as in a religious ritual)

[1]**cen•sor** \ˈsen-sər\ *n* **1** : one of two early Roman magistrates whose duties included taking the census **2** : an official who inspects printed matter or sometimes motion pictures with power to suppress anything objectionable — **cen•so•ri•al** \sen-ˈsōr-ē-əl\ *adj*

[2]**censor** *vb* : to subject to censorship

cen•so•ri•ous \sen-ˈsōr-ē-əs\ *adj* : marked by or given to censure : CRITICAL — **cen•so•ri•ous•ly** *adv* — **cen•so•ri•ous•ness** *n*

cen•sor•ship \ˈsen-sər-ˌship\ *n* **1** : the action of a censor especially in stopping the transmission or publication of matter considered objectionable **2** : the office of a Roman censor

cen•sur•able *adj* ♦ : deserving or open to censure

♦ blamable, blameworthy, culpable, reprehensible ♦ objectionable, obnoxious, offensive, reprehensible

[1]**cen•sure** \ˈsen-chər\ *n* **1** : the act of blaming or condemning sternly **2** ♦ : an official reprimand

♦ denunciation, rebuke, reprimand, reproach, reproof, stricture *Ant* citation, commendation, endorsement

²**censure** *vb* **cen•sured; cen•sur•ing** ♦ **:** to find fault with and criticize as blameworthy

♦ condemn, damn, decry, denounce, reprehend, reprobate ♦ blame, condemn, criticize, denounce, fault, knock, pan, reprehend ♦ condemn, denounce, rebuke, reprimand, reproach, reprove *Ant* cite, commend, endorse

cen•sur•er *n* ♦ **:** one that censures

♦ carper, castigator, caviler, critic, faultfinder, nitpicker, railer, scold

cen•sus \ˈsen-səs\ *n* **1 :** a periodic governmental count of population **2 :** COUNT, TALLY — **census** *vb*

¹**cent** \ˈsent\ *n* **1 :** a monetary unit equal to 1/100 of a basic unit of value (as of a dollar) **2 :** a coin, token, or note representing one cent

²**cent** *abbr* **1** centigrade **2** central **3** century

cen•taur \ˈsen-ˌtȯr\ *n* **:** any of a race of creatures in Greek mythology half man and half horse

cen•te•nar•i•an \ˌsent-ᵊn-ˈer-ē-ən\ *n* **:** a person who is 100 or more years old

cen•te•na•ry \sen-ˈte-nə-rē, ˈsent-ᵊn-ˌer-ē\ *n, pl* **-ries :** CENTENNIAL — **centenary** *adj*

cen•ten•ni•al \sen-ˈte-nē-əl\ *n* **:** a 100th anniversary or its celebration — **centennial** *adj*

¹**cen•ter** *or Can and Brit* **cen•tre** \ˈsen-tər\ *n* **1** ♦ **:** the point that is equally distant from all points on the circumference of a circle or surface of a sphere; *also* **:** MIDDLE **2** ♦ **:** the point about which an activity concentrates or from which something originates **3 :** a region of concentrated population **4 :** a middle part **5** *often cap* **:** political figures holding moderate views especially between those of conservatives and liberals **6 :** a player occupying a middle position (as in football or basketball)

♦ [1] core, midpoint, midst *Ant* perimeter, periphery ♦ [2] base, core, cynosure, eye, focus, heart, hub, mecca, nucleus, seat

²**center** *or Can and Brit* **cen•tre** *vb* **centered** *or* **centred; centering** *or* **centring 1** ♦ **:** to place or fix at or around a center or central area **2** ♦ **:** to give a central focus or basis **:** CONCENTRATE **3 :** to have a center **:** FOCUS

♦ centralize, concentrate, consolidate, unify, unite

cen•ter•board *or Can and Brit* **cen•tre•board** \ˈsen-tər-ˌbōrd\ *n* **:** a retractable keel used especially in sailboats

cen•ter•piece \-ˌpēs\ *or Can and Brit* **cen•tre•piece** *n* **1 :** an object in a central position; *esp* **:** an adornment in the center of a table **2 :** one that is of central importance or interest in a larger whole

cen•tes•i•mal \sen-ˈte-sə-məl\ *adj* **:** marked by or relating to division into hundredths

cen•ti•grade \ˈsen-tə-ˌgrād, ˈsän-\ *adj* **:** relating to, conforming to, or having a thermometer scale on which the interval between the freezing and boiling points of water is divided into 100 degrees with 0° representing the freezing point and 100° the boiling point ⟨10° ~⟩

cen•ti•gram \-ˌgram\ *n* **:** a metric unit of measure equal to 1/100 gram

cen•ti•li•ter \ˈsen-ti-ˌlē-tər\ *or Can and Brit* **cen•ti•li•tre** *n* **:** a metric unit of measure equal to 1/100 liter

cen•ti•me•ter \ˈsen-tə-ˌmē-tər, ˈsän-\ *or Can and Brit* **cen•ti•me•tre** *n* **:** a metric unit of measure equal to 1/100 meter

centimeter–gram–second *adj* **:** of, relating to, or being a system of units based on the centimeter as the unit of length, the gram as the unit of mass, and the second as the unit of time

cen•ti•pede \ˈsen-tə-ˌpēd\ *n* **:** any of a class of long flattened segmented arthropods with one pair of legs on each segment except the first which has a pair of poison fangs

¹**cen•tral** \ˈsen-trəl\ *adj* **1 :** constituting a center **2** ♦ **:** belonging to the center as the most important part **:** PRINCIPAL **3 :** situated at, in, or near the center **4 :** centrally placed and superseding separate units ⟨~ heating⟩ — **cen•tral•ly** *adv*

♦ arch, cardinal, chief, dominant, first, foremost, grand, key, main, paramount, predominant, preeminent, premier, primary, principal, sovereign, supreme

²**central** *n* **:** a central controlling office

cen•tral•ise *Brit var of* CENTRALIZE

cen•tral•ize \ˈsen-trə-ˌlīz\ *vb* **-ized; -iz•ing** ♦ **:** to bring to a central point or under central control — **cen•tral•i•za•tion** \ˌsen-trə-lə-ˈzā-shən\ *n* — **cen•tral•iz•er** \ˈsen-trə-ˌlī-zər\ *n*

♦ center (*or* centre), concentrate, consolidate, unify, unite *Ant* decentralize, spread (out)

central nervous system *n* **:** the part of the nervous system which integrates nervous function and activity and which in vertebrates consists of the brain and spinal cord

cen•tre *Can and Brit var of* CENTER

cen•trif•u•gal \sen-ˈtri-fyə-gəl, -fi-\ *adj* **1 :** proceeding or acting in a direction away from a center or axis **2 :** using or acting by centrifugal force

centrifugal force *n* **:** the apparent force felt by an object moving in a curved path and acting outward from a center of rotation

cen•tri•fuge \ˈsen-trə-ˌfyüj\ *n* **:** a machine using centrifugal force (as for separating substances of different densities or for removing moisture)

cen•trip•e•tal \sen-ˈtri-pət-ᵊl\ *adj* **:** proceeding or acting in a direction toward a center or axis

centripetal force *n* **:** the force needed to keep an object revolving about a point moving in a circular path

cen•trist \ˈsen-trist\ *n* **1** *often cap* **:** a member of a center party **2 :** one who holds moderate views

cen•tu•ri•on \sen-ˈtu̇r-ē-ən, -ˈtyu̇r-\ *n* **:** an officer commanding a Roman century

cen•tu•ry \ˈsen-chə-rē\ *n, pl* **-ries 1 :** a subdivision of a Roman legion **2 :** a group or sequence of 100 like things **3 :** a period of 100 years

century plant *n* **:** a Mexican agave maturing and flowering only once in many years and then dying

CEO \ˌsē-(ˌ)ē-ˈō\ *n* **:** the executive with the chief decision-making authority in an organization or business

ce•phal•ic \sə-ˈfa-lik\ *adj* **1 :** of or relating to the head **2 :** directed toward or situated on or in or near the head

ce•ram•ic \sə-ˈra-mik\ *n* **1** *pl* **:** the art or process of making articles from a nonmetallic mineral (as clay) by firing **2 :** a product produced by ceramics — **ceramic** *adj*

ce•ra•mist \sə-ˈra-mist\ *or* **ce•ram•i•cist** \sə-ˈra-mə-sist\ *n* **:** one who engages in ceramics

¹**ce•re•al** \ˈsir-ē-əl\ *adj* **:** relating to grain or to the plants that produce it; *also* **:** made of grain

²**cereal** *n* **1 :** a grass (as wheat) yielding grain suitable for food; *also* **:** its grain **2 :** a food and especially a breakfast food prepared from the grain of a cereal

cer•e•bel•lum \ˌser-ə-ˈbe-ləm\ *n, pl* **-bellums** *or* **-bel•la** \-lə\ **:** a part of the brain that projects over the medulla and is concerned especially with coordination of muscular action and with bodily balance — **cer•e•bel•lar** \-lər\ *adj*

ce•re•bral \sə-ˈrē-brəl, ˈser-ə-\ *adj* **1** ♦ **:** of or relating to the brain, intellect, or cerebrum **2** ♦ **:** appealing to or involving the intellect — **ce•re•bral•ly** *adv*

♦ [1, 2] inner, intellectual, mental, psychological

cerebral cortex *n* **:** the surface layer of gray matter of the cerebrum that functions chiefly in coordination of sensory and motor information

cerebral palsy *n* **:** a disorder caused by brain damage usually before, during, or shortly after birth and marked especially by defective muscle control

cer•e•brate \ˈser-ə-ˌbrāt\ *vb* **-brat•ed; -brat•ing :** THINK — **cer•e•bra•tion** \ˌser-ə-ˈbrā-shən\ *n*

ce•re•brum \sə-ˈrē-brəm, ˈser-ə-\ *n, pl* **-brums** *or* **-bra** \-brə\ **:** the enlarged front and upper part of the brain that contains the higher nervous centers

cere•ment \ˈser-ə-mənt, ˈsir-mənt\ *n* **:** a shroud for the dead

¹**cer•e•mo•ni•al** \ˌser-ə-ˈmō-nē-əl\ *adj* **1** ♦ **:** of, relating to, or forming a ceremony **2 :** stressing careful attention to form and detail — **cer•e•mo•ni•al•ly** *adv*

♦ ceremonious, conventional, formal, orthodox, regular, routine

²**ceremonial** *n* **:** a ceremonial act or system **:** RITUAL, FORM

cer•e•mo•ni•ous \ˌser-ə-ˈmō-nē-əs\ *adj* **1 :** devoted to forms and ceremony **2 :** of, relating to, or constituting a ceremony **:** CEREMONIAL **3** ♦ **:** according to formal usage or procedure **4** ♦ **:** marked by ceremony — **cer•e•mo•ni•ous•ly** *adv* — **cer•e•mo•ni•ous•ness** *n*

♦ [3, 4] correct, decorous, formal, proper, starchy *Ant* casual, easygoing, informal, laid-back

cer•e•mo•ny \ˈser-ə-ˌmō-nē\ *n, pl* **-nies 1** ♦ **:** a formal act or series of acts prescribed by law, ritual, or convention **2 :** a conventional act of politeness **3 :** a mere outward form with no deeper significance **4 :** FORMALITY

♦ ceremonial, form, formality, observance, rite, ritual, solemnity

ce·re·us \ˈsir-ē-əs\ *n* : any of various cacti of the western U.S. and tropical America
ce·rise \sə-ˈrēs\ *n* : a moderate red color
ce·ri·um \ˈsir-ē-əm\ *n* : a malleable metallic chemical element used especially in alloys
cer·met \ˈsər-ˌmet\ *n* : a strong alloy of a heat-resistant compound and a metal used especially for turbine blades
cert *abbr* certificate; certification; certified; certify
1**cer·tain** \ˈsərt-ᵊn\ *adj* **1** ♦ : not subject to change or fluctuation : FIXED, SETTLED **2** ♦ : of a specific but unspecified character <~ people in authority> **3 a** : capable of being depended on : DEPENDABLE, RELIABLE **b** ♦ : incapable of failing **4** : INDISPUTABLE, UNDENIABLE **5** ♦ : assured in mind or action **6** : INEVITABLE

♦ [1] determinate, final, firm, fixed, flat, frozen, hard, hard-and-fast, set, settled, stable ♦ [2] anonymous, one, some, unidentified, unnamed, unspecified ♦ [3b] sure, surefire, unfailing ♦ [5] assured, clear, cocksure, confident, doubtless, positive, sanguine, sure *Ant* doubtful, dubious, uncertain, unsure

2**certain** *pron* : certain ones
cer·tain·ly *adv* **1** ♦ : in a manner that is certain : with certainty **2** : it is certain that

♦ definitely, doubtless, incontestably, indeed, indisputably, really, surely, truly, undeniably, undoubtedly, unquestionably

cer·tain·ty \-tē\ *n, pl* **-ties** **1** : something that is certain **2** ♦ : the quality or state of being certain

♦ assurance, certitude, confidence, conviction, positiveness, sureness

cer·tif·i·cate \sər-ˈti-fi-kət\ *n* **1** : a document testifying to the truth of a fact **2** : a document testifying that one has fulfilled certain requirements (as of a course or school) **3** : a document giving evidence of ownership or debt <a stock ~>
certificate of deposit : a money-market bond redeemable without penalty only on maturity
cer·ti·fi·ca·tion \ˌsər-tə-fə-ˈkā-shən\ *n* **1** : the act of certifying : the state of being certified **2** : a certified statement
certified mail *n* : first class mail for which proof of delivery may be secured but no indemnity value is claimed
certified public accountant *n* : an accountant who has met the requirements of a state law and has been granted a certificate
cer·ti·fy \ˈsər-tə-ˌfī\ *vb* **-fied; -fy·ing** **1** ♦ : to attest as being true **2** : to endorse officially **3** : to guarantee (a bank check) as good by a statement to that effect stamped on its face **4** ♦ : to provide with a usually professional certificate or license — **cer·ti·fi·able** \-ə-bəl\ *adj* — **cer·ti·fi·ably** \-blē\ *adv* — **cer·ti·fi·er** *n*

♦ [1] attest, authenticate, avouch, testify, vouch, witness ♦ [4] accredit, authorize, commission, empower, enable, invest, license, qualify

cer·ti·tude \ˈsər-tə-ˌtüd, -ˌtyüd\ *n* ♦ : the state of being or feeling certain

♦ assurance, certainty, confidence, conviction, positiveness, sureness

ce·ru·le·an \sə-ˈrü-lē-ən\ *adj* : AZURE
ce·ru·men \sə-ˈrü-mən\ *n* : EARWAX
cer·vi·cal \ˈsər-vi-kəl\ *adj* : of or relating to a neck or cervix
cervical cap *n* : a contraceptive device in the form of a thimble-shaped molded cap that fits over the uterine cervix and blocks sperm from entering the uterus
cer·vix \ˈsər-viks\ *n, pl* **cer·vi·ces** \-və-ˌsēz\ *or* **cer·vix·es** **1** : NECK; *esp* : the back part of the neck **2** : a constricted portion of an organ or part; *esp* : the narrow outer end of the uterus
ce·sar·e·an *or* **cae·sar·e·an** *also* **ce·sar·i·an** \si-ˈzar-ē-ən\ *n, often cap* : CESAREAN SECTION — **cesarean** *or* **caesarean** *also* **cesarian** *adj, often cap*
cesarean section *also* **caesarean section** *n, often cap C* : surgical incision of the walls of the abdomen and uterus for delivery of offspring
ce·si·um \ˈsē-zē-əm\ *n* : a silver-white soft ductile chemical element
ces·sa·tion \se-ˈsā-shən\ *n* ♦ : a temporary or final ceasing (as of action)

♦ close, closure, conclusion, end, ending, expiration, finish, halt, lapse, shutdown, stop, stoppage, termination

ces·sion \ˈse-shən\ *n* : a yielding (as of rights) to another
cess·pool \ˈses-ˌpül\ *n* : an underground pit or tank for receiving household sewage
ce·ta·cean \si-ˈtā-shən\ *n* : any of an order of aquatic mostly marine mammals that includes whales, porpoises, dolphins, and related forms — **cetacean** *adj*

cf *abbr* compare
Cf *symbol* californium
CF *abbr* cystic fibrosis
CFC *abbr* chlorofluorocarbon
cg *abbr* centigram
CG *abbr* **1** coast guard **2** commanding general
cgs *abbr* centimeter-gram-second
ch *abbr* **1** chain **2** champion **3** chapter **4** church
CH *abbr* **1** clearinghouse **2** courthouse **3** customhouse
Cha·blis \sha-ˈblē, shə-, shä-; ˈsha-ˌblē\ *n, pl* **Cha·blis** \-ˈblēz, -(ˌ)blēz\ **1** : a dry sharp white Burgundy wine **2** : a white California wine
cha–cha \ˈchä-ˌchä\ *n* : a fast rhythmic ballroom dance of Latin American origin
Chad·ian \ˈcha-dē-ən\ *n* : a native or inhabitant of Chad — **Chadian** *adj*
chafe \ˈchāf\ *vb* **chafed; chaf·ing** **1** ♦ : to bring trouble or distress to : cause agitation or anxiety to : IRRITATE, VEX **2** : FRET **3** : to warm by rubbing **4** ♦ : to rub so as to wear away **5** ♦ : to make sore by rubbing

♦ [1] aggravate, annoy, bother, bug, exasperate, gall, get, grate, irk, irritate, nettle, peeve, persecute, pique, put out, rasp, rile, vex ♦ [4] abrade, erode, fray, fret, gall, rub, wear ♦ [5] abrade, gall, irritate

cha·fer \ˈchā-fər\ *n* : any of various scarab beetles
1**chaff** \ˈchaf\ *n* **1** : debris (as husks) separated from grain in threshing **2** ♦ : something comparatively worthless

♦ deadwood, dust, garbage, junk, litter, refuse, riffraff, rubbish, scrap, trash, waste

2**chaff** *n* ♦ : light jesting talk : BANTER

♦ banter, persiflage, raillery, repartee

3**chaff** *vb* ♦ : to tease good-naturedly

♦ jive, josh, kid, rally, razz, rib, ride, roast, tease

chaf·fer \ˈcha-fər\ *vb* ♦ : to discuss terms : haggle especially over a price — **chaf·fer·er** *n*

♦ bargain, deal, dicker, haggle, negotiate, palter

chaf·finch \ˈcha-ˌfinch\ *n* : a common European finch with a cheerful song
chaffy *adj* ♦ : of little importance or worth

♦ empty, junky, no-good, null, valueless, worthless

chaf·ing dish \ˈchā-fiŋ-\ *n* : a utensil for cooking food at the table
1**cha·grin** \shə-ˈgrin\ *n* : mental uneasiness or annoyance caused by failure, disappointment, or humiliation
2**chagrin** *vb* **cha·grined** \-ˈgrind\; **cha·grin·ing** : to cause to feel chagrin
1**chain** \ˈchān\ *n* **1** : a flexible series of connected links **2** : a chainlike surveying instrument; *also* : a unit of length equal to 66 feet (about 20 meters) **3** ♦ : something that confines, restrains, or secures : BOND, FETTER **4** ♦ : a series of things linked, connected, or associated together <a ~ of events> <a mountain ~>

♦ [3] band, bond, fetter, irons, ligature, manacle, shackle ♦ [4] progression, sequence, string, train

2**chain** *vb* **1** ♦ : to fasten, bind, or connect with a chain; *also* : FETTER **2** ♦ : to join together so as to make a chain

♦ [1] bind, enchain, fetter, handcuff, manacle, shackle, trammel ♦ [2] compound, connect, couple, hitch, hook, join, link, yoke

chain gang *n* : a gang of convicts chained together
chain letter *n* : a letter sent to several persons with a request that each send copies to an equal number of persons
chain mail *n* : flexible armor of interlocking metal rings
chain reaction *n* **1** : a series of events in which each event initiates the succeeding one **2** : a chemical or nuclear reaction yielding products that cause further reactions of the same kind
chain saw *n* : a portable power saw that has teeth linked together to form an endless chain — **chain·saw** \ˈchān-ˌsȯ\ *vb*
chain–smoke \ˈchān-ˈsmōk\ *vb* : to smoke especially cigarettes continuously
chain store *n* : any of numerous stores under the same ownership that sell the same lines of goods
1**chair** \ˈcher\ *n* **1** : a seat with a back for one person **2** : ELECTRIC CHAIR **3** ♦ : an official seat or a seat of authority, state, or dignity; *also* : an office or position of authority or dignity **4** : the presiding officer of a meeting or event : CHAIRMAN

♦ head, headship, helm, rein

2**chair** *vb* : to act as chairman of

chair•lift \'cher-,lift\ *n* **:** a motor-driven conveyor for skiers consisting of seats hung from a moving cable
chair•man \-mən\ *n* ♦ **:** the presiding officer of a meeting or of a committee — **chair•man•ship** *n*

♦ chair, moderator, president, speaker

chair•per•son \-,pər-sən\ *n* **:** the presiding officer of a meeting or assembly **:** CHAIRMAN
chair•wom•an \-,wu̇-mən\ *n* **:** a woman who serves as chairman
chaise \'shāz\ *n* **:** a 2-wheeled horse-drawn carriage with a folding top
chaise longue \'shāz-'lȯŋ\ *n, pl* **chaise longues** *same or* -'lȯŋz\ **:** a long reclining chair
chaise lounge \-'lau̇nj\ *n* **:** CHAISE LONGUE
chal•ced•o•ny \kal-'sed-ᵊn-ē\ *n, pl* **-nies :** a translucent pale blue or gray quartz
chal•co•py•rite \,kal-kə-'pī-,rīt\ *n* **:** a yellow mineral constituting an important ore of copper
cha•let \sha-'lā\ *n* **1 :** a herdsman's cabin in the Swiss mountains **2 a :** a building in the style of a Swiss cottage with a wide roof overhang **b** ♦ **:** a cottage or house in chalet style

♦ cabin, camp, cottage, lodge

chal•ice \'cha-ləs\ *n* **:** a drinking cup; *esp* **:** the eucharistic cup
[1]**chalk** \'chȯk\ *n* **1 :** a soft limestone **2 :** chalk or chalky material especially when used as a crayon — **chalky** *adj*
[2]**chalk** *vb* **1 :** to rub or mark with chalk **2 :** to record with or as if with chalk — usually used with *up*
chalk•board \'chȯk-,bȯrd\ *n* **:** BLACKBOARD
chalk up *vb* **1 :** ASCRIBE, CREDIT **2 :** ATTAIN, ACHIEVE
[1]**chal•lenge** \'cha-lənj\ *vb* **chal•lenged; chal•leng•ing 1 :** to order to halt and prove identity **2** ♦ **:** to dispute especially as being unjust, invalid, or untrue **:** to take exception to **:** DISPUTE **3** ♦ **:** to issue an invitation to compete against one especially in single combat **:** DARE, DEFY

♦ [2] contest, dispute, query, question ***Ant*** accept, believe, embrace, swallow ♦ [3] dare, defy

[2]**challenge** *n* **1 :** a summons to a duel **2 :** an invitation to compete in a sport **3** ♦ **:** a calling to account or into question **4 :** an exception taken to a juror **5 :** a sentry's command to halt and prove identity **6 :** a stimulating or interesting task or problem

♦ complaint, demur, expostulation, fuss, kick, objection, protest, question, remonstrance

challenged *adj* ♦ **:** presented with difficulties (as by a disability)

♦ disabled, handicapped

chal•leng•er *n* ♦ **:** one that challenges; *specif* **:** a contender for a championship (as boxing)

♦ competition, competitor, contender, contestant, rival

challenging *adj* ♦ **:** arousing competitive interest, thought, or action ⟨a ~ course of study⟩

♦ arduous, burdensome, demanding, exacting, grueling, laborious, onerous, taxing, toilsome

chal•lis \'sha-lē\ *n, pl* **chal•lises** \-lēz\ **:** a lightweight clothing fabric of wool, cotton, or synthetic yarns
cham•ber \'chām-bər\ *n* **1** ♦ **:** a partitioned part of the inside of a building **:** ROOM **2** ♦ **:** an enclosed space or cavity **3 :** a hall for meetings of a legislative body **4 :** a judge's consultation room — usually used in plural **5 :** a legislative or judicial body; *also* **:** a council for a business purpose **6 :** the part of a firearm that holds the cartridge or powder charge during firing — **cham•bered** \-bərd\ *adj*

♦ [1, 2] bay, cabin, cell, compartment, cubicle

cham•ber•lain \'chām-bər-lən\ *n* **1 :** a chief officer in the household of a king or nobleman **2 :** TREASURER
cham•ber•maid \-,mād\ *n* **:** a maid who takes care of bedrooms
chamber music *n* **:** music intended for performance by a few musicians before a small audience
cham•bray \'sham-,brā\ *n* **:** a lightweight clothing fabric of white and colored threads
cha•me•leon \kə-'mēl-yən\ *n* **:** a small lizard whose skin changes color especially according to its surroundings
[1]**cham•fer** \'cham-fər\ *vb* **1 :** to cut a furrow in (as a column) **:** GROOVE **2 :** to make a chamfer on **:** BEVEL
[2]**chamfer** *n* **:** a beveled edge
cham•ois \'sha-mē\ *n, pl* **cham•ois** *same or* -mēz\ **1 :** a small goatlike antelope of Europe and the Caucasus region of Russia **2** *also* **cham•my** \'sha-mē\ **:** a soft leather made especially from the skin of the sheep or goat **3 :** a cotton fabric made in imitation of chamois leather
cham•o•mile \'ka-mə-,mīl, -,mēl\ *n* **:** any of a genus of strong-scented herbs related to the daisies and having flower heads that yield a bitter substance used especially in tonics and teas
[1]**champ** \'champ, 'chämp\ *vb* **1 :** to chew noisily **2 :** to show impatience of delay or restraint
[2]**champ** \'champ\ *n* ♦ **:** a winner of first prize or first place in competition **:** CHAMPION; *also* **:** one who shows marked superiority

♦ champion, victor, winner

cham•pagne \sham-'pān\ *n* **:** a white effervescent wine
[1]**cham•pi•on** \'cham-pē-ən\ *n* **1** ♦ **:** a militant advocate or defender **2** ♦ **:** one that wins first prize or place in a contest **3 :** one that is acknowledged to be better than all others

♦ [1] advocate, apostle, backer, booster, exponent, friend, promoter, proponent, supporter ♦ [2] champ, victor, winner

[2]**champion** *vb* ♦ **:** to protect or fight for as a champion

♦ advocate, back, endorse, patronize, support

cham•pi•on•ship \-,ship\ *n* **1 :** the position or title of a champion **2 :** the act of championing **:** DEFENSE **3 :** a contest held to determine a champion
[1]**chance** \'chans\ *n* **1 :** something that happens without apparent cause **2** ♦ **:** the unpredictable element in existence **:** LUCK **3** ♦ **:** a situation favoring some purpose **:** OPPORTUNITY **4** ♦ **:** the likelihood of a particular outcome in an uncertain situation **:** PROBABILITY **5** ♦ **:** a gamble or risk taken in hopes of a favorable outcome with a real possibility of loss **6 :** a raffle ticket — **by chance :** in the haphazard course of events

♦ [2] accident, circumstance, hazard, luck ♦ [3] occasion, opening, opportunity, room ♦ [4] odds, percentage, probability ♦ [5] enterprise, flier, gamble, speculation, venture

[2]**chance** *vb* **chanced; chanc•ing 1** ♦ **:** to take place by chance **:** HAPPEN **2** ♦ **:** to encounter or discover by chance — used with *upon* **3 :** to leave the outcome of to chance **4** ♦ **:** to accept the risk of

♦ [1] be, befall, betide, come, go, happen, occur, pass, transpire ♦ *usu* **chance upon** [2] encounter, find, happen (on *or* upon), hit, meet, stumble ♦ [4] gamble, hazard, risk, venture

[3]**chance** *adj* ♦ **:** happening, experienced, or encountered by chance, without forethought, plan, or intention

♦ accidental, casual, fluky, fortuitous, incidental, unintended, unintentional, unplanned, unpremeditated, unwitting

chan•cel \'chan-səl\ *n* **:** the part of a church including the altar and choir
chan•cel•lery *or* **chan•cel•lory** \'chan-sə-lə-rē\ *n, pl* **-ler•ies** *or* **-lor•ies 1 :** the position or office of a chancellor **2 :** the building or room where a chancellor works **3 :** the office or staff of an embassy or consulate
chan•cel•lor \'chan-sə-lər\ *n* **1 :** a high state official in various countries **2 :** the head of a university **3 :** a judge in the equity court in various states of the U.S. **4 :** the chief minister of state in some European countries — **chan•cel•lor•ship** *n*
chan•cery \'chan-sə-rē\ *n, pl* **-cer•ies 1 :** any of various courts of equity in the U.S. and Britain **2 :** a record office for public or diplomatic archives **3 :** a chancellor's court or office **4 :** the office of an embassy
chan•cre \'shaŋ-kər\ *n* **:** a primary sore or ulcer at the site of entry of an infective agent (as of syphilis)
chan•croid \'chaŋ-,krȯid\ *n* **:** a sexually transmitted disease caused by a bacterium and characterized by chancres that differ from those of syphilis in lacking hardened margins
chancy \'chan-sē\ *adj* **chanc•i•er; -est 1** *Scot* **:** AUSPICIOUS **2 :** RISKY
chan•de•lier \,shan-də-'lir\ *n* **:** a branched lighting fixture suspended from a ceiling
chan•dler \'chand-lər\ *n* **:** a dealer in provisions and supplies of a specified kind ⟨ship's ~⟩ — **chan•dlery** *n*
[1]**change** \'chānj\ *vb* **changed; chang•ing 1** ♦ **:** to make or become different **:** ALTER **2** ♦ **:** to replace with another **3 :** to give or receive an equivalent sum in notes or coins of usually smaller denominations or of another currency **4 :** to put fresh clothes or covering on ⟨~ a bed⟩ **5 :** to put on different clothes **6** ♦ **:** to switch to or with another **:** EXCHANGE ⟨neither liked his seat so they ~*ed* with each other⟩ — **chang•er** *n*

♦ [1] alter, make over, modify, recast, redo, refashion, remake, remodel, revamp, revise, rework, vary ***Ant*** fix, freeze, set, stabilize ♦ [1] fluctuate, mutate, shift, vary ***Ant*** stabilize ♦ [2, 6] commute, exchange, shift, substitute, swap, switch, trade

[2]**change** *n* **1** ♦ **:** the act, process, or result of changing **2 :** a fresh set of clothes **3 :** money given in exchange for other money of higher denomination **4 :** money returned when a payment exceeds the sum due **5 :** coins especially of small denominations

♦ alteration, difference, modification, revise, revision, variation *Ant* fixation, stabilization

change•able *adj* **1** ♦ **:** subject to change ⟨~ plans⟩ **2** ♦ **:** able or apt to vary ⟨~ weather⟩

♦ [1] adaptable, adjustable, elastic, flexible, fluid, malleable, variable ♦ [2] capricious, fickle, fluid, inconstant, mercurial, mutable, temperamental, uncertain, unpredictable, unsettled, unstable, unsteady, variable, volatile

change•ful *adj* **:** notably variable **:** UNCERTAIN

change•ling \ˈchānj-liŋ\ *n* **:** a child secretly exchanged for another in infancy

change•over \ˈchānj-ˌō-vər\ *n* ♦ **:** the action of changing over **:** CONVERSION

♦ conversion, metamorphosis, transfiguration, transformation

change ringing *n* **:** the art or practice of ringing a set of tuned bells in continually varying order

[1]**chan•nel** \ˈchan-^{ə}l\ *n* **1 :** the bed of a stream **2 :** the deeper part of a waterway **3** ♦ **:** a comparatively narrow passageway connecting two large bodies of water **:** STRAIT **4 :** a means of passage or transmission **5 :** a range of frequencies of sufficient width for a single radio or television transmission **6** ♦ **:** a usually tubular enclosed passage **:** CONDUIT **7** ♦ **:** a long gutter, groove, or furrow usually for the passage of water

♦ [3] narrows, sound, strait ♦ [6] conduit, duct, leader, line, penstock, pipe, tube ♦ [6, 7] aqueduct, canal, conduit, flume, raceway, watercourse

[2]**channel** *vb* **-neled** *or* **-nelled; -neling** *or* **-nel•ling 1 :** to make a channel in **2** ♦ **:** to direct into or through a channel

♦ conduct, direct, funnel, pipe, siphon

chan•nel•ize \ˈchan-^{ə}l-ˌīz\ *vb* **-ized; -iz•ing :** to direct through or into a channel or restricted area **:** CHANNEL — **chan•nel•iza•tion** \ˌchan-^{ə}l-ə-ˈzā-shən\ *n*

chan•son \shä^{n}-ˈsō^{n}\ *n, pl* **chan•sons** *same or* -ˈsō^{n}z\ **:** SONG; *esp* **:** a cabaret song

[1]**chant** \ˈchant\ *vb* **1** ♦ **:** to make melodic sounds with the voice **:** SING; *esp* **:** to sing a chant **2 :** to utter or recite in the manner of a chant **3 :** to celebrate or praise in song — **chant•er** *n*

♦ carol, descant, sing, vocalize

[2]**chant** *n* **1 :** a repetitive melody in which several words are sung to one tone **:** SONG; *esp* **:** a liturgical melody **2 :** a manner of singing or speaking in musical monotones

chan•te•relle \ˌshan-tə-ˈrel\ *n* **:** a fragrant edible mushroom

chan•teuse \shä^{n}-ˈtərz, shan-ˈtüz\ *n, pl* **chan•teuses** *same or* -ˈtər-zəz, -ˈtü-zəz\ **:** a woman who is a concert or nightclub singer

chan•tey *or* **chan•ty** \ˈshan-tē, ˈchan-\ *n, pl* **chanteys** *or* **chanties :** a song sung by sailors in rhythm with their work

chan•ti•cleer \ˌchan-tə-ˈklir, ˌshan-\ *n* **:** ROOSTER

Chanukah *var of* HANUKKAH

cha•os \ˈkā-ˌäs\ *n* **1** *often cap* **:** the confused unorganized state existing before the creation of distinct forms **2 :** the inherent unpredictability in the behavior of a natural system (as the atmosphere or the beating heart) **3** ♦ **:** a state of utter confusion or disorder

♦ confusion, disarray, disorder, disorganization, havoc, hell, jumble, mess, muddle, shambles *Ant* order, orderliness

chaos theory *n* **:** a branch of mathematical and physical theory concerned with chaotic systems

cha•ot•ic \kā-ˈä-tik\ *adj* ♦ **:** completely confused or disordered — **cha•ot•i•cal•ly** \-ti-k(ə-)lē\ *adv*

♦ confused, disheveled, disordered, messy, muddled, sloppy, unkempt, untidy

[1]**chap** \ˈchap\ *vb* **chapped; chap•ping :** to dry and crack open usually from wind and cold ⟨*chapped* lips⟩

[2]**chap** *n* **:** a jaw with its fleshy covering — usually used in plural

[3]**chap** *n* ♦ **:** an adult male individual **:** FELLOW

♦ buck, dude, fellow, gent, gentleman, guy, hombre, jack, joker, lad, male, man

[4]**chap** *abbr* chapter

chap•ar•ral \ˌsha-pə-ˈral\ *n* **1** ♦ **:** a dense impenetrable thicket of shrubs or dwarf trees **2 :** an ecological community especially of southern California composed of shrubby plants

♦ brake, brushwood, coppice, covert, thicket

chap•book \ˈchap-ˌbu̇k\ *n* **:** a small book of ballads, tales, or tracts

cha•peau \sha-ˈpō\ *n, pl* **cha•peaus** \-ˈpōz\ *or* **cha•peaux** \-ˈpō, -ˈpōz\ **:** HAT

cha•pel \ˈcha-pəl\ *n* **1 :** a private or subordinate place of worship **2 :** an assembly at an educational institution usually including devotional exercises **3 :** a place of worship used by a Christian group other than an established church

[1]**chap•er•one** *or* **chap•er•on** \ˈsha-pə-ˌrōn\ *n* **1 :** a person (as a matron) who accompanies young unmarried women in public for propriety **2 :** an older person who accompanies young people at a social gathering to ensure proper behavior

[2]**chaperone** *or* **chaperon** *vb* **-oned; -on•ing 1** ♦ **:** to attend upon **:** ESCORT **2** ♦ **:** to act as a chaperone to or for — **chap•er•on•age** \-ˌrō-nij\ *n*

♦ [1, 2] accompany, attend, convoy, escort, squire

chap•fall•en \ˈchap-ˌfȯ-lən, ˈchäp-\ *adj* **1 :** having the lower jaw hanging loosely **2 :** DEJECTED, DEPRESSED

chap•lain \ˈcha-plən\ *n* **1 :** a member of the clergy officially attached to a special group (as the army) **2 :** a person chosen to conduct religious exercises (as for a club) — **chap•lain•cy** \-sē\ *n*

chap•let \ˈcha-plət\ *n* **1 :** a wreath for the head **2 :** a string of beads **:** NECKLACE

chap•man \ˈchap-mən\ *n, Brit* **:** an itinerant dealer **:** PEDDLER

chaps \ˈshaps, ˈchaps\ *n pl* **:** leather leggings resembling trousers without a seat that are worn especially by western ranch hands

chap•ter \ˈchap-tər\ *n* **1 :** a main division of a book **2 :** a body of canons (as of a cathedral) **3** ♦ **:** a local branch of a society or fraternity

♦ affiliate, branch, local

[1]**char** \ˈchär\ *n, pl* **char** *or* **chars :** any of a genus of trouts (as the common brook trout) with small scales

[2]**char** *vb* **charred; char•ring 1 :** to burn or become burned to charcoal **2** ♦ **:** to burn slightly or partly **:** SCORCH

♦ scorch, sear, singe

[3]**char** *vb* **charred; char•ring :** to work as a cleaning woman

char•ac•ter \ˈkar-ik-tər\ *n* **1 :** a graphic symbol (as a letter) used in writing or printing **2 :** a symbol that represents information; *also* **:** a representation of such a character that may be accepted by a computer **3 :** a distinguishing feature **:** ATTRIBUTE **4** ♦ **:** the complex of mental and ethical traits marking a person or a group **5** ♦ **:** a person marked by conspicuous often peculiar traits **6 :** one of the persons in a novel or play **7** ♦ **:** reputation especially when good **:** good name **:** REPUTATION **8** ♦ **:** moral excellence

♦ [4] complexion, constitution, genius, identity, nature, personality, tone ♦ [5] crackpot, crank, eccentric, kook, nut, oddball, screwball, weirdo ♦ [7] mark, name, note, report, reputation ♦ [8] decency, goodness, honesty, honor (*or* honour), integrity, morality, probity, rectitude, righteousness, uprightness, virtue

[1]**char•ac•ter•is•tic** \ˌkar-ik-tə-ˈris-tik\ *n* ♦ **:** a distinguishing trait, quality, or property

♦ attribute, character, feature, mark, peculiarity, point, property, quality, trait

[2]**characteristic** *adj* ♦ **:** serving to mark individual character — **char•ac•ter•is•ti•cal•ly** \-ti-k(ə-)lē\ *adv*

♦ classic, distinct, distinctive, individual, peculiar, proper, symptomatic, typical *Ant* atypical, nontypical

char•ac•ter•ize \ˈkar-ik-tə-ˌrīz\ *vb* **-ized; -iz•ing 1** ♦ **:** to describe the character of **2 :** to be a characteristic of — **char•ac•ter•iza•tion** \ˌkar-ik-tə-rə-ˈzā-shən\ *n*

♦ define, depict, describe, portray, represent

cha•rades \shə-ˈrādz\ *n sing or pl* **:** a game in which some of the players try to guess a word or phrase from the actions of another player who may not speak

char•coal \ˈchär-ˌkōl\ *n* **1 :** a porous carbon prepared from vegetable or animal substances **2 :** a piece of fine charcoal used in drawing; *also* **:** a drawing made with charcoal

chard \ˈchärd\ *n* **:** SWISS CHARD

char•don•nay \ˌshard-^{ə}n-ˈā\ *n, often cap* **:** a dry white wine made from a single variety of white grape

[1]**charge** \ˈchärj\ *n* **1 :** a quantity (as of fuel or ammunition) required to fill something to capacity **2 :** a store or accumulation of force **3 :** an excess or deficiency of electrons in a body **4 :** THRILL,

KICK **5** ♦ **:** a task or duty imposed **6 :** a person or thing committed to the care of another **:** CARE **7** ♦ **:** control of the acts, workings, or disposition of something **8 a** ♦ **:** a direction or order calling for compliance **b :** instructions from a judge to a jury **9** ♦ **:** the price demanded for something **:** COST, PRICE; *also* **:** a debit to an account **10** ♦ **:** a formal assertion of illegality **:** INDICTMENT **11 :** a violent rush forward (as to attack) **:** ATTACK, ASSAULT

♦ [5] assignment, job, mission, operation, post ♦ [7] care, guidance, headship, oversight, regulation, superintendence, supervision ♦ [8a] behest, command, commandment, decree, dictate, direction, directive, edict, instruction, order, word ♦ [9] cost, fee, figure, price ♦ [10] complaint, count, indictment, rap

[2]**charge** *vb* **charged; charg•ing 1 :** to load or fill to capacity **2 :** to give an electric charge to; *also* **:** to restore the activity of (a storage battery) by means of an electric current **3** ♦ **:** to impose a task or responsibility on **4 :** to command, instruct, or exhort with authority **:** COMMAND, ORDER ⟨I ∼ you not to go⟩ **5 :** to make an assertion against especially by ascribing guilt or blame **:** ACCUSE **6** ♦ **:** to rush against **:** rush forward in assault **7** ♦ **:** to make liable for payment; *also* **:** to record a debt or liability against **8** ♦ **:** to fix as a price — **charge•able** *adj*

♦ [3] assign, commission, entrust, trust ♦ [6] assail, assault, attack, beset, descend, jump, pounce (on *or* upon), raid, rush, storm, strike ♦ [7] assess, exact, fine, impose, lay, levy, put ♦ [8] ask, command, demand

charge–coupled device *n* **:** a semiconductor device used especially as an optical sensor

charged \ˈchärjd\ *adj* **1** ♦ **:** possessing or showing strong emotion **2 :** capable of arousing strong emotion; *also* **:** EXCITING

♦ ardent, burning, emotional, fervent, fiery, hot-blooded, impassioned, passionate, red-hot, vehement

char•gé d'af•faires \shär-ˌzhā-də-ˈfar\ *n, pl* **chargés d'affaires** \-ˌzhā-, -ˌzhāz-\ **:** a diplomat who substitutes for an ambassador or minister

[1]**char•ger** \ˈchär-jər\ *n* **:** a large platter

[2]**charg•er** *n* **1 :** a device or a worker that charges something **2 :** WARHORSE

char•i•ness \ˈcher-ē-nəs\ *n* the quality or state of being chary

char•i•ot \ˈchar-ē-ət\ *n* **:** a 2-wheeled horse-drawn vehicle of ancient times used especially in war and in races — **char•i•o•teer** \ˌchar-ē-ə-ˈtir\ *n*

cha•ris•ma \kə-ˈriz-mə\ *n* ♦ **:** a personal quality of leadership arousing popular loyalty or enthusiasm — **char•is•mat•ic** \ˌkar-əz-ˈma-tik\ *adj*

♦ allure, appeal, attractiveness, captivation, charm, enchantment, fascination, glamour, magic, magnetism

char•i•ta•ble \ˈchar-ə-tə-bəl\ *adj* **1** ♦ **:** liberal in giving to needy people **2** ♦ **:** merciful or lenient in judging others — **char•i•ta•ble•ness** *n* — **char•i•ta•bly** \-blē\ *adv*

♦ [1] bountiful, free, generous, liberal, munificent, openhanded, unselfish, unsparing ♦ [2] altruistic, beneficent, benevolent, humanitarian, philanthropic ***Ant*** self-centered, selfish

char•i•ty \ˈchar-ə-tē\ *n, pl* **-ties 1 :** a disposition to goodwill, kindliness, and sympathy **2** ♦ **:** an act or feeling of generosity **3** ♦ **:** the giving of aid to the poor; *also* **:** ALMS **4 :** an institution engaged in relief of the poor **5 :** leniency in judging others

♦ [2, 3] alms, benefaction, beneficence, contribution, donation, philanthropy

char•la•tan \ˈshär-lə-tən\ *n* ♦ **:** a person making usually showy pretenses to knowledge or ability **:** FRAUD

♦ fake, fraud, hoaxer, humbug, mountebank, phony, pretender, quack

Charles•ton \ˈchärl-stən\ *n* **:** a lively dance in which the knees are swung in and out and the heels are turned sharply outward on each step

char•ley horse \ˈchär-lē-ˌhȯrs\ *n* **:** a muscular pain, cramping, or stiffness from a strain or bruise

[1]**charm** \ˈchärm\ *n* **1** ♦ **:** a practice or expression believed to have magic power **2** ♦ **:** something worn about the person to ward off evil or bring good fortune **:** AMULET **3 :** a trait that fascinates or allures **4** ♦ **:** physical grace or attraction **5 :** a small ornament worn on a bracelet or chain **6 :** a quark with a charge of $+\frac{2}{3}$ and a measured energy of approximately 1.5 billion electron volts

♦ [1] bewitchment, conjuration, enchantment, incantation, spell ♦ [2] amulet, fetish, mascot, talisman ***Ant*** hoodoo, jinx ♦ [4] allure, appeal, attractiveness, captivation, charisma, enchantment, fascination, glamour, magic, magnetism ***Ant*** repulsion, repulsiveness

[2]**charm** *vb* **1** ♦ **:** to affect by or as if by a magic spell **2 :** to protect by or as if by charms **3 :** to please, soothe, or delight by compelling attraction **:** FASCINATE, ENCHANT ⟨∼*s* customers with his suave manner⟩ — **charm•er** *n*

♦ allure, beguile, bewitch, captivate, enchant, fascinate, wile ♦ bewitch, enchant, hex, spell

charmed \ˈchärmd\ *adj* **:** extremely lucky or prosperous ⟨a ∼ life⟩

charm•er *n* **1 :** one that charms **:** ENCHANTER, MAGICIAN **2 :** one that pleases, intrigues, or fascinates

charm•ing \ˈchär-miŋ\ *adj* ♦ **:** marked by compelling attraction or appeal — **charm•ing•ly** *adv*

♦ alluring, attractive, captivating, elfin, engaging, fascinating, fetching, glamorous, magnetic, seductive

char•nel house \ˈchärn-ᵊl-\ *n* **:** a building or chamber in which bodies or bones are deposited

[1]**chart** \ˈchärt\ *n* **1 :** an outline map detailing certain geographical aspects of an area **:** MAP **2 :** a sheet giving information in the form of a table, list, or diagram; *also* **:** GRAPH

[2]**chart** *vb* **1 :** to make a chart of **2** ♦ **:** to lay out a plan for **:** PLAN

♦ arrange, blueprint, calculate, design, frame, lay out, map, plan, project, scheme

[1]**char•ter** \ˈchär-tər\ *n* **1 :** an official document granting rights or privileges (as to a colony, town, or college) from a sovereign or a governing body **2 :** CONSTITUTION **3 :** a written instrument from a society creating a branch **4 :** a mercantile lease of a ship

[2]**charter** *vb* **1 :** to grant a charter to **2** *Brit* **:** CERTIFY ⟨∼*ed* engineer⟩ **3 :** to hire, rent, or lease for temporary use — **char•ter•er** *n*

charter member *n* **:** an original member of an organization

char•treuse \shär-ˈtrüz, -ˈtrüs\ *n* **:** a brilliant yellow green

char•wom•an \ˈchär-ˌwu̇-mən\ *n* **:** a cleaning woman especially in large buildings

chary \ˈchar-ē\ *adj* **chari•er; -est 1 :** CAUTIOUS, CIRCUMSPECT **2 :** SPARING — **char•i•ly** \-ə-lē\ *adv*

[1]**chase** \ˈchās\ *n* **1 a** ♦ **:** the act of chasing **:** PURSUIT **b :** HUNTING **2 :** something pursued **:** QUARRY **3 :** a tract of unenclosed land used as a game preserve

♦ following, pursuit, tracing

[2]**chase** *vb* **chased; chas•ing 1** ♦ **:** to follow rapidly **:** PURSUE **2 :** to pursue for food or in sport **:** HUNT **3 :** to seek out ⟨*chasing* down clues⟩ **4** ♦ **:** to cause to depart or flee **:** drive away **5 :** RUSH, HASTEN

♦ [1] dog, follow, hound, pursue, shadow, tag, tail, trace, track, trail ♦ [4] banish, boot (out), bounce, dismiss, drum, eject, expel, oust, rout, run off

[3]**chase** *vb* **chased; chas•ing :** to decorate (a metal surface) by embossing or engraving

[4]**chase** *n* **:** FURROW, GROOVE

chas•er \ˈchā-sər\ *n* **1 :** one that chases **2 :** a mild drink (as beer) taken after hard liquor

chasm \ˈka-zəm\ *n* **:** a deep cleft in the surface (as of a planet) **:** GORGE 2

chas•sis \ˈcha-sē, ˈsha-sē\ *n, pl* **chas•sis** \-sēz\ **:** the supporting frame of a structure (as an automobile or television set)

chaste \ˈchāst\ *adj* **chast•er; chast•est 1** ♦ **:** innocent of unlawful sexual intercourse **:** VIRTUOUS, PURE **2 :** CELIBATE **3** ♦ **:** pure in thought **:** MODEST **4 :** severe or simple in design

♦ [1, 3] clean, decent, immaculate, modest, pure, virtuous ***Ant*** immodest, impure, indecent, unchaste, unclean

chaste•ly *adv* ♦ **:** in a chaste manner

♦ modestly, purely, righteously, virtuously

chas•ten \ˈchās-ᵊn\ *vb* **1** ♦ **:** to correct through punishment or suffering **:** DISCIPLINE **2 :** PURIFY — **chas•ten•er** *n*

♦ castigate, chastise, correct, discipline, penalize, punish

chaste•ness *n* **:** the state or quality of being chaste

chas•tise \chas-ˈtīz\ *vb* **chas•tised; chas•tis•ing 1** ♦ **:** to punish especially bodily **2** ♦ **:** to censure severely **:** CASTIGATE

♦ [1, 2] castigate, chasten, correct, discipline, penalize, punish

chas•tise•ment \-mənt, ˈchas-təz-\ *n* ♦ **:** the action, an act, or the means of chastising; *esp* **:** PUNISHMENT

♦ castigation, correction, desert, discipline, nemesis, penalty, punishment, wrath

chas•ti•ty \ˈchas-tə-tē\ *n* ♦ **:** the quality or state of being chaste; *esp* **:** sexual purity

♦ modesty, purity ***Ant*** immodesty, impurity, unchastity

cha•su•ble \ˈcha-zə-bəl, -sə-\ *n* **:** the outer vestment of the priest at mass

chat \ˈchat\ *n* **1** ♦ **:** light familiar informal talk **2 :** online discussion in a chat room — **chat** *vb*

♦ chatter, chitchat, gabfest, gossip, palaver, rap, talk

chat *vb* ♦ **:** to talk in a light and familiar manner

♦ converse, gab, jaw, palaver, patter, prattle, rattle, talk, visit ♦ *usu* **chat with** speak, talk

châ•teau \sha-ˈtō\ *n, pl* **châ•teaus** \-ˈtōz\ *or* **châ•teaux** \-ˈtō, -ˈtōz\ **1 :** a feudal castle in France **2 :** a large country house **3 :** a French vineyard estate

chat•e•laine \ˈshat-ᵊl-ˌān\ *n* **1 :** the mistress of a chateau **2 :** a clasp or hook for a watch, purse, or keys

chat room *n* **:** a real-time online interactive discussion group

chat•tel \ˈchat-ᵊl\ *n* **1** ♦ **:** an item of tangible property other than real estate **2 :** a person held in servitude **:** SLAVE, BONDMAN

♦ *usu* **chattels** effects, holdings, paraphernalia, possessions, things

¹chat•ter \ˈcha-tər\ *vb* **1** ♦ **:** to utter speechlike but meaningless sounds **2** ♦ **:** to talk idly, incessantly, or fast **3 :** to click repeatedly or uncontrollably

♦ [1] babble, drivel, gabble, gibber, jabber, prattle, sputter ♦ [2] chat, converse, gab, jaw, palaver, patter, prattle, rattle, talk, visit

²chatter *n* **:** idle talk

chat•ter•box \ˈcha-tər-ˌbäks\ *n* ♦ **:** one who talks incessantly

♦ jabberer, magpie, talker

chat•ter•er *n* **:** a person who rambles on and on

chat•ty \ˈcha-tē\ *adj* **chat•ti•er; -est 1** ♦ **:** fond of chatting **:** TALKATIVE ⟨a ∼ neighbor⟩ **2** ♦ **:** having the style and manner of light familiar conversation ⟨a ∼ letter⟩ — **chat•ti•ly** \-tə-lē\ *adv* — **chat•ti•ness** \-tē-nəs\ *n*

♦ [1] conversational, gabby, garrulous, loquacious, talkative ♦ [2] colloquial, conversational, newsy ***Ant*** bookish, literary

¹chauf•feur \ˈshō-fər, shō-ˈfər\ *n* **:** a person employed to drive an automobile

²chauffeur *vb* **chauf•feured; chauf•feur•ing 1 :** to do the work of a chauffeur **2 :** to transport in the manner of a chauffeur

chau•vin•ism \ˈshō-və-ˌni-zəm\ *n* **1 :** excessive or blind patriotism **2 :** an attitude of superiority toward members of the opposite sex — **chau•vin•is•tic** \ˌshō-və-ˈnis-tik\ *adj* — **chau•vin•is•ti•cal•ly** \-ti-k(ə-)lē\ *adv*

chau•vin•ist *n or adj* **:** one who practices chauvinism

cheap \ˈchēp\ *adj* **1** ♦ **:** of small cost **:** INEXPENSIVE **2 :** costing little effort to obtain **3** ♦ **:** of inferior quality or worth **:** SHODDY **4 :** worthy of scorn **5 :** not generous or liberal in using, giving, or spending **:** STINGY — **cheap** *adv* — **cheap•ly** *adv*

♦ [1] cut-rate, inexpensive, low, reasonable ***Ant*** costly, dear, expensive, high, premium ♦ [3] bad, bum, coarse, common, cut-rate, execrable, inferior, junky, lousy, mediocre, miserable, poor, rotten, second-rate, shoddy, sleazy, terrible, trashy, wretched ***Ant*** excellent, fine, first-rate, good, superior, top-notch

cheap•en \ˈchē-pən\ *vb* **1** ♦ **:** to make or become cheap or cheaper in price or value **2 :** to make tawdry

♦ depreciate, depress, mark down, write off

cheap•ness *n* ♦ **:** the quality or state of being cheap

♦ closeness, miserliness, parsimony, stinginess, tightness

cheap•skate \ˈchēp-ˌskāt\ *n* ♦ **:** a miserly or stingy person; *esp* **:** one who tries to avoid paying a fair share of costs

♦ miser, niggard, skinflint, tightwad

¹cheat \ˈchēt\ *vb* **1** ♦ **:** to deprive of something through fraud or deceit **2 :** to practice fraud or trickery **3 :** to violate rules (as of a game) dishonestly — **cheat•er** *n*

♦ bleed, chisel, cozen, defraud, fleece, gyp, hustle, mulct, rook, shortchange, skin, squeeze, stick, sting, swindle, victimize

²cheat *n* **1 :** the act of deceiving **:** FRAUD, DECEPTION **2** ♦ **:** one that cheats **:** a dishonest person

♦ dodger, hoaxer, shark, sharper, swindler, trickster

¹check \ˈchek\ *n* **1 :** exposure of a chess king to an attack **2 :** a sudden stoppage of progress **3 :** a sudden pause or break **4** ♦ **:** something that stops or restrains **5 :** a standard for testing or evaluation **6** ♦ **:** a strict or close inspection **:** a study of by close examination **:** EXAMINATION **7 :** the act of testing or verifying **8** *or Can and Brit* **cheque :** a written order directing a bank to pay money as instructed **:** DRAFT **9 :** a ticket or token showing ownership or identity **10** ♦ **:** a slip indicating an amount due **11 :** a pattern in squares; *also* **:** a fabric in such a pattern **12 :** a mark typically ✓ placed beside an item to show that it has been noted **13 :** CRACK, SPLIT

♦ [4] condition, constraint, curb, fetter, limitation, restraint, restriction ♦ [6] audit, checkup, examination, inspection, review, scan, scrutiny, survey ♦ [10] account, bill, invoice, statement, tab

²check *vb* **1 :** to put (a chess king) in check **2** ♦ **:** to slow down or stop **3** ♦ **:** to restrain the action or force of **:** CURB **4 :** to compare with a source, original, or authority **:** VERIFY — often used with *out* **5** ♦ **:** to inspect or test for satisfactory condition **6 :** to mark with a check as examined **7 :** to consign for shipment for one holding a passenger ticket **8 :** to mark into squares **9 :** to leave or accept for safekeeping in a checkroom **10 :** to prove to be consistent or truthful **11 :** CRACK, SPLIT **12** ♦ **:** to correspond often detail for detail

♦ [2] arrest, catch, draw up, fetch up, halt, hold up, stall, stay, still, stop ♦ [3] bridle, constrain, contain, control, curb, govern, inhibit, regulate, rein, restrain, tame ♦ *usu* **check out** [5] audit, examine, inspect, review, scan, scrutinize, survey ♦ [12] accord, agree, answer, coincide, comport, conform, correspond, dovetail, fit, go, harmonize, jibe, square, tally ***Ant*** differ (from), disagree (with)

check•book \ˈchek-ˌbu̇k\ *n* **:** a book containing blank checks

¹check•er \ˈche-kər\ *n* **:** a piece in the game of checkers

²checker *vb* **1 :** to variegate with different colors or shades **2 :** to vary with contrasting elements ⟨a ∼*ed* career⟩ **3 :** to mark into squares

³checker *n* **:** one that checks; *esp* **:** one who checks out purchases in a supermarket

check•er•ber•ry \ˈche-kər-ˌber-ē\ *n* **:** WINTERGREEN 1; *also* **:** the spicy red fruit of this plant

check•er•board \-ˌbōrd\ *n* **:** a board of 64 squares of alternate colors used in various games

check•ered \ˈche-kərd\ *adj* **:** marked by inconsistent fortune or recurring problems ⟨his ∼ past⟩

check•ers \ˈche-kərz\ *n* **:** a game for two played on a checkerboard with each player having 12 pieces

check in *vb* **:** to report one's presence or arrival (as at a hotel)

check•list \ˈchek-ˌlist\ *n* **1** ♦ **:** a list of things to be checked or done **2** ♦ **:** a comprehensive list

♦ [1, 2] catalog, list, listing, menu, register, registry, roll, roster, schedule, table

check•mate \ˈchek-ˌmāt\ *vb* **1** ♦ **:** to thwart completely **:** FRUSTRATE **2 :** to attack (an opponent's king) in chess so that escape is impossible — **checkmate** *n*

♦ baffle, balk, beat, foil, frustrate, thwart

check•off \ˈche-ˌkȯf\ *n* **:** the deduction of union dues from a worker's paycheck by the employer

check•out \ˈche-ˌkau̇t\ *n* **1 :** the action or an instance of checking out **2 :** a counter at which checking out is done **3 :** the process of examining and testing something as to readiness for intended use

check out *vb* **1 :** to settle one's account (as at a hotel) and leave **2 :** to total or have totaled the cost of purchases in a store and to make or receive payment for them

check•point \ˈchek-ˌpȯint\ *n* **:** a point at which a check is performed

check•room \-ˌrüm, -ˌru̇m\ *n* **:** a room at which baggage, parcels, or clothing is left for safekeeping

checks and balances *n pl* **:** a system allowing each branch of a government to restrict the actions of another branch (as by a veto)

check•up \ˈche-ˌkəp\ *n* ♦ **:** the act of checking something or someone **:** EXAMINATION; *esp* **:** a general physical examination

♦ audit, check, examination, inspection, review, scan, scrutiny, survey

ched•dar \ˈche-dər\ *n, often cap* **:** a hard mild to sharp white or yellow cheese of smooth texture

cheek \ˈchēk\ *n* **1 :** the fleshy side part of the face **2** ♦ **:** insolent boldness and self-assurance : IMPUDENCE, AUDACITY **3 :** BUTTOCK 1 — **cheeked** \ˈchēkt\ *adj*

♦ audacity, brass, brazenness, chutzpah, effrontery, gall, impertinence, impudence, nerve, presumption, sauce, sauciness, temerity

cheek•bone \ˈchēk-ˌbōn\ *n* **:** the bone or bony ridge below the eye
cheek•i•ness \-kē-nəs\ *n* **:** insolence or impudence of speech or behavior
cheeky \ˈchē-kē\ *adj* **cheek•i•er; -est** ♦ **:** insolently bold **:** IMPUDENT, SAUCY — **cheek•i•ly** \-kə-lē\ *adv*

♦ arch, bold, brash, brazen, cocky, fresh, impertinent, impudent, insolent, nervy, sassy, saucy

cheep \ˈchēp\ *vb* ♦ **:** to utter faint shrill sounds **:** PEEP — **cheep** *n*

♦ chirp, peep, pipe, tweet, twitter

[1]**cheer** \ˈchir\ *n* **1** ♦ **:** state of mind or heart **:** SPIRIT **2** ♦ **:** lightness of mind and feeling **3 :** hospitable entertainment **:** WELCOME **4 :** food and drink for a feast **5 :** something that gladdens **6 :** a shout of applause or encouragement

♦ [1] frame, humor (*or* humour), mode, mood, spirit, temper ♦ [2] comfort, consolation, relief, solace ♦ [2] cheerfulness, cheeriness, glee, hilarity, joviality, merriment, mirth

[2]**cheer** *vb* **1** ♦ **:** to give hope or courage to **:** COMFORT — usually used with *up* **2 :** to make glad **3 :** to urge on especially by shouts **4** ♦ **:** to applaud or show approval of especially with shouts **5 :** to grow or be cheerful — usually used with *up* — **cheer•er** *n*

♦ *usu* **cheer up** [1] buoy (up), comfort, embolden, encourage, hearten, inspire, steel ♦ [4] acclaim, applaud, crack up, hail, laud, praise, salute, tout

cheer•ful \ˈchir-fəl\ *adj* **1** ♦ **:** having or showing good spirits **2** ♦ **:** conducive to good spirits **:** pleasant and bright

♦ [1] blithe, bright, buoyant, cheery, chipper, gay, lightsome, sunny, upbeat ***Ant*** dour, gloomy, glum, morose, saturnine, sulky, sullen ♦ [2] bright, cheery, gay, glad ***Ant*** bleak, cheerless, dark, depressing, dismal, dreary, gloomy, gray

cheer•ful•ly *adv* ♦ **:** in a cheerful manner

♦ gaily, happily, heartily, jovially, merrily, mirthfully

cheer•ful•ness *n* ♦ **:** the quality or state of being cheerful

♦ cheer, cheeriness, glee, hilarity, joviality, merriment, mirth

cheer•i•ness \-ē-nəs\ *n* ♦ **:** the quality or state of being cheery

♦ cheer, cheerfulness, glee, hilarity, joviality, merriment, mirth, mirthfulness

cheer•lead•er \ˈchir-ˌlē-dər\ *n* **:** a person who directs organized cheering especially at a sports event
cheer•less \ˈchir-ləs\ *adj* **:** lacking qualities that cheer **:** BLEAK, DISPIRITING — **cheer•less•ly** *adv* — **cheer•less•ness** *n*
cheery \ˈchir-ē\ *adj* **cheer•i•er; -est 1** ♦ **:** marked by cheerfulness or good spirits **:** CHEERFUL **2** ♦ **:** causing or suggesting cheerfulness ⟨~ music⟩ — **cheer•i•ly** \-ə-lē\ *adv*

♦ [1] blithe, bright, buoyant, cheerful, chipper, gay, lightsome, sunny, upbeat ♦ [2] bright, cheerful, gay, glad

cheese \ˈchēz\ *n* **:** the curd of milk usually pressed into cakes and cured for use as food
cheese•burg•er \-ˌbər-gər\ *n* **:** a hamburger topped with cheese
cheese•cake \-ˌkāk\ *n* **1 :** a dessert consisting of a creamy filling usually containing cheese baked in a shell **2 :** photographs of shapely scantily clad women
cheese•cloth \-ˌklȯth\ *n* **:** a lightweight coarse cotton gauze
cheese•par•ing \-ˌpar-iŋ\ *n* **:** miserly economizing — **cheeseparing** *adj*
cheese•steak \-ˌstāk\ *n* **:** a sandwich of thinly sliced beef topped with melted cheese
cheesy \ˈchē-zē\ *adj* **chees•i•er; -est 1 :** resembling, suggesting, or containing cheese **2** *slang* **:** CHEAP 3
chee•tah \ˈchē-tə\ *n* **:** a large long-legged swift-moving spotted cat of Africa and southwestern Asia
chef \ˈshef\ *n* **1 :** a cook who manages the kitchen (as of a restaurant) **2 :** a person who prepares food for eating **:** COOK
chef d'oeu•vre \shā-ˈdœvrᵊ\ *n, pl* **chefs d'oeuvre** *same*\ **:** MASTERPIECE
chem *abbr* chemical; chemist; chemistry
[1]**chem•i•cal** \ˈke-mi-kəl\ *adj* **1 :** of, relating to, used in, or produced by chemistry **2 :** acting or operated or produced by chemicals — **chem•i•cal•ly** \-k(ə-)lē\ *adv*
[2]**chemical** *n* **:** a substance obtained by a chemical process or used for producing a chemical effect
chemical engineering *n* **:** engineering dealing with the industrial application of chemistry
chemical warfare *n* **:** warfare using incendiary mixtures, smokes, or irritant, burning, or asphyxiating gases
chemical weapon *n* **:** a weapon used in chemical warfare
che•mise \shə-ˈmēz\ *n* **1 :** a woman's one-piece undergarment **2 :** a loose straight-hanging dress
chem•ist \ˈke-mist\ *n* **1 :** one trained in chemistry **2** *Brit* **:** PHARMACIST
chem•is•try \ˈke-mə-strē\ *n, pl* **-tries 1 :** the science that deals with the composition, structure, and properties of substances and of the changes they undergo **2 :** chemical composition or properties ⟨the ~ of gasoline⟩ **3 :** a strong mutual attraction; *also* **:** harmonious interaction among people (as on a team)
che•mo \ˈkē-mō\ *n* **:** CHEMOTHERAPY
che•mo•ther•a•py \ˌkē-mō-ˈther-ə-pē\ *n* **:** the use of chemicals in the treatment or control of disease — **che•mo•ther•a•peu•tic** \-ˌther-ə-ˈpyü-tik\ *adj*
che•nille \shə-ˈnēl\ *n* **:** a fabric with a deep fuzzy pile often used for bedspreads and rugs
cheque *Can and Brit var of* [1]CHECK 8
cher•ish \ˈcher-ish\ *vb* **1** ♦ **:** to hold dear **:** feel or treat with care and affection **2** ♦ **:** to keep deeply in mind — **cher•ish•able** *adj* — **cher•ish•er** *n*

♦ [1] adore, love, worship ♦ [1] appreciate, love, prize, treasure, value ♦ [2] bear, entertain, harbor (*or* harbour), have, hold, nurse

Cher•o•kee \ˈcher-ə-(ˌ)kē\ *n, pl* **Cherokee** *or* **Cherokees :** a member of an American Indian people orig. of Tennessee and No. Carolina; *also* **:** their language
che•root \shə-ˈrüt\ *n* **:** a cigar cut square at both ends
cher•ry \ˈcher-ē\ *n, pl* **cherries 1 :** the small fleshy pale yellow to deep blackish red fruit of a tree related to the roses; *also* **:** the tree or its wood **2 :** a moderate red
chert \ˈchərt, ˈchat\ *n* **:** a rock resembling flint and consisting essentially of fine crystalline quartz and fibrous chalcedony — **cherty** *adj*
cher•ub \ˈcher-əb\ *n* **1** *pl* **cher•u•bim** \ˈcher-ə-ˌbim\ **:** an angel of the 2d highest rank **2** *pl* **cherubs :** a chubby rosy person — **che•ru•bic** \chə-ˈrü-bik\ *adj*
chess \ˈches\ *n* **:** a game for two played on a chessboard with each player having 16 pieces — **chess•man** \-ˌman, -mən\ *n*
chess•board \ˈches-ˌbōrd\ *n* **:** a checkerboard used in the game of chess
chest \ˈchest\ *n* **1** ♦ **:** a box, case, or boxlike receptacle for storage or shipping **2 :** the part of the body enclosed by the ribs and sternum — **chest•ed** \ˈches-təd\ *adj* — **chest•ful** \ˈchest-ˌfu̇l\ *n*

♦ box, caddy, case, casket, locker, trunk

ches•ter•field \ˈches-tər-ˌfēld\ *n* **1 :** an overcoat with a velvet collar **2 :** a large sofa usually with upright armrests
chest•nut \ˈches-(ˌ)nət\ *n* **1 :** the edible nut of any of a genus of trees related to the beech and oaks; *also* **:** this tree **2 :** a grayish to reddish brown **3 :** an old joke or story
che•val glass \shə-ˈval-\ *n* **:** a full-length mirror that may be tilted in a frame
che•va•lier \ˌshe-və-ˈlir, shə-ˈval-ˌyā\ *n* **:** a member of one of various orders of knighthood or of merit
chev•i•ot \ˈshe-vē-ət\ *n, often cap* **1 :** a twilled fabric with a rough nap **2 :** a sturdy soft-finished cotton fabric
chev•ron \ˈshe-vrən\ *n* **:** a sleeve badge of one or more V-shaped or inverted V-shaped stripes worn to indicate rank or service (as in the armed forces)
[1]**chew** \ˈchü\ *vb* ♦ **:** to crush, grind, or gnaw (as food) with the teeth — **chew•able** *adj* — **chew•er** *n* — **chew on :** to think about **:** PONDER ⟨*chew on* the proposals⟩ — **chew the fat :** to make conversation **:** CHAT

♦ bite, champ, chomp, crunch, gnaw, nibble

[2]**chew** *n* **1 :** an act of chewing **2 :** something for chewing
chew out *vb* ♦ **:** to bawl out **:** to criticize severely

♦ admonish, chide, lecture, rail (at *or* against), rate, rebuke, reprimand, scold

chew over *vb* ♦ **:** to meditate on **:** think about reflectively

♦ cogitate, consider, contemplate, debate, deliberate, entertain, meditate, mull, ponder, question, ruminate, study, think, weigh

chewy \ˈchü-ē\ *adj* **:** requiring much chewing ⟨~ candy⟩
Chey•enne \shī-ˈan, -ˈen\ *n, pl* **Cheyenne** *or* **Cheyennes :** a

member of an American Indian people of the western plains of the U.S.; *also* : their language

chg *abbr* **1** change **2** charge

chi \ˈkī\ *n* : the 22d letter of the Greek alphabet — Χ or χ

Chi•an•ti \kē-ˈän-tē, -ˈan-\ *n* : a dry usually red wine

chiar•oscu•ro \kē-ˌär-ə-ˈskůr-ō, -ˈskyůr-\ *n, pl* **-ros** **1** : pictorial representation in terms of light and shade without regard to color **2** : the arrangement or treatment of light and dark parts in a pictorial work of art

[1]**chic** \ˈshēk\ *n* : STYLISHNESS

[2]**chic** *adj* ♦ : cleverly stylish : SMART; *also* : currently fashionable

♦ à la mode, fashionable, in, modish, sharp, smart, snappy, stylish

Chi•ca•na \chi-ˈkä-nə*also* shi-\ *n* : an American woman or girl of Mexican descent — **Chicana** *adj*

chi•cane \shi-ˈkān\ *n* : CHICANERY

chi•ca•nery \-ˈka-nə-rē\ *n, pl* **-ner•ies** ♦ : deception by artful subterfuge or sophistry : TRICKERY

♦ artifice, hanky-panky, subterfuge, trickery, wile

Chi•ca•no \chi-ˈkä-nō\ *n, pl* **-nos** : an American of Mexican descent — **Chicano** *adj*

chi•chi \ˈshē-(ˌ)shē, ˈchē-(ˌ)chē\ *adj* **1** : SHOWY, FRILLY **2** : ARTY, PRECIOUS **3** : CHIC — **chichi** *n*

chick \ˈchik\ *n* **1** : a young chicken; *also* : a young bird **2** *slang* : a young woman

chick•a•dee \ˈchi-kə-(ˌ)dē\ *n* : any of several small grayish American birds with black or brown caps

Chick•a•saw \ˈchi-kə-ˌsȯ\ *n, pl* **Chickasaw** *or* **Chickasaws** : a member of an American Indian people of Mississippi and Alabama

[1]**chick•en** \ˈchi-kən\ *n* **1** : a common domestic fowl especially when young; *also* : its flesh used as food **2** ♦ : one who is easily frightened and easily daunted : COWARD

♦ coward, craven, dastard, poltroon, recreant, sissy

[2]**chicken** *adj* **1** ♦ : being or behaving like a coward : COWARDLY **2** *slang* : insistent on petty especially military discipline

♦ cowardly, craven, dastardly, pusillanimous, recreant, spineless, yellow

chicken feed *n, slang* : an insignificant sum of money

chick•en•heart•ed \ˌchi-kən-ˈhär-təd\ *adj* : being or behaving like a coward : COWARDLY

chicken out *vb* : to lose one's courage

chicken pox *n* : an acute contagious virus disease especially of children characterized by a low fever and vesicles

chicken wire *n* : a light wire netting of hexagonal mesh

chick•pea \ˈchik-ˌpē\ *n* : an Asian herb of the legume family cultivated for its short pods with one or two edible seeds; *also* : its seed

chick•weed \ˈchik-ˌwēd\ *n* : any of several low-growing small-leaved weeds related to the pinks

chi•cle \ˈchi-kəl\ *n* : a gum from the latex of a tropical tree used as the chief ingredient of chewing gum

chic•o•ry \ˈchi-kə-rē\ *n, pl* **-ries** : a usually blue-flowered herb related to the daisies and grown for its root and for use in salads; *also* : its dried ground root used to flavor or adulterate coffee

chide \ˈchīd\ *vb* **chid** \ˈchid\ *or* **chid•ed** \ˈchī-dəd\; **chid** *or* **chid•den** \ˈchid-ᵊn\ *or* **chided; chid•ing** ♦ : to speak disapprovingly to

♦ admonish, rebuke, reprimand, reproach, reprove admonish, lecture, rail (at *or* against), rate, rebuke, scold

[1]**chief** \ˈchēf\ *adj* **1** ♦ : highest in rank **2** ♦ : most important

♦ [1] first, foremost, head, high, lead, preeminent, premier, primary, prime, principal, supreme ♦ [2] arch, cardinal, central, dominant, first, foremost, grand, key, main, paramount, predominant

[2]**chief** *n* **1** ♦ : the leader of a body or organization : HEAD **2** : the principal or most valuable part — **chief•dom** *n*

♦ boss, captain, foreman, head, headman, helmsman, kingpin, leader, master, taskmaster

chief•ly *adv* ♦ : for the most part : most importantly

♦ altogether, basically, generally, largely, mainly, mostly, overall, predominantly, primarily, principally

chief master sergeant *n* : a noncommissioned officer of the highest rank in the air force

chief petty officer *n* : an enlisted man in the navy ranking next below a senior chief petty officer

chief•tain \ˈchēf-tən\ *n* : a chief especially of a band, tribe, or clan — **chief•tain•cy** \-sē\ *n* — **chief•tain•ship** *n*

chief warrant officer *n* : a warrant officer of senior rank

chif•fon \shi-ˈfän, ˈshi-ˌ\ *n* : a sheer fabric especially of silk

chif•fo•nier \ˌshi-fə-ˈnir\ *n* : a high narrow chest of drawers

chig•ger \ˈchi-gər\ *n* : a bloodsucking larval mite that causes intense itching

chi•gnon \ˈshēn-ˌyän\ *n* : a knot of hair worn at the back of the head

Chi•hua•hua \chə-ˈwä-ˌwä\ *n* : any of a breed of very small large-eared dogs that originated in Mexico

chil•blain \ˈchil-ˌblān\ *n* : a sore or inflamed swelling (as on the feet or hands) caused by exposure to cold

child \ˈchīld\ *n, pl* **chil•dren** \ˈchil-drən\ **1** ♦ : an unborn or recently born person **2** ♦ : a young person between the periods of infancy and youth **3** : a male or female offspring : SON, DAUGHTER **4** : one strongly influenced by another or by a place or state of affairs — **child•less** *adj* — **child•less•ness** *n* — **child•like** *adj*

♦ [1] baby, infant, newborn ♦ [2] cub, juvenile, kid, youngster, youth ***Ant*** adult, grown-up

child•bear•ing \ˈchīld-ˌbar-iŋ\ *n* : of or relating to the process of conceiving, being pregnant with, and giving birth to children : CHILDBIRTH — **childbearing** *adj*

child•birth \-ˌbərth\ *n* ♦ : the act or process of giving birth to offspring

♦ delivery, labor (*or* labour)

child•hood \-ˌhůd\ *n* : the state or period of being a child

child•ish *adj* ♦ : marked by or suggestive of immaturity and lack of poise — **child•ish•ly** *adv* — **child•ish•ness** *n*

♦ adolescent, babyish, immature, infantile, juvenile, kiddish ***Ant*** adult, grown-up, mature

[1]**child•proof** \-ˌprüf\ *adj* **1** : made to prevent opening or use by children ⟨~ lighters⟩ **2** : made safe for children

[2]**childproof** *vb* : to make childproof ⟨~ a house⟩

child's play *n* **1** ♦ : an extremely simple task or act **2** : something that is insignificant

♦ breeze, cinch, picnic, pushover, snap

Chil•ean \ˈchi-lē-ən, chə-ˈlā-ən\ *n* : a native or inhabitant of Chile — **Chilean** *adj*

chili *or* **chile** *or* **chil•li** \ˈchi-lē\ *n, pl* **chil•ies** *or* **chil•es** *or* **chil•lies** **1** : a pungent pepper related to the tomato **2** : a thick sauce of meat and chilies **3** : CHILI CON CARNE

chili con car•ne \ˌchi-lē-kän-ˈkär-nē\ *n* : a spiced stew of ground beef and chilies or chili powder usually with beans

chili powder *n* : a seasoning made of ground chilies and other spices

chili sauce *n* : a spiced tomato sauce usually made with red and green peppers

[1]**chill** \ˈchil\ *n* **1** : a feeling of coldness accompanied by shivering **2** ♦ : moderate coldness **3** : a check to enthusiasm or warmth of feeling

♦ bite, bitterness, bleakness, nip, rawness, sharpness

[2]**chill** *adj* **1** : moderately cold **2** : affected by a penetrating cold : benumbed or shivering with cold : COLD, RAW **3** : cool in manner or feeling : lacking warmth : UNFRIENDLY ⟨a ~ reception⟩ **4** : DEPRESSING, DISPIRITING

[3]**chill** *vb* **1** : to make or become cold or chilly **2** : to make cool especially without freezing — **chill•er** *n*

chill•i•ness *n* : the quality or state of being chilly

chill•ing \ˈchi-liŋ\ *adj* : gravely disturbing or frightening ⟨a ~ scene⟩

chill out *vb, slang* ♦ : to calm down : RELAX

♦ de-stress, relax, unwind

chilly \ˈchi-lē\ *adj* **chill•i•er; -est** **1** ♦ : noticeably cold **2** : unpleasantly affected by cold **3** ♦ : lacking warmth of feeling

♦ [1] bitter, bleak, chill, nippy, raw, sharp ♦ [3] chill, cold, cold-blooded, cool, frigid, frosty, glacial, icy, unfriendly, unsympathetic, wintry

[1]**chime** \ˈchīm\ *n* **1** : a set of bells musically tuned **2** : the sound of a set of bells — usually used in plural **3** : a musical sound suggesting bells

[2]**chime** *vb* **chimed; chim•ing** **1** ♦ : to make bell-like sounds **2** : to indicate (as the time of day) by chiming **3** : to be or act in accord : be in harmony

♦ knell, peal, ring, toll

chime in *vb* ♦ : to break into or join in a conversation

♦ break, cut in, interpose, interrupt, intrude

chi•me•ra \kī-ˈmir-ə, kə-\ *n* **1 :** an imaginary monster made up of incongruous parts **2 a** ♦ **:** an illusion or fabrication of the mind **b :** an impossible dream

♦ conceit, daydream, delusion, dream, fancy, fantasy, figment, hallucination, illusion, phantasm, pipe dream, unreality, vision

chi•me•ri•cal \ki-ˈmer-i-kəl\ *also* **chi•me•ric** \-ik\ *adj* **1** ♦ **:** existing only as the product of unchecked imagination **:** fantastically visionary or improbable **2 :** given to fantastic schemes

♦ fabulous, fanciful, fantastic, fictitious, imaginary, made-up, mythical, phantom, pretend, unreal

chim•ney \ˈchim-nē\ *n, pl* **chimneys 1 :** a vertical structure extending above the roof of a building for carrying off smoke **2 :** a glass tube around a lamp flame

chimp \ˈchimp\ *n* **:** CHIMPANZEE

chim•pan•zee \ˌchim-ˌpan-ˈzē, chim-ˈpan-zē\ *n* **:** an African ape related to the much larger gorilla

[1]**chin** \ˈchin\ *n* **:** the part of the face below the lower lip including the prominence of the lower jaw — **chin•less** *adj*

[2]**chin** *vb* **chinned; chin•ning :** to raise (oneself) while hanging by the hands until the chin is level with the support

chi•na \ˈchī-nə\ *n* **:** porcelain ware; *also* **:** domestic pottery in general

Chi•na•town \-ˌtau̇n\ *n* **:** the Chinese quarter of a city

chinch bug \ˈchinch-\ *n* **:** a small black and white bug destructive to cereal grasses

chin•chil•la \chin-ˈchi-lə\ *n* **1 :** either of two small So. American rodents with soft pearl-gray fur; *also* **:** this fur **2 :** a heavy long-napped woolen cloth

chine \ˈchīn\ *n* **:** the back or spine of an animal or man **:** BACKBONE, SPINE; *also* **:** a cut of meat including all or part of the backbone

Chi•nese \chī-ˈnēz, -ˈnēs\ *n, pl* **Chinese 1 :** a native or inhabitant of China **2 :** any of a group of related languages of China — **Chinese** *adj*

Chinese cabbage *n* **1 :** BOK CHOY **2 :** an Asian garden plant related to the cabbage and widely grown in the U.S. for its tight elongate cylindrical heads of pale green to cream-colored leaves

Chinese checkers *n* **:** a game in which each player in turn transfers a set of marbles from a home point to the opposite point of a pitted 6-pointed star

Chinese gooseberry *n* **:** a subtropical vine that bears kiwifruit; *also* **:** KIWIFRUIT

Chinese lantern *n* **:** a collapsible translucent cover for a light

[1]**chink** \ˈchiŋk\ *n* ♦ **:** a small crack or fissure

♦ cleft, crack, cranny, crevice, fissure, rift, split

[2]**chink** *vb* **:** to fill the chinks of **:** stop up

[3]**chink** *n* **:** a slight sharp metallic sound

[4]**chink** *vb* ♦ **:** to make a slight sharp metallic sound

♦ jingle, tinkle

chi•no \ˈchē-nō\ *n, pl* **chinos 1 :** a usually khaki cotton twill **2** *pl* **:** an article of clothing made of chino

Chi•nook \shə-ˈnu̇k, chə-, -ˈnük\ *n, pl* **Chinook** *or* **Chinooks :** a member of an American Indian people of Oregon

chintz \ˈchints\ *n* **:** a usually glazed printed cotton cloth

chintzy \ˈchint-sē\ *adj* **chintz•i•er; -est 1 :** decorated with or as if with chintz **2 :** GAUDY, CHEAP **3 :** STINGY

chin–up \ˈchi-ˌnəp\ *n* **:** the act of chinning oneself

[1]**chip** \ˈchip\ *n* **1** ♦ **:** a small usually thin and flat piece (as of wood) cut or broken off **2 :** a thin crisp morsel of food **3 :** a counter used in games (as poker) **4** *pl, slang* **:** something generally accepted as a means of payment **:** MONEY **5** ♦ **:** a flaw left after a chip is removed **6 :** INTEGRATED CIRCUIT **7 :** a very small slice of silicon containing electronic circuits

♦ [1] flake, splinter ♦ [5] hack, indentation, nick, notch

[2]**chip** *vb* **chipped; chip•ping 1 :** to cut or break chips from **2 :** to break off in small pieces at the edges **3 :** to play a chip shot

chip in *vb* ♦ **:** to give money or assistance to an enterprise **:** CONTRIBUTE

♦ contribute, kick in, pitch in

chip•munk \ˈchip-ˌməŋk\ *n* **:** any of a genus of small striped No. American and Asian rodents closely related to the squirrels and marmots

chi•pot•le \chə-ˈpōt-lā\ *n* **:** a smoked and usually dried jalapeño pepper

chipped beef \ˈchipt-\ *n* **:** smoked dried beef sliced thin

[1]**chip•per** \ˈchi-pər\ *n* **:** one that chips

[2]**chipper** *adj* **1** ♦ **:** being high in spirits **:** CHEERFUL **2** ♦ **:** being in good health **:** being in a state of physical well-being

♦ [1] blithe, bright, buoyant, cheerful, cheery, gay, lightsome, sunny, upbeat ♦ [2] able-bodied, fit, hale, healthy, hearty, robust, sound, well, whole, wholesome

Chip•pe•wa \ˈchi-pə-ˌwȯ, -ˌwä, -ˌwā, -wə\ *n, pl* **Chippewa** *or* **Chippewas :** OJIBWA

chip shot *n* **:** a short usually low shot to the green in golf

chi•rog•ra•phy \kī-ˈrä-grə-fē\ *n* **:** HANDWRITING, PENMANSHIP — **chi•ro•graph•ic** \ˌkī-rə-ˈgra-fik\ *adj*

chi•rop•o•dy \kə-ˈrä-pə-dē, shə-\ *n* **:** PODIATRY — **chi•rop•o•dist** \-dist\ *n*

chi•ro•prac•tic \ˈkī-rə-ˌprak-tik\ *n* **:** a system of therapy based especially on manipulation of body structures — **chi•ro•prac•tor** \-tər\ *n*

[1]**chirp** \ˈchərp\ *n* **:** a short sharp sound characteristic of a small bird or cricket

[2]**chirp** *vb* ♦ **:** to make a usually repetitive short sharp sound

♦ cheep, peep, pipe, tweet, twitter

[1]**chis•el** \ˈchi-zəl\ *n* **:** a metal tool with a sharpened edge at one end used to chip, carve, or cut into a solid material (as wood or stone)

[2]**chisel** *vb* **-eled** *or* **-elled; -el•ing** *or* **-el•ling 1 :** to work with or as if with a chisel **2 a** ♦ **:** to obtain something from by unfair practices **:** CHEAT **b :** to obtain by shrewd often unfair methods — **chis•el•er** *n*

♦ bleed, cheat, cozen, defraud, fleece, gyp, hustle, mulct, rook, shortchange, skin, squeeze, stick, sting, swindle, victimize

[1]**chit** \ˈchit\ *n* **1 :** CHILD **2 :** a pert young woman

[2]**chit** *n* **:** a signed voucher for a small debt

chit•chat \ˈchit-ˌchat\ *n* ♦ **:** casual or trifling conversation — **chitchat** *vb*

♦ chat, chatter, gabfest, gossip, palaver, rap, talk

chi•tin \ˈkīt-ᵊn\ *n* **:** a sugar polymer that forms part of the hard outer integument especially of insects — **chi•tin•ous** *adj*

chit•ter•lings *or* **chit•lins** \ˈchit-lənz\ *n pl* **:** the intestines of hogs especially when prepared as food

chi•val•ric \shə-ˈval-rik\ *adj* **:** relating to chivalry **:** CHIVALROUS

chiv•al•rous \ˈshi-vəl-rəs\ *adj* **1 :** of or relating to chivalry **2** ♦ **:** marked by honor, courtesy, and generosity **3 :** marked by gracious courtesy especially to women — **chiv•al•rous•ly** *adv* — **chiv•al•rous•ness** *n*

♦ gallant, great, greathearted, high, high-minded, lofty, lordly, magnanimous, noble, sublime

chiv•al•ry \ˈshi-vəl-rē\ *n, pl* **-ries 1 :** mounted men-at-arms **2 :** the system or practices of knighthood **3 :** the spirit or character of the ideal knight

chive \ˈchīv\ *n* **:** an herb related to the onion that has leaves used for flavoring

chla•myd•ia \klə-ˈmi-dē-ə\ *n, pl* **-i•ae** \-dē-ˌē\ **1 :** any of a genus of bacteria that cause various diseases of the eye and urogenital tract **2 :** a disease or infection caused by chlamydiae

chlo•ral hydrate \ˈklōr-əl-\ *n* **:** a white crystalline compound used as a hypnotic and sedative

chlor•dane \ˈklōr-ˌdān\ *n* **:** a highly chlorinated persistent insecticide

chlo•ride \ˈklōr-ˌīd\ *n* **:** a compound of chlorine with another element or group

chlo•ri•nate \ˈklōr-ə-ˌnāt\ *vb* **-nat•ed; -nat•ing :** to treat or combine with chlorine or a chlorine compound — **chlo•ri•na•tion** \ˌklōr-ə-ˈnā-shən\ *n* — **chlo•ri•na•tor** \ˈklōr-ə-ˌnā-tər\ *n*

chlo•rine \ˈklōr-ˌēn\ *n* **:** a nonmetallic chemical element that is found alone as a strong-smelling greenish yellow irritating gas and is used as a bleach, oxidizing agent, and disinfectant

chlo•rite \ˈklōr-ˌīt\ *n* **:** a usually green mineral found with and resembling mica

chlo•ro•flu•o•ro•car•bon \ˌklōr-ə-ˈflōr-ə-ˌkär-bən, -ˈflu̇r-\ *n* **:** any of several gaseous compounds that contain carbon, chlorine, fluorine, and sometimes hydrogen and are used especially as solvents, refrigerants, and aerosol propellants

[1]**chlo•ro•form** \ˈklōr-ə-ˌfȯrm\ *n* **:** a colorless heavy fluid with etherlike odor used as a solvent and anesthetic

[2]**chloroform** *vb* **:** to treat with chloroform to produce anesthesia or death

chlo•ro•phyll \-ˌfil\ *n* **:** the green coloring matter of plants that functions in photosynthesis

chm *abbr* chairman

chock \ˈchäk\ *n* **:** a wedge for steadying something or for blocking the movement of a wheel — **chock** *vb*

chock•a•block \'chä-kə-ˌbläk\ *adj* : very full : CROWDED
chock–full *or* **chock•ful** \'chək-'fu̇l, 'chäk-\ *adj* ♦ : full to the limit : CRAMMED

♦ brimful, crowded, fat, fraught, full, loaded, packed, replete

choc•o•late \'chä-k(ə-)lət, 'chȯ-\ *n* **1 :** a food prepared from ground roasted cacao beans; *also* : a drink prepared from this **2 :** a candy made of or with a coating of chocolate **3 :** a dark brown color — **choc•o•laty** *or* **choc•o•lat•ey** \-k(ə-)lə-tē\ *adj*
Choc•taw \'chäk-ˌtȯ\ *n, pl* **Choctaw** *or* **Choctaws :** a member of an American Indian people of Mississippi, Alabama, and Louisiana; *also* : their language
¹choice \'chȯis\ *n* **1** ♦ **:** the act of choosing : SELECTION **2** ♦ **:** the power or opportunity of choosing : OPTION **3** ♦ **:** the best part **4 :** a person or thing selected **5 :** a variety offered for selection

♦ [1] election, selection ♦ [2] alternative, discretion, option, pick, preference, way ♦ [3] best, cream, elect, elite, fat, flower, pick, prime

²choice *adj* **choic•er; choic•est** **1 :** worthy of being chosen **2 :** selected with care **3** ♦ **:** of high quality

♦ dainty, delicate, elegant, exquisite, rare, select

choir \'kwī(-ə)r\ *n* **1** ♦ **:** an organized company of singers (as in a church service) **2 :** the part of a church occupied by the singers or by the clergy

♦ chorale, chorus

choir•boy \'kwī(-ə)r-ˌbȯi\ *n* : a boy member of a church choir
choir•mas•ter \-ˌmas-tər\ *n* : the director of a choir (as in a church)
¹choke \'chōk\ *vb* **choked; chok•ing** **1** ♦ **:** to hinder breathing (as by obstructing the trachea) : STRANGLE **2 :** to check the growth or action of **3** ♦ **:** to obstruct by filling up or clogging : CLOG, OBSTRUCT **4 :** to enrich the fuel mixture of (a motor) by restricting the carburetor air intake **5 :** to perform badly in a critical situation

♦ [1] smother, stifle, strangle, suffocate ♦ [1] garrote, strangle, throttle ♦ [3] block, clog, close (off), congest, dam, jam, obstruct, plug (up), stop (up), stuff

²choke *n* **1 :** the act of choking **2 :** a narrowing in size toward the muzzle in the bore of a gun **3 :** a valve for choking a gasoline engine
chok•er \'chō-kər\ *n* : something (as a necklace) worn tightly around the neck
cho•ler \'kä-lər, 'kō-\ *n* : a tendency toward anger : IRASCIBILITY
chol•era \'kä-lə-rə\ *n* : any of several bacterial diseases usually marked by severe vomiting and dysentery
cho•ler•ic \'kä-lə-rik, kə-'ler-ik\ *adj* **1** ♦ **:** easily moved to often unreasonable or excessive anger : hot-tempered **2 :** ANGRY, IRATE

♦ crabby, cranky, cross, crotchety, grouchy, grumpy, irascible, irritable, peevish, perverse, petulant, short-tempered, snappish, snappy, snippy, testy, waspish

cho•les•ter•ol \kə-'les-tə-ˌrȯl\ *n* : a physiologically important waxy steroid alcohol found in animal tissues and in high concentrations implicated as a cause of arteriosclerosis
chomp \'chämp, 'chȯmp\ *vb* ♦ : to chew or bite on something heavily

♦ bite, champ, chew, crunch, gnaw, nibble

choose \'chüz\ *vb* **chose** \chōz\; **cho•sen** \'chōz-ᵊn\; **choos•ing** \chü-ziŋ\ **1** ♦ **:** to select especially after consideration **2** ♦ **:** to make a final choice or judgment about : DECIDE **3 :** to have a preference for — **choos•er** *n*

♦ [1] cull, elect, handpick, name, opt, pick, prefer, select, single, take *Ant* decline, refuse, reject, turn down ♦ [2] conclude, decide, determine, figure, opt, resolve

choosy *or* **choos•ey** \'chü-zē\ *adj* **choos•i•er; -est** ♦ : very particular in making choices

♦ demanding, exacting, particular, picky, selective

¹chop \'chäp\ *vb* **chopped; chop•ping** **1** ♦ **:** to cut or sever usually by repeated blows **2** ♦ **:** to cut into small pieces : MINCE **3 :** to strike (a ball) with a short quick downward stroke

♦ [1] cut, fell, hew ♦ [2] hash, mince

²chop *n* **1 :** a sharp downward blow or stroke **2 :** a small cut of meat often including part of a rib **3 :** a short abrupt motion (as of a wave)
³chop *n* **1 :** an official seal or stamp **2 :** a mark on goods to indicate quality or kind; *also* : QUALITY, GRADE
chop•house \'chäp-ˌhau̇s\ *n* : RESTAURANT
chop•per \'chä-pər\ *n* **1 :** one that chops **2** *pl, slang* : TEETH **3 :** HELICOPTER
chop•pi•ness \'chä-pē-nəs\ *n* : the quality or state of being choppy
¹chop•py \'chä-pē\ *adj* **chop•pi•er; -est** **1 :** rough with small waves **2** ♦ **:** interrupted by ups and downs : moving along with fits and starts **3** ♦ **:** lacking orderly continuity, arrangement, or relevance : DISCONNECTED — **chop•pi•ly** \-pə-lē\ *adv*

♦ [2] casual, discontinuous, erratic, fitful, intermittent, irregular, occasional, spasmodic, sporadic, spotty, unsteady ♦ [3] disconnected, disjointed, unconnected

²choppy *adj* **chop•pi•er; -est :** CHANGEABLE, VARIABLE ⟨a ~ wind⟩
chops \'chäps\ *n pl* **1 :** the fleshy covering of the jaws **2 :** expertise in a particular field or activity ⟨acting ~⟩
chop•stick \'chäp-ˌstik\ *n* : one of a pair of sticks used chiefly in Asian countries for lifting food to the mouth
chop su•ey \chäp-'sü-ē\ *n, pl* **chop sueys :** a dish made of vegetables (as bean sprouts, bamboo shoots, water chestnuts, onions, mushrooms) and meat or fish and served with rice
cho•ral \'kōr-əl\ *adj* : of, relating to, or sung by a choir or chorus or in chorus — **cho•ral•ly** *adv*
cho•rale \kə-'ral, -'räl\ *n* **1** ♦ **:** a hymn or psalm sung in church; *also* : a harmonization of a traditional melody **2 :** a group formed to sing church music : CHORUS, CHOIR

♦ anthem, canticle, carol, hymn, psalm, spiritual

¹chord \'kȯrd\ *n* : three or more musical tones sounded simultaneously
²chord *n* **1 :** CORD 2 **2 :** a straight line joining two points on a curve
chore \'chōr\ *n* **1** *pl* : the daily light work of a household or farm **2** ♦ **:** a routine task or job **3 :** a difficult or disagreeable task

♦ assignment, duty, job, stint, task

cho•rea \kə-'rē-ə\ *n* : a nervous disorder marked by spasmodic uncontrolled movements
cho•re•og•ra•phy \ˌkōr-ē-'ä-grə-fē\ *n, pl* **-phies :** the art of composing and arranging dances and especially ballets — **cho•reo•graph** \'kōr-ē-ə-ˌgraf\ *vb* — **cho•re•og•ra•pher** \ˌkōr-ē-'ä-grə-fər\ *n* — **cho•reo•graph•ic** \ˌkōr-ē-ə-'gra-fik\ *adj* — **cho•reo•graph•i•cal•ly** \-fi-k(ə-)lē\ *adv*
cho•ris•ter \'kōr-ə-stər\ *n* : a singer in a choir
¹chor•tle \'chȯrt-ᵊl\ *vb* **chor•tled; chor•tling :** to laugh or chuckle especially in satisfaction or exultation
²chortle *n* ♦ : a sound expressive of pleasure or exultation

♦ cackle, laugh, laughter, snicker, titter

¹chorus \'kōr-əs\ *n* **1** ♦ **:** an organized company of singers : CHOIR **2 :** a group of dancers and singers (as in a musical comedy) **3 :** a part of a song repeated at intervals **4 :** a composition to be sung by a chorus; *also* : group singing **5 :** sounds uttered by a number of persons or animals together ⟨a ~ of boos⟩

♦ choir, chorale

²chorus *vb* : to sing or utter in chorus
chose *past of* CHOOSE
cho•sen \'chōz-ᵊn\ *adj* ♦ : selected or marked for special favor or privilege

♦ elect, select

¹chow \'chau̇\ *n* ♦ : material that is taken or absorbed into the body in order to sustain growth and to furnish energy : FOOD

♦ fare, food, grub, meat, provender, provisions, viands, victuals

²chow *vb* : EAT — often used with *down*
³chow *n* : CHOW CHOW
chow•chow \'chau̇-ˌchau̇\ *n* : chopped mixed pickles in mustard sauce
chow chow \'chau̇-ˌchau̇\ *n* : any of a breed of thick-coated straight-legged muscular dogs of Chinese origin with a blue-black tongue and a short tail curled close to the back
chow•der \'chau̇-dər\ *n* : a soup or stew made from seafood or vegetables and containing milk or tomatoes
chow mein \'chau̇-'mān\ *n* : a seasoned stew of shredded or diced meat, mushrooms, and vegetables that is usually served with fried noodles
chrism \'kri-zəm\ *n* : consecrated oil used especially in baptism, confirmation, and ordination
Christ \'krīst\ *n* : Jesus especially as the Messiah — **Christ•like** *adj* — **Christ•ly** *adj*

chris•ten \ˈkris-ᵊn\ *vb* **1 :** BAPTIZE **2 ♦ :** to name at baptism **3 ♦ :** to name or dedicate (as a ship) by a ceremony suggestive of baptism — **chris•ten•ing** *n*

♦ [2, 3] baptize, call, denominate, designate, dub, entitle, label, name, style, term, title

Chris•ten•dom \ˈkris-ᵊn-dəm\ *n* **1 :** CHRISTIANITY **2 :** the part of the world in which Christianity prevails
[1]**Chris•tian** \ˈkris-chən\ *n* **:** an adherent of Christianity
[2]**Christian** *adj* **1 :** of or relating to Christianity **2 :** based on or conforming with Christianity **3 :** of or relating to a Christian **4 :** professing Christianity
chris•ti•an•ia \ˌkris-chē-ˈa-nē-ə, ˌkris-tē-\ *n* **:** CHRISTIE
Chris•ti•an•i•ty \ˌkris-chē-ˈa-nə-tē\ *n* **:** the religion derived from Jesus Christ, based on the Bible as sacred scripture, and professed by Christians
Chris•tian•ize \ˈkris-chə-ˌnīz\ *vb* **-ized; -iz•ing :** to make Christian
Christian name *n* **:** a name that precedes one's surname **:** GIVEN NAME
Christian Science *n* **:** a religion and system of healing founded by Mary Baker Eddy and taught by the Church of Christ, Scientist — **Christian Scientist** *n*
chris•tie *or* **chris•ty** \ˈkris-tē\ *n, pl* **christies :** a skiing turn made by shifting body weight forward and skidding into a turn with parallel skis
Christ•mas \ˈkris-məs\ *n* **:** December 25 celebrated as a church festival in commemoration of the birth of Christ and observed as a legal holiday
Christmas club *n* **:** a savings account in which regular deposits are made to provide money for Christmas shopping
Christ•mas•time \-ˌtīm\ *n* **♦ :** the Christmas season

♦ Christmastide, Noel, yuletide

Christ•mas•tide \ˈkris-məs-ˌtīd\ *n* **♦ :** the season of Christmas

♦ Christmastime, Noel, yuletide

chro•mat•ic \krō-ˈma-tik\ *adj* **1 :** of or relating to color **2 :** proceeding by half steps of the musical scale — **chro•mat•i•cism** \-tə-ˌsi-zəm\ *n*
chro•mato•graph \krō-ˈma-tə-ˌgraf\ *n* **:** an instrument used in chromatography
chro•ma•tog•ra•phy \ˌkrō-mə-ˈtä-grə-fē\ *n* **:** the separation of a complex mixture into its component compounds as a result of the different rates at which the compounds travel through or over a stationary substance due to differing affinities for the substance — **chro•mato•graph•ic** \krō-ˌma-tə-ˈgra-fik\ *adj* — **chro•mato•graph•i•cal•ly** \-fi-k(ə-)lē\ *adv*
chrome \ˈkrōm\ *n* **1 :** CHROMIUM **2 :** a chromium pigment **3 :** something plated with an alloy of chromium
chro•mi•um \ˈkrō-mē-əm\ *n* **:** a bluish white metallic element used especially in alloys and chrome plating
chro•mo•some \ˈkrō-mə-ˌsōm, -ˌzōm\ *n* **:** any of the rod-shaped or threadlike DNA-containing structures of cellular organisms that contain most or all of the genes of the organism — **chro•mo•som•al** \ˌkrō-mə-ˈsō-məl, -ˈzō-\ *adj*
chro•mo•sphere \ˈkrō-mə-ˌsfir\ *n* **:** the lower part of a star's atmosphere
chron *abbr* **1** chronicle **2** chronological; chronology
Chron *abbr* Chronicles
chron•ic \ˈkrä-nik\ *adj* **1 :** marked by long duration or frequent recurrence ⟨a ~ disease⟩ **2 ♦ :** being such habitually **:** HABITUAL ⟨a ~ grumbler⟩ — **chron•i•cal•ly** \-ni-k(ə-)lē\ *adv*

♦ confirmed, habitual, inveterate

chronic fatigue syndrome *n* **:** a disorder of unknown cause that is characterized by persistent profound fatigue
[1]**chron•i•cle** \ˈkrä-ni-kəl\ *n* **♦ :** an account of events arranged in the order of time **:** HISTORY, NARRATIVE

♦ account, history, narrative, record, report, story

[2]**chronicle** *vb* **-cled; -cling :** to record in or as if in a chronicle
chron•i•cler *n* **:** a writer or compiler of a chronicle
Chronicles *n* **:** either of two books of the Jewish and Christian Scripture
chro•no•graph \ˈkrä-nə-ˌgraf\ *n* **:** an instrument for measuring and recording time intervals with accuracy — **chro•no•graph•ic** \ˌkrä-nə-ˈgra-fik\ *adj* — **chro•nog•ra•phy** \krə-ˈnä-grə-fē\ *n*
chro•nol•o•gy \krə-ˈnä-lə-jē\ *n, pl* **-gies 1 :** the science that deals with measuring time and dating events **2 :** a chronological list or table **3 :** arrangement of events in the order of their occurrence — **chron•o•log•i•cal** \ˌkrän-ᵊl-ˈä-ji-kəl\ *adj* — **chron•o•log•i•cal•ly** \-k(ə-)lē\ *adv* — **chro•nol•o•gist** \krə-ˈnä-lə-jist\ *n*
chro•nom•e•ter \krə-ˈnä-mə-tər\ *n* **:** a very accurate timepiece
chrys•a•lid \ˈkri-sə-ləd\ *n* **:** CHRYSALIS
chrys•a•lis \ˈkri-sə-ləs\ *n, pl* **chry•sal•i•des** \kri-ˈsa-lə-ˌdēz\ *or* **chrys•a•lis•es :** an insect pupa in a firm case without a cocoon
chry•san•the•mum \kri-ˈsan-thə-məm\ *n* **:** any of various plants related to the daisies including some grown for their showy flowers or for medicinal products or insecticides; *also* **:** a flower of a chrysanthemum
chub \ˈchəb\ *n, pl* **chub** *or* **chubs :** any of various small freshwater fishes related to the carp
chub•bi•ness *n* **:** the quality or state of being chubby
chub•by \ˈchə-bē\ *adj* **chub•bi•er; -est ♦ :** short, thick, and well-rounded **:** PLUMP

♦ corpulent, fat, fleshy, full, gross, obese, overweight, plump, portly, rotund, round

[1]**chuck** \ˈchək\ *vb* **1 :** to give a pat or tap **2 ♦ :** to throw with a short action of the arm or hand **:** TOSS **3 :** DISCARD; *also* **:** EJECT **4 :** to have done with

♦ cast, catapult, dash, fire, fling, heave, hurl, hurtle, launch, peg, pelt, pitch, sling, throw, toss

[2]**chuck** *n* **1 :** a light pat under the chin **2 :** TOSS
[3]**chuck** *n* **1 :** a cut of beef including most of the neck and the parts around the shoulder blade and the first three ribs **2 :** a device for holding work or a tool in a machine (as a lathe)
chuck•hole \ˈchək-ˌhōl\ *n* **:** POTHOLE
[1]**chuck•le** \ˈchə-kəl\ *vb* **chuck•led; chuck•ling :** to laugh in a quiet hardly audible manner
[2]**chuckle** *n* **:** a quiet hardly audible laugh
chuck wagon *n* **:** a wagon equipped with a stove and food supplies
[1]**chug** \ˈchəg\ *n* **:** a dull explosive sound made by or as if by a laboring engine
[2]**chug** *vb* **chugged; chug•ging :** to move or go with chugs
chuk•ka \ˈchə-kə\ *n* **:** a usually ankle-length leather boot
chuk•ker \ˈchə-kər\ *also* **chuk•ka** \ˈchə-kə\ *n* **:** a playing period of a polo game
[1]**chum** \ˈchəm\ *n* **♦ :** a close friend

♦ buddy, comrade, crony, familiar, friend, intimate, pal

[2]**chum** *vb* **chummed; chum•ming 1 :** to room together **2 ♦ :** to be a close friend

♦ associate, consort, fraternize, hang around, hobnob, pal

chum•mi•ness \-mē-nəs\ *n* **:** the quality or state of being chummy
chum•my \ˈchə-mē\ *adj* **chum•mi•er; -est ♦ :** quite friendly **:** INTIMATE — **chum•mi•ly** \-mə-lē\ *adv* — **chum•mi•ness** \-mē-nəs\ *n*

♦ bosom, close, familiar, friendly, intimate, thick

chump \ˈchəmp\ *n* **:** stupid lout **:** FOOL, BLOCKHEAD
chunk \ˈchəŋk\ *n* **1 ♦ :** a short thick piece **2 :** a sizable amount

♦ blob, clod, clump, glob, gob, hunk, lump, nub, wad

chunky \ˈchəŋ-kē\ *adj* **chunk•i•er; -est 1 ♦ :** compact, sturdy, and thick in build **:** STOCKY **2 :** containing chunks

♦ dumpy, heavyset, squat, stocky, stout, stubby, stumpy, thickset

church \ˈchərch\ *n* **1 :** a building for public and especially Christian worship **2** *often cap* **:** the whole body of Christians **3 :** DENOMINATION **4 :** a group of persons assembled for worship **:** CONGREGATION **5 :** public divine worship
church•go•er \ˈchərch-ˌgō(-ə)r\ *n* **:** one who habitually attends church — **church•go•ing** *adj or n*
church•less \ˈchərch-ləs\ *adj* **:** not affiliated with a church
church•man \ˈchərch-mən\ *n* **1 :** CLERGYMAN **2 :** a member of a church
church•war•den \ˈchərch-ˌwȯrd-ᵊn\ *n* **:** WARDEN 5
church•yard \-ˌyärd\ *n* **:** a yard that belongs to a church and is often used as a burial ground
churl \ˈchərl\ *n* **1 :** a medieval peasant **2 :** RUSTIC **3 ♦ :** a rude ill-bred person — **churl•ish** *adj* — **churl•ish•ly** *adv* — **churl•ish•ness** *n*

♦ beast, boor, clown, creep, cretin, cur, heel, jerk, joker, louse, lout, skunk, slob, snake

churl•ish *adj* **♦ :** marked by a lack of civility or graciousness — **churl•ish•ly** *adv* — **churl•ish•ness** *n*

♦ boorish, clownish, loutish, uncouth

[1]**churn** \ˈchərn\ *n* **:** a container in which milk or cream is violently agitated in making butter

²**churn** *vb* **1 :** to stir in a churn; *also* **:** to make (butter) by such stirring **2** ♦ **:** to stir or shake around especially violently **3** ♦ **:** to experience violent motion or agitation

♦ [2] agitate, stir, swirl, whirl ♦ [3] boil, roil, seethe

churn out *vb* **:** to produce mechanically or in large quantity
chute \ˈshüt\ *n* **1 :** an inclined surface, trough, or passage down or through which something may pass ⟨a coal ~⟩ ⟨a mail ~⟩ **2 :** PARACHUTE
chut•ney \ˈchət-nē\ *n, pl* **chutneys :** a thick sauce containing fruits, vinegar, sugar, and spices
chutz•pah \ˈhu̇t-spə, ˈk̲u̇t-, -(ˌ)spä\ *n* ♦ **:** supreme self-confidence

♦ audacity, brass, brazenness, cheek, effrontery, gall, nerve, presumption, sauce, sauciness, temerity

CIA *abbr* Central Intelligence Agency
cía *abbr* company
ciao \ˈchau̇\ *interj* — used to express greeting or farewell
ci•ca•da \sə-ˈkā-də\ *n* **:** any of a family of stout-bodied insects related to the aphids and having wide blunt heads and large transparent wings
ci•ca•trix \ˈsi-kə-ˌtriks\ *n, pl* **ci•ca•tri•ces** \ˌsi-kə-ˈtrī-ˌsēz\ **:** a scar resulting from formation and contraction of fibrous tissue in a wound
ci•ce•ro•ne \ˌsi-sə-ˈrō-nē, ˌchē-chə-\ *n, pl* **-ni** \-(ˌ)nē\ **:** a guide who conducts sightseers
CID *abbr* Criminal Investigation Department
ci•der \ˈsī-dər\ *n* **:** juice pressed from fruit (as apples) and used as a beverage, vinegar, or flavoring
cie *abbr* company
ci•gar \si-ˈgär\ *n* **:** a roll of tobacco for smoking
cig•a•rette \ˌsi-gə-ˈret, ˈsi-gə-ˌret\ *n* **:** a slender roll of cut tobacco enclosed in paper for smoking
cig•a•ril•lo \ˌsi-gə-ˈri-lō, -ˈrē-ō\ *n, pl* **-los 1 :** a very small cigar **2 :** a cigarette wrapped in tobacco rather than paper
ci•lan•tro \si-ˈlän-trō, -ˈlan-\ *n* **:** leaves of coriander used as a flavoring or garnish; *also* **:** the coriander plant
cil•i•ate \ˈsi-lē-ˌāt\ *n* **:** any of a group of protozoans characterized by cilia
cil•i•um \ˈsi-lē-əm\ *n, pl* **-ia** \-lē-ə\ **1 :** a minute short hairlike process; *esp* **:** one of a cell **2 :** EYELASH
C in C *abbr* commander in chief
¹**cinch** \ˈsinch\ *n* **1 :** a girth for a pack or saddle **2** ♦ **:** a thing done with ease

♦ breeze, child's play, picnic, pushover, snap *Ant* chore, headache, labor

²**cinch** *vb* ♦ **:** to make certain **:** ASSURE

♦ assure, ensure, guarantee, guaranty, insure, secure

cin•cho•na \siŋ-ˈkō-nə\ *n* **:** any of a genus of So. American trees related to the madder; *also* **:** the bitter quinine-containing bark of a cinchona
cinc•ture \ˈsiŋk-chər\ *n* ♦ **:** an article of dress encircling the body usually at the waist **:** BELT, SASH

♦ belt, cummerbund, girdle, sash

cin•der \ˈsin-dər\ *n* **1 :** SLAG **2** *pl* **:** ASHES **3 :** a hot piece of partly burned wood or coal **4 :** a fragment of lava from an erupting volcano — **cinder** *vb* — **cin•dery** *adj*
cinder block *n* **:** a building block made of cement and coal cinders
cin•e•ma \ˈsi-nə-mə\ *n* **1 :** a motion-picture theater **2 :** the film industry **:** MOVIES — **cin•e•mat•ic** \ˌsi-nə-ˈma-tik\ *adj*
cin•e•ma•theque \ˌsi-nə-mə-ˈtek\ *n* **:** a small movie house specializing in avant-garde films
cin•e•ma•tog•ra•phy \ˌsi-nə-mə-ˈtä-grə-fē\ *n* **:** motion-picture photography — **cin•e•ma•tog•ra•pher** *n* — **cin•e•mat•o•graph•ic** \-ˌma-tə-ˈgra-fik\ *adj*
cin•e•plex \ˈsi-nə-ˌpleks\ *n* **:** a complex that houses several movie theaters
cin•er•ar•i•um \ˌsi-nə-ˈrer-ē-əm\ *n, pl* **-ia** \-ē-ə\ **:** a place to receive the ashes of the cremated dead — **cin•er•ary** \ˈsi-nə-ˌrer-ē\ *adj*
cin•na•bar \ˈsi-nə-ˌbär\ *n* **:** a red mineral that is the only important ore of mercury
cin•na•mon \ˈsi-nə-mən\ *n* **:** a spice prepared from the highly aromatic bark of any of several trees related to the true laurel; *also* **:** a tree that yields cinnamon
cinque•foil \ˈsiŋk-ˌfȯil, ˈsaŋk-\ *n* **:** any of a genus of plants related to the roses with leaves having five lobes
¹**ci•pher** \ˈsī-fər\ *n* **1** ♦ **:** the symbol 0 denoting the absence of all magnitude or quantity **:** ZERO, NAUGHT **2 :** a method of secret writing

♦ aught, naught, nil, nothing, zero, zip

²**cipher** *vb* **:** to compute arithmetically
cir *or* **circ** *abbr* circular
cir•ca \ˈsər-kə\ *prep* **:** ABOUT ⟨~ 1600⟩
cir•ca•di•an \ˌsər-ˈka-dē-ən, ˌsər-kə-ˈdī-ən\ *adj* **:** being, having, characterized by, or occurring in approximately 24-hour intervals (as of biological activity)
¹**cir•cle** \ˈsər-kəl\ *n* **1** ♦ **:** a closed curve every point of which is equally distant from a fixed point within it **2** ♦ **:** something circular **3 :** an area of action or influence **4 :** a series ending at its starting point **:** CYCLE **5** ♦ **:** a group bound by a common tie

♦ [1, 2] band, hoop, ring, round ♦ [5] clan, clique, coterie, crowd, fold, gang, ring, set

²**circle** *vb* **cir•cled; cir•cling 1** ♦ **:** to enclose in a circle **2** ♦ **:** to move or revolve around; *also* **:** to move in a circle

♦ [1] encircle, enclose, encompass, ring, surround ♦ [2] circumnavigate, coil, compass, encircle, girdle, loop, orbit, ring, round

cir•clet \ˈsər-klət\ *n* **:** a small circle; *esp* **:** a circular ornament
cir•cuit \ˈsər-kət\ *n* **1 :** a boundary around an enclosed space **2 :** a course around a periphery **3 :** a regular tour (as by a judge) around an assigned territory **4 :** the complete path of an electric current; *also* **:** an assemblage of electronic components **5 :** LEAGUE; *also* **:** a chain of theaters — **cir•cuit•al** \-ᵊl\ *adj*
circuit breaker *n* **:** a switch that automatically interrupts an electric circuit under an abnormal condition
circuit court *n* **:** a court that sits at two or more places within one judicial district
cir•cu•i•tous \ˌsər-ˈkyü-ə-təs\ *adj* **1** ♦ **:** having a circular or winding course **2** ♦ **:** not being forthright or direct in language or action

♦ [1] circular, indirect, roundabout ♦ [2] diffuse, long-winded, prolix, rambling, verbose, windy, wordy

cir•cuit•ry \ˈsər-kə-trē\ *n, pl* **-ries :** the plan or the components of an electric circuit
cir•cu•ity \ˌsər-ˈkyü-ə-tē\ *n, pl* **-ities :** INDIRECTION
¹**cir•cu•lar** \ˈsər-kyə-lər\ *adj* **1 :** having the form of a circle **:** ROUND **2 :** moving in or around a circle **3** ♦ **:** not forthright or direct in language or action **:** CIRCUITOUS **4 :** intended for circulation ⟨a ~ letter⟩ — **cir•cu•lar•i•ty** \ˈsər-kyə-ˈlar-ə-tē\ *n*

♦ circuitous, indirect, roundabout

²**circular** *n* ♦ **:** a paper (as a leaflet) intended for wide distribution

♦ booklet, brochure, folder, leaflet, pamphlet

cir•cu•lar•ise *Brit var of* CIRCULARIZE
cir•cu•lar•ize \ˈsər-kyə-lə-ˌrīz\ *vb* **-ized; -iz•ing 1 :** to send circulars to **2 :** to poll by questionnaire
circular saw *n* **:** a power saw with a round cutting blade
cir•cu•late \ˈsər-kyə-ˌlāt\ *vb* **-lat•ed; -lat•ing 1 :** to move or cause to move in a circle, circuit, or orbit **2** ♦ **:** to pass from place to place or from person to person **3** ♦ **:** to become well-known or widespread — **cir•cu•la•tion** \ˌsər-kyə-ˈlā-shən\ *n*

♦ broadcast, disseminate, propagate, spread, strew

cir•cu•la•to•ry \ˈsər-kyə-lə-ˌtōr-ē\ *adj* **:** of or relating to circulation or the circulatory system
circulatory system *n* **:** the system of blood, blood vessels, lymphatic vessels, and heart concerned with the circulation of the blood and lymph
cir•cum•am•bu•late \ˌsər-kəm-ˈam-byə-ˌlāt\ *vb* **-lat•ed; -lat•ing :** to circle on foot especially as part of a ritual
cir•cum•cise \ˈsər-kəm-ˌsīz\ *vb* **-cised; -cis•ing :** to cut off the foreskin of — **cir•cum•ci•sion** \ˌsər-kəm-ˈsi-zhən\ *n*
cir•cum•fer•ence \sər-ˈkəm-f(ə-)rəns\ *n* **1 :** the perimeter of a circle **2** ♦ **:** the external boundary or surface of a figure or object

♦ border, bound, boundary, compass, confines, edge, end, fringe, margin, perimeter, periphery, rim, skirt, verge

cir•cum•flex \ˈsər-kəm-ˌfleks\ *n* **:** the mark ˆ over a vowel
cir•cum•lo•cu•tion \ˌsər-kəm-lō-ˈkyü-shən\ *n* ♦ **:** the use of an unnecessarily large number of words to express an idea

♦ prolixity, redundancy, verbiage, wordiness

cir•cum•lu•nar \-ˈlü-nər\ *adj* **:** revolving about or surrounding the moon
cir•cum•nav•i•gate \-ˈna-və-ˌgāt\ *vb* ♦ **:** to go completely around

(as the earth) especially by water — **cir•cum•nav•i•ga•tion** \-ˌna-və-ˈgā-shən\ *n*

♦ circle, coil, compass, encircle, girdle, loop, orbit, ring, round

cir•cum•po•lar \-ˈpō-lər\ *adj* **1 :** continually visible above the horizon ⟨a ~ star⟩ **2 :** surrounding or found near a pole of the earth

cir•cum•scribe \ˈsər-kəm-ˌskrīb\ *vb* **1** ♦ **:** to constrict the range or activity of **2 :** to draw a line around — **cir•cum•scrip•tion** \ˌsər-kəm-ˈskrip-shən\ *n*

♦ check, confine, control, curb, inhibit, limit, restrain, restrict ♦ bound, define, delimit, demarcate, limit, mark, terminate

cir•cum•spect \ˈsər-kəm-ˌspekt\ *adj* ♦ **:** careful to consider all circumstances and consequences **:** PRUDENT — **cir•cum•spec•tion** \ˌsər-kəm-ˈspek-shən\ *n*

♦ alert, careful, cautious, considerate, gingerly, guarded, heedful, prudent, safe, wary

cir•cum•spec•tion \ˌsər-kəm-ˈspek-shən\ *n* ♦ **:** careful consideration to minimize risk

♦ alertness, care, carefulness, caution, heedfulness

cir•cum•stance \ˈsər-kəm-ˌstans\ *n* **1 :** a condition, fact, or event accompanying, conditioning, or determining another **2 :** surrounding conditions **3 a** ♦ **:** an inevitable and often adverse end **:** FATE **b** ♦ **:** something that happens unpredictably **:** CHANCE **4** *pl* **:** situation with regard to wealth **5 :** CEREMONY

♦ [3a] destiny, doom, fate, fortune, lot, portion ♦ [3b] accident, chance, hazard, luck

cir•cum•stan•tial \ˌsər-kəm-ˈstan-chəl\ *adj* **1 :** consisting of or depending on circumstances **2 :** INCIDENTAL **3** ♦ **:** containing full details — **cir•cum•stan•tial•ly** *adv*

♦ detailed, elaborate, full, minute, thorough

cir•cum•vent \ˌsər-kəm-ˈvent\ *vb* **1 a** ♦ **:** to go around **:** make a full circuit around or bypass without going through **b** ♦ **:** to manage to get around especially by ingenuity or stratagem **2 :** to check or defeat especially by stratagem — **cir•cum•ven•tion** \-ˈvent-shən\ *n*

♦ [1a, 1b] dodge, sidestep, skirt ***Ant*** comply (with), follow, keep, obey, observe ♦ [1a, 1b] bypass, detour, skirt

cir•cus \ˈsər-kəs\ *n* **1** ♦ **:** a large arena enclosed by tiers of seats on three or all four sides and used especially for sports or spectacles **2 :** a usually traveling show that features feats of physical skill, wild animal acts, and performances by clowns **3 :** a circus performance; *also* **:** the equipment, livestock, and personnel of a circus **4** ♦ **:** something suggestive of a circus (as in frenzied activity or razzle-dazzle) ⟨a media ~⟩

♦ [1] bowl, coliseum, stadium ♦ [4] bedlam, hell, madhouse

cirque \ˈsərk\ *n* **:** a deep steep-walled mountain basin usually forming the blunt end of a valley

cir•rho•sis \sə-ˈrō-səs\ *n, pl* **-rho•ses** \-ˌsēz\ **:** fibrosis of the liver — **cir•rhot•ic** \-ˈrä-tik\ *adj or n*

cir•rus \ˈsir-əs\ *n, pl* **cir•ri** \ˈsir-ˌī\ **:** a wispy white cloud usually of minute ice crystals at high altitudes

cis•lu•nar \(ˌ)sis-ˈlü-nər\ *adj* **:** lying between the earth and the moon or the moon's orbit

cis•tern \ˈsis-tərn\ *n* **:** an often underground tank for storing water

cit *abbr* **1** citation; cited **2** citizen

cit•a•del \ˈsi-tə-dəl, -ˌdel\ *n* **1** ♦ **:** a fortress commanding a city **2** ♦ **:** a place of security or survival **:** STRONGHOLD

♦ [1, 2] bastion, fastness, fort, fortification, fortress, hold, stronghold

ci•ta•tion \sī-ˈtā-shən\ *n* **1 :** an official summons to appear (as before a court) **2 a :** something that is quoted **b :** a passage referred to or given as an example **:** QUOTATION **3** ♦ **:** a formal statement of the achievements of a person; *also* **:** a specific reference in a military dispatch to meritorious performance of duty

♦ accolade, commendation, encomium, eulogy, homage, paean, panegyric, salutation, tribute

cite \ˈsīt\ *vb* **cit•ed; cit•ing 1 :** to summon to appear before a court **2** ♦ **:** to quote by way of example, authority, or proof **:** QUOTE **3 :** to refer to especially in commendation or praise **4** ♦ **:** to bring forward or call to another's attention especially as an example

♦ [2] advert (to), instance, mention, name, note, notice, quote, refer (to), specify, touch (*on* or *upon*) ♦ [4] adduce, instance, mention, quote

cit•i•fied \ˈsi-ti-ˌfīd\ *adj* **:** of, relating to, or characterized by an urban style of living

cit•i•zen \ˈsi-tə-zən\ *n* **1 :** an inhabitant of a city or town **2 :** a person who owes allegiance to a government and is entitled to its protection — **cit•i•zen•ship** *n*

cit•i•zen•ry \-rē\ *n, pl* **-ries :** a whole body of citizens

citizens band *n* **:** a range of radio frequencies set aside for private radio communications

cit•ric acid \ˈsi-trik-\ *n* **:** a sour organic acid obtained from lemon and lime juices or by fermentation of sugars and used as a flavoring

cit•ron \ˈsi-trən\ *n* **1 :** the oval lemonlike fruit of an Asian citrus tree; *also* **:** the tree **2 :** a small hard-fleshed watermelon used especially in pickles and preserves

cit•ro•nel•la \ˌsi-trə-ˈne-lə\ *n* **:** a lemon-scented oil obtained from a fragrant grass of southern Asia and used in perfumes and as an insect repellent

cit•rus \ˈsi-trəs\ *n, pl* **citrus** *or* **cit•rus•es :** any of a genus of often thorny evergreen trees or shrubs grown for their fruits (as the orange, lemon, lime, and grapefruit); *also* **:** the fruit

city \ˈsi-tē\ *n, pl* **cit•ies 1** ♦ **:** an inhabited place larger or more important than a town **2 :** a municipality in the U.S. governed under a charter granted by the state; *also* **:** an incorporated municipal unit of the highest class in Canada

♦ metropolis, municipality

city manager *n* **:** an official employed by an elected council to direct the administration of a city government

city–state \ˈsi-tē-ˌstāt\ *n* **:** an autonomous state consisting of a city and surrounding territory

civ *abbr* **1** civil; civilian **2** civilization

civ•et \ˈsi-vət\ *n* **:** a yellowish strong-smelling substance obtained from a catlike mammal (**civet cat**) of Africa or Asia and used in making perfumes

civ•ic \ˈsi-vik\ *adj* **:** of or relating to a city, citizenship, or civil affairs

civ•ics \-viks\ *n* **:** a social science dealing with the rights and duties of citizens

civ•il \ˈsi-vəl\ *adj* **1** ♦ **:** of or relating to citizens or to the state as a political body **2** ♦ **:** adequate in courtesy and politeness **:** COURTEOUS, POLITE **3 :** of or relating to legal proceedings in connection with private rights and obligations ⟨the ~ code⟩ **4 :** of or relating to the general population **:** not military or ecclesiastical

♦ [1] national, public, state ♦ [2] courteous, genteel, gracious, mannerly, polite, well-bred

civil defense *n* **:** protective measures and emergency relief activities conducted by civilians in case of enemy attack or natural disaster

civil disobedience *n* **:** refusal to obey governmental commands especially as a nonviolent means of protest

civil engineer *n* **:** an engineer whose training or occupation is in the design and construction especially of public works (as roads or harbors) — **civil engineering** *n*

ci•vil•ian \sə-ˈvil-yən\ *n* **:** a person not on active duty in a military, police, or fire-fighting force

ci•vil•i•ty \sə-ˈvi-lə-tē\ *n, pl* **-ties 1** ♦ **:** civilized conduct **:** POLITENESS, COURTESY **2** ♦ **:** a polite act or expression

♦ [1] courtesy, gentility, graciousness, mannerliness, politeness ♦ [2] amenity, courtesy, formality, gesture

civ•i•li•za•tion \ˌsi-və-lə-ˈzā-shən\ *n* **1** ♦ **:** a relatively high level of cultural and technological development **2** ♦ **:** the culture characteristic of a time or place — **civ•i•li•za•tion•al** \-shə-nᵊl\ *adj*

♦ [1] cultivation, culture, polish, refinement ♦ [2] culture, life, lifestyle, society

civ•i•lize \ˈsi-və-ˌlīz\ *vb* **-lized; -liz•ing 1 :** to raise from a primitive state to an advanced and ordered stage of cultural development **2 :** REFINE

civ•i•lized *adj* **1 :** characteristic of a state of civilization **2** ♦ **:** characterized by taste, refinement, or restraint

♦ cultivated, cultured, genteel, polished, refined

civil liberty *n* **:** freedom from arbitrary governmental interference specifically by denial of governmental power — usually used in plural

civ•il•ly \ˈsi-vəl-lē\ *adv* **1 :** in terms of civil rights, matters, or law ⟨~ dead⟩ **2 :** in a civil manner **:** POLITELY

civil rights *n pl* **:** the nonpolitical rights of a citizen; *esp* **:** those guaranteed by the 13th and 14th amendments to the Constitution and by acts of Congress

civil servant *n* **:** a member of a civil service

civil service *n* : the administrative service of a government
civil war *n* : a war between opposing groups of citizens of the same country
civ•vies \ˈsi-vēz\ *n pl* : civilian clothes as distinguished from a military uniform
CJ *abbr* chief justice
ck *abbr* **1** cask **2** check
cl *abbr* **1** centiliter **2** class
Cl *symbol* chlorine
¹clack \ˈklak\ *vb* **1** : CHATTER, PRATTLE **2** : to make an abrupt striking sound or series of sounds
²clack *n* **1** : rapid continuous talk : CHATTER **2** : a sound of clacking ⟨the ~ of a typewriter⟩
clad \ˈklad\ *adj* **1** : CLOTHED, COVERED **2** : being or consisting of coins made of outer layers of one metal bonded to a core of a different metal
¹claim \ˈklām\ *vb* **1** ♦ : to ask for especially as a right **2** : to call for : REQUIRE **3** ♦ : to state as a fact : MAINTAIN

♦ [1] call, clamor (*or* clamour), command, demand, enjoin, exact, insist, press, quest, stipulate (for) ♦ [3] affirm, allege, assert, aver, avouch, avow, contend, declare, insist, maintain, profess, protest, warrant ***Ant*** deny, gainsay

²claim *n* **1** ♦ : a demand for something due or believed to be due **2** ♦ : a right to something usually in another's possession **3** ♦ : an assertion open to challenge **4** ♦ : something claimed (as a tract of land)

♦ [1] demand, dun, requisition ♦ [2] call, pretense, pretension, right ♦ [3] affirmation, assertion, avowal, declaration, profession, protestation ♦ [4] interest, share, stake

claim•ant \ˈklā-mənt\ *n* : a person making a claim
clair•voy•ance \-əns\ *n* : the power or faculty of discerning objects not present to the senses
clair•voy•ant \klar-ˈvȯi-ənt\ *adj* **1** : unusually perceptive **2** : having the power of discerning objects not present to the senses — **clairvoyant** *n*
clam \ˈklam\ *n* **1** : any of numerous bivalve mollusks including many that are edible **2** : DOLLAR
clam•bake \-ˌbāk\ *n* : a party or gathering (as at the seashore) at which food is cooked usually on heated rocks covered by seaweed
clam•ber \ˈklam-bər\ *vb* : to climb awkwardly — **clam•ber•er** *n*
clam•my \ˈkla-mē\ *adj* **clam•mi•er; -est** : being damp, soft, sticky, and usually cool — **clam•mi•ness** *n*
¹clam•or \ˈkla-mər\ *or Can and Brit* **clam•our** *n* **1** ♦ : a noisy shouting **2** ♦ : a loud continuous noise **3** : insistent public expression (as of support or protest)

♦ [1] howl, hubbub, hue and cry, hullabaloo, noise, outcry, roar, tumult, uproar ♦ [2] bluster, cacophony, din, noise, racket, roar

²clamor *or Can and Brit* **clamour** *vb* ♦ : to appeal, demand, or protest by sustained noisy outcry : to become loudly insistent — usually used with *for*

♦ *usu* **clamor for** call, claim, demand, enjoin, exact, insist, press, quest, stipulate (for)

clam•or•ous *or Can and Brit* **clamourous** *adj* **1** ♦ : marked by confused din or outcry **2** ♦ : full of noise : noisily insistent

♦ [1] blatant, obstreperous, vociferous ♦ [2] booming, deafening, earsplitting, loud, piercing, resounding, ringing, roaring, sonorous, stentorian, thunderous

¹clamp \ˈklamp\ *n* : a device that holds or presses parts together firmly
²clamp *vb* ♦ : to fasten with or as if with a clamp

♦ anchor, fasten, fix, hitch, moor, secure, set

clamp down *vb* ♦ : to impose restrictions : become repressive — **clamp•down** \ˈklamp-ˌdau̇n\ *n*

♦ *usu* **clamp down on** crack down, crush, put down, quash, quell, repress, silence, snuff, squash, squelch, subdue, suppress

clam•shell \ˈklam-ˌshel\ *n* **1** : the shell of a clam **2** : a bucket or grapnel (as on a dredge) having two hinged jaws
clam up *vb* ♦ : to become silent

♦ hush, pipe down, quiet (down), shut up

clan \ˈklan\ *n* **1** ♦ : a group of people tracing descent from a common ancestor **2** ♦ : a group united by a common interest or common characteristics — **clan•nish** *n* — **clan•nish•ness** *n*

♦ [1] blood, family, folks, house, kin, kindred, kinfolk, line, lineage, people, race, stock, tribe ♦ [2] circle, clique, coterie, crowd, fold, gang, ring, set

clan•des•tine \klan-ˈdes-tən\ *adj* ♦ : held in or conducted with secrecy

♦ covert, furtive, hugger-mugger, private, secret, sneak, sneaky, stealthy, surreptitious, undercover, underground, underhanded

clang \ˈklaŋ\ *n* ♦ : a loud metallic ringing sound — **clang** *vb*

♦ clash

clan•gor *or Can and Brit* **clan•gour** \ˈklaŋ-ər, -gər\ *n* : a loud deeply resounding sound made especially by metal objects struck together
clank \ˈklaŋk\ *n* : a sharp brief metallic ringing sound — **clank** *vb*
clan•nish *n* : tending to associate only with a select group of similar background or status — **clan•nish•ness** *n*
¹clap \ˈklap\ *vb* **clapped; clap•ping** **1** : to strike noisily **2** : APPLAUD
²clap *n* **1** ♦ : a loud noisy crash **2** : a sudden sometimes resounding blow or stroke **3** : the noise made by clapping the hands

♦ bang, blast, boom, crack, crash, pop, report, slam, smash, snap, thwack, whack

³clap *n* : GONORRHEA
clap•board \ˈkla-bərd, -ˌbōrd; ˈklap-ˌbōrd\ *n* : a narrow board thicker at one edge than the other used for siding — **clap•board** *vb*
clap•per \ˈkla-pər\ *n* : one that claps; *esp* : the tongue of a bell
clap•trap \ˈklap-ˌtrap\ *n* ♦ : pretentious nonsense

♦ bunk, drivel, fiddlesticks, folly, foolishness, fudge, hogwash, humbug, nonsense, piffle, rot, silliness, slush, stupidity, trash

claque \ˈklak\ *n* **1** : a group hired to applaud at a performance **2** : a group of sycophants
clar•et \ˈklar-ət\ *n* : a dry red wine
clar•i•fi•ca•tion \ˌklar-ə-fə-ˈkā-shən\ *n* ♦ : the act or process of clarifying; *also* : something that clarifies

♦ construction, elucidation, explanation, explication, exposition, illumination, illustration, interpretation

clar•i•fy \ˈklar-ə-ˌfī\ *vb* **-fied; -fy•ing** ♦ : to make or become clear

♦ clear (up), construe, demonstrate, elucidate, explain, explicate, expound, illuminate, illustrate, interpret, spell out ♦ clear, distill, filter, purify

clar•i•net \ˌklar-ə-ˈnet\ *n* : a single-reed woodwind instrument in the form of a cylindrical tube with a moderately flaring end — **clar•i•net•ist** *or* **clar•i•net•tist** \-ˈne-tist\ *n*
clar•i•on \ˈklar-ē-ən\ *adj* : brilliantly clear ⟨a ~ call⟩
clar•i•ty \ˈklar-ə-tē\ *n* ♦ : the quality or state of being clear : LUCIDITY

♦ explicitness, lucidity, perspicuity, simplicity

¹clash \ˈklash\ *vb* **1** : to make or cause to make a clash **2** ♦ : to be incompatible **3** ♦ : to come into conflict

♦ [2] collide, conflict, jar ***Ant*** blend, harmonize, match ♦ *usu* **clash with** [3] battle, combat, fight, scrimmage, skirmish, war

²clash *n* **1** ♦ : a noisy usually metallic sound of collision **2** ♦ : a hostile encounter; *also* : a conflict of opinion

♦ [1] clang ♦ [2] battle, combat, conflict, contest, fight, fracas, fray, hassle, scrap, scrimmage, scuffle, skirmish, struggle, tussle

¹clasp \ˈklasp\ *n* **1** : a device (as a hook) for holding objects or parts together **2** : a holding or enveloping with or as if with the hands or arms : EMBRACE, GRASP
²clasp *vb* ♦ : to enclose and hold with the arms or hands

♦ caress, embrace, enfold, grasp, hug ♦ grasp, grip, hold, take

¹class \ˈklas\ *n* **1** : a group of students meeting regularly in a course; *also* : a group graduating together **2** : a course of instruction; *also* : the period when such a course is taught **3 a** ♦ : social rank; *esp* : high social rank **b** ♦ : high quality : ELEGANCE **4** ♦ : a group of the same general status or nature; *esp* : a major category in biological classification that is above the order and below the phylum **5** ♦ : a division or rating based on grade or quality — **class•less** *adj*

♦ [3a] caste, estate, folk, order, place, position, rank, standing, status, stratum ♦ [3b] elegance, grace, handsomeness, majesty, refinement, stateliness ♦ [4] breed, description, feather, ilk, kind, like, manner, nature, order, sort, species, type ♦ [5] bracket, category, division, family, grade, group, kind, order, set, species, type

²class *vb* ♦ : to arrange in classes : CLASSIFY

♦ assort, break down, categorize, classify, grade, group, peg, place, range, rank, separate, sort

class action *n* : a legal action undertaken in behalf of the plaintiffs and all others having an identical interest in the alleged wrong

[1]**clas•sic** \ˈkla-sik\ *adj* **1** ♦ : serving as a standard of excellence; *also* : TRADITIONAL **2** : CLASSICAL 2 **3** : notable especially as the best example **4** : AUTHENTIC **5** ♦ : typical or regarded as typical : ideally illustrative

♦ [1] model, paradigmatic, quintessential, traditional ♦ [5] characteristic, distinct, distinctive, individual, peculiar, proper, symptomatic, typical

[2]**classic** *n* **1** : a work of enduring excellence and especially of ancient Greece or Rome; *also* : its author **2** ♦ : a typical or perfect example **3** : a traditional event

♦ beau ideal, epitome, exemplar, ideal, perfection, quintessence

clas•si•cal \ˈkla-si-kəl\ *adj* **1** : CLASSIC **2** : of or relating to the ancient Greek and Roman classics **3** : of or relating to a form or system of primary significance before modern times ⟨~ economics⟩ **4** : concerned with a general study of the arts and sciences **5** ♦ : handed down (as beliefs or customs) by example from one generation to another — **clas•si•cal•ly** \-k(ə-)lē\ *adv*

♦ conventional, customary, traditional

clas•si•cism \ˈkla-sə-ˌsi-zəm\ *n* **1** : the principles or style of the literature or art of ancient Greece and Rome **2** : adherence to traditional standards believed to be universally valid — **clas•si•cist** \-sist\ *n*

clas•si•fi•ca•tion \ˌkla-sə-fə-ˈkā-shən\ *n* ♦ : a group of the same general status or nature : CLASS, CATEGORY

♦ bracket, category, class, division, family, grade, group, kind, order, rank, set, species, type

clas•si•fied \ˈkla-sə-ˌfīd\ *adj* : withheld from general circulation for reasons of national security

clas•si•fieds \-ˌfīdz\ *n pl* : advertisements grouped by subject

clas•si•fy \ˈkla-sə-ˌfī\ *vb* **-fied; -fy•ing** ♦ : to arrange in or assign to classes — **clas•si•fi•able** *adj* — **clas•si•fi•ca•tion** \ˌkla-sə-fə-ˈkā-shən\ *n* — **clas•si•fi•er** *n*

♦ arrange, array, codify, dispose, draw up, marshal, order, organize, range, systematize ♦ assort, break down, categorize, class, grade, group, peg, place, range, rank, separate, sort

class•less \ˈklas-ləs\ *adj* ♦ : having the qualities or behavior of a boor : BOORISH

♦ boorish, churlish, clownish, loutish, uncouth

class•mate \ˈklas-ˌmāt\ *n* : a member of the same class (as in a college)

class•room \-ˌrüm, -ˌru̇m\ *n* : a place where classes meet

classy \ˈkla-sē\ *adj* **class•i•er; -est** : ELEGANT, STYLISH — **class•i•ness** *n*

clat•ter \ˈkla-tər\ *n* **1** : a rattling sound ⟨the ~ of dishes⟩ **2** : an agitated disturbance or noisy confusion

clatter *vb* : to make a rattling sound

clause \ˈklȯz\ *n* **1** : a group of words having its own subject and predicate but forming only part of a compound or complex sentence **2** : a separate part of an article or document

claus•tro•pho•bia \ˌklȯ-strə-ˈfō-bē-ə\ *n* : abnormal dread of being in closed or narrow spaces — **claus•tro•pho•bic** \-bik\ *adj*

clav•i•chord \ˈkla-və-ˌkȯrd\ *n* : an early keyboard instrument in use before the piano

clav•i•cle \ˈkla-vi-kəl\ *n* : COLLARBONE

cla•vier \klə-ˈvir; ˈklā-vē-ər\ *n* **1** : the keyboard of a musical instrument **2** : an early keyboard instrument

[1]**claw** \ˈklȯ\ *n* **1** : a sharp usually curved nail on the toe of an animal **2** : a sharp curved process (as on the foot of an insect); *also* : a pincerlike organ at the end of a limb of some arthropods (as a lobster) — **clawed** \ˈklȯd\ *adj*

[2]**claw** *vb* : to rake, seize, or dig with or as if with claws

clay \ˈklā\ *n* **1** : an earthy material that is plastic when moist but hard when fired and is used in making pottery; *also* : finely divided soil consisting largely of such clay **2** : EARTH, MUD **3** : a plastic substance used for modeling **4** : the mortal human body — **clay•ey** \ˈklā-ē\ *adj*

clay•more \ˈklā-ˌmōr\ *n* : a large 2-edged sword formerly used by Scottish Highlanders

clay pigeon *n* : a saucer-shaped target thrown from a trap in trapshooting

[1]**clean** \ˈklēn\ *adj* **1** ♦ : free from dirt or disease **2 a** ♦ : free from moral taint or corruption : PURE **b** ♦ : observing the rules : FAIR **3** ♦ : so decisive and complete as to leave no loose ends or uncertainty : THOROUGH ⟨made a ~ break with the past⟩ **4** : TRIM ⟨a ship with ~ lines⟩; *also* : EVEN **5** : habitually neat — **clean•ly** \ˈklēn-lē\ *adv* — **clean•ness** \ˈklēn-nəs\ *n*

♦ [1] immaculate, spick-and-span, spotless, stainless, unsoiled, unsullied *Ant* dirty, filthy, foul, grubby, soiled, spotted, stained, sullied, unclean ♦ [2a] chaste, decent, immaculate, modest, pure ♦ [2b] fair, legal, sportsmanlike ♦ [3] all-out, complete, comprehensive, exhaustive, full-scale, out-and-out, thorough, thoroughgoing, total

[2]**clean** *adv* ♦ : all the way : COMPLETELY

♦ absolutely, all, altogether, completely, entirely, fully, quite, totally, utterly, wholly

[3]**clean** *vb* **1** : to make or become clean **2** ♦ : to remove the entrails from **3** ♦ : to exhaust the stock of — usually used with *out*

♦ [2] draw, eviscerate, gut ♦ *usu* **clean out** [3] consume, deplete, drain, exhaust, expend, spend, use up

clean–cut \ˈklēn-ˈkət\ *adj* **1** : cut so that the surface or edge is smooth and even **2** : sharply defined or outlined **3** : giving an effect of wholesomeness

clean•er *n* ♦ : a preparation for cleaning

♦ detergent, soap

clean•ly \ˈklen-lē\ *adj* **clean•li•er; -est** **1** : careful to keep clean **2** : habitually kept clean — **clean•li•ness** *n*

clean room \ˈklēn-ˌrüm, -ˌru̇m\ *n* : an uncontaminated room maintained for the manufacture or assembly of objects (as precision parts)

cleanse \ˈklenz\ *vb* **cleansed; cleans•ing** **1** : to make clean **2** : to rid of impurities by or as if by washing

cleans•er *vb* : a preparation (as a scouring powder or a skin cream) used for cleaning

cleansing *n* : the action or an act of cleansing especially morally or spiritually

[1]**clean•up** \ˈklē-ˌnəp\ *n* **1** : an act or instance of cleaning **2** : a very large profit

[2]**cleanup** *adj* : being 4th in the batting order of a baseball team

clean up *vb* **1** : to make a spectacular business profit **2** : rid of debasing or harmful features or elements

[1]**clear** \ˈklir\ *adj* **1 a** : shining brightly : entirely light **b** : UNTROUBLED, SERENE **2** ♦ : having the sky free from clouds : CLOUDLESS **3 a** : CLEAN, PURE **b** ♦ : easily seen through : TRANSPARENT **4 a** ♦ : easily heard, seen, or understood **b** : easy to perceive or determine with certainty **5 a** : capable of sharp discernment **b** : free from doubt **6** ♦ : free from guile or guilt : INNOCENT **7** ♦ : free from restriction, obstruction, or entanglement — **clear** *adv* — **clear•ly** \ˈklir-lē\ *adv* — **clear•ness** *n*

♦ [2] cloudless, fair, sunny, sunshiny, unclouded ♦ [3b] limpid, liquid, lucent, pellucid, transparent *Ant* cloudy, opaque ♦ [4a] apparent, broad, clear-cut, distinct, evident, lucid, manifest, obvious, palpable, patent, perspicuous, plain, transparent, unambiguous, unequivocal, unmistakable *Ant* dark, enigmatic, indistinct, mysterious, obscure, unclear; ambiguous, equivocal ♦ [6] blameless, faultless, guiltless, impeccable, innocent, irreproachable ♦ [7] free, open, unobstructed

[2]**clear** *vb* **1** ♦ : to make or become clear **2** : to go away : DISPERSE **3 a** ♦ : to free from accusation or blame **b** ♦ : to accept officially as satisfactory **c** : to certify as trustworthy **4** ♦ : to explain or make understandable — often used with *up* **5** : to get free from obstruction **6** ♦ : to make clear or free from debt or obligation : SETTLE **7** : NET **8** : to get rid of : REMOVE **9 a** ♦ : to free (as from contact or entanglement) : DISENTANGLE **b** : to jump or go by without touching; *also* : PASS

♦ [1] clarify, distill, filter, purify ♦ [3a] absolve, acquit, exculpate, exonerate, vindicate ♦ [3b] approve, authorize, OK, ratify, sanction, warrant ♦ *usu* **clear up** [4] clarify, construe, demonstrate, elucidate, explain, explicate, expound, illuminate, illustrate, interpret, spell out ♦ [6] discharge, foot, liquidate, pay, pay off, quit, recompense, settle, spring, stand ♦ [9a] disengage, disentangle, extricate, free, liberate, release, untangle

[3]**clear** *n* : a clear space or part

clear•ance \ˈklir-əns\ *n* **1** : an act or process of clearing **2** : the distance by which one object clears another **3** ♦ : certification as clear of objection : AUTHORIZATION

♦ allowance, authorization, concurrence, consent, leave, license (*or* licence), permission, sanction, sufferance

clear–cut \ˈklir-ˈkət\ *adj* **1** : sharply outlined : DISTINCT **2** ♦ : free from ambiguity or uncertainty : DEFINITE, UNEQUIVOCAL

♦ definite, definitive, explicit, express, specific, unambiguous, unequivocal

clear•head•ed \-ˈhe-dəd\ *adj* ♦ : having a clear understanding : able to think clearly

♦ balanced, lucid, normal, right, sane, stable

clear•ing \ˈklir-iŋ\ *n* **1** : a tract of land cleared of wood and brush **2** : the passage of checks and claims through a clearinghouse **3** : the act or process of becoming clear

clear•ing•house \-ˌhau̇s\ *n* : an institution maintained by banks for making an exchange of checks and claims held by each bank against other banks; *also* : an informal channel for information or assistance

clear out *vb* **1** ♦ : to drive out or away usually by force **2** ♦ : to go away or run from : DEPART

♦ [1] disband, disperse, dissipate, scatter ♦ [2] abscond, escape, flee, fly, get out, lam, run away, run off ♦ [2] depart, exit, get off, go, move, pull, quit, sally, shove, take off

cleat \ˈklēt\ *n* : a piece of wood or metal fastened on or projecting from something to give strength, provide a grip, or prevent slipping

cleav•age \ˈklē-vij\ *n* **1** : a splitting apart : SPLIT **2** : the depression between a woman's breasts especially when exposed by a low-cut dress

¹cleave \ˈklēv\ *vb* **cleaved** \ˈklēvd\ *or* **clove** \ˈklōv\; **cleaved; cleav•ing** : to adhere firmly and closely or loyally and unwaveringly : ADHERE, CLING

²cleave *vb* **cleaved** \ˈklēvd\ *also* **cleft** \ˈkleft\ *or* **clove** \ˈklōv\; **cleaved** *also* **cleft** *or* **clo•ven** \ˈklō-vən\; **cleav•ing** **1** : to divide by force : split asunder **2** : DIVIDE

cleav•er \ˈklē-vər\ *n* : a heavy chopping knife for cutting meat

clef \ˈklef\ *n* : a sign placed on the staff in music to show what pitch is represented by each line and space

cleft \ˈkleft\ *n* ♦ : a space or opening made by or as if by splitting : FISSURE, CRACK

♦ chink, crack, cranny, crevice, fissure, rift, split

cleft palate *n* : a split in the roof of the mouth that appears as a birth defect

clem•a•tis \ˈkle-mə-təs; kli-ˈma-təs\ *n* : any of a genus of vines or herbs related to the buttercups that have showy usually white or purple flowers

clem•en•cy \ˈkle-mən-sē\ *n, pl* **-cies** **1** ♦ : disposition to be merciful **2** : mildness of weather

♦ charity, leniency, mercy, quarter

clem•ent \ˈkle-mənt\ *adj* **1** : MERCIFUL, LENIENT **2** ♦ : not severe in temperature : TEMPERATE, MILD

♦ balmy, equable, gentle, mild, moderate, temperate *Ant* harsh, inclement, intemperate, severe

clem•en•tine \ˈkle-mən-ˌtēn\ *n* : a small citrus fruit that is probably a hybrid between a tangerine and an orange

clench \ˈklench\ *vb* **1** : CLINCH 1 **2** ♦ : to hold fast : CLUTCH **3** : to set or close tightly

♦ cling, clutch, grip, hang on, hold, hold on

clere•sto•ry \ˈklir-ˌstōr-ē\ *n* : an outside wall of a room or building that rises above an adjoining roof and contains windows

cler•gy \ˈklər-jē\ *n* : a body of religious officials authorized to conduct services

cler•gy•man \-mən\ *n* ♦ : a member of the clergy

♦ divine, ecclesiastic, father, minister, preacher, priest, reverend *Ant* layman

cler•ic \ˈkler-ik\ *n* : a member of the clergy

cler•i•cal \ˈkler-i-kəl\ *adj* **1** ♦ : of or relating to the clergy **2** : of or relating to a clerk

♦ ministerial, pastoral, priestly, sacerdotal *Ant* lay, nonclerical

cler•i•cal•ism \ˈkler-i-kə-ˌli-zəm\ *n* : a policy of maintaining or increasing the power of a religious hierarchy

clerk \ˈklərk, *Brit* ˈklärk\ *n* **1** : CLERIC **2 a** ♦ : an official responsible for correspondence, records, and accounts **b** : a person employed to perform general office work **3** : a store salesperson — **clerk** *vb* — **clerk•ship** *n*

♦ register, registrar, scribe

clev•er \ˈkle-vər\ *adj* **1** ♦ : showing skill or resourcefulness **2** ♦ : marked by wit or ingenuity — **clev•er•ly** *adv*

♦ [1] alert, brainy, bright, intelligent, keen, nimble, quick, quick-witted, sharp, smart ♦ [1] adroit, artful, creative, deft, imaginative, ingenious, innovative *Ant* uncreative, unimaginative ♦ [2] facetious, humorous, jocular, smart, witty

clev•er•ness *n* ♦ : the quality of being clever

♦ adeptness, adroitness, art, artfulness, artifice, artistry, craft, cunning, deftness, masterfulness, skill

clev•is \ˈkle-vəs\ *n* : a U-shaped shackle used for fastening

¹clew \ˈklü\ *n* **1** : CLUE **2** : a metal loop on a lower corner of a sail

²clew *vb* : to haul (a sail) up or down by ropes through the clews

cli•ché \kli-ˈshā\ *n* ♦ : a trite phrase or expression — **cli•chéd** \-ˈshād\ *adj*

♦ banality, commonplace, platitude, shibboleth

¹click \ˈklik\ *vb* **1** : to make or cause to make a click **2** : to fit together : hit it off **3** ♦ : to function or operate smoothly or successfully **4** : to select or make a selection on a computer by pressing a button on a control device (as a mouse) — **click•able** \ˈkli-kə-bəl\ *adj*

♦ deliver, go over, pan out, succeed, work out

²click *n* : a slight sharp noise

click•er \ˈkli-kər\ *n* : a remote control device (as for a television)

cli•ent \ˈklī-ənt\ *n* **1** : DEPENDENT **2** : a person who engages the professional services of another; *also* : PATRON, CUSTOMER **3** : a computer in a network that uses the services (as access to files) provided by a server

cli•en•tele \ˌklī-ən-ˈtel, ˌklē-\ *n* : a body of clients and especially customers

cliff \ˈklif\ *n* ♦ : a high steep face of rock, earth, or ice

♦ bluff, crag, escarpment, palisade, precipice, scarp

cliff–hang•er \-ˌhaŋ-ər\ *n* **1** : an adventure serial or melodrama usually presented in installments each of which ends in suspense **2** : a contest whose outcome is in doubt up to the very end

cli•mac•ter•ic \klī-ˈmak-tə-rik\ *n* **1** : a major turning point or critical stage **2** : MENOPAUSE; *also* : a corresponding period in the male

cli•mate \ˈklī-mət\ *n* **1** : a region having specific climatic conditions **2** : the average weather conditions at a place over a period of years **3** : the prevailing set of conditions (as temperature and humidity) indoors **4** ♦ : a prevailing atmosphere or environment ⟨the ~ of opinion⟩ — **cli•mat•ic** \klī-ˈma-tik\ *adj* — **cli•mat•i•cal•ly** \-ti-k(ə-)lē\ *adv*

♦ air, atmosphere, aura, flavor (*or* flavour), mood, note, temper ♦ atmosphere, environment, environs, medium, milieu, setting, surroundings

cli•ma•tol•o•gy \ˌklī-mə-ˈtä-lə-jē\ *n* : the science that deals with climates — **cli•ma•to•log•i•cal** \-mət-ᵊl-ˈä-ji-kəl\ *adj* — **cli•ma•to•log•i•cal•ly** \-k(ə-)lē\ *adv* — **cli•ma•tol•o•gist** \-mə-ˈtä-lə-jist\ *n*

¹cli•max \ˈklī-ˌmaks\ *n* **1** : a series of ideas or statements so arranged that they increase in force and power from the first to the last; *also* : the last member of such a series **2** ♦ : the highest point **3** : ORGASM — **cli•mac•tic** \klī-ˈmak-tik\ *adj*

♦ acme, apex, crown, culmination, head, height, meridian, peak, pinnacle, summit, tip-top, top, zenith

²climax *vb* : to come or bring to a climax : provide a culminating event for

¹climb \ˈklīm\ *vb* **1** ♦ : to rise to a higher point **2** ♦ : to go up or down especially by use of hands and feet; *also* : to ascend in growing — **climb•er** *n*

♦ [1, 2] arise, ascend, lift, mount, rise, soar, up

²climb *n* **1** : a place where climbing is necessary **2** ♦ : the act of climbing : ascent by climbing

♦ ascent, rise, soar

clime \ˈklīm\ *n* : CLIMATE

¹clinch \ˈklinch\ *vb* **1** : to turn over or flatten the end of something sticking out ⟨~ a nail⟩; *also* : to fasten by clinching **2** : to make final : SETTLE **3** : to hold fast or firmly

²clinch *n* **1** : a fastening by means of a clinched nail, rivet, or bolt **2** : an act or instance of clinching in boxing

clinch•er \ˈklin-chər\ *n* : one that clinches; *esp* : a decisive fact, argument, act, or remark

cling \ˈkliŋ\ *vb* **clung** \ˈkləŋ\; **cling•ing** **1 a** ♦ : to adhere as if glued **b** ♦ : to hold or hold on tightly **2** : to have a strong emotional attachment **3** ♦ : to give support or maintain loyalty

♦ [1a] adhere, hew, stick ♦ *usu* **cling to** [1b] clench, clutch, grip, hang on, hold, hold on ♦ *usu* **cling to** [3] adhere, hew, keep, stick

cling•stone \ˈkliŋ-ˌstōn\ *n* **:** any of various fruits (as some peaches) whose flesh adheres strongly to the pit
clin•ic \ˈkli-nik\ *n* **1 :** a medical class in which patients are examined and discussed **2 :** a group meeting for teaching a certain skill and working on individual problems ⟨a reading ~⟩ **3 :** a facility (as of a hospital) for diagnosis and treatment of outpatients
clin•i•cal \ˈkli-ni-kəl\ *adj* **1 :** of, relating to, or typical of a clinic; *esp* **:** involving direct observation of the patient **2 :** scientifically dispassionate — **clin•i•cal•ly** \-k(ə-)lē\ *adv*
cli•ni•cian \kli-ˈni-shən\ *n* **:** a person qualified in the clinical practice of medicine, psychiatry, or psychology as distinguished from one specializing in laboratory or research techniques or in theory
1clink \ˈkliŋk\ *vb* **:** to make or cause to make a sharp short metallic sound
2clink *n* **:** a clinking sound
clin•ker \ˈkliŋ-kər\ *n* **:** stony matter fused together **:** SLAG
1clip \ˈklip\ *vb* **clipped; clip•ping :** to fasten with a clip
2clip *n* **1 :** a device that grips, clasps, or hooks **2 :** a cartridge holder for a rifle
3clip *vb* **clipped; clip•ping 1** ♦ **:** to cut or cut off with shears **2 :** CURTAIL, DIMINISH **3 :** HIT, PUNCH **4 :** to illegally block (an opponent) in football

♦ bob, crop, cut, cut back, dock, lop, nip, prune, shave, shear, trim

4clip *n* **1 :** a 2-bladed instrument for cutting especially the nails **2 :** a sharp blow **3 :** a rapid pace
clip•board \ˈklip-ˌbōrd\ *n* **:** a small writing board with a spring clip at the top for holding papers
clip joint *n, slang* **:** an establishment (as a nightclub) that makes a practice of defrauding its customers
clip•per \ˈkli-pər\ *n* **1 :** an implement for clipping especially the hair or nails — usually used in plural **2 :** a fast sailing ship
clip•ping \ˈkli-piŋ\ *n* **:** a piece clipped from something (as a newspaper)
clique \ˈklēk, ˈklik\ *n* ♦ **:** a small exclusive group of people **:** COTERIE — **cliqu•ey** \ˈklē-kē, ˈkli-\ *adj* — **cliqu•ish** \-kish\ *adj*

♦ circle, clan, community, coterie, crowd, fold, gang, ring, set

cli•to•ris \ˈkli-tə-rəs\ *n, pl* **cli•to•ris•es :** a small erectile organ at the anterior or ventral part of the vulva homologous to the penis — **cli•to•ral** \-rəl\ *adj*
clk *abbr* clerk
clo *abbr* clothing
1cloak \ˈklōk\ *n* **1 :** a loose outer garment **2** ♦ **:** something that conceals

♦ curtain, hood, mantle, mask, shroud, veil

2cloak *vb* ♦ **:** to cover or hide with a cloak

♦ blanket, blot out, conceal, cover, curtain, enshroud, hide, mask, obscure, occult, screen, shroud, veil

cloak–and–dagger *adj* **:** involving or suggestive of espionage
clob•ber \ˈklä-bər\ *vb* **1 :** to pound mercilessly **2 :** to hit with force **3** ♦ **:** to defeat overwhelmingly

♦ drub, rout, skunk, thrash, trim, trounce, wallop, whip

cloche \ˈklōsh\ *n* **:** a woman's small close-fitting hat
1clock \ˈkläk\ *n* **:** a timepiece not intended to be carried on the person
2clock *vb* **1 :** to time (a person or a performance) by a timing device **2 :** to register (as speed) on a mechanical recording device — **clock•er** *n*
3clock *n* **:** an ornamental figure on a stocking or sock
clock•wise \ˈkläk-ˌwīz\ *adv* **:** in the direction in which the hands of a clock move — **clockwise** *adj*
clock•work \-ˌwərk\ *n* **1 :** the machinery that runs a mechanical device (as a clock or toy) **2 :** the precision or regularity associated with a clock
clod \ˈkläd\ *n* **1** ♦ **:** a lump especially of earth or clay **2** ♦ **:** a dull or insensitive person

♦ [1] blob, chunk, clump, glob, gob, hunk, lump, nub, wad ♦ [2] hulk, lout, lubber, lug, oaf

clod•hop•per \-ˌhä-pər\ *n* **1** ♦ **:** an uncouth rustic **2 :** a large heavy shoe

♦ bumpkin, hick, hillbilly, provincial, rustic, yokel

1clog \ˈkläg\ *n* **1 a :** a weight attached to an animal to impede motion **b :** something that shackles or impedes **2 :** a thick-soled shoe
2clog *vb* **clogged; clog•ging 1 a :** to impede with a clog **:** HINDER **b** ♦ **:** to halt or retard the progress, operation, or growth of **:** ENCUMBER **2** ♦ **:** to obstruct passage through **3 :** to become filled with extraneous matter

♦ [1b] encumber, hamper, hinder, hold up, impede, inhibit, interfere with, obstruct, tie up ♦ [2] block, choke, close (off), congest, dam, jam, obstruct, plug (up), stop (up), stuff ***Ant*** clear, free, open (up), unclog

cloi•son•né \ˌklȯiz-ᵊn-ˈā\ *adj* **:** a colored decoration made of enamels poured into the divided areas in a design outlined with wire or metal strips
1clois•ter \ˈklȯi-stər\ *n* **1** ♦ **:** a monastic establishment **2 :** a covered usually colonnaded passage on the side of a court — **clois•tral** \-strəl\ *adj*

♦ abbey, friary, monastery, priory

2cloister *vb* **:** to shut away from the world
clois•tered \ˈklȯ-stərd\ *adj* **1 :** being or living in or as if in a cloister **2** ♦ **:** providing shelter from contact with the outside world

♦ covert, isolated, quiet, remote, secluded, secret

clone \ˈklōn\ *n* **1 :** the collection of genetically identical cells or organisms produced asexually from a single ancestral cell or organism; *also* **:** an individual grown from a single cell and genetically identical to it ⟨a sheep ~⟩ **2 :** a group of replicas of a biological molecule (as DNA) **3 :** one that appears to be a copy of an original form — **clon•al** \ˈklō-nᵊl\ *adj* — **clone** *vb*
clop \ˈkläp\ *n* **:** a sound made by or as if by a hoof or wooden shoe against pavement — **clop** *vb*
1close \ˈklōz\ *vb* **closed; clos•ing 1 :** to bar passage through **:** SHUT **2 :** to suspend the operations (as of a school) **3** ♦ **:** to bring or come to an end or period **:** END, TERMINATE **4 :** to bring together the parts or edges of; *also* **:** to fill up **5** ♦ **:** to come near or approach close **6 :** GRAPPLE ⟨~ with the enemy⟩ **7 :** to enter into an agreement — **clos•able** *or* **close•able** *adj*

♦ [3] conclude, end, finish, round, terminate, wind up, wrap up ***Ant*** begin, commence, inaugurate, open, start ♦ [5] approach, near

2close \ˈklōz\ *n* ♦ **:** a coming or bringing of something to a conclusion or an end **:** CONCLUSION, END

♦ conclusion, consummation, end, ending, finale, finis, finish, windup ♦ cessation, closure, conclusion, end, ending, expiration, finish, halt, lapse, shutdown, stop, stoppage, termination

3close \ˈklōs\ *n* ♦ **:** an enclosed space

♦ court, courtyard, quadrangle, yard

4close \ˈklōs\ *adj* **clos•er; clos•est 1 :** having no openings **:** CLOSED **2 :** narrowly restricting or restricted **3 :** limited to a privileged class **4 a :** SECLUDED **b** ♦ **:** marked by a disposition to secrecy or extreme discreetness about divulging information **:** SECRETIVE **5 :** RIGOROUS **6** ♦ **:** hot and stuffy **:** causing a sensation of being slightly smothered or stifled **7 :** not generous in giving or spending **:** STINGY **8** ♦ **:** having little space between items or units **9 :** fitting tightly; *also* **:** SHORT ⟨~ haircut⟩ **10** ♦ **:** being near in time, space, effect, or degree **:** NEAR **11** ♦ **:** marked by a warm friendship developing through long association **:** INTIMATE ⟨~ friends⟩ **12 :** very precise and attentive to details **:** ACCURATE **13** ♦ **:** decided by a narrow margin ⟨a ~ game⟩ — **close•ly** *adv*

♦ [4b] closemouthed, dark, reticent, secretive, uncommunicative ♦ [6] breathless, stuffy ♦ [8] compact, crowded, dense, packed, serried, thick, tight ***Ant*** loose, uncrowded ♦ [10] immediate, near, nearby, nigh ***Ant*** distant, far, faraway, far-off, remote ♦ [11] bosom, chummy, familiar, friendly, intimate, thick ♦ [13] narrow, neck and neck, nip and tuck, tight

5close *adv* ♦ **:** in proximity of space or time

♦ around, by, hard, in, near, nearby, nigh

closed–cir•cuit \ˈklōzd-ˈsər-kət\ *adj* **:** used in, shown on, or being a television installation in which the signal is transmitted by wire to a limited number of receivers
closed shop *n* **:** an establishment having only members of a labor union on the payroll
close•fist•ed \ˈklōz-ˈfis-təd, ˈklōs-\ *adj* **:** not openhanded or liberal especially in giving **:** STINGY
close–knit \ˈklōs-ˈnit\ *adj* **:** closely bound together by social, cultural, economic, or political ties
close•mouthed \ˈklōz-ˈmau̇t͟hd, ˈklōs-ˈmau̇tht\ *adj* **1** ♦ **:** cautious or reticent in speaking **2** ♦ **:** disposed to secrecy about one's personal affairs

♦ [1] laconic, reserved, reticent, silent, taciturn, uncommunicative ♦ [2] close, dark, reticent, secretive, uncommunicative

close•ness *n* ♦ **:** the quality or state of being close

♦ familiarity, intimacy, nearness ♦ contiguity, immediacy, nearness, proximity

close•out \ˈklō-ˌzau̇t\ *n* **:** a sale of a business's entire stock at low prices
close out *vb* **1 :** to dispose of by a closeout **2 :** to dispose of a business **:** SELL OUT
[1]**clos•et** \ˈklä-zət, ˈklȯ-\ *n* **1** ♦ **:** a small room for privacy **2** ♦ **:** a small compartment for household utensils or clothing **3 :** a state or condition of secrecy ⟨came out of the ∼⟩

♦ [1] cell, chamber, room ♦ [2] buffet, cabinet, cupboard, hutch, locker, sideboard

[2]**closet** *vb* **1 :** to shut up in or as if in a closet **2 :** to take into a private room for an interview
close–up \ˈklō-ˌsəp\ *n* **1 :** a photograph or movie shot taken at close range **2 :** an intimate view or examination
clo•sure \ˈklō-zhər\ *n* **1** ♦ **:** an act of closing **:** the condition of being closed **2 :** a bringing to a point of completion **3 :** something that closes **4 :** CLOTURE

♦ cessation, close, conclusion, end, ending, expiration, finish, halt, lapse, shutdown, stop, stoppage, termination

[1]**clot** \ˈklät\ *n* **:** a mass formed by a portion of liquid (as blood) thickening and sticking together
[2]**clot** *vb* ♦ **:** to become a clot

♦ coagulate, congeal, gel, jell, set

cloth \ˈklȯth\ *n, pl* **cloths** \ˈklȯt͟hz, ˈklȯths\ **1 :** a pliable fabric made usually by weaving or knitting natural or synthetic fibers and filaments **2 :** TABLECLOTH **3 :** distinctive dress of the clergy; *also* **:** CLERGY
clothe \ˈklōt͟h\ *vb* **clothed** *or* **clad** \ˈklad\; **cloth•ing 1** ♦ **:** to provide with clothes **:** cover with clothes **:** DRESS **2** ♦ **:** to express by suitably significant language

♦ [1] apparel, array, attire, caparison, deck, dress, garb, invest, rig, suit ***Ant*** disrobe, strip, unclothe, undress ♦ [2] articulate, couch, express, formulate, phrase, put, say, state, word

clothes \ˈklōt͟hz, ˈklōz\ *n pl* **1 :** covering for the human body or garments in general **:** CLOTHING **2 :** BEDCLOTHES
clothes•horse \-ˌhȯrs\ *n* **1 :** a frame on which to hang clothes **2 :** a conspicuously dressy person
clothes•line \-ˌlīn\ *n* **:** a rope or cord on which clothes are hung to dry
clothes moth *n* **:** any of several small pale moths whose larvae eat wool, fur, and feathers
clothes•pin \ˈklōt͟hz-ˌpin, ˈklōz-\ *n* **:** a device for fastening clothes on a line
clothes•press \-ˌpres\ *n* **:** a receptacle for clothes
cloth•ier \ˈklōt͟h-yər, ˈklō-t͟hē-ər\ *n* **:** a maker or seller of clothing
cloth•ing \ˈklō-t͟hiŋ\ *n* ♦ **:** garments in general

♦ apparel, attire, dress, duds, raiment, wear

clo•ture \ˈklō-chər\ *n* **:** the closing or limitation (as by calling for a vote) of debate in a legislative body
[1]**cloud** \ˈklau̇d\ *n* **1 :** a visible mass of particles of condensed vapor (as water or ice) suspended in the atmosphere **2 :** a usually visible mass of minute airborne particles; *also* **:** a mass of obscuring matter in interstellar space **3 :** CROWD, SWARM ⟨a ∼ of mosquitoes⟩ **4 :** something having a dark or threatening aspect — **cloud•i•ness** \ˈklau̇-dē-nəs\ *n*
[2]**cloud** *vb* **1** ♦ **:** to darken or hide with or as if with a cloud **:** OBSCURE **2** ♦ **:** to make unclear or confused **:** CONFUSE **3 :** TAINT, SULLY

♦ [1] becloud, befog, blur, darken, dim, fog, haze, mist, obscure, overshadow, shroud ***Ant*** brighten, illuminate, illumine, lighten ♦ [2] becloud, befog, blur, confuse, fog, muddy

cloud•burst \-ˌbərst\ *n* ♦ **:** a sudden heavy rainfall

♦ deluge, downpour, rain, rainstorm, storm, wet

cloud•less *adj* ♦ **:** free from any cloud

♦ clear, fair, sunny, sunshiny, unclouded

cloud•let \-lət\ *n* **:** a small cloud
cloud nine *n* **:** a feeling of extreme well-being or elation — usually used with *on*
cloudy *adj* **1** ♦ **:** having a cloudy or overcast sky **2** ♦ **:** dimmed or dulled as if by clouds **3** ♦ **:** having visible material in suspension **:** MURKY

♦ [1] dull, hazy, heavy, overcast ♦ [2] foggy, hazy, misty, murky, smoggy, soupy ♦ [3] muddy, murky, turbid ***Ant*** clear

[1]**clout** \ˈklau̇t\ *n* **1** ♦ **:** a blow especially with the hand **2** ♦ **:** the power to sway people **:** special influence

♦ [1] bat, belt, blow, box, hit, punch, slug, thump, wallop, whack ♦ [2] authority, influence, pull, sway, weight

[2]**clout** *vb* **:** to hit forcefully
[1]**clove** \ˈklōv\ *n* **:** one of the small bulbs that grows at the base of the scales of a large bulb ⟨a ∼ of garlic⟩
[2]**clove** *past of* CLEAVE
[3]**clove** *n* **:** the dried flower bud of an East Indian tree used especially as a spice
clo•ven \ˈklō-vən\ *past part of* CLEAVE
cloven foot *n* **:** CLOVEN HOOF — **cloven–foot•ed** \-ˈfu̇-təd\ *adj*
cloven hoof *n* **:** a foot (as of a sheep) with the front part divided into two parts — **cloven–hoofed** \-ˈhu̇ft, -ˈhu̇vd\ *adj*
clo•ver \ˈklō-vər\ *n* **:** any of a genus of leguminous herbs with usually 3-parted leaves and dense flower heads
clo•ver•leaf \-ˌlēf\ *n, pl* **cloverleafs** \-ˌlēfs\ *or* **clo•ver•leaves** \-ˌlēvz\ **:** an interchange between two major highways that from above resembles a four-leaf clover
[1]**clown** \ˈklau̇n\ *n* **1** ♦ **:** a rude ill-bred person **:** BOOR **2** ♦ **:** a fool or comedian in an entertainment (as a circus)

♦ [1] beast, boor, churl, creep, cretin, cur, heel, jerk, joker, louse, lout, skunk, slob, snake ♦ [2] buffoon, harlequin, zany

[2]**clown** *vb* ♦ **:** to act like a clown ⟨always ∼*ing* around⟩

♦ *usu* **clown around** act up, cut up, fool around, monkey, show off, skylark

clown•ish *adj* ♦ **:** resembling or befitting a clown (as in ignorance and lack of sophistication) — **clown•ish•ly** *adv* — **clown•ish•ness** *n*

♦ boorish, churlish, loutish, uncouth ***Ant*** cultivated, polished, refined, well-bred; courtly, genteel, gentlemanly, ladylike; civil, courteous, polite

cloy \ˈklȯi\ *vb* **:** to disgust or nauseate with excess of something orig. pleasing — **cloy•ing•ly** *adv*
clr *abbr* clear
[1]**club** \ˈkləb\ *n* **1** ♦ **:** a heavy wooden stick or staff used as a weapon; *also* **:** BAT **2 :** any of a suit of playing cards marked with a black figure resembling a clover leaf **3 a** ♦ **:** a group of persons associated for a common purpose **b :** the meeting place of a group or association

♦ [1] bat, billy club, bludgeon, cudgel, nightstick, staff, truncheon ♦ [3a] association, brotherhood, college, congress, council, fellowship, fraternity, guild, institute, institution, league, order, organization, society

[2]**club** *vb* **clubbed; club•bing 1 :** to strike with a club **2** ♦ **:** to unite or combine for a common cause

♦ ally, associate, band, confederate, conjoin, cooperate, federate, league, unite

club•foot \ˈkləb-ˈfu̇t\ *n* **:** a misshapen foot twisted out of position from birth; *also* **:** this deformed condition — **club•foot•ed** \-ˈfu̇-təd\ *adj*
club•house \ˈkləb-ˌhau̇s\ *n* **1 :** a house occupied by a club **2 :** locker rooms used by an athletic team **3 :** a building at a golf course with locker rooms and usually a pro shop and a restaurant
club sandwich *n* **:** a sandwich of three slices of bread with two layers of meat (as turkey) and lettuce, tomato, and mayonnaise
club soda *n* **:** SODA WATER
cluck \ˈklək\ *n* **:** the call of a hen especially to her chicks — **cluck** *vb*
[1]**clue** \ˈklü\ *n* **1** ♦ **:** something that guides through an intricate procedure or maze; *esp* **:** a piece of evidence leading to the solution of a problem **2** ♦ **:** an indication that properly interpreted may lead to full understanding of something **:** IDEA, NOTION ⟨has no ∼ what he's doing⟩

♦ [1, 2] cue, hint, idea, indication, inkling, intimation, lead, notion, suggestion

[2]**clue** *vb* **clued; clue•ing** *or* **clu•ing 1 :** to provide with a clue **2** ♦ **:** to give information to ⟨∼ me in⟩

♦ *usu* **clue in** acquaint, advise, apprise, brief, enlighten, familiarize, fill in, inform, instruct, tell, wise

¹clump \ˈkləmp\ *n* **1** ♦ **:** a group of things clustered together **2** ♦ **:** a compact mass **3 :** a heavy tramping sound

♦ array, assemblage, bank, batch, block, bunch, cluster, collection, group, huddle, knot, lot, package, parcel, set, suite

²clump *vb* **:** to tread clumsily and noisily

clum•sy \ˈkləm-zē\ *adj* **clum•si•er; -est 1** ♦ **:** lacking dexterity, nimbleness, or grace **2** ♦ **:** not tactful or subtle **3** ♦ **:** awkward or inefficient in use or construction **:** UNWIELDY — **clum•si•ly** \-zə-lē\ *adv* — **clum•si•ness** \-zē-nəs\ *n*

♦ [1] awkward, gawky, graceless, heavy-handed, lubberly, lumpish, ungainly, unhandy *Ant* deft, dexterous, graceful, handy ♦ [2] awkward, inept, inexpert, maladroit ♦ [3] awkward, cranky, cumbersome, ungainly, unhandy, unwieldy

clung *past and past part of* CLING

clunk•er \ˈkləŋ-kər\ *n* **1 :** a dilapidated automobile **2 :** a notable failure

¹clus•ter \ˈkləs-tər\ *n* ♦ **:** a number of similar things that occur together **:** GROUP, BUNCH

♦ array, assemblage, bank, batch, block, bunch, clump, collection, group, huddle, knot, lot, package, parcel, set, suite

²cluster *vb* ♦ **:** to grow or gather in a cluster

♦ assemble, collect, concentrate, conglomerate, congregate, convene, forgather, gather, meet, rendezvous ♦ bunch, crowd, huddle, press

¹clutch \ˈkləch\ *vb* ♦ **:** to grasp with or as if with the hand

♦ clench, cling, grip, hang on, hold, hold on

²clutch *n* **1 a :** the claws or a hand in the act of grasping **b** ♦ **:** an often cruel or unrelenting control, power, or possession **:** CONTROL, POWER **2 :** a device for gripping an object **3 :** a coupling used to connect and disconnect a driving and a driven part of a mechanism; *also* **:** a lever or pedal operating such a coupling **4** ♦ **:** a crucial situation

♦ [1b] arm, authority, command, control, dominion, grip, hold, mastery, power, sway ♦ [4] crisis, crunch, emergency, head, juncture

³clutch *adj* **:** made, done, or successful in a crucial situation

⁴clutch *n* **1 :** a nest or batch of eggs; *also* **:** a brood of chicks **2 :** GROUP, BUNCH

¹clut•ter \ˈklə-tər\ *vb* **:** to fill or cover with a disorderly scattering of things

²clutter *n* ♦ **:** a crowded mass

♦ assortment, jumble, medley, mélange, miscellany, motley, muddle, variety, welter

cm *abbr* centimeter

Cm *symbol* curium

CM *abbr* Northern Mariana Islands

cmdr *abbr* commander

cml *abbr* commercial

CMSgt *abbr* chief master sergeant

CNO *abbr* chief of naval operations

CNS *abbr* central nervous system

co *abbr* **1** company **2** county

Co *symbol* cobalt

CO *abbr* **1** Colorado **2** commanding officer **3** conscientious objector

c/o *abbr* care of

¹coach \ˈkōch\ *n* **1 :** a large closed 4-wheeled carriage with an elevated outside front seat for the driver **2 :** a railroad passenger car especially for day travel **3 :** BUS **4 a :** a private tutor **b :** one who instructs or trains; *esp* **:** one who instructs players in a sport ⟨a soccer ~⟩

²coach *vb* ♦ **:** to instruct, direct, or prompt as a coach

♦ counsel, guide, lead, mentor, pilot, shepherd, show, tutor

coach•man \-mən\ *n* **:** a man who drives a coach or carriage

co•ad•ju•tor \ˌkō-ə-ˈjü-tər, kō-ˈa-jə-tər\ *n* **:** one who works together with another **:** ASSISTANT; *esp* **:** an assistant bishop having the right of succession

co•ag•u•lant \kō-ˈa-gyə-lənt\ *n* **:** something that produces coagulation

co•ag•u•late \-ˌlāt\ *vb* **-lat•ed; -lat•ing** ♦ **:** to cause to become viscous or thickened into a coherent mass **:** CLOT — **co•ag•u•la•tion** \kō-ˌa-gyə-ˈlā-shən\ *n*

♦ clot, congeal, gel, jell, set

¹coal \ˈkōl\ *n* **1 :** EMBER **2 :** a black solid combustible mineral used as fuel

²coal *vb* **1 :** to supply with coal **2 :** to take in coal

co•a•lesce \ˌkō-ə-ˈles\ *vb* **co•a•lesced; co•a•lesc•ing 1 :** to grow together **2** ♦ **:** to unite into a whole **:** FUSE — **co•a•les•cence** \-ᵊns\ *n*

♦ associate, combine, conjoin, connect, couple, fuse, join, link, marry, unify, unite

coal•field \ˈkōl-ˌfēld\ *n* **:** a region rich in coal deposits

coal gas *n* **:** gas from coal; *esp* **:** gas distilled from bituminous coal and used for heating

co•a•li•tion \ˌkō-ə-ˈli-shən\ *n* **1 :** UNION **2** ♦ **:** a temporary alliance of distinct parties, persons, or states for a common purpose — **co•a•li•tion•ist** *n*

♦ alliance, bloc, combination, combine, confederacy, confederation, federation, league, union ♦ bloc, body, combination, combine, faction, party, sect, set, side, wing

coal oil *n* **:** KEROSENE

coal tar *n* **:** tar distilled from bituminous coal and used in dyes and drugs

co–an•chor \ˈkō-ˈaŋ-kər\ *n* **:** a newscaster who shares the duties of head broadcaster

coarse \ˈkȯrs\ *adj* **coars•er; coars•est 1** ♦ **:** of ordinary or inferior quality **2** ♦ **:** composed of large parts or particles ⟨~ sand⟩ **3** ♦ **:** crude or unrefined in taste, manners, or language **:** CRUDE ⟨~ manners⟩ **4 :** harsh or rough in tone or texture **:** ROUGH, HARSH — **coarse•ly** *adv*

♦ [1] bad, bum, cheap, common, cut-rate, inferior, junky, lousy, mediocre, poor, second-rate, shoddy, sleazy, trashy ♦ [2] grainy, granular *Ant* dusty, fine, floury, powdery ♦ [3] common, crass, crude, gross, ill-bred, low, rough, rude, tasteless, uncouth, uncultivated, uncultured, unpolished, unrefined, vulgar *Ant* cultivated, cultured, genteel, polished, refined, smooth, tasteful, well-bred

coars•en \ˈkȯr-sᵊn\ *vb* **:** to make or become coarse

coarse•ness *n* ♦ **:** the quality or state of being coarse

♦ grossness, indelicacy, lowness, rudeness, vulgarity

¹coast \ˈkōst\ *n* **1 :** SEASHORE **2 :** a slide down a slope **3 :** the immediate area of view — used in the phrase *the coast is clear* — **coast•al** *adj*

²coast *vb* **1 :** to sail along the shore **2** ♦ **:** to move (as downhill on a sled) without effort

♦ bowl, breeze, drift, flow, glide, roll, sail, skim, slide, slip, stream, sweep, whisk

coast•er *n* **1 :** one that coasts **2 :** a shallow container or a plate or mat to protect a surface

coaster brake *n* **:** a brake in the hub of the rear wheel of a bicycle

coast guard *n* **:** a military force employed in guarding or patrolling a coast — **coast•guards•man** \ˈkōst-ˌgärdz-mən\ *n*

coast•line \ˈkōst-ˌlīn\ *n* **:** the outline or shape of a coast

¹coat \ˈkōt\ *n* **1 :** an outer garment for the upper part of the body **2** ♦ **:** an external growth (as of fur or feathers) on an animal **3 :** a covering layer ⟨a ~ of paint⟩ — **coat•ed** \ˈkō-təd\ *adj*

♦ fleece, fur, hair, pelage, pile, wool

²coat *vb* ♦ **:** to cover usually with a finishing or protective coat or layer

♦ blanket, carpet, cover, overlay, overlie, overspread

coat•ing \ˈkō-tiŋ\ *n* **:** COAT, COVERING

coat of arms : a shield or similar device for displaying the insignia of a family or group

co•au•thor \ˈkō-ˈȯ-thər\ *n* **:** a joint or associate author — **coauthor** *vb*

coax \ˈkōks\ *vb* ♦ **:** to gain by gentle urging or flattery **:** WHEEDLE

♦ cajole, wheedle

co•ax•i•al \ˈkō-ˈak-sē-əl\ *adj* **:** having coincident axes — **co•ax•i•al•ly** *adv*

coaxial cable *n* **:** a cable that consists of a tube of electrically conducting material surrounding a central conductor

cob \ˈkäb\ *n* **1 :** a male swan **2 :** CORNCOB **3 :** a short-legged stocky horse

co•balt \ˈkō-ˌbȯlt\ *n* **:** a tough shiny silver-white magnetic metallic chemical element found with iron and nickel

cob•ble \ˈkä-bəl\ *vb* **cob•bled; cob•bling :** to make or put together roughly or hastily — often used with *together* or *up* ⟨~ together a solution⟩

cob•bler \ˈkä-blər\ *n* **1 :** a mender or maker of shoes **2 :** a deep-dish fruit pie with a thick crust

cob•ble•stone \ˈkä-bəl-ˌstōn\ *n* **:** a naturally rounded stone larger than a pebble and smaller than a boulder

co•bra \ˈkō-brə\ *n* **:** any of several venomous snakes of Asia and Africa that when excited expand the skin of the neck into a broad hood

cob•web \ˈkäb-ˌweb\ *n* **1 :** SPIDERWEB; *also* **:** a thread spun by a spider or insect larva **2 :** something flimsy or entangling — **cob•web•by** \-ˌwe-bē\ *adj*

co•caine \kō-ˈkān, ˈkō-ˌkān\ *n* **:** a drug obtained from the leaves of a So. American shrub (**co•ca** \ˈkō-kə\) that can result in severe psychological dependence and is sometimes used in medicine as a local anesthetic and illegally as a stimulant of the central nervous system

coc•cus \ˈkä-kəs\ *n, pl* **coc•ci** \ˈkäk-ˌsī\ **:** a spherical bacterium

coc•cyx \ˈkäk-siks\ *n, pl* **coc•cy•ges** \ˈkäk-sə-ˌjēz\ *also* **coc•cyx•es** \ˈkäk-sik-səz\ **:** the end of the spinal column beyond the sacrum especially in humans

co•chi•neal \ˈkä-chə-ˌnēl\ *n* **:** a red dye made from the dried bodies of females of a tropical American insect (**cochineal insect**)

co•chlea \ˈkō-klē-ə, ˈkä-\ *n, pl* **co•chle•as** *or* **co•chle•ae** \-klē-ˌē, -ˌī\ **:** the usually spiral part of the inner ear containing nerve endings which carry information about sound to the brain — **co•chle•ar** \-klē-ər\ *adj*

[1]**cock** \ˈkäk\ *n* **1 :** the adult male of a bird and especially of the common domestic chicken **2** ♦ **:** a device (as a faucet or valve) for regulating the flow of a liquid **:** VALVE, FAUCET **3 :** LEADER **4 a :** the hammer of a firearm **b :** the position of the hammer when ready for firing

♦ faucet, gate, spigot, tap, valve

[2]**cock** *vb* **1 :** to draw back the hammer of a firearm **2 :** to set or draw back in readiness for some action ⟨~ your arm to throw⟩ **3** ♦ **:** to turn or tilt usually to one side

♦ angle, cant, heel, incline, lean, list, slant, slope, tilt, tip

[3]**cock** *n* ♦ **:** the act of tilting **:** the state or position of being tilted

♦ bend, inclination, list, slant, tilt, tip

[4]**cock** *n* **:** a small pile (as of hay)

cock•ade \kä-ˈkād\ *n* **:** an ornament worn on the hat as a badge

cock•a•tiel \ˌkä-kə-ˈtēl\ *n* **:** a small crested gray parrot often kept as a cage bird

cock•a•too \ˈkä-kə-ˌtü\ *n, pl* **-toos :** any of various large noisy crested parrots chiefly of Australia

cock•a•trice \ˈkä-kə-trəs, -ˌtrīs\ *n* **:** a legendary serpent with a deadly glance

cock•crow \ˈkäk-ˌkrō\ *n* ♦ **:** the first appearance of light in the morning followed by sunrise **:** DAWN

♦ aurora, dawn, morning, sunrise

cocked hat \ˈkäkt-\ *n* **:** a hat with the brim turned up on two or three sides

cock•er•el \ˈkä-kə-rəl\ *n* **:** a young male domestic chicken

cock•er spaniel \ˈkä-kər-\ *n* **:** any of a breed of small spaniels with long ears, square muzzle, and silky coat

cock•eyed \ˈkä-ˈkīd\ *adj* **1** ♦ **:** turned or tilted to one side **2 :** slightly crazy **:** FOOLISH

♦ askew, awry, crooked, listing, lopsided, slantwise, uneven

cock•fight \ˈkäk-ˌfīt\ *n* **:** a contest of gamecocks usually fitted with metal spurs

[1]**cock•le** \ˈkä-kəl\ *n* **:** any of several weedy plants related to the pinks

[2]**cockle** *n* **:** a bivalve mollusk with a heart-shaped shell

cock•le•shell \-ˌshel\ *n* **1 :** the shell of a cockle **2 :** a light flimsy boat

cock•ney \ˈkäk-nē\ *n, pl* **cockneys :** a native of London and especially of the East End of London; *also* **:** the dialect of a cockney

cock•pit \ˈkäk-ˌpit\ *n* **1 :** a pit for cockfights **2 :** a space or compartment in a vehicle from which it is steered, piloted, or driven

cock•roach \ˈkäk-ˌrōch\ *n* **:** any of an order or suborder of active nocturnal insects including some which infest houses and ships

cock•sure \ˈkäk-ˈshu̇r\ *adj* **1** ♦ **:** perfectly sure **:** CERTAIN **2 :** COCKY

♦ assured, certain, clear, confident, doubtless, positive, sanguine, sure

cock•tail \ˈkäk-ˌtāl\ *n* **1 :** an iced drink made of liquor and flavoring ingredients **2 :** an appetizer (as tomato juice) served as a first course of a meal

cocky \ˈkä-kē\ *adj* **cock•i•er; -est** ♦ **:** boldly and brashly self-confident — **cock•i•ly** \-kə-lē\ *adv* — **cock•i•ness** \-kē-nəs\ *n*

♦ arch, bold, brash, brazen, cheeky, fresh, impertinent, impudent, insolent, nervy, sassy, saucy

co•coa \ˈkō-kō\ *n* **1 :** CACAO **2 :** chocolate deprived of some of its fat and powdered; *also* **:** a drink made of this heated with water or milk

cocoa butter *n* **:** a pale vegetable fat obtained from cacao beans

co•co•nut \ˈkō-kə-(ˌ)nət\ *n* **:** a large edible nut produced by a tall tropical palm (**coconut palm**)

co•coon \kə-ˈkün\ *n* **1 :** a case usually of silk formed by some insect larvae for protection during the pupal stage **2** ♦ **:** something suggesting a cocoon especially in providing protection or in producing isolation

♦ armor, capsule, case, casing, cover, housing, husk, jacket, pod, sheath, shell

cod \ˈkäd\ *n, pl* **cod** *also* **cods :** a bottom-dwelling bony fish of the No. Atlantic that is an important food fish; *also* **:** a related fish of the Pacific Ocean

COD *abbr* **1** cash on delivery **2** collect on delivery

co•da \ˈkō-də\ *n* **:** a closing section in a musical composition that is formally distinct from the main structure

cod•dle \ˈkäd-ᵊl\ *vb* **cod•dled; cod•dling 1 :** to cook slowly in water below the boiling point **2** ♦ **:** to treat with extreme or excessive care or kindness **:** PAMPER

♦ baby, mollycoddle, nurse, pamper, spoil

[1]**code** \ˈkōd\ *n* **1 :** a systematic statement of a body of law **2 :** a system of principles or rules ⟨moral ~⟩ **3 :** a system of signals **4 :** a system of symbols (as in secret communication) with special meanings **5 :** GENETIC CODE

[2]**code** *vb* **cod•ed; cod•ing :** to put into the form or symbols of a code

co•deine \ˈkō-ˌdēn\ *n* **:** a narcotic drug obtained from opium and used especially as an analgesic and cough suppressant

co•dex \ˈkō-ˌdeks\ *n, pl* **co•di•ces** \ˈkō-də-ˌsēz, ˈkä-\ **:** a manuscript book (as of the Scriptures or classics)

cod•fish \ˈkäd-ˌfish\ *n* **:** COD

cod•ger \ˈkä-jər\ *n* **:** an odd or cranky and usually elderly fellow

cod•i•cil \ˈkä-də-səl, -ˌsil\ *n* **:** a legal instrument modifying an earlier will

cod•i•fy \ˈkä-də-ˌfī, ˈkō-\ *vb* **-fied; -fy•ing** ♦ **:** to arrange in a systematic form — **cod•i•fi•ca•tion** \ˌkä-də-fə-ˈkā-shən, ˌkō-\ *n*

♦ arrange, array, classify, dispose, draw up, marshal, order, organize, range, systematize

co•ed \ˈkō-ˌed\ *n* **:** a female student in a coeducational institution — **coed** *adj*

co•ed•u•ca•tion \ˌkō-ˌe-jə-ˈkā-shən\ *n* **:** the education of male and female students at the same institution — **co•ed•u•ca•tion•al** \-shə-nəl\ *adj* — **co•ed•u•ca•tion•al•ly** *adv*

co•ef•fi•cient \ˌkō-ə-ˈfi-shənt\ *n* **1 :** a constant factor as distinguished from a variable in a mathematical term **2 :** a number that serves as a measure of some property (as of a substance, device, or process)

coe•len•ter•ate \si-ˈlen-tə-ˌrāt, -rət\ *n* **:** any of a phylum of radially symmetrical invertebrate animals including the corals, sea anemones, and jellyfishes

co•equal \kō-ˈē-kwəl\ *adj* **:** equal with another — **coequal** *n* — **co•equal•i•ty** \ˌkō-ē-ˈkwä-lə-tē\ *n* — **co•equal•ly** *adv*

co•erce \kō-ˈərs\ *vb* **co•erced; co•erc•ing 1 :** RESTRAIN, REPRESS **2** ♦ **:** to compel to an act or choice **3 :** ENFORCE — **co•er•cive** \-ˈər-siv\ *adj*

♦ compel, constrain, drive, force, make, muscle, obligate, oblige, press, pressure

co•er•cion \-ˈər-zhən, -shən\ *n* ♦ **:** the act, process, or power of coercing

♦ compulsion, constraint, duress, force, pressure

co•eval \kō-ˈē-vəl\ *adj* ♦ **:** of the same age

♦ concurrent, contemporary, simultaneous, synchronous

coeval *n* **:** one of the same age

co•ex•ist \ˌkō-ig-ˈzist\ *vb* **1 :** to exist together or at the same time **2 :** to live in peace with each other

co•ex•is•tence \-ˈzis-təns\ *n* **:** the quality or state of coexisting

co•ex•ten•sive \ˌkō-ik-ˈsten-siv\ *adj* **:** having the same scope or extent in space or time

C of C *abbr* Chamber of Commerce

cof•fee \ˈkȯ-fē\ *n* **:** a drink made from the roasted and ground seeds of a fruit of a tropical shrub or tree; *also* **:** these seeds (**coffee beans**) or a plant producing them

cof•fee•house \-ˌhau̇s\ *n* **:** a place where refreshments (as coffee) are sold
coffee klatch \-ˌklach\ *n* **:** KAFFEEKLATSCH
cof•fee•pot \-ˌpät\ *n* **:** a pot for brewing or serving coffee
coffee shop *n* **:** a small restaurant
coffee table *n* **:** a low table customarily placed in front of a sofa
cof•fer \ˈkȯ-fər\ *n* **:** a chest or box used especially for valuables
cof•fer•dam \-ˌdam\ *n* **:** a watertight enclosure from which water is pumped to expose the bottom of a body of water and permit construction
cof•fin \ˈkȯ-fən\ *n* **:** a box or chest for a corpse to be buried in
C of S *abbr* chief of staff
[1]**cog** \ˈkäg\ *n* **:** a tooth on the rim of a wheel or gear — **cogged** \ˈkägd\ *adj*
[2]**cog** *abbr* cognate
co•gen•cy \-jən-sē\ *n* ♦ **:** the quality or state of being cogent

♦ effectiveness, force, impact, persuasiveness, pertinence, punch, relevance, soundness, strength ***Ant*** ineffectiveness

co•gen•e•ra•tion \ˌkō-ˌje-nə-ˈrā-shən\ *n* **:** the simultaneous generation of electricity and heat from the same fuel
co•gent \ˈkō-jənt\ *adj* ♦ **:** having power to compel or constrain **:** CONVINCING

♦ compelling, conclusive, convincing, decisive, effective, forceful, persuasive, pertinent, relevant, satisfying, sound, strong, telling, valid ***Ant*** inconclusive, indecisive, ineffective, unconvincing

cog•i•tate \ˈkä-jə-ˌtāt\ *vb* **-tat•ed; -tat•ing** ♦ **:** to ponder or meditate on usually intently **:** THINK, PONDER — **cog•i•ta•tion** \ˌkä-jə-ˈtā-shən\ *n* — **cog•i•ta•tive** \ˈkä-jə-ˌtā-tiv\ *adj*

♦ chew over, consider, contemplate, debate, deliberate, entertain, meditate, mull, ponder, question, ruminate, study, think, weigh

co•gnac \ˈkōn-ˌyak\ *n* **:** a French brandy
cog•nate \ˈkäg-ˌnāt\ *adj* **1 :** of the same or similar nature **2 :** RELATED; *esp* **:** related by descent from the same ancestral language — **cognate** *n*
cog•ni•tive \ˈkäg-nə-tiv\ *adj* **:** of, relating to, or being conscious intellectual activity (as thinking, remembering, reasoning, or using language) — **cog•ni•tion** \käg-ˈni-shən\ *n* — **cog•ni•tive•ly** *adv*
cog•ni•zance \ˈkäg-nə-zəns\ *n* **1** ♦ **:** apprehension by the mind **:** AWARENESS **2 :** NOTICE, HEED **3 :** particular knowledge **:** conscious recognition

♦ attention, awareness, ear, eye, heed, notice, observance, observation

cog•ni•zant \ˈkäg-nə-zənt\ *adj* ♦ **:** knowledgeable of something especially through personal experience

♦ alive, aware, conscious, mindful, sensible, sentient, witting

cog•no•men \käg-ˈnō-mən, ˈkäg-nə-\ *n, pl* **cognomens** *or* **cog•no•mi•na** \käg-ˈnä-mə-nə, -ˈnō-\ ♦ **:** a word or phrase that constitutes the distinctive designation of a person or thing **:** NAME; *esp* **:** NICKNAME

♦ alias, nickname ♦ appellation, denotation, designation, handle, name, title

co•gno•scen•te \ˌkän-yə-ˈshen-tē\ *n, pl* **-scen•ti** \-tē\ **:** CONNOISSEUR
cog•wheel \ˈkäg-ˌhwēl\ *n* **:** a wheel with cogs or teeth
co•hab•it \kō-ˈha-bət\ *vb* **:** to live together as husband and wife — **co•hab•i•ta•tion** \-ˌha-bə-ˈtā-shən\ *n*
co•here \kō-ˈhir\ *vb* **co•hered; co•her•ing 1 :** to stick together **2 :** to become united in principles, relationships, or interests
co•her•ence \-əns\ *n* ♦ **:** the quality or state of being coherent

♦ balance, consonance, harmony, proportion, symmetry, symphony, unity

co•her•ent \kō-ˈhir-ənt\ *adj* **1 :** having the quality of cohering **2** ♦ **:** logically consistent — **co•her•ent•ly** *adv*

♦ analytic, good, logical, rational, reasonable, sensible, sober, sound, valid

co•he•sion \kō-ˈhē-zhən\ *n* **1** ♦ **:** a sticking together **2 :** molecular attraction by which the particles of a body are united — **co•he•sive** \-siv\ *adj* — **co•he•sive•ly** *adv* — **co•he•sive•ness** *n*

♦ adherence, adhesion

co•ho \ˈkō-ˌhō\ *n, pl* **cohos** *or* **coho :** a rather small Pacific salmon with light-colored flesh
co•hort \ˈkō-ˌhȯrt\ *n* **1 :** a group of warriors or followers **2** ♦ **:** one that keeps company with another **:** COMPANION, ACCOMPLICE

♦ accomplice, associate, companion, comrade, crony, fellow, mate

coif \ˈkȯif; *2 usu* ˈkwäf\ *n* **1 :** a close-fitting hat **2 :** COIFFURE
coif•feur \kwä-ˈfər\ *n* **:** HAIRDRESSER
coif•feuse \kwä-ˈfərz, -ˈfəz, -ˈfüz, -ˈfyüz\ *n* **:** a female hairdresser
coif•fure \kwä-ˈfyu̇r\ *n* **:** a manner of arranging the hair
[1]**coil** \ˈkȯil\ *vb* ♦ **:** to wind in a spiral shape

♦ curl, entwine, spiral, twine, twist, wind

[2]**coil** *n* **:** a series of rings or loops (as of coiled rope, wire, or pipe) **:** RING, LOOP
[1]**coin** \ˈkȯin\ *n* **1 :** a piece of metal issued by government authority as money **2 :** metal money
[2]**coin** *vb* **1 :** to make (a coin) especially by stamping **:** MINT **2 :** CREATE, INVENT ⟨~ a phrase⟩ — **coin•er** *n*
coin•age \ˈkȯi-nij\ *n* **1 :** the act or process of coining **2 a** ♦ **:** something that has been coined **b :** COINS

♦ concoction, contrivance, creation, innovation, invention, wrinkle

co•in•cide \ˌkō-ən-ˈsīd, ˈkō-ən-ˌsīd\ *vb* **-cid•ed; -cid•ing 1 :** to occupy the same place in space or time **2** ♦ **:** to correspond or agree exactly

♦ accord, agree, answer, check, comport, conform, correspond, dovetail, fit, go, harmonize, jibe, square, tally

co•in•ci•dence \kō-ˈin-sə-dəns\ *n* **1 :** exact agreement **2 :** occurrence together apparently without reason; *also* **:** an event that so occurs
co•in•ci•dent \-sə-dənt\ *adj* **1 :** of similar nature **2** ♦ **:** occupying the same space or time

♦ attendant, concomitant, concurrent

co•in•ci•den•tal \kō-ˌin-sə-ˈdent-ᵊl\ *adj* **:** occurring or existing at the same time
co•i•tus \ˈkō-ə-təs\ *n* **:** physical union of male and female genitalia **:** SEXUAL INTERCOURSE — **co•i•tal** \-ᵊl\ *adj*
[1]**coke** \ˈkōk\ *n* **:** a hard gray porous fuel made by heating soft coal to drive off most of its volatile material
[2]**coke** *n* **:** COCAINE
[1]**col** *abbr* **1** colonial; colony **2** column
[2]**col** *or* **coll** *abbr* **1** collect, collected, collection **2** college, collegiate
Col *abbr* **1** colonel **2** Colorado **3** Colossians
COL *abbr* **1** colonel **2** cost of living
co•la \ˈkō-lə\ *n* **:** a carbonated soft drink usually containing sugar, caffeine, caramel, and special flavoring
col•an•der \ˈkə-lən-dər, ˈkä-\ *n* **:** a perforated utensil for draining food
[1]**cold** \ˈkōld\ *adj* **1** ♦ **:** having a low or decidedly subnormal temperature **2** ♦ **:** lacking warmth of feeling **3 :** suffering or uncomfortable from lack of warmth **4 :** giving the appearance of being dead **:** UNCONSCIOUS — **cold•ly** *adv* — **cold•ness** *n* — **in cold blood :** with premeditation **:** DELIBERATELY

♦ [1] arctic, bitter, chill, chilly, cool, freezing, frigid, frosty, glacial, icy, nippy, polar, raw, snappy, wintry ***Ant*** broiling, burning, fiery, hot, piping hot, red-hot, roasting, scalding, scorching, searing, sultry, summery, sweltering, torrid, tropical, warm, warming ♦ [2] aloof, antisocial, cool, detached, distant, frosty, remote, standoffish, unsociable ♦ [2] chill, chilly, cold-blooded, cool, frigid, frosty, glacial, icy, unfriendly, unsympathetic, wintry ***Ant*** cordial, friendly, genial, hearty, sympathetic, warm, warm-blooded, warmhearted

[2]**cold** *n* **1 a :** a condition marked by low temperature **b :** cold weather **2 :** a chilly feeling **3 :** a bodily disorder popularly associated with chilling; *esp* **:** COMMON COLD
[3]**cold** *adv* **:** TOTALLY, FINALLY
cold–blood•ed \ˈkōld-ˈblə-dəd\ *adj* **1** ♦ **:** lacking normal human feelings **2 :** having a body temperature not internally regulated but close to that of the environment **3 :** sensitive to cold

♦ callous, hard, heartless, inhuman, inhumane, pitiless, soulless, unfeeling, unsympathetic ♦ apathetic, impassive, phlegmatic, stoic, stolid, unemotional

cold feet *n pl* **:** doubt or fear that prevents action
cold front *n* **:** an advancing edge of a cold air mass
cold shoulder *n* ♦ **:** cold or unsympathetic behavior — **cold–shoul•der** *vb*

♦ brush-off, rebuff, repulse, snub

cold sore *n* : a group of fluid-filled blisters appearing in or about the mouth in the oral form of herpes simplex
cold sweat *n* : concurrent perspiration and chill usually associated with fear, pain, or shock
[1]**cold turkey** *n* : abrupt complete cessation of the use of an addictive drug
[2]**cold turkey** *adv* **1 :** without a period of adjustment **2 :** without preparation
cold war *n* : a conflict characterized by the use of means short of sustained overt military action
cole•slaw \ˈkōl-ˌslȯ\ *n* : a salad made of raw cabbage
col•ic \ˈkä-lik\ *n* **1 :** sharp sudden abdominal pain **2 :** a condition marked by recurrent episodes of crying and irritability in an otherwise healthy infant — **col•icky** \ˈkä-li-kē\ *adj*
col•i•se•um \ˌkä-lə-ˈsē-əm\ *n* ♦ **:** a large structure especially for athletic contests

♦ bowl, circus, stadium

co•li•tis \kō-ˈlī-təs\ *n* : inflammation of the colon
col•lab•o•rate \kə-ˈla-bə-ˌrāt\ *vb* **-rat•ed; -rat•ing 1** ♦ **:** to work jointly with others (as in writing a book) **2 :** to cooperate with an enemy force occupying one's country — **col•lab•o•ra•tive** \-ˈla-bə-ˌrā-tiv, -b(ə-)rə-\ *adj* — **col•lab•o•ra•tor** \-ˈla-bə-ˌrā-tər\ *n*

♦ concert, cooperate, join, team

col•lab•o•ra•tion \-ˌla-bə-ˈrā-shən\ *n* ♦ **:** the act of collaborating or a situation marked by collaborating

♦ affiliation, alliance, association, confederation, connection, cooperation, hookup, liaison, partnership, relation, relationship, union ♦ cooperation, coordination, teamwork

col•lage \kə-ˈläzh\ *n* **:** an artistic composition of fragments (as of printed matter) pasted on a surface
col•la•gen \ˈkä-lə-jən\ *n* **:** any of a group of fibrous proteins widely found in vertebrate connective tissue
[1]**col•lapse** \kə-ˈlaps\ *vb* **col•lapsed; col•laps•ing 1** ♦ **:** to fall or shrink together abruptly **2 :** to break down completely **:** DISINTEGRATE; *also* **:** to fall in **:** give way **3 a :** to break down physically or mentally; *esp* **:** to fall helpless or unconscious **b :** to suddenly lose force, significance, effectiveness, or worth **4 :** to fold down compactly — **col•laps•ible** *adj*

♦ cave in, crumple, give, go, yield

[2]**collapse** *n* ♦ **:** sudden failure **:** a failure to function

♦ burnout, exhaustion, fatigue, lassitude, prostration, tiredness, weariness ♦ crash, cropper, defeat, failure, fizzle, nonsuccess

[1]**col•lar** \ˈkä-lər\ *n* **1 :** a band, strip, or chain worn around the neck or the neckline of a garment **2 :** something resembling a collar — **col•lar•less** *adj*
[2]**collar** *vb* **1 :** to seize by the collar **2** ♦ **:** to take or seize by or as if by a sudden motion or grasp **:** GRAB **3** ♦ **:** to take or get control of

♦ [2, 3] bag, capture, catch, corral, get, grab, grapple, hook, land, nab, seize, snare, trap

col•lar•bone \-ˌbōn\ *n* **:** the bone of the shoulder that joins the breastbone and the shoulder blade
col•lard \ˈkä-lərd\ *n* **:** a stalked smooth-leaved kale — usually used in plural
col•late \kə-ˈlāt; ˈkä-ˌlāt, ˈkō-\ *vb* **col•lat•ed; col•lat•ing 1 :** to compare (as two texts) carefully and critically **2 :** to assemble in proper order
[1]**col•lat•er•al** \kə-ˈla-tə-rəl\ *adj* **1 :** associated but of secondary importance **2 :** descended from the same ancestors but not in the same line **3 :** PARALLEL **4 :** of, relating to, or being collateral used as security; *also* **:** secured by collateral
[2]**collateral** *n* **:** property (as stocks) used as security for the repayment of a loan
col•la•tion \kä-ˈlā-shən, kō-\ *n* **1 :** a light meal **2 :** the act, process, or result of collating
col•league \ˈkä-ˌlēg\ *n* **:** an associate especially in a profession
[1]**col•lect** \ˈkä-likt, -ˌlekt\ *n* **:** a short prayer comprising an invocation, petition, and conclusion
[2]**col•lect** \kə-ˈlekt\ *vb* **1 a** ♦ **:** to bring or come together into one body or place **:** GATHER **b :** to gather or exact from a number of persons or sources **2** ♦ **:** to gain control of ⟨~ his thoughts⟩ **3 :** to receive payment of **4** ♦ **:** to form a layer, heap, or mass — **col•lect•ible** *or* **col•lect•able** *adj or n* — **col•lec•tor** \-ˈlek-tər\ *n*

♦ [1a] accumulate, amass, assemble, concentrate, garner, gather, group, lump, pick up, round up, scrape ♦ [2] calm, compose, control, settle ♦ [4] accumulate, conglomerate, gather, heap, pile up

[3]**col•lect** \kə-ˈlekt\ *adv or adj* **:** to be paid for by the receiver
col•lect•ed \kə-ˈlek-təd\ *adj* ♦ **:** possessed of calmness and composure often through concentrated effort **:** SELF-POSSESSED, CALM

♦ calm, composed, cool, placid, self-possessed, serene, tranquil, undisturbed, unperturbed, unshaken, untroubled, unworried

col•lec•tion \kə-ˈlek-shən\ *n* **1 :** the act or process of collecting ⟨garbage ~⟩ **2** ♦ **:** something collected ⟨a stamp ~⟩ **3** ♦ **:** a number of individuals or objects brought together as a unit **:** GROUP

♦ [2, 3] accumulation, assemblage, gathering ♦ [3] array, assemblage, bank, batch, block, bunch, clump, cluster, group, huddle, knot, lot, package, parcel, set, suite

[1]**col•lec•tive** \kə-ˈlek-tiv\ *adj* **1 :** of, relating to, or denoting a group of individuals considered as a whole **2** ♦ **:** involving all members of a group as distinct from its individuals **3** ♦ **:** shared or assumed by all members of the group

♦ [2, 3] common, communal, concerted, conjoint, joint, mutual, public, united *Ant* individual, single, sole

[2]**collective** *n* **1 :** GROUP **2 :** a cooperative unit or organization
collective bargaining *n* **:** negotiation between an employer and a labor union
col•lec•tive•ly \kə-ˈlek-tiv-lē\ *adv* ♦ **:** in a collective sense or manner

♦ all around, altogether, overall, together

col•lec•tiv•ise *chiefly Brit var of* COLLECTIVIZE
col•lec•tiv•ism \kə-ˈlek-ti-ˌvi-zəm\ *n* **:** a political or economic theory advocating collective control especially over production and distribution
col•lec•tiv•ize \-ˌvīz\ *vb* **-ized; -iz•ing :** to organize under collective control — **col•lec•tiv•i•za•tion** \-ˌlek-ti-və-ˈzā-shən\ *n*
col•leen \kä-ˈlēn, ˈkä-ˌlēn\ *n* : an Irish girl
col•lege \ˈkä-lij\ *n* **1 :** a building used for an educational or religious purpose **2 :** an institution of higher learning or division of a university granting a bachelor's degree; *also* **:** an institution offering instruction especially in a vocational or technical field ⟨barber ~⟩ **3** ♦ **:** an organized body of persons having common interests or duties ⟨~ of cardinals⟩ — **col•le•giate** \kə-ˈlē-jət\ *adj*

♦ association, brotherhood, club, congress, council, fellowship, fraternity, guild, institute, institution, league, order, organization, society

col•le•gi•al•i•ty \kə-ˌlē-jē-ˈa-lə-tē\ *n* **:** the relationship of colleagues
col•le•gian \kə-ˈlē-jən\ *n* **:** a college student or recent college graduate
col•le•gi•um \kə-ˈle-gē-əm, -ˈlā-\ *n, pl* **-gia** \-gē-ə\ *or* **-giums :** a group in which each member has approximately equal power
col•lide \kə-ˈlīd\ *vb* **col•lid•ed; col•lid•ing 1** ♦ **:** to come together with solid impact **2** ♦ **:** to come into conflict **:** CLASH

♦ [1] bang, bash, bump, crash, hit, impact, knock, ram, slam, smash, strike, swipe, thud ♦ [2] clash, conflict, jar

col•lid•er \kə-ˈlī-dər\ *n* **:** a particle accelerator in which two beams of particles are made to collide
col•lie \ˈkä-lē\ *n* **:** any of a breed of large dogs developed in Scotland for herding sheep that occur in rough-coated and smooth-coated varieties
col•lier \ˈkäl-yər\ *n* **1 :** a coal miner **2 :** a ship for carrying coal
col•liery \ˈkäl-yə-rē\ *n, pl* **-lier•ies :** a coal mine and its associated buildings
col•li•mate \ˈkä-lə-ˌmāt\ *vb* **-mat•ed; -mat•ing :** to make (as light rays) parallel
col•li•sion \kə-ˈli-zhən\ *n* ♦ **:** an act or instance of colliding

♦ bump, concussion, crash, impact, jar, jolt, shock, smash, strike, wallop ♦ crack-up, crash, smash, wreck

col•lo•ca•tion \ˌkä-lə-ˈkā-shən\ *n* **:** the act or result of placing or arranging together; *esp* **:** a noticeable arrangement or conjoining of linguistic elements (as words)
col•loid \ˈkä-ˌlȯid\ *n* **:** a substance in the form of submicroscopic particles that when in solution or suspension do not settle out; *also* **:** such a substance together with the medium in which it is dispersed — **col•loi•dal** \kə-ˈlȯid-ᵊl\ *adj*
colloq *abbr* colloquial
col•lo•qui•al \kə-ˈlō-kwē-əl\ *adj* ♦ **:** of, relating to, or characteristic of conversation and especially of familiar and informal conversation

♦ conversational, informal, nonliterary, vernacular, vulgar *Ant* bookish, formal, learned, literary

col·lo·qui·al·ism \-ˈlō-kwē-ə-ˌli-zəm\ *n* **:** a colloquial expression
col·lo·qui·um \kə-ˈlō-kwē-əm\ *n, pl* **-qui·ums** *or* **-quia** \-ə\ **:** CONFERENCE, SEMINAR
col·lo·quy \ˈkä-lə-kwē\ *n, pl* **-quies** ♦ **:** a usually formal conversation or conference

♦ forum, panel, parley, powwow, seminar, symposium ♦ argument, conference, deliberation, discourse, discussion, give-and-take, parley, talk

col·lu·sion \kə-ˈlü-zhən\ *n* ♦ **:** secret agreement or cooperation for an illegal or deceitful purpose — **col·lu·sive** \-siv\ *adj*

♦ connivance, conspiracy

Colo *abbr* Colorado
co·logne \kə-ˈlōn\ *n* **:** a perfumed liquid — **co·logned** \-ˈlōnd\ *adj*
Co·lom·bi·an \kə-ˈləm-bē-ən\ *n* **:** a native or inhabitant of Colombia — **Colombian** *adj*
¹co·lon \ˈkō-lən\ *n, pl* **colons** *or* **co·la** \-lə\ **:** the part of the large intestine extending from the cecum to the rectum — **co·lon·ic** \kō-ˈlä-nik\ *adj*
²colon *n, pl* **colons :** a punctuation mark : used especially to direct attention to following matter (as a list)
col·o·nel \ˈkərn-ᵊl\ *n* **:** a commissioned officer (as in the army) ranking next below a brigadier general
¹co·lo·nial \kə-ˈlō-nē-əl\ *adj* **1 :** of, relating to, or characteristic of a colony; *also* **:** possessing or composed of colonies **2** *often cap* **:** of or relating to the original 13 colonies forming the U.S.
²colonial *n* **:** a member or inhabitant of a colony
co·lo·nial·ism \-ə-ˌli-zəm\ *n* **:** control by one power over a dependent area or people; *also* **:** a policy advocating or based on such control — **co·lo·nial·ist** \-list\ *n or adj*
col·o·nise *Brit var of* COLONIZE
col·o·nist \ˈkä-lə-nist\ *n* **1** ♦ **:** a member or inhabitant of a colony **:** COLONIAL **2** ♦ **:** one that colonizes or settles in a new country

♦ [1, 2] frontiersman, homesteader, pioneer, settler

col·o·nize \ˈkä-lə-ˌnīz\ *vb* **-nized; -niz·ing 1 :** to establish a colony in or on **2 :** SETTLE — **col·o·ni·za·tion** \ˌkä-lə-nə-ˈzā-shən\ *n*
col·o·niz·er *n* **:** one that colonizes or settles in a new country
col·on·nade \ˌkä-lə-ˈnād\ *n* **:** an evenly spaced row of columns usually supporting the base of a roof structure
co·lo·nos·co·py \ˌkō-lə-ˈnäs-kə-pē\ *n, pl* **-pies :** endoscopic examination of the colon — **co·lon·o·scope** \kō-ˈlä-nə-ˌskōp\ *n*
col·o·ny \ˈkä-lə-nē\ *n, pl* **-nies 1 :** a body of people living in a new territory; *also* **:** the territory inhabited by these people **2 :** a localized population of organisms ⟨a ~ of bees⟩ **3 :** a group with common interests situated in close association ⟨a writers' ~⟩; *also* **:** the area occupied by such a group
col·o·phon \ˈkä-lə-fən, -ˌfän\ *n* **1 :** an inscription placed at the end of a book with facts relative to its production **2 :** a distinctive symbol used by a printer or publisher
¹col·or *or Can and Brit* **col·our** \ˈkə-lər\ *n* **1** ♦ **:** a phenomenon of light (as red or blue) or visual perception that enables one to differentiate otherwise identical objects; *also* **:** a hue as contrasted with black, white, or gray **2 :** APPEARANCE **3 :** complexion tint **4** *pl* ♦ **:** an identifying badge, pennant, or flag; *also* **:** military service ⟨a call to the ~*s*⟩ **5 :** VIVIDNESS, INTEREST **6** ♦ **:** something used to give color

♦ [1] cast, hue, shade, tinge, tint, tone ♦ *usu* **colors** [4] banner, ensign, flag, jack, pennant, standard, streamer ♦ [6] dye, pigment, stain

²color *or Can and Brit* **colour** *vb* **1 a** ♦ **:** to give color to **b** ♦ **:** to change the color of (as by dyeing, staining, or painting) **2** ♦ **:** to become red in the face **:** BLUSH **3** ♦ **:** to give a false or misleading representation of the facts

♦ [1a, 1b] dye, paint, stain, tinge, tint ♦ [2] bloom, blush, crimson, flush, glow, redden ♦ [3] distort, falsify, garble, misinterpret, misrepresent, misstate, pervert, twist, warp ♦ [3] elaborate, embroider, exaggerate, magnify, pad, stretch

Col·o·ra·do potato beetle \ˌkä-lə-ˈra-dō-, -ˈrä-\ *n* **:** a black-and-yellow striped beetle that feeds on the leaves of the potato
col·or·ation \ˌkə-lə-ˈrā-shən\ *n* **:** use or arrangement of colors
col·or·a·tu·ra \ˌkə-lə-rə-ˈtür-ə, -ˈtyür-\ *n* **1 :** elaborate ornamentation in vocal music **2 :** a soprano specializing in coloratura
col·or–blind *or Can and Brit* **col·our–blind** \ˈkə-lər-ˌblīnd\ *adj* **1 :** partially or totally unable to distinguish one or more chromatic colors **2 :** not influenced by differences of race — **col·or blind·ness** *n*
col·ored *or Can and Brit* **col·oured** \ˈkə-lərd\ *adj* **1 :** having color **2 :** SLANTED, BIASED
col·or·fast *or Can and Brit* **col·our·fast** \ˈkə-lər-ˌfast\ *adj* **:** having color that does not fade or run — **col·or·fast·ness** *n*
col·or·ful *or Can and Brit* **col·our·ful** *adj* ♦ **:** having striking colors

♦ multicolored (*or* multicoloured), variegated *Ant* colorless; monochromatic

col·or·ize *or Can* **col·our·ize** *or Brit* **-ise** \ˈkə-lə-ˌrīz\ *vb* **-ized; -iz·ing :** to add color to by means of a computer — **col·or·i·za·tion** \ˌkə-lə-rə-ˈzā-shən\ *n*
col·or·less *or Can and Brit* **col·our·less** *adj* ♦ **:** lacking color

♦ uncolored (*or* uncoloured, unpainted, white *Ant* colored, dyed, painted, stained, tinged, tinted

co·los·sal \kə-ˈlä-səl\ *adj* ♦ **:** of very great size or degree

♦ astronomical, enormous, giant, gigantic, ginormous, grand, huge, mammoth, massive, monumental, tremendous

Co·los·sians \kə-ˈlä-shənz\ *n* **:** a book of the New Testament of Christian Scripture
co·los·sus \kə-ˈlä-səs\ *n, pl* **co·los·si** \-ˌsī\ **1 :** a gigantic statue **2** ♦ **:** something of great size or scope

♦ behemoth, blockbuster, giant, jumbo, leviathan, mammoth, monster, titan, whale, whopper

col·our *Can and Brit var of* COLOR
col·por·teur \ˈkäl-ˌpōr-tər\ *n* **:** a peddler of religious books
colt \ˈkōlt\ *n* **1 :** FOAL; *also* **:** a young male horse, ass, or zebra **2 :** a young untried person
colt·ish *adj* ♦ **:** full of play **:** inclined to friskiness or liveliness

♦ antic, elfish, fay, frisky, frolicsome, playful, sportive

col·um·bine \ˈkä-ləm-ˌbīn\ *n* **:** any of a genus of plants with showy spurred flowers that are related to the buttercups
co·lum·bi·um \kə-ˈləm-bē-əm\ *n* **:** NIOBIUM
Columbus Day \kə-ˈləm-bəs-\ *n* **:** the 2d Monday in October or formerly October 12 observed as a legal holiday in many states in commemoration of the landing of Columbus
col·umn \ˈkä-ləm\ *n* **1 :** one of two or more vertical sections of a printed page; *also* **:** one in a usually regular series of articles (as in a newspaper) **2** ♦ **:** a supporting pillar; *esp* **:** one consisting of a usually round shaft, a capital, and a base **3 :** something resembling a column ⟨a ~ of water⟩ **4** ♦ **:** a long row (as of soldiers) — **co·lum·nar** \kə-ˈləm-nər\ *adj*

♦ [2] pier, pillar, post, stanchion ♦ [4] cue, file, line, queue, range, string, train

col·um·nist \ˈkä-ləm-nist\ *n* **:** a person who writes a newspaper or magazine column
com *abbr* **1** comedy; comic **2** comma **3** commercial organization
co·ma \ˈkō-mə\ *n* **:** a state of deep unconsciousness caused by disease, injury, or poison — **co·ma·tose** \ˈkō-mə-ˌtōs, ˈkä-\ *adj*
Co·man·che \kə-ˈman-chē\ *n, pl* **Comanche** *or* **Comanches :** a member of an American Indian people ranging from Wyoming and Nebraska south into New Mexico and Texas
¹comb \ˈkōm\ *n* **1 :** a toothed instrument for arranging the hair or for separating and cleaning textile fibers **2 :** a fleshy crest on the head of a fowl **3 :** HONEYCOMB — **combed** \ˈkōmd\ *adj*
²comb *vb* **1 :** to draw a comb through for the purpose of arranging or cleaning **2 :** to pass across with a scraping or raking action **3 :** to eliminate (as with a comb) by a thorough going-over **4 :** to search or examine systematically
³comb *abbr* combination; combining
¹com·bat \ˈkäm-ˌbat\ *n* ♦ **:** a fight or contest between individuals or groups

♦ battle, conflict, confrontation, contest, duel, face-off, rivalry, struggle, tug-of-war, warfare ♦ battle, clash, conflict, contest, fight, fracas, fray, hassle, scrap, scrimmage, scuffle, skirmish, struggle, tussle

²combat \kəm-ˈbat, ˈkäm-ˌbat\ *vb* **-bat·ed** *or* **-bat·ted; -bat·ing** *or* **-bat·ting 1** ♦ **:** to fight with **:** FIGHT, CONTEND **2** ♦ **:** to struggle against **:** OPPOSE **3 :** to engage in battle during war — **com·bat·ant** \kəm-ˈbat-ᵊnt, ˈkäm-bə-tənt\ *n*

♦ battle, contend, counter, fight, oppose

combat fatigue *n* **:** a traumatic psychological reaction occurring under wartime conditions (as combat) that cause intense stress

com•bat•ive \kəm-ˈba-tiv\ *adj* ♦ **:** marked by eagerness to fight or contend

♦ aggressive, argumentative, bellicose, belligerent, contentious, discordant, disputatious, militant, pugnacious, quarrelsome, scrappy, truculent, warlike

comb•er \ˈkō-mər\ *n* **1 :** one that combs **2 :** a long curling wave of the sea
com•bi•na•tion \ˌkäm-bə-ˈnā-shən\ *n* **1 a** ♦ **:** a result or product of combining **b** ♦ **:** an alliance of individuals, corporations, or states united to achieve a social, political, or economic end **c** ♦ **:** two or more persons working as a team **2 :** a sequence of letters or numbers chosen in setting a lock **3 a** ♦ **:** the act or process of combining **b :** the quality or state of being combined

♦ [1a] admixture, amalgam, blend, composite, compound, fusion, intermixture, mix, mixture ♦ [1b] alliance, bloc, coalition, combine, confederacy, confederation, federation, league, union ♦ [1b, 1c] bloc, body, coalition, combine, faction, party, sect, set, side, wing ♦ [3a] connection, consolidation, coupling, junction, unification, union

1**com•bine** \kəm-ˈbīn\ *vb* **com•bined; com•bin•ing 1** ♦ **:** to become one **:** UNITE **2** ♦ **:** to cause (as two or more things or ideas) to mix together

♦ [1] associate, coalesce, conjoin, connect, couple, fuse, join, link, marry, unify, unite ♦ [2] amalgamate, blend, commingle, fuse, incorporate, integrate, intermingle, merge, mingle, mix

2**com•bine** \ˈkäm-ˌbīn\ *n* **1** ♦ **:** a combination especially of business or political interests **2 :** a machine that harvests and threshes grain while moving over a field

♦ alliance, bloc, coalition, combination, confederacy, confederation, federation, league, union ♦ cartel, combination, syndicate, trust ♦ bloc, body, coalition, combination, faction, party, sect, set, side, wing

comb•ings \ˈkō-miŋz\ *n pl* **:** loose hairs or fibers removed by a comb
combining form *n* **:** a linguistic form that occurs only in compounds or derivatives
com•bo \ˈkäm-bō\ *n, pl* **combos :** a small jazz or dance band
com•bus•ti•ble \kəm-ˈbəs-tə-bəl\ *adj* ♦ **:** capable of being burned — **com•bus•ti•bil•i•ty** \-ˌbəs-tə-ˈbi-lə-tē\ *n* — **combustible** *n*

♦ flammable, ignitable, inflammable ***Ant*** fireproof, incombustible, noncombustible, nonflammable, noninflammable

com•bus•tion \kəm-ˈbəs-chən\ *n* **1 :** an act or instance of burning **2 :** slow oxidation (as in the animal body)
comdg *abbr* commanding
comdr *abbr* commander
comdt *abbr* commandant
come \ˈkəm\ *vb* **came** \ˈkām\; **come; com•ing** \ˈkə-miŋ\ **1** ♦ **:** to move toward something **:** APPROACH **2** ♦ **:** to arrive at a particular place, end, result, or conclusion **:** ARRIVE **3 :** to reach the point of being or becoming ⟨∼ to a boil⟩ **4 a** ♦ **:** to reach a total **:** add up **:** AMOUNT ⟨the bill *came* to $10⟩ **b** ♦ **:** to be equal or nearly equal in or at the end **5** ♦ **:** to come to pass **:** take place **6 :** ORIGINATE, ARISE **7 :** to be available **8 :** REACH, EXTEND — **come across 1 :** to make a specified impression ⟨*came across* as rude⟩ **2 :** to find especially by chance ⟨*came across* an intriguing story⟩ — **come clean :** CONFESS — **come into :** ACQUIRE, ACHIEVE — **come of age :** MATURE — **come to grips with :** to meet or deal with frankly — **come to pass :** HAPPEN — **come to terms :** to reach an agreement

♦ [1] advance, approach, near ***Ant*** go, retreat, withdraw ♦ [2] arrive, land, show up, turn up ***Ant*** go ♦ *usu* **come to** [4a, 4b] add up, amount, equal, number, sum, total ♦ [5] be, befall, betide, chance, go, happen, occur, pass, transpire

come around *vb* **1 :** to come round **2** ♦ **:** to recover consciousness

♦ come round, come to, revive

come•back \ˈkəm-ˌbak\ *n* **1** ♦ **:** a sharp or witty reply **:** RETORT **2** ♦ **:** a return to a former position or condition — **come back** *vb*

♦ [1] repartee, retort, riposte ♦ [1] answer, reply, response, retort, return ♦ [2] convalescence, rally, recovery, recuperation, rehabilitation

come by *vb* ♦ **:** to make a brief visit

♦ call, drop (by *or* in), pop (in), stop (by *or* in), visit

co•me•di•an \kə-ˈmē-dē-ən\ *n* **1 :** an actor in comedy **2** ♦ **:** a comic person; *esp* **:** an entertainer specializing in comedy

♦ card, comic, humorist, jester, joker, wag, wit

co•me•di•enne \-ˌmē-dē-ˈen\ *n* **:** a woman who is a comedian
come•down \ˈkəm-ˌdau̇n\ *n* ♦ **:** a descent in rank or dignity

♦ decline, descent, down, downfall, fall ***Ant*** aggrandizement, ascent, exaltation, rise, up

come down *vb* **1 :** to lose or fall in estate or condition **2 a :** to pass by tradition **b :** to pass from a usually high source **3 :** to reduce itself **:** AMOUNT ⟨it *comes down* to this⟩ **4** ♦ **:** to become ill ⟨*come down* with measles⟩

♦ catch, contract, get, sicken, take

com•e•dy \ˈkä-mə-dē\ *n, pl* **-dies 1 :** a light amusing play with a happy ending **2 :** a literary work treating a comic theme or written in a comic style **3** ♦ **:** humorous entertainment — **co•me•dic** \kə-ˈmē-dik\ *adj*

♦ farce, humor (*or* humour), slapstick

come•li•ness *n* ♦ **:** the condition of being comely especially with respect to grace or beauty of external form

♦ attractiveness, beauty, handsomeness, looks, loveliness, prettiness

come•ly \ˈkəm-lē\ *adj* **come•li•er; -est :** having a pleasing appearance **:** ATTRACTIVE, HANDSOME
come off *vb* **:** SUCCEED
come–on \ˈkə-ˌmȯn, -ˌmän\ *n* **:** INDUCEMENT, LURE
come out *vb* **1 a** ♦ **:** to come into view **b** ♦ **:** to become public **2 :** to declare oneself **3** ♦ **:** to turn out in an outcome **:** end up **:** TURN OUT 5 ⟨everything *came out* all right⟩ — **come out with :** SAY 1

♦ [1a] appear, materialize, show up, turn up ♦ [1b] get out, leak out, out, spread ♦ [3] pan out, prove, turn out

com•er \ˈkə-mər\ *n* **1 :** one that comes ⟨all ∼*s*⟩ **2 :** a promising beginner
come round *vb* **1 :** to change direction **2** ♦ **:** to recover consciousness **3** ♦ **:** to accede to a particular opinion or course of action

♦ [2] come around, come to, revive ♦ [3] accede, acquiesce, agree, assent, consent, subscribe (to)

1**co•mes•ti•ble** \kə-ˈmes-tə-bəl\ *adj* **:** EDIBLE
2**comestible** *n* **:** FOOD — usually used in plural
com•et \ˈkä-mət\ *n* **:** a small bright celestial body that develops a long tail when near the sun
come to *vb* ♦ **:** to regain consciousness

♦ come around, come round, revive

come•up•pance \kə-ˈmə-pəns\ *n* **:** a deserved rebuke or penalty
com•fit \ˈkəm-fət\ *n* **:** a candied fruit or nut
1**com•fort** \ˈkəm-fərt\ *vb* **1** ♦ **:** to give strength and hope to **2** ♦ **:** to ease the grief or trouble of **:** CONSOLE

♦ [1] buoy (up), cheer, embolden, encourage, hearten, inspire, steel ♦ [2] assure, cheer, console, reassure, solace, soothe ***Ant*** distress, torment, torture, trouble

2**comfort** *n* **1 :** the act or an instance of consoling **:** the state of being consoled **2** ♦ **:** freedom from pain, trouble, or anxiety **3** ♦ **:** something that consoles **:** something that gives freedom or ease **4** ♦ **:** one that gives or brings comfort ⟨all the ∼*s* of home⟩

♦ [2] alleviation, ease, relief ♦ [2] cheer, consolation, relief, solace ♦ [3, 4] amenity, convenience, luxury ***Ant*** burden, millstone, weight

com•fort•able \ˈkəm-fər-tə-bəl, ˈkəmf-tər-\ *adj* **1** ♦ **:** providing comfort or security **2** ♦ **:** feeling at ease **3** ♦ **:** affording an ease with money and a secure way of living without great wealth — **com•fort•ably** \-blē\ *adv*

♦ [1] easy, snug, soft ***Ant*** uncomfortable ♦ [2] content, contented, peaceful, pleased, relaxed, untroubled ***Ant*** uncomfortable ♦ [3] abundant, ample, bountiful, generous, liberal, plentiful

com•fort•er \ˈkəm-fər-tər\ *n* **1 :** one that comforts **2 :** QUILT
comforting *adj* ♦ **:** providing or intended to provide comfort

♦ encouraging, gratifying, heartening, heartwarming, rewarding, satisfying ♦ dreamy, narcotic, sedative, soothing

com•fy \ˈkəm-fē\ *adj* **:** COMFORTABLE
1**com•ic** \ˈkä-mik\ *adj* **1 :** relating to comedy or comic strips **2 :** provoking laughter or amusement

2**comic** *n* **1** ♦ **:** a comical individual especially a professional entertainer who uses any of various physical or verbal means to be amusing **:** COMEDIAN **2** *pl* **:** the part of a newspaper devoted to comic strips

♦ card, comedian, humorist, jester, joker, wag, wit

com•i•cal *adj* ♦ **:** causing laughter

♦ antic, comic, droll, farcical, funny, hilarious, humorous, hysterical, laughable, ludicrous, ridiculous, riotous, risible, screaming, uproarious ♦ absurd, derisive, farcical, laughable, ludicrous, preposterous, ridiculous, risible, silly

comic book *n* **:** a magazine containing sequences of comic strips
comic strip *n* ♦ **:** a group of cartoons in narrative sequence

♦ cartoon

coming \ˈkə-miŋ\ *adj* **1** ♦ **:** immediately due in sequence or development **:** APPROACHING, NEXT **2 :** gaining importance

♦ forthcoming, imminent, impending, oncoming, pending ♦ following, next, succeeding

co•mi•ty \ˈkä-mə-tē, ˈkō-\ *n, pl* **-ties :** friendly civility **:** COURTESY
coml *abbr* commercial
comm *abbr* **1** command; commander **2** commerce; commercial **3** commission; commissioner **4** committee **5** common **6** commonwealth
com•ma \ˈkä-mə\ *n* **:** a punctuation mark, used especially as a mark of separation within the sentence
1**com•mand** \kə-ˈmand\ *vb* **1** ♦ **:** to direct authoritatively **:** ORDER **2** ♦ **:** to exercise a dominating influence over **:** have command of **3 :** to overlook from a strategic position **4** ♦ **:** to demand or receive as one's due ⟨~*s* a high fee⟩

♦ [1] bid, boss, charge, direct, enjoin, instruct, order, tell *Ant* mind, obey ♦ [2] boss, captain, control, govern, preside, rule ♦ [2] dominate, head, lead, spearhead ♦ [4] ask, charge, demand

2**command** *n* **1** ♦ **:** an order given **2 a** ♦ **:** ability to control **:** MASTERY **b :** facility in use ⟨a good ~ of French⟩ **3 :** the act of commanding **4 :** a signal that actuates a device (as a computer); *also* **:** the activation of a device by means of a signal **5 a :** a body of troops under a commander **b :** an area or position that one commands **6 :** a position of highest authority

♦ [1] behest, charge, commandment, decree, dictate, direction, directive, edict, instruction, order, word ♦ [2a] arm, authority, clutch, control, dominion, grip, hold, mastery, power, sway

com•man•dant \ˈkä-mən-ˌdant, -ˌdänt\ *n* **:** an officer in command
com•man•deer \ˌkä-mən-ˈdir\ *vb* ♦ **:** to take possession of by force

♦ appropriate, arrogate, preempt, usurp

com•mand•er \kə-ˈman-dər\ *n* **1 a** ♦ **:** one in an official position of command or control **b** ♦ **:** an officer commanding an army or subdivision of an army **2 :** a commissioned officer in the navy ranking next below a captain

♦ [1a, 1b] captain

com•mand•ment \kə-ˈmand-mənt\ *n* ♦ **:** something that is commanded **:** COMMAND, ORDER; *esp* **:** any of the Ten Commandments

♦ behest, charge, command, decree, dictate, direction, directive, edict, instruction, order, word

command module *n* **:** a space vehicle module designed to carry the crew and reentry equipment
com•man•do \kə-ˈman-dō\ *n, pl* **-dos** *or* **-does :** a member of a military unit trained for surprise raids
command sergeant major *n* **:** a noncommissioned officer in the army ranking above a sergeant major
com•mem•o•rate \kə-ˈme-mə-ˌrāt\ *vb* **-rat•ed; -rat•ing 1 :** to call or recall to mind **2 :** to serve as a memorial of **3** ♦ **:** to mark by some ceremony or observation **:** OBSERVE — **com•mem•o•ra•tion** \-ˌme-mə-ˈrā-shən\ *n*

♦ celebrate, keep, observe

com•mem•o•ra•tive \kə-ˈmem-rə-tiv, -ˈme-mə-ˌrā-tiv\ *adj* **:** intended to commemorate an event
com•mence \kə-ˈmens\ *vb* **com•menced; com•menc•ing** ♦ **:** to have or make a beginning **:** BEGIN, START

♦ arise, begin, dawn, form, materialize, originate, spring, start ♦ begin, embark (on *or* upon), enter, get off, launch, open, start, strike

com•mence•ment \-mənt\ *n* **1** ♦ **:** the act or time of a beginning **2 :** the graduation exercises of a school or college

♦ beginning, birth, dawn, genesis, launch, morning, onset, outset, start, threshold

com•mend \kə-ˈmend\ *vb* **1** ♦ **:** to entrust for care or preservation **2 :** RECOMMEND **3 :** PRAISE — **com•mend•ably** \-blē\ *adv* — **com•men•da•tion** \ˌkä-mən-ˈdā-shən, -ˌmen-\ *n* — **com•mend•er** *n*

♦ commit, consign, delegate, deliver, entrust, give, hand over, leave, pass, transfer, transmit, trust, turn over, vest

com•mend•able \-ˈmen-də-bəl\ *adj* ♦ **:** worthy of being commended

♦ admirable, creditable, laudable, meritorious, praiseworthy

com•men•da•tion \ˌkä-mən-ˈdā-shən, -ˌmen-\ *n* ♦ **:** the act of commending **:** the expression of approval

♦ accolade, citation, encomium, eulogy, homage, paean, panegyric, salutation, tribute

com•men•su•ra•ble \kə-ˈmen-sə-rə-bəl\ *adj* **:** having a common measure or a common divisor
com•men•su•rate \kə-ˈmen-sə-rət, -ˈmen-chə-\ *adj* **:** equal in measure or extent; *also* **:** PROPORTIONAL, CORRESPONDING ⟨a job ~ with her abilities⟩
com•ment \ˈkä-ˌment\ *n* **1** ♦ **:** an expression of opinion **2** ♦ **:** an explanatory, illustrative, or critical note or observation **:** REMARK

♦ note, observation, reflection, remark

comment *vb* ♦ **:** to explain or interpret something by comment **:** OBSERVE

♦ note, observe, opine, remark

com•men•tary \ˈkä-mən-ˌter-ē\ *n, pl* **-tar•ies** ♦ **:** a systematic series of comments

♦ analysis, comment, exposition

com•men•ta•tor \-ˌtā-tər\ *n* **:** one who comments; *esp* **:** a person who discusses news events on radio or television
com•merce \ˈkä-(ˌ)mərs\ *n* ♦ **:** the buying and selling of commodities **:** TRADE

♦ business, marketplace, trade, traffic

1**com•mer•cial** \kə-ˈmər-shəl\ *adj* **1 :** having to do with commerce **2 :** designed for profit or for mass appeal — **com•mer•cial•ly** *adv*
2**commercial** *n* **:** an advertisement broadcast on radio or television
com•mer•cial•ise *Brit var of* COMMERCIALIZE
com•mer•cial•ism \kə-ˈmər-shə-ˌli-zəm\ *n* **1 :** a spirit, method, or practice characteristic of business **2 :** excessive emphasis on profit
com•mer•cial•ize *or Brit* **com•mer•cial•ise** \-ˌlīz\ *vb* **-ized; -iz•ing 1 :** to manage on a business basis for profit **2 :** to exploit for profit
com•mi•na•tion \ˌkä-mə-ˈnā-shən\ *n* **:** DENUNCIATION — **com•mi•na•to•ry** \ˈkä-mə-nə-ˌtōr-ē\ *adj*
com•min•gle \kə-ˈmiŋ-gəl\ *vb* ♦ **:** to mingle or mix together **:** MINGLE, BLEND

♦ amalgamate, blend, combine, fuse, incorporate, integrate, intermingle, merge, mingle, mix

com•mis•er•ate \kə-ˈmi-zə-ˌrāt\ *vb* **-at•ed; -at•ing** ♦ **:** to feel or express pity **:** SYMPATHIZE

♦ bleed, feel, pity, sympathize

com•mis•er•a•tion \-ˌmi-zə-ˈrā-shən\ *n* ♦ **:** the act of commiserating **:** the feeling or showing of sorrow or the expression of condolence for the wants or distresses of another

♦ charity, compassion, feeling, heart, humanity, kindliness, kindness, mercy, pity, sympathy

com•mis•sar \ˈkä-mə-ˌsär\ *n* **:** a Communist party official
com•mis•sar•i•at \ˌkä-mə-ˈser-ē-ət\ *n* **1 :** a system for supplying troops with food **2 :** a department headed by a commissar
com•mis•sary \ˈkä-mə-ˌser-ē\ *n, pl* **-sar•ies 1 :** a store for equipment and provisions especially for military personnel **2** ♦ **:** one delegated by a superior to execute a duty or an office

♦ agent, attorney, delegate, deputy, envoy, factor, proxy, representative

1**com•mis•sion** \kə-ˈmi-shən\ *n* **1** ♦ **:** a warrant granting certain powers and imposing certain duties; *also* **:** the fact of granting these powers or duties **2 :** a certificate conferring military rank and authority **3** ♦ **:** authority to act as agent for another; *also*

: something to be done by an agent **4 :** a body of persons charged with performing a duty **5** ♦ **:** the doing of some act; *also* **:** the thing done **6 :** the allowance made to an agent for transacting business for another

♦ [1] authorization, delegation, license (*or* licence), mandate ♦ [3] appointment, assignment, designation ♦ [5] accomplishment, achievement, discharge, enactment, execution, fulfillment, implementation, performance ***Ant*** nonfulfillment, nonperformance

[2]**commission** *vb* **1** ♦ **:** to give a commission to **2 :** to order to be made **3 :** to put (a ship) into a state of readiness for service

♦ assign, charge, entrust, trust ♦ accredit, authorize, certify, delegate, empower, enable, invest, license, qualify ♦ appoint, assign, attach, constitute, designate, detail, name

commissioned officer *n* **:** an officer of the armed forces holding rank by a commission from the president

com•mis•sion•er \kə-ˈmi-shə-nər\ *n* **1 :** a member of a commission **2 :** an official in charge of a department of public service **3 :** the administrative head of a professional sport — **com•mis•sion•er•ship** *n*

com•mit \kə-ˈmit\ *vb* **com•mit•ted; com•mit•ting 1 a :** to put into charge or trust **:** ENTRUST **b** ♦ **:** to put into a place for disposal or safekeeping **2** ♦ **:** to put in a prison or mental institution **3 :** TRANSFER, CONSIGN **4** ♦ **:** to carry into action ⟨∼ a crime⟩ **5** ♦ **:** to pledge or assign to some particular course or use — **com•mit•tal** *n*

♦ [1b] commend, consign, delegate, deliver, entrust, give, hand over, leave, pass, transfer, transmit, trust, turn over, vest ♦ [2] confine, immure, imprison, jail ♦ [4] accomplish, achieve, carry out, compass, do, execute, follow through, fulfill, make, perform ♦ [5] engage, pledge, troth

com•mit•ment *n* ♦ **:** an agreement or pledge to do something in the future

♦ burden, charge, duty, need, obligation, responsibility

com•mit•tee \kə-ˈmi-tē\ *n* **:** a body of persons selected to consider and act or report on some matter — **com•mit•tee•man** \-mən\ *n* — **com•mit•tee•wom•an** \-ˌwu̇-mən\ *n*

commo *abbr* commodore

com•mode \kə-ˈmōd\ *n* **1 :** a movable washstand with cupboard below **2 :** TOILET 3

com•mo•di•ous \kə-ˈmō-dē-əs\ *adj* ♦ **:** comfortably spacious **:** ROOMY

♦ ample, capacious, roomy, spacious

com•mod•i•ty \kə-ˈmä-də-tē\ *n, pl* **-ties 1 :** a product of agriculture or mining **2** ♦ **:** an article of commerce — often used in plural **3 :** something useful or valued ⟨that valuable ∼ patience⟩

♦ *usu* **commodities** merchandise, wares

com•mo•dore \ˈkä-mə-ˌdōr\ *n* **1 :** a commissioned officer in the navy ranking next below a rear admiral **2 :** an officer commanding a group of merchant ships **3 :** the chief officer of a yacht club

[1]**com•mon** \ˈkä-mən\ *adj* **1** ♦ **:** belonging to or serving the community **:** PUBLIC **2** ♦ **:** shared by a number in a group **3** ♦ **:** widely or generally known, found, or observed **:** FAMILIAR ⟨∼ knowledge⟩ **4 :** VERNACULAR 3 ⟨∼ names of plants⟩ **5** ♦ **:** not above the average especially in social status **6** ♦ **:** lacking refinement **:** COARSE **7** ♦ **:** falling below ordinary standards

♦ [1] blanket, general, generic, global, overall, public, universal ♦ [2] collective, communal, concerted, conjoint, joint, mutual, public, united ♦ [3] commonplace, customary, everyday, familiar, frequent, normal, ordinary, regular, routine, standard, usual ***Ant*** extraordinary, infrequent, rare, uncommon, unfamiliar, unusual ♦ [5] humble, ignoble, inferior, low, lowly, mean, plebeian, vulgar ♦ [6] coarse, crass, crude, gross, ill-bred, low, rough, rude, tasteless, uncouth, uncultivated, uncultured, unpolished, unrefined, vulgar ♦ [7] fair, indifferent, mediocre, medium, middling, ordinary, passable, run-of-the-mill, second-rate, so-so

[2]**common** *n* **1** *pl* **:** the common people **2** *pl* **:** a dining hall **3** *pl, cap* **:** the lower house of the British and Canadian parliaments **4 :** a piece of land subject to common use — **in common :** shared together

com•mon•al•ty \ˈkä-mən-ᵊl-tē\ *n, pl* **-ties :** the common people

common cold *n* **:** a contagious respiratory disease caused by a virus and characterized by a sore, swollen, and inflamed nose and throat, usually by much mucus, and by coughing and sneezing

common denominator *n* **1 :** a common multiple of the denominators of a group of fractions **2 :** a common trait or theme

common divisor *n* **:** a number or expression that divides two or more numbers or expressions without remainder

com•mon•er \ˈkä-mə-nər\ *n* ♦ **:** one of the common people **:** a person having no rank of nobility

♦ *usu* **commoners** herd, masses, mob, people, plebeians, populace, rank and file

common fraction *n* **:** a fraction (as $\frac{1}{2}$ or $\frac{3}{4}$) in which the numerator and denominator are both integers and are separated by a horizontal or slanted line

common law *n* **:** a group of legal practices and traditions based on judges' decisions and social customs and usually having the same force as laws passed by legislative bodies

common logarithm *n* **:** a logarithm whose base is 10

com•mon•ly *adv* ♦ **:** as a general thing **:** often in the usual course of events

♦ generally, ordinarily, typically, usually

common market *n* **:** an economic association formed to remove trade barriers among members

common multiple *n* **:** a multiple of each of two or more numbers or expressions

[1]**com•mon•place** \ˈkä-mən-ˌplās\ *n* ♦ **:** something that is ordinary or trite

♦ banality, cliché, platitude, shibboleth

[2]**commonplace** *adj* ♦ **:** commonly found or seen **:** ORDINARY

♦ average, common, everyday, normal, ordinary, prosaic, routine, run-of-the-mill, standard, unexceptional, unremarkable, usual, workaday

common sense *n* ♦ **:** ordinary good sense and judgment — **com•mon•sen•si•cal** \ˈkä-mən-ˈsen-si-kəl\ *adj*

♦ horse sense, sense, wisdom, wit

com•mon•weal \ˈkä-mən-ˌwēl\ *n* **1** *archaic* **:** COMMONWEALTH **2 :** the general welfare

com•mon•wealth \-ˌwelth\ *n* **1** ♦ **:** the body of people politically organized into a state **2 :** a state especially conceived as a body politic founded on law and united by compact or by tacit agreement of the people for the common good; *also* **:** an association or federation of autonomous states

♦ country, land, nation, sovereignty, state

com•mo•tion \kə-ˈmō-shən\ *n* **1** ♦ **:** violent or sharp disturbance **:** noisy, unruly, or tumultuous stir **2 :** mental excitement, uncertainty, or confusion

♦ disturbance, furor, fuss, hubbub, hullabaloo, pandemonium, tumult, turmoil, uproar

com•mu•nal \kə-ˈmyün-ᵊl, ˈkäm-yən-ᵊl\ *adj* **1 :** of or relating to a commune or community **2 :** marked by collective ownership and use of property **3** ♦ **:** shared or used in common

♦ collective, common, concerted, conjoint, joint, mutual, public, united

[1]**com•mune** \kə-ˈmyün\ *vb* **com•muned; com•mun•ing :** to communicate intimately

[2]**com•mune** \ˈkäm-ˌyün; kə-ˈmyün\ *n* **1 :** the smallest administrative district in some European countries **2 :** a community organized on a communal basis

com•mu•ni•ca•ble \kə-ˈmyü-ni-kə-bəl\ *adj* ♦ **:** capable of being communicated ⟨∼ diseases⟩ — **com•mu•ni•ca•bil•i•ty** \-ˌmyü-ni-kə-ˈbi-lə-tē\ *n*

♦ catching, contagious, transmittable

com•mu•ni•cant \-ˈmyü-ni-kənt\ *n* **1 :** a church member entitled to receive Communion **2 :** one that communicates; *esp* **:** INFORMANT

com•mu•ni•cate \kə-ˈmyü-nə-ˌkāt\ *vb* **-cat•ed; -cat•ing 1 :** to make known **2** ♦ **:** to pass from one to another **:** TRANSMIT **3 :** to receive Communion **4 :** to be in communication **5 :** JOIN, CONNECT — **com•mu•ni•cat•or** \-ˌkā-tər\ *n*

♦ convey, impart, spread, transfer, transfuse, transmit

com•mu•ni•ca•tion \kə-ˌmyü-nə-ˈkā-shən\ *n* **1 :** an act of transmitting **2 :** information communicated **:** a verbal or written message **3 :** exchange of information or opinions **4 :** a means of communicating — **com•mu•ni•ca•tive** \-ˈmyü-nə-ˌkā-tiv, -ni-kə-tiv\ *adj*

com•mu•nion \kə-ˈmyü-nyən\ *n* **1 :** a sharing of something with others **2** *cap* **:** a Christian sacrament in which bread and wine are consumed as the substance or symbols of Christ's body and blood in commemoration of the death of Christ **3 :** intimate fellowship or rapport **4 :** a body of Christians having a common faith and discipline

com•mu•ni•qué \kə-ˈmyü-nə-ˌkā, -ˌmyü-nə-ˈkā\ *n* ♦ **:** a brief public report intended for immediate release on a matter of public interest **:** BULLETIN

♦ advertisement, announcement, bulletin, notice, notification, release

com•mu•nism \ˈkäm-yə-ˌni-zəm\ *n* **1 :** social organization in which goods are held in common **2 :** a theory of social organization advocating common ownership of means of production and a distribution of products of industry based on need **3** *cap* **:** a political doctrine based on revolutionary Marxist socialism that was the official ideology of the U.S.S.R. and some other countries; *also* **:** a system of government in which one party controls state-owned means of production — **com•mu•nist** \-nist\ *n or adj, often cap* — **com•mu•nis•tic** \ˌkäm-yə-ˈnis-tik\ *adj, often cap*

com•mu•ni•ty \kə-ˈmyü-nə-tē\ *n, pl* **-ties 1 :** a body of people living in the same place under the same laws; *also* **:** a natural population of plants and animals that interact ecologically and live in one place (as a pond) **2 :** society at large **3 :** joint ownership **4** ♦ **:** common character **:** SIMILARITY, LIKENESS **5 :** the people with common interests living in a particular area **6** ♦ **:** a body of persons of common and especially professional interests scattered through a larger society

♦ [4] correspondence, likeness, parallelism, resemblance, similarity, similitude ♦ [6] brotherhood, corps, fellowship, fraternity

community college *n* **:** a 2-year government-supported college that offers an associate degree

community property *n* **:** property held jointly by husband and wife

com•mu•ta•tion \ˌkäm-yə-ˈtā-shən\ *n* ♦ **:** substitution of one form of payment or penalty for another

♦ barter, exchange, swap, trade, truck

com•mu•ta•tive \ˈkäm-yə-ˌtā-tiv, kə-ˈmyü-tə-\ *adj* **:** of, having, or being the property that the result obtained using a mathematical operation on any two elements of a set does not differ with the order in which the elements are used ⟨*a* × *b* = *b* × *a* because multiplication is ~⟩ — **com•mu•ta•tiv•i•ty** \kə-ˌmyü-tə-ˈti-və-tē, ˌkäm-yə-tə-\ *n*

com•mu•ta•tor \ˈkäm-yə-ˌtā-tər\ *n* **:** a device (as on a generator or motor) for changing the direction of electric current

[1]**com•mute** \kə-ˈmyüt\ *vb* **com•mut•ed; com•mut•ing 1** ♦ **:** to give in exchange for another **:** EXCHANGE **2 :** to revoke (a sentence) and impose a milder penalty **3 :** to travel back and forth regularly — **com•mut•er** *n*

♦ change, exchange, shift, substitute, swap, switch, trade

[2]**commute** *n* **:** a trip made in commuting

comp *abbr* **1** comparative; compare **2** compensation **3** compiled; compiler **4** composition; compositor **5** compound **6** comprehensive **7** comptroller

[1]**com•pact** \kəm-ˈpakt, ˈkäm-ˌpakt\ *adj* **1** ♦ **:** having a dense structure or parts or units closely packed or joined **:** SOLID, DENSE **2** ♦ **:** not diffuse or verbose **:** BRIEF, SUCCINCT **3** ♦ **:** occupying a small volume by efficient use of space ⟨a ~ formation of troops⟩

♦ [1] dense, firm, hard, rigid, solid, stiff, unyielding ♦ [2] brief, compendious, concise, crisp, epigrammatic, laconic, pithy, succinct, summary, terse ♦ [3] close, crowded, dense, packed, serried, thick, tight

[2]**compact** *vb* **1** ♦ **:** to pack together **:** COMPRESS **2 :** to knit or draw together **:** CONSOLIDATE — **com•pac•tor** \kəm-ˈpak-tər, ˈkäm-ˌpak-\ *n*

♦ compress, condense, constrict, contract, squeeze

[3]**com•pact** \ˈkäm-ˌpakt\ *n* **1 :** a small case for cosmetics **2 :** a small automobile

[4]**com•pact** \ˈkäm-ˌpakt\ *n* ♦ **:** an agreement or covenant between two or more parties

♦ accord, agreement, bargain, contract, convention, covenant, deal, pact, settlement, understanding

com•pact disc \ˈkäm-ˌpakt-\ *n* **:** CD

com•pact•ly *adv* ♦ **:** in a compact manner

♦ concisely, crisply, laconically, shortly, succinctly, summarily, tersely

com•pact•ness *n* ♦ **:** the quality or state of being compact

♦ brevity, briefness, conciseness, crispness, succinctness, terseness

com•pa•dre \kəm-ˈpä-drā\ *n* ♦ **:** a close friend **:** BUDDY

♦ buddy, chum, comrade, crony, familiar, friend, intimate, pal

[1]**com•pan•ion** \kəm-ˈpan-yən\ *n* **1 a** ♦ **:** one that accompanies another **:** COMRADE **b** ♦ **:** an intimate friend or associate **2** ♦ **:** one that is closely connected with something similar

♦ [1a, 1b] associate, cohort, comrade, crony, fellow, mate ♦ [2] half, match, mate, twin

[2]**companion** *n* **:** COMPANIONWAY

com•pan•ion•able *adj* ♦ **:** marked by, conducive to, or suggestive of companionship

♦ amicable, comradely, cordial, friendly, genial, hearty, neighborly, warm, warmhearted ♦ boon, convivial, extroverted, gregarious, outgoing, sociable, social

com•pan•ion•ship *n* ♦ **:** the fellowship existing among companions **:** COMPANY

♦ camaraderie, company, comradeship, fellowship, society

com•pan•ion•way *n* **:** a ship's stairway from one deck to another

com•pa•ny \ˈkəm-pə-nē\ *n, pl* **-nies 1** ♦ **:** association with another or others **:** FELLOWSHIP; *also* **:** COMPANIONS **2 :** GUESTS **3** ♦ **:** a group of persons or things **4 :** an infantry unit consisting of two or more platoons and normally commanded by a captain **5 :** a group of musical or dramatic performers **6 :** the officers and crew of a ship **7** ♦ **:** an association of persons for carrying on a business

♦ [1] camaraderie, companionship, comradeship, fellowship, society ♦ [3] band, crew, gang, outfit, party, squad, team ♦ [7] business, concern, enterprise, establishment, firm, house, outfit

com•pa•ra•ble \ˈkäm-pə-rə-bəl, -prə-\ *adj* ♦ **:** capable of being compared — **com•pa•ra•bil•i•ty** \ˌkäm-pə-rə-ˈbi-lə-tē\ *n*

♦ akin, alike, analogous, correspondent, like, parallel, similar, such

[1]**com•par•a•tive** \kəm-ˈpar-ə-tiv\ *adj* **1 :** of, relating to, or constituting the degree of grammatical comparison that denotes increase in quality, quantity, or relation **2** ♦ **:** considered as if in comparison to something else as a standard not quite attained **:** RELATIVE ⟨a ~ stranger⟩ — **com•par•a•tive•ly** *adv*

♦ approximate, near, relative *Ant* absolute, complete, downright, out-and-out, outright, perfect, pure, unqualified

[2]**comparative** *n* **:** the comparative degree or form in a language

[1]**com•pare** \kəm-ˈpar\ *vb* **com•pared; com•par•ing 1** ♦ **:** to represent as similar **:** LIKEN **2 a :** to examine for likenesses and differences **b** ♦ **:** to view in relation to **3 :** to inflect or modify (an adjective or adverb) according to the degrees of comparison

♦ [1] bracket, equate, liken *Ant* contrast ♦ *usu* **compare with** [2b] approach, approximate, measure up, stack up

[2]**compare** *n* **:** the possibility of comparing ⟨beauty beyond ~⟩

com•par•i•son \kəm-ˈpar-ə-sən\ *n* **1 :** the act of comparing **2 :** change in the form of an adjective or adverb to show different levels of quality, quantity, or relation

com•part•ment \kəm-ˈpärt-mənt\ *n* **1 :** a separate division **2** ♦ **:** a section of an enclosed space

♦ bay, cabin, cell, chamber, cubicle

com•part•men•tal•ise *Brit var of* COMPARTMENTALIZE

com•part•men•tal•ize \kəm-ˌpärt-ˈment-ᵊl-ˌīz\ *vb* **-ized; -iz•ing :** to separate into compartments

[1]**com•pass** \ˈkəm-pəs, ˈkäm-\ *vb* **1 :** CONTRIVE, PLOT **2** ♦ **:** to lie around **:** ENCIRCLE **3** ♦ **:** to bring about **:** ACHIEVE

♦ [2] circle, circumnavigate, coil, encircle, girdle, loop, orbit, ring, round ♦ [3] accomplish, achieve, carry out, commit, do, execute, follow through, fulfill, make, perform

[2]**compass** *n* **1** ♦ **:** an often rounded or curved boundary limit **:** BOUNDARY, CIRCUMFERENCE **2 :** an enclosed space **3** ♦ **:** range or limit of perception, knowledge, interest, or concern **:** RANGE, SCOPE **4 :** a device for determining direction by means of a magnetic needle swinging freely and pointing to the magnetic north; *also* **:** a nonmagnetic device that indicates direction **5 :** an instrument for drawing circles or transferring measurements consisting of two legs joined by a pivot

♦ [1] border, bound, boundary, circumference, confines, edge, end, fringe, margin, perimeter, periphery, rim, skirt, verge ♦ [3] amplitude, breadth, extent, range, reach, realm, scope, sweep, width

com•pas•sion \kəm-ˈpa-shən\ *n* ♦ : sympathetic feeling : PITY, MERCY

♦ charity, commiseration, feeling, heart, humanity, kindliness, kindness, mercy, pity, sympathy

com•pas•sion•ate \-shə-nət\ *adj* ♦ : having or showing compassion — **com•pas•sion•ate•ly** *adv*

♦ beneficent, benevolent, good-hearted, humane, kind, kindly, sympathetic, tender, tenderhearted, warmhearted

com•pat•i•bil•i•ty \-ˌpa-tə-ˈbi-lə-tē\ *n* ♦ : the quality or state of being compatible

♦ concord, harmony, peace

com•pat•i•ble \kəm-ˈpa-tə-bəl\ *adj* ♦ : able to exist or act together harmoniously ⟨~ colors⟩ ⟨~ drugs⟩

♦ agreeable, amicable, congenial, harmonious, kindred, unanimous, united ♦ conformable (to), congruous, consistent, consonant, correspondent, harmonious

com•pa•tri•ot \kəm-ˈpā-trē-ət, -ˌät\ *n* : a fellow countryman
com•peer \ˈkäm-ˌpir\ *n* : EQUAL, PEER
com•pel \kəm-ˈpel\ *vb* **com•pelled; com•pel•ling** ♦ : to drive or urge with force

♦ coerce, constrain, drive, force, make, muscle, obligate, oblige, press, pressure

compelling *adj* **1** : demanding and holding one's attention ⟨a ~ novel⟩ **2** ♦ : tending to convince or convert by or as if by forcefulness of evidence

♦ cogent, conclusive, convincing, decisive, effective, forceful, persuasive, satisfying, strong, telling

com•pen•di•ous \kəm-ˈpen-dē-əs\ *adj* **1** ♦ : marked by brief expression of a comprehensive matter : concise and comprehensive **2** ♦ : covering completely or broadly : COMPREHENSIVE

♦ [1] brief, compact, concise, crisp, epigrammatic, laconic, pithy, succinct, summary, terse ♦ [2] complete, comprehensive, encyclopedic, full, global, inclusive, omnibus, panoramic, universal

com•pen•di•um \kəm-ˈpen-dē-əm\ *n, pl* **-di•ums** *or* **-dia** \-ə\ **1** : a brief summary of a larger work or of a field of knowledge **2** : COLLECTION
com•pen•sate \ˈkäm-pən-ˌsāt\ *vb* **-sat•ed; -sat•ing** **1 a** : to be equivalent to **b** ♦ : to make up for : COUNTERBALANCE **2** ♦ : to make an appropriate and usually counterbalancing payment to : PAY, REMUNERATE — **com•pen•sa•to•ry** \kəm-ˈpen-sə-ˌtōr-ē\ *adj*

♦ *usu* **compensate for** [1b] annul, cancel, correct, counteract, counterbalance, make up, neutralize, offset ♦ [2] indemnify, pay, recompense, recoup, remunerate, requite

com•pen•sa•tion \ˌkäm-pən-ˈsā-shən\ *n* **1** ♦ : the act or action of making up, making good, or counterbalancing : rendering equal **2** ♦ : something that constitutes an equivalent or recompense

♦ [1] disbursement, payment, remittance, remuneration ♦ [2] damages, indemnity, quittance, recompense, redress, remuneration, reparation, requital, restitution, satisfaction ♦ [2] consideration, pay, payment, remittance, remuneration, requital

com•pete \kəm-ˈpēt\ *vb* **com•pet•ed; com•pet•ing** ♦ : to seek or strive for something (as a position, possession, reward) for which others are also contending : CONTEND, VIE

♦ battle, contend, fight, race, vie

com•pe•tence \ˈkäm-pə-təns\ *n* **1** : adequate means for subsistence **2** ♦ : the quality or state of being functionally adequate or of having sufficient knowledge, judgment, skill, or strength : ABILITY

♦ ability, capability, capacity, faculty

com•pe•ten•cy \-tən-sē\ *n, pl* **-cies** : the quality or state of being competent
com•pe•tent \-tənt\ *adj* ♦ : having requisite or adequate ability or qualities : CAPABLE, FIT, QUALIFIED

♦ able, capable, fit, good, qualified, suitable *Ant* incompetent, inept, poor, unfit, unqualified

com•pe•ti•tion \ˌkäm-pə-ˈti-shən\ *n* **1** : the act of competing : RIVALRY **2 a** ♦ : a contest between rivals : CONTEST, MATCH **b** : one that competes; *also* : one's competitors — **com•pet•i•tive** \kəm-ˈpe-tə-tiv\ *adj* — **com•pet•i•tive•ly** *adv* — **com•pet•i•tive•ness** *n*

♦ bout, contest, event, game, match, meet, tournament

com•pet•i•tor \kəm-ˈpe-tə-tər\ *n* ♦ : one that competes : RIVAL

♦ challenger, competition, contender, contestant, rival

com•pi•la•tion \ˌkäm-pə-ˈlā-shən\ *n* ♦ : something that is a product of the putting together of two or more items

♦ album, anthology, miscellany

com•pile \kəm-ˈpīl\ *vb* **com•piled; com•pil•ing** **1** : to compose out of materials from other documents **2** : to collect and edit into a volume **3** : to translate (a computer program) with a compiler **4** : to build up gradually ⟨~ a record of four wins and two losses⟩
com•pil•er \kəm-ˈpī-lər\ *n* **1** : one that compiles **2** : a computer program that translates any program correctly written in a specific programming language into machine language
com•pla•cence \kəm-ˈplās-ᵊns\ *n* ♦ : the quality or state of being self-satisfied

♦ conceit, ego, egotism, pride, self-conceit, self-esteem, self-importance, self-satisfaction, smugness, vainglory, vanity *Ant* humbleness, humility, modesty

com•pla•cen•cy \-ᵊn-sē\ *n, pl* **-cies** **1** : SATISFACTION **2** : the quality or state of being self-satisfied
com•pla•cent \-ᵊnt\ *adj* ♦ : marked by complacency : SELF-SATISFIED — **com•pla•cent•ly** *adv*

♦ conceited, egotistic, important, overweening, pompous, prideful, proud, self-important, self-satisfied, smug, stuck-up, vain

com•plain \kəm-ˈplān\ *vb* **1** ♦ : to express grief, pain, or discontent **2** : to make a formal accusation

♦ beef, bellyache, carp, crab, croak, fuss, gripe, grouse, growl, grumble, kick, moan, murmur, mutter, repine, squawk, wail, whine *Ant* rejoice

com•plain•ant *n* **1** : the party who makes the complaint in a legal action or proceeding : **2** : one who complains
com•plain•er *n* ♦ : one that complains

♦ bear, crab, crank, curmudgeon, grouch, grumbler, whiner

com•plaint \kəm-ˈplānt\ *n* **1** ♦ : expression of grief, pain, or dissatisfaction **2** ♦ : a bodily ailment or disease **3** ♦ : a formal accusation against a person

♦ [1] challenge, demur, expostulation, fuss, kick, objection, protest, question, remonstrance ♦ [1] beef, fuss, grievance, gripe, grumble, murmur, plaint, squawk ♦ [2] ailment, complication, condition, disease, disorder, fever, ill, illness, infirmity, malady, sickness, trouble ♦ [3] charge, count, indictment, rap

com•plai•sance \kəm-ˈplās-ᵊns, ˌkäm-plā-ˈzans\ *n* : disposition to please — **com•plai•sant** \-ᵊnt, -ˈzant\ *adj*
com•pleat \kəm-ˈplēt\ *adj* : PROFICIENT
com•plect•ed \kəm-ˈplek-təd\ *adj* : having a specified facial complexion ⟨dark-*complected*⟩
¹**com•ple•ment** \ˈkäm-plə-mənt\ *n* **1 a** : something that fills up or completes **b** : the full quantity, number, or amount that makes a thing complete **2** : an added word by which a predicate is made complete **3** : a group of proteins in blood that combines with antibodies to destroy antigens
²**com•ple•ment** \-ˌment\ *vb* : to be complementary to : fill out
com•ple•men•ta•ry \ˌkäm-plə-ˈmen-t(ə-)rē\ *adj* : serving to fill out or complete : being complements of each other
complementary medicine *n* : ALTERNATIVE MEDICINE
¹**com•plete** \kəm-ˈplēt\ *adj* **com•plet•er; -est** **1** ♦ : having all parts or elements **2** ♦ : brought to an end **3** ♦ : fully carried out **4** : fully realized : carried to the ultimate : ABSOLUTE 2 ⟨~ silence⟩ — **com•plete•ness** *n* — **com•ple•tion** \-ˈplē-shən\ *n*

♦ [1] compendious, comprehensive, encyclopedic, full, global, inclusive, omnibus, panoramic, universal ♦ [1] comprehensive, entire, full, grand, intact, integral, perfect, plenary, total, whole *Ant* imperfect, incomplete, partial ♦ [2] done, down, over, through, up *Ant* continuing, incomplete, ongoing, unfinished ♦ [3] all-out, clean, comprehensive, exhaustive, full-scale, out-and-out, thorough, thoroughgoing, total

²**complete** *vb* **com•plet•ed; com•plet•ing** **1** ♦ : to bring to an end and especially into a perfected state : FINISH **2** ♦ : to make whole or perfect ⟨the hat ~*s* the outfit⟩

♦ [1, 2] consummate, finalize, finish, perfect

com•plete•ly *adv* **1** ♦ **:** so as to be complete **:** FULLY **2** ♦ **:** to a complete degree

♦ [1, 2] altogether, dead, entirely, fast, flat, full, fully, perfectly, quite, thoroughly, well, wholly

1com•plex \ˈkäm-ˌpleks\ *n* **1 :** a whole made up of or involving intricately interrelated elements **2 :** a group of repressed desires and memories that exert a dominating influence on one's personality and behavior ⟨a guilt ~⟩ **3** ♦ **:** a building or group of buildings housing related units

♦ establishment, facility, installation

2com•plex \käm-ˈpleks, ˈkäm-ˌpleks\ *adj* **1** ♦ **:** composed of two or more parts **2 :** consisting of a main clause and one or more subordinate clauses ⟨~ sentence⟩ **3** ♦ **:** hard to separate, analyze, solve, or do **4** ♦ **:** marked by an involvement of many parts, aspects, or details necessitating careful study or attention — **com•plex•ly** *adv*

♦ [1, 4] complicated, convoluted, elaborate, intricate, involved, knotty, sophisticated *Ant* plain, simple ♦ [3] complicated, detailed, elaborate, fancy, intricate, involved, sophisticated

complex fraction *n* **:** a fraction with a fraction or mixed number in the numerator or denominator or both

com•plex•ion \kəm-ˈplek-shən\ *n* **1 :** the hue or appearance of the skin especially of the face **2** ♦ **:** overall aspect or character — **com•plex•ioned** \-shənd\ *adj*

♦ character, constitution, genius, nature, personality, tone

com•plex•i•ty \käm-ˈplek-sə-tē\ *n* **1** ♦ **:** something complex **2** ♦ **:** the quality or state of being complex

♦ [1] complication, difficulty, intricacy ♦ [2] elaborateness, intricacy, sophistication *Ant* plainness, simpleness, simplicity

complex number *n* **:** a number of the form $a + b\sqrt{-1}$ where *a* and *b* are real numbers

com•pli•ance \kəm-ˈplī-əns\ *n* **1** ♦ **:** the act of complying to a demand or proposal **2** ♦ **:** a disposition to yield

♦ [1] conformity, obedience, observance, submission, subordination ♦ [2] deference, docility, obedience *Ant* defiance, disobedience, recalcitrance

com•pli•ant \-ənt\ *adj* ♦ **:** ready or disposed to comply

♦ amenable, conformable, docile, obedient, submissive, tractable

com•pli•cate \ˈkäm-plə-ˌkāt\ *vb* **-cat•ed; -cat•ing :** to make or become complex or intricate

com•pli•cat•ed \ˈkäm-plə-ˌkā-təd\ *adj* **1** ♦ **:** consisting of parts intricately combined **2** ♦ **:** difficult to analyze, understand, or explain **3 :** not simple or easy to fabricate or comprehend — **com•pli•cat•ed•ly** *adv*

♦ complex, convoluted, detailed, elaborate, intricate, involved, knotty, sophisticated

com•pli•ca•tion \ˌkäm-plə-ˈkā-shən\ *n* **1 a :** the quality or state of being complicated **b** ♦ **:** a complex feature **2** ♦ **:** a disease or condition that develops during and affects the course of a primary disease or condition

♦ [1b] complexity, difficulty, intricacy ♦ [2] ailment, bug, complaint, condition, disease, disorder, fever, ill, illness, infirmity, malady, sickness, trouble

com•plic•i•ty \kəm-ˈpli-sə-tē\ *n, pl* **-ties :** the state of being an accomplice

1com•pli•ment \ˈkäm-plə-ment\ *n* **1 :** an expression of approval or admiration; *esp* **:** a flattering remark **2** *pl* ♦ **:** best wishes **:** REGARDS

♦ *usu* **compliments** greetings, regards, respects

2com•pli•ment \-ˌment\ *vb* **:** to pay a compliment to

com•pli•men•ta•ry \ˌkäm-plə-ˈmen-t(ə-)rē\ *adj* **1** ♦ **:** containing or expressing a compliment **2** ♦ **:** given free as a courtesy ⟨~ ticket⟩

♦ [1] appreciative, favorable (*or* favourable), friendly, good, positive ♦ [2] free, gratuitous

com•ply \kəm-ˈplī\ *vb* **com•plied; com•ply•ing** ♦ **:** to conform, submit, or adapt (as to a regulation or to another's wishes) as required or requested

♦ *usu* **comply with** conform, follow, mind, obey, observe ♦ *usu* **comply with** answer, fill, fulfill, keep, meet, redeem, satisfy

1com•po•nent \kəm-ˈpō-nənt, ˈkäm-ˌpō-\ *n* ♦ **:** a component part

♦ constituent, element, factor, ingredient, member

2component *adj* **:** serving to form a part of **:** CONSTITUENT

com•port \kəm-ˈpōrt\ *vb* **1** ♦ **:** to be fitting **:** AGREE, ACCORD **2** ♦ **:** to behave in a manner conformable to what is right, proper, or expected **:** CONDUCT

♦ [1] accord, agree, answer, check, coincide, conform, correspond, dovetail, fit, go, harmonize, jibe, square, tally ♦ [2] acquit, bear, behave, conduct, demean, deport, quit

com•port•ment *n* ♦ **:** manner of bearing **:** DEMEANOR

♦ actions, bearing, behavior (*or* behaviour), conduct, demeanor (*or* demeanour), deportment

com•pose \kəm-ˈpōz\ *vb* **com•posed; com•pos•ing 1 a :** to form by putting together **b** ♦ **:** to form the substance of **2** ♦ **:** to produce (as pages of type) by composition **3 :** ADJUST, ARRANGE **4** ♦ **:** to free from agitation **:** CALM, QUIET **5 :** to practice composition ⟨~ music⟩

♦ [1b] comprise, constitute, form, make up ♦ [2] cast, craft, draft, draw, formulate, frame, prepare ♦ [4] allay, calm, quiet, settle, soothe, still, tranquilize ♦ [4] calm, collect, control, settle

composed *adj* ♦ **:** free from agitation

♦ calm, collected, cool, placid, self-possessed, serene, tranquil, undisturbed, unperturbed, unshaken, untroubled, unworried

com•pos•er *n* **:** one that composes **:** a person who writes music

1com•pos•ite \käm-ˈpä-zət\ *adj* **1 :** made up of distinct parts or elements **2 :** of, relating to, or being a large family of flowering plants (as a daisy or aster) that bear many small flowers united into compact heads resembling single flowers

2composite *n* **1** ♦ **:** something composite **2 :** a plant of the composite family

♦ admixture, amalgam, blend, combination, compound, fusion, intermixture, mix, mixture

com•po•si•tion \ˌkäm-pə-ˈzi-shən\ *n* **1 a :** the act or process of composing **b** ♦ **:** arrangement especially in artistic form **2 :** the arrangement or production of type for printing **3 :** general makeup **4 :** a product of mixing various elements or ingredients **5 a** ♦ **:** a literary, musical, or artistic product **b** ♦ **:** a brief piece of writing **:** ESSAY

♦ [1b] arrangement, configuration, design, form, format, layout, makeup, pattern ♦ [5a] opus, piece, work ♦ [5b] article, essay, paper, theme

com•pos•i•tor \kəm-ˈpä-zə-tər\ *n* **:** one who sets type

com•post \ˈkäm-ˌpōst\ *n* **:** a fertilizing material consisting largely of decayed organic matter

com•po•sure \kəm-ˈpō-zhər\ *n* ♦ **:** a calmness or repose especially of mind, bearing, or appearance **:** CALMNESS, SELF-POSSESSION

♦ aplomb, calmness, coolness, equanimity, placidity, self-possession, serenity, tranquillity

com•pote \ˈkäm-ˌpōt\ *n* **1 :** fruits cooked in syrup **2 :** a bowl (as of glass) usually with a base and stem for serving especially fruit or compote

1com•pound \käm-ˈpau̇nd, ˈkäm-ˌ\ *vb* **1** ♦ **:** to put together (parts) so as to form a whole **:** COMBINE **2 :** to form by combining parts ⟨~ a medicine⟩ **3 :** SETTLE ⟨~ a dispute⟩; *also* **:** to refrain from prosecuting (an offense) in return for a consideration **4 a :** to increase (as interest) by an amount that can itself vary **b** ♦ **:** to add to

♦ [1] chain, combine, connect, couple, hitch, hook, join, link, yoke ♦ [4b] add, aggrandize, amplify, augment, boost, enlarge, escalate, expand, extend, increase, multiply, raise, swell, up

2com•pound \ˈkäm-ˌpau̇nd\ *adj* **1 :** made up of individual parts **2 :** composed of united similar parts especially of a kind usually independent ⟨a ~ plant ovary⟩ **3 :** formed by the combination of two or more otherwise independent elements ⟨~ sentence⟩

3com•pound \ˈkäm-ˌpau̇nd\ *n* **1 :** a word consisting of parts that are words **2** ♦ **:** something formed from a union of elements or parts; *esp* **:** a distinct substance formed by the union of two or more chemical elements

♦ admixture, amalgam, blend, combination, composite, fusion, intermixture, mix, mixture

4com•pound \ˈkäm-ˌpau̇nd\ *n* **:** an enclosure containing buildings

compound interest *n* **:** interest computed on the sum of an original principal and accrued interest

com•pre•hend \ˌkäm-pri-ˈhend\ *vb* **1** ♦ **:** to grasp the nature, significance, or meaning of **:** UNDERSTAND **2** ♦ **:** to contain or hold within a total scope, significance, or amount : INCLUDE — **com•pre•hen•si•ble** \-ˈhen-sə-bəl\ *adj*

♦ [1] appreciate, apprehend, catch, catch on (to), get, grasp, make, make out, perceive, see, seize, understand ***Ant*** miss ♦ [2] carry, contain, embrace, encompass, entail, include, involve, number, take in

com•pre•hen•sion \-ˈhen-chən\ *n* ♦ **:** knowledge gained by comprehending

♦ appreciation, apprehension, grasp, grip, perception, understanding

com•pre•hen•sive \-siv\ *adj* ♦ **:** covering completely or broadly **:** covering all possibilities — **com•pre•hen•sive•ly** *adv* — **com•pre•hen•sive•ness** *n*

♦ compendious, complete, encyclopedic, full, global, inclusive, omnibus, panoramic, universal ♦ complete, entire, full, grand, intact, integral, perfect, plenary, total, whole

¹**com•press** \kəm-ˈpres\ *vb* **1** ♦ **:** to press or squeeze together **2** ♦ **:** to reduce in size, quantity, or volume as if by squeezing — **com•pres•sor** \-ˈpre-sər\ *n*

♦ [1] condense, constrict, contract, shrink ♦ [2] compact, condense, constrict, contract, squeeze ***Ant*** expand, open, outspread

²**com•press** \ˈkäm-ˌpres\ *n* **:** a folded pad or cloth used to press upon a body part

compressed air *n* **:** air under pressure greater than that of the atmosphere

com•pres•sion \-ˈpre-shən\ *n* **1** ♦ **:** the act or process of compressing **2 :** the process of compressing the fuel mixture in an internal combustion engine **3 :** conversion (as of data) in order to reduce the space occupied or the bandwidth required

♦ condensation, constriction, contraction ***Ant*** expansion

com•prise \kəm-ˈprīz\ *vb* **com•prised; com•pris•ing 1 :** INCLUDE, CONTAIN **2 :** to consist of **:** to be made up of **3** ♦ **:** to make up **:** COMPOSE, CONSTITUTE

♦ compose, constitute, form, make up

¹**com•pro•mise** \ˈkäm-prə-ˌmīz\ *n* ♦ **:** a settlement of differences reached by mutual concessions

♦ accommodation, concession, give-and-take, negotiation

²**compromise** *vb* **-mised; -mis•ing 1 :** to settle by compromise **2 a :** to expose to suspicion or loss of reputation **b** ♦ **:** to put in jeopardy **:** endanger by some act that cannot be recalled

♦ adventure, gamble with, hazard, imperil, jeopardize, menace, risk, venture

comp•trol•ler \kən-ˈtrō-lər, ˈkämp-ˌtrō-\ *n* **:** an official who audits and supervises expenditures and accounts

com•pul•sion \kəm-ˈpəl-shən\ *n* **1** ♦ **:** an act of compelling **2 :** a force that compels **3 :** an irresistible persistent impulse to perform an act

♦ coercion, constraint, duress, force, pressure

com•pul•sive \-siv\ *adj* **:** of, having to do with, caused by, or suggestive of psychological compulsion or obsession

com•pul•so•ry \-sə-rē\ *adj* ♦ **:** demanded, directed, or designated by authority

♦ imperative, incumbent, involuntary, mandatory, necessary, nonelective, obligatory, peremptory

com•punc•tion \kəm-ˈpəŋk-shən\ *n* ♦ **:** anxiety arising from guilt

♦ misgiving, qualm, scruple

com•pu•ta•tion \ˌkäm-pyu̇-ˈtā-shən\ *n* ♦ **:** the act or action of computing — **com•pu•ta•tion•al** *adj*

♦ arithmetic, calculation, reckoning

com•pute \kəm-ˈpyüt\ *vb* **com•put•ed; com•put•ing** ♦ **:** to determine or ascertain especially by mathematical means **:** arrive at an answer to or sum for **:** CALCULATE, RECKON

♦ calculate, figure, reckon, work out

computed tomography *n* **:** radiography in which a three-dimensional image of a body structure is constructed by computer from a series of plane cross-sectional images made along an axis

com•put•er \kəm-ˈpyü-tər\ *n* **:** a programmable electronic device that can store, retrieve, and process data

com•put•er•ise *chiefly Brit var of* COMPUTERIZE

com•put•er•ize \kəm-ˈpyü-tə-ˌrīz\ *vb* **-ized; -iz•ing 1 :** to carry out, control, or produce by means of a computer **2 :** to provide with computers **3 :** to store in a computer; *also* **:** put into a form that a computer can use — **com•put•er•iza•tion** \-ˌpyü-tə-rə-ˈzā-shən\ *n*

computerized axial tomography *n* **:** COMPUTED TOMOGRAPHY

com•rade \ˈkäm-ˌrad\ *n* ♦ **:** an intimate friend or associate **:** COMPANION, ASSOCIATE

♦ associate, cohort, companion, crony, fellow, mate ♦ buddy, chum, crony, familiar, friend, intimate, pal

com•rade•ly *adj* ♦ **:** of or like a comrade or partner

♦ amicable, companionable, cordial, friendly, genial, hearty, neighborly, warm, warmhearted

com•rade•ship *n* ♦ **:** association as comrades

♦ camaraderie, companionship, company, fellowship, society

¹**con** \ˈkän\ *vb* **conned; con•ning 1 :** to commit to memory by vocal or mental repetition **:** MEMORIZE **2 :** STUDY

²**con** *adv* **:** in opposition **:** AGAINST

³**con** *n* **:** an opposing argument, person, or position ⟨pros and ~*s*⟩

⁴**con** *vb* **conned; con•ning 1 :** SWINDLE **2 :** PERSUADE, CAJOLE

⁵**con** *n* **:** CONVICT

conc *abbr* concentrated

con•cat•e•nate \kän-ˈka-tə-ˌnāt\ *vb* **-nat•ed; -nat•ing :** to link together in a series or chain — **con•cat•e•na•tion** \(ˌ)kän-ˌka-tə-ˈnā-shən\ *n*

con•cave \kän-ˈkāv, ˈkän-ˌ\ *adj* ♦ **:** curved or rounded inward like the inside of a bowl

♦ depressed, hollow, sunken

con•cav•i•ty \kän-ˈka-və-tē\ *n* ♦ **:** a concave line, surface, or space

♦ cavity, dent, depression, hole, hollow, indentation, pit, recess

con•ceal \kən-ˈsēl\ *vb* ♦ **:** to place out of sight **:** HIDE

♦ bury, cache, ensconce, hide, secrete

con•ceal•ment *n* **1** ♦ **:** the act or practice of concealing **2** ♦ **:** a hiding place

♦ [1] secretion ***Ant*** display, exhibition, exposure, parading, showing ♦ [2] covert, den, hideout, lair, nest

con•cede \kən-ˈsēd\ *vb* **con•ced•ed; con•ced•ing 1** ♦ **:** to admit to be true **2** ♦ **:** to make concession **:** GRANT, YIELD

♦ [1] acknowledge, admit, agree, allow, confess, grant, own ♦ [2] bow, budge, capitulate, give in, grant, knuckle under, quit, submit, succumb, surrender, yield

con•ceit \kən-ˈsēt\ *n* **1** ♦ **:** excessively high opinion of one's self or ability **:** VANITY **2 :** an elaborate or strained metaphor **3** ♦ **:** a fanciful idea

♦ [1] complacence, ego, egotism, pride, self-conceit, self-esteem, self-importance, self-satisfaction, smugness, vainglory, vanity ♦ [3] chimera, daydream, delusion, dream, fancy, fantasy, figment, hallucination, illusion, phantasm, pipe dream, unreality, vision

con•ceit•ed *adj* ♦ **:** having or showing an excessively high opinion of oneself — **con•ceit•ed•ly** *adv* — **con•ceit•ed•ness** *n*

♦ complacent, egotistic, important, overweening, pompous, prideful, proud, self-important, self-satisfied, smug, stuck-up, vain ***Ant*** humble, modest

con•ceiv•ably \-blē\ *adv* ♦ **:** it may be conceived **:** POSSIBLY

♦ maybe, perchance, perhaps, possibly

con•ceive \kən-ˈsēv\ *vb* **con•ceived; con•ceiv•ing 1 :** to become pregnant or pregnant with ⟨~ a child⟩ **2** ♦ **:** to form an idea of **:** IMAGINE — **con•ceiv•able** \-ˈsē-və-bəl\ *adj*

♦ dream, envisage, fancy, imagine, picture, vision, visualize

con•cel•e•brant \kən-ˈse-lə-brənt\ *n* **:** one that jointly participates in celebrating the Eucharist

¹**con•cen•trate** \ˈkän-sən-ˌtrāt\ *vb* **-trat•ed; -trat•ing 1** ♦ **:** to gather into one body, mass, or force **2 :** to make less dilute **3** ♦ **:** to fix one's powers, efforts, or attentions

♦ [1] center (*or* centre), centralize, consolidate, unify, unite ♦ [1] accumulate, amass, assemble, collect, garner, gather, group, lump, pick up, round up, scrape ♦ [3] fasten, focus, rivet, train

²**concentrate** *n* **:** something concentrated

concentrated *adj* **1** ♦ **:** rich in respect to a particular or essential element **2** ♦ **:** not scattered or dispersed

♦ [1] full, full-bodied, potent, rich, robust, strong ♦ [2] all, entire, undivided, whole

con•cen•tra•tion \ˌkän-sən-ˈtrā-shən\ *n* **1** ♦ **:** the act or process of concentrating **:** the state of being concentrated; *esp* **:** direction of attention on a single object **2 :** the amount of a component in a given area or volume

♦ absorption, attention

concentration camp *n* **:** a camp where persons (as prisoners of war or political prisoners) are confined

con•cen•tric \kən-ˈsen-trik\ *adj* **1 :** having a common center ⟨~ circles⟩ **2 :** COAXIAL

¹con•cept \ˈkän-ˌsept\ *n* ♦ **:** something conceived in the mind **:** THOUGHT, NOTION, IDEA

♦ idea, image, impression, notion, picture, thought

²concept *adj* **1 :** organized around a main idea or theme ⟨a ~ album⟩ **2 :** created to illustrate a concept ⟨a ~ car⟩

con•cep•tion \kən-ˈsep-shən\ *n* **1 :** the process of conceiving or being conceived **2 :** the power to form or understand ideas or concepts **3 :** a general idea **:** CONCEPT **4 :** the originating of something

con•cep•tu•al \kən-ˈsep-chə-wəl\ *adj* **:** of, relating to, or consisting of concepts — **con•cep•tu•al•ly** *adv*

con•cep•tu•al•ise *Brit var of* CONCEPTUALIZE

con•cep•tu•al•ize \-ˈsep-chə-wə-ˌlīz\ *vb* **-ized; -iz•ing :** to form a conception of

¹con•cern \kən-ˈsərn\ *vb* **1** ♦ **:** to relate to **:** be about ⟨the novel ~*s* three soldiers⟩ **2** ♦ **:** to be the business of **:** INVOLVE **3 :** ENGAGE, OCCUPY **4** ♦ **:** to be a care, trouble, or distress to

♦ [1] cover, deal, pertain, treat ♦ [2] affect, interest, involve, touch ♦ [4] agitate, bother, discompose, disquiet, distress, disturb, exercise, freak out, perturb, undo, unhinge, unsettle, upset, worry

²concern *n* **1** ♦ **:** an uneasy state of blended interest, uncertainty, and apprehension **:** ANXIETY **2 :** AFFAIR, MATTER **3** ♦ **:** a business organization

♦ [1] agitation, anxiety, apprehension, care, disquiet, nervousness, perturbation, uneasiness, worry ♦ [3] business, company, enterprise, establishment, firm, house, outfit

con•cerned *adj* **1 :** ANXIOUS, UNEASY **2 :** INVOLVED

con•cern•ing *prep* ♦ **:** relating to **:** REGARDING

♦ about, apropos of, of, on, regarding, respecting, toward

con•cern•ment \kən-ˈsərn-mənt\ *n* **1 :** something in which one is concerned **2 :** IMPORTANCE, CONSEQUENCE

¹con•cert \ˈkän-(ˌ)sərt\ *n* **1 :** agreement in a plan or design **2 :** a concerted action **3 :** a public performance (as of music)

²con•cert \kən-ˈsərt\ *vb* **1** ♦ **:** to plan together **2** ♦ **:** to settle or adjust by conferring and reaching an agreement

♦ [1] collaborate, cooperate, join, team ♦ [2] arrange, conclude, negotiate

con•cert•ed \kən-ˈsər-təd\ *adj* **1 :** mutually agreed on **2** ♦ **:** performed in unison

♦ collective, common, communal, conjoint, joint, mutual, public, united

con•cer•ti•na \ˌkän-sər-ˈtē-nə\ *n* **:** an instrument of the accordion family

concertina wire *n* **:** a coiled wire with sharp points for use as an obstacle

con•cert•mas•ter \ˈkän-sərt-ˌmas-tər\ *or* **con•cert•meis•ter** \-ˌmī-stər\ *n* **:** the leader of the first violins of an orchestra and assistant to the conductor

con•cer•to \kən-ˈcher-tō\ *n, pl* **-ti** \-(ˌ)tē\ *or* **-tos :** a piece for one or more solo instruments and orchestra in three movements

con•ces•sion \kən-ˈse-shən\ *n* **1** ♦ **:** an act of conceding or yielding **2** ♦ **:** something yielded **3 :** a grant by a government of land or of a right to use it **4 :** a grant of a portion of premises for some specific purpose; *also* **:** the activities or enterprise carried on — **con•ces•sion•ary** \-ˈse-shə-ˌner-ē\ *adj*

♦ [1] acknowledgment, admission, avowal, confession ♦ [1, 2] accommodation, compromise, give-and-take, negotiation

con•ces•sion•aire \kən-ˌse-shə-ˈnar, -ˈner\ *n* **:** one that owns or operates a concession

conch \ˈkäŋk, ˈkänch\ *n, pl* **conchs** \ˈkäŋks\ *or* **conch•es** \ˈkän-chəz\ **:** a large spiral-shelled marine gastropod mollusk; *also* **:** its shell

con•cierge \kōⁿ-ˈsyerzh\ *n, pl* **con•cierges** *same or* -ˈsyerzhəz\ **1 :** a resident in an apartment building who performs services for the tenants **2 :** a usually multilingual hotel staff member who usually handles mail and reservations

con•cil•i•ate \kən-ˈsi-lē-ˌāt\ *vb* **-at•ed; -at•ing 1** ♦ **:** to bring into agreement **:** RECONCILE **2 :** to gain the goodwill of — **con•cil•i•a•tion** \-ˌsi-lē-ˈā-shən\ *n*

♦ accommodate, conform, coordinate, harmonize, key, reconcile

con•cil•ia•to•ry \-ˈsi-lē-ə-ˌtōr-ē\ *adj* ♦ **:** tending to conciliate

♦ pacific, propitiatory

con•cise \kən-ˈsīs\ *adj* ♦ **:** expressing much in few words **:** BRIEF

♦ brief, compact, compendious, crisp, epigrammatic, laconic, pithy, succinct, summary, terse *Ant* diffuse, long-winded, prolix, rambling, verbose, wordy

con•cise•ly *adv* ♦ **:** in a concise manner

♦ compactly, crisply, laconically, shortly, succinctly, summarily, tersely

con•cise•ness *n* ♦ **:** the quality or state of being concise

♦ brevity, briefness, compactness, crispness, succinctness, terseness

con•clave \ˈkän-ˌklāv\ *n* **:** a private gathering; *also* **:** CONVENTION

con•clude \kən-ˈklüd\ *vb* **con•clud•ed; con•clud•ing 1** ♦ **:** to bring or come to a close **:** END **2 a** ♦ **:** to reach as a logically necessary end by reasoning **:** JUDGE **b** ♦ **:** to make a decision about **:** DECIDE **3 :** to bring about as a result

♦ [1] close, end, finish, round, terminate, wind up, wrap up ♦ [2a] deduce, extrapolate, gather, infer, judge, reason, understand ♦ [2b] choose, decide, determine, figure, opt, resolve

con•clu•sion \kən-ˈklü-zhən\ *n* **1** ♦ **:** the logical consequence of a reasoning process **2** ♦ **:** the last part of anything **:** END **3** ♦ **:** a final decision or settlement **:** OUTCOME, RESULT

♦ [1, 3] aftermath, consequence, corollary, development, effect, issue, outcome, outgrowth, product, result, resultant, sequence, upshot ♦ [2] close, consummation, end, ending, finale, finis, finish, windup

con•clu•sive \-siv\ *adj* ♦ **:** putting an end to debate or question especially by reason of irrefutability — **con•clu•sive•ly** *adv*

♦ absolute, clear, decisive, definitive *Ant* inconclusive, indecisive, unclear

con•clu•sive•ness *adj* ♦ **:** the quality or state of being conclusive

♦ authority, cogency, effectiveness, force, persuasion, persuasiveness

con•coct \kən-ˈkäkt, kän-\ *vb* **1 :** to prepare by combining raw materials **2 a** ♦ **:** to formulate by thought **b :** to put together usually for the purposes of deception **:** DEVISE

♦ contrive, cook up, devise, fabricate, invent, make up, manufacture, think up

con•coc•tion \-ˈkäk-shən\ *n* **1** ♦ **:** something that is concocted (as a food or scheme) **2 :** something that suggests origin by concoction (as by mingling of diverse elements)

♦ coinage, contrivance, creation, innovation, invention, wrinkle

¹con•com•i•tant \-ˈkä-mə-tənt\ *adj* ♦ **:** accompanying especially in a subordinate or incidental way

♦ attendant, coincident, concurrent

²concomitant *n* **:** something that accompanies or is collaterally connected with something else

con•cord \ˈkän-ˌkȯrd, ˈkäŋ-\ *n* ♦ **:** a state of agreement **:** HARMONY

♦ compatibility, harmony, peace

con•cor•dance \kən-ˈkȯr-dᵊns\ *n* **1 :** an alphabetical index of words in a book or in an author's works with the passages in which they occur **2 :** AGREEMENT, COVENANT

con•cor•dant \-dᵊnt\ *adj* **:** ♦ **:** marked by accord in sentiment or action **:** HARMONIOUS

♦ compatible, conformable (to), congruous, consistent, consonant, correspondent, harmonious

con•cor•dat \kən-ˈkȯr-ˌdat\ *n* **:** CONCORDANCE 2

con•course \ˈkän-ˌkōrs\ *n* **1 :** a spontaneous coming together **:** GATHERING **2 :** an open space or hall (as in a bus terminal) where crowds gather

¹con•crete \kän-ˈkrēt, ˈkän-ˌkrēt\ *adj* **1 :** naming a real thing or class of things **:** not abstract **2** ♦ **:** not theoretical **:** ACTUAL

3 : made of or relating to concrete **4 ♦ :** formed by coalition of particles into one solid mass

♦ [2] actual, existent, factual, real, true, very ♦ [4] material, physical, substantial

²con•crete \ˈkän-ˌkrēt, kän-ˈkrēt\ *vb* **con•cret•ed; con•cret•ing** **1 :** to form into a solid mass : SOLIDIFY **2 :** to cover with concrete

³con•crete \ˈkän-ˌkrēt, kän-ˈkrēt\ *n* **:** a hard building material made by mixing cement, sand, and gravel with water

con•cre•tion \kän-ˈkrē-shən\ *n* **:** a hard mass especially when formed abnormally in the body

con•cu•bine \ˈkäŋ-kyu̇-ˌbīn\ *n* **:** a woman who is not legally a wife but lives with a man and sometimes has a recognized position in his household; *also* : MISTRESS — **con•cu•bi•nage** \kän-ˈkyü-bə-nij\ *n*

con•cu•pis•cence \kän-ˈkyü-pə-səns\ *n* **:** ardent sexual desire : LUST

con•cur \kən-ˈkər\ *vb* **con•curred; con•cur•ring** **1 :** to act together **2 :** to express agreement : AGREE **3 :** to happen together : COINCIDE

con•cur•rence \-ˈkər-əns\ *n* **1 ♦ :** agreement in action or opinion **2 :** occurrence together

♦ accord, agreement, consensus, unanimity

con•cur•rent \-ˈkər-ənt\ *adj* **1 ♦ :** happening or operating at the same time **2 :** joint and equal in authority

♦ coeval, contemporary, simultaneous, synchronous ♦ attendant, coincident, concomitant

con•cus•sion \kən-ˈkə-shən\ *n* **1 ♦ :** a hard blow or collision; *also* : bodily injury (as to the brain) resulting from a sudden jar **2 :** AGITATION, SHAKING

♦ bump, collision, crash, impact, jar, jolt, shock, smash, strike, wallop

con•demn \kən-ˈdem\ *vb* **1 ♦ :** to declare to be wrong, reprehensible, or evil **2 :** to pronounce guilty **3 ♦ :** to sentence judicially **4 ♦ :** to pronounce unfit for use or consumption ⟨~ a building⟩ **5 :** to declare forfeited or taken for public use **6 ♦ :** to pronounce judgment on the faults of — **con•dem•na•tion** \kän-dem-ˈnā-shən\ *n*

♦ [1] censure, damn, decry, denounce, reprehend, reprobate *Ant* bless ♦ [3] damn, doom, sentence ♦ [4] censure, denounce, rebuke, reprimand, reproach, reprove ♦ [6] blame, censure, criticize, denounce, fault, knock, pan, reprehend

con•den•sate \ˈkän-dən-ˌsāt, kən-ˈden-\ *n* **:** a product of condensation

con•den•sa•tion \ˌkän-den-ˈsā-shən\ *n* **1 ♦ :** the act or process of condensing **2 ♦ :** abridgment and usually compression of a literary work

♦ [1] compression, constriction, contraction ♦ [2] abbreviation, digest

con•dense \kən-ˈdens\ *vb* **con•densed; con•dens•ing** **1 ♦ :** to make or become more compact or dense : compress or concentrate into a smaller scope or volume **2 :** to change from vapor to liquid

♦ compact, compress, constrict, contract, squeeze

condensed *adj* **:** reduced to a more compact form

con•dens•er \kən-ˈden-sər\ *n* **1 :** one that condenses **2 :** CAPACITOR

con•de•scend \ˌkän-di-ˈsend\ *vb* **1 :** to descend to a less formal or dignified level **2 :** to assume an air of superiority — **con•de•scend•ing•ly** \-ˈsen-diŋ-lē\ *adv* — **con•de•scen•sion** \-ˈsen-chən\ *n*

con•dign \kən-ˈdīn, ˈkän-ˌdīn\ *adj* **:** DESERVED, APPROPRIATE ⟨~ punishment⟩

con•di•ment \ˈkän-də-mənt\ *n* **:** something used to make food savory; *esp* **:** a pungent seasoning (as pepper)

¹con•di•tion \kən-ˈdi-shən\ *n* **1 ♦ :** something essential to the occurrence of some other thing **2 ♦ :** state of being **3 :** social status **4** *pl* **:** state of affairs : CIRCUMSTANCES **5 :** a bodily state in which something is wrong ⟨a heart ~⟩ **6 ♦ :** a state of health, fitness, or working order ⟨in good ~⟩ **7 ♦ :** a restricting or modifying factor

♦ [1] essential, must, necessity, provision, proviso, qualification, requirement, stipulation ♦ [2, 6] estate, fettle, form, order, repair, shape, trim ♦ [7] check, constraint, curb, fetter, limitation, restraint, restriction

²condition *vb* **1 ♦ :** to put into proper condition for action or use **2 ♦ :** to adapt, modify, or mold to respond in a particular way **3 :** to modify so that an act or response previously associated with one stimulus becomes associated with another

♦ [1, 2] acclimate, accommodate, adapt, adjust, conform, fit, shape

con•di•tion•al \kən-ˈdi-shə-nəl\ *adj* **♦ :** containing, implying, or depending on a condition — **con•di•tion•al•ly** *adv*

♦ contingent, dependent, subject

con•di•tioned *adj* **:** determined or established by conditioning

con•di•tion•er \-ˈdi-shə-nər\ *n* **:** a preparation used to improve the condition of hair

con•do \ˈkän-(ˌ)dō\ *n* **:** CONDOMINIUM 3

con•dole \kən-ˈdōl\ *vb* **con•doled; con•dol•ing** **:** to express sympathetic sorrow — **con•do•lence** \kən-ˈdō-ləns\ *n*

con•dom \ˈkän-dəm, ˈkən-\ *n* **:** a usually rubber sheath worn over the penis (as to prevent pregnancy or venereal infection during sexual intercourse)

con•do•min•i•um \ˌkän-də-ˈmi-nē-əm\ *n, pl* **-ums** **1 :** joint sovereignty (as by two or more nations) **2 :** a politically dependent territory under condominium **3 :** individual ownership of a unit (as an apartment) in a multiunit structure; *also* **:** a unit so owned

con•done \kən-ˈdōn\ *vb* **con•doned; con•don•ing ♦ :** to overlook or forgive especially by treating (an offense) as harmless or trivial — **con•do•na•tion** \ˌkän-də-ˈnā-shən\ *n*

♦ disregard, excuse, gloss over, ignore, pardon, pass over, shrug off, wink at

con•dor \ˈkän-dər, -ˌdȯr\ *n* **:** a very large American vulture of the high Andes; *also* **:** a related nearly extinct vulture of southern California

con•duce \kən-ˈdüs, -ˈdyüs\ *vb* **con•duced; con•duc•ing** **:** to lead or contribute to a particular result — **con•du•cive** *adj*

¹con•duct \ˈkän-(ˌ)dəkt\ *n* **1 ♦ :** the act, manner, or process of carrying on : MANAGEMENT, DIRECTION **2 ♦ :** a mode or standard of personal behavior especially as based on moral principles : BEHAVIOR

♦ [1] administration, control, direction, government, guidance, management, operation, oversight, regulation, running, superintendence, supervision ♦ [2] actions, bearing, behavior (*or* behaviour), comportment, demeanor (*or* demeanour), deportment

²con•duct \kən-ˈdəkt\ *vb* **1 ♦ :** to bring by or as if by leading : GUIDE **2 ♦ :** to direct or take part in the operation or management of : MANAGE, DIRECT **3 ♦ :** to convey in a channel **4 ♦ :** to cause (oneself) to act or behave in a particular and especially in a controlled manner : BEHAVE — **con•duc•tion** \-ˈdək-shən\ *n*

♦ [1] direct, guide, lead, marshal, pilot, route, show, steer, usher ♦ [2] administer, carry on, control, direct, govern, guide, handle, manage, operate, oversee, regulate, run, superintend, supervise ♦ [3] channel, direct, funnel, pipe, siphon ♦ [4] acquit, bear, behave, comport, demean, deport, quit

con•duc•tance \kən-ˈdək-təns\ *n* **:** the readiness with which a conductor transmits an electric current

con•duc•tive \kən-ˈdək-tiv\ *adj* **:** having the power to conduct (as heat or electricity) — **con•duc•tiv•i•ty** \ˌkän-ˌdək-ˈti-və-tē\ *n*

con•duc•tor \kən-ˈdək-tər\ *n* **1 :** one that conducts; *esp* **:** a material that permits an electric current to flow easily **2 :** a collector of fares in a public conveyance **3 :** the leader of a musical ensemble

con•duit \ˈkän-ˌdü-ət, ˌdyü-, -dwət\ *n* **1 ♦ :** a natural or artificial channel through which something (as a fluid) is conveyed **2 :** a tube or trough for protecting electric wires or cables **3 :** a means of transmitting or distributing

♦ channel, duct, leader, line, penstock, pipe, tube ♦ aqueduct, canal, channel, flume, raceway, watercourse

con•dyle \ˈkän-ˌdīl, -dᵊl\ *n* **:** an articular prominence of a bone — **con•dy•lar** \-də-lər\ *adj*

cone \ˈkōn\ *n* **1 :** the scaly fruit of trees of the pine family **2 :** a solid figure formed by rotating a right triangle about one of its legs **3 :** a solid figure that slopes evenly to a point from a usually circular base **4 :** any of the conical light-sensitive receptor cells of the retina that function in color vision **5 :** something shaped like a cone

Con•es•to•ga wagon \ˌkä-nə-ˈstō-gə-\ *n* **:** a broad-wheeled covered wagon used especially for transporting freight across the prairies

co•ney \ˈkō-nē\ *n, pl* **coneys** **1 :** RABBIT; *also* **:** its fur **2 :** PIKA

conf *abbr* **1** conference **2** confidential

con•fab \ˈkän-ˌfab, kən-ˈfab\ *n* **:** CONFABULATION 1

con•fab•u•la•tion \kən-ˌfab-yə-ˈlā-shən\ *n* **1 :** CHAT; *also* **:** CONFERENCE **2 :** a filling in of gaps in memory by fabrication

con•fec•tion \kən-ˈfek-shən\ *n* **:** a fancy dish or sweet; *also* **:** CANDY

con•fec•tion•er \-sh(ə-)nər\ *n* **:** a maker of or dealer in confections

con•fec•tion•ery \-shə-ˌner-ē\ *n, pl* **-er•ies** **1 :** sweet foods **2 :** a confectioner's place of business

Confed *abbr* Confederate

con•fed•er•a•cy \kən-ˈfe-də-rə-sē\ *n, pl* **-cies** **1** ♦ **:** a league or compact for mutual support or common action **:** LEAGUE, ALLIANCE **2** *cap* **:** the 11 southern states that seceded from the U.S. in 1860 and 1861

♦ alliance, bloc, coalition, combination, combine, confederation, federation, league, union

1**con•fed•er•ate** \kən-ˈfe-də-rət\ *adj* **1 :** united in a league **:** ALLIED **2** *cap* **:** of or relating to the Confederacy

2**confederate** *n* **1** ♦ **:** one that is associated with another as a helper **2** *cap* **:** an adherent of the Confederacy

♦ abettor, accessory, accomplice, cohort ♦ abettor, ally, backer, supporter, sympathizer

3**con•fed•er•ate** \-ˈfe-də-ˌrāt\ *vb* **-at•ed; -at•ing** ♦ **:** to unite in a confederacy

♦ ally, associate, band, club, conjoin, cooperate, federate, league, unite

con•fed•er•a•tion \kən-ˌfe-də-ˈrā-shən\ *n* **1 :** an act of confederating **:** ALLIANCE **2** ♦ **:** as association of parties for mutual assistance **:** LEAGUE

♦ alliance, bloc, coalition, combination, combine, confederacy, federation, league, union

con•fer \kən-ˈfər\ *vb* **con•ferred; con•fer•ring** **1** ♦ **:** to give or grant from or as if from a position of superiority **:** BESTOW **2** ♦ **:** to exchange views **:** CONSULT — **con•fer•ee** \ˌkän-fə-ˈrē\ *n*

♦ [1] accord, award, bestow, give, grant ♦ [2] advise, consult, counsel, parley

con•fer•ence \ˈkän-f(ə-)rəns\ *n* **1 a** ♦ **:** an interchange of views **b** ♦ **:** a meeting for an exchange of views **2 :** an association of athletic teams

♦ [1a] argument, colloquy, deliberation, discourse, discussion, give-and-take, parley, talk ♦ [1b] assembly, congress, convention, convocation, council, gathering, get-together, huddle, meeting, powwow, seminar

con•fer•enc•ing \ˈkän-f(ə-)rən-siŋ\ *n* **:** the holding of conferences especially by means of electronic devices

con•fess \kən-ˈfes\ *vb* **1** ♦ **:** to tell or make known (as something wrong or damaging to oneself) **2 :** to acknowledge one's sins to God or to a priest **3 :** to receive the confession of (a penitent)

♦ acknowledge, admit, agree, allow, concede, grant, own

con•fessed•ly \-ˈfe-səd-lē\ *adv* **:** by confession **:** ADMITTEDLY

con•fes•sion \-ˈfe-shən\ *n* **1** ♦ **:** an act of confessing (as in the sacrament of penance) **2** ♦ **:** an acknowledgment of guilt **3 :** a formal statement of religious beliefs **4 :** a religious body having a common creed — **con•fes•sion•al** *adj*

♦ [1, 2] acknowledgment, admission, avowal, concession

con•fes•sion•al \-ˈfe-shə-nəl\ *n* **:** a place where a priest hears confessions

con•fes•sor \kən-ˈfe-sər\ *n* **1 :** one that confesses **2 :** a priest who hears confessions

con•fet•ti \kən-ˈfe-tē\ *n* **:** bits of colored paper or ribbon for throwing (as at weddings)

con•fi•dant \ˈkän-fə-ˌdänt, -ˌdant\ *n* **:** one to whom secrets are confided

con•fi•dante \-ˌdänt, -ˌdant\ *n* **:** CONFIDANT; *esp* **:** one who is a woman

con•fide \kən-ˈfīd\ *vb* **con•fid•ed; con•fid•ing** **1 :** to have or show faith **:** TRUST ⟨~ in a friend⟩ **2 :** to tell confidentially ⟨~ a secret⟩ **3 :** ENTRUST

1**con•fi•dence** \ˈkän-fə-dəns\ *n* **1 :** faith or belief that one will act in a right, proper, or effective way **:** TRUST **2** ♦ **:** a feeling or consciousness of one's powers or of reliance on one's circumstances **:** SELF-ASSURANCE **3** ♦ **:** a state of trust or intimacy **4 :** a communication made in confidence **:** SECRET 2 **5** ♦ **:** the quality or state of being certain **:** CERTITUDE

♦ [2] aplomb, assurance, self-assurance, self-confidence, self-esteem *Ant* diffidence, self-doubt ♦ [3] credence, faith, stock, trust ♦ [5] assurance, certainty, certitude, conviction, positiveness, sureness *Ant* doubt, incertitude, uncertainty

2**confidence** *adj* **:** of or relating to swindling by false promises ⟨a ~ game⟩

con•fi•dent \-dənt\ *adj* **1** ♦ **:** full of conviction **:** CERTAIN **2** ♦ **:** having or showing assurance and self-reliance — **con•fi•dent•ly** *adv*

♦ [1] assured, certain, clear, cocksure, doubtless, positive, sanguine, sure ♦ [2] assured, secure, self-assured, self-confident *Ant* diffident, insecure

con•fi•den•tial \ˌkän-fə-ˈden-shəl\ *adj* **1** ♦ **:** known only to a limited few **:** SECRET, PRIVATE **2 :** entrusted with confidences ⟨~ clerk⟩ — **con•fi•den•tial•ly** \-ˈden-shə-lē\ *adv*

♦ hushed, inside, intimate, private, secret

con•fig•u•ra•tion \kən-ˌfi-gyə-ˈrā-shən\ *n* ♦ **:** relative arrangement of parts or elements **:** SHAPE

♦ arrangement, composition, design, form, format, layout, makeup, pattern, shape

con•fig•ure \kən-ˈfi-gyər\ *vb* **-ured; -ur•ing** **:** to set up for operation especially in a particular way

con•fine \kən-ˈfīn\ *vb* **con•fined; con•fin•ing** **1** ♦ **:** to hold within a location; *also* **:** IMPRISON **2** ♦ **:** to keep within limits ⟨will ~ my remarks to one subject⟩ — **con•fin•er** *n*

♦ [1] commit, immure, imprison, jail ♦ [2] check, circumscribe, control, curb, inhibit, limit, restrain, restrict

con•fine•ment *n* ♦ **:** an act of confining **:** the state of being confined

♦ captivity, imprisonment, incarceration, internment

con•fines \ˈkän-ˌfīnz\ *n pl* ♦ **:** something (as borders or walls) that encloses **:** something that restrains

♦ boundary, ceiling, end, extent, limit, limitation, line, termination ♦ border, boundary, circumference, compass, edge, end, fringe, margin, perimeter, periphery, rim, skirt, verge

con•firm \kən-ˈfərm\ *vb* **1 :** to give approval to **:** RATIFY **2 :** to make firm or firmer **3 :** to administer the rite of confirmation to **4** ♦ **:** to give new assurance of the validity of **:** VERIFY, CORROBORATE

♦ bear out, corroborate, substantiate, support, validate, verify, vindicate *Ant* disprove, rebut, refute

con•fir•ma•tion \ˌkän-fər-ˈmā-shən\ *n* **1 :** a religious ceremony admitting a person to full membership in a church or synagogue **2** ♦ **:** an act of ratifying or corroborating; *also* **:** PROOF

♦ attestation, corroboration, documentation, evidence, proof, substantiation, testament, testimony, validation, witness

con•fir•ma•to•ry \-ˈfər-mə-ˌtōr-ē\ *adj* ♦ **:** serving to confirm

♦ corroborative

confirmed *adj* **1** ♦ **:** marked by long continuance and likely to persist **2** ♦ **:** fixed in habit and unlikely to change

♦ [1] deep-rooted, deep-seated, inveterate, settled ♦ [2] chronic, habitual, inveterate

con•fis•cate \ˈkän-fə-ˌskāt\ *vb* **-cat•ed; -cat•ing** **:** to take possession of by or as if by public authority — **con•fis•ca•tion** \ˌkän-fə-ˈskā-shən\ *n* — **con•fis•ca•to•ry** \kən-ˈfis-kə-ˌtōr-ē\ *adj*

con•fit \kōn-ˈfē\ *n* **:** a garnish of fruit or vegetables cooked in a seasoned liquid

con•fla•gra•tion \ˌkän-flə-ˈgrā-shən\ *n* ♦ **:** FIRE; *esp* **:** a large disastrous fire

♦ fire, holocaust, inferno

1**con•flict** \ˈkän-ˌflikt\ *n* **1** ♦ **:** prolonged fighting especially with weapons **:** WAR **2** ♦ **:** a clash between hostile or opposing elements, ideas, or forces

♦ [1] battle, clash, combat, contest, fight, fracas, fray, hassle, scrap, scrimmage, scuffle, skirmish, struggle, war, warfare ♦ [1, 2] battle, combat, confrontation, contest, duel, face-off, rivalry, struggle, tug-of-war, warfare ♦ [2] conflict, discord, dissension, dissent, disunity, friction, schism, strife, variance, war, warfare

2**con•flict** \kən-ˈflikt\ *vb* ♦ **:** to show opposition or irreconcilability **:** CLASH

♦ clash, collide, jar

con•flu•ence \ˈkän-ˌflü-əns, kən-ˈflü-\ *n* **1** ♦ **:** a coming together at one point **2 :** the meeting or place of meeting of two or more streams — **con•flu•ent** \-ənt\ *adj*

♦ conjunction, convergence, meeting

con•flux \ˈkän-ˌfləks\ *n* **:** CONFLUENCE

con•form \kən-ˈfȯrm\ *vb* **1 a :** to be similar or identical **b** ♦ **:** to be in agreement or harmony **:** AGREE **2** ♦ **:** to be obedient or compliant — usually used with *to*; *also* **:** COMPLY **3** ♦ **:** to make like **:** shape to fit — **con•form•ist** \-ˈfȯr-mist\ *adj*

♦ [1b] accord, agree, answer, check, coincide, comport, correspond, dovetail, fit, go, harmonize, jibe, square, tally ♦ *usu* **conform to** [2] comply, follow, mind, obey, observe ♦ [3] acclimate, accommodate, adapt, adjust, condition, fit, shape

con•form•able *adj* **1** ♦ **:** corresponding or consistent in form or character **2** ♦ **:** giving compliance or obedience

♦ *usu* **conformable to** [1] compatible, congruous, consistent, consonant, correspondent, harmonious ♦ [2] amenable, compliant, docile, obedient, submissive, tractable

con•for•mance \kən-ˈfȯr-məns\ *n* **:** CONFORMITY

con•for•ma•tion \ˌkän-fȯr-ˈmā-shən\ *n* ♦ **:** formation of something by appropriate arrangement of parts or elements **:** an assembling into a whole

♦ arrangement, configuration, format, layout, setup

con•for•mi•ty \kən-ˈfȯr-mə-tē\ *n, pl* **-ties** **1** ♦ **:** correspondence in form, manner, or character **:** HARMONY, AGREEMENT **2** ♦ **:** action in accordance with some specified standard or authority **:** COMPLIANCE, OBEDIENCE

♦ [1] accord, agreement, consonance, harmony, tune *Ant* conflict, disagreement ♦ [2] compliance, obedience, observance, submission, subordination

con•found \kən-ˈfau̇nd, kän-\ *vb* **1** ♦ **:** to throw (a person) into confusion or perplexity **2** ♦ **:** to put to shame **:** CONFUSE 2

♦ [1] addle, baffle, befog, befuddle, bemuse, bewilder, confuse, disorient, muddle, muddy, mystify, perplex, puzzle ♦ [2] abash, confuse, discomfit, disconcert, discountenance, embarrass, faze, fluster, mortify, rattle

con•fra•ter•ni•ty \ˌkän-frə-ˈtər-nə-tē\ *n* **:** a society devoted especially to a religious or charitable cause

con•frere \ˈkän-ˌfrer, ˈkōⁿ-\ *n* **:** COLLEAGUE, COMRADE

con•front \kən-ˈfrənt\ *vb* **1 a** ♦ **:** to face especially in challenge **b** ♦ **:** to deal unflinchingly with ⟨~*ed* the issue⟩ **2 :** to cause to face or meet

♦ [1a, 1b] beard, brave, brazen, dare, defy, face

con•fron•ta•tion \ˌkän-frən-ˈtā-shən\ *n* ♦ **:** the act of confronting **:** the state of being confronted — **con•fron•ta•tion•al** \-shə-nᵊl\ *adj*

♦ battle, combat, conflict, contest, duel, face-off, rivalry, struggle, tug-of-war, warfare

Con•fu•cian \kən-ˈfyü-shən\ *adj* **:** of or relating to the Chinese philosopher Confucius or his teachings — **Con•fu•cian•ism** \-shə-ˌni-zəm\ *n*

con•fuse \kən-ˈfyüz\ *vb* **con•fused; con•fus•ing** **1 a** ♦ **:** to make mentally unclear or uncertain **b** ♦ **:** to disturb the composure of **2 :** to mix up **:** JUMBLE **3** ♦ **:** to fail to make clear or distinct — **con•fus•ed•ly** \-ˈfyü-zəd-lē\ *adv*

♦ [1a] addle, baffle, befog, befuddle, bemuse, bewilder, confound, disorient, muddle, muddy, mystify, perplex, puzzle ♦ [1b] abash, confound, discomfit, disconcert, discountenance, embarrass, faze, fluster, mortify, rattle ♦ [3] becloud, befog, blur, cloud, fog, muddy *Ant* clarify

confused *adj* **1** ♦ **:** being perplexed or disconcerted **2** ♦ **:** being disordered or mixed up

♦ [1] dizzy, stunned ♦ [2] chaotic, disheveled, disordered, messy, muddled, sloppy, unkempt, untidy

con•fu•sion \-ˈfyü-zhən\ *n* **1 :** an act or instance of confusing **2** ♦ **:** the quality or state of being confused **3** ♦ **:** a confused mass or mixture

♦ [2] bafflement, bewilderment, distraction, muddle, mystification, perplexity, puzzlement, whirl ♦ [3] chaos, disarray, disorder, disorganization, havoc, hell, jumble, mess, muddle, shambles

con•fu•ta•tion \ˌkän-fyu̇-ˈtā-shən\ *n* ♦ **:** something (as an argument or statement) that refutes

♦ rebuttal, refutation *Ant* proof

con•fute \kən-ˈfyüt\ *vb* **con•fut•ed; con•fut•ing** ♦ **:** to overwhelm by argument **:** refute conclusively

♦ belie, disprove, rebut, refute

cong *abbr* congress; congressional

con•ga \ˈkäŋ-gə\ *n* **:** a Cuban dance of African origin performed by a group usually in single file

con•geal \kən-ˈjēl\ *vb* **1** ♦ **:** to change from a fluid to a solid state by or as if by cold **:** FREEZE **2** ♦ **:** to make or become hard or thick

♦ [1] clot, coagulate, gel, jell, set ♦ [1, 2] concrete, firm, freeze, harden, set, solidify

con•gee \ˈkän-jē\ *n* **:** porridge made from rice

con•ge•ner \ˈkän-jə-nər\ *n* **:** one related to another; *esp* **:** a plant or animal of the same taxonomic genus as another — **con•ge•ner•ic** \ˌkän-jə-ˈner-ik\ *adj*

con•ge•nial \kən-ˈjē-nyəl\ *adj* **1** ♦ **:** having the same nature, disposition, or tastes **:** KINDRED **2** ♦ **:** agreeably suited to one's nature, tastes, or outlook **:** AGREEABLE — **con•ge•ni•al•i•ty** \-ˌjē-nē-ˈa-lə-tē\ *n* — **con•ge•nial•ly** *adv*

♦ [1] agreeable, amicable, compatible, harmonious, kindred, unanimous, united ♦ [2] agreeable, delectable, delicious, delightful, dreamy, felicitous, good, grateful, gratifying, nice, palatable, pleasant, pleasurable, satisfying

con•gen•i•tal \kən-ˈje-nə-tᵊl\ *adj* **:** existing at or dating from birth

con•ger eel \ˈkän-gər-\ *n* **:** a large edible marine eel of the Atlantic

con•ge•ries \ˈkän-jə-(ˌ)rēz\ *n, pl* **congeries** **:** AGGREGATION, COLLECTION

con•gest \kən-ˈjest\ *vb* **1 :** to cause excessive fullness of the blood vessels of (as a lung) **2** ♦ **:** to obstruct by overcrowding **3 :** to concentrate in a small or narrow space — **con•ges•tion** \-ˈjes-chən\ *n* — **con•ges•tive** \-ˈjes-tiv\ *adj*

♦ block, choke, clog, close (off), dam, jam, obstruct, plug (up), stop (up), stuff

congestive heart failure *n* **:** heart failure in which the heart is unable to keep enough blood circulating in the tissues or is unable to pump out the blood returned to it by the veins

¹con•glom•er•ate \kən-ˈglä-mə-rət\ *adj* **:** made up of parts from various sources

²con•glom•er•ate \-ˌrāt\ *vb* **-at•ed; -at•ing** ♦ **:** to gather into a mass **:** form a coherent whole — **con•glom•er•a•tion** \-ˌglä-mə-ˈrā-shən\ *n*

♦ accumulate, collect, gather, heap, pile up

³con•glom•er•ate \-rət\ *n* **1 :** a mass formed of fragments from various sources; *esp* **:** a rock composed of fragments varying from pebbles to boulders held together by a cementing material **2 :** a widely diversified corporation

Con•go•lese \ˌkäŋ-gə-ˈlēz, -ˈlēs\ *n* **:** a native or inhabitant of Congo — **Congolese** *adj*

con•grat•u•late \kən-ˈgra-chə-ˌlāt\ *vb* **-lat•ed; -lat•ing** **:** to express sympathetic pleasure to on account of success or good fortune **:** FELICITATE — **con•grat•u•la•to•ry** \-ˈgra-chə-lə-ˌtōr-ē\ *adj*

con•grat•u•la•tion \-ˌgra-chə-ˈlā-shən\ *n* **1 :** the act of congratulating **2 :** a congratulatory expression — usually used in plural

con•gre•gate \ˈkäŋ-gri-ˌgāt\ *vb* **-gat•ed; -gat•ing** ♦ **:** to collect into a group or crowd **:** ASSEMBLE

♦ assemble, cluster, collect, concentrate, conglomerate, convene, forgather, gather, meet, rendezvous

con•gre•ga•tion \ˌkäŋ-gri-ˈgā-shən\ *n* **1** ♦ **:** an assembly of persons met especially for worship; *also* **:** a group that habitually so meets **2 :** a religious community or order **3 :** the act or an instance of congregating

♦ assemblage, assembly, conference, convocation, gathering, meeting, muster

con•gre•ga•tion•al \-shə-nəl\ *adj* **1 :** of or relating to a congregation **2** *cap* **:** observing the faith and practice of certain Protestant churches which recognize the independence of each congregation in church matters — **con•gre•ga•tion•al•ism** \-nə-ˌli-zəm\ *n, often cap* — **con•gre•ga•tion•al•ist** \-list\ *n, often cap*

con•gress \ˈkäŋ-grəs\ *n* **1** ♦ **:** an assembly especially of delegates for discussion and usually action on some question **2 :** the body of senators and representatives constituting a nation's legislature **3 :** the body of persons coming together for a common purpose — **con•gres•sio•nal** \kən-ˈgre-shə-nəl\ *adj*

♦ assembly, conference, convention, convocation, council, gathering, get-together, huddle, meeting, powwow, seminar

con•gress•man \ˈkäŋ-grəs-mən\ *n* : a member of a congress
con•gress•wom•an \-ˌwu̇-mən\ *n* : a woman who is a member of a congress
con•gru•ence \kən-ˈgrü-əns, ˈkäŋ-grü-\ *n* : the quality of agreeing or coinciding : CONGRUITY — **con•gru•ent** \kən-ˈgrü-ənt, ˈkäŋ-grü-\ *adj*
con•gru•en•cy \-sē\ *n, pl* **-cies** : CONGRUENCE
con•gru•ity \kän-ˈgrü-ə-tē\ *n, pl* **-ities** : correspondence between things
con•gru•ous \ˈkäŋ-grü-əs\ *adj* ♦ : being in agreement, harmony, or correspondence

♦ balanced, consonant, harmonious ♦ compatible, conformable (to), consistent, consonant, correspondent, harmonious

con•ic \ˈkä-nik\ *adj* **1** : of or relating to a cone **2** : CONICAL
con•i•cal \ˈkä-ni-kəl\ *adj* : resembling a cone especially in shape
co•ni•fer \ˈkä-nə-fər, ˈkō-\ *n* : any of an order of shrubs or trees (as the pines) that usually are evergreen and bear cones — **co•nif•er•ous** \kō-ˈni-fə-rəs\ *adj*
conj *abbr* conjunction
con•jec•tur•al \-chə-rəl\ *adj* ♦ : of the nature of or involving or based on conjecture

♦ hypothetical, speculative, theoretical

[1]**con•jec•ture** \kən-ˈjek-chər\ *n* **1** ♦ : a conclusion deduced by surmise or guesswork : GUESS, SURMISE **2** ♦ : inference from defective or presumptive evidence

♦ [1, 2] guess, supposition, surmise ♦ [2] hypothesis, proposition, supposition, theory

[2]**conjecture** *vb* ♦ : to arrive at or deduce by conjecture : GUESS

♦ calculate, call, estimate, figure, gauge, guess, judge, make, place, put, reckon, suppose ♦ assume, guess, presume, speculate, suppose, surmise, suspect

con•join \kən-ˈjȯin\ *vb* ♦ : to join together — **con•joint** \-ˈjȯint\ *adj*

♦ associate, coalesce, combine, connect, couple, fuse, join, link, marry, unify, unite

con•joint \-ˈjȯint\ *adj* ♦ : related to, made up of, or carried on by two or more in combination

♦ collective, common, communal, concerted, joint, mutual, public, united

con•ju•gal \ˈkän-ji-gəl\ *adj* ♦ : of or relating to marriage : MATRIMONIAL

♦ connubial, marital, matrimonial, nuptial

[1]**con•ju•gate** \ˈkän-ji-gət, -jə-ˌgāt\ *adj* **1** : united especially in pairs : COUPLED **2** : of kindred origin and meaning ‹*sing* and *song* are ~› — **con•ju•gate•ly** *adv*
[2]**con•ju•gate** \-jə-ˌgāt\ *vb* **-gat•ed; -gat•ing** **1** : INFLECT ‹~ a verb› **2** : to join together : COUPLE
con•ju•ga•tion \ˌkän-jə-ˈgā-shən\ *n* **1** : an arrangement of the inflectional forms of a verb **2** : the act of conjugating : the state of being conjugated
con•junct \kän-ˈjəŋkt\ *adj* : JOINED, UNITED
con•junc•tion \kən-ˈjəŋk-shən\ *n* **1** ♦ : the act or an instance of conjoining : the state of being combined **2** : occurrence at the same time **3** : a word that joins together sentences, clauses, phrases, or words

♦ confluence, convergence, meeting

con•junc•ti•va \ˌkän-ˌjəŋk-ˈtī-və\ *n, pl* **-vas** *or* **-vae** \-(ˌ)vē\ : the mucous membrane lining the inner surface of the eyelids and continuing over the forepart of the eyeball
con•junc•tive \kən-ˈjəŋk-tiv\ *adj* **1** : CONNECTIVE **2** : CONJUNCT **3** : being or functioning like a conjunction
con•junc•ti•vi•tis \kən-ˌjəŋk-ti-ˈvī-təs\ *n* : inflammation of the conjunctiva
con•junc•ture \kən-ˈjəŋk-chər\ *n* **1** : CONJUNCTION, UNION **2** : JUNCTURE 3
con•jun•to \kōn-ˈhün-tō\ *n* : Mexican-American music influenced by the music of German immigrants to Texas
con•ju•ra•tion \ˌkän-jü-ˈrā-shən, ˌkən-\ *n* ♦ : a magic expression used in conjuring

♦ bewitchment, charm, enchantment, incantation, spell

con•jure \ˈkän-jər, ˈkən- *for 1, 2;* kən-ˈju̇r *for 3*\ *vb* **con•jured; con•jur•ing** **1** : to implore earnestly or solemnly **2** : to practice magic; *esp* : to summon (as a devil) by sorcery **3** : to practice sleight of hand **4 a** : to summon by or as if by invocation or incantation **b** : to affect or effect by or as if by magic
con•jur•er *or* **con•ju•ror** \ˈkän-jər-ər, ˈkən-\ *n* **1** ♦ : one that practices magic arts : WIZARD **2** ♦ : one that performs feats of sleight of hand and illusion : MAGICIAN

♦ [1] enchanter, magician, necromancer, sorcerer, voodoo, witch, wizard ♦ [2] illusionist, magician, trickster

conk \ˈkäŋk\ *vb* ♦ : to become inoperative or ineffective : BREAK DOWN; *esp* : STALL ‹the motor ~*ed* out›

♦ break, break down, crash, cut out, die, fail, stall

Conn *abbr* Connecticut
con•nect \kə-ˈnekt\ *vb* **1** ♦ : to join or fasten together in a single relationship often by something intervening : JOIN, LINK **2** ♦ : to associate in one's mind **3** : to establish a communications connection ‹~ to the Internet› — **con•nect•able** *adj* — **con•nec•tor** *n*

♦ [1] chain, compound, couple, hitch, hook, join, link, yoke *Ant* disconnect, disjoin, separate, unchain, uncouple, unhitch, unyoke ♦ [2] associate, correlate, identify, link, relate

con•nec•tion \kə-ˈnek-shən\ *n* **1 a** ♦ : the act of connecting : a coming into or being put in contact : JUNCTION, UNION **b** ♦ : the state of being connected or linked **c** ♦ : the place where a connection occurs **2** ♦ : logical relationship; *esp* : relation of a word to other words in a sentence **3** : family relationship **4** : something that connects or the point of the connecting **5** : a person related by blood or marriage **6** ♦ : relationship in social affairs or in business **7** : a set or group of persons connected or associated together in a common interest; *esp* : a religious denomination

♦ [1a] combination, consolidation, coupling, junction, unification, union ♦ [1b] association, bearing, kinship, liaison, linkage, relation, relationship ♦ [1c] coupling, joint, junction, juncture ♦ [2] applicability, bearing, pertinence, relevance ♦ [6] affiliation, alliance, association, collaboration, confederation, cooperation, hookup, liaison, partnership, relation, relationship, union

[1]**con•nec•tive** \kə-ˈnek-tiv\ *adj* : serving to connect — **con•nec•tiv•i•ty** \ˌkä-ˌnek-ˈti-və-tē\ *n*
[2]**connective** *n* : a word (as a conjunction) that connects words or word groups
connective tissue *n* : a tissue (as bone or cartilage) that forms a supporting framework for the body or its parts
con•nex•ion *chiefly Brit var of* CONNECTION
con•ning tower \ˈkä-niŋ-\ *n* : a raised structure on the deck of a submarine
con•nip•tion \kə-ˈnip-shən\ *n* : a fit of rage, hysteria, or alarm
con•niv•ance *n* ♦ : knowledge of and active or passive consent to wrongdoing

♦ collusion, conspiracy

con•nive \kə-ˈnīv\ *vb* **con•nived; con•niv•ing** **1** : to pretend ignorance of something one ought to oppose as wrong **2** : to cooperate secretly : give secret aid — **con•niv•er** *n*
con•nois•seur \ˌkä-nə-ˈsər\ *n* : a critical judge in matters of art or taste
con•no•ta•tion \ˌkä-nə-ˈtā-shən\ *n* : a meaning in addition to or apart from the thing explicitly named or described by a word
con•no•ta•tive \ˈkä-nə-ˌtā-tiv, kə-ˈnō-tə-\ *adj* **1** : connoting or tending to connote **2** : relating to connotation
con•note \kə-ˈnōt\ *vb* **con•not•ed; con•not•ing** : to suggest or mean as a connotation
con•nu•bi•al \kə-ˈnü-bē-əl, -ˈnyü-\ *adj* ♦ : of or relating to the married state : CONJUGAL

♦ conjugal, marital, matrimonial, nuptial

con•quer \ˈkäŋ-kər\ *vb* **1** ♦ : to gain by force of arms : WIN **2** ♦ : to get the better of : OVERCOME

♦ [1] prevail, triumph, win ♦ [2] beat, crush, defeat, dominate, overcome, overpower, subdue, subject, vanquish

con•quer•or \-ər\ *n* ♦ : one that conquers

♦ master, victor, winner

con•quest \ˈkän-ˌkwest, ˈkäŋ-\ *n* **1** ♦ : an act of conquering **2** : something conquered

♦ domination, subjection

con•quis•ta•dor \kȯŋ-ˈkēs-tə-ˌdȯr, kän-ˈkwis-\ *n, pl* **-do•res** \-ˌkēs-tə-ˈdȯr-ēz, -ˌkwis-\ *or* **-dors** : CONQUEROR; *esp* : a leader in the Spanish conquest of the Americas in the 16th century
cons *abbr* consonant

con•san•guin•i•ty \ˌkän-ˌsan-ˈgwi-nə-tē, -ˌsaŋ-\ *n, pl* **-ties** : blood relationship — **con•san•guin•e•ous** \-nē-əs\ *adj*

con•science \ˈkän-chəns\ *n* : consciousness of the moral right and wrong of one's own acts or motives — **con•science•less** *adj*

con•sci•en•tious \ˌkän-chē-ˈen-chəs\ *adj* **1** ♦ : guided by one's own sense of right and wrong **2** ♦ : marked by or done with exact or thoughtful attention — **con•sci•en•tious•ly** *adv*

♦ [1] ethical, honest, honorable (*or* honourable), just, moral, principled, scrupulous ***Ant*** cutthroat, dishonest, dishonorable, immoral, unethical, unjust, unprincipled, unscrupulous ♦ [2] careful, fussy, meticulous, painstaking

conscientious objector *n* : a person who refuses to serve in the armed forces or to bear arms on moral or religious grounds

¹con•scious \ˈkän-chəs\ *adj* **1** ♦ : perceiving, apprehending, or noticing with a degree of controlled thought or observation : AWARE **2** : known or felt by one's inner self **3** : mentally awake or alert : not asleep or unconscious **4** : INTENTIONAL — **con•scious•ness** *n*

♦ alive, aware, cognizant, mindful, sensible, sentient, witting ***Ant*** insensible, unaware, unconscious, unmindful

²conscious *n* : the upper level of mental life of which a person is aware : CONSCIOUSNESS

con•scious•ly *adv* ♦ : in a conscious manner

♦ deliberately, intentionally, knowingly, purposely, willfully

¹con•script \kən-ˈskript\ *vb* : to enroll by compulsion for military or naval service — **con•scrip•tion** \kən-ˈskrip-shən\ *n*

²conscript \ˈkän-ˌskript\ *n* : a conscripted person (as a military recruit)

con•se•crate \ˈkän-sə-ˌkrāt\ *vb* **-crat•ed; -crat•ing 1** : to induct (as a bishop) into an office with a religious rite **2** ♦ : to make or declare sacred ⟨~ a church⟩ **3** ♦ : to devote solemnly to a purpose

♦ [2] bless, hallow, sanctify ♦ [3] allocate, dedicate, devote, earmark, reserve, save

con•se•cra•tion \ˌkän-sə-ˈkrā-shən\ *n* ♦ : the act or ceremony of consecrating

♦ blessing, sanctification

con•sec•u•tive \kən-ˈse-kyə-tiv\ *adj* ♦ : following in regular order : SUCCESSIVE — **con•sec•u•tive•ly** *adv*

♦ sequential, successive

con•sen•su•al \kən-ˈsen-chə-wəl\ *adj* : involving or based on mutual consent

con•sen•sus \kən-ˈsen-səs\ *n* **1** ♦ : agreement in opinion, testimony, or belief **2** : collective opinion

♦ accord, agreement, concurrence, unanimity

¹con•sent \kən-ˈsent\ *vb* ♦ : to give assent or approval

♦ accede, acquiesce, agree, assent, come round, subscribe (to)

²consent *n* ♦ : approval or acceptance of something done or proposed by another

♦ allowance, authorization, clearance, concurrence, leave, license (*or* licence), permission, sanction, sufferance

con•se•quence \ˈkän-sə-ˌkwens\ *n* **1** ♦ : something produced by a cause or necessarily following from a set of conditions : RESULT **2** ♦ : importance with respect to power to produce an effect

♦ [1] aftermath, conclusion, corollary, development, effect, issue, outcome, outgrowth, product, result, resultant, sequence, upshot ♦ [2] import, magnitude, moment, significance, weight

con•se•quent \-kwənt, -ˌkwent\ *adj* ♦ : following as a result or effect

♦ attendant, consequential, due, resultant

con•se•quen•tial \ˌkän-sə-ˈkwen-chəl\ *adj* **1** ♦ : having significant consequences : IMPORTANT **2** : showing self-importance **3** : following as a result

♦ big, eventful, important, major, material, meaningful, momentous, significant, substantial, weighty

con•se•quent•ly \ˈkän-sə-ˌkwent-lē, -kwənt-\ *adv* ♦ : as a result : ACCORDINGLY

♦ accordingly, ergo, hence, so, therefore, thus, wherefore

con•ser•van•cy \kən-ˈsər-vən-sē\ *n, pl* **-cies** : an organization or area designated to conserve natural resources

con•ser•va•tion \ˌkän-sər-ˈvā-shən\ *n* ♦ : a careful preservation and protection of something : PRESERVATION; *esp* : planned management of natural resources

♦ maintenance, preservation, upkeep

con•ser•va•tion•ist \-shə-nist\ *n* : a person who advocates conservation especially of natural resources

con•ser•va•tism \kən-ˈsər-və-ˌti-zəm\ *n* : disposition to keep to established ways : opposition to change

¹con•ser•va•tive \kən-ˈsər-və-tiv\ *adj* **1** : PRESERVATIVE **2** ♦ : disposed to maintain existing views, conditions, or institutions **3** : MODERATE, CAUTIOUS **4** ♦ : marked by or relating to traditional norms of taste, elegance, style, or manners — **con•ser•va•tive•ly** *adv*

♦ [2] old-fashioned, orthodox, reactionary, traditional ***Ant*** liberal, nonorthodox, nontraditional, progressive, unorthodox ♦ [4] muted, quiet, restrained, subdued, unpretentious

²conservative *n* : a person who is conservative especially in politics

♦ reactionary, rightist, Tory ***Ant*** leftist, liberal, progressive

con•ser•va•tor \kən-ˈsər-və-tər, ˈkän-sər-ˌvā-\ *n* **1** : PROTECTOR, GUARDIAN **2** : one named by a court to protect the interests of an incompetent (as a child)

con•ser•va•to•ry \kən-ˈsər-və-ˌtōr-ē\ *n, pl* **-ries 1** : a greenhouse for growing or displaying plants **2** : a place of instruction in one of the fine arts (as music)

¹con•serve \kən-ˈsərv\ *vb* **con•served; con•serv•ing** ♦ : to keep from losing or wasting : preserve in a sound state

♦ keep up, maintain, preserve, save

²con•serve \ˈkän-ˌsərv\ *n* **1** : CONFECTION; *esp* : a candied fruit **2** : PRESERVE; *esp* : one prepared from a mixture of fruits

con•sid•er \kən-ˈsi-dər\ *vb* **1** ♦ : to reflect on : think about with a degree of care or caution **2** ♦ : to be of the opinion : REGARD **3** ♦ : to think of : come to view, judge, or classify — **con•sid•ered** *adj*

♦ [1] chew over, cogitate, contemplate, debate, deliberate, entertain, meditate, mull, ponder, question, ruminate, study, think, weigh ♦ [2, 3] account, count, esteem, hold, rate, reckon, regard, take

con•sid•er•able \-ˈsi-dər-ə-bəl, -ˈsi-drə-bəl\ *adj* **1** : worthy of consideration : of consequence or distinction **2** ♦ : large in extent, amount, or degree

♦ good, goodly, healthy, respectable, significant, sizable, substantial, tidy ***Ant*** inconsiderable, insignificant, insubstantial

con•sid•er•ably \-blē\ *adv* ♦ : to a notable extent or degree

♦ broadly, greatly, hugely, largely, massively, monstrously, much, sizably, stupendously, tremendously, utterly, vastly

con•sid•er•ate \kən-ˈsi-də-rət\ *adj* **1** ♦ : observant of the rights and feelings of others **2** ♦ : marked by or given to careful consideration

♦ [1] attentive, kind, solicitous, thoughtful ♦ [2] alert, careful, cautious, circumspect, gingerly, guarded, heedful, safe, wary

con•sid•er•ation \kən-ˌsi-də-ˈrā-shən\ *n* **1** ♦ : careful thought : DELIBERATION **2** : a matter taken into account **3** : thoughtful attention **4** : JUDGMENT, OPINION **5** ♦ : something given as recompense

♦ [1] debate, deliberation, thought ♦ [5] compensation, pay, payment, recompense, remittance, remuneration, requital

con•sid•er•ing *prep* : in view of : taking into account

con•sign \kən-ˈsīn\ *vb* **1** ♦ : to give over to another's charge, custody, or care : ENTRUST, COMMIT **2** : to deliver formally **3** : to send (goods) to an agent for sale — **con•sign•ee** \ˌkän-sə-ˈnē, -ˌsī-; kən-ˌsī-\ *n* — **con•sign•or** \ˌkän-sə-ˈnȯr, -ˌsī-; kən-ˌsī-\ *n*

♦ commend, commit, delegate, deliver, entrust, give, hand over, leave, pass, transfer, transmit, trust, turn over, vest

con•sign•ment \kən-ˈsīn-mənt\ *n* : something consigned especially in a single shipment

con•sist \kən-ˈsist\ *vb* **1** : to be inherent : LIE — usually used with *in* **2** : to be composed or made up — usually used with *of*

con•sis•tence \kən-ˈsis-təns\ *n* : CONSISTENCY

con•sis•ten•cy \-tən-sē\ *n, pl* **-cies 1** : COHESIVENESS, FIRMNESS **2** : agreement or harmony in parts or of different things **3** : UNIFORMITY ⟨~ of behavior⟩ **4** ♦ : degree of firmness, density, viscosity, or resistance to movement or separation of constituent particles

♦ thickness, viscosity

con•sis•tent \-tənt\ *adj* ♦ : marked by agreement

♦ compatible, conformable (to), congruous, consonant, correspondent, harmonious *Ant* conflicting, incompatible, incongruous, inconsistent, inharmonious

con•sis•tent•ly *adv* : in a consistent manner
con•sis•to•ry \kən-ˈsis-tə-rē\ *n, pl* **-ries** : a solemn assembly (as of Roman Catholic cardinals)
consol *abbr* consolidated
con•so•la•tion \ˌkän-sə-ˈlā-shən\ *n* ♦ : the act or an instance of consoling : the state of being consoled

♦ cheer, comfort, relief, solace ♦ comforting, solace

[1]**con•sole** \ˈkän-ˌsōl\ *n* **1** : the desklike part of an organ at which the organist sits **2** : the combination of displays and controls of a device or system **3** : a cabinet for a radio or television set resting directly on the floor **4** : a small storage cabinet between bucket seats in an automobile
[2]**con•sole** \kən-ˈsōl\ *vb* **con•soled; con•sol•ing** ♦ : to soothe the grief of : COMFORT, SOLACE — **con•so•la•to•ry** \kən-ˈsō-lə-ˌtōr-ē, -ˈsä-\ *adj*

♦ assure, cheer, comfort, reassure, solace, soothe

con•sol•i•date \kən-ˈsä-lə-ˌdāt\ *vb* **-dat•ed; -dat•ing** **1** ♦ : to unite or become united into one whole : COMBINE **2** : to make stronger or more secure **3** ♦ : to form into a compact mass

♦ [1, 3] center (*or* centre), centralize, combine, compact, concentrate, unify, unite

con•sol•i•da•tion \-ˌsä-lə-ˈdā-shən\ *n* ♦ : the act or process of consolidating : the state of being consolidated

♦ combination, connection, coupling, junction, unification, union

con•som•mé \ˌkän-sə-ˈmā\ *n* : a clear soup made from well-seasoned stock
con•so•nance \ˈkän-sə-nəns\ *n* **1** ♦ : harmony or agreement among components **2** : repetition of consonants especially as an alternative to rhyme in verse

♦ balance, coherence, harmony, proportion, symmetry, symphony, unity

[1]**con•so•nant** \-nənt\ *adj* ♦ : having consonance, harmony, or agreement — **con•so•nant•ly** *adv*

♦ compatible, conformable (to), congruous, consistent, correspondent, harmonious

[2]**consonant** *n* **1** : a speech sound (as p, g, n, l, s, r) characterized by constriction or closure at one or more points in the breath channel **2** : a letter other than *a, e, i, o,* and *u* — **con•so•nan•tal** \ˌkän-sə-ˈnant-ᵊl\ *adj*
[1]**con•sort** \ˈkän-ˌsȯrt\ *n* **1** : a ship accompanying another **2** : a wife or husband : SPOUSE, MATE
[2]**con•sort** \kən-ˈsȯrt\ *vb* **1** ♦ : to spend time in the company of **2** : ACCORD, HARMONIZE

♦ associate, chum, fraternize, hang around, hobnob, pal

con•sor•tium \kən-ˈsȯr-shəm; -shē-əm, -tē-\ *n, pl* **-sor•tia** \-shə-; -shē-ə, -tē-\ : an agreement or combination (as of companies) formed to undertake a large enterprise
con•spec•tus \kən-ˈspek-təs\ *n* **1** : a brief survey or summary **2** : SUMMARY
con•spic•u•ous \kən-ˈspi-kyə-wəs\ *adj* **1** ♦ : obvious to the eye or mind : PROMINENT **2** ♦ : attracting attention : STRIKING **3** ♦ : marked by a noticeable violation of good taste — **con•spic•u•ous•ly** *adv*

♦ [1, 2] bold, catchy, emphatic, marked, noticeable, prominent, pronounced, remarkable, striking ♦ [3] blatant, egregious, flagrant, glaring, gross, obvious, patent, prominent, pronounced, rank, striking

con•spir•a•cy \kən-ˈspir-ə-sē\ *n, pl* **-cies** **1** ♦ : an agreement among conspirators : PLOT **2** ♦ : a group of conspirators

♦ [1] design, intrigue, machination, plot, scheme ♦ [2] cabal, gang, mob, ring, syndicate

con•spir•a•tor \kən-ˈspir-ə-tər\ *n* : one that conspires — **con•spir•a•to•ri•al** \-ˌspir-ə-ˈtōr-ē-əl\ *adj*
con•spire \kən-ˈspīr\ *vb* **conspired; con•spir•ing** ♦ : to plan secretly an unlawful act : PLOT

♦ contrive, intrigue, machinate, plot, scheme

const *abbr* **1** constant **2** constitution; constitutional
con•sta•ble \ˈkän-stə-bəl, ˈkən-\ *n* ♦ : a public officer responsible for keeping the peace

♦ cop, officer, police officer

con•stab•u•lary \kən-ˈsta-byə-ˌler-ē\ *n, pl* **-lar•ies** **1** : the police of a particular district or country **2** : a police force organized like the military
con•stan•cy \ˈkän-stən-sē\ *n, pl* **-cies** **1** ♦ : firmness of mind **2** ♦ : a state of being constant or unchanging

♦ [1] allegiance, dedication, devotion, faith, faithfulness, fastness, fealty, fidelity, loyalty, steadfastness ♦ [2] fixedness, immutability, stability, steadiness *Ant* instability, mutability, unsteadiness, variability

[1]**con•stant** \-stənt\ *adj* **1** ♦ : marked by firm steadfast resolution or faithfulness : STEADFAST, FAITHFUL **2** ♦ : fixed and invariable : remaining unchanged : UNCHANGING **3** ♦ : continually recurring : REGULAR

♦ [1] devoted, faithful, fast, good, loyal, pious, staunch, steadfast, steady, true, true-blue ♦ [2] stable, stationary, steady, unchanging, unvarying *Ant* changeful, changing, fluctuating, inconstant, varying, unstable, unsteady ♦ [3] frequent, habitual, periodic, regular, repeated, steady

[2]**constant** *n* : something unchanging
con•stant•ly *adv* ♦ : with regular occurrence

♦ continually, frequently, often, repeatedly ♦ always, continually, ever, forever, incessantly, invariably, perpetually, unfailingly

con•stel•la•tion \ˌkän-stə-ˈlā-shən\ *n* : any of 88 groups of stars forming patterns
con•ster•na•tion \ˌkän-stər-ˈnā-shən\ *n* : amazement or dismay that hinders or throws into confusion
con•sti•pa•tion \ˌkän-stə-ˈpā-shən\ *n* : abnormally difficult or infrequent bowel movements — **con•sti•pate** \ˈkän-stə-ˌpāt\ *vb*
con•stit•u•en•cy \kən-ˈsti-chə-wən-sē\ *n, pl* **-cies** : a body of constituents; *also* : an electoral district
[1]**con•stit•u•ent** \-wənt\ *n* **1** : a person entitled to vote for a representative for a district **2** ♦ : a component part

♦ component, element, factor, ingredient, member

[2]**constituent** *adj* **1** : COMPONENT **2** : having power to create a government or frame or amend a constitution
con•sti•tute \ˈkän-stə-ˌtüt, -ˌtyüt\ *vb* **-tut•ed; -tut•ing** **1** ♦ : to appoint to an office or duty **2** ♦ : to set up : ESTABLISH ⟨~ a law⟩ **3** ♦ : to make up (the element or elements of which a thing, person, or idea is made up) : COMPOSE

♦ [1] appoint, assign, attach, commission, designate, detail, name ♦ [2] establish, found, inaugurate, initiate, innovate, institute, introduce, launch, pioneer, set up, start ♦ [3] compose, comprise, form, make up

con•sti•tu•tion \ˌkän-stə-ˈtü-shən, -ˈtyü-\ *n* **1** : an established law or custom **2** ♦ : the physical makeup of the individual **3** ♦ : the structure, composition, or makeup of something ⟨~ of the sun⟩ **4** : the basic law in a politically organized body; *also* : a document containing such law

♦ [2] build, figure, form, frame, physique, shape ♦ [3] character, complexion, genius, nature, personality, tone

[1]**con•sti•tu•tion•al** \-shə-nəl\ *adj* **1** : of or relating to the constitution of body or mind **2** : being in accord with the constitution of a state or society; *also* : of or relating to such a constitution
[2]**constitutional** *n* : an exercise (as a walk) taken for one's health
con•sti•tu•tion•al•i•ty \-ˌtü-shə-ˈna-lə-tē, -ˌtyü-\ *n* : the quality or state of being constitutional
con•sti•tu•tion•al•ly *adv* ♦ : with respect to mental or spiritual makeup : with respect to bodily makeup

♦ inherently, innately, intrinsically, naturally

con•sti•tu•tive \ˈkän-stə-ˌtü-tiv, -tyü-; kən-ˈsti-chə-tiv\ *adj* **1** : CONSTRUCTIVE **2** : CONSTITUENT, ESSENTIAL
constr *abbr* construction
con•strain \kən-ˈstrān\ *vb* **1** ♦ : to force by imposed stricture, restriction, or limitation : COMPEL **2** : CONFINE **3** ♦ : to withhold or restrain by force

♦ [1] coerce, compel, drive, force, make, muscle, obligate, oblige, press, pressure ♦ [3] bridle, check, contain, control, curb, govern, inhibit, regulate, rein, restrain, tame

con•straint \-ˈstrānt\ *n* **1 a** : the state of being checked, restricted, or compelled to avoid or perform some action : COMPULSION **b** ♦ : the act or action of using force or threat of force to prevent or condition an action **c** ♦ : a constraining condition, agency, or force : RESTRAINT **2** ♦ : repression of one's natural feelings

♦ [1b] coercion, compulsion, duress, force, pressure ♦ [1c] check, condition, curb, fetter, limitation, restraint, restriction ♦ [2] reserve, restraint, self-control

con•strict \kən-ˈstrikt\ *vb* **1** ♦ **:** to draw together **:** SQUEEZE **2** ♦ **:** to become constricted — **con•stric•tion** \-ˈstrik-shən\ *n* — **con•stric•tive** \-ˈstrik-tiv\ *adj*

♦ [1, 2] compact, compress, condense, contract, squeeze

con•stric•tion \-ˈstrik-shən\ *n* ♦ **:** the act or product of constricting

♦ compression, condensation, contraction

con•stric•tor \kən-ˈstrik-tər\ *n* **:** a snake that coils around and compresses its prey

con•struct \kən-ˈstrəkt\ *vb* ♦ **:** to make or form by combining or arranging parts or elements **:** BUILD, MAKE — **con•struc•tor** \-ˈstrək-tər\ *n*

♦ assemble, build, erect, fabricate, make, make up, piece, put up, raise, rear, set up

con•struc•tion \kən-ˈstrək-shən\ *n* **1** ♦ **:** the act or result of construing, interpreting, or explaining **2 a :** the art, process, or manner of building **b :** something built, created, or established **:** STRUCTURE **3 :** syntactical arrangement of words in a sentence

♦ clarification, elucidation, explanation, explication, exposition, illumination, illustration, interpretation

con•struc•tion•ist \-shə-nist\ *n* **:** a person who construes a legal document (as the U.S. Constitution) in a specific way ⟨a strict ∼⟩

con•struc•tive \-tiv\ *adj* **:** of or relating to construction or creation

con•strue \kən-ˈstrü\ *vb* **con•strued; con•stru•ing 1 :** to analyze the mutual relations of words in a sentence; *also* **:** TRANSLATE **2** ♦ **:** to understand or explain the sense or intention of usually in a particular way or with respect to a given set of circumstances **:** EXPLAIN, INTERPRET — **con•stru•able** *adj*

♦ clarify, clear (up), demonstrate, elucidate, explain, explicate, expound, illuminate, illustrate, interpret, spell out

con•sub•stan•ti•a•tion \ˌkän-səb-ˌstan-chē-ˈā-shən\ *n* **:** the actual substantial presence and combination of the body and blood of Christ with the eucharistic bread and wine

con•sul \ˈkän-səl\ *n* **1 :** a chief magistrate of the Roman republic **2 :** an official appointed by a government to reside in a foreign country to care for the commercial interests of the appointing government's citizens — **con•sul•ar** \-sə-lər\ *adj* — **con•sul•ate** \-lət\ *n* — **con•sul•ship** *n*

con•sult \kən-ˈsəlt\ *vb* **1 :** to ask the advice or opinion of **2** ♦ **:** to deliberate together **:** CONFER — **con•sul•ta•tion** \ˌkän-səl-ˈtā-shən\ *n*

♦ advise, confer, counsel, parley, powwow

con•sul•tant \-ᵊnt\ *n* **:** one who gives professional advice or services

con•sume \kən-ˈsüm\ *vb* **con•sumed; con•sum•ing 1 :** to do away with completely ⟨*consumed* by fire⟩ **2 a :** to spend wastefully **b** ♦ **:** to use up **3 :** to eat up **:** DEVOUR **4 :** to absorb the attention of **:** ENGROSS — **con•sum•able** *adj* — **con•sum•er** *n*

♦ clean, deplete, drain, exhaust, expend, spend, use up

con•sum•er•ism \kən-ˈsü-mə-ˌri-zəm\ *n* **:** the promotion of consumers' interests (as against false advertising)

consumer price index *n* **:** an index measuring the change in the cost of widely purchased goods and services from the cost in some base period

¹con•sum•mate \ˈkän-sə-mət, kən-ˈsə-\ *adj* **1 :** complete in every detail **:** PERFECT **2** ♦ **:** extremely skilled and accomplished **3** ♦ **:** of the highest degree

♦ [2] accomplished, adept, crack, crackerjack, expert, good, great, master, masterful, masterly, proficient, skilled, skillful, virtuoso ♦ [3] maximum, most, nth, paramount, supreme, top, ultimate, utmost

²con•sum•mate \ˈkän-sə-ˌmāt\ *vb* **-mat•ed; -mat•ing** ♦ **:** to make complete **:** FINISH

♦ complete, finalize, finish, perfect

con•sum•ma•tion \ˌkän-sə-ˈmā-shən\ *n* ♦ **:** the ultimate end

♦ close, conclusion, end, ending, finale, finis, finish, windup ♦ accomplishment, achievement, actuality, attainment, fruition, fulfillment, realization

con•sump•tion \kən-ˈsəmp-shən\ *n* **1 :** progressive bodily wasting away; *also* **:** TUBERCULOSIS **2 :** the act of consuming or using up **3 :** the use of economic goods

¹con•sump•tive \-ˈsəmp-tiv\ *adj* **1 :** tending to consume **2 :** relating to or affected with consumption

²consumptive *n* **:** a person who has consumption

cont *abbr* **1** containing **2** contents **3** continent; continental **4** continued **5** control

¹con•tact \ˈkän-ˌtakt\ *n* **1 :** a touching or meeting of bodies **2 :** association or relationship (as in physical or mental or business or social meeting or communication) **:** CONNECTION **3 :** a person serving as a go-between or source of information **4 :** CONTACT LENS

²contact *vb* **1 :** to come or bring into contact **:** TOUCH **2 :** to get in communication with

contact lens *n* **:** a thin lens fitting over the cornea usually to correct vision

con•ta•gion \kən-ˈtā-jən\ *n* **1 :** a contagious disease; *also* **:** the transmission of such a disease **2 :** a disease-producing agent (as a virus) **3 :** transmission of an influence on the mind or emotions

con•ta•gious \-jəs\ *adj* **1** ♦ **:** able to be passed by contact between individuals ⟨colds are ∼⟩ ⟨∼ disease⟩; *also* **:** capable of passing on a contagious disease **2** ♦ **:** communicated or transmitted like a contagious disease; *esp* **:** exciting similar emotion or conduct in others

♦ [1] catching, communicable, transmittable ♦ [2] catching, infectious

con•tain \kən-ˈtān\ *vb* **1** ♦ **:** to keep within limits **:** hold back or hold down **2 :** to have within **:** HOLD **3** ♦ **:** to consist of wholly or in part **:** COMPRISE, INCLUDE — **con•tain•able** \-ˈtā-nə-bəl\ *adj* — **con•tain•ment** *n*

♦ [1] bridle, check, constrain, control, curb, govern, inhibit, regulate, rein, restrain, tame ♦ [3] carry, comprehend, comprise, embrace, encompass, entail, include, involve, number, take in

con•tain•er \kən-ˈtā-nər\ *n* ♦ **:** a receptacle (as a box or jar) for holding goods; *esp* **:** one for shipment of goods

♦ holder, receptacle, vessel

con•tam•i•nant \kən-ˈta-mə-nənt\ *n* ♦ **:** something that contaminates

♦ adulterant, defilement, impurity, pollutant

con•tam•i•nate \kən-ˈta-mə-ˌnāt\ *vb* **-nat•ed; -nat•ing** ♦ **:** to soil, stain, or infect by contact or association — **con•tam•i•na•tion** \-ˌta-mə-ˈnā-shən\ *n*

♦ befoul, defile, foul, poison, pollute, taint ***Ant*** decontaminate, purify

contd *abbr* continued

con•temn \kən-ˈtem\ *vb* **:** to view or treat with contempt **:** DESPISE

con•tem•plate \ˈkän-təm-ˌplāt\ *vb* **-plat•ed; -plat•ing 1** ♦ **:** to view or consider with continued attention **2** ♦ **:** to view as contingent or probable or as an end or intention **:** INTEND

♦ [1] chew over, cogitate, consider, debate, deliberate, entertain, meditate, mull, ponder, question, ruminate, study, think, weigh ♦ [2] aim, aspire, design, intend, mean, meditate, plan, propose

con•tem•pla•tion \ˌkän-təm-ˈplā-shən\ *n* **:** an act of considering with attention

con•tem•pla•tive \kən-ˈtem-plə-tiv, ˈkän-təm-ˌplā-\ *adj* ♦ **:** marked by or given to contemplation

♦ meditative, melancholy, pensive, reflective, ruminant, thoughtful ***Ant*** unreflective

con•tem•po•ra•ne•ous \kən-ˌtem-pə-ˈrā-nē-əs\ *adj* **:** existing, occurring, or originating during the same time **:** CONTEMPORARY

¹con•tem•po•rary \kən-ˈtem-pə-ˌrer-ē\ *adj* **1** ♦ **:** occurring or existing at the same time **2** ♦ **:** marked by characteristics of the present period

♦ [1] coeval, concurrent, simultaneous, synchronous ♦ [2] current, hot, mod, modern, new, newfangled, red-hot, space-age, ultramodern, up-to-date

²contemporary *n* **:** one of the same or nearly the same age as another

con•tempt \kən-ˈtempt\ *n* **1** ♦ **:** the act of despising **:** the state of mind of one who despises **2 :** the state of being despised **3 :** disobedience to or open disrespect of a court or legislature

♦ despite, disdain, scorn ***Ant*** admiration, esteem, regard, respect

con•tempt•ible \kən-ˈtemp-tə-bəl\ *adj* ♦ : deserving contempt : DESPICABLE — **con•tempt•ibly** \-blē\ *adv*

♦ base, despicable, detestable, dirty, dishonorable (*or* dishonourable), ignoble, low, mean, snide, sordid, vile, wretched ♦ despicable, lousy, nasty, pitiful, scabby, scurvy, sorry, wretched ***Ant*** admirable

con•temp•tu•ous \-ˈtemp-chə-wəs\ *adj* ♦ : manifesting, feeling, or expressing contempt — **con•temp•tu•ous•ly** *adv*

♦ degrading, derogatory, disdainful, scornful, uncomplimentary

con•tend \kən-ˈtend\ *vb* **1** ♦ : to strive or vie in contest or rivalry or against difficulties — often used with *with* **2** : to strive in debate : ARGUE **3** ♦ : to affirm in or as if in argument : MAINTAIN, ASSERT

♦ [1] battle, compete, fight, race, vie ♦ *usu* **contend with** [1] cope with, grapple with, handle, manage, maneuver (*or* manoeuvre), negotiate, swing, treat ♦ [3] affirm, allege, argue, assert, aver, avouch, avow, claim, declare, insist, maintain, profess, protest, warrant

con•tend•er *n* ♦ : one that contends

♦ applicant, aspirant, campaigner, candidate, hopeful, prospect, seeker ♦ challenger, competition, competitor, contestant, rival

¹con•tent \kən-ˈtent\ *adj* ♦ : having desires limited to whatever one has : SATISFIED

♦ contented, happy, pleased ***Ant*** discontent, discontented, displeased, dissatisfied, malcontent, unhappy

²content *vb* ♦ : to appease the desires of : SATISFY; *esp* : to limit (oneself) in requirements or actions

♦ delight, gladden, gratify, please, rejoice, satisfy, suit, warm

³content *n* : the quality or state of being contented : CONTENTMENT

⁴con•tent \ˈkän-ˌtent\ *n* **1** : something contained ⟨~*s* of a room⟩ **2** ♦ : subject matter or topics treated (as in a book) **3** : material (as text or music) offered by a Web site **4** : essential meaning or significance **5** : the amount of material contained **6** : the ability to hold, receive, or accommodate

♦ matter, motif, question, subject, theme, topic

con•tent•ed \kən-ˈten-təd\ *adj* ♦ : easy in mind : satisfied especially with one's lot in life — **con•tent•ed•ly** *adv*

♦ content, happy, pleased

con•tent•ed•ness *n* ♦ : the quality or state of being contented

♦ content, contentment, gratification, happiness, pleasure, satisfaction

con•ten•tion \kən-ˈten-chən\ *n* **1** : CONTEST, STRIFE **2** ♦ : an idea or point for which a person argues

♦ argument, assertion, thesis

con•ten•tious \-chəs\ *adj* ♦ : exhibiting an often perverse and wearisome tendency to quarrels and disputes — **con•ten•tious•ly** *adv*

♦ argumentative, disputatious, quarrelsome, scrappy

con•tent•ment \kən-ˈtent-mənt\ *n* ♦ : ease of mind : SATISFACTION

♦ delectation, delight, enjoyment, gladness, gratification, pleasure, relish, satisfaction

con•ter•mi•nous \kän-ˈtər-mə-nəs\ *adj* : having the same or a common boundary — **con•ter•mi•nous•ly** *adv*

¹con•test \kən-ˈtest\ *vb* **1** : to engage in a struggle or competition : COMPETE, VIE **2** ♦ : to make the subject of dispute, contention, or litigation : CHALLENGE, DISPUTE

♦ challenge, dispute, query, question

²con•test \ˈkän-ˌtest\ *n* ♦ : a struggle for superiority or victory

♦ bout, competition, event, game, match, meet, tournament ♦ battle, combat, conflict, confrontation, duel, face-off, rivalry, struggle, tug-of-war, warfare

con•tes•tant \-ˈtes-tənt\ *n* ♦ : one that participates in a contest

♦ challenger, competition, competitor, contender, rival

con•text \ˈkän-ˌtekst\ *n* : the parts of a discourse that surround a word or passage and help to explain its meaning; *also* : the circumstances surrounding an act or event — **con•tex•tu•al•ly** *adv*

con•ti•gu•i•ty \ˌkän-tə-ˈgyü-ə-tē\ *n* ♦ : the quality or state of being contiguous

♦ closeness, immediacy, nearness, proximity

con•tig•u•ous \kən-ˈti-gyə-wəs\ *adj* ♦ : being in contact : TOUCHING; *also* : ADJOINING

♦ adjacent, adjoining, touching

con•ti•nence \ˈkänt-ᵊn-əns\ *n* **1** : SELF-RESTRAINT; *esp* : a refraining from sexual intercourse **2** : the ability to retain urine or feces voluntarily

¹con•ti•nent \ˈkänt-ᵊn-ənt\ *adj* : exercising continence

²continent *n* **1** : any of the great divisions of land on the globe **2** *cap* : the continent of Europe

¹con•ti•nen•tal \ˌkän-tə-ˈnent-ᵊl\ *adj* **1** : of or relating to a continent; *esp, often cap* : of or relating to the continent of Europe **2** *often cap* : of or relating to the colonies later forming the U.S. **3** : of or relating to cuisine based on classical European cooking

²continental *n* **1** *often cap* : a soldier in the Continental army **2** : EUROPEAN

continental drift *n* : a hypothetical slow movement of the continents over a fluid layer deep within the earth

continental shelf *n* : a shallow submarine plain forming a border to a continent

continental slope *n* : a usually steep slope from a continental shelf to the ocean floor

con•tin•gen•cy \kən-ˈtin-jən-sē\ *n, pl* **-cies** ♦ : a chance or possible event

♦ case, event, eventuality, possibility

¹con•tin•gent \-jənt\ *adj* **1** : liable but not certain to happen : POSSIBLE **2** : happening by chance : not planned **3** ♦ : dependent on something that may or may not occur — used with *on* or *upon*

♦ *usu* **contingent on** *or* **contingent upon** conditional, dependent, subject

²contingent *n* : a quota (as of troops) supplied from an area or group

con•tin•u•al \kən-ˈtin-yə-wəl\ *adj* **1** ♦ : continuing indefinitely in time without interruption : CONTINUOUS, UNBROKEN **2** ♦ : steadily recurring

♦ [1] ceaseless, continuous, incessant, unbroken, unceasing, uninterrupted ♦ [2] intermittent, periodic, recurrent

con•tin•u•al•ly *adv* ♦ : in a continual way : in an unceasing or regular way

♦ always, constantly, ever, forever, incessantly, invariably, perpetually, unfailingly

con•tin•u•ance \-yə-wəns\ *n* **1** : unbroken succession **2** : the extent of continuing : DURATION **3** : adjournment of legal proceedings

♦ continuation, duration, endurance, persistence, subsistence

con•tin•u•a•tion \kən-ˌtin-yə-ˈwā-shən\ *n* **1** ♦ : extension or prolongation of a state or activity **2** : resumption after an interruption; *also* : something that carries on after a pause or break

♦ continuance, duration, endurance, persistence, subsistence ***Ant*** ending, termination

con•tin•ue \kən-ˈtin-yü\ *vb* **-tin•ued; -tinu•ing** **1** : to maintain without interruption **2** ♦ : to remain in existence : ENDURE, LAST **3** : to remain in a place or condition **4** ♦ : to resume (as a story) after an intermission **5** : EXTEND; *also* : to persist in **6** : to allow to remain **7** : to keep (a legal case) on the calendar or undecided

♦ [2] abide, endure, hold, keep up, last, persist, run on ***Ant*** cease, desist, discontinue, quit, stop ♦ [4] renew, reopen, restart, resume

con•tin•u•ing *adj* ♦ : needing no renewal : ENDURING

♦ abiding, ageless, dateless, enduring, eternal, everlasting, immortal, imperishable, lasting, perennial, perpetual, timeless, undying

con•ti•nu•i•ty \ˌkän-tə-ˈnü-ə-tē, -ˈnyü-\ *n, pl* **-ties** **1** : the state of being continuous **2** : something that has or provides continuity

con•tin•u•ous \kən-ˈtin-yə-wəs\ *adj* ♦ : continuing without interruption — **con•tin•u•ous•ly** *adv*

♦ ceaseless, continual, incessant, unbroken, unceasing, uninterrupted ***Ant*** noncontinuous

con•tin•u•um \-yə-wəm\ *n, pl* **-ua** \-yə-wə\ *also* **-u•ums** : something that is the same throughout or consists of a series of variations or of a sequence of things in regular order

con•tort \kən-ˈtȯrt\ *vb* ♦ : to twist out of shape

♦ deform, distort, screw, warp

con•tor•tion \-ˈtȯr-shən\ *n* ♦ **:** a twisting into abnormal or grotesque shape

♦ deformation, distortion

con•tor•tion•ist \-ˈtȯr-shə-nist\ *n* **:** an acrobat able to twist the body into unusual postures

con•tour \ˈkän-ˌtu̇r\ *n* **1** ♦ **:** an outline especially of a curving or irregular figure **:** OUTLINE **2 :** SHAPE, FORM — often used in plural ⟨the ~*s* of a statue⟩

♦ outline, silhouette

contr *abbr* contract; contraction

con•tra•band \ˈkän-trə-ˌband\ *n* **:** goods legally prohibited in trade; *also* **:** smuggled goods

con•tra•cep•tion \ˌkän-trə-ˈsep-shən\ *n* **:** intentional prevention of conception and pregnancy — **con•tra•cep•tive** \-ˈsep-tive\ *adj or n*

¹con•tract \ˈkän-ˌtrakt\ *n* **1** ♦ **:** a binding agreement **2 :** an undertaking to win a specified number of tricks in bridge — **con•trac•tu•al** \kən-ˈtrak-chə-wəl\ *adj* — **con•trac•tu•al•ly** *adv*

♦ bond, covenant, guarantee, guaranty, surety, warranty ♦ accord, agreement, bargain, compact, convention, covenant, deal, pact, settlement, understanding

²con•tract \kən-ˈtrakt, *2 usu* ˈkän-ˌtrakt\ *vb* **1** ♦ **:** to become affected with ⟨~ a disease⟩ **2 :** to establish or undertake by contract **3 a** ♦ **:** to reduce to smaller size by or as if by squeezing or forcing together **:** SHRINK, LESSEN; *esp* **:** to draw together especially so as to shorten ⟨~ a muscle⟩ **b** ♦ **:** to become reduced in size or volume **4 :** to shorten (a word) by omitting letters or sounds in the middle — **con•tract•ible** \kən-ˈtrak-tə-bəl, ˈkän-ˌ\ *adj* — **con•trac•tor** \ˈkän-ˌtrak-tər, kən-ˈtrak-\ *n*

♦ [1] catch, come down, get, sicken, take ♦ [3a, 3b] compress, condense, constrict, lessen, shrink *Ant* expand, swell

con•trac•tile \kən-ˈtrakt-ᵊl\ *adj* **:** able to contract — **con•trac•til•i•ty** \ˌkän-ˌtrak-ˈti-lə-tē\ *n*

con•trac•tion \kən-ˈtrak-shən\ *n* ♦ **:** the action or process of contracting

♦ compression, condensation, constriction

con•tra•dict \ˌkän-trə-ˈdikt\ *vb* ♦ **:** to assert the contrary of **:** deny the truth of

♦ deny, disallow, disavow, disclaim, gainsay, negate, negative, reject, repudiate

con•tra•dic•tion \-ˈdik-shən\ *n* ♦ **:** the act or an instance of contradicting

♦ denial, disallowance, disavowal, disclaimer, negation, rejection, repudiation

con•tra•dic•to•ry \-ˈdik-tə-rē\ *adj* ♦ **:** involving, causing, or constituting a contradiction

♦ antipodal, antithetical, contrary, diametric, opposite, polar

con•tra•dis•tinc•tion \ˌkän-trə-dis-ˈtiŋk-shən\ *n* **:** distinction by contrast

con•trail \ˈkän-ˌtrāl\ *n* **:** a streak of condensed water vapor created by an airplane or rocket at high altitudes

con•tra•in•di•cate \ˌkän-trə-ˈin-də-ˌkāt\ *vb* **:** to make (a treatment or procedure) inadvisable — **con•tra•in•di•ca•tion** \-ˌin-də-ˈkā-shən\ *n*

con•tral•to \kən-ˈtral-tō\ *n, pl* **-tos :** the lowest female voice; *also* **:** a singer having such a voice

con•trap•tion \kən-ˈtrap-shən\ *n* ♦ **:** something devised or contrived **:** CONTRIVANCE

♦ contrivance, gadget, gimmick, gizmo, jigger

con•tra•pun•tal \ˌkän-trə-ˈpənt-ᵊl\ *adj* **:** of or relating to counterpoint

con•tra•ri•ety \ˌkän-trə-ˈrī-ə-tē\ *n, pl* **-eties :** the state of being contrary **:** DISAGREEMENT, INCONSISTENCY

con•trari•wise \ˈkän-ˌtrer-ē-ˌwīz, kən-ˈtrer-\ *adv* **1 :** on the contrary **2 :** VICE VERSA

con•trary \ˈkän-ˌtrer-ē; *4 often* kən-ˈtrer-ē\ *adj* **1** ♦ **:** opposite in nature or position **2 :** COUNTER, OPPOSED **3 :** UNFAVORABLE — used of wind or weather **4** ♦ **:** unwilling to accept control or advice — **con•trari•ly** \-ˌtrer-ə-lē, -ˈtrer-\ *adv* — **con•trary** *n is* ˈkän-ˌtrer-ē, *adv is like adj*\ *n or adv*

♦ [1] antipodal, antithetical, contradictory, diametric, opposite, polar ♦ [4] defiant, disobedient, froward, intractable, rebellious, recalcitrant, refractory, unruly, untoward, wayward, willful

¹con•trast \kən-ˈtrast\ *vb* **1 :** to show differences when compared **2 :** to compare in such a way as to show differences

²con•trast \ˈkän-ˌtrast\ *n* **1 :** diversity of adjacent parts in color, emotion, tone, or brightness ⟨the ~ of a photograph⟩ **2** ♦ **:** unlikeness as shown when things are compared **:** DIFFERENCE

♦ difference, disagreement, discrepancy, disparity, distinction, diversity, unlikeness

con•tra•vene \ˌkän-trə-ˈvēn\ *vb* **-vened; -ven•ing 1 :** to go or act contrary to ⟨~ a law⟩ **2 :** CONTRADICT

con•tre•temps \ˈkän-trə-ˌtäⁿ, kōⁿ-trə-ˈtäⁿ\ *n, pl* **con•tre•temps** \-ˌtäⁿ, -ˌtäⁿz\ **:** an inopportune or embarrassing occurrence

contrib *abbr* contribution; contributor

con•trib•ute \kən-ˈtri-byət\ *vb* **-ut•ed; -ut•ing 1** ♦ **:** to give along with others (as to a fund) **2 :** HELP, ASSIST — **con•trib•u•tor** \kən-ˈtri-byə-tər\ *n* — **con•trib•u•to•ry** \-byə-ˌtōr-ē\ *adj*

♦ bestow, chip in, donate, give, kick in, pitch in, present

con•tri•bu•tion \ˌkän-trə-ˈbyü-shən\ *n* **1 :** the act of contributing **2** ♦ **:** the thing contributed

♦ alms, benefaction, beneficence, charity, donation, philanthropy

con•trite \ˈkän-ˌtrīt, kən-ˈtrīt\ *adj* ♦ **:** feeling or showing sorrow and remorse for a sin or shortcoming **:** PENITENT, REPENTANT — **con•trite•ly** *adv*

♦ apologetic, penitent, regretful, remorseful, repentant, rueful, sorry *Ant* impenitent, remorseless, unapologetic, unrepentant

con•tri•tion \kən-ˈtri-shən\ *n* ♦ **:** the state of being contrite

♦ guilt, penitence, remorse, repentance, self-reproach, shame

con•triv•ance \kən-ˈtrī-vəns\ *n* **1** ♦ **:** a mechanical device; *broadly* **:** something contrived, invented, or devised **2 :** SCHEME, PLAN **3 :** the act or faculty of contriving **:** the state of being contrived

♦ contraption, creation, gadget, gimmick, gizmo, invention, jigger

con•trive \kən-ˈtrīv\ *vb* **con•trived; con•triv•ing 1** ♦ **:** to form or create in an artistic or ingenious manner **:** PLAN, DEVISE **2** ♦ **:** to make devices **:** form plans, schemes, or designs **3 :** to bring about with difficulty

♦ [1] concoct, cook up, devise, fabricate, invent, make up, manufacture, plan, think up ♦ [2] conspire, intrigue, machinate, plot, scheme

con•trived \-ˈtrīvd\ *adj* ♦ **:** lacking in natural or spontaneous quality

♦ affected, artificial, assumed, bogus, factitious, fake, false, feigned, mechanical, mock, phony, put-on, sham, spurious, unnatural

con•triv•er *n* **:** one that contrives

¹con•trol \kən-ˈtrōl\ *vb* **con•trolled; con•trol•ling 1** ♦ **:** to exercise restraining or directing influence over **:** REGULATE **2** ♦ **:** to have power over **:** RULE

♦ [1] bridle, check, constrain, contain, curb, govern, inhibit, regulate, rein, restrain, tame ♦ [1] check, circumscribe, confine, curb, inhibit, limit, restrain, restrict ♦ [2] boss, captain, command, govern, preside, rule ♦ [2] administer, carry on, conduct, direct, govern, guide, handle, manage, operate, oversee, regulate, run, superintend, supervise

²control *n* **1** ♦ **:** power to direct or regulate **2 :** the condition of being restrained, checked, or controlled; *also* **:** RESERVE, RESTRAINT **3 :** a device for regulating a mechanism

♦ arm, authority, clutch, command, dominion, grip, hold, mastery, power, sway

con•trol•ler \kən-ˈtrō-lər, ˈkän-ˌtrō-lər\ *n* **1 :** COMPTROLLER **2 :** one that controls

con•tro•ver•sy \ˈkän-trə-ˌvər-sē\ *n, pl* **-sies 1** ♦ **:** a clash of opposing views **2 :** strife through expression of opposing views or claims **:** DISPUTE — **con•tro•ver•sial** \ˌkän-trə-ˌvər-shəl, -sē-əl\ *adj*

♦ difference, disagreement, dispute, dissension

con•tro•vert \ˈkän-trə-ˌvərt, ˌkän-trə-ˈvərt\ *vb* **:** DENY, CONTRADICT — **con•tro•vert•ible** *adj*

con•tu•ma•cious \ˌkän-tü-ˈmā-shəs, -tyü-\ *adj* **:** stubbornly disobedient — **con•tu•ma•cy** \kən-ˈtü-mə-sē, -ˈtyü-; ˈkän-tyə-\ *n* — **con•tu•ma•cious•ly** *adv*

con•tu•me•ly \kən-ˈtü-mə-lē, -ˈtyü-; ˈkän-tə-ˌmē-lē, -tyə-\ *n, pl* **-lies :** contemptuous treatment **:** INSULT

con•tu•sion \kən-ˈtü-zhən, -ˈtyü-\ *n* : BRUISE — **con•tuse** \-ˈtüz, -ˈtyüz\ *vb*
co•nun•drum \kə-ˈnən-drəm\ *n* ♦ : an intricate and difficult problem : RIDDLE

♦ enigma, mystery, mystification, puzzle, puzzlement, riddle, secret

conv *abbr* **1** convention **2** convertible
con•va•lesce \ˌkän-və-ˈles\ *vb* **-lesced; -lesc•ing** ♦ : to recover health gradually — **con•va•les•cent** \-ᵊnt\ *adj or n*

♦ gain, heal, mend, rally, recover, recuperate, snap back

con•va•les•cence \-ᵊns\ *n* ♦ : gradual recovery of health and strength after disease

♦ comeback, rally, recovery, recuperation, rehabilitation

con•vec•tion \kən-ˈvek-shən\ *n* : circulatory motion in a fluid due to warmer portions rising and cooler denser portions sinking; *also* : the transfer of heat by such motion — **con•vec•tion•al** \-shə-nəl\ *adj* — **con•vec•tive** \-ˈvek-tiv\ *adj*
convection oven *n* : an oven with a fan that circulates hot air uniformly and continuously around the food
con•vene \kən-ˈvēn\ *vb* **con•vened; con•ven•ing** **1** ♦ : to come together, meet, or assemble in a group or body : ASSEMBLE, MEET **2** ♦ : to cause (persons) to assemble in a group or body : call or gather together

♦ [1] assemble, cluster, collect, concentrate, conglomerate, congregate, forgather, gather, meet, rendezvous ♦ [2] assemble, call, convoke, muster, summon

con•ve•nience \kən-ˈvē-nyəns\ *n* **1** : SUITABLENESS **2** : a labor-saving device **3** : a suitable time ⟨at your ~⟩ **4** ♦ : personal comfort : EASE

♦ amenity, comfort, luxury

convenience store *n* : a small market that is open long hours
con•ve•nient \-nyənt\ *adj* **1** : suited to personal comfort or ease **2** ♦ : placed near at hand — **con•ve•nient•ly** *adv*

♦ accessible, handy, reachable *Ant* inaccessible, inconvenient, unhandy, unreachable

con•vent \ˈkän-vənt, -ˌvent\ *n* : a local community or house of a religious order especially of nuns — **con•ven•tu•al** \kän-ˈven-chə-wəl\ *adj*
con•ven•ti•cle \kən-ˈven-ti-kəl\ *n* : MEETING; *esp* : a secret meeting for worship
con•ven•tion \kən-ˈven-chən\ *n* **1** ♦ : an agreement especially between states on a matter of common concern **2** : MEETING, ASSEMBLY **3** ♦ : an assembly of delegates convened for some purpose **4** : generally accepted custom, practice, or belief

♦ [1] accord, agreement, bargain, compact, contract, covenant, deal, pact, settlement, understanding ♦ [3] assembly, conference, congress, convocation, council, gathering, get-together, huddle, meeting, powwow, seminar

con•ven•tion•al \-chə-nəl\ *adj* **1** ♦ : sanctioned by general custom **2** : COMMONPLACE, ORDINARY — **con•ven•tion•al•i•ty** \-ˌven-chə-ˈna-lə-tē\ *n* — **con•ven•tion•al•ize** \-ˈven-chə-nə-ˌlīz\ *vb* — **con•ven•tion•al•ly** *adv*

♦ current, customary, popular, standard, stock, usual ♦ classical, customary, traditional

con•verge \kən-ˈvərj\ *vb* **con•verged; con•verg•ing** : to approach one common center or single point — **con•ver•gent** \-jənt\ *adj*
con•ver•gence \kən-ˈvər-jəns\ *n* ♦ : the act of converging

♦ confluence, conjunction, meeting *Ant* divergence

con•ver•sant \kən-ˈvərs-ᵊnt\ *adj* ♦ : having knowledge and experience — used with *with*

♦ *usu* **conversant with** abreast, familiar, informed, knowledgeable, up, up-to-date, versed

con•ver•sa•tion \ˌkän-vər-ˈsā-shən\ *n* ♦ : an informal talking together — **con•ver•sa•tion•al•ly** *adv*

♦ colloquy, dialogue, discourse, discussion, exchange

con•ver•sa•tion•al \-shə-nəl\ *adj* **1** ♦ : inclined to converse : fond of or given to conversation **2** ♦ : of, for, characteristic of, or suited to conversation or oral communication

♦ [1] chatty, gabby, garrulous, loquacious, talkative ♦ [2] colloquial, informal, nonliterary, vernacular, vulgar

con•ver•sa•tion•al•ist \-shə-nᵊl-ist\ *n* : a person who converses a great deal or who excels in conversation

[1]**con•verse** \ˈkän-ˌvərs\ *n* : CONVERSATION
[2]**con•verse** \kən-ˈvərs\ *vb* **con•versed; con•vers•ing** : to engage in conversation
[3]**con•verse** \ˈkän-ˌvərs\ *n* : a statement related to another statement by having its hypothesis and conclusion or its subject and predicate reversed or interchanged
[4]**con•verse** \kən-ˈvərs, ˈkän-ˌvers\ *adj* : reversed in order or relation — **con•verse•ly** *adv*
con•ver•sion \kən-ˈvər-zhən\ *n* **1** ♦ : a change in nature or form **2** : an experience associated with a decisive adoption of religion

♦ changeover, metamorphosis, transfiguration, transformation

[1]**con•vert** \kən-ˈvərt\ *vb* **1** : to turn from one belief or party to another **2** ♦ : to change from one form or function to another : TRANSFORM **3** : MISAPPROPRIATE **4** : EXCHANGE — **con•vert•er** *or* **con•ver•tor** \-ˈvər-tər\ *n*

♦ make over, metamorphose, transfigure, transform

[2]**con•vert** \ˈkän-ˌvərt\ *n* ♦ : one that is converted

♦ adherent, disciple, follower, partisan, pupil, votary

[1]**con•vert•ible** \kən-ˈvər-tə-bəl\ *adj* : capable of being converted
[2]**convertible** *n* : an automobile with a top that may be lowered or removed
con•vex \kän-ˈveks, ˈkän-ˌveks\ *adj* : curved or rounded like the exterior of a sphere or circle — **con•vex•i•ty** \kän-ˈvek-sə-tē\ *n*
con•vey \kən-ˈvā\ *vb* **1** ♦ : to bear from one place to another : CARRY, TRANSPORT **2** ♦ : to transfer or deliver (as property) to another : TRANSMIT, TRANSFER — **con•vey•or** *also* **con•vey•er** \-ər\ *n*

♦ [1] bear, carry, cart, ferry, haul, lug, pack, tote, transport ♦ [2] communicate, impart, spread, transfer, transfuse, transmit

con•vey•ance \-ˈvā-əns\ *n* **1** : the act of conveying **2** : a legal paper transferring ownership of property **3** ♦ : a means of transport : VEHICLE

♦ transport, vehicle

[1]**con•vict** \kən-ˈvikt\ *vb* : to prove or find guilty
[2]**con•vict** \ˈkän-ˌvikt\ *n* : a person serving a prison sentence
con•vic•tion \kən-ˈvik-shən\ *n* **1** : the act of convicting especially in a court **2** ♦ : the state of being convinced **3** ♦ : a strong persuasion or belief

♦ [2] assurance, certainty, certitude, confidence, positiveness, sureness ♦ [3] belief, eye, feeling, judgment (*or* judgement), mind, notion, opinion, persuasion, sentiment, verdict, view

con•vince \kən-ˈvins\ *vb* **con•vinced; con•vinc•ing** ♦ : to bring (as by argument) to belief or action — **con•vinc•ing•ly** *adv*

♦ argue, get, induce, move, persuade, prevail, satisfy, talk, win

con•vinc•ing *adj* ♦ : satisfying or assuring by argument or proof

♦ cogent, compelling, conclusive, decisive, effective, forceful, persuasive, satisfying, strong, telling

con•viv•ial \kən-ˈvi-vē-əl\ *adj* ♦ : enjoying companionship and the pleasures of feasting and drinking — **con•viv•ial•ly** *adv*

♦ boon, companionable, extroverted, gregarious, outgoing, sociable, social *Ant* antisocial, introverted, unsociable

con•viv•i•al•i•ty \-ˌvi-vē-ˈa-lə-tē\ *n* ♦ : convivial activities or behavior

♦ festivity, gaiety, jollification, merriment, merrymaking, revelry

con•vo•ca•tion \ˌkän-və-ˈkā-shən\ *n* **1 a** : a ceremonial assembly (as of the clergy) **b** ♦ : an assembly of persons convoked **2** : the act of convoking

♦ assemblage, assembly, conference, congregation, gathering, meeting, muster

con•voke \kən-ˈvōk\ *vb* **con•voked; con•vok•ing** ♦ : to call together to a meeting

♦ assemble, call, convene, muster, summon

con•vo•lut•ed \ˈkän-və-ˌlü-təd\ *adj* **1** : folded in curved or tortuous windings **2** ♦ : marked by extreme and often needless or excessive complexity : INVOLVED, INTRICATE

♦ complex, complicated, elaborate, intricate, involved, knotty, sophisticated

con•vo•lu•tion \ˌkän-və-ˈlü-shən\ *n* : a tortuous or sinuous structure; *esp* : one of the ridges of the brain
[1]**con•voy** \ˈkän-ˌvȯi, kən-ˈvȯi\ *vb* ♦ : to accompany for protection

♦ accompany, attend, escort, squire

[2]**con·voy** \ˈkän-ˌvȯi\ *n* **1 :** one that convoys; *esp* **:** a protective escort (as for ships) **2 :** the act of convoying **3 :** a group of moving vehicles

con·vulse \kən-ˈvəls\ *vb* **con·vulsed; con·vuls·ing** ♦ **:** to agitate violently

♦ agitate, jolt, jounce, quake, quiver, shake, shudder, vibrate, wobble

con·vul·sion \kən-ˈvəl-shən\ *n* **1 :** an abnormal and violent involuntary contraction or series of contractions of muscle **2** ♦ **:** a violent disturbance

♦ cataclysm, paroxysm, storm, tempest, tumult, upheaval, uproar

con·vul·sive \-siv\ *adj* ♦ **:** resembling a convulsion in being violent, sudden, frantic, or spasmodic — **con·vul·sive·ly** *adv*

♦ stormy, tempestuous, tumultuous

cony *var of* CONEY

coo \ˈkü\ *n* **:** a soft low sound made by doves or pigeons; *also* **:** a sound like this — **coo** *vb*

COO *abbr* chief operating officer

[1]**cook** \ˈku̇k\ *n* **:** a person who prepares food for eating

[2]**cook** *vb* **1 :** to prepare food for eating **2 :** to subject to heat or fire **3** ♦ **:** to devise by thinking **:** FABRICATE — usually used with *up* — **cook·er** *n* — **cook·ware** \-ˌwar\ *n*

♦ *usu* **cook up** concoct, contrive, devise, fabricate, invent, make up, manufacture, think up

cook·book \-ˌbu̇k\ *n* **:** a book of cooking directions and recipes

cook·ery \ˈku̇-kə-rē\ *n, pl* **-er·ies :** the art or practice of cooking

cook·ie *or* **cooky** \ˈku̇-kē\ *n, pl* **cook·ies 1 :** a small sweet flat cake **2** *cookie* **:** a file containing information about a Web site user created and read by a Web site server and stored on the user's computer

cookie–cutter *adj* **:** marked by a lack of originality or distinction ⟨~ malls⟩

cook·out \ˈku̇k-ˌau̇t\ *n* **:** an outing at which a meal is cooked and served in the open

[1]**cool** \ˈkül\ *adj* **1 :** moderately cold **2** ♦ **:** not excited **:** CALM **3** ♦ **:** not friendly **4 :** IMPUDENT **5 :** protecting from heat **6** *slang* **:** very good — **cool·ly** *adv*

♦ [2] calm, collected, composed, placid, self-possessed, serene, tranquil, undisturbed, unperturbed, unshaken, untroubled, unworried ♦ [3] aloof, antisocial, chilly, cold, detached, distant, frosty, remote, standoffish, unfriendly, unsociable *Ant* cordial, friendly, sociable, warm

[2]**cool** *vb* ♦ **:** to make or become cool **:** lose or cause to lose heat, warmth, or passion — sometimes used with *off* or *down*

♦ *sometimes* **cool off** *or* **cool down** calm (down), hush, quiet, settle (down)

[3]**cool** *n* **1 :** a cool time or place **2 :** INDIFFERENCE; *also* **:** SELF-ASSURANCE, COMPOSURE ⟨kept his ~⟩

cool·ant \ˈkü-lənt\ *n* **:** a usually fluid cooling agent

cool·er \ˈkü-lər\ *n* **1 :** a container for keeping food or drink cool **2 :** JAIL, PRISON **3 :** a tall iced drink

coo·lie \ˈkü-lē\ *n* **:** an unskilled laborer usually in or from the Far East

cool·ness *n* ♦ **:** the quality or state of being cool

♦ aplomb, calmness, composure, equanimity, placidity, self-possession, serenity, tranquillity

coon \ˈkün\ *n* **:** RACCOON

coon·hound \-ˌhau̇nd\ *n* **:** a sporting dog trained to hunt raccoons

coon·skin \-ˌskin\ *n* **:** the pelt of a raccoon; *also* **:** something (as a cap) made of this

[1]**coop** \ˈküp, ˈku̇p\ *n* ♦ **:** a small enclosure or building usually for poultry

♦ cage, corral, pen, pound

[2]**coop** *vb* ♦ **:** to confine in or as if in a coop — usually used with *up*

♦ *usu* **coop up** cage, closet, corral, encase, enclose, envelop, fence, hedge, hem, house, immure, pen, wall

co–op \ˈkō-ˌäp\ *n* **:** COOPERATIVE

coo·per \ˈkü-pər, ˈku̇-\ *n* **:** one who makes or repairs barrels or casks — **cooper** *vb* — **coo·per·age** \-pə-rij\ *n*

co·op·er·ate \kō-ˈä-pə-ˌrāt\ *vb* ♦ **:** to act jointly with another or others — **co·op·er·a·tor** \-ˈä-pə-ˌrā-tər\ *n*

♦ affiliate, ally, associate, band, collaborate, combine, concert, confederate, join, league, team, unite

co·op·er·a·tion \-ˌä-pə-ˈrā-shən\ *n* ♦ **:** the act of cooperating **:** a condition marked by cooperating

♦ collaboration, coordination, teamwork

[1]**co·op·er·a·tive** \kō-ˈä-prə-tiv, -ˈä-pə-ˌrā-\ *adj* **1 :** willing to work with others **2 :** of or relating to an association formed to enable its members to buy or sell to better advantage by eliminating middlemen's profits **3** ♦ **:** marked by cooperation

♦ collective, common, communal, concerted, conjoint, joint, mutual, public, united

[2]**cooperative** *n* **:** a cooperative association

co–opt \kō-ˈäpt\ *vb* **1 :** to choose or elect as a colleague **2 :** ABSORB, ASSIMILATE; *also* **:** TAKE OVER

[1]**co·or·di·nate** \kō-ˈȯrd-ᵊn-ət\ *adj* **1 :** equal in rank or order **2 :** of equal rank in a compound sentence ⟨~ clause⟩ **3 :** joining words or word groups of the same rank — **co·or·di·nate·ly** *adv*

[2]**co·or·di·nate** \-ˈȯrd-ᵊn-ˌāt\ *vb* **-nat·ed; -nat·ing 1** ♦ **:** to make or become coordinate **2** ♦ **:** to work or act together harmoniously — **co·or·di·na·tor** \-ˈȯrd-ᵊn-ˌā-tər\ *n*

♦ accommodate, agree, blend, conciliate, conform, harmonize, key, reconcile

[3]**co·or·di·nate** \-ˈȯrd-ᵊn-ət\ *n* **1 :** one of a set of numbers used in specifying the location of a point on a surface or in space **2** *pl* **:** articles (as of clothing) designed to be used together and to attain their effect through pleasing contrast **3** ♦ **:** one who is of equal rank, authority, or importance with another

♦ counterpart, equal, equivalent, fellow, like, match, parallel, peer, rival

co·or·di·na·tion \-ˌȯrd-ᵊn-ˈā-shən\ *n* ♦ **:** the harmonious functioning of parts for effective results

♦ collaboration, cooperation, teamwork

coot \ˈküt\ *n* **1 :** a dark-colored ducklike bird related to the rails **2 :** any of several No. American sea ducks **3 :** a harmless simple person

coo·tie \ˈkü-tē\ *n* **:** a body louse

[1]**cop** \ˈkäp\ *n* ♦ **:** a member of a police force **:** POLICE OFFICER

♦ constable, officer, police officer

[2]**cop** *vb* **1** *slang* **:** to take surreptitiously ⟨~ a glance⟩ **2** *slang* **:** ADMIT — used with *to* ⟨~ to the charges⟩ **3 :** to take up and practice or use **:** ADOPT ⟨~ an attitude⟩

co–pay \ˈkō-ˈpā\ *n* **:** CO-PAYMENT

co–pay·ment \ˈkō-ˌpā-mənt, ˌkō-ˈ\ *n* **:** a fixed fee required of a patient by a health insurer (as an HMO) at the time of each outpatient service or filling of a prescription

[1]**cope** \ˈkōp\ *n* **:** a long cloaklike ecclesiastical vestment

[2]**cope** *vb* **coped; cop·ing** ♦ **:** to struggle to overcome problems or difficulties — usually used with *with*

♦ do, fare, get along, make out, manage, shift ♦ *usu* **cope with** contend with, grapple with, handle, manage, maneuver (*or* manoeuvre), negotiate, swing, treat

copi·er \ˈkä-pē-ər\ *n* **:** one that copies; *esp* **:** a machine for making copies

co·pi·lot \ˈkō-ˌpī-lət\ *n* **:** an assistant pilot of an aircraft or spacecraft

cop·ing \ˈkō-piŋ\ *n* **:** the top layer of a wall

co·pi·ous \ˈkō-pē-əs\ *adj* ♦ **:** present in large quantity **:** LAVISH — **co·pi·ous·ly** *adv* — **co·pi·ous·ness** *n*

♦ lavish, profuse, riotous

cop–out \ˈkäp-ˌau̇t\ *n* ♦ **:** an excuse for copping out; *also* **:** an act of copping out

♦ avoidance, escape, evasion, out

cop out *vb* ♦ **:** to back out (as of an unwanted responsibility)

♦ back down, renege

cop·per \ˈkä-pər\ *n* **1 :** a malleable reddish metallic chemical element that is one of the best conductors of heat and electricity **2 :** a coin or token made of copper — **cop·pery** *adj*

cop·per·head \ˈkä-pər-ˌhed\ *n* **:** a largely coppery brown pit viper especially of the eastern and central U.S.

cop·pice \ˈkä-pəs\ *n* ♦ **:** a thicket, grove, or growth of small trees **:** THICKET

♦ brake, brushwood, chaparral, covert, thicket

co·pra \ˈkō-prə\ *n* **:** dried coconut meat yielding coconut oil

copse \ˈkäps\ *n* **:** a thicket, grove, or growth of small trees **:** THICKET

cop·ter \ˈkäp-tər\ *n* **:** HELICOPTER

cop•u•la \ˈkä-pyə-lə\ *n* : LINKING VERB — **cop•u•la•tive** \-lə-tiv, -ˌlā-\ *adj*
cop•u•late \ˈkä-pyə-ˌlāt\ *vb* **-lat•ed; -lat•ing** : to engage in sexual intercourse — **cop•u•la•to•ry** \ˈkä-pyə-lə-ˌtōr-ē\ *adj*
cop•u•la•tion \ˌkä-pyə-ˈlā-shən\ *n* ♦ : sexual union

♦ intercourse, sexual intercourse

¹copy \ˈkä-pē\ *n, pl* **cop•ies** **1** ♦ : an imitation or reproduction of an original work **2** : material to be set in type

♦ carbon copy, duplicate, duplication, facsimile, imitation, replica, replication, reproduction ***Ant*** original

²copy *vb* **cop•ied; copy•ing** **1** ♦ : to make a copy of **2** ♦ : to attempt to resemble : IMITATE — **copy•ist** *n*

♦ [1] duplicate, imitate, replicate, reproduce ***Ant*** originate ♦ [2] ape, emulate, imitate, mime, mimic

copy•book \ˈkä-pē-ˌbu̇k\ *n* : a book formerly used to teach handwriting containing examples to be copied
copy•boy \-ˌbȯi\ *n* : a person who carries copy and runs errands (as in a newspaper office)
copy•cat \-ˌkat\ *n* : a slavish imitator
copy•desk \-ˌdesk\ *n* : the desk at which newspaper copy is edited
copy editor *n* : one who edits newspaper copy and writes headlines; *also* : one who reads and corrects manuscript copy in a publishing house
copy•read•er \-ˌrē-dər\ *n* : COPY EDITOR
¹copy•right \-ˌrīt\ *n* : the sole right to reproduce, publish, and sell a literary or artistic work
²copyright *vb* : to secure a copyright on
copy•writ•er \ˈkä-pē-ˌrī-tər\ *n* : a writer of advertising copy
co•quet *or* **co•quette** \kō-ˈket\ *vb* **co•quet•ted; co•quet•ting** : FLIRT — **co•quet•ry** \ˈkō-kə-trē, kō-ˈke-trē\ *n*
co•quette \kō-ˈket\ *n* : FLIRT
co•quett•ish *adj* ♦ : having the air or nature of a coquette

♦ coy, demure, kittenish

cor *abbr* corner
Cor *abbr* Corinthians
cor•a•cle \ˈkȯr-ə-kəl\ *n* : a boat made of a frame covered usually with hide or tarpaulin
cor•al \ˈkȯr-əl\ *n* **1** : a stony or horny material that forms the skeleton of colonies of tiny sea polyps and includes a red form used in jewelry; *also* : a coral-forming polyp or polyp colony **2** : a deep pink color — **coral** *adj*
coral snake *n* : any of several venomous chiefly tropical New World snakes brilliantly banded in red, black, and yellow or white
cor•bel \ˈkȯr-bəl\ *n* : a bracket-shaped architectural member that projects from a wall and supports a weight
¹cord \ˈkȯrd\ *n* **1** ♦ : a usually heavy string consisting of several strands woven or twisted together **2** : a long slender anatomical structure (as a tendon or nerve) **3** : a small flexible insulated electrical cable used to connect an appliance with a receptacle **4** : a cubic measure used especially for firewood and equal to a stack 4×4×8 feet **5** : a rib or ridge on cloth

♦ cable, lace, line, rope, string, wire

²cord *vb* **1** : to tie or furnish with a cord **2** : to pile (wood) in cords
cord•age \ˈkȯr-dij\ *n* : ROPES, CORDS; *esp* : ropes in the rigging of a ship
¹cor•dial \ˈkȯr-jəl\ *adj* ♦ : warmly receptive or welcoming — **cor•dial•ly** *adv*

♦ amicable, companionable, comradely, friendly, genial, hearty, neighborly, warm, warmhearted ♦ affable, genial, gracious, hospitable, sociable

²cordial *n* **1** : a stimulating medicine or drink **2** : LIQUEUR
cor•di•al•i•ty \ˌkȯr-jē-ˈa-lə-tē, kȯr-ˈja-\ *n* ♦ : sincere affection and kindness

♦ amity, benevolence, fellowship, friendliness, friendship, goodwill, kindliness

cor•dil•le•ra \ˌkȯr-dəl-ˈyer-ə, -də-ˈler-\ *n* : a series of parallel mountain ranges
cord•less \ˈkȯrd-ləs\ *adj* : having no cord; *esp* : powered by a battery ⟨a ~ phone⟩ — **cord•less** *n*
cor•don \ˈkȯrd-ᵊn\ *n* **1** : an ornamental cord or ribbon **2** : an encircling line (as of troops or police) — **cordon** *vb*
cor•do•van \ˈkȯr-də-vən\ *n* : a soft fine-grained leather
cor•du•roy \ˈkȯr-də-ˌrȯi\ *n, pl* **-roys** : a heavy ribbed fabric; *also, pl* : trousers of this material
cord•wain•er \ˈkȯrd-ˌwā-nər\ *n* : SHOEMAKER
¹core \ˈkōr\ *n* **1 a** : the central usually inedible part of some fruits (as the apple) **b** ♦ : an inmost part of something **2** ♦ : the essential meaning : GIST **3** ♦ : a central or most important part distinct from the enveloping part

♦ [1b, 2] crux, gist, heart, nub, pith, pivot ♦ [3] base, center (*or* centre), cynosure, eye, focus, heart, hub, mecca, nucleus, seat ♦ [3] body, bulk, generality, main, mass ♦ [3] center (*or* centre), midpoint

²core *vb* **cored; cor•ing** : to take out the core of — **cor•er** *n*
CORE \ˈkōr\ *abbr* Congress of Racial Equality
co•re•op•sis \ˌkȯr-ē-ˈäp-səs\ *n, pl* **coreopsis** : any of a genus of widely cultivated composite herbs with showy often yellow flower heads
co•re•spon•dent \ˌkō-ri-ˈspän-dənt\ *n* : a person named as guilty of adultery with the defendant in a divorce suit
co•ri•an•der \ˈkōr-ē-ˌan-dər\ *n* : an herb related to the carrot; *also* : its aromatic dried fruit used as a flavoring
Cor•in•thi•ans \kə-ˈrin-thē-ənz\ *n* : either of two letters written by St. Paul to the Christians of Corinth and included as books in the New Testament
¹cork \ˈkȯrk\ *n* **1** : the tough elastic bark of a European oak (**cork oak**) used especially for stoppers and insulation; *also* : a stopper of this **2** : a tissue of a woody plant making up most of the bark — **corky** *adj*
²cork *vb* : to furnish with or stop up with cork or a cork
cork•screw \ˈkȯrk-ˌskrü\ *n* : a device for drawing corks from bottles
corm \ˈkȯrm\ *n* : a solid bulblike underground part of a stem (as of the crocus or gladiolus)
cor•mo•rant \ˈkȯr-mə-rənt, -ˌrant\ *n* : any of a family of dark-colored water birds with a long neck, hooked bill, and distensible throat pouch
¹corn \ˈkȯrn\ *n* **1** : the seeds of a cereal grass and especially of the chief cereal crop of a region (as wheat in Britain and Indian corn in the U.S.); *also* : a cereal grass **2** : sweet corn served as a vegetable
²corn *vb* : to salt (as beef) in brine and preservatives
³corn *n* : a local hardening and thickening of skin (as on a toe)
¹corn•ball \ˈkȯrn-ˌbȯl\ *n* : an unsophisticated person; *also* : something corny
²cornball *adj* : CORNY
corn bread *n* : bread made with cornmeal
corn•cob \-ˌkäb\ *n* : the woody core on which the kernels of Indian corn are arranged
corn•crib \-ˌkrib\ *n* : a crib for storing ears of Indian corn
cor•nea \ˈkȯr-nē-ə\ *n* : the transparent part of the coat of the eyeball covering the iris and the pupil — **cor•ne•al** *adj*
corn ear•worm \-ˈir-ˌwərm\ *n* : a moth whose larva is destructive especially to Indian corn
¹cor•ner \ˈkȯr-nər\ *n* **1** : the point or angle formed by the meeting of lines, edges, or sides **2** ♦ : the place where two streets come together **3** : a quiet secluded place **4** ♦ : a position from which retreat or escape is impossible **5** : control of enough of the available supply (as of a commodity) to permit manipulation of the price — **cor•nered** *adj* — **around the corner** : ready to take place : about to happen ⟨has a birthday just *around the corner*⟩

♦ [2] crossing, crossroad, intersection ♦ [4] fix, hole, jam, pickle, predicament, spot

²cor•ner *vb* **1** : to drive into a corner **2** : to get a corner on ⟨~ the wheat market⟩ **3** : to turn a corner
cor•ner•stone \ˈkȯr-nər-ˌstōn\ *n* **1** : a stone forming part of a corner in a wall; *esp* : such a stone laid at a formal ceremony **2** ♦ : something of basic importance

♦ base, basis, bedrock, footing, foundation, ground, groundwork, keystone, underpinning

cor•net \kȯr-ˈnet\ *n* : a brass band instrument resembling the trumpet
corn flour *n, Brit* : CORNSTARCH
corn•flow•er \ˈkȯrn-ˌflau̇(-ə)r\ *n* : BACHELOR'S BUTTON
cor•nice \ˈkȯr-nəs\ *n* : the horizontal projecting part crowning the wall of a building
corn•meal \ˈkȯrn-ˌmēl\ *n* : meal ground from corn
corn•row \-ˌrō\ *n* : a section of hair braided flat to the scalp in rows — **cornrow** *vb*
corn•stalk \-ˌstȯk\ *n* : a stalk of Indian corn
corn•starch \-ˌstärch\ *n* : a starch made from corn and used in cookery as a thickening agent
corn syrup *n* : a sweet syrup obtained from cornstarch
cor•nu•co•pia \ˌkȯr-nə-ˈkō-pē-ə, -nyə-\ *n* : a horn-shaped container filled with fruits and grain emblematic of abundance

corny \ˈkȯr-nē\ *adj* **corn•i•er; -est** ♦ **:** tiresomely simple or sentimental

♦ maudlin, mawkish, mushy, saccharine, sappy, schmaltzy, sentimental *Ant* unsentimental

co•rol•la \kə-ˈrä-lə, -ˈrō-\ *n* **:** the petals of a flower
cor•ol•lary \ˈkȯr-ə-ˌler-ē\ *n, pl* **-lar•ies** **1 :** a deduction from a proposition already proved true **2** ♦ **:** something that naturally follows **:** CONSEQUENCE, RESULT

♦ aftermath, conclusion, consequence, development, effect, issue, outcome, outgrowth, product, result, resultant, sequence, upshot

co•ro•na \kə-ˈrō-nə\ *n* **1 :** a colored circle often seen around and close to a luminous body (as the sun or moon) **2 :** the outermost part of the atmosphere of a star (as the sun) — **co•ro•nal** \ˈkȯr-ən-ᵊl, kə-ˈrōn-ᵊl\ *adj*
cor•o•nal \ˈkȯr-ən-ᵊl\ *n* **:** a circlet for the head
¹cor•o•nary \ˈkȯr-ə-ˌner-ē\ *adj* **:** of or relating to the heart or its blood vessels
²coronary *n, pl* **-nar•ies** **1 :** a coronary blood vessel **2 :** CORONARY THROMBOSIS; *also* **:** HEART ATTACK
coronary thrombosis *n* **:** the blocking by a thrombus of one of the arteries supplying the heart tissues
cor•o•na•tion \ˌkȯr-ə-ˈnā-shən\ *n* **:** the act or ceremony of crowning a monarch
cor•o•ner \ˈkȯr-ə-nər\ *n* **:** a public official who investigates causes of deaths possibly not due to natural causes
cor•o•net \ˌkȯr-ə-ˈnet\ *n* **1 :** a small crown **2 :** an ornamental band worn around the temples
corp *abbr* **1** corporal **2** corporation
¹cor•po•ral \ˈkȯr-p(ə-)rəl\ *adj* ♦ **:** of or relating to the body ⟨~ punishment⟩

♦ animal, bodily, carnal, fleshly, material, physical, somatic

²corporal *n* **:** a noncommissioned officer (as in the army) ranking next below a sergeant
cor•po•rate \ˈkȯr-p(ə-)rət\ *adj* **1 :** INCORPORATED; *also* **:** belonging to an incorporated body **2 :** combined into one body
cor•po•ra•tion \ˌkȯr-pə-ˈrā-shən\ *n* **1 :** the municipal authorities of a town or city **2 :** a legal creation authorized to act with the rights and liabilities of a person ⟨a business ~⟩
cor•po•rat•ize \ˈkȯr-pə-rə-ˌtīz\ *vb* **-ized; -iz•ing** **:** to subject to corporate control ⟨~ education⟩
cor•po•re•al \kȯr-ˈpōr-ē-əl\ *adj* **1 :** having, consisting of, or relating to a physical material body **:** PHYSICAL, MATERIAL **2** *archaic* **:** BODILY — **cor•po•re•al•i•ty** \kȯr-ˌpōr-ē-ˈa-lə-tē\ *n* — **cor•po•re•al•ly** *adv*
corps \ˈkōr\ *n, pl* **corps** \ˈkōrz\ **1 :** an organized subdivision of a country's military forces **2** ♦ **:** a group acting under common direction

♦ brotherhood, community, fellowship, fraternity

corpse \ˈkȯrps\ *n* **:** a dead body
corps•man \ˈkōr-mən, ˈkōrz-\ *n* **:** an enlisted man trained to give first aid
cor•pu•lence \ˈkȯr-pyə-ləns\ *n* ♦ **:** excessive fatness **:** OBESITY

♦ fatness, grossness, obesity, plumpness *Ant* leanness, thinness

cor•pu•lent \-lənt\ *adj* ♦ **:** having a large bulky body **:** OBESE

♦ chubby, fat, fleshy, full, gross, obese, overweight, plump, portly, rotund, round

cor•pus \ˈkȯr-pəs\ *n, pl* **cor•po•ra** \-pə-rə\ **1 :** BODY; *esp* **:** CORPSE **2 :** a body of writings or works
cor•pus•cle \ˈkȯr-pə-səl, -ˌpə-\ *n* **1 :** a minute particle **2 :** a living cell (as in blood or cartilage) not aggregated into continuous tissues — **cor•pus•cu•lar** \kȯr-ˈpəs-kyə-lər\ *adj*
cor•pus de•lic•ti \ˌkȯr-pəs-di-ˈlik-ˌtī, -tē\ *n, pl* **corpora delicti** **1 :** the substantial fact proving that a crime has been committed **2 :** the body of a victim of murder
corr *abbr* **1** correct; corrected; correction **2** correspondence; correspondent; corresponding
cor•ral \kə-ˈral\ *n* **1** ♦ **:** an enclosure for confining or capturing animals **2 :** an enclosure of wagons for defending a camp

♦ cage, coop, pen, pound

corral *vb* **corralled; corralling** **1** ♦ **:** to enclose in a corral **2** ♦ **:** to gain or regain control of

♦ [1] cage, closet, coop up, encase, enclose, envelop, fence, hedge, hem, house, immure, pen, wall ♦ [2] bag, capture, catch, collar, get, grab, grapple, hook, land, nab, seize, snare, trap

¹cor•rect \kə-ˈrekt\ *vb* **1** ♦ **:** to make right **2** ♦ **:** to punish (as a child) with a view to reforming or improving **:** CHASTISE **3** ♦ **:** to counteract the activity or effect of — **cor•rect•able** \-ˈrek-tə-bəl\ *adj*

♦ [1] amend, debug, emend, rectify, reform, remedy ♦ [2] castigate, chasten, chastise, discipline, penalize, punish ♦ [3] annul, cancel, compensate, counteract, counterbalance, make up, neutralize, offset

²correct *adj* **1** ♦ **:** conforming to a conventional standard **2** ♦ **:** agreeing with fact or truth **3 :** conforming to the standards of a specific ideology ⟨environmentally ~⟩ — **cor•rect•ness** *n*

♦ [1] decent, decorous, genteel, nice, polite, proper, respectable, seemly ♦ [2] accurate, exact, precise, proper, right, so, true *Ant* false, improper, inaccurate, incorrect, inexact, untrue, wrong

cor•rec•tion \-ˈrek-shən\ *n* **1** ♦ **:** the action or an instance of correcting **2** ♦ **:** a reproving or punishing of faults or deviations from proper actions

♦ [1, 2] castigation, chastisement, desert, discipline, nemesis, penalty, punishment, wrath

cor•rec•tion•al \-ˈrek-sh(ə-)nəl\ *adj* **:** of or relating to correction
cor•rec•tive \-ˈrek-tiv\ *adj* ♦ **:** tending to correct

♦ disciplinary, penal, punitive ♦ reformative, remedial

cor•rect•ly *adv* ♦ **:** in a correct manner

♦ appropriately, fittingly, happily, properly, rightly, suitably

cor•re•late \ˈkȯr-ə-ˌlāt\ *vb* **-lat•ed; -lat•ing** ♦ **:** to connect in a systematic way **:** establish the mutual relations of — **cor•re•late** \-lət, -ˌlāt\ *n* — **cor•re•la•tion** \ˌkȯr-ə-ˈlā-shən\ *n*

♦ associate, connect, identify, link, relate

cor•rel•a•tive \kə-ˈre-lə-tiv\ *adj* **1 :** reciprocally related **2 :** regularly used together (as *either* and *or*) — **correlative** *n* — **cor•rel•a•tive•ly** *adv*
cor•re•spond \ˌkȯr-ə-ˈspänd\ *vb* **1** ♦ **:** to be in agreement **2 :** to communicate by letter **3** ♦ **:** to compare closely — usually used with *to* or *with*

♦ [1] accord, agree, answer, check, coincide, comport, conform, dovetail, fit, go, harmonize, jibe, square, tally ♦ *usu* **correspond to** [3] equal, match, parallel

cor•re•spon•dence \-ˈspän-dəns\ *n* **1** ♦ **:** agreement between particular things **2 :** communication by letters; *also* **:** the letters exchanged

♦ community, likeness, parallelism, resemblance, similarity, similitude

¹cor•re•spon•dent \-dənt\ *adj* **1** ♦ **:** having or participating in the same relationship (as kind, degree, position, correspondence, or function) **:** SIMILAR **2** ♦ **:** of a kind appropriate to the situation — used with *with* or *to*

♦ [1] akin, alike, analogous, comparable, like, parallel, similar, such ♦ *usu* **correspondent with** *or* **correspondent to** [2] compatible, conformable (to), congruous, consistent, consonant, harmonious

²correspondent *n* **1 :** something that corresponds **2 :** a person with whom one communicates by letter **3** ♦ **:** a person employed to contribute news regularly from a place

♦ journalist, newsman, reporter

cor•re•spond•ing•ly *adv* ♦ **:** in a corresponding manner

♦ alike, also, likewise, similarly, so

cor•ri•dor \ˈkȯr-ə-dər, -ˌdȯr\ *n* **1** ♦ **:** a passageway into which compartments or rooms open (as in a hotel or school) **2 :** a narrow strip of land especially through foreign-held territory **3 :** a densely populated strip of land including two or more major cities

♦ gallery, hall, hallway, passage

cor•ri•gen•dum \ˌkȯr-ə-ˈjen-dəm\ *n, pl* **-da** \-də\ **:** an error in a printed work discovered after printing and shown with its correction on a separate sheet
cor•ri•gi•ble \ˈkȯr-ə-jə-bəl\ *adj* **:** CORRECTABLE
cor•rob•o•rate \kə-ˈrä-bə-ˌrāt\ *vb* **-rat•ed; -rat•ing** ♦ **:** to support with evidence **:** CONFIRM

♦ bear out, confirm, substantiate, support, validate, verify, vindicate

cor•rob•o•ra•tion \-ˌrä-bə-ˈrā-shən\ *n* ♦ **:** something that corroborates

♦ attestation, confirmation, documentation, evidence, proof, substantiation, testament, testimony, validation, witness

cor·rob·o·ra·tive \-ˈrä-bə-ˌrā-tiv, -ˈrä-brə-\ *adj* ♦ **:** serving or tending to corroborate

♦ confirmatory *Ant* confuting, disproving, refuting

cor·rob·o·ra·to·ry \-ˈrä-bə-rə-ˌtōr-ē\ *adj* **:** serving or tending to corroborate

cor·rode \kə-ˈrōd\ *vb* **cor·rod·ed; cor·rod·ing** ♦ **:** to wear or be worn away gradually (as by chemical action) — **cor·ro·sion** \-ˈrō-zhən\ *n* — **cor·ro·sive** \-ˈrō-siv\ *adj or n*

♦ bite, eat, erode, fret

cor·ru·gate \ˈkȯr-ə-ˌgāt\ *vb* **-gat·ed; -gat·ing :** to form into wrinkles or ridges and grooves — **cor·ru·gat·ed** *adj* — **cor·ru·ga·tion** \ˌkȯr-ə-ˈgā-shən\ *n*

[1]**cor·rupt** \kə-ˈrəpt\ *vb* **1 a** ♦ **:** to make evil **:** DEPRAVE **b :** BRIBE **2** ♦ **:** to undergo decomposition from the action of bacteria or fungi **:** ROT, SPOIL

♦ [1a] debase, degrade, demean, demoralize, humble, subvert, warp ♦ [2] break down, decay, decompose, disintegrate, molder, putrefy, rot, spoil

[2]**corrupt** *adj* ♦ **:** morally degenerate; *also* **:** characterized by improper conduct ⟨~ officials⟩

♦ debauched, decadent, degenerate, dissolute, perverse, perverted, reprobate

cor·rupt·ible *adj* ♦ **:** capable of being corrupted

♦ bribable, purchasable, venal

cor·rup·tion \-ˈrəp-shən\ *n* **1** ♦ **:** impairment of integrity, virtue, or moral principle **2** ♦ **:** the process of rotting

♦ [1] debasement, debauchery, decadence, degeneracy, degeneration, degradation, demoralization, depravity, dissipation, dissoluteness, perversion ♦ [2] breakdown, decay, decomposition, putrefaction, rot, spoilage

cor·sage \kȯr-ˈsäzh, -ˈsäj\ *n* **1 :** the waist or bodice of a dress **2 :** a bouquet to be worn or carried

cor·sair \ˈkȯr-ˌsar\ *n* ♦ **:** one who commits or practices piracy **:** PIRATE

♦ buccaneer, freebooter, pirate, rover

cor·set \ˈkȯr-sət\ *n* **:** a stiffened undergarment worn for support or to give shape to the waist and hips

cor·tege *also* **cor·tège** \kȯr-ˈtezh, ˈkȯr-ˌtezh\ *n* **1 :** PROCESSION; *esp* **:** a funeral procession **2** ♦ **:** a train of attendants

♦ following, retinue, suite, train

cor·tex \ˈkȯr-ˌteks\ *n, pl* **cor·ti·ces** \ˈkȯr-tə-ˌsēz\ *or* **cor·tex·es :** an outer or covering layer of an organism or one of its parts ⟨the adrenal ~⟩ ⟨~ of a plant stem⟩; *esp* **:** CEREBRAL CORTEX — **cor·ti·cal** \ˈkȯr-ti-kəl\ *adj*

cor·ti·co·ste·roid \ˌkȯr-ti-kō-ˈstir-ˌȯid, -ˈster-\ *n* **:** any of various steroids made in the adrenal cortex and used medically as anti-inflammatory agents

cor·ti·sone \ˈkȯr-tə-ˌsōn, -ˌzōn\ *n* **:** an adrenal hormone used in treating rheumatoid arthritis

co·run·dum \kə-ˈrən-dəm\ *n* **:** a very hard aluminum-containing mineral used as an abrasive or as a gem

cor·us·cate \ˈkȯr-ə-ˌskāt\ *vb* **-cat·ed; -cat·ing :** FLASH, SPARKLE — **cor·us·ca·tion** \ˌkȯr-ə-ˈskā-shən\ *n*

cor·vette \kȯr-ˈvet\ *n* **1 :** a naval sailing ship smaller than a frigate **2 :** an armed escort ship smaller than a destroyer

co·ry·za \kə-ˈrī-zə\ *n* **:** an inflammatory disorder of the upper respiratory tract; *esp* **:** COMMON COLD

cos *abbr* cosine

COS *abbr* **1** cash on shipment **2** chief of staff

co·sig·na·to·ry \kō-ˈsig-nə-ˌtōr-ē\ *n* **:** a joint signer

co·sign·er \ˈkō-ˌsī-nər\ *n* **:** COSIGNATORY; *esp* **:** a joint signer of a promissory note

co·sine \ˈkō-ˌsīn\ *n* **:** the trigonometric function that is the ratio between the side next to an acute angle in a right triangle and the hypotenuse

[1]**cos·met·ic** \käz-ˈme-tik\ *adj* **1 :** intended to beautify the hair or complexion **2 :** correcting physical defects especially to improve appearance ⟨~ dentistry⟩ **3 :** SUPERFICIAL

[2]**cosmetic** *n* **:** a cosmetic preparation

cos·me·tol·o·gist \ˌkäz-mə-ˈtä-lə-jist\ *n* **:** one who gives beauty treatments — **cos·me·tol·o·gy** \-jē\ *n*

cos·mic \ˈkäz-mik\ *also* **cos·mi·cal** \-mi-kəl\ *adj* **1 :** of or relating to the cosmos **2 :** characterized by greatness especially in extent, intensity, or comprehensiveness **:** VAST, GRAND — **cos·mi·cal·ly** *adv*

cosmic ray *n* **:** a stream of very penetrating atomic nuclei that enter the earth's atmosphere from outer space

cos·mog·o·ny \käz-ˈmä-gə-nē\ *n, pl* **-nies :** the origin or creation of the world or universe

cos·mol·o·gy \-ˈmä-lə-jē\ *n, pl* **-gies :** a branch of astronomy dealing with the origin and structure of the universe — **cos·mo·log·i·cal** \ˌkäz-mə-ˈlä-ji-kəl\ *adj* — **cos·mol·o·gist** \käz-ˈmä-lə-jist\ *n*

cos·mo·naut \ˈkäz-mə-ˌnȯt\ *n* **:** a Soviet or Russian astronaut

cos·mo·pol·i·tan \ˌkäz-mə-ˈpä-lət-ᵊn\ *adj* ♦ **:** belonging to all the world **:** not local — **cosmopolitan** *n*

♦ smart, sophisticated, worldly, worldly-wise

cos·mos \ˈkäz-məs, *1 also* -ˌmōs, -ˌmäs\ *n* **1** ♦ **:** the whole body of things and phenomena observed or postulated **:** UNIVERSE **2 :** a tall garden herb related to the daisies

♦ creation, macrocosm, nature, universe, world

co·spon·sor \ˈkō-ˌspän-sər, -ˈspän-\ *n* **:** a joint sponsor — **cosponsor** *vb*

Cos·sack \ˈkä-ˌsak, -sək\ *n* **:** a member of one of several autonomous communities drawn from various ethnic groups in southern Russia; *also* **:** a mounted soldier from one of these communities

[1]**cost** \ˈkȯst\ *n* **1** ♦ **:** the amount paid or charged for something **2 :** the loss or penalty incurred in gaining something ⟨knowledge is gained at the ~ of innocence⟩ **3** *pl* **:** expenses incurred in a law suit — **at all costs :** regardless of consequences ⟨win *at all costs*⟩

♦ disbursement, expenditure, expense, outgo, outlay ♦ charge, fee, figure, price

[2]**cost** *vb* **cost; cost·ing 1 :** to require a specified amount in payment **2 :** to cause to pay, suffer, or lose **3** ♦ **:** to have a price of

♦ bring, fetch, go, sell

co–star \ˈkō-ˌstär\ *n* **:** one of two leading players in a motion picture or play — **co–star** *vb*

Cos·ta Ri·can \ˌkäs-tə-ˈrē-kən\ *n* **:** a native or inhabitant of Costa Rica — **Costa Rican** *adj*

cos·tive \ˈkäs-tiv\ *adj* **:** affected with or causing constipation

cost·ly \ˈkȯst-lē\ *adj* **cost·li·er; -est 1** ♦ **:** of great cost or value **:** not cheap **2 :** done at great expense or sacrifice ⟨a ~ error⟩ — **cost·li·ness** *n*

♦ dear, expensive, high, precious, valuable *Ant* cheap, inexpensive

cos·tume \ˈkäs-ˌtüm, -ˌtyüm\ *n* **1 :** the style of attire characteristic of a period or country **2 :** an outfit worn to create the appearance characteristic of a particular period, person, place, or thing ⟨Halloween ~*s*⟩ — **cos·tum·er** \ˈkäs-ˌtü-mər, -ˌtyü-\ *n*

costume jewelry *n* **:** inexpensive jewelry

cosy *chiefly Brit var of* COZY

[1]**cot** \ˈkät\ *n* **:** a small house **:** COTTAGE

[2]**cot** *n* **:** a small often collapsible bed

cote \ˈkōt, ˈkät\ *n* **:** a small shed or coop (as for sheep or doves)

co·te·rie \ˈkō-tə-ˌrē, ˌkō-tə-ˈrē\ *n* ♦ **:** an intimate often exclusive group of persons with a common interest

♦ circle, clan, clique, crowd, fold, gang, ring, set

co·ter·mi·nous \ˌko-ˈtər-mə-nəs\ *adj* **:** having the same scope or duration

co·til·lion \kō-ˈtil-yən, kə-\ *n* **:** a formal ball

cot·tage \ˈkä-tij\ *n* ♦ **:** a small house — **cot·tag·er** *n*

♦ cabin, camp, chalet, lodge

cottage cheese *n* **:** a soft uncured cheese made from soured skim milk

cot·ter *or* **cot·tar** \ˈkä-tər\ *n* **:** a peasant or farm laborer occupying a cottage and often a small holding

cotter pin *n* **:** a metal strip bent into a pin whose ends can be spread apart after insertion through a hole or slot

cot·ton \ˈkä-tᵊn\ *n* **1 :** a soft fibrous usually white substance composed of hairs attached to the seeds of various tropical plants related to the mallow; *also* **:** this plant **2 :** thread or cloth made of cotton

cotton candy *n* **:** a candy made of spun sugar

cot·ton·mouth \ˈkät-ᵊn-ˌmau̇th\ *n* **:** WATER MOCCASIN

cot·ton·seed \-ˌsēd\ *n* **:** the seed of the cotton plant yielding a protein-rich meal and a fatty oil (**cottonseed oil**) used especially in cooking

cot•ton•tail \-ˌtāl\ *n* **:** a No. American rabbit with a white-tufted tail
cot•ton•wood \-ˌwu̇d\ *n* **:** a poplar having seeds with cottony hairs
cot•tony *adj* ♦ **:** resembling cotton in appearance or character

♦ downy, satiny, silken, soft, velvety

cot•y•le•don \ˌkä-tə-ˈlēd-ᵊn\ *n* **:** the first leaf or one of the first pair or whorl of leaves developed by a seed plant
¹couch \ˈkau̇ch\ *vb* **1 :** to lie or place on a couch **2** ♦ **:** to phrase in a specified manner

♦ articulate, clothe, express, formulate, phrase, put, say, state, word

²couch *n* ♦ **:** a piece of furniture (as a bed or sofa) that one can sit or lie on

♦ davenport, divan, lounge, settee, sofa

couch•ant \ˈkau̇-chənt\ *adj* **:** lying down with the head raised ⟨coat of arms with lion ~⟩
couch potato *n* **:** one who spends a great deal of time watching television
cou•gar \ˈkü-gər\ *n, pl* **cougars** *also* **cougar** ♦ **:** a large powerful tawny brown wild American cat

♦ mountain lion, panther

cough \ˈkȯf\ *vb* **:** to force air from the lungs with short sharp noises; *also* **:** to expel by coughing — **cough** *n*
could \kəd, ˈku̇d\ *past of* CAN — used as an auxiliary in the past or as a polite or less forceful alternative to *can* in the present
cou•lee \ˈkü-lē\ *n* **1 :** a small stream **2 :** a dry streambed **3 :** GULLY
cou•lomb \ˈkü-ˌläm, -ˌlōm\ *n* **:** a unit of electric charge equal to the electricity transferred by a current of one ampere in one second
coun•cil \ˈkau̇n-səl\ *n* **1** ♦ **:** an assembly or meeting for consultation, advice, or discussion **2 :** an official body of lawmakers ⟨city ~⟩ **3** ♦ **:** an association of persons for some common object usually jointly supported and meeting periodically — **coun•cil•lor** *or* **coun•cil•or** \-sə-lər\ *n* — **coun•cil•man** \-səl-mən\ *n* — **coun•cil•wom•an** \-ˌwu̇-mən\ *n*

♦ [1] assembly, conference, congress, convention, convocation, gathering, get-together, huddle, meeting, powwow, seminar ♦ [3] association, brotherhood, club, college, congress, fellowship, fraternity, guild, institute, institution, league, order, organization, society

¹coun•sel \ˈkau̇n-səl\ *n* **1 :** ADVICE **2 :** a plan of action **3 :** deliberation together **4** *pl* **counsel** ♦ **:** one who gives professional advice or services **:** LAWYER

♦ advocate, attorney, lawyer

²counsel *vb* **-seled** *or* **-selled; -sel•ing** *or* **-sel•ling 1** ♦ **:** to give advice to **2** ♦ **:** to ask the advice or opinion of **:** CONSULT

♦ [1] coach, guide, lead, mentor, pilot, shepherd, show, tutor ♦ [2] advise, confer, consult, parley

coun•sel•or *or* **coun•sel•lor** \ˈkau̇n-sə-lər\ *n* **1 :** a person who gives advice or counseling **:** ADVISER **2 :** one that gives advice in law and manages cases for clients in court **:** LAWYER **3 :** one who has supervisory duties at a summer camp
¹count \ˈkau̇nt\ *vb* **1** ♦ **:** to name or indicate one by one in order to find the total number **2 :** to recite numbers in order **3** ♦ **:** to take into account **:** CONSIDER, ACCOUNT **4** ♦ **:** to rely or depend on someone or something **:** RELY — used with *on* ⟨you can ~ on me⟩ **5** ♦ **:** to be of value or account **6** ♦ **:** to exclude by or as if by counting — used with *out* ⟨~ him *out*⟩ **7 :** to include by as if by counting — used with *in* ⟨~ me *in*⟩ — **count•able** *adj*

♦ [1] enumerate, number, tell ♦ [3] account, consider, esteem, hold, rate, reckon, regard, take ♦ *usu* **count on** [4] depend, lean, reckon, rely ♦ [5] import, matter, mean, signify, weigh ♦ *usu* **count out** [6] ban, bar, debar, eliminate, except, exclude, rule out

²count *n* **1 :** the act of counting; *also* **:** the total obtained by counting **2** ♦ **:** a particular charge in an indictment or legal declaration

♦ charge, complaint, indictment, rap

³count *n* **:** a European nobleman whose rank corresponds to that of a British earl
count•down \ˈkau̇nt-ˌdau̇n\ *n* **:** a backward counting in fixed units (as seconds) to indicate the time remaining before an event (as the launching of a rocket) — **count down** *vb*

¹coun•te•nance \ˈkau̇nt-ᵊn-əns\ *n* **1** ♦ **:** the human face **2 :** FAVOR, APPROVAL **3** ♦ **:** the expression of the face

♦ [1] face, mug, visage ♦ [3] cast, expression, face, look, visage

²countenance *vb* **-nanced; -nanc•ing** ♦ **:** to extend approval or toleration to **:** SANCTION, TOLERATE

♦ accept, approve, care, favor (*or* favour), OK, sanction, subscribe ♦ abide, bear, brook, endure, meet, stand, stick out, stomach, support, sustain, take, tolerate

¹count•er \ˈkau̇n-tər\ *n* **1 :** a piece (as of metal or plastic) used in reckoning or in games **2 :** a level surface over which business is transacted, food is served, or work is conducted
²count•er *n* **:** a device for recording a number or amount
³coun•ter *vb* ♦ **:** to act in opposition to

♦ battle, combat, contend, fight, oppose

⁴coun•ter *adv* **:** in an opposite direction **:** CONTRARY
⁵coun•ter *n* **1 :** OPPOSITE, CONTRARY **2 :** an answering or offsetting force or blow
⁶coun•ter *adj* **:** marked by or tending toward or in an opposite direction or effect **:** CONTRARY, OPPOSITE
coun•ter•act \ˌkau̇n-tər-ˈakt\ *vb* ♦ **:** to lessen the force of **:** OFFSET — **coun•ter•ac•tive** \-ˈak-tiv\ *adj*

♦ annul, cancel, compensate, correct, counterbalance, make up, neutralize, offset

coun•ter•at•tack \ˈkau̇n-tər-ə-ˌtak\ *n* **:** an attack made to oppose an enemy's attack — **counterattack** *vb*
¹coun•ter•bal•ance \ˈkau̇n-tər-ˌba-ləns\ *n* ♦ **:** a weight or influence that balances another

♦ balance, canceler, counterweight, equipoise, offset

²counterbalance \ˌkau̇n-tər-ˈba-ləns\ *vb* **:** to oppose with equal weight or influence
coun•ter•claim \ˈkau̇n-tər-ˌklām\ *n* **:** an opposing claim especially in law
coun•ter•clock•wise \ˌkau̇n-tər-ˈkläk-ˌwīz\ *adv* **:** in a direction opposite to that in which the hands of a clock rotate — **counterclockwise** *adj*
coun•ter•cul•ture \ˈkau̇n-tər-ˌkəl-chər\ *n* **:** a culture especially of the young with values and mores that run counter to those of established society
coun•ter•es•pi•o•nage \ˌkau̇n-tər-ˈes-pē-ə-ˌnäzh, -nij\ *n* **:** activities intended to discover and defeat enemy espionage
¹coun•ter•feit \ˈkau̇n-tər-ˌfit\ *adj* **1 :** not genuine or real **2** ♦ **:** made in imitation of something else with intent to deceive

♦ bogus, fake, false, inauthentic, phony, sham, spurious, unauthentic *Ant* authentic, bona fide, genuine, real

²counterfeit *vb* **1 :** to copy or imitate in order to deceive **2** ♦ **:** to imitate or feign especially with intent to deceive **:** PRETEND, FEIGN — **coun•ter•feit•er** *n*

♦ affect, assume, fake, feign, pretend, profess, put on, sham, simulate

³counterfeit *n* ♦ **:** something counterfeit **:** FORGERY

♦ fake, forgery, hoax, humbug, phony, sham

coun•ter•in•sur•gen•cy \ˌkau̇n-tər-in-ˈsər-jən-sē\ *n* **:** military activity designed to deal with insurgents
coun•ter•in•tel•li•gence \-in-ˈte-lə-jəns\ *n* **:** organized activities of an intelligence service designed to counter the activities of an enemy's intelligence service
coun•ter•in•tu•i•tive \-in-ˈtü-ə-tiv, -ˈtyü-\ *adj* **:** contrary to what would intuitively be expected
coun•ter•man \ˈkau̇n-tər-ˌman, -mən\ *n* **:** one who tends a counter
coun•ter•mand \ˈkau̇nt-ər-ˌmand\ *vb* **:** to withdraw (an order already given) by a contrary order
coun•ter•mea•sure \-ˌme-zhər\ *n* **:** an action or device designed to counter another
coun•ter•of•fen•sive \-ə-ˌfen-siv\ *n* **:** a large-scale counterattack
coun•ter•pane \-ˌpān\ *n* ♦ **:** a usually ornamental cloth cover for a bed **:** BEDSPREAD

♦ bedspread, spread

coun•ter•part \-ˌpärt\ *n* ♦ **:** a person or thing very closely like or corresponding to another person or thing

♦ coordinate, equal, equivalent, fellow, like, match, parallel, peer, rival ♦ carbon copy, double, duplicate, duplication, facsimile, image, likeness, match, picture, replica, ringer, spit

coun•ter•point \-ˌpȯint\ *n* : music in which one melody is accompanied by one or more other melodies all woven into a harmonious whole

coun•ter•poise \-ˌpȯiz\ *n* : a force or influence that offsets or checks an opposing force : COUNTERBALANCE

coun•ter•rev•o•lu•tion \ˌkau̇n-tər-ˌre-və-ˈlü-shən\ *n* : a revolution opposed to a current or earlier one — **coun•ter•rev•o•lu•tion•ary** \-shə-ˌner-ē\ *adj or n*

coun•ter•sign \ˈkau̇n-tər-ˌsīn\ *n* **1** : a confirmatory signature added to a writing already signed by another person **2** : a military secret signal that must be given by a person who wishes to pass a guard — **countersign** *vb*

coun•ter•sink \-ˌsiŋk\ *vb* **-sunk** \-ˌsəŋk\; **-sink•ing** **1** : to form a funnel-shaped enlargement at the outer end of a drilled hole **2** : to set the head of (as a screw) at or below the surface — **countersink** *n*

coun•ter•spy \-ˌspī\ *n* : a spy engaged in counterespionage

coun•ter•ten•or \-ˌte-nər\ *n* : a tenor with an unusually high range

coun•ter•vail \ˌkau̇n-tər-ˈvāl\ *vb* : COUNTERACT

coun•ter•weight \ˈkau̇n-tər-ˌwāt\ *n* ♦ : a force or influence that offsets or checks an opposing force : COUNTERBALANCE

♦ balance, canceler, counterbalance, equipoise, offset

count•ess \ˈkau̇n-təs\ *n* **1** : the wife or widow of a count or an earl **2** : a woman holding the rank of a count or an earl in her own right

count•ing•house \ˈkau̇n-tiŋ-ˌhau̇s\ *n* : a building or office for keeping books and conducting business

count•less \ˈkau̇nt-ləs\ *adj* ♦ : too numerous to be counted : INNUMERABLE

♦ innumerable, numberless, uncountable, unnumbered, untold ***Ant*** countable

coun•tri•fied *also* **coun•try•fied** \ˈkən-tri-ˌfīd\ *adj* **1** : RURAL, RUSTIC **2** : UNSOPHISTICATED **3** : played or sung in the manner of country music

[1]coun•try \ˈkən-trē\ *n, pl* **countries** **1** : REGION, DISTRICT **2** ♦ : the land of a person's birth, residence, or citizenship : FATHERLAND **3** ♦ : a nation or its territory **4** : rural regions as opposed to towns and cities **5** : COUNTRY MUSIC

♦ [2] fatherland, home, homeland, motherland, sod ♦ [3] commonwealth, land, nation, sovereignty, state

[2]country *adj* **1** ♦ : of, relating to, or characteristic of the country : RURAL **2** : of or relating to country music ⟨a ~ singer⟩

♦ bucolic, pastoral, rural, rustic

country and western *n* : COUNTRY MUSIC

country club *n* : a suburban club for social life and recreation; *esp* : one having a golf course — **country–club** *adj*

coun•try–dance \ˈkən-trē-ˌdans\ *n* : an English dance in which partners face each other especially in rows

coun•try•man \ˈkən-trē-mən, *2 often* -ˌman\ *n* **1** : an inhabitant of a specified country **2** : COMPATRIOT **3** : one raised or living in the country : RUSTIC

country music *n* : music derived from or imitating the folk style of the southern U.S. or of the Western cowboy

coun•try•side \ˈkən-trē-ˌsīd\ *n* : a rural area or its people

coun•ty \ˈkau̇n-tē\ *n, pl* **counties** **1** : the domain of a count **2** : a territorial division of a country or state for purposes of local government

coup \ˈkü\ *n, pl* **coups** \ˈküz\ **1** ♦ : a highly successful stroke, action, plan, or stratagem **2** : COUP D'ÉTAT

♦ accomplishment, achievement, attainment, success, triumph

coup de grace \ˌkü-də-ˈgräs\ *n, pl* **coups de grace** *same*\ : DEATHBLOW; *also* : a final decisive stroke or event

coup d'état \ˌkü-də-ˈtä\ *n, pl* **coups d'état** *same or* -ˈtäz\ : a sudden violent overthrow of a government by a small group

cou•pé *or* **coupe** \kü-ˈpā, *2 often* ˈküp\ *n* **1** : a closed horse-drawn carriage for two persons inside with an outside seat for the driver **2** *usu coupe* : a 2-door automobile with an enclosed body

[1]cou•ple \ˈkə-pəl\ *n* **1** : two persons closely associated; *esp* : a man and a woman married or otherwise paired **2** ♦ : two of the same kind considered together : PAIR **3** : BOND, TIE **4** : an indefinite small number : FEW ⟨a ~ of days ago⟩

♦ brace, duo, pair, twain, twosome

[2]couple *vb* **cou•pled; cou•pling** ♦ : to link together

♦ associate, combine, conjoin, connect, hitch, hook, join, link, marry, unify, unite, yoke

cou•plet \ˈkə-plət\ *n* : two successive rhyming lines of verse

cou•pling \ˈkə-pliŋ (*usual for 2*), -pə-liŋ\ *n* **1** ♦ : the act of bringing or coming together : CONNECTION; *also* : the point at which things are connected **2** : a device for connecting two parts or things

♦ combination, connection, consolidation, junction, unification, union

cou•pon \ˈkü-ˌpän, ˈkyü-\ *n* **1** : a statement attached to a bond showing interest due and designed to be cut off and presented for payment **2** : a form surrendered in order to obtain an article, service, or accommodation **3** : a printed document or slip used to submit orders or inquiries or to obtain a discount on merchandise or services

cour•age \ˈkər-ij\ *n* ♦ : ability to conquer fear or despair : BRAVERY, VALOR

♦ bravery, daring, fearlessness, gallantry, guts, hardihood, heart, heroism, nerve, stoutness, valor ***Ant*** cowardice

cou•ra•geous \kə-ˈrā-jəs\ *adj* ♦ : having or characterized by courage — **cou•ra•geous•ly** *adv*

♦ brave, dauntless, doughty, fearless, gallant, greathearted, heroic, intrepid, lionhearted, manful, stalwart, stout, undaunted, valiant, valorous

cou•ri•er \ˈku̇r-ē-ər, ˈkər-ē-\ *n* ♦ : one who bears messages or information especially for the diplomatic or military services

♦ go-between, messenger, page, runner

[1]course \ˈkōrs\ *n* **1 a** : the act or action of moving in a path from point to point : PROGRESS, PASSAGE **b** ♦ : direction of progress **2** : the ground or path over which something moves **3 a** ♦ : method of procedure **b** : CONDUCT, BEHAVIOR **4** ♦ : an ordered series of acts or proceedings : sequence of events **5** : a series of instruction periods dealing with a subject **6** : the series of studies leading to graduation from a school or college **7** : the part of a meal served at one time — **of course** : as might be expected

♦ [1b] line, path, route, track, way ♦ [3a] line, policy, procedure, program ♦ [4] operation, procedure, proceeding, process

[2]course *vb* **coursed; cours•ing** **1** : to hunt with dogs **2** ♦ : to run or go speedily

♦ barrel, career, dash, fly, hurry, pelt, race, rip, rocket, run, rush, shoot, speed, tear, zip, zoom

cours•er \ˈkōr-sər\ *n* : a swift or spirited horse

[1]court \ˈkōrt\ *n* **1** : the residence of a sovereign or similar dignitary **2** : a sovereign's formal assembly of officials and advisers as a governing power **3** : an assembly of the retinue of a sovereign **4** ♦ : an open space enclosed by a building or buildings **5** : a space walled or marked off for playing a game (as tennis or basketball) **6** : the place where justice is administered; *also* : a judicial body or a meeting of a judicial body **7** : attention intended to win favor **8** ♦ : a judge or judges in session

♦ [4] close, courtyard, quadrangle, yard ♦ [8] bench, judge, justice, magistrate

[2]court *vb* **1** : to try to gain the favor of **2** ♦ : to seek to gain or achieve : WOO **3** : ATTRACT, TEMPT

♦ ask, woo

cour•te•ous \ˈkər-tē-əs\ *adj* ♦ : marked by respect for others : CIVIL, POLITE

♦ civil, genteel, gracious, mannerly, polite, well-bred

cour•te•ous•ly *adv* ♦ : in a courteous manner

♦ kindly, nicely, thoughtfully, well

cour•te•san \ˈkōr-tə-zən, -ˌzan\ *n* : PROSTITUTE

cour•te•sy \ˈkər-tə-sē\ *n, pl* **-sies** **1** ♦ : courteous behavior **2** ♦ : a favor courteously performed

♦ [1] amenity, civility, formality, gesture ♦ [1] civility, gentility, graciousness, mannerliness, politeness ♦ [2] boon, favor (*or* favour), grace, indulgence, kindness, mercy, service, turn

court•house \ˈkōrt-ˌhau̇s\ *n* : a building in which courts of law are held or county offices are located

court•ier \ˈkōr-tē-ər\ *n* : a person in attendance at a royal court

court•li•ness *n* ♦ : the quality of being courtly

♦ class, elegance, grace, gracefulness, handsomeness, majesty, refinement, stateliness

court•ly \ˈkōrt-lē\ *adj* **court•li•er; -est** : of a quality befitting the court : REFINED, ELEGANT

court–mar•tial \ˈkōrt-ˌmär-shəl\ *n, pl* **courts–martial** : a military or naval court for trial of offenses against military or naval law; *also* : a trial by this court — **court–martial** *vb*
court•room \-ˌrüm, -ˌru̇m\ *n* : a room in which a court of law is held
court•ship \-ˌship\ *n* : the act of courting : the act of wooing
court•yard \-ˌyärd\ *n* ♦ : an enclosure next to a building

♦ close, court, quadrangle, yard

cous•cous \ˈküs-ˌküs\ *n* : a No. African dish of steamed semolina usually served with meat or vegetables; *also* : the semolina itself
cous•in \ˈkə-zən\ *n* : a child of one's uncle or aunt
cou•ture \kü-ˈtu̇r, -ˈtu̅e̅r\ *n* : the business of designing fashionable custom-made women's clothing; *also* : the designers and establishments engaged in this business
cou•tu•ri•er \kü-ˈtu̇r-ē-ər, -ē-ˌā\ *n* : the owner of an establishment engaged in couture
cove \ˈkōv\ *n* ♦ : a small sheltered inlet or bay

♦ bay, bight, estuary, fjord, gulf, inlet

co•ven \ˈkə-vən\ *n* : an assembly or band of witches
cov•e•nant \ˈkə-və-nənt\ *n* ♦ : a formal binding agreement : COMPACT

♦ accord, agreement, bargain, compact, contract, convention, deal, pact, settlement, understanding ♦ bond, contract, guarantee, surety, warranty

cov•e•nant \-nənt, -ˌnant\ *vb* ♦ : to promise by a covenant

♦ pledge, promise, swear, vow

¹cov•er \ˈkə-vər\ *vb* **1** : to bring or hold within range of a firearm **2** ♦ : to afford protection or security to : PROTECT, SHIELD **3** ♦ : to hide from sight or knowledge : HIDE, CONCEAL **4** ♦ : to place something over or upon **5** : INCLUDE, COMPRISE **6** : to have as one's field of activity ⟨one salesman ∼*s* the state⟩ **7** : to buy (stocks) in order to have them for delivery on a previous short sale **8** ♦ : to deal with **9** ♦ : to pass over **10** ♦ : to act as a substitute or replacement during an absence

♦ [2] defend, guard, protect, safeguard, screen, secure, shield, ward ♦ [3] blanket, blot out, cloak, conceal, curtain, enshroud, hide, mask, obscure, occult, screen, shroud, veil ♦ [4] blanket, carpet, coat, overlay, overlie, overspread ♦ [8] concern, deal, pertain, treat ♦ [9] crisscross, cross, cut, follow, go, pass, proceed, travel, traverse ♦ [10] fill in, pinch-hit, stand in, sub, substitute, take over

²cover *n* **1** ♦ : something that protects or shelters **2** ♦ : a movable cover for the opening of a hollow container : LID, TOP **3** : CASE, BINDING **4** : TABLECLOTH **5** : a cloth used on a bed **6** : SCREEN, DISGUISE **7** : an envelope or wrapper for mail

♦ [1] aegis, armor, defense (*or* defence), guard, protection, safeguard, screen, security, shield, wall, ward ♦ [1] armor, capsule, case, casing, cocoon, housing, husk, jacket, pod, sheath, shell ♦ [2] cap, lid, top

cov•er•age \ˈkə-və-rij\ *n* **1** : the act or fact of covering **2** : the total group covered : SCOPE
cov•er•all \ˈkə-vər-ˌȯl\ *n* : a one-piece outer garment worn to protect one's clothes — usually used in plural
cover charge *n* : a charge made by a restaurant or nightclub in addition to the charge for food and drink
cover crop *n* : a crop planted to prevent soil erosion and to provide humus
cov•er•ing *n* : something that covers or conceals
cov•er•let \ˈkə-vər-lət\ *n* : a usually ornamental cloth cover for a bed : BEDSPREAD
¹co•vert \ˈkō-ˌvərt, ˈkə-vərt\ *adj* **1** ♦ : not openly shown, engaged in, or avowed : SECRET **2** : SHELTERED — **co•vert•ly** *adv*

♦ cloistered, isolated, quiet, remote, secluded, secret ♦ clandestine, furtive, hugger-mugger, private, secret, sneak, sneaky, stealthy, surreptitious, undercover, underground, underhanded

²co•vert \ˈkə-vərt, ˈkō-\ *n* **1** ♦ : a secret or sheltered place; *esp* : a thicket sheltering game **2** : a feather covering the bases of the quills of the wings and tail of a bird

♦ concealment, den, hideout, lair, nest ♦ brake, brushwood, chaparral, coppice, thicket

cov•er–up \ˈkə-vər-ˌəp\ *n* **1** : a device for masking or concealing **2** : a usually concerted effort to keep an illegal or unethical act or situation from being made public
cov•et \ˈkə-vət\ *vb* ♦ : to desire enviously (what belongs to another)

♦ ache for, crave, desire, die for, hanker for, hunger for, long for, lust (for *or* after), pine for, repine for, thirst for, want, wish for, yearn for

cov•et•ous *adj* ♦ : marked by inordinate desire for wealth or possessions or for another's possessions

♦ acquisitive, avaricious, avid, grasping, greedy, mercenary, rapacious

cov•et•ous•ness *n* ♦ : the state of being covetous

♦ acquisitiveness, avarice, avidity, cupidity, greed, rapaciousness

cov•ey \ˈkə-vē\ *n, pl* **coveys** **1** : a bird with her brood of young **2** : a small flock (as of quail)
¹cow \ˈkau̇\ *n* **1** : the mature female of cattle or of an animal (as the moose, elephant, or whale) of which the male is called *bull* **2** : any domestic bovine animal irrespective of sex or age
²cow *vb* ♦ : to destroy the resolve or courage of : INTIMIDATE

♦ browbeat, bully, hector, intimidate

cow•ard \ˈkau̇(-ə)rd\ *n* ♦ : one who lacks courage or shows shameful fear or timidity — **coward** *adj* — **cow•ard•ice** \ˈkau̇-ər-dəs\ *n*

♦ chicken, craven, dastard, poltroon, recreant, sissy ***Ant*** hero, stalwart, valiant

cow•ard•ly *adv or adj* ♦ : being, resembling, or befitting a coward

♦ chicken, craven, dastardly, pusillanimous, recreant, spineless, yellow ***Ant*** brave, courageous, daring, dauntless, doughty, fearless, gallant, greathearted, gutsy, hardy, heroic, intrepid, lionhearted, stalwart, stout, valiant, valorous

cow•bird \ˈkau̇-ˌbərd\ *n* : a small No. American blackbird that lays its eggs in the nests of other birds
cow•boy \-ˌbȯi\ *n* : one (as a mounted ranch hand) who tends cattle or horses
cow•er \ˈkau̇(-ə)r\ *vb* ♦ : to shrink or crouch down from fear or cold : QUAIL

♦ cringe, grovel, quail

cow•girl \ˈkau̇-ˌgərl\ *n* : a girl or woman who tends cattle or horses
cow•hand \ˈkau̇-ˌhand\ *n* : one who tends cattle or horses : COWBOY
cow•hide \-ˌhīd\ *n* **1** : the hide of a cow; *also* : leather made from it **2** : a coarse whip of braided rawhide
cowl \ˈkau̇l\ *n* : a monk's hood
cow•lick \ˈkau̇-ˌlik\ *n* : a turned-up tuft of hair that resists control
cowl•ing \ˈkau̇-liŋ\ *n* : a usually metal covering for the engine or another part of an airplane
cow•man \ˈkau̇-mən, -ˌman\ *n* : one who tends cattle or horses : COWBOY; *also* : a cattle owner or rancher
co•work•er \ˈkō-ˌwər-kər\ *n* : a fellow worker
cow•poke \ˈkau̇-ˌpōk\ *n* : one who tends cattle or horses : COWBOY
cow pony *n* : a strong and agile horse trained for herding cattle
cow•pox \ˈkau̇-ˌpäks\ *n* : a mild disease of the cow that when communicated to humans protects against smallpox
cow•punch•er \-ˌpən-chər\ *n* : one who tends cattle or horses : COWBOY
cow•slip \ˈkau̇-ˌslip\ *n* **1** : a yellow-flowered European primrose **2** : MARSH MARIGOLD
cox•comb \ˈkäks-ˌkōm\ *n* : a conceited foolish person : FOP
cox•swain \ˈkäk-sən, -ˌswān\ *n* : the steersman of a ship's boat or a racing shell
coy \ˈkȯi\ *adj* **1** ♦ : shrinking from contact or familiarity : BASHFUL, SHY **2** ♦ : marked by artful playfulness : COQUETTISH — **coy•ly** *adv* — **coy•ness** *n*

♦ [1] bashful, demure, diffident, introverted, modest, retiring, sheepish, shy ♦ [2] coquettish, demure, kittenish

coy•ote \ˈkī-ˌōt, kī-ˈō-tē\ *n, pl* **coyotes** *or* **coyote** : a mammal of No. America smaller than the related wolves
coy•pu \ˈkȯi-pü\ *n* : NUTRIA 2
coz•en \ˈkəz-ᵊn\ *vb* ♦ : to deceive, win over, or induce to do something by artful coaxing and wheedling or shrewd trickery — **coz•en•age** \-ij\ *n* — **coz•en•er** *n*

♦ beguile, bluff, deceive, delude, dupe, fool, gull, have, hoax, hoodwink, humbug, misinform, mislead, string along, take in, trick ♦ bleed, cheat, chisel, defraud, fleece, gyp, hustle, mulct, rook, shortchange, skin, squeeze, stick, sting, swindle, victimize

¹co•zy \ˈkō-zē\ *adj* **co•zi•er; -est** : enjoying or affording warmth and ease : SNUG, COMFORTABLE — **co•zi•ly** \-zə-lē\ *adv* — **co•zi•ness** \-zē-nəs\ *n*

[2]**cozy** *n, pl* **co•zies :** a padded covering for a vessel (as a teapot) to keep the contents hot
cp *abbr* **1** compare **2** coupon
CP *abbr* **1** cerebral palsy **2** chemically pure **3** command post **4** communist party
CPA *abbr* certified public accountant
CPB *abbr* Corporation for Public Broadcasting
cpd *abbr* compound
CPI *abbr* consumer price index
Cpl *abbr* corporal
CPO *abbr* chief petty officer
CPOM *abbr* master chief petty officer
CPOS *abbr* senior chief petty officer
CPR *abbr* cardiopulmonary resuscitation
CPT *abbr* captain
CPU \ˌsē-ˌpē-ˈyü\ *n* **:** the part of a computer that performs its basic operations, manages its components, and exchanges data with memory or peripherals
CQ *abbr* charge of quarters
cr *abbr* credit; creditor
Cr *symbol* chromium
[1]**crab** \ˈkrab\ *n* **:** any of various crustaceans with a short broad shell and small abdomen
[2]**crab** *n* ♦ **:** an ill-natured person

♦ bear, complainer, crank, grouch, grumbler, whiner

[3]**crab** *vb* **crabbed; crab•bing** ♦ **:** to complain about peevishly **:** COMPLAIN, GROUSE

♦ beef, bellyache, carp, complain, croak, fuss, gripe, grouse, growl, grumble, kick, moan, murmur, mutter, repine, squawk, wail, whine

crab apple *n* **:** a small often highly colored sour apple; *also* **:** a tree that produces crab apples
crab•bed \ˈkra-bəd\ *adj* **1 :** MOROSE, PEEVISH **2 :** CRAMPED, IRREGULAR
crab•by \ˈkra-bē\ *adj* **crab•bi•er; -est** ♦ **:** marked by typically transitory bad temper **:** CROSS

♦ choleric, cranky, cross, crotchety, grouchy, grumpy, irascible, irritable, peevish, perverse, petulant, short-tempered, snappish, snappy, snippy, testy, waspish

crab•grass \ˈkrab-ˌgras\ *n* **:** a weedy grass with creeping or sprawling stems that root freely at the nodes
crab louse *n* **:** a louse infesting the pubic region in humans
[1]**crack** \ˈkrak\ *vb* **1 :** to break with a sharp sudden sound **2 :** to break with or without completely separating into parts **3 :** to fail in tone or become harsh ⟨her voice ~*ed*⟩ **4 :** to subject (as a petroleum oil) to heat for breaking down into lighter products (as gasoline) **5 :** to strike with a sharp noise **6** ♦ **:** to puzzle out and expose, solve, or reveal the mystery of **7** ♦ **:** to lose control or effectiveness under pressure

♦ [6] answer, break, decode, dope, figure out, puzzle, resolve, riddle, solve, unravel, work, work out ♦ [7] break, flip, freak

[2]**crack** *n* **1** ♦ **:** a sudden sharp noise **2** ♦ **:** a witty or sharp remark **3** ♦ **:** a narrow break or opening **:** FISSURE **4** ♦ **:** a sharp blow **5** ♦ **:** an attempt or opportunity to do something **6 :** a potent form of cocaine in small chips used illicitly for smoking

♦ [1] bang, blast, boom, clap, crash, pop, report, slam, smash, snap, thwack, whack ♦ [2] gag, jest, joke, laugh, pleasantry, quip, sally, waggery, wisecrack, witticism ♦ [3] chink, cleft, cranny, crevice, fissure, rift, split ♦ [4] bat, belt, blow, box, clout, hit, punch, slug, thump, wallop, whack ♦ [5] attempt, bid, endeavor (*or* endeavour), essay, fling, go, pass, shot, stab, trial, try, whack, whirl

[3]**crack** *adj* ♦ **:** extremely proficient

♦ accomplished, adept, consummate, crackerjack, expert, good, great, master, masterful, masterly, proficient, skilled, skillful, virtuoso

crack•down \ˈkrak-ˌdau̇n\ *n* **:** an act or instance of taking positive disciplinary action ⟨a ~ on gambling⟩
crack down *vb* ♦ **:** to take positive regulatory or disciplinary action — used with *on*

♦ *usu* **crack down on** clamp down, crush, put down, quash, quell, repress, silence, snuff, squash, squelch, subdue, suppress

cracked *adj* ♦ **:** mentally disturbed

♦ balmy, crazy, deranged, insane, loco, lunatic, mad, nuts, nutty, screwy, unsound

crack•er \ˈkra-kər\ *n* **1 :** FIRECRACKER **2 :** a dry thin crispy baked bread product made of flour and water
crack•er•jack \-ˌjak\ *n* ♦ **:** a person or thing of marked excellence

♦ ace, adept, artist, authority, expert, maestro, master, scholar, shark, virtuoso, whiz, wizard

crackerjack *adj* ♦ **:** of striking ability or excellence

♦ accomplished, adept, consummate, crack, expert, good, great, master, masterful, masterly, proficient, skilled, skillful, virtuoso

crack•le \ˈkra-kəl\ *vb* **crack•led; crack•ling 1 :** to make small sharp snapping noises **2 :** to develop fine cracks in a surface — **crackle** *n* — **crack•ly** \-k(ə-)lē\ *adj*
crack•pot \ˈkrak-ˌpät\ *n* ♦ **:** an eccentric person

♦ character, crank, eccentric, kook, nut, oddball, screwball, weirdo

crack–up \ˈkrak-ˌəp\ *n* **1** ♦ **:** a wrecking or smashing especially of a vehicle **:** CRASH, WRECK **2 :** BREAKDOWN

♦ collision, crash, smash, wreck

crack up *vb* **1** ♦ **:** to express a favorable judgment of **:** PRAISE ⟨isn't all it's *cracked up* to be⟩ **2 :** to laugh or cause to laugh out loud **3 :** to crash a vehicle

♦ acclaim, applaud, cheer, hail, laud, praise, salute, tout

[1]**cra•dle** \ˈkrād-ᵊl\ *n* **1 :** a baby's bed or cot **2 :** a framework or support (as for a telephone receiver) **3 :** INFANCY ⟨from ~ to the grave⟩ **4** ♦ **:** a place of origin

♦ birthplace, home

[2]**cradle** *vb* **cra•dled; cra•dling 1 :** to place in or as if in a cradle **2 :** SHELTER, REAR
craft \ˈkraft\ *n* **1 a** ♦ **:** skill in planning, making, or executing **b** ♦ **:** an occupation requiring special skill **2** ♦ **:** skill in deceiving to gain an end **:** CUNNING, GUILE **3** *pl usu* **craft** ♦ **:** a boat especially of small size; *also* **:** AIRCRAFT, SPACECRAFT

♦ [1a] adeptness, adroitness, art, artfulness, artifice, artistry, cleverness, cunning, deftness, masterfulness, skill ♦ [1b] handicraft, trade ♦ [2] artfulness, artifice, caginess, canniness, craftiness, cunning, guile, slyness, wiliness ♦ [3] boat, bottom, vessel

craft *vb* ♦ **:** to make or produce with care, skill, or ingenuity

♦ cast, compose, draft, draw, formulate, frame, prepare

craft•i•ness \-tē-nəs\ *n* ♦ **:** the quality or state of being crafty

♦ artfulness, artifice, caginess, canniness, craft, cunning, guile, slyness, wiliness

crafts•man \ˈkrafts-mən\ *n* ♦ **:** a skilled artisan — **crafts•man•ship** *n*

♦ artificer, artisan, handicrafter

crafty \ˈkraf-tē\ *adj* **craft•i•er; -est** ♦ **:** adept in the use of subtlety and cunning **:** CUNNING, SUBTLE — **craft•i•ly** \-tə-lē\ *adv*

♦ artful, cagey, cunning, devious, foxy, guileful, slick, sly, subtle, wily

crag \ˈkrag\ *n* ♦ **:** a steep rugged cliff or rock

♦ bluff, cliff, escarpment, palisade, precipice, scarp

crag•gy *adj* ♦ **:** having a broken, uneven, or bumpy surface

♦ broken, jagged, ragged, scraggly

cram \ˈkram\ *vb* **crammed; cram•ming 1** ♦ **:** to pack in tight **:** JAM **2 :** to eat greedily **3 :** to study rapidly under pressure for an examination

♦ crowd, jam, ram, sandwich, squeeze, stuff, wedge ♦ charge, fill, heap, jam, jam-pack, load, pack, stuff

[1]**cramp** \ˈkramp\ *n* **1** ♦ **:** a sudden painful contraction of muscle **2 :** sharp abdominal pain — usually used in plural

♦ spasm

[2]**cramp** *vb* **1 :** to affect with a cramp or cramps **2** ♦ **:** to restrain from free action **:** HAMPER

♦ encumber, hamper, hinder, hold up, impede, inhibit, interfere with, obstruct, tie up

cran•ber•ry \ˈkran-ˌber-ē, -bə-rē\ *n* **:** the red acid berry of any of several trailing plants related to the heaths; *also* **:** one of these plants
[1]**crane** \ˈkrān\ *n* **1 :** any of a family of tall wading birds related to the rails; *also* **:** any of several herons **2 :** a machine for lifting and carrying heavy objects

2crane *vb* **craned; cran•ing** **1 :** to stretch one's neck to see better **2** ♦ **:** to raise or lift by or as if by a crane

♦ boost, elevate, heave, heft, heighten, hike, hoist, jack, lift, pick up, raise, up, uphold

crane fly *n* **:** any of a family of long-legged slender dipteran flies that resemble large mosquitoes but do not bite
cranial nerve *n* **:** any of the nerves that arise in pairs from the lower surface of the brain and pass through openings in the skull to the periphery of the body
cra•ni•um \ˈkrā-nē-əm\ *n, pl* **-ni•ums** *or* **-nia** \-ə\ **:** SKULL; *esp* **:** the part enclosing the brain — **cra•ni•al** \-əl\ *adj*
1crank \ˈkraŋk\ *n* **1 :** a bent part of an axle or shaft or an arm at right angles to the end of a shaft by which circular motion is imparted to or received from it **2** ♦ **:** an eccentric person **3** ♦ **:** a bad-tempered person **:** GROUCH

♦ [2] character, crackpot, eccentric, kook, nut, oddball, screwball, weirdo ♦ [3] bear, complainer, crab, curmudgeon, grouch, grumbler, whiner

2crank *vb* ♦ **:** to start or operate by or as if by turning a crank — usually used with *up*

♦ *usu* **crank up** activate, actuate, drive, move, propel, run, set off, spark, start, touch off, trigger, turn on

crank•case \ˈkraŋk-ˌkās\ *n* **:** the housing of a crankshaft
crank out *vb* **:** to produce in a mechanical manner
crank•shaft \ˈkraŋk-ˌshaft\ *n* **:** a shaft turning or driven by a crank
cranky \ˈkraŋ-kē\ *adj* **crank•i•er; -est** **1** ♦ **:** given to fretful fussiness **:** IRRITABLE **2** ♦ **:** operating uncertainly or imperfectly

♦ [1] choleric, crabby, cross, crotchety, fussy, grouchy, grumpy, irascible, irritable, peevish, perverse, petulant, short-tempered, snappish, snappy, snippy, testy, waspish ♦ [2] awkward, clumsy, cumbersome, ungainly, unhandy, unwieldy

cran•ny \ˈkra-nē\ *n, pl* **crannies** ♦ **:** a small break or slit **:** CREVICE, CHINK

♦ chink, cleft, crack, crevice, fissure, rift, split

craps \ˈkraps\ *n* **:** a gambling game played with two dice
crap•shoot•er \ˈkrap-ˌshü-tər\ *n* **:** a person who plays craps
1crash \ˈkrash\ *vb* **1** ♦ **:** to break noisily **:** SMASH **2 :** to damage an airplane in landing **3 :** to enter or attend without invitation or without paying ⟨∼ a party⟩ **4 :** to decline suddenly and steeply **5** ♦ **:** to suffer a sudden major failure usually with loss of data ⟨my computer ∼*ed*⟩

♦ [1] bang, bash, bump, collide, hit, impact, knock, ram, slam, smash, strike, swipe, thud ♦ [5] break, break down, conk, cut out, die, fail, stall

2crash *n* **1** ♦ **:** a loud sound (as of things smashing) **2** ♦ **:** an instance of crashing ⟨a plane ∼⟩; *also* **:** COLLISION **3** ♦ **:** a sudden failure (as of a business)

♦ [1] bang, blast, boom, clap, crack, pop, report, slam, smash, snap, thwack, whack ♦ [2] collision, crack-up, smash, wreck ♦ [3] collapse, cropper, defeat, failure, fizzle, nonsuccess

3crash *adj* **:** marked by concerted effort over the shortest possible time
4crash *n* **:** coarse linen fabric used for towels and draperies
crash–land \ˈkrash-ˈland\ *vb* **:** to land an aircraft or spacecraft under emergency conditions usually with damage to the craft — **crash landing** *n*
crass \ˈkras\ *adj* ♦ **:** coarse in nature or behavior **:** GROSS — **crass•ly** *adv*

♦ coarse, common, crude, gross, ill-bred, low, rough, rude, tasteless, uncouth, uncultivated, uncultured, unpolished, unrefined, vulgar

crate \ˈkrāt\ *n* **:** a container often of wooden slats — **crate** *vb*
cra•ter \ˈkrā-tər\ *n* **1 :** the depression around the opening of a volcano **2 :** a depression formed by the impact of a meteorite or by the explosion of a bomb or shell
cra•vat \krə-ˈvat\ *n* **:** NECKTIE
crave \ˈkrāv\ *vb* **craved; crav•ing** **1 :** to ask for earnestly **:** BEG **2** ♦ **:** to long for **:** DESIRE

♦ ache for, covet, desire, die for, hanker for, hunger for, long for, lust (for *or* after), pine for, repine for, thirst for, want, wish for, yearn for

cra•ven \ˈkrā-vən\ *adj* ♦ **:** lacking the least bit of courage **:** contemptibly fainthearted

♦ chicken, cowardly, dastardly, pusillanimous, recreant, spineless, yellow

craven *n* **:** an avowed coward
crav•ing \ˈkrā-viŋ\ *n* ♦ **:** an urgent or abnormal desire

♦ appetite, desire, drive, hankering, hunger, itch, longing, lust, passion, thirst, urge, yearning, yen

craw•fish \ˈkrȯ-ˌfish\ *n* **1 :** CRAYFISH 1 **2 :** SPINY LOBSTER
1crawl \ˈkrȯl\ *vb* **1** ♦ **:** to move slowly by drawing the body along the ground **2** ♦ **:** to advance feebly, cautiously, or slowly **3** ♦ **:** to be swarming with or feel as if swarming with creeping things ⟨a place ∼*ing* with ants⟩ ⟨her flesh ∼*ed*⟩

♦ [1] creep, grovel, slither, snake, worm ♦ [2] creep, drag, inch, plod, poke *Ant* fly, race, speed, whiz, zip ♦ [3] abound, brim, bulge, burst, swarm, teem

2crawl *n* **1 :** a very slow pace **2 :** a prone speed swimming stroke
cray•fish \ˈkrā-ˌfish\ *n* **1 :** any of numerous freshwater crustaceans usually much smaller than the related lobsters **2 :** SPINY LOBSTER
cray•on \ˈkrā-ˌän, -ən\ *n* **:** a stick of chalk or wax used for writing, drawing, or coloring; *also* **:** a drawing made with such material — **crayon** *vb*
1craze \ˈkrāz\ *vb* **crazed; craz•ing** ♦ **:** to make or become insane

♦ derange, madden, unhinge

2craze *n* ♦ **:** an exaggerated and often transient enthusiasm **:** FAD

♦ fad, mode, rage, style, trend, vogue

cra•zi•ness \-zē-nəs\ *n* ♦ **:** the quality or state of being crazy

♦ absurdity, asininity, balminess, daftness, fatuity, folly, foolishness, inanity, insanity, lunacy, madness, silliness, simplicity, zaniness

cra•zy \ˈkrā-zē\ *adj* **cra•zi•er; -est** **1** ♦ **:** mentally disordered **:** INSANE **2** ♦ **:** not characterized by common sense **:** wildly impractical; *also* **:** ERRATIC **3** ♦ **:** distracted with desire or excitement **4** ♦ **:** absurdly fond — usually used with *about* or *over* — **cra•zi•ly** \-zə-lē\ *adv*

♦ [1, 2] absurd, cuckoo, fatuous, foolish, mad, nonsensical, nutty, senseless, silly, stupid ♦ [3] agog, anxious, ardent, athirst, avid, eager, enthusiastic, gung ho, hot, hungry, keen, nuts, raring, solicitous, thirsty, voracious ♦ *usu* **crazy about** *or* **crazy over** [4] mad, nuts

CRC *abbr* Civil Rights Commission
creak \ˈkrēk\ *vb* **:** to make a prolonged squeaking or grating sound — **creak** *n* — **creaky** *adj*
1cream \ˈkrēm\ *n* **1 :** the yellowish fat-rich part of milk **2 :** a thick smooth sauce, confection, or cosmetic **3** ♦ **:** the choicest part **4 :** a pale yellow color — **creamy** *adj*

♦ best, choice, elect, elite, fat, flower, pick, prime

2cream *vb* **1 :** to prepare with a cream sauce **2 :** to beat or blend into creamy consistency **3 :** to defeat decisively
cream cheese *n* **:** a cheese made from whole milk enriched with cream
cream•ery \ˈkrē-mə-rē\ *n, pl* **-er•ies** **:** an establishment where butter and cheese are made or milk and cream are prepared for sale
1crease \ˈkrēs\ *n* ♦ **:** a mark or line made by or as if by folding

♦ crimp, crinkle, furrow, wrinkle

2crease *vb* **:** to become creased
cre•ate \krē-ˈāt\ *vb* **cre•at•ed; cre•at•ing** ♦ **:** to bring into being **:** cause to exist

♦ bring about, cause, effect, effectuate, generate, induce, make, produce, prompt, result, work, yield

♦ engender, generate, induce, make, produce, spawn

cre•a•tion \krē-ˈā-shən\ *n* **1 :** the act of creating or producing ⟨∼ of the world⟩ **2** ♦ **:** something that is created **3** ♦ **:** all created things **:** WORLD

♦ [2] coinage, concoction, contrivance, innovation, invention, wrinkle ♦ [3] cosmos, macrocosm, nature, universe, world

cre•a•tion•ism \krē-ˈā-shə-ˌni-zəm\ *n* **:** a doctrine or theory holding that matter, the various forms of life, and the world were created by God out of nothing — **cre•a•tion•ist** \-nist\ *n or adj*
cre•a•tive \-ˈā-tiv\ *adj* ♦ **:** marked by the ability or power to create — **cre•a•tive•ness** *n*

♦ artful, clever, imaginative, ingenious, innovative, inventive, original *Ant* uncreative, unimaginative, unoriginal

cre•a•tiv•i•ty \ˌkre-(ˌ)ā-ˈti-və-tē\ *n* ♦ **:** the ability to create

♦ ingenuity, invention, inventiveness, originality

cre•a•tor \krē-ˈā-tər\ *n* **1** ♦ **:** one that creates **:** MAKER, AUTHOR **2** *cap* **:** GOD 1

♦ author, father, founder, riginator

crea•ture \ˈkrē-chər\ *n* **1** ♦ **:** a lower animal **2** ♦ **:** a human being

♦ [1] animal, beast, brute, critter ♦ [2] being, body, human, individual, man, mortal, person

crèche \ˈkresh\ *n* **:** a representation of the Nativity scene
cre•dence \ˈkrēd-ᵊns\ *n* ♦ **:** mental acceptance as true or real

♦ confidence, faith, stock, trust ♦ belief, credit, faith

cre•den•tial \kri-ˈden-chəl\ *n* ♦ **:** something that gives a basis for credit or confidence — used in plural

♦ *usu* **credentials** capability, qualification, stuff

cre•den•za \kri-ˈden-zə\ *n* **:** a sideboard, buffet, or bookcase usually without legs
cred•i•ble \ˈkre-də-bəl\ *adj* ♦ **:** offering reasonable grounds for being believed **:** BELIEVABLE — **cred•i•bil•i•ty** \ˌkre-də-ˈbi-lə-tē\ *n*

♦ believable, likely, plausible, probable

¹cred•it \ˈkre-dət\ *vb* **1** ♦ **:** to trust in the truth of **:** BELIEVE **2** ♦ **:** to give credit to

♦ [1] accept, believe, swallow, trust ♦ [2] accredit, ascribe, attribute, impute

²credit *n* **1 :** the balance (as in a bank) in a person's favor **2 :** time given for payment for goods sold on trust **3 :** an accounting entry of payment received **4** ♦ **:** reliance on the truth or reality of something **:** BELIEF, FAITH **5 :** financial trustworthiness **6** ♦ **:** good name **7** ♦ **:** a source of honor or distinction **8 :** a unit of academic work

♦ [4] belief, credence, faith ♦ [6] acclaim, accolade, distinction, glory, homage, honor (*or* honour), laurels ♦ [7] boast, glory, honor (*or* honour), jewel, pride, treasure

cred•it•able \ˈkre-də-tə-bəl\ *adj* ♦ **:** worthy of esteem or praise **cred•it•ably** \-blē\ *adv*

♦ admirable, commendable, laudable, meritorious, praiseworthy

credit card *n* **:** a card authorizing purchases on credit
cred•i•tor \ˈkre-də-tər\ *n* **:** a person to whom money is owed
cre•do \ˈkrē-dō, ˈkrā-\ *n, pl* **credos 1 :** a set of fundamental beliefs **:** CREED **2 :** a guiding principle
cred•u•lous \ˈkre-jə-ləs\ *adj* **:** inclined to believe especially on slight evidence — **cre•du•li•ty** \kri-ˈdü-lə-tē, -ˈdyü-\ *n* — **cred•u•lous•ly** *adv*
Cree \ˈkrē\ *n, pl* **Cree** *or* **Crees :** a member of an American Indian people of Canada
creed \ˈkrēd\ *n* **1** ♦ **:** a statement of the essential beliefs of a religious faith; *also* **:** the body of such beliefs **2** ♦ **:** a guiding principle

♦ [1] cult, faith, persuasion, religion ♦ [2] doctrine, gospel, ideology, philosophy

creek \ˈkrēk, ˈkrik\ *n* **1** *chiefly Brit* **:** a small inlet **2** ♦ **:** a stream smaller than a river

♦ brook, rill, rivulet, streamlet

Creek \ˈkrēk\ *n* **:** a member of an American Indian people of Alabama, Georgia, and Florida
creel \ˈkrēl\ *n* **:** a wicker basket especially for carrying fish
¹creep \ˈkrēp\ *vb* **crept** \ˈkrept\; **creep•ing 1** ♦ **:** to move along with the body prone and close to the ground **:** CRAWL **2 :** to feel as though insects were crawling on the skin **3 :** to grow over a surface like ivy **4** ♦ **:** to go very slowly **5 :** to enter, advance, or progress gradually so as to be almost unnoticed ⟨the cost of living keeps *∼ing* up⟩ — **creep•er** *n*

♦ [1] crawl, grovel, slither, snake, worm ♦ [4] crawl, drag, inch, plod, poke

²creep *n* ♦ **:** an unpleasant or obnoxious person

♦ beast, boor, churl, clown, cretin, cur, heel, jerk, joker, louse, lout, skunk, slob, snake

creep•ing \ˈkrē-piŋ\ *adj* ♦ **:** developing or advancing by imperceptible degrees

♦ dilatory, laggard, languid, poky, slow, sluggish, tardy

creepy \ˈkrē-pē\ *adj* **creep•i•er; -est** ♦ **:** having or producing a nervous shivery fear

♦ eerie, haunting, spooky, uncanny, unearthly, weird

cre•mate \ˈkrē-ˌmāt\ *vb* **cre•mat•ed; cre•mat•ing :** to reduce (a dead body) to ashes with fire — **cre•ma•tion** \kri-ˈmā-shən\ *n*
cre•ma•to•ry \ˈkrē-mə-ˌtōr-ē, ˈkre-\ *n, pl* **-ries :** a furnace for cremating; *also* **:** a structure containing such a furnace
crème \ˈkrem, ˈkrēm\ *n, pl* **crèmes** *same or* ˈkremz, ˈkrēmz\ **:** a sweet liqueur
cren•el•lat•ed *or* **cren•el•at•ed** \ˈkren-ᵊl-ˌā-təd\ *adj* **:** having battlements — **cren•el•la•tion** \ˌkren-ᵊl-ˈā-shən\ *n*
Cre•ole \ˈkrē-ˌōl\ *n* **1 :** a descendant of early French or Spanish settlers of the U.S. Gulf states preserving their speech and culture; *also* **:** a person of mixed French or Spanish and black descent speaking a dialect of French or Spanish **2** *not cap* **:** a language that has evolved from a pidgin but serves as the native language of a speech community
cre•o•sote \ˈkrē-ə-ˌsōt\ *n* **:** an oily liquid obtained by distillation of coal tar and used in preserving wood
crepe *or* **crêpe** \ˈkrāp\ *n* **:** a light crinkled fabric of any of various fibers
crêpe su•zette \ˌkrāp-sü-ˈzet\ *n, pl* **crêpes suzette** *same or* ˌkrāps-\ *or* **crêpe suzettes** \-sü-ˈzets\ *often cap S* **:** a thin folded or rolled pancake in a hot orange-butter sauce that is sprinkled with a liqueur and set ablaze for serving
cre•pus•cu•lar \kri-ˈpəs-kyə-lər\ *adj* **1 :** of, relating to, or resembling twilight **2 :** occurring or active during twilight ⟨∼ insects⟩
cre•scen•do \krə-ˈshen-dō\ *adv or adj* **:** increasing in loudness — used as a direction in music — **crescendo** *n*
cres•cent \ˈkres-ᵊnt\ *n* **:** the moon at any stage between new moon and first quarter and between last quarter and new moon; *also* **:** something shaped like the figure of the crescent moon with a convex and a concave edge — **cres•cen•tic** \kre-ˈsen-tik\ *adj*
cress \ˈkres\ *n* **:** any of several salad plants related to the mustards
¹crest \ˈkrest\ *n* **1 :** a tuft or process on the head of an animal (as a bird) **2 :** a heraldic device **3 :** an upper part, edge, or limit ⟨the ∼ of a hill⟩ — **crest•ed** \ˈkres-təd\ *adj* — **crest•less** *adj*
²crest *vb* **1 :** CROWN **2 :** to reach the crest of **3 :** to rise to a crest
crest•fall•en \ˈkrest-ˌfȯ-lən\ *adj* **:** feeling shame or humiliation; *also* **:** feeling low in spirit **:** DISPIRITED, DEJECTED
Cre•ta•ceous \kri-ˈtā-shəs\ *adj* **:** of, relating to, or being the latest period of the Mesozoic era marked by great increase in flowering plants, diversification of mammals, and extinction of the dinosaurs — **Cretaceous** *n*
cre•tin \ˈkrēt-ᵊn\ *n* **1 :** one affected with cretinism **2** ♦ **:** a stupid, vulgar, or insensitive person

♦ blockhead, dope, dummy, idiot, imbecile, jackass, moron, numskull

cre•tin•ism \-ˌi-zəm\ *n* **:** a usually congenital abnormal condition characterized by physical stunting and mental retardation
cre•tonne \ˈkrē-ˌtän\ *n* **:** a strong unglazed cotton cloth for curtains and upholstery
cre•vasse \kri-ˈvas\ *n* **:** a deep fissure especially in a glacier
crev•ice \ˈkre-vəs\ *n* ♦ **:** a narrow fissure

♦ chink, cleft, crack, cranny, fissure, rift, split

¹crew \ˈkrü\ *chiefly Can and Brit past of* CROW
²crew *n* **1** ♦ **:** a body of people trained to work together for certain purposes **2 :** a group of people who operate a ship, train, aircraft, or spacecraft **3 :** the rowers and coxswain of a racing shell; *also* **:** the sport of rowing engaged in by a crew — **crew•man** \-mən\ *n*

♦ band, company, gang, outfit, party, squad, team

crew cut *n* **:** a very short bristly haircut
crew•el \ˈkrü-əl\ *n* **:** slackly twisted worsted yarn used for embroidery — **crew•el•work** \-ˌwərk\ *n*
¹crib \ˈkrib\ *n* **1 :** a manger for feeding animals **2 :** a child's bedstead with high sides **3 :** a building or bin for storage (as of grain) **4 :** something used for cheating in an exam
²crib *vb* **cribbed; crib•bing 1 :** to put in a crib **2 :** STEAL, PLAGIARIZE — **crib•ber** *n*
crib•bage \ˈkri-bij\ *n* **:** a card game usually played by two players and scored on a board (**cribbage board**)
crib death *n* **:** SUDDEN INFANT DEATH SYNDROME
crick \ˈkrik\ *n* **:** a painful spasm of muscles (as of the neck)
¹crick•et \ˈkri-kət\ *n* **:** any of a family of leaping insects related to the grasshoppers and noted for the chirping noises of the male
²cricket *n* **:** a game played with a bat and ball by two teams on a field centering upon two wickets each defended by a batsman

cri•er \ˈkrī(-ə)r\ *n* **:** one who calls out proclamations and announcements

crime \ˈkrīm\ *n* **1** ♦ **:** a serious offense against the public law **2** ♦ **:** something reprehensible, foolish, or disgraceful

♦ [1] error, malefaction, misdeed, misdoing, offense, sin, transgression, violation, wrongdoing ♦ [2] disgrace, outrage, pity, scandal, shame, sin

1**crim•i•nal** \ˈkri-mən-ᵊl\ *adj* **1** ♦ **:** involving or being a crime **2 :** relating to crime or its punishment — **crim•i•nal•i•ty** \ˌkri-mə-ˈna-lə-tē\ *n* — **crim•i•nal•ly** *adv*

♦ illegal, illegitimate, illicit, unlawful, wrongful

2**criminal** *n* ♦ **:** one who has committed a crime

♦ crook, culprit, felon, lawbreaker, malefactor, offender

crim•i•nol•o•gy \ˌkri-mə-ˈnä-lə-jē\ *n* **:** the scientific study of crime and criminals — **crim•i•nol•o•gist** \ˌkri-mə-ˈnä-lə-jist\ *n*

1**crimp** \ˈkrimp\ *vb* **:** to cause to become crinkled, wavy, or bent

2**crimp** *n* **1 :** something (as a curl in hair) produced by or as if by crimping **2** ♦ **:** a bend or crease formed in something **3** ♦ **:** something that cramps or inhibits

♦ [2] crease, crinkle, furrow, wrinkle ♦ [3] bar, block, encumbrance, hindrance, inhibition, obstacle

1**crim•son** \ˈkrim-zən\ *n* **:** a deep purplish red color — **crimson** *adj*

2**crimson** *vb* ♦ **:** to make or become crimson

♦ bloom, blush, color (*or* colour), flush, glow, redden

cringe \ˈkrinj\ *vb* **cringed; cring•ing** ♦ **:** to shrink in fear **:** COWER

♦ cower, grovel, quail

1**crin•kle** \ˈkriŋ-kəl\ *vb* **crin•kled; crin•kling** ♦ **:** to form many short bends or curves; *also* **:** WRINKLE — **crin•kly** \-kə-lē\ *adj*

♦ crease, furrow, rumple, wrinkle

2**crinkle** *n* **:** a line, mark, or ridge made by or as if by folding a pliable substance

crin•o•line \ˈkrin-ᵊl-ən\ *n* **1 :** an open-weave cloth used for stiffening and lining **2 :** a full stiff skirt or underskirt made of crinoline

1**crip•ple** \ˈkri-pəl\ *n* **:** one that is disabled or deficient in a specified manner ⟨a social ~⟩

2**cripple** *vb* **crip•pled; crip•pling** **1** ♦ **:** to make lame **2** ♦ **:** to make useless or imperfect

♦ [1] disable, lame, maim, mutilate ♦ [2] blemish, break, damage, deface, disfigure, flaw, harm, hurt, injure, mar, spoil, vitiate ♦ [2] disable, hamstring, immobilize, incapacitate, paralyze, prostrate

cri•sis \ˈkrī-səs\ *n, pl* **cri•ses** \-ˌsēz\ **1 :** the turning point for better or worse in an acute disease or fever **2** ♦ **:** a decisive or critical moment

♦ clutch, crunch, emergency, head, juncture

crisp \ˈkrisp\ *adj* **1 :** CURLY, WAVY **2** ♦ **:** easily crumbled **:** BRITTLE **3 :** FIRM, FRESH ⟨~ lettuce⟩ **4** ♦ **:** being sharp and clear; *also* **:** concise and to the point **5 :** LIVELY, SPARKLING **6 :** FROSTY, SNAPPY; *also* **:** INVIGORATING **7** ♦ **:** noticeably neat — **crisp** *vb*

♦ [2] brittle, crumbly, flaky, friable ♦ [4] brief, compact, compendious, concise, epigrammatic, laconic, pithy, succinct, summary, terse ♦ [7] neat, orderly, shipshape, snug, tidy, trim, uncluttered

crisp•ly *adv* ♦ **:** in a crisp manner

♦ compactly, concisely, laconically, shortly, succinctly, summarily, tersely

crisp•ness *n* ♦ **:** the quality or state of being crisp

♦ brevity, briefness, compactness, conciseness, succinctness, terseness

crispy *adj* **:** easily crumbled

1**criss•cross** \ˈkris-ˌkrȯs\ *vb* **1 :** to mark with crossed lines **2** ♦ **:** to go or pass back and forth through or over

♦ cover, cross, cut, follow, go, pass, proceed, travel, traverse

2**crisscross** *adj* **:** marked or characterized by crisscrossing — **crisscross** *adv*

3**crisscross** *n* **:** a pattern formed by crossed lines

crit *abbr* critical; criticism

cri•te•ri•on \krī-ˈtir-ē-ən\ *n, pl* **-ria** \-ē-ə\ ♦ **:** a standard on which a judgment may be based

♦ grade, mark, measure, par, standard, touchstone, yardstick

crit•ic \ˈkri-tik\ *n* **1 :** a person who judges literary or artistic works **2** ♦ **:** one inclined to find fault

♦ carper, castigator, caviler, censurer, faultfinder, nitpicker, railer, scold

crit•i•cal \ˈkri-ti-kəl\ *adj* **1 :** being or relating to a condition or disease involving danger of death **2** ♦ **:** being a crisis **3** ♦ **:** inclined to criticize **4 :** relating to criticism or critics **5 :** requiring careful judgment **6 :** UNCERTAIN **7** ♦ **:** marked by or indicative of significant worth or consequence — **crit•i•cal•ly** \-k(ə-)lē\ *adv*

♦ [2] acute, dire, imperative, imperious, instant, pressing, urgent ♦ [3] captious, carping, hypercritical, overcritical ***Ant*** uncritical ♦ [7] crucial, key, pivotal, vital

crit•i•cise *Brit var of* CRITICIZE

crit•i•cism \ˈkri-tə-ˌsi-zəm\ *n* **1 :** the act of criticizing; *esp* **:** CENSURE **2 :** a judgment or review **3 :** the art of judging works of literature or art

crit•i•cize \ˈkri-tə-ˌsīz\ *vb* **-cized; -ciz•ing** **1 :** to judge as a critic **:** EVALUATE **2** ♦ **:** to find fault **:** express criticism

♦ blame, censure, condemn, denounce, fault, knock, pan, reprehend ***Ant*** extol, laud, praise

cri•tique \krə-ˈtēk\ *n* **:** a critical estimate or discussion

crit•ter \ˈkri-tər\ *n* ♦ **:** a lower animal **:** CREATURE

♦ animal, beast, brute, creature

1**croak** \ˈkrōk\ *n* **:** a hoarse harsh cry (as of a frog)

2**croak** *vb* ♦ **:** to mutter in discontent

♦ beef, bellyache, carp, complain, crab, fuss, gripe, grouse, growl, grumble, kick, moan, murmur, mutter, repine, squawk, wail, whine

Croat \ˈkrō-ˌat\ *n* **:** CROATIAN

Cro•atian \krō-ˈā-shən\ *n* **:** a native or inhabitant of Croatia — **Croatian** *adj*

cro•chet \krō-ˈshā\ *n* **:** needlework done with a single thread and hooked needle — **crochet** *vb*

crock \ˈkräk\ *n* **:** a thick earthenware pot or jar

crock•ery \ˈkrä-kə-rē\ *n* **:** EARTHENWARE

croc•o•dile \ˈkrä-kə-ˌdīl\ *n* **:** any of several thick-skinned long-bodied carnivorous reptiles of tropical and subtropical waters

cro•cus \ˈkrō-kəs\ *n, pl* **cro•cus•es** *also* **crocus** *or* **cro•ci** \-ˌkī\ **:** any of a large genus of low herbs related to the irises and having brightly colored flowers borne singly in early spring

Crohn's disease \ˈkrōnz\ *n* **:** a chronic inflammatory disease of the gastrointestinal tract and especially the ileum

crois•sant \krō-ˈsänt, krwä-ˈsä^{n}\ *n, pl* **croissants** *same or* -ˈsänts, -ˈsä^{n}z\ **:** a rich crescent-shaped roll

Cro–Ma•gnon \krō-ˈmag-nən, -ˈman-yən\ *n* **:** any of a tall erect human race known from skeletal remains found chiefly in southern France and usually classified as the same species as present-day human beings — **Cro–Magnon** *adj*

crone \ˈkrōn\ *n* ♦ **:** a withered old woman **:** HAG

♦ hag, witch

cro•ny \ˈkrō-nē\ *n, pl* **cronies** ♦ **:** a close friend especially of long standing

♦ associate, cohort, companion, comrade, fellow, mate ♦ buddy, chum, comrade, familiar, friend, intimate, pal

1**crook** \ˈkru̇k\ *vb* ♦ **:** to curve or bend sharply

♦ arc, arch, bend, bow, curve, hook, round, sweep, swerve, wheel

2**crook** *n* **1 :** a bent or curved implement **2 :** a bent or curved part; *also* **:** BEND, CURVE **3 :** a person who engages in fraudulent or criminal practices **:** SWINDLER, THIEF

crook•ed \ˈkru̇-kəd\ *adj* **1** ♦ **:** having a crook **2** ♦ **:** characterized by lack of truth, honesty, or trustworthiness **:** DISHONEST — **crook•ed•ly** *adv*

♦ [1] devious, serpentine, sinuous, tortuous, winding ***Ant*** straight, straightaway ♦ [2] deceptive, dishonest, fast, fraudulent, shady, sharp, shifty, underhanded

crook•ed•ness *n* ♦ **:** the quality or state of being crooked

♦ artifice, craft, craftiness, cunning, deceit, deceitfulness, dishonesty, dissimulation, double-dealing, duplicity, guile, wiliness

croon \ˈkrün\ *vb* **:** to sing or hum in a gentle murmuring voice — **croon•er** *n*

1**crop** \ˈkräp\ *n* **1 :** the handle of a whip; *also* **:** a short riding whip **2 :** a pouch in the throat of many birds and insects where food is received **3 :** something that can be harvested; *also* **:** the yield at harvest **4 :** two or more figures forming a complete unit in a composition

[2]**crop** *vb* **cropped; crop•ping 1 ♦ :** to remove the tips of **:** cut off short; *also* **:** TRIM **2 :** to feed on by cropping **3 a :** to devote (land) to crops **b ♦ :** to grow as a crop **:** yield a crop **4 ♦ :** to appear unexpectedly — often used with *up*

♦ [1] bob, clip, cut, cut back, dock, lop, nip, prune, shave, shear, trim ♦ [3b] cultivate, grow, promote, raise, rear, tend ♦ *usu* **crop up** [4] arise, emerge, materialize, spring, surface

crop duster *n* **:** a person who uses an airplane to spray crops with insecticidal dusts; *also* **:** an airplane so used

crop•land \\-ˌland\\ *n* **:** land devoted to the production of plant crops

crop•per \\ˈkrä-pər\\ *n* **:** a raiser of crops; *esp* **:** SHARECROPPER

crop•per \\ˈkrä-pər\\ *n* **♦ :** a sudden or violent failure or collapse

♦ collapse, crash, defeat, failure, fizzle, nonsuccess

cro•quet \\krō-ˈkā\\ *n* **:** a game in which mallets are used to drive wooden balls through a series of wickets set out on a lawn

cro•quette \\krō-ˈket\\ *n* **:** a small often rounded mass of minced meat, fish, or vegetables fried in deep fat

cro•sier \\ˈkrō-zhər\\ *n* **:** a staff carried by bishops and abbots

[1]**cross** \\ˈkrȯs\\ *n* **1 :** a structure consisting of an upright beam and a crossbar used especially by the ancient Romans for execution **2 :** a figure of the cross on which Christ was crucified used as a Christian symbol **3 :** a hybridizing of unlike individuals or strains; *also* **:** a product of this **4 :** a punch delivered with a circular motion over an opponent's lead **5 ♦ :** an affliction that tries one's virtue, steadfastness, or patience

♦ gauntlet, ordeal, trial

[2]**cross** *vb* **1 :** to lie or place across; *also* **:** INTERSECT **2 :** to cancel by marking a cross on or by lining through **3 :** THWART, OBSTRUCT **4 ♦ :** to go or extend across **:** TRAVERSE **5 :** HYBRIDIZE **6 :** to meet and pass on the way

♦ cover, crisscross, cut, follow, go, pass, proceed, travel, traverse

[3]**cross** *adj* **1 :** lying across **2 :** CONTRARY, OPPOSED **3 ♦ :** marked by bad temper **4 :** HYBRID — **cross•ly** *adv*

♦ choleric, crabby, cranky, crotchety, grouchy, grumpy, irascible, irritable, peevish, perverse, petulant, short-tempered, snappish, snappy, snippy, testy, waspish

cross•bar \\ˈkrȯs-ˌbär\\ *n* **:** a transverse bar or piece

cross•bow \\-ˌbō\\ *n* **:** a short bow mounted crosswise at the end of a wooden stock that shoots short arrows

cross•breed \\ˈkrȯs-ˌbrēd, -ˈbrēd\\ *vb* **-bred** \\-ˈbred\\; **-breed•ing :** HYBRIDIZE

cross–coun•try \\-ˈkən-trē\\ *adj* **1 :** extending or moving across a country **2 :** proceeding over the countryside (as fields and woods) and not by roads **3 :** of or relating to racing or skiing over the countryside instead of over a track or run — **cross–country** *adv*

cross•cur•rent \\-ˈkər-ənt\\ *n* **1 :** a current running counter to another **2 :** a conflicting tendency — usually used in plural

[1]**cross•cut** \\-ˌkət\\ *vb* **:** to cut or saw crosswise especially of the grain of wood

[2]**crosscut** *adj* **1 :** made or used for crosscutting 〈a ∼ saw〉 **2 :** cut across the grain

[3]**crosscut** *n* **:** something that cuts through transversely

cross–ex•am•ine \\ˌkrȯ-sig-ˈza-mən\\ *vb* **:** to examine with questions to check the answers to previous questions — **cross–ex•am•i•na•tion** \\-ˌza-mə-ˈnā- shən\\ *n*

cross–eyed \\ˈkrȯ-ˌsīd\\ *adj* **:** having one or both eyes turned inward toward the nose

cross–fer•til•i•za•tion \\-ˌfərt-ᵊl-ə-ˈzā-shən\\ *n* **1 :** fertilization between sex cells produced by separate individuals or sometimes by individuals of different kinds; *also* **:** CROSS-POLLINATION **2 :** a broadening or productive interchange (as between cultures) — **cross–fer•til•ize** \\-ˈfərt-ᵊl-ˌīz\\ *vb*

cross fire *n* **1 :** crossing lines of fire in combat **2 :** rapid or angry interchange

cross•hair \\ˈkrȯs-ˌhar\\ *n* **:** a fine wire or thread in the eyepiece of an optical instrument used as a reference line

cross•hatch \\ˈkrȯs-ˌhach\\ *vb* **:** to mark with two series of parallel lines that intersect — **cross–hatch•ing** *n*

cross•ing \\ˈkrȯ-siŋ\\ *n* **1 :** a place or structure for crossing something (as a river) **2 ♦ :** a point of intersection (as of a street and a railroad track) **3 ♦ :** the act or action of crossing

♦ [2] corner, crossroad, intersection ♦ [3] cruise, passage, sail, voyage

cross•over \\ˈkrȯs-ˌō-vər\\ *n* **1 :** CROSSING **2 :** a member of a political party who votes in the primary of the other party **3 :** a broadening of the popular appeal of an artist (as a musician) by a change in the artist's style, genre, or medium **4 :** an instance of breaking into another category

cross over *vb* **:** to achieve broader popularity by a change of medium or style

cross•piece \\ˈkrȯs-ˌpēs\\ *n* **:** a horizontal member

cross–pol•li•na•tion \\ˌkrȯs-ˌpä-lə-ˈnā- shən\\ *n* **:** transfer of pollen from one flower to the stigma of another — **cross–pol•li•nate** \\ˈkrȯs-ˈpä-lə-ˌnāt\\ *vb*

cross–pur•pose \\ˈkrȯs-ˈpər-pəs\\ *n* **:** a purpose contrary to another purpose 〈working at *cross-purposes*〉

cross–ques•tion \\-ˈkwes-chən\\ *vb* **:** CROSS-EXAMINE — **cross–question** *n*

cross–re•fer \\ˌkrȯs-ri-ˈfər\\ *vb* **:** to refer by a notation or direction from one place to another (as in a book or list) — **cross–ref•er•ence** \\ˈkrȯs-ˈre-frəns\\ *n*

cross•road \\ˈkrȯs-ˌrōd\\ *n* **1 :** a road that crosses a main road or runs between main roads **2 ♦ :** a place where roads meet — usually used in plural **3 :** a crucial point where a decision must be made

♦ *usu* **crossroads** corner, crossing, intersection

cross section *n* **1 :** a section cut across something; *also* **:** a representation made by or as if by such cutting **2 :** a number of persons or things selected from a group that show the general nature of the whole group — **cross–sec•tion•al** *adj*

cross•walk \\ˈkrȯs-ˌwȯk\\ *n* **:** a marked path for pedestrians crossing a street

cross•ways \\-ˌwāz\\ *adv* **:** so as to cross something **:** CROSSWISE

cross•wind \\-ˌwind\\ *n* **:** a wind not parallel to a course (as of an airplane)

cross•wise \\-ˌwīz\\ *adv* **♦ :** so as to cross something — **crosswise** *adj*

♦ athwart, obliquely, transversely

cross•word \\ˈkrȯs-ˌwərd\\ *n* **:** a puzzle in which words are put into a pattern of numbered squares in answer to clues

cros•ti•ni \\krȯ-ˈstē-nē\\ *n pl* **:** small slices of toasted bread served with a topping

crotch \\ˈkräch\\ *n* **:** an angle formed by the parting of two legs, branches, or members

crotch•et \\ˈkrä-chət\\ *n* **1 :** an odd notion **:** WHIM **2 ♦ :** a highly individual and usually eccentric opinion or preference

♦ eccentricity, idiosyncrasy, mannerism, oddity, peculiarity, quirk, singularity, trick

crotch•ety *adj* **♦ :** given to crotchets **:** subject to whims, crankiness, or ill temper

♦ choleric, crabby, cranky, cross, grouchy, grumpy, irascible, irritable, peevish, perverse, petulant, short-tempered, snappish, snappy, snippy, testy, waspish

crouch \\ˈkrau̇ch\\ *vb* **1 ♦ :** to stoop or bend low **2 :** CRINGE, COWER — **crouch** *n*

♦ huddle, hunch, squat

croup \\ˈkrüp\\ *n* **:** laryngitis especially of infants marked by a hoarse ringing cough and difficult breathing — **croupy** *adj*

crou•pi•er \\ˈkrü-pē ər, -pē-ˌā\\ *n* **:** an employee of a gambling casino who collects and pays bets at a gaming table

crou•ton \\ˈkrü-ˌtän\\ *n* **:** a small cube of bread toasted or fried crisp

[1]**crow** \\ˈkrō\\ *n* **1 :** any of various large glossy black birds related to the jays **2** *cap* **:** a member of an American Indian people of a region in Montana and Wyoming; *also* **:** the language of the Crow people

[2]**crow** *vb* **1 :** to make the loud shrill sound characteristic of the cock **2 ♦ :** to utter a sound expressive of pleasure **3 ♦ :** to exult gloatingly especially over the distress of another **:** EXULT **4 ♦ :** to brag exultantly or blatantly **:** BRAG, BOAST

♦ [2, 3] delight, exult, glory, joy, rejoice, triumph ♦ [4] boast, brag, plume, swagger

[3]**crow** *n* **:** the cry of the cock

crow•bar \\ˈkrō-ˌbär\\ *n* **:** a metal bar usually wedge-shaped at the end for use as a pry or lever

[1]**crowd** \\ˈkrau̇d\\ *vb* **1 ♦ :** to press close **2 ♦ :** to gather in numbers **:** THRONG **3 ♦ :** to press, force, or thrust into a small space **:** CRAM, STUFF

♦ [1, 3] cram, jam, ram, sandwich, squeeze, stuff, wedge ♦ [2] flock, mob, swarm, throng

[2]**crowd** *n* **1** ♦ **:** a large number of people gathered together at random **:** THRONG **2** ♦ **:** a group of people having something (as a habit, interest, or occupation) in common

♦ [1] army, crush, drove, flock, horde, host, legion, mob, multitude, press, swarm, throng ♦ [2] circle, clan, clique, coterie, fold, gang, ring, set

crowded *adj* **1** ♦ **:** filled with numerous things or people often overly compacted or concentrated **2** ♦ **:** pressed together

♦ [1] brimful, chock-full, fat, fraught, full, loaded, packed, replete ♦ [2] close, compact, dense, packed, serried, thick, tight

[1]**crown** \ˈkrau̇n\ *n* **1 :** a mark of victory or honor; *esp* **:** the title of a champion in a sport **2 :** a royal headdress **3 :** the top of the head **4** ♦ **:** the highest part (as of a tree or tooth) **5** *often cap* **:** sovereign power; *also* **:** MONARCH **6 :** a formerly used British silver coin — **crowned** \ˈkrau̇nd\ *adj*

♦ acme, apex, climax, culmination, head, height, meridian, peak, pinnacle, summit, tip-top, top, zenith

[2]**crown** *vb* **1 :** to place a crown on **2 :** HONOR **3 :** TOP, SURMOUNT **4 :** to fit (a tooth) with an artificial crown

crown vetch *n* **:** a European leguminous herb with umbels of pink-and-white flowers and sharp-angled pods

crow's–foot \ˈkrōz-ˌfu̇t\ *n, pl* **crow's–feet** \-ˌfēt\ **:** any of the wrinkles around the outer corners of the eyes — usually used in plural

crow's nest *n* **:** a partly enclosed platform high on a ship's mast for use as a lookout

crozier *var of* CROSIER

[1]**CRT** \ˌsē-(ˌ)är-ˈtē\ *n, pl* **CRTs** *or* **CRT's :** CATHODE-RAY TUBE; *also* **:** a display device incorporating a cathode-ray tube

[2]**CRT** *abbr* carrier route

cru•cial \ˈkrü-shəl\ *adj* **1** ♦ **:** important or essential as resolving a crisis **:** DECISIVE **2 :** IMPORTANT, SIGNIFICANT

♦ critical, decisive, essential, indispensable, key, necessary, pivotal, pressing, requisite, urgent, vital

cru•ci•ate \ˈkrü-shē-ˌāt\ *adj* **:** CRUCIFORM

cru•ci•ble \ˈkrü-sə-bəl\ *n* **1 :** a heat-resistant container in which material can be subjected to great heat **2 :** a severe test

cru•ci•fix \ˈkrü-sə-ˌfiks\ *n* **:** a representation of Christ on the cross

cru•ci•fix•ion \ˌkrü-sə-ˈfik-shən\ *n* **1** *cap* **:** the crucifying of Christ **2 :** the act of crucifying

cru•ci•form \ˈkrü-sə-ˌfȯrm\ *adj* **:** shaped like a cross

cru•ci•fy \ˈkrü-sə-ˌfī\ *vb* **-fied; -fy•ing 1 :** to put to death by nailing or binding the hands and feet to a cross **2 :** MORTIFY 1 **3 :** TORTURE, PERSECUTE

[1]**crude** \ˈkrüd\ *adj* **crud•er; crud•est 1** ♦ **:** not refined **:** RAW 〈~ oil〉 〈~ statistics〉 **2** ♦ **:** lacking grace, taste, tact, or polish **3** ♦ **:** rough or inexpert in plan or execution — **crude•ly** *adv* — **cru•di•ty** \ˈkrü-də-tē\ *n*

♦ [1] native, natural, raw, undressed, unprocessed, unrefined, untreated *Ant* processed, refined, treated ♦ [2] coarse, common, crass, gross, ill-bred, low, rough, rude, tasteless, uncouth, uncultivated, uncultured, unpolished, unrefined, vulgar ♦ [3] artless, clumsy, rough, rude, unrefined

[2]**crude** *n* **:** unrefined petroleum

cru•el \ˈkrü-əl\ *adj* **cru•el•er** *or* **cru•el•ler; cru•el•est** *or* **cru•el•lest 1** ♦ **:** causing pain and suffering to others **2** ♦ **:** extremely painful — **cru•el•ly** *adv*

♦ [1] barbarous, brutal, heartless, inhumane, sadistic, savage, vicious, wanton *Ant* benign, benignant, compassionate, goodhearted, humane, kind, kindhearted, sympathetic, tenderhearted ♦ [2] agonizing, bitter, excruciating, galling, grievous, harrowing, harsh, hurtful, painful, tortuous

cru•el•ty \-tē\ *n* ♦ **:** the quality or state of being cruel

♦ barbarity, brutality, inhumanity, sadism, savagery, viciousness, wantonness *Ant* benignity, compassion, humanity, kindness, sympathy

cru•et \ˈkrü-ət\ *n* **:** a small usually glass bottle for vinegar, oil, or sauce

[1]**cruise** \ˈkrüz\ *vb* **cruised; cruis•ing 1 :** to sail about touching at a series of ports **2 :** to travel for enjoyment **3 :** to travel about the streets at random **4 :** to travel at the most efficient operating speed 〈the *cruising* speed of an airplane〉

[2]**cruise** *n* ♦ **:** an act or an instance of cruising; *esp* **:** a tour by ship

♦ crossing, passage, sail, voyage

cruis•er \ˈkrü-zər\ *n* **1 :** SQUAD CAR **2 :** a large fast moderately armored and gunned warship **3 :** a motorboat equipped for living aboard

crul•ler \ˈkrə-lər\ *n* **1 :** a small sweet cake in the form of a twisted strip fried in deep fat **2** *Northern & Midland* **:** an unraised doughnut

[1]**crumb** \ˈkrəm\ *n* **1** ♦ **:** a small fragment **2** ♦ **:** a small piece or quantity of some material thing

♦ atom, bit, fleck, flyspeck, grain, granule, molecule, morsel, mote, particle, patch, scrap, scruple, speck, tittle

[2]**crumb** *vb* **1 :** to break into crumbs **2 :** to cover with crumbs

crum•ble \ˈkrəm-bəl\ *vb* **crum•bled; crum•bling 1 :** to break into small pieces **:** DISINTEGRATE **2 :** to break down completely

crum•bly *adj* ♦ **:** easily crumbled

♦ brittle, crisp, flaky, friable

crum•my \ˈkrə-mē\ *adj* **crum•mi•er; -est** ♦ **:** very poor or inferior **:** LOUSY

♦ bad, deficient, inferior, lousy, off, poor, punk, rotten, substandard, unacceptable, unsatisfactory, wanting, wretched, wrong

crum•pet \ˈkrəm-pət\ *n* **:** a small round unsweetened bread cooked on a griddle

crum•ple \ˈkrəm-pəl\ *vb* **crum•pled; crum•pling 1** ♦ **:** to crush together **:** RUMPLE **2** ♦ **:** fall into a jumbled or flattened mass through the force of external pressure **:** COLLAPSE

♦ [1] crinkle, rumple, wrinkle *Ant* iron out, smooth ♦ [2] cave in, collapse, give, go, yield

[1]**crunch** \ˈkrənch\ *vb* **1** ♦ **:** to chew with a grinding noise **2** ♦ **:** to grind or press with a crushing noise

♦ *usu* **crunch on** [1] bite, champ, chew, chomp, gnaw, nibble ♦ [2] gnash, grate, grind, grit, scrape

[2]**crunch** *n* **1 :** an act of or a sound made by crunching **2** ♦ **:** a tight or critical situation — **crunchy** *adj*

♦ clutch, crisis, emergency, head, juncture

cru•sade \krü-ˈsād\ *n* **1** *cap* **:** any of the expeditions in the 11th, 12th, and 13th centuries undertaken by Christian countries to take the Holy Land from the Muslims **2** ♦ **:** a reforming enterprise undertaken with zeal — **crusade** *vb*

♦ bandwagon, campaign, cause, drive, movement

cru•sad•er *n* ♦ **:** one engaged in a crusade

♦ fanatic, militant, partisan, zealot

cruse \ˈkrüz, ˈkrüs\ *n* **:** a jar for water or oil

[1]**crush** \ˈkrəsh\ *vb* **1** ♦ **:** to squeeze out of shape **2 :** HUG, EMBRACE **3** ♦ **:** to grind or pound to small bits **4** ♦ **:** to suppress or overwhelm as if by pressure or weight **:** SUPPRESS **5** ♦ **:** to subdue completely

♦ [1] mash, squash ♦ [3] atomize, grind, powder, pulverize ♦ [4, 5] clamp down, crack down, put down, quash, quell, repress, silence, snuff, squash, squelch, subdue, suppress ♦ [4, 5] carry away, devastate, floor, oppress, overcome, overpower, overwhelm, prostrate, snow under, swamp

[2]**crush** *n* **1 :** an act of crushing **2** ♦ **:** a violent crowding **3 :** INFATUATION

♦ army, crowd, drove, flock, horde, host, legion, mob, multitude, press, swarm, throng

crust \ˈkrəst\ *n* **1 :** the outside part of bread; *also* **:** a piece of old dry bread **2 :** the cover of a pie **3 :** a hard surface layer — **crustal** *adj*

crus•ta•cean \ˌkrəs-ˈtā-shən\ *n* **:** any of a large class of mostly aquatic arthropods (as lobsters or crabs) having a firm crustlike shell — **crustacean** *adj*

crusty *adj* **crust•i•er; -est 1 :** having or being a crust **2 :** giving an effect of surly incivility in address or disposition **:** CROSS, GRUMPY

crutch \ˈkrəch\ *n* **:** a supporting device; *esp* **:** a support fitting under the armpit for use by the disabled in walking

crux \ˈkrəks, ˈkru̇ks\ *n, pl* **crux•es 1 :** a puzzling or difficult problem **2** ♦ **:** a crucial point

♦ core, gist, heart, nub, pith, pivot

[1]**cry** \ˈkrī\ *vb* **cried; cry•ing 1** ♦ **:** to call out **:** SHOUT **2 :** to proclaim publicly **:** ADVERTISE **3** ♦ **:** to shed tears often noisily **:** WEEP **4** ♦ **:** to protest or complain loudly or vigorously — often used with *out*

♦ [1] bawl, call, holler, shout, vociferate, yell ♦ [3] bawl, blubber, sob, weep ♦ *usu* **cry out** [4] blurt, bolt, ejaculate, spout

[2]**cry** *n, pl* **cries** **1** ♦ **:** a loud outcry **2** ♦ **:** an earnest plea **:** APPEAL, ENTREATY **3 :** a fit of weeping **4 :** the characteristic sound uttered by an animal **5 :** DISTANCE — usually used in the phrase *a far cry* **6** ♦ **:** a loud shout **7** ♦ **:** a word or motto that embodies a principle or guide to action of an individual or group

♦ [1, 6] holler, hoot, howl, shout, whoop, yell, yowl ♦ [2] appeal, entreaty, petition, plea, prayer, solicitation, suit, supplication ♦ [7] shibboleth, slogan, watchword

cry•ba•by \ˈkrī-ˌbā-bē\ *n* ♦ **:** one who cries or complains easily or often

♦ complainer, grumbler, whiner

cry down *vb* ♦ **:** to lower in rank or reputation

♦ belittle, decry, deprecate, depreciate, diminish, discount, disparage, minimize, put down, write off

cryo•gen•ic \ˌkrī-ə-ˈje-nik\ *adj* **:** of or relating to the production of very low temperatures; *also* **:** involving the use of a very low temperature — **cryo•gen•i•cal•ly** \-ni-k(ə-)lē\ *adv*
cryo•gen•ics \-niks\ *n* **:** a branch of physics that relates to the production and effects of very low temperatures
cryo•lite \ˈkrī-ə-ˌlīt\ *n* **:** a usually white mineral used in making aluminum
crypt \ˈkript\ *n* **:** a chamber wholly or partly underground
cryp•tic \ˈkrip-tik\ *adj* **1** ♦ **:** meant to be puzzling or mysterious **2** ♦ **:** having or seeming to have a hidden or ambiguous meaning

♦ ambiguous, dark, darkling, deep, enigmatic, equivocal, inscrutable, murky, mysterious, mystic, nebulous, obscure, occult

cryp•to•gram \ˈkrip-tə-ˌgram\ *n* **:** a communication in cipher or code
cryp•tog•ra•phy \krip-ˈtä-grə-fē\ *n* **:** the coding and decoding of secret messages — **cryp•tog•ra•pher** \-fər\ *n*
crys•tal \ˈkrist-ᵊl\ *n* **1 :** transparent quartz **2 :** something resembling crystal (as in transparency); *esp* **:** a clear glass used for table articles **3 :** a body that is formed by solidification of a substance and has a regular repeating arrangement of atoms and often of external plane faces ⟨a salt ∼⟩ **4 :** the transparent cover of a watch dial
crystal clear *adj* **:** perfectly or transparently clear
crys•tal•line \ˈkris-tə-lən\ *adj* **1 :** made of or resembling crystal **2 :** very clear or sparkling
crys•tal•lise *Brit var of* CRYSTALLIZE
crys•tal•lize \ˈkris-tə-ˌlīz\ *vb* **-lized; -liz•ing 1 :** to assume or cause to assume a crystalline form **2** ♦ **:** to take or cause to take a definite form — **crys•tal•li•za•tion** \ˌkris-tə-lə-ˈzā-shən\ *n*

♦ form, jell, shape, solidify

crys•tal•log•ra•phy \ˌkris-tə-ˈlä-grə-fē\ *n* **:** the science dealing with the forms and structures of crystals — **crys•tal•log•ra•pher** *n*
cs *abbr* case; cases
Cs *symbol* cesium
CS *abbr* **1** civil service **2** county seat
CSA *abbr* Confederate States of America
C–section \ˈsē-ˌsek-shən\ *n* **:** CESAREAN SECTION
CSM *abbr* command sergeant major
CST *abbr* central standard time
ct *abbr* **1** carat **2** cent **3** count **4** county **5** court
CT *abbr* **1** central time **2** Connecticut
ctn *abbr* carton
ctr *abbr* **1** center **2** counter
CT scan \ˌsē-ˈtē-\ *n* **:** CAT SCAN
cu *abbr* cubic
Cu *symbol* copper
cub \ˈkəb\ *n* **1 :** a young individual of some animals (as a fox, bear, or lion) **2** ♦ **:** a young person

♦ child, juvenile, kid, kiddo, moppet, whelp, youngster, youth

Cu•ban \ˈkyü-bən\ *n* **:** a native or inhabitant of Cuba — **Cuban** *adj*
Cu•ban sandwich \ˈkyü-bən-\ *n* **:** a usually grilled and pressed sandwich served on a long split roll
cub•by•hole \ˈkə-bē-ˌhōl\ *n* **:** a snug place (as for storing things)
[1]**cube** \ˈkyüb\ *n* **1 :** a solid having 6 equal square sides **2 :** the product obtained by taking a number 3 times as a factor ⟨27 is the ∼ of 3⟩
[2]**cube** *vb* **cubed; cub•ing 1 :** to raise to the third power **2 :** to form into a cube **3 :** to cut into cubes
cube root *n* **:** a number whose cube is a given number
cu•bic \ˈkyü-bik\ *also* **cu•bi•cal** *adj* **1 :** having the form of a cube **2 :** being the volume of a cube whose edge is a specified unit **3 :** having length, width, and height

cu•bi•cle \ˈkyü-bi-kəl\ *n* ♦ **:** a small separate space (as for sleeping or studying)

♦ bay, cabin, cell, chamber, compartment

cubic measure *n* **:** a unit (as cubic inch) for measuring volume
cubic zir•co•nia \-ˌzər-ˈkō-nē-ə\ *also* **cubic zirconium** *n* **:** a synthetic gemstone resembling a diamond made from an oxide of zirconium
cub•ism \ˈkyü-ˌbi-zəm\ *n* **:** a style of art characterized by the abstraction of natural forms into fragmented geometric shapes — **cub•ist** \-bist\ *n or adj*
cu•bit \ˈkyü-bət\ *n* **:** an ancient unit of length equal to about 18 inches (46 centimeters)
Cub Scout *n* **:** a member of the program of the Boy Scouts for boys in the first through fifth grades in school
cuck•old \ˈkə-kəld, ˈku̇-\ *n* **:** a man whose wife is unfaithful — **cuckold** *vb*
[1]**cuck•oo** \ˈkü-kü, ˈku̇-\ *n, pl* **cuckoos :** a largely grayish brown European bird that lays its eggs in the nests of other birds for them to hatch
[2]**cuckoo** *n* **:** a silly or foolish person
[3]**cuckoo** *adj* ♦ **:** being one that is silly or foolish

♦ absurd, crazy, fatuous, foolish, mad, nonsensical, nutty, senseless, silly, stupid

cu•cum•ber \ˈkyü-(ˌ)kəm-bər\ *n* **:** the long fleshy many-seeded fruit of a vine of the gourd family that is grown as a garden vegetable; *also* **:** this vine
cud \ˈkəd\ *n* **:** food brought up into the mouth by some animals (as cows) from the rumen to be chewed again
cud•dle \ˈkəd-ᵊl\ *vb* **cud•dled; cud•dling 1** ♦ **:** to lie close **:** SNUGGLE **2** ♦ **:** to hold close for warmth or comfort or in affection

♦ nestle, nuzzle, snug, snuggle

cud•gel \ˈkə-jəl\ *n* ♦ **:** a short heavy club — **cudgel** *vb*

♦ bat, billy club, bludgeon, club, staff, truncheon

[1]**cue** \ˈkyü\ *n* **1 :** a word, phrase, or action in a play serving as a signal for the next actor to speak or act **2** ♦ **:** a hint, intimation, or suggestion as to what course of action to take or when to take it **:** HINT — **cue** *vb*

♦ clue, hint, indication, inkling, intimation, lead, suggestion

[2]**cue** *n* **:** a tapered rod for striking the balls in billiards or pool
[3]**cue** *n* **:** a waiting line especially of persons or vehicles
cue ball *n* **:** the ball a player strikes with a cue in billiards or pool
[1]**cuff** \ˈkəf\ *n* **1 :** a part (as of a sleeve or glove) encircling the wrist **2 :** the folded hem of a trouser leg
[2]**cuff** *vb* **:** to strike especially with the open hand **:** SLAP
[3]**cuff** *n* **:** to strike especially with or as if with the palm of the hand
cui•sine \kwi-ˈzēn\ *n* **:** style of cooking; *also* **:** the food prepared
cuke \ˈkyük\ *n* **:** CUCUMBER
cul–de–sac \ˌkəl-di-ˈsak, ˌku̇l-\ *n, pl* **culs–de–sac** *same or* ˌkəlz-, ˌku̇lz-\ *also* **cul–de–sacs** \ˌkəl-də-ˈsaks, ˌku̇l-\ **:** a street or passage closed at one end
cu•li•nary \ˈkə-lə-ˌner-ē, ˈkyü-\ *adj* **:** of or relating to the kitchen or cookery
[1]**cull** \ˈkəl\ *vb* ♦ **:** to pick out from a group

♦ choose, elect, handpick, name, opt, pick, prefer, select, single, take

[2]**cull** *n* ♦ **:** something rejected from a group or lot as worthless or inferior

♦ discard, reject, rejection

cul•mi•nate \ˈkəl-mə-ˌnāt\ *vb* **-nat•ed; -nat•ing :** to reach the highest point
cul•mi•na•tion \ˌkəl-mə-ˈnā-shən\ *n* ♦ **:** culminating position

♦ acme, apex, climax, crown, head, height, meridian, peak, pinnacle, summit, tip-top, top, zenith

cu•lotte \ˈkü-ˌlät, ˌkyü-, ku̇-ˌlät, kyu̇-\ *n* **:** a divided skirt; *also* **:** a garment having a divided skirt — often used in plural
cul•pa•bil•i•ty \ˌkəl-pə-ˈbi-lə-tē\ *n* ♦ **:** the quality or state of being culpable

♦ blame, fault, guilt, rap

cul•pa•ble \ˈkəl-pə-bəl\ *adj* ♦ **:** deserving blame

♦ blamable, blameworthy, censurable, reprehensible

cul•prit \ˈkəl-prət\ *n* ♦ **:** one accused or guilty of a crime

♦ criminal, crook, felon, lawbreaker, malefactor, offender

cult \ˈkəlt\ *n* **1 :** formal religious veneration **2** ♦ **:** a religious system or its adherents **3 :** faddish devotion; *also* **:** a group of persons showing such devotion — **cult·ish** \ˈkəl-tish\ *adj* — **cult·ist** \-tist\ *n*

♦ creed, faith, persuasion, religion

cul·ti·va·ble \ˈkəl-tə-və-bəl\ *adj* **:** capable of being cultivated
cul·ti·var \ˈkəl-tə-ˌvär, -ver\ *n* **:** a plant variety originating and persisting under cultivation
cul·ti·vate \ˈkəl-tə-ˌvāt\ *vb* **-vat·ed; -vat·ing 1** ♦ **:** to prepare for the raising of crops **2** ♦ **:** to foster the growth of by tilling or by labor and care ⟨~ vegetables⟩ **3** ♦ **:** to improve by labor, care, or study **4 :** to help forward **:** ENCOURAGE, FURTHER

♦ [1] farm, tend ♦ [2] advance, encourage, forward, foster, further, nourish, nurture, promote ♦ [3] crop, grow, promote, raise, rear, tend

cul·ti·va·ted \ˈkəl-tə-ˌvāt-əd\ *adj* ♦ **:** having an education; *esp* **:** trained in the arts and social graces

♦ civilized, cultured, genteel, polished, refined *Ant* philistine, uncivilized, uncultured, unpolished, unrefined

cul·ti·va·tion \ˌkəl-tə-ˈvā-shən\ *n* ♦ **:** enlightenment and excellence of taste acquired by intellectual and aesthetic training

♦ civilization, culture, polish, refinement

cul·ti·va·tor \ˈkəl-tə-ˌvā-tər\ *n* ♦ **:** one that cultivates

♦ agriculturist, farmer, grower, planter, tiller

cul·ture \ˈkəl-chər\ *n* **1 :** TILLAGE, CULTIVATION **2 :** the act of developing by education and training **3** ♦ **:** refinement of intellectual and artistic taste **4** ♦ **:** the customary beliefs, social forms, and material traits of a racial, religious, or social group — **cul·tur·al** \ˈkəl-chə-rəl\ *adj* — **cul·tur·al·ly** *adv*

♦ [3] civilization, cultivation, polish, refinement ♦ [4] civilization, life, lifestyle, society

cul·tured \-chərd\ *adj* ♦ **:** having an education; *esp* **:** having an education beyond the average

♦ civilized, cultivated, genteel, polished, refined

cul·vert \ˈkəl-vərt\ *n* **:** a drain crossing under a road or railroad
cum *abbr* cumulative
cum·ber \ˈkəm-bər\ *vb* **:** to weigh down **:** BURDEN, HINDER
cum·ber·some \ˈkəm-bər-səm\ *adj* ♦ **:** hard to handle or manage because of size or weight

♦ awkward, clumsy, cranky, ungainly, unhandy, unwieldy *Ant* handy

cum·brous \ˈkəm-brəs\ *adj* **:** unwieldy because of heaviness and bulk **:** CUMBERSOME — **cum·brous·ly** *adv* — **cum·brous·ness** *n*
cum·in \ˈkə-mən, ˈkyü-\ *n* **:** the seedlike fruit of a small annual herb related to the carrot that is used as a spice; *also* **:** this herb
cum·mer·bund \ˈkə-mər-ˌbənd, ˈkəm-bər-\ *n* ♦ **:** a broad sash worn as a waistband

♦ belt, cincture, girdle, sash

cu·mu·la·tive \ˈkyü-myə-lə-tiv, -ˌlā-\ *adj* **:** increasing in force or value by successive additions
cu·mu·lo·nim·bus \ˌkyü-myə-lō-ˈnim-bəs\ *n* **:** an anvil-shaped cumulus cloud extending to great heights
cu·mu·lus \ˈkyü-myə-ləs\ *n, pl* **-li** \-ˌlī, -ˌlē\ **:** a massive cloud having a flat base and rounded outlines
cu·ne·i·form \kyu̇-ˈnē-ə-ˌfȯrm\ *adj* **1 :** wedge-shaped **2 :** composed of wedge-shaped characters
cun·ni·lin·gus \ˌkə-ni-ˈliŋ-gəs\ *also* **cun·ni·linc·tus** \-ˈliŋk-təs\ *n* **:** oral stimulation of the vulva or clitoris
¹cun·ning \ˈkə-niŋ\ *adj* **1** ♦ **:** dexterous or crafty in the use of special resources (as skill or knowledge) or in attaining an end **:** DEXTEROUS **2** ♦ **:** marked by wiliness and trickery **3 :** CUTE — **cun·ning·ly** *adv*

♦ [1] clever, deft, dexterous, handy ♦ [2] artful, cagey, crafty, devious, foxy, guileful, slick, sly, subtle, wily

²cunning *n* **1** ♦ **:** skill in planning, making, or executing **:** SKILL **2** ♦ **:** skill in deceiving to gain an end

♦ [1] adeptness, adroitness, art, artfulness, artifice, artistry, cleverness, craft, deftness, masterfulness, skill ♦ [2] artfulness, artifice, caginess, canniness, craft, craftiness, guile, slyness, wiliness

¹cup \ˈkəp\ *n* **1 :** a small bowl-shaped drinking vessel **2 :** the contents of a cup **3 :** the consecrated wine of the Communion **4 :** something resembling a cup **:** a small bowl or hollow **5 :** a half pint — **cup·ful** *n* — **cup·like** \-ˌlīk\ *adj*
²cup *vb* **cupped; cup·ping :** to curve into the shape of a cup
cup·board \ˈkə-bərd\ *n* ♦ **:** a small closet with shelves for food or dishes

♦ buffet, cabinet, closet, hutch, locker, sideboard

cup·cake \ˈkəp-ˌkāk\ *n* **:** a small cake baked in a cuplike mold
cu·pid \ˈkyü-pəd\ *n* **:** a winged naked figure of an infant often with a bow and arrow that represents the god Cupid
cu·pid·i·ty \kyu̇-ˈpi-də-tē\ *n, pl* **-ties** ♦ **:** excessive desire for money

♦ acquisitiveness, avarice, avidity, covetousness, greed, rapaciousness

cu·po·la \ˈkyü-pə-lə, -ˌlō\ *n* **:** a small structure on top of a roof or building
¹cur \ˈkər\ *n* **1 :** a mongrel dog **2** ♦ **:** a surly or cowardly fellow

♦ beast, boor, churl, clown, creep, cretin, heel, jerk, joker, louse, lout, skunk, slob, snake

²cur *abbr* **1** currency **2** current
cu·rate \ˈkyu̇r-ət\ *n* **1 :** a member of the clergy who is in charge of a parish **2 :** a member of the clergy who assists a rector or vicar — **cu·ra·cy** \-ə-sē\ *n*
cu·ra·tive \-ə-tiv\ *adj* **:** relating to or used in the cure of diseases — **curative** *n*
cu·ra·tor \ˈkyu̇r-ˌā-tər, kyu̇-ˈrā-\ *n* **:** CUSTODIAN; *esp* **:** one in charge of a place of exhibit (as a museum or zoo)
¹curb \ˈkərb\ *n* **1 :** a bit that exerts pressure on a horse's jaws **2** ♦ **:** one that arrests, limits, or restrains **:** CHECK, RESTRAINT **3 :** a raised edging (as of stone or concrete) along a paved street

♦ check, condition, constraint, fetter, limitation, restraint, restriction

²curb *vb* ♦ **:** to hold in or back **:** RESTRAIN

♦ bridle, check, constrain, contain, control, govern, inhibit, regulate, rein, restrain, tame

curb·ing \ˈkər-biŋ\ *n* **1 :** the material for a curb **2 :** CURB
curd \ˈkərd\ *n* **:** the thick protein-rich part of coagulated milk
cur·dle \ˈkərd-ᵊl\ *vb* **cur·dled; cur·dling :** to form curds; *also* **:** SPOIL, SOUR
¹cure \ˈkyu̇r\ *n* **1 :** spiritual care **2 :** recovery or relief from disease **3** ♦ **:** a curative agent **:** REMEDY **4 :** a course or period of treatment

♦ drug, medicine, pharmaceutical, remedy, specific

²cure *vb* **cured; cur·ing 1** ♦ **:** to restore to health **:** HEAL; *also* **:** to become cured **2 :** to process for storage or use ⟨~ bacon⟩ — **cur·able** *adj*

♦ heal, mend, rehabilitate

cu·ré \kyu̇-ˈrā\ *n* **:** a parish priest
cure–all \ˈkyu̇r-ˌȯl\ *n* **:** a remedy for all ills **:** PANACEA
cu·ret·tage \ˌkyu̇r-ə-ˈtäzh\ *n* **:** a surgical scraping or cleaning of a body part (as the uterus)
cur·few \ˈkər-ˌfyü\ *n* **:** a regulation that specified persons (as children) be off the streets at a set hour of the evening; *also* **:** the sounding of a signal (as a bell) at this hour
cu·ria \ˈkyu̇r-ē-ə, ˈku̇r-\ *n, pl* **cu·ri·ae** \ˈkyu̇r-ē-ˌē, ˈku̇r-ē-ˌī\ *often cap* **:** the body of congregations, tribunals, and offices through which the pope governs the Roman Catholic Church
cu·rie \ˈkyu̇r-ē\ *n* **:** a unit of radioactivity equal to 37 billion disintegrations per second
cu·rio \ˈkyu̇r-ē-ˌō\ *n, pl* **cu·ri·os :** an object or article valued because it is strange or rare
cu·ri·os·i·ty \ˌkyu̇r-ē-ˈä-sə-tē\ *n* **1** ♦ **:** one that arouses interest especially for uncommon or exotic characteristics **2** ♦ **:** an unusual knickknack

♦ [1] exotic, oddity, rarity ♦ [2] bauble, gewgaw, knickknack, novelty, trinket

cu·ri·ous \ˈkyu̇r-ē-əs\ *adj* **1** ♦ **:** having a desire to investigate and learn **2** ♦ **:** exciting attention as strange, novel, or unexpected **:** STRANGE, UNUSUAL, ODD

♦ [1] inquisitive, nosy, prying *Ant* incurious, uncurious ♦ [2] extraordinary, funny, odd, peculiar, rare, singular, strange, unaccustomed, uncommon, uncustomary, unique, unusual, weird

cu·ri·ous·ly *adv* **1 :** in a curious manner **2 :** as is curious
cu·ri·um \ˈkyu̇r-ē-əm\ *n* **:** a metallic radioactive element produced artificially

¹curl \ˈkərl\ *vb* **1 :** to form into ringlets **2** ♦ **:** to move or progress in curves or spirals **:** COIL — **curl•er** *n*

♦ coil, entwine, spiral, twine, twist, wind

²curl *n* **1 :** a lock of hair that coils **:** RINGLET **2 :** something having a spiral or twisted form — **curly** *adj*
cur•lew \ˈkər-lü, ˈkərl-yü\ *n, pl* **curlews** *or* **curlew :** any of various long-legged brownish birds that have a down-curved bill and are related to the sandpipers and snipes
curli•cue \ˈkər-li-ˌkyü\ *n* **:** a fancifully curved or spiral figure
curl up *vb* ♦ **:** to arrange oneself in or as if in a ball or curl

♦ nestle, snug, snuggle

cur•mud•geon \(ˌ)kər-ˈmə-jən\ *n* ♦ **:** a crusty, ill-tempered, and usually old man

♦ bear, complainer, crab, crank, grouch, grumbler, whiner

cur•rant \ˈkər-ənt\ *n* **1 :** a small seedless raisin **2 :** the acid berry of a shrub related to the gooseberry; *also* **:** this plant
cur•ren•cy \ˈkər-ən-sē\ *n, pl* **-cies 1 :** general use or acceptance **2** ♦ **:** something that is in circulation as a medium of exchange **:** MONEY

♦ cash, dough, lucre, money, pelf, tender

¹cur•rent \ˈkər-ənt\ *adj* **1** ♦ **:** occurring in or belonging to the present **2 :** used as a medium of exchange **3** ♦ **:** generally accepted or practiced

♦ [1] contemporary, hot, mod, modern, new, newfangled, red-hot, space-age, ultramodern, up-to-date ♦ [3] conventional, customary, popular, standard, stock, usual *Ant* nonstandard, unconventional, unpopular, unusual

²current *n* **1 :** the part of a body of fluid moving continuously in a certain direction; *also* **:** the swiftest part of a stream **2 :** a flow of electric charge; *also* **:** the rate of such flow **3** ♦ **:** a tendency or course of events that is usually the result of an interplay of forces

♦ drift, leaning, run, tendency, tide, trend, wind

cur•ric•u•lum \kə-ˈri-kyə-ləm\ *n, pl* **-la** \-lə\ *also* **-lums :** the courses offered by an educational institution
¹cur•ry \ˈkər-ē\ *vb* **cur•ried; cur•ry•ing 1 :** to clean the coat of (a horse) with a currycomb **2 :** to treat (tanned leather) especially by incorporating oil or grease — **curry favor :** to seek to gain favor by flattery or attention
²cur•ry *n, pl* **cur•ries :** a powder of pungent spices used in cooking; *also* **:** a food seasoned with curry
cur•ry•comb \-ˌkōm\ *n* **:** a comb used especially to curry horses — **currycomb** *vb*
¹curse \ˈkərs\ *n* **1** ♦ **:** a prayer for harm to come upon one **2 :** something that is cursed **3 :** evil or misfortune coming as if in response to a curse

♦ anathema, execration, imprecation, malediction *Ant* benediction, benison, blessing

²curse *vb* **cursed; curs•ing 1 :** to call on divine power to send injury upon **2 :** BLASPHEME **3** ♦ **:** to bring great evil upon **:** AFFLICT

♦ afflict, agonize, bedevil, harrow, martyr, persecute, plague, rack, torment, torture

cur•sive \ˈkər-siv\ *adj* **:** written with the strokes of the letters joined together and the angles rounded
cur•sor \ˈkər-sər\ *n* **:** a visual cue (as a pointer) on a computer screen that indicates position (as for data entry)
cur•so•ri•ly \-rə-lē\ *adj* ♦ **:** in a cursory manner

♦ hastily, headlong, hurriedly, pell-mell, precipitately, rashly

cur•so•ry \ˈkər-sə-rē\ *adj* ♦ **:** rapidly and often superficially done **:** HASTY

♦ hasty, headlong, pell-mell, precipitate, precipitous, rash

curt \ˈkərt\ *adj* ♦ **:** rudely short or abrupt — **curt•ly** *adv* — **curt•ness** *n*

♦ abrupt, bluff, blunt, brusque, snippy

cur•tail \(ˌ)kər-ˈtāl\ *vb* ♦ **:** to cut off the end of **:** SHORTEN — **cur•tail•ment** *n*

♦ abbreviate, abridge, cut back, shorten

¹cur•tain \ˈkərt-ᵊn\ *n* **1 :** a hanging screen that can be drawn back especially at a window **2 :** the screen between the stage and auditorium of a theater
²curtain *vb* ♦ **:** to veil with or as if with a curtain

♦ blanket, blot out, cloak, conceal, cover, enshroud, hide, mask, obscure, occult, screen, shroud, veil

curt•sy *also* **curt•sey** \ˈkərt-sē\ *n, pl* **curtsies** *or* **curtseys :** a courteous bow made by women chiefly by bending the knees — **curtsy** *also* **curtsey** *vb*
cur•va•ceous *also* **cur•va•cious** \ˌkər-ˈvā-shəs\ *adj* **:** having curves suggestive of a well-proportioned feminine figure
cur•va•ture \ˈkər-və-ˌchu̇r\ *n* **1 :** a measure or amount of curving **:** BEND **2 :** curved part
¹curve \ˈkərv\ *vb* **curved; curv•ing** ♦ **:** to bend from a straight line or course

♦ arc, arch, bend, bow, crook, hook, round, sweep, swerve, wheel *Ant* straighten

²curve *n* **1 :** a line especially when curved **2** ♦ **:** something that bends or curves without angles ⟨a ~ in the road⟩ **3 :** a baseball pitch thrown so that it swerves especially downward and to one side

♦ angle, arc, arch, bend, bow, crook, turn, wind

cur•vet \(ˌ)kər-ˈvet\ *n* **:** a prancing leap of a horse — **curvet** *vb*
¹cush•ion \ˈku̇-shən\ *n* **1 :** a soft pillow or pad to rest on or against **2 :** the springy pad inside the rim of a billiard table **3** ♦ **:** something soft that prevents discomfort or protects against injury

♦ buffer, bumper, fender, pad

²cushion *vb* **1 :** to provide (as a seat) with a cushion **2** ♦ **:** to soften or lessen the force or shock of

♦ buffer, gentle, soften

cusp \ˈkəsp\ *n* ♦ **:** a pointed end or part (as of a tooth)

♦ apex, end, pike, point, tip

cus•pid \ˈkəs-pəd\ *n* **:** a canine tooth
cus•pi•dor \ˈkəs-pə-ˌdȯr\ *n* **:** SPITTOON
cus•tard \ˈkəs-tərd\ *n* **:** a sweetened cooked mixture of milk and eggs
cus•to•di•al \ˌkəs-ˈtō-dē-əl\ *adj* **:** marked by watching and protecting rather than seeking to cure ⟨~ care⟩
cus•to•di•an \ˌkəs-ˈtō-dē-ən\ *n* ♦ **:** one that protects and maintains; *esp* **:** one who has custody (as of a building)

♦ caretaker, guardian, janitor, keeper, warden, watchman ♦ defender, defense (*or* defence), guard, protection, protector

cus•to•dy \ˈkəs-tə-dē\ *n, pl* **-dies** ♦ **:** immediate charge and control

♦ care, guardianship, keeping, safekeeping, trust, ward

¹cus•tom \ˈkəs-təm\ *n* **1** ♦ **:** habitual course of action **:** recognized usage **2** *pl* **:** taxes levied on imports **3 :** business patronage

♦ fashion, habit, pattern, practice, trick, way, wont

²custom *adj* **1 :** made to personal order **2 :** doing work only on order
cus•tom•ary \ˈkəs-tə-ˌmer-ē\ *adj* **1** ♦ **:** based on or established by custom **2** ♦ **:** commonly practiced or observed — **cus•tom•ar•i•ly** *adv*

♦ [1] classical, conventional, traditional ♦ [2] conventional, current, popular, standard, stock, usual

cus•tom–built \ˈkəs-təm-ˈbilt\ *adj* **:** built to individual order
cus•tom•er \ˈkəs-tə-mər\ *n* **1** ♦ **:** one that purchases a commodity or service; *esp* **:** a regular or frequent buyer **2 :** an individual usually having some specified distinctive trait

♦ guest, patron

cus•tom•house \ˈkəs-təm-ˌhau̇s\ *n* **:** the building where customs are paid
cus•tom•ise *Brit var of* CUSTOMIZE
cus•tom•ize \ˈkəs-tə-ˌmīz\ *vb* **-ized; -iz•ing :** to build, fit, or alter according to individual specifications
cus•tom–made \ˈkəs-təm-ˈmād\ *adj* ♦ **:** made to individual order

♦ custom, tailored *Ant* mass-produced, ready-made

¹cut \ˈkət\ *vb* **cut; cut•ting 1** ♦ **:** to penetrate or divide with a sharp edge **:** CLEAVE, GASH; *also* **:** to experience the growth of (a tooth) through the gum **2 :** to hurt the feelings of **3 :** to strike sharply **4** ♦ **:** to diminish or reduce by or as if by paring **:** SHORTEN, REDUCE **5 :** to remove by severing or paring **6 :** INTERSECT, CROSS **7 :** to divide into parts **8 a :** to go quickly or change direction abruptly **b :** to veer from a direct line **9 :** to cause to stop **10** ♦ **:** to proceed obliquely from a straight course — often used with *across*

♦ [1] rip, slash, slice, slit ♦ [4] bob, clip, crop, cut back, dock, lop, nip, prune, reduce, shave, shear, shorten, trim ♦ *usu* **cut**

across [10] cover, crisscross, cross, follow, go, pass, proceed, travel, traverse

²cut *n* **1 :** something made by cutting **:** GASH, CLEFT **2** ♦ **:** a portion belonging to, due to, or contributed by an individual or group **:** SHARE **3 :** a segment or section of a meat carcass **4 :** an excavated channel or roadway **5 :** a sharp stroke or blow **6 :** REDUCTION ⟨∼ in wages⟩ **7 :** the shape or manner in which a thing is cut **8** ♦ **:** a grade or step

♦ [2] allotment, allowance, part, portion, proportion, quota, share ♦ [8] degree, grade, inch, notch, peg, phase, point, stage, step

cut–and–dried \ˌkət-ᵊn-ˈdrīd\ *also* **cut–and–dry** \-ˈdrī\ *adj* **:** according to a plan, set procedure, or formula

cu•ta•ne•ous \kyu̇-ˈtā-nē-əs\ *adj* **:** of, relating to, or affecting the skin

cut•back \ˈkət-ˌbak\ *n* **1 :** something cut back **2 :** REDUCTION

cut back *vb* **1** ♦ **:** to shorten by cutting **2** ♦ **:** to remake in a smaller size

♦ [1] bob, clip, crop, cut, dock, lop, nip, prune, shave, shear, trim ♦ [2] abbreviate, abridge, curtail, shorten

cut down *vb* ♦ **:** to strike to the ground with or as if with a sharp blow

♦ chop, fell, hew

cute \ˈkyüt\ *adj* **cut•er; cut•est 1 :** CLEVER, SHREWD **2** ♦ **:** daintily attractive **:** PRETTY

♦ attractive, beautiful, bonny, fair, pretty

cu•ti•cle \ˈkyü-ti-kəl\ *n* **1 :** an outer layer (as of skin or a leaf) **2 :** dead or horny epidermis especially around a fingernail — **cu•tic•u•lar** \kyu̇-ˈti-kyə-lər\ *adj*

cut in *vb* **1** ♦ **:** to thrust oneself between others **2 :** to interrupt a dancing couple and take one as one's partner

♦ break, chime in, interpose, interrupt, intrude

cut•lass \ˈkət-ləs\ *n* **:** a short heavy curved sword

cut•ler \ˈkət-lər\ *n* **:** one who makes, deals in, or repairs cutlery

cut•lery \ˈkət-lə-rē\ *n* **:** edged or cutting tools; *esp* **:** implements for cutting and eating food

cut•let \ˈkət-lət\ *n* **1 :** a slice of meat (as veal) for broiling or frying **2** ♦ **:** a flat croquette of chopped meat or fish

♦ fritter, patty

cut•off \ˈkət-ˌȯf\ *n* **1 :** the channel formed when a stream cuts through the neck of an oxbow; *also* **:** SHORTCUT **2 :** a device for cutting off **3** *pl* **:** shorts orig. made from jeans with the legs cut off at the knees or higher

cut off *vb* ♦ **:** to set apart from others

♦ insulate, isolate, seclude, segregate, separate, sequester

cut•out \ˈkət-ˌau̇t\ *n* **:** something cut out or prepared for cutting out from something else ⟨a page of animal ∼*s*⟩

¹cut out *vb* **1 :** to determine or assign through necessity ⟨had her work *cut out* for her⟩ **2 :** DISCONNECT **3** ♦ **:** to cease operating ⟨the engine *cut out*⟩ **4 :** ELIMINATE ⟨*cut out* unnecessary expense⟩ **5 :** to put an end to

♦ break, break down, conk, crash, die, fail, stall

cut–rate \ˈkət-ˈrāt\ *adj* **1** ♦ **:** relating to or dealing in goods sold at reduced rates **2** ♦ **:** of second or inferior quality or value

♦ [1] cheap, low, reasonable ♦ [2] bad, bum, cheap, coarse, common, execrable, inferior, junky, lousy, mediocre, miserable, poor, rotten, second-rate, shoddy, sleazy, terrible, trashy, wretched

cut•ter \ˈkə-tər\ *n* **1 :** a tool or a machine for cutting **2 :** a ship's boat for carrying stores and passengers **3 :** a small armed vessel in government service **4 :** a light sleigh

¹cut•throat \ˈkət-ˌthrōt\ *n* **:** MURDERER

²cutthroat *adj* **1 :** MURDEROUS, CRUEL **2** ♦ **:** marked by unprincipled practices ⟨∼ competition⟩

♦ immoral, Machiavellian, unconscionable, unethical, unprincipled, unscrupulous

cutthroat trout *n* **:** a large American trout with a red mark under the jaw

¹cut•ting \ˈkə-tiŋ\ *n* **:** a piece of a plant able to grow into a new plant

²cutting *adj* **1** ♦ **:** made for cutting, severing, or dividing **:** SHARP, EDGED **2** ♦ **:** marked by piercing cold **3** ♦ **:** likely to hurt the feelings **:** SARCASTIC ⟨a ∼ remark⟩

♦ [1] edgy, ground, keen, sharp ♦ [2] biting, bitter, keen, penetrating, piercing, raw, sharp ♦ [3] acrid, biting, caustic, mordant, pungent, sarcastic, satiric, scathing, sharp, tart

cut•tle•fish \ˈkə-tᵊl-ˌfish\ *n* **:** any of various marine mollusks having eight arms and two usually longer tentacles and an internal shell (**cut•tle•bone** \-ˌbōn\) composed of calcium compounds

cut•up \ˈkət-ˌəp\ *n* **:** a person who clowns or acts boisterously

cut up *vb* ♦ **:** to behave in a comic, boisterous, or unruly manner

♦ act up, clown, fool, monkey, show off, skylark

cut•worm \-ˌwərm\ *n* **:** any of various smooth-bodied moth larvae that feed on plants at night

cw *abbr* clockwise

CWO *abbr* **1** cash with order **2** chief warrant officer

cwt *abbr* hundredweight

-cy \sē\ *n suffix* **1 :** action **:** practice ⟨mendican*cy*⟩ **2 :** rank **:** office ⟨chaplain*cy*⟩ **3 :** body **:** class ⟨constituen*cy*⟩ **4 :** state **:** quality ⟨accura*cy*⟩

cy•an \ˈsī-ˌan, -ən\ *n* **:** a greenish blue color

cy•a•nide \ˈsī-ə-ˌnīd, -nəd\ *n* **:** a poisonous compound of carbon and nitrogen with another element (as potassium)

cy•ber \ˈsī-bər\ *adj* **:** of, relating to, or involving computers or computer networks

cyber- *comb form* **:** computer **:** computer network

cy•ber•ca•fe \ˈsī-bər-ka-ˈfā\ *n* **:** a small restaurant offering use of computers with Internet access

cy•ber•net•ics \ˌsī-bər-ˈne-tiks\ *n* **:** the science of communication and control theory that is concerned especially with the comparative study of automatic control systems — **cy•ber•net•ic** *adj*

cy•ber•punk \ˈsī-bər-ˌpəŋk\ *n* **1 :** science fiction dealing with computer-dominated future societies **2 :** HACKER 3

cy•ber•sex \ˈsī-bər-ˌseks\ *n* **1 :** online sex-oriented conversations **2 :** sex-oriented material available on a computer

cy•ber•space \ˈsī-bər-ˌspās\ *n* **:** the on-line world of computer networks

cy•cla•men \ˈsī-klə-mən\ *n* **:** any of a genus of plants related to the primroses and grown for their showy nodding flowers

¹cy•cle \ˈsī-kəl\ *n* **1 :** a period of time occupied by a series of events that repeat themselves regularly and in the same order **2 :** a recurring round of operations or events **3 :** one complete occurrence of a periodic process (as a vibration or current alternation) **4 :** a circular or spiral arrangement **5** ♦ **:** a long period of time **:** AGE **6 :** BICYCLE **7 :** MOTORCYCLE — **cy•clic** \ˈsī-klik, ˈsi-\ *or* **cy•cli•cal** \-kli-kəl\ *adj* — **cy•cli•cal•ly** \-k(ə-)lē\ *also* **cy•clic•ly** *adv*

♦ aeon (*or* eon), age, eternity

²cy•cle \ˈsī-kəl\ *vb* **cy•cled; cy•cling :** to ride a cycle — **cy•clist** \ˈsī-klist, -kə-list\ *n*

cy•clone \ˈsī-ˌklōn\ *n* **1 :** a storm or system of winds that rotates about a center of low atmospheric pressure and advances at 20 to 30 miles (about 30 to 50 kilometers) an hour **2 :** TORNADO — **cy•clon•ic** \sī-ˈklä-nik\ *adj*

cy•clo•pe•dia *or* **cy•clo•pae•dia** \ˌsī-klə-ˈpē-dē-ə\ *n* **:** ENCYCLOPEDIA

cy•clo•tron \ˈsī-klə-ˌträn\ *n* **:** a device for giving high speed to charged particles by magnetic and electric fields

cyg•net \ˈsig-nət\ *n* **:** a young swan

cyl *abbr* cylinder

cyl•in•der \ˈsi-lən-dər\ *n* **:** the solid figure formed by turning a rectangle about one side as an axis; *also* **:** a body or space of this form ⟨an engine ∼⟩ ⟨a bullet in the ∼ of a revolver⟩ — **cy•lin•dri•cal** \sə-ˈlin-dri-kəl\ *adj*

cyn•ic \ˈsi-nik\ *n* **:** one who attributes all actions to selfish motives — **cyn•i•cal** \-ni-kəl\ *adj* — **cyn•i•cal•ly** \-k(ə-)lē\ *adv* — **cyn•i•cism** \si-nə-ˌsi-zəm\ *n*

cy•no•sure \ˈsī-nə-ˌshu̇r, ˈsi-\ *n* ♦ **:** a center of attraction or attention

♦ base, center (*or* centre), core, eye, focus, heart, hub, mecca, nucleus, seat

CYO *abbr* Catholic Youth Organization

cy•pher *chiefly Brit var of* CIPHER

cy•press \ˈsī-prəs\ *n* **1 :** any of a genus of scaly-leaved evergreen trees and shrubs **2 :** BALD CYPRESS **3 :** the wood of a cypress

Cyp•ri•ot \ˈsi-prē-ət, -ˌät\ *or* **Cyp•ri•ote** \-ˌōt, -ət\ *n* **:** a native or inhabitant of Cyprus — **Cypriot** *adj*

cyst \ˈsist\ *n* **:** an abnormal closed bodily sac usually containing liquid — **cys•tic** \ˈsis-tik\ *adj*

cystic fibrosis *n* **:** a common hereditary disease marked especially by deficiency of pancreatic enzymes, by respiratory symptoms, and by excessive loss of salt in the sweat

cy•tol•o•gy \sī-ˈtä-lə-jē\ *n* : a branch of biology dealing with cells — **cy•to•log•i•cal** \ˌsīt-ᵊl-ˈä-ji-kəl\ *or* **cy•to•log•ic** \-jik\ *adj* — **cy•tol•o•gist** \sī-ˈtä-lə-jist\ *n*
cy•to•plasm \ˈsī-tə-ˌpla-zəm\ *n* : the protoplasm of a cell that lies external to the nucleus — **cy•to•plas•mic** \ˌsī-tə-ˈplaz-mik\ *adj*
cy•to•sine \ˈsī-tə-ˌsēn\ *n* : a chemical base that is a pyrimidine coding genetic information in DNA and RNA
CZ *abbr* Canal Zone
czar \ˈzär, ˈtsär\ *n* **1** : the ruler of Russia until 1917 **2** ♦ : one having great authority — **czar•ist** \-ist\ *n or adj*

♦ baron, king, magnate, mogul, prince, tycoon

cza•ri•na \zä-ˈrē-nə\ *n* : the wife of a czar
Czech \ˈchek\ *n* **1** : a native or inhabitant of Czechoslovakia or the Czech Republic **2** : the language of the Czechs — **Czech** *adj*

D

¹d \ˈdē\ *n, pl* **d's** *or* **ds** \ˈdēz\ *often cap* **1** : the 4th letter of the English alphabet **2** : a grade rating a student's work as poor
²d *abbr, often cap* **1** date **2** daughter **3** day **4** dead **5** deceased **6** degree **7** Democrat **8** penny; pence **9** depart; departure **10** diameter
D *symbol* deuterium
DA *abbr* **1** deposit account **2** district attorney **3** don't answer
¹dab \ˈdab\ *n* **1 a** ♦ : a sudden blow or thrust : POKE **b** : PECK **2** ♦ : a small amount **3** : a gentle touch or stroke : PAT **4** : DAUB

♦ [1a] dig, jab, poke ♦ [2] bit, hint, lick, little, particle, spot, touch

²dab *vb* **dabbed; dab•bing** **1** : to strike or touch gently : PAT **2** : to apply lightly or irregularly : DAUB — **dab•ber** *n*
dab•ble \ˈda-bəl\ *vb* **dab•bled; dab•bling** **1** : to wet by splashing : SPATTER **2** : to paddle or play in or as if in water **3** : to work or involve oneself without serious effort — **dab•bler** *n*
da ca•po \dä-ˈkä-(ˌ)pō\ *adv or adj* : from the beginning — used as a direction in music to repeat
dace \ˈdās\ *n, pl* **dace** : any of various small No. American freshwater fishes related to the carp
da•cha \ˈdä-chə\ *n* : a Russian country house
dachs•hund \ˈdäks-ˌhůnt\ *n, pl* **dachshunds** : any of a breed of long-bodied short-legged dogs of German origin
dac•tyl \ˈdakt-ᵊl\ *n* : a metrical foot of one accented syllable followed by two unaccented syllables — **dac•tyl•ic** \dak-ˈti-lik\ *adj or n*
dad \ˈdad\ *n* : a male parent : FATHER 1
Da•da \ˈdä-(ˌ)dä\ *n* : a movement in art and literature based on deliberate irrationality and negation of traditional artistic values — **da•da•ism** \-ˌi-zəm\ *n, often cap* — **da•da•ist** \-ˌist\ *n or adj, often cap*
dad•dy \ˈda-dē\ *n, pl* **daddies** ♦ : a male human parent : FATHER 1

♦ father, papa, pop

dad•dy long•legs \ˌda-dē-ˈlȯŋ-ˌlegz\ *n, pl* **daddy longlegs** : any of an order of arachnids resembling the true spiders but having small rounded bodies and long slender legs
daemon *var of* DEMON
daf•fo•dil \ˈda-fə-ˌdil\ *n* : any of various bulbous herbs with usually large flowers having a trumpetlike center
daf•fy \ˈda-fē\ *adj* **daf•fi•er; -est** **1** : exhibiting or indicative of a lack of common sense or sound judgment : FOOLISH **2** : disordered in mind : INSANE
daft \ˈdaft\ *adj* **1** ♦ : exhibiting or indicative of a lack of common sense or sound judgment : FOOLISH **2** ♦ : disordered in mind : INSANE

♦ [1] absurd, crazy, cuckoo, fatuous, foolish, mad, nonsensical, nutty, senseless, silly, stupid ♦ [2] cracked, crazy, deranged, insane, loco, lunatic, mad, maniacal, nuts, nutty, screwy, unsound

daft•ness \-nəs\ *n* ♦ : the quality or state of being daft

♦ absurdity, asininity, balminess, craziness, fatuity, folly, foolishness, inanity, insanity, lunacy, madness, silliness, simplicity, zaniness

dag *abbr* dekagram
dag•ger \ˈda-gər\ *n* **1** : a sharp pointed knife for stabbing **2** : a character † used as a reference mark or to indicate a death date
da•guerre•o•type \də-ˈger-(ē-)ə-ˌtīp\ *n* : an early photograph produced on a silver or a silver-covered copper plate
dahl•ia \ˈdal-yə, ˈdäl-\ *n* : any of a genus of tuberous herbs related to the daisies and having showy flowers
¹dai•ly \ˈdā-lē\ *adj* **1** : occurring, done, or used every day or every weekday **2** : of or relating to every day ⟨~ visitors⟩ **3** : computed in terms of one day ⟨~ wages⟩ — **dai•li•ness** \-lē-nəs\ *n* — **daily** *adv*
²daily *n, pl* **dailies** : a newspaper published every weekday
daily double *n* : a system of betting on races in which the bettor must pick the winners of two stipulated races in order to win
dain•ti•ness \ˈdān-tē-nəs\ *n* ♦ : the quality or state of being dainty

♦ delicacy, fineness, fragility

¹dain•ty \ˈdān-tē\ *n, pl* **dainties** ♦ : something delicious or pleasing to the taste : DELICACY

♦ delicacy, goody, tidbit, treat

²dainty *adj* **dain•ti•er; -est** **1** ♦ : pleasing to taste **2** : delicately pretty **3** ♦ : marked by fastidious discrimination or finicky taste — **dain•ti•ly** \-ti-lē\ *adv*

♦ [1] choice, delicate, elegant, exquisite, rare, select ♦ [3] choosy, delicate, demanding, exacting, fastidious, finicky, fussy, nice, old-maidish, particular, picky

dai•qui•ri \ˈdī-kə-rē, ˈda-kə-rē\ *n* : a cocktail made of usually rum, lime juice, and sugar
dairy \ˈder-ē\ *n, pl* **dair•ies** **1** : CREAMERY **2** : a farm specializing in milk production
dairy•ing \ˈder-ē-iŋ\ *n* : the business of operating a dairy
dairy•maid \-ˌmād\ *n* : a woman employed in a dairy
dairy•man \-mən, -ˌman\ *n* : a person who operates a dairy farm or works in a dairy
da•is \ˈdā-əs\ *n* ♦ : a raised platform usually above the floor of a hall or large room

♦ platform, podium, rostrum, stage, stand

dai•sy \ˈdā-zē\ *n, pl* **daisies** : any of numerous composite plants having flower heads in which the marginal flowers resemble petals
dai•sy–chain \-ˌchān\ *vb* : to link (as computer components) together in series — **daisy chain** *n*
daisy wheel *n* : a disk with spokes bearing type that serves as the printing element of an electric typewriter or printer; *also* : a printer that uses such a disk
Da•ko•ta \də-ˈkō-tə\ *n, pl* **Dakotas** *also* **Dakota** : a member of an American Indian people of the northern Mississippi valley; *also* : their language
dal *abbr* dekaliter
dale \ˈdāl\ *n* ♦ : a long depression between ranges of hills or mountains : VALLEY

♦ hollow, valley

dal•li•ance \ˈda-lē-əns\ *n* ♦ : an act of dallying

♦ frolic, fun, play, relaxation, sport

dal•ly \ˈda-lē\ *vb* **dal•lied; dal•ly•ing** **1** ♦ : to act playfully; *esp* : to play amorously **2** ♦ : to waste time **3** : to move slowly : LINGER

♦ [1] disport, frolic, play, recreate, rollick, sport ♦ [2] dawdle, dillydally, hang around, hang out, idle, loaf, loll, lounge

dal•ma•tian \dal-ˈmā-shən\ *n, often cap* : any of a breed of medium-sized dogs having a white short-haired coat with many black or brown spots
¹dam \ˈdam\ *n* : the female parent of an animal and especially of a domestic animal
²dam *n* ♦ : a barrier (as across a stream) to stop the flow of water

♦ dike, embankment, levee

[3]dam *vb* **1 :** to provide or restrain with a dam **2** ♦ **:** to stop up **:** BLOCK

♦ block, choke, clog, close (off), congest, jam, obstruct, plug (up), stop (up), stuff

[4]dam *abbr* dekameter

[1]dam•age \ˈda-mij\ *n* **1** ♦ **:** loss or harm due to injury to persons, property, or reputation **2** *pl* ♦ **:** compensation in money imposed by law for loss or injury ⟨bring a suit for ∼*s*⟩

♦ [1] detriment, harm, hurt, injury ♦ *usu* **damages** [2] fine, forfeit, mulct, penalty ♦ *usu* **damages** [2] compensation, indemnity, quittance, recompense, redress, remuneration, reparation, requital, restitution, satisfaction

[2]damage *vb* **dam•aged; dam•ag•ing** ♦ **:** to cause damage to

♦ blemish, break, cripple, deface, disfigure, flaw, harm, hurt, injure, mar, spoil, vitiate ***Ant*** fix, mend, patch, rebuild, recondition, reconstruct, renovate, repair, revamp

dam•ag•ing *adj* ♦ **:** causing or able to cause damage

♦ adverse, bad, baleful, baneful, deleterious, detrimental, evil, harmful, hurtful, ill, injurious, mischievous, noxious, pernicious, prejudicial

dam•a•scene \ˈda-mə-ˌsēn\ *vb* **-scened; -scen•ing :** to ornament (as iron or steel) with wavy patterns or with inlaid work of precious metals

dam•ask \ˈda-məsk\ *n* **1 :** a firm lustrous reversible figured fabric used for household linen **2 :** a tough steel having decorative wavy lines

dame \ˈdām\ *n* **1** ♦ **:** a woman of rank, station, or authority **2** ♦ **:** an elderly woman **3 :** WOMAN

♦ [1] gentlewoman, lady, noblewoman ♦ [2] dowager, matriarch, matron

damn \ˈdam\ *vb* **1 :** to condemn to a punishment or fate; *esp* **:** to condemn especially to hell **2** ♦ **:** to condemn as invalid, illegal, immoral, bad, or harmful **3 :** CURSE — **damned** *adj*

♦ censure, condemn, decry, denounce, reprehend, reprobate

dam•na•ble \ˈdam-nə-bəl\ *adj* **1 :** liable to or deserving punishment **2 :** DETESTABLE ⟨∼ weather⟩ — **dam•na•bly** \-blē\ *adv*

dam•na•tion \dam-ˈnā-shən\ *n* **1 :** the act of damning **2 :** the state of being damned

[1]damp \ˈdamp\ *n* **1 :** a noxious gas **2 :** the small amount of liquid that causes dampness **:** MOISTURE

[2]damp *vb* **:** to check or diminish the activity or vigor of **:** DAMPEN

[3]damp *adj* **:** MOIST

damp•en \ˈdam-pən\ *vb* **1** ♦ **:** to check or diminish in activity or vigor **2 :** to make or become damp

♦ blunt, deaden, dull, numb

damp•er \ˈdam-pər\ *n* **1 :** a dulling or deadening influence ⟨put a ∼ on the party⟩ **2 :** one that damps; *esp* **:** a valve or movable plate (as in the flue of a stove, furnace, or fireplace) to regulate the draft

damp•ness \ˈdamp-nəs\ *n* **:** the quality or state of being damp

dam•sel \ˈdam-zəl\ *n* **:** a young woman **:** MAIDEN

dam•sel•fly \-ˌflī\ *n* **:** any of a group of insects that are closely related to the dragonflies but fold their wings above the body when at rest

dam•son \ˈdam-zən\ *n* **:** a plum with acid purple fruit; *also* **:** its fruit

Dan *abbr* Daniel

[1]dance \ˈdans\ *vb* **danced; danc•ing 1** ♦ **:** to glide, step, or move through a set series of movements usually to music **2** ♦ **:** to move quickly up and down or about **3 :** to perform or take part in as a dancer — **danc•er** *n*

♦ [1] foot, step ♦ [2] dart, flit, flutter, zip

[2]dance *n* **1 :** an act or instance of dancing **2** ♦ **:** a social gathering for dancing **3 :** a piece of music (as a waltz) by which dancing may be guided **4 :** the art of dancing

♦ ball, formal, hop, prom

D & C *n* **:** a surgical procedure that involves stretching the cervix and scraping the inside walls of the uterus (as to test for cancer or to perform an abortion)

dan•de•li•on \ˈdan-də-ˌlī-ən, -dē-\ *n* **:** any of a genus of common yellow-flowered composite herbs

dan•der \ˈdan-dər\ *n* **:** ANGER, TEMPER

dan•di•fy \ˈdan-di-ˌfī\ *vb* **-fied; -fy•ing :** to cause to resemble a dandy

dan•dle \ˈdand-^{ə}l\ *vb* **dan•dled; dan•dling 1 :** to move up and down in one's arms or on one's knee in affectionate play **2 :** to treat with extreme or excessive care and attention

dan•druff \ˈdan-drəf\ *n* **:** scaly white or grayish flakes of dead skin cells that come off the scalp — **dan•druffy** \-drə-fē\ *adj*

[1]dan•dy \ˈdan-dē\ *n, pl* **dandies 1** ♦ **:** a man unduly attentive to personal appearance **2** ♦ **:** something excellent in its class

♦ [1] buck, dude, fop, gallant ♦ [2] beauty, crackerjack, jim-dandy, knockout, pip

[2]dandy *adj* **dan•di•er; -est :** very good **:** FIRST-RATE

Dane \ˈdān\ *n* **1 :** a native or inhabitant of Denmark **2 :** GREAT DANE

dan•ger \ˈdān-jər\ *n* **1** ♦ **:** exposure or liability to injury, harm, or evil **2** ♦ **:** something that may cause injury or harm

♦ [1] distress, jeopardy, peril, risk, trouble ***Ant*** safety, security
♦ [2] hazard, menace, peril, pitfall, risk, threat, trouble

dan•ger•ous \ˈdān-jə-rəs\ *adj* **1** ♦ **:** exposing to or involving danger **:** HAZARDOUS **2 :** able or likely to inflict injury — **dan•ger•ous•ly** *adv*

♦ grave, grievous, hazardous, menacing, parlous, perilous, risky, serious, unhealthy, unsafe, venturesome ***Ant*** harmless, innocent, innocuous, safe

dan•gle \ˈdaŋ-gəl\ *vb* **dan•gled; dan•gling 1** ♦ **:** to hang loosely especially with a swinging motion **:** SWING **2 :** to be a hanger-on or dependent **3 :** to be left without proper grammatical connection in a sentence **4 :** to keep hanging uncertainly **5 :** to offer as an inducement

♦ hang, sling, suspend, swing

Dan•iel \ˈdan-yəl\ *n* **:** a book of Jewish and Christian Scripture

Dan•ish \ˈdā-nish\ *n* **:** the language of the Danes — **Danish** *adj*

Danish pastry *n* **:** a pastry made of a rich yeast-raised dough

dank \ˈdaŋk\ *adj* **:** disagreeably wet or moist **:** DAMP — **dank•ness** *n*

dan•seuse \dän^{n}-ˈsərz, -ˈsəz; dän-ˈsüz\ *n* **:** a female ballet dancer

dap•per \ˈda-pər\ *adj* **1** ♦ **:** neat and trim in style or appearance **:** SPRUCE **2 :** being alert and lively in movement and manners **:** JAUNTY

♦ natty, sharp, smart, spruce

dap•ple \ˈda-pəl\ *vb* **dap•pled; dap•pling** ♦ **:** to mark with different-colored spots

♦ blotch, dot, fleck, freckle, mottle, pepper, speck, spot, sprinkle, stipple

dap•pled *adj* ♦ **:** marked with small spots or patches contrasting with the background

♦ mottled, piebald, pied, spotted ♦ mottled, spotted, spotty, variegated

DAR *abbr* Daughters of the American Revolution

[1]dare \ˈder\ *vb* **dared; dar•ing 1 :** to have sufficient courage **:** be bold enough to **2** ♦ **:** to challenge to perform an action especially as a proof of courage **3** ♦ **:** to confront boldly

♦ [2] challenge, defy ♦ [3] beard, brave, brazen, confront, defy, face

[2]dare *n* **:** an act or instance of daring **:** CHALLENGE

dare•dev•il \-ˌde-vəl\ *n* ♦ **:** a recklessly bold person — **daredevil** *adj*

♦ devil, madcap

[1]daring \ˈder-iŋ\ *adj* ♦ **:** venturesomely bold in action or thought — **dar•ing•ly** *adv*

♦ adventurous, audacious, bold, enterprising, gutsy, hardy, nervy, venturesome

[2]dar•ing *n* ♦ **:** venturesome boldness

♦ bravery, courage, fearlessness, gallantry, guts, hardihood, heart, heroism, nerve, stoutness, valor

[1]dark \ˈdärk\ *adj* **1** ♦ **:** being without light or without much light **2 :** not light in color ⟨a ∼ suit⟩ **3 a :** showing or causing gloom or depression **:** GLOOMY **b** ♦ **:** lacking knowledge or culture **4** ♦ **:** not clear to the understanding **5** *often cap* **:** being a period of stagnation or decline ⟨the *Dark* Ages⟩ **6 :** tending to keep secrets or to act secretly **:** SECRETIVE — **dark•ly** *adv*

♦ [1] darkling, dim, dusky, gloomy, murky, obscure, somber (*or* sombre) ***Ant*** bright, brightened, brilliant, illumined, illuminated, light, lighted, lucent, lucid, luminous ♦ [3b] ignorant, illiterate, simple, uneducated, unlearned, untaught ♦ [4] am-

◆ ambiguous, cryptic, darkling, deep, enigmatic, equivocal, inscrutable, murky, mysterious, mystic, nebulous, obscure, occult

[2]**dark** *n* **1 a** ◆ **:** a place or time of little or no light **b** ◆ **:** absence of light **:** DARKNESS; *esp* **:** NIGHT **2 :** a dark or deep color — **in the dark 1 :** in secrecy **2 :** in ignorance ⟨kept *in the dark* about the plans⟩

◆ darkness, dusk, gloaming, gloom, murk, night, semidarkness, shade, shadows, twilight ***Ant*** blaze, brightness, brilliance, day, daylight, glare, glow, light, lightness

dark•en \ˈdär-kən\ *vb* **1 a** ◆ **:** to make or grow dark or darker **b** ◆ **:** to make or become less clear **:** DIM **3 :** BESMIRCH, TARNISH **4** ◆ **:** to make or become gloomy or forbidding

◆ [1a, 1b] becloud, befog, blur, cloud, dim, fog, haze, mist, obscure, overcast, overshadow, shroud ◆ [4] gloom, glower, lower ***Ant*** brighten, cheer (up), lighten, perk (up)

dark horse *n* **:** a contestant or a political figure whose abilities and chances as a contender are not known

dark•ling \ˈdär-kliŋ\ *adj* **1 :** DARK: as **a :** devoid or partially devoid of light **b** ◆ **:** not clear to the understanding **:** MYSTERIOUS **2 :** done or taking place in the dark

◆ ambiguous, cryptic, dark, deep, enigmatic, equivocal, inscrutable, murky, mysterious, mystic, nebulous, obscure, occult

dark•ness \-nəs\ *n* ◆ **:** the quality or state of being dark

◆ dark, dusk, gloaming, gloom, murk, night, semidarkness, shade, shadows, twilight ◆ ambiguity, murkiness, obscurity, opacity

dark•room \ˈdärk-ˌrüm, -ˌru̇m\ *n* **:** a lightproof room in which photographic materials are processed

[1]**dar•ling** \ˈdär-liŋ\ *n* **1** ◆ **:** a dearly loved person **2** ◆ **:** one that is treated or regarded with special favor or liking **:** FAVORITE

◆ [1] beloved, dear, flame, honey, love, sweet, sweetheart ◆ [2] favorite (*or* favourite), minion, pet, preference

[2]**darling** *adj* **1** ◆ **:** dearly loved **:** FAVORITE **2** ◆ **:** very pleasing **:** CHARMING

◆ [1] adorable, dear, endearing, lovable, precious, sweet, winning ◆ [2] agreeable, charming, delectable, delicious, delightful, enjoyable, heavenly, luscious, pleasurable

darm•stadt•i•um \ˌdärm-ˈsta-tē-əm\ *n* **:** a short-lived radioactive chemical element produced artificially

[1]**darn** \ˈdärn\ *vb* **:** to mend with interlacing stitches — **darn•er** *n*

[2]**darn** *or* **darned** \ˈdärnd\ *adv* **:** VERY, EXTREMELY ⟨a ~ good job⟩

darning needle *n* **1 :** a needle for darning **2 :** DRAGONFLY

[1]**dart** \ˈdärt\ *n* **1 :** a small missile with a point on one end and feathers on the other; *also, pl* **:** a game in which darts are thrown at a target **2** ◆ **:** something causing a sudden pain or distress **3 :** a stitched tapering fold in a garment **4 :** a quick movement

◆ affront, barb, dig, indignity, insult, name, offense, outrage, put-down, sarcasm, slight, slur, wound

[2]**dart** *vb* **1 :** to throw with a sudden movement **2** ◆ **:** to thrust or move suddenly or rapidly **3 :** to shoot with a dart containing a usually tranquilizing drug

◆ dance, flit, flutter, zip

dart•er \ˈdär-tər\ *n* **:** any of numerous small No. American freshwater fishes related to the perches

Dar•win•ism \ˈdär-wə-ˌni-zəm\ *n* **:** a theory explaining the origin and continued existence of new species of plants and animals by means of natural selection acting on chance variations — **Dar•win•ist** \-nist\ *n or adj*

[1]**dash** \ˈdash\ *vb* **1 :** SMASH **2** ◆ **:** to knock, hurl, or thrust violently **3 :** to soil or stain with splashed liquid **:** SPLASH **4 :** RUIN **5 :** DEPRESS, SADDEN **6 :** to perform or finish hastily **7** ◆ **:** to move with sudden speed **:** move rapidly

◆ [2] cast, catapult, chuck, fire, fling, heave, hurl, hurtle, launch, peg, pelt, pitch, sling, throw, toss ◆ [7] career, course, fly, hasten, hurry, race, rip, rocket, run, rush, shoot, speed, tear, zip, zoom

[2]**dash** *n* **1 :** a sudden burst or splash **2 :** a stroke of a pen **3 :** a punctuation mark — that is used especially to indicate a break in the thought or structure of a sentence **4 :** a small addition ⟨a ~ of salt⟩ **5 :** flashy showiness **6** ◆ **:** animation in style and action **7 :** a sudden rush or attempt ⟨made a ~ for the door⟩ **8 :** a short foot race **9 :** DASHBOARD

◆ energy, life, pep, vigor (*or* vigour), vim, vitality

dash•board \-ˌbȯrd\ *n* **:** a panel in an automobile or aircraft below the windshield usually containing dials and controls

dash•er \ˈda-shər\ *n* **:** a device (as in a churn) for agitating something

da•shi•ki \də-ˈshē-kē\ *also* **dai•shi•ki** \dī-\ *n* **:** a usually brightly colored loose-fitting pullover garment

dash•ing \ˈda-shiŋ\ *adj* **1 :** marked by vigorous action **2 :** marked by smartness especially in dress and manners

das•tard \ˈdas-tərd\ *n* **1** ◆ **:** one who shows disgraceful fear or timidity **:** COWARD **2 :** a person who acts treacherously

◆ chicken, coward, craven, poltroon, recreant, sissy

das•tard•ly \-lē\ *adj* ◆ **:** showing disgraceful fear or timidity **:** COWARDLY

◆ chicken, cowardly, craven, pusillanimous, recreant, spineless, yellow

dat *abbr* dative

da•ta \ˈdā-tə, ˈda-, ˈdä-\ *n sing or pl* **:** factual information (as measurements or statistics) used as a basis for reasoning, discussion, or calculation

da•ta•base \-ˌbās\ *n* **:** a usually large collection of data organized especially for rapid search and retrieval (as by a computer) — **database** *vb*

data processing *n* **:** the action or process of supplying a computer with information and having the computer use it to produce a desired result

[1]**date** \ˈdāt\ *n* **:** the oblong edible fruit of a tall palm; *also* **:** this palm

[2]**date** *n* **1 :** the day, month, or year of an event **2 :** a statement giving the time of execution or making (as of a coin or check) **3** ◆ **:** the period to which something belongs **4** ◆ **:** an appointment to meet at a specified time; *esp* **:** a social engagement between two persons that often has a romantic character **5 :** a person with whom one has a usually romantic date — **to date :** up to the present moment

◆ [3] duration, life, lifetime, run, standing, time ◆ [4] appointment, engagement, rendezvous, tryst

[3]**date** *vb* **dat•ed; dat•ing 1 :** to record the date of or on **2 :** to determine, mark, or reveal the date, age, or period of **3 :** to make or have a date with **4 :** ORIGINATE ⟨~s from ancient times⟩ **5 :** EXTEND ⟨*dating* back to childhood⟩ **6 :** to show qualities typical of a past period

dat•ed \ˈdā-təd\ *adj* **1 :** provided with a date **2** ◆ **:** no longer acceptable, stylish, current, or usable

◆ antiquated, archaic, obsolete, outdated, outmoded, outworn, passé

date•less \ˈdāt-ləs\ *adj* **1 :** being or seeming to be without end **:** ENDLESS **2 :** having no date **3** ◆ **:** too ancient to be dated **4 :** not limited or affected by time **:** TIMELESS

◆ age-old, ancient, antediluvian, antique, hoary, old, venerable

date•line \ˈdāt-ˌlīn\ *n* **:** a line in a publication giving the date and place of composition or issue — **dateline** *vb*

date rape *n* **:** rape committed by the victim's date

da•tive \ˈdā-tiv\ *adj* **:** of, relating to, or constituting a grammatical case marking typically the indirect object of a verb — **dative** *n*

da•tum \ˈdā-təm, ˈda-, ˈdä-\ *n, pl* **da•ta** \-tə\ *or* **datums :** a single piece of data **:** FACT

dau *abbr* daughter

[1]**daub** \ˈdȯb\ *vb* **1** ◆ **:** to cover or smear with something sticky or dirty **2 :** to apply paint or color crudely — **daub•er** *n*

◆ smear

[2]**daub** *n* **1 :** something daubed on **:** SMEAR **2 :** a crude picture

daugh•ter \ˈdȯ-tər\ *n* **1 :** a female offspring especially of human beings **2 :** a female adopted child **3 :** a human female descendant — **daughter** *adj* — **daugh•ter•less** \-ləs\ *adj*

daugh•ter–in–law \ˈdȯ-tə-rən-ˌlȯ\ *n, pl* **daugh•ters–in–law** \-tər-zən-\ **:** the wife of one's son

daunt \ˈdȯnt\ *vb* ◆ **:** to lessen the courage of

◆ demoralize, discourage, dishearten, dismay, dispirit, unman, unnerve

daunt•ing \ˈdȯn-tiŋ\ *adj* **:** tending to overwhelm or intimidate ⟨a ~ task⟩

daunt•less \-ləs\ *adj* ◆ **:** marked by courageous resolution **:** FEARLESS — **daunt•less•ly** *adv*

◆ brave, courageous, doughty, fearless, gallant, greathearted, heroic, intrepid, lionhearted, manful, stalwart, stout, undaunted, valiant, valorous

dau•phin \ˈdō-fən\ *n, often cap* **:** the eldest son of a king of France
DAV *abbr* Disabled American Veterans
dav•en•port \ˈda-vən-ˌpōrt\ *n* ♦ **:** a large upholstered sofa

♦ couch, divan, lounge, settee, sofa

da•vit \ˈdā-vət, ˈda-\ *n* **:** a small crane on a ship used in pairs especially to raise or lower boats
daw•dle \ˈdȯd-ᵊl\ *vb* **daw•dled; daw•dling 1** ♦ **:** to spend time wastefully or idly **2** ♦ **:** to move lackadaisically — **daw•dler** *n*

♦ [1] dally, dillydally, hang around, hang out, idle, loaf, loll, lounge ♦ [2] crawl, creep, dally, delay, dillydally, drag, lag, linger, loiter, poke, tarry

¹dawn \ˈdȯn\ *vb* **1 :** to begin to grow light as the sun rises **2** ♦ **:** to begin to appear or develop **3 :** to begin to be understood ⟨the solution ~*ed* on him⟩

♦ arise, begin, commence, form, materialize, originate, spring, start

²dawn *n* **1** ♦ **:** the first appearance of light in the morning **2** ♦ **:** a first appearance **:** BEGINNING ⟨the ~ of a new era⟩

♦ [1] aurora, cockcrow, morning, sunrise ***Ant*** nightfall, sundown, sunset ♦ [2] beginning, birth, commencement, genesis, launch, morning, onset, outset, start, threshold

day \ˈdā\ *n* **1 :** the period of light between one night and the next; *also* **:** DAYLIGHT, DAYTIME **2 :** the period of rotation of a planet (as earth) or a moon on its axis **3 :** a period of 24 hours beginning at midnight **4 :** a specified day or date ⟨wedding ~⟩ **5 :** a specified time or period **:** AGE ⟨in olden ~*s*⟩ **6 :** the conflict or contention of the day **7 :** the time set apart by usage or law for work ⟨the 8-hour ~⟩
day•bed \ˈdā-ˌbed\ *n* **:** a couch that can be converted into a bed
day•book \-ˌbu̇k\ *n* **:** DIARY, JOURNAL
day•break \-ˌbrāk\ *n* **:** the first appearance of light in the morning followed by sunrise **:** DAWN
day care *n* **:** supervision of and care for children or disabled adults provided during the day; *also* **:** a program offering day care
day•dream \ˈdā-ˌdrēm\ *n* ♦ **:** a pleasant reverie — **daydream** *vb*

♦ chimera, conceit, delusion, dream, fancy, fantasy, figment, hallucination, illusion, phantasm, pipe dream, unreality, vision

day•light \ˈdā-ˌlīt\ *n* **1 :** the light of day **2 :** the time during which there is daylight **:** DAYTIME **3 :** the first appearance of light in the morning followed by sunrise **:** DAWN **4 :** understanding of something that has been obscure **5** *pl* **:** CONSCIOUSNESS; *also* **:** WITS **6 :** a perceptible space, gap, or difference
daylight saving time *n* **:** time usually one hour ahead of standard time
Day of Atonement : YOM KIPPUR
day school *n* **:** a private school without boarding facilities
day student *n* **:** a student who attends regular classes at a college or preparatory school but does not live there
day•time \ˈdā-ˌtīm\ *n* **:** the period of daylight
¹daze \ˈdāz\ *vb* **dazed; daz•ing 1 :** to stupefy especially by a blow **2 :** to dazzle with light **:** DAZZLE — **da•zed•ly** \ˈdā-zəd-lē\ *adv*
²daze *n* ♦ **:** the state of being dazed

♦ fog, haze, muddle, spin

¹daz•zle \ˈda-zəl\ *vb* **daz•zled; daz•zling 1** ♦ **:** to overpower with light **2 :** to impress greatly or confound with brilliance

♦ daze

²dazzle *n* ♦ **:** the action of dazzling

♦ brilliance, effulgence, illumination, lightness, lucidity, luminosity, radiance, refulgence, splendor

dB *abbr* decibel
Db *symbol* dubnium
d/b/a *abbr* doing business as
dbl *or* **dble** *abbr* double
DC *abbr* **1** from the beginning **2** direct current **3** District of Columbia **4** doctor of chiropractic
DD *abbr* **1** days after date **2** demand draft **3** dishonorable discharge **4** doctor of divinity
D–day *n* **:** a day set for launching an operation (as an invasion)
DDS *abbr* doctor of dental surgery
DDT \ˌdē-(ˌ)dē-ˈtē\ *n* **:** a persistent insecticide poisonous to many higher animals
DE *abbr* Delaware
dea•con \ˈdē-kən\ *n* **:** a subordinate officer in a Christian church
dea•con•ess \ˈdē-kə-nəs\ *n* **:** a woman chosen to assist in the church ministry
de•ac•ti•vate \dē-ˈak-tə-ˌvāt\ *vb* ♦ **:** to make inactive or ineffective

♦ kill, shut off, turn off ***Ant*** activate, actuate, crank (up), drive, move, propel, run, set off, spark, start, touch off, trigger, turn on

¹dead \ˈded\ *adj* **1** ♦ **:** deprived of life **:** LIFELESS **2 :** having the appearance of death **:** DEATHLIKE ⟨in a ~ faint⟩ **3 :** lacking power to move, feel, or respond **:** NUMB **4** ♦ **:** very tired **5 :** UNRESPONSIVE **6 :** EXTINGUISHED ⟨~ coals⟩ **7 :** INANIMATE, INERT **8** ♦ **:** no longer active or functioning ⟨a ~ battery⟩ **9 :** lacking power, significance, or effect ⟨a ~ custom⟩ **10** ♦ **:** no longer in use ⟨a ~ language⟩ **11 :** lacking in gaiety or animation ⟨a ~ party⟩ **12 :** QUIET, IDLE, UNPRODUCTIVE ⟨~ capital⟩ **13 :** lacking elasticity ⟨a ~ tennis ball⟩ **14 :** not circulating **:** STAGNANT ⟨~ air⟩ **15 :** lacking warmth, vigor, or taste ⟨~ wine⟩ **16 :** absolutely uniform ⟨~ level⟩ **17 :** UNERRING, EXACT ⟨a ~ shot⟩ **18 :** ABRUPT ⟨a ~ stop⟩ **19 :** having no exceptions or restrictions **:** COMPLETE ⟨a ~ loss⟩

♦ [1] breathless, deceased, defunct, gone, late, lifeless ***Ant*** alive, breathing, living ♦ [4] beat, bushed, drained, effete, jaded, limp, prostrate, spent, tired, weary, worn-out ♦ [8] dormant, fallow, free, idle, inactive, inert, inoperative, latent, off, vacant ♦ [10] bygone, defunct, extinct, gone

²dead *n, pl* **dead 1 :** one that is dead — usually used collectively ⟨the living and the ~⟩ **2 :** the time of greatest quiet ⟨the ~ of the night⟩
³dead *adv* **1** ♦ **:** in an absolute manner or condition ⟨~ right⟩ **2 :** in a sudden and complete manner ⟨stopped ~⟩ **3 :** in a direct manner **:** DIRECTLY ⟨~ ahead⟩

♦ altogether, completely, entirely, fast, flat, full, fully, perfectly, quite, thoroughly, well, wholly

dead•beat \-ˌbēt\ *n* **:** a person who persistently fails to pay personal debts or expenses
dead duck *n* **:** GONER
dead•en \ˈded-ᵊn\ *vb* **1** ♦ **:** to impair in vigor or sensation **:** BLUNT ⟨~ pain⟩ **2 :** to lessen the luster or spirit of **3 :** to make (as a wall) soundproof

♦ blunt, dampen, dull, numb

dead end *n* **1 :** an end (as of a street) without an exit **2 :** a position, situation, or course of action that leads to nothing further — **dead–end** \ˌded-ˌend\ *adj*
dead heat *n* ♦ **:** a contest in which two or more contestants tie (as by crossing the finish line simultaneously)

♦ draw, stalemate, standoff, tie

dead horse *n* **:** an exhausted topic or issue
dead letter *n* **1 :** something that has lost its force or authority without being formally abolished **2 :** a letter that cannot be delivered or returned
dead•line \ˈded-ˌlīn\ *n* **:** a date or time before which something must be done
dead•lock \ˈded-ˌläk\ *n* **1** ♦ **:** a stoppage of action because neither faction in a struggle will give in **2 :** a tie score — **deadlock** *vb*

♦ halt, impasse, stalemate, standstill

¹dead•ly \ˈded-lē\ *adj* **dead•li•er; -est 1** ♦ **:** likely to cause or capable of causing death **2 :** HOSTILE, IMPLACABLE **3 :** very accurate **:** UNERRING **4 :** tending to deprive of force or vitality ⟨a ~ habit⟩ **5 :** suggestive of death **6 :** very great **:** EXTREME — **dead•li•ness** *n*

♦ baleful, deathly, fatal, fell, lethal, mortal, murderous, pestilent, vital ***Ant*** healthful, healthy, nonfatal, nonlethal, wholesome

²deadly *adv* **1 :** suggesting death ⟨~ pale⟩ **2 :** to a high degree **:** EXTREMELY ⟨~ dull⟩
deadly sin *n* **:** one of seven sins of pride, covetousness, lust, anger, gluttony, envy, and sloth held to be fatal to spiritual progress
dead meat *n* **:** one that is doomed
¹dead•pan \ˈded-ˌpan\ *adj* ♦ **:** marked by an impassive manner or expression — **deadpan** *vb* — **deadpan** *adv*

♦ blank, expressionless, impassive, inexpressive, stolid, vacant

²deadpan *n* **:** a completely expressionless face
dead reckoning *n* **:** the determination of the position of a ship or aircraft solely from the record of the direction and distance of its course
dead•weight \ˈded-ˈwāt\ *n* **1 :** the unrelieved weight of an inert mass **2 :** a ship's load including the weight of cargo, fuel, crew, and passengers

dead•wood \-ˌwu̇d\ *n* **1 :** wood dead on the tree **2** ♦ **:** useless personnel or material

♦ chaff, dust, garbage, junk, litter, refuse, riffraff, rubbish, scrap, trash, waste

deaf \ˈdef\ *adj* **1 :** unable to hear **2 :** unwilling to hear or listen ⟨~ to all suggestions⟩ — **deaf•ness** *n*
deaf•en \ˈde-fən\ *vb* **:** to make deaf
deaf•en•ing \-iŋ\ *adj* ♦ **:** very loud

♦ booming, clamorous (*or* clamourous), earsplitting, loud, piercing, resounding, ringing, roaring, sonorous, stentorian, thunderous

deaf–mute \ˈdef-ˌmyüt\ *n, often offensive* **:** a deaf person who has never learned to speak
¹**deal** \ˈdēl\ *n* **1 :** a usually large or indefinite quantity or degree ⟨a great ~ of support⟩ **2 :** the act or right of distributing cards to players in a card game; *also* **:** HAND
²**deal** *vb* **dealt** \ˈdelt\; **deal•ing 1 a** ♦ **:** to give as one's portion **:** DISTRIBUTE **b :** to distribute playing cards to players in a game **2 :** ADMINISTER, DELIVER ⟨*dealt* him a blow⟩ **3** ♦ **:** to concern itself **:** TREAT ⟨the book ~*s* with crime⟩ **4 :** to take action in regard to something ⟨~ with offenders⟩ **5 a :** TRADE **b** ♦ **:** to sell or distribute something as a business ⟨~ in used cars⟩ **6 :** to reach a state of acceptance ⟨~ with her child's death⟩ **7 :** to engage in bargaining

♦ [1a] administer, allocate, apportion, dispense, distribute, mete, parcel, portion, prorate ♦ [3] concern, cover, pertain, treat ♦ [5b] market, merchandise, put up, retail, sell, vend

³**deal** *n* **1** ♦ **:** an act of buying and selling **:** TRANSACTION **2 :** treatment received ⟨a raw ~⟩ **3** ♦ **:** an often secret agreement or arrangement for mutual advantage **4** ♦ **:** something acquired by or as if by bargaining; *esp* **:** an advantageous purchase **:** BARGAIN

♦ [1] sale, trade, transaction ♦ [3] accord, agreement, bargain, compact, contract, convention, covenant, pact, settlement, understanding ♦ [4] bargain, buy, steal

⁴**deal** *n* **:** wood or a board of fir or pine
deal•er \ˈdē-lər\ *n* ♦ **:** one that deals; *esp* **:** a person who makes a business of buying and selling goods

♦ merchant, trader, trafficker ♦ seller, vendor

deal•er•ship \ˈdē-lər-ˌship\ *n* **:** an authorized sales agency
deal•ing \ˈdē-liŋ\ *n* **1 :** a way of acting or of doing business **2** *pl* ♦ **:** friendly or business transactions

♦ *usu* **dealings** intercourse, relations

dean \ˈdēn\ *n* **1 :** a clergyman who is head of a group of canons or of joint pastors of a church **2 :** the head of a division, faculty, college, or school of a university **3 :** a college or secondary school administrator in charge of counseling and disciplining students **4** ♦ **:** the senior member of a body or group ⟨the ~ of a diplomatic corps⟩ — **dean•ship** *n*

♦ elder, senior *Ant* baby

dean•ery \ˈdē-nə-rē\ *n, pl* **-er•ies :** the office, jurisdiction, or official residence of a clerical dean
¹**dear** \ˈdir\ *adj* **1** ♦ **:** highly valued **:** PRECIOUS **2 :** AFFECTIONATE, FOND **3** ♦ **:** high in price **:** EXPENSIVE **4 :** HEARTFELT — **dear•ly** *adv* — **dear•ness** *n*

♦ [1] beloved, darling, favorite (*or* favourite), loved, pet, precious, special, sweet ♦ [3] costly, expensive, high, precious, valuable

²**dear** *n* ♦ **:** a loved one **:** DARLING

♦ beloved, darling, honey, love, sweet, sweetheart

Dear John \-ˈjän\ *n* **:** a letter (as to a soldier) in which a woman breaks off a marital or romantic relationship
dearth \ˈdərth\ *n* **1** ♦ **:** scarcity that makes dear **:** FAMINE **2** ♦ **:** an inadequate supply **:** LACK

♦ deficiency, deficit, failure, famine, inadequacy, insufficiency, lack, paucity, poverty, scantiness, scarcity, shortage, want

death \ˈdeth\ *n* **1** ♦ **:** the end of life **2 :** the cause of loss of life **3 :** the state of being dead **4** ♦ **:** the passing or destruction of something inanimate **5 :** SLAUGHTER

♦ [1] decease, demise, doom, end, passing, quietus *Ant* birth ♦ [4] demise, expiration, termination *Ant* beginning, creation, start

death•bed \-ˌbed\ *n* **1 :** the bed in which a person dies **2 :** the last hours of life
death•blow \-ˌblō\ *n* **:** a destructive or killing stroke or event
death grip *n* **:** an extremely tight grip or hold
death•less \-ləs\ *adj* ♦ **:** not subject to death or destruction **:** IMMORTAL ⟨~ fame⟩

♦ ceaseless, dateless, endless, eternal, everlasting, immortal, permanent, perpetual, undying, unending

death•like \-ˌlīk\ *adj* **:** of, relating to, or suggestive of death **:** DEATHLY
death•ly \-lē\ *adj* **1** ♦ **:** causing death **:** FATAL **2** ♦ **:** of, relating to, or suggesting death ⟨a ~ pallor⟩ — **deathly** *adv*

♦ [1] baleful, deadly, fatal, fell, lethal, mortal, murderous, pestilent, vital ♦ [2] dead, mortal

death rattle *n* **:** a sound produced by air passing through mucus in the lungs and air passages of a dying person
death's–head \ˈdeths-ˌhed\ *n* **:** a human skull emblematic of death
death•watch \ˈdeth-ˌwäch\ *n* **:** a vigil kept over the dead or dying
deb \ˈdeb\ *n* **:** DEBUTANTE
de•ba•cle \di-ˈbä-kəl, -ˈba-\ *also* **dé•bâ•cle** *same or* dā-ˈbäk\ *n* **1** ♦ **:** a great disaster **2** ♦ **:** a complete failure **:** FIASCO

♦ [1] calamity, cataclysm, catastrophe, disaster, tragedy ♦ [2] bummer, bust, catastrophe, dud, failure, fiasco, fizzle, flop, lemon, loser, turkey, washout

de•bar \di-ˈbär\ *vb* ♦ **:** to bar from having or doing something

♦ ban, bar, count out, eliminate, except, exclude, rule out

de•bark \di-ˈbärk\ *vb* **:** DISEMBARK — **de•bar•ka•tion** \ˌdē-ˌbär-ˈkā-shən\ *n*
de•base \di-ˈbās\ *vb* ♦ **:** to lower in character, quality, or value

♦ abase, corrupt, debauch, degrade, demean, demoralize, deprave, pervert, poison, profane, prostitute, subvert, vitiate, warp *Ant* elevate, ennoble, uplift ♦ discredit, disgrace, dishonor (*or* dishonour), humble, humiliate, lower, shame, smirch, take down

de•base•ment \-mənt\ *n* **1** ♦ **:** the act or process of debasing **2 :** the state of being debased

♦ corruption, debauchery, decadence, degeneracy, degeneration, degradation, demoralization, depravity, dissipation, dissoluteness, perversion

de•bat•able \di-ˈbā-tə-bəl\ *adj* ♦ **:** open to dispute **:** giving reason for being doubted, questioned, or challenged

♦ arguable, disputable, doubtful, moot, questionable *Ant* incontestable, incontrovertible, indisputable, indubitable, undeniable, unquestionable ♦ doubtful, equivocal, problematic, questionable, suspect, suspicious

¹**de•bate** \di-ˈbāt\ *n* **1** ♦ **:** a contention by words or arguments **2** ♦ **:** consideration of or reflection upon a problem ⟨after a moment of ~, she went forward⟩

♦ [1] controversy, disagreement, dissension ♦ [2] consideration, deliberation, thought

²**debate** *vb* **de•bat•ed; de•bat•ing 1** ♦ **:** to discuss a question by considering opposed arguments **2 :** to take part in a debate **3** ♦ **:** to reflect upon (a question or problem)

♦ [1] argue, chew over, discuss, dispute, hash, moot, talk over ♦ [3] chew over, cogitate, consider, contemplate, deliberate, entertain, meditate, mull, ponder, question, ruminate, study, think, weigh

de•bat•er \-ˈbā-tər\ *n* ♦ **:** one that debates

♦ arguer, contender, disputant, disputer

de•bauch \di-ˈbȯch\ *vb* ♦ **:** to lead away from virtue or excellence **:** CORRUPT

♦ debase, degrade, demean, demoralize, humble, subvert, warp

de•bauched \-ˈbȯcht\ *adj* ♦ **:** having or showing looseness in morals or conduct

♦ corrupt, decadent, degenerate, dissolute, perverse, perverted, reprobate

de•bauch•ery \-ˈbȯ-chə-rē\ *n* ♦ **:** extreme indulgence in sensuality

♦ corruption, debasement, decadence, degeneracy, degeneration, degradation, demoralization, depravity, dissipation, dissoluteness, perversion ♦ corruption, depravity, immorality, iniquity, licentiousness, sin, vice

de•ben•ture \di-ˈben-chər\ *n* **:** BOND; *esp* **:** one secured by the general credit of the issuer rather than a lien on particular assets

de·bil·i·tate \di-ˈbi-lə-ˌtāt\ *vb* **-tat·ed; -tat·ing** ◆ **:** to impair the health or strength of

◆ enervate, enfeeble, prostrate, sap, soften, tire, waste, weaken

de·bil·i·ty \di-ˈbi-lə-tē\ *n, pl* **-ties** ◆ **:** an infirm or weakened state

◆ delicacy, enfeeblement, faintness, feebleness, frailty, infirmity, languor, lowness, weakness

1deb·it \ˈde-bət\ *vb* **:** to enter as a debit **:** charge with or as a debit
2debit *n* **1 :** an entry in an account showing money paid out or owed **2 :** DISADVANTAGE, SHORTCOMING
debit card *n* **:** a card by which money may be withdrawn or the cost of purchases paid directly from the holder's bank account
deb·o·nair \ˌde-bə-ˈnar\ *adj* **1** ◆ **:** smoothly gracious and sophisticated **:** SUAVE **2 :** LIGHTHEARTED

◆ smooth, sophisticated, suave, urbane

de·bouch \di-ˈbau̇ch, -ˈbüsh\ *vb* **:** to come out into an open area **:** EMERGE
de·brief \di-ˈbrēf\ *vb* **1 :** to question (as a pilot back from a mission) in order to obtain useful information **2 :** to review carefully upon completion
de·bris \də-ˈbrē, dā-; ˈdā-ˌbrē\ *n, pl* **debris** \-ˈbrēz, -ˌbrēz\ **1** ◆ **:** the remains of something broken down or destroyed **2 :** an accumulation of rock fragments **3 :** RUBBISH

◆ remains, rubble, ruins, wreck, wreckage

debt \ˈdet\ *n* **1 :** an offense against religious or moral law **:** SIN **2 :** something owed **:** OBLIGATION **3 :** a condition of owing
debt·or \ˈde-tər\ *n* **1 :** one guilty of neglect or violation of duty **2 :** one that owes a debt
de·bug \(ˌ)dē-ˈbəg\ *vb* ◆ **:** to eliminate errors in

◆ amend, correct, emend, rectify, reform, remedy

de·bunk \dē-ˈbəŋk\ *vb* ◆ **:** to expose the sham or falseness of ⟨~ a legend⟩

◆ expose, show up, uncloak, uncover, unmask

1de·but \ˈdā-ˌbyü, dā-ˈbyü\ *n* **1 :** a first appearance **2 :** a formal entrance into society
2debut *vb* **:** to make a debut; *also* **:** INTRODUCE
deb·u·tante \ˈde-byu̇-ˌtänt\ *n* **:** a young woman making her formal entrance into society
dec *abbr* **1** deceased **2** decrease
Dec *abbr* December
de·cade \ˈde-ˌkād, de-ˈkād\ *n* **:** a period of 10 years
dec·a·dence \ˈde-kə-dəns, di-ˈkād-ᵊns\ *n* **1** ◆ **:** the process of becoming decadent **:** the quality or state of being decadent **2** ◆ **:** a period of decline

◆ [1, 2] corruption, debasement, debauchery, degeneracy, degeneration, degradation, demoralization, depravity, dissipation, dissoluteness, perversion

1dec·a·dent \ˈde-kə-dənt, di-ˈkād-ᵊnt\ *adj* **1** ◆ **:** marked by decay or decline **2** ◆ **:** characterized by or appealing to self-indulgence

◆ [1] degenerate, effete, overripe ◆ [1, 2] corrupt, debauched, degenerate, dissolute, perverse, perverted, reprobate

2decadent *n* ◆ **:** one that is decadent

◆ degenerate, libertine, pervert, profligate

de·caf \ˈdē-ˌkaf\ *n* **:** decaffeinated coffee
de·caf·fein·at·ed \(ˌ)dē-ˈka-fə-nā-təd\ *adj* **:** having the caffeine removed ⟨~ coffee⟩
deca·gon \ˈde-kə-ˌgän\ *n* **:** a plane polygon of 10 angles and 10 sides
de·cal \ˈdē-ˌkal\ *n* **:** a picture, design, or label made to be transferred (as to glass) from specially prepared paper
de·cal·co·ma·nia \di-ˌkal-kə-ˈmā-nē-ə\ *n* **:** DECAL
Deca·logue \ˈde-kə-ˌlȯg\ *n* **:** TEN COMMANDMENTS
de·camp \di-ˈkamp\ *vb* **1 :** to break up a camp **2 :** to depart suddenly
de·cant \di-ˈkant\ *vb* **:** to pour (as wine) gently from one vessel into another
de·cant·er \di-ˈkan-tər\ *n* **:** an ornamental glass bottle for serving wine
de·cap·i·tate \di-ˈka-pə-ˌtāt\ *vb* **-tat·ed; -tat·ing :** BEHEAD — **de·cap·i·ta·tion** \-ˌka-pə-ˈtā-shən\ *n* — **de·cap·i·ta·tor** \-ˈka-pə-ˌtā-tər\ *n*
deca·syl·lab·ic \ˌde-kə-sə-ˈla-bik\ *adj* **:** having or composed of verses having 10 syllables — **decasyllabic** *n*
de·cath·lon \di-ˈkath-lən, -ˌlän\ *n* **:** a 10-event athletic contest
1de·cay \di-ˈkā\ *vb* **1** ◆ **:** to decline from a sound or prosperous condition **2** ◆ **:** to cause or undergo decomposition ⟨radium ~*s* slowly⟩; *esp* **:** to break down while spoiling **:** ROT

◆ [1] decline, degenerate, descend, deteriorate, ebb, rot, sink, worsen ◆ [2] break down, corrupt, decompose, disintegrate, molder, putrefy, rot, spoil

2decay *n* **1** ◆ **:** gradual decline in strength, soundness, or prosperity or in degree of excellence or perfection **2** ◆ **:** the process of rotting **:** the state of being rotten

◆ [1] decline, degeneration, deterioration ◆ [2] breakdown, corruption, decomposition, putrefaction, rot, spoilage

decd *abbr* deceased
de·cease \di-ˈsēs\ *n* ◆ **:** a permanent cessation of all vital functions **:** DEATH

◆ death, demise, doom, end, passing, quietus

1de·ceased \-ˈsēst\ *adj* ◆ **:** no longer alive; *esp* **:** recently dead

◆ breathless, dead, defunct, gone, late, lifeless

2deceased *n, pl* **deceased :** a dead person
de·ce·dent \di-ˈsēd-ᵊnt\ *n* **:** a deceased person
de·ceit \di-ˈsēt\ *n* **1 :** the act or practice of deceiving **:** DECEPTION **2 :** an attempt or device to deceive **:** TRICK **3** ◆ **:** the quality of being deceitful **:** DECEITFULNESS

◆ artifice, craft, craftiness, crookedness, cunning, deceitfulness, dishonesty, dissimulation, double-dealing, duplicity, guile, wiliness *Ant* artlessness, forthrightness, good faith, guilelessness, sincerity

de·ceit·ful \-fəl\ *adj* **1** ◆ **:** practicing or tending to practice deceit **2** ◆ **:** tending or having power to deceive **:** DECEPTIVE ⟨a ~ answer⟩ — **de·ceit·ful·ly** *adv*

◆ [1] crooked, dishonest, double-dealing, false, fraudulent ◆ [2] deceptive, delusive, fallacious, false, misleading, specious

de·ceit·ful·ness \-nəs\ *n* ◆ **:** the quality or state of being deceitful

◆ artifice, craft, craftiness, crookedness, cunning, deceit, dishonesty, dissimulation, double-dealing, duplicity, guile, wiliness

de·ceive \di-ˈsēv\ *vb* **de·ceived; de·ceiv·ing 1** ◆ **:** to cause to believe an untruth **2 :** to use or practice deceit — **de·ceiv·er** *n*

◆ beguile, bluff, cozen, delude, dupe, fool, gull, have, hoax, hoodwink, humbug, misinform, mislead, string along, take in, trick *Ant* undeceive

de·cel·er·ate \dē-ˈse-lə-ˌrāt\ *vb* **-at·ed; -at·ing** ◆ **:** to slow down

◆ brake, retard, slow

De·cem·ber \di-ˈsem-bər\ *n* **:** the 12th month of the year
de·cen·cy \ˈdēs-ᵊn-sē\ *n, pl* **-cies 1** ◆ **:** the quality or state of being decent **:** PROPRIETY **2** ◆ **:** conformity to standards of taste, propriety, or quality **3 :** a standard of propriety — usually used in plural

◆ [1] decorum, form, propriety *Ant* impropriety, indecency ◆ [2] character, goodness, honesty, honor (*or* honour), integrity, morality, probity, rectitude, righteousness, uprightness, virtue

de·cen·ni·al \di-ˈse-nē-əl\ *adj* **1 :** consisting of 10 years **2 :** happening every 10 years ⟨~ census⟩
de·cent \ˈdē-sᵊnt\ *adj* **1** ◆ **:** conforming to standards of propriety, good taste, or morality **2 :** modestly clothed **3** ◆ **:** free from immodesty or obscenity **4** ◆ **:** ADEQUATE ⟨~ housing⟩ — **de·cent·ly** *adv*

◆ [1] ethical, good, honest, honorable (*or* honourable), just, moral, right, righteous, straight, upright, virtuous ◆ [1] correct, decorous, genteel, nice, polite, proper, respectable, seemly ◆ [3] chaste, clean, immaculate, modest, pure ◆ [4] acceptable, adequate, all right, fine, OK, passable, respectable, satisfactory, tolerable

de·cen·tral·i·za·tion \dē-ˌsen-trə-lə-ˈzā-shən\ *n* **1 :** the distribution of powers from a central authority to regional and local authorities **2 :** the redistribution of population and industry from urban centers to outlying areas — **de·cen·tral·ize** \-ˈsen-trə-ˌlīz\ *vb*
de·cep·tion \di-ˈsep-shən\ *n* **1 :** the act of deceiving **2 :** the fact or condition of being deceived **3 :** FRAUD, TRICK
de·cep·tive \di-ˈsep-tiv\ *adj* ◆ **:** tending or having power to deceive — **de·cep·tive·ly** *adv* — **de·cep·tive·ness** *n*

◆ deceitful, delusive, fallacious, false, misleading, specious *Ant* aboveboard, forthright, straightforward

deci·bel \ˈde-sə-ˌbel, -bəl\ *n* : a unit for measuring the relative loudness of sounds

de·cide \di-ˈsīd\ *vb* **de·cid·ed; de·cid·ing** **1** ♦ : to arrive at a solution that ends uncertainty or dispute about **2** : to bring to a definitive end ⟨one blow *decided* the fight⟩ **3** : to induce to come to a choice **4** ♦ : to make a choice or judgment

♦ [1] arrange, fix, set, settle ♦ [4] choose, conclude, determine, figure, opt, resolve ♦ [4] adjudicate, arbitrate, determine, judge, referee, rule, settle, umpire

de·cid·ed \di-ˈsī-dəd\ *adj* **1** : UNQUESTIONABLE **2** : FIRM, DETERMINED — **de·cid·ed·ly** *adv*

de·cid·u·ous \di-ˈsi-jə-wəs\ *adj* **1** : falling off or out usually at the end of a period of growth or function ⟨∼ leaves⟩ ⟨a ∼ tooth⟩ **2** : having deciduous parts ⟨∼ trees⟩

deci·gram \ˈde-sə-ˌgram\ *n* : a metric unit of measure equal to $^1/_{10}$ gram

deci·li·ter \-ˌlē-tər\ *n* : a metric unit of measure equal to $^1/_{10}$ liter

[1]**dec·i·mal** \ˈde-sə-məl\ *adj* : based on the number 10 : reckoning by tens

[2]**decimal** *n* : any number expressed in base 10; *esp* : DECIMAL FRACTION

decimal fraction *n* : a fraction or mixed number in which the denominator is a power of 10 and that is usually expressed with a decimal point ⟨the *decimal fraction* .25 is equivalent to the common fraction $^{25}/_{100}$⟩

decimal place *n* : the position of a digit as counted to the right of the decimal point in a decimal fraction

decimal point *n* : a period, centered dot, or in some countries a comma at the left of a decimal fraction (as .678) less than one or between a whole number and a decimal fraction in a mixed number (as 3.678)

dec·i·mate \ˈde-sə-ˌmāt\ *vb* **-mat·ed; -mat·ing** **1** : to take or destroy the 10th part of **2** : to cause great destruction or harm to

dec·i·me·ter \ˈde-sə-ˌmē-tər\ *n* : a metric unit of measure equal to $^1/_{10}$ meter

de·ci·pher \di-ˈsī-fər\ *vb* **1** : to convert (as a coded message) into intelligible form : DECODE **2** : to make out the meaning of despite indistinctness — **de·ci·pher·able** *adj*

de·ci·sion \di-ˈsi-zhən\ *n* **1** ♦ : the act or result of deciding **2** ♦ : promptness and firmness in deciding

♦ [1] conclusion, determination, diagnosis, judgment (*or* judgement), opinion, resolution, verdict ♦ [2] decisiveness, determination, firmness, granite, resolution, resolve

de·ci·sive \-ˈsī-siv\ *adj* **1** : having the power to decide ⟨the ∼ vote⟩ **2** ♦ : marked by firm determination : RESOLUTE **3** ♦ : not questionable : CONCLUSIVE ⟨a ∼ victory⟩ — **de·ci·sive·ly** *adv*

♦ [2] bound, determined, firm, intent, purposeful, resolute, set, single-minded ♦ [3] absolute, clear, conclusive, definitive

de·ci·sive·ness \-nəs\ *n* ♦ : the quality or state of being decisive

♦ decision, determination, firmness, granite, resolution, resolve

[1]**deck** \ˈdek\ *n* **1** : a floorlike platform of a ship; *also* : something resembling the deck of a ship **2** : a pack of playing cards

[2]**deck** *vb* **1** ♦ : to clothe in a striking or elegant manner : ARRAY **2** ♦ : to furnish with something ornamental : DECORATE **3** : to furnish with a deck **4** : KNOCK DOWN, FLOOR

♦ [1] apparel, array, attire, caparison, clothe, dress, garb, invest, rig, suit ♦ [2] adorn, array, beautify, bedeck, decorate, do, dress, embellish, enrich, garnish, grace, ornament, trim

deck·hand \ˈdek-ˌhand\ *n* : a sailor who performs manual duties

deck·le edge \ˈdek-əl-\ *n* : the rough untrimmed edge of paper — **deck·le–edged** \-ˈejd\ *adj*

de·claim \di-ˈklām\ *vb* ♦ : to speak or deliver in the manner of a formal speech — **de·clam·a·to·ry** \di-ˈkla-mə-ˌtōr-ē\ *adj*

♦ descant, discourse, harangue, lecture, orate, speak, talk

dec·la·ma·tion \ˌde-klə-ˈmā-shən\ *n* ♦ : the act or art of declaiming

♦ address, harangue, oration, speech, talk

dec·la·ra·tion \ˌde-klə-ˈrā-shən\ *n* **1** ♦ : the act of declaring **2** : something that is declared

♦ affirmation, assertion, avowal, claim, profession, protestation

de·clar·a·tive \di-ˈklar-ə-tiv\ *adj* : making a declaration ⟨∼ sentence⟩

de·clare \di-ˈklar\ *vb* **de·clared; de·clar·ing** **1** ♦ : to make known formally, officially, or explicitly : ANNOUNCE ⟨∼ war⟩ **2** ♦ : to state emphatically : AFFIRM **3** : to make a full statement of — **de·clar·a·to·ry** \di-ˈklar-ə-ˌtōr-ē\ *adj* — **de·clar·er** *n*

♦ [1] advertise, announce, blaze, broadcast, enunciate, placard, post, proclaim, promulgate, publicize, publish, sound ♦ [2] affirm, allege, assert, aver, avouch, avow, claim, contend, insist, maintain, profess, protest, warrant

de·clas·si·fy \dē-ˈkla-sə-ˌfī\ *vb* : to remove the security classification of — **de·clas·si·fi·ca·tion** \-ˌkla-sə-fə-ˈkā-shən\ *n*

de·clen·sion \di-ˈklen-chən\ *n* **1** : the inflectional forms of a noun, pronoun, or adjective **2** : a falling off or away especially from a standard or a high point of development **3** : a bending or sloping downward

[1]**de·cline** \di-ˈklīn\ *vb* **de·clined; de·clin·ing** **1** ♦ : to slope downward : DESCEND **2** : DROOP **3** : WANE **4** ♦ : to tend toward an inferior state or weaker condition **5** ♦ : to withhold consent; *also* : REFUSE **6** : INFLECT 2 ⟨∼ a noun⟩ — **de·clin·able** *adj* — **dec·li·na·tion** \ˌde-klə-ˈnā-shən\ *n*

♦ [1] descend, dip, drop, fall, lower, plummet, plunge, sink, tumble ♦ [4] decay, degenerate, descend, deteriorate, ebb, rot, sink, worsen ♦ [5] disallow, disapprove, negative, refuse, reject, repudiate, spurn, turn down ***Ant*** accept, agree (to), approve

[2]**decline** *n* **1** ♦ : a gradual sinking and wasting away **2** ♦ : a change to a lower state or level **3** : the time when something is approaching its end **4** : a descending slope

♦ [1] decay, degeneration, deterioration ***Ant*** improvement, recovery, revitalization ♦ [2] degradation, fall ***Ant*** ascent, rise, upswing

de·cliv·i·ty \di-ˈkli-və-tē\ *n, pl* **-ties** : a steep downward slope

de·code \dē-ˈkōd\ *vb* ♦ : to convert (a coded message) into ordinary language — **de·cod·er** *n*

♦ break, crack ***Ant*** cipher, code, encode

dé·col·le·tage \dā-ˌkä-lə-ˈtäzh\ *n* : the low-cut neckline of a dress

dé·col·le·té \dā-ˌkäl-ˈtā\ *adj* **1** : wearing a strapless or low-necked gown **2** : having a low-cut neckline

de·com·mis·sion \ˌdē-kə-ˈmi-shən\ *vb* : to remove from service

de·com·pose \ˌdē-kəm-ˈpōz\ *vb* **1** : to separate into constituent parts **2** ♦ : to break down in decay : ROT

♦ break down, corrupt, decay, disintegrate, molder, putrefy, rot, spoil

de·com·po·si·tion \dē-ˌkäm-pə-ˈzi-shən\ *n* ♦ : the act or process of decomposing

♦ breakdown, corruption, decay, putrefaction, rot, spoilage

de·com·press \ˌdē-kəm-ˈpres\ *vb* : to release from pressure or compression — **de·com·pres·sion** \-ˈpre-shən\ *n*

de·con·ges·tant \ˌdē-kən-ˈjes-tənt\ *n* : an agent that relieves congestion (as of mucous membranes)

de·con·struc·tion \ˌdē-kən-ˈstrək-shən\ *n* : the analysis of something (as language or literature) by the separation and individual examination of its basic elements — **de·con·struct** \-ˈstrəkt\ *vb*

de·con·tam·i·nate \ˌdē-kən-ˈta-mə-ˌnāt\ *vb* : to rid of contamination (as radioactive material) — **de·con·tam·i·na·tion** \-ˌta-mə-ˈnā-shən\ *n*

de·con·trol \ˌdē-kən-ˈtrōl\ *vb* : to end control of ⟨∼ prices⟩ — **decontrol** *n*

de·cor *or* **dé·cor** \dā-ˈkȯr, ˈdā-ˌkȯr\ *n* : DECORATION; *esp* : the style and layout of interior furnishings

dec·o·rate \ˈde-kə-ˌrāt\ *vb* **-rat·ed; -rat·ing** **1** ♦ : to furnish with something ornamental ⟨∼ a room⟩ **2** : to award a mark of honor (as a medal) to

♦ adorn, array, beautify, bedeck, deck, do, dress, embellish, enrich, garnish, grace, ornament, trim ***Ant*** blemish, deface, disfigure, mar, scar, spoil

dec·o·ra·tion \ˌde-kə-ˈrā-shən\ *n* **1** : the act or process of decorating **2** ♦ : something that adorns, enriches, or beautifies : ORNAMENT **3** ♦ : a badge of honor

♦ [2] adornment, caparison, embellishment, frill, garnish, ornament, trim ♦ [3] award, distinction, honor (*or* honour), plume, prize

dec·o·ra·tive \ˈde-kə-rə-tiv\ *adj* : serving to decorate : ORNAMENTAL

dec·o·ra·tor \ˈde-kə-ˌrā-tər\ *n* : one that decorates; *esp* : a person who designs or executes interiors and their furnishings

dec·o·rous \ˈde-kə-rəs, di-ˈkōr-əs\ *adj* ♦ : marked by propriety and good taste : PROPER

♦ correct, decent, genteel, nice, polite, proper, respectable, seemly

de•co•rum \di-ˈkōr-əm\ *n* **1** ♦ **:** conformity to accepted standards of conduct **2 :** ORDERLINESS

♦ decency, form, propriety

¹de•coy \ˈdē-ˌkȯi, di-ˈkȯi\ *n* **1 :** something that lures or entices; *esp* **:** an artificial bird used to attract live birds within shot **2 :** something used to draw attention away from another

²de•coy \di-ˈkȯi, ˈdē-ˌkȯi\ *vb* ♦ **:** to lure by or as if by a decoy **:** ENTICE

♦ allure, beguile, entice, lead on, lure, seduce, tempt

¹de•crease \di-ˈkrēs\ *vb* **de•creased; de•creas•ing** ♦ **:** to grow or cause to grow less **:** DIMINISH

♦ abate, de-escalate, decline, die, diminish, dwindle, ebb, fall, lessen, let up, lower, moderate, recede, relent, shrink, subside, taper, wane ***Ant*** accumulate, balloon, build, burgeon, enlarge, escalate, expand, grow, increase, intensify, mount, mushroom, pick up, rise, snowball, soar, swell, wax

²de•crease \ˈdē-ˌkrēs\ *n* **1 :** the process of decreasing **2** ♦ **:** an amount of diminution **:** REDUCTION

♦ abatement, decline, decrement, diminution, drop, fall, loss, reduction, shrinkage ***Ant*** boost, enlargement, gain, increase, increment, raise, rise

¹de•cree \di-ˈkrē\ *n* **1** ♦ **:** an order usually having the force of law **:** EDICT **2 :** a judicial decision

♦ behest, charge, command, commandment, dictate, direction, directive, edict, instruction, order, word

²decree *vb* **de•creed; de•cree•ing** **1** ♦ **:** to direct authoritatively **:** COMMAND **2 :** to determine or order judicially

♦ command, dictate, direct, ordain, order

dec•re•ment \ˈde-krə-mənt\ *n* **1 :** gradual decrease **2** ♦ **:** the quantity lost by diminution or waste

♦ abatement, decline, decrease, diminution, drop, fall, loss, reduction, shrinkage

de•crep•it \di-ˈkre-pət\ *adj* **:** broken down with age **:** WORN-OUT — **de•crep•i•tude** \-pə-ˌtüd, -ˌtyüd\ *n*

de•cre•scen•do \ˌdā-krə-ˈshen-dō\ *adv or adj* **:** with a decrease in volume — used as a direction in music

de•crim•i•nal•ize \dē-ˈkri-mən-ᵊl-ˌīz\ *vb* **:** to remove or reduce the criminal status of

de•cry \di-ˈkrī\ *vb* ♦ **:** to express strong disapproval of

♦ belittle, cry down, deprecate, depreciate, diminish, discount, disparage, minimize, put down, write off ***Ant*** acclaim, applaud, exalt, extol, glorify, laud, magnify, praise

ded•i•cate \ˈde-di-ˌkāt\ *vb* **-cat•ed; -cat•ing** **1 :** to devote to the worship of a divine being especially with sacred rites **2** ♦ **:** to set apart for a definite purpose **3 :** to inscribe or address as a compliment — **ded•i•ca•tor** \ˈde-di-ˌkā-tər\ *n* — **ded•i•ca•to•ry** \-kə-ˌtōr-ē\ *adj*

♦ allocate, consecrate, devote, earmark, reserve, save

ded•i•ca•tion \ˌde-di-ˈkā-shən\ *n* **1 :** an act or rite of dedicating especially to a sacred use **2 :** a setting aside for a particular purpose **3** ♦ **:** self-sacrificing devotion

♦ allegiance, constancy, devotion, faith, faithfulness, fastness, fealty, fidelity, loyalty, steadfastness

de•duce \di-ˈdüs, -ˈdyüs\ *vb* **de•duced; de•duc•ing** **1** ♦ **:** to derive by reasoning **:** INFER **2 :** to trace the course of

♦ conclude, extrapolate, gather, infer, judge, reason, understand

de•duct \di-ˈdəkt\ *vb* **:** SUBTRACT — **de•duct•ible** *adj*

de•duc•tion \di-ˈdək-shən\ *n* **1 :** an act of taking away **:** SUBTRACTION **2** ♦ **:** something that is or may be subtracted **3 :** the deriving of a conclusion by reasoning **:** the conclusion so reached — **de•duc•tive** \-ˈdək-tiv\ *adj* — **de•duc•tive•ly** *adv*

♦ abatement, discount, reduction ***Ant*** accession, addition

¹deed \ˈdēd\ *n* **1** ♦ **:** something done **2** ♦ **:** a usually illustrious act or action **:** FEAT **3 :** a document containing some legal transfer, bargain, or contract

♦ exploit, feat, thing

²deed *vb* ♦ **:** to convey or transfer by deed

♦ alienate, assign, cede, make over, transfer

dee•jay \ˈdē-ˌjā\ *n* **:** DISC JOCKEY

deem \ˈdēm\ *vb* ♦ **:** to come to think or judge

♦ believe, consider, feel, figure, guess, hold, imagine, suppose, think

de–em•pha•size \dē-ˈem-fə-ˌsīz\ *vb* **:** to reduce in relative importance; *also* **:** to attach little importance to — **de–em•pha•sis** \-səs\ *n*

¹deep \ˈdēp\ *adj* **1 :** extending far down, back, within, or outward **2 :** having a specified extension downward or backward **3** ♦ **:** difficult to understand; *also* **:** MYSTERIOUS ⟨a ~ dark secret⟩ **4 :** WISE **5 :** ENGROSSED, INVOLVED ⟨~ in thought⟩ **6** ♦ **:** characterized by profundity of feeling or quality **:** INTENSE ⟨~ grief⟩ ⟨~ sleep⟩ **7 :** dark and rich in color ⟨a ~ red⟩ **8** ♦ **:** having a low musical pitch or range ⟨a ~ voice⟩ **9 :** situated well within **10 :** covered, enclosed, or filled often to a specified degree — **deep•ly** *adv*

♦ [3] ambiguous, cryptic, dark, darkling, enigmatic, equivocal, inscrutable, murky, mysterious, mystic, nebulous, obscure, occult ♦ [6] explosive, exquisite, fearful, ferocious, fierce, furious, hard, heavy, intense, profound, terrible, vehement, vicious, violent ♦ [8] bass, low, throaty ***Ant*** acute, high, piping, sharp, shrill, treble

²deep *adv* **1 :** DEEPLY **2 :** far on **:** LATE ⟨~ in the night⟩

³deep *n* **1** ♦ **:** an extremely deep place or part; *esp* **:** the whole body of salt water that covers nearly three fourths of the surface of the earth **:** OCEAN **2** ♦ **:** the middle or most intense part ⟨the ~ of winter⟩

♦ [1] blue, brine, ocean, sea ♦ [2] depth, height, middle, midst, thick

deep•en \ˈdē-pən\ *vb* ♦ **:** to make or become deep or deeper

♦ amplify, beef, boost, consolidate, enhance, heighten, intensify, magnify, redouble, step up, strengthen

deep–freeze \ˈdēp-ˈfrēz\ *vb* **-froze** \-ˈfrōz\; **-fro•zen** \-ˈfrōz-ᵊn\ **:** QUICK-FREEZE

deep–fry *vb* **:** to cook in enough oil to cover the food being fried

deep pocket *n* **1 :** one having substantial financial resources **2** *pl* **:** substantial financial resources

deep–root•ed \ˈdēp-ˈrü-təd, -ˈru̇-\ *adj* ♦ **:** deeply implanted or established

♦ confirmed, deep-seated, inveterate, settled

deep–sea \ˈdēp-ˈsē\ *adj* **:** of, relating to, or occurring in the deeper parts of the sea ⟨~ fishing⟩

deep–seat•ed \ˈdēp-ˈsē-təd\ *adj* **1 :** situated far below the surface **2** ♦ **:** firmly established ⟨~ convictions⟩

♦ confirmed, deep-rooted, inveterate, settled

deer \ˈdir\ *n, pl* **deer :** any of numerous ruminant mammals with cloven hoofs and usually antlers especially in the males

deer•fly \-ˌflī\ *n* **:** any of numerous small horseflies

deer•skin \-ˌskin\ *n* **:** leather made from the skin of a deer; *also* **:** a garment of such leather

deer tick *n* **:** a tick that transmits the bacterium causing Lyme disease

de–es•ca•late \dē-ˈes-kə-ˌlāt\ *vb* ♦ **:** to decrease in extent, volume, or scope — **de–es•ca•la•tion** \-ˌes-kə-ˈlā-shən\ *n*

♦ abate, decline, decrease, die, diminish, dwindle, ebb, fall, lessen, let up, lower, moderate, recede, relent, shrink, subside, taper, wane

deet \ˈdēt\ *n, often all cap* **:** a colorless oily liquid insect and tick repellent

¹def \ˈdef\ *adj* **def•fer; def•fest** *slang* **:** very good **:** COOL

²def *abbr* **1** defendant **2** definite **3** definition

de•face \di-ˈfās\ *vb* ♦ **:** to destroy or mar the appearance of — **de•face•ment** *n* — **de•fac•er** *n*

♦ blemish, break, cripple, damage, disfigure, flaw, harm, hurt, injure, mar, spoil, vitiate

de fac•to \di-ˈfak-tō, dā-\ *adj or adv* **1 :** actually existing ⟨*de facto* segregation⟩ **2 :** actually exercising power ⟨*de facto* government⟩

de•fal•ca•tion \ˌdē-ˌfal-ˈkā-shən, -ˌfȯl-; ˌde-fəl-\ *n* **:** EMBEZZLEMENT

def•a•ma•tion \ˌde-fə-ˈmā-shən\ *n* ♦ **:** the act of defaming another

♦ libel, slander, vilification

de•fam•a•to•ry \di-ˈfa-mə-ˌtōr-ē\ *adj* ♦ **:** containing defamation **:** injurious to reputation

♦ libelous, scandalous, slanderous

de•fame \di-ˈfām\ *vb* **de•famed; de•fam•ing** ♦ **:** to injure or destroy the reputation of by libel or slander

♦ blacken, libel, malign, slander, smear, traduce, vilify

de•fault \di-ˈfȯlt\ *n* **1** ♦ **:** failure to do something required by duty or law; *also* **:** failure to appear for a legal proceeding **2 :** failure to compete in or to finish an appointed contest ⟨lose a race by ~⟩ **3 :** a choice made without active consideration due to lack of viable alternatives **4 :** a selection made automatically by a computer in the absence of a choice by the user — **default** *vb* — **de•fault•er** *n*

♦ delinquency, dereliction, failure, neglect, negligence, oversight

¹de•feat \di-ˈfēt\ *vb* **1 :** FRUSTRATE, NULLIFY **2** ♦ **:** to win victory over **:** BEAT

♦ beat, conquer, master, overcome, prevail, rout, subdue, surmount, triumph, win

²defeat *n* **1** ♦ **:** frustration by nullification or by prevention of success **:** the state or face of being defeated ⟨the bill suffered ~ in the Senate⟩ **2 :** an overthrow of an army in battle **3** ♦ **:** loss of a contest

♦ [1] collapse, crash, cropper, failure, fizzle, nonsuccess ♦ [3] loss, rout, shellacking ***Ant*** success, triumph, victory, win

de•feat•ism \-ˈfē-ˌti-zəm\ *n* **:** acceptance of or resignation to defeat — **de•feat•ist** \-tist\ *n*

defeatist *adj* ♦ **:** characterized by defeatism

♦ despairing, hopeless, pessimistic

def•e•cate \ˈde-fi-ˌkāt\ *vb* **-cat•ed; -cat•ing** **1 :** to free from impurity or corruption **2 :** to discharge feces from the bowels — **def•e•ca•tion** \ˌde-fi-ˈkā-shən\ *n*

¹de•fect \ˈdē-ˌfekt, di-ˈfekt\ *n* ♦ **:** an imperfection that impairs worth or utility **:** BLEMISH

♦ blemish, deformity, disfigurement, fault, flaw, imperfection, mark, pockmark, scar

²de•fect \di-ˈfekt\ *vb* **:** to desert a cause or party especially in order to espouse another — **de•fec•tion** \-ˈfek-shən\ *n*

de•fec•tive \di-ˈfek-tiv\ *adj* ♦ **:** imperfect in form or function **:** FAULTY — **defective** *n*

♦ bad, faulty, imperfect

de•fec•tor \di-ˈfek-tər\ *n* ♦ **:** one that defects

♦ deserter, recreant, renegade

de•fence *Can and Brit var of* DEFENSE

de•fend \di-ˈfend\ *vb* **1** ♦ **:** to repel danger or attack from **2 :** to act as attorney for **3 :** to oppose the claim of another in a lawsuit **:** CONTEST **4** ♦ **:** to maintain against opposition ⟨~ an idea⟩

♦ [1] cover, guard, protect, safeguard, screen, secure, shield, ward ***Ant*** assail, assault, attack ♦ [4] justify, maintain, support, uphold

de•fen•dant \di-ˈfen-dənt\ *n* **:** a person required to make answer in a legal action or suit

de•fend•er \di-ˈfen-dər\ *n* ♦ **:** one that defends

♦ custodian, defense (*or* defence), guard, protection, protector

de•fense *or Can and Brit* **de•fence** \di-ˈfens\ *n* **1 :** the act of defending **:** resistance against attack **2** ♦ **:** means, method, or capability of defending **3** ♦ **:** an argument in support or justification **4 :** the answer made by the defendant in a legal action **5 :** a defending party, group, or team

♦ [2] aegis, armor, cover, guard, protection, safeguard, screen, security, shield, wall, ward ♦ [3] alibi, excuse, justification, plea, reason

de•fense•less *or Can and Brit* **de•fence•less** \-ləs\ *adj* ♦ **:** being without defense

♦ exposed, helpless, susceptible, undefended, unguarded, unprotected, unresistant, vulnerable

defense mechanism *n* **:** an often unconscious mental process (as repression) that assists in reaching compromise solutions to personal problems

de•fen•si•ble \di-ˈfen(t)-si-bəl\ *adj* ♦ **:** capable of being defended

♦ justifiable, maintainable, supportable, sustainable, tenable

¹de•fen•sive \di-ˈfen-siv\ *adj* **1 :** serving or intended to defend or protect **2 :** of or relating to the attempt to keep an opponent from scoring (as in a game) — **de•fen•sive•ly** *adv* — **de•fen•sive•ness** *n*

²defensive *n* **:** a defensive position

¹de•fer \di-ˈfər\ *vb* **de•ferred; de•fer•ring** ♦ **:** to put off to a later time **:** POSTPONE

♦ delay, hold up, postpone, put off, shelve

²defer *vb* **deferred; deferring :** to submit or yield to the opinion or wishes of another

def•er•ence \ˈde-fər-əns\ *n* ♦ **:** courteous, respectful, or ingratiating regard for another's wishes

♦ compliance, docility, obedience

def•er•en•tial \ˌde-fə-ˈren-chəl\ *adj* ♦ **:** showing or expressing deference

♦ dutiful, regardful, respectful

de•fer•ment \di-ˈfər-mənt\ *n* **:** the act of delaying; *esp* **:** official postponement of military service

de•fi•ance \di-ˈfī-əns\ *n* **1** ♦ **:** the act or an instance of defying **2 :** disposition to resist or contend

♦ disobedience, insubordination, rebelliousness, recalcitrance, refractoriness, unruliness

de•fi•ant \-ənt\ *adj* ♦ **:** full of defiance — **de•fi•ant•ly** *adv*

♦ contrary, disobedient, froward, intractable, rebellious, recalcitrant, refractory, unruly, untoward, wayward, willful

de•fi•bril•la•tor \dē-ˈfi-brə-ˌlā-tər\ *n* **:** an electronic device that applies an electric shock to restore the rhythm of a fibrillating heart — **de•fi•bril•late** \-ˌlāt\ *vb* — **de•fi•bril•la•tion** \-ˌfi-brə-ˈlā-shən\ *n*

de•fi•cien•cy \di-ˈfi-shən-sē\ *n* ♦ **:** the quality or state of being deficient

♦ dearth, deficit, failure, famine, inadequacy, insufficiency, lack, paucity, poverty, scantiness, scarcity, shortage, want ***Ant*** abundance, adequacy, amplitude, plenitude, plenty, sufficiency

deficiency disease *n* **:** a disease (as scurvy or beriberi) caused by a lack of essential dietary elements and especially a vitamin or mineral

de•fi•cient \di-ˈfi-shənt\ *adj* ♦ **:** lacking in something necessary; *also* **:** not up to a normal standard

♦ inadequate, insufficient, scarce, short, shy, wanting ♦ bad, inferior, lousy, off, poor, punk, rotten, substandard, unacceptable, unsatisfactory, wanting, wretched, wrong

def•i•cit \ˈde-fə-sət\ *n* ♦ **:** a deficiency in amount; *esp* **:** an excess of expenditures over revenue

♦ dearth, deficiency, failure, famine, inadequacy, insufficiency, lack, paucity, poverty, scantiness, scarcity, shortage, want

¹de•file \di-ˈfīl\ *vb* **de•filed; de•fil•ing** **1** ♦ **:** to corrupt the purity or perfection of **2** ♦ **:** to make physically unclean especially with something unpleasant or contaminating **3 :** to violate the chastity of **4** ♦ **:** to violate the sanctity of **:** DESECRATE **5 :** DISHONOR

♦ [1, 2] befoul, contaminate, foul, poison, pollute, taint ♦ [4] desecrate, profane, violate

²de•file \di-ˈfīl, ˈdē-ˌfīl\ *n* ♦ **:** a narrow passage or gorge

♦ canyon, flume, gap, gorge, gulch, notch, pass, ravine

de•file•ment \-mənt\ *n* **1** ♦ **:** the act of defiling or state of being defiled **2** ♦ **:** something that defiles

♦ [1] blasphemy, desecration, impiety, irreverence, sacrilege ♦ [2] adulterant, contaminant, impurity, pollutant

de•fine \di-ˈfīn\ *vb* **de•fined; de•fin•ing** **1 :** to set forth the meaning of ⟨~ a word⟩ **2** ♦ **:** to fix or mark the limits of **3** ♦ **:** to clarify in outline or character — **de•fin•able** *adj* — **de•fin•er** *n*

♦ [2] bound, circumscribe, delimit, demarcate, limit, mark, terminate ♦ [3] delineate, outline, silhouette, sketch, trace ♦ [3] characterize, depict, describe, portray, represent

def•i•nite \ˈde-fə-nət\ *adj* **1** ♦ **:** having distinct limits **2** ♦ **:** clear in meaning **3 :** typically designating an identified or immediately identifiable person or thing — **def•i•nite•ness** *n*

♦ [1] determinate, finite, limited, measured, narrow, restricted ♦ [2] clear-cut, definitive, explicit, express, specific, unambiguous, unequivocal

def•i•nite•ly \-lē\ *adv* ♦ **:** in a definite way or manner

♦ certainly, doubtless, incontestably, indeed, indisputably, really, surely, truly, undeniably, undoubtedly, unquestionably

def•i•ni•tion \ˌde-fə-ˈni-shən\ *n* **1 :** an act of determining or settling **2 :** a statement of the meaning of a word or word group; *also* **:** the action or process of defining **3 :** the action or the power of making definite and clear **:** CLARITY, DISTINCTNESS
de•fin•i•tive \di-ˈfi-nə-tiv\ *adj* **1** ♦ **:** serving to provide a final solution or to end a situation **:** DECISIVE **2 :** authoritative and apparently exhaustive **3** ♦ **:** serving to define or specify precisely

♦ [1] absolute, clear, conclusive, decisive ♦ [3] clear-cut, definite, explicit, express, specific, unambiguous, unequivocal

de•flate \di-ˈflāt\ *vb* **de•flat•ed; de•flat•ing 1 :** to release air or gas from **2 :** to reduce in size, importance, or effectiveness; *also* **:** to reduce from a state of inflation **3 :** to become deflated
de•fla•tion \-ˈflā-shən\ *n* **1 :** an act or instance of deflating **:** the state of being deflated **2 :** reduction in the volume of available money or credit resulting in a decline of the general price level
de•flect \di-ˈflekt\ *vb* ♦ **:** to turn aside — **de•flec•tion** \-ˈflek-shən\ *n*

♦ divert, swerve, swing, turn, veer, wheel, whip

de•flo•ra•tion \ˌde-flə-ˈrā-shən\ *n* **:** rupture of the hymen
de•flow•er \dē-ˈflau̇(-ə)r\ *vb* **:** to deprive of virginity
de•fog \dē-ˈfȯg, -ˈfäg\ *vb* **:** to remove fog or condensed moisture from — **de•fog•ger** *n*
de•fo•li•ant \dē-ˈfō-lē-ənt\ *n* **:** a chemical spray or dust used to defoliate plants
de•fo•li•ate \-ˌāt\ *vb* **:** to deprive of leaves especially prematurely — **de•fo•li•a•tion** \dē-ˌfō-lē-ˈā-shən\ *n* — **de•fo•li•a•tor** \dē-ˈfō-lē-ˌā-tər\ *n*
de•for•es•ta•tion \dē-ˌfȯr-ə-ˈstā-shən\ *n* **:** the action or process of clearing an area of forests; *also* **:** the state of having been cleared of forests — **de•for•est** \(ˌ)dē-ˈfȯr-əst, -ˈfär-\ *vb*
de•form \di-ˈfȯrm\ *vb* **1 :** DISFIGURE, DEFACE **2** ♦ **:** to make or become misshapen or changed in shape

♦ contort, distort, screw, warp

de•for•ma•tion \ˌdē-ˌfȯr-ˈmā-shən, ˌde-fər-\ *n* ♦ **:** the action of deforming

♦ contortion, distortion

de•formed *adj* ♦ **:** distorted or unshapely in form

♦ distorted, malformed, misshapen, monstrous, shapeless

de•for•mi•ty \di-ˈfȯr-mə-tē\ *n, pl* **-ties 1 :** the state of being deformed **2** ♦ **:** a physical blemish or distortion

♦ blemish, defect, disfigurement, fault, flaw, imperfection, mark, pockmark, scar

de•fraud \di-ˈfrȯd\ *vb* ♦ **:** to deprive of something by deception or fraud **:** CHEAT

♦ bleed, cheat, chisel, cozen, fleece, gyp, hustle, mulct, rook, shortchange, skin, squeeze, stick, sting, swindle, victimize

de•fray \di-ˈfrā\ *vb* **:** to provide for the payment of **:** PAY — **de•fray•al** *n*
de•frock \(ˌ)dē-ˈfräk\ *vb* **:** to deprive (as a priest) of the right to exercise the functions of office
de•frost \di-ˈfrȯst\ *vb* **1 :** to thaw out **2 :** to free from ice — **de•frost•er** *n*
deft \ˈdeft\ *adj* ♦ **:** characterized by facility and skill — **deft•ly** *adv*

♦ clever, cunning, dexterous, handy

deft•ness \-nəs\ *n* ♦ **:** the quality or state of being deft

♦ agility, dexterity, nimbleness, sleight ♦ adeptness, adroitness, art, artfulness, artifice, artistry, cleverness, craft, cunning, masterfulness, skill

de•funct \di-ˈfəŋkt\ *adj* ♦ **:** no longer living, existing, or functioning

♦ bygone, dead, extinct, gone

de•fuse \dē-ˈfyüz\ *vb* **1 :** to remove the fuse from (as a bomb) **2 :** to make less harmful, potent, or tense
de•fy \di-ˈfī\ *vb* **de•fied; de•fy•ing 1** ♦ **:** to challenge to do something considered impossible **:** DARE **2** ♦ **:** to refuse boldly to obey or to yield to ⟨∼ the law⟩ **3** ♦ **:** to resist attempts at **:** WITHSTAND ⟨a scene that *defies* description⟩

♦ [1] challenge, dare ♦ [2] beard, brave, brazen, confront, dare, face ♦ [3] buck, fight, oppose, repel, resist, withstand

deg *abbr* degree
de•gas \dē-ˈgas\ *vb* **:** to remove gas from
de•gen•er•a•cy \di-ˈje-nə-rə-sē\ *n, pl* **-cies 1 :** the state of being degenerate **2** ♦ **:** the process of becoming degenerate **3 :** PERVERSION

♦ corruption, debasement, debauchery, decadence, degeneration, degradation, demoralization, depravity, dissipation, dissoluteness, perversion

¹de•gen•er•ate \di-ˈje-nə-rət\ *adj* ♦ **:** fallen or deteriorated from a former, higher, or normal condition — **de•gen•er•a•tive** \-ˈje-nə-ˌrā-tiv\ *adj*

♦ corrupt, debauched, decadent, dissolute, perverse, perverted, reprobate

²de•gen•er•ate \di-ˈje-nə-ˌrāt\ *vb* ♦ **:** to undergo deterioration (as in morality, intelligence, structure, or function)

♦ decay, decline, descend, deteriorate, ebb, rot, sink, worsen

³de•gen•er•ate \-rət\ *n* ♦ **:** a degenerate person; *esp* **:** a sexual pervert

♦ decadent, libertine, pervert, profligate

de•gen•er•a•tion \di-ˌje-nə-ˈrā-shən\ *n* ♦ **:** the process of passing from a higher to a lower type

♦ decay, decline, deterioration ♦ corruption, debasement, debauchery, decadence, degeneracy, degradation, demoralization, depravity, dissipation, dissoluteness, perversion

de•grad•able \di-ˈgrā-də-bəl\ *adj* **:** capable of being chemically degraded
deg•ra•da•tion \ˌde-grə-ˈdā-shən\ *n* **1 :** the act or process of degrading **2 a** ♦ **:** decline to a low, destitute, or demoralized state **b** ♦ **:** moral or intellectual decadence

♦ [2a] decline, fall ♦ [2b] corruption, debasement, debauchery, decadence, degeneracy, degeneration, demoralization, depravity, dissipation, dissoluteness, perversion

de•grade \di-ˈgrād\ *vb* **1** ♦ **:** to reduce from a higher to a lower rank or degree **2 a** ♦ **:** to bring to low esteem or into disrepute **b** ♦ **:** to drag down in moral or intellectual character **:** DEBASE **3 :** DECOMPOSE

♦ [1] break, bust, demote, downgrade, reduce ♦ [2a] abase, debase, demean, discredit, disgrace, dishonor (*or* dishonour), humble, humiliate, lower, shame, smirch, take down ♦ [2b] debase, degrade, demean, demoralize, humble, subvert, warp

degrading *adj* ♦ **:** that degrades

♦ contemptuous, derogatory, disdainful, scornful, uncomplimentary

de•gree \di-ˈgrē\ *n* **1** ♦ **:** a step in a series **2** ♦ **:** a rank or grade of official, ecclesiastical, or social position; *also* **:** the civil condition of a person **3 :** the extent, intensity, or scope of something especially as measured by a graded series **4 :** one of the forms or sets of forms used in the comparison of an adjective or adverb **5 :** a title conferred upon students by a college, university, or professional school on completion of a program of study **6 :** a line or space of the musical staff; *also* **:** a note or tone of a musical scale **7 :** a unit of measure for angles that is equal to an angle with its vertex at the center of a circle and its sides cutting off $\frac{1}{360}$ of the circumference; *also* **:** a unit of measure for arcs of a circle that is equal to the amount of arc extending $\frac{1}{360}$ of the circumference **8 :** any of various units for measuring temperature

♦ [1] cut, grade, inch, notch, peg, phase, point, stage, step ♦ [2] footing, level, place, position, rank, situation, standing, station, status

de•horn \dē-ˈhȯrn\ *vb* **:** to deprive of horns
de•hu•man•ize \dē-ˈhyü-mə-ˌnīz\ *vb* **:** to deprive of human qualities, personality, or spirit — **de•hu•man•i•za•tion** \ˌdē-ˌhyü-mə-nə-ˈzā-shən\ *n*
de•hu•mid•i•fy \ˌdē-hyü-ˈmi-də-ˌfī\ *vb* **:** to remove moisture from (as the air) — **de•hu•mid•i•fi•er** *n*
de•hy•drate \dē-ˈhī-ˌdrāt\ *vb* ♦ **:** to remove water from; *also* **:** to lose liquid — **de•hy•dra•tion** \ˌdē-hī-ˈdrā-shən\ *n*

♦ dry, parch, sear

de•hy•dro•ge•na•tion \ˌdē-(ˌ)hī-ˌdrä-jə-ˈnā-shən, -drə-\ *n* **:** the removal of hydrogen from a chemical compound — **de•hy•dro•ge•nate** \ˌdē-(ˌ)hī-ˈdrä-jə-ˌnāt, dē-ˈhī-drə-jə-\ *vb*
de•ice \dē-ˈīs\ *vb* **:** to keep free or rid of ice — **de•ic•er** *n*
de•i•fi•ca•tion \ˌdē-ə-fə-ˈkā-shən\ *n* ♦ **:** the act or an instance of deifying

♦ adulation, idolatry, worship

de•i•fy \ˈdē-ə-ˌfī\ *vb* **-fied; -fy•ing 1 a :** to make a god of **b** ♦ **:** to treat as an object of worship **2** ♦ **:** to glorify as of supreme worth; *also* **:** WORSHIP

♦ [1b] adore, canonize, dote on, idolize, worship ♦ [2] adore, glorify, revere, venerate, worship

deign \ˈdān\ *vb* : CONDESCEND
de•ion•ize \dē-ˈī-ə-ˌnīz\ *vb* : to remove ions from
de•ism \ˈdē-ˌi-zəm\ *n, often cap* : a system of thought advocating natural religion based on human morality and reason rather than divine revelation — **de•ist** \ˈdē-ist\ *n, often cap* — **de•is•tic** \dē-ˈis-tik\ *adj*
de•i•ty \ˈde-ə-tē, ˈdā-\ *n, pl* **-ties** **1** ♦ : the quality or state of being divine : DIVINITY **2** *cap* ♦ : the Being worshipped as the creator and ruler of the universe : GOD 1 **3** : a god or goddess

♦ [1] divinity, godhead ♦ **Deity** [2] Almighty, Jehovah, Supreme Being

dé•jà vu \ˌdā-ˌzhä-ˈvü\ *n* : the feeling that one has seen or heard something before
de•ject•ed \di-ˈjek-təd\ *adj* ♦ : low in spirits : SAD — **de•ject•ed•ly** *adv*

♦ bad, blue, depressed, despondent, disconsolate, down, forlorn, gloomy, glum, low, melancholy, miserable, mournful, sad, unhappy

de•jec•tion \di-ˈjek-shən\ *n* ♦ : lowness of spirits

♦ blues, depression, desolation, despondency, doldrums, dumps, forlornness, gloom, heartsickness, melancholy, sadness

de ju•re \dē-ˈju̇r-ē\ *adv or adj* : by legal right
deka•gram \ˈde-kə-ˌgram\ *n* : a metric unit of measure equal to 10 grams
deka•li•ter \-ˌlē-tər\ *n* : a metric unit of measure equal to 10 liters
deka•me•ter \-ˌmē-tər\ *n* : a metric unit of measure equal to 10 meters
del *abbr* delegate; delegation
Del *abbr* Delaware
Del•a•ware \ˈde-lə-ˌwar\ *n, pl* **Delaware** *or* **Delawares** : a member of an American Indian people orig. of the Delaware valley; *also* : their language
¹de•lay \di-ˈlā\ *n* **1** : the act of delaying : the state of being delayed **2** : the time for which something is delayed
²delay *vb* **1** ♦ : to put off to a later time : POSTPONE **2** ♦ : to stop, detain, or hinder for a time **3** ♦ : to move or act slowly

♦ [1] defer, hold up, postpone, put off, shelve ♦ [2] encumber, hamper, hinder, hold up, impede, inhibit, interfere with, obstruct, tie up ♦ [3] crawl, creep, dally, dawdle, dillydally, drag, lag, linger, loiter, poke, tarry ***Ant*** hurry, run, rush, speed

de•lec•ta•ble \di-ˈlek-tə-bəl\ *adj* **1** ♦ : highly pleasing : DELIGHTFUL **2** ♦ : very pleasing to the taste or smell : DELICIOUS

♦ [1] agreeable, congenial, delicious, delightful, dreamy, felicitous, good, grateful, gratifying, nice, palatable, pleasant, pleasurable, satisfying ♦ [2] ambrosial, appetizing, delicious, flavorful (*or* flavourful), luscious, palatable, savory, scrumptious, tasty, toothsome, yummy

de•lec•ta•tion \ˌdē-ˌlek-ˈtā-shən\ *n* **1** ♦ : a high degree of gratification **2** ♦ : something that gives great pleasure : DELIGHT

♦ contentment, delight, enjoyment, gladness, gratification, pleasure, relish, satisfaction

¹del•e•gate \ˈde-li-gət, -ˌgāt\ *n* **1** ♦ : a person acting for another **2** : a member of the lower house of the legislature of Maryland, Virginia, or West Virginia

♦ ambassador, emissary, envoy, legate, minister, representative ♦ agent, attorney, commissary, deputy, envoy, factor, proxy, representative

²del•e•gate \-ˌgāt\ *vb* **-gat•ed; -gat•ing** **1** : to assign (as responsibility or power to act or make decisions) to another ⟨~ authority⟩ **2** ♦ : to appoint as one's delegate

♦ commission, deputize

del•e•ga•tion \ˌde-li-ˈgā-shən\ *n* **1** ♦ : the act of delegating **2** : one or more persons chosen to represent others

♦ authorization, commission, license (*or* licence), mandate

de•lete \di-ˈlēt\ *vb* **de•let•ed; de•let•ing** : to eliminate especially by blotting out, cutting out, or erasing — **de•le•tion** \-ˈlē-shən\ *n*
del•e•te•ri•ous \ˌde-lə-ˈtir-ē-əs\ *adj* ♦ : harmful often in a subtle or unexpected way : NOXIOUS

♦ adverse, bad, baleful, baneful, damaging, detrimental, evil, harmful, hurtful, ill, injurious, mischievous, noxious, pernicious, prejudicial

delft \ˈdelft\ *n* **1** : a Dutch pottery with an opaque white glaze and predominantly blue decoration **2** : glazed pottery especially when blue and white
delft•ware \-ˌwer\ *n* : DELFT
deli \ˈde-lē\ *n, pl* **del•is** : DELICATESSEN
¹de•lib•er•ate \di-ˈli-bə-ˌrāt\ *vb* **-at•ed; -at•ing** ♦ : to consider carefully — **de•lib•er•a•tive** \-ˈli-bə-ˌrā-tiv, -brə-tiv\ *adj* — **de•lib•er•a•tive•ly** *adv*

♦ chew over, cogitate, consider, contemplate, debate, entertain, meditate, mull, ponder, question, ruminate, study, think, weigh

²de•lib•er•ate \di-ˈli-bə-rət, -ˈli-brət\ *adj* **1** ♦ : determined after careful thought **2** ♦ : done or said intentionally **3** : UNHURRIED, SLOW — **de•lib•er•ate•ness** *n*

♦ [1] advised, calculated, measured, reasoned, studied, thoughtful, thought-out ***Ant*** casual ♦ [2] freewill, intentional, purposeful, voluntary, willful, willing ***Ant*** coerced, forced, involuntary, unintentional

de•lib•er•ate•ly \-lē\ *adv* ♦ : in a deliberate manner

♦ consciously, intentionally, knowingly, purposely, willfully

de•lib•er•a•tion \di-ˌli-bə-ˈrā-shən\ *n* **1** ♦ : the act of deliberating **2** : the quality or state of being deliberate

♦ consideration, debate, thought ♦ argument, colloquy, conference, discourse, discussion, give-and-take, parley, talk

del•i•ca•cy \ˈde-li-kə-sē\ *n, pl* **-cies** **1** ♦ : something pleasing to eat and considered rare or luxurious **2 a** ♦ : the quality or state of being dainty : FINENESS **b** : the quality or state of being frail : FRAILTY **3** : nicety or expressiveness of touch **4 a** : precise perception and discrimination **b** ♦ : extreme sensitivity and precision **5** : sensibility in feeling or conduct; *also* : SQUEAMISHNESS **6** : the quality or state of requiring delicate handling

♦ [1] dainty, goody, tidbit, treat ♦ [2a] daintiness, fineness, fragility ***Ant*** coarseness, crudity, roughness, rudeness ♦ [4b] accuracy, closeness, exactness, fineness, precision, veracity

del•i•cate \ˈde-li-kət\ *adj* **1** : pleasing to the senses of taste or smell especially in a mild or subtle way **2** ♦ : marked by daintiness or charm : EXQUISITE **3 a** : difficult to please : FASTIDIOUS **b** : SQUEAMISH **4 a** ♦ : easily damaged : FRAGILE **b** : not robust in health or constitution : SICKLY **5** ♦ : requiring skill or tact **6** ♦ : marked by care, skill, or tact **7** ♦ : marked by minute precision : very sensitive — **del•i•cate•ly** *adv*

♦ [2] dainty, exquisite, gentle, mild, refined, subtle ***Ant*** robust, strong, sturdy ♦ [2] choice, dainty, elegant, exquisite, rare, select ♦ [4a] breakable, fragile, frail ♦ [5] catchy, difficult, knotty, problematic, spiny, thorny, ticklish, touchy, tough, tricky ♦ [6] exact, fine, minute, nice, refined, subtle ♦ [7] acute, keen, perceptive, sensitive, sharp

del•i•ca•tes•sen \ˌde-li-kə-ˈtes-ᵊn\ *n pl* **1** : ready-to-eat food products (as cooked meats and prepared salads) **2** *sing, pl* **delicatessens** : a store where delicatessen are sold
de•li•cious \di-ˈli-shəs\ *adj* **1** : affording great pleasure : DELIGHTFUL **2** ♦ : appealing to one of the bodily senses especially of taste or smell

♦ ambrosial, appetizing, delectable, flavorful (*or* flavourful), luscious, palatable, savory, scrumptious, tasty, toothsome, yummy ***Ant*** flat, flavorless, insipid, stale, tasteless, unappetizing, unpalatable

de•li•cious•ly \-lē\ *adv* **1** : in a delicious manner **2** : so as to produce delight
de•li•cious•ness \-nəs\ *n* ♦ : the quality or state of being delicious

♦ lusciousness, palatability, savor, tastiness

¹de•light \di-ˈlīt\ *n* **1** ♦ : great pleasure or satisfaction **2** ♦ : something that gives great pleasure

♦ [1] delectation, joy, kick, manna, pleasure, treat ♦ [1, 2] contentment, delectation, enjoyment, gladness, gratification, pleasure, relish, satisfaction

²delight *vb* **1** ♦ : to take great pleasure **2** ♦ : to satisfy greatly : PLEASE

♦ [1] crow, exult, glory, joy, rejoice, triumph ♦ *usu* **delight in** [1] adore, dig, enjoy, fancy, groove, like, love, relish, revel ♦ [2] content, gladden, gratify, please, rejoice, satisfy, suit, warm

de•light•ed *adj* ♦ : highly pleased : GRATIFIED — **de•light•ed•ly** *adv*

♦ blissful, glad, happy, joyful, pleased

de•light•ful \-fəl\ *adj* ♦ : affording great pleasure and satisfaction

♦ agreeable, congenial, delectable, delicious, dreamy, felicitous, good, grateful, gratifying, nice, palatable, pleasant, pleasurable, satisfying ♦ amusing, diverting, enjoyable, entertaining, fun, pleasurable

de•light•ful•ly \-fə-lē\ *adv* ♦ : in a delightful manner

♦ agreeably, favorably (*or* favourably), felicitously, gloriously, nicely, pleasantly, pleasingly, satisfyingly, splendidly, well

de•lim•it \di-ˈli-mət\ *vb* ♦ : to mark the limits of

♦ bound, circumscribe, define, demarcate, limit, mark, terminate

de•lin•eate \di-ˈli-nē-ˌāt\ *vb* **-eat•ed; -eat•ing** **1** ♦ : to mark the outline of : SKETCH **2** ♦ : to picture in words : DESCRIBE

♦ [1] define, outline, silhouette, sketch, trace ♦ [2] depict, describe, draw, image, paint, picture, portray, sketch

de•lin•ea•tion \di-ˌli-nē-ˈā-shən\ *n* **1** : the act of delineating **2** ♦ : something made by delineating

♦ cartoon, drawing, sketch ♦ depiction, description, picture, portrait, portrayal, sketch

de•lin•quen•cy \di-ˈliŋ-kwən-sē\ *n, pl* **-cies** ♦ : the quality or state of being delinquent

♦ default, dereliction, failure, neglect, negligence, oversight

¹de•lin•quent \-kwənt\ *n* : a delinquent person

²delinquent *adj* **1** : offending by neglect or violation of duty or of law **2** ♦ : being overdue in payment

♦ behind, belated, late, overdue, tardy

del•i•quesce \ˌde-li-ˈkwes\ *vb* **-quesced; -quesc•ing** ♦ : to dissolve or melt away — **del•i•ques•cent** \-ˈkwes-ᵊnt\ *adj*

♦ flux, fuse, liquefy, melt, run, thaw

de•lir•i•ous \-ē-əs\ *adj* **1** : of, relating to, or characteristic of delirium **2** ♦ : affected with or marked by delirium — **de•lir•i•ous•ly** *adv*

♦ feverish, fierce, frantic, frenetic, frenzied, furious, mad, rabid, violent, wild

de•lir•i•um \di-ˈlir-ē-əm\ *n* **1** : mental disturbance marked by confusion, disordered speech, and hallucinations **2** ♦ : frenzied excitement

♦ agitation, distraction, frenzy, furor, fury, hysteria, rage, rampage, uproar

delirium tre•mens \-ˈtrē-mənz, -ˈtre-\ *n* : a violent delirium with tremors that is induced by excessive and prolonged use of alcoholic liquors

de•liv•er \di-ˈli-vər\ *vb* **-ered; -er•ing** **1** ♦ : to set free : rescue from actual or feared evil : SAVE **2** ♦ : to take and hand over to or leave for another : TRANSFER ⟨~ a letter⟩ **3** : to assist in giving birth or at the birth of; *also* : to give birth to **4** : UTTER, COMMUNICATE **5** : to send to an intended target or destination **6** ♦ : to produce the promised, desired, or expected results — **de•liv•er•able** \-ˈli-v(ə-)rə-bəl\ *adj*

♦ [1] rescue, save ♦ [2] commend, commit, consign, entrust, give, hand over, leave, pass, transfer, transmit, trust, turn over, vest ♦ [6] click, go over, pan out, succeed, work out

de•liv•er•ance \di-ˈli-v(ə-)rən(t)s\ *n* **1** : the act of delivering someone or something : the state of being delivered **2** : something delivered; *esp* : an opinion or decision (as the verdict of a jury) expressed publicly

♦ rescue, salvation

de•liv•er•er \-ər\ *n* ♦ : one that delivers

♦ redeemer, rescuer, savior

de•liv•ery \di-ˈli-və-rē\ *n, pl* **-er•ies** ♦ : the act or manner of delivering something; *also* : something delivered — **de•liv•ery•man** \-ˌman\ *n*

♦ discharge, quietus, quittance, release ♦ childbirth, labor (*or* labour)

dell \ˈdel\ *n* : a small secluded valley

de•louse \dē-ˈlau̇s\ *vb* : to remove lice from

del•phin•i•um \del-ˈfi-nē-əm\ *n* : any of a genus of mostly perennial herbs related to the buttercups with tall branching spikes of irregular flowers

del•ta \ˈdel-tə\ *n* **1** : the 4th letter of the Greek alphabet — Δ or δ **2** : something shaped like a capital Δ; *esp* : the triangular silt-formed land at the mouth of a river — **del•ta•ic** \del-ˈtā-ik\ *adj*

del•toid \ˈdel-ˌtȯid\ *n* : a large triangular muscle that covers the shoulder joint and raises the arm laterally

de•lude \di-ˈlüd\ *vb* **de•lud•ed; de•lud•ing** ♦ : to mislead the mind or judgment of : DECEIVE

♦ beguile, bluff, cozen, deceive, dupe, fool, gull, have, hoax, hoodwink, humbug, misinform, mislead, string along, take in, trick

¹del•uge \ˈdel-yüj\ *n* **1** ♦ : a flooding of land by water **2** ♦ : a drenching rain **3** : a great amount or number

♦ [1] cataclysm, cataract, flood, inundation, overflow, spate, torrent ♦ [2] cloudburst, downpour, rain, rainstorm, storm, wet

²deluge *vb* **del•uged; del•ug•ing** **1** ♦ : to overflow with water : INUNDATE **2** : to overwhelm as if with a deluge

♦ drown, engulf, flood, inundate, overflow, overwhelm, submerge, swamp

de•lu•sion \di-ˈlü-zhən\ *n* ♦ : a deluding or being deluded; *esp* : a persistent false psychotic belief — **de•lu•sion•al** \-ˈlü-zhə-nəl\ *adj*

♦ chimera, conceit, daydream, dream, fancy, fantasy, figment, hallucination, illusion, phantasm, pipe dream, unreality, vision

de•lu•sive \di-ˈlü-siv\ *adj* **1** ♦ : likely to delude **2** : constituting a delusion

♦ deceitful, deceptive, fallacious, false, misleading, specious

de•luxe \di-ˈlu̇ks, -ˈləks, -ˈlüks\ *adj* ♦ : notably luxurious or elegant

♦ lavish, luxuriant, luxurious, opulent, palatial, plush, sumptuous

delve \ˈdelv\ *vb* **delved; delv•ing** **1** : to dig or labor with or as if with a spade **2** ♦ : to seek laboriously for information

♦ *usu* **delve into** dig, explore, go, inquire into, investigate, look, probe, research

dely *abbr* delivery

Dem *abbr* Democrat; Democratic

de•mag•ne•tize \dē-ˈmag-nə-ˌtīz\ *vb* : to cause to lose magnetic properties — **de•mag•ne•ti•za•tion** \dē-ˌmag-nə-tə-ˈzā-shən\ *n*

dem•a•gogue *also* **dem•a•gog** \ˈde-mə-ˌgäg\ *n* ♦ : a person who appeals to the emotions and prejudices of people especially in order to gain political power — **dem•a•gogu•ery** \-ˌgä-gə-rē\ *n* — **dem•a•gogy** \-ˌgä-gē, -ˌgä-jē\ *n*

♦ agitator, firebrand, incendiary, inciter, rabble-rouser

¹de•mand \di-ˈmand\ *n* **1** ♦ : an act of demanding; *also* : something claimed as due or just **2** : the ability and desire to buy goods or services; *also* : the quantity of goods wanted at a stated price **3** : a seeking or being sought after : urgent need **4** ♦ : a pressing need or requirement

♦ [1] claim, dun, requisition ♦ [4] condition, essential, must, necessity, need, requirement, requisite

²demand *vb* **1** ♦ : to ask for with authority : claim as due or just **2** : to ask earnestly or in the manner of a command **3** ♦ : to call for as useful or necessary : REQUIRE ⟨a patient who ~*s* constant care⟩

♦ [1] call, claim, clamor (*or* clamour), command, enjoin, exact, insist, press, quest, stipulate (for) ♦ [3] necessitate, need, require, take, want, warrant

de•mand•ing *adj* **1** ♦ : requiring much time, effort, or attention **2** ♦ : difficult in making demands

♦ [1] arduous, burdensome, challenging, exacting, grueling, laborious, onerous, taxing, toilsome ***Ant*** light, undemanding ♦ [2] choosy, dainty, delicate, exacting, fastidious, finicky, fussy, nice, old-maidish, particular, picky

de•mar•cate \di-ˈmär-ˌkāt, ˈdē-ˌmär-\ *vb* **-cat•ed; -cat•ing** **1** ♦ : to fix or define the limits of : DELIMIT **2** : to set apart : DISTINGUISH

♦ bound, circumscribe, define, delimit, limit, mark, terminate

de•mar•ca•tion \ˌdē-ˌmär-ˈkā-shən\ *n* ♦ : the act or process of demarcating; *also* : the result of demarcating

♦ discrimination, distinction, separation

dé·marche *or* **de·marche** \dā-ˈmärsh\ *n* : a course of action : MANEUVER

[1]**de·mean** \di-ˈmēn\ *vb* **de·meaned; de·mean·ing** ♦ : to behave or conduct (oneself) usually in a proper manner

♦ acquit, bear, behave, comport, conduct, deport, quit

[2]**demean** *vb* **de·meaned; de·mean·ing** ♦ : to lower in character, status, or reputation : DEGRADE

♦ debase, degrade, demean, demoralize, humble, subvert, warp

de·mean·or *of Can and Brit* **de·mean·our** \di-ˈme-nər\ *n* ♦ : behavior toward others : BEARING

♦ actions, bearing, behavior (*or* behaviour), comportment, conduct, deportment

de·ment·ed \di-ˈmen-təd\ *adj* : disordered in mind : INSANE — **de·ment·ed·ly** *adv*

de·men·tia \di-ˈmen-chə\ *n* **1** : deterioration of cognitive functioning (as in Alzheimer's disease) **2** ♦ : a deranged state of the mind : INSANITY

♦ aberration, derangement, insanity, lunacy, madness, mania

de·mer·it \di-ˈmer-ət\ *n* **1** ♦ : a quality that deserves blame or lacks merit : FAULT **2** : a mark placed against a person's record for some fault or offense

♦ failing, fault, foible, frailty, shortcoming, vice, weakness

de·mesne \di-ˈmān, -ˈmēn\ *n* **1** : manorial land actually possessed by the lord and not held by free tenants **2 a** ♦ : the land attached to a mansion **b** : ESTATE **3** ♦ : an indeterminate geographic area : REGION **4** : a sphere of knowledge, influence, or activity : REALM

♦ [2a] grounds, park, premises, yard ♦ [3] area, field, region, zone

demi·god \ˈde-mi-ˌgäd\ *n* : a mythological being with more power than a mortal but less than a god

demi·john \ˈde-mi-ˌjän\ *n* : a large narrow-necked bottle usually enclosed in wickerwork

de·mil·i·ta·rize \dē-ˈmi-lə-tə-ˌrīz\ *vb* : to strip of military forces, weapons, or fortifications — **de·mil·i·tar·i·za·tion** \dē-ˌmi-lə-tə-rə-ˈzā-shən\ *n*

demi·mon·daine \ˌde-mi-ˌmän-ˈdān\ *n* : a woman of the demimonde

demi·monde \ˈde-mi-ˌmänd\ *n* **1** : a class of women on the fringes of respectable society supported by wealthy lovers **2** : a distinct isolated group having low reputation or prestige

de·min·er·al·ize \dē-ˈmi-nə-rə-ˌlīz\ *vb* : to remove the mineral matter from — **de·min·er·al·i·za·tion** \-ˌmi-nə-rə-lə-ˈzā-shən\ *n*

de·mise \di-ˈmīz\ *n* **1** : LEASE **2** : transfer of sovereignty to a successor ⟨~ of the crown⟩ **3 a** ♦ : a permanent cessation of all vital functions : DEATH **b** ♦ : a cessation of existence or activity **4** : loss of status

♦ [3a] death, expiration, termination ♦ [3b] death, decease, doom, end, passing, quietus

demi·tasse \ˈde-mi-ˌtas\ *n* : a small cup of black coffee; *also* : the cup used to serve it

demo \ˈde-mō\ *n, pl* **demos** **1** : DEMONSTRATION **2** : a product used to show performance or merits to prospective buyers **3** : a recording used to show off a song or performer

de·mo·bi·lize \di-ˈmō-bə-ˌlīz, dē-\ *vb* **1** : DISBAND **2** : to discharge from military service — **de·mo·bi·li·za·tion** \di-ˌmō-bə-lə-ˈzā-shən, dē-\ *n*

de·moc·ra·cy \di-ˈmä-krə-sē\ *n, pl* **-cies** **1** : government by the people; *esp* : rule of the majority **2** : a government in which the supreme power is held by the people **3** : a political unit that has a democratic government **4** *cap* : the principles and policies of the Democratic party in the U.S. **5** : the common people especially when constituting the source of political authority **6** : the absence of hereditary or arbitrary class distinctions or privileges

dem·o·crat \ˈde-mə-ˌkrat\ *n* **1** : one who believes in or practices democracy **2** *cap* : a member of the Democratic party of the U.S.

dem·o·crat·ic \ˌde-mə-ˈkra-tik\ *adj* **1** ♦ : of, relating to, or favoring democracy **2** *often cap* : of or relating to one of the two major political parties in the U.S. associated in modern times with policies of broad social reform and internationalism **3** : relating to or appealing to the common people ⟨~ art⟩ **4** : not snobbish — **dem·o·crat·i·cal·ly** \-ti-k(ə-)lē\ *adv*

♦ popular, republican, self-governing ***Ant*** undemocratic

de·moc·ra·tize \di-ˈmä-krə-ˌtīz\ *vb* **-tized; -tiz·ing** : to make democratic

dé·mo·dé \ˌdā-mō-ˈdā\ *adj* : no longer fashionable : OUT-OF-DATE

de·mo·graph·ics \ˌde-mə-ˈgra-fiks, ˌdē-\ *n pl* : the statistical characteristics of human populations

de·mog·ra·phy \di-ˈmä-grə-fē\ *n* : the statistical study of human populations and especially their size and distribution and the number of births and deaths — **de·mog·ra·pher** \-fər\ *n* — **de·mo·graph·ic** \ˌde-mə-ˈgra-fik, ˌdē-\ *adj* — **de·mo·graph·i·cal·ly** \-fi-k(ə-)lē\ *adv*

dem·oi·selle \ˌdem-wə-ˈzel\ *n* : a young woman

de·mol·ish \di-ˈmä-lish\ *vb* **1** ♦ : to destroy to the ground : RAZE **2** ♦ : to break to pieces : SMASH **3** ♦ : to put an end to

♦ [1, 3] annihilate, blot out, desolate, destroy, devastate, do in, exterminate, extinguish, obliterate, pulverize, ruin, shatter, smash, tear down, waste, wipe out, wreck ♦ [2] blast, blow up, burst, explode, pop, shatter, smash

de·mo·li·tion \ˌde-mə-ˈli-shən, ˌdē-\ *n* ♦ : the act of demolishing; *esp* : destruction by means of explosives

♦ annihilation, desolation, destruction, devastation, havoc, loss, obliteration, ruin, wastage, wreckage

de·mon *or* **dae·mon** \ˈdē-mən\ *n* **1** ♦ : an evil spirit : DEVIL **2** *usu daemon* : an attendant power or spirit **3** : one that has unusual drive or effectiveness

♦ devil, fiend, ghoul, imp

de·mon·e·tize \dē-ˈmä-nə-ˌtīz, -ˈmə-\ *vb* : to stop using as money or as a monetary standard ⟨~ silver⟩ — **de·mon·e·ti·za·tion** \dē-ˌmä-nə-tə-ˈzā-shən, -ˌmə-\ *n*

de·mo·ni·ac \di-ˈmō-nē-ˌak\ *also* **de·mo·ni·a·cal** \ˌdē-mə-ˈnī-ə-kəl\ *adj* **1** : possessed or influenced by a demon **2** : of, relating to, or suggestive of a demon : DEVILISH

de·mon·ic \di-ˈmä-nik\ *also* **de·mon·i·cal** \-ni-kəl\ *adj* ♦ : of, relating to, or suggestive of a demon : FIENDISH

♦ devilish, diabolical, fiendish, satanic

de·mon·ize \ˈdē-mə-ˌnīz\ *vb* **-ized; -iz·ing** **1** : to convert into a demon **2** : to characterize or treat as evil or harmful

de·mon·ol·o·gy \ˌdē-mə-ˈnä-lə-jē\ *n* **1** : the study of demons **2** : belief in demons

de·mon·stra·ble \di-ˈmän-strə-bəl\ *adj* **1** ♦ : capable of being demonstrated **2** : APPARENT, EVIDENT — **de·mon·stra·bly** \-blē\ *adv*

♦ provable, supportable, sustainable, verifiable

dem·on·strate \ˈde-mən-ˌstrāt\ *vb* **-strat·ed; -strat·ing** **1** ♦ : to show clearly **2** ♦ : to prove or make clear by reasoning or evidence **3** ♦ : to explain especially with many examples **4** : to show publicly ⟨~ a new car⟩ **5** : to make a public display ⟨~ in protest⟩ — **dem·on·stra·tor** \ˈde-mən-ˌstrā-tər\ *n*

♦ [1] establish, prove, show, substantiate ♦ [2] document, establish, prove, substantiate, validate ♦ [3] clarify, clear (up), construe, elucidate, explain, explicate, expound, illuminate, illustrate, interpret, spell out

dem·on·stra·tion \ˌde-mən-ˈstrā-shən\ *n* **1** : an act, process, or means of demonstrating to the intelligence **2** ♦ : an outward expression or display

♦ display, exhibition, show

[1]**de·mon·stra·tive** \di-ˈmän-strə-tiv\ *adj* **1** : demonstrating as real or true **2** : characterized by demonstration **3** : pointing out the one referred to and distinguishing it from others of the same class ⟨~ pronoun⟩ **4** ♦ : marked by display of feeling : EFFUSIVE — **de·mon·stra·tive·ly** *adv* — **de·mon·stra·tive·ness** *n*

♦ effusive, emotional, uninhibited, unreserved, unrestrained ***Ant*** inhibited, reserved, restrained, undemonstrative, unemotional

[2]**demonstrative** *n* : a demonstrative word and especially a pronoun

de·mor·al·i·za·tion \di-ˌmȯr-ə-lə-ˈzā-shən\ *n* ♦ : the act or process of demoralizing : a demoralized state

♦ corruption, debasement, debauchery, decadence, degeneracy, degeneration, degradation, depravity, dissipation, dissoluteness, perversion ♦ despair, despondency, discouragement, dismay

de·mor·al·ize \di-ˈmȯr-ə-ˌlīz\ *vb* **1** ♦ : to corrupt in morals **2** ♦ : to weaken in discipline or spirit

♦ [1] debase, degrade, demean, demoralize, humble, subvert, warp ♦ [2] daunt, discourage, dishearten, dismay, dispirit, unman, unnerve

de·mote \di-ˈmōt\ *vb* **de·mot·ed; de·mot·ing** ♦ : to reduce to a lower grade or rank — **de·mo·tion** \-ˈmō-shən\ *n*

♦ break, bust, degrade, downgrade, reduce *Ant* advance, elevate, promote, raise

de•mot•ic \di-ˈmä-tik\ *adj* **:** COMMON, POPULAR

[1]**de•mur** \di-ˈmər\ *vb* **de•murred; de•mur•ring** ♦ **:** to take exception **:** OBJECT

♦ kick, object, protest, remonstrate

[2]**demur** *n* **1 :** hesitation (as in doing or accepting) usually based on doubt of the acceptability of something offered or proposed **2** ♦ **:** the act or an instance of objecting — **de•mur•ral** \-əl\ *n*

♦ challenge, complaint, expostulation, fuss, kick, objection, protest, question, remonstrance

de•mure \di-ˈmyůr\ *adj* **1** ♦ **:** quietly modest **2** ♦ **:** affectedly modest, reserved, or serious — **de•mure•ly** *adv*

♦ [1] humble, lowly, meek, modest, retiring, shy, unassuming, unpretentious ♦ [2] coquettish, coy, kittenish

de•mur•rer \di-ˈmər-ər\ *n* **:** a claim by the defendant in a legal action that the plaintiff does not have sufficient grounds to proceed

den \ˈden\ *n* **1** ♦ **:** the lair of a wild usually predatory animal **2** ♦ **:** a refuge or place for hiding **:** HIDEOUT ⟨a robber's ~⟩; *also* **:** a place like a hideout or a center of secret activity ⟨opium ~⟩ ⟨a ~ of iniquity⟩ **3 :** a cozy private little room

♦ [1] burrow, hole, lair, lodge ♦ [2] concealment, covert, hideout, lair, nest

Den *abbr* Denmark

de•na•ture \dē-ˈnā-chər\ *vb* **de•na•tured; de•na•tur•ing :** to remove or change the natural qualities of; *esp* **:** to make (alcohol) unfit for drinking

den•drol•o•gy \den-ˈdrä-lə-jē\ *n* **:** the study of trees — **den•drol•o•gist** \-jist\ *n*

den•gue \ˈdeŋ-gē, -ˌgā\ *n* **:** an acute infectious disease characterized by headache, severe joint pain, and rash

de•ni•al \di-ˈnī-əl\ *n* **1** ♦ **:** rejection of a request **2** ♦ **:** refusal to admit the truth of a statement or charge; *also* **:** assertion that something alleged is false **3 :** DISAVOWAL **4 :** restriction on one's own activity or desires

♦ [1] disallowance, nay, no, refusal, rejection *Ant* allowance, grant ♦ [2] contradiction, disallowance, disavowal, disclaimer, negation, rejection, repudiation *Ant* acknowledgment, admission, avowal, confirmation

de•nier \ˈden-yər\ *n* **:** a unit of fineness for yarn

den•i•grate \ˈde-ni-ˌgrāt\ *vb* **-grat•ed; -grat•ing :** to cast aspersions on **:** DEFAME — **den•i•gra•tion** \ˌde-ni-ˈgrā-shən\ *n*

den•im \ˈde-nəm\ *n* **1 :** a firm durable twilled usually cotton fabric woven with colored warp and white filling threads **2** *pl* **:** overalls or pants of usually blue denim

den•i•zen \ˈde-nə-zən\ *n* ♦ **:** one that occupies a particular place regularly, routinely, or for a period of time **:** INHABITANT

♦ dweller, inhabitant, occupant, resident

de•nom•i•nate \di-ˈnä-mə-ˌnāt\ *vb* ♦ **:** to assign a name to **:** DESIGNATE

♦ baptize, call, christen, designate, dub, entitle, label, name, style, term, title

de•nom•i•na•tion \di-ˌnä-mə-ˈnā-shən\ *n* **1 :** an act of denominating **2 :** a value or size of a series of related values (as of money) **3 :** a word or phrase that constitutes the distinctive designation of a person or thing **:** NAME; *esp* **:** a general name for a category **4 :** a religious organization uniting local congregations in a single body — **de•nom•i•na•tion•al** \-shə-nəl\ *adj*

de•nom•i•na•tor \di-ˈnä-mə-ˌnā-tər\ *n* **:** the part of a fraction that is below the line indicating division

de•no•ta•tion \ˌdē-nō-ˈtā-shən\ *n* **1 :** an act or process of denoting **2** ♦ **:** the thing one conveys or intends to convey especially by language; *esp* **:** a direct specific meaning as distinct from an implied or associated idea **3** ♦ **:** a denoting term **:** NAME

♦ [2] drift, import, intent, meaning, purport, sense, significance, signification ♦ [3] appellation, cognomen, designation, handle, name, title

de•no•ta•tive \ˈdē-nō-ˌtā-tiv, di-ˈnō-tə-tiv\ *adj* **1** ♦ **:** denoting or tending to denote **2 :** relating to denotation

♦ indicative, significant, telltale

de•note \di-ˈnōt\ *vb* **1 :** to mark out plainly **:** INDICATE **2 :** to make known **3** ♦ **:** to serve as a linguistic expression of the notion of **:** MEAN

♦ express, import, mean, signify, spell

de•noue•ment \ˌdā-ˌnü-ˈmäⁿ\ *n* **:** the final outcome of the dramatic complications in a literary work

de•nounce \di-ˈnaůns\ *vb* **de•nounced; de•nounc•ing 1** ♦ **:** to pronounce especially publicly to be blameworthy or evil **2 :** to inform against **:** ACCUSE **3 :** to announce formally the termination of (as a treaty) — **de•nounce•ment** *n*

♦ censure, condemn, damn, decry, reprehend, reprobate ♦ blame, criticize, fault, knock, pan

de no•vo \di-ˈnō-vō\ *adv or adj* **:** over again **:** ANEW

dense \ˈdens\ *adj* **dens•er; dens•est 1** ♦ **:** marked by compactness or crowding together of parts **:** THICK ⟨~ forest⟩ ⟨a ~ fog⟩ **2** ♦ **:** slow to understand **:** STUPID — **dense•ly** *adv*

♦ [1] close, compact, crowded, packed, serried, thick, tight ♦ [2] dull, dumb, obtuse, simple, slow, stupid, thick

dense•ness \-nəs\ *n* ♦ **:** the quality or state of being dense

♦ dopiness, obtuseness, stupidity

den•si•ty \ˈden-sə-tē\ *n, pl* **-ties 1 :** the quality or state of being dense **2 :** the quantity of something per unit volume, unit area, or unit length

dent \ˈdent\ *n* **1** ♦ **:** a small depressed place made by a blow or by pressure **2 :** an impression or weakening effect made usually against resistance **3 :** initial progress — **dent** *vb*

♦ cavity, concavity, depression, hole, hollow, indentation, pit, recess

den•tal \ˈdent-ᵊl\ *adj* **:** of or relating to teeth or dentistry — **den•tal•ly** *adv*

dental floss *n* **:** a thread used to clean between the teeth

dental hygienist *n* **:** a person licensed to clean and examine teeth

den•tate \ˈden-ˌtāt\ *adj* **:** having pointed projections **:** NOTCHED

den•ti•frice \ˈden-tə-frəs\ *n* **:** a powder, paste, or liquid for cleaning the teeth

den•tin \ˈdent-ᵊn\ *or* **den•tine** \ˈden-ˌtēn, den-ˈtēn\ *n* **:** a calcareous material like bone but harder and denser that composes the principal mass of a tooth

den•tist \ˈden-tist\ *n* **:** a person licensed in the care, treatment, and replacement of teeth — **den•tist•ry** *n*

den•ti•tion \den-ˈti-shən\ *n* **:** the number, kind, and arrangement of teeth (as of a person or animal); *also* **:** TEETH

den•ture \ˈden-chər\ *n* **:** a set of teeth; *esp* **:** a partial or complete set of false teeth

de•nude \di-ˈnüd, -ˈnyüd\ *vb* **de•nud•ed; de•nud•ing :** to strip the covering from — **de•nu•da•tion** \ˌdē-nü-ˈdā-shən, -nyü-\ *n*

de•nun•ci•a•tion \di-ˌnən-sē-ˈā-shən\ *n* ♦ **:** the act of denouncing; *esp* **:** a public condemnation

♦ censure, rebuke, reprimand, reproach, reproof, stricture

de•ny \di-ˈnī\ *vb* **de•nied; de•ny•ing 1** ♦ **:** to declare untrue **2 :** to refuse to recognize or acknowledge **:** DISAVOW **3** ♦ **:** to refuse to grant ⟨~ a request⟩ **4 :** to reject as false ⟨~ a theory⟩

♦ [1] contradict, disallow, disavow, disclaim, gainsay, negate, negative, reject, repudiate *Ant* acknowledge, admit, allow, avow, concede, confirm, own ♦ [3] decline, disallow, refuse, reject, withhold *Ant* allow, concede, grant, let, permit

de•o•dar \ˈdē-ə-ˌdär\ *n* **:** a Himalayan cedar

de•odor•ant \dē-ˈō-də-rənt\ *n* **:** a preparation that destroys or masks unpleasant odors

de•odor•ize \dē-ˈō-də-ˌrīz\ *vb* **:** to eliminate the offensive odor of

de•ox•i•dize \dē-ˈäk-sə-ˌdīz\ *vb* **:** to remove oxygen from

de•oxy•ri•bo•nu•cle•ic acid \dē-ˈäk-si-ˌrī-bō-nů-ˌklē-ik-, -nyů-\ *n* **:** DNA

de•oxy•ri•bose \dē-ˌäk-si-ˈrī-ˌbōs\ *n* **:** a sugar with five carbon and four oxygen atoms in each molecule that is part of DNA

dep *abbr* **1** depart; departure **2** deposit **3** deputy

de•part \di-ˈpärt\ *vb* **1** ♦ **:** to go away **:** go away from **2 :** to cease living **:** DIE **3 :** to turn aside **:** DEVIATE

♦ clear out, exit, get off, go, move, pull, quit, sally, shove, take off

de•part•ment \di-ˈpärt-mənt\ *n* **1** ♦ **:** a distinct sphere or category especially of an activity or attribute **2** ♦ **:** a functional or territorial division (as of a government, business, or college) — **de•part•men•tal** \di-ˌpärt-ˈment-ᵊl, ˌdē-\ *adj* — **de•part•men•tal•ly** *adv*

♦ [1] area, arena, demesne, discipline, domain, field, line, province, realm, specialty, sphere ♦ [2] bureau, desk, division, office

department store *n* **:** a store having separate sections for a wide variety of goods

de•par•ture \di-ˈpär-chər\ *n* **1** ♦ **:** the act of going away **2 :** a starting out (as on a journey) **3 :** DIVERGENCE

♦ exit, farewell, leave-taking, parting *Ant* arrival

de•pend \di-ˈpend\ *vb* **1** ♦ **:** to be determined, based, or contingent ⟨life ~*s* on food⟩ **2** ♦ **:** to place reliance or trust ⟨you can ~ on me⟩ **3 :** to be dependent especially for financial support **4 :** to hang down ⟨a vine ~*ing* from a tree⟩

♦ [1] base, hang, rest ♦ [2] count, lean, reckon, rely

de•pend•abil•i•ty \di-ˌpen-də-ˈbi-lə-tē\ *n* ♦ **:** the quality or state of being dependable

♦ reliability, solidity, sureness, trustworthiness

de•pend•able \di-ˈpen-də-bəl\ *adj* ♦ **:** capable of being depended on **:** RELIABLE

♦ good, reliable, responsible, safe, solid, steady, sure, tried, true, trustworthy *Ant* irresponsible, undependable, unreliable, untrustworthy

de•pen•dence *also* **de•pen•dance** \di-ˈpen-dəns\ *n* **1 :** the quality or state of being dependent; *esp* **:** the quality or state of being influenced by or subject to another **2 :** RELIANCE, TRUST **3** ♦ **:** something on which one relies **4 :** drug addiction; *also* **:** HABITUATION 2

♦ buttress, mainstay, pillar, reliance, standby, support

de•pen•den•cy \-dən-sē\ *n, pl* **-cies 1 :** DEPENDENCE **2 :** a territory under the jurisdiction of a nation but not formally annexed by it

¹de•pen•dent \-dənt\ *adj* **1** ♦ **:** hanging down **2 a** ♦ **:** determined or conditioned by another **b :** affected with drug dependence **3 :** relying on another for support **4 :** subject to another's jurisdiction **5 :** SUBORDINATE 4

♦ [1] pendulous ♦ [2a] conditional, contingent, subject *Ant* independent

²dependent *also* **de•pen•dant** \-dənt\ *n* **:** one that is dependent; *esp* **:** a person who relies on another for support

de•pict \di-ˈpikt\ *vb* **1** ♦ **:** to represent by a picture **2** ♦ **:** to describe in words

♦ [1] image, picture, portray, represent ♦ [2] delineate, describe, draw, image, paint, picture, portray, sketch

de•pic•tion \di-ˈpik-shən\ *n* ♦ **:** a descriptive statement

♦ delineation, description, picture, portrait, portrayal, sketch

de•pil•a•to•ry \di-ˈpi-lə-ˌtōr-ē\ *n, pl* **-ries :** a preparation for removing hair, wool, or bristles

de•plane \dē-ˈplān\ *vb* **:** to get out of an airplane

de•plete \di-ˈplēt\ *vb* **de•plet•ed; de•plet•ing** ♦ **:** to exhaust especially of strength or resources — **de•ple•tion** \-ˈplē-shən\ *n*

♦ clean, consume, drain, exhaust, expend, spend, use up *Ant* renew, replace

de•plor•able \di-ˈplōr-ə-bəl\ *adj* **1** ♦ **:** that is to be regretted or lamented **:** LAMENTABLE **2 :** deserving censure or contempt **:** WRETCHED — **de•plor•ably** *adv*

♦ distressful, grievous, heartbreaking, lamentable, regrettable, unfortunate, woeful

de•plore \-ˈplōr\ *vb* **de•plored; de•plor•ing 1** ♦ **:** to feel or express grief for **2** ♦ **:** to regret strongly **3 :** to consider unfortunate or deserving of disapproval

♦ [1] bemoan, bewail, grieve, lament, mourn, wail ♦ [2] bemoan, lament, regret, repent, rue

de•ploy \di-ˈplȯi\ *vb* **:** to spread out (as troops or ships) in order for battle — **de•ploy•ment** \-mənt\ *n*

de•po•nent \di-ˈpō-nənt\ *n* **:** one who gives evidence

de•pop•u•late \dē-ˈpä-pyə-ˌlāt\ *vb* **:** to reduce greatly the population of — **de•pop•u•la•tion** \-ˌpä-pyə-ˈlā-shən\ *n*

de•port \di-ˈpōrt\ *vb* **1** ♦ **:** to behave or comport (oneself) especially in accord with a code **:** CONDUCT **2** ♦ **:** to send out of the country **:** BANISH

♦ [1] acquit, bear, behave, comport, conduct, demean, quit ♦ [2] banish, displace, exile, expatriate, transport

de•por•ta•tion \ˌdē-ˌpōr-ˈtā-shən\ *n* ♦ **:** an act or instance of deporting

♦ banishment, displacement, exile, expulsion

de•port•ment \di-ˈpōrt-mənt\ *n* ♦ **:** the manner in which one conducts oneself **:** BEHAVIOR

♦ actions, bearing, behavior (*or* behaviour), comportment, conduct, demeanor (*or* demeanour)

de•pose \di-ˈpōz\ *vb* **de•posed; de•pos•ing 1** ♦ **:** to remove from high office (as of king) **2** ♦ **:** to testify under oath or by affidavit

♦ [1] oust *Ant* crown, enthrone, throne ♦ [2] attest, swear, testify, witness

¹de•pos•it \di-ˈpä-zət\ *vb* **de•pos•it•ed** \-zə-təd\; **de•pos•it•ing 1** ♦ **:** to place for safekeeping or as a pledge; *esp* **:** to put money in a bank **2** ♦ **:** to lay down **:** PLACE **3 :** to let fall or sink ⟨silt ~*ed* by a flood⟩ — **de•pos•i•tor** \-zə-tər\ *n*

♦ [1] bank, cache, lay away, store *Ant* withdraw ♦ [2] dispose, fix, lay, place, position, put, set, set up, stick

²deposit *n* **1 :** the state of being deposited ⟨money on ~⟩ **2** ♦ **:** something placed for safekeeping; *esp* **:** money deposited in a bank **3 :** money given as a pledge **4 :** an act of depositing **5** ♦ **:** something laid down ⟨a ~ of silt⟩ **6 :** a natural accumulation (as of a mineral)

♦ [2] cache, hoard, reserve, store ♦ [2] account, budget, fund, kitty, nest egg, pool ♦ [5] dregs, grounds, lees, precipitate, sediment

de•po•si•tion \ˌde-pə-ˈzi-shən, ˌdē-\ *n* **1 :** an act of removing from a position of authority **2 :** TESTIMONY **3 :** the process of depositing **4 :** something deposited **:** DEPOSIT

de•pos•i•to•ry \di-ˈpä-zə-ˌtōr-ē\ *n, pl* **-ries** ♦ **:** a place where something is deposited especially for safekeeping

♦ repository, storage, storehouse, warehouse

de•pot *1, 2 usu* ˈde-pō, *3 usu* ˈdē-\ *n* **1 :** a place for storing goods or motor vehicles **:** STOREHOUSE **2** ♦ **:** a place where military supplies or replacements are kept or assembled **3 :** a building for railroad or bus passengers

♦ armory, arsenal, dump, magazine

depr *abbr* depreciation

de•prave \di-ˈprāv\ *vb* **de•praved; de•prav•ing** ♦ **:** to make bad **:** CORRUPT

♦ debase, degrade, demean, demoralize, humble, subvert, warp

de•praved *adj* **:** marked by corruption or evil

de•prav•i•ty \di-ˈpra-və-tē\ *n* **1** ♦ **:** a corrupt act or practice **2** ♦ **:** the quality or state of being depraved

♦ [1] corruption, debasement, debauchery, decadence, degeneracy, degeneration, degradation, demoralization, dissipation, dissoluteness, perversion ♦ [1] immorality, iniquity, licentiousness, sin, vice ♦ [2] atrociousness, atrocity, enormity, heinousness, monstrosity, vileness, wickedness

dep•re•cate \ˈde-pri-ˌkāt\ *vb* **-cat•ed; -cat•ing 1** ♦ **:** to express disapproval of **2** ♦ **:** to speak slightingly of **:** BELITTLE

♦ [1] disapprove, discountenance, disfavor (*or* disfavour), dislike, frown, reprove ♦ [2] belittle, cry down, decry, depreciate, diminish, discount, disparage, minimize, put down, write off

dep•re•ca•tion \ˌde-pri-ˈkā-shən\ *n* ♦ **:** an act of deprecating

♦ disapproval, disfavor (*or* disfavour), dislike, displeasure

dep•re•ca•to•ry \ˈde-pri-kə-ˌtōr-ē\ *adj* **1 :** APOLOGETIC **2 :** serving to deprecate **:** DISAPPROVING

de•pre•ci•ate \di-ˈprē-shē-ˌāt\ *vb* **-at•ed; -at•ing 1 :** to speak slightingly of **:** DISPARAGE **2** ♦ **:** to lessen in price or value

♦ cheapen, depress, mark down, write off *Ant* appreciate, mark up

de•pre•ci•a•tion \di-ˌprē-shē-ˈā-shən\ *n* ♦ **:** the act of reducing in value or esteem

♦ deprecation, detraction, disparagement, put-down *Ant* aggrandizement, ennoblement, exaltation, glorification, magnification

dep•re•da•tion \ˌde-prə-ˈdā-shən\ *n* **:** a laying waste or plundering — **dep•re•date** \ˈde-prə-ˌdāt\ *vb*

de•press \di-ˈpres\ *vb* **1** ♦ **:** to press down **:** cause to sink to a lower position **2 :** to lessen the activity or force of **3** ♦ **:** to make sad **:** SADDEN **4** ♦ **:** to lessen in price or value — **de•pres•sor** \-ˈpre-sər\ *n*

♦ [1] bear, press, shove, weigh ♦ [3] burden, oppress, sadden *Ant* brighten, buoy, cheer, gladden ♦ [4] cheapen, depreciate, mark down, write off

de•pres•sant \di-ˈpres-ᵊnt\ *n* **:** one that depresses; *esp* **:** a chemical substance (as a drug) that reduces bodily functional activity — **depressant** *adj*

de·pressed *adj* **1** ♦ : low in spirits; *also* : affected with psychological depression **2** ♦ : having the central part lower than the margin **3** : suffering from economic depression

♦ [1] bad, blue, down, gloomy, glum, low, melancholy, miserable, mournful, sad, sorrowful, sorry, unhappy ♦ [2] concave, hollow, sunken

de·press·ing *adj* ♦ : that depresses; *esp* : causing emotional depression

♦ bleak, dark, dismal, dreary, gloomy, gray (*or* grey), somber (*or* sombre), wretched

de·pres·sion \di-ˈpre-shən\ *n* **1** : an act of depressing : a state of being depressed **2** : a pressing down : LOWERING **3** ♦ : a state of feeling sad **4** : a psychological disorder marked especially by sadness, inactivity, difficulty in thinking and concentration, and feelings of dejection **5** ♦ : a depressed area or part **6** : a period of low general economic activity with widespread unemployment

♦ [3] blues, dejection, desolation, despondency, doldrums, dumps, forlornness, gloom, heartsickness, melancholy, sadness ♦ [5] cavity, concavity, dent, hole, hollow, indentation, pit, recess

[1]**de·pres·sive** \di-ˈpre-siv\ *adj* **1** : tending to depress **2** : characterized or affected by psychological depression

[2]**depressive** *n* : a person affected with or prone to psychological depression

de·pres·sur·ize \(ˌ)dē-ˈpre-shə-ˌrīz\ *vb* : to release pressure from

dep·ri·va·tion \ˌde-prə-ˈvā-shən\ *n* **1** : an act or instance of depriving : LOSS **2** : PRIVATION 2

de·prive \di-ˈprīv\ *vb* **de·prived; de·priv·ing** **1** : to take something away from **2** : to stop from having something

deprived *adj* : marked by deprivation especially of the necessities of life

de·pro·gram \(ˌ)dē-ˈprō-ˌgram, -grəm\ *vb* : to dissuade from convictions usually of a religious nature often by coercive means

dept *abbr* department

depth \ˈdepth\ *n, pl* **depths** \ˈdepths\ **1** : something that is deep; *esp* : the deep part of a body of water **2** : a part that is far from the outside or surface; *also* : the middle or innermost part **3** : ABYSS **4** ♦ : a profound or intense state ⟨the ~*s* of reflection⟩; *also* : the worst part ⟨during the ~*s* of the depression⟩ **5** : a reprehensibly low condition **6** : the distance from top to bottom or from front to back **7** : the quality of being deep **8** : the degree of intensity

♦ deep, height, middle, midst, thick

depth charge *n* : an explosive device for use underwater especially against submarines

dep·u·ta·tion \ˌde-pyə-ˈtā-shən\ *n* **1** : the act of appointing a deputy **2** : DELEGATION

de·pute \di-ˈpyüt\ *vb* **de·put·ed; de·put·ing** : to appoint as one's representative : DELEGATE

dep·u·tize \ˈde-pyə-ˌtīz\ *vb* **-tized; -tiz·ing** ♦ : to appoint or act as deputy

♦ commission, delegate

dep·u·ty \ˈde-pyə-tē\ *n, pl* **-ties** **1** ♦ : a person appointed to act for or in place of another **2** : a second in command or assistant who usually takes charge when his or her superior is absent **3** : a member of a lower house of a legislative assembly

♦ agent, attorney, commissary, delegate, envoy, factor, proxy, representative

der *or* **deriv** *abbr* derivation; derivative

de·rail \di-ˈrāl\ *vb* : to leave or cause to leave the rails — **de·rail·ment** *n*

de·rail·leur \di-ˈrā-lər\ *n* : a device for shifting gears on a bicycle by moving the chain from one set of exposed gears to another

de·range \di-ˈrānj\ *vb* **de·ranged; de·rang·ing** **1** : to disturb the arrangement or order of : DISARRANGE **2** ♦ : to make insane

♦ craze, madden, unhinge

deranged *adj* ♦ : mentally disordered

♦ crazy, insane, lunatic, mad, maniacal, mental, unsound

de·range·ment \-mənt\ *n* ♦ : the state of being deranged

♦ aberration, dementia, insanity, lunacy, madness, mania

der·by \ˈdər-bē, *Brit* ˈdär-\ *n, pl* **derbies** **1** : a horse race usually for three-year-olds held annually **2** : a race or contest open to all **3** : a stiff felt hat with dome-shaped crown and narrow brim

de·reg·u·la·tion \(ˌ)dē-ˌre-gyü-ˈlā-shən\ *n* : the act of removing restrictions or regulations — **de·reg·u·late** \-ˈre-gyü-ˌlāt\ *vb*

[1]**der·e·lict** \ˈder-ə-ˌlikt\ *adj* **1** ♦ : abandoned by the owner or occupant **2** ♦ : failing to exercise the care expected : NEGLIGENT ⟨~ in his duty⟩

♦ [1] abandoned, deserted, forsaken ♦ [2] careless, lax, negligent, remiss, slack

[2]**derelict** *n* **1** : something voluntarily abandoned; *esp* : a ship abandoned on the high seas **2** : a destitute homeless social misfit : VAGRANT, BUM

der·e·lic·tion \ˌder-ə-ˈlik-shən\ *n* **1** ♦ : the act of abandoning : the state of being abandoned **2** ♦ : a failure in duty

♦ [1] abandonment, desertion *Ant* reclamation ♦ [2] default, delinquency, failure, neglect, negligence, oversight

de·ride \di-ˈrīd\ *vb* **de·rid·ed; de·rid·ing** ♦ : to laugh at scornfully : RIDICULE

♦ gibe, jeer, laugh, mock, ridicule, scout

de ri·gueur \də-rē-ˈgər\ *adj* : prescribed or required by fashion, etiquette, or custom : PROPER

de·ri·sion \də-ˈri-zhən\ *n* **1** : RIDICULE **2** : an object of ridicule or scorn

de·ri·sive \də-ˈrī-siv\ *adj* ♦ : expressing or causing derision — **de·ri·sive·ly** *adv* — **de·ri·sive·ness** *n*

♦ absurd, comical, farcical, laughable, ludicrous, preposterous, ridiculous, risible, silly

de·ri·so·ry \də-ˈrī-sə-rē\ *adj* : worthy of derision

der·i·va·tion \ˌder-ə-ˈvā-shən\ *n* **1** : the formation of a word from an earlier word or root; *also* : an act of ascertaining or stating the derivation of a word **2** : ETYMOLOGY **3** : SOURCE, ORIGIN; *also* : DESCENT **4** : an act or process of deriving

de·riv·a·tive \di-ˈri-və-tiv\ *n* **1** : a word formed by derivation **2** ♦ : something derived — **derivative** *adj*

♦ offshoot, outgrowth, spin-off *Ant* origin, root, source

de·rive \di-ˈrīv\ *vb* **de·rived; de·riv·ing** **1** : to receive or obtain from a source **2** : to obtain from a parent substance **3** ♦ : to come to as a conclusion from facts or premises : INFER, DEDUCE **4** : to trace the derivation of **5** : to come from a certain source

♦ conclude, deduce, extrapolate, gather, infer, judge, reason, understand

der·mal \ˈdər-məl\ *adj* : of or relating to the skin : CUTANEOUS

der·ma·ti·tis \ˌdər-mə-ˈtī-təs\ *n, pl* **-tit·i·des** \-ˈti-tə-ˌdēz\ *or* **-ti·tis·es** : inflammation of the skin

der·ma·tol·o·gy \-ˈtä-lə-jē\ *n* : a branch of medical science dealing with the structure, functions, and diseases of the skin — **der·ma·tol·o·gist** \-jist\ *n*

der·mis \ˈdər-məs\ *n* : the sensitive vascular inner layer of the skin

der·o·gate \ˈder-ə-ˌgāt\ *vb* **-gat·ed; -gat·ing** **1** : to cause to seem inferior : DISPARAGE **2** : DETRACT — **der·o·ga·tion** \ˌder-ə-ˈgā-shən\ *n* — **de·rog·a·tive** \di-ˈrä-gə-tiv\ *adj*

de·rog·a·to·ry \di-ˈrä-gə-ˌtōr-ē\ *adj* ♦ : intended to lower the reputation of a person or thing : DISPARAGING — **de·rog·a·to·ri·ly** \-ˌrä-gə-ˈtōr-ə-lē\ *adv*

♦ contemptuous, degrading, disdainful, scornful, uncomplimentary *Ant* complimentary

der·rick \ˈder-ik\ *n* **1** : a hoisting apparatus : CRANE **2** : a framework over a drill hole (as for oil) for supporting machinery

der·ri·ere *or* **der·ri·ère** \ˌder-ē-ˈer\ *n* : BUTTOCKS

der·ring–do \ˌder-iŋ-ˈdü\ *n* : DARING

der·rin·ger \ˈder-ən-jər\ *n* : a short-barreled pocket pistol

der·vish \ˈdər-vish\ *n* : a member of a Muslim religious order noted for devotional exercises (as bodily movements leading to a trance)

de·sal·i·nate \dē-ˈsa-lə-ˌnāt\ *vb* **-nat·ed; -nat·ing** : DESALT — **de·sal·i·na·tion** \-ˌsa-lə-ˈnā-shən\ *n*

de·sal·i·nize \dē-ˈsa-lə-ˌnīz\ *vb* **-nized; -niz·ing** : DESALT — **de·sal·i·ni·za·tion** \-ˌsa-lə-nə-ˈzā-shən\ *n*

de·salt \dē-ˈsölt\ *vb* : to remove salt from ⟨~ seawater⟩ — **de·salt·er** *n*

des·cant \ˈdes-ˌkant\ *vb* **1** ♦ : to sing or play part music : SING **2** : to discourse or write at length

♦ carol, chant, sing, vocalize

de·scend \di-ˈsend\ *vb* **1** ♦ : to pass from a higher to a lower place or level : pass, move, or climb down or down along **2** : DE-

RIVE ⟨~*ed* from royalty⟩ **3 :** to pass by inheritance or transmission **4** ♦ **:** to incline, lead, or extend downward **5** ♦ **:** to swoop down or appear suddenly (as in an attack)

♦ [1, 4] decline, dip, drop, fall, plunge ***Ant*** ascend, climb, rise ♦ [5] assail, assault, attack, beset, charge, jump, pounce (on *or* upon), raid, rush, storm, strike

¹de•scen•dant *also* **de•scen•dent** \di-ˈsen-dənt\ *adj* **1 :** moving or directed downward **2 :** proceeding from an ancestor or source

²descendant *also* **descendent** *n* **1 :** one descended from another or from a common stock **2 :** one deriving directly from a precursor or prototype

de•scent \di-ˈsent\ *n* **1** ♦ **:** derivation from an ancestor **:** LINEAGE **2** ♦ **:** the act or process of descending **3 :** SLOPE **4 :** a descending way (as a downgrade) **5** ♦ **:** a sudden hostile raid or assault **6** ♦ **:** a downward step (as in station or value) **:** DECLINE

♦ [1] ancestry, birth, blood, bloodline, breeding, extraction, family tree, genealogy, line, lineage, origin, parentage, pedigree, stock, strain ♦ [2] dip, dive, down, drop, fall, plunge ***Ant*** ascent, climb, rise, upswing, upturn ♦ [5] aggression, assault, attack, charge, offense (*or* offence), offensive, onset, onslaught, raid, rush, strike ♦ [6] comedown, decline, down, downfall, fall

de•scribe \di-ˈskrīb\ *vb* **de•scribed; de•scrib•ing 1 a** ♦ **:** to represent or give an account of in words **b** ♦ **:** to communicate an account of salient identifying features of **2 :** to trace the outline of — **de•scrib•able** *adj*

♦ delineate, depict, draw, image, narrate, paint, picture, portray, recount, sketch

de•scrip•tion \di-ˈskrip-shən\ *n* **1** ♦ **:** an account of something; *esp* **:** an account that presents a picture to a person who reads or hears it **2** ♦ **:** kind or character especially as determined by prominent features **:** SORT — **de•scrip•tive** \-ˈskrip-tiv\ *adj*

♦ [1] delineation, depiction, picture, portrait, portrayal, sketch ♦ [2] breed, class, feather, ilk, kind, like, manner, nature, order, sort, species, type

de•scry \di-ˈskrī\ *vb* **de•scried; de•scry•ing 1** ♦ **:** to catch sight of **2 :** to discover by observation or investigation

♦ behold, discern, distinguish, espy, eye, look, note, notice, observe, perceive, regard, remark, see, sight, spy, view, witness

des•e•crate \ˈde-si-ˌkrāt\ *vb* **-crat•ed; -crat•ing** ♦ **:** to violate the sanctity of **:** PROFANE

♦ defile, profane, violate

des•e•cra•tion \ˌde-si-ˈkrā-shən\ *n* ♦ **:** an act or instance of desecrating

♦ blasphemy, defilement, impiety, irreverence, sacrilege

de•seg•re•gate \dē-ˈse-gri-ˌgāt\ *vb* **:** to eliminate segregation in; *esp* **:** to free of any law or practice requiring isolation on the basis of race — **de•seg•re•ga•tion** \-ˌse-gri-ˈgā-shən\ *n*

de•sen•si•tize \dē-ˈsen-sə-ˌtīz\ *vb* **:** to make (a sensitized or hypersensitive individual) insensitive or nonreactive to a sensitizing agent — **de•sen•si•ti•za•tion** \-ˌsen-sə-tə-ˈzā-shən\ *n*

¹des•ert \ˈde-zərt\ *n* ♦ **:** dry land with few plants and little rainfall

♦ barren, desolation, waste, wasteland

²des•ert \ˈde-zərt\ *adj* **:** of, relating to, or resembling a desert; *esp* **:** being barren and without life ⟨a ~ island⟩

³de•sert \di-ˈzərt\ *n* **1 :** the quality or fact of deserving reward or punishment **2** ♦ **:** a just reward or punishment

♦ castigation, chastisement, correction, discipline, nemesis, penalty, punishment, wrath

⁴de•sert \di-ˈzərt\ *vb* **1** ♦ **:** to withdraw from and leave especially permanently **2** ♦ **:** to leave in the lurch **:** ABANDON

♦ [1, 2] abandon, forsake, maroon, quit

de•sert•ed \di-ˈzər-təd\ *adj* ♦ **:** left without the accustomed occupants, company, or support

♦ abandoned, derelict, forsaken

de•sert•er \di-ˈzər-tər\ *n* ♦ **:** one who forsakes a duty or cause

♦ defector, recreant, renegade

de•ser•tion \di-ˈzər-shən\ *n* ♦ **:** an act of deserting

♦ abandonment, dereliction

de•serve \di-ˈzərv\ *vb* **de•served; de•serv•ing** ♦ **:** to be worthy of **:** MERIT

♦ earn, merit, rate

de•serv•ed•ly \-ˈzər-vəd-lē\ *adv* **:** according to merit **:** JUSTLY

deserving *adj* ♦ **:** deserving of honor or esteem

♦ good, meritorious, worthy

des•ic•cate \ˈde-si-ˌkāt\ *vb* **-cat•ed; -cat•ing :** DRY, DEHYDRATE — **des•ic•ca•tion** \ˌde-si-ˈkā-shən\ *n* — **des•ic•ca•tor** \ˈde-si-ˌkā-tər\ *n*

de•sid•er•a•tum \di-ˌsi-də-ˈrä-təm, -ˌzi-, -ˈrā-\ *n, pl* **-ta** \-tə\ **:** something desired as essential

¹de•sign \di-ˈzīn\ *vb* **1** ♦ **:** to conceive and plan out in the mind **2** ♦ **:** to have as a purpose **:** INTEND **3 :** to devise for a specific function or end **4 :** to make a pattern or sketch of **5 :** to conceive and draw the plans for

♦ [1] arrange, blueprint, calculate, chart, frame, lay out, map, plan, project, scheme ♦ [2] aim, aspire, contemplate, intend, mean, meditate, plan, propose

²design *n* **1** ♦ **:** a particular purpose **:** deliberate planning **2** ♦ **:** a mental project or scheme **:** PLAN **3** ♦ **:** a secret project or scheme **:** PLOT **4** *pl* **:** aggressive or evil intent — used with *on* or *against* **5 :** a preliminary sketch or plan **6 :** an underlying scheme that governs functioning, developing, or unfolding **:** MOTIF **7** ♦ **:** the arrangement of elements or details in a product or a work of art **8** ♦ **:** a decorative pattern **9 :** the art of executing designs

♦ [1] arrangement, blueprint, game, plan, project, scheme, strategy, system ♦ [2] aim, ambition, aspiration, dream, end, goal, intent, mark, meaning, object, objective, plan, pretension, purpose, thing ♦ [3] conspiracy, intrigue, machination, plot, scheme ♦ [7] arrangement, composition, configuration, form, format, layout, makeup, pattern ♦ [8] figure, motif, motive, pattern

¹des•ig•nate \ˈde-zig-ˌnāt, -nət\ *adj* **:** chosen but not yet installed ⟨ambassador ~⟩

²des•ig•nate \-ˌnāt\ *vb* **-nat•ed; -nat•ing 1** ♦ **:** to appoint and set apart for a special purpose **2 :** to mark or point out **:** INDICATE; *also* **:** SPECIFY, STIPULATE **3** ♦ **:** to call by a name or title

♦ [1] appoint, assign, attach, commission, constitute, detail, name ♦ [3] baptize, call, christen, denominate, dub, entitle, label, name, style, term, title

designated driver *n* **:** a person chosen to abstain from alcohol so as to transport others safely

designated hitter *n* **:** a baseball player designated at the start of the game to bat in place of the pitcher without causing the pitcher to be removed from the game

des•ig•na•tion \ˌde-zig-ˈnā-shən\ *n* **1 :** the act of indicating or identifying **2** ♦ **:** appointment to or selection for an office, post, or service **3** ♦ **:** a distinguishing name, sign, or title

♦ [2] appointment, assignment, commission ♦ [3] appellation, cognomen, denotation, handle, name, title

de•sign•er \di-ˈzī-nər\ *n* ♦ **:** one that designs: as **a :** one who creates plans for a project or structure **b :** one who designs and manufactures a new product style or design; *esp* **:** one who designs and manufactures high-fashion clothing — **designer** *adj*

♦ developer, innovator, inventor, originator

designer drug *n* **:** a synthetic version of an illicit drug that has been chemically altered to avoid its prohibition

de•sign•ing \di-ˈzī-niŋ\ *adj* ♦ **:** adept in the use of subtlety and cunning **:** CRAFTY, SCHEMING

♦ artful, cagey, crafty, cunning, devious, foxy, guileful, scheming, slick, sly, subtle, wily

de•sir•able \di-ˈzī-rə-bəl\ *adj* **1 :** PLEASING, ATTRACTIVE **2** ♦ **:** worth seeking or doing as advantageous, beneficial, or wise **:** ADVISABLE ⟨~ legislation⟩ — **de•sir•abil•i•ty** \-ˌzī-rə-ˈbi-lə-tē\ *n* — **de•sir•able•ness** *n*

♦ advisable, expedient, judicious, politic, prudent, tactical, wise

¹de•sire \di-ˈzīr\ *vb* **de•sired; de•sir•ing 1** ♦ **:** to long or hope for **:** exhibit or feel desire for **2 :** REQUEST

♦ ache for, covet, crave, die for, hanker for, hunger for, long for, lust (for *or* after), pine for, repine for, thirst for, want, wish for, yearn for

²desire *n* **1** ♦ **:** a strong wish **:** LONGING **2 :** sexual urge or appetite **3 :** a usually formal request for action **4 :** something desired

♦ appetite, craving, drive, hankering, hunger, itch, longing, lust, passion, thirst, urge, yearning, yen

de•sir•ous \di-ˈzīr-əs\ *adj* **:** impelled or governed by desire

de•sist \di-ˈzist, -ˈsist\ *vb* ♦ **:** to cease to proceed, act, or continue

◆ *usu* **desist from** break, break off, cease, cut, discontinue, drop, end, halt, knock off, layoff, leave off, quit, shut off, stop

desk \ˈdesk\ *n* **1 :** a table, frame, or case especially for writing and reading **2 :** a counter, stand, or booth at which a person performs duties **3** ◆ **:** a specialized division of an organization (as a newspaper) ⟨city ~⟩

◆ bureau, department, division, office

desk•top publishing \ˈdesk-ˌtäp-\ *n* **:** the production of printed matter by means of a microcomputer

[1]**des•o•late** \ˈde-sə-lət, -zə-\ *adj* **1 :** DESERTED, ABANDONED **2** ◆ **:** joyless, disconsolate, and sorrowful through or as if through separation from a loved one **:** LONELY **3 :** DILAPIDATED **4 :** BARREN, LIFELESS **5** ◆ **:** devoid of warmth, comfort, or hope **:** CHEERLESS — **des•o•late•ly** *adv* — **des•o•late•ness** *n*

◆ [2] forlorn, lonely, lonesome ◆ [5] bleak, dark, dismal, dreary, gloomy, gray (*or* grey), somber (*or* sombre), wretched

[2]**des•o•late** \-ˌlāt\ *vb* **-lat•ed; -lat•ing :** to make desolate **:** destroy the activity, vitality, or sound condition or contentment of **:** make wretched

des•o•la•tion \ˌde-sə-ˈlā-shən, -zə-\ *n* **1** ◆ **:** the action of desolating **:** state of being desolated **2 :** the quality or state of being sad **:** SADNESS **3 :** LONELINESS **4** ◆ **:** a condition of neglect leading to confusion and disintegration or of natural barrenness and bleakness **5** ◆ **:** barren wasteland

◆ [1] annihilation, demolition, destruction, devastation, havoc, loss, obliteration, ruin, wastage, wreckage ◆ [4] dilapidation, disrepair, neglect ◆ [5] barren, desert, waste, wasteland

des•oxy•ri•bo•nu•cle•ic acid \de-ˌzäk-sē-ˈrī-bō-nu̇-ˌklē-ik-, -nyu̇-\ *n* **:** DNA

[1]**de•spair** \di-ˈspar\ *vb* **:** to lose all hope or confidence

[2]**despair** *n* **1** ◆ **:** utter destruction of hope **2 :** a cause of hopelessness

◆ desperation, despondency, forlornness, hopelessness *Ant* hope, hopefulness

de•spair•ing *adj* ◆ **:** given to, arising from, or marked by despair **:** having no hope — **de•spair•ing•ly** *adv*

◆ defeatist, hopeless, pessimistic

des•per•a•do \ˌdes-pə-ˈrä-dō, -ˈrā-\ *n, pl* **-does** *or* **-dos :** a bold or reckless criminal

des•per•ate \ˈdes-pə-rət, -prət\ *adj* **1 :** being beyond or almost beyond hope **:** causing despair **2 :** RASH **3 :** extremely intense — **des•per•ate•ly** *adv* — **des•per•ate•ness** *n*

des•per•a•tion \ˌdes-pə-ˈrā-shən\ *n* **1** ◆ **:** a loss of hope and surrender to despair **2 :** a state of hopelessness leading to rashness

◆ despair, despondency, forlornness, hopelessness

de•spi•ca•ble \di-ˈspi-kə-bəl, ˈdes-pi-\ *adj* ◆ **:** deserving to be despised — **de•spi•ca•bly** \-blē\ *adv*

◆ contemptible, lousy, nasty, pitiful, scabby, scurvy, sorry, wretched ◆ base, contemptible, detestable, dirty, dishonorable (*or* dishonourable), ignoble, low, mean, snide, sordid, vile, wretched

de•spise \di-ˈspīz\ *vb* **de•spised; de•spis•ing** **1** ◆ **:** to look down on with contempt or aversion **:** DETEST **2** ◆ **:** to regard as negligible, worthless, or distasteful

◆ [1] abhor, abominate, detest, execrate, hate, loathe ◆ [2] disregard, flout, scorn

[1]**de•spite** \di-ˈspīt\ *prep* ◆ **:** in spite of

◆ notwithstanding, regardless of, with

[2]**despite** *n* **:** the act of despising **:** CONTEMPT

de•spoil \di-ˈspȯil\ *vb* ◆ **:** to strip of belongings, possessions, or value — **de•spoil•er** *n* — **de•spoil•ment** *n*

◆ loot, maraud, pillage, plunder, ransack, sack, strip

de•spo•li•a•tion \di-ˌspō-lē-ˈā-shən\ *n* **:** the act of plundering **:** the state of being despoiled

[1]**de•spond** \di-ˈspänd\ *vb* **:** to become discouraged or disheartened

[2]**despond** *n* **:** DESPONDENCY

de•spon•den•cy \-ˈspän-dən-sē\ *n* ◆ **:** the state of being despondent

◆ blues, dejection, depression, desolation, doldrums, dumps, forlornness, gloom, heartsickness, melancholy, sadness ◆ despair, desperation, forlornness, hopelessness

de•spon•dent \-dənt\ *adj* ◆ **:** feeling or showing extreme discouragement, dejection, or depression — **de•spon•dent•ly** *adv*

◆ brokenhearted, dejected, depressed, disconsolate, heartsick, miserable, sad, wretched

des•pot \ˈdes-pət, -ˌpät\ *n* **1 :** a ruler with absolute power and authority **2** ◆ **:** a person exercising power tyrannically

◆ autocrat, dictator, oppressor, tyrant

des•pot•ic \des-ˈpä-tik\ *adj* ◆ **:** of, relating to, or characteristic of a despot

◆ authoritarian, autocratic, bossy, dictatorial, domineering, imperious, masterful, overbearing, peremptory, tyrannical, tyrannous

des•po•tism \ˈdes-pə-ˌti-zəm\ *n* ◆ **:** a system of government in which the ruler has unlimited power

◆ autocracy, dictatorship, totalitarianism, tyranny

des•sert \di-ˈzərt\ *n* **:** a course of sweet food, fruit, or cheese served at the close of a meal

des•ti•na•tion \ˌdes-tə-ˈnā-shən\ *n* **1 :** a purpose for which something is destined **2 :** an act of appointing, setting aside for a purpose, or predetermining **3 :** a place to which one is journeying or to which something is sent

des•tine \ˈdes-tən\ *vb* **des•tined; des•tin•ing** **1 :** to settle in advance **2** ◆ **:** to designate, assign, or dedicate in advance **3 :** to direct or set apart for a specific purpose or place

◆ doom, foredoom, foreordain, ordain, predestine

des•ti•ny \ˈdes-tə-nē\ *n, pl* **-nies** **1** ◆ **:** something to which a person or thing is destined **:** FATE **2 :** a predetermined course of events

◆ circumstance, doom, fate, fortune, lot, portion

des•ti•tute \ˈdes-tə-ˌtüt, -ˌtyüt\ *adj* **1 :** lacking something needed or desirable **2** ◆ **:** suffering extreme poverty

◆ broke, devoid, impecunious, indigent, needy, penniless, penurious, poor, poverty-stricken

des•ti•tu•tion \ˌdes-tə-ˈtü-shən, -ˈtyü-\ *n* ◆ **:** the state of being destitute

◆ beggary, impecuniousness, impoverishment, indigence, need, pauperism, penury, poverty, want

de–stress \ˈdē-ˈstres\ *vb* ◆ **:** to release bodily or mental tension **:** UNWIND

◆ chill out, relax, unwind

de•stroy \di-ˈstrȯi\ *vb* **1** ◆ **:** to put an end to **:** RUIN **2** ◆ **:** to deprive of life **:** KILL

◆ [1] annihilate, blot out, demolish, desolate, devastate, do in, exterminate, extinguish, obliterate, pulverize, ruin, shatter, smash, tear down, waste, wipe out, wreck *Ant* build, construct, erect, put up, raise ◆ [2] dispatch, do in, fell, kill, slay

de•stroy•er \di-ˈstrȯi-ər\ *n* **1 :** one that destroys **2 :** a small speedy warship

de•struc•ti•ble \di-ˈstrək-tə-bəl\ *adj* **:** capable of being destroyed — **de•struc•ti•bil•i•ty** \-ˌstrək-tə-ˈbi-lə-tē\ *n*

de•struc•tion \di-ˈstrək-shən\ *n* **1** ◆ **:** the state or fact of being destroyed **:** RUIN **2 :** the action or process of destroying something **3 :** a destroying agency

◆ annihilation, demolition, desolation, devastation, havoc, loss, obliteration, ruin, wastage, wreckage *Ant* building, construction, erection, raising

de•struc•tive \di-ˈstrək-tiv\ *adj* **1** ◆ **:** causing destruction **:** RUINOUS **2** ◆ **:** designed or tending to destroy — **de•struc•tive•ly** *adv* — **de•struc•tive•ness** *n*

◆ calamitous, devastating, disastrous, ruinous *Ant* constructive

de•sue•tude \ˈde-swi-ˌtüd, -ˌtyüd\ *n* **:** DISUSE

des•ul•to•ry \ˈde-səl-ˌtōr-ē\ *adj* ◆ **:** passing aimlessly from one thing or subject to another

◆ aimless, arbitrary, erratic, haphazard, random, scattered, stray

det *abbr* **1** detached; detachment **2** detail

de•tach \di-ˈtach\ *vb* **1 :** to separate especially from a larger mass **2 :** DISENGAGE, WITHDRAW — **de•tach•able** *adj*

de•tached \di-ˈtacht\ *adj* **1** ◆ **:** not joined or connected **:** SEPARATE **2** ◆ **:** exhibiting an aloof objectivity ⟨a ~ attitude⟩

◆ [1] disconnected, discrete, freestanding, separate, single, unattached, unconnected ◆ [2] aloof, antisocial, cold, cool, distant, frosty, remote, standoffish, unsociable

de•tach•ment \di-ˈtach-mənt\ *n* **1 :** SEPARATION **2 :** the dispatching of a body of troops or part of a fleet from the main body for special service; *also* **:** the portion so dispatched **3 :** a small permanent military unit of special composition **4 :** indifference to worldly concerns **:** ALOOFNESS **5** ♦ **:** freedom from bias or prejudice **:** IMPARTIALITY

♦ disinterestedness, impartiality, neutrality, objectivity ***Ant*** bias, favor, favoritism, partiality, partisanship, prejudice

1de·tail \di-ˈtāl, ˈdē-ˌtāl\ *n* **1 :** a dealing with something item by item ⟨go into ∼⟩ **2** ♦ **:** a part of a whole ⟨the ∼*s* of a story⟩ **3 :** selection (as of soldiers) for special duty; *also* **:** the persons thus selected

♦ fact, particular, point

2detail *vb* **1** ♦ **:** to report minutely and distinctly **2** ♦ **:** to assign to a special duty

♦ [1] enumerate, itemize, list, numerate, rehearse, tick (off) ♦ [2] appoint, assign, attach, commission, constitute, designate, name

de·tailed \di-ˈtāld, ˈdē-ˌtāld\ *adj* ♦ **:** marked by abundant detail

♦ circumstantial, elaborate, full, minute, thorough ***Ant*** compendious, summary ♦ complex, complicated, elaborate, fancy, intricate, involved, sophisticated

de·tail·ing \ˈdē-ˌtāl-iŋ\ *n* **:** the meticulous cleaning and refurbishing of an automobile

de·tain \di-ˈtān\ *vb* **1 :** to hold in or as if in custody **2 :** STOP, DELAY

de·tect \di-ˈtekt\ *vb* ♦ **:** to discover the nature, existence, presence, or fact of — **de·tec·tor** \-ˈtek-tər\ *n*

♦ determine, dig up, discover, ferret out, find, hit on, locate, track down

de·tect·able \di-tek-tə-bəl\ *adj* ♦ **:** capable of being detected

♦ appreciable, discernible, distinguishable, palpable, perceptible, sensible

de·tec·tion \di-ˈtek-shən\ *n* ♦ **:** the act of detecting

♦ discovery, finding

1de·tec·tive \di-ˈtek-tiv\ *adj* **1 :** fitted or used for detection **2 :** of or relating to detectives

2detective *n* ♦ **:** a person employed or engaged in detecting lawbreakers or getting information that is not readily accessible

♦ investigator, operative, shadow, sleuth, tail

dé·tente *or* **de·tente** \dā-ˈtänt\ *n* **:** a relaxation of strained relations or tensions (as between nations)

de·ten·tion \di-ˈten-chən\ *n* **1 :** the act or fact of detaining **:** CONFINEMENT; *esp* **:** a period of temporary custody prior to disposition by a court **2 :** a forced delay

de·ter \di-ˈtər\ *vb* **de·terred; de·ter·ring 1** ♦ **:** to turn aside, discourage, or prevent from acting (as by fear) **2 :** INHIBIT

♦ discourage, dissuade, inhibit

de·ter·gent \di-ˈtər-jənt\ *n* ♦ **:** a cleansing agent; *esp* **:** a chemical product similar to soap in its cleaning ability

♦ cleaner, soap

de·te·ri·o·rate \di-ˈtir-ē-ə-ˌrāt\ *vb* **-rat·ed; -rat·ing** ♦ **:** to make or become worse in quality or condition

♦ decay, decline, degenerate, descend, ebb, rot, sink, worsen ***Ant*** ameliorate, improve, meliorate

de·te·ri·o·ra·tion \di-ˌtir-ē-ə-ˈrā-shən\ *n* ♦ **:** the action or process of deteriorating

♦ decay, decline, degeneration

de·ter·min·able \-ˈtər-mə-nə-bəl\ *adj* **:** capable of being determined; *esp* **:** ASCERTAINABLE

de·ter·mi·nant \-mə-nənt\ *n* **1 :** something that determines or conditions **2 :** GENE

de·ter·mi·nate \di-ˈtər-mə-nət\ *adj* **1** ♦ **:** having fixed limits **:** DEFINITE **2** ♦ **:** definitely settled — **de·ter·mi·nate·ness** *n*

♦ [1] definite, finite, limited, measured, narrow, restricted ♦ [2] certain, final, firm, fixed, flat, frozen, hard, hard-and-fast, set, settled, stable

de·ter·mi·na·tion \di-ˌtər-mə-ˈnā-shən\ *n* **1 a :** the act of coming to a decision **b** ♦ **:** the decision or conclusion reached **2 :** a fixing of the extent, position, or character of something **3 :** accurate measurement (as of length or volume) **4** ♦ **:** firm or fixed purpose

♦ [1b] conclusion, decision, deliverance, diagnosis, judgment (*or* judgement), opinion, resolution, verdict ♦ [4] decision, decisiveness, firmness, granite, resolution, resolve ***Ant*** hesitation, indecision, irresolution, vacillation

de·ter·mine \di-ˈtər-mən\ *vb* **-mined; -min·ing 1** ♦ **:** to fix conclusively or authoritatively **2** ♦ **:** to come to a decision **:** RESOLVE **3 :** to fix the form or character of beforehand **:** ORDAIN; *also* **:** REGULATE **4 :** to find out the limits, nature, dimensions, or scope of ⟨∼ a position at sea⟩ **5 :** to find out or come to a decision about by investigation, reasoning, or calculation **6 :** to bring about as a result

♦ [1] adjudicate, arbitrate, decide, judge, referee, rule, settle, umpire ♦ [2] choose, conclude, decide, figure, opt, resolve

de·ter·mined \-ˈtər-mənd\ *adj* **1** ♦ **:** firmly resolved **2** ♦ **:** characterized by or showing determination — **de·ter·mined·ness** \-mənd-nəs\ *n*

♦ [1] bound, decisive, firm, intent, purposeful, resolute, set, single-minded ***Ant*** faltering, hesitant, indecisive, irresolute, undetermined, unresolved, vacillating, wavering ♦ [2] dogged, grim, implacable, relentless, unflinching, unrelenting, unyielding

de·ter·mined·ly \di-ˈtər-mənd-lē, -mə-nəd-lē\ *adv* ♦ **:** in a determined manner

♦ diligently, hard, hardly, laboriously, mightily, slavishly, strenuously, tirelessly

de·ter·min·ism \di-ˈtər-mə-ˌni-zəm\ *n* **:** a doctrine that acts of the will, natural events, or social changes are determined by preceding events or natural causes — **de·ter·min·ist** \-nist\ *n or adj*

de·ter·rence \di-ˈtər-əns\ *n* **:** the inhibition of criminal behavior by fear especially of punishment

de·ter·rent \-ənt\ *adj* **1 :** serving to deter **2 :** relating to deterrence — **deterrent** *n*

de·test \di-ˈtest\ *vb* ♦ **:** to feel intense and often violent antipathy toward **:** LOATHE — **de·tes·ta·tion** \ˌdē-ˌtes-ˈtā-shən\ *n*

♦ abhor, abominate, despise, execrate, hate, loathe

de·test·able \di-ˈtes-tə-bəl\ *adj* ♦ **:** arousing or meriting intense dislike

♦ base, contemptible, despicable, dirty, dishonorable (*or* dishonourable), ignoble, low, mean, snide, sordid, vile, wretched

de·throne \di-ˈthrōn\ *vb* **:** to remove from a throne **:** DEPOSE — **de·throne·ment** *n*

det·o·nate \ˈdet-ᵊn-ˌāt\ *vb* **-nat·ed; -nat·ing** ♦ **:** to explode or cause to explode with violence

♦ blow up, burst, explode, go off, pop

det·o·na·tion \ˌdet-ᵊn-ˈā-shən\ *n* ♦ **:** the action or process of detonating

♦ blast, eruption, explosion

det·o·na·tor \ˈdet-ᵊn-ˌā-tər\ *n* **:** a device for detonating an explosive

1de·tour \ˈdē-ˌtu̇r\ *n* **:** an indirect way replacing part of a route

2detour *vb* ♦ **:** to go by detour

♦ bypass, circumvent, skirt ♦ deviate, sheer, swerve, swing, turn, turn off, veer

de·tox \ˈdē-ˌtäks, di-ˈtäks\ *n* **:** detoxification from an intoxicating or addictive substance — **detox** *vb*

de·tox·i·fy \dē-ˈtäk-sə-ˌfī\ *vb* **-fied; -fy·ing 1 :** to remove a poison or toxin or the effect of such from **2 :** to free (as a drug user) from an intoxicating or addictive substance or from dependence on it — **de·tox·i·fi·ca·tion** \dē-ˌtäk-sə-fə-ˈkā-shən\ *n*

de·tract \di-ˈtrakt\ *vb* **1 :** to take away or diminish the value or effect of something **2 :** DIVERT — **de·trac·tor** \-ˈtrak-tər\ *n*

de·trac·tion \di-ˈtrak-shən\ *n* ♦ **:** a lessening of reputation or esteem especially by envious, malicious, or petty criticism

♦ deprecation, depreciation, disparagement, put-down

de·train \dē-ˈtrān\ *vb* **:** to leave or cause to leave a railroad train

det·ri·ment \ˈde-trə-mənt\ *n* **1 :** hurt, damage, or loss sustained **2** ♦ **:** a cause of injury or damage

♦ damage, harm, hurt, injury

det·ri·men·tal \ˌde-trə-ˈment-ᵊl\ *adj* ♦ **:** obviously harmful — **det·ri·men·tal·ly** *adv*

♦ adverse, bad, baleful, baneful, damaging, deleterious, evil, harmful, hurtful, ill, injurious, mischievous, noxious, pernicious, prejudicial

de·tri·tus \di-ˈtrī-təs\ *n, pl* **de·tri·tus :** fragments resulting from disintegration (as of rocks) **:** DEBRIS

deuce \ˈdüs, ˈdyüs\ *n* **1 :** a two in cards or dice **2 :** a tie in a tennis game with both sides at 40 **3 :** DEVIL — used chiefly as a mild oath
Deut *abbr* Deuteronomy
deu•te•ri•um \dü-ˈtir-ē-əm, dyü-\ *n* **:** an isotope of hydrogen that has twice the mass of ordinary hydrogen
Deu•ter•on•o•my \ˌdü-tə-ˈrä-nə-mē, ˌdyü-\ *n* **:** a book of Jewish and Christian Scripture
deut•sche mark \ˈdȯi-chə-ˌmärk\ *n* **:** a former monetary unit of Germany
dev *abbr* deviation
de•val•ue \dē-ˈval-yü\ *vb* **:** to reduce the international exchange value of ⟨~ a currency⟩ — **de•val•u•a•tion** \-ˌval-yə-ˈwā-shən\ *n*
dev•as•tate \ˈde-və-ˌstāt\ *vb* **-tat•ed; -tat•ing** **1** ♦ **:** to bring to ruin **2** ♦ **:** to reduce to chaos or helplessness

♦ [1] destroy, ravage, ruin, scourge ♦ [2] carry away, crush, floor, oppress, overcome, overpower, overwhelm, prostrate, snow under, swamp

devastating *adj* ♦ **:** serving, tending, or having the power to devastate

♦ calamitous, destructive, disastrous, ruinous

dev•as•ta•tion \ˌde-və-ˈstā-shən\ *n* ♦ **:** the action of devastating or state of being devastated

♦ annihilation, demolition, desolation, destruction, havoc, loss, obliteration, ruin, wastage, wreckage

de•vel•op \di-ˈve-ləp\ *vb* **1** ♦ **:** to unfold gradually or in detail **2 :** to place (exposed photographic material) in chemicals to produce a visible image **3 :** to bring out the possibilities of **4 :** to make more available or usable ⟨~ land⟩ **5** ♦ **:** to acquire gradually ⟨~ a taste for olives⟩ **6** ♦ **:** to go through a natural process of growth, differentiation, or evolution **7 :** to come into being gradually

♦ [1] amplify, elaborate (on), enlarge (on), expand ♦ [5] acquire, cultivate, form *Ant* lose ♦ [6] age, grow, grow up, mature, progress, ripen

de•vel•op•er \-lə-pər\ *n* ♦ **:** one that develops something new

♦ designer, innovator, inventor, originator

de•vel•op•ment \-ləp-mənt\ *n* ♦ **:** the act, process, or result of developing — **de•vel•op•men•tal** \-ˌve-ləp-ˈment-ᵊl\ *adj* — **de•vel•op•men•tal•ly** \-tᵊl-ē\ *adv*

♦ elaboration, evolution, expansion, growth, maturation, progress, progression *Ant* regression, retrogression ♦ aftermath, conclusion, consequence, corollary, effect, issue, outcome, outgrowth, product, result, resultant, sequence, upshot

¹de•vi•ant \ˈdē-vē-ənt\ *adj* ♦ **:** deviating especially from some accepted norm ⟨~ behavior⟩ — **de•vi•ance** \-əns\ *n* — **de•vi•an•cy** \-ən-sē\ *n*

♦ aberrant, abnormal, anomalous, atypical, irregular, unnatural *Ant* natural, normal, regular, standard, typical

²deviant *n* ♦ **:** one that is deviant

♦ bohemian, individualist, loner, maverick, nonconformist

de•vi•ate \ˈdē-vē-ˌāt\ *vb* **-at•ed; -at•ing** ♦ **:** to turn aside from a course, standard, principle, or topic — **de•vi•ate** \-vē-ət, -vē-ˌāt\ *n* — **de•vi•a•tion** \ˌdē-vē-ˈā-shən\ *n*

♦ detour, sheer, swerve, swing, turn, turn off, veer

de•vice \di-ˈvīs\ *n* **1** ♦ **:** a scheme to deceive **:** STRATAGEM **2** ♦ **:** a piece of equipment or a mechanism for a special purpose **3** ♦ **:** a particular disposition of mind or character **:** INCLINATION — used in plural ⟨left to my own ~*s*⟩ **4 :** an emblematic design

♦ [1] artifice, dodge, gimmick, jig, ploy, scheme, sleight, stratagem, trick, wile ♦ [2] implement, instrument, tool, utensil ♦ *usu* **devices** [3] affinity, bent, disposition, genius, inclination, leaning, partiality, penchant, predilection, predisposition, proclivity, propensity, talent, tendency, turn

¹dev•il \ˈde-vəl\ *n* **1** *often cap* **:** the personal supreme spirit of evil **2** ♦ **:** an evil spirit **:** DEMON **3** ♦ **:** a wicked person **4 a** ♦ **:** an energetic, reckless, or dashing person **b** ♦ **:** a person prone to mischief **5 :** an individual human **:** FELLOW ⟨poor ~⟩ ⟨lucky ~⟩

♦ [2] demon, fiend, ghoul, imp ♦ [3] beast, evildoer, fiend, nogood, reprobate, rogue, varlet, villain, wretch ♦ [4a] daredevil, madcap ♦ [4b] hellion, imp, mischief, monkey, rapscallion, rascal, rogue, scamp, urchin

²devil *vb* **-iled** *or* **-illed; -il•ing** *or* **-il•ling** **1 :** to season highly ⟨~*ed* eggs⟩ **2 :** TEASE, ANNOY
dev•il•ish \ˈde-və-lish\ *adj* **1** ♦ **:** befitting a devil **:** EVIL; *also* **:** MISCHIEVOUS **2 :** exceeding the ordinary, usual, or expected **:** EXTREME

♦ demonic, diabolical, evil, fiendish, satanic ♦ impish, knavish, mischievous, rascally, roguish, sly, waggish, wicked

dev•il•ish•ly \-lē\ *adv* ♦ **:** in a devilish manner

♦ excessively, inordinately, monstrously, overly, overmuch, too

dev•il•ish•ness \-nəs\ *n* ♦ **:** the quality or state of being devilish

♦ impishness, knavery, mischief, mischievousness, rascality, shenanigans, waggery, wickedness

dev•il•ment \ˈde-vəl-mənt, -ˌment\ *n* **:** MISCHIEF
dev•il•ry \-rē\ *or* **dev•il•try** \-trē\ *n, pl* **-il•ries** *or* **-il•tries** **1 :** action performed with the help of the devil **2 :** action that annoys or irritates **:** MISCHIEF
de•vi•ous \ˈdē-vē-əs\ *adj* **1** ♦ **:** deviating from a straight line **2 :** ERRANT 3 **3 a :** deviating from a right, accepted, or common course **b** ♦ **:** not straightforward **:** CUNNING ⟨a ~ politician⟩; *also* **:** tending or having power to deceive ⟨a ~ trick⟩

♦ [1] crooked, serpentine, sinuous, tortuous, winding ♦ [3b] artful, cagey, crafty, cunning, foxy, guileful, slick, sly, subtle, wily

¹de•vise \di-ˈvīz\ *vb* **de•vised; de•vis•ing** **1** ♦ **:** to form in the mind by new combinations or applications of ideas or principles **:** INVENT **2 :** PLOT **3 :** to give (real estate) by will

♦ concoct, contrive, cook up, fabricate, invent, make up, manufacture, think up

²devise *n* **1 :** a disposing of real property by will **2 :** a will or clause of a will disposing of real property **3 :** property given by will
de•vi•tal•ize \dē-ˈvīt-ᵊl-ˌīz\ *vb* **:** to deprive of life or vitality
de•void \di-ˈvȯid\ *adj* ♦ **:** being without **:** VOID ⟨a book ~ of interest⟩

♦ bare, blank, empty, stark, vacant, void ♦ bereft, destitute, empty, void *Ant* replete

de•voir \də-ˈvwär\ *n* **1 :** DUTY **2 :** a formal act of civility or respect
de•volve \di-ˈvälv\ *vb* **de•volved; de•volv•ing** **:** to pass (as rights or responsibility) from one to another usually by succession or transmission — **dev•o•lu•tion** \ˌde-və-ˈlü-shən, ˌdē-\ *n*
De•vo•ni•an \di-ˈvō-nē-ən\ *adj* **:** of, relating to, or being the period of the Paleozoic era between the Silurian and the Mississippian — **Devonian** *n*
de•vote \di-ˈvōt\ *vb* **de•vot•ed; de•vot•ing** **1** ♦ **:** to commit to wholly or chiefly **2** ♦ **:** to set apart for a special purpose **:** DEDICATE

♦ [1] address, apply, bend, buckle, give ♦ [2] allocate, consecrate, dedicate, earmark, reserve, save

de•vot•ed \-ˈvō-təd\ *adj* ♦ **:** characterized by loyalty and devotion **:** FAITHFUL

♦ constant, faithful, fast, good, loyal, pious, staunch, steadfast, steady, true, true-blue

dev•o•tee \ˌde-və-ˈtē, -ˈtā\ *n* ♦ **:** an ardent follower, supporter, or enthusiast

♦ addict, aficionado, buff, bug, enthusiast, fan, fanatic, fancier, fiend, freak, lover, maniac, nut

de•vo•tion \di-ˈvō-shən\ *n* **1** ♦ **:** religious fervor **2 :** an act of prayer or private worship — usually used in plural **3 :** a religious exercise for private use **4** ♦ **:** the fact or state of being dedicated and loyal ⟨~ to the cause⟩; *also* **:** the act of devoting

♦ [1] faith, piety, religion ♦ [4] allegiance, constancy, dedication, faith, faithfulness, fastness, fealty, fidelity, loyalty, steadfastness ♦ [4] affection, attachment, fondness, love, passion

de•vo•tion•al \-shə-nəl\ *adj* ♦ **:** of, relating to, or characterized by devotion

♦ religious, sacred, spiritual

de•vour \di-ˈvau̇r\ *vb* **1** ♦ **:** to eat up greedily or ravenously **2 :** WASTE, ANNIHILATE **3 :** to enjoy avidly ⟨~ a book⟩ — **de•vour•er** *n*

♦ bolt, gobble, gorge, gormandize, gulp, scarf

de•vout \di-ˈvau̇t\ *adj* **1** ♦ **:** devoted to religion **:** PIOUS **2 :** expressing devotion or piety **3 :** EARNEST, SERIOUS — **de•vout•ly** *adv*

♦ faithful, godly, holy, pious, religious, sainted, saintly

de•vout•ness \-nəs\ *n* ♦ : the quality or state of being devout

♦ blessedness, godliness, holiness, piety, sainthood, sanctity

dew \ˈdü, ˈdyü\ *n* : moisture that condenses on the surfaces of cool bodies at night — **dewy** *adj*

dew•ber•ry \ˈdü-ˌber-ē, ˈdyü-\ *n* : any of several sweet edible berries related to and resembling blackberries; *also* : a trailing bramble bearing these

dew•claw \-ˌklȯ\ *n* : a digit on the foot of a mammal that does not reach the ground; *also* : its claw or hoof

dew•lap \-ˌlap\ *n* : loose skin hanging under the neck of an animal

dew point *n* : the temperature at which the moisture in the air begins to condense

dex•ter•i•ty \dek-ˈster-ə-tē\ *n, pl* **-ties** **1** ♦ : quickness and skill in managing any complicated or difficult affair **2** ♦ : readiness and grace in physical activity; *esp* : skill and ease in using the hands

♦ [1] adroitness, cleverness, craft, finesse, sleight ♦ [2] agility, deftness, nimbleness, sleight ***Ant*** awkwardness, clumsiness

dex•ter•ous *also* **dex•trous** \ˈdek-strəs\ *adj* **1** : CLEVER **2** ♦ : done with skillfulness **3** ♦ : skillful and competent with the hands — **dex•ter•ous•ly** *adv*

♦ [2] adroit, artful, masterful, practiced, skillful, virtuoso ♦ [3] clever, cunning, deft, handy ***Ant*** butterfingered, heavy-handed, unhandy

dex•trose \ˈdek-ˌstrōs\ *n* : the naturally occurring form of glucose found in plants and blood

DFC *abbr* Distinguished Flying Cross

dg *abbr* decigram

DG *abbr* **1** by the grace of God **2** director general

DH \ˌdē-ˈāch\ *n* : DESIGNATED HITTER

dhow \ˈdau̇\ *n* : an Arab sailing ship usually having a long overhang forward and a high poop

DI *abbr* drill instructor

dia *abbr* diameter

di•a•be•tes \ˌdī-ə-ˈbē-tēz, -təs\ *n* : an abnormal state marked by passage of excessive amounts of urine; *esp* : one (**diabetes mel•li•tus** \-ˈme-lə-təs\) characterized by deficient insulin, by excess sugar in the blood and urine, and by thirst, hunger, and loss of weight — **di•a•bet•ic** \-ˈbe-tik\ *adj or n*

di•a•bol•ical \ˌdī-ə-ˈbä-li-kəl\ *or* **di•a•bol•ic** \-lik\ *adj* ♦ : of, relating to, or characteristic of the devil : DEVILISH — **di•a•bol•i•cal•ly** \-k(ə-)lē\ *adv*

♦ demonic, devilish, fiendish, satanic

di•a•bol•i•cal•ness \ˌdī-ə-ˈbä-li-kəl-nəs\ *n* : the quality or state of being diabolical

di•a•crit•ic \ˌdī-ə-ˈkri-tik\ *n* : a mark accompanying a letter and indicating a sound value different from that of the same letter when unmarked — **di•a•crit•i•cal** \-ti-kəl\ *adj*

di•a•dem \ˈdī-ə-ˌdem\ *n* : CROWN; *esp* : a royal headband

di•aer•e•sis *or* **di•er•e•sis** \dī-ˈer-ə-səs\ *n, pl* **-e•ses** \-ˌsēz\ : a mark ¨ placed over a vowel to show that it is pronounced in a separate syllable (as in *naïve*)

diag *abbr* **1** diagonal **2** diagram

di•ag•no•sis \ˌdī-ig-ˈnō-səs\ *n, pl* **-no•ses** \-ˌsēz\ **1** : the art or act of identifying a disease from its signs and symptoms; *also* : the decision reached by diagnosis **2 a** : investigation or analysis of the cause or nature of a condition, situation, or problem **b** ♦ : a statement or conclusion from an investigation or analysis — **di•ag•nose** \ˈdī-ig-ˌnōs\ *vb* — **di•ag•nos•tic** \ˌdī-ig-ˈnäs-tik\ *adj* — **di•ag•nos•ti•cian** \-ˌnäs-ˈti-shən\ *n*

♦ conclusion, decision, deliverance, determination, judgment (*or* judgement), opinion, resolution, verdict

1di•ag•o•nal \dī-ˈa-gə-nəl\ *adj* **1** : extending from one corner to the opposite corner in a 4-sided figure **2** ♦ : running in a slanting direction ⟨~ stripes⟩ **3** : having slanting markings or parts ⟨a ~ weave⟩ — **di•ag•o•nal•ly** *adv*

♦ canted, inclined, listing, oblique, slantwise

2diagonal *n* **1** : a diagonal line or plane **2** : a diagonal row, pattern, or direction **3** : a mark / used especially to mean "or," "and or," or "per"

1di•a•gram \ˈdī-ə-ˌgram\ *n* ♦ : a design and especially a drawing that makes something easier to understand — **di•a•gram•ma•ble** \-ˌgra-mə-bəl\ *adj* — **di•a•gram•mat•ic** \ˌdī-ə-grə-ˈma-tik\ *adj* — **di•a•gram•mat•i•cal•ly** \-ti-k(ə-)lē\ *adv*

♦ figure, graphic, illustration, plate

2diagram *vb* **-grammed** *or* **-gramed** \-ˌgramd\; **-gram•ming** *or* **-gram•ing** : to represent by a diagram

1di•al \ˈdī(-ə)l\ *n* **1** : the face of a sundial **2** : the face of a timepiece **3** : a face with a pointer and numbers that indicate something ⟨the ~ of a gauge⟩ **4** : a device used for making electrical connections or for regulating operation (as of a radio)

2dial *vb* **di•aled** *or* **di•alled; di•al•ing** *or* **di•al•ling** **1** : to manipulate a dial so as to operate or select **2** ♦ : to make a telephone call or connection

♦ call, telephone

3dial *abbr* dialect

di•a•lect \ˈdī-ə-ˌlekt\ *n* ♦ : a regional variety of a language

♦ argot, cant, jargon, language, lingo, patois, patter, slang, vocabulary

di•a•lec•tic \ˌdī-ə-ˈlek-tik\ *n* : the process or art of reasoning by discussion of conflicting ideas; *also* : the tension between opposing elements — **di•a•lec•ti•cal** \-ti-kəl\ *adj*

dialog box *n* : a window on a computer screen for choosing options or inputting information

di•a•logue \ˈdī-ə-ˌlȯg\ *also* **di•a•log** *n* **1** ♦ : a conversation between two or more parties **2** : the parts of a literary or dramatic work that represent conversation

♦ colloquy, conversation, discourse, discussion, exchange

di•al•y•sis \dī-ˈa-lə-səs\ *n, pl* **-y•ses** \-ˌsēz\ **1** : the separation of substances from solution by means of their unequal diffusion through semipermeable membranes **2** : the medical procedure of removing blood from an artery, purifying it by dialysis, and returning it to a vein

diam *abbr* diameter

di•am•e•ter \dī-ˈa-mə-tər\ *n* **1** : a straight line passing through the center of a figure or body; *esp* : one that divides a circle in half **2** : the length of a diameter

di•a•met•ric \ˌdī-ə-ˈme-trik\ *or* **di•a•met•ri•cal** \-tri-kəl\ *adj* **1** : of, relating to, or constituting a diameter **2** ♦ : completely opposed or opposite — **di•a•met•ri•cal•ly** \-k(ə-)lē\ *adv*

♦ antipodal, antithetical, contradictory, contrary, opposite, polar

di•a•mond \ˈdī-mənd, ˈdī-ə-\ *n* **1** : a hard brilliant mineral that consists of crystalline carbon and is used as a gem **2** : a flat figure having four equal sides, two acute angles, and two obtuse angles **3** : any of a suit of playing cards marked with a red diamond **4** : INFIELD; *also* : the entire playing field in baseball

di•a•mond•back rattlesnake \-ˌbak-\ *n* : either of two large and deadly rattlesnakes of the southern U.S.

di•an•thus \dī-ˈan-thəs\ *n* : 1 PINK 1

di•a•pa•son \ˌdī-ə-ˈpāz-ᵊn, -ˈpās-\ *n* **1** : the organ stop governing the flue pipes that form the primary basis of organ tone **2** : the entire range of musical tones

1di•a•per \ˈdī-pər, ˈdī-ə-\ *n* **1** : a cotton or linen fabric woven in a simple geometric pattern **2** : a garment for a baby drawn up between the legs and fastened about the waist

2diaper *vb* **1** : to ornament with diaper designs **2** : to put a diaper on

di•aph•a•nous \dī-ˈa-fə-nəs\ *adj* : of so fine a texture as to be transparent

di•a•pho•ret•ic \ˌdī-ə-fə-ˈre-tik\ *adj* : having the power to increase perspiration — **diaphoretic** *n*

di•a•phragm \ˈdī-ə-ˌfram\ *n* **1** : a sheet of muscle between the chest and abdominal cavities of a mammal **2** : a vibrating disk (as in a microphone) **3** : a cup-shaped device usually of thin rubber fitted over the uterine cervix to act as a mechanical contraceptive barrier — **di•a•phrag•mat•ic** \ˌdī-ə-frəg-ˈma-tik, -ˌfrag-\ *adj*

di•a•rist \ˈdī-ə-rist\ *n* : one who keeps a diary

di•ar•rhea *or chiefly Brit* **di•ar•rhoea** \ˌdī-ə-ˈrē-ə\ *n* : abnormally frequent and watery bowel movements

di•a•ry \ˈdī-ə-rē\ *n, pl* **-ries** : a daily record especially of personal experiences; *also* : a book used as a diary

di•as•po•ra \dī-ˈas-pə-rə\ *n* **1** *cap* : the settling of scattered colonies of Jews outside Palestine after the Babylonian exile **2** *cap* : the Jews living outside Palestine or modern Israel **3** : the migration or scattering of a people away from an ancestral homeland

di•as•to•le \dī-ˈas-tə-(ˌ)lē\ *n* : the stretching of the chambers of the heart during which they fill with blood — **di•a•stol•ic** \ˌdī-ə-ˈstä-lik\ *adj*

dia•ther•my \ˈdī-ə-ˌthər-mē\ *n* : the generation of heat in tissue by electric currents for medical purposes

di•a•tom \ˈdī-ə-ˌtäm\ *n* : any of a class of planktonic one-celled or colonial algae with skeletons of silica

di•atom•ic \ˌdī-ə-ˈtä-mik\ *adj* : having two atoms in the molecule

di•a•tribe \ˈdī-ə-ˌtrīb\ *n* ♦ : biting or abusive speech or writing

♦ harangue, rant, tirade

di•az•e•pam \dī-ˈa-zə-ˌpam\ *n* **:** a tranquilizer used especially to relieve anxiety, tension, and muscle spasms
dib•ble \ˈdi-bəl\ *n* **:** a pointed hand tool for making holes (as for planting bulbs) in the ground — **dibble** *vb*
1**dice** \ˈdīs\ *n, pl* **dice :** DIE 1
2**dice** *vb* **diced; dic•ing 1 :** to cut into small cubes ⟨∼ carrots⟩ **2 :** to play games with dice
di•chot•o•my \dī-ˈkä-tə-mē\ *n, pl* **-mies :** a division or the process of dividing into two especially mutually exclusive or contradictory groups — **di•chot•o•mous** \-məs\ *adj*
dick•er \ˈdi-kər\ *vb* ♦ **:** to negotiate over the terms of a purchase, agreement, or contract **:** BARGAIN

♦ bargain, chaffer, deal, haggle, negotiate, palter

dick•ey *or* **dicky** \ˈdi-kē\ *n, pl* **dickeys** *or* **dick•ies :** a small fabric insert worn to fill in the neckline
di•cot•y•le•don \ˌdī-ˌkät-ᵊl-ˈēd-ᵊn\ *n* **:** any of a group of seed plants having an embryo with two cotyledons — **di•cot•y•le•don•ous** *adj*
dict *abbr* dictionary
1**dic•tate** \ˈdik-ˌtāt\ *vb* **dic•tat•ed; dic•tat•ing 1 :** to speak or read for a person to transcribe or for a machine to record **2 :** to issue as an order **:** COMMAND — **dic•ta•tion** \dik-ˈtā-shən\ *n*
2**dic•tate** \ˈdik-ˌtāt\ *n* ♦ **:** an authoritative rule, prescription, or injunction **:** COMMAND ⟨the ∼*s* of conscience⟩

♦ behest, charge, command, commandment, decree, direction, directive, edict, instruction, order, word

dic•ta•tor \ˈdik-ˌtā-tər\ *n* **1** ♦ **:** a person ruling absolutely and often brutally and oppressively **2 :** one that dictates

♦ autocrat, despot, oppressor, tyrant

dic•ta•to•ri•al \ˌdik-tə-ˈtōr-ē-əl\ *adj* ♦ **:** of, relating to, or characteristic of a dictator or a dictatorship

♦ arbitrary, authoritarian, autocratic, bossy, despotic, domineering, imperious, masterful, overbearing, peremptory, tyrannical, tyrannous

dic•ta•tor•ship \dik-ˈtā-tər-ˌship, ˈdik-ˌtā-\ *n* **1 :** the office of a dictator **2 :** autocratic rule, control, or leadership **3** ♦ **:** a government or country in which absolute power is held by a dictator or a small clique

♦ autocracy, despotism, totalitarianism, tyranny

dic•tion \ˈdik-shən\ *n* **1** ♦ **:** choice of words especially with regard to correctness, clearness, or effectiveness **:** WORDING **2 :** ENUNCIATION

♦ language, phraseology, phrasing, wording

dic•tio•nary \ˈdik-shə-ˌner-ē\ *n, pl* **-nar•ies :** a reference book containing words usually alphabetically arranged along with information about their forms, pronunciations, functions, etymologies, meanings, and syntactical and idiomatic uses
dic•tum \ˈdik-təm\ *n, pl* **dic•ta** \-tə\ *also* **dictums :** a noteworthy, formal, or authoritative statement or observation
did *past of* DO
di•dac•tic \dī-ˈdak-tik\ *adj* **1 :** intended to instruct, inform, or teach a moral lesson **2 :** making moral observations
di•do \ˈdī-dō\ *n, pl* **didoes** *or* **didos :** a mischievous act **:** PRANK
1**die** \ˈdī\ *vb* **died; dy•ing** \ˈdī-iŋ\ **1** ♦ **:** to cease living **:** EXPIRE **2** ♦ **:** to pass out of existence ⟨a *dying* race⟩ **3** ♦ **:** to disappear or subside gradually ⟨the wind *died* down⟩ **4** ♦ **:** to long keenly — usu. used with *to* or *for* ⟨*dying* to go⟩ ⟨*dying* for a snack⟩ **5 :** to cease functioning **:** STOP ⟨the motor *died*⟩

♦ [1] depart, expire, pass, pass away, perish, succumb *Ant* breathe, live ♦ [2] break off, break up, cease, close, conclude, discontinue, elapse, end, expire, finish, halt, lapse, leave off, let up, pass, quit, stop, terminate, wind up ♦ *usu* **die down** [3] abate, decline, decrease, de-escalate, diminish, dwindle, ebb, fall, lessen, let up, lower, moderate, recede, relent, shrink, subside, taper, wane ♦ *usu* **die for** [4] ache for, crave, desire, hanker for, hunger for, long for, lust (for *or* after), pine for, repine for, thirst for, want, wish for, yearn for

2**die** \ˈdī\ *n* **1** *pl* **dice** \ˈdīs\ **:** a small cube marked on each face with one to six spots and used usually in pairs in games and gambling **2** *pl* **dies** \ˈdīz\ **:** a device used to shape, finish, or impress an object
die•hard \ˈdī-ˌhärd\ *n* **:** one who is strongly devoted or determined
dieresis *var of* DIAERESIS
die•sel \ˈdē-zəl, -səl\ *n* **1 :** DIESEL ENGINE **2 :** a vehicle driven by a diesel engine **3 :** DIESEL FUEL
diesel engine *n* **:** an internal combustion engine in whose cylinders air is compressed to a temperature sufficiently high to ignite the fuel
diesel fuel *n* **:** a heavy mineral oil used as fuel in diesel engines
die•sel•ing \ˈdē-zə-liŋ\ *n* **:** the continued operation of an internal combustion engine after the ignition has been turned off
1**di•et** \ˈdī-ət\ *n* **1 :** food and drink regularly consumed **:** FARE **2 :** an allowance of food prescribed for a special reason (as to lose weight) — **di•e•tary** \-ə-ˌter-ē\ *adj or n*
2**diet** *vb* **:** to eat or cause to eat or drink less or according to a prescribed rule — **di•et•er** *n*
dietary supplement *n* **:** a product taken orally that contains ingredients (as vitamins or amino acids) intended to supplement one's diet
di•e•tet•ics \ˌdī-ə-ˈte-tiks\ *n sing or pl* **:** the science or art of applying the principles of nutrition to diet — **di•e•tet•ic** *adj*
di•e•ti•tian *or* **di•e•ti•cian** \ˌdī-ə-ˈti-shən\ *n* **:** a specialist in dietetics
dif *or* **diff** *abbr* difference
dif•fer \ˈdi-fər\ *vb* **dif•fered; dif•fer•ing 1 :** to be unlike **2 :** VARY **3 :** DISAGREE
dif•fer•ence \ˈdi-frəns, ˈdi-fə-rəns\ *n* **1** ♦ **:** the quality or state of being different **:** UNLIKENESS ⟨∼ in their looks⟩ **2 :** distinction or discrimination in preference **3** ♦ **:** disagreement in opinion; *also* **:** an instance or cause of disagreement ⟨unable to settle their ∼*s*⟩ **4 :** the amount by which one number or quantity differs from another

♦ [1] contrast, disagreement, discrepancy, disparity, distinction, diversity, unlikeness *Ant* community, likeness, resemblance, sameness, similarity ♦ [3] controversy, disagreement, dispute, dissension

dif•fer•ent \ˈdi-frənt, ˈdi-fə-rənt\ *adj* **1** ♦ **:** unlike in nature or quality **2** ♦ **:** not the same ⟨∼ age groups⟩; *also* **:** VARIOUS ⟨∼ members of the club⟩ **3 :** ANOTHER ⟨try a ∼ channel⟩ **4 :** UNUSUAL, SPECIAL

♦ disparate, dissimilar, distinct, distinctive, distinguishable, diverse, other, unalike, unlike *Ant* alike, indistinguishable, like, parallel, same, similar

1**dif•fer•en•tial** \ˌdi-fə-ˈren-chəl\ *adj* **:** showing, creating, or relating to a difference
2**differential** *n* **1 :** the amount or degree by which things differ **2 :** DIFFERENTIAL GEAR
differential gear *n* **:** an arrangement of gears in an automobile that allows one wheel to turn faster than another (as in rounding curves)
dif•fer•en•ti•ate \ˌdi-fə-ˈren-chē-ˌāt\ *vb* **-at•ed; -at•ing 1 :** to make or become different **2 :** to attain a specialized adult form and function during development **3** ♦ **:** to recognize or state the difference ⟨∼ between them⟩ — **dif•fer•en•ti•a•tion** \-ˌren-chē-ˈā-shən\ *n*

♦ discern, discriminate, distinguish, separate

dif•fer•ent•ly \-lē\ *adv* ♦ **:** in a different manner

♦ else, other, otherwise

dif•fi•cult \ˈdi-fi-(ˌ)kəlt\ *adj* **1** ♦ **:** hard to do or make **2** ♦ **:** hard to understand or deal with ⟨∼ reading⟩ ⟨a ∼ child⟩

♦ [1] arduous, demanding, exacting, formidable, grueling, hard, herculean, laborious, murderous, rough, stiff, strenuous, tall, toilsome, tough ♦ [2] catchy, delicate, knotty, problematic, spiny, thorny, ticklish, touchy, tough, tricky

dif•fi•cul•ty \-(ˌ)kəl-tē\ *n, pl* **-ties 1 :** difficult nature ⟨the ∼ of a task⟩ **2 :** DISAGREEMENT ⟨settled their *difficulties*⟩ **3** ♦ **:** something that is difficult or serves to impede ⟨overcome *difficulties*⟩ **4 :** an instance of trouble ⟨in financial *difficulties*⟩

♦ adversity, asperity, hardness, hardship, rigor ♦ complexity, complication, intricacy

dif•fi•dent \ˈdi-fə-dənt\ *adj* **1** ♦ **:** lacking confidence **2 :** RESERVED 1 — **dif•fi•dence** \-dəns\ *n* — **dif•fi•dent•ly** *adv*

♦ bashful, coy, demure, introverted, modest, retiring, sheepish, shy

dif•frac•tion \di-ˈfrak-shən\ *n* **:** the bending or spreading of waves (as of light) especially when passing through narrow slits
1**dif•fuse** \di-ˈfyüs\ *adj* **1** ♦ **:** being at once verbose and ill-organized ⟨∼ writing⟩ **2 :** not concentrated or localized ⟨∼ light⟩

♦ circuitous, long-winded, prolix, rambling, verbose, windy, wordy

2**dif•fuse** \di-ˈfyüz\ *vb* **dif•fused; dif•fus•ing 1 :** to pour out or spread widely **2 :** to undergo or cause to undergo diffusion **3 :** to break up light by diffusion

dif·fu·sion \di-ˈfyü-zhən\ *n* **1 :** a diffusing or a being diffused **2 :** movement of particles (as of a gas) from a region of high to one of lower concentration **3 :** the reflection of light from a rough surface or the passage of light through a translucent material

¹dig \ˈdig\ *vb* **dug** \ˈdəg\; **dig·ging** **1 :** to turn up the soil (as with a spade) **2 :** to hollow out or form by removing earth ⟨~ a hole⟩ **3 a :** to uncover or seek by turning up earth ⟨~ potatoes⟩ **b** ♦ **:** to penetrate below the surface in search of something hidden or buried — used with *into* **c** ♦ **:** to advance by or as if by removing or pushing aside material ⟨~ through the toy box⟩ **4** ♦ **:** to come upon by searching or effort **:** DISCOVER ⟨~ up information⟩ **5 :** POKE, THRUST ⟨~ a person in the ribs⟩ **6 :** to work hard **7 a :** UNDERSTAND, APPRECIATE **b** ♦ **:** to feel attraction toward or take pleasure in **:** LIKE

♦ *usu* **dig into** [3b] delve, explore, go, inquire into, investigate, look, probe, research ♦ *usu* **dig through** [3c] dredge, hunt, rake, ransack, rifle, rummage, scour, search ♦ *usu* **dig up** [4] detect, determine, discover, ferret out, find, hit on, locate, track down ♦ [7b] adore, delight, enjoy, fancy, groove, like, love, relish, revel

²dig *n* **1 a :** a quick thrust **:** POKE **b** ♦ **:** a cutting remark **2** *pl* **:** living accommodations

♦ affront, barb, dart, indignity, insult, name, offense, outrage, put-down, sarcasm, slight, slur, wound

³dig *abbr* digest

¹di·gest \ˈdī-ˌjest\ *n* ♦ **:** a summation or condensation of a body of information; *esp* **:** a summarized or shortened version especially of a literary work

♦ abbreviation, condensation ♦ abstract, encapsulation, epitome, outline, précis, recapitulation, résumé (*or* resume), roundup, sum, summary, synopsis, wrap-up

²di·gest \dī-ˈjest, də-\ *vb* **1 :** to think over and arrange in the mind **2 :** to convert (food) into simpler forms that can be absorbed by the body **3** ♦ **:** to compress into a short summary — **di·gest·ibil·i·ty** \-ˌjes-tə-ˈbi-lə-tē\ *n* — **di·gest·ible** *adj* — **di·ges·tion** \-ˈjes-chən\ *n* — **di·ges·tive** \-ˈjes-tiv\ *adj*

♦ abstract, encapsulate, epitomize, outline, recapitulate, sum up, summarize, wrap up

di·ges·tif \ˌdē-zhes-ˈtēf\ *n* **:** an alcoholic drink taken after a meal

dig in *vb* **1 :** to take a defensive stand especially by digging trenches **2 :** to firmly set to work **3 :** to begin eating

dig·it \ˈdi-jət\ *n* **1** ♦ **:** any of the Arabic numerals 1 to 9 and usually the symbol 0 **2 :** FINGER, TOE

♦ figure, integer, number, numeral, whole number

dig·i·tal \ˈdi-jə-tᵊl\ *adj* **1 :** of, relating to, or done with a finger or toe **2 :** of, relating to, or using calculation by numerical methods or by discrete units **3 :** relating to or employing communications signals in the form of binary digits ⟨a ~ broadcast⟩ **4 :** providing a readout in numerical digits ⟨a ~ watch⟩ **5 :** ELECTRONIC; *also* **:** characterized by computerized technology ⟨the ~ age⟩ — **dig·i·tal·ly** *adv*

digital camera *n* **:** a camera that records images as digital data instead of on film

dig·i·tal·is \ˌdi-jə-ˈta-ləs\ *n* **:** a drug from the common foxglove that is a powerful heart stimulant; *also* **:** FOXGLOVE

digital versatile disc *n* **:** DVD

digital video disc *n* **:** DVD

dig·ni·fied \ˈdig-nə-ˌfīd\ *adj* ♦ **:** showing or expressing dignity

♦ august, imposing, solemn, staid, stately ***Ant*** flighty, frivolous, giddy, goofy, silly, undignified

dig·ni·fy \-ˌfī\ *vb* **-fied; -fy·ing** ♦ **:** to give dignity, distinction, or attention to

♦ aggrandize, ennoble, exalt, glorify, magnify

dig·ni·tary \ˈdig-nə-ˌter-ē\ *n, pl* **-tar·ies :** a person of high position or honor

dig·ni·ty \ˈdig-nə-tē\ *n, pl* **-ties** **1 :** the quality or state of being worthy, honored, or esteemed **2 :** high rank, office, or position **3 :** formal reserve of manner, language, or appearance

di·graph \ˈdī-ˌgraf\ *n* **:** a group of two successive letters whose phonetic value is a single sound (as *ea* in *bread*)

di·gress \dī-ˈgres, də-\ *vb* **:** to turn aside especially from the main subject or argument — **di·gres·sion** \dī-ˈgre-shən\ *n*

di·gres·sive \dī-ˈgre-siv\ *adj* ♦ **:** characterized by digressions

♦ desultory, discursive, rambling

Di·jon mustard \ˈdē-ˌzhän-, di-ˈzhän-\ *n* **:** a mustard made from dark mustard seeds, white wine, and spices

dike \ˈdīk\ *n* **1** ♦ **:** an artificial watercourse **:** DITCH **2** ♦ **:** a bank of earth constructed to control water **:** LEVEE

♦ [1] ditch, gutter, trench ♦ [2] dam, embankment, levee

dil *abbr* dilute

di·lap·i·dat·ed \də-ˈla-pə-ˌdā-təd\ *adj* ♦ **:** fallen into partial ruin or decay

♦ grungy, mean, neglected, ratty, seedy, shabby

di·lap·i·da·tion \də-ˌla-pə-ˈdā-shən\ *n* ♦ **:** the act of dilapidating or the state of being dilapidated

♦ desolation, disrepair, neglect

di·late \dī-ˈlāt, ˈdī-ˌlāt\ *vb* **di·lat·ed; di·lat·ing :** SWELL, DISTEND, EXPAND — **dil·a·ta·tion** \ˌdi-lə-ˈtā-shən\ *n* — **di·la·tion** \dī-ˈlā-shən\ *n*

dil·a·to·ry \ˈdi-lə-ˌtōr-ē\ *adj* **1 :** DELAYING **2** ♦ **:** characterized by procrastination **:** TARDY

♦ creeping, laggard, languid, poky, slow, sluggish, tardy

di·lem·ma \də-ˈle-mə\ *n* **1 :** a usually undesirable or unpleasant choice; *also* **:** a situation involving such a choice **2 :** PREDICAMENT

dil·et·tante \ˌdi-lə-ˈtänt, -ˈtant\ *n, pl* **-tantes** *or* **-tan·ti** \-ˈtän-tē, -ˈtan-\ **:** a person having a superficial interest in an art or a branch of knowledge

dil·i·gence \ˈdi-lə-jəns\ *n* ♦ **:** persevering application

♦ assiduity, industry

dil·i·gent \ˈdi-lə-jənt\ *adj* ♦ **:** characterized by steady, earnest, and energetic effort

♦ active, assiduous, busy, engaged, laborious, occupied, sedulous, working

dil·i·gent·ly \-lē\ *adv* ♦ **:** in a diligent manner

♦ determinedly, hard, laboriously, strenuously, tirelessly

dill \ˈdil\ *n* **:** an herb related to the carrot with aromatic leaves and seeds used as seasoning and in pickles

dil·ly \ˈdi-lē\ *n, pl* **dil·lies :** one that is remarkable or outstanding

dil·ly·dal·ly \ˈdi-lē-ˌda-lē\ *vb* ♦ **:** to waste time by loitering or delaying

♦ crawl, creep, dally, dawdle, delay, drag, lag, linger, loiter, poke, tarry

¹di·lute \dī-ˈlüt, də-\ *vb* **di·lut·ed; di·lut·ing** ♦ **:** to lessen the consistency or strength of by mixing with something else — **di·lu·tion** \-ˈlü-shən\ *n*

♦ adulterate, thin, water, weaken

²dilute *adj* ♦ **:** having the consistency or strength of lessened by mixing with something else

♦ impure, polluted ♦ thin, watery, weak

¹dim \ˈdim\ *adj* **dim·mer; dim·mest** **1** ♦ **:** lacking brilliance or luster **:** DULL **2** ♦ **:** not bright or distinct **:** OBSCURE **3 :** not seeing or understanding clearly **4** ♦ **:** perceived by the senses or mind indistinctly or weakly — **dim·ly** *adv* — **dim·ness** *n*

♦ [1] dull, flat, lusterless ♦ [2] dark, darkling, dusky, gloomy, murky, obscure, somber (*or* sombre) ♦ [4] bleary, faint, foggy, fuzzy, hazy, indefinite, indistinct, indistinguishable, murky, nebulous, obscure, opaque, shadowy, unclear, undefined, undetermined, vague

²dim *vb* **dimmed; dim·ming** **1** ♦ **:** to make or become dim or lusterless **2** ♦ **:** to reduce the light from

♦ becloud, befog, blur, cloud, darken, fog, haze, mist, obscure, overcast, overshadow, shroud

³dim *abbr* **1** dimension **2** diminished **3** diminutive

dime \ˈdīm\ *n* **:** a U.S. or Canadian coin worth ten cents

di·men·sion \də-ˈmen-chən, dī-\ *n* **1 :** the physical property of length, breadth, or thickness; *also* **:** a measure of this **2 a** ♦ **:** the quality of spatial extension **:** EXTENT **b :** the range over which or the degree to which something extends **:** SCOPE — usually used in plural — **di·men·sion·al** \-ˈmen-chə-nəl\ *adj* — **di·men·sion·al·i·ty** \-ˌmen-chə-ˈna-lə-tē\ *n*

♦ extent, magnitude, measure, measurement, proportion, size

di·min·ish \də-ˈmi-nish\ *vb* **1 :** to make less or cause to appear less **2** ♦ **:** to lessen the authority, dignity, or reputation of **:** BELITTLE **3** ♦ **:** to become gradually less (as in size or importance) **:** DWINDLE **4** ♦ **:** to diminish gradually **:** TAPER

♦ [2] belittle, cry down, decry, deprecate, depreciate, discount, disparage, minimize, put down, write off ♦ [3, 4] abate, de-escalate, decline, decrease, die, dwindle, ebb, fall, lessen, let up, lower, moderate, recede, relent, shrink, subside, taper, wane

di•min•u•en•do \də-ˌmin-yə-ˈwen-dō\ *adv or adj* **:** DECRESCENDO

dim•i•nu•tion \ˌdi-mə-ˈnü-shən, -ˈnyü-\ *n* ♦ **:** the act, process, or an instance of diminishing

♦ abatement, decline, decrease, decrement, drop, fall, loss, reduction, shrinkage

¹di•min•u•tive \də-ˈmin-yə-tiv\ *n* **1 :** a diminutive word or affix **2 :** a diminutive individual

²diminutive *adj* **1 :** indicating small size and sometimes the state or quality of being lovable, pitiable, or contemptible ⟨the ∼ suffixes *-ette* and *-ling*⟩ **2 :** extremely small **:** TINY

dim•i•ty \ˈdi-mə-tē\ *n, pl* **-ties :** a thin usually corded cotton fabric

dim•mer \ˈdi-mər\ *n* **:** a device for controlling the amount of light from an electric lighting unit

di•mor•phic \(ˌ)dī-ˈmȯr-fik\ *adj* **:** occurring in two distinct forms — **di•mor•phism** \-ˌfi-zəm\ *n*

¹dim•ple \ˈdim-pəl\ *n* **:** a small depression especially in the cheek or chin

²dimple *vb* **dim•pled; dim•pling :** to form dimples (as in smiling)

din \ˈdin\ *n* ♦ **:** a loud confused mixture of noises

♦ bluster, cacophony, clamor (*or* clamour), noise, racket, roar

dine \ˈdīn\ *vb* **dined; din•ing 1** ♦ **:** to eat dinner **2** ♦ **:** to give a dinner to

♦ [1] eat, fare, feed ♦ [2] banquet, feast, junket, regale

din•er \ˈdī-nər\ *n* **1 :** one that dines **2 :** a railroad dining car **3** ♦ **:** a restaurant usually resembling a dining car

♦ café, grill, restaurant

di•nette \dī-ˈnet\ *n* **:** an alcove or small room used for dining

ding \ˈdiŋ\ *vb* **:** to cause minor damage to a surface — **ding** *n*

din•ghy \ˈdiŋ-ē\ *n, pl* **dinghies 1 :** a small boat **2 :** LIFE RAFT

din•gi•ness \ˈdin-jē-nəs\ *n* ♦ **:** the quality or state of being dingy

♦ dirtiness, filthiness, foulness, grubbiness, nastiness, uncleanliness

din•gle \ˈdiŋ-gəl\ *n* **:** a small wooded valley

din•go \ˈdiŋ-gō\ *n, pl* **dingoes :** a reddish brown wild dog of Australia

din•gus \ˈdiŋ-gəs, -əs\ *n* **:** DOODAD

din•gy \ˈdin-jē\ *adj* **din•gi•er; -est 1 :** not clean or pure **:** DIRTY **2 :** SHABBY

dink \ˈdiŋk\ *n, often all cap* **:** a couple with two incomes and no children; *also* **:** a member of such a couple

din•ky \ˈdiŋ-kē\ *adj* **din•ki•er; -est :** overly or unattractively small

din•ner \ˈdi-nər\ *n* **1 :** the main meal of the day **2** ♦ **:** a formal banquet

♦ banquet, feast, feed, spread

din•ner•ware \ˈdi-nər-ˌwar\ *n* **:** tableware other than flatware

di•no \ˈdī-nō\ *n, pl* **dinos :** DINOSAUR

di•no•fla•gel•late \ˌdī-nō-ˈfla-jə-lət, -ˌlāt\ *n* **:** any of an order of planktonic plantlike unicellular flagellates of which some cause red tide

di•no•saur \ˈdī-nə-ˌsȯr\ *n* **:** any of a group of extinct long-tailed Mesozoic reptiles often of huge size

dint \ˈdint\ *n* **1 :** FORCE ⟨by ∼ of sheer grit⟩ **2 :** a depression or hollow made by a blow or by pressure **:** DENT

di•o•cese \ˈdī-ə-səs, -ˌsēz, -ˌsēs\ *n, pl* **-ces•es** \-sə-səz, -ˌsē-zəz, -ˌsē-səz\ **:** the territorial jurisdiction of a bishop — **di•oc•e•san** \dī-ˈä-sə-sən, ˌdī-ə-ˈsēz-ᵊn\ *adj or n*

di•ode \ˈdī-ˌōd\ *n* **:** an electronic device with two electrodes or terminals used especially as a rectifier

di•ox•in \dī-ˈäk-sən\ *n* **:** a persistent toxic hydrocarbon that occurs especially as a by-product of industrial processes and waste incineration

¹dip \ˈdip\ *vb* **dipped; dip•ping 1** ♦ **:** to plunge temporarily or partially under the surface (as of a liquid) **2 :** to thrust in a way to suggest immersion **3** ♦ **:** to scoop up or out **:** LADLE **4 :** to lower and then raise quickly ⟨∼ a flag in salute⟩ **5** ♦ **:** to drop or slope down especially suddenly ⟨the moon *dipped* below the crest⟩ **6** ♦ **:** to decrease moderately and usually temporarily ⟨prices *dipped*⟩ **7 :** to reach inside or as if inside or below a surface ⟨*dipped* into their savings⟩ **8** ♦ **:** to examine or read something casually or superficially ⟨∼ into a book⟩

♦ [1] douse, duck, dunk, immerse, souse, submerge ♦ [3] ladle, scoop, spoon ♦ [5, 6] decline, descend, drop, fall, lower, plummet, plunge, sink, tumble ♦ [8] browse, glance, glimpse, peek, skim

²dip *n* **1 :** an act of dipping; *esp* **:** a short swim **2** ♦ **:** inclination downward **:** DROP **3 :** something obtained by or used in dipping **4 :** a sauce or soft mixture into which food may be dipped **5 :** a liquid into which something may be dipped (as for cleansing or coloring)

♦ descent, dive, down, drop, fall, plunge

diph•the•ria \dif-ˈthir-ē-ə\ *n* **:** an acute contagious bacterial disease marked by fever and by coating of the air passages with a membrane that interferes with breathing

diph•thong \ˈdif-ˌthȯŋ\ *n* **:** two vowel sounds joined in one syllable to form one speech sound (as *ou* in *out*)

dip•loid \ˈdi-ˌplȯid\ *adj* **:** having two haploid sets of chromosomes ⟨∼ somatic cells⟩ — **diploid** *n*

di•plo•ma \də-ˈplō-mə\ *n, pl* **diplomas :** an official record of graduation from or of a degree conferred by a school

di•plo•ma•cy \də-ˈplō-mə-sē\ *n* **1 :** the art and practice of conducting negotiations between nations **2 :** TACT

dip•lo•mat \ˈdi-plə-ˌmat\ *n* **:** one employed or skilled in diplomacy — **dip•lo•mat•ic** \ˌdi-plə-ˈma-tik\ *adj*

di•plo•ma•tist \də-ˈplō-mə-tist\ *n* **:** DIPLOMAT

dip•per \ˈdi-pər\ *n* **1 :** any of a genus of birds that are related to the thrushes and are skilled in diving **2 :** something (as a ladle or scoop) that dips or is used for dipping **3** *cap* **:** BIG DIPPER **4** *cap* **:** LITTLE DIPPER

dip•so•ma•nia \ˌdip-sə-ˈmā-nē-ə\ *n* **:** an uncontrollable craving for alcoholic liquors — **dip•so•ma•ni•ac** \-nē-ˌak\ *n*

dip•stick \ˈdip-ˌstik\ *n* **:** a graduated rod for indicating depth

dip•ter•an \ˈdip-tə-rən\ *adj* **:** of, relating to, or being a fly (sense 2) — **dipteran** *n* — **dip•ter•ous** \-rəs\ *adj*

dir *abbr* **1** direction **2** director

dire \ˈdīr\ *adj* **dir•er; dir•est 1** ♦ **:** very horrible **:** DREADFUL **2** ♦ **:** warning of disaster **3 :** EXTREME **4** ♦ **:** demanding immediate action to fend off disastrous consequences

♦ [1] dreadful, fearful, fearsome, forbidding, formidable, frightful, hair-raising, horrible, redoubtable, scary, shocking, terrible, terrifying ♦ [2] baleful, foreboding, menacing, ominous, portentous, sinister ♦ [4] acute, critical, imperative, imperious, instant, pressing, urgent

¹di•rect \də-ˈrekt, dī-\ *vb* **1 :** ADDRESS ⟨∼ a letter⟩; *also* **:** to impart orally **:** AIM ⟨∼ a remark to the gallery⟩ **2** ♦ **:** to regulate the activities or course of **:** guide the supervision, organizing, or performance of **3** ♦ **:** to cause to turn, move, or point or to follow a certain course **4 :** to point, extend, or project in a specified line or course **5** ♦ **:** to request or instruct with authority **6** ♦ **:** to show or point out the way

♦ [2] administer, carry on, conduct, control, govern, guide, handle, manage, operate, oversee, regulate, run, superintend, supervise ♦ [3] aim, bend, cast, head, level, set, train ♦ [5] command, decree, dictate, ordain, order ♦ [5] bid, boss, charge, command, enjoin, instruct, order, tell ♦ [6] conduct, guide, lead, marshal, pilot, route, show, steer, usher

²direct *adj* **1** ♦ **:** stemming immediately from a source ⟨∼ result⟩ **2 :** being or passing in a straight line of descent **:** LINEAL ⟨∼ ancestor⟩ **3 :** leading from one point to another in time or space without turn or stop **:** STRAIGHT **4** ♦ **:** free from evasiveness or obscurity **:** STRAIGHTFORWARD ⟨a ∼ manner⟩ **5 :** operating without an intervening agency or step ⟨∼ action⟩ **6 :** effected by the action of the people or the electorate and not by representatives ⟨∼ democracy⟩ **7 :** consisting of or reproducing the exact words of a speaker or writer

♦ [1] firsthand, immediate, primary ***Ant*** indirect, secondhand ♦ [4] candid, forthright, foursquare, frank, honest, open, outspoken, plain, straight, straightforward, unguarded, unreserved

³direct *adv* ♦ **:** in a direct way

♦ dead, directly, due, plump, right, straight

direct broadcast satellite *n* **:** a television broadcasting system in which satellite transmissions are received at the viewing location

direct current *n* **:** an electric current flowing in one direction only

direct deposit *n* **:** a method of payment in which money is transferred to the payee's account without the use of checks or cash

di•rec•tion \də-ˈrek-shən, dī-\ *n* **1** ♦ **:** guidance or supervision of action or conduct **:** MANAGEMENT **2 :** an explicit instruction **:** COMMAND **3 :** the course or line along which something moves, lies, or points **4 :** TENDENCY, TREND — **di•rec•tion•al** \-shə-nəl\ *adj*

♦ administration, conduct, control, government, guidance, management, operation, oversight, regulation, running, superintendence, supervision

di•rec•tive \də-ˈrek-tiv, dī-\ *n* ♦ **:** something that directs and usually impels toward an action or goal; *esp* **:** an order issued by a high-level body or official

♦ decree, edict, fiat, ruling ♦ behest, charge, command, commandment, decree, dictate, direction, edict, instruction, order, word

di•rect•ly \-lē\ *adv* **1** ♦ **:** in a direct manner **2** ♦ **:** without delay

♦ [1] dead, direct, due, plump, right, straight *Ant* indirectly ♦ [2] forthwith, immediately, instantly, now, promptly, pronto, right away, right now

direct mail *n* **:** printed matter used for soliciting business or contributions and mailed direct to individuals

di•rect•ness \-nəs\ *n* **1 :** the character of being accurate in course or aim **2** ♦ **:** strict pertinence **:** FORTHRIGHTNESS

♦ candor (*or* candour), forthrightness, frankness, openness, plainness

di•rec•tor \də-ˈrek-tər, dī-\ *n* **1** ♦ **:** one that directs **:** MANAGER **2 :** one of a group of persons who direct the affairs of an organized body — **di•rec•tor•ship** *n*

♦ administrator, executive, manager, superintendent, supervisor

di•rec•tor•ate \-tə-rət\ *n* **1 :** the office or position of director **2 :** a board of directors; *also* **:** membership on such a board **3 :** an executive staff

di•rec•to•ri•al \də-ˌrek-ˈtōr-ē-əl\ *adj* ♦ **:** serving to direct

♦ executive, managerial, supervisory

director's cut *n* **:** a version of a motion picture that is edited according to the director's wishes

di•rec•to•ry \-tə-rē\ *n, pl* **-ries :** an alphabetical or classified list especially of names and addresses

dire•ful \ˈdīr-fəl\ *adj* **1 :** causing great and oppressive fear **:** DREADFUL **2 :** OMINOUS

dirge \ˈdərj\ *n* ♦ **:** a song of lamentation; *also* **:** a slow mournful piece of music

♦ elegy, lament, requiem, threnody

di•ri•gi•ble \ˈdir-ə-jə-bəl, də-ˈri-jə-\ *n* **:** AIRSHIP

dirk \ˈdərk\ *n* **:** DAGGER 1

dirndl \ˈdərnd-ᵊl\ *n* **:** a full skirt with a tight waistband

dirt \ˈdərt\ *n* **1** ♦ **:** a filthy or soiling substance (as mud, dust, or grime) **2** ♦ **:** loose or packed earth **:** SOIL **3 :** moral uncleanness **4 :** scandalous gossip **5 :** embarrassing or incriminating information

♦ [1] filth, grime, muck, smut, soil ♦ [2] earth, ground, soil

dirt•i•ness \ˈdər-tē-nəs\ *n* ♦ **:** the quality or state of being dirty

♦ dinginess, filthiness, foulness, grubbiness, nastiness, uncleanliness *Ant* cleanliness

¹dirty \ˈdər-tē\ *adj* **dirt•i•er; -est 1** ♦ **:** not clean **:** SOILED **2** ♦ **:** morally unclean or corrupt **:** INDECENT ⟨∼ jokes⟩ **3 a** ♦ **:** lacking honor **:** BASE ⟨a ∼ trick⟩ **b** ♦ **:** not characteristic of or exhibiting good sportsmanship **4** ♦ **:** relating to, characterized by, or indicative of a storm ⟨∼ weather⟩ **5 :** not clear in color **:** DULL ⟨a ∼ red⟩ — **dirty** *adv*

♦ [1] dusty, filthy, foul, grubby, grungy, mucky, muddy, nasty, smutty, sordid, unclean *Ant* clean, cleanly, immaculate, spick-and-span, spotless, stainless, unsoiled, unstained, unsullied ♦ [2] bawdy, coarse, crude, filthy, foul, gross, indecent, lascivious, lewd, nasty, obscene, pornographic, ribald, smutty, unprintable, vulgar, wanton ♦ [3a] base, contemptible, despicable, detestable, dishonorable (*or* dishonourable), ignoble, low, mean, snide, sordid, vile, wretched ♦ [3b] foul, illegal, unfair, unsportsmanlike ♦ [4] bleak, foul, inclement, nasty, raw, rough, squally, stormy, tempestuous, turbulent

²dirty *vb* **dirt•ied; dirty•ing** ♦ **:** to make or become dirty

♦ befoul, begrime, besmirch, blacken, foul, grime, mire, muddy, smirch, soil, stain *Ant* clean, cleanse

dis•able \di-ˈsā-bəl\ *vb* **dis•abled; dis•abling 1 :** to disqualify legally **2** ♦ **:** to make unable to perform by or as if by illness, injury, or malfunction — **dis•abil•i•ty** \ˌdi-sə-ˈbi-lə-tē\ *n*

♦ cripple, hamstring, immobilize, incapacitate, paralyze, prostrate

dis•abled *adj* ♦ **:** incapacitated by illness, injury, or wounds; *also* **:** physically or mentally impaired

♦ challenged, handicapped *Ant* able-bodied

dis•abuse \ˌdi-sə-ˈbyüz\ *vb* **:** to free from error, fallacy, or misconception

dis•ad•van•tage \ˌdi-səd-ˈvan-tij\ *n* **1 :** loss or damage especially to reputation or finances **2 a :** an unfavorable, inferior, or prejudicial condition **b** ♦ **:** a quality or circumstance that makes achievement unusually difficult **:** HANDICAP

♦ drawback, handicap, liability, minus, penalty, strike *Ant* advantage, asset, edge, plus

dis•ad•van•taged \-tijd\ *adj* **:** lacking in basic resources or conditions believed necessary for an equal position in society

dis•ad•van•ta•geous \di-ˌsad-ˌvan-ˈta-jəs, -vən-\ *adj* ♦ **:** constituting a disadvantage

♦ adverse, counter, hostile, inimical, negative, prejudicial, unfavorable (*or* unfavourable), unfriendly, unsympathetic

dis•af•fect \ˌdi-sə-ˈfekt\ *vb* ♦ **:** to alienate the affection or loyalty of

♦ alienate, disgruntle, estrange, sour ♦ discontent, disgruntle, displease, dissatisfy

dis•af•fec•tion \ˌdi-sə-ˈfek-shən\ *n* ♦ **:** alienation of affection

♦ alienation, estrangement

dis•agree \ˌdi-sə-ˈgrē\ *vb* **1 :** to fail to agree **2 :** to differ in opinion **3 :** to cause discomfort or distress ⟨fried foods ∼ with her⟩

dis•agree•able \-ə-bəl\ *adj* **1** ♦ **:** causing discomfort **:** UNPLEASANT **2** ♦ **:** marked by ill temper **:** ILL-TEMPERED — **dis•agree•able•ness** *n* — **dis•agree•ably** \-blē\ *adv*

♦ [1] bad, distasteful, nasty, rotten, sour, uncongenial, unlovely, unpleasant, unwelcome ♦ [2] bearish, bilious, cantankerous, dyspeptic, ill-humored, ill-tempered, ornery, splenetic, surly

dis•agree•ment \-mənt\ *n* **1** ♦ **:** the act or instance of disagreeing **2 a** ♦ **:** the state of being at variance **:** DISPARITY **b** ♦ **:** a usually verbal conflict between antagonists **:** QUARREL

♦ [1] controversy, difference, dispute, dissension *Ant* accord, agreement, harmony ♦ [2a] contrast, difference, discrepancy, disparity, distinction, diversity, unlikeness ♦ [2b] altercation, argument, bicker, brawl, dispute, fight, hassle, misunderstanding, quarrel, row, scrap, spat, squabble, wrangle

dis•al•low \ˌdi-sə-ˈlau̇\ *vb* **1** ♦ **:** to deny the force, truth, or validity of **:** REJECT ⟨∼ a claim⟩ **2** ♦ **:** to refuse to allow

♦ contradict, deny, disavow, disclaim, gainsay, negate, negative, reject, repudiate

dis•al•low•ance \ˌdi-sə-ˈlau̇-ən(t)s\ *n* ♦ **:** the act of disallowing

♦ contradiction, denial, disavowal, disclaimer, negation, rejection, repudiation

dis•ap•pear \ˌdi-sə-ˈpir\ *vb* **1** ♦ **:** to pass out of sight **2 :** to cease to be **:** become lost — **dis•ap•pear•ance** *n*

♦ dissolve, evaporate, fade, flee, go, melt, vanish *Ant* appear, materialize

dis•ap•point \ˌdi-sə-ˈpȯint\ *vb* ♦ **:** to fail to fulfill the expectation or hope of

♦ cheat, dissatisfy, fail, let down *Ant* satisfy

dis•ap•point•ment \-mənt\ *n* ♦ **:** the act or an instance of disappointing **:** the state or emotion of being disappointed

♦ dismay, dissatisfaction, frustration, letdown *Ant* contentment, gratification, satisfaction

dis•ap•pro•ba•tion \di-ˌsa-prə-ˈbā-shən\ *n* **:** the act or state of disapproving **:** the state of being disapproved **:** DISAPPROVAL

dis•ap•prov•al \ˌdi-sə-ˈprü-vəl\ *n* ♦ **:** the act or state of disapproving **:** the state of being disapproved

♦ deprecation, disfavor (*or* disfavour), dislike, displeasure *Ant* approbation, approval, favor

dis•ap•prove \-ˈprüv\ *vb* **1** ♦ **:** to pass unfavorable judgment on **2 :** to feel or express disapproval ⟨∼*s* of smoking⟩ **3** ♦ **:** to refuse approval to **:** REJECT — **dis•ap•prov•ing•ly** \-ˈprü-viŋ-lē\ *adv*

♦ *usu* **disapprove of** [1] deprecate, discountenance, disfavor (*or* disfavour), dislike, frown, reprove *Ant* approve, favor, like ♦ [3] decline, disallow, negative, refuse, reject, repudiate, spurn, turn down

dis•arm \di-ˈsärm\ *vb* **1 :** to take arms or weapons from **2 :** to reduce the size and strength of the armed forces of a country **3** ♦ **:** to make harmless, peaceable, or friendly **:** win over ⟨a ∼*ing* smile⟩ — **dis•ar•ma•ment** \-ˈsär-mə-mənt\ *n*

♦ appease, conciliate, mollify, pacify, placate, propitiate

dis•ar•range \ˌdi-sə-ˈrānj\ *vb* **:** to disturb the arrangement or order of
dis•ar•range•ment \-mənt\ *n* **:** the act of disarranging or the state of being disarranged
dis•ar•ray \-ˈrā\ *n* **1** ◆ **:** a lack of order or sequence **:** DISORDER **2 :** disorderly or careless dress

◆ chaos, confusion, disorder, disorganization, havoc, hell, jumble, mess, muddle, shambles

dis•as•sem•ble \ˌdi-sə-ˈsem-bəl\ *vb* ◆ **:** to take apart

◆ dismantle, knock down, strike, take down ***Ant*** assemble, construct, put together

dis•as•so•ci•ate \-ˈsō-shē-ˌāt, -sē-\ *vb* **:** to detach from association
di•sas•ter \di-ˈzas-tər, -ˈsas-\ *n* ◆ **:** a sudden or great misfortune — **di•sas•trous•ly** *adv*

◆ calamity, cataclysm, catastrophe, debacle, tragedy

di•sas•trous \di-ˈzas-trəs\ *adj* ◆ **:** attended by or causing suffering or disaster

◆ calamitous, catastrophic, destructive, fatal, fateful, ruinous, unfortunate

dis•avow \ˌdi-sə-ˈvau̇\ *vb* **1** ◆ **:** to deny responsibility for **:** REPUDIATE **2** ◆ **:** to refuse to acknowledge or accept **:** DISCLAIM

◆ [1, 2] contradict, deny, disallow, disclaim, gainsay, negate, negative, reject, repudiate

dis•avow•al \ˌdi-sə-ˈvau̇-əl\ *n* ◆ **:** the act or an instance of disavowing

◆ contradiction, denial, disallowance, disclaimer, negation, rejection, repudiation

dis•band \dis-ˈband\ *vb* ◆ **:** to break up the organization of **:** DISPERSE

◆ break up, disperse, dissolve ***Ant*** band, join, unite

dis•bar \dis-ˈbär\ *vb* **:** to expel from the legal profession — **dis•bar•ment** *n*
dis•be•lieve \ˌdis-bə-ˈlēv\ *vb* **1 :** to hold not worthy of belief **:** not believe **2 :** to withhold or reject belief — **dis•be•lief** \-ˈlēf\ *n*
dis•be•liev•er \ˌdis-bə-ˈlē-vər\ *n* ◆ **:** one that is not a believer

◆ doubter, questioner, skeptic, unbeliever

dis•bur•den \dis-ˈbərd-ᵊn\ *vb* ◆ **:** to rid of a burden

◆ clear, disencumber, free, relieve, rid, unburden

dis•burse \dis-ˈbərs\ *vb* **dis•bursed; dis•burs•ing 1** ◆ **:** to pay out **:** EXPEND **2 :** DISTRIBUTE

◆ expend, give, lay out, pay, spend

dis•burse•ment \-mənt\ *n* **1** ◆ **:** the act of disbursing **2** ◆ **:** funds paid out

◆ [1] compensation, payment, remittance, remuneration ◆ [2] cost, expenditure, expense, outgo, outlay

[1]disc *var of* DISK
[2]disc *abbr* discount
[1]dis•card \dis-ˈkärd, ˈdis-ˌkärd\ *vb* **1 :** to let go a playing card from one's hand; *also* **:** to play (a card) from a suit other than a trump but different from the one led **2** ◆ **:** to get rid of as unwanted

◆ cast, ditch, dump, fling, jettison, junk, lose, reject, scrap, shed, shuck, slough, throw away, throw out, unload

[2]discard \ˈdis-ˌkärd\ *n* ◆ **:** one that is cast off or rejected

◆ cull, reject, rejection

disc brake *n* **:** a brake that operates by the friction of a pair of plates pressing against the sides of a rotating disc
dis•cern \di-ˈsərn, -ˈzərn\ *vb* **1** ◆ **:** to detect with the eyes **:** DISTINGUISH **2** ◆ **:** to recognize or identify as separate and distinct **:** DISCRIMINATE **3 :** to come to know or recognize mentally

◆ [1] behold, descry, distinguish, espy, eye, look, note, notice, observe, perceive, regard, remark, see, sight, spy, view, witness ◆ [2] differentiate, discriminate, distinguish, separate

dis•cern•ible \di-ˈsər-nə-bəl, -ˈzər-\ *n* ◆ **:** capable of being discerned

◆ appreciable, detectable, distinguishable, palpable, perceptible, sensible

dis•cern•ing *adj* ◆ **:** revealing insight and understanding

◆ insightful, perceptive, sagacious, sage, sapient, wise

dis•cern•ment \-mənt\ *n* ◆ **:** the ability to grasp and comprehend what is obscure

◆ insight, perception, sagacity, sapience, wisdom

[1]dis•charge \dis-ˈchärj, ˈdis-ˌchärj\ *vb* **1** ◆ **:** to relieve of a charge, load, or burden **:** UNLOAD; *esp* **:** to remove the electrical energy from 〈~ a storage battery〉 **2** ◆ **:** to let or put off 〈~ passengers〉 **3** ◆ **:** to drive (as an arrow or bullet) forward quickly or forcibly **:** SHOOT **4 :** to set free 〈~ a prisoner〉 **5** ◆ **:** to give outlet or vent to 〈~ emotions〉 〈~ fumes〉 **6 :** to dismiss from service or employment, service, or duty 〈~ a soldier〉 **7** ◆ **:** to get rid of by paying or doing 〈~ a debt〉 **8 :** to give forth fluid 〈the river ~*s* into the ocean〉

◆ [1, 2] disburden, disencumber, unburden, unload ◆ [3] blast, fire, loose, shoot ◆ [5] cast, emit, exhale, expel, issue, release, shoot, vent ◆ [7] clear, foot, liquidate, pay, pay off, quit, recompense, settle, spring, stand

[2]dis•charge \ˈdis-ˌchärj, dis-ˈchärj\ *n* **1** ◆ **:** the act of discharging, unloading, releasing, or relieving **2 :** something that discharges; *esp* **:** a certification of release or payment **3 :** a firing off (as of a gun) **4 :** a flowing out (as of blood from a wound); *also* **:** something that is emitted 〈a purulent ~〉 **5** ◆ **:** release or dismissal especially from an office or employment; *also* **:** complete separation from military service **6 :** a flow of electricity (as through a gas)

◆ [1] delivery, quietus, quittance, release ◆ [5] dismissal, layoff

dis•ci•ple \di-ˈsī-pəl\ *n* **1** ◆ **:** one who accepts and helps to spread the teachings of another; *also* **:** a convinced adherent **2** *cap* **:** a member of the Disciples of Christ

◆ adherent, convert, follower, partisan, pupil, votary

dis•ci•pli•nar•i•an \ˌdi-sə-plə-ˈner-ē-ən\ *n* **:** one who enforces order
dis•ci•plin•ary \ˈdi-sə-plə-ˌner-ē\ *adj* ◆ **:** of or relating to discipline; *also* **:** CORRECTIVE 〈take ~ action〉

◆ corrective, penal, punitive

[1]dis•ci•pline \ˈdi-sə-plən\ *n* **1 :** suffering, pain, or loss that serves as retribution **:** PUNISHMENT **2** ◆ **:** a field of study **3 :** training that corrects, molds, or perfects **4 :** control gained by obedience or training **:** orderly conduct **5 :** a system of rules governing conduct

◆ area, arena, demesne, department, domain, field, line, province, realm, specialty, sphere

[2]discipline *vb* **-plined; -plin•ing 1** ◆ **:** to punish or penalize for the sake of discipline **:** PUNISH **2 :** to train or develop by instruction and exercise especially in self-control **3 :** to bring under control 〈~ troops〉; *also* **:** to impose order upon

◆ castigate, chasten, chastise, correct, penalize, punish

disc jockey *or* **disk jockey** *n* **:** an announcer of a radio show of popular recorded music
dis•claim \dis-ˈklām\ *vb* **1 :** to declare untrue **:** DENY **2** ◆ **:** to refuse to admit or acknowledge **:** DISAVOW

◆ disavow, disown, repudiate ***Ant*** acknowledge, avow, claim, own, recognize

dis•claim•er \dis-ˈklā-mər\ *n* **1 :** a denial or disavowal of legal claim; *also* **:** a writing that embodies a legal disclaimer **2** ◆ **:** a refusal to acknowledge or accept

◆ contradiction, denial, disallowance, disavowal, negation, rejection, repudiation

dis•close \dis-ˈklōz\ *vb* **1 :** to expose to view **2** ◆ **:** to make known or public — **dis•clo•sure** \-ˈklō-zhər\ *n*

◆ bare, discover, divulge, expose, reveal, spill, tell, unbosom, uncloak, uncover, unmask, unveil

dis•co \ˈdis-kō\ *n, pl* **discos 1** ◆ **:** a nightclub for dancing to live or recorded music **2 :** popular dance music characterized by hypnotic rhythm, repetitive lyrics, and electronically produced sounds

◆ café, discotheque, nightclub

dis•col•or *or Can and Brit* **dis•col•our** \dis-ˈkə-lər\ *vb* **:** to alter or change in hue or color especially for the worse — **dis•col•or•ation** \-ˌkə-lə-ˈrā-shən\ *n*
dis•com•bob•u•late \ˌdis-kəm-ˈbä-byu̇-ˌlāt\ *vb* **-lat•ed; -lat•ing** ◆ **:** to disturb the composure of **:** CONFUSE

◆ addle, baffle, befog, befuddle, bemuse, bewilder, confound, confuse, disorient, muddle, muddy, mystify, perplex, puzzle

dis·com·fit \dis-ˈkəm-fət, *esp Southern* ˌdis-kəm-ˈfit\ *vb* ♦ **:** to put into a state of perplexity and embarrassment

♦ abash, confound, confuse, disconcert, discountenance, embarrass, faze, fluster, mortify, rattle

dis·com·fi·ture \dis-ˈkəm-fə-ˌchu̇r\ *n* ♦ **:** the act of discomfiting **:** the state of being discomfited

♦ abashment, confusion, embarrassment, fluster, mortification

[1]dis·com·fort \dis-ˈkəm-fərt\ *vb* **:** to make uncomfortable or uneasy

[2]discomfort *n* **:** mental or physical uneasiness

dis·com·mode \ˌdis-kə-ˈmōd\ *vb* **-mod·ed; -mod·ing** ♦ **:** to cause inconvenience to **:** TROUBLE

♦ disoblige, disturb, inconvenience, trouble

dis·com·pose \-kəm-ˈpōz\ *vb* **1** ♦ **:** to destroy the composure of **:** AGITATE **2 :** to disturb the order of **:** DISARRANGE — **dis·com·po·sure** \-ˈpō-zhər\ *n*

♦ agitate, bother, concern, disquiet, distress, disturb, exercise, freak out, perturb, undo, unhinge, unsettle, upset, worry

dis·con·cert \ˌdis-kən-ˈsərt\ *vb* ♦ **:** to disturb the composure of **:** CONFUSE

♦ abash, confound, confuse, discomfit, discountenance, embarrass, faze, fluster, mortify, rattle

dis·con·cert·ing *adj* ♦ **:** causing loss of composure or self-possession

♦ awkward, embarrassing, uncomfortable

dis·con·nect \ˌdis-kə-ˈnekt\ *vb* ♦ **:** to undo the connection of — **dis·con·nec·tion** \-ˈnek-shən\ *n*

♦ break up, disjoint, dissever, dissociate, disunite, divide, divorce, part, resolve, separate, sever, split, sunder, unyoke

dis·con·nect·ed *adj* **1** ♦ **:** not connected **:** SEPARATE **2** ♦ **:** lacking orderly continuity, arrangement, or relevance **:** INCOHERENT — **dis·con·nect·ed·ly** *adv* — **dis·con·nect·ed·ness** *n*

♦ [1] detached, discrete, freestanding, separate, single, unattached, unconnected ♦ [2] disjointed, incoherent, unconnected

dis·con·so·late \dis-ˈkän-sə-lət\ *adj* **1 :** CHEERLESS **2** ♦ **:** hopelessly sad — **dis·con·so·late·ly** *adv*

♦ brokenhearted, despondent, forlorn, heartsick, miserable, sad, unhappy, wretched

[1]dis·con·tent \ˌdis-kən-ˈtent\ *n* ♦ **:** uneasiness of mind **:** DISSATISFACTION

♦ displeasure, disquiet, dissatisfaction *Ant* contentedness, contentment, pleasure, satisfaction

[2]discontent *vb* ♦ **:** to make dissatisfied or displeased

♦ disaffect, disgruntle, displease, dissatisfy *Ant* content, gratify, please, satisfy

dis·con·tent·ed *adj* ♦ **:** expressing or showing lack of satisfaction

♦ aggrieved, discontent, dissatisfied, malcontent *Ant* content, contented, gratified, pleased, satisfied

dis·con·tin·u·ance \ˌdis-kən-ˈtin-yə-wəns\ *n* **:** the act or an instance of discontinuing

dis·con·tin·ue \ˌdis-kən-ˈtin-yü\ *vb* **1** ♦ **:** to break the continuity of **:** cease to operate, use, or take **2** ♦ **:** to come or bring to an end

♦ [1, 2] break, break off, cease, cut, desist, drop, end, halt, knock off, lay off, leave off, quit, shut off, stop

dis·con·ti·nu·i·ty \dis-ˌkän-tə-ˈnü-ə-tē, -ˈnyü-\ *n* **1 :** lack of continuity or cohesion **2** ♦ **:** a break in continuity **:** GAP

♦ gap, hiatus, interim, interlude, intermission, interruption, interval

dis·con·tin·u·ous \ˌdis-kən-ˈtin-yə-wəs\ *adj* ♦ **:** not continuous

♦ casual, choppy, erratic, fitful, intermittent, irregular, occasional, spasmodic, sporadic, spotty, unsteady

dis·cord \ˈdis-ˌkȯrd\ *n* **1** ♦ **:** lack of agreement or harmony **:** DISSENSION **2 :** a harsh combination of musical sounds **3 :** a harsh or unpleasant sound

♦ conflict, dissent, disunity, friction, schism, strife, variance, war, warfare *Ant* accord, agreement, concord, concordance, harmony, peace

dis·cor·dant \dis-ˈkȯrd-ᵊnt\ *adj* **1 a** ♦ **:** being at variance ⟨~ opinions⟩ **b :** apt or disposed to quarrel in an often petty manner **:** QUARRELSOME **2** ♦ **:** relating to a discord ⟨a ~ tone⟩ — **dis·cor·dant·ly** *adv*

♦ [1a] discrepant, incompatible, incongruous, inharmonious ♦ [2] dissonant, inharmonious, unmelodious, unmusical

dis·co·theque *or* **discothèque** \ˈdis-kə-ˌtek\ *n* ♦ **:** a nightclub for dancing to live or recorded music **:** DISCO 1

♦ café, disco, nightclub

[1]dis·count \ˈdis-ˌkau̇nt\ *n* **1** ♦ **:** a reduction made from a regular or list price **2** ♦ **:** a deduction of interest in advance when lending money

♦ [1, 2] abatement, deduction, reduction

[2]dis·count \ˈdis-ˌkau̇nt, dis-ˈkau̇nt\ *vb* **1 :** to deduct from the amount of a bill, debt, or charge usually for cash or prompt payment; *also* **:** to sell or offer for sale at a discount **2 :** to lend money after deducting the discount ⟨~ a note⟩ **3 a :** DISREGARD **b** ♦ **:** to minimize the importance of **4 :** to make allowance for bias or exaggeration **5 :** to take into account (as a future event) in present calculations — **dis·count·able** *adj* — **dis·count·er** *n*

♦ belittle, cry down, decry, deprecate, depreciate, diminish, disparage, minimize, put down, write off

[3]dis·count \ˈdis-ˌkau̇nt\ *adj* **:** selling goods or services at a discount; *also* **:** sold at or reflecting a discount

dis·coun·te·nance \dis-ˈkau̇nt-ᵊn-ənts\ *vb* **1** ♦ **:** to disturb the composure of **:** DISCONCERT **2** ♦ **:** to look with disfavor on

♦ [1] abash, confound, confuse, discomfit, disconcert, embarrass, faze, fluster, mortify, rattle ♦ [2] deprecate, disapprove, disfavor (*or* disfavour), dislike, frown, reprove

dis·cour·age \dis-ˈkər-ij\ *vb* **-aged; -ag·ing 1** ♦ **:** to deprive of courage or confidence **:** DISHEARTEN **2 :** to hinder by disfavoring **3** ♦ **:** to dissuade or attempt to dissuade — **dis·cour·ag·ing·ly** *adv*

♦ [1] daunt, demoralize, dishearten, dismay, dispirit, unman, unnerve *Ant* embolden, encourage, hearten, nerve, steel ♦ [3] deter, dissuade, inhibit *Ant* encourage, persuade

dis·cour·age·ment \-mənt\ *n* ♦ **:** the act of discouraging **:** the state of being discouraged

♦ demoralization, despair, despondency, dismay *Ant* encouragement

[1]dis·course \ˈdis-ˌkōrs\ *n* **1** ♦ **:** verbal interchange of ideas **2 :** formal and usually extended expression of thought on a subject

♦ colloquy, conversation, dialogue, discussion, exchange

[2]dis·course \dis-ˈkōrs\ *vb* **dis·coursed; dis·cours·ing 1** ♦ **:** to express oneself in especially oral discourse **2 :** TALK, CONVERSE

♦ declaim, descant, harangue, lecture, orate, speak, talk

dis·cour·te·ous \(ˌ)dis-ˈkər-tē-əs\ *adj* ♦ **:** lacking courtesy **:** RUDE — **dis·cour·te·ous·ly** *adv*

♦ ill-bred, ill-mannered, impertinent, impolite, inconsiderate, rude, thoughtless, uncivil, ungracious, unmannerly

dis·cour·te·sy \-ˈkər-tə-sē\ *n* ♦ **:** the quality or state of being rude **:** RUDENESS; *also* **:** a rude act

♦ brazenness, disrespect, impertinence, impudence, incivility, insolence, rudeness *Ant* civility, consideration, courtesy, genteelness, gentility, graciousness, politeness, thoughtfulness

dis·cov·er \dis-ˈkə-vər\ *vb* **1** ♦ **:** to make known or visible **2 a** ♦ **:** to obtain sight or knowledge of for the first time **b** ♦ **:** to learn by study, observation, or search **:** FIND OUT — **dis·cov·er·er** *n*

♦ [1] bare, disclose, divulge, expose, reveal, spill, tell, unbosom, uncloak, uncover, unmask, unveil ♦ [2a] ascertain, catch on, find out, hear, learn, realize, see ♦ [2b] detect, determine, dig up, ferret out, find, hit on, locate, track down

dis·cov·ery \dis-ˈkə-və-rē\ *n, pl* **-er·ies 1** ♦ **:** the act or process of discovering **2 :** something discovered **3 :** the disclosure usually before a civil trial of pertinent facts or documents

♦ detection, finding

[1]dis·cred·it \(ˌ)dis-ˈkre-dət\ *vb* **1 :** DISBELIEVE **2 :** to cause disbelief in the accuracy or authority of **3** ♦ **:** to deprive of good repute **:** DISGRACE

♦ abase, debase, degrade, demean, disgrace, dishonor (*or* dishonour), humble, humiliate, lower, shame, smirch, take down

²discredit *n* **1** ♦ **:** loss of reputation **2 :** lack or loss of belief or confidence

♦ disgrace, dishonor (*or* dishonour), disrepute, ignominy, infamy, odium, opprobrium, reproach, shame

dis•cred•it•able \-tə-bəl\ *adj* ♦ **:** not reputable or decent **:** injurious to a reputation for decency

♦ disgraceful, dishonorable (*or* dishonourable), disreputable, ignominious, infamous, notorious, shameful

dis•creet \dis-ˈkrēt\ *adj* **:** showing good judgment; *esp* **:** capable of observing prudent silence — **dis•creet•ly** *adv*

dis•crep•an•cy \dis-ˈkre-pən-sē\ *n, pl* **-cies** **1** ♦ **:** the quality or state of being discrepant **:** DIFFERENCE **2 :** an instance of being discrepant

♦ contrast, difference, disagreement, disparity, distinction, diversity, unlikeness

dis•crep•ant \-pənt\ *adj* ♦ **:** being at variance

♦ discordant, incompatible, incongruous, inharmonious

dis•crete \dis-ˈkrēt, ˈdis-ˌkrēt\ *adj* **1** ♦ **:** individually distinct **2 :** NONCONTINUOUS

♦ detached, disconnected, freestanding, separate, single, unattached, unconnected

dis•cre•tion \dis-ˈkre-shən\ *n* **1** ♦ **:** the quality of being discreet **:** PRUDENCE **2** ♦ **:** individual choice or judgment **3 :** power of free decision or latitude of choice

♦ [1] common sense, horse sense, prudence ♦ [2] alternative, choice, option, pick, preference, way

dis•cre•tion•ary \-ˈkre-shə-ˌner-ē\ *adj* **1** ♦ **:** left to discretion **:** exercised at one's own discretion **2 :** available for discretionary use

♦ elective, optional, voluntary

dis•crim•i•nate \dis-ˈkri-mə-ˌnāt\ *vb* **-nat•ed; -nat•ing** **1** ♦ **:** to recognize or give expression to a difference **:** DISTINGUISH **2 :** to make a difference in treatment on a basis other than individual merit

♦ differentiate, discern, distinguish, separate

dis•crim•i•nat•ing *adj* **:** marked by discrimination; *esp* **:** DISCERNING, JUDICIOUS

dis•crim•i•na•tion \dis-ˌkri-mə-ˈnā-shən\ *n* **1 a :** the quality or power of finely distinguishing **b** ♦ **:** recognition, perception, or identification especially of differences **2 a :** the act, practice, or an instance of discriminating categorically rather than individually **b :** prejudiced or prejudicial outlook, action, or treatment

♦ demarcation, distinction, separation

dis•crim•i•na•to•ry \dis-ˈkri-mə-nə-ˌtōr-ē\ *adj* **:** marked by especially unjust discrimination ⟨~ treatment⟩

dis•cur•sive \dis-ˈkər-siv\ *adj* ♦ **:** moving from topic to topic without order **:** RAMBLING — **dis•cur•sive•ly** *adv* — **dis•cur•sive•ness** *n*

♦ desultory, digressive, rambling

dis•cus \ˈdis-kəs\ *n, pl* **dis•cus•es** **:** a disk that is hurled for distance in a track-and-field contest

dis•cuss \di-ˈskəs\ *vb* **1** ♦ **:** to argue or consider carefully by presenting the various sides **2 :** to talk about

♦ argue, chew over, debate, dispute, hash, moot, talk over

dis•cus•sant \di-ˈskəs-ᵊnt\ *n* **:** one who takes part in a formal discussion

dis•cus•sion \di-ˈskə-shən\ *n* ♦ **:** consideration of a question in open and usually informal debate

♦ argument, colloquy, conference, deliberation, discourse, give-and-take, parley, talk

¹dis•dain \dis-ˈdān\ *n* ♦ **:** a feeling of contempt for someone or something regarded as unworthy or inferior **:** SCORN

♦ contempt, despite, scorn

²disdain *vb* **1** ♦ **:** to look on with scorn **2 :** to reject or refrain from because of disdain

♦ high-hat, scorn, slight, sniff at, snub

dis•dain•ful \dis-ˈdān-fəl\ *adj* ♦ **:** full of or expressing disdain — **dis•dain•ful•ly** *adv*

♦ haughty, highfalutin, lofty, lordly, prideful, proud, superior ♦ contemptuous, degrading, derogatory, scornful, uncomplimentary

dis•ease \di-ˈzēz\ *n* ♦ **:** an abnormal bodily condition that impairs normal functioning and can usually be recognized by signs and symptoms **:** SICKNESS — **dis•eased** \-ˈzēzd\ *adj*

♦ ailment, bug, complaint, complication, condition, disorder, fever, ill, illness, infirmity, malady, sickness, trouble *Ant* health, wellness

dis•em•bark \ˌdi-səm-ˈbärk\ *vb* ♦ **:** to go or put ashore from a ship — **dis•em•bar•ka•tion** \di-ˌsem-ˌbär-ˈkā-shən\ *n*

♦ dock, land, moor, tie up

dis•em•body \ˌdi-səm-ˈbä-dē\ *vb* **:** to deprive of bodily existence

dis•em•bow•el \-ˈbau̇-əl\ *vb* **:** to take out the bowels of **:** EVISCERATE — **dis•em•bow•el•ment** *n*

dis•em•power \ˌdis-im-ˈpau̇(-ə)r\ *vb* **:** to deprive of power, authority, or influence

dis•en•chant \ˌdis-ᵊn-ˈchant\ *vb* ♦ **:** to free from illusion **:** DISILLUSION — **dis•en•chant•ment** *n*

♦ disillusion, undeceive

dis•en•chant•ed \-ˈchan-təd\ *adj* **:** DISAPPOINTED, DISSATISFIED

dis•en•cum•ber \ˌdis-ᵊn-ˈkəm-bər\ *vb* ♦ **:** to free from something that burdens

♦ disburden, discharge, unburden, unload

dis•en•fran•chise \ˌdis-in-ˈfran-ˌchīz\ *vb* **:** to deprive of a franchise, a legal right, or a privilege; *esp* **:** to deprive of the right to vote — **dis•en•fran•chise•ment** *n*

dis•en•gage \ˌdis-ᵊn-ˈgāj\ *vb* ♦ **:** to release from something that engages or involves **:** EXTRICATE — **dis•en•gage•ment** *n*

♦ clear, disentangle, extricate, free, liberate, release, untangle

dis•en•gaged \-ˈgājd\ *adj* **:** IMPARTIAL, DETACHED ⟨a ~ observer⟩

dis•en•tan•gle \ˌdis-ᵊn-ˈtaŋ-gəl\ *vb* ♦ **:** to free from entanglement

♦ unravel, untangle, untwine

dis•equi•lib•ri•um \di-ˌsē-kwə-ˈli-brē-əm\ *n* **:** loss or lack of equilibrium

dis•es•tab•lish \ˌdi-sə-ˈsta-blish\ *vb* **:** to end the establishment of; *esp* **:** to deprive of the status of an established church — **dis•es•tab•lish•ment** *n*

dis•es•teem \ˌdi-sə-ˈstēm\ *n* **:** lack of esteem **:** DISFAVOR, DISREPUTE

dis•fa•vor *or Can and Brit* **dis•fa•vour** \(ˌ)dis-ˈfā-vər\ *n* **1** ♦ **:** a feeling of aversion or disapproval **:** DISLIKE **2 :** the state or fact of being no longer favored

♦ aversion, disinclination, dislike ♦ deprecation, disapproval, dislike, displeasure

dis•fig•ure \dis-ˈfi-gyər\ *vb* ♦ **:** to spoil the appearance of ⟨*disfigured* by a scar⟩

♦ blemish, break, cripple, damage, deface, flaw, harm, hurt, injure, mar, spoil, vitiate

dis•fig•ure•ment \-mənt\ *n* **1 :** the act of disfiguring or the state of being disfigured **2** ♦ **:** something that disfigures

♦ blemish, defect, deformity, fault, flaw, imperfection, mark, pockmark, scar

dis•fran•chise \dis-ˈfran-ˌchīz\ *vb* **:** DISENFRANCHISE — **dis•fran•chise•ment** *n*

disfunction *var of* DYSFUNCTION

dis•gorge \-ˈgȯrj\ *vb* **1 :** to discharge by the throat and mouth **:** VOMIT **2** ♦ **:** to discharge forcefully or confusedly

♦ belch, eject, erupt, expel, jet, spew, spout, spurt

¹dis•grace \di-ˈskrās, dis-ˈgrās\ *vb* ♦ **:** to bring reproach or shame to

♦ abase, debase, degrade, demean, discredit, dishonor (*or* dishonour), humble, humiliate, lower, shame, smirch, take down

²disgrace *n* **1 a** ♦ **:** the condition of one fallen from grace or honor **:** SHAME **b** ♦ **:** a source of shame **2 :** the condition of being out of favor **:** loss of respect

♦ [1a] discredit, dishonor (*or* dishonour), disrepute, ignominy, infamy, odium, opprobrium, reproach, shame *Ant* esteem, honor, respect ♦ [1b] dishonor, reflection, reproach, scandal *Ant* credit, honor

dis•grace•ful \-fəl\ *adj* ♦ **:** bringing or involving disgrace — **dis•grace•ful•ly** *adv*

♦ discreditable, dishonorable (*or* dishonourable), disreputable, ignominious, infamous, notorious, shameful

dis•grun•tle \dis-ˈgrənt-ᵊl\ *vb* **dis•grun•tled; dis•grun•tling** ♦ : to put in bad humor — usually used as a participial adjective ⟨they were a very *disgruntled* crew⟩

♦ alienate, disaffect, estrange, sour ♦ disaffect, discontent, displease, dissatisfy

[1]**dis•guise** \dis-ˈgīz\ *vb* **dis•guised; dis•guis•ing 1** ♦ : to change the appearance of to conceal the identity or to resemble another **2 :** HIDE, CONCEAL

♦ camouflage, cloak, dress up, mask

[2]**disguise** *n* **1** ♦ : clothing put on to conceal one's identity or counterfeit another's **2 :** an outward appearance that hides what something really is

♦ camouflage, guise

[1]**dis•gust** \dis-ˈgəst\ *n* ♦ : marked aversion aroused by something highly distasteful : REPUGNANCE — **dis•gust•ful** \-fəl\ *adj*

♦ distaste, loathing, nausea, repugnance, repulsion, revulsion

[2]**disgust** *vb* ♦ : to provoke to loathing, repugnance, or aversion : be offensive to — **dis•gust•ing** \-ˈgəs-tiŋ\ *adj* — **dis•gust•ing•ly** *adv*

♦ nauseate, repel, repulse, revolt, sicken, turn off

dis•gust•ed *adj* ♦ : affected by disgust — **dis•gust•ed•ly** *adv*

♦ sick, squeamish

[1]**dish** \ˈdish\ *n* **1 :** a vessel used for serving food **2 :** the food served in a dish ⟨a ∼ of berries⟩ **3 :** food prepared in a particular way **4 :** something resembling a dish especially in being shallow and concave **5 :** SATELLITE DISH **6 :** GOSSIP 2

[2]**dish** *vb* **1 :** to put into a dish **2 :** to make concave like a dish **3 :** GOSSIP

dis•ha•bille \ˌdi-sə-ˈbēl\ *n* : the state of being dressed in a casual or careless manner

dis•har•mo•ny \(ˌ)dis-ˈhär-mə-nē\ *n* : lack of harmony — **dis•har•mo•ni•ous** \ˌdis-(ˌ)här-ˈmō-nē-əs\ *adj*

dish•cloth \ˈdish-ˌklȯth\ *n* : a cloth for washing dishes

dis•heart•en \dis-ˈhärt-ᵊn\ *vb* ♦ : to cause to lose spirit or morale : DISCOURAGE

♦ daunt, demoralize, discourage, dismay, dispirit, unman, unnerve

dished \ˈdisht\ *adj* : CONCAVE

di•shev•el \di-ˈshe-vəl\ *vb* **-shev•eled** *or* **-shev•elled; -shev•el•ing** *or* **-shev•el•ling** ♦ : to throw into disorder or disarray

♦ derange, disarray, disorder, disrupt, disturb, mess, mix, muddle, rumple, upset

di•shev•eled *or* **di•shev•elled** *adj* ♦ : marked by disorder or disarray

♦ disordered, messy, muddled, unkempt, untidy

dis•hon•est \di-ˈsä-nəst\ *adj* ♦ : not honest — **dis•hon•est•ly** *adv*

♦ lying, mendacious ***Ant*** honest, truthful, veracious ♦ crooked, deceptive, fast, fraudulent, shady, sharp, shifty, underhanded ***Ant*** aboveboard, honest, straight

dis•hon•es•ty \di-ˈsä-nə-stē\ *n* ♦ : lack of honesty or integrity

♦ artifice, craft, craftiness, crookedness, cunning, deceit, deceitfulness, dissimulation, double-dealing, duplicity, guile, wiliness

[1]**dis•hon•or** *or Can and Brit* **dis•hon•our** \di-ˈsä-nər\ *vb* **1** ♦ : to bring reproach or shame on : DISGRACE **2 :** to refuse to accept or pay ⟨∼ a check⟩

♦ abase, debase, degrade, demean, discredit, disgrace, humble, humiliate, lower, shame, smirch, take down

[2]**dishonor** *or Can and Brit* **dishonour** *n* **1 :** lack or loss of honor **2** ♦ : the state of one who has lost honor or prestige : SHAME **3** ♦ : a cause of disgrace **4 :** the act of dishonoring a negotiable instrument when presented for payment

♦ [2] discredit, disgrace, disrepute, ignominy, infamy, odium, opprobrium, reproach, shame ♦ [3] disgrace, reflection, reproach, scandal

dis•hon•or•able *or Can and Brit* **dis•hon•our•able** \di-ˈsä-nə-rə-bəl\ *adj* ♦ : lacking honor — **dis•hon•or•ably** \-blē\ *adv*

♦ base, contemptible, despicable, detestable, dirty, ignoble, low, mean, snide, sordid, vile, wretched ♦ discreditable, disgraceful, disreputable, ignominious, infamous, notorious, shameful

dish out *vb* : to give freely

dish•rag \ˈdish-ˌrag\ *n* : DISHCLOTH

dish•wash•er \-ˌwȯ-shər, -ˌwä-\ *n* : a person or machine that washes dishes

dish•wa•ter \-ˌwȯ-tər, -ˌwä-\ *n* : water used for washing dishes

dis•il•lu•sion \ˌdi-sə-ˈlü-zhən\ *vb* ♦ : to leave without illusion or naive faith and trust — **dis•il•lu•sion•ment** *n*

♦ disenchant, undeceive

dis•il•lu•sioned *adj* : DISAPPOINTED, DISSATISFIED

dis•in•cli•na•tion \di-ˌsin-klə-ˈnā-shən\ *n* ♦ : a preference for avoiding something : slight aversion

♦ hesitancy, reluctance, reticence

dis•in•cline \ˌdis-ᵊn-ˈklīn\ *vb* : to make unwilling

dis•in•clined *adj* : unwilling because of dislike or disapproval

dis•in•fect \ˌdis-ᵊn-ˈfekt\ *vb* : to cleanse of infection-causing germs — **dis•in•fec•tant** \-ˈfek-tənt\ *n* — **dis•in•fec•tion** \-ˈfek-shən\ *n*

dis•in•for•ma•tion \-ˌin-fər-ˈmā-shən\ *n* : false information deliberately and often covertly spread

dis•in•gen•u•ous \ˌdis-ᵊn-ˈjen-yə-wəs\ *adj* : lacking in candor; *also* : giving a false appearance of simple frankness

dis•in•her•it \ˌdis-ᵊn-ˈher-ət\ *vb* : to deprive of the right to inherit

dis•in•te•grate \di-ˈsin-tə-ˌgrāt\ *vb* **1** ♦ : to break or decompose into constituent parts or small particles **2 :** to destroy the unity or integrity of — **dis•in•te•gra•tion** \-ˌsin-tə-ˈgrā-shən\ *n*

♦ break down, corrupt, decay, decompose, molder, putrefy, rot, spoil

dis•in•ter \ˌdis-ᵊn-ˈtər\ *vb* **1 :** to take from the grave or tomb **2 :** UNEARTH

dis•in•ter•est•ed \(ˌ)dis-ˈin-tə-rəs-təd, -ˌres-\ *adj* **1** ♦ : not interested **2** ♦ : free from selfish motive or interest : UNBIASED

♦ [1] apathetic, casual, indifferent, insouciant, nonchalant, perfunctory, unconcerned, uncurious, uninterested ♦ [2] dispassionate, equal, equitable, fair, impartial, just, nonpartisan, objective, square, unbiased, unprejudiced

dis•in•ter•est•ed•ness \(ˌ)dis-ˈin-tə-rəs-təd-nəs, -ˌres-\ *n* ♦ : the quality or state of being objective or impartial

♦ detachment, impartiality, neutrality, objectivity

dis•join \(ˌ)dis-ˈjȯin\ *vb* : to end the joining of : SEPARATE

dis•joint \(ˌ)dis-ˈjȯint\ *vb* **1 :** to disturb the orderly arrangement of **2** ♦ : to separate at the joints

♦ break up, disconnect, dissever, dissociate, disunite, divide, divorce, part, resolve, separate, sever, split, sunder, unyoke

dis•joint•ed *adj* **1** ♦ : lacking coherence or orderly sequence **2 :** separated at or as if at the joint

♦ disconnected, incoherent, unconnected

disk *or* **disc** \ˈdisk\ *n* **1 :** something round and flat; *esp* : a flat rounded anatomical structure (as the central part of the flower head of a composite plant or a pad of cartilage between vertebrae) **2** *usu disc* : a phonograph record **3 :** a round flat plate coated with a magnetic substance on which data for a computer is stored **4** *usu disc* : OPTICAL DISK

disk drive *n* : a device for accessing or storing data on a magnetic disk

dis•kette \ˌdis-ˈket\ *n* : FLOPPY DISK

disk jockey *var of* DISC JOCKEY

[1]**dis•like** \(ˌ)dis-ˈlīk\ *n* ♦ : a feeling of aversion or disapproval

♦ deprecation, disapproval, disfavor (*or* disfavour), displeasure ♦ aversion, disfavor (*or* disfavour), disinclination ***Ant*** appetite, fondness, like, liking, partiality, preference, taste

[2]**dislike** *vb* ♦ : to regard with dislike : DISAPPROVE

♦ deprecate, disapprove, discountenance, disfavor (*or* disfavour), frown, reprove

dis•lo•cate \ˈdis-lō-ˌkāt, dis-ˈlō-\ *vb* **1** ♦ : to put out of place; *esp* : to displace (a bone or joint) from normal connections ⟨∼ a shoulder⟩ **2 :** to force a change in the usual status, relationship, or order of : DISRUPT

♦ budge, displace, disturb, move, remove, shift, transfer

dis•lo•ca•tion \ˌdis-(ˌ)lō-ˈkā-shən\ *n* ♦ : the act of dislocating : the state of being dislocated

♦ disruption, disturbance, upset

dis•lodge \(ˌ)dis-ˈläj\ *vb* : to force out of a place especially of rest, hiding, or defense

dis•loy•al \(ˌ)dis-ˈlȯi-əl\ *adj* ♦ : lacking in loyalty

♦ faithless, false, fickle, inconstant, loose, perfidious, recreant, traitorous, treacherous, unfaithful, untrue

dis•loy•al•ty \(ˌ)dis-ˈlȯi-əl-tē\ *n* ♦ **:** lack of loyalty

♦ betrayal, double cross, faithlessness, falseness, falsity, infidelity, perfidy, treachery, treason, unfaithfulness

dis•mal \ˈdiz-məl\ *adj* **1** ♦ **:** showing or causing gloom or depression **2 :** lacking merit — **dis•mal•ly** *adv*

♦ bleak, dark, dreary, gloomy, gray (*or* grey), somber (*or* sombre), wretched

dis•man•tle \(ˌ)dis-ˈmant-ᵊl\ *vb* **-tled; -tling 1** ♦ **:** to take apart **2 :** to strip of furniture and equipment — **dis•man•tle•ment** *n*

♦ disassemble, knock down, strike, take down

1**dis•may** \dis-ˈmā\ *vb* ♦ **:** to cause to lose courage or resolution from alarm or fear **:** DAUNT — **dis•may•ing•ly** *adv*

♦ daunt, demoralize, discourage, dishearten, dispirit, unman, unnerve

2**dismay** *n* **1** ♦ **:** sudden loss of courage or resolution from alarm or fear **2** ♦ **:** sudden disappointment

♦ [1] demoralization, despair, despondency, discouragement ♦ [2] disappointment, dissatisfaction, frustration, letdown

dis•mem•ber \dis-ˈmem-bər\ *vb* **1 :** to cut off or separate the limbs or parts of **2 :** to break up or tear into pieces — **dis•mem•ber•ment** *n*

dis•miss \dis-ˈmis\ *vb* **1** ♦ **:** to send away **2** ♦ **:** to dismiss from service or employment **3 :** to put aside or out of mind **4 :** to put out of judicial consideration ⟨~*ed* all charges⟩ — **dis•mis•sive** \-ˈmi-siv\ *adj* — **dis•mis•sive•ly** *adv*

♦ [1] banish, boot (out), bounce, cast, chase, drum, eject, expel, oust, rout, run off, throw out ♦ [2] cashier, fire, remove, retire, sack ***Ant*** employ, hire

dis•miss•al \ˈmi-səl\ *n* ♦ **:** the act of dismissing **:** the fact or state of being dismissed

♦ discharge, layoff

dis•mount \dis-ˈmau̇nt\ *vb* **1 :** to get down from something (as a horse or bicycle) **2 :** UNHORSE **3 :** DISASSEMBLE

dis•obe•di•ence \ˌdi-sə-ˈbē-dē-əns\ *n* ♦ **:** neglect or refusal to obey

♦ defiance, insubordination, rebelliousness, recalcitrance, refractoriness, unruliness ***Ant*** compliance, docility, obedience

dis•obe•di•ent \-ənt\ *adj* ♦ **:** refusing or neglecting to obey

♦ contrary, defiant, froward, intractable, rebellious, recalcitrant, refractory, unruly, untoward, wayward, willful ***Ant*** amenable, compliant, docile, obedient, tractable

dis•obey \ˌdi-sə-ˈbā\ *vb* **:** to fail to obey **:** be disobedient

dis•oblige \ˌdi-sə-ˈblīj\ *vb* **1 :** to go counter to the wishes of **2** ♦ **:** to subject to inconvenience

♦ discommode, disturb, inconvenience, trouble

1**dis•or•der** \di-ˈsȯr-dər\ *vb* **1** ♦ **:** to disturb the order of **2 :** to disturb the regular or normal functions of

♦ confuse, derange, disarray, discompose, dishevel, dislocate, disrupt, disturb, jumble, mess, mix, muddle, rumple, scramble, shuffle, tumble, upset ***Ant*** arrange, array, draw up, marshal, order, organize, range, regulate, straighten (up), tidy

2**disorder** *n* **1** ♦ **:** lack of order **:** CONFUSION **2 :** breach of the peace or public order **:** TUMULT **3** ♦ **:** an abnormal physical or mental condition **:** AILMENT

♦ [1] chaos, confusion, disarray, disorganization, havoc, hell, jumble, mess, muddle, shambles ♦ [3] ailment, bug, complaint, condition, disease, fever, ill, illness, infirmity, malady, sickness, trouble

dis•or•dered *adj* **1** ♦ **:** marked by disorder **2 :** not functioning in a normal orderly healthy way

♦ chaotic, confused, disheveled, messy, muddled, sloppy, unkempt, untidy

dis•or•der•ly \-lē\ *adj* **1** ♦ **:** offensive to public order **2 :** marked by disorder ⟨a ~ desk⟩ — **dis•or•der•li•ness** *n*

♦ anarchic, lawless, unruly

dis•or•ga•ni•za•tion \di-ˌsȯr-gə-nə-ˈzā-shən\ *n* ♦ **:** the act of disorganizing or the quality or state of being disorganized

♦ chaos, confusion, disarray, disorder, havoc, hell, jumble, mess, muddle, shambles

dis•or•ga•nize \di-ˈsȯr-gə-ˌnīz\ *vb* **:** to break up the regular system of **:** throw into disorder

dis•ori•ent \di-ˈsōr-ē-ˌent\ *vb* ♦ **:** to cause to be confused or lost — **dis•ori•en•ta•tion** \di-ˌsōr-ē-ən-ˈtā-shən\ *n*

♦ addle, baffle, befog, befuddle, bemuse, bewilder, confound, confuse, muddle, muddy, mystify, perplex, puzzle

dis•own \di-ˈsōn\ *vb* ♦ **:** to repudiate any connection or identification with **:** DISCLAIM

♦ disavow, disclaim, repudiate

dis•par•age \di-ˈspar-ij\ *vb* **-aged; -ag•ing 1 :** to lower in rank or reputation **:** DEGRADE **2** ♦ **:** to depreciate by indirect means (as invidious comparison) **:** BELITTLE — **dis•par•ag•ing•ly** *adv*

♦ belittle, cry down, decry, deprecate, depreciate, diminish, discount, minimize, put down, write off

dis•par•age•ment \-mənt\ *n* ♦ **:** diminution of esteem or standing

♦ deprecation, depreciation, detraction, put-down

dis•pa•rate \ˈdis-pə-rət, dis-ˈpar-ət\ *adj* ♦ **:** distinct in quality or character

♦ different, dissimilar, distinct, distinctive, distinguishable, diverse, other, unalike, unlike

dis•par•i•ty \di-ˈspar-ə-tē\ *n* ♦ **:** the state of being disparate

♦ contrast, difference, disagreement, discrepancy, distinction, diversity, unlikeness

dis•pas•sion•ate \(ˌ)dis-ˈpa-shə-nət\ *adj* ♦ **:** not influenced by strong feeling **:** IMPARTIAL — **dis•pas•sion** \-ˈpa-shən\ *n* — **dis•pas•sion•ate•ly** *adv*

♦ disinterested, equal, equitable, fair, impartial, just, nonpartisan, objective, square, unbiased, unprejudiced

1**dis•patch** \di-ˈspach\ *vb* **1** ♦ **:** to send off or away with promptness or speed especially on official business **2** ♦ **:** to put to death **3 :** to attend to rapidly or efficiently **4 :** DEFEAT — **dis•patch•er** *n*

♦ [1] consign, pack, send, ship, transfer, transmit, transport ♦ [2] do in, execute, kill, liquidate, murder, slay

2**dis•patch** \di-ˈspach, ˈdis-ˌpach\ *n* **1** ♦ **:** a message sent with speed **2 :** a news item sent in by a correspondent to a newspaper **3 :** the act of dispatching; *esp* **:** SHIPMENT **4 :** the act of putting to death **5 :** promptness and efficiency in performing a task

♦ letter, memorandum, missive, note

dis•pel \di-ˈspel\ *vb* **dis•pelled; dis•pel•ling :** to drive away by scattering **:** DISSIPATE

dis•pens•able \di-ˈspen-sə-bəl\ *adj* **:** capable of being dispensed with

dis•pen•sa•ry \di-ˈspen-sə-rē\ *n, pl* **-ries :** a place where medicine or medical or dental aid is dispensed

dis•pen•sa•tion \ˌdis-pən-ˈsā-shən\ *n* **1 :** a system of rules for ordering affairs **2 :** a particular arrangement or provision especially of nature **3 :** an exemption from a rule or from a vow or oath **4** ♦ **:** the act of dispensing **5 :** something dispensed or distributed

♦ allocation, distribution, division, issuance

dis•pense \di-ˈspens\ *vb* **dis•pensed; dis•pens•ing 1** ♦ **:** to portion out **2 :** ADMINISTER ⟨~ justice⟩ **3 :** EXEMPT **4 :** to make up and give out (remedies) — **dis•pens•er** *n* — **dispense with 1 :** SUSPEND **2 :** to do without

♦ administer, allocate, apportion, deal, distribute, mete, parcel, portion, prorate

dis•per•sal \-ˈspər-səl\ *n* **:** the act or result of dispersing

dis•perse \di-ˈspərs\ *vb* **dis•persed; dis•pers•ing** ♦ **:** to break up and scatter about

♦ clear out, disband, dissipate, scatter ♦ break up, disband, dissolve

dis•per•sion \-ˈspər-zhən\ *n* **:** the act or process of dispersing **:** the state of being dispersed

dis•pir•it \dis-ˈpir-ət\ *vb* ♦ **:** to deprive of morale or enthusiasm **:** DISCOURAGE

♦ daunt, demoralize, discourage, dishearten, dismay, unman, unnerve

dis•place \dis-ˈplās\ *vb* **1** ♦ **:** to remove from the usual or proper place; *esp* **:** to expel or force to flee from home or native land ⟨*displaced* persons⟩ **2 :** to move out of position ⟨water *displaced* by a floating object⟩ **3** ♦ **:** to take the place of **:** REPLACE

♦ [1] budge, dislocate, disturb, move, remove, shift, transfer ♦ [1] banish, deport, exile, expatriate, transport ♦ [3] replace, substitute, supersede, supplant

dis•place•ment \-mənt\ *n* **1** ♦ **:** the act of displacing **:** the state of being displaced **2 :** the volume or weight of a fluid (as water) displaced by a floating body (as a ship) **3 :** the difference between the initial position of an object and a later position

♦ banishment, deportation, exile, expulsion

¹dis•play \di-ˈsplā\ *vb* ♦ **:** to present to view **:** make evident

♦ disport, exhibit, expose, flash, flaunt, parade, show, show off, sport, strut, unveil

²display *n* **1** ♦ **:** a displaying of something **2 :** an electronic device (as a cathode-ray tube) that gives information in visual form; *also* **:** the visual information

♦ demonstration, exhibition, show ♦ exhibit, exhibition, exposition, fair, show

dis•please \(ˌ)dis-ˈplēz\ *vb* **1** ♦ **:** to arouse the disapproval and dislike of **2 :** to be offensive to **:** give displeasure

♦ disaffect, discontent, disgruntle, dissatisfy

dis•plea•sure \-ˈple-zhər\ *n* ♦ **:** a feeling of dislike and irritation **:** a display of disapproval

♦ deprecation, disapproval, disfavor (*or* disfavour), dislike

dis•port \di-ˈspōrt\ *vb* **1** ♦ **:** to entertain or occupy in a light, playful, or pleasant manner **:** AMUSE **2** ♦ **:** to amuse oneself in light or lively fashion **:** FROLIC **3 :** to make evident **:** DISPLAY

♦ [1] amuse, divert, entertain, regale ♦ [2] caper, cavort, frisk, frolic, gambol, lark, rollick, romp, sport

dis•pos•able \di-ˈspō-zə-bəl\ *adj* **1 :** remaining after deduction of taxes ⟨∼ income⟩ **2 :** designed to be used once and then thrown away ⟨∼ diapers⟩ — **disposable** *n*

dis•pos•al \di-ˈspō-zəl\ *n* **1 :** CONTROL, COMMAND **2** ♦ **:** an orderly arrangement **3** ♦ **:** a getting rid of **4 :** MANAGEMENT, ADMINISTRATION **5 :** presenting or bestowing something ⟨∼ of favors⟩ **6 :** a device used to reduce waste matter (as by grinding)

♦ [2] arrangement, array, disposition, distribution, order, sequence, setup ♦ [3] disposition, dumping, jettison, removal, riddance

dis•pose \di-ˈspōz\ *vb* **dis•posed; dis•pos•ing** **1 :** to give a tendency to **:** INCLINE ⟨*disposed* to accept⟩ **2** ♦ **:** to put in place ⟨troops *disposed* for withdrawal⟩ **3 :** SETTLE — **dis•pos•er** *n* — **dispose of** **1 :** to transfer to the control of another **2 :** to get rid of **3 :** to deal with conclusively

♦ deposit, fix, lay, place, position, put, set, set up, stick ♦ arrange, array, classify, codify, draw up, marshal, order, organize, range, systematize

dis•posed *adj* ♦ **:** having a particular temperament, disposition, or tendency **:** being in a particular frame of mind

♦ amenable, game, glad, inclined, ready, willing

dis•po•si•tion \ˌdis-pə-ˈzi-shən\ *n* **1 :** the act or power of disposing **:** DISPOSAL **2 :** RELINQUISHMENT **3** ♦ **:** orderly arrangement **4** ♦ **:** prevailing tendency, mood, or inclination **5 :** natural attitude toward things ⟨a cheerful ∼⟩

♦ [3] arrangement, array, disposal, distribution, order, sequence, setup ♦ [4] affinity, bent, devices, genius, inclination, leaning, partiality, penchant, predilection, predisposition, proclivity, propensity, talent, tendency, turn ♦ [4] grain, nature, temper, temperament

dis•pos•sess \ˌdis-pə-ˈzes\ *vb* **:** to put out of possession or occupancy — **dis•pos•ses•sion** \-ˈze-shən\ *n*

dis•praise \(ˌ)dis-ˈprāz\ *vb* **:** DISPARAGE — **dispraise** *n* — **dis•prais•er** *n*

dis•proof \(ˌ)dis-ˈprüf\ *n* **:** evidence that disproves

dis•pro•por•tion \ˌdis-prə-ˈpōr-shən\ *n* **:** lack of proportion, symmetry, or proper relation — **dis•pro•por•tion•ate** \-shə-nət\ *adj*

dis•prove \(ˌ)dis-ˈprüv\ *vb* ♦ **:** to prove to be false or wrong

♦ belie, confute, rebut, refute *Ant* confirm, prove, verify

dis•put•able \di-ˈspyü-tə-bəl, ˈdis-pyə-tə-bəl\ *adj* ♦ **:** capable of being disputed or contested

♦ arguable, debatable, doubtful, moot, questionable

dis•pu•tant \di-ˈspyüt-ᵊnt, ˈdis-pyə-tənt\ *n* ♦ **:** one that is engaged in a dispute

♦ arguer, contender, debater, disputer

dis•pu•ta•tion \ˌdis-pyu̇-ˈtā-shən\ *n* **1 :** the action of disputing **:** DEBATE **2 :** an oral defense of an academic thesis

dis•pu•ta•tious \-shəs\ *adj* ♦ **:** inclined to dispute **:** ARGUMENTATIVE

♦ argumentative, contentious, quarrelsome, scrappy

¹dis•pute \di-ˈspyüt\ *vb* **dis•put•ed; dis•put•ing** **1** ♦ **:** to engage in argument **:** ARGUE **2 :** WRANGLE **3** ♦ **:** to question the truth or rightness of **4 :** to struggle against or over **:** OPPOSE

♦ [1] argue, chew over, debate, discuss, hash, moot, talk over ♦ [3] challenge, contest, query, question

²dis•pute *n* **1** ♦ **:** verbal controversy **2** ♦ **:** a usually verbal conflict between antagonists **:** QUARREL

♦ [1] controversy, difference, disagreement, dissension ♦ [2] altercation, argument, bicker, brawl, disagreement, fight, hassle, misunderstanding, quarrel, row, scrap, spat, squabble, wrangle

dis•put•er *n* ♦ **:** one that disputes

♦ arguer, contender, debater, disputant

dis•qual•i•fy \(ˌ)dis-ˈkwä-lə-ˌfī\ *vb* **:** to make or declare unfit or not qualified — **dis•qual•i•fi•ca•tion** \-ˌkwä-lə-fə-ˈkā-shən\ *n*

¹dis•qui•et \(ˌ)dis-ˈkwī-ət\ *vb* ♦ **:** to make uneasy or restless **:** DISTURB

♦ agitate, bother, concern, discompose, distress, disturb, exercise, freak out, perturb, undo, unhinge, unsettle, upset, worry

²disquiet *n* ♦ **:** lack of peace or tranquillity

♦ agitation, anxiety, apprehension, care, concern, nervousness, perturbation, uneasiness, worry

dis•qui•etude \(ˌ)dis-ˈkwī-ə-ˌtüd, -ˌtyüd\ *n* **:** AGITATION, ANXIETY

dis•qui•si•tion \ˌdis-kwə-ˈzi-shən\ *n* **:** a formal inquiry or discussion

¹dis•re•gard \ˌdis-ri-ˈgärd\ *vb* ♦ **:** to pay no attention to **:** treat as unworthy of notice or regard

♦ forget, ignore, neglect, overlook, pass over, slight, slur ♦ condone, excuse, gloss over, ignore, pardon, pass over, shrug off, wink at

²disregard *n* ♦ **:** the act of disregarding **:** the state of being disregarded — **dis•re•gard•ful** *adj*

♦ apathy, disinterestedness, indifference, insouciance, nonchalance

dis•re•pair \ˌdis-ri-ˈpar\ *n* ♦ **:** the state of being in need of repair

♦ desolation, dilapidation, neglect

dis•rep•u•ta•ble \dis-ˈre-pyu̇-tə-bəl\ *adj* ♦ **:** having a bad reputation

♦ discreditable, disgraceful, dishonorable (*or* dishonourable), ignominious, infamous, notorious, shameful *Ant* honorable, reputable, respectable

dis•re•pute \ˌdis-ri-ˈpyüt\ *n* ♦ **:** lack or decline of reputation **:** a state of being held in low esteem

♦ discredit, disgrace, dishonor (*or* dishonour), ignominy, infamy, odium, opprobrium, reproach, shame

dis•re•spect \ˌdis-ri-ˈspekt\ *n* ♦ **:** lack of respect **:** DISCOURTESY

♦ brazenness, discourtesy, impertinence, impudence, incivility, insolence, rudeness

dis•re•spect•ful \ˌdis-ri-ˈspekt-fəl\ *adj* ♦ **:** lacking proper respect in speech or action

♦ discourteous, ill-bred, ill-mannered, impertinent, impolite, inconsiderate, rude, thoughtless, uncivil, ungracious, unmannerly

dis•robe \dis-ˈrōb\ *vb* **:** to strip of clothing or covering **:** UNDRESS

dis•rupt \dis-ˈrəpt\ *vb* **1 :** to break apart **2** ♦ **:** to throw into disorder **3 :** INTERRUPT — **dis•rup•tive** \-ˈrəp-tiv\ *adj*

♦ discompose, disorder, disturb, upset

dis•rup•tion \-ˈrəp-shən\ *n* ♦ **:** the act or process of disrupting **:** the state of being disrupted

♦ dislocation, disturbance, upset

dis•sat•is•fac•tion \di-ˌsa-təs-ˈfak-shən\ *n* ♦ : the quality or state of being dissatisfied

♦ disappointment, dismay, frustration, letdown

dis•sat•is•fied \-fīd\ ♦ : expressing or showing lack of satisfaction : not pleased or satisfied

♦ aggrieved, discontent, discontented, malcontent

dis•sat•is•fy \di-ˈsa-təs-ˌfī\ *vb* ♦ : to fail to satisfy

♦ disappoint, fail, let down

dis•sect \di-ˈsekt\ *vb* **1** ♦ : to divide into parts especially for examination and study **2** ♦ : to analyze and interpret minutely — **dis•sec•tor** \-ˈsek-tər\ *n*

♦ analyze, anatomize, assay, break down, break up

dis•sect•ed *adj* : cut deeply into narrow lobes ⟨a ~ leaf⟩

dis•sec•tion \-ˈsek-shən\ *n* ♦ : the act or process of dissecting : the state of being dissected

♦ analysis, assay, breakdown, breakup

dis•sem•ble \di-ˈsem-bəl\ *vb* **-bled; -bling** **1** ♦ : to hide under or put on a false appearance : conceal facts, intentions, or feelings under some pretense **2** : SIMULATE — **dis•sem•bler** *n*

♦ dissimulate, let on, pretend

dis•sem•i•nate \di-ˈse-mə-ˌnāt\ *vb* **-nat•ed; -nat•ing** ♦ : to spread abroad as if sowing seed ⟨~ ideas⟩ — **dis•sem•i•na•tion** \-ˌse-mə-ˈnā-shən\ *n*

♦ broadcast, circulate, propagate, spread, strew

dis•sen•sion \di-ˈsen-chən\ *n* ♦ : disagreement in opinion

♦ controversy, difference, disagreement, dispute

¹dis•sent \di-ˈsent\ *vb* **1** : to withhold assent **2** : to differ in opinion

²dissent *n* **1 a** ♦ : difference of opinion; *esp* : religious nonconformity **b** ♦ : contentious quarreling **2** : a written statement in which a justice disagrees with the opinion of the majority

♦ [1a] heresy, heterodoxy, nonconformity ♦ [1a, b] conflict, discord, disunity, friction, schism, strife, variance, war, warfare

dis•sent•er \di-ˈsen-tər\ *n* **1** ♦ : one that dissents **2** *cap* : an English Nonconformist

♦ dissident, heretic, nonconformist

dis•ser•ta•tion \ˌdi-sər-ˈtā-shən\ *n* : an extended usually written treatment of a subject; *esp* : one submitted for a doctorate

dis•ser•vice \di-ˈsər-vəs\ *n* ♦ : ill service : INJURY

♦ injury, injustice, raw deal, wrong *Ant* justice

dis•sev•er \di-ˈse-vər\ *vb* ♦ : to set or keep apart : SEPARATE

♦ break up, disconnect, disjoint, dissociate, disunite, divide, divorce, part, resolve, separate, sever, split, sunder, unyoke

dis•si•dence \ˈdi-sə-dəns\ *n* : difference of opinion : DISSENT

¹dis•si•dent \-dənt\ *adj* ♦ : disagreeing especially with an established religious or political system, organization, or belief

♦ heretical, heterodox, nonconforming, nonconformist, nonorthodox, unconventional, unorthodox

²dissident *n* : one that is dissident

dis•sim•i•lar \di-ˈsi-mə-lər\ *adj* ♦ : not like : UNLIKE

♦ different, disparate, distinct, distinctive, distinguishable, diverse, other, unalike, unlike

dis•sim•i•lar•i•ty \di-ˌsi-mə-ˈlar-ə-tē\ *n* : the quality or state of being dissimilar

dis•sim•u•late \di-ˈsi-myə-ˌlāt\ *vb* ♦ : to hide under a false appearance : DISSEMBLE

♦ dissemble, let on, pretend

dis•sim•u•la•tion \di-ˌsi-myə-ˈlā-shən\ *n* ♦ : the act of dissembling or the fact of being dissembled

♦ artifice, craft, craftiness, crookedness, cunning, deceit, deceitfulness, dishonesty, double-dealing, duplicity, guile, wiliness

dis•si•pate \ˈdi-sə-ˌpāt\ *vb* **-pat•ed; -pat•ing** **1** ♦ : to break up and drive off : DISPERSE ⟨the breeze *dissipated* the fog⟩ **2** ♦ : to spend or use up wastefully or foolishly : SQUANDER **3** : to break up and vanish **4** : to be dissolute; *esp* : to drink alcoholic beverages to excess — **dis•si•pat•ed** *adj*

♦ [1] clear out, disband, disperse, scatter ♦ [2] blow, fritter, lavish, misspend, run through, spend, squander, throw away, waste

dis•si•pa•tion \di-sə-ˈpā-shən\ *n* **1** : the action or process of dissipating : the state of being dissipated **2** ♦ : self-indulgence and intemperate living

♦ corruption, debasement, debauchery, decadence, degeneracy, degeneration, degradation, demoralization, depravity, dissoluteness, perversion

dis•so•ci•ate \di-ˈsō-shē-ˌāt\ *vb* **-at•ed; -at•ing** ♦ : to set or keep apart : DISCONNECT — **dis•so•ci•a•tion** \di-ˌsō-shē-ˈā-shən\ *n* — **dis•so•cia•tive** \di-ˈsō-shē-ˌā-tiv\ *adj*

♦ break up, disconnect, disjoint, dissever, disunite, divide, divorce, part, resolve, separate, sever, split, sunder, unyoke

dis•so•lute \ˈdi-sə-ˌlüt\ *adj* ♦ : loose in morals or conduct — **dis•so•lute•ly** *adv*

♦ corrupt, debauched, decadent, degenerate, perverse, perverted, reprobate

dis•so•lute•ness \-nəs\ *n* ♦ : the quality or state of being dissolute

♦ corruption, debasement, debauchery, decadence, degeneracy, degeneration, degradation, demoralization, depravity, dissipation, perversion

dis•so•lu•tion \ˌdi-sə-ˈlü-shən\ *n* **1** : the action or process of dissolving **2** ♦ : separation of a thing into its parts **3** : DECAY; *also* : DEATH **4** : the termination or breaking up of (as an assembly)

♦ breakup, division, partition, schism, separation, split

dis•solve \di-ˈzälv\ *vb* **1** ♦ : to separate into component parts **2** : to pass or cause to pass into solution ⟨sugar ~*s* in water⟩ **3** ♦ : to bring or come to an end ⟨~ parliament⟩ ⟨the organization *dissolved*⟩ **4** : to waste or fade away ⟨his courage *dissolved*⟩ **5** : to be overcome emotionally ⟨~ in tears⟩ **6** : to resolve itself as if by dissolution **7** ♦ : to disperse or disappear or cause to disperse or disappear

♦ [1] break up, disband, disperse ♦ [3] abolish, abrogate, annul, cancel, invalidate, negate, nullify, quash, repeal, rescind, void ♦ [7] disappear, evaporate, fade, flee, go, melt, vanish

dis•so•nance \ˈdi-sə-nəns\ *n* : DISCORD

dis•so•nant \-nənt\ *adj* ♦ : marked by dissonance : DISCORDANT

♦ discordant, inharmonious, unmelodious, unmusical *Ant* harmonious, harmonizing, melodious, musical

dis•suade \di-ˈswād\ *vb* **dis•suad•ed; dis•suad•ing** ♦ : to advise against a course of action : persuade or try to persuade not to do something — **dis•sua•sion** \-ˈswā-zhən\ *n* — **dis•sua•sive** \-ˈswā-siv\ *adj*

♦ deter, discourage, inhibit

dist *abbr* **1** distance **2** district

¹dis•taff \ˈdis-ˌtaf\ *n, pl* **distaffs** \-ˌtafs, -ˌtavz\ **1** : a staff for holding the flax, tow, or wool in spinning **2** : a woman's work or domain **3** : the female branch or side of a family

²distaff *adj* **1** : MATERNAL 2 **2** : FEMALE 1

dis•tal \ˈdist-ᵊl\ *adj* **1** : situated away from the point of attachment or origin especially on the body **2** : of, relating to, or being the surface of a tooth that is farthest from the middle of the front of the jaw — **dis•tal•ly** *adv*

¹dis•tance \ˈdis-təns\ *n* **1** ♦ : measure of separation in space or time **2** : EXPANSE **3** : the full length ⟨go the ~⟩ **4** : spatial remoteness **5** : COLDNESS, RESERVE **6** : DIFFERENCE, DISPARITY **7** : a distant point

♦ lead, length, remove, spread, stretch, way

²distance *vb* **dis•tanced; dis•tanc•ing** : to leave far behind : OUTSTRIP

³distance *adj* : taking place via electronic media linking instructors and students ⟨~ learning⟩

dis•tant \ˈdis-tənt\ *adj* **1** : separate in space : AWAY **2** ♦ : situated at a great distance : FAR-OFF **3** : far apart or behind **4** : not close in relationship ⟨a ~ cousin⟩ **5** : different in kind **6** ♦ : reserved or aloof in personal relationship : COLD ⟨~ politeness⟩ **7** : going a long distance — **dis•tant•ly** *adv* — **dis•tant•ness** *n*

♦ [2] away, far, far-off, remote *Ant* close, near, nearby, nigh ♦ [6] aloof, antisocial, cold, cool, detached, frosty, remote, standoffish, unsociable

dis•taste \(ˌ)dis-ˈtāst\ *n* ♦ : a settled dislike

♦ disgust, loathing, nausea, repugnance, repulsion, revulsion

dis•taste•ful \-fəl\ *adj* **1** ♦ : objectionable because inappropriate, unethical, or offensive to taste **2** ♦ : unpleasant to the sense of taste ⟨~ fruit⟩

♦ [1] bad, disagreeable, nasty, offensive, rotten, sour, uncongenial, unlovely, unpleasant, unwelcome ♦ [2] unappetizing, unsavory *Ant* appetizing, delectable, delicious, palatable, savory, tasty

dis•tem•per \(ˌ)dis-ˈtem-pər\ *n* **:** a bodily disorder usually of a domestic animal; *esp* **:** a contagious often fatal virus disease of dogs
dis•tend \di-ˈstend\ *vb* **:** EXPAND, SWELL — **dis•ten•si•ble** \-ˈsten-sə-bəl\ *adj* — **dis•ten•sion** *or* **dis•ten•tion** \-chən\ *n*
dis•tich \ˈdis-(ˌ)tik\ *n* **:** a unit of two lines of poetry
dis•till *also* **dis•til** \di-ˈstil\ *vb* **dis•tilled; dis•till•ing 1 :** to fall or let fall in drops **2** ♦ **:** to obtain or purify by distillation — **dis•till•er** *n* — **dis•till•ery** \-ˈsti-lə-rē\ *n*

♦ clarify, clear, filter, purify

dis•til•late \ˈdis-tə-ˌlāt, -lət\ *n* **:** a liquid product condensed from vapor during distillation
dis•til•la•tion \ˌdis-tə-ˈlā-shən\ *n* **:** the process of purifying a liquid by successive evaporation and condensation
dis•tinct \di-ˈstiŋkt\ *adj* **1 :** distinguishable to the eye or mind as discrete **:** SEPARATE **2** ♦ **:** presenting a clear unmistakable impression — **dis•tinct•ly** *adv*

♦ apparent, broad, clear, clear-cut, evident, lucid, manifest, obvious, palpable, patent, perspicuous, plain, transparent, unambiguous, unequivocal, unmistakable

dis•tinc•tion \di-ˈstiŋk-shən\ *n* **1** ♦ **:** the distinguishing of a difference; *also* **:** the difference distinguished **2 :** something that distinguishes **3** ♦ **:** special honor or recognition **4** ♦ **:** the quality or state of being distinguished or worthy

♦ [1] contrast, difference, disagreement, discrepancy, disparity, diversity, unlikeness ♦ [1] demarcation, discrimination, separation ♦ [3] acclaim, accolade, award, credit, glory, homage, honor (*or* honour), laurels ♦ [4] excellence, merit, value, virtue

dis•tinc•tive \di-ˈstiŋk-tiv\ *adj* **1 a** ♦ **:** serving to distinguish **b** ♦ **:** set apart from others **2** ♦ **:** having or giving style or distinction — **dis•tinc•tive•ly** *adv*

♦ [1a, 2] characteristic, classic, distinct, individual, peculiar, proper, symptomatic, typical ♦ [1b] different, disparate, dissimilar, distinct, distinguishable, diverse, other, unalike, unlike

dis•tinc•tive•ness \-nəs\ *n* **:** the quality or state of being distinctive
dis•tinct•ness \-nəs\ *n* **:** the quality or state of being distinct
dis•tin•guish \di-ˈstiŋ-gwish\ *vb* **1** ♦ **:** to recognize by some mark or characteristic **2** ♦ **:** to hear or see clearly **:** DISCERN **3** ♦ **:** to make distinctions ⟨∼ between right and wrong⟩ **4 :** to give prominence or distinction to; *also* **:** to take special notice of

♦ [1] behold, descry, discern, espy, eye, look, note, notice, observe, perceive, regard, remark, see, sight, spy, view, witness ♦ [2, 3] differentiate, discern, discriminate, separate *Ant* confuse, mistake, mix (up)

dis•tin•guish•able \di-ˈstiŋ-gwi-shə-bəl\ *adj* ♦ **:** capable of being distinguished

♦ appreciable, detectable, discernible, palpable, perceptible, sensible

dis•tin•guished \-gwisht\ *adj* **1** ♦ **:** marked by eminence or excellence **2 :** befitting an eminent person

♦ eminent, illustrious, noble, notable, noteworthy, outstanding, preeminent, prestigious, signal, star, superior

dis•tort \di-ˈstȯrt\ *vb* **1** ♦ **:** to twist out of the true meaning **2** ♦ **:** to twist out of a natural, normal, or original shape or condition **3 :** to cause to be perceived unnaturally

♦ [1] color (*or* colour), falsify, garble, misinterpret, misrepresent, misstate, pervert, twist, warp ♦ [2] contort, deform, screw, warp

distorted *adj* ♦ **:** twisted or deformed in shape or condition

♦ deformed, malformed, misshapen, monstrous, shapeless

dis•tor•tion \di-ˈstȯr-shən\ *n* **1** ♦ **:** the act of distorting **2 :** the quality or state of being distorted **:** a product of distorting

♦ contortion, deformation

distr *abbr* distribute; distribution
dis•tract \di-ˈstrakt\ *vb* **1 :** to draw (the attention or mind) to a different object **:** DIVERT **2 :** to stir up or confuse with conflicting emotions or motives
dis•tract•ed \di-ˈstrakt-əd\ *adj* ♦ **:** mentally confused, troubled, or remote

♦ absent, absentminded, abstracted, preoccupied

dis•trac•tion \-ˈstrak-shən\ *n* **1** ♦ **:** the act of distracting or the state of being distracted; *esp* **:** mental confusion ⟨driven to ∼⟩ **2** ♦ **:** something that distracts; *esp* **:** AMUSEMENT ⟨a harmless ∼⟩

♦ [1] bafflement, bewilderment, confusion, muddle, mystification, perplexity, puzzlement, whirl ♦ [2] amusement, diversion, entertainment

dis•trait \di-ˈstrā\ *adj* **:** apprehensively divided or withdrawn in attention
dis•traught \di-ˈstrȯt\ *adj* **1** ♦ **:** agitated with doubt or mental conflict **2 :** INSANE

♦ agitated, delirious, frantic, frenzied, hysterical

¹dis•tress \di-ˈstres\ *n* **1** ♦ **:** suffering of body or mind **:** PAIN **2 :** TROUBLE, MISFORTUNE **3** ♦ **:** a condition of danger or desperate need

♦ [1] affliction, agony, anguish, misery, pain, torment, torture, tribulation, woe ♦ [3] danger, jeopardy, peril, risk, trouble

²distress *vb* **1 :** to subject to great strain or difficulties **2** ♦ **:** to cause to worry or be troubled **:** UPSET

♦ agitate, bother, concern, discompose, disquiet, disturb, exercise, freak out, perturb, undo, unhinge, unsettle, upset, worry

dis•tress•ed \-ˈstrest\ *adj* **:** experiencing economic decline or difficulty
dis•tress•ful \-fəl\ *adj* ♦ **:** causing distress **:** full of distress

♦ anxious, nervous, restless, tense, unsettling, upsetting, worrisome

dis•trib•ute \di-ˈstri-byüt\ *vb* **-ut•ed; -ut•ing 1** ♦ **:** to divide among several or many **2 :** to spread out **:** SCATTER; *also* **:** DELIVER **3 :** CLASSIFY

♦ administer, allocate, apportion, deal, dispense, mete, parcel, portion, prorate

dis•tri•bu•tion \ˌdis-trə-ˈbyü-shən\ *n* **1** ♦ **:** the act or process of distributing **2** ♦ **:** the position, arrangement, or frequency of occurrence (as of the members of a group) over an area or throughout a space or unit of time

♦ [1] allocation, dispensation, division, issuance ♦ [2] arrangement, array, disposal, disposition, order, sequence, setup

dis•trib•u•tive \di-ˈstri-byů-tiv\ *adj* **1 :** of or relating to distribution **2 :** of, having, or being the property of producing the same value when an operation is carried out on a whole expression and when it is carried out on each part of an expression with the results then collected together ⟨$a(b + c) = ab + ac$ because multiplication is ∼⟩ — **dis•trib•u•tive•ly** *adv*
dis•trib•u•tor \di-ˈstri-byů-tər\ *n* **1 :** one that distributes **2 :** one that markets goods **3 :** a device for directing current to the spark plugs of an engine
dis•trict \ˈdis-(ˌ)trikt\ *n* **1** ♦ **:** a fixed territorial division (as for administrative or electoral purposes) **2** ♦ **:** an area, region, or section with a distinguishing character

♦ neighborhood (*or* neighbourhood), quarter, section

district attorney *n* **:** the prosecuting attorney of a judicial district
¹dis•trust \dis-ˈtrəst\ *n* ♦ **:** a lack or absence of trust

♦ doubt, incertitude, misgiving, mistrust, skepticism, suspicion, uncertainty

²distrust *vb* ♦ **:** to hold as untrustworthy or unreliable

♦ doubt, mistrust, question, suspect *Ant* trust

dis•trust•ful \-fəl\ *adj* ♦ **:** having or showing distrust

♦ incredulous, leery, mistrustful, skeptical, suspicious ♦ doubtful, dubious, mistrustful, skeptical, suspicious, uncertain, undecided, unsettled, unsure

dis•trust•ful•ly \-fə-lē\ *adv* ♦ **:** in a distrustful manner

♦ askance, dubiously, mistrustfully, suspiciously

dis•turb \di-ˈstərb\ *vb* **1 :** to interfere with **:** INTERRUPT **2** ♦ **:** to alter the position or arrangement of; *also* **:** to upset the natural and especially the ecological balance of **3** ♦ **:** to destroy the tranquillity or composure of **:** make uneasy **4 :** to throw into disorder **5** ♦ **:** to put to inconvenience — **dis•turb•er** *n* — **dis•turb•ing•ly** \-ˈstər-biŋ-lē\ *adv*

♦ [2] budge, dislocate, displace, move, remove, shift, transfer ♦ [3] agitate, bother, concern, discompose, disquiet, distress, exercise, freak out, perturb, undo, unhinge, unsettle, upset, worry *Ant* calm, compose, quiet, settle, soothe, tranquilize ♦ [5] discommode, disoblige, inconvenience, trouble

dis•tur•bance \-ˈstər-bəns\ *n* ♦ : the act of disturbing : the state of being disturbed

♦ dislocation, disruption, upset ♦ commotion, furor, fuss, hubbub

dis•turbed \-ˈstərbd\ *adj* : showing symptoms of emotional illness

dis•unite \ˌdis-yü-ˈnīt\ *vb* ♦ : to destroy the unity of : DIVIDE

♦ break up, disconnect, disjoint, dissever, dissociate, divide, divorce, part, resolve, separate, sever, split, sunder, unyoke

dis•uni•ty \dis-ˈyü-nə-tē\ *n* ♦ : lack of unity; *esp* : DISSENSION

♦ conflict, discord, dissent, friction, schism, strife, variance, war, warfare

dis•use \-ˈyüs\ *n* : a cessation of use or practice

dis•used \-ˈyüzd\ *adj* : no longer used or occupied

¹ditch \ˈdich\ *n* ♦ : a long narrow channel or trench dug in the earth

♦ dike, gutter, trench

²ditch *vb* **1** : to enclose with a ditch; *also* : to dig a ditch in **2** ♦ : to get rid of : DISCARD **3** : to make a forced landing of an airplane on water

♦ cast, discard, dump, fling, jettison, junk, lose, reject, scrap, shed, shuck, slough, throw away, throw out, unload

dith•er \ˈdi-th̲ər\ *n* ♦ : a highly nervous, excited, or agitated state

♦ fluster, fret, fuss, huff, lather, pother, stew, tizzy, twitter

dit•sy *or* **dit•zy** \ˈdit-sē\ *adj* **dits•i•er** *or* **ditz•i•er; -est** : eccentrically silly, giddy, or inane

dit•to \ˈdi-tō\ *n, pl* **dittos** **1** : a thing mentioned previously or above — used to avoid repeating a word **2** : a mark " or " used as a symbol for the word *ditto*

dit•ty \ˈdi-tē\ *n, pl* **ditties** : a short simple song

dit•zy *or* **dit•sy** \ˈdit-sē\ *adj* **ditz•i•er** *or* **dits•i•er; -est** : eccentrically silly, giddy, or inane

di•uret•ic \ˌdī-yə-ˈre-tik\ *adj* : tending to increase urine flow — **diuretic** *n*

di•ur•nal \dī-ˈərn-ᵊl\ *adj* **1** : DAILY **2** : of, relating to, occurring, or active in the daytime

div *abbr* **1** divided **2** dividend **3** division **4** divorced

di•va \ˈdē-və\ *n, pl* **divas** *or* **di•ve** \-ˌvā\ **1** : PRIMA DONNA **2** : a usually glamorous and successful female performer or personality ⟨the current ~ of the popular music world⟩

di•va•gate \ˈdī-və-ˌgāt\ *vb* **-gat•ed; -gat•ing** : to wander or stray from a course or subject : DIVERGE — **di•va•ga•tion** \ˌdī-və-ˈgā-shən\ *n*

di•van \ˈdī-ˌvan, di-ˈvan\ *n* ♦ : a large couch usually without back or arms often designed for use as a bed

♦ couch, davenport, lounge, settee, sofa

¹dive \ˈdīv\ *vb* **dived** \ˈdīvd\ *or* **dove** \ˈdōv\; **dived; div•ing** **1** ♦ : to plunge into water headfirst **2** : SUBMERGE **3** : to come or drop down precipitously **4** : to descend in an airplane at a steep angle **5** : to plunge into some matter or activity **6** : DART, LUNGE — **div•er** *n*

♦ pitch, plunge, sound

²dive *n* **1** ♦ : the act or an instance of diving **2** ♦ : a sharp decline **3** : a disreputable bar or place of amusement

♦ descent, dip, down, drop, fall, plunge

di•verge \də-ˈvərj, dī-\ *vb* **di•verged; di•verg•ing** **1** ♦ : to move or extend in different directions from a common point : draw apart **2** : to differ in character, form, or opinion **3** : DEVIATE **4** : DEFLECT — **di•ver•gence** \-ˈvər-jəns\ *n* — **di•ver•gent** \-jənt\ *adj*

♦ branch, fan, radiate ♦ branch, divide, fork, separate

di•vers \ˈdī-vərz\ *adj* : of differing kinds : VARIOUS

di•verse \dī-ˈvərs, də-, ˈdī-ˌvərs\ *adj* **1** ♦ : differing from one another : UNLIKE **2** : composed of distinct forms or qualities — **di•verse•ly** *adv*

♦ different, disparate, dissimilar, distinct, distinctive, distinguishable, other, unalike, unlike

di•ver•si•fy \də-ˈvər-sə-ˌfī, dī-\ *vb* **-fied; -fy•ing** : to make different or various in form or quality — **di•ver•si•fi•ca•tion** \-ˌvər-sə-fə-ˈkā-shən\ *n*

di•ver•sion \də-ˈvər-zhən, dī-\ *n* **1** : a turning aside from a course, activity, or use : DEVIATION **2** ♦ : something that diverts or amuses

♦ delight, entertainment, fun, pleasure ♦ amusement, distraction, entertainment

di•ver•si•ty \də-ˈvər-sə-tē, dī-\ *n, pl* **-ties** **1** ♦ : the condition of being diverse **2** : an instance of being diverse

♦ assortment, variety ♦ contrast, difference, disagreement, discrepancy, disparity, distinction, unlikeness

di•vert \də-ˈvərt, dī-\ *vb* **1** ♦ : to turn from a course or purpose : DEFLECT **2** : DISTRACT **3** ♦ : to give pleasure to especially by distracting the attention from what burdens or distresses : ENTERTAIN

♦ [1] deflect, swerve, swing, turn, veer, wheel, whip ♦ [3] amuse, disport, entertain, regale

di•vert•ing \də-ˈvər-tiŋ, dī-\ *adj* ♦ : providing amusement or entertainment

♦ amusing, delightful, enjoyable, entertaining, fun, pleasurable

di•vest \dī-ˈvest, də-\ *vb* **1** : to deprive or dispossess especially of property, authority, or rights **2** : to strip especially of clothing, ornament, or equipment

¹di•vide \də-ˈvīd\ *vb* **di•vid•ed; di•vid•ing** **1 a** : to separate into two or more parts, areas, or groups **b** : CLASSIFY **2** : CLEAVE, PART **3** : DISTRIBUTE, APPORTION **4** : to possess or make use of in common : share in **5** ♦ : to cause to be separate, distinct, or apart from one another **6** : to separate into opposing sides or parties **7** : to mark divisions on **8** : to subject to or use in mathematical division; *also* : to be used as a divisor with respect to **9** ♦ : to branch out

♦ [5] break up, disconnect, disjoint, dissever, dissociate, disunite, divorce, part, resolve, separate, sever, split, sunder, unyoke ♦ [9] branch, diverge, fork, separate

²divide *n* : WATERSHED 1

div•i•dend \ˈdi-və-ˌdend\ *n* **1** : an individual share of something distributed **2** ♦ : something in addition to what is expected or strictly due : BONUS **3** : a number to be divided **4** : a sum or fund to be divided or distributed

♦ bonus, extra, lagniappe, perquisite, tip

di•vid•er \də-ˈvī-dər\ *n* **1** : one that divides (as a partition) ⟨room ~⟩ **2** *pl* : COMPASS 5

div•i•na•tion \ˌdi-və-ˈnā-shən\ *n* **1** : the art or practice of using omens or magic powers to foretell the future **2** : unusual insight or intuitive perception

¹di•vine \də-ˈvīn\ *adj* **di•vin•er; -est** **1** ♦ : of, relating to, or being God or a god **2** : supremely good : SUPERB; *also* : HEAVENLY — **di•vine•ly** *adv*

♦ blessed, godlike, heavenly, holy

²divine *n* **1** : a member of the clergy : CLERGYMAN **2** : THEOLOGIAN

³divine *vb* **di•vined; di•vin•ing** **1** : INFER, CONJECTURE **2** ♦ : to predict with assurance or on the basis of mystic knowledge **3** : DOWSE

♦ anticipate, foreknow, foresee

di•vin•er \də-ˈvī-nər\ *n* ♦ : a person who practices divination

♦ augur, forecaster, fortune-teller, futurist, prognosticator, prophet, seer, soothsayer

divining rod *n* : a forked rod believed to reveal the presence of water or minerals by dipping downward when held over a vein

di•vin•i•ty \də-ˈvi-nə-tē\ *n, pl* **-ties** **1** : THEOLOGY **2** ♦ : the quality or state of being divine **3** : a divine being; *esp* : GOD 1

♦ deity, godhead

di•vis•i•ble \də-ˈvi-zə-bəl\ *adj* : capable of being divided — **di•vis•i•bil•i•ty** \-ˌvi-zə-ˈbi-lə-tē\ *n*

di•vi•sion \də-ˈvi-zhən\ *n* **1 a** ♦ : the act or process of dividing : SEPARATION **b** ♦ : the act, process, or an instance of distributing among a number : DISTRIBUTION **2** ♦ : one of the parts or groupings into which a whole is divided **3** : DISAGREEMENT, DISUNITY **4** : something that divides or separates **5** : the mathematical operation of finding how many times one number is contained in another **6** : a large self-contained military unit **7** ♦ : an administrative or operating unit of a governmental, business, or educational organization — **di•vi•sion•al** \-ˈvi-zhə-nəl\ *adj*

♦ [1a] breakup, dissolution, partition, schism, separation, split ♦ [1b] allocation, dispensation, distribution, issuance ♦ [2] bracket, category, class, family, grade, group, kind, order, set, species, type ♦ [7] bureau, department, desk, office

di•vi•sive \də-ˈvī-siv, -ˈvi-ziv\ *adj* : creating disunity or dissension — **di•vi•sive•ly** *adv* — **di•vi•sive•ness** *n*

di•vi•sor \də-ˈvī-zər\ *n* : the number by which a dividend is divided

¹di•vorce \də-ˈvōrs\ *n* **1 :** an act or instance of legally dissolving a marriage **2 :** SEPARATION, SEVERANCE — **di•vorce•ment** *n*
²divorce *vb* **1 :** to end marriage with (one's spouse) by divorce ⟨*divorced* his wife⟩ **2 :** to dissolve the marriage contract between ⟨they were *divorced* last year⟩ **3** ♦ **:** to make or keep separate

♦ break up, disconnect, disjoint, dissever, dissociate, disunite, divide, part, resolve, separate, sever, split, sunder, unyoke

di•vor•cé \də-ˌvōr-ˈsā\ *n* **:** a divorced man
di•vor•cée \də-ˌvōr-ˈsā, -ˈsē\ *n* **:** a divorced woman
div•ot \ˈdi-vət\ *n* **:** a piece of turf dug from a golf fairway in making a stroke
di•vulge \də-ˈvəlj, dī-\ *vb* **di•vulged; di•vulg•ing** ♦ **:** to make known (as a confidence or secret) **:** REVEAL

♦ bare, disclose, discover, expose, reveal, spill, tell, unbosom, uncloak, uncover, unmask, unveil

Dix•ie•land \ˈdik-sē-ˌland\ *n* **:** jazz music in duple time played in a style developed in New Orleans
diz•zy \ˈdi-zē\ *adj* **diz•zi•er; -est 1 :** FOOLISH, SILLY **2** ♦ **:** having a sensation of whirling **:** GIDDY **3 a :** causing or caused by giddiness **b** ♦ **:** confusing or feeling confused mentally **4** ♦ **:** extremely rapid — **diz•zi•ly** \-zə-lē\ *adv* — **diz•zi•ness** \-zē-nəs\ *n*

♦ [2] giddy, light-headed ♦ [3b] confused, stunned ***Ant*** clear-headed ♦ [4] breakneck, breathless, brisk, fast, fleet, hasty, lightning, nippy, quick, rapid, rattling, snappy, speedy, swift

DJ *n, often not cap* **:** DISC JOCKEY
dk *abbr* **1** dark **2** deck **3** dock
dl *abbr* deciliter
DLitt *or* **DLit** *abbr* doctor of letters; doctor of literature
DLO *abbr* dead letter office
dm *abbr* decimeter
DMD *abbr* doctor of dental medicine
DMZ *abbr* demilitarized zone
dn *abbr* down
DNA \ˌdē-(ˌ)en-ˈā\ *n* **:** any of various nucleic acids that are usually the molecular basis of heredity and are localized especially in cell nuclei
DNR *abbr* do not resuscitate
¹do \ˈdü\ *vb* **did** \ˈdid\; **done** \ˈdən\; **do•ing; does** \ˈdəz\ **1** ♦ **:** to bring to pass **:** ACCOMPLISH **2 :** ACT, BEHAVE ⟨~ as I say⟩ **3 :** to be active or busy ⟨up and ~*ing*⟩ **4 :** HAPPEN ⟨what's ~*ing*?⟩ **5 :** to be engaged in the study or practice of **:** work at ⟨he *does* tailoring⟩ **6 :** COOK ⟨steak *done* rare⟩ **7 :** to put in order (as by cleaning or arranging) ⟨~ the dishes⟩ **8 :** to furnish with something ornamental **:** DECORATE ⟨*did* the hall in blue⟩ **9 :** GET ALONG ⟨~ well in school⟩ **10** ♦ **:** to deal with something successfully **:** MANAGE **11 :** RENDER ⟨sleep will ~ you good⟩ **12 :** to bring to an end **:** FINISH ⟨when he had *done*⟩ **13 :** EXERT ⟨*did* my best⟩ **14 :** PRODUCE ⟨*did* a poem⟩ **15 :** to play the part of **16 :** CHEAT ⟨*did* him out of his share⟩ **17 :** TRAVERSE, TOUR **18 :** TRAVEL **19 :** to spend or serve out a period of time ⟨*did* ten years in prison⟩ **20** ♦ **:** to serve the needs of **21** ♦ **:** to be fitting or proper **22 :** USE ⟨doesn't ~ drugs⟩ **23** — used as an auxiliary verb (1) before the subject in an interrogative sentence ⟨*does* he work?⟩ and after some adverbs ⟨never *did* she say so⟩, (2) in a negative statement ⟨I *don't* know⟩, (3) for emphasis ⟨you ~ know⟩, and (4) as a substitute for a preceding predicate ⟨he works harder than I ~⟩ — **do away with 1 :** to put an end to **2 :** DESTROY, KILL — **do by :** to deal with **:** TREAT ⟨*did* right *by* her⟩ — **do for :** to bring about the death or ruin of — **do the trick :** to produce a desired result

♦ [1] accomplish, achieve, carry out, commit, compass, execute, follow through, make, perform ♦ [10] cope, fare, get along, make out, manage, shift ♦ [20, 21] befit, fit, go, serve, suit

²do *n* **1 :** AFFAIR, PARTY **2 :** a command or entreaty to do something ⟨list of ~*s* and don'ts⟩ **3 :** HAIRDO
³do *abbr* ditto
DOA *abbr* dead on arrival
do•able \ˈdü-ə-bəl\ *adj* ♦ **:** that can be done **:** PRACTICABLE

♦ achievable, attainable, feasible, possible, practicable, realizable, viable, workable

DOB *abbr* date of birth
dob•bin \ˈdä-bən\ *n* **1 :** a farm horse **2 :** a quiet plodding horse
Do•ber•man pin•scher \ˈdō-bər-mən-ˈpin-chər\ *n* **:** any of a German breed of short-haired medium-sized dogs
¹doc \ˈdäk\ *n* **:** DOCTOR
²doc *abbr* document

do•cent \ˈdōs-ᵊnt, dōt-ˈsent\ *n* **:** TEACHER, LECTURER; *also* **:** a person who leads a guided tour
doc•ile \ˈdä-səl\ *adj* ♦ **:** easily taught, led, or managed **:** TRACTABLE

♦ amenable, compliant, conformable, obedient, submissive, tractable

do•cil•i•ty \dä-ˈsi-lə-tē\ *n* ♦ **:** the quality or state of being docile

♦ compliance, deference, obedience

¹dock \ˈdäk\ *n* **:** any of a genus of coarse weedy herbs related to buckwheat
²dock *vb* **1 :** to cut off the end of **:** cut short **2 :** to take away a part of **:** deduct from ⟨~ a worker's wages⟩
³dock *n* **1 :** an artificial basin to receive ships **2 :** ²SLIP 2 **3** ♦ **:** a wharf or platform for loading or unloading materials

♦ float, jetty, landing, levee, pier, quay, wharf

⁴dock *vb* **1** ♦ **:** to bring or come into dock **2 :** to join (as two spacecraft) mechanically in space

♦ disembark, land, moor, tie up

⁵dock *n* **:** the place in a court where a prisoner stands or sits during trial
dock•age \ˈdä-kij\ *n* **:** docking facilities
dock•et \ˈdä-kət\ *n* **1 :** a formal abridged record of the proceedings in a legal action; *also* **:** a register of such records **2 :** a list of legal causes to be tried **3** ♦ **:** a calendar of matters to be acted on **:** AGENDA **4 :** a label attached to a document containing identification or directions — **docket** *vb*

♦ agenda, calendar, program, schedule, timetable

dock•hand \ˈdäk-ˌhand\ *n* **:** LONGSHOREMAN
dock•work•er \-ˌwər-kər\ *n* **:** LONGSHOREMAN
dock•yard \-ˌyärd\ *n* **:** SHIPYARD
¹doc•tor \ˈdäk-tər\ *n* **1 :** a person holding one of the highest academic degrees (as a PhD) conferred by a university **2 :** a person skilled in healing arts; *esp* **:** one (as a physician, dentist, or veterinarian) academically and legally qualified to practice **3 :** a person who restores or repairs things — **doc•tor•al** \-tə-rəl\ *adj*
²doctor *vb* **1 :** to give medical treatment to **2 :** to practice medicine **3** ♦ **:** to restore to good condition **:** REPAIR **4 :** to adapt or modify for a desired end **5 :** to alter deceptively

♦ fix, mend, patch, recondition, renovate, repair, revamp

doc•tor•ate \ˈdäk-tə-rət\ *n* **:** the degree, title, or rank of a doctor
doc•tri•naire \ˌdäk-trə-ˈnar\ *n* **:** one who attempts to put an abstract theory into effect without regard to practical difficulties — **doctrinaire** *adj*
doc•trine \ˈdäk-trən\ *n* **1 :** something that is taught **2** ♦ **:** a principle or position or the body of principles in a branch of knowledge or system of belief — **doc•tri•nal** \-trən-ᵊl\ *adj*

♦ creed, gospel, ideology, philosophy

docu•dra•ma \ˈdä-kyə-ˌdrä-mə, -ˌdra-\ *n* **:** a drama for television, motion pictures, or theater that deals freely with historical events
¹doc•u•ment \ˈdä-kyə-mənt\ *n* **1 :** a paper that furnishes information, proof, or support of something else **2 :** a computer file containing information input by a computer user usually via a word processor
²doc•u•ment \-ˌment\ *vb* ♦ **:** to furnish documentary evidence of — **doc•u•ment•er** *n*

♦ demonstrate, establish, prove, substantiate, validate

doc•u•men•ta•ry \ˌdä-kyə-ˈmen-tə-rē\ *adj* **1 :** consisting of documents; *also* **:** being in writing ⟨~ proof⟩ **2 a :** giving a factual presentation in artistic form ⟨a ~ movie⟩ **b** ♦ **:** of or relating to facts — **documentary** *n*

♦ factual, hard, historical, literal, matter-of-fact, nonfictional, objective, true

doc•u•men•ta•tion \ˌdä-kyə-mən-ˈtā-shən\ *n* **1 :** the act or an instance of furnishing or authenticating with documents **2 a :** the provision of documents in substantiation **b** ♦ **:** documentary evidence

♦ attestation, confirmation, corroboration, evidence, proof, substantiation, testament, testimony, validation, witness

DOD *abbr* Department of Defense
¹dod•der \ˈdä-dər\ *n* **:** any of a genus of leafless parasitic twining vines that are highly deficient in chlorophyll
²dodder *vb* **dod•dered; dod•der•ing 1 :** to tremble or shake usually from age **2** ♦ **:** to progress feebly and unsteadily

♦ careen, lurch, reel, stagger, teeter, totter

[1]dodge \ˈdäj\ *n* **1 :** an act of evading by sudden bodily movement **2** ♦ **:** an artful device to evade, deceive, or trick **3 :** EXPEDIENT

♦ artifice, device, gimmick, jig, ploy, scheme, sleight, stratagem, trick, wile

[2]dodge *vb* **dodged; dodg•ing 1** ♦ **:** to evade usually by trickery **2** ♦ **:** to move suddenly aside; *also* **:** to avoid or evade by so doing

♦ [1] avoid, duck, elude, escape, eschew, evade, shake, shirk, shun ♦ [2] duck, sidestep

dodg•er \ˈdä-jər\ *n* ♦ **:** one that dodges; *esp* **:** one who uses tricky devices

♦ cheat, hoaxer, shark, sharper, swindler, trickster

do•do \ˈdō-dō\ *n, pl* **dodoes** *or* **dodos 1 :** an extinct heavy flightless bird of the island of Mauritius related to the pigeons and larger than a turkey **2** ♦ **:** one hopelessly behind the times **3** ♦ **:** a stupid person

♦ [2] antediluvian, fogy, fossil, fuddy-duddy, reactionary ♦ [3] blockhead, dope, dummy, idiot, imbecile, jackass, moron, numskull

doe \ˈdō\ *n, pl* **does** *or* **doe :** an adult female of various mammals (as a deer, rabbit, or kangaroo) of which the male is called *buck*
DOE *abbr* Department of Energy
do•er \ˈdü-ər\ *n* **:** one that does
does *pres 3d sing of* DO; *pl of* DOE
doff \ˈdäf\ *vb* **1 :** to take off (the hat) in greeting or as a sign of respect **2 :** to rid oneself of **3** ♦ **:** to remove (an article of wear) from the body

♦ peel, put off, remove, take off

[1]dog \ˈdȯg\ *n* **1 :** a flesh-eating domestic mammal related to the wolves; *esp* **:** a male of this animal **2 :** a worthless or contemptible person **3 :** FELLOW, CHAP ⟨you lucky ~⟩ **4 :** a mechanical device for holding something **5 :** uncharacteristic or affected stylishness or dignity ⟨put on the ~⟩ **6** *pl* **:** RUIN ⟨gone to the ~*s*⟩
[2]dog *vb* **dogged; dog•ging 1** ♦ **:** to hunt or track like a hound **2 :** to worry as if by pursuit with dogs **:** PLAGUE

♦ chase, follow, hound, pursue, shadow, tag, tail, trace, track, trail

dog•bane \ˈdȯg-ˌbān\ *n* **:** any of a genus of mostly poisonous herbs with milky juice and often showy flowers
dog•cart \-ˌkärt\ *n* **:** a light one-horse carriage with two seats back to back
dog•catch•er \-ˌka-chər, -ˌke-\ *n* **:** a community official assigned to catch and dispose of stray dogs
dog–ear \ˈdȯg-ˌir\ *n* **:** the turned-down corner of a leaf of a book — **dog–ear** *vb*
dog–eared \ˈdȯg-ˌird\ *adj* **:** ill-kept **:** SHABBY
dog•fight \ˈdȯg-ˌfīt\ *n* **:** a fight between fighter planes at close range
dog•fish \-ˌfish\ *n* **:** any of various small usually bottom-dwelling sharks
dog•ged \ˈdȯ-gəd\ *adj* ♦ **:** stubbornly determined — **dog•ged•ly** *adv*

♦ insistent, patient, persevering, persistent, pertinacious, tenacious ♦ determined, grim, implacable, relentless, unflinching, unrelenting, unyielding

dog•ged•ness \-nəs\ *n* **:** the quality or state of being dogged
dog•ger•el \ˈdȯ-gə-rəl\ *n* **:** verse that is loosely styled and irregular in measure especially for comic effect
dog•gie bag *or* **doggy bag** \ˈdȯ-gē-\ *n* **:** a container for carrying home leftover food from a restaurant meal
[1]dog•gy *or* **dog•gie** \ˈdȯ-gē\ *n, pl* **doggies :** a usually small dog
[2]dog•gy *adj* **dog•gi•er; -est :** of or resembling a dog ⟨a ~ odor⟩
dog•house \ˈdȯg-ˌhau̇s\ *n* **:** a shelter for a dog — **in the doghouse :** in a state of disfavor
do•gie \ˈdō-gē\ *n, chiefly West* **:** a motherless calf in a range herd
dog•leg \ˈdȯg-ˌleg\ *n* **:** a sharp bend or angle (as in a road or a golf fairway) — **dogleg** *vb*
dog•ma \ˈdȯg-mə\ *n, pl* **dogmas** *also* **dog•ma•ta** \-mə-tə\ **1 :** a tenet or code of tenets **2 :** a doctrine or body of doctrines formally proclaimed by a church
dog•ma•tism \ˈdȯg-mə-ˌti-zəm\ *n* **:** positiveness in stating matters of opinion especially when unwarranted or arrogant — **dog•mat•ic** \dȯg-ˈma-tik\ *adj* — **dog•mat•i•cal•ly** \-ti-k(ə-)lē\ *adv*
do–good•er \ˈdü-ˌgu̇-dər\ *n* **:** an earnest often naive humanitarian or reformer

dog•tooth violet \ˈdȯg-ˌtüth-\ *n* **:** any of a genus of small spring-flowering bulbous herbs related to the lilies
dog•trot \ˈdȯg-ˌträt\ *n* **:** a gentle trot — **dogtrot** *vb*
dog•wood \ˈdȯg-ˌwu̇d\ *n* **:** any of a genus of trees and shrubs having heads of small flowers often with showy white, pink, or red bracts
doi•ly \ˈdȯi-lē\ *n, pl* **doilies :** a small often decorative mat
do in *vb* **1 :** to bring about the defeat or destruction of **:** RUIN **2** ♦ **:** to deprive of life **:** KILL **3** ♦ **:** to tire extremely or completely **:** EXHAUST ⟨the climb *did* him *in*⟩ **4 :** CHEAT

♦ [2] destroy, dispatch, fell, kill, slay ♦ [3] burn out, drain, exhaust, fag, fatigue, tire, tucker, wash out, wear, wear out, weary

do•ing \ˈdü-iŋ\ *n* **1** ♦ **:** the act or result of performing, executing, or creating ⟨to achieve those plans will take some ~⟩ **2 do•ings** \ˈdü-iŋz\ *pl* **:** things that go on or occur ⟨the daily ~*s* in the market⟩

♦ deed, exploit, feat, thing

do–it–yourself *n* **:** the activity of doing or making something without professional training or help — **do–it–your•self•er** *n*
dol *abbr* dollar
dol•drums \ˈdōl-drəmz, ˈdäl-\ *n pl* **1** ♦ **:** a spell of listlessness or despondency **2** *often cap* **:** a part of the ocean near the equator known for calms **3 :** a state or period of inactivity, stagnation, or slump

♦ blues, dejection, depression, desolation, despondency, dumps, forlornness, gloom, heartsickness, melancholy, sadness ♦ boredom, ennui, listlessness, restlessness, tedium, tiredness, weariness

[1]dole \ˈdōl\ *n* **1** ♦ **:** a distribution especially of food, money, or clothing to the needy; *also* **:** something so distributed **2 :** a grant of government funds to the unemployed

♦ charity, philanthropy

[2]dole *vb* **doled; dol•ing :** to give or distribute as a charity — usually used with *out*
dole•ful \ˈdōl-fəl\ *adj* **:** full of grief **:** SAD — **dole•ful•ly** *adv*
dole out *vb* **1** ♦ **:** to give or deliver in small portions **2 :** to give or dispense freely **:** DISH OUT

♦ administer, allocate, apportion, deal, dispense, distribute, mete, parcel, portion, prorate

doll \ˈdäl, ˈdȯl\ *n* **1 :** a small figure of a human being used especially as a child's plaything **2** ♦ **:** a pretty woman **3 :** an attractive person — **doll•ish** \ˈdä-lish, ˈdȯ-\ *adj*

♦ girl, lass, maid, maiden, miss

dol•lar \ˈdä-lər\ *n* **1 :** a basic monetary unit of any of several countries (as the U.S., Canada, Australia, and Singapore) **2 :** a coin, note, or token representing one dollar
dol•lop \ˈdä-ləp\ *n* **1 :** LUMP, GLOB **2 :** PORTION 1 — **dollop** *vb*
doll up *vb* **1 :** to dress elegantly or extravagantly **2 :** to make more attractive **3 :** to get dolled up
dol•ly \ˈdä-lē\ *n, pl* **dollies :** a small cart or wheeled platform (as for a television or movie camera)
dol•men \ˈdōl-mən, ˈdäl-\ *n* **:** a prehistoric monument consisting of two or more upright stones supporting a horizontal stone slab
do•lo•mite \ˈdō-lə-ˌmīt, ˈdä-\ *n* **:** a mineral found in broad layers as a compact limestone
do•lor *or Can and Brit* **do•lour** \ˈdō-lər, ˈdä-\ *n* ♦ **:** mental suffering or anguish **:** SORROW

♦ affliction, anguish, grief, heartache, sorrow, woe

do•lor•ous \ˈdō-lə-rəs, ˈdä-\ *adj* ♦ **:** causing, marked by, or expressing misery or grief — **do•lor•ous•ly** *adv*

♦ funeral, lugubrious, mournful, plaintive, regretful, rueful, sorrowful, weeping, woeful

dol•phin \ˈdäl-fən\ *n* **1 :** any of various small whales with conical teeth and an elongated beaklike snout **2 :** either of two active food fishes of tropical and temperate seas
dolt \ˈdōlt\ *n* ♦ **:** a stupid individual

♦ blockhead, dope, dummy, idiot, imbecile, jackass, moron, numskull

dolt•ish \ˈdōl-tish\ *adj* **:** like a dolt **:** STUPID
dolt•ish•ness \-nəs\ *n* **:** the quality or state of being doltish **:** STUPIDITY
dom *abbr* **1** domestic **2** dominant **3** dominion
-dom *n suffix* **1 :** dignity **:** office ⟨duke*dom*⟩ **2 :** realm **:** jurisdiction ⟨king*dom*⟩ **3 :** state or fact of being ⟨free*dom*⟩ **4 :** those

having a (specified) office, occupation, interest, or character ⟨official*dom*⟩

do·main \dō-ˈmān\ *n* **1 :** complete and absolute ownership of land **2 :** land completely owned **3 :** a territory over which dominion is exercised **4** ♦ **:** a sphere of knowledge, influence, or activity ⟨the ~ of science⟩ **5 :** a subdivision of the Internet made up of computers whose URLs share a characteristic abbreviation (as *com* or *gov*)

♦ area, arena, demesne, department, discipline, field, line, province, realm, specialty, sphere

domain name *n* **:** a sequence of characters (as Merriam-Webster.com) that specifies a group of online resources and forms part of its URL

dome \ˈdōm\ *n* **1 :** a large hemispherical roof or ceiling **2 :** a structure or natural formation that resembles the dome of a building **3 :** a roofed sports stadium — **dome** *vb*

¹do·mes·tic \də-ˈmes-tik\ *adj* **1 :** living near or about human habitations **2 :** reduced from a state of native wildness especially so as to be tractable and useful to humans **:** DOMESTICATED **3 :** relating and limited to one's own country or the country under consideration **4 :** of or relating to the household or the family **5 :** devoted to home duties and pleasures **6 :** INDIGENOUS — **do·mes·ti·cal·ly** \-ti-k(ə-)lē\ *adv*

²domestic *n* ♦ **:** a household servant

♦ girl, housemaid, maid, maidservant

do·mes·ti·cate \də-ˈmes-ti-ˌkāt\ *vb* **-cat·ed; -cat·ing :** to adapt to life in association with and to the use of humans — **do·mes·ti·ca·tion** \-ˌmes-ti-ˈkā-shən\ *n*

do·mes·tic·i·ty \ˌdō-ˌmes-ˈti-sə-tē, də-\ *n, pl* **-ties** **1 :** the quality or state of being domestic or domesticated **2 :** domestic activities or life

domestic violence *n* **:** the inflicting of injury by one family or household member on another

¹do·mi·cile \ˈdä-mə-ˌsīl, ˈdō-; ˈdä-mə-səl\ *n* ♦ **:** a dwelling place **:** HOME — **dom·i·cil·i·ary** \ˌdä-mə-ˈsi-lē-ˌer-ē, ˌdō-\ *adj*

♦ abode, dwelling, home, house, lodging, quarters, residence

²domicile *vb* ♦ **:** to establish in or provide with a domicile

♦ accommodate, billet, chamber, harbor (*or* harbour), house, lodge, put up, quarter, roof, shelter, take in

dom·i·nance \ˈdä-mə-nəns\ *n* **1** ♦ **:** dominant position especially in a social hierarchy **2 :** the property of one of a pair of alleles or traits that suppresses expression of the other when both are present

♦ ascendancy, dominion, predominance, preeminence, supremacy

¹dom·i·nant \-nənt\ *adj* **1** ♦ **:** controlling or prevailing over all others **2 :** overlooking from a high position **3 :** exhibiting genetic dominance

♦ arch, cardinal, central, chief, first, foremost, grand, key, main, paramount, predominant, preeminent, premier, primary, principal, sovereign, supreme

²dominant *n* **:** a dominant gene or trait

dom·i·nate \ˈdä-mə-ˌnāt\ *vb* **-nat·ed; -nat·ing** **1** ♦ **:** to exert control, direction, or influence on **2** ♦ **:** to have a commanding position or controlling power over **3 :** to rise high above in a position suggesting power to dominate — **dom·i·na·tor** \-ˌnā-tər\ *n*

♦ [1] conquer, overpower, subdue, subject, vanquish ♦ [2] boss, captain, command, head, lead, spearhead

dom·i·na·tion \ˌdä-mə-ˈnā-shən\ *n* **1 :** supremacy or preeminence over another **2** ♦ **:** exercise of mastery, ruling power, or preponderant influence

♦ conquest, subjection

dom·i·na·trix \ˌdä-mə-ˈnā-triks\ *n, pl* **-trices** \-ˈnā-trə-ˌsēz, -nə-ˈtrī-sēz\ **:** a woman who dominates her sexual partner; *also* **:** a dominating woman

dom·i·neer \ˌdä-mə-ˈnir\ *vb* **1 :** to rule in an arrogant manner **2 :** to be overbearing

dom·i·neer·ing \-ˈnir-iŋ\ *adj* ♦ **:** inclined to exercise arbitrary and overbearing control over others

♦ authoritarian, autocratic, bossy, despotic, dictatorial, imperious, masterful, overbearing, peremptory, tyrannical, tyrannous

do·mi·nie *1 usu* ˈdä-mə-nē, *2 usu* ˈdō-\ *n* **1** *chiefly Scot* **:** SCHOOLMASTER **2 :** a member of the clergy **:** CLERGYMAN

do·min·ion \də-ˈmin-yən\ *n* **1 :** DOMAIN **2** ♦ **:** supreme authority **3** *often cap* **:** a self-governing nation of the Commonwealth

♦ ascendancy, dominance, predominance, preeminence, supremacy

dom·i·no \ˈdä-mə-ˌnō\ *n, pl* **-noes** *or* **-nos** **1 :** a long loose hooded cloak usually worn with a half mask as a masquerade costume **2 :** a flat rectangular block used as a piece in a game (**dominoes**)

¹don \ˈdän\ *vb* **donned; don·ning** ♦ **:** to put on (as clothes)

♦ put on, slip, throw

²don *n* **1 :** a Spanish nobleman or gentleman — used as a title prefixed to the first name **2 :** a head, tutor, or fellow in an English university

do·ña \ˈdō-nyə\ *n* **:** a Spanish woman of rank — used as a title prefixed to the first name

do·nate \ˈdō-ˌnāt\ *vb* **do·nat·ed; do·nat·ing** **1** ♦ **:** to make a gift of **:** CONTRIBUTE **2 :** to make a donation

♦ bestow, contribute, give, present

do·na·tion \dō-ˈnā-shən\ *n* **1 :** the making of a gift especially to a charity **2** ♦ **:** a free contribution

♦ alms, benefaction, beneficence, charity, contribution, philanthropy ♦ bestowal, freebie, gift, lagniappe, largesse, present

¹done \ˈdən\ *past part of* DO

²done *adj* **1 :** doomed to failure, defeat, or death **2** ♦ **:** gone by **:** OVER ⟨when day is ~⟩ **3 :** cooked sufficiently **4 :** conformable to social convention

♦ complete, down, over, through, up

done deal *n* **:** FAIT ACCOMPLI

don·key \ˈdäŋ-kē, ˈdəŋ-\ *n, pl* **donkeys** **1** ♦ **:** a sturdy and patient domestic mammal classified with the asses **2 :** a stupid or obstinate person

♦ ass, jackass

don·ny·brook \ˈdä-nē-ˌbrůk\ *n, often cap* **:** an uproarious brawl

do·nor \ˈdō-nər\ *n* **:** one that gives, donates, or presents

donut *var of* DOUGHNUT

doo·dad \ˈdü-ˌdad\ *n* **:** an often small article whose common name is unknown or forgotten

doo·dle \ˈdü-dᵊl\ *vb* **doo·dled; doo·dling :** to draw or scribble aimlessly while occupied with something else — **doodle** *n* — **doo·dler** *n*

¹doom \ˈdüm\ *n* **1** ♦ **:** a judicial decision; *esp* **:** a judicial condemnation or sentence **2** ♦ **:** something to which a person or thing is destined **:** DESTINY **3 a :** RUIN **b :** a permanent cessation of all vital functions **:** DEATH

♦ [1] finding, holding, judgment (*or* judgement), ruling, sentence ♦ [2] circumstance, destiny, fate, fortune, lot, portion

²doom *vb* **1** ♦ **:** to give judgment against **:** CONDEMN **2** ♦ **:** to fix the fate of **:** DESTINE

♦ [1] condemn, damn, sentence ♦ [2] destine, foredoom, foreordain, ordain, predestine

dooms·day \ˈdümz-ˌdā\ *n* **:** JUDGMENT DAY

door \ˈdōr\ *n* **1** ♦ **:** a usually swinging or sliding barrier by which an entry is closed and opened; *also* **:** a similar part of a piece of furniture **2** ♦ **:** the opening that a door closes **:** DOORWAY **3 :** a means of access or participation **:** OPPORTUNITY

♦ [1] gate, hatch, portal ♦ [2] doorway, entrance, gate, gateway, way

door·keep·er \-ˌkē-pər\ *n* ♦ **:** a person who tends a door

♦ gatekeeper, janitor

door·knob \-ˌnäb\ *n* **:** a knob that when turned releases a door latch

door·man \-ˌman, -mən\ *n* **:** a usually uniformed attendant at the door of a building (as a hotel)

door·mat \-ˌmat\ *n* **:** a mat placed before or inside a door for wiping dirt from the shoes

door·plate \-ˌplāt\ *n* **:** a nameplate on a door

door·step \-ˌstep\ *n* **:** a step or series of steps before an outer door

door·way \-ˌwā\ *n* **1** ♦ **:** the opening that a door closes **2** ♦ **:** a means of access or participation

♦ [1] door, entrance, gate, gateway, way ♦ [2] access, admission, entrance, entrée, gateway

do·pa \ˈdō-pə\ *n* **:** a form of an amino acid that is used especially in the treatment of Parkinson's disease

do·pa·mine \ˈdō-pə-ˌmēn\ *n* **:** an organic compound that occurs especially as a neurotransmitter in the brain

¹dope \ˈdōp\ *n* **1 :** a preparation for giving a desired quality **2 :** an illicit, habit-forming, or narcotic drug; *esp* : MARIJUANA **3** ♦ : a stupid person **4** ♦ : information especially from a reliable source

♦ [3] blockhead, dummy, idiot, imbecile, jackass, moron, numskull ♦ [4] lowdown, scoop, tip

²dope *vb* **doped; dop•ing 1** : to treat with dope; *esp* : to give a narcotic to **2** ♦ : to find a solution, explanation, or answer for : FIGURE OUT — usually used with *out* **3** : to take dope

♦ *usu* **dope out** answer, break, crack, figure out, puzzle, resolve, riddle, solve, unravel, work, work out

dop•er *n* ♦ : an habitual or frequent drug user

♦ addict, fiend, user

dop•ey *also* **dopy** \ˈdō-pē\ *adj* **dop•i•er; -est 1** : dulled by alcohol or a narcotic **2** : SLUGGISH **3** : slow of mind : STUPID; *also* : complacently or inanely foolish

dop•i•ness \-nəs\ *n* ♦ : the quality or state of being dopey

♦ denseness, foolishness, imbecility, mindlessness, obtuseness, stupidity, vacuity

doping *n* : the use of a substance or technique to illegally improve athletic performance

Dopp•ler effect \ˈdä-plər-\ *n* : a change in the frequency at which waves (as of sound) reach an observer from a source in motion with respect to the observer

do–rag \ˈdü-ˌrag\ *n* ♦ : a kerchief worn especially to cover the hair

♦ babushka, bandanna, kerchief, mantilla

dork \ˈdȯrk\ *n, slang* : NERD; *also* : JERK 2

dorm \ˈdȯrm\ *n* : DORMITORY

dor•man•cy \-mən-sē\ *n* ♦ : the quality or state of being dormant

♦ abeyance, doldrums, latency, quiescence, suspension ♦ idleness, inaction, inactivity, inertness, quiescence

dor•mant \ˈdȯr-mənt\ *adj* **1** ♦ : marked by a suspension of activity **2** ♦ : sleeping or drowsing

♦ [1] dead, fallow, free, idle, inactive, inert, inoperative, latent, off, vacant ♦ [2] asleep

dor•mer \ˈdȯr-mər\ *n* : a window built upright in a sloping roof; *also* : the roofed structure containing such a window

dor•mi•to•ry \ˈdȯr-mə-ˌtōr-ē\ *n, pl* **-ries 1** : a room for sleeping; *esp* : a large room containing a number of beds **2** : a residence hall providing sleeping rooms

dor•mouse \ˈdȯr-ˌmau̇s\ *n* : any of numerous Old World rodents that resemble small squirrels

dor•sal \ˈdȯr-səl\ *adj* : of, relating to, or located near or on the surface of the body that in humans is the back but in most other animals is the upper surface — **dor•sal•ly** *adv*

do•ry \ˈdōr-ē\ *n, pl* **dories** : a flat-bottomed boat with high flaring sides and a sharp bow

DOS *abbr* disk operating system

¹dose \ˈdōs\ *n* **1** : a measured quantity (as of medicine) to be taken or administered at one time **2** : the quantity of radiation administered or absorbed — **dos•age** \ˈdō-sij\ *n*

²dose *vb* **dosed; dos•ing 1** : to give in doses **2** : to give medicine to

do•sim•e•ter \dō-ˈsi-mə-tər\ *n* : a device for measuring doses of radiations (as X-rays) — **do•sim•e•try** \-mə-trē\ *n*

dos•sier \ˈdȯs-ˌyā, ˈdȯ-sē-ˌā\ *n* : a file containing detailed records on a particular person or subject

¹dot \ˈdät\ *n* **1** ♦ : a small spot : SPECK **2** : a small round mark **3** : a precise point especially in time ⟨be here on the ~⟩

♦ blotch, fleck, mottle, patch, point, speck, spot

²dot *vb* **dot•ted; dot•ting 1** : to mark with a dot ⟨~ an *i*⟩ **2** ♦ : to cover with or as if with dots — **dot•ter** *n*

♦ blotch, dapple, fleck, freckle, mottle, pepper, speck, spot, sprinkle, stipple

DOT *abbr* Department of Transportation

dot•age \ˈdō-tij\ *n* : feebleness of mind especially in old age : SENILITY

dot•ard \-tərd\ *n* : a person in dotage

dot–com \ˈdät-ˌkäm\ *n* : a company that markets its products or services usually exclusively via a Web site

dote \ˈdōt\ *vb* **dot•ed; dot•ing 1** : to be feebleminded especially from old age **2** ♦ : to be lavish or excessive in one's attention, affection, or fondness ⟨*doted* on her niece⟩

♦ *usu* **dote on** adore, canonize, deify, idolize, worship

dot matrix *n* : a rectangular arrangement of dots from which alphanumeric characters can be formed (as by a computer printer)

Dou•ay Version \dü-ˈā-\ *n* : an English translation of the Vulgate used by Roman Catholics

¹dou•ble \ˈdə-bəl\ *adj* **1** : TWOFOLD, DUAL **2** ♦ : consisting of two members or parts **3** : being twice as great or as many **4** : folded in two **5** : having more than one whorl of petals ⟨~ roses⟩

♦ binary, bipartite, dual, duplex, twin ***Ant*** single

²double *vb* **dou•bled; dou•bling 1** : to make, be, or become twice as great or as many **2** : to make a call in bridge that increases the trick values and penalties of (an opponent's bid) **3** : FOLD **4** : CLENCH **5** : to be or cause to be bent over **6** : to take the place of another **7** : to hit a double **8** : to turn sharply and suddenly; *esp* : to turn back on one's course

³double *adv* **1** : DOUBLY **2** : two together

⁴double *n* **1** : something twice another in size, strength, speed, quantity, or value **2** : a base hit that enables the batter to reach second base **3** ♦ : one that is the counterpart of another : DUPLICATE; *esp* : a person who closely resembles another **4** : UNDERSTUDY, SUBSTITUTE **5** : a sharp turn : REVERSAL **6** : FOLD **7** : a combined bet placed on two different contests **8** *pl* : a game between two pairs of players **9** : an act of doubling in a card game

♦ carbon copy, counterpart, duplicate, duplication, facsimile, image, likeness, match, picture, replica, ringer, spit

double bond *n* : a chemical bond in which two atoms in a molecule share two pairs of electrons

double cross *n* ♦ : an act of betraying or cheating especially an associate — **dou•ble–cross** \ˌdə-bəl-ˈkrȯs\ *vb*

♦ betrayal, disloyalty, faithlessness, falseness, falsity, infidelity, perfidy, treachery, treason, unfaithfulness

dou•ble–cross•er *n* ♦ : one that double-crosses

♦ apostate, betrayer, quisling, recreant, traitor, turncoat

¹dou•ble–deal•ing \ˌdə-bəl-ˈdē-liŋ\ *n* ♦ : action contradictory to a professed attitude : DUPLICITY — **dou•ble–deal•er** \-ˈdē-lər\ *n*

♦ artifice, craft, craftiness, crookedness, cunning, deceit, deceitfulness, dishonesty, dissimulation, duplicity, guile, wiliness

²double–dealing *adj* ♦ : given to or marked by duplicity

♦ crooked, deceitful, dishonest, false, fraudulent

dou•ble–deck•er \-ˈde-kər\ *n* : something having two decks, levels, or layers — **dou•ble–deck** \-ˌdek\ *or* **dou•ble–decked** \-ˌdekt\ *adj*

dou•ble–dig•it \ˌdə-bəl-ˈdi-jət\ *adj* : amounting to 10 percent or more

dou•ble en•ten•dre \ˌdüb-əl-äⁿ-ˈtäⁿd, ˌdə-bəl-, -ˈtänd-rə\ *n, pl* **double entendres** *same or* -ˈtän-drəz\ : a word or expression capable of two interpretations with one usually risqué

dou•ble•head•er \ˌdə-bəl-ˈhe-dər\ *n* : two games played consecutively on the same day

double helix *n* : a helix or spiral consisting of two strands (as of DNA) in the surface of a cylinder which coil around its axis

dou•ble–hung \ˌdə-bəl-ˈhəŋ\ *adj, of a window* : having an upper and a lower sash that can slide past each other

dou•ble–joint•ed \-ˈjȯin-təd\ *adj* : having a joint that permits an exceptional degree of freedom of motion of the parts joined ⟨a ~ finger⟩

dou•ble–park \ˌdə-bəl-ˈpärk\ *vb* : to park a vehicle beside a row of vehicles already parked parallel to the curb

double play *n* : a play in baseball by which two players are put out

double pneumonia *n* : pneumonia affecting both lungs

double standard *n* : a set of principles that applies differently and usually more rigorously to one group of people or circumstances than to another

dou•blet \ˈdə-blət\ *n* **1** : a man's close-fitting jacket worn in Europe especially in the 16th century **2** : one of two similar or identical things

dou•ble take \ˈdə-bəl-ˌtāk\ *n* : a delayed reaction to a surprising or significant situation after an initial failure to notice anything unusual

dou•ble–talk \-ˌtȯk\ *n* ♦ : language that appears to be meaningful but in fact is a mixture of sense and nonsense

♦ babble, bunk, claptrap, drivel, fudge, gabble, gibberish, gobbledygook, hogwash, jabber, jabberwocky, jazz, moonshine, mumbo jumbo, nonsense, piffle, prattle

double up *vb* : to share accommodations designed for one

double whammy *n* : a combination of two usually adverse forces, circumstances, or effects

dou•bloon \ˌdə-ˈblün\ *n* : a former gold coin of Spain and Spanish America

dou•bly \ˈdə-blē\ *adv* **1** : in a twofold manner **2** : to twice the degree

¹doubt \ˈdau̇t\ *vb* **1 :** to be uncertain about **2** ♦ **:** to lack confidence in : DISTRUST **3 :** to consider unlikely

♦ distrust, mistrust, question, suspect

²doubt *n* **1 :** uncertainty of belief or opinion **2 :** a condition causing uncertainty, hesitation, or suspense ⟨the outcome was in ∼⟩ **3** ♦ **:** a lack of confidence : DISTRUST **4 :** an inclination not to believe or accept

♦ distrust, incertitude, misgiving, mistrust, skepticism, suspicion, uncertainty ***Ant*** assurance, belief, certainty, certitude, confidence, conviction, sureness, surety, trust

doubt•able \ˈdau̇-tə-bəl\ *adj* **:** capable of being doubted : QUESTIONABLE

doubt•er \ˈdau̇-tər\ *n* ♦ **:** one that doubts

♦ disbeliever, questioner, skeptic, unbeliever

doubt•ful \ˈdau̇t-fəl\ *adj* **1** ♦ **:** giving rise to doubt : open to question **2 a :** lacking a definite opinion, conviction, or determination **b :** uncertain in outcome ⟨the outcome of the election is ∼⟩ **3** ♦ **:** marked by qualities that raise doubts about worth, honesty, or validity — **doubt•ful•ness** *n*

♦ [1, 3] debatable, disputable, dubious, equivocal, fishy, problematic, questionable, shady, shaky, suspect, suspicious ***Ant*** certain, incontestable, indisputable, indubitable, sure, undeniable, undoubted, unquestionable ♦ [3] distrustful, dubious, mistrustful, skeptical, suspicious, uncertain, undecided, unsettled, unsure ***Ant*** certain, convinced, positive, sure

doubt•ful•ly \-fə-lē\ *adv* **:** in a doubtful manner

¹doubt•less \ˈdau̇t-ləs\ *adv* **1** ♦ **:** without doubt **2 :** without much doubt : PROBABLY

♦ certainly, definitely, incontestably, indeed, indisputably, really, surely, truly, undeniably, undoubtedly, unquestionably

²doubtless *adj* ♦ **:** free from doubt : CERTAIN — **doubt•less•ly** *adv*

♦ assured, certain, clear, cocksure, confident, positive, sanguine, sure

douche \ˈdüsh\ *n* **1 :** a jet of fluid (as water) directed against a part or into a cavity of the body; *also* **:** a cleansing with a douche **2 :** a device for giving douches — **douche** *vb*

dough \ˈdō\ *n* **1 :** a mixture that consists of flour or meal and a liquid (as milk or water) and is stiff enough to knead or roll **2 :** something resembling dough especially in consistency **3** ♦ **:** something generally accepted as a medium of exchange, a measure of value, or a means of payment : MONEY — **doughy** \ˈdō-ē\ *adj*

♦ cash, currency, lucre, money, pelf, tender

dough•boy \-ˌbȯi\ *n* **:** an American infantryman especially in World War I

dough•nut *also* **do•nut** \-(ˌ)nət\ *n* **:** a small usually ring-shaped cake fried in fat

dough•ty \ˈdau̇-tē\ *adj* **dough•ti•er; -est** ♦ **:** marked by fearless resolution : VALIANT

♦ brave, courageous, dauntless, fearless, gallant, greathearted, heroic, intrepid, lionhearted, manful, stalwart, stout, undaunted, valiant, valorous

Doug•las fir \ˈdə-gləs-\ *n* **:** a tall evergreen timber tree of the western U.S.

dou•la \ˈdü-lə\ *n* **:** a woman who provides assistance to a mother before, during, and just after childbirth

do up *vb* **1 :** to prepare (as by cleaning) for use **2 :** to wrap up **3 :** CLOTHE, DECORATE **4 :** FASTEN

dour \ˈdau̇(-ə)r, ˈdu̇r\ *adj* **1** ♦ **:** marked by harsh sternness or severity **2 :** OBSTINATE **3 :** SULLEN — **dour•ly** *adv*

♦ austere, fierce, flinty, forbidding, grim, gruff, rough, rugged, severe, stark, steely, stern

douse \ˈdau̇s, ˈdau̇z\ *vb* **doused; dous•ing 1** ♦ **:** to plunge into water **2** ♦ **:** to throw a liquid on : DRENCH **3** ♦ **:** to cause to cease burning : EXTINGUISH

♦ [1] dip, duck, dunk, immerse, souse, submerge ♦ [2] bathe, drench, soak, sop, souse, wash, water, wet ♦ [3] extinguish, put out, quench, snuff

¹dove \ˈdəv\ *n* **1 :** any of numerous pigeons; *esp* **:** a small wild pigeon **2 :** an advocate of peace or of a peaceful policy **3** ♦ **:** a gentle woman or child — **dov•ish** \ˈdə-vish\ *adj*

♦ angel, innocent, lamb, sheep

²dove \ˈdōv\ *past of* DIVE

¹dove•tail \ˈdəv-ˌtāl\ *n* **:** something that resembles a dove's tail; *esp* **:** a flaring tenon and a mortise into which it fits tightly

²dovetail *vb* **1 :** to join by means of dovetails **2** ♦ **:** to fit skillfully together to form a whole ⟨our plans ∼ nicely⟩

♦ accord, agree, answer, check, coincide, comport, conform, correspond, fit, go, harmonize, jibe, square, tally

dow•a•ger \ˈdau̇-i-jər\ *n* **1 :** a widow owning property or a title from her deceased husband **2** ♦ **:** a dignified elderly woman

♦ dame, matriarch, matron

dowdy \ˈdau̇-dē\ *adj* **dowd•i•er; -est 1** ♦ **:** lacking neatness and charm : UNTIDY **2** ♦ **:** lacking smartness or taste

♦ [1] frowsy, sloppy, slovenly, unkempt, untidy ♦ [2] inelegant, tacky, tasteless, trashy, unfashionable, unstylish

dow•el \ˈdau̇(-ə)l\ *n* **1 :** a pin used for fastening together two pieces of wood **2 :** a round rod (as of wood) — **dowel** *vb*

¹dow•er \ˈdau̇(-ə)r\ *n* **1 :** the part of a deceased husband's real estate which the law gives for life to his widow **2 :** DOWRY

²dower *vb* **:** to supply with a dower or dowry : ENDOW

dow•itch•er \ˈdau̇-i-chər\ *n* **:** any of several long-billed wading birds related to the sandpipers

¹down \ˈdau̇n\ *adv* **1** ♦ **:** toward or in a lower physical position **2 :** to a lying or sitting position **3 :** toward or to the ground, floor, or bottom **4 :** as a down payment ⟨paid $5 ∼⟩ **5 :** on paper ⟨put ∼ what he says⟩ **6 :** in a direction that is the opposite of up **7 :** SOUTH **8 :** to or in a lower or worse condition or status **9 :** from a past time **10 :** to or in a state of less activity **11 :** into defeat ⟨voted the motion ∼⟩

♦ below, downward, over ***Ant*** up, upward, upwardly

²down *prep* **:** down in, on, along, or through : toward the bottom of

³down *vb* **1** ♦ **:** to go or cause to go or come down **2 :** DEFEAT **3 :** to cause (a football) to be out of play

♦ bowl, drop, fell, floor, knock, level

⁴down *adj* **1 :** occupying a low position; *esp* **:** lying on the ground **2** ♦ **:** directed or going downward **3 :** being in a state of reduced or low activity **4 :** low in spirits : DEJECTED **5** ♦ **:** affected with disease or ill health : SICK ⟨∼ with a cold⟩ **6 :** arrived at or brought to an end : DONE **7 :** completely mastered ⟨got her lines ∼⟩ **8 :** being on record ⟨you're ∼ for two tickets⟩

♦ [2] downcast, downward ♦ [5] bad, ill, indisposed, peaked, punk, sick, unhealthy, unsound, unwell

⁵down *n* **1** ♦ **:** a low or falling period (as in activity, emotional life, or fortunes) **2 :** one of a series of attempts to advance a football **3 :** an instance of putting down **4 :** a quark with a charge of -⅓ that is one of the constituents of the proton and neutron

♦ comedown, decline, descent, downfall, fall

⁶down *n* ♦ **:** a rolling usually treeless upland with sparse soil — usually used in plural

♦ *usu* **downs** grassland, plain, prairie, savanna, steppe, veld

⁷down *n* **1 :** a covering of soft fluffy feathers; *also* **:** such feathers **2** ♦ **:** a downlike covering or material

♦ floss, fluff, fur, fuzz, lint, nap, pile

down•beat \ˈdau̇n-ˌbēt\ *n* **:** the downward stroke of a conductor indicating the principally accented note of a measure of music

down•burst \-ˌbərst\ *n* **:** a powerful downdraft usually associated with a thunderstorm that is a hazard for low flying aircraft; *also* **:** MICROBURST

down•cast \-ˌkast\ *adj* **1 :** low in spirit : DEJECTED **2** ♦ **:** directed down ⟨a ∼ glance⟩

♦ down, downward

down•draft \-ˌdraft\ *n* **:** a downward current of gas (as air)

down•er \ˈdau̇-nər\ *n* **1 :** a depressant drug; *esp* **:** BARBITURATE **2 :** someone or something depressing

down•fall \ˈdau̇n-ˌfȯl\ *n* **1** ♦ **:** a sudden fall (as from high rank) **2 :** something that causes a downfall — **down•fall•en** \-ˌfȯ-lən\ *adj*

♦ comedown, decline, descent, down, fall

¹down•grade \ˈdau̇n-ˌgrād\ *n* **1 :** a downward slope (as of a road) **2 :** a decline toward a worse condition

²downgrade *vb* ♦ **:** to lower in quality, value, extent, or status

♦ break, bust, degrade, demote, reduce

down•heart•ed \-ˈhär-təd\ *adj* **:** low in spirit : DEJECTED

¹down•hill \ˈdau̇n-ˈhil\ *adv* **:** toward the bottom of a hill — **downhill** \-ˌhil\ *adj*

²down·hill \-ˌhil\ *n* : the sport of skiing downhill usually in a race against time
¹down·load \ˈdau̇n-ˌlōd\ *n* : an act or instance of downloading something; *also* : the item downloaded
²download *vb* : to transfer (data) from a computer to another device — **down·load·able** \-ˌlō-də-bəl\ *adj*
down payment *n* : a part of the full price paid at the time of purchase or delivery with the balance to be paid later
down·play \ˈdau̇n-ˌplā\ *vb* : DE-EMPHASIZE ⟨~*ed* the allegations⟩
down·pour \ˈdau̇n-ˌpōr\ *n* ♦ : a heavy rain

♦ cloudburst, deluge, rain, rainstorm, storm, wet

down·range \-ˈrānj\ *adv* : away from a launching site
¹down·right \-ˌrīt\ *adv* : THOROUGHLY
²downright *adj* **1** : being completely or exactly what is stated : ABSOLUTE ⟨a ~ lie⟩ **2** : abrupt in speech or manner : BLUNT ⟨a ~ man⟩
down·shift \-ˌshift\ *vb* : to shift an automotive vehicle into a lower gear
down·size \-ˌsīz\ *vb* ♦ : to reduce or undergo reduction in size or numbers

♦ abate, de-escalate, decrease, diminish, dwindle, lessen, lower, reduce

down·spout \-ˌspau̇t\ *n* : a vertical pipe used to drain rainwater from a roof
Down's syndrome \ˈdau̇nz-\ *or* **Down syndrome** \ˈdau̇n-\ *n* : a birth defect characterized by mental retardation, slanting eyes, a broad short skull, broad hands with short fingers, and the presence of an extra chromosome
down·stage \ˈdau̇n-ˈstāj\ *adv or adj* : toward or at the front of a theatrical stage
down·stairs \-ˈstarz\ *adv* : on or to a lower floor and especially the main or ground floor — **down·stairs** \-ˌstarz\ *adj or n*
down·stream \-ˈstrēm\ *adv or adj* : in the direction of flow of a stream
down·stroke \-ˌstrōk\ *n* : a downward stroke
down·swing \-ˌswiŋ\ *n* **1** : a swing downward **2** : DOWNTURN
down–to–earth *adj* ♦ : having or showing concern for fact or reality and rejection of the impractical and visionary

♦ earthy, hardheaded, matter-of-fact, practical, pragmatic, realistic

down·town \ˈdau̇n-ˌtau̇n\ *n* : the main business district of a town or city — **downtown** \ˈdau̇n-ˈtau̇n\ *adj or adv*
down·trod·den \ˈdau̇n-ˈträ-dᵊn\ *adj* : suffering oppression
down·turn \-ˌtərn\ *n* : a downward turn especially in economic activity
¹down·ward \ˈdau̇n-wərd\ *or* **down·wards** \-wərdz\ *adv* **1** ♦ : from a higher to a lower place or condition **2** : from an earlier time **3** : from an ancestor or predecessor

♦ below, down, over

²downward *adj* ♦ : directed toward or situated in a lower place or condition

♦ down, downcast

down·wind \ˈdau̇n-ˈwind\ *adv or adj* : in the direction that the wind is blowing
downy \ˈdau̇-nē\ *adj* **down·i·er; -est** ♦ : resembling or covered with down

♦ cottony, satiny, silken, soft, velvety

downy mildew *n* : any of various parasitic fungi producing whitish masses especially on the underside of plant leaves; *also* : a plant disease caused by downy mildew
downy woodpecker *n* : a small black-and-white woodpecker of No. America
dow·ry \ˈdau̇r-ē\ *n, pl* **dowries** : the property that a woman brings to her husband in marriage
dowse \ˈdau̇z\ *vb* **dowsed; dows·ing** : to use a divining rod especially to find water — **dows·er** *n*
dox·ol·o·gy \däk-ˈsä-lə-jē\ *n, pl* **-gies** : a usually short hymn of praise to God
doy·en \ˈdȯi-ən, ˈdwä-ˌyaⁿ\ *n* : the senior or most experienced person in a group
doy·enne \dȯi-ˈyen, dwä-ˈyen\ *n* : a woman who is a doyen
doy·ley *chiefly Brit var of* DOILY
doz *abbr* dozen
¹doze \ˈdōz\ *vb* **dozed; doz·ing** ♦ : to sleep lightly

♦ catnap, drowse, nap, slumber, snooze

²doze *n* ♦ : a light sleep

♦ catnap, drowse, forty winks, nap, siesta, snooze, wink

doz·en \ˈdə-zᵊn\ *n, pl* **dozens** *or* **dozen** : a group of twelve — **doz·enth** \-zᵊnth\ *adj*
¹DP \ˌdē-ˈpē\ *n, pl* **DP's** *or* **DPs** **1** : a displaced person **2** : DOUBLE PLAY
²DP *abbr* data processing
dpt *abbr* department
DPT *abbr* diphtheria-pertussis-tetanus (vaccines)
dr *abbr* **1** debtor **2** dram **3** drive **4** drum
Dr *abbr* doctor
DR *abbr* **1** dead reckoning **2** dining room
drab \ˈdrab\ *adj* **drab·ber; drab·best** **1** : being of a light olive-brown color **2** ♦ : characterized by dullness and monotony — **drab·ly** *adv* — **drab·ness** *n*

♦ dreary, dry, dull, monotonous, uninteresting

dra·co·ni·an \drā-ˈkō-nē-ən, drə-\ *adj, often cap* : CRUEL; *also* : SEVERE
¹draft \ˈdraft, ˈdråft\ *n* **1** : the act of drawing or hauling **2 a** : the act or an instance of drinking or inhaling **b** ♦ : the portion drunk or inhaled in one such act **3** : DOSE, POTION **4** : DELINEATION, PLAN, DESIGN; *also* : a preliminary sketch, outline, or version ⟨a rough ~ of a speech⟩ **5** : the act of drawing (as from a cask); *also* : a portion of liquid so drawn **6** : the depth of water a ship draws especially when loaded **7** : a system for or act of selecting persons (as for compulsory military service or sports teams); *also* : the persons so selected **8** : an order for the payment of money drawn by one person or bank on another **9** : a heavy demand : STRAIN **10** : a current of air; *also* : a device to regulate air supply (as in a stove) — **on draft** : ready to be drawn from a receptacle ⟨beer *on draft*⟩

♦ drag, drink, nip, quaff, shot, slug, snort, swallow, swig

²draft *adj* **1** : used or adapted for drawing loads ⟨~ horses⟩ **2** : being or having been on draft ⟨~ beer⟩
³draft *vb* **1** : to select usually on a compulsory basis; *esp* : to conscript for military service **2** : to draw the preliminary sketch, version, or plan of **3** ♦ : to put into written form : COMPOSE **4** : to draw off or away — **draft·ee** \draf-ˈtē, dråf-\ *n*

♦ cast, compose, craft, draw, formulate, frame, prepare

draft·ee \draf-ˈtē, ˈdräf-\ *n* : a person who is drafted
drafts·man \ˈdraft-smən, ˈdråft-\ *n* : a person who draws plans (as for buildings or machinery)
drafty \ˈdraf-tē, ˈdräf-\ *adj* **draft·i·er; -est** : exposed to or abounding in drafts of air
¹drag \ˈdrag\ *n* **1** : a device pulled along under water for detecting or gathering **2** : something (as a harrow or sledge) that is dragged along over a surface **3 a** : the act or an instance of dragging **b** : a draft of liquid **4** ♦ : something that hinders progress; *also* : something boring **5** : an open way for vehicles, persons, and animals : STREET ⟨the main ~⟩ **6** : clothing typical of one sex worn by a member of the opposite sex

♦ bar, block, clog, crimp, embarrassment, hindrance, let, obstacle, stop, stumbling block

²drag *vb* **dragged; drag·ging** **1** ♦ : to draw slowly or heavily : HAUL **2** ♦ : to move with painful or undue slowness or difficulty **3** : to force into or out of some situation, condition, or course of action **4** : PROTRACT ⟨~ a story out⟩ **5** : to hang or lag behind **6** : to explore, search, or fish with a drag **7** : to trail along on the ground **8** : DRAW, PUFF ⟨~ on a cigarette⟩ **9** : to move (items on a computer screen) especially by using a mouse — **drag·ger** *n* — **drag one's feet** *also* **drag one's heels** : to act slowly or with hesitation

♦ [1] draw, hale, haul, lug, pull, tow, tug ♦ [2] crawl, creep, dally, dawdle, delay, dillydally, lag, linger, loiter, poke, tarry

drag·net \-ˌnet\ *n* **1** : NET, TRAWL **2** : a network of planned actions for pursuing and catching ⟨a police ~⟩
drag·o·man \ˈdra-gə-mən\ *n, pl* **-mans** *or* **-men** \-mən\ : an interpreter employed especially in the Near East
drag·on \ˈdra-gən\ *n* : a fabulous animal usually represented as a huge winged scaly serpent with a crested head and large claws
drag·on·fly \-ˌflī\ *n* : any of a group of large harmless 4-winged insects that hold the wings horizontal and unfolded in repose
¹dra·goon \drə-ˈgün, dra-\ *n* : a heavily armed mounted soldier
²dragoon *vb* : to force or attempt to force into submission : COERCE
drag race *n* : an acceleration contest between vehicles — **drag racer** *n*
drag·ster \ˈdrag-stər\ *n* : a usually high-powered vehicle used in a drag race
drag strip *n* : a site for drag races
¹drain \ˈdrān\ *vb* **1** : to draw off or flow off gradually or completely **2** ♦ : to exhaust physically or emotionally **3** : to make or

become gradually dry or empty **4** ♦ **:** to carry away the surface water of **:** discharge surface or surplus water **5** ♦ **:** to deplete or empty by or as if by drawing off by degrees or in increments **:** EXHAUST — **drain•er** *n*

♦ [2] burn out, do in, exhaust, fag, fatigue, tire, tucker, wash out, wear, wear out, weary ♦ [4] bleed, draw off, pump, siphon, tap ***Ant*** fill ♦ [5] clean, consume, deplete, exhaust, expend, spend, use up

[2]**drain** *n* **1 :** a means (as a channel or sewer) of draining **2 :** the act of draining **3 :** a gradual outflow; *also* **:** something causing an outflow ⟨a ~ on our savings⟩
drain•age \ˈdrā-nij\ *n* **1 :** the act or process of draining; *also* **:** something that is drained off **2 :** a means for draining **:** DRAIN, SEWER **3 :** an area drained
drained *adj* ♦ **:** exhausted physically or emotionally

♦ beat, bushed, dead, effete, jaded, limp, prostrate, spent, tired, weary, worn-out

drain•pipe \ˈdrān-ˌpīp\ *n* **:** a pipe for drainage
drake \ˈdrāk\ *n* **:** a male duck
dram \ˈdram\ *n* **1 :** a unit of measure equal to $\frac{1}{16}$ ounce **2 :** FLUID DRAM **3 :** a small drink
dra•ma \ˈdrä-mə, ˈdra-\ *n* **1 a :** a literary composition designed for theatrical presentation **b :** a play, movie, or television production with a serious tone or subject **2 :** dramatic art, literature, or affairs **3 :** a series of events involving conflicting forces — **dra•ma•tist** \ˈdra-mə-tist, ˈdrä-\ *n*
dra•mat•ic \drə-ˈma-tik\ *adj* **1 :** of or relating to the drama **2 a** ♦ **:** suitable to or characteristic of the drama **b** ♦ **:** striking in appearance or effect — **dra•mat•i•cal•ly** \-ti-k(ə-)lē\ *adv*

♦ [2a] histrionic, melodramatic, theatrical ♦ [2b] catchy, conspicuous, flamboyant, showy, striking

dram•a•ti•sa•tion, dra•ma•tise *Brit var of* DRAMATIZATION, DRAMATIZE
dra•ma•tize \ˈdra-mə-ˌtīz, ˈdrä-\ *vb* **-tized; -tiz•ing 1 :** to adapt for or be suitable for theatrical presentation **2 :** to present or represent in a dramatic manner — **dram•a•ti•za•tion** \ˌdra-mə-tə-ˈzā-shən, ˌdrä-\ *n*
dra•me•dy \ˈdrä-mə-dē, ˈdra-\ *n* **:** a comedy having dramatic moments
drank *past and past part of* DRINK
[1]**drape** \ˈdrāp\ *vb* **draped; drap•ing 1 :** to cover or adorn with or as if with folds of cloth **2 :** to cause to hang or stretch out loosely or carelessly **3 :** to arrange or become arranged in flowing lines or folds
[2]**drape** *n* **1 :** CURTAIN **2 :** arrangement in or of folds **3 :** the cut or hang of clothing
drap•er \ˈdrā-pər\ *n, chiefly Brit* **:** a dealer in cloth and sometimes in clothing and dry goods
drap•ery \ˈdrā-pə-rē\ *n, pl* **-er•ies 1** *Brit* **:** DRY GOODS **2 :** a decorative fabric especially when hung loosely and in folds; *also* **:** hangings of heavy fabric used as a curtain
dras•tic \ˈdras-tik\ *adj* **:** HARSH, RIGOROUS, SEVERE ⟨~ punishment⟩ — **dras•ti•cal•ly** \-ti-k(ə-)lē\ *adv*
draught \ˈdräft\, **draughty** \ˈdräf-tē\ *chiefly Brit var of* DRAFT, DRAFTY
draughts \ˈdräfts\ *n, Brit* **:** CHECKERS
[1]**draw** \ˈdrȯ\ *vb* **drew** \ˈdrü\; **drawn** \ˈdrȯn\; **draw•ing 1** ♦ **:** to cause to move toward a force exerted **2 :** to cause to go in a certain direction ⟨*drew* him aside⟩ **3 :** to move or go steadily or gradually ⟨night ~*s* near⟩ **4 :** ATTRACT, ENTICE **5 :** PROVOKE, ROUSE ⟨*drew* enemy fire⟩ **6 :** INHALE ⟨~ a deep breath⟩ **7 :** to bring or pull out ⟨*drew* a gun⟩ **8 :** to cause to come out of a container ⟨~ water for a bath⟩ **9 :** to take out the entrails of **:** EVISCERATE **10 :** to require (a specified depth) to float in **11 :** ACCUMULATE, GAIN ⟨~*ing* interest⟩ **12 :** to take money from a place of deposit **:** WITHDRAW **13** ♦ **:** to receive regularly ⟨~ a salary⟩ **14 :** to take (cards) from a stack or the dealer **15 :** to receive or take at random ⟨~ a winning number⟩ **16 :** to bend (a bow) by pulling back the string **17 :** WRINKLE, SHRINK **18 :** to change shape by or as if by pulling or stretching ⟨a face *drawn* with sorrow⟩ **19 :** to leave (a contest) undecided **:** TIE **20** ♦ **:** to give a portrayal of **:** DELINEATE **21 :** to write out in due form **:** DRAFT ⟨~ up a will⟩ **22 :** FORMULATE ⟨~ comparisons⟩ **23 :** INFER ⟨~ a conclusion⟩ **24 :** to spread or elongate (metal) by hammering or by pulling through dies **25 :** to produce or allow a draft or current of air ⟨the chimney ~*s* well⟩ **26 :** to swell out in a wind ⟨all sails ~*ing*⟩ — **draw the line** *or* **draw a line :** to fix an arbitrary boundary usually between two things

♦ [1] drag, hale, haul, lug, pull, tow, tug ♦ [13] acquire, attain, capture, carry, earn, gain, garner, get, land, make, obtain, procure, realize, secure, win ♦ [20] delineate, depict, describe, image, paint, picture, portray, sketch

[2]**draw** *n* **1** ♦ **:** the act, process, or result of drawing **2 :** a lot or chance drawn at random **3** ♦ **:** a contest left undecided or deadlocked **:** TIE **4** ♦ **:** one that draws attention or patronage

♦ [1] haul, jerk, pluck, pull, tug, wrench ♦ [3] dead heat, stalemate, standoff, tie ♦ [4] attraction, lodestone, magnet

draw•back \ˈdrȯ-ˌbak\ *n* ♦ **:** an unfavorable, inferior, or prejudicial condition **:** DISADVANTAGE

♦ disadvantage, handicap, liability, minus, penalty, strike

draw•bridge \-ˌbrij\ *n* **:** a bridge made to be raised, lowered, or turned to permit or deny passage
draw•er \ˈdrȯr, ˈdrȯ-ər\ *n* **1 :** one that draws **2** *pl* **:** an undergarment for the lower part of the body **3 :** a sliding boxlike compartment (as in a table or desk)
draw•ing \ˈdrȯ-iŋ\ *n* **1 :** an act or instance of drawing; *esp* **:** an occasion when something is decided by drawing lots ⟨tonight's lottery ~⟩ **2 :** the act or art of making a figure, plan, or sketch by means of lines **3** ♦ **:** a representation made by drawing **:** SKETCH

♦ cartoon, delineation, sketch

drawing card *n* **:** DRAW 4
drawing room *n* **:** a formal reception room
drawl \ˈdrȯl\ *vb* **:** to speak or utter slowly with vowels greatly prolonged — **drawl** *n*
draw off *vb* ♦ **:** to remove especially from an environment or container

♦ bleed, drain, pump, siphon, tap

draw on *vb* **:** to draw nearer **:** APPROACH ⟨night *draws on*⟩
draw out *vb* **1** ♦ **:** to extend beyond a minimum in time **:** PROLONG **2 :** to cause to speak freely

♦ elongate, extend, lengthen, prolong, protract, stretch

draw•string \ˈdrȯ-ˌstriŋ\ *n* **:** a string, cord, or tape for use in closing a bag or controlling fullness in garments or curtains
draw up *vb* **1** ♦ **:** to prepare a draft or version of **2 :** to pull oneself erect **3** ♦ **:** to bring or come to a stop **4** ♦ **:** to bring (as troops) into array

♦ [1] cast, compose, craft, draft, formulate, frame, prepare ♦ [3] arrest, catch, check, fetch up, halt, hold up, stall, stay, still, stop ♦ [4] arrange, array, classify, codify, dispose, marshal, order, organize, range, systematize

dray \ˈdrā\ *n* **:** a strong low cart for carrying heavy loads
[1]**dread** \ˈdred\ *vb* **1 :** to fear greatly **2 :** to feel extreme reluctance to meet or face
[2]**dread** *n* ♦ **:** great fear especially of some harm to come

♦ alarm, anxiety, apprehension, fear, fright, horror, panic, terror, trepidation

[3]**dread** *adj* **1 :** causing great fear or anxiety **2 :** inspiring awe
dread•ful \ˈdred-fəl\ *adj* **1** ♦ **:** inspiring dread or awe **:** FRIGHTENING **2** ♦ **:** extremely distasteful, unpleasant, or shocking — **dread•ful•ly** *adv*

♦ [1] dire, fearful, fearsome, forbidding, formidable, frightful, hair-raising, horrible, redoubtable, scary, shocking, terrible, terrifying ♦ [2] appalling, atrocious, awful, frightful, ghastly, grisly, gruesome, hideous, horrible, horrid, lurid, macabre, monstrous, nightmarish, shocking, terrible

dread•locks \ˈdred-ˌläks\ *n pl* **:** long braids of hair over the entire head
dread•nought \ˈdred-ˌnȯt\ *n* **:** BATTLESHIP
[1]**dream** \ˈdrēm\ *n* **1 :** a series of thoughts, images, or emotions occurring during sleep **2** ♦ **:** a dreamlike vision **3** ♦ **:** something notable for its beauty, excellence, or enjoyable quality **4 a** ♦ **:** a strongly desired goal or purpose **b :** IDEAL — **dream•like** \-ˌlīk\ *adj*

♦ [2] chimera, conceit, daydream, delusion, fancy, fantasy, figment, hallucination, illusion, phantasm, pipe dream, unreality, vision ♦ [3] beauty, enchantress, fox, goddess, knockout, queen ♦ [4a] aim, ambition, aspiration, design, end, goal, intent, mark, meaning, object, objective, plan, pretension, purpose, thing

[2]**dream** \ˈdrēm\ *vb* **dreamed** \ˈdremt, ˈdrēmd\ *or* **dreamt** \ˈdremt\; **dream•ing 1 :** to have a dream of **2 :** to indulge in daydreams or fantasies **:** pass (time) in reverie or inaction **3** ♦ **:** to consider as a possibility **:** IMAGINE

♦ conceive, envisage, fancy, imagine, picture, vision, visualize

dream•boat \ˈdrēm-ˌbōt\ *n, slang* **:** something highly desirable; *esp* **:** a very attractive person
dream•er \ˈdrē-mər\ *n* **1 :** one that dreams **2** ♦ **:** one who lives in a world of fancy and imagination **3** ♦ **:** one who has ideas or conceives projects regarded as impractical

♦ idealist, romantic, utopian, visionary

dream•land \ˈdrēm-ˌland\ *n* **:** an unreal delightful country that exists in imagination or in dreams
dream up *vb* **:** INVENT, CONCOCT
dream•world \-ˌwərld\ *n* **:** a world of illusion or fantasy
dreamy \ˈdrē-mē\ *adj* ♦ **:** quiet and soothing; *also* **:** pleasant

♦ comforting, narcotic, sedative, soothing ♦ agreeable, congenial, delectable, delicious, delightful, felicitous, good, grateful, gratifying, nice, palatable, pleasant, pleasurable, satisfying

drear \ˈdrir\ *adj* **:** DREARY
drea•ry \ˈdrir-ē\ *adj* **drea•ri•er; -est 1 :** feeling, displaying, or reflecting listlessness or discouragement **2** ♦ **:** having nothing likely to provide cheer, comfort, or interest — **drea•ri•ly** \-ə-lē\ *adv*

♦ bleak, dark, dismal, gloomy, gray (*or* grey), somber (*or* sombre), wretched

1**dredge** \ˈdrej\ *vb* **dredged; dredg•ing** ♦ **:** to gather or search with or as if with a dredge; *esp* **:** to bring to light or gather by deep searching — often used with *up* — **dredg•er** *n*

♦ dig, hunt, rake, ransack, rifle, rummage, scour, search ♦ *often* **dredge up** detect, determine, dig up, discover, ferret out, find, hit on, locate, track down

2**dredge** *n* **:** a machine or barge for removing earth or silt
3**dredge** *vb* **dredged; dredg•ing :** to coat (food) by sprinkling (as with flour)
dregs \ˈdregz\ *n pl* **1** ♦ **:** the matter that settles to the bottom of a liquid **:** SEDIMENT **2 :** the most undesirable part ⟨the ~ of humanity⟩

♦ deposit, grounds, lees, precipitate, sediment

drench \ˈdrench\ *vb* ♦ **:** to wet thoroughly

♦ bathe, douse, soak, sop, souse, wash, water, wet

1**dress** \ˈdres\ *vb* **1 :** to make or set straight **:** ALIGN **2 :** to prepare for use; *esp* **:** BUTCHER **3** ♦ **:** to add decorative details or accessories to **:** EMBELLISH ⟨~ a store window⟩ **4** ♦ **:** to put clothes on **:** CLOTHE; *also* **:** to put on or wear formal or fancy clothes **5 :** to apply dressings or medicine to **6 :** to arrange (the hair) by combing, brushing, or curling **7 :** to apply fertilizer to **8** ♦ **:** to put through a finishing process **:** SMOOTH ⟨~ leather⟩

♦ [3] adorn, array, beautify, bedeck, deck, decorate, do, embellish, enrich, garnish, grace, ornament, trim ♦ [4] apparel, array, attire, caparison, clothe, deck, garb, invest, rig, suit ♦ [8] buff, burnish, gloss, grind, polish, rub, shine, smooth

2**dress** *n* **1** ♦ **:** personal attire **:** CLOTHING **2 :** a garment usually consisting of a one-piece bodice and skirt **3** ♦ **:** covering, adornment, or appearance appropriate or peculiar to a particular time — **dress•mak•er** \-ˌmā-kər\ *n* — **dress•mak•ing** \-ˌmā-kiŋ\ *n*

♦ [1] apparel, attire, clothing, duds, raiment, wear ♦ [3] garb, getup, guise, outfit

3**dress** *adj* **:** suitable for a formal occasion; *also* **:** requiring formal dress
dres•sage \drə-ˈsäzh\ *n* **:** the execution by a trained horse of complex movements in response to barely perceptible signals from its rider
dress down *vb* ♦ **:** to scold severely

♦ admonish, chide, lecture, rail (at *or* against), rate, rebuke, reprimand, scold

1**dress•er** \ˈdre-sər\ *n* **:** a chest of drawers or bureau with a mirror
2**dresser** *n* **:** one that dresses
dress•ing \ˈdre-siŋ\ *n* **1 :** the act or process of one who dresses **2 :** a sauce for adding to a dish (as a salad) **3 :** a seasoned mixture usually used as stuffing **4 :** material used to cover an injury
dressing gown *n* **:** a loose robe worn especially while dressing or resting
dress up *vb* **1 :** to change the customary dress or appearance of **2** ♦ **:** furnish with a false appearance

♦ camouflage, cloak, disguise, mask

dressy \ˈdre-sē\ *adj* **dress•i•er; -est 1 :** showy in dress **2 :** STYLISH, SMART
drew *past of* DRAW

1**drib•ble** \ˈdri-bəl\ *vb* **drib•bled; drib•bling 1** ♦ **:** to fall or flow in drops **:** TRICKLE **2** ♦ **:** to let saliva trickle from the corner of the mouth **:** DROOL **3 :** to propel by successive slight taps or bounces

♦ [1] gurgle, lap, plash, ripple, slosh, splash, trickle, wash ♦ [2] drivel, drool, salivate, slaver, slobber

2**dribble** *n* **1 :** a small trickling stream or flow **2 :** a drizzling shower **3 :** the dribbling of a ball or puck
drib•let \ˈdri-blət\ *n* **1 :** a trifling amount **2** ♦ **:** a drop of liquid

♦ blob, drip, drop, droplet, glob

dri•er *or* **dry•er** \ˈdrī-ər\ *n* **1 :** a substance that speeds drying (as of paint or ink) **2** *usu dryer* **:** a device for drying
1**drift** \ˈdrift\ *n* **1** ♦ **:** the motion or course of something drifting; *also* **:** a gradual shift of position **2** ♦ **:** a mass of matter (as snow or sand) piled up especially by wind **3 :** earth, gravel, and rock deposited by a glacier **4** ♦ **:** a general underlying design or tendency **:** MEANING ⟨if you catch my ~⟩

♦ [1] current, leaning, run, tendency, tide, trend, wind ♦ [2] bank, bar, mound ♦ [4] denotation, import, intent, meaning, purport, sense, significance, signification

2**drift** *vb* **1** ♦ **:** to float or be driven along by or as if by a current of water or air; *also* **:** to move along smoothly as if drifting on a current of water or air **2 :** to become piled up by wind or water

♦ float, glide, hang, hover, poise, ride, sail, waft

drift•er \ˈdrif-tər\ *n* ♦ **:** a person without aim, ambition, or initiative

♦ nomad, rambler, rover, stroller, vagabond, wanderer

drift net *n* **:** a fishing net often miles in extent arranged to drift with the tide or current
drift•wood \ˈdrift-ˌwu̇d\ *n* **:** wood drifted or floated by water
1**drill** \ˈdril\ *n* **1 :** a tool for boring holes **2 :** the training of soldiers in marching and the handling of arms **3** ♦ **:** a regularly practiced exercise

♦ exercise, practice, routine, training, workout

2**drill** *vb* **1 :** to instruct and exercise by repetition **2 :** to train in or practice military drill **3** ♦ **:** to bore or drive a hole in **4 :** to shoot with or as if with a gun — **drill•er** *n*

♦ bore, hole, perforate, pierce, punch, puncture

3**drill** *n* **1 :** a shallow furrow or trench in which seed is sown **2 :** an agricultural implement for making furrows and dropping seed into them
4**drill** *n* **:** a firm cotton twilled fabric
drill•mas•ter \ˈdril-ˌmas-tər\ *n* **:** an instructor in military drill
drill press *n* **:** an upright drilling machine in which the drill is pressed to the work usually by a hand lever
drily *var of* DRYLY
1**drink** \ˈdriŋk\ *vb* **drank** \ˈdraŋk\; **drunk** \ˈdrəŋk\ *or* **drank; drink•ing 1** ♦ **:** to swallow liquid **:** IMBIBE **2** ♦ **:** to take in or suck up **:** ABSORB **3 :** to take in through the senses ⟨~ in the beautiful scenery⟩ **4 :** to give or join in a toast **5 :** to drink alcoholic beverages especially to excess — **drink•able** *adj* — **drink•er** *n*

♦ [1] guzzle, imbibe, quaff, sup, swig, toss ♦ [2] absorb, imbibe, soak, sponge, suck

2**drink** *n* **1 a** ♦ **:** a liquid suitable for swallowing **:** BEVERAGE **b** ♦ **:** an alcoholic beverage **2** ♦ **:** a draft or portion of liquid **3 :** excessive consumption of alcoholic beverages

♦ [1a] beverage, libation, quencher ♦ [1b] alcohol, booze, intoxicant, liquor, moonshine, spirits ♦ [2] draft, drag, nip, quaff, shot, slug, snort, swallow, swig

1**drip** \ˈdrip\ *vb* **dripped; drip•ping 1 :** to fall or let fall in drops **2 :** to let fall drops of moisture or liquid ⟨a *dripping* faucet⟩ **3 :** to overflow with or as if with moisture
2**drip** *n* **1 :** a falling in drops **2** ♦ **:** liquid that falls, overflows, or is extruded in drops **3 :** the sound made by or as if by falling drops

♦ blob, driblet, drop, droplet, glob

1**drive** \ˈdrīv\ *vb* **drove** \ˈdrōv\; **driv•en** \ˈdri-vən\; **driv•ing 1** ♦ **:** to urge, push, or force onward **2 :** to carry through strongly ⟨~ a bargain⟩ **3** ♦ **:** to set or keep in motion or operation **4 :** to direct the movement or course of **5 :** to convey in a vehicle **6 :** to bring into a specified condition ⟨the noise ~*s* me crazy⟩ **7** ♦ **:** to exert inescapable or coercive pressure on **:** FORCE ⟨*driven* by hunger to steal⟩ **8 :** to project, inject, or impress forcefully ⟨*drove* the lesson home⟩ **9 :** to produce by opening a way ⟨~ a well⟩ **10 :** to progress with strong momentum ⟨a *driving* rain⟩

11 : to propel an object of play (as a golf ball) by a hard blow — **driv•er** *n*

♦ [1] propel, push, shove, thrust ♦ [1] herd, punch, run ♦ [3] activate, actuate, crank, move, propel, run, set off, spark, start, touch off, trigger, turn on ♦ [7] coerce, compel, constrain, force, make, muscle, obligate, oblige, press, pressure

²drive *n* **1 :** a trip in a carriage or automobile **2 :** a driving or collecting of animals ⟨a cattle ~⟩ **3 :** the guiding of logs downstream to a mill **4 :** the act of driving a ball; *also* **:** the flight of a ball **5 :** DRIVEWAY **6 :** a public road for driving (as in a park) **7 :** the state of being hurried and under pressure **8** ♦ **:** a strong systematic group effort ⟨membership ~⟩ **9 :** the apparatus by which motion is imparted to a machine **10 :** an offensive or aggressive move **:** a military attack **11 a** ♦ **:** an urgent, basic, or instinctual need **b** ♦ **:** an impelling culturally acquired concern, interest, or longing **12** ♦ **:** dynamic quality **13 :** a device for reading and writing on magnetic media (as magnetic tape or disks)

♦ [8] bandwagon, campaign, cause, crusade, movement ♦ [11a, 11b] appetite, craving, desire, hankering, hunger, itch, longing, lust, passion, thirst, urge, yearning, yen ♦ [12] aggressiveness, ambition, enterprise, go, hustle, initiative

drive–in \ˈdrī-ˌvin\ *adj* **:** accommodating patrons while they remain in their automobiles — **drive–in** *n*

¹driv•el \ˈdri-vəl\ *vb* **-eled** *or* **-elled; -el•ing** *or* **-el•ling 1 :** to let saliva dribble from the mouth **:** DROOL **2** ♦ **:** to talk or utter stupidly, carelessly, or in an infantile way — **driv•el•er** *n*

♦ babble, chatter, gabble, gibber, jabber, prattle, sputter

²drivel *n* ♦ **:** language, conduct, or an idea that is absurd or contrary to good sense **:** NONSENSE

♦ bunk, claptrap, fiddlesticks, folly, foolishness, fudge, hogwash, humbug, nonsense, piffle, rot, silliness, slush, stupidity, trash

drive•shaft \ˈdrīv-ˌshaft\ *n* **:** a shaft that transmits mechanical power

drive–through *also* **drive–thru** \ˈdrīv-ˌthrü\ *adj* **:** designed for the service of patrons remaining in their automobiles — **drive–through** *also* **drive–thru** *n*

drive•way \-ˌwā\ *n* **:** a short private road leading from the street to a house, garage, or parking lot

¹driz•zle \ˈdri-zəl\ *n* **:** a fine misty rain

²drizzle *vb* **driz•zled; driz•zling :** to rain in very small drops

drogue \ˈdrōg\ *n* **:** a small parachute for slowing down or stabilizing something (as a space capsule)

droll \ˈdrōl\ *adj* ♦ **:** having a humorous, whimsical, or odd quality ⟨a ~ expression⟩ — **droll•ery** \ˈdrō-lə-rē\ *n* — **drol•ly** *adv*

♦ antic, comic, comical, farcical, funny, hilarious, humorous, hysterical, laughable, ludicrous, ridiculous, riotous, risible, screaming, uproarious

drom•e•dary \ˈdrä-mə-ˌder-ē\ *n, pl* **-dar•ies :** CAMEL; *esp* **:** a domesticated one-humped camel of western Asia and northern Africa

¹drone \ˈdrōn\ *n* **1 :** a male honeybee **2 :** one that lives on the labors of others **:** PARASITE **3 :** an unmanned aircraft or ship guided by remote control

²drone *vb* **droned; dron•ing** ♦ **:** to sound with a low dull monotonous murmuring sound; *also* **:** speak monotonously

♦ buzz, hum, whir, whish, whiz, zip, zoom

³drone *n* ♦ **:** a deep monotonous sound

♦ buzz, hum, purr, whir, whiz, zoom

drool \ˈdrül\ *vb* **1** ♦ **:** to let liquid flow from the mouth **2 :** to talk foolishly

♦ dribble, drivel, salivate, slaver, slobber

¹droop \ˈdrüp\ *vb* **1** ♦ **:** to hang or incline downward **2 :** to sink gradually **3** ♦ **:** to become depressed or weakened **:** LANGUISH

♦ [1] flag, hang, loll, sag, wilt ♦ [3] decay, fail, flag, go, lag, languish, sag, waste, weaken, wilt

²droop *n* ♦ **:** the condition or appearance of drooping — **droopy** *adj*

♦ sag, slack, slackness

droopy \ˈdrü-pē\ *adj* **1 :** low in spirits **2** ♦ **:** drooping or tending to droop

♦ pendulous ♦ flaccid, floppy, lank, limp, slack, yielding

¹drop \ˈdräp\ *n* **1** ♦ **:** the quantity of fluid that falls in one spherical mass **2** *pl* **:** a dose of medicine measured by drops **3 :** a small quantity of drink **4 :** the smallest practical unit of liquid measure **5 :** something (as a pendant or a small round candy) that resembles a liquid drop **6** ♦ **:** the act or an instance of dropping **:** FALL **7** ♦ **:** a decline in quantity or quality **8 :** a descent by parachute **9 :** the distance through which something drops **10 :** a slot into which something is to be dropped **11 :** something that drops or has dropped **12** ♦ **:** an advantage or superiority over an opponent — usually used in the phrase *get the drop on*

♦ [1] blob, driblet, drip, droplet, glob ♦ [6] descent, dip, dive, down, fall, plunge ♦ [7] abatement, decline, decrease, decrement, diminution, fall, loss, reduction, shrinkage ♦ [12] advantage, better, edge, jump, upper hand, vantage

²drop *vb* **dropped; drop•ping 1 :** to fall or let fall in drops **2 :** to let fall **:** LOWER ⟨~ a glove⟩ ⟨*dropped* his voice⟩ **3 :** SEND ⟨~ me a note⟩ **4 :** to let go **:** DISMISS ⟨~ the subject⟩ **5 :** to knock down **:** cause to fall **6** ♦ **:** to go lower **:** become less ⟨prices *dropped*⟩ **7 :** to come or go unexpectedly or informally ⟨~ in to call⟩ **8 :** to pass from one state into a less active one ⟨~ off to sleep⟩ **9** ♦ **:** to move downward or with a current **10** ♦ **:** to desist from **:** QUIT **11 :** to give birth to — **drop back :** to move toward the rear — **drop behind :** to fail to keep up

♦ [6] decline, descend, dip, fall, lower, plummet, plunge, sink, tumble *Ant* arise, lift, rise, soar ♦ [9] decline, descend, dip, fall, plunge ♦ [10] discontinue, give up, knock off, lay off, quit

drop by *vb* ♦ **:** to pay a brief casual visit

♦ **drop by** *or* **drop in** call, pop (in), stop (by *or* in), visit

drop in *vb* **:** to pay an unexpected or casual visit

♦ call, pop (in), stop (by *or* in), visit

drop•kick \-ˈkik\ *n* **:** a kick made by dropping a ball to the ground and kicking it at the moment it starts to rebound — **drop–kick** *vb*

drop•let \ˈdrä-plət\ *n* ♦ **:** a tiny drop

♦ blob, driblet, drip, drop, glob

drop–off \ˈdräp-ˌȯf\ *n* **1 :** a steep or perpendicular descent **2 :** a marked decline ⟨a ~ in attendance⟩

drop off *vb* **:** to fall asleep

drop out *vb* **:** to withdraw from participation or membership; *esp* **:** to leave school before graduation — **drop•out** \ˈdräp-ˌau̇t\ *n*

drop•per \ˈdrä-pər\ *n* **1 :** one that drops **2 :** a short glass tube with a rubber bulb used to measure out liquids by drops

drop•pings *n pl* ♦ **:** the feces of an animal **:** DUNG

♦ dung, slops, waste

drop•sy \ˈdräp-sē\ *n* **:** EDEMA — **drop•si•cal** \-si-kəl\ *adj*

dross \ˈdräs\ *n* **1 :** the scum that forms on the surface of a molten metal **2 :** waste matter **:** REFUSE

drought \ˈdrau̇t\ *also* **drouth** \ˈdrau̇th\ *n* **:** a long spell of dry weather

¹drove \ˈdrōv\ *n* **1 :** a group of animals driven or moving in a body **2** ♦ **:** a large number **:** CROWD — usually used in plural ⟨tourists arriving in ~*s*⟩

♦ *usu* **droves** army, crowd, crush, flock, horde, host, legion, mob, multitude, press, swarm, throng

²drove *past of* DRIVE

drov•er \ˈdrō-vər\ *n* **:** one that drives domestic animals usually to market

drown \ˈdrau̇n\ *vb* **drowned** \ˈdrau̇nd\; **drown•ing 1 :** to suffocate by submersion especially in water **2 :** to become drowned **3** ♦ **:** to cover with water; *also* **:** to soak, drench, or cover with a liquid **4 :** to cause to be muted (as a sound) by a loud noise **5 :** OVERPOWER, OVERWHELM

♦ deluge, engulf, flood, inundate, overflow, overwhelm, submerge, swamp ♦ drench, impregnate, saturate, soak, sop, souse, steep

¹drowse \ˈdrau̇z\ *vb* **drowsed; drows•ing** ♦ **:** to fall into a light slumber **:** DOZE

♦ catnap, doze, nap, slumber, snooze

²drowse *n* ♦ **:** the act or an instance of drowsing

♦ catnap, doze, forty winks, nap, siesta, snooze, wink

drowsy \ˈdrau̇-zē\ *adj* **drows•i•er; -est 1** ♦ **:** ready to fall asleep **2** ♦ **:** making one sleepy — **drows•i•ly** \-zə-lē\ *adv* — **drows•i•ness** \-zē-nəs\ *n*

♦ [1] sleepy, slumberous ♦ [2] hypnotic, narcotic, opiate, slumberous

drub \ˈdrəb\ *vb* **drubbed; drub•bing** **1** ♦ **:** to beat severely **2** ♦ **:** to defeat decisively

♦ [1] bash, bat, batter, beat, pound ♦ [2] clobber, rout, skunk, thrash, trim, trounce, wallop, whip

¹drudge \ˈdrəj\ *vb* **drudged; drudg•ing** ♦ **:** to do hard, menial, or monotonous work

♦ endeavor (*or* endeavour), fag, grub, hustle, labor (*or* labour), peg, plod, plug, slave, slog, strain, strive, struggle, sweat, toil, work

²drudge *n* ♦ **:** one whose work is menial or routine and boring

♦ fag, peon, slave, toiler, worker

drudg•ery \ˈdrə-jə-rē\ *n* ♦ **:** dull, irksome, and fatiguing work

♦ grind, labor (*or* labour), slavery, sweat, toil, travail

¹drug \ˈdrəg\ *n* **1** ♦ **:** a substance used as or in medicine **2 :** a substance (as heroin or marijuana) that can cause addiction, habituation, or a marked change in mental status

♦ cure, medicine, pharmaceutical, remedy, specific

²drug *vb* **drugged; drug•ging :** to affect with or as if with drugs; *esp* **:** to stupefy with a narcotic

drug•gist \ˈdrə-gist\ *n* **:** a dealer in drugs and medicines; *also* **:** PHARMACIST

drug•store \ˈdrəg-ˌstōr\ *n* **:** a retail shop where medicines and miscellaneous articles are sold

dru•id \ˈdrü-əd\ *n, often cap* **:** one of an ancient Celtic priesthood appearing in Irish, Welsh, and Christian legends as magicians and wizards

¹drum \ˈdrəm\ *n* **1 :** a percussion instrument usually consisting of a hollow cylinder with a skin or plastic head stretched over one or both ends that is beaten with the hands or with a stick **2 :** the sound of a drum; *also* **:** a similar sound **3** ♦ **:** a drum-shaped object

♦ can, canister, tin

²drum *vb* **drummed; drum•ming** **1 :** to beat a drum **2 :** to sound rhythmically **:** THROB, BEAT **3 :** to summon or enlist by or as if by beating a drum ⟨*drummed* into service⟩ **4** ♦ **:** to dismiss ignominiously **:** EXPEL — usually used with *out* **5 :** to drive or force by steady effort ⟨~ the facts into memory⟩ **6** ♦ **:** to strike or tap repeatedly so as to produce rhythmic sounds

♦ [4] banish, boot (out), bounce, cast, chase, dismiss, eject, expel, oust, rout, run off, throw out ♦ [6] beat, rap, tap

drum•beat \ˈdrəm-ˌbēt\ *n* **:** a stroke on a drum or its sound

drum major *n* **:** the leader of a marching band

drum ma•jor•ette \-ˌmā-jə-ˈret\ *n* **:** a girl or woman who leads a marching band; *also* **:** a baton twirler who accompanies a marching band

drum•mer \ˈdrə-mər\ *n* **1 :** one that plays a drum **2 :** a traveling salesman

drum•stick \ˈdrəm-ˌstik\ *n* **1 :** a stick for beating a drum **2 :** the lower segment of a fowl's leg

drum up *vb* **1 :** to bring about by persistent effort ⟨*drum up* business⟩ **2 :** INVENT, ORIGINATE

¹drunk *past part of* DRINK

²drunk \ˈdrəŋk\ *adj* **1** ♦ **:** having the faculties impaired by alcohol ⟨~ drivers⟩ **2 :** dominated by an intense feeling ⟨~ with power⟩ **3 :** of, relating to, or caused by intoxication

♦ high, inebriate, intoxicated, tipsy ***Ant*** sober

³drunk *n* **1 :** a period of excessive drinking **2** ♦ **:** a drunken person

♦ inebriate, soak, sot, souse, tippler

drunk•ard \ˈdrəŋ-kərd\ *n* **:** one who is habitually drunk

♦ inebriate, soak, sot, souse, tippler

drunk•en \ˈdrəŋ-kən\ *adj* **1 :** being under the influence of alcohol **:** DRUNK **2 :** given to habitual excessive use of alcohol **3 :** of, relating to, or resulting from intoxication ⟨a ~ brawl⟩ **4 :** unsteady or lurching as if from intoxication — **drunk•en•ly** *adv* — **drunk•en•ness** *n*

drupe \ˈdrüp\ *n* **:** a partly fleshy fruit (as a plum or cherry) having one seed enclosed in a hard inner shell

¹dry \ˈdrī\ *adj* **dri•er** \ˈdrī-ər\; **dri•est** \-əst\ **1 :** free or freed from water or liquid ⟨~ fruits⟩; *also* **:** not being in or under water **2** ♦ **:** characterized by lack of water or moisture ⟨~ climate⟩ **3 :** lacking freshness **:** STALE **4 :** devoid of natural moisture; *also* **:** THIRSTY **5 :** no longer liquid or sticky ⟨the ink is ~⟩ **6 :** not giving milk ⟨a ~ cow⟩ **7 :** marked by the absence of alcoholic beverages **8 :** prohibiting the making or distributing of alcoholic beverages **9 :** not sweet ⟨~ wine⟩ **10 :** solid as opposed to liquid ⟨~ groceries⟩ **11 :** containing or employing no liquid **12 a :** not showing or communicating warmth, enthusiasm, or tender feeling **:** SEVERE **b :** causing weariness or lack of interest **:** UNINTERESTING **13 :** not productive **14 :** marked by a matter-of-fact, ironic, or terse manner of expression ⟨~ humor⟩ — **dry•ly** *or* **dri•ly** *adv* — **dry•ness** *n*

♦ arid, sere, thirsty ***Ant*** damp, dank, humid, moist, wet

²dry *vb* **dried; dry•ing** ♦ **:** to make or become dry

♦ dehydrate, parch, sear ***Ant*** hydrate, wet

³dry *n, pl* **drys :** PROHIBITIONIST

dry•ad \ˈdrī-əd, -ˌad\ *n* **:** WOOD NYMPH

dry cell *n* **:** a battery whose contents are not spillable

dry–clean \ˈdrī-ˌklēn\ *vb* **:** to clean (fabrics) chiefly with solvents other than water — **dry cleaning** *n*

dry dock \ˈdrī-ˌdäk\ *n* **:** a dock that can be kept dry during ship construction or repair

dryer *var of* DRIER

dry farm•ing *n* **:** farming without irrigation in areas of limited rainfall — **dry–farm** *vb* — **dry farm•er** *n*

dry goods \ˈdrī-ˌgu̇dz\ *n pl* **:** cloth goods (as fabrics, ribbon, and ready-to-wear clothing)

dry ice *n* **:** solid carbon dioxide

dry measure *n* **:** a series of units of capacity for dry commodities

dry rot *n* **:** decay of timber in which fungi consume the wood's cellulose

dry run *n* ♦ **:** a practice exercise **:** REHEARSAL

♦ practice, rehearsal, trial

dry•wall \ˈdrī-ˌwȯl\ *n* **:** a wallboard consisting of fiberboard, paper, or felt over a plaster core

Ds *symbol* darmstadtium

DSC *abbr* **1** Distinguished Service Cross **2** doctor of surgical chiropody

DSM *abbr* Distinguished Service Medal

DST *abbr* daylight saving time

DTP *abbr* diphtheria, tetanus, pertussis (vaccines)

d.t.'s \ˌdē-ˈtēz\ *n pl, often cap D&T* **:** DELIRIUM TREMENS

du•al \ˈdü-əl, ˈdyü-\ *adj* **1** ♦ **:** consisting of two parts or elements or having two like parts **:** DOUBLE **2 :** having a double character or nature — **du•al•ism** \-ə-ˌli-zəm\ *n* — **du•al•i•ty** \dü-ˈa-lə-tē, dyü-\ *n*

♦ binary, bipartite, double, duplex, twin

¹dub \ˈdəb\ *vb* **dubbed; dub•bing** **1 :** to confer knighthood upon **2** ♦ **:** to call by a distinctive title, epithet, or nickname **:** NAME

♦ baptize, call, christen, denominate, designate, entitle, label, name, style, term, title

²dub *n* **:** a clumsy person **:** DUFFER

³dub *vb* **dubbed; dub•bing :** to add (sound effects) to a motion picture or to a radio or television production

du•bi•ety \dü-ˈbī-ə-tē, dyü-\ *n, pl* **-eties** **1 :** UNCERTAINTY **2 :** a matter of doubt

du•bi•ous \ˈdü-bē-əs, ˈdyü-\ *adj* **1** ♦ **:** of doubtful promise or outcome **2** ♦ **:** questionable or suspect as to true nature or quality **:** QUESTIONABLE **3** ♦ **:** feeling doubt — **du•bi•ous•ness** *n*

♦ [1] doubtful, flimsy, improbable, questionable, unlikely ♦ [2] debatable, disputable, doubtful, equivocal, fishy, problematic, questionable, shady, shaky, suspect, suspicious ♦ [3] distrustful, doubtful, mistrustful, skeptical, suspicious, uncertain, undecided, unsettled, unsure

du•bi•ous•ly \-lē\ *adv* ♦ **:** in a manner expressive of doubt, hesitation, or suspicion

♦ askance, distrustfully, mistrustfully, suspiciously

dub•ni•um \ˈdüb-nē-əm, ˈdəb-\ *n* **:** a short-lived radioactive chemical element produced artificially

du•cal \ˈdü-kəl, ˈdyü-\ *adj* **:** of or relating to a duke or dukedom

duc•at \ˈdə-kət\ *n* **:** a gold coin formerly used in various European countries

duch•ess \ˈdə-chəs\ *n* **1 :** the wife or widow of a duke **2 :** a woman holding the rank of duke in her own right

duchy \ˈdə-chē\ *n, pl* **duch•ies :** the territory of a duke or duchess **:** DUKEDOM

¹duck \ˈdək\ *n, pl* **ducks :** any of various swimming birds related to but smaller than geese and swans

²duck *vb* **1** ♦ **:** to thrust or plunge under water **2 a :** to lower the head or body suddenly **:** BOW **b** ♦ **:** to make a sudden movement in a new direction : DODGE **3** ♦ : to evade a duty, question, or responsibility ⟨~ the issue⟩

♦ [1] dip, douse, dunk, immerse, souse, submerge ♦ [2b] dodge, sidestep ♦ [3] avoid, dodge, elude, escape, eschew, evade, shake, shirk, shun

[3]**duck** *n* **1** : a durable closely woven usually cotton fabric **2** *pl* : light clothes made of duck
duck•bill \ˈdək-ˌbil\ *n* : PLATYPUS
duck•ling \-liŋ\ *n* : a young duck
duck•pin \-ˌpin\ *n* **1** : a small bowling pin shorter and wider in the middle than a tenpin **2** *pl but sing in constr* : a bowling game using duckpins
duck sauce *n* : a thick sweet sauce made with fruits and seasonings and used in Chinese cuisine
duct \ˈdəkt\ *n* **1** : a tube or canal for conveying a bodily fluid **2** ♦ : a pipe or tube through which a fluid (as air) flows — **duct•less** *adj*

♦ channel, conduit, leader, line, penstock, pipe, tube

duc•tile \ˈdəkt-ᵊl\ *adj* **1** : capable of being drawn out into wire or thread **2** : easily led : DOCILE — **duc•til•i•ty** \ˌdək-ˈti-lə-tē\ *n*
ductless gland *n* : an endocrine gland
duct tape *n* : a cloth adhesive tape orig. designed for sealing certain ducts and joints — **duct tape** *vb*
dud \ˈdəd\ *n* **1** *pl* ♦ : personal attire : CLOTHING **2** ♦ : one that fails completely; *also* : a bomb or missile that fails to explode

♦ **duds** [1] apparel, attire, clothing, dress, raiment, wear ♦ [2] bummer, bust, catastrophe, debacle, failure, fiasco, fizzle, flop, lemon, loser, turkey, washout

dude \ˈdüd, ˈdyüd\ *n* **1** ♦ : a man who gives exaggerated attention to personal appearance : DANDY **2** : a city dweller; *esp* : an Easterner in the West **3** ♦ : a male human : GUY — sometimes used as an informal form of address

♦ [1] buck, dandy, fop, gallant ♦ [3] buck, chap, fellow, gent, gentleman, guy, hombre, jack, joker, lad, male, man

dude ranch *n* : a vacation resort offering activities (as horseback riding) typical of western ranches
dud•geon \ˈdə-jən\ *n* ♦ : a fit or state of indignation ⟨in high ~⟩

♦ huff, offense, peeve, pique, resentment, umbrage

[1]**due** \ˈdü, ˈdyü\ *adj* **1** : owed or owing as a debt **2** : owed or owing as a right **3** : APPROPRIATE, FITTING **4** : SUFFICIENT, ADEQUATE **5** ♦ : being in accordance with some established rule, law, or principle ⟨~ process of law⟩ **6** ♦ : capable of being attributed — used with *to* ⟨~ to negligence⟩ **7** : PAYABLE ⟨a bill ~ today⟩ **8** : SCHEDULED ⟨~ to arrive soon⟩

♦ [5] just, right ♦ *usu* **due to** [6] attendant, consequent, consequential, resultant

[2]**due** *n* **1** : something that rightfully belongs to one ⟨give everyone their ~⟩ **2** : DEBT **3** *pl* : FEES, CHARGES
[3]**due** *adv* ♦ : in a direct manner : DIRECTLY ⟨~ north⟩

♦ dead, direct, directly, plump, right, straight

du•el \ˈdü-əl, ˈdyü-\ *n* **1** : a combat between two persons; *esp* : one fought with weapons in the presence of witnesses **2** ♦ : a conflict between antagonistic persons, ideas, or forces; *also* : a hard-fought contest between two opponents — **duel** *vb* — **du•el•ist** \-ə-list\ *n*

♦ battle, combat, conflict, confrontation, contest, face-off, rivalry, struggle, tug-of-war, warfare

du•en•de \dü-ˈen-dā\ *n* : the power to attract through personal magnetism and charm
du•en•na \dü-ˈe-nə, dyü-\ *n* **1** : an elderly woman in charge of the younger ladies in a Spanish or Portuguese family **2** : CHAPERONE
du•et \dü-ˈet, dyü-\ *n* : a musical composition for two performers
due to *prep* ♦ : as a result of : BECAUSE OF

♦ because of, owing to, through, with

duf•fel bag \ˈdə-fəl-\ *n* : a large cylindrical bag for personal belongings
duf•fer \ˈdə-fər\ *n* : an incompetent or clumsy person
dug *past and past part of* DIG
dug•out \ˈdəg-ˌau̇t\ *n* **1** : a boat made by hollowing out a log **2** : a shelter dug in the ground **3** : a low shelter facing a baseball diamond that contains the players' bench
DUI *n* : the act or crime of driving while under the influence of alcohol
duke \ˈdük, ˈdyük\ *n* **1** : a sovereign ruler of a continental European duchy **2** : a nobleman of the highest rank; *esp* : a member of the highest grade of the British peerage **3** *slang* : FIST 1 ⟨put up your ~*s*⟩ — **duke•dom** *n*
dul•cet \ˈdəl-sət\ *adj* **1** : pleasing to the ear **2** : AGREEABLE, SOOTHING
dul•ci•mer \ˈdəl-sə-mər\ *n* **1** : a stringed instrument of trapezoidal shape played with light hammers held in the hands **2** *or* **dul•ci•more** \-ˌmōr\ : an American folk instrument with three or four strings that is held on the lap and played by plucking or strumming
[1]**dull** \ˈdəl\ *adj* **1** : mentally slow : STUPID **2** : slow in perception or sensibility **3** : LISTLESS **4** : slow in action : SLUGGISH ⟨a ~ market⟩ **5** : lacking in force or intensity; *also* : not resonant or ringing **6** ♦ : lacking sharpness of edge or point : BLUNT **7** ♦ : lacking brilliance or luster **8** ♦ : low in saturation and lightness ⟨~ color⟩ **9** : overcast with clouds : CLOUDY **10** ♦ : causing weariness or lack of interest : UNINTERESTING — **dul•ly** *adv*

♦ [6] blunt, obtuse *Ant* keen, pointed, sharp, whetted ♦ [7] dim, flat, lusterless ♦ [8] light, pale, pastel, washed-out ♦ [10] dry, flat, monotonous, uninteresting, weary

[2]**dull** *vb* ♦ : to make or become dull

♦ blunt, dampen, deaden, numb *Ant* sharpen, whet

dull•ard \ˈdə-lərd\ *n* : a stupid person
dull•ness *also* **dul•ness** \ˈdəl-nəs\ *n* : the quality or state of being dull
du•ly \ˈdü-lē, ˈdyü-\ *adv* : in a due manner or time
dumb \ˈdəm\ *adj* **1** *often offensive* : lacking the power of speech **2** ♦ : making no utterance : SILENT **3** ♦ : not having or showing intelligence : STUPID — **dumb•ly** *adv*

♦ [2] mum, mute, silent, speechless, uncommunicative ♦ [3] mindless, senseless, simple, stupid, unintelligent

dumb•bell \ˈdəm-ˌbel\ *n* **1** : a bar with weights at the end used for exercise **2** : one who is stupid : DUMMY
dumb down *vb* : to lower the level of difficulty or intellectual content of
dumb•found *also* **dum•found** \ˌdəm-ˈfau̇nd\ *vb* ♦ : to confound briefly and usually with astonishment : ASTONISH

♦ amaze, astonish, astound, bowl, flabbergast, floor, shock, startle, stun, stupefy, surprise

dumb•wait•er \ˈdəm-ˌwā-tər\ *n* : a small elevator for conveying food and dishes from one floor to another
dum•my \ˈdə-mē\ *n, pl* **dummies** **1 a** : a person who cannot speak **b** ♦ : a stupid person **2** : the exposed hand in bridge played by the declarer in addition to that player's own hand; *also* : a bridge player whose hand is a dummy **3 a** : an imitative substitute for something **b** ♦ : a form representing the human figure used especially for displaying clothes : MANNEQUIN **4** : one seeming to act alone but really acting for another **5** : a mock-up of matter to be reproduced especially by printing

♦ [1b] blockhead, dope, idiot, imbecile, jackass, moron, numskull ♦ [3b] figure, form, manikin, mannequin

[1]**dump** \ˈdəmp\ *vb* **1** : to let fall in a pile **2** ♦ : to get rid of unceremoniously

♦ cast, discard, ditch, fling, jettison, junk, lose, reject, scrap, shed, shuck, slough, throw away, throw out, unload

[2]**dump** *n* **1** : a place for dumping something (as refuse) **2 a** : a reserve supply **b** ♦ : a place where reserve supplies are kept ⟨an ammunition ~⟩ **3** : a messy or objectionable place

♦ armory, arsenal, depot, magazine

dump•ing \ˈdəm-piŋ\ *n* ♦ : the act of one that dumps; *esp* : the selling of goods in quantity at below market price

♦ disposal, disposition, jettison, removal, riddance

dump•ling \ˈdəm-pliŋ\ *n* **1** : a small mass of boiled or steamed dough **2** : a dessert of fruit baked in biscuit dough
dumps \ˈdəmps\ *n pl* ♦ : a gloomy state of mind : low spirits ⟨in the ~⟩

♦ blues, dejection, depression, desolation, despondency, doldrums, forlornness, gloom, heartsickness, melancholy, sadness

dump truck *n* : a truck for transporting and dumping bulk material
dumpy \ˈdəm-pē\ *adj* **dump•i•er; -est** **1** ♦ : short and thick in build **2** : SHABBY

♦ chunky, heavyset, squat, stocky, stout, stubby, stumpy, thickset

¹dun \ˈdən\ *n* : a brownish dark gray
²dun *vb* **dunned; dun•ning** **1** : to make persistent demands for payment **2** : PLAGUE, PESTER — **dun** *n*
³dun *n* ♦ : an urgent request

♦ claim, demand, requisition

dunce \ˈdəns\ *n* ♦ : a slow stupid person

♦ blockhead, dope, dummy, idiot, imbecile, jackass, moron, numskull

dun•der•head \ˈdən-dər-ˌhed\ *n* : DUNCE, BLOCKHEAD
dune \ˈdün, ˈdyün\ *n* : a hill or ridge of sand piled up by the wind
dune buggy *n* : a motor vehicle with oversize tires for use on sand
¹dung \ˈdəŋ\ *n* ♦ : the feces of an animal : MANURE

♦ droppings, slops, waste

²dung *vb* : to dress (land) with dung
dun•ga•ree \ˌdəŋ-gə-ˈrē\ *n* **1** : a heavy coarse cotton twill; *esp* : blue denim **2** *pl* : clothes made of blue denim
dun•geon \ˈdən-jən\ *n* : a dark prison commonly underground
dung•hill \ˈdəŋ-ˌhil\ *n* : a manure pile
dunk \ˈdəŋk\ *vb* **1** ♦ : to dip or submerge temporarily in liquid **2** : to submerge oneself in water **3** : to shoot a basketball into the basket from above the rim

♦ dip, douse, duck, immerse, souse, submerge

duo \ˈdü-(ˌ)ō, ˈdyü-\ *n, pl* **du•os** **1** : DUET **2** ♦ : two similar or associated things : PAIR

♦ brace, couple, pair, twain, twosome

duo•dec•i•mal \ˌdü-ə-ˈde-sə-məl, ˌdyü-\ *adj* : of, relating to, or being a system of numbers with a base of 12
du•o•de•num \ˌdü-ə-ˈdē-nəm, ˌdyü-, dü-ˈäd-ᵊn-əm, dyü-\ *n, pl* **-de•na** \-ˈdē-nə, -ᵊn-ə\ *or* **-denums** : the first part of the small intestine extending from the stomach to the jejunum — **du•o•de•nal** \-ˈdēn-ᵊl, -ᵊn-əl\ *adj*
dup *abbr* **1** duplex **2** duplicate
¹dupe \ˈdüp, ˈdyüp\ *n* ♦ : one who is easily deceived or cheated

♦ gull, pigeon, sap, sucker, tool

²dupe *vb* **duped; dup•ing** ♦ : to make a dupe of : DECEIVE

♦ beguile, bluff, cozen, deceive, delude, fool, gull, have, hoax, hoodwink, humbug, misinform, mislead, string along, take in, trick

du•ple \ˈdü-pəl, ˈdyü-\ *adj* : having two beats or a multiple of two beats to the measure ⟨~ time⟩
¹du•plex \ˈdü-ˌpleks, ˈdyü-\ *adj* ♦ : having two principal elements or parts : DOUBLE

♦ binary, bipartite, double, dual, twin

²duplex *n* : something duplex; *esp* : a 2-family house
¹du•pli•cate \ˈdü-pli-kət, ˈdyü-\ *adj* **1** : consisting of or existing in two corresponding or identical parts or examples **2** ♦ : being the same as another

♦ equal, even, identical, indistinguishable, same

²du•pli•cate \ˈdü-pli-ˌkāt, ˈdyü-\ *vb* **-cat•ed; -cat•ing** **1** : to make double or twofold **2** ♦ : to make a copy of

♦ copy, imitate, replicate, reproduce

³du•pli•cate \-kət\ *n* ♦ : a thing that exactly resembles another in appearance, pattern, or content : COPY

♦ carbon copy, copy, duplication, facsimile, imitation, replica, replication, reproduction

du•pli•ca•tion \ˌdü-pli-ˈkā-shən, ˌdyü-\ *n* **1** : the act or process of duplicating **2** ♦ : a thing that exactly resembles another in appearance, pattern, or content

♦ carbon copy, counterpart, double, duplicate, facsimile, image, likeness, match, picture, replica, ringer, spit

du•pli•ca•tor \ˈdü-pli-ˌkā-tər, ˈdyü-\ *n* : COPIER
du•plic•i•ty \dü-ˈpli-sə-tē, dyü-\ *n, pl* **-ties** ♦ : the disguising of true intentions by deceptive words or action — **du•plic•i•tous** \-təs\ *adj* — **du•plic•i•tous•ly** *adv*

♦ artifice, craft, craftiness, crookedness, cunning, deceit, deceitfulness, dishonesty, dissimulation, double-dealing, guile, wiliness

du•ra•bil•i•ty \ˌdür-ə-ˈbi-lə-tē, ˌdyür-\ *n* ♦ : the quality or state of being durable

♦ endurance, persistence

du•ra•ble \ˈdür-ə-bəl, ˈdyür-\ *adj* : able to exist for a long time without significant deterioration of qualities or capabilities ⟨~ goods⟩
du•rance \ˈdür-əns, ˈdyür-\ *n* : restraint by or as if by physical force ⟨held in ~ vile⟩
du•ra•tion \dü-ˈrā-shən, dyü-\ *n* **1** ♦ : continuance in time **2** ♦ : the time during which something exists or lasts

♦ [1] continuance, continuation, endurance, persistence, subsistence ♦ [2] date, life, lifetime, run, standing, time

du•ress \dü-ˈres, dyü-\ *n* ♦ : compulsion by threat ⟨confession made under ~⟩

♦ coercion, compulsion, constraint, force, pressure

dur•ing \ˈdür-iŋ, ˈdyür-\ *prep* **1** ♦ : throughout the duration of ⟨swims every day ~ the summer⟩ **2** : at some point in ⟨broke in ~ the night⟩

♦ over, through, throughout

dusk \ˈdəsk\ *n* **1** ♦ : the darker part of twilight especially at night **2** : partial darkness

♦ evening, gloaming, nightfall, sundown, sunset, twilight *Ant* aurora, cockcrow, dawn, dawning, daybreak, daylight, morn, morning, sunrise, sunup

dusky \ˈdəs-kē\ *adj* **dusk•i•er; -est** **1** : somewhat dark in color **2** ♦ : marked by slight or deficient light — **dusk•i•ness** *n*

♦ dark, darkling, dim, gloomy, murky, obscure, somber (*or* sombre)

¹dust \ˈdəst\ *n* **1** : fine particles of matter **2** : the particles into which something disintegrates **3** ♦ : something worthless **4** ♦ : the surface of the ground — **dust•less** *adj*

♦ [3] chaff, deadwood, garbage, junk, litter, refuse, riffraff, rubbish, scrap, trash, waste ♦ [4] dirt, earth, ground, land, soil

²dust *vb* **1** : to make free of or remove dust **2** : to sprinkle with fine particles **3** : to sprinkle in the form of dust
dust bowl *n* : a region suffering from long droughts and dust storms
dust devil *n* : a small whirlwind containing sand or dust
dust•er \ˈdəs-tər\ *n* **1** : one that removes dust **2** : a dress-length housecoat **3** : one that scatters fine particles; *esp* : a device for applying insecticides to crops
dust•pan \ˈdəst-ˌpan\ *n* : a flat-ended pan for sweepings
dust storm *n* : a violent wind carrying dust across a dry region
dusty \ˈdəs-tē\ *adj* **1** ♦ : consisting of dust : POWDERY **2** : covered or abounding with dust

♦ fine, floury, powdery

dutch \ˈdəch\ *adv, often cap* : with each person paying his or her own way ⟨go ~⟩
Dutch \ˈdəch\ *n* **1 Dutch** *pl* : the people of the Netherlands **2** : the language of the Netherlands — **Dutch** *adj* — **Dutch•man** \-mən\ *n*
Dutch elm disease *n* : a fungus disease of elms characterized by yellowing of the foliage, defoliation, and death
dutch treat *n, often cap D* : an entertainment (as a meal) for which each person pays his or her own way — **dutch treat** *adv, often cap D*
du•te•ous \ˈdü-tē-əs, ˈdyü-\ *adj* : DUTIFUL, OBEDIENT
du•ti•able \ˈdü-tē-ə-bəl, ˈdyü-\ *adj* : subject to a duty ⟨~ imports⟩
du•ti•ful \ˈdü-ti-fəl, ˈdyü-\ *adj* **1** : motivated by a sense of duty ⟨a ~ son⟩ **2** ♦ : coming from or showing a sense of duty ⟨~ affection⟩ — **du•ti•ful•ly** *adv* — **du•ti•ful•ness** *n*

♦ deferential, regardful, respectful

du•ty \ˈdü-tē, ˈdyü-\ *n, pl* **duties** **1** ♦ : conduct or action required by one's occupation or position; *also* : obligatory tasks, conduct, or functions required by order or usage **2** : assigned service or business; *esp* : active military service **3** ♦ : a moral or legal obligation **4** ♦ : a charge usually of money imposed by authority on persons or property for public purposes : TAX **5** : the service required (as of a machine) : USE ⟨a heavy-*duty* tire⟩

♦ [1] assignment, chore, job, stint, task ♦ [3] burden, charge, commitment, need, obligation, responsibility ♦ [4] assessment, impost, levy, tax

DV *abbr* **1** God willing **2** Douay Version
DVD \ˌdē-ˌvē-ˈdē\ *n* : a high-capacity optical disk format; *also* : an optical disk using such a format
DVM *abbr* doctor of veterinary medicine
¹dwarf \ˈdwȯrf\ *n, pl* **dwarfs** \ˈdwȯrfs\ *also* **dwarves** \ˈdwȯrvz\ **1** ♦ : one that is much below normal size **2** ♦ : a small legendary

manlike being who is usually misshapen and ugly and skilled as a craftsman

♦ [1] midget, mite, peewee, pygmy, runt, scrub, shrimp *Ant* behemoth, colossus, giant, jumbo, leviathan, mammoth, monster, titan ♦ [2] brownie, elf, fairy, fay, gnome, hobgoblin, leprechaun, pixie, puck, troll

²**dwarf** *vb* **1 :** to restrict the growth or development of **:** STUNT **2 :** to cause to appear smaller ⟨*dwarfed* by comparison⟩
³**dwarf** *adj* **:** characterized by smallness or insignificance of size, proportion, scope, strength, or power
dwarf•ish \ˈdwȯr-fish\ *adj* ♦ **:** of or like a dwarf

♦ dwarf, fine, little, pocket, pygmy, slight, small, undersized

dwell \ˈdwel\ *vb* **dwelt** \ˈdwelt\ *or* **dwelled** \ˈdweld, ˈdwelt\; **dwell•ing 1** ♦ **:** to remain for a time **:** ABIDE **2** ♦ **:** to live as a resident **:** RESIDE **3 :** to keep the attention directed **4 :** to write or speak insistently — used with *on* or *upon*

♦ [1] abide, hang around, remain, stay, stick around, tarry ♦ [2] abide, live, reside

dwell•er \ˈdwe-lər\ *n* ♦ **:** one that dwells **:** INHABITANT

♦ denizen, inhabitant, occupant, resident

dwell•ing \ˈdwe-liŋ\ *n* ♦ **:** a shelter (as a house) in which people live **:** RESIDENCE

♦ abode, domicile, home, house, lodging, quarters, residence

DWI \ˌdē-ˌdəb-əl-(ˌ)yü-ˈī\ *n* **:** DUI
dwin•dle \ˈdwin-dᵊl\ *vb* **dwin•dled; dwin•dling** ♦ **:** to make or become steadily less

♦ abate, de-escalate, decline, decrease, die, diminish, ebb, fall, lessen, let up, lower, moderate, recede, relent, shrink, subside, taper, wane

dwt *abbr* pennyweight
Dy *symbol* dysprosium
dyb•buk \ˈdi-bək\ *n, pl* **dyb•bu•kim** \ˌdi-bu̇-ˈkēm\ *also* **dyb•buks :** a wandering soul believed in Jewish folklore to enter and possess a person
¹**dye** \ˈdī\ *n* **1 :** color produced by dyeing **2** ♦ **:** material used for coloring or staining

♦ color (*or* colour), pigment, stain

²**dye** *vb* **dyed; dye•ing 1** ♦ **:** to impart a new color to especially by impregnating with a dye **2 :** to take up or impart color in dyeing — **dy•er** \ˈdī(-ə)r\ *n*

♦ color (*or* colour), paint, stain, tinge, tint

dye•stuff \ˈdī-ˌstəf\ *n* **:** material used for coloring or staining **:** DYE
dying *pres part of* DIE
dy•nam•ic \dī-ˈna-mik\ *also* **dy•nam•i•cal** \-mi-kəl\ *adj* **1 :** of or relating to physical force producing motion **2** ♦ **:** operating with or marked by vigor or effect **:** ENERGETIC

♦ energetic, flush, lusty, peppy, robust, strenuous, vigorous, vital ♦ aggressive, assertive, emphatic, forceful, resounding, vehement

dy•nam•i•cal•ly \dī-ˈna-mi-kə-lē\ *adv* ♦ **:** in a dynamic manner

♦ energetically, firmly, forcefully, forcibly, hard, mightily, powerfully, stiffly, stoutly, strenuously, strongly, sturdily, vigorously

¹**dy•na•mite** \ˈdī-nə-ˌmīt\ *n* **:** an explosive made of nitroglycerin absorbed in a porous material; *also* **:** an explosive made without nitroglycerin
²**dynamite** *vb* **-mit•ed; -mit•ing :** to blow up with dynamite
³**dynamite** *adj* **:** TERRIFIC, WONDERFUL
dy•na•mo \ˈdī-nə-ˌmō\ *n, pl* **-mos 1 :** an electrical generator **2 :** a forceful energetic individual
dy•na•mom•e•ter \ˌdī-nə-ˈmä-mə-tər\ *n* **:** an instrument for measuring mechanical power (as of an engine)
dy•nas•ty \ˈdī-nəs-tē, -ˌnas-\ *n, pl* **-ties 1 :** a succession of rulers of the same family **2 :** a powerful group or family that maintains its position for a long time — **dy•nas•tic** \dī-ˈnas-tik\ *adj*
dys•en•tery \ˈdis-ᵊn-ˌter-ē\ *n, pl* **-ter•ies :** a disease marked by diarrhea with blood and mucus in the feces; *also* **:** DIARRHEA
dys•func•tion *also* **dis•func•tion** \dis-ˈfəŋk-shən\ *n* **1 :** impaired or abnormal functioning ⟨liver ∼⟩ **2 :** abnormal or unhealthy behavior within a group ⟨family ∼⟩ — **dys•func•tion•al** \-shə-nəl\ *adj*
dys•lex•ia \dis-ˈlek-sē-ə\ *n* **:** a learning disability marked by difficulty in reading, writing, and spelling — **dys•lex•ic** \-sik\ *adj or n*
dys•pep•sia \dis-ˈpep-shə, -sē-ə\ *n* **:** INDIGESTION — **dys•pep•tic** \-ˈpep-tik\ *n*
dys•pep•tic *adj* ♦ **:** having or showing ill humor

♦ bearish, bilious, cantankerous, disagreeable, ill-humored, ill-tempered, ornery, splenetic, surly

dys•pla•sia \dis-ˈplā-zh(ē-)ə\ *n* **:** abnormal growth or development
dys•pro•si•um \dis-ˈprō-zē-əm\ *n* **:** a metallic chemical element that forms highly magnetic compounds
dys•tro•phy \ˈdis-trə-fē\ *n, pl* **-phies :** a disorder involving atrophy of muscular tissue; *esp* **:** MUSCULAR DYSTROPHY
dz *abbr* dozen

E

¹**e** \ˈē\ *n, pl* **e's** *or* **es** \ˈēz\ *often cap* **1 :** the 5th letter of the English alphabet **2 :** the base of the system of natural logarithms having the approximate value 2.71828 **3 :** a grade rating a student's work as poor or failing
²**e** *abbr, often cap* **1** east; eastern **2** error **3** excellent
e- *comb form* **:** electronic ⟨*e*-commerce⟩
ea *abbr* each
¹**each** \ˈēch\ *adj* **:** being one of the class named ⟨∼ player⟩
²**each** *pron* **:** every individual one
³**each** *adv* **:** to or for each **:** APIECE ⟨cost five cents ∼⟩
each other *pron* **:** each of two or more in reciprocal action or relation ⟨looked at *each other*⟩
ea•ger \ˈē-gər\ *adj* ♦ **:** marked by urgent or enthusiastic desire or interest ⟨∼ to learn⟩ — **ea•ger•ly** *adv*

♦ avid, enthusiastic, hungry, keen, raring, thirsty *Ant* apathetic, indifferent

ea•ger•ness *n* ♦ **:** the quality or state of being eager; *also* **:** an act or instance of being eager

♦ alacrity, ambition, appetite, ardor, avidity, enthusiasm, excitement, hunger, impatience, keenness, quickness, thirst *Ant* apathy, indifference

¹**ea•gle** \ˈē-gəl\ *n* **1 :** a large bird of prey related to the hawks **2 :** a score of two under par on a hole in golf
²**eagle** *vb* **ea•gled; ea•gling :** to score an eagle on a golf hole
ea•glet \ˈē-glət\ *n* **:** a young eagle
-ean — see -AN
E and OE *abbr* errors and omissions excepted
¹**ear** \ˈir\ *n* **1 :** the organ of hearing; *also* **:** the outer part of this in a vertebrate **2 :** something resembling a mammal's ear in shape, position, or function **3 :** an ability to understand and appreciate something heard ⟨a good ∼ for music⟩ **4** ♦ **:** sympathetic attention

♦ attention, awareness, cognizance, eye, heed, notice, observance, observation

²**ear** *n* **:** the fruiting spike of a cereal (as wheat)
ear•ache \-ˌāk\ *n* **:** an ache or pain in the ear
ear•drum \-ˌdrəm\ *n* **:** a thin membrane that receives and transmits sound waves in the ear
eared \ˈird\ *adj* **:** having ears especially of a specified kind or number ⟨a long-*eared* dog⟩
ear•ful \ˈir-ˌfu̇l\ *n* **:** a verbal outpouring (as of news, gossip, anger, or complaint)
earl \ˈərl\ *n* **:** a member of the British peerage ranking below a marquess and above a viscount — **earl•dom** \-dəm\ *n*
ear•lobe \ˈir-ˌlōb\ *n* **:** the pendent part of the ear
¹**ear•ly** \ˈər-lē\ *adv* **ear•li•er; -est** ♦ **:** at an ealy time

♦ beforehand, precociously, prematurely, unseasonably *Ant* late

²early *adj* **ear·li·er; -est** **1** ♦ **:** of, relating to, or occurring near the beginning; *also* **:** ANCIENT, PRIMITIVE **2** ♦ **:** occurring before the usual time ⟨an ~ breakfast⟩; *also* **:** occurring in the near future

♦ [1] ancient, primal, primeval, primitive *Ant* late ♦ [2] precocious, premature, unseasonable, untimely *Ant* late

¹ear·mark \ˈir-ˌmärk\ *n* **:** an identification mark (as on the ear of an animal); *also* **:** a distinguishing mark ⟨~*s* of poverty⟩

²earmark *vb* **1 :** to mark with an earmark **2** ♦ **:** to designate for a specific purpose

♦ allocate, consecrate, dedicate, devote, reserve, save

ear·muff \-ˌməf\ *n* **:** one of a pair of ear coverings worn to protect against cold

earn \ˈərn\ *vb* **1** ♦ **:** to receive as a return for service **2** ♦ **:** to make or come to be duly worthy of **:** DESERVE, MERIT — **earn·er** *n*

♦ [1] acquire, attain, draw, gain, garner, get, land, make, secure, win *Ant* forfeit, lose ♦ [2] deserve, merit, rate

earned run *n* **:** a run in baseball that scores without benefit of an error before the fielding team has had a chance to make the third putout of the inning

earned run average *n* **:** the average number of earned runs per game scored against a pitcher in baseball

¹ear·nest \ˈər-nəst\ *n* ♦ **:** an intensely serious state of mind ⟨spoke in ~⟩

♦ earnestness, gravity, intentness, seriousness, sobriety, solemnity

²earnest *adj* **1** ♦ **:** seriously intent and sober ⟨an ~ face⟩ ⟨an ~ attempt⟩ **2** ♦ **:** marked by importance **:** GRAVE — **ear·nest·ly** *adv*

♦ [1, 2] grave, humorless (*or* humourless), serious, severe, sober, solemn, staid, unsmiling, weighty

³earnest *n* **1 :** something of value given by a buyer to a seller to bind a bargain **2 :** PLEDGE

ear·nest·ness *n* ♦ **:** intent and serious state or quality (as of mind)

♦ gravity, intentness, seriousness, sobriety, solemnity *Ant* frivolity, levity, lightheartedness

earn·ings \ˈər-niŋz\ *n pl* **1** ♦ **:** something (as wages) earned **2** ♦ **:** the balance of revenue after deduction of costs and expenses

♦ [1] income, proceeds, profit, return, revenue, yield ♦ [2] gain, lucre, net, payoff, proceeds, profit, return

ear·phone \ˈir-ˌfōn\ *n* **:** a device that reproduces sound and is worn over or in the ear

ear·piece \-ˌpēs\ *n* **:** a part of an instrument which is placed against or in the ear; *esp* **:** EARPHONE

ear·plug \-ˌpləg\ *n* **:** a protective device for insertion into the opening of the ear

ear·ring \-ˌriŋ\ *n* **:** an ornament for the earlobe

ear·shot \-ˌshät\ *n* ♦ **:** range of hearing

♦ hail, hearing, sound

ear·split·ting \-ˌspli-tiŋ\ *adj* ♦ **:** intolerably loud or shrill

♦ booming, clamorous (*or* clamourous), deafening, loud, piercing, roaring, thunderous

earth \ˈərth\ *n* **1** ♦ **:** the fragmental material composing part of the surface of the globe **:** SOIL, DIRT **2** ♦ **:** areas of land as distinguished from sea and air **:** LAND, GROUND **3** *often cap* ♦ **:** the planet on which we live that is 3d in order from the sun

♦ [1, 2] dirt, dust, ground, land, soil ♦ [3] planet, world

earth·en \ˈər-thən\ *adj* **:** made of earth or baked clay

earth·en·ware \-ˌwar\ *n* **:** slightly porous opaque pottery fired at low heat

earth·ling \ˈərth-liŋ\ *n* **:** an inhabitant of the earth

earth·ly \ˈərth-lē\ *adj* ♦ **:** characteristic of or belonging to this earth; *also* **:** relating to the human race's actual life on this earth — **earth·li·ness** *n*

♦ material, mundane, temporal, terrestrial, worldly *Ant* heavenly, nontemporal

earth·quake \-ˌkwāk\ *n* **:** a shaking or trembling of a portion of the earth

earth science *n* **:** any of the sciences (as geology or meteorology) that deal with the earth or one of its parts

earth·shak·ing \ˈərth-ˌshā-kiŋ\ *adj* **:** of great importance **:** MOMENTOUS

earth·ward \-wərd\ *also* **earth·wards** \-wərdz\ *adv* **:** toward the earth

earth·work \ˈərth-ˌwərk\ *n* **:** an embankment or fortification of earth

earth·worm \-ˌwərm\ *n* **:** a long segmented worm found in damp soil

earthy \ˈər-thē\ *adj* **earth·i·er; -est** **1 :** of, relating to, or consisting of earth; *also* **:** suggesting earth ⟨~ flavors⟩ **2** ♦ **:** not theoretical or ideal **:** PRACTICAL **3 :** COARSE, GROSS — **earth·i·ness** *n*

♦ down-to-earth, hardheaded, matter-of-fact, practical, pragmatic, realistic

ear·wax \ˈir-ˌwaks\ *n* **:** the yellow waxy secretion from the ear

ear·wig \-ˌwig\ *n* **:** any of numerous insects with slender many-jointed antennae and a pair of appendages resembling forceps at the end of the body

¹ease \ˈēz\ *n* **1** ♦ **:** comfort of body or mind **:** freedom from pain, discomfort, or concern **2 :** naturalness of manner **3** ♦ **:** freedom from difficulty or effort

♦ [1] alleviation, comfort, decrease, relief ♦ [3] leisure, relaxation, repose, rest

²ease *vb* **eased; eas·ing** **1** ♦ **:** to relieve from distress **2** ♦ **:** to lessen the pressure or tension of **3** ♦ **:** to make or become less difficult ⟨~ credit⟩

♦ [1] allay, alleviate, assuage, help, mitigate, mollify, palliate, relieve, soothe ♦ [2] loosen, relax, slack, slacken ♦ [3] assist, facilitate, further, hasten, help, improve, loosen, promote *Ant* complicate

ea·sel \ˈē-zəl\ *n* **:** a frame for supporting something (as an artist's canvas)

eas·i·ly \ˈē-zə-lē\ *adv* ♦ **:** in an easy manner **:** without difficulty

♦ effortlessly, fluently, freely, handily, lightly, painlessly, readily, smoothly *Ant* arduously, laboriously

¹east \ˈēst\ *adv* **:** to or toward the east

²east *adj* **1 :** situated toward or at the east **2 :** coming from the east

³east *n* **1 :** the general direction of sunrise **2 :** the compass point directly opposite to west **3** *cap* **:** regions or countries east of a specified or implied point — **east·er·ly** \ˈē-stər-lē\ *adv or adj* — **east·ward** *adv or adj* — **east·wards** *adv*

Eas·ter \ˈē-stər\ *n* **:** a church feast observed on a Sunday in March or April in commemoration of Christ's resurrection

east·ern \ˈē-stərn\ *adj* **1** *often cap* **:** of, relating to, or characteristic of a region designated East **2** *cap* **:** of, relating to, or being the Christian churches originating in the Church of the Eastern Roman Empire **3 :** lying toward or coming from the east — **East·ern·er** *n*

easy \ˈē-zē\ *adj* **eas·i·er; -est** **1** ♦ **:** marked by ease ⟨an ~ life⟩; *esp* **:** not causing distress or difficulty ⟨~ tasks⟩ **2 :** MILD, LENIENT ⟨be ~ on him⟩ **3 :** GRADUAL ⟨an ~ slope⟩ **4 :** free from pain, trouble, or worry ⟨rest ~⟩ **5 :** LEISURELY ⟨an ~ pace⟩ **6 :** NATURAL ⟨an ~ manner⟩ **7** ♦ **:** giving ease, comfort, or relaxation **:** COMFORTABLE ⟨an ~ chair⟩ **8** ♦ **:** readily taken advantage of — **eas·i·ness** \-zē-nəs\ *n*

♦ [1] effortless, facile, fluent, fluid, light, painless, ready, simple, smooth, snap, soft *Ant* arduous, difficult, hard, labored ♦ [7] comfortable, snug, soft ♦ [8] gullible, susceptible

easy·go·ing \ˌē-zē-ˈgō-iŋ\ *adj* ♦ **:** relaxed and casual in style or manner

♦ affable, breezy, carefree, happy-go-lucky, informal, laid-back *Ant* uptight ♦ flexible, lax, loose, relaxed, slack, unrestrained, unrestricted *Ant* rigorous ♦ carefree, careless, cavalier, gay, happy-go-lucky, insouciant, lighthearted, unconcerned

eat \ˈēt\ *vb* **ate** \ˈāt\; **eat·en** \ˈēt-ᵊn\; **eat·ing** **1** ♦ **:** to take in as food **:** take food **2 :** to use up **:** DEVOUR **3** ♦ **:** to consume gradually **:** CORRODE — **eat·able** *adj or n* — **eat·er** *n*

♦ [1] dine, fare, feed ♦ [3] bite, corrode, erode, fret

eat·ery \ˈē-tə-rē\ *n, pl* **-er·ies** **:** LUNCHEONETTE, RESTAURANT

eaves \ˈēvz\ *n pl* **:** the overhanging lower edge of a roof

eaves·drop \ˈēvz-ˌdräp\ *vb* **:** to listen secretly — **eaves·drop·per** *n*

¹ebb \ˈeb\ *n* **1 :** the flowing back from shore of water brought in by the tide **2 :** a point or state of decline

²ebb *vb* **1 :** to recede from the flood **2** ♦ **:** to fall from a higher to a lower level or from a better to a worse state **:** DECLINE ⟨his fortunes ~*ed*⟩

♦ abate, decline, decrease, diminish, dwindle, fall, lessen, recede, subside, taper

EBCDIC \ˈeb-sə-ˌdik\ *n* **:** a computer code for representing alphanumeric information
Ebo·la \ē-bō-lə\ *n* **:** an often fatal hemorrhagic fever caused by a virus (**Ebola virus**) of African origin
¹eb·o·ny \ˈe-bə-nē\ *n, pl* **-nies :** a hard heavy wood of Old World tropical trees related to the persimmon
²ebony *adj* **1 :** made of or resembling ebony **2** ♦ **:** of the color black

♦ black, raven

ebul·lient \i-ˈbu̇l-yənt, -ˈbəl-\ *adj* **1 :** BOILING, AGITATED **2 :** EXUBERANT — **ebul·lience** \-yəns\ *n*
EC *abbr* European Community
¹ec·cen·tric \ik-ˈsen-trik\ *adj* **1 :** deviating from a usual or accepted pattern **2 :** deviating from a circular path ⟨~ orbits⟩ **3 :** set with axis or support off center ⟨an ~ cam⟩; *also* **:** being off center — **ec·cen·tri·cal·ly** \-tri-k(ə-)lē\ *adv*
²eccentric *n* ♦ **:** an eccentric person

♦ character, crackpot, crank, kook, nut, oddball, screwball, weirdo

ec·cen·tric·i·ty \ˌek-ˌsen-ˈtri-sə-tē\ *n* ♦ **:** the quality or state of being eccentric; *also* **:** odd or whimsical behavior

♦ crotchet, idiosyncrasy, mannerism, oddity, peculiarity, quirk, singularity, trick

Eccles *abbr* Ecclesiastes
Ec·cle·si·as·tes \i-ˌklē-zē-ˈas-tēz\ *n* **:** a book of wisdom literature in canonical Jewish and Christian Scripture
ec·cle·si·as·tic \i-ˌklē-zē-ˈas-tik\ *n* ♦ **:** a member of the clergy **:** CLERGYMAN

♦ clergyman, divine, father, minister, preacher, priest, reverend

ec·cle·si·as·ti·cal \-ti-kəl\ *or* **ec·cle·si·as·tic** \-tik\ *adj* **:** of or relating to a church especially as an institution ⟨~ art⟩ — **ec·cle·si·as·ti·cal·ly** \-ti-k(ə-)lē\ *adv*
Ec·cle·si·as·ti·cus \i-ˌklē-zē-ˈas-ti-kəs\ *n* **:** a didactic book included in the Protestant Apocrypha and as Sirach in the Roman Catholic canon of the Old Testament
Ecclus *abbr* Ecclesiasticus
ECG *abbr* electrocardiogram
ech·e·lon \ˈe-shə-ˌlän\ *n* **1 :** a steplike arrangement (as of troops or airplanes) **2** ♦ **:** a level (as of authority or responsibility) within an organization

♦ degree, footing, level, place, position, rank, situation, standing, station, status — see RANK

ech·i·na·cea \ˌe-ki-ˈnā-sē-ə, -shə\ *n* **:** the dried root of three composite herbs that is used primarily in herbal remedies to boost the immune system; *also* **:** any of these herbs
echi·no·derm \i-ˈkī-nə-ˌdərm\ *n* **:** any of a phylum of marine animals (as starfishes and sea urchins) having similar body parts (as the arms of a starfish) arranged around a central axis and often having a calcium-containing outer skeleton
¹echo \ˈe-kō\ *n, pl* **ech·oes** *also* **ech·os 1 :** repetition of a sound caused by a reflection of the sound waves; *also* **:** the reflection of a radar signal by an object **2 :** one who closely imitates or repeats another's words, ideas, or acts — **echo·ic** \e-ˈkō-ik\ *adj*
²echo *vb* ♦ **:** to produce an echo; *also* **:** to repeat or imitate (as a sound)

♦ repeat, resonate, resound, reverberate

echo·lo·ca·tion \ˌe-kō-lō-ˈkā-shən\ *n* **:** a process for locating distant or invisible objects by sound waves reflected back to the sender (as a bat) from the objects
echt \ˈekt\ *adj* **:** TRUE, GENUINE ⟨an ~ New Yorker⟩
éclair \ā-ˈklar\ *n* **:** an oblong shell of light pastry with whipped cream or custard filling
éclat \ā-ˈklä\ *n* **1 :** a dazzling effect or success **2 :** ACCLAIM
eclec·tic \e-ˈklek-tik\ *adj* **1 :** selecting or made up of what seems best of varied sources **2** ♦ **:** composed of elements drawn from various sources; *also* **:** consisting of dissimilar ingredients or constituents — **eclectic** *n* — **eclec·ti·cism** \-ˈklek-tə-ˌsi-zəm\ *n*

♦ assorted, heterogeneous, miscellaneous, mixed, motley, varied

¹eclipse \i-ˈklips\ *n* **1 :** the total or partial obscuring of one heavenly body by another; *also* **:** a passing into the shadow of a heavenly body **2 :** a falling into obscurity or decline
²eclipse *vb* **eclipsed; eclips·ing 1 :** to cause an eclipse of **2** ♦ **:** to go beyond in accomplishment **:** SURPASS

♦ beat, better, excel, outdistance, outdo, outshine, outstrip, surpass, top, transcend

eclip·tic \i-ˈklip-tik\ *n* **:** the great circle of the celestial sphere that is the apparent path of the sun
ec·logue \ˈek-ˌlȯg, -ˌläg\ *n* **:** a pastoral poem
ECM *abbr* European Common Market
ecol *abbr* ecological; ecology
E. coli \ˌē-ˈkō-ˌlī\ *n, pl* **E. coli :** a rod-shaped bacterium that sometimes causes intestinal illness
ecol·o·gy \i-ˈkä-lə-jē, e-\ *n, pl* **-gies 1 :** a branch of science concerned with the relationships between organisms and their environment **2 :** the pattern of relations between one or more organisms and the environment — **eco·log·i·cal** \ˌē-kə-ˈlä-ji-kəl, ˌe-\ *also* **eco·log·ic** \-jik\ *adj* — **eco·log·i·cal·ly** \-ji-k(ə-)lē\ *adv* — **ecol·o·gist** \i-ˈkä-lə-jist, e-\ *n*
e–com·merce \ˈē-ˌkä-(ˌ)mərs\ *n* **:** commerce conducted via the Internet
econ *abbr* economics; economist; economy
eco·nom·ic \ˌe-kə-ˈnä-mik, ˌē-\ *adj* **:** of or relating to the production, distribution, and consumption of goods and services
eco·nom·i·cal \-ˈnä-mi-kəl\ *adj* **1** ♦ **:** marked by careful use of resources **:** THRIFTY **2 :** operating with little waste or at a saving — **ec·o·nom·i·cal·ly** \-k(ə-)lē\ *adv*

♦ frugal, provident, sparing, thrifty

eco·nom·ics \ˌe-kə-ˈnä-miks, ˌē-\ *n sing or pl* **:** a social science dealing with the production, distribution, and consumption of goods and services — **econ·o·mist** \i-ˈkä-nə-mist\ *n*
econ·o·mise *Brit var of* ECONOMIZE
econ·o·mize \i-ˈkä-nə-ˌmīz\ *vb* **-mized; -miz·ing** ♦ **:** to practice economy **:** be frugal — **econ·o·miz·er** *n*

♦ save, scrimp, skimp *Ant* waste

¹econ·o·my \i-ˈkä-nə-mē\ *n, pl* **-mies 1** ♦ **:** thrifty and efficient use of resources; *also* **:** an instance of this **2 :** manner of arrangement or functioning **:** ORGANIZATION **3 :** an economic system ⟨a money ~⟩

♦ frugality, husbandry, providence, thrift *Ant* wastefulness

²economy *adj* **:** ECONOMICAL ⟨~ cars⟩
eco·sys·tem \ˈē-kō-ˌsis-təm, ˈe-\ *n* **:** the complex of an ecological community and its environment functioning as a unit in nature
eco·tour·ism \ˌē-kō-ˈtu̇r-ˌi-zəm, ˌe-\ *n* **:** the touring of natural habitats in a manner meant to minimize ecological impact — **eco·tour·ist** \-ˈtu̇r-ist\ *n*
ecru \ˈe-krü, ˈā-\ *n* **:** BEIGE — **ecru** *adj*
ec·sta·sy \ˈek-stə-sē\ *n, pl* **-sies 1** ♦ **:** extreme and usually rapturous emotional excitement **2** *often cap* **:** an illicit drug with hallucinogenic properties that is chemically related to amphetamine

♦ elation, euphoria, exhilaration, heaven, intoxication, paradise, rapture, rhapsody, transport *Ant* depression

ec·stat·ic \ek-ˈsta-tik, ik-\ *adj* ♦ **:** of, relating to, or marked by ecstasy — **ec·stat·i·cal·ly** \-ti-k(ə-)lē\ *adv*

♦ elated, euphoric, intoxicated, rapturous, rhapsodic *Ant* depressed

Ecua *abbr* Ecuador
Ec·ua·dor·an \ˌe-kwə-ˈdȯr-ən\ *or* **Ec·ua·dor·ean** *or* **Ec·ua·dor·ian** \-ē-ən\ *n* **:** a native or inhabitant of Ecuador — **Ecuadorean** *or* **Ecuadorian** *adj*
ec·u·men·i·cal \ˌe-kyu̇-ˈme-ni-kəl\ *adj* **:** general in extent or influence; *esp* **:** promoting or tending toward worldwide Christian unity — **ec·u·men·i·cal·ly** \-k(ə-)lē\ *adv*
ec·ze·ma \ig-ˈzē-mə, ˈeg-zə-mə, ˈek-sə-\ *n* **:** an itching skin inflammation with oozing and then crusted lesions — **ec·zem·a·tous** \ig-ˈze-mə-təs\ *adj*
ed *abbr* **1** edited; edition; editor **2** education
¹-ed \d *after a vowel or* b, g, j, l, m, n, ŋ, r, t͟h, v, z, zh; əd, id *after* d, t; t *after other sounds*\ *vb suffix or adj suffix* **1** — used to form the past participle of regular weak verbs ⟨end*ed*⟩ ⟨fad*ed*⟩ ⟨tri*ed*⟩ ⟨patt*ed*⟩ **2 :** having **:** characterized by ⟨cultur*ed*⟩ ⟨2-legg*ed*⟩; *also* **:** having the characteristics of ⟨bigot*ed*⟩
²-ed *vb suffix* — used to form the past tense of regular weak verbs ⟨judg*ed*⟩ ⟨deni*ed*⟩ ⟨dropp*ed*⟩
Edam \ˈē-dəm, -ˌdam\ *n* **:** a yellow Dutch pressed cheese made in balls
ed·dy \ˈe-dē\ *n, pl* **eddies :** WHIRLPOOL — **eddy** *vb*
edel·weiss \ˈād-ᵊl-ˌwīs, -ˌvīs\ *n* **:** a small perennial woolly composite herb that grows high in the Alps
ede·ma \i-ˈdē-mə\ *n* **:** abnormal accumulation of watery fluid in connective tissue or in a serous cavity — **edem·a·tous** \-ˈde-mə-təs\ *adj*
Eden \ˈēd-ᵊn\ *n* ♦ **:** a place or state of bliss or delight **:** PARADISE

♦ Elysium, heaven, paradise, utopia

¹edge \ˈej\ *n* **1 :** the cutting side of a blade **2 :** a noticeably harsh or sharp quality; *also* **:** FORCE, EFFECTIVENESS **3** ♦ **:** the line where something begins or ends; *also* **:** the area adjoining such an edge **4** ♦ **:** a favorable margin **:** ADVANTAGE — **edged** \ˈejd\ *adj*

♦ [3] border, bound, boundary, fringe, margin, perimeter, periphery, rim, skirt, verge ♦ [4] advantage, better, drop, jump, upper hand, vantage

²edge *vb* **edged; edg•ing 1** ♦ **:** to give or form an edge **2 :** to move or force gradually ⟨~ into a crowd⟩ **3 :** to defeat by a small margin ⟨*edged* out her opponent⟩ — **edg•er** *n*

♦ grind, hone, sharpen, strop, whet

edge•wise \ˈej-ˌwīz\ *adv* **:** SIDEWAYS

edg•ing \ˈe-jiŋ\ *n* **:** something that forms an edge or border ⟨a lace ~⟩

edgy \ˈe-jē\ *adj* **edg•i•er; -est 1** ♦ **:** having an edge **:** SHARP ⟨an ~ tone⟩ **2** ♦ **:** being on edge **:** TENSE, NERVOUS **3 :** having a bold, provocative, or unconventional quality — **edg•i•ness** *n*

♦ [1] cutting, ground, keen, sharp ♦ [2] aflutter, anxious, jittery, jumpy, nervous, nervy, tense, troubled, upset, worried

ed•i•ble \ˈe-də-bəl\ *adj* **:** fit or safe to be eaten — **ed•i•bil•i•ty** \ˌe-də-ˈbi-lə-tē\ *n* — **edible** *n*

edict \ˈē-ˌdikt\ *n* ♦ **:** a proclamation having the force of law; *also* **:** ORDER, DECREE

♦ decree, directive, fiat, order, ruling

ed•i•fi•ca•tion \ˌe-də-fə-ˈkā-shən\ *n* **:** instruction and improvement especially in morality

ed•i•fice \ˈe-də-fəs\ *n* **:** a usually large building

ed•i•fy \ˈe-də-ˌfī\ *vb* ♦ **:** to instruct and improve especially in moral and religious knowledge

♦ educate, enlighten, nurture

ed•it \ˈe-dət\ *vb* **1** ♦ **:** to revise, assemble, or prepare for publication or release (as a motion picture) **2 :** to direct the publication and policies of (as a newspaper) **3 :** DELETE — **ed•i•tor** \ˈe-də-tər\ *n* — **ed•i•tor•ship** *n* — **ed•i•tress** \-trəs\ *n*

♦ redraft, revamp, revise, rework

edi•tion \i-ˈdi-shən\ *n* **1 :** the form in which a text is published **2 :** the total number of copies (as of a book) published at one time **3 :** VERSION

¹ed•i•to•ri•al \ˌe-də-ˈtōr-ē-əl\ *adj* **1 :** of or relating to an editor or editing **2 :** being or resembling an editorial — **ed•i•to•ri•al•ly** *adv*

²editorial *n* **:** an article (as in a newspaper) giving the views of the editors or publishers; *also* **:** an expression of opinion resembling an editorial ⟨a television ~⟩

ed•i•to•ri•al•ize \ˌe-də-ˈtōr-ē-ə-ˌlīz\ *vb* **-ized; -iz•ing 1 :** to express an opinion in an editorial **2 :** to introduce opinions into factual reporting **3 :** to express an opinion — **ed•i•to•ri•al•i•za•tion** \-ˌtōr-ē-ə-lə-ˈzā-shən\ *n* — **ed•i•to•ri•al•iz•er** *n*

EDP *abbr* electronic data processing

EDT *abbr* Eastern daylight (saving) time

educ *abbr* education; educational

ed•u•ca•ble \ˈe-jə-kə-bəl\ *adj* **:** capable of being educated

ed•u•cate \ˈe-jə-ˌkāt\ *vb* **-cat•ed; -cat•ing 1** ♦ **:** to provide with schooling **2** ♦ **:** to develop mentally and morally; *also* **:** to provide with information

♦ [1] indoctrinate, instruct, school, teach, train, tutor ♦ [2] edify, enlighten, nurture

educated *adj* ♦ **:** having an education; *esp* **:** having an education beyond the average

♦ erudite, knowledgeable, learned, literate, scholarly, well-read *Ant* ignorant, illiterate, uneducated

ed•u•ca•tion \ˌe-jə-ˈkā-shən\ *n* **1** ♦ **:** the action or process of educating or being educated; *also* **:** the knowledge and development resulting from an educational process **2 :** a field of study dealing with methods of teaching and learning

♦ instruction, teaching, training, tutelage ♦ erudition, knowledge, learning, scholarship, science

ed•u•ca•tion•al \-shə-nəl\ *adj* ♦ **:** of, relating to, or concerned with education; *also* **:** serving to further education — **ed•u•ca•tion•al•ly** *adv*

♦ informative, instructive

educational television *n* **:** PUBLIC TELEVISION

ed•u•ca•tor \-ˌkā-tər\ *n* ♦ **:** one skilled in teaching

♦ instructor, pedagogue, schoolteacher, teacher

educe \i-ˈdüs, -ˈdyüs\ *vb* **educed; educ•ing 1 :** to bring out (as something latent) **:** ELICIT, EVOKE **2 :** DEDUCE

ed•u•tain•ment \ˌe-jə-ˈtān-mənt\ *n* **:** entertainment that is designed to be educational

¹-ee \ˈē, (ˌ)ē\ *n suffix* **1 :** one that receives or benefits from (a specified action or thing) ⟨grant*ee*⟩ ⟨patent*ee*⟩ **2 :** a person who does (a specified action) ⟨escap*ee*⟩

²-ee *n suffix* **1 :** a particular especially small kind of ⟨boot*ee*⟩ **2 :** one resembling or suggestive of ⟨goat*ee*⟩

EE *abbr* electrical engineer

EEC *abbr* European Economic Community

EEG *abbr* **1** electroencephalogram **2** electroencephalograph

eel \ˈēl\ *n* **:** any of numerous snakelike bony fishes with a smooth slimy skin

EEO *abbr* equal employment opportunity

ee•rie *also* **ee•ry** \ˈir-ē\ *adj* **ee•ri•er; -est** ♦ **:** so mysterious, strange, or unexpected as to send a chill up the spine **:** WEIRD, UNCANNY — **ee•ri•ly** \ˈir-ə-lē\ *adv*

♦ creepy, haunting, odd, spooky, strange, uncanny, unearthly, weird

eff *abbr* efficiency

ef•face \i-ˈfās, e-\ *vb* **ef•faced; ef•fac•ing :** to obliterate or obscure by or as if by rubbing out — **ef•face•able** *adj* — **ef•face•ment** *n*

¹ef•fect \i-ˈfekt\ *n* **1 :** MEANING, INTENT **2** ♦ **:** something that inevitably follows an antecedent **:** RESULT **3 :** APPEARANCE **4** ♦ **:** power to bring about a result **:** INFLUENCE **5** *pl* ♦ **:** movable property **:** GOODS, POSSESSIONS **6 :** the quality or state of being operative **:** OPERATION

♦ [2] aftermath, conclusion, consequence, issue, outcome, outgrowth, product, result, upshot *Ant* antecedent, cause, occasion, reason ♦ [4] impact, influence, mark, repercussion, sway ♦ *usu* **effects** [5] belongings, chattels, holdings, paraphernalia, possessions, things

²effect *vb* ♦ **:** to cause to happen ⟨~ repairs⟩ ⟨~ changes⟩

♦ bring about, cause, create, effectuate, generate, induce, make, produce, prompt, result

ef•fec•tive \i-ˈfek-tiv\ *adj* **1** ♦ **:** producing a decisive or desired effect; *also* **:** marked by the quality of being influential or exerting positive influence ⟨an ~ presentation⟩ **2 :** IMPRESSIVE, STRIKING **3 :** ready for service or action **4 :** being in effect — **ef•fec•tive•ly** *adv*

♦ convincing, decisive, effectual, efficacious, efficient, forceful, fruitful, persuasive, potent, productive *Ant* ineffective, ineffectual, inefficient, fruitless, unproductive

ef•fec•tive•ness *n* ♦ **:** the quality or state of being effective; *also* **:** power to be effective

♦ efficacy, efficiency, force, impact, productiveness

ef•fec•tu•al \i-ˈfek-chə-wəl\ *adj* ♦ **:** producing an intended effect — **ef•fec•tu•al•ly** *adv*

♦ effective, efficacious, efficient, fruitful, potent, productive

ef•fec•tu•ate \i-ˈfek-chə-ˌwāt\ *vb* **-at•ed; -at•ing** ♦ **:** to cause to come into being **:** BRING ABOUT, EFFECT

♦ bring about, cause, create, effect, generate, induce, make, produce, prompt, result, work, yield

ef•fem•i•nate \ə-ˈfe-mə-nət\ *adj* ♦ **:** marked by qualities more typical of women than men — **ef•fem•i•na•cy** \-nə-sē\ *n*

♦ feminine, girlish, unmanly, womanly *Ant* manly, mannish, masculine

ef•fen•di \e-ˈfen-dē\ *n* **:** a man of property, authority, or education in an eastern Mediterranean country

ef•fer•ent \ˈe-fə-rənt\ *adj* **:** bearing or conducting outward from a more central part ⟨~ nerves⟩

ef•fer•vesce \ˌe-fər-ˈves\ *vb* **-vesced; -vesc•ing 1 :** to bubble and hiss as gas escapes **2 :** to show liveliness or exhilaration — **ef•fer•ves•cence** \-ˈve-sᵊns\ *n*

ef•fer•ves•cent \-ᵊnt\ *adj* ♦ **:** impossible or difficult to restrain or suppress — **ef•fer•ves•cent•ly** *adv*

♦ bubbly, buoyant, exuberant, frolicsome, high-spirited, vivacious

ef•fete \e-ˈfēt\ *adj* **1** ♦ **:** having lost character, vitality, or strength; *also* **:** DECADENT **2 :** EFFEMINATE

♦ decadent, degenerate, soft, weak

ef•fi•ca•cious \ˌe-fə-ˈkā-shəs\ *adj* ♦ **:** producing an intended effect ⟨~ remedies⟩

♦ effective, effectual, efficient, fruitful, potent, productive

ef•fi•ca•cy \ˈe-fi-kə-sē\ *n* ♦ **:** the power to produce an effect

♦ effectiveness, efficiency, productiveness ***Ant*** ineffectiveness, inefficiency

ef•fi•cien•cy \-shən-sē\ *n* ♦ **:** the quality or degree of being efficient; *also* **:** efficient operation

♦ effectiveness, efficacy, productiveness

ef•fi•cient \i-ˈfi-shənt\ *adj* ♦ **:** productive of desired effects especially without waste — **ef•fi•cient•ly** *adv*

♦ effective, effectual, efficacious, fruitful, potent, productive

ef•fi•gy \ˈe-fə-jē\ *n, pl* **-gies :** IMAGE; *esp* **:** a crude figure of a hated person
ef•flo•res•cence \ˌe-flə-ˈres-ᵊns\ *n* **1 :** the period or state of flowering **2 :** the action or process of developing **3 :** fullness of development **:** FLOWERING
ef•flu•ence \ˈe-ˌflü-əns\ *n* **:** something that flows out
ef•flu•ent \ˈe-ˌflü-ənt\ *n* **:** something that flows out; *esp* **:** a fluid (as sewage) discharged as waste — **effluent** *adj*
ef•flu•vi•um \e-ˈflü-vē-əm\ *n, pl* **-via** \-vē-ə\ *also* **-vi•ums 1 :** a usually unpleasant emanation **2 :** a by-product usually in the form of waste
ef•fort \ˈe-fərt\ *n* **1** ♦ **:** hard work **:** EXERTION; *also* **:** a product of effort **2 :** active or applied force

♦ exertion, expenditure, labor (*or* labour), pains, sweat, trouble, work

ef•fort•less *adj* ♦ **:** showing or requiring little or no effort

♦ easy, facile, fluent, fluid, light, painless, ready, smooth, snap

ef•fort•less•ly *adv* ♦ **:** in an effortless manner

♦ easily, fluently, freely, handily, lightly, painlessly, readily, smoothly

ef•fron•tery \i-ˈfrən-tə-rē\ *n, pl* **-ter•ies** ♦ **:** shameless and offensive boldness

♦ audacity, brass, brazenness, cheek, chutzpah, gall, nerve, presumption, temerity

ef•ful•gence \i-ˈfu̇l-jəns, -ˈfəl-\ *n* ♦ **:** radiant splendor **:** BRILLIANCE

♦ brilliance, dazzle, illumination, luminosity, radiance, splendor

ef•ful•gent \-jənt\ *adj* ♦ **:** extremely radiant

♦ beaming, bright, brilliant, glowing, incandescent, luminous, lustrous, radiant

ef•fu•sion \i-ˈfyü-zhən, e-\ *n* **:** a gushing forth; *also* **:** unrestrained utterance — **ef•fuse** \-ˈfyüz, e-\ *vb*
ef•fu•sive \i-ˈfyü-siv, e-\ *adj* ♦ **:** marked by the expression of great or excessive emotion or enthusiasm — **ef•fu•sive•ly** *adv*

♦ demonstrative, emotional, uninhibited, unreserved, unrestrained

eft \ˈeft\ *n* **:** NEWT
EFT *or* **EFTS** *abbr* electronic funds transfer (system)
e.g. *abbr* for example
Eg *abbr* Egypt; Egyptian
egal•i•tar•i•an•ism \i-ˌga-lə-ˈter-ē-ə-ˌni-zəm\ *n* **:** a belief in human equality especially in social, political, and economic affairs — **egal•i•tar•i•an** *adj or n*
¹egg \ˈeg\ *vb* ♦ **:** to urge to action — usually used with *on*

♦ *usu* **egg on** encourage, exhort, goad, press, prod, prompt, urge

²egg *n* **1 :** a rounded usually hard-shelled reproductive body especially of birds and reptiles from which the young hatches; *also* **:** the egg of the common domestic chicken as an article of food **2 :** a germ cell produced by a female
egg•beat•er \ˈeg-ˌbē-tər\ *n* **:** a hand-operated kitchen utensil for beating, stirring, or whipping
egg cell *n* **:** EGG 2
egg•head \-ˌhed\ *n* ♦ **:** an intellectual person **:** INTELLECTUAL, HIGHBROW

♦ highbrow, intellectual, nerd

egg•nog \-ˌnäg\ *n* **:** a drink consisting of eggs beaten with sugar, milk or cream, and often alcoholic liquor
egg•plant \-ˌplant\ *n* **:** the edible usually large and purplish fruit of a plant related to the potato; *also* **:** the plant
egg roll *n* **:** a thin egg-dough casing filled with minced vegetables and often bits of meat and usually deep-fried
egg•shell \ˈeg-ˌshel\ *n* **:** the hard exterior covering of an egg
egis *var of* AEGIS
eg•lan•tine \ˈe-glən-ˌtīn, -ˌtēn\ *n* **:** SWEETBRIER
ego \ˈē-gō\ *n, pl* **egos 1 :** the self as distinguished from others **2 :** the one of the three divisions of the psyche in psychoanalytic theory that is the organized conscious mediator between the person and reality **3** ♦ **:** an exaggerated sense of self-importance; *also* **:** a confidence and satisfaction in oneself

♦ complacence, conceit, pride, self-importance, self-regard, self-respect, self-satisfaction, smugness, vainglory, vanity

ego•cen•tric \ˌē-gō-ˈsen-trik\ *adj* ♦ **:** concerned or overly concerned with the self; *esp* **:** SELF-CENTERED

♦ egotistic, self-seeking, selfish ***Ant*** selfless

ego•ism \ˈē-gō-ˌi-zəm\ *n* **1 :** a doctrine holding self-interest to be the motive or the valid end of action **2** ♦ **:** excessive concern for oneself with or without exaggerated feelings of self-importance — **ego•ist** \-ist\ *n*

♦ egotism, self-centeredness, self-interest, self-regard, selfishness ***Ant*** selflessness

ego•is•tic \ˌē-gō-ˈis-tik\ *adj* **:** having an exaggerated sense of self-importance — **ego•is•ti•cal•ly** *adv*
ego•tism \ˈē-gə-ˌti-zəm\ *n* **1 :** the practice of talking about oneself too much **2** ♦ **:** an exaggerated sense of self-importance **:** CONCEIT — **ego•tist** \-tist\ *n*

♦ complacence, conceit, pride, self-esteem, self-importance, self-satisfaction, smugness, vainglory, vanity

ego•tis•tic \ˌē-gə-ˈtis-tik\ *or* **ego•tis•ti•cal** \-ti-kəl\ *adj* ♦ **:** an exaggerated sense of self-importance — **ego•tis•ti•cal•ly** *adv*

♦ complacent, conceited, important, prideful, proud, self-important, self-satisfied, smug, stuck-up, vain

ego trip *n* **:** an act that enhances and satisfies one's ego
egre•gious \i-ˈgrē-jəs\ *adj* ♦ **:** notably bad **:** FLAGRANT — **egre•gious•ly** *adv* — **egre•gious•ness** *n*

♦ blatant, flagrant, glaring, gross, obvious, patent, pronounced, rank, striking

egress \ˈē-ˌgres\ *n* ♦ **:** a way out **:** EXIT

♦ exit, issue, outlet

egret \ˈē-grət, i-ˈgret\ *n* **:** any of various herons that bear long plumes during the breeding season
Egyp•tian \i-ˈjip-shən\ *n* **1 :** a native or inhabitant of Egypt **2 :** the language of the ancient Egyptians from earliest times to about the 3d century A.D. — **Egyptian** *adj*
ei•der \ˈī-dər\ *n* **:** any of several northern sea ducks that yield a soft down
ei•der•down \-ˌdau̇n\ *n* **1 :** the down of the eider **2 :** a comforter filled with eiderdown
ei•do•lon \ī-ˈdō-lən\ *n, pl* **-lons** *or* **-la** \-lə\ **1 :** PHANTOM **2 :** IDEAL
eight \ˈāt\ *n* **1 :** one more than seven **2 :** the 8th in a set or series **3 :** something having eight units — **eight** *adj or pron* — **eighth** \ˈātth\ *adj or adv or n*
eight ball *n* **:** a black pool ball numbered 8 — **behind the eight ball :** in a highly disadvantageous position
eigh•teen \ˈāt-ˈtēn\ *n* **:** one more than 17 — **eighteen** *adj or pron* — **eigh•teenth** \-ˈtēnth\ *adj or n*
eighty \ˈā-tē\ *n, pl* **eight•ies :** eight times 10 — **eight•i•eth** \ˈā-tē-əth\ *adj or n* — **eighty** *adj or pron*
ein•stei•ni•um \īn-ˈstī-nē-əm\ *n* **:** an artificially produced radioactive element
¹ei•ther \ˈē-t͟hər, ˈī-\ *adj* **1 :** being the one and the other of two **:** EACH ⟨trees on ~ side⟩ **2 :** being the one or the other of two ⟨take ~ road⟩
²either *pron* **:** the one or the other
³either *conj* — used as a function word before the first of two or more words or word groups of which the last is preceded by *or* to indicate that they represent alternatives ⟨a statement is ~ true or false⟩
ejac•u•late \i-ˈja-kyə-ˌlāt\ *vb* **-lat•ed; -lat•ing 1 :** to eject a fluid (as semen) **2** ♦ **:** to utter suddenly **:** EXCLAIM — **ejac•u•la•to•ry** \-ˈja-kyə-lə-ˌtōr-ē\ *adj*

♦ blurt, bolt, cry, spout

ejac•u•la•tion \i-ˌja-kyə-ˈlā-shən\ *n* **:** something ejaculated; *esp* ♦ **:** a short sudden emotional utterance

♦ cry, exclamation, interjection

eject \i-ˈjekt\ *vb* ♦ : to drive or throw out or off — **ejec•tion** \-ˈjek-shən\ *n*

♦ banish, boot (out), bounce, cast, expel, oust, rout, run off, throw out ♦ belch, disgorge, erupt, jet, spew, spout, spurt

eke \ˈēk\ *vb* **eked; ek•ing** ♦ : to gain, supplement, or extend usually with effort — usually used with *out* ⟨∼ out a living⟩

♦ *usu* **eke out** scrape, squeeze, wrest, wring

EKG *abbr* electrocardiogram; electrocardiograph
el *abbr* elevation
¹elab•o•rate \i-ˈla-bə-rət, -ˈla-brət\ *adj* **1** ♦ : planned or carried out with great care **2** ♦ : being complex and usually ornate — **elab•o•rate•ly** *adv*

♦ [1, 2] complex, complicated, detailed, fancy, intricate, involved, sophisticated *Ant* simple

²elab•o•rate \i-ˈla-bə-ˌrāt\ *vb* **-rat•ed; -rat•ing** **1** : to build up from simpler ingredients **2** ♦ : to work out in detail : develop fully

♦ *usu* **elaborate on** amplify, develop, embellish, enlarge (on), expand

elab•o•rate•ness *n* ♦ : the state or quality of being elaborate

♦ complexity, intricacy, sophistication

elab•o•ra•tion \-ˌla-bə-ˈrā-shən\ *n* **1** ♦ : the act or process of elaborating **2** : something produced by elaborating

♦ development, evolution, expansion, growth, progress, progression

élan \ā-ˈlän\ *n* : ARDOR, SPIRIT
eland \ˈē-lənd, -ˌland\ *n, pl* **eland** *also* **elands** : either of two large African antelopes with spirally twisted horns in both sexes
elapse \i-ˈlaps\ *vb* **elapsed; elaps•ing** ♦ : to slip by : PASS

♦ cease, end, expire, finish, pass, quit, stop, terminate, wind up

¹elas•tic \i-ˈlas-tik\ *adj* **1** ♦ : capable of recovering size and shape after deformation : SPRINGY **2** ♦ : capable of ready change or easy expansion or contraction : FLEXIBLE; *also* ADAPTABLE — **elas•tic•i•ty** \-ˌlas-ˈti-sə-tē, ˌē-ˌlas-\ *n*

♦ [1] flexible, resilient, rubbery, springy, stretch, supple *Ant* inelastic, inflexible, rigid, stiff ♦ [2] adaptable, adjustable, changeable, flexible, fluid, malleable, variable

²elastic *n* **1** : elastic material **2** : a rubber band
elate \i-ˈlāt\ *vb* **elat•ed; elat•ing** ♦ : to fill with joy

♦ elevate, enrapture, exhilarate, transport *Ant* depress

elated *adj* ♦ : marked by high spirits

♦ ecstatic, euphoric, intoxicated, rapturous, rhapsodic

ela•tion \-ˈlā-shən\ *n* ♦ : the quality or state of being elated

♦ ecstasy, euphoria, exhilaration, heaven, intoxication, paradise, rapture, rhapsody, transport

¹el•bow \ˈel-ˌbō\ *n* **1** : the joint of the arm; *also* : the outer curve of the bent arm **2** : a bend or joint resembling an elbow in shape
²elbow *vb* ♦ : to push aside with the elbow; *also* : to make one's way by elbowing

♦ bulldoze, muscle, press, push

elbow room \ˈel-ˌbō-ˌrüm, -ˌrům\ *n* : enough space for work or operation
¹el•der \ˈel-dər\ *n* : ELDERBERRY 2
²elder *adj* **1** : being the older one **2** : EARLIER, FORMER **3** : of higher rank : SENIOR
³elder *n* **1** ♦ : an older individual : SENIOR **2** ♦ : one having authority by reason of age and experience **3** : a church officer

♦ [1] ancient, golden-ager, oldster, senior citizen ♦ [2] dean, senior

el•der•ber•ry \ˈel-dər-ˌber-ē\ *n* **1** : the edible black or red fruit of a shrub or tree related to the honeysuckle and bearing flat clusters of small white or pink flowers **2** : a tree or shrub bearing elderberries
el•der•ly \ˈel-dər-lē\ *adj* **1** ♦ : rather old; *esp* : past middle age **2** : of, relating to, or characteristic of later life

♦ ancient, geriatric, old, senior *Ant* young, youthful

el•dest \ˈel-dəst\ *adj* : of the greatest age
El Do•ra•do \ˌel-də-ˈrä-dō, -ˈrā-\ *n* : a place of vast riches, abundance, or opportunity
elec *abbr* electric; electrical; electricity

¹elect \i-ˈlekt\ *adj* **1** ♦ : carefully selected : CHOSEN **2** : elected but not yet installed in office ⟨the president-*elect*⟩

♦ chosen, select

²elect *n, pl* **elect** **1** : a selected person **2** *pl* ♦ : a select or exclusive group

♦ best, choice, cream, elite, fat, flower, pick, prime

³elect *vb* **1** : to select by vote (as for office or membership) **2** ♦ : to select or choose especially by preference : PICK

♦ choose, cull, handpick, name, opt, pick, prefer, select, single, take

elec•tion \i-ˈlek-shən\ *n* **1** ♦ : an act or process of electing **2** : the fact of being elected

♦ choice, selection

elec•tion•eer \i-ˌlek-shə-ˈnir\ *vb* : to work for the election of a candidate or party
¹elec•tive \i-ˈlek-tiv\ *adj* **1** : chosen or filled by election **2** ♦ : permitting a choice : OPTIONAL

♦ discretionary, optional, voluntary

²elective *n* : an elective course or subject of study
elec•tor \i-ˈlek-tər\ *n* **1** : one qualified to vote in an election **2** : one elected to an electoral college — **elec•tor•al** \i-ˈlek-tə-rəl\ *adj*
electoral college *n* : a body of electors who elect the president and vice president of the U.S.
elec•tor•ate \i-ˈlek-tə-rət\ *n* : a body of persons entitled to vote
elec•tric \i-ˈlek-trik\ *adj* **1** *or* **elec•tri•cal** \-tri-kəl\ : of, relating to, operated by, or produced by electricity **2** ♦ : exciting as if by electric shock : ELECTRIFYING, THRILLING; *also* : charged with strong emotion — **elec•tri•cal•ly** *adv*

♦ breathtaking, exciting, exhilarating, rousing, stirring, thrilling

electrical storm *n* : THUNDERSTORM
electric chair *n* : a chair used to carry out the death penalty by electrocution
electric eye *n* : PHOTOELECTRIC CELL
elec•tri•cian \i-ˌlek-ˈtri-shən\ *n* : a person who installs, operates, or repairs electrical equipment
elec•tric•i•ty \i-ˌlek-ˈtri-sə-tē\ *n, pl* **-ties** **1** : a form of energy that occurs naturally (as in lightning) or is produced (as in a generator) and that is expressed in terms of the movement and interaction of electrons **2** : electric current
elec•tri•fy \i-ˈlek-trə-ˌfī\ *vb* **-fied; -fy•ing** **1** : to charge with electricity **2** : to equip for use of electric power **3** ♦ : to excite intensely or suddenly : THRILL — **elec•tri•fi•ca•tion** \i-ˌlek-trə-fə-ˈkā-shən\ *n*

♦ excite, exhilarate, galvanize, intoxicate, thrill, titillate, turn on

elec•tro•car•dio•gram \i-ˌlek-trō-ˈkär-dē-ə-ˌgram\ *n* : the tracing made by an electrocardiograph
elec•tro•car•dio•graph \-ˌgraf\ *n* : a device for recording the changes of electrical potential occurring during the heartbeat — **elec•tro•car•dio•graph•ic** \-ˌkär-dē-ə-ˈgra-fik\ *adj* — **elec•tro•car•di•og•ra•phy** \-dē-ˈä-grə-fē\ *n*
elec•tro•chem•is•try \-ˈke-mə-strē\ *n* : a branch of chemistry that deals with the relation of electricity to chemical changes — **elec•tro•chem•i•cal** \-ˈke-mi-kəl\ *adj*
elec•tro•cute \i-ˈlek-trə-ˌkyüt\ *vb* **-cut•ed; -cut•ing** **1** : to kill (a criminal) by electricity **2** : to kill by electric shock — **elec•tro•cu•tion** \-ˌlek-trə-ˈkyü-shən\ *n*
elec•trode \i-ˈlek-ˌtrōd\ *n* : a conductor used to establish electrical contact with a nonmetallic part of a circuit
elec•tro•en•ceph•a•lo•gram \i-ˌlek-trō-in-ˈse-fə-lə-ˌgram\ *n* : the tracing made by an electroencephalograph
elec•tro•en•ceph•a•lo•graph \-ˌgraf\ *n* : an apparatus for detecting and recording brain waves — **elec•tro•en•ceph•a•lo•graph•ic** \-ˌse-fə-lə-ˈgra-fik\ *adj* — **elec•tro•en•ceph•a•log•ra•phy** \-ˈlä-grə-fē\ *n*
elec•trol•o•gist \i-ˌlek-ˈträ-lə-jist\ *n* : one that uses electrical means to remove hair, warts, moles, and birthmarks from the body
elec•trol•y•sis \i-ˌlek-ˈträ-lə-səs\ *n* **1** : the production of chemical changes by passage of an electric current through an electrolyte **2** : the destruction of hair roots with an electric current — **elec•tro•lyt•ic** \-trə-ˈli-tik\ *adj*
elec•tro•lyte \i-ˈlek-trə-ˌlīt\ *n* : a nonmetallic electric conductor in which current is carried by the movement of ions; *also* : a substance whose solution or molten form is such a conductor
elec•tro•mag•net \i-ˌlek-trō-ˈmag-nət\ *n* : a core of magnetic

material (as iron) surrounded by a coil of wire through which an electric current is passed to magnetize the core
elec•tro•mag•net•ic \-mag-ˈne-tik\ *adj* **:** of, relating to, or produced by electromagnetism — **elec•tro•mag•net•i•cal•ly** *adv*
electromagnetic radiation *n* **:** energy in the form of electromagnetic waves; *also* **:** a series of electromagnetic waves
electromagnetic wave *n* **:** a wave (as a radio wave, an X-ray, or a wave of visible light) that consists of associated electric and magnetic effects and that travels at the speed of light
elec•tro•mag•ne•tism \i-ˌlek-trō-ˈmag-nə-ˌti-zəm\ *n* **1 :** magnetism developed by a current of electricity **2 :** a natural force responsible for interactions between charged particles which result from their charge
elec•tro•mo•tive force \i-ˌlek-trə-ˈmō-tiv-\ *n* **:** the potential difference derived from an electrical source per unit quantity of electricity passing through the source
elec•tron \i-ˈlek-ˌträn\ *n* **:** a negatively charged elementary particle
elec•tron•ic \i-ˌlek-ˈträ-nik\ *adj* **1 :** of or relating to electrons or electronics **2 :** involving a computer — **elec•tron•i•cal•ly** \-ni-k(ə-)lē\ *adv*
electronic mail *n* **:** E-MAIL
elec•tron•ics \i-ˌlek-ˈträ-niks\ *n* **1 :** the physics of electrons and electronic devices **2 :** electronic components, devices, or equipment
electron microscope *n* **:** an instrument in which a beam of electrons is used to produce an enlarged image of a minute object
electron tube *n* **:** a device in which electrical conduction by electrons takes place within a sealed container and which is used for the controlled flow of electrons
electron volt *n* **:** a unit of energy equal to 1.60×10^{-19} joule
elec•tro•pho•re•sis \i-ˌlek-trə-fə-ˈrē-səs\ *n* **:** the movement of suspended particles through a medium (as paper or gel) by an electromotive force — **elec•tro•pho•ret•ic** \-ˈre-tik\ *adj*
elec•tro•plate \i-ˈlek-trə-ˌplāt\ *vb* **:** to coat (as with metal) by electrolysis
elec•tro•shock therapy \i-ˈlek-trō-ˌshäk-\ *n* **:** the treatment of mental disorder by applying electric current to the head and inducing convulsions
elec•tro•stat•ics \i-ˌlek-trə-ˈsta-tiks\ *n* **:** physics dealing with the interactions of stationary electric charges
el•ee•mos•y•nary \ˌe-li-ˈmäs-ᵊn-ˌer-ē\ *adj* **:** CHARITABLE
el•e•gance \ˈe-li-gəns\ *n* **1 a ♦ :** refined gracefulness **b ♦ :** tasteful richness (as of design) **2 :** something marked by elegance — **el•e•gant•ly** *adv*

♦ [1a, 1b] class, grace, handsomeness, majesty, refinement, stateliness

el•e•gant \-gənt\ *adj* **♦ :** marked by elegance; *also* **:** of a high grade or quality

♦ graceful, handsome, majestic, refined, stately, tasteful *Ant* graceless, inelegant, tasteless, unhandsome ♦ choice, dainty, delicate, exquisite, rare, select

ele•giac \ˌe-lə-ˈjī-ək, -ˌak\ *adj* **:** of or relating to an elegy
el•e•gy \ˈe-lə-jē\ *n, pl* **-gies ♦ :** a song, poem, or speech expressing grief for one who is dead; *also* **:** a reflective poem usually melancholy in tone

♦ dirge, lament, requiem, threnody

elem *abbr* elementary
el•e•ment \ˈe-lə-mənt\ *n* **1** *pl* **:** weather conditions; *esp* **:** severe weather ⟨boards exposed to the ~*s*⟩ **2 :** natural environment ⟨in her ~⟩ **3 ♦ :** a constituent part **4** *pl* **♦ :** the simplest principles (as of an art or science) **:** RUDIMENTS **5 :** a member of a mathematical set **6 :** any of more than 100 fundamental substances that consist of atoms of only one kind

♦ [3] component, constituent, factor, ingredient, member *Ant* whole ♦ *usu* **elements** [4] essentials, principles, rudiments

el•e•men•tal \ˌe-lə-ˈment-ᵊl\ *adj* **♦ :** of, relating to, or being an element

♦ basic, elementary, essential, fundamental, rudimentary, underlying

el•e•men•ta•ry \ˌe-lə-ˈmen-trē, -tə-rē\ *adj* **1 ♦ :** of, relating to, or dealing with the simplest elements or principles of something **:** RUDIMENTARY **2 :** of, relating to, or teaching the basic subjects of education

♦ basic, elemental, essential, fundamental, rudimentary, underlying *Ant* advanced

elementary particle *n* **:** a subatomic particle of matter and energy that does not appear to be made up of other smaller particles
elementary school *n* **:** a school usually including the first six or the first eight grades
el•e•phant \ˈe-lə-fənt\ *n, pl* **elephants** *also* **elephant :** any of a family of huge thickset nearly hairless mammals that have the snout lengthened into a trunk and two long curving pointed ivory tusks
el•e•phan•ti•a•sis \ˌe-lə-fən-ˈtī-ə-səs\ *n, pl* **-a•ses** \-ˌsēz\ **:** enlargement and thickening of tissues in response especially to infection by minute parasitic worms
el•e•phan•tine \ˌe-lə-ˈfan-ˌtēn, -ˌtīn, ˈe-lə-fən-\ *adj* **1 ♦ :** of great size or strength **2 :** CLUMSY, PONDEROUS

♦ enormous, giant, gigantic, ginormous, huge, jumbo, mammoth, monumental, titanic, tremendous, vast, whopping

elev *abbr* elevation
el•e•vate \ˈe-lə-ˌvāt\ *vb* **-vat•ed; -vat•ing 1 ♦ :** to lift up **:** RAISE **2 ♦ :** to raise in rank or status **3 ♦ :** to raise the spirits of **:** ELATE

♦ [1] boost, hike, hoist, jack, lift, raise ♦ [2] advance, promote, raise, upgrade ♦ [3] elate, enrapture, exhilarate, transport

el•e•va•tion \ˌe-lə-ˈvā-shən\ *n* **1 :** the height to which something is raised (as above sea level) **2 ♦ :** a lifting up **3 ♦ :** something (as a hill or swelling) that is elevated

♦ [2] advancement, ascent, promotion, rise, upgrade ♦ [3] eminence, height, highland, hill, mound, prominence, rise

el•e•va•tor \ˈe-lə-ˌvā-tər\ *n* **1 :** a cage or platform for conveying people or things from one level to another **2 :** a building for storing and discharging grain **3 :** a movable surface on an airplane to produce motion up or down
elev•en \i-ˈle-vən\ *n* **1 :** one more than 10 **2 :** the 11th in a set or series **3 :** something having 11 units; *esp* **:** a football team — **eleven** *adj or pron* — **elev•enth** \-vənth\ *adj or n*
elf \ˈelf\ *n, pl* **elves** \ˈelvz\ **♦ :** a mischievous fairy

♦ brownie, dwarf, fairy, fay, gnome, hobgoblin, leprechaun, pixie, puck, troll

ELF *abbr* extremely low frequency
elf•in \ˈel-fən\ *adj* **1 :** of, relating to, or resembling an elf **2 ♦ :** having an otherworldly or magical quality or charm

♦ alluring, attractive, charming, engaging, fascinating, fetching

elf•ish \ˈel-fish\ *adj* **♦ :** of, relating to, or like an elf; *also* **:** irresponsibly playful

♦ antic, coltish, fay, frisky, frolicsome, playful, sportive

elic•it \i-ˈli-sət\ *vb* **♦ :** to draw out or forth

♦ evoke, raise

elide \i-ˈlīd\ *vb* **elid•ed; elid•ing :** to suppress or alter by elision
el•i•gi•ble \ˈe-lə-jə-bəl\ *adj* **:** qualified to participate or to be chosen — **el•i•gi•bil•i•ty** \ˌe-lə-jə-ˈbi-lə-tē\ *n* — **eligible** *n*
elim•i•nate \i-ˈli-mə-ˌnāt\ *vb* **-nat•ed; -nat•ing 1 :** REMOVE, ERADICATE **2 :** to pass (wastes) from the body **3 :** to leave out **4 ♦ :** to bar from participation, enjoyment, consideration, or inclusion — **elim•i•na•tion** \-ˌli-mə-ˈnā-shən\ *n*

♦ ban, bar, count out, debar, except, exclude, rule out

eli•sion \i-ˈli-zhən\ *n* **:** the omission of a final or initial sound or a word; *esp* **:** the omission of an unstressed vowel or syllable in a verse to achieve a uniform rhythm
elite \ā-ˈlēt, ē-\ *n* **1 ♦ :** the choice part; *also* **:** a superior group **2 :** a typewriter type providing 12 characters to the inch — **elite** *adj*

♦ best, choice, cream, elect, fat, flower, pick, prime

elit•ism \-ˈlē-ˌti-zəm\ *n* **:** leadership or rule by an elite; *also* **:** advocacy of such elitism — **elit•ist** \-tist\ *n or adj*
elix•ir \i-ˈlik-sər\ *n* **1 :** a substance held capable of prolonging life indefinitely; *also* **:** PANACEA **2 :** a sweetened alcoholic medicinal solution
Eliz•a•be•than \i-ˌli-zə-ˈbē-thən\ *adj* **:** of, relating to, or characteristic of Elizabeth I of England or her times
elk \ˈelk\ *n, pl* **elk** *or* **elks 1 :** MOOSE — used for one of the Old World **2 :** a large gregarious deer of No. America, Europe, Asia, and northwestern Africa with curved antlers having many branches
ell *n* **:** an extension at right angles to a building
el•lipse \i-ˈlips, e-\ *n* **:** a closed curve of oval shape
el•lip•sis \i-ˈlip-səs, e-\ *n, pl* **el•lip•ses** \-ˌsēz\ **1 :** omission from an expression of a word clearly implied **2 :** marks (as . . .) to show omission
el•lip•soid \i-ˈlip-ˌsȯid, e-\ *n* **:** a surface all plane sections of which are circles or ellipses — **el•lip•soi•dal** \-ˌlip-ˈsȯid-ᵊl\ *also* **ellipsoid** *adj*

el•lip•ti•cal \i-ˈlip-ti-kəl, e-\ *or* **el•lip•tic** \-tik\ *adj* **1 :** of, relating to, or shaped like an ellipse **2 :** of, relating to, or marked by ellipsis — **el•lip•ti•cal•ly** \-ti-k(ə-)lē\ *adv*
elm \ˈelm\ *n* **:** any of a genus of large trees that have toothed leaves and nearly circular one-seeded winged fruits and are often grown as shade trees; *also* **:** the wood of an elm
El Ni•ño \el-ˈnē-nyō\ *n* **:** a flow of unusually warm Pacific Ocean water moving toward and along the west coast of So. America
el•o•cu•tion \ˌe-lə-ˈkyü-shən\ *n* **:** the art of effective public speaking — **el•o•cu•tion•ist** \-shə-nist\ *n*
elon•gate \i-ˈlȯŋ-ˌgāt\ *vb* **-gat•ed; -gat•ing** ♦ **:** to make or grow longer

♦ draw out, extend, lengthen, prolong, protract, stretch

elon•ga•tion \(ˌ)ē-ˌlȯŋ-ˈgā-shən\ *n* ♦ **:** the state of being elongated or lengthened; *also* **:** the process of growing or increasing in length

♦ extension, prolongation

elope \i-ˈlōp\ *vb* **eloped; elop•ing :** to run away especially to be married — **elope•ment** *n* — **elop•er** *n*
el•o•quence \-kwəns\ *n* ♦ **:** forceful and persuasive expression; *also* **:** the art or power of using such expression

♦ articulateness, persuasiveness, poetry, power, rhetoric

el•o•quent \ˈe-lə-kwənt\ *adj* **1** ♦ **:** having or showing clear and forceful expression **2** ♦ **:** clearly showing some feeling or meaning — **el•o•quent•ly** *adv*

♦ [1] articulate, fluent, well-spoken ♦ [2] expressive, meaning, meaningful, pregnant, significant, suggestive

[1]**else** \ˈels\ *adv* **1** ♦ **:** in a different or additional manner or place or at a different or additional time ⟨where ~ can we meet⟩ **2 :** if not ⟨obey or ~ you'll be sorry⟩

♦ differently, other, otherwise

[2]**else** *adj* ♦ **:** being another **:** OTHER; *esp* **:** being in addition ⟨what ~ do you want⟩

♦ additional, another, farther, further, more, other

else•where \-ˌhwer\ *adv* **:** in or to another place
elu•ci•date \i-ˈlü-sə-ˌdāt\ *vb* **-dat•ed; -dat•ing** ♦ **:** to make clear usually by explanation

♦ clarify, clear (up), demonstrate, explain, explicate, expound, illuminate, illustrate, interpret, spell out

elu•ci•da•tion \-ˌlü-sə-ˈdā-shən\ *n* ♦ **:** the act, process, or means of elucidating

♦ clarification, explanation, explication, exposition, illumination, illustration, interpretation

elude \ē-ˈlüd\ *vb* **elud•ed; elud•ing** **1** ♦ **:** to avoid adroitly **:** EVADE **2 :** to escape the notice of

♦ avoid, dodge, duck, escape, eschew, evade, shake, shirk, shun

elu•sive \ē-ˈlü-siv\ *adj* ♦ **:** tending to elude **:** EVASIVE — **elu•sive•ly** *adv* — **elu•sive•ness** *n*

♦ evasive, fugitive, slippery

el•ver \ˈel-vər\ *n* **:** a young eel
elves *pl of* ELF
Ely•sian \-ˈli-zhən\ *adj* ♦ **:** of or relating to Elysium; *esp* **:** full of bliss or delight

♦ celestial, empyrean, heavenly, supernal

Ely•si•um \i-ˈli-zhē-əm, -zē-\ *n, pl* **-si•ums** *or* **-sia** \-zhē-ə, -zē-\ ♦ **:** a place or state of bliss or delight **:** PARADISE

♦ Eden, heaven, paradise, utopia

em \ˈem\ *n* **:** a length approximately the width of the letter *M*
EM *abbr* **1** electromagnetic **2** electron microscope **3** enlisted man
ema•ci•ate \i-ˈmā-shē-ˌāt\ *vb* **-at•ed; -at•ing :** to become or cause to become very thin — **ema•ci•a•tion** \-ˌmā-shē-ˈā-shən, -sē-\ *n*
e–mail \ˈē-ˌmāl\ *n* **1 :** a system for transmitting messages between computers on a network **2 :** a message or messages sent and received through an e-mail system
em•a•nate \ˈe-mə-ˌnāt\ *vb* **-nat•ed; -nat•ing :** to come out from a source — **em•a•na•tion** \ˌe-mə-ˈnā-shən\ *n*
eman•ci•pate \i-ˈman-sə-ˌpāt\ *vb* **-pat•ed; -pat•ing** ♦ **:** to set free — **eman•ci•pa•tor** \-ˈman-sə-ˌpā-tər\ *n*

♦ discharge, enfranchise, free, liberate, loose, loosen, manumit, release, spring, unbind, unchain, unfetter

eman•ci•pa•tion \-ˌman-sə-ˈpā-shən\ *n* ♦ **:** the act or process of emancipating

♦ enfranchisement, liberation, manumission

emas•cu•late \i-ˈmas-kyu̇-ˌlāt\ *vb* **-lat•ed; -lat•ing** **1 :** to deprive of virility **:** CASTRATE **2 :** to deprive of strength or spirit **:** WEAKEN — **emas•cu•la•tion** \-ˌmas-kyu̇-ˈlā-shən\ *n*
em•balm \im-ˈbäm, -ˈbälm\ *vb* **:** to treat (a corpse) so as to protect from decay — **em•balm•er** *n*
em•bank•ment \im-ˈbaŋk-mənt\ *n* ♦ **:** a raised structure (as of earth) to hold back water or carry a roadway

♦ dam, dike, levee

em•bar•go \im-ˈbär-gō\ *n, pl* **-goes** ♦ **:** a prohibition on commerce — **embargo** *vb*

♦ ban, interdict, interdiction, prohibition, proscription, veto

em•bark \im-ˈbärk\ *vb* **1 :** to put or go on board a ship or airplane **2** ♦ **:** to make a start — **em•bar•ka•tion** \ˌem-ˌbär-ˈkā-shən\ *n*

♦ begin, commence, enter, launch, open, start

em•bar•rass \im-ˈbar-əs\ *vb* **1 :** CONFUSE, DISCONCERT **2 :** to involve in financial difficulties **3** ♦ **:** to cause to experience self-conscious distress **4** ♦ **:** to hamper or impede the movement or freedom of movement of **:** HINDER, IMPEDE — **em•bar•rass•ing•ly** *adv*

♦ [3] abash, confound, confuse, discomfit, disconcert, discountenance, faze, fluster, mortify, rattle ♦ [4] encumber, hamper, hinder, hold up, impede, inhibit, interfere with, obstruct, tie up

em•bar•rass•ing *adj* ♦ **:** causing embarrassment

♦ awkward, disconcerting, uncomfortable

em•bar•rass•ment *n* **1 :** something that embarrasses; *esp* **:** a burden that impedes action or renders it difficult **2 :** the state of being embarrassed: as **a** ♦ **:** confusion or disturbance of mind **b** ♦ **:** difficulty in making progress or functioning (as from lack of resources or from disease)

♦ [2a] abashment, confusion, discomfiture, fluster, mortification
♦ [2b] bar, block, encumbrance, hindrance, inhibition, obstacle

em•bas•sy \ˈem-bə-sē\ *n, pl* **-sies** **1 :** a group of representatives headed by an ambassador **2 :** the function, position, or mission of an ambassador **3 :** the official residence and offices of an ambassador
em•bat•tle \im-ˈbat-ᵊl\ *vb* **:** to arrange in order for battle; *also* **:** FORTIFY
em•bat•tled *adj* **1 :** engaged in battle, conflict, or controversy **2 :** being a site of battle, conflict, or controversy **3 :** characterized by conflict or controversy
em•bed \im-ˈbed\ *vb* **em•bed•ded; em•bed•ding** **1** ♦ **:** to enclose closely in a surrounding mass **2 :** to make something an integral part of

♦ entrench, fix, implant, ingrain, lodge, root

em•bel•lish \im-ˈbe-lish\ *vb* **1** ♦ **:** to make beautiful with ornamentation **:** DECORATE **2** ♦ **:** to heighten the attractiveness of by adding decorative or fanciful details

♦ [1, 2] adorn, array, beautify, decorate, dress, enrich, garnish, grace, ornament, trim ♦ [2] color (*or* colour), elaborate, embroider, exaggerate, magnify, pad, stretch

em•bel•lish•ment *n* ♦ **:** the act or process of embellishing; *also* **:** something serving to embellish

♦ adornment, caparison, decoration, frill, garnish, ornament, trim
♦ elaboration, exaggeration, hyperbole, overstatement, padding

em•ber \ˈem-bər\ *n* **1 :** a glowing or smoldering fragment from a fire **2** *pl* **:** the smoldering remains of a fire
em•bez•zle \im-ˈbe-zəl\ *vb* **-zled; -zling :** to steal (as money) by falsifying records — **em•bez•zle•ment** *n* — **em•bez•zler** *n*
em•bit•ter \im-ˈbi-tər\ *vb* **1 :** to arouse bitter feelings in **2 :** to make bitter
em•bla•zon \-ˈblāz-ᵊn\ *vb* **1 :** to adorn with heraldic devices **2 :** to display conspicuously
em•blem \ˈem-bləm\ *n* ♦ **:** something (as an object or picture) suggesting another object or an idea **:** SYMBOL — **em•blem•at•ic** \ˌem-blə-ˈma-tik\ *also* **em•blem•at•i•cal** \-ti-kəl\ *adj*

♦ hallmark, logo, symbol, trademark

em•bodi•ment \-di-mənt\ *n* **1** ♦ **:** a thing in which something (as a soul, idea, principle, or type) is embodied **2 :** the act of embodying; *also* **:** the state of being embodied

♦ epitome, incarnation, manifestation, personification

em•body \im-ˈbä-dē\ *vb* **em•bod•ied; em•body•ing** **1 :** INCARNATE **2 :** to express in definite form **3** ♦ **:** to incorporate into a system or body **4** ♦ **:** to represent in human or animal form **:** PERSONIFY

♦ [3] assimilate, incorporate, integrate ♦ [4] epitomize, manifest, materialize, personify, substantiate

em•bold•en \im-ˈbōl-dən\ *vb* ♦ **:** to inspire with courage

♦ buoy (up), cheer, comfort, encourage, hearten, inspire, steel

em•bo•lism \ˈem-bə-ˌli-zəm\ *n* **:** the obstruction of a blood vessel by a foreign or abnormal particle
em•bon•point \äⁿ-bōⁿ-ˈpwaⁿ\ *n* **:** plumpness of person **:** STOUTNESS
em•boss \im-ˈbäs, -ˈbȯs\ *vb* **:** to ornament with raised work
em•bou•chure \ˈäm-bü-ˌshu̇r, ˌäm-bü-ˈshu̇r\ *n* **:** the position and use of the lips, tongue, and teeth in playing a wind instrument
em•bow•er \im-ˈbau̇(-ə)r\ *vb* **:** to shelter or enclose in a bower
1**em•brace** \im-ˈbrās\ *vb* **em•braced; em•brac•ing** **1** ♦ **:** to clasp in the arms; *also* **:** CHERISH, LOVE **2 :** to surround or close in **3** ♦ **:** to take up especially readily or gladly **:** ADOPT ⟨*embraced* the cause⟩; *also* **:** WELCOME ⟨*embraced* the opportunity⟩ **4** ♦ **:** to take in or include as a part of a whole **5 :** to participate in an embrace

♦ [1] caress, clasp, enfold, grasp, hug ♦ [3] adopt, borrow, take up ♦ [4] carry, comprehend, contain, encompass, entail, include, involve, number, take in

2**embrace** *n* **:** an encircling with the arms
em•bra•sure \im-ˈbrā-zhər\ *n* **1 :** an opening in a wall through which a cannon is fired **2 :** a recess of a door or window
em•bro•ca•tion \ˌem-brə-ˈkā-shən\ *n* **:** LINIMENT
em•broi•der \im-ˈbrȯi-dər\ *vb* **1 :** to ornament with or do needlework **2** ♦ **:** to elaborate with exaggerated detail

♦ color (*or* colour), elaborate, embellish, exaggerate, magnify, stretch

em•broi•dery \im-ˈbrȯi-də-rē\ *n, pl* **-der•ies** **1 :** the forming of decorative designs with needlework **2 :** something embroidered
em•broil \im-ˈbrȯil\ *vb* **1 :** to throw into confusion or disorder **2 :** to involve in conflict or difficulties — **em•broil•ment** *n*
em•bryo \ˈem-brē-ˌō\ *n, pl* **embryos :** a living thing in its earliest stages of development — **em•bry•on•ic** \ˌem-brē-ˈä-nik\ *adj*
em•bry•ol•o•gy \ˌem-brē-ˈä-lə-jē\ *n* **:** a branch of biology dealing with embryos and their development — **em•bry•o•log•i•cal** \-brē-ə-ˈlä-ji-kəl\ *adj* — **em•bry•ol•o•gist** \-brē-ˈä-lə-jist\ *n*
em•cee \ˌem-ˈsē\ *n* **:** MASTER OF CEREMONIES — **emcee** *vb*
emend \ē-ˈmend\ *vb* ♦ **:** to correct usually by altering the text of — **emen•da•tion** \ˌē-ˌmen-ˈdā-shən\ *n*

♦ amend, correct, debug, rectify, reform, remedy

emer *abbr* emeritus
1**em•er•ald** \ˈem-rəld, ˈe-mə-\ *n* **:** a green beryl prized as a gem
2**emerald** *adj* **:** brightly or richly green
emerge \i-ˈmərj\ *vb* **emerged; emerg•ing** ♦ **:** to rise, come forth, or come out into view — **emer•gence** \-ˈmər-jəns\ *n* — **emer•gent** \-jənt\ *adj*

♦ arise, crop, materialize, spring, surface

emer•gen•cy \i-ˈmər-jən-sē\ *n, pl* **-cies** ♦ **:** an unforeseen event or condition requiring prompt action

♦ clutch, crisis, crunch, fix, hole, jam

emergency room *n* **:** a hospital room for receiving and treating persons needing immediate medical care
emer•i•ta \i-ˈmer-ə-tə\ *adj* **:** EMERITUS — used of a woman
emer•i•tus \i-ˈmer-ə-təs\ *adj* **:** retired from active duty ⟨professor ～⟩
em•ery \ˈe-mə-rē\ *n, pl* **em•er•ies :** a dark granular mineral consisting primarily of corundum and used as an abrasive
emet•ic \i-ˈme-tik\ *n* **:** an agent that induces vomiting — **emetic** *adj*
emf *n* **:** POTENTIAL DIFFERENCE
em•i•grant \-mi-grənt\ *n* ♦ **:** one who emigrates

♦ émigré, immigrant, migrant, settler

em•i•grate \ˈe-mə-ˌgrāt\ *vb* **-grat•ed; -grat•ing :** to leave a place (as a country) to settle elsewhere — **em•i•gra•tion** \ˌe-mə-ˈgrā-shən\ *n*
émi•gré *also* **emi•gré** \ˈe-mi-ˌgrā, ˌe-mi-ˈgrā\ *n* ♦ **:** a person who emigrates especially because of political conditions

♦ emigrant, evacuee, exile, expatriate, refugee

em•i•nence \ˈe-mə-nəns\ *n* **1** ♦ **:** high rank or position; *also* **:** a person of high rank or attainments **2** ♦ **:** a lofty place

♦ [1] distinction, dominance, preeminence, superiority ♦ [2] elevation, height, highland, hill, mound, prominence, rise

em•i•nent \ˈe-mə-nənt\ *adj* **1 :** CONSPICUOUS, EVIDENT **2** ♦ **:** exhibiting eminence especially in standing above others in some quality or position **:** DISTINGUISHED, PROMINENT — **em•i•nent•ly** *adv*

♦ distinguished, illustrious, noble, notable, noteworthy, outstanding, preeminent, prestigious, prominent, superior

eminent domain *n* **:** a right of a government to take private property for public use
emir *or* **amir** \ə-ˈmir, ā-\ *n* **:** a ruler, chief, or commander in Islamic countries — **emir•ate** \ˈe-mər-ət\ *n*
em•is•sary \ˈe-mə-ˌser-ē\ *n, pl* **-sar•ies** **1** ♦ **:** one designated as the agent of another **2 :** a secret agent

♦ ambassador, delegate, envoy, legate, minister, representative

emis•sion \ē-ˈmi-shən\ *n* **:** something emitted; *esp* **:** substances discharged into the air
emit \ē-ˈmit\ *vb* **emit•ted; emit•ting** **1** ♦ **:** to give off or out ⟨～ light⟩; *also* **:** EJECT **2 :** EXPRESS, UTTER — **emit•ter** *n*

♦ cast, discharge, eject, exhale, expel, issue, release, shoot, vent

emol•lient \i-ˈmäl-yənt\ *adj* **:** making soft or supple; *also* **:** soothing especially to the skin or mucous membrane — **emol•lient** *n*
emol•u•ment \i-ˈmäl-yə-mənt\ *n* ♦ **:** the product (as salary or fees) of an employment

♦ hire, pay, payment, salary, stipend, wage

emote \i-ˈmōt\ *vb* **emot•ed; emot•ing :** to give expression to emotion in or as if in a play
emo•ti•con \i-ˈmō-ti-ˌkän\ *n* **:** a group of keyboard characters (as :-)) that represents a facial expression especially in online communications
emo•tion \i-ˈmō-shən\ *n* ♦ **:** a usually intense feeling (as of love, hate, or despair)

♦ feeling, passion, sentiment ♦ ardor, fervency, fervor, heat, intensity, passion, vehemence, warmth

emo•tion•al \-shə-nəl\ *adj* **1 :** of or relating to emotion **2** ♦ **:** dominated by or prone to emotion **3** ♦ **:** appealing to or arousing emotion **4** ♦ **:** markedly aroused or agitated in feeling or sensibilities — **emo•tion•al•ly** *adv*

♦ [2] demonstrative, effusive, uninhibited, unreserved, unrestrained ♦ [3] affecting, impressive, moving, poignant, stirring, touching ♦ [4] ardent, burning, charged, fervent, fiery, impassioned, passionate, red-hot, vehement

emot•ive \i-ˈmō-tiv\ *adj* **1 :** of or relating to the emotions **2 :** appealing to or expressing emotion
emp *abbr* emperor; empress
empanel *var of* IMPANEL
em•pa•thy \ˈem-pə-thē\ *n* **:** the experiencing as one's own of the feelings of another; *also* **:** the capacity for this — **em•path•ic** \em-ˈpa-thik\ *adj*
em•pen•nage \ˌäm-pə-ˈnäzh, ˌem-\ *n* **:** the tail assembly of an airplane
em•per•or \ˈem-pər-ər\ *n* **:** the sovereign male ruler of an empire
em•pha•sis \ˈem-fə-səs\ *n, pl* **-pha•ses** \-ˌsēz\ ♦ **:** a forcefulness of expression that gives special significance or prominence (as to a syllable in speaking or to a phase of action)

♦ accent, accentuation, stress, weight

em•pha•sise *Brit var of* EMPHASIZE
em•pha•size \-ˌsīz\ *vb* **-sized; -siz•ing** ♦ **:** to place emphasis on **:** STRESS

♦ accent, accentuate, feature, highlight, play, point, stress, underline, underscore *Ant* play (down)

em•phat•ic \im-ˈfa-tik, em-\ *adj* **1** ♦ **:** uttered with emphasis **2** ♦ **:** attracting special attention — **em•phat•i•cal•ly** \-ˈti-k(ə-)lē\ *adv*

♦ [1] aggressive, assertive, dynamic, energetic, forceful, resounding, strenuous, vehement, vigorous *Ant* unemphatic ♦ [2] bold, catchy, conspicuous, marked, noticeable, prominent, pronounced, remarkable, striking

em•phy•se•ma \ˌem-fə-ˈzē-mə, -ˈsē-\ *n* **:** a condition marked especially by abnormal expansion of the air spaces of the lungs and often by impairment of heart action
em•pire \ˈem-ˌpī(-ə)r\ *n* **1 :** a large state or a group of states under a single sovereign who is usually an emperor; *also* **:** some-

thing resembling a political empire **2 :** imperial sovereignty or dominion
em•pir•i•cal \im-ˈpir-i-kəl\ *also* **em•pir•ic** \-ik\ *adj* **:** based on observation; *also* **:** subject to verification by observation or experiment ⟨~ laws⟩ — **em•pir•i•cal•ly** \-i-k(ə-)lē\ *adv*
em•pir•i•cism \im-ˈpir-ə-ˌsi-zəm, em-\ *n* **:** the practice of relying on observation and experiment especially in the natural sciences — **em•pir•i•cist** \-sist\ *n*
em•place•ment \im-ˈplās-mənt\ *n* **1 :** a prepared position for weapons or military equipment **2 :** PLACEMENT
1**em•ploy** \im-ˈplȯi\ *vb* **1** ♦ **:** to make use of **2** ♦ **:** to use the services of **3 :** OCCUPY, DEVOTE — **em•ploy•er** *n*

♦ [1] apply, exercise, exploit, harness, operate, use, utilize ♦ [2] engage, hire, retain, take on *Ant* discharge, dismiss, fire, sack

2**em•ploy** \im-ˈplȯi; ˈim-ˌplȯi, ˈem-\ *n* ♦ **:** the state of being employed **:** EMPLOYMENT

♦ employment, engagement, hire

em•ploy•ee *also* **em•ploye** \im-ˌplȯi-ˈē, ˌem-; im-ˈplȯi-ˌē, em-\ *n* ♦ **:** a person who works for another

♦ hand, hireling, jobholder, worker *Ant* employer

em•ploy•ment \im-ˈplȯi-mənt\ *n* **1** ♦ **:** activity in which one engages or is employed **:** OCCUPATION **2** ♦ **:** the act of employing **:** the condition of being employed

♦ [1] calling, line, occupation, profession, trade, vocation, work ♦ [2] application, exercise, operation, play, use ♦ [2] employ, engagement, hire

em•po•ri•um \im-ˈpȯr-ē-əm, em-\ *n, pl* **-ri•ums** *also* **-ria** \-ē-ə\ ♦ **:** a commercial center; *esp* **:** a store carrying varied articles

♦ shop, store

em•pow•er \im-ˈpau̇(-ə)r\ *vb* ♦ **:** to give authority or power to; *also* **:** ENABLE — **em•pow•er•ment** \-mənt\ *n*

♦ accredit, authorize, certify, commission, enable, invest, license, qualify

em•press \ˈem-prəs\ *n* **1 :** the wife or widow of an emperor **2 :** a sovereign female ruler of an empire
emp•ti•ness *n* ♦ **:** the quality or state of being empty

♦ blank, blankness, vacancy, vacuity, void

1**emp•ty** \ˈemp-tē\ *adj* **emp•ti•er; -est 1** ♦ **:** containing nothing **2 :** UNOCCUPIED, UNINHABITED **3** ♦ **:** lacking value, force, sense, or purpose **4** ♦ **:** feeling the need for food

♦ [1] bare, blank, devoid, stark, vacant, void *Ant* full ♦ [3] meaningless, pointless, senseless, worthless ♦ [3] fruitless, futile, ineffective, unproductive, unsuccessful ♦ [4] famished, hungry

2**empty** *vb* **emp•tied; emp•ty•ing 1 :** to make or become empty **2** ♦ **:** to discharge contents; *also* **:** to remove from what holds or encloses

♦ clear, evacuate, vacate, void *Ant* fill, load

3**empty** *n, pl* **empties :** an empty bottle or can
emp•ty–hand•ed \ˌemp-tē-ˈhan-dəd\ *adj* **1 :** having or bringing nothing **2 :** having acquired or gained nothing
1**em•py•re•an** \ˌem-ˌpī-ˈrē-ən, -pə-\ *n* **1 :** the highest heaven; *also* **:** FIRMAMENT **2 :** an ideal place or state
2**empyrean** *adj* ♦ **:** of or relating to the empyrean

♦ celestial, Elysian, heavenly, supernal

EMT \ˌē-(ˌ)em-ˈtē\ *n* **:** a specially trained medical technician certified to provide basic medical services before and during transport to a hospital
1**emu** \ˈē-myü, -mü\ *n* **:** a swift-running flightless Australian bird smaller than the related ostrich
2**emu** *abbr* electromagnetic unit
em•u•late \ˈem-yu̇-ˌlāt\ *vb* **-lat•ed; -lat•ing** ♦ **:** to strive to equal or excel **:** IMITATE — **em•u•la•tion** \ˌem-yu̇-ˈlā-shən\ *n* — **em•u•lous** \ˈem-yu̇-ləs\ *adj*

♦ ape, copy, imitate, mime, mimic

emul•si•fi•er \i-ˈməl-sə-ˌfī(-ə)r\ *n* **:** a substance (as a soap) that helps to form and stabilize an emulsion
emul•si•fy \-ˌfī\ *vb* **-fied; -fy•ing :** to disperse (as an oil) in an emulsion — **emul•si•fi•ca•tion** \i-ˌməl-sə-fə-ˈkā-shən\ *n*
emul•sion \i-ˈməl-shən\ *n* **1 :** a mixture of mutually insoluble liquids in which one is dispersed in droplets throughout the other ⟨an ~ of oil in water⟩ **2 :** a light-sensitive coating on photographic film or paper

en \ˈen\ *n* **:** a length approximately half the width of the letter *M*
1**-en** *also* **-n** *adj suffix* **:** made of **:** consisting of ⟨earth*en*⟩
2**-en** *vb suffix* **1 :** become or cause to be ⟨sharp*en*⟩ **2 :** cause or come to have ⟨length*en*⟩
en•able \i-ˈnā-bəl\ *vb* **en•abled; en•abling 1** ♦ **:** to make able or feasible **2** ♦ **:** to give legal power, capacity, or sanction to

♦ [1] allow, let, permit *Ant* prevent ♦ [2] accredit, authorize, certify, commission, empower, invest, license, qualify

en•act \i-ˈnakt\ *vb* **1** ♦ **:** to make into law **2 :** to act out

♦ lay down, legislate, make, pass *Ant* repeal, rescind, revoke

en•act•ment *n* ♦ **:** the act of enacting; *also* **:** something (as a law) that has been enacted

♦ act, law, ordinance, statute ♦ accomplishment, achievement, commission, discharge, execution, fulfillment, implementation, performance

enam•el \i-ˈna-məl\ *n* **1 :** a glasslike substance used to coat the surface of metal or pottery **2 :** the hard outer layer of a tooth **3 :** a usually glossy paint that forms a hard coat — **enamel** *vb*
enam•el•ware \-ˌwer\ *n* **:** metal utensils coated with enamel
en•am•or *or Can and Brit* **en•am•our** \i-ˈna-mər\ *vb* **:** to inflame with love
en bloc \äⁿ-ˈbläk\ *adv or adj* **:** as a whole **:** in a mass
enc *or* **encl** *abbr* enclosure
en•camp \in-ˈkamp\ *vb* **:** to make camp
en•camp•ment *n* ♦ **:** the place where a group (as a body of troops) is encamped

♦ bivouac, camp

en•cap•su•late \in-ˈkap-sə-ˌlāt\ *vb* **-lat•ed; -lat•ing 1 :** to encase or become encased in a capsule **2** ♦ **:** to give an abstract of **:** SUMMARIZE

♦ abstract, digest, outline, recapitulate, sum up, summarize, wrap up

en•cap•su•la•tion \-ˌkap-sə-ˈlā-shən\ *n* ♦ **:** an act, instance, or result of encapsulating

♦ abstract, digest, outline, précis, résumé (*or* resume), summary, synopsis, wrap-up

en•case \in-ˈkās\ *vb* ♦ **:** to enclose in or as if in a case — **en•case•ment** \-ˈkā-smənt\ *n*

♦ cage, coop up, corral, enclose, fence, hedge, hem, house, pen, wall

-ence *n suffix* **1 :** action or process ⟨emerg*ence*⟩ **:** instance of an action or process ⟨refer*ence*⟩ **2 :** quality or state ⟨depend*ence*⟩
en•ceinte \äⁿn-ˈsant\ *adj* **:** PREGNANT 1
en•ceph•a•li•tis \in-ˌse-fə-ˈlī-təs\ *n, pl* **-lit•i•des** \-ˈli-tə-ˌdēz\ **:** inflammation of the brain — **en•ceph•a•lit•ic** \-ˈli-tik\ *adj*
en•ceph•a•lop•a•thy \in-ˌse-fə-ˈlä-pə-thē\ *n, pl* **-thies :** a disease of the brain
en•chain \in-ˈchān\ *vb* ♦ **:** to bind or hold with or as if with chains **:** FETTER, CHAIN

♦ bind, chain, fetter, handcuff, manacle, shackle, trammel

en•chant \in-ˈchant\ *vb* **1** ♦ **:** to influence by or as if by charms and incantation **:** BEWITCH **2** ♦ **:** to attract and move deeply — **en•chant•ing•ly** *adv*

♦ [1] allure, beguile, bewitch, captivate, charm, fascinate, wile ♦ [2] arrest, enthrall, fascinate, grip, hypnotize, mesmerize

en•chant•er *n* ♦ **:** one that enchants

♦ conjurer, magician, necromancer, sorcerer, voodoo, witch, wizard

en•chant•ment *n* **1** ♦ **:** the act or art of enchanting; *also* **:** the quality or state of being enchanted **2** ♦ **:** something that enchants

♦ [1] allure, appeal, attractiveness, captivation, charisma, charm, fascination, glamour, magic, magnetism ♦ [2] bewitchment, charm, conjuration, incantation, spell

en•chant•ress \-ˈchan-trəs\ *n* **1** ♦ **:** a woman who practices magic **2** ♦ **:** a fascinating or beautiful woman

♦ [1] hag, hex, witch ♦ [2] beauty, fox, goddess, knockout, queen

en•chi•la•da \ˌen-chə-ˈlä-də\ *n* **:** a rolled filled tortilla covered with chili sauce and usually baked
en•ci•pher \in-ˈsī-fər, en-\ *vb* **:** ENCODE
en•cir•cle \in-ˈsər-kəl\ *vb* ♦ **:** to pass completely around **:** SURROUND — **en•cir•cle•ment** *n*

♦ circle, circumnavigate, coil, compass, enclose, encompass, girdle, ring, round, surround

en•clave \ˈen-ˌklāv; ˈän-ˌklāv\ *n* **:** a distinct territorial, cultural, or social unit enclosed within or as if within foreign territory
en•close \in-ˈklōz\ *vb* **1** ♦ **:** to shut up or in; *esp* **:** to surround with a fence **2 :** to include along with something else in a parcel or envelope ⟨~ a check⟩ — **en•clo•sure** \-ˈklō-zhər\ *n*

♦ cage, coop up, corral, encase, envelop, fence, hedge, hem, pen ♦ circle, encircle, encompass, ring, surround

en•code \in-ˈkōd, en-\ *vb* **:** to convert (a message) into code
en•co•mi•um \en-ˈkō-mē-əm\ *n, pl* **-mi•ums** *also* **-mia** \-mē-ə\ ♦ **:** high or glowing praise

♦ accolade, citation, commendation, eulogy, homage, paean, panegyric, salutation, tribute

en•com•pass \in-ˈkəm-pəs\ *vb* **1** ♦ **:** to form a circle about **:** ENCIRCLE **2 :** to enclose or enfold completely with or as if with a covering **:** ENVELOP, INCLUDE **3** ♦ **:** to contain or hold within a total scope, significance, or amount

♦ [1] circle, encircle, enclose, ring, surround ♦ [3] carry, comprehend, contain, embrace, entail, include, involve, number, take in

en•core \ˈän-ˌkȯr\ *n* **1 :** a demand for repetition or reappearance **2 :** a further performance or appearance demanded by an audience **3 :** a second achievement that usually surpasses the first — **encore** *vb*
1en•coun•ter \in-ˈkau̇n-tər\ *vb* **1 :** to meet as an enemy **:** FIGHT **2** ♦ **:** to meet usually unexpectedly

♦ chance, find, happen (on *or* upon), hit, meet, stumble

2encounter *n* **1** ♦ **:** a hostile meeting **:** COMBAT **2 :** a chance meeting **3 :** an experience shared with another ⟨a romantic ~⟩

♦ brush, run-in, scrape, skirmish

en•cour•age \in-ˈkər-ij\ *vb* **-aged; -ag•ing 1** ♦ **:** to inspire with courage and hope **2** ♦ **:** to spur on **:** STIMULATE, INCITE; *also* **:** to attempt to persuade **3** ♦ **:** to give help or patronage to **:** FOSTER

♦ [1] buoy (up), cheer, comfort, embolden, hearten, inspire, steel *Ant* daunt, discourage, dishearten, dispirit ♦ [2] arouse, excite, fire, incite, instigate, move, pique, provoke, stimulate, stir ♦ [2] egg on, exhort, goad, press, prod, prompt, urge ♦ [3] advance, cultivate, forward, foster, further, nourish, nurture, promote

en•cour•age•ment *n* ♦ **:** the act of encouraging **:** the state of being encouraged; *also* **:** something that encourages

♦ boost, goad, impetus, impulse, incentive, instigation, motivation, provocation, spur, stimulus

en•cour•ag•ing \-i-jiŋ, -ri-jiŋ\ *adj* ♦ **:** giving hope or promise — **en•cour•ag•ing•ly** *adv*

♦ auspicious, bright, fair, golden, heartening, hopeful, likely, promising, propitious, rosy, upbeat ♦ comforting, gratifying, heartening, heartwarming, rewarding, satisfying

en•croach \in-ˈkrōch\ *vb* **:** to enter gradually or stealthily upon another's property or rights — **en•croach•er** *n* — **en•croach•ment** *n*
en•crust *also* **in•crust** \in-ˈkrəst\ *vb* **:** to provide with or form a crust
en•crus•ta•tion \(ˌ)in-ˌkrəs-ˈtā-shən, ˌen-\ *var of* INCRUSTATION
en•cum•ber \in-ˈkəm-bər\ *vb* **1** ♦ **:** to weigh down **:** BURDEN **2** ♦ **:** to hinder the function or activity of

♦ [1] burden, load, lumber, saddle, weight ♦ [2] hamper, hinder, hobble, hold back, hold up, impede, inhibit, interfere with, obstruct, tie up

en•cum•brance \-brəns\ *n* **1** ♦ **:** something that encumbers **2 :** a claim (as a mortgage) against property

♦ bar, block, hindrance, inhibition, obstacle

ency *or* **encyc** *abbr* encyclopedia
-en•cy *n suffix* **:** quality or state ⟨despond*ency*⟩
1en•cyc•li•cal \in-ˈsi-kli-kəl, en-\ *adj* **:** addressed to all the individuals of a group
2encyclical *n* **:** an encyclical letter; *esp* **:** a papal letter to the bishops of the church
en•cy•clo•pe•dia *also* **en•cy•clo•pae•dia** \in-ˌsī-klə-ˈpē-dē-ə\ *n* **:** a work treating the various branches of learning
en•cy•clo•pe•dic *also* **en•cy•clo•pae•dic** \-ˈpē-dik\ *adj* ♦ **:** of, relating to, or suggestive of an encyclopedia or its methods of treating or covering a subject

♦ compendious, complete, comprehensive, full, global, inclusive, omnibus, panoramic, universal

en•cyst \in-ˈsist, en-\ *vb* **:** to form or become enclosed in a cyst — **en•cyst•ment** *n*
1end \ˈend\ *n* **1** ♦ **:** the part of an area that lies at the boundary; *also* **:** a point which marks the extent or limit of something or at which something ceases to exist **2** ♦ **:** a ceasing of a course (as of action or activity); *also* **:** DEATH **3 :** the ultimate state; *also* **:** RESULT, ISSUE **4** ♦ **:** something incomplete, fragmentary, or undersized **:** REMNANT **5** ♦ **:** an outcome worked toward **:** PURPOSE, OBJECTIVE **6 :** a player stationed at the extremity of a line (as in football) **7 :** a share, operation, or aspect of an undertaking

♦ [1] bound, boundary, ceiling, confines, extent, limit, limitation, line, termination ♦ [2] death, decease, demise, doom, passing, quietus ♦ [2] cessation, close, closure, conclusion, finish, halt, lapse, shutdown, stop, stoppage, termination *Ant* continuation ♦ [4] fag end, leftover, remainder, remnant, scrap ♦ [5] aim, ambition, aspiration, goal, intent, mark, meaning, object, objective, plan, purpose

2end *vb* **1** ♦ **:** to bring or come to an end **2 :** DESTROY; *also* **:** DIE **3 :** to form or be at the end of

♦ close, conclude, finish, round, terminate, wind up, wrap up ♦ break, break off, cease, cut, desist, discontinue, drop, halt, knock off, layoff, leave off, quit, shut off, stop

en•dan•ger \in-ˈdān-jər\ *vb* ♦ **:** to bring into danger; *also* **:** to create danger

♦ compromise, gamble with, hazard, imperil, jeopardize, menace, risk, venture

en•dan•gered *adj* **:** being or relating to an endangered species
endangered species *n* **:** a species threatened with extinction
en•dear \in-ˈdir\ *vb* **:** to cause to become beloved or admired
endearing *adj* ♦ **:** arousing affection, tenderness, or admiration

♦ adorable, darling, dear, lovable, precious, sweet, winning

en•dear•ment \-mənt\ *n* **:** a sign of affection **:** CARESS
1en•deav•or *or Can and Brit* **en•deavour** \in-ˈde-vər\ *vb* ♦ **:** to attempt (as the fulfillment of an obligation) by exertion of effort; *also* **:** to work with set purpose

♦ assay, attempt, essay, seek, strive, try

2endeavor *or Can and Brit* **endeavour** *n* ♦ **:** serious determined effort; *also* **:** activity directed toward a goal

♦ attempt, bid, crack, essay, fling, go, pass, shot, stab, trial, try, whack, whirl

en•dem•ic \en-ˈde-mik, in-\ *adj* ♦ **:** restricted to a particular place ⟨~ plants⟩ ⟨an ~ disease⟩ — **endemic** *n*

♦ aboriginal, born, indigenous, native

end•ing \ˈen-diŋ\ *n* **1** ♦ **:** something that forms an end **2 :** SUFFIX

♦ close, conclusion, consummation, end, finale, finis, finish, windup

en•dive \ˈen-ˌdīv\ *n* **1 :** an herb related to chicory and grown as a salad plant **2 :** the blanched shoot of chicory
end•less \ˈend-ləs\ *adj* **1** ♦ **:** having or seeming to have no end **:** ETERNAL **2 :** united at the ends **:** CONTINUOUS ⟨an ~ belt⟩ — **end•less•ly** *adv*

♦ boundless, illimitable, immeasurable, indefinite, infinite, limitless, measureless, unbounded, unfathomable, unlimited ♦ ceaseless, dateless, deathless, eternal, everlasting, immortal, permanent, perpetual, undying, unending

end•most \-ˌmōst\ *adj* **:** situated at the very end
end•note \-ˌnōt\ *n* **:** a note placed at the end of a text
en•do•crine \ˈen-də-krən, -ˌkrīn, -ˌkrēn\ *adj* **:** producing secretions that are distributed by way of the bloodstream ⟨~ glands⟩ — **endocrine** *n* — **en•do•cri•nol•o•gist** \-kri-ˈnä-lə-jist\ *n* — **en•do•cri•nol•o•gy** \-jē\ *n*
en•dog•e•nous \en-ˈdä-jə-nəs\ *adj* **:** caused or produced by factors inside the organism or system ⟨~ psychic depression⟩ — **en•dog•e•nous•ly** *adv*
en•do•me•tri•um \ˌen-dō-ˈmē-trē-əm\ *n, pl* **-tria** \-trē-ə\ **:** the mucous membrane lining the uterus — **en•do•me•tri•al** \-trē-əl\ *adj*
en•dor•phin \en-ˈdȯr-fən\ *n* **:** any of a group of endogenous morphinelike proteins found especially in the brain
en•dorse *also* **in•dorse** \in-ˈdȯrs\ *vb* **en•dorsed; en•dors•ing 1 :** to sign one's name on the back of (as a check) **2** ♦ **:** to express support or approval of publicly and definitely; *esp* **:** to recom-

mend (as a product) usually for financial compensation — **en·dorse·ment** *also* **in·dorse·ment** *n*

♦ advocate, back, champion, patronize, support

en·do·scope \ˈen-də-ˌskōp\ *n* **:** an illuminated usually fiber-optic instrument for visualizing the interior of a hollow organ or part (as the colon or esophagus) — **en·do·scop·ic** \ˌen-də-ˈskä-pik\ *adj* — **en·dos·co·py** \en-ˈdäs-kə-pē\ *n*

en·do·ther·mic \ˌen-də-ˈthər-mik\ *adj* **:** characterized by or formed with absorption of heat

en·dow \in-ˈdau̇\ *vb* **1** ♦ **:** to furnish with funds for support ⟨~ a school⟩ **2** ♦ **:** to furnish with something freely or naturally

♦ [1] finance, fund, subsidize ♦ [2] invest

en·dow·ment *n* **:** something that is endowed: as **a :** the part of an institution's income derived from donations **b** ♦ **:** natural capacity, power, or ability

♦ aptitude, faculty, flair, genius, gift, knack, talent

en·due \in-ˈdü, -ˈdyü\ *vb* **en·dued; en·du·ing :** PROVIDE, ENDOW

en·dur·able *adj* ♦ **:** capable of being borne or endured

♦ bearable, sufferable, supportable, sustainable, tolerable

en·dur·ance \in-ˈdu̇r-əns, -ˈdyu̇r-\ *n* **1** ♦ **:** continuation in the same state **:** DURATION **2 :** the ability to withstand hardship or stress **:** FORTITUDE

♦ continuance, continuation, duration, persistence, subsistence

en·dure \in-ˈdu̇r, -ˈdyu̇r\ *vb* **en·dured; en·dur·ing** **1** ♦ **:** to continue in the same state **:** LAST, PERSIST **2** ♦ **:** to suffer firmly or patiently **:** BEAR **3 :** TOLERATE

♦ [1] abide, continue, hold, keep up, last, persist, run on ♦ [2] abide, bear, brook, countenance, meet, stand, stick out, stomach, support, sustain, take, tolerate

enduring *adj* ♦ **:** existing or continuing a long while **:** LASTING

♦ abiding, ageless, continuing, dateless, eternal, everlasting, immortal, imperishable, lasting, perennial, perpetual, timeless, undying

end·ways \ˈend-ˌwāz\ *adv or adj* **1 :** LENGTHWISE **2 :** with the end forward **3 :** on end

end·wise \-ˌwīz\ *adv or adj* **:** ENDWAYS

ENE *abbr* east-northeast

en·e·ma \ˈe-nə-mə\ *n, pl* **enemas** *also* **ene·ma·ta** \ˌe-nə-ˈmä-tə, ˈe-nə-mə-tə\ **:** injection of liquid into the rectum; *also* **:** material so injected

en·e·my \ˈe-nə-mē\ *n, pl* **-mies** ♦ **:** one that attacks or tries to harm another **:** FOE; *esp* **:** a military opponent

♦ adversary, antagonist, foe, opponent ***Ant*** friend

en·er·get·ic \ˌe-nər-ˈje-tik\ *adj* ♦ **:** marked by energy **:** ACTIVE, VIGOROUS

♦ active, animated, jaunty, lively, peppy, spirited, sprightly, springy, vigorous, vital, vivacious

en·er·get·i·cal·ly \-ti-k(ə-)lē\ *adv* ♦ **:** in an energetic manner

♦ forcefully, powerfully, strongly, sturdily, vigorously

en·er·gise *chiefly Brit var of* ENERGIZE

en·er·gize \ˈe-nər-ˌjīz\ *vb* **-gized; -giz·ing** ♦ **:** to give energy to

♦ animate, brace, enliven, fire, invigorate, jazz up, liven up, pep up, quicken, stimulate, vitalize, vivify, zip (up)

en·er·gy \ˈe-nər-jē\ *n, pl* **-gies** **1 :** vigorous action **:** EFFORT **2** ♦ **:** capacity for action **3** ♦ **:** capacity for performing work **4 :** usable power (as heat or electricity); *also* **:** the resources for producing such power

♦ [2] force, main, might, muscle, potency, power, strength, vigor (*or* vigour) ♦ [2, 3] force, main, might, muscle, potency, power, strength, vigor (*or* vigour) ♦ [3] dash, life, pep, vigor (*or* vigour), vim, vitality

energy level *n* **:** one of the stable states of constant energy that may be assumed by a physical system (as the electrons in an atom)

en·er·vate \ˈe-nər-ˌvāt\ *vb* **-vat·ed; -vat·ing** ♦ **:** to lessen the strength or vigor of **:** weaken in mind or body — **en·er·vat·ing·ly** \-ˌvā-tiŋ-lē\ *adv* — **en·er·va·tion** \ˌe-nər-ˈvā-shən\ *n*

♦ debilitate, enfeeble, prostrate, sap, soften, tire, waste, weaken

en·er·vat·ed \ˈe-nər-ˌvāt-əd\ ♦ **:** lacking physical, mental, or moral vigor

♦ lackadaisical, languid, languorous, limp, listless, spiritless

en·fee·ble \in-ˈfē-bəl\ *vb* **-bled; -bling** ♦ **:** to make feeble

♦ debilitate, enervate, prostrate, sap, soften, tire, waste, weaken

en·fee·ble·ment *n* ♦ **:** the action of enfeebling; *also* **:** the quality or state of being enfeebled

♦ debility, delicacy, faintness, feebleness, frailty, infirmity, languor, lowness, weakness

en·fi·lade \ˈen-fə-ˌlād, -ˌläd\ *n* **:** gunfire directed along the length of an enemy battle line — **enfilade** *vb*

en·fold \in-ˈfōld\ *vb* **1** ♦ **:** to cover with or as if with folds **:** ENVELOP **2** ♦ **:** to clasp within the arms **:** EMBRACE

♦ [1] caress, clasp, embrace, grasp, hug ♦ [2] enclose, encompass, enshroud, envelop, invest, lap, mantle, shroud, swathe, veil, wrap

en·force \in-ˈfȯrs\ *vb* **1 :** COMPEL ⟨~ obedience by threats⟩ **2** ♦ **:** to execute effectively ⟨~ the law⟩ — **en·force·able** *adj* — **en·force·ment** *n*

♦ administer, apply, execute, implement

en·forc·er \in-ˈfȯr-sər\ *n* **:** one that enforces; *esp* **:** an aggressive player (as in ice hockey) known for rough play

en·fran·chise \in-ˈfran-ˌchīz\ *vb* **-chised; -chis·ing** **1** ♦ **:** to set free (as from slavery) **2 :** to admit to the rights of citizenship; *also* **:** to grant the vote to

♦ discharge, emancipate, free, liberate, loose, loosen, manumit, release, spring, unbind, unchain, unfetter

en·fran·chise·ment \-ˌchīz-mənt, -chəz-\ *n* **:** the act or result of enfranchising: as **a** ♦ **:** the releasing from slavery or custody **b** ♦ **:** admission to citizenship and its rights

♦ [a] emancipation, liberation, manumission ♦ [b] franchise, suffrage, vote

eng *abbr* engine; engineer; engineering

Eng *abbr* England; English

en·gage \in-ˈgāj\ *vb* **en·gaged; en·gag·ing** **1** ♦ **:** to bind (as oneself) by a pledge to do something; *esp* **:** to bind by a pledge to marry **2** ♦ **:** to use the services of **:** EMPLOY, HIRE **3** ♦ **:** to attract and hold especially by interesting; *also* **:** to cause to participate **4 :** to commence or take part in a venture **5** ♦ **:** to bring or enter into conflict **6 :** to connect or interlock with **:** MESH; *also* **:** to cause to mesh

♦ [1] commit, pledge, troth ♦ [2] employ, hire, retain, take on ♦ [3] absorb, busy, engross, enthrall, fascinate, grip, immerse, interest, intrigue, involve, occupy ♦ [5] battle, encounter, face, meet, take on

en·gaged \in-ˈgājd, en-\ **1** ♦ **:** involved in activity **2 :** pledged to be married

♦ active, assiduous, busy, diligent, laborious, occupied, sedulous, working

en·gage·ment \in-ˈgāj-mənt\ *n* **1** ♦ **:** an arrangement to meet or be present at a specified time and place **2** ♦ **:** a job or period of employment especially as a performer **3** ♦ **:** a mutual promise to marry **4 :** a hostile encounter

♦ [1] appointment, date, rendezvous, tryst ♦ [2] employ, employment, hire ♦ [3] espousal, troth ***Ant*** disengagement

en·gag·ing *adj* ♦ **:** tending to draw favorable attention or interest **:** ATTRACTIVE — **en·gag·ing·ly** *adv*

♦ alluring, attractive, captivating, charming, fascinating, fetching, glamorous ♦ absorbing, engrossing, enthralling, fascinating, interesting, intriguing

en·gen·der \in-ˈjen-dər\ *vb* **1 :** BEGET **2** ♦ **:** to cause to exist or to develop **:** CREATE

♦ create, generate, induce, make, produce, spawn

en·gine \ˈen-jən\ *n* **1 :** a mechanical device **2 :** a machine for converting energy into mechanical motion **3 :** LOCOMOTIVE **4 :** software that performs a fundamental function especially of a larger program — **en·gine·less** *adj*

[1]**en·gi·neer** \ˌen-jə-ˈnir\ *n* **1 :** a member of a military unit specializing in engineering work **2 :** a designer or builder of engines **3 :** one trained in engineering **4 :** one that operates an engine

[2]**engineer** *vb* **1 :** to lay out or manage as an engineer **2 :** to guide the course of

en·gi·neer·ing *n* **:** the practical applications of scientific and mathematical principles

En·glish \ˈiŋ-glish\ *n* **1 :** the language of England, the U.S., and many areas now or formerly under British rule **2 English** *pl* **:** the people of England **3 :** spin imparted to a ball that is driven or

rolled — **English** *adj* — **En•glish•man** \-mən\ *n* — **En•glish•wom•an** \-ˌwu̇-mən\ *n*
English horn *n* : a woodwind instrument longer than and having a range lower than the oboe
English setter *n* : any of a breed of hunting dogs with a flat silky coat of white or white with color
English sparrow *n* : HOUSE SPARROW
English system *n* : a system of weights and measures in which the foot is the principal unit of length and the pound is the principal unit of weight
engr *abbr* **1** engineer **2** engraved
en•gram \ˈen-ˌgram\ *n* : a hypothetical change in neural tissue postulated in order to account for persistence of memory
en•grave \in-ˈgrāv\ *vb* **en•graved; en•grav•ing** **1** ♦ : to produce (as letters or lines) by incising a surface **2** : to cut figures, letters, or designs on for printing; *also* : to print from an engraved plate **3** : PHOTOENGRAVE **4** ♦ : to impress deeply as if with an engraving tool — **en•grav•er** *n*

♦ [1] etch, grave, inscribe ♦ [4] etch, impress, imprint, ingrain, inscribe

en•grav•ing \in-ˈgrā-viŋ\ *n* **1** : the art of one who engraves **2** : an engraved plate; *also* : a print made from it
en•gross \in-ˈgrōs\ *vb* ♦ : to take up the whole interest or attention of

♦ absorb, busy, engage, enthrall, fascinate, grip, immerse, interest, intrigue, involve, occupy

en•grossed \in-ˈgrōst\ *adj* ♦ : completely occupied or absorbed

♦ absorbed, attentive, intent, observant, rapt

en•gross•ing *adj* ♦ : taking up the time or attention completely

♦ absorbing, engaging, enthralling, fascinating, interesting, intriguing

en•gulf \in-ˈgəlf\ *vb* ♦ : to flow over and enclose

♦ deluge, drown, flood, inundate, overflow, overwhelm, submerge, swamp

en•hance \in-ˈhans\ *vb* **en•hanced; en•hanc•ing** ♦ : to increase or improve (as in value or desirability)

♦ ameliorate, amend, better, enrich, improve, perfect, refine

en•hance•ment *n* ♦ : the act of enhancing or state of being enhanced

♦ advance, advancement, breakthrough, improvement, refinement

enig•ma \i-ˈnig-mə\ *n* ♦ : something obscure or hard to understand

♦ conundrum, mystery, mystification, puzzle, puzzlement, riddle, secret

enig•mat•ic \ˌen-ig-ˈma-tik\ *adj* ♦ : resembling an enigma — **en•ig•mat•i•cal•ly** \-ti-k(ə-)lē\ *adv*

♦ ambiguous, cryptic, deep, equivocal, inscrutable, murky, mysterious, mystic, nebulous, obscure, occult

en•join \in-ˈjȯin\ *vb* **1** ♦ : to direct or impose by authoritative order or with urgent warning : COMMAND **2** ♦ : to forbid by authority

♦ [1] call, charge, command, demand, direct, exact, insist, instruct, order, press, stipulate (for) ♦ [1, 2] ban, bar, forbid, interdict, outlaw, prohibit, proscribe

en•joy \in-ˈjȯi\ *vb* **1** ♦ : to have for one's benefit or use ⟨∼ good health⟩ **2** ♦ : to take pleasure or satisfaction in ⟨∼*ed* the concert⟩

♦ [1] command, have, hold, occupy, own, possess, retain ♦ [2] adore, delight, dig, fancy, like, love, relish, revel

en•joy•able *adj* ♦ : being a source of pleasure or enjoyment

♦ agreeable, amusing, delectable, delicious, delightful, entertaining, fun, heavenly, luscious, pleasurable

en•joy•ment *n* **1** ♦ : the action or state of enjoying **2** : something that gives keen satisfaction

♦ contentment, delectation, delight, gladness, gratification, pleasure, relish, satisfaction

enl *abbr* **1** enlarged **2** enlisted
en•large \in-ˈlärj\ *vb* **en•larged; en•larg•ing** **1** ♦ : to make or grow larger **2** ♦ : to give greater scope to; *also* : to speak or write at length : ELABORATE — often used with *on* or *upon* — **en•large•ment** *n*

♦ [1] add, aggrandize, amplify, augment, boost, compound, escalate, expand, extend, increase, multiply, raise, swell, up ♦ *usu* **enlarge on** [2] amplify, develop, elaborate (on), expand

en•light•en \in-ˈlīt-ᵊn\ *vb* **1** ♦ : to give knowledge to : INSTRUCT, INFORM **2** ♦ : to give spiritual insight to — **en•light•en•ment** *n*

♦ [1] acquaint, advise, apprise, brief, clue, familiarize, fill in, inform, instruct, tell, wise ♦ [2] edify, educate, nurture

en•list \in-ˈlist\ *vb* **1** : to secure the aid or support of **2** ♦ : to engage for service in the armed forces **3** ♦ : to participate heartily (as in a cause or effort) ⟨∼*ed* in the cause of world peace⟩ — **en•list•ee** \-ˌlis-ˈtē\ *n* — **en•list•ment** \-ˈlist-mənt\ *n*

♦ *usu* **enlist in** [2, 3] enroll, enter, join, sign on, sign up

en•list•ed \in-ˈlis-təd\ *adj* : of, relating to, or forming the part of a military force below commissioned or warrant officers
enlisted man *n* : a man or woman in the armed forces ranking below a commissioned or warrant officer
en•liv•en \in-ˈlī-vən\ *vb* ♦ : to give life, action, or spirit to : ANIMATE

♦ animate, brace, energize, fire, invigorate, jazz up, liven up, pep up, quicken, stimulate, vitalize, vivify, zip (up)

en masse \äⁿ-ˈmas\ *adv* : in a body : as a whole
en•mesh \in-ˈmesh\ *vb* ♦ : to catch or entangle in or as if in meshes

♦ ensnare, entangle, entrap, mesh, snare, tangle, trap

en•mi•ty \ˈen-mə-tē\ *n, pl* **-ties** ♦ : positive, active, and typically mutual hatred or ill will

♦ animosity, antagonism, antipathy, bitterness, gall, grudge, hostility, rancor ***Ant*** amity

en•no•ble \i-ˈnō-bəl\ *vb* **-bled; -bling** ♦ : to raise in rank or status : EXALT; *esp* : to raise to noble rank — **en•no•ble•ment** *n*

♦ aggrandize, dignify, exalt, glorify, magnify

en•nui \ˌän-ˈwē\ *n* ♦ : a feeling of weariness and dissatisfaction : BOREDOM

♦ boredom, doldrums, listlessness, restlessness, tedium, tiredness, weariness

enor•mi•ty \i-ˈnȯr-mə-tē\ *n, pl* **-ties** **1** : an outrageous, vicious, or immoral act **2** ♦ : great wickedness **3** ♦ : the quality or state of being huge : IMMENSITY

♦ [2] atrociousness, atrocity, depravity, heinousness, monstrosity, vileness, wickedness ♦ [3] hugeness, immensity, magnitude, massiveness, vastness

enor•mous \i-ˈnȯr-məs\ *adj* **1** : exceedingly wicked **2** ♦ : great in size, number, or degree : HUGE — **enor•mous•ly** *adv*

♦ astronomical, colossal, elephantine, giant, gigantic, ginormous, huge, jumbo, mammoth, massive, prodigious, titanic, tremendous, whopping

¹enough \i-ˈnəf\ *adj* : SUFFICIENT
²enough *adv* **1** ♦ : in or to a degree or quantity that suffices : SUFFICIENTLY **2** : FULLY, QUITE **3** ♦ : in a tolerable degree

♦ [1] adequately, satisfactorily ***Ant*** inadequately, insufficiently ♦ [3] fairly, kind of, moderately, so-so, somewhat, sort of

³enough *pron* : a sufficient number, quantity, or amount
en•quire \in-ˈkwī(-ə)r\, **en•qui•ry** \ˈin-ˌkwī(-ə)r-ē, in-ˈ; ˈin-kwə-rē, ˈiŋ-\ *chiefly Brit var of* INQUIRE, INQUIRY
en•rage \in-ˈrāj\ *vb* ♦ : to fill with rage

♦ anger, antagonize, incense, inflame, infuriate, madden, outrage, rankle, rile, roil

en•raged \in-ˈrājd\ *adj* ♦ : full of fury or rage

♦ angry, boiling, furious, irate

en•rap•ture \in-ˈrap-chər\ *vb* **en•rap•tured; en•rap•tur•ing** ♦ : to fill with delight

♦ carry away, elate, elevate, enthrall, exhilarate, transport

en•rich \in-ˈrich\ *vb* **1 a** : to make rich or richer **b** ♦ : to add to or improve with additions **2** ♦ : to add beauty to : ORNAMENT, ADORN — **en•rich•ment** *n*

♦ [1b] ameliorate, amend, better, enhance, improve, perfect, refine ♦ [2] adorn, array, beautify, bedeck, deck, decorate, do, dress, embellish, garnish, grace, ornament, trim

en•roll *or Can and Brit* **en•rol** \in-ˈrōl\ *vb* **en•rolled; en•roll•ing** **1** ♦ : to enter or register on a roll or list **2** ♦ : to offer (oneself) for enrolling — **en•roll•ment** *n*

♦ [1] inscribe, itemize, list, matriculate, register ♦ [1] catalog, enter, index, inscribe, list, put down, record ♦ [2] enlist, enter, join, sign on, sign up

en•roll•ment *or chiefly Can and Brit* **en•rol•ment** *n* **1 :** the act or process of enrolling (as at enlistment or registration) **2 :** the number enrolled

en route \än-ˈrüt, en-\ *adv or adj* **:** on or along the way

ENS *abbr* ensign

en•sconce \in-ˈskäns\ *vb* **en•sconced; en•sconc•ing 1** ♦ **:** to place out of sight **:** CONCEAL **2** ♦ **:** to settle snugly or securely

♦ [1] bury, cache, conceal, hide, secrete ♦ [2] install, lodge, perch, roost, settle

en•sem•ble \än-ˈsäm-bəl\ *n* **:** a group (as of singers, dancers, or players) or a set (as of clothes) producing a single effect

en•sheathe \in-ˈshēth\ *vb* **:** to cover with or as if with a sheath

en•shrine \in-ˈshrīn\ *vb* **1 :** to enclose in or as if in a shrine **2 :** to cherish as sacred — **en•shrine•ment** \-mənt\ *n*

en•shroud \in-ˈshraud\ *vb* ♦ **:** to cover or enclose with or as if with a shroud **:** OBSCURE

♦ blanket, blot out, cloak, conceal, cover, curtain, hide, mask, obscure, occult, screen, shroud, veil

en•sign \ˈen-sən, *1 also* ˈen-ˌsīn\ *n* **1** ♦ **:** a flag that is flown (as by a ship) as the symbol of nationality and that may also be flown with a distinctive badge added to its design; *also* **:** BADGE, EMBLEM **2 :** a commissioned officer in the navy ranking next below a lieutenant junior grade

♦ banner, colors (*or* colours), flag, jack, pennant, standard, streamer

en•slave \in-ˈslāv\ *vb* **:** to make a slave of

en•slave•ment *n* **1 :** the act or process of enslaving **2** ♦ **:** the state of being enslaved

♦ bondage, servitude, slavery, thrall, yoke

en•snare \in-ˈsnar\ *vb* ♦ **:** to take in or as if in a snare **:** TRAP

♦ enmesh, entangle, entrap, mesh, snare, tangle, trap

en•sue \in-ˈsü\ *vb* **en•sued; en•su•ing :** to follow in time or as a result ⟨the birds escaped and chaos *ensued*⟩

en•sure \in-ˈshur\ *vb* **en•sured; en•sur•ing** ♦ **:** to give security to **:** INSURE, GUARANTEE

♦ assure, cinch, guarantee, guaranty, insure, secure

en•tail \in-ˈtāl\ *vb* **1 :** to limit the inheritance of (property) to the owner's lineal descendants or to a class thereof **2** ♦ **:** to include or involve as a necessary step or result — **en•tail•ment** *n*

♦ carry, comprehend, contain, embrace, encompass, include, involve, number, take in

en•tan•gle \in-ˈtaŋ-gəl\ *vb* **1** ♦ **:** to wrap or twist together **:** TANGLE; *also* **:** to make complicated **2** ♦ **:** to take in or as if in a snare; *also* **:** to involve in a perplexing or troublesome situation

♦ [1] interlace, intertwine, interweave, knot, snarl, tangle ♦ [2] enmesh, ensnare, entrap, mesh, snare, tangle, trap *Ant* disentangle

en•tan•gle•ment *n* **1 :** the action of entangling **:** the state of being entangled **2** ♦ **:** something that entangles, confuses, or ensnares

♦ net, snare, web

en•tente \än-ˈtänt\ *n* **:** an understanding providing for joint action; *also* **:** parties linked by such an entente

en•ter \ˈen-tər\ *vb* **1 :** to go or come in or into **2** ♦ **:** to become a member of **:** JOIN ⟨~ the ministry⟩ **3** ♦ **:** to make a beginning **:** to begin to consider a subject — usually used with *into* or *upon* **4 :** to take part in **:** CONTRIBUTE **5 :** to go into or upon and take possession **6** ♦ **:** to set down (as in a list) **:** REGISTER ⟨~ the data⟩ **7 :** to place (a complaint) before a court; *also* **:** to put on record ⟨~ a complaint⟩

♦ [2] enlist, enroll, join, sign on, sign up ♦ *usu* **enter into** *or* **enter upon** [3] begin, commence, embark (on *or* upon), get off, launch, open, start, strike ♦ [6] catalog, enroll, index, inscribe, list, put down, record, register, schedule, slate

en•ter•i•tis \ˌen-tə-ˈrī-təs\ *n* **:** intestinal inflammation; *also* **:** a disease marked by this

en•ter•prise \ˈen-tər-ˌprīz\ *n* **1** ♦ **:** a project or undertaking that is especially difficult, complicated, or risky **2** ♦ **:** readiness for daring action **:** INITIATIVE **3** ♦ **:** a business organization

♦ [1] chance, flier, gamble, speculation, venture ♦ [2] aggressiveness, ambition, drive, go, hustle, initiative ♦ [3] business, company, concern, establishment, firm, house, outfit

en•ter•pris•ing \-ˌprī-ziŋ\ *adj* ♦ **:** bold and vigorous in action

♦ adventurous, audacious, bold, daring, gutsy, hardy, nervy, venturesome

en•ter•tain \ˌen-tər-ˈtān\ *vb* **1 :** to treat or receive as a guest **2** ♦ **:** to provide entertainment for **:** AMUSE, DIVERT **3** ♦ **:** to hold in mind; *also* **:** to receive and take into consideration — **en•ter•tain•er** *n*

♦ [2] amuse, disport, divert, regale ♦ [3] consider, contemplate, debate, deliberate, meditate, mull, ponder, question, ruminate, study, think, weigh

en•ter•tain•ing \-ˈtā-niŋ\ *adj* ♦ **:** providing entertainment

♦ amusing, delightful, diverting, enjoyable, fun, pleasurable

en•ter•tain•ment *n* **1** ♦ **:** the act of entertaining **2** ♦ **:** amusement or diversion provided especially by performers; *also* **:** something or someone diverting or engaging

♦ [1] amusement, distraction, diversion ♦ [2] delight, diversion, fun, pleasure

en•thrall *or* **en•thral** \in-ˈthrȯl\ *vb* **en•thralled; en•thrall•ing 1 :** ENSLAVE **2** ♦ **:** to hold the attention of as if under a spell **:** hold spellbound

♦ arrest, enchant, fascinate, grip, hypnotize, interest, intrigue, involve, mesmerize

en•thrall•ing *adj* ♦ **:** capable of holding spellbound **:** intensely absorbing or interesting

♦ absorbing, engaging, engrossing, fascinating, interesting, intriguing

en•throne \in-ˈthrōn\ *vb* **1 :** to seat on or as if on a throne **2 :** EXALT

en•thuse \in-ˈthüz, -ˈthyüz\ *vb* **en•thused; en•thus•ing 1 :** to make enthusiastic **2** ♦ **:** to show enthusiasm

♦ fuss, gush, rave, rhapsodize

en•thu•si•asm \in-ˈthü-zē-ˌa-zəm, -ˈthyü-\ *n* **1** ♦ **:** strong warmth of feeling **:** keen interest **:** FERVOR **2** ♦ **:** something that inspires or is pursued or regarded with ardent zeal or fervor

♦ [1] appetite, ardor, avidity, eagerness, excitement, fervor, hunger, impatience, keenness, thirst ♦ [2] craze, fad, fashion, go, mode, rage, sensation, style, trend, vogue

en•thu•si•ast \-ˌast, -əst\ *n* ♦ **:** a person filled with enthusiasm

♦ addict, aficionado, buff, bug, devotee, fan, fancier, lover, nut

en•thu•si•as•tic \in-ˌthü-zē-ˈas-tik, -ˌthyü-\ *adj* ♦ **:** filled with or marked by enthusiasm — **en•thu•si•as•ti•cal•ly** \-ti-k(ə-)lē\ *adv*

♦ ardent, athirst, avid, eager, gung ho, keen, nuts, raring, thirsty

en•tice \in-ˈtīs\ *vb* **en•ticed; en•tic•ing** ♦ **:** to attract cunningly or by arousing hope or desire **:** ALLURE, TEMPT

♦ allure, beguile, decoy, lead on, lure, seduce, tempt

en•tice•ment *n* **1** ♦ **:** the act of enticing **2** ♦ **:** something that entices **:** a means or method of enticing

♦ lure, seduction, solicitation, temptation

en•tire \in-ˈtī(-ə)r\ *adj* ♦ having no element or part left out **:** COMPLETE, WHOLE

♦ complete, comprehensive, full, grand, intact, integral, perfect, plenary, total, undivided, whole

en•tire•ly *adv* ♦ **:** to the full or entire extent

♦ altogether, completely, dead, fast, flat, full, fully, perfectly, quite, thoroughly, well, wholly

en•tire•ty \in-ˈtī-rə-tē, -ˈtī(-ə)r-tē\ *n, pl* **-ties 1 :** COMPLETENESS **2 :** WHOLE, TOTALITY

en•ti•tle \in-ˈtī-tᵊl\ *vb* **en•ti•tled; en•ti•tling 1** ♦ **:** to give a title to **:** DESIGNATE **2** ♦ **:** to furnish with proper grounds for seeking or claiming something ⟨*entitled* to a fair trial⟩

♦ [1] baptize, call, christen, denominate, designate, dub, label, name, style, term, title ♦ [2] authorize, qualify *Ant* disqualify

en•ti•tle•ment \in-ˈtīt-ᵊl-mənt\ *n* **:** a government program providing benefits to members of a specified group

en•ti•ty \ˈen-tə-tē\ *n, pl* **-ties 1 :** EXISTENCE, BEING **2** ♦ **:** something with separate and real existence

♦ being, individual, object, substance, thing

en•tomb \in-ˈtüm\ *vb* **:** to place in a tomb **:** BURY

en•tomb•ment *n* ♦ **:** the act or process of entombing

♦ burial, interment, sepulture

en•to•mol•o•gy \ˌen-tə-ˈmä-lə-jē\ *n* **:** a branch of zoology that deals with insects — **en•to•mo•log•i•cal** \-mə-ˈlä-ji-kəl\ *adj* — **en•to•mol•o•gist** \-jist\ *n*
en•tou•rage \ˌän-tu̇-ˈräzh\ *n* **:** RETINUE
en•tr'acte \ˈä^{n}n-ˌtrakt\ *n* **1 :** something (as a dance) performed between two acts of a play **2 :** the interval between two acts of a play
en•trails \ˈen-ˌtrālz\ *n pl* **:** the internal organs especially in the trunk of the body **:** VISCERA; *esp* **:** the tubular part of the alimentary canal that extends from the stomach to the anus
¹en•trance \ˈen-trəns\ *n* **1** ♦ **:** permission or right to enter **2 :** the act of entering **3** ♦ **:** a means or place of entry

♦ [1] access, admission, doorway, entrée, entry, gateway ♦ [3] door, doorway, gate, gateway, way

²en•trance \in-ˈtrans\ *vb* **en•tranced; en•tranc•ing** ♦ **:** to carry away with delight, wonder, or rapture

♦ carry away, enrapture, enthrall, ravish, transport

en•trant \ˈen-trənt\ *n* **:** one that enters especially as a competitor
en•trap \in-ˈtrap\ *vb* ♦ **:** to catch in or as if in a trap **:** ENSNARE, TRAP — **en•trap•ment** *n*

♦ enmesh, ensnare, entangle, mesh, snare, tangle, trap

en•treat \in-ˈtrēt\ *vb* ♦ **:** to ask urgently **:** BESEECH

♦ appeal, beg, beseech, implore, importune, petition, plead, pray, solicit, supplicate

en•treaty \-ˈtrē-tē\ *n* ♦ **:** an act of entreating

♦ appeal, cry, petition, plea, prayer, solicitation, suit, supplication

en•trée *or* **en•tree** \ˈän-ˌtrā\ *n* **1** ♦ **:** freedom of entry or access **2 :** the main course of a meal in the U.S.

♦ access, admission, doorway, entrance, entry, gateway

en•trench \in-ˈtrench\ *vb* **1 a :** to place within or surround with a trench especially for defense **b** ♦ **:** to establish solidly ⟨~*ed* customs⟩ **2 :** ENCROACH, TRESPASS — **en•trench•ment** *n*

♦ embed, fix, implant, ingrain, lodge, root *Ant* dislodge, root (out), uproot

en•tre•pre•neur \ˌän-trə-prə-ˈnər, -ˈnu̇r, -ˈnyu̇r\ *n* **:** one who organizes and assumes the risk of a business or enterprise — **en•tre•pre•neur•ial** \-ˈnu̇r-ē-əl, -ˈnyu̇r-, -ˈnər-\ *adj* — **en•tre•pre•neur•ship** \-ˌship\ *n*
en•tro•py \ˈen-trə-pē\ *n, pl* **-pies 1 :** the degree of disorder in a system **2 :** an ultimate state of inert uniformity
en•trust \in-ˈtrəst\ *vb* **1** ♦ **:** to commit something to as a trust **2** ♦ **:** to commit to another with confidence

♦ [1] assign, charge, commission, trust ♦ [2] commend, commit, consign, delegate, deliver, give, hand over, leave, pass, transfer, transmit, trust, turn over, vest

en•try \ˈen-trē\ *n, pl* **entries 1** ♦ **:** a place of entrance; *also* **:** the act, means, right, or privilege of entering **2 :** an entering in a record; *also* **:** an item so entered **3 :** a headword with its definition or identification; *also* **:** VOCABULARY ENTRY **4 :** one entered in a contest

♦ foyer, hall, lobby, vestibule ♦ access, admission, doorway, entrée, entrance, gateway

en•twine \in-ˈtwīn\ *vb* ♦ **:** to twine together or around

♦ coil, curl, spiral, twine, twist, wind

enu•mer•ate \i-ˈnü-mə-ˌrāt, -ˈnyü-\ *vb* **-at•ed; -at•ing 1** ♦ **:** to determine the number of **:** COUNT **2** ♦ **:** to specify one after another **:** LIST — **enu•mer•a•tion** \-ˌnü-mə-ˈrā-shən, -ˌnyü-\ *n*

♦ [1] count, number, tell ♦ [2] detail, itemize, list, numerate, rehearse, tick (off)

enun•ci•ate \ē-ˈnən-sē-ˌāt\ *vb* **-at•ed; -at•ing 1 a :** to state definitely **b** ♦ **:** to make known publicly **:** ANNOUNCE, PROCLAIM **2 :** to say clearly and effectively **:** PRONOUNCE, ARTICULATE — **enun•ci•a•tion** \-ˌnən-sē-ˈā-shən\ *n*

♦ advertise, announce, blaze, broadcast, declare, placard, post, proclaim, promulgate, publicize, publish, sound

en•ure•sis \ˌen-yu̇-ˈrē-səs\ *n* **:** involuntary discharge of urine **:** BED-WETTING
env *abbr* envelope
en•vel•op \in-ˈve-ləp\ *vb* ♦ **:** to enclose completely with or as if with a covering — **en•vel•op•ment** *n*

♦ embrace, enclose, encompass, enfold, enshroud, invest, lap, mantle, shroud, swathe, veil, wrap

en•ve•lope \ˈen-və-ˌlōp, ˈän-\ *n* **1 :** a usually paper container for a letter **2 :** WRAPPER, COVERING **3 :** a conventionally accepted limit ⟨fashions that push the ~⟩
en•ven•om \in-ˈve-nəm\ *vb* **1 :** to make poisonous **2 :** EMBITTER
en•vi•able \ˈen-vē-ə-bəl\ *adj* **:** highly desirable — **en•vi•ably** \-blē\ *adv*
en•vi•ous \ˈen-vē-əs\ *adj* ♦ **:** feeling or showing envy — **en•vi•ous•ly** *adv*

♦ covetous, jaundiced, jealous, resentful

en•vi•ous•ness *n* ♦ **:** the quality or state of being envious

♦ covetousness, envy, jealousy, resentment

en•vi•ron•ment \in-ˈvī-rən-mənt, -ˈvī(-ə)rn-\ *n* **1** ♦ **:** the circumstances, objects, or conditions surrounding someone or something **:** SURROUNDINGS **2 :** the whole complex of factors (as soil, climate, and living things) that influence the form and the ability to survive of a plant or animal or ecological community — **en•vi•ron•men•tal** \-ˌvī-rən-ˈment-^{ə}l, -ˌvī(-ə)rn-\ *adj* — **en•vi•ron•men•tal•ly** \-t^{ə}l-ē\ *adv*

♦ atmosphere, climate, environs, medium, milieu, setting, surroundings

en•vi•ron•men•tal•ist \-ˌvī-rən-ˈment-^{ə}l-ist, -ˌvīrn-\ *n* **:** a person concerned about environmental quality especially with respect to control of pollution
en•vi•rons \in-ˈvī-rənz\ *n pl* **1** ♦ **:** the districts around a city **2** ♦ **:** the circumstances, conditions, or objects by which one is surrounded **:** SURROUNDINGS; *also* **:** VICINITY

♦ [1] exurbia, outskirts, suburbia ♦ [2] atmosphere, climate, environment, medium, milieu, setting, surroundings

en•vis•age \in-ˈvi-zij\ *vb* **-aged; -ag•ing** ♦ **:** to have a mental picture of

♦ conceive, dream, fancy, imagine, picture, vision, visualize

en•vi•sion \in-ˈvi-zhən, en-\ *vb* **:** to picture to oneself ⟨~*s* world peace⟩
en•voy \ˈen-ˌvȯi, ˈän-\ *n* **1** ♦ **:** a diplomatic agent **2** ♦ **:** one who bears a message or does an errand **:** REPRESENTATIVE

♦ [1] ambassador, delegate, emissary, legate, minister, representative ♦ [2] agent, attorney, commissary, delegate, deputy, factor, proxy, representative

¹en•vy \ˈen-vē\ *n, pl* **envies** ♦ **:** painful or resentful awareness of another's advantages; *also* **:** an object of envy

♦ covetousness, enviousness, jealousy, resentment

²envy *vb* **en•vied; en•vy•ing :** to feel envy toward or on account of
en•zyme \ˈen-ˌzīm\ *n* **:** any of various complex proteins produced by living cells that catalyze specific biochemical reactions at body temperatures — **en•zy•mat•ic** \ˌen-zə-ˈma-tik\ *adj*
Eo•cene \ˈē-ə-ˌsēn\ *adj* **:** of, relating to, or being the epoch of the Tertiary between the Paleocene and the Oligocene — **Eocene** *n*
EOE *abbr* equal opportunity employer
eo•lian \ē-ˈō-lē-ən\ *adj* **:** borne, deposited, or produced by the wind
EOM *abbr* end of month
eon *var of* AEON
EP *abbr* European plan
EPA *abbr* Environmental Protection Agency
ep•au•let *also* **ep•au•lette** \ˌe-pə-ˈlet\ *n* **:** a shoulder ornament especially on a coat or military uniform
épée \ˈe-ˌpā, ā-ˈpā\ *n* **:** a fencing or dueling sword
Eph *or* **Ephes** *abbr* Ephesians
ephed•rine \i-ˈfe-drən\ *n* **:** a stimulant drug used to treat asthma and nasal congestion
ephem•era \i-ˈfe-mər-ə\ *n pl* **:** collectibles (as posters or tickets) not intended to have lasting value
ephem•er•al \i-ˈfe-mə-rəl\ *adj* ♦ **:** lasting a very short time **:** SHORT-LIVED, TRANSITORY — **ephem•er•al•i•ty** \i-ˌfe-mə-ˈra-lə-tē\ *n*

♦ evanescent, flash, fleeting, impermanent, momentary, short-lived, transient

Ephe•sians \i-ˈfē-zhənz\ *n* **:** a letter addressed to early Christians and included as a book in the New Testament
ep•ic \ˈe-pik\ *n* **:** a long poem in elevated style narrating the deeds of a hero — **epic** *adj*

epi•cen•ter *or Can and Brit* **epi•cen•tre** \ˈe-pi-ˌsen-tər\ *n* : the point on the earth's surface directly above the point of origin of an earthquake
ep•i•cure \ˈe-pi-ˌkyu̇r\ *n* ♦ : a person with sensitive and discriminating tastes especially in food and wine

♦ epicurean, gourmand, gourmet

ep•i•cu•re•an \ˌe-pi-kyu̇-ˈrē-ən, -ˈkyu̇r-ē-\ *n* ♦ : a person with sensitive and discriminating tastes especially in food and wine : EPICURE — **epicurean** *adj*

♦ epicure, gourmand, gourmet

¹**ep•i•dem•ic** \ˌe-pə-ˈde-mik\ *adj* : affecting many persons at one time ⟨~ disease⟩; *also* : excessively prevalent
²**epidemic** *n* : an epidemic outbreak especially of disease
ep•i•de•mi•ol•o•gy \ˌep-ə-ˌdē-mē-ˈä-lə-jē\ *n* : the study of the incidence, distribution, and control of disease in a population — **ep•i•de•mi•o•log•i•cal** \-ˌdē-mē-ə-ˈlä-ji-kəl\ *also* **ep•i•de•mi•o•log•ic** \-jik\ *adj* — **ep•i•de•mi•ol•o•gist** \-ˈä-lə-jist\ *n*
epi•der•mis \ˌe-pə-ˈdər-məs\ *n* : an outer layer especially of skin — **epi•der•mal** \-məl\ *adj*
epi•du•ral \ˌe-pi-ˈd(y)u̇r-əl\ *adj* : administered into the space outside the membrane that envelops the spinal cord ⟨~ anesthesia⟩ — **epidural** *n*
epi•glot•tis \ˌe-pə-ˈglä-təs\ *n* : a thin plate of flexible tissue protecting the tracheal opening during swallowing
ep•i•gram \ˈe-pə-ˌgram\ *n* **1** : a short often satirical poem **2** ♦ : a terse, sage, or witty often paradoxical saying

♦ adage, aphorism, byword, maxim, proverb, saying

ep•i•gram•mat•ic \ˌe-pə-grə-ˈma-tik\ *adj* ♦ : of, relating to, or resembling an epigram; *also* : marked by or given to the use of epigrams

♦ brief, compact, compendious, concise, crisp, laconic, pithy, succinct, summary, terse

ep•i•lep•sy \ˈe-pə-ˌlep-sē\ *n, pl* **-sies** : a disorder marked by abnormal electrical discharges in the brain and typically manifested by sudden periods of diminished consciousness or by convulsions — **ep•i•lep•tic** \ˌe-pə-ˈlep-tik\ *adj or n*
ep•i•logue *also* **ep•i•log** \ˈe-pə-ˌlȯg, -ˌläg\ *n* **1** : a concluding section of a literary work **2** : a speech addressed to the spectators by an actor at the end of a play
epi•neph•rine \ˌe-pə-ˈne-frən\ *n* : an adrenal hormone used medicinally especially as a heart stimulant, a muscle relaxant, and a vasoconstrictor
epiph•a•ny \i-ˈpi-fə-nē\ *n, pl* **-nies** **1** *cap* : January 6 observed as a church festival in commemoration of the coming of the Magi to Jesus at Bethlehem **2** : a sudden striking understanding of something
epis•co•pa•cy \i-ˈpis-kə-pə-sē\ *n, pl* **-cies** **1** : government of a church by bishops **2** : EPISCOPATE
epis•co•pal \i-ˈpis-kə-pəl\ *adj* **1** : of or relating to a bishop or episcopacy **2** *cap* : of or relating to the Protestant Episcopal Church
Epis•co•pa•lian \i-ˌpis-kə-ˈpāl-yən\ *n* : a member of the Protestant Episcopal Church
epis•co•pate \i-ˈpis-kə-pət, -ˌpāt\ *n* **1** : the rank, office, or term of a bishop **2** : a body of bishops
ep•i•sode \ˈe-pə-ˌsōd\ *n* **1** : a unit of action in a dramatic or literary work **2** ♦ : an incident in a course of events : OCCURRENCE ⟨a feverish ~⟩

♦ affair, circumstance, event, happening, incident, occasion, occurrence, thing

ep•i•sod•ic \ˌe-pə-ˈsä-dik\ *adj* ♦ : made up of separate especially loosely connected episodes

♦ periodic, serial

epis•tle \i-ˈpi-səl\ *n* **1** *cap* : one of the letters of the New Testament **2** : a direct or personal written or printed message addressed to a person or organization : LETTER; *esp* : a formal or elegant letter — **epis•to•lary** \i-ˈpis-tə-ˌler-ē\ *adj*
ep•i•taph \ˈe-pə-ˌtaf\ *n* : an inscription in memory of a dead person
ep•i•tha•la•mi•um \ˌe-pə-thə-ˈlā-mē-əm\ *or* **ep•i•tha•la•mi•on** \-mē-ən\ *n, pl* **-mi•ums** *or* **-mia** \-mē-ə\ : a song or poem in honor of a bride and bridegroom
ep•i•the•li•um \ˌe-pə-ˈthē-lē-əm\ *n, pl* **-lia** \-lē-ə\ : a cellular membrane covering a bodily surface or lining a cavity — **ep•i•the•li•al** \-lē-əl\ *adj*
ep•i•thet \ˈe-pə-ˌthet, -thət\ *n* : a characterizing and often abusive word or phrase
epit•o•me \i-ˈpi-tə-mē\ *n* **1** ♦ : a brief presentation or statement of something : ABSTRACT, SUMMARY **2** ♦ : a typical or ideal example : EMBODIMENT

♦ [1] abstract, digest, encapsulation, outline, précis, recapitulation, résumé (*or* resume), roundup, sum, summary, synopsis, wrap-up ♦ [2] embodiment, exemplar, ideal, incarnation, manifestation, personification, quintessence

epit•o•mize \-ˌmīz\ *vb* **1** ♦ : to make or give an epitome of **2** ♦ : to serve as the typical or ideal example of

♦ [1] abstract, digest, encapsulate, outline, recapitulate, sum up, summarize, wrap up ♦ [2] embody, manifest, materialize, personify

ep•och \ˈe-pək, -ˌpäk\ *n* ♦ : a usually extended period : ERA, AGE — **ep•och•al** \-pə-kəl, -ˌpä-\ *adj*

♦ age, era, period, time

ep•onym \ˈe-pə-ˌnim\ *n* **1** : one for whom something is or is believed to be named **2** : a name (as of a disease) based on or derived from an eponym — **epon•y•mous** \i-ˈpä-nə-məs\ *adj*
ep•oxy \i-ˈpäk-sē\ *vb* **ep•ox•ied** *or* **ep•oxyed; ep•oxy•ing** : to glue, fill, or coat with epoxy resin
epoxy resin *n* : a synthetic resin used in coatings and adhesives
ep•si•lon \ˈep-sə-ˌlän, -lən\ *n* : the 5th letter of the Greek alphabet — Ε or ϵ
Ep•som salts \ˈep-səm-\ *n* : a bitter colorless or white magnesium salt with cathartic properties
eq *abbr* **1** equal **2** equation
equa•ble \ˈe-kwə-bəl, ˈē-\ *adj* ♦ : showing regular or consistent movement, occurrence, operation, or character; *esp* : free from unpleasant extremes — **eq•ua•bil•i•ty** \ˌe-kwə-ˈbi-lə-tē, ˌē-\ *n* — **eq•ua•bly** \ˈe-kwə-blē, ˈē-\ *adv*

♦ balmy, clement, gentle, mild, moderate, temperate

¹**equal** \ˈē-kwəl\ *adj* **1** ♦ : of the same measure, quantity, value, quality, number, degree, or status as another **2** ♦ : regarding or affecting all objects in the same way : IMPARTIAL ⟨all citizens are due ~ treatment under the law⟩ **3** : free from extremes **4** : able to cope with a situation or task — **equal•ly** *adv*

♦ [1] duplicate, even, identical, indistinguishable, same ♦ [2] disinterested, dispassionate, equitable, fair, impartial, just, nonpartisan, objective, square, unbiased, unprejudiced

²**equal** *vb* **equaled** *or* **equalled; equal•ing** *or* **equal•ling** **1** ♦ : to be or become equal to; *also* : to be identical in value to **2** ♦ : to make or produce something equal to

♦ [1, 2] correspond, match, parallel ♦ [1, 2] add up, amount, come, correspond, meet, rival, tie, touch

³**equal** *n* ♦ : one that is equal

♦ coordinate, counterpart, equivalent, fellow, like, match, parallel, peer, rival

equal•ise, equal•is•er *Brit var of* EQUALIZE, EQUALIZER
equal•i•ty \i-ˈkwä-lə-tē\ *n* ♦ : the quality or state of being equal

♦ equivalence, par, parity, sameness

equal•ize \ˈē-kwə-ˌlīz\ *vb* **-ized; -iz•ing** ♦ : to make equal, uniform, or constant — **equal•i•za•tion** \ˌē-kwə-lə-ˈzā-shən\ *n* — **equal•iz•er** *n*

♦ balance, equate, even, level

equals sign *or* **equal sign** *n* : a sign = indicating equivalence
equa•nim•i•ty \ˌē-kwə-ˈni-mə-tē, ˌe-\ *n, pl* **-ties** ♦ : evenness of mind especially under stress : COMPOSURE

♦ aplomb, calmness, composure, coolness, placidity, self-possession, serenity, tranquillity *Ant* agitation, discomposure, perturbation

equate \i-ˈkwāt\ *vb* **equat•ed; equat•ing** **1** ♦ : to make, treat, or regard as equal or comparable **2** : show the relationship between

♦ balance, equalize, even, level ♦ bracket, compare, liken

equa•tion \i-ˈkwā-zhən\ *n* **1** : an act of equating : the state of being equated **2** : a usually formal statement of equivalence especially of mathematical expressions
equa•tor \i-ˈkwā-tər, ˈē-ˌ\ *n* : an imaginary circle around the earth that is everywhere equally distant from the two poles — **equa•to•ri•al** \ˌē-kwə-ˈtōr-ē-əl, ˌe-\ *adj*
equer•ry \ˈe-kwə-rē, i-ˈkwer-ē\ *n, pl* **-ries** **1** : an officer in charge of the horses of a prince or noble **2** : a personal attendant of a member of the British royal family
¹**eques•tri•an** \i-ˈkwes-trē-ən\ *adj* : of or relating to horseback riding; *also* : representing a person on horseback ⟨an ~ statue⟩
²**equestrian** *n* : one who rides a horse

eques•tri•enne \i-ˌkwes-trē-ˈen\ *n* : a female rider on horseback
equi•dis•tant \ˌē-kwə-ˈdis-tənt\ *adj* : equally distant
equi•lat•er•al \ˌē-kwə-ˈla-tə-rəl\ *adj* : having all sides or faces equal ⟨~ triangles⟩
equi•lib•ri•um \ˌē-kwə-ˈli-brē-əm, ˌe-\ *n, pl* **-ri•ums** *or* **-ria** \-brē-ə\ **1 :** a state of intellectual or emotional balance **2** ♦ **:** a state of balance between opposing forces or actions

♦ balance, equipoise, poise

¹equine \ˈē-ˌkwīn, ˈe-\ *adj* : of or relating to the horse
²equine *n* : a member of the family of hoofed mammals consisting of the horses, asses, and zebras and extinct related animals; *specif* : HORSE
equi•noc•tial \ˌē-kwə-ˈnäk-shəl, ˌe-\ *adj* : relating to an equinox
equi•nox \ˈē-kwə-ˌnäks, ˈe-\ *n* : either of the two times each year when the sun appears directly overhead at the equator and day and night are everywhere of equal length
equip \i-ˈkwip\ *vb* **equipped; equip•ping 1** ♦ **:** to supply with needed resources **2** ♦ **:** to make ready : PREPARE

♦ [1] accoutre, fit, furnish, outfit, rig, supply ♦ [2] fit, prepare, qualify, ready, season

eq•ui•page \ˈe-kwə-pij\ *n* : a horse-drawn carriage usually with its servants
equip•ment \i-ˈkwip-mənt\ *n* **1** ♦ **:** things used in equipping : OUTFIT **2 :** the equipping of a person or thing : the state of being equipped

♦ accoutrements (*or* accouterments), apparatus, gear, matériel, outfit, paraphernalia, tackle

equi•poise \ˈe-kwə-ˌpȯiz, ˈē-\ *n* **1** ♦ **:** a state of equilibrium : BALANCE **2** ♦ **:** a weight or force that offsets another : COUNTERBALANCE

♦ [1] balance, equilibrium, poise ♦ [2] balance, counterbalance, counterweight, offset

eq•ui•ta•ble \ˈe-kwə-tə-bəl\ *adj* ♦ **:** having or exhibiting equity : JUST, FAIR — **eq•ui•ta•bly** \-blē\ *adv*

♦ disinterested, dispassionate, equal, fair, impartial, just, nonpartisan, objective, square, unbiased, unprejudiced

eq•ui•ta•tion \ˌe-kwə-ˈtā-shən\ *n* : the act or art of riding on horseback
eq•ui•ty \ˈe-kwə-tē\ *n, pl* **-ties 1 :** JUSTNESS, IMPARTIALITY **2 :** value of a property or of an interest in it in excess of claims against it
equiv *abbr* equivalent
equiv•a•lence \-ləns\ *n* ♦ **:** the state or property of being equivalent

♦ equality, par, parity, sameness ***Ant*** inequality

¹equiv•a•lent \i-ˈkwi-və-lənt\ *adj* : EQUAL; *also* : virtually identical
²equivalent *n* ♦ **:** one that is equivalent (as in value, meaning, or effect)

♦ coordinate, counterpart, equal, fellow, like, match, parallel, peer, rival

equiv•o•cal \i-ˈkwi-və-kəl\ *adj* **1** ♦ **:** subject to two or more interpretations and usually used to mislead or confuse : AMBIGUOUS **2 :** UNCERTAIN, UNDECIDED **3** ♦ **:** of doubtful advantage, genuineness, or morality : SUSPICIOUS, DUBIOUS ⟨~ behavior⟩ — **equiv•o•cal•ly** *adv*

♦ [1] ambiguous, cryptic, enigmatic, inscrutable, mysterious, mystic, nebulous, obscure, occult ♦ [3] debatable, disputable, doubtful, dubious, fishy, problematic, questionable, shady, shaky, suspect, suspicious

equiv•o•cate \i-ˈkwi-və-ˌkāt\ *vb* **-cat•ed; -cat•ing 1 :** to use misleading language **2** ♦ **:** to avoid committing oneself in what one says

♦ fudge, hedge, pussyfoot

equiv•o•ca•tion \-ˌkwi-və-ˈkā-shən\ *n* : an equivocal state or character; *esp* : the state of having more than one meaning
¹-er \ər\ *adj suffix or adv suffix* — used to form the comparative degree of adjectives and adverbs of one or two syllables ⟨hott*er*⟩ ⟨dri*er*⟩ ⟨silli*er*⟩ and sometimes of longer ones
²-er \ər\ *also* **-ier** \ē-ər, yər\ *or* **-yer** \yər\ *n suffix* **1 :** a person occupationally connected with ⟨hatt*er*⟩ ⟨lawy*er*⟩ **2 :** a person or thing belonging to or associated with ⟨old-tim*er*⟩ **3 :** a native of : resident of ⟨New Zealand*er*⟩ **4 :** one that has ⟨double-deck*er*⟩ **5 :** one that produces or yields ⟨pork*er*⟩ **6 :** one that does or performs (a specified action) ⟨report*er*⟩ **7 :** one that is a suitable object of (a specified action) ⟨broil*er*⟩ **8 :** one that is ⟨foreign*er*⟩
Er *symbol* erbium
ER *abbr* emergency room
era \ˈir-ə, ˈer-ə, ˈē-rə\ *n* **1 :** a chronological order or system of notation reckoned from a given date as basis **2** ♦ **:** a period identified by some special feature **3 :** any of the four major divisions of geologic time

♦ age, epoch, period, time

ERA *abbr* **1** earned run average **2** Equal Rights Amendment
erad•i•cate \i-ˈra-də-ˌkāt\ *vb* **-cat•ed; -cat•ing 1 :** to pull up (as a weed) by the roots : UPROOT **2** ♦ **:** destroy completely : ELIMINATE — **erad•i•ca•ble** \-di-kə-bəl\ *adj* — **erad•i•ca•tion** \-ˌra-də-ˈkā-shən\ *n*

♦ annihilate, blot out, demolish, eliminate, exterminate, liquidate, obliterate, root, rub out, snuff, stamp, wipe out

erase \i-ˈrās\ *vb* **erased; eras•ing :** to rub or scratch out (as written words); *also* : OBLITERATE — **eras•er** *n* — **era•sure** \i-ˈrā-shər\ *n*
er•bi•um \ˈər-bē-əm\ *n* : a rare metallic element found with yttrium
¹ere \ˌer\ *prep* ♦ **:** preceding in time : BEFORE

♦ ahead of, before, of, previous to, prior to, to

²ere *conj* : BEFORE
¹erect \i-ˈrekt\ *adj* **1** ♦ **:** not leaning or lying down : UPRIGHT **2 :** being in a state of physiological erection

♦ perpendicular, standing, upright, upstanding, vertical ***Ant*** flat, recumbent

²erect *vb* **1** ♦ **:** to put up by the fitting together of materials or parts : BUILD **2** ♦ **:** to fix or set in an upright position **3 :** SET UP; *also* : ESTABLISH, DEVELOP

♦ [1] assemble, build, construct, fabricate, make, make up, piece, put up, raise ♦ [2] pitch, put up, raise, rear, set up

erec•tile \i-ˈrekt-ᵊl, -ˈrek-ˌtīl\ *adj* : capable of becoming erect ⟨~ tissue⟩ ⟨~ feathers of a bird⟩
erec•tion \i-ˈrek-shən\ *n* **1 :** the turgid state of a previously flaccid bodily part when it becomes dilated with blood **2 :** CONSTRUCTION
ere•long \er-ˈlȯŋ\ *adv* : before long
er•e•mite \ˈer-ə-ˌmīt\ *n* : a religious recluse : HERMIT
er•go \ˈer-gō, ˈər-\ *adv* ♦ **:** because of a preceding fact or premise : THEREFORE

♦ accordingly, consequently, hence, so, therefore, thus, wherefore

er•go•nom•ics \ˌər-gə-ˈnä-miks\ *n sing or pl* : an applied science concerned with designing and arranging things people use in order to improve efficiency and safety — **er•go•nom•ic** \-mik\ *adj*
er•got \ˈər-gət, -ˌgät\ *n* **1 :** a disease of rye and other cereals caused by a fungus; *also* : this fungus **2 :** a medicinal compound or preparation derived from an ergot fungus
Er•i•tre•an \ˌer-ə-ˈtrē-ən, -ˈtrā-\ *n* : a native or inhabitant of Eritrea — **Eritrean** *adj*
er•mine \ˈər-mən\ *n, pl* **ermines 1 :** any of several weasels with winter fur mostly white; *also* : this white fur **2 :** a rank or office whose official robe is ornamented with ermine
erode \i-ˈrōd\ *vb* **erod•ed; erod•ing** ♦ **:** to diminish or destroy by degrees; *esp* : to gradually eat into or wear away ⟨soil *eroded* by wind and water⟩ — **erod•ible** *also* **erod•able** \-ˈrō-də-bəl\ *adj*

♦ abrade, bite, chafe, corrode, eat, fray, fret, gall, rub, wear

erog•e•nous \i-ˈrä-jə-nəs\ *adj* **1 :** sexually sensitive ⟨~ zones⟩ **2 :** of, relating to, or arousing sexual feelings
ero•sion \i-ˈrō-zhən\ *n* : the process or state of being eroded — **ero•sion•al** \-ˈrō-zhə-nəl\ *adj* — **ero•sion•al•ly** *adv*
ero•sive \i-ˈrō-siv\ *adj* : tending to erode — **ero•sive•ness** *n*
erot•ic \i-ˈrä-tik\ *adj* ♦ **:** relating to or dealing with sexual love : AMATORY — **erot•i•cal•ly** \-ti-k(ə-)lē\ *adv* — **erot•i•cism** \-tə-ˌsi-zəm\ *n*

♦ amatory, amorous, sexy

err \ˈər, ˈer\ *vb* ♦ **:** to be or do wrong

♦ offend, sin, transgress, trespass

er•rand \ˈer-ənd\ *n* : a short trip taken to do something; *also* : the object or purpose of such a trip
er•rant \ˈer-ənt\ *adj* **1** ♦ **:** traveling or given to traveling : WANDERING ⟨an ~ knight⟩ **2 :** straying outside proper bounds ⟨an

~ throw⟩ **3** ♦ : deviating from an accepted pattern or standard (as of behavior) ⟨an ~ child⟩

♦ [1] itinerant, nomad, peripatetic, roaming, vagabond, vagrant ♦ [3] bad, contrary, froward, mischievous, naughty

er•ra•ta \e-ˈrä-tə\ *n* : a list of corrigenda
er•rat•ic \i-ˈra-tik\ *adj* **1** : having no fixed course **2 a** ♦ : characterized by lack of consistency, regularity, or uniformity : INCONSISTENT **b** : ECCENTRIC — **er•rat•i•cal•ly** \-ti-k(ə-)lē\ *adv*

♦ aimless, arbitrary, desultory, haphazard, random, scattered, stray ♦ choppy, discontinuous, fitful, intermittent, irregular, occasional, spasmodic, sporadic, spotty, uneven, unsteady

er•ra•tum \e-ˈrä-təm\ *n, pl* **-ta** \-tə\ : CORRIGENDUM
er•ro•ne•ous \i-ˈrō-nē-əs, e-ˈrō-\ *adj* ♦ : containing or characterized by error : INCORRECT

♦ false, inaccurate, incorrect, inexact, invalid, off, unsound, untrue, wrong

er•ro•ne•ous•ly *adv* ♦ : in an erroneous manner

♦ amiss, faultily, improperly, inaptly, incorrectly, mistakenly, wrongly

er•ror \ˈer-ər\ *n* **1** ♦ : a usually ignorant or unintentional deviating from accuracy or truth ⟨made an ~ in adding⟩ **2** : a defensive misplay in baseball **3** : the state of one that errs ⟨to be in ~⟩ **4** : a product of mistake ⟨a typographical ~⟩ **5** ♦ : an act or condition of ignorant or imprudent deviation from a code of behavior **6** ♦ : an instance of false belief : a mistaken idea or system of ideas

♦ [1] blunder, fault, flub, fumble, goof, lapse, misstep, mistake, oversight, slip, stumble ♦ [5] crime, malefaction, misdeed, misdoing, offense, sin, transgression, violation, wrongdoing ♦ [6] fallacy, falsehood, falsity, illusion, misconception, untruth

er•ror•less *adj* : done, played, or performed without an error
er•satz \ˈer-ˌzäts\ *adj* : being usually an artificial and inferior substitute
erst \ˈərst\ *adv, archaic* : ERSTWHILE
[1]**erst•while** \-ˌhwīl\ *adv* : in the past : FORMERLY
[2]**erstwhile** *adj* ♦ : having been or existed at some past time : FORMER

♦ former, late, old, onetime, past, sometime, whilom

er•u•dite \ˈer-ə-ˌdīt, ˈer-yə-\ *adj* ♦ : possessing or displaying erudition

♦ educated, knowledgeable, learned, literate, scholarly, well-read ♦ bookish, learned, literary

er•u•di•tion \ˌer-ə-ˈdi-shən, ˌer-yə-\ *n* ♦ : extensive knowledge acquired chiefly from books : SCHOLARSHIP, LEARNING

♦ education, knowledge, learning, scholarship, science

erupt \i-ˈrəpt\ *vb* **1 a** ♦ : to burst forth : emerge with a sudden often violent rush **b** ♦ : to cause to burst forth : force out or release usually suddenly and violently **2** : to break through a surface ⟨teeth ~*ing* through the gum⟩ **3** : to break out with or as if with a skin rash — **erup•tive** \-tiv\ *adj*

♦ [1a] break out, burst, explode, flame, flare, go off ♦ [1b] belch, disgorge, eject, expel, jet, spew, spout, spurt

erup•tion \-ˈrəp-shən\ *n* ♦ : an act, process, or instance of erupting; *also* : a product of erupting (as a skin rash)

♦ agony, burst, explosion, fit, flare, flush, gush, outburst, paroxysm, spasm, storm ♦ blast, detonation, explosion

-ery *n suffix* **1** : qualities collectively : character : -NESS ⟨snob*bery*⟩ **2** : art : practice ⟨cook*ery*⟩ **3** : place of doing, keeping, producing, or selling (the thing specified) ⟨fish*ery*⟩ ⟨bak*ery*⟩ **4** : collection : aggregate ⟨fin*ery*⟩ **5** : state or condition ⟨slav*ery*⟩
ery•sip•e•las \ˌer-ə-ˈsi-pə-ləs, ˌir-\ *n* : an acute bacterial disease marked by fever and severe skin inflammation
er•y•the•ma \ˌer-ə-ˈthē-mə\ *n* : abnormal redness of the skin due to capillary congestion (as in inflammation)
eryth•ro•cyte \i-ˈri-thrə-ˌsīt\ *n* : RED BLOOD CELL
Es *symbol* einsteinium
[1]**-es** \əz, iz *after* s, z, sh, ch; z *after* v *or a vowel*\ *n pl suffix* — used to form the plural of most nouns that end in *s* ⟨glass*es*⟩, *z* ⟨fuzz*es*⟩, *sh* ⟨bush*es*⟩, *ch* ⟨peach*es*⟩, or a final *y* that changes to *i* ⟨lad*ies*⟩ and of some nouns ending in *f* that changes to *v* ⟨loav*es*⟩
[2]**-es** *vb suffix* — used to form the third person singular present of most verbs that end in *s* ⟨bless*es*⟩, *z* ⟨fizz*es*⟩, *sh* ⟨hush*es*⟩, *ch* ⟨catch*es*⟩, or a final *y* that changes to *i* ⟨def*ies*⟩
es•ca•late \ˈes-kə-ˌlāt\ *vb* **-lat•ed; -lat•ing** ♦ : to increase in extent, volume, number, intensity, or scope — **es•ca•la•tion** \ˌes-kə-ˈlā-shən\ *n*

♦ accumulate, appreciate, balloon, build, burgeon, enlarge, expand, increase, mount, multiply, mushroom, proliferate, rise, snowball, swell, wax

es•ca•la•tor \ˈes-kə-ˌlā-tər\ *n* : a moving set of stairs
es•ca•pade \ˈes-kə-ˌpād\ *n* ♦ : a mischievous adventure

♦ antic, caper, frolic, monkeyshine, practical joke, prank, trick

[1]**es•cape** \is-ˈkāp\ *vb* **es•caped; es•cap•ing** **1** ♦ : to get free or away **2** : to avoid a threatening evil **3** ♦ : miss or succeed in averting : AVOID 2 ⟨~ injury⟩ ⟨*escaped* punishment⟩ **4** : to fail to be noticed or recallable by : ELUDE ⟨his name ~*s* me⟩ **5** : to be produced or uttered involuntarily by ⟨let a sob ~ him⟩

♦ [1] abscond, clear out, flee, fly, get out, lam, run away, run off ♦ [3] avoid, dodge, duck, elude, eschew, evade, shake, shirk, shun

[2]**escape** *n* **1** ♦ : flight from or avoidance of something unpleasant **2** : LEAKAGE **3** ♦ : a means of escape

♦ [1] avoidance, cop-out, evasion, out ♦ [3] flight, getaway, lam, slip

[3]**escape** *adj* : providing a means or way of escape
es•cap•ee \is-ˌkā-ˈpē, ˌes-(ˌ)kā-\ *n* : one that has escaped especially from prison
escape velocity *n* : the minimum velocity needed by a body (as a rocket) to escape from the gravitational field of a celestial body (as the earth)
es•cap•ism \is-ˈkā-ˌpi-zəm\ *n* : diversion of the mind to imaginative activity as an escape from routine — **es•cap•ist** \-pist\ *adj or n*
es•car•got \ˌes-ˌkär-ˈgō\ *n, pl* **-gots** \-ˈgō(z)\ : a snail prepared for use as food
es•ca•role \ˈes-kə-ˌrōl\ *n* : ENDIVE 1
es•carp•ment \es-ˈkärp-mənt\ *n* **1** : a steep slope in front of a fortification **2** ♦ : a long cliff

♦ bluff, cliff, crag, palisade, precipice, scarp

es•chew \is-ˈchü\ *vb* ♦ : to avoid habitually especially on moral or practical grounds : SHUN, AVOID

♦ avoid, dodge, duck, elude, escape, evade, shake, shirk, shun

[1]**es•cort** \ˈes-ˌkȯrt\ *n* ♦ : one (as a person or warship) accompanying another especially as a protection or courtesy

♦ attendant, companion, guard, guide

[2]**es•cort** \is-ˈkȯrt, es-\ *vb* ♦ : to accompany as an escort

♦ accompany, attend, convoy, squire

es•crow \ˈes-ˌkrō\ *n* : something (as a deed or a sum of money) delivered by one person to another to be delivered to a third party only upon the fulfillment of a condition; *also* : a fund or deposit serving as an escrow
es•cutch•eon \is-ˈkə-chən\ *n* : the usually shield-shaped surface on which a coat of arms is shown
Esd *abbr* Esdras
Es•dras \ˈez-drəs\ *n* **1** : either of two books of the Roman Catholic canon of the Old Testament: **a** : a narrative book of canonical Jewish and Christian Scripture **b** : narrative and historical book of canonical Jewish and Christian Scripture **2** : either of two uncanonical books of Scripture included in the Protestant Apocrypha
ESE *abbr* east-southeast
Es•ki•mo \ˈes-kə-ˌmō\ *n* **1** : a member of a group of peoples of northern Canada, Greenland, Alaska, and eastern Siberia **2** : any of the languages of the Eskimo peoples
Eskimo dog *n* : a sled dog of American origin
ESL *abbr* English as a second language
esoph•a•gus \i-ˈsä-fə-gəs\ *n, pl* **-gi** \-ˌgī, -ˌjī\ : a muscular tube that leads from the cavity behind the mouth to the stomach — **esoph•a•geal** \-ˌsä-fə-ˈjē-əl\ *adj*
es•o•ter•ic \ˌe-sə-ˈter-ik\ *adj* **1** ♦ : designed for or understood only by the specially initiated; *broadly* : difficult to understand **2** : PRIVATE, SECRET

♦ abstruse, deep, profound

esp *abbr* especially
ESP \ˌē-(ˌ)es-ˈpē\ *n* : EXTRASENSORY PERCEPTION

es•pa•drille \ˈes-pə-ˌdril\ *n* : a flat sandal usually having a fabric upper and a flexible sole
es•pal•ier \is-ˈpal-yər, -ˌyā\ *n* : a plant (as a fruit tree) trained to grow flat against a support — **espalier** *vb*
es•pe•cial \is-ˈpe-shəl\ *adj* ♦ : being distinctive : SPECIAL

♦ distinct, express, precise, set, special, specific

es•pe•cial•ly *adv* **1** : in a special manner; *also* : in particular **2** ♦ : in a particularly strong or good way — used as an intensive

♦ extra, extremely, greatly, highly, hugely, mightily, mighty, mortally, most, much, real, right, so, very

Es•pe•ran•to \ˌes-pə-ˈran-tō, -ˈrän-\ *n* : an artificial international language based especially on words common to the chief European languages
es•pi•o•nage \ˈes-pē-ə-ˌnäzh, -nij\ *n* : the practice of spying
es•pla•nade \ˈes-plə-ˌnäd\ *n* : a level open stretch or area; *esp* : one for walking or driving along a shore
es•pous•al \i-ˈspau̇-zəl\ *n* **1** ♦ : the act of betrothing or fact of being betrothed : BETROTHAL; *also* : WEDDING **2** : a taking up (as of a cause) as a supporter — **es•pouse** \-ˈspau̇z\ *vb*

♦ marriage, wedding ♦ betrothal, engagement, troth

espres•so \e-ˈspre-sō\ *n, pl* **-sos** : coffee brewed by forcing steam through finely ground darkly roasted coffee beans
es•prit \i-ˈsprē\ *n* ♦ : sprightly wit

♦ bounce, dash, drive, pep, punch, snap, spirit, verve, vim, zing, zip

es•prit de corps \i-ˌsprē-də-ˈkȯr\ *n* : the common spirit existing in the members of a group
es•py \i-ˈspī\ *vb* **es•pied; es•py•ing** ♦ : to catch sight of

♦ discern, eye, notice, observe, perceive, regard, see, sight, spy, view

Esq *or* **Esqr** *abbr* esquire
es•quire \ˈes-ˌkwī(-ə)r\ *n* **1** : a man of the English gentry ranking next below a knight **2** : a candidate for knighthood serving as attendant to a knight **3** — used as a title of courtesy
-ess \əs, ˌes\ *n suffix* : female ⟨author*ess*⟩
[1]**es•say** \e-ˈsā, ˈe-ˌsā\ *vb* ♦ : to make an often tentative or experimental effort to perform : ATTEMPT, TRY

♦ assay, attempt, endeavor (*or* endeavour), seek, strive, try

[2]**es•say** *n* **1** \ˈe-ˌsā, e-ˈsā\ ♦ : an initial tentative effort : ATTEMPT **2** \ˈe-ˌsā\ ♦ : a literary composition usually dealing with a subject from a limited or personal point of view — **es•say•ist** \ˈe-ˌsā-ist\ *n*

♦ [1] attempt, bid, crack, endeavor (*or* endeavour), fling, go, pass, shot, stab, trial, try, whack, whirl ♦ [2] article, composition, paper, theme

es•sence \ˈes-ᵊns\ *n* **1** ♦ : fundamental nature or quality **2** : a substance distilled or extracted from another substance (as a plant or drug) and having the special qualities of the original substance **3** : PERFUME **4** ♦ : the most significant element or aspect of something ⟨the ~ of the issue⟩

♦ [1, 4] nature, quintessence, soul, stuff, substance

[1]**es•sen•tial** \i-ˈsen-chəl\ *adj* **1** ♦ : of, relating to, or constituting an essence ⟨voting is an ~ right of citizenship⟩ ⟨~ oils⟩ **2** ♦ : of the utmost importance : INDISPENSABLE; *also* : of, relating to, or forming the base or essence **3** : being a substance that must be obtained from the diet because it is not sufficiently produced by the body ⟨~ amino acids⟩ — **es•sen•tial•ly** *adv*

♦ [1] ingrained, inherent, innate, integral, intrinsic, natural ♦ [1] basic, elemental, elementary, fundamental, underlying ♦ [2] imperative, indispensable, integral, necessary, needful, requisite, vital *Ant* dispensable, needless, nonessential

[2]**essential** *n* ♦ : something indispensable

♦ condition, demand, must, necessity, need, requirement, requisite *Ant* nonessential ♦ *usu* **essentials** elements, principles, rudiments

est *abbr* **1** established **2** estimate; estimated
EST *abbr* eastern standard time
[1]**-est** \əst, ist\ *adj suffix or adv suffix* — used to form the superlative degree of adjectives and adverbs of one or two syllables ⟨fat*test*⟩ ⟨lat*est*⟩ ⟨luck*iest*⟩ ⟨often*est*⟩ and less often of longer ones
[2]**-est** \əst, ist\ *or* **-st** \st\ *vb suffix* — used to form the archaic second person singular of English verbs (with *thou*) ⟨did*st*⟩
es•tab•lish \i-ˈsta-blish\ *vb* **1** : to institute permanently ⟨~ a law⟩ **2** ♦ : to bring into existence : FOUND ⟨~ a settlement⟩; *also* : EFFECT **3** : to make firm or stable **4** : to put on a firm basis : SET UP ⟨~ a son in business⟩ **5** ♦ : to gain acceptance or recognition of ⟨the movie ~*ed* her as a star⟩; *also* : PROVE

♦ [2] constitute, effect, found, inaugurate, initiate, innovate, institute, introduce, launch, pioneer, set up, start ♦ [5] demonstrate, prove, show, substantiate *Ant* disprove

es•tab•lish•ment \-mənt\ *n* **1** : something established: as **a** ♦ : a permanent civil or military organization **b** ♦ : a public or private institution **2** : a place of residence or business with its furnishings and staff **3** : an established ruling or controlling group ⟨the literary ~⟩ **4** : the act or state of establishing or being established

♦ [1a, 1b] foundation, institute, institution ♦ [1b] business, company, concern, enterprise, firm, house, outfit

es•tate \i-ˈstāt\ *n* **1 a** ♦ : mode or condition of being : STATE **b** : social standing : STATUS **2** ♦ : a social or political class ⟨the three ~*s* of nobility, clergy, and commons⟩ **3** : a person's possessions : FORTUNE **4** ♦ : a landed property

♦ [1a] condition, fettle, form, order, repair, shape, state, trim ♦ [2] caste, class, folk, order, stratum ♦ [4] castle, hall, manor, mansion, palace, villa

[1]**es•teem** \i-ˈstēm\ *n* ♦ : high regard

♦ admiration, appreciation, estimation, favor (*or* favour), regard, respect

[2]**esteem** *vb* **1** ♦ : to view as : REGARD **2** ♦ : to set a high value on

♦ [1] account, call, consider, count, hold, rate, reckon, regard, take ♦ [2] admire, appreciate, regard, respect

es•ter \ˈes-tər\ *n* : an often fragrant organic compound formed by the reaction of an acid and an alcohol
Esth *abbr* Esther
Es•ther \ˈes-tər\ *n* : a narrative book of canonical Jewish and Christian Scripture
esthete, esthetic, esthetically, esthetics *var of* AESTHETE, aesthetic, AESTHETICALLY, AESTHETICS
es•ti•ma•ble \ˈes-tə-mə-bəl\ *adj* : worthy of esteem
[1]**es•ti•mate** \ˈes-tə-ˌmāt\ *vb* **-mat•ed; -mat•ing** **1** ♦ : to give or form an approximation (as of value, size, or cost) **2** : JUDGE, CONCLUDE — **es•ti•ma•tor** \-ˌmā-tər\ *n*

♦ appraise, assess, evaluate, rate, set, value ♦ calculate, call, conjecture, figure, gauge, guess, judge, make, place, put, reckon, suppose

[2]**es•ti•mate** \ˈes-tə-mət\ *n* **1** ♦ : an opinion or judgment of the nature, character, or quality of a person or thing **2** ♦ : a rough or approximate calculation **3** : a statement of the cost of work to be done

♦ [1] appraisal, assessment, estimation, evaluation, judgment (*or* judgement) ♦ [2] calculation, computation, measurement, reckoning, valuation

es•ti•ma•tion \ˌes-tə-ˈmā-shən\ *n* **1** ♦ : a view, judgment, or appraisal formed in the mind about a particular matter : JUDGMENT **2** ♦ : the value, amount, or size arrived at in an estimate : ESTIMATE; *also* : the act of estimating something **3** ♦ : high regard : ESTEEM

♦ [1] appraisal, assessment, estimate, evaluation, judgment (*or* judgement), reckoning, valuation ♦ [2] appraisal, assessment, estimate, evaluation, judgment (*or* judgement) ♦ [3] admiration, appreciation, esteem, favor (*or* favour), regard, respect

es•ti•vate \ˈes-tə-ˌvāt\ *vb* **-vat•ed; -vat•ing** : to pass the summer in an inactive or resting state — **es•ti•va•tion** \ˌes-tə-ˈvā-shən\ *n*
Es•to•nian \e-ˈstō-nē-ən\ *n* : a native or inhabitant of Estonia — **Estonian** *adj*
es•trange \i-ˈstrānj\ *vb* **es•tranged; es•trang•ing** ♦ : to alienate the affections or confidence of

♦ alienate, disaffect, disgruntle, sour *Ant* reconcile

es•trange•ment *n* ♦ : the act of estranging or the condition of being estranged : alienation especially in friendship

♦ alienation, disaffection *Ant* reconciliation

es•tro•gen \ˈes-trə-jən\ *n* : a steroid (as a sex hormone) that tends to cause estrus and the development of female secondary sex characteristics — **es•tro•gen•ic** \ˌes-trə-ˈje-nik\ *adj*
estrous cycle *n* : the cycle of changes in the endocrine and reproductive systems of a female mammal from the beginning of one period of estrus to the beginning of the next
es•trus \ˈes-trəs\ *n* : a periodic state of sexual excitability during which the female of most mammals is willing to mate with the

male and is capable of becoming pregnant : HEAT — **es•trous** \ˈtrəs\ *adj*

es•tu•ary \ˈes-chü-ˌwer-ē\ *n, pl* **-ar•ies** ♦ : an arm of the sea at the mouth of a river

♦ bay, bight, cove, gulf, inlet

ET *abbr* eastern time

eta \ˈā-tə\ *n* : the 7th letter of the Greek alphabet — Η or η

ETA *abbr* estimated time of arrival

et al \et-ˈal\ *abbr* and others

etc *abbr* et cetera

et cet•era \et-ˈset-ə-rə\ : and others especially of the same kind — used to imply that other items are to be understood

etch \ˈech\ *vb* **1** ♦ : to produce (as a design) on a hard material by corroding its surface (as by acid) **2** ♦ : to delineate or impress clearly — **etch•er** *n*

♦ [1] engrave, grave, inscribe ♦ [2] engrave, impress, imprint, ingrain, inscribe

etch•ing *n* **1** : the action, process, or art of etching **2** : a design produced on or print made from an etched plate

ETD *abbr* estimated time of departure

eter•nal \i-ˈtərn-ᵊl\ *adj* ♦ : having infinite duration : EVERLASTING, PERPETUAL

♦ ceaseless, dateless, deathless, endless, everlasting, immortal, permanent, perpetual, undying, unending

eter•nal•ly *adv* ♦ : throughout eternity

♦ always, ever, everlastingly, forever, permanently, perpetually

eter•ni•ty \i-ˈtər-nə-tē\ *n, pl* **-ties** **1** : infinite duration **2** ♦ : the state after death : IMMORTALITY **3** ♦ : a seemingly endless or immeasurable time

♦ [2] afterlife, hereafter, immortality ♦ [3] aeon (*or* eon), age, cycle

¹-eth \əth, ith\ *or* **-th** \th\ *vb suffix* — used to form the archaic third person singular present of verbs ⟨do*th*⟩

eth•ane \ˈe-ˌthān\ *n* : a colorless odorless gaseous hydrocarbon found in natural gas and used especially as a fuel

eth•a•nol \ˈe-thə-ˌnȯl\ *n* : ALCOHOL 1

ether \ˈē-thər\ *n* **1** : the upper regions of space; *also* : the gaseous element formerly held to fill these regions **2** : a light flammable liquid used as an anesthetic and solvent

ethe•re•al \i-ˈthir-ē-əl\ *adj* **1** : CELESTIAL, HEAVENLY **2** ♦ : exceptionally delicate : AIRY, DAINTY — **ethe•re•al•ly** *adv* — **ethe•re•al•ness** *n*

♦ airy, dainty, fluffy, light

Ether•net \ˈē-thər-ˌnet\ *n* : a computer network architecture for local area networks

eth•i•cal \ˈe-thi-kəl\ *adj* **1** : of or relating to ethics **2** ♦ : conforming to accepted and especially professional standards of conduct — **eth•i•cal•ly** *adv*

♦ decent, good, honest, honorable (*or* honourable), just, moral, principled, right, straight, upright, virtuous ♦ conscientious, honest, honorable (*or* honourable), just, moral, principled, scrupulous

eth•ics \ˈe-thiks\ *n sing or pl* **1** : a discipline dealing with good and evil and with moral duty **2** ♦ : moral principles or practice

♦ morality, morals, principles, standards

Ethi•o•pi•an \ˌē-thē-ˈō-pē-ən\ *n* : a native or inhabitant of Ethiopia — **Ethiopian** *adj*

¹eth•nic \ˈeth-nik\ *adj* : of or relating to races or large groups of people classed according to common traits and customs — **eth•ni•cal•ly** *adv*

²ethnic *n* : a member of a minority ethnic group who retains its customs, language, or social views

eth•nol•o•gy \eth-ˈnä-lə-jē\ *n* : a science dealing with the races of human beings, their origin, distribution, characteristics, and relations — **eth•no•log•i•cal** \ˌeth-nə-ˈlä-ji-kəl\ *adj* — **eth•nol•o•gist** \eth-ˈnä-lə-jist\ *n*

ethol•o•gy \ē-ˈthä-lə-jē\ *n* : the scientific and objective study of animal behavior — **etho•log•i•cal** \ˌē-thə-ˈlä-ji-kəl, ˌe-\ *adj* — **ethol•o•gist** \ē-ˈthä-lə-jist\ *n*

ethos \ˈē-ˌthäs\ *n* : the distinguishing character, sentiment, moral nature, or guiding beliefs of a person, group, or institution

ethyl alcohol *n* : ALCOHOL 1

eth•yl•ene \ˈe-thə-ˌlēn\ *n* : a colorless flammable gas found in coal gas or obtained from petroleum

eti•ol•o•gy \ˌē-tē-ˈä-lə-jē\ *n* : the causes of a disease or abnormal condition; *also* : a branch of medicine concerned with the causes and origins of diseases — **eti•o•log•ic** \ˌē-tē-ə-ˈlä-jik\ *or* **eti•o•log•i•cal** \-ji-kəl\ *adj*

et•i•quette \ˈe-ti-kət, -ˌket\ *n* ♦ : the forms prescribed by custom or authority to be observed in social, official, or professional life

♦ manners, mores

Etrus•can \i-ˈtrəs-kən\ *n* **1** : the language of the Etruscans **2** : an inhabitant of ancient Etruria — **Etruscan** *adj*

et seq *abbr* and the following one and the following ones

-ette \ˈet, ˌet, ət, it\ *n suffix* **1** : little one ⟨din*ette*⟩ **2** : female ⟨usher*ette*⟩

étude \ˈā-ˌtüd, -ˌtyüd\ *n* : a musical composition for practice to develop technical skill

et•y•mol•o•gy \ˌe-tə-ˈmä-lə-jē\ *n, pl* **-gies** **1** : the history of a linguistic form (as a word) shown by tracing its development and relationships **2** : a branch of linguistics dealing with etymologies — **et•y•mo•log•i•cal** \-mə-ˈlä-ji-kəl\ *adj* — **et•y•mol•o•gist** \-ˈmä-lə-jist\ *n*

Eu *symbol* europium

eu•ca•lyp•tus \ˌyü-kə-ˈlip-təs\ *n, pl* **-ti** \-ˌtī\ *or* **-tus•es** : any of a genus of mostly Australian evergreen trees widely grown for shade or their wood, oils, resins, and gums

Eu•cha•rist \ˈyü-kə-rəst\ *n* : COMMUNION 2 — **eu•cha•ris•tic** \ˌyü-kə-ˈris-tik\ *adj, often cap*

¹eu•chre \ˈyü-kər\ *n* : a card game in which the side naming the trump must take three of five tricks to win

²euchre *vb* **eu•chred; eu•chring** : CHEAT, TRICK

eu•clid•e•an *also* **eu•clid•i•an** \yü-ˈkli-dē-ən\ *adj, often cap* : of or relating to the geometry of Euclid or a geometry based on similar axioms

eu•gen•ics \yü-ˈje-niks\ *n* : a science dealing with the improvement (as by selective breeding) of hereditary qualities especially of human beings — **eu•gen•ic** \-nik\ *adj*

eu•lo•gy \ˈyü-lə-jē\ *n, pl* **-gies** **1** ♦ : a speech in praise of some person or thing especially in honor of a deceased person **2** : high praise — **eu•lo•gis•tic** \ˌyü-lə-ˈjis-tik\ *adj* — **eu•lo•gize** \ˈyü-lə-ˌjīz\ *vb*

♦ accolade, citation, commendation, encomium, homage, paean, panegyric, salutation, tribute

eu•nuch \ˈyü-nək\ *n* : a castrated man

eu•phe•mism \ˈyü-fə-ˌmi-zəm\ *n* : the substitution of a mild or pleasant expression for one offensive or unpleasant; *also* : the expression substituted — **eu•phe•mis•tic** \ˌyü-fə-ˈmis-tik\ *adj* — **eu•phe•mis•ti•cal•ly** \-ti-k(ə-)lē\ *adv*

eu•pho•ni•ous \yü-ˈfō-nē-əs\ *adj* ♦ : pleasing to the ear — **eu•pho•ni•ous•ly** *adv*

♦ harmonious, lyric, melodious, musical, symphonic, tuneful

eu•pho•ny \ˈyü-fə-nē\ *n, pl* **-nies** : the effect produced by words so combined as to please the ear

eu•pho•ria \yü-ˈfȯr-ē-ə\ *n* ♦ : a marked feeling of well-being or elation

♦ ecstasy, elation, exhilaration, heaven, intoxication, paradise, rapture, rhapsody, transport

eu•phor•ic \-ˈfȯr-ik\ *adj* ♦ : characterized by or based on euphoria

♦ ecstatic, elated, intoxicated, rapturous, rhapsodic

Eur *abbr* Europe; European

Eur•asian \yü-ˈrā-zhən, -shən\ *adj* **1** : of mixed European and Asian origin **2** : of or relating to Europe and Asia — **Eurasian** *n*

eu•re•ka \yü-ˈrē-kə\ *interj* — used to express triumph on a discovery

eu•ro \ˈyu̇r-ō\ *n, pl* **euros** : the common basic monetary unit of most countries of the European Union

Eu•ro–Amer•i•can \ˌyu̇r-ō-ə-ˈmer-ə-kən\ *n* **1** : a person of mixed European and American ancestry **2** : CAUCASIAN

Eu•ro•bond \ˈyu̇r-ō-ˌbänd\ *n* : a bond of a U.S. corporation that is sold outside the U.S. but that is valued and paid for in dollars and yields interest in dollars

Eu•ro•cur•ren•cy \ˌyu̇r-ō-ˈkər-ən-sē\ *n* : moneys (as of the U.S. and Japan) held outside their countries of origin and used in the money markets of Europe

Eu•ro•dol•lar \ˈyu̇r-ō-ˌdä-lər\ *n* : a U.S. dollar held as Eurocurrency

Eu•ro•pe•an \ˌyu̇r-ə-ˈpē-ən\ *n* **1** : a native or inhabitant of Europe **2** : a person of European descent — **European** *adj* — **Eu•ro•pe•an•ize** \-ə-ˌnīz\ *vb*

European–American *n* : EURO-AMERICAN

Eu•ro•pe•an•ism \yu̇r-ˌō-ˈpē-ə-ni-zəm\ *n* **1** : allegiance to the traditions, interests, or ideals of Europeans **2** : advocacy of polit-

ical and economic integration of Europe — **eu•ro•pe•an•ist** \-nist\ *n*
European plan *n* : a hotel plan whereby the daily rates cover only the cost of the room
eu•ro•pi•um \yu̇-ˈrō-pē-əm\ *n* : a rare metallic chemical element
eu•sta•chian tube \yu̇-ˈstā-shən-\ *n, often cap E* : a tube connecting the inner cavity of the ear with the throat and equalizing air pressure on both sides of the eardrum
eu•tha•na•sia \ˌyü-thə-ˈnā-zhə\ *n* : the act or practice of killing or permitting the death of hopelessly sick or injured persons or animals with as little pain as possible for reasons of mercy
EVA *abbr* extravehicular activity
evac•u•ate \i-ˈva-kyə-ˌwāt\ *vb* **-at•ed; -at•ing** **1** ♦ : to to make empty : empty out **2** : to discharge wastes from the body **3** : to remove or withdraw from : VACATE — **evac•u•a•tion** \-ˌva-kyə-ˈwā-shən\ *n*

♦ clear, empty, vacate, void

evac•u•ee \i-ˌva-kyə-ˈwē\ *n* ♦ : a person removed from a dangerous place

♦ émigré, exile, expatriate, refugee

evade \i-ˈvād\ *vb* **evad•ed; evad•ing** ♦ : to manage to avoid especially by dexterity or slyness : ELUDE, ESCAPE

♦ avoid, dodge, duck, elude, escape, eschew, shake, shirk, shun

eval•u•ate \i-ˈval-yu̇-ˌwāt\ *vb* **-at•ed; -at•ing** ♦ : to determine or fix the value of : APPRAISE, VALUE; *also* : to determine the significance, worth, or condition of usually by careful appraisal and study

♦ appraise, assess, estimate, rate, set, value

eval•u•a•tion \-ˌval-yu̇-ˈwā-shən\ *n* ♦ : the act or result of evaluating

♦ appraisal, assessment, estimate, estimation, judgment (*or* judgement)

ev•a•nes•cent \ˌe-və-ˈnes-ᵊnt\ *adj* ♦ : tending to vanish like vapor — **ev•a•nes•cence** \-ᵊns\ *n*

♦ ephemeral, flash, fleeting, impermanent, momentary, short-lived, transient

evan•gel•i•cal \ˌē-ˌvan-ˈje-li-kəl, ˌe-vən-\ *adj* **1** : of or relating to the Christian gospel especially as presented in the four Gospels **2** : of or relating to certain Protestant churches emphasizing the authority of Scripture and the importance of preaching as contrasted with ritual **3** : ZEALOUS ⟨~ fervor⟩ — **Evangelical** *n* — **Evan•gel•i•cal•ism** \-kə-ˌli-zəm\ *n* — **evan•gel•i•cal•ly** *adv*
evan•ge•lism \i-ˈvan-jə-ˌli-zəm\ *n* **1** : the winning or revival of personal commitments to Christ **2** : militant or crusading zeal — **evan•ge•lis•tic** \-ˌvan-jə-ˈlis-tik\ *adj* — **evan•ge•lis•ti•cal•ly** *adv*
evan•ge•list \i-ˈvan-jə-list\ *n* **1** *often cap* : the writer of any of the four Gospels **2** : a person who evangelizes; *esp* : a Protestant minister or layman who preaches at special services
evan•ge•lize \i-ˈvan-jə-ˌlīz\ *vb* **-lized; -liz•ing** **1** : to preach the gospel **2** : to convert to Christianity
evap *abbr* evaporate
evap•o•rate \i-ˈva-pə-ˌrāt\ *vb* **-rat•ed; -rat•ing** **1** : to pass off or cause to pass off in vapor **2** ♦ : to disappear quickly **3** : to drive out the moisture from (as by heat) — **evap•o•ra•tion** \-ˌva-pə-ˈrā-shən\ *n* — **evap•o•ra•tor** \-ˌrā-tər\ *n*

♦ disappear, dissolve, fade, flee, go, melt, vanish

evap•o•rite \i-ˈva-pə-ˌrīt\ *n* : a sedimentary rock that originates by the evaporation of seawater in an enclosed basin
eva•sion \i-ˈvā-zhən\ *n* **1** ♦ : a means of evading **2** ♦ : an act or instance of evading — **eva•sive•ness** *n*

♦ [1, 2] avoidance, cop-out, escape, out

eva•sive \i-ˈvā-siv\ *adj* ♦ : tending or intended to evade; *also* : not easily caught

♦ elusive, fugitive, slippery

eve \ˈēv\ *n* **1** : EVENING **2** : the period just before some important event
[1]**even** \ˈē-vən\ *adj* **1** ♦ : having a horizontal surface : LEVEL, FLAT **2** : REGULAR, SMOOTH **3** : EQUAL, FAIR **4** : BALANCED; *also* : fully revenged **5** : divisible by two **6** ♦ : having no fraction either lacking or in excess : EXACT — **even•ly** *adv* — **even•ness** *n*

♦ [1] flat, flush, level, plane, smooth ♦ [6] exact, flat, precise, round

[2]**even** *adv* **1** : EXACTLY, PRECISELY **2** : FULLY, QUITE **3** : at the very time **4** ♦ — used as an intensive to stress the identity or character of something ⟨~ I know that⟩ ⟨he looked content, ~ happy⟩ **5** — used as an intensive to emphasize something extreme or highly unlikely ⟨so simple ~ a child can do it⟩ **6** — used as an intensive to stress the comparative degree ⟨did ~ better⟩ **7** — used as an intensive to indicate a small or minimum degree ⟨didn't ~ try⟩

♦ indeed, nay, truly, verily, yea

[3]**even** *vb* ♦ : to make or become even

♦ balance, equalize, equate, level ♦ level, plane, smooth ***Ant*** rough, roughen

even•hand•ed \ˌē-vən-ˈhan-dəd\ *adj* ♦ : marked by justice, honesty, and freedom from bias : FAIR, IMPARTIAL — **even•hand•ed•ly** *adv*

♦ disinterested, dispassionate, equal, equitable, fair, impartial, just, nonpartisan, objective, square, unbiased, unprejudiced

eve•ning \ˈēv-niŋ\ *n* **1** ♦ : the end of the day and early part of the night **2** *chiefly Southern & Midland* : AFTERNOON

♦ dusk, gloaming, nightfall, sundown, sunset, twilight

evening primrose *n* : a coarse biennial herb with yellow flowers that open in the evening
evening star *n* : a bright planet (as Venus) seen especially in the western sky at or after sunset
even•song \ˈē-vən-ˌsȯŋ\ *n, often cap* **1** : VESPERS **2** : evening prayer especially when sung
event \i-ˈvent\ *n* **1** ♦ : something that happens : OCCURRENCE **2** ♦ : a noteworthy happening; *also* : a social occasion or activity **3** ♦ : a postulated outcome, condition, or eventuality : CONTINGENCY ⟨in the ~ of rain⟩ **4** ♦ : a contest in a program of sports

♦ [1] affair, circumstance, deed, episode, experience, occurrence ♦ [2] affair, fete, function, get-together, party ♦ [3] case, contingency, eventuality, possibility ♦ [4] bout, competition, contest, game, match, meet, tournament

event•ful *adj* **1** : full of or rich in events **2** ♦ : very important

♦ big, consequential, important, major, material, meaningful, momentous, significant, substantial, weighty

even•tide \ˈē-vən-ˌtīd\ *n* : the time of evening : EVENING
even•tu•al \i-ˈven-chü-wəl\ *adj* : coming at some later time : ULTIMATE
even•tu•al•i•ty \i-ˌven-chü-ˈwa-lə-tē\ *n, pl* **-ties** ♦ : a possible event or outcome

♦ case, contingency, event, possibility

even•tu•al•ly *adv* ♦ : at an unspecified later time : in the end

♦ someday, sometime, ultimately, yet

even•tu•ate \i-ˈven-chü-ˌwāt\ *vb* **-at•ed; -at•ing** : to result finally
ev•er \ˈe-vər\ *adv* **1** ♦ : at all times : ALWAYS **2** ♦ : at any time **3** : in any way : AT ALL

♦ [1] always, eternally, everlastingly, forever, permanently, perpetually ***Ant*** never, nevermore ♦ [2] always, invariably, unfailingly

ev•er•glade \ˈe-vər-ˌglād\ *n* : a low-lying tract of swampy or marshy land
ev•er•green \-ˌgrēn\ *adj* : having foliage that remains green ⟨most coniferous trees are ~⟩ — **evergreen** *n*
[1]**ev•er•last•ing** \ˌe-vər-ˈlas-tiŋ\ *adj* **1** ♦ : enduring forever : ETERNAL **2** : having or being flowers or foliage that retain form or color for a long time when dried

♦ ceaseless, dateless, deathless, endless, eternal, immortal, permanent, perpetual, undying, unending ***Ant*** impermanent, mortal, temporary

[2]**everlasting** *n* **1** : ETERNITY ⟨from ~⟩ **2** : a plant with everlasting flowers; *also* : its flower
ev•er•last•ing•ly *adv* ♦ : in an everlasting manner

♦ always, eternally, ever, forever, permanently, perpetually

ev•er•more \ˌe-vər-ˈmōr\ *adv* : for a limitless time : FOREVER
ev•ery \ˈev-rē\ *adj* **1** : being each one of a group **2** : all possible ⟨given ~ chance⟩; *also* : COMPLETE ⟨have ~ confidence⟩
ev•ery•body \ˈev-ri-ˌbä-dē, -bə-\ *pron* : every person
ev•ery•day \ˈev-rē-ˌdā\ *adj* ♦ : encountered or used routinely : ORDINARY

♦ average, common, commonplace, customary, familiar, normal, ordinary, prosaic, routine, run-of-the-mill, standard, unexceptional, unremarkable, usual, workaday

ev•ery•one \-(ˌ)wən\ *pron* : every person : EVERYBODY
ev•ery•thing \ˈev-rē-ˌthiŋ\ *pron* **1** : all that exists **2** : all that is relevant
ev•ery•where \ˈev-rē-ˌhwer\ *adv* : in every place or part
evg *abbr* evening
evict \i-ˈvikt\ *vb* **1** : to put (a person) out from a property by legal process **2** : EXPEL — **evic•tion** \-ˈvik-shən\ *n*
¹ev•i•dence \ˈe-və-dəns\ *n* **1** : an outward sign **2** ♦ : something that furnishes proof : PROOF, TESTIMONY; *esp* : matter submitted in court to determine the truth of alleged facts

♦ attestation, confirmation, corroboration, documentation, proof, substantiation, testament, testimony, validation, witness

²evidence *vb* : PROVE, EVINCE
ev•i•dent \-dənt\ *adj* ♦ : clear to the vision and understanding

♦ apparent, broad, clear, clear-cut, distinct, lucid, manifest, obvious, palpable, patent, perspicuous, plain, transparent, unambiguous, unequivocal, unmistakable

ev•i•dent•ly \ˈe-və-dənt-lē, ˌe-və-ˈdent-\ *adv* **1** : in an evident manner **2** ♦ : on the basis of available evidence ⟨he was born ~ in Texas⟩

♦ apparently, ostensibly, presumably, seemingly, supposedly

¹evil \ˈē-vəl\ *adj* **evil•er** *or* **evil•ler; evil•est** *or* **evil•lest** **1** ♦ : morally reprehensible : WICKED **2** ♦ : causing or threatening distress or harm : PERNICIOUS — **evil•ly** *adv*

♦ [1] bad, black, immoral, iniquitous, nefarious, rotten, sinful, vicious, vile, villainous, wicked, wrong ♦ [2] bad, damaging, deleterious, detrimental, harmful, hurtful, injurious, noxious, pernicious

²evil *n* **1** ♦ : the fact of suffering, misfortune, and wrongdoing; *also* : evil actions or deeds **2** : a source of sorrow, distress, or calamity

♦ bad, ill, immorality, iniquity, sin, villainy, wrong ***Ant*** good, morality, right, virtue

evil•do•er \ˌē-vəl-ˈdü-ər\ *n* ♦ : one who does evil

♦ beast, devil, fiend, no-good, reprobate, rogue, varlet, villain, wretch ♦ malefactor, sinner, wrongdoer

evil–mind•ed \-ˈmīn-dəd\ *adj* : having an evil disposition or evil thoughts — **evil–mind•ed•ly** *adv*
evince \i-ˈvins\ *vb* **evinced; evinc•ing** ♦ : to constitute outward evidence of : SHOW, REVEAL

♦ bespeak, betray, demonstrate, display, expose, give away, manifest, reveal, show

evis•cer•ate \i-ˈvi-sə-ˌrāt\ *vb* **-at•ed; -at•ing** **1** ♦ : to remove the entrails of **2** : to deprive of vital content or force — **evis•cer•a•tion** \-ˌvi-sə-ˈrā-shən\ *n*

♦ clean, draw, gut

evoke \i-ˈvōk\ *vb* **evoked; evok•ing** ♦ : to call forth or up — **evo•ca•tion** \ˌē-vō-ˈkā-shən, ˌe-və-\ *n* — **evoc•a•tive** \i-ˈvä-kə-tiv\ *adj*

♦ elicit, raise

evo•lu•tion \ˌe-və-ˈlü-shən\ *n* **1** : one of a set of prescribed movements (as in a dance) **2** ♦ : a process of change in a particular direction **3** : a theory that the various kinds of plants and animals are descended from other kinds that lived in earlier times and that the differences are due to inherited changes that occurred over many generations — **evo•lu•tion•ary** \-shə-ˌner-ē\ *adj* — **evo•lu•tion•ist** \-shə-nist\ *n*

♦ development, elaboration, expansion, growth, progress, progression

evolve \i-ˈvälv\ *vb* **evolved; evolv•ing** : to develop or change by or as if by evolution
EW *abbr* enlisted woman
ewe \ˈyü\ *n* : a female sheep
ew•er \ˈyü-ər\ *n* ♦ : a water pitcher

♦ flagon, jug, pitcher

¹ex \ˈeks\ *prep* : out of : FROM
²ex *n* : a former spouse
³ex *abbr* **1** example **2** express **3** extra
Ex *abbr* Exodus
ex- \e *also occurs in this prefix where only* i *is shown below (as in "express") and* ks *sometimes occurs where only* gz *is shown (as in "exact")*\ *prefix* **1** : out of : outside **2** : former ⟨*ex*-president⟩
ex•ac•er•bate \ig-ˈza-sər-ˌbāt\ *vb* **-bat•ed; -bat•ing** : to make more violent, bitter, or severe — **ex•ac•er•ba•tion** \-ˌza-sər-ˈbā-shən\ *n*
¹ex•act \ig-ˈzakt\ *vb* **1** ♦ : to demand and force or compel (as payment, surrender, concession, performance, or compliance) **2** : to call for or establish as suitable or necessary — **ex•ac•tion** \-ˈzak-shən\ *n*

♦ call, claim, command, demand, enjoin, extort, insist, press ♦ assess, charge, fine, impose, lay, levy, put

²exact *adj* ♦ : precisely accurate or correct

♦ accurate, correct, precise, proper, right, so, true ♦ delicate, fine, minute, nice, refined, subtle

ex•act•ing \ig-ˈzak-tiŋ\ *adj* **1** ♦ : greatly demanding ⟨an ~ taskmaster⟩ **2** ♦ : requiring close attention and precision

♦ [1] choosy, demanding, fastidious, finicky, particular, picky ♦ [1] inflexible, rigid, rigorous, strict, stringent, uncompromising ♦ [2] arduous, burdensome, challenging, demanding, grueling, laborious, onerous, taxing, toilsome

ex•ac•ti•tude \ig-ˈzak-tə-ˌtüd, -ˌtyüd\ *n* : the quality or state of being exact
ex•act•ly *adv* **1** ♦ : in a manner or measure or to a degree or number that strictly conforms to a fact or condition; *also* : in every respect **2** : quite so : as you say or state — used to express agreement

♦ accurately, just, precisely, right, sharp, squarely, strictly

ex•act•ness *n* ♦ : the quality or an instance of being exact

♦ accuracy, closeness, delicacy, fineness, precision, veracity

ex•ag•ger•ate \ig-ˈza-jə-ˌrāt\ *vb* **-at•ed; -at•ing** ♦ : to enlarge (as a statement) beyond normal — **ex•ag•ger•at•ed•ly** *adv* — **ex•ag•ger•a•tor** \-ˈza-jə-ˌrā-tər\ *n*

♦ color (*or* colour), elaborate, embellish, embroider, magnify, pad, stretch

ex•ag•ger•a•tion \-ˌza-jə-ˈrā-shən\ *n* ♦ : the act of exaggerating; *also* : the state or an instance of being exaggerated

♦ elaboration, embellishment, hyperbole, magnification, overstatement, padding ***Ant*** understatement

ex•alt \ig-ˈzȯlt\ *vb* **1** ♦ : to raise up especially in rank, power, or dignity **2** ♦ : to elevate in estimation : GLORIFY — **ex•al•ta•tion** \ˌeg-ˌzȯl-ˈtā-shən, ˌek-ˌsȯl-\ *n*

♦ [1, 2] aggrandize, dignify, ennoble, glorify, magnify ***Ant*** abase, debase, degrade, demean, humble, humiliate

ex•am \ig-ˈzam\ *n* : an exercise or a series of exercises designed to examine progress or test qualification : EXAMINATION
ex•am•i•na•tion \-ˌza-mə-ˈnā-shən\ *n* **1** ♦ : the act or process of examining; *also* : the state of being examined **2** ♦ : an exercise designed to examine progress or test qualification or knowledge **3** : a formal interrogation

♦ [1] check, checkup, examination, inspection, review, scan, scrutiny, survey ♦ [1] exploration, inquiry, investigation, probe, research, study ♦ [2] quiz, test

ex•am•ine \ig-ˈza-mən\ *vb* **ex•am•ined; ex•am•in•ing** **1** ♦ : to inspect closely **2** ♦ : to attempt to determine or test by questioning

♦ [1] audit, check, inspect, review, scan, scrutinize, survey ♦ [2] grill, interrogate, pump, query, question, quiz

ex•am•ple \ig-ˈzam-pəl\ *n* **1** : something forming a model to be followed or avoided **2** ♦ : a representative sample **3** : a problem to be solved in order to show the application of some rule

♦ case, exemplar, illustration, instance, representative, sample, specimen

ex•as•per•ate \ig-ˈzas-pə-ˌrāt\ *vb* **-at•ed; -at•ing** ♦ : to excite the anger of : VEX, IRRITATE

♦ aggravate, annoy, bother, bug, grate, irk, irritate, vex

ex•as•per•a•ting *adj* ♦ : causing irritation : ANNOYING

♦ aggravating, annoying, frustrating, irksome, irritating, pesty, vexatious

ex•as•per•a•tion \ig-ˌzas-pə-ˈrā-shən\ *n* ♦ : the state of being exasperated; *also* : the act or source of being exasperated

♦ aggravation, annoyance, bother, frustration, hassle, headache, irritant, nuisance, problem, thorn, vexation

exc *abbr* **1** excellent **2** except
ex•ca•vate \ˈek-skə-ˌvāt\ *vb* **-vat•ed; -vat•ing** **1** : to hollow out;

also **:** to form by hollowing out **2 :** to dig out and remove (as earth) **3 :** to reveal to view by digging away a covering — **ex•ca•va•tion** \ˌek-skə-ˈvā-shən\ *n* — **ex•ca•va•tor** \ˈek-skə-ˌvā-tər\ *n*

ex•ceed \ik-ˈsēd\ *vb* **1** ♦ **:** to go or be beyond the limit of **2** ♦ **:** to be greater than or superior to **:** SURPASS

♦ [1, 2] overreach, overrun, overshoot, overstep, surpass

ex•ceed•ing \-ˈsē-diŋ\ *adj* ♦ **:** exceptional in amount, quality, or degree

♦ aberrant, abnormal, atypical, exceptional, extraordinary, freak, odd, peculiar, phenomenal, rare, singular, uncommon, uncustomary, unique, unusual, unwonted

ex•ceed•ing•ly \-ˈsē-diŋ-lē\ *also* **ex•ceed•ing** *adv* **:** to an extreme degree **:** EXTREMELY, VERY

ex•cel \ik-ˈsel\ *vb* **ex•celled; ex•cel•ling** ♦ **:** to be superior to **:** SURPASS, OUTDO

♦ beat, better, eclipse, outdistance, outdo, outshine, outstrip, surpass, top, transcend

ex•cel•lence \ˈek-sə-ləns\ *n* **1** ♦ **:** the quality of being excellent **2** ♦ **:** an excellent or valuable quality **:** VIRTUE **3 :** EXCELLENCY 2

♦ [1] distinction, greatness, preeminence, superiority, supremacy ♦ [2] distinction, merit, value, virtue ***Ant*** deficiency

ex•cel•len•cy \-lən-sē\ *n, pl* **-cies 1 :** outstanding or valuable quality **:** EXCELLENCE **2** — used as a title of honor

ex•cel•lent \-lənt\ *adj* ♦ **:** very good of its kind — **ex•cel•lent•ly** *adv*

♦ A1, bang-up, banner, fabulous, fine, grand, great, marvelous (*or* marvellous), prime, sensational, splendid, superb, superior, unsurpassed, wonderful ***Ant*** poor

ex•cel•si•or \ik-ˈsel-sē-ər\ *n* **:** fine curled wood shavings used especially for packing fragile items

¹ex•cept \ik-ˈsept\ *also* **ex•cept•ing** *prep* ♦ **:** with the exclusion or exception of ⟨daily ~ Sundays⟩

♦ aside from, bar, barring, besides, but, except for, exclusive of, outside (of), save

²except *vb* **1** ♦ **:** to take or leave out **2 :** OBJECT

♦ ban, bar, count out, debar, eliminate, exclude, rule out

³except *also* **excepting** *conj* **1 :** UNLESS ⟨~ you repent⟩ **2** ♦ **:** were it not that **:** ONLY ⟨I'd go, ~ it's too far⟩

♦ but, only, yet

except for *prep* **1** ♦ **:** with the exception of ⟨everyone was gone *except for* me⟩ **2 :** were it not for ⟨*except for* you I would be dead⟩

♦ aside from, bar, barring, besides, but, exclusive of, other than, outside (of), save

ex•cep•tion \ik-ˈsep-shən\ *n* **1 :** the act of excepting **2 :** something excepted **3 :** OBJECTION

ex•cep•tion•able \ik-ˈsep-shə-nə-bəl\ *adj* **:** being likely to cause objection **:** OBJECTIONABLE

ex•cep•tion•al \ik-ˈsep-shə-nəl\ *adj* **1** ♦ **:** forming an exception **:** UNUSUAL ⟨an ~ number of rainy days⟩ **2 :** SUPERIOR ⟨~ skill⟩ — **ex•cep•tion•al•ly** *adv*

♦ abnormal, atypical, rare, singular, uncommon, uncustomary, unique, unusual, unwonted ***Ant*** common, customary, normal, ordinary, typical

ex•cerpt \ˈek-ˌsərpt, ˈeg-ˌzərpt\ *n* **:** a passage selected or copied **:** EXTRACT — **excerpt** \ek-ˈsərpt, eg-ˈzərpt; ˈek-ˌsərpt, ˈeg-ˌzərpt\ *vb*

¹ex•cess \ik-ˈses, ˈek-ˌses\ *n* **1** ♦ **:** the state or an instance of surpassing usual, proper, or specified limits **:** SUPERFLUITY, SURPLUS **2 :** the amount by which one quantity exceeds another **3 :** INTEMPERANCE; *also* **:** an instance of intemperance

♦ fat, overabundance, overflow, superfluity, surfeit, surplus ***Ant*** deficiency, deficit, insufficiency

²excess *adj* ♦ **:** more than the usual, proper, or specified amount

♦ extra, spare, superfluous, supernumerary, surplus

ex•ces•sive \ik-ˈse-siv\ *adj* ♦ **:** exceeding what is usual, proper, necessary, or normal

♦ extravagant, extreme, immoderate, inordinate, lavish, overmuch, steep, stiff ***Ant*** moderate, modest, reasonable, temperate

ex•ces•sive•ly *adv* ♦ **:** to an exceptional or even improper degree

♦ inordinately, overly, overmuch, too

exch *abbr* exchange; exchanged

¹ex•change \iks-ˈchānj\ *n* **1** ♦ **:** the giving or taking of one thing in return for another **:** TRADE **2 :** a substituting of one thing for another **3 :** interchange of valuables and especially of bills of exchange or money of different countries **4 :** a place where things and services are exchanged; *esp* **:** a marketplace for securities **5 :** a central office in which telephone lines are connected for communication **6** ♦ **:** a reciprocal interchange (as of things or ideas); *also* **:** the act of such an interchange

♦ [1] barter, commutation, swap, trade, truck ♦ [6] colloquy, conversation, dialogue, discourse, discussion

²exchange *vb* **ex•changed; ex•chang•ing** ♦ **:** to transfer in return for some equivalent **:** SWAP — **ex•change•able** \iks-ˈchān-jə-bəl\ *adj*

♦ change, commute, shift, substitute, swap, switch, trade

ex•che•quer \ˈeks-ˌche-kər\ *n* **:** TREASURY; *esp* **:** a national treasury

ex•cise \ˈek-ˌsīz\ *n* **:** a tax on the manufacture, sale, or consumption of a commodity

ex•ci•sion \ik-ˈsi-zhən\ *n* **:** removal by or as if by cutting out especially by surgical means — **ex•cise** \ik-ˈsīz\ *vb*

ex•cit•able \ik-ˈsī-tə-bəl\ *adj* ♦ **:** easily excited — **ex•cit•abil•i•ty** \-ˌsī-tə-ˈbi-lə-tē\ *n*

♦ flighty, fluttery, high-strung, jittery, jumpy, nervous, skittish, spooky ***Ant*** unflappable

ex•cite \ik-ˈsīt\ *vb* **ex•cit•ed; ex•cit•ing 1** ♦ **:** to stir up the emotions of **2** ♦ **:** to increase the activity of **:** STIMULATE — **ex•ci•ta•tion** \ˌek-ˌsī-ˈtā-shən, ˌek-sə-\ *n* — **ex•cit•ed•ly** *adv* — **ex•cit•ing•ly** *adv*

♦ [1] electrify, exhilarate, galvanize, intoxicate, thrill, titillate, turn on ♦ [2] arouse, encourage, fire, incite, instigate, move, pique, provoke, stimulate, stir

ex•cite•ment \ik-ˈsīt-mənt\ *n* **1** ♦ **:** something that excites or rouses **2** ♦ **:** the action of exciting **:** the state of being excited

♦ [1] incitement, instigation, provocation, stimulus ♦ [2] appetite, ardor, avidity, eagerness, enthusiasm, hunger, impatience, keenness, thirst

ex•cit•ing *adj* ♦ **:** producing excitement

♦ breathtaking, electric, exhilarating, rousing, stirring, thrilling ***Ant*** unexciting

ex•claim \iks-ˈklām\ *vb* **:** to cry out, speak, or utter sharply or vehemently — **ex•clam•a•to•ry** \iks-ˈkla-mə-ˌtōr-ē\ *adj*

ex•cla•ma•tion \ˌeks-klə-ˈmā-shən\ *n* ♦ **:** a sharp or sudden utterance

♦ cry, ejaculation, interjection

exclamation point *n* **:** a punctuation mark ! used especially after an interjection or exclamation

ex•clude \iks-ˈklüd\ *vb* **ex•clud•ed; ex•clud•ing 1** ♦ **:** to prevent from using or participating **:** BAR **2 :** to put out **:** EXPEL — **ex•clu•sion** \-ˈklü-zhən\ *n*

♦ ban, bar, count out, debar, eliminate, except, rule out ***Ant*** admit, include

ex•clud•ing *adj* **:** being prevented from using or participating

ex•clu•sive \iks-ˈklü-siv\ *adj* **1 :** reserved for particular persons **2 :** snobbishly aloof; *also* **:** STYLISH **3 :** having no sharer **:** SOLE ⟨~ rights⟩; *also* **:** UNDIVIDED — **exclusive** *n* — **ex•clu•sive•ness** *n* — **ex•clu•siv•i•ty** \ˌeks-ˌklü-si-və-tē, iks-, -zi-\ *n*

ex•clu•sive•ly *adv* ♦ **:** in an exclusive manner

♦ alone, just, only, simply, solely

exclusive of *prep* ♦ **:** not taking into account

♦ aside from, bar, barring, besides, but, except for, other than, outside (of), save

ex•cog•i•tate \ek-ˈskä-jə-ˌtāt\ *vb* **:** to think out **:** DEVISE

ex•com•mu•ni•cate \ˌek-skə-ˈmyü-nə-ˌkāt\ *vb* **:** to cut off officially from the rites of the church — **ex•com•mu•ni•ca•tion** \-ˌmyü-nə-ˈkā-shən\ *n*

ex•co•ri•ate \ek-ˈskōr-ē-ˌāt\ *vb* **-at•ed; -at•ing** ♦ **:** to criticize severely

♦ abuse, assail, attack, belabor, blast, castigate, jump, lambaste, slam, vituperate

ex•co•ri•a•tion \(ˌ)ek-ˌskōr-ē-ˈā-shən\ *n* ♦ **:** a harsh and usually public criticism

♦ denunciation, rebuke, reprimand, reproach, reproof, stricture

ex•cre•ment \ˈek-skrə-mənt\ *n* : waste discharged from the body and especially from the alimentary canal; *esp* : FECES — **ex•cre•men•tal** \ˌek-skrə-ˈment-ᵊl\ *adj*

ex•cres•cence \ik-ˈskres-ᵊns\ *n* : OUTGROWTH; *esp* ♦ : an abnormal outgrowth (as a wart)

♦ growth, lump, neoplasm, tumor

ex•cre•ta \ik-ˈskrē-tə\ *n pl* : waste matter separated or eliminated from an organism

ex•crete \ik-ˈskrēt\ *vb* **ex•cret•ed; ex•cret•ing** : to separate and eliminate wastes from the body especially in urine or sweat — **ex•cre•tion** \-ˈskrē-shən\ *n* — **ex•cre•to•ry** \ˈek-skrə-ˌtōr-ē\ *adj*

ex•cru•ci•at•ing \ik-ˈskrü-shē-ˌā-tiŋ\ *adj* ♦ : intensely painful, distressing, or difficult to bear — **ex•cru•ci•at•ing•ly** *adv*

♦ agonizing, harrowing

ex•cul•pate \ˈek-(ˌ)skəl-ˌpāt\ *vb* **-pat•ed; -pat•ing** ♦ : to clear from alleged fault or guilt

♦ absolve, acquit, clear, exonerate, vindicate *Ant* incriminate

ex•cul•pa•tion \ˌek-(ˌ)skəl-ˈpā-shən\ *n* ♦ : the act or fact of exculpating from alleged fault or crime

♦ acquittal, exoneration, vindication

ex•cur•sion \ik-ˈskər-zhən\ *n* **1 a** : EXPEDITION **b** ♦ : a pleasure trip **2** : deviation from a direct, definite, or proper course : DIGRESSION

♦ jaunt, junket, outing, sally

ex•cur•sion•ist \-zhə-nist\ *n* ♦ : a person who goes on an excursion

♦ sightseer, tourist, traveler

ex•cur•sive \-ˈskər-siv\ *adj* : constituting or characterized by digression

ex•cus•able *adj* ♦ : capable of or fit for being excused, forgiven, justified, or acquitted of blame

♦ forgivable, pardonable, venial

¹ex•cuse \ik-ˈskyüz\ *vb* **ex•cused; ex•cus•ing** **1 a** : to make excuse for : offer apology for **b** : to try to remove blame from **2** ♦ : to forgive entirely or overlook as of little consequence : PARDON **3** : to release from an obligation **4** : JUSTIFY

♦ disregard, forgive, gloss over, pardon, pass over, shrug off, wink at

²excuse \ik-ˈskyüs\ *n* **1** : an act of excusing **2** ♦ : something that excuses or is a reason for excusing : JUSTIFICATION

♦ alibi, defense (*or* defence), justification, plea, reason

exec *n* : EXECUTIVE

ex•e•cra•ble \ˈek-si-krə-bəl\ *adj* **1** : DETESTABLE **2** ♦ : very bad ⟨∼ spelling⟩

♦ atrocious, awful, lousy, punk, rotten, terrible, wretched

ex•e•crate \ˈek-sə-ˌkrāt\ *vb* **-crat•ed; -crat•ing** ♦ : to denounce as evil or detestable; *also* : DETEST

♦ condemn, damn, denounce *Ant* bless ♦ abhor, abominate, despise, detest, hate, loathe

ex•e•cra•tion \ˌek-sə-ˈkrā-shən\ *n* **1** ♦ : the act of cursing or denouncing; *also* : the curse so uttered **2** : an object of curses : something detested

♦ anathema, curse, imprecation, malediction

ex•e•cute \ˈek-si-ˌkyüt\ *vb* **-cut•ed; -cut•ing** **1** ♦ : to carry out fully : put completely into effect **2** ♦ : to do what is called for by (as a law) **3** ♦ : to put to death especially in accordance with a legal sentence **4** : to produce by carrying out a design **5** : to do what is needed to give validity to ⟨∼ a deed⟩ — **ex•e•cu•tion•er** *n*

♦ [1] accomplish, achieve, carry out, commit, compass, do, follow through, make, perform ♦ [1, 2] administer, apply, enforce, implement ♦ [3] dispatch, do in, liquidate, murder, slay

ex•e•cu•tion \ˌek-si-ˈkyü-shən\ *n* ♦ : the act or process of executing

♦ accomplishment, achievement, commission, discharge, enactment, fulfillment, implementation, performance, perpetration

¹ex•ec•u•tive \ig-ˈze-kyə-tiv\ *adj* **1** ♦ : of or relating to the enforcement of laws and the conduct of affairs **2** : designed for or related to carrying out plans or purposes

♦ directorial, managerial, supervisory

²executive *n* **1** : the branch of government with executive duties **2** ♦ : one having administrative or managerial responsibility

♦ administrator, director, manager, superintendent, supervisor

ex•ec•u•tor \ig-ˈze-kyə-tər\ *n* : the person named in a will to execute it

ex•ec•u•trix \ig-ˈze-kyə-ˌtriks\ *n, pl* **ex•ec•u•tri•ces** \-ˌze-kyə-ˈtrī-ˌsēz\ *or* **ex•ec•u•trix•es** \-ˈze-kyə-ˌtrik-səz\ : a woman who is an executor

ex•e•ge•sis \ˌek-sə-ˈjē-səs\ *n, pl* **-ge•ses** \-ˈjē-ˌsēz\ : explanation or critical interpretation of a text

ex•e•gete \ˈek-sə-ˌjēt\ *n* : one who practices exegesis — **ex•e•get•i•cal** \ˌek-sə-ˈje-ti-kəl\ *adj*

ex•em•plar \ig-ˈzem-ˌplär, -plər\ *n* **1** ♦ : one that serves as a model or example; *esp* : an ideal model **2** ♦ : a typical instance or example

♦ [1] beau ideal, classic, epitome, ideal, model, nonpareil, paragon, perfection, quintessence ♦ [2] case, example, illustration, instance, representative, sample, specimen

ex•em•pla•ry \ig-ˈzem-plə-rē\ *adj* : serving as a pattern; *also* : COMMENDABLE

ex•em•pli•fy \ig-ˈzem-plə-ˌfī\ *vb* **-fied; -fy•ing** ♦ : to illustrate by example : serve as an example of — **ex•em•pli•fi•ca•tion** \-ˌzem-plə-fə-ˈkā-shən\ *n*

♦ demonstrate, illustrate, instance

¹ex•empt \ig-ˈzempt\ *adj* : free from some liability to which others are subject

²exempt *vb* : to make exempt : EXCUSE — **ex•emp•tion** \ig-ˈzemp-shən\ *n*

¹ex•er•cise \ˈek-sər-ˌsīz\ *n* **1** ♦ : the act of bringing into play or realizing in action : EMPLOYMENT, USE ⟨∼ of authority⟩ **2** ♦ : exertion made for the sake of training or physical fitness **3** ♦ : a task or problem done to develop skill **4** *pl* : a public exhibition or ceremony

♦ [1] application, employment, operation, play, use ♦ [2] activity, exertion ♦ [3] drill, practice, routine, training, workout

²exercise *vb* **-cised; -cis•ing** **1** ♦ : to make effective in action; *also* : to bring to bear : EXERT ⟨∼ control⟩ **2** : to train by or engage in exercise **3** : to cause anxiety, alarm, or indignation in : WORRY, DISTRESS — **ex•er•cis•er** *n*

♦ [1] apply, exert, put out, wield ♦ [1] apply, employ, exploit, harness, operate, use, utilize

ex•ert \ig-ˈzərt\ *vb* ♦ : to bring or put into action ⟨∼ influence⟩ ⟨∼*ed* himself⟩

♦ apply, exercise, put out, wield

ex•er•tion \-ˈzər-shən\ *n* ♦ : the act or an instance of exerting; *esp* : a laborious or perceptible effort

♦ activity, exercise ♦ effort, labor (*or* labour), pains, sweat, trouble, work

ex•fo•li•ate \eks-ˈfō-lē-ˌāt\ *vb* **-at•ed; -at•ing** : to cast off in scales, layers, or splinters — **ex•fo•lia•tion** \-ˌfō-lē-ˈā-shən\ *n*

ex•hale \eks-ˈhāl\ *vb* **ex•haled; ex•hal•ing** **1** ♦ : to breathe out **2** ♦ : to give or pass off in the form of vapor — **ex•ha•la•tion** \ˌeks-hə-ˈlā-shən\ *n*

♦ [1] blow, breathe, expire *Ant* inhale, inspire ♦ [2] cast, discharge, emit, expel, issue, release, shoot, vent

¹ex•haust \ig-ˈzȯst\ *vb* **1** ♦ : to use up wholly **2** ♦ : to tire or wear out **3** : to draw off or let out completely; *also* : EMPTY **4** : to develop (a subject) completely

♦ [1] clean, consume, deplete, drain, expend, spend, use up ♦ [2] burn out, do in, drain, fag, fatigue, tire, tucker, wash out, wear, wear out, weary

²exhaust *n* **1** : the escape of used vapor or gas from an engine; *also* : the gas that escapes **2** : a system of pipes through which exhaust escapes

ex•haust•ed *adj* : being tired, worn out, or completely used up

♦ bushed, dead, drained, prostrate, spent, weary, worn-out

ex•haus•tion \ig-ˈzȯs-chən\ *n* ♦ : extreme weariness : FATIGUE

♦ burnout, collapse, fatigue, lassitude, prostration, tiredness, weariness

ex•haus•tive \ig-ˈzȯ-stiv\ *adj* ♦ : covering all possibilities : THOROUGH

♦ all-out, clean, complete, comprehensive, full-scale, out-and-out, thorough, thoroughgoing, total

ex•haus•tive•ly *adv* ♦ **:** in a thorough or exhaustive manner

♦ completely, fully, minutely, roundly, thoroughly, totally

[1]**ex•hib•it** \ig-ˈzi-bət\ *vb* **1 :** to display especially publicly **2 :** to present to a court in legal form — **ex•hib•i•tor** \ig-ˈzi-bə-tər\ *n*

[2]**exhibit** *n* **1** ♦ **:** an act or instance of exhibiting; *also* **:** something exhibited **2 :** something produced and identified in court for use as evidence

♦ display, exhibition, exposition, fair, show

ex•hi•bi•tion \ˌek-sə-ˈbi-shən\ *n* ♦ **:** an act or instance of exhibiting; *also* **:** a public showing (as of works of art, objects of manufacture, or athletic skill)

♦ demonstration, display, show ♦ display, exhibit, exposition, fair, show

ex•hi•bi•tion•ism \ˌek-sə-ˈbi-shə-ˌni-zəm\ *n* **1 :** a perversion marked by a tendency to indecently expose one's genitals **2 :** the act or practice of behaving so as to attract attention to oneself — **ex•hi•bi•tion•ist** \-nist\ *n or adj*

ex•hil•a•rate \ig-ˈzi-lə-ˌrāt\ *vb* **-rat•ed; -rat•ing** ♦ **:** to make cheerful and excited

♦ elate, elevate, enrapture, thrill, transport

exhilarating *adj* ♦ **:** serving to exhilarate

♦ breathtaking, exciting, rousing, stirring, thrilling

ex•hil•a•ra•tion \-ˌzi-lə-ˈrā-shən\ *n* **1 :** the action of exhilarating **2** ♦ **:** the feeling or the state of being exhilarated

♦ ecstasy, elation, euphoria, heaven, intoxication, paradise, rapture, rhapsody, thrill, transport

ex•hort \ig-ˈzȯrt\ *vb* ♦ **:** to urge, advise, or warn earnestly — **ex•hor•ta•tion** \ˌek-ˌsȯr-ˈtā-shən, ˌeg-ˌzȯr-, -zər-\ *n*

♦ egg on, encourage, goad, press, prod, prompt, urge

ex•hume \ig-ˈzüm, iks-ˈhyüm\ *vb* **ex•humed; ex•hum•ing :** DISINTER — **ex•hu•ma•tion** \ˌeks-hyü-ˈmā-shən, ˌeg-zü-\ *n*

ex•i•gen•cy \ˈek-sə-jən-sē, ig-ˈzi-jən-\ *n, pl* **-cies** **1** *pl* **:** REQUIREMENTS **2 :** urgent need — **ex•i•gent** \ˈek-sə-jənt\ *adj*

ex•ig•u•ous \ig-ˈzi-gyə-wəs\ *adj* **:** scanty in amount — **ex•i•gu•i•ty** \ˌeg-zi-ˈgyü-ə-tē\ *n*

[1]**ex•ile** \ˈeg-ˌzīl, ˈek-ˌsīl\ *n* **1** ♦ **:** the state or a period of forced absence from one's country or home **:** BANISHMENT; *also* **:** voluntary absence from one's country or home **2** ♦ **:** a person driven from his or her native place

♦ [1] banishment, deportation, displacement, expulsion ♦ [2] émigré, evacuee, expatriate, refugee

[2]**exile** *vb* **ex•iled; ex•il•ing** ♦ **:** to expel from one's own country or home **:** BANISH

♦ banish, deport, displace, expatriate, transport

ex•ist \ig-ˈzist\ *vb* **1 :** to have being **2** ♦ **:** to continue to be **:** LIVE

♦ be, breathe, live, subsist

ex•is•tence \ig-ˈzis-təns\ *n* **1 :** continuance in living **2** ♦ **:** actual or present occurrence ⟨~ of a state of war⟩ **3 :** something existing

♦ actuality, reality, subsistence ***Ant*** nonexistence

ex•is•tent \-tənt\ *adj* ♦ **:** having being; *also* **:** existing now

♦ actual, concrete, factual, real, true, very ♦ alive, extant, living

ex•is•ten•tial \ˌeg-zis-ˈten-chəl, ˌek-sis-\ *adj* **1 :** of or relating to existence **2 :** EMPIRICAL **3 :** having being in time and space **4 :** of or relating to existentialism or existentialists

ex•is•ten•tial•ism \ˌeg-zis-ˈten-chə-ˌli-zəm\ *n* **:** a philosophy centered on individual existence and personal responsibility for acts of free will in the absence of certain knowledge of what is right or wrong — **ex•is•ten•tial•ist** \-list\ *adj or n*

[1]**ex•it** \ˈeg-zət, ˈek-sət\ *n* **1 :** a departure from a stage **2** ♦ **:** a going out or away; *also* **:** DEATH **3** ♦ **:** a way out of an enclosed space **4 :** a point of departure from an expressway

♦ [2] departure, farewell, leave-taking, parting ♦ [3] egress, issue, outlet ***Ant*** entrance, entry; ingress

[2]**exit** *vb* ♦ **:** to go out or away from

♦ clear out, depart, get off, go, move, pull, quit, sally, shove, take off

exo•bi•ol•o•gy \ˌek-sō-bī-ˈä-lə-jē\ *n* **:** biology concerned with life originating or existing outside the earth or its atmosphere — **exo•bi•ol•o•gist** \-jist\ *n*

exo•crine gland \ˈek-sə-krən-, -ˌkrīn-, -ˌkrēn-\ *n* **:** a gland (as a salivary gland) that releases a secretion externally by means of a canal or duct

Exod *abbr* Exodus

ex•o•dus \ˈek-sə-dəs\ *n* **1** *cap* **:** the mainly narrative second book of canonical Jewish and Christian Scripture **2 :** a mass departure **:** EMIGRATION

ex of•fi•cio \ˌek-sə-ˈfi-shē-ˌō\ *adv or adj* **:** by virtue of or because of an office ⟨*ex officio* chairman⟩

ex•og•e•nous \ek-ˈsä-jə-nəs\ *adj* **:** caused or produced by factors outside the organism or system — **ex•og•e•nous•ly** *adv*

ex•on•er•ate \ig-ˈzä-nə-ˌrāt\ *vb* **-at•ed; -at•ing** ♦ **:** to free from blame

♦ absolve, acquit, clear, exculpate, vindicate

ex•on•er•a•tion \-ˌzä-nə-ˈrā-shən\ *n* ♦ **:** the act or state of exonerating

♦ acquittal, exculpation, vindication

ex•or•bi•tant \ig-ˈzȯr-bə-tənt\ *adj* ♦ **:** exceeding what is usual or proper

♦ excessive, extravagant, extreme, immoderate, inordinate, lavish, steep, stiff

ex•or•cise \ˈek-ˌsȯr-ˌsīz, -sər-\ *vb* **-cised; -cis•ing** **1 :** to get rid of by or as if by solemn command **2 :** to free of an evil spirit — **ex•or•cism** \-ˌsi-zəm\ *n* — **ex•or•cist** \-ˌsist\ *n*

exo•sphere \ˈek-sō-ˌsfir\ *n* **:** the outermost region of the atmosphere

exo•ther•mic \ˌek-sō-ˈthər-mik\ *adj* **:** characterized by or formed with evolution of heat

ex•ot•ic \ig-ˈzä-tik\ *adj* **1 :** introduced from another country **2** ♦ **:** strikingly, excitingly, or mysteriously different or unusual

♦ fantastic, glamorous, marvelous (*or* marvellous), outlandish, romantic, strange

exp *abbr* **1** expense **2** experiment **3** export **4** express

ex•pand \ik-ˈspand\ *vb* **1** ♦ **:** to open up **:** UNFOLD **2** ♦ **:** to increase in extent, number, volume, or scope **:** ENLARGE **3** ♦ **:** to develop in detail — **ex•pand•er** *n*

♦ [1] extend, fan, flare, open, spread, stretch, unfold ♦ [2] add, aggrandize, amplify, augment, boost, compound, enlarge, escalate, extend, increase, multiply, raise, swell, up ♦ [3] amplify, develop, elaborate (on), enlarge (on) ***Ant*** abbreviate, abridge, condense, shorten

ex•panse \ik-ˈspans\ *n* ♦ **:** a broad extent (as of land or sea)

♦ breadth, extent, reach, spread, stretch

ex•pan•sion \ik-ˈspan-chən\ *n* **1** ♦ **:** the act or process of expanding **2 :** the quality or state of being expanded **3** ♦ **:** an expanded part or thing

♦ [1] development, elaboration, evolution, growth, progress, progression ♦ [3] accretion, addition, augmentation, boost, gain, increase, increment, plus, proliferation, raise, rise, supplement

expansion slot *n* **:** a socket on a motherboard for a circuit board (**expansion card**) offering additional capabilities

ex•pan•sive \ik-ˈspan-siv\ *adj* **1 :** tending to expand or to cause expansion **2 :** warmly benevolent, generous, or ready to talk **3** ♦ **:** of large extent or scope — **ex•pan•sive•ly** *adv* — **ex•pan•sive•ness** *n*

♦ broad, extended, extensive, far-flung, far-reaching, wide, widespread

ex par•te \eks-ˈpär-tē\ *adv or adj* **:** from a one-sided point of view

ex•pa•ti•ate \ek-ˈspā-shē-ˌāt\ *vb* **-at•ed; -at•ing :** to talk or write at length — **ex•pa•ti•a•tion** \ek-ˌspā-shē-ˈā-shən\ *n*

[1]**ex•pa•tri•ate** \ek-ˈspā-trē-ˌāt\ *vb* **-at•ed; -at•ing** **1 :** to leave one's native country to live elsewhere **:** EXILE **2** ♦ **:** to drive into exile

♦ banish, deport, displace, exile, transport

[2]**ex•pa•tri•ate** \ek-ˈspā-trē-ˌāt, -trē-ət\ *adj* **:** living in a foreign country

[3]**expatriate** *n* **:** one who lives in a foreign country; *specif* **:** one who has renounced his native country

ex•pa•tri•a•tion \ek-ˌspā-trē-ˈā-shən\ *n* **:** the act or action of expatriating

ex•pect \ik-ˈspekt\ *vb* **1 :** SUPPOSE, THINK **2** ♦ **:** to look forward to **:** ANTICIPATE **3 :** to consider reasonable, due, or necessary **4 :** to consider to be obliged

♦ anticipate, await, hope, watch

ex•pec•tan•cy \-ˈspek-tən-sē\ *n, pl* **-cies** **1 :** EXPECTATION **2 :** the expected amount (as of years of life)

ex•pec•tant \-tənt\ *adj* ♦ **:** marked by expectation; *esp* **:** expecting the birth of a child — **ex•pec•tant•ly** *adv*

♦ agape, agog, anticipatory

ex•pec•ta•tion \ˌek-ˌspek-ˈtā-shən\ *n* **1 :** the act or state of expecting **2 :** prospect of good or bad fortune — usually used in plural **3 :** something expected

ex•pec•to•rant \ik-ˈspek-tə-rənt\ *n* **:** an agent that promotes the discharge or expulsion of mucus from the respiratory tract — **expectorant** *adj*

ex•pec•to•rate \-ˌrāt\ *vb* **-rat•ed; -rat•ing :** SPIT — **ex•pec•to•ra•tion** \-ˌspek-tə-ˈrā-shən\ *n*

ex•pe•di•ence \ik-ˈspē-dē-əns\ *n* **:** EXPEDIENCY

ex•pe•di•en•cy \-ən-sē\ *n, pl* **-cies** **1 :** fitness to some end **2 :** use of expedient means and methods; *also* **:** something expedient

[1]**ex•pe•di•ent** \-ənt\ *adj* **1** ♦ **:** adapted for achieving a particular end **2 :** marked by concern with what is advantageous; *esp* **:** governed by self-interest

♦ advisable, desirable, judicious, politic, prudent, tactical, wise *Ant* imprudent, inadvisable, inexpedient, injudicious, unwise

[2]**expedient** *n* ♦ **:** something expedient; *esp* **:** a temporary means to an end

♦ measure, move, shift, step ♦ recourse, resort, resource

ex•pe•dite \ˈek-spə-ˌdīt\ *vb* **-dit•ed; -dit•ing :** to carry out promptly; *also* **:** to speed up

ex•pe•dit•er \-ˌdī-tər\ *n* **:** one that expedites; *esp* **:** one employed to ensure efficient movement of goods or supplies in a business

ex•pe•di•tion \ˌek-spə-ˈdi-shən\ *n* **1** ♦ **:** a journey for a particular purpose; *also* **:** the persons making it **2 :** efficient promptness

♦ journey, passage, peregrination, trek, trip

ex•pe•di•tion•ary \-ˈdi-shə-ˌner-ē\ *adj* **:** of, relating to, or constituting an expedition; *also* **:** sent on military service abroad

ex•pe•di•tious \-ˈdi-shəs\ *adj* ♦ **:** marked by or acting with prompt efficiency

♦ alert, prompt, quick, ready, willing

ex•pel \ik-ˈspel\ *vb* **ex•pelled; ex•pel•ling** ♦ **:** to drive or force out

♦ banish, boot (out), bounce, cast, chase, dismiss, drum, eject, oust, rout, run off, throw out ♦ belch, disgorge, eject, erupt, jet, spew, spout, spurt

ex•pend \ik-ˈspend\ *vb* **1** ♦ **:** to pay out **:** SPEND **2** ♦ **:** to make use of; *also* **:** USE UP — **ex•pend•able** *adj*

♦ [1] disburse, give, lay out, pay, spend ♦ [2] clean, consume, deplete, drain, exhaust, spend, use up

ex•pen•di•ture \ik-ˈspen-di-chər, -ˌchu̇r\ *n* **1 :** the act or process of expending **2** ♦ **:** something expended

♦ cost, disbursement, expense, outgo, outlay

ex•pense \ik-ˈspens\ *n* **1** ♦ **:** something expended to secure a benefit or bring about a result **:** EXPENDITURE **2 :** COST **3 :** a cause of expenditure **4 :** a loss, detriment, or embarrassment that results from some action or gain ⟨had a laugh at my ~⟩

♦ cost, disbursement, expenditure, outgo, outlay

ex•pen•sive \ik-ˈspen-siv\ *adj* ♦ **:** involving high cost or sacrifice **:** COSTLY, DEAR

♦ costly, dear, high, precious, valuable

ex•pen•sive•ly *adv* ♦ **:** in an expensive manner

♦ extravagantly, grandly, high, lavishly, luxuriously, opulently, richly

[1]**ex•pe•ri•ence** \ik-ˈspir-ē-əns\ *n* **1 :** observation of or participation in events resulting in or tending toward knowledge **2** ♦ **:** knowledge, practice, or skill derived from observation or participation in events; *also* **:** the length of such participation **3** ♦ **:** something encountered, undergone, or lived through (as by a person or community)

♦ [2] expertise, know-how, proficiency, savvy *Ant* inexperience ♦ [3] adventure, happening, time

[2]**experience** *vb* **-enced; -enc•ing** **1 :** FIND OUT, DISCOVER **2** ♦ **:** to have experience of **:** UNDERGO

♦ endure, feel, have, know, see, suffer, sustain, taste, undergo

ex•pe•ri•enced *adj* ♦ **:** made capable through experience

♦ accomplished, adept, expert, masterful, masterly, practiced, proficient, seasoned, skilled, skillful, versed *Ant* amateurish, inexperienced, inexpert, unseasoned, unskilled

[1]**ex•per•i•ment** \ik-ˈsper-ə-mənt\ *n* ♦ **:** a controlled procedure carried out to discover, test, or demonstrate something; *also* **:** the process of testing

♦ test, trial

[2]**ex•per•i•ment** \-ˌment\ *vb* **:** to make experiments — **ex•per•i•men•ter** *n*

ex•per•i•men•tal \-ˌsper-ə-ˈment-ᵊl\ *adj* **:** of, relating to, or based on experience or experiment; *also* **:** serving the ends of or used as a means of experimentation — **ex•per•i•men•tal•ly** \-ˈmen-tᵊl-ē\ *adv*

ex•per•i•men•ta•tion \ik-ˌsper-ə-mən-ˈtā-shən\ *n* **:** the act, process, or practice of making experiments; *also* **:** an instance of experimentation

[1]**ex•pert** \ˈek-ˌspərt\ *adj* ♦ **:** showing special skill or knowledge — **ex•pert•ness** *n*

♦ accomplished, ace, adept, crack, experienced, master, masterful, masterly, practiced, proficient, seasoned, skilled, skillful, versed

[2]**ex•pert** \ˈek-ˌspərt\ *n* ♦ **:** an expert person

♦ ace, artist, authority, master, scholar, shark, virtuoso, whiz, wizard *Ant* amateur

ex•per•tise \ˌek-(ˌ)spər-ˈtēz\ *n* ♦ **:** the skill of an expert

♦ experience, know-how, proficiency, savvy

ex•pert•ly *adv* ♦ **:** in an expert manner

♦ ably, adeptly, capably, masterfully, proficiently, skillfully, well

expert system *n* **:** computer software that attempts to mimic the reasoning of a human specialist

ex•pi•ate \ˈek-spē-ˌāt\ *vb* **-at•ed; -at•ing :** to give satisfaction for **:** ATONE — **ex•pi•a•tion** \ˌek-spē-ˈā-shən\ *n*

ex•pi•a•to•ry \ˈek-spē-ə-ˌtōr-ē\ *adj* **:** serving to expiate

ex•pi•ra•tion \ˌek-spə-ˈrā-shən\ *n* **1 :** the last emission of breath; *also* **:** the act or process of releasing air from the lungs through the nose or mouth **2** ♦ **:** the fact of coming to an end or the point at which something ends

♦ death, demise, termination ♦ cessation, close, conclusion, end, ending, finish, shutdown, stop, stoppage, termination

expiration date *n* **1 :** the date after which something is no longer in effect **2 :** the date after which a product is expected to decline in quality or effectiveness

ex•pire \ik-ˈspīr, ek-\ *vb* **ex•pired; ex•pir•ing** **1** ♦ **:** to breathe one's last breath **:** DIE **2** ♦ **:** to come to an end **3** ♦ **:** to breathe out from or as if from the lungs

♦ [1] decease, depart, die, pass, pass away, perish, succumb ♦ [2] cease, close, conclude, die, discontinue, end, finish, halt, pass, quit, stop, terminate ♦ [3] blow, breathe, exhale

ex•plain \ik-ˈsplān\ *vb* **1** ♦ **:** to make clear **2** ♦ **:** to give the reason for — **ex•plan•a•to•ry** \ik-ˈspla-nə-ˌtōr-ē\ *adj*

♦ [1] clarify, clear (up), construe, demonstrate, elucidate, explicate, expound, illuminate, illustrate, interpret, spell out *Ant* obscure ♦ [2] account, rationalize

explain away *vb* **:** to get rid of by or as if by explanation; *also* **:** to minimize the significance of by or as if by explanation

ex•pla•na•tion \ˌek-splə-ˈnā-shən\ *n* **1 :** the act or process of explaining **2** ♦ **:** something that explains

♦ clarification, construction, elucidation, explication, exposition, illumination, illustration, interpretation ♦ argument, case, defense (*or* defence), rationale, reason

ex•ple•tive \ˈek-splə-tiv\ *n* **:** a usually profane exclamation

ex•pli•ca•ble \ek-ˈspli-kə-bəl, ˈek-(ˌ)spli-\ *adj* ♦ **:** capable of being explained

♦ answerable, resolvable, soluble, solvable

ex•pli•cate \ˈek-splə-ˌkāt\ *vb* **-cat•ed; -cat•ing** ♦ **:** to give a detailed explanation of; *esp* **:** to interpret the meaning or sense of

♦ clarify, clear (up), construe, demonstrate, elucidate, explain, expound, illuminate, illustrate, interpret, spell out

ex•pli•ca•tion \ˌek-spli-ˈkā-shən\ *n* **1 :** the act or process of explicating **2** ♦ **:** something that explicates or that results from the act or process of explicating

♦ clarification, construction, elucidation, explanation, exposition, illumination, illustration, interpretation

ex•plic•it \ik-ˈspli-sət\ *adj* ♦ **:** clearly and precisely expressed — **ex•plic•it•ly** *adv*

♦ clear-cut, definite, definitive, express, specific, unambiguous, unequivocal ***Ant*** implicit, implied, inferred; ambiguous, circuitous

ex•plic•it•ness *n* ♦ **:** the quality or state of being explicit

♦ clarity, lucidity, perspicuity, simplicity

ex•plode \ik-ˈsplōd\ *vb* **ex•plod•ed; ex•plod•ing** **1 :** DISCREDIT 〈∼ a belief〉 **2** ♦ **:** to burst or cause to burst violently and noisily 〈∼ a bomb〉 〈the boiler *exploded*〉 **3 :** to undergo a rapid chemical or nuclear reaction with production of heat and violent expansion of gas 〈dynamite ∼*s*〉 **4 :** to give forth a sudden strong and noisy outburst of emotion **5 :** to increase rapidly 〈the city's population *exploded*〉 **6** ♦ **:** to suggest an explosion (as in appearance or effect)

♦ [2] blow up, burst, detonate, go off, pop ***Ant*** implode ♦ [6] break out, burst, erupt, flame, flare, go off

ex•plod•ed *adj* **:** showing the parts separated but in correct relationship to each other 〈an ∼ view of a carburetor〉

¹ex•ploit \ˈek-ˌsplȯit\ *n* ♦ **:** something that is done; *esp* **:** a notable or heroic act

♦ deed, feat, stunt, trick

²ex•ploit \ik-ˈsplȯit\ *vb* **1** ♦ **:** to make productive use of **:** UTILIZE **2** ♦ **:** to use unfairly for one's own advantage — **ex•ploi•ta•tion** \ˌek-ˌsplȯi-ˈtā-shən\ *n*

♦ [1] apply, employ, exercise, harness, operate, use, utilize ♦ [2] abuse, capitalize, cash in, impose, play, use

ex•plo•ra•tion \ˌek-splə-ˈrā-shən\ *n* ♦ **:** the act or an instance of exploring

♦ examination, inquiry, investigation, probe, research, study

ex•plore \ik-ˈsplōr\ *vb* **ex•plored; ex•plor•ing** **1** ♦ **:** to look into or travel over thoroughly **2** ♦ **:** to examine carefully 〈∼ a wound〉 — **ex•plor•ato•ry** \ik-ˈsplōr-ə-ˌtōr-ē\ *adj* — **ex•plor•er** *n*

♦ [1] hunt, probe, prospect, search ♦ [2] delve, dig, go, inquire into, investigate, look, probe, research

ex•plo•sion \ik-ˈsplō-zhən\ *n* ♦ **:** the act or an instance of exploding

♦ agony, burst, fit, flash, flush, outburst, paroxysm, spasm, storm ♦ blast, detonation, eruption ***Ant*** implosion

ex•plo•sive \ik-ˈsplō-siv\ *adj* **1 a :** relating to or able to cause explosion **b :** characterized by or like an explosion **2** ♦ **:** tending to explode; *also* **:** likely to erupt in or produce hostile reaction or violence — **explosive** *n* — **ex•plo•sive•ly** *adv*

♦ ferocious, fierce, furious, hot, rabid, rough, stormy, tempestuous, turbulent, violent, volcanic

ex•po \ˈek-ˌspō\ *n, pl* **expos :** EXPOSITION 2

ex•po•nent \ik-ˈspō-nənt, ˈek-ˌspō-\ *n* **1 :** a symbol written above and to the right of a mathematical expression (as ³ in a^3) to signify how many times it is to be used as a factor **2 :** INTERPRETER, EXPOUNDER **3** ♦ **:** one that champions, practices, or exemplifies **:** ADVOCATE — **ex•po•nen•tial** \ˌek-spə-ˈnen-chəl\ *adj* — **ex•po•nen•tial•ly** *adv*

♦ advocate, apostle, backer, booster, champion, friend, promoter, proponent, supporter ***Ant*** adversary, antagonist, opponent

ex•po•nen•ti•a•tion \ˌek-spə-ˌnen-chē-ˈā-shen\ *n* **:** the mathematical operation of raising a quantity to a power

¹ex•port \ek-ˈspōrt, ˈek-ˌspōrt\ *vb* **:** to send (as merchandise) to foreign countries — **ex•por•ta•tion** \ˌek-ˌspōr-ˈtā-shən, -spər-\ *n* — **ex•port•er** *n*

²ex•port \ˈek-ˌspōrt\ *n* **1 :** something exported especially for trade **2 :** the act of exporting

ex•pose \ik-ˈspōz\ *vb* **ex•posed; ex•pos•ing** **1 :** to deprive of shelter or protection **2 :** to submit or subject to an action or influence; *esp* **:** to subject (as photographic film) to radiant energy (as light) **3** ♦ **:** to bring to light; *esp* **:** to disclose or reveal the true nature of **4** ♦ **:** to cause to be open to view

♦ [3] bare, disclose, discover, divulge, reveal, spill, tell ♦ [3] debunk, show up, uncloak, uncover, unmask ***Ant*** camouflage, cloak, disguise, mask ♦ [4] display, exhibit, show, unveil

ex•po•sé \ˌek-spō-ˈzā\ *n* **:** an exposure of something discreditable

ex•posed \ik-ˈspōzd\ *adj* ♦ **:** open to view; *also* **:** not shielded or protected

♦ liable, open, sensitive, subject, susceptible, unprotected, vulnerable ♦ bald, bare, naked, open, uncovered

ex•po•si•tion \ˌek-spə-ˈzi-shən\ *n* **1** ♦ **:** a setting forth of the meaning or purpose (as of a writing); *also* **:** discourse designed to convey information **2** ♦ **:** a public exhibition

♦ [1] clarification, construction, elucidation, explanation, explication, illumination, illustration, interpretation ♦ [1] analysis, comment, commentary ♦ [2] display, exhibit, exhibition, fair, show

ex•pos•i•tor \ik-ˈspä-zə-tər\ *n* **:** one who explains **:** COMMENTATOR

ex•pos•i•tory \ik-ˈspä-zə-tə-rē\ *adj* **:** serving to explain

ex post fac•to \ˌeks-ˈpōst-ˌfak-tō\ *adv or adj* **:** after the fact

ex•pos•tu•late \ik-ˈspäs-chə-ˌlāt\ *vb* **:** to reason earnestly with a person especially in dissuading **:** REMONSTRATE

ex•pos•tu•la•tion \-ˌspäs-chə-ˈlā-shən\ *n* ♦ **:** an act or an instance of expostulating

♦ challenge, complaint, demur, fuss, kick, objection, protest, question, remonstrance

ex•po•sure \ik-ˈspō-zhər\ *n* **1** ♦ **:** the fact or condition of being exposed **2 :** the act or an instance of exposing **3 :** the length of time for which a film is exposed **4 :** a section of a photographic film for one picture

♦ liability, openness, vulnerability

ex•pound \ik-ˈspau̇nd\ *vb* **1 :** STATE **2** ♦ **:** to explain by setting forth in careful and often elaborate detail **:** INTERPRET — **ex•pound•er** *n*

♦ clarify, clear (up), construe, demonstrate, elucidate, explain, explicate, illuminate, illustrate, interpret, spell out

¹ex•press \ik-ˈspres\ *adj* **1** ♦ **:** directly, firmly, and explicitly stated; *also* **:** EXACT, PRECISE **2** ♦ **:** of a particular sort **:** SPECIFIC 〈this ∼ purpose〉 **3 :** traveling at high speed and especially with few stops 〈an ∼ train〉; *also* **:** adapted to high speed use 〈∼ roads〉 — **ex•press•ly** *adv*

♦ [1] clear-cut, definite, definitive, explicit, specific, unambiguous, unequivocal ♦ [1, 2] distinct, especial, exact, precise, set, special, specific ***Ant*** nonspecific

²express *adv* **:** by express 〈ship it ∼〉

³express *n* **1 :** a system for the prompt transportation of goods; *also* **:** a company operating such a service or the shipments so transported **2 :** an express vehicle

⁴express *vb* **1** ♦ **:** to make known **:** STATE 〈∼ regret〉; *also* **:** to represent by a sign or symbol **2** ♦ **:** to squeeze out **:** extract by pressing **3 :** to send by express **4 :** to manifest or produce by a genetic process

♦ [1] denote, import, mean, signify, spell ♦ [1] articulate, clothe, couch, formulate, phrase, put, say, state, word ♦ [1] air, give, sound, state, voice ***Ant*** stifle, suppress ♦ [2] crush, mash, press, squeeze

ex•pres•sion \ik-ˈspre-shən\ *n* **1** ♦ **:** an act, process, or instance of representing in a medium (as words) **:** UTTERANCE **2 :** something that represents or symbolizes **:** SIGN; *esp* **:** a mathematical symbol or combination of signs and symbols representing a quantity or operation **3 :** a significant word or phrase; *also* **:** manner of expressing (as in writing or music) **4** ♦ **:** facial aspect or vocal intonation indicative of feeling

♦ [1] articulation, formulation, statement, utterance, voice ♦ [4] cast, countenance, face, look, visage

ex•pres•sion•ism \ik-ˈspre-shə-ˌni-zəm\ *n* **:** a theory or practice in art of seeking to depict the artist's subjective responses to objects and events — **ex•pres•sion•ist** \-nist\ *n or adj* — **ex•pres•sion•is•tic** \-ˌspre-shə-ˈnis-tik\ *adj*

ex•pres•sion•less *adj* ♦ **:** lacking expression

♦ blank, deadpan, impassive, inexpressive, stolid, vacant

ex•pres•sive \ik-ˈspre-siv\ *adj* **1 :** of or relating to expression **2** ♦ **:** serving to express — **ex•pres•sive•ly** *adv* — **ex•pres•sive•ness** *n*

♦ eloquent, meaning, meaningful, pregnant, significant, suggestive

ex•press•way \ik-ˈspres-ˌwā\ *n* **:** a divided superhighway with limited access

ex•pro•pri•ate \ek-ˈsprō-prē-ˌāt\ *vb* **-at•ed; -at•ing :** to deprive

of possession or the right to own — **ex•pro•pri•a•tion** \(ˌ)ek-ˌsprō-prē-ˈā-shən\ *n*
expt *abbr* experiment
ex•pul•sion \ik-ˈspəl-shən\ *n* ♦ : an expelling or being expelled

♦ banishment, deportation, displacement, exile

ex•punge \ik-ˈspənj\ *vb* **ex•punged; ex•pung•ing** : to efface completely : OBLITERATE
ex•pur•gate \ˈek-spər-ˌgāt\ *vb* **-gat•ed; -gat•ing** : to clear (as a book) of objectionable passages — **ex•pur•ga•tion** \ˌek-spər-ˈgā-shən\ *n*
ex•qui•site \ek-ˈskwi-zət, ˈek-(ˌ)skwi-\ *adj* **1** : marked by flawless form or workmanship **2** : keenly appreciative or sensitive **3** ♦ : pleasingly beautiful or delicate **4** : characterized by sharpness or severity : INTENSE ⟨~ pain⟩

♦ dainty, delicate, refined, subtle

ext *abbr* **1** extension **2** exterior **3** external **4** extra **5** extract
ex•tant \ˈek-stənt; ek-ˈstant\ *adj* ♦ : currently or actually existing; *esp* : not lost or destroyed

♦ current, ongoing, present ♦ alive, existent, living ***Ant*** dead, extinct

ex•tem•po•ra•ne•ous \ek-ˌstem-pə-ˈrā-nē-əs\ *adj* ♦ : not planned beforehand : IMPROMPTU — **ex•tem•po•ra•ne•ous•ly** *adv*

♦ ad-lib, impromptu, informal, offhand, spontaneous, unplanned, unprepared, unrehearsed ***Ant*** considered, planned, premeditated, prepared, rehearsed

ex•tem•po•rary \ik-ˈstem-pə-ˌrer-ē\ *adj* : EXTEMPORANEOUS
ex•tem•po•re \ik-ˈstem-pə-(ˌ)rē\ *adv* : EXTEMPORANEOUSLY
ex•tem•po•rise *chiefly Brit var of* EXTEMPORIZE
ex•tem•po•rize \ik-ˈstem-pə-ˌrīz\ *vb* **-rized; -riz•ing** : to do something extemporaneously
ex•tend \ik-ˈstend\ *vb* **1** ♦ : to spread or stretch forth or out (as in reaching) **2** : to exert or cause to exert to full capacity **3** ♦ : to make the offer of : PROFFER ⟨~ credit⟩ **4** : PROLONG ⟨~ a note⟩ **5** : to make greater or broader ⟨~ knowledge⟩ ⟨~ a business⟩ **6** : to stretch out or reach across a distance, space, or time — **extend•able** *also* **ex•tend•ible** \-ˈsten-də-bəl\ *adj*

♦ [1] expand, fan, flare, open, spread, stretch, unfold ♦ [1] draw out, elongate, lengthen, prolong, protract, stretch ***Ant*** abbreviate, abridge, curtail, cut, cut back, shorten ♦ [3] give, offer, proffer, tender

ex•tend•ed *adj* **1** ♦ : drawn out in length especially of time **2** : fully stretched out **3** ♦ : having wide or considerable extent

♦ [1] far, great, lengthy, long, marathon ♦ [3] broad, expansive, extensive, far-flung, far-reaching, wide, widespread

ex•ten•sion \ik-ˈsten-chən\ *n* **1** ♦ : an extending or being extended **2** : a program that geographically extends the educational resources of an institution **3** ♦ : an additional part; *also* : an extra telephone connected to a line

♦ [1] elongation, prolongation ***Ant*** abbreviation, abridgment, curtailment, cutback, shortening ♦ [3] addition, annex, penthouse

ex•ten•sive \ik-ˈsten-siv\ *adj* ♦ : of considerable extent : FAR-REACHING, BROAD — **ex•ten•sive•ly** *adv*

♦ broad, expansive, extended, far-flung, far-reaching, wide, widespread ***Ant*** narrow

ex•tent \ik-ˈstent\ *n* **1** ♦ : the range or space over which something extends ⟨a property of large ~⟩ **2** ♦ : the point or degree to which something extends ⟨to the fullest ~ of the law⟩ ⟨exerting the full ~ of his power⟩

♦ [1] amplitude, breadth, compass, range, reach, realm, scope, sweep, width ♦ [1] dimension, magnitude, measure, measurement, proportion, size ♦ [2] bound, boundary, ceiling, confines, end, limit, limitation, line, termination

ex•ten•u•ate \ik-ˈsten-yu̇-ˌwāt\ *vb* **-at•ed; -at•ing** : to lessen the seriousness of — **ex•ten•u•a•tion** \-ˌsten-yu̇-ˈwā-shən\ *n*
¹ex•te•ri•or \ek-ˈstir-ē-ər\ *adj* **1** ♦ : being on an outside surface : EXTERNAL **2** : suitable for use on an outside surface ⟨~ paint⟩

♦ external, outer, outside, outward

²exterior *n* ♦ : an exterior part or surface

♦ face, outside, skin, surface, veneer ***Ant*** inside, interior

ex•ter•mi•nate \ik-ˈstər-mə-ˌnāt\ *vb* **-nat•ed; -nat•ing** ♦ : to get rid of completely usually by killing off — **ex•ter•mi•na•tor** \-ˈstər-mə-ˌnā-tər\ *n*

♦ annihilate, blot out, demolish, eradicate, liquidate, obliterate, root, rub out, snuff, stamp, wipe out

ex•ter•mi•na•tion \-ˌstər-mə-ˈnā-shən\ *n* : the act of exterminating or the condition of being exterminated
¹ex•ter•nal \ek-ˈstərn-ᵊl\ *adj* **1** : outwardly perceivable; *also* : SUPERFICIAL **2** ♦ : of, relating to, or located on the outside or an outer part **3** : arising or acting from without; *also* : FOREIGN ⟨~ affairs⟩ — **ex•ter•nal•ly** *adv*

♦ exterior, outer, outside, outward

²external *n* : an external feature
ex•tinct \ik-ˈstiŋkt\ *adj* **1** : EXTINGUISHED; *also* : no longer active ⟨an ~ volcano⟩ **2** ♦ : no longer existing or in use ⟨dinosaurs are ~⟩ ⟨~ languages⟩

♦ bygone, dead, defunct, gone ***Ant*** alive, existent, existing, extant, living

ex•tinc•tion \ik-ˈstiŋk-shən\ *n* **1** : the act of making extinct or causing to be extinguished **2** : the condition or fact of being extinct or extinguished; *also* : the process of becoming extinct
ex•tin•guish \ik-ˈstiŋ-gwish\ *vb* **1** ♦ : to cause to stop burning **2** ♦ : to bring to an end : cause to die out ⟨disease that *extinguished* an entire population⟩ ⟨*extinguishing* the last glimmer of hope⟩ — **ex•tin•guish•able** *adj* — **ex•tin•guish•er** *n*

♦ [1] douse, put out, quench, snuff ***Ant*** fire, ignite, inflame, kindle ♦ [2] annihilate, blot out, demolish, desolate, destroy, devastate, do in, obliterate, ruin, shatter, smash, wipe out, wreck

ex•tir•pate \ˈek-stər-ˌpāt\ *vb* **-pat•ed; -pat•ing** **1** : to destroy completely **2** : UPROOT — **ex•tir•pa•tion** \ˌek-stər-ˈpā-shən\ *n*
ex•tol *also* **ex•toll** \ik-ˈstōl\ *vb* **ex•tolled; ex•tol•ling** ♦ : to praise highly : GLORIFY

♦ bless, glorify, laud, magnify, praise

ex•tort \ik-ˈstȯrt\ *vb* ♦ : to obtain by force or improper pressure ⟨~ a bribe⟩ — **ex•tor•tion** \-ˈstȯr-shən\ *n* — **ex•tor•tion•er** *n*

♦ exact, wrest, wring

ex•tor•tion•ate \ik-ˈstȯr-shə-nət\ *adj* : EXCESSIVE, EXORBITANT — **ex•tor•tion•ate•ly** *adv*
ex•tor•tion•ist *n* ♦ : one that practices or is given to extortion

♦ racketeer

¹ex•tra \ˈek-strə\ *adj* **1** ♦ : more than is due, usual, or necessary **2** : SUPERIOR

♦ excess, spare, superfluous, supernumerary, surplus

²extra *n* ♦ : one that is extra or additional: as **a** : a special edition of a newspaper **b** : an added charge **c** : an additional worker or performer (as in a motion picture)

♦ amenity, comfort, frill, indulgence, luxury, superfluity ♦ bonus, dividend, lagniappe, perquisite, tip

³extra *adv* ♦ : beyond what is usual

♦ extremely, greatly, highly, hugely, mightily, mighty, mortally, most, much, real, right, so, very

¹ex•tract \ik-ˈstrakt, *esp for 3* ˈek-ˌstrakt\ *vb* **1** ♦ : to draw out; *esp* : to pull out forcibly ⟨~ a tooth⟩ **2** : to withdraw (as a juice or a constituent) by a physical or chemical process **3** : to select for citation : QUOTE — **ex•tract•able** *adj* — **ex•trac•tor** \-tər\ *n*

♦ prize, pry, pull, root, tear, uproot, wrest

²ex•tract \ˈek-ˌstrakt\ *n* **1** : EXCERPT, CITATION **2** : a product (as a juice or concentrate) obtained by extracting
ex•trac•tion \ik-ˈstrak-shən\ *n* **1** : the act or process of extracting something **2** ♦ : line of descent

♦ ancestry, birth, descent, line, lineage, origin, parentage

ex•tra•cur•ric•u•lar \ˌek-strə-kə-ˈri-kyə-lər\ *adj* : lying outside the regular curriculum; *esp* : of or relating to school-connected activities (as sports) usually carrying no academic credit
ex•tra•dite \ˈek-strə-ˌdīt\ *vb* **-dit•ed; -dit•ing** : to obtain by or deliver up to extradition
ex•tra•di•tion \ˌek-strə-ˈdi-shən\ *n* : the surrender of an alleged criminal to a different jurisdiction for trial
ex•tra•mar•i•tal \ˌek-strə-ˈmar-ət-ᵊl\ *adj* : of or relating to sexual intercourse by a married person with someone other than his or her spouse
ex•tra•mu•ral \-ˈmyu̇r-əl\ *adj* : existing or functioning beyond the bounds of an organized unit
ex•tra•ne•ous \ek-ˈstrā-nē-əs\ *adj* **1** : coming from without **2** ♦ : not forming a vital part; *also* : IRRELEVANT — **ex•tra•ne•ous•ly** *adv*

♦ immaterial, irrelevant

ex•tra•net \ˈek-strə-ˌnet\ *n* **:** a network like an intranet but also allowing access by certain outside parties

ex•traor•di•nary \ik-ˈstrȯr-də-ˌner-ē, ˌek-strə-ˈȯr-\ *adj* **1** ♦ **:** notably unusual or exceptional ⟨did ~ work on the project⟩ **2 :** employed on special service ⟨an ambassador ~⟩ — **ex•traor•di•nari•ly** \-ˌstrȯr-də-ˈner-ə-lē, ˌek-strə-ˌȯr-\ *adv*

♦ atypical, exceptional, phenomenal, rare, uncustomary, unique, unusual

ex•trap•o•late \ik-ˈstra-pə-ˌlāt\ *vb* **-lat•ed; -lat•ing** ♦ **:** to infer (unknown data) from known data — **ex•trap•o•la•tion** \-ˌstra-pə-ˈlā-shən\ *n*

♦ conclude, deduce, gather, infer, judge, reason, understand

ex•tra•sen•so•ry \ˌek-strə-ˈsen-sə-rē\ *adj* **:** not acting or occurring through the known senses

extrasensory perception *n* **:** perception (as in telepathy) of events external to the self not gained through the senses and not deducible from previous experience

ex•tra•ter•res•tri•al \-tə-ˈres-trē-əl\ *adj* **:** originating or existing outside the earth or its atmosphere ⟨~ life⟩ — **extraterrestrial** *n*

ex•tra•ter•ri•to•ri•al \-ˌter-ə-ˈtōr-ē-əl\ *adj* **:** existing or taking place outside the territorial limits of a jurisdiction

ex•tra•ter•ri•to•ri•al•i•ty \-ˌtōr-ē-ˈa-lə-tē\ *n* **:** exemption from the application or jurisdiction of local law or tribunals ⟨diplomats enjoy ~⟩

ex•trav•a•gance \-gəns\ *n* ♦ **:** an instance of excess or prodigality; *specif* **:** an excessive outlay of money

♦ lavishness, prodigality, wastefulness ***Ant*** economy, frugality

ex•trav•a•gant \ik-ˈstra-vi-gənt\ *adj* **1** ♦ **:** exceeding the limits of reason or necessity **:** EXCESSIVE ⟨~ claims⟩ **2** ♦ **:** spending or tending to spend much more than necessary **:** spending lavishly, recklessly, or wastefully **3 :** too costly

♦ [1] excessive, extreme, immoderate, inordinate, lavish, overmuch, steep, stiff ♦ [2] prodigal, profligate, spendthrift, thriftless, unthrifty, wasteful

ex•trav•a•gant•ly *adv* ♦ **:** in an extravagant manner

♦ expensively, grandly, high, lavishly, luxuriously, opulently, richly

ex•trav•a•gan•za \ik-ˌstra-və-ˈgan-zə\ *n* **1 :** a literary or musical work marked by extreme freedom of style and structure **2 :** a spectacular show

ex•tra•ve•hic•u•lar \ˌek-strə-vē-ˈhi-kyə-lər\ *adj* **:** taking place outside a vehicle (as a spacecraft) ⟨~ activity⟩

¹ex•treme \ik-ˈstrēm\ *adj* **1 :** very great or intense ⟨~ cold⟩ **2 :** very severe or radical ⟨~ measures⟩ **3** ♦ **:** going to great lengths or beyond normal limits ⟨politically ~⟩ **4** ♦ **:** most remote ⟨the ~ end⟩ **5 :** UTMOST; *also* **:** MAXIMUM

♦ [3] excessive, immoderate, inordinate, overmuch, unconscionable ♦ [3] extremist, fanatic, rabid, radical, revolutionary, ultra ***Ant*** middle-of-the-road ♦ [4] farthest, furthest, outermost, ultimate, utmost ***Ant*** inmost, innermost

²extreme *n* **1 :** something located at one end or the other of a range or series **2 :** EXTREMITY 4

ex•treme•ly *adv* ♦ **:** in an extreme manner **:** to an extreme extent

♦ extra, greatly, highly, hugely, mightily, mighty, mortally, most, much, real, right, so, very

extremely low frequency *n* **:** a radio frequency in the lowest range of the radio spectrum

ex•trem•ism \ik-ˈstrē-ˌmi-zəm\ *n* **:** the quality or state of being extreme; *esp* **:** advocacy of extreme political measures

¹ex•trem•ist \-mist\ *n* ♦ **:** an adherent or advocate of extremism

♦ radical, revolutionary

²extremist *adj* ♦ **:** of, relating to, or favoring extremism or extremists

♦ extreme, fanatic, rabid, radical, revolutionary, ultra

ex•trem•i•ty \ik-ˈstre-mə-tē\ *n, pl* **-ties 1** ♦ **:** the most remote part or point **2 :** a limb of the body; *esp* **:** a human hand or foot **3 :** the greatest need or danger **4 :** the utmost degree; *also* **:** a drastic or desperate measure

♦ depth, extremity, limit

ex•tri•cate \ˈek-strə-ˌkāt\ *vb* **-cat•ed; -cat•ing** ♦ **:** to free from an entanglement or difficulty — **ex•tri•ca•ble** \ik-ˈstri-kə-bəl, ek-; ˈek-(ˌ)stri-\ *adj* — **ex•tri•ca•tion** \ˌek-strə-ˈkā-shən\ *n*

♦ clear, disengage, disentangle, free, liberate, release, untangle ***Ant*** embroil, entangle

ex•trin•sic \ek-ˈstrin-zik, -sik\ *adj* **1** ♦ **:** not forming part of or belonging to a thing **2 :** EXTERNAL — **ex•trin•si•cal•ly** \-zi-k(ə-)lē, -si-\ *adv*

♦ adventitious, alien, extraneous, foreign ***Ant*** inherent, innate, intrinsic

ex•tro•vert *also* **ex•tra•vert** \ˈek-strə-ˌvərt\ *n* **:** a gregarious and unreserved person — **ex•tro•ver•sion** *or* **ex•tra•ver•sion** \ˌek-strə-ˈvər-zhən\ *n*

ex•tro•vert•ed *also* **ex•tra•vert•ed** *adj* ♦ **:** having the characteristics of an extrovert **:** marked by extroversion

♦ boon, companionable, convivial, gregarious, outgoing, sociable, social

ex•trude \ik-ˈstrüd\ *vb* **ex•trud•ed; ex•trud•ing 1 :** to force, press, or push out **2 :** to shape (as plastic) by forcing through a die — **ex•tru•sion** \-ˈstrü-zhən\ *n* — **ex•trud•er** *n*

ex•u•ber•ance \-rəns\ *n* **1** ♦ **:** the quality or state of being exuberant **2 :** an exuberant act or expression

♦ [1] animation, briskness, liveliness, lustiness, robustness, sprightliness, vibrancy, vitality

ex•u•ber•ant \ig-ˈzü-bə-rənt\ *adj* **1** ♦ **:** unrestrained in enthusiasm or style **2 :** PROFUSE

♦ bubbly, buoyant, effervescent, frolicsome, high-spirited, vivacious ***Ant*** sullen

ex•u•ber•ant•ly *adv* ♦ **:** in an exuberant manner

♦ gaily, jauntily, sprightly

ex•ude \ig-ˈzüd\ *vb* **ex•ud•ed; ex•ud•ing 1** ♦ **:** to discharge slowly through pores or cuts **:** OOZE **2 :** to display conspicuously or abundantly ⟨~*s* charm⟩ — **ex•u•date** \ˈek-sü-ˌdāt, -syü-\ *n* — **ex•u•da•tion** \ˌek-sü-ˈdā-shən, -syü-\ *n*

♦ bleed, ooze, percolate, seep, strain, sweat, weep

ex•ult \ig-ˈzəlt\ *vb* ♦ **:** to be extremely joyful **:** REJOICE, GLORY — **ex•ul•tant•ly** *adv* — **ex•ul•ta•tion** \ˌek-(ˌ)səl-ˈtā-shən, ˌeg-(ˌ)zəl-\ *n*

♦ crow, delight, glory, joy, rejoice, triumph

ex•ul•tant \-ˈzəlt-ᵊnt\ *adj* ♦ **:** filled with or expressing great joy or triumph

♦ jubilant, rejoicing, triumphant

ex•urb \ˈek-ˌsərb, ˈeg-ˌzərb\ *n* **:** a region outside a city and its suburbs inhabited chiefly by well-to-do families — **ex•ur•ban** \ek-ˈsər-bən, eg-ˈzər-\ *adj*

ex•ur•ban•ite \ek-ˈsər-bə-ˌnīt; eg-ˈzər-\ *n* **:** one who lives in an exurb

ex•ur•bia \ek-ˈsər-bē-ə, eg-ˈzer-\ *n* ♦ **:** the generalized region of exurbs

♦ environs, outskirts, suburbia

-ey — see -Y

¹eye \ˈī\ *n* **1 :** an organ of sight typically consisting in vertebrates of a globular structure that is located in a socket of the skull, is lined with a sensitive retina, and is normally paired **2 :** skill or ability dependent upon eyesight **:** VISION, PERCEPTION; *also* **:** faculty of discrimination ⟨an ~ for bargains⟩ **3 a** ♦ **:** a way of looking at or thinking about something **:** JUDGMENT — often used in plural ⟨in the ~*s* of the law⟩ **b** ♦ **:** an attentive or critical observation **4 a :** something having an appearance suggesting an eye ⟨the ~ of a needle⟩ **b :** an undeveloped bud (as on a potato) **5 a :** the calm center of a cyclone **b** ♦ **:** an important or pivotal point — **eyed** \ˈīd\ *adj*

♦ [3a] belief, conviction, feeling, judgment (*or* judgement), mind, notion, opinion, persuasion, sentiment, verdict, view ♦ [3b] cast, gander, glance, glimpse, look, regard, sight, view ♦ [5b] base, center (*or* centre), core, cynosure, focus, heart, hub, mecca, nucleus, seat

²eye *vb* **eyed; eye•ing** *or* **ey•ing** ♦ **:** to look at

♦ distinguish, espy, look, note, notice, observe, perceive, regard, remark, see, sight, spy, view, witness

¹eye•ball \ˈī-ˌbȯl\ *n* **:** the globular capsule of the vertebrate eye

²eyeball *vb* **:** to look at intently

eye•brow \-ˌbrau̇\ *n* **:** the ridge over the eye or the hair growing on it

eye•drop•per \-ˌdrä-pər\ *n* **:** DROPPER 2

eye•glass \-ˌglas\ *n* ♦ **:** a lens worn to aid vision; *also, pl* **:** GLASSES

♦ **eyeglasses** glasses, spectacles

eye•lash \-ˌlash\ *n* **1 :** the fringe of hair edging the eyelid — usually used in plural **2 :** a single hair of the eyelashes
eye•let \-lət\ *n* **1 :** a small hole intended for ornament or for passage of a cord or lace **2 :** a typically metal ring for reinforcing an eyelet **:** GROMMET
eye•lid \-ˌlid\ *n* **:** either of the movable folds of skin and muscle that can be closed over the eyeball
eye•lin•er \-ˌlī-nər\ *n* **:** makeup used to emphasize the contour of the eyes
eye–open•er \-ˌō-pə-nər\ *n* **:** something startling or surprising
eye–open•ing *adj* ♦ **:** that which opens the eyes (as with astonishment) **:** surprising or enlightening

♦ amazing, astonishing, astounding, startling, stunning, surprising

eye•piece \-ˌpēs\ *n* **:** the lens or combination of lenses at the eye end of an optical instrument
eye shadow *n* **:** a colored cosmetic applied to the eyelids to accent the eyes
eye•sight \-ˌsīt\ *n* **:** the process, power, or function of seeing **:** SIGHT, VISION
eye•sore \-ˌsōr\ *n* ♦ **:** something offensive to view

♦ fright, horror, mess, monstrosity, sight

eye•strain \-ˌstrān\ *n* **:** weariness or a strained state of the eye
eye•tooth \-ˈtüth\ *n* **:** a canine tooth of the upper jaw
eye•wash \-ˌwȯsh, -ˌwäsh\ *n* **1 :** an eye lotion **2 :** misleading or deceptive statements, actions, or procedures
eye•wit•ness \-ˈwit-nəs\ *n* **:** a person who actually sees something happen
Ez *or* **Ezr** *abbr* Ezra
Ezech *abbr* Ezechiel
Eze•chiel \i-ˈzē-kyəl\ *n* **:** EZEKIEL
Ezek *abbr* Ezekiel
Eze•kiel \i-ˈzē-kyəl\ *n* **:** a book of Jewish and Christian Scripture
e–zine \ˈē-ˌzēn\ *n* **:** an online magazine
Ez•ra \ˈez-rə\ *n* **:** a book of Jewish and Christian Scripture

F

¹f \ˈef\ *n, pl* **f's** *or* **fs** \ˈefs\ *often cap* **1 :** the 6th letter of the English alphabet **2 :** a grade rating a student's work as failing
²f *abbr, often cap* **1** Fahrenheit **2** false **3** family **4** farad **5** female **6** feminine **7** forte **8** French **9** frequency **10** Friday
³f *symbol* focal length
F *symbol* fluorine
FAA *abbr* Federal Aviation Administration
fab \ˈfab\ *adj* **:** FABULOUS
Fa•bi•an \ˈfā-bē-ən\ *adj* **:** of, relating to, or being a society of socialists organized in England in 1884 to spread socialist principles gradually — **Fabian** *n* — **Fa•bi•an•ism** *n*
fa•ble \ˈfā-bəl\ *n* **1 :** a legendary story of supernatural happenings **2 :** a narration intended to teach a lesson; *esp* **:** one in which animals speak and act like people **3 :** FALSEHOOD **4 :** the plot, story, or connected series of events forming the theme of a literary work
fa•bled \ˈfā-bəld\ *adj* **1 :** FICTITIOUS **2** ♦ **:** told or celebrated in fable

♦ fabulous, legendary, mythical

fab•ric \ˈfa-brik\ *n* **1 :** STRUCTURE, FRAMEWORK ⟨the ~ of society⟩ **2 :** CLOTH; *also* **:** a material that resembles cloth
fab•ri•cate \ˈfa-bri-ˌkāt\ *vb* **-cat•ed; -cat•ing 1** ♦ **:** to think up or imagine **:** concoct mentally **:** INVENT **2** ♦ **:** to make up for the sake of deception **3 :** to form, make, or create by combining parts or elements **:** CONSTRUCT **4** ♦ **:** to form by art and labor

♦ [1] concoct, contrive, cook up, devise, invent, make up, manufacture, think up ♦ [2] fib, lie, prevaricate ♦ [4] fashion, form, frame, make, manufacture, produce

fab•ri•ca•tion *n* **1** ♦ **:** the invention or utterance of something calculated to deceive **2** ♦ **:** a product of the imagination

♦ [1] falsehood, fib, lie, story, tale, untruth, whopper ♦ [2] fantasy, fiction, figment, invention

fab•u•lous \ˈfa-byə-ləs\ *adj* **1 :** resembling a fable **2** ♦ **:** told in or based on fable **3 :** like the contents of fables in being so marvelous, incredible, absurd, extreme, exaggerated, or approaching the impossible **4 :** not real, actual, or historical **5** ♦ **:** outstanding or remarkable especially in some acceptable or pleasing quality — **fab•u•lous•ly** *adv*

♦ [2] fabled, legendary, mythical ♦ [5] excellent, grand, great, sensational, splendid, superb, superior, swell, terrific, unsurpassed, wonderful

fac *abbr* **1** facsimile **2** faculty
fa•cade *also* **fa•çade** \fə-ˈsäd\ *n* **1 :** the principal face or front of a building **2** ♦ **:** a false, superficial, or artificial appearance or effect ⟨a ~ of composure⟩ **3** ♦ **:** a surface or front

♦ [2] act, airs, front, guise, masquerade, pose, pretense, put-on, semblance, show ♦ [3] face, front

¹face \ˈfās\ *n* **1 :** the front part of the head **2 :** PRESENCE ⟨in the ~ of danger⟩ **3** ♦ **:** facial expression **:** LOOK ⟨put a sad ~ on⟩ **4** ♦ **:** a deliberate or involuntary distortion of the countenance expressive of some feeling **:** GRIMACE ⟨made a ~⟩ **5 :** outward appearance ⟨looks easy on the ~ of it⟩ **6 :** CONFIDENCE; *also* **:** BOLDNESS **7 :** DIGNITY, PRESTIGE ⟨afraid to lose ~⟩ **8** ♦ **:** a front, upper, or outer surface or a surface presented to view or regarded as principal **:** SURFACE; *esp* **:** a front, principal, or bounding surface ⟨~ of a cliff⟩ ⟨the ~*s* of a cube⟩ — **faced** \ˈfāst, ˈfā-səd\ *adj*

♦ [3] cast, countenance, expression, look, visage ♦ [4] frown, grimace, pout, scowl ♦ [8] facade, front ♦ [8] exterior, outside, skin, surface, veneer

²face *vb* **faced; fac•ing 1** ♦ **:** to confront brazenly **2 :** to line near the edge especially with a different material; *also* **:** to cover the front or surface of ⟨~ a building with marble⟩ **3** ♦ **:** to meet or bring in direct contact or confrontation ⟨*faced* the problem⟩ **4** ♦ **:** to stand or sit with the face toward ⟨~ the sun⟩ **5 :** to have the front oriented toward ⟨a house *facing* the park⟩ **6 :** to have as or be a prospect ⟨~ a grim future⟩ **7 :** to turn the face or body in a specified direction **8 :** to bring directly to the attention of — **face the music :** to meet the unpleasant consequences of one's actions

♦ [1] beard, brave, brazen, confront, dare, defy ♦ [3] battle, encounter, engage, meet, take on ♦ [4] front, look, point

face•down \ˌfās-ˈdau̇n\ *adv* **:** with the face downward
face•less \-ləs\ *n* **1 :** lacking a face **2 :** lacking character or individuality
face–lift \ˈfās-ˌlift\ *n* **1 :** plastic surgery on the face and neck to remove defects (as wrinkles) typical of aging **:** a cosmetic surgical operation for removal of facial defects (as wrinkles) typical of aging **2 :** MODERNIZATION — **face–lift** *vb*
face–off \ˈfās-ˌȯf\ *n* **1 :** a method of beginning play by dropping a ball or puck (as in hockey) between two opposing players each of whom attempts to control it **2** ♦ **:** the clashing of forces or ideas **:** CONFRONTATION

♦ battle, combat, conflict, confrontation, contest, duel, rivalry, struggle

face off *vb* ♦ **:** to be or come into opposition or competition

♦ battle, compete, contend, fight, race, vie

fac•et \ˈfa-sət\ *n* **1 :** a small plane surface of a cut gem **2** ♦ **:** any of the definable aspects that make up a subject (as of contemplation) or an object (as of consideration) **:** ASPECT, PHASE

♦ [2] angle, aspect, hand, phase, side

fa•ce•tious \fə-ˈsē-shəs\ *adj* **1** ♦ **:** joking often inappropriately **2** ♦ **:** characterized by pleasantry or levity **:** exciting laughter **:** JOCULAR — **fa•ce•tious•ly** *adv*

♦ [1] flip, flippant, pert, smart ♦ [2] clever, humorous, jocular, smart, witty

fa•ce•tious•ness *n* ♦ **:** the quality or state of being facetious

♦ flightiness, flippancy, frivolity, levity, lightness

¹fa•cial \ˈfā-shəl\ *adj* **1 :** of or relating to the face **2 :** used to improve the appearance of the face
²facial *n* **:** a facial treatment
fac•ile \ˈfa-səl\ *adj* **1** ♦ **:** easily accomplished, handled, or attained **2 :** SIMPLISTIC **3 :** readily manifested and often insincere ⟨~ prose⟩ **4 :** READY, FLUENT ⟨a ~ writer⟩

♦ easy, effortless, fluent, fluid, light, painless, ready, simple, smooth, snap, soft

fa•cil•i•tate \fə-ˈsi-lə-ˌtāt\ *vb* **-tat•ed; -tat•ing** ♦ **:** to make easier — **fa•cil•i•ta•tion** \-ˌsi-lə-ˈtā-shən\ *n* — **fa•cil•i•ta•tor** \-ˈsi-lə-ˌtā-tər\ *n*

♦ ease, loosen, smooth, unclog

fa•cil•i•ty \fə-ˈsi-lə-tē\ *n, pl* **-ties 1 :** the quality of being easily performed **2 :** ease in performance **:** APTITUDE **3 :** PLIANCY **4 :** something that makes easier an action, operation, or course of conduct; *also* **:** REST ROOM — often used in plural **5** ♦ **:** something (as a hospital) built or installed for a particular purpose

♦ complex, establishment, installation

fac•ing \ˈfā-siŋ\ *n* **1 :** a lining at the edge especially of a garment **2** *pl* **:** the collar, cuffs, and trimmings of a uniform coat **3 :** an ornamental or protective layer **4 :** material for facing
fac•sim•i•le \fak-ˈsi-mə-lē\ *n* **1** ♦ **:** an exact copy **2 :** a system of transmitting and reproducing printed matter or pictures by means of signals sent over telephone lines

♦ carbon copy, double, duplicate, image, match, replica, reproduction

fact \ˈfakt\ *n* **1 :** DEED; *esp* **:** CRIME ⟨accessory after the ~⟩ **2 :** the quality of being actual **3 :** something that exists or occurs **4** ♦ **:** a piece of information — **in fact :** in truth

♦ detail, particular, point

fac•tion \ˈfak-shən\ *n* ♦ **:** a group or combination (as in a government) acting together within and usually against a larger body — **fac•tion•al•ism** \-shə-nə-ˌli-zəm\ *n*

♦ bloc, body, coalition, combination, combine, party, sect, set, side, wing

fac•tious \ˈfak-shəs\ *adj* **1 :** of, relating to, or caused by faction **2 :** inclined to faction or the formation of factions **:** causing dissension
fac•ti•tious \fak-ˈti-shəs\ *adj* **1 a** ♦ **:** produced by human art, skill, or effort **b** ♦ **:** not natural or real **:** SHAM ⟨a ~ display of grief⟩ **2 :** not natural or spontaneous

♦ artificial, fake, faux, imitation, mock, sham, synthetic

fac•toid \ˈfak-ˌtȯid\ *n* **1 :** an invented fact believed to be true because of its appearance in print **2 :** a brief usually trivial fact
¹fac•tor \ˈfak-tər\ *n* **1** ♦ **:** a person that acts or transacts business for another **:** AGENT **2** ♦ **:** something that actively contributes to a result ⟨a ~ in her decision⟩ **3 :** GENE **4 :** any of the numbers or symbols in mathematics that when multiplied together form a product; *esp* **:** any of the integers that divide a given integer without a remainder

♦ [1] agent, attorney, delegate, deputy, representative ♦ [2] component, constituent, element, ingredient, member

²factor *vb* **1 :** to work as a factor **2 :** to find the mathematical factors of and especially the prime mathematical factors of
¹fac•to•ri•al \fak-ˈtȯr-ē-əl\ *adj* **:** of, relating to, or being a factor
²factorial *n* **:** the product of all the positive integers from 1 to a given integer *n*
fac•to•ry \ˈfak-trē, -tə-rē\ *n, pl* **-ries 1 :** a trading post where resident brokers trade **2** ♦ **:** a building or group of buildings used for manufacturing

♦ mill, plant, shop, works, workshop

fac•to•tum \fak-ˈtō-təm\ *n* **:** a person (as a servant) having numerous or varied duties
facts of life : the physiological processes and behavior involved in sex and reproduction
fac•tu•al \ˈfak-chə-wəl\ *adj* **1** ♦ **:** of or relating to facts **2** ♦ **:** based on fact — **fac•tu•al•ly** *adv*

♦ [1] actual, concrete, existent, real, true, very ♦ [2] documentary, literal, nonfictional, objective, true

fac•ul•ty \ˈfa-kəl-tē\ *n, pl* **-ties 1 a** ♦ **:** ability to act or do **b** ♦ **:** natural aptitude **2 :** one of the powers of the mind or body ⟨the ~ of hearing⟩ **3 :** the teachers in a school or college or one of its divisions

♦ [1a] ability, capability, capacity, competence ♦ [1b] aptitude, endowment, flair, genius, gift, knack, talent

fad \ˈfad\ *n* ♦ **:** a practice or interest followed for a time with exaggerated zeal **:** CRAZE — **fad•dist** *n*

♦ craze, mode, rage, style, trend, vogue

fad•dish \ˈfa-dish\ *adj* ♦ **:** constituting or resembling a fad — **fad•dish•ly** *adv*

♦ fashionable, hot, in, modish, popular, vogue

¹fade \ˈfād\ *vb* **fad•ed; fad•ing 1 :** WITHER **2** ♦ **:** to lose or cause to lose freshness or brilliance of color **3** ♦ **:** to sink away **:** VANISH **4 :** to grow dim or faint

♦ [2] blanch, bleach, blench, dull, pale, wash out, whiten ♦ [3] disappear, dissolve, evaporate, flee, go, melt, vanish

²fade *n* **:** a short haircut in which hair on top of the head stands high
FADM *abbr* fleet admiral
fae•cal, fae•ces *chiefly Brit var of* FECAL, FECES
fa•er•ie *also* **fa•ery** \ˈfā-rē, ˈfar-ē\ *n, pl* **fa•er•ies 1 :** FAIRYLAND **2 :** FAIRY
¹fag \ˈfag\ *vb* **fagged; fag•ging 1 :** to work hard **:** DRUDGE **2 :** to act as a fag **3** ♦ **:** to tire by strenuous activity **:** TIRE, EXHAUST

♦ burn out, do in, drain, exhaust, fatigue, tire, tucker, wash out, wear, wear out, weary

²fag *n* ♦ **:** one who is obliged to do menial work **:** DRUDGE

♦ drudge, peon, slave, toiler, worker

³fag *n* **:** an English public-school boy who acts as servant to another
⁴fag *vb* **:** to act as a fag
⁵fag *n* **:** CIGARETTE
fag end *n* **1** ♦ **:** a worn, poor, or useless ending or remnant unlikely to afford either pleasure or profit **:** REMNANT **2 :** the extreme end **3 :** the last part or coarser end of a web of cloth **4 :** the untwisted end of a rope

♦ end, leftover, remainder, remnant, scrap

fag•ot *or* **fag•got** \ˈfa-gət\ *n* **:** a bundle of sticks or twigs
fag•ot•ing *or* **fag•got•ing** *n* **:** an embroidery produced by tying threads in hourglass-shaped clusters
Fah *or* **Fahr** *abbr* Fahrenheit
Fahr•en•heit \ˈfar-ən-ˌhīt\ *adj* **:** relating to, conforming to, or having a thermometer scale with the boiling point of water at 212 degrees and the freezing point at 32 degrees above zero
fa•ience *or* **fa•ïence** \fā-ˈäns\ *n* **:** earthenware decorated with opaque colored glazes
¹fail \ˈfāl\ *vb* **1** ♦ **:** to become feeble; *esp* **:** to decline in health **2 :** to die away **3** ♦ **:** to stop functioning **4** ♦ **:** to fall short ⟨~*ed* in his duty⟩ **5 :** to be or become absent or inadequate **6** ♦ **:** to be unsuccessful **7 :** to become bankrupt **8** ♦ **:** to disappoint the expectations or trust of **9 :** NEGLECT

♦ [1] decay, droop, flag, go, lag, languish, sag, waste, weaken, wilt ♦ [3] break, break down, conk, crash, cut out, die, stall ***Ant*** start (up) ♦ [4, 8] cheat, disappoint, dissatisfy, let down ♦ [6] collapse, flop, flunk, fold, wash out ***Ant*** succeed

²fail *n* **:** FAILURE ⟨without ~⟩
¹fail•ing \ˈfā-liŋ\ *n* ♦ **:** a usually slight or insignificant defect in character, conduct, or ability **:** WEAKNESS, SHORTCOMING

♦ demerit, fault, foible, frailty, shortcoming, vice, weakness

²failing *prep* **:** in the absence or lack of
faille \ˈfī(-ə)l\ *n* **:** a somewhat shiny closely woven ribbed fabric (as silk)
fail–safe \ˈfāl-ˌsāf\ *adj* **1 :** incorporating a counteractive feature for a possible source of failure **2 :** having no chance of failure — **fail–safe** *n*
fail•ure \ˈfāl-yər\ *n* **1** ♦ **:** a failing to do or perform **2 :** a state of inability to perform a normal function adequately ⟨heart ~⟩; *also* **:** an abrupt cessation of functioning ⟨a power ~⟩ **3 :** a fracturing or giving way under stress **4** ♦ **:** a lack of success **5 :** BANKRUPTCY **6** ♦ **:** a falling short **:** DEFICIENCY **7 :** DETERIORATION, DECAY **8** ♦ **:** one that has failed

♦ [1] default, delinquency, dereliction, neglect, negligence, oversight ♦ [4] collapse, crash, cropper, defeat, fizzle, nonsuccess ***Ant*** accomplishment, achievement, success ♦ [6] dearth, deficiency, deficit, famine, inadequacy, insufficiency, lack, paucity, poverty, scantiness, scarcity, shortage, want ♦ [8] bust, catastrophe, debacle, dud, fiasco, fizzle, flop, loser, washout ***Ant*** hit, smash, success, winner

[1]**fain** \ˈfān\ *adj* **1** *archaic* **:** GLAD; *also* **:** INCLINED **2 :** being obliged or compelled

[2]**fain** *adv* **1 :** with pleasure **2 :** by preference

[1]**faint** \ˈfānt\ *adj* **1 :** COWARDLY, SPIRITLESS **2 :** weak, dizzy, and likely to faint **3** ♦ **:** lacking vigor or strength **:** FEEBLE ⟨∼ praise⟩ **4** ♦ **:** hardly perceptible **:** INDISTINCT, DIM — **faint•ly** *adv*

♦ [3] delicate, feeble, frail, infirm, slight, soft, wasted, weak ♦ [4] bleary, dim, foggy, fuzzy, hazy, indistinct, obscure, opaque, shadowy, unclear, vague *Ant* clear, definite

[2]**faint** *vb* ♦ **:** to lose consciousness

♦ black out, pass out, swoon *Ant* come around, come round, come to, revive

[3]**faint** *n* **1 :** the action of fainting **2** ♦ **:** the condition of one who has fainted

♦ blackout, knockout, swoon

faint•heart•ed \ˌfānt-ˈhär-təd\ *adj* ♦ **:** lacking courage **:** TIMID

♦ fearful, mousy, shy, skittish, timid

faint•ness *n* ♦ **:** the quality or state of being faint; *esp* **:** a loss of strength or near loss of consciousness

♦ debility, feebleness, frailty, infirmity, languor, weakness

[1]**fair** \ˈfer\ *adj* **1** ♦ **:** pleasing in appearance **:** BEAUTIFUL **2 :** superficially pleasing **:** SPECIOUS **3 :** CLEAN, PURE **4 :** CLEAR, LEGIBLE **5** ♦ **:** not stormy or cloudy **6** ♦ **:** marked by impartiality and honesty **:** free from self-interest, prejudice, or favoritism **:** JUST **7 :** conforming with the rules **:** ALLOWED; *also* **:** being within the foul lines ⟨∼ ball⟩ **8 :** open to legitimate pursuit or attack ⟨∼ game⟩ **9 :** giving promise of success or excellence **:** PROMISING, LIKELY ⟨a ∼ chance of winning⟩ **10 :** favorable to a ship's course ⟨a ∼ wind⟩ **11** ♦ **:** light colored **12** ♦ **:** of middling quality **13 :** significant in size ⟨a ∼ amount of traffic⟩ — **fairness** *n*

♦ [1] attractive, beautiful, cute, handsome, lovely, pretty ♦ [5] clear, cloudless, sunny, sunshiny, unclouded *Ant* bleak, cloudy, overcast, stormy, sunless ♦ [6] disinterested, dispassionate, equal, equitable, impartial, just, nonpartisan, objective, square, unbiased, unprejudiced *Ant* biased, partisan, prejudiced, unequal, unjust ♦ [11] blond, flaxen, golden, sandy, straw ♦ [12] common, indifferent, mediocre, medium, middling, ordinary, passable, run-of-the-mill, second-rate, so-so

[2]**fair** *adv* **1 :** in a fair manner ⟨play ∼⟩ **2** *chiefly Brit* **:** FAIRLY 4

[3]**fair** *n* **1** ♦ **:** a gathering of buyers and sellers at a stated time and place for trade **2** ♦ **:** a competitive exhibition (as of farm products) **3** ♦ **:** a sale of assorted articles usually for a charitable purpose **4** ♦ **:** an exhibition designed to promote available or planned products or services ⟨a book ∼⟩ ⟨a job ∼⟩

♦ [1, 2, 3, 4] display, exhibit, exhibition, exposition, show

fair•ground \-ˌgrau̇nd\ *n* **:** an area where outdoor fairs, circuses, or exhibitions are held

fair•ing \ˈfar-iŋ\ *n* **:** a structure for producing a smooth outline and reducing drag (as on an airplane)

fair•ly \ˈfar-lē\ *adv* **1 :** HANDSOMELY **2 :** in a manner of speaking ⟨∼ bursting with pride⟩ **3 :** without bias **4 :** to a full degree or extent **:** PLAINLY, DISTINCTLY **5** ♦ **:** moderately well **:** SOMEWHAT, RATHER ⟨a ∼ easy job⟩

♦ enough, kind of, moderately, pretty, quite, rather, so-so, somewhat, sort of

fair–spo•ken \ˈfar-ˈspō-kən\ *adj* **:** pleasant and courteous in speech

fair–trade \-ˈtrād\ *adj* **:** of, relating to, or being an agreement between a producer and a seller that branded merchandise will be sold at or above a specified price — **fair–trade** *vb*

fair•way \-ˌwā\ *n* **:** the mowed part of a golf course between tee and green

fairy \ˈfer-ē\ *n, pl* **fair•ies** ♦ **:** an imaginary being of folklore and romance usually having diminutive human form and magic powers — **fairy** *adj*

♦ brownie, dwarf, elf, fay, gnome, hobgoblin, leprechaun, pixie, puck, troll

fairy•land \-ˌland\ *n* **1 :** the land of fairies **2 :** a beautiful or charming place

fairy tale *n* **1 :** a children's story usually about mythical beings (as fairies) **2** ♦ **:** an implausible, incredible, or lying story **:** a statement designed to delude or mislead **:** FIB

♦ fabrication, falsehood, falsity, fib, lie, story, untruth

fait ac•com•pli \ˈfāt-ˌa-ˌkōⁿ-ˈplē\ *n, pl* **faits accomplis** *same or* -ˈplēz\ **:** a thing accomplished and presumably irreversible

faith \ˈfāth\ *n, pl* **faiths** \ˈfāths, ˈfāt͟hz\ **1** ♦ **:** allegiance to duty or a person **:** LOYALTY **2** ♦ **:** belief and trust in God **3** ♦ **:** complete trust **4** ♦ **:** a system of religious beliefs

♦ [1] allegiance, constancy, dedication, devotion, faithfulness, fastness, fealty, fidelity, loyalty, steadfastness ♦ [2] devotion, piety, religion *Ant* atheism, godlessness ♦ [3] confidence, credence, stock, trust ♦ [4] creed, cult, persuasion, religion

faith•ful \-fəl\ *adj* **1** ♦ **:** true and constant in affection or allegiance **2** ♦ **:** conforming to the facts or to an original — **faith•ful•ly** *adv*

♦ [1] constant, devoted, loyal, pious, staunch, steadfast, steady, true, true-blue *Ant* disloyal, false, fickle, inconstant, perfidious, traitorous, treacherous ♦ [2] accurate, authentic, exact, precise, right, strict, true, veracious *Ant* false, imprecise, inaccurate, inexact

faith•ful•ness *n* ♦ **:** the quality or state of being faithful

♦ allegiance, constancy, dedication, devotion, fealty, fidelity, loyalty, steadfastness

faith•less \ˈfāth-ləs\ *adj* **1** ♦ **:** false to promises or agreements **:** DISLOYAL **2 :** not to be relied on — **faith•less•ly** *adv*

♦ disloyal, false, fickle, inconstant, perfidious, traitorous, treacherous, unfaithful, untrue *Ant* constant, devoted, loyal, staunch, steadfast, steady, true

faith•less•ness *n* ♦ **:** the quality or condition of being faithless

♦ betrayal, disloyalty, falsity, infidelity, perfidy, treachery, treason

fa•ji•ta \fə-ˈhē-tə\ *n* **:** a marinated strip usually of beef or chicken grilled or broiled and served usually with a flour tortilla and savory fillings

[1]**fake** \ˈfāk\ *adj* ♦ **:** one that is not what it purports to be **:** SHAM

♦ bogus, counterfeit, false, inauthentic, phony, sham, spurious ♦ artificial, faux, imitation, mock, sham, synthetic

[2]**fake** *n* **1 a** ♦ **:** someone or something that is not genuine **b** ♦ **:** one that assumes false identity or title for the purpose of deception **2 :** a simulated move in sports (as a pretended pass)

♦ [1a] counterfeit, forgery, hoax, humbug, phony, sham ♦ [1b] charlatan, fraud, hoaxer, humbug, phony, pretender, quack

[3]**fake** *vb* **faked; fak•ing** **1 :** to treat so as to falsify **2** ♦ **:** to counterfeit or make a counterfeit of in order to deceive **3 :** to deceive (an opponent) in a sports contest by making a fake — **fak•er** *n*

♦ affect, assume, counterfeit, feign, pretend, profess, put on, sham, simulate

fa•kir \fə-ˈkir\ *n* **1 :** a Muslim mendicant **:** DERVISH **2 :** a wandering Hindu ascetic

fal•con \ˈfal-kən, ˈfȯl-\ *n* **1 :** a hawk trained for use in falconry **2 :** any of various swift long-winged long-tailed hawks having a notched beak and usually inhabiting open areas

fal•con•ry \ˈfal-kən-rē, ˈfȯl-\ *n* **1 :** the art of training hawks to hunt in cooperation with a person **2 :** the sport of hunting with hawks — **fal•con•er** *n*

[1]**fall** \ˈfȯl\ *vb* **fell** \ˈfel\; **fall•en** \ˈfȯ-lən\; **fall•ing** **1** ♦ **:** to descend freely by the force of gravity **2 :** to hang freely **3 :** to come or go as if by falling ⟨darkness *fell*⟩ **4 :** to become uttered **5** ♦ **:** to lower or become lowered **:** DROP ⟨her eyes *fell*⟩ **6** ♦ **:** to leave an erect position suddenly and involuntarily **7 :** STUMBLE, STRAY **8 :** to drop down wounded or dead especially in battle **9** ♦ **:** to become captured ⟨the city *fell* to the enemy⟩ **10 :** to suffer ruin, defeat, or failure **11 :** to commit an immoral act **12 :** to move or extend in a downward direction **13** ♦ **:** to become quiet or less **:** SUBSIDE, ABATE **14 :** to decline in quality, activity, quantity, or value **15 :** to assume a look of shame or dejection ⟨her face *fell*⟩ **16 :** to occur at a certain time **17 :** to come by chance **18 :** DEVOLVE ⟨the duties *fell* to him⟩ **19 :** to have the proper place or station ⟨the accent ∼*s* on the first syllable⟩ **20 :** to come within the scope of something **21 :** to pass from one condition to another ⟨*fell* ill⟩ **22 :** to set about heartily or actively ⟨∼ to work⟩ — **fall all over oneself** *or* **fall over backward :** to display excessive eagerness — **fall flat :** to produce no response or result — **fall for 1 :** to fall in love with **2 :** to become a victim of — **fall foul :** to have a quarrel **:** CLASH — **fall from grace :** BACKSLIDE — **fall into line :** to comply with a certain course of action — **fall short 1 :** to be deficient **2 :** to fail to attain

♦ [1, 5] decline, descend, drop, lower, settle, sink *Ant* rise ♦ [6] slip, stumble, topple, trip, tumble *Ant* get up, rise, stand (up) ♦ [9] capitulate, give up, knuckle under, submit, succumb, surrender *Ant* stand ♦ [13] abate, decline, decrease, diminish, dwindle, ebb, lessen, recede, subside, wane

[2]**fall** *n* **1** ♦ **:** the act of falling **2 :** a falling out, off, or away **:** DROPPING **3 :** AUTUMN **4 :** a thing or quantity that falls ⟨a light ~ of snow⟩ ⟨a ~ of 20% in the value of the stock⟩ **5** ♦ **:** loss of greatness, power, status, influence, or dominion **6 :** the surrender or capture of a besieged place **7 :** departure from virtue or goodness **8 :** SLOPE **9 :** WATERFALL — usually used in plural **10** ♦ **:** a decrease in size, quantity, degree, or value ⟨a ~ in price⟩ **11 :** the distance which something falls **12 :** an act of forcing a wrestler's shoulders to the mat; *also* **:** a bout of wrestling

♦ [1] descent, dip, dive, down, drop, plunge ♦ [1] slip, spill, stumble, tumble ♦ [5] comedown, decline, descent, down, downfall ♦ [5] decline, degradation ♦ [10] decline, decrease, drop, loss, reduction, shrinkage

fal•la•cious \fə-ˈlā-shəs\ *adj* **1** ♦ **:** embodying a fallacy ⟨a ~ argument⟩ **2** ♦ **:** tending to deceive or mislead

♦ [1] illogical, invalid, irrational, unsound, weak ♦ [2] deceptive, false, misleading, specious

fal•la•cy \ˈfa-lə-sē\ *n, pl* **-cies 1** ♦ **:** a false or mistaken idea **2 :** an often plausible argument using false or illogical reasoning **3 :** erroneous or fallacious character

♦ error, falsehood, falsity, illusion, misconception, myth, untruth *Ant* truth, verity

fall back *vb* ♦ **:** to give way **:** RETREAT, RECEDE

♦ back, recede, retire, retreat, withdraw

fall guy *n* **1 :** one that is easily duped **2 :** one who assumes or on whom is placed the blame or responsibility **:** SCAPEGOAT

fal•li•ble \ˈfa-lə-bəl\ *adj* **1 :** liable to be erroneous **2 :** capable of making a mistake — **fal•li•bly** \-blē\ *adv*

fall•ing–out \ˌfȯ-liŋ-ˈau̇t\ *n, pl* **fallings–out** *or* **falling–outs :** QUARREL

falling star *n* **:** METEOR

fal•lo•pi•an tube \fə-ˈlō-pē-ən-\ *n, often cap F* **:** either of the pair of anatomical tubes that carry the eggs from the ovary to the uterus

fall•out \ˈfȯ-ˌlau̇t\ *n* **1 :** the often radioactive particles that result from a nuclear explosion and descend through the air **2 :** a secondary and often lingering effect or result

fall out *vb* ♦ **:** to have a quarrel **:** QUARREL

♦ argue, bicker, dispute, quarrel, row, scrap, spat, squabble, wrangle

[1]**fal•low** \ˈfa-(ˌ)lō\ *n* **:** fallow land; *also* **:** the state or period of being fallow — **fallow** *vb*

[2]**fallow** *adj* **1 :** left without tilling or sowing after plowing **2** ♦ **:** characterized by a state of creative or recuperative rest or dormancy **:** DORMANT, INACTIVE ⟨a writer's ~ period⟩

♦ dead, dormant, idle, inactive, inert, inoperative

false \ˈfȯls\ *adj* **fals•er; fals•est 1** ♦ **:** not genuine **:** artificially made or assumed **2 :** intentionally untrue **3** ♦ **:** adjusted or made so as to deceive ⟨~ scales⟩ **4 a** ♦ **:** tending to mislead **:** DECEPTIVE ⟨~ promises⟩ **b** ♦ **:** assumed or designed to deceive **5** ♦ **:** not true ⟨~ concepts⟩ **6** ♦ **:** not faithful or loyal **:** TREACHEROUS **7 :** not essential or permanent ⟨~ front⟩ **8 :** inaccurate in pitch **9 :** based on mistaken ideas — **false•ly** *adv*

♦ [1] artificial, bogus, fake, imitation, mechanical, mock, phony, sham, synthetic, unnatural ♦ [3, 4b] counterfeit, crooked, deceitful, dishonest, fraudulent, phony, sham, spurious ♦ [4a] deceitful, deceptive, misleading, specious ♦ [5] erroneous, inaccurate, incorrect, inexact, untrue, wrong *Ant* accurate, correct, right, sound, true ♦ [6] disloyal, faithless, traitorous, treacherous, unfaithful

false•hood \ˈfȯls-ˌhu̇d\ *n* **1** ♦ **:** something that is untrue; *esp* **:** an untrue statement **:** LIE **2 :** absence of truth or accuracy **3 :** the practice of lying

♦ error, fallacy, falsity, illusion, misconception, myth, untruth ♦ fabrication, fairy tale, falsity, fib, lie, mendacity, prevarication, story, tale, untruth, whopper

false•ness *n* **1** ♦ **:** the quality or state of being false **2** ♦ **:** an instance of treachery **:** an act of perfidy or treason

♦ [1] fallacy, falsity, untruth ♦ [2] betrayal, disloyalty, infidelity, perfidy, treachery, treason, unfaithfulness

fal•set•to \fȯl-ˈse-tō\ *n, pl* **-tos :** an artificially high voice; *esp* **:** an artificial singing voice that overlaps and extends above the range of the full voice especially of a tenor

fal•si•fy \ˈfȯl-sə-ˌfī\ *vb* **-fied; -fy•ing 1 :** to prove to be false **2** ♦ **:** to alter so as to deceive **3 :** LIE; *also* **:** MISREPRESENT — **fal•si•fi•able** \ˌfȯl-sə-ˈfī-ə-bəl\ *adj* — **fal•si•fi•ca•tion** \ˌfȯl-sə-fə-ˈkā-shən\ *n*

♦ color (*or* colour), distort, garble, misinterpret, misrepresent, misstate, pervert, twist, warp

fal•si•ty \ˈfȯl-sə-tē\ *n* **1** ♦ **:** something false **2** ♦ **:** the quality or state of being false

♦ [1] fallacy, falsehood, fib, lie, myth, tale, untruth ♦ [2] betrayal, disloyalty, infidelity, perfidy, treachery, treason, unfaithfulness

fal•ter \ˈfȯl-tər\ *vb* **1** ♦ **:** to move unsteadily **:** TOTTER **2 :** to hesitate in speech **:** STAMMER **3** ♦ **:** to hesitate in purpose or action **:** WAVER **4 :** to lose effectiveness ⟨a *~ing* business⟩ — **fal•ter•ing•ly** *adv*

♦ [1] seesaw, sway, teeter, totter, waver, wobble ♦ [3] hesitate, shilly-shally, teeter, vacillate, waver

fam *abbr* **1** familiar **2** family

fame \ˈfām\ *n* ♦ **:** public reputation **:** RENOWN

♦ celebrity, notoriety, renown *Ant* anonymity, obscurity

famed \ˈfāmd\ *adj* ♦ **:** known widely and well

♦ celebrated, famous, noted, prominent, renowned, well-known

fa•mil•ial \fə-ˈmil-yəl\ *adj* **1 :** of, relating to, or suggestive of a family **2 :** tending to occur in more members of a family than expected by chance alone ⟨a ~ disorder⟩

[1]**fa•mil•iar** \fə-ˈmil-yər\ *n* **1** ♦ **:** an intimate associate **2 :** a spirit held to attend and serve or guard a person **3 :** one who frequents a place

♦ comrade, friend, intimate

[2]**familiar** *adj* **1** ♦ **:** closely acquainted **:** INTIMATE **2 :** of or relating to a family **3 :** INFORMAL **4** ♦ **:** overly free and unrestrained **:** PRESUMPTUOUS **5** ♦ **:** frequently seen or experienced **6 :** of everyday occurrence **7** ♦ **:** having personal or intimate knowledge — often used with *with* — **fa•mil•iar•ly** *adv*

♦ [1] chummy, close, friendly, intimate, thick *Ant* distant ♦ [4] bold, forward, free, immodest, presumptuous ♦ [5] common, customary, everyday, frequent, ordinary, routine, usual ♦ [7] conversant, informed, knowledgeable, up-to-date *Ant* ignorant, unacquainted, unfamiliar, uninformed

fa•mil•iar•ise *Brit var of* FAMILIARIZE

fa•mil•iar•i•ty \fə-ˌmil-ˈyar-ə-tē, -ˌmi-lē-ˈar-\ *n, pl* **-ties 1** ♦ **:** close friendship **:** INTIMACY **2 :** INFORMALITY **3** ♦ **:** an unduly bold or forward act or expression **:** IMPROPRIETY **4 :** close acquaintance with something

♦ [1] closeness, intimacy, nearness *Ant* distance ♦ [3] gaffe, impropriety, indiscretion

fa•mil•iar•ize \fə-ˈmil-yə-ˌrīz\ *vb* **-ized; -iz•ing 1 :** to make known through experience or repetition **:** remove strangeness from **2** ♦ **:** to make (someone) thoroughly acquainted

♦ acquaint, apprise, brief, clue, enlighten, fill in, inform, instruct, tell

fam•i•ly \ˈfam-lē, ˈfa-mə-\ *n, pl* **-lies 1 :** a group of individuals living under one roof and under one head **:** HOUSEHOLD **2** ♦ **:** a group of persons of common ancestry **:** CLAN **3** ♦ **:** a group of things having common characteristics; *esp* **:** a group of related plants or animals ranking in biological classification above a genus and below an order **4 :** a social unit usually consisting of one or two parents and their children

♦ [2] blood, clan, folks, house, kin, kindred, kinfolk, line, lineage, people, race, stock, tribe ♦ [3] category, class, division, group, kind, set, type

family planning *n* **:** planning intended to determine the number and spacing of one's children by using birth control

family tree *n* ♦ **:** an account or history of the descent of a person, family, or group from an ancestor or ancestors or from older forms **:** GENEALOGY; *also* **:** a genealogical diagram

♦ ancestry, bloodline, descent, genealogy, lineage, origin

fam•ine \ˈfa-mən\ *n* **1 :** an extreme scarcity of food **2** ♦ **:** a great shortage

♦ dearth, deficiency, deficit, failure, inadequacy, insufficiency, lack, paucity, poverty, scantiness, scarcity, shortage, want

fam•ish \ˈfa-mish\ *vb* **1 :** STARVE **2 :** to suffer for lack of something necessary
fam•ished *adj* ♦ **:** intensely hungry

♦ empty, hungry

fa•mous \ˈfā-məs\ *adj* **1** ♦ **:** widely known **2 :** honored for achievement **3 :** EXCELLENT, FIRST-RATE

♦ celebrated, famed, noted, notorious, prominent, renowned, well-known *Ant* anonymous, obscure, unknown

fa•mous•ly *adv* **:** SPLENDIDLY, EXCELLENTLY
1fan \ˈfan\ *n* **:** a device (as a hand-waved triangular piece or a mechanism with blades) for producing a current of air
2fan *vb* **fanned; fan•ning 1 :** to drive away the chaff from grain by winnowing **2 :** to move (air) with or as if with a fan **3 :** to direct a current of air upon ⟨~ a fire⟩ **4 :** to stir up to activity **:** STIMULATE **5** ♦ **:** to spread like a fan — often used with *out* **6 :** to strike out in baseball

♦ *usu* **fan out** expand, extend, flare, open, radiate, spread, unfold

3fan *n* ♦ **:** an enthusiastic follower or admirer

♦ addict, aficionado, buff, devotee, enthusiast, fancier, lover

1fa•nat•ic \fə-ˈna-tik\ *or* **fa•nat•i•cal** \-ti-kəl\ *adj* ♦ **:** marked by excessive enthusiasm and often intense uncritical devotion — **fa•nat•i•cism** \-tə-ˌsi-zəm\ *n*

♦ extreme, extremist, rabid, radical, revolutionary, ultra

2fa•nat•ic *n* ♦ **:** a person who is ardently attached to a cause, object, or pursuit; *esp* **:** a person exhibiting excessive enthusiasm and intense uncritical devotion usually toward some controversial matter

♦ crusader, militant, partisan, zealot

fan•ci•er \ˈfan-sē-ər\ *n* **1** ♦ **:** one that has a special liking or interest **2 :** a person who breeds or grows some kind of animal or plant for points of excellence

♦ aficionado, buff, devotee, enthusiast, fan, lover

fan•ci•ful \ˈfan-si-fəl\ *adj* **1** ♦ **:** marked by, existing in, or given to unrestrained imagination or whim rather than reason **2 :** curiously made or shaped — **fan•ci•ful•ly** *adv*

♦ fantastic, fictitious, imaginary, made-up, pretend, unreal

1fan•cy \ˈfan-sē\ *vb* **fan•cied; fan•cy•ing 1** ♦ **:** to be pleased with especially on account of external appearance or manners **:** LIKE **2** ♦ **:** to form a conception of **:** IMAGINE **3 :** to believe without evidence or certainty **4 :** to visualize or interpret as

♦ [1] delight, enjoy, like, love, relish ♦ [2] conceive, imagine, picture, visualize

2fancy *n, pl* **fancies 1** ♦ **:** amorous fondness **:** love or desire; *also* **:** LOVE **2** ♦ **:** an opinion or notion formed without much reflection **:** WHIM, NOTION ⟨a passing ~⟩ **3** ♦ **:** an image or representation of something formed in the mind **4 :** TASTE, JUDGMENT

♦ [1] favor (*or* favour), fondness, like, liking, love, partiality, preference ♦ [2] caprice, notion, whim ♦ [3] chimera, conceit, delusion, dream, fantasy, figment, hallucination, illusion, phantasm, pipe dream, unreality, vision

3fancy *adj* **fan•ci•er; -est 1 :** WHIMSICAL **2 :** not plain **:** ornamented and often elegant **3 :** of particular excellence **4 :** bred especially for a showy appearance **5 :** EXCESSIVE **6** ♦ **:** executed with technical skill and style — **fan•ci•ly** \ˈfan-sə-lē\ *adv*

♦ complex, complicated, detailed, elaborate, intricate

fancy dress *n* **:** a costume (as for a masquerade) chosen to suit a fancy
fan•cy–free \ˌfan-sē-ˈfrē\ *adj* **:** free from amorous attachment; *also* **:** free to imagine
fan•cy•work \ˈfan-sē-ˌwərk\ *n* **:** ornamental needlework (as embroidery)
fan•dan•go \fan-ˈdaŋ-gō\ *n, pl* **-gos 1 :** a lively Spanish or Spanish-American dance **2 :** TOMFOOLERY
fane \ˈfān\ *n* **1 :** TEMPLE **2 :** CHURCH
fan•fare \ˈfan-ˌfar\ *n* **1 :** a flourish of trumpets **2 :** a showy display
fang \ˈfaŋ\ *n* **:** a long sharp tooth; *esp* **:** a grooved or hollow tooth of a venomous snake — **fanged** \ˈfaŋd\ *adj*
fan•light \ˈfan-ˌlīt\ *n* **:** a semicircular window with radiating bars like a fan that is set over a door or window
fan•ny \ˈfa-nē\ *n, pl* **fannies :** BUTTOCKS
fan•tail \ˈfan-ˌtāl\ *n* **1 :** a fan-shaped tail or end **2 :** an overhang at the stern of a ship

fan•ta•sia \fan-ˈtā-zhə, -zhē-ə, -zē-ə; ˌfan-tə-ˈzē-ə\ *n* **:** a musical composition free and fanciful in form
fan•ta•sise *chiefly Brit var of* FANTASIZE
fan•ta•size \ˈfan-tə-ˌsīz\ *vb* **-sized; -siz•ing :** IMAGINE, DAYDREAM
fan•tas•tic \fan-ˈtas-tik\ *also* **fan•tas•ti•cal** \-ti-kəl\ *adj* **1** ♦ **:** based on fantasy rather than reason **:** IMAGINARY, UNREAL **2** ♦ **:** conceived by unrestrained fancy **3** ♦ **:** exceedingly or unbelievably great **4** ♦ **:** exhibiting strange, grotesque, inappropriate, or startlingly novel characteristics — **fan•tas•ti•cal•ly** \-ti-k(ə-)lē\ *adv*

♦ [1] fanciful, imaginary, made-up, unreal ♦ [2] absurd, bizarre, crazy, fanciful, foolish, preposterous, unreal *Ant* realistic, reasonable ♦ [3] inconceivable, incredible, unbelievable, unimaginable ♦ [4] exotic, glamorous, marvelous (*or* marvellous), outlandish, romantic, strange

fan•ta•sy *also* **phan•ta•sy** \ˈfan-tə-sē\ *n, pl* **-sies 1** ♦ **:** the free play of creative imagination as it affects perception and productivity usually as expressed in an art form or as elicited by projective techniques of formal psychology **:** IMAGINATION, FANCY **2** ♦ **:** a product of the imagination **:** ILLUSION **3** ♦ **:** a chimerical or fantastic notion — **fantasy** *vb*

♦ [1] creativity, fancy, imagination, invention ♦ [2, 3] chimera, conceit, delusion, dream, fancy, fantasy, figment, hallucination, illusion, phantasm, pipe dream, unreality, vision

FAQ *abbr* frequently asked question
1far \ˈfär\ *adv* **far•ther** \-t͟hər\ *or* **fur•ther** \ˈfər-\; **far•thest** *or* **fur•thest** \-t͟həst\ **1 :** at or to a considerable distance in space or time ⟨~ from home⟩ **2 :** by a broad interval **:** WIDELY, MUCH ⟨~ better⟩ **3 :** to or at a definite distance, point, or degree ⟨as ~ as I know⟩ **4 :** to an advanced point or extent ⟨go ~ in his field⟩ **5 :** to a great extent — **by far :** by a considerable margin — **far and away :** DECIDEDLY — **so far :** until now
2far *adj* **farther** *or* **further; farthest** *or* **furthest 1** ♦ **:** remote in space or time **2 :** DIFFERENT **3 :** involving a long distance ⟨a ~ journey⟩ **4 :** being the more distant of two ⟨on the ~ side of the lake⟩

♦ distant, far-off, remote *Ant* close, near, nearby

far•ad \ˈfar-ˌad, -əd\ *n* **:** a unit of capacitance equal to the capacitance of a capacitor having a potential difference of one volt between its plates when it is charged with one coulomb of electricity
far•away \ˈfär-ə-ˌwā\ *adj* **1 :** distant in space or time **:** DISTANT, REMOTE **2 :** DREAMY
farce \ˈfärs\ *n* **1** ♦ **:** a broadly satirical comedy with an improbable plot **2 :** the humor characteristic of farce or pretense **3** ♦ **:** a ridiculous or empty display

♦ [1] comedy, humor (*or* humour), slapstick ♦ [3] caricature, joke, mockery, parody, sham, travesty

far•ci•cal \ˈfär-si-kəl\ *adj* ♦ **:** of, relating to, or resembling farce

♦ absurd, comical, funny, humorous, laughable, ludicrous, ridiculous, silly

far cry *n* **1 :** a long distance **2 :** something notably different ⟨a *far cry* from what we expected⟩
1fare \ˈfar\ *vb* **fared; far•ing 1** ♦ **:** to go or travel **:** GO, TRAVEL **2** ♦ **:** to get along **:** make out or turn out **:** GET ALONG **3 :** to consume food **:** EAT, DINE

♦ [1] advance, go, proceed, progress, travel ♦ [2] cope, do, get along, make out, manage

2fare *n* **1 a** ♦ **:** a range or stock of food **b :** material provided for use, consumption, or enjoyment ⟨fine theatrical ~⟩ **2 :** the price charged to transport a person **3 :** a person paying a fare **:** PASSENGER

♦ food, provender, provisions, viands, victuals

1fare•well \far-ˈwel\ *vb imper* **:** get along well — used interjectionally to or by one departing
2farewell *n* **1** ♦ **:** a wish of well-being at parting **:** GOOD-BYE **2** ♦ **:** act of departure **:** LEAVE-TAKING

♦ [1] adieu, au revoir, bon voyage, good-bye ♦ [2] departure, leave-taking, parting

3fare•well \ˈfar-ˌwel\ *adj* **:** PARTING, FINAL ⟨a ~ concert⟩
far–fetched \ˈfär-ˈfecht\ *adj* **:** not easily or naturally deduced or introduced **:** IMPROBABLE ⟨~ story⟩
far–flung \-ˈfləŋ\ *adj* ♦ **:** widely spread or distributed

♦ broad, expansive, extensive, far-reaching, widespread

fa·ri·na \fə-ˈrē-nə\ *n* **:** a fine meal (as of wheat) used in puddings or as a breakfast cereal

far·i·na·ceous \ˌfar-ə-ˈnā-shəs\ *adj* **1 :** having a mealy texture or surface **2 :** containing or rich in starch

[1]**farm** \ˈfärm\ *n* **1 :** a tract of land used for raising crops or livestock **2 :** a minor-league subsidiary of a major-league team

[2]**farm** *vb* ♦ **:** to use (land) as a farm ⟨~*ed* 200 acres⟩; *also* **:** to raise crops or livestock

♦ cultivate, tend

farm·er *n* ♦ **:** a person who cultivates land or crops or raises livestock

♦ agriculturist, cultivator, grower, planter, tiller

farm·hand \ˈfärm-ˌhand\ *n* **:** a farm laborer

farm·house \-ˌhau̇s\ *n* **:** a dwelling on a farm

farm·ing \ˈfär-miŋ\ *n* **:** the occupation or business of a person who farms

farm·land \ˈfärm-ˌland\ *n* **:** land used or suitable for farming

farm out *vb* **:** to turn over (as a task) to another

farm·stead \ˈfärm-ˌsted\ *n* **:** a farm with its buildings

farm·yard \-ˌyärd\ *n* **:** land around or enclosed by farm buildings

far–off \ˈfär-ˈȯf\ *adj* ♦ **:** remote in time or space **:** DISTANT

♦ distant, remote

fa·rouche \fə-ˈrüsh\ *adj* **1 :** WILD **2 :** marked by shyness and lack of polish

far–out \ˈfär-ˈau̇t\ *adj* ♦ **:** very unconventional ⟨~ clothes⟩

♦ bizarre, odd, outlandish, outré, peculiar, strange, wacky, weird, wild

far·ra·go \fə-ˈrä-gō, -ˈrā-\ *n, pl* **-goes :** a confused collection **:** MIXTURE

far–reach·ing \ˈfär-ˈrē-chiŋ\ *adj* ♦ **:** having a wide range or effect

♦ broad, extensive, widespread

far·ri·er \ˈfer-ē-ər\ *n* **:** a person who shoes horses

[1]**far·row** \ˈfar-ō\ *vb* **:** to give birth to a litter of pigs

[2]**farrow** *n* **:** a litter of pigs

far·see·ing \ˈfär-ˌsē-iŋ\ *adj* **1 :** FARSIGHTED 1 **2 :** FARSIGHTED 2

far·sight·ed \ˈfär-ˌsī-təd\ *adj* **1 a :** seeing or able to see to a great distance **b** ♦ **:** having foresight **:** able to anticipate and plan for the future **2 :** JUDICIOUS, WISE, SHREWD **3 :** affected with an eye condition in which vision is better for distant than near objects — **far·sight·ed·ness** *n*

♦ foresighted, prescient, provident

[1]**far·ther** \ˈfär-t͟hər\ *adv* **1** ♦ **:** at or to a greater distance or more advanced point **2 :** to a greater degree or extent

♦ beyond, further, yonder

[2]**farther** *adj* **1 :** more distant **2** ♦ **:** going or extending beyond what exists **:** ADDITIONAL

♦ additional, another, more

far·ther·most \-ˌmōst\ *adj* **:** most remote **:** FARTHEST

[1]**far·thest** \ˈfär-t͟həst\ *adj* ♦ **:** most distant

♦ extreme, outermost, ultimate, utmost

[2]**farthest** *adv* **1 :** to or at the greatest distance **:** REMOTEST **2 :** to the most advanced point **3 :** by the greatest degree or extent **:** MOST

fas·cia *1 is usu* ˈfā-sh(ē-)ə, *2 is usu* ˈfa-\ *n, pl* **-ci·ae** \-shē-ˌē\ *or* **-cias 1 :** a flat usually horizontal part (as a band or board) of or on a building **2 :** a sheet of connective tissue covering body structures (as muscles)

fas·ci·cle \ˈfa-si-kəl\ *n* **1 :** a small or slender bundle (as of pine needles or nerve fiber) **2 :** one of the divisions of a book published in parts — **fas·ci·cled** \-kəld\ *adj*

fas·ci·nate \ˈfas-ᵊn-ˌāt\ *vb* **-nat·ed; -nat·ing 1 :** to transfix and hold spellbound by an irresistible power **2 a** ♦ **:** to have or exercise the power of charming, alluring, or enthralling **b** ♦ **:** engage and powerfully hold the attention or interest **3 :** to be irresistibly attractive

♦ [2a, 2b] allure, beguile, captivate, charm, enchant, enthrall ♦ [2b] engage, engross, grip, interest, intrigue, involve, occupy

fascinating ♦ **:** holding the interest as if by a spell

♦ alluring, attractive, captivating, charming, engaging, enthralling, interesting, intriguing *Ant* repellant, repelling, repugnant

fas·ci·na·tion \ˌfas-ᵊn-ˈā-shən\ *n* ♦ **:** the quality of fascinating **:** the ability to enthrall

♦ allure, appeal, attractiveness, charisma, charm, enchantment, glamour

fas·cism \ˈfa-ˌshi-zəm\ *n, often cap* **:** a political philosophy, movement, or regime that exalts nation and often race and stands for a centralized autocratic often militaristic government — **fas·cist** \-shist\ *n or adj, often cap* — **fas·cis·tic** \fa-ˈshis-tik\ *adj, often cap*

[1]**fash·ion** \ˈfa-shən\ *n* **1 :** the make or form of something **2** ♦ **:** a distinctive or peculiar and often habitual manner or way **:** MANNER, WAY **3** ♦ **:** a prevailing usually short-lived custom, usage, or style **4 :** the prevailing style (as in dress)

♦ [2] custom, habit, manner, pattern, practice, way ♦ [3] craze, enthusiasm, fad, mode, rage, sensation, style, trend, vogue

[2]**fashion** *vb* **1** ♦ **:** to make or construct usually with the use of imagination and ingenuity **2 :** FIT, ADAPT

♦ fabricate, form, frame, make, manufacture, produce

fash·ion·able \ˈfa-shə-nə-bəl\ *adj* **1** ♦ **:** dressing or behaving according to fashion **2** ♦ **:** of, relating to, or being something in fashion ⟨~ resorts⟩ — **fash·ion·ably** \-blē\ *adv*

♦ [1] à la mode, chic, in, modish, sharp, smart, snappy, stylish ♦ [2] hot, in, popular

[1]**fast** \ˈfast\ *adj* **1** ♦ **:** firmly fixed **2 :** tightly shut **3 :** adhering firmly **4 :** STUCK **5** ♦ **:** firmly loyal **:** STAUNCH ⟨~ friends⟩ **6 a** ♦ **:** characterized by quick motion, operation, or effect ⟨a ~ trip⟩ ⟨a ~ track⟩ **b** ♦ **:** unusually quick and ingenious or cunning in finding or recognizing and profiting by easy and often shady ways of making or acquiring money **7 :** indicating ahead of the correct time ⟨the clock is ~⟩ **8** ♦ **:** not easily disturbed **:** SOUND ⟨a ~ sleep⟩ **9 :** permanently dyed; *also* **:** being proof against fading ⟨colors ~ to sunlight⟩ **10 :** DISSIPATED, WILD **11 :** sexually promiscuous

♦ [1, 8] firm, secure, set, snug, sound, stable, tight ♦ [5] constant, devoted, faithful, loyal, staunch, steadfast, steady, true ♦ [6a] brisk, fleet, hasty, quick, rapid, speedy, swift *Ant* slow ♦ [6b] deceptive, dishonest, shady, sharp, shifty

[2]**fast** *adv* **1** ♦ **:** in a fast manner ⟨stuck ~ in the mud⟩ ⟨~ asleep⟩ **2** ♦ **:** in a rapid manner **:** SWIFTLY **3 :** RECKLESSLY

♦ [1] completely, entirely, fully, thoroughly, well, wholly ♦ [2] briskly, hastily, presto, pronto, quick, quickly, rapidly, speedily, swiftly *Ant* slow, slowly

[3]**fast** *vb* **1 :** to abstain from food **2 :** to eat sparingly or abstain from some foods

[4]**fast** *n* **1 :** the act or practice of fasting **2 :** a time of fasting

fast·back \ˈfast-ˌbak\ *n* **:** an automobile having a roof with a long slope to the rear

fast·ball \-ˌbȯl\ *n* **:** a baseball pitch thrown at full speed

fas·ten \ˈfas-ᵊn\ *vb* **1** ♦ **:** to attach or join by or as if by pinning, tying, or nailing **2** ♦ **:** to make fast **:** fix securely **3 :** to become fixed or joined **4** ♦ **:** to focus attention ⟨~*ed* onto the newest trends⟩ — **fas·ten·er** *n*

♦ [1, 2] attach, fix, secure, tie *Ant* detach, loose, loosen, undo ♦ [4] concentrate, focus, rivet, train

fas·ten·ing *n* **:** something that fastens **:** FASTENER

fast–food \ˌfast-ˈfüd\ *adj* **:** specializing in food that is prepared and served quickly ⟨a ~ restaurant⟩

fast–for·ward \-ˈfȯr-wərd\ *n* **1 :** a function of an electronic device that advances a recording rapidly **2 :** a state of rapid advancement — **fast–forward** *vb*

fas·tid·i·ous \fa-ˈsti-dē-əs\ *adj* **1** ♦ **:** overly difficult to please **2** ♦ **:** showing a meticulous or demanding attitude ⟨~ workmanship⟩ — **fas·tid·i·ous·ly** *adv* — **fas·tid·i·ous·ness** *n*

♦ [1, 2] choosy, demanding, exacting, finicky, fussy, particular, picky

fast·ness \ˈfast-nəs\ *n* **1 a :** the quality or state of being fast **b :** fixed attachment **c** ♦ **:** the quality or state of being swift **2** ♦ **:** a fortified or secure place **:** STRONGHOLD

♦ [1c] celerity, fleetness, haste, hurry, quickness, rapidity, speed, swiftness, velocity ♦ [2] bastion, citadel, fort, fortification, fortress, stronghold

fast–talk \ˈfast-ˌtȯk\ *vb* **:** to influence by persuasive and usually deceptive talk

fast–track \ˈfast-ˌtrak\ *vb* ♦ **:** to speed up the processing or production of

♦ accelerate, hasten, hurry, quicken, rush, speed (up), whisk

fast track *n* : a course leading to rapid advancement or success
[1]**fat** \ˈfat\ *adj* **fat·ter; fat·test** **1** ♦ : notable for having an unusual amount of fat : PLUMP, OBESE **2** : OILY, GREASY **3** ♦ : well filled out : unusually large **4** ♦ : well furnished, filled, or stocked : ABUNDANT **5** ♦ : richly rewarding **6** ♦ : having the quality or power of producing especially in abundance

♦ [1] chubby, corpulent, obese, overweight, plump, portly, rotund, round *Ant* lean, slender, slim, spare, thin ♦ [3] broad, thick, wide ♦ [4] abundant, chock-full, full, packed, replete ♦ [5] gainful, lucrative, profitable, remunerative ♦ [6] fertile, fruitful, productive, prolific, rich

[2]**fat** *n* **1** : animal tissue rich in greasy or oily matter **2** : any of various energy-rich esters that occur naturally in animal fats and in plants and are soluble in organic solvents (as ether) but not in water **3** ♦ : the best or richest portion ⟨lived on the ~ of the land⟩ **4** : OBESITY **5** ♦ : something in excess or expendable

♦ [3] best, choice, elite, pick, prime ♦ [5] excess, overflow, surfeit, surplus

fa·tal \ˈfāt-ᵊl\ *adj* **1** : FATEFUL ⟨that ~ day⟩ **2** ♦ : causing death or ruin ⟨a ~ mistake⟩ — **fa·tal·ly** *adv*

♦ deadly, deathly, lethal, mortal, murderous, pestilent ♦ calamitous, catastrophic, destructive, disastrous, fateful, ruinous

fa·tal·ism \-ˌi-zəm\ *n* : the belief that events are determined by fate — **fa·tal·ist** \-ist\ *n* — **fa·tal·is·tic** \ˌfāt-ᵊl-ˈis-tik\ *adj* — **fa·tal·is·ti·cal·ly** \-ti-k(ə-)lē\ *adv*
fa·tal·i·ty \fā-ˈta-lə-tē, fə-\ *n, pl* **-ties** **1** : DEADLINESS **2** : FATE **3 a** : death resulting from a disaster or accident **b** ♦ : one who suffers a death from a disaster or accident

♦ casualty, loss, victim

fat·back \ˈfat-ˌbak\ *n* : a fatty strip from the back of the hog usually cured by salting and drying
fat cat *n* **1** : a wealthy contributor to a political campaign **2** : a wealthy privileged person
fate \ˈfāt\ *n* **1** ♦ : the cause or will that is held to determine events : DESTINY **2** ♦ : LOT, FORTUNE **3** : DISASTER; *esp* : DEATH **4** : ultimate lot or disposition : final outcome **5** *cap, pl* : the three goddesses of classical mythology who determine the course of human life

♦ [1, 2] circumstance, destiny, doom, fortune, lot

fat·ed \ˈfā-təd\ *adj* : decreed, controlled, or marked by fate
fate·ful \ˈfāt-fəl\ *adj* **1** : OMINOUS, PROPHETIC **2** : IMPORTANT, DECISIVE **3** ♦ : bringing on adverse fate : DESTRUCTIVE **4** : determined by fate — **fate·ful·ly** *adv*

♦ calamitous, catastrophic, destructive, disastrous, fatal, ruinous

fath *abbr* fathom
fat·head \ˈfat-ˌhed\ *n* ♦ : a stupid person — **fat·head·ed** \-ˈhe-dəd\ *adj*

♦ blockhead, dope, dummy, idiot, imbecile, jackass, moron, numskull

[1]**fa·ther** \ˈfä-t͟hər\ *n* **1** ♦ : a male parent **2** *cap* : God especially as the first person of the Trinity **3** ♦ : a male ancestor more remote than a parent : FOREFATHER **4** : one deserving the respect and love given to a father **5** *often cap* : an early Christian writer accepted by the church as an authoritative witness to its teaching and practice **6** ♦ : one that originates or institutes : ORIGINATOR ⟨the ~ of modern radio⟩; *also* : SOURCE **7** ♦ : a priest of the regular clergy : PRIEST — used especially as a title **8** : one of the leading men ⟨city ~*s*⟩ — **fa·ther·hood** \-ˌhu̇d\ *n* — **fa·ther·less** *adj* — **fa·ther·ly** *adj*

♦ [1] daddy, papa, pop ♦ [3] ancestor, forefather, grandfather ♦ [6] author, creator, founder, originator ♦ [7] clergyman, minister, preacher, priest, reverend

[2]**father** *vb* **1** ♦ : to make oneself the father of : BEGET **2** : to be the founder, producer, or author of **3** : to treat or care for as a father

♦ beget, get, produce, sire

father–in–law \ˈfä-t͟hə-rən-ˌlȯ\ *n, pl* **fa·thers–in–law** \-t͟hər-zən-\ : the father of one's husband or wife
fa·ther·land \ˈfä-t͟hər-ˌland\ *n* **1** : the native land of one's ancestors **2** ♦ : one's native land

♦ country, home, homeland

[1]**fath·om** \ˈfa-t͟həm\ *n* : a unit of length equal to 6 feet (about 1.8 meters) used especially for measuring the depth of water
[2]**fathom** *vb* **1** : to measure by a sounding line **2** : PROBE **3** : to penetrate and come to understand — **fath·om·able** \ˈfa-t͟hə-mə-bəl\ *adj*
fath·om·less \ˈfa-t͟həm-ləs\ *adj* : incapable of being fathomed
[1]**fa·tigue** \fə-ˈtēg\ *n* **1** : manual or menial work performed by military personnel **2** *pl* : the uniform or work clothing worn on fatigue and in the field **3** ♦ : weariness from labor or stress **4** : the tendency of a material to break under repeated stress

♦ burnout, collapse, exhaustion, lassitude, prostration, tiredness, weariness *Ant* refreshment, rejuvenation, revitalization

[2]**fatigue** *vb* **fa·tigued; fa·tigu·ing** ♦ : to weary with labor or exertion : WEARY, TIRE

♦ burn out, do in, drain, exhaust, tire, wear out, weary

fat·ness *n* ♦ : the quality or state of being fat or rich in fats : fullness of flesh

♦ corpulence, obesity, plumpness

fat·ten \ˈfat-ᵊn\ *vb* : to make or grow fat
Fat Tuesday *n* : MARDI GRAS
[1]**fat·ty** \ˈfa-tē\ *adj* **fat·ti·er; -est** **1** : containing fat especially in unusual amounts **2** : GREASY
[2]**fatty** *n, pl* **fat·ties** : a fat person
fatty acid *n* : any of numerous acids that contain only carbon, hydrogen, and oxygen and that occur naturally in fats and various oils
fa·tu·ity \fə-ˈtü-ə-tē, -ˈtyü-\ *n, pl* **-ities** **1** ♦ : something foolish or stupid **2** ♦ : the quality or state of being stupid

♦ [1] absurdity, folly, foolery, foolishness, idiocy, inanity, madness, stupidity ♦ [2] absurdity, foolishness, inanity, insanity, lunacy, madness, silliness, simplicity, stupidity

fat·u·ous \ˈfa-chu̇-wəs\ *adj* ♦ : marked by lack of intelligence and rational consideration — **fat·u·ous·ly** *adv*

♦ dense, dull, dumb, obtuse, stupid, unintelligent, vacuous, witless

fau·bourg \fō-ˈbu̇r\ *n* **1** : a suburb especially of a French city **2** : a city quarter
fau·ces \ˈfȯ-ˌsēz\ *n pl* : the narrow passage located between the soft palate and the base of the tongue that joins the mouth to the pharynx
fau·cet \ˈfȯ-sət, ˈfä-\ *n* ♦ : a fixture for drawing off a liquid (as from a pipe)

♦ cock, gate, spigot, tap, valve

[1]**fault** \ˈfȯlt\ *n* **1** ♦ : a weakness in character : FAILING **2** ♦ : a physical or intellectual imperfection or impairment : IMPERFECTION, DEFECT **3** : an error especially in service in a net or racket game **4** ♦ : a failure to do what is right : an unintentional error : MISTAKE **5** ♦ : responsibility for something wrong **6** : a fracture in the earth's crust accompanied by a displacement of one side relative to the other

♦ [1] demerit, failing, foible, frailty, shortcoming, vice, weakness *Ant* merit, virtue ♦ [2] blemish, defect, flaw, imperfection ♦ [4] blunder, error, fumble, goof, misstep, mistake, oversight, slip ♦ [5] blame, culpability, guilt, rap

[2]**fault** *vb* **1** : to commit a fault : ERR **2** : to fracture so as to produce a geologic fault **3** ♦ : to find a fault in

♦ blame, condemn, criticize, denounce, knock, pan

fault·find·er \ˈfȯlt-ˌfīn-dər\ *n* ♦ : a person who tends to find fault or complain — **fault·find·ing** *n or adj*

♦ carper, castigator, censurer, critic, nitpicker, scold

fault·i·ly \ˈfȯl-tə-lē\ *adv* ♦ : in a faulty or blamable manner

♦ erroneously, improperly, incorrectly, wrongly

fault·less *adj* ♦ : having no fault : free from defect, imperfection, failing, blemish, or error

♦ flawless, impeccable, perfect, unblemished ♦ blameless, innocent, irreproachable

fault·less·ly *adv* ♦ : in a manner having no fault

♦ flawlessly, ideally, impeccably, perfectly

faulty *adj* ♦ : marked by a fault : having a fault, blemish, or defect

♦ bad, defective, imperfect *Ant* faultless, flawless, perfect

faun \ˈfȯn\ *n* : a Roman god similar to but gentler than a satyr
fau·na \ˈfȯ-nə\ *n, pl* **faunas** *also* **fau·nae** \-ˌnē, -ˌnī\ : animals or animal life especially of a region, period, or environment — **fau·nal** \-nəl\ *adj*
fau·vism \ˈfō-ˌvi-zəm\ *n, often cap* : a movement in painting

characterized by vivid colors, free treatment of form, and a vibrant and decorative effect — **fau•vist** \-vist\ *n, often cap*

faux \ˈfō\ *adj* ♦ : resembling something else that is usually genuine and of better quality

♦ artificial, fake, imitation, mock, sham, synthetic

faux pas \ˈfō-ˌpä, fō-ˈ\ *n, pl* **faux pas** *same or* -ˌpäz, -ˈpäz\ : BLUNDER; *esp* : a social blunder

fa•va bean \ˈfä-və-\ *n* : the large flat edible seed of an Old World vetch; *also* : this plant

¹fa•vor *or Can and Brit* **fa•vour** \ˈfā-vər\ *n* **1** ♦ : friendly regard shown toward another especially by a superior **2** ♦ : the act of approving or the state of being approved of : APPROVAL **3** ♦ : bias in favor : PARTIALITY **4** : POPULARITY **5** : gracious kindness; *also* : an act of such kindness **6** *pl* ♦ : effort in one's behalf : ATTENTION **7** : a token of love (as a ribbon) usually worn conspicuously **8** : a small gift or decorative item given out at a party **9** : a special privilege **10** : sexual privileges — usually used in plural **11** : BEHALF, INTEREST

♦ [1] admiration, appreciation, esteem, estimation, regard, respect ♦ [2] approbation, approval, blessing, imprimatur, OK ♦ [3] bias, partiality, partisanship, prejudice ♦ [6] boon, courtesy, grace, indulgence, kindness, mercy, service, turn

²favor *or Can and Brit* **favour** *vb* **1** ♦ : to regard or treat with favor **2** : to do a kindness for or oblige especially with a gift : OBLIGE **3** : ENDOW ⟨~*ed* by nature⟩ **4** : to treat gently or carefully : SPARE ⟨~ a lame leg⟩ **5** ♦ : to show partiality toward : PREFER **6** : SUPPORT, SUSTAIN **7** : FACILITATE ⟨darkness ~*s* attack⟩ **8** : RESEMBLE ⟨he ~*s* his father⟩

♦ [1] accept, approve, care, countenance, OK, subscribe ♦ [5] lean, like, prefer

fa•vor•able *or Can and Brit* **fa•vour•able** \ˈfā-və-rə-bəl\ *adj* **1** ♦ : expressing approval : APPROVING **2** ♦ : tending to promote or facilitate : HELPFUL, ADVANTAGEOUS ⟨~ weather⟩ **3** ♦ : marked by success

♦ [1] appreciative, complimentary, friendly, good, positive ***Ant*** adverse, disapproving, negative ♦ [2] advantageous, beneficial, helpful, profitable, salutary ♦ [3] auspicious, bright, encouraging, hopeful, promising, propitious ***Ant*** discouraging, inauspicious, unfavorable, unpromising

fa•vor•ably *or Can and Brit* **fa•vour•ably** \-blē\ *adv* ♦ : in a favorable manner

♦ agreeably, nicely, pleasantly, pleasingly, satisfyingly, well

¹fa•vor•ite *or Can and Brit* **fa•vour•ite** \ˈfā-və-rət, -vrət\ *n* **1** ♦ : a person or a thing that is favored above others **2** : a competitor regarded as most likely to win

♦ darling, pet, preference, prize, treasure

²favorite *or Can and Brit* **favourite** *adj* ♦ : being a favorite

♦ dear, loved, precious, special

favorite son *n* : a candidate supported by the delegates of his state at a presidential nominating convention

fa•vor•it•ism \ˈfā-və-rə-ˌti-zəm\ *or Can and Brit* **fa•vour•it•ism** *n* : PARTIALITY, BIAS

¹fawn \ˈfȯn, ˈfän\ *vb* **1** : to show affection ⟨a dog ~*ing* on its master⟩ **2** ♦ : to court favor by a cringing or flattering manner

♦ fuss, kowtow, toady

²fawn *n* **1** : a young deer **2** : a light grayish brown — **fawny** \ˈfȯ-nē, ˈfä-\ *adj*

fax \ˈfaks\ *n* **1** : FACSIMILE 2 **2** : a device used to send or receive facsimile communications; *also* : such a communication — **fax** *vb*

¹fay \ˈfā\ *n* ♦ : a mythical being of folklore and romance usually having diminutive human form and magic powers and given to beneficial or mischievous interference in human affairs

♦ brownie, dwarf, elf, fairy, gnome, hobgoblin, leprechaun, pixie, puck, troll

²fay *adj* ♦ : like an elf

♦ antic, elfish, frisky, frolicsome, playful

faze \ˈfāz\ *vb* **fazed; faz•ing** ♦ : to disturb the composure or courage of

♦ confound, confuse, disconcert, embarrass, fluster, rattle

FBI *abbr* Federal Bureau of Investigation

FCC *abbr* Federal Communications Commission

FD *abbr* fire department

FDA *abbr* Food and Drug Administration

FDIC *abbr* Federal Deposit Insurance Corporation

Fe *symbol* iron

fe•al•ty \ˈfēl-tē\ *n, pl* **-ties** ♦ : intense fidelity : LOYALTY, ALLEGIANCE

♦ allegiance, constancy, dedication, devotion, faith, faithfulness, fastness, fidelity, loyalty, steadfastness

¹fear \ˈfir\ *vb* **1** : to have a reverent awe of ⟨~ God⟩ **2** : to be afraid of : have fear ⟨~*s* spiders⟩ **3** ♦ : to be apprehensive

♦ bother, fret, stew, sweat, trouble, worry

²fear *n* **1** ♦ : an unpleasant often strong emotion caused by expectation or awareness of danger; *also* : an instance of or a state marked by this emotion **2** : anxious concern : SOLICITUDE **3** : profound reverence especially toward God

♦ alarm, anxiety, apprehension, dread, fright, trepidation

fear•ful \-fəl\ *adj* **1** ♦ : causing fear **2** ♦ : filled with fear **3** ♦ : showing or caused by fear **4** ♦ : extremely bad, intense, or large — **fear•ful•ly** *adv*

♦ [1] dire, dreadful, fearsome, forbidding, formidable, frightful, hair-raising, horrible, redoubtable, scary, shocking, terrible, terrifying ♦ [2, 3] afraid, scared, skittish, timid ♦ [4] deep, fierce, furious, hard, intense, profound, terrible, violent

fear•less \-ləs\ *adj* ♦ : free from fear : BRAVE — **fear•less•ly** *adv*

♦ brave, courageous, heroic, intrepid, lionhearted, stalwart, stout, undaunted, valiant

fear•less•ness *n* ♦ : the quality or state of being without fear

♦ bravery, courage, daring, heroism, nerve, stoutness, valor

fear•some \-səm\ *adj* **1** ♦ : causing fear **2** : TIMID **3** : INTENSE ⟨~ determination⟩

♦ fearful, formidable, hair-raising, scary, shocking, terrifying

fea•si•ble \ˈfē-zə-bəl\ *adj* **1** ♦ : capable of being done or carried out ⟨a ~ plan⟩ **2** : SUITABLE **3** : REASONABLE, LIKELY — **fea•si•bil•i•ty** \ˌfē-zə-ˈbi-lə-tē\ *n* — **fea•si•bly** \ˈfē-zə-blē\ *adv*

♦ achievable, attainable, doable, possible, practicable, viable, workable

¹feast \ˈfēst\ *n* **1** ♦ : an elaborate meal : BANQUET **2** : ABUNDANCE ⟨a ~ of good books⟩ **3** : FESTIVAL 1

♦ banquet, dinner, feed, spread

²feast *vb* **1 a** : to take part in a feast **b** ♦ : to give a feast for **2** : to enjoy some unusual pleasure or delight **3** : DELIGHT, GRATIFY

♦ banquet, dine, junket, regale

feat \ˈfēt\ *n* ♦ : a deed notable especially for courage : a heroic achievement; *esp* : an act notable for courage, skill, endurance, or ingenuity

♦ deed, exploit, stunt, trick

¹feath•er \ˈfe-t͟hər\ *n* **1** : any of the light horny outgrowths that form the external covering of the body of a bird **2** : the vane of an arrow **3** : the entire clothing of feathers of a bird : PLUMAGE **4** ♦ : a group united by common traits or interests ⟨birds of a ~⟩ **5** ♦ : elaborate, showy, or ceremonial dress ⟨in full ~⟩ **6** : CONDITION, MOOD ⟨in fine ~⟩ — **feath•ered** \-t͟hərd\ *adj* — **feath•er•less** *adj* — **a feather in one's cap** : a mark of distinction : HONOR

♦ [4] class, ilk, kind, like, sort, type ♦ [5] array, best, finery, full dress, regalia

²feather *vb* **1** : to furnish with a feather ⟨~ an arrow⟩ **2** : to cover, clothe, line, or adorn with or as if with feathers — **feather one's nest** : to provide for oneself financially especially while exploiting a position of trust

feath•er•bed•ding \ˈfe-t͟hər-ˌbe-diŋ\ *n* : the requiring of an employer usually under a union rule or safety statute to employ more workers than are needed

feath•er•edge \-ˌej\ *n* : a very thin sharp edge

feath•er•weight \-ˌwāt\ *n* : one that is very light in weight; *esp* : a boxer weighing more than 118 but not over 126 pounds

feath•ery *adj* ♦ : light and delicate

♦ airy, light

¹fea•ture \ˈfē-chər\ *n* **1** : the shape or appearance of the face or its parts **2** : a part of the face : LINEAMENT **3** ♦ : a prominent part or characteristic **4** : a special attraction (as in a newspaper) **5** : something offered to the public or advertised as particularly attractive — **fea•ture•less** *adj*

♦ attribute, character, characteristic, mark, peculiarity, point, property, quality, trait

2**feature** *vb* **1 :** to picture in the mind : IMAGINE **2** ♦ **:** to give special prominence to ⟨the show ~*s* new artists⟩ **3 :** to play an important part

♦ accent, accentuate, emphasize, highlight, stress, underline, underscore

Feb *abbr* February
fe•brile \ˈfe-ˌbrī(-ə)l\ *adj* **:** FEVERISH
Feb•ru•ary \ˈfe-b(y)ə-ˌwer-ē, ˈfe-brə-\ *n* **:** the 2d month of the year
fe•ces \ˈfē-ˌsēz\ *n pl* **:** bodily waste discharged from the intestine : EXCREMENT — **fe•cal** \-kəl\ *adj*
feck•less \ˈfek-ləs\ *adj* **1 :** WEAK, INEFFECTIVE **2 :** WORTHLESS, IRRESPONSIBLE
fe•cund \ˈfe-kənd, ˈfē-\ *adj* ♦ **:** fruitful in offspring or vegetation : FRUITFUL, PROLIFIC — **fe•cun•di•ty** \fi-ˈkən-də-tē, fe-\ *n*

♦ fat, fertile, fruitful, luxuriant, productive, prolific, rich

fe•cun•date \ˈfe-kən-ˌdāt, ˈfē-\ *vb* **-dat•ed; -dat•ing 1 :** to make fecund **2 :** IMPREGNATE — **fe•cun•da•tion** \ˌfe-kən-ˈdā-shən, ˌfē-\ *n*
fed *abbr* federal; federation
fed•er•al \ˈfe-də-rəl, -drəl\ *adj* **1 :** formed by a compact between political units that surrender individual sovereignty to a central authority but retain certain limited powers **2 :** of or constituting a form of government in which power is distributed between a central authority and constituent territorial units **3 :** of or relating to the central government of a federation **4** *cap* **:** FEDERALIST **5** *often cap* **:** of, relating to, or loyal to the federal government or the Union armies of the U.S. in the American Civil War — **fed•er•al•ly** *adv*
Federal *n* **:** a supporter of the U.S. government in the Civil War; *esp* **:** a soldier in the federal armies
federal district *n* **:** a district (as the District of Columbia) set apart as the seat of the central government of a federation
fed•er•al•ism \ˈfe-də-rə-ˌli-zəm, -drə-\ *n* **1** *often cap* **:** the distribution of power in an organization (as a government) between a central authority and the constituent units **2 :** support or advocacy of federalism **3** *cap* **:** the principles of the Federalists
fed•er•al•ist \-list\ *n* **1 :** an advocate of federalism **2** *often cap* **:** an advocate of a federal union between the American colonies after the Revolution and of adoption of the U.S. Constitution **3** *cap* **:** a member of a major political party in the early years of the U.S. favoring a strong centralized national government — **federalist** *adj, often cap*
fed•er•al•ize \ˈfe-də-rə-ˌlīz, -drə-\ *vb* **-ized; -iz•ing 1 :** to unite in or under a federal system **2 :** to bring under the jurisdiction of a federal government
fed•er•ate \ˈfe-də-ˌrāt\ *vb* **-at•ed; -at•ing** ♦ **:** to join in a federation

♦ ally, associate, band, club, confederate, conjoin, cooperate, league, unite

fed•er•a•tion \ˌfe-də-ˈrā-shən\ *n* **1 :** a political or societal entity formed by uniting smaller entities **2 :** a federal government **3** ♦ **:** a union of organizations **4 :** the forming of a federal union

♦ alliance, bloc, coalition, combination, combine, confederacy, confederation, league, union

fedn *abbr* federation
fe•do•ra \fi-ˈdōr-ə\ *n* **:** a low soft felt hat with the crown creased lengthwise
fed up *adj* ♦ **:** satiated, tired, or disgusted beyond endurance

♦ jaded, sick, tired, weary

fee \ˈfē\ *n* **1 :** an estate in land held from a feudal lord **2 :** an inherited or heritable estate in land **3** ♦ **:** a fixed charge; *also* **:** a charge for a service

♦ charge, cost, figure, price

fee•ble \ˈfē-bəl\ *adj* **fee•bler** \-bə-lər\; **fee•blest** \-bə-ləst\ **1** ♦ **:** markedly lacking in strength : FRAIL **2 :** INEFFECTIVE, INADEQUATE ⟨a ~ protest⟩ — **fee•bly** \-blē\ *adv*

♦ faint, frail, infirm, wasted, weak

fee•ble•mind•ed \ˌfē-bəl-ˈmīn-dəd\ *adj* **:** lacking normal intelligence — **fee•ble•mind•ed•ness** *n*
fee•ble•ness *n* ♦ **:** the quality or state of being feeble

♦ debility, frailty, infirmity, weakness

1**feed** \ˈfēd\ *vb* **fed** \ˈfed\; **feed•ing 1** ♦ **:** to give food to; *also* **:** to give as food **2 a** ♦ **:** to consume food : EAT 1 **b :** to seize and devour prey — used with *on, upon,* or *off* **3 :** to furnish what is necessary to the growth or function of **4 :** to supply for use or consumption — **feed•er** *n*

♦ [1] board, cater, provision, victual ♦ [2a] dine, eat, fare

2**feed** *n* **1 a** ♦ **:** a usually large meal; *esp* **:** a sumptuous meal **b** ♦ **:** the portion or serving of food eaten at a meal **2 :** food for livestock **3 :** a mechanism for feeding material to a machine

♦ [1a] banquet, dinner, feast, spread ♦ [1b] board, chow, meal, mess, repast, table

feed•back \ˈfēd-ˌbak\ *n* **1 :** the return to the input of a part of the output of a machine, system, or process **2 :** response especially to one in authority about an activity or policy **3 :** sound (as whistling) resulting from the retransmission of an amplified or broadcast signal
feed•lot \ˈfēd-ˌlät\ *n* **:** land on which cattle are fattened for market
feed•stuff \-ˌstəf\ *n* **:** FEED 2
1**feel** \ˈfēl\ *vb* **felt** \ˈfelt\; **feel•ing 1 :** to perceive or examine through physical contact : TOUCH, HANDLE **2** ♦ **:** to undergo passive experience of : EXPERIENCE; *also* **:** to suffer from **3 :** to ascertain by cautious trial ⟨~ out public sentiment⟩ **4** ♦ **:** to be aware of **5 :** to be conscious of an inward impression, state of mind, or physical condition **6** ♦ **:** to be aware of by instinct or inference : BELIEVE, THINK ⟨say what you ~⟩ **7** ♦ **:** to search for something with the fingers : GROPE **8 :** SEEM ⟨it ~*s* like spring⟩ **9** ♦ **:** to have sympathy or pity ⟨I ~ for you⟩

♦ [2] endure, experience, have, know, see, suffer, sustain, taste, undergo ♦ [4] perceive, scent, see, sense, smell, taste [6] believe, consider, deem, figure, guess, hold, imagine, suppose, think ♦ [7] fish, fumble, grope ♦ *usu* **feel for** [9] commiserate, pity, sympathize

2**feel** *n* **1 :** the sense of touch **2** ♦ **:** a sensation experienced through the sense of feeling **3 :** the quality of a thing as imparted through touch

♦ [2] feeling, sensation, sense

feel•er \ˈfē-lər\ *n* **1 :** one that feels; *esp* **:** a tactile organ (as on the head of an insect) **2 :** a proposal or remark made to find out the views of other people
1**feel•ing** \ˈfē-liŋ\ *n* **1 a :** the sense of touch **b** ♦ **:** a sensation perceived by touch **2** ♦ **:** a state of mind ⟨a ~ of loneliness⟩ **3** *pl* **:** general emotional condition : SENSIBILITIES ⟨hurt their ~*s*⟩ **4** ♦ **:** often unreasoned opinion or belief : OPINION, BELIEF **5** ♦ **:** capacity to respond emotionally

♦ [1b] feel, sensation, sense ♦ [2] emotion, sentiment ♦ [4] belief, conviction, eye, judgment (*or* judgement), mind, notion, opinion, persuasion, sentiment, verdict, view ♦ [5] compassion, heart, humanity, kindness, sympathy

2**feeling** *adj* **1 :** having the capacity to feel or respond emotionally : SENSITIVE; *esp* **:** easily moved emotionally **2 :** expressing emotion or sensitivity — **feel•ing•ly** *adv*
feet *pl of* FOOT
feign \ˈfān\ *vb* **1** ♦ **:** to give a false appearance of : SHAM ⟨~ illness⟩ **2 :** to assert as if true : PRETEND

♦ affect, assume, fake, pretend, put on, sham, simulate

feigned \ˈfānd\ *adj* **1 :** not genuine or real **2** ♦ **:** not genuinely felt

♦ artificial, hypocritical, insincere, two-faced

feint \ˈfānt\ *n* **:** something feigned; *esp* **:** a mock blow or attack intended to distract attention from the real point of attack — **feint** *vb*
feisty \ˈfī-stē\ *adj* **feist•i•er; -est :** having or showing a lively aggressiveness ⟨a ~ heroine⟩
feld•spar \ˈfeld-ˌspär\ *n* **:** any of a group of crystalline minerals consisting of silicates of aluminum with another element (as potassium or sodium)
fe•lic•i•tate \fi-ˈli-sə-ˌtāt\ *vb* **-tat•ed; -tat•ing :** to offer congratulations to : CONGRATULATE
fe•lic•i•ta•tion \fi-ˌli-sə-ˈtā-shən\ *n* **:** the act or an instance of congratulating : CONGRATULATION
fe•lic•i•tous \fi-ˈli-sə-təs\ *adj* **1** ♦ **:** suitably expressed : APT **2** ♦ **:** highly pleasing : affording great pleasure and satisfaction : PLEASANT, DELIGHTFUL

♦ [1] applicable, appropriate, apt, fit, fitting, proper, right, suitable ♦ [2] agreeable, congenial, delightful, pleasant, pleasurable, satisfying

fe•lic•i•tous•ly *adv* ♦ **:** in a felicitous manner

◆ agreeably, favorably (*or* favourably), nicely, pleasantly, pleasingly, satisfyingly, splendidly, well

fe•lic•i•ty \fi-ˈli-sə-tē\ *n, pl* **-ties** **1** ◆ **:** the quality or state of being happy; *esp* **:** great happiness **2** ◆ **:** something that causes happiness **3 :** a pleasing manner or quality especially in art or language **4 :** an apt expression

◆ [1] blessedness, bliss, gladness, happiness, joy ◆ [2] benefit, blessing, boon, godsend, good, manna, windfall

fe•line \ˈfē-ˌlīn\ *adj* **1 :** of or relating to cats or their kin **2 :** SLY, TREACHEROUS **3 :** STEALTHY

feline *n* ◆ **:** a feline animal

◆ cat, kitty, puss

¹fell \ˈfel\ *n* **:** SKIN, HIDE, PELT

²fell *vb* **1 a** ◆ **:** to cut, beat, or knock down **b :** to deprive of life **2 :** to sew (a seam) by folding one raw edge under the other

◆ chop, cut, hew

³fell *past of* FALL

⁴fell *adj* **1** ◆ **:** violently hostile or aggressive in temperament **:** FIERCE **2** ◆ **:** killing or markedly sickening or destroying **:** DEADLY — **in one fell swoop** *also* **at one fell swoop :** all at once **:** with a single effort

◆ [1] ferocious, fierce, grim, savage, vicious ◆ [2] deadly, fatal, lethal, mortal, murderous, pestilent, vital

fel•lah \ˈfe-lə, fə-ˈlä\ *n, pl* **fel•la•hin** *or* **fel•la•heen** \ˌfe-lə-ˈhēn\ **:** a peasant or agricultural laborer in Arab countries (as Egypt or Syria)

fel•la•tio \fə-ˈlā-shē-ˌō\ *also* **fel•la•tion** \-shən\ *n* **:** oral stimulation of the penis

fel•low \ˈfe-lō\ *n* **1** ◆ **:** one that accompanies or is in the company of another **:** one much in the company of another **2** ◆ **:** an equal in rank, power, or character **:** EQUAL, PEER **3 :** one of a pair **:** MATE **4 :** a member of an incorporated literary or scientific society **5** ◆ **:** an individual human **:** an adult male human **:** MAN **6** ◆ **:** a frequent, regular, or favorite escort or male companion **:** BOYFRIEND **7 :** a person granted a stipend for advanced study

◆ [1] associate, cohort, companion, comrade, crony, mate ◆ [2] equal, like, match, parallel, peer ◆ [5] buck, chap, dude, gent, gentleman, guy, hombre, jack, joker, lad, male, man ◆ [6] beau, boyfriend, man, swain

fel•low man \ˌfe-lō-ˈman\ *n* **:** a kindred human being

fel•low•ship \ˈfe-lō-ˌship\ *n* **1** ◆ **:** the condition of friendly relationship existing among persons **2** ◆ **:** a community of interest or feeling **3** ◆ **:** a group with similar interests **4 :** the position of a fellow (as of a university) **5 :** the stipend granted a fellow

◆ [1] camaraderie, companionship, company, comradeship, society ◆ [2] brotherhood, community, corps, fraternity ◆ [3] association, club, college, congress, council, fraternity, league, order, organization, society

fellow traveler *n* **:** a sympathetic supporter of another's cause; *esp* **:** a person who sympathizes with and often furthers the ideals and program of an organized group (as the Communist party) without joining it

fel•on \ˈfe-lən\ *n* **1** ◆ **:** one who has committed a felony **2 :** WHITLOW

◆ criminal, crook, culprit, lawbreaker, malefactor, offender

fe•lo•ni•ous \fə-ˈlō-nē-əs\ *adj* **:** of, relating to, or having the nature of a felony

fel•o•ny \ˈfe-lə-nē\ *n, pl* **-nies :** a serious crime punishable by a heavy sentence

fel•spar *chiefly Brit var of* FELDSPAR

¹felt \ˈfelt\ *n* **1 :** a cloth made of wool and fur often mixed with natural or synthetic fibers **2 :** a material resembling felt

²felt *past and past part of* FEEL

fem *abbr* **1** female **2** feminine

fe•male \ˈfē-ˌmāl\ *adj* **1 :** of, relating to, or being the sex that bears young; *also* **:** PISTILLATE **2** ◆ **:** characteristic of girls or women ⟨~ voices⟩

◆ feminine, womanly

female *n* **:** a female person **:** a woman

¹fem•i•nine \ˈfe-mə-nən\ *adj* **1 a :** of the female sex **b** ◆ **:** characteristic of or appropriate or peculiar to women **2 :** of, relating to, or constituting the gender that includes most words or grammatical forms referring to females — **fem•i•nin•i•ty** \ˌfe-mə-ˈni-nə-tē\ *n*

◆ female, womanly *Ant* male, manly, mannish, masculine

²feminine *n* **:** a noun, pronoun, adjective, or inflectional form or class of the feminine gender; *also* **:** the feminine gender

fem•i•nism \ˈfe-mə-ˌni-zəm\ *n* **1 :** the theory of the political, economic, and social equality of the sexes **2 :** organized activity on behalf of women's rights and interests — **fem•i•nist** \-nist\ *n or adj*

femme fa•tale \ˌfem-fə-ˈtal\ *n, pl* **femmes fa•tales** *same or* -ˈtalz\ **:** a seductive woman

fe•mur \ˈfē-mər\ *n, pl* **fe•murs** *or* **fem•o•ra** \ˈfe-mə-rə\ **:** the long leg bone extending from the hip to the knee — **fem•o•ral** \ˈfe-mə-rəl\ *adj*

fen \ˈfen\ *n* ◆ **:** low swampy land

◆ bog, marsh, mire, morass, slough, swamp

¹fence \ˈfens\ *n* **1** ◆ **:** a barrier (as of wood or wire) to prevent escape or entry or to mark a boundary **2 :** a person who receives stolen goods; *also* **:** a place where stolen goods are disposed of — **on the fence :** in a position of neutrality or indecision

◆ barrier, hedge, wall

²fence *vb* **fenced; fenc•ing** **1** ◆ **:** to enclose with a fence **2 :** to keep in or out with a fence **3 :** to practice fencing **4 :** to use tactics of attack and defense especially in debate — **fenc•er** *n*

◆ *usu* **fence in** cage, corral, enclose, hedge, pen

fenc•ing *n* **1 :** the art or practice of attack and defense with the foil, épée, or saber **2 :** the fences of a property or region **3 :** material used for building fences

fend \ˈfend\ *vb* **1** ◆ **:** to keep or ward off **:** REPEL **2 :** SHIFT ⟨~ for yourself⟩

◆ *usu* **fend off** repel, repulse, stave off

fend•er \ˈfen-dər\ *n* ◆ **:** a protective device (as a guard over the wheel of an automobile)

◆ buffer, bumper, cushion, pad

fen•es•tra•tion \ˌfe-nə-ˈstrā-shən\ *n* **:** the arrangement and design of windows and doors in a building

Fe•ni•an \ˈfē-nē-ən\ *n* **:** a member of a secret 19th century Irish and Irish-American organization dedicated to overthrowing British rule in Ireland

fen•nel \ˈfen-ᵊl\ *n* **:** a garden plant related to the carrot and grown for its aromatic foliage and seeds

FEPC *abbr* Fair Employment Practices Commission

fe•ral \ˈfir-əl, ˈfer-\ *adj* **1 :** SAVAGE **2** ◆ **:** not domesticated or cultivated **:** WILD 1 **3 :** having escaped from domestication and become wild

◆ savage, unbroken, undomesticated, untamed, wild

fer–de–lance \ˈfer-də-ˈlans\ *n, pl* **fer–de–lance :** a large venomous pit viper of Central and So. America

¹fer•ment \fər-ˈment\ *vb* **1 :** to cause or undergo fermentation **2 :** to be or cause to be in a state of agitation or intense activity

²fer•ment \ˈfər-ˌment\ *n* **1 :** a living organism (as a yeast) causing fermentation by its enzymes; *also* **:** ENZYME **2** ◆ **:** a state of unrest

◆ restlessness, turmoil, uneasiness, unrest

fer•men•ta•tion \ˌfər-mən-ˈtā-shən, -ˌmen-\ *n* **1 :** chemical decomposition of an organic substance (as in the souring of milk or the formation of alcohol from sugar) by enzymatic action in the absence of oxygen often with formation of gas **2 :** FERMENT 2

fer•mi•um \ˈfer-mē-əm, ˈfər-\ *n* **:** an artificially produced radioactive metallic chemical element

fern \ˈfərn\ *n* **:** any of an order of vascular plants resembling seed plants in having roots, stems, and leaflike fronds but reproducing by spores instead of by flowers and seeds

fern•ery \ˈfər-nə-rē\ *n, pl* **-er•ies** **1 :** a place for growing ferns **2 :** a collection of growing ferns

fe•ro•cious \fə-ˈrō-shəs\ *adj* **1** ◆ **:** exhibiting or given to extreme fierceness and unrestrained violence and brutality **2** ◆ **:** extremely intense — **fe•ro•cious•ly** *adv* — **fe•ro•cious•ness** *n*

◆ [1] fell, fierce, grim, savage, vicious ◆ [2] deep, fearful, heavy, intense, profound

fe•roc•i•ty \fə-ˈrä-sə-tē\ *n* **:** the quality or state of being ferocious

¹fer•ret \ˈfer-ət\ *n* **:** a partially domesticated usually white European mammal related to the weasels

²ferret *vb* **1 :** to hunt game with ferrets **2 :** to drive out of a hiding place **3** ◆ **:** to find and bring to light by searching — usually used with *out* ⟨~ out the truth⟩

◆ *usu* **ferret out** detect, determine, dig up, discover, find, hit on, locate, track down

fer•ric \ˈfer-ik\ *adj* **:** of, relating to, or containing iron

ferric oxide *n* **:** an oxide of iron found in nature as hematite and as rust and used especially as a pigment, for polishing, and in magnetic materials

Fer·ris wheel \ˈfer-əs-\ *n* **:** an amusement device consisting of a large upright power-driven wheel with seats that remain horizontal around its rim

fer·ro·mag·net·ic \ˌfer-ō-mag-ˈne-tik\ *adj* **:** of or relating to substances that are easily magnetized

fer·rous \ˈfer-əs\ *adj* **:** of, relating to, or containing iron

fer·rule \ˈfer-əl\ *n* **:** a metal ring or cap around a slender wooden shaft to prevent splitting

[1]**fer·ry** \ˈfer-ē\ *vb* **fer·ried; fer·ry·ing** **1 :** to carry by boat across a body of water **2 :** to cross by a ferry **3** ♦ **:** to convey from one place to another

♦ bear, carry, convey, haul, transport

[2]**ferry** *n, pl* **ferries** **1 :** a place where persons or things are ferried **2 :** FERRYBOAT

fer·ry·boat \ˈfer-ē-ˌbōt\ *n* **:** a boat used in ferrying

fer·tile \ˈfərt-ᵊl\ *adj* **1** ♦ **:** producing plentifully **:** PRODUCTIVE ⟨~ soils⟩ ⟨a ~ mind⟩ **2 :** capable of developing or reproducing ⟨~ seed⟩ ⟨a ~ bull⟩ — **fer·til·i·ty** \(ˌ)fər-ˈti-lə-tē\ *n*

♦ fecund, fruitful, luxuriant, productive, prolific, rich ***Ant*** barren, infertile, sterile, unfruitful, unproductive

fer·til·ize \ˈfərt-ᵊl-ˌīz\ *vb* **-ized; -iz·ing** **1 :** to unite with in the process of fertilization ⟨a sperm ~*s* an egg⟩ **2 :** to apply fertilizer to — **fer·til·iza·tion** \ˌfərt-ᵊl-ə-ˈzā-shən\ *n*

fer·til·iz·er \-ˌī-zər\ *n* **:** material (as manure or a chemical mixture) for enriching land

fer·ule \ˈfer-əl\ *n* **:** a rod or ruler used to punish children

fer·ven·cy \ˈfər-vən-sē\ *n, pl* **-cies** ♦ **:** deep interest in or enthusiasm for something **:** FERVOR

♦ ardor, emotion, fervor, heat, intensity, passion, vehemence, warmth

fer·vent \ˈfər-vənt\ *adj* **1 :** very hot **:** GLOWING **2** ♦ **:** marked by great intensity of feeling — **fer·vent·ly** *adv*

♦ ardent, burning, charged, emotional, fiery, hot-blooded, impassioned, passionate, red-hot, vehement ***Ant*** cold, cool, dispassionate, impassive, unemotional

fer·vid \-vəd\ *adj* **1 :** very hot **2** ♦ **:** marked by often extreme fervor **:** ARDENT — **fer·vid·ly** *adv*

♦ ardent, burning, charged, emotional, fervent, fiery, hot-blooded, impassioned, intense, passionate, red-hot, vehement

fer·vor *or Can and Brit* **fer·vour** \ˈfər-vər\ *n* **1 :** intense heat **2** ♦ **:** intensity of feeling or expression

♦ ardor, emotion, fervency, heat, intensity, passion, vehemence, warmth

fes·cue \ˈfes-kyü\ *n* **:** any of a genus of tufted perennial grasses

fes·tal \ˈfest-ᵊl\ *adj* **:** FESTIVE

fester \ˈfes-tər\ *vb* **1 :** to form pus **2 :** PUTREFY, ROT **3 :** RANKLE

fes·ti·val \ˈfes-tə-vəl\ *n* **1** ♦ **:** a time of celebration marked by special observances; *esp* **:** an occasion marked with religious ceremonies **2 :** a periodic season or program of cultural events or entertainment ⟨a dance ~⟩

♦ carnival, celebration, festivity, fete, fiesta, gala, jubilee

fes·tive \ˈfes-tiv\ *adj* **1 :** of, relating to, or suitable for a feast or festival **2** ♦ **:** marked by gaiety, conviviality, or revelry — **fes·tive·ly** *adv*

♦ gay, gleeful, jolly, jovial, merry, mirthful, sunny

fes·tiv·i·ty \fes-ˈti-və-tē\ *n, pl* **-ties** **1** ♦ **:** a time of celebration marked by special observances **:** FESTIVAL 1 **2 :** the quality or state of being festive **3** ♦ **:** festive activity

♦ [1] carnival, celebration, festival, fete, fiesta, gala, jubilee ♦ [3] conviviality, gaiety, jollification, merriment, merrymaking, revelry

[1]**fes·toon** \fes-ˈtün\ *n* **1 :** a decorative chain or strip hanging between two points **2 :** a carved, molded, or painted ornament representing a decorative chain

[2]**festoon** *vb* **1 :** to hang or form festoons on **2 :** to shape into festoons

fe·ta \ˈfe-tə\ *n* **:** a white crumbly Greek cheese made from sheep's or goat's milk

fe·tal \ˈfēt-ᵊl\ *adj* **:** of, relating to, or being a fetus

fetch \ˈfech\ *vb* **1 :** to go or come after and bring or take back ⟨teach a dog to ~ a stick⟩ **2** ♦ **:** to have as a price **3 :** to cause to come **:** bring out ⟨~*ed* tears from the eyes⟩ **4 :** to give by striking ⟨~ him a blow⟩

♦ bring, cost, go, sell

fetch·ing *adj* ♦ **:** tending to win interest or admiration **:** ATTRACTIVE — **fetch·ing·ly** *adv*

♦ alluring, attractive, charming, engaging, fascinating

fetch up *vb* ♦ **:** to bring to a stop

♦ draw up, halt, hold up, stay, still, stop

[1]**fete** *or* **fête** \ˈfāt, ˈfet\ *n* **1** ♦ **:** a festive celebration or entertainment **:** FESTIVAL **2** ♦ **:** a large elaborate entertainment or party

♦ [1] carnival, celebration, festival, festivity, fiesta, gala, jubilee ♦ [2] affair, blowout, event, function, get-together, party

[2]**fete** *or* **fête** *vb* **fet·ed** *or* **fêt·ed; fet·ing** *or* **fêt·ing** **1 :** to honor or commemorate with a fete **2 :** to pay high honor to

fet·id \ˈfe-təd\ *adj* ♦ **:** having an offensive smell

♦ foul, malodorous, noisome, rank, reeky, smelly, strong

fe·tish *also* **fe·tich** \ˈfe-tish\ *n* **1** ♦ **:** an object (as an idol or image) believed to have magical powers (as in curing disease) **2** ♦ **:** an object of unreasoning devotion or concern **3 :** an object whose real or fantasied presence is psychologically necessary for sexual gratification

♦ [1] amulet, charm, mascot, talisman ♦ [2] fixation, mania, obsession, preoccupation, prepossession

fe·tish·ism \-ti-ˌshi-zəm\ *n* **1 :** belief in or devotion to fetishes **2 :** the pathological transfer of sexual interest and gratification to a fetish — **fe·tish·ist** \-shist\ *n* — **fe·tish·is·tic** \ˌfe-ti-ˈshis-tik\ *adj*

fe·tish·ize \-ti-ˌshīz\ *vb* **-ized; -iz·ing** **:** to make a fetish of

fet·lock \ˈfet-ˌläk\ *n* **:** a projection on the back of a horse's leg above the hoof; *also* **:** a tuft of hair on this

fet·ter \ˈfe-tər\ *n* **1** ♦ **:** a chain or shackle for the feet **2** ♦ **:** something that confines

♦ [1] band, bond, chain, irons, ligature, manacle, shackle ♦ [2] check, condition, constraint, curb, limitation, restraint, restriction

fetter *vb* **1** ♦ **:** to put fetters on **2** ♦ **:** to restrain from motion, action, or progress

♦ [1] bind, chain, enchain, handcuff, manacle, shackle, trammel ♦ [2] delay, encumber, hamper, handicap, hinder, hobble, hold back, impede, inhibit, interfere with, obstruct

fet·tle \ˈfet-ᵊl\ *n* ♦ **:** a state of fitness or order **:** CONDITION ⟨in fine ~⟩

♦ condition, form, order, repair, shape, trim

fe·tus \ˈfē-təs\ *n* **:** an unborn or unhatched vertebrate especially after its basic structure is laid down; *esp* **:** a developing human in the uterus from usually three months after conception to birth

feud \ˈfyüd\ *n* **:** a prolonged quarrel; *esp* **:** a lasting conflict between families or clans marked by violent attacks made for revenge — **feud** *vb*

feu·dal \ˈfyü-dᵊl\ *adj* **1 :** of, relating to, or having the characteristics of a medieval fee **2 :** of, relating to, or characteristic of feudalism

feu·dal·ism \ˈfyü-də-ˌli-zəm\ *n* **:** a system of political organization prevailing in medieval Europe in which a vassal renders service to a lord and receives protection and land in return; *also* **:** a similar political or social system — **feu·dal·is·tic** \ˌfyüd-ᵊl-ˈis-tik\ *adj*

[1]**feu·da·to·ry** \ˈfyü-də-ˌtōr-ē\ *adj* **:** owing feudal allegiance

[2]**feudatory** *n, pl* **-ries** **1 :** FIEF **2 :** a person who holds lands by feudal law or usage

fe·ver \ˈfē-vər\ *n* **1 a :** a rise in body temperature above the normal **b** ♦ **:** an abnormal bodily state characterized by increased heat, accelerated pulse, and systemic debility **c** ♦ **:** a disease of which a high body temperature is a chief symptom **2 :** a state of heightened emotion or activity **3 :** CRAZE — **fe·ver·ish·ly** *adv*

♦ [1b, 1c] ailment, bug, complaint, condition, disease, disorder, ill, illness, infirmity, malady, sickness, trouble

fe·ver·ish *adj* ♦ **:** marked by intense emotion, activity, or instability

♦ agitated, frenzied, heated, hectic, overactive, overwrought ♦ delirious, fierce, frantic, frenetic, frenzied, furious, mad, violent, wild

[1]**few** \ˈfyü\ *pron* **:** not many **:** a small number

[2]**few** *adj* **1 :** consisting of or amounting to a small number **2 :** not

many but some ⟨caught a ~ fish⟩ — **few•ness** *n* — **few and far between** : RARE 3

³few *n* **1** ♦ **:** a small number of units or individuals ⟨a ~ of them⟩ **2 :** a special limited number ⟨among the ~⟩

♦ handful, smattering, sprinkle, sprinkling *Ant* crowd, horde, many

few•er \ˈfyü-ər\ *pron* **:** a smaller number of persons or things

fey \ˈfā\ *adj* **1** *chiefly Scot* **:** fated to die; *also* **:** marked by a foreboding of death or calamity **2 :** able to see into the future : VISIONARY **3 :** marked by an otherworldly air or attitude **4 :** CRAZY, TOUCHED

fez \ˈfez\ *n, pl* **fez•zes** *also* **fez•es :** a round red felt hat that has a flat top and a tassel but no brim

ff *abbr* **1** folios **2** and the following ones **3** fortissimo

FHA *abbr* Federal Housing Administration

fi•an•cé \ˌfē-ˌän-ˈsā\ *n* **:** a man engaged to be married

fi•an•cée \ˌfē-ˌän-ˈsā\ *n* **:** a woman engaged to be married

fi•as•co \fē-ˈas-kō\ *n, pl* **-coes** ♦ **:** a complete failure

♦ bust, catastrophe, debacle, failure, flop, washout

fi•at \ˈfē-ət, -ˌat, -ˌät; ˈfī-ət, -ˌat\ *n* ♦ **:** an authoritative and often arbitrary order or decree

♦ decree, directive, edict, ruling

¹fib \ˈfib\ *n* ♦ **:** a trivial or childish lie

♦ fabrication, falsehood, falsity, lie, story, tale, untruth

²fib *vb* **fibbed; fib•bing** ♦ **:** to tell a fib

♦ fabricate, lie, prevaricate

fib•ber *n* ♦ **:** one that tells fibs

♦ liar, prevaricator

fi•ber *or Can and Brit* **fi•bre** \ˈfī-bər\ *n* **1 :** a threadlike substance or structure (as a muscle cell or fine root); *esp* **:** a natural (as wool or flax) or artificial (as rayon) filament capable of being spun or woven **2 :** indigestible material in human food that stimulates the intestine to move its contents along **3 :** an element that gives texture or substance **4** ♦ **:** basic toughness : STRENGTH — **fi•brous** \-brəs\ *adj*

♦ backbone, fortitude, grit, guts, pluck, spunk

fi•ber•board *or Can and Brit* **fi•bre•board** \ˈfī-bər-ˌbōrd\ *n* **:** a material made by compressing fibers (as of wood) into stiff sheets

fi•ber•fill *or Can and Brit* **fi•bre•fill** \-ˌfil\ *n* **:** synthetic fibers used as a filling material (as for cushions)

fi•ber•glass *or Can and Brit* **fi•bre•glass** \-ˌglas\ *n* **:** glass in fibrous form used in making various products (as insulation)

fiber optics *n* **1** *pl* **:** thin transparent fibers of glass or plastic that are enclosed by a less refractive material and that transmit light by internal reflection; *also* **:** a bundle of such fibers used in an instrument **2 :** the technique of the use of fiber optics — **fiber–optic** *adj*

fi•bril \ˈfī-brəl, ˈfi-\ *n* **:** a small fiber

fi•bril•la•tion \ˌfi-brə-ˈlā-shən, ˌfī-\ *n* **:** rapid irregular contractions of the heart muscle fibers resulting in a lack of synchronism between heartbeat and pulse — **fib•ril•late** \ˈfi-brə-ˌlāt, ˈfī-\ *vb*

fi•brin \ˈfī-brən\ *n* **:** a white insoluble fibrous protein formed in the clotting of blood

fi•broid \ˈfī-ˌbrȯid, ˈfi-\ *adj* **:** resembling, forming, or consisting of fibrous tissue ⟨~ tumors⟩

fi•bro•my•al•gia \ˌfī-ˌbrō-ˌmī-ˈal-jə\ *n* **:** any of a group of rheumatic disorders affecting soft tissues (as muscles or tendons)

fi•bro•sis \fī-ˈbro-səs\ *n* **:** a condition marked by abnormal increase of fiber-containing tissue

fib•u•la \ˈfi-byə-lə\ *n, pl* **-lae** \-lē, -lī\ *or* **-las :** the outer and usually the smaller of the two bones between the knee and ankle — **fib•u•lar** \-lər\ *adj*

FICA *abbr* Federal Insurance Contributions Act

-fication *n comb form* **:** making : production ⟨simpli*fication*⟩

fiche \ˈfēsh\ *n, pl* **fiche :** MICROFICHE

fi•chu \ˈfi-shü\ *n* **:** a woman's light triangular scarf draped over the shoulders and fastened in front

fick•le \ˈfi-kəl\ *adj* ♦ **:** not firm or steadfast in disposition or character : INCONSTANT — **fick•le•ness** *n*

♦ capricious, changeable, inconstant, mercurial, uncertain, unpredictable, unsteady, variable *Ant* certain, constant, steady, unchangeable ♦ disloyal, faithless, false, inconstant, unfaithful, untrue

fic•tion \ˈfik-shən\ *n* **1** ♦ **:** something (as a story) invented by the imagination **2** ♦ **:** fictitious literature (as novels)

♦ [1, 2] fabrication, fantasy, figment, invention *Ant* fact

fic•tion•al \ˈfik-shə-nəl\ *adj* **:** of, relating to, or characteristic of fiction — **fic•tion•al•ly** *adv*

fic•ti•tious \fik-ˈti-shəs\ *adj* **1** ♦ **:** of, relating to, or characteristic of fiction : IMAGINARY **2 :** FALSE, ASSUMED ⟨a ~ name⟩ **3 :** FEIGNED

♦ imaginary, made-up, mythical, pretend, unreal

¹fid•dle \ˈfid-ᵊl\ *n* **:** VIOLIN

²fiddle *vb* **fid•dled; fid•dling 1 :** to play on a fiddle **2** ♦ **:** to move the hands or fingers restlessly **3** ♦ **:** to move or act aimlessly or idly — often used with *around* **4** ♦ **:** to interest oneself in what is not one's concern — **fid•dler** *n*

♦ [2] fidget, jerk, squirm, twitch, wiggle ♦ *usu* **fiddle around** [3] fool, mess, monkey, play, putter ♦ *usu* **fiddle with** [4] fool, mess, monkey, play, tamper, tinker

fid•dle•head \ˈfi-dᵊl-ˌhed\ *n* **:** one of the young unfurling fronds of some ferns that are often eaten as greens

fiddler crab *n* **:** any of a genus of burrowing crabs with one claw much enlarged in the male

fid•dle•stick \ˈfid-ᵊl-ˌstik\ *n* **1** *archaic* **:** a violin bow **2** *pl* ♦ **:** language, conduct, or an idea that is absurd or contrary to good sense : NONSENSE — used as an interjection

♦ **fiddlesticks** foolishness, hogwash, humbug, nonsense, silliness

fi•del•i•ty \fə-ˈde-lə-tē, fī-\ *n, pl* **-ties 1** ♦ **:** the quality or state of being faithful **2 :** ACCURACY ⟨~ in sound reproduction⟩

♦ allegiance, constancy, dedication, devotion, faith, faithfulness, fastness, fealty, loyalty, steadfastness *Ant* disloyalty, infidelity, perfidy, treachery

¹fidg•et \ˈfi-jət\ *n* **1 :** uneasiness or restlessness as shown by nervous movements — usually used in plural **2 :** one that fidgets — **fidg•ety** *adj*

²fidget *vb* ♦ **:** to move or cause to move or act restlessly or nervously

♦ fiddle, jerk, squirm, twitch, wiggle

fi•du•cia•ry \fə-ˈdü-shē-ˌer-ē, -ˈdyü-, -shə-rē\ *adj* **1 :** involving a confidence or trust **2 :** held or holding in trust for another ⟨~ accounts⟩ — **fiduciary** *n*

fie \ˈfī\ *interj* — used to express disgust or disapproval

fief \ˈfēf\ *n* **:** a feudal estate : FEE

¹field \ˈfēld\ *n* **1** ♦ **:** open country **2 :** a piece of cleared land for cultivation or pasture **3 :** a piece of land yielding some special product **4 :** the place where a battle is fought; *also* **:** BATTLE **5** ♦ **:** an area, division, or sphere of activity ⟨the ~ of science⟩ ⟨salesmen in the ~⟩ **6 :** an area for military exercises **7 :** an area for sports **8 :** a background on which something is drawn or projected ⟨a flag with white stars on a ~ of blue⟩ **9 :** a region or space in which a given effect (as magnetism) exists — **field** *adj*

♦ [1] ground, lot, parcel, plat, plot, tract ♦ [5] area, arena, department, discipline, domain, line, province, realm, specialty, sphere

²field *vb* **1 :** to handle a batted or thrown baseball while on defense **2 :** to put into the field **3 :** to answer satisfactorily ⟨~ a tough question⟩ — **field•er** *n*

field day *n* **1 :** a day devoted to outdoor sports and athletic competition **2 :** a time of extraordinary pleasure or opportunity

field event *n* **:** a track-and-field event (as weight-throwing) other than a race

field glass *n* **:** a hand-held binocular telescope — usually used in plural

field guide *n* **:** a manual for identifying natural objects, plants, or animals

field hockey *n* **:** a field game played between two teams of 11 players each whose object is to knock a ball into the opponent's goal with a curved stick

field marshal *n* **:** an officer (as in the British army) of the highest rank

field–test \-ˌtest\ *vb* **:** to test (as a new product) in actual situations reflecting intended use — **field test** *n*

fiend \ˈfēnd\ *n* **1 :** DEVIL 1 **2** ♦ **:** an infernal being : DEMON **3** ♦ **:** an extremely wicked or cruel person **4** ♦ **:** a person excessively devoted to a pursuit ⟨a golf ~⟩ **5** ♦ **:** one who is addicted especially to a substance : ADDICT ⟨dope ~⟩

♦ [2] demon, devil, ghoul, imp ♦ [3] beast, devil, evildoer, no-good, reprobate, rogue, varlet, villain, wretch ♦ [4] addict, enthusiast, fan, fanatic, freak, lover, maniac, nut ♦ [5] addict, doper, user

fiend•ish *adj* ♦ **:** perversely diabolical — **fiend•ish•ly** *adv*

♦ demonic, devilish, diabolical, satanic *Ant* angelic

fierce \ˈfirs\ *adj* **fierc•er; fierc•est** **1** ♦ : violently hostile or aggressive in temperament **2** : given to fighting or killing : PUGNACIOUS **3** ♦ : marked by unrestrained zeal or vehemence : INTENSE **4** ♦ : furiously active or determined **5** ♦ : wild or menacing in appearance — **fierce•ly** *adv*

♦ [1] fell, ferocious, grim, savage, vicious ***Ant*** gentle, mild ♦ [3] explosive, ferocious, furious, intense, terrible, vehement, vicious, violent ♦ [4] aggressive, ambitious, assertive, enterprising, go-getting, high-pressure, militant, self-assertive ♦ [5] austere, forbidding, grim, rough, rugged, severe, steely, stern

fierce•ness *n* ♦ : the quality or state of being fierce

♦ aggressiveness, assertiveness, emphasis, intensity, vehemence

fi•ery \ˈfī-ə-rē\ *adj* **fi•er•i•er; -est** **1** : consisting of fire **2** ♦ : on fire : BURNING, BLAZING **3** : FLAMMABLE **4** ♦ : hot like a fire **5** : RED ⟨a ~ sunset⟩ **6** ♦ : full of emotion or spirit **7** : IRRITABLE — **fi•eri•ness** \-rē-nəs\ *n*

♦ [2] ablaze, afire, burning ♦ [4] broiling, burning, hot, torrid ♦ [6] ardent, emotional, fervent, feverish, hot-blooded, impassioned, passionate, red-hot, vehement

fi•es•ta \fē-ˈes-tə\ *n* ♦ : a time of celebration marked by special observances : FESTIVAL

♦ carnival, celebration, festival, festivity, fete, gala, jubilee

fife \ˈfīf\ *n* : a small flute
FIFO *abbr* first in, first out
fif•teen \fif-ˈtēn\ *n* : one more than 14 — **fifteen** *adj or pron* — **fif•teenth** \-ˈtēnth\ *adj or n*
fifth \ˈfifth\ *n* **1** : one that is number five in a countable series **2** : one of five equal parts of something **3** : a unit of measure for liquor equal to ⅕ U.S. gallon — **fifth** *adj or adv*
fifth column *n* : a group of secret supporters of a nation's enemy that engage in espionage or sabotage within the country — **fifth columnist** *n*
fifth wheel *n* : one that is unnecessary and often burdensome
fif•ty \ˈfif-tē\ *n, pl* **fifties** : five times 10 — **fif•ti•eth** \-tē-əth\ *adj or n* — **fifty** *adj or pron*
fif•ty–fif•ty \ˌfif-tē-ˈfif-tē\ *adj* **1** : shared equally ⟨a ~ proposition⟩ **2** : half favorable and half unfavorable
¹fig \ˈfig\ *n* : a soft usually pear-shaped edible fruit of a tree related to the mulberry; *also* : a tree bearing figs
²fig *abbr* **1** figurative; figuratively **2** figure
¹fight \ˈfīt\ *vb* **fought** \ˈfȯt\; **fight•ing** **1** ♦ : to contend against another in battle or physical combat **2** : BOX **3** : to put forth a determined effort **4** ♦ : to contend in disagreement or competition **5** ♦ : to attempt to prevent the success or effectiveness of **6** : WAGE **7** : to gain by struggle

♦ [1] battle, clash, combat, scrimmage, skirmish, war ♦ [4] battle, compete, contend, race, vie ♦ [4] argue, brawl, dispute, quarrel, row, scrap, spat, squabble ♦ [5] battle, combat, contend, counter, oppose ***Ant*** advance, encourage, promote

²fight *n* **1** ♦ : a hostile encounter : BATTLE **2** : a boxing match **3** ♦ : a verbal disagreement **4** ♦ : a struggle for a goal or an objective **5** ♦ : strength or disposition for fighting ⟨full of ~⟩

♦ [1] battle, clash, combat, conflict, contest, skirmish, struggle ♦ [3] argument, brawl, disagreement, dispute, quarrel, row, scrap, spat, squabble ♦ [4] battle, fray, scrabble, struggle ♦ [5] aggression, aggressiveness, belligerence, militancy, pugnacity, truculence

fight•er \ˈfī-tər\ *n* **1** ♦ : one that fights; *esp* : WARRIOR **2** ♦ : one that engages in the sport of boxing : BOXER **3** : a fast maneuverable warplane for destroying enemy aircraft

♦ [1] legionnaire, man-at-arms, regular, serviceman, soldier, warrior ♦ [2] boxer, prizefighter, pugilist

fig•ment \ˈfig-mənt\ *n* ♦ : something imagined or made up

♦ chimera, conceit, delusion, dream, fancy, fantasy, hallucination, illusion, phantasm, pipe dream, unreality, vision

fig•u•ra•tion \ˌfi-gyə-ˈrā-shən, -gə-\ *n* **1** : FORM, OUTLINE **2** : an act or instance of representation in figures and shapes
fig•u•ra•tive \ˈfi-gyə-rə-tiv, -gə-\ *adj* **1** : EMBLEMATIC **2** : expressing one thing in terms normally denoting another with which it may be regarded as analogous : SYMBOLIC, METAPHORICAL ⟨~ language⟩ — **fig•u•ra•tive•ly** *adv*
¹fig•ure \ˈfi-gyər, -gər\ *n* **1** ♦ : a number symbol : NUMERAL **2** : a written or printed character **3** ♦ : value especially as expressed in numbers : PRICE **4** : a combination of points, lines, or surfaces in geometry ⟨a circle is a closed plane ~⟩ **5** ♦ : a body apparent chiefly in outline : an object significant or noticeable only in its form : SHAPE, FORM, OUTLINE **6 a** : the graphic representation of a form especially of a person **b** : a representation of the human figure used especially for displaying clothes **7** ♦ : a diagram or pictorial illustration of textual matter **8** : an often repetitive pattern or design in a manufactured article (as cloth) or natural product (as wood) : PATTERN, DESIGN **9** : appearance made or impression produced ⟨they cut quite a ~⟩ **10** : a series of movements (as in a dance) **11** ♦ : a prominent personality : PERSONAGE **12** ♦ : the shape of the human body

♦ [1] digit, integer, number, numeral, whole number ♦ [3] charge, cost, fee, price ♦ [5] cast, configuration, form, outline, shape ♦ [7] diagram, graphic, illustration, plate ♦ [11] celebrity, notable, personage, personality ♦ [12] build, constitution, form, frame, physique, shape

²figure *vb* **fig•ured; fig•ur•ing** **1** : to represent by or as if by a figure or outline **2** : to decorate with a pattern **3** : to indicate or represent by numerals **4** ♦ : to think of especially with regard to taking some action **5** : to be or appear important or conspicuous **6** ♦ : to determine especially by mathematical means : COMPUTE, CALCULATE **7** : to reckon by exercise of practical judgment **8** ♦ : to take as granted or true

♦ [4] choose, conclude, decide, determine, opt, resolve ♦ [6] calculate, compute, reckon, work out ♦ [8] believe, consider, feel, imagine, suppose, think

fig•ure•head \ˈfi-gyər-ˌhed, -gər-\ *n* **1** : a figure on the bow of a ship **2** : a head or chief in name only
figure of speech : a form of expression (as a simile or metaphor) that often compares or identifies one thing with another to convey meaning or heighten effect
figure out *vb* **1** : FIND OUT, DISCOVER **2** ♦ : to find a solution, explanation, or answer for : SOLVE

♦ answer, puzzle, resolve, riddle, solve, unravel, work, work out

figure skating *n* : skating that includes various jumps, spins, and dance movements
fig•u•rine \ˌfi-gyə-ˈrēn, -gə-\ *n* : a small carved or molded figure
Fi•ji•an \ˈfē-jē-ən, fi-ˈjē-ən\ *n* : a native or inhabitant of the Pacific island country of Fiji — **Fijian** *adj*
fil•a•ment \ˈfi-lə-mənt\ *n* : a fine thread or threadlike object, part, or process — **fil•a•men•tous** \ˌfi-lə-ˈmen-təs\ *adj*
fil•bert \ˈfil-bərt\ *n* : the sweet thick-shelled nut of either of two European hazels; *also* : a shrub or small tree bearing filberts
filch \ˈfilch\ *vb* ♦ : to steal furtively

♦ appropriate, pilfer, pocket, steal, swipe, thieve

¹file \ˈfīl\ *n* : a usually steel tool with a ridged or toothed surface used especially for smoothing a hard substance
²file *vb* **filed; fil•ing** ♦ : to rub, smooth, or cut away with a file

♦ buff, grind, hone, rasp, rub, sand

³file *vb* **filed; fil•ing** **1** : to arrange in order **2** : to enter or record officially or as prescribed by law ⟨~ a lawsuit⟩ **3** : to send (copy) to a newspaper
⁴file *n* **1** : a device (as a folder or cabinet) by means of which papers may be kept in order **2** : a collection of papers or publications usually arranged or classified **3** : a collection of data (as text) treated by a computer as a unit
⁵file *n* ♦ : a row of persons, animals, or things arranged one behind the other

♦ column, cue, line, queue, range, string, train

⁶file *vb* **filed; fil•ing** ♦ : to march or proceed in file

♦ march, pace, parade, stride

fi•let mi•gnon \ˌfi-(ˌ)lā-mēn-ˈyōⁿ, fi-ˌlā-\ *n, pl* **filets mignons** \-(ˌ)lā-mēn-ˈyōⁿz, -ˌlā-\ : a thick slice of beef cut from the narrow end of a beef tenderloin
fil•ial \ˈfi-lē-əl, ˈfil-yəl\ *adj* : of, relating to, or befitting a son or daughter
fil•i•bus•ter \ˈfi-lə-ˌbəs-tər\ *n* **1** : a military adventurer; *esp* : an American engaged in fomenting 19th century Latin American uprisings **2** : the use of delaying tactics (as extremely long speeches) especially in a legislative assembly; *also* : an instance of this practice — **filibuster** *vb* — **fil•i•bus•ter•er** *n*
fil•i•gree \ˈfi-lə-ˌgrē\ *n* : ornamental openwork (as of fine wire) — **fil•i•greed** \-ˌgrēd\ *adj*
fil•ing \ˈfī-liŋ\ *n* **1** : the act or instance of using a file **2** : a small piece scraped off by a file ⟨iron ~*s*⟩
Fil•i•pi•no \ˌfi-lə-ˈpē-nō\ *n, pl* **Filipinos** : a native or inhabitant of the Philippines — **Filipino** *adj*
¹fill \ˈfil\ *vb* **1** ♦ : to make or become full **2** ♦ : to stop up : PLUG

⟨~ a cavity⟩ **3 :** FEED, SATIATE **4** ♦ **:** to carry out the terms of (as a contract) **:** SATISFY, FULFILL ⟨~ all requirements⟩ **5 :** to occupy fully **6 :** to spread through ⟨laughter ~*ed* the room⟩ **7 :** OCCUPY ⟨~ the office of president⟩ **8 :** to put a person in ⟨~ a vacancy⟩ **9 :** to supply as directed ⟨~ a prescription⟩

♦ [1] charge, cram, heap, jam, jam-pack, load, pack, stuff *Ant* empty ♦ [2] block, dam, pack, plug, stop, stuff ♦ [4] answer, comply, fulfill, keep, meet, redeem, satisfy

²fill *n* **1 :** a full supply; *esp* **:** a quantity that satisfies or satiates **2 :** material used especially for filling a low place

fill•er \ˈfi-lər\ *n* **1 :** one that fills **2** ♦ **:** a substance added to another substance (as to increase bulk or weight) **3 :** a material used for filling cracks and pores in wood before painting

♦ fill, filling, padding, stuffing

¹fil•let \ˈfi-lət, *in sense 2* fi-ˈlā, ˈfi-(ˌ)lā\ *also* **fi•let** \fi-ˈlā, ˈfi-(ˌ)lā\ *n* **1 :** a narrow band, strip, or ribbon **2 :** a piece or slice of boneless meat or fish; *esp* **:** the tenderloin of beef

²fil•let \ˈfi-lət, *in sense 2 also* fi-ˈlā, ˈfi-(ˌ)lā\ *vb* **1 :** to bind or adorn with or as if with a fillet **2 :** to cut into fillets

fill in *vb* **1** ♦ **:** to provide necessary or recent information **2** ♦ **:** to serve as a temporary substitute

♦ [1] acquaint, brief, enlighten, familiarize, inform, instruct ♦ [2] cover, pinch-hit, stand in, sub, substitute, take over

fill•ing \ˈfi-liŋ\ *n* **1** ♦ **:** material used to fill something ⟨a ~ for a tooth⟩ **2 :** the yarn interlacing the warp in a fabric **3 :** a food mixture used to fill pastry or sandwiches

♦ fill, filler, padding, stuffing

filling station *n* **:** a retail station for servicing motor vehicles especially with gasoline and oil

fil•lip \ˈfi-ləp\ *n* **1 :** a blow or gesture made by a flick or snap of the finger across the thumb **2 :** something that serves to arouse or excite — **fillip** *vb*

fill–up \ˈfil-ˌəp\ *n* **:** an act or instance of filling something

fil•ly \ˈfi-lē\ *n, pl* **fillies :** a young female horse usually less than four years old

¹film \ˈfilm\ *n* **1 :** a thin skin or membrane **2 :** a thin coating or layer **3 :** a flexible strip of chemically treated material used in taking pictures **4** ♦ **:** a representation (as of a story) by means of motion pictures

♦ motion picture, movie, picture

²film *vb* **1 :** to cover with a film **2 :** to make a motion picture of

film•dom \ˈfilm-dəm\ *n* **:** the motion-picture industry

film•og•ra•phy \fil-ˈmä-grə-fē\ *n, pl* **-phies :** a list of motion pictures featuring the work of a film figure or a particular topic

film•strip \ˈfilm-ˌstrip\ *n* **:** a strip of film bearing a sequence of images for projection as still pictures

filmy *adj* **:** light, transparent, and fluffy

fils \ˈfēs\ *n* **:** SON — used after a family name to distinguish a son from his father

¹fil•ter \ˈfil-tər\ *n* **1 :** a porous material through which a fluid is passed to separate out matter in suspension; *also* **:** a device containing such material **2 :** a device for suppressing waves of certain frequencies; *esp* **:** one (as for a camera) that absorbs light of certain colors **3 :** software for sorting or blocking certain online material

²filter *vb* **1** ♦ **:** to remove by means of a filter **2 :** to pass through a filter — **fil•ter•able** *also* **fil•tra•ble** \-tə-rə-bəl, -trə-\ *adj* — **fil•tra•tion** \fil-ˈtrā-shən\ *n*

♦ clarify, clear, distill, purify

filth \ˈfilth\ *n* **1** ♦ **:** foul matter; *esp* **:** loathsome dirt or refuse **2** ♦ **:** moral corruption **3 :** something that tends to corrupt or disgust **:** OBSCENITY

♦ [1] dirt, grime, muck, refuse, smut, soil ♦ [2] coarseness, dirt, grossness, indecency, lewdness, obscenity, smut, vulgarity

filth•i•ness *n* ♦ **:** the quality or state of being filthy

♦ dinginess, dirtiness, foulness, grubbiness, nastiness, uncleanliness

¹filthy \ˈfil-thē\ *adj* **1** ♦ **:** covered with, having the appearance of, or containing filth **:** very dirty **2** ♦ **:** abhorrent to morality or virtue **:** designed to incite to lust or depravity

♦ [1] dirty, grubby, grungy, mucky, muddy, unclean ♦ [2] bawdy, coarse, crude, dirty, gross, indecent, lewd, obscene, pornographic, vulgar

²filthy *adv* **:** VERY, EXTREMELY ⟨~ dirty⟩ ⟨~ rich⟩

fil•trate \ˈfil-ˌtrāt\ *n* **:** fluid that has passed through a filter

¹fin \ˈfin\ *n* **1 :** one of the thin external processes by which an aquatic animal (as a fish) moves through water **2 :** a fin-shaped part (as on an airplane) **3 :** FLIPPER 2 — **finned** \ˈfind\ *adj*

²fin *abbr* **1** finance; financial **2** finish

fi•na•gle \fə-ˈnā-gəl\ *vb* **-gled; -gling 1** ♦ **:** to obtain by indirect or dishonest means **:** WANGLE **2** ♦ **:** to use devious dishonest methods to achieve one's ends — **fi•na•gler** *n*

♦ [1, 2] contrive, finesse, frame, machinate, maneuver, wangle

¹fi•nal \ˈfī-ᵊl\ *adj* **1** ♦ **:** not to be altered or undone **2** ♦ **:** coming at the end **:** being the last in a series, process, or progress **3 :** relating to or occurring at the end or conclusion — **fi•nal•i•ty** \fī-ˈna-lə-tē, fə-\ *n* — **fi•nal•ly** *adv*

♦ [1] certain, firm, fixed, hard, hard-and-fast, set, settled, stable ♦ [2] hindmost, last, latter, terminal, ultimate

²final *n* **1 :** a deciding match or game — usually used in plural **2 :** the last examination in a course — often used in plural

fi•na•le \fə-ˈna-lē, fi-ˈnä-\ *n* ♦ **:** the close or end of something; *esp* **:** the last section of a musical composition

♦ close, conclusion, consummation, end, ending, finis, finish, windup *Ant* beginning, dawn, opening, start

fi•nal•ise *Brit var of* FINALIZE

fi•nal•ist \ˈfī-ᵊl-əst\ *n* **:** a contestant in the finals of a competition

fi•nal•ize \ˈfī-ᵊl-ˌīz\ *vb* **-ized; -iz•ing** ♦ **:** to put in final or finished form

♦ complete, consummate, finish, perfect

¹fi•nance \fə-ˈnans, ˈfī-ˌnans\ *n* **1** *pl* ♦ **:** money resources available especially to a government or business **2 :** management of money affairs

♦ *usu* **finances** funds, resources, wherewithal

²finance *vb* **fi•nanced; fi•nanc•ing 1** ♦ **:** to raise or provide funds for **2** ♦ **:** to furnish with necessary funds **3 :** to sell or supply on credit

♦ [1] capitalize, endow, fund, stake, subsidize, underwrite ♦ [1, 2] endow, fund, subsidize

finance company *n* **:** a company that makes usually small short-term loans usually to individuals

fi•nan•cial \fə-ˈnan-chəl, fī-\ *adj* ♦ **:** relating to finance or financiers — **fi•nan•cial•ly** *adv*

♦ fiscal, monetary, pecuniary

fi•nan•cials \-shəlz\ *n pl* **:** financial statistics

fi•nan•cier \ˌfi-nən-ˈsir, ˌfī-ˌnan-\ *n* **1 :** a person skilled in managing public moneys **2 :** a person who deals with large-scale finance and investment

finch \ˈfinch\ *n* **:** any of numerous songbirds with strong conical bills

¹find \ˈfīnd\ *vb* **found** \ˈfau̇nd\; **find•ing 1** ♦ **:** to meet with either by chance or by searching or study **2 :** to obtain by effort or management ⟨~ time to read⟩ **3 :** to arrive at **:** REACH ⟨the bullet *found* its mark⟩ **4 :** EXPERIENCE, FEEL ⟨*found* happiness⟩ **5 :** to gain or regain the use of ⟨*found* his voice again⟩ **6 :** to determine and make a statement about ⟨~ a verdict⟩

♦ detect, determine, dig up, discover, ferret out, hit on, locate, track down *Ant* miss, overlook, pass over

²find *n* **1 :** an act or instance of finding **2 :** something found; *esp* **:** a valuable item of discovery

find•er \ˈfīn-dər\ *n* **:** one that finds; *esp* **:** VIEWFINDER

fin de siè•cle \ˌfaⁿ-də-sē-ˈeklᵊ\ *adj* **1 :** of, relating to, or characteristic of the close of the 19th century **2 :** of or relating to the end of a century

find•ing \ˈfīn-diŋ\ *n* **1** ♦ **:** the act of finding **2 :** FIND 2 **3 :** the result of a judicial proceeding or inquiry

♦ detection, discovery

find out *vb* ♦ **:** to learn by study, observation, or search **:** DISCOVER

♦ ascertain, catch on, discover, hear, learn, realize, see

¹fine \ˈfīn\ *n* ♦ **:** money exacted as a penalty for an offense

♦ damages, forfeit, mulct, penalty

²fine *vb* **fined; fin•ing** ♦ **:** to impose a fine on **:** punish by a fine

♦ assess, charge, exact, impose, lay, levy, put

³fine *adj* **fin•er; fin•est 1** ♦ **:** free from impurity **2 a** ♦ **:** very thin in gauge or texture **b** ♦ **:** very small **3 :** not coarse **4 :** SUBTLE, SENSITIVE ⟨a ~ distinction⟩ **5** ♦ **:** superior in quality or appearance **:** eminently good **6** ♦ **:** very precise or accurate **:** REFINED **7** ♦ **:** very well — **fine•ly** *adv*

♦ [1] pure, refined, unadulterated, undiluted ♦ [2a] dusty, floury, powdery *Ant* coarse, grainy, granular ♦ [2b] narrow, skinny, slender, slim, thin ♦ [5] A1, excellent, grand, great, heavenly, prime, splendid, superb, superior, unsurpassed, wonderful ♦ [6] delicate, exact, minute, precise, refined, subtle *Ant* coarse, inexact, rough ♦ [7] agreeable, all right, alright, good, OK, satisfactory

4fine *adv* **1** ♦ **:** very well **2** — used to express agreement

♦ all right, good, nicely, OK, satisfactorily, well

fine art *n* **:** art (as painting, sculpture, or music) concerned primarily with the creation of beautiful objects — usually used in plural

fine•ness *n* **1** ♦ **:** exquisite perfection or elaborateness of form, texture, or construction **:** superior quality **2** ♦ **:** delicate, subtle, or sensitive in quality, perception, or discrimination

♦ [1] accuracy, closeness, delicacy, exactness, precision, veracity ♦ [2] daintiness, delicacy, fragility

fin•ery \ˈfī-nə-rē\ *n, pl* **-er•ies** **1 :** ORNAMENT, DECORATION **2** ♦ **:** showy clothing and jewels

♦ array, best, feather, frippery, full dress, regalia

fine•spun \ˈfīn-ˈspən\ *adj* **:** developed with extremely or excessively fine delicacy or detail

1fi•nesse \fə-ˈnes\ *n* **1 :** refinement or delicacy of workmanship, structure, or texture **2** ♦ **:** skillful handling of a situation **:** adroit maneuvering

♦ adroitness, cleverness, craft, dexterity, sleight

2finesse *vb* ♦ **:** to bring about, direct, or manage by adroit maneuvering

♦ finagle, maneuver, mastermind, negotiate, wangle

fine–tune \ˈfīn-ˈtün\ *vb* **:** to adjust so as to bring to the highest level of performance or effectiveness

fin•fish \ˈfin-ˌfish\ *n* **:** FISH 2

1fin•ger \ˈfiŋ-gər\ *n* **1 :** any of the five divisions at the end of the hand; *esp* **:** one other than the thumb **2 :** something that resembles or does the work of a finger **3 :** a part of a glove into which a finger is inserted

2finger *vb* **fin•gered; fin•ger•ing** **1 :** to touch or feel with the fingers **:** HANDLE **2 :** to perform with the fingers or with a certain fingering **3 :** to mark the notes of a piece of music as a guide in playing **4 :** to point out

fin•ger•board \ˈfiŋ-gər-ˌbōrd\ *n* **:** the part of a stringed instrument against which the fingers press the strings to vary the pitch

finger bowl *n* **:** a small water bowl for rinsing the fingers at the table

fin•ger•ing \ˈfiŋ-gə-riŋ\ *n* **1 :** handling or touching with the fingers **2 :** the act or method of using the fingers in playing an instrument **3 :** the marking of the method of fingering

fin•ger•ling \ˈfiŋ-gər-liŋ\ *n* **:** a small fish

fin•ger•nail \ˈfiŋ-gər-ˌnāl\ *n* **:** the nail of a finger

fin•ger•print \-ˌprint\ *n* **:** the pattern of marks made by pressing the tip of a finger or thumb on a surface; *esp* **:** an ink impression of such a pattern taken for the purpose of identification — **fingerprint** *vb*

fin•ger•tip \-ˌtip\ *n* **:** the tip of a finger

fin•i•al \ˈfi-nē-əl\ *n* **:** an ornamental projection or end (as on a spire)

fin•ick•ing \ˈfi-ni-kiŋ\ *adj* **:** FINICKY

fin•icky \ˈfi-ni-kē\ *adj* ♦ **:** excessively particular in taste or standards

♦ choosy, dainty, delicate, demanding, exacting, fastidious, fussy, particular, picky *Ant* undemanding, unfussy

fi•nis \ˈfi-nəs\ *n* **1 :** a point that marks the extent of something **2** ♦ **:** cessation of a course of action, pursuit, or activity **:** END, CONCLUSION

♦ close, conclusion, consummation, end, ending, finale, finish, windup

1fin•ish \ˈfi-nish\ *vb* **1** ♦ **:** to come to an end **:** TERMINATE **2 :** to use or dispose of entirely **3** ♦ **:** to bring to completion **4 :** to put a final coat or surface on — **fin•ish•er** *n*

♦ [1] break off, cease, close, conclude, die, end, expire, quit, stop, terminate ♦ [3] complete, consummate, finalize, perfect

2finish *n* **1** ♦ **:** final stage **:** END, CONCLUSION **2 :** something that completes or perfects **3 :** the final treatment or coating of a surface

♦ close, conclusion, consummation, end, ending, finale, finis, windup

fi•nite \ˈfī-ˌnīt\ *adj* **1** ♦ **:** having definite or definable limits; *also* **:** having a limited nature or existence **2 :** being less than some positive integer in number or measure and greater than its negative **3 :** showing distinction of grammatical person and number ⟨a ~ verb⟩

♦ definite, determinate, limited, measured, narrow, restricted

fink \ˈfiŋk\ *n* **1 :** a contemptible person **2 :** STRIKEBREAKER **3 :** INFORMER

Finn \ˈfin\ *n* **:** a native or inhabitant of Finland

fin•nan had•die \ˌfi-nən-ˈha-dē\ *n* **:** smoked haddock

1Finn•ish \ˈfi-nish\ *adj* **:** of or relating to Finland, the Finns, or Finnish

2Finnish *n* **:** the language of the Finns

fin•ny \ˈfi-nē\ *adj* **1 :** having or characterized by fins **2 :** relating to or being fish

fiord *var of* FJORD

fir \ˈfər\ *n* **:** any of a genus of usually large evergreen trees related to the pines; *also* **:** the light soft wood of a fir

fiord *var of* FJORD

1fire \ˈfīr\ *n* **1 :** the light or heat and especially the flame of something burning **2 :** ENTHUSIASM, ZEAL **3 :** fuel that is burning (as in a stove or fireplace) **4** ♦ **:** destructive burning (as of a house) **5 :** the firing of weapons — **fire•less** *adj*

♦ conflagration, holocaust, inferno

2fire *vb* **fired; fir•ing** **1** ♦ **:** to set on fire **:** set fire to **:** KINDLE, IGNITE ⟨~ a house⟩ **2 a** ♦ **:** to give life or spirit to **:** STIR, ENLIVEN ⟨~ the imagination⟩ **b** ♦ **:** to become irritated **:** become angry or inflamed with passion **3** ♦ **:** to dismiss from employment **4** ♦ **:** to cause to be driven forward with force from a bow, sling, or similar device or from a firearm **:** SHOOT ⟨~ a gun⟩ ⟨~ an arrow⟩ **5 :** BAKE ⟨*firing* pottery in a kiln⟩ **6 :** to apply fire or fuel to something ⟨~ a furnace⟩ **7** ♦ **:** to throw with speed or force

♦ [1] burn, ignite, inflame, kindle, light ♦ [2a] animate, brace, energize, enliven, invigorate, jazz up, liven up, pep up, quicken, stimulate, vitalize, vivify, zip (up) ♦ *usu* **fire (up)** [2b] arouse, encourage, excite, incite, instigate, move, pique, provoke, stimulate, stir ♦ [3] cashier, dismiss, remove, retire, sack ♦ [4] blast, discharge, loose, shoot ♦ [7] dash, fling, heave, hurl, hurtle, launch, pitch, sling, throw, toss

fire ant *n* **:** either of two small fiercely stinging So. American ants introduced into the southeastern U.S. where they are agricultural pests

fire•arm \ˈfī(-ə)r-ˌärm\ *n* ♦ **:** a weapon (as a pistol) from which a shot is discharged by gunpowder

♦ arm, gun, piece

fire•ball \-ˌbȯl\ *n* **1 :** a ball of fire **2 :** a very bright meteor **3 :** the highly luminous cloud of vapor and dust created by a nuclear explosion **4 :** a highly energetic person

fire•boat \-ˌbōt\ *n* **:** a boat equipped for fighting fires

fire•bomb \-ˌbäm\ *n* **:** an incendiary bomb — **firebomb** *vb*

fire•box \-ˌbäks\ *n* **1 :** a chamber (as of a furnace) that contains a fire **2 :** a box containing a fire alarm

fire•brand \-ˌbrand\ *n* **1 :** a piece of burning wood **2** ♦ **:** a person who creates unrest or strife **:** AGITATOR

♦ agitator, demagogue, incendiary, inciter, rabble-rouser

fire•break \-ˌbrāk\ *n* **:** a barrier of cleared or plowed land intended to check a forest or grass fire

fire•bug \-ˌbəg\ *n* **:** a person who deliberately sets destructive fires

fire•crack•er \-ˌkra-kər\ *n* **:** a paper tube containing an explosive and a fuse and set off to make a noise

fire department *n* **:** an organization for preventing or extinguishing fires; *also* **:** its members

fire engine *n* **:** a motor vehicle with equipment for extinguishing fires

fire escape *n* **:** a stairway or ladder for escape from a burning building

fire•fight•er \ˈfī(-ə)r-ˌfī-tər\ *n* **:** a person who fights fires; *esp* **:** a member of a fire department

fire•fly \-ˌflī\ *n* **:** any of various small night-flying beetles that produce flashes of light for courtship purposes

fire•house \-ˌhau̇s\ *n* **:** FIRE STATION

fire irons *n pl* **:** tools for tending a fire especially in a fireplace

fire•man \ˈfī(-ə)r-mən\ *n* **1 :** STOKER **2 :** FIREFIGHTER

fire off *vb* **:** to write and send

fire•place \-ˌplās\ *n* **1 :** a framed opening made in a chimney to

hold an open fire **2 :** an outdoor structure of brick or stone for an open fire
fire•plug \-ˌpləg\ *n* **:** HYDRANT
fire•pow•er \-ˌpau̇(-ə)r\ *n* **:** the ability to deliver gunfire or warheads on a target
¹fire•proof \-ˈprüf\ *adj* ♦ **:** resistant to fire

♦ noncombustible, nonflammable, noninflammable

²fireproof *vb* **:** to make fireproof
fire–sale \-ˌsāl\ *adj* **:** heavily discounted ⟨~ prices⟩
fire screen *n* **:** a protective screen before a fireplace
¹fire•side \ˈfī(-ə)r-ˌsīd\ *n* **1 :** a place near the fire or hearth **2** ♦ **:** one's place of residence **:** HOME

♦ abode, domicile, dwelling, home, house, lodging

²fireside *adj* **:** having an informal or intimate quality
fire station *n* **:** a building housing fire engines and usually firefighters
fire•storm \ˈfī(-ə)r-ˌstȯrm\ *n* **1 :** a large destructive very hot fire **2 :** a sudden or violent outburst ⟨~ of criticism⟩
fire tower *n* **:** a tower (as in a forest) from which a watch for fires is kept
fire•trap \ˈfī(-ə)r-ˌtrap\ *n* **:** a building or place apt to catch on fire or difficult to escape from in case of fire
fire truck *n* **:** FIRE ENGINE
fire•wall \-ˌwȯl\ *n* **:** computer hardware or software for preventing unauthorized access to data
fire•wa•ter \ˈfī(-ə)r-ˌwȯ-tər, -ˌwä-\ *n* **:** intoxicating liquor
fire•wood \-ˌwu̇d\ *n* **:** wood used for fuel
fire•work \-ˌwərk\ *n* **1 :** a device designed to produce a striking display by the burning of explosive or flammable materials — usually used in plural ⟨a display of ~*s* at the end of the festival⟩ **2** ♦ **:** *pl* a display of temper or intense conflict

♦ *usu* **fireworks** blowup, dudgeon, explosion, fit, huff, scene, tantrum

firing line *n* **1 :** a line from which fire is delivered against a target **2 :** the forefront of an activity
¹firm \ˈfərm\ *adj* **1** ♦ **:** securely fixed in place **2 :** SOLID, VIGOROUS ⟨a ~ handshake⟩ **3** ♦ **:** having a solid or compact texture **4** ♦ **:** not subject to change or fluctuation **:** STEADY ⟨~ prices⟩ **5** ♦ **:** not easily moved or disturbed **:** STEADFAST **6** ♦ **:** indicating firmness or resolution

♦ [1] fast, frozen, secure, set, snug, tight ♦ [3] compact, hard, rigid, solid, stiff, unyielding ***Ant*** flabby, soft, spongy ♦ [4] certain, fixed, hard, hard-and-fast, set, settled, stable ♦ [5] fast, sound, stable, stalwart, steady, strong, sturdy ♦ [6] decisive, determined, intent, purposeful, resolute, set, single-minded

²firm *vb* ♦ **:** to make or become firm

♦ *usu* **firm up** concrete, congeal, freeze, harden, set, solidify

³firm *n* **1 :** the name under which a company transacts business **2 :** a business partnership of two or more persons **3** ♦ **:** a business enterprise

♦ business, company, concern, enterprise, establishment, house, outfit

fir•ma•ment \ˈfər-mə-mənt\ *n* **:** the arch of the sky **:** HEAVENS
firm•ly *adv* ♦ **:** in a firm manner

♦ forcefully, forcibly, hard, stoutly, strenuously, strongly, vigorously

firm•ness *n* ♦ **:** the quality or state of being firm

♦ decision, decisiveness, determination, resolution, resolve, stability, strength

firm•ware \ˈfirm-ˌwer\ *n* **:** computer programs contained permanently in a hardware device
¹first \ˈfərst\ *adj* ♦ **:** preceding all others as in time, order, or importance

♦ chief, dominant, foremost, key, paramount, predominant, primary, principal ♦ initial, original, pioneer, premier ***Ant*** final, last, terminal, ultimate

²first *adv* **1 :** before any other **2 :** for the first time **3** ♦ **:** in preference to something else

♦ preferably, rather, readily, soon

³first *n* **1 :** number one in a countable series **2 :** something that is first **3 :** the lowest forward gear in an automotive vehicle **4 :** the winning or highest place in a competition or examination
first aid *n* **:** emergency care or treatment given an injured or ill person
first•born \ˈfərst-ˈbȯrn\ *adj* **:** ELDEST — **firstborn** *n*
first class *n* **:** the best or highest group in a classification — **first–class** *adj or adv*
first•hand \ˈfərst-ˈhand\ *adj* ♦ **:** coming from direct personal observation or experience — **firsthand** *adv*

♦ direct, immediate, primary

first lady *n, often cap F&L* **:** the wife or hostess of the chief executive of a political unit (as a country)
first lieutenant *n* **:** a commissioned officer (as in the army) ranking next below a captain
first•ling \ˈfərst-liŋ\ *n* **:** one that comes or is produced first
first•ly \-lē\ *adv* ♦ **:** in the first place **:** FIRST

♦ first, initially, originally, primarily

¹first–rate \-ˈrāt\ *adj* ♦ **:** of the first order of size, importance, or quality

♦ excellent, fabulous, fantastic, great, superb, terrific, wonderful

²first–rate *adv* **:** very well
first sergeant *n* **1 :** a noncommissioned officer serving as the chief assistant to the commander of a military unit **2 :** a rank in the army below a sergeant major and in the marine corps below a master gunnery sergeant
first strike *n* **:** a preemptive nuclear attack
first–string \ˈfərst-ˈstriŋ\ *adj* **:** being a regular as distinguished from a substitute — **first–string•er** \-ˌstriŋ-ər\ *n*
firth \ˈfərth\ *n* **:** a narrow arm of the sea **:** the opening of a river into the sea **:** ESTUARY
fis•cal \ˈfis-kəl\ *adj* **1 :** of or relating to taxation, public revenues, or public debt **2** ♦ **:** of or relating to financial matters — **fis•cal•ly** *adv*

♦ financial, monetary, pecuniary

¹fish \ˈfish\ *n, pl* **fish** *or* **fish•es** **1 :** a water-dwelling animal — usually used in combination ⟨star*fish*⟩ ⟨shell*fish*⟩ **2 :** any of numerous cold-blooded water-breathing vertebrates with fins, gills, and usually scales that include the bony fishes and usually the cartilaginous and jawless fishes **3 :** the flesh of fish used as food
²fish *vb* **1 :** to attempt to catch fish **2 :** to seek something by roundabout means ⟨~ for praise⟩ **3 :** to search for something underwater **4** ♦ **:** to engage in a search by groping **5 :** to draw forth

♦ feel, fumble, grope

fish–and–chips *n pl* **:** fried fish and french fried potatoes
fish•bowl \ˈfish-ˌbōl\ *n* **1 :** a bowl for the keeping of live fish **2 :** a place or condition that affords no privacy
fish•er \ˈfi-shər\ *n* **1 :** one that fishes **2 :** a dark brown No. American carnivorous mammal related to the weasels
fish•er•man \-mən\ *n* **1 :** a person engaged in fishing **2 :** a fish ing boat
fish•ery \ˈfi-shə-rē\ *n, pl* **-er•ies** **1 :** the business of catching fish **2 :** a place for catching fish
fish•hook \ˈfish-ˌhu̇k\ *n* **:** a usually barbed hook for catching fish
fish ladder *n* **:** an arrangement of pools in steps by which fish can pass over a dam in going upstream
fish•net \ˈfish-ˌnet\ *n* **1 :** netting for catching fish **2 :** a coarse open-mesh fabric
fish•tail \-ˌtāl\ *vb* **:** to have the rear end slide from side to side out of control while moving forward
fish•wife \-ˌwīf\ *n* **1 :** a woman who sells fish **2 :** a vulgar abusive woman
fishy \ˈfi-shē\ *adj* **fish•i•er; -est** **1 :** of or resembling fish **2** ♦ **:** inspiring doubt or suspicion **:** QUESTIONABLE ⟨the story sounds ~ to me⟩

♦ debatable, doubtful, problematic, questionable, shady, shaky, suspect, suspicious

fis•sion \ˈfi-shən, -zhən\ *n* **1 :** a cleaving into parts **2 :** a method of reproduction in which a living cell or body divides into two or more parts each of which grows into a whole new individual **3 :** the splitting of an atomic nucleus resulting in the release of large amounts of energy — **fis•sion•able** \ˈfi-shə-nə-bəl, -zhə-\ *adj*
fis•sure \ˈfi-shər\ *n* ♦ **:** a narrow opening or crack

♦ chink, cleft, crack, cranny, crevice, rift, split

fist \ˈfist\ *n* **1 :** the hand with fingers folded into the palm **2 :** INDEX 6
fist•ful \ˈfist-ˌfu̇l\ *n* **:** HANDFUL
fist•i•cuffs \ˈfis-ti-ˌkəfs\ *n pl* **:** a fight with the fists
fis•tu•la \ˈfis-chə-lə\ *n, pl* **-las** *or* **-lae** **:** an abnormal passage leading from an abscess or hollow organ — **fis•tu•lous** \-ləs\ *adj*
¹fit \ˈfit\ *adj* **fit•ter; fit•test** **1** ♦ **:** adapted to a purpose **2 :** PROPER, RIGHT ⟨a movie ~ for children⟩ **3** ♦ **:** put into a suitable state **:** made ready **4** ♦ **:** physically and mentally sound — **fit•ly** *adv*

◆ [1] appropriate, apt, good, happy, proper, right, suitable *Ant* inapplicable, inappropriate, unsuitable, wrong ◆ [1, 3] go, ready, set ◆ [3] available, functional, operable, practicable, serviceable, usable, useful ◆ [4] able-bodied, hale, healthy, hearty, robust, sound, well

²fit *n* **1** ◆ **:** a sudden violent attack (as in epilepsy) **2** ◆ **:** a sudden outburst

◆ [1] attack, bout, case, seizure, siege, spell ◆ [2] blowup, dudgeon, explosion, fireworks, huff, outburst, scene, tantrum

³fit *vb* **fit·ted** *also* **fit; fit·ting 1** ◆ **:** to be suitable for or to **2 :** to be correctly adjusted to or shaped for **3** ◆ **:** to insert or adjust until correctly in place **4** ◆ **:** to make a place or room for **5** ◆ **:** to be in agreement or accord with **6** ◆ **:** to put into a condition of readiness **:** PREPARE **7** ◆ **:** to make or adjust to the right shape and size **:** ADJUST **8 :** to supply with something that is adjusted or designed for the use required — usually used with *out* **9 :** to be in harmony or accord **:** BELONG — **fit·ter** *n*

◆ [1] befit, do, go, serve, suit ◆ [1, 6] equip, prepare, qualify, ready, season ◆ *usu* **fit in** *or* **fit into** [3] inject, insert, insinuate, interject, interpose, introduce ◆ [4] accommodate, hold, take ◆ [5] agree, answer, check, conform, correspond, dovetail, go, harmonize ◆ [7] acclimate, accommodate, adapt, adjust, condition, conform, shape

⁴fit *n* **:** the fact, condition, or manner of fitting or being fitted

fit·ful \ˈfit-fəl\ *adj* ◆ **:** not regular **:** INTERMITTENT ⟨∼ sleep⟩ — **fit·ful·ly** *adv*

◆ erratic, intermittent, irregular, occasional, spasmodic, sporadic, spotty, unsteady *Ant* constant, continuous, regular, steady

fit·ness *n* ◆ **:** the quality or state of being fit

◆ health, robustness, soundness, wellness ◆ appropriateness, aptness, rightness, suitability

¹fit·ting \ˈfi-tiŋ\ *adj* ◆ **:** of a kind appropriate to the situation **:** APPROPRIATE, SUITABLE

◆ applicable, appropriate, apt, fit, proper, right, suitable

²fitting *n* **1 :** the action or act of one that fits; *esp* **:** a trying on of clothes being made or altered **2 :** a small often standardized part ⟨a plumbing ∼⟩

fit·ting·ly *adv* ◆ **:** in a fitting manner

◆ appropriately, correctly, happily, properly, rightly, suitably

fit·ting·ness *n* **:** the quality or state of being appropriate to the situation

five \ˈfīv\ *n* **1 :** one more than four **2 :** the 5th in a set or series **3 :** something having five units; *esp* **:** a basketball team **4 :** a 5-dollar bill — **five** *adj or pron*

¹fix \ˈfiks\ *vb* **1 :** to make firm, stable, or fast **2 :** to give a permanent or final form to **3** ◆ **:** to attach physically **:** AFFIX, ATTACH **4 :** to hold or direct steadily ⟨∼*es* his eyes on the horizon⟩ **5** ◆ **:** to set or place definitely **:** SET **6 :** ASSIGN ⟨∼ the blame⟩ **7 :** to set in order **:** ADJUST **8 :** to get ready **:** PREPARE **9** ◆ **:** to make whole or sound again **10 :** to get even with **11 :** to influence by improper or illegal methods ⟨∼ a race⟩ **12** ◆ **:** to assign precisely **:** settle on **:** arrange — **fix·er** *n*

◆ [3] affix, attach, fasten ◆ [5] deposit, place, position, put, set, set up, stick ◆ [9] doctor, mend, patch, recondition, renovate, repair, revamp ◆ [12] arrange, decide, set, settle

²fix *n* **1** ◆ **:** a position of difficulty or embarrassment **:** PREDICAMENT **2 :** a determination of position (as of a ship) **3 :** an accurate determination or understanding **4 :** an act of improper influence **5 :** a supply or dose of something (as an addictive drug) strongly desired or craved **6 :** something that fixes or restores

◆ corner, hole, jam, pickle, predicament, spot

fix·a·tion \fik-ˈsā-shən\ *n* ◆ **:** an obsessive or unhealthy preoccupation or attachment — **fix·ate** \ˈfik-ˌsāt\ *vb*

◆ fetish, mania, obsession, preoccupation, prepossession

fix·a·tive \ˈfik-sə-tiv\ *n* **:** something that stabilizes or sets

fixed \ˈfikst\ *adj* **1 :** securely placed or fastened **:** STATIONARY **2 :** not volatile **3** ◆ **:** not subject to change or fluctuation **4 :** INTENT, CONCENTRATED ⟨a ∼ stare⟩ **5 :** supplied with a definite amount of something needed (as money) — **fixed·ly** \ˈfik-səd-lē\ *adv*

◆ certain, determinate, final, firm, flat, frozen, hard, hard-and-fast, set, settled, stable ◆ fast, hard-and-fast, immutable, inflexible, unalterable, unchangeable

fixed·ness \ˈfik-səd-nəs\ *n* ◆ **:** the quality or state of being fixed

◆ constancy, immutability, stability, steadiness

fix·i·ty \ˈfik-sə-tē\ *n, pl* **-ties :** the quality or state of being fixed or stable

fix·ture \ˈfiks-chər\ *n* **1 :** something firmly attached as a permanent part of some other thing **2 :** a familiar feature in a particular setting; *esp* **:** a person associated with a place or activity

¹fizz \ˈfiz\ *vb* ◆ **:** to make a hissing or sputtering sound

◆ hiss, sizzle, swish, whish, whiz

²fizz *n* **1 :** a hissing sound **2 :** an effervescent beverage

¹fiz·zle \ˈfi-zəl\ *vb* **fiz·zled; fiz·zling 1 :** FIZZ **2 :** to fail after a good start — often used with *out*

²fizzle *n* ◆ **:** lack of satisfactory performance or effect **:** FAILURE

◆ collapse, crash, cropper, defeat, failure, nonsuccess

fjord *or* **fiord** \fē-ˈȯrd\ *n* ◆ **:** a narrow inlet of the sea between cliffs or steep slopes

◆ bay, bight, cove, estuary, gulf, inlet

fl *abbr* **1** flourished **2** fluid

FL *or* **Fla** *abbr* Florida

flab \ˈflab\ *n* **:** soft flabby body tissue

flab·ber·gast \ˈfla-bər-ˌgast\ *vb* ◆ **:** to overwhelm with shock, surprise, or wonder **:** ASTOUND

◆ amaze, astonish, astound, bowl, dumbfound, floor, shock, startle, stun, stupefy, surprise

flab·by \ˈfla-bē\ *adj* **flab·bi·er; -est** ◆ **:** lacking firmness **:** FLACCID ⟨∼ muscles⟩ — **flab·bi·ness** \-bē-nəs\ *n*

◆ flaccid, mushy, pulpy, soft, spongy

flac·cid \ˈflak-səd\ *adj* ◆ **:** lacking firmness ⟨∼ muscles⟩

◆ droopy, floppy, lank, limp, slack, yielding

¹flag \ˈflag\ *n* **:** any of various irises; *esp* **:** a wild iris

²flag *n* **1 :** a usually rectangular piece of fabric of distinctive design that is used as a symbol (as of a nation) or as a signaling device **2** ◆ **:** something used like a flag to signal or attract attention **3 :** one of the cross strokes of a musical note less than a quarter note in value

◆ banner, colors (*or* colours), ensign, pennant, standard, streamer

³flag *vb* **flagged; flag·ging 1** ◆ **:** to signal with or as if with a flag; *esp* **:** to signal to stop ⟨∼ a taxi⟩ **2 :** to mark or identify with or as if with a flag **3 :** to call a penalty on

◆ gesture, motion, signal, wave

⁴flag *vb* **flagged; flag·ging 1** ◆ **:** to hang loose or limp **2** ◆ **:** to become unsteady, feeble, or spiritless **3 :** to decline in interest or attraction ⟨the topic *flagged*⟩

◆ [1] droop, hang, loll, sag, wilt ◆ [2] decay, droop, fail, go, lag, languish, sag, waste, weaken, wilt

⁵flag *n* **:** a hard flat stone suitable for paving

flag·el·late \ˈfla-jə-ˌlāt\ *vb* **-lat·ed; -lat·ing :** to punish by whipping — **flag·el·la·tion** \ˌfla-jə-ˈlā-shən\ *n*

fla·gel·lum \flə-ˈje-ləm\ *n, pl* **-la** \-lə\ *also* **-lums :** a long whiplike process that is the primary organ of motion of many microorganisms — **fla·gel·lar** \-lər\ *adj*

fla·geo·let \ˌfla-jə-ˈlet, -ˈlā\ *n* **:** a small woodwind instrument belonging to the flute class

fla·gi·tious \flə-ˈji-shəs\ *adj* **:** grossly wicked **:** VILLAINOUS

flag·on \ˈfla-gən\ *n* ◆ **:** a container for liquids usually with a handle, spout, and lid

◆ ewer, jug, pitcher

flag·pole \ˈflag-ˌpōl\ *n* **:** a pole on which to raise a flag

fla·grant \ˈflā-grənt\ *adj* ◆ **:** conspicuously bad ⟨∼ abuse of power⟩ — **fla·grant·ly** *adv*

◆ blatant, conspicuous, egregious, gross, pronounced, rank, striking

fla·gran·te de·lic·to \flə-ˌgran-tē-di-ˈlik-tō\ *adv* **:** the act of committing a misdeed — used in the phrase *in flagrante delicto*

flag·ship \ˈflag-ˌship\ *n* **1 :** the ship that carries the commander of a fleet or subdivision thereof and flies his flag **2 :** the most important one of a group

flag·staff \-ˌstaf\ *n* **:** FLAGPOLE

flag·stone \-ˌstōn\ *n* **:** ⁵FLAG

¹flail \ˈflāl\ *n* **:** a tool for threshing grain by hand

²flail *vb* ◆ **:** to strike or swing with or as if with a flail

◆ flog, hide, lash, switch, thrash, whale, whip

flair \ˈflar\ *n* **1** ♦ **:** ability to appreciate or make good use of something **:** TALENT **2 :** a unique style

♦ aptitude, endowment, faculty, genius, gift, knack, talent

flak \ˈflak\ *n, pl* **flak** **1 :** antiaircraft guns or bursting shells fired from them **2 :** CRITICISM, OPPOSITION

¹flake \ˈflāk\ *n* **1 :** a small loose mass or bit **2** ♦ **:** a thin flattened piece or layer **:** CHIP

♦ chip, splinter

²flake *vb* **flaked; flak•ing :** to form or separate into flakes

³flake *n* **:** a markedly eccentric person **:** ODDBALL — **flak•i•ness** \ˈflā-kē-nəs\ *n* — **flaky** *adj*

flaky *adj* ♦ **:** tending to flake

♦ brittle, crisp, crumbly, friable

flam•beau \ˈflam-ˌbō\ *n, pl* **flambeaux** \-ˌbōz\ *or* **flambeaus :** a flaming torch

flam•boy•ance \-əns\ *n* ♦ **:** the quality or state of being flamboyant

♦ flashiness, gaudiness, glitz, ostentation, pretentiousness, showiness, swank

flam•boy•ant \flam-ˈbȯi-ənt\ *adj* ♦ **:** marked by or given to strikingly elaborate or colorful display or behavior — **flam•boy•an•cy** \-ən-sē\ *n*

♦ flashy, garish, gaudy, glitzy, loud, ostentatious, swank, tawdry

flam•boy•ant•ly *adv* ♦ **:** in a flamboyant manner **:** with flamboyance

♦ flashily, gaily, jauntily, rakishly

flame \ˈflām\ *n* **1 :** the glowing gaseous part of a fire **2 :** a state of blazing combustion **3 :** a flamelike condition **4 :** burning zeal or passion **5 :** BRILLIANCE **6** ♦ **:** a person beloved **:** SWEETHEART **7 :** an angry, hostile, or abusive electronic message

♦ beloved, darling, dear, honey, love, sweet, sweetheart

flame *vb* **1** ♦ **:** to burn with a flame **2** ♦ **:** to burst or break out violently or passionately **3** ♦ **:** to shine brightly

♦ [1] blaze, burn, glow ♦ [2] break out, burst, erupt, explode, flare, go off ♦ [3] beat, blaze, burn, glare

fla•men•co \flə-ˈmeŋ-kō\ *n, pl* **-cos :** a vigorous rhythmic dance style of the Spanish Gypsies

flame•throw•er \ˈflām-ˌthrō-ər\ *n* **:** a device that expels from a nozzle a burning stream of liquid or semiliquid fuel under pressure

fla•min•go \flə-ˈmiŋ-gō\ *n, pl* **-gos** *also* **-goes :** any of several long-legged long-necked tropical water birds with scarlet wings and a broad bill bent downward

flam•ma•ble \ˈfla-mə-bəl\ *adj* ♦ **:** easily ignited and quick-burning — **flam•ma•bil•i•ty** \ˌfla-mə-ˈbi-lə-tē\ *n* — **flammable** *n*

♦ combustible, ignitable, inflammable

flan \ˈflan, ˈflän\ *n* **1 :** an open pie with a sweet or savory filling **2 :** custard baked with a caramel glaze

flange \ˈflanj\ *n* **:** a rim used for strengthening or guiding something or for attachment to another object

¹flank \ˈflaŋk\ *n* **1 :** the fleshy part of the side between the ribs and the hip; *also* **:** the side of a quadruped **2 :** SIDE **3 :** the right or left of a formation

²flank *vb* **1 :** to attack or threaten the flank of **2** ♦ **:** to be situated on the side of

♦ abut, adjoin, border (on), fringe, join, skirt, touch, verge (on)

flank•er \ˈflaŋ-kər\ *n* **:** a football player stationed wide of the formation slightly behind the line of scrimmage as a pass receiver

flan•nel \ˈflan-ᵊl\ *n* **1 :** a soft twilled wool or worsted fabric with a napped surface **2 :** a stout cotton fabric napped on one side **3** *pl* **:** flannel underwear or pants

¹flap \ˈflap\ *n* **1 :** a stroke with something broad **:** SLAP **2 :** something broad, limber, or flat and usually thin that hangs loose **3 :** the motion or sound of something broad and limber as it swings to and fro **4 :** a state of excitement or confusion

²flap *vb* **flapped; flap•ping 1 :** to beat with something broad and flat **2 :** FLING **3** ♦ **:** to move (as wings) with a beating motion **4 :** to sway loosely usually with a noise of striking

♦ beat, flail, flop, flutter, whip

flap•jack \ˈflap-ˌjak\ *n* ♦ **:** a flat cake made of thin batter and cooked (as on a griddle) on both sides **:** PANCAKE

♦ griddle cake, pancake

flap•per \ˈfla-pər\ *n* **1 :** one that flaps **2 :** a young woman of the 1920s who showed freedom from conventions (as in conduct)

¹flare \ˈflar\ *n* **1** ♦ **:** a blaze of light used especially to signal or illuminate; *also* **:** a device for producing such a blaze **2 :** an unsteady glaring light **3** ♦ **:** a sudden outburst (as of sound, excitement, or anger)

♦ [1] blaze, illumination, incandescence, light, luminescence, radiance, shine ♦ [3] agony, burst, eruption, explosion, fit, flare-up, flash, outburst, spasm, storm

²flare *vb* **flared; flar•ing 1** ♦ **:** to flame with a sudden unsteady light **2** ♦ **:** to spread outward ⟨her skirt *flaring* at the bottom⟩ ⟨a boat with the gunwales *flaring* out⟩ **3 :** to become suddenly excited or angry — usually used with *up* ⟨she ∼*s* up at the slightest provocation⟩ **4** ♦ **:** to break out or intensify usually suddenly or violently — often used with *up* ⟨fighting *flared* up after a 2-week lull⟩

♦ [1] beat, blaze, burn, flame, glare ♦ *usu* **flare out** [2] expand, extend, fan, open, spread, stretch, unfold ♦ *usu* **flare up** [4] break out, burst, erupt, explode, flame, go off

flare–up \-ˌəp\ *n* ♦ **:** a sudden outburst or intensification

♦ burst, flare, flash, outbreak, outburst, spurt

¹flash \ˈflash\ *vb* **1 :** to break forth in or like a sudden flame **2 :** to appear or pass suddenly or with great speed **3** ♦ **:** to send out in or as if in flashes ⟨∼ a message⟩ **4 :** to make a sudden display (as of brilliance or feeling) **5 :** to gleam or glow intermittently **6 :** to fill by a sudden rush of water **7 :** to expose to view very briefly ⟨∼ a badge⟩ — **flash•er** *n*

♦ flame, gleam, glimmer, glisten, glitter, shimmer, sparkle, twinkle, wink

²flash *n* **1 :** a sudden burst of light **2 :** a movement of a flag or light in signaling **3 :** a sudden and brilliant burst (as of wit) **4** ♦ **:** a brief time **5 :** SHOW, DISPLAY; *esp* **:** ostentatious display **6** ♦ **:** something or someone that attracts notice; *esp* **:** an outstanding athlete **7 :** GLIMPSE, LOOK **8 :** a first brief news report **9 :** FLASHLIGHT **10 :** a device for producing a brief and very bright flash of light for taking photographs **11 :** a quick-spreading flame or momentary intense outburst of radiant heat

♦ [4] instant, jiffy, minute, moment, second, shake, twinkling, wink ♦ [6] marvel, miracle, phenomenon, prodigy, sensation, wonder

³flash *adj* **:** of sudden origin and short duration ⟨a ∼ flood⟩

♦ fleeting, momentary, short-lived, transient

⁴flash *adv* **:** by very brief exposure to an intense agent (as heat or cold) ⟨∼ freeze⟩

flash•back \ˈflash-ˌbak\ *n* **1 :** interruption of the chronological sequence (as of a film or literary work) by an event of earlier occurrence **2 :** a past event remembered vividly

flash back *vb* **1 :** to vividly remember a past incident **2 :** to employ a flashback

flash•bulb \-ˌbəlb\ *n* **:** an electric bulb that can be used only once to produce a brief and very bright flash of light for taking photographs

flash card *n* **:** a card bearing words, numbers, or pictures briefly displayed usually as a learning aid

flash•cube \ˈflash-ˌkyüb\ *n* **:** a cubical device incorporating four flashbulbs

flash•gun \-ˌgən\ *n* **:** a device for producing a bright flash of light for photography

flash•i•ly \-shə-lē\ *adv* ♦ **:** in a flashy manner or style

♦ flamboyantly, gaily, jauntily, rakishly

flash•i•ness \-shē-nəs\ *n* ♦ **:** the quality or state of being flashy

♦ flamboyance, gaudiness, glitz, ostentation, pretentiousness, showiness, swank

flash•ing \ˈfla-shiŋ\ *n* **:** sheet metal used in waterproofing (as at the angle between a chimney and a roof)

flash•light \ˈflash-ˌlīt\ *n* **:** a battery-operated portable electric light

flash memory *n* **:** a computer memory chip not requiring connection to a power source to retain its data

flashy \ˈfla-shē\ *adj* **flash•i•er; -est 1 :** momentarily dazzling **2** ♦ **:** superficially attractive or impressive **:** SHOWY

♦ flamboyant, garish, gaudy, glitzy, loud, ostentatious, showy, swank, tawdry

flask \ˈflask\ *n* **:** a flattened bottle-shaped container ⟨a whiskey ∼⟩

¹flat \ˈflat\ *adj* **flat•ter; flat•test 1 :** spread out along a surface;

also : being or characterized by a horizontal line **2** ♦ **:** having a smooth, level, or even surface **3 :** having a broad smooth surface and little thickness **4 :** clearly unmistakable : DOWNRIGHT ⟨a ~ refusal⟩ **5 :** not varying : FIXED ⟨charge a ~ rate⟩ **6** ♦ **:** having no fraction either lacking or in excess : EXACT, PRECISE ⟨in four minutes ~⟩ **7 a** ♦ **:** lacking in animation, zest, or vigor : DULL, UNINTERESTING **b** ♦ **:** lacking savor : INSIPID **8 :** DEFLATED ⟨a ~ tire⟩ **9 :** lower than the true pitch; *also* : lower by a half step **10** ♦ **:** free from gloss ⟨a ~ paint⟩ **11 :** lacking depth of characterization — **flat·ly** *adv* — **flat·ness** *n*

♦ [2] even, flush, level, plane, smooth ♦ [6] even, exact, precise, round ♦ [7a] dull, monotonous, uninteresting ♦ [7b] flavorless (*or* flavourless), insipid, tasteless ♦ [10] dim, dull, lusterless

[2]**flat** *n* **1 :** a level surface of land : PLAIN **2 :** a flat part or surface **3 :** a character ♭ that indicates that a specified note is to be lowered by a half step; *also* : the resulting note **4 :** something flat **5 :** an apartment on one floor **6 :** a deflated tire

[3]**flat** *adv* **1 :** FLATLY **2** ♦ **:** without qualification or reservation : COMPLETELY ⟨~ broke⟩ **3 :** below the true musical pitch

♦ completely, entirely, fully, perfectly, quite, thoroughly, wholly

[4]**flat** *vb* **flat·ted; flat·ting 1 :** FLATTEN **2 :** to lower in pitch especially by a half step

flat·bed \ˈflat-ˌbed\ *n* **:** a truck or trailer with a body in the form of a platform or shallow box

flat·boat \-ˌbōt\ *n* **:** a flat-bottomed boat used especially for carrying bulky freight

flat·car \-ˌkär\ *n* **:** a railroad freight car without sides or roof

flat·fish \-ˌfish\ *n* **:** any of an order of flattened marine bony fishes with both eyes on the upper side

flat·foot \-ˌfu̇t, -ˈfu̇t\ *n, pl* **flat·feet** \-ˌfēt, -ˈfēt\ **:** a condition in which the arch of the foot is flattened so that the entire sole rests upon the ground — **flat–foot·ed** \-ˈfu̇-təd\ *adj*

Flat·head \-ˌhed\ *n, pl* **Flatheads** *or* **Flathead :** a member of an American Indian people of Montana

flat·iron \-ˌī(-ə)rn\ *n* **:** IRON 3

flat·land \-ˌland\ *n* **:** land lacking significant variation in elevation

flat–out \ˈflat-ˌau̇t\ *adj* **1 :** being or going at maximum effort or speed **2 :** OUT-AND-OUT, DOWNRIGHT ⟨it was a ~ lie⟩

flat out *adv* **1 :** BLUNTLY, DIRECTLY **2 :** at top speed **3** *usu* **flat–out :** to the greatest degree : COMPLETELY ⟨is just *flat-out* confusing⟩

flat–pan·el \-ˈpa-nᵊl\ *adj* **:** relating to or being a thin flat video display

flat·ten \ˈflat-ᵊn\ *vb* **:** to make or become flat

flat·ter \ˈfla-tər\ *vb* **1** ♦ **:** to praise too much or without sincerity **2 :** to represent too favorably ⟨the portrait ~*s* him⟩ **3 :** to display to advantage **4 :** to judge (oneself) favorably or too favorably — **flat·ter·er** *n*

♦ blarney, overpraise

flat·tery \ˈfla-tə-rē\ *n, pl* **-ter·ies** ♦ **:** flattering speech or attentions : insincere or excessive praise

♦ adulation, blarney, overpraise

flat·top \ˈflat-ˌtäp\ *n* **1 :** AIRCRAFT CARRIER **2 :** CREW CUT

flat·u·lent \ˈfla-chə-lənt\ *adj* **1 :** full of gas ⟨a ~ stomach⟩ **2 :** INFLATED, POMPOUS — **flat·u·lence** \-ləns\ *n*

fla·tus \ˈflā-təs\ *n* **:** gas formed in the intestine or stomach

flat·ware \ˈflat-ˌwer\ *n* ♦ **:** eating and serving utensils

♦ silver, tableware

flat·worm \-ˌwərm\ *n* **:** any of a phylum of flattened mostly parasitic segmented worms (as trematodes and tapeworms)

flaunt \ˈflȯnt\ *vb* **1** ♦ **:** to display oneself to public notice **2 :** to wave or flutter showily **3 :** to display ostentatiously or impudently : PARADE — **flaunt** *n*

♦ display, disport, exhibit, flash, parade, show, show off

flau·ta \ˈflau̇-tə\ *n* **:** a tortilla rolled around a filling and deep-fried

flau·tist \ˈflȯ-tist, ˈflau̇-\ *n* **:** FLUTIST

[1]**fla·vor** *or Can and Brit* **fla·vour** \ˈflā-vər\ *n* **1 :** the quality of something that affects the sense of taste or of taste and smell **2** ♦ **:** a substance that adds flavor **3** ♦ **:** characteristic or predominant quality — **fla·vored** \-vərd\ *adj* — **fla·vor·some** *adj*

♦ [2] seasoning, spice ♦ [3] air, atmosphere, aura, climate, mood, note, temper

[2]**flavor** *or Can and Brit* **flavour** *vb* ♦ **:** to give or add flavor to

♦ savor, season, spice

fla·vor·ful *or Can and Brit* **flavourful** *adj* ♦ **:** full of flavor

♦ appetizing, delectable, delicious, savory, tasty, toothsome, yummy

fla·vor·ing *or Can and Brit* **flavouring** *n* **:** a substance that flavors : FLAVOR 2

fla·vor·less *or Can and Brit* **flavourless** *adj* ♦ **:** lacking in flavor

♦ flat, insipid, tasteless

flaw \ˈflȯ\ *n* ♦ **:** a small often hidden defect — **flaw·less·ness** *n*

♦ blemish, defect, fault, imperfection, mark

flaw·less *adj* ♦ **:** lacking any flaw or imperfection

♦ absolute, faultless, ideal, impeccable, letter-perfect, perfect, unblemished

flaw·less·ly \-lē\ *adv* ♦ **:** in a flawless manner

♦ faultlessly, ideally, impeccably, perfectly

flax \ˈflaks\ *n* **:** a fiber that is the source of linen; *also* **:** a blue-flowered plant grown for this fiber and its oily seeds

flax·en \ˈflak-sən\ *adj* **1 :** made of flax **2** ♦ **:** resembling flax especially in pale soft straw color

♦ blond, fair, golden, sandy, straw

flay \ˈflā\ *vb* **1** ♦ **:** to strip off the skin or surface of **2** ♦ **:** to criticize harshly

♦ [1] bark, hull, husk, peel, shell, skin ♦ [2] admonish, chide, lecture, rail (at *or* against), rate, rebuke, reprimand, scold

fl dr *abbr* fluid dram

flea \ˈflē\ *n* **:** any of an order of small wingless leaping blood-sucking insects

flea·bane \ˈflē-ˌbān\ *n* **:** any of various plants of the daisy family once believed to drive away fleas

flea–bit·ten \-ˌbit-ᵊn\ *adj* **:** bitten by or infested with fleas

flea market *n* **:** a usually open-air market for secondhand articles and antiques

[1]**fleck** \ˈflek\ *vb* **:** to mark in or with spots : STREAK, SPOT

[2]**fleck** *n* **1** ♦ **:** a small area visibly different (as in color, finish, or material) from the surrounding area : SPOT, MARK **2** ♦ **:** a small loose mass or bit : PARTICLE

♦ [1] blotch, dapple, dot, mark, speck, spot ♦ [2] atom, bit, crumb, grain, granule, molecule, particle, speck

fledge \ˈflej\ *vb* **fledged; fledg·ing :** to develop the feathers necessary for flying or independent activity

fledg·ling \ˈflej-liŋ\ *n* **1 :** a young bird with flight feathers newly developed **2** ♦ **:** an immature or inexperienced person

♦ beginner, greenhorn, neophyte, newcomer, novice, tyro

flee \ˈflē\ *vb* **fled** \ˈfled\; **flee·ing 1** ♦ **:** to run away often from danger or evil **2** ♦ **:** to pass away swiftly from perception

♦ [1] clear out, escape, fly, get out, lam, run away, run off ♦ [2] disappear, dissolve, evaporate, fade, go, melt, vanish

[1]**fleece** \ˈflēs\ *n* **1** ♦ **:** the woolly coat of an animal and especially a sheep **2 :** a soft or woolly covering

♦ coat, fur, hair, pelage, pile, wool

[2]**fleece** *vb* **fleeced; fleec·ing 1** ♦ **:** to strip of money or property by fraud or extortion **2 :** SHEAR

♦ cheat, defraud, rook, shortchange, skin, squeeze, stick, sting, swindle, victimize

fleecy *adj* ♦ **:** covered with, made of, or resembling fleece

♦ furry, hairy, unshorn, woolly

[1]**fleet** \ˈflēt\ *vb* **:** to pass rapidly

[2]**fleet** *n* **1 :** a group of warships under one command **2** ♦ **:** a group (as of ships, planes, or trucks) under one management

♦ armada, caravan, cavalcade, motorcade, train

[3]**fleet** *adj* **1** ♦ **:** swift in motion : SWIFT, NIMBLE **2 :** not enduring : FLEETING

♦ breakneck, fast, hasty, lightning, nimble, nippy, quick, rapid, speedy, swift

fleet admiral *n* **:** an admiral of the highest rank in the navy

fleet·ing \ˈflē-tiŋ\ *adj* ♦ **:** passing swiftly

♦ ephemeral, evanescent, momentary, short-lived, transient

fleet·ness *n* ♦ **:** the quality or state of being fleet

♦ celerity, fastness, haste, hurry, quickness, rapidity, speed, swiftness, velocity

Flem•ing \ˈfle-miŋ\ *n* **:** a member of a Germanic people inhabiting chiefly northern Belgium

Flem•ish \ˈfle-mish\ *n* **1 :** the Dutch language as spoken by the Flemings **2 Flemish** *pl* **:** FLEMINGS — **Flemish** *adj*

¹**flesh** \ˈflesh\ *n* **1 :** the soft parts of an animal's body; *esp* **:** muscular tissue **2 :** MEAT **3 :** the physical nature of humans as distinguished from the soul **4 :** human beings; *also* **:** living beings **5 :** STOCK, KINDRED **6 :** fleshy plant tissue (as fruit pulp) — **fleshed** \ˈflesht\ *adj*

²**flesh** *vb* ♦ **:** to make fuller or more nearly complete — usually used with *out*

♦ *usu* **flesh out** amplify, develop, elaborate (on), enlarge (on), expand

flesh fly *n* **:** a dipteran fly whose maggots feed on flesh

flesh•ly \ˈflesh-lē\ *adj* **1** ♦ **:** of or relating to the flesh or body **:** CORPOREAL, BODILY **2** ♦ **:** not spiritual **:** WORLDLY **3** ♦ **:** of or relating to bodily appetites **:** CARNAL, SENSUAL

♦ [1] animal, bodily, carnal, corporal, material, physical, somatic ♦ [2] carnal, earthly, material, mundane, temporal, terrestrial, worldly ♦ [3] carnal, luscious, sensual, sensuous, voluptuous

flesh•pot \ˈflesh-ˌpät\ *n* **1** *pl* **:** bodily comfort **:** LUXURY **2 :** a place of lascivious entertainment — usually used in plural

fleshy \ˈfle-shē\ *adj* **flesh•i•er; -est 1 :** consisting of or resembling animal flesh **2** ♦ **:** marked by abundant flesh **:** PLUMP, FAT **3** ♦ **:** full of juice

♦ [2] chubby, fat, plump, portly, rotund, round ♦ [3] juicy, pulpy, succulent

flew *past of* ¹FLY

flex \ˈfleks\ *vb* **:** to bend especially repeatedly — **flex** *n*

flex•i•ble \ˈflek-sə-bəl\ *adj* **1** ♦ **:** capable of being flexed **2** ♦ **:** yielding to influence **3** ♦ **:** readily changed or changing — **flex•i•bil•i•ty** \ˌflek-sə-ˈbi-lə-tē\ *n*

♦ [1] limber, lissome, lithe, pliable, supple, willowy ♦ [1] elastic, resilient, rubbery, springy, stretch, supple ♦ [2, 3] easygoing, relaxed, unrestrained, unrestricted ♦ [3] adaptable, adjustable, changeable, elastic, fluid, malleable, variable *Ant* established, fixed, immutable

flex•or \ˈflek-sər, -ˌsȯr\ *n* **:** a muscle serving to bend a body part

flex•ure \ˈflek-shər\ *n* **:** TURN, FOLD

flib•ber•ti•gib•bet \ˌfli-bər-tē-ˈji-bət\ *n* **:** a silly flighty person

¹**flick** \ˈflik\ *n* **1 :** a light sharp jerky stroke or movement **2 :** a sound produced by a flick **3 :** ²FLICKER

²**flick** *vb* **1 :** to strike lightly with a quick sharp motion **2 :** FLUTTER, FLIT

³**flick** *n* **:** MOVIE <can't wait to catch the new *flick* at the theater>

¹**flick•er** \ˈfli-kər\ *vb* **1 :** to move irregularly or unsteadily **:** FLUTTER **2 :** to burn fitfully or with a fluctuating light — **flick•er•ing•ly** *adv*

²**flicker** *n* **1 :** an act of flickering **2 :** a sudden brief movement <a ~ of an eyelid> **3 :** a momentary stirring <a ~ of interest> **4 :** a slight indication **:** HINT **5 :** a wavering light

³**flicker** *n* **:** a large barred and spotted No. American woodpecker with a brown back that occurs as an eastern form with yellow on the underside of the wings and tail and a western form with red in these areas

flied *past and past part of* ³FLY

fli•er \ˈflī-ər\ *n* **1** ♦ **:** one that flies; *esp* **:** PILOT **2** ♦ **:** a reckless or speculative undertaking **3** *usu* **fly•er** ♦ **:** an advertising circular

♦ [1] airman, aviator, pilot ♦ [2] chance, enterprise, gamble, speculation, venture ♦ *usu* **flyer** [3] circular, leaflet, pamphlet

¹**flight** \ˈflīt\ *n* **1 :** an act or instance of flying **2 :** the ability to fly **3 :** a passing through air or space **4 :** the distance covered in a flight **5 :** swift movement **6 :** a trip made by or in an airplane or spacecraft **7 :** a group of similar individuals (as birds or airplanes) flying as a unit **8 :** a passing (as of the imagination) beyond ordinary limits **9 :** a series of stairs from one landing to another — **flight•less** *adj*

²**flight** *n* ♦ **:** an act or instance of running away

♦ escape, getaway, lam, slip

flight bag *n* **1 :** a lightweight traveling bag with zippered outside pockets **2 :** a small canvas satchel

flight•i•ness \-tē-nəs\ *n* ♦ **:** the quality or state of being flighty

♦ facetiousness, flippancy, frivolity, levity, lightness

flight line *n* **:** a parking and servicing area for airplanes

flighty \ˈflī-tē\ *adj* **flight•i•er; -est 1 :** easily upset **:** VOLATILE **2** ♦ **:** easily excited **:** SKITTISH **3** ♦ **:** governed or characterized by caprice **:** CAPRICIOUS, SILLY

♦ [2] excitable, fluttery, high-strung, jittery, jumpy, nervous, skittish, spooky ♦ [3] capricious, frivolous, giddy, harebrained, scatterbrained, silly

flim-flam \ˈflim-ˌflam\ *n* **:** DECEPTION, FRAUD — **flim•flam•mery** \-ˌfla-mə-rē\ *n*

flim•sy \ˈflim-zē\ *adj* **flim•si•er; -est 1** ♦ **:** lacking strength or substance **2** ♦ **:** of inferior materials and workmanship **3** ♦ **:** having little worth or plausibility <a ~ excuse> — **flim•si•ly** \-zə-lē\ *adv* — **flim•si•ness** \-zē-nəs\ *n*

♦ [1, 2] gauzy, insubstantial, unsubstantial *Ant* sturdy, substantial ♦ [3] doubtful, dubious, improbable, questionable, unlikely

flinch \ˈflinch\ *vb* ♦ **:** to shrink from or as if from pain **:** WINCE — **flinch** *n*

♦ blench, quail, recoil, shrink, wince

¹**fling** \ˈfliŋ\ *vb* **flung** \ˈfləŋ\; **fling•ing 1 :** to move hastily, brusquely, or violently <*flung* out of the room> **2 :** to kick or plunge vigorously **3 a :** to throw with force or recklessness **b** ♦ **:** to cast as if by throwing **4 :** to put suddenly into a state or condition

♦ cast, catapult, chuck, hurl, hurtle, launch, pitch, sling, throw, toss

²**fling** *n* **1 :** an act or instance of flinging **2** ♦ **:** a casual try **:** ATTEMPT **3** ♦ **:** a period of self-indulgence

♦ [2] attempt, bid, endeavor (*or* endeavour), essay, go, pass, shot, stab, trial, try, whack, whirl ♦ [3] frolic, gambol, lark, revel, rollick, romp

flint \ˈflint\ *n* **1 :** a hard quartz that produces a spark when struck by steel **2 :** an alloy used for producing a spark in lighters

flint glass *n* **:** heavy glass containing an oxide of lead and used in lenses and prisms

flint•lock \ˈflint-ˌläk\ *n* **1 :** a lock for a gun using a flint to ignite the charge **2 :** a firearm fitted with a flintlock

flinty *adj* ♦ **:** harsh and unyielding **:** rigorous and stern

♦ austere, authoritarian, hard, harsh, rigorous, severe, stern, strict

¹**flip** \ˈflip\ *vb* **flipped; flip•ping 1 :** to turn by tossing <~ a coin> **2** ♦ **:** to turn over; *also* **:** to leaf through **3 :** FLICK, JERK <~ a light switch> **4** ♦ **:** to lose self-control — **flip** *n*

♦ [2] reverse, turn ♦ [4] break, crack, freak

²**flip** *adj* **:** glib or pert in speech **:** FLIPPANT

flip•pan•cy \ˈfli-pən-sē\ *n* ♦ **:** the quality or state of being flippant

♦ facetiousness, flightiness, frivolity, levity, lightness

flip•pant \ˈfli-pənt\ *adj* ♦ **:** lacking proper respect or seriousness

♦ facetious, flip, pert, smart *Ant* earnest, sincere

flip•per \ˈfli-pər\ *n* **1 :** a broad flat limb (as of a seal) adapted for swimming **2 :** a paddlelike shoe used in skin diving

flip side *n* **:** the reverse and usually less popular side of a phonograph record

¹**flirt** \ˈflərt\ *vb* **1 :** to move erratically **:** FLIT **2 :** to behave amorously without serious intent **3 :** to show casual interest <~*ed* with the idea>; *also* **:** to come close to <~ with danger> — **flir•ta•tion** \ˌflər-ˈtā-shən\ *n* — **flir•ta•tious** \-shəs\ *adj*

²**flirt** *n* **1 :** an act or instance of flirting **2 :** a person who flirts

flit \ˈflit\ *vb* **flit•ted; flit•ting** ♦ **:** to pass or move quickly or abruptly from place to place **:** DART — **flit** *n*

♦ dance, dart, flutter, zip

flitch \ˈflich\ *n* **:** a side of cured meat; *esp* **:** a side of bacon

fliv•ver \ˈfli-vər\ *n* **:** a small cheap usually old automobile

¹**float** \ˈflōt\ *n* **1** ♦ **:** something (as a raft) that floats; *also* **:** a floating platform anchored near a shoreline for use by swimmers or boats **2 :** a cork buoying up the baited end of a fishing line **3 :** a hollow ball that floats at the end of a lever in a cistern or tank and regulates the liquid level **4 :** a vehicle with a platform to carry an exhibit **5 :** a soft drink with ice cream floating in it

♦ dock, jetty, landing, levee, pier, quay, wharf

²**float** *vb* **1 :** to rest on the surface of or be suspended in a fluid **2** ♦ **:** to move gently on or through a fluid **3 :** to cause to float **4 :** WANDER **5 :** to offer (securities) in order to finance an enterprise **6 :** to finance by floating an issue of stocks or bonds **7 :** to arrange for <~ a loan> — **float•er** *n*

♦ drift, glide, hang, hover, poise, ride, sail, waft *Ant* settle, sink

[1]flock \ˈfläk\ *n* **1 :** a group of birds or mammals assembled or herded together **2 :** a group of people under the guidance of a leader; *esp* **:** CONGREGATION **3** ♦ **:** a large number ⟨a ∼ of tourists⟩

♦ army, crowd, crush, drove, horde, host, legion, mob, multitude, press, swarm, throng

[2]flock *vb* ♦ **:** to gather or move in a flock ⟨people ∼*ed* to the beach⟩

♦ crowd, mob, swarm, throng

floe \ˈflō\ *n* **:** a flat mass of floating ice

flog \ˈfläg\ *vb* **flogged; flog•ging 1** ♦ **:** to beat with or as if with a rod or whip **2 :** SELL ⟨∼ encyclopedias⟩ — **flog•ger** *n*

♦ bash, bat, batter, beat, belt, bludgeon, buffet, club, drub, hammer, hide, lace, lambaste, lick, maul, pelt, pound, thrash, thump, wallop, whale, whip

[1]flood \ˈfləd\ *n* **1** ♦ **:** a great flow of water over the land **2 :** the flowing in of the tide **3** ♦ **:** an overwhelming volume

♦ [1, 3] cataclysm, cataract, deluge, inundation, overflow, spate, torrent ***Ant*** drought

[2]flood *vb* **1** ♦ **:** to cover or become filled with a flood **2 :** to fill abundantly or excessively; *esp* **:** to supply an excess of fuel to ⟨∼*ed* the engine⟩ **3 :** to pour forth in a flood — **flood•er** *n*

♦ deluge, drown, engulf, inundate, overflow, overwhelm, submerge, swamp ***Ant*** drain

flood•gate \ˈfləd-ˌgāt\ *n* **:** a gate for controlling a body of water **:** SLUICE

flood•light \-ˌlīt\ *n* **:** a lamp that throws a broad beam of light; *also* **:** the beam itself — **floodlight** *vb*

flood•plain \-ˌplān\ *n* **:** a plain along a river or stream subject to periodic flooding

flood tide *n* **1 :** a rising tide **2 :** an overwhelming quantity **3 :** a high point

flood•wa•ter \ˈfləd-ˌwȯ-tər, -ˌwä-\ *n* **:** the water of a flood

[1]floor \ˈflōr\ *n* **1 :** the bottom of a room on which one stands **2 :** a ground surface **3 :** a story of a building **4 :** a main level space (as in a legislative chamber) distinguished from a platform or gallery **5 :** AUDIENCE **6 :** the right to address an assembly **7 :** a lower limit ⟨put a ∼ under wheat prices⟩ — **floor•ing** *n*

[2]floor *vb* **1 :** to furnish with a floor **2** ♦ **:** to knock down **3** ♦ **:** to overwhelm with shock, surprise, or wonder **4 :** to press (a vehicle's accelerator) to the floorboard especially rapidly

♦ [2] bowl, down, drop, fell, knock, level ♦ [3] amaze, astonish, astound, bowl, dumbfound, flabbergast, overwhelm, shock, startle, stun, surprise

floor•board \-ˌbȯrd\ *n* **1 :** a board in a floor **2 :** the floor of an automobile

floor leader *n* **:** a member of a legislative body who has charge of a party's organization and strategy on the floor

floor show *n* **:** a series of acts presented in a nightclub

floor•walk•er \ˈflȯr-ˌwȯ-kər\ *n* **:** a person employed in a retail store to oversee the sales force and aid customers

floo•zy *or* **floo•zie** \ˈflü-zē\ *n, pl* **floozies :** a usually young woman of loose morals

[1]flop \ˈfläp\ *vb* **flopped; flop•ping 1** ♦ **:** to swing or move loosely **:** FLAP **2** ♦ **:** to throw oneself down heavily, clumsily, or in a relaxed manner ⟨*flopped* into a chair⟩ **3** ♦ **:** to fall short of success **:** FAIL ⟨the show *flopped*⟩ — **flop** *adv* — **flop•per** *n*

♦ [1] beat, flail, flap, flutter, whip ♦ [2] plop, plump, plunk ♦ [3] collapse, fail, flunk, fold, wash out

[2]flop *n* ♦ **:** something that is a failure

♦ bust, debacle, dud, failure, fiasco, fizzle, loser, washout

flop•house \ˈfläp-ˌhau̇s\ *n* **:** a cheap hotel

[1]flop•py \ˈflä-pē\ *adj* **flop•pi•er; -est** ♦ **:** tending to flop; *esp* **:** soft and flexible — **flop•pi•ly** \-pə-lē\ *adv*

♦ droopy, flaccid, lank, limp, slack, yielding

[2]floppy *n, pl* **flop•pies :** FLOPPY DISK

floppy disk *n* **:** a thin plastic disk with a magnetic coating on which computer data can be stored

flop sweat *n* **:** sweat caused by the fear of failing

flo•ra \ˈflōr-ə\ *n, pl* **floras** *also* **flo•rae** \-ˌē, -ˌī\ ♦ **:** plants or plant life especially of a region or period

♦ foliage, green, greenery, herbage, leafage, vegetation, verdure

flo•ral \ˈflōr-əl\ *adj* **:** of, relating to, or depicting flowers ⟨a ∼ design⟩

flo•res•cence \flȯ-ˈres-ᵊns, flə-\ *n* **:** a state or period of being in bloom or flourishing — **flo•res•cent** \-ᵊnt\ *adj*

flor•id \ˈflȯr-əd\ *adj* **1** ♦ **:** very flowery in style ⟨∼ prose⟩ **2** ♦ **:** tinged with red **:** RUDDY **3 :** marked by emotional or sexual fervor

♦ [1] flowery, grandiloquent, high-flown, highfalutin ♦ [2] flush, glowing, rosy, ruddy, sanguine

flo•rin \ˈflȯr-ən\ *n* **1 :** an old gold coin first struck at Florence, Italy, in 1252 **2 :** a gold coin of a European country patterned after the florin of Florence **3 :** any of several modern silver coins issued in Commonwealth countries

flo•rist \ˈflōr-ist\ *n* **:** a person who sells flowers or ornamental plants

[1]floss \ˈfläs\ *n* **1 :** soft thread of silk or mercerized cotton for embroidery **2 :** DENTAL FLOSS **3** ♦ **:** fluffy fibrous material

♦ down, fluff, fur, fuzz, lint, nap, pile

[2]floss *vb* **:** to use dental floss on (one's teeth)

flossy \ˈflä-sē\ *adj* **floss•i•er; -est 1 :** of, relating to, or having the characteristics of floss **2 :** STYLISH, GLAMOROUS — **floss•i•ly** \-sə-lē\ *adv*

flo•ta•tion \flō-ˈtā-shən\ *n* **:** the process or an instance of floating

flo•til•la \flō-ˈti-lə\ *n* **:** a fleet especially of small ships

flot•sam \ˈflät-səm\ *n* **:** floating wreckage of a ship or its cargo

[1]flounce \ˈflau̇ns\ *vb* **flounced; flounc•ing 1 :** to move with exaggerated jerky or bouncy motions **2 :** to go with sudden determination

[2]flounce *n* **:** an act or instance of flouncing — **flouncy** \ˈflau̇n-sē\ *adj*

[3]flounce *n* ♦ **:** a strip of fabric attached by one edge; *also* **:** a wide ruffle

♦ frill, furbelow, ruffle

[1]floun•der \ˈflau̇n-dər\ *n, pl* **flounder** *or* **flounders :** FLATFISH; *esp* **:** any of various important marine food fishes

[2]flounder *vb* **1 :** to struggle to move or obtain footing **2** ♦ **:** to proceed clumsily ⟨∼*ed* through the speech⟩

♦ limp, lumber, plod, stumble

[1]flour \ˈflau̇r\ *n* **:** finely ground and sifted meal of a grain (as wheat); *also* **:** a fine soft powder

[2]flour *vb* **:** to coat with or as if with flour

[1]flour•ish \ˈflər-ish\ *vb* **1** ♦ **:** to grow luxuriantly **:** THRIVE, PROSPER **2 :** to be in a state of activity or production ⟨∼*ed* about 1850⟩ **3** ♦ **:** to reach a height of development or influence **4 :** to make bold and sweeping gestures **5 :** BRANDISH

♦ [1] burgeon, prosper, thrive ♦ [3] prosper, succeed, thrive

[2]flourish *n* **1 :** a florid bit of speech or writing; *also* **:** an ornamental touch or decorative detail **2 :** FANFARE **3 :** WAVE ⟨with a ∼ of his cane⟩ **4 :** showiness in doing something

floury *adj* ♦ **:** of or resembling flour especially in fine powdery texture

♦ dusty, fine, powdery

[1]flout \ˈflau̇t\ *vb* ♦ **:** to treat with contemptuous disregard ⟨∼ the law⟩ — **flout•er** *n*

♦ despise, disregard, scorn

[2]flout *n* **:** TAUNT

[1]flow \ˈflō\ *vb* **1** ♦ **:** to issue or move in a stream **2 :** RISE ⟨the tide ebbs and ∼*s*⟩ **3 :** ABOUND **4** ♦ **:** to proceed smoothly and readily **5 :** to have a smooth continuity **6 :** to hang loose and billowing **7 :** COME, ARISE **8 :** MENSTRUATE

♦ [1] pour, roll, run, stream ***Ant*** back up ♦ [4] breeze, coast, glide, roll, sail, slide, slip, stream, sweep ***Ant*** flounder, struggle

[2]flow *n* **1 :** an act of flowing **2 :** FLOOD 1, 2 **3 :** a smooth uninterrupted movement **4 :** STREAM; *also* **:** a mass of material that has flowed when molten **5 :** the quantity that flows in a certain time **6 :** MENSTRUATION **7 :** a continuous transfer of energy — **flow•age** \ˈflō-ij\ *n*

flow•chart \ˈflō-ˌchärt\ *n* **:** a symbolic diagram showing step-by-step progression through a procedure

flow diagram *n* **:** FLOWCHART

[1]flow•er \ˈflau̇(-ə)r\ *n* **1 :** a plant shoot modified for reproduction and bearing leaves specialized into floral organs; *esp* **:** one of a seed plant consisting of a calyx, corolla, stamens, and carpels **2 :** a plant cultivated for its blossoms **3** ♦ **:** the best part or example **4** ♦ **:** the finest most vigorous period **5 :** a state of blooming or flourishing — **flow•ered** \ˈflau̇(-ə)rd\ *adj* — **flow•er•less** *adj* — **flow•er•like** \-ˌlīk\ *adj*

◆ [3] best, choice, cream, elite, pick, prime ◆ [4] bloom, blossom, flush, heyday, prime

²flower *vb* **1 :** DEVELOP; *also* **:** FLOURISH **2** ◆ **:** to produce flowers **:** BLOOM

◆ bloom, blossom, blow, burgeon, unfold

flower girl *n* **:** a little girl who carries flowers at a wedding
flower head *n* **:** a compact cluster of small flowers without stems suggesting a single flower
flowering plant *n* **:** any of a major group of vascular plants (as magnolias, grasses, or roses) that produce flowers and fruit and have the seeds enclosed in an ovary
flow•er•pot \ˈflau̇(-ə)r-ˌpät\ *n* **:** a pot in which to grow plants
flow•ery \ˈflau̇(-ə)r-ē\ *adj* **1 :** of, relating to, or resembling flowers **2** ◆ **:** full of fine words or phrases — **flow•er•i•ly** \-ə-lē\ *adv* — **flow•er•i•ness** \-ē-nəs\ *n*

◆ florid, grandiloquent, high-flown, highfalutin

flown \ˈflōn\ *past part of* ¹FLY
fl oz *abbr* fluid ounce
flu \ˈflü\ *n* **1 :** INFLUENZA **2 :** any of several virus diseases marked especially by respiratory or intestinal symptoms — **flu–like** \-ˌlīk\ *adj*
¹flub \ˈfləb\ *vb* **flubbed; flub•bing** ◆ **:** to make a mess of **:** BOTCH

◆ bobble, botch, bungle, foul up, fumble, mangle, mess up, screw up

²flub *n* ◆ **:** a clumsy or stupid failure

◆ blunder, error, fault, fumble, goof, mistake, slip, stumble

fluc•tu•ate \ˈflək-chə-ˌwāt\ *vb* **-at•ed; -at•ing 1** ◆ **:** to become wavering, unsteady, irresolute, or undetermined **2 :** to move up and down or back and forth — **fluc•tu•a•tion** \ˌflək-chə-ˈwā-shən\ *n*

◆ change, mutate, shift, vary

flue \ˈflü\ *n* **:** a passage (as in a chimney) for directing a current (as of smoke or gases)
flu•ent \ˈflü-ənt\ *adj* **1 :** capable of flowing **:** FLUID **2** ◆ **:** ready or facile in speech ⟨~ in French⟩; *also* **:** having or showing mastery in a subject or skill **3** ◆ **:** effortlessly smooth and rapid ⟨~ speech⟩ — **flu•en•cy** \-ən-sē\ *n*

◆ [2] articulate, eloquent, well-spoken ◆ [3] easy, effortless, facile, fluid, ready, simple, smooth

flu•ent•ly \-lē\ *adv* ◆ **:** in a fluent manner

◆ easily, effortlessly, freely, handily, lightly, painlessly, readily, smoothly

flue pipe *n* **:** an organ pipe whose tone is produced by an air current striking the beveled opening of the pipe
¹fluff \ˈfləf\ *n* **1 :** ⁷DOWN 1 ⟨~ from a pillow⟩ **2** ◆ **:** something fluffy **3 :** something inconsequential **4 :** BLUNDER; *esp* **:** an actor's lapse of memory

◆ down, floss, fur, fuzz, lint, nap, pile

²fluff *vb* **1 :** to make or become fluffy ⟨~ up a pillow⟩ **2 :** to make a mistake
fluffy \ˈflə-fē\ *adj* **fluff•i•er; -est 1 :** covered with or resembling fluff **2** ◆ **:** being light and soft or airy **3 :** lacking in meaning or substance — **fluff•i•ly** \-fə-lē\ *adv*

◆ airy, ethereal, light

¹flu•id \ˈflü-əd\ *adj* **1** ◆ **:** capable of flowing **2** ◆ **:** subject to change or movement **3** ◆ **:** showing a smooth easy style ⟨~ movements⟩ **4 :** available for a different use; *esp* **:** LIQUID 5 ⟨~ assets⟩ — **flu•id•i•ty** \flü-ˈi-də-tē\ *n* — **flu•id•ly** *adv*

◆ [1] fluent, liquid, runny ***Ant*** hard, solid ◆ [2] adaptable, adjustable, changeable, elastic, flexible, malleable, variable ◆ [3] easy, effortless, facile, fluent, light, ready, smooth

²fluid *n* **:** a substance (as a liquid or gas) tending to flow or take the shape of its container
fluid dram *or* **flu•i•dram** \ˌflü-ə-ˈdram\ *n* **:** a unit of liquid measure equal to ⅛ fluid ounce
fluid ounce *n* **:** a unit of liquid measure equal to $^1/_{16}$ pint in the U.S. or $^1/_{20}$ pint in the U.K.
¹fluke \ˈflük\ *n* **:** any of various trematode flatworms
²fluke *n* **1 :** the part of an anchor that fastens in the ground **2 :** a lobe of a whale's tail
³fluke *n* **:** a stroke of luck
fluky *also* **fluk•ey** \ˈflü-kē\ *adj* **1** ◆ **:** happening or depending on chance rather than skill **2 :** light and uncertain

◆ accidental, casual, chance, fortuitous, incidental, unplanned

flume \ˈflüm\ *n* **1** ◆ **:** an inclined channel for carrying water **2** ◆ **:** a ravine or gorge with a stream running through it

◆ [1] aqueduct, canal, channel, conduit, raceway, watercourse ◆ [2] canyon, defile, gap, gorge, gulch, notch, pass, ravine

flung *past and past part of* FLING
flunk \ˈfləŋk\ *vb* ◆ **:** to fail especially in an examination or course — **flunk** *n*

◆ collapse, fail, flop, fold, wash out

flun•ky *also* **flun•key** *or* **flun•kie** \ˈfləŋ-kē\ *n, pl* **flunkies** *also* **flunkeys 1 a :** a liveried servant **b** ◆ **:** one performing menial or miscellaneous duties **2 :** YES-MAN

◆ domestic, lackey, menial, retainer, servant, steward

fluo•res•cence \flo̍-ˈres-ᵊns\ *n* **1 :** luminescence caused by radiation absorption that ceases almost immediately after the incident radiation has stopped **2** ◆ **:** visible emitted radiation — **fluo•resce** \-ˈres\ *vb* — **fluo•res•cent** \-ˈres-ᵊnt\ *adj*

◆ glow, illumination, incandescence, light, luminescence, radiance, shine

fluorescent lamp *n* **:** a tubular electric lamp in which light is produced by the action of ultraviolet light on a fluorescent material that coats the inner surface of the lamp
fluo•ri•date \ˈflo̍r-ə-ˌdāt\ *vb* **-dat•ed; -dat•ing :** to add a fluoride to (as drinking water) to reduce tooth decay — **fluo•ri•da•tion** \ˌflo̍r-ə-ˈdā-shən\ *n*
fluo•ride \ˈflo̍r-ˌīd\ *n* **:** a compound of fluorine
fluo•ri•nate \ˈflo̍r-ə-ˌnāt\ *vb* **-nat•ed; -nat•ing :** to treat or cause to combine with fluorine or a compound of fluorine — **fluo•ri•na•tion** \ˌflo̍r-ə-ˈnā-shən\ *n*
fluo•rine \ˈflo̍r-ˌēn, -ən\ *n* **:** a pale yellowish flammable irritating toxic gaseous chemical element
fluo•rite \ˈflo̍r-ˌīt\ *n* **:** a mineral that consists of the fluoride of calcium used as a flux and in making glass
fluo•ro•car•bon \ˌflo̍r-ō-ˈkär-bən\ *n* **:** a compound containing fluorine and carbon used chiefly as a lubricant, refrigerant, or nonstick coating; *also* **:** CHLOROFLUOROCARBON
fluo•ro•scope \ˈflo̍r-ə-ˌskōp\ *n* **:** an instrument for observing the internal structure of an opaque object (as the living body) by means of X-rays — **fluo•ro•scop•ic** \ˌflo̍r-ə-ˈskä-pik\ *adj* — **fluo•ros•co•py** \-ˈä-skə-pē\ *n*
fluo•ro•sis \ˌflü-ˈrō-səs, ˌflo̍-\ *n* **:** an abnormal condition (as spotting of the teeth) caused by fluorine or its compounds
flu•ox•e•tine \flü-ˈäk-sə-ˌtēn\ *n* **:** an antidepressant drug that enhances serotonin activity
flur•ry \ˈflər-ē\ *n, pl* **flurries 1** ◆ **:** a gust of wind **2 :** a brief light snowfall **3 :** COMMOTION, BUSTLE **4** ◆ **:** a brief outburst of activity ⟨a ~ of trading⟩ — **flurry** *vb*

◆ [1] blast, blow, gust, williwaw ◆ [4] burst, flash, outbreak, outburst, spurt

¹flush \ˈfləsh\ *vb* **:** to cause (a bird) to fly away suddenly
²flush *n* **:** a hand of cards all of the same suit
³flush *n* **1 :** a sudden flow (as of water) **2 :** a surge especially of emotion ⟨a ~ of triumph⟩ **3 :** a tinge of red **:** BLUSH **4** ◆ **:** a fresh and vigorous state ⟨in the ~ of youth⟩ **5 :** a passing sensation of extreme heat

◆ bloom, blossom, flower, heyday, prime

⁴flush *vb* **1 :** to flow and spread suddenly and freely **2 :** to glow brightly **3** ◆ **:** to become red in the face especially from shame, modesty, or confusion **:** BLUSH **4** ◆ **:** to wash out with a rush of fluid **5 :** INFLAME, EXCITE **6 :** to cause to blush

◆ [3] bloom, blush, color (*or* colour), crimson, glow, redden ◆ [4] irrigate, rinse, sluice, wash

⁵flush *adj* **1** ◆ **:** of a ruddy healthy color **2 :** full of life and vigor **3** ◆ **:** filled to overflowing **4** ◆ **:** fully or generously supplied usually with money **:** AFFLUENT **5 :** readily available **:** ABUNDANT **6** ◆ **:** having an unbroken or even surface **7 :** directly abutting **:** immediately adjacent **8 :** set even with an edge of a type page or column — **flush•ness** *n*

◆ [1] florid, glowing, rosy, ruddy ◆ [3] fraught, replete, rife, thick ◆ [4] affluent, loaded, moneyed, opulent, rich, wealthy, well-fixed, well-heeled, well-off, well-to-do ◆ [6] even, flat, level, plane, smooth

⁶flush *adv* **1 :** in a flush manner **2 :** SQUARELY ⟨a blow ~ on the chin⟩
⁷flush *vb* **:** to make flush
¹flus•ter \ˈfləs-tər\ *vb* ♦ **:** to put into a state of agitated confusion

♦ abash, confound, confuse, discomfit, disconcert, embarrass, rattle

²fluster *n* ♦ **:** a state of agitated confusion

♦ abashment, confusion, discomfiture, dither, embarrassment, fret

flute \ˈflüt\ *n* **1 :** a hollow pipelike musical instrument **2 :** a grooved pleat **3 :** GROOVE — **flute** *vb* — **flut•ed** *adj*
flut•ing *n* **:** fluted decoration
flut•ist \ˈflü-tist\ *n* **:** a flute player
¹flut•ter \ˈflə-tər\ *vb* **1 :** to flap the wings rapidly **2** ♦ **:** to move with quick wavering or flapping motions **3 :** to vibrate in irregular spasms **4 :** to move about or behave in an agitated aimless manner

♦ beat, flail, flap, flop, whip

²flutter *n* **1 :** an act of fluttering **2 :** a state of nervous confusion **3 :** a sudden but usually slight stir **:** FLURRY
flut•tery \-tə-rē\ *adj* ♦ **:** given to or characterized by fluttering

♦ excitable, flighty, high-strung, jittery, jumpy, nervous, skittish, spooky

¹flux \ˈfləks\ *n* **1 :** an act of flowing **2 :** a state of continuous change **3 :** a substance used to aid in fusing metals
²flux *vb* ♦ **:** to become or cause to become fluid

♦ deliquesce, fuse, liquefy, melt, run, thaw

¹fly \ˈflī\ *vb* **flew** \ˈflü\; **flown** \ˈflōn\; **fly•ing 1** ♦ **:** to move in or pass through the air with wings **2 :** to move through the air or before the wind **3 :** to float or cause to float, wave, or soar in the air **4** ♦ **:** to take flight **:** FLEE **5 :** to fade and disappear **:** VANISH **6** ♦ **:** to move or pass swiftly **7 :** to become expended or dissipated rapidly **8 :** to operate or travel in an aircraft or spacecraft **9 :** to journey over by flying **10 :** AVOID, SHUN **11 :** to transport by flying

♦ [1] glide, plane, soar, wing ♦ [4] abscond, clear out, escape, flee, get out, lam, run away, run off ♦ [6] barrel, bolt, career, course, dash, hasten, hurry, pelt, race, run, rush, speed, tear, zip, zoom

²fly *n, pl* **flies 1 :** the action or process of flying **:** FLIGHT **2** *pl* **:** the space over a theater stage **3 :** a garment closing concealed by a fold of cloth **4 :** the length of an extended flag from its staff or support **5 :** a baseball hit high into the air **6 :** the outer canvas of a tent with a double top — **on the fly :** while still in the air
³fly *vb* **flied; fly•ing :** to hit a fly in baseball
⁴fly *n, pl* **flies 1 :** a winged insect — usually used in combination ⟨butter*fly*⟩ **2 :** any of a large order of insects mostly with one pair of functional wings and another pair that if present are reduced to balancing organs and often with larvae without a head, eyes, or legs; *esp* **:** one (as a housefly) that is large and stout-bodied **3 :** a fishhook dressed to suggest an insect
fly•able \ˈflī-ə-bəl\ *adj* **:** suitable for flying or being flown
fly ball *n* **:** ² FLY 5
fly•blown \ˈflī-ˌblōn\ *adj* **:** not pure **:** TAINTED, CORRUPT
fly•by \-ˌbī\ *n, pl* **flybys 1 :** a usually low-altitude flight by an aircraft over a public gathering **2 :** a flight of a spacecraft past a heavenly body (as Jupiter) close enough to obtain scientific data
fly–by–night \-bī-ˌnīt\ *adj* **1 :** seeking a quick profit usually by shady acts **2 :** TRANSITORY, PASSING
fly casting *n* **:** the casting of artificial flies in fly-fishing or as a competitive sport
fly•catch•er \-ˌka-chər, -ˌke-\ *n* **:** any of various passerine birds that feed on insects caught in flight
flyer *var of* FLIER
fly–fish•ing \ˈflī-ˌfi-shiŋ\ *n* **:** a method of fishing in which an artificial fly is used for bait
flying boat *n* **:** a seaplane with a hull designed for floating
flying buttress *n* **:** a projecting arched structure to support a wall or building
flying fish *n* **:** any of numerous marine bony fishes capable of long gliding flights out of water by spreading their large fins like wings
flying saucer *n* **:** an unidentified flying object reported to be saucer-shaped or disk-shaped
flying squirrel *n* **:** either of two small nocturnal No. American squirrels with folds of skin connecting the forelegs and hind legs that enable them to make long gliding leaps

fly•leaf \ˈflī-ˌlēf\ *n, pl* **fly•leaves** \-ˌlēvz\ **:** a blank leaf at the beginning or end of a book
fly•pa•per \-ˌpā-pər\ *n* **:** paper poisoned or coated with a sticky substance for killing or catching flies
fly•speck \-ˌspek\ *n* **1 :** a speck of fly dung **2** ♦ **:** something small and insignificant

♦ atom, bit, crumb, fleck, grain, particle, speck

fly•way \-ˌwā\ *n* **:** an established air route of migratory birds
fly•wheel \-ˌhwēl\ *n* **:** a heavy wheel for regulating the speed of machinery
fm *abbr* fathom
Fm *symbol* fermium
FM \ˈef-ˌem\ *n* **:** a broadcasting system using frequency modulation; *also* **:** a radio receiver of such a system
fn *abbr* footnote
fo *or* **fol** *abbr* folio
FO *abbr* foreign office
¹foal \ˈfōl\ *n* **:** a young horse or related animal; *esp* **:** one under one year
²foal *vb* **:** to give birth to a foal
¹foam \ˈfōm\ *n* **1** ♦ **:** a mass of bubbles formed on the surface of a liquid **:** FROTH, SPUME **2 :** material (as rubber) in a lightweight cellular form — **foamy** *adj*

♦ froth, head, lather, spume

²foam *vb* **:** to form foam **:** FROTH
fob \ˈfäb\ *n* **1 :** a short strap, ribbon, or chain attached especially to a pocket watch **2 :** a small ornament worn on a fob
FOB *abbr* free on board
fob off *vb* **1 :** to put off with a trick, excuse, or inferior substitute **2 :** to pass or offer as genuine **3 :** to put aside
FOC *abbr* free of charge
focal length *n* **:** the distance of a focus from a lens or curved mirror
fo'c'sle *var of* FORECASTLE
¹fo•cus \ˈfō-kəs\ *n, pl* **fo•ci** \-ˌsī\ *also* **fo•cus•es 1 :** a point at which rays (as of light, heat, or sound) meet or diverge or appear to diverge; *esp* **:** the point at which an image is formed by a mirror, lens, or optical system **2 :** FOCAL LENGTH **3 :** adjustment (as of eyes or eyeglasses) that gives clear vision **4** ♦ **:** a central point **:** CENTER — **fo•cal** \ˈfō-kəl\ *adj* — **fo•cal•ly** *adv*

♦ base, center (*or* centre), core, heart, hub, nucleus, seat

²focus *vb* **-cused** *also* **-cussed; -cus•ing** *also* **-cus•sing 1 :** to bring or come to a focus ⟨~ rays of light⟩ **2** ♦ **:** to cause to be concentrated ⟨~ attention on a problem⟩ **3 :** to adjust the focus of

♦ concentrate, fasten, rivet, train

fod•der \ˈfä-dər\ *n* **1 :** coarse dry food (as cornstalks) for livestock **2 :** available material used to supply a heavy demand
foe \ˈfō\ *n* ♦ **:** one who has personal enmity for another **:** ENEMY

♦ adversary, antagonist, enemy, opponent

FOE *abbr* Fraternal Order of Eagles
foehn *or* **föhn** \ˈfərn, ˈfœn, ˈfān\ *n* **:** a warm dry wind blowing down a mountainside
foe•man \ˈfō-mən\ *n* **:** FOE
foe•tal, foe•tus *chiefly Brit var of* FETAL, FETUS
¹fog \ˈfȯg, ˈfäg\ *n* **1** ♦ **:** fine particles of water suspended in the lower atmosphere **2** ♦ **:** mental confusion

♦ [1] haze, murk, smog, soup ♦ [2] daze, haze, muddle, spin

²fog *vb* **fogged; fog•ging** ♦ **:** to obscure or be obscured with or as if with fog

♦ blur, cloud, confuse, dim, haze, mist, obscure ♦ becloud, befog, blur, cloud, confuse, muddy

fog•gy \ˈfȯ-gē, ˈfä-\ *adj* **1 a :** filled or abounding with fog **b** ♦ **:** covered or made opaque by moisture or grime **2** ♦ **:** blurred or obscured as if by fog

♦ [1b] cloudy, hazy, misty, murky, smoggy, soupy ♦ [2] bleary, dim, faint, fuzzy, hazy, indefinite, indistinct, murky, obscure, unclear

fog•horn \ˈfȯg-ˌhȯrn, ˈfäg-\ *n* **:** a horn sounded in a fog to give warning
fo•gy *also* **fo•gey** \ˈfō-gē\ *n, pl* **fogies** *also* **fogeys** ♦ **:** a person with old-fashioned ideas ⟨an old ~⟩

♦ antediluvian, dodo, fossil, fuddy-duddy, reactionary ***Ant*** modern

foi•ble \ˈfȯi-bəl\ *n* ♦ **:** a minor failing or weakness in character or behavior

♦ demerit, failing, fault, frailty, shortcoming, vice, weakness

foie gras \ˈfwä-ˈgrä\ *n* **:** the fattened liver of an animal and especially of a goose usually served as a pâté
¹foil \ˈfȯil\ *vb* **1** ♦ **:** to prevent from attaining an end **2** ♦ **:** to bring to naught **:** THWART

♦ [1, 2] baffle, balk, beat, checkmate, frustrate, thwart

²foil *n* **1 :** a very thin sheet of metal ⟨aluminum ~⟩ **2 :** one that serves as a contrast to another ⟨acted as a ~ for a comedian⟩
³foil *n* **:** a light fencing sword with a flexible blade tapering to a blunt point
foist \ˈfȯist\ *vb* **:** to pass off (something false or worthless) as genuine
¹fold \ˈfōld\ *n* **1 :** an enclosure for sheep **2** ♦ **:** a group of people with a common faith, belief, or interest

♦ body, circle, clan, clique, community, coterie, set

²fold *vb* **:** to house (sheep) in a fold
³fold *vb* **1 :** to lay one part over or against another part **2 :** to clasp together **3 :** EMBRACE **4 :** to bend (as a layer of rock) into folds **5 :** to incorporate into a mixture by overturning repeatedly without stirring or beating **6 :** to become doubled or pleated **7** ♦ **:** to fail completely **:** FAIL, COLLAPSE

♦ collapse, fail, flop, flunk, wash out

⁴fold *n* **1 :** a doubling or folding over **2 :** a part doubled or laid over another part
fold•away \ˈfōl-də-ˌwā\ *adj* **:** designed to fold out of the way or out of sight
fold•er \ˈfōl-dər\ *n* **1 :** one that folds **2** ♦ **:** a folded printed circular **3 :** a folded cover or large envelope for loose papers **4 :** an object in a computer operating system used to organize files or other folders

♦ booklet, brochure, circular, leaflet, pamphlet

fol•de•rol \ˈfäl-də-ˌräl\ *n* **1 :** a useless trifle **2 :** NONSENSE
fold•out \ˈfōl-ˌdau̇t\ *n* **:** a folded leaf (as in a magazine) larger in some dimension than the page
fo•liage \ˈfō-lē-ij\ *n* ♦ **:** a mass of leaves (as of a plant or forest)

♦ flora, green, greenery, herbage, leafage, vegetation, verdure

fo•li•at•ed \ˈfō-lē-ˌā-təd\ *adj* **:** composed of or separable into layers
fo•lic acid \ˌfō-lik-\ *n* **:** a vitamin of the vitamin B complex used especially to treat nutritional anemias
fo•lio \ˈfō-lē-ˌō\ *n, pl* **fo•li•os** **1 :** a leaf of a book; *also* **:** a page number **2 :** the size of a piece of paper cut two from a sheet **3 :** a book printed on folio pages
¹folk \ˈfōk\ *n, pl* **folk** *or* **folks** **1 :** the largest number or most characteristic part of a group of people forming a tribe or nation **2 a** *pl* ♦ **:** a certain kind, class, or group of people **:** PEOPLE, PERSONS ⟨country ~⟩ ⟨old ~*s*⟩ **b** ♦ **:** people generally **3** *folks pl* ♦ **:** the persons of one's own family

♦ *usu* **folks** [2a, 2b] humanity, humankind, people, persons, public, society, world ♦ *usu* **folks** [3] blood, clan, family, house, kin, kindred, kinfolk, line, lineage, people, race, stock, tribe

²folk *adj* **:** of, relating to, or originating among the common people ⟨~ music⟩
folk art *n* **:** the traditional anonymous art of usually untrained people
folk•lore \ˈfōk-ˌlȯr\ *n* ♦ **:** customs, beliefs, stories, and sayings of a people handed down from generation to generation — **folk•lor•ic** \-ˌlȯr-ik\ *adj* — **folk•lor•ist** \-ist\ *n*

♦ legend, lore, myth, mythology, tradition

folk mass *n* **:** a mass in which traditional liturgical music is replaced by folk music
folk•sing•er \ˈfōk-ˌsiŋ-ər\ *n* **:** a singer of folk songs — **folk•sing•ing** *n*
folksy \ˈfōk-sē\ *adj* **folks•i•er; -est** **1 :** SOCIABLE, FRIENDLY **2 :** informal, casual, or familiar in manner or style
folk•way \ˈfōk-ˌwā\ *n* **:** a way of thinking, feeling, or acting common to a given group of people; *esp* **:** a traditional social custom
fol•li•cle \ˈfä-li-kəl\ *n* **1 :** a small anatomical cavity or gland ⟨a hair ~⟩ **2 :** a small fluid-filled cavity in the ovary of a mammal enclosing a developing egg
fol•low \ˈfä-lō\ *vb* **1** ♦ **:** to go or come after **2** ♦ **:** to proceed along **3 :** to engage in as a way of life ⟨~ the sea⟩ ⟨~ a profession⟩ **4** ♦ **:** to be or act in accordance with **:** to accept as authority **:** OBEY **5** ♦ **:** to pursue in an effort to overtake **:** PURSUE **6 :** to come after in order or rank or natural sequence **7** ♦ **:** to keep one's attention fixed on **8 :** to result from — **follow suit** **1 :** to play a card of the same suit as the card led **2 :** to follow an example set

♦ [1] succeed *Ant* antedate, precede, predate ♦ [2] go, pass, proceed, travel, traverse ♦ [4] comply, conform, mind, obey, observe ♦ [5] chase, pursue, tail, trace, track, trail *Ant* guide, lead, pilot ♦ [7] heed, listen, mind, note, observe, regard, watch

fol•low•er *n* ♦ **:** one that follows the opinions or teachings of another

♦ adherent, convert, disciple, partisan, pupil, votary *Ant* leader

¹fol•low•ing \ˈfä-lə-wiŋ\ *adj* **1** ♦ **:** next after **:** SUCCEEDING ⟨the ~ day⟩ **2 :** that immediately follows ⟨trains will leave at the ~ times⟩

♦ coming, next, succeeding

²following *n* ♦ **:** a group of followers, adherents, or partisans

♦ cortege, retinue, suite, train

³following *prep* **:** subsequent to **:** AFTER
follow through *vb* ♦ **:** to press on in an activity or process especially to a conclusion

♦ accomplish, achieve, carry out, commit, compass, do, execute, fulfill, make, perform

fol•low–up \ˈfä-lə-ˌwəp\ *n* **:** a system or instance of pursuing an initial effort by supplementary action
fol•ly \ˈfä-lē\ *n, pl* **follies** **1 :** lack of good sense **2** ♦ **:** a foolish act or idea **3 :** an excessively costly or unprofitable undertaking

♦ absurdity, fatuity, foolery, foolishness, idiocy, inanity, madness, stupidity

fo•ment \fō-ˈment\ *vb* ♦ **:** to promote the growth or development of **:** INCITE

♦ abet, ferment, incite, instigate, provoke, raise, stir, whip

fo•men•ta•tion \ˌfō-mən-ˈtā-shən, -ˌmen-\ *n* **1 :** a hot moist material (as a damp cloth) applied to the body to ease pain **2 :** the act of fomenting **:** INSTIGATION
fond \ˈfänd\ *adj* **1 :** FOOLISH, SILLY ⟨~ pride⟩ **2 :** prizing highly **:** DESIROUS ⟨~ of praise⟩ **3** ♦ **:** strongly attracted or predisposed ⟨~ of music⟩ **4 a :** foolishly tender **:** INDULGENT **b** ♦ **:** feeling or expressing love **:** LOVING, AFFECTIONATE **5 :** CHERISHED, DEAR ⟨his ~*est* hopes⟩ — **fond•ly** *adv*

♦ [3] inclined, partial *Ant* averse, disinclined ♦ [4b] affectionate, devoted, loving, tender, tenderhearted

fon•dant \ˈfän-dənt\ *n* **:** a creamy preparation of sugar used as a basis for candies or icings
fon•dle \ˈfänd-ᵊl\ *vb* **fon•dled; fon•dling** ♦ **:** to touch or handle lovingly **:** CARESS

♦ caress, love, pat, pet, stroke

fond•ness \ˈfän(d)-nəs\ *n* **1** ♦ **:** tender affection **2** ♦ **:** enjoyment of or delight in something that satisfies one's tastes, inclinations, or desires

♦ [1] affection, attachment, devotion, love, passion ♦ [1, 2] appetite, fancy, favor (*or* favour), like, liking, love, partiality, preference

fon•due *also* **fon•du** \fän-ˈdü, -ˈdyü\ *n* **:** a preparation of melted cheese often flavored with white wine
¹font \ˈfänt\ *n* **1 :** a receptacle for baptismal or holy water **2 :** FOUNTAIN, SOURCE
²font *n* **:** an assortment of printing type of one size and style
food \ˈfüd\ *n* **1 :** material taken into an organism and used for growth, repair, and vital processes and as a source of energy; *also* **:** organic material produced by green plants and used by them as food **2** ♦ **:** nourishment in solid form **3 :** something that nourishes, sustains, or supplies ⟨~ for thought⟩

♦ chow, fare, meat, provisions, viands, victuals

food chain *n* **1 :** a hierarchical arrangement of organisms in an ecological community such that each uses the next usually lower member as a food source **2 :** a hierarchy based on power or importance
food court *n* **:** an area (as within a shopping mall) set apart for food concessions
food poisoning *n* **:** a digestive illness caused by bacteria or by chemicals in food
food•stuff \ˈfüd-ˌstəft\ *n* **:** a substance with food value; *esp* **:** a specific nutrient (as fat or protein)

[1]fool \ˈfül\ *n* **1** ♦ **:** a person who lacks sense or judgment **2 :** JESTER **3 :** DUPE **4 :** IDIOT

♦ booby, goose, jackass, lunatic, nitwit, nut, simpleton

[2]fool *vb* **1** ♦ **:** to meddle or tamper thoughtlessly or ignorantly **2** ♦ **:** to speak in jest **:** JOKE **3** ♦ **:** to make a fool of **:** DECEIVE **4 :** FRITTER ⟨~*ed* away his time⟩

♦ [1] fiddle (around), mess, monkey, play, tamper, tinker ♦ [2] banter, fun, jest, jive, joke, josh, kid, quip, wisecrack ♦ [3] deceive, delude, dupe, gull, hoodwink, mislead, take in, trick

fool around *vb* **1** ♦ **:** to spend time idly, aimlessly, or frivolously **2 :** to engage in casual sexual activity

♦ fiddle (around), monkey, play, trifle

fool•ery \ˈfü-lə-rē\ *n, pl* **-er•ies 1** ♦ **:** a foolish act, utterance, or belief **2** ♦ **:** foolish behavior

♦ [1] absurdity, fatuity, folly, foolishness, idiocy, inanity, madness, stupidity ♦ [2] high jinks, horseplay, monkeyshines, shenanigans, tomfoolery

fool•har•dy \ˈfül-ˌhär-dē\ *adj* ♦ **:** foolishly daring **:** RASH — **fool•har•di•ness** \-dē-nəs\ *n*

♦ brash, madcap, overbold, overconfident, rash, reckless *Ant* careful, cautious, heedful, prudent

fool•ish \ˈfü-lish\ *adj* **1** ♦ **:** showing or arising from folly or lack of judgment **2** ♦ **:** ridiculously unreasonable, unsound, or incongruous **:** ABSURD **3 :** ABASHED — **fool•ish•ly** *adv*

♦ [1] absurd, bizarre, crazy, fanciful, fantastic, insane, nonsensical, preposterous, unreal, wild ♦ [2] absurd, asinine, crazy, cuckoo, daft, fatuous, insane, kooky, mad, nonsensical, nutty, preposterous, senseless, silly, stupid *Ant* judicious, prudent, sensible, sound, wise

fool•ish•ness *n* **1** ♦ **:** foolish behavior **2** ♦ **:** a foolish act or idea

♦ folly, nonsense, piffle, rot, silliness

fool•proof \ˈfül-ˌprüf\ *adj* **:** so simple or reliable as to leave no opportunity for error, misuse, or failure ⟨a ~ plan⟩
fools•cap \ˈfül-ˌskap\ *n* **:** a size of paper typically 16×13 inches
fool's gold *n* **:** PYRITE
[1]foot \ˈfu̇t\ *n, pl* **feet** \ˈfēt\ *also* **foot 1 :** the end part of a leg below the ankle of a vertebrate animal **2 :** a unit of measure equal to 12 inches **3 :** a group of syllables forming the basic unit of verse meter **4 :** something resembling an animal's foot in position or use **5** ♦ **:** the lowest part **:** BOTTOM **6 :** the part at the opposite end from the head **7 :** the part (as of a stocking) that covers the foot

♦ base, bottom

[2]foot *vb* **1** ♦ **:** to tread to music **:** DANCE **2** ♦ **:** to go on foot **3 :** to add up **4** ♦ **:** to pay or provide for paying

♦ *usu* **foot it** [1] dance, step ♦ *usu* **foot it** [2] leg, pad, step, traipse, tread, walk ♦ [4] clear, discharge, liquidate, pay, recompense, settle, spring, stand

foot•age \ˈfu̇-tij\ *n* **1 :** length expressed in feet **2 :** the length of film used for a scene; *also* **:** the material contained on such footage
foot–and–mouth disease *n* **:** an acute contagious viral disease especially of cattle
foot•ball \ˈfu̇t-ˌbȯl\ *n* **1 :** any of several games played by two teams on a rectangular field with goalposts at each end in which the object is to get the ball over the goal line or between goalposts by running, passing, or kicking **2 :** the ball used in football
foot•board \-ˌbōrd\ *n* **1 :** a narrow platform on which to stand or brace the feet **2 :** a board forming the foot of a bed
foot•bridge \-ˌbrij\ *n* **:** a bridge for pedestrians
foot•ed \ˈfu̇-təd\ *adj* **:** having a foot or feet of a specified kind or number ⟨flat-*footed*⟩ ⟨four-*footed*⟩
-foot•er \ˈfu̇-tər\ *comb form* **:** one that is a specified number of feet in height, length, or breadth ⟨a six-*footer*⟩
foot•fall \ˈfu̇t-ˌfȯl\ *n* **:** the sound of a footstep
foot•hill \-ˌhil\ *n* **:** a hill at the foot of higher hills or mountains
foot•hold \-ˌhōld\ *n* **1 :** a hold for the feet **:** FOOTING **2 :** a position usable as a base for further advance
foot•ing *n* **1 :** the placing of one's feet in a stable position **2 :** the act of moving on foot **3 :** a place or space for standing **:** FOOTHOLD **4** ♦ **:** position with respect to one another **:** STATUS **5** ♦ **:** an underlying condition or state of affairs **:** BASIS

♦ [4] degree, level, place, position, rank, situation, standing, station, status ♦ [5] base, basis, bedrock, cornerstone, foundation, ground, groundwork, keystone, underpinning

foot•less \ˈfu̇t-ləs\ *adj* **1 :** having no feet **2 :** INEPT, INEFFECTUAL
foot•lights \-ˌlīts\ *n pl* **1 :** a row of lights along the front of a stage floor **2 :** the stage as a profession
foo•tling \ˈfüt-liŋ\ *adj* **1 :** INEPT **2 :** TRIVIAL
foot•lock•er \ˈfu̇t-ˌlä-kər\ *n* **:** a small trunk designed to be placed at the foot of a bed (as in a barracks)
foot•loose \-ˌlüs\ *adj* ♦ **:** having no ties **:** FREE

♦ free, loose, unbound, unconfined, unrestrained

foot•man \-mən\ *n* **:** a male servant who attends a carriage or waits on table, admits visitors, and runs errands
foot•note \-ˌnōt\ *n* **1 :** a note of reference, explanation, or comment placed usually at the bottom of a page **2 :** COMMENTARY
foot•pad \-ˌpad\ *n* **:** a round somewhat flat foot on the leg of a spacecraft for distributing weight to minimize sinking into a surface
foot•path \-ˌpath, -ˌpȧth\ *n* ♦ **:** a narrow path for pedestrians

♦ path, trace, track, trail

foot•print \-ˌprint\ *n* **1 :** an impression of the foot **2 :** the area on a surface covered by something
foot•race \-ˌrās\ *n* **:** a race run on foot
foot•rest \-ˌrest\ *n* **:** a support for the feet
foot•sore \-ˌsōr\ *adj* **:** having sore or tender feet (as from much walking)
foot•step \-ˌstep\ *n* **1 :** the mark of the foot **:** TRACK **2 :** TREAD **3 :** distance covered by a step **:** PACE **4 :** a step on which to ascend or descend **5 :** a way of life, conduct, or action
foot•stool \-ˌstül\ *n* **:** a low stool to support the feet
foot•wear \-ˌwar\ *n* **:** apparel (as shoes or boots) for the feet
foot•work \-ˌwərk\ *n* **:** the management of the feet (as in boxing)
fop \ˈfäp\ *n* ♦ **:** a man who is devoted to or vain about his appearance or dress **:** DANDY — **fop•pery** \ˈfä-pə-rē\ *n* — **fop•pish** *adj*

♦ buck, dandy, dude, gallant

[1]for \fər, ˈfȯr\ *prep* **1 :** as a preparation toward ⟨dress ~ dinner⟩ **2 :** toward the purpose or goal of ⟨need time ~ study⟩ ⟨money ~ a trip⟩ **3 :** so as to reach or attain ⟨run ~ cover⟩ **4 :** as being ⟨took him ~ a fool⟩ **5 :** because of ⟨cry ~ joy⟩ **6** — used to indicate a recipient ⟨a letter ~ you⟩ **7 :** in support of ⟨fought ~ his country⟩ **8 :** directed at **:** AFFECTING ⟨a cure ~ what ails you⟩ **9** — used with a noun or pronoun followed by an infinitive to form the equivalent of a noun clause ⟨~ you to go would be silly⟩ **10 :** in exchange as equal to **:** so as to return the value of ⟨a lot of trouble ~ nothing⟩ ⟨pay $10 ~ a hat⟩ **11 :** CONCERNING ⟨a stickler ~ detail⟩ **12 :** CONSIDERING ⟨tall ~ her age⟩ **13 :** through the period of ⟨served ~ three years⟩ **14 :** in honor of
[2]for *conj* ♦ **:** for the reason that **:** BECAUSE

♦ because, now, since, whereas

[3]for *abbr* **1** foreign **2** forestry
fora *pl of* FORUM
[1]for•age \ˈfȯr-ij\ *n* **1 :** food for animals especially when taken by browsing or grazing **2 :** a search for food or supplies
[2]forage *vb* **for•aged; for•ag•ing 1 :** to collect forage from **2 :** to search for food or supplies **3 :** to get by foraging **4** ♦ **:** to make a search **:** RUMMAGE

♦ *usu* **forage for** cast about, hunt, pursue, quest, rummage, search (for *or* out), seek

for•ay \ˈfȯr-ˌā, fȯ-ˈrā\ *vb* ♦ **:** to raid especially in search of plunder

♦ *usu* **foray into** invade, overrun, raid

foray *n* ♦ **:** a sudden or irregular incursion for war or spoils

♦ descent, incursion, invasion, irruption, raid

[1]for•bear \fȯr-ˈber\ *vb* **-bore** \-ˈbȯr\; **-borne** \-ˈbȯrn\; **-bear•ing 1** ♦ **:** to refrain from **:** ABSTAIN **2 :** to be patient

♦ abstain (from), forgo, keep, refrain *Ant* give in (to), succumb (to), yield (to)

[2]forbear *var of* FOREBEAR
for•bear•ance \-ˈber-əns\ *n* ♦ **:** the act of forbearing

♦ long-suffering, patience, sufferance, tolerance

forbearing *adj* ♦ **:** marked by calm patience

♦ long-suffering, patient, stoic, tolerant, uncomplaining

for•bid \fər-ˈbid\ *vb* **-bade** \-ˈbad, -ˈbād\ *also* **-bad** \-ˈbad\; **-bid•den** \-ˈbi-dᵊn\; **-bid•ding 1** ♦ **:** to command against **:** PROHIBIT **2 :** HINDER, PREVENT

♦ ban, bar, enjoin, interdict, outlaw, prohibit, proscribe *Ant* allow, let, permit, suffer

forbidden *adj* ♦ : not allowed : not permitted

♦ impermissible, taboo

forbidding *adj* **1 :** causing discomfort **2** ♦ **:** presenting, suggesting, or constituting a menace

♦ austere, grim, menacing, scary, severe

[1]**force** \ˈfōrs\ *n* **1** ♦ **:** strength or energy especially of an exceptional degree **:** active power **2** ♦ **:** capacity to persuade or convince **3 :** military strength; *also, pl* **:** the whole military strength (as of a nation) **4** ♦ **:** a body (as of persons or ships) available for a particular purpose **5** ♦ **:** violence, compulsion, or constraint used on or against a person or thing **:** COMPULSION **6 :** an influence (as a push or pull) that causes motion or a change of motion — **in force 1 :** in great numbers **2 :** VALID, OPERATIVE

♦ [1] energy, main, might, muscle, potency, power, strength, vigor (*or* vigour) ♦ [2] cogency, effectiveness, persuasiveness ♦ [4] help, personnel, pool, staff ♦ [5] coercion, compulsion, constraint, duress, pressure

[2]**force** *vb* **forced; forc•ing 1** ♦ **:** to compel by physical, moral, or intellectual means **:** COERCE **2 :** to cause through necessity ⟨*forced* to admit defeat⟩ **3 :** to press, attain to, or effect against resistance or inertia ⟨~ your way through⟩ **4 :** to raise or accelerate to the utmost ⟨~ the pace⟩ **5 :** to produce with unnatural or unwilling effort ⟨*forced* a smile⟩ **6 :** to hasten (as in growth) by artificial means

♦ coerce, compel, constrain, drive, make, muscle, obligate, oblige, press, pressure

force•ful \ˈfōrs-fəl\ *adj* ♦ **:** possessing or filled with force — **force•ful•ness** \-nəs\ *n*

♦ cogent, compelling, convincing, decisive, emphatic, persuasive, strong ♦ authoritative, influential, weighty

force•ful•ly \-fə-lē\ *adv* ♦ **:** in a forceful manner

♦ firmly, forcibly, hard, mightily, powerfully, strongly, vigorously

for•ceps \ˈfȯr-səps\ *n, pl* **forceps :** a hand-held instrument for grasping, holding, or pulling objects especially for delicate operations (as by a surgeon)

forc•ible \ˈfōr-sə-bəl\ *adj* **1 :** obtained or done by force **2 :** showing force or energy **:** POWERFUL

forc•i•bly \-blē\ *adv* ♦ **:** in a forcible manner

♦ energetically, firmly, forcefully, hard, mightily, powerfully, vigorously

[1]**ford** \ˈfōrd\ *n* **:** a place where a stream may be crossed by wading

[2]**ford** *vb* **:** to cross (a body of water) by wading

[1]**fore** \ˈfōr\ *adv* **:** in, toward, or adjacent to the front **:** FORWARD

[2]**fore** *adj* **:** being or coming before in time, order, or space

[3]**fore** *n* **:** something that occupies a front position

[4]**fore** *interj* — used by a golfer to warn anyone within range of the probable line of flight of the ball

fore–and–aft \ˌfōr-ə-ˈnaft\ *adj* **:** lying, running, or acting along the length of a structure (as a ship)

[1]**fore•arm** \(ˌ)fōr-ˈärm\ *vb* ♦ **:** to arm in advance **:** PREPARE

♦ brace, fortify, nerve, prepare, psych (up), ready, steel, strengthen

[2]**fore•arm** \ˈfōr-ˌärm\ *n* **:** the part of the arm between the elbow and the wrist

fore•bear \-ˌbar\ *n* ♦ **:** one from whom a person is descended and who is usually more remote in the line of descent than a grandparent **:** ANCESTOR, FOREFATHER

♦ ancestor, father, forefather, grandfather

fore•bode \fōr-ˈbōd\ *vb* **1 :** to give promise of **2 :** FORETELL, PREDICT

fore•bod•ing *n* ♦ **:** an omen, prediction, or presentiment especially of coming evil — **fore•bod•ing•ly** *adv*

♦ omen, portent, premonition, presage, presentiment ♦ alarm, apprehension, dread, misgiving

[1]**fore•cast** \ˈfōr-ˌkast\ *vb* **-cast** *also* **-cast•ed; -cast•ing 1** ♦ **:** to calculate or predict (some future event or condition) **:** PREDICT ⟨~ weather conditions⟩ **2** ♦ **:** to indicate as likely to occur

♦ [1, 2] augur, foretell, predict, presage, prognosticate, prophesy

[2]**forecast** *n* ♦ **:** a prophecy, estimate, or prediction of a future happening or condition

♦ prediction, prognostication, prophecy

fore•cast•er *n* ♦ **:** one that forecasts

♦ diviner, fortune-teller, futurist, prognosticator, prophet, seer

fore•cas•tle *or* **fo'•c'sle** \ˈfōk-səl\ *n* **1 :** the forward part of the upper deck of a ship **2 :** the crew's quarters usually in a ship's bow

fore•close \fōr-ˈklōz\ *vb* **1 :** to shut out **:** PRECLUDE **2 :** to take legal measures to terminate a mortgage and take possession of the mortgaged property

fore•clo•sure \-ˈklō-zhər\ *n* **:** the act of foreclosing; *esp* **:** the legal procedure of foreclosing a mortgage

fore•doom \fōr-ˈdüm\ *vb* ♦ **:** to doom beforehand

♦ destine, doom, foreordain, ordain, predestine

fore•fa•ther \ˈfōr-ˌfä-t͟hər\ *n* **1** ♦ **:** one from whom a person is descended and who is usually more remote in the line of descent than a grandparent **:** ANCESTOR **2 :** a person of an earlier period and common heritage

♦ ancestor, father, forebear, grandfather

forefend *var of* FORFEND

fore•fin•ger \-ˌfiŋ-gər\ *n* **:** INDEX FINGER

fore•foot \-ˌfu̇t\ *n* **:** either of the front feet of a quadruped; *also* **:** the front part of the human foot

fore•front \-ˌfrənt\ *n* **:** the foremost part or place

foregather *var of* FORGATHER

[1]**fore•go** \fōr-ˈgō\ *vb* **-went** \-ˈwent\; **-gone** \-ˈgȯn\; **-go•ing** ♦ **:** to go before **:** PRECEDE

♦ antedate, precede

[2]**forego** *var of* FORGO

fore•go•ing *adj* ♦ **:** listed, mentioned, or occurring before **:** PRECEDING

♦ antecedent, anterior, preceding, previous, prior

fore•gone \ˈfōr-ˌgȯn\ *adj* **:** determined in advance ⟨a ~ conclusion⟩

fore•ground \-ˌgrau̇nd\ *n* **1 :** the part of a scene or representation that appears nearest to and in front of the spectator **2 :** a position of prominence

fore•hand \-ˌhand\ *n* **:** a stroke (as in tennis) made with the palm of the hand turned in the direction in which the hand is moving; *also* **:** the side on which such a stroke is made — **forehand** *adj*

fore•hand•ed \(ˌ)fōr-ˈhan-dəd\ *adj* ♦ **:** mindful of the future **:** PRUDENT

♦ farsighted, foresighted, prescient, provident, prudent

fore•head \ˈfȯr-əd, ˈfōr-ˌhed\ *n* **:** the part of the face above the eyes

for•eign \ˈfȯr-ən\ *adj* **1 :** situated outside a place or country and especially one's own country **2 :** born in, belonging to, or characteristic of some place or country other than the one under consideration ⟨~ language⟩ **3** ♦ **:** not connected, pertinent, or characteristically present **4 :** related to or dealing with other nations ⟨~ affairs⟩ **5 :** occurring in an abnormal situation in the living body ⟨a ~ body in the eye⟩

♦ alien, extraneous, extrinsic

for•eign•er \ˈfȯr-ə-nər\ *n* **:** a person belonging to or owing allegiance to a foreign country

foreign minister *n* **:** a governmental minister for foreign affairs

fore•know \fōr-ˈnō\ *vb* **-knew** \-ˈnü, -ˈnyü\; **-known** \-ˈnōn\; **-know•ing** ♦ **:** to have previous knowledge of — **fore•knowl•edge** \ˈfōr-ˌnä-lij, fōr-ˈnä-\ *n*

♦ anticipate, divine, foresee

fore•la•dy \ˈfōr-ˌlā-dē\ *n* **:** FOREWOMAN

fore•leg \-ˌleg\ *n* **:** a front leg

fore•limb \-ˌlim\ *n* **:** a front or upper limb (as a wing, arm, fin, or leg)

fore•lock \-ˌläk\ *n* **:** a lock of hair growing from the front part of the head

fore•man \-mən\ *n* **1 :** a spokesperson of a jury **2** ♦ **:** a person in charge of a group of workers

♦ boss, captain, chief, head, headman, leader, master, taskmaster

fore•mast \-ˌmast\ *n* **:** the mast nearest the bow of a ship

fore•most \-ˌmōst\ *adj* ♦ **:** first in time, place, or order **:** most important **:** PREEMINENT — **foremost** *adv*

♦ chief, dominant, first, key, main, predominant, preeminent, primary, principal *Ant* last, least

fore•name \-ˌnām\ *n* : a first name
fore•named \-ˌnāmd\ *adj* : previously named : AFORESAID
fore•noon \-ˌnün\ *n* : MORNING
¹**fo•ren•sic** \fə-ˈren-sik\ *adj* **1 :** belonging to, used in, or suitable to courts of law or to public speaking or debate **2 :** relating to the application of scientific knowledge to legal problems ⟨~ medicine⟩
²**forensic** *n* **1 :** an argumentative exercise **2** *pl* **:** the art or study of argumentative discourse **3** *pl* **:** scientific analysis of physical evidence (as from a crime scene)
fore•or•dain \ˌfōr-ȯr-ˈdān\ *vb* ♦ **:** to ordain or decree beforehand **:** PREDESTINE

♦ destine, doom, foredoom, ordain, predestine

fore•part \ˈfōr-ˌpärt\ *n* **1 :** the anterior part of something **2 :** the earlier part of a period of time
fore•quar•ter \-ˌkwȯr-tər\ *n* **:** the front half of a lateral half of the body or carcass of a quadruped ⟨a ~ of beef⟩
fore•run•ner \-ˌrə-nər\ *n* **1** ♦ **:** one that goes before to give notice of the approach of others **:** HARBINGER **2** ♦ **:** something belonging to a relatively early developmental period of a contemporary or fully developed object or phenomenon **:** PREDECESSOR, ANCESTOR

♦ [1] angel, harbinger, herald, precursor ♦ [2] ancestor, antecedent, precursor

fore•sail \-ˌsāl, -səl\ *n* **1 :** the lowest sail on the foremast of a square-rigged ship or schooner **2 :** the principal sail forward of the foremast (as of a sloop)
fore•see \fōr-ˈsē\ *vb* **-saw** \-ˈsȯ\; **-seen** \-ˈsēn\; **-see•ing** ♦ **:** to see or realize beforehand — **fore•see•able** *adj*

♦ anticipate, divine, foreknow

fore•shad•ow \-ˈsha-dō\ *vb* ♦ **:** to give a hint or suggestion of beforehand

♦ harbinger, prefigure

fore•short•en \fōr-ˈshȯrt-ᵊn\ *vb* **:** to shorten (a detail) in a drawing or painting so that it appears to have depth
fore•sight \ˈfōr-ˌsīt\ *n* **1 :** the act or power of foreseeing **2** ♦ **:** care or provision for the future **:** PRUDENCE **3 :** an act of looking forward; *also* **:** a view forward

♦ forethought, prescience, providence, prudence *Ant* improvidence, shortsightedness

fore•sight•ed \-ˌsī-təd\ *adj* ♦ **:** having foresight — **fore•sight•ed•ness** *n*

♦ farsighted, prescient, provident, prudent *Ant* improvident, shortsighted

fore•skin \-ˌskin\ *n* **:** a fold of skin enclosing the end of the penis
for•est \ˈfȯr-əst\ *n* ♦ **:** a large thick growth of trees and underbrush — **for•est•ed** \ˈfȯr-ə-stəd\ *adj* — **for•est•land** \ˈfȯr-əst-ˌland\ *n*

♦ timberland, woodland

fore•stall \fōr-ˈstȯl, fȯr-\ *vb* **1** ♦ **:** to keep out, hinder, or prevent by measures taken in advance **2 :** ANTICIPATE

♦ avert, help, obviate, preclude, prevent

forest ranger *n* **:** a person in charge of the management and protection of a portion of a forest
for•est•ry \ˈfȯr-ə-strē\ *n* **:** the science of growing and caring for forests — **for•est•er** \ˈfȯr-ə-stər\ *n*
foreswear *var of* FORSWEAR
¹**fore•taste** \ˈfōr-ˌtāst\ *n* **:** an advance indication, warning, or notion
²**fore•taste** \fōr-ˈtāst\ *vb* **:** to taste beforehand **:** ANTICIPATE
fore•tell \fōr-ˈtel\ *vb* **-told** \-ˈtōld\; **-tell•ing** ♦ **:** to tell of beforehand **:** PREDICT

♦ augur, forecast, predict, presage, prognosticate, prophesy

fore•thought \ˈfōr-ˌthȯt\ *n* **1 :** PREMEDITATION **2** ♦ **:** consideration for the future

♦ foresight, prescience, providence

fore•to•ken \fōr-ˈtō-kən\ *vb* **:** to indicate in advance
fore•top \ˈfōr-ˌtäp\ *n* **:** a platform near the top of a ship's foremast
for•ev•er \fȯr-ˈe-vər\ *adv* **1** ♦ **:** for a limitless time **2** ♦ **:** at all times **:** ALWAYS

♦ [1] always, eternally, ever, everlastingly, permanently, perpetually ♦ [2] always, constantly, continually, incessantly, invariably, unfailingly

for•ev•er•more \-ˌe-vər-ˈmōr\ *adv* **:** for a limitless time or endless ages **:** FOREVER

fore•warn \fōr-ˈwȯrn\ *vb* ♦ **:** to warn beforehand

♦ alert, caution, warn

forewent *past of* FOREGO
fore•wing \ˈfōr-ˌwiŋ\ *n* **:** either of the anterior wings of a 4-winged insect
fore•wom•an \ˈfōr-ˌwu̇-mən\ *n* **:** a woman having the responsibilities of a foreman
fore•word \-ˌwərd\ *n* ♦ **:** prefatory comments (as for a book) especially when written by someone other than the author **:** PREFACE

♦ introduction, preamble, preface, prologue

¹**for•feit** \ˈfȯr-fət\ *n* **1** ♦ **:** something forfeited **:** PENALTY, FINE **2 :** FORFEITURE **3 :** something deposited and then redeemed on payment of a fine **4** *pl* **:** a game in which forfeits are exacted

♦ damages, fine, mulct, penalty

²**forfeit** *vb* **:** to lose or lose the right to by some error, offense, or crime
for•fei•ture \ˈfȯr-fə-ˌchu̇r\ *n* **1 :** the act of forfeiting **2 :** something forfeited **:** PENALTY
for•fend \fȯr-ˈfend\ *vb* **1 :** PREVENT **2 :** PROTECT, PRESERVE
for•gath•er \fȯr-ˈga-t͟hər\ *vb* **1** ♦ **:** to come together **:** ASSEMBLE **2 :** to meet someone usually by chance

♦ assemble, collect, congregate, convene, gather, meet, rendezvous

¹**forge** \ˈfōrj\ *n* **:** a furnace or shop with its furnace where metal is heated and worked
²**forge** *vb* **forged; forg•ing 1** ♦ **:** to form (metal) by heating and hammering **2** ♦ **:** to form or bring into being especially by an expenditure of effort **:** FASHION, SHAPE ⟨~ an agreement⟩ **3 :** to make or imitate falsely especially with intent to defraud ⟨~ a signature⟩ — **forg•er** *n*

♦ [1] beat, hammer, pound ♦ [2] build, carve, fashion, grind, hammer, shape, work out

³**forge** *vb* **forged; forg•ing** ♦ **:** to move ahead steadily but gradually

♦ advance, fare, get along, go, march, proceed, progress

forg•ery \ˈfōr-jə-rē\ *n* ♦ **:** something forged

♦ counterfeit, fake, hoax, humbug, phony, sham

for•get \fər-ˈget\ *vb* **-got** \-ˈgät\; **-got•ten** \-ˈgät-ᵊn\ *or* **-got; -get•ting 1 :** to be unable to think of or recall **2** ♦ **:** to fail to become mindful of at the proper time **3** ♦ **:** to treat with inattention or disregard **:** NEGLECT, DISREGARD **4 :** to give up hope for or expectation of

♦ [2] fail, neglect, omit ♦ [3] disregard, ignore, neglect, overlook, pass over, slight, slur

for•get•ful \-ˈget-fəl\ *adj* **:** likely to forget — **for•get•ful•ly** *adv* — **for•get•ful•ness** *n*
for•get–me–not \fər-ˈget-mē-ˌnät\ *n* **:** any of a genus of small herbs with bright blue or white flowers
forg•ing *n* **:** a piece of forged work
for•giv•able *adj* ♦ **:** being of a kind that can be forgiven

♦ excusable, pardonable, venial

for•give \fər-ˈgiv\ *vb* **-gave** \-ˈgāv\; **-giv•en** \-ˈgi-vən\; **-giv•ing 1 :** to give up resentment of or claim to requital for **2 :** to give up resentment of **:** PARDON, ABSOLVE **3 :** to grant relief from payment of
for•give•ness *n* ♦ **:** an act of forgiving or state of being forgiven

♦ absolution, amnesty, pardon, remission

for•giv•ing *adj* **1 :** willing or able to forgive **2 :** allowing room for error or weakness
for•go \fōr-ˈgō\ *vb* **-went** \-ˈwent\; **-gone** \-ˈgȯn\; **-go•ing** ♦ **:** to give up the enjoyment or advantage of **:** do without

♦ abstain (from), forbear, keep, refrain

¹**fork** \ˈfȯrk\ *n* **1 :** an implement with two or more prongs for taking up (as in eating), pitching, or digging **2 :** a forked part, tool, or piece of equipment **3 :** a dividing into branches or a place where something branches; *also* **:** a branch of such a fork
²**fork** *vb* **1** ♦ **:** to divide into two or more branches **2 :** to give the form of a fork to ⟨~*ing* her fingers⟩ **3 :** to raise or pitch with a fork ⟨~ hay⟩ **4** ♦ **:** to make a disposal or transfer of **:** PAY — used with *over, out,* or *up*

♦ [1] branch, diverge, divide, separate ♦ *usu* **fork over** *or* **fork out** [4] disburse, expend, give, lay out, pay

forked \ˈfȯrkt, ˈfȯr-kəd\ *adj* **:** having a fork **:** shaped like a fork ⟨~ lightning⟩
fork•lift \ˈfōrk-ˌlift\ *n* **:** a machine for lifting heavy objects by means of steel fingers inserted under the load
for•lorn \fər-ˈlȯrn, fȯr-\ *adj* **1** ♦ **:** sad and lonely because of isolation or desertion **2 :** being in poor condition **:** WRETCHED **3 :** nearly hopeless — **for•lorn•ly** *adv*

♦ desolate, lonely, lonesome, sad

for•lorn•ness *n* ♦ **:** forlorn quality or state

♦ blues, dejection, desolation, melancholy, sadness

¹form \ˈfȯrm\ *n* **1 :** SHAPE, STRUCTURE **2** ♦ **:** a body especially of a person **:** FIGURE **3 :** the essential nature of a thing **4** ♦ **:** an established manner of doing or saying something **5 :** FORMULA **6** ♦ **:** a document with blank spaces for insertion of information ⟨tax ~⟩ **7** ♦ **:** conduct regulated by extraneous controls (as of custom or etiquette) **:** CEREMONY **8 :** manner of performing according to recognized standards **9 :** a long seat **:** BENCH **10** ♦ **:** a model of the human figure used for displaying clothes **11 :** MOLD ⟨a ~ for concrete⟩ **12 :** type or plates in a frame ready for printing **13 :** one of the different modes of existence, action, or manifestation of a particular thing or substance **:** MODE, KIND, VARIETY ⟨coal is a ~ of carbon⟩ **14 :** orderly method of arrangement; *also* **:** a particular kind or instance of such arrangement ⟨the sonnet ~ in poetry⟩ **15** ♦ **:** the structural element, plan, or design of a work of art **16 :** a bounded surface or volume **17 :** a grade in a British school or in some American private schools **18 :** RACING FORM **19 a :** known ability to perform **b** ♦ **:** condition (as of an athlete) suitable for performing **20 :** one of the ways in which a word is changed to show difference in use ⟨the plural ~ of a noun⟩

♦ [2] build, constitution, figure, frame, physique, shape ♦ [4] manner, method, style, system, technique, way ♦ [6] blank, document, paper ♦ [7] ceremonial, ceremony, formality, observance, rite ♦ [10] dummy, figure, mannequin ♦ [15] arrangement, composition, configuration, design, format, layout, makeup, pattern ♦ [19b] condition, estate, fettle, order, repair, shape, trim

²form *vb* **1** ♦ **:** to give form or shape to **:** FASHION, MAKE **2 :** TRAIN, INSTRUCT **3** ♦ **:** to serve to make up or constitute **:** CONSTITUTE, COMPOSE **4** ♦ **:** to acquire gradually **:** DEVELOP, ACQUIRE ⟨~ a habit⟩ **5 :** to arrange in order ⟨~ a battle line⟩ **6** ♦ **:** to take form **:** ARISE ⟨clouds are ~*ing*⟩ **7 :** to take a definite form, shape, or arrangement

♦ [1] fabricate, fashion, frame, make, manufacture, produce ♦ [3] compose, comprise, constitute, make up ♦ [4] acquire, cultivate, develop ♦ [6] arise, begin, materialize, originate

¹for•mal \ˈfȯr-məl\ *adj* **1** ♦ **:** according with conventional forms and rules ⟨a ~ dinner party⟩ **2 :** done in due or lawful form ⟨a ~ contract⟩ **3** ♦ **:** rigidly ceremonious **:** CEREMONIOUS ⟨a ~ manner⟩ **4** ♦ **:** having the appearance without the substance **:** NOMINAL — **for•mal•ly** *adv*

♦ [1, 3] ceremonial, ceremonious, conventional, correct, decorous, proper, regular ***Ant*** informal, irregular, unceremonious ♦ [4] nominal, paper, titular

²formal *n* ♦ **:** something (as a social event) formal in character

♦ ball, dance, prom

form•al•de•hyde \fȯr-ˈmal-də-ˌhīd\ *n* **:** a colorless pungent gas used in water solution as a preservative and disinfectant
for•mal•ise *chiefly Brit var of* FORMALIZE
for•mal•ism \ˈfȯr-mə-ˌli-zəm\ *n* **:** strict adherence to set forms
for•mal•i•ty \fȯr-ˈma-lə-tē\ *n, pl* **-ties 1** ♦ **:** compliance with formal or conventional rules **2 :** the quality or state of being formal **3** ♦ **:** an established form that is required or conventional

♦ [1, 3] ceremonial, ceremony, form, observance, rite, ritual, solemnity ♦ [3] amenity, civility, courtesy, gesture

for•mal•ize \ˈfȯr-mə-ˌlīz\ *vb* **-ized; -iz•ing 1** ♦ **:** to give a certain or definite form to **2 :** to make formal; *also* **:** to give formal status or approval to

♦ homogenize, normalize, regularize, standardize

¹for•mat \ˈfȯr-ˌmat\ *n* **1** ♦ **:** the general composition or style of a publication **2** ♦ **:** the general plan or arrangement of something **3** ♦ **:** a method of organizing data ⟨various file ~*s*⟩

♦ arrangement, composition, configuration, design, form, layout, makeup, pattern

²format *vb* **for•mat•ted; for•mat•ting :** to arrange (as material to be printed) in a particular format — **for•mat•ter** *n*
for•ma•tion \fȯr-ˈmā-shən\ *n* **1 :** an act of giving form to something **:** DEVELOPMENT **2 :** something that is formed **3 :** the manner in which a thing is formed **:** STRUCTURE, SHAPE **4 :** an arrangement of persons or things in a prescribed manner or for a certain purpose
for•ma•tive \ˈfȯr-mə-tiv\ *adj* **1 :** giving or capable of giving form **:** CONSTRUCTIVE **2 :** of, relating to, or characterized by important growth or formation ⟨a child's ~ years⟩
for•mer \ˈfȯr-mər\ *adj* **1 :** PREVIOUS, EARLIER **2 :** FOREGOING **3 :** being first mentioned or in order of two or more things **4** ♦ **:** having been previously

♦ erstwhile, late, old, onetime, past, sometime

for•mer•ly \-lē\ *adv* **:** in time past **:** PREVIOUSLY
form•fit•ting \ˈfȯrm-ˌfi-tiŋ\ *adj* **:** conforming to the outline of the body
for•mi•da•ble \ˈfȯr-mə-də-bəl, fȯr-ˈmi-\ *adj* **1** ♦ **:** exciting fear, dread, or awe **2** ♦ **:** imposing serious difficulties — **for•mi•da•bly** \-blē\ *adv*

♦ [1] dreadful, fearful, fearsome, forbidding, frightful, redoubtable, scary ♦ [2] arduous, demanding, difficult, exacting, hard, strenuous, tall, toilsome, tough

form•less *adj* ♦ **:** having no regular form or shape

♦ amorphous, shapeless, unformed, unshaped, unstructured ***Ant*** formed, shaped, structured

form letter *n* **1 :** a letter on a frequently recurring topic that can be sent to different people at different times **2 :** a letter for mass circulation sent out in many printed copies
for•mu•la \ˈfȯr-myə-lə\ *n, pl* **-las** *or* **-lae** \-ˌlē, -ˌlī\ **1 :** a set form of words for ceremonial use **2 :** RECIPE, PRESCRIPTION **3 :** a milk mixture or substitute for a baby **4 :** a group of symbols or figures joined to express information concisely **5 :** a customary or set form or method
for•mu•late \-ˌlāt\ *vb* **-lat•ed; -lat•ing 1 :** to express in a formula **2** ♦ **:** to put into a systematized statement or expression ⟨~ a policy⟩ **3 :** to prepare according to a formula

♦ articulate, clothe, couch, express, phrase, put, say, state, word ♦ cast, compose, craft, draft, draw, frame, prepare

for•mu•la•tion \ˌfȯr-myə-ˈlā-shən\ *n* ♦ **:** an act or the product of formulating

♦ articulation, expression, statement, utterance, voice

for•ni•ca•tion \ˌfȯr-nə-ˈkā-shən\ *n* **:** consensual sexual intercourse between two persons not married to each other — **for•ni•cate** \ˈfȯr-nə-ˌkāt\ *vb* — **for•ni•ca•tor** \-ˌkā-tər\ *n*
for•sake \fər-ˈsāk, fȯr-\ *vb* **for•sook** \-ˈsu̇k\; **for•sak•en** \-ˈsā-kən\; **for•sak•ing** ♦ **:** to renounce or turn away from entirely

♦ abandon, desert, leave, quit

forsaken *adj* ♦ **:** left desolate or empty

♦ abandoned, derelict, deserted

for•swear \fȯr-ˈswar\ *vb* **-swore** \-ˈswōr\; **-sworn** \-ˈswōrn\; **-swear•ing 1 :** to swear falsely **:** commit perjury **2 :** to renounce earnestly or under oath **3 :** to deny under oath
for•syth•ia \fər-ˈsi-thē-ə\ *n, pl* **-ias** *also* **-ia :** any of a genus of shrubs related to the olive and having yellow bell-shaped flowers appearing before the leaves in early spring
fort \ˈfōrt\ *n* **1** ♦ **:** a fortified place **2 :** a permanent army post

♦ bastion, bulwark, citadel, fastness, fortification, fortress, hold, stronghold

¹forte \ˈfōrt, ˈfȯr-ˌtā\ *n* **:** one's strong point
²for•te \ˈfȯr-ˌtā\ *adv or adj* **:** LOUD — used as a direction in music
forth \ˈfōrth\ *adv* **1** ♦ **:** onward in time, place, or order **:** FORWARD, ONWARD ⟨from that day ~⟩ **2 :** out into view or notice ⟨put ~ leaves⟩

♦ ahead, along, forward, on, onward

forth•com•ing \fōrth-ˈkə-miŋ\ *adj* **1** ♦ **:** coming or available soon ⟨the ~ holidays⟩ **2 :** marked by openness and candor **:** OUTGOING

♦ coming, imminent, impending, oncoming, pending ***Ant*** late, recent

forth•right \ˈfōrth-ˌrīt\ *adj* **1** ♦ **:** free from ambiguity or evasiveness **2** ♦ **:** going straight to the point ⟨a ~ answer⟩

♦ candid, direct, frank, honest, open, plain, straight, straightforward, unreserved

forth·right·ly *adv* ♦ **:** in a forthright manner

♦ directly, foursquare, plain, plainly, straight, straightforward

forth·right·ness *n* ♦ **:** the quality or state of being forthright

♦ candor (*or* candour), directness, frankness, openness, plainness

forth·with \ˌfōrth-ˈwith\ *adv* ♦ **:** with dispatch **:** without delay **:** IMMEDIATELY

♦ directly, immediately, instantly, now, promptly, pronto, right away, right now

for·ti·fi·ca·tion \ˌfȯr-tə-fə-ˈkā-shən\ *n* ♦ **:** something that fortifies, defends, or strengthens; *esp* **:** works erected to defend a place or position

♦ bastion, citadel, fastness, fort, fortress, hold, stronghold

for·ti·fy \ˈfȯr-tə-ˌfī\ *vb* **-fied; -fy·ing 1 :** to strengthen by military defenses **2** ♦ **:** to give physical strength or endurance to **3** ♦ **:** to add mental or moral strength to **:** ENCOURAGE **4 :** to strengthen or enrich with a material ⟨∼ bread with vitamins⟩

♦ [2] harden, season, steel, strengthen, toughen ♦ [3] brace, encourage, forearm, nerve, psych (up), ready, steel, strengthen

for·tis·si·mo \fȯr-ˈti-sə-ˌmō\ *adv or adj* **:** very loud — used as a direction in music

for·ti·tude \ˈfȯr-tə-ˌtüd, -ˌtyüd\ *n* ♦ **:** strength of mind that enables one to meet danger or bear pain or adversity with courage

♦ backbone, fiber (*or* fibre), grit, guts, pluck, spunk

fort·night \ˈfōrt-ˌnīt\ *n* **:** two weeks — **fort·night·ly** \-lē\ *adj or adv*

for·tress \ˈfȯr-trəs\ *n* ♦ **:** a fortified place **:** FORT

♦ bastion, citadel, fastness, fort, fortification, hold, stronghold

for·tu·itous \fȯr-ˈtü-ə-təs, -ˈtyü-\ *adj* **1** ♦ **:** happening by chance **2** ♦ **:** producing or resulting in good by chance **:** FORTUNATE

♦ [1] accidental, casual, chance, fluky, unplanned ♦ [2] fortunate, happy, lucky, providential

for·tu·ity \-ə-tē\ *n, pl* **-ities 1 :** the quality or state of being fortuitous **2 :** a chance event or occurrence

for·tu·nate \ˈfȯr-chə-nət\ *adj* **1** ♦ **:** bringing some good thing not foreseen **2 :** receiving some unforeseen or unexpected good

♦ fluky, fortuitous, happy, lucky, providential *Ant* luckless, unfortunate, unhappy, unlucky

for·tu·nate·ly \-lē\ *adv* **1 :** in a fortunate manner **2 :** it is fortunate that

for·tune \ˈfȯr-chən\ *n* **1 :** prosperity attained partly through luck; *also* **:** CHANCE, LUCK **2 :** what happens to a person **:** good or bad luck **3** ♦ **:** a predetermined course of events often held to be an irresistible power or agency **:** FATE, DESTINY **4** ♦ **:** abundance of valuable material possessions or resources **:** RICHES, WEALTH

♦ [3] circumstance, destiny, doom, fate, lot, portion ♦ [4] assets, capital, means, opulence, riches, substance, wealth, wherewithal

fortune hunter *n* **:** a person who seeks wealth especially by marriage

for·tune–tell·er \-ˌte-lər\ *n* ♦ **:** a person who professes to foretell future events — **for·tune–tell·ing** *n or adj*

♦ augur, diviner, forecaster, futurist, prognosticator, prophet, seer, soothsayer

for·ty \ˈfȯr-tē\ *n, pl* **forties :** four times 10 — **for·ti·eth** \ˈfȯr-tē-əth\ *adj or n* — **forty** *adj or pron*

for·ty–five \ˌfȯr-tē-ˈfīv\ *n* **1 :** a .45 caliber handgun — usually written .45 **2 :** a phonograph record designed to be played at 45 revolutions per minute

for·ty–nin·er \-ˈnī-nər\ *n* **:** a person in the rush to California for gold in 1849

forty winks *n sing or pl* ♦ **:** a short sleep

♦ catnap, doze, drowse, nap, siesta, snooze, wink

fo·rum \ˈfōr-əm\ *n, pl* **forums** *also* **fo·ra** \-ə\ **1 :** the marketplace or central meeting place of an ancient Roman city **2 :** a medium (as a publication) of open discussion **3 :** COURT **4** ♦ **:** a public assembly, lecture, or program involving audience or panel discussion

♦ colloquy, panel, parley, powwow, seminar, symposium

[1]**for·ward** \ˈfȯr-wərd\ *adj* **1 :** being near or at or belonging to the front **2 :** EAGER, READY **3** ♦ **:** lacking modesty or reserve **:** BOLD **4 :** notably advanced or developed **:** PRECOCIOUS **5 :** moving, tending, or leading toward a position in front **6 :** EXTREME, RADICAL **7 :** of, relating to, or getting ready for the future — **for·ward·ness** *n*

♦ bold, familiar, free, immodest, presumptuous

[2]**forward** *adv* ♦ **:** to or toward what is ahead or in front

♦ ahead, along, forth, on, onward

[3]**forward** *vb* **1** ♦ **:** to help onward **:** ADVANCE **2 :** to send forward **:** TRANSMIT **3 :** to send or ship onward

♦ advance, cultivate, encourage, foster, further, nourish, nurture, promote

[4]**forward** *n* **:** a player who plays at the front of a team's offensive formation near the opponent's goal

for·ward·er \-wər-dər\ *n* **:** one that forwards; *esp* **:** an agent who forwards goods

for·wards \ˈfȯr-wərdz\ *adv* **:** to or toward what is ahead or in front **:** FORWARD

forwent *past of* FORGO

[1]**fos·sil** \ˈfä-səl\ *adj* **1 :** preserved from a past geologic age ⟨∼ plants⟩ **2 :** of or relating to fossil fuels

[2]**fossil** *n* **1 :** a trace or impression or the remains of a plant or animal of a past geologic age preserved in the earth's crust **2** ♦ **:** a person whose ideas are out-of-date — **fos·sil·ize** \ˈfä-sə-ˌlīz\ *vb*

♦ antediluvian, dodo, fogy, fuddy-duddy, reactionary

fossil fuel *n* **:** a fuel (as coal or oil) that is formed in the earth from plant or animal remains

[1]**fos·ter** \ˈfȯs-tər\ *adj* **:** affording, receiving, or sharing nourishment or parental care though not related by blood or legal ties ⟨∼ parent⟩ ⟨∼ child⟩

[2]**foster** *vb* **1** ♦ **:** to give parental care to **2** ♦ **:** to promote the growth or development of **:** ENCOURAGE

♦ [1] breed, bring up, raise, rear ♦ [2] advance, cultivate, encourage, forward, further, nourish, nurture, promote *Ant* discourage, frustrate, hinder, inhibit

foster home *n* **:** a household in which an orphaned, neglected, or delinquent child is placed for care

fos·ter·ling \-tər-liŋ\ *n* **:** a foster child

Fou·cault pendulum \ˌfü-ˈkō-\ *n* **:** a device that consists of a heavy weight hung by a long wire and that swings in a constant direction which appears to change showing that the earth rotates

fought *past and past part of* FIGHT

[1]**foul** \ˈfau̇(-ə)l\ *adj* **1 a** ♦ **:** offensive to the senses **b** ♦ **:** clogged with dirt **2** ♦ **:** arousing or deserving hatred or repugnance **:** ODIOUS **3** ♦ **:** abhorrent to morality or virtue **:** OBSCENE **4** ♦ **:** being wet and stormy **:** STORMY ⟨∼ weather⟩ **5 :** characterized by or manifesting treachery **:** DISHONORABLE, UNFAIR **6 :** marking the bounds of a playing field ⟨∼ lines⟩; *also* **:** being outside the foul line ⟨∼ ball⟩ ⟨∼ territory⟩ **7 :** containing marked-up corrections **8 :** ENTANGLED — **foul·ly** *adv*

♦ [1a] fetid, malodorous, noisome, rank, reeky, smelly, strong ♦ [1b] dirty, filthy, muddy, unclean ♦ [2, 3] abhorrent, awful, distasteful, obnoxious, odious, offensive, repellent, repugnant, repulsive ♦ [4] bleak, dirty, inclement, nasty, raw, rough, squally, stormy, tempestuous, turbulent *Ant* clement, fair

[2]**foul** *n* **1 :** an entanglement or collision in fishing or sailing **2 :** an infraction of the rules in a game or sport; *also* **:** a baseball hit outside the foul line

[3]**foul** *vb* **1** ♦ **:** to make or become foul or filthy **2 :** to entangle or become entangled **3 :** OBSTRUCT, BLOCK **4 :** to collide with **5 :** to make or hit a foul

♦ befoul, blacken, contaminate, dirty, muddy, smirch, soil, stain, taint

[4]**foul** *adv* **:** in a foul manner

fou·lard \fu̇-ˈlärd\ *n* **:** a lightweight silk of plain or twill weave usually decorated with a printed pattern

foul·mouthed \ˈfau̇(-ə)l-ˈmau̇t͟hd, -ˈmau̇tht\ *adj* **:** given to the use of obscene, profane, or abusive language

foul·ness *n* ♦ **:** the quality or state of being foul

♦ dirtiness, filth, filthiness, grossness, nastiness, obscenity, smut, vulgarity

foul play *n* **1 :** unfair, dishonest, or treacherous conduct or dealing **:** VIOLENCE **2 :** the crime of unlawfully killing a person especially with malice aforethought **:** MURDER

foul–up \ˈfau̇(-ə)l-ˌəp\ *n* **1 :** a state of being fouled up **2 :** a mechanical difficulty

foul up *vb* **1** ♦ **:** to spoil by mistakes or poor judgment **2 :** to cause a foul-up **:** BUNGLE

♦ bobble, botch, bungle, butcher, flub, fumble, mangle, mess up, screw up

1found \ˈfau̇nd\ *past and past part of* FIND

2found *vb* **1 :** to take the first steps in building **2 :** to set or ground on something solid **:** BASE **3** ♦ **:** to establish (as an institution) often with provision for future maintenance

♦ establish, inaugurate, initiate, institute, introduce, launch, pioneer, set up, start *Ant* close (down), phase out, shut (up)

foun•da•tion \fau̇n-ˈdā-shən\ *n* **1 :** the act of founding **2** ♦ **:** a basis upon which something stands or is supported ⟨suspicions without ∼⟩ **3 a :** funds given for the permanent support of an institution or cause **:** ENDOWMENT **b** ♦ **:** an endowed institution **4 :** supporting structure **:** BASE **5 :** CORSET — **foun•da•tion•al** \-shə-nəl\ *adj*

♦ [2] base, basis, bedrock, cornerstone, footing, ground, groundwork, keystone, underpinning ♦ [3b] establishment, institute, institution

foun•der \ˈfau̇n-dər\ *vb* **1 :** to make or become lame ⟨the horse ∼*ed*⟩ **2 :** COLLAPSE **3 :** SINK ⟨a ∼*ing* ship⟩ **4 :** FAIL

found•er *n* ♦ **:** one that founds or establishes

♦ author, creator, father, originator

found•ling \ˈfau̇nd-liŋ\ *n* **:** an infant found after its unknown parents have abandoned it

found•ry \ˈfau̇n-drē\ *n, pl* **foundries :** a building or works where metal is cast

fount \ˈfau̇nt\ *n* **:** SOURCE, FOUNTAIN

foun•tain \ˈfau̇nt-ᵊn\ *n* **1 :** a spring of water **2 :** SOURCE **3 :** an artificial jet of water **4 :** a container for liquid that can be drawn off as needed

foun•tain•head \-ˌhed\ *n* **:** SOURCE

fountain pen *n* **:** a pen with a reservoir that feeds the writing point with ink

four \ˈfōr\ *n* **1 :** one more than three **2 :** the 4th in a set or series **3 :** something having four units — **four** *adj or pron*

4x4 *also* **four–by–four** \ˈfȯr-bī-ˌfȯr\ *n* **:** a four-wheel automobile with four-wheel drive

four flush \-ˌfləsh\ *vb* **:** to make a false claim **:** BLUFF

four–flush•er *n* **:** one that cannot back up his pretensions

four•fold \-ˌfōld, -ˈfōld\ *adj* **1 :** being four times as great or as many **2 :** having four units or members — **four•fold** \-ˈfōld\ *adv*

4–H \ˈfōr-ˈāch\ *adj* **:** of or relating to a program set up by the U.S. Department of Agriculture to help young people become productive citizens — **4–H'•er** *n*

Four Hundred *or* **400** *n* **:** the exclusive social set of a community — used with *the*

four–in–hand \ˈfōr-ən-ˌhand\ *n* **1 :** a team of four horses driven by one person; *also* **:** a vehicle drawn by such a team **2 :** a necktie tied in a slipknot with long ends overlapping vertically in front

four–o'clock \ˈfōr-ə-ˌkläk\ *n* **:** a garden plant with fragrant yellow, red, or white flowers without petals that open late in the afternoon

four–post•er \ˌfōr-ˈpō-stər\ *n* **:** a bed with tall corner posts orig. designed to support curtains or a canopy

four•score \ˈfōr-ˈskōr\ *adj* **:** being four times twenty **:** EIGHTY

four•some \ˈfōr-səm\ *n* **1 :** a group of four persons or things **2 :** a golf match between two pairs of partners

1four•square \-ˈskwer\ *adj* **1 :** SQUARE **2** ♦ **:** marked by boldness and conviction **:** FORTHRIGHT

♦ candid, direct, forthright, frank, honest, open, outspoken, plain, straightforward, unreserved

2foursquare *adv* ♦ **:** in a foursquare manner

♦ directly, forthrightly, plain, plainly, straight, straightforward

four•teen \fōr-ˈtēn\ *n* **:** one more than 13 — **fourteen** *adj or pron* — **four•teenth** \-ˈtēnth\ *adj or n*

fourth \ˈfōrth\ *n* **1 :** one that is number four in a countable series **2 :** one of four equal parts of something — **fourth** *adj or adv*

fourth estate *n, often cap F&E* **:** the public press

fourth wall *n* **:** an imaginary wall that keeps performers from recognizing or directly addressing their audience

4WD *abbr* four-wheel drive

four–wheel \ˈfōr-ˌhwēl\ *or* **four•wheeled** \-ˌhwēld\ *adj* **:** acting on or by means of four wheels of a motor vehicle

four–wheel drive *n* **:** an automotive drive mechanism that acts on all four wheels of the vehicle; *also* **:** a vehicle with such a drive

1fowl \ˈfau̇(-ə)l\ *n, pl* **fowl** *or* **fowls 1 :** BIRD **2 :** a cock or hen of the domestic chicken; *also* **:** the flesh of these used as food

2fowl *vb* **:** to hunt wildfowl

1fox \ˈfäks\ *n, pl* **fox•es** *also* **fox 1 :** any of various flesh-eating mammals related to the wolves but smaller and with shorter legs and a more pointed muzzle; *also* **:** the fur of a fox **2 :** a clever crafty person **3** *cap* **:** a member of an American Indian people formerly living in what is now Wisconsin **4** ♦ **:** a good-looking young woman

♦ beauty, dream, enchantress, knockout, queen

2fox *vb* ♦ **:** to trick by ingenuity or cunning **:** OUTWIT

♦ outfox, outmaneuver, outsmart, outwit, overreach

fox•glove \ˈfäks-ˌgləv\ *n* **:** a common plant related to the snapdragons that is grown for its showy spikes of dotted white or purple tubular flowers and as a source of digitalis

fox•hole \-ˌhōl\ *n* **:** a pit dug for protection against enemy fire

fox•hound \-ˌhau̇nd\ *n* **:** any of various large swift powerful hounds used in hunting foxes

fox•ing \ˈfäk-siŋ\ *n* **:** brownish spots on old paper

fox terrier *n* **:** a small lively terrier that occurs in varieties with smooth dense coats or with harsh wiry coats

fox–trot \ˈfäks-ˌträt\ *n* **1 :** a short broken slow trotting gait **2 :** a ballroom dance in duple time

foxy \ˈfäk-sē\ *adj* **fox•i•er; -est 1 :** resembling or suggestive of a fox **2** ♦ **:** cunningly shrewd **:** WILY **3 :** physically attractive

♦ artful, cagey, crafty, cunning, devious, guileful, slick, sly, subtle, wily

foy•er \ˈfȯi-ər, ˈfȯi-ˌyā\ *n* **1** ♦ **:** an anteroom or lobby especially of a theater **2** ♦ **:** an entrance hallway

♦ [1, 2] entry, hall, lobby, vestibule

fpm *abbr* feet per minute

FPO *abbr* fleet post office

fps *abbr* feet per second

fr *abbr* **1** father **2** franc **3** friar **4** from

1Fr *abbr* **1** France; French **2** Friday

2Fr *symbol* francium

fra•cas \ˈfrā-kəs, ˈfra-\ *n, pl* **fra•cas•es** \-kə-səz\ ♦ **:** a noisy quarrel

♦ brawl, fray, free-for-all, melee, row

frac•tal \ˈfrak-tᵊl\ *n* **:** an irregular curve or shape that repeats itself at any scale on which it is examined — **fractal** *adj*

frac•tion \ˈfrak-shən\ *n* **1 :** a numerical representation (as ½, ¾, or 3.323) indicating the quotient of two numbers **2 :** FRAGMENT **3 :** PORTION — **frac•tion•al** \-shə-nəl\ *adj* — **frac•tion•al•ly** *adv*

frac•tious \ˈfrak-shəs\ *adj* **1 :** tending to be troublesome **:** hard to handle or control **2 :** QUARRELSOME, IRRITABLE

1frac•ture \ˈfrak-chər\ *n* **1 :** a breaking of something and especially a bone **2 :** CRACK, CLEFT

2fracture *vb* ♦ **:** to break or cause to break

♦ break, bust, fragment

frag•ile \ˈfra-jəl, -ˌjīl\ *adj* ♦ **:** easily broken **:** DELICATE

♦ breakable, delicate, frail *Ant* nonbreakable, strong, sturdy, tough, unbreakable

fra•gil•i•ty \frə-ˈji-lə-tē\ *n* ♦ **:** the quality or state of being fragile

♦ daintiness, delicacy, fineness

1frag•ment \ˈfrag-mənt\ *n* ♦ **:** a part broken off, detached, or incomplete

♦ piece, scrap

2frag•ment \-ˌment\ *vb* ♦ **:** to break into fragments — **frag•men•ta•tion** \ˌfrag-mən-ˈtā-shən, -ˌmən-\ *n*

♦ break, bust, fracture

frag•men•tary \ˈfrag-mən-ˌter-ē\ *adj* ♦ **:** made up of fragments **:** INCOMPLETE

♦ deficient, halfway, incomplete, partial

fra•grance \-grəns\ *n* ♦ **:** a sweet or delicate odor

♦ aroma, bouquet, incense, perfume, redolence, scent, spice *Ant* reek, stench, stink

fra•grant \ˈfrā-grənt\ *adj* ♦ **:** sweet or agreeable in smell — **fra•grant•ly** *adv*

♦ ambrosial, aromatic, redolent, savory, scented *Ant* fetid, foul, malodorous, noisome, putrid, smelly, stinking

frail \ˈfrāl\ *adj* **1** ♦ **:** morally or physically weak **2** ♦ **:** easily broken or destroyed **:** FRAGILE, DELICATE

♦ [1] delicate, feeble, infirm, tender, wasted, weak ♦ [2] breakable, delicate, fragile

frail•ty \ˈfrāl-tē\ *n, pl* **frailties** **1** ♦ **:** the quality or state of being frail **2** ♦ **:** a fault due to weakness

♦ [1] debility, delicacy, faintness, feebleness, infirmity, weakness ♦ [2] demerit, failing, fault, foible, shortcoming, vice, weakness

¹frame \ˈfrām\ *vb* **framed; fram•ing** **1** ♦ **:** to make plans **2** ♦ **:** to form, make, or create by combining parts or elements **:** SHAPE, CONSTRUCT **3** ♦ **:** to give expression to **:** FORMULATE **4** ♦ **:** to make a draft of or draw up ⟨~ a constitution⟩ **5 :** to make appear guilty **6 :** to fit or adjust for a purpose **:** ARRANGE **7 :** to provide with or enclose in a frame — **fram•er** *n*

♦ [1] arrange, blueprint, calculate, chart, design, lay out, map, plan, project, scheme ♦ [2] construct, fabricate, fashion, form, make, manufacture, produce, shape ♦ [3, 4] cast, compose, craft, draft, draw, formulate, prepare

²frame *n* **1 :** something made of parts fitted and joined together **2** ♦ **:** the physical makeup of the body **3** ♦ **:** an arrangement of structural parts that gives form or support **4 :** a supporting or enclosing border or open case (as for a window or picture) **5 :** one picture of a series (as on a length of film) **6 :** FRAME-UP

♦ [2] build, constitution, figure, form, physique, shape ♦ [3] configuration, framework, shell, skeleton, structure

³frame *adj* **:** having a wood frame
frame of mind *n* **:** mental attitude or outlook **:** MOOD
frame–up \ˈfrā-ˌməp\ *n* **1 :** an act or series of actions in which someone is framed **2 :** an action that is planned, contrived, or formulated
frame•work \ˈfrām-ˌwərk\ *n* ♦ **:** a basic supporting part or structure

♦ configuration, frame, shell, skeleton, structure

franc \ˈfraŋk\ *n* **1 :** any of various former basic monetary units (as of Belgium, France, and Luxembourg) **2 :** a basic monetary unit of any of several countries especially in Africa
fran•chise \ˈfran-ˌchīz\ *n* **1 :** a right or license granted to an individual or group ⟨a ~ to operate a ferry⟩ **2 a :** a constitutional or statutory right or privilege **b** ♦ **:** the right to vote **3 :** the right of membership in a professional sports league; *also* **:** a team having such membership

♦ enfranchisement, suffrage, vote

fran•chi•see \ˌfran-ˌchī-ˈzē, -chə-\ *n* **:** one granted a franchise
fran•chis•er \ˈfran-ˌchī-zər\ *n* **1 :** FRANCHISEE **2 :** FRANCHISOR
fran•chi•sor \ˌfran-ˌchī-ˈzȯr, -chə-\ *n* **:** one that grants a franchise
fran•ci•um \ˈfran-sē-əm\ *n* **:** a radioactive metallic chemical element
Fran•co–Amer•i•can \ˌfraŋ-kō-ə-ˈmer-ə-kən\ *n* **:** an American of French or especially French-Canadian descent — **Franco–American** *adj*
fran•gi•ble \ˈfran-jə-bəl\ *adj* **:** BREAKABLE — **fran•gi•bil•i•ty** \ˌfran-jə-ˈbi-lə-tē\ *n*
¹frank \ˈfraŋk\ *adj* ♦ **:** marked by free, forthright, and sincere expression

♦ candid, direct, forthright, honest, open, outspoken, plain, straight, straightforward ***Ant*** dissembling

²frank *vb* **:** to mark (a piece of mail) with an official sign so that it can be mailed free; *also* **:** to mail free
³frank *n* **1 :** the signature or mark on a piece of mail indicating free or paid postage **2 :** the privilege of sending mail free
⁴frank *n* **:** FRANKFURTER
Fran•ken•stein \ˈfraŋ-kən-ˌstīn\ *n* **1 :** a monstrous creation that usually ruins its originator **2 :** a monster in the shape of a man
frank•furt•er \ˈfraŋk-fər-tər, -ˌfər-\ *or* **frank•furt** \-fərt\ *n* **:** a seasoned sausage (as of beef or beef and pork)
frank•in•cense \ˈfraŋ-kən-ˌsens\ *n* **:** a fragrant resin burned as incense
frank•ly \ˈfraŋ-klē\ *adv* **1 :** in a frank manner **2** ♦ **:** in truth

♦ actually, honestly, really, truly, truthfully, verily

frank•ness *n* ♦ **:** the quality or state of being frank

♦ candor (*or* candour), directness, forthrightness, openness, plainness

fran•tic \ˈfran-tik\ *adj* ♦ **:** marked by or showing uncontrolled emotion or disordered anxious activity

♦ agitated, distraught, feverish, frenetic, frenzied, hysterical ***Ant*** collected, composed, self-possessed

fran•ti•cal•ly \-ti-k(ə-)lē\ *adv* ♦ **:** in a frantic manner

♦ berserk, hectically, helter-skelter, madly, pell-mell, wild, wildly

frap•pé \fra-ˈpā\ *or* **frappe** *same or* ˈfrap\ *n* **1 :** an iced or frozen drink **2 :** a thick milk shake — **frap•pé** \fra-ˈpā\ *adj*
fra•ter•nal \frə-ˈtərn-ᵊl\ *adj* **1 :** of, relating to, or involving brothers **2 :** of, relating to, or being a fraternity or society **3 :** derived from two ova ⟨~ twins⟩ **4 :** FRIENDLY, BROTHERLY — **fra•ter•nal•ly** *adv*
fra•ter•ni•ty \frə-ˈtər-nə-tē\ *n, pl* **-ties** **1** ♦ **:** a social, honorary, or professional group; *esp* **:** a men's student organization **2 :** BROTHERLINESS **3 :** persons of the same class, profession, or tastes

♦ association, brotherhood, club, council, fellowship, guild, league, order, organization, society

frat•er•nize \ˈfra-tər-ˌnīz\ *vb* **-nized; -niz•ing** **1** ♦ **:** to mingle as friends **2 :** to associate on close terms with members of a hostile group — **frat•er•ni•za•tion** \ˌfra-tər-nə-ˈzā-shən\ *n*

♦ associate, chum, consort, hang around, hobnob, pal

frat•ri•cide \ˈfra-trə-ˌsīd\ *n* **1 :** one that kills a sibling or countryman **2 :** the act of a fratricide — **frat•ri•cid•al** \ˌfra-trə-ˈsīd-ᵊl\ *adj*
fraud \ˈfrȯd\ *n* **1 :** DECEIT, TRICKERY **2 :** TRICK **3** ♦ **:** a person who is not what he or she pretends to be **:** IMPOSTOR

♦ charlatan, fake, hoaxer, humbug, impostor, mountebank, phony, pretender, quack

fraud•ster \ˈfrȯd-stər\ *n, chiefly Brit* **:** a person who engages in fraud
fraud•u•lent \ˈfrȯ-jə-lənt\ *adj* ♦ **:** characterized by, based on, or done by fraud — **fraud•u•lent•ly** *adv*

♦ crooked, deceitful, deceptive, dishonest, double-dealing, false, misleading, specious ***Ant*** aboveboard, honest, truthful

fraught \ˈfrȯt\ *adj* ♦ **:** full of or accompanied by something specified ⟨~ with danger⟩

♦ flush, replete, rife

¹fray \ˈfrā\ *n* ♦ **:** a usually disorderly or protracted fight, struggle, or dispute **:** FIGHT, STRUGGLE

♦ battle, clash, combat, conflict, contest, fight, fracas, hassle, struggle

²fray *vb* **1** ♦ **:** to wear (as an edge of cloth) by rubbing **2 :** to separate the threads at the edge of **3 :** STRAIN, IRRITATE ⟨~*ed* nerves⟩

♦ abrade, chafe, erode, fret, gall, rub, wear

fraz•zle \ˈfra-zəl\ *vb* **fraz•zled; fraz•zling** **1 :** FRAY **2 :** to put in a state of extreme physical or nervous fatigue — **frazzle** *n*
¹freak \ˈfrēk\ *n* **1** ♦ **:** a sudden and odd or seemingly pointless idea or turn of the mind **:** a seemingly capricious action or event **2** ♦ **:** a strange, abnormal, or unusual person or thing **3** *slang* **:** a person who uses an illicit drug **4** ♦ **:** an ardent enthusiast — **freaky** \ˈfrē-kē\ *adj*

♦ [1] caprice, fancy, notion, vagary, whim ♦ [2] abnormality, monster, monstrosity ***Ant*** average, norm ♦ [4] addict, aficionado, buff, bug, devotee, enthusiast, fan, fanatic, fancier, fiend, lover, maniac, nut

²freak *vb* **1 :** to experience the effects (as hallucinations) of taking illicit drugs — often used with *out* **2** ♦ **:** to distress or become distressed — often used with *out* — **freak–out** \ˈfrē-ˌkau̇t\ *n*

♦ *usu* **freak out** agitate, bother, concern, distress, disturb, exercise, perturb, unsettle, upset, worry

³freak *adj* ♦ **:** having the character of a freak

♦ aberrant, abnormal, atypical, exceeding, exceptional, extraordinary, odd, peculiar, phenomenal, rare, singular, uncommon, uncustomary, unique, unusual, unwonted

¹freck•le \ˈfre-kəl\ *n* **:** a brownish spot on the skin
²freckle *vb* ♦ **:** to sprinkle or mark with freckles or small spots

♦ dot, fleck, pepper, speck, spot, sprinkle

¹free \ˈfrē\ *adj* **fre•er; fre•est** **1** ♦ **:** having liberty **2** ♦ **:** enjoying political or personal independence; *also* **:** not subject to or allowing slavery **3 :** made or done voluntarily **:** SPONTANEOUS **4 :** relieved from or lacking something unpleasant **5 :** not subject to a duty, tax, or charge **6** ♦ **:** not obstructed **:** CLEAR **7 :** not being used or occupied **8 :** not fastened **9 :** LAVISH **10 :** OPEN, FRANK **11 a** ♦ **:** given without charge **b** ♦ **:** made, done, or given voluntarily or spontaneously **12 :** not literal or exact **13 :** not restricted by conventional forms **14** ♦ **:** overly familiar or forward in action or attitude

♦ [1] footloose, loose, unbound, unconfined, unrestrained ***Ant*** bound, confined, restrained, unfree ♦ [2] autonomous, independent, self-governing, separate, sovereign ***Ant*** dependent, subject, unfree ♦ [6] clear, open, unobstructed ♦ [11a] complimentary, gratuitous ♦ [11b] bountiful, charitable, generous, liberal, munificent, openhanded, unselfish, unsparing ♦ [14] bold, familiar, forward, immodest, presumptuous

²free *vb* **freed; free•ing 1** ♦ **:** to set free **2** ♦ **:** to relieve or rid of what restrains, confines, restricts, or embarrasses **3** ♦ **:** to clear from what obstructs or is unneeded **:** CLEAR

♦ [1, 2] discharge, emancipate, enfranchise, liberate, manumit, release, unchain, unfetter ***Ant*** bind, confine, enchain, fetter, restrain ♦ [2] clear, disburden, disencumber, relieve, rid, unburden ♦ [2, 3] clear, disengage, disentangle, extricate, liberate, release, untangle ♦ [3] clear, open, unclog, unstop

³free *adv* **1 :** FREELY **2 :** without charge

free•base \ˈfrē-ˌbās\ *n* **:** purified cocaine smoked as crack or heated to produce vapors for inhalation — **freebase** *vb*

free•bie *or* **free•bee** \ˈfrē-bē\ *n* ♦ **:** something given without charge

♦ bestowal, donation, gift, lagniappe, present

free•board \ˈfrē-ˌbōrd\ *n* **:** the vertical distance between the waterline and the upper edge of the side of a boat

free•boo•ter \-ˌbü-tər\ *n* ♦ **:** one who commits or practices piracy **:** PIRATE

♦ buccaneer, corsair, pirate, rover

free•born \-ˈbȯrn\ *adj* **1 :** not born in vassalage or slavery **2 :** of, relating to, or befitting one that is freeborn

freed•man \ˈfrēd-mən, -ˌman\ *n* **:** a person freed from slavery

free•dom \ˈfrē-dəm\ *n* **1** ♦ **:** the quality or state of being free **:** INDEPENDENCE **2 :** EXEMPTION, RELEASE **3 :** EASE, FACILITY **4 :** FRANKNESS **5 :** unrestricted use **6 :** a political right; *also* **:** FRANCHISE, PRIVILEGE **7** ♦ **:** the ability or capacity to act without undue hindrance or restraint

♦ [1] autonomy, independence, liberty, self-government, sovereignty ***Ant*** dependence, subjection ♦ [7] authorization, latitude, license (*or* licence), run

freedom fighter *n* **:** a person who takes part in a resistance movement against an oppressive political or social establishment

free enterprise *n* **:** freedom of private business to operate with little regulation by the government

¹free–for–all \ˈfrē-fə-ˌrȯl\ *adj* ♦ **:** unrestricted as to entries, participants, or users

♦ open, public, unrestricted

²free–for–all *n* ♦ **:** a competition or fight open to all comers and usually with no rules **:** BRAWL

♦ brawl, fracas, fray, melee, row

free•hand \-ˌhand\ *adj* **:** done without mechanical aids or devices

free•hold \ˈfrē-ˌhōld\ *n* **:** ownership of an estate for life usually with the right to bequeath it to one's heirs; *also* **:** an estate thus owned — **free•hold•er** *n*

free•lance \-ˌlans\ *n* **:** one who pursues a profession (as writing) without a long-term commitment to any one employer — **freelance** *adj or vb*

free–liv•ing \ˈfrē-ˈli-viŋ\ *adj* **1 :** unrestricted in pursuing personal pleasures **2 :** being neither parasitic nor symbiotic ⟨~ organisms⟩

free•load \ˈfrē-ˌlōd\ *vb* **:** to impose upon another's hospitality — **free•load•er** *n*

free love *n* **1 :** the practice of living openly with one of the opposite sex without marriage **2 :** sexual relations without any commitments by either partner

free•ly *adv* ♦ **:** in a free manner

♦ easily, effortlessly, fluently, handily, lightly, painlessly, readily, smoothly

free•man \ˈfrē-mən, -ˌman\ *n* **1 :** one who has civil or political liberty **2 :** one having the full rights of a citizen

Free•ma•son \-ˌmās-ᵊn\ *n* **:** a member of a secret fraternal society called Free and Accepted Masons — **Free•ma•son•ry** \-rē\ *n*

free radical *n* **:** an especially reactive atom or group of atoms with one or more unpaired electrons; *esp* **:** one that can cause bodily damage (as by altering the chemical structure of cells)

free–range \ˈfrē-ˌrānj\ *adj* **:** allowed to range and forage with relative freedom ⟨~ chickens⟩; *also* **:** produced by free-range animals ⟨~ eggs⟩

free speech *n* **:** speech that is protected by the First Amendment to the U.S. Constitution

free spirit *n* **:** NONCONFORMIST

free•stand•ing \ˈfrē-ˈstan-diŋ\ *adj* ♦ **:** standing alone or on its own foundation free of support

♦ detached, disconnected, discrete, separate, single, unattached, unconnected

free•stone \ˈfrē-ˌstōn\ *n* **1 :** a stone that may be cut freely without splitting **2 :** a fruit stone to which the flesh does not cling; *also* **:** a fruit (as a peach or cherry) having such a stone

free•think•er \-ˈthiŋ-kər\ *n* **:** one who forms opinions on the basis of reason independently of authority; *esp* **:** one who doubts or denies religious dogma — **free•think•ing** *n or adj*

free trade *n* **:** trade between nations without restrictions (as high taxes on imports)

free verse *n* **:** verse whose meter is irregular or whose rhythm is not metrical

free•ware \ˈfrē-ˌwer\ *n* **:** software that is free or that has a small usually optional cost

free•way \ˈfrē-ˌwā\ *n* **:** an expressway without tolls

free•wheel \-ˈhwēl\ *vb* **:** to move, live, or play freely or irresponsibly

free•wheel•ing \ˌfrē-ˈhwē-liŋ\ *adj* **:** free and loose in form or manner

free•will \ˈfrē-ˌwil\ *adj* ♦ **:** produced in or by an act of choice

♦ deliberate, intentional, purposeful, voluntary, willful, willing

free will *n* ♦ **:** voluntary choice or decision

♦ accord, choice, option, self-determination, volition, will

¹freeze \ˈfrēz\ *vb* **froze** \ˈfrōz\; **fro•zen** \ˈfrōz-ᵊn\ **1** ♦ **:** to harden or cause to harden into a solid (as ice) by loss of heat **2 :** to withstand freezing **3 :** to chill or become chilled with cold **4 :** to damage by frost **5 :** to adhere solidly by or as if by freezing **6 :** to become fixed, motionless, or incapable of speech **7 :** to cause to grip tightly **8 :** to become clogged with ice **9 :** to fix at a certain stage or level

♦ concrete, congeal, firm, harden, set, solidify

²freeze *n* **1 :** an act or instance of freezing **2 :** the state of being frozen **3 :** a state of weather marked by low temperature

freeze–dry \ˈfrēz-ˈdrī\ *vb* **:** to dry in a frozen state under vacuum especially for preservation — **freeze–dried** *adj*

freez•er \ˈfrē-zər\ *n* **:** a compartment, device, or room for freezing food or keeping it frozen

freez•ing *adj* ♦ **:** very cold

♦ arctic, cold, frigid, frosty, glacial, icy, polar, wintry

¹freight \ˈfrāt\ *n* **1 :** payment for carrying goods **2** ♦ **:** something that is loaded for transportation **:** CARGO **3 :** BURDEN **4 :** the carrying of goods by a common carrier **5 :** a train that carries freight

♦ burden, cargo, haul, lading, load, payload, weight

²freight *vb* **1 :** to load with goods for transportation **2 :** BURDEN, CHARGE **3 :** to ship or transport by freight

freight•er \ˈfrā-tər\ *n* **:** a ship or airplane used chiefly to carry freight

French \ˈfrench\ *n* **1 :** the language of France **2 French** *pl* **:** the people of France **3 :** strong language — **French** *adj* — **French•man** \-mən\ *n* — **French•wom•an** \-ˌwu̇-mən\ *n*

French Canadian *n* **:** one of the descendants of French settlers in Lower Canada — **French–Canadian** *adj*

French door *n* **:** a door with small panes of glass extending the full length

French dressing *n* **1 :** a thin salad dressing usually made of vinegar and oil with spices **2 :** a creamy salad dressing flavored with tomatoes

french fry *n, often cap 1st F* **:** a strip of potato fried in deep fat until brown — **french fry** *vb, often cap 1st F*

French horn *n* **:** a curved brass instrument with a funnel-shaped mouthpiece and a flaring bell

French press *n* **:** a coffeepot in which ground beans are infused and then pressed by a plunger

French toast *n* **:** bread dipped in a mixture of eggs and milk and fried at a low heat

French twist *n* **:** a woman's hairstyle in which the hair is coiled at the rear and secured in place

fre•net•ic \fri-ˈne-tik\ *adj* ♦ **:** marked by fast and nervous, disordered, or anxiety-driven activity : FRANTIC — **fre•net•i•cal•ly** \-ti-k(ə-)lē\ *adv*

♦ delirious, feverish, fierce, frantic, frenzied, furious, mad, rabid, violent, wild

fren•zied \ˈfren-zēd\ *adj* ♦ : feeling or showing great or abnormal excitement or emotional disturbance

♦ delirious, feverish, frantic, frenetic, furious, hectic, hysterical

fren•zy \ˈfren-zē\ *n, pl* **frenzies** **1** ♦ : temporary madness or a violently agitated state **2** ♦ : intense often disordered activity

♦ [1, 2] agitation, chaos, confusion, disorder, furor, fury, hysteria, rage, rampage, tumult, turmoil, uproar

freq *abbr* frequency; frequent; frequently

fre•quen•cy \ˈfrē-kwən-sē\ *n, pl* **-cies** **1** : the fact or condition of occurring frequently **2** : rate of occurrence **3** : the number of cycles per second of an alternating current **4** : the number of waves (as of sound or electromagnetic energy) that pass a fixed point each second

frequency modulation *n* : variation of the frequency of a carrier wave according to another signal; *also* : FM

¹fre•quent \frē-ˈkwent, ˈfrē-kwənt\ *vb* ♦ : to associate with, be in, or resort to habitually

♦ hang around, hang out, haunt, resort, visit ***Ant*** avoid, shun

²fre•quent \ˈfrē-kwənt\ *adj* **1** ♦ : happening often or at short intervals **2** ♦ : done or happening on a regular or recurring basis

♦ [1] common, commonplace, customary, everyday, familiar, ordinary, routine, usual ♦ [2] constant, habitual, periodic, regular, repeated, steady

fre•quent•er *n* : one that frequents

fre•quent–fli•er \ˈfrē-kwənt-ˈflī-ər\ *adj* : of, relating to, or being an airline program offering awards for specified numbers of air miles traveled

fre•quent•ly *adv* ♦ : at frequent or short intervals

♦ constantly, continually, often, repeatedly

fres•co \ˈfres-kō\ *n, pl* **frescoes** : the art of painting on fresh plaster; *also* : a painting done by this method

fresh \ˈfresh\ *adj* **1** : VIGOROUS, REFRESHED **2** : not containing salt **3** : not altered by processing (as freezing or canning) **4** : free from taint : PURE **5** : fairly strong : BRISK ⟨~ breeze⟩ **6** ♦ : not stale, sour, or decayed ⟨~ bread⟩ **7** : not faded **8** ♦ : not worn or rumpled **9** ♦ : experienced, made, or received newly or anew **10** : ADDITIONAL, ANOTHER ⟨made a ~ start⟩ **11** : ORIGINAL, VIVID **12** : INEXPERIENCED **13** : newly come or arrived ⟨~ from school⟩ **14** ♦ : disposed to take liberties : IMPUDENT

♦ [6, 8] brand-new, pristine, virgin ***Ant*** stale ♦ [9] new, novel, original, unfamiliar ♦ [14] bold, brash, brazen, cheeky, impudent, insolent, nervy, sassy, saucy

fresh•en \ˈfre-shən\ *vb* ♦ : to make, grow, or become fresh

♦ refresh, rejuvenate, renew, restore, revitalize, revive

fresh•et \ˈfre-shət\ *n* : an overflowing of a stream (as by heavy rains)

fresh•ly *adv* ♦ : in a fresh manner

♦ just, late, lately, new, newly, now, only, recently

fresh•man \ˈfresh-mən\ *n* **1** : a 1st-year student **2** ♦ : one that begins something; *esp* : an inexperienced person

♦ beginner, greenhorn, neophyte, newcomer, novice, recruit, rookie, tenderfoot, tyro

fresh•ness *n* ♦ : the quality or state of being fresh

♦ newness, novelty, originality

fresh•wa•ter \-ˌwȯ-tər, -ˌwä-\ *n* : water that is not salty — **freshwater** *adj*

¹fret \ˈfret\ *vb* **fret•ted; fret•ting** **1** : to eat or gnaw into **2** ♦ : to chafe with or as if with friction : RUB **3** : to make by wearing away **4** ♦ : to become irritated : WORRY **5** : GRATE; *also* : AGITATE

♦ [2] abrade, chafe, erode, fray, gall, rub, wear ♦ [4] bother, fear, stew, sweat, trouble, worry

²fret *n* ♦ : an irritated or worried state ⟨in a ~ about the interview⟩

♦ dither, fluster, fuss, huff, lather, pother, stew, tizzy, twitter

³fret *n* : ornamental work especially of straight lines in symmetrical patterns

⁴fret *n* : one of a series of ridges across the fingerboard of a stringed musical instrument — **fret•ted** *adj*

fret•ful \ˈfret-fəl\ *adj* : IRRITABLE — **fret•ful•ly** *adv* — **fret•ful•ness** *n*

fret•saw \-ˌsȯ\ *n* : a narrow-bladed saw used for cutting curved outlines

fret•work \-ˌwərk\ *n* **1** : decoration consisting of frets **2** : ornamental openwork or work in relief

Fri *abbr* Friday

fri•a•ble \ˈfrī-ə-bəl\ *adj* ♦ : easily crumbled or pulverized ⟨~ soil⟩

♦ brittle, crisp, crumbly, flaky

fri•ar \ˈfrī-ər\ *n* : a member of a religious order that orig. lived by alms

fri•ary \ˈfrī-ər-ē\ *n, pl* **-ar•ies** ♦ : a monastery of friars

♦ abbey, cloister, monastery, priory

¹fric•as•see \ˈfri-kə-ˌsē, ˌfri-kə-ˈsē\ *n* : a dish made of meat (as chicken) cut into pieces, stewed in stock, and served in sauce

²fricassee *vb* **-seed; -see•ing** : to cook as a fricassee

fric•tion \ˈfrik-shən\ *n* **1** : the rubbing of one body against another **2** : the force that resists motion between bodies in contact **3** ♦ : clash in opinions between persons or groups : DISAGREEMENT — **fric•tion•al** *adj*

♦ conflict, discord, dissent, disunity, schism, strife, variance

friction tape *n* : a usually cloth adhesive tape impregnated with insulating material and used especially to protect and insulate electrical conductors

Fri•day \ˈfrī-dē, -(ˌ)dā\ *n* : the sixth day of the week

fridge \ˈfrij\ *n* : REFRIGERATOR

fried•cake \ˈfrīd-ˌkāk\ *n* : DOUGHNUT, CRULLER

fried rice *n* : a dish of boiled or steamed rice that is stir-fried with soy sauce and typically includes egg, meat, and vegetables

friend \ˈfrend\ *n* **1** ♦ : one attached to another by respect or affection **2** : ACQUAINTANCE **3** : one who is not hostile **4** ♦ : one who supports or favors something ⟨a ~ of art⟩ **5** *cap* : a member of the Society of Friends : QUAKER — **friend•less** *adj*

♦ [1] buddy, chum, comrade, crony, familiar, intimate, pal ***Ant*** enemy, foe ♦ [4] advocate, apostle, backer, booster, champion, exponent, promoter, proponent, supporter

friend•li•ness \-lē-nəs\ *n* ♦ : the quality or state of being friendly

♦ amity, benevolence, cordiality, fellowship, friendship, goodwill, kindliness

friend•ly \ˈfren(d)-lē\ *adj* ♦ : of, relating to, or befitting a friend

♦ appreciative, complimentary, favorable (*or* favourable), good, positive ♦ amicable, companionable, comradely, cordial, genial, hearty, neighborly, warm, warmhearted ***Ant*** antagonistic, hostile, unfriendly

friend•ship \-ˌship\ *n* ♦ : the state of being friends

♦ amity, benevolence, cordiality, fellowship, friendliness, goodwill, kindliness

frieze \ˈfrēz\ *n* : an ornamental often sculptured band extending around something (as a building or room)

frig•ate \ˈfri-gət\ *n* **1** : a square-rigged warship **2** : a warship smaller than a destroyer

fright \ˈfrīt\ *n* **1** ♦ : sudden terror : ALARM **2** ♦ : something that is ugly or shocking

♦ [1] alarm, anxiety, apprehension, dread, fear, horror, panic, terror, trepidation ♦ [2] eyesore, horror, mess, monstrosity, sight

fright•en \ˈfrīt-ᵊn\ *vb* **1** ♦ : to make afraid **2** : to drive away or out by frightening **3** : to become frightened — **fright•en•ing** *adj* — **fright•en•ing•ly** *adv*

♦ alarm, horrify, panic, scare, shock, spook, startle, terrify, terrorize ***Ant*** reassure

fright•ful \ˈfrīt-fəl\ *adj* **1** ♦ : causing intense fear or alarm : TERRIFYING **2** : startling especially in being bad or objectionable **3** : EXTREME ⟨~ thirst⟩

♦ fearful, fearsome, forbidding, formidable, hair-raising, scary, shocking, terrifying

fright•ful•ly *adv* ♦ : in a frightful manner

♦ especially, extremely, greatly, highly, hugely, mightily, mighty, mortally, most, much, real, right, so, very

fright•ful•ness *n* ♦ : the quality or state of being frightful

♦ atrociousness, atrocity, hideousness, horror, monstrosity, repulsiveness

frig•id \ˈfri-jəd\ *adj* **1** ♦ **:** intensely cold **2** ♦ **:** lacking warmth or ardor **:** INDIFFERENT **3 :** abnormally averse to or unable to achieve orgasm during sexual intercourse — used especially of women — **fri•gid•i•ty** \fri-ˈji-də-tē\ *n*

♦ [1] arctic, bitter, cold, freezing, frosty, glacial, icy, polar, wintry ♦ [2] chill, chilly, cold, cool, frosty, icy, indifferent, unfriendly, wintry

frigid zone *n* **:** the area or region between the arctic circle and the north pole or between the antarctic circle and the south pole

frill \ˈfril\ *n* **1** ♦ **:** a gathered, pleated, or ruffled edging **2** ♦ **:** something unessential — **frilly** *adj*

♦ [1] flounce, furbelow, ruffle ♦ [2] amenity, comfort, extra, indulgence, luxury, superfluity

¹fringe \ˈfrinj\ *n* **1 :** an ornamental border consisting of short threads or strips hanging from an edge or band **2** ♦ **:** something that resembles a fringe **:** EDGE **3 :** something that is additional or secondary to an activity, process, or subject

♦ border, boundary, edge, margin, perimeter, periphery

²fringe *vb* **1 :** to furnish or adorn with a fringe **2** ♦ **:** to serve as a border or fringe for

♦ border, bound, margin, rim, skirt

fringe benefit *n* **1 :** an employment benefit paid for by an employer without affecting basic wage rates **2 :** any additional benefit

frip•pery \ˈfri-pə-rē\ *n, pl* **-per•ies** **1 a** ♦ **:** dressy or showy clothing and jewels **:** FINERY **b** ♦ **:** something showy, frivolous, or nonessential **2 :** pretentious display

♦ [1a] array, best, bravery, caparison, feather, finery, full dress, gaiety, regalia ♦ [1b] child's play, nothing, trifle, triviality

frisk \ˈfrisk\ *vb* **1** ♦ **:** to leap, skip, or dance in a lively or playful way **:** GAMBOL **2 :** to search (a person) especially for concealed weapons by running the hand rapidly over the clothing

♦ caper, cavort, disport, frolic, gambol, lark, rollick, romp, sport

frisk•i•ness \-kē-nəs\ *n* ♦ **:** the quality or state of being inclined to frisk

♦ impishness, mischief, mischievousness, playfulness

frisky \ˈfris-kē\ *adj* **frisk•i•er; -est** ♦ **:** inclined to frisk **:** PLAYFUL — **frisk•i•ly** \-kə-lē\ *adv*

♦ antic, coltish, elfish, fay, frolicsome, playful, sportive ♦ active, animated, energetic, lively, peppy, perky, spirited, sprightly

¹frit•ter \ˈfri-tər\ *n* **:** a small lump of fried batter often containing fruit or meat

²fritter *vb* **1** ♦ **:** to reduce or waste piecemeal — usually used with *away* **2 :** to break into small fragments

♦ *usu* **fritter away** blow, dissipate, lavish, misspend, run through, spend, squander, throw away, waste

fritz \ˈfrits\ *n* **:** a state of disorder or disrepair — used in the phrase *on the fritz*

fri•vol•i•ty \fri-ˈvä-lə-tē\ *n* ♦ **:** the quality or state of being frivolous

♦ facetiousness, flightiness, flippancy, levity, lightness *Ant* gravity, seriousness, soberness, sobriety

friv•o•lous \ˈfri-və-ləs\ *adj* **1** ♦ **:** of little importance **:** TRIVIAL **2** ♦ **:** lacking in seriousness — **friv•o•lous•ly** *adv*

♦ [1] insignificant, little, minor, minute, negligible, slight, small, trifling, trivial, unimportant ♦ [2] flighty, giddy, goofy, harebrained, light-headed, scatterbrained, silly

frizz \ˈfriz\ *vb* **:** to form into small tight curls — **frizz** *n* — **frizzy** *adj*

friz•zies \ˈfri-zēz\ *n pl* **:** hair which has become difficult to manage (as due to humidity)

¹friz•zle \ˈfri-zəl\ *vb* **friz•zled; friz•zling** **:** FRIZZ, CURL — **frizzle** *n*

²frizzle *vb* **friz•zled; friz•zling** **1 :** to fry until crisp and curled **2 :** to cook with a sizzling noise

fro \ˈfrō\ *adv* **:** BACK, AWAY — used in the phrase *to and fro*

frock \ˈfräk\ *n* **1 :** an outer garment worn by monks and friars **2 :** an outer garment worn especially by men **3 :** a woman's or girl's dress

frock coat *n* **:** a man's knee-length usually double-breasted coat with knee-length skirts

frog \ˈfrȯg, ˈfräg\ *n* **1 :** any of various largely aquatic smooth-skinned tailless leaping amphibians **2 :** an ornamental braiding for fastening the front of a garment by a loop through which a button passes **3 :** a condition in the throat causing hoarseness **4 :** a small holder (as of metal, glass, or plastic) with perforations or spikes that is placed in a bowl or vase to keep cut flowers in position

frog•man \ˈfrȯg-ˌman, ˈfräg-, -mən\ *n* **:** a swimmer equipped to work underwater for long periods of time

¹frol•ic \ˈfrä-lik\ *vb* **frol•icked; frol•ick•ing** **1** ♦ **:** to make merry **2** ♦ **:** to play about happily **:** ROMP

♦ caper, cavort, disport, frisk, gambol, lark, play, rollick, romp, sport

²frolic *n* **1** ♦ **:** a playful or mischievous action **2** ♦ **:** an occasion or scene of fun

♦ [1] dalliance, fun, play, relaxation, sport ♦ [1] antic, caper, escapade, monkeyshine, practical joke, prank, trick ♦ [2] binge, fling, gambol, lark, revel, rollick, romp

frol•ic•some \-səm\ *adj* ♦ **:** full of gaiety

♦ antic, coltish, elfish, fay, frisky, playful, sportive

from \ˈfrəm, ˈfräm\ *prep* **1** — used to show a starting point ⟨a letter ~ home⟩ **2** — used to show removal or separation ⟨subtract 3 ~ 9⟩ **3** — used to show a material, source, or cause ⟨suffering ~ a cold⟩

frond \ˈfränd\ *n* **:** a usually large divided leaf especially of a fern or palm tree

¹front \ˈfrənt\ *n* **1 :** FOREHEAD; *also* **:** the whole face **2** ♦ **:** external and often feigned appearance **3 :** a region of active fighting; *also* **:** a sphere of activity **4 :** a political coalition **5 :** the side of a building containing the main entrance **6** ♦ **:** the forward part or surface **7 :** FRONTAGE **8 :** a boundary between two dissimilar air masses **9 :** a position directly before or ahead of something else **10 :** a person, group, or thing used to mask the identity of the actual controlling agent

♦ [2] act, airs, facade, guise, masquerade, pose, pretense, put-on, semblance, show ♦ [6] facade, face *Ant* back, rear, reverse

²front *vb* **1 :** to have the principal side adjacent to something **2 :** to serve as a front **3 :** CONFRONT

front•age \ˈfrən-tij\ *n* **1 :** a piece of land lying adjacent (as to a street or the ocean) **2 :** the length of a frontage **3 :** the front side of a building

front•al \ˈfrənt-ᵊl\ *adj* **1 :** of, relating to, or next to the forehead **2 :** of, relating to, or directed at the front ⟨a ~ attack⟩ — **fron•tal•ly** *adv*

fron•tier \ˌfrən-ˈtir\ *n* **1** ♦ **:** a border between two countries **2** ♦ **:** a region that forms the margin of settled territory **3 :** the outer limits of knowledge or achievement ⟨the ~s of science⟩

♦ [1] border, borderland, march ♦ [2] backwoods, bush, hinterland, sticks, up-country

fron•tiers•man \-ˈtirz-mən\ *n* ♦ **:** a person who lives or works on a frontier

♦ colonist, homesteader, pioneer, settler

fron•tis•piece \ˈfrən-tə-ˌspēs\ *n* **:** an illustration preceding and usually facing the title page of a book

front man *n* **:** a person serving as a front or figurehead

front•ward \ˈfrənt-wərd\ *or* **front•wards** \-wərdz\ *adv or adj* **:** toward the front

¹frost \ˈfrȯst\ *n* **1 :** freezing temperature **2 :** a covering of tiny ice crystals on a cold surface

²frost *vb* **1 :** to cover with frost **2 :** to put icing on (as a cake) **3 :** to produce a slightly roughened surface on (as glass) **4 :** to injure or kill by frost

¹frost•bite \ˈfrȯst-ˌbīt\ *vb* **-bit** \-ˌbit\; **-bit•ten** \-ˌbit-ᵊn\; **-bit•ing** **:** to injure by frost or frostbite

²frostbite *n* **:** the freezing or the local effect of a partial freezing of some part of the body

frost heave *n* **:** an upthrust of pavement caused by freezing of moist soil

frost•ing \ˈfrȯ-stiŋ\ *n* **1 :** ICING **2 :** dull finish on metal or glass

frosty *adj* **1** ♦ **:** briskly cold **2 :** covered or appearing as if covered with frost **3** ♦ **:** marked by coolness or extreme reserve in manner

♦ [1] chill, chilly, cold, cool, nippy, raw, snappy, wintry ♦ [3] aloof, antisocial, cold, cool, detached, distant, remote, standoffish, unfriendly, unsociable

froth \ˈfrȯth\ *n, pl* **froths** \ˈfrȯths, ˈfrȯt͟hz\ **1** ♦ **:** bubbles formed in or on a liquid **2 :** something light or worthless — **frothy** *adj*

♦ foam, head, lather, spume

frou•frou \ˈfrü-ˌfrü\ *n* **1 :** a rustling especially of a woman's skirts **2 :** showy or frilly ornamentation
fro•ward \ˈfrō-wərd\ *adj* ♦ **:** habitually disposed to disobedience and opposition

♦ contrary, defiant, disobedient, headstrong, intractable, rebellious, unruly, untoward, wayward, willful

¹frown \ˈfrau̇n\ *vb* **1 :** to wrinkle the forehead (as in displeasure or thought) **2** ♦ **:** to look with disapproval — usually used with *on* in transitive senses **3 :** to express with a frown

♦ glare, gloom, glower, lower, scowl ***Ant*** beam, smile ♦ *usu* **frown on** deprecate, disapprove, discountenance, disfavor (*or* disfavour), dislike, reprove

²frown *n* ♦ **:** a wrinkling of the brow especially in a severe, reproving, or stern look

♦ face, grimace, lower, mouth, pout, scowl

frow•sy *or* **frow•zy** \ˈfrau̇-zē\ *adj* **frow•si•er** *or* **frow•zi•er; -est** ♦ **:** having a slovenly or uncared-for appearance

♦ dowdy, sloppy, slovenly, unkempt, untidy

froze *past of* FREEZE
fro•zen \ˈfrōz-ᵊn\ *adj* **1 :** treated, affected, or crusted over by freezing **2 :** subject to long and severe cold **3** ♦ **:** incapable of being changed, moved, or undone ⟨~ wages⟩ **4 :** not available for present use ⟨~ capital⟩ **5 :** expressing or characterized by cold unfriendliness

♦ certain, determinate, final, firm, fixed, flat, hard, hard-and-fast, set, settled, stable

FRS *abbr* Federal Reserve System
frt *abbr* freight
fruc•ti•fy \ˈfrək-tə-ˌfī, ˈfru̇k-\ *vb* **-fied; -fy•ing 1 :** to bear fruit **2 :** to make fruitful or productive
fruc•tose \ˈfrək-ˌtōs, ˈfrük-\ *n* **:** a very sweet soluble sugar that occurs especially in fruit juices and honey
fru•gal \ˈfrü-gəl\ *adj* ♦ **:** characterized by or reflecting economy in the use of resources **:** ECONOMICAL, THRIFTY — **fru•gal•ly** *adv*

♦ economical, provident, sparing, thrifty ***Ant*** prodigal, wasteful

fru•gal•i•ty \frü-ˈga-lə-tē\ *n* ♦ **:** the quality or state of being frugal

♦ economy, husbandry, providence, thrift

¹fruit \ˈfrüt\ *n* **1 :** a product of plant growth; *esp* **:** a usually edible and sweet reproductive body (as a strawberry or apple) of a seed plant **2 :** a product of fertilization in a plant; *esp* **:** the ripe ovary of a seed plant with its contents and appendages **3 :** the effect or consequence of an action or operation — **fruit•ed** \ˈfrü-təd\ *adj*
²fruit *vb* **:** to bear or cause to bear fruit
fruit•cake \ˈfrüt-ˌkāk\ *n* **:** a rich cake containing nuts, dried or candied fruits, and spices
fruit fly *n* **:** any of various small dipteran flies whose larvae feed on fruit or decaying vegetable matter
fruit•ful \ˈfrüt-fəl\ *adj* **1** ♦ **:** yielding or producing fruit **2** ♦ **:** very productive ⟨a ~ soil⟩; *also* **:** bringing results ⟨a ~ idea⟩ — **fruit•ful•ly** *adv* — **fruit•ful•ness** *n*

♦ [1] fat, fecund, fertile, luxuriant, productive, prolific, rich ♦ [2] effective, effectual, efficacious, efficient, potent, productive

fru•ition \frü-ˈi-shən\ *n* **1 :** ENJOYMENT **2 :** the state of bearing fruit **3** ♦ **:** the state of being realized **:** REALIZATION, ACCOMPLISHMENT

♦ accomplishment, achievement, actuality, attainment, consummation, fulfillment, realization ***Ant*** naught, nonfulfillment

fruit•less \ˈfrüt-ləs\ *adj* **1 :** not bearing fruit **2** ♦ **:** not successful **:** UNSUCCESSFUL ⟨a ~ attempt⟩ — **fruit•less•ly** *adv*

♦ futile, ineffective, unproductive, unsuccessful

fruity \ˈfrü-tē\ *adj* **fruit•i•er; -est :** resembling a fruit especially in flavor
frumpy \ˈfrəm-pē\ *adj* **frump•i•er; -est :** DOWDY, DRAB
frus•trate \ˈfrəs-ˌtrāt\ *vb* **frus•trat•ed; frus•trat•ing 1** ♦ **:** to balk or defeat in an endeavor **2 :** to induce feelings of insecurity, discouragement, or dissatisfaction in **3 :** to bring to nothing — **frus•trat•ing•ly** *adv*

♦ baffle, balk, beat, checkmate, foil, thwart

frus•trat•ing *adj* ♦ **:** tending to produce or characterized by frustration

♦ aggravating, annoying, bothersome, galling, irksome, irritating, pesty, vexatious

frus•tra•tion \ˌfrəs-ˈtrā-shən\ *n* **1** ♦ **:** the state or an instance of being frustrated **2** ♦ **:** something that frustrates

♦ [1] disappointment, dismay, dissatisfaction, letdown ♦ [2] aggravation, annoyance, bother, exasperation, vexation

frus•tum \ˈfrəs-təm\ *n, pl* **frustums** *or* **frus•ta** \-tə\ **:** the part of a cone or pyramid formed by cutting off the top by a plane parallel to the base
frwy *abbr* freeway
¹fry \ˈfrī\ *vb* **fried; fry•ing 1 :** to cook in a pan or on a griddle over heat especially with the use of fat **2 :** to undergo frying
²fry *n, pl* **fries 1 :** a social gathering where fried food is eaten **2 :** a dish of something fried; *esp, pl* **:** FRENCH FRIES
³fry *n, pl* **fry 1 :** recently hatched fishes; *also* **:** very small adult fishes **2 :** members of a group or class ⟨small ~⟩
fry•er \ˈfrī-ər\ *n* **1 :** something (as a young chicken) suitable for frying **2 :** a deep utensil for frying foods
FSLIC *abbr* Federal Savings and Loan Insurance Corporation
ft *abbr* **1** feet; foot **2** fort
FTC *abbr* Federal Trade Commission
FTP \ˌef-ˌtē-ˈpē\ *n* **:** a system for transferring computer files especially via the Internet — **FTP** *vb*
fuch•sia \ˈfyü-shə\ *n* **1 :** any of a genus of shrubs related to the evening primrose and grown for their showy nodding often red or purple flowers **2 :** a vivid reddish purple color
fud•dle \ˈfəd-ᵊl\ *vb* **fud•dled; fud•dling :** MUDDLE, CONFUSE
fud•dy–dud•dy \ˈfə-dē-ˌdə-dē\ *n, pl* **-dies** ♦ **:** one that is old-fashioned, unimaginative, or conservative

♦ antediluvian, dodo, fogy, fossil, reactionary

¹fudge \ˈfəj\ *vb* **fudged; fudg•ing 1 :** to exceed the proper bounds of something **2 :** to act dishonestly **:** CHEAT; *also* **:** FALSIFY **3** ♦ **:** to fail to come to grips with

♦ equivocate, hedge, pussyfoot

²fudge *n* **1** ♦ **:** a piece of foolish nonsense **2 :** a soft candy of milk, sugar, butter, and flavoring

♦ bunk, folly, foolishness, hogwash, humbug, nonsense, piffle, rot, silliness

¹fu•el \ˈfyü-əl, ˈfyül\ *n* **:** a material used to produce heat or power by burning; *also* **:** a material from which nuclear energy can be liberated
²fuel *vb* **-eled** *or* **-elled; -el•ing** *or* **-el•ling :** to provide with or take in fuel
fuel cell *n* **:** a device that continuously changes the chemical energy of a fuel directly into electrical energy
fuel injection *n* **:** a system for injecting a precise amount of atomized fuel into an internal combustion engine — **fuel–in•ject•ed** \ˈfyül-in-ˈjek-təd\ *adj*
¹fu•gi•tive \ˈfyü-jə-tiv\ *n* **1 :** one who flees or tries to escape **2 :** something elusive or hard to find
²fugitive *adj* **1 :** running away or trying to escape **2** ♦ **:** likely to vanish suddenly **:** not fixed or lasting

♦ ephemeral, evanescent, flash, fleeting, impermanent, momentary, short-lived, transient

fugue \ˈfyüg\ *n* **1 :** a musical composition in which different parts successively repeat the theme **2 :** a disturbed state of consciousness characterized by acts that are not recalled upon recovery
füh•rer *or* **fueh•rer** \ˈfyu̇r-ər, ˈfir-\ *n* **:** LEADER; *esp* **:** TYRANT
¹-ful \fəl\ *adj suffix, sometimes* **-ful•ler** *sometimes* **-ful•lest 1 :** full of ⟨pride*ful*⟩ **2 :** characterized by ⟨peace*ful*⟩ **3 :** having the qualities of ⟨master*ful*⟩ **4 :** tending, given, or liable to ⟨help*ful*⟩
²-ful \ˌfu̇l\ *n suffix* **:** number or quantity that fills or would fill ⟨room*ful*⟩
ful•crum \ˈfu̇l-krəm, ˈfəl-\ *n, pl* **ful•crums** *or* **ful•cra** \-krə\ **:** the support on which a lever turns
ful•fill *or* **ful•fil** \fu̇l-ˈfil\ *vb* **ful•filled; ful•fill•ing 1 :** to put into effect **2** ♦ **:** to bring to an end **3** ♦ **:** to meet the requirements of **:** SATISFY

♦ [2] accomplish, achieve, carry out, commit, compass, do, execute, follow through, make, perform ♦ [3] answer, comply, fill, keep, meet, redeem, satisfy ***Ant*** breach, break, violate

ful•fill•ment *n* ♦ **:** the act or process of fulfilling

♦ accomplishment, achievement, actuality, attainment, consummation, fruition, realization

¹full \ˈfu̇l\ *adj* **1** ♦ **:** containing as much or as many as is possible or normal **:** FILLED **2** ♦ **:** complete especially in detail, number, or duration **3** ♦ **:** having all the distinguishing characteristics ⟨a ~ member⟩ **4** ♦ **:** being at the highest or greatest degree **:** MAXIMUM **5 :** rounded in outline **:** being full or plump in form ⟨a ~ figure⟩ **6 :** possessing or containing an abundance ⟨~ of wrinkles⟩ **7 :** having an abundance of material ⟨a ~ skirt⟩ **8** ♦ **:** satisfied especially with food or drink **9 :** having volume or depth of sound **10 :** completely occupied with a thought or plan — **full·ness** *also* **ful·ness** *n*

♦ [1] brimful, crowded, loaded, packed, replete, rife ***Ant*** bare, empty, stark, vacant ♦ [2] complete, comprehensive, detailed, encyclopedic, inclusive, universal ♦ [3] complete, comprehensive, entire, total, whole ♦ [4] maximum, top, utmost ***Ant*** least, lowest, minimal, minimum ♦ [8] sated, satiate, satiated ***Ant*** empty, hungry, starving

²full *adv* **1 :** to a high degree **:** VERY, EXTREMELY **2** ♦ **:** to a complete degree **:** ENTIRELY **3 :** STRAIGHT, SQUARELY ⟨hit him ~ in the face⟩

♦ altogether, completely, entirely, fully, perfectly, quite, thoroughly, well, wholly

³full *n* **1 :** the highest or fullest state or degree **2 :** the utmost extent **3** ♦ **:** the requisite or complete amount

♦ aggregate, sum, total, totality, whole

⁴full *vb* **:** to shrink and thicken (woolen cloth) by moistening, heating, and pressing — **full·er** *n*

full·back \ˈfu̇l-ˌbak\ *n* **:** a football back stationed between the halfbacks

full–blood·ed \ˈfu̇l-ˈblə-dəd\ *adj* ♦ **:** of unmixed ancestry **:** PUREBRED

♦ purebred, thoroughbred

full–blown \-ˈblōn\ *adj* **1 :** being at the height of bloom **2** ♦ **:** fully mature or developed

♦ adult, full-fledged, mature, ripe

full–bod·ied \-ˈbä-dēd\ *adj* ♦ **:** marked by richness and fullness

♦ concentrated, full, potent, rich, robust, strong ***Ant*** light, mild, thin, weak

full dress *n* ♦ **:** the style of dress worn for ceremonial or formal occasions

♦ array, best, bravery, caparison, feather, finery, frippery, gaiety, regalia

full–fledged \ˈfu̇l-ˈflejd\ *adj* **1** ♦ **:** fully developed **2 :** having attained complete status ⟨a ~ lawyer⟩

♦ adult, full-blown, mature, ripe

full house *n* **:** a poker hand containing three of a kind and a pair

full moon *n* **:** the moon with its whole disk illuminated

full–on \-ˌȯn, -ˌän\ *adj* **:** COMPLETE, FULL-FLEDGED

full–scale \ˈfu̇l-ˈskāl\ *adj* **1 :** identical to an original in proportion and size ⟨~ drawing⟩ **2** ♦ **:** involving full use of available resources ⟨a ~ revolt⟩

♦ all-out, clean, complete, comprehensive, exhaustive, out-and-out, thorough, thoroughgoing, total

full–term \-ˌtərm\ *adj* **:** retained in the uterus for the normal period of gestation before birth ⟨a ~ baby⟩

full tilt *adv* ♦ **:** at high speed **:** with a rush

♦ fast, hastily, posthaste, rapidly, speedily, swiftly

full–time \ˈfu̇l-ˈtīm\ *adj or adv* **:** involving or working a normal or standard schedule

ful·ly \ˈfu̇-lē\ *adv* **1** ♦ **:** in a full manner or degree **:** COMPLETELY **2 :** at least

♦ altogether, chiefly, completely, entirely, generally, largely, mainly, mostly, perfectly, primarily, principally, quite, thoroughly, well, wholly ***Ant*** partially, partly

ful·mi·nate \ˈfu̇l-mə-ˌnāt, ˈfəl-\ *vb* **-nat·ed; -nat·ing** ♦ **:** to utter or send out censure or invective **:** condemn severely

♦ bluster, rant, rave, spout

ful·mi·na·tion \ˌfu̇l-mə-ˈnā-shən, ˌfəl-\ *n* ♦ **:** vehement menace or censure

♦ abuse, invective, vitriol, vituperation

ful·some \ˈfu̇l-səm\ *adj* **1 :** COPIOUS, ABUNDANT ⟨~ detail⟩ **2 :** generous in amount or extent ⟨a ~ victory⟩ **3** ♦ **:** excessively flattering ⟨~ praise⟩

♦ adulatory, unctuous

fu·ma·role \ˈfyü-mə-ˌrōl\ *n* **:** a hole in a volcanic region from which hot gases issue

¹fum·ble \ˈfəm-bəl\ *vb* **fum·bled; fum·bling 1 a** ♦ **:** to grope about clumsily **b :** make awkward attempts to do or find something **2** ♦ **:** to fail to hold, catch, or handle properly

♦ [1a] feel, fish, grope ♦ [2] bobble, botch, bungle, flub, foul up, mangle, mess up, screw up

²fumble *n* **:** an act or instance of fumbling

¹fume \ˈfyüm\ *n* **:** a usually irritating smoke, vapor, or gas

²fume *vb* **fumed; fum·ing 1 :** to treat with fumes **2 :** to give off fumes **3 a** ♦ **:** to express anger or annoyance **b** ♦ **:** to be in a state of excited irritation or anger

♦ [3a] rage, storm ♦ [3b] boil, burn, rage, seethe, steam

fu·mi·gant \ˈfyü-mi-gənt\ *n* **:** a substance used for fumigation

fu·mi·gate \ˈfyü-mə-ˌgāt\ *vb* **-gat·ed; -gat·ing :** to treat with fumes to disinfect or destroy pests — **fu·mi·ga·tion** \ˌfyü-mə-ˈgā-shən\ *n* — **fu·mi·ga·tor** \ˈfyü-mə-ˌgā-tər\ *n*

¹fun \ˈfən\ *n* **1** ♦ **:** something that provides amusement or enjoyment **2 :** the action or state of enjoying **:** ENJOYMENT **3** ♦ **:** a mood for finding or making amusement

♦ [1] delight, diversion, entertainment, pleasure ***Ant*** bore, bummer, downer, drag ♦ [1] frolic, fun, play, relaxation, sport ♦ [3] game, jest, play, sport ***Ant*** earnest

²fun *adj* ♦ **:** full of fun ⟨a ~ person⟩ ⟨had a ~ time⟩

♦ amusing, delightful, diverting, enjoyable, entertaining, pleasurable

¹func·tion \ˈfəŋk-shən\ *n* **1** ♦ **:** professional or official position of employment **2 :** special purpose **3** ♦ **:** the particular purpose for which a person or thing is specially fitted or used or for which a thing exists ⟨the ~ of a hammer⟩; *also* **:** the natural or proper action of a bodily part in a living thing ⟨the ~ of the heart⟩ **4** ♦ **:** a formal ceremony or social affair **5 :** a mathematical relationship that assigns to each element of a set one and only one element of the same or another set **6 :** a variable (as a quality, trait, or measurement) that depends on and varies with another ⟨height is a ~ of age in children⟩ **7 :** a computer subroutine that performs a calculation with variables provided by a program — **func·tion·al·ly** *adv*

♦ [1] appointment, billet, capacity, job, place, position, post, situation ♦ [3] capacity, job, part, place, position, purpose, role, task, work ♦ [4] affair, blowout, event, fete, get-together, party

²function *vb* ♦ **:** to have or carry on a function

♦ act, perform, serve, work

func·tion·al \-shə-nəl\ *adj* **1** ♦ **:** performing or able to perform a regular function **2 :** of, connected with, or being a function

♦ active, alive, living, on, operational, operative, running, working ♦ applicable, practicable, practical, serviceable, usable, useful, workable

func·tion·ary \ˈfəŋk-shə-ˌner-ē\ *n, pl* **-ar·ies** ♦ **:** one who performs a certain function; *esp* **:** one who holds a public office

♦ officeholder, officer, official, public servant

function word *n* **:** a word (as a preposition, auxiliary verb, or conjunction) expressing the grammatical relationship between other words

¹fund \ˈfənd\ *n* **1** ♦ **:** a sum of money or resources intended for a special purpose **2 :** STORE, SUPPLY **3 a** *pl* ♦ **:** available money **b** ♦ **:** an available quantity of material or intangible resources **4 :** an organization administering a special fund

♦ [1] account, budget, deposit, kitty, nest egg, pool ♦ *usu* **funds** [3a] finances, pocket, resources, wherewithal ♦ [3b] budget, pool, supply

²fund *vb* **1** ♦ **:** to provide funds for **2 :** to convert (a short-term obligation) into a long-term interest-bearing debt — **fund·er** *n*

♦ capitalize, endow, finance, stake, subsidize, underwrite

fun·da·men·tal \ˌfən-də-ˈment-ᵊl\ *adj* **1 :** serving as an origin **:** PRIMARY **2** ♦ **:** serving as a basis supporting existence or determining essential structure or function **:** BASIC, ESSENTIAL **3 :** RADICAL ⟨~ change⟩ **4 :** of central importance **:** PRINCIPAL — **fundamental** *n* — **fun·da·men·tal·ly** *adv*

♦ basic, elemental, elementary, essential, rudimentary, underlying

fun·da·men·tal·ism \-tə-ˌli-zəm\ *n* **1** *often cap* **:** a Protestant religious movement emphasizing the literal infallibility of the Bible **2 :** a movement or attitude stressing strict adherence to a set of basic principles — **fun·da·men·tal·ist** \-ist\ *adj or n*

[1]**fu•ner•al** \ˈfyü-nə-rəl\ *adj* **1 :** of, relating to, or constituting a funeral **2** ♦ **:** befitting or suggesting a funeral : FUNEREAL

♦ dolorous, funereal, lugubrious, mournful, plaintive, sorrowful, woeful

[2]**funeral** *n* **:** the ceremonies held for a dead person usually before burial

fu•ner•ary \ˈfyü-nə-ˌrer-ē\ *adj* **:** of, used for, or associated with burial

fu•ne•re•al \fyu̇-ˈnir-ē-əl\ *adj* **1 :** of or relating to a funeral **2** ♦ **:** suggesting a funeral

♦ bleak, dark, dismal, dreary, gloomy, gray (*or* grey), somber (*or* sombre), wretched

fun•gi•cide \ˈfən-jə-ˌsīd, ˈfəŋ-gə-\ *n* **:** an agent that kills or checks the growth of fungi — **fun•gi•cid•al** \ˌfən-jə-ˈsīd-ᵊl, ˌfən-gə-\ *adj*

fun•gus \ˈfəŋ-gəs\ *n, pl* **fun•gi** \ˈfən-ˌjī, ˈfəŋ-ˌgī\ *also* **fun•gus•es** \ˈfəŋ-gə-səz\ **:** any of a kingdom of parasitic spore-producing organisms (as molds, mildews, and mushrooms) formerly classified as plants — **fun•gal** \-gəl\ *adj* — **fun•gous** \-gəs\ *adj*

fu•nic•u•lar \fyu̇-ˈni-kyə-lər, fə-\ *n* **:** a cable railway ascending a mountain

[1]**funk** \ˈfəŋk\ *n* **:** a strong offensive smell

[2]**funk** *n* **:** a depressed state of mind

funky \ˈfəŋ-kē\ *adj* **funk•i•er; -est** **1 :** having an earthy unsophisticated style and feeling; *esp* **:** having the style and feeling of older black American music **2 :** odd or quaint in appearance or style

[1]**fun•nel** \ˈfən-ᵊl\ *n* **1 :** a cone-shaped utensil with a tube used for catching and directing a downward flow (as of liquid) **2 :** FLUE, SMOKESTACK

[2]**funnel** *vb* **-neled** *also* **-nelled; -nel•ing** *also* **-nel•ling** **1 :** to pass through or as if through a funnel **2** ♦ **:** to move to a central point or into a central channel

♦ channel, conduct, direct, pipe, siphon

fun•nies \ˈfə-nēz\ *n pl* **:** a comic strip or a comic section (as of a newspaper) — used with *the*

[1]**fun•ny** \ˈfə-nē\ *adj* **fun•ni•er; -est** **1** ♦ **:** affording light mirth and laughter **2** ♦ **:** seeking or intended to amuse **3** ♦ **:** differing from the ordinary in a suspicious, perplexing, quaint, or eccentric way **:** PECULIAR **4 :** UNDERHANDED — **funny** *adv*

♦ [1, 2] amusing, antic, comic, comical, droll, farcical, hilarious, humorous, laughable, ludicrous, mirthful, risible ***Ant*** humorless, lame, uncomic, unfunny ♦ [3] bizarre, curious, odd, peculiar, quaint, queer, quirky, strange, weird

[2]**funny** *n, pl* **funnies** **:** a comic strip or a comic section (as of a newspaper)

funny bone *n* **:** a place at the back of the elbow where a blow easily compresses a nerve and causes a painful tingling sensation

fun•plex \ˈfən-ˌpleks\ *n* **:** a center containing various entertainment facilities

[1]**fur** \ˈfər\ *n* **1 :** an article of clothing made of or with fur **2** ♦ **:** the hairy coat of a mammal especially when fine, soft, and thick **3** ♦ **:** an animal's coat dressed for use **4 :** a coating resembling fur — **fur** *adj* — **furred** \ˈfərd\ *adj*

♦ [2] coat, fleece, hair, pelage, pile, wool ♦ [3] hide, pelt, skin

[2]**fur** *abbr* furlong

fur•be•low \ˈfər-bə-ˌlō\ *n* **1** ♦ **:** a pleated or gathered piece of material **2 :** showy trimming

♦ flounce, frill, ruffle

fur•bish \ˈfər-bish\ *vb* **1 :** to make lustrous **:** POLISH **2 :** to give a new look to **:** RENOVATE

fu•ri•ous \ˈfyu̇r-ē-əs\ *adj* **1** ♦ **:** exhibiting or goaded by anger **:** indicative of or proceeding from anger **2 :** BOISTEROUS **3** ♦ **:** existing in an extreme degree **:** INTENSE **4** ♦ **:** full of activity — **fu•ri•ous•ly** *adv*

♦ [1] angry, enraged, irate ♦ [3] deep, ferocious, fierce, hard, heavy, intense, profound, terrible ♦ [4] crazy, delirious, excessive, extreme, feverish, fierce, frantic, frenetic, frenzied, inordinate, insane, intense, irrational, mad, rabid, vehement, violent, wild ***Ant*** relaxed

furl \ˈfərl\ *vb* **1 :** to wrap or roll (as a sail or a flag) close to or around something **2 :** to curl in furls — **furl** *n*

fur•long \ˈfər-ˌlȯŋ\ *n* **:** a unit of distance equal to 220 yards (about 201 meters)

fur•lough \ˈfər-lō\ *n* **1 :** a leave of absence from duty granted especially to a soldier **2 :** a leave of absence granted by an employer to an employee — **furlough** *vb*

fur•nace \ˈfər-nəs\ *n* **:** an enclosed structure in which heat is produced

fur•nish \ˈfər-nish\ *vb* **1** ♦ **:** to provide with what is needed **:** EQUIP **2** ♦ **:** to make available for use **:** SUPPLY, GIVE

♦ [1] accoutre, allocate, allot, assign, bestow, deal, dispense, distribute, donate, equip, fit, give, outfit, present, rig, store, supply ♦ [2] deliver, feed, give, hand, hand over, provide, supply ***Ant*** hold (back), keep (back), reserve, retain, withhold

fur•nish•ings \-ni-shiŋz\ *n pl* **1 :** articles or accessories of dress **2 :** an object that tends to increase comfort or utility; *esp* **:** an article of furniture

fur•ni•ture \ˈfər-ni-chər\ *n* **1 :** equipment that is necessary or desirable **2 :** movable articles (as chairs or beds) for a room

fu•ror \ˈfyu̇r-ˌȯr\ *n* **1** ♦ **:** an angry or maniacal fit **:** RAGE **2 :** a contagious excitement; *esp* **:** a fashionable craze **3** ♦ **:** furious or hectic activity **:** UPROAR

♦ [1] anger, fury, indignation, ire, outrage, rage, spleen, wrath, wrathfulness ♦ [3] commotion, disturbance, pandemonium, tumult, turmoil, uproar

fu•rore \-ˌōr\ *n* **1 :** a contagious excitement; *esp* **:** a fashionable craze **2 :** furious or hectic activity **:** UPROAR

fur•ri•er \ˈfər-ē-ər\ *n* **:** one who prepares or deals in fur

fur•ring \ˈfər-iŋ\ *n* **:** wood or metal strips applied to a wall or ceiling to form a level surface or an air space

[1]**fur•row** \ˈfər-ō\ *n* **1 :** a trench in the earth made by a plow **2** ♦ **:** a narrow groove or wrinkle

♦ crease, crimp, crinkle, wrinkle

[2]**furrow** *vb* **:** to make or form furrows, grooves, wrinkles, or lines

fur•ry \ˈfər-ē\ *adj* **fur•ri•er; -est** **1** ♦ **:** resembling or consisting of fur **2** ♦ **:** covered with fur

♦ [1] fuzzy, hairy, rough, shaggy, woolly ♦ [2] fleecy, hairy, hirsute, rough, shaggy, unshorn, woolly

[1]**fur•ther** \ˈfər-t͟hər\ *adv* **1** ♦ **:** at or to a greater distance or more advanced point **:** FARTHER **2** ♦ **:** in addition **:** MOREOVER **3 :** to a greater extent or degree

♦ [1] beyond, farther, yonder ♦ [2] additionally, again, also, besides, more, moreover, then, too

[2]**further** *vb* ♦ **:** to promote or help advance

♦ advance, cultivate, encourage, forward, foster, nourish, nurture, promote

[3]**further** *adj* **1 :** FARTHER 1 **2** ♦ **:** going or extending beyond what exists **:** ADDITIONAL

♦ additional, another, else, farther, more, other

fur•ther•ance \ˈfər-t͟hə-rəns\ *n* ♦ **:** the act of furthering

♦ advance, advancement, passage, process, procession, progress, progression

fur•ther•more \ˈfər-t͟hər-ˌmōr\ *adv* ♦ **:** in addition to what precedes **:** BESIDES

♦ additionally, again, also, besides, more, too, withal, yet

fur•ther•most \-ˌmōst\ *adj* **:** most distant **:** FARTHEST

fur•thest \ˈfər-t͟həst\ *adv or adj* ♦ **:** to or at the greatest distance in space **:** FARTHEST

♦ extreme, farthest, outermost, ultimate, utmost

fur•tive \ˈfər-tiv\ *adj* ♦ **:** done by stealth — **fur•tive•ly** *adv* — **fur•tive•ness** *n*

♦ clandestine, covert, secret, sneaky, stealthy, surreptitious, undercover

fu•ry \ˈfyu̇r-ē\ *n, pl* **furies** **1** ♦ **:** intense and often destructive rage **2 :** extreme fierceness or violence **3** ♦ **:** a state of inspired exaltation **:** FRENZY **4** ♦ **:** one who resembles an avenging spirit; *esp* **:** a spiteful woman

♦ [1] anger, furor, indignation, ire, outrage, rage, spleen, wrath, wrathfulness ♦ [3] agitation, delirium, distraction, frenzy, furor, hysteria, rage, rampage, uproar ♦ [4] harpy, shrew, termagant, virago

furze \ˈfərz\ *n* **:** GORSE

[1]**fuse** \ˈfyüz\ *vb* **fused; fus•ing** **1** ♦ **:** to reduce to a liquid or plastic state by heat **:** MELT **2** ♦ **:** to unite by or as if by melting together — **fus•ible** *adj*

♦ [1] deliquesce, flux, liquefy, melt, run, thaw ♦ [2] associate, coalesce, combine, couple, join, link, marry, unify, unite ♦ [2] amalgamate, blend, commingle, merge, mingle

[2]**fuse** *n* **:** an electrical safety device having a metal wire or strip that melts and interrupts the circuit when the current becomes too strong

[3]**fuse** *n* **1 :** a cord or cable that is set afire to ignite an explosive charge **2** *usu* **fuze :** a mechanical or electrical device for setting off the explosive charge of a projectile, bomb, or torpedo

[4]**fuse** *also* **fuze** \ˈfyüz\ *vb* **fused** *or* **fuzed; fus•ing** *or* **fuz•ing :** to equip with a fuse

fu•se•lage \ˈfyü-sə-ˌläzh, -zə-\ *n* **:** the central body portion of an aircraft

fu•sil•lade \ˈfyü-sə-ˌläd, -ˌlād\ *n* **1 :** a number of shots fired simultaneously or in rapid succession **2 ♦ :** something that gives the effect of a fusillade

♦ barrage, bombardment, cannonade, hail, salvo, shower, storm, volley

fu•sion \ˈfyü-zhən\ *n* **1 :** the act or process of melting or making plastic by heat **2 ♦ :** union by or as if by melting **3 :** the union of light atomic nuclei to form heavier nuclei with the release of huge quantities of energy

♦ [2] admixture, amalgam, blend, combination, composite, compound, intermixture, mix, mixture

[1]**fuss** \ˈfəs\ *n* **1 ♦ :** needless bustle or excitement **:** COMMOTION **2 :** effusive praise **3 ♦ :** a state of agitation **4 ♦ :** an act of objecting **5 :** DISPUTE

♦ [1] bother, bustle, commotion, furor, hubbub, hullabaloo, pandemonium, stir, tumult, turmoil, uproar ♦ [3] dither, fluster, fret, huff, lather, pother, stew, tizzy, twitter ♦ [4] challenge, complaint, demur, expostulation, kick, objection, protest, question, remonstrance

[2]**fuss** *vb* **1 :** to make a fuss **2 a ♦ :** to give flattering or doting attention to **b :** to pay close or undue attention to small details **3 ♦ :** to express annoyance or complaint

♦ [2a] enthuse, fawn, gush, rave, rhapsodize, slobber ♦ [3] beef, carp, complain, crab, gripe, grouse, moan, squawk

fuss•bud•get \ˈfəs-ˌbə-jət\ *n* **:** one who fusses or is fussy about trifles

fussy \ˈfə-sē\ *adj* **fuss•i•er; -est 1 ♦ :** nervous or easily upset **2 :** overly decorated **3 ♦ :** requiring or giving close attention or concern to details or niceties; *also* **:** overly difficult to please — **fuss•i•ly** \-sə-lē\ *adv* — **fuss•i•ness** \-sē-nəs\ *n*

♦ [1] crabby, cranky, grouchy, grumpy, querulous *Ant* uncomplaining ♦ [3] choosy, dainty, delicate, demanding, exacting, fastidious, finicky, meticulous, painstaking, particular, picky

fus•tian \ˈfəs-chən\ *n* **1 :** a strong usually cotton fabric **2 :** pretentious writing or speech — **fustian** *adj*

fus•ty \ˈfəs-tē\ *adj* **fus•ti•er; -est 1 ♦ :** saturated with dust and stale odors **:** MUSTY **2 :** OLD-FASHIONED

♦ malodorous, musty, smelly

fut *abbr* future

fu•tile \ˈfyüt-ᵊl, ˈfyü-ˌtīl\ *adj* **1 ♦ :** serving no useful purpose **:** USELESS, VAIN **2 :** FRIVOLOUS, TRIVIAL — **fu•tile•ly** *adv* — **fu•til•i•ty** \fyü-ˈti-lə-tē\ *n*

♦ empty, fruitless, hopeless, ineffective, meaningless, pointless, unproductive, unsuccessful, useless, vain *Ant* effective, fruitful, productive, profitable, successful

fu•ton \ˈfü-ˌtän\ *n* **:** a usually cotton-filled mattress used on the floor or in a frame as a bed, couch, or chair

[1]**fu•ture** \ˈfyü-chər\ *adj* **1 :** of, relating to, or constituting a verb tense that expresses time yet to come **2 :** coming after the present

[2]**future** *n* **1 ♦ :** time that is to come **2 :** what is going to happen **3 :** an expectation of advancement or progressive development **4 :** the future tense; *also* **:** a verb form in it

♦ hereafter *Ant* past

fu•tur•ism \ˈfyü-chə-ˌri-zəm\ *n* **:** a modern movement in art, music, and literature that tries especially to express the energy and activity of mechanical processes

fu•tur•ist \ˈfyü-chə-rist\ *n* **♦ :** one who studies and predicts the future especially on the basis of current trends

♦ augur, diviner, forecaster, fortune-teller, prognosticator, prophet, seer, soothsayer

fu•tur•is•tic \ˌfyü-chə-ˈris-tik\ *adj* **:** of or relating to the future or to futurism; *also* **:** very modern

fu•tu•ri•ty \fyü-ˈtu̇r-ə-tē, -ˈtyu̇r-\ *n, pl* **-ties 1 :** time that is to come **:** FUTURE **2 :** the quality or state of being future **3** *pl* **:** future events or prospects

fuze *var of* FUSE

fuzz \ˈfəz\ *n* **♦ :** fine light particles or fibers (as of down or fluff)

♦ down, floss, fluff, fur, lint, nap, pile

fuzzy \ˈfə-zē\ *adj* **fuzz•i•er; -est 1 ♦ :** having or resembling fuzz **2 ♦ :** lacking in clarity or definition **3 :** being or relating to pleasant usually sentimental emotions ⟨~ feelings⟩ — **fuzz•i•ness** \-zē-nəs\ *n*

♦ [1] furry, hairy, rough, shaggy, woolly ♦ [2] indefinite, unclear, vague

fuzzy logic *n* **:** a system of logic in which a statement can be true, false, or any of a continuum of values in between

fwd *abbr* forward

FWD *abbr* front-wheel drive

FY *abbr* fiscal year

-fy *vb suffix* **:** make **:** form into ⟨dandi*fy*⟩

FYI *abbr* for your information

G

[1]**g** \ˈjē\ *n, pl* **g's** *or* **gs** \ˈjēz\ *often cap* **1 :** the 7th letter of the English alphabet **2 :** a unit of force equal to the force exerted by gravity on a body at rest and used to indicate the force to which a body is subjected when accelerated **3** *slang* **:** a sum of $1000

[2]**g** *abbr, often cap* **1** game **2** gauge **3** good **4** gram **5** gravity

ga *abbr* gauge

[1]**Ga** *abbr* Georgia

[2]**Ga** *symbol* gallium

GA *abbr* **1** general assembly **2** general average **3** general of the army **4** Georgia

gab \ˈgab\ *vb* **gabbed; gab•bing ♦ :** to talk in a rapid or thoughtless manner **:** CHATTER — **gab** *n*

♦ chat, converse, gab, jaw, palaver, patter, prattle, rattle, talk, visit

gab•ar•dine \ˈga-bər-ˌdēn\ *n* **1 :** GABERDINE 1 **2 :** a firm durable twilled fabric having diagonal ribs and made of various fibers; *also* **:** a garment of gabardine

gab•ble \ˈga-bəl\ *vb* **gab•bled; gab•bling ♦ :** to talk fast or foolishly **:** JABBER, BABBLE

♦ babble, chatter, drivel, gibber, jabber, prattle, sputter

gab•by \ˈga-bē\ *adj* **gab•bi•er; -est ♦ :** pointlessly or annoyingly talkative **:** GARRULOUS

♦ chatty, conversational, garrulous, loquacious, talkative

gab•er•dine \ˈga-bər-ˌdēn\ *n* **1 :** a long loose outer garment worn in medieval times and associated especially with Jews **2 :** GABARDINE 2

gab•fest \ˈgab-ˌfest\ *n* **1 :** an informal gathering for general talk **2 ♦ :** an extended conversation

♦ chat, chatter, chitchat, gossip, palaver, rap, talk

ga•ble \ˈgā-bəl\ *n* **:** the vertical triangular end of a building formed by the sides of the roof sloping from the ridge down to the eaves — **ga•bled** \-bəld\ *adj*

Gab•o•nese \ˌga-bə-ˈnēz, -ˈnēs\ *n* **:** a native or inhabitant of Gabon — **Gabonese** *adj*

gad \ˈgad\ *vb* **gad•ded; gad•ding ♦ :** to be constantly active without specific purpose — usually used with *about* — **gad•der** *n*

♦ *usu* **gad about** gallivant, knock, meander, rove, traipse, wander

gad•about \ˈga-də-ˌbau̇t\ *n* : a person who flits about in social activity

gad•fly \ˈgad-ˌflī\ *n* **1** : a fly that bites or harasses livestock **2** ♦ : a person who annoys especially by persistent criticism

♦ annoyance, bother, nuisance, persecutor, pest, tease

gad•get \ˈga-jət\ *n* ♦ : an often small mechanical or electronic device with a practical use but often thought of as a novelty : CONTRIVANCE — **gad•get•ry** \ˈga-jə-trē\ *n*

♦ contraption, contrivance, gimmick, gizmo, jigger

gad•o•lin•i•um \ˌga-də-ˈli-nē-əm\ *n* : a magnetic metallic chemical element

[1]Gael \ˈgāl\ *n* : a Celtic inhabitant of Ireland or Scotland

[2]Gael *abbr* Gaelic

Gael•ic \ˈgā-lik\ *adj* : of or relating to the Gaels or their languages — **Gaelic** *n*

gaff \ˈgaf\ *n* **1** : a spear used in taking fish or turtles; *also* : a metal hook for holding or lifting heavy fish **2** : the spar supporting the top of a fore-and-aft sail **3** : rough treatment : ABUSE — **gaff** *vb*

gaffe \ˈgaf\ *n* **1** ♦ : a usually social blunder **2** ♦ : a noticeable mistake

♦ [1] familiarity, impropriety, indiscretion ♦ [2] blunder, error, fault, flub, fumble, goof, lapse, miscue, misstep, mistake, oversight, screwup, slip, stumble, trip

gaf•fer \ˈga-fər\ *n* **1** : an old man **2** : a lighting electrician on a motion-picture or television set

[1]gag \ˈgag\ *vb* **gagged; gag•ging** **1** : to restrict use of the mouth with a gag **2** : to prevent from speaking freely **3** ♦ : to retch or cause to retch **4** : OBSTRUCT, CHOKE **5** : BALK **6** : to make quips — **gag•ger** *n*

♦ heave, spit up, throw up, vomit

[2]gag *n* **1** : something thrust into the mouth especially to prevent speech or outcry **2** : an official check or restraint on free speech **3** ♦ : a laugh-provoking remark or act **4** : PRANK, TRICK

♦ crack, jest, joke, laugh, pleasantry, quip, sally, waggery, wisecrack, witticism

[1]gage \ˈgāj\ *n* **1** : a token of defiance; *esp* : a glove or cap cast on the ground as a pledge of combat **2** ♦ : something deposited as a pledge of performance : SECURITY

♦ guarantee, guaranty, pawn, pledge, security

[2]gage *var of* GAUGE

gag•gle \ˈga-gəl\ *n* **1** : a flock of geese **2** : an unorganized group

gai•ety \ˈgā-ə-tē\ *n, pl* **-eties** **1** ♦ : festive activity : MERRYMAKING **2** : MERRIMENT **3** ♦ : dressy or showy clothing and jewels : FINERY

♦ [1] conviviality, festivity, jollification, merriment, merrymaking, revelry ♦ [3] array, best, bravery, caparison, feather, finery, frippery, full dress, regalia

gai•ly \ˈgā-lē\ *adv* ♦ : in a gay manner

♦ cheerfully, happily, heartily, jovially, merrily, mirthfully ***Ant*** bleakly, cheerlessly, darkly, heavily, miserably, morosely, unhappily ♦ exuberantly, jauntily, sprightly ***Ant*** dully, inanimately, sluggishly, tardily ♦ flamboyantly, flashily, jauntily, rakishly ***Ant*** conservatively, plain, quietly

[1]gain \ˈgān\ *n* **1** ♦ : resources or advantage acquired or increased : PROFIT **2** : ACQUISITION, ACCUMULATION **3** ♦ : an increase in amount, magnitude, or degree

♦ [1] earnings, lucre, net, payoff, proceeds, profit, return ♦ [3] accretion, addition, augmentation, boost, expansion, increase, increment, plus, proliferation, raise, rise, supplement

[2]gain *vb* **1** ♦ : to get possession of usually by effort, merit, or craft : EARN **2** : WIN ⟨~ a victory⟩ **3** ♦ : to increase in ⟨~ momentum⟩ **4** : PERSUADE **5** : to arrive at **6** : ACHIEVE ⟨~ strength⟩ **7** : to run fast ⟨the watch ~*s* a minute a day⟩ **8** : PROFIT **9** : INCREASE **10** ♦ : to improve in health — **gain•er** *n*

♦ [1] acquire, attain, capture, carry, draw, earn, garner, get, land, make, obtain, procure, realize, secure, win ♦ [3] build, gather, grow, pick up ***Ant*** decrease (in), lose ♦ [10] convalesce, heal, mend, rally, recover, recuperate, snap back

gain•ful \ˈgān-fəl\ *adj* ♦ : productive of gain : PROFITABLE — **gain•ful•ly** *adv*

♦ fat, lucrative, profitable, remunerative

gain•say \ˌgān-ˈsā\ *vb* **-said** \-ˈsād, -ˈsed\; **-say•ing; -says** \-ˈsāz, -ˈsez\ **1** ♦ : to declare to be untrue or invalid : DENY **2** : to speak against — **gain•say•er** *n*

♦ contradict, deny, disallow, disavow, disclaim, negate, negative, reject, repudiate

gait \ˈgāt\ *n* : manner of moving on foot; *also* : a particular pattern or style of such moving — **gait•ed** *adj*

gai•ter \ˈgā-tər\ *n* **1** : a leg covering reaching from the instep to ankle, mid-calf, or knee **2** : an overshoe with a fabric upper **3** : an ankle-high shoe with elastic gores in the sides

[1]gal \ˈgal\ *n* : a young unmarried woman : GIRL

[2]gal *abbr* gallon

Gal *abbr* Galatians

ga•la \ˈgā-lə, ˈga-, ˈgä-\ *n* ♦ : a festive celebration : FESTIVITY — **gala** *adj*

♦ carnival, celebration, festival, festivity, fete, fiesta, jubilee

ga•lac•tic \gə-ˈlak-tik\ *adj* : of or relating to a galaxy

Ga•la•tians \gə-ˈlā-shənz\ *n* : an argumentative letter of St. Paul written to the Christians of Galatia and included as a book in the New Testament

gal•axy \ˈga-lək-sē\ *n, pl* **-ax•ies** **1** *often cap* : MILKY WAY GALAXY — used with *the* **2** : a very large group of stars **3** : an assemblage of brilliant or famous persons or things

gale \ˈgāl\ *n* **1** : a strong wind **2** ♦ : an emotional outburst ⟨~*s* of laughter⟩

♦ agony, burst, eruption, explosion, fit, flare, flare-up, flash, flush, gush, gust, outburst, paroxysm, spasm, storm

ga•le•na \gə-ˈlē-nə\ *n* : a lustrous bluish gray mineral that consists of the sulfide of lead and is the chief ore of lead

[1]gall \ˈgȯl\ *n* **1** : BILE **2** : something bitter to endure **3** ♦ : bitterness of spirit : RANCOR **4** ♦ : brazen boldness coupled with impudent assurance and insolence : IMPUDENCE

♦ [3] animosity, antagonism, antipathy, bitterness, enmity, grudge, hostility, rancor ♦ [4] audacity, brass, brazenness, cheek, chutzpah, effrontery, impudence, nerve, presumption, sauce, sauciness, temerity

[2]gall *n* : a skin sore caused by chafing

[3]gall *vb* **1** ♦ : to make or become sore or worn by rubbing : CHAFE **2** ♦ : to provoke impatience, anger, or displeasure in : VEX

♦ [1] abrade, chafe, erode, fray, fret, rub, wear ♦ [2] aggravate, annoy, bother, bug, chafe, exasperate, get, grate, irk, irritate, nettle, peeve, persecute, pique, put out, rasp, rile, vex

[4]gall *n* : an abnormal outgrowth of plant tissue usually due to parasites

[1]gal•lant \gə-ˈlant, -ˈlänt; ˈga-lənt\ *n* **1** ♦ : a young man of fashion **2** : a man who shows a marked fondness for the company of women and who is especially attentive to them **3** : one who courts a woman or seeks to marry her : SUITOR

♦ buck, dandy, dude, fop

[2]gal•lant \ˈga-lənt (*usual for 2, 3, 4*); gə-ˈlant, -ˈlänt (*usual for 5*)\ *adj* **1** : showy in dress or bearing : SMART **2** : impressive in size or splendor : SPLENDID, STATELY **3** ♦ : full of energy, animation, or courage : SPIRITED, BRAVE **4** ♦ : nobly chivalrous and often self-sacrificing **5** : polite and attentive to women

♦ [3] brave, courageous, dauntless, doughty, fearless, heroic, intrepid, spirited, stalwart, stout, undaunted, valiant, valorous ♦ [4] chivalrous, great, greathearted, high, high-minded, lofty, lordly, magnanimous, noble, sublime

gal•lant•ly *adv* ♦ : in a gallant manner

♦ grandly, greatly, heroically, honorably (*or* honourably), magnanimously, nobly

gal•lant•ry \ˈga-lən-trē\ *n, pl* **-ries** **1** *archaic* : gallant appearance **2** : an act of marked courtesy **3** : courteous attention to a woman **4** ♦ : conspicuous bravery

♦ bravery, courage, daring, fearlessness, guts, hardihood, heart, heroism, nerve, stoutness, valor

gall•blad•der \ˈgȯl-ˌbla-dər\ *n* : a membranous muscular sac attached to the liver and serving to store bile

gal•le•on \ˈga-lē-ən\ *n* : a large square-rigged sailing ship formerly used especially by the Spanish

gal•le•ria \ˌga-lə-ˈrē-ə\ *n* : a roofed and usually glass-enclosed promenade or court

gal•lery \ˈga-lə-rē\ *n, pl* **-ler•ies** **1** : an outdoor balcony; *also* : PORCH, VERANDA **2** ♦ : a long narrow passage, apartment, or hall **3** : a narrow passage (as one made underground by a miner or through wood by an insect) **4** : a room where works of art are exhibited; *also* : an organization dealing in works of art **5** : a balcony in a theater, auditorium, or church; *esp* : the highest one in a theater **6 :** the spectators at a tennis or golf match **7 :** a photographer's studio — **gal•ler•ied** \-rēd\ *adj*

♦ corridor, hall, hallway, passage

gal•ley \ˈga-lē\ *n, pl* **galleys 1 :** a long low ship propelled especially by oars and formerly used especially in the Mediterranean Sea **2 :** the kitchen especially of a ship or airplane **3 :** a proof of typeset matter especially in a single column
Gal•lic \ˈga-lik\ *adj* **:** of or relating to Gaul or France
gal•li•mau•fry \ˌga-lə-ˈmȯ-frē\ *n, pl* **-fries :** HODGEPODGE
gall•ing \ˈgȯ-liŋ\ ♦ **:** markedly irritating

♦ aggravating, annoying, bothersome, frustrating, irksome, irritating, pesty, vexatious

gal•li•nule \ˈga-lə-ˌnül, -ˌnyül\ *n* **:** any of several aquatic birds related to the rails
gal•li•um \ˈga-lē-əm\ *n* **:** a bluish white metallic chemical element
gal•li•vant \ˈga-lə-ˌvant\ *vb* ♦ **:** to travel, roam, or move about for pleasure

♦ gad, knock, maunder, meander, mope, ramble, range, roam, rove, traipse, wander

gal•lon \ˈga-lən\ *n* **:** a unit of liquid capacity equal to 231 cubic inches or four quarts
¹gal•lop \ˈga-ləp\ *vb* **1 :** to go or cause to go at a gallop **2** ♦ **:** to run fast — **gal•lop•er** *n*

♦ dash, jog, run, scamper, sprint, trip

²gallop *n* **1 :** a bounding gait of a quadruped; *esp* **:** a fast 3-beat gait of a horse **2 :** a ride or run at a gallop
gal•lows \ˈga-lōz\ *n, pl* **gallows** *or* **gal•lows•es :** a frame usually of two upright posts and a crosspiece from which criminals are hanged; *also* **:** the punishment of hanging
gall•stone \ˈgȯl-ˌstōn\ *n* **:** an abnormal concretion occurring in the gallbladder or bile passages
gal•lus•es \ˈga-lə-səz\ *n pl* **:** SUSPENDERS
ga•lore \gə-ˈlōr\ *adj* **:** amply supplied **:** characterized by, constituting, or existing in plenty
ga•losh \gə-ˈläsh\ *n* **:** a high overshoe
galv *abbr* galvanized
gal•va•nise *chiefly Brit var of* GALVANIZE
gal•va•nize \ˈgal-və-ˌnīz\ *vb* **-nized; -niz•ing 1** ♦ **:** to stimulate as if by an electric shock **2 :** to coat (iron or steel) with zinc — **gal•va•ni•za•tion** \ˌgal-və-nə-ˈzā-shən\ *n* — **gal•va•niz•er** *n*

♦ electrify, excite, exhilarate, intoxicate, thrill, titillate, turn on

gal•va•nom•e•ter \ˌgal-və-ˈnä-mə-tər\ *n* **:** an instrument for detecting or measuring a small electric current
Gam•bi•an \ˈgam-bē-ən\ *n* **:** a native or inhabitant of Gambia — **Gambian** *adj*
gam•bit \ˈgam-bət\ *n* **1 :** a chess opening in which a player risks one or more minor pieces to gain an advantage in position **2 :** a calculated move **:** STRATAGEM
¹gam•ble \ˈgam-bəl\ *vb* **gam•bled; gam•bling 1 :** to play a game for money or property **2** ♦ **:** to bet on an uncertain outcome **:** WAGER **3** ♦ **:** to expose to hazard **:** VENTURE, HAZARD

♦ [2] bet, go, lay, stake, wager ♦ *usu* **gamble on** [2] chance, hazard, risk, venture ♦ *usu* **gamble with** [3] adventure, compromise, hazard, imperil, jeopardize, menace, risk, venture

²gamble *n* ♦ **:** something chancy

♦ chance, enterprise, flier, speculation, venture

gam•bol \ˈgam-bəl\ *vb* **-boled** *or* **-bolled; -bol•ing** *or* **-bol•ling** ♦ **:** to skip about in play **:** FRISK

♦ caper, cavort, disport, frisk, frolic, lark, rollick, romp, sport

gambol *n* **:** a skipping or leaping about in play
gam•brel roof \ˈgam-brəl-\ *n* **:** a roof with a lower steeper slope and an upper flatter one on each side
¹game \ˈgām\ *n* **1 :** AMUSEMENT, DIVERSION **2** ♦ **:** often derisive or mocking jesting **:** SPORT, FUN **3** ♦ **:** a procedure or strategy for gaining an end **:** SCHEME, PROJECT **4 :** a line of work **:** PROFESSION **5** ♦ **:** a physical or mental competition conducted according to rules with the participants in direct opposition to each other **:** CONTEST **6 :** animals hunted for sport or food; *also* **:** the flesh of a game animal

♦ [2] fun, jest, play, sport ♦ [3] arrangement, blueprint, design, plan, project, scheme, strategy, system ♦ [5] bout, competition, contest, event, match, meet, tournament

²game *vb* **gamed; gam•ing :** to play for a stake **:** GAMBLE
³game *adj* ♦ **:** having or showing a resolute unyielding spirit; *also* **:** willing or ready to proceed — **game•ly** *adv*

♦ amenable, disposed, glad, inclined, ready, willing

⁴game *adj* **:** LAME ⟨a ~ leg⟩
game•cock \ˈgām-ˌkäk\ *n* **:** a rooster trained for fighting
game fish *n* **:** SPORT FISH
game•keep•er \ˈgām-ˌkē-pər\ *n* **:** a person in charge of the breeding and protection of game animals or birds on a private preserve
game•ness *n* ♦ **:** the state or quality of being game

♦ alacrity, goodwill, willingness

game•some \ˈgām-səm\ *adj* **:** MERRY
game•ster \ˈgām-stər\ *n* **:** a person who gambles
gam•ete \ˈga-ˌmēt\ *n* **:** a mature germ cell — **ga•met•ic** \gə-ˈme-tik\ *adj*
game theory *n* **:** the analysis of a situation involving conflicting interests (as in business) in terms of gains and losses among opposing players
gam•in \ˈga-mən\ *n* **1 :** a boy who hangs around on the streets **2 :** GAMINE 2
ga•mine \ga-ˈmēn\ *n* **1 :** a girl who hangs around on the streets **2 :** a small playfully mischievous girl
gam•ma \ˈga-mə\ *n* **:** the 3d letter of the Greek alphabet — Γ *or* γ
gamma globulin *n* **:** a blood protein fraction rich in antibodies; *also* **:** a solution of this from human blood donors that is given to provide immunity against some infectious diseases (as measles)
gamma ray *n* **:** a photon emitted by a radioactive substance; *also* **:** a high-energy photon — usually used in plural
gam•mer \ˈga-mər\ *n, archaic* **:** an old woman
gam•mon \ˈga-mən\ *n, chiefly Brit* **:** a cured ham or side of bacon
gam•ut \ˈga-mət\ *n* ♦ **:** an entire range or series

♦ range, scale, spectrum, spread, stretch

gamy *or* **gam•ey** \ˈgā-mē\ *adj* **gam•i•er; -est 1 :** GAME, PLUCKY **2 :** having the flavor of game especially when near tainting **3 :** SCANDALOUS; *also* **:** DISREPUTABLE — **gam•i•ness** \-mē-nəs\ *n*
¹gan•der \ˈgan-dər\ *n* **:** a male goose
²gander *n* ♦ **:** the act of looking **:** GLANCE

♦ cast, eye, glance, glimpse, look, peek, peep, regard, sight, view

¹gang \ˈgaŋ\ *n* **1 :** a set of implements or devices arranged to operate together **2 a** ♦ **:** a group of persons working or associated together **b** ♦ **:** a group of criminals or young delinquents

♦ [2a] band, company, crew, outfit, party, squad, team
♦ [2a] circle, clan, clique, coterie, crowd, fold, ring, set
♦ [2b] cabal, conspiracy, mob, ring, syndicate

²gang *vb* **1 :** to attack in a gang — usually used with *up* **2 :** to form into or move or act as a gang
gang•land \ˈgaŋ-ˌland\ *n* **:** the world of organized crime
gan•gling \ˈgaŋ-gliŋ\ *adj* ♦ **:** loosely and awkwardly built **:** LANKY

♦ lanky, rangy, spindly

gan•gli•on \ˈgaŋ-glē-ən\ *n, pl* **-glia** \-ə\ *also* **-gli•ons :** a mass of nerve tissue containing cell bodies of neurons outside the central nervous system; *also* **:** NUCLEUS 3 — **gan•gli•on•ic** \ˌgaŋ-glē-ˈä-nik\ *adj*
gan•gly \ˈgaŋ-glē\ *adj* **:** GANGLING
gang•plank \ˈgaŋ-ˌplaŋk\ *n* **:** a movable bridge from a ship to the shore
gang•plow \-ˌplau̇\ *n* **:** a plow that turns two or more furrows at one time
gan•grene \ˈgaŋ-ˌgrēn, gaŋ-ˈgrēn\ *n* **:** the death of soft tissues in a local area of the body due to loss of the blood supply — **gangrene** *vb* — **gan•gre•nous** \ˈgaŋ-grə-nəs\ *adj*
gang•ster \ˈgaŋ-stər\ *n* ♦ **:** a member of a gang of criminals **:** RACKETEER

♦ bully, goon, hood, hoodlum, mobster, mug, punk, rowdy, ruffian, thug, tough

gang•way \ˈgaŋ-ˌwā\ *n* **1 :** PASSAGEWAY; *also* **:** GANGPLANK **2 :** clear passage through a crowd
gan•net \ˈga-nət\ *n, pl* **gannets** *also* **gannet :** any of several large fish-eating usually white and black seabirds that breed chiefly on offshore islands
gantlet *var of* GAUNTLET
gan•try \ˈgan-trē\ *n, pl* **gantries :** a frame structure on side supports over or around something
GAO *abbr* General Accounting Office
gaol \ˈjāl\, **gaol•er** \ˈjā-lər\ *chiefly Brit var of* JAIL, JAILER
gap \ˈgap\ *n* **1 :** BREACH, CLEFT **2** ♦ **:** a mountain pass **3** ♦ **:** a blank space; *also* **:** an incomplete or deficient area **4 :** a wide dif-

ference in character or attitude **5 :** a problem caused by a disparity ⟨credibility ~⟩

♦ [2] canyon, defile, flume, gorge, gulch, notch, pass, ravine ♦ [3] breach, break, gulf, hole, opening, rent, rift, separation ♦ [3] discontinuity, hiatus, interim, interlude, intermission, interruption, interval ***Ant*** continuation, continuity

gape \ˈgāp\ *vb* **gaped; gap•ing 1 :** to open the mouth wide **2 :** to open or part widely **3** ♦ **:** to stare with mouth open **4 :** YAWN — **gape** *n*

♦ gawk, gaze, goggle, peer, rubberneck, stare

1gar \ˈgär\ *n* **:** any of several fishes that have a long body resembling that of a pike and long narrow jaws
2gar *abbr* garage
GAR *abbr* Grand Army of the Republic
1ga•rage \gə-ˈräzh, -ˈräj\ *n* **:** a shelter or repair shop for automobiles
2garage *vb* **ga•raged; ga•rag•ing :** to keep or put in a garage
garage sale *n* **:** a sale of used household or personal articles held on the seller's own premises
1garb \ˈgärb\ *n* **1** ♦ **:** style of dress **2 :** outward form **:** APPEARANCE

♦ dress, getup, guise, outfit

2garb *vb* ♦ **:** to cover with or as if with clothing

♦ apparel, array, attire, caparison, clothe, deck, dress, invest, rig, suit

gar•bage \ˈgär-bij\ *n* **1 :** food waste **2** ♦ **:** unwanted or useless material — **gar•bage•man** \-ˌman\ *n*

♦ chaff, deadwood, dust, junk, litter, refuse, riffraff, rubbish, scrap, trash, waste ***Ant*** find, prize

gar•ble \ˈgär-bəl\ *vb* **gar•bled; gar•bling** ♦ **:** to distort the meaning of ⟨~ a story⟩

♦ color (*or* colour), distort, falsify, misinterpret, misrepresent, misstate, pervert, twist, warp

gar•çon \gär-ˈsōⁿ\ *n, pl* **garçons** *same or* -ˈsōⁿz\ **:** WAITER
1gar•den \ˈgär-dᵊn\ *n* **1 :** a plot for growing fruits, flowers, or vegetables **2 :** a public recreation area; *esp* **:** one for displaying plants or animals
2garden *vb* **:** to lay out or work in a garden — **gar•den•er** *n*
gar•de•nia \gär-ˈdē-nyə\ *n* **:** any of a genus of tropical trees or shrubs that are related to the madder and have fragant white or yellow flowers; *also* **:** one of these trees
garden–variety *adj* **:** COMMONPLACE, ORDINARY
gar•fish \ˈgär-ˌfish\ *n* **:** GAR
gar•gan•tuan \gär-ˈgan-chə-wən\ *adj, often cap* ♦ **:** of tremendous size or volume

♦ colossal, enormous, giant, ginormous, huge, jumbo, mammoth, massive, prodigious, titanic, tremendous

gar•gle \ˈgär-gəl\ *vb* **gar•gled; gar•gling :** to rinse the throat with liquid agitated by air forced through it from the lungs — **gargle** *n*
gar•goyle \ˈgär-ˌgȯ(-ə)il\ *n* **1 :** a waterspout in the form of a grotesque human or animal figure projecting from the roof or eaves of a building **2 :** a grotesquely carved figure
gar•ish \ˈgar-ish\ *adj* **1 :** clothed in vivid colors **:** excessively or disturbingly vivid **2** ♦ **:** tastelessly showy **:** FLASHY, GAUDY

♦ flamboyant, flashy, gaudy, glitzy, loud, ostentatious, swank, tawdry

gar•ish•ness *n* **:** the quality or state of being garish
1gar•land \ˈgär-lənd\ *n* **:** WREATH, CHAPLET
2garland *vb* **:** to form into or deck with a garland
gar•lic \ˈgär-lik\ *n* **:** an herb related to the lilies and grown for its pungent bulbs used in cooking; *also* **:** its bulb — **gar•licky** \-li-kē\ *adj*
gar•ment \ˈgär-mənt\ *n* **:** an article of clothing
gar•ner \ˈgär-nər\ *vb* **1 :** to gather into storage **2** ♦ **:** to acquire by effort **3** ♦ **:** to pick up **:** ACCUMULATE, COLLECT

♦ [2] acquire, attain, capture, carry, draw, earn, gain, get, land, make, obtain, procure, realize, secure, win ♦ [3] accumulate, amass, assemble, collect, concentrate, gather, group, lump, pick up, round up, scrape

gar•net \ˈgär-nət\ *n* **:** a transparent deep red mineral sometimes used as a gem
1gar•nish \ˈgär-nish\ *vb* **1** ♦ **:** to furnish with something ornamental **:** DECORATE, EMBELLISH **2 :** to add decorative or savory touches to (food) **3 :** GARNISHEE

♦ adorn, array, beautify, bedeck, deck, decorate, do, dress, embellish, enrich, grace, ornament, trim

2garnish *n* **1** ♦ **:** something that lends grace or beauty **2 :** something (as lemon wedges or parsley) used to garnish food or drink

♦ adornment, caparison, decoration, embellishment, frill, ornament, trim

gar•nish•ee \ˌgär-nə-ˈshē\ *vb* **-eed; -ee•ing 1 :** to serve with a garnishment **2 :** to take (as a debtor's wages) by legal authority
gar•nish•ment \ˈgär-nish-mənt\ *n* **1 :** GARNISH **2 :** a legal warning concerning the attachment of property to satisfy a debt; *also* **:** the attachment of such property
gar•ni•ture \-ni-chər, -ˌchu̇r\ *n* **:** EMBELLISHMENT, TRIMMING
gar•ret \ˈgar-ət\ *n* **:** the part of a house just under the roof **:** ATTIC
gar•ri•son \ˈgar-ə-sən\ *n* **1 :** a military post; *esp* **:** a permanent military installation **2 :** the troops stationed at a garrison — **garrison** *vb*
garrison state *n* **:** a state organized on a primarily military basis
1gar•rote *or* **ga•rotte** \gə-ˈrät, -ˈrōt\ *n* **1 :** a method of execution by strangulation; *also* **:** the apparatus used **2 :** an implement (as a wire with handles) for strangulation
2garrote *or* **garotte** *vb* ♦ **:** to strangle with or as if with a garrote

♦ choke, strangle, throttle

gar•ru•lous \ˈgar-ə-ləs\ *adj* **1 :** WORDY **2** ♦ **:** pointlessly or annoyingly talkative — **gar•ru•li•ty** \gə-ˈrü-lə-tē\ *n* — **gar•ru•lous•ly** *adv* — **gar•ru•lous•ness** *n*

♦ chatty, conversational, gabby, loquacious, talkative

gar•ter \ˈgär-tər\ *n* **:** a band or strap worn to hold up a stocking or sock
garter snake *n* **:** any of a genus of harmless American snakes with longitudinal stripes on the back
1gas \ˈgas\ *n, pl* **gas•es** *also* **gas•ses 1 :** a fluid (as hydrogen or air) that tends to expand indefinitely **2 :** a gas or mixture of gases used as a fuel or anesthetic **3 :** a substance that can be used to produce a poisonous, asphyxiating, or irritant atmosphere **4 :** GASOLINE **5** ♦ **:** empty talk

♦ bombast, grandiloquence, hot air, rhetoric, wind

2gas *vb* **gassed; gas•sing 1 :** to treat with gas; *also* **:** to poison with gas **2 :** to fill with gasoline ⟨~ up the car⟩ **3 :** to talk idly or garrulously
gas•eous \ˈga-sē-əs, -shəs\ *adj* **1 :** having the form of or being gas **2** ♦ **:** characterized by many words but little content

♦ bombastic, grandiloquent, oratorical, rhetorical, windy

1gash \ˈgash\ *n* ♦ **:** a deep long cut

♦ laceration, rent, rip, slash, slit, tear

2gash *vb* **:** to make a gash in
gas•ket \ˈgas-kət\ *n* **:** material (as rubber) or a part used to seal a joint
gas•light \ˈgas-ˌlīt\ *n* **1 :** light made by burning illuminating gas **2 :** a gas flame; *also* **:** a gas lighting fixture
gas mask *n* **:** a mask with a chemical air filter used to protect the face and lungs against poison gas
gas•o•line \ˈga-sə-ˌlēn, ˌga-sə-ˈlēn\ *n* **:** a flammable liquid mixture made from petroleum and used especially as a motor fuel
gasp \ˈgasp\ *vb* **1 :** to catch the breath audibly (as with shock) **2** ♦ **:** to breathe laboriously **:** PANT **3 :** to utter in a gasping manner — **gasp** *n*

♦ blow, pant, puff, wheeze

gas•tric \ˈgas-trik\ *adj* **:** of or relating to the stomach
gastric juice *n* **:** the acid digestive secretion of the stomach
gas•tri•tis \gas-ˈtrī-təs\ *n* **:** inflammation of the lining of the stomach
gas•tro•en•ter•ol•o•gy \ˌgas-trō-ˌen-tə-ˈrä-lə-jē\ *n* **:** a branch of medicine concerned with the structure, functions, and diseases of the stomach and intestines — **gas•tro•en•ter•ol•o•gist** \-jist\ *n*
gas•tro•in•tes•ti•nal \ˌgas-trō-in-ˈtes-tən-ᵊl\ *adj* **:** of, relating to, affecting, or including both the stomach and intestine ⟨~ tract⟩ ⟨~ distress⟩
gas•tron•o•my \gas-ˈträ-nə-mē\ *n* **:** the art of good eating — **gas•tro•nom•ic** \ˌgas-trə-ˈnä-mik\ *also* **gas•tro•nom•i•cal** \-mi-kəl\ *adj*
gas•tro•pod \ˈgas-trə-ˌpäd\ *n* **:** any of a large class of mollusks (as snails and slugs) with a muscular foot and a spiral shell or none — **gastropod** *adj*
gas•works \ˈgas-ˌwərks\ *n sing or pl* **:** a plant for manufacturing gas
gate \ˈgāt\ *n* **1** ♦ **:** an opening for passage in a wall or fence **2 :** a

city or castle entrance often with defensive structures **3 :** the frame or door that closes a gate **4** ♦ **:** a device (as a valve) for controlling the passage of a fluid or signal **5 :** the total admission receipts or the number of people at an event

♦ [1] door, hatch, portal ♦ [1] door, doorway, entrance, way ♦ [4] cock, faucet, spigot, tap, valve

-gate \ˌgāt\ *n comb form* **:** usually political scandal often involving the concealment of wrongdoing
gate–crash•er \ˈgāt-ˌkra-shər\ *n* **:** a person who enters without paying admission or attends without invitation
gate•keep•er \-ˌkē-pər\ *n* ♦ **:** a person who tends or guards a gate

♦ doorkeeper, janitor

gate•post \-ˌpōst\ *n* **:** the post to which a gate is hung or the one against which it closes
gate•way \-ˌwā\ *n* **1 :** an opening for a gate **2** ♦ **:** a means of entrance or exit

♦ access, admission, doorway, entrance, entry, entrée

¹gath•er \ˈga-thər\ *vb* **1** ♦ **:** to bring or come together **:** COLLECT **2** ♦ **:** to bring in a crop **:** PICK, HARVEST **3** ♦ **:** to pick up little by little **4 :** to gain or win by gradual increase **:** ACCUMULATE ⟨~ speed⟩ **5 :** to summon up ⟨~ courage to dive⟩ **6 :** to draw about or close to something **7 :** to pull (fabric) along a line of stitching into puckers **8** ♦ **:** to reach a conclusion often intuitively from hints or through inferences **:** DEDUCE, INFER **9 :** ASSEMBLE **10 :** to swell out and fill with pus **11 :** GROW, INCREASE — **gath•er•er** *n*

♦ [1] accumulate, amass, assemble, collect, concentrate, garner, group, lump, pick up, round up, scrape *Ant* dispel, disperse, dissipate, scatter ♦ [1] assemble, congregate, convene, forgather, meet, rendezvous ♦ [2] harvest, pick, reap ♦ [3] build, gain, grow, pick up ♦ [8] conclude, deduce, extrapolate, infer, judge, reason, understand

²gather *n* **:** a puckering in cloth made by gathering
gathering *n* **1** ♦ **:** a company of persons gathered for deliberation and legislation, worship, or entertainment **2** ♦ **:** something compiled

♦ [1] assemblage, assembly, conference, congregation, convocation, meeting, muster ♦ [2] accumulation, assemblage, collection

GATT \ˈgat\ *abbr* General Agreement on Tariffs and Trade
gauche \ˈgōsh\ *adj* **1** ♦ **:** lacking social experience or grace; *also* **:** not tactful **2 :** crudely made or done

♦ awkward, clumsy, graceless, inelegant, stiff, stilted, uncomfortable, uneasy, ungraceful, wooden

gau•che•rie \ˌgō-shə-ˈrē\ *n* **:** a tactless or awkward action
gau•cho \ˈgau̇-chō\ *n, pl* **gauchos :** a cowboy of the So. American pampas
gaud \ˈgȯd\ *n* **:** a small ornament (as a jewel or ring)
gaud•i•ness \-dē-nəs\ *n* ♦ **:** the quality or state of being gaudy

♦ flamboyance, flashiness, glitz, ostentation, pretentiousness, showiness, swank

gaudy \ˈgȯ-dē\ *adj* **gaud•i•er; -est 1** ♦ **:** ostentatiously or tastelessly ornamented **2 :** marked by showiness or extravagance — **gaud•i•ly** \-də-lē\ *adv*

♦ flamboyant, flashy, garish, glitzy, loud, ostentatious, swank, tawdry *Ant* conservative, quiet, understated

¹gauge *also* **gage** \ˈgāj\ *n* **1 :** measurement according to some standard or system **2 :** DIMENSIONS, SIZE **3** *usu gage* **:** an instrument for measuring, testing, or registering
²gauge *also* **gage** *vb* **gauged** *also* **gaged; gaug•ing** *also* **gag•ing 1** ♦ **:** to measure precisely the size, dimensions, or other measurable quantity of **2 :** to determine the capacity or contents of **3** ♦ **:** to determine roughly the size, extent, or nature of **:** ESTIMATE, JUDGE

♦ [1] measure, scale, span ♦ [3] calculate, call, conjecture, estimate, figure, guess, judge, make, place, put, reckon, suppose

gaunt \ˈgȯnt\ *adj* **1** ♦ **:** excessively thin and angular **2 :** BARREN, DESOLATE — **gaunt•ness** *n*

♦ cadaverous, haggard, skeletal, wasted

¹gaunt•let \ˈgȯnt-lət\ *n* **1 :** a protective glove **2 :** an open challenge (as to combat) **3 :** a dress glove extending above the wrist
²gauntlet *n* **1** ♦ **:** a severe trial **:** ORDEAL **2 :** a double file of men armed with weapons (as clubs) with which to strike at an individual who is made to run between them

♦ cross, ordeal, trial

gauze \ˈgȯz\ *n* **:** a very thin often transparent fabric used especially for draperies and surgical dressings
gauzy *adj* **gauz•i•er; -est** ♦ **:** made of or resembling gauze; *also* **:** marked by vagueness, elusiveness, or fuzziness

♦ flimsy, insubstantial, sheer, unsubstantial

gave *past of* GIVE
gav•el \ˈga-vəl\ *n* **:** the mallet of a presiding officer or auctioneer
ga•votte \gə-ˈvät\ *n* **:** a dance of French peasant origin marked by the raising rather than sliding of the feet
gawk \ˈgȯk\ *vb* ♦ **:** to gape or stare stupidly — **gawk•er** *n*

♦ gape, gaze, goggle, peer, rubberneck, stare

gawky \ˈgȯ-kē\ *adj* **gawk•i•er; -est** ♦ **:** lacking ease or grace (as of movement or expression) **:** AWKWARD, CLUMSY — **gawk•i•ly** \-kə-lē\ *adv*

♦ awkward, clumsy, graceless, heavy-handed, lubberly, lumpish, ungainly, unhandy

gay \ˈgā\ *adj* **1** ♦ **:** happily excited **:** MERRY **2** ♦ **:** bright and lively in appearance **3 :** brilliant in color **4 :** given to social pleasures; *also* **:** LICENTIOUS **5 :** HOMOSEXUAL; *also* **:** of, relating to, or used by homosexuals

♦ [1] active, animate, animated, brisk, energetic, frisky, jaunty, jazzy, lively, peppy, perky, pert, racy, snappy, spirited, sprightly, springy, vital, vivacious ♦ [1] blithe, boon, festive, gleeful, jocund, jolly, jovial, merry, mirthful, sunny ♦ [2] bright, cheerful, cheery, glad, upbeat

gayety, gayly *var of* GAIETY, GAILY
gaz *abbr* gazette
gaze \ˈgāz\ *vb* **gazed; gaz•ing** ♦ **:** to fix the eyes in a steady intent look — **gaze** *n* — **gaz•er** *n*

♦ gape, gawk, goggle, peer, rubberneck, stare

ga•ze•bo \gə-ˈzē-bō\ *n, pl* **-bos 1 :** BELVEDERE **2 :** a freestanding roofed structure usually open on the sides
ga•zelle \gə-ˈzel\ *n, pl* **gazelles** *also* **gazelle :** any of numerous small swift graceful antelopes
ga•zette \gə-ˈzet\ *n* **1 :** NEWSPAPER **2 :** an official journal
gaz•et•teer \ˌga-zə-ˈtir\ *n* **:** a geographical dictionary
ga•zil•lion \gə-ˈzil-yən\ *n* **:** ZILLION — **gazillion** *adj* — **ga•zil•li•onth** \-yənth\ *adj*
gaz•pa•cho \gəz-ˈpä-(ˌ)chō, gə-ˈspä-\ *n, pl* **-chos :** a spicy soup usually made from raw vegetables and served cold
GB *abbr* Great Britain
GCA *abbr* ground-controlled approach
gd *abbr* good
Gd *symbol* gadolinium
GDR *abbr* German Democratic Republic
Ge *symbol* germanium
gear \ˈgir\ *n* **1 :** CLOTHING **2 :** movable property **:** GOODS **3** ♦ **:** the implements used in an operation or activity **:** EQUIPMENT ⟨fishing ~⟩ **4 :** a mechanism that performs a specific function ⟨steering ~⟩ **5 :** a toothed wheel **6 :** working adjustment of gears ⟨in ~⟩ **7 :** an adjustment of transmission gears (as of an automobile or bicycle) that determines speed and direction of travel — **gear** *vb*

♦ accoutrements (*or* accouterments), apparatus, equipment, matériel, outfit, paraphernalia, tackle

gear•box \ˈgir-ˌbäks\ *n* **:** TRANSMISSION 3
gear•shift \-ˌshift\ *n* **:** a mechanism by which transmission gears are shifted
gear•wheel \-ˌhwēl\ *n* **:** GEAR 5
gecko \ˈge-kō\ *n, pl* **geck•os** *also* **geck•oes :** any of numerous small chiefly tropical insect-eating lizards
GED *abbr* **1** General Educational Development (tests) **2** general equivalency diploma
geek \ˈgēk\ *n* **:** a person of an intellectual bent who is often disliked — **geeky** *adj*
geese *pl of* GOOSE
gee•zer \ˈgē-zər\ *n* **:** an odd or eccentric person usually of old age
Gei•ger counter \ˈgī-gər-\ *n* **:** an electronic instrument for detecting the presence of cosmic rays or radioactive substances
gei•sha \ˈgā-shə, ˈgē-\ *n, pl* **geisha** *or* **geishas :** a Japanese girl or woman who is trained to provide entertaining company for men
¹gel \ˈjel\ *n* **:** a solid jellylike colloid (as gelatin dessert)
²gel *vb* ♦ **:** to change into or take on the form of a gel

♦ clot, coagulate, congeal, jell, set

gel•a•tin *also* **gel•a•tine** \ˈje-lət-ᵊn\ *n* **:** glutinous material and especially protein obtained from animal tissues by boiling and used as a food, in dyeing, and in photography; *also* **:** an edible jelly formed with gelatin

ge•lat•i•nous \jə-ˈlat-ᵊn-əs\ *adj* ♦ **:** resembling gelatin or jelly

♦ adhesive, gluey, glutinous, gooey, gummy, sticky, viscid, viscous

geld \ˈgeld\ *vb* **:** CASTRATE

geld•ing *n* **:** a castrated male horse

gel•id \ˈje-ləd\ *adj* **:** extremely cold

gem \ˈjem\ *n* **1** ♦ **:** a usually valuable stone cut and polished for ornament **2** ♦ **:** something valued for beauty or perfection

♦ [1] brilliant, gemstone, jewel ♦ [2] catch, jewel, pearl, plum, prize, treasure

Gem•i•ni \ˈje-mə-(ˌ)nē, -ˌnī; ˈge-mə-ˌnē\ *n* **1 :** a zodiacal constellation between Taurus and Cancer usually pictured as twins sitting together **2 :** the 3d sign of the zodiac in astrology; *also* **:** one born under this sign

gem•ol•o•gy *or* **gem•mol•o•gy** \je-ˈmä-lə-jē, jə-\ *n* **:** the science of gems — **gem•olog•i•cal** \ˌje-mə-ˈlä-ji-kəl\ *adj* — **gem•ol•o•gist** *also* **gem•mol•o•gist** \je-ˈmä-lə-jist\ *n*

gem•stone \ˈjem-ˌstōn\ *n* **:** a mineral or petrified material that when cut and polished can be used in jewelry

gen *abbr* **1** general **2** genitive

Gen *abbr* Genesis

Gen AF *abbr* general of the air force

gen•darme \ˈzhän-ˌdärm, ˈjän-\ *n* **:** a member of a body of soldiers especially in France serving as an armed police force

gen•der \ˈjen-dər\ *n* **1 :** any of two or more divisions within a grammatical class that determine agreement with and selection of other words or grammatical forms **2 :** SEX 1

gene \ˈjēn\ *n* **:** a part of DNA or RNA that contains chemical information needed to make a particular protein (as an enzyme) controlling or influencing an inherited bodily trait (as eye color) or activity or that influences or controls the activity of another gene or genes — **gen•ic** \ˈjē-nik, ˈje-\ *adj*

ge•ne•al•o•gy \ˌjē-nē-ˈä-lə-jē, ˌje-, -ˈa-\ *n, pl* **-gies** ♦ **:** an ancestral line **:** PEDIGREE, LINEAGE; *also* **:** the study of family pedigrees — **ge•ne•a•log•i•cal** \ˌjē-nē-ə-ˈlä-ji-kəl, ˌje-\ *adj* — **ge•ne•a•log•i•cal•ly** \-k(ə-)lē\ *adv* — **ge•ne•al•o•gist** \ˌjē-nē-ˈä-lə-jist, ˌje-; -ˈa-\ *n*

♦ ancestry, birth, blood, bloodline, breeding, descent, extraction, family tree, line, lineage, origin, parentage, pedigree, stock, strain

genera *pl of* GENUS

¹gen•er•al \ˈje-nə-rəl, ˈjen-rəl\ *adj* **1** ♦ **:** of or relating to the whole **2 :** taken as a whole **3 :** relating to or covering all instances **4** ♦ **:** not special or specialized **5** ♦ **:** common to many ⟨a ~ custom⟩ **6 :** not limited in meaning **:** not specific **7 :** holding superior rank ⟨inspector ~⟩

♦ [1] blanket, common, generic, global, overall, universal *Ant* individual, particular ♦ [4] broad, nonspecific, overall, unlimited, wide *Ant* delineated, detailed, particularized, specific ♦ [5] characteristic, common, communal, contemporary, current, dominant, everyday, familiar, household, popular, predominant, present, public, rife, typical, universal, usual, well-known, widespread *Ant* uncommon, unpopular

²general *n* **1 :** something that involves or is applicable to the whole **2 :** a commissioned officer ranking next below a general of the army or a general of the air force **3 :** a commissioned officer of the highest rank in the marine corps — **in general :** for the most part

general assembly *n* **1 :** a legislative assembly; *esp* **:** a U.S. state legislature **2** *cap G&A* **:** the supreme deliberative body of the United Nations

gen•er•al•i•sa•tion, gen•er•al•ise *chiefly Brit var of* GENERALIZATION, GENERALIZE

gen•er•a•lis•si•mo \ˌje-nə-rə-ˈli-sə-ˌmō\ *n, pl* **-mos :** the chief commander of an army

gen•er•al•i•ty \ˌje-nə-ˈra-lə-tē\ *n, pl* **-ties 1 :** the quality or state of being general **2 :** a general statement, law, principle, or proposition **:** GENERALIZATION 2 **3 :** a vague or inadequate statement **4** ♦ **:** the greatest part **:** BULK

♦ body, bulk, core, main, mass, staple, weight

gen•er•al•i•za•tion \ˌje-nə-rə-lə-ˈzā-shən, ˌjen-rə-\ *n* **1 :** the act or process of generalizing **2 :** a general statement, law, principle, or proposition

gen•er•al•ize \ˈje-nə-rə-ˌlīz, ˈjen-rə-\ *vb* **-ized; -iz•ing 1 :** to make general **2 :** to draw general conclusions from **3 :** to reach a general conclusion especially on the basis of particular instances **4 :** to extend throughout the body

gen•er•al•ly \ˈjen-rə-lē, ˈje-nə-\ *adv* **1 :** in a general manner **2** ♦ **:** as a rule

♦ commonly, ordinarily, typically, usually ♦ altogether, basically, chiefly, largely, mainly, mostly, overall, predominantly, primarily, principally

general of the air force : a commissioned officer of the highest rank in the air force

general of the army : a commissioned officer of the highest rank in the army

general practitioner *n* **:** a physician or veterinarian whose practice is not limited to a specialty

gen•er•al•ship \ˈje-nə-rəl-ˌship, ˈjen-rəl-\ *n* **1 :** office or tenure of office of a general **2 :** LEADERSHIP **3 :** military skill as a high commander

general store *n* **:** a retail store that carries a wide variety of goods but is not divided into departments

gen•er•ate \ˈje-nə-ˌrāt\ *vb* **-at•ed; -at•ing** ♦ **:** to bring into existence **:** PRODUCE

♦ create, engender, induce, make, produce, spawn

gen•er•a•tion \ˌje-nə-ˈrā-shən\ *n* **1 :** a body of living beings constituting a single step in the line of descent from an ancestor; *also* **:** the average period between generations **2 :** PRODUCTION

Generation X *n* **:** the generation of Americans born in the 1960s and 1970s

gen•er•a•tive \ˈje-nə-rə-tiv, -ˌrā-tiv\ *adj* **:** having the power or function of generating, originating, producing, or reproducing ⟨~ organs⟩

gen•er•a•tor \ˈje-nə-ˌrā-tər\ *n* **1 :** one that generates **2 :** a machine by which mechanical energy is changed into electrical energy

ge•ner•ic \jə-ˈner-ik\ *adj* **1** ♦ **:** not specific **:** GENERAL **2 :** not protected by a trademark ⟨a ~ drug⟩ **3 :** of or relating to a biological genus — **generic** *n* — **ge•ner•i•cal•ly** \-i-k(ə-)lē\ *adv*

♦ blanket, common, general, global, overall, universal

gen•er•os•i•ty \ˌje-nə-ˈrä-sə-tē\ *n* **1** ♦ **:** the quality or fact of being generous **2 :** a generous act

♦ bounty, liberality, philanthropy, unselfishness

gen•er•ous \ˈje-nə-rəs\ *adj* **1** ♦ **:** free in giving or sharing **2 :** HIGH-MINDED, NOBLE **3** ♦ **:** marked by abundance or ample proportions **:** COPIOUS — **gen•er•ous•ness** *n*

♦ [1] bountiful, charitable, free, liberal, munificent, openhanded, unselfish, unsparing *Ant* cheap, close, closefisted, miserly, niggardly, parsimonious, penurious, selfish, stingy, tight, tightfisted, uncharitable ♦ [3] abundant, ample, bountiful, comfortable, copious, liberal, plentiful

gen•er•ous•ly \ˈje-nə-rəs-lē\ *adv* ♦ **:** in a generous manner

♦ bountifully, handsomely, liberally, well

gen•e•sis \ˈje-nə-səs\ *n, pl* **-e•ses** \-ˌsēz\ ♦ **:** the origin or coming into existence of something

♦ beginning, birth, commencement, dawn, launch, morning, onset, outset, start, threshold

Genesis *n* **:** the mainly narrative first book of canonical Jewish and Christian Scriptures

gene–splic•ing \-ˌsplī-siŋ\ *n* **:** the process of preparing recombinant DNA

gene therapy *n* **:** the insertion of normal or altered genes into cells usually to replace defective genes especially in the treatment of genetic disorders

ge•net•ic \jə-ˈne-tik\ *adj* **1 :** of or relating to the origin, development, or causes of something **2 a :** of or relating to genetics **b** ♦ **:** of, relating to, caused by, or controlled by genes — **ge•net•i•cal•ly** \-ti-k(ə-)lē\ *adv*

♦ hereditary, heritable, inborn, inherited

genetic code *n* **:** the chemical code that is the basis of genetic inheritance and consists of units of three linked chemical groups in DNA and RNA which specify particular amino acids used to make proteins or which start or stop the process of making proteins

genetic engineering *n* **:** the alteration of genetic material especially by cutting up and joining together DNA from one or more species of organism and inserting the result into an organism — **genetically engineered** *adj*

ge•net•ics \jə-ˈne-tiks\ *n* **:** a branch of biology dealing with heredity and variation — **ge•net•i•cist** \-tə-sist\ *n*

ge•nial \ˈjē-nyəl, ˈjē-nē-əl\ *adj* **1 :** favorable to growth or comfort ⟨~ sunshine⟩ **2** ♦ **:** marked by or diffusing sympathy or friendliness ⟨a ~ host⟩ — **ge•nial•ly** *adv*

♦ affable, agreeable, amiable, good-natured, gracious, nice, sweet, well-disposed ♦ amicable, companionable, comradely, cordial, friendly, hearty, hospitable, neighborly, sociable, warm, warmhearted

ge•nial•i•ty \ˌjē-nē-ˈa-lə-tē, jēn-ˈya-\ *n* ♦ **:** the quality of being genial; *esp* **:** warmth of disposition and manners

♦ agreeableness, amenity, amiability, graciousness, niceness, pleasantness, sweetness

-gen•ic \ˈje-nik\ *adj comb form* **1 :** producing **:** forming **2 :** produced by **:** formed from **3 :** suitable for production or reproduction by (such) a medium
ge•nie \ˈjē-nē\ *n, pl* **ge•nies** *also* **ge•nii** \-nē-ˌī\ **:** a supernatural spirit that often takes human form usually serving the person who calls on it
gen•i•tal \ˈje-nə-tᵊl\ *adj* **1 :** concerned with reproduction ⟨~ organs⟩ **2 :** of, relating to, or characterized by the stage of psychosexual development in psychoanalytic theory in which oral and anal impulses are subordinated to adaptive interpersonal mechanisms — **gen•i•tal•ly** *adv*
gen•i•ta•lia \ˌje-nə-ˈtāl-yə\ *n pl* **:** reproductive organs; *esp* **:** the external genital organs — **gen•i•ta•lic** \-ˈta-lik, -ˈtā-\ *adj*
gen•i•tals \ˈje-nə-tᵊlz\ *n pl* **:** GENITALIA
gen•i•tive \ˈje-nə-tiv\ *adj* **:** of, relating to, or constituting a grammatical case marking typically a relationship of possessor or source — **genitive** *n*
gen•i•to•uri•nary \ˌje-nə-tō-ˈyu̇r-ə-ˌner-ē\ *adj* **:** of or relating to the genital and urinary organs or functions
ge•nius \ˈjē-nyəs\ *n, pl* **ge•nius•es** *or* **ge•nii** \-nē-ˌī\ **1** *pl genii* **:** an attendant spirit of a person or place; *also* **:** a person who influences another for good or evil **2** ♦ **:** a strong leaning or inclination **3** ♦ **:** a peculiar or distinctive character or spirit (as of a nation or a language) **4** *pl usu genii* **:** SPIRIT, GENIE **5** *pl usu geniuses* ♦ **:** a single strongly marked capacity or aptitude **6 a :** extraordinary intellectual power **b** ♦ **:** a person having extraordinary intellectual power

♦ [2] affinity, bent, devices, disposition, inclination, leaning, partiality, penchant, predilection, predisposition, proclivity, propensity, talent, tendency, turn ♦ [3] character, complexion, constitution, nature, personality, tone ♦ [5] aptitude, endowment, faculty, flair, gift, knack, talent ♦ [6b] brain, intellect, thinker, whiz, wizard *Ant* dumbbell, dummy, dunce, idiot, imbecile, moron

genl *abbr* general
geno•cide \ˈje-nə-ˌsīd\ *n* **:** the deliberate and systematic destruction of a racial, political, or cultural group
ge•nome \ˈjē-ˌnōm\ *n* **1 :** one haploid set of chromosomes **2 :** the genetic material of an organism
ge•no•mics \jē-ˈnō-miks\ *n* **:** a branch of biotechnology concerned especially with investigating and collecting data about the structure and function of all or part of an organism's genome
-genous \jə-nəs\ *adj comb form* **1 :** producing **:** yielding ⟨eroge*nous*⟩ **2 :** having (such) an origin ⟨endo*genous*⟩
genre \ˈzhän-rə, ˈzhäⁿ-; ˈzhäⁿr; ˈjän-rə\ *n* **1 :** a distinctive type or category especially of literary composition **2 :** a style of painting in which everyday subjects are treated realistically
gens \ˈjenz, ˈgens\ *n, pl* **gen•tes** \ˈjen-ˌtēz, ˈgen-ˌtās\ **:** a Roman clan embracing the families of the same stock in the male line
gent *n* ♦ **:** a man of any social class or condition **:** GENTLEMAN

♦ buck, chap, dude, fellow, gentleman, guy, hombre, jack, joker, lad, male, man

gen•teel \jen-ˈtēl\ *adj* **1** ♦ **:** having an aristocratic quality or flavor; *also* **:** of or relating to the gentry or upper class **2 :** ELEGANT, STYLISH **3** ♦ **:** free from vulgarity or rudeness **:** POLITE **4 :** maintaining the appearance of superior social status **5 :** marked by false delicacy, prudery, or affectation — **gen•teel•ly** *adv* — **gen•teel•ness** *n*

♦ [1] aristocratic, gentle, grand, highborn, noble, patrician, wellborn ♦ [1] civilized, cultivated, cultured, polished, refined ♦ [3] civil, courteous, gracious, mannerly, polite, well-bred ♦ [3] correct, decent, decorous, nice, polite, proper, respectable, seemly

gen•tian \ˈjen-chən\ *n* **:** any of numerous herbs with opposite leaves and showy usually blue flowers in the fall
gen•tile \ˈjen-ˌtī(-ə)l\ *n* **1** *often cap* **:** a person who is not Jewish; *esp* **:** a Christian as distinguished from a Jew **2 :** a person who does not acknowledge the God of the Bible **:** HEATHEN, PAGAN — **gentile** *adj, often cap*
gen•til•i•ty \jen-ˈti-lə-tē\ *n, pl* **-ties** **1 :** good birth and family **2** ♦ **:** the qualities characteristic of a well-bred person **3 :** good manners **4 :** superior social status shown in manners or mode of life

♦ civility, courtesy, graciousness, mannerliness, politeness

¹gen•tle \ˈjen-tᵊl\ *adj* **gen•tler** \ˈjent-lər, -tᵊl-ər\; **gen•tlest** \ˈjent-ləst, -tᵊl-əst\ **1** ♦ **:** belonging to a family of high social station **2 :** of, relating to, or characteristic of a gentleman **3 :** KIND, AMIABLE **4 :** TRACTABLE, DOCILE **5** ♦ **:** not harsh, stern, or violent **6 :** SOFT, DELICATE **7** ♦ **:** marked by moderation **:** MODERATE — **gen•tle•ness** *n* — **gen•tly** *adv*

♦ [1] aristocratic, genteel, grand, highborn, noble, patrician, wellborn ♦ [5] balmy, benign, bland, delicate, light, mellow, mild, soft, soothing, tender *Ant* abrasive, caustic, coarse, hard, harsh, rough ♦ [7] balmy, clement, equable, mild, moderate, temperate

²gentle *vb* **gen•tled; gen•tling** **1 :** to make or become mild, docile, soft, or moderate **2 :** MOLLIFY, PLACATE
gen•tle•folk \ˈjen-tᵊl-ˌfōk\ *also* **gen•tle•folks** \-ˌfōks\ *n* **:** persons of good family and breeding
gen•tle•man \-mən\ *n* **1** ♦ **:** a man of good family **2 :** a well-bred man **3** ♦ **:** an adult male human being **:** MAN — used in plural as a form of address — **gen•tle•man•ly** *adj*

♦ [1] aristocrat, grandee, noble, patrician ♦ [3] buck, chap, dude, fellow, gent, guy, hombre, jack, joker, lad, male, man

gen•tle•wom•an \-ˌwu̇-mən\ *n* **1** ♦ **:** a woman of good family **2 :** a woman attending a lady of rank **3 :** a woman with very good manners **:** LADY

♦ dame, lady, noblewoman

gen•tri•fi•ca•tion \ˌjen-trə-fə-ˈkā-shən\ *n* **:** the process of renewal accompanying the influx of middle-class people into deteriorating areas that often displaces earlier usually poorer residents — **gen•tri•fy** \ˈjen-trə-fī\ *vb*
gen•try \ˈjen-trē\ *n, pl* **gentries** **1 :** people of good birth, breeding, and education **:** ARISTOCRACY **2 :** the class of English people between the nobility and the yeomanry **3 :** persons of a designated class
gen•u•flect \ˈjen-yu̇-ˌflekt\ *vb* **:** to bend the knee especially in worship — **gen•u•flec•tion** \ˌjen-yu̇-ˈflek-shən\ *n*
gen•u•ine \ˈjen-yə-wən\ *adj* **1** ♦ **:** actually having the reputed or apparent qualities or character **:** AUTHENTIC, REAL **2** ♦ **:** free from hypocrisy or pretense **:** SINCERE, HONEST — **gen•u•ine•ness** *n*

♦ [1] authentic, bona fide, real, right, true ♦ [2] artless, honest, ingenuous, innocent, naive, natural, real, simple, sincere, true, unaffected, unpretentious

gen•u•ine•ly *adv* ♦ **:** in a genuine manner **:** ACTUALLY

♦ actually, authentically, really, veritably, very

ge•nus \ˈjē-nəs\ *n, pl* **gen•era** \ˈje-nə-rə\ **:** a category of biological classification that ranks between the family and the species and contains related species
geo•cen•tric \ˌjē-ō-ˈsen-trik\ *adj* **1 :** relating to or measured from the earth's center **2 :** having or relating to the earth as a center
geo•chem•is•try \-ˈke-mə-strē\ *n* **:** a branch of geology that deals with the chemical composition of and chemical changes in the earth — **geo•chem•i•cal** \-mi-kəl\ *adj* — **geo•chem•ist** \-mist\ *n*
ge•ode \ˈjē-ˌōd\ *n* **:** a nodule of stone having a cavity lined with mineral matter
¹geo•de•sic \ˌjē-ə-ˈde-sik\ *adj* **:** made of light straight structural elements ⟨a ~ dome⟩
²geodesic *n* **:** the shortest line between two points on a surface
geo•det•ic \ˌjē-ə-ˈde-tik\ *adj* **:** of, relating to, or being precise measurement of the earth and its features ⟨a ~ survey⟩
geog *abbr* geographic; geographical; geography
ge•og•ra•phy \jē-ˈä-grə-fē\ *n, pl* **-phies** **1 :** a science that deals with the natural features of the earth and the climate, products, and inhabitants **2 :** the natural features of a region — **ge•og•ra•pher** \-fər\ *n* — **geo•graph•ic** \ˌjē-ə-ˈgra-fik\ *or* **geo•graph•i•cal** \-fi-kəl\ *adj* — **geo•graph•i•cal•ly** \-fi-k(ə-)lē\ *adv*
geol *abbr* geologic; geological; geology
ge•ol•o•gy \jē-ˈä-lə-jē\ *n, pl* **-gies** **1 :** a science that deals with the history of the earth and its life especially as recorded in rocks; *also* **:** a study of the features of a celestial body (as the moon) **2 :** the geologic features of an area — **geo•log•ic** \ˌjē-ə-ˈlä-jik\

or **geo·log·i·cal** \-ji-kəl\ *adj* — **geo·log·i·cal·ly** \-ji-k(ə-)lē\ *adv* — **ge·ol·o·gist** \jē-ˈä-lə-jist\ *n*
geom *abbr* geometric; geometrical; geometry
geo·mag·net·ic \ˌjē-ō-mag-ˈne-tik\ *adj* : of or relating to the magnetism of the earth — **geo·mag·ne·tism** \-ˈmag-nə-ˌti-zəm\ *n*
geometric mean *n* : the *n*th root of the product of *n* numbers; *esp* : a number that is the second term of three consecutive terms of a geometric progression ⟨the *geometric mean* of 9 and 4 is 6⟩
geometric progression *n* : a progression (as 1, ½, ¼) in which the ratio of a term to its predecessor is always the same
ge·om·e·try \jē-ˈä-mə-trē\ *n, pl* **-tries** **1** : a branch of mathematics dealing with the relations, properties, and measurements of solids, surfaces, lines, points, and angles **2** ♦ : relative arrangement of parts or elements — **ge·om·e·ter** \-tər\ *n* — **ge·o·met·ric** \ˌjē-ə-ˈme-trik\ *or* **ge·o·met·ri·cal** \-tri-kəl\ *adj*

♦ cast, configuration, conformation, figure, form, shape

geo·phys·ics \ˌjē-ō-ˈfi-ziks\ *n* : the physics of the earth — **geo·phys·i·cal** \-zi-kəl\ *adj* — **geo·phys·i·cist** \-zə-sist\ *n*
geo·pol·i·tics \-ˈpä-lə-ˌtiks\ *n* : a combination of political and geographic factors relating to a state — **geo·po·lit·i·cal** \-pə-ˈli-ti-kəl\ *adj*
geo·ther·mal \ˌjē-ō-ˈthər-məl\ *adj* : of, relating to, or using the heat of the earth's interior
ger *abbr* gerund
Ger *abbr* German; Germany
ge·ra·ni·um \jə-ˈrā-nē-əm\ *n* : any of a genus of herbs with usually deeply cut leaves and typically pink, purple, or white flowers; *also* : any of a related genus of herbs that are native to southern Africa and are widely grown for their clusters of showy usually red, pink, or white flowers
ger·bil *also* **ger·bile** \ˈjər-bəl\ *n* : any of numerous Old World burrowing desert rodents with long hind legs
ge·ri·at·ric \ˌjer-ē-ˈa-trik\ *adj* **1** : of or relating to geriatrics or the process of aging **2** : of, relating to, or appropriate for elderly people **3** ♦ : advanced in years or age : OLD

♦ ancient, elderly, old, senior

ge·ri·at·rics \-triks\ *n* : a branch of medicine dealing with the problems and diseases of old age and aging
germ \ˈjərm\ *n* **1** : a bit of living matter capable of growth and development (as into an organism) **2** : SOURCE, RUDIMENTS **3** : MICROORGANISM; *esp* : one causing disease
Ger·man \ˈjər-mən\ *n* **1** : a native or inhabitant of Germany **2** : the language of Germany, Austria, and parts of Switzerland — **German** *adj* — **Ger·man·ic** \jər-ˈma-nik\ *adj*
ger·mane \jər-ˈmān\ *adj* ♦ : being at once relevant and appropriate

♦ applicable, apposite, apropos, material, pertinent, pointed, relative, relevant

ger·ma·ni·um \jər-ˈmā-nē-əm\ *n* : a grayish white hard chemical element used especially in semiconductors
German measles *n sing or pl* : an acute contagious virus disease milder than typical measles but damaging to the fetus when occurring early in pregnancy
German shepherd *n* : any of a breed of intelligent responsive working dogs of German origin often used in police work and as guide dogs for the blind
germ cell *n* : an egg or sperm or one of their antecedent cells
ger·mi·cide \ˈjər-mə-ˌsīd\ *n* : an agent that destroys germs — **ger·mi·cid·al** \ˌjər-mə-ˈsīd-ᵊl\ *adj*
ger·mi·nal \ˈjər-mə-nəl\ *adj* : of or relating to a germ or germ cell; *also* : EMBRYONIC
ger·mi·nate \ˈjər-mə-ˌnāt\ *vb* **-nat·ed; -nat·ing** **1** : to cause to develop : begin to develop : SPROUT **2** : to come into being : EVOLVE — **ger·mi·na·tion** \ˌjər-mə-ˈnā-shən\ *n*
ger·on·tol·o·gy \ˌjer-ən-ˈtä-lə-jē\ *n* : a scientific study of aging and the problems of the aged — **ge·ron·to·log·i·cal** \jə-ˌränt-ᵊl-ˈä-ji-kəl\ *adj* — **ger·on·tol·o·gist** \ˌjer-ən-ˈtä-lə-jist\ *n*
ger·ry·man·der \ˈjer-ē-ˌman-dər\ *vb* : to divide into election districts so as to give one political party an advantage — **gerrymander** *n*
ger·und \ˈjer-ənd\ *n* : a word having the characteristics of both verb and noun
ge·sta·po \gə-ˈstä-pō\ *n, pl* **-pos** : a usually terrorist secret-police organization operating against persons suspected of disloyalty
ges·ta·tion \je-ˈstā-shən\ *n* : PREGNANCY, INCUBATION — **gestate** \ˈjes-ˌtāt\ *vb*
ges·tic·u·late \je-ˈsti-kyə-ˌlāt\ *vb* **-lat·ed; -lat·ing** : to make gestures especially when speaking
ges·tic·u·la·tion \-ˌsti-kyə-ˈlā-shən\ *n* : the act of making gestures; *also* : an expressive gesture made in showing strong feeling or in enforcing an argument
¹ges·ture \ˈjes-chər\ *n* **1** ♦ : a movement usually of the body or limbs that expresses or emphasizes an idea, sentiment, or attitude **2** ♦ : something said or done by way of formality or courtesy, as a symbol or token, or for its effect on the attitudes of others — **ges·tur·al** \-chə-rəl\ *adj*

♦ [1] pantomime, sign, signal ♦ [2] amenity, civility, courtesy, formality

²gesture *vb* ♦ : to make a gesture; *also* : to express or direct by a gesture

♦ flag, motion, signal, wave

ge·sund·heit \gə-ˈzu̇nt-ˌhīt\ *interj* — used to wish good health especially to one who has just sneezed
¹get \ˈget\ *vb* **got** \ˈgät\; **got** *or* **got·ten** \ˈgät-ᵊn\; **get·ting** **1** ♦ : to gain possession of (as by receiving, acquiring, earning, buying, or winning) : PROCURE, OBTAIN **2** : to succeed in coming or going ⟨*got* away to the lake⟩ **3** : to cause to come or go ⟨*got* the car to the station⟩ **4** ♦ : to become the father of : BEGET **5** : to cause to be in a certain condition or position ⟨don't ~ wet⟩ **6** ♦ : to undergo change or development : BECOME ⟨~ sick⟩ **7** : to make ready : PREPARE **8** ♦ : to take possession of : SEIZE **9** : to move emotionally; *also* : IRRITATE **10** : BAFFLE, PUZZLE **11** : KILL **12** : HIT **13** ♦ : to be subjected to ⟨~ the measles⟩ **14** : to receive as punishment **15** ♦ : to find out especially by calculation **16 a** : HEAR **b** ♦ : to grasp the meaning of : UNDERSTAND **17** : to prevail on : PERSUADE, INDUCE **18** : HAVE ⟨he's *got* no money⟩ **19** : to have as an obligation or necessity ⟨you have *got* to come⟩ **20** : to establish communication with **21** : to be able ⟨finally *got* to go to med school⟩ **22** : to come to be ⟨*got* talking about old times⟩ **23** : to leave at once

♦ [1] acquire, attain, capture, carry, draw, earn, gain, garner, land, make, obtain, procure, realize, secure, win ♦ [4] beget, father, produce, sire ♦ [6] become, come, go, grow, run, turn, wax ♦ [8] bag, capture, catch, collar, corral, grab, grapple, hook, land, nab, seize, snare, trap ♦ [13] catch, come down, contract, sicken, take ♦ [15] detect, determine, dig up, discover, ferret out, find, hit on, locate, track down ♦ [16b] appreciate, apprehend, catch, catch on (to), comprehend, grasp, make, make out, perceive, see, seize, understand

²get \ˈget\ *n* : OFFSPRING, PROGENY
get across *vb* ♦ : to make clear or convincing

♦ clarify, clear (up), construe, demonstrate, elucidate, explain, explicate, expound, illuminate, illustrate, interpret, spell out

get along *vb* **1** ♦ : to meet one's needs **2** : to be on friendly terms **3** ♦ : to proceed toward a destination

♦ [1] cope, do, fare, make out, manage, shift ♦ [3] advance, fare, forge, go, march, proceed, progress

get around *vb* **1** ♦ : to manage to avoid the intent, effect, or force of something especially by ingenuity or stratagem : CIRCUMVENT **2** ♦ : to become known or current

♦ [1] circumvent, dodge, shortcut, sidestep, skirt ♦ [2] circulate, come out, get out, leak out, out, spread

get·away \ˈge-tə-ˌwā\ *n* **1** ♦ : an act or instance of getting away : ESCAPE **2** : START

♦ escape, flight, lam, slip

get by *vb* : to meet one's needs : GET ALONG
get off *vb* ♦ : to go away from; *also* : to do or experience the first stages or actions of ⟨*got off* on the trip early⟩

♦ clear out, depart, exit, go, move, pull, quit, sally, shove, take off ♦ begin, commence, embark (on *or* upon), enter, launch, open, start, strike

get on *vb* **1** : to proceed toward a destination **2** : to meet one's needs : GET ALONG
get out *vb* **1** ♦ : to become known; *also* : to produce or release for distribution **2** ♦ : to get away (as by flight); *also* : to cause to leave or escape

♦ [1] come out, leak out, out, spread ♦ [1] issue, print, publish ♦ [2] abscond, clear out, escape, flee, fly, lam, run away, run off

get–to·geth·er \ˈget-tə-ˌge-t͟hər\ *n* ♦ : an assembly for a common purpose; *esp* : an informal social gathering

♦ assembly, conference, congress, convention, convocation, council, gathering, huddle, meeting, powwow, seminar

get·up \ˈget-ˌəp\ *n* **1** ♦ : a clothing ensemble often for a special occasion or activity : OUTFIT, COSTUME **2 :** general composition or structure

♦ dress, garb, guise, outfit

gew•gaw \ˈgü-ˌgȯ, ˈgyü-\ *n* ♦ **:** a showy trifle : BAUBLE, TRINKET

♦ bauble, curiosity, knickknack, novelty, trinket

gey•ser \ˈgī-zər\ *n* **:** a spring that intermittently shoots up hot water and steam

g–force \ˈjē-ˌfȯrs\ *n* **:** the force of gravity or acceleration on a body

Gha•na•ian \gä-ˈnā-ən\ *n* **:** a native or inhabitant of Ghana — **Ghanaian** *adj*

ghast•ly \ˈgast-lē\ *adj* **ghast•li•er; -est 1** ♦ **:** terrifyingly horrible to the senses : SHOCKING **2 :** resembling a ghost : DEATHLIKE, PALE

♦ appalling, atrocious, awful, dreadful, frightful, horrible, horrid, nightmarish, shocking, terrible

ghat \ˈgȯt\ *n* **:** a broad flight of steps on an Indian riverbank that provides access to the water

gher•kin \ˈgər-kən\ *n* **1 :** a small prickly fruit of a vine related to the cucumber used to make pickles **2 :** an immature cucumber

ghet•to \ˈge-tō\ *n, pl* **ghettos** *or* **ghettoes :** a quarter of a city in which members of a minority group live because of social, legal, or economic pressure

¹ghost \ˈgōst\ *n* **1 :** the seat of life : SOUL **2** ♦ **:** a disembodied soul; *esp* **:** the soul of a dead person believed to be an inhabitant of the unseen world or to appear in bodily form to living people **3 :** SPIRIT, DEMON **4 :** a faint trace ⟨a ~ of a smile⟩ **5 :** a false image in a photographic negative or on a television screen — **ghost•ly** *adv*

♦ apparition, bogey, phantasm, phantom, poltergeist, shade, shadow, specter, spirit, spook, vision, wraith

²ghost *vb* **:** GHOSTWRITE

ghost•write \-ˌrīt\ *vb* **-wrote** \-ˌrōt\; **-writ•ten** \-ˌri-tᵊn\ **:** to write for and in the name of another — **ghost•writ•er** *n*

ghoul \ˈgül\ *n* ♦ **:** a legendary evil being that robs graves and feeds on corpses — **ghoul•ish** *adj*

♦ demon, devil, fiend, imp

GHQ *abbr* general headquarters

gi *abbr* gill

¹GI \ˌjē-ˈī\ *adj* **1 :** provided by an official U.S. military supply department ⟨~ shoes⟩ **2 :** of, relating to, or characteristic of U.S. military personnel **3 :** conforming to military regulations or customs ⟨a ~ haircut⟩

²GI *n, pl* **GIs** *or* **GI's** \-ˈīz\ **:** a member or former member of the U.S. armed forces; *esp* **:** an enlisted man

³GI *abbr* **1** galvanized iron **2** gastrointestinal **3** general issue **4** government issue

¹gi•ant \ˈjī-ənt\ *n* **1 :** a legendary humanlike being of great size and strength **2** ♦ **:** a living being or thing of extraordinary size or powers

♦ behemoth, blockbuster, colossus, jumbo, leviathan, mammoth, monster, titan, whale, whopper *Ant* dwarf, midget, mini, miniature, peewee, pygmy, runt, shrimp

²giant *adj* ♦ **:** having extremely large size, proportion, or power

♦ astronomical, colossal, enormous, gigantic, ginormous, grand, huge, jumbo, mammoth, massive, monumental, prodigious, titanic, tremendous

gi•ant•ess \ˈjī-ən-təs\ *n* **:** a female giant

giant panda *n* **:** PANDA 2

gib•ber \ˈji-bər\ *vb* ♦ **:** to speak rapidly, inarticulately, and often foolishly

♦ babble, chatter, drivel, gabble, jabber, prattle, sputter

gib•ber•ish \ˈji-bə-rish\ *n* ♦ **:** unintelligible or confused speech or language

♦ babble, bunk, claptrap, drivel, gabble, gobbledygook, hogwash, nonsense, piffle, prattle, rot

¹gib•bet \ˈji-bət\ *n* **:** GALLOWS

²gibbet *vb* **1 :** to hang on a gibbet **2 :** to expose to public scorn **3 :** to execute by hanging

gib•bon \ˈgi-bən\ *n* **:** any of several tailless apes of southeastern Asia

gib•bous \ˈji-bəs, ˈgi-\ *adj* **1 :** rounded like the exterior of a sphere or circle **2 :** seen with more than half but not all of the apparent disk illuminated ⟨~ moon⟩ **3 :** having a hump : HUMP-BACKED

gibe *or* **jibe** \ˈjīb\ *vb* **gibed** *or* **jibed; gib•ing** *or* **jib•ing** ♦ **:** to utter taunting words : SNEER — **gibe** *or* **jibe** *n*

♦ deride, jeer, laugh, mock, ridicule, scout

gib•lets \ˈjib-ləts\ *n pl* **:** the edible viscera of a fowl

Gib•son girl \ˈgib-sən-\ *adj* **:** of or relating to a style in women's clothing characterized by high necks, full sleeves, and slender waistlines

gid•dy \ˈgi-dē\ *adj* **gid•di•er; -est 1** ♦ **:** having a whirling sensation in the head with a tendency to fall : DIZZY **2 :** causing dizziness **3** ♦ **:** not serious : FRIVOLOUS, SILLY — **gid•di•ness** \-dē-nəs\ *n*

♦ [1] dizzy, light-headed ♦ [3] flighty, frivolous, goofy, harebrained, light-headed, scatterbrained, silly *Ant* earnest, serious, sober

GIF \ˈgif, ˈjif\ *n* **:** a computer file format for digital images; *also* **:** the image itself

gift \ˈgift\ *n* **1** ♦ **:** a special ability : TALENT **2** ♦ **:** something given : PRESENT **3 :** the act or power of giving

♦ [1] aptitude, endowment, faculty, flair, genius, knack, talent ♦ [2] bestowal, donation, freebie, lagniappe, present

gift•ed \ˈgif-təd\ *adj* **:** TALENTED

¹gig \ˈgig\ *n* **1 :** a long light ship's boat **2 :** a light 2-wheeled one-horse carriage

²gig *n* **:** a pronged spear for catching fish — **gig** *vb*

³gig *n* **:** a job for a specified time; *esp* **:** an entertainer's engagement

⁴gig *n* **:** a military demerit — **gig** *vb*

giga•byte \ˈji-gə-ˌbīt, ˈgi-\ *n* **:** 1024 megabytes or 1,073,741,824 bytes; *also* **:** one billion bytes

gi•gan•tic \jī-ˈgan-tik\ *adj* ♦ **:** exceeding the usual (as in size or force)

♦ colossal, enormous, giant, ginormous, huge, jumbo, mammoth, massive, prodigious, titanic, tremendous

gig•gle \ˈgi-gəl\ *vb* **gig•gled; gig•gling :** to laugh with repeated short catches of the breath — **gig•gly** \-gə-lē\ *adj*

giggle *n* **:** the act of giggling

GIGO *abbr* garbage in, garbage out

gig•o•lo \ˈji-gə-ˌlō\ *n, pl* **-los 1 :** a man supported by a woman usually in return for his attentions **2 :** a professional dancing partner or male escort

Gi•la monster \ˈhē-lə-\ *n* **:** a large orange and black venomous lizard of the southwestern U.S.

¹gild \ˈgild\ *vb* **gild•ed** *or* **gilt** \ˈgilt\; **gild•ing 1 :** to overlay with or as if with a thin covering of gold **2 :** to give an attractive but often deceptive appearance to

²gild *var of* GUILD

¹gill \ˈjil\ *n* **:** a British measure of capacity equal to 5 fluid ounces; *also* **:** a U.S. measure of capacity equal to 5 fluid ounces

²gill \ˈgil\ *n* **:** an organ (as of a fish) for obtaining oxygen from water

¹gilt \ˈgilt\ *adj* **:** of the color of gold

²gilt *n* **:** gold or a substance resembling gold laid on the surface of an object

³gilt *n* **:** a young female swine

gim•crack \ˈjim-ˌkrak\ *n* **:** a showy object of little use or value

²gimcrack *adj* **:** CHEAP, SHODDY

gim•let \ˈgim-lət\ *n* **:** a small tool with screw point and cross handle for boring holes

gim•mick \ˈgi-mik\ *n* **1** ♦ **:** an ingenious or novel mechanical device : CONTRIVANCE, GADGET **2 :** an important feature that is not immediately apparent : CATCH **3** ♦ **:** a new and ingenious scheme — **gim•micky** \-mi-kē\ *adj*

♦ [1] contraption, contrivance, gadget, gizmo, jigger ♦ [3] artifice, device, dodge, jig, ploy, scheme, sleight, stratagem, trick, wile

gim•mick•ry \ˈgi-mi-krē\ *n, pl* **-ries :** an array of or the use of gimmicks

gimpy \ˈgim-pē\ *adj* **:** LAME 1

¹gin \ˈjin\ *n* **1 :** TRAP, SNARE **2 :** a machine to separate seeds from cotton — **gin** *vb*

²gin *n* **:** a liquor distilled from a grain mash and flavored with juniper berries

gin•ger \ˈjin-jər\ *n* **1 :** the pungent aromatic rootstock of a tropical plant used especially as a spice and in medicine; *also* **:** the spice or the plant **2 :** brisk energy or initiative and high spirits

ginger ale *n* **:** a carbonated soft drink flavored with ginger

gin•ger•bread \ˈjin-jər-ˌbred\ *n* **1 :** a cake made with molasses and flavored with ginger **2 :** lavish or superfluous ornament

gin•ger•ly \ˈjin-jər-lē\ *adj* ♦ : very cautious or careful — **gingerly** *adv*

♦ alert, careful, cautious, circumspect, considerate, guarded, heedful, safe, wary

gin•ger•snap \-ˌsnap\ *n* : a thin brittle molasses cookie flavored with ginger

ging•ham \ˈgiŋ-əm\ *n* : a clothing fabric usually of yarn-dyed cotton in plain weave

gin•gi•vi•tis \ˌjin-jə-ˈvī-təs\ *n* : inflammation of the gums

gink•go *also* **ging•ko** \ˈgiŋ-(ˌ)kō\ *n, pl* **ginkgoes** *or* **ginkgos** : a tree of eastern China with fan-shaped leaves often grown as a shade tree

ginkgo bi•lo•ba \-ˌbī-ˈlō-bə\ *n* : an extract of the leaves of ginkgo that is held to enhance mental functioning

gi•nor•mous \jī-ˈnȯr-məs\ *n* ♦ : extremely large : HUGE

♦ colossal, enormous, giant, huge, jumbo, mammoth, massive, prodigious, titanic, tremendous

gin•seng \ˈjin-ˌseŋ\ *n* : an aromatic root of a Chinese or No. American herb used especially in Chinese medicine; *also* : one of these herbs

Gip•sy *chiefly Brit var of* GYPSY

gi•raffe \jə-ˈraf\ *n, pl* **giraffes** : an African ruminant mammal with a very long neck and a short coat with dark blotches

gird \ˈgərd\ *vb* **gird•ed** *or* **girt** \ˈgərt\; **gird•ing** **1** ♦ : to encircle or fasten (as a sword) with or as if with a belt **2** : to invest especially with power or authority **3** : PREPARE, BRACE

♦ band, belt, girdle, wrap ***Ant*** unwrap ♦ band, bind, tie, truss

gird•er \ˈgər-dər\ *n* : a horizontal main supporting beam

¹gir•dle \ˈgər-dᵊl\ *n* **1** : something (as a belt or sash) that encircles or confines **2** : a woman's supporting undergarment that extends from the waist to below the hips

²girdle *vb* **gir•dled gir•dling** \ˈgər-dᵊl-iŋ\ **1** ♦ : to encircle with or as if with a girdle **2** ♦ : to move around

♦ [1] band, belt, gird, wrap ♦ [2] circle, circumnavigate, coil, compass, encircle, loop, orbit, ring, round

girl \ˈgərl\ *n* **1** : a female child **2** ♦ : a young woman **3** : SWEETHEART — **girl•hood** \-ˌhu̇d\ *n*

♦ doll, lass, maid, maiden, miss

girl Friday *n* : a female assistant (as in an office) entrusted with a wide variety of tasks

girl•friend \ˈgərl-ˌfrend\ *n* **1** : a female friend **2** : a regular female companion in a romantic or sexual relationship

girl•ish *adj* ♦ : of, relating to, or having the characteristics of a girl or girlhood

♦ effeminate, feminine, unmanly, womanly

Girl Scout *n* : a member of any of the scouting programs of the Girl Scouts of the United States of America

girth \ˈgərth\ *n* **1** : a band around an animal by which something (as a saddle) may be fastened on its back **2** : a measure around something

gist \ˈjist\ *n* ♦ : the main point or part

git *dial var of* GET

♦ core, crux, heart, nub, pith, pivot

¹give \ˈgiv\ *vb* **gave** \ˈgāv\; **giv•en** \ˈgi-vən\; **giv•ing** **1** ♦ : to make a present of **2** : to bestow by formal action **3** : to accord or yield to another **4** ♦ : to yield to force, strain, or pressure **5** ♦ : to put into the possession or keeping of another **6** ♦ : to offer to the action of another : PROFFER **7** : to put into the possession of another : DELIVER **8** ♦ : to present in public performance or to view **9** : PROVIDE ⟨~ a party⟩ **10** : ATTRIBUTE **11** : to make, form, or yield as a product or result ⟨cows ~ milk⟩ **12** : to yield possession of by way of exchange : PAY **13** : to deliver by some bodily action ⟨*gave* me a push⟩ **14** : to offer as a pledge ⟨I ~ you my word⟩ **15** : to apply freely or fully : DEVOTE **16** : to cause to have or receive

♦ [1] bestow, contribute, donate, present ♦ [4] cave in, collapse, crumple, go, yield ♦ [5] commend, commit, consign, delegate, deliver, entrust, hand over, leave, pass, transfer, transmit, trust, turn over, vest ***Ant*** hold, keep, retain ♦ [6] extend, offer, proffer, tender ♦ [8] carry, mount, offer, present, stage

²give *n* **1** : capacity or tendency to yield to force or strain **2** : the quality or state of being springy

give–and–take \ˌgiv-ən-ˈtāk\ *n* **1** ♦ : the practice of making mutual concessions : COMPROMISE **2** ♦ : a usually good-natured exchange (as of remarks or ideas)

♦ [1] accommodation, compromise, concession, negotiation ♦ [2] argument, colloquy, conference, deliberation, discourse, discussion, parley, talk

give•away \ˈgi-və-ˌwā\ *n* **1** : an unintentional revelation or betrayal **2** : something given away free; *esp* : PREMIUM

give away *vb* **1** : to make a present of **2** : to deliver (a bride) ceremonially to the bridegroom at a wedding **3** ♦ : to reveal or make known sometimes unintentionally

♦ bespeak, betray, demonstrate, display, evince, expose, manifest, reveal, show

give in *vb* ♦ : to yield under insistence or entreaty : SUBMIT, SURRENDER

♦ bow, budge, capitulate, concede, knuckle under, quit, submit, succumb, surrender, yield

¹giv•en \ˈgi-vən\ *adj* **1** ♦ : having a tendency or inclination : INCLINED ⟨~ to swearing⟩ **2** : SPECIFIED, PARTICULAR ⟨at a ~ time⟩

♦ apt, inclined, prone ♦ accustomed, used, wont

²given *prep* : CONSIDERING

given name *n* : a name that precedes one's surname

give out *vb* **1** : EMIT **2** : BREAK DOWN **3** : to become exhausted : COLLAPSE

give up *vb* **1** ♦ : to yield control or possession of : SURRENDER **2** : to abandon (oneself) to a feeling, influence, or activity **3** ♦ : to cease doing or attempting something especially as an admission of defeat : QUIT

♦ [1] cede, deliver, hand over, leave, relinquish, render, surrender, turn over, yield ♦ [3] discontinue, drop, knock off, lay off, quit

giz•mo *also* **gis•mo** \ˈgiz-mō\ *n, pl* **gizmos** *also* **gismos** ♦ : an often small mechanical or electronic device with a practical use but often thought of as a novelty : GADGET

♦ contraption, contrivance, gadget, gimmick, jigger

giz•zard \ˈgi-zərd\ *n* : the muscular usually horny-lined enlargement of the alimentary canal of a bird used for churning and grinding up food

gla•cial \ˈglā-shəl\ *adj* **1** : suggestive of ice: as **a** ♦ : extremely cold **b** ♦ : devoid of warmth and cordiality **2** : of or relating to glaciers **3** : being or relating to a past period of time when a large part of the earth was covered by glaciers **4** *cap* : PLEISTOCENE **5** : very slow ⟨a ~ pace⟩ — **gla•cial•ly** *adv*

♦ [1a] arctic, bitter, cold, freezing, frigid, polar, raw, wintry ♦ [1b] chill, chilly, cold, cold-blooded, cool, frigid, frosty, icy, unfriendly, unsympathetic, wintry

gla•ci•ate \ˈglā-shē-ˌāt\ *vb* **-at•ed; -at•ing** **1** : to subject to glacial action **2** : to produce glacial effects in or on — **gla•ci•a•tion** \ˌglā-shē-ˈā-shən, -sē-\ *n*

gla•cier \ˈglā-shər\ *n* : a large body of ice moving slowly down a slope or spreading outward on a land surface

¹glad \ˈglad\ *adj* **glad•der; glad•dest** **1** ♦ : experiencing pleasure, joy, or delight **2** : PLEASED **3** ♦ : very willing **4** : PLEASANT, JOYFUL **5** ♦ : causing happiness and joy : CHEERFUL — **glad•ly** *adv*

♦ [1] blissful, delighted, happy, joyful, pleased ***Ant*** displeased, joyless, sad, unhappy, unsatisfied ♦ [3] amenable, disposed, game, inclined, ready, willing ♦ [5] bright, cheerful, cheery, gay

²glad *n* : GLADIOLUS

glad•den \ˈglad-ᵊn\ *vb* ♦ : to make glad

♦ content, delight, gratify, please, rejoice, satisfy, suit, warm

glade \ˈglād\ *n* : a grassy open space surrounded by woods

glad•i•a•tor \ˈgla-dē-ˌā-tər\ *n* **1** : a person engaged in a fight to the death for public entertainment in ancient Rome **2** : a person engaging in a public fight or controversy; *also* : PRIZEFIGHTER

glad•i•a•to•ri•al \ˌgla-dē-ə-ˈtȯr-ē-əl\ *adj* **1** : of, relating to, or suggestive of gladiators or the combats of gladiators **2** : inclined toward controversy or contention

glad•i•o•lus \ˌgla-dē-ˈō-ləs\ *n, pl* **-o•li** \-(ˈ)ō-(ˌ)lē, -ˌlī\ *or* **-olus** : any of a genus of chiefly African plants related to the irises and having erect sword-shaped leaves and stalks of bright colored flowers

glad•ness *n* ♦ : the quality or state of being glad

♦ blessedness, bliss, felicity, happiness, joy ♦ contentment, delectation, delight, enjoyment, gratification, pleasure, relish, satisfaction

glad•some \ˈglad-səm\ *adj* : giving or showing joy : CHEERFUL
glad•stone \ˈglad-ˌstōn\ *n, often cap* : a suitcase with flexible sides on a rigid frame that opens flat into two compartments
glam \ˈglam\ *n* : extravagantly showy glamour — **glam** *adj*
glam•or•ise *chiefly Brit var of* GLAMORIZE
glam•or•ize *also* **glam•our•ize** \ˈgla-mə-ˌrīz\ *vb* **-ized; -iz•ing** ♦ : to make or look upon as glamorous; *also* : treat as idealized or heroic

♦ dream, glorify, idealize

glam•or•ous \-mə-rəs\ *adj* ♦ : full of glamour : excitingly attractive

♦ exotic, fantastic, marvelous (*or* marvellous), outlandish, romantic, strange ♦ alluring, attractive, captivating, charming, elfin, engaging, fascinating, fetching, magnetic, seductive

glam•our \ˈgla-mər\ *n* ♦ : an exciting and often illusory and romantic attractiveness; *esp* : alluring personal attraction

♦ allure, appeal, attractiveness, captivation, charisma, charm, enchantment, fascination, magic, magnetism

¹glance \ˈglans\ *vb* **glanced; glanc•ing** **1** ♦ : to strike and fly off to one side **2** ♦ : to flash or gleam with quick intermittent rays of light **3** ♦ : to give a quick look

♦ [1] bounce, carom, rebound, ricochet, skim, skip ♦ [2] flame, flash, gleam, glimmer, glisten, glitter, scintillate, shimmer, sparkle, twinkle, wink ♦ [3] browse, dip, glimpse, peek, skim ***Ant*** stare, gaze

²glance *n* **1** : a quick intermittent flash or gleam **2** : a deflected impact or blow **3** ♦ : a quick look

♦ cast, eye, gander, glimpse, look, peek, peep, regard, sight, view

gland \ˈgland\ *n* : a cell or group of cells that prepares and secretes a substance (as saliva or sweat) for further use in or discharge from the body
glan•du•lar \ˈglan-jə-lər\ *adj* : of, relating to, or involving glands
glans \ˈglanz\ *n, pl* **glan•des** \ˈglan-ˌdēz\ : a conical vascular body forming the extremity of the penis or clitoris
¹glare \ˈgler\ *vb* **glared; glar•ing** **1** ♦ : to shine with a harsh dazzling light **2** ♦ : to stare fiercely or angrily

♦ [1] beat, blaze, burn, flame, flare ♦ [2] frown, gloom, glower, lower, scowl

²glare *n* **1** : a harsh dazzling light **2** : an angry or fierce stare
glaring *adj* ♦ : very conspicuous ⟨a ~ error⟩ — **glar•ing•ly** *adv*

♦ blatant, conspicuous, egregious, flagrant, gross, obvious, patent, prominent, pronounced, rank, striking

glass \ˈglas\ *n* **1** : a hard brittle amorphous usually transparent or translucent material consisting typically of silica **2** : something made of glass; *esp* : TUMBLER 2 **3** *pl* ♦ : a pair of lenses used to correct defects of vision : SPECTACLES **4** : the quantity held by a glass container — **glass** *adj* — **glass•ful** \-ˌfu̇l\ *n* — **glassy** *adj*

♦ **glasses** eyeglasses, spectacles

glass•blow•ing \-ˌblō-iŋ\ *n* : the art of shaping a mass of glass that has been softened by heat by blowing air into it through a tube — **glass•blow•er** *n*
glass•ware \-ˌwer\ *n* : articles made of glass
glau•co•ma \glau̇-ˈkō-mə, glȯ-\ *n* : a disease of the eye marked by increased pressure within the eyeball resulting in damage to the retina and gradual loss of vision
¹glaze \ˈglāz\ *vb* **glazed; glaz•ing** **1** : to furnish (as a window frame) with glass **2** : to apply glaze to
²glaze *n* : a glassy coating or surface
gla•zier \ˈglā-zhər\ *n* : a person who sets glass in window frames
¹gleam \ˈglēm\ *n* **1** : a transient subdued or partly obscured light **2 a** ♦ : a small bright light **b** : GLINT **3** : a faint trace ⟨a ~ of hope⟩

♦ blaze, flare, fluorescence, glare, glow, illumination, incandescence, light, luminescence, radiance, shine

²gleam *vb* **1** ♦ : to shine with subdued light or moderate brightness **2** : to appear briefly or faintly

♦ flame, flash, glance, glimmer, glisten, glitter, scintillate, shimmer, sparkle, twinkle, wink

glean \ˈglēn\ *vb* **1** : to gather grain left by reapers **2** : to collect little by little or with patient effort — **glean•able** *adj* — **glean•er** *n*
glean•ings \ˈglē-niŋz\ *n pl* : things acquired by gleaning

glee \ˈglē\ *n* **1** ♦ : exultant high-spirited joy : HILARITY **2** : a part-song for three usually male voices

♦ cheer, cheerfulness, hilarity, joviality, merriment, mirth

glee club *n* : a chorus organized for singing usually short choral pieces
glee•ful *adj* ♦ : full of glee

♦ blithe, boon, festive, gay, jocund, jolly, jovial, merry, mirthful, sunny

glen \ˈglen\ *n* : a narrow hidden valley
glen•gar•ry \glen-ˈgar-ē\ *n, pl* **-ries** *often cap* : a woolen cap of Scottish origin
glib \ˈglib\ *adj* **glib•ber; glib•best** : speaking or spoken with careless ease — **glib•ly** *adv*
glide \ˈglīd\ *vb* **glid•ed; glid•ing** **1** ♦ : to move smoothly and effortlessly **2** ♦ : to descend gradually without engine power ⟨~ in an airplane⟩ — **glide** *n*

♦ [1] bowl, breeze, coast, drift, flow, roll, sail, skim, slide, slip, stream, sweep, whisk ♦ [2] fly, plane, soar, wing

glid•er \ˈglī-dər\ *n* **1** : one that glides **2** : an aircraft resembling an airplane but having no engine **3** : a porch seat suspended from an upright frame
¹glim•mer \ˈgli-mər\ *vb* ♦ : to shine faintly or unsteadily

♦ flame, flash, glance, gleam, glisten, glitter, scintillate, shimmer, sparkle, twinkle, wink

²glimmer *n* **1** : a faint unsteady light **2** : INKLING **3** ♦ : a small amount : HINT

♦ hint, little, mite, particle, touch, trace

¹glimpse \ˈglimps\ *vb* **glimpsed; glimps•ing** ♦ : to take a brief look : see momentarily or incompletely

♦ browse, dip, glance, peek, skim

²glimpse *n* **1** : a faint idea : GLIMMER **2** ♦ : a short hurried look

♦ cast, eye, gander, glance, look, peek, peep, regard, sight, view

glint \ˈglint\ *vb* **1** : to shine by reflection : SPARKLE, GLEAM **2** : to appear briefly or faintly — **glint** *n*
glis•san•do \gli-ˈsän-(ˌ)dō\ *n, pl* **-di** \-(ˌ)dē\ *or* **-dos** : a rapid sliding up or down the musical scale
¹glis•ten \ˈgli-sᵊn\ *vb* ♦ : to shine by reflection with a soft luster or sparkle

♦ flame, flash, glance, gleam, glimmer, glitter, scintillate, shimmer, sparkle, twinkle, wink

²glisten *n* : GLITTER, SPARKLE
glis•ter \ˈglis-tər\ *vb* : to shine by reflection with many small flashes of brilliant light : GLITTER
glitch \ˈglich\ *n* : MALFUNCTION; *also* : SNAG 2
¹glit•ter \ˈgli-tər\ *vb* **1** ♦ : to shine with brilliant or metallic luster : SPARKLE **2** : to shine with strong emotion : FLASH ⟨eyes ~*ing* in anger⟩ **3** : to be brilliantly attractive especially in a superficial way

♦ flame, flash, glance, gleam, glimmer, glisten, scintillate, shimmer, sparkle, twinkle, wink

²glitter *n* **1** : sparkling brilliancy, showiness, or attractiveness **2** : small glittering objects used for ornamentation — **glit•tery** \ˈgli-tə-rē\ *adj*
glitz \ˈglits\ *n* ♦ : extravagant showiness

♦ flamboyance, flashiness, gaudiness, ostentation, pretentiousness, showiness, swank

glitzy \ˈglit-sē\ *adj* ♦ : having glitz

♦ flamboyant, flashy, garish, gaudy, loud, ostentatious, swank, tawdry

gloam•ing \ˈglō-miŋ\ *n* ♦ : the light from the sky between full night and sunrise or between sunset and full night : TWILIGHT, DUSK

♦ dusk, evening, nightfall, sundown, sunset, twilight

gloat \ˈglōt\ *vb* : to think about something with triumphant and often malicious delight
glob \ˈgläb\ *n* **1** ♦ : a small drop **2** ♦ : a large rounded mass

♦ [1] blob, driblet, drip, drop, droplet ♦ [2] blob, chunk, clod, clump, gob, hunk, lump, nub, wad

glob•al \ˈglō-bəl\ *adj* **1** : of, relating to, or involving the entire world : WORLDWIDE **2** ♦ : of, relating to, or applying to a whole : COMPREHENSIVE, GENERAL — **glob•al•ly** *adv*

♦ blanket, common, general, generic, overall, universal ♦ compendious, complete, comprehensive, encyclopedic, full, inclusive, omnibus, panoramic, universal

glob•al•i•za•tion \ˌglō-bə-lə-ˈzā-shən\ *n* **:** the development of an increasingly integrated global economy

Global Positioning System *n* **:** GPS

global warming *n* **:** an increase in the earth's atmospheric and oceanic temperatures due to an increase in the greenhouse effect

globe \ˈglōb\ *n* **1 :** a round body **:** BALL, SPHERE **2 :** the planet on which we live that is third in order from the sun **:** EARTH; *also* **:** a spherical representation of the earth

globe–trot•ter \ˈglōb-ˌträ-tər\ *n* **:** a person who travels widely — **globe–trot•ting** *n or adj*

glob•u•lar \ˈglä-byə-lər\ *adj* **:** having the shape of a globe or globule

glob•ule \ˈglä-(ˌ)byül\ *n* **:** a tiny globe or ball especially of a liquid

glob•u•lin \ˈglä-byə-lən\ *n* **:** any of a class of simple proteins insoluble in pure water but soluble in dilute salt solutions that occur widely in plant and animal tissues

glock•en•spiel \ˈglä-kən-ˌshpēl, -ˌspēl\ *n* **:** a percussion musical instrument consisting of a series of metal bars played with two hammers

gloom \ˈglüm\ *n* **1** ♦ **:** partial or total darkness **2** ♦ **:** lowness of spirits **:** DEJECTION **3 :** an atmosphere of despondency

♦ [1] dark, darkness, dusk, gloaming, murk, night, semidarkness, shade, shadows, twilight ♦ [2] blues, dejection, depression, doldrums, dumps, melancholy, sadness

gloom•i•ness \-mē-nəs\ *n* **:** the quality or state of being gloomy

gloomy \ˈglü-mē\ *adj* **gloom•i•er; -est 1** ♦ **:** partially or totally dark **2** ♦ **:** causing gloom; *also* **:** lacking in promise or hopefulness **3** ♦ **:** low in spirits — **gloom•i•ly** \ˈglü-mə-lē\ *adv*

♦ [1] dark, darkling, dim, dusky, murky, obscure, somber (*or* sombre) ♦ [2] bleak, dark, depressing, desolate, dismal, dreary, glum, gray (*or* grey), miserable, murky, somber (*or* sombre) ***Ant*** bright, cheerful, gay, festive, friendly, heartwarming, sunshiny ♦ [3] blue, dejected, depressed, down, downcast, forlorn, glum, low, melancholy, miserable, sad, sorrowful, unhappy

Gloomy Gus \-ˈgəs\ *n, pl* **Gloomy Gus•es :** a person who is habitually gloomy

glop \ˈgläp\ *n* **:** a messy mass or mixture

glo•ri•fy \ˈglȯr-ə-ˌfī\ *vb* **-fied; -fy•ing 1 :** to raise to heavenly glory **2 :** to light up brilliantly **3** ♦ **:** to represent as glorious **:** EXTOL **4** ♦ **:** to give glory to (as in worship) **5** ♦ **:** to cause to be or seem to be better than the actual condition **6** ♦ **:** to make glorious by bestowing honor, praise, or admiration — **glo•ri•fi•ca•tion** \ˌglȯr-ə-fə-ˈkā-shən\ *n*

♦ [3] bless, extol, laud, magnify, praise ♦ [4] adore, deify, revere, venerate, worship ♦ [5] dream, glamorize, idealize ♦ [6] aggrandize, dignify, ennoble, exalt, magnify

glo•ri•ous \ˈglȯr-ē-əs\ *adj* **1 :** possessing or deserving glory **:** PRAISEWORTHY **2 :** conferring glory **3** ♦ **:** marked by great beauty or splendor **:** MAGNIFICENT **4 :** DELIGHTFUL, WONDERFUL

♦ august, baronial, gallant, grand, grandiose, heroic, imposing, magnificent, majestic, monumental, noble, proud, regal, royal, splendid, stately

glo•ri•ous•ly *adv* ♦ **:** in a glorious manner

♦ agreeably, delightfully, favorably (*or* favourably), felicitously, nicely, pleasantly, pleasingly, satisfyingly, splendidly, well

¹glo•ry \ˈglȯr-ē\ *n, pl* **glories 1** ♦ **:** praise, honor, or distinction extended by common consent **:** RENOWN **2 :** honor and praise rendered in worship **3** ♦ **:** something that secures praise or renown **4 :** a distinguishing quality or asset **5** ♦ **:** great beauty and splendor **:** RESPLENDENCE, MAGNIFICENCE **6 :** heavenly bliss **7 :** a height of prosperity or achievement

♦ [1] acclaim, accolade, credit, distinction, fame, homage, honor (*or* honour), laurels, praise, renown ♦ [3] boast, credit, honor (*or* honour), jewel, pride, treasure ♦ [5] augustness, brilliance, grandeur, grandness, magnificence, majesty, nobility, nobleness, resplendence, splendor, stateliness

²glory *vb* **glo•ried; glo•ry•ing** ♦ **:** to rejoice proudly **:** EXULT

♦ crow, delight, exult, joy, rejoice, triumph

¹gloss \ˈgläs, ˈglȯs\ *n* **1** ♦ **:** a surface luster or brightness **:** SHEEN **2 :** outward show

♦ luster (*or* lustre), polish, sheen, shine

²gloss *vb* **1** ♦ **:** to give a false appearance of acceptableness to ⟨∼ over inadequacies⟩ **2** ♦ **:** to deal with too lightly or not at all — usually used with *over* **3** ♦ **:** to give a gloss to

♦ *usu* **gloss over** [1] excuse, palliate, whitewash ♦ *usu* **gloss over** [2] condone, disregard, excuse, forgive, ignore, pardon, pass over, shrug off, wink at ♦ [3] buff, burnish, dress, grind, polish, rub, shine, smooth

³gloss *n* **1 :** an explanatory note (as in the margin of a text) **2 :** GLOSSARY **3 :** an interlinear translation **4 :** a continuous commentary accompanying a text

⁴gloss *vb* **:** to furnish glosses for

glos•sa•ry \ˈglä-sə-rē, ˈglȯ-\ *n, pl* **-ries :** a collection of difficult or specialized terms with their meanings — **glos•sar•i•al** \glä-ˈser-ē-əl, glȯ-\ *adj*

glos•so•la•lia \ˌglä-sə-ˈlā-lē-ə, ˌglȯ-\ *n* **:** TONGUE 6

¹glossy \ˈglä-sē, ˈglȯ-\ *adj* **gloss•i•er; -est** ♦ **:** having a surface luster or brightness — **gloss•i•ly** \-sə-lē\ *adv* — **gloss•i•ness** \-sē-nəs\ *n*

♦ lustrous, polished, satiny, sleek ***Ant*** dim, dull, flat, lusterless, matte

²glossy *n, pl* **gloss•ies :** a photograph printed on smooth shiny paper

glot•tis \ˈglä-təs\ *n, pl* **glot•tis•es** *or* **glot•ti•des** \-tə-ˌdēz\ **:** the slitlike opening between the vocal cords in the larynx — **glot•tal** \ˈglä-tᵊl\ *adj*

glove \ˈgləv\ *n* **1 :** a covering for the hand having separate sections for each finger **2 :** a padded leather covering for the hand for use in a sport

¹glow \ˈglō\ *vb* **1** ♦ **:** to shine with or as if with intense heat **2** ♦ **:** to have a rich warm usually ruddy color **:** FLUSH, BLUSH **3 :** to feel hot **4 :** to show exuberance or elation ⟨∼ with pride⟩

♦ [1] blaze, burn, flame ♦ [2] bloom, blush, color (*or* colour), crimson, flush, redden

²glow *n* **1 :** brightness or warmth of color; *esp* **:** REDNESS **2 :** warmth of feeling or emotion **3 :** a sensation of warmth **4** ♦ **:** light such as is emitted from a heated substance

♦ blaze, flare, fluorescence, glare, gleam, illumination, incandescence, light, luminescence, radiance, shine

glow•er \ˈglau̇(-ə)r\ *vb* ♦ **:** to stare angrily **:** SCOWL — **glower** *n*

♦ frown, glare, gloom, lower, scowl

glowing *adj* **1** ♦ **:** giving off light especially because of heat **2** ♦ **:** marked by a rich warm coloration; *also* **:** marked by a radiant healthfully ruddy coloration **3 :** highly enthusiastic

♦ [1] beaming, bright, brilliant, effulgent, incandescent, lambent, lucent, lucid, luminous, lustrous, radiant, refulgent, shiny ♦ [2] florid, flush, rosy, ruddy, sanguine

glow•worm \ˈglō-ˌwərm\ *n* **:** any of various insect larvae or adults that give off light

glox•in•ia \gläk-ˈsi-nē-ə\ *n* **:** any of a genus of tropical herbs related to the African violets; *esp* **:** one with showy bell-shaped or slipper-shaped flowers

gloze \ˈglōz\ *vb* **glozed; gloz•ing :** to make appear right or acceptable **:** GLOSS

glu•cose \ˈglü-ˌkōs\ *n* **1 :** a form of crystalline sugar; *esp* **:** DEXTROSE **2 :** a sweet light-colored syrup made from cornstarch

glue \ˈglü\ *n* ♦ **:** a jellylike protein substance made from animal materials and used for sticking things together; *also* **:** any of various other strong adhesives — **glue** *vb*

♦ adhesive, cement, size

glu•ey \ˈglü-ē\ *adj* **1** ♦ **:** having the quality of glue; *also* **:** resembling or suggestive of glue (as in stickiness or consistency) **2 :** daubed, smeared, or covered with glue

♦ adhesive, gelatinous, glutinous, gooey, gummy, sticky, viscid, viscous

glum \ˈgləm\ *adj* **glum•mer; glum•mest 1** ♦ **:** broodingly morose **:** SULLEN **2** ♦ **:** having nothing likely to provide cheer, comfort, or interest **:** DREARY, GLOOMY

♦ [1] moody, morose, sulky, sullen, surly ♦ [1, 2] bleak, dark, dismal, dreary, gloomy, gray (*or* grey), somber (*or* sombre), wretched

¹glut \ˈglət\ *vb* **glut•ted; glut•ting 1 :** to supply with more than is needed or than can be handled **2** ♦ **:** to fill especially with food to satiety **:** SATIATE

♦ gorge, sate, satiate, stuff, surfeit

[2]**glut** *n* **:** an excessive supply
glu·ten \ˈglüt-ᵊn\ *n* **:** a gluey protein substance that causes dough to be sticky
glu·ti·nous \ˈglü-tə-nəs\ *adj* ♦ **:** having the quality of glue **:** STICKY

♦ adhesive, gelatinous, gluey, gooey, gummy, sticky, viscid, viscous

glut·ton \ˈglə-tᵊn\ *n* **:** one that eats to excess — **glut·tony** \ˈglə-tə-nē\ *n*
glut·ton·ous \ˈglət-ᵊn-əs\ *adj* ♦ **:** marked by or given to excessive eating or drinking

♦ greedy, hoggish, piggish, rapacious, ravenous, voracious

glyc·er·in *or* **glyc·er·ine** \ˈgli-sə-rən\ *n* **:** GLYCEROL
glyc·er·ol \ˈgli-sə-ˌrȯl, -ˌrōl\ *n* **:** a sweet syrupy alcohol usually obtained from fats and used especially as a solvent
gly·co·gen \ˈglī-kə-jən\ *n* **:** a white tasteless substance that is the chief storage carbohydrate of animals
gm *abbr* gram
GM *abbr* **1** general manager **2** guided missile
G–man \ˈjē-ˌman\ *n* **:** a special agent of the Federal Bureau of Investigation
GMT *abbr* Greenwich mean time
gnarled \ˈnärld\ *adj* **1 :** KNOTTY **2 :** GLOOMY, SULLEN
gnash \ˈnash\ *vb* ♦ **:** to grind (as teeth) together

♦ crunch, grate, grind, grit, scrape

gnat \ˈnat\ *n* **:** any of various small usually biting dipteran flies
gnaw \ˈnȯ\ *vb* **1** ♦ **:** to consume, wear away, or make by persistent biting or nibbling **2 :** to affect as if by gnawing

♦ *usu* **gnaw on** bite, champ, chew, chomp, crunch, nibble

gnaw·er *n* **:** one that gnaws
gneiss \ˈnīs\ *n* **:** a layered rock similar in composition to granite
gnome \ˈnōm\ *n* ♦ **:** a dwarf of folklore who lives inside the earth and guards precious ore or treasure — **gnom·ish** *adj*

♦ brownie, dwarf, elf, fairy, fay, hobgoblin, leprechaun, pixie, puck, troll

GNP *abbr* gross national product
gnu \ˈnü\ *n, pl* **gnu** *or* **gnus :** WILDEBEEST
[1]**go** \ˈgō\ *vb* **went** \ˈwent\; **gone** \ˈgȯn, ˈgän\; **go·ing; goes** \ˈgōz\ **1** ♦ **:** to move on a course **:** PROCEED ⟨∼ slow⟩ **2** ♦ **:** to move out of or away from a place expressed or implied **:** LEAVE, DEPART **3 :** to take a certain course or follow a certain procedure ⟨reports ∼ through department channels⟩ **4** ♦ **:** to extend from point to point or in a certain direction **:** RUN ⟨his land ∼*es* to the river⟩; *also* **:** LEAD ⟨that door ∼*es* to the cellar⟩ **5 :** to be habitually in a certain state ⟨∼*es* armed after dark⟩ **6 :** to become lost, consumed, or spent; *also* **:** DIE **7 :** ELAPSE, PASS **8** ♦ **:** to pass by sale ⟨*went* for a good price⟩ **9 :** to become impaired or weakened **10 :** to give way under force or pressure **11 :** to move along in a specified manner ⟨it *went* well⟩ **12 :** to be in general or on an average ⟨cheap, as yachts ∼⟩ **13 :** to become especially as the result of a contest ⟨the decision *went* against him⟩ **14 :** to put or subject oneself ⟨∼ to great expense⟩ **15** ♦ **:** to have recourse to another **:** RESORT ⟨*went* to court to recover damages⟩ **16 :** to begin or maintain an action or motion ⟨here ∼*es*⟩ **17 :** to function properly ⟨the clock doesn't ∼⟩ **18 :** to be known ⟨∼*es* by an alias⟩ **19 :** to be or act in accordance ⟨a good rule to ∼ by⟩ **20 :** to come to be applied **21 :** to pass by award, assignment, or lot **22 :** to contribute to a result ⟨qualities that ∼ to make a hero⟩ **23 :** to be about, intending, or expecting something ⟨is ∼*ing* to leave town⟩ **24 :** to arrive at a certain state or condition ⟨∼ to sleep⟩ **25 :** to come to be ⟨the tire *went* flat⟩ **26 :** to be capable of being sung or played ⟨the tune ∼*es* like this⟩ **27 :** to be suitable or becoming **:** HARMONIZE **28 :** to be capable of passing, extending, or being contained or inserted ⟨this coat will ∼ in the trunk⟩ **29 :** to have a usual or proper place or position **:** BELONG ⟨these books ∼ on the top shelf⟩ **30 :** to be capable of being divided ⟨3 ∼*es* into 6 twice⟩ **31 :** to have a tendency ⟨that ∼*es* to show that he is honest⟩ **32 :** to be acceptable, satisfactory, or adequate **33 :** to empty the bladder or bowels **34 :** to proceed along or according to **:** FOLLOW **35** ♦ **:** to travel through or along **:** TRAVERSE **36 :** to make a wager or offer of **:** BET, BID ⟨willing to ∼ $50⟩ **37 :** to assume the function or obligation of ⟨∼ bail for a friend⟩ **38 :** to participate to the extent of ⟨∼ halves⟩ **39 :** WEIGH **40 :** ENDURE, TOLERATE **41 :** AFFORD ⟨can't ∼ the price⟩ **42 :** SAY — used chiefly in oral narration of speech **43 :** to engage in ⟨don't ∼ telling everyone⟩ — **go at 1 :** ATTACK, ATTEMPT **2 :** UNDERTAKE — **go back on 1 :** ABANDON **2 :** BETRAY **3 :** FAIL — **go by the board :** to be discarded — **go for 1 :** to pass for or serve as **2 :** to try to secure **3 :** FAVOR — **go one better :** OUTDO, SURPASS — **go over 1 :** EXAMINE **2 :** REPEAT **3 :** STUDY, REVIEW — **go places :** to be on the way to success — **go steady :** to date one person exclusively — **go to bat for :** DEFEND, CHAMPION — **go to town 1 :** to work or act efficiently **2 :** to be very successful

♦ [1] advance, fare, forge, get along, march, proceed, progress *Ant* remain, stand, stay, stop ♦ [2] clear out, depart, exit, get off, leave, move, pull, quit, sally, shove, take off *Ant* arrive, come, show up, turn up ♦ [4] extend, head, lead, lie, run ♦ *usu* **go for** [8] bring, cost, fetch, sell ♦ *usu* **go to** [15] refer, resort, turn ♦ [35] cover, crisscross, cross, cut, follow, pass, proceed, travel, traverse

[2]**go** *n, pl* **goes 1 :** the act or manner of going **2 :** the height of fashion ⟨boots are all the ∼⟩ **3 :** a turn of affairs **:** OCCURRENCE **4 :** active bodily or mental strength or force **:** ENERGY, VIGOR **5** ♦ **:** an experimental trial or attempt **6 :** a spell of activity — **no go :** USELESS, HOPELESS — **on the go :** constantly active

♦ attempt, bid, crack, endeavor (*or* endeavour), essay, fling, pass, shot, stab, trial, try, whack, whirl

[3]**go** *adj* ♦ **:** functioning properly

♦ fit, ready, set

[1]**goad** \ˈgōd\ *n* **1 :** a pointed rod used to urge on an animal **2** ♦ **:** something that urges

♦ boost, encouragement, impetus, impulse, incentive, incitement, instigation, momentum, motivation, provocation, spur, stimulus, yeast

[2]**goad** *vb* ♦ **:** to incite or rouse as if with a goad

♦ egg on, encourage, exhort, press, prod, prompt, urge

go–ahead \ˈgō-ə-ˌhed\ *n* **:** authority to proceed
goal \ˈgōl\ *n* **1 :** the mark set as limit to a race; *also* **:** an area to be reached safely in children's games **2** ♦ **:** the end toward which effort is directed **:** AIM, PURPOSE **3 :** an area or object toward which play is directed to score; *also* **:** a successful attempt to score

♦ aim, ambition, aspiration, design, dream, end, intent, mark, meaning, object, objective, plan, pretension, purpose, thing

goal·ie \ˈgō-lē\ *n* **:** GOALKEEPER
goal·keep·er \ˈgōl-ˌkē-pər\ *n* **:** a player who defends the goal in various games
goal·post \-ˌpōst\ *n* **:** one of the two vertical posts with a crossbar that constitute the goal in various games
goat \ˈgōt\ *n, pl* **goats** *or* **goat :** any of various hollow-horned ruminant mammals related to the sheep that have backward-curving horns, a short tail, and usually straight hair
goa·tee \gō-ˈtē\ *n* **:** a small trim pointed or tufted beard on a man's chin
goat·herd \ˈgōt-ˌhərd\ *n* **:** a person who tends goats
goat·skin \-ˌskin\ *n* **:** the skin of a goat or a leather made from it
[1]**gob** \ˈgäb\ *n* **1** ♦ **:** a piece or mass of indefinite size and shape **:** LUMP, MASS **2** ♦ **:** a large amount — usually used in plural ⟨∼*s* of money⟩

♦ [1] blob, chunk, clod, clump, glob, hunk, lump, mass, nub, wad ♦ *usu* **gobs** [2] abundance, deal, heap, loads, lot, pile, plenty, quantity, scads

[2]**gob** *n* ♦ **:** a member of a ship's crew **:** SAILOR

♦ jack, jack-tar, mariner, sailor, seaman, swab, tar

gob·bet \ˈgä-bət\ *n* **:** a piece or mass of indefinite size and shape **:** LUMP, MASS
[1]**gob·ble** \ˈgä-bəl\ *vb* **gob·bled; gob·bling 1** ♦ **:** to swallow or eat greedily **2 :** to take eagerly **:** GRAB

♦ bolt, devour, gorge, gormandize, gulp, scarf, scoff, wolf

[2]**gobble** *vb* **gob·bled; gob·bling :** to make the natural guttural noise of a male turkey
gob·ble·dy·gook *also* **gob·ble·de·gook** \ˈgä-bəl-dē-ˌgu̇k, -ˌgük\ *n* ♦ **:** generally unintelligible jargon

♦ babble, gabble, gibberish, hogwash, jabber, jabberwocky, nonsense

gob·bler \ˈgä-blər\ *n* **:** a male turkey
go–be·tween \ˈgō-bə-ˌtwēn\ *n* ♦ **:** an intermediate agent **:** BROKER

♦ arbiter, arbitrator, broker, intercessor, intermediary, mediator, middleman, peacemaker

gob·let \ˈgä-blət\ *n* **:** a drinking glass with a foot and stem

gob•lin \ˈgä-blən\ *n* : an ugly or grotesque sprite that is mischievous and sometimes evil and malicious
go•by \ˈgō-bē\ *n, pl* **gobies** *also* **goby** : any of numerous spiny-finned fishes usually having the pelvic fins united to form a ventral sucking disk
god \ˈgäd, ˈgȯd\ *n* **1** *cap* : the supreme reality; *esp* : the Being worshiped as the creator and ruler of the universe **2** : a being or object believed to have supernatural attributes and powers and to require worship **3** : a thing of supreme value **4** : an extraordinarily attractive person
god•child \ˈgäd-ˌchīld, ˈgȯd-\ *n* : a person for whom another person stands as sponsor at baptism
god•daugh•ter \-ˌdȯ-tər\ *n* : a female godchild
god•dess \ˈgä-dəs, ˈgȯ-\ *n* **1** : a female god **2** ♦ : a woman whose charm or beauty arouses adoration

♦ beauty, enchantress, fox, knockout, queen

god•fa•ther \ˈgäd-ˌfä-t͟hər, ˈgȯd-\ *n* **1** : a man who sponsors a person at baptism **2** : the leader of an organized crime syndicate
god•head \-ˌhed\ *n* **1** ♦ : divine nature or essence **2** *cap* : GOD 1; *also* : the nature of God especially as existing in three persons

♦ deity, divinity

god•hood \-ˌhu̇d\ *n* : the quality or state of being a god : DIVINITY
god•less \-ləs\ *adj* : not acknowledging a deity or divine law — **god•less•ness** *n*
god•like \-ˌlīk\ *adj* ♦ : resembling or having the qualities of God or a god

♦ blessed, divine, heavenly, holy

god•li•ness *n* ♦ : the quality or state of living a godly life

♦ blessedness, devoutness, holiness, piety, sainthood, sanctity

god•ly \-lē\ *adj* **god•li•er; -est** **1** : DIVINE **2** ♦ : marked by or showing reverence for deity and devotion to divine worship : PIOUS, DEVOUT

♦ devout, faithful, holy, pious, religious, sainted, saintly

god•moth•er \-ˌmə-t͟hər\ *n* : a woman who sponsors a person at baptism
god•par•ent \-ˌpar-ənt\ *n* : a sponsor at baptism
god•send \-ˌsend\ *n* ♦ : a desirable or needed thing or event that comes unexpectedly

♦ benefit, blessing, boon, felicity, good, manna, windfall

god•son \-ˌsən\ *n* : a male godchild
God•speed \-ˈspēd\ *n* : a prosperous journey : SUCCESS ⟨bade him ~⟩
go•fer *or* **go•pher** \ˈgō-fər\ *n* : an employee whose duties include running errands
go–get•ter \ˈgō-ˌge-tər\ *n* ♦ : an aggressively enterprising person — *adj or n*

♦ hustler, live wire, powerhouse, self-starter

go–get•ting *adj* ♦ : marked by driving forceful energy, ambition, or initiative — **go-getting** *n*

♦ aggressive, ambitious, assertive, enterprising, fierce, high-pressure, militant, self-assertive

gog•gle \ˈgä-gəl\ *vb* **gog•gled; gog•gling** ♦ : to stare with wide or protuberant eyes

♦ gape, gawk, gaze, peer, rubberneck, stare

gog•gles \ˈgä-gəlz\ *n pl* : protective glasses set in a flexible frame that fits snugly against the face
go–go \ˈgō-ˌgō\ *adj* **1** : related to, being, or employed to entertain in a disco ⟨~ dancers⟩ **2** : aggressively enterprising and energetic
go•ings–on \ˌgō-iŋ-ˈzȯn, -ˈzän\ *n pl* : ACTIONS, EVENTS
goi•ter *or Can and Brit* **goi•tre** \ˈgȯi-tər\ *n* : an abnormally enlarged thyroid gland visible as a swelling at the base of the neck — **goi•trous** \-trəs, -tə-rəs\ *adj*
go–kart \ˈgō-ˌkärt\ *n* : a small motorized vehicle used especially for racing
gold \ˈgōld\ *n* **1** : a malleable yellow metallic chemical element used especially for coins and jewelry **2** : gold coins; *also* : MONEY **3** : a yellow color
gold•brick \ˈgōld-ˌbrik\ *n* : a person who shirks assigned work — **goldbrick** *vb*
gold coast *n, often cap G&C* : an exclusive residential district
gold digger *n* : a person who uses charm to extract money or gifts from others
gold•en \ˈgōl-dən\ *adj* **1** : made of or relating to gold **2** ♦ : having the color of gold; *also* : BLOND **3** : SHINING, LUSTROUS **4** : SUPERB **5** ♦ : marked by success or economic well-being : PROSPEROUS **6** : radiantly youthful and vigorous **7** ♦ : tending to promote or facilitate : FAVORABLE, ADVANTAGEOUS ⟨a ~ opportunity⟩ **8** : rich and full but free from garishness or stridency : MELLOW, RESONANT

♦ [2] blond, fair, flaxen, sandy, straw ♦ [5] booming, palmy, prosperous, roaring, successful ♦ [7] advantageous, auspicious, bright, encouraging, favorable (*or* favourable), heartening, hopeful, promising, propitious

gold•en–ag•er \ˈgōl-dən-ˈā-jər\ *n* ♦ : an elderly and often retired person usually engaging in club activities

♦ ancient, elder, oldster, senior citizen

golden hamster *n* : a small tawny hamster often kept as a pet
golden handcuffs *n pl* : special benefits offered to an employee as an inducement to continue service
golden handshake *n* : a generous severance agreement given especially as an inducement to early retirement
golden retriever *n* : any of a breed of retrievers with a flat golden coat
gold•en•rod \ˈgōl-dən-ˌräd\ *n* : any of numerous herbs related to the daisies that have tall slender stalks with many tiny usually yellow flower heads
golden years *n pl* : the advanced years in a lifetime
gold•finch \-ˌfinch\ *n* **1** : a small largely red, black, and yellow Old World finch often kept in a cage **2** : any of three small related American finches of which the males usually become bright yellow and black in summer
gold•fish \-ˌfish\ *n* : a small usually golden-orange carp often kept as an aquarium or pond fish
gold•smith \-ˌsmith\ *n* : a person who makes or deals in articles of gold
golf \ˈgälf, ˈgȯlf\ *n* : a game played with a small ball and various clubs on a course having 9 or 18 holes — **golf** *vb* — **golf•er** *n*
-gon \ˌgän\ *n comb form* : figure having (so many) angles ⟨hexa*gon*⟩
go•nad \ˈgō-ˌnad\ *n* : a sperm- or egg-producing gland : OVARY, TESTIS — **go•nad•al** \gō-ˈna-dᵊl\ *adj*
go•nad•o•trop•ic \gō-ˌna-də-ˈträ-pik\ *also* **go•nad•o•tro•phic** \-ˈtrō-fik, -ˈträ-\ *adj* : acting on or stimulating the gonads
go•nad•o•tro•pin \-ˈtrō-pən\ *also* **go•nad•o•tro•phin** \-fən\ *n* : a gonadotropic hormone
gon•do•la \ˈgän-də-lə (*usual for 1*), gän-ˈdō-\ *n* **1** : a long narrow boat used on the canals of Venice **2** : a railroad car used for hauling loose freight (as coal) **3** : an enclosure beneath an airship or balloon **4** : an enclosed car suspended from a cable and used especially for transporting skiers
gon•do•lier \ˌgän-də-ˈlir\ *n* : a person who propels a gondola
¹gone \ˈgȯn\ *past part of* GO
²gone *adj* **1** ♦ : no longer alive : DEAD **2** : no longer possessed : LOST, RUINED **3** : SINKING, WEAK **4** : INVOLVED, ABSORBED **5** : INFATUATED **6** : PREGNANT **7** : having existed or taken place in a period before the present : PAST

♦ bygone, dead, deceased, defunct, extinct

gon•er \ˈgȯ-nər\ *n* : one whose case is hopeless
gong \ˈgäŋ, ˈgȯŋ\ *n* : a metallic disk that produces a resounding tone when struck
gono•coc•cus \ˌgä-nə-ˈkä-kəs\ *n, pl* **-coc•ci** \-ˈkäk-ˌsī, -(ˌ)sē, -ˈkä-ˌkī, -(ˌ)kē\ : a pus-producing bacterium causing gonorrhea — **gono•coc•cal** \-ˈkä-kəl\ *adj*
gon•or•rhea \ˌgä-nə-ˈrē-ə\ *n* : a contagious sexually transmitted inflammation of the genital tract caused by the gonococcus — **gon•or•rhe•al** \-ˈrē-əl\ *adj*
goo \ˈgü\ *n* **1** : a viscid or sticky substance **2** : sentimental tripe
goo•ber \ˈgü-bər, ˈgu̇-\ *n, Southern & Midland* : PEANUT
¹good \ˈgu̇d\ *adj* **bet•ter** \ˈbe-tər\; **best** \ˈbest\ **1** ♦ : of a favorable character or tendency **2** : BOUNTIFUL, FERTILE **3** : COMELY, ATTRACTIVE **4** ♦ : adapted to a use or purpose : SUITABLE, FIT **5** : SOUND, WHOLE **6** ♦ : having qualities that tend to give pleasure : AGREEABLE, PLEASANT **7** : SALUTARY, WHOLESOME **8** : of a noticeably large size or quantity : CONSIDERABLE **9** : FULL **10** ♦ : based on excellent reasoning, information, judgment, or grounds **11** : TRUE ⟨holds ~ for everybody⟩ **12** : legally valid or effectual **13** : sufficient for a specific requirement : SATISFACTORY **14** ♦ : conforming to a standard **15** : DISCRIMINATING **16** : worthy of being commended **17** : KIND **18** : UPPER-CLASS **19** ♦ : having or displaying competence or skill **20** : unswerving in allegiance : LOYAL, CLOSE — **good•ish** *adj* — **good–look•ing** \-ˈlu̇-kiŋ\ *adj*

♦ [1] appreciative, complimentary, favorable (*or* favourable), friendly, positive ♦ [4] applicable, appropriate, apt, felicitous, fit, fitting, happy, meet, proper, right, suitable ♦ [6] agreeable, congenial, delightful, felicitous, grateful, gratifying, nice, palatable, pleasant, pleasurable, satisfying ♦ [10] hard, informed, just, logical, rational, reasonable, reasoned, sensible, solid, valid, well-founded ***Ant*** baseless, illogical, invalid, unfounded, uninformed, unreasonable, unsound ♦ [14] decent, ethical, honest, honorable (*or* honourable), just, moral, right, straight, virtuous ***Ant*** bad, evil, unethical, wrong ♦ [19] accomplished, adept, capable, competent, proficient, skilled, skillful

[2]**good** *n* **1** ♦ **:** something good **2 :** GOODNESS **3** ♦ **:** advancement of prosperity or well-being **:** BENEFIT, WELFARE ⟨for the ~ of mankind⟩ **4 :** something that has economic utility **5** *pl* **:** personal property **6** *pl* **:** CLOTH **7** *pl* **:** something manufactured or produced for sale **:** WARES, MERCHANDISE **8 :** good persons ⟨the ~ die young⟩ **9** *pl* **:** proof of wrongdoing — **for good :** FOREVER, PERMANENTLY — **to the good :** in a position of net gain or profit ⟨$10 *to the good*⟩

♦ [1] blessing, boon, felicity, godsend, manna, windfall ♦ [3] benefit, interest, weal, welfare, well-being

[3]**good** *adv* ♦ **:** in a good or proper manner **:** WELL

♦ OK, adequately, all right, fine, nicely, passably, satisfactorily, so-so, tolerably, well

good–bye *or* **good–by** \gu̇d-ˈbī, gə-\ *n* ♦ **:** a concluding remark at parting

♦ adieu, au revoir, bon voyage, farewell ***Ant*** hello

good cholesterol *n* **:** HDL

good–for–noth•ing \ˈgu̇d-fər-ˌnə-thiŋ\ *adj* **:** of no use or value — **good–for–nothing** *n*

Good Friday *n* **:** the Friday before Easter observed as the anniversary of the crucifixion of Christ

good–heart•ed \-ˈhär-təd\ *adj* ♦ **:** having a kindly generous disposition

♦ beneficent, benevolent, compassionate, humane, kind, kindly, sympathetic, tender, tenderhearted, warmhearted

good•ly \ˈgu̇d-lē\ *adj* **good•li•er; -est 1 :** of pleasing appearance **2** ♦ **:** significantly large **:** CONSIDERABLE

♦ considerable, good, healthy, respectable, significant, sizable, substantial, tidy

good•man \ˈgu̇d-mən\ *n, archaic* **:** MR.

good–na•tured \ˈgu̇d-ˈnā-chərd\ *adj* ♦ **:** of a cheerful disposition — **good–na•tured•ly** \-chərd-lē\ *adv*

♦ affable, agreeable, amiable, genial, gracious, nice, sweet, well-disposed

good•ness \-nəs\ *n* ♦ **:** the quality or state of being good **:** VIRTUE

♦ character, decency, honesty, honor (*or* honour), integrity, morality, probity, rectitude, righteousness, uprightness, virtue

good–tem•pered \-ˈtem-pərd\ *adj* **:** not easily angered or upset

good•wife \-ˌwīf\ *n, archaic* **:** MRS.

good•will \-ˈwil\ *n* **1** ♦ **:** kindly feeling of approval and support **:** BENEVOLENCE **2 :** the value of the trade a business has built up over time **3 :** cheerful consent **4** ♦ **:** willing effort

♦ [1] amity, benevolence, cordiality, fellowship, friendliness, friendship, kindliness ***Ant*** ill will, malevolence ♦ [4] alacrity, gameness, willingness

goody *or* **good•ie** \ˈgu̇-dē\ *n, pl* **good•ies** ♦ **:** something that is good especially to eat

♦ dainty, delicacy, tidbit, treat

goody–goody \ˌgu̇-dē-ˈgu̇-dē\ *adj* **:** affectedly good — **goody–goody** *n*

goo•ey \ˈgü-ē\ *adj* ♦ **:** having a sticky or thick quality

♦ adhesive, gelatinous, gluey, glutinous, gummy, sticky, viscid, viscous

[1]**goof** \ˈgüf\ *vb* **1** ♦ **:** to spend time idly or foolishly — usually used with *off* **2 :** BLUNDER — often used with *up*

♦ *usu* **goof off** ♦ dally, dawdle, dillydally, hang around, hang out, idle, loaf, loll, lounge

[2]**goof** *n* **1 :** a silly or stupid person **2** ♦ **:** a gross error or mistake resulting usually from stupidity, ignorance, or carelessness

♦ blunder, error, fault, flub, fumble, lapse, miscue, misstep, mistake, oversight, slip, stumble

goof•ball \ˈgüf-ˌbȯl\ *n* **1** *slang* **:** a barbiturate sleeping pill **2 :** a goofy person

go off *vb* **1** ♦ **:** to burst forth with sudden violence or noise from internal energy **:** EXPLODE **2 :** to follow a course ⟨the party *went off* well⟩

♦ blow up, burst, detonate, explode, pop

goof–off \ˈgü-ˌfȯf\ *n* **:** one who evades work or responsibility

goofy \ˈgü-fē\ *adj* **goof•i•er; -est** ♦ **:** being crazy, ridiculous, or mildly ludicrous **:** SILLY — **goof•i•ness** \-fē-nəs\ *n*

♦ flighty, frivolous, giddy, harebrained, light-headed, scatterbrained, silly

goon \ˈgün\ *n* **1** ♦ **:** a man hired to terrorize or kill opponents **2** ♦ **:** a stupid person

♦ [1] bully, gangster, hood, hoodlum, mobster, mug, punk, rowdy, ruffian, thug, tough ♦ [2] blockhead, dope, dummy, idiot, imbecile, jackass, moron, numskull

go on *vb* **1 :** to continue in a course of action **2** ♦ **:** to take place **:** HAPPEN

♦ be, befall, betide, chance, come, happen, occur, pass, transpire

goose \ˈgüs\ *n, pl* **geese** \ˈgēs\ **1 :** any of numerous long-necked web-footed birds related to the swans and ducks; *also* **:** a female goose as distinguished from a gander **2** ♦ **:** a foolish person **3** *pl* **goos•es :** a tailor's smoothing iron

♦ booby, fool, half-wit, jackass, lunatic, nitwit, nut, simpleton, turkey

goose•ber•ry \ˈgüs-ˌber-ē, ˈgüz-, -bə-rē\ *n* **:** the acid berry of any of several shrubs related to the currant and used especially in jams and pies

goose bumps *n pl* **:** roughening of the skin caused usually by cold, fear, or a sudden feeling of excitement

goose•flesh \-ˌflesh\ *n* **:** GOOSE BUMPS

goose pimples *n pl* **:** GOOSE BUMPS

go out *vb* **1 :** to become extinguished **2 :** to become a candidate ⟨*went out* for the football team⟩

go over *vb* ♦ **:** to win approval **:** SUCCEED

♦ click, deliver, pan out, succeed, work out

GOP *abbr* Grand Old Party (Republican)

[1]**go•pher** \ˈgō-fər\ *n* **1 :** a burrowing American land tortoise **2 :** any of a family of No. American burrowing rodents with large cheek pouches opening beside the mouth **3 :** any of several small ground squirrels of the prairie region of No. America

[2]**gopher** *var of* GOFER

[1]**gore** \ˈgȯr\ *n* **1 :** BLOOD **2 :** vivid gruesomeness

[2]**gore** *n* **:** a tapering or triangular piece (as of cloth in a skirt)

[3]**gore** *vb* **gored; gor•ing** ♦ **:** to pierce or wound with something pointed

♦ harpoon, impale, lance, pierce, puncture, skewer, spear, spike, stab, stick, transfix

[1]**gorge** \ˈgȯrj\ *n* **1 :** THROAT **2** ♦ **:** a narrow ravine **3 :** a mass of matter that chokes up a passage

♦ canyon, defile, flume, gap, gulch, notch, pass, ravine

[2]**gorge** *vb* **gorged; gorg•ing** ♦ **:** to eat greedily, hurridly, or to capacity

♦ glut, sate, stuff, surfeit ♦ bolt, devour, gobble, gormandize, gulp, scarf, scoff, wolf

gor•geous \ˈgȯr-jəs\ *adj* ♦ **:** resplendently beautiful

♦ attractive, beautiful, cute, fair, handsome, knockout, lovely, pretty, ravishing, stunning

Gor•gon•zo•la \ˌgȯr-gən-ˈzō-lə\ *n* **:** a blue cheese of Italian origin

go•ril•la \gə-ˈri-lə\ *n* **:** an African anthropoid ape related to but much larger than the chimpanzee

gor•man•dise *chiefly Brit var of* GORMANDIZE

gor•man•dize \ˈgȯr-mən-ˌdīz\ *vb* **-dized; -diz•ing** ♦ **:** to eat ravenously

♦ bolt, devour, gobble, gorge, gulp, scarf, scoff, wolf

gor•man•diz•er \ˌdī-zə(r)\ *n* **:** one who eats gluttonously or ravenously

gorp \ˈgȯrp\ *n* **:** a snack consisting of high-calorie food (as raisins and nuts)

gorse \ˈgȯrs\ *n* **:** a spiny yellow-flowered European evergreen shrub of the legume family

gory \ˈgōr-ē\ *adj* **gor•i•er; -est 1 :** BLOODSTAINED **2 :** HORRIBLE, SENSATIONAL

gos•hawk \ˈgäs-ˌhȯk\ *n* **:** any of several long-tailed hawks with short rounded wings

gos•ling \ˈgäz-liŋ, ˈgȯz-\ *n* **:** a young goose

¹gos•pel \ˈgäs-pəl\ *n* **1 :** the teachings of Christ and the apostles **2** *cap* **:** any of the first four books of the New Testament **3** ♦ **:** something accepted as infallible truth

♦ creed, doctrine, ideology, philosophy

²gospel *adj* **1 :** of, relating to, or emphasizing the gospel **2 :** relating to or being American religious songs associated with evangelism

gos•sa•mer \ˈgä-sə-mər\ *n* **1 :** a film of cobwebs floating in the air **2 :** something light, delicate, or tenuous

¹gos•sip \ˈgä-səp\ *n* **1 :** a person who habitually reveals personal or sensational facts **2 :** rumor or report of an intimate nature **3** ♦ **:** an informal conversation

♦ chat, chatter, chitchat, gabfest, palaver, rap, talk

²gossip *vb* ♦ **:** to spread gossip

♦ blab, talk, tattle

gos•sipy *adj* **:** characterized by, full of, or given to gossip

got *past and past part of* GET

Goth \ˈgäth\ *n* **:** a member of a Germanic people that early in the Christian era overran the Roman Empire

¹Goth•ic \ˈgä-thik\ *adj* **1 :** of or relating to the Goths **2 :** of or relating to a style of architecture prevalent in western Europe from the middle 12th to the early 16th century

²Gothic *n* **1 :** the Germanic language of the Goths **2 :** the Gothic architectural style or decoration

gotten *past part of* GET

Gou•da \ˈgü-də\ *n* **:** a mild Dutch milk cheese shaped in balls

¹gouge \ˈgau̇j\ *n* **1 :** a rounded troughlike chisel **2 :** a hole or groove made with or as if with a gouge

²gouge *vb* **gouged; goug•ing 1 :** to cut holes or grooves in with or as if with a gouge **2** ♦ **:** to charge too much or too fully

♦ overcharge, soak, sting

gou•lash \ˈgü-ˌläsh, -ˌlash\ *n* **:** a stew made with meat, assorted vegetables, and paprika

go under *vb* **:** to be overwhelmed, defeated, or destroyed **:** FAIL

gourd \ˈgȯrd, ˈgu̇rd\ *n* **1 :** any of a family of tendril-bearing vines including the cucumber, squash, and melon **2 :** the fruit of a gourd; *esp* **:** any of various inedible hard-shelled fruits used especially for ornament or implements

gour•mand \ˈgu̇r-ˌmänd\ *n* **1 :** one who is excessively fond of eating and drinking **2** ♦ **:** a connoisseur of food and drink **:** GOURMET

♦ epicure, epicurean, gourmet

gour•met \ˈgu̇r-ˌmā, gu̇r-ˈmā\ *n* ♦ **:** a connoisseur of food and drink

♦ epicure, epicurean, gourmand

gout \ˈgau̇t\ *n* **:** a metabolic disease marked by painful inflammation and swelling of the joints — **gouty** *adj*

gov *abbr* **1** government **2** governor

gov•ern \ˈgə-vərn\ *vb* **1** ♦ **:** to control and direct the making and administration of policy in **:** RULE **2** ♦ **:** to prevail or have decisive influence over **:** CONTROL, DIRECT **3 :** DETERMINE, REGULATE **4** ♦ **:** to hold in check **:** RESTRAIN

♦ [1] boss, captain, command, control, preside, rule ♦ [2] administer, carry on, conduct, control, direct, guide, handle, manage, operate, oversee, regulate, run, superintend, supervise ♦ [4] bridle, check, constrain, contain, control, curb, inhibit, regulate, rein, restrain, tame

gov•er•nance \-vər-nəns\ *n* **:** the act or process of governing; *specif* **:** authoritative direction or control

gov•ern•ess \ˈgə-vər-nəs\ *n* **:** a woman who teaches and trains a child especially in a private home

gov•ern•ment \ˈgə-vərn-mənt\ *n* **1** ♦ **:** authoritative direction or control **:** RULE **2** ♦ **:** the making of policy **3 :** the organization or agency through which a political unit exercises authority **4 :** the complex of institutions, laws, and customs through which a political unit is governed **5 :** the governing body — **gov•ern•men•tal** \ˌgə-vərn-ˈment-ᵊl\ *adj*

♦ [1] administration, authority, jurisdiction, regime, rule ♦ [2] conduct, control, direction, guidance, management, operation, oversight, regulation, running, superintendence, supervision

gov•er•nor \ˈgə-vər-nər\ *n* **1 :** one that governs; *esp* **:** a ruler, chief executive, or head of a political unit (as a state) **2 :** an attachment to a machine for automatic control of speed — **gov•er•nor•ship** *n*

govt *abbr* government

¹gown \ˈgau̇n\ *n* **1 :** a loose flowing outer garment **2 :** an official robe worn especially by a judge, clergyman, or teacher **3 :** a woman's dress ⟨evening ∼*s*⟩ **4 :** a loose robe

²gown *vb* **:** to dress in or invest with a gown

gp *abbr* group

GP *abbr* general practitioner

GPO *abbr* **1** general post office **2** Government Printing Office

GPS \ˌjē-ˌpē-ˈes\ *n* **:** a navigation system that uses satellite signals to fix location; *also* **:** the signal receiver itself

GQ *abbr* general quarters

gr *abbr* **1** grade **2** grain **3** gram **4** gravity **5** gross

¹grab \ˈgrab\ *vb* **grabbed; grab•bing** ♦ **:** to take hastily **:** SNATCH

♦ bag, capture, catch, collar, corral, get, grapple, hook, land, nab, seize, snare, trap

²grab *n* **1 :** something grabbed; *also* **:** an act or instance of grabbing **2** ♦ **:** an unlawful or unscrupulous seizure

♦ rip-off, theft

¹grace \ˈgrās\ *n* **1 :** unmerited help given to people by God (as in overcoming temptation) **2 :** freedom from sin through divine grace **3 :** a virtue coming from God **4** — used as a title for a duke, a duchess, or an archbishop **5 :** a short prayer at a meal **6 :** a temporary respite (as from the payment of a debt) **7 :** APPROVAL, ACCEPTANCE ⟨in his good ∼*s*⟩ **8 :** CHARM **9 :** ATTRACTIVENESS, BEAUTY **10** ♦ **:** fitness or proportion of line or expression **11 :** ease of movement **12 :** a musical trill or ornament **13** ♦ **:** disposition to or an act or instance of kindness, courtesy, or clemency — **grace•ful•ly** *adv* — **grace•ful•ness** *n*

♦ [10] class, elegance, handsomeness, majesty, refinement, stateliness ♦ [13] boon, courtesy, favor (*or* favour), indulgence, kindness, mercy, service, turn

²grace *vb* **graced; grac•ing 1 :** HONOR **2** ♦ **:** to endow with grace **:** ADORN, EMBELLISH

♦ adorn, array, beautify, bedeck, deck, decorate, do, dress, embellish, enrich, garnish, ornament, trim

grace•ful \-fəl\ *adj* ♦ **:** displaying grace in form or action **:** pleasing or attractive in line, proportion, or movement

♦ elegant, handsome, majestic, refined, stately, tasteful ♦ agile, light, lissome, lithe, nimble, spry ***Ant*** awkward, clumsy, gawky, graceless, lumbering, ungainly, ungraceful

grace•ful•ness *n* **:** the quality or state of being graceful

grace•less *adj* **1** ♦ **:** artistically inept or unbeautiful **2** ♦ **:** lacking a sense of propriety

♦ [1] awkward, clumsy, gawky, heavy-handed, lubberly, lumpish, ungainly, unhandy ♦ [1] gauche, inelegant, stiff, stilted, uncomfortable, uneasy, ungraceful, wooden ♦ [2] improper, inappropriate, inapt, infelicitous, unbecoming, unfit, unseemly, unsuitable, wrong

gra•cious \ˈgrā-shəs\ *adj* **1** ♦ **:** marked by kindness and courtesy **2 :** GRACEFUL **3 :** characterized by charm and good taste **4 :** MERCIFUL — **gra•cious•ly** *adv*

♦ affable, agreeable, amiable, congenial, convivial, cordial, friendly, genial, hospitable, kind, kindly, sociable ***Ant*** inhospitable, ungracious, unsociable ♦ civil, courteous, genteel, mannerly, polite, well-bred

gra•cious•ness *n* ♦ **:** the quality or state of being gracious

♦ civility, courtesy, gentility, mannerliness, politeness ♦ agreeableness, amenity, amiability, geniality, niceness, pleasantness, sweetness

grack•le \ˈgra-kəl\ *n* **:** any of several large American blackbirds with glossy iridescent plumage

grad *abbr* graduate; graduated

gra•da•tion \grā-ˈdā-shən, grə-\ *n* **1 :** a series forming successive stages **2 :** a step, degree, or stage in a series **3 :** an advance by regular degrees **4 :** the act or process of grading

¹grade \ˈgrād\ *vb* **grad•ed; grad•ing 1** ♦ **:** to arrange in grades **:** SORT; *also* **:** to arrange in a scale or series **2 :** to make level or evenly sloping ⟨∼ a highway⟩ **3 :** to give a grade to ⟨∼ a pupil in history⟩ **4 :** to assign to a grade

♦ assort, break down, categorize, class, classify, group, peg, place, range, rank, rate, separate, sort

²grade *n* **1** ♦ **:** a degree or stage in a series, order, or ranking **2** ♦ **:** a position in a scale of rank, quality, or order **3** ♦ **:** a class of persons or things of the same rank or quality **4 :** a division of the school course representing one year's work; *also* **:** the pupils in such a division **5** *pl* **:** the elementary school system **6 :** a mark or rating especially of accomplishment in school **7** ♦ **:** the degree of slope (as of a road); *also* **:** SLOPE **8** ♦ **:** a reference level or starting point used for measuring or calculating

♦ [1] cut, degree, inch, notch, peg, phase, point, stage, step ♦ [2] caliber (*or* calibre), class, quality, rate ♦ [3] bracket, category, class, division, family, group, kind, order, set, species, type ♦ [7] cant, diagonal, inclination, incline, lean, pitch, slant, slope, tilt, upgrade ♦ [8] criterion, mark, measure, par, standard, touchstone, yardstick

grad•er \ˈgrā-dər\ *n* **:** a machine for leveling earth
grade school *n* **:** ELEMENTARY SCHOOL
gra•di•ent \ˈgrā-dē-ənt\ *n* **:** the rate of regular or graded ascent or descent **:** SLOPE, GRADE
grad•u•al \ˈgra-jə-wəl\ *adj* ♦ **:** proceeding or changing by steps or degrees — **grad•u•al•ly** *adv*

♦ imperceptible, progressive *Ant* sudden

grad•u•al•ism \-wə-ˌli-zəm\ *n* **:** the policy of approaching a desired end gradually
¹grad•u•ate \ˈgra-jə-wət\ *n* **1 :** a holder of an academic degree or diploma **2 :** a graduated container for measuring contents
²graduate *adj* **1 :** holding an academic degree or diploma **2 :** of or relating to studies beyond the first or bachelor's degree ⟨~ school⟩
³grad•u•ate \ˈgra-jə-ˌwāt\ *vb* **-at•ed; -at•ing 1 :** to grant or receive an academic degree or diploma **2 :** to divide into grades, classes, or intervals **3 :** to admit to a particular standing or grade
grad•u•a•tion \ˌgra-jə-ˈwā-shən\ *n* **1 :** a mark that graduates something **2** ♦ **:** arrangement in degrees or ranks **3 :** COMMENCEMENT 2

♦ ladder, scale

graf•fi•ti \grə-ˈfē-(ˌ)tē\ *n* **:** unauthorized writing or drawing on a public surface
graf•fi•to \grə-ˈfē-tō, grə-\ *n, pl* **-ti** \-(ˌ)tē\ **:** an inscription or drawing made on a public surface (as a wall)
¹graft \ˈgraft\ *n* **1 :** a grafted plant; *also* **:** the point of union in this **2 :** material (as skin) used in grafting **3 :** the getting of money or advantage dishonestly; *also* **:** the money or advantage so gained
²graft *vb* **1 :** to insert a shoot from one plant into another so that they join and grow; *also* **:** to join one thing to another as in plant grafting ⟨~ skin over a burn⟩ **2 :** to get (as money) dishonestly — **graft•er** *n*
gra•ham cracker \ˈgrā-əm-, ˈgram-\ *n* **:** a slightly sweet cracker made chiefly of whole wheat flour
Grail \ˈgrāl\ *n* **:** the cup or platter used according to medieval legend by Christ at the Last Supper and thereafter the object of knightly quests
grain \ˈgrān\ *n* **1 :** a seed or fruit of a cereal grass **2 :** seeds or fruits of various food plants and especially cereal grasses; *also* **:** a plant (as wheat) producing grain **3** ♦ **:** a small hard particle **4 :** a unit of weight based on the weight of a grain of wheat **5 :** TEXTURE; *also* **:** the arrangement of fibers in wood **6** ♦ **:** natural disposition — **grained** \ˈgrānd\ *adj*

♦ [3] bit, granule, molecule, particle ♦ [6] disposition, nature, temper, temperament

grain alcohol *n* **:** ALCOHOL 1
grainy \ˈgrā-nē\ *adj* **grain•i•er; -est 1** ♦ **:** resembling or having some characteristic of grain **:** not smooth or fine **2** *of a photograph* **:** appearing to be composed of grain-like particles

♦ coarse, granular

¹gram \ˈgram\ *n* **:** a metric unit of mass and weight equal to $^1/_{1000}$ kilogram
²gram *abbr* grammar; grammatical
-gram \ˌgram\ *n comb form* **:** drawing **:** writing **:** record ⟨tele*gram*⟩
gram•mar \ˈgra-mər\ *n* **1 :** the study of the classes of words, their inflections, and their functions and relations in the sentence **2 :** a study of what is to be preferred and what avoided in inflection and syntax **3 :** speech or writing evaluated according to its conformity to grammatical rules — **gram•mar•i•an** \grə-ˈmer-ē-ən, -ˈmar-\ *n* — **gram•mat•i•cal** \-ˈma-ti-kəl\ *adj* — **gram•mat•i•cal•ly** \-k(ə-)lē\ *adv*
grammar school *n* **1 :** a secondary school emphasizing Latin and Greek in preparation for college; *also* **:** a British college preparatory school **2 :** a school intermediate between the primary grades and high school **3 :** ELEMENTARY SCHOOL
gramme \ˈgram\ *chiefly Brit var of* GRAM
gram•o•phone \ˈgra-mə-ˌfōn\ *n* **:** PHONOGRAPH

gra•na•ry \ˈgrā-nə-rē, ˈgra-\ *n, pl* **-ries 1 :** a storehouse for grain **2 :** a region producing grain in abundance
¹grand \ˈgrand\ *adj* **1** ♦ **:** higher in rank or importance **:** FOREMOST, CHIEF **2** ♦ **:** large and striking in size, scope, extent, or conception **3** ♦ **:** covering or intended to cover all items, costs, or services **:** COMPLETE ⟨a ~ total⟩ **4 :** MAGNIFICENT, SPLENDID **5** ♦ **:** showing wealth or high social standing **6 :** fine or imposing in appearance or impression **:** IMPRESSIVE, STATELY **7 :** very good **:** FINE

♦ [1] chief, dominant, first, foremost, key, main, paramount, predominant, preeminent, premier, primary, principal ♦ [2] august, baronial, gallant, glorious, grandiose, heroic, imposing, magnificent, majestic, monumental, noble, proud, regal, royal, splendid, stately *Ant* humble, unheroic, unimposing, unimpressive ♦ [2] big, considerable, goodly, great, large, outsize, oversize, sizable, substantial ♦ [3] complete, comprehensive, entire, full, intact, integral, perfect, plenary, total, whole ♦ [5] aristocratic, genteel, gentle, highborn, noble, patrician, wellborn

²grand *n, pl* **grand** *slang* **:** a thousand dollars
gran•dam \ˈgran-ˌdam, -dəm\ *or* **gran•dame** \-ˌdām, -dəm\ *n* **:** an old woman
grand•child \ˈgrand-ˌchī(-ə)ld\ *n* **:** a child of one's son or daughter
grand•daugh•ter \ˈgran-ˌdȯ-tər\ *n* **:** a daughter of one's son or daughter
grande dame \ˈgrän-ˈdäm\ *n, pl* **grandes dames :** a usually elderly woman of great prestige or ability
gran•dee \gran-ˈdē\ *n* ♦ **:** a high-ranking Spanish or Portuguese nobleman

♦ aristocrat, gentleman, noble, patrician

gran•deur \ˈgran-jər\ *n* **1** ♦ **:** the quality or state of being grand **:** MAGNIFICENCE **2 :** something that is grand

♦ augustness, brilliance, glory, grandness, magnificence, majesty, nobility, nobleness, resplendence, splendor, stateliness

grand•fa•ther \ˈgrand-ˌfä-t͟hər\ *n* ♦ **:** the father of one's father or mother; *also* **:** ANCESTOR

♦ ancestor, father, forebear, forefather

grandfather clock *n* **:** a tall clock that stands on the floor
gran•dil•o•quence \gran-ˈdi-lə-kwəns\ *n* ♦ **:** pompous eloquence

♦ bombast, gas, hot air, rhetoric, wind

gran•dil•o•quent \-kwənt\ *adj* ♦ **:** marked by a lofty, extravagantly colorful, pompous, or bombastic style, manner, or quality especially in language

♦ florid, flowery, high-flown, highfalutin ♦ bombastic, gaseous, oratorical, rhetorical, windy

gran•di•ose \ˈgran-dē-ˌōs, ˌgran-dē-ˈōs\ *adj* ♦ **:** impressive because of uncommon largeness, scope, effect, or grandeur **:** IMPOSING; *also* **:** affectedly splendid — **gran•di•ose•ly** *adv*

♦ august, baronial, gallant, glorious, grand, heroic, imposing, magnificent, majestic, monumental, noble, proud, regal, royal, splendid, stately ♦ affected, highfalutin, ostentatious, pompous, pretentious

gran•di•os•i•ty \ˌgran-dē-ˈä-sə-tē\ *n* **:** the quality or state of being grandiose
grand jury *n* **:** a jury that examines accusations of crime against persons and makes formal charges on which the persons are later tried
grand•ly \-ndlē, -lī\ *adv* ♦ **:** in a grand manner

♦ expensively, extravagantly, high, lavishly, luxuriously, opulently, richly ♦ gallantly, greatly, heroically, honorably (*or* honourably), magnanimously, nobly

grand mal \ˈgrän-ˌmäl; ˈgrand-ˌmal\ *n* **:** severe epilepsy
grand•moth•er \ˈgrand-ˌmə-t͟hər\ *n* **:** the mother of one's father or mother; *also* **:** a female ancestor
grand•ness \ˈgran(d)nəs\ *n* ♦ **:** the quality or state of being grand

♦ augustness, brilliance, glory, grandeur, magnificence, majesty, nobility, nobleness, resplendence, splendor, stateliness ♦ bigness, greatness, largeness

grand•par•ent \-ˌpar-ənt\ *n* **:** a parent of one's father or mother
grand piano *n* **:** a piano with horizontal frame and strings
grand prix \ˈgräⁿ-ˈprē\ *n, pl* **grand prix** *same or* -ˈprēz\ *often cap G&P* **:** a long-distance auto race over a road course

grand slam *n* **1 :** a total victory or success **2 :** a home run hit with three runners on base
grand•son \ˈgrand-ˌsən\ *n* **:** a son of one's son or daughter
grand•stand \-ˌstand\ *n* **:** a usually roofed stand for spectators at a racecourse or stadium
grange \ˈgrānj\ *n* **1 :** a farm or farmhouse with its various buildings **2** *cap* **:** one of the lodges of a national association originally made up of farmers; *also* **:** the association itself — **grang•er** \ˈgrān-jər\ *n*
gran•ite \ˈgra-nət\ *n* **1 :** a hard granular igneous rock used especially for building **2** ♦ **:** unyielding firmness or endurance — **gra•nit•ic** \gra-ˈni-tik\ *adj*

♦ decision, decisiveness, determination, firmness, resolution, resolve

gran•ite•ware \ˈgra-nət-ˌwar\ *n* **:** ironware with mottled enamel
gra•no•la \grə-ˈnō-lə\ *n* **:** a cereal made of rolled oats and usually raisins and nuts
¹grant \ˈgrant\ *vb* **1 :** to consent to **:** ALLOW, PERMIT **2** ♦ **:** to bestow or transfer formally **:** GIVE **3** ♦ **:** to admit as true — **grant•er** *n* — **grant•or** \ˈgran-tər, -ˌtȯr\ *n*

♦ [2] accord, award, confer, give ♦ [3] acknowledge, admit, agree, allow, concede, confess, own

²grant *n* **1 :** the act of granting **2** ♦ **:** something granted; *esp* **:** a gift for a particular purpose ⟨a ~ for study abroad⟩ **3 :** a transfer of property by deed or writing; *also* **:** the instrument by which such a transfer is made **4 :** the property transferred by grant — **grant•ee** \gran-ˈtē\ *n*

♦ allocation, allotment, appropriation, subsidy

gran•u•lar \ˈgra-nyə-lər\ *adj* ♦ **:** consisting of or appearing to consist of granules — **gran•u•lar•i•ty** \ˌgra-nyə-ˈlar-ə-tē\ *n*

♦ coarse, grainy

gran•u•late \ˈgra-nyə-ˌlāt\ *vb* **-lat•ed; -lat•ing :** to form into grains or crystals — **gran•u•la•tion** \ˌgra-nyə-ˈlā-shən\ *n*
gran•ule \ˈgra-nyül\ *n* ♦ **:** a small grain or particle

♦ bit, grain, molecule, particle

grape \ˈgrāp\ *n* **1 :** a smooth-skinned juicy edible greenish white, deep red, or purple berry that is the chief source of wine **2 :** any of numerous woody vines widely grown for their bunches of grapes
grape•fruit \ˈgrāp-ˌfrüt\ *n* **1** *pl* **grapefruit** *or* **grapefruits :** a large edible yellow-skinned citrus fruit **2 :** a tree bearing grapefruit
grape hyacinth *n* **:** any of several small bulbous spring-flowering herbs with clusters of usually blue flowers that are related to the lilies
grape•shot \ˈgrāp-ˌshät\ *n* **:** a cluster of small iron balls formerly fired at people from short range by a cannon
grape•vine \-ˌvīn\ *n* **1 :** GRAPE 2 **2 :** RUMOR; *also* **:** an informal means of circulating information or gossip
graph \ˈgraf\ *n* **:** a diagram that usually by means of dots and lines shows change in one variable factor in comparison with one or more other factors — **graph** *vb*
-graph \ˌgraf\ *n comb form* **1 :** something written ⟨auto*graph*⟩ **2 :** instrument for making or transmitting records ⟨seismo*graph*⟩
¹graph•ic \ˈgra-fik\ *also* **graph•i•cal** \-fi-kəl\ *adj* **1 :** being written, drawn, or engraved **2 :** vividly described **3 :** of or relating to the arts (**graphic arts**) of representation, decoration, and printing on flat surfaces — **graph•i•cal•ly** \-fi-k(ə-)lē\ *adv*
²graphic *n* **1** ♦ **:** a picture, map, or graph used for illustration **2** *pl* **:** a pictorial image displayed on a computer screen

♦ diagram, figure, illustration, plate

graphical user interface *n* **:** a computer program designed to allow easy user interaction especially by having graphic menus or icons
graph•ics tablet \-fiks-\ *n* **:** a computer input device for entering pictorial information by drawing or tracing
graph•ite \ˈgra-ˌfīt\ *n* **:** a soft black form of carbon used especially for lead pencils and lubricants
grap•nel \ˈgrap-nəl\ *n* **:** a small anchor with usually four claws used especially in dragging or grappling operations
¹grap•ple \ˈgra-pəl\ *n* ♦ **:** the act of grappling

♦ clasp, grasp, grip, hold

²grapple *vb* **grap•pled; grap•pling 1** ♦ **:** to seize or hold with or as if with a hooked implement **2** ♦ **:** to engage in a hand-to-hand struggle **:** WRESTLE **3** ♦ **:** to attempt to deal with something — used with *with*

♦ [1] bag, capture, catch, collar, corral, get, grab, hook, land, nab, seize, snare, trap ♦ [2] scuffle, tussle, wrestle ♦ *usu* **grapple with** [3] contend with, cope with, handle, manage, maneuver (*or* manoeuvre), negotiate, swing, treat

¹grasp \ˈgrasp\ *vb* **1 :** to make the motion of seizing **2 :** to take or seize firmly **3** ♦ **:** to enclose and hold with the fingers or arms **4** ♦ **:** to lay hold of with the mind **:** COMPREHEND

♦ [3] clasp, grip, hold, take ♦ [4] appreciate, apprehend, catch, catch on (to), comprehend, get, make, make out, perceive, see, seize, understand

²grasp *n* **1 :** HANDLE **2 :** EMBRACE **3 :** HOLD, CONTROL **4 :** the reach of the arms **5 a** ♦ **:** the act or manner of holding **b :** the power of seizing and holding **6** ♦ **:** mental hold or comprehension especially when broad

♦ [5a] clasp, grapple, grip, hold ♦ [6] appreciation, apprehension, comprehension, grip, perception, understanding

grasp•ing *adj* ♦ **:** desiring material possessions urgently and excessively and often to the point of ruthlessness **:** GREEDY, AVARICIOUS

♦ acquisitive, avaricious, avid, covetous, greedy, mercenary, rapacious

grass \ˈgras\ *n* **1 :** herbage for grazing animals **2 :** any of a large family of plants (as wheat, bamboo, or sugarcane) with jointed stems and narrow leaves **3 :** grass-covered land **4 :** MARIJUANA — **grassy** *adj*
grass•hop•per \-ˌhä-pər\ *n* **:** any of numerous leaping plant-eating insects
grass•land \-ˌland\ *n* ♦ **:** land covered naturally or under cultivation with grasses and low-growing herbs

♦ down, plain, prairie, savanna, steppe, veld

grass roots *n pl* **:** society at the local level as distinguished from the centers of political leadership
¹grate \ˈgrāt\ *vb* **grat•ed; grat•ing 1 :** to pulverize by rubbing against something rough **2** ♦ **:** to grind or rub against with a rasping noise **3** ♦ **:** to provoke impatience, anger, or displeasure in **:** IRRITATE — **grat•er** *n* — **grat•ing•ly** *adv*

♦ [2] grind, rasp, scrape, scratch ♦ [3] aggravate, annoy, bother, exasperate, irk, irritate, nettle, peeve, put out, vex

²grate *n* **1 :** GRATING **2 :** a frame of iron bars for holding fuel while it burns
grate•ful \ˈgrāt-fəl\ *adj* **1** ♦ **:** appreciative of benefits received **:** THANKFUL; *also* **:** expressing gratitude **2 :** giving pleasure or contentment **:** PLEASING — **grate•ful•ly** *adv*

♦ appreciative, obliged, thankful ***Ant*** thankless, unappreciative, ungrateful

grate•ful•ness *n* ♦ **:** the quality or state of being grateful

♦ appreciation, gratitude, thanks

grat•i•fi•ca•tion \ˌgra-tə-fə-ˈkā-shən\ *n* ♦ **:** the act of gratifying **:** the state of being gratified

♦ contentment, delectation, delight, enjoyment, gladness, pleasure, relish, satisfaction

grat•i•fy \ˈgra-tə-ˌfī\ *vb* **-fied; -fy•ing 1** ♦ **:** to afford pleasure to **2** ♦ **:** to give in to

♦ [1] content, delight, gladden, please, rejoice, satisfy, suit, warm ♦ [2] cater to, humor (*or* humour), indulge

grat•i•fy•ing *adj* ♦ **:** giving pleasure or satisfaction

♦ agreeable, felicitous, good, grateful, pleasant, pleasurable, satisfying ♦ comforting, encouraging, heartening, heartwarming, rewarding, satisfying

grat•ing \ˈgrā-tiŋ\ *n* **:** a framework with parallel bars or crossbars
gra•tis \ˈgra-təs, ˈgrā-\ *adv or adj* **:** without charge or recompense **:** FREE
grat•i•tude \ˈgra-tə-ˌtüd, -ˌtyüd\ *n* ♦ **:** the state of being grateful **:** THANKFULNESS

♦ appreciation, gratefulness, thanks

gra•tu•itous \grə-ˈtü-ə-təs, -ˈtyü-\ *adj* **1** ♦ **:** done or provided without recompense **:** FREE **2 :** UNWARRANTED

♦ complimentary, free

gra•tu•ity \-ə-tē\ *n, pl* **-ities :** something given voluntarily or beyond obligation usually for some service **:** TIP
gra•va•men \grə-ˈvā-mən\ *n, pl* **-va•mens** *or* **-vam•i•na** \-ˈva-mə-nə\ **:** the basic or significant part of a grievance or complaint

¹grave \ˈgrāv\ *vb* **graved; grav·en** \ˈgrā-vən\ *or* **graved; grav·ing** **1 :** to carve or shape with a chisel **:** SCULPTURE **2 :** to carve or cut (as letters or figures) into a hard surface **:** ENGRAVE

²grave *n* **:** an excavation in the earth as a place of burial; *also* **:** TOMB

³grave \ˈgrāv; *5 also* ˈgräv\ *adj* **1** ♦ **:** deserving serious consideration **2** ♦ **:** threatening great harm or danger **3** ♦ **:** having a serious and dignified quality or demeanor **:** SOLEMN **4 :** drab in color **:** SOMBER **5 :** of, marked by, or being an accent mark having the form ˋ — **grave·ly** *adv* — **grave·ness** *n*

♦ [1] heavy, serious, weighty ♦ [2] dangerous, grievous, hazardous, menacing, parlous, perilous, risky, serious, unhealthy, unsafe, venturesome ♦ [3] earnest, humorless (*or* humourless), serious, severe, sober, solemn, staid, unsmiling, weighty

grav·el \ˈgra-vəl\ *n* **:** pebbles and small pieces of rock larger than grains of sand

grav·el·ly *adj* **1 :** of, containing, or covered with gravel **2** ♦ **:** having a rough or grating sound

♦ coarse, gruff, hoarse, husky, scratchy, throaty

Graves' disease \ˈgrāvz-\ *n* **:** hyperthyroidism characterized by goiter and often protrusion of the eyeballs

grave·stone \ˈgrāv-ˌstōn\ *n* ♦ **:** a burial monument

♦ headstone, monument, tombstone

grave·yard \-ˌyärd\ *n* **:** CEMETERY

grav·id \ˈgra-vəd\ *adj* **:** PREGNANT

gra·vi·me·ter \gra-ˈvi-mə-tər, ˈgra-və-ˌmē-\ *n* **:** a device for measuring variations in a gravitational field

grav·i·tate \ˈgra-və-ˌtāt\ *vb* **-tat·ed; -tat·ing :** to move or tend to move toward something

grav·i·ta·tion \ˌgra-və-ˈtā-shən\ *n* **1 :** a natural force of attraction that tends to draw bodies together and that occurs because of the mass of the bodies **2 :** the action or process of gravitating — **grav·i·ta·tion·al** \-shə-nəl\ *adj* — **grav·i·ta·tion·al·ly** *adv*

grav·i·ty \ˈgra-və-tē\ *n, pl* **-ties** **1 a :** IMPORTANCE **b** ♦ **:** the quality or state of being serious **2 :** ²MASS 5 **3 :** the gravitational attraction of the mass of a celestial object (as earth) for bodies close to it; *also* **:** GRAVITATION 1

♦ earnest, earnestness, intentness, seriousness, sobriety, solemnity

gra·vure \grə-ˈvyu̇r\ *n* **:** PHOTOGRAVURE

gra·vy \ˈgrā-vē\ *n, pl* **gravies** **1 :** a sauce made from the thickened and seasoned juices of cooked meat **2 :** unearned or illicit gain **:** GRAFT

¹gray *or chiefly Can and Brit* **grey** \ˈgrā\ *adj* **1** ♦ **:** of the color gray; *also* **:** dull in color **2 :** having gray hair **3** ♦ **:** lacking cheer or brightness in mood, outlook, style, or flavor **:** CHEERLESS, DISMAL **4 :** intermediate in position or character — **gray·ness** *n*

♦ [1] leaden, pewter, silver, silvery, slate, steely ♦ [3] bleak, dark, dismal, dreary, gloomy, somber (*or* sombre), wretched

²gray *or chiefly Can and Brit* **grey** *n* **1 :** something of a gray color **2 :** a neutral color ranging between black and white

³gray *or chiefly Can and Brit* **grey** *vb* **:** to make or become gray

gray·beard *or chiefly Can and Brit* **greybeard** \ˈgrā-ˌbird\ *n* **:** an old man

gray·ish *or chiefly Can and Brit* **grey·ish** *adj* **:** somewhat gray

gray·ling \ˈgrā-liŋ\ *n, pl* **grayling** *also* **graylings :** any of several slender freshwater food and sport fishes related to the trouts

gray matter *n* **1 :** the grayish part of nervous tissue consisting mostly of nerve cell bodies **2** ♦ **:** capacity for knowledge and learning **:** INTELLIGENCE

♦ brains, intellect, intelligence, reason, sense

gray wolf *n* **:** a large wolf of northern No. America and Asia that is usually gray

¹graze \ˈgrāz\ *vb* **grazed; graz·ing** **1** ♦ **:** to feed on herbage or pasture **2 :** to feed (livestock) on grass or pasture — **graz·er** *n*

♦ browse, forage, pasture

²graze *vb* **grazed; graz·ing** **1** ♦ **:** to touch lightly in passing **2** ♦ **:** to irritate or roughen by rubbing **:** SCRATCH, ABRADE

♦ [1] brush, kiss, nick, shave, skim ♦ [2] abrade, scrape, scratch, scuff

¹grease \ˈgrēs\ *n* **1 :** rendered animal fat **2 :** oily material **3 :** a thick lubricant

²grease \ˈgrēs, ˈgrēz\ *vb* **greased; greas·ing** ♦ **:** to smear or lubricate with grease

♦ lubricate, oil, slick, wax

grease·paint \ˈgrēs-ˌpānt\ *n* **:** theater makeup

greasy \ˈgrē-sē, -zē\ *adj* **1 :** smeared or soiled with grease; *also* **:** oily in appearance, texture, or manner **2** ♦ **:** causing or tending to cause something to slide or fall **3 :** containing an unusual amount of grease

♦ slick, slippery, slithery

great \ˈgrāt\ *adj* **1** ♦ **:** large in size **:** BIG **2 :** ELABORATE, AMPLE **3 :** large in number **:** NUMEROUS **4 :** being beyond the average **:** MIGHTY, INTENSE ⟨a ~ weight⟩ ⟨in ~ pain⟩ **5 :** EMINENT, GRAND **6** ♦ **:** long continued ⟨a ~ while⟩ **7 :** MAIN, PRINCIPAL **8 :** more distant in a family relationship by one generation ⟨a *great*-grandfather⟩ **9** ♦ **:** markedly superior in character, quality, or skill ⟨~ at bridge⟩ **10** ♦ **:** very good of its kind **:** EXCELLENT, FINE ⟨had a ~ time⟩

♦ [1] big, hefty, large, outsize, oversize, sizable, substantial ♦ [6] extended, far, lengthy, long, marathon ♦ [9] accomplished, adept, consummate, crack, crackerjack, expert, good, master, masterful, masterly, proficient, skilled, skillful, virtuoso ♦ [10] excellent, fabulous, fine, grand, splendid, superb, superior, swell, terrific, wonderful

great ape *n* **:** any of a family of primates including the gorilla, orangutan, and chimpanzees

great blue heron *n* **:** a large crested grayish blue American heron

great circle *n* **:** a circle on the surface of a sphere that has the same center as the sphere; *esp* **:** one on the surface of the earth an arc of which is the shortest travel distance between two points

great·coat \ˈgrāt-ˌkōt\ *n* **:** a heavy overcoat

Great Dane *n* **:** any of a breed of tall massive powerful smooth-coated dogs

great·heart·ed \ˈgrāt-ˈhär-təd\ *adj* **1** ♦ **:** characterized by bravery **:** COURAGEOUS **2 :** characterized by a noble or forbearing spirit **:** MAGNANIMOUS

♦ brave, courageous, dauntless, doughty, fearless, gallant, heroic, intrepid, lionhearted, manful, stalwart, stout, undaunted, valiant, valorous

great·ly *adv* **1** ♦ **:** to a great extent or degree **:** very much **2** ♦ **:** in a great manner

♦ [1] broadly, considerably, extremely, highly, hugely, largely, much, sizably, tremendously, very *Ant* slightly ♦ [2] gallantly, grandly, heroically, honorably (*or* honourably), magnanimously, nobly *Ant* basely, dishonorably, ignobly

great·ness *n* ♦ **:** the quality or state of being great

♦ distinction, excellence, preeminence, superiority, supremacy ♦ bigness, grandness, largeness

great power *n, often cap G&P* **:** one of the nations that figure most decisively in international affairs

great white shark *n* **:** a large and dangerous shark of warm seas that has large saw-edged teeth and is whitish below and bluish or brownish above

grebe \ˈgrēb\ *n* **:** any of a family of lobe-toed diving birds related to the loons

Gre·cian \ˈgrē-shən\ *adj* **:** GREEK

greed \ˈgrēd\ *n* ♦ **:** acquisitive or selfish desire beyond reason — **greed·i·ly** \ˈgrē-də-lē\ *adv*

♦ acquisitiveness, avarice, avidity, covetousness, cupidity, rapaciousness

greed·i·ness \-dē-nəs\ *n* **:** the quality or state of being greedy; *esp* **:** extreme or excessive desire for wealth or gain

greedy \ˈgrē-dē\ *adj* **1** ♦ **:** having a strong desire for food or drink **2** ♦ **:** marked by greed **:** having or showing a selfish desire for wealth and possessions

♦ [1] gluttonous, hoggish, piggish, rapacious, ravenous, voracious ♦ [2] acquisitive, avaricious, avid, covetous, grasping, mercenary, rapacious

¹Greek \ˈgrēk\ *n* **1 :** a native or inhabitant of Greece **2 :** the ancient or modern language of Greece

²Greek *adj* **1 :** of, relating to, or characteristic of Greece, the Greeks, or Greek **2 :** ORTHODOX 3

¹green \ˈgrēn\ *adj* **1 :** of the color green **2** ♦ **:** covered with verdure; *also* **:** consisting of green plants or of the leafy parts of plants ⟨a ~ salad⟩ **3 :** UNRIPE; *also* **:** IMMATURE **4** ♦ **:** having a sickly appearance **5 :** not fully processed or treated ⟨~ liquor⟩ ⟨~ hides⟩ **6** ♦ **:** lacking in training, knowledge, or experience **:** INEXPERIENCED; *also* **:** NAIVE **7 :** concerned with or supporting environmentalism — **green·ish** *adj*

♦ [2] leafy, lush, luxuriant, verdant ♦ [4] cadaverous, lurid, pale, pasty, peaked, sallow, sickly ♦ [6] adolescent, callow, immature, inexperienced, juvenile, raw ♦ [6] ingenuous, innocent, naive, simple, unknowing, unsophisticated, unwary, unworldly

²**green** *vb* : to make or become green

³**green** *n* **1** : a color between blue and yellow in the spectrum : the color of growing fresh grass or of the emerald **2** : something of a green color **3** : green vegetation; *esp, pl* : leafy herbs or leafy parts of a vegetable ⟨collard ~*s*⟩ ⟨beet ~*s*⟩ **4** : a grassy plot; *esp* : a smooth grassy area around the hole into which the ball must be played in golf

green•back \ˈgrēn-ˌbak\ *n* : a U.S. legal-tender note

green bean *n* : a kidney bean that is used as a snap bean when the pods are colored green

green•belt \ˈgrēn-ˌbelt\ *n* : a belt of parks or farmlands around a community

green card *n* : an identity card attesting the permanent resident status of an alien in the U.S.

green•ery \ˈgrē-nə-rē\ *n, pl* **-er•ies** ♦ : green foliage or plants

♦ flora, foliage, green, herbage, leafage, vegetation, verdure

green–eyed \ˈgrē-ˈnīd\ *adj* : JEALOUS

green•gro•cer \ˈgrēn-ˌgrō-sər\ *n* : a retailer of fresh vegetables and fruit

green•horn \-ˌhȯrn\ *n* ♦ : an inexperienced person; *also* : NEWCOMER

♦ beginner, fledgling, freshman, neophyte, newcomer, novice, recruit, rookie, tenderfoot, tyro

green•house \-ˌhau̇s\ *n* : a glass structure for the growing of tender plants

greenhouse effect *n* : warming of a planet's atmosphere that occurs when the sun's radiation passes through the atmosphere, is absorbed by the planet, and is reradiated as radiation of longer wavelength that can be absorbed by atmospheric gases

green manure *n* : an herbaceous crop (as clover) plowed under when green to enrich the soil

green•ness *n* ♦ : the quality or state of being green; *esp* : being unaffectedly simple and candid

♦ artlessness, ingenuousness, innocence, naturalness, naïveté, simplicity, unworldliness

green onion *n* : a young onion pulled before the bulb has enlarged and used especially in salads; *also* : SCALLION

green pepper *n* : a sweet pepper before it turns red at maturity

green•room \ˈgrēn-ˌrüm, -ˌru̇m\ *n* : a room in a theater or concert hall where actors or musicians relax before, between, or after appearances

green•sward \-ˌswȯrd\ *n* : turf that is green with growing grass

green thumb *n* : an unusual ability to make plants grow

green•wash•ing \ˈgrēn-ˌwȯ-shiŋ, -ˌwä-\ *n* : expressions of environmentalist concerns as a cover for products, policies, or activities deleterious to the environment

Green•wich mean time \ˈgri-nij-, ˈgre-, -nich-\ *n* : the time of the meridian of Greenwich used as the basis of worldwide standard time

Greenwich time *n* : GREENWICH MEAN TIME

green•wood \ˈgrēn-ˌwu̇d\ *n* : a forest green with foliage

greet \ˈgrēt\ *vb* **1** : to address with expressions of kind wishes **2** : to meet or react to in a specified manner **3** : to be perceived by — **greet•er** *n*

greet•ing *n* **1** ♦ : a salutation on meeting **2** *pl* ♦ : best wishes : REGARDS

♦ [1] hello, salutation, salute ♦ **greetings** [2] compliments, regards, respects

greeting card *n* : a card that bears a message usually sent on a special occasion

gre•gar•i•ous \gri-ˈgar-ē-əs\ *adj* **1** ♦ : marked by or indicating a liking for companionship : SOCIAL, COMPANIONABLE **2** : tending to flock together — **gre•gar•i•ous•ly** *adv* — **gre•gar•i•ous•ness** *n*

♦ boon, companionable, convivial, extroverted, outgoing, sociable, social

grem•lin \ˈgrem-lən\ *n* : a cause of error or equipment malfunction conceived of as a small gnome

gre•nade \grə-ˈnād\ *n* : a small bomb that is thrown by hand or launched (as by a rifle)

gren•a•dier \ˌgre-nə-ˈdir\ *n* : a member of a European regiment formerly armed with grenades

gren•a•dine \ˌgre-nə-ˈdēn, ˈgre-nə-ˌdēn\ *n* : a syrup flavored with pomegranates and used in mixed drinks

grew *past of* GROW

grey *var of* GRAY

grey•hound \ˈgrā-ˌhau̇nd\ *n* : any of a breed of tall slender dogs noted for speed and keen sight

grid \ˈgrid\ *n* **1** : GRATING **2** : a network of conductors for distributing electric power **3** : a network of horizontal and perpendicular lines (as for locating points on a map) **4** : GRIDIRON 2; *also* : FOOTBALL

grid•dle \ˈgrid-ᵊl\ *n* : a flat usually metal surface for cooking food

griddle cake *n* ♦ : a flat cake made of thin batter and cooked (as on a griddle) on both sides : PANCAKE

♦ flapjack, pancake

grid•iron \ˈgrid-ˌīrn, -ˌī-ərn\ *n* **1** : a grate for broiling food **2** : a football field

grid•lock \-ˌläk\ *n* : a traffic jam in which an intersection is so blocked that vehicles cannot move

grief \ˈgrēf\ *n* **1** ♦ : emotional distress caused by or as if by bereavement; *also* : a cause of such distress **2** : MISHAP **3** : DISASTER

♦ affliction, anguish, dolor, heartache, sorrow, woe

griev•ance \ˈgrē-vəns\ *n* **1** ♦ : a cause of distress affording reason for complaint or resistance **2** ♦ : the formal expression of a grievance : COMPLAINT

♦ [1] grudge, resentment, score ♦ [2] beef, complaint, fuss, gripe, grumble, murmur, plaint, squawk

grieve \ˈgrēv\ *vb* **grieved; griev•ing** **1** : to cause grief or sorrow to : DISTRESS **2** ♦ : to feel grief

♦ agonize, bleed, feel, hurt, mourn, sorrow, suffer ♦ *usu* **grieve for** bemoan, bewail, deplore, lament, mourn, wail

griev•ous \ˈgrē-vəs\ *adj* **1** ♦ : causing or characterized by severe suffering, grief, or sorrow : SEVERE ⟨a ~ wound⟩ **2** ♦ : unreasonably burdensome or severe : OPPRESSIVE, ONEROUS **3** ♦ : having important or dangerous possible consequences : SERIOUS, GRAVE

♦ [1, 2] bitter, brutal, burdensome, cruel, excruciating, grim, hard, harsh, heavy, onerous, oppressive, rough, rugged, severe, stiff, tough, trying ♦ [3] dangerous, grave, hazardous, menacing, parlous, perilous, risky, serious, unhealthy, unsafe, venturesome

griev•ous•ly *adv* **1** ♦ : in a grievous manner : in a manner characterized by sorrow or grief **2** : to a grievous degree

♦ agonizingly, bitterly, hard, hardly, sadly, sorrowfully, unhappily, woefully, wretchedly

¹**grill** \ˈgril\ *vb* **1** : to broil on a grill; *also* : to fry or toast on a griddle **2** ♦ : to question intensely

♦ examine, interrogate, pump, query, question, quiz

²**grill** *n* **1** : a cooking utensil of parallel bars on which food is grilled **2** ♦ : an informal restaurant

♦ café, diner, restaurant

grille *or* **grill** \ˈgril\ *n* : a grating that forms a barrier or screen

grill•work \ˈgril-ˌwərk\ *n* : work constituting or resembling a grille

grim \ˈgrim\ *adj* **grim•mer; grim•mest** **1** ♦ : fierce in disposition or action : CRUEL **2** ♦ : harsh and forbidding in appearance **3** : ghastly or repellent in character **4** ♦ : not flinching or shrinking : RELENTLESS — **grim•ly** *adv* — **grim•ness** *n*

♦ [1] cruel, fell, ferocious, fierce, savage, vicious ♦ [2] austere, dour, fierce, flinty, forbidding, gruff, rough, rugged, severe, stark, steely, stern *Ant* benign, benignant, gentle, mild, tender ♦ [4] determined, dogged, implacable, relentless, unflinching, unrelenting, unyielding

¹**gri•mace** \ˈgri-məs, gri-ˈmās\ *n* ♦ : a facial expression usually of disgust or disapproval — **grimace** *vb*

♦ face, frown, lower, mouth, pout, scowl

grime \ˈgrīm\ *n* ♦ : soot, smut, or dirt adhering to or embedded in a surface; *also* : accumulated dirtiness and disorder

♦ dirt, filth, muck, smut, soil

grimy *adj* : full of or covered with grime

grin \ˈgrin\ *vb* **grinned; grin•ning** : to draw back the lips so as to show the teeth especially in amusement — **grin** *n*

¹**grind** \ˈgrīnd\ *vb* **ground** \ˈgrau̇nd\; **grind•ing** **1** ♦ : to reduce to small particles **2** ♦ : to wear down, polish, or sharpen by friction **3** : OPPRESS **4** ♦ : to press with a grating noise : GRIT ⟨~ the teeth⟩ **5** : to operate or produce by turning a crank **6** : DRUDGE;

esp : to study hard **7** : to move with difficulty or friction ⟨gears *~ing*⟩

♦ [1] atomize, crush, powder, pulverize ♦ [2] buff, burnish, edge, file, hone, plane, polish, rasp, rub, sand, sharpen, whet ♦ [4] crunch, gnash, grate, grit, rasp, scrape, scratch

2grind *n* **1** ♦ : dreary monotonous labor, routine, or study **2** : one who works or studies excessively **3** ♦ : the act or sound of grinding

♦ [1] drudgery, labor (*or* labour), slavery, sweat, toil, travail ♦ [3] rasp, scrape, scratch

grind•er \ˈgrīn-dər\ *n* **1** : MOLAR **2** *pl* : TEETH **3** : one that grinds **4** ♦ : a large sandwich on a long split roll : SUBMARINE 2

♦ hoagie, poor boy, sub, submarine

grind out *vb* ♦ : to produce in a mechanical way

♦ build, carve, forge, hammer, work out

grind•stone \ˈgrīnd-ˌstōn\ *n* : a flat circular stone of natural sandstone that revolves on an axle and is used for grinding, shaping, or smoothing

1grip \ˈgrip\ *vb* **gripped; grip•ping 1** ♦ : to seize or hold firmly **2** ♦ : to hold the interest of strongly

♦ [1] clasp, clench, cling, clutch, grasp, hang on, hold, hold on ♦ [2] absorb, busy, engage, engross, enthrall, fascinate, immerse, interest, intrigue, involve, occupy

2grip *n* **1** : GRASP; *also* : strength in gripping **2** ♦ : a firm tenacious hold typically giving control, mastery, or understanding **3** ♦ : mental grasp : UNDERSTANDING **4** : a device for gripping **5** ♦ : portable case designed to hold a traveler's clothing and personal articles : TRAVELING BAG

♦ [2] arm, authority, clutch, command, control, dominion, hold, mastery, power, sway ♦ [3] appreciation, apprehension, comprehension, grasp, perception, understanding ♦ [5] carryall, handbag, portmanteau, suitcase, traveling bag

1gripe \ˈgrīp\ *vb* **griped; grip•ing 1** : IRRITATE, VEX **2** : to cause or experience spasmodic pains in the bowels **3** ♦ : to complain with grumbling

♦ beef, bellyache, carp, complain, crab, croak, fuss, grouse, growl, grumble, kick, moan, murmur, mutter, repine, squawk, wail, whine

2gripe *n* ♦ : expression of grief, pain, or dissatisfaction

♦ beef, complaint, fuss, grievance, grumble, murmur, plaint, squawk

grippe \ˈgrip\ *n* : INFLUENZA

gris–gris \ˈgrē-ˌgrē\ *n, pl* **gris–gris** \-ˌgrēz\ : an amulet or incantation used chiefly by people of black African ancestry

gris•ly \ˈgriz-lē\ *adj* **gris•li•er; -est** ♦ : inspiring horror, intense fear, disgust, or distaste : HORRIBLE, GRUESOME

♦ appalling, atrocious, awful, dreadful, frightful, ghastly, gruesome, hideous, horrible, horrid, lurid, macabre, monstrous, nightmarish, shocking, terrible

grist \ˈgrist\ *n* : grain to be ground or already ground

gris•tle \ˈgri-səl\ *n* : CARTILAGE — **gris•tly** \ˈgris-lē\ *adj*

grist•mill \ˈgrist-ˌmil\ *n* : a mill for grinding grain

1grit \ˈgrit\ *n* **1** : a hard sharp granule (as of sand); *also* : material composed of such granules **2** ♦ : unyielding courage — **grit•ty** *adj*

♦ backbone, fiber (*or* fibre), fortitude, guts, pluck, spunk

2grit *vb* **grit•ted; grit•ting** : to give forth a grating sound : GRIND, GRATE

grits \ˈgrits\ *n pl* : coarsely ground hulled grain ⟨hominy ~⟩

griz•zled \ˈgri-zəld\ *adj* : streaked or mixed with gray

griz•zly \ˈgriz-lē\ *adj* **griz•zli•er; -est** : GRIZZLED

grizzly bear *n* : a large pale-coated bear of western No. America

gro *abbr* gross

groan \ˈgrōn\ *vb* **1** ♦ : to utter a deep moan indicative of pain, grief, or annoyance : MOAN **2** : to make a harsh sound under sudden or prolonged strain ⟨the chair *~ed* under his weight⟩ — **groan** *n*

♦ howl, keen, lament, moan, plaint, wail

groat \ˈgrōt\ *n* : an old British coin worth four pennies

gro•cer \ˈgrō-sər\ *n* : a dealer especially in staple foodstuffs — **gro•cery** \ˈgrōs-rē, ˈgrōsh-, ˈgrō-sə-\ *n*

grog \ˈgräg\ *n* : alcoholic liquor; *esp* : liquor (as rum) mixed with water

grog•gy \ˈgrä-gē\ *adj* **grog•gi•er; -est** : weak and unsteady on the feet or in action — **grog•gi•ly** \-gə-lē\ *adv* — **grog•gi•ness** \-gē-nəs\ *n*

groin \ˈgröin\ *n* **1** : the juncture of the lower abdomen and inner part of the thigh; *also* : the region of this juncture **2** : the curved line or rib on a ceiling along which two vaults meet

grok \ˈgräk\ *vb* **grokked grok•king** : to understand profoundly and intuitively

grom•met \ˈgrä-mət, ˈgrə-\ *n* **1** : a ring of rope **2** : an eyelet of firm material to strengthen or protect an opening

1groom \ˈgrüm, ˈgru̇m\ *n* **1** : a person responsible for the care of horses **2** : BRIDEGROOM

2groom *vb* **1** : to clean and care for (an animal) **2** : to make neat or attractive **3** : PREPARE

grooms•man \ˈgrümz-mən, ˈgru̇mz-\ *n* : a male friend who attends a bridegroom at his wedding

1groove \ˈgrüv\ *n* **1** : a long narrow channel **2** ♦ : a fixed routine

♦ pattern, rote, routine, rut, treadmill

2groove *vb* **1** ♦ : to make a groove in; *also* : to form a groove **2** ♦ : to enjoy oneself intensely

♦ [1] score, scribe ♦ *usu* **groove on** [2] adore, delight, dig, enjoy, fancy, like, love, relish, revel

groovy \ˈgrü-vē\ *adj* **groov•i•er; -est 1** : unusually good : EXCELLENT **2** : HIP

grope \ˈgrōp\ *vb* **groped; grop•ing 1** ♦ : to feel about or search for blindly or uncertainly ⟨~ for the right word⟩ **2** : to feel one's way by groping

♦ feel, fish, fumble

gros•beak \ˈgrōs-ˌbēk\ *n* : any of several finches of Europe or America with large stout conical bills

gros•grain \ˈgrō-ˌgrān\ *n* : a silk or rayon fabric with crosswise cotton ribs

1gross \ˈgrōs\ *adj* **1** ♦ : glaringly noticeable **2** : OUT-AND-OUT, UTTER **3** ♦ : physically large : BIG, BULKY; *esp* : excessively fat **4** : GENERAL, BROAD **5** : consisting of an overall total exclusive of deductions ⟨~ earnings⟩ **6** : CARNAL, EARTHY ⟨~ pleasures⟩ **7** ♦ : coarse in nature or behavior : UNREFINED; *also* : crudely vulgar **8** : lacking knowledge — **gross•ly** *adv*

♦ [1] blatant, conspicuous, egregious, flagrant, glaring, obvious, patent, prominent, pronounced, rank, striking ♦ [3] chubby, corpulent, fat, fleshy, full, obese, overweight, plump, portly, rotund, round ♦ [7] coarse, common, crass, crude, ill-bred, low, rough, rude, tasteless, uncouth, uncultivated, uncultured, unpolished, unrefined, vulgar

2gross *n* : an overall total exclusive of deductions — **gross** *vb*

3gross *n, pl* **gross** : a total of 12 dozen things ⟨a ~ of pencils⟩

gross domestic product *n* : the gross national product excluding the value of net income earned abroad

gross national product *n* : the total value of the goods and services produced in a nation during a year

gross•ness *n* ♦ : the quality or state of being gross

♦ corpulence, fatness, obesity, plumpness ♦ coarseness, indelicacy, lowness, rudeness, vulgarity

grot \ˈgrät\ *n* : a natural underground chamber or series of chambers open to the surface : GROTTO

gro•tesque \grō-ˈtesk\ *adj* **1** : FANCIFUL, BIZARRE **2** ♦ : absurdly incongruous **3** ♦ : departing markedly from the natural, the expected, or the typical — **gro•tesque•ly** *adv*

♦ [2] harsh, unaesthetic ♦ [3] hideous, ugly, unappealing, unattractive

grot•to \ˈgrä-tō\ *n, pl* **grottoes** *also* **grottos 1** : a natural underground chamber or series of chambers open to the surface : CAVE **2** : an artificial cavelike structure

grouch \ˈgrau̇ch\ *n* **1** : a fit of bad temper **2** ♦ : an habitually irritable or complaining person — **grouch** *vb*

♦ bear, complainer, crab, crank, curmudgeon, grumbler, whiner

grouchy *adj* ♦ : given to grumbling : marked by ill temper

♦ choleric, cross, crotchety, irascible, irritable, peevish, snappy, snippy, testy, waspish ♦ crabby, cranky, fussy, grumpy, querulous

1ground \ˈgrau̇nd\ *n* **1** : the bottom of a body of water **2** *pl* ♦ : sediment at the bottom of a liquid **3** ♦ : a basis for belief, action, or argument **4** : a surrounding area : BACKGROUND **5** ♦ : the surface of the earth; *also* : SOIL **6** : an area with a particular use ⟨fishing *~s*⟩ **7** *pl* ♦ : the area about and belonging to a building **8** : a conductor that makes electrical connection with the earth

♦ **grounds** [2] deposit, dregs, lees, precipitate, sediment ♦ [3] base, basis, bedrock, cornerstone, footing, foundation, groundwork, keystone, underpinning ♦ *usu* **grounds** [3] motive, reason, wherefore, why ♦ [5] dirt, earth, soil ♦ **grounds** [7] demesne, park, premises, yard

²ground *vb* **1 :** to bring to or place on the ground **2 :** to run or cause to run aground **3** ♦ **:** to provide a reason or justification for **4 :** to furnish with a foundation of knowledge **5 :** to connect electrically with a ground **6 :** to restrict to the ground; *also* **:** prohibit from some activity

♦ base, rest

³ground *past and past part of* GRIND
ground ball *n* **:** a batted baseball that rolls or bounces along the ground
ground cover *n* **:** low plants that grow over and cover the soil; *also* **:** a plant suitable for use as ground cover
ground•ed \ˈgrau̇n-dəd\ *adj* **:** mentally and emotionally stable
ground•er \ˈgrau̇n-dər\ *n* **:** GROUND BALL
ground•hog \ˈgrau̇nd-ˌhȯg, -ˌhäg\ *n* **:** WOODCHUCK
ground•less \ˈgrau̇n(d)-ləs\ *adj* ♦ **:** having no ground or foundation

♦ baseless, invalid, unfounded, unreasonable, unsubstantiated, unsupported, unwarranted

ground•ling \ˈgrau̇nd-liŋ\ *n* **:** a spectator in the pit of an Elizabethan theater
ground rule *n* **1 :** a sports rule adopted to modify play on a particular field, court, or course **2 :** a rule of procedure
ground squirrel *n* **:** any of various burrowing rodents of No. America and Eurasia that are related to the squirrels and live in colonies in open areas
ground swell *n* **1 :** a broad deep ocean swell caused by an often distant gale or earthquake **2** *usu* **ground•swell :** a rapid spontaneous growth (as of political opinion)
ground•wa•ter \ˈgrau̇nd-ˌwȯ-tər, -ˌwä-\ *n* **:** water within the earth that supplies wells and springs
ground•work \-ˌwərk\ *n* ♦ **:** something that forms a foundation or support **:** BASIS; *also* **:** preparation made beforehand

♦ base, basis, bedrock, footing, foundation, ground, keystone, underpinning

ground zero *n* **1 :** the point above, below, or at which a nuclear explosion occurs **2 :** the center or origin of rapid, intense, or violent activity
¹group \ˈgrüp\ *n* **1** ♦ **:** a number of individuals related by a common factor (as physical association, community of interests, or blood) **2 :** a combination of atoms commonly found together in a molecule ⟨a methyl ~⟩

♦ bracket, category, class, division, family, grade, kind, order, set, species, type

²group *vb* ♦ **:** to associate in groups

♦ assort, break down, categorize, class, classify, grade, peg, place, range, rank, separate, sort ♦ accumulate, amass, assemble, collect, concentrate, garner, gather, lump, pick up, round up, scrape

grou•per \ˈgrü-pər\ *n, pl* **groupers** *also* **grouper :** any of numerous large solitary bottom fishes of warm seas
group home *n* **:** a residence for persons requiring care or supervision
group•ie \ˈgrü-pē\ *n* **:** a fan of a rock group who usually follows the group around on concert tours; *also* **:** ENTHUSIAST, FAN
group•ing \ˈgrü-piŋ\ *n* **1 :** the act or process of combining in groups **2 :** a set of objects combined in a group
group therapy *n* **:** therapy in the presence of a therapist in which several patients discuss their personal problems
groupware \ˈgrüp-ˌwer\ *n* **:** software that enables users to work jointly via a network on projects or files
¹grouse \ˈgrau̇s\ *n, pl* **grouse** *or* **grouses :** any of numerous ground-dwelling game birds that have feathered legs and are usually of reddish brown or other protective color
²grouse *vb* **groused; grous•ing** ♦ **:** to mutter in discontent **:** COMPLAIN, GRUMBLE

♦ beef, bellyache, carp, complain, crab, fuss, gripe, grumble, kick, moan, squawk, wail, whine

grout \ˈgrau̇t\ *n* **:** material (as mortar) used for filling spaces — **grout** *vb*
grove \ˈgrōv\ *n* **:** a small wood usually without underbrush
grov•el \ˈgrä-vəl, ˈgrə-\ *vb* **-eled** *or* **-elled; -el•ing** *or* **-el•ling** **1** ♦ **:** to creep or lie with the body prostrate in fear or humility **2 :** to abase oneself

♦ crawl, creep, slither, snake, worm

grow \ˈgrō\ *vb* **grew** \ˈgrü\; **grown** \ˈgrōn\; **grow•ing** **1** ♦ **:** to spring up and develop to maturity **2 :** to be able to grow **:** THRIVE **3 :** to take on some relation through or as if through growth ⟨tree limbs *grown* together⟩ **4** ♦ **:** to become progressively greater **5 :** to develop from a parent source **6** ♦ **:** to pass into a condition **:** BECOME **7 :** to have an increasing influence **8** ♦ **:** to cause to grow

♦ [1] age, develop, grow up, mature, progress, ripen ♦ *usu* **grow in** [4] build, gain, gather, pick up ♦ [6] become, come, get, go, run, turn, wax ♦ [8] crop, cultivate, culture, promote, raise, rear, tend

grow•er *n* **1 :** one that grows especially in a specified way **2** ♦ **:** a person who grows a specified fruit or other product

♦ agriculturist, cultivator, farmer, planter, tiller

growing pains *n pl* **1 :** pains in the legs of growing children having no known relation to growth **2 :** the stresses and strains attending a new project or development
growl \ˈgrau̇l\ *vb* **1 :** RUMBLE **2** ♦ **:** to utter a deep throaty sound **3 :** to complain angrily **:** GRUMBLE — **growl** *n*

♦ bellow, boom, roar, thunder

grown–up \ˈgrō-ˌnəp\ *adj* **:** not childish **:** ADULT — **grown–up** *n*
growth \ˈgrōth\ *n* **1 :** stage or condition attained in growing **2** ♦ **:** a process of growing especially through progressive development or increase **3 a :** a result or product of growing ⟨a fine ~ of hair⟩ **b** ♦ **:** an abnormal mass of tissue (as a tumor)

♦ [2] development, elaboration, evolution, expansion, maturation, progress, progression ♦ [3b] excrescence, lump, neoplasm, tumor

growth hormone *n* **:** a vertebrate hormone that is secreted by the pituitary gland and regulates growth
growth industry *n* **:** a business, interest, or activity that is increasingly popular, profitable, or trendy
grow up *vb* ♦ **:** to grow toward or arrive at full stature or physical or mental maturity

♦ age, develop, grow, mature, progress, ripen

¹grub \ˈgrəb\ *vb* **grubbed; grub•bing** **1 :** to clear or root out by digging **2 :** to dig in the ground usually for a hidden object **3 :** to search about **4 :** to work hard and long
²grub *n* **1 :** a soft thick wormlike insect larva ⟨beetle ~*s*⟩ **2 :** DRUDGE; *also* **:** a slovenly person **3** ♦ **:** nourishment in solid form **:** FOOD

♦ chow, fare, food, meat, provender, provisions, viands, victuals

grub•bi•ness \-bē-nəs\ *n* ♦ **:** the state of being grubby

♦ dinginess, dirtiness, filthiness, foulness, nastiness, uncleanliness

grub•by \ˈgrə-bē\ *adj* **grub•bi•er; -est** ♦ **:** full of or covered with grime **:** DIRTY, SLOVENLY

♦ dirty, filthy, foul, grungy, mucky, muddy, slovenly, unclean

grub•stake \ˈgrəb-ˌstāk\ *n* **:** supplies or funds furnished a mining prospector in return for a share in his finds
¹grudge \ˈgrəj\ *vb* **grudged; grudg•ing :** to be reluctant to give **:** BEGRUDGE
²grudge *n* ♦ **:** a feeling of deep-seated resentment or ill will

♦ animosity, antagonism, antipathy, bitterness, enmity, gall, hostility, rancor ♦ grievance, resentment, score

gru•el \ˈgrü-əl\ *n* **:** a thin porridge
gru•el•ing *or* **gru•el•ling** \ˈgrü-liŋ, ˈgrü-ə-\ *adj* ♦ **:** requiring extreme effort **:** EXHAUSTING

♦ arduous, demanding, difficult, exacting, formidable, hard, herculean, laborious, murderous, rough, stiff, strenuous, tall, toilsome, tough

grue•some \ˈgrü-səm\ *adj* ♦ **:** inspiring horror or repulsion

♦ appalling, atrocious, awful, dreadful, frightful, ghastly, grisly, hideous, horrible, horrid, lurid, macabre, monstrous, nightmarish, shocking, terrible

gruff \ˈgrəf\ *adj* **1** ♦ **:** rough in speech or manner **2** ♦ **:** being deep and harsh **:** HOARSE — **gruff•ly** *adv*

♦ [1] flinty, grim, rough, rugged, severe, stark, steely, stern ♦ [2] coarse, gravelly, hoarse, husky, scratchy, throaty

grum•ble \ˈgrəm-bəl\ *vb* **grum•bled; grum•bling 1 ♦ :** to mutter in discontent **2 ♦ :** to utter a growl : GROWL, RUMBLE

♦ [1] beef, bellyache, complain, fuss, gripe, grouse, kick, moan, squawk, wail, whine ♦ [2] growl, lumber, roll, rumble

grum•bler *n* **♦ :** one that grumbles

♦ bear, complainer, crab, crank, curmudgeon, grouch, whiner

grump•i•ness \-pē-nəs\ *n* **♦ :** the quality or state of being grumpy

♦ biliousness, irritability, peevishness, perverseness, perversity

grumpy \ˈgrəm-pē\ *adj* **grump•i•er; -est ♦ :** moodily cross : SURLY — **grump•i•ly** \-pə-lē\ *adv*

♦ choleric, crabby, cranky, cross, crotchety, grouchy, irascible, irritable, peevish, petulant, short-tempered, surly, testy, waspish

grunge \ˈgrənj\ *n* **1 :** one that is grungy **2 :** heavy metal rock music expressing alienation and discontent **3 :** untidy or tattered clothing typically worn by grunge fans

grun•gy \ˈgrən-jē\ *adj* **grun•gi•er; -est ♦ :** shabby or dirty in character or condition

♦ dirty, grubby, mucky, muddy, unclean ♦ dilapidated, mean, neglected, ratty, seedy, shabby

grun•ion \ˈgrən-yən\ *n* **:** a fish of the California coast which comes inshore to spawn at nearly full moon

¹grunt \ˈgrənt\ *n* **:** a deep throaty sound (as that of a hog)

²grunt *vb* **:** to utter a grunt; *also* **:** to utter with a grunt

GSA *abbr* **1** General Services Administration **2** Girl Scouts of America

G suit *n* **:** a suit for a pilot or astronaut designed to counteract the physiological effects of acceleration

GSUSA *abbr* Girl Scouts of the United States of America

gt *abbr* great

Gt Brit *abbr* Great Britain

gtd *abbr* guaranteed

GU *abbr* Guam

gua•ca•mo•le \ˌgwä-kə-ˈmō-lē\ *n* **:** mashed and seasoned avocado

gua•nine \ˈgwä-ˌnēn\ *n* **:** a purine base that codes genetic information in the molecular chain of DNA and RNA

gua•no \ˈgwä-nō\ *n* **:** excrement especially of seabirds or bats; *also* **:** a fertilizer composed chiefly of this excrement

¹guar•an•tee \ˌgar-ən-ˈtē\ *n* **1 :** GUARANTOR **2 :** GUARANTY 1 **3 ♦ :** an agreement by which one person undertakes to secure another in the possession or enjoyment of something **4 :** an assurance of the quality of or of the length of use to be expected from a product offered for sale **5 ♦ :** something given as security : GUARANTY

♦ [3] bond, contract, covenant, guaranty, surety, warranty ♦ [5] gage, guaranty, pawn, pledge, security

²guarantee *vb* **-teed; -tee•ing 1 :** to undertake to answer for the debt, failure to perform, or faulty performance of (another) **2 :** to undertake an obligation to establish, perform, or continue **3 ♦ :** to give security to

♦ assure, cinch, ensure, guaranty, insure, secure

guar•an•tor \ˌgar-ən-ˈtȯr\ *n* **♦ :** one who gives a guarantee

♦ backer, patron, sponsor, surety

¹guar•an•ty \ˈgar-ən-tē\ *n, pl* **-ties 1 :** an undertaking to answer for another's failure to pay a debt or perform a duty **2 ♦ :** an agreement by which one person undertakes to secure another in the possession or enjoyment of something : GUARANTEE **3 :** GUARANTOR **4 ♦ :** something given as security : PLEDGE

♦ [2] bond, contract, covenant, guarantee, surety, warranty ♦ [4] gage, guarantee, pawn, pledge, security

²guaranty *vb* **-tied; -ty•ing :** to give security to : GUARANTEE

¹guard \ˈgärd\ *n* **1 ♦ :** a person or a body of persons on sentinel duty **2** *pl* **:** troops assigned to protect a sovereign **3 :** a defensive position (as in boxing) **4 ♦ :** the act or duty of protecting or defending **5 ♦ :** one that protects : PROTECTION **6 :** a protective or safety device **7 :** a football lineman playing between center and tackle; *also* **:** a basketball player stationed toward the rear — **on guard :** WATCHFUL, ALERT

♦ [1] custodian, guardian, keeper, lookout, picket, sentry, warden, warder, watch, watchman ♦ [4] aegis, armor, cover, defense (*or* defence), protection, safeguard, screen, security, shield, wall, ward ♦ [5] custodian, defender, defense (*or* defence), protection, protector

²guard *vb* **1 ♦ :** to protect from danger especially by watchful attention : DEFEND **2 :** to watch over **3 ♦ :** to be on guard

♦ [1] cover, defend, protect, safeguard, screen, secure, shield, ward ♦ *usu* **guard against** [3] beware (of), mind, watch out (for)

guard•ed \ˈgär-dəd\ *adj* **♦ :** careful to consider all circumstances and possible consequences

♦ alert, careful, cautious, circumspect, considerate, gingerly, heedful, safe, wary

guard•house \ˈgärd-ˌhau̇s\ *n* **1 :** a building occupied by a guard or used as a headquarters by soldiers on guard duty **2 :** a military jail

guard•ian \ˈgär-dē-ən\ *n* **1 ♦ :** one that guards : CUSTODIAN **2 ♦ :** one who has the care of the person or property of another

♦ caretaker, custodian, janitor, keeper, warden, watchman

guard•ian•ship *n* **♦ :** supervision or support of one that is smaller and weaker; *specif* **:** the relationship existing between guardian and ward

♦ care, custody, keeping, safekeeping, trust, ward

guard•room \ˈgärd-ˌrüm\ *n* **1 :** a room used by a military guard while on duty **2 :** a room where military prisoners are confined

guards•man \ˈgärdz-mən\ *n* **:** a member of a military body called *guard* or *guards*

Gua•te•ma•lan \ˌgwä-tə-ˈmä-lən\ *n* **:** a native or inhabitant of Guatemala — **Guatemalan** *adj*

gua•va \ˈgwä-və\ *n* **:** the sweet yellow or pink acid fruit of a shrubby tropical American tree used especially for making jam and jelly; *also* **:** the tree

gu•ber•na•to•ri•al \ˌgü-bər-nə-ˈtōr-ē-əl\ *adj* **:** of or relating to a governor

guer•don \ˈgərd-ᵊn\ *n* **:** REWARD, RECOMPENSE

Guern•sey \ˈgərn-zē\ *n, pl* **Guernseys :** any of a breed of usually reddish brown and white dairy cattle that produce rich yellowish milk

guer•ril•la *or* **gue•ril•la** \gə-ˈri-lə\ *n* **:** one who engages in irregular warfare especially as a member of an independent unit

¹guess \ˈges\ *vb* **1 ♦ :** to form an opinion from little or no evidence **2 ♦ :** to hold as an opinion : BELIEVE, SUPPOSE **3 ♦ :** to conjecture correctly about

♦ [1] assume, conjecture, presume, speculate, suppose, surmise, suspect ♦ [2] believe, consider, deem, feel, figure, hold, imagine, suppose, think ♦ [3] calculate, call, conjecture, estimate, figure, gauge, judge, make, place, put, reckon, suppose

²guess *n* **♦ :** a conclusion deduced by surmise or guesswork

♦ conjecture, supposition, surmise

guest \ˈgest\ *n* **1 :** a person to whom hospitality (as of a house or a club) is extended **2 ♦ :** a patron of a commercial establishment (as a hotel) **3 :** a person not a regular member of a cast who appears on a program

♦ customer, patron

guest•house \ˈgest-ˌhau̇s\ *n* **:** a house run as a boarding house or bed-and-breakfast

guf•faw \(ˌ)gə-ˈfȯ\ *n* **:** a loud burst of laughter — **guf•faw** *vb*

guid•ance \ˈgīd-ᵊns\ *n* **1 ♦ :** the act or process of guiding **2 :** the direction provided by a guide : ADVICE

♦ administration, conduct, control, direction, government, management, operation, oversight, regulation, running, superintendence, supervision

¹guide \ˈgīd\ *n* **1 ♦ :** one who leads or directs another's course **2 ♦ :** one who shows and explains points of interest **3 :** something that provides guiding information; *also* **:** SIGNPOST **4 :** a device to direct the motion of something

♦ [1, 2] attendant, companion, escort, guard

²guide *vb* **guid•ed; guid•ing 1 ♦ :** to act as a guide to **2 ♦ :** to direct, supervise, or influence usually to a particular end **3 :** to superintend the training of — **guid•able** \ˈgī-də-bəl\ *adj*

♦ [1] conduct, direct, lead, marshal, pilot, route, show, steer, usher ♦ [1, 2] administer, carry on, conduct, control, direct, govern, handle, manage, operate, oversee, regulate, run, superintend, supervise ♦ [2] coach, counsel, lead, mentor, pilot, shepherd, show, tutor

guide•book \ˈgīd-ˌbu̇k\ *n* **:** a book of information for travelers

guided missile *n* **:** a missile whose course may be altered during flight

guide dog *n* : a dog trained to lead the blind
guide•line \ˈgīd-ˌlīn\ *n* : an indication or outline of policy or conduct
guide word *n* : a term at the head of a page of an alphabetical reference work that indicates the alphabetically first or last word on that page
gui•don \ˈgī-ˌdän, ˈgīd-ᵊn\ *n* : a small flag (as of a military unit)
guild \ˈgild\ *n* ♦ : an association of people with common aims and interests; *esp* : a medieval association of merchants or craftsmen — **guild•hall** \-ˌhȯl\ *n*

♦ association, brotherhood, club, college, congress, council, fellowship, fraternity, institute, institution, league, order, organization, society

guile \ˈgīl\ *n* ♦ : deceitful cunning : DUPLICITY

♦ artfulness, artifice, caginess, canniness, craft, craftiness, cunning, slyness, wiliness ♦ craft, craftiness, crookedness, deceit, deceitfulness, dishonesty, dissimulation, double-dealing, duplicity

guile•ful *adj* ♦ : full of guile : characterized by cunning, deceit, or treachery

♦ artful, cagey, crafty, cunning, devious, foxy, slick, sly, subtle, wily

guil•lo•tine \ˈgi-lə-ˌtēn, ˌgē-ə-ˈtēn\ *n* : a machine for beheading persons — **guillotine** *vb*
guilt \ˈgilt\ *n* **1** : the fact of having committed an offense especially against the law **2** ♦ : the state of one who has committed an offense especially consciously **3** ♦ : a feeling of responsibility for wrongdoing

♦ [2] blame, culpability, fault, rap ♦ [3] contrition, penitence, remorse, repentance, self-reproach, shame

guilt•less *adj* ♦ : free from guilt or evil

♦ blameless, clear, faultless, impeccable, innocent, irreproachable

guilt-trip \ˈgilt-ˌtrip\ *vb* : to cause feelings of guilt in
guilty \ˈgil-tē\ *adj* **guilt•i•er; -est** **1** ♦ : having committed a breach of conduct or a crime **2** : suggesting or involving guilt **3** ♦ : aware of or suffering from guilt — **guilt•i•ly** \-tə-lē\ *adv* — **guilt•i•ness** \-tē-nəs\ *n*

♦ [1] accountable, answerable, blamable, blameworthy, censurable, culpable, reprehensible ***Ant*** blameless, guiltless, innocent ♦ [3] ashamed, contrite, hangdog, penitent, remorseful, repentant, shamefaced ***Ant*** impenitent, remorseless, shameless, unashamed, unrepentant

guin•ea \ˈgi-nē\ *n* **1** : a British gold coin no longer issued worth 21 shillings **2** : a unit of value equal to 21 shillings
guinea fowl *n* : a gray and white spotted West African bird related to the pheasants and widely raised for food; *also* : any of several related birds
guinea hen *n* : a female guinea fowl; *also* : GUINEA FOWL
Guin•ean \ˈgi-nē-ən\ *n* : a native or inhabitant of Guinea — **Guinean** *adj*
guinea pig *n* **1** : a small stocky short-eared and nearly tailless So. American rodent often kept as a pet or used in lab research **2** : a subject of research or testing
guise \ˈgīz\ *n* **1** ♦ : a form or style of dress : COSTUME **2** ♦ : external appearance : SEMBLANCE

♦ [1] dress, garb, getup, outfit ♦ [2] appearance, face, name, semblance, show

gui•tar \gi-ˈtär\ *n* : a musical instrument with usually six strings plucked with a pick or with the fingers
gulch \ˈgəlch\ *n* ♦ : a deep or precipitous cleft : RAVINE

♦ canyon, defile, flume, gap, gorge, notch, pass, ravine

gulf \ˈgəlf\ *n* **1** ♦ : a part of an ocean or sea partly or mostly surrounded by land **2** : ABYSS, CHASM **3** : a wide separation

♦ bay, bight, cove, estuary, fjord, inlet

¹gull \ˈgəl\ *n* : any of numerous mostly white or gray long-winged web-footed seabirds
²gull *vb* ♦ : to make a dupe of : DECEIVE

♦ deceive, delude, dupe, fool, misinform, mislead, take in, trick

³gull *n* : a person who is easily deceived or cheated : DUPE
gul•let \ˈgə-lət\ *n* : ESOPHAGUS; *also* : THROAT
gull•ible \ˈgə-lə-bəl\ *adj* ♦ : easily duped or cheated

♦ easy, susceptible

gul•ly \ˈgə-lē\ *n, pl* **gullies** : a trench worn in the earth by and often filled with running water after rains
¹gulp \ˈgəlp\ *vb* **1** ♦ : to swallow hurriedly or greedily **2** : SUPPRESS ⟨~ down a sob⟩ **3** : to catch the breath as if in taking a long drink

♦ gobble, bolt, devour, gorge, gormandize, scarf, scoff, wolf

²gulp *n* **1** : the act or an instance of gulping **2** : the amount taken in a single large swallow
¹gum \ˈgəm\ *n* : the oral tissue that surrounds the necks of the teeth
²gum *n* **1** : a sticky plant exudate; *esp* : one that hardens on drying **2** : a sticky substance **3** : a preparation usually of a plant gum sweetened and flavored and used for chewing
gum arabic *n* : a water-soluble gum obtained from several acacias and used especially in making inks, adhesives, confections, and pharmaceuticals
gum•bo \ˈgəm-bō\ *n* : a rich thick soup usually thickened with okra
gum•drop \ˈgəm-ˌdräp\ *n* : a candy made usually from corn syrup with gelatin and coated with sugar crystals
gum•my *adj* ♦ : having a thick or sticky quality; *also* : consisting, containing, or covered with gum

♦ adhesive, gelatinous, gluey, glutinous, gooey, sticky, viscid, viscous

gump•tion \ˈgəmp-shən\ *n* **1** : shrewd common sense **2** : ENTERPRISE, INITIATIVE
gum•shoe \ˈgəm-ˌshü\ *n* : DETECTIVE — **gumshoe** *vb*
¹gun \ˈgən\ *n* **1** : CANNON **2** ♦ : a portable firearm **3** : a discharge of a gun **4** : something suggesting a gun in shape or function **5** : THROTTLE — **gunned** \ˈgənd\ *adj*

♦ arm, firearm, piece

²gun *vb* **gunned; gun•ning** **1** : to hunt with a gun **2** : to hit with a missile (as a bullet) from a gun : SHOOT **3** : to open up the throttle of so as to increase speed
gun•boat \ˈgən-ˌbōt\ *n* : a small lightly armed ship for use in shallow waters
gun•fight \-ˌfīt\ *n* : a duel with guns — **gun•fight•er** *n*
gun•fire \-ˌfīr\ *n* : the firing of guns
gung ho \ˈgəŋ-ˈhō\ *adj* ♦ : extremely zealous or enthusiastic

♦ avid, eager, enthusiastic, keen, nuts, raring

gun•man \-mən\ *n* : a man armed with a gun; *esp* : a professional killer
gun•ner \ˈgə-nər\ *n* **1** : a soldier or airman who operates or aims a gun **2** : one who hunts with a gun
gun•nery \ˈgə-nə-rē\ *n* : the use of guns; *esp* : the science of the flight of projectiles and effective use of guns
gunnery sergeant *n* : a noncommissioned officer in the marine corps ranking next below a master sergeant
gun•ny•sack \ˈgə-nē-ˌsak\ *n* : a sack made of a coarse heavy fabric (as burlap)
gun•point \ˈgən-ˌpȯint\ *n* : the muzzle of a gun — **at gunpoint** : under a threat of death by being shot
gun•pow•der \-ˌpau̇-dər\ *n* : an explosive powder used in guns and blasting
gun•shot \-ˌshät\ *n* **1** : shot fired from a gun **2** : the range of a gun ⟨within ~⟩
gun–shy \-ˌshī\ *adj* **1** : afraid of a loud noise **2** : markedly distrustful
gun•sling•er \-ˌsliŋ-ər\ *n* : a skilled gunman especially in the old West
gun•smith \-ˌsmith\ *n* : one who designs, makes, or repairs firearms
gun•wale *also* **gun•nel** \ˈgən-ᵊl\ *n* : the upper edge of a ship's or boat's side
gup•py \ˈgə-pē\ *n, pl* **guppies** : a small brightly colored tropical fish
gur•gle \ˈgər-gəl\ *vb* **gur•gled; gur•gling** **1** : to make a sound like that of an irregularly flowing or gently splashing liquid **2** ♦ : to flow in a broken irregular current — **gurgle** *n*

♦ dribble, lap, plash, ripple, slosh, splash, trickle, wash ***Ant*** roll, pour, stream

Gur•kha \ˈgu̇r-kə, ˈgər-\ *n* : a soldier from Nepal in the British or Indian army
gur•ney \ˈgər-nē\ *n, pl* **gurneys** : a wheeled cot or stretcher
gu•ru \ˈgu̇r-ü\ *n, pl* **gurus** **1** : a personal religious and spiritual teacher in Hinduism **2** : a teacher in matters of fundamental concern **3** ♦ : a person who has knowledge or skills acquired through actual practice : EXPERT ⟨a fitness ~⟩

♦ ace, adept, artist, authority, crackerjack, expert, hand, hotshot, maestro, master, scholar, shark, virtuoso, whiz, wizard

gush \ˈgəsh\ *vb* **1** ♦ **:** to issue or pour forth copiously or violently **:** SPOUT **2** ♦ **:** to make an effusive display of affection or enthusiasm

♦ [1] jet, pour, rush, spew, spout, spurt, squirt *Ant* dribble, drip, drop, trickle ♦ [2] enthuse, fuss, rave, rhapsodize, slobber

gush•er \ˈgə-shər\ *n* **:** one that gushes; *esp* **:** an oil well with a large natural flow
gushy \ˈgə-shē\ *adj* **gush•i•er; -est :** marked by effusive sentimentality
gus•set \ˈgə-sət\ *n* **:** a triangular insert (as in a seam of a sleeve) to give width or strength — **gusset** *vb*
gus•sy up \ˈgə-sē-\ *vb* **1 :** to dress up in best or formal clothes **2 :** to make more attractive, glamorous or fancy
¹gust \ˈgəst\ *n* **1** ♦ **:** a sudden brief rush of wind **2 :** a sudden outburst **:** SURGE

♦ blast, blow, flurry, williwaw

²gust *vb* **:** to blow in gusts
gus•ta•to•ry \ˈgəs-tə-ˌtōr-ē\ *adj* **:** relating to or associated with the sense of taste
gus•to \ˈgə-ˌstō\ *n* **:** enthusiastic and vigorous enjoyment, appreciation, or delight
gusty *adj* ♦ **:** blowing in gusts

♦ blowy, blustery, breezy, windy

¹gut \ˈgət\ *n* **1** *pl* **:** internal organs of the body **:** BOWELS, ENTRAILS **2** ♦ **:** the alimentary canal or a part of it (as the intestine); *also* **:** BELLY, ABDOMEN **3** *pl* **:** the inner essential parts **4** *pl* ♦ **:** fortitude and stamina in coping with what alarms, repels, or discourages **:** COURAGE, PLUCK

♦ [2] abdomen, belly, solar plexus, stomach, tummy ♦ **guts** [4] bravery, courage, daring, fearlessness, hardihood, nerve, stoutness ♦ **guts** [4] backbone, fiber (*or* fibre), fortitude, grit, pluck, spunk

²gut *vb* **gut•ted; gut•ting 1** ♦ **:** to take out the entrails of **:** EVISCERATE **2 :** to destroy the inside of

♦ clean, draw, eviscerate

gut check *n* **:** a test of courage, character, or determination
gutsy \ˈgət-sē\ *adj* **guts•i•er; -est** ♦ **:** marked by courage and determination

♦ adventurous, audacious, bold, daring, enterprising, hardy, nervy, venturesome

gut•ter \ˈgə-tər\ *n* ♦ **:** a groove or channel for carrying off especially rainwater

♦ dike, ditch, trench

gut•ter•snipe \-ˌsnīp\ *n* **:** a street urchin
gut•tur•al \ˈgə-tə-rəl\ *adj* **1 :** sounded in the throat **2 :** being or marked by an utterance that is strange, unpleasant, or disagreeable — **guttural** *n*
gut•ty \ˈgə-tē\ *adj* **gut•ti•er; -est 1 :** GUTSY **2 :** having a vigorous challenging quality
gut–wrench•ing \ˈgət-ˌren-chiŋ\ *adj* **:** causing emotional anguish
¹guy \ˈgī\ *n* **:** a rope, chain, or rod attached to something as a brace or guide
²guy *vb* **:** to steady or reinforce with a guy
³guy *n* ♦ **:** an adult male human **:** MAN, FELLOW; *also, pl* **:** PERSONS ⟨all the ∼*s* came⟩

♦ buck, chap, dude, fellow, gent, gentleman, hombre, jack, joker, lad, male, man

⁴guy *vb* **:** to make fun of **:** RIDICULE
Guy•a•nese \ˌgī-ə-ˈnēz\ *n, pl* **Guyanese :** a native or inhabitant of Guyana — **Guyanese** *adj*
guz•zle \ˈgə-zəl\ *vb* **guz•zled; guz•zling** ♦ **:** to drink greedily

♦ drink, imbibe, quaff, sup, swig, toss

gym \ˈjim\ *n* **:** GYMNASIUM
gym•kha•na \jim-ˈkä-nə\ *n* **:** a meet featuring sports contests; *esp* **:** a contest of automobile-driving skill
gym•na•si•um *for 1* jim-ˈnā-zē-əm, -zhəm, *for 2* gim-ˈnä-zē-əm\ *n, pl* **-na•si•ums** *or* **-na•sia** \-ˈnā-zē-ə, -ˈnā-zhə; -ˈnä-zē-ə\ **1 :** a room or building for indoor sports **2 :** a European secondary school that prepares students for the university
gym•nas•tics \jim-ˈnas-tiks\ *n* **:** a competitive sport developed from physical exercises designed to demonstrate strength, balance, and body control — **gym•nast** \ˈjim-ˌnast\ *n* — **gym•nas•tic** *adj*
gym•no•sperm \ˈjim-nə-ˌspərm\ *n* **:** any of a class or subdivision of woody vascular seed plants (as conifers) that produce naked seeds not enclosed in an ovary
gyn *or* **gynecol** *abbr* gynecology
gy•nae•col•o•gy *chiefly Brit var of* GYNECOLOGY
gy•ne•col•o•gy \ˌgī-nə-ˈkä-lə-jē\ *n* **:** a branch of medicine dealing with the diseases and hygiene of women — **gy•ne•co•log•ic** \-ni-kə-ˈlä-jik\ *or* **gy•ne•co•log•i•cal** \-ji-kəl\ *adj* — **gy•ne•col•o•gist** \-nə-ˈkä-lə-jist\ *n*
gy•no•cen•tric \ˌgī-nə-ˈsen-trik\ *adj* **:** emphasizing feminine interests or a feminine point of view
¹gyp \ˈjip\ *n* **1 :** CHEAT, SWINDLER **2 :** FRAUD, SWINDLE
²gyp *vb* ♦ **:** to deprive of something valuable by the use of deceit or fraud

♦ bleed, cheat, chisel, cozen, defraud, fleece, hustle, mulct, rook, shortchange, skin, squeeze, stick, sting, swindle, victimize

gyp•sum \ˈjip-səm\ *n* **:** a calcium-containing mineral used in making plaster of paris
Gyp•sy \ˈjip-sē\ *n, pl* **Gypsies :** a member of a traditionally traveling people coming orig. from India and living chiefly in Europe, Asia, and No. America; *also* **:** the language of the Gypsies
gypsy moth *n* **:** an Old World moth that was introduced into the U.S. where its caterpillar is a destructive defoliator of many trees
gy•rate \ˈjī-ˌrāt\ *vb* **gy•rat•ed; gy•rat•ing 1** ♦ **:** to revolve around a point or axis **2 :** to oscillate with or as if with a circular or spiral motion

♦ pirouette, revolve, roll, rotate, spin, turn, twirl, wheel, whirl

gy•ra•tion \jī-ˈrā-shən\ *n* **:** an act or instance of gyrating

♦ pirouette, reel, revolution, roll, rotation, spin, twirl, wheel, whirl

gyr•fal•con \ˈjər-ˌfal-kən, -ˌfȯl-\ *n* **:** an arctic falcon with several color forms that is the largest of all falcons
¹gy•ro \ˈjī-rō\ *n, pl* **gyros :** GYROSCOPE
²gy•ro \ˈyē-ˌrō, ˈzhir-ō\ *n, pl* **gyros :** a sandwich especially of lamb and beef, tomato, onion, and yogurt sauce on pita bread
gy•ro•scope \ˈjī-rō-ˌskōp\ *n* **:** a wheel or disk mounted to spin rapidly about an axis that is free to turn in various directions
Gy Sgt *abbr* gunnery sergeant
gyve \ˈjīv, ˈgiv\ *n* **:** FETTER — **gyve** *vb*

H

¹h \ˈāch\ *n, pl* **h's** *or* **hs** \ˈā-chəz\ *often cap* **:** the 8th letter of the English alphabet
²h *abbr, often cap* **1** hard; hardness **2** heroin **3** hit **4** husband
H *symbol* hydrogen
¹ha \ˈhä\ *interj* — used especially to express surprise or joy
²ha *abbr* hectare
Hab *abbr* Habacuc; Habakkuk
Ha•ba•cuc \ˈha-bə-ˌkək, hə-ˈba-kək\ *n* **:** HABAKKUK
Ha•bak•kuk \ˈha-bə-ˌkək, hə-ˈba-kək\ *n* **:** a book of the canonical Jewish and Christian Scriptures
ha•ba•ne•ra \ˌhä-bə-ˈner-ə\ *n* **:** a Cuban dance in slow time; *also* **:** the music for this dance
ha•ba•ne•ro *also* **ha•ba•ñe•ro** \ˌ(h)ä-bə-ˈn(y)er-ō\ *n* **:** a very hot chili pepper that is usually orange when mature
ha•be•as cor•pus \ˈhā-bē-əs-ˈkȯr-pəs\ *n* **:** a writ issued to bring a party before a court

hab•er•dash•er \ˈha-bər-ˌda-shər\ *n* : a dealer in men's clothing and accessories
hab•er•dash•ery \-ˌda-shə-rē\ *n, pl* **-er•ies** **1 :** goods sold by a haberdasher **2 :** a haberdasher's shop
ha•bil•i•ment \hə-ˈbi-lə-mənt\ *n* **1** *pl* **:** TRAPPINGS, EQUIPMENT **2 :** DRESS; *esp* **:** the dress characteristic of an occupation or occasion — usually used in plural
hab•it \ˈha-bət\ *n* **1 :** DRESS, GARB **2 :** BEARING, CONDUCT **3 :** PHYSIQUE **4 :** mental makeup **5** ♦ **:** a usual manner of behavior **:** CUSTOM **6 :** a behavior pattern acquired by frequent repetition **7 :** ADDICTION **8 :** mode of growth or occurrence ⟨trees with a spreading ~⟩
♦ custom, fashion, pattern, practice, trick, way, wont

hab•it•able \ˈha-bə-tə-bəl\ *adj* **:** capable of being lived in — **hab•it•abil•i•ty** \ˌha-bə-tə-ˈbi-lə-tē\ *n*
hab•i•tat \ˈha-bə-ˌtat\ *n* ♦ **:** the place or environment where a plant or animal naturally occurs
♦ home, niche, range, territory

hab•i•ta•tion \ˌha-bə-ˈtā-shən\ *n* **1 :** OCCUPANCY **2** ♦ **:** a dwelling place **:** RESIDENCE **3 :** SETTLEMENT
♦ abode, domicile, dwelling, home, house, lodging, quarters, residence

hab•it–form•ing \ˈha-bət-ˌfȯr-miŋ\ *adj* **:** causing addiction **:** ADDICTIVE
ha•bit•u•al \hə-ˈbi-chə-wəl\ *adj* **1** ♦ **:** having the nature of a habit **2** ♦ **:** doing, practicing, or acting by force of habit ⟨~ drunkards⟩ **3 :** inherent in an individual — **ha•bit•u•al•ly** *adv* — **ha•bit•u•al•ness** *n*
♦ [1] constant, frequent, periodic, regular, repeated, steady ♦ [2] chronic, confirmed, inveterate

ha•bit•u•ate \hə-ˈbi-chə-ˌwāt\ *vb* **-at•ed; -at•ing** **1 :** ACCUSTOM **2 :** to cause or undergo habituation
ha•bit•u•a•tion \hə-ˌbi-chə-ˈwā-shən\ *n* **1 :** the process of becoming or state of being accustomed to or dependent on something **2 :** psychological dependence on a drug after a period of use
ha•bi•tué *also* **ha•bi•tue** \hə-ˈbi-chə-ˌwā\ *n* **:** one who may be regularly found in or at (as a place of entertainment)
ha•ci•en•da \ˌhä-sē-ˌen-də\ *n* **1 :** a large estate in a Spanish-speaking country **2 :** the main building of a farm or ranch
¹hack \ˈhak\ *vb* **1 :** to cut or sever with repeated irregular blows **2 :** to cough in a short dry manner **3 :** to manage successfully; *also* **:** TOLERATE
²hack *n* **1 :** an implement for hacking **2 :** a short dry cough **3 :** a hacking blow **4** ♦ **:** a V-shaped indentation
♦ chip, indentation, nick, notch

³hack *n* **1 :** a horse hired or used for varied work **2 :** a horse worn out in service **3 :** a light easy often 3-gaited saddle horse **4 a :** HACKNEY **b :** an automobile that carries passengers for a fare usually determined by the distance traveled **:** TAXICAB **5 :** a person who works solely for mercenary reasons; *esp* **:** a writer working solely for commercial success — **hack** *adj*
⁴hack *vb* **:** to operate a taxicab
hack•er \ˈha-kər\ *n* **1 :** one that hacks; *also* **:** a person unskilled at something **2 :** an expert at using a computer **3 :** a person who illegally gains access to and sometimes tampers with information in a computer system
hack•ie \ˈha-kē\ *n* **:** a taxicab driver
hack•le \ˈha-kəl\ *n* **1 :** one of the long feathers on the neck or back of a bird **2** *pl* **:** hairs (as on a dog's neck) that can be erected **3** *pl* **:** TEMPER, DANDER
hack•man \ˈhak-mən\ *n* **:** HACKIE
¹hack•ney \ˈhak-nē\ *n, pl* **hackneys** **1 :** a horse for riding or driving **2 :** a carriage or automobile kept for hire
²hackney *vb* **:** to make trite
hack•neyed \ˈhak-nēd\ *adj* ♦ **:** lacking in freshness or originality
♦ banal, commonplace, musty, stale, stereotyped, threadbare, tired, trite

hack•saw \ˈhak-ˌsȯ\ *n* **:** a fine-tooth saw in a frame for cutting metal
hack•work \-ˌwərk\ *n* **:** work done on order usually according to a formula
had *past and past part of* HAVE
had•dock \ˈha-dək\ *n, pl* **haddock** *also* **haddocks :** an Atlantic food fish usually smaller than the related cod
Ha•des \ˈhā-(ˌ)dēz\ *n* **1 :** the abode of the dead in Greek mythology **2** *often not cap* **:** HELL

hae•ma•tite *chiefly Brit var of* HEMATITE
haf•ni•um \ˈhaf-nē-əm\ *n* **:** a gray metallic chemical element
haft \ˈhaft\ *n* **:** the handle of a weapon or tool
hag \ˈhag\ *n* **1** ♦ **:** an ugly or evil-looking old woman **2 :** a woman that is credited with usually malignant supernatural powers
♦ crone, witch

Hag *abbr* Haggai
Hag•gai \ˈha-gē-ˌī, ˈha-ˌgī\ *n* **:** a book of the canonical Jewish and Christian Scriptures
hag•gard \ˈha-gərd\ *adj* ♦ **:** having a worn or emaciated appearance — **hag•gard•ly** *adv* — **hag•gard•ness** *n*
♦ cadaverous, gaunt, skeletal, wasted

hag•gis \ˈha-gəs\ *n* **:** a traditionally Scottish dish made of the heart, liver, and lungs of a sheep or a calf minced with suet, onions, oatmeal, and seasonings
hag•gle \ˈha-gəl\ *vb* **hag•gled; hag•gling** ♦ **:** to argue in bargaining — **hag•gler** *n*
♦ bargain, chaffer, deal, dicker, negotiate, palter

Ha•gi•og•ra•pha \ˌha-gē-ˈä-grə-fə, ˌhā-jē-\ *n pl* **:** the third part of the Jewish Scriptures
ha•gio•graph•ic \ˌha-gē-ə-ˈgra-fik, ˌhā-, -jē-\ *adj* **:** of or relating to hagiography; *esp* **:** excessively flattering
ha•gi•og•ra•phy \ˌha-gē-ˈä-grə-fē, ˌhā-jē-\ *n* **1 :** biography of saints or venerated persons **2 :** idealizing or idolizing biography — **ha•gi•og•ra•pher** \-fər\ *n*
hai•ku \ˈhī-(ˌ)kü\ *n, pl* **haiku :** an unrhymed Japanese verse form of three lines containing usually 5, 7, and 5 syllables respectively; *also* **:** a poem in this form
¹hail \ˈhāl\ *n* **1 :** precipitation in the form of small lumps of ice **2** ♦ **:** something that gives the effect of falling hail
♦ rain, shower, storm ♦ barrage, bombardment, cannonade, fusillade, salvo, shower, storm, volley

²hail *vb* **1 :** to precipitate hail **2 :** to pour down and strike like hail
³hail *interj* — used to express acclamation
⁴hail *vb* **1 a :** SALUTE, GREET **b** ♦ **:** to greet with enthusiastic approval **:** ACCLAIM **2 :** SUMMON
♦ acclaim, applaud, cheer, crack up, laud, praise, salute, tout

⁵hail *n* **1 :** an expression of greeting, approval, or praise **2** ♦ **:** hearing distance
♦ earshot, hearing, sound ♦ hearing, sound

Hail Mary *n* **:** a salutation and prayer to the Virgin Mary
hail•stone \ˈhāl-ˌstōn\ *n* **:** a pellet of hail
hail•storm \-ˌstȯrm\ *n* **:** a storm accompanied by hail
hair \ˈhar\ *n* **1 a :** a threadlike outgrowth especially from the skin of a mammal **b** ♦ **:** a covering or growth of hairs of an animal or a body part **2** ♦ **:** a minute distance or amount — **haired** \ˈhard\ *adj* — **hair•less** *adj*
♦ [1b] coat, fleece, fur, pelage, pile, wool ♦ [2] ace, inch, step, stone's throw

hair•breadth \ˈhar-ˌbredth\ *or* **hairs•breadth** \ˈharz-\ *n* ♦ **:** a very small distance or margin
♦ *or* **hairsbreadth** ♦ ace, hair, inch, step, stone's throw

hair•brush \-ˌbrəsh\ *n* **:** a brush for the hair
hair•cloth \-ˌklȯth\ *n* **:** a stiff wiry fabric used especially for upholstery
hair•cut \-ˌkət\ *n* **:** the act, process, or style of cutting and shaping the hair
hair•do \-ˌdü\ *n, pl* **hairdos :** a way of wearing the hair
hair•dress•er \-ˌdre-sər\ *n* **:** one who dresses or cuts hair — **hair•dress•ing** *n*
hair•line \-ˌlīn\ *n* **1 :** a very thin line **2 :** the outline of the hair on the head
hair•piece \-ˌpēs\ *n* **1 :** supplementary hair (as a switch) used in some women's hairdos **2 :** TOUPEE
hair•pin \-ˌpin\ *n* **1 :** a U-shaped pin to hold the hair in place **2 :** a sharp U-shaped turn in a road — **hairpin** *adj*
hair–rais•ing \ˈhar-ˌrā-ziŋ\ *adj* ♦ **:** causing terror or astonishment
♦ fearful, fearsome, forbidding, formidable, frightful, scary, shocking, terrible, terrifying

hair•split•ter \-ˌspli-tər\ *n* **:** a person who makes excessively fine distinctions in reasoning — **hair•split•ting** \-ˌspli-tiŋ\ *n*
hair•split•ting *adj* **:** made or done with extreme care and accuracy

hair•spray \ˈher-ˌsprā\ *n* : a liquid sprayed onto the hair to hold it in place
hair•style \-ˌstī(-ə)l\ *n* : HAIRDO — **hair•styl•ing** *n*
hair•styl•ist \-ˌstī-list\ *n* : HAIRDRESSER
hair–trigger *adj* : immediately responsive to the slightest stimulus
hairy \ˈhar-ē\ *adj* **hair•i•er; -est** **1** ♦ : covered with or as if with hair **2** : tending to cause nervous tension ⟨a few ~ moments⟩ **3** ♦ : composed of or being like hair — **hair•i•ness** \-ē-nəs\ *n*

♦ [1] fleecy, furry, hirsute, rough, shaggy, unshorn, woolly ***Ant*** bald, hairless, shorn, smooth ♦ [3] furry, fuzzy, rough, shaggy, woolly

hairy woodpecker *n* : a common No. American woodpecker with a white back that is larger than the similarly marked downy woodpecker
Hai•tian \ˈhā-shən\ *n* : a native or inhabitant of Haiti — **Haitian** *adj*
hajj \ˈhaj\ *n* : a pilgrimage to Mecca prescribed as a religious duty for Muslims
hajji \ˈha-jē\ *n* : one who has made a pilgrimage to Mecca — often used as a title
hake \ˈhāk\ *n* : any of several marine food fishes related to the cod
hal•berd \ˈhal-bərd, ˈhȯl-\ *also* **hal•bert** \-bərt\ *n* : a weapon especially of the 15th and 16th centuries consisting of a battle-ax and pike on a long handle
hal•cy•on \ˈhal-sē-ən\ *adj* ♦ : marked by calm : PEACEFUL

♦ calm, hushed, peaceful, placid, quiet, serene, still, tranquil, untroubled

¹hale \ˈhāl\ *adj* ♦ : free from defect, disease, or infirmity

♦ able-bodied, chipper, fit, healthy, hearty, robust, sound, well, whole, wholesome

²hale *vb* **haled; hal•ing** **1** ♦ : to exert force upon so as to cause or tend to cause motion toward the force : HAUL, PULL **2** : to compel to go

♦ drag, draw, haul, lug, pull, tow, tug

¹half \ˈhaf, ˈhȧf\ *n, pl* **halves** \ˈhavz, ˈhȧvz\ **1** : either of two equal parts that compose something **2** ♦ : one of a pair

♦ companion, match, mate, twin

²half *adj* **1** : being one of two equal parts **2** : amounting to nearly half **3** : PARTIAL, INCOMPLETE
³half *adv* **1 a** : in an equal part or degree **b** : not completely **2** : by any means : AT ALL
half–and–half \ˌhaf-ᵊn-ˈhaf, ˌhȧf-ᵊn-ˈhȧf\ *n* : something that is half one thing and half another
half•back \ˈhaf-ˌbak, ˈhȧf-\ *n* **1** : a football back stationed on or near the flank **2** : a player stationed immediately behind the forward line
half–baked \-ˈbākt\ *adj* **1** : not thoroughly baked **2** ♦ : poorly planned; *also* : lacking common sense

♦ absurd, crazy, cuckoo, fatuous, foolish, mad, nonsensical, nutty, senseless, silly, stupid

half–breed \-ˌbrēd\ *n, often disparaging* : one of mixed racial descent — **half–breed** *adj, often disparaging*
half brother *n* : a brother related through one parent only
half–caste \ˈhaf-ˌkast, ˈhȧf-\ *n* : one of mixed racial descent : HALF-BREED — **half–caste** *adj*
half–dol•lar \-ˈdä-lər\ *n* **1** : a coin representing one half of a dollar **2** : the sum of fifty cents
half•heart•ed \-ˈhär-təd\ *adj* ♦ : lacking spirit or interest — **half•heart•ed•ly** *adv* — **half•heart•ed•ness** *n*

♦ tepid, uneager, unenthusiastic

half–life \-ˌlīft\ *n* : the time required for half of something (as atoms or a drug) to undergo a process
half–mast \-ˈmast\ *n* : a point about halfway down from the top of a mast or staff
half note *n* : a musical note equal in time to one half of a whole note
half•pen•ny \ˈhāp-nē\ *n, pl* **half•pence** \ˈhā-pəns\ *or* **halfpen•nies** : a formerly used British coin representing one half of a penny
half–pint \ˈhaf-ˌpīnt, ˈhȧf-\ *adj* : of less than average size — **half–pint** *n*
half sister *n* : a sister related through one parent only
half sole *n* : a shoe sole extending from the shank forward — **half–sole** *vb*
half–staff \ˈhaf-ˈstaf, ˈhȧf-\ *n* : HALF-MAST
half step *n* : a musical interval equivalent to one twelfth of an octave
half•time \ˈhaf-ˌtīm, ˈhȧf-\ *n* : an intermission between halves of a game
half–track \-ˌtrak\ *n* : a motor vehicle propelled by an endless chain-track drive system; *esp* : such a vehicle lightly armored for military use
half–truth \-ˌtrüth\ *n* : a statement that is only partially true; *esp* : one that deliberately mixes truth and falsehood
half•way \-ˈwā\ *adj* **1** ♦ : midway between two points **2** : of or relating to a part rather than the whole : not general or total : PARTIAL — **halfway** *adv*

♦ intermediary, intermediate, median, medium, middle, midmost

half–wit \-ˌwit\ *n* ♦ : a foolish or imbecilic person

♦ booby, fool, goose, jackass, lunatic, nitwit, nut, simpleton, turkey ♦ blockhead, dope, dummy, idiot, imbecile, jackass, moron, numskull

half–wit•ted \-ˈwi-təd\ *adj* **1** : exhibiting or indicative of a lack of common sense or sound judgment **2** : mentally deficient — **half–wit•ted•ness** *n*
hal•i•but \ˈha-lə-bət\ *n, pl* **halibut** *also* **halibuts** : any of several large edible marine flatfishes
ha•lite \ˈha-ˌlīt, ˈhā-\ *n* : ROCK SALT
hal•i•to•sis \ˌha-lə-ˈtō-səs\ *n* : the condition of having fetid breath
hall \ˈhȯl\ *n* **1** : the residence of a medieval king or noble; *also* : the house of a landed proprietor **2** : a large public building **3** : a college or university building; *also* : DORMITORY **4 a** ♦ : the entrance room of a building : LOBBY **b** ♦ : a corridor or passage in a building **5** : a large room for assembly : AUDITORIUM **6** ♦ : a place used for public entertainment

♦ [4a] entry, foyer, lobby, vestibule ♦ [4b] corridor, gallery, hallway, passage ♦ [6] arena, theater

hal•le•lu•jah \ˌha-lə-ˈlü-yə\ *interj* — used to express praise, joy, or thanks
hall•mark \ˈhȯl-ˌmärk\ *n* **1** ♦ : a mark put on an article to indicate origin, purity, or genuineness **2** : a distinguishing characteristic

♦ emblem, logo, symbol, trademark

hal•low \ˈha-lō\ *vb* **1** ♦ : to make holy or set apart for holy use **2** : REVERE

♦ bless, consecrate, sanctify

hal•lowed \ˈha-lōd, -lə-wəd\ *adj* **1** ♦ : made or declared sacred **2** ♦ : regarded as worthy of great honor

♦ [1] blessed, holy, sacred, sacrosanct, sanctified ♦ [2] reverend, venerable

Hal•low•een *also* **Hal•low•e'en** \ˌha-lə-ˈwēn, ˌhä-\ *n* : the evening of October 31 observed especially by children in merrymaking and masquerading
hal•lu•ci•nate \hə-ˈlüs-ᵊn-ˌāt\ *vb* **-nat•ed; -nat•ing** : to have hallucinations or experience as a hallucination
hal•lu•ci•na•tion \hə-ˌlüs-ᵊn-ˈā-shən\ *n* **1** : perception of objects with no reality due usually to use of drugs or to disorder of the nervous system **2** ♦ : something perceived by hallucination — **hal•lu•ci•na•to•ry** \-ᵊn-ə-ˌtōr-ē\ *adj*

♦ chimera, conceit, daydream, delusion, dream, fancy, fantasy, figment, illusion, phantasm, pipe dream, unreality, vision

hal•lu•ci•no•gen \hə-ˈlüs-ᵊn-ə-jən\ *n* : a substance that induces hallucinations — **hal•lu•ci•no•gen•ic** \-ˌlüs-ᵊn-ə-ˈje-nik\ *adj or n*
hall•way \ˈhȯl-ˌwā\ *n* **1** : an entrance hall **2** ♦ : a passageway into which compartments or rooms open : CORRIDOR

♦ corridor, gallery, hall, passage

ha•lo \ˈhā-lō\ *n, pl* **halos** *or* **haloes** **1** : a circle of light appearing to surround a shining body (as the sun) **2** : the aura of glory surrounding an idealized person or thing
¹hal•o•gen \ˈha-lə-jən\ *n* : any of the five elements fluorine, chlorine, bromine, iodine, and astatine
²hal•o•gen *adj* : containing, using, or being a halogen ⟨a ~ lamp⟩
¹halt \ˈhȯlt\ *adj* : LAME
²halt *n* ♦ : a stop in an action or process

♦ cessation, close, closure, conclusion, end, ending, expiration, finish, lapse, shutdown, stop, stoppage, termination

³halt *vb* **1** : to stop marching or traveling **2** ♦ : to come or bring to an end : DISCONTINUE

♦ break, break off, cease, cut, desist, discontinue, drop, end, knock off, lay off, leave off, quit, shut off, stop ♦ arrest, catch, check, draw up, fetch up, hold up, stall, stay, still, stop

[1]hal•ter \ˈhȯl-tər\ *n* **1 :** a rope or strap for leading or tying an animal; *also* **:** HEADSTALL **2 :** NOOSE **3 :** a brief blouse held in place by straps around the neck and across the back

[2]halter *vb* **hal•tered; hal•ter•ing 1 :** to catch with or as if with a halter; *also* **:** to put a halter on (as a horse) **2 :** HANG **3 :** IMPEDE, RESTRAIN

halt•ing \ˈhȯl-tiŋ\ *adj* **:** UNCERTAIN, FALTERING — **halt•ing•ly** *adv*

halve \ˈhav, ˈhȧv\ *vb* **halved; halv•ing 1 :** to divide into two equal parts **2 :** to reduce to one half

halv•ers \ˈha-vərz, ˈhȧ-\ *n pl* **:** half shares **:** HALVES

halves *pl of* HALF

hal•yard \ˈhal-yərd\ *n* **:** a rope or tackle for hoisting and lowering (as sails)

[1]ham \ˈham\ *n* **1 :** a buttock with its associated thigh — usually used in plural **2 :** a cut of meat and especially pork from the thigh **3 :** a showy performer **4 :** an operator of an amateur radio station — **ham** *adj*

[2]ham *vb* **hammed; ham•ming :** to overplay a part **:** OVERACT

ham•burg•er \ˈham-ˌbər-gər\ *or* **ham•burg** \-ˌbərg\ *n* **1 :** ground beef **2 :** a sandwich consisting of a ground-beef patty in a round roll

ham•let \ˈham-lət\ *n* **:** a small village

[1]ham•mer \ˈha-mər\ *n* **1 :** a hand tool used for pounding; *also* **:** something resembling a hammer in form or function **2 :** the part of a gun whose striking action causes explosion of the charge **3 :** a metal sphere hurled for distance in a track-and-field event (**hammer throw**) **4 :** ACCELERATOR 2

[2]hammer *vb* **1** ♦ **:** to beat, drive, or shape with or as if with repeated blows of a hammer **:** POUND **2 :** to produce or bring about as if by repeated blows — usually used with *out* **3 :** to criticize severely

♦ beat, forge, pound

ham•mer•head \ˈha-mər-ˌhed\ *n* **1 :** the striking part of a hammer **2 :** any of a family of medium-sized sharks with eyes at the ends of lateral extensions of the flattened head

ham•mer•lock \-ˌläk\ *n* **:** a wrestling hold in which an opponent's arm is held bent behind the back

hammer out *vb* ♦ **:** to produce or bring about as if by repeated blows

♦ build, carve, forge, grind, work out

ham•mer•toe \-ˌtō\ *n* **:** a toe deformed by having one or more joints permanently flexed

[1]ham•mock \ˈha-mək\ *n* **:** a swinging couch hung by cords at each end

[2]hammock *n* **:** a fertile elevated area of the southern U.S. and especially Florida with hardwood vegetation and soil rich in humus

[1]ham•per \ˈham-pər\ *vb* **1** ♦ **:** to restrict the movement or operation of **:** IMPEDE **2 :** RESTRAIN

♦ clog, cramp, delay, embarrass, encumber, fetter, handicap, hinder, hobble, hold back, hold up, impede, inhibit, interfere with, manacle, obstruct, shackle, tie up, trammel *Ant* aid, assist, facilitate, help

[2]hamper *n* **:** a large usually lidded basket

ham•ster \ˈham-stər\ *n* **:** any of a subfamily of small Old World rodents with large cheek pouches

[1]ham•string \ˈham-ˌstriŋ\ *n* **:** any of several muscles at the back of the thigh or tendons at the back of the knee

[2]hamstring *vb* **-strung** \-ˌstrəŋ\; **-string•ing 1 :** to cripple by cutting the leg tendons **2** ♦ **:** to make ineffective or powerless

♦ cripple, disable, immobilize, incapacitate, paralyze, prostrate

[1]hand \ˈhand\ *n* **1 :** the end of a front limb when modified (as in humans) for grasping **2** ♦ **:** an indicator or pointer on a dial **3** ♦ **:** personal possession — usually used in plural and in the phrase *in one's hands*; *also* **:** CONTROL **4** ♦ **:** a position regarded as opposite to another **:** SIDE — usually used in the phrase *on the other hand* **5 :** a pledge especially of betrothal **6 :** style of penmanship **:** HANDWRITING **7 :** SKILL, ABILITY; *also* **:** a significant part **8 :** ASSISTANCE; *also* **:** PARTICIPATION **9 :** an outburst of applause **10 :** a single round in a card game; *also* **:** the cards held by a player after a deal **11** ♦ **:** one employed by another usually for wages or salary and in a position below the executive level **:** WORKER, EMPLOYEE; *also* **:** a member of a ship's crew — **handless** *adj* — **at hand :** near in time or place — **on hand :** in present possession or readily available

♦ [2] index, indicator, needle, pointer ♦ *usu* **hands** [3] control, keeping, possession ♦ [4] angle, aspect, facet, phase, side ♦ [11] employee, hireling, jobholder, worker

[2]hand *vb* **1 :** to lead, guide, or assist with the hand **2** ♦ **:** to give, pass, or transmit with the hand

♦ deliver, feed, furnish, give, hand over, provide, supply ♦ hand over, pass, reach, transfer

hand•bag \ˈhand-ˌbag\ *n* ♦ **:** a bag for carrying small personal articles and money

♦ bag, pocketbook, purse

hand•ball \-ˌbȯl\ *n* **:** a game played by striking a small rubber ball against a wall with the hand

hand•bill \-ˌbil\ *n* **:** a small printed sheet for distribution by hand

hand•book \-ˌbu̇k\ *n* ♦ **:** a concise reference book **:** MANUAL

♦ manual, primer, textbook

hand•car \-ˌkär\ *n* **:** a small 4-wheeled railroad car propelled by hand or by a small motor

hand•clasp \-ˌklasp\ *n* **:** HANDSHAKE

hand•craft \-ˌkraft\ *vb* **:** to fashion by manual skill

[1]hand•cuff \-ˌkəf\ *n* **:** a metal fastening that can be locked around a wrist and is usually connected with another such fastening — usually used in plural

[2]handcuff *vb* **1** ♦ **:** to apply handcuffs to **:** MANACLE **2** ♦ **:** to hold in check **:** make ineffective or powerless

♦ [1, 2] bind, chain, enchain, fetter, manacle, shackle, trammel

hand•ed \ˈhan-dəd\ *adj* **:** having or using such or so many hands ⟨a left-*handed* person⟩ — **hand•ed•ness** *n*

hand•ful \ˌhand-ˌfu̇l\ *n, pl* **hand•fuls** \-ˌfu̇lz\ *also* **hands•ful** \ˈhandz-ˌfu̇l\ **1 :** as much or as many as the hand will grasp **2** ♦ **:** a small number **3 :** as much as one can manage

♦ few, smattering, sprinkle, sprinkling

hand•gun \-ˌgən\ *n* **:** a firearm held and fired with one hand

[1]hand•i•cap \ˈhan-di-ˌkap\ *n* **1 :** a contest in which an artificial advantage is given or disadvantage imposed on a contestant to equalize chances of winning; *also* **:** the advantage given or disadvantage imposed **2** ♦ **:** a disadvantage that makes achievement difficult

♦ disadvantage, drawback, liability, minus, penalty, strike

[2]handicap *vb* **-capped; -cap•ping 1 :** to give a handicap to **2** ♦ **:** to put at a disadvantage

♦ encumber, hamper, hinder, hold up, impede, inhibit, interfere with, obstruct, tie up

hand•i•capped *adj, sometimes offensive* ♦ **:** having a physical or mental disability

♦ challenged, disabled

hand•i•cap•per \-ˌka-pər\ *n* **:** a person who predicts the winners in a horse race usually for a publication

hand•i•craft \ˈhan-di-ˌkraft\ *n* **1 :** manual skill **2** ♦ **:** an occupation requiring manual skill **3 :** the articles fashioned by those engaged in handicraft — **hand•i•crafts•man** \-ˌkrafts-mən\ *n*

♦ craft, trade

hand•i•craft•er \ˈhan-di-ˌkraf-tər\ *n* ♦ **:** one that engages in a handicraft usually as a hobby or avocation

♦ artificer, artisan, craftsman

hand•i•ly \ˈhan-də-lē\ *adv* ♦ **:** in an easy manner **:** without difficulty

♦ easily, effortlessly, fluently, freely, lightly, painlessly, readily, smoothly

hand in glove *or* **hand and glove** *adv* **:** in an extremely close relationship

hand•i•work \ˈhan-di-ˌwərk\ *n* **1 :** work done personally or by the hands **2** ♦ **:** the product of handiwork

♦ affair, fruit, output, produce, product, thing, work, yield

hand•ker•chief \ˈhaŋ-kər-chəf, -ˌchēft\ *n, pl* **-chiefs** \-chəfs, -ˌchēfs\ *also* **-chieves** \-ˌchēvz\ **:** a small piece of cloth used for various personal purposes (as the wiping of the face)

[1]han•dle \ˈhand-ᵊl\ *n* **1 :** a part (as of a tool) designed to be grasped by the hand **2 :** a word or phrase that constitutes the distinctive designation of a person or thing **:** NAME — **han•dled** \-ᵊld\ *adj* — **off the handle :** into a state of sudden and violent anger — usually used with *fly*

[2]handle *vb* **han•dled; han•dling 1 :** to touch, hold, or manage with the hands **2** ♦ **:** to have responsibility for **3 :** to deal or trade in **4 :** to behave in a certain way when managed or directed ⟨a car that ∼*s* well⟩ **5** ♦ **:** to act on or perform a required function with regard to — **han•dler** *n*

♦ [2] contend with, cope with, grapple with, manage, maneuver (*or* manoeuvre), negotiate, swing, treat *Ant* fumble, muddle (through) ♦ [2] administer, carry on, conduct, control, direct, govern, guide, manage, operate, oversee, regulate, run, superintend, supervise ♦ [5] act, be, deal, serve, treat, use

han•dle•bar \ˈhand-ᵊl-bär\ *n* : a usually bent bar with a grip at each end (as for steering a bicycle) — usually used in plural
hand•made \ˈhand-ˈmād\ *adj* : made by hand or by a hand process
hand•maid•en \-ˌmād-ᵊn\ *also* **hand•maid** \-ˌmād\ *n* : a female attendant
hand–me–down \-me-ˌdau̇n\ *adj* : used by one person after having been used by another — **hand–me–down** *n*
hand•out \ˈhan-ˌdau̇t\ *n* **1 :** a portion (as of food) given to a beggar **2 :** a piece of printed information for free distribution; *also* : a prepared statement released to the press
hand over *vb* ♦ **:** to yield control of

♦ cede, deliver, give up, leave, relinquish, render, surrender, turn over, yield ♦ hand, pass, reach, transfer

hand•pick \ˈhand-ˈpik\ *vb* ♦ **:** to select personally ⟨a ~*ed* candidate⟩

♦ choose, cull, elect, name, opt, pick, prefer, select, single, take

hand•rail \-ˌrāl\ *n* : a narrow rail for grasping as a support
hand•saw \-ˌsȯ\ *n* : a saw designed to be used with one hand
hands down *adv* **1 :** with little effort **2 :** without question
hand•sel \ˈhan-səl\ *n* **1 :** a gift made as a token of good luck **2 :** a first installment : earnest money
hand•set \ˈhand-ˌset\ *n* : a combined telephone transmitter and receiver mounted on a handle
hand•shake \-ˌshāk\ *n* : a clasping usually of right hands by two people
hands–off \ˈhandz-ˈȯf\ *adj* : characterized by noninterference
hand•some \ˈhan-səm\ *adj* **hand•som•er; -est** **1 :** moderately large : SIZABLE **2 :** GENEROUS, LIBERAL **3** ♦ **:** pleasing and usually impressive in appearance

♦ attractive, beautiful, fair, gorgeous, knockout, lovely, pretty, ravishing, stunning

hand•some•ly \-lē\ *adv* ♦ **:** in a handsome manner

♦ bountifully, generously, liberally, well

hand•some•ness \-nəs\ *n* ♦ **:** the quality or state of being handsome

♦ class, elegance, grace, majesty, refinement, stateliness ♦ attractiveness, beauty, comeliness, looks, loveliness, prettiness

hands–on \ˈhandz-ˈȯn, -ˈän\ *adj* **1 :** being or providing direct practical experience in the operation of something **2 :** characterized by active personal involvement ⟨~ management⟩
hand•spring \ˈhand-ˌspriŋ\ *n* : an acrobatic feat in which the body turns in a full circle from a standing position and lands first on the hands and then on the feet
hand•stand \-ˌstand\ *n* : an act of supporting the body on the hands with the trunk and legs balanced in the air
hand–to–hand *adj* : involving physical contact or very close range ⟨~ fighting⟩ — **hand to hand** *adv*
hand–to–mouth *adj* : having or providing nothing to spare
hand•wo•ven \ˈhand-ˌwō-vən\ *adj* : produced on a hand-operated loom
hand•writ•ing \-ˌrī-tiŋ\ *n* **1** ♦ **:** writing done by hand **2** ♦ **:** the form of writing peculiar to a person — **hand•writ•ten** \-ˌrit-ᵊn\ *adj*

♦ [1] manuscript, penmanship, script *Ant* print, type ♦ [2] hand, penmanship, script

handy \ˈhan-dē\ *adj* **hand•i•er; -est** **1** ♦ **:** conveniently near **2 :** easily used **3** ♦ **:** clever in using the hands : DEXTEROUS — **hand•i•ness** \-dē-nəs\ *n*

♦ [1] accessible, convenient, reachable ♦ [3] clever, cunning, deft, dexterous

handy•man \-ˌman\ *n* **1 :** one who does odd jobs **2 :** one competent in a variety of small skills or repair work
¹hang \ˈhaŋ\ *vb* **hung** \ˈhəŋ\ *also* **hanged; hang•ing** **1** ♦ **:** to fasten or remain fastened to an elevated point without support from below; *also* : to fasten or be fastened so as to allow free motion on the point of suspension ⟨~ a door⟩ **2 :** to suspend by the neck until dead; *also* : to die by hanging **3 :** to hold or bear in a suspended or inclined manner : DROOP ⟨*hung* his head in shame⟩ **4 :** to fasten to a wall ⟨~ wallpaper⟩ **5 :** to prevent (a jury) from coming to a decision **6 :** to display (pictures) in a gallery **7** ♦ **:** to remain stationary in the air **8** ♦ **:** to be imminent : IMPEND ⟨doom *hung* over the nation⟩ **9 :** DEPEND **10 :** to take hold for support **11 :** to be burdensome **12 :** to undergo delay **13 :** to incline downward; *also* : to fit or fall from the figure in easy lines **14 :** to be raptly attentive **15 :** LINGER, LOITER — **hang•er** *n*

♦ [1] dangle, sling, suspend, swing ♦ [7] drift, float, glide, hover, poise, ride, sail, waft ♦ *usu* **hang over** [8] hover, menace, overhang, threaten

²hang *n* **1 :** the manner in which a thing hangs **2 :** an understanding of something
han•gar \ˈhaŋ-ər\ *n* : a covered and usually enclosed area for housing and repairing aircraft
hang around *vb* **1** ♦ **:** to pass time or stay aimlessly in or at **2** ♦ **:** to spend one's time in company especially idly

♦ *usu* **hang around in** [1] frequent, hang out, haunt, resort, visit ♦ [1] abide, dwell, remain, stay, stick around, tarry ♦ [2] associate, chum, consort, fraternize, hobnob, pal

hang back *vb* ♦ **:** to be reluctant

♦ falter, hesitate, shilly-shally, stagger, teeter, vacillate, waver, wobble

hang•dog \ˈhaŋ-ˌdȯg\ *adj* **1** ♦ **:** affected by or showing embarrassment caused by consciousness of a fault : ASHAMED, GUILTY **2 :** ABJECT, COWED

♦ ashamed, contrite, guilty, penitent, remorseful, repentant, shamefaced

hang•er \ˈhaŋ-ər\ *n* **1 :** one that hangs **2 :** a device that fits inside or around a garment for hanging from a hook or rod
hang•er–on \ˈhaŋ-ər-ˈȯn, -ˈän\ *n, pl* **hangers–on** ♦ **:** one who hangs around a person or place especially for personal gain

♦ leech, parasite, sponge

hang in *vb* : to persist tenaciously
hang•ing *n* **1 :** an execution by strangling or snapping the neck by a suspended noose **2 :** something hung
hang•man \ˈhaŋ-mən\ *n* : a public executioner **2 :** a game in which players must identify an unknown word by guessing the letters that comprise it within a designated number of chances
hang•nail \-ˌnāl\ *n* : a bit of skin hanging loose at the edge of a fingernail
hang on *vb* **1 :** HANG IN **2 :** to keep a telephone connection open **3** ♦ **:** to keep hold onto something

♦ *usu* **hang on to** hold, keep, reserve, retain, withhold ♦ *usu* **hang on to** clench, cling, clutch, grip, hold, hold on

hang•out \ˈhaŋ-ˌau̇t\ *n* ♦ **:** a favorite place for spending time

♦ haunt, rendezvous, resort

hang out *vb* ♦ **:** to spend time idly or in loitering around or in a particular place

♦ *usu* **hang out at** frequent, hang around, haunt, resort, visit ♦ dally, dawdle, dillydally, hang around, idle, loaf, loll, lounge

hang•over \-ˌō-vər\ *n* **1 :** something that remains from what is past **2 :** disagreeable physical effects following heavy drinking or the use of drugs
hang–up \ˈhaŋ-ˌəp\ *n* : a source of mental or emotional difficulty
hang up *vb* **1 :** to place on a hook or hanger **2 :** to end a telephone conversation by breaking the connection **3 :** to keep delayed or suspended
hank \ˈhaŋk\ *n* : COIL, LOOP
han•ker \ˈhaŋ-kər\ *vb* ♦ **:** to desire strongly or persistently — often used with *for* or *after*

♦ *usu* **hanker for** *or* **hanker after** ache for, covet, crave, desire, die for, hunger for, long for, lust (for *or* after), pine for, repine for, thirst for, want, wish for, yearn for

han•ker•ing *n* ♦ **:** the experience of one that hankers : strong desire

♦ appetite, craving, desire, drive, hunger, itch, longing, lust, passion, thirst, urge, yearning, yen

han•kie *or* **han•ky** \ˈhaŋ-kē\ *n, pl* **hankies** **:** HANDKERCHIEF
han•ky–pan•ky \ˌhaŋ-kē-ˈpaŋ-kē\ *n* **1** ♦ **:** questionable or underhanded activity **2 :** sexual dalliance

♦ artifice, chicanery, subterfuge, trickery, wile

hansel *var of* HANDSEL
han•som \ˈhan-səm\ *n* : a 2-wheeled covered carriage with the driver's seat elevated at the rear
han•ta•virus \ˈhän-tə-ˌvī-rəs, ˈhən-, ˈhan-\ *n* : any of a genus of

viruses including some transmitted by rodents that cause pneumonia or hemorrhagic fevers

Ha•nuk•kah \ˈkä-nə-kə, ˈhä-\ *n* : an 8-day Jewish holiday commemorating the rededication of the Temple of Jerusalem after its defilement by Antiochus of Syria

hap \ˈhap\ *n* **1** : something that happens : HAPPENING **2** : a force which shapes events unpredictably : CHANCE

¹hap•haz•ard \hap-ˈha-zərd\ *n* : CHANCE

²haphazard *adj* ♦ : marked by lack of plan or order — **hap•haz•ard•ly** *adv* — **hap•haz•ard•ness** *n*

♦ aimless, arbitrary, desultory, erratic, random, scattered, stray

hap•less \ˈhap-ləs\ *adj* ♦ : having no luck : UNFORTUNATE — **hap•less•ly** *adv* — **hap•less•ness** *n*

♦ ill-fated, ill-starred, luckless, unfortunate, unhappy, unlucky

hap•loid \ˈhap-ˌlȯid\ *adj* : having the number of chromosomes characteristic of gametic cells — **haploid** *n*

hap•ly \ˈhap-lē\ *adv* : by chance

hap•pen \ˈha-pən\ *vb* **1** : to occur by chance **2** ♦ : to come into being or occur as an event, process, or result **3** ♦ : to come casually or unexpectedly : CHANCE 2 — used with *on* or *upon*

♦ [2] be, befall, betide, chance, come, go, occur, pass, transpire ♦ *usu* **happen on** *or* **happen upon** [3] chance, encounter, find, hit, meet, stumble

¹hap•pen•ing *n* **1** ♦ : something that happens : OCCURRENCE **2** ♦ : an event that is especially interesting, entertaining, or important

♦ [1] affair, circumstance, episode, event, incident, occasion, occurrence, thing ♦ [2] adventure, experience, time

²happening *adj* **1** : very fashionable **2** : offering much stimulating activity ⟨a ∼ nightclub⟩

hap•pi•ly \ˈha-pə-lē\ *adv* **1** : LUCKILY **2** ♦ : in a happy manner or state ⟨lived ∼ ever after⟩ **3** ♦ : in an adequate or fitting manner

♦ [2] cheerfully, gaily, heartily, jovially, merrily, mirthfully ♦ [3] appropriately, correctly, fittingly, properly, rightly, suitably

hap•pi•ness \ˈha-pē-nəs\ *n* **1 a** ♦ : a state of well-being and contentment **b** ♦ : a pleasurable satisfaction **2** : APTNESS

♦ [1a] blessedness, bliss, felicity, gladness, joy ***Ant*** misery, sadness, unhappiness, wretchedness ♦ [1b] content, contentedness, contentment, gratification, pleasure, satisfaction

hap•py \ˈha-pē\ *adj* **hap•pi•er; -est** **1** ♦ : favored by luck or fortune : FORTUNATE **2** ♦ : notably fitting, effective, or well adapted : APT, FELICITOUS **3** : enjoying well-being and contentment **4 a** : PLEASANT **b** ♦ : made pleased, satisfied, or grateful

♦ [1] fluky, fortuitous, fortunate, lucky, providential ♦ [2] applicable, appropriate, apt, felicitous, fit, fitting, good, meet, proper, right, suitable ♦ [4b] blissful, content, delighted, glad, joyful, pleased

hap•py–go–lucky \ˌha-pē-gō-ˈlə-kē\ *adj* ♦ : blithely unconcerned

♦ carefree, careless, cavalier, easygoing, gay, insouciant, lighthearted, unconcerned

happy hour *n* : a period of time when the price of drinks at a bar is reduced

hara–kiri \ˌhar-i-ˈkir-ē, -ˈkar-ē\ *n* : ritual suicide by disembowelment

¹ha•rangue \hə-ˈraŋ\ *n* **1** ♦ : a ranting speech or writing **2** ♦ : a speech addressed to a public assembly

♦ [1] diatribe, rant, tirade ♦ [2] address, declamation, oration, speech, talk

²harangue *vb* ♦ : to make a harangue — **ha•rangu•er** *n*

♦ declaim, descant, discourse, lecture, orate, speak, talk

ha•rass \hə-ˈras, ˈhar-əs\ *vb* **1** : EXHAUST, FATIGUE **2** : to worry and impede by repeated raids **3** : to annoy continually

ha•rass•ment \-mənt\ *n* **1** ♦ : the act or an instance of harassing **2** : the condition of being harassed

♦ aggravation, annoyance, disturbance, vexation

¹har•bin•ger \ˈhär-bən-jər\ *n* **1** ♦ : one that announces or foreshadows what is coming : PRECURSOR **2** : PORTENT

♦ angel, forerunner, herald, precursor

²harbinger *vb* ♦ : to be a harbinger of

♦ foreshadow, prefigure

¹har•bor *or Can and Brit* **har•bour** \ˈhär-bər\ *n* **1** ♦ : a place of security and comfort **2** ♦ : a part of a body of water protected and deep enough to furnish anchorage : PORT

♦ [1] asylum, haven, refuge, retreat, sanctuary, shelter ♦ [2] anchorage, haven, port

²harbor *or Can and Brit* **harbour** *vb* **1** : to give or take refuge : SHELTER **2 a** ♦ : to be the home or habitat of **b** : LIVE **3** ♦ : to hold a thought or feeling ⟨∼ a grudge⟩

♦ [2a] accommodate, billet, chamber, domicile, house, lodge, put up, quarter, roof, shelter, take in ♦ [3] bear, cherish, entertain, have, hold, nurse

har•bor•age *or Can and Brit* **har•bour•age** \ˈhär-bə-rij\ *n* **1** : a place of security and comfort **2** : a part of a body of water protected and deep enough to furnish anchorage : HARBOR

¹hard \ˈhärd\ *adj* **1** ♦ : not easily penetrated : not easily yielding to pressure **2** : high in alcoholic content **3** : containing salts that prevent lathering with soap ⟨∼ water⟩ **4** : stable in value ⟨∼ currency⟩ **5 a** : physically fit **b** ♦ : resistant to stress or disease **6 a** ♦ : not subject to change or revision : FIRM ⟨∼ agreement⟩ **b** ♦ : based on clear fact ⟨∼ evidence⟩ **7** : CLOSE, SEARCHING ⟨∼ look⟩ **8** : free from sentimentality or illusion : REALISTIC ⟨good ∼ sense⟩ **9** ♦ : lacking in responsiveness : OBDURATE, UNFEELING ⟨∼ heart⟩ **10** : difficult to bear ⟨∼ times⟩; *also* : HARSH, SEVERE **11** ♦ : caused or marked by resentment : RESENTFUL ⟨∼ feelings⟩ **12 a** ♦ : making no concession : STRICT **b** : rigidly firm in will or purpose : UNRELENTING **13** : INCLEMENT ⟨∼ winter⟩ **14** : intense in force, manner, or degree ⟨∼ blow⟩ **15** ♦ : demanding the exertion of considerable effort : ARDUOUS, STRENUOUS ⟨∼ work⟩ **16** : sounding as in *arcing* and *geese* respectively — used of *c* and *g* **17** : TROUBLESOME ⟨∼ problem⟩ **18** : having difficulty in doing something ⟨∼ of hearing⟩ **19** : addictive and gravely detrimental to health ⟨∼ drugs⟩ **20** : of or relating to the natural sciences and especially the physical sciences

♦ [1] compact, firm, rigid, solid, stiff, unyielding ♦ [5b] hard-bitten, hardy, rugged, stout, strong, sturdy, tough, vigorous ♦ [6a] certain, determinate, final, firm, fixed, flat, frozen, hard-and-fast, set, settled, stable ♦ [6b] documentary, factual, historical, literal, matter-of-fact, nonfictional, objective, true ♦ [9] callous, cold-blooded, heartless, inhuman, inhumane, merciless, obdurate, pitiless, ruthless, soulless, stony, uncharitable, unfeeling, unsparing, unsympathetic ***Ant*** charitable, compassionate, humane, merciful, sensitive, sympathetic, tender, tenderhearted, warm, warmhearted ♦ [11] acrid, acrimonious, bitter, rancorous, resentful, sore ♦ [12a] austere, authoritarian, flinty, harsh, heavy-handed, ramrod, rigid, rigorous, severe, stern, strict ♦ [15] arduous, demanding, difficult, exacting, formidable, grueling, herculean, laborious, murderous, rough, stiff, strenuous, tall, toilsome, tough ***Ant*** easy, effortless, facile, simple, soft, undemanding

²hard *adv* **1 a** ♦ : with great or utmost effort or energy **b** ♦ : in a fierce or violent manner **2 a** ♦ : in such a manner as to cause hardship, difficulty, or pain **b** ♦ : with rancor, bitterness, or grief **3** ♦ : close in time or space

♦ [1a] determinedly, diligently, hardly, laboriously, mightily, slavishly, strenuously, tirelessly ♦ [1b] energetically, firmly, forcefully, forcibly, mightily, powerfully, stiffly, stoutly, strenuously, strongly, sturdily, vigorously ***Ant*** feebly, gently, softly, weakly ♦ [2a] hardly, harshly, ill, oppressively, roughly, severely, sternly, stiffly ♦ [2b] agonizingly, bitterly, grievously, hardly, sadly, sorrowfully, unhappily, woefully, wretchedly ***Ant*** gladly, happily, joyfully, joyously ♦ [3] around, by, close, in, near, nearby, nigh

hard–and–fast *adj* ♦ : rigidly binding ⟨a ∼ rule⟩

♦ certain, determinate, final, firm, fixed, flat, frozen, hard, set, settled, stable ♦ fast, fixed, immutable, inflexible, unalterable, unchangeable

hard•back \ˈhärd-ˌbak\ *n* : a hardcover book

hard•ball \-ˌbȯl\ *n* **1** : BASEBALL **2** : forceful uncompromising methods

hard–bit•ten \-ˈbit-ᵊn\ *adj* ♦ : seasoned or steeled by difficult experience : TOUGH ⟨∼ campaigners⟩

♦ hard, hardy, rugged, stout, strong, sturdy, tough, vigorous

hard•board \-ˌbōrd\ *n* : a very dense fiberboard

hard–boiled \-ˈbȯi(-ə)ld\ *adj* **1** *of an egg* : boiled until both white and yolk have solidified **2 a** : lacking sentiment **b** : HARDHEADED 2

hard•bound \-ˌbau̇nd\ *adj* : HARDCOVER

hard copy *n* **:** copy of textual or graphic information (as from computer storage) produced on paper
hard–core \ˈhärd-ˈkōr\ *adj* **1 :** extremely resistant to solution or improvement **2 :** being the most determined or dedicated members of a specified group **3 :** containing explicit depictions of sex acts — **hard core** *n*
hard•cov•er \-ˈkə-vər\ *adj* **:** having rigid boards on the sides covered in cloth or paper ⟨∼ books⟩
hard disk *n* **:** a sealed rigid metal disk used as a computer storage device
hard–drive *n* **:** a data-storage device consisting of a drive and one or more hard disks
hard–driv•ing \ˈhär(d)-ˈdrī-viŋ\ *adj* ♦ **:** intensely ambitious, energetic, or hardworking

♦ ambitious, go-getting, self-seeking

hard•en \ˈhärd-ᵊn\ *vb* **1** ♦ **:** to make or become hard or harder **2 :** to confirm or become confirmed in disposition or action **3** ♦ **:** to make hardy or robust — **hard•en•er** *n*

♦ [1] concrete, congeal, firm, freeze, set, solidify ***Ant*** soften ♦ [3] fortify, season, steel, strengthen, toughen ***Ant*** soften

hard•hack \ˈhärd-ˌhak\ *n* **:** an American spirea with dense clusters of pink or white flowers and leaves having a hairy rusty yellow underside
hard hat *n* **1 :** a protective hat worn especially by construction workers **2 :** a construction worker
hard•head•ed \ˈhärd-ˈhe-dəd\ *adj* **1** ♦ **:** unreasonably or perversely unyielding **:** STUBBORN, WILLFUL **2** ♦ **:** concerned with or involving practical considerations — **hard•head•ed•ly** *adv*

♦ [1] dogged, headstrong, mulish, obdurate, obstinate, opinionated, peevish, pertinacious, perverse, pigheaded, stubborn, unyielding, willful ♦ [2] astute, canny, knowing, sharp, shrewd, smart ♦ [2] down-to-earth, earthy, matter-of-fact, practical, pragmatic, realistic

hard•head•ed•ness \-nəs\ *n* ♦ **:** the quality or state of being hardheaded

♦ mulishness, obduracy, obstinacy, peevishness, pertinacity, self-will, stubbornness, tenacity

hard–heart•ed \-ˈhär-təd\ *adj* **:** PITILESS, CRUEL — **hard–heart•ed•ly** *adv* — **hard–heart•ed•ness** *n*
har•di•hood \ˈhär-de-ˌhu̇d\ *n* **1 :** resolute courage and fortitude **2 :** active bodily or mental strength or force **:** VIGOR

♦ bravery, courage, daring, fearlessness, gallantry, guts, heart, heroism, nerve, stoutness, valor

hard–line \ˈhärd-ˈlīn\ *adj* **:** advocating or involving a rigidly uncompromising course of action — **hard–lin•er** \-ˈlī-nər\ *n*
hard–luck \-ˌlək\ *adj* ♦ **:** marked by or relating to bad luck ⟨∼ losing teams⟩

♦ hapless, ill-fated, ill-starred, luckless, unfortunate, unhappy, unlucky

hard•ly \ˈhärd-lē\ *adv* **1 :** with force **2 a** ♦ **:** in a severe manner **:** HARSHLY **b :** with great or excessive grief or resentment **3** ♦ **:** with difficulty **:** by hard work or struggle **4** ♦ **:** only just **:** BARELY **5** ♦ **:** certainly not

♦ [2a] hard, harshly, ill, oppressively, roughly, severely, sternly, stiffly ***Ant*** gently, leniently, lightly, mildly, softly ♦ [3] determinedly, diligently, hard, laboriously, mightily, slavishly, strenuously, tirelessly ♦ [4] barely, just, marginally, scarcely, slightly ♦ [5] no, none, scarcely ***Ant*** absolutely, certainly, completely, definitely, positively, surely

hard•ness \-nəs\ *n* **1** ♦ **:** the quality or state of being hard **2** ♦ **:** a condition that makes life difficult, challenging, or uncomfortable

♦ [1] harshness, inflexibility, rigidity, severity, sternness, strictness ♦ [2] adversity, asperity, difficulty, hardship, rigor

hard–nosed \ˈhärd-ˈnōzd\ *adj* **:** TOUGH, UNCOMPROMISING; *also* **:** HARDHEADED 2
hard palate *n* **:** the bony anterior part of the palate forming the roof of the mouth
hard•pan \ˈhärd-ˌpan\ *n* **:** a compact layer in soil that is impenetrable by roots
hard–pressed \-ˈprest\ *adj* **:** HARD PUT; *esp* **:** being under financial strain
hard put *adj* **1 :** barely able **2 :** faced with difficulty or perplexity
hard rock *n* **:** rock music marked by a heavy beat, high amplification, and usually frenzied performances
hard–shell \ˈhärd-ˌshel\ *adj* **:** HIDEBOUND, UNCOMPROMISING ⟨a ∼ conservative⟩
hard•ship \-ˌship\ *n* **1 :** SUFFERING, PRIVATION **2** ♦ **:** something that causes suffering or privation

♦ adversity, asperity, difficulty, hardness, rigor

hard•tack \-ˌtak\ *n* **:** a saltless hard biscuit, bread, or cracker
hard•top \-ˌtäp\ *n* **:** an automobile having a permanent rigid top
hard up *adj* ♦ **:** short of money

♦ broke, destitute, impecunious, impoverished, indigent, needy, penniless, penurious, poor, poverty-stricken

hard•ware \-ˌwar\ *n* **1 :** ware (as cutlery or tools) made of metal **2** ♦ **:** major items of equipment or their components used for a particular purpose **3 :** the physical components (as electronic devices) of a vehicle (as a spacecraft) or an apparatus (as a computer)

♦ accoutrements (*or* accouterments), apparatus, equipment, gear, matériel, outfit, paraphernalia, stuff, tackle

hard•wired \-ˌwī(-ə)rd\ *adj* **1 :** connected or incorporated by or as if by permanent electrical connections **2 :** genetically or innately determined or predisposed ⟨∼ reactions⟩ ⟨is ∼ to avoid change⟩
hard•wood \-ˌwu̇d\ *n* **:** the wood of a broad-leaved usually deciduous tree as distinguished from that of a conifer; *also* **:** such a tree — **hardwood** *adj*
hard•work•ing \-ˈwər-kiŋ\ *adj* **:** INDUSTRIOUS
har•dy \ˈhär-dē\ *adj* **har•di•er; -est 1 :** BOLD, BRAVE **2** ♦ **:** intrepidly daring **:** AUDACIOUS **3 a :** ROBUST **b** ♦ **:** able to withstand adverse conditions ⟨∼ shrubs⟩ — **har•di•ly** \-də-lē\ *adv* — **har•di•ness** \-dē-nəs\ *n*

♦ [2] adventurous, audacious, bold, daring, enterprising, gutsy, nervy, venturesome ♦ [3b] hard, hard-bitten, rugged, stout, strong, sturdy, tough, vigorous ***Ant*** delicate, soft, tender, weak

hare \ˈhar\ *n, pl* **hare** *or* **hares :** any of various swift timid long-eared mammals like the related rabbits but born with open eyes and fur
hare•bell \ˈhar-ˌbel\ *n* **:** a slender herb with bright blue bell-shaped flowers
hare•brained \-ˈbrānd\ *adj* ♦ **:** lacking in sense, judgment, or discretion

♦ absurd, crazy, cuckoo, fatuous, foolish, mad, nonsensical, nutty, senseless, silly, stupid

hare•lip \-ˈlip\ *n, sometimes offensive* **:** a birth defect characterized by one or more clefts in the upper lip — **hare•lipped** \-ˈlipt\ *adj*
ha•rem \ˈhar-əm\ *n* **1 :** a house or part of a house allotted to women in a Muslim household **2 :** the women and servants occupying a harem **3 :** a group of females associated with one male
hark \ˈhärk\ *vb* ♦ **:** to pay close attention **:** LISTEN

♦ attend, hear, heed, listen, mind

harken *var of* HEARKEN
har•le•quin \ˈhär-li-kən, -kwən\ *n* **1** *cap* **:** a character (as in comedy) with a shaved head, masked face, variegated tights, and wooden sword **2** ♦ **:** a fool or comedian in an entertainment (as a circus) **:** CLOWN

♦ buffoon, clown, zany

har•lot \ˈhär-lət\ *n* **:** a woman who engages in sexual activities especially for money **:** PROSTITUTE
[1]**harm** \ˈhärm\ *n* **1** ♦ **:** physical or mental damage **:** INJURY **2 :** MISCHIEF, HURT

♦ damage, detriment, hurt, injury

[2]**harm** *vb* ♦ **:** to cause harm to **:** INJURE

♦ damage, hurt, injure, wound

harm•ful \-fəl\ *adj* ♦ **:** of a kind likely to be damaging — **harm•ful•ly** *adv* — **harm•ful•ness** *n*

♦ adverse, bad, baleful, baneful, damaging, deleterious, detrimental, evil, hurtful, ill, injurious, mischievous, noxious, pernicious, prejudicial ***Ant*** harmless, innocent, innocuous, inoffensive, safe

harm•less \-ləs\ *adj* ♦ **:** lacking capacity or intent to injure — **harm•less•ly** *adv* — **harm•less•ness** *n*

♦ innocent, innocuous, safe, white ***Ant*** adverse, bad, harmful, hurtful, ill, injurious

[1]**har•mon•ic** \här-ˈmä-nik\ *adj* **1 :** of or relating to musical har-

mony or harmonics **2 :** pleasing to the ear — **har•mon•i•cal•ly** \-ni-k(ə-)lē\ *adv*

²harmonic *n* **:** a musical overtone

har•mon•i•ca \här-ˈmä-ni-kə\ *n* **:** a small wind instrument in which the sound is produced by metal reeds

har•mo•ni•ous \här-ˈmō-nē-əs\ *adj* **1** ♦ **:** musically concordant **2** ♦ **:** having the parts agreeably related **:** CONGRUOUS **3** ♦ **:** marked by accord in sentiment or action — **har•mo•ni•ous•ly** *adv* — **har•mo•ni•ous•ness** *n*

♦ [1] euphonious, melodious, musical, symphonic, tuneful *Ant* discordant, dissonant, inharmonious, unmelodious, unmusical ♦ [2] balanced, congruous, consonant *Ant* incongruous, inharmonious, unbalanced ♦ [3] agreeable, amicable, compatible, congenial, kindred, unanimous, united *Ant* disagreeable, disunited, incompatible, inharmonious, uncongenial

har•mo•nise *chiefly Brit var of* HARMONIZE

har•mo•ni•um \här-ˈmō-nē-əm\ *n* **:** a keyboard wind instrument in which the wind acts on a set of metal reeds

har•mo•nize \ˈhär-mə-ˌnīz\ *vb* **-nized; -niz•ing 1 :** to play or sing in harmony **2** ♦ **:** to be in harmony **3** ♦ **:** to bring into consonance or accord — **har•mo•ni•za•tion** \ˌhär-mə-nə-ˈzā-shən\ *n*

♦ [2, 3] agree, blend, conform, coordinate *Ant* clash, collide, conflict ♦ [3] accommodate, conciliate, conform, coordinate, key, reconcile *Ant* alienate, disjoin

har•mo•ny \ˈhär-mə-nē\ *n, pl* **-nies 1 :** musical agreement of sounds; *esp* **:** the combination of tones into chords and progressions of chords **2 a** ♦ **:** a pleasing arrangement of parts **b** ♦ **:** balanced interrelationship **3 :** internal calm

♦ [2a] balance, coherence, consonance, proportion, symmetry, symphony, unity *Ant* asymmetry, disproportion, disunity, imbalance, incoherence ♦ [2b] compatibility, concord, peace *Ant* conflict, discord, dissension

¹har•ness \ˈhär-nəs\ *n* **1 :** the gear other than a yoke of a draft animal **2 :** something that resembles a harness

²harness *vb* **1 :** to put a harness on; *also* **:** YOKE **2** ♦ **:** to make use of **:** UTILIZE

♦ apply, employ, exercise, exploit, operate, use, utilize

¹harp \ˈhärp\ *n* **:** a musical instrument consisting of a triangular frame set with strings plucked by the fingers — **harp•ist** \ˈhär-pist\ *n*

²harp *vb* **1 :** to play on a harp **2 :** to dwell on a subject tiresomely — **harp•er** *n*

¹har•poon \här-ˈpün\ *n* **:** a barbed spear used especially in hunting whales

²harpoon *vb* ♦ **:** to strike or capture with or as if with a harpoon — **har•poon•er** *n*

♦ gore, impale, lance, pierce, puncture, skewer, spear, spike, stab, stick, transfix

harp•si•chord \ˈhärp-si-ˌkȯrd\ *n* **:** a keyboard instrument producing tones by the plucking of its strings with quills or with leather or plastic points

har•py \ˈhär-pē\ *n, pl* **harpies 1 :** a predatory person **:** LEECH **2** ♦ **:** a shrewish woman

♦ fury, shrew, termagant, virago

har•ri•dan \ˈhar-əd-ᵊn\ *n* **:** SHREW 2

¹har•ri•er \ˈhar-ē-ər\ *n* **1 :** any of a breed of medium-sized foxhounds **2 :** a runner on a cross-country team

²harrier *n* **:** a slender long-legged hawk

¹har•row \ˈhar-ō\ *n* **:** a cultivating tool that has spikes, spring teeth, or disks and is used especially to pulverize and smooth the soil

²harrow *vb* **1 :** to cultivate with a harrow **2** ♦ **:** to cause distress or suffering to **:** TORMENT

♦ afflict, agonize, bedevil, curse, martyr, persecute, plague, rack, torment, torture

harrowing *adj* ♦ **:** acutely distressing or painful

♦ agonizing, bitter, cruel, excruciating, galling, grievous, harsh, hurtful, painful, tortuous

har•rumph \hə-ˈrəmf\ *vb* **:** to comment disapprovingly as though clearing the throat

har•ry \ˈhar-ē\ *vb* **har•ried; har•ry•ing 1 :** RAID, PILLAGE **2 :** to torment by or as if by constant attack

harsh \ˈhärsh\ *adj* **1 :** disagreeably rough **2** ♦ **:** causing discomfort or pain **3** ♦ **:** unduly exacting **:** SEVERE **4** ♦ **:** lacking in aesthetic appeal or refinement

♦ [2] bitter, brutal, burdensome, cruel, excruciating, grievous, grim, hard, heavy, inhuman, murderous, onerous, oppressive, rough, rugged, severe, stiff, tough, trying *Ant* easy, light, soft ♦ [3] austere, authoritarian, flinty, hard, heavy-handed, ramrod, rigid, rigorous, severe, stern, strict ♦ [4] grotesque, unaesthetic *Ant* aesthetic

harsh•en \ˈhär-shən\ *vb* **:** to make or become harsh ⟨~*ed* his voice⟩

harsh•ly \-lē\ *adv* ♦ **:** in a harsh manner

♦ hard, hardly, ill, oppressively, roughly, severely, sternly, stiffly

harsh•ness \-nəs\ *n* ♦ **:** the quality or state of being harsh

♦ bite, bitterness, pungency, sharpness, tartness ♦ hardness, inflexibility, rigidity, severity, sternness, strictness

hart \ˈhärt\ *n, chiefly Brit* **:** STAG

¹har•um–scar•um \ˌhar-əm-ˈskar-əm\ *adj* ♦ **:** having or showing a lack of concern for the consequences of one's actions **:** RECKLESS, IRRESPONSIBLE

♦ daredevil, foolhardy, irresponsible, reckless

²harum–scarum *adv* ♦ **:** in a rash or heedless way

♦ amok, berserk, frantically, hectically, helter-skelter, madly, pell-mell, wild, wildly

¹har•vest \ˈhär-vəst\ *n* **1 :** the season for gathering in crops; *also* **:** the act of gathering in a crop **2 :** a mature crop **3 :** the product or reward of effort

²harvest *vb* **1** ♦ **:** to gather in a crop **:** REAP **2 :** to gather, hunt, or kill (as deer) for human use or population control — **har•vest•er** *n*

♦ gather, pick, reap

has *pres 3d sing of* HAVE

has–been \ˈhaz-ˌbin\ *n* **:** one that has passed the peak of ability, power, effectiveness, or popularity

¹hash \ˈhash\ *vb* **1** ♦ **:** to chop into small pieces **2** ♦ **:** to talk about — often used with *over* or *out* **3 :** to make a confused muddle of

♦ [1] chop, mince ♦ *usu* **hash over** [2] argue, chew over, debate, discuss, dispute, moot, talk over

²hash *n* **1 :** chopped meat mixed with potatoes and browned **2** ♦ **:** a mass of things mingled together without order or plan **:** HODGEPODGE, JUMBLE

♦ assortment, clutter, jumble, medley, mélange, miscellany, motley, muddle, variety, welter

³hash *n* **:** HASHISH

hash browns *n pl* **:** boiled potatoes that have been diced, mixed with chopped onions and shortening, and fried

hash•ish \ˈha-ˌshēsh, ha-ˈshēsh\ *n* **:** the intoxicating concentrated resin from the flowering tops of the female hemp plant

hasp \ˈhasp\ *n* **:** a fastener (as for a door) consisting of a hinged metal strap that fits over a staple and is secured by a pin or padlock

has•si•um \ˈha-sē-əm\ *n* **:** an artificially produced radioactive metallic chemical element

¹has•sle \ˈha-səl\ *n* **1 a** ♦ **:** a heated often protracted argument **b :** a violent skirmish **:** FIGHT **2** ♦ **:** an annoying or troublesome concern

♦ [1a] altercation, argument, bicker, brawl, disagreement, dispute, fight, misunderstanding, quarrel, row, scrap, spat, squabble, wrangle ♦ [2] aggravation, annoyance, bother, exasperation, frustration, headache, inconvenience, irritant, nuisance, peeve, pest, problem, thorn

²hassle *vb* **1** ♦ **:** to contend or disagree in words **2 :** to annoy persistently or acutely

♦ argue, bicker, brawl, dispute, fall out, fight, quarrel, row, scrap, spat, squabble, wrangle

has•sock \ˈha-sək\ *n* **:** a cushion that serves as a seat or leg rest; *also* **:** a cushion to kneel on in prayer

haste \ˈhāst\ *n* **1** ♦ **:** rapidity of motion or action **:** SPEED **2** ♦ **:** rash or headlong action **3 :** excessive eagerness

♦ [1] celerity, fastness, fleetness, hurry, quickness, rapidity, speed, swiftness, velocity ♦ [2] hurry, hustle, precipitation, rush

has•ten \ˈhās-ᵊn\ *vb* **1 :** to urge on **2** ♦ **:** to move or act quickly **:** HURRY; *also* **:** to cause to move or act faster

♦ accelerate, hurry, quicken, rush, speed (up), step up, whisk

hast•i•ly \ˈhā-stə-lē\ *adv* ♦ : in haste

♦ cursorily, headlong, hurriedly, pell-mell, precipitately, rashly *Ant* deliberately ♦ apace, briskly, fast, full tilt, posthaste, presto, pronto, quick, quickly, rapidly, soon, speedily, swift, swiftly

hast•i•ness \ˈhā-stē-nəs\ *n* : the quality or state of being hasty
hasty \ˈhā-stē\ *adj* ♦ : made, done, or acting in haste

♦ cursory, headlong, pell-mell, precipitate, precipitous, rash *Ant* deliberate, unhurried

hat \ˈhat\ *n* ♦ : a covering for the head usually having a shaped crown and brim

♦ cap, headgear

hat•box \ˈhat-ˌbäks\ *n* : a round piece of luggage especially for carrying hats
¹hatch \ˈhach\ *n* **1** ♦ : a small door or opening **2** : a door or cover for access down into a compartment of a ship

♦ door, gate, portal

²hatch *vb* **1 a** : to produce by incubation **b** ♦ : to incubate eggs **2** : to emerge from an egg or pupa; *also* : to give forth young **3** : ORIGINATE — **hatch•ery** \ˈha-chə-rē\ *n*

♦ brood, incubate, set, sit

hatch•back \ˈhach-ˌbak\ *n* : an automobile with a rear hatch that opens upward
hatch•et \ˈha-chət\ *n* **1** : a short-handled ax with a hammerlike part opposite the blade **2** : TOMAHAWK
hatchet man *n* : a person hired for murder, coercion, or unscrupulous attack
hatch•ing \ˈha-chiŋ\ *n* : the engraving or drawing of closely spaced fine lines chiefly to give an effect of shading; *also* : the pattern so created
hatch•way \ˈhach-ˌwā\ *n* : a hatch giving access usually by a ladder or stairs
¹hate \ˈhāt\ *n* **1** ♦ : intense hostility and aversion **2** ♦ : an object of hatred

♦ [1] abhorrence, abomination, execration, hatred, loathing *Ant* affection, love, devotion, fondness ♦ [2] abhorrence, abomination, anathema, antipathy, aversion, bête noire *Ant* love

²hate *vb* **hat•ed; hat•ing** **1** ♦ : to express or feel extreme enmity **2** : to find distasteful — **hat•er** *n*

♦ abhor, abominate, despise, detest, execrate, loathe *Ant* love

hate•ful \-fəl\ *adj* ♦ : full of hate : MALICIOUS

♦ catty, cruel, malevolent, malicious, malign, malignant, mean, nasty, spiteful, virulent *Ant* benevolent, benign, benignant, loving, unmalicious

hate•ful•ly \-fə-lē\ *adv* ♦ : in a hateful manner

♦ maliciously, meanly, nastily, spitefully, viciously, wickedly

hate•ful•ness \-nəs\ *n* ♦ : the quality or state of being hateful

♦ cattiness, despite, malice, malignity, meanness, nastiness, spite, spleen, venom, viciousness

ha•tred \ˈhā-trəd\ *n* ♦ : intense hostility and aversion : HATE; *also* : prejudiced hostility or animosity

♦ abhorrence, abomination, execration, hate, loathing

hat•ter \ˈha-tər\ *n* : one that makes, sells, or cleans and repairs hats
hau•berk \ˈhò-bərk\ *n* : a coat of mail
haugh•ti•ness \ˈhò-tē-nəs\ *n* ♦ : the quality or state of being haughty

♦ arrogance, loftiness, pretense, pretension, pretentiousness, self-importance, superiority

haugh•ty \ˈhò-tē\ *adj* **haugh•ti•er; -est** ♦ : disdainfully proud — **haugh•ti•ly** \-tə-lē\ *adv*

♦ disdainful, highfalutin, lofty, lordly, prideful, proud, superior

¹haul \ˈhòl\ *vb* **1** ♦ : to exert traction on : DRAW, PULL **2** ♦ : to furnish transportation : CART — **haul•er** *n*

♦ [1] drag, draw, hale, lug, pull, tow, tug ♦ [2] bear, carry, cart, convey, ferry, lug, pack, tote, transport

²haul *n* **1** : the act or process of hauling : PULL, TUG **2** ♦ : the result of an effort to obtain, collect, or win **3 a** : the length or course of a transportation route **b** ♦ : a quantity transported : LOAD

♦ [2] catch, take, yield ♦ [3b] burden, cargo, freight, lading, load, payload, weight

haul•age \ˈhò-lij\ *n* **1** : the act or process of hauling **2** : a charge for hauling
haunch \ˈhònch\ *n* **1** : ²HIP 1 **2** : HINDQUARTER 2 — usually used in plural **3** : HINDQUARTER 1
¹haunt \ˈhònt\ *vb* **1** ♦ : to visit often : FREQUENT **2** : to have a disquieting effect on; *also* : to reappear continually in **3** : to visit or inhabit as a ghost — **haunt•er** *n*

♦ frequent, hang around, hang out, resort, visit

²haunt \ˈhònt, *2 is usu* ˈhant\ *n* **1** ♦ : a place habitually frequented **2** *chiefly dial* : GHOST

♦ hangout, rendezvous, resort

haunting *adj* ♦ : having a disquieting effect — **haunt•ing•ly** *adv*

♦ creepy, eerie, spooky, uncanny, unearthly, weird

haute cou•ture \ˌōt-kü-ˈtu̇r\ *n* : the establishments or designers that create exclusive and often trend-setting fashions for women; *also* : the fashions created
haute cui•sine \-kwi-ˈzēn\ *n* : artful or elaborate cuisine
hau•teur \hò-ˈtər, ō-, hō-\ *n* : ARROGANCE, HAUGHTINESS
¹have \ˈhav, həv, v; *in sense 2 before "to" usu* ˈhaf\ *vb* **had** \ˈhad, həd\; **hav•ing; has** \ˈhaz, həz, *in sense 2 before "to" usu* ˈhas\ **1** ♦ : to hold in possession; *also* : to hold in one's use, service, or regard **2** ♦ : to be compelled or forced — usually used with an infinitive with *to* ⟨~ to go now⟩ **3** : to stand in relationship to ⟨*has* many enemies⟩ **4** : OBTAIN; *also* : RECEIVE, ACCEPT **5** : to be marked by **6** : SHOW; *also* : USE, EXERCISE **7 a** ♦ : to experience especially by submitting to, undergoing, or suffering ⟨~ a cold⟩ **b** : TAKE ⟨~ a look⟩ **8** ♦ : to entertain in the mind ⟨~ an idea⟩ **9** : to cause to **10** : to consent to : ALLOW ⟨I won't ~ you jumping on the bed⟩ **11** : to be competent in **12 a** : to hold in a disadvantageous position **b** ♦ : to take advantage of : TRICK **13** : to give birth to **14** : to partake of **15** — used as an auxiliary with the past participle to form the present perfect, past perfect, or future perfect — **have at** : ATTACK — **have coming** : DESERVE — **have done with** : to be finished with — **have had it** : to have endured all one will permit or can stand — **have to do with** : to have in the way of relation with or effect on

♦ [1] command, enjoy, hold, occupy, own, possess, retain *Ant* lack, want ♦ *usu* **have to** [2] must, need, ought, shall, should ♦ [7a] endure, experience, feel, know, see, suffer, sustain, taste, undergo ♦ [8] bear, cherish, entertain, harbor (*or* harbour), hold, nurse ♦ [12b] beguile, bluff, cozen, deceive, delude, dupe, fool, gull, hoax, hoodwink, humbug, misinform, mislead, string along, take in, trick

²have \ˈhav\ *n* : one that has material wealth
ha•ven \ˈhā-vən\ *n* **1** ♦ : a part of a body of water protected and deep enough to furnish anchorage : HARBOR, PORT **2** ♦ : a place of safety **3** : a place offering favorable conditions ⟨a tourist's ~⟩

♦ [1] anchorage, harbor (*or* harbour), port ♦ [2] asylum, refuge, retreat, sanctuary, shelter

have–not \ˈhav-ˌnät, -ˈnät\ *n* : one that is poor in material wealth
hav•er•sack \ˈha-vər-ˌsak\ *n* : a bag similar to a knapsack but worn over one shoulder
hav•oc \ˈha-vək\ *n* **1** ♦ : wide and general destruction **2** ♦ : great confusion and disorder

♦ [1] annihilation, demolition, desolation, destruction, devastation, loss, obliteration, ruin, wastage, wreckage ♦ [2] chaos, confusion, disarray, disorder, disorganization, hell, jumble, mess, muddle, shambles

haw \ˈhò\ *n* : a hawthorn berry; *also* : HAWTHORN
Ha•wai•ian \hə-ˈwä-yən\ *n* : the Polynesian language of Hawaii
¹hawk \ˈhòk\ *n* **1** : any of numerous mostly small or medium-sized day-flying birds of prey (as a falcon or kite) **2** : a supporter of a war or a warlike policy — **hawk•ish** *adj*
²hawk *vb* : to offer goods for sale by calling out in the street — **hawk•er** *n*
³hawk *vb* : to make a harsh coughing sound in or as if in clearing the throat; *also* : to raise by hawking
hawk•weed \ˈhòk-ˌwēd\ *n* : any of several plants related to the daisies usually having yellow flowers
haw•ser \ˈhò-zər\ *n* : a large rope for towing, mooring, or securing a ship
haw•thorn \ˈhò-ˌthòrn\ *n* : any of a genus of spiny spring-flowering shrubs or small trees related to the apple
¹hay \ˈhā\ *n* **1** : herbage (as grass) mowed and cured for fodder **2** : REWARD **3** *slang* : BED ⟨hit the ~⟩ **4** : a small amount of money
²hay *vb* : to cut, cure, and store for hay

hay•cock \ˈhā-ˌkäk\ *n* : a small conical pile of hay
hay fever *n* : an acute allergic reaction especially to plant pollen that resembles a cold
hay•loft \ˈhā-ˌlȯft\ *n* : a loft for hay
hay•mow \-ˌmau̇\ *n* : a mow of or for hay
hay•rick \-ˌrik\ *n* : a large sometimes thatched outdoor stack of hay
hay•seed \-ˌsēd\ *n, pl* **hayseed** *or* **hayseeds** **1** : clinging bits of straw or chaff from hay **2** : BUMPKIN, YOKEL
hay•stack \-ˌstak\ *n* : a stack of hay
hay•wire \-ˌwī(-ə)r\ *adj* : being out of order or control : CRAZY
[1]**haz•ard** \ˈha-zərd\ *n* **1** ♦ : a source of danger **2** ♦ : the assumed impersonal purposeless determiner of unaccountable happenings : CHANCE; *also* : ACCIDENT **3** : an obstacle on a golf course

♦ [1] danger, menace, peril, pitfall, risk, threat, trouble ♦ [2] accident, chance, circumstance, luck

[2]**hazard** *vb* **1** : to expose to possible risk of loss or damage : VENTURE, RISK **2** ♦ : to undertake the risks and dangers of **3** : to offer at the risk of rebuff, rejection, or censure

♦ chance, gamble, risk, venture

haz•ard•ous \ˈha-zər-dəs\ *adj* ♦ : involving or exposing one to risk (as of loss or harm)

♦ dangerous, grave, grievous, menacing, parlous, perilous, risky, serious, unhealthy, unsafe, venturesome

[1]**haze** \ˈhāz\ *n* **1** ♦ : fine dust, smoke, or light vapor causing lack of transparency in the air **2** ♦ : vagueness of mind or perception

♦ [1] fog, murk, smog, soup ♦ [2] daze, fog, muddle, spin

[2]**haze** *vb* : to make or become hazy, dull, or cloudy
[3]**haze** *vb* **hazed; haz•ing** : to harass by abusive and humiliating tricks usually by way of initiation
ha•zel \ˈhā-zəl\ *n* **1** : any of a genus of shrubs or small trees related to the birches and bearing edible brown nuts (**ha•zel•nuts** \-ˌnəts\) **2** : a light brown color
hazy \ˈhā-zē\ *adj* **haz•i•er; -est** **1** ♦ : obscured or darkened by haze **2** ♦ : not clearly perceived or understood : VAGUE, INDEFINITE — **haz•i•ly** \-zə-lē\ *adv* — **haz•i•ness** \-zē-nəs\ *n*

♦ [1] cloudy, foggy, misty, murky, smoggy, soupy ***Ant*** clear, cloudless, limpid, pellucid, unclouded ♦ [2] bleary, dim, faint, foggy, fuzzy, indefinite, indistinct, indistinguishable, murky, nebulous, obscure, opaque, shadowy, unclear, undefined, undetermined, vague

Hb *abbr* hemoglobin
HBM *abbr* Her Britannic Majesty; His Britannic Majesty
H–bomb \ˈāch-ˌbäm\ *n* : HYDROGEN BOMB
HC *abbr* **1** Holy Communion **2** House of Commons
hd *abbr* head
HD *abbr* heavy-duty
hdbk *abbr* handbook
hdkf *abbr* handkerchief
HDL \ˌāch-(ˌ)dē-ˈel\ *n* : a cholesterol-poor protein-rich lipoprotein of blood plasma correlated with reduced risk of atherosclerosis
hdwe *abbr* hardware
he \ˈhē\ *pron* **1** : that male one **2** : a person : the person ⟨~ who hesitates is lost⟩
He *symbol* helium
HE *abbr* **1** Her Excellency **2** His Eminence **3** His Excellency
[1]**head** \ˈhed\ *n* **1** ♦ : the front or upper part of the body containing the brain, the chief sense organs, and the mouth **2 a** ♦ : the seat of the intellect : MIND; *also* : mental or emotional control **b** : natural aptitude **3** : POISE **4** : the obverse of a coin **5** : a single human being : INDIVIDUAL; *also, pl* **head** : one of a number (as of cattle) **6** : the end that is upper or higher or opposite the foot; *also* : either end of something (as a drum) whose two ends need not be distinguished **7** : the source of a stream **8** ♦ : a person who leads : LEADER; *also* : a leading element (as of a procession) **9** : a projecting part; *also* : the striking part of a weapon **10** ♦ : the place of leadership or honor **11** : a separate part or topic **12** ♦ : the foam on a fermenting or effervescing liquid **13** : culminating point of action : CRISIS — **head•ed** \ˈhe-dəd\ *adj* — **head•less** *adj*

♦ [1] noggin, pate, poll ♦ [2a] mind, reason, sanity, wit ♦ [8] boss, captain, chief, foreman, headman, helmsman, kingpin, leader, master, taskmaster ♦ [10] chair, headship, helm, rein ♦ [12] foam, froth, lather, spume

[2]**head** *adj* ♦ : most important, consequential, or influential : PRINCIPAL, CHIEF

♦ chief, first, foremost, high, lead, preeminent, premier, primary, prime, principal, supreme

[3]**head** *vb* **1** : to provide with or form a head; *also* : to form the head of **2** ♦ : to act as leader or head to **3** : to get in front of especially so as to stop; *also* : SURPASS **4** : to put or stand at the head **5** ♦ : to point or proceed in a certain direction

♦ [2] boss, captain, command, dominate, lead, spearhead, supervise ♦ [5] extend, go, lead, lie, run

head•ache \ˈhe-ˌdāk\ *n* **1** : pain in the head **2** ♦ : a vexatious or baffling situation or problem

♦ aggravation, annoyance, bother, exasperation, frustration, hassle, inconvenience, irritant, nuisance, peeve, pest, problem, thorn

head•band \ˈhed-ˌband\ *n* : a band worn on or around the head
head•bang•er \-ˌbaŋ-ər\ *n* : one who performs or enjoys hard rock
head•board \-ˌbōrd\ *n* : a board forming the head (as of a bed)
head cold *n* : a common cold centered in the nasal passages and adjacent mucous tissues
head•dress \ˈhed-ˌdres\ *n* : an often elaborate covering for the head
head•first \-ˈfərst\ *adv* : HEADLONG 1 — **headfirst** *adj*
head•gear \-ˌgir\ *n* ♦ : a covering or protective device for the head

♦ cap, hat

head–hunt•ing \-ˌhən-tiŋ\ *n* : the practice of seeking out and decapitating enemies and preserving their heads as trophies — **head•hunt•er** \-tər\ *n*
head•ing \ˈhe-diŋ\ *n* **1** : the compass direction in which the longitudinal axis of a ship or airplane points **2** ♦ : something that forms or serves as a head; *esp* : an inscription, headline, or title standing at the top or beginning (as of a letter or chapter)

♦ title

head•land \ˈhed-lənd, -ˌland\ *n* ♦ : a high point of land or rock projecting into a body of water : PROMONTORY

♦ cape, peninsula, point, promontory, spit

head•light \-ˌlīt\ *n* : a light mounted on the front of a vehicle to illuminate the road ahead
[1]**head•line** \-ˌlīn\ *n* : a head of a newspaper story or article usually printed in large type
[2]**headline** *vb* **1** : to provide with a headline **2** : to publicize highly **3** : to be a leading performer in
head•lock \-ˌläk\ *n* : a wrestling hold in which one encircles the opponent's head with one arm
[1]**head•long** \-ˈlȯŋ\ *adv* **1** : with the head foremost **2** ♦ : without deliberation : RASHLY **3** : without delay

♦ cursorily, hastily, hurriedly, pell-mell, precipitately, rashly

[2]**head•long** \-ˌlȯŋ\ *adj* **1** ♦ : lacking in calmness or restraint : PRECIPITATE, RASH **2** : plunging with the head foremost

♦ cursory, hasty, pell-mell, precipitate, precipitous, rash

head•man \ˈhed-ˈman, -ˌman\ *n* ♦ : one who is a leader : CHIEF

♦ boss, captain, chief, foreman, head, helmsman, kingpin, leader, master, taskmaster

head•mas•ter \-ˌmas-tər\ *n* : a man who is head of a private school
head•mis•tress \-ˌmis-trəs\ *n* : a woman who is head of a private school
head of stream : strong driving force : MOMENTUM
head–on \ˈhed-ˈȯn, -ˈän\ *adj* : having the front facing in the direction of initial contact or line of sight ⟨~ collision⟩ — **head–on** *adv*
head•phone \-ˌfōn\ *n* : an earphone held on by a band over the head
head•piece \-ˌpēs\ *n* : a covering for the head
head•pin \-ˌpin\ *n* : a bowling pin that stands foremost in the arrangement of pins
head•quar•ters \-ˌkwȯr-tərz\ *n sing or pl* **1** : a place from which a commander exercises command **2** : the administrative center of an enterprise
head•rest \-ˌrest\ *n* **1** : a support for the head **2** : a pad at the top of the back of an automobile seat
head•room \-ˌrüm, -ˌru̇m\ *n* : vertical space in which to stand, sit, or move
head–scratcher \-ˌskra-chər\ *n* : PUZZLE, MYSTERY
head•set \-ˌset\ *n* : a pair of headphones

head•ship \-ˌship\ *n* ♦ : the position, office, or dignity of a head

♦ care, charge, guidance, oversight, regulation, superintendence, supervision ♦ chair, head, helm, rein

heads•man \ˈhedz-mən\ *n* : EXECUTIONER

head•stall \ˈhed-ˌstȯl\ *n* : a part of a bridle or halter that encircles the head

head•stone \-ˌstōn\ *n* ♦ : a memorial stone at the head of a grave

♦ gravestone, monument, tombstone

head•strong \-ˌstrȯŋ\ *adj* **1** ♦ : not easily restrained **2** ♦ : directed by ungovernable will

♦ [1] froward, intractable, recalcitrant, refractory, uncontrollable, unmanageable, unruly, untoward, wayward, willful ♦ [2] dogged, hardheaded, mulish, obdurate, obstinate, opinionated, peevish, pertinacious, perverse, pigheaded, stubborn, unyielding, willful

heads–up \ˈhedz-ˈəp\ *n* : WARNING

head•wait•er \-ˈwā-tər\ *n* : the head of the dining-room staff of a restaurant or hotel

head•wa•ter \-ˌwȯ-tər, -ˌwä-\ *n* : the source of a stream — usually used in plural

head•way \-ˌwā\ *n* ♦ : forward motion; *also* : PROGRESS

♦ advance, advancement, furtherance, march, onrush, passage, process, procession, progress, progression

head wind *n* : a wind blowing in a direction opposite to a course especially of a ship or aircraft

head•word \ˈhed-ˌwərd\ *n* **1** : a word or term placed at the beginning **2** : a word qualified by a modifier

head•work \-ˌwərk\ *n* : mental work or effort : THINKING

heady \ˈhe-dē\ *adj* **head•i•er; -est** **1** : WILLFUL, RASH; *also* : IMPETUOUS **2** : INTOXICATING **3** : SHREWD

heal \ˈhēl\ *vb* **1** ♦ : to make or become healthy, sound, or whole **2** ♦ : to restore to health : CURE — **heal•er** *n*

♦ [1] convalesce, gain, mend, rally, recover, recuperate, snap back ♦ [2] cure, mend, rehabilitate

health \ˈhelth\ *n* **1** ♦ : sound physical or mental condition; *also* : overall condition of the body ⟨in poor ~⟩ **2** : WELL-BEING **3** : a toast to someone's health or prosperity

♦ fitness, heartiness, robustness, soundness, wellness, wholeness, wholesomeness *Ant* illness, sickness, unsoundness

health care *n* : efforts made to maintain or restore health — usually hyphenated when used attributively

health club *n* : a commercial establishment providing health and fitness facilities and equipment for members

health•ful \ˈhelth-fəl\ *adj* **1** ♦ : beneficial to health **2** : enjoying good health — **health•ful•ly** *adv* — **health•ful•ness** *n*

♦ healthy, restorative, salubrious, salutary, wholesome *Ant* insalubrious, noxious, unhealthful, unhealthy, unwholesome

health•i•ness \ˈhel-thē-nəs\ *n* : the quality or state of being healthy

health maintenance organization *n* : HMO

healthy \ˈhel-thē\ *adj* **health•i•er; -est** **1** ♦ : enjoying or typical of good health : WELL **2** ♦ : evincing or conducive to health **3 a** : PROSPEROUS **b** ♦ : not small or feeble : CONSIDERABLE — **health•i•ly** \-thə-lē\ *adv*

♦ [1] able-bodied, chipper, fit, hale, hearty, robust, sound, well, whole, wholesome *Ant* ailing, diseased, ill, sick, unfit, unhealthy, unsound, unwell ♦ [2] healthful, restorative, salubrious, salutary, wholesome ♦ [3b] considerable, good, goodly, respectable, significant, sizable, substantial, tidy

¹heap \ˈhēp\ *n* **1** ♦ : a collection of things thrown one on another : PILE **2** ♦ : a great number or large quantity : LOT

♦ [1] cock, hill, mound, mountain, pile, rick, stack ♦ [2] abundance, deal, gobs, loads, lot, pile, plenty, quantity, scads

²heap *vb* **1** ♦ : to throw or lay in a heap : pile or collect in great quantity **2 a** ♦ : to give in large quantities **b** ♦ : to load heavily

♦ [1] accumulate, collect, conglomerate, gather, pile up ♦ [1] hill, mound, pile, stack ♦ [2a] lavish, pour, rain, shower ♦ [2b] charge, cram, fill, jam, jam-pack, load, pack, stuff

hear \ˈhir\ *vb* **heard** \ˈhərd\; **hear•ing** **1** : to perceive by the ear **2** ♦ : to gain knowledge of by hearing : LEARN **3** ♦ : to listen to with attention : HEED; *also* : ATTEND **4** : to give a legal hearing to or take testimony from — **hear•er** *n*

♦ [2] ascertain, catch on, discover, find out, learn, realize, see ♦ [3] attend, hark, heed, listen, mind

hear•ing *n* **1** : the process, function, or power of perceiving sound; *esp* : the special sense by which noises and tones are received as stimuli **2** ♦ : range of hearing : EARSHOT **3** : opportunity to be heard **4** : a listening to arguments (as in a court); *also* : a session (as of a legislative committee) in which testimony is taken from witnesses

♦ earshot, hail, sound

hear•ken \ˈhär-kən\ *vb* : to give attention : LISTEN

hear•say \ˈhir-ˌsā\ *n* : RUMOR

hearse \ˈhərs\ *n* : a vehicle for carrying the dead to the grave

heart \ˈhärt\ *n* **1** : a hollow muscular organ that by rhythmic contraction keeps up the circulation of the blood in the body; *also* : something resembling a heart in shape **2** : any of a suit of playing cards marked with a red figure of a heart; *also, pl* : a card game in which the object is to avoid taking tricks containing hearts **3 a** : the whole personality **b** : the emotional or moral as distinguished from the intellectual nature **c** ♦ : generous disposition : COMPASSION **4** ♦ : mental or moral strength to venture, persevere, and withstand danger, fear, or difficulty : COURAGE **5** ♦ : one's innermost being **6 a** : CENTER **b** ♦ : the essential part **7** : the younger central part of a compact leafy cluster (as of lettuce) **8** : a single human being ⟨dear ~⟩ — **heart•ed** \ˈhär-təd\ *adj* — **by heart** : by rote or from memory

♦ [3c] charity, commiseration, compassion, feeling, humanity, kindliness, kindness, mercy, pity, sympathy *Ant* inhumanity ♦ [4] bravery, courage, daring, fearlessness, gallantry, guts, hardihood, heroism, nerve, stoutness, valor ♦ [5] core, quick, soul ♦ [6b] core, crux, gist, nub, pith, pivot

heart•ache \-ˌāk\ *n* ♦ : anguish of mind

♦ affliction, anguish, dolor, grief, sorrow, woe

heart attack *n* : an acute episode of heart disease due to insufficient blood supply to the heart muscle

heart•beat \ˈhärt-ˌbēt\ *n* : one complete pulsation of the heart

heart•break \-ˌbrāk\ *n* : crushing grief

heart•break•ing \-ˌbrā-kiŋ\ *adj* ♦ : causing extreme sorrow or distress — **heart•break•er** \-ˌbrā-kər\ *n*

♦ depressing, dismal, dreary, melancholy, pathetic, sad, sorry, tearful ♦ deplorable, distressful, grievous, lamentable, regrettable, unfortunate, woeful

heart•bro•ken \-ˌbrō-kən\ *adj* : overcome by sorrow

heart•burn \-ˌbərn\ *n* : a burning distress behind the sternum due to the backward flow of acid from the stomach to the esophagus

heart disease *n* : an abnormal organic condition of the heart or of the heart and circulation

heart•en \ˈhärt-ᵊn\ *vb* ♦ : to give heart to : ENCOURAGE, CHEER

♦ buoy (up), cheer, comfort, embolden, encourage, inspire, steel

heartening *adj* ♦ : tending or serving to hearten, inspire, or give fresh courage

♦ auspicious, bright, encouraging, fair, golden, hopeful, likely, promising, propitious, rosy, upbeat ♦ comforting, encouraging, gratifying, heartwarming, rewarding, satisfying

heart•felt \ˈhärt-ˌfelt\ *adj* : deeply felt : SINCERE

hearth \ˈhärth\ *n* **1** : an area (as of brick) in front of a fireplace; *also* : the floor of a fireplace **2** ♦ : one's place of residence : HOME

♦ abode, domicile, dwelling, home, house, lodging, quarters, residence

hearth•stone \ˈhärth-ˌstōn\ *n* **1** : stone forming a hearth **2** : one's place of residence : HOME

heart•i•ly \ˈhär-tə-lē\ *adv* ♦ : in a hearty manner

♦ cheerfully, gaily, happily, jovially, merrily, mirthfully

heart•i•ness \ˈhär-tē-nəs\ *n* ♦ : the quality or state of being hearty

♦ fitness, health, robustness, soundness, wellness, wholeness, wholesomeness

heart•less \ˈhärt-ləs\ *adj* ♦ : lacking feeling or affection

♦ callous, hard, inhuman, inhumane, pitiless, soulless, unfeeling, unsympathetic

heart•rend•ing \-ˌren-diŋ\ *adj* : causing extreme sorrow or distress : HEARTBREAKING

heart•sick \-ˌsik\ *adj* ♦ : very despondent

♦ bad, blue, brokenhearted, dejected, depressed, despondent, disconsolate, miserable, mournful, sad, wretched

heart•sick•ness \-nəs\ *n* ♦ : the quality or state of being heartsick

♦ blues, dejection, depression, desolation, despondency, doldrums, dumps, forlornness, gloom, melancholy, sadness

heart–stop•ping \-ˌstä-piŋ\ *adj* : extremely shocking or exciting
heart•strings \-ˌstriŋz\ *n pl* : the deepest emotions or affections
heart•throb \-ˌthräb\ *n* **1** : the throb of a heart **2** : sentimental emotion **3** : SWEETHEART **4** : an entertainer noted for his sex appeal
heart–to–heart *adj* : SINCERE, FRANK
heart•warm•ing \ˈhärt-ˌwȯr-miŋ\ *adj* ♦ : inspiring sympathetic feeling

♦ comforting, encouraging, gratifying, heartening, rewarding, satisfying *Ant* depressing, discouraging, disheartening, dispiriting

heart•wood \-ˌwu̇d\ *n* : the older harder nonliving and usually darker wood of the central part of a tree trunk
¹hearty \ˈhär-tē\ *adj* **heart•i•er; -est** **1 a** : giving full support **b** ♦ : enthusiastically or exuberantly cordial **2** ♦ : vigorously healthy **3** : ABUNDANT; *also* : NOURISHING **4** ♦ : carried out forcefully and energetically

♦ [1b] amicable, companionable, comradely, cordial, friendly, genial, neighborly, warm, warmhearted ♦ [2] able-bodied, chipper, fit, hale, healthy, robust, sound, well, whole, wholesome ♦ [4] firm, forceful, lusty, robust, solid, stout, strong, sturdy, vigorous

²hearty *n, pl* **heart•ies** : an enthusiastic jovial fellow; *also* : SAILOR
¹heat \ˈhēt\ *vb* **1** : to make or become warm or hot **2** : EXCITE — **heat•ed•ly** *adv* — **heat•er** *n*
²heat *n* **1** : a condition of being hot : WARMTH **2** : a form of energy that when added to a body causes the body to rise in temperature, to fuse, to evaporate, or to expand **3** : high temperature **4 a** ♦ : intensity of feeling **b** : sexual excitement especially in a female mammal **5** : a preliminary race for narrowing the competition **6** : pungency of flavor **7** *slang* : POLICE **8** : PRESSURE, COERCION; *also* : ABUSE, CRITICISM

♦ ardor, emotion, fervency, fervor, intensity, passion, vehemence, warmth

heat•ed \ˈhē-təd\ *adj* ♦ : marked by anger or passion

♦ agitated, feverish, frenzied, hectic, overactive, overwrought

heat exchanger *n* : a device (as an automobile radiator) for transferring heat from one fluid to another without allowing them to mix
heat exhaustion *n* : a condition marked by weakness, nausea, dizziness, and profuse sweating resulting from physical exertion in a hot environment
heath \ˈhēth\ *n* **1** : any of a large family of often evergreen shrubby plants (as a blueberry or heather) of wet acid soils **2** : a tract of wasteland — **heathy** *adj*
¹hea•then \ˈhē-t͟hən\ *adj* **1** : of or relating to heathens, their religions, or their customs **2** ♦ : not civilized

♦ Neanderthal, barbarous, heathenish, rude, savage, uncivil, uncivilized, uncultivated, wild

²heathen *n, pl* **heathens** *or* **heathen** **1** : an unconverted member of a people or nation that does not acknowledge the God of the Bible **2** : an uncivilized or irreligious person — **hea•then•dom** *n* — **hea•then•ism** *n*
hea•then•ish \ˈhē-t͟hə-nish\ *adj* ♦ : resembling or characteristic of heathens : BARBAROUS

♦ Neanderthal, barbarous, heathen, rude, savage, uncivil, uncivilized, uncultivated, wild

heath•er \ˈhe-t͟hər\ *n* : a northern and alpine evergreen heath with usually lavender flowers — **heath•ery** *adj*
heat lightning *n* : flashes of light without thunder ascribed to distant lightning reflected by high clouds
heat•stroke \ˈhēt-ˌstrōk\ *n* : a disorder marked especially by high body temperature without sweating and by collapse that follows prolonged exposure to excessive heat
¹heave \ˈhēv\ *vb* **heaved** *or* **hove** \ˈhōv\; **heav•ing** **1** ♦ : to rise or lift upward **2** ♦ : to propel through the air by a forward motion of the hand and arm : THROW **3** : to rise and fall rhythmically; *also* : PANT **4** : to disgorge the stomach contents through the mouth; *also* : to make an effort to vomit **5** : PULL, PUSH — **heav•er** *n*

♦ [1] boost, heft, hoist, jack ♦ [2] cast, catapult, chuck, dash, fire, fling, hurl, hurtle, launch, peg, pelt, pitch, sling, throw, toss

²heave *n* **1** : an effort to lift or raise **2** : THROW, CAST **3** : an upward motion **4** *pl* : a chronic lung disease of horses marked by difficult breathing and persistent cough
heav•en \ˈhe-vən\ *n* **1** : FIRMAMENT — usually used in plural **2** *often cap* : the abode of the Deity and of the blessed dead; *also* : a spiritual state of everlasting communion with God **3** *cap* : GOD 1 **4** ♦ : a place or condition of supreme happiness — **heav•en•ward** *adv or adj*

♦ Eden, Elysium, paradise, utopia ♦ ecstasy, elation, euphoria, exhilaration, intoxication, paradise, rapture, rhapsody, transport

heav•en•ly \-lē\ *adj* **1** ♦ : of or relating to heaven or the heavens **2 a** : suggesting the blessed state of heaven **b** ♦ : highly pleasing

♦ [1] Elysian, celestial, empyrean, supernal ♦ [2b] agreeable, darling, delectable, delicious, delightful, enjoyable, luscious, pleasurable

heavi•ly \ˈhe-və-lē\ *adv* : to a large degree
¹heavy \ˈhe-vē\ *adj* **heavi•er; -est** **1** ♦ : having great weight **2** ♦ : hard to bear **3** : of weighty import : SERIOUS **4** : characterized by intensity of quality : DEEP, PROFOUND **5** : burdened with something oppressive; *also* : PREGNANT **6** : SLUGGISH **7 a** : lacking sparkle or vivacity : DRAB **b** : DOLEFUL **8** : DROWSY **9** : greater than the average of its kind or class **10** : very rich and hard to digest; *also* : not properly raised or leavened **11** : producing goods (as steel) used in the production of other goods **12** ♦ : threatening to rain or snow — **heavi•ness** \-vē-nəs\ *n*

♦ [1] hefty, massive, ponderous, weighty *Ant* light, lightweight, weightless ♦ [2] bitter, brutal, burdensome, cruel, excruciating, grievous, grim, hard, harsh, inhuman, murderous, onerous, oppressive, rough, rugged, severe, stiff, tough, trying ♦ [12] cloudy, dull, hazy, overcast

²heavy *n, pl* **heav•ies** **1** : a theatrical role representing a dignified or imposing person **2** : a villain especially in a story
heavy–du•ty \ˌhe-vē-ˈdü-tē, -ˈdyü-\ *adj* : able to withstand unusual strain
heavy–hand•ed \-ˈhan-dəd\ *adj* **1** ♦ : lacking dexterity, nimbleness, or grace : CLUMSY **2** ♦ : unduly exacting : HARSH

♦ [1] awkward, clumsy, gawky, graceless, lubberly, lumpish, ungainly, unhandy ♦ [2] austere, authoritarian, flinty, hard, harsh, ramrod, rigid, rigorous, severe, stern, strict

heavy•heart•ed \-ˈhär-təd\ *adj* : SADDENED, DESPONDENT
heavy lifting *n* : a burdensome or laborious duty
heavy metal *n* : energetic and highly amplified electronic rock music
heavy•set \ˌhe-vē-ˈset\ *adj* ♦ : stocky and compact in build

♦ chunky, dumpy, squat, stocky, stout, stubby, stumpy, thickset

heavy water *n* : water enriched in deuterium
heavy•weight \ˈhe-vē-ˌwāt\ *n* : one above average in weight; *esp* : a boxer weighing over 175 pounds
Heb *abbr* Hebrews
He•bra•ism \ˈhē-brā-ˌi-zəm\ *n* : the thought, spirit, or practice characteristic of the Hebrews — **He•bra•ic** \hi-ˈbrā-ik\ *adj*
He•bra•ist \ˈhē-ˌbrā-ist\ *n* : a specialist in Hebrew and Hebraic studies
He•brew \ˈhē-brü\ *n* **1** : the language of the Hebrews **2** : a member of or descendant from a group of Semitic peoples; *esp* : ISRAELITE — **Hebrew** *adj*
He•brews \ˈhē-(ˌ)brüz\ *n* : a book of the New Testament in Christian Scriptures
hec•a•tomb \ˈhe-kə-ˌtōm\ *n* : an ancient Greek and Roman sacrifice of 100 oxen or cattle
heck•le \ˈhe-kəl\ *vb* **heck•led; heck•ling** ♦ : to harass with questions or gibes

♦ bait, bug, hassle, needle, ride, taunt, tease

heck•ler \ˈhe-k(ə-)lər\ *n* ♦ : one that heckles

♦ oppressor, persecutor, taunter, tormentor, torturer

hect•are \ˈhek-ˌtar\ *n* : a metric measure equal to 10,000 square meters
hec•tic \ˈhek-tik\ *adj* **1** : being hot and flushed **2** ♦ : filled with excitement, activity, or confusion

♦ agitated, feverish, frenzied, heated, overactive, overwrought

hec•ti•cal•ly \ˈhek-ti-k(ə-)lē\ *adv* ♦ : in a hectic manner

♦ amok, berserk, frantically, harum-scarum, helter-skelter, madly, pell-mell, wild, wildly

hec•to•gram \ˈhek-tə-ˌgram\ *n* : a metric measure equal to 100 grams

hec•to•li•ter \ˈhek-tə-ˌlē-tər\ *n* : a metric measure equal to 100 liters
hec•to•me•ter \ˈhek-tə-ˌmē-tər, hek-ˈtä-mə-tər\ *n* : a metric measure equal to 100 meters
hec•tor \ˈhek-tər\ *vb* **1** : SWAGGER **2** ♦ : to intimidate by bluster or personal pressure

♦ browbeat, bully, cow, intimidate

¹hedge \ˈhej\ *n* **1** : a fence or boundary formed of shrubs or small trees **2** ♦ : something that impedes or separates : BARRIER **3** : a means of protection (as against financial loss)

♦ barrier, fence, wall

²hedge *vb* **hedged; hedg•ing** **1** ♦ : to enclose or protect with or as if with a hedge **2** : HINDER **3** : to protect oneself financially by a counterbalancing action **4** ♦ : to evade the risk of commitment — **hedg•er** *n*

♦ [1] cage, closet, coop up, corral, encase, enclose, envelop, fence, hem, house, immure, pen, wall ♦ [4] equivocate, fudge, pussyfoot

hedge•hog \ˈhej-ˌhȯg, -ˌhäg\ *n* : a small Old World insect-eating mammal covered with spines; *also* : PORCUPINE
hedge•hop \-ˌhäp\ *vb* : to fly an airplane very close to the ground
hedge•row \-ˌrō\ *n* : a row of shrubs or trees bounding or separating fields
he•do•nism \ˈhēd-ᵊn-ˌi-zəm\ *n* : the doctrine that pleasure is the chief good in life; *also* : a way of life based on this — **he•do•nist** \-ist\ *n* — **he•do•nis•tic** \ˌhēd-ᵊn-ˈi-stik\ *adj*
¹heed \ˈhēd\ *vb* ♦ : to pay attention

♦ attend, hark, hear, listen, mind ♦ follow, listen, mind, note, observe, regard, watch *Ant* disregard, ignore, tune out

²heed *n* ♦ : the act or state of attending or noticing

♦ attention, awareness, cognizance, ear, eye, notice, observance, observation

heed•ful \ˈhēd-fəl\ *adj* ♦ : taking heed — **heed•ful•ly** *adv*

♦ alert, careful, cautious, circumspect, considerate, gingerly, guarded, safe, wary

heed•ful•ness \-nəs\ *n* ♦ : the quality or state of being heedful

♦ alertness, care, carefulness, caution, circumspection ♦ care, carefulness, heed, pains, scrupulousness

heed•less \-ləs\ *adj* ♦ : not taking heed — **heed•less•ly** *adv*

♦ careless, mindless, unguarded, unsafe, unwary

heed•less•ness \-ləs-nəs\ *n* ♦ : the quality or state of being heedless

♦ carelessness, dereliction, laxness, negligence, remissness, slackness

¹heel \ˈhēl\ *n* **1** : the hind part of the foot **2** : one of the crusty ends of a loaf of bread **3** : a solid attachment forming the back of the sole of a shoe **4** : a rear, low, or bottom part **5** ♦ : a contemptible person

♦ beast, boor, churl, clown, creep, cretin, cur, jerk, joker, louse, lout, skunk, slob, snake

²heel *vb* : to tilt to one side : LIST
¹heft \ˈheft\ *n* : WEIGHT, HEAVINESS
²heft *vb* **1** ♦ : to heave up : HOIST **2** : to test the weight of by lifting

♦ boost, heave, hoist, jack

hefty \ˈhef-tē\ *adj* **heft•i•er; -est** **1** : marked by bigness, bulk, and usually strength **2** ♦ : impressively large **3** ♦ : quite heavy

♦ [2] big, large, outsize, oversize, sizable, substantial ♦ [3] heavy, massive, ponderous, weighty

he•ge•mo•ny \hi-ˈje-mə-nē\ *n* : preponderant influence or authority over others : DOMINATION
he•gi•ra \hi-ˈjī-rə\ *n* : a journey especially when undertaken to escape a dangerous or undesirable environment
heif•er \ˈhe-fər\ *n* : a young cow; *esp* : one that has not had a calf
height \ˈhīt\ *n* **1** ♦ : the highest or most advanced part or point **2** ♦ : the distance from the bottom to the top of something standing upright **3** : ALTITUDE **4** ♦ : an extent of land rising to a considerable degree above the surrounding country

♦ [1] acme, apex, climax, crown, culmination, head, meridian, peak, pinnacle, summit, tip-top, top, zenith *Ant* bottom, nadir ♦ [1] depth, limit ♦ [2] altitude, elevation ♦ [4] elevation, eminence, highland, hill, mound, prominence, rise *Ant* lowland

height•en \ˈhīt-ᵊn\ *vb* **1** ♦ : to increase in amount or degree **2** ♦ : to make or become high or higher

♦ [1] amplify, beef, boost, consolidate, deepen, enhance, intensify, magnify, redouble, step up, strengthen ♦ [2] boost, crane, elevate, heave, heft, hike, hoist, jack, lift, pick up, raise, up, uphold

Heim•lich maneuver \ˈhīm-lik-\ *n* : the manual application of sudden upward pressure on the upper abdomen of a choking victim to force a foreign object from the trachea
hei•nous \ˈhā-nəs\ *adj* : hatefully or shockingly evil — **hei•nous•ly** *adv*
hei•nous•ness \-nəs\ *n* ♦ : the state or quality of being heinous

♦ atrociousness, atrocity, depravity, enormity, monstrosity, vileness, wickedness

heir \ˈar\ *n* : one who inherits or is entitled to inherit property, rank, title, or office — **heir•ship** *n*
heir apparent *n, pl* **heirs apparent** : an heir whose right to succeed (as to a title) cannot be taken away if he or she survives the present holder
heir•ess \ˈar-əs\ *n* : a female heir especially to great wealth
heir•loom \ˈar-ˌlüm\ *n* **1** : a piece of personal property that descends by inheritance **2** : something handed on from one generation to another
heir presumptive *n, pl* **heirs presumptive** : an heir whose present right to inherit could be lost through the birth of a nearer relative
heist \ˈhīst\ *vb, slang* : to commit armed robbery on; *also* : STEAL — **heist** *n, slang*
held *past and past part of* HOLD
he•li•cal \ˈhe-li-kəl, ˈhē-\ *adj* ♦ : of, relating to, or having the form of a helix : SPIRAL

♦ spiral, winding

he•li•cop•ter \ˈhe-lə-ˌkäp-tər, ˈhē-\ *n* : an aircraft that is supported in the air by one or more rotors revolving on substantially vertical axes
he•lio•cen•tric \ˌhē-lē-ō-ˈsen-trik\ *adj* : having or relating to the sun as center
he•li•o•sphere \ˈhē-lē-ə-ˌsfir, -ō-\ *n* : the region in space influenced by the sun or solar wind
he•lio•trope \ˈhē-lē-ə-ˌtrōp\ *n* : any of a genus of herbs or shrubs related to the forget-me-not that have small white or purple flowers
he•li•port \ˈhe-lə-ˌpōrt\ *n* : a landing and takeoff place for a helicopter
he•li•um \ˈhē-lē-əm\ *n* : a very light nonflammable gaseous chemical element occurring in various natural gases
he•lix \ˈhē-liks\ *n, pl* **he•li•ces** \ˈhe-lə-ˌsēz, ˈhē-\ *also* **he•lix•es** \ˈhē-lik-səz\ : something spiral in form
hell \ˈhel\ *n* **1** : a nether world in which the dead continue to exist **2** : the realm of the devil in which the damned suffer everlasting punishment **3** ♦ : a place or state of torment or wickedness **4** ♦ : a place or state of turmoil, disorder, or destruction — **hell•ish** *adj*

♦ [3] agony, horror, misery, murder, nightmare, torment, torture *Ant* heaven, paradise ♦ [4] bedlam, circus, madhouse ♦ [4] chaos, confusion, disarray, disorder, disorganization, havoc, jumble, mess, muddle, shambles

hel•la•cious \ˌhe-ˈlā-shəs\ *adj* **1** : exceptionally powerful or violent **2** : remarkably good **3** : extremely difficult **4** : extraordinarily large
hell–bent \ˈhel-ˌbent\ *adj* ♦ : stubbornly determined

♦ bound, decisive, determined, firm, intent, purposeful, resolute, set, single-minded

hell•cat \-ˌkat\ *n* **1** : WITCH 2 **2** : a violently temperamental person; *esp* : an ill-tempered woman
hel•le•bore \ˈhe-lə-ˌbōr\ *n* **1** : any of a genus of poisonous herbs related to the buttercups; *also* : the dried root of a hellebore **2** : a poisonous plant related to the lilies; *also* : its dried roots used in medicine and insecticides
Hel•lene \ˈhe-ˌlēn\ *n* : GREEK
Hel•le•nism \ˈhe-lə-ˌni-zəm\ *n* : a body of humanistic and classical ideals associated with ancient Greece — **Hel•len•ic** \he-ˈle-nik\ *adj* — **Hel•le•nist** \ˈhe-lə-nist\ *n*
Hel•le•nis•tic \ˌhe-lə-ˈnis-tik\ *adj* : of or relating to Greek history, culture, or art after Alexander the Great
hell–for–leather *adv* : at full speed
hell•gram•mite \ˈhel-grə-ˌmīt\ *n* : an aquatic insect larva that is used as bait in fishing

hell•hole \ˈhel-ˌhōl\ *n* : a place of extreme misery or squalor
hel•lion \ˈhel-yən\ *n* ♦ : a troublesome or mischievous person

♦ devil, imp, mischief, monkey, rapscallion, rascal, rogue, scamp, urchin

hel•lo \hə-ˈlō, he-\ *n, pl* **hellos** ♦ : an expression of greeting — used interjectionally

♦ greeting, salutation, salute ***Ant*** adieu, bon voyage, farewell, Godspeed, good-bye

helm \ˈhelm\ *n* **1** : a lever or wheel for steering a ship **2** ♦ : a position of control

♦ chair, head, headship, rein

hel•met \ˈhel-mət\ *n* : a protective covering for the head
helms•man \ˈhelmz-mən\ *n* ♦ : the person at the helm

♦ boss, captain, chief, foreman, head, headman, kingpin, leader, master, taskmaster

hel•ot \ˈhe-lət\ *n* : SLAVE, SERF
¹help \ˈhelp\ *vb* **1** ♦ : to give assistance or support to : AID **2** ♦ : to make more pleasant or bearable **3** : to be of use; *also* : PROMOTE **4** : to change for the better **5 a** : to refrain from **b** : to keep from occurring : PREVENT **6** : to serve with food or drink ⟨~ yourself⟩

♦ [1] abet, aid, assist, back, prop, support ***Ant*** hinder ♦ [2] allay, alleviate, assuage, ease, mitigate, mollify, palliate, relieve, soothe ***Ant*** aggravate

²help *n* **1 a** ♦ : the act of helping : help given **b** ♦ : a source of aid **2** : REMEDY, RELIEF **3** : one who assists another **4** ♦ : one employed by another usually for wages or salary and in a position below the executive level — often used collectively

♦ [1a] aid, assist, assistance, backing, boost, lift, support ***Ant*** hindrance ♦ [1b] advantage, aid, benefit, boon ***Ant*** disadvantage, drawback, hindrance, impediment ♦ [4] force, personnel, pool, staff

help•er \ˈhel-pər\ *n* ♦ : one that helps

♦ aid, apprentice, assistant, deputy, helpmate, mate, sidekick

helper T cell *n* : a T cell that participates in the immune response by recognizing foreign antigens and has a protein on its surface to which HIV attaches
help•ful \-fəl\ *adj* ♦ : of service or assistance — **help•ful•ly** *adv* — **help•ful•ness** *n*

♦ advantageous, beneficial, favorable (*or* favourable), profitable, salutary

help•ing *n* : a portion of food
help•less \-ləs\ *adj* **1** ♦ : lacking protection or support : DEFENSELESS **2** ♦ : marked by an inability to act or react — **help•less•ly** *adv* — **help•less•ness** *n*

♦ [1] defenseless (*or* defenceless), exposed, susceptible, undefended, unguarded, unprotected, unresistant, vulnerable ***Ant*** guarded, invulnerable, protected, resistant, shielded ♦ [2] impotent, powerless, weak

help•mate \ˈhelp-ˌmāt\ *n* **1** ♦ : one that helps : HELPER **2** ♦ : a female partner in a marriage : WIFE

♦ [1] aid, apprentice, assistant, deputy, helper, mate, sidekick ♦ [2] lady, old lady, wife

help•meet \-ˌmēt\ *n* **1** : one that helps : HELPMATE **2** : a female partner in a marriage : WIFE
hel•ter–skel•ter \ˌhel-tər-ˈskel-tər\ *adv* **1** : in undue haste or disorder **2** ♦ : in a haphazard manner

♦ amok, berserk, frantically, harum-scarum, hectically, madly, pell-mell, wild, wildly

helve \ˈhelv\ *n* : a handle of a tool or weapon
Hel•ve•tian \hel-ˈvē-shən\ *adj* : SWISS — **Helvetian** *n*
¹hem \ˈhem\ *n* **1** : a border of an article (as of cloth) doubled back and stitched down **2** : RIM, MARGIN
²hem *vb* **hemmed; hem•ming** **1** : to make a hem in sewing; *also* : BORDER, EDGE **2** ♦ : to surround restrictively

♦ cage, closet, coop up, corral, encase, enclose, envelop, fence, hedge, house, immure, pen, wall

he–man \ˈhē-ˌman\ *n* : a strong virile man
he•ma•tite \ˈhē-mə-ˌtīt\ *n* : a mineral that consists of an oxide of iron and that constitutes an important iron ore
he•ma•tol•o•gy \ˌhē-mə-ˈtä-lə-jē\ *n* : a branch of biology that deals with the blood and blood-forming organs — **he•ma•to•log•ic** \-tə-ˈlä-jik\ *also* **he•ma•to•log•i•cal** \-ji-kəl\ *adj* — **he•ma•tol•o•gist** \-ˈtä-lə-jist\ *n*
he•ma•to•ma \-ˈtō-mə\ *n, pl* **mas** *also* **-ma•ta** \-mə-tə\ : a usually clotted mass of blood forming as a result of a broken blood vessel
heme \ˈhēm\ *n* : the deep red iron-containing part of hemoglobin
hemi•sphere \ˈhe-mə-ˌsfir\ *n* **1** : one of the halves of the earth as divided by the equator into northern and southern parts or by a meridian into eastern and western parts **2** : either of two half spheres formed by a plane through the sphere's center — **hemi•spher•ic** \ˌhe-mə-ˈsfir-ik, -ˈsfer-\ *or* **hemi•spher•i•cal** \-ˈsfir-i-kəl, -ˈsfer-\ *adj*
hem•line \ˈhem-ˌlīn\ *n* : the line formed by the lower edge of a garment
hem•lock \ˈhem-ˌläk\ *n* **1** : any of several poisonous herbs related to the carrot **2** : an evergreen tree related to the pines; *also* : its soft light wood
he•mo•glo•bin \ˈhē-mə-ˌglō-bən\ *n* : an iron-containing compound found in red blood cells that carries oxygen from the lungs to the body tissues
he•mo•phil•ia \ˌhē-mə-ˈfi-lē-ə\ *n* : a hereditary blood defect usually of males that slows blood clotting with resulting difficulty in stopping bleeding — **he•mo•phil•i•ac** \-lē-ˌak\ *adj or n*
hem•or•rhage \ˈhem-rij, ˈhe-mə-\ *n* : a large discharge of blood from the blood vessels — **hemorrhage** *vb* — **hem•or•rhag•ic** \ˌhe-mə-ˈra-jik\ *adj*
hem•or•rhoid \ˈhem-ˌrȯid, ˈhe-mə-\ *n* : a swollen mass of dilated veins at or just within the anus — usually used in plural
hemp \ˈhemp\ *n* : a tall widely grown Asian herb related to the mulberry that is the source of a tough fiber used in rope and of marijuana and hashish from its flowers and leaves; *also* : the fiber — **hemp•en** \ˈhem-pən\ *adj*
hem•stitch \ˈhem-ˌstich\ *vb* : to embroider (fabric) by drawing out parallel threads and stitching the exposed threads in groups to form designs
hen \ˈhen\ *n* : a female chicken especially over a year old; *also* : a female bird
hence \ˈhens\ *adv* **1** : AWAY **2** : from this time **3** ♦ : because of a preceding fact or premise : CONSEQUENTLY **4** : from this source or origin

♦ accordingly, consequently, ergo, so, therefore, thus, wherefore

hence•forth \hens-ˌfōrth\ *adv* : from this point on
hence•for•ward \-ˈfȯr-wərd\ *adv* : HENCEFORTH
hench•man \ˈhench-mən\ *n* : a trusted follower or supporter
hen•na \ˈhe-nə\ *n* **1** : an Old World tropical shrub with fragrant white flowers; *also* : a reddish brown dye obtained from its leaves and used especially on hair **2** : the color of henna dye
hen•peck \ˈhen-ˌpek\ *vb* ♦ : to nag and boss one's husband

♦ hound, nag, needle

hep \ˈhep\ *adj* : HIP
hep•a•rin \ˈhe-pə-rən\ *n* : a compound found especially in liver that slows the clotting of blood and is used medically
he•pat•ic \hi-ˈpa-tik\ *adj* : of, relating to, or associated with the liver
he•pat•i•ca \hi-ˈpa-ti-kə\ *n* : any of a genus of herbs related to the buttercups that have lobed leaves and delicate white, pink, or bluish flowers
hep•a•ti•tis \ˌhe-pə-ˈtī-təs\ *n, pl* **-tit•i•des** \-ˈti-tə-ˌdēz\ : inflammation of the liver; *also* : a virus disease of which this is a feature
hep•tam•e•ter \hep-ˈta-mə-tər\ *n* : a line of verse containing seven metrical feet
hep•tath•lon \hep-ˈtath-lən, -ˌlän\ *n* : a 7-event athletic contest for women
¹her \ˈhər\ *adj* : of or relating to her or herself
²her *pron, objective case of* SHE
¹her•ald \ˈher-əld\ *n* **1** : an official crier or messenger **2** ♦ : one that precedes or foreshadows : HARBINGER **3** : ANNOUNCER **4** : ADVOCATE

♦ angel, forerunner, harbinger, precursor

²herald *vb* **1** : to give notice of **2** : HAIL, GREET; *also* : PUBLICIZE
he•ral•dic \he-ˈral-dik, hə-\ *adj* : of or relating to heralds or heraldry
her•ald•ry \ˈher-əl-drē\ *n, pl* **-ries** **1** : the practice of devising and granting armorial insignia and of tracing genealogies **2** : INSIGNIA **3** : PAGEANTRY
herb \ˈərb, ˈhərb\ *n* **1** : a seed plant that lacks woody tissue and dies to the ground at the end of a growing season **2** : a plant or plant part valued for medicinal or savory qualities — **her•ba•ceous** \ˌər-ˈbā-shəs, ˌhər-\ *adj*
herb•age \ˈər-bij, ˈhər-\ *n* ♦ : green plants especially when used or fit for grazing

♦ flora, foliage, green, greenery, leafage, vegetation, verdure

herb•al \ˈər-bəl, ˈhər-\ *adj* : of, relating to, utilizing, or made of herbs
herb•al•ist \ˈər-bə-list, ˈhər-\ *n* **1** : a person who practices healing by the use of herbs **2** : a person who collects or grows herbs
her•bar•i•um \ˌər-ˈbar-ē-əm, ˌhər-\ *n, pl* **-ia** \-ē-ə\ **1** : a collection of dried plant specimens **2** : a place that houses an herbarium
her•bi•cide \ˈər-bə-ˌsīd, ˈhər-\ *n* : an agent used to destroy or inhibit plant growth — **her•bi•cid•al** \ˌər-bə-ˈsīd-ᵊl, ˌhər-\ *adj*
her•biv•o•rous \ˌər-ˈbi-və-rəs, ˌhər-\ *adj* : feeding on plants — **her•bi•vore** \ˈər-bə-ˌvōr, ˈhər-\ *n*
her•cu•le•an \ˌhər-kyə-ˈlē-ən, ˌhər-ˈkyü-lē-\ *adj, often cap* ♦ : of extraordinary power, size, or difficulty

♦ arduous, demanding, difficult, exacting, formidable, grueling, hard, laborious, murderous, rough, stiff, strenuous, tall, toilsome, tough

¹herd \ˈhərd\ *n* **1** : a group of animals of one kind kept or living together **2** : a group of people with a common bond **3** ♦ : the undistinguished masses : MOB

♦ commoners, masses, mob, people, plebeians, populace, rank and file

²herd *vb* ♦ : to assemble or move in or as if in a herd — **herd•er** *n*

♦ drive, punch, run

herds•man \ˈhərdz-mən\ *n* : one who manages, breeds, or tends livestock
¹here \ˈhir\ *adv* **1** : in or at this place; *also* : NOW **2** : at or in this point, particular, or case **3** : in the present life or state **4** : to this place
²here *n* : this place <get away from ~>
here•abouts \ˈhir-ə-ˌbau̇ts\ *or* **here•about** \-ˌbau̇t\ *adv* : in this vicinity
¹here•af•ter \hir-ˈaf-tər\ *adv* **1** : after this in sequence or in time **2** : in some future time or state
²hereafter *n, often cap* **1** : time that is to come : FUTURE **2** ♦ : an existence beyond earthly life

♦ afterlife, eternity, immortality

here•by \hir-ˈbī\ *adv* : by means of this
he•red•i•tary \hə-ˈre-də-ˌter-ē\ *adj* **1** ♦ : genetically passed or passable from parent to offspring **2** : passing by inheritance; *also* : having title or possession through inheritance **3** : of a kind established by tradition

♦ genetic, heritable, inborn, inherited

he•red•i•ty \-də-tē\ *n* : the characteristics and potentialities genetically derived from one's ancestors; *also* : the passing of these from ancestor to descendant
Her•e•ford \ˈhər-fərd\ *n* : any of a breed of red-coated beef cattle with white faces and markings
here•in \hir-ˈin\ *adv* : in this
here•of \-ˈəv, -ˈäv\ *adv* : of this
here•on \-ˈȯn, -ˈän\ *adv* : on this
her•e•sy \ˈher-ə-sē\ *n, pl* **-sies** **1** : adherence to a religious opinion contrary to church dogma **2** : an opinion or doctrine contrary to church dogma **3** ♦ : dissent from a dominant theory, opinion, or practice

♦ dissent, heterodoxy, nonconformity *Ant* conformity, orthodoxy

her•e•tic \ˈher-ə-ˌtik\ *n* ♦ : one who dissents from an accepted belief or doctrine

♦ dissenter, dissident, nonconformist

he•ret•i•cal \hə-ˈre-ti-kəl\ *adj* ♦ : of, relating to, or characterized by departure from accepted beliefs or standards

♦ dissident, heterodox, nonconforming, nonconformist, nonorthodox, unconventional, unorthodox *Ant* conforming, conventional, orthodox

here•to \hir-ˈtü\ *adv* : to this document
here•to•fore \ˈhir-tə-ˌfōr\ *adv* ♦ : up to this time

♦ hitherto, yet

here•un•der \hir-ˈən-dər\ *adv* : under this or according to this writing
here•un•to \hir-ˈən-tü\ *adv* : to this
here•upon \ˈhir-ə-ˌpȯn, -ˌpän\ *adv* : on this or immediately after this
here•with \ˈhir-ˈwith, -ˈwith\ *adv* **1** : with this **2** : HEREBY
her•i•ta•ble \ˈher-ə-tə-bəl\ *adj* ♦ : capable of being inherited

♦ genetic, hereditary, inborn, inherited

her•i•tage \ˈher-ə-tij\ *n* **1** : property that descends to an heir **2** ♦ : something transmitted by or acquired from a predecessor : LEGACY **3** : BIRTHRIGHT

♦ bequest, birthright, inheritance, legacy

her•maph•ro•dite \(ˌ)hər-ˈma-frə-ˌdīt\ *n* : an animal or plant having both male and female reproductive organs — **hermaphrodite** *adj* — **her•maph•ro•dit•ic** \(ˌ)hər-ˌma-frə-ˈdi-tik\ *adj*
her•met•ic \hər-ˈme-tik\ *also* **her•met•i•cal** \-ti-kəl\ *adj* : AIRTIGHT — **her•met•i•cal•ly** \-ti-k(ə-)lē\ *adv*
her•mit \ˈhər-mət\ *n* ♦ : one who lives in solitude especially for religious reasons

♦ anchorite, recluse, solitary

her•mit•age \-mə-tij\ *n* **1** : the dwelling of a hermit **2** : a secluded dwelling
hermit crab *n* : any of numerous crabs that occupy empty mollusk shells
her•nia \ˈhər-nē-ə\ *n, pl* **-ni•as** *or* **-ni•ae** \-nē-ˌē, -nē-ˌī\ : a protrusion of a bodily part (as a loop of intestine) into a pouch of the weakened wall of a cavity in which it is normally enclosed — **her•ni•ate** \-nē-ˌāt\ *vb* — **her•ni•a•tion** \ˌhər-nē-ˈā-shən\ *n*
he•ro \ˈhē-rō\ *n, pl* **heroes** **1** : a mythological or legendary figure of great strength or ability **2** : a man admired for his achievements and qualities **3** : the chief male character in a literary or dramatic work **4** *pl usu* **heros** : a large sandwich on a long split roll : SUBMARINE 2
he•ro•ic \hi-ˈrō-ik\ *adj* **1** : of, relating to, resembling, or suggesting heroes especially of antiquity **2** ♦ : exhibiting or marked by courage and daring **3** ♦ : of impressive size, power, extent, or effect

♦ [2] brave, courageous, dauntless, doughty, fearless, gallant, greathearted, intrepid, lionhearted, manful, stalwart, stout, undaunted, valiant, valorous ♦ [3] august, baronial, gallant, glorious, grand, grandiose, imposing, magnificent, majestic, monumental, noble, proud, regal, royal, splendid, stately

he•ro•i•cal•ly \hi-ˈrō-i-k(ə-)lē\ *adv* ♦ : in a heroic manner

♦ gallantly, grandly, greatly, honorably (*or* honourably), magnanimously, nobly

heroic couplet *n* : a rhyming couplet in iambic pentameter
he•ro•ics \hi-ˈrō-iks\ *n pl* : heroic or showy behavior
her•o•in \ˈher-ə-wən\ *n* : an illicit addictive narcotic drug made from morphine
her•o•ine \ˈher-ə-wən\ *n* **1** : a woman admired for her achievements and qualities **2** : the chief female character in a literary or dramatic work
her•o•ism \ˈher-ə-ˌwi-zəm\ *n* **1** ♦ : heroic conduct **2** : the qualities of a hero

♦ bravery, courage, daring, fearlessness, gallantry, guts, hardihood, heart, nerve, stoutness, valor

her•on \ˈher-ən\ *n, pl* **herons** *also* **heron** : any of various long-legged long-billed wading birds with soft plumage
her•pes \ˈhər-pēz\ *n* : any of several virus diseases characterized by the formation of blisters on the skin or mucous membranes
herpes sim•plex \-ˈsim-ˌpleks\ *n* : either of two virus diseases marked in one by watery blisters above the waist (as on the mouth and lips) and in the other on the sex organs
herpes zos•ter \-ˈzäs-tər\ *n* : SHINGLES
her•pe•tol•o•gy \ˌhər-pə-ˈtä-lə-jē\ *n* : a branch of zoology dealing with reptiles and amphibians — **her•pe•tol•o•gist** \ˌhər-pə-ˈtä-lə-jist\ *n*
her•ring \ˈher-iŋ\ *n, pl* **herring** *or* **herrings** : a valuable narrow-bodied food fish of the north Atlantic; *also* : a related fish of the north Pacific harvested especially for its roe
her•ring•bone \ˈher-iŋ-ˌbōn\ *n* : a pattern made up of rows of parallel lines with adjacent rows slanting in reverse directions; *also* : a twilled fabric with this pattern
hers \ˈhərz\ *pron* : one or the ones belonging to her
her•self \hər-ˈself\ *pron* : SHE, HER — used reflexively, for emphasis, or in absolute constructions
hertz \ˈhərts, ˈherts\ *n, pl* **hertz** : a unit of frequency equal to one cycle per second
hes•i•tance \ˈhe-zə-təns\ *n* : HESITANCY
hes•i•tan•cy \ˈhe-zə-tən-sē\ *n* **1** ♦ : the quality or state of being hesitant **2** ♦ : an act or instance of hesitating

♦ [1] disinclination, reluctance, reticence ♦ [2] hesitation, indecision, irresolution, vacillation

hes•i•tant \ˈhe-zə-tənt\ *adj* ♦ : tending to hesitate — **hes•i•tant•ly** *adv*

♦ afraid, dubious, indisposed, reluctant *Ant* disposed, inclined

hes•i•tate \ˈhe-zə-ˌtāt\ *vb* **-tat•ed; -tat•ing** **1** ♦ **:** to hold back (as in doubt) **2 :** PAUSE

♦ falter, hang back, shilly-shally, stagger, teeter, vacillate, waver, wobble *Ant* dive (in), plunge (in)

hes•i•ta•tion \ˌhe-zə-ˈtā-shən\ *n* ♦ **:** an act or instance of hesitating

♦ hesitancy, indecision, irresolution, vacillation

het•ero•dox \ˈhe-tə-rə-ˌdäks\ *adj* **1** ♦ **:** differing from an acknowledged standard **2** ♦ **:** holding unorthodox opinions

♦ [1, 2] dissident, heretical, nonconforming, nonconformist, nonorthodox, unconventional, unorthodox

het•er•o•doxy \ˈhe-tə-rə-ˌdäk-sē\ *n* ♦ **:** the quality or state of being heterodox

♦ dissent, heresy, nonconformity

het•er•o•ge•neous \ˌhe-tə-rə-ˈjē-nē-əs, -nyəs\ *adj* ♦ **:** consisting of dissimilar ingredients or constituents **:** MIXED — **het•er•o•ge•ne•ity** \-jə-ˈnē-ə-tē\ *n* — **het•er•o•ge•neous•ly** *adv*

♦ assorted, miscellaneous, mixed, motley, varied

het•ero•glos•sia \ˌhe-tə-rō-ˈglä-sē-ə, -ˈglȯ-\ *n* **:** a diversity of voices, styles of discourse, or points of view in a literary work

het•ero•sex•ism \ˌhe-tə-rō-ˈsek-si-zəm\ *n* **:** discrimination or prejudice by heterosexuals against homosexuals

het•ero•sex•u•al \ˌhe-tə-rō-ˌsek-shə-wəl\ *adj* **1 :** of, relating to, or marked by sexual interest in the opposite sex; *also* **:** of, relating to, or involving sexual intercourse between members of opposite sex **2 :** of or relating to different sexes — **heterosexual** *n* — **het•ero•sex•u•al•i•ty** \-ˌsek-shə-ˈwa-lə-tē\ *n*

hew \ˈhyü\ *vb* **hewed; hewed** *or* **hewn** \ˈhyün\; **hew•ing** **1** ♦ **:** to cut or fell with blows (as of an ax) **2 :** to give shape to with or as if with an ax **3** ♦ **:** to conform or adhere strictly ⟨∼ to tradition⟩ — **hew•er** *n*

♦ [1] chop, cut, fell ♦ *usu* **hew to** [3] adhere, cling, stick

HEW *abbr* Department of Health, Education, and Welfare

¹hex \ˈheks\ *vb* **1 :** to practice witchcraft **2 :** JINX **3** ♦ **:** to put a hex on

♦ bewitch, charm, enchant, spell

²hex *n* **1** ♦ **:** a person who practices witchcraft **:** WITCH **2 :** SPELL, JINX

♦ enchantress, hag, witch

³hex *adj* **:** HEXAGONAL

⁴hex *abbr* hexagon

hexa•gon \ˈhek-sə-ˌgän\ *n* **:** a polygon having six angles and six sides — **hex•ag•o•nal** \hek-ˈsa-gən-ᵊl\ *adj*

hex•am•e•ter \hek-ˈsa-mə-tər\ *n* **:** a line of verse containing six metrical feet

hey \ˈhā\ *interj* — used especially to call attention or to express doubt, surprise, or joy

hey•day \ˈhā-ˌdā\ *n* ♦ **:** a period of greatest strength, vigor, or prosperity

♦ bloom, blossom, flower, flush, prime

hf *abbr* half

Hf *symbol* hafnium

HF *abbr* high frequency

hg *abbr* hectogram

Hg *symbol* mercury

hgt *abbr* height

hgwy *abbr* highway

HH *abbr* **1** Her Highness **2** His Highness **3** His Holiness

HHS *abbr* Department of Health and Human Services

HI *abbr* **1** Hawaii **2** humidity index

hi•a•tus \hī-ˈā-təs\ *n* **1 :** a break in an object **:** GAP **2** ♦ **:** a lapse in continuity

♦ discontinuity, gap, interim, interlude, intermission, interruption, interval

hi•ba•chi \hi-ˈbä-chē\ *n* **:** a charcoal brazier

hi•ber•nate \ˈhī-bər-ˌnāt\ *vb* **-nat•ed; -nat•ing** **:** to pass the winter in a torpid or resting state — **hi•ber•na•tion** \ˌhī-bər-ˈnā-shən\ *n* — **hi•ber•na•tor** \ˈhī-bər-ˌnā-tər\ *n*

hi•bis•cus \hī-ˈbis-kəs, hə-\ *n* **:** any of a genus of herbs, shrubs, and trees related to the mallows and noted for large showy flowers

hic•cup *also* **hic•cough** \ˈhi-(ˌ)kəp\ *n* **1 :** a spasmodic breathing movement checked by sudden closing of the glottis accompanied by a peculiar sound; *also, pl* **:** an attack of hiccuping **2 :** a slight irregularity, error, or malfunction **3 :** a brief minor interruption or change — **hiccup** *vb*

hick \ˈhik\ *n* ♦ **:** an awkward provincial person — **hick** *adj*

♦ bumpkin, clodhopper, hillbilly, provincial, rustic, yokel *Ant* cosmopolitan

hick•o•ry \ˈhi-kə-rē\ *n, pl* **-ries** **:** any of a genus of No. American hardwood trees related to the walnuts; *also* **:** the wood of a hickory — **hickory** *adj*

hi•dal•go \hi-ˈdal-gō\ *n, pl* **-gos** *often cap* **:** a member of the lower nobility of Spain

hidden tax *n* **1 :** a tax ultimately paid by someone other than the person on whom it is formally levied **2 :** an economic injustice that reduces one's income or buying power

¹hide \ˈhīd\ *vb* **hid** \ˈhid\; **hid•den** \ˈhid-ᵊn\ *or* **hid; hid•ing** **1** ♦ **:** to put or remain out of sight **2 :** to conceal for shelter or protection; *also* **:** to seek protection **3** ♦ **:** to keep secret **4 :** to turn away in shame or anger — **hid•er** *n*

♦ [1] bury, cache, conceal, ensconce, secrete *Ant* display, exhibit ♦ [3] blanket, blot out, cloak, conceal, cover, curtain, enshroud, mask, obscure, occult, screen, shroud, veil *Ant* bare, disclose, display, divulge, expose, reveal, show, uncloak, uncover, unmask, unveil

²hide *n* ♦ **:** the skin of an animal

♦ fur, pelt, skin

³hide *vb* **:** to give a beating to

hide–and–seek \ˌhīd-ᵊn-ˈsēk\ *n* **:** a children's game in which everyone hides from one player who tries to find them

hide•away \ˈhī-də-ˌwā\ *n* **:** a place of refuge, retreat, or concealment **:** HIDEOUT

hide•bound \ˈhīd-ˌbau̇nd\ *adj* ♦ **:** being inflexible or conservative

♦ conservative, old-fashioned, orthodox, reactionary, traditional

hid•eous \ˈhi-dē-əs\ *adj* **1** ♦ **:** offensive to one of the senses **:** UGLY **2** ♦ **:** morally offensive **:** SHOCKING — **hid•eous•ly** *adv*

♦ [1] grotesque, ugly, unappealing, unattractive, unlovely, unsightly, vile ♦ [2] appalling, atrocious, awful, dreadful, frightful, ghastly, grisly, gruesome, horrible, horrid, lurid, macabre, monstrous, nightmarish, shocking, terrible

hid•eous•ness \-nəs\ *n* ♦ **:** the quality or state of being hideous

♦ atrociousness, atrocity, frightfulness, horror, monstrosity, repulsiveness

hide•out \ˈhī-ˌdau̇t\ *n* ♦ **:** a place of refuge or concealment

♦ concealment, covert, den, lair, nest

hie \ˈhī\ *vb* **hied; hy•ing** *or* **hie•ing** ♦ **:** to move or act quickly **:** HASTEN

♦ accelerate, fast-track, hasten, hurry, quicken, rush, speed, whisk

hi•er•ar•chy \ˈhī-ə-ˌrär-kē\ *n, pl* **-chies** **1 :** a ruling body of clergy organized into ranks **2 :** persons or things arranged in a graded series — **hi•er•ar•chi•cal** \ˌhī-ə-ˈrär-ki-kəl\ *adj* — **hi•er•ar•chi•cal•ly** \-k(ə-)lē\ *adv*

hi•er•o•glyph•ic \ˌhī-ə-rə-ˈgli-fik\ *n* **1 :** a character in a system of picture writing (as of the ancient Egyptians) **2 :** a symbol or sign difficult to decipher

hi–fi \ˈhī-ˈfī\ *n* **1 :** HIGH FIDELITY **2 :** equipment for reproduction of sound with high fidelity

¹hig•gle•dy–pig•gle•dy \ˌhi-gəl-dē-ˈpi-gəl-dē\ *adv* **:** in confusion

²higgledy–piggledy *adj* ♦ **:** lacking order

♦ chaotic, disheveled, disordered, disorderly, hugger-mugger, messy, pell-mell, topsy-turvy, unkempt, untidy

¹high \ˈhī\ *adj* **1 a** ♦ **:** having large extension upward ⟨a ∼ wall⟩ **b :** having a specified elevation **:** TALL ⟨six feet ∼⟩ **2 :** advanced toward fullness or culmination; *also* **:** slightly tainted **3 :** advanced especially in complexity ⟨∼*er* mathematics⟩ **4 :** long past **5 :** SHRILL, SHARP **6 :** far from the equator ⟨∼ latitudes⟩ **7 :** exalted in character **8** ♦ **:** of greater degree, size, or amount than average ⟨∼ in cholesterol⟩ ⟨∼ prices⟩ **9** ♦ **:** of relatively great importance **10 :** FORCIBLE, STRONG ⟨∼ winds⟩ **11 :** showing elation or excitement **12** ♦ **:** excited or stupefied by alcohol or a drug **:** INTOXICATED; *also* **:** excited or stupefied as if by a drug **13** ♦ **:** dear in price **:** EXPENSIVE

♦ [1a] lofty, tall, towering *Ant* low, short, squat ♦ [8] advanced, up *Ant* down, low ♦ [9] chief, first, foremost, head, lead, preeminent, premier, primary, prime, principal, supreme

◆ [12] drunk, inebriate, intoxicated, tipsy ◆ [13] costly, dear, expensive, precious, valuable

²**high** *adv* **1 :** at or to a high place or degree **2** ◆ **:** in a luxurious manner ⟨living ~⟩

◆ expensively, extravagantly, grandly, lavishly, luxuriously, opulently, richly ***Ant*** austerely, humbly, modestly, plainly, simply

³**high** *n* **1 a :** an elevated place **b :** the space overhead **:** SKY **2 :** a region of high barometric pressure **3 :** a high point or level **4 :** the gear of a vehicle giving the highest speed **5 :** an excited or stupefied state produced by or as if by a drug

high•ball \ˈhī-ˌbȯl\ *n* **:** a usually tall drink of liquor mixed with water or a carbonated beverage

high beam *n* **:** the long-range focus of a vehicle headlight

high•born \ˈhī-ˈbȯrn\ *adj* ◆ **:** of noble birth

◆ aristocratic, genteel, gentle, grand, noble, patrician, wellborn

high•boy \-ˌbȯi\ *n* **:** a high chest of drawers mounted on a base with legs

high•bred \-ˈbred\ *adj* **:** coming from superior stock

high•brow \-ˌbrau̇\ *n* ◆ **:** a person of superior learning or culture — **highbrow** *adj* — **high•brow•ism** \-ˌbrau̇-ˌi-zəm\ *n*

◆ egghead, intellectual, nerd

high–definition *adj* **:** being or relating to a television system with twice as many scan lines per frame as a conventional system

high–density li•po•pro•tein \-ˌlī-pō-ˈprō-tēn, -ˌli-\ *n* **:** HDL

high•er–up \ˌhī-ər-ˈəp\ *n* **:** a superior officer or official

high•fa•lu•tin \ˌhī-fə-ˈlüt-ᵊn\ *adj* **1** ◆ **:** characterized by or reflecting an attitude of self-importance or superciliousness **2** ◆ **:** expressed in or marked by the use of high-flown bombastic language

◆ [1] disdainful, haughty, lofty, lordly, prideful, proud, superior ◆ [1, 2] affected, grandiose, ostentatious, pompous, pretentious ◆ [2] florid, flowery, grandiloquent, high-flown

high fashion *n* **1 :** HIGH STYLE **2 :** HAUTE COUTURE

high fidelity *n* **:** the reproduction of sound or image with a high degree of faithfulness to the original

high five *n* **:** a slapping of upraised right hands by two people (as in celebration) — **high–five** *vb*

high–flown \ˈhī-ˈflōn\ *adj* **1** ◆ **:** exceedingly or excessively high or favorable **2** ◆ **:** having an excessively embellished or inflated character

◆ [1] eloquent, formal, lofty, majestic, stately, towering ◆ [2] florid, flowery, grandiloquent, highfalutin

high frequency *n* **:** a radio frequency between 3 and 30 megahertz

high gear *n* **1 :** HIGH 4 **2 :** a state of intense or maximum activity

high–hand•ed \ˈhī-ˈhan-dəd\ *adj* ◆ **:** having or showing no regard for the rights, concerns, or feelings of others — **high–hand•ed•ly** *adv* — **high–hand•ed•ness** *n*

◆ arbitrary, dictatorial, imperious, peremptory, willful

¹**high–hat** \-ˈhat\ *adj* ◆ **:** assuming an attitude of superiority **:** SUPERCILIOUS

◆ arrogant, cavalier, haughty, high-handed, highfalutin, imperious, important, lofty, lordly, masterful, overweening, peremptory, pompous, presumptuous, pretentious, supercilious, superior, uppity

²**high–hat** *vb* ◆ **:** to treat snobbishly

◆ disdain, scorn, slight, sniff at, snub

high jinks \ˈhī-ˌjiŋks\ *n pl* ◆ **:** boisterous or rambunctious carryings-on

◆ foolery, horseplay, monkeyshines, roughhouse, shenanigans, tomfoolery

high•land \ˈhī-lənd\ *n* ◆ **:** elevated or mountainous land

◆ elevation, eminence, height, hill, mound, prominence, rise

high•land•er \-lən-dər\ *n* **1 :** an inhabitant of a highland **2** *cap* **:** an inhabitant of the Scottish Highlands

high–lev•el \ˈhī-ˈle-vəl\ *adj* **1 :** being of high importance or rank **2 :** being or relating to highly concentrated and environmentally hazardous nuclear waste

¹**high•light** \-ˌlīt\ *n* **:** an event or detail of major importance

²**highlight** *vb* **1** ◆ **:** to center attention on **:** EMPHASIZE **2 :** to constitute a highlight of

◆ accent, accentuate, emphasize, feature, play, point, stress, underline, underscore

high•light•er \-ˌlī-tər\ *n* **:** a pen with transparent ink used for marking text passages

high•ly \ˈhī-lē\ *adv* **1 :** in or to a high place, level, or rank **2** ◆ **:** in or to a high degree or amount **3 :** with approval **:** FAVORABLY

◆ especially, extremely, greatly, hugely, mightily, mighty, mortally, most, much, real, right, so, very

high–mind•ed \-ˈmīn-dəd\ *adj* ◆ **:** marked by elevated principles and feelings — **high–mind•ed•ness** *n*

◆ chivalrous, gallant, great, greathearted, high, lofty, lordly, magnanimous, noble, sublime

high•ness \ˈhī-nəs\ *n* **1 :** the quality or state of being high **2** — used as a title (as for kings)

high–pres•sure \-ˈpre-shər\ *adj* ◆ **:** using or involving aggressive and insistent sales techniques

◆ aggressive, ambitious, assertive, enterprising, fierce, go-getting, militant, self-assertive

high–rise \-ˈrīz\ *adj* **:** having several stories and being equipped with elevators ⟨~ apartments⟩; *also* **:** of or relating to high-rise buildings

high road *n* **:** HIGHWAY

high school *n* **:** a school usually including grades 9 to 12 or 10 to 12

high sea *n* **:** the open sea outside territorial waters — usually used in plural

high–sound•ing \ˈhī-ˈsau̇n-diŋ\ *adj* **:** POMPOUS, IMPOSING

high–spir•it•ed \-ˈspir-ə-təd\ *adj* ◆ **:** characterized by a bold or energetic spirit

◆ bubbly, buoyant, effervescent, exuberant, frolicsome, vivacious ◆ fiery, mettlesome, peppery, spirited, spunky

high–strung \-ˈstrəŋ\ *adj* ◆ **:** having an extremely nervous or sensitive temperament

◆ excitable, flighty, fluttery, jittery, jumpy, nervous, skittish, spooky

high style *n* **:** the newest in fashion or design

high•tail \ˈhī-ˌtāl\ *vb* **:** to retreat at full speed

high tech \-ˈtek\ *n* **:** HIGH TECHNOLOGY

high technology *n* **:** technology involving the use of advanced devices

high–ten•sion \ˈhī-ˈten-chən\ *adj* **:** having or using a high voltage

high–test \-ˈtest\ *adj* **:** having a high octane number

high–tick•et \-ˈti-kət\ *adj* **:** EXPENSIVE

high–toned \-ˈtōnd\ *adj* **1 :** high in social, moral, or intellectual quality **2 :** PRETENTIOUS, POMPOUS

high•way \ˈhī-ˌwā\ *n* ◆ **:** a main direct road

◆ artery, pike, road, thoroughfare, turnpike, way

high•way•man \ˈhī-ˌwā-mən\ *n* **:** a person who robs travelers on a road

hi•jack *also* **high•jack** \ˈhī-ˌjak\ *vb* **:** to steal especially by stopping a vehicle on the highway; *also* **:** to commandeer a flying airplane — **hijack** *n* — **hi•jack•er** *n*

¹**hike** \ˈhīk\ *vb* **hiked; hik•ing 1** ◆ **:** to move or raise with a sudden motion **2 :** to take a long walk — **hik•er** *n*

◆ boost, crane, elevate, heave, heft, heighten, hoist, jack, lift, pick up, raise, up, uphold

²**hike** *n* **1 :** a long walk **2 :** RISE, INCREASE

hi•lar•i•ous \hi-ˈlar-ē-əs, hī-\ *adj* ◆ **:** marked by or providing boisterous merriment — **hi•lar•i•ous•ly** *adv*

◆ antic, comic, comical, droll, farcical, funny, humorous, hysterical, laughable, ludicrous, ridiculous, riotous, risible, screaming, uproarious

hi•lar•i•ty \hi-ˈlar-ə-tē, hī-\ *n* ◆ **:** boisterous and high-spirited merriment or laughter

◆ cheer, cheerfulness, cheeriness, glee, joviality, merriment, mirth

hill \ˈhil\ *n* **1** ◆ **:** a usually rounded elevation of land **2** ◆ **:** a little heap or mound (as of earth) — **hilly** *adj*

◆ [1] elevation, eminence, height, highland, mound, prominence, rise ◆ [2] cock, heap, mound, mountain, pile, rick, stack

hill•bil•ly \ˈhil-ˌbi-lē\ *n, pl* **-lies** ◆ **:** a person from a backwoods area

◆ bumpkin, clodhopper, hick, provincial, rustic, yokel

hill•ock \ˈhi-lək\ *n* **:** a small hill

hill•side \ˈhil-ˌsīd\ *n* **:** the part of a hill between the summit and the foot
hill•top \-ˌtäp\ *n* **:** the top of a hill
hilt \ˈhilt\ *n* **:** a handle especially of a sword or dagger
him \ˈhim\ *pron, objective case of* HE
Hi•ma•la•yan \ˌhi-mə-ˈlā-ən, hi-ˈmäl-yən\ *adj* **:** of, relating to, or characteristic of the Himalaya mountains or the people living there
him•self \him-ˈself\ *pron* **:** HE, HIM — used reflexively, for emphasis, or in absolute constructions
[1]**hind** \ˈhīnd\ *n, pl* **hinds** *also* **hind :** a female of a common Eurasian deer
[2]**hind** *adj* ♦ **:** of or forming the part that follows or is behind **:** REAR

♦ back, hindmost, posterior, rear

[1]**hin•der** \ˈhin-dər\ *vb* **1** ♦ **:** to impede the progress of **2 :** to hold back

♦ encumber, hamper, hold up, impede, inhibit, interfere with, obstruct, tie up

[2]**hind•er** \ˈhīn-dər\ *adj* **:** HIND
Hin•di \ˈhin-dē\ *n* **:** a literary and official language of northern India
hind•most \ˈhīnd-ˌmōst\ *adj* ♦ **:** farthest to the rear

♦ final, last, latter, terminal, ultimate

hind•quar•ter \-ˌkwȯr-tər\ *n* **1 :** one side of the back half of the carcass of a quadruped **2** *pl* **:** the part of the body of a quadruped behind the junction of hind limbs and trunk
hin•drance \ˈhin-drəns\ *n* **1 :** the state of being hindered; *also* **:** the action of hindering **2** ♦ **:** something that impedes **:** IMPEDIMENT

♦ bar, block, encumbrance, inhibition, obstacle

hind•sight \ˈhīnd-ˌsīt\ *n* **:** understanding of an event after it has happened
Hindu–Arabic *adj* **:** relating to, being, or composed of Arabic numerals
Hin•du•ism \ˈhin-dü-ˌi-zəm\ *n* **:** a body of religious beliefs and practices native to India — **Hin•du** *n or adj*
hind wing *n* **:** either of the posterior wings of a 4-winged insect
[1]**hinge** \ˈhinj\ *n* **:** a jointed device on which a swinging part (as a door, gate, or lid) turns
[2]**hinge** *vb* **hinged; hing•ing 1 :** to attach by or furnish with hinges **2 :** to be contingent on a single consideration
[1]**hint** \ˈhint\ *n* **1** ♦ **:** an indirect or summary suggestion **2** ♦ **:** a slight indication of the existence, approach, or nature of something **:** CLUE **3** ♦ **:** a very small amount

♦ [1, 2] clue, cue, indication, inkling, intimation, lead, suggestion ♦ [3] bit, dab, little, particle, suspicion, touch, trace

[2]**hint** *vb* ♦ **:** to give a hint

♦ allude, imply, indicate, infer, insinuate, intimate, suggest

hin•ter•land \ˈhin-tər-ˌland\ *n* **1 :** a region behind a coast **2** ♦ **:** a region remote from cities

♦ backwoods, bush, frontier, sticks, up-country

[1]**hip** \ˈhip\ *n* **:** the fruit of a rose
[2]**hip** *n* **1 :** the part of the body on either side below the waist consisting of the side of the pelvis and the upper thigh **2 :** HIP JOINT
[3]**hip** *adj* **hip•per; hip•pest :** keenly aware of or interested in the newest developments or styles — **hip•ness** *n*
[4]**hip** *vb* **hipped; hip•ping :** TELL, INFORM
hip•bone \ˈhip-ˈbōn, -ˌbōn\ *n* **:** the large flaring bone that makes a lateral half of the pelvis in mammals
hip–hop \ˈhip-ˌhäp\ *n* **1 :** a subculture especially of inner-city youths who are devotees of rap music **2 :** the stylized rhythmic music that accompanies rap
hip–hug•gers \ˈhip-ˌhə-gərz\ *n pl* **:** low-slung close-fitting pants that rest on the hips
hip joint *n* **:** the articulation between the femur and the hipbone
hipped \ˈhipt\ *adj* **:** having hips especially of a specified kind ⟨broad-*hipped*⟩
hip•pie *or* **hip•py** \ˈhi-pē\ *n, pl* **hippies :** a usually young person who rejects established mores and advocates nonviolence; *also* **:** a long-haired unconventionally dressed young person
hip•po \ˈhi-pō\ *n, pl* **hippos :** HIPPOPOTAMUS
hip•po•drome \ˈhi-pə-ˌdrōm\ *n* **:** an arena for equestrian performances
hip•po•pot•a•mus \ˌhi-pə-ˈpä-tə-məs\ *n, pl* **-mus•es** *or* **-mi** \-ˌmī\ **:** a large thick-skinned aquatic mammal of sub-Saharan Africa that is related to the swine

[1]**hire** \ˈhīr\ *n* **1 :** payment for labor or personal services **:** WAGES **2** ♦ **:** the state of being hired **:** EMPLOYMENT **3 :** one who is hired

♦ employ, employment, engagement *Ant* unemployment

[2]**hire** *vb* **hired; hir•ing 1** ♦ **:** to employ for pay **2** ♦ **:** to engage the temporary use of for pay **3 :** to take employment

♦ [1] employ, engage, retain, take on ♦ [2] engage, lease, let, rent

hire•ling \ˈhīr-liŋ\ *n* ♦ **:** a hired person; *esp* **:** one with mercenary motives

♦ employee, hand, jobholder, worker

hir•sute \ˈhər-ˌsüt, ˈhir-\ *adj* ♦ **:** covered with hair or hairlike material **:** HAIRY

♦ fleecy, furry, hairy, rough, shaggy, unshorn, woolly

[1]**his** \ˈhiz\ *adj* **:** of or relating to him or himself
[2]**his** *pron* **:** one or the ones belonging to him
His•pan•ic \hi-ˈspa-nik\ *adj* **:** of, relating to, or being a person of Latin-American descent living in the U.S. — **Hispanic** *n*
[1]**hiss** \ˈhis\ *vb* **:** to make a sharp sibilant sound; *also* **:** to express disapproval of by hissing
[2]**hiss** *n* **1** ♦ **:** a prolonged sibilant sound **2** ♦ **:** a hiss used to express disapproval

♦ [1] fizz, sizzle, swish, whish, whiz ♦ [2] boo, catcall, hoot, jeer, raspberry, snort

hissy fit \ˈhi-sē-\ *n* ♦ **:** a fit of bad temper **:** TANTRUM

♦ blowup, explosion, fireworks, fit, huff, scene, tantrum

hist *abbr* historian; historical; history
his•ta•mine \ˈhis-tə-ˌmēn, -mən\ *n* **:** a compound widespread in animal tissues that plays a major role in allergic reactions (as hay fever)
his•to•gram \ˈhis-tə-ˌgram\ *n* **:** a representation of statistical data by rectangles whose widths represent class intervals and whose heights usually represent corresponding frequencies
his•tol•o•gy \his-ˈtä-lə-jē\ *n, pl* **-gies 1 :** a branch of anatomy dealing with tissue structure **2 :** tissue structure or organization — **his•to•log•i•cal** \ˌhis-tə-ˈlä-ji-kəl\ *or* **his•to•log•ic** \-ˈlä-jik\ *adj* — **his•tol•o•gist** \-ˈtä-lə-jist\ *n*
his•to•ri•an \hi-ˈstōr-ē-ən\ *n* **:** a student or writer of history
his•tor•i•cal \hi-ˈstȯr-i-kəl\ *adj* **1 :** of, relating to, or having the character of history **2** ♦ **:** based on history — **his•tor•i•cal•ly** \-k(ə-)lē\ *adv*

♦ documentary, factual, hard, literal, matter-of-fact, nonfictional, objective, true

his•to•ric•i•ty \ˌhis-tə-ˈri-sə-tē\ *n* **:** historical actuality
his•to•ri•og•ra•pher \hi-ˌstōr-ē-ˈä-grə-fər\ *n* **:** HISTORIAN
his•to•ry \ˈhis-tə-rē\ *n, pl* **-ries 1** ♦ **:** a chronological record of significant events often with an explanation of their causes **2 :** a branch of knowledge that records and explains past events **3** ♦ **:** events that form the subject matter of history **4 :** an established record ⟨a convict's ~ of violence⟩ — **his•tor•ic** \hi-ˈstȯr-ik\ *adj*

♦ [1] annals, chronicle, record ♦ [1] account, chronicle, narrative, record, report, story ♦ [3] past, yesteryear, yore

his•tri•on•ic \ˌhis-trē-ˈä-nik\ *adj* **1** ♦ **:** deliberately affected **2 :** of or relating to actors, acting, or the theater — **his•tri•on•i•cal•ly** \-ni-k(ə-)lē\ *adv*

♦ dramatic, melodramatic, theatrical

his•tri•on•ics \-niks\ *n pl* **1 :** theatrical performances **2 :** deliberate display of emotion for effect
[1]**hit** \ˈhit\ *vb* **hit; hit•ting 1** ♦ **:** to reach with a blow **:** STRIKE; *also* **:** to arrive with a force like a blow ⟨the storm ~⟩ **2** ♦ **:** to make or bring into contact **:** COLLIDE **3 :** to affect detrimentally ⟨was ~ by the flu⟩ **4 :** to make a request of **5** ♦ **:** to come upon **:** to discover or meet especially by chance **6 :** to accord with **:** SUIT **7** ♦ **:** to reach as an end **:** ATTAIN **8 :** to indulge in often to excess **9** ♦ **:** to succeed in attaining or coming up with something — often used with *on* or *upon* — **hit•ter** *n*

♦ [1] bang, bash, bat, belt, clout, crack, knock, pound, punch, slug, strike, swat, wallop, whack ♦ [2] bang, bash, bump, collide, crash, impact, knock, ram, slam, smash, strike, swipe, thud ♦ *usu* **hit upon** [5] chance, encounter, find, happen (on *or* upon), meet, stumble ♦ [7] achieve, attain, make, score, win ♦ *often* **hit on** *or* **hit upon** [9] detect, determine, dig up, discover, ferret out, find, locate, track down

[2]**hit** *n* **1** ♦ **:** an act or instance of hitting or being hit **2** ♦ **:** a great

success **3 :** BASE HIT **4 :** a dose of a drug **5 :** a murder committed by a gangster **6 :** a successful match in a search (as of the Internet)

♦ [1] bat, blow, box, clout, punch, slug, thump, wallop, whack ♦ [2] blockbuster, smash, success, winner ***Ant*** bummer, bust, catastrophe, debacle, dud, failure, fiasco, flop, turkey, washout

1**hitch** \ˈhich\ *vb* **1** ♦ **:** to move by jerks **2** ♦ **:** to catch or fasten especially by a hook or knot **3 :** HITCHHIKE

♦ [1] buck, jerk, jolt, twitch ♦ [2] anchor, catch, clamp, fasten, fix, moor, secure, set

2**hitch** *n* **1 :** JERK, PULL **2 :** a sudden halt **3 :** a connection between something towed and its mover **4 :** KNOT **5** ♦ **:** a delimited period especially of military service

♦ stint, tenure, term, tour

hitch•hike \ˈhich-ˌhīk\ *vb* **:** to travel by securing free rides from passing vehicles — **hitch•hik•er** *n*

1**hith•er** \ˈhi-t͟hər\ *adv* **:** to this place

2**hither** *adj* **:** being on the near or adjacent side

hith•er•to \-ˌtü\ *adv* ♦ **:** up to this time

♦ heretofore, yet ***Ant*** henceforth, henceforward, hereafter, thenceforth, thenceforward, thereafter

HIV \ˌāch-(ˌ)ī-ˈvē\ *n* **:** any of several retroviruses that infect and destroy helper T cells causing the great reduction in their numbers that is diagnostic of AIDS

hive \ˈhīv\ *n* **1 :** a container for housing honeybees **2 :** a colony of bees **3 :** a place swarming with busy occupants — **hive** *vb*

hives \ˈhīvz\ *n sing or pl* **:** an allergic disorder marked by raised itching patches on the skin or mucous membranes

hl *abbr* hectoliter

HL *abbr* House of Lords

hm *abbr* hectometer

HM *abbr* **1** Her Majesty; Her Majesty's **2** His Majesty; His Majesty's

HMO \ˌāch-(ˌ)em-ˈō\ *n* **:** a comprehensive health-care organization financed by periodic fixed payments by voluntarily enrolled individuals and families

HMS *abbr* **1** Her Majesty's ship **2** His Majesty's ship

Ho *symbol* holmium

hoa•gie *also* **hoa•gy** \ˈhō-gē\ *n, pl* **hoagies** ♦ **:** a large sandwich on a long split roll **:** SUBMARINE

♦ grinder, poor boy, sub, submarine

1**hoard** \ˈhōrd\ *n* ♦ **:** a hidden accumulation

♦ cache, reserve, stash, stockpile, store

2**hoard** *vb* ♦ **:** to lay up a hoard — **hoard•er** *n*

♦ cache, lay away, lay up, put by, salt away, stash, stockpile, store

hoar•frost \ˈhōr-ˌfrȯst\ *n* **:** FROST 2

hoarse \ˈhōrs\ *adj* **hoars•er; hoars•est 1** ♦ **:** rough and harsh in sound **2 :** having a grating voice — **hoarse•ly** *adv* — **hoarse•ness** *n*

♦ coarse, gravelly, gruff, husky, scratchy, throaty

hoary \ˈhōr-ē\ *adj* **hoar•i•er; -est 1 :** gray or white with or as if with age **2** ♦ **:** extremely old **:** ANCIENT — **hoar•i•ness** \ˈhōr-ē-nəs\ *n*

♦ age-old, ancient, antediluvian, antique, dateless, old, venerable

1**hoax** \ˈhōks\ *vb* ♦ **:** to trick into believing or accepting as genuine something that is false

♦ beguile, bluff, cozen, deceive, delude, dupe, fool, gull, have, hoodwink, humbug, misinform, mislead, string along, take in, trick

2**hoax** *n* **1 :** an act intended to trick or dupe **2** ♦ **:** something accepted or established by fraud

♦ counterfeit, fake, forgery, humbug, phony, sham

hoax•er *n* ♦ **:** one that hoaxes another

♦ cheat, dodger, shark, sharper, swindler, trickster ♦ charlatan, fake, fraud, humbug, mountebank, phony, pretender, quack

hob \ˈhäb\ *n* **:** action that annoys or irritates **:** MISCHIEF — used with *play* and *raise* 〈always raising ~〉

1**hob•ble** \ˈhä-bəl\ *vb* **hob•bled, hob•bling 1 :** to limp along; *also* **:** to make lame **2 :** to fasten together the legs of (as a horse) to prevent straying **:** FETTER **3** ♦ **:** to place under handicap **:** HAMPER

♦ encumber, hamper, hinder, hold up, impede, inhibit, interfere with, obstruct, tie up

2**hobble** *n* **1 :** a hobbling movement **2 :** something used to hobble an animal

hob•by \ˈhä-bē\ *n, pl* **hobbies :** a pursuit or interest engaged in for relaxation — **hob•by•ist** \-ist\ *n*

hob•by•horse \ˈhä-bē-ˌhȯrs\ *n* **1 :** a stick with a horse's head on which children pretend to ride **2 :** a toy horse mounted on rockers **3 :** a topic to which one constantly reverts

hob•gob•lin \ˈhäb-ˌgäb-lən\ *n* **1** ♦ **:** a mischievous goblin **2** ♦ **:** a source of fear, perplexity, or harassment **:** BOGEY

♦ [1] brownie, dwarf, elf, fairy, fay, gnome, leprechaun, pixie, puck, troll ♦ [2] bête noire, bogey, bugbear, ogre

hob•nail \-ˌnāl\ *n* **:** a short large-headed nail for studding shoe soles — **hob•nailed** \-ˌnāld\ *adj*

hob•nob \-ˌnäb\ *vb* **hob•nobbed; hob•nob•bing** ♦ **:** to associate familiarly

♦ associate, chum, consort, fraternize, hang around, pal ♦ associate, fraternize, mingle, mix, socialize

ho•bo \ˈhō-bō\ *n, pl* **hoboes** *also* **hobos** ♦ **:** a homeless and usually penniless vagabond **:** TRAMP

♦ bum, tramp, vagabond, vagrant

1**hock** \ˈhäk\ *n* **:** a joint or region in the hind limb of a quadruped just above the foot and corresponding to the human ankle

2**hock** *n* **:** PAWN; *also* **:** DEBT 3 — **hock** *vb*

hock•ey \ˈhä-kē\ *n* **1 :** FIELD HOCKEY **2 :** ICE HOCKEY

ho•cus–po•cus \ˌhō-kəs-ˈpō-kəs\ *n* **1 :** SLEIGHT OF HAND **2 :** nonsense or sham used to conceal deception

hod \ˈhäd\ *n* **:** a long-handled carrier for mortar or bricks

hodge•podge \ˈhäj-ˌpäj\ *n* ♦ **:** a heterogeneous mixture **:** JUMBLE

♦ assortment, clutter, jumble, medley, mélange, miscellany, motley, muddle, variety, welter

Hodgkin's disease \ˈhäj-kinz-\ *n* **:** a neoplastic disease of lymphoid tissue characterized especially by enlargement of lymph nodes, spleen, and liver

hoe \ˈhō\ *n* **:** a long-handled implement with a thin flat blade used especially for cultivating, weeding, or loosening the earth around plants — **hoe** *vb*

hoe•cake \ˈhō-ˌkāk\ *n* **:** a small cornmeal cake

hoe•down \-ˌdau̇n\ *n* **1 :** SQUARE DANCE **2 :** a gathering featuring hoedowns

1**hog** \ˈhȯg, ˈhäg\ *n, pl* **hogs** *also* **hog 1 :** a domestic swine especially when grown **2 :** a selfish, gluttonous, or filthy person

2**hog** *vb* **hogged; hog•ging :** to take or hold selfishly

ho•gan \ˈhō-ˌgän\ *n* **:** a Navajo Indian dwelling usually made of logs and mud

hog•back \ˈhȯg-ˌbak, ˈhäg-\ *n* **:** a ridge with a sharp summit and steep sides

hog•gish \ˈhȯ-gish, ˈhä-\ *adj* ♦ **:** grossly selfish, gluttonous, or filthy

♦ gluttonous, greedy, piggish, rapacious, ravenous, voracious

hog•nose snake \ˈhȯg-ˌnōz-, ˈhäg-\ *or* **hog•nosed snake** \-ˌnōzd-\ *n* **:** any of a genus of rather small harmless stout-bodied No. American snakes that seldom bite but hiss wildly and often play dead when disturbed

hogs•head \ˈhȯgz-ˌhed, ˈhägz-\ *n* ♦ **:** a large cask or barrel

♦ barrel, cask, keg, pipe, puncheon

hog–tie \ˈhȯg-ˌtī, ˈhäg-\ *vb* **1 :** to tie together the feet of 〈~ a calf〉 **2 :** to make helpless

hog•wash \-ˌwȯsh, -ˌwäsh\ *n* **1 :** SWILL, SLOP **2** ♦ **:** language, conduct, or an idea that is absurd or contrary to good sense **:** NONSENSE

♦ bunk, claptrap, drivel, fiddlesticks, folly, foolishness, fudge, humbug, nonsense, piffle, rot, silliness, slush, stupidity, trash

hog–wild \-ˈwīld\ *adj* **:** lacking in restraint

hoi pol•loi \ˌhȯi-pə-ˈlȯi\ *n pl* **:** the general populace

hoi•sin sauce \ˈhȯi-ˌsin-\ *n* **:** a thick reddish sauce of soybeans, spices, and garlic used in Asian cookery

1**hoist** \ˈhȯist\ *vb* ♦ **:** to raise from a lower to a higher position

♦ boost, crane, elevate, heave, heft, heighten, hike, jack, lift, pick up, raise, up, uphold

2**hoist** *n* **1 :** LIFT **2 :** an apparatus for hoisting

hoke \ˈhōk\ *vb* **hoked; hok•ing :** FAKE — usually used with *up*

hok•ey \ˈhō-kē\ *adj* **hok•i•er; -est :** CORNY; *also* **:** PHONY

ho•kum \ˈhō-kəm\ *n* **:** NONSENSE

[1]**hold** \ˈhōld\ *vb* **held** \ˈheld\; **hold·ing** **1** ♦ **:** to have possession or ownership of or have at one's disposal **2 :** RESTRAIN **3** ♦ **:** to have a grasp on **4 :** to support, remain, or keep in a particular situation or position **5 :** SUSTAIN; *also* **:** RESERVE **6 :** BEAR, COMPORT **7 :** to maintain in being or action **:** PERSIST **8 :** to enclose and keep in a container or within bounds **:** ACCOMMODATE **9 a** ♦ **:** to have in the mind or express as a judgment, opinion, or belief **b** ♦ **:** to think of in a particular way **:** CONSIDER, REGARD **10 :** to carry on by concerted action; *also* **:** CONVOKE **11 :** to occupy especially by appointment or election **12 :** to be valid **13 :** HALT, PAUSE — **hold forth :** to speak at length — **hold to :** to adhere to **:** MAINTAIN — **hold with :** to agree with or approve of

♦ [1] hang on, keep, reserve, retain, withhold ♦ [1] command, enjoy, have, occupy, own, possess, retain ♦ [3] clench, cling, clutch, grip, hang on, hold on ♦ [9a] believe, consider, deem, feel, figure, guess, imagine, suppose, think ♦ [9a] bear, cherish, entertain, harbor (*or* harbour), have, nurse ♦ [9b] account, call, consider, count, esteem, rate, reckon, regard, take

[2]**hold** *n* **1** ♦ **:** a fortified place **:** STRONGHOLD **2 :** CONFINEMENT; *also* **:** PRISON **3** ♦ **:** the act or manner of holding **:** GRIP **4** ♦ **:** a restraining, dominating, or controlling influence **5 :** something that may be grasped as a support **6 :** an order or indication that something is to be reserved or delayed — **on hold :** in a temporary state of waiting (as during a phone call); *also* **:** in a state of postponement ⟨plans *on hold*⟩

♦ [1] bastion, citadel, fastness, fort, fortification, fortress, stronghold ♦ [3] clasp, grapple, grasp, grip ♦ [4] arm, authority, clutch, command, control, dominion, grip, mastery, power, sway

[3]**hold** *n* **1 :** the interior of a ship below decks; *esp* **:** a ship's cargo deck **2 :** an airplane's cargo compartment

hold back *vb* ♦ **:** to hinder the progress or achievement of

♦ encumber, hamper, hinder, hold up, impede, inhibit, interfere with, obstruct, tie up

hold·er *n* **1** ♦ **:** a person that holds **2** ♦ **:** a device that holds

♦ [1] owner, possessor, proprietor ♦ [2] container, receptacle, vessel

hold·ing *n* **1** ♦ **:** land or other property owned — usually used in plural **2** ♦ **:** a ruling of a court especially on an issue of law

♦ *usu* **holdings** [1] belongings, chattels, effects, paraphernalia, possessions, things ♦ [2] doom, finding, judgment (*or* judgement), ruling, sentence

holding pattern *n* **1 :** a course flown by an aircraft waiting to land **2** ♦ **:** a state of waiting or suspended activity or progress

♦ abeyance, doldrums, dormancy, latency, moratorium, quiescence, suspension

hold on *vb* **1** ♦ **:** to maintain a condition or position **:** PERSIST **2** ♦ **:** to maintain a grasp on something **3** ♦ **:** to await something (as a telephone connection) desired or requested

♦ [1] endure, hold, last, persist ♦ *usu* **hold on to** [2] clench, cling, clutch, grip, hang on, hold ♦ [3] await, bide, stay, wait

hold out *vb* **1** ♦ **:** to continue to fight or work **2 :** to refuse to come to an agreement — **hold·out** \ˈhōl-ˌdau̇t\ *n*

♦ hold, keep up, last, prevail, survive *Ant* fail, fizzle, give out, go out, peter (out), run out

hold·over \ˈhōl-ˌdō-vər\ *n* **:** one that is held over

hold·up \ˈhōl-ˌdəp\ *n* **1 :** DELAY **2 :** robbery at the point of a gun

hold up *vb* **1 :** to rob at gunpoint **2** ♦ **:** to stop, delay, or impede the course or advance of **3 :** to call attention to **4** ♦ **:** to continue in the same condition without failing or losing effectiveness or force

♦ [2] arrest, catch, check, draw up, fetch up, halt, stall, stay, still, stop ♦ [2] encumber, hamper, hinder, impede, inhibit, interfere with, obstruct, tie up ♦ [4] abide, continue, endure, keep up, last, persist, run on

[1]**hole** \ˈhōl\ *n* **1** ♦ **:** an opening into or through something **2** ♦ **:** a hollow place (as a pit or cave) **3 :** the resting or living place of a wild animal **:** DEN, BURROW **4 :** a wretched or dingy place **5 :** a unit of play from tee to cup in golf **6** ♦ **:** an awkward position

♦ [1] breach, break, discontinuity, gap, gulf, interval, opening, rent, rift, separation ♦ [1] aperture, opening, orifice, perforation ♦ [2] cavity, concavity, dent, depression, hollow, indentation, pit, recess *Ant* bulge, convexity, protrusion, protuberance ♦ [6] corner, fix, jam, pickle, predicament, spot

[2]**hole** *vb* ♦ **:** to make a hole in

♦ bore, drill, perforate, pierce, punch, puncture

hol·i·day \ˈhä-lə-ˌdā\ *n* **1 :** a day set aside for special religious observance **2 :** a day of freedom from work; *esp* **:** one in commemoration of an event **3 :** VACATION — **holiday** *vb*

ho·li·ness \ˈhō-lē-nəs\ *n* ♦ **:** the quality or state of being holy — used as a title for various high religious officials

♦ blessedness, devoutness, godliness, piety, sainthood, sanctity *Ant* godlessness, impiety, ungodliness, unholiness

ho·lis·tic \hō-ˈlis-tik\ *adj* **:** relating to or concerned with integrated wholes or complete systems rather than with the analysis or treatment of separate parts ⟨~ medicine⟩ ⟨~ ecology⟩

hol·lan·daise \ˌhä-lən-ˈdāz\ *n* **:** a rich sauce made basically of butter, egg yolks, and lemon juice or vinegar

[1]**hol·ler** \ˈhä-lər\ *vb* **:** to cry out **:** SHOUT

[2]**holler** *n* ♦ **:** a loud cry or call

♦ cry, hoot, howl, shout, whoop, yell, yowl

[1]**hol·low** \ˈhä-lō\ *n* **1 :** CAVITY, HOLE **2** ♦ **:** a surface depression

♦ dale, valley ♦ cavity, concavity, dent, depression, hole, indentation, pit, recess

[2]**hollow** *adj* **hol·low·er** \ˈhä-lə-wər\; **hol·low·est** \-lə-wəst\ **1** ♦ **:** having an indentation or inward curve **:** CONCAVE, SUNKEN **2 :** having a cavity within **3 :** lacking in real value, sincerity, or substance; *also* **:** FALSE **4 :** MUFFLED ⟨a ~ sound⟩ — **hol·low·ness** *n*

♦ concave, depressed, sunken *Ant* convex, bulging, protruding, protuberant

[3]**hollow** *vb* **:** to make or become hollow

hol·low·ware *or* **hol·lo·ware** \ˈhä-lə-ˌwar\ *n* **:** vessels (as bowls or cups) with a significant depth and volume

hol·ly \ˈhä-lē\ *n, pl* **hollies :** either of two trees or shrubs with branches of usually evergreen glossy spiny-margined leaves and red berries

hol·ly·hock \ˈhä-lē-ˌhäk, -ˌhȯk\ *n* **:** a biennial or perennial herb related to the mallows that is widely grown for its tall stalks of showy flowers

hol·mi·um \ˈhōl-mē-əm\ *n* **:** a metallic chemical element

ho·lo·caust \ˈhä-lə-ˌkȯst, ˈhō-\ *n* **1** ♦ **:** a thorough destruction especially by fire **2** *often cap* **:** the killing of European Jews by the Nazis during World War II; *also* **:** GENOCIDE

♦ conflagration, fire, inferno

Ho·lo·cene \ˈhō-lə-ˌsēn\ *adj* **:** of, relating to, or being the present geologic epoch — **Holocene** *n*

ho·lo·gram \ˈhō-lə-ˌgram, ˈhä-\ *n* **:** a three-dimensional image produced by an interference pattern of light (as laser light)

ho·lo·graph \ˈhō-lə-ˌgraf, ˈhä-\ *n* **:** a document wholly in the handwriting of its author

ho·log·ra·phy \hō-ˈlä-grə-fē\ *n* **:** the process of making a hologram — **ho·lo·graph·ic** \ˌhō-lə-ˈgra-fik, ˌhä-\ *adj*

Hol·stein \ˈhōl-ˌstēn, -ˌstīn\ *n* **:** any of a breed of large black-and-white dairy cattle that produce large quantities of comparatively low-fat milk

Hol·stein–Frie·sian \-ˈfrē-zhən\ *n* **:** HOLSTEIN

hol·ster \ˈhōl-stər\ *n* **:** a usually leather case for a firearm

ho·ly \ˈhō-lē\ *adj* **ho·li·er; -est** **1** ♦ **:** worthy of absolute devotion **2** ♦ **:** to be treated with veneration or the utmost respect **:** SACRED **3** ♦ **:** having a divine quality **4** ♦ **:** devoted to the deity or the work of the deity — **ho·li·ly** \-lə-lē\ *adv*

♦ [1, 2] inviolable, sacred, sacrosanct ♦ [1, 2] blessed, hallowed, sacred, sacrosanct, sanctified *Ant* unconsecrated, unhallowed ♦ [3] blessed, divine, godlike, heavenly ♦ [4] devout, faithful, godly, pious, religious, sainted, saintly *Ant* faithless, godless, impious, irreligious, ungodly, unholy

Holy Spirit *n* **:** the third person of the Christian Trinity

ho·ly·stone \ˈhō-lē-ˌstōn\ *n* **:** a soft sandstone used to scrub a ship's wooden decks — **holystone** *vb*

hom·age \ˈä-mij, ˈhä-\ *n* ♦ **:** expression of high regard; *also* **:** TRIBUTE

♦ accolade, citation, commendation, encomium, eulogy, paean, panegyric, salutation, tribute ♦ acclaim, accolade, credit, distinction, glory, honor (*or* honour), laurels

hom·bre \ˈäm-brē, ˈəm-, -ˌbrā\ *n* ♦ **:** an adult male human **:** GUY, FELLOW

♦ buck, chap, dude, fellow, gent, gentleman, guy, jack, joker, lad, male, man

hom•burg \ˈhäm-ˌbərg\ *n* **:** a man's felt hat with a stiff curled brim and a high crown creased lengthwise

¹**home** \ˈhōm\ *n* **1** ♦ **:** one's residence; *also* **:** HOUSE **2 :** the social unit formed by a family living together **3 :** a congenial environment; *also* **:** HABITAT **4** ♦ **:** a place of origin **5 :** the objective in various games **6** ♦ **:** the place or environment where a plant or animal naturally or normally lives and grows

♦ [1] abode, domicile, dwelling, fireside, habitation, hearth, house, lodging, pad, place, quarters, residence, roof ♦ [4] country, fatherland, homeland, motherland, sod ♦ [6] habitat, niche, range, territory

²**home** *vb* **homed; hom•ing 1 :** to go or return home **2 :** to proceed to or toward a source of radiated energy used as a guide

home•body \ˈhōm-ˌbä-dē\ *n* **:** one whose life centers on home

home•boy \-ˌbȯi\ *n* **1 :** a boy or man from one's neighborhood, hometown, or region **2 :** a fellow member of a youth gang **3 :** an inner-city youth

home•bred \-ˈbred\ *adj* **:** produced at home **:** INDIGENOUS

home•com•ing \-ˌkə-miŋ\ *n* **1 :** a return home **2 :** an annual celebration for alumni at a college or university

home computer *n* **:** a small inexpensive microcomputer

home economics *n* **:** the theory and practice of homemaking

home•girl \ˈhōm-gərl\ *n* **1 :** a girl or woman from one's neighborhood, hometown, or region **2 :** a girl or woman who is a member of one's peer group **3 :** an inner-city girl or woman

home•grown \ˈhōm-ˈgrōn\ *adj* **1 :** grown domestically **2 :** LOCAL, INDIGENOUS

home•land \-ˌland\ *n* **1** ♦ **:** native land **2 :** an area set aside to be a state for a people of a particular national, cultural, or racial origin

♦ country, fatherland, home, motherland, sod

¹**home•less** \-ləs\ *adj* **:** having no home or permanent residence

²**homeless** *n pl* **:** persons especially in urban areas that have no home

home•ly \ˈhōm-lē\ *adj* **home•li•er; -est 1 :** FAMILIAR **2 :** unaffectedly natural **3 :** lacking beauty or proportion — **home•li•ness** \-lē-nəs\ *n*

home•made \ˈhōm-ˌmād\ *adj* **:** made in the home, on the premises, or by one's own efforts

home•mak•er \-ˌmā-kər\ *n* **:** one who manages a household especially as a wife and mother — **home•mak•ing** \-kiŋ\ *n*

ho•me•op•a•thy \ˌhō-mē-ˈä-pə-thē\ *n* **:** a system of medical practice that treats disease especially with minute doses of a remedy that would in healthy persons produce symptoms similar to those of the disease treated — **ho•meo•path** \ˈhō-mē-ə-ˌpath\ *n* — **ho•meo•path•ic** \ˌhō-mē-ə-ˈpa-thik\ *adj*

ho•meo•sta•sis \ˌhō-mē-ō-ˈstā-səs\ *n* **:** the maintence of a relatively stable state of equilibrium between interrelated physiological, psychological, or social factors characteristic of an individual or group — **ho•meo•stat•ic** \-ˈsta-tik\ *adj*

home page *n* **:** the page usually encountered first at a Web site that usually contains hyperlinks to the other pages of the site

home plate *n* **:** a slab at the apex of a baseball diamond that a base runner must touch in order to score

hom•er \ˈhō-mər\ *n* **:** HOME RUN — **homer** *vb*

home•room \ˈhōm-ˌrüm, -ˌrům\ *n* **:** a classroom where pupils report at the beginning of each school day

home run *n* **:** a hit in baseball that enables the batter to go around all the bases and score a run

home•school \ˈhōm-ˌskül\ *vb* **:** to teach school subjects to one's children at home — **home•school•er** \-ˌskü-lər\ *n*

home•sick \ˈhōm-ˌsik\ *adj* **:** longing for home and family while absent from them — **home•sick•ness** *n*

home•spun \-ˌspən\ *adj* **1 :** spun or made at home; *also* **:** made of a loosely woven usually woolen or linen fabric **2 :** SIMPLE, HOMELY

¹**home•stead** \-ˌsted\ *n* **:** the home and land occupied by a family

²**homestead** *vb* **:** to acquire or settle on public land

home•stead•er \ˌste-dər\ *n* ♦ **:** one who seeks, establishes, or possesses a homestead under a homestead law

♦ colonist, frontiersman, pioneer, settler

home•stretch \-ˈstrech\ *n* **1 :** the part of a racecourse between the last curve and the winning post **2** ♦ **:** a final stage (as of a project)

♦ close, conclusion, consummation, end, ending, finale, finis, finish, windup

home theater *n* **:** an entertainment system (as a television with surround sound and a DVD player) for the home

home video *n* **:** prerecorded videocassettes or videodiscs for home viewing

¹**home•ward** \-wərd\ *or* **home•wards** \-wərdz\ *adv* **:** toward home

²**homeward** *adj* **:** being or going toward home

home•work \-ˌwərk\ *n* **1 :** an assignment given a student to be completed outside the classroom **2 :** preparatory reading or research

¹**hom•ey** \ˈhō-mē\ *adj* **hom•i•er; -est :** characteristic of home

²**homey** *or* **hom•ie** \ˈhō-mē\ *n, pl* **homeys** *or* **homies :** HOMEBOY

hom•i•cid•al \ˌhä-mə-ˈsīd-ᵊl\ *adj* ♦ **:** of, relating to, or tending toward homicide

♦ bloodthirsty, bloody, murderous, sanguinary, sanguine

ho•mi•cide \ˈhä-mə-ˌsīd, ˈhō-\ *n* **1 :** a person who kills another **2** ♦ **:** a killing of one human being by another

♦ murder

hom•i•ly \ˈhä-mə-lē\ *n, pl* **-lies :** SERMON — **hom•i•let•ic** \ˌhä-mə-ˈle-tik\ *adj*

homing pigeon *n* **:** a racing pigeon trained to return home

hom•i•nid \ˈhä-mə-nəd, -ˌnid\ *n* **:** any of a family of primate mammals that comprise all living humans and extinct ancestral and related forms — **hominid** *adj*

hom•i•ny \ˈhä-mə-nē\ *n* **:** hulled corn with the germ removed

ho•mo•cys•te•ine \ˌhō-mō-ˈsis-tə-ˌēn\ *n* **:** an amino acid associated with an increased risk of heart disease when occurring at high levels in the blood

ho•mo•erot•ic \ˌhō-mō-i-ˈrä-tik\ *adj* **:** marked by or portraying homosexual desire — **ho•mo•erot•i•cism** \-ˈrä-tə-ˌsi-zəm\ *n*

ho•mo•ge•neous \ˌhō-mə-ˈjē-nē-əs, -nyəs\ *adj* **:** of the same or a similar kind; *also* **:** of uniform structure — **ho•mo•ge•ne•i•ty** \-jə-ˈnē-ə-tē\ *n* — **ho•mo•ge•neous•ly** *adv*

ho•mog•e•ni•sa•tion, ho•mog•e•nise *chiefly Brit var of* HOMOGENIZATION, HOMOGENIZE

ho•mog•e•nize \hō-ˈmä-jə-ˌnīz, hə-\ *vb* **-nized; -niz•ing 1** ♦ **:** to make homogeneous **2 :** to reduce the particles in (as milk) to uniform size and distribute them evenly throughout the liquid — **ho•mog•e•ni•za•tion** \-ˌmä-jə-nə-ˈzā-shən\ *n* — **ho•mog•e•niz•er** *n*

♦ formalize, normalize, regularize, standardize

ho•mo•graph \ˈhä-mə-ˌgraf, ˈhō-\ *n* **:** one of two or more words spelled alike but different in origin, meaning, or pronunciation (as the *bow* of a ship, a *bow* and arrow)

ho•mol•o•gy \hō-ˈmä-lə-jē, hə-\ *n, pl* **-gies 1 :** structural likeness between corresponding parts of different plants or animals due to evolution from a common ancestor **2 :** structural likeness between different parts of the same individual — **ho•mol•o•gous** \-ˈmä-lə-gəs\ *adj*

hom•onym \ˈhä-mə-ˌnim, ˈhō-\ *n* **1 :** HOMOPHONE, HOMOGRAPH **2 :** one of two or more words spelled and pronounced alike but different in meaning (as *pool* of water and *pool* the game)

ho•mo•pho•bia \ˈhō-mə-ˈfō-bē-ə\ *n* **:** irrational fear of, aversion to, or discrimination against homosexuality or homosexuals — **ho•mo•phobe** \ˈhō-mə-ˌfōb\ *n* — **ho•mo•pho•bic** \-ˈfō-bik\ *adj*

ho•mo•phone \ˈhä-mə-ˌfōn, ˈhō-\ *n* **:** one of two or more words (as *to, too, two*) pronounced alike but different in meaning or derivation or spelling

Ho•mo sa•pi•ens \ˌhō-mō-ˈsā-pē-ənz, -ˈsa-\ *n* ♦ **:** the human race **:** HUMANKIND

♦ humanity, humankind, man, mankind

ho•mo•sex•u•al \ˌhō-mō-ˈsek-shə-wəl\ *adj* **:** of, relating to, or marked by sexual interest in the same sex as oneself; *also* **:** of, relating to, or involving sexual intercourse between members of the same sex — **homosexual** *n* — **ho•mo•sex•u•al•i•ty** \-ˌsek-shə-ˈwa-lə-tē\ *n*

hon *abbr* honor; honorable; honorary

Hon•du•ran \hän-ˈdůr-ən\ *or* **Hon•du•ra•ne•an** *or* **Hon•du•ra•ni•an** \ˌhan-dů-ˈrā-nē-ən, -dyů-\ *n* **:** a native or inhabitant of Honduras — **Honduran** *or* **Honduranean** *or* **Honduranian** *adj*

¹**hone** \ˈhōn\ *n* **:** WHETSTONE

²**hone** *vb* **1** ♦ **:** to sharpen or smooth with a whetstone **2 :** to make more acute, intense, or effective — **hon•er** *n*

♦ edge, grind, sharpen, strop, whet

hone in *vb* **:** to move toward or direct attention to an objective

¹**hon•est** \ˈä-nəst\ *adj* **1** ♦ **:** free from deception **:** TRUTHFUL; *also* **:** GENUINE, REAL **2 :** REPUTABLE **3 :** CREDITABLE **4** ♦ **:** marked by integrity **5** ♦ **:** marked by free, forthright, and sincere expression **:** FRANK

◆ [1] artless, genuine, ingenuous, innocent, naive, natural, real, simple, sincere, true, unaffected, unpretentious ◆ [4] decent, ethical, good, honorable (*or* honourable), just, moral, principled, right, righteous, straight, upright, virtuous ◆ [4] conscientious, honorable (*or* honourable), just, moral, principled, scrupulous ◆ [5] candid, direct, forthright, foursquare, frank, open, outspoken, plain, straight, straightforward, unguarded, unreserved

2**honest** *adv* **:** HONESTLY; *also* **:** with all sincerity ⟨I didn't do it, ~⟩
hon•est•ly \ˈä-nəst-lē\ *adv* **1 :** in an honest manner **2** ◆ **:** to be honest ⟨~, I don't know⟩

◆ actually, frankly, really, truly, truthfully, verily

hon•es•ty \ˈä-nə-stē\ *n* **1** ◆ **:** fairness and straightforwardness of conduct **2** ◆ **:** adherence to the facts

◆ [1] character, decency, goodness, honor (*or* honour), integrity, morality, probity, rectitude, righteousness, uprightness, virtue ◆ [2] integrity, probity, truthfulness, veracity, verity ***Ant*** deceit, deceitfulness, dishonesty, lying, mendacity

hon•ey \ˈhə-nē\ *n, pl* **honeys 1 :** a sweet sticky substance made by honeybees from the nectar of flowers **2** ◆ **:** a loved one

◆ beloved, darling, dear, flame, love, sweet, sweetheart

hon•ey•bee \ˈhə-nē-ˌbē\ *n* **:** a social and colonial 4-winged insect often kept in hives for the honey it produces
1**hon•ey•comb** \-ˌkōm\ *n* **:** a mass of 6-sided wax cells built by honeybees; *also* **:** something of similar structure or appearance
2**honeycomb** *vb* **:** to make or become full of cavities like a honeycomb
hon•ey•dew \-ˌdü, -ˌdyü\ *n* **:** a sweetish deposit secreted on plants by aphids, scale insects, or fungi
honeydew melon *n* **:** a smooth-skinned muskmelon with sweet green flesh
honey locust *n* **:** a tall usually spiny No. American leguminous tree with hard durable wood and long twisted pods
hon•ey•moon \ˈhə-nē-ˌmün\ *n* **1 :** a period of harmony especially just after marriage **2 :** a holiday taken by a newly married couple — **honeymoon** *vb*
hon•ey•suck•le \ˈhə-nē-ˌsə-kəl\ *n* **:** any of a genus of shrubs with fragrant tube-shaped flowers rich in nectar
honk \ˈhäŋk, ˈhȯŋk\ *n* **:** the cry of a goose; *also* **:** a similar sound (as of a horn) — **honk** *vb* — **honk•er** *n*
hon•ky–tonk \ˈhäŋ-kē-ˌtäŋk, ˈhȯŋ-kē-ˌtȯŋk\ *n* **:** a tawdry nightclub or dance hall — **honky–tonk** *adj*
1**hon•or** \ˈä-nər\ *or Can and Brit* **hon•our** *n* **1** ◆ **:** good name **:** REPUTATION; *also* **:** outward respect **2** ◆ **:** an exclusive or special right, power, or privilege **3 :** a person of superior standing — used especially as a title **4 :** one that brings respect or fame **5** ◆ **:** an evidence or symbol of distinction **6 :** CHASTITY, PURITY **7** ◆ **:** a keen sense of ethical conduct **:** INTEGRITY

◆ [1] boast, credit, glory, jewel, pride, treasure ◆ [2] boon, concession, privilege ◆ [5] acclaim, accolade, credit, distinction, glory, homage, laurels ◆ [5] award, decoration, distinction, plume, prize ◆ [7] honesty, integrity, probity, rectitude, righteousness, uprightness ***Ant*** baseness, lowness

2**honor** *or Can and Brit* **honour** *vb* **1 :** to regard or treat with honor **2 :** to confer honor on **3 :** to fulfill the terms of; *also* **:** to accept as payment — **hon•or•ee** \ˌä-nə-ˈrē\ *n* — **hon•or•er** *n*
hon•or•able \ˈä-nə-rə-bəl\ *or Can and Brit* **hon•our•able** *adj* **1 :** deserving of honor **2 :** of great renown **3 :** accompanied with marks of honor **4 :** doing credit to the possessor **5** ◆ **:** characterized by integrity — **hon•or•able•ness** *n*

◆ decent, ethical, good, honest, just, moral, right, righteous, straight, upright, virtuous ◆ decent, ethical, honest, just, noble, principled, respectable, righteous, upright, upstanding ***Ant*** base, dishonest, ignoble, low, unethical, unjust, unprincipled, unrighteous ◆ conscientious, honest, just, moral, principled, scrupulous

hon•or•ably \ˈä-nə-rə-blē\ *or Can and Brit* **hon•our•ably** *adv* ◆ **:** in an honorable manner

◆ gallantly, grandly, greatly, heroically, magnanimously, nobly

hon•o•rar•i•um \ˌä-nə-ˈrer-ē-əm\ *n, pl* **-ia** \-ē-ə\ *also* **-i•ums :** a reward usually for services on which custom or propriety forbids a price to be set
hon•or•ary \ˈä-nə-ˌrer-ē\ *adj* **1 :** having or conferring distinction **2 :** conferred in recognition of achievement without the usual prerequisites ⟨~ degree⟩ **3 :** UNPAID, VOLUNTARY — **hon•or•ari•ly** \ˌä-nə-ˈrer-ə-lē\ *adv*
hon•or•if•ic \ˌä-nə-ˈri-fik\ *adj* **:** conferring or conveying honor ⟨~ titles⟩

hon•our, hon•our•able *Can and Brit var of* HONOR, HONORABLE
1**hood** \ˈhu̇d\ *n* **1 :** a covering for the head and neck and sometimes the face **2 :** an ornamental fold (as at the back of an ecclesiastical vestment) **3 a** ◆ **:** something resembling a hood in form or use **b :** a cover for parts of mechanisms; *esp* **:** the covering over an automobile engine — **hood•ed** \ˈhu̇-dəd\ *adj*

◆ cloak, curtain, mantle, mask, shroud, veil

2**hood** \ˈhu̇d, ˈhüd\ *n* **:** a brutal ruffian **:** HOODLUM
3**hood** \ˈhu̇d\ *n* **:** an inner-city neighborhood
-hood \ˌhu̇d\ *n suffix* **1 :** state **:** condition **:** quality **:** character ⟨boy*hood*⟩ ⟨hardi*hood*⟩ **2 :** instance of a (specified) state or quality ⟨false*hood*⟩ **3 :** individuals sharing a (specified) state or character ⟨brother*hood*⟩
hood•ie \ˈhu̇-dē\ *n* **:** a hooded sweatshirt
hood•lum \ˈhüd-ləm, ˈhu̇d-\ *n* **1** ◆ **:** a brutal ruffian **:** THUG **2 :** a young ruffian or loafer

◆ bully, gangster, goon, hood, mobster, mug, punk, rowdy, ruffian, thug, tough

hoo•doo \ˈhü-dü\ *n, pl* **hoodoos 1 :** a body of magical practices traditional especially among blacks in the southern U.S. **2 :** something that brings bad luck — **hoodoo** *vb*
hood•wink \ˈhu̇d-ˌwiŋk\ *vb* ◆ **:** to deceive by false appearance

◆ beguile, bluff, cozen, deceive, delude, dupe, fool, gull, have, hoax, humbug, misinform, mislead, string along, take in, trick

hoo•ey \ˈhü-ē\ *n* **:** NONSENSE
hoof \ˈhu̇f, ˈhüf\ *n, pl* **hooves** \ˈhu̇vz, ˈhüvz\ *or* **hoofs :** a horny covering that protects the ends of the toes of ungulate mammals (as horses or cattle); *also* **:** a hoofed foot — **hoofed** \ˈhu̇ft, ˈhüft\ *adj*
1**hook** \ˈhu̇k\ *n* **1 :** a curved or bent device for catching, holding, or pulling **2 :** something curved or bent like a hook **3 :** a flight of a ball (as in golf) that curves in a direction opposite to the dominant hand of the player propelling it **4 :** a short punch delivered with a circular motion and with the elbow bent and rigid
2**hook** *vb* **1** ◆ **:** to form into a hook **:** CURVE, CROOK **2 a :** to seize or make fast with a hook **b** ◆ **:** to connect by or as if by a hook — often used with *up* **3** ◆ **:** to take the property of another wrongfully **:** STEAL **4 :** to work as a prostitute

◆ [1] arc, arch, bend, bow, crook, curve, round, sweep, swerve, wheel ◆ [2b] chain, compound, connect, couple, hitch, join, link, yoke ◆ [3] appropriate, filch, misappropriate, nip, pilfer, pocket, purloin, snitch, steal, swipe, thieve

hoo•kah \ˈhu̇-kə, ˈhü-\ *n* **:** WATER PIPE
hook•er \ˈhu̇-kər\ *n* **1 :** one that hooks **2 :** PROSTITUTE
hook•up \ˈhu̇-ˌkəp\ *n* **1** ◆ **:** a state of cooperation or alliance **2 :** an assemblage (as of apparatus or circuits) used for a specific purpose (as in radio)

◆ affiliation, alliance, association, collaboration, confederation, connection, cooperation, liaison, partnership, relation, relationship, union

hook•worm \ˈhu̇k-ˌwərm\ *n* **:** any of several parasitic intestinal nematode worms having hooks or plates around the mouth; *also* **:** infestation with or disease caused by hookworms
hoo•li•gan \ˈhü-li-gən\ *n* ◆ **:** a brutal person **:** RUFFIAN, HOODLUM

◆ bully, gangster, goon, homeboy, hood, hoodlum, mobster, mug, punk, rowdy, ruffian, thug, tough

hoop \ˈhu̇p, ˈhüp\ *n* **1 :** a circular strip used especially for holding together the staves of a barrel **2** ◆ **:** a circular figure or object **:** RING **3 :** a circle of flexible material for expanding a woman's skirt **4 :** BASKETBALL — usually used in plural

◆ band, circle, ring, round

hoop•la \ˈhüp-ˌlä, ˈhu̇p-\ *n* **:** TO-DO; *also* **:** BALLYHOO
hoop•ster \ˈhüp-stər\ *n* **:** a basketball player
hoo•ray \hu̇-ˈrā\ *interj* — used to express joy, approval, or encouragement
hoose•gow \ˈhüs-ˌgau̇\ *n* **:** JAIL
1**hoot** \ˈhüt\ *vb* **1 :** to shout or laugh usually in contempt **2 :** to make the natural throat noise of an owl — **hoot•er** *n*
2**hoot** *n* **1** ◆ **:** a sound of hooting **2** ◆ **:** the least bit ⟨don't give a ~⟩ **3 :** something or someone amusing ⟨the play is a real ~⟩

◆ [1] cry, holler, howl, shout, whoop, yell, yowl ◆ [1] boo, catcall, hiss, jeer, raspberry, snort ◆ [2] jot, lick, modicum, rap, tittle, whit

hoot•e•nan•ny \ˈhü-tə-ˌna-nē\ *n, pl* **-nies :** a gathering at which folksingers entertain often with the audience joining in
1**hop** \ˈhäp\ *vb* **hopped; hop•ping 1** ◆ **:** to move by a quick

springy leap or in a series of leaps **2 :** to make a quick trip **3 :** to ride on especially surreptitiously and without authorization

♦ bound, jump, leap, spring, vault

²hop *n* **1** ♦ **:** a short brisk leap especially on one leg **2 :** a social gathering for dancing **:** DANCE **3 :** a short trip by air

♦ bound, jump, leap, spring, vault

³hop *n* **:** a vine related to the mulberry whose ripe dried pistillate catkins are used especially in flavoring malt liquors; *also, pl* **:** its pistillate catkins

¹hope \ˈhōp\ *vb* **hoped; hop•ing** ♦ **:** to desire with expectation of fulfillment ⟨*hopes* for a promotion⟩

♦ *usu* **hope for** anticipate, await, expect, watch

²hope *n* **1 :** TRUST, RELIANCE **2 :** desire accompanied by expectation of fulfillment; *also* **:** something hoped for **3 :** one that gives promise for the future

HOPE *abbr* Health Opportunity for People Everywhere

hope•ful \ˈhōp-fəl\ *adj* **1** ♦ **:** having qualities which inspire hope **2 :** full of hope — **hope•ful•ness** *n*

♦ auspicious, bright, encouraging, fair, golden, heartening, likely, promising, propitious, rosy, upbeat *Ant* bleak, dark, desperate, discouraging, disheartening, dismal, dreary, gloomy, hopeless, inauspicious, pessimistic, unlikely, unpromising

hope•ful•ly \ˈhōp-fə-lē\ *adv* **1 :** in a hopeful manner **2 :** it is hoped

hope•less \ˈhō-pləs\ *adj* **1** ♦ **:** having no expectation of good or success **2 a** ♦ **:** incapable of solution, management, or accomplishment **:** IMPOSSIBLE **b** ♦ **:** not susceptible to remedy or cure; *also* **:** incapable of redemption or improvement — **hope•less•ly** *adv*

♦ [1] defeatist, despairing, pessimistic ♦ [2a] impossible, unattainable, unsolvable, unworkable ♦ [2b] incorrigible, incurable, irredeemable, irremediable, unrecoverable, unredeemable *Ant* curable, correctable, reclaimable, recoverable, redeemable, reformable, remediable, retrievable

hope•less•ness \-nəs\ *n* ♦ **:** the quality or state of being hopeless

♦ despair, desperation, despondency, forlornness

Ho•pi \ˈhō-pē\ *n, pl* **Hopi** *or* **Hopis :** a member of an American Indian people of Arizona; *also* **:** the language of the Hopi people

hopped–up \ˈhäpt-ˈəp\ *adj* **1 :** being under the influence of a narcotic; *also* **:** full of enthusiasm or excitement **2 :** having more power than usual ⟨a ~ engine⟩

hop•per \ˈhä-pər\ *n* **1 :** a usually immature hopping insect (as a grasshopper) **2 :** a usually funnel-shaped container for delivering material (as grain) **3 :** a freight car with hinged doors in a sloping bottom **4 :** a box into which a bill to be considered by a legislative body is dropped **5 :** a tank holding a liquid and having a device for releasing its contents through a pipe

hop•scotch \ˈhäp-ˌskäch\ *n* **:** a child's game in which a player tosses an object (as a stone) into areas of a figure drawn on the ground and hops through the figure to pick up the object

hor *abbr* horizontal

horde \ˈhōrd\ *n* ♦ **:** a teeming crowd or throng **:** SWARM

♦ army, crowd, crush, drove, flock, host, legion, mob, multitude, press, swarm, throng

ho•ri•zon \hə-ˈrī-zᵊn\ *n* **1 :** the apparent junction of earth and sky **2 :** range of outlook or experience

hor•i•zon•tal \ˌhȯr-ə-ˈzänt-ᵊl\ *adj* **:** parallel to the horizon **:** LEVEL — **horizontal** *n* — **hor•i•zon•tal•ly** *adv*

hor•mon•al \hȯr-ˈmōn-ᵊl\ *adj* **:** of, relating to, or effected by hormones

hor•mone \ˈhȯr-ˌmōn\ *n* **:** a product of living cells that circulates in body fluids and has a specific effect on the activity of cells remote from its point of origin

horn \ˈhȯrn\ *n* **1 :** one of the hard projections of bone or keratin on the head of many hoofed mammals **2 :** something resembling or suggesting a horn **3 :** a brass wind instrument **4 :** a usually electrical device that makes a noise ⟨automobile ~⟩ — **horned** \ˈhȯrnd\ *adj* — **horn•less** *adj*

horn•book \ˈhȯrn-ˌbu̇k\ *n* **1 :** a child's primer consisting of a sheet of parchment or paper protected by a sheet of transparent horn **2 :** a rudimentary treatise

horned toad *n* **:** any of several small harmless insect-eating lizards with spines on the head resembling horns and spiny scales on the body

hor•net \ˈhȯr-nət\ *n* **:** any of the larger social wasps

horn in *vb* **:** to participate without invitation **:** INTRUDE

horn•pipe \ˈhȯrn-ˌpīp\ *n* **:** a lively folk dance of the British Isles

horny \ˈhȯr-nē\ *adj* **horn•i•er; -est 1 :** of or made of horn; *also* **:** HARD, CALLOUS **2 :** having horns **3 :** desiring sexual gratification; *also* **:** excited sexually

ho•rol•o•gy \hə-ˈrä-lə-jē\ *n* **:** the science of measuring time or constructing time-indicating instruments — **hor•o•log•ic** \ˌhȯr-ə-ˈlä-jik\ *adj* — **ho•rol•o•gist** \hə-ˈrä-lə-jist\ *n*

horo•scope \ˈhȯr-ə-ˌskōp\ *n* **1 :** a diagram of the relative positions of planets and signs of the zodiac at a particular time for use by astrologers to foretell events of a person's life **2 :** an astrological forecast

hor•ren•dous \hȯ-ˈren-dəs\ *adj* **:** inspiring horror **:** DREADFUL, HORRIBLE

hor•ri•ble \ˈhȯr-ə-bəl\ *adj* **1** ♦ **:** marked by or arousing horror **2** ♦ **:** highly disagreeable — **hor•ri•ble•ness** *n* — **hor•ri•bly** \-blē\ *adv*

♦ [1] dreadful, fearful, fearsome, hair-raising, scary, terrifying ♦ [2] abhorrent, abominable, distasteful, horrid, obnoxious, odious, offensive, repellent, repugnant, repulsive, revolting, scandalous, ugly ♦ [2] appalling, atrocious, awful, dreadful, frightful, ghastly, grisly, gruesome, hideous, horrid, lurid, macabre, monstrous, nightmarish, shocking, terrible

hor•rid \ˈhȯr-əd\ *adj* **1 :** inspiring horror **:** HIDEOUS **2** ♦ **:** highly disagreeable — **hor•rid•ly** *adv*

♦ abhorrent, abominable, appalling, awful, distasteful, dreadful, horrible, obnoxious, offensive, repugnant, repulsive, revolting, scandalous, shocking, ugly

hor•rif•ic \hȯ-ˈri-fik\ *adj* **:** having the power to horrify — **hor•rif•i•cal•ly** \-fi-k(ə-)lē\ *adv*

hor•ri•fy \ˈhȯr-ə-ˌfī\ *vb* **-fied; -fy•ing** ♦ **:** to cause to feel horror

♦ alarm, frighten, panic, scare, shock, spook, startle, terrify, terrorize

hor•ror \ˈhȯr-ər\ *n* **1** ♦ **:** painful and intense fear, dread, or dismay **2 :** intense repugnance **3 a** ♦ **:** something that horrifies **b :** a repulsive or dismal quality or character **4** ♦ **:** the quality of inspiring horror

♦ [1] alarm, anxiety, apprehension, dread, fear, fright, panic, terror, trepidation ♦ [3a] agony, hell, misery, murder, nightmare, torment, torture ♦ [4] atrociousness, atrocity, frightfulness, hideousness, monstrosity, repulsiveness

horror story *n* **:** an account of an unsettling or unfortunate occurrence

hors de com•bat \ˌȯr-də-kōⁿ-ˈbä\ *adv or adj* **:** in a disabled condition

hors d'oeuvre \ȯr-ˈdərv\ *n, pl* **hors d'oeuvres** *same or* -ˈdərvz\ *also* **hors d'oeuvre :** any of various savory foods usually served as appetizers

horse \ˈhȯrs\ *n, pl* **hors•es** *also* **horse 1 :** a large solid-hoofed herbivorous mammal domesticated as a draft and saddle animal **2 :** a supporting framework usually with legs — **horse•less** *adj*

¹horse•back \ˈhȯrs-ˌbak\ *n* **:** the back of a horse

²horseback *adv* **:** on horseback

horse chestnut *n* **:** a large tree with palmate leaves, erect conical clusters of showy flowers, and large glossy brown seeds enclosed in a prickly bur; *also* **:** its seed

horse•flesh \ˈhȯrs-ˌflesh\ *n* **:** horses for riding, driving, or racing

horse•fly \-ˌflī\ *n* **:** any of a family of large dipteran flies with bloodsucking females

horse•hair \-ˌhar\ *n* **1 :** the hair of a horse especially from the mane or tail **2 :** cloth made from horsehair

horse•hide \-ˌhīd\ *n* **1 :** the dressed or raw hide of a horse **2 :** the ball used in baseball

horse latitudes *n pl* **:** either of two calm regions near 30°N and 30°S latitude

horse•laugh \ˈhȯrs-ˌlaf, -ˌlȧf\ *n* **:** a loud boisterous laugh

horse•man \-mən\ *n* **1 :** one who rides horseback; *also* **:** one skilled in managing horses **2 :** a breeder or raiser of horses — **horse•man•ship** *n*

horse•play \-ˌplā\ *n* ♦ **:** rough boisterous play

♦ foolery, high jinks, monkeyshines, roughhouse, shenanigans, tomfoolery

horse•play•er \-ər\ *n* **:** a bettor on horse races

horse•pow•er \ˈhȯrs-ˌpau̇(-ə)r\ *n* **:** a unit of power equal in the U.S. to 746 watts

horse•rad•ish \-ˌra-dish\ *n* **:** a tall white-flowered herb related to the mustards whose pungent root is used as a condiment; *also* **:** the pungent condiment

horse sense *n* ♦ **:** sound and prudent judgment based on a simple perception of the situation or facts

♦ common sense, prudence, sense, wisdom, wit

horse•shoe \ˈhȯrs-ˌshü\ *n* **1 :** a usually U-shaped protective metal plate fitted to the rim of a horse's hoof **2** *pl* **:** a game in which horseshoes are pitched at a fixed object — **horse•shoe** *vb* — **horse•sho•er** *n*

horseshoe crab *n* **:** any of several marine arthropods with a broad crescent-shaped combined head and thorax

horse•tail \ˈhȯrs-ˌtāl\ *n* **:** any of a genus of primitive spore-producing plants with hollow jointed stems and leaves reduced to sheaths about the joints

horse•whip \-ˌhwip\ *vb* **:** to flog with a whip made to be used on a horse

horse•wom•an \-ˌwu̇-mən\ *n* **:** a woman skilled in riding horseback or in caring for or managing horses; *also* **:** a woman who breeds or raises horses

hors•ey *also* **horsy** \ˈhȯr-sē\ *adj* **hors•i•er; -est** **1 :** of, relating to, or suggesting a horse **2 :** having to do with horses or horse racing

hort *abbr* horticultural; horticulture

hor•ta•tive \ˈhȯr-tə-tiv\ *adj* **:** giving exhortation

hor•ta•to•ry \ˈhȯr-tə-ˌtōr-ē\ *adj* **:** HORTATIVE

hor•ti•cul•ture \ˈhȯr-tə-ˌkəl-chər\ *n* **:** the science and art of growing fruits, vegetables, flowers, and ornamental plants — **hor•ti•cul•tur•al** \ˌhȯr-tə-ˈkəl-chə-rəl\ *adj* — **hor•ti•cul•tur•ist** \-rist\ *n*

Hos *abbr* Hosea

ho•san•na \hō-ˈza-nə, -ˈzä-\ *interj* — used as a cry of acclamation and adoration — **hosanna** *n*

¹hose \ˈhōz\ *n, pl* **hose** *or* **hos•es** **1** *pl hose* **:** STOCKING, SOCK; *also* **:** a close-fitting garment covering the legs and waist **2 :** a flexible tube for conveying fluids (as from a faucet)

²hose *vb* **hosed; hos•ing :** to spray, water, or wash with a hose

Ho•sea \hō-ˈzā-ə, -ˈzē-\ *n* **:** a book of the canonical Jewish and Christian Scriptures

ho•siery \ˈhō-zhə-rē, -zə-\ *n* **:** STOCKINGS, SOCKS

hosp *abbr* hospital

hos•pice \ˈhäs-pəs\ *n* **1** ♦ **:** a lodging for travelers or for young persons or the underprivileged **2 :** a facility or program for caring for dying persons

♦ hotel, inn, lodge, public house, tavern

hos•pi•ta•ble \hä-ˈspi-tə-bəl, ˈhäs-(ˌ)pi-\ *adj* **1** ♦ **:** given to generous and cordial reception of guests **2 :** readily receptive — **hos•pi•ta•bly** \-blē\ *adv*

♦ affable, cordial, genial, gracious, sociable

hos•pi•tal \ˈhäs-ˌpit-ᵊl\ *n* **:** an institution where the sick or injured receive medical or surgical care

hos•pi•tal•ise *chiefly Brit var of* HOSPITALIZE

hos•pi•tal•i•ty \ˌhäs-pə-ˈta-lə-tē\ *n, pl* **-ties :** hospitable treatment, reception, or disposition

hos•pi•tal•ize \ˈhäs-ˌpit-ᵊl-ˌīz\ *vb* **-ized; -iz•ing :** to place in a hospital as a patient — **hos•pi•tal•i•za•tion** \ˌhäs-ˌpit-ᵊl-ə-ˈzā-shən\ *n*

¹host \ˈhōst\ *n* **1 :** a large organized body of armed personnel trained for war especially on land **:** ARMY **2** ♦ **:** a very large number **:** MULTITUDE

♦ army, crowd, crush, drove, flock, horde, legion, mob, multitude, press, swarm, throng

²host *n* **1 :** one who receives or entertains guests **2 :** an animal or plant on or in which a parasite lives — **host** *vb*

³host *n, often cap* **:** the eucharistic bread

hos•tage \ˈhäs-tij\ *n* **1 :** a person kept as a pledge pending the fulfillment of an agreement **2 :** a person taken by force to secure the taker's demands

hos•tel \ˈhäst-ᵊl\ *n* **1 :** an establishment for the lodging and entertaining of travelers **:** INN **2 :** a supervised lodging for youth — **hos•tel•er** *n*

hos•tel•ry \-rē\ *n, pl* **-ries :** an establishment for the lodging and entertaining of travelers **:** INN, HOTEL

host•ess \ˈhō-stəs\ *n* **:** a woman who acts as host

hos•tile \ˈhäst-ᵊl, ˈhäs-ˌtīl\ *adj* ♦ **:** marked by usually overt antagonism **:** UNFRIENDLY — **hostile** *n* — **hos•tile•ly** *adv*

♦ antagonistic, inhospitable, inimical, jaundiced, negative, unfriendly, unsympathetic *Ant* friendly, hospitable, sympathetic

hos•til•i•ty \hä-ˈsti-lə-tē\ *n, pl* **-ties** **1** ♦ **:** an unfriendly state or action **2** *pl* **:** overt acts of war

♦ animosity, antagonism, antipathy, bitterness, enmity, gall, grudge, rancor

hos•tler \ˈhäs-lər, ˈäs-\ *n* **:** one who takes care of horses or mules

hot \ˈhät\ *adj* **hot•ter; hot•test** **1** ♦ **:** marked by a high temperature or an uncomfortable degree of body heat **2 :** giving a sensation of heat or of burning **3 :** ARDENT, FIERY **4 :** sexually excited **5** ♦ **:** marked by enthusiastic or impatient desire or interest **:** EAGER **6** ♦ **:** newly made or received **7 :** PUNGENT **8 :** unusually lucky or favorable ⟨~ dice⟩ **9 :** recently and illegally obtained ⟨~ jewels⟩ **10** ♦ **:** currently popular or in demand **11** ♦ **:** marked by extreme force or sudden intense activity **:** VIOLENT — **hot** *adv* — **hot•ly** *adv*

♦ [1] broiling, burning, fiery, red-hot, scorching, sultry, torrid *Ant* arctic, chill, chilled, cold, freezing, frigid, frozen, glacial, iced, icy ♦ [5] agog, anxious, ardent, athirst, avid, crazy, eager, enthusiastic, gung ho, hungry, keen, nuts, raring, solicitous, thirsty, voracious ♦ [6] contemporary, current, mod, modern, new, newfangled, red-hot, space-age, ultramodern, up-to-date ♦ [10] fashionable, in, modish, popular, vogue ♦ [11] explosive, ferocious, fierce, furious, rabid, rough, stormy, tempestuous, turbulent, violent, volcanic

hot air *n* ♦ **:** empty talk

♦ bombast, gas, grandiloquence, rhetoric, wind

hot•bed \-ˌbed\ *n* **1 :** a glass-covered bed of soil heated (as by fermenting manure) and used especially for raising seedlings **2 :** an environment that favors rapid growth or development

hot–blood•ed \-ˈblə-dəd\ *adj* ♦ **:** easily roused or excited

♦ ardent, burning, charged, emotional, fervent, fiery, impassioned, passionate, red-hot, vehement

hot•box \-ˌbäks\ *n* **:** a bearing (as of a railroad car) overheated by friction

hot button *n* **:** an emotional issue or concern that triggers immediate intense reaction

hot•cake \-ˌkāk\ *n* **:** a flat cake made of thin batter and cooked (as on a griddle) on both sides **:** PANCAKE

hot dog *n* **:** a cooked frankfurter usually served in a long split roll

ho•tel \hō-ˈtel\ *n* ♦ **:** a building where lodging and usually meals, entertainment, and various personal services are provided for the public

♦ hospice, inn, lodge, public house, tavern

hot flash *n* **:** a sudden brief flushing and sensation of heat usually associated with menopausal endocrine imbalance

hot•head•ed \ˈhät-ˈhe-dəd\ *adj* **:** FIERY, IMPETUOUS — **hot•head** \-ˌhed\ *n* — **hot•head•ed•ly** *adv* — **hot•head•ed•ness** *n*

hot•house \-ˌhau̇s\ *n* **:** a heated greenhouse especially for raising tropical plants

hot•line \ˈhät-ˌlīn\ *n* **:** a telephone line for emergency use (as between governments or to a counseling service)

hot•ness \-nəs\ *n* **:** the quality or state of being hot

hot pants *n pl* **:** very short shorts

hot pepper *n* **:** a small usually thin-walled pepper with a pungent taste; *also* **:** a plant bearing hot peppers

hot plate *n* **:** a simple portable appliance for heating or for cooking

hot potato *n* **:** an embarrassing or controversial issue

hot rod *n* **:** an automobile modified for high speed and fast acceleration — **hot–rod•der** \-ˈrä-dər\ *n*

hots \ˈhäts\ *n pl* **:** strong sexual desire — usually used with *the*

hot seat *n* **:** a position of anxiety or embarrassment

hot•shot \ˈhät-ˌshät\ *n* ♦ **:** a showily skillful person

♦ ace, adept, artist, authority, crackerjack, expert, guru, hand, maestro, master, scholar, shark, virtuoso, whiz, wizard

hot tub *n* **:** a large tub of hot water for one or more bathers

hot water *n* **:** TROUBLE, DIFFICULTY

hot–wire \ˈhät-ˌwī(-ə)r\ *vb* **:** to start (an automobile) by short-circuiting the ignition system

¹hound \ˈhau̇nd\ *n* **1 :** a domestic mammal closely related to the gray wolf; *esp* **:** any of various hunting dogs that track prey by scent or sight **2 :** FAN, ADDICT

²hound *vb* ♦ **:** to pursue relentlessly

♦ chase, dog, follow, pursue, shadow, tag, tail, trace, track, trail ♦ henpeck, nag, needle

hour \ˈau̇(-ə)r\ *n* **1 :** the 24th part of a day **:** 60 minutes **2 :** the time of day **3 :** a particular or customary time **4 :** a class session — **hour•ly** *adv or adj*

hour•glass \ˈau̇(-ə)r-ˌglas\ *n* **:** a glass vessel for measuring time in which sand runs from an upper compartment to a lower compartment in an hour

hou•ri \ˈhu̇r-ē\ *n* **:** one of the beautiful maidens of the Muslim paradise

¹house \ˈhau̇s\ *n, pl* **hous•es** \ˈhau̇-zəz\ **1** ♦ **:** a building for human habitation **2 :** an animal shelter (as a den or nest) **3 :** a building in which something is stored **4 a :** those who dwell under the same roof and compose a family : HOUSEHOLD **b** ♦ **:** a family including ancestors, descendants, and kindred : FAMILY **5 :** a residence for a religious community or for students; *also* **:** those in residence **6 :** a legislative body **7 :** a place of business or entertainment **8** ♦ **:** a business organization **9 :** the audience in a theater or concert hall — **house•ful** *n*

♦ [1] abode, domicile, dwelling, home, lodging, quarters, residence ♦ [4b] blood, clan, family, folks, kin, kindred, kinfolk, line, lineage, people, race, stock, tribe ♦ [8] business, company, concern, enterprise, establishment, firm, outfit

²**house** \ˈhau̇z\ *vb* **housed; hous•ing 1** ♦ **:** to provide with or take shelter : LODGE **2** ♦ **:** to encase, enclose, or shelter as if by putting in a house

♦ [1] accommodate, billet, chamber, domicile, harbor (*or* harbour), lodge, put up, quarter, roof, shelter, take in ♦ [2] cage, closet, coop up, corral, encase, enclose, envelop, fence, hedge, hem, immure, pen, wall

house•boat \ˈhau̇s-ˌbōt\ *n* **:** a pleasure boat fitted for use as a dwelling or for leisurely cruising
house•boy \-ˌbȯi\ *n* **:** a boy or man hired to act as a household servant
house•break \-ˌbrāk\ *vb* **-broke; -bro•ken; -break•ing :** to train (a pet) in excretory habits acceptable in indoor living
house•break•ing \-ˌbrā-kiŋ\ *n* **:** the act of breaking into a dwelling with the intent of committing a felony
house•clean \-ˌklēn\ *vb* **:** to clean a house and its furniture — **house•clean•ing** *n*
house•coat \-ˌkōt\ *n* **:** a woman's often long-skirted informal garment for wear around the house
house•fly \-ˌflī\ *n* **:** a dipteran fly that is common about human habitations
¹**house•hold** \-ˌhōld\ *n* ♦ **:** those who dwell as a family under the same roof — **house•hold•er** *n*

♦ house

²**household** *adj* **1 :** DOMESTIC **2** ♦ **:** frequently seen or experienced : FAMILIAR, COMMON ⟨a ~ name⟩

♦ common, commonplace, customary, everyday, familiar, frequent, ordinary, routine, usual

house•keep•er \-ˌkē-pər\ *n* **:** a woman employed to take care of a house
house•keep•ing \-ˌkē-piŋ\ *n* **:** the care and management of a house or institutional property
house•lights \-ˌlīts\ *n pl* **:** the lights that illuminate the auditorium of a theater
house•maid \-ˌmād\ *n* ♦ **:** a female servant employed to do housework

♦ domestic, girl, maid, maidservant

house•moth•er \-ˌmə-t͟hər\ *n* **:** a woman acting as hostess, chaperone, and often housekeeper in a group residence
House of Commons : the lower house of the British or Canadian parliaments
house•plant \-ˌplant\ *n* **:** a plant grown or kept indoors
house sparrow *n* **:** a Eurasian sparrow widely introduced in urban and agricultural areas
house•top \ˈhau̇s-ˌtäp\ *n* **:** ROOF
house•wares \-ˌwarz\ *n pl* **:** small articles of household equipment
house•warm•ing \-ˌwȯr-miŋ\ *n* **:** a party to celebrate the taking possession of a house or premises
house•wife \-ˌwīf\ *n* **:** a married woman in charge of a household — **house•wife•ly** *adj* — **house•wif•ery** \-ˌwī-fə-rē\ *n*
house•work \-ˌwərk\ *n* **:** the work of housekeeping
¹**hous•ing** \ˈhau̇-ziŋ\ *n* **1 :** SHELTER; *also* **:** dwellings provided for people **2** ♦ **:** something that covers or protects

♦ armor, capsule, case, casing, cocoon, cover, husk, jacket, pod, sheath, shell

²**housing** *n* **:** CAPARISON 1
HOV *abbr* high-occupancy vehicle
hove *past and past part of* HEAVE
hov•el \ˈhə-vəl, ˈhä-\ *n* **:** a small, wretched, and often dirty house **:** HUT
hov•er \ˈhə-vər, ˈhä-\ *vb* **hov•ered; hov•er•ing 1 a :** FLUTTER **b** ♦ **:** to remain suspended over a place or object **2 :** to move to and fro **3** ♦ **:** to be in an uncertain state of uncertainty, irresolution, or suspense

♦ [1b] drift, float, glide, hang, poise, ride, sail, waft ♦ [3] hang, menace, overhang, threaten

hov•er•craft \-ˌkraft\ *n* **:** a vehicle that rides on a cushion of air over a surface
¹**how** \ˈhau̇\ *adv* **1 :** in what way or manner ⟨~ was it done⟩ **2 :** with what meaning ⟨~ do we interpret such behavior⟩ **3 :** for what reason ⟨~ could you have done such a thing⟩ **4 :** to what extent or degree ⟨~ deep is it⟩ **5 :** in what state or condition ⟨~ are you⟩ — **how about :** what do you say to or think of ⟨*how about* coming with me⟩ — **how come :** why is it that
²**how** *conj* **1 :** the way or manner in which ⟨remember ~ they fought⟩ **2 :** HOWEVER ⟨do it ~ you like⟩
¹**how•be•it** \hau̇-ˈbē-ət\ *conj* ♦ **:** even though : ALTHOUGH

♦ albeit, although, though, when, while

²**howbeit** *adv* ♦ **:** on the other hand : NEVERTHELESS

♦ but, however, nevertheless, nonetheless, notwithstanding, still, though, withal, yet

how•dah \ˈhau̇-də\ *n* **:** a seat or covered pavilion on the back of an elephant or camel
¹**how•ev•er** \hau̇-ˈe-vər\ *conj* **:** in whatever manner that
²**however** *adv* **1 :** to whatever degree; *also* **:** in whatever manner **2** ♦ **:** on the other hand

♦ but, howbeit, nevertheless, nonetheless, notwithstanding, still, though, withal, yet

how•it•zer \ˈhau̇-ət-sər\ *n* **:** a short cannon that shoots shells at a high angle
¹**howl** \ˈhau̇(-ə)l\ *vb* **1** ♦ **:** to emit a loud long doleful sound characteristic of dogs **2** ♦ **:** to cry loudly

♦ [1] bay, keen, wail, yowl ♦ [2] scream, shriek, shrill, squeal, yell, yelp

²**howl** *n* **1 :** a loud protracted mournful cry characteristic of dogs **2 a** ♦ **:** a prolonged cry of distress **b** ♦ **:** a yell or outcry of disappointment, rage, or protest

♦ [2a] groan, keen, lament, moan, plaint, wail ♦ [2b] cry, holler, hoot, shout, whoop, yell, yowl ♦ [2b] clamor (*or* clamour), hubbub, hue and cry, hullabaloo, noise, outcry, roar, tumult, uproar

howl•er \ˈhau̇-lər\ *n* **1 :** one that howls **2 :** a humorous and ridiculous blunder
howl•ing *adj* **1 :** DESOLATE, WILD **2 :** very great ⟨a ~ success⟩
how•so•ev•er \ˌhau̇-sə-ˈwe-vər\ *adv* **:** HOWEVER 1
hoy•den \ˈhȯid-ᵊn\ *n* **:** a girl or woman of saucy, boisterous, or carefree behavior
hoy•den•ish \-ish\ *adj* **:** being or acting as a hoyden
hp *abbr* horsepower
HP *abbr* high pressure
HPF *abbr* highest possible frequency
HQ *abbr* headquarters
hr *abbr* **1** here **2** hour
HR *abbr* House of Representatives
HRH *abbr* **1** Her Royal Highness **2** His Royal Highness
hrzn *abbr* horizon
Hs *symbol* hassium
HS *abbr* high school
HST *abbr* Hawaiian standard time
ht *abbr* height
HT *abbr* **1** Hawaii time **2** high-tension
HTML \ˌāch-ˌtē-ˌem-ˈel\ *n* **:** a computer language used to create World Wide Web documents
http *abbr* hypertext transfer protocol
hua•ra•che \wə-ˈrä-chē\ *n* **:** a sandal with an upper made of interwoven leather strips
hub \ˈhəb\ *n* **1 :** the central part of a circular object (as a wheel) **2 a** ♦ **:** a center of activity **b :** an airport or city through which an airline routes most of its traffic

♦ base, center (*or* centre), core, cynosure, eye, focus, heart, mecca, nucleus, seat

hub•bub \ˈhə-bəb\ *n* **1** ♦ **:** a noisy confusion of sound : UPROAR **2** ♦ **:** a state of tumultuous confusion or excitement : TURMOIL

♦ [1] clamor (*or* clamour), howl, hue and cry, hullabaloo, noise, outcry, roar, tumult, uproar ♦ [2] commotion, disturbance, furor, fuss, pandemonium, tumult, turmoil

hub•cap \ˈhəb-ˌkap\ *n* **:** a removable metal cap over the end of an axle
hu•bris \ˈhyü-brəs\ *n* **:** exaggerated pride or self-confidence
huck•le•ber•ry \ˈhə-kəl-ˌber-ē\ *n* **1 :** any of a genus of American

shrubs of the heath family; *also* : its edible dark blue berry **2** : BLUEBERRY

huck•ster \ˈhək-stər\ *n* : PEDDLER, HAWKER — **huckster** *vb*

HUD *abbr* Department of Housing and Urban Development

[1]**hud•dle** \ˈhəd-ᵊl\ *vb* **hud•dled; hud•dling 1** ♦ **:** to crowd together **2** : CONFER **3** ♦ **:** to curl up : CROUCH

♦ [1] bunch, cluster, crowd, press ♦ [3] crouch, hunch, squat

[2]**huddle** *n* **1** ♦ **:** a closely packed group **2** ♦ **:** an assembly for a common purpose : MEETING, CONFERENCE

♦ [1] array, assemblage, bank, batch, block, bunch, clump, cluster, collection, group, knot, lot, package, parcel, set, suite ♦ [2] assembly, conference, congress, convention, convocation, council, gathering, get-together, meeting, powwow, seminar

hue \ˈhyü\ *n* **1** ♦ **:** a phenomenon of light or visual perception that enables one to differentiate otherwise identical objects : COLOR; *also* : gradation of color **2 :** the attribute of colors that permits them to be classed as red, yellow, green, blue, or an intermediate color — **hued** \ˈhyüd\ *adj*

♦ cast, color (*or* colour), shade, tinge, tint, tone

hue and cry *n* ♦ **:** a clamor of pursuit or protest

♦ clamor (*or* clamour), howl, hubbub, hullabaloo, noise, outcry, roar, tumult, uproar

huff \ˈhəf\ *n* ♦ **:** a fit of anger or pique — **huff** *vb* — **huffy** *adj*

♦ dither, fluster, fret, fuss, lather, pother, stew, tizzy, twitter ♦ dudgeon, offense, peeve, pique, resentment, umbrage

hug \ˈhəg\ *vb* **hugged; hug•ging 1** ♦ **:** to press tightly especially in the arms : EMBRACE **2 :** to stay close to — **hug** *n*

♦ caress, clasp, embrace, enfold, grasp

huge \ˈhyüj\ *adj* **hug•er; hug•est** ♦ **:** very large or extensive

♦ astronomical, colossal, enormous, giant, gigantic, grand, jumbo, mammoth, massive, prodigious, titanic, tremendous, vast, whopping ***Ant*** diminutive, microscopic, minute, teeny, tiny, wee

huge•ly *adv* ♦ **:** to a great extent or degree

♦ broadly, considerably, greatly, largely, massively, monstrously, much, sizably, stupendously, tremendously, utterly, vastly

huge•ness \-nəs\ *n* ♦ **:** the quality or state of being huge

♦ enormity, immensity, magnitude, massiveness, vastness

[1]**hug•ger–mug•ger** \ˈhə-gər-ˌmə-gər\ *n* **1 :** SECRECY **2 :** CONFUSION, MUDDLE

[2]**hugger–mugger** *adj* **1** ♦ **:** kept from knowledge or view **2** ♦ **:** of a confused or disorderly nature

♦ [1] clandestine, covert, furtive, private, secret, sneak, sneaky, stealthy, surreptitious, undercover, underground, underhanded ♦ [2] chaotic, disheveled, disordered, disorderly, higgledy-piggledy, messy, pell-mell, topsy-turvy, unkempt, untidy

Hu•gue•not \ˈhyü-gə-ˌnät\ *n* **:** a French Protestant of the 16th and 17th centuries

hu•la \ˈhü-lə\ *n* **:** a sinuous Polynesian dance usually accompanied by chants

hulk \ˈhəlk\ *n* **1 :** a heavy clumsy ship **2 :** an old ship unfit for service **3** ♦ **:** a bulky or unwieldy person or thing

♦ clod, lout, lubber, lug, oaf

hulk•ing \ˈhəl-kiŋ\ *adj* : BURLY, MASSIVE

[1]**hull** \ˈhəl\ *n* **1 :** the outer covering of a fruit or seed **2 :** the frame or body especially of a ship or boat

[2]**hull** *vb* ♦ **:** to remove the hulls of — **hull•er** *n*

♦ bark, flay, husk, peel, shell, skin

hul•la•ba•loo \ˈhə-lə-bə-ˌlü\ *n, pl* **-loos** ♦ **:** a confused noise : UPROAR

♦ clamor (*or* clamour), howl, hubbub, hue and cry, noise, outcry, roar, tumult, uproar

hul•lo \ˌhə-ˈlō\ *chiefly Brit variant of* HELLO

[1]**hum** \ˈhəm\ *vb* **hummed; hum•ming 1 :** to utter a sound like that of the speech sound m prolonged **2** ♦ **:** to make the natural noise of an insect in motion or a similar sound : DRONE **3 :** to be busily active **4 :** to run smoothly **5 :** to sing with closed lips

♦ buzz, drone, whir, whish, whiz, zip, zoom

[2]**hum** *n* ♦ **:** the act of humming or the sound made by humming

♦ buzz, drone, purr, whir, whiz, zoom

[1]**hu•man** \ˈhyü-mən, ˈyü-\ *adj* **1 :** of, relating to, being, or characteristic of humans **2 :** having human form or attributes — **hu•man•ly** *adv* — **hu•man•ness** *n*

[2]**human** *n* ♦ **:** any of a species of bipedal primate mammals comprising all living persons and their recent ancestors; *also* : HOMINID

♦ being, body, creature, individual, man, mortal, person, stiff

hu•mane \hyü-ˈmān, yü-\ *adj* **1** ♦ **:** marked by compassion, sympathy, or consideration for others **2** : HUMANISTIC — **hu•mane•ly** *adv* — **hu•mane•ness** *n*

♦ beneficent, benevolent, compassionate, good-hearted, kind, kindly, sympathetic, tender, tenderhearted, warmhearted ***Ant*** barbarous, bestial, brutal, brutish, callous, cold-blooded, cruel, heartless, inhuman, inhumane, insensate, savage, unfeeling, unkind, unkindly, unsympathetic

human immunodeficiency virus *n* : HIV

hu•man•ism \ˈhyü-mə-ˌni-zəm, ˈyü-\ *n* **1 :** devotion to the humanities; *also* : the revival of classical letters characteristic of the Renaissance **2 :** a doctrine or way of life centered on human interests or values — **hu•man•ist** \-nist\ *n or adj* — **hu•man•is•tic** \ˌhyü-mə-ˈnis-tik, ˌyü-\ *adj*

[1]**hu•man•i•tar•i•an** \hyü-ˌma-nə-ˈter-ē-ən, yü-\ *n* **:** one who practices philanthropy — **hu•man•i•tar•i•an•ism** *n*

[2]**humanitarian** *adj* ♦ **:** concerned for or active in the promotion of human welfare

♦ altruistic, beneficent, benevolent, charitable, philanthropic

hu•man•i•ty \hyü-ˈma-nə-tē, yü-\ *n, pl* **-ties 1** ♦ **:** the quality or state of being human or humane **2** *pl* **:** the branches of learning dealing with human concerns (as philosophy) as opposed to natural processes (as physics) **3** ♦ **:** the human race

♦ [1] charity, commiseration, compassion, feeling, heart, kindliness, kindness, mercy, pity, sympathy ♦ [3] folks, humankind, people, persons, public, society, world

hu•man•ize \ˈhyü-mə-ˌnīz, ˈyü-\ *vb* **-ized; -iz•ing :** to make human or humane — **hu•man•iza•tion** \ˌhyü-mə-nə-ˈzā-shən, ˌyü-\ *n* — **hu•man•iz•er** *n*

hu•man•kind \ˈhyü-mən-ˌkīnd, ˈyü-\ *n* ♦ **:** the human race

♦ Homo sapiens, humanity, man, mankind

hu•man•oid \ˈhyü-mə-ˌnȯid, ˈyü-\ *adj* **:** having human form or characteristics — **humanoid** *n*

human pap•il•lo•ma•virus \-ˌpa-pə-ˈlō-mə-ˌvī-rəs\ *n* **:** any of numerous DNA-containing viruses that cause various human warts

[1]**hum•ble** \ˈhəm-bəl\ *adj* **hum•bler** \-bə-lər\; **hum•blest** \-bə-ləst\ **1 :** not proud or haughty **2** ♦ **:** not pretentious : UNASSUMING **3** ♦ **:** ranking low in a hierarchy or scale

♦ [2] demure, lowly, meek, modest, retiring, unassuming, unpretentious ***Ant*** arrogant, conceited, presumptuous, proud, self-important ♦ [3] common, ignoble, inferior, low, lowly, mean, plebeian, vulgar

[2]**humble** *vb* **hum•bled; hum•bling 1 :** to make humble **2** ♦ **:** to destroy the power or prestige of — **hum•bler** *n*

♦ abase, debase, degrade, demean, discredit, disgrace, dishonor (*or* dishonour), humiliate, lower, shame, smirch, take down ***Ant*** aggrandize, elevate, exalt

hum•ble•ness \-nəs\ *n* ♦ **:** the quality or state of being humble

♦ humility, lowliness, meekness, modesty

hum•bly \ˈhəm-blē\ *adv* ♦ **:** in a humble manner

♦ lowly, meekly, modestly, sheepishly

[1]**hum•bug** \ˈhəm-ˌbəg\ *n* **1** ♦ **:** something designed to deceive and mislead : HOAX **2** ♦ **:** language, conduct, or an idea that is absurd or contrary to good sense : NONSENSE **3** ♦ **:** a willfully false, deceptive, or insincere person

♦ [1] counterfeit, fake, forgery, hoax, phony, sham ♦ [2] bunk, claptrap, drivel, fiddlesticks, folly, foolishness, fudge, hogwash, nonsense, piffle, rot, silliness, slush, stupidity, trash ♦ [3] charlatan, fake, fraud, hoaxer, mountebank, phony, pretender, quack

[2]**humbug** *vb* **hum•bugged; hum•bug•ging** ♦ **:** to cause to accept as true or valid what is false or invalid : DECEIVE

♦ beguile, bluff, cozen, deceive, delude, dupe, fool, gull, have, hoax, hoodwink, misinform, mislead, string along, take in, trick

hum•ding•er \ˈhəm-ˈdiŋ-ər\ *n* **:** a person or thing of striking excellence

hum•drum \ˈhəm-ˌdrəm\ *adj* ♦ : tediously uniform or unvarying : MONOTONOUS, DULL — **humdrum** *n*

♦ drab, dull, flat, monotonous, ponderous, stuffy, uninteresting

hu•mer•us \ˈhyü-mə-rəs\ *n, pl* **hu•meri** \ˈhyü-mə-ˌrī, -ˌrē\ : the long bone extending from shoulder to elbow

hu•mid \ˈhyü-məd, ˈyü-\ *adj* ♦ : containing or characterized by perceptible moisture — **hu•mid•ly** *adv*

♦ muggy, sticky, sultry ***Ant*** dry

hu•mid•i•fy \hyü-ˈmi-də-ˌfī\ *vb* **-fied; -fy•ing** : to make humid — **hu•mid•i•fi•ca•tion** \-ˌmi-də-fə-ˈkā-shən\ *n* — **hu•mid•i•fi•er** \-ˈmi-də-ˌfī-ər\ *n*

hu•mid•i•ty \hyü-ˈmi-də-tē, yü-\ *n, pl* **-ties** : the amount of atmospheric moisture

hu•mi•dor \ˈhyü-mə-ˌdȯr, ˈyü-\ *n* : a case (as for storing cigars) in which the air is kept properly humidified

hu•mil•i•ate \hyü-ˈmi-lē-ˌāt, yü-\ *vb* **-at•ed; -at•ing** ♦ : to injure the self-respect of — **hu•mil•i•at•ing•ly** *adv* — **hu•mil•i•a•tion** \-ˌmi-lē-ˈā-shən\ *n*

♦ abase, debase, degrade, demean, discredit, disgrace, dishonor (*or* dishonour), humble, lower, shame, smirch, take down

hu•mil•i•ty \hyü-ˈmi-lə-tē, yü-\ *n* ♦ : the quality or state of being humble

♦ humbleness, lowliness, meekness, modesty ***Ant*** arrogance, conceit, egoism, egotism, haughtiness, pretense, pretension, pretentiousness, pride, superiority

hum•mer \ˈhə-mər\ *n* : one that hums

hum•ming•bird \ˈhə-miŋ-ˌbərd\ *n* : any of a family of tiny brightly colored American birds related to the swifts

hum•mock \ˈhə-mək\ *n* : a rounded mound : KNOLL — **hum•mocky** \-mə-kē\ *adj*

hum•mus \ˈhə-məs, ˈhu̇-\ *n* : a paste of pureed chickpeas usually mixed with sesame oil or paste

hu•mon•gous \hyü-ˈməŋ-gəs, -ˈmäŋ-\ *adj* : extremely large

[1]**hu•mor** *or Can and Brit* **hu•mour** \ˈhyü-mər, ˈyü-\ *n* **1** : TEMPERAMENT **2** ♦ : a conscious state of mind or predominant emotion : MOOD **3** : WHIM **4** : a quality that appeals to a sense of the ludicrous or incongruous; *also* : a keen perception of the ludicrous or incongruous **5** ♦ : comical or amusing entertainment

♦ [2] cheer, frame, mode, mood, spirit, temper ♦ [5] comedy, farce, slapstick

[2]**humor** *or Can and Brit* **humour** *vb* ♦ : to comply with the wishes or mood of

♦ cater to, gratify, indulge

hu•mor•ist \ˈhyü-mə-rist, ˈyü-\ *n* ♦ : a person specializing in or noted for humor

♦ card, comedian, comic, jester, joker, wag, wit

hu•mor•less *or Can and Brit* **hu•mour•less** \ˈhyü-mər-ləs, ˈyü-\ *adj* **1** ♦ : lacking a sense of humor **2** : lacking humorous characteristics — **hu•mor•less•ly** *adv* — **hu•mor•less•ness** *n*

♦ earnest, grave, serious, severe, sober, solemn, staid, unsmiling, weighty

hu•mor•ous \ˈhyü-mə-rəs, ˈyü-\ *adj* **1** ♦ : full of or characterized by humor **2** ♦ : indicating or expressive of a sense of humor — **hu•mor•ous•ly** *adv*

♦ [1] antic, comic, comical, droll, farcical, funny, hilarious, hysterical, laughable, ludicrous, ridiculous, riotous, risible, screaming, uproarious ♦ [2] clever, facetious, jocular, smart, witty

hu•mor•ous•ness *n* : the quality or state of being humorous

humour *Can and Brit var of* HUMOR

hump \ˈhəmp\ *n* **1** : a rounded protuberance (as on the back of a camel) **2** : a difficult phase or obstacle ⟨over the ~⟩ — **humped** *adj*

hump•back \ˈhəmp-ˌbak; *1 also* -ˈbak\ *n* **1** : HUNCHBACK **2** : HUMPBACK WHALE — **hump•backed** *adj*

humpback whale *n* : a large baleen whale having very long flippers

hu•mus \ˈhyü-məs, ˈyü-\ *n* : the dark organic part of soil formed from decaying matter

Hun \ˈhən\ *n* : a member of an Asian people that invaded Europe about A.D. 450

[1]**hunch** \ˈhənch\ *vb* **1** : to thrust oneself forward **2** ♦ : to assume or cause to assume a bent or crooked posture

♦ crouch, huddle, squat

[2]**hunch** *n* **1** : PUSH **2** : a strong intuitive feeling about what will happen

hunch•back \ˈhənch-ˌbak\ *n* : a person with a crooked back; *also* : a back with a hump — **hunch•backed** *adj*

hun•dred \ˈhən-drəd\ *n, pl* **hundreds** *or* **hundred** : 10 times 10 — **hundred** *adj* — **hun•dredth** \-drədth\ *adj or n*

hun•dred•weight \-ˌwāt\ *n, pl* **hundredweight** *or* **hundredweights** : a unit of measurement typically equal to 100 pounds

[1]**hung** *past and past part of* HANG

[2]**hung** *adj* : unable to reach a decision or verdict ⟨a ~ jury⟩

Hung *abbr* Hungarian; Hungary

Hun•gar•i•an \ˌhəŋ-ˈger-ē-ən\ *n* **1** : a native or inhabitant of Hungary **2** : the language of the Hungarians — **Hungarian** *adj*

[1]**hun•ger** \ˈhəŋ-gər\ *n* **1** : a craving or urgent need for food **2** ♦ : a strong desire

♦ appetite, craving, desire, drive, hankering, itch, longing, lust, passion, thirst, urge, yearning, yen ♦ appetite, ardor, avidity, eagerness, enthusiasm, excitement, impatience, keenness, thirst

[2]**hunger** *vb* **1** : to feel or suffer hunger **2** ♦ : to have an eager desire

♦ ache, die, hanker, itch, long, pant, pine, sigh, thirst, yearn ♦ *usu* **hunger for** ache for, covet, crave, desire, die for, hanker for, long for, lust (for *or* after), pine for, repine for, thirst for, want, wish for, yearn for

hung•over \ˈhəŋ-ˈō-vər\ *adj* : having a hangover

hun•gry \ˈhəŋ-grē\ *adj* **1** ♦ : feeling hunger **2** ♦ : marked by enthusiastic or impatient desire or interest — **hun•gri•ly** *adv*

♦ [1] empty, famished ***Ant*** full, satisfied ♦ [2] agog, anxious, ardent, athirst, avid, crazy, eager, enthusiastic, gung ho, hot, keen, nuts, raring, solicitous, thirsty, voracious

hung up *adj* **1** : DELAYED **2** : ENTHUSIASTIC; *also* : PREOCCUPIED **3** : anxiously nervous

hunk \ˈhəŋk\ *n* **1** ♦ : a large piece **2** : an attractive well-built man — **hunky** *adj*

♦ blob, chunk, clod, clump, glob, gob, lump, nub, wad

hun•ker \ˈhəŋ-kər\ *vb* **1** : CROUCH, SQUAT — usually used with *down* **2** : to settle in for a sustained period — used with *down*

hun•ky–do•ry \ˌhəŋ-kē-ˈdōr-ē\ *adj* : quite satisfactory : FINE

[1]**hunt** \ˈhənt\ *vb* **1** : to pursue for food or in sport; *also* : to take part in a hunt **2** ♦ : to try to find : SEEK **3** : to drive or chase especially by harrying **4** : to traverse or go over in search of prey or quarry **5** ♦ : to find, uncover, or obtain after diligent search — used with *through, up,* or *down* — **hunt•er** *n*

♦ [2] cast about, forage, pursue, quest, search (for *or* out), seek ♦ *usu* **hunt through** [5] dig, dredge, rake, ransack, rifle, rummage, scour, search ♦ *usu* **hunt down** *or* **hunt up** [5] detect, determine, dig up, discover, ferret out, find, hit on, locate, track down

[2]**hunt** *n* : an act, practice, or instance of hunting

Hun•ting•ton's disease \ˈhən-tiŋ-tənz-\ *n* : a chorea that usually begins in middle age and leads to dementia

hunt•ress \ˈhən-trəs\ *n* : a woman who hunts game

hunts•man \ˈhənts-mən\ *n* **1** : HUNTER **2** : a person who manages a hunt and looks after the hounds

hur•dle \ˈhərd-ᵊl\ *n* **1** : a barrier to leap over in a race **2** : something that impedes progress or achievement : OBSTACLE — **hurdle** *vb* — **hur•dler** *n*

hur•dy–gur•dy \ˌhər-dē-ˈgər-dē, ˈhər-dē-ˌgər-dē\ *n, pl* **-gurdies** : a musical instrument in which the sound is produced by turning a crank

hurl \ˈhərl\ *vb* **1** : to move or cause to move vigorously **2** : to throw down with violence **3 a** ♦ : to throw forcefully : FLING **b** : to throw (a baseball) to a batter : PITCH — **hurl** *n* — **hurl•er** *n*

♦ cast, catapult, chuck, dash, fire, fling, heave, hurtle, launch, peg, pelt, pitch, sling, throw, toss

hur•ly–bur•ly \ˌhər-lē-ˈbər-lē\ *n* : a state of commotion, excitement, or violent disturbance : UPROAR

Hu•ron \ˈhyu̇r-ən, ˈhyu̇r-ˌän\ *n, pl* **Hurons** *or* **Huron** : a member of a confederacy of American Indian peoples formerly living between Georgian Bay and Lake Ontario

hur•rah \hu̇-ˈrō, -ˈrä\ *also* **hur•ray** \hu̇-ˈrā\ *interj* — used to express joy, approval, or encouragement

hur•ri•cane \ˈhər-ə-ˌkān\ *n* : a tropical cyclone with winds of 74 miles (118 kilometers) per hour or greater that is usually accompanied by rain, thunder, and lightning

hur•ried•ly \ˈhər-əd-lē\ *adv* ♦ : in a hurried manner

♦ cursorily, hastily, headlong, pell-mell, precipitately, rashly

[1]**hur·ry** \ˈhər-ē\ *vb* **hur·ried; hur·ry·ing** **1** ♦ **:** to carry or cause to go with haste **2 :** to impel to a greater speed **3** ♦ **:** to move or act with haste — **hur·ried·ness** *n*

♦ [1, 3] accelerate, hasten, quicken, rush, speed (up), step up, whisk *Ant* decelerate, retard, slow (down) ♦ [3] course, dash, fly, hasten, hurtle, hustle, pelt, race, rocket, run, rush, shoot, speed, step, tear, zip, zoom *Ant* crawl, creep, poke

[2]**hurry** *n* ♦ **:** extreme haste or eagerness

♦ celerity, fastness, fleetness, haste, quickness, rapidity, speed, swiftness, velocity ♦ haste, hustle, precipitation, rush *Ant* deliberateness, deliberation

[1]**hurt** \ˈhərt\ *vb* **hurt; hurt·ing** **1** ♦ **:** to feel or cause to feel physical or emotional pain **2** ♦ **:** to do harm to **:** DAMAGE **3 :** OFFEND **4 :** HAMPER **5 :** to be in need — usually used with *for* — **hurt** *adj*

♦ [1] agonize, bleed, feel, grieve, mourn, sorrow, suffer ♦ [1] ache, pain, smart ♦ [2] damage, harm, injure, wound ♦ [2] blemish, break, cripple, damage, deface, disfigure, flaw, harm, injure, mar, spoil, vitiate

[2]**hurt** *n* **1 :** a bodily injury or wound **2 :** SUFFERING **3** ♦ **:** physical or mental damage **:** HARM

♦ damage, detriment, harm, injury

hurt·ful \ˈhərt-fəl\ *adj* ♦ **:** causing injury, detriment, or suffering — **hurt·ful·ness** *n*

♦ adverse, bad, baleful, baneful, damaging, deleterious, detrimental, evil, harmful, ill, injurious, mischievous, noxious, pernicious, prejudicial

hur·tle \ˈhərt-ᵊl\ *vb* **hur·tled; hur·tling** **1** ♦ **:** to move rapidly or forcefully **2 :** to throw forcefully **:** HURL, FLING

♦ dash, fly, hasten, hurry, rocket, run, rush, speed, tear, zip, zoom

[1]**hus·band** \ˈhəz-bənd\ *n* **:** a male partner in a marriage
[2]**husband** *vb* **:** to manage prudently
hus·band·man \ˈhəz-bənd-mən\ *n* **:** FARMER
hus·band·ry \ˈhəz-bən-drē\ *n* **1** ♦ **:** the control or judicious use of resources **2 :** AGRICULTURE **3 :** the production and care of domestic animals

♦ economy, frugality, providence, thrift

[1]**hush** \ˈhəsh\ *vb* **1** ♦ **:** to make or become quiet or calm **2 :** SUPPRESS

♦ calm (down), cool (off *or* down), quiet, settle (down) ♦ mute, quell, settle, silence, still

[2]**hush** *n* ♦ **:** a silence or calm especially following noise

♦ calm, calmness, peace, placidity, quiet, quietness, repose, serenity, still, stillness, tranquillity

hushed \ˈhəsht\ *adj* **1** ♦ **:** free of noise or agitation **2** ♦ **:** marked by secrecy or caution

♦ [1] calm, halcyon, peaceful, placid, quiet, serene, still, tranquil, untroubled ♦ [1] muted, noiseless, quiet, silent, soundless, still ♦ [2] confidential, inside, intimate, private, secret

hush–hush \ˈhəsh-ˌhəsh\ *adj* **:** SECRET, CONFIDENTIAL
[1]**husk** \ˈhəsk\ *n* **1 :** a usually thin dry outer covering of a seed or fruit **2** ♦ **:** an outer layer **:** SHELL

♦ armor, capsule, case, casing, cocoon, cover, housing, jacket, pod, sheath, shell

[2]**husk** *vb* ♦ **:** to strip the husk from — **husk·er** *n*

♦ bark, flay, hull, peel, shell, skin

[1]**hus·ky** \ˈhəs-kē\ *adj* **hus·ki·er; -est** ♦ **:** hoarse with or as if with emotion — **hus·ki·ly** \-kə-lē\ *adv* — **hus·ki·ness** \-kē-nəs\ *n*

♦ coarse, gravelly, gruff, hoarse, scratchy, throaty

[2]**husky** *adj* **1** ♦ **:** strongly formed or constructed **:** BURLY **2 :** LARGE

♦ beefy, brawny, burly

[3]**husky** *n, pl* **huskies :** a heavy-coated working dog of the New World arctic region
hus·sar \(ˌ)hə-ˈzär\ *n* **:** a member of any of various European cavalry units
hus·sy \ˈhə-zē, -sē\ *n, pl* **hussies** **1 :** a lewd or brazen woman **2 :** a pert or mischievous girl
hus·tings \ˈhəs-tiŋz\ *n pl* **:** a place where political campaign speeches are made; *also* **:** the proceedings in an election campaign

[1]**hus·tle** \ˈhə-səl\ *vb* **hus·tled; hus·tling** **1 :** JOSTLE, SHOVE **2 :** to move or act quickly **:** HASTEN, HURRY **3 :** to work energetically **4** ♦ **:** to sell something to or obtain something from by energetic and especially underhanded activity

♦ bleed, cheat, chisel, cozen, defraud, fleece, gyp, mulct, rook, shortchange, skin, squeeze, stick, sting, swindle, victimize

[2]**hustle** *n* **1** ♦ **:** energetic activity **2** ♦ **:** an act or instance of fraud

♦ [1] haste, hurry, precipitation, rush ♦ [2] racket, swindle

hus·tler \ˈhəs-lər\ *n* ♦ **:** one that hustles

♦ go-getter, live wire, powerhouse, self-starter

hut \ˈhət\ *n* ♦ **:** an often small and temporary dwelling of simple construction **:** SHACK

♦ cabin, camp, hutch, shack, shanty

hutch \ˈhəch\ *n* **1 :** a chest or compartment for storage **2** ♦ **:** a cupboard usually surmounted with open shelves **3 :** a pen or coop for an animal **4 :** a small and often temporary dwelling **:** HUT

♦ buffet, cabinet, closet, cupboard, locker, sideboard

huz·zah *or* **huz·za** \(ˌ)hə-ˈzä\ *n* **:** a shout of acclaim — often used interjectionally to express joy or approbation
HV *abbr* **1** high velocity **2** high voltage
HVAC *abbr* heating, ventilating and air-conditioning
hvy *abbr* heavy
HW *abbr* hot water
hwy *abbr* highway
hy·a·cinth \ˈhī-ə-(ˌ)sinth\ *n* **:** a bulbous Mediterranean herb related to the lilies that is widely grown for its spikes of fragrant bell-shaped flowers
[1]**hy·brid** \ˈhī-brəd\ *n* **1** ♦ **:** an offspring of genetically differing parents (as members of different breeds or species) **2 :** one of mixed origin or composition — **hy·brid·i·za·tion** \ˌhī-brə-də-ˈzā-shən\ *n* — **hy·brid·ize** \ˈhī-brə-ˌdīz\ *vb* — **hy·brid·iz·er** *n*

♦ cross, mongrel

[2]**hybrid** *adj* ♦ **:** of, relating to, or being a hybrid

♦ mixed, mongrel

hy·dra \ˈhī-drə\ *n* **:** any of numerous small tubular freshwater coelenterates that are polyps having at one end a mouth surrounded by tentacles
hy·dran·gea \hī-ˈdrān-jə\ *n* **:** any of a genus of shrubs related to the currants and grown for their showy clusters of white or tinted flowers
hy·drant \ˈhī-drənt\ *n* **:** a pipe with a valve and spout at which water may be drawn from a main pipe
hy·drate \ˈhī-ˌdrāt\ *n* **:** a compound formed by union of water with some other substance — **hydrate** *vb*
hy·drau·lic \hī-ˈdrȯ-lik\ *adj* **1 :** operated, moved, or effected by means of water **2 :** of or relating to hydraulics **3 :** operated by the resistance offered or the pressure transmitted when a quantity of liquid is forced through a small orifice or through a tube **4 :** hardening or setting under water
hy·drau·lics \-liks\ *n* **:** a science that deals with practical applications of liquid (as water) in motion
hydro \ˈhī-drō\ *n* **:** HYDROPOWER
hy·dro·car·bon \ˈhī-drō-ˌkär-bən\ *n* **:** an organic compound containing only carbon and hydrogen
hy·dro·ceph·a·lus \ˌhī-drō-ˈse-fə-ləs\ *n* **:** abnormal increase in the amount of fluid in the cranial cavity accompanied by enlargement of the skull and atrophy of the brain
hy·dro·chlo·ric acid \ˌhī-drə-ˈklōr-ik-\ *n* **:** a sharp-smelling corrosive acid used in the laboratory and in industry and present in dilute form in gastric juice
hy·dro·dy·nam·ics \ˌhī-drō-dī-ˈna-miks\ *n* **:** a science that deals with the motion of fluids and the forces acting on moving bodies immersed in fluids — **hy·dro·dy·nam·ic** *adj*
hy·dro·elec·tric \ˌhī-drō-i-ˈlek-trik\ *adj* **:** of or relating to production of electricity by waterpower — **hy·dro·elec·tric·i·ty** \-ˌlek-ˈtri-sə-tē\ *n*
hy·dro·foil \ˈhī-drə-ˌfȯi(-ə)l\ *n* **:** a boat that has fins attached to the bottom by struts for lifting the hull clear of the water to allow faster speeds
hy·dro·gen \ˈhī-drə-jən\ *n* **:** a gaseous colorless odorless highly flammable chemical element that is the lightest of the elements — **hy·drog·e·nous** \hī-ˈdrä-jə-nəs\ *adj*
hy·dro·ge·nate \hī-ˈdrä-jə-ˌnāt, ˈhī-drə-\ *vb* **-nat·ed; -nat·ing** **:** to combine or treat with hydrogen; *esp* **:** to add hydrogen to the molecule of — **hy·dro·ge·na·tion** \hī-ˌdrä-jə-ˈnā-shən, ˌhī-drə-\ *n*
hydrogen bomb *n* **:** a bomb whose violent explosive power is due

to the sudden release of atomic energy resulting from the fusion of light nuclei (as of hydrogen atoms)

hydrogen peroxide *n* : an unstable compound of hydrogen and oxygen used especially as an oxidizing and bleaching agent, an antiseptic, and a propellant

hy•dro•graph•ic \ˌhī-drə-ˈgra-fik\ *adj* : of or relating to the description and study of bodies of water — **hy•drog•ra•pher** *n* — **hy•drog•ra•phy** \hī-ˈdrä-grə-fē\ *n*

hy•drol•o•gy \hī-ˈdrä-lə-jē\ *n* : a science dealing with the properties, distribution, and circulation of water — **hy•dro•log•ic** \ˌhī-drə-ˈlä-jik\ *or* **hy•dro•log•i•cal** \-ji-kəl\ *adj* — **hy•drol•o•gist** \hī-ˈdrä-lə-jist\ *n*

hy•dro•ly•sis \hī-ˈdrä-lə-səs\ *n* : a chemical decomposition involving the addition of the elements of water

hy•drom•e•ter \hī-ˈdrä-mə-tər\ *n* : a floating instrument for determining specific gravities of liquids and hence the strength (as of alcoholic liquors)

hy•dro•pho•bia \ˌhī-drə-ˈfō-bē-ə\ *n* : RABIES

hy•dro•phone \ˈhī-drə-ˌfōn\ *n* : an underwater listening device

1**hy•dro•plane** \ˈhī-drə-ˌplān\ *n* **1** : a powerboat designed for racing that skims the surface of the water **2** : SEAPLANE

2**hydroplane** *vb* : to skid on a wet road due to loss of contact between the tires and road

hy•dro•pon•ics \ˌhī-drə-ˈpä-niks\ *n* : the growing of plants in nutrient solutions — **hy•dro•pon•ic** *adj*

hy•dro•pow•er \ˈhī-drə-ˌpau̇(-ə)r\ *n* : hydroelectric power

hy•dro•sphere \ˈhī-drə-ˌsfir\ *n* : the water (as vapor or lakes) of the earth

hy•dro•stat•ic \ˌhī-drə-ˈsta-tik\ *adj* : of or relating to fluids at rest or to the pressures they exert or transmit

hy•dro•ther•a•py \ˌhī-drə-ˈther-ə-pē\ *n* : the use of water especially externally in the treatment of disease or disability

hy•dro•ther•mal \ˌhī-drə-ˈthər-məl\ *adj* : of or relating to hot water

hy•drous \ˈhī-drəs\ *adj* : containing water

hy•drox•ide \hī-ˈdräk-ˌsīd\ *n* **1** : a negatively charged ion consisting of one atom of oxygen and one atom of hydrogen **2** : a compound of hydroxide with an element or group

hy•e•na \hī-ˈē-nə\ *n* : any of several large doglike carnivorous mammals of Asia and Africa

hy•giene \ˈhī-ˌjēn\ *n* **1** : a science concerned with establishing and maintaining good health **2** : conditions or practices conducive to health — **hy•gien•i•cal•ly** \-ni-k(ə-)lē\ *adv* — **hy•gien•ist** \hī-ˈjē-nist, ˈhī-ˌjē-, hī-ˈje-\ *n*

hy•gien•ic \hī-ˈje-nik, -ˈjē-\ *adj* ♦ : having or showing good hygiene

♦ aseptic, sanitary, sterile

hy•grom•e•ter \hī-ˈgrä-mə-tər\ *n* : any of several instruments for measuring the humidity of the atmosphere

hy•gro•scop•ic \ˌhī-grə-ˈskä-pik\ *adj* : readily taking up and retaining moisture

hying *pres part of* HIE

hy•men \ˈhī-mən\ *n* : a fold of mucous membrane partly closing the opening of the vagina

hy•me•ne•al \ˌhī-mə-ˈnē-əl\ *adj* : NUPTIAL

hymn \ˈhim\ *n* ♦ : a song of praise especially to God — **hymn** *vb*

♦ anthem, canticle, carol, chorale, psalm, spiritual

hym•nal \ˈhim-nəl\ *n* : a book of hymns

hyp *abbr* hypothesis; hypothetical

1**hype** \ˈhīp\ *vb* **hyped; hyp•ing** **1** : STIMULATE — usually used with *up* **2** : INCREASE — **hyped–up** *adj*

2**hype** *vb* **hyped; hyping** **1** : DECEIVE **2** : PUBLICIZE

3**hype** *n* **1** : DECEPTION, PUT-ON **2** : PUBLICITY

hy•per \ˈhī-pər\ *adj* **1** : HIGH-STRUNG, EXCITABLE **2** : extremely active

hy•per•acid•i•ty \ˌhī-pər-ə-ˈsi-də-tē\ *n* : the condition of containing excessive acid especially in the stomach — **hy•per•ac•id** \-ˈa-səd\ *adj*

hy•per•ac•tive \-ˈak-tiv\ *adj* ♦ : excessively or pathologically active — **hy•per•ac•tiv•i•ty** \-ˌak-ˈti-və-tē\ *n*

♦ agitated, feverish, frenzied, heated, hectic, overactive, overwrought

hy•per•bar•ic \ˌhī-pər-ˈbar-ik\ *adj* : of, relating to, or utilizing greater than normal pressure (as of oxygen)

hy•per•bo•la \hī-ˈpər-bə-lə\ *n, pl* **-las** *or* **-lae** \-(ˌ)lē\ : a curve formed by the intersection of a double right circular cone with a plane that cuts both halves of the cone — **hy•per•bol•ic** \ˌhī-pər-ˈbä-lik\ *adj*

hy•per•bo•le \hī-ˈpər-bə-(ˌ)lē\ *n* ♦ : extravagant exaggeration used as a figure of speech

♦ caricature, elaboration, embellishment, exaggeration, magnification, overstatement, padding

hy•per•crit•i•cal \ˌhī-pər-ˈkri-ti-kəl\ *adj* ♦ : excessively critical — **hy•per•crit•i•cal•ly** \-k(ə-)lē\ *adv*

♦ captious, carping, critical, overcritical

hy•per•drive \ˈhī-pər-ˌdrīv\ *n* : a state of extremely heightened activity

hy•per•ex•tend \ˌhī-pər-ik-ˈstend\ *vb* : to extend beyond the normal range of motion — **hy•per•ex•ten•sion** \-ˈsten-shən\ *n*

hy•per•gly•ce•mia \ˌhī-pər-glī-ˈsē-mē-ə\ *n* : excess of sugar in the blood — **hy•per•gly•ce•mic** \-mik\ *adj*

hy•per•ki•net•ic \-kə-ˈne-tik\ *adj* : characterized by fast-paced or frenetic activity

hy•per•link \ˈhī-pər-ˌliŋk\ *n* : a connecting element (as highlighted text) between one place in a hypertext or hypermedia document and another

hy•per•me•dia \ˈhī-pər-ˌmē-dē-ə\ *n* : a database format offering direct access to text, sound, or images related to that on display

hy•per•opia \ˌhī-pə-ˈrō-pē-ə\ *n* : a condition in which visual images come to focus behind the retina resulting especially in defective vision for near objects — **hy•per•opic** \-ˈrō-pik, -ˈrä-\ *adj*

hy•per•sen•si•tive \-ˈsen-sə-tiv\ *adj* **1** : excessively or abnormally sensitive **2** : abnormally susceptible physiologically to a specific agent (as a drug) — **hy•per•sen•si•tive•ness** *n* — **hy•per•sen•si•tiv•i•ty** \-ˌsen-sə-ˈti-və-tē\ *n*

hy•per•ten•sion \ˈhī-pər-ˌten-chən\ *n* : high blood pressure — **hy•per•ten•sive** \ˌhī-pər-ˈten-siv\ *adj or n*

hy•per•text \ˈhī-pər-ˌtekst\ *n* : a database format in which information related to that on display can be accessed directly from the display

hy•per•thy•roid•ism \ˌhī-pər-ˈthī-ˌrȯi-ˌdi-zəm\ *n* : excessive activity of the thyroid gland; *also* : the resulting bodily condition — **hy•per•thy•roid** \-ˈthī-ˌrȯid\ *adj*

hy•per•tro•phy \hī-ˈpər-trə-fē\ *n, pl* **-phies** : excessive development of a body part — **hy•per•tro•phic** \ˌhī-pər-ˈtrō-fik\ *adj* — **hypertrophy** *vb*

hy•per•ven•ti•late \ˌhī-pər-ˈven-tə-ˌlāt\ *vb* : to breathe rapidly and deeply especially to the point of losing an abnormal amount of carbon dioxide from the blood — **hy•per•ven•ti•la•tion** \-ˌven-tə-ˈlā-shən\ *n*

hy•phen \ˈhī-fən\ *n* : a punctuation mark - used especially to divide or to compound words or word parts — **hyphen** *vb*

hy•phen•ate \ˈhī-fə-ˌnāt\ *vb* **-at•ed; -at•ing** : to connect or divide with a hyphen — **hy•phen•ation** \ˌhī-fə-ˈnā-shən\ *n*

hyp•no•sis \hip-ˈnō-səs\ *n, pl* **-no•ses** \-ˌsēz\ : an induced state that resembles sleep and in which the subject is responsive to suggestions of the inducer (**hyp•no•tist** \ˈhip-nə-tist\) — **hyp•no•tism** \ˈhip-nə-ˌti-zəm\ *n*

1**hyp•not•ic** \hip-ˈnä-tik\ *adj* **1** ♦ : inducing sleep **2** : of or relating to hypnosis or hypnotism **3** : readily holding the attention — **hyp•not•i•cal•ly** \-ti-k(ə-)lē\ *adv*

♦ drowsy, narcotic, opiate, slumberous *Ant* stimulant

2**hypnotic** *n* : a sleep-inducing drug

hyp•no•tise *chiefly Brit var of* HYPNOTIZE

hyp•no•tize \ˈhip-nə-ˌtīz\ *vb* **1** : to induce hypnosis in **2** ♦ : to dazzle or overcome by or as if by suggestion — **hyp•no•tiz•able** \ˈhip-nə-ˌtī-zə-bəl\ *adj*

♦ arrest, enchant, enthrall, fascinate, grip, mesmerize

hy•po \ˈhī-pō\ *n, pl* **hypos** : SODIUM THIOSULFATE

hy•po•al•ler•gen•ic \ˌhī-pō-ˌa-lər-ˈje-nik\ *adj* : having little likelihood of causing an allergic response

hy•po•cen•ter \ˈhī-pə-ˌsen-tər\ *n* : the point of origin of an earthquake

hy•po•chon•dria \ˌhī-pə-ˈkän-drē-ə\ *n* : depression of mind often centered on imaginary physical ailments — **hy•po•chon•dri•ac** \-drē-ˌak\ *adj or n*

hy•poc•ri•sy \hi-ˈpä-krə-sē\ *n, pl* **-sies** ♦ : a feigning to be what one is not or to believe what one does not; *esp* : the false assumption of an appearance of virtue or religion

♦ cant, dissimulation, insincerity, piety *Ant* genuineness, sincerity

hyp•o•crit•i•cal \ˌhi-pə-ˈkri-ti-kəl\ *adj* ♦ : characterized by hypocrisy; *also* : being a hypocrite — **hyp•o•crite** \ˈhi-pə-ˌkrit\ *n* — **hyp•o•crit•i•cal•ly** \-k(ə-)lē\ *adv*

♦ artificial, double-dealing, feigned, insincere, left-handed, mealy, mealymouthed, two-faced, unctuous

1hy·po·der·mic \ˌhī-pə-ˈdər-mik\ *adj* **:** administered by or used in making an injection beneath the skin

2hypodermic *n* **:** a small syringe with a hollow needle for injecting material into or through the skin **:** HYPODERMIC SYRINGE; *also* **:** an injection made with this

hypodermic needle *n* **1 :** NEEDLE 3 **2 :** a small syringe with a hollow needle for injecting material into or through the skin **:** HYPODERMIC SYRINGE

hypodermic syringe *n* ♦ **:** a small syringe with a hollow needle for injecting material into or through the skin

♦ needle, syringe

hy·po·gly·ce·mia \ˌhī-pō-glī-ˈsē-mē-ə\ *n* **:** abnormal decrease of sugar in the blood — **hy·po·gly·ce·mic** \-mik\ *adj*

hy·pot·e·nuse \hī-ˈpät-ᵊn-ˌüs, -ˌyüs, -ˌüz, -ˌyüz\ *n* **:** the side of a triangle having a right angle that is opposite the right angle; *also* **:** its length

hy·po·thal·a·mus \ˌhī-pō-ˈtha-lə-məs\ *n* **:** a part of the brain that lies beneath the thalamus and is a control center for the autonomic nervous system

hy·poth·e·sis \hī-ˈpä-thə-səs\ *n, pl* **-e·ses** \-ˌsēz\ ♦ **:** an assumption made especially in order to test its logical or empirical consequences

♦ conjecture, proposition, supposition, theory

hy·poth·e·size \-ˌsīz\ *vb* **-sized; -siz·ing :** to adopt as a hypothesis

hy·po·thet·i·cal \ˌhī-pə-ˈthe-ti-kəl\ *adj* ♦ **:** being or involving a hypothesis — **hy·po·thet·i·cal·ly** \-k(ə-)lē\ *adv*

♦ conjectural, speculative, theoretical

hy·po·thy·roid·ism \ˌhī-pō-ˈthī-ˌròi-ˌdi-zəm\ *n* **:** deficient activity of the thyroid gland; *also* **:** a resultant lowered metabolic rate and general loss of vigor — **hy·po·thy·roid** *adj*

hys·sop \ˈhi-səp\ *n* **:** a European mint sometimes used as a potherb

hys·ter·ec·to·my \ˌhis-tə-ˈrek-tə-mē\ *n, pl* **-mies :** surgical removal of the uterus

hys·te·ria \hi-ˈster-ē-ə, -ˈstir-\ *n* **1 :** a nervous disorder marked especially by defective emotional control **2** ♦ **:** unmanageable fear or outburst of emotion — **hys·ter·ic** \-ˈster-ik\ *n* — **hys·ter·i·cal·ly** \-k(ə-)lē\ *adv*

♦ agitation, delirium, distraction, frenzy, furor, fury, rage, rampage, uproar

hys·ter·i·cal \-ˈster-i-kəl\ *also* **hysteric** *adj* **1 :** of, relating to, or marked by hysteria **2** ♦ **:** exhibiting unrestrained emotionalism

♦ agitated, delirious, distraught, frantic, frenzied

hys·ter·ics \-ˈster-iks\ *n pl* **:** a fit of uncontrollable laughter or crying

Hz *abbr* hertz

I

1i \ˈī\ *n, pl* **i's** *or* **is** \ˈīz\ *often cap* **:** the 9th letter of the English alphabet

2i *abbr, often cap* island; isle

3i *symbol* imaginary unit

1I \ˈī, ə\ *pron* **:** the one speaking or writing

2I *abbr* interstate

3I *symbol* iodine

Ia *or* **IA** *abbr* Iowa

-ial *adj suffix* **:** 1-AL ⟨manor*ial*⟩

iamb \ˈī-ˌam\ *or* **iam·bus** \ī-ˈam-bəs\ *n, pl* **iambs** \ˈī-ˌamz\ *or* **iam·bus·es :** a metrical foot of one unaccented syllable followed by one accented syllable — **iam·bic** \ī-ˈam-bik\ *adj or n*

-i·at·ric \ē-ˈa-trik\ *also* **-i·at·ri·cal** \-tri-kəl\ *adj comb form* **:** of or relating to (such) medical treatment or healing ⟨ped*iatric*⟩

-i·at·rics \ē-ˈa-triks\ *n pl comb form* **:** medical treatment ⟨ped*iatrics*⟩

ib *or* **ibid** *abbr* ibidem

ibex \ˈī-ˌbeks\ *n, pl* **ibex** *or* **ibex·es :** any of several Old World wild goats with large curved horns

ibi·dem \ˈi-bə-ˌdem, i-ˈbī-dəm\ *adv* **:** in the same place

ibis \ˈī-bəs\ *n, pl* **ibis** *or* **ibis·es :** any of various wading birds related to the herons but having a downwardly curved bill

ibu·pro·fen \ˌī-byu̇-ˈprō-fən\ *n* **:** a nonsteroidal anti-inflammatory drug used to relieve pain and fever

IC \ˌī-ˈsē\ *n* **:** INTEGRATED CIRCUIT

1-ic \ik\ *adj suffix* **1 :** of, relating to, or having the form of **:** being ⟨panoram*ic*⟩ **2 :** related to, derived from, or containing ⟨alcohol*ic*⟩ **3 :** in the manner of **:** like that of **:** characteristic of **4 :** associated or dealing with **:** utilizing ⟨electron*ic*⟩ **5 :** characterized by **:** exhibiting ⟨nostalg*ic*⟩ **:** affected with ⟨allerg*ic*⟩ **6 :** caused by **7 :** tending to produce ⟨analges*ic*⟩

2-ic *n suffix* **:** one having the character or nature of **:** one belonging to or associated with **:** one exhibiting or affected by **:** one that produces

-i·cal \i-kəl\ *adj suffix* **:** -IC ⟨symmetr*ical*⟩ ⟨geolog*ical*⟩ — **-i·cal·ly** \i-kə-lē, -klē\ *adv suffix*

ICBM \ˌī-ˌsē-(ˌ)bē-ˈem\ *n, pl* **ICBM's** *or* **ICBMs** \-ˈemz\ **:** an intercontinental ballistic missile

ICC *abbr* Interstate Commerce Commission

1ice \ˈīs\ *n* **1 :** frozen water **2 :** a substance resembling ice **3 :** a state of coldness (as from formality or reserve) **4 :** a flavored frozen dessert; *esp* **:** one containing no milk or cream

2ice *vb* **iced; ic·ing 1 :** FREEZE **2 :** CHILL **3 :** to cover with or as if with icing

ice age *n* **:** a time of widespread glaciation

ice bag *n* **:** a waterproof bag to hold ice for local application of cold to the body

ice·berg \ˈīs-ˌbərg\ *n* **:** a large floating mass of ice broken off from a glacier

iceberg lettuce *n* **:** any of various crisp light green lettuces that form a compact head like a cabbage

ice·boat \ˈīs-ˌbōt\ *n* **:** a boatlike frame on runners propelled on ice by sails

ice·bound \-ˌbau̇nd\ *adj* **:** surrounded, obstructed, or covered by ice

ice·box \-ˌbäks\ *n* **:** REFRIGERATOR

ice·break·er \-ˌbrā-kər\ *n* **:** a ship equipped to make a channel through ice

ice cap *n* **:** a glacier forming on relatively level land and flowing outward from its center

ice cream *n* **:** a frozen food containing sweetened or flavored cream or butterfat

ice hockey *n* **:** a game in which two teams of ice-skating players try to shoot a puck into the opponent's goal

ice·house \ˈīs-ˌhau̇s\ *n* **:** a building in which ice is made or stored

Ice·land·er \-ˌlan-dər, -lən-\ *n* **:** a native or inhabitant of Iceland

1Ice·lan·dic \īs-ˈlan-dik\ *adj* **:** of, relating to, or characteristic of Iceland, the Icelanders, or their language

2Icelandic *n* **:** the language of Iceland

ice·man \ˈīs-ˌman\ *n* **:** one who sells or delivers ice

ice milk *n* **:** a sweetened frozen food made of skim milk

ice pick *n* **:** a hand tool ending in a spike for chipping ice

ice–skate \ˈīs-ˌskāt\ *vb* **:** to skate on ice — **ice–skater** *n*

ice storm *n* **:** a storm in which falling rain freezes on contact

ice water *n* **:** chilled or iced water especially for drinking

ich·thy·ol·o·gy \ˌik-thē-ˈä-lə-jē\ *n* **:** a branch of zoology dealing with fishes — **ich·thy·ol·o·gist** \-jist\ *n*

ici·cle \ˈī-ˌsi-kəl\ *n* **:** a hanging mass of ice formed by the freezing of dripping water

ic·ing \ˈī-siŋ\ *n* **:** a sweet usually creamy mixture used to coat baked goods

ICJ *abbr* International Court of Justice

icky \ˈi-kē\ *adj* **ick·i·er; -est :** OFFENSIVE, DISTASTEFUL — **ick·i·ness** *n*

icon \ˈī-ˌkän\ *n* **1 :** IMAGE; *esp* **:** a religious image painted on a wood panel **2** ♦ **:** a sign (as a word or graphic symbol) whose form suggests its meaning **3 :** a small picture on a computer display that suggests the purpose of an available function

♦ character, sign, symbol

icon·o·clasm \ī-ˈkä-nə-ˌkla-zəm\ *n* **:** the doctrine, practice, or attitude of an iconoclast

icon·o·clast \-ˌklast\ *n* **1 :** one who destroys religious images or opposes their veneration **2 :** one who attacks cherished beliefs or institutions

-ics \iks\ *n sing or pl suffix* **1 :** study : knowledge : skill : practice ⟨linguis*tics*⟩ ⟨electron*ics*⟩ **2 :** characteristic actions or activities ⟨acrobat*ics*⟩ **3 :** characteristic qualities, operations, or phenomena ⟨mechan*ics*⟩

ic•tus \ˈik-təs\ *n* **:** the recurring stress or beat in a rhythmic or metrical series of sounds

ICU *abbr* intensive care unit

icy \ˈī-sē\ *adj* **ic•i•er; -est 1 :** covered with, abounding in, or consisting of ice **2 ♦ :** intensely cold **3 ♦ :** being cold and unfriendly — **ic•i•ly** \ˈī-sə-lē\ *adv* — **ic•i•ness** \-sē-nəs\ *n*

♦ [2] arctic, bitter, chill, cold, freezing, frigid, frosty, glacial, polar, raw, wintry ♦ [3] chill, chilly, cold, cold-blooded, cool, frigid, frosty, glacial, unfriendly, unsympathetic, wintry

¹id \ˈid\ *n* **:** the part of the psyche in psychoanalytic theory that is completely unconscious and concerned with instinctual needs and drives

²id *abbr* idem

¹ID \ˈī-ˈdē\ *vb* **ID'd** *or* **IDed; ID'ing** *or* **IDing :** IDENTIFY

²ID *abbr* **1** Idaho **2** identification

idea \ī-ˈdē-ə\ *n* **1 :** a plan for action **:** DESIGN **2 ♦ :** something (as a thought, concept, sensation, or image) present in the mind **3 :** a central meaning or purpose

♦ concept, image, impression, notion, picture, thought

¹ide•al \ī-ˈdēl\ *adj* **1 :** existing only in the mind **:** IMAGINARY; *also* **:** lacking practicality **2 ♦ :** of or relating to an ideal or to perfection **:** PERFECT

♦ absolute, faultless, flawless, impeccable, letter-perfect, perfect, unblemished

²ideal *n* **1 ♦ :** a standard of excellence **2 ♦ :** one regarded as a model worthy of imitation **3 :** GOAL

♦ [1] classic, epitome, exemplar, perfection, quintessence ♦ [2] beau ideal, classic, exemplar, model, nonpareil, paragon

ide•al•ise *chiefly Brit var of* IDEALIZE

ide•al•ism \ī-ˈdē-ə-ˌli-zəm\ *n* **:** the practice of forming ideals or living under their influence; *also* **:** an idealized representation — **ide•al•is•tic** \ī-ˌdē-ə-ˈlis-tik\ *adj* — **ide•al•is•ti•cal•ly** \-ti-k(ə-)lē\ *adv*

ide•al•ist \-list\ *n* **♦ :** one guided by ideals; *also* **:** one that places ideals before practical considerations

♦ dreamer, romantic, utopian, visionary ***Ant*** realist

ide•al•ize \ī-ˈdē-ə-ˌlīz\ *vb* **-ized; -iz•ing ♦ :** to think of or represent as ideal — **ide•al•i•za•tion** \-ˌdē-ə-lə-ˈzā-shən\ *n*

♦ dream, glamorize, glorify

ide•al•ly \ī-ˈdē-lē, -ˈdē-ə-lē\ *adv* **1 :** in idea or imagination **:** MENTALLY **2 ♦ :** in agreement with an ideal **:** PERFECTLY

♦ faultlessly, flawlessly, impeccably, perfectly

ide•a•tion \ˌī-dē-ˈā-shən\ *n* **:** the forming of ideas — **ide•ate** \ˈī-dē-ˌāt\ *vb* — **ide•a•tion•al** \ˌī-dē-ˈā-shə-nəl\ *adj*

idem \ˈī-ˌdem, ˈē-, ˈi-\ *pron* **:** the same as something previously mentioned

iden•ti•cal \ī-ˈden-ti-kəl\ *adj* **1 ♦ :** being the same **2 ♦ :** essentially alike

♦ duplicate, equal, even, indistinguishable, same

iden•ti•fi•ca•tion \ī-ˌden-tə-fə-ˈkā-shən\ *n* **1 :** an act of identifying **:** the state of being identified **2 :** evidence of identity **3 :** an unconscious psychological process by which an individual models thoughts, feelings, and actions after another person or an object

iden•ti•fy \ī-ˈden-tə-ˌfī\ *vb* **-fied; -fy•ing 1 :** to regard as identical **2 ♦ :** to think of as united (as in spirit, outlook, or principle) **:** ASSOCIATE **3 ♦ :** to establish the identity of **4 :** to practice psychological identification — **iden•ti•fi•able** \-ˌden-tə-ˈfī-ə-bəl\ *adj* — **iden•ti•fi•ably** \-blē\ *adv* — **iden•ti•fi•er** \-ˌfī(-ə)r\ *n*

♦ [2] associate, connect, correlate, link, relate ♦ [3] distinguish, pinpoint, single

iden•ti•ty \ī-ˈden-tə-tē\ *n, pl* **-ties 1 :** sameness of essential character **2 ♦ :** the distinguishing character or personality of an individual **:** INDIVIDUALITY **3 :** the fact of being the same person or thing as claimed

♦ character, individuality, personality, self-identity

identity crisis *n* **:** psychological conflict especially in adolescence involving confusion about one's social role and one's personality

identity theft *n* **:** the illegal use of someone else's personal information to obtain money or credit

ideo•gram \ˈī-dē-ə-ˌgram, ˈi-\ *n* **1 :** a picture or symbol used in a system of writing to represent a thing or an idea **2 :** a character or symbol used in a system of writing to represent an entire word

ideo•logue *also* **idea•logue** \ˈī-dē-ə-ˌlȯg\ *n* **:** a partisan advocate or adherent of a particular ideology

ide•ol•o•gy \ˌī-dē-ˈä-lə-jē, ˌi-\ *also* **ide•al•o•gy** \-ˈä-lə-jē, -ˈa-\ *n, pl* **-gies 1 ♦ :** the body of ideas characteristic of a particular individual, group, or culture **2 :** the assertions, theories, and aims that constitute a political, social, and economic program — **ide•o•log•i•cal** \ˌī-dē-ə-ˈlä-ji-kəl, ˌi-\ *adj* — **ide•ol•o•gist** \-dē-ˈä-lə-jist\ *n*

♦ creed, doctrine, gospel, philosophy

ides \ˈīdz\ *n sing or pl* **:** the 15th day of March, May, July, or October or the 13th day of any other month in the ancient Roman calendar

id•i•o•cy \ˈi-dē-ə-sē\ *n, pl* **-cies 1** *usu offensive* **:** extreme mental retardation **2 ♦ :** something notably stupid or foolish

♦ absurdity, fatuity, folly, foolery, foolishness, inanity, madness, stupidity

id•i•om \ˈi-dē-əm\ *n* **1 :** the language peculiar to a person or group **2 :** the characteristic form or structure of a language **3 :** an expression that cannot be understood from the meanings of its separate words (as *give way*) — **id•i•o•mat•ic** \ˌi-dē-ə-ˈma-tik\ *adj* — **id•i•o•mat•i•cal•ly** \-ti-k(ə-)lē\ *adv*

id•i•o•path•ic \ˌi-dē-ə-ˈpa-thik\ *adj* **:** arising spontaneously or from an obscure or unknown cause ⟨an ~ disease⟩

id•i•o•syn•cra•sy \ˌi-dē-ə-ˈsiŋ-krə-sē\ *n, pl* **-sies ♦ :** personal peculiarity — **id•i•o•syn•crat•ic** \ˌi-dē-ō-sin-ˈkra-tik\ *adj* — **id•i•o•syn•crat•i•cal•ly** \-ˈkra-ti-k(ə-)lē\ *adv*

♦ crotchet, eccentricity, mannerism, oddity, peculiarity, quirk, singularity, trick

id•i•ot \ˈi-dē-ət\ *n* **1** *usu offensive* **:** a person affected with extreme mental retardation **2 ♦ :** a foolish or stupid person — **id•i•ot•ic** \ˌi-dē-ˈä-tik\ *adj* — **id•i•ot•i•cal•ly** \-ti-k(ə-)lē\ *adv*

♦ blockhead, cretin, dodo, dolt, dope, dummy, imbecile, jackass, moron, nitwit, numskull, simpleton ***Ant*** brain, genius

id•i•ot•proof \ˈi-dē-ət-ˌprüf\ *adj* **:** extremely easy to operate or maintain

¹idle \ˈīd-ᵊl\ *adj* **idler** \ˈī-də-lər\; **idlest** \ˈī-də-ləst\ **1 :** GROUNDLESS, WORTHLESS, USELESS ⟨~ talk⟩ **2 ♦ :** not occupied or employed **:** INACTIVE **3 ♦ :** lacking in ambition or incentive **:** LAZY — **idly** \ˈīd-lē\ *adv*

♦ [2] dead, dormant, fallow, free, inactive, inert, inoperative, latent, off, vacant ♦ [3] indolent, lazy, shiftless, slothful

²idle *vb* **idled; idling 1 ♦ :** to spend time doing nothing **2 :** to make idle **3 :** to run without being connected so that power is not used for useful work

♦ dally, dawdle, dillydally, hang around, hang out, loaf, loll, lounge

idle•ness *n* **♦ :** the quality or state of being idle (as through lack of worth, occupation, employment, industry)

♦ indolence, inertia, laziness, sloth ♦ dormancy, inaction, inactivity, inertness, quiescence

idler *n* **♦ :** one that idles or is unoccupied **:** a lazy person

♦ lazybones, loafer, slouch, slug, sluggard

idol \ˈīd-ᵊl\ *n* **1 :** an image worshipped as a god; *also* **:** a false god **2 :** an object of passionate devotion

idol•a•ter *or* **idol•a•tor** \ī-ˈdä-lə-tər\ *n* **:** a worshiper of idols

idol•a•try \-trē\ *n, pl* **-tries 1 :** the worship of a physical object as a god **2 ♦ :** excessive devotion — **idol•a•trous** \-trəs\ *adj*

♦ adulation, deification, worship

idol•i•za•tion \ˌīd-ᵊl-ə-ˈzā-shən\ *n* **:** the act of idolizing or state of being idolized

idol•ize \ˈīd-ᵊl-ˌīz\ *vb* **-ized; -iz•ing ♦ :** to make an idol of

♦ adore, canonize, deify, dote on, worship

idyll \ˈīd-ᵊl\ *n* **1 :** a simple work of writing or poetry that describes country life or suggests a peaceful setting **2 ♦ :** a lighthearted carefree episode that is a fit subject for an idyll — **idyl•lic** \ī-ˈdi-lik\ *adj*

♦ binge, fling, frolic, gambol, lark, revel, rollick, romp

i.e. \ˈī-ˈē\ *abbr* that is
IE *abbr* industrial engineer
if \ˈif\ *conj* **1 :** in the event that ⟨~ he stays, I leave⟩ **2 :** WHETHER ⟨ask ~ he left⟩ **3** — used as a function word to introduce an exclamation expressing a wish ⟨~ it would only rain⟩ **4 :** even though ⟨an interesting ~ untenable argument⟩
IF *abbr* intermediate frequency
if•fy \ˈi-fē\ *adj* **:** full of contingencies or unknown conditions
-i•fy \ə-ˌfī\ *vb suffix* **:** -FY
IG *abbr* inspector general
ig•loo \ˈi-glü\ *n, pl* **igloos :** an Eskimo house or hut often made of snow blocks and in the shape of a dome
ig•ne•ous \ˈig-nē-əs\ *adj* **1 :** FIERY **2 :** formed by solidification of molten rock
ig•nit•able \-ˈnī-tə-bəl\ *adj* ♦ **:** capable of being ignited

♦ combustible, flammable, inflammable

ig•nite \ig-ˈnīt\ *vb* **ig•nit•ed; ig•nit•ing** ♦ **:** to set afire or catch fire

♦ burn, fire, inflame, kindle, light

ig•ni•tion \ig-ˈni-shən\ *n* **1 :** a setting on fire **2 :** the process or means (as an electric spark) of igniting the fuel mixture in an engine
ig•no•ble \ig-ˈnō-bəl\ *adj* **1** ♦ **:** of common birth **2** ♦ **:** not honorable **:** BASE, MEAN — **ig•no•bly** *adv*

♦ [1] common, humble, inferior, low, lowly, mean, plebeian, vulgar *Ant* aristocratic, high, highborn, lofty, noble, wellborn ♦ [2] base, contemptible, despicable, detestable, dirty, dishonorable (*or* dishonourable), low, mean, snide, sordid, vile, wretched *Ant* high, high-minded, honorable, lofty, noble, straight, upright, venerable, virtuous

ig•no•min•i•ous \ˌig-nə-ˈmi-nē-əs\ *adj* **1** ♦ marked with or characterized by disgrace or shame **:** DISHONORABLE **2 :** DESPICABLE **3 :** HUMILIATING, DEGRADING — **ig•no•min•i•ous•ly** *adv*

♦ discreditable, disgraceful, dishonorable (*or* dishonourable), disreputable, infamous, notorious, shameful

ig•no•mi•ny \ˈig-nə-ˌmi-nē, ig-ˈnä-mə-nē\ *n* **1** ♦ **:** deep personal humiliation and disgrace **2 :** disgraceful or dishonorable conduct, quality, or action

♦ discredit, disgrace, dishonor (*or* dishonour), disrepute, infamy, odium, opprobrium, reproach, shame

ig•no•ra•mus \ˌig-nə-ˈrā-məs\ *n* **:** an utterly ignorant person
ig•no•rance \ˈig-nə-rəns\ *n* ♦ **:** the state of being ignorant

♦ obliviousness, unawareness *Ant* acquaintance, awareness, familiarity

ig•no•rant \ˈig-nə-rənt\ *adj* **1** ♦ **:** lacking knowledge **2 :** resulting from or showing lack of knowledge or intelligence **3** ♦ **:** not aware **:** UNAWARE, UNINFORMED — **ig•no•rant•ly** *adv*

♦ [1] dark, illiterate, simple, uneducated, unlearned, untaught *Ant* educated, knowledgeable, literate, schooled ♦ [3] oblivious, unaware, unconscious, uninformed, unknowing, unwitting *Ant* acquainted, aware, cognizant, conscious, conversant, grounded, informed, knowing, mindful, witting

ig•nore \ig-ˈnōr\ *vb* **ig•nored; ig•nor•ing** ♦ **:** to refuse to take notice of

♦ disregard, forget, neglect, overlook, pass over, slight, slur ♦ condone, disregard, excuse, gloss over, pardon, pass over, shrug off, wink at

igua•na \i-ˈgwä-nə\ *n* **:** any of various large tropical American lizards
ihp *abbr* indicated horsepower
IHS \ˌī-ˌāch-ˈes\ — used as a Christian symbol and monogram for *Jesus*
ikon *var of* ICON
IL *abbr* Illinois
il•e•itis \ˌi-lē-ˈī-təs\ *n* **:** inflammation of the ileum
il•e•um \ˈi-lē-əm\ *n, pl* **il•ea** \-lē-ə\ **:** the part of the small intestine between the jejunum and the large intestine
il•i•ac \ˈi-lē-ˌak\ *adj* **:** of, relating to, or located near the ilium
il•i•um \ˈi-lē-əm\ *n* **:** the uppermost and largest of the three bones making up either side of the pelvis
ilk \ˈilk\ *n* ♦ **:** a group set up on the basis of any characteristic in common **:** SORT, KIND

♦ breed, class, description, feather, kind, like, manner, nature, order, sort, species, type

¹ill \ˈil\ *adj* **worse** \ˈwərs\; **worst** \ˈwərst\ **1** ♦ **:** attended or caused by an evil intent ⟨~ deeds⟩ **2 a :** not normal or sound ⟨~ health⟩ **b** ♦ **:** not in good health **:** SICK; *also* **:** feeling nauseated **3 :** BAD, UNLUCKY ⟨~ omen⟩ **4 :** not right or proper ⟨~ manners⟩ **5 :** UNFRIENDLY, HOSTILE ⟨~ feeling⟩

♦ [1] adverse, bad, baleful, baneful, damaging, deleterious, detrimental, evil, harmful, hurtful, injurious, mischievous, noxious, pernicious, prejudicial ♦ [2b] nauseous, queasy, queer, sick, squeamish ♦ [2b] bad, down, indisposed, peaked, punk, sick, unhealthy, unsound, unwell

²ill *adv* **worse; worst 1 :** with displeasure **2** ♦ **:** in a harsh manner **3 :** probably not **:** HARDLY ⟨can ~ afford it⟩ **4 :** BADLY, UNLUCKILY **5 :** in a faulty way

♦ hard, hardly, harshly, oppressively, roughly, severely, sternly, stiffly

³ill *n* **1** ♦ **:** the reverse of good **:** EVIL **2 :** MISFORTUNE, DISTRESS **3 :** AILMENT, SICKNESS; *also* **:** TROUBLE

♦ bad, evil, immorality, iniquity, sin, villainy, wrong

⁴ill *abbr* illustrated; illustration; illustrator
Ill *abbr* Illinois
ill–ad•vised \ˌil-əd-ˈvīzd\ *adj* ♦ **:** not well counseled ⟨~ efforts⟩ — **ill–ad•vis•ed•ly** \-ˈvī-zəd-lē\ *adv*

♦ imprudent, indiscreet, tactless, unwise

ill–bred \-ˈbred\ *adj* ♦ **:** showing bad upbringing **:** IMPOLITE

♦ discourteous, ill-mannered, impertinent, impolite, inconsiderate, rude, thoughtless, uncivil, ungracious, unmannerly

il•le•gal \il-ˈlē-gəl\ *adj* ♦ **:** not lawful; *also* **:** not sanctioned by official rules — **il•le•gal•i•ty** \ˌi-li-ˈga-lə-tē\ *n* — **il•le•gal•ly** *adv*

♦ criminal, illegitimate, illicit, unlawful, wrongful *Ant* lawful, legal, legitimate ♦ dirty, foul, unfair, unsportsmanlike

il•leg•i•ble \il-ˈle-jə-bəl\ *adj* **:** not legible — **il•leg•i•bil•i•ty** \il-ˌle-jə-ˈbi-lə-tē\ *n* — **il•leg•i•bly** \il-ˈle-jə-blē\ *adv*
il•le•git•i•mate \ˌi-li-ˈji-tə-mət\ *adj* **1** ♦ **:** born of unmarried parents **2 :** ILLOGICAL **3** ♦ **:** not sanctioned by law **:** ILLEGAL — **il•le•git•i•ma•cy** \-ˈji-tə-mə-sē\ *n* — **il•le•git•i•mate•ly** *adv*

♦ [1] natural *Ant* legitimate ♦ [3] criminal, illegal, illicit, unlawful, wrongful

ill–fat•ed \ˈil-ˈfā-təd\ *adj* ♦ **:** having or destined to a hapless fate **:** UNFORTUNATE

♦ hapless, ill-starred, luckless, unfortunate, unhappy, unlucky

ill–fa•vored \-ˈfā-vərd\ *adj* **:** unattractive in physical appearance **:** UGLY
ill–got•ten \-ˈgät-ᵊn\ *adj* **:** acquired by improper means ⟨~ gains⟩
ill–hu•mored \-ˈhyü-mərd, -ˈyü-\ *adj* ♦ **:** irritably sullen and churlish in mood or manner **:** SURLY

♦ bearish, bilious, cantankerous, disagreeable, dyspeptic, ill-tempered, ornery, splenetic, surly

il•lib•er•al \il-ˈli-bə-rəl\ *adj* **:** not liberal **:** NARROW, BIGOTED
il•lic•it \il-ˈli-sət\ *adj* ♦ **:** not permitted **:** UNLAWFUL — **il•lic•it•ly** *adv*

♦ criminal, illegal, illegitimate, unlawful, wrongful

il•lim•it•able \il-ˈli-mə-tə-bəl\ *adj* ♦ **:** incapable of being limited or bounded **:** BOUNDLESS, MEASURELESS — **il•lim•it•ably** \-blē\ *adv*

♦ boundless, endless, immeasurable, indefinite, infinite, limitless, measureless, unbounded, unfathomable, unlimited

Il•li•nois \ˌi-lə-ˈnȯi *also* -ˈnȯiz\ *n, pl* **Illinois :** a member of an American Indian people of Illinois, Iowa, and Wisconsin
il•lit•er•ate \il-ˈli-tə-rət\ *adj* **1** ♦ **:** having little or no education; *esp* **:** unable to read or write **2 :** showing a lack of familiarity with the fundamentals of a particular field of knowledge — **il•lit•er•a•cy** \-ˈli-tə-rə-sē\ *n* — **illiterate** *n*

♦ dark, ignorant, simple, uneducated, unlearned, untaught

ill–man•nered \ˈil-ˈma-nərd\ *adj* ♦ **:** marked by bad manners **:** RUDE

♦ discourteous, ill-bred, impertinent, impolite, inconsiderate, rude, thoughtless, uncivil, ungracious, unmannerly

ill–na•tured \-ˈnā-chərd\ *adj* **:** having a bad disposition **:** CROSS, SURLY — **ill–na•tured•ly** *adv*
ill•ness \ˈil-nəs\ *n* ♦ **:** an unhealthy condition of body or mind **:** SICKNESS; *also* **:** a specific disease

♦ ailment, bug, complaint, complication, condition, disease, disorder, fever, infirmity, malady, sickness, trouble

il•log•i•cal \il-ˈlä-ji-kəl\ *adj* ♦ : lacking sound reasoning; *also* : SENSELESS — **il•log•i•cal•ly** \-ji-k(ə-)lē\ *adv*

♦ fallacious, invalid, irrational, senseless, unreasonable, unsound, weak

ill–starred \ˈil-ˈstärd\ *adj* ♦ : having or meeting with misfortune : UNLUCKY

♦ hapless, ill-fated, luckless, unfortunate, unhappy, unlucky

ill–tem•pered \-ˈtem-pərd\ *adj* ♦ : having a bad disposition : CROSS

♦ bearish, bilious, cantankerous, cross, disagreeable, dyspeptic, ill-humored, ornery, splenetic, surly *Ant* amiable, good-natured, good-tempered

ill–treat \-ˈtrēt\ *vb* ♦ : to treat cruelly or improperly : MALTREAT — **ill–treat•ment** *n*

♦ abuse, maltreat, manhandle, mishandle, mistreat, misuse

il•lu•mi•nate \i-ˈlü-mə-ˌnāt\ *vb* **-nat•ed; -nat•ing 1** ♦ : to supply or brighten with light : light up **2** ♦ : to make clear : ELUCIDATE **3** : to decorate (as a manuscript) with designs or pictures in gold or colors — **il•lu•mi•nat•ing•ly** *adv* — **il•lu•mi•na•tor** \-ˈlü-mə-ˌnā-tər\ *n*

♦ [1] light *Ant* blacken, darken ♦ [2] clarify, clear (up), construe, demonstrate, elucidate, explain, explicate, expound, illustrate, interpret, spell out

il•lu•mi•na•tion \-ˌlü-mə-ˈnā-shən\ *n* **1** ♦ : the action of illuminating **2** ♦ : the state of being illuminated

♦ [1] blaze, flare, fluorescence, glare, gleam, glow, incandescence, light, luminescence, radiance, shine ♦ [2] brilliance, dazzle, effulgence, lightness, lucidity, luminosity, radiance, refulgence, splendor

il•lu•mine \i-ˈlü-mən\ *vb* **-mined; -min•ing** : to make clear or bright : ILLUMINATE

ill–us•age \ˈil-ˈyü-sij\ *n* : harsh, unkind, or abusive treatment

ill–use \-ˈyüz\ *vb* : to use badly : MALTREAT, ABUSE

il•lu•sion \i-ˈlü-zhən\ *n* **1** ♦ : a mistaken idea : MISCONCEPTION **2** ♦ : a misleading visual image; *also* : HALLUCINATION

♦ [1] error, fallacy, falsehood, falsity, misconception, myth, untruth ♦ [2] chimera, conceit, daydream, delusion, dream, fancy, fantasy, figment, hallucination, phantasm, pipe dream, unreality, vision

il•lu•sion•ist \i-ˈlü-zhə-nist\ *n* ♦ : one that produces illusions; *esp* : a sleight-of-hand performer

♦ conjurer, magician, trickster

il•lu•sive \i-ˈlü-siv\ *adj* : DECEPTIVE

il•lu•so•ry \i-ˈlü-sə-rē, -zə-\ *adj* : DECEPTIVE

illust *or* **illus** *abbr* illustrated; illustration

il•lus•trate \ˈi-ləs-ˌtrāt\ *vb* **-trat•ed; -trat•ing 1** ♦ : to explain by use of examples; *also* : DEMONSTRATE **2** : to provide with pictures or figures that explain or decorate **3** : to serve to explain or decorate — **il•lus•tra•tor** \ˈi-lə-ˌstrā-tər\ *n*

♦ demonstrate, exemplify, instance

il•lus•tra•tion \ˌi-lə-ˈstrā-shən\ *n* **1** : the act of illustrating : the condition of being illustrated **2** ♦ : an example or instance that helps make something clear **3** ♦ : a picture or diagram that explains or decorates

♦ [2] clarification, construction, elucidation, explanation, explication, exposition, illumination, interpretation ♦ [3] diagram, figure, graphic, plate

il•lus•tra•tive \i-ˈləs-trə-tiv, ˈi-lə-ˌstrā-\ *adj* : serving, tending, or designed to illustrate — **il•lus•tra•tive•ly** *adv*

il•lus•tri•ous \i-ˈləs-trē-əs\ *adj* ♦ : notably outstanding because of rank or achievement — **il•lus•tri•ous•ness** *n*

♦ distinguished, eminent, noble, notable, noteworthy, outstanding, preeminent, prestigious, signal, star, superior

ill will *n* : unfriendly feeling

ILS *abbr* instrument landing system

¹im•age \ˈi-mij\ *n* **1** : a likeness or imitation of a person or thing; *esp* : STATUE **2** : a picture of an object formed by a device (as a mirror or lens) **3** ♦ : a person strikingly like another person ⟨he is the ∼ of his father⟩ **4** ♦ : a mental picture or conception : IMPRESSION, IDEA, CONCEPT **5** : a vivid representation or description

♦ [3] carbon copy, counterpart, double, duplicate, duplication, facsimile, likeness, match, picture, replica, ringer, spit ♦ [4] concept, idea, impression, notion, picture, thought

²image *vb* **im•aged; im•ag•ing 1** : to call up a mental picture of **2** ♦ : to describe or portray in words **3** ♦ : to create a representation of **4** : REFLECT, MIRROR **5** : to make appear : PROJECT

♦ [2] delineate, depict, describe, draw, paint, picture, portray, sketch ♦ [3] depict, picture, portray, represent

im•ag•ery \ˈi-mij-rē\ *n, pl* **-er•ies 1** : IMAGES; *also* : the art of making images **2** : figurative language **3** : mental images; *esp* : the products of imagination

imag•in•able \i-ˈma-jə-nə-bəl\ *adj* : capable of being imagined : CONCEIVABLE — **imag•in•ably** *adv*

imag•i•nary \i-ˈma-jə-ˌner-ē\ *adj* **1** ♦ : existing only in the imagination **2** : containing or relating to a quantity (**imaginary unit**) that is the positive square root of minus 1 ($\sqrt{-1}$)

♦ chimerical, fabulous, fanciful, fantastic, fictitious, made-up, mythical, phantom, pretend, unreal *Ant* actual, existent, existing, real

imaginary number *n* : a complex number (as 2 + 3*i*) with a nonzero term (**imaginary part**) containing the imaginary unit as a factor

imag•i•na•tion \i-ˌma-jə-ˈnā-shən\ *n* **1** ♦ : the act or power of forming a mental image of something not present to the senses or not previously known or experienced **2** : creative ability **3** : RESOURCEFULNESS **4** : a mental image : a creation of the mind

♦ creativity, fancy, fantasy, invention, inventiveness

imag•i•na•tive \i-ˈma-jə-nə-tiv, -ˌnā-\ *adj* ♦ : of, relating to, or characterized by imagination — **imag•i•na•tive•ly** *adv*

♦ creative, ingenious, innovative, inventive, original

imag•ine \i-ˈma-jən\ *vb* **imag•ined; imag•in•ing 1** ♦ : to form a mental picture of something not present **2** ♦ : to hold as an opinion : THINK, GUESS ⟨I ∼ it will rain⟩

♦ [1] conceive, dream, envisage, fancy, picture, vision, visualize ♦ [2] believe, consider, deem, feel, figure, guess, hold, suppose, think

imag•in•ings \-ˈmaj-niŋz, -ˈma-jə-\ *n pl* : products of the imagination

im•ag•ism \ˈi-mi-ˌji-zəm\ *n, often cap* : a movement in poetry advocating free verse and the expression of ideas and emotions through clear precise images — **im•ag•ist** \-jist\ *n*

ima•go \i-ˈmā-gō, -ˈmä-\ *n, pl* **imagoes** *or* **ima•gi•nes** \-ˈmā-gə-ˌnēz, -ˈmä-\ : an insect in its final adult stage — **ima•gi•nal** \i-ˈmā-gən-ᵊl, -ˈmä-\ *adj*

im•bal•ance \ˈim-ˈba-ləns\ *n* : lack of balance : the state of being out of equilibrium or out of proportion

im•be•cile \ˈim-bə-səl, -ˌsil\ *n* **1** *usu offensive* : a person affected with moderate mental retardation **2** ♦ : a person lacking in judgment or prudence : IDIOT — **imbecile** *or* **im•be•cil•ic** \ˌim-bə-ˈsi-lik\ *adj*

♦ blockhead, dope, dummy, idiot, jackass, nitwit, numskull, simpleton

im•be•cil•i•ty \ˌim-bə-ˈsi-lə-tē\ *n* **1** : the quality or state of being imbecile or an imbecile **2** : something that is foolish or nonsensical

imbed *var of* EMBED

im•bibe \im-ˈbīb\ *vb* **im•bibed; im•bib•ing 1** : to receive and retain in the mind **2** ♦ : to take through the mouth and esophagus into the stomach : DRINK **3** ♦ : to take in or up : ABSORB — **im•bib•er** *n*

♦ [2] drink, guzzle, quaff, sup, swig, toss ♦ [3] absorb, drink, soak, sponge, suck

im•bri•ca•tion \ˌim-brə-ˈkā-shən\ *n* **1** : an overlapping of edges (as of tiles) **2** : a pattern showing imbrication — **im•bri•cate** \ˈim-bri-kət\ *adj*

im•bro•glio \im-ˈbrōl-yō\ *n, pl* **-glios 1** : a confused mass **2** : a complicated situation; *also* : a serious or embarrassing misunderstanding

im•brue \im-ˈbrü\ *vb* **im•brued; im•bru•ing** : STAIN ⟨hands *imbrued* with blood⟩

im•bue \-ˈbyü\ *vb* **im•bued; im•bu•ing 1** ♦ : to permeate or influence as if by dyeing **2** : to tinge or dye deeply

♦ inculcate, infuse, ingrain, invest, steep, suffuse

IMF *abbr* International Monetary Fund

imit *abbr* imitative

im•i•ta•ble \ˈi-mə-tə-bəl\ *adj* : capable or worthy of being imitated or copied

im•i•tate \ˈi-mə-ˌtāt\ *vb* **-tat•ed; -tat•ing 1** ♦ : to follow as a model **2 :** RESEMBLE **3 ♦ :** to produce a copy of **:** REPRODUCE **4 ♦ :** to copy or feign especially with intent to deceive **:** MIMIC

♦ [1] ape, copy, emulate, mime, mimic ♦ [3] copy, duplicate, replicate, reproduce ♦ [4] burlesque, caricature, mimic, mock, parody, take off, travesty

1im•i•ta•tion \ˌi-mə-ˈtā-shən\ *n* **1 :** an act of imitating **2 ♦ :** something produced as a copy **3 :** a literary work that reproduces the style of another author

♦ carbon copy, copy, duplicate, duplication, facsimile, replica, replication, reproduction

2imitation *adj* **♦ :** resembling something else that is usually genuine and of better quality **:** not real

♦ artificial, bogus, factitious, fake, false, mimic, mock, sham, substitute, synthetic ***Ant*** genuine, natural, real

im•i•ta•tive \ˈi-mə-ˌtā-tiv\ *adj* **1 ♦ :** marked by imitation **2 :** inclined to imitate **3 :** COUNTERFEIT

♦ mimic, slavish, unoriginal ***Ant*** original

im•i•ta•tor \-ˌtā-tər\ *n* **♦ :** one that imitates

♦ impersonator, impressionist, mimic

im•mac•u•late \i-ˈma-kyə-lət\ *adj* **1 ♦ :** being without stain or blemish **:** PURE **2 ♦ :** spotlessly clean ⟨~ linen⟩ — **im•mac•u•late•ly** *adv*

♦ [1] chaste, clean, decent, modest, pure ♦ [2] clean, spick-and-span, spotless, stainless, unsoiled, unsullied

im•ma•nent \ˈi-mə-nənt\ *adj* **1 :** INHERENT **2 :** being within the limits of experience or knowledge — **im•ma•nence** \-nəns\ *n* — **im•ma•nen•cy** \-nən-sē\ *n*

im•ma•te•ri•al \ˌi-mə-ˈtir-ē-əl\ *adj* **1 ♦ :** not consisting of matter **:** SPIRITUAL **2 :** of no substantial consequence **:** UNIMPORTANT, TRIFLING **3 ♦ :** not material or essential — **im•ma•te•ri•al•i•ty** \-ˌtir-ē-ˈa-lə-tē\ *n*

♦ [1] bodiless, incorporeal, insubstantial, nonmaterial, nonphysical, spiritual, unsubstantial ***Ant*** bodily, corporeal, material, physical, substantial ♦ [3] extraneous, irrelevant

im•ma•ture \ˌi-mə-ˈtu̇r, -ˈtyu̇r\ *adj* **♦ :** lacking complete development **:** not yet mature — **im•ma•tu•ri•ty** \-ˈtu̇r-ə-tē, -ˈtyu̇r-\ *n*

♦ adolescent, babyish, childish, infantile, juvenile, kiddish ♦ adolescent, callow, green, inexperienced, juvenile, raw

im•mea•sur•able \(ˌ)i-ˈme-zhə-rə-bəl\ *adj* **♦ :** not capable of being measured **:** indefinitely extensive — **im•mea•sur•ably** \-blē\ *adv*

♦ boundless, endless, illimitable, indefinite, infinite, limitless, measureless, unbounded, unfathomable, unlimited

im•me•di•a•cy \i-ˈmē-dē-ə-sē\ *n, pl* **-cies 1 ♦ :** the quality or state of being immediate **2 :** something that is of immediate importance

♦ closeness, contiguity, nearness, proximity

im•me•di•ate \i-ˈmē-dē-ət\ *adj* **1 ♦ :** acting directly and alone **:** DIRECT ⟨the ~ cause of death⟩ **2 :** being next in line or relation ⟨members of the ~ family⟩ **3 ♦ :** not distant **:** CLOSE **4 ♦ :** made or done at once ⟨an ~ response⟩ **5 ♦ :** near to or related to the present time ⟨the ~ future⟩

♦ [1] direct, firsthand, primary ♦ [3, 5] close, near, nearby, nigh ♦ [4] prompt, punctual, timely ♦ [4] instant, instantaneous, straightaway

im•me•di•ate•ly *adv* **1 :** in direct connection or relation **2 ♦ :** without interval of time

♦ directly, forthwith, instantly, now, promptly, pronto, right away, right now

im•me•mo•ri•al \ˌi-mə-ˈmōr-ē-əl\ *adj* **♦ :** extending beyond the reach of memory, record, or tradition

♦ age-old, ancient, antediluvian, antique, dateless, hoary, old, venerable

im•mense \i-ˈmens\ *adj* **1 :** very great in size or degree **:** VAST **2 :** EXCELLENT — **im•mense•ly** *adv*

im•men•si•ty \-ˈmen-sə-tē\ *n* **1 ♦ :** the quality or state of being immense **2 :** something immense

♦ enormity, hugeness, magnitude, massiveness, vastness ***Ant*** minuteness

im•merse \i-ˈmərs\ *vb* **im•mersed; im•mers•ing 1 ♦ :** to plunge or dip especially into a fluid **2 ♦ :** to take or engage the whole attention of **:** ENGROSS, ABSORB **3 :** to baptize by immersing

♦ [1] dip, douse, duck, dunk, souse, submerge ♦ [2] absorb, busy, engage, engross, enthrall, fascinate, grip, interest, intrigue, involve, occupy

im•mer•sion \-ˈmər-zhən\ *n* **:** the act of immersing or the state of being immersed; *esp* **:** absorbing involvement

im•mi•grant \ˈi-mi-grənt\ *n* **1 ♦ :** a person who immigrates **2 :** a plant or animal that becomes established where it did not previously occur

♦ emigrant, émigré, migrant, settler

im•mi•grate \ˈi-mə-ˌgrāt\ *vb* **-grat•ed; -grat•ing :** to come into a foreign country and take up residence — **im•mi•gra•tion** \ˌi-mə-ˈgrā-shən\ *n*

im•mi•nent \ˈi-mə-nənt\ *adj* **♦ :** ready to take place; *esp* **:** hanging threateningly over one's head — **im•mi•nence** \-nəns\ *n* — **im•mi•nent•ly** *adv*

♦ coming, forthcoming, impending, oncoming, pending ♦ impending, pending

im•mis•ci•ble \(ˌ)i-ˈmi-sə-bəl\ *adj* **:** incapable of mixing — **im•mis•ci•bil•i•ty** \-ˌmi-sə-ˈbi-lə-tē\ *n*

im•mis•er•a•tion \(ˌ)i-ˌmi-zə-ˈrā-shən\ *n* **:** IMPOVERISHMENT

im•mo•bile \(ˌ)i-ˈmō-bəl\ *adj* **♦ :** incapable of moving or being moved **:** IMMOVABLE — **im•mo•bil•i•ty** \ˌi-mō-ˈbi-lə-tē\ *n*

♦ immovable, standing, static, stationary, unmovable

im•mo•bi•lize \i-ˈmō-bə-ˌlīz\ *vb* **♦ :** to make immobile — **im•mo•bi•li•za•tion** \i-ˌmō-bə-lə-ˈzā-shən\ *n*

♦ cripple, disable, hamstring, incapacitate, paralyze, prostrate

im•mod•er•ate \(ˌ)i-ˈmä-də-rət\ *adj* **♦ :** lacking in moderation **:** EXCESSIVE — **im•mod•er•a•cy** \-rə-sē\ *n* — **im•mod•er•ate•ly** *adv*

♦ devilish, excessive, exorbitant, extravagant, extreme, inordinate, lavish, overmuch, overweening, steep, stiff, towering, unconscionable

im•mod•est \(ˌ)i-ˈmä-dəst\ *adj* **♦ :** not modest ⟨~ conduct⟩; *specif* **:** not conforming to the sexual mores of a particular time or place ⟨an ~ dress⟩ — **im•mod•est•ly** *adv* — **im•mod•es•ty** \-də-stē\ *n*

♦ bold, familiar, forward, free, presumptuous

im•mo•late \ˈi-mə-ˌlāt\ *vb* **-lat•ed; -lat•ing :** to offer in sacrifice; *esp* **:** to kill as a sacrificial victim

im•mo•la•tion \ˌi-mə-ˈlā-shən\ *n* **1 :** the act of immolating **:** the state of being immolated **2 :** something that is immolated

im•mor•al \(ˌ)i-ˈmȯr-əl\ *adj* **♦ :** not moral — **im•mor•al•ly** *adv*

♦ bad, black, evil, iniquitous, nefarious, rotten, sinful, unethical, unsavory, vicious, vile, villainous, wicked, wrong ♦ cutthroat, Machiavellian, unconscionable, unethical, unprincipled, unscrupulous

im•mo•ral•i•ty \ˌi-mȯ-ˈra-lə-tē, ˌi-mə-\ *n* **1 ♦ :** the quality or state of being immoral; *esp* **:** UNCHASTITY **2 ♦ :** an immoral act or practice

♦ [1] bad, evil, ill, iniquity, sin, villainy, wrong ♦ [2] corruption, debauchery, depravity, iniquity, licentiousness, sin, vice

1im•mor•tal \(ˌ)i-ˈmȯrt-ᵊl\ *adj* **1 ♦ :** not mortal **:** exempt from death ⟨~ gods⟩ **2 ♦ :** destined to be remembered forever ⟨those ~ words⟩ — **im•mor•tal•ly** *adv*

♦ [1, 2] ceaseless, dateless, deathless, endless, eternal, everlasting, permanent, perpetual, undying, unending

2immortal *n* **1 :** one exempt from death **2** *pl, often cap* **:** the gods in Greek and Roman mythology **3 :** a person whose fame is lasting ⟨an ~ of baseball⟩

im•mor•tal•ise *chiefly Brit var of* IMMORTALIZE

im•mor•tal•i•ty \ˌi-ˌmȯr-ˈta-lə-tē\ *n* **♦ :** the quality or state of being immortal; *esp* **:** unending existence

♦ afterlife, eternity, hereafter, immortality

im•mor•tal•ize \i-ˈmȯrt-ᵊl-ˌīz\ *vb* **-ized; -iz•ing :** to make immortal

im•mov•able \(ˌ)i-ˈmü-və-bəl\ *adj* **1 ♦ :** firmly fixed, settled, or fastened ⟨~ mountains⟩ **2 :** firm in belief, determination, or adherence **:** UNYIELDING **3 :** IMPASSIVE — **im•mov•abil•ity** \-ˌmü-və-ˈbi-lə-tē\ *n* — **im•mov•ably** \-blē\ *adv*

♦ immobile, nonmotile, unbudging, unmovable ***Ant*** mobile, motile, movable, moving

im•mune \i-ˈmyün\ *adj* **1 :** EXEMPT **2 :** having a special capacity for resistance (as to a disease) **3 :** containing or producing antibodies — **im•mu•ni•ty** \-ˈmyü-nə-tē\ *n*

immune response *n* **:** a response of the body to an antigen resulting in the formation of antibodies and cells designed to react with the antigen and render it harmless

immune system *n* **:** the bodily system that protects the body from foreign substances, cells, and tissues by producing the immune response and that includes especially the thymus, spleen, lymph nodes, and lymphocytes

im•mu•nize \ˈi-myə-ˌnīz\ *vb* **-nized; -niz•ing :** to make immune — **im•mu•ni•za•tion** \ˌi-myə-nə-ˈzā-shən\ *n*

im•mu•no•de•fi•cien•cy \ˌi-myə-nō-di-ˈfi-shən-sē\ *n* **:** inability to produce the normal number of antibodies or immunologically sensitized cells especially in response to specific antigens — **im•mu•no•de•fi•cient** \-ˈfi-shənt\ *adj*

im•mu•no•glob•u•lin \ˌi-myə-nō-ˈglä-byə-lən\ *n* **:** ANTIBODY

im•mu•nol•o•gy \ˌi-myə-ˈnä-lə-jē\ *n* **:** a science that deals with the immune system, immunity, and the immune response — **im•mu•no•log•ic** \-nə-ˈlä-jik\ *or* **im•mu•no•log•i•cal** \-ji-kəl\ *adj* — **im•mu•no•log•i•cal•ly** \-ji-k(ə-)lē\ *adv* — **im•mu•nol•o•gist** \-ˈnä-lə-jist\ *n*

im•mu•no•sup•pres•sion \ˌi-myə-nō-sə-ˈpre-shən\ *n* **:** suppression (as by drugs) of natural immune responses — **im•mu•no•sup•press** \-ˈpres\ *vb* — **im•mu•no•sup•pres•sive** \-ˈpre-siv\ *adj*

im•mu•no•ther•a•py \-ˈther-ə-pē\ *n* **:** treatment or prevention of disease by attempting to induce immunity

im•mure \i-ˈmyu̇r\ *vb* **im•mured; im•mur•ing 1** ◆ **:** to enclose within or as if within walls; *also* **:** IMPRISON **2 :** to build into a wall; *esp* **:** to entomb in a wall

◆ cage, closet, coop up, corral, encase, enclose, envelop, fence, hedge, hem, house, pen, wall ◆ commit, confine, imprison, jail

im•mu•ta•bil•i•ty \-ˌmyü-tə-ˈbi-lə-tē\ *n* ◆ **:** the quality or state of being immutable

◆ constancy, fixedness, stability, steadiness

im•mu•ta•ble \(ˌ)i-ˈmyü-tə-bəl\ *adj* ◆ **:** not capable of or susceptible to change **:** UNCHANGEABLE, UNCHANGING — **im•mu•ta•bly** \-ˈmyü-tə-blē\ *adv*

◆ fast, fixed, hard-and-fast, inflexible, unalterable, unchangeable, unchanging

[1]**imp** \ˈimp\ *n* **1** ◆ **:** a small demon **:** FIEND **2** ◆ **:** a mischievous child

◆ [1] demon, devil, fiend, ghoul ◆ [2] devil, hellion, mischief, monkey, rapscallion, rascal, rogue, scamp, urchin

[2]**imp** *abbr* **1** imperative **2** imperfect **3** imperial **4** import; imported

[1]**im•pact** \im-ˈpakt\ *vb* **1 :** to press together **2** ◆ **:** to have an impact on **3** ◆ **:** to strike forcefully

◆ [2] affect, impress, influence, move, strike, sway, tell, touch ◆ [3] bang, bash, bump, collide, crash, hit, knock, ram, slam, smash, strike, swipe, thud

[2]**im•pact** \ˈim-ˌpakt\ *n* **1** ◆ **:** a forceful contact, collision, or onset; *also* **:** the impetus communicated in or as if in a collision **2** ◆ **:** the force of impression of one thing on another **:** EFFECT

◆ [1] bump, collision, concussion, crash, jar, jolt, shock, smash, strike, wallop ◆ [2] effect, influence, mark, repercussion, sway

im•pact•ed \im-ˈpak-təd\ *adj* **1 :** packed or wedged in **2 :** wedged between the jawbone and another tooth

im•pair \im-ˈpar\ *vb* **:** to diminish in quantity, value, excellence, or strength **:** DAMAGE, LESSEN — **im•pair•ment** *n*

im•paired \-ˈpard\ *adj* ◆ **:** being in a less than perfect or whole condition; *esp* **:** disabled or functionally defective — often used in combination ⟨hearing-*impaired*⟩

◆ challenged, disabled, impaired

im•pa•la \im-ˈpa-lə\ *n, pl* **impalas** *or* **impala :** a large brownish African antelope that in the male has slender curved horns with ridges

im•pale \im-ˈpāl\ *vb* **im•paled; im•pal•ing** ◆ **:** to pierce with or as if with something pointed — **im•pale•ment** *n*

◆ gore, harpoon, lance, pierce, puncture, skewer, spear, spike, stab, stick, transfix

im•pal•pa•ble \(ˌ)im-ˈpal-pə-bəl\ *adj* **1 :** unable to be felt by touch **:** INTANGIBLE **2** ◆ **:** not easily seen or understood — **im•pal•pa•bly** \-blē\ *adv*

◆ imperceptible, inappreciable, indistinguishable

im•pan•el \im-ˈpan-ᵊl\ *vb* **:** to enter in or on a panel **:** ENROLL ⟨∼ a jury⟩

im•part \im-ˈpärt\ *vb* **1** ◆ **:** to give from one's store or abundance ⟨the sun ∼*s* warmth⟩ **2** ◆ **:** to make known

◆ [1, 2] communicate, convey, spread, transfer, transfuse, transmit

im•par•tial \(ˌ)im-ˈpär-shəl\ *adj* ◆ **:** not partial **:** UNBIASED, JUST — **im•par•tial•ly** *adv*

◆ disinterested, dispassionate, equal, equitable, fair, just, nonpartisan, objective, square, unbiased, unprejudiced

im•par•tial•i•ty \-ˌpär-shē-ˈa-lə-tē\ *n* ◆ **:** the quality or state of being impartial **:** freedom from bias or favoritism

◆ detachment, disinterestedness, neutrality, objectivity

im•pass•able \(ˌ)im-ˈpa-sə-bəl\ *adj* ◆ **:** incapable of being passed, traversed, or crossed ⟨∼ roads⟩ — **im•pass•ably** \-blē\ *adv*

◆ impenetrable, impervious

im•passe \ˈim-ˌpas\ *n* **1 :** an impassable road or way **2** ◆ **:** a predicament from which there is no obvious escape

◆ deadlock, halt, stalemate, standstill

im•pas•si•ble \(ˌ)im-ˈpa-sə-bəl\ *adj* **:** incapable of feeling **:** IMPASSIVE

im•pas•sioned \im-ˈpa-shənd\ *adj* ◆ **:** filled with passion or zeal **:** showing great warmth or intensity of feeling

◆ ardent, burning, charged, emotional, fervent, fiery, hot-blooded, passionate, red-hot, vehement

im•pas•sive \(ˌ)im-ˈpa-siv\ *adj* ◆ **:** showing no signs of feeling, emotion, or interest **:** EXPRESSIONLESS; *also* **:** lacking or not feeling emotion — **im•pas•sive•ly** *adv*

◆ blank, deadpan, expressionless, inexpressive, stolid, vacant ◆ apathetic, cold-blooded, phlegmatic, stoic, stolid, unemotional *Ant* demonstrative, emotional, fervent, fervid, hot-blooded, impassioned, passionate

im•pas•siv•i•ty \ˌim-ˌpa-ˈsi-və-tē\ *n* ◆ **:** the quality or state of being impassive **:** lack or absence of feeling or expression

◆ apathy, numbness, phlegm, stupor

im•pas•to \im-ˈpas-tō, -ˈpäs-\ *n* **:** the thick application of a pigment to a canvas or panel in painting; *also* **:** the body of pigment so applied

im•pa•tience \-shəns\ *n* ◆ **:** the quality or state of being impatient

◆ appetite, ardor, avidity, eagerness, enthusiasm, excitement, hunger, keenness, thirst

im•pa•tiens \im-ˈpā-shənz, -shəns\ *n* **:** any of a genus of herbs with usually spurred flowers and seed capsules that readily split open

im•pa•tient \(ˌ)im-ˈpā-shənt\ *adj* **1 :** not patient **:** restless or short of temper especially under irritation, delay, or opposition **2 :** INTOLERANT ⟨∼ of poverty⟩ **3 :** prompted or marked by impatience **4 :** eagerly desirous **:** ANXIOUS — **im•pa•tient•ly** *adv*

im•peach \im-ˈpēch\ *vb* **1 :** to charge (a public official) before an authorized tribunal with misconduct in office **2 :** to challenge the credibility or validity of **3 :** to remove from public office for misconduct — **im•peach•ment** *n*

im•pec•ca•bil•i•ty \(ˌ)im-ˌpe-kə-ˈbi-lə-tē\ *n* **:** the quality or state of being impeccable

im•pec•ca•ble \(ˌ)im-ˈpe-kə-bəl\ *adj* **1 :** not capable of sinning or wrongdoing **2** ◆ **:** free from fault or blame **:** FAULTLESS ⟨a man of ∼ character⟩

◆ faultless, flawless, irreproachable *Ant* censurable, defective, faulty, reproachable ◆ absolute, ideal, letter-perfect, perfect, unblemished

im•pec•ca•bly \(ˌ)im-ˈpe-kə-blē\ *adv* ◆ **:** in an impeccable manner

◆ faultlessly, flawlessly, ideally, perfectly

im•pe•cu•nious \ˌim-pi-ˈkyü-nyəs, -nē-əs\ *adj* ◆ **:** having little or no money

◆ broke, destitute, indigent, needy, penniless, penurious, poor, poverty-stricken

im•pe•cu•nious•ness *n* ◆ **:** the quality or state of being impecunious

◆ beggary, destitution, impoverishment, indigence, need, pauperism, penury, poverty, want

im•ped•ance \im-ˈpēd-ᵊns\ *n* **:** the opposition in an electrical circuit to the flow of an alternating current
im•pede \im-ˈpēd\ *vb* **im•ped•ed; im•ped•ing** ♦ **:** to interfere with the progress of

♦ encumber, fetter, hamper, hinder, hold back, hold up, inhibit, interfere with, obstruct

im•ped•i•ment \im-ˈpe-də-mənt\ *n* **1 :** something that impedes, hinders, or obstructs **2 :** a speech defect
im•ped•i•men•ta \im-ˌpe-də-ˈmen-tə\ *n pl* **:** things that impede
im•pel \im-ˈpel\ *vb* **im•pelled; im•pel•ling** ♦ **:** to urge or drive forward or on; *also* **:** PROPEL

♦ actuate, drive, move, propel, work

im•pel•ler *also* **im•pel•lor** \im-ˈpe-lər\ *n* **:** a rotor especially in a pump
im•pend \im-ˈpend\ *vb* **1 :** to hover or hang over threateningly **:** MENACE **2 :** to be about to occur
impending *adj* ♦ **:** that is about to occur

♦ coming, forthcoming, imminent, oncoming, pending

im•pen•e•tra•ble \(ˌ)im-ˈpe-nə-trə-bəl\ *adj* **1** ♦ **:** incapable of being penetrated or pierced ⟨an ~ jungle⟩ **2** ♦ **:** incapable of being comprehended **:** INSCRUTABLE ⟨an ~ mystery⟩ — **im•pen•e•tra•bil•i•ty** \-ˌpe-nə-trə-ˈbi-lə-tē\ *n* — **im•pen•e•tra•bly** \-ˈpe-nə-trə-blē\ *adv*

♦ [1] impervious, tight ♦ [2] cryptic, darkling, deep, enigmatic, inscrutable, mysterious, mystic, occult, uncanny ♦ [2] incomprehensible, unfathomable

im•pen•i•tent \(ˌ)im-ˈpe-nə-tənt\ *adj* **:** not penitent **:** not repenting of sin — **im•pen•i•tence** \-təns\ *n*
im•per•a•tive \im-ˈper-ə-tiv\ *adj* **1 :** expressing a command, request, or encouragement ⟨~ sentence⟩ **2** ♦ **:** having power to restrain, control, or direct **3** ♦ **:** not to be avoided or evaded — **imperative** *n* — **im•per•a•tive•ly** *adv*

♦ [2] compulsory, incumbent, involuntary, mandatory, necessary, nonelective, obligatory, peremptory ♦ [3] acute, critical, dire, imperious, instant, pressing, urgent

im•per•cep•ti•ble \ˌim-pər-ˈsep-tə-bəl\ *adj* ♦ **:** not perceptible; *esp* **:** too slight to be perceived ⟨~ changes⟩ — **im•per•cep•ti•bly** \-blē\ *adv*

♦ impalpable, inappreciable, indistinguishable *Ant* appreciable, discernible, palpable, perceptible, sensible

im•per•cep•tive \ˌim-pər-ˈsep-tiv\ *adj* **:** not perceptive
imperf *abbr* imperfect
[1]**im•per•fect** \(ˌ)im-ˈpər-fikt\ *adj* **1** ♦ **:** not perfect especially by having a fault or a lack **2 :** of, relating to, or being a verb tense used to designate a continuing state or an incomplete action especially in the past — **im•per•fect•ly** *adv*

♦ bad, defective, faulty

[2]**imperfect** *n* **:** the imperfect tense; *also* **:** a verb form in it
im•per•fec•tion \ˌim-pər-ˈfek-shən\ *n* **1 :** the quality or state of being imperfect **2** ♦ **:** the quality or aspect which makes something incomplete or defective **:** FAULT, BLEMISH

♦ blemish, defect, deformity, disfigurement, fault, flaw, mark, pockmark, scar

im•pe•ri•al \im-ˈpir-ē-əl\ *adj* **1 :** of, relating to, or befitting an empire or an emperor; *also* **:** of or relating to the United Kingdom or to the Commonwealth or British Empire **2 :** ROYAL, SOVEREIGN; *also* **:** REGAL, IMPERIOUS **3** ♦ **:** of unusual size or excellence

♦ august, baronial, gallant, glorious, grand, grandiose, heroic, imposing, magnificent, majestic, monumental, noble, proud, regal, royal, splendid, stately

im•pe•ri•al•ism \im-ˈpir-ē-ə-ˌli-zəm\ *n* **:** the policy of seeking to extend the power, dominion, or territories of a nation — **im•pe•ri•al•ist** \-list\ *n or adj* — **im•pe•ri•al•is•tic** \-ˌpir-ē-ə-ˈlis-tik\ *adj* — **im•pe•ri•al•is•ti•cal•ly** \-ti-k(ə-)lē\ *adv*
im•per•il \im-ˈper-əl\ *vb* **-iled** *or* **-illed; -il•ing** *or* **-il•ling** ♦ **:** to bring into peril **:** ENDANGER

♦ adventure, compromise, gamble with, hazard, jeopardize, menace, risk, venture

im•pe•ri•ous \im-ˈpir-ē-əs\ *adj* **1 :** befitting or characteristic of one of eminent rank or attainments **:** COMMANDING, LORDLY **2** ♦ **:** marked by arrogant assurance **:** DOMINEERING **3** ♦ **:** intensely compelling **:** IMPERATIVE, URGENT — **im•pe•ri•ous•ly** *adv*

♦ [2] authoritarian, autocratic, bossy, despotic, dictatorial, domineering, masterful, overbearing, peremptory, tyrannical, tyrannous ♦ [2] arbitrary, dictatorial, high-handed, peremptory, willful ♦ [3] acute, critical, dire, imperative, instant, pressing, urgent

im•per•ish•able \(ˌ)im-ˈper-i-shə-bəl\ *adj* **:** not perishable or subject to decay
im•per•ma•nent \(ˌ)im-ˈpər-mə-nənt\ *adj* ♦ **:** not permanent — **im•per•ma•nent•ly** *adv*

♦ interim, provisional, short-term, temporary ♦ ephemeral, evanescent, flash, fleeting, momentary, short-lived, transient

im•per•me•able \(ˌ)im-ˈpər-mē-ə-bəl\ *adj* **:** not permitting passage (as of a fluid) through its substance
im•per•mis•si•ble \ˌim-pər-ˈmi-sə-bəl\ *adj* ♦ **:** not permissible

♦ forbidden, taboo *Ant* allowable, permissible, permissive, sufferable

im•per•son•al \(ˌ)im-ˈpər-sə-nəl\ *adj* **1 :** not referring to any particular person or thing **2 :** not involving human emotions — **im•per•son•al•i•ty** \-ˌpər-sə-ˈna-lə-tē\ *n* — **im•per•son•al•ly** *adv*
im•per•son•ate \im-ˈpər-sə-ˌnāt\ *vb* **-at•ed; -at•ing** ♦ **:** to assume or act the character of — **im•per•son•a•tion** \-ˌpər-sə-ˈnā-shən\ *n*

♦ act, perform, play, portray ♦ masquerade, play, pose

im•per•son•a•tor \-ˈpər-sə-ˌnā-tər\ *n* ♦ **:** one that impersonates; *esp* **:** an entertainer who impersonates an individual, a type of person, an animal, or an inanimate object

♦ imitator, impressionist, mimic

im•per•ti•nence \(ˌ)im-ˈpərt-ᵊn-əns\ *n* ♦ **:** the quality or state of being impertinent; *also* **:** an instance of impertinence

♦ brazenness, discourtesy, disrespect, impudence, incivility, insolence, rudeness

im•per•ti•nent \(ˌ)im-ˈpərt-ᵊn-ənt\ *adj* **1 :** IRRELEVANT **2** ♦ **:** not restrained within due or proper bounds — **im•per•ti•nent•ly** *adv*

♦ arch, bold, brash, brazen, cheeky, cocky, fresh, impudent, insolent, nervy, sassy, saucy ♦ discourteous, ill-bred, ill-mannered, impolite, inconsiderate, rude, thoughtless, uncivil, ungracious, unmannerly

im•per•turb•able \ˌim-pər-ˈtər-bə-bəl\ *adj* ♦ **:** marked by extreme calm, impassivity, and steadiness

♦ nerveless, unflappable, unshakable

im•per•vi•ous \(ˌ)im-ˈpər-vē-əs\ *adj* **1** ♦ **:** incapable of being penetrated (as by moisture) **2 :** not capable of being affected or disturbed ⟨~ to criticism⟩

♦ impenetrable, tight

im•pe•ti•go \ˌim-pə-ˈtē-gō, -ˈtī-\ *n* **:** a contagious skin disease characterized by vesicles, pustules, and yellowish crusts
im•pet•u•ous \im-ˈpe-chə-wəs\ *adj* **1 :** marked by impulsive vehemence ⟨~ temper⟩ **2 :** marked by force and violence ⟨with ~ speed⟩ — **im•pet•u•os•i•ty** \(ˌ)im-ˌpe-chə-ˈwä-sə-tē\ *n* — **im•pet•u•ous•ly** *adv*
im•pe•tus \ˈim-pə-təs\ *n* **1** ♦ **:** a driving force **:** IMPULSE; *also* **:** INCENTIVE **2 :** MOMENTUM

♦ boost, encouragement, goad, impulse, incentive, incitement, instigation, momentum, motivation, provocation, spur, stimulus, yeast

im•pi•e•ty \(ˌ)im-ˈpī-ə-tē\ *n, pl* **-ties 1 :** the quality or state of being impious **2** ♦ **:** an impious act

♦ blasphemy, defilement, desecration, irreverence, sacrilege

im•pinge \im-ˈpinj\ *vb* **im•pinged; im•ping•ing 1 :** to strike or dash especially with a sharp collision **2 :** ENCROACH, INFRINGE — **im•pinge•ment** *n*
im•pi•ous \ˈim-pē-əs, (ˌ)im-ˈpī-\ *adj* **:** not pious **:** IRREVERENT, PROFANE
imp•ish \ˈim-pish\ *adj* ♦ **:** of, relating to, or befitting an imp; *esp* **:** MISCHIEVOUS — **imp•ish•ly** *adv*

♦ devilish, knavish, mischievous, rascally, roguish, sly, waggish, wicked

imp•ish•ness *n* ♦ **:** the quality or state of being impish

♦ friskiness, mischief, mischievousness, playfulness

im•pla•ca•ble \(ˌ)im-ˈpla-kə-bəl, -ˈplā-\ *adj* ♦ **:** not capable of being appeased, pacified, mitigated, or changed ⟨an ~ enemy⟩ — **im•pla•ca•bil•i•ty** \-ˌpla-kə-ˈbi-lə-tē, -ˌplā-\ *n* — **im•pla•ca•bly** \-ˈpla-kə-blē\ *adv*

◆ adamant, hard, immovable, inflexible, pat, rigid, unbending, uncompromising, unrelenting, unyielding

im·plant \im-ˈplant\ *vb* **1** ◆ **:** to set firmly or deeply **2 :** to fix in the mind or spirit **3 :** to insert in living tissue (as for growth or absorption) — **im·plant** \ˈim-ˌplant\ *n* — **im·plan·ta·tion** \ˌim-ˌplan-ˈtā-shən\ *n*

◆ embed, entrench, fix, ingrain, lodge, root

im·plau·si·ble \(ˌ)im-ˈplȯ-zə-bəl\ *adj* ◆ **:** not plausible — **im·plau·si·bil·i·ty** \-ˌplȯ-zə-ˈbi-lə-tē\ *n* — **im·plau·si·bly** \-ˈplȯ-zə-blē\ *adv*

◆ fantastic, inconceivable, incredible, unbelievable, unconvincing, unimaginable, unthinkable

1im·ple·ment \ˈim-plə-mənt\ *n* ◆ **:** a device used in the performance of a task **:** TOOL, UTENSIL

◆ device, instrument, tool, utensil

2im·ple·ment \-ˌment\ *vb* **1** ◆ **:** to put into execution or bring to completion **2 :** to provide implements for

◆ administer, apply, enforce, execute

im·ple·men·ta·tion \ˌim-plə-mən-ˈtā-shən\ *n* ◆ **:** the act of implementing or the state of being implemented

◆ accomplishment, achievement, commission, discharge, enactment, execution, fulfillment, performance, perpetration

im·pli·cate \ˈim-plə-ˌkāt\ *vb* **-cat·ed; -cat·ing 1 :** IMPLY **2 :** INVOLVE — **im·pli·ca·tion** \ˌim-plə-ˈkā-shən\ *n*

im·plic·it \im-ˈpli-sət\ *adj* **1** ◆ **:** understood though not directly stated or expressed **:** IMPLIED; *also* **:** POTENTIAL **2 :** COMPLETE, UNQUESTIONING, ABSOLUTE ⟨~ faith⟩ — **im·plic·it·ly** *adv*

◆ potential, tacit, unexpressed, unspoken, unvoiced, wordless *Ant* explicit, express, expressed, spoken, stated

im·plode \im-ˈplōd\ *vb* **im·plod·ed; im·plod·ing 1** ◆ **:** to burst or collapse inward **2 :** SELF-DESTRUCT — **im·plo·sion** \-ˈplō-zhən\ *n* — **im·plo·sive** \-siv\ *adj*

◆ buckle, cave in, collapse, crumple, give, go, yield

im·plore \im-ˈplōr\ *vb* **im·plored; im·plor·ing** ◆ **:** to call upon in supplication **:** BESEECH, ENTREAT

◆ appeal, beg, beseech, entreat, importune, petition, plead, pray, solicit, supplicate

im·ply \im-ˈplī\ *vb* **im·plied; im·ply·ing 1 :** to involve or indicate by inference, association, or necessary consequence rather than by direct statement ⟨war *implies* fighting⟩ **2** ◆ **:** to express indirectly **:** hint at

◆ allude, hint, indicate, infer, insinuate, intimate, suggest

im·po·lite \ˌim-pə-ˈlīt\ *adj* ◆ **:** not polite **:** RUDE, DISCOURTEOUS

◆ discourteous, ill-bred, ill-mannered, impertinent, inconsiderate, rude, thoughtless, uncivil, ungracious, unmannerly *Ant* civil, considerate, courteous, genteel, gracious, mannerly, polite, thoughtful, well-bred

im·pol·i·tic \(ˌ)im-ˈpä-lə-ˌtik\ *adj* **:** not politic **:** UNWISE

im·pon·der·a·ble \(ˌ)im-ˈpän-də-rə-bəl\ *adj* **:** incapable of being weighed or evaluated with exactness — **imponderable** *n*

1im·port \im-ˈpōrt\ *vb* **1 :** to bear or convey as meaning or portent **:** MEAN **2 :** to bring (as merchandise) into a place or country from a foreign or external source — **im·port·er** *n*

2im·port \ˈim-ˌpōrt\ *n* **1 :** IMPORTANCE, SIGNIFICANCE **2** ◆ **:** meaning conveyed, professed, or implied **:** SIGNIFICATION **3 :** something (as merchandise) brought in from another country

◆ denotation, drift, intent, meaning, purport, sense, significance, signification

im·por·tance \im-ˈpȯrt-ᵊns\ *n* **:** the quality or state of being important **:** MOMENT, SIGNIFICANCE

im·por·tant \im-ˈpȯrt-ᵊnt\ *adj* **1** ◆ **:** marked by importance **:** SIGNIFICANT **2** ◆ **:** giving an impression of self-importance — **im·por·tant·ly** *adv*

◆ [1] big, consequential, eventful, major, material, meaningful, momentous, significant, substantial, weighty *Ant* insignificant, little, minor, slight, small, trivial, unimportant ◆ [1] influential, mighty, potent, powerful, significant, strong *Ant* impotent, insignificant, little, powerless, unimportant, weak ◆ [2] complacent, conceited, egotistic, overweening, pompous, prideful, proud, self-important, self-satisfied, smug, stuck-up, vain

im·por·ta·tion \ˌim-ˌpōr-ˈtā-shən, -pər-\ *n* **1 :** the act or practice of importing **2 :** something imported

im·por·tu·nate \im-ˈpȯr-chə-nət\ *adj* **1 :** troublesomely urgent or persistent **2 :** BURDENSOME, TROUBLESOME

im·por·tune \ˌim-pər-ˈtün, -ˈtyün; im-ˈpȯr-chən\ *vb* **-tuned; -tun·ing** ◆ **:** to urge or beg with troublesome persistence — **im·por·tu·ni·ty** \-pər-ˈtü-nə-tē, -ˈtyü-\ *n*

◆ appeal, beg, beseech, entreat, implore, petition, plead, pray, solicit, supplicate

im·pose \im-ˈpōz\ *vb* **im·posed; im·pos·ing 1** ◆ **:** to establish or apply by authority ⟨~ a tax⟩; *also* **:** to establish by force ⟨*imposed* a government⟩ **2 :** OBTRUDE ⟨*imposed* herself on others⟩ **3 :** to take unwarranted advantage of something ⟨~ on her good nature⟩

◆ assess, charge, exact, fine, lay, levy, put *Ant* remit

im·pos·ing *adj* ◆ **:** impressive because of size, bearing, dignity, or grandeur — **im·pos·ing·ly** *adv*

◆ august, baronial, gallant, glorious, grand, grandiose, heroic, magnificent, majestic, monumental, noble, proud, regal, royal, splendid, stately

im·po·si·tion \ˌim-pə-ˈzi-shən\ *n* **:** something imposed: as **a :** an amount levied **b :** an excessive or uncalled-for requirement or burden

im·pos·si·ble \(ˌ)im-ˈpä-sə-bəl\ *adj* **1 :** incapable of being or of occurring **2** ◆ **:** enormously difficult **:** felt to be incapable of being done, attained, or fulfilled **3 :** extremely undesirable **:** UNACCEPTABLE — **im·pos·si·bil·i·ty** \-ˌpä-sə-ˈbi-lə-tē\ *n* — **im·pos·si·bly** \-ˈpä-sə-blē\ *adv*

◆ hopeless, unattainable, unsolvable, unworkable *Ant* achievable, attainable, doable, feasible, possible, realizable, workable

1im·post \ˈim-ˌpōst\ *n* ◆ **:** something imposed or levied **:** TAX, DUTY

◆ assessment, duty, levy, tax

2impost *n* **:** a block, capital, or molding from which an arch springs

im·pos·tor *or* **im·pos·ter** \im-ˈpäs-tər\ *n* **:** one that assumes an identity or title not one's own in order to deceive

im·pos·ture \im-ˈpäs-chər\ *n* **:** DECEPTION; *esp* **:** fraudulent impersonation

im·po·tence \-təns\ *n* ◆ **:** the quality or state of being impotent

◆ inability, inadequacy, incapability, incompetence, ineptitude

im·po·tent \ˈim-pə-tənt\ *adj* **1** ◆ **:** lacking in power or strength **:** deficient in capacity **2 a :** unable to copulate **b** ◆ **:** failing to produce or incapable of producing offspring **:** STERILE — **im·po·ten·cy** \-tən-sē\ *n* — **im·po·tent·ly** *adv*

◆ [1] helpless, powerless, weak ◆ [2b] barren, infertile, sterile

im·pound \im-ˈpau̇nd\ *vb* **1 :** CONFINE, ENCLOSE ⟨~ stray dogs⟩ **2 :** to seize and hold in legal custody **3 :** to collect in a reservoir ⟨~ water⟩ — **im·pound·ment** *n*

im·pov·er·ish \im-ˈpä-və-rish\ *vb* **:** to make poor; *also* **:** to deprive of strength, richness, or fertility

impoverished *adj* **1** *of a fauna or flora* **:** represented by few species or individuals **2 :** deprived of strength, richness, or fertility

im·pov·er·ish·ment *n* ◆ **:** the act of impoverishing or the state of being impoverished

◆ beggary, destitution, impecuniousness, indigence, need, pauperism, penury, poverty, want

im·prac·ti·ca·ble \(ˌ)im-ˈprak-ti-kə-bəl\ *adj* **:** not practicable **:** incapable of being put into practice or use

im·prac·ti·cal \(ˌ)im-ˈprak-ti-kəl\ *adj* **1 :** not practical **2** ◆ **:** incapable of being done by the means available **:** IMPRACTICABLE

◆ inoperable, unusable, unworkable, useless *Ant* practicable, practical, usable, useful, workable

im·pre·cate \ˈim-pri-ˌkāt\ *vb* **-cat·ed; -cat·ing :** CURSE

im·pre·ca·tion \ˌim-pri-ˈkā-shən\ *n* ◆ **:** a prayer or invocation for harm or injury to come upon one; *also* **:** the act of imprecating

◆ anathema, curse, execration, malediction

im·pre·cise \ˌim-pri-ˈsīs\ *adj* ◆ **:** not precise — **im·pre·cise·ly** *adv* — **im·pre·cise·ness** *n* — **im·pre·ci·sion** \-ˈsi-zhən\ *n*

◆ inaccurate, inexact, loose

im·preg·na·ble \im-ˈpreg-nə-bəl\ *adj* **1** ◆ **:** incapable of being taken by assault **:** UNCONQUERABLE **2 :** not liable to doubt, attack, or question — **im·preg·na·bil·i·ty** \(ˌ)im-ˌpreg-nə-ˈbi-lə-tē\ *n*

◆ indomitable, insurmountable, invincible, invulnerable, unbeatable, unconquerable

im•preg•nate \im-ˈpreg-ˌnāt\ *vb* **-nat•ed; -nat•ing** **1 :** to fertilize or make pregnant **2** ♦ **:** to cause to be filled, permeated, or saturated — **im•preg•na•tion** \ˌim-ˌpreg-ˈnā-shən\ *n*

♦ drench, drown, saturate, soak, sop, souse, steep

im•pre•sa•rio \ˌim-prə-ˈsär-ē-ˌō\ *n, pl* **-ri•os** **1 :** the manager or conductor of an opera or concert company **2 :** one who puts on an entertainment **3 :** MANAGER, PRODUCER

¹im•press \im-ˈpres\ *vb* **1 :** to apply with or produce (as a mark) by pressure **:** IMPRINT **2 :** to press, stamp, or print in or upon **3** ♦ **:** to imprint a vivid impression of (as on the memory) **4** ♦ **:** to affect especially forcibly or deeply — **im•press•ible** *adj*

♦ [3] engrave, etch, imprint, ingrain, inscribe ♦ [4] affect, impact, influence, move, strike, sway, tell, touch

²im•press \ˈim-ˌpres\ *n* **1 :** a characteristic or distinctive mark **2 :** IMPRESSION, EFFECT **3 :** IMPRESSION 2 **4 :** an image of something formed by or as if by pressure; *esp* **:** SEAL **5 :** a product of pressure or influence

³im•press \im-ˈpres\ *vb* **1 :** to force into naval service **2 :** to get the aid or services of by forcible argument or persuasion — **im•press•ment** *n*

im•pres•sion \im-ˈpre-shən\ *n* **1 :** a characteristic trait or feature resulting from influence **:** IMPRESS **2** ♦ **:** a stamp, form, or figure made by impressing **:** IMPRINT **3 :** an especially marked influence or effect on feeling, sense, or mind **4 :** a single print or copy (as from type or from an engraved plate or book) **5 :** all the copies of a publication (as a book) printed for one issue **:** PRINTING **6** ♦ **:** a usually vague notion or remembrance **7 :** an imitation in caricature of a noted personality as a form of entertainment

♦ [2] impress, imprint, print, stamp ♦ [6] concept, idea, image, notion, picture, thought

im•pres•sion•able \im-ˈpre-shə-nə-bəl\ *adj* **:** capable of being easily impressed **:** easily molded or influenced

im•pres•sion•ism \im-ˈpre-shə-ˌni-zəm\ *n, often cap* **:** a theory or practice in modern art of depicting the natural appearances of objects by dabs or strokes of primary unmixed colors in order to simulate actual reflected light — **im•pres•sion•is•tic** \-ˌpre-shə-ˈnis-tik\ *adj*

im•pres•sion•ist \im-ˈpre-shə-nist\ *n* **1** *often cap* **:** a painter who practices impressionism **2** ♦ **:** an entertainer who does impressions

♦ imitator, impersonator, impressionist, mimic

im•pres•sive \im-ˈpre-siv\ *adj* ♦ **:** making or tending to make a marked impression ⟨an ~ speech⟩ — **im•pres•sive•ly** *adv* — **im•pres•sive•ness** *n*

♦ affecting, emotional, moving, poignant, stirring, touching

im•pri•ma•tur \ˌim-prə-ˈmä-ˌtu̇r\ *n* **1 :** a license to print or publish; *also* **:** official approval of a publication by a censor **2** ♦ **:** explicit or official approval, permission, or ratification

♦ approbation, approval, blessing, favor (*or* favour), OK

¹im•print \im-ˈprint, ˈim-ˌprint\ *vb* **1 :** to stamp or mark by or as if by pressure **:** IMPRESS **2** ♦ **:** to fix firmly (as on the memory)

♦ engrave, etch, impress, ingrain, inscribe

²im•print \ˈim-ˌprint\ *n* **1** ♦ **:** something imprinted or printed; *also* **:** a mark or depression made by pressure **2 :** a publisher's name printed at the foot of a title page **3 :** an indelible distinguishing effect or influence

♦ trace, track, trail ♦ impress, impression, print, stamp

im•pris•on \im-ˈpriz-ᵊn\ *vb* ♦ **:** to put in or as if in prison **:** CONFINE

♦ commit, confine, immure, jail ***Ant*** discharge, free, liberate, release

im•pris•on•ment *n* ♦ **:** the act of imprisoning or the state of being imprisoned

♦ captivity, confinement, incarceration, internment

im•prob•a•ble \(ˌ)im-ˈprä-bə-bəl\ *adj* ♦ **:** unlikely to be true or to occur — **im•prob•a•bil•i•ty** \-ˌprä-bə-ˈbi-lə-tē\ *n* — **im•prob•a•bly** \-ˈprä-bə-blē\ *adv*

♦ doubtful, dubious, flimsy, questionable, unlikely ***Ant*** likely, probable

im•promp•tu \im-ˈprämp-tü, -tyü\ *adj* **1 :** made or done on or as if on the spur of the moment **2** ♦ **:** composed or uttered without previous preparation **:** EXTEMPORANEOUS, UNREHEARSED — **impromptu** *adv or n*

♦ ad-lib, extemporaneous, offhand, snap, unplanned, unpremeditated, unprepared, unrehearsed

im•prop•er \(ˌ)im-ˈprä-pər\ *adj* **1** ♦ **:** not proper, fit, or suitable **2 :** INCORRECT, INACCURATE **3 :** not in accord with propriety, modesty, or good manners

♦ inappropriate, inapt, infelicitous, unbecoming, unfit, unseemly, unsuitable, wrong

improper fraction *n* **:** a fraction whose numerator is equal to or larger than the denominator

im•prop•er•ly *adv* ♦ **:** in an improper manner

♦ amiss, erroneously, faultily, inaptly, incorrectly, mistakenly, wrongly

im•pro•pri•e•ty \ˌim-prə-ˈprī-ə-tē\ *n, pl* **-ties** **1** ♦ **:** an improper act or remark; *esp* **:** an unacceptable use of a word or of language **2** ♦ **:** the quality or state of being improper

♦ [1] familiarity, gaffe, indiscretion ***Ant*** amenity, civility, courtesy, formality, gesture ♦ [2] incorrectness, indecency ***Ant*** appropriateness, correctness, decency, fitness, propriety, rightness, suitability

im•prov \ˈim-ˌpräv\ *adj* **:** of, relating to, or being an improvised comedy routine — **improv** *n*

im•prove \im-ˈprüv\ *vb* **im•proved; im•prov•ing** **1** ♦ **:** to enhance or increase in value or quality **2 :** to grow or become better ⟨your work is *improving*⟩ **3 :** to make good use of ⟨~ the time by reading⟩ — **im•prov•able** \-ˈprü-və-bəl\ *adj*

♦ ameliorate, amend, better, enhance, enrich, perfect, refine ***Ant*** worsen

im•prove•ment \im-ˈprüv-mənt\ *n* **1 :** the act or process of improving **2 :** increased value or excellence of something **3** ♦ **:** something that adds to the value or appearance of a thing

♦ advance, advancement, breakthrough, enhancement, refinement

im•prov•i•dent \(ˌ)im-ˈprä-və-dənt\ *adj* **:** not providing for the future — **im•prov•i•dence** \-dəns\ *n*

im•pro•vise \ˈim-prə-ˌvīz\ *vb* **-vised; -vis•ing** **1 :** to compose, recite, play, or sing on the spur of the moment **:** EXTEMPORIZE ⟨~ on the piano⟩ **2 :** to make, invent, or arrange offhand ⟨~ a sail out of shirts⟩ — **im•pro•vi•sa•tion** \im-ˌprä-və-ˈzā-shən, ˌim-prə-və-\ *n* — **im•pro•vis•er** *or* **im•pro•vi•sor** \ˌim-prə-ˈvī-zər, ˈim-prə-ˌvī-\ *n*

im•pru•dent \(ˌ)im-ˈprüd-ᵊnt\ *adj* ♦ **:** not prudent **:** lacking discretion — **im•pru•dence** \-ᵊns\ *n*

♦ ill-advised, indiscreet, tactless, unwise

im•pu•dence \-dəns\ *n* ♦ **:** the quality or state of being impudent; *also* **:** an impudent remark or act

♦ brazenness, discourtesy, disrespect, impertinence, incivility, insolence, rudeness

im•pu•dent \ˈim-pyu̇-dənt\ *adj* ♦ **:** marked by contemptuous boldness or disregard of others — **im•pu•dent•ly** *adv*

♦ arch, bold, brash, brazen, cheeky, cocky, fresh, impertinent, insolent, nervy, sassy, saucy

im•pugn \im-ˈpyün\ *vb* **:** to attack by words or arguments **:** oppose or attack as false or as lacking integrity

im•puis•sance \im-ˈpwis-ᵊns, -ˈpyü-ə-səns\ *n* **:** the quality or state of being powerless **:** WEAKNESS

im•pulse \ˈim-ˌpəls\ *n* **1 :** a force that starts a body into motion; *also* **:** the motion produced by such a force **2** ♦ **:** an arousing of the mind and spirit to some usually unpremeditated action **3 :** NERVE IMPULSE

♦ boost, encouragement, goad, impetus, incentive, incitement, instigation, momentum, motivation, provocation, spur, stimulus, yeast

im•pul•sion \im-ˈpəl-shən\ *n* **1 :** the act of impelling **:** the state of being impelled **2 :** a force that impels **3 :** IMPULSE 2; *also* **:** COMPULSION 3

im•pul•sive \im-ˈpəl-siv\ *adj* **1 :** having the power of or actually driving or impelling **2** ♦ **:** acting or prone to act on impulse ⟨~ buying⟩ — **im•pul•sive•ly** *adv* — **im•pul•sive•ness** *n*

♦ capricious, whimsical

im•pu•ni•ty \im-ˈpyü-nə-tē\ *n* **:** exemption from punishment, harm, or loss

im•pure \(ˌ)im-ˈpyu̇r\ *adj* **1 :** not pure **:** UNCHASTE, OBSCENE **2 :** DIRTY, FOUL **3** ♦ **:** mixed or impregnated with an extraneous and usually unwanted substance **:** ADULTERATED

♦ dilute, polluted *Ant* pure, unadulterated, unalloyed, uncontaminated, undiluted, unpolluted, untainted

im•pu•ri•ty \-ˈpyu̇r-ə-tē\ *n* ♦ **:** something that is impure or makes something else impure; *also* **:** the quality or state of being impure

♦ adulterant, contaminant, defilement, pollutant

im•pute \im-ˈpyüt\ *vb* **im•put•ed; im•put•ing** **1 :** to lay the responsibility or blame for often falsely or unjustly **2** ♦ **:** to credit to a person or a cause **:** ATTRIBUTE — **im•put•able** \-ˈpyü-tə-bəl\ *adj* — **im•pu•ta•tion** \ˌim-pyu̇-ˈtā-shən\ *n*

♦ accredit, ascribe, attribute, credit

[1]in \ˈin\ *prep* **1** — used to indicate physical surroundings ⟨swim ~ the lake⟩ **2 :** INTO 1 ⟨ran ~ the house⟩ **3 :** DURING ⟨~ the summer⟩ **4 :** WITH ⟨written ~ pencil⟩ **5** — used to indicate one's situation or state of being ⟨~ luck⟩ ⟨~ love⟩ **6** — used to indicate manner or purpose ⟨~ a hurry⟩ ⟨said ~ reply⟩ **7 :** INTO 2 ⟨broke ~ pieces⟩

[2]in *adv* **1 :** to or toward the inside ⟨come ~⟩; *also* **:** to or toward some destination or place ⟨flew ~ from the South⟩ **2** ♦ **:** at close quarters **:** NEAR ⟨the enemy closed ~⟩ **3 :** into the midst of something ⟨mix ~ the flour⟩ **4 :** to or at its proper place ⟨fit a piece ~⟩ **5 :** WITHIN ⟨locked ~⟩ **6 :** in vogue or season **7 :** in one's presence, possession, or control ⟨the results are ~⟩

♦ around, by, close, hard, near, nearby, nigh

[3]in *adj* **1 :** located inside or within **2 :** that is in position, operation, or power ⟨the ~ party⟩ **3 :** directed inward **:** INCOMING ⟨the ~ train⟩ **4** ♦ **:** keenly aware of and responsive to what is new and fashionable ⟨the ~ crowd⟩; *also* **:** extremely fashionable ⟨the ~ thing to do⟩

♦ à la mode, chic, fashionable, modish, popular, sharp, smart, snappy, stylish

[4]in *n* **1 :** one who is in office or power or on the inside **2 :** INFLUENCE, PULL ⟨he has an ~ with the owner⟩

[5]in *abbr* **1** inch **2** inlet

In *symbol* indium

IN *abbr* Indiana

in- \(ˌ)in\ *prefix* **:** not **:** absence of **:** NON-, UN-

inadmissibility
inadmissible
inadvisability
inadvisable
inapparent
inapplicable
inapposite
inapproachable
inaptitude
inarguable
inartistic
inaudible
inaudibly
incautious
incombustible
incomprehension
inconclusive
incongruent
inconsistency
incoordination
indecipherable
indemonstrable
indestructible
indeterminable
indiscernible
inedible
ineducable
ineffaceable
inefficacious
inefficacy
inelastic
inelasticity
inequitable
inequity
ineradicable
inerrant
inexpedient
inextinguishable
infeasible
injudicious
inoffensive
insanitary
insensitive
insensitivity
insignificance
insolvable
insusceptible

in•abil•i•ty \ˌi-nə-ˈbi-lə-tē\ *n* ♦ **:** the quality or state of being unable

♦ impotence, inadequacy, incapability, incompetence, ineptitude *Ant* ability, adequacy, capability, capacity, competence, potency

in ab•sen•tia \ˌin-ab-ˈsen-chə, -chē-ə\ *adv* **:** in one's absence

in•ac•ces•si•ble \ˌi-nik-ˈse-sə-bəl, (ˌ)i-ˌnak-\ *adj* ♦ **:** not accessible — **in•ac•ces•si•bil•i•ty** \-ˌse-sə-ˈbi-lə-tē\ *n*

♦ inconvenient, unapproachable, unattainable, unavailable, unobtainable, unreachable, untouchable *Ant* accessible, approachable, attainable, convenient, obtainable, reachable

in•ac•cu•ra•cy \(ˌ)i-ˈna-kyə-rə-sē, -k(ə-)rə-sē\ *n, pl* **-cies** **1 :** the quality or state of being inaccurate **2 :** something (as a statement or act) that is inaccurate

in•ac•cu•rate \-ˈa-kyə-rət, -k(ə-)rət\ *adj* ♦ **:** not accurate

♦ erroneous, false, incorrect, inexact, invalid, off, unsound, untrue, wrong

in•ac•tion \(ˌ)i-ˈnak-shən\ *n* ♦ **:** not occupied or employed

♦ dormancy, idleness, inactivity, inertness, quiescence *Ant* action, activeness, activity

in•ac•ti•vate \(ˌ)i-ˈnak-tə-ˌvāt\ *vb* **:** to make inactive — **in•ac•ti•va•tion** \(ˌ)i-ˌnak-tə-ˈvā-shən\ *n*

in•ac•tive \(ˌ)i-ˈnak-tiv\ ♦ **:** not active, energetic, or in use

♦ dull, inert, lethargic, quiescent, sleepy, sluggish, torpid *Ant* active ♦ dead, dormant, fallow, free, idle, inert, inoperative, latent, off, vacant *Ant* active, alive, busy, employed, functioning, on, operating, operative, running, working

in•ac•tiv•i•ty \-ˌnak-ˈti-və-tē\ *n* ♦ **:** the quality or state of being inactive

♦ dormancy, idleness, inaction, inertness, quiescence

in•ad•e•qua•cy \-kwə-sē\ *n* ♦ **:** the quality or state of being inadequate or insufficient

♦ dearth, deficiency, deficit, failure, famine, insufficiency, lack, paucity, poverty, scantiness, scarcity, shortage, want ♦ impotence, inability, incapability, incompetence, ineptitude

in•ad•e•quate \(ˌ)i-ˈna-di-kwət\ *adj* ♦ **:** not adequate **:** INSUFFICIENT — **in•ad•e•quate•ly** *adv* — **in•ad•e•quate•ness** *n*

♦ deficient, insufficient, scarce, short, shy, wanting

in•ad•ver•tent \ˌi-nəd-ˈvərt-ᵊnt\ *adj* **1 :** HEEDLESS, INATTENTIVE **2 :** not intentional **:** UNINTENTIONAL — **in•ad•ver•tence** \-ᵊns\ *n* — **in•ad•ver•ten•cy** \-ᵊn-sē\ *n* — **in•ad•ver•tent•ly** *adv*

in•alien•able \(ˌ)i-ˈnāl-yə-nə-bəl, -ˈnā-lē-ə-\ *adj* **:** incapable of being alienated, surrendered, or transferred ⟨~ rights⟩ — **in•alien•abil•i•ty** \(ˌ)i-ˌnāl-yə-nə-ˈbi-lə-tē, -ˌnā-lē-ə-\ *n* — **in•alien•ably** *adv*

in•amo•ra•ta \i-ˌnä-mə-ˈrä-tə\ *n* **:** a woman with whom one is in love

inane \i-ˈnān\ *adj* **inan•er; -est** **1 :** EMPTY, INSUBSTANTIAL **2 :** lacking significance, meaning, or point

in•an•i•mate \(ˌ)i-ˈna-nə-mət\ *adj* **:** not animate or animated **:** lacking the qualities of living things — **in•an•i•mate•ly** *adv* — **in•an•i•mate•ness** *n*

inan•i•ty \i-ˈna-nə-tē\ *n* **1** ♦ **:** the quality or state of being inane **2** ♦ **:** something that is inane

♦ [1, 2] absurdity, asininity, balminess, craziness, daftness, fatuity, folly, foolishness, insanity, lunacy, madness, silliness, simplicity, zaniness ♦ [2] absurdity, fatuity, folly, foolery, foolishness, idiocy, madness, stupidity

in•ap•pre•cia•ble \ˌi-nə-ˈprē-shə-bəl\ *adj* ♦ **:** too small to be perceived — **in•ap•pre•cia•bly** \-blē\ *adv*

♦ impalpable, imperceptible, indistinguishable

in•ap•pro•pri•ate \ˌi-nə-ˈprō-prē-ˌət\ *adj* **:** not in good taste or suitale for a particular occasion or situation

♦ amiss, graceless, improper, inapt, incongruous, incorrect, indecorous, inept, infelicitous, unapt, unbecoming, unfit, unhappy, unseemly, unsuitable, wrong *Ant* appropriate, becoming, befitting, correct, fit, fitting, proper, right, seemly, suitable

in•apt \(ˌ)i-ˈnapt\ *adj* **1** ♦ **:** not suitable **2** ♦ **:** inappropriate or incompetent often to an absurd degree **:** INEPT — **in•apt•ness** *n*

♦ [1, 2] improper, inappropriate, infelicitous, unbecoming, unfit, unseemly, unsuitable, wrong

in•apt•ly *adv* ♦ **:** in an inapt manner

♦ amiss, erroneously, faultily, improperly, incorrectly, mistakenly, wrongly

in•ar•tic•u•late \ˌi-när-ˈti-kyə-lət\ *adj* **1 :** not understandable as spoken words **2** ♦ **:** incapable of speech especially under stress of emotion **:** MUTE **3 :** incapable of being expressed by speech; *also* **:** UNSPOKEN **4 :** not having the power of distinct utterance or effective expression — **in•ar•tic•u•late•ly** *adv*

♦ dumb, mute, speechless, voiceless

in•as•much as \ˌi-nəz-ˈməch-\ *conj* **:** seeing that **:** SINCE

in•at•ten•tion \ˌi-nə-ˈten-chən\ *n* **:** failure to pay attention **:** DISREGARD

in•at•ten•tive \-ˈten-tiv\ *adj* **:** not paying attention **:** not attentive

[1]in•au•gu•ral \i-ˈnȯ-gyə-rəl, -gə-\ *adj* **1 :** of or relating to an inauguration **2** ♦ **:** marking a beginning

♦ first, initial, maiden, original, pioneer, premier

²inaugural *n* **1 :** an inaugural address **2 :** an act of inaugurating **:** INAUGURATION; *esp* **:** a ceremonial induction into office
in•au•gu•rate \i-ˈnȯ-gyə-ˌrāt, -gə-\ *vb* **-rat•ed; -rat•ing** **1** ♦ **:** to introduce into an office with suitable ceremonies **:** INSTALL **2 :** to dedicate ceremoniously **3** ♦ **:** to bring about the beginning of **:** INITIATE

♦ [1] baptize, induct, initiate, install, invest ♦ [3] constitute, establish, found, initiate, innovate, institute, introduce, launch, pioneer, set up, start

in•au•gu•ra•tion \-ˌnȯ-gyə-ˈrā-shən, -gə-\ *n* ♦ **:** an act of inaugurating; *also* **:** a ceremonial induction into office

♦ inaugural, induction, installation, investiture

in•aus•pi•cious \ˌi-ˌnȯ-ˈspi-shəs\ *adj* ♦ **:** not auspicious

♦ foreboding, ominous, portentous, prophetic

in•au•then•tic \ˌi-ˌnȯ-ˈthen-tik\ *adj* ♦ **:** not authentic

♦ bogus, counterfeit, fake, false, phony, sham, spurious, unauthentic

in•board \ˈin-ˌbōrd\ *adv* **1 :** inside the hull of a ship **2 :** close or closest to the center line of a vehicle or craft — **inboard** *adj*
in•born \ˈin-ˈbȯrn\ *adj* **1** ♦ **:** present from or as if from birth **2** ♦ **:** genetically transmitted or transmittable from parent to offspring **:** HEREDITARY, INHERITED

♦ [1] essential, ingrained, inherent, innate, integral, intrinsic, natural ♦ [2] genetic, hereditary, heritable, inherited

in•bound \ˈin-ˌbau̇nd\ *adj* **:** inward bound ⟨~ traffic⟩
in–box \ˈin-ˌbäks\ *n* **:** a receptacle for incoming interoffice letters; *also* **:** a computer folder for incoming e-mail
in•bred \ˈin-ˈbred\ *adj* **1 :** ingrained in one's nature as deeply as if by heredity **2 :** subjected to or produced by inbreeding
in•breed•ing \ˈin-ˌbrē-diŋ\ *n* **1 :** the interbreeding of closely related individuals especially to preserve and fix desirable characters of and to eliminate unfavorable characters from a stock **2 :** confinement to a narrow range or a local or limited field of choice — **in•breed** \-ˈbrēd\ *vb*
inc *abbr* **1** incomplete **2** incorporated **3** increase
In•ca \ˈiŋ-kə\ *n* **1 :** a noble or a member of the ruling family of an Indian empire of Peru, Bolivia, and Ecuador until the Spanish conquest **2 :** a member of any people under Inca influence
in•cal•cu•la•ble \(ˌ)in-ˈkal-kyə-lə-bəl\ *adj* **:** not capable of being calculated; *esp* **:** too large or numerous to be calculated — **in•cal•cu•la•bly** \-blē\ *adv*
in•can•des•cence \ˌin-kən-ˈdes-ᵊns\ *n* ♦ **:** the quality or state of being incandescent; *esp* **:** emission by a hot body of radiation that makes it visible

♦ blaze, flare, fluorescence, glare, gleam, glow, illumination, light, luminescence, radiance, shine

in•can•des•cent \ˌin-kən-ˈdes-ᵊnt\ *adj* **1 :** glowing with heat **2** ♦ **:** strikingly bright, radiant, or clear **:** SHINING, BRILLIANT

♦ beaming, bright, brilliant, effulgent, glowing, lambent, lucent, lucid, luminous, lustrous, radiant, refulgent, shiny

incandescent lamp *n* **:** a lamp in which an electrically heated filament emits light
in•can•ta•tion \ˌin-ˌkan-ˈtā-shən\ *n* ♦ **:** a use of spells or verbal charms spoken or sung as a part of a ritual of magic; *also* **:** a formula of words used in or as if in such a ritual

♦ bewitchment, charm, conjuration, enchantment, incantation, spell

in•ca•pa•bil•i•ty \(ˌ)in-ˌkā-pə-ˈbi-lə-tē\ *n* ♦ **:** the quality or state of being incapable

♦ impotence, inability, inadequacy, incompetence, ineptitude

in•ca•pa•ble \(ˌ)in-ˈkā-pə-bəl\ *adj* ♦ **:** lacking ability or qualification for a particular purpose; *also* **:** UNQUALIFIED

♦ incompetent, inept, inexpert, unfit, unqualified, unskilled, unskillful

in•ca•pac•i•tate \ˌin-kə-ˈpa-sə-ˌtāt\ *vb* **-tat•ed; -tat•ing** ♦ **:** to make incapable or unfit **:** DISABLE

♦ cripple, disable, hamstring, immobilize, paralyze, prostrate

in•ca•pac•i•ty \ˌin-kə-ˈpa-sə-tē\ *n, pl* **-ties :** the quality or state of being incapable
in•car•cer•ate \in-ˈkär-sə-ˌrāt\ *vb* **-at•ed; -at•ing :** to put in prison **:** IMPRISON, CONFINE
in•car•cer•a•tion \(ˌ)in-ˌkär-sə-ˈrā-shən\ *n* ♦ **:** a confining or state of being confined

♦ captivity, confinement, imprisonment, internment

in•car•na•dine \in-ˈkär-nə-ˌdīn, -ˌdēn\ *vb* **-dined; -din•ing** **:** REDDEN
¹in•car•nate \in-ˈkär-nət, -ˌnāt\ *adj* **1 :** having bodily and especially human form and substance **2 :** PERSONIFIED
²in•car•nate \-ˌnāt\ *vb* **:** to make incarnate: as **a :** to give bodily form and substance to **b :** to give a concrete or actual form to
in•car•na•tion \ˌin-ˌkär-ˈnā-shən\ *n* **1 a :** the embodiment of a deity or spirit in an earthly form **b** ♦ **:** a concrete or actual form of a quality or concept **2** *cap* **:** the union of divine and human natures in Jesus Christ **3 :** a person showing a trait or typical character to a marked degree **4 :** the act of incarnating **:** the state of being incarnate

♦ embodiment, epitome, manifestation, personification

¹in•cen•di•ary \in-ˈsen-dē-ˌer-ē\ *adj* **1 :** of or relating to a deliberate burning of property **2 :** tending to excite or inflame **3 :** designed to start fires ⟨an ~ bomb⟩
²incendiary *n* **1 a :** a person who commits arson **b :** an incendiary agent (as a bomb) **2** ♦ **:** a person who excites factions, quarrels, or sedition

♦ agitator, demagogue, firebrand, inciter, rabble-rouser

¹in•cense \ˈin-ˌsens\ *n* **1 :** material used to produce a fragrant odor when burned **2** ♦ **:** the perfume or smoke from some spices and gums when burned

♦ aroma, bouquet, fragrance, perfume, redolence, scent, spice

²in•cense \in-ˈsens\ *vb* **in•censed; in•cens•ing** ♦ **:** to make extremely angry

♦ anger, antagonize, enrage, inflame, infuriate, madden, outrage, rankle, rile, roil

in•cen•tive \in-ˈsen-tiv\ *n* ♦ **:** something that incites or is likely to incite to determination or action

♦ boost, encouragement, goad, impetus, impulse, incitement, instigation, momentum, motivation, provocation, spur, stimulus, yeast

in•cep•tion \in-ˈsep-shən\ *n* **:** an act, process, or instance of beginning **:** COMMENCEMENT
in•cer•ti•tude \(ˌ)in-ˈsər-tə-ˌtüd, -ˌtyüd\ *n* **1** ♦ **:** absence of assurance or confidence **:** UNCERTAINTY, DOUBT **2 :** INSECURITY, INSTABILITY

♦ distrust, doubt, misgiving, mistrust, skepticism, suspicion, uncertainty

in•ces•sant \(ˌ)in-ˈses-ᵊnt\ *adj* ♦ **:** continuing or flowing without interruption ⟨~ rains⟩

♦ ceaseless, continual, continuous, unbroken, unceasing, uninterrupted

in•ces•sant•ly *adv* ♦ **:** in an unceasing manner or course **:** without intermission or relief

♦ always, constantly, continually, ever, forever, invariably, perpetually, unfailingly

in•cest \ˈin-ˌsest\ *n* **:** sexual intercourse between persons so closely related that marriage is illegal — **in•ces•tu•ous** \in-ˈses-chü-wəs\ *adj*
¹inch \ˈinch\ *n* **1 :** a unit of length equal to ¹⁄₃₆ yard **2** ♦ **:** a small amount, distance, or degree

♦ ace, hair, step, stone's throw

²inch *vb* ♦ **:** to move by small degrees

♦ crawl, creep, drag, plod, poke

in•cho•ate \in-ˈkō-ət, ˈin-kə-ˌwāt\ *adj* **:** being only partly in existence or operation **:** INCOMPLETE, INCIPIENT
inch•worm \ˈinch-ˌwərm\ *n* **:** LOOPER
in•ci•dence \ˈin-sə-dəns\ *n* **:** rate of occurrence or effect
¹in•ci•dent \-dənt\ *n* **1** ♦ **:** an occurrence of an action or situation that is a separate unit of experience **:** HAPPENING **2 :** an action likely to lead to grave consequences especially in diplomatic matters

♦ affair, circumstance, episode, event, happening, occasion, occurrence, thing

²incident *adj* **1 :** occurring or likely to occur especially in connection with some other happening **2 :** falling or striking on something ⟨~ light rays⟩
¹in•ci•den•tal \ˌin-sə-ˈdent-ᵊl\ *adj* **1 :** subordinate, nonessential, or attendant in position or significance ⟨~ expenses⟩ **2** ♦ **:** oc-

curring merely by chance or without intention or planning : CASUAL, CHANCE

♦ accidental, casual, chance, fluky, fortuitous, unintended, unintentional, unplanned, unpremeditated, unwitting

²**incidental** *n* **1** *pl* **:** minor items (as of expense) that are not individually accounted for **2 :** something incidental
in•ci•den•tal•ly \ˌin-sə-ˈden-tə-lē, -ˈdent-lē\ *adv* **1 :** in an incidental manner **2 :** by the way
in•cin•er•ate \in-ˈsi-nə-ˌrāt\ *vb* **-at•ed; -at•ing :** to burn to ashes
in•cin•er•a•tor \in-ˈsi-nə-ˌrā-tər\ *n* **:** a furnace for burning waste
in•cip•i•ent \in-ˈsi-pē-ənt\ *adj* **:** beginning to be or become apparent
in•cise \in-ˈsīz\ *vb* **in•cised; in•cis•ing 1 :** to cut into **2 :** to carve figures, letters, or devices into **:** ENGRAVE
in•ci•sion \in-ˈsi-zhən\ *n* **:** a wound made by something sharp **:** GASH; *esp* **:** a surgical cut
in•ci•sive \in-ˈsī-siv\ *adj* **:** impressively direct and decisive — **in•ci•sive•ly** *adv*
in•ci•sor \in-ˈsī-zər\ *n* **:** a front tooth typically adapted for cutting
in•cite \in-ˈsīt\ *vb* **in•cit•ed; in•cit•ing ♦ :** to arouse to action

♦ abet, ferment, foment, instigate, provoke, raise, stir, whip ♦ arouse, encourage, excite, fire, instigate, move, pique, provoke, stimulate, stir

in•cite•ment *n* **♦ :** the act of inciting or the state of being incited

♦ excitement, instigation, provocation, stimulus

in•cit•er *n* **♦ :** one that incites

♦ agitator, demagogue, firebrand, incendiary, rabble-rouser

in•ci•vil•i•ty \ˌin-sə-ˈvi-lə-tē\ *n* **1 ♦ :** the quality or state of being uncivil **:** RUDENESS, DISCOURTESY **2 :** a rude or discourteous act

♦ brazenness, discourtesy, disrespect, impertinence, impudence, insolence, rudeness

incl *abbr* include; included; including; inclusive
in•clem•ent \(ˌ)in-ˈkle-mənt\ *adj* **♦ :** lacking mildness; *esp* **:** physically severe **:** STORMY ⟨~ weather⟩ — **in•clem•en•cy** \-mən-sē\ *n*

♦ bleak, dirty, foul, nasty, raw, rough, squally, stormy, tempestuous, turbulent

in•cli•na•tion \ˌin-klə-ˈnā-shən\ *n* **1 ♦ :** a particular disposition of mind or character **:** PROPENSITY; *esp* **:** LIKING **2 :** BOW, NOD ⟨an ~ of the head⟩ **3 :** a tilting of something **4 ♦ :** the degree of deviation from the true vertical or horizontal **:** SLANT, SLOPE

♦ [1] affinity, bent, devices, disposition, genius, leaning, partiality, penchant, predilection, predisposition, proclivity, propensity, talent, tendency, turn ♦ [4] cant, diagonal, grade, incline, lean, pitch, slant, slope, tilt, upgrade

¹**in•cline** \in-ˈklīn\ *vb* **in•clined; in•clin•ing 1 :** BOW, BEND **2 ♦ :** to be drawn toward an opinion or course of action **3 ♦ :** to deviate from the vertical or horizontal **:** SLOPE **4 :** INFLUENCE, PERSUADE — **in•clin•er** *n*

♦ [2] lean, run, tend, trend ♦ [3] angle, cant, cock, heel, lean, list, slant, slope, tilt, tip

²**in•cline** \ˈin-ˌklīn\ *n* **:** an inclined plane **:** SLOPE
in•clined *adj* **1 ♦ :** having inclination, disposition, or tendency **2 a ♦ :** having a leaning or slope **b ♦ :** making an angle with a line or plane

♦ [1] amenable, disposed, game, glad, ready, willing ♦ [1] apt, given, prone ♦ [2a, b] canted, diagonal, listing, oblique, slantwise

inclose, inclosure *var of* ENCLOSE, ENCLOSURE
in•clude \in-ˈklüd\ *vb* **in•clud•ed; in•clud•ing ♦ :** to take in or comprise as a part of a whole ⟨the price ~*s* tax⟩ — **in•clu•sion** \in-ˈklü-zhən\ *n*

♦ carry, comprehend, contain, embrace, encompass, entail, involve, number, take in ***Ant*** exclude, omit

in•clu•sive \-ˈklü-siv\ *adj* **1 :** comprehending stated limits or extremes **2 ♦ :** broad in orientation or scope; *also* **:** covering or intended to cover all items, costs, or services

♦ compendious, complete, comprehensive, encyclopedic, full, global, omnibus, panoramic, universal

incog *abbr* incognito
¹**in•cog•ni•to** \ˌin-ˌkäg-ˈnē-tō, in-ˈkäg-nə-ˌtō\ *n, pl* **-tos 1 :** one appearing or living incognito **2 :** the state or disguise of an incognito
²**incognito** *adv or adj* **:** with one's identity concealed

in•co•her•ent \ˌin-kō-ˈhir-ənt, -ˈher-\ *adj* **1 :** not sticking closely or compactly together **:** LOOSE **2 ♦ :** not clearly or logically connected **:** RAMBLING — **in•co•her•ence** \-əns\ *n* — **in•co•her•ent•ly** *adv*

♦ disconnected, disjointed, rambling, unconnected ***Ant*** coherent, connected

in•come \ˈin-ˌkəm\ *n* **♦ :** a gain usually measured in money that derives from labor, business, or property

♦ earnings, proceeds, profit, return, revenue, yield

income tax *n* **:** a tax on the net income of an individual or business concern
in•com•ing \ˈin-ˌkə-miŋ\ *adj* **:** coming in ⟨the ~ tide⟩ ⟨~ freshmen⟩
in•com•men•su•rate \ˌin-kə-ˈmen-sə-rət, -ˈmen-chə-\ *adj* **:** not commensurate; *esp* **:** INADEQUATE
in•com•mode \ˌin-kə-ˈmōd\ *vb* **-mod•ed; -mod•ing :** to give inconvenience or distress to **:** DISTURB
in•com•mu•ni•ca•ble \ˌin-kə-ˈmyü-ni-kə-bəl\ *adj* **:** not capable of being communicated or imparted; *also* **:** UNCOMMUNICATIVE
in•com•mu•ni•ca•do \ˌin-kə-ˌmyü-nə-ˈkä-dō\ *adv or adj* **:** without means of communication; *also* **:** in solitary confinement ⟨a prisoner held ~⟩
in•com•pa•ra•ble \(ˌ)in-ˈkäm-pə-rə-bəl, -prə-\ *adj* **1 ♦ :** eminent beyond comparison **:** MATCHLESS **2 :** not suitable for comparison — **in•com•pa•ra•bly** \-blē\ *adv*

♦ inimitable, matchless, nonpareil, only, peerless, unequaled, unmatched, unparalleled, unrivaled, unsurpassed

in•com•pat•i•ble \ˌin-kəm-ˈpa-tə-bəl\ *adj* **♦ :** incapable of or unsuitable for association or use together ⟨~ colors⟩ ⟨temperamentally ~⟩ — **in•com•pat•i•bil•i•ty** \ˌin-kəm-ˌpa-tə-ˈbi-lə-tē\ *n*

♦ discordant, discrepant, incongruous, inharmonious

in•com•pe•tence \-təns\ *n* **♦ :** the state or fact of being incompetent

♦ impotence, inability, inadequacy, incapability, ineptitude

in•com•pe•tent \(ˌ)in-ˈkäm-pə-tənt\ *adj* **1 :** not legally qualified **2 ♦ :** not competent **:** lacking sufficient knowledge, skill, or ability — **in•com•pe•ten•cy** \-tən-sē\ *n* — **incompetent** *n*

♦ incapable, inept, inexpert, unfit, unqualified, unskilled, unskillful ***Ant*** able, capable, competent, expert, fit, qualified, skilled, skillful

in•com•plete \ˌin-kəm-ˈplēt\ *adj* **♦ :** lacking a part or parts **:** UNFINISHED, IMPERFECT — **in•com•plete•ness** *n*

♦ deficient, fragmentary, halfway, imperfect, partial ***Ant*** complete, entire, full, intact, whole

in•com•plete•ly *adv* **:** in an incomplete manner or to an incomplete degree **:** not wholly, perfectly, or fully
in•com•pre•hen•si•ble \ˌin-ˌkäm-prē-ˈhen-sə-bəl\ *adj* **♦ :** impossible to comprehend **:** UNINTELLIGIBLE

♦ impenetrable, unfathomable ***Ant*** fathomable, intelligible, understandable

in•con•ceiv•able \ˌin-kən-ˈsē-və-bəl\ *adj* **1 :** impossible to comprehend **2 ♦ :** impossible to believe **:** UNBELIEVABLE

♦ fantastic, implausible, incredible, unbelievable, unconvincing, unimaginable, unthinkable

in•con•gru•ous \(ˌ)in-ˈkäŋ-grü-wəs\ *adj* **1 :** not consistent with or suitable to the surroundings or associations **2 ♦ :** lacking harmony — **in•con•gru•i•ty** \ˌin-kən-ˈgrü-ə-tē, -ˌkän-\ *n* — **in•con•gru•ous•ly** *adv*

♦ discordant, discrepant, incompatible, inharmonious

in•con•se•quen•tial \ˌin-ˌkän-sə-ˈkwen-chəl\ *adj* **1 :** ILLOGICAL; *also* **:** IRRELEVANT **2 ♦ :** of no significance **:** UNIMPORTANT — **in•con•se•quence** \(ˌ)in-ˈkän-sə-ˌkwens\ *n* — **in•con•se•quen•tial•ly** *adv*

♦ frivolous, inconsiderable, insignificant, little, minor, minute, negligible, slight, small, trifling, trivial, unimportant

in•con•sid•er•able \ˌin-kən-ˈsi-də-rə-bəl\ *adj* **♦ :** not considerable **:** SLIGHT, TRIVIAL

♦ inconsequential, insignificant, measly, minute, negligible, nominal, paltry, petty, slight, trifling, trivial

in•con•sid•er•ate \ˌin-kən-ˈsi-də-rət\ *adj* **♦ :** not taking heed **:** THOUGHTLESS; *esp* **:** not respecting the rights or feelings of others — **in•con•sid•er•ate•ly** *adv* — **in•con•sid•er•ate•ness** *n*

♦ discourteous, ill-bred, ill-mannered, impertinent, impolite, rude, thoughtless, uncivil, ungracious, unmannerly

in•con•sis•tent \ˌin-kən-ˈsis-tənt\ : lacking consistency : not compatible with facts or claims
in•con•sol•able \ˌin-kən-ˈsō-lə-bəl\ *adj* : incapable of being consoled — **in•con•sol•ably** \-blē\ *adv*
in•con•spic•u•ous \ˌin-kən-ˈspi-kyə-wəs\ *adj* : not readily noticeable — **in•con•spic•u•ous•ly** *adv*
in•con•stan•cy \-stən-sē\ *n* ♦ : the quality or state of being inconstant

♦ disloyalty, faithlessness, falseness, falsity, infidelity, perfidy, unfaithfulness

in•con•stant \(ˌ)in-ˈkän-stənt\ *adj* ♦ : not constant : CHANGEABLE — **in•con•stant•ly** *adv*

♦ capricious, changeable, fickle, fluid, mercurial, mutable, temperamental, uncertain, unpredictable, unsettled, unstable, unsteady, variable, volatile

in•con•test•able \ˌin-kən-ˈtes-tə-bəl\ *adj* ♦ : not contestable : INDISPUTABLE

♦ indisputable, indubitable, irrefutable, unanswerable, undeniable, unquestionable

in•con•test•ably \-ˈtes-tə-blē\ *adv* ♦ : in an incontestable manner or to an incontestable degree or level : with certainty

♦ certainly, definitely, doubtless, indeed, indisputably, really, surely, truly, undeniably, undoubtedly, unquestionably

in•con•ti•nent \(ˌ)in-ˈkänt-ᵊn-ənt\ *adj* **1** : lacking self-restraint **2** : unable to retain urine or feces voluntarily — **in•con•ti•nence** \-əns\ *n*
in•con•tro•vert•ible \ˌin-ˌkän-trə-ˈvər-tə-bəl\ *adj* : not open to question : INDISPUTABLE ⟨~ evidence⟩
in•con•tro•vert•ibly \-blē\ *adv* : not open to question
¹**in•con•ve•nience** \ˌin-kən-ˈvē-nyəns\ *n* **1** ♦ : something that is inconvenient **2** : the quality or state of being inconvenient

♦ aggravation, annoyance, bother, exasperation, frustration, hassle, headache, irritant, nuisance, peeve, pest, problem, thorn

²**inconvenience** *vb* **-nienced; -niencing** ♦ : to subject to inconvenience

♦ discommode, disoblige, disturb, trouble *Ant* accommodate, oblige

in•con•ve•nient \ˌin-kən-ˈvē-nyənt\ *adj* **1** ♦ : not convenient **2** ♦ : causing trouble or annoyance — **in•con•ve•nient•ly** *adv*

♦ [1] inaccessible, unapproachable, unattainable, unavailable, unobtainable, unreachable, untouchable ♦ [2] awkward *Ant* convenient

in•cor•po•rate \in-ˈkȯr-pə-ˌrāt\ *vb* **-rat•ed; -rat•ing** **1** ♦ : to unite closely or so as to form one body **2** : to form, form into, or become a corporation **3** : to give material form to : EMBODY — **in•cor•po•ra•tion** \-ˌkȯr-pə-ˈrā-shən\ *n*

♦ assimilate, commingle, integrate, intermingle, merge

in•cor•po•re•al \ˌin-kȯr-ˈpōr-ē-əl\ *adj* ♦ : having no material body or form

♦ bodiless, immaterial, insubstantial, nonmaterial, nonphysical, spiritual, unsubstantial

in•cor•rect \ˌin-kə-ˈrekt\ *adj* **1** : marked by fault or defect : INACCURATE **2** ♦ : not true : WRONG **3** ♦ : not according with appropriate standards : UNBECOMING, IMPROPER

♦ [2] erroneous, false, inaccurate, inexact, invalid, off, unsound, untrue, wrong ♦ [3] improper, inappropriate, inapt, infelicitous, unbecoming, unfit, unseemly, unsuitable, wrong

in•cor•rect•ly *adv* ♦ : in an incorrect manner

♦ amiss, erroneously, faultily, improperly, inaptly, mistakenly, wrongly

in•cor•rect•ness *n* ♦ : the quality or state of being incorrect

♦ impropriety, indecency

in•cor•ri•gi•ble \(ˌ)in-ˈkȯr-ə-jə-bəl\ *adj* ♦ : incapable of being corrected, amended, or reformed — **in•cor•ri•gi•bil•i•ty** \(ˌ)in-ˌkȯr-ə-jə-ˈbi-lə-tē\ *n* — **in•cor•ri•gi•bly** \-ˈkōr-ə-jə-blē\ *adv*

♦ hopeless, incurable, irredeemable, irremediable, unrecoverable, unredeemable

in•cor•rupt•ible \ˌin-kə-ˈrəp-tə-bəl\ *adj* **1** : not subject to decay or dissolution **2** : incapable of being bribed or morally corrupted — **in•cor•rupt•ibil•i•ty** \-ˌrəp-tə-ˈbi-lə-tē\ *n* — **in•cor•rupt•ibly** \-ˈrəp-tə-blē\ *adv*
incr *abbr* increase; increased
¹**in•crease** \in-ˈkrēs, ˈin-ˌkrēs\ *vb* **in•creased; in•creas•ing** **1** ♦ : to become greater : GROW **2** : to multiply by the production of young ⟨rabbits ~ rapidly⟩ **3** ♦ : to make greater — **in•creas•ing•ly** \-ˈkrē-siŋ-lē\ *adv*

♦ [1] accumulate, appreciate, balloon, build, burgeon, enlarge, escalate, expand, grow, mount, multiply, mushroom, proliferate, rise, snowball, swell, wax *Ant* contract, decrease, diminish, lessen, wane ♦ [3] add, aggrandize, amplify, augment, boost, compound, enlarge, escalate, expand, extend, multiply, raise, swell, up *Ant* abate, contract, decrease, diminish, lessen, lower, reduce, subtract (from)

²**in•crease** \ˈin-ˌkrēs, in-ˈkrēs\ *n* **1** ♦ : addition or enlargement in size, extent, or quantity : GROWTH **2** ♦ : something that is added to an original stock or amount (as by growth)

♦ accretion, addition, augmentation, boost, expansion, gain, growth, increment, plus, proliferation, raise, rise, supplement *Ant* abatement, decrease, lessening, lowering, reduction

in•cred•i•ble \(ˌ)in-ˈkre-də-bəl\ *adj* ♦ : too extraordinary and improbable to be believed; *also* : hard to believe — **in•cred•i•bil•i•ty** \(ˌ)in-ˌkre-də-ˈbi-lə-tē\ *n*

♦ fantastic, implausible, inconceivable, unbelievable, unconvincing, unimaginable, unthinkable *Ant* believable, conceivable, convincing, credible, imaginable, plausible

in•cred•i•bly \(ˌ)in-ˈkre-də-blē\ *adv* ♦ : in an incredible manner : to an incredible extent : EXTREMELY

♦ extremely, greatly, highly, hugely, mightily, mighty, mortally, most, much, real, right, so, very

in•cred•u•lous \-ˈkre-jə-ləs\ *adj* **1** ♦ : unwilling to admit or accept what is offered as true : SKEPTICAL **2** : expressing disbelief — **in•cre•du•li•ty** \ˌin-kri-ˈdü-lə-tē, -ˈdyü-\ *n* — **in•cred•u•lous•ly** *adv*

♦ distrustful, leery, mistrustful, skeptical, suspicious

in•cre•ment \ˈiŋ-krə-mənt, ˈin-\ *n* **1** : the action or process of increasing especially in quantity or value : ENLARGEMENT; *also* : QUANTITY **2** ♦ : something gained or added; *esp* : one of a series of regular consecutive additions

♦ accretion, addition, augmentation, boost, expansion, gain, increase, plus, proliferation, raise, rise, supplement

in•cre•men•tal \ˌiŋ-krə-ˈment-ᵊl, ˌin-\ *adj* : of, relating to, being, or occurring in especially small increments — **in•cre•men•tal•ly** *adv*
in•crim•i•nate \in-ˈkri-mə-ˌnāt\ *vb* **-nat•ed; -nat•ing** ♦ : to charge with or prove involvement in a crime or fault : ACCUSE — **in•crim•i•na•tion** \-ˌkri-mə-ˈnā-shən\ *n* — **in•crim•i•na•to•ry** \-ˈkri-mə-nə-ˌtōr-ē\ *adj*

♦ accuse, charge, indict

incrust *var of* ENCRUST
in•crus•ta•tion \ˌin-ˌkrəs-ˈtā-shən\ *n* **1** : CRUST; *also* : an accumulation (as of habits, opinions, or customs) resembling a crust **2** : the act of encrusting : the state of being encrusted
in•cu•bate \ˈiŋ-kyu̇-ˌbāt, ˈin-\ *vb* **-bat•ed; -bat•ing** ♦ : to sit on (eggs) to hatch by the warmth of the body; *also* : to keep (as an embryo) under conditions favorable for development — **in•cu•ba•tion** \ˌiŋ-kyu̇-ˈbā-shən, ˌin-\ *n*

♦ brood, hatch, set, sit

in•cu•ba•tor \ˈiŋ-kyu̇-ˌbāt-ər, ˈin-\ *n* : one that incubates; *esp* : an apparatus providing suitable conditions (as of warmth and moisture) for incubating something (as a premature baby)
in•cu•bus \ˈiŋ-kyə-bəs, ˈin-\ *n, pl* **-bi** \-ˌbī, -ˌbē\ *also* **-bus•es** **1** : a spirit supposed to work evil on persons in their sleep **2** : NIGHTMARE 1 **3** : one that oppresses like a nightmare
in•cul•cate \in-ˈkəl-ˌkāt, ˈin-(ˌ)kəl-\ *vb* **-cat•ed; -cat•ing** ♦ : to teach and impress by frequent repetitions or admonitions — **in•cul•ca•tion** \ˌin-(ˌ)kəl-ˈkā-shən\ *n*

♦ imbue, infuse, ingrain, invest, steep, suffuse

in•cul•pa•ble \(ˌ)in-ˈkəl-pə-bəl\ *adj* : free from guilt : INNOCENT
in•cul•pate \in-ˈkəl-ˌpāt, ˈin-(ˌ)kəl-\ *vb* **-pat•ed; -pat•ing** : INCRIMINATE
in•cum•ben•cy \in-ˈkəm-bən-sē\ *n, pl* **-cies** **1** : something that is incumbent **2** : the quality or state of being incumbent **3** : the office or period of office of an incumbent

¹in·cum·bent \in-ˈkəm-bənt\ *n* **:** the holder of an office or position
²incumbent *adj* **1** ♦ **:** imposed as a duty **2 :** occupying a specified office **3 :** lying or resting on something else

♦ compulsory, imperative, involuntary, mandatory, necessary, nonelective, obligatory, peremptory

in·cu·nab·u·lum \ˌin-kyə-ˈna-byə-ləm, iŋ-\ *n, pl* **-la** \-lə\ **:** a book printed before 1501
in·cur \in-ˈkər\ *vb* **in·curred; in·cur·ring :** to become liable or subject to **:** bring down upon oneself
in·cur·able \(ˌ)in-ˈkyu̇r-ə-bəl\ *adj* **1** ♦ **:** not curable **2** ♦ **:** not likely to be changed — **incurable** *n* — **in·cur·ably** \(ˌ)in-ˈkyu̇r-ə-blē\ *adv*

♦ [1, 2] hopeless, incorrigible, irredeemable, irremediable, unrecoverable, unredeemable

in·cu·ri·ous \(ˌ)in-ˈkyu̇r-ē-əs\ *adj* **:** lacking a normal or usual curiosity
in·cur·sion \in-ˈkər-zhən\ *n* **1** ♦ **:** a sudden hostile invasion **:** RAID **2 :** an entering in or into (as an activity)

♦ descent, foray, invasion, irruption, raid

in·cus \ˈiŋ-kəs\ *n, pl* **in·cu·des** \iŋ-ˈkyü-(ˌ)dēz\ **:** the middle bone of a chain of three small bones in the middle ear of a mammal
ind *abbr* **1** independent **2** index **3** industrial; industry
Ind *abbr* **1** Indian **2** Indiana
in·debt·ed \in-ˈde-təd\ *adj* **1** ♦ **:** owing gratitude or recognition to another **2** ♦ **:** owing money — **in·debt·ed·ness** *n*

♦ [1, 2] beholden, obligated, obliged

in·de·cen·cy \(ˌ)in-ˈdēs-ᵊn-sē\ *n* ♦ **:** the quality or state of being indecent

♦ impropriety, incorrectness

in·de·cent \(ˌ)in-ˈdēs-ᵊnt\ *adj* ♦ **:** not decent; *esp* **:** morally offensive — **in·de·cent·ly** *adv*

♦ bawdy, coarse, crude, dirty, filthy, foul, gross, lascivious, lewd, nasty, obscene, pornographic, ribald, smutty, unprintable, vulgar, wanton

in·de·ci·sion \ˌin-di-ˈsi-zhən\ *n* ♦ **:** a wavering between two or more possible courses of action **:** IRRESOLUTION

♦ hesitancy, hesitation, irresolution, vacillation

in·de·ci·sive \ˌin-di-ˈsī-siv\ *adj* **1 :** leading to no conclusion or definite result **2 :** marked by or prone to indecision **3 :** INDEFINITE — **in·de·ci·sive·ly** *adv* — **in·de·ci·sive·ness** *n*
in·de·co·rous \(ˌ)in-ˈde-kə-rəs; ˌin-di-ˈkōr-əs\ *adj* ♦ **:** not decorous — **in·de·co·rous·ly** *adv* — **in·de·co·rous·ness** *n*

♦ improper, inappropriate, inapt, infelicitous, unbecoming, unfit, unseemly, unsuitable, wrong

in·deed \in-ˈdēd\ *adv* **1** ♦ **:** without any question — often used interjectionally to express irony, disbelief, or surprise **2** ♦ **:** in reality **3 :** all things considered

♦ [1] certainly, definitely, doubtless, incontestably, indisputably, really, surely, truly, undeniably, undoubtedly, unquestionably ♦ [2] even, nay, truly, verily, yea

indef *abbr* indefinite
in·de·fat·i·ga·ble \ˌin-di-ˈfa-ti-gə-bəl\ *adj* ♦ **:** incapable of being fatigued **:** UNTIRING

♦ inexhaustible, tireless, unflagging, untiring

in·de·fat·i·ga·bly \-blē\ *adv* **:** in an indefatigable manner
in·de·fea·si·ble \-ˈfē-zə-bəl\ *adj* **:** not capable of being annulled or voided — **in·de·fea·si·bly** \-blē\ *adv*
in·de·fen·si·ble \-ˈfen-sə-bəl\ *adj* **1 :** incapable of being maintained as right or valid **2** ♦ **:** incapable of being justified or excused **:** INEXCUSABLE **3 :** incapable of being protected against physical attack

♦ inexcusable, unforgivable, unjustifiable, unpardonable, unwarrantable

in·de·fin·able \-ˈfī-nə-bəl\ *adj* **:** incapable of being precisely described or analyzed — **in·de·fin·ably** \-blē\ *adv*
in·def·i·nite \(ˌ)in-ˈde-fə-nət\ *adj* **1 :** not defining or identifying ⟨*an* is an ~ article⟩ **2** ♦ **:** not precise **:** VAGUE **3** ♦ **:** having no fixed limit — **in·def·i·nite·ly** *adv* — **in·def·i·nite·ness** *n*

♦ [2] bleary, dim, faint, foggy, fuzzy, hazy, indistinct, indistinguishable, murky, nebulous, obscure, opaque, shadowy, unclear, undefined, undetermined, vague ♦ [3] boundless, endless, illimitable, immeasurable, infinite, limitless, measureless, unbounded, unfathomable, unlimited

in·del·i·ble \in-ˈde-lə-bəl\ *adj* **1 :** not capable of being removed or erased **2 :** making marks that cannot be erased **3 :** LASTING, UNFORGETTABLE — **in·del·i·bly** \in-ˈde-lə-blē\ *adv*
in·del·i·ca·cy \in-ˈde-lə-kə-sē\ *n* **1** ♦ **:** the quality or state of being indelicate **2 :** something that is indelicate

♦ coarseness, grossness, lowness, rudeness, vulgarity

in·del·i·cate \(ˌ)in-ˈde-li-kət\ *adj* **:** not delicate; *esp* **:** IMPROPER, COARSE, TACTLESS
in·dem·ni·fi·ca·tion \-ˌdem-nə-fə-ˈkā-shən\ *n* **1 :** the action of indemnifying; *also* **:** the condition of being indemnified **2 :** something that indemnifies
in·dem·ni·fy \in-ˈdem-nə-ˌfī\ *vb* **-fied; -fy·ing 1 :** to secure against hurt, loss, or damage **2** ♦ **:** to make compensation to for hurt, loss, or damage

♦ compensate, recompense, recoup, remunerate, requite

in·dem·ni·ty \in-ˈdem-nə-tē\ *n, pl* **-ties 1 :** security against hurt, loss, or damage; *also* **:** exemption from incurred penalties or liabilities **2** ♦ **:** something that indemnifies

♦ compensation, damages, quittance, recompense, redress, remuneration, reparation, requital, restitution, satisfaction

¹in·dent \in-ˈdent\ *vb* **1 :** to notch the edge of **2 :** INDENTURE **3 :** to set (as a line of a paragraph) in from the margin
²indent *vb* **1 :** to force inward so as to form a depression **2 :** to form a dent in
in·den·ta·tion \ˌin-ˌden-ˈtā-shən\ *n* **1** ♦ **:** a V-shaped cut usually on an edge or a surface **:** NOTCH; *also* **:** a usually deep recess (as in a coastline) **2 :** the action of indenting **:** the condition of being indented **3** ♦ **:** a depression or hollow made by a blow or by pressure **:** DENT **4 :** INDENTION 2

♦ [1] chip, hack, nick, notch ♦ [3] cavity, concavity, dent, depression, hole, hollow, pit, recess

in·den·tion \in-ˈden-chən\ *n* **1 :** INDENTATION 2 **2 :** the blank space produced by indenting
¹in·den·ture \in-ˈden-chər\ *n* **1 :** a written certificate or agreement; *esp* **:** a contract binding one person (as an apprentice) to work for another for a given period of time — usually used in plural **2 :** INDENTATION 1 **3 :** DENT
²indenture *vb* **in·den·tured; in·den·tur·ing :** to bind (as an apprentice) by indentures
in·de·pen·dence \ˌin-də-ˈpen-dəns\ *n* ♦ **:** the quality or state of being independent **:** FREEDOM

♦ autonomy, freedom, liberty, self-government, sovereignty

Independence Day *n* **:** July 4 observed as a legal holiday in commemoration of the adoption of the Declaration of Independence in 1776
in·de·pen·dent \ˌin-də-ˈpen-dənt\ *adj* **1** ♦ **:** not subject to control by others **:** SELF-GOVERNING; *also* **:** not affiliated with a larger controlling unit **2** ♦ **:** not requiring or relying on something else or somebody else ⟨an ~ conclusion⟩ ⟨~ of her parents⟩ **3 :** not easily influenced **:** showing self-reliance and personal freedom ⟨an ~ mind⟩ **4 :** not committed to a political party ⟨an ~ voter⟩ **5 :** MAIN ⟨an ~ clause⟩ — **independent** *n*

♦ [1] autonomous, free, self-governing, separate, sovereign ♦ [2] self-reliant, self-sufficient, self-supporting

in·de·pen·dent·ly *adv* ♦ **:** in an independent manner **:** without dependence on another

♦ alone, singly, solely, unaided, unassisted

independent variable *n* **:** a variable whose value is not determined by that of any other variable in a function
in·de·scrib·able \ˌin-di-ˈskrī-bə-bəl\ *adj* **1** ♦ **:** that cannot be described **2 :** being too intense or great for description — **in·de·scrib·ably** \-blē\ *adv*

♦ ineffable, inexpressible, nameless, unspeakable, unutterable *Ant* communicable, definable

in·de·ter·mi·nate \ˌin-di-ˈtər-mə-nət\ *adj* **1 :** VAGUE; *also* **:** not known in advance **2 :** not limited in advance; *also* **:** not leading to a definite end or result — **in·de·ter·mi·na·cy** \-nə-sē\ *n* — **in·de·ter·mi·nate·ly** *adv*
¹in·dex \ˈin-ˌdeks\ *n, pl* **in·dex·es** *or* **in·di·ces** \-də-ˌsēz\ **1** ♦ **:** a device (as the pointer on a scale) that serves to indicate a value or quantity **2 :** SIGN, INDICATION ⟨an ~ of character⟩ **3 :** a guide for facilitating references; *esp* **:** an alphabetical list of items treated in a printed work with the page number where each item may be found **4 :** a list of restricted or prohibited material **5** *pl usu in-*

dices : a number or symbol or expression (as an exponent) associated with another to indicate a mathematical operation or use or position in an arrangement or expansion **6 :** a character ☞ used to direct attention (as to a note) **7 :** INDEX NUMBER

♦ index, indicator, needle, pointer

²**index** *vb* **1** ♦ **:** to provide with or put into an index **2 :** to serve as an index of **3 :** to regulate by indexation

♦ catalog, enroll, enter, inscribe, list, put down, record, register, schedule, slate

in•dex•ation \ˌin-ˌdek-ˈsā-shən\ *n* **:** a system of economic control in which a body of variables (as wages and interest) rise or fall at the same rate as an index of the cost of living
index finger *n* **:** the finger next to the thumb
in•dex•ing *n* **:** INDEXATION
index number *n* **:** a number used to indicate change in magnitude (as of cost) as compared with the magnitude at some specified time usually taken as 100
index of refraction : REFRACTIVE INDEX
in•dia ink \ˈin-dē-ə-\ *n, often cap 1st I* **1 :** a solid black pigment used in drawing **2 :** a fluid made from india ink
In•di•an \ˈin-dē-ən\ *n* **1 :** a native or inhabitant of India or of the East Indies **2 :** a person of Indian descent **3 :** a member of any of the native peoples of the western hemisphere except often the Eskimos **:** AMERICAN INDIAN — **Indian** *adj*
Indian corn *n* **:** a tall widely grown American cereal grass bearing seeds on long ears; *also* **:** its ears or seeds
Indian meal *n* **:** CORNMEAL
Indian paintbrush *n* **:** any of a genus of herbaceous plants related to the snapdragon that have brightly colored bracts
Indian pipe *n* **:** a waxy white leafless saprophytic herb of Asia and the U.S.
Indian summer *n* **:** a period of mild weather in late autumn or early winter
In•dia paper \ˈin-dē-ə-\ *n* **1 :** a thin absorbent paper used especially for taking impressions (as of steel engravings) **2 :** a thin tough opaque printing paper
indic *abbr* indicative
in•di•cate \ˈin-də-ˌkāt\ *vb* **-cat•ed; -cat•ing** **1 :** to point out or to **2** ♦ **:** to show indirectly **3 :** to state briefly

♦ allude, hint, imply, infer, insinuate, intimate, suggest

in•di•ca•tion \ˌin-də-ˈkā-shən\ *n* **1** ♦ **:** something that serves to indicate; *also* **:** something that is indicated as advisable or necessary **2 :** the action of indicating

♦ clue, cue, hint, inkling, intimation, lead, suggestion

¹**in•dic•a•tive** \in-ˈdi-kə-tiv\ *adj* **1 :** of, relating to, or being a verb form that represents an act or state as a fact ⟨~ mood⟩ **2** ♦ **:** serving to indicate ⟨actions ~ of fear⟩

♦ denotative, significant, telltale

²**indicative** *n* **1 :** the indicative mood of a language **2 :** a form in the indicative mood
in•di•ca•tor \ˈin-də-ˌkā-tər\ *n* ♦ **:** one that indicates; *esp* **:** an index hand (as on a dial)

♦ hand, index, needle, pointer

in•di•cia \in-ˈdi-shə, -shē-ə\ *n pl* **1 :** distinctive marks **2 :** postal markings often imprinted on mail or mailing labels
in•dict \in-ˈdīt\ *vb* **1** ♦ **:** to charge with a fault or offense **2 :** to charge with a crime by the finding of a jury — **in•dict•able** *adj*

♦ accuse, charge, incriminate, indict

in•dict•ment \-mənt\ *n* ♦ **:** the action or the legal process of indicting

♦ charge, complaint, count, rap

in•die \ˈin-dē\ *n* **1 :** one that is independent; *esp* **:** an unaffiliated record or motion-picture production company **2 :** something produced by an indie — **indie** *adj*
in•dif•fer•ence \-frəns, -fə-rəns\ *n* ♦ **:** the quality, state, or fact of being indifferent; *also* **:** absence of compulsion to or toward one thing or another

♦ apathy, disinterestedness, disregard, insouciance, nonchalance *Ant* concern, interest, regard

in•dif•fer•ent \in-ˈdi-frənt, -fə-rənt\ *adj* **1 :** UNBIASED, UNPREJUDICED **2 :** of no importance one way or the other **3** ♦ **:** marked by no special liking for or dislike of something **4 :** being neither excessive nor inadequate **5** ♦ **:** being neither good nor bad **:** PASSABLE, MEDIOCRE **6 :** being neither right nor wrong — **in•dif•fer•ent•ly** *adv*

♦ [3] apathetic, casual, disinterested, insouciant, nonchalant, perfunctory, unconcerned, uncurious, uninterested *Ant* concerned, interested ♦ [5] common, fair, mediocre, medium, middling, ordinary, passable, run-of-the-mill, second-rate, so-so

in•di•gence \-jəns\ *n* ♦ **:** a level of poverty in which real hardship and deprivation are suffered and comforts of life are wholly lacking

♦ beggary, destitution, impecuniousness, impoverishment, need, pauperism, penury, poverty, want

in•dig•e•nous \in-ˈdi-jə-nəs\ *adj* ♦ **:** produced, growing, or living naturally in a particular region

♦ aboriginal, born, endemic, native

in•di•gent \ˈin-di-jənt\ *adj* ♦ **:** suffering from indigence **:** NEEDY

♦ broke, destitute, impecunious, needy, penniless, penurious, poor, poverty-stricken

in•di•gest•ible \ˌin-dī-ˈjes-tə-bəl, -də-\ *adj* **:** not readily digested
in•di•ges•tion \-ˈjes-chən\ *n* **:** inadequate or difficult digestion **:** DYSPEPSIA
in•dig•nant \in-ˈdig-nənt\ *adj* **:** filled with or marked by indignation — **in•dig•nant•ly** *adv*
in•dig•na•tion \ˌin-dig-ˈnā-shən\ *n* ♦ **:** anger aroused by something unjust, unworthy, or mean

♦ anger, furor, fury, ire, outrage, rage, spleen, wrath, wrathfulness

in•dig•ni•ty \in-ˈdig-nə-tē\ *n, pl* **-ties** ♦ **:** an offense against personal dignity or self-respect; *also* **:** humiliating treatment

♦ affront, barb, dart, dig, insult, name, offense, outrage, put-down, sarcasm, slight, slur, wound

in•di•go \ˈin-di-ˌgō\ *n, pl* **-gos** *or* **-goes** **1 :** a blue dye obtained from plants or synthesized **2 :** a deep reddish blue color
in•di•rect \ˌin-də-ˈrekt, -dī-\ *adj* **1 :** not straight ⟨an ~ route⟩ **2** ♦ **:** not straightforward and open ⟨~ methods⟩ **3 :** not having a plainly seen connection ⟨an ~ cause⟩ **4 :** not directly to the point ⟨an ~ answer⟩ — **in•di•rec•tion** \-ˈrek-shən\ *n* — **in•di•rect•ly** *adv* — **in•di•rect•ness** *n*

♦ circuitous, circular, roundabout *Ant* direct, straight, straightforward

in•dis•creet \ˌin-di-ˈskrēt\ *adj* ♦ **:** not discreet **:** IMPRUDENT — **in•dis•creet•ly** *adv*

♦ ill-advised, imprudent, tactless, unwise *Ant* advisable, discreet, judicious, prudent, tactful, wise

in•dis•cre•tion \ˌin-di-ˈskre-shən\ *n* **1 :** IMPRUDENCE **2** ♦ **:** something marked by lack of discretion; *esp* **:** an act deviating from accepted morality

♦ familiarity, gaffe, impropriety

in•dis•crim•i•nate \ˌin-di-ˈskri-mə-nət\ *adj* **1 :** not marked by discrimination or careful distinction **2 :** HAPHAZARD, RANDOM **3 :** UNRESTRAINED **4 :** MOTLEY — **in•dis•crim•i•nate•ly** *adv*
in•dis•pens•able \ˌin-di-ˈspen-sə-bəl\ *adj* ♦ **:** absolutely essential **:** REQUISITE — **in•dis•pens•abil•i•ty** \-ˌspen-sə-ˈbi-lə-tē\ *n* — **indispensable** *n* — **in•dis•pens•ably** \-ˈspen-sə-blē\ *adv*

♦ essential, imperative, integral, necessary, needful, requisite, vital

in•dis•posed \-ˈspōzd\ *adj* **1** ♦ **:** slightly ill **2** ♦ **:** having an active feeling of reluctance or dislike **:** AVERSE

♦ [1] bad, down, ill, peaked, punk, sick, unhealthy, unsound, unwell ♦ [2] afraid, dubious, hesitant, reluctant

in•dis•po•si•tion \(ˌ)in-ˌdis-pə-ˈzi-shən\ *n* **:** the condition of being indisposed: as **a :** slight aversion **b :** a usually slight illness
in•dis•put•able \ˌin-di-ˈspyü-tə-bəl, (ˌ)in-ˈdis-pyə-\ *adj* ♦ **:** not disputable **:** UNQUESTIONABLE ⟨~ proof⟩

♦ incontestable, indubitable, irrefutable, unanswerable, undeniable, unquestionable

in•dis•put•ably \-blē\ *adv* ♦ **:** not open to question

♦ certainly, definitely, doubtless, incontestably, indeed, really, surely, truly, undeniably, undoubtedly, unquestionably

in•dis•sol•u•ble \ˌin-di-ˈsäl-yə-bəl\ *adj* **:** not capable of being dissolved, undone, or broken **:** PERMANENT
in•dis•tinct \ˌin-di-ˈstiŋkt\ *adj* **1 :** not sharply outlined or separable **:** BLURRED, FAINT, DIM **2** ♦ **:** not readily distinguishable — **in•dis•tinct•ly** *adv* — **in•dis•tinct•ness** *n*

♦ bleary, dim, faint, foggy, fuzzy, hazy, indefinite, indistinguishable, murky, nebulous, obscure, opaque, shadowy, unclear, undefined, undetermined, vague

in·dis·tin·guish·able \ˌin-di-ˈstiŋ-gwi-shə-bəl, -ˈstiŋ-wi-\ *adj* : not distinguishable: as **a** : indeterminate in shape or structure **b** ♦ : not clearly recognizable or understandable **c** ♦ : lacking identifying or individualizing qualities

♦ [b] impalpable, imperceptible, inappreciable ♦ [c] duplicate, equal, even, identical, same

in·dite \in-ˈdīt\ *vb* **in·dit·ed; in·dit·ing** : COMPOSE ⟨~ a poem⟩; *also* : to put in writing ⟨~ a letter⟩
in·di·um \ˈin-dē-əm\ *n* : a malleable silvery metallic chemical element
indiv *abbr* individual
1in·di·vid·u·al \ˌin-də-ˈvi-jə-wəl\ *adj* **1** ♦ : of, relating to, or associated with an individual ⟨~ traits⟩ **2** : being an individual : existing as an indivisible whole **3** : intended for one person **4** : SEPARATE ⟨~ copies⟩ **5** ♦ : having marked individuality ⟨an ~ style⟩ — **in·di·vid·u·al·ly** *adv*

♦ [1] particular, peculiar, personal, private, separate, singular, unique *Ant* general, generic, public, popular, shared, universal ♦ [5] different, respective, separate

2individual *n* **1** ♦ : a single member of a category : a particular person, animal, or thing **2** ♦ : a single human being ⟨a disagreeable ~⟩

♦ [1] being, entity, object, substance, thing ♦ [2] being, body, creature, human, man, mortal, person

in·di·vid·u·al·ise *chiefly Brit var of* INDIVIDUALIZE
in·di·vid·u·al·ism \ˌin-də-ˈvi-jə-wə-ˌli-zəm\ *n* **1** : a doctrine that the interests of the individual are primary **2** : a doctrine holding that the individual has political or economic rights with which the state must not interfere **3** : INDIVIDUALITY
in·di·vid·u·al·ist \-list\ *n* **1** ♦ : one that pursues a markedly independent course in thought or action **2** : one that advocates or practices individualism — **individualist** *or* **in·di·vid·u·al·is·tic** \-ˌvi-jə-wə-ˈlis-tik\ *adj*

♦ bohemian, deviant, loner, maverick, nonconformist

in·di·vid·u·al·i·ty \-ˌvi-jə-ˈwa-lə-tē\ *n, pl* **-ties** **1** ♦ : the sum of qualities that characterize and distinguish an individual from all others; *also* : PERSONALITY **2** : separate or distinct existence **3** : INDIVIDUAL, PERSON

♦ character, identity, personality, self-identity

in·di·vid·u·al·ize \-ˈvi-jə-wə-ˌlīz\ *vb* **-ized; -iz·ing** **1** : to make individual in character **2** : to treat or notice individually : PARTICULARIZE **3** : to adapt to the needs of an individual
individual retirement account *n* : IRA
in·di·vid·u·ate \ˌin-də-ˈvi-jə-ˌwāt\ *vb* **-at·ed; -at·ing** : to give individuality to : form into an individual — **in·di·vid·u·a·tion** \-ˌvi-jə-ˈwā-shən\ *n*
in·di·vis·i·ble \ˌin-də-ˈvi-zə-bəl\ *adj* : impossible to divide or separate — **in·di·vis·i·bil·i·ty** \-ˌvi-zə-ˈbi-lə-tē\ *n* — **in·di·vis·i·bly** *adv*
In·do–Ar·y·an \ˌin-dō-ˈer-ē-ən\ *n* : a branch of the Indo-European language family that includes Hindi and other languages of south Asia
in·doc·tri·nate \in-ˈdäk-trə-ˌnāt\ *vb* **-nat·ed; -nat·ing** **1** ♦ : to instruct especially in fundamentals or rudiments : TEACH **2** : to teach the beliefs and doctrines of a particular group — **in·doc·tri·na·tion** \(ˌ)in-ˌdäk-trə-ˈnā-shən\ *n* — **in·doc·tri·na·tor** *n*

♦ educate, instruct, school, teach, train, tutor

In·do–Eu·ro·pe·an \ˌin-dō-ˌyu̇r-ə-ˈpē-ən\ *adj* : of, relating to, or constituting a family of languages comprising those spoken in most of Europe and in the parts of the world colonized by Europeans since 1500 and also in Persia, the subcontinent of India, and some other parts of Asia
in·do·lence \-ləns\ *n* ♦ : inclination to laziness

♦ idleness, inertia, laziness, sloth

in·do·lent \ˈin-də-lənt\ *adj* **1** : slow to develop or heal ⟨~ ulcers⟩ **2** ♦ : averse to activity, effort, or movement : LAZY — **in·do·lent·ly** *adv*

♦ idle, lazy, shiftless, slothful

in·dom·i·ta·ble \in-ˈdä-mə-tə-bəl\ *adj* ♦ : incapable of being subdued : UNCONQUERABLE ⟨~ courage⟩ — **in·dom·i·ta·bly** \-blē\ *adv*

♦ impregnable, insurmountable, invincible, invulnerable, unbeatable, unconquerable

In·do·ne·sian \ˌin-də-ˈnē-zhən\ *n* : a native or inhabitant of the Republic of Indonesia — **Indonesian** *adj*

in·door \ˈin-ˈdōr\ *adj* **1** : of or relating to the inside of a building **2** : living, located, or carried on within a building
in·doors \in-ˈdōrz\ *adv* : in or into a building
indorse, indorsement *var of* ENDORSE, ENDORSEMENT
in·du·bi·ta·ble \(ˌ)in-ˈdü-bə-tə-bəl, -ˈdyü-\ *adj* ♦ : too evident to be doubted : UNQUESTIONABLE — **in·du·bi·ta·bly** \-blē\ *adv*

♦ incontestable, indisputable, irrefutable, unanswerable, undeniable, unquestionable

in·duce \in-ˈdüs, -ˈdyüs\ *vb* **in·duced; in·duc·ing** **1** ♦ : to move by persuasion or influence : PERSUADE **2** : to serve as the cause of : BRING ABOUT **3** : to produce (as an electric current) by induction **4** : to determine by induction; *esp* : to infer from particulars — **in·duc·er** *n*

♦ argue, convince, get, move, persuade, prevail, satisfy, talk, win

in·duce·ment \-mənt\ *n* **1** : something that induces : MOTIVE **2** ♦ : the act or process of inducing

♦ convincing, persuasion

in·duct \in-ˈdəkt\ *vb* **1** ♦ : to place in office **2** ♦ : to admit as a member **3** : to enroll for military training or service — **in·duct·ee** \-ˌdək-ˈtē\ *n*

♦ [1, 2] baptize, inaugurate, initiate, install, invest

in·duc·tance \in-ˈdək-təns\ *n* : a property of an electric circuit by which a varying current produces an electromotive force in that circuit or in a nearby circuit; *also* : the measure of this property
in·duc·tion \in-ˈdək-shən\ *n* **1** ♦ : the act or process of inducting; *also* : INITIATION **2** : the formality by which a civilian is inducted into military service **3** : inference of a generalized conclusion from particular instances; *also* : a conclusion so reached **4** : the act of causing or bringing on or about **5** : the process by which an electric current, an electric charge, or magnetism is produced in a body by the proximity of an electric or magnetic field

♦ inaugural, inauguration, installation, investiture

in·duc·tive \in-ˈdək-tiv\ *adj* : of, relating to, or employing induction
in·duc·tor \in-ˈdək-tər\ *n* : an electrical component that acts upon another or is itself acted upon by induction
in·dulge \in-ˈdəlj\ *vb* **in·dulged; in·dulg·ing** **1** ♦ : to give free rein to : GRATIFY **2** : HUMOR **3** : to gratify one's taste or desire for ⟨~ in alcohol⟩

♦ cater to, gratify, humor (*or* humour)

in·dul·gence \in-ˈdəl-jəns\ *n* **1** : remission of temporal punishment due in Roman Catholic doctrine for sins whose eternal punishment has been remitted by reception of the sacrament of penance **2** : the act of indulging : the state of being indulgent **3** : an indulgent act **4** ♦ : the thing indulged in **5** : SELF-INDULGENCE

♦ amenity, comfort, extra, frill, luxury, superfluity

in·dul·gent \in-ˈdəl-jənt\ *adj* ♦ : indulging or characterized by indulgence — **in·dul·gent·ly** *adv*

♦ accommodating, friendly, obliging

in·du·rat·ed \ˈin-dyu̇-ˌrā-təd, -du̇-\ *adj* : physically or emotionally hardened — **in·du·ra·tion** \ˌin-dyu̇-ˈrā-shən, -du̇-\ *n*
in·dus·tri·al \in-ˈdəs-trē-əl\ *adj* **1** : of or relating to industry; *also* : HEAVY-DUTY **2** : characterized by highly developed industries — **in·dus·tri·al·ly** *adv*
in·dus·tri·al·ise *chiefly Brit var of* INDUSTRIALIZE
in·dus·tri·al·ist \-ə-list\ *n* : a person owning or engaged in the management of an industry
in·dus·tri·al·ize \in-ˈdəs-trē-ə-ˌlīz\ *vb* **-ized; -iz·ing** : to make or become industrial — **in·dus·tri·al·i·za·tion** \-ˌdəs-trē-ə-lə-ˈzā-shən\ *n*
in·dus·tri·ous \in-ˈdəs-trē-əs\ *adj* : constantly, regularly, or habitually active or occupied : DILIGENT, BUSY
in·dus·tri·ous·ly *adv* : in an industrious manner
in·dus·tri·ous·ness *n* : the quality or state of being industrious
in·dus·try \ˈin-(ˌ)dəs-trē\ *n, pl* **-tries** **1** ♦ : steady or habitual effort : DILIGENCE **2** : a department or branch of a craft, art, business, or manufacture; *esp* : one that employs a large personnel and capital **3** : a distinct group of productive enterprises **4** : manufacturing activity as a whole

♦ assiduity, diligence

in·dwell \(ˌ)in-ˈdwel\ *vb* : to exist within as an activating spirit or force

In•dy car \ˈin-dē-\ *n* **:** a single-seat, open-cockpit racing car with the engine in the rear

1in•ebri•ate \i-ˈnē-brē-ˌāt\ *vb* **-at•ed; -at•ing :** to make drunk : INTOXICATE — **in•ebri•a•tion** \-ˌnē-brē-ˈā-shən\ *n*

2in•ebri•ate \-ət\ *n* ♦ **:** one that is drunk; *esp* : DRUNKARD

♦ drunk, drunkard, soak, sot, souse, tippler

in•ef•fa•ble \(ˌ)in-ˈe-fə-bəl\ *adj* **1** ♦ **:** incapable of being expressed in words : INDESCRIBABLE ⟨~ joy⟩ **2 :** UNSPEAKABLE ⟨~ disgust⟩ **3 :** not to be uttered : TABOO — **in•ef•fa•bly** \-blē\ *adv*

♦ indescribable, inexpressible, nameless, unspeakable, unutterable

in•ef•fec•tive \ˌi-nə-ˈfek-tiv\ *adj* **1 :** not producing an intended effect : INEFFECTUAL **2 :** incapable of performing efficiently — **in•ef•fec•tive•ly** *adv* — **in•ef•fec•tive•ness** *n*

in•ef•fec•tu•al \-ˈfek-chə-wəl\ *adj* **:** INEFFECTIVE — **in•ef•fec•tu•al•ly** *adv*

in•ef•fi•cient \ˌi-nə-ˈfi-shənt\ *adj* **1 :** not producing the desired effect **2 :** wasteful of time or energy **3 :** INCAPABLE, INCOMPETENT — **in•ef•fi•cien•cy** \-ˈfi-shən-sē\ *n* — **in•ef•fi•cient•ly** *adv*

in•el•e•gant \(ˌ)i-ˈne-li-gənt\ *adj* ♦ **:** lacking in refinement, grace, or good taste — **in•el•e•gance** \-gəns\ *n* — **in•el•e•gant•ly** *adv*

♦ awkward, clumsy, gauche, graceless, stiff, stilted, uncomfortable, uneasy, ungraceful, wooden ♦ dowdy, tacky, tasteless, trashy, unfashionable, unstylish

in•el•i•gi•ble \(ˌ)i-ˈne-lə-jə-bəl\ *adj* **:** not qualified for an office or position — **in•el•i•gi•bil•i•ty** \(ˌ)i-ˌne-lə-jə-ˈbi-lə-tē\ *n*

in•eluc•ta•ble \ˌi-ni-ˈlək-tə-bəl\ *adj* **:** not to be avoided, changed, or resisted — **in•eluc•ta•bly** \-blē\ *adv*

in•ept \i-ˈnept\ *adj* **1** ♦ **:** lacking in fitness or aptitude : UNFIT **2 :** FOOLISH **3** ♦ **:** inappropriate to the time or circumstances **4** ♦ **:** generally incompetent : BUNGLING — **in•ept•ly** *adv* — **in•ept•ness** *n*

♦ [1, 4] incapable, incompetent, inexpert, unfit, unqualified, unskilled, unskillful ♦ [3] improper, inappropriate, inapt, infelicitous, unbecoming, unfit, unseemly, unsuitable, wrong

in•ep•ti•tude \(ˌ)i-ˈnep-ti-ˌtüd, -ˌtyüd\ *n* ♦ **:** the quality or state of being inept; *esp* : INCOMPETENCE

♦ impotence, inability, inadequacy, incapability, incompetence

in•equal•i•ty \ˌi-ni-ˈkwä-lə-tē\ *n* **1 :** the quality of being unequal or uneven; *esp* : UNEVENNESS, DISPARITY **2 :** an instance of being unequal

in•ert \i-ˈnərt\ *adj* **1** ♦ **:** powerless to move **2** ♦ **:** averse to activity or exertion : SLUGGISH **3 :** lacking in active properties ⟨chemically ~⟩ — **in•ert•ly** *adv*

♦ [1] dead, dormant, fallow, free, idle, inactive, inoperative, latent, off, vacant ♦ [2] dull, inactive, lethargic, quiescent, sleepy, sluggish, torpid

in•er•tia \i-ˈnər-shə, -shē-ə\ *n* **1 :** a property of matter whereby it remains at rest or continues in uniform motion unless acted upon by some outside force **2** ♦ **:** indisposition to motion, exertion, or change — **in•er•tial** \-shəl\ *adj*

♦ idleness, indolence, laziness, sloth

in•ert•ness *n* ♦ **:** the quality or state of being inert : lack of activity

♦ dormancy, idleness, inaction, inactivity, quiescence

in•es•cap•able \ˌi-nə-ˈskā-pə-bəl\ *adj* **:** incapable of being escaped : INEVITABLE

in•es•cap•ably \-blē\ *adv* **:** in an inevitable way

in•es•ti•ma•ble \(ˌ)i-ˈnes-tə-mə-bəl\ *adj* **1 :** incapable of being estimated or computed ⟨~ errors⟩ **2 :** too valuable or excellent to be fully appreciated — **in•es•ti•ma•bly** \-blē\ *adv*

in•ev•i•ta•ble \i-ˈne-və-tə-bəl\ *adj* ♦ **:** incapable of being avoided or evaded : bound to happen — **in•ev•i•ta•bil•i•ty** \(ˌ)i-ˌne-və-tə-ˈbi-lə-tē\ *n*

♦ certain, necessary, sure, unavoidable *Ant* avoidable, uncertain, unsure

in•ev•i•ta•bly \-blē\ *adv* **1 :** in an inevitable way **2** ♦ **:** as is to be expected

♦ necessarily, needs, perforce, unavoidably

in•ex•act \ˌi-nig-ˈzakt\ *adj* **1** ♦ **:** not precisely correct or true : INACCURATE **2 :** not rigorous and careful — **in•ex•act•ly** *adv* — **in•ex•act•ness** *n*

♦ erroneous, false, inaccurate, incorrect, invalid, off, unsound, untrue, wrong ♦ imprecise, inaccurate, loose *Ant* accurate, dead, exact, precise

in•ex•cus•able \ˌi-nik-ˈskyü-zə-bəl\ *adj* ♦ **:** being without excuse or justification — **in•ex•cus•ably** \-blē\ *adv*

♦ indefensible, unforgivable, unjustifiable, unpardonable, unwarrantable *Ant* defensible, excusable, forgivable, justifiable, pardonable

in•ex•haust•ible \ˌi-nig-ˈzȯ-stə-bəl\ *adj* **1 :** incapable of being used up ⟨an ~ supply⟩ **2** ♦ **:** incapable of being wearied or worn out : UNTIRING — **in•ex•haust•ibly** \-blē\ *adv*

♦ indefatigable, tireless, unflagging, untiring

in•ex•o•ra•ble \(ˌ)i-ˈnek-sə-rə-bəl\ *adj* **:** not to be moved by entreaty : RELENTLESS — **in•ex•o•ra•bly** *adv*

in•ex•pen•sive \ˌi-nik-ˈspen(t)-siv\ *adj* **:** reasonable in price

in•ex•pe•ri•ence \ˌi-nik-ˈspir-ē-əns\ *n* **:** lack of experience or of knowledge gained by experience

in•ex•pe•ri•enced \-ənst\ *adj* ♦ **:** lacking practical experience

♦ amateur, amateurish, inexpert, nonprofessional, unprofessional, unskilled, unskillful

in•ex•pert \(ˌ)i-ˈnek-ˌspərt\ *adj* ♦ **:** not expert : UNSKILLED — **in•ex•pert•ly** *adv*

♦ amateur, amateurish, inexperienced, nonprofessional, unprofessional, unskilled, unskillful

in•ex•pi•a•ble \(ˌ)i-ˈnek-spē-ə-bəl\ *adj* **:** not capable of being atoned for

in•ex•pli•ca•ble \ˌi-nik-ˈspli-kə-bəl, (ˌ)i-ˈnek-(ˌ)spli-\ *adj* **:** incapable of being explained or accounted for — **in•ex•pli•ca•bly** \-blē\ *adv*

in•ex•press•ible \-ˈspre-sə-bəl\ *adj* ♦ **:** not capable of being expressed — **in•ex•press•ibly** \-blē\ *adv*

♦ indescribable, ineffable, nameless, unspeakable, unutterable

in•ex•pres•sive \-ˈspre-siv\ *adj* ♦ **:** lacking expression or meaning

♦ blank, deadpan, expressionless, impassive, stolid, vacant

in ex•tre•mis \ˌin-ik-ˈstrā-məs, -ˈstrē-\ *adv* **:** in extreme circumstances; *esp* : at the point of death

in•ex•tri•ca•ble \ˌi-nik-ˈstri-kə-bəl, (ˌ)i-ˈnek-(ˌ)stri-\ *adj* **1 :** forming a maze or tangle from which it is impossible to get free **2 :** incapable of being disentangled or untied — **in•ex•tri•ca•bly** \-blē\ *adv*

inf *abbr* **1** infantry **2** infinitive

in•fal•li•ble \(ˌ)in-ˈfa-lə-bəl\ *adj* **1 :** incapable of error : UNERRING **2** ♦ **:** not liable to mislead, deceive, or disappoint : SURE, CERTAIN ⟨an ~ remedy⟩ — **in•fal•li•bil•i•ty** \(ˌ)in-ˌfa-lə-ˈbi-lə-tē\ *n* — **in•fal•li•bly** \(ˌ)in-ˈfa-lə-blē\ *adv*

♦ certain, sure, unfailing *Ant* fallible

in•fa•mous \ˈin-fə-məs\ *adj* **1** ♦ **:** having a reputation of the worst kind **2** ♦ **:** causing or bringing infamy : DISGRACEFUL — **in•fa•mous•ly** *adv*

♦ [1, 2] discreditable, disgraceful, dishonorable (*or* dishonourable), disreputable, ignominious, notorious, shameful

in•fa•my \-mē\ *n, pl* **-mies 1 :** evil reputation brought about by something grossly criminal, shocking, or brutal **2 :** an extreme and publicly known criminal or evil act **3** ♦ **:** the state of being infamous

♦ discredit, disgrace, dishonor (*or* dishonour), disrepute, ignominy, odium, opprobrium, reproach, shame

in•fan•cy \ˈin-fən-sē\ *n, pl* **-cies 1 :** early childhood **2 :** a beginning or early period of existence

in•fant \ˈin-fənt\ *n* ♦ **:** a child in the first period of life : BABY; *also* : a person who is a legal minor

♦ baby, child, newborn

in•fan•ti•cide \in-ˈfan-tə-ˌsīd\ *n* **:** the killing of an infant

in•fan•tile \ˈin-fən-ˌtīl, -tᵊl, -ˌtēl\ *adj* ♦ **:** of or relating to infants; *also* : CHILDISH

♦ adolescent, babyish, childish, immature, juvenile, kiddish

infantile paralysis *n* **:** POLIOMYELITIS

in•fan•try \ˈin-fən-trē\ *n, pl* **-tries :** soldiers trained, armed, and equipped to fight on foot — **in•fan•try•man** \-mən\ *n*

in•farct \ˈin-ˌfärkt\ *n* **:** an area of dead tissue (as of the heart wall) caused by blocking of local blood circulation — **in•farc•tion** \in-ˈfärk-shən\ *n*

in•fat•u•ate \in-ˈfa-chə-ˌwāt\ *vb* **-at•ed; -at•ing :** to inspire with a foolish or extravagant love or admiration — **in•fat•u•a•tion** \-ˌfa-chə-ˈwā-shən\ *n*

in•fect \in-ˈfekt\ *vb* **1 :** to contaminate with disease-producing matter **2 :** to communicate a pathogen or disease to **3 :** to cause to share one's feelings

in•fec•tion \in-ˈfek-shən\ *n* **1 :** a disease or condition caused by a germ or parasite; *also* **:** such a germ or parasite **2 :** an act or process of infecting — **in•fec•tive** \-ˈfek-tiv\ *adj*

in•fec•tious \-shəs\ *adj* **1 :** capable of causing infection; *also* **:** communicable by infection **2** ♦ **:** spreading or capable of spreading rapidly to others

♦ catching, contagious

infectious mononucleosis *n* **:** an acute infectious disease characterized by fever, swelling of lymph glands, and increased numbers of lymph cells in the blood

in•fe•lic•i•tous \ˌin-fi-ˈli-sə-təs\ *adj* ♦ **:** not appropriate in application or expression — **in•fe•lic•i•ty** \-sə-tē\ *n*

♦ improper, inappropriate, inapt, unbecoming, unfit, unseemly, unsuitable, wrong

in•fer \in-ˈfər\ *vb* **in•ferred; in•fer•ring 1** ♦ **:** to derive as a conclusion from facts or premises **2 :** GUESS, SURMISE **3 :** to lead to as a conclusion or consequence **4** ♦ **:** to convey indirectly and by allusion rather than explicitly **:** HINT, SUGGEST

♦ [1] conclude, deduce, extrapolate, gather, judge, reason, understand ♦ [4] allude, hint, imply, indicate, insinuate, intimate, suggest

¹in•fe•ri•or \in-ˈfir-ē-ər\ *adj* **1 :** situated lower down **2** ♦ **:** of low or lower degree or rank **3** ♦ **:** of lesser quality **4** ♦ **:** of little or less importance, value, or merit — **in•fe•ri•or•i•ty** \(ˌ)in-ˌfir-ē-ˈȯr-ə-tē\ *n*

♦ [2] common, humble, ignoble, low, lowly, mean, plebeian, vulgar ♦ [3] cheap, cut-rate, junky, lousy, mediocre, shoddy, sleazy, trashy ♦ [4] junior, less, lesser, lower, minor, subordinate, under ♦ [4] mean, minor, second-rate, secondary *Ant* superior

²inferior *n* ♦ **:** a person or thing inferior to another (as in worth, status, or importance)

♦ junior, subordinate, underling

in•fer•nal \in-ˈfərn-ᵊl\ *adj* **1 :** of or relating to hell **2 :** HELLISH, FIENDISH ⟨~ schemes⟩ **3 :** DAMNABLE ⟨an ~ pest⟩ — **in•fer•nal•ly** *adv*

in•fer•no \in-ˈfər-nō\ *n, pl* **-nos** ♦ **:** a place or a state that resembles or suggests hell; *also* **:** intense heat

♦ conflagration, fire, holocaust

in•fer•tile \(ˌ)in-ˈfərt-ᵊl\ *adj* ♦ **:** not fertile or productive **:** BARREN — **in•fer•til•i•ty** \ˌin-fər-ˈti-lə-tē\ *n*

♦ barren, impotent, sterile, unproductive

in•fest \in-ˈfest\ *vb* **:** to trouble by spreading or swarming in or over; *also* **:** to live in or on as a parasite — **in•fes•ta•tion** \ˌin-ˌfes-ˈtā-shən\ *n*

in•fi•del \ˈin-fəd-ᵊl, -fə-ˌdel\ *n* **1 :** one who is not a Christian or opposes Christianity **2 :** an unbeliever especially with respect to a particular religion

in•fi•del•i•ty \ˌin-fə-ˈde-lə-tē, -fī-\ *n, pl* **-ties 1 :** lack of belief in a religion **2** ♦ **:** unfaithfulness to a moral obligation **:** DISLOYALTY **3** ♦ **:** marital unfaithfulness or an instance of it

♦ [2, 3] betrayal, disloyalty, double cross, treachery, treason ♦ [3] disloyalty, faithlessness, falseness, falsity, inconstancy, perfidy, unfaithfulness *Ant* allegiance, constancy, devotion, faith, faithfulness, fealty, fidelity, loyalty

in•field \ˈin-ˌfēld\ *n* **:** the part of a baseball field inside the baselines — **in•field•er** *n*

in•fight•ing \ˈin-ˌfī-tiŋ\ *n* **1 :** fighting at close quarters **2 :** dissension or rivalry among members of a group

in•fil•trate \in-ˈfil-ˌtrāt, ˈin-(ˌ)fil-\ *vb* **-trat•ed; -trat•ing 1 :** to enter or filter into or through something **2** ♦ **:** to pass into or through by or as if by filtering or permeating — **in•fil•tra•tion** \ˌin-(ˌ)fil-ˈtrā-shən\ *n* — **in•fil•tra•tor** *n*

♦ insinuate, slip, sneak, work, worm

in•fi•nite \ˈin-fə-nət\ *adj* **1** ♦ **:** extending indefinitely **:** LIMITLESS, ENDLESS ⟨~ space⟩ ⟨~ patience⟩ **2 :** VAST, IMMENSE; *also* **:** INEXHAUSTIBLE ⟨~ wealth⟩ **3 :** greater than any preassigned finite value however large ⟨~ number of positive integers⟩; *also* **:** extending to infinity ⟨~ plane surface⟩ — **infinite** *n* — **in•fi•nite•ly** *adv*

♦ boundless, endless, illimitable, immeasurable, indefinite, limitless, measureless, unbounded, unfathomable, unlimited *Ant* bounded, circumscribed, confined, definite, finite, limited, restricted

in•fin•i•tes•i•mal \(ˌ)in-ˌfi-nə-ˈte-sə-məl\ *adj* ♦ **:** immeasurably or incalculably small — **in•fin•i•tes•i•mal•ly** *adv*

♦ atomic, microscopic, miniature, minute, teeny, tiny, wee

in•fin•i•tive \in-ˈfi-nə-tiv\ *n* **:** a verb form having the characteristics of both verb and noun and in English usually being used with *to*

in•fin•i•tude \in-ˈfi-nə-ˌtüd, -ˌtyüd\ *n* **1 :** the quality or state of being infinite **2 :** something that is infinite especially in extent

in•fin•i•ty \in-ˈfi-nə-tē\ *n, pl* **-ties 1 :** the quality of being infinite **2 :** unlimited extent of time, space, or quantity **:** BOUNDLESSNESS **3 :** an indefinitely great number or amount

in•firm \in-ˈfərm\ *adj* **1** ♦ **:** deficient in vitality; *esp* **:** feeble from age **2 :** weak of mind, will, or character **:** IRRESOLUTE **3 :** not solid or stable **:** INSECURE

♦ delicate, faint, feeble, frail, wasted, weak

in•fir•ma•ry \in-ˈfər-mə-rē\ *n, pl* **-ries :** a place for the care of the infirm or sick

in•fir•mi•ty \in-ˈfər-mə-tē\ *n, pl* **-ties 1** ♦ **:** the condition of being feeble **:** FEEBLENESS **2** ♦ **:** a disease or disorder of the animal body **:** AILMENT **3 :** a personal failing **:** FOIBLE

♦ [1] debility, delicacy, enfeeblement, faintness, feebleness, frailty, languor, lowness, weakness ♦ [2] ailment, bug, complaint, complication, condition, disease, disorder, fever, illness, malady, sickness, trouble

infl *abbr* influenced

in fla•gran•te de•lic•to \ˌin-flə-ˈgrän-tē-di-ˈlik-tō, -ˈgran-\ *adv* **1 :** in the very act of committing a misdeed **2 :** in the midst of sexual activity

in•flame \in-ˈflām\ *vb* **in•flamed; in•flam•ing 1** ♦ **:** to set on fire **:** KINDLE **2** ♦ **:** to excite to excessive or uncontrollable action or feeling; *also* **:** INTENSIFY **3 :** to affect or become affected with inflammation

♦ [1] burn, fire, ignite, kindle, light ♦ [2] anger, antagonize, enrage, incense, infuriate, intensify, madden, outrage, rankle, rile, roil

in•flam•ma•ble \in-ˈfla-mə-bəl\ *adj* **1** ♦ **:** capable of being easily ignited and of burning quickly **:** FLAMMABLE **2 :** easily inflamed, excited, or angered **:** IRASCIBLE

♦ combustible, flammable, ignitable

in•flam•ma•tion \ˌin-flə-ˈmā-shən\ *n* **:** a bodily response to injury in which an affected area becomes red, hot, and painful and congested with blood

in•flam•ma•to•ry \in-ˈfla-mə-ˌtōr-ē\ *adj* **1 :** tending to excite the senses or to arouse anger, disorder, or tumult **:** SEDITIOUS **2 :** causing or accompanied by inflammation ⟨an ~ disease⟩

in•flate \in-ˈflāt\ *vb* **in•flat•ed; in•flat•ing 1 :** to swell with air or gas ⟨~ a balloon⟩ **2 :** to puff up **:** ELATE **3 :** to expand or increase abnormally ⟨~ prices⟩ — **in•flat•able** *adj*

in•fla•tion \in-ˈflā-shən\ *n* **1 :** an act of inflating **:** the state of being inflated **2 :** empty pretentiousness **:** POMPOSITY **3 :** a continuing rise in the general price level usually attributed to an increase in the volume of money and credit

in•fla•tion•ary \-shə-ˌner-ē\ *adj* **:** of, characterized by, or productive of inflation

in•flect \in-ˈflekt\ *vb* **1 :** to turn from a direct line or course **:** CURVE **2 :** to vary a word by inflection **3 :** to change or vary the pitch of the voice

in•flec•tion \in-ˈflek-shən\ *n* **1 :** the act or result of curving or bending **2 :** a change in pitch or loudness of the voice **3 :** the change of form that words undergo to mark case, gender, number, tense, person, mood, or voice — **in•flec•tion•al** \-shə-nəl\ *adj*

in•flex•i•bil•i•ty \-ˌflek-sə-ˈbi-lə-tē\ *n* ♦ **:** the quality or state of being inflexible

♦ hardness, harshness, rigidity, severity, sternness, strictness

in•flex•i•ble \(ˌ)in-ˈflek-sə-bəl\ *adj* **1** ♦ **:** rigidly firm in will or purpose **:** UNYIELDING **2** ♦ **:** not readily bent **:** RIGID **3** ♦ **:** incapable of change — **in•flex•i•bly** \-ˈflek-sə-blē\ *adv*

♦ [1, 2] adamant, hard, immovable, implacable, pat, rigid, steadfast, unbending, uncompromising, unflinching, unrelenting, unyielding *Ant* acquiescent, agreeable, amenable, compliant, flexible, pliant, pliable ♦ [3] fast, fixed, hard-and-fast, immutable, unalterable, unchangeable *Ant* changeable, flexible, mutable, variable

in•flex•ion \in-ˈflek-shən\ *chiefly Brit var of* INFLECTION

in·flict \in-ˈflikt\ *vb* : AFFLICT; *also* : to give by or as if by striking — **in·flic·tion** \-ˈflik-shən\ *n*
in·flo·res·cence \ˌin-flə-ˈres-ᵊns\ *n* : the manner of development and arrangement of flowers on a stem; *also* : a flowering stem with its appendages : a flower cluster
in·flow \ˈin-ˌflō\ *n* : a flowing in
[1]**in·flu·ence** \ˈin-ˌflü-əns\ *n* **1** ♦ : the act or power of producing an effect without apparent force or direct authority **2** ♦ : the power or capacity of causing an effect in indirect or intangible ways ⟨under the ~ of liquor⟩ **3** : a person or thing that exerts influence

♦ [1] authority, clout, pull, sway, weight ♦ [2] effect, impact, mark, repercussion, sway

[2]**influence** *vb* **-enced; -enc·ing 1** ♦ : to affect or alter by influence : SWAY **2** : to have an effect on the condition or development of : MODIFY

♦ affect, impact, impress, move, strike, sway, tell, touch

in·flu·en·tial \ˌin-flü-ˈen-chəl\ *adj* ♦ : exerting or possessing influence; *also* : having authority or ascendancy

♦ important, mighty, potent, powerful, significant, strong ♦ authoritative, forceful, weighty

in·flu·en·za \ˌin-flü-ˈen-zə\ *n* : an acute and highly contagious virus disease marked by fever, prostration, aches and pains, and respiratory inflammation; *also* : any of various feverish usually virus diseases typically with respiratory symptoms
in·flux \ˈin-ˌfləks\ *n* : a coming in
in·fo \ˈin-(ˌ)fō\ *n* : INFORMATION
in·fold \in-ˈfōld\ *vb* **1** : ENFOLD **2** : to fold inward or toward one another
in·fo·mer·cial \ˈin-fō-ˌmər-shəl\ *n* : a television program that is an extended advertisement often including a discussion or demonstration
in·form \in-ˈfȯrm\ *vb* **1** ♦ : to communicate knowledge to : TELL **2** : to give information or knowledge **3** ♦ : to act as an informer

♦ [1] acquaint, advise, apprise, brief, clue, enlighten, familiarize, fill in, instruct, tell, wise ♦ [3] snitch, squeal, talk, tell

in·for·mal \(ˌ)in-ˈfȯr-məl\ *adj* **1** ♦ : conducted or carried out without formality or ceremony ⟨an ~ party⟩ **2** ♦ : characteristic of or appropriate to ordinary, casual, or familiar use ⟨~ clothes⟩ — **in·for·mal·i·ty** \ˌin-fȯr-ˈma-lə-tē, -fər-\ *n* — **in·for·mal·ly** \(ˌ)in-ˈfȯr-mə-lē\ *adv*

♦ [1] irregular, unceremonious, unconventional, unorthodox ***Ant*** ceremonial, ceremonious, conventional, formal, orthodox, regular, routine ♦ [2] casual, everyday, workaday

in·for·mant \in-ˈfȯr-mənt\ *n* : a person who gives information : INFORMER
in·for·ma·tion \ˌin-fər-ˈmā-shən\ *n* **1** : the communication or reception of knowledge or intelligence **2** : knowledge obtained from investigation, study, or instruction : FACTS, DATA
in·for·ma·tion·al \-shə-nəl\ *adj* : relating to or giving information
information superhighway *n* : INTERNET
in·for·ma·tive \in-ˈfȯr-mə-tiv\ *adj* ♦ : imparting knowledge : INSTRUCTIVE

♦ educational, instructive ***Ant*** uninstructive

in·formed \in-ˈfȯrmd\ *adj* **1** ♦ : having or based on information **2** ♦ : having an education : KNOWLEDGEABLE

♦ [1] good, hard, just, levelheaded, logical, rational, reasonable, reasoned, sensible, sober, solid, valid, well-founded ♦ [2] abreast, conversant, familiar, knowledgeable, up, up-to-date, versed

informed consent *n* : consent to a medical procedure by someone who understands what is involved
in·form·er \-ˈfȯr-mər\ *n* ♦ : one that informs; *esp* : a person who informs against others for illegalities especially for financial gain

♦ betrayer, blabbermouth, rat, snitch, stool pigeon, tattler, tattletale

in·fo·tain·ment \ˌin-fō-ˈtān-mənt\ *n* : a television program that presents information (as news) in a manner intended to be entertaining
in·frac·tion \in-ˈfrak-shən\ *n* ♦ : the act of infringing : VIOLATION

♦ breach, infringement, offense, transgression, trespass, violation

in·fra dig \ˌin-frə-ˈdig\ *adj* : being beneath one's dignity
in·fra·red \ˌin-frə-ˈred\ *adj* : being, relating to, or using radiation having wavelengths longer than those of red light — **infrared** *n*
in·fra·struc·ture \ˈin-frə-ˌstrək-chər\ *n* **1** : the underlying foundation or basic framework (as of a system or organization) **2** : the system of public works of a country, state, or region; *also* : the resources (as buildings or equipment) required for an activity
in·fre·quent \(ˌ)in-ˈfrē-kwənt\ *adj* **1** ♦ : seldom happening : RARE **2** : placed or occurring at wide intervals in space or time

♦ occasional, rare, sporadic ***Ant*** frequent

in·fre·quent·ly \-lē\ *adv* ♦ : in an infrequent manner

♦ little, rarely, seldom

in·fringe \in-ˈfrinj\ *vb* **in·fringed; in·fring·ing 1** : to encroach upon in a way that violates law or the rights of another : VIOLATE, TRANSGRESS ⟨~ a patent⟩ **2** : ENCROACH, TRESPASS
in·fringe·ment *n* ♦ : the act of infringing; *also* : an encroachment or trespass on a right or privilege

♦ breach, infraction, offense, transgression, trespass, violation

in·fu·ri·ate \in-ˈfyu̇r-ē-ˌāt\ *vb* **-at·ed; -at·ing** ♦ : to make furious : ENRAGE — **in·fu·ri·at·ing·ly** *adv*

♦ anger, antagonize, enrage, incense, inflame, madden, outrage, rankle, rile, roil

in·fuse \in-ˈfyüz\ *vb* **in·fused; in·fus·ing 1** ♦ : to instill a principle or quality in **2** : INSPIRE, ANIMATE **3** : to steep (as tea) without boiling — **in·fu·sion** \-ˈfyü-zhən\ *n*

♦ imbue, inculcate, ingrain, invest, steep, suffuse

[1]**-ing** \iŋ\ *n suffix* **1** : action or process ⟨sleep*ing*⟩ : instance of an action or process ⟨a meet*ing*⟩ **2** : product or result of an action or process ⟨an engrav*ing*⟩ ⟨earn*ings*⟩ **3** : something used in an action or process ⟨a bed cover*ing*⟩ **4** : something connected with, consisting of, or used in making (a specified thing) ⟨scaffold*ing*⟩ **5** : something related to (a specified concept) ⟨off*ing*⟩
[2]**-ing** *n suffix* : one of a (specified) kind
[3]**-ing** *vb suffix or adj suffix* — used to form the present participle ⟨sail*ing*⟩ and sometimes to form an adjective resembling a present participle but not derived from a verb ⟨swashbuckl*ing*⟩
in·ga·ther \ˈin-ˌga-t͟hər\ *vb* : to gather in : ASSEMBLE
in·ge·nious \in-ˈjēn-yəs\ *adj* **1** ♦ : marked by special aptitude at discovering, inventing, or contriving **2** ♦ : marked by originality, resourcefulness, and cleverness in conception or execution — **in·ge·nious·ly** *adv*

♦ [1, 2] creative, imaginative, innovative, inventive, original ♦ [2] artful, clever, creative, imaginative

in·ge·nious·ness *n* : the power or quality of ready invention
in·ge·nue *or* **in·gé·nue** \ˈan-jə-ˌnü, ˈän-; ˈaⁿ-zhə-, ˈäⁿ-\ *n* : a naive girl or young woman; *esp* : an actress portraying such a person
in·ge·nu·i·ty \ˌin-jə-ˈnü-ə-tē, -ˈnyü-\ *n, pl* **-ties** ♦ : skill or cleverness in planning or inventing : INVENTIVENESS

♦ creativity, invention, inventiveness, originality

in·gen·u·ous \in-ˈjen-yə-wəs\ *adj* **1** : STRAIGHTFORWARD, FRANK **2** ♦ : showing innocent or childlike simplicity and candidness : NAIVE

♦ green, innocent, naive, simple, unknowing, unsophisticated, unwary, unworldly

in·gen·u·ous·ly *adv* ♦ : in an ingenuous manner

♦ artlessly, naively, naturally, unaffectedly

in·gen·u·ous·ness *n* ♦ : the quality of being ingenuous : absence of guile, reserve, or disguise

♦ artlessness, greenness, innocence, naïveté, naturalness, simplicity, unworldliness

in·gest \in-ˈjest\ *vb* : to take in for or as if for digestion — **in·ges·tion** \-ˈjes-chən\ *n*
in·gle·nook \ˈiŋ-gəl-ˌnu̇k\ *n* : a nook by a large open fireplace; *also* : a bench occupying this nook
in·glo·ri·ous \(ˌ)in-ˈglōr-ē-əs\ *adj* **1** : SHAMEFUL **2** : not glorious : lacking fame or honor — **in·glo·ri·ous·ly** *adv*
in·got \ˈiŋ-gət\ *n* : a mass of metal cast in a form convenient for storage or transportation
[1]**in·grain** \(ˌ)in-ˈgrān\ *vb* ♦ : to work indelibly into the natural texture or mental or moral constitution

♦ imbue, inculcate, infuse, invest, steep, suffuse

[2]**in·grain** \ˈin-ˌgrān\ *adj* **1** : made of fiber that is dyed before being spun into yarn **2** : made of yarn that is dyed before being woven or knitted **3** : INNATE — **in·grain** *n*

in•grained *adj* **1 :** worked into the grain or fiber **2** ♦ **:** forming a part of the essence or inmost being

♦ essential, inborn, inherent, innate, integral, intrinsic, natural

in•grate \ˈin-ˌgrāt\ *n* **:** an ungrateful person

in•gra•ti•ate \in-ˈgrā-shē-ˌāt\ *vb* **-at•ed; -at•ing :** to gain favor by deliberate effort

in•gra•ti•at•ing *adj* **1** ♦ **:** capable of winning favor ⟨an ~ smile⟩ **2 :** FLATTERING ⟨an ~ manner⟩

♦ endearing, winning, winsome

in•grat•i•tude \(ˌ)in-ˈgra-tə-ˌtüd, -ˌtyüd\ *n* **:** lack of gratitude **:** UNGRATEFULNESS

in•gre•di•ent \in-ˈgrē-dē-ənt\ *n* ♦ **:** one of the substances that make up a mixture or compound **:** CONSTITUENT

♦ component, constituent, element, factor, member

in•gress \ˈin-ˌgres\ *n* **:** ♦ **:** a means or place of entry **:** ENTRANCE, ACCESS — **in•gres•sion** \in-ˈgre-shən\ *n*

♦ access, admission, doorway, entrance, entrée, entry, gateway

in•grow•ing \ˈin-ˌgrō-iŋ\ *adj* **:** growing or tending inward

in•grown \-ˌgrōn\ *adj* **:** grown in; *esp* **:** having the free tip or edge embedded in the flesh ⟨~ toenail⟩

in•gui•nal \ˈiŋ-gwən-ᵊl\ *adj* **:** of, relating to, or situated in or near the region of the groin

in•hab•it \in-ˈha-bət\ *vb* **:** to live or dwell in — **in•hab•it•able** *adj*

in•hab•i•tant \in-ˈha-bə-tənt\ *n* ♦ **:** a permanent resident in a place

♦ denizen, dweller, occupant, resident *Ant* transient

in•hal•ant \in-ˈhā-lənt\ *n* **:** something (as a medicine) that is inhaled

in•ha•la•tor \ˈin-hə-ˌlā-tər\ *n* **:** a device that provides a mixture of carbon dioxide and oxygen for breathing

in•hale \in-ˈhāl\ *vb* **in•haled; in•hal•ing :** to breathe in — **in•ha•la•tion** \ˌin-hə-ˈlā-shən\ *n*

in•hal•er \in-ˈhā-lər\ *n* **:** a device by means of which medicinal material is inhaled

in•har•mo•ni•ous \-ˈmō-nē-əs\ *adj* **1** ♦ **:** not harmonious **2** ♦ **:** not fitting or congenial

♦ discordant, discrepant, incompatible, incongruous, inharmonious

in•here \in-ˈhir\ *vb* **in•hered; in•her•ing :** to be inherent

in•her•ent \in-ˈhir-ənt, -ˈher-\ *adj* ♦ **:** established as an essential part of something **:** INTRINSIC

♦ essential, inborn, ingrained, innate, integral, intrinsic, natural *Ant* adventitious, extraneous, extrinsic

in•her•ent•ly \-lē\ *adv* ♦ **:** in an inherent manner

♦ constitutionally, innately, intrinsically, naturally

in•her•it \in-ˈher-ət\ *vb* **1 :** to receive especially from one's ancestors **2 :** to receive by genetic transmission — **in•her•i•tor** \-ə-tər\ *n*

in•her•it•able \-ə-tə-bəl\ *adj* **1 :** capable of being inherited **2 :** capable of taking by inheritance

in•her•i•tance \-ə-təns\ *n* **1 :** the act of inheriting **2** ♦ **:** something that is or may be passed on to another generation

♦ bequest, birthright, heritage, legacy

inherited *adj* ♦ **:** being something received by inheritance

♦ genetic, hereditary, heritable, inborn, inherited

in•hib•it \in-ˈhi-bət\ *vb* **1 :** PROHIBIT, FORBID **2** ♦ **:** to hold in check

♦ bridle, check, constrain, contain, control, curb, govern, regulate, rein, restrain, tame

in•hi•bi•tion \ˌin-hə-ˈbi-shən\ *n* **1 :** something that forbids or restricts **2** ♦ **:** a usually inner check on free activity, expression, or functioning

♦ repression, restraint, self-control, self-restraint, suppression

in•hos•pi•ta•ble \ˌin-(ˌ)hä-ˈspi-tə-bəl, (ˌ)in-ˈhäs-(ˌ)pi-\ *adj* **1** ♦ **:** not showing hospitality **:** not friendly or receptive **2 :** providing no shelter or sustenance

♦ antagonistic, hostile, inimical, jaundiced, negative, unfriendly, unsympathetic

in–house \ˈin-ˌhau̇s, -ˈhau̇s\ *adj* **:** existing, originating, or carried on within a group or organization

in•hu•man \(ˌ)in-ˈhyü-mən, -ˈyü-\ *adj* **1** ♦ **:** lacking pity, kindness, or mercy **2 :** not engaging the human personality or emotions **3** ♦ **:** not worthy of or conforming to the needs of human beings ⟨~ conditions⟩ **4 :** of or suggesting a nonhuman class of beings — **in•hu•man•ly** *adv* — **in•hu•man•ness** *n*

♦ [1] callous, hard, heartless, inhumane, pitiless, soulless, unfeeling, unsympathetic ♦ [3] bitter, brutal, burdensome, cruel, excruciating, grievous, grim, hard, harsh, heavy, murderous, onerous, oppressive, rough, rugged, severe, stiff, tough, trying

in•hu•mane \ˌin-hyü-ˈmān, -yü-\ *adj* ♦ **:** not humane **:** not devoted or sympathetic to humans or human needs

♦ barbarous, brutal, cruel, heartless, sadistic, savage, vicious, wanton

in•hu•man•i•ty \-ˈma-nə-tē\ *n, pl* **-ties 1** ♦ **:** the quality or state of being cruel or barbarous **2 :** a cruel or barbarous act

♦ barbarity, brutality, cruelty, sadism, savagery, viciousness, wantonness

in•im•i•cal \i-ˈni-mi-kəl\ *adj* **1 :** being adverse often by reason of hostility **2** ♦ **:** having the disposition of an enemy **:** HOSTILE, UNFRIENDLY — **in•im•i•cal•ly** *adv*

♦ antagonistic, hostile, inhospitable, jaundiced, negative, unfriendly, unsympathetic

in•im•i•ta•ble \(ˌ)i-ˈni-mə-tə-bəl\ *adj* ♦ **:** not capable of being imitated

♦ incomparable, matchless, nonpareil, only, peerless, unequaled, unmatched, unparalleled, unrivaled, unsurpassed

in•iq•ui•tous \i-ˈni-kwə-təs\ *adj* ♦ **:** characterized by iniquity

♦ bad, black, evil, immoral, nefarious, rotten, sinful, unethical, unsavory, vicious, vile, villainous, wicked, wrong

in•iq•ui•ty \i-ˈni-kwə-tē\ *n, pl* **-ties 1 :** gross injustice **:** WICKEDNESS **2** ♦ **:** a wicked act

♦ corruption, debauchery, depravity, immorality, licentiousness, sin, vice

¹ini•tial \i-ˈni-shəl\ *adj* **1 :** of or relating to the beginning **:** INCIPIENT **2** ♦ **:** placed at the beginning **:** FIRST

♦ first, inaugural, maiden, original, pioneer, premier

²initial *n* **:** the first letter of a word or name

³initial *vb* **-tialed** *or* **-tialled; -tial•ing** *or* **-tial•ling :** to affix an initial to

ini•tial•ly *adv* ♦ **:** in the first place **:** at the beginning

♦ firstly, originally, primarily

¹ini•ti•ate \i-ˈni-shē-ˌāt\ *vb* **-at•ed; -at•ing 1** ♦ **:** set going **:** START, BEGIN **2** ♦ **:** to induct into membership by or as if by special ceremonies **3** ♦ **:** to instruct in the rudiments or principles of something

♦ [1] begin, constitute, establish, found, inaugurate, innovate, institute, introduce, launch, pioneer, set up, start ♦ [2] baptize, inaugurate, induct, install, invest ♦ [3] acquaint, familiarize, introduce, orient

²ini•tiate \i-ˈni-shē-ət\ *n* **1 :** a person who is undergoing or has passed an initiation **2 :** a person who is instructed or adept in some special field

ini•ti•a•tion \-ˌni-shē-ˈā-shən\ *n* **1 :** the act or an instance of initiating **2 :** the process of being initiated; *specif* **:** the rites, ceremonies, ordeals, or instructions with which one is made a member of a sect or society or is invested with a particular function or status

ini•tia•tive \i-ˈni-shə-tiv\ *n* **1 :** an introductory step **2** ♦ **:** self-reliant enterprise ⟨showed great ~⟩ **3 :** a process by which laws may be introduced or enacted directly by vote of the people

♦ aggressiveness, ambition, drive, enterprise, go, hustle

ini•tia•to•ry \i-ˈni-shē-ə-ˌtōr-ē\ *adj* **1 :** INTRODUCTORY **2 :** tending or serving to initiate ⟨~ rites⟩

in•ject \in-ˈjekt\ *vb* **1 :** to force into something ⟨~ serum with a needle⟩ **2** ♦ **:** to introduce as an element into some situation or subject ⟨~ a note of suspicion⟩ — **in•jec•tion** \-ˈjek-shən\ *n*

♦ fit, insert, insinuate, interject, interpose, introduce

in•junc•tion \in-ˈjəŋk-shən\ *n* **1 :** ORDER, ADMONITION **2 :** a court writ whereby one is required to do or to refrain from doing a specified act

in•jure \ˈin-jər\ *vb* **in•jured; in•jur•ing 1 :** to do an injustice to **:** WRONG **2** ♦ **:** to inflict bodily hurt on **:** HURT; *also* **:** to impair the soundness of

♦ damage, harm, hurt, wound

in•ju•ri•ous \in-ˈju̇r-ē-əs\ *adj* ♦ : inflicting or tending to inflict injury

♦ adverse, bad, baleful, baneful, damaging, deleterious, detrimental, evil, harmful, hurtful, ill, mischievous, noxious, pernicious, prejudicial

in•ju•ry \ˈin-jə-rē\ *n, pl* **-ries** **1** ♦ : an act that damages or hurts **2** : hurt, damage, or loss sustained

♦ damage, detriment, harm, hurt

in•jus•tice \(ˌ)in-ˈjəs-təs\ *n* **1** ♦ : violation of a person's rights : UNFAIRNESS **2** ♦ : an unjust act or deed : WRONG

♦ [1, 2] disservice, injury, raw deal, wrong

¹ink \ˈiŋk\ *n* : a usually liquid and colored material for writing and printing — **inky** *adj*

²ink *vb* : to put ink on; *esp* : SIGN

ink•blot test \ˈiŋk-ˌblät-\ *n* : any of several psychological tests based on the interpretation of irregular figures

ink•horn \-ˌhȯrn\ *n* : a small bottle (as of horn) for holding ink

in–kind \ˈin-ˈkīnd\ *adj* : consisting of something (as goods) other than money

ink–jet *n* : a computer printer that sprays electrically charged droplets of ink onto paper — **ink–jet** *adj*

in•kling \ˈiŋ-kliŋ\ *n* **1** ♦ : a slight indication or suggestion : HINT, INTIMATION **2** : a vague idea

♦ clue, cue, hint, indication, intimation, lead, suggestion

ink•stand \ˈiŋk-ˌstand\ *n* : INKWELL; *also* : a pen and ink stand

ink•well \-ˌwel\ *n* : a container for ink

in•laid \ˈin-ˈlād\ *adj* : decorated with material set into a surface

¹in•land \ˈin-ˌland, -lənd\ *adj* **1** *chiefly Brit* : not foreign : DOMESTIC ⟨~ revenue⟩ **2** : of or relating to the interior of a country

²inland *n* : the interior of a country

³inland *adv* : into or toward the interior

in–law \ˈin-ˌlȯ\ *n* : a relative by marriage

¹in•lay \(ˌ)in-ˈlā, ˈin-ˌlā\ *vb* **in•laid** \-ˈlād\; **in•lay•ing** : to set (a material) into a surface or ground material especially for decoration

²in•lay \ˈin-ˌlā\ *n* **1** : inlaid work **2** : a shaped filling cemented into a tooth

in•let \ˈin-ˌlet, -lət\ *n* **1** ♦ : a small or narrow bay **2** : an opening for intake especially of a fluid

♦ bay, bight, cove, estuary, fjord, gulf

in–line skate *n* : a roller skate whose four wheels are set in a straight line

in•mate \ˈin-ˌmāt\ *n* : any of a group occupying a single place of residence; *esp* : a person confined (as in a hospital or prison)

in me•di•as res \in-ˌmā-dē-əs-ˈrās\ *adv* : in or into the middle of a narrative or plot

in me•mo•ri•am \ˌin-mə-ˈmōr-ē-əm\ *prep* : in memory of

in•most \ˈin-ˌmōst\ *adj* : deepest within : INNERMOST

inn \ˈin\ *n* ♦ : an establishment for the lodging and entertaining of travelers : HOTEL, TAVERN

♦ hospice, hotel, lodge, public house, tavern

in•nards \ˈi-nərdz\ *n pl* **1** : the internal organs of a human being or animal; *esp* : VISCERA **2** : the internal parts of a structure or mechanism

in•nate \i-ˈnāt\ *adj* **1** : existing in, belonging to, or determined by factors present in an individual from birth : NATIVE **2** ♦ : belonging to the essential nature of something : INHERENT, INTRINSIC

♦ essential, inborn, ingrained, inherent, integral, intrinsic, natural

in•nate•ly *adv* ♦ : in an innate manner

♦ constitutionally, inherently, intrinsically, naturally

in•ner \ˈi-nər\ *adj* **1** ♦ : located farther in ⟨the ~ bark⟩ **2** : near a center especially of influence ⟨the ~ circle⟩ **3** ♦ : of or relating to the mind or spirit

♦ [1] inside, interior, internal, inward ***Ant*** exterior, external, outer, outside, outward ♦ [3] cerebral, intellectual, mental, psychological

inner city *n* : the usually older, poorer, and more densely populated section of a city — **inner–city** *adj*

in•ner–di•rect•ed \ˌi-nər-də-ˈrek-təd, -(ˌ)dī-\ *adj* : directed in thought and action by one's own scale of values as opposed to external norms

inner ear *n* : the part of the ear that is most important for hearing, is located in a cavity in the temporal bone, and contains sense organs of hearing and of awareness of position in space

in•ner•most \ˈi-nər-ˌmōst\ *adj* : farthest inward : INMOST

in•ner•sole \ˈi-nər-ˈsōl\ *n* : INSOLE

in•ner•spring \ˈi-nər-ˈspriŋ\ *adj* : having coil springs inside a padded casing

inner tube *n* : an airtight rubber tube inside a tire to hold air under pressure

in•ning \ˈi-niŋ\ *n* **1** *sing or pl* : a division of a cricket match **2** : a baseball team's turn at bat; *also* : a division of a baseball game consisting of a turn at bat for each team

inn•keep•er \ˈin-ˈkē-pər\ *n* **1** : a proprietor of an inn **2** : a hotel manager

in•no•cence \ˈi-nə-səns\ *n* **1** ♦ : freedom from guilt or sin through being unacquainted with evil : BLAMELESSNESS; *also* : freedom from legal guilt **2** ♦ : freedom from guile or cunning : SIMPLICITY; *also* : IGNORANCE

♦ [1] decency, goodness, honesty, integrity, righteousness ***Ant*** blameworthiness, culpability, guilt, guiltiness ♦ [2] artlessness, greenness, ignorance, ingenuousness, naïveté, naturalness, simplicity, unworldliness

¹in•no•cent \-sənt\ *adj* **1** ♦ : free from guilt or sin : BLAMELESS **2** ♦ : harmless in effect or intention; *also* : CANDID **3** : free from legal guilt or fault : LAWFUL **4** ♦ : lacking or reflecting a lack of sophistication, guile, or self-consciousness : INGENUOUS **5** : UNAWARE

♦ [1] blameless, clear, faultless, guiltless, impeccable, irreproachable ***Ant*** guilty ♦ [2] candid, harmless, innocuous, safe, white ♦ [4] green, ingenuous, naive, simple, unknowing, unsophisticated, unwary, unworldly

²innocent *n* ♦ : an innocent one

♦ angel, dove, lamb, sheep

in•no•cent•ly \-lē\ *adv* : in an innocent manner

in•noc•u•ous \i-ˈnä-kyə-wəs\ *adj* **1** ♦ : producing no injury : HARMLESS **2** : not offensive; *also* : INSIPID

♦ harmless, innocent, safe, white

in•nom•i•nate \i-ˈnä-mə-nət\ *adj* : having no name; *also* : ANONYMOUS

in•no•vate \ˈi-nə-ˌvāt\ *vb* **-vat•ed; -vat•ing** ♦ : to introduce as or as if new; *also* : to make changes

♦ constitute, establish, found, inaugurate, initiate, institute, introduce, launch, pioneer, set up, start

in•no•va•tion \ˌi-nə-ˈvā-shən\ *n* **1** : the introduction of something new **2** ♦ : a new idea, method, or device

♦ coinage, concoction, contrivance, creation, invention, wrinkle

in•no•va•tive \-ˌvā-tiv\ *adj* ♦ : characterized by, tending to, or introducing innovations

♦ creative, imaginative, ingenious, inventive, original

in•no•va•tor \-ˌvā-tər\ *n* ♦ : one that innovates

♦ designer, developer, inventor, originator

in•nu•en•do \ˌin-yə-ˈwen-dō\ *n, pl* **-dos** *or* **-does** : HINT, INSINUATION; *esp* : a veiled reflection on character or reputation

in•nu•mer•a•ble \i-ˈnü-mə-rə-bəl, -ˈnyü-\ *adj* ♦ : too many to be numbered

♦ countless, numberless, uncountable, unnumbered, untold

in•oc•u•late \i-ˈnä-kyə-ˌlāt\ *vb* **-lat•ed; -lat•ing** : to introduce something into: as **a** : to introduce a serum or antibody into (an organism) to treat or prevent a disease **b** : to introduce information to — **in•oc•u•la•tion** \-ˌnä-kyə-ˈlā-shən\ *n*

in•op•er•a•ble \(ˌ)i-ˈnä-pə-rə-bəl\ *adj* **1** : not suitable for surgery **2** ♦ : not operable

♦ inoperative, nonfunctional ***Ant*** functional, functioning, operable, operating, operational, operative, running, working ♦ impractical, unusable, unworkable, useless

in•op•er•a•tive \-ˈnä-pə-rə-tiv, -ˈnä-pə-ˌrā-\ *adj* ♦ : not functioning

♦ dead, dormant, fallow, free, idle, inactive, inert, latent, off, vacant

in•op•por•tune \(ˌ)i-ˌnä-pər-ˈtün, -ˈtyün\ *adj* : not opportune : INCONVENIENT

in•op•por•tune•ly \-lē\ *adv* : in an inopportune manner

in•or•di•nate \i-ˈnȯrd-ᵊn-ət\ *adj* ♦ : exceeding reasonable limits : IMMODERATE ⟨an ~ curiosity⟩

♦ devilish, excessive, exorbitant, extravagant, extreme, immoderate, lavish, overmuch, overweening, steep, stiff, towering, unconscionable

in•or•di•nate•ly *adv* ♦ : to an excessive or unreasonable degree

♦ devilishly, excessively, monstrously, overly, overmuch, too

in•or•gan•ic \ˌi-ˌnȯr-ˈga-nik\ *adj* : being or composed of matter of other than plant or animal origin : MINERAL
in•pa•tient \ˈin-ˌpā-shənt\ *n* : a hospital patient who receives lodging and food as well as treatment
in•put \ˈin-ˌpu̇t\ *n* **1** : something put in **2** : power or energy put into a machine or system **3** : information fed into a computer or data processing system **4** ♦ : recommendation with regard to a course of action : ADVICE — **input** *vb*

♦ advice, counsel, guidance

in•quest \ˈin-ˌkwest\ *n* **1** : an official inquiry or examination especially before a jury **2** : a systematic investigation : INQUIRY, INVESTIGATION
in•qui•etude \(ˌ)in-ˈkwī-ə-ˌtüd, -ˌtyüd\ *n* : UNEASINESS, RESTLESSNESS
in•quire \in-ˈkwīr\ *vb* **in•quired; in•quir•ing** **1** ♦ : to ask or ask about **2** ♦ : to make investigation or inquiry : INVESTIGATE — often used with *into* — **in•quir•er** *n* — **in•quir•ing•ly** *adv*

♦ *usu* **inquire of** [1] ask, query, question, quiz ♦ *usu* **inquire into** [2] delve, dig, explore, go, investigate, look, probe, research

in•qui•ry \ˈin-ˌkwīr-ē, in-ˈkwīr-ē; ˈin-kwə-rē, ˈiŋ-\ *n, pl* **-ries** **1** ♦ : a request for information; *also* : RESEARCH **2** ♦ : a systematic investigation of a matter of public interest

♦ [1] query, question, request ♦ [2] examination, exploration, investigation, probe, research, study

in•qui•si•tion \ˌin-kwə-ˈzi-shən, ˌiŋ-\ *n* **1** : a judicial or official inquiry usually before a jury **2** *cap* : a former Roman Catholic tribunal for the discovery and punishment of heresy **3** : a severe questioning **4** : the act of inquiring — **in•quis•i•tor** \in-ˈkwi-zə-tər\ *n* — **in•quis•i•to•ri•al** \-ˌkwi-zə-ˈtōr-ē-əl\ *adj*
in•quis•i•tive \in-ˈkwi-zə-tiv\ *adj* **1** : given to examination or investigation ⟨an ~ mind⟩ **2** ♦ : unduly curious — **in•quis•i•tive•ly** *adv*

♦ curious, nosy, prying

in•quis•i•tive•ness *n* : the quality or state of being inquisitive
in re \in-ˈrā, -ˈrē\ *prep* : in the matter of
INRI *abbr* Jesus of Nazareth, King of the Jews
in•road \ˈin-ˌrōd\ *n* **1** : a sudden hostile incursion : INVASION, RAID **2** : an advance made usually at the expense of another
in•rush \ˈin-ˌrəsh\ *n* : a crowding or flooding in
ins *abbr* **1** inches **2** insurance
INS *abbr* Immigration and Naturalization Service
in•sa•lu•bri•ous \ˌin-sə-ˈlü-brē-əs\ *adj* : UNWHOLESOME, NOXIOUS
ins and outs *n pl* **1** : characteristic peculiarities **2** : RAMIFICATIONS
in•sane \(ˌ)in-ˈsān\ *adj* **1** ♦ : exhibiting serious and debilitating mental disorder; *also* : used by or for the insane **2** ♦ : ridiculously unreasonable, unsound, or incongruous : ABSURD — **in•sane•ly** *adv*

♦ [1] crazy, cuckoo, deranged, loco, lunatic, mad, nuts, nutty, screwy, unsound, wacky ***Ant*** balanced, sane, sound ♦ [2] absurd, bizarre, crazy, fanciful, fantastic, foolish, nonsensical, preposterous, unreal, wild

in•san•i•ty \in-ˈsa-nə-tē\ *n* **1** ♦ : a deranged state of the mind usually occurring as a specific disorder (as schizophrenia) **2** ♦ : extreme folly or unreasonableness; *also* : something utterly foolish or unreasonable

♦ [1] aberration, dementia, derangement, lunacy, madness, mania ***Ant*** mind, sanity ♦ [2] absurdity, asininity, balminess, craziness, daftness, fatuity, folly, foolishness, inanity, lunacy, madness, silliness, simplicity, zaniness

in•sa•tia•ble \(ˌ)in-ˈsā-shə-bəl\ *adj* : incapable of being satisfied — **in•sa•tia•bil•i•ty** \(ˌ)in-ˌsā-shə-ˈbi-lə-tē\ *n* — **in•sa•tia•bly** *adv*
in•sa•tiate \(ˌ)in-ˈsā-shē-ət, -shət\ *adj* : INSATIABLE — **in•sa•tiate•ly** *adv*
in•scribe \in-ˈskrīb\ *vb* **1** : to write, engrave, or print as a lasting record **2** ♦ : to enter on a list : ENROLL **3** ♦ : to write, engrave, or print characters upon **4** : to dedicate to someone **5** : to draw within a figure so as to touch in as many places as possible — **in•scrip•tion** \-ˈskrip-shən\ *n*

♦ [2] catalog, enroll, enter, index, list, put down, record, register, schedule, slate ♦ [3] engrave, etch, grave, inscribe

in•scru•ta•ble \in-ˈskrü-tə-bəl\ *adj* ♦ : not readily comprehensible : MYSTERIOUS — **in•scru•ta•bly** \-blē\ *adv*

♦ cryptic, darkling, deep, enigmatic, impenetrable, mysterious, mystic, occult, uncanny

in•seam \ˈin-ˌsēm\ *n* : the seam on the inside of the leg of a pair of pants; *also* : the length of this seam
in•sect \ˈin-ˌsekt\ *n* : any of a class of small usually winged arthropod animals (as flies, bees, beetles, and moths) with usually three pairs of legs as adults
in•sec•ti•cide \in-ˈsek-tə-ˌsīd\ *n* : an agent for destroying insects — **in•sec•ti•cid•al** \(ˌ)in-ˌsek-tə-ˈsīd-ˈl\ *adj*
in•sec•tiv•o•rous \ˌin-ˌsek-ˈti-və-rəs\ *adj* : feeding on insects
in•se•cure \ˌin-si-ˈkyu̇r\ *adj* **1** : UNCERTAIN **2** : not protected : UNSAFE **3** ♦ : not firmly fastened or fixed : LOOSE **4** : not highly stable; *also* : lacking assurance : ANXIOUS, FEARFUL — **in•se•cure•ly** *adv*

♦ lax, loose, relaxed, slack

in•se•cu•ri•ty \-ˈkyu̇r-ə-tē\ *n* ♦ : the quality or state of being insecure

♦ instability, precariousness, shakiness, unsteadiness

in•sem•i•nate \in-ˈse-mə-ˌnāt\ *vb* **-nat•ed; -nat•ing** : to introduce semen into the genital tract of (a female) — **in•sem•i•na•tion** \-ˌse-mə-ˈnā-shən\ *n*
in•sen•sate \(ˌ)in-ˈsen-ˌsāt, -sət\ *adj* **1** : lacking sense or understanding; *also* : FOOLISH **2** : INANIMATE **3** : lacking humane feeling : INHUMAN ⟨~ rage⟩
in•sen•si•bil•i•ty \-ˌsen-sə-ˈbi-lə-tē\ *n* : the quality or state of being insensible: as **a** : lack of mental or emotional feeling or response **b** : an unconscious or comatose state
in•sen•si•ble \(ˌ)in-ˈsen-sə-bəl\ *adj* **1** : not perceptible by a sense or by the mind : IMPERCEPTIBLE; *also* : SLIGHT, GRADUAL **2** : INANIMATE **3** : not knowing or perceiving : UNCONSCIOUS **4** : lacking sensory perception or ability to react ⟨~ to pain⟩ **5** : APATHETIC, INDIFFERENT; *also* : UNAWARE ⟨~ of their danger⟩ **6** : MEANINGLESS **7** : lacking delicacy or refinement — **in•sen•si•bly** \-ˈsen-sə-blē\ *adv*
in•sen•tient \(ˌ)in-ˈsen-chē-ənt\ *adj* : lacking perception, consciousness, or animation — **in•sen•tience** \-chē-əns\ *n*
in•sep•a•ra•bil•i•ty \-ˌse-prə-ˈbi-lə-tē, -pə-rə-\ *n* : the quality or state of being inseparable
in•sep•a•ra•ble \(ˌ)in-ˈse-prə-bəl, -pə-rə-\ *adj* **1** : incapable of being separated or disjoined **2** very close or intimate — **inseparable** *n* — **in•sep•a•ra•bly** \-ˈse-prə-blē, -pə-rə-\ *adv*
¹in•sert \in-ˈsərt\ *vb* **1** : to put or thrust in ⟨~ a key in a lock⟩ ⟨~ a comma⟩ **2** ♦ : to put or introduce into the body of something : INTERPOLATE **3** : to set in (as a piece of fabric) and make fast

♦ fit, inject, insinuate, interject, interpose, introduce

²in•sert \ˈin-ˌsərt\ *n* : something that is inserted or is for insertion; *esp* : written or printed material inserted (as between the leaves of a book)
in•ser•tion \in-ˈsər-shən\ *n* **1** : something that is inserted **2** : the act or process of inserting
in•set \ˈin-ˌset\ *vb* **inset** *or* **in•set•ted; in•set•ting** : to set in : INSERT — **inset** *n*
¹in•shore \ˈin-ˈshōr\ *adj* **1** : situated, living, or carried on near shore **2** : moving toward shore
²inshore *adv* : to or toward shore
¹in•side \in-ˈsīd, ˈin-ˌsīd\ *n* **1** : an inner side or surface : INTERIOR **2** : inward nature, thoughts, or feeling **3** *pl* : VISCERA, ENTRAILS **4** : a position of power, trust, or familiarity
²inside *adv* **1** : on the inner side **2** : in or into the interior
³inside *prep* **1** : in or into the inside of **2** : WITHIN ⟨~ an hour⟩
⁴inside *adj* **1** ♦ : of, relating to, or being on or near the inside **2** ♦ : relating or known to a select group

♦ [1] inner, interior, internal, inward ♦ [2] confidential, hushed, intimate, private, secret

inside of *prep* : INSIDE
inside out *adv* **1** : in such a manner that the inner surface becomes the outer ⟨turned the shirt *inside out*⟩ **2** : in a state of disarray or reorganization ⟨turned her life *inside out*⟩
in•sid•er \in-ˈsī-dər\ *n* : a person who is in a position of power or has access to confidential information
in•sid•i•ous \in-ˈsi-dē-əs\ *adj* **1** : SLY, TREACHEROUS **2** : SEDUCTIVE **3** : having a gradual and cumulative effect : SUBTLE — **in•sid•i•ous•ly** *adv* — **in•sid•i•ous•ness** *n*
in•sight \ˈin-ˌsīt\ *n* ♦ : the power, act, or result of seeing into a situation

♦ discernment, perception, sagacity, sapience, wisdom

in·sight·ful \ˈin-ˌsīt-fəl, in-ˈsīt-\ *adj* ♦ : exhibiting or characterized by insight

♦ discerning, perceptive, sagacious, sage, sapient, wise

in·sig·nia \in-ˈsig-nē-ə\ *also* **in·sig·ne** \-(ˌ)nē\ *n, pl* **-nia** *or* **-ni·as** : a distinguishing mark especially of authority or honor : BADGE

in·sig·nif·i·cant \-kənt\ *adj* : not significant: as **a** ♦ : lacking meaning or import **b** ♦ : not worth considering

♦ frivolous, inconsequential, inconsiderable, little, minor, minute, negligible, slight, small, trifling, trivial, unimportant

in·sin·cere \ˌin-sin-ˈsir\ *adj* ♦ : not sincere : HYPOCRITICAL — **in·sin·cere·ly** *adv*

♦ artificial, double-dealing, feigned, hypocritical, left-handed, mealy, mealymouthed, two-faced, unctuous ***Ant*** genuine, heartfelt, honest, sincere, unfeigned

in·sin·cer·i·ty \-ˈser-ə-tē\ *n* ♦ : the quality or state of being insincere

♦ cant, dissimulation, hypocrisy, piety

in·sin·u·ate \in-ˈsin-yə-ˌwāt\ *vb* **-at·ed; -at·ing** **1** ♦ : to introduce gradually or in a subtle, indirect, or artful way **2** ♦ : to imply in a subtle or devious way — **in·sin·u·a·tion** \(ˌ)in-ˌsin-yə-ˈwā-shən\ *n*

♦ [1] infiltrate, insert, interpose, introduce, slip, sneak, work, worm ♦ [2] allude, hint, imply, indicate, infer, intimate, suggest

in·sin·u·at·ing *adj* **1** : winning favor and confidence by imperceptible degrees **2** : tending gradually to cause doubt, distrust, or change of outlook

in·sip·id \in-ˈsi-pəd\ *adj* **1** ♦ : lacking taste or savor **2** ♦ : lacking in qualities that interest, stimulate, or challenge : FLAT — **in·si·pid·i·ty** \ˌin-sə-ˈpi-də-tē\ *n*

♦ [1] flat, flavorless (*or* flavourless), tasteless ***Ant*** flavorful, savory, tasty ♦ [2] banal, flat, wishy-washy

in·sist \in-ˈsist\ *vb* ♦ : to take a resolute stand

♦ affirm, allege, assert, aver, avouch, avow, claim, contend, declare, maintain, profess, protest, warrant ♦ *usu* **insist on** call, claim, clamor (*or* clamour), command, demand, enjoin, exact, press, quest, stipulate (for)

in·sis·tence \in-ˈsis-təns\ *n* : the act of insisting; *also* : an insistent attitude or quality : URGENCY

in·sis·tent \in-ˈsis-tənt\ *adj* ♦ : disposed to insist — **in·sis·tent·ly** *adv*

♦ dogged, patient, persevering, persistent, pertinacious, tenacious

in si·tu \in-ˈsī-tü, -ˈsē-\ *adv or adj* : in the natural or original position

in·so·far as \ˌin-sə-ˈfär-\ *conj* : to the extent or degree that

insol *abbr* insoluble

in·so·la·tion \ˌin-(ˌ)sō-ˈlā-shən\ *n* : solar radiation that has been received

in·sole \ˈin-ˌsōl\ *n* **1** : an inside sole of a shoe **2** : a loose thin strip placed inside a shoe for warmth or comfort

in·so·lence \-ləns\ *n* **1** : the quality or state of being insolent **2** ♦ : an instance of insolent conduct or treatment

♦ back talk, cheek, impertinence, impudence, sauce ♦ brazenness, discourtesy, disrespect, impertinence, impudence, incivility, rudeness

in·so·lent \ˈin-sə-lənt\ *adj* ♦ : contemptuous, rude, disrespectful, or bold in behavior or language

♦ bold, brash, fresh, impertinent, impudent, nervy, sassy, saucy

in·sol·u·ble \(ˌ)in-ˈsäl-yə-bəl\ *adj* **1** ♦ : having or admitting of no solution or explanation **2** : difficult or impossible to dissolve — **in·sol·u·bil·i·ty** \-ˌsäl-yə-ˈbi-lə-tē\ *n*

♦ hopeless, impossible, unattainable, unsolvable

in·sol·vent \(ˌ)in-ˈsäl-vənt\ *adj* **1** : unable or insufficient to pay all debts ⟨an ~ estate⟩ **2** : IMPOVERISHED, DEFICIENT — **in·sol·ven·cy** \-vən-sē\ *n*

in·som·nia \in-ˈsäm-nē-ə\ *n* : prolonged and usually abnormal sleeplessness — **in·som·ni·ac** \-nē-ˌak\ *n*

in·so·much as \ˌin-sə-ˈməch-\ *conj* : INASMUCH AS

insomuch that *conj* : to such a degree that : SO

in·sou·ci·ance \in-ˈsü-sē-əns, a^{n}-süs-ˈyä^{n}s\ *n* ♦ : lighthearted unconcern

♦ apathy, disinterestedness, disregard, indifference, nonchalance

in·sou·ci·ant \in-ˈsü-sē-ənt, a^{n}-süs-ˈyä^{n}\ *adj* ♦ : exhibiting or characterized by insouciance

♦ carefree, careless, cavalier, easygoing, gay, happy-go-lucky, lighthearted, nonchalant, unconcerned

insp *abbr* inspector

in·spect \in-ˈspekt\ *vb* ♦ : to view closely and critically : EXAMINE — **in·spec·tor** \-tər\ *n*

♦ audit, check, examine, review, scan, scrutinize, survey

in·spec·tion \-ˈspek-shən\ *n* **1** : the act of inspecting **2** ♦ : a checking or testing of an individual against established standards

♦ audit, check, checkup, examination, review, scan, scrutiny, survey

inspector general *n* : the head of a system of inspection (as of an army)

in·spi·ra·tion \ˌin-spə-ˈrā-shən\ *n* **1** : the act or power of moving the intellect or emotions **2** : INHALATION **3** : the quality or state of being inspired; *also* : something that is inspired **4** : an inspiring agent or influence — **in·spi·ra·tion·al** \-shə-nəl\ *adj*

in·spire \in-ˈspīr\ *vb* **in·spired; in·spir·ing** **1** : to influence, move, or guide by divine or supernatural inspiration **2** ♦ : to exert an animating, enlivening, or exalting influence upon; *also* : AFFECT **3** : to communicate to an agent supernaturally; *also* : to bring out or about **4** : INHALE **5** : INCITE **6** : to spread by indirect means — **in·spir·er** *n*

♦ buoy (up), cheer, comfort, embolden, encourage, hearten, steel

in·spir·it \in-ˈspir-ət\ *vb* : ENCOURAGE, HEARTEN

inst *abbr* **1** instant **2** institute; institution; institutional

in·sta·bil·i·ty \ˌin-stə-ˈbi-lə-tē\ *n* ♦ : lack of steadiness; *esp* : lack of emotional or mental stability

♦ insecurity, precariousness, shakiness, unsteadiness ***Ant*** fixedness, security, stability, steadiness

in·stall *or* **in·stal** \in-ˈstȯl\ *vb* **in·stalled; in·stall·ing** **1** ♦ : to place formally in office : induct into an office, rank, or order **2** ♦ : to establish in an indicated place, condition, or status **3** : to set up for use or service

♦ [1] baptize, inaugurate, induct, initiate, invest ♦ [2] ensconce, lodge, perch, roost, settle

in·stal·la·tion \ˌin-stə-ˈlā-shən\ *n* **1** ♦ : the act of installing : the state of being installed **2** ♦ : a military camp, fort, or base

♦ [1] inaugural, inauguration, induction, investiture ♦ [2] complex, establishment, facility

[1]in·stall·ment *also* **in·stal·ment** \in-ˈstȯl-mənt\ *n* : INSTALLATION

[2]installment *also* **instalment** *n* **1** : one of the parts into which a debt or sum is divided for payment **2** : one of several parts presented at intervals

[1]in·stance \ˈin-stəns\ *n* **1** : INSTIGATION, REQUEST **2** ♦ : an individual illustrative of a category or brought forward in support or disproof of a generalization : EXAMPLE ⟨for ~⟩ **3** : an event or step that is part of a process or series

♦ case, example, exemplar, illustration, representative, sample, specimen

[2]instance *vb* **in·stanced; in·stanc·ing** **1** ♦ : to mention as a case or example **2** ♦ : to explain by reference to examples

♦ [1] advert (to), cite, mention, name, note, notice, quote, refer (to), specify, touch (*on* or *upon*) ♦ [2] demonstrate, exemplify, illustrate

[1]in·stant \ˈin-stənt\ *n* **1** ♦ : an immeasurably small space of time : MOMENT ⟨the ~ we met⟩ **2** : the present or current month

♦ flash, jiffy, minute, moment, second, shake, trice, twinkle, twinkling, wink

[2]instant *adj* **1** : calling for immediate attention : URGENT **2** : PRESENT, CURRENT **3** : occurring, acting, or accomplished without loss or interval of time : IMMEDIATE ⟨~ relief⟩ **4** : premixed or precooked for easy final preparation ⟨~ cake mix⟩; *also* : immediately soluble in water ⟨~ coffee⟩

in·stan·ta·neous \ˌin-stən-ˈtā-nē-əs\ *adj* ♦ : done or occurring in an instant or without delay — **in·stan·ta·neous·ly** *adv*

♦ immediate, instant, straightaway

in·stan·ter \in-ˈstan-tər\ *adv* : at once

in·stan·ti·ate \in-ˈstan-chē-ˌāt\ *vb* **-at·ed; -at·ing** : to represent

(an abstraction) by a concrete example — **in•stan•ti•a•tion** \-ˌstan-chē-ˈā-shən\ *n*
in•stant•ly \ˈin-stənt-lē\ *adv* ♦ : at once : IMMEDIATELY

♦ directly, forthwith, immediately, now, promptly, pronto, right away, right now

in•state \in-ˈstāt\ *vb* : to establish in a rank or office : INSTALL
in•stead \in-ˈsted\ *adv* **1** : as a substitute or equivalent **2** : as an alternative : RATHER
instead of *prep* : as a substitute for or alternative to
in•step \ˈin-ˌstep\ *n* : the arched part of the human foot in front of the ankle joint; *esp* : its upper surface
in•sti•gate \ˈin-stə-ˌgāt\ *vb* **-gat•ed; -gat•ing** ♦ : to goad or urge forward : PROVOKE, INCITE ⟨~ a revolt⟩

♦ abet, ferment, foment, incite, provoke, raise, stir, whip

in•sti•ga•tion \ˌin-stə-ˈgā-shən\ *n* **1** : an act of instigating or the state of being instigated **2** ♦ : something that instigates

♦ boost, encouragement, goad, impetus, impulse, incentive, incitement, momentum, motivation, provocation, spur, stimulus, yeast

in•sti•ga•tor \ˈin-stə-ˌgā-tər\ *n* : one that instigates
in•stil *chiefly Brit var of* INSTILL
in•still \in-ˈstil\ *vb* **in•stilled; in•still•ing** **1** : to cause to enter drop by drop **2** : to impart gradually
¹in•stinct \ˈin-ˌstiŋkt\ *n* **1** : a natural aptitude **2** : a largely inheritable and unalterable tendency of an organism to make a complex and specific response to environmental stimuli without involving reason; *also* : behavior originating below the conscious level
²in•stinct \in-ˈstiŋkt, ˈin-ˌstiŋkt\ *adj* : IMBUED, INFUSED
in•stinc•tive \in-ˈstiŋk-tiv\ *adj* **1** : of, relating to, or being instinct **2** : prompted by natural instinct or propensity : arising spontaneously — **in•stinc•tive•ly** *adv*
in•stinc•tu•al \in-ˈstiŋk-chə-wəl\ *adj* : of, relating to, or based on instinct
¹in•sti•tute \ˈin-stə-ˌtüt, -ˌtyüt\ *vb* **-tut•ed; -tut•ing** **1** : to establish in a position or office **2** : ORGANIZE **3** ♦ : to bring about the beginning of : INAUGURATE, INITIATE

♦ constitute, establish, found, inaugurate, initiate, innovate, introduce, launch, pioneer, set up, start

²institute *n* **1** : an elementary principle recognized as authoritative; *also, pl* : a collection of such principles and precepts **2** ♦ : an organization for the promotion of a cause : ASSOCIATION **3** : an educational institution **4** : a brief course of instruction on a particular field

♦ association, brotherhood, club, college, congress, council, fellowship, fraternity, guild, institution, league, order, organization, society

in•sti•tu•tion \ˌin-stə-ˈtü-shən, -ˈtyü-\ *n* **1** : an act of originating, setting up, or founding **2** : an established practice, law, or custom **3** ♦ : a society or corporation especially of a public character ⟨a charitable ~⟩ **4** : ASYLUM 3 — **in•sti•tu•tion•al** \-ˈtü-shə-nəl, -ˈtyü-\ *adj* — **in•sti•tu•tion•al•ize** \-nə-ˌlīz\ *vb* — **in•sti•tu•tion•al•ly** *adv*

♦ establishment, foundation, institute

instr *abbr* **1** instructor **2** instrument; instrumental
in•struct \in-ˈstrəkt\ *vb* **1** ♦ : to give knowledge to : TEACH **2** ♦ : to provide with authoritative information or advice : INFORM **3** ♦ : to give an order or a command to

♦ [1] educate, indoctrinate, school, teach, train, tutor ♦ [2] acquaint, advise, apprise, brief, clue, enlighten, familiarize, fill in, inform, tell, wise ♦ [3] bid, boss, charge, command, direct, enjoin, order, tell

in•struc•tion \in-ˈstrək-shən\ *n* **1** : LESSON, PRECEPT **2** ♦ : a direction calling for compliance : COMMAND, ORDER **3** *pl* : DIRECTIONS **4** ♦ : the action, practice, or profession of a teacher

♦ [2] behest, charge, command, commandment, decree, dictate, direction, directive, edict, order, word ♦ [4] education, teaching, training, tutelage

in•struc•tion•al \-shə-nəl\ *adj* **1** : relating to, serving for, or promoting instruction **2** : containing or conveying instruction or information
in•struc•tive \in-ˈstrək-tiv\ *adj* ♦ : carrying a lesson

♦ educational, informative

in•struc•tor \in-ˈstrək-tər\ *n* ♦ : one that instructs; *esp* : a college teacher below professorial rank — **in•struc•tor•ship** *n*

♦ educator, pedagogue, schoolteacher, teacher

in•stru•ment \ˈin-strə-mənt\ *n* **1** : a device used to produce music **2** ♦ : a means by which something is done **3** ♦ : a device for doing work and especially precision work **4** : a legal document (as a deed) **5** : a device used in navigating an airplane — **in•stru•ment** \-ˌment\ *vb*

♦ [2] agency, agent, instrumentality, machinery, means, medium, organ, vehicle ♦ [3] device, implement, tool, utensil

in•stru•men•tal \ˌin-strə-ˈment-ᵊl\ *adj* **1** : acting as a crucial agent or means **2** : of, relating to, or done with an instrument **3** : relating to, composed for, or performed on a musical instrument
in•stru•men•tal•ist \-ˈmen-tə-list\ *n* : a player on a musical instrument
in•stru•men•tal•i•ty \ˌin-strə-mən-ˈta-lə-tē, -ˌmen-\ *n, pl* **-ties** **1** : the quality or state of being instrumental **2** ♦ : something useful or helpful to a desired end : MEANS, AGENCY

♦ agency, agent, instrument, machinery, means, medium, organ, vehicle

in•stru•men•ta•tion \ˌin-strə-mən-ˈtā-shən, -ˌmen-\ *n* **1** : ORCHESTRATION **2** : instruments for a particular purpose
instrument panel *n* : DASHBOARD
in•sub•or•di•nate \ˌin-sə-ˈbȯrd-ᵊn-ət\ *adj* : disobedient to authority
in•sub•or•di•na•tion \-ˌbȯrd-ᵊn-ˈā-shən\ *n* ♦ : the quality or state of being insubordinate : defiance of authority

♦ defiance, disobedience, rebelliousness, recalcitrance, refractoriness, unruliness

in•sub•stan•tial \ˌin-səb-ˈstan-chəl\ *adj* **1** : lacking substance or reality **2** ♦ : lacking firmness or solidity

♦ flimsy, gauzy, unsubstantial

in•suf•fer•able \(ˌ)in-ˈsə-fə-rə-bəl\ *adj* ♦ : not to be endured : INTOLERABLE ⟨an ~ bore⟩ — **in•suf•fer•ably** \-blē\ *adv*

♦ insupportable, intolerable, unbearable, unendurable, unsupportable

in•suf•fi•cien•cy \-shən-sē\ *n* : the quality or state of being insufficient: as **a** : lack of mental or moral fitness **b** ♦ : lack of adequate supply

♦ dearth, deficiency, deficit, failure, famine, inadequacy, lack, paucity, poverty, scantiness, scarcity, shortage, want

in•suf•fi•cient \ˌin-sə-ˈfi-shənt\ *adj* ♦ : not sufficient — **in•suf•fi•cient•ly** *adv*

♦ deficient, inadequate, scarce, short, shy, wanting

in•su•lar \ˈin-sə-lər, -syə-\ *adj* **1** : of, relating to, or forming an island **2** : dwelling or situated on an island **3** ♦ : being, having, or reflecting a narrow provincial viewpoint : NARROW-MINDED — **in•su•lar•i•ty** \ˌin-sə-ˈlar-ə-tē, -syə-\ *n*

♦ little, narrow, narrow-minded, parochial, petty, provincial, sectarian, small

in•su•late \ˈin-sə-ˌlāt\ *vb* **-lat•ed; -lat•ing** **1** ♦ : to place in a detached situation : ISOLATE **2** : to separate a conductor of electricity, heat, or sound from other conducting bodies by means of a nonconductor — **in•su•la•tor** \ˈin-sə-ˌlā-tər\ *n*

♦ cut off, isolate, seclude, segregate, separate, sequester

in•su•la•tion \ˌin-sə-ˈlā-shən\ *n* **1 a** : the action of insulating **b** ♦ : the state of being insulated **2** : material used in insulating

♦ isolation, seclusion, segregation, sequestration, solitude

in•su•lin \ˈin-sə-lən\ *n* : a pancreatic hormone essential especially for the metabolism of carbohydrates and the regulation of glucose in the blood
¹in•sult \in-ˈsəlt\ *vb* ♦ : to treat with insolence or contempt : AFFRONT — **in•sult•ing•ly** *adv*

♦ affront, offend, outrage, slight, wound

²in•sult \ˈin-ˌsəlt\ *n* ♦ : a gross indignity

♦ affront, barb, dart, dig, indignity, name, offense, outrage, put-down, sarcasm, slight, slur, wound

in•su•per•a•ble \(ˌ)in-ˈsü-pə-rə-bəl\ *adj* ♦ : incapable of being surmounted, overcome, passed over, or solved — **in•su•per•a•bly** \-blē\ *adv*

♦ impregnable, indomitable, insurmountable, invincible, invulnerable, unbeatable, unconquerable

in•sup•port•able \ˌin-sə-ˈpōr-tə-bəl\ *adj* **1** ♦ : more than can be endured : UNENDURABLE **2** : UNJUSTIFIABLE

♦ insufferable, intolerable, unbearable, unendurable, unsupportable

in•sur•able \in-ˈshu̇-rə-bəl\ *adj* : capable of being or proper to be insured
in•sur•ance \in-ˈshu̇r-əns\ *n* **1** : the business of insuring persons or property **2** : coverage by contract whereby one party agrees to guarantee another against a specified loss **3** : the sum for which something is insured **4** : a means of guaranteeing protection or safety
in•sure \in-ˈshu̇r\ *vb* **in•sured; in•sur•ing** **1** : to provide or obtain insurance on or for : UNDERWRITE **2** ♦ : to make certain : ENSURE

♦ assure, cinch, ensure, guarantee, guaranty, secure

in•sured \in-ˈshu̇rd\ *n* : a person whose life or property is insured
in•sur•er \in-ˈshu̇r-ər\ *n* : one that insures; *esp* : an insurance company
in•sur•gen•cy \-jən-sē\ *n* : the quality or state of being insurgent; *specif* : a condition of revolt against a government that is less than an organized revolution and that is not recognized as belligerency
[1]**in•sur•gent** \in-ˈsər-jənt\ *n* **1** : a person who revolts against civil authority or an established government : REBEL **2** : a member of a political party who rebels against it — **in•sur•gence** \-jəns\ *n*
[2]**in•sur•gent** *adj* ♦ : rising in opposition to civil authority or established leadership

♦ mutinous, rebellious, revolutionary

in•sur•mount•able \ˌin-sər-ˈmau̇n-tə-bəl\ *adj* ♦ : incapable of being surmounted, overcome, passed over, or solved — **in•sur•mount•ably** \-blē\ *adv*

♦ impregnable, indomitable, invincible, invulnerable, unbeatable, unconquerable

in•sur•rec•tion \ˌin-sə-ˈrek-shən\ *n* ♦ : an act or instance of revolting against civil authority or an established government

♦ mutiny, rebellion, revolt, revolution, uprising

in•sur•rec•tion•ist \-shə-nist\ *n* ♦ : a favorer of or participant in insurrection

♦ insurgent, mutineer, rebel, red, revolter, revolutionary

int *abbr* **1** interest **2** interior **3** intermediate **4** internal **5** international **6** intransitive
in•tact \in-ˈtakt\ *adj* **1** : untouched especially by anything that harms or diminishes **2** ♦ : being complete or entire

♦ complete, comprehensive, entire, full, grand, integral, perfect, plenary, total, whole

in•ta•glio \in-ˈtal-yō\ *n, pl* **-glios** : an engraving cut deeply into the surface of a hard material (as stone)
in•take \ˈin-ˌtāk\ *n* **1** : an opening through which fluid enters **2** : the act of taking in **3** : something taken in
in•tan•gi•ble \(ˌ)in-ˈtan-jə-bəl\ *adj* : incapable of being touched : IMPALPABLE — **intangible** *n* — **in•tan•gi•bly** \-blē\ *adv*
in•te•ger \ˈin-ti-jər\ *n* ♦ : a number (as 1, 2, 3, 12, 432) that is not a fraction and does not include a fraction, is the negative of such a number, or is 0

♦ digit, figure, number, numeral, whole number

in•te•gral \ˈin-ti-grəl\ *adj* **1** ♦ : essential to completeness **2** : formed as a unit with another part **3** : composed of parts that make up a whole **4** ♦ : lacking nothing essential : ENTIRE **5** ♦ : being or involved in the essential nature of a thing

♦ [1] essential, imperative, indispensable, necessary, needful, requisite, vital ♦ [4] complete, comprehensive, entire, full, grand, intact, perfect, plenary, total, whole ♦ [5] essential, inborn, ingrained, inherent, innate, intrinsic, natural

integral calculus *n* : calculus concerned especially with advanced methods of finding lengths, areas, and volumes
in•te•grate \ˈin-tə-ˌgrāt\ *vb* **-grat•ed; -grat•ing** **1** ♦ : to form, coordinate, or blend into a functioning whole **2** ♦ : to incorporate into a larger unit **3** : to end the segregation of and bring into equal membership in society or an organization; *also* : DESEGREGATE — **in•te•gra•tion** \ˌin-tə-ˈgrā-shən\ *n*

♦ [1] assimilate, embody, incorporate ♦ [2] amalgamate, blend, combine, commingle, fuse, incorporate, intermingle, merge, mingle, mix

integrated circuit *n* : a group of tiny electronic components and their connections that is produced in or on a small slice of material (as silicon)
in•teg•ri•ty \in-ˈte-grə-tē\ *n* **1** ♦ : adherence to a code of values **2** : SOUNDNESS **3** : COMPLETENESS

♦ character, decency, goodness, honesty, honor (*or* honour), morality, probity, rectitude, righteousness, uprightness, virtue

in•teg•u•ment \in-ˈte-gyə-mənt\ *n* : a covering layer (as a skin or cuticle) of an organism or one of its parts
in•tel•lect \ˈin-tə-ˌlekt\ *n* **1** : the power of knowing : the capacity for knowledge **2** : the capacity for rational or intelligent thought especially when highly developed **3** ♦ : a person with great intellectual powers

♦ brain, genius, thinker, whiz, wizard

[1]**in•tel•lec•tu•al** \ˌin-tə-ˈlek-chə-wəl\ *adj* **1** ♦ : of, relating to, or performed by the intellect **2** ♦ : given to study, reflection, and speculation **3** : engaged in activity requiring the creative use of the intellect — **in•tel•lec•tu•al•ly** *adv*

♦ [1] cerebral, inner, mental, psychological ♦ [2] cerebral, erudite, learned, literate, scholarly *Ant* lowbrow, nonintellectual

[2]**intellectual** *n* ♦ : an intellectual person

♦ egghead, highbrow, nerd *Ant* lowbrow, philistine

in•tel•lec•tu•al•ism \-chə-wə-ˌli-zəm\ *n* : devotion to the exercise of intellect or to intellectual pursuits
in•tel•lec•tu•al•i•ty \ˌin-tə-ˌlek-chə-ˈwa-lə-tē\ *n* : the quality or state of being intellectual
in•tel•li•gence \in-ˈte-lə-jəns\ *n* **1** ♦ : ability to learn and understand or to deal with new or trying situations **2** : mental acuteness **3** : INFORMATION, NEWS **4** : an agency engaged in obtaining information especially concerning an enemy or possible enemy; *also* : the information so gained

♦ brains, gray matter (*or* grey matter), intellect, reason, sense

intelligence quotient *n* : IQ
in•tel•li•gent \in-ˈte-lə-jənt\ *adj* ♦ : having or showing intelligence or intellect — **in•tel•li•gent•ly** *adv*

♦ alert, brainy, bright, brilliant, clever, keen, nimble, quick, quick-witted, sharp, smart *Ant* brainless, dumb, mindless, stupid, thick, unintelligent ♦ rational, reasonable, reasoning

in•tel•li•gen•tsia \in-ˌte-lə-ˈjent-sē-ə, -ˈgent-\ *n* : intellectuals forming a vanguard or elite
in•tel•li•gi•ble \in-ˈte-lə-jə-bəl\ *adj* : capable of being understood or comprehended — **in•tel•li•gi•bil•i•ty** \-ˌte-lə-jə-ˈbi-lə-tē\ *n* — **in•tel•li•gi•bly** \-ˈte-lə-jə-blē\ *adv*
in•tem•per•ance \(ˌ)in-ˈtem-pə-rəns\ *n* : lack of moderation; *esp* : habitual or excessive drinking of intoxicants — **in•tem•per•ate•ness** *n*
in•tem•per•ate \-pə-rət\ *adj* ♦ : not temperate; *also* : given to excessive use of intoxicating liquors

♦ rampant, unbridled, unchecked, uncontrolled, ungoverned, unhampered, unhindered, unrestrained

in•tend \in-ˈtend\ *vb* **1** ♦ : to have in mind as a purpose or aim **2** : to design for a specified use or future

♦ aim, aspire, contemplate, design, mean, meditate, plan, propose

in•ten•dant \in-ˈten-dənt\ *n* : an official (as a governor) especially under the French, Spanish, or Portuguese monarchies
[1]**in•tend•ed** *adj* **1** : expected to be such in the future; *esp* : BETROTHED **2** : INTENTIONAL
[2]**intended** *n* ♦ : an engaged person

♦ betrothed

in•tense \in-ˈtens\ *adj* **1** ♦ : existing in an extreme degree **2** : marked by great zeal, energy, or eagerness **3** : showing strong feeling; *also* : deeply felt

♦ deep, explosive, exquisite, fearful, ferocious, fierce, furious, hard, heavy, profound, terrible, vehement, vicious, violent *Ant* light, moderate, soft

in•tense•ly \-lē\ *adv* : in an intense manner
in•ten•si•fy \in-ˈten-sə-ˌfī\ *vb* **-fied; -fy•ing** **1** ♦ : to make or become intense or more intensive **2** : to make more acute : SHARPEN — **in•ten•si•fi•ca•tion** \-ˌten-sə-fə-ˈkā-shən\ *n*

♦ amplify, beef, boost, consolidate, deepen, enhance, heighten, magnify, redouble, step up, strengthen *Ant* abate, moderate

in•ten•si•ty \in-ˈten-sə-tē\ *n, pl* **-ties** ♦ : the quality or state of being intense; *esp* : degree of strength, energy, or force

♦ ardor, emotion, fervency, fervor, heat, passion, vehemence, warmth

[1]**in•ten•sive** \in-ˈten-siv\ *adj* **1** : marked by intensity : highly concentrated **2** : serving to give emphasis

[2]**intensive** *n* : an intensive word, particle, or prefix

intensive care *n* : continuous monitoring and treatment of seriously ill patients; *also* : an area of a hospital providing this treatment

in•ten•sive•ly \-lē\ *adv* : in an intensive manner

[1]**in•tent** \in-ˈtent\ *n* **1** : the state of mind with which an act is done : VOLITION **2** ♦ : a usually clearly formulated or planned intention : PURPOSE, AIM **3** ♦ : the thing that is conveyed or intended to be conveyed especially by language : MEANING, SIGNIFICANCE

♦ [2] aim, ambition, aspiration, design, dream, end, goal, mark, meaning, object, objective, plan, pretension, purpose, thing ♦ [3] denotation, drift, import, meaning, purport, sense, significance, signification

[2]**intent** *adj* **1** : directed with keen attention ⟨an ~ gaze⟩ **2** ♦ : having the mind, attention, or will concentrated on something or some end or purpose

♦ bound, decisive, determined, firm, purposeful, resolute, set, single-minded ♦ absorbed, attentive, engrossed, observant, rapt

in•ten•tion \in-ˈten-chən\ *n* **1** : a determination to act in a certain way **2** : what one intends to do or bring about : PURPOSE, AIM

in•ten•tion•al \in-ˈten-chə-nəl\ *adj* ♦ : done by intention or design : INTENDED

♦ deliberate, freewill, purposeful, voluntary, willful, willing

in•ten•tion•al•ly *adv* ♦ : in an intentional manner : with intention

♦ consciously, deliberately, knowingly, purposely, willfully *Ant* inadvertently, unconsciously, unintentionally, unknowingly, unwittingly

in•tent•ly *adv* : in an intent manner

in•tent•ness *n* ♦ : the quality or state of being intent

♦ earnest, earnestness, gravity, seriousness, sobriety, solemnity

in•ter \in-ˈtər\ *vb* **in•terred; in•ter•ring** : BURY

in•ter•ac•tion \ˌin-tər-ˈak-shən\ *n* : mutual or reciprocal action or influence — **in•ter•act** \-ˈakt\ *vb*

in•ter•ac•tive \-ˈak-tiv\ *adj* **1** : mutually or reciprocally active **2** : allowing two-way electronic communications (as between a person and a computer) — **in•ter•ac•tive•ly** *adv*

in•ter alia \ˌin-tər-ˈā-lē-ə, -ˈä-\ *adv* : among other things

in•ter•atom•ic \ˌin-tər-ə-ˈtä-mik\ *adj* : existing or acting between atoms

in•ter•breed \-ˈbrēd\ *vb* **-bred** \-ˈbred\; **-breed•ing** : to breed together

in•ter•ca•la•ry \in-ˈtər-kə-ˌler-ē\ *adj* **1** : INTERCALATED ⟨February 29 is an ~ day⟩ **2** : INTERPOLATED

in•ter•ca•late \-ˌlāt\ *vb* **-lat•ed; -lat•ing** **1** : to insert (as a day) in a calendar **2** : to insert between or among existing elements or layers — **in•ter•ca•la•tion** \-ˌtər-kə-ˈlā-shən\ *n*

in•ter•cede \ˌin-tər-ˈsēd\ *vb* **-ced•ed; -ced•ing** ♦ : to act between parties with a view to reconciling differences

♦ interpose, intervene, mediate

[1]**in•ter•cept** \ˌin-tər-ˈsept\ *vb* **1** : to stop or interrupt the progress or course of **2** : to include (as part of a curve or solid) between two points, curves, or surfaces **3** : to gain possession of (an opponent's pass in football) — **in•ter•cep•tion** \-ˈsep-shən\ *n*

[2]**in•ter•cept** \ˈin-tər-ˌsept\ *n* : INTERCEPTION; *esp* : the interception of a target by an interceptor or missile

in•ter•cep•tor \ˌin-tər-ˈsep-tər\ *n* : a fighter plane designed for defense against attacking bombers

in•ter•ces•sion \ˌin-tər-ˈse-shən\ *n* **1** : MEDIATION **2** : prayer or petition in favor of another — **in•ter•ces•so•ry** \-ˈse-sə-rē\ *adj*

in•ter•ces•sor \-ˈse-sər\ *n* ♦ : one who intercedes

♦ arbiter, arbitrator, broker, go-between, intermediary, mediator, middleman, peacemaker

[1]**in•ter•change** \ˌin-tər-ˈchānj\ *vb* **1** : to put each in the place of the other **2** : EXCHANGE **3** : to change places mutually — **in•ter•change•able** \-ˈchān-jə-bəl\ *adj* — **in•ter•change•ably** \-blē\ *adv*

[2]**in•ter•change** \ˈin-tər-ˌchānj\ *n* **1** : EXCHANGE **2** : a highway junction that by separated levels permits passage between highways without crossing traffic streams

in•ter•col•le•giate \ˌin-tər-kə-ˈlē-jət\ *adj* : existing or carried on between colleges

in•ter•com \ˈin-tər-ˌkäm\ *n* : a two-way system for localized communication

in•ter•con•nect \ˌin-tər-kə-ˈnekt\ *vb* ♦ : to connect with one another — **in•ter•con•nec•tion** \-ˈnek-shən\ *n*

♦ chain, compound, connect, couple, hitch, hook, join, link, yoke

in•ter•con•ti•nen•tal \-ˌkänt-ᵊn-ˈent-ᵊl\ *adj* **1** : extending among or carried on between continents ⟨~ trade⟩ **2** : capable of traveling between continents ⟨~ ballistic missiles⟩

in•ter•course \ˈin-tər-ˌkōrs\ *n* **1** ♦ : connection or dealings between persons or nations **2** ♦ : physical sexual contact between individuals that involves the genitalia of at least one person ⟨anal ~⟩; *esp* : SEXUAL INTERCOURSE

♦ [1] dealings, relations ♦ [2] copulation, sexual intercourse

in•ter•de•nom•i•na•tion•al \ˌin-tər-di-ˌnä-mə-ˈnā-shə-nəl\ *adj* : involving different denominations

in•ter•de•part•men•tal \ˌin-tər-di-ˌpärt-ˈment-ᵊl, -ˌdē-\ *adj* : carried on between or involving different departments (as of a college)

in•ter•de•pen•dent \ˌin-tər-di-ˈpen-dənt\ *adj* : dependent upon one another — **in•ter•de•pen•dence** \-dəns\ *n*

in•ter•dict \ˌin-tər-ˈdikt\ *vb* **1** ♦ : to prohibit by decree **2** : to destroy, cut off, or damage (as an enemy line of supply) **3** : INTERCEPT

♦ ban, bar, enjoin, forbid, outlaw, prohibit, proscribe

in•ter•dic•tion \-ˈdik-shən\ *n* ♦ : the act of interdicting or state of being interdicted; *also* : a prohibitory decree

♦ barring, forbidding, prohibition, proscription

in•ter•dis•ci•plin•ary \-ˈdi-sə-plə-ˌner-ē\ *adj* : involving two or more academic, scientific, or artistic disciplines

[1]**in•ter•est** \ˈin-trəst; ˈin-tə-rəst, -ˌrest\ *n* **1** ♦ : right, title, or legal share in something **2** : a charge for borrowed money that is generally a percentage of the amount borrowed; *also* : the return received by capital on its investment **3 a** ♦ : a benefit resulting from some course of action : WELFARE **b** : SELF-INTEREST **4** : CURIOSITY, CONCERN **5** : readiness to be concerned with or moved by an object or class of objects **6** : a quality in a thing that arouses interest

♦ [1] claim, share, stake ♦ [3a] good, weal, welfare, well-being

[2]**interest** *vb* **1** : to persuade to participate or engage **2** ♦ : to engage the attention of

♦ absorb, busy, engage, engross, enthrall, fascinate, grip, immerse, intrigue, involve, occupy

in•ter•est•ing *adj* ♦ : holding the attention — **in•ter•est•ing•ly** *adv*

♦ absorbing, engaging, engrossing, enthralling, fascinating, intriguing *Ant* boring, drab, dry, dull, heavy, monotonous, tedious, uninteresting

[1]**in•ter•face** \ˈin-tər-ˌfās\ *n* **1** : a surface forming a common boundary of two bodies, spaces, or phases ⟨an oil-water ~⟩ **2** : the place at which two independent systems meet and act on or communicate with each other ⟨the man-machine ~⟩ **3** : the means by which interaction or communication is achieved at an interface — **in•ter•fa•cial** \ˌin-tər-ˈfā-shəl\ *adj*

[2]**interface** *vb* **-faced; -fac•ing** **1** : to connect by means of an interface **2** : to serve as an interface

in•ter•faith \ˌin-tər-ˈfāth\ *adj* : involving persons of different religious faiths

in•ter•fere \ˌin-tər-ˈfir\ *vb* **-fered; -fer•ing** **1** ♦ : to come in collision or be in opposition : to interpose in a way that hinders or impedes **2** ♦ : to take an unwarranted active part in the affairs of others **3** : to affect one another

♦ *usu* **interfere with** [1] encumber, hamper, hinder, hold up, impede, inhibit, obstruct, tie up ♦ [2] butt in, intrude, meddle, mess, nose, obtrude, poke, pry, snoop

in•ter•fer•ence \-ˈfir-əns\ *n* **1** : the act or process of interfering **2** ♦ : something that interferes : OBSTRUCTION **3** : the mutual effect on meeting of two waves resulting in areas of increased and decreased amplitude **4** : the blocking of an opponent in football to make way for the ballcarrier **5** : the illegal hindering of an opponent in sports

♦ bar, block, encumbrance, hindrance, inhibition, obstacle

in•ter•fer•om•e•ter \ˌin-tər-fə-ˈrä-mə-tər\ *n* : an apparatus that uses the interference of waves (as of light) for making precise measurements — **in•ter•fer•om•e•try** \-fə-ˈrä-mə-trē\ *n*

in•ter•fer•on \ˌin-tər-ˈfir-ˌän\ *n* : any of a group of antiviral proteins of low molecular weight produced usually by animal cells in response to a virus, a parasite in the cell, or a chemical

in·ter·ga·lac·tic \ˌin-tər-gə-ˈlak-tik\ *adj* **:** relating to or situated in the spaces between galaxies
in·ter·gen·er·a·tion·al \-ˌje-nə-ˈrā-shə-nəl\ *adj* **:** existing or occurring between generations
in·ter·gla·cial \-ˈglā-shəl\ *n* **:** a warm period between successive glaciations
in·ter·gov·ern·men·tal \-ˌgə-vərn-ˈment-ᵊl\ *adj* **:** existing or occurring between two governments or levels of government
¹in·ter·im \ˈin-tə-rəm\ *n* ♦ **:** a time intervening **:** INTERVAL

♦ discontinuity, gap, hiatus, interlude, intermission, interruption, interval

²interim *adj* **:** done, made, appointed, or occurring for an interim

♦ impermanent, provisional, short-term, temporary

¹in·te·ri·or \in-ˈtir-ē-ər\ *adj* **1** ♦ **:** lying, occurring, or functioning within the limiting boundaries **:** INSIDE **2 :** remote from the surface, border, or shore **:** INLAND

♦ inner, inside, internal, inward

²interior *n* **1 :** the inland part (as of a country) **2 :** INSIDE **3 :** the internal affairs of a state or nation **4 :** a scene or view of the interior of a building
interior decoration *n* **:** INTERIOR DESIGN — **interior decorator** *n*
interior design *n* **:** the art or practice of planning and supervising the design and execution of architectural interiors and their furnishings — **interior designer** *n*
interj *abbr* interjection
in·ter·ject \ˌin-tər-ˈjekt\ *vb* ♦ **:** to throw in between or among other things

♦ fit, inject, insert, insinuate, interpose, introduce

in·ter·jec·tion \ˌin-tər-ˈjek-shən\ *n* ♦ **:** an exclamatory word or phrase (as *ouch*) — **in·ter·jec·tion·al·ly** \-shə-nə-lē\ *adv*

♦ cry, ejaculation, exclamation

in·ter·lace \ˌin-tər-ˈlās\ *vb* ♦ **:** to unite by or as if by lacing together **:** INTERWEAVE

♦ intersperse, intertwine, interweave, lace, thread, weave, wreathe

in·ter·lard \ˌin-tər-ˈlärd\ *vb* **:** to vary by inserting or interjecting something
in·ter·leave \ˌin-tər-ˈlēv\ *vb* **-leaved; -leav·ing :** to arrange in alternate layers
in·ter·leu·kin \ˌin-tər-ˈlü-kən\ *n* **:** any of several proteins of low molecular weight that are produced by cells of the body and regulate the immune system and immune responses
¹in·ter·line \ˌin-tər-ˈlīn\ *vb* **:** to insert between lines already written or printed
²interline *vb* **:** to provide (as a coat) with an interlining
in·ter·lin·ear \ˌin-tər-ˈli-nē-ər\ *adj* **:** inserted between lines already written or printed ⟨an ~ translation of a text⟩
in·ter·lin·gual \ˌin-tər-ˈliŋ-gwəl\ *adj* **:** of, relating to, or existing between two or more languages
in·ter·lin·ing \ˈin-tər-ˌlī-niŋ\ *n* **:** a lining (as of a coat) between the ordinary lining and the outside fabric
in·ter·link \ˌin-tər-ˈliŋk\ *vb* **:** to link together
in·ter·lock \ˌin-tər-ˈläk\ *vb* **1 :** to engage or interlace together **:** lock together **:** UNITE **2 :** to connect so that action of one part affects action of another part — **in·ter·lock** \ˈin-tər-ˌläk\ *n*
in·ter·loc·u·tor \ˌin-tər-ˈlä-kyə-tər\ *n* **:** one who takes part in dialogue or conversation
in·ter·loc·u·to·ry \-ˌtōr-ē\ *adj* **:** made during the progress of a legal action and not final or definite ⟨an ~ decree⟩
in·ter·lope \ˌin-tər-ˈlōp\ *vb* **-loped; -lop·ing 1 :** to encroach on the rights (as in trade) of others **2 :** INTRUDE, INTERFERE
in·ter·lop·er *n* ♦ **:** one who interlopes; *esp* **:** one that intrudes in a place or sphere of activity

♦ busybody, intruder, kibitzer, meddler

in·ter·lude \ˈin-tər-ˌlüd\ *n* **1 :** a usually short simple play or dramatic entertainment **2** ♦ **:** an intervening period, space, or event **3 :** a piece of music inserted between the parts of a longer composition or a religious service

♦ discontinuity, gap, hiatus, interim, intermission, interruption, interval

in·ter·mar·riage \ˌin-tər-ˈmar-ij\ *n* **1 :** marriage within one's own group as required by custom **2 :** marriage between members of different groups
in·ter·mar·ry \-ˈmar-ē\ *vb* **1 :** to marry each other **2 :** to marry within a group **3 :** to become connected by intermarriage
¹in·ter·me·di·ary \ˌin-tər-ˈmē-dē-ˌer-ē\ *adj* **1 :** being or occurring at the middle place, stage, or degree or between extremes **:** INTERMEDIATE **2 :** acting as a mediator
²intermediary *n, pl* **-ar·ies** ♦ **:** one that mediates **:** MEDIATOR, GO-BETWEEN

♦ arbiter, arbitrator, broker, go-between, intercessor, mediator, middleman, peacemaker

¹in·ter·me·di·ate \ˌin-tər-ˈmē-dē-ət\ *adj* ♦ **:** being or occurring at the middle place or degree or between extremes

♦ halfway, intermediary, median, medium, middle, midmost

²intermediate *n* **1 :** one that is intermediate **2 :** INTERMEDIARY
intermediate school *n* **1 :** JUNIOR HIGH SCHOOL **2 :** a school usually comprising grades 4–6
in·ter·ment \in-ˈtər-mənt\ *n* ♦ **:** the act or ceremony of interring **:** BURIAL

♦ burial, entombment, sepulture

in·ter·mez·zo \ˌin-tər-ˈmet-sō, -ˈmed-zō\ *n, pl* **-zi** \-sē, -zē\ *or* **-zos :** a short movement connecting major sections of an extended musical work (as a symphony); *also* **:** a short independent instrumental composition
in·ter·mi·na·ble \(ˌ)in-ˈtər-mə-nə-bəl\ *adj* **:** ENDLESS; *esp* **:** wearisomely protracted — **in·ter·mi·na·bly** \-blē\ *adv*
in·ter·min·gle \ˌin-tər-ˈmiŋ-gəl\ *vb* ♦ **:** to mingle or mix together

♦ amalgamate, blend, combine, commingle, fuse, incorporate, integrate, merge, mingle, mix

in·ter·mis·sion \ˌin-tər-ˈmi-shən\ *n* **1** ♦ **:** the act of intermitting **:** the state of being intermitted **:** INTERRUPTION **2 :** a temporary halt especially in a public performance

♦ discontinuity, gap, hiatus, interim, interlude, interruption, interval

in·ter·mit \-ˈmit\ *vb* **-mit·ted; -mit·ting :** DISCONTINUE; *also* **:** to be intermittent
in·ter·mit·tent \-ˈmit-ᵊnt\ *adj* ♦ **:** coming and going at intervals — **in·ter·mit·tent·ly** *adv*

♦ casual, choppy, discontinuous, erratic, fitful, irregular, occasional, spasmodic, sporadic, spotty, unsteady

in·ter·mix \ˌin-tər-ˈmiks\ *vb* **:** to mix together **:** INTERMINGLE
in·ter·mix·ture \-ˈmiks-chər\ *n* ♦ **:** a mass formed by mixture **:** a mass of ingredients mixed

♦ admixture, amalgam, blend, combination, composite, compound, fusion, mix, mixture

in·ter·mo·lec·u·lar \-mə-ˈle-kyə-lər\ *adj* **:** existing or acting between molecules
in·ter·mon·tane \ˌin-tər-ˈmän-ˌtān\ *adj* **:** situated between mountains
¹in·tern \ˈin-ˌtərn, in-ˈtərn\ *vb* **:** to confine or impound especially during a war
²in·tern *also* **in·terne** \ˈin-ˌtərn\ *n* **:** an advanced student or recent graduate (as in medicine) gaining supervised practical experience — **in·tern·ship** *n*
³in·tern \ˈin-ˌtərn\ *vb* **:** to work as an intern
in·ter·nal \in-ˈtərn-ᵊl\ *adj* **1** ♦ **:** existing or situated within the limits or surface of something **2 :** relating to or located in the inside of the body ⟨~ pain⟩ **3 :** of, relating to, or occurring within the confines of an organized structure ⟨~ affairs⟩ **4 :** of, relating to, or existing within the mind **5 :** INTRINSIC, INHERENT — **in·ter·nal·ly** *adv*

♦ inner, inside, interior, inward

internal combustion engine *n* **:** an engine in which the fuel is ignited within the engine cylinder
in·ter·nal·ise *chiefly Brit var of* INTERNALIZE
in·ter·nal·ize \in-ˈtər-nə-ˌlīz\ *vb* **-ized; -iz·ing :** to incorporate (as values) within the self through learning or socialization — **in·ter·nal·i·za·tion** \-ˌtər-nə-lə-ˈzā-shən\ *n*
internal medicine *n* **:** a branch of medicine that deals with the diagnosis and treatment of diseases not requiring surgery
¹in·ter·na·tion·al \ˌin-tər-ˈna-shə-nəl\ *adj* **1 :** common to or affecting two or more nations ⟨~ trade⟩ **2 :** of, relating to, or constituting a group having members in two or more nations — **in·ter·na·tion·al·ly** *adv*
²international *n* **:** one that is international; *esp* **:** an organization of international scope
in·ter·na·tion·al·ise *chiefly Brit var of* INTERNATIONALIZE
in·ter·na·tion·al·ism \-ˈna-shə-nə-ˌli-zəm\ *n* **:** a policy of cooperation among nations; *also* **:** an attitude favoring such a policy
in·ter·na·tion·al·ize \-ˈna-shə-nə-ˌlīz\ *vb* **:** to make international; *esp* **:** to place under international control

International System of Units *n* **:** a system of units based on the metric system and used by international convention especially for scientific work

in•ter•ne•cine \ˌin-tər-ˈne-ˌsēn, -ˈnē-ˌsīn\ *adj* **1 :** DEADLY; *esp* **:** mutually destructive **2 :** of, relating to, or involving conflict within a group ⟨∼ feuds⟩

in•tern•ee \(ˌ)in-ˌtər-ˈnē\ *n* ◆ **:** a person interned

◆ captive, capture, prisoner

In•ter•net \ˈin-tər-ˌnet\ *n* **:** an electronic communications network that connects computer networks worldwide

in•ter•nist \ˈin-ˌtər-nist\ *n* **:** a physician who specializes in internal medicine

in•tern•ment \in-ˈtərn-mənt\ *n* ◆ **:** the act of interning or the state of being interned

◆ captivity, confinement, imprisonment, incarceration

in•ter•nun•cio \ˌin-tər-ˈnən-sē-ˌō, -ˈnůn-\ *n* **:** a papal legate of lower rank than a nuncio

in•ter•of•fice \-ˈȯ-fəs\ *adj* **:** functioning or communicating between the offices of an organization

in•ter•per•son•al \-ˈpərs-ᵊn-əl\ *adj* **:** being, relating to, or involving relations between persons — **in•ter•per•son•al•ly** *adv*

in•ter•plan•e•tary \ˌin-tər-ˈpla-nə-ˌter-ē\ *adj* **:** existing, carried on, or operating between planets ⟨∼ space⟩

in•ter•play \ˈin-tər-ˌplā\ *n* **:** INTERACTION

in•ter•po•late \in-ˈtər-pə-ˌlāt\ *vb* **-lat•ed; -lat•ing 1 :** to change (as a text) by inserting new or foreign matter **2 :** to insert (as words) into a text or into a conversation **3 :** to estimate values of (data or a function) between two known values **4 :** to insert between other things or parts — **in•ter•po•la•tion** \-ˌtər-pə-ˈlā-shən\ *n*

in•ter•pose \ˌin-tər-ˈpōz\ *vb* **-posed; -pos•ing 1** ◆ **:** to place between **2** ◆ **:** to thrust in **:** INTRUDE, INTERRUPT **3 :** to inject between parts of a conversation or argument **4 :** to come or be between — **in•ter•po•si•tion** \-pə-ˈzi-shən\ *n*

◆ [1] fit, inject, insert, insinuate, interject, introduce ◆ [2] break, chime in, cut in, interrupt, intrude

in•ter•pret \in-ˈtər-prət\ *vb* **1** ◆ **:** to explain the meaning of; *also* **:** to act as an interpreter **2 :** to understand according to individual belief, judgment, or interest **3 :** to represent artistically — **in•ter•pret•er** *n* — **in•ter•pre•tive** \-ˈtər-prə-tiv\ *adj*

◆ clarify, clear (up), construe, demonstrate, elucidate, explain, explicate, expound, illuminate, illustrate, spell out

in•ter•pre•ta•tion \in-ˌtər-prə-ˈtā-shən\ *n* **1** ◆ **:** the act or the result of interpreting **:** EXPLANATION **2 :** an instance of artistic interpretation in performance or adaptation

◆ clarification, construction, elucidation, explanation, explication, exposition, illumination, illustration

in•ter•pre•ta•tive \in-ˈtər-prə-ˌtā-tiv\ *adj* **:** designed or fitted to interpret **:** EXPLANATORY

in•ter•ra•cial \-ˈrā-shəl\ *adj* **:** of, involving, or designed for members of different races

in•ter•reg•num \ˌin-tə-ˈreg-nəm\ *n, pl* **-nums** *or* **-na** \-nə\ **1 :** the time during which a throne is vacant between two successive reigns or regimes **2 :** a pause in a continuous series

in•ter•re•late \ˌin-tər-ri-ˈlāt\ *vb* **:** to bring into or have a mutual relationship — **in•ter•re•lat•ed•ness** \-lā-təd-nəs\ *n* — **in•ter•re•la•tion** \-ˈlā-shən\ *n* — **in•ter•re•la•tion•ship** *n*

interrog *abbr* interrogative

in•ter•ro•gate \in-ˈter-ə-ˌgāt\ *vb* **-gat•ed; -gat•ing** ◆ **:** to question especially formally and systematically — **in•ter•ro•ga•tion** \-ˌter-ə-ˈgā-shən\ *n* — **in•ter•ro•ga•tor** \-ˈter-ə-ˌgā-tər\ *n*

◆ ask, examine, grill, pump, query, question, quiz

in•ter•rog•a•tive \ˌin-tə-ˈrä-gə-tiv\ *adj* **:** asking a question ⟨∼ sentence⟩ — **interrogative** *n* — **in•ter•rog•a•tive•ly** *adv*

in•ter•rog•a•to•ry \ˌin-tə-ˈrä-gə-ˌtōr-ē\ *adj* **:** INTERROGATIVE

in•ter•rupt \ˌin-tə-ˈrəpt\ *vb* **1 :** to stop or hinder by breaking in **2 :** to break the uniformity or continuity of **3** ◆ **:** to break in by speaking while another is speaking — **in•ter•rupt•er** *n* — **in•ter•rup•tive** \-ˈrəp-tiv\ *adv*

◆ break, chime in, cut in, interpose, intrude

in•ter•rup•tion \-ˈrəp-shən\ *n* ◆ **:** an act of interrupting or state of being interrupted; *also* **:** temporary cessation

◆ discontinuity, gap, hiatus, interim, interlude, intermission, interval ◆ break, breather, lull, pause

in•ter•scho•las•tic \ˌin-tər-skə-ˈlas-tik\ *adj* **:** existing or carried on between schools

in•ter•sect \ˌin-tər-ˈsekt\ *vb* **1 :** to divide by passing through or across **2 :** to meet and cross (as at a point); *also* **:** OVERLAP

in•ter•sec•tion \-ˈsek-shən\ *n* ◆ **:** a place or area where two or more things (as streets) intersect

◆ corner, crossing, crossroad

in•ter•sperse \ˌin-tər-ˈspərs\ *vb* **-spersed; -spers•ing 1 :** to place something at intervals in or among **2** ◆ **:** to insert at intervals among other things — **in•ter•sper•sion** \-ˈspər-zhən\ *n*

◆ interlace, intertwine, interweave, lace, thread, weave, wreathe

¹in•ter•state \ˌin-tər-ˈstāt\ *adj* **:** relating to, including, or connecting two or more states especially of the U.S.

²in•ter•state \ˈin-tər-ˌstāt\ *n* **:** an interstate highway

in•ter•stel•lar \ˌin-tər-ˈste-lər\ *adj* **:** located or taking place among the stars

in•ter•stice \in-ˈtər-stəs\ *n, pl* **-stic•es** \-stə-ˌsēz, -stə-səz\ ◆ **:** a space that intervenes between things — **in•ter•sti•tial** \ˌin-tər-ˈsti-shəl\ *adj*

◆ breach, break, discontinuity, gap, gulf, hiatus, hole, interval, opening, rent, rift, separation

in•ter•tid•al \ˌin-tər-ˈtīd-ᵊl\ *adj* **:** of, relating to, or being the area that is above low-tide mark but exposed to tidal flooding ⟨life in the ∼ mud⟩

in•ter•twine \-ˈtwīn\ *vb* ◆ **:** to twine or cause to twine about one another **:** INTERLACE — **in•ter•twine•ment** *n*

◆ interlace, interweave, lace

in•ter•twist \-ˈtwist\ *vb* **:** INTERTWINE

in•ter•ur•ban \-ˈər-bən\ *adj* **:** connecting cities or towns

in•ter•val \ˈin-tər-vəl\ *n* **1** ◆ **:** a space of time between events or states **:** PAUSE **2** ◆ **:** a space between objects, units, or states **3 :** the difference in pitch between two tones

◆ [1] discontinuity, gap, hiatus, interim, interlude, intermission, interruption ◆ [2] breach, break, discontinuity, gap, gulf, hole, opening, rent, rift, separation

in•ter•vene \ˌin-tər-ˈvēn\ *vb* **-vened; -ven•ing 1 :** to occur, fall, or come between points of time or between events **2 :** to enter or appear as an unrelated feature or circumstance ⟨rain *intervened* and we postponed the trip⟩ **3** ◆ **:** to come in or between in order to stop, settle, or modify ⟨∼ in a quarrel⟩ **4 :** to occur or lie between two things — **in•ter•ven•tion** \-ˈven-chən\ *n*

◆ intercede, interpose, mediate

in•ter•ven•tion•ism \-ˈven-chə-ˌni-zəm\ *n* **:** interference by one country in the political affairs of another — **in•ter•ven•tion•ist** \-ˈven-chə-nist\ *n or adj*

in•ter•view \ˈin-tər-ˌvyü\ *n* **1 :** a formal consultation usually to evaluate qualifications **2 :** a meeting at which a writer or reporter obtains information from a person; *also* **:** the recorded or written account of such a meeting — **interview** *vb* — **in•ter•view•ee** \ˌin-tər-(ˌ)vyü-ˈē\ *n* — **in•ter•view•er** *n*

in•ter•vo•cal•ic \ˌin-tər-vō-ˈka-lik\ *adj* **:** immediately preceded and immediately followed by a vowel

in•ter•weave \ˌin-tər-ˈwēv\ *vb* **-wove** \-ˈwōv\ *also* **-weaved; -wo•ven** \-ˈwō-vən\ *also* **-weaved; -weav•ing** ◆ **:** to weave or blend together — **interwoven** *adj*

◆ interlace, intersperse, intertwine, lace, thread, weave, wreathe

in•tes•tate \in-ˈtes-ˌtāt, -tət\ *adj* **1 :** having made no valid will ⟨died ∼⟩ **2 :** not disposed of by will ⟨∼ estate⟩

in•tes•tine \in-ˈtes-tən\ *n* **:** the tubular part of the alimentary canal that extends from stomach to anus and consists of a long narrow upper part (**small intestine**) followed by a broader shorter lower part (**large intestine**) — **in•tes•ti•nal** \-tən-ᵊl\ *adj*

in•ti•fa•da \ˌin-tə-ˈfä-də\ *n* **:** an armed uprising of Palestinians against Israeli occupation of the West Bank and Gaza Strip

in•ti•ma•cy \ˈin-tə-mə-sē\ *n* **1** ◆ **:** the state of being intimate **2 :** something of a personal or private nature

◆ closeness, familiarity, nearness

¹in•ti•mate \ˈin-tə-ˌmāt\ *vb* **-mat•ed; -mat•ing 1 :** ANNOUNCE, NOTIFY **2** ◆ **:** to communicate indirectly **:** HINT

◆ allude, hint, imply, indicate, infer, insinuate, suggest

²in•ti•mate \ˈin-tə-mət\ *adj* **1 :** INTRINSIC; *also* **:** INNERMOST **2** ◆ **:** marked by very close association, contact, or familiarity **3 :** marked by a warm friendship **4 :** suggesting informal warmth or privacy **5** ◆ **:** of a very personal or private nature — **in•ti•mate•ly** *adv*

◆ [2] bosom, chummy, close, familiar, friendly, thick ◆ [5] confidential, hushed, inside, private, secret

3**in•ti•mate** \ˈin-tə-mət\ *n* ♦ : an intimate friend, associate, or confidant

♦ buddy, chum, comrade, crony, familiar, friend, pal

in•ti•ma•tion \ˌin-tə-ˈmā-shən\ *n* ♦ : an indirect usually hinted suggestion or notice; *also* : something intimated

♦ clue, cue, hint, indication, inkling, lead, suggestion

in•tim•i•date \in-ˈti-mə-ˌdāt\ *vb* **-dat•ed; -dat•ing** ♦ : to make timid or fearful; *esp* : to compel or deter by or as if by threats — **in•tim•i•dat•ing•ly** *adv* — **in•tim•i•da•tion** \-ˌti-mə-ˈdā-shən\ *n*

♦ browbeat, bully, cow, hector

intl *or* **intnl** *abbr* international

in•to \ˈin-tü\ *prep* **1** : to the inside of ⟨ran ~ the house⟩ **2** : to the state, condition, or form of ⟨got ~ trouble⟩ **3** : AGAINST ⟨ran ~ a wall⟩

in•tol•er•a•ble \(ˌ)in-ˈtä-lə-rə-bəl\ *adj* **1** ♦ : not tolerable : UNBEARABLE **2** : EXCESSIVE — **in•tol•er•a•bly** \-blē\ *adv*

♦ insufferable, insupportable, unbearable, unendurable, unsupportable

in•tol•er•ant \(ˌ)in-ˈtä-lə-rənt\ *adj* **1** : unable or unwilling to tolerate **2** ♦ : unwilling to grant equality, freedom, or other social rights : BIGOTED — **in•tol•er•ance** \-rəns\ *n*

♦ bigoted, narrow, narrow-minded, prejudiced ***Ant*** liberal, broad-minded, open-minded, tolerant, unprejudiced

in•to•na•tion \ˌin-tō-ˈnā-shən\ *n* **1** : the act of intoning and especially of chanting **2** : something that is intoned **3** : the manner of singing, playing, or uttering tones **4** : the rise and fall in pitch of the voice in speech

in•tone \in-ˈtōn\ *vb* **in•toned; in•ton•ing** : to utter in musical or prolonged tones : CHANT

in to•to \in-ˈtō-tō\ *adv* : TOTALLY, ENTIRELY

in•tox•i•cant \in-ˈtäk-si-kənt\ *n* ♦ : something that intoxicates; *esp* : an alcoholic drink — **intoxicant** *adj*

♦ alcohol, booze, drink, liquor, moonshine, spirits

in•tox•i•cate \-sə-ˌkāt\ *vb* **-cat•ed; -cat•ing** **1** : to affect by a drug (as alcohol or cocaine) especially to the point of physical or mental impairment **2** ♦ : to excite to enthusiasm or frenzy

♦ electrify, excite, exhilarate, galvanize, thrill, titillate, turn on

in•tox•i•cat•ed \-sə-ˌkā-təd\ *adj* ♦ : affected by or as if by alcohol

♦ drunk, high, inebriate, tipsy ♦ ecstatic, elated, euphoric, rapturous, rhapsodic

in•tox•i•ca•tion \-ˌtäk-sə-ˈkā-shən\ *n* ♦ : the condition of being drunk; *also* : a strong excitement or elation

♦ ecstasy, elation, euphoria, exhilaration, heaven, paradise, rapture, rhapsody, transport

in•trac•ta•ble \(ˌ)in-ˈtrak-tə-bəl\ *adj* ♦ : not easily controlled

♦ froward, headstrong, recalcitrant, refractory, uncontrollable, unmanageable, unruly, untoward, wayward, willful

in•tra•mu•ral \-ˈmyu̇r-əl\ *adj* : being or occurring within the walls or limits (as of a city or college) ⟨~ sports⟩

in•tra•mus•cu•lar \-ˈməs-kyə-lər\ *adj* : situated within, occurring in, or administered by entering a muscle — **in•tra•mus•cu•lar•ly** *adv*

in•tra•net \ˈin-trə-ˌnet\ *n* : a network similar to the World Wide Web but having access limited to certain authorized users

intrans *abbr* intransitive

in•tran•si•gent \-jənt\ *adj* : UNCOMPROMISING; *also* : IRRECONCILABLE — **in•tran•si•gence** \-jəns\ *n* — **intransigent** *n*

in•tran•si•tive \(ˌ)in-ˈtran-sə-tiv, -zə-\ *adj* : not transitive; *esp* : not having or containing an object ⟨an ~ verb⟩ — **in•tran•si•tive•ly** *adv* — **in•tran•si•tive•ness** *n*

in•tra•state \ˌin-trə-ˈstāt\ *adj* : existing or occurring within a state

in•tra•uter•ine device \-ˈyü-tə-rən-, -ˌrīn-\ *n* : a device inserted into and left in the uterus to prevent pregnancy

in•tra•ve•nous \ˌin-trə-ˈvē-nəs\ *adj* : being within or entering by way of the veins; *also* : used in or using intravenous procedures — **in•tra•ve•nous•ly** *adv*

intrench *var of* ENTRENCH

in•trep•id \in-ˈtre-pəd\ *adj* ♦ : characterized by resolute fearlessness, fortitude, and endurance

♦ brave, courageous, dauntless, doughty, fearless, gallant, greathearted, heroic, lionhearted, manful, stalwart, stout, undaunted, valiant, valorous

in•tre•pid•i•ty \ˌin-trə-ˈpi-də-tē\ *n* : the quality or state of being intrepid : resolute bravery

in•tri•ca•cy \-tri-kə-sē\ *n* ♦ : the quality or state of being intricate; *also* : something intricate

♦ complexity, complication, difficulty, intricacy ♦ complexity, elaborateness, sophistication

in•tri•cate \ˈin-tri-kət\ *adj* **1** ♦ : having many complexly interrelated parts : COMPLICATED **2** ♦ : involving or done with precision; *also* : difficult to follow, understand, or solve — **in•tri•cate•ly** *adv*

♦ complex, complicated, convoluted, detailed, elaborate, involved, knotty, sophisticated

1**in•trigue** \in-ˈtrēg\ *vb* **in•trigued; in•trigu•ing** **1** : to accomplish by intrigue **2** ♦ : to carry on an intrigue; *esp* : PLOT, SCHEME **3** ♦ : to arouse the interest, desire, or curiosity of

♦ [2] conspire, contrive, machinate, plot, scheme ♦ [3] absorb, busy, engage, engross, enthrall, fascinate, grip, immerse, interest, involve, occupy

2**in•trigue** \ˈin-ˌtrēg, in-ˈtrēg\ *n* **1** ♦ : a secret scheme : MACHINATION **2** : a clandestine love affair

♦ conspiracy, design, machination, plot, scheme

intriguing *adj* ♦ : engaging the interest to a marked degree

♦ absorbing, engaging, engrossing, enthralling, fascinating, interesting

in•trin•sic \in-ˈtrin-zik, -sik\ *adj* ♦ : belonging to the essential nature or constitution of a thing

♦ essential, inborn, ingrained, inherent, innate, integral, natural

in•trin•si•cal•ly \in-ˈtrin-zi-k(ə-)lē, -si-\ *adv* ♦ : in an intrinsic manner : having an intrinsic quality

♦ constitutionally, inherently, innately, naturally

introd *abbr* introduction

in•tro•duce \ˌin-trə-ˈdüs, -ˈdyüs\ *vb* **-duced; -duc•ing** **1** : to lead or bring in especially for the first time **2** ♦ : to bring into practice or use **3** ♦ : to cause to be acquainted **4** ♦ : to present for discussion **5** ♦ : to put in : INSERT — **in•tro•duc•to•ry** \-ˈdək-tə-rē\ *adj*

♦ [2] constitute, establish, found, inaugurate, initiate, innovate, institute, launch, pioneer, set up, start ♦ [3] acquaint, familiarize, initiate, orient ♦ [4] bring up, broach, moot, raise ♦ [5] fit, inject, insert, insinuate, interject, interpose

in•tro•duc•tion \-ˈdək-shən\ *n* **1** ♦ : something that introduces **2** : the act or process of introducing : the state of being introduced; *also* : something introduced

♦ foreword, preamble, preface, prologue ***Ant*** epilogue

in•troit \ˈin-ˌtrȯit, -ˌtrō-ət\ *n* **1** *often cap* : the first part of the traditional proper of the Mass **2** : a piece of music sung or played at the beginning of a worship service

in•tro•spec•tion \-ˈspek-shən\ *n* : a reflective looking inward : an examination of one's own thoughts or feelings — **in•tro•spect** \ˌin-trə-ˈspekt\ *vb* — **in•tro•spec•tive** \-ˈspek-tiv\ *adj* — **in•tro•spec•tive•ly** *adv*

in•tro•vert \ˈin-trə-ˌvərt\ *n* : a reserved or shy person — **in•tro•ver•sion** \ˌin-trə-ˈvər-zhən\ *n* — **introvert** *adj*

in•tro•vert•ed \ˈin-trə-ˌvər-təd\ *adj* ♦ : turned in upon itself; *specif* : marked by being wholly or predominantly concerned with and interested in one's own mental life

♦ bashful, coy, demure, diffident, modest, retiring, sheepish, shy

in•trude \in-ˈtrüd\ *vb* **in•trud•ed; in•trud•ing** **1** ♦ : to thrust, enter, or force in or upon **2** : ENCROACH, TRESPASS — **in•tru•sion** \-ˈtrü-zhən\ *n*

♦ break, chime in, cut in, interpose, interrupt ♦ butt in, interfere, meddle, mess, nose, obtrude, poke, pry, snoop ♦ *usu* **intrude upon** bother, bug, disturb, pester

in•trud•er *n* ♦ : one that intrudes

♦ busybody, interloper, kibitzer, meddler

in•tru•sive \-ˈtrü-siv\ *adj* ♦ : characterized by intrusion : intruding where one is not welcome or invited — **in•tru•sive•ness** *n*

♦ meddlesome, nosy, obtrusive, officious, presumptuous, prying ***Ant*** unobtrusive

intrust *var of* ENTRUST

in•tu•it \in-ˈtü-ət, -ˈtyü-\ *vb* : to know, sense, or understand by intuition

in•tu•ition \ˌin-tü-ˈwi-shən, -tyü-\ *n* **1 :** quick and ready insight **2 :** the power or faculty of knowing things without conscious reasoning — **in•tu•i•tive** \in-ˈtü-ə-tiv, -ˈtyü-\ *adj* — **in•tu•i•tive•ly** *adv*

In•u•it \ˈi-nü-wət, ˈin-yü-\ *n* **1** *pl* **Inuit** *or* **Inuits :** a member of the Eskimo people of No. America and Greenland **2 :** the language of the Inuit people

in•un•date \ˈi-nən-ˌdāt\ *vb* **-dat•ed; -dat•ing** ♦ **:** to cover with or as if with a flood : OVERFLOW

♦ deluge, drown, engulf, flood, overflow, overwhelm, submerge, swamp

in•un•da•tion \ˌi-nən-ˈdā-shən\ *n* ♦ **:** an overflowing of the land by water; *also* **:** an overwhelming amount or number

♦ cataclysm, cataract, deluge, flood, overflow, spate, torrent

in•ure \i-ˈnür, -ˈnyür\ *vb* **in•ured; in•ur•ing 1 :** to accustom to accept something undesirable **2 :** to become of advantage

in utero \in-ˈyü-tə-ˌrō\ *adv or adj* **:** in the uterus **:** before birth

inv *abbr* **1** inventor **2** invoice

in vac•uo \in-ˈva-kyü-ˌwō\ *adv* **:** in a vacuum

in•vade \in-ˈvād\ *vb* **in•vad•ed; in•vad•ing 1** ♦ **:** to enter in a hostile manner **2 :** to encroach upon **3 :** to spread through and usually harm ⟨germs ~ the tissues⟩ — **in•vad•er** *n*

♦ foray, overrun, raid

¹in•val•id \(ˌ)in-ˈva-ləd\ *adj* ♦ **:** being without foundation or force in fact, reason, or law — **in•va•lid•i•ty** \ˌin-və-ˈli-də-tē\ *n* — **in•val•id•ly** *adv*

♦ baseless, groundless, unfounded, unreasonable, unsubstantiated, unsupported, unwarranted ♦ null, void ♦ erroneous, false, inaccurate, incorrect, inexact, off, unsound, untrue, wrong

²in•va•lid \ˈin-və-ləd\ *adj* **:** being in ill health : SICKLY

³invalid \ˈin-və-ləd\ *n* **:** a person in usually chronic ill health — **in•va•lid•ism** \-lə-ˌdi-zəm\ *n*

⁴in•va•lid \ˈin-və-ləd, -ˌlid\ *vb* **1 :** to remove from active duty by reason of sickness or disability **2 :** to make sickly or disabled

in•val•i•date \(ˌ)in-ˈva-lə-ˌdāt\ *vb* ♦ **:** to make invalid; *esp* **:** to weaken or make valueless — **in•val•i•da•tion** \in-ˌva-lə-ˈdā-shən\ *n*

♦ abolish, abrogate, annul, cancel, dissolve, negate, nullify, quash, repeal, rescind, void

in•valu•able \-ˈval-yə-bəl, -yə-wə-bəl\ *adj* **:** valuable beyond estimation

in•vari•able \-ˈver-ē-ə-bəl\ *adj* **:** not changing or capable of change : CONSTANT

in•vari•ably \-blē\ *adv* ♦ **:** on every occasion

♦ always, constantly, continually, ever, forever, incessantly, perpetually, unfailingly

in•va•sion \in-ˈvā-zhən\ *n* ♦ **:** an act or instance of invading; *esp* **:** entry of an army into a country for conquest

♦ descent, foray, incursion, irruption, raid

in•va•sive \in-ˈvā-siv, -ziv\ *adj* **1 :** tending to spread ⟨~ cancer cells⟩ **2 :** involving entry into the living body (as by surgery) ⟨~ therapy⟩

in•vec•tive \in-ˈvek-tiv\ *n* **1 :** an abusive expression or speech **2** ♦ **:** abusive language — **invective** *adj*

♦ abuse, fulmination, vitriol, vituperation

in•veigh \in-ˈvā\ *vb* **:** to protest or complain bitterly or vehemently : RAIL

in•vei•gle \in-ˈvā-gəl, -ˈvē-\ *vb* **in•vei•gled; in•vei•gling 1 :** to win over by flattery : ENTICE **2 :** to acquire by ingenuity or flattery

in•vent \in-ˈvent\ *vb* **1** ♦ **:** to think up **2** ♦ **:** to create or produce for the first time

♦ [1, 2] concoct, contrive, cook up, devise, fabricate, make up, manufacture, think up

in•ven•tion \in-ˈven-chən\ *n* **1** ♦ **:** productive imagination : INVENTIVENESS **2** ♦ **:** a creation of the imagination; *esp* **:** a false conception **3** ♦ **:** a device, contrivance, or process originated after study and experiment **4 :** the act or process of inventing

♦ [1] creativity, fancy, fantasy, imagination, inventiveness ♦ [2] fabrication, fantasy, fiction, figment, invention ♦ [3] coinage, concoction, contrivance, creation, innovation, wrinkle

in•ven•tive \in-ˈven-tiv\ *adj* **1** ♦ **:** adept or prolific at producing inventions : CREATIVE, INGENIOUS ⟨an ~ composer⟩ **2 :** characterized by invention ⟨an ~ turn of mind⟩

♦ creative, imaginative, ingenious, innovative, original

in•ven•tive•ness *n* ♦ **:** the quality or state of being inventive

♦ creativity, ingenuity, invention, originality

in•ven•tor \-ˈven-tər\ *n* ♦ **:** one that invents: as **a :** one that conceives by creative imagination **b :** one that creates a new device or process

♦ designer, developer, innovator, originator

¹in•ven•to•ry \ˈin-vən-ˌtōr-ē\ *n, pl* **-ries 1 :** an itemized list of current goods or assets **2 :** SURVEY, SUMMARY **3 :** STOCK, SUPPLY **4 :** the act or process of taking an inventory

²inventory *vb* **-ried; -ry•ing** ♦ **:** to make an inventory of

♦ enumerate, itemize, list, numerate

¹in•verse \(ˌ)in-ˈvərs, ˈin-ˌvərs\ *adj* **:** opposite in order, nature, or effect : REVERSED — **in•verse•ly** *adv*

²inverse *n* **:** something inverse or resulting in or from inversion : OPPOSITE

in•ver•sion \in-ˈvər-zhən\ *n* **1 :** a reversal of position, order, or relationship; *esp* **:** an increase of temperature with altitude through a layer of air **2 :** the act or process of inverting

in•vert \in-ˈvərt\ *vb* **1 :** to reverse in position, order, or relationship **2 :** to turn upside down or inside out **3 :** to turn inward

in•ver•te•brate \(ˌ)in-ˈvər-tə-brət, -ˌbrāt\ *adj* **1 :** lacking a backbone; *also* **:** of or relating to invertebrate animals **2 :** lacking in strength or vitality — **invertebrate** *n*

¹in•vest \in-ˈvest\ *vb* **1** ♦ **:** to install formally in an office or honor **2** ♦ **:** to furnish with power or authority **3 :** to cover completely : ENVELOP **4 :** to cover with or as if with cloth or clothing : CLOTHE, ADORN **5 :** to surround with troops or ships so as to prevent escape or entry : BESIEGE **6** ♦ **:** to endow with a quality or characteristic

♦ [1] baptize, inaugurate, induct, initiate, install ♦ [2] accredit, authorize, certify, commission, empower, enable, license, qualify ♦ [6] imbue, inculcate, infuse, ingrain, steep, suffuse

²invest *vb* **1 :** to commit (money) in order to earn a financial return **2 :** to expend for future benefits or advantages **3 :** to make an investment — **in•ves•tor** \-ˈves-tər\ *n*

in•ves•ti•gate \in-ˈves-tə-ˌgāt\ *vb* **-gat•ed; -gat•ing** ♦ **:** to study by close examination and systematic inquiry — **in•ves•ti•ga•tive** \-ˈves-tə-ˌgā-tiv\ *adj*

♦ delve, dig, explore, go, inquire into, look, probe, research

in•ves•ti•ga•tion \-ˌves-tə-ˈgā-shən\ *n* ♦ **:** the action or process of investigating; *esp* **:** detailed examination or a searching inquiry

♦ examination, exploration, inquiry, probe, research, study

in•ves•ti•ga•tor \-ˌgā-tər\ *n* ♦ **:** one that investigates; *esp* **:** one employed or engaged in detecting lawbreakers or in getting information that is not readily or publicly accessible

♦ detective, operative, shadow, sleuth, tail

in•ves•ti•ture \in-ˈves-tə-ˌchür, -chər\ *n* **1** ♦ **:** the act of ratifying or establishing in office **2 :** something that covers or adorns

♦ inaugural, inauguration, induction, installation

¹in•vest•ment \in-ˈvest-mənt\ *n* **1 :** an outer layer : ENVELOPE **2 :** INVESTITURE 1 **3 :** BLOCKADE, SIEGE

²investment *n* **:** the outlay of money for income or profit; *also* **:** the sum invested or the property purchased

in•vet•er•ate \in-ˈve-tə-rət\ *adj* **1** ♦ **:** firmly established by age or long persistence **2** ♦ **:** confirmed in a habit

♦ [1] confirmed, deep-rooted, deep-seated, settled ♦ [2] chronic, confirmed, habitual

in•vi•a•ble \(ˌ)in-ˈvī-ə-bəl\ *adj* **:** incapable of surviving

in•vid•i•ous \in-ˈvi-dē-əs\ *adj* **1 :** tending to cause discontent, animosity, or envy **2 :** feeling or showing envy : ENVIOUS **3 :** OBNOXIOUS — **in•vid•i•ous•ly** *adv*

in•vig•o•rate \in-ˈvi-gə-ˌrāt\ *vb* **-rat•ed; -rat•ing** ♦ **:** to give life and energy to : ANIMATE — **in•vig•o•ra•tion** \-ˌvi-gə-ˈrā-shən\ *n*

♦ animate, brace, energize, enliven, fire, jazz up, liven up, pep up, quicken, stimulate, vitalize, vivify, zip (up)

invigorating *adj* ♦ **:** having an enlivening effect

♦ bracing, refreshing, restorative, stimulative, tonic

in•vin•ci•ble \(ˌ)in-ˈvin-sə-bəl\ *adj* ♦ **:** incapable of being conquered, overcome, or subdued — **in•vin•ci•bil•i•ty** \-ˌvin-sə-ˈbi-lə-tē\ *n* — **in•vin•ci•bly** \-ˈvin-sə-blē\ *adv*

♦ impregnable, indomitable, insurmountable, invulnerable, unbeatable, unconquerable *Ant* vulnerable

in•vi•o•la•ble \-ˈvī-ə-lə-bəl\ *adj* **1** ♦ **:** safe from violation or profanation **2 :** secure from assault or trespass **:** UNASSAILABLE — **in•vi•o•la•bil•i•ty** \-ˌvī-ə-lə-ˈbi-lə-tē\ *n*

♦ holy, sacred, sacrosanct

in•vi•o•late \-ˈvī-ə-lət\ *adj* **:** not violated or profaned **:** PURE

in•vis•i•ble \-ˈvi-zə-bəl\ *adj* **1 :** incapable of being seen ⟨∼ to the naked eye⟩ **2 :** HIDDEN **3 :** IMPERCEPTIBLE, INCONSPICUOUS — **in•vis•i•bil•i•ty** \-ˌvi-zə-ˈbi-lə-tē\ *n* — **in•vis•i•bly** \-ˈvi-zə-blē\ *adv*

invisible hand *n* **:** a hypothetical economic force that works for the benefit of all

in•vi•ta•tion•al \ˌin-və-ˈtā-shə-nəl\ *adj* **:** limited to invited participants ⟨an ∼ tournament⟩ — **invitational** *n*

in•vite \in-ˈvīt\ *vb* **in•vit•ed; in•vit•ing 1 :** ENTICE, TEMPT **2 :** to increase the likelihood of **3 :** to request the presence or participation of **:** ASK **4 :** to request formally **5 :** ENCOURAGE — **in•vi•ta•tion** \ˌin-və-ˈtā-shən\ *n*

in•vit•ing *adj* **:** ATTRACTIVE, TEMPTING

in vi•tro \in-ˈvē-trō, -ˈvī-, -ˈvi-\ *adv or adj* **:** outside the living body and in an artificial environment ⟨*in vitro* fertilization⟩

in•vo•ca•tion \ˌin-və-ˈkā-shən\ *n* **1 :** SUPPLICATION; *esp* **:** a prayer at the beginning of a service **2 :** a formula for conjuring **:** INCANTATION

¹in•voice \ˈin-ˌvȯis\ *n* ♦ **:** an itemized list of goods shipped usually specifying the price and the terms of sale **:** BILL

♦ account, bill, check, statement, tab

²invoice *vb* **in•voiced; in•voic•ing :** to send an invoice to or for **:** BILL

in•voke \in-ˈvōk\ *vb* **in•voked; in•vok•ing 1 :** to petition for help or support **2 :** to appeal to or cite as authority ⟨∼ a law⟩ **3 :** to call forth by incantation **:** CONJURE ⟨∼ spirits⟩ **4 :** to make an earnest request for **:** SOLICIT **5 :** to put into effect or operation **6 :** to bring about **:** CAUSE

in•vol•un•tary \(ˌ)in-ˈvä-lən-ˌter-ē\ *adj* **1** ♦ **:** done contrary to or without choice **2** ♦ **:** dictated by authority or circumstance **:** COMPULSORY **3** ♦ **:** not controlled by the will ⟨∼ contractions⟩ — **in•vol•un•tari•ly** \-ˌvä-lən-ˈter-ə-lē\ *adv*

♦ [1] unintended, unintentional *Ant* deliberate, intentional, unforced, voluntary, willful, willing ♦ [2] compulsory, imperative, incumbent, mandatory, necessary, nonelective, obligatory, peremptory ♦ [3] automatic, mechanical, spontaneous

in•vo•lute \ˈin-və-ˌlüt\ *adj* **:** INVOLVED, INTRICATE

in•vo•lu•tion \ˌin-və-ˈlü-shən\ *n* **1 :** the act or an instance of enfolding or entangling **2 :** the quality or state of being complex **:** COMPLEXITY, INTRICACY

in•volve \in-ˈvälv\ *vb* **in•volved; in•volv•ing 1** ♦ **:** to draw in as a participant **2 :** ENVELOP **3** ♦ **:** to occupy (as oneself) absorbingly; *esp* **:** to commit oneself emotionally **4 :** to relate closely **:** CONNECT **5** ♦ **:** to have as part of itself **:** INCLUDE **6 :** ENTAIL, IMPLY **7 :** to have an effect on — **in•volve•ment** *n*

♦ [1] affect, concern, interest, touch ♦ [3] absorb, busy, engage, engross, enthrall, fascinate, grip, immerse, interest, intrigue, occupy ♦ [5] carry, comprehend, contain, embrace, encompass, entail, include, number, take in

in•volved \-ˈvälvd\ *adj* ♦ **:** marked by extreme and often needless or excessive complexity **:** INTRICATE, COMPLEX ⟨an ∼ plot⟩

♦ complex, complicated, convoluted, detailed, elaborate, intricate, knotty, sophisticated

in•vul•ner•a•ble \(ˌ)in-ˈvəl-nə-rə-bəl\ *adj* **1 :** incapable of being wounded, injured, or damaged **2** ♦ **:** immune to or proof against attack — **in•vul•ner•a•bil•i•ty** \-ˌvəl-nə-rə-ˈbi-lə-tē\ *n* — **in•vul•ner•a•bly** \-ˈvəl-nə-rə-blē\ *adv*

♦ impregnable, indomitable, insurmountable, invincible, unbeatable, unconquerable

¹in•ward \ˈin-wərd\ *adj* **1** ♦ **:** situated on the inside **2 :** MENTAL; *also* **:** SPIRITUAL **3 :** directed toward the interior

♦ inner, inside, interior, internal

²inward *or* **in•wards** \-wərdz\ *adv* **1 :** toward the inside, center, or interior **2 :** toward the inner being

in•ward•ly \ˈin-wərd-lē\ *adv* **1 :** MENTALLY, SPIRITUALLY **2 :** INTERNALLY ⟨bled ∼⟩ **3 :** to oneself ⟨cursed ∼⟩

IOC *abbr* International Olympic Committee

io•dide \ˈī-ə-ˌdīd\ *n* **:** a compound of iodine with another element or group

io•dine \ˈī-ə-ˌdīn, -əd-ᵊn\ *n* **1 :** a nonmetallic chemical element used especially in medicine and photography **2 :** a solution of iodine used as a local antiseptic

io•dise *chiefly Brit var of* IODIZE

io•dize \ˈī-ə-ˌdīz\ *vb* **io•dized; io•diz•ing :** to treat with iodine or an iodide

ion \ˈī-ən, ˈī-ˌän\ *n* **:** an electrically charged particle, atom, or group of atoms — **ion•ic** \ī-ˈä-nik\ *adj*

-ion *n suffix* **:** act, process, state, or condition ⟨validat*ion*⟩

ion•ise *chiefly Brit var of* IONIZE

ion•ize \ˈī-ə-ˌnīz\ *vb* **ion•ized; ion•iz•ing 1 :** to convert wholly or partly into ions **2 :** to become ionized — **ion•iz•able** \ˌī-ə-ˈnī-zə-bəl\ *adj* — **ion•iza•tion** \ˌī-ə-nə-ˈzā-shən\ *n* — **ion•iz•er** \ˈī-ə-ˌnī-zər\ *n*

ion•o•sphere \ī-ˈä-nə-ˌsfir\ *n* **:** the part of the earth's atmosphere extending from about 30 miles (50 kilometers) to the exosphere that contains ionized atmospheric gases — **ion•o•spher•ic** \ī-ˌä-nə-ˈsfir-ik, -ˈsfer-\ *adj*

IOOF *abbr* Independent Order of Odd Fellows

io•ta \ī-ˈō-tə\ *n* **1 :** the 9th letter of the Greek alphabet — Ι or ι **2 :** a very small quantity **:** JOT

IOU \ˌī-(ˌ)ō-ˈyü\ *n* **:** an acknowledgment of a debt

IP *abbr* innings pitched

IP address \ˈī-ˈpē-\ *n* **:** the numeric address of a computer on the Internet

ip•e•cac \ˈi-pi-ˌkak\ *n* **:** an emetic and expectorant drug used especially as a syrup in treating accidental poisoning; *also* **:** either of two tropical American plants or their rhizomes and roots used to make ipecac

IPO \ˌī-ˌpē-ˈō\ *n, pl* **IPOs :** an initial public offering of a company's stock

ip•so fac•to \ˌip-sō-ˈfak-tō\ *adv* **:** by the very nature of the case

iq *abbr* the same as

IQ \ˈī-ˈkyü\ *n* **:** a number used to express a person's relative intelligence as determined by a standardized test

¹Ir *abbr* Irish

²Ir *symbol* iridium

IR *abbr* infrared

¹IRA \ˌī-(ˌ)är-ˈā; ˈī-rə\ *n* **:** a retirement savings account in which income taxes are deferred until withdrawals are made

²IRA *abbr* Irish Republican Army

Ira•ni•an \i-ˈrā-nē-ən *also* -ˈrä-\ *n* **:** a native or inhabitant of Iran — **Iranian** *adj*

Iraqi \i-ˈrä-kē, -ˈra-\ *n* **:** a native or inhabitant of Iraq — **Iraqi** *adj*

iras•ci•bil•i•ty \-ˌra-sə-ˈbi-lə-tē\ *n* **:** the quality or state of being irascible **:** proneness to anger

iras•ci•ble \i-ˈra-sə-bəl\ *adj* ♦ **:** marked by hot temper and easily provoked anger

♦ choleric, crabby, cranky, cross, irritable, short-tempered, snappish, snappy, snippy, testy, waspish

irate \ī-ˈrāt\ *adj* **1** ♦ **:** roused to ire **2 :** arising from anger — **irate•ly** *adv*

♦ angry, boiling, enraged, furious, rabid, sore

¹ire \ˈīr\ *n* ♦ **:** intense and usually openly displayed anger **:** ANGER, WRATH

♦ anger, furor, fury, indignation, outrage, rage, spleen, wrath, wrathfulness

²ire *vb* **ired; iring** ♦ **:** to provoke to anger

♦ anger, antagonize, enrage, incense, inflame, infuriate, madden, outrage, rankle, rile, roil

Ire *abbr* Ireland

ire•ful *adj* **:** full of ire **:** marked by ire; *also* **:** easily angered

ire•nic \ī-ˈre-nik\ *adj* **:** favoring, conducive to, or operating toward peace or conciliation

ir•i•des•cence \ˌir-ə-ˈdes-ᵊns\ *n* **:** a rainbowlike play of colors — **ir•i•des•cent** \-ᵊnt\ *adj*

irid•i•um \ir-ˈi-dē-əm\ *n* **:** a hard brittle heavy metallic chemical element

iris \ˈī-rəs\ *n, pl* **iris•es** *also* **iri•des** \ˈī-rə-ˌdēz, ˈir-ə-\ **1 :** the colored part around the pupil of the eye **2 :** any of a large genus of plants with linear basal leaves and large showy flowers

Irish \ˈīr-ish\ *n* **1 Irish** *pl* **:** the people of Ireland **2 :** the Celtic language of Ireland — **Irish** *adj* — **Irish•man** \-mən\ *n* — **Irish•wom•an** \-ˌwu̇-mən\ *n*

Irish bull *n* **:** an incongruous statement (as "it was hereditary in his family to have no children")

Irish coffee *n* **:** hot sugared coffee with Irish whiskey and whipped cream

Irish moss *n* **:** the dried and bleached plants of a red alga that is a source of carrageenan; *also* **:** this red alga
Irish setter *n* **:** any of a breed of hunting dogs with a mahogany-red coat
irk \'ərk\ *vb* ♦ **:** to make weary, irritated, or bored **:** ANNOY

♦ aggravate, annoy, bother, bug, chafe, exasperate, gall, get, grate, irritate, nettle, peeve, persecute, pique, put out, rasp, rile, vex

irk•some \'ərk-səm\ *adj* ♦ **:** tending to irk **:** ANNOYING — **irk•some•ly** *adv*

♦ aggravating, annoying, bothersome, frustrating, galling, irritating, pesty, vexatious

¹iron \'īrn, 'ī-ərn\ *n* **1 :** a heavy malleable magnetic metallic chemical element that rusts easily and is vital to biological processes **2 a :** something made of metal and especially iron **b** *pl* ♦ **:** something (as handcuffs) used to bind or restrain ⟨put them in ~*s*⟩ **3 :** a household device with a flat base that is heated and used for pressing cloth **4 :** STRENGTH, HARDNESS

♦ *usu* **irons** band, bond, chain, fetter, ligature, manacle, shackle

²iron *vb* **1 :** to press or smooth with or as if with a heated iron **2 :** to remove (as wrinkles) by ironing — **iron•er** *n*
¹iron•clad \-'klad\ *adj* **1 :** sheathed in iron armor **2 :** so firm or secure as to be unbreakable
²iron•clad \-ˌklad\ *n* **:** an armored naval vessel especially of the 19th century
iron curtain *n* **:** a political, military, and ideological barrier that isolates an area; *esp, often cap* **:** one formerly isolating an area under Soviet control
iron•ic \ī-'rä-nik\ *also* **iron•i•cal** \-ni-kəl\ *adj* **1 :** of, relating to, or marked by irony **2 :** given to irony
iron•i•cal•ly \-ni-k(ə-)lē\ *adv* **1 :** in an ironic manner **2 :** it is ironic
iron•ing *n* **:** clothes ironed or to be ironed
iron lung *n* **:** a device for artificial respiration that encloses the chest in a chamber in which changes of pressure force air into and out of the lungs
iron out *vb* **:** to remove or lessen difficulties in or extremes of
iron oxide *n* **:** FERRIC OXIDE
iron•stone \'ī(-ə)rn-ˌstōn, 'ī-ərn-\ *n* **1 :** a hard iron-rich sedimentary rock **2 :** a hard heavy durable pottery developed in England in the 19th century
iron•ware \-ˌwar\ *n* **:** articles made of iron
iron•weed \-ˌwēd\ *n* **:** any of a genus of mostly weedy plants related to the asters that have terminal heads of red, purple, or white flowers
iron•wood \-ˌwu̇d\ *n* **:** any of numerous trees or shrubs with exceptionally hard wood; *also* **:** the wood
iron•work \-ˌwərk\ *n* **1 :** work in iron **2** *pl* **:** a mill or building where iron or steel is smelted or heavy iron or steel products are made — **iron•work•er** *n*
iro•ny \'ī-rə-nē\ *n, pl* **-nies 1 :** the use of words to express the opposite of what one really means **2 :** incongruity between the actual result of a sequence of events and the expected result
Ir•o•quois \'ir-ə-ˌkwȯi\ *n, pl* **Iroquois** *same or* -ˌkwȯiz\ **1** *pl* **:** an American Indian confederacy orig. of New York that consisted of the Cayuga, Mohawk, Oneida, Onondaga, and Seneca and later included the Tuscarora **2 :** a member of any of the Iroquois peoples
ir•ra•di•ate \i-'rā-dē-ˌāt\ *vb* **-at•ed; -at•ing 1 :** to supply or brighten with light **:** ILLUMINATE **2 :** ENLIGHTEN **3 :** to treat by exposure to radiation **4 :** RADIATE — **ir•ra•di•a•tion** \-ˌrā-de-'ā-shən\ *n*
¹ir•ra•tio•nal \(ˌ)i-'ra-shə-nəl\ *adj* **1 :** incapable of reasoning ⟨~ beasts⟩; *also* **:** defective in mental power ⟨~ with fever⟩ **2** ♦ **:** not based on reason ⟨~ fears⟩ **3 :** being or numerically equal to an irrational number — **ir•ra•tio•nal•i•ty** \(ˌ)i-ˌra-shə-'na-lə-tē\ *n* — **ir•ra•tio•nal•ly** *adv*

♦ fallacious, illogical, invalid, unreasonable, unsound, weak

²irrational *n* **:** IRRATIONAL NUMBER
irrational number *n* **:** a real number that cannot be expressed as the quotient of two integers
ir•rec•on•cil•able \(ˌ)i-ˌre-kən-'sī-lə-bəl, -'re-kən-ˌsī-\ *adj* **:** impossible to reconcile, adjust, or harmonize — **ir•rec•on•cil•abil•i•ty** \(ˌ)i-ˌre-kən-ˌsī-lə-'bi-lə-tē\ *n*
ir•re•cov•er•able \ˌir-i-'kə-və-rə-bəl\ *adj* **:** not capable of being recovered or rectified **:** IRREPARABLE — **ir•re•cov•er•ably** \-blē\ *adv*
ir•re•deem•able \ˌir-i-'dē-mə-bəl\ *adj* **1 :** not redeemable; *esp* **:** not terminable by payment of the principal ⟨an ~ bond⟩ **2 :** not convertible into gold or silver at the will of the holder **3** ♦ **:** being beyond remedy

♦ hopeless, incorrigible, incurable, irremediable, irreparable, unrecoverable, unredeemable

ir•re•den•tism \-'den-ˌti-zəm\ *n* **:** a principle or policy directed toward the incorporation of a territory historically or ethnically part of another into that other — **ir•re•den•tist** \-tist\ *n or adj*
ir•re•duc•ible \ˌir-i-'dü-sə-bəl, -'dyü-\ *adj* **:** not reducible — **ir•re•duc•ibly** \-blē\ *adv*
ir•re•fut•able \ˌir-i-'fyü-tə-bəl, (ˌ)i-'re-fyət-\ *adj* ♦ **:** impossible to refute

♦ incontestable, indisputable, indubitable, unanswerable, undeniable, unquestionable *Ant* answerable, debatable, disputable, questionable

irreg *abbr* irregular
ir•reg•u•lar \(ˌ)i-'re-gyə-lər\ *adj* **1** ♦ **:** not regular **:** not natural or uniform **2 :** not conforming to the normal or usual manner of inflection ⟨~ verbs⟩ **3 :** not belonging to a regular or organized army ⟨~ troops⟩ — **irregular** *n* — **ir•reg•u•lar•ly** *adv*

♦ aberrant, abnormal, anomalous, atypical, deviant, unnatural
♦ informal, unceremonious, unconventional, unorthodox

ir•reg•u•lar•i•ty \i-ˌre-gyə-'lar-ə-tē\ *n, pl* **-ties 1 :** something that is irregular **2 :** the quality or state of being irregular **3 :** occasional constipation
ir•rel•e•vant \(ˌ)i-'re-lə-vənt\ *adj* ♦ **:** not relevant — **ir•rel•e•vance** \-vəns\ *n*

♦ extraneous, immaterial

ir•re•li•gious \ˌir-i-'li-jəs\ *adj* ♦ **:** lacking religious emotions, doctrines, or practices

♦ blasphemous, nonreligious, sacrilegious *Ant* religious

ir•re•me•di•a•ble \ˌir-i-'mē-dē-ə-bəl\ *adj* ♦ **:** impossible to remedy or correct

♦ hopeless, incorrigible, incurable, irredeemable, unrecoverable, unredeemable

ir•re•mov•able \-'mü-və-bəl\ *adj* **:** not removable
ir•rep•a•ra•ble \(ˌ)i-'re-pə-rə-bəl\ *adj* ♦ **:** impossible to make good, undo, repair, or remedy ⟨~ damage⟩

♦ irredeemable, irremediable, unrecoverable, unredeemable *Ant* redeemable, remediable, retrievable

ir•re•place•able \ˌir-i-'plā-sə-bəl\ *adj* **:** not replaceable
ir•re•press•ible \-'pre-sə-bəl\ *adj* **:** impossible to repress or control
ir•re•proach•able \-'prō-chə-bəl\ *adj* ♦ **:** not reproachable

♦ blameless, clear, faultless, guiltless, impeccable, innocent, irreproachable

ir•re•sist•ible \ˌir-i-'zis-tə-bəl\ *adj* **:** impossible to successfully resist — **ir•re•sist•ibly** \-blē\ *adv*
ir•res•o•lute \(ˌ)i-'re-zə-ˌlüt\ *adj* **:** uncertain how to act or proceed **:** VACILLATING — **ir•res•o•lute•ly** \-ˌlüt-lē; (ˌ)i-ˌre-zə-'lüt-\ *adv*
ir•res•o•lu•tion \(ˌ)i-ˌre-zə-'lü-shən\ *n* ♦ **:** lack of resolution **:** a fluctuation of mind (as in doubt or between hope and fear)

♦ hesitancy, hesitation, indecision, vacillation

ir•re•spec•tive of \ˌir-i-'spek-tiv-\ *prep* **:** without regard to
ir•re•spon•si•ble \-'spän-sə-bəl\ *adj* ♦ **:** not responsible — **ir•re•spon•si•bil•i•ty** \-ˌspän-sə-'bi-lə-tē\ *n* — **ir•re•spon•si•bly** \-'spän-sə-blē\ *adv*

♦ foolhardy, reckless

ir•re•triev•able \ˌir-i-'trē-və-bəl\ *adj* **:** not retrievable **:** IRRECOVERABLE
ir•rev•er•ence \(ˌ)i-'re-və-rəns\ *n* **1 :** lack of reverence **2** ♦ **:** an irreverent act or utterance

♦ blasphemy, defilement, desecration, impiety, sacrilege

ir•rev•er•ent \-rənt\ *adj* **:** lacking proper respect or seriousness; *also* **:** SATIRIC — **ir•rev•er•ent•ly** *adv*
ir•re•vers•ible \ˌir-i-'vər-sə-bəl\ *adj* **:** incapable of being reversed
ir•rev•o•ca•ble \(ˌ)i-'re-və-kə-bəl\ *adj* **:** incapable of being revoked or recalled — **ir•rev•o•ca•bly** \-blē\ *adv*
ir•ri•gate \'ir-ə-ˌgāt\ *vb* **-gat•ed; -gat•ing** ♦ **:** to supply (as land) with water by artificial means; *also* **:** to flush with liquid — **ir•ri•ga•tion** \ˌir-ə-'gā-shən\ *n*

♦ flush, rinse, sluice, wash

ir•ri•ta•bil•i•ty \ˌir-ə-tə-'bi-lə-tē\ *n* **1 :** the property of living things and of protoplasm that enables reaction to stimuli

2 ♦ **:** the quality or state of being irritable; *esp* **:** readiness to become annoyed or angry

♦ grumpiness, peevishness

ir•ri•ta•ble \ˈir-ə-tə-bəl\ *adj* ♦ **:** capable of being irritated; *esp* **:** readily or easily irritated — **ir•ri•ta•bly** \-blē\ *adv*

♦ choleric, crabby, cranky, cross, crotchety, grouchy, grumpy, irascible, peevish, perverse, petulant, short-tempered, snappish, snappy, snippy, testy, waspish

ir•ri•tant \ˈir-ə-tənt\ *n* ♦ **:** something that irritates or excites — **irritant** *adj*

♦ aggravation, annoyance, bother, exasperation, frustration, hassle, headache, inconvenience, nuisance, peeve, pest, problem, thorn

ir•ri•tate \ˈir-ə-ˌtāt\ *vb* **-tat•ed; -tat•ing 1** ♦ **:** to excite to anger **:** EXASPERATE **2** ♦ **:** to make sore or inflamed — **ir•ri•tat•ing•ly** *adv*

♦ [1] aggravate, annoy, bother, bug, chafe, exasperate, gall, get, grate, irk, nettle, peeve, persecute, pique, put out, rasp, rile, vex ♦ [2] abrade, chafe, gall

irritating *adj* ♦ **:** causing displeasure or annoyance

♦ aggravating, annoying, bothersome, frustrating, galling, irksome, pesty, vexatious

ir•ri•ta•tion \ˌir-ə-ˈtā-shən\ *n* **:** the act of irritating **:** the state of being irritated; *also* **:** something that irritates

ir•rupt \(ˌ)i-ˈrəpt\ *vb* **1 :** to rush in forcibly or violently **2 :** to increase suddenly in numbers ⟨rabbits ~ in cycles⟩

ir•rup•tion \-ˈrəp-shən\ *n* ♦ **:** an act or instance of irrupting; *esp* **:** a sudden violent or forcible entry

♦ descent, foray, incursion, invasion, raid

IRS *abbr* Internal Revenue Service

is *pres 3d sing of* BE

Isa *or* **Is** *abbr* Isaiah

Isa•iah \ī-ˈzā-ə\ *n* **1 :** a major Hebrew prophet in Judah about 740 to 701 B.C. **2 :** a book of Jewish and Christian Scripture

Isa•ias \ī-ˈzā-əs\ *n* **:** ISAIAH

ISBN *abbr* International Standard Book Number

is•che•mia \is-ˈkē-mē-ə\ *n* **:** deficient supply of blood to a body part (as the brain) — **is•che•mic** \-mik\ *adj*

-ish \ish\ *adj suffix* **1 :** of, relating to, or being ⟨Finn*ish*⟩ **2 :** characteristic of ⟨boy*ish*⟩ ⟨mul*ish*⟩ **3 :** inclined or liable to ⟨book*ish*⟩ **4 :** having a touch or trace of **:** somewhat ⟨purpl*ish*⟩ **5 :** having the approximate age of ⟨forty*ish*⟩

isin•glass \ˈīz-ᵊn-ˌglas, ˈī-ziŋ-\ *n* **1 :** a gelatin obtained from various fish **2 :** mica especially in thin sheets

isl *abbr* island

Is•lam \is-ˈläm, iz-, -ˈlam, ˈis-ˌ, ˈiz-ˌ\ *n* **:** the religious faith of Muslims including belief in Allah as the sole deity and in Muhammad as his prophet; *also* **:** the civilization built on this faith — **Is•lam•ic** \is-ˈlä-mik, iz-, -ˈla-\ *adj*

is•land \ˈī-lənd\ *n* **1** ♦ **:** a body of land smaller than a continent surrounded by water **2 :** something resembling an island in its isolation

♦ cay, isle, key

is•land•er \ˈī-lən-dər\ *n* **:** a native or inhabitant of an island

isle \ˈī(-ə)l\ *n* ♦ **:** a small island

♦ cay, island, key

is•let \ˈī-lət\ *n* **:** a small island

ism \ˈi-zəm\ *n* **:** a distinctive doctrine, cause, or theory

-ism \ˌi-zəm\ *n suffix* **1 :** act **:** practice **:** process ⟨critic*ism*⟩ **2 :** manner of action or behavior characteristic of a (specified) person or thing ⟨fanatic*ism*⟩ **3 :** state **:** condition **:** property ⟨dual*ism*⟩ **4 :** abnormal state or condition ⟨alcohol*ism*⟩ **5 :** doctrine **:** theory **:** cult ⟨Buddh*ism*⟩ **6 :** adherence to a set of principles ⟨stoic*ism*⟩ **7 :** prejudice or discrimination on the basis of a (specified) attribute ⟨rac*ism*⟩ ⟨sex*ism*⟩ **8 :** characteristic or peculiar feature or trait ⟨colloquial*ism*⟩

iso•bar \ˈī-sə-ˌbär\ *n* **:** a line on a map connecting places of equal barometric pressure — **iso•bar•ic** \ˌī-sə-ˈbär-ik, -ˈbar-\ *adj*

iso•late \ˈī-sə-ˌlāt\ *vb* **-lat•ed; -lat•ing** ♦ **:** to place or keep by itself **:** separate from others

♦ cut off, insulate, seclude, segregate, separate, sequester *Ant* desegregate, integrate

iso•lat•ed *adj* **1 :** occurring alone or once **:** UNIQUE **2 :** SPORADIC **3** ♦ **:** placed alone or apart

♦ cloistered, covert, quiet, remote, secluded, secret

iso•la•tion \ˌī-sə-ˈlā-shən\ *n* ♦ **:** the action of isolating **:** the condition of being isolated

♦ insulation, seclusion, segregation, sequestration, solitude

iso•la•tion•ism \ˌī-sə-ˈlā-shə-ˌni-zəm\ *n* **:** a policy of national isolation by abstention from international political and economic relations — **iso•la•tion•ist** \-shə-nist\ *n or adj*

iso•mer \ˈī-sə-mər\ *n* **:** any of two or more chemical compounds that contain the same numbers of atoms of the same elements but differ in structural arrangement and properties — **iso•mer•ic** \ˌī-sə-ˈmer-ik\ *adj* — **isom•er•ism** \ī-ˈsä-mə-ˌri-zəm\ *n*

iso•met•rics \ˌī-sə-ˈme-triks\ *n sing or pl* **:** exercise involving a series of brief and intense contractions of muscles against each other or against an immovable resistance — **iso•met•ric** *adj*

iso•prene \ˈī-sə-ˌprēn\ *n* **:** a hydrocarbon used especially in making synthetic rubber

isos•ce•les \ī-ˈsä-sə-ˌlēz\ *adj* **:** having two equal sides ⟨an ~ triangle⟩

iso•therm \ˈī-sə-ˌthərm\ *n* **:** a line on a map connecting points having the same temperature

iso•ther•mal \ˌī-sə-ˈthər-məl\ *adj* **:** of, relating to, or marked by equality of temperature

iso•tope \ˈī-sə-ˌtōp\ *n* **:** any of the forms of a chemical element that differ chiefly in the number of neutrons in an atom — **iso•to•pic** \ˌī-sə-ˈtä-pik, -ˈtō-\ *adj* — **iso•to•pi•cal•ly** \-ˈtä-pi-k(ə-)lē, -ˈtō-\ *adv*

Isr *abbr* Israel; Israeli

Is•rae•li \iz-ˈrā-lē\ *n, pl* **Israelis** *also* **Israeli :** a native or inhabitant of Israel — **Israeli** *adj*

Is•ra•el•ite \ˈiz-rē-ə-ˌlīt\ *n* **:** a member of the Hebrew people descended from Jacob

is•su•ance \ˈi-shü-wəns\ *n* ♦ **:** the act of issuing or giving out especially officially

♦ allocation, dispensation, distribution, division

¹is•sue \ˈi-shü\ *n* **1 :** the action of going, coming, or flowing out **:** EGRESS, EMERGENCE **2 :** a means or place of going out **:** EXIT, OUTLET **3** ♦ **:** the product of the reproductive processes of an animal or plant **:** OFFSPRING, PROGENY **4 :** OUTCOME, RESULT **5 :** a point of debate or controversy; *also* **:** the point at which an unsettled matter is ready for a decision **6 :** a discharge (as of blood) from the body **7 :** something coming forth from a specified source **8 :** the act of officially giving out or printing **:** PUBLICATION; *also* **:** the quantity of things given out at one time

♦ offspring, posterity, progeny, seed, spawn

²issue *vb* **is•sued; is•su•ing 1 :** to go, come, or flow out **2** ♦ **:** to come forth or cause to come forth **:** EMIT **3 :** ACCRUE **4 :** to descend from a specified parent or ancestor **5 :** to result in **6 :** to put forth or distribute officially **7** ♦ **:** to send out for sale or circulation **:** PUBLISH **8 :** EMANATE, RESULT — **is•su•er** *n*

♦ [2] cast, discharge, emit, exhale, expel, release, shoot, vent ♦ [7] get out, print, publish

¹-ist \ist\ *n suffix* **1 :** one that performs a (specified) action ⟨cycl*ist*⟩ **:** one that makes or produces ⟨novel*ist*⟩ **2 :** one that plays a (specified) musical instrument ⟨harp*ist*⟩ **3 :** one that operates a (specified) mechanical instrument or contrivance ⟨machin*ist*⟩ **4 :** one that specializes in a (specified) art or science or skill ⟨geolog*ist*⟩ **5 :** one that adheres to or advocates a (specified) doctrine or system or code of behavior ⟨social*ist*⟩ or that of a (specified) individual ⟨Darwin*ist*⟩

²-ist *adj suffix* **:** -ISTIC

isth•mi•an \ˈis-mē-ən\ *adj* **:** of, relating to, or situated in or near an isthmus

isth•mus \ˈis-məs\ *n* **:** a narrow strip of land connecting two larger portions of land

-is•tic \ˈis-tik\ *or* **-is•ti•cal** \ˈis-ti-kəl\ *adj suffix* **:** of, relating to, or characteristic of ⟨altru*istic*⟩

¹it \ˈit\ *pron* **1 :** that one — used of a lifeless thing, a plant, a person or animal, or an abstract entity ⟨~'s a big building⟩ ⟨~'s a shade tree⟩ ⟨who is ~⟩ ⟨beauty is everywhere and ~ is a source of joy⟩ **2** — used as a subject of an impersonal verb that expresses a condition or action without reference to an agent ⟨~ is raining⟩ **3** — used as an anticipatory subject or object ⟨~'s good to see you⟩

²it \ˈit\ *n* **:** the player in a game who performs the principal action of the game (as trying to find others in hide-and-seek)

It *abbr* Italian; Italy

ital *abbr* italic; italicized

Ital *abbr* Italian

Ital•ian \i-ˈtal-yən\ *n* **1 :** a native or inhabitant of Italy **2 :** the language of Italy — **Italian** *adj*

ital·ic \i-ˈta-lik, ī-\ *adj* **:** relating to type in which the letters slope up toward the right (as in "*italic*") — **italic** *n*
ital·i·cise *Brit var of* ITALICIZE
ital·i·cize \i-ˈta-lə-ˌsīz, ī-\ *vb* **-cized; -ciz·ing :** to print in italics — **ital·i·ci·za·tion** \-ˌta-lə-sə-ˈzā-shən\ *n*
1itch \ˈich\ *n* **1 :** an uneasy irritating skin sensation that evokes a desire to scratch the affected area **2 :** a skin disorder accompanied by an itch **3 ♦ :** a persistent desire — **itchy** *adj*

♦ appetite, craving, desire, drive, hankering, hunger, longing, lust, passion, thirst, urge, yearning, yen

2itch *vb* **1 :** to have an itch; *also* **:** to produce an itchy sensation **2 ♦ :** to have a restless desire or hankering for something — usu. used with *for*

♦ *usu* **itch for** ache for, crave, desire, die for, hanker for, hunger for, long for, lust (for *or* after), pine for, repine for, thirst for, want, wish for, yearn for

-ite \ˌīt\ *n suffix* **1 :** native **:** resident ⟨suburban*ite*⟩ **2 :** adherent **:** follower ⟨Lenin*ite*⟩ **3 :** product ⟨metabol*ite*⟩ **4 :** mineral **:** rock ⟨quartz*ite*⟩
item \ˈī-təm\ *n* **1 ♦ :** a separate particular in a list, account, or series **:** ARTICLE **2 ♦ :** a separate piece of news (as in a newspaper)

♦ [1] article, constituent, detail, element, feature, ingredient, particular, point ♦ [2] intelligence, news, story, tidings, word

item·ise *chiefly Brit var of* ITEMIZE
item·ize \ˈī-tə-ˌmīz\ *vb* **-ized; -iz·ing ♦ :** to set down in detail — **item·i·za·tion** \ˌī-tə-mə-ˈzā-shən\ *n*

♦ detail, enumerate, inventory, list, numerate

it·er·ate \ˈi-tə-ˌrāt\ *vb* **-at·ed; -at·ing :** REITERATE, REPEAT
it·er·a·tion \ˌi-tə-ˈrā-shən\ *n* **1 :** REPETITION; *esp* **:** a computational process in which a series of operations is repeated until a condition is met **2 :** one repetition of the series of operations in iteration
itin·er·ant \ī-ˈti-nə-rənt, ə-\ *adj* **♦ :** traveling from place to place; *esp* **:** covering a circuit ⟨an ~ preacher⟩

♦ errant, nomad, peripatetic, roaming, vagabond, vagrant

itin·er·ary \ī-ˈti-nə-ˌrer-ē, ə-\ *n, pl* **-ar·ies 1 :** the route of a journey or the proposed outline of one **2 :** a travel diary **3 :** GUIDEBOOK
its \ˈits\ *adj* **:** of or relating to it or itself
it·self \it-ˈself\ *pron* **:** that identical one — used reflexively, for emphasis, or in absolute constructions
-ity \ə-tē\ *n suffix* **:** quality **:** state **:** degree ⟨alkalin*ity*⟩
IUD \ˌī-(ˌ)yü-ˈdē\ *n* **:** INTRAUTERINE DEVICE
IV \ˌī-ˈvē\ *n* **:** an apparatus used to administer a fluid (as of nutrients) intravenously; *also* **:** a fluid administered by IV
-ive \iv\ *adj suffix* **:** that performs or tends toward an (indicated) action ⟨correct*ive*⟩
ivo·ry \ˈī-vrē, -və-rē\ *n, pl* **-ries 1 :** the hard creamy-white material composing the tusks of an elephant or walrus **2 :** a pale yellow color **3 :** something made of ivory or of a similar substance
ivory tower *n* **1 :** an impractical lack of concern with urgent problems **2 :** a place of learning
ivy \ˈī-vē\ *n, pl* **ivies :** a trailing woody evergreen vine with small black berries that is related to ginseng
IWW *abbr* Industrial Workers of the World
-ize \ˌīz\ *vb suffix* **1 :** cause to be or conform to or resemble ⟨American*ize*⟩ **:** cause to be formed into ⟨union*ize*⟩ **2 :** subject to a (specified) action ⟨satir*ize*⟩ **3 :** saturate, treat, or combine with ⟨macadam*ize*⟩ **4 :** treat like ⟨idol*ize*⟩ **5 :** become **:** become like ⟨crystall*ize*⟩ **6 :** be productive in or of **:** engage in a (specified) activity ⟨philosoph*ize*⟩ **7 :** adopt or spread the manner of activity or the teaching of ⟨Christian*ize*⟩

J

1j \ˈjā\ *n, pl* **j's** *or* **js** \ˈjāz\ *often cap* **:** the 10th letter of the English alphabet
2j *abbr, often cap* **1** jack **2** journal **3** judge **4** justice
1jab \ˈjab\ *vb* **jabbed; jab·bing :** to thrust quickly or abruptly **:** POKE
2jab *n* **♦ :** a usually short straight punch

♦ dab, dig, poke

1jab·ber \ˈja-bər\ *vb* **♦ :** to talk rapidly, indistinctly, or unintelligibly **:** CHATTER

♦ babble, chatter, drivel, gabble, gibber, prattle, sputter

2jabber *n* **:** unintelligible or meaningless language
jab·ber·er *n* **:** one that jabbers

♦ chatterbox, magpie, talker

jab·ber·wocky \ˈja-bər-ˌwä-kē\ *n* **♦ :** meaningless speech or writing

♦ babble, gabble, gibberish, gobbledygook, hogwash, jabber, nonsense, piffle, prattle

ja·bot \zha-ˈbō, ˈja-ˌbō\ *n* **:** a ruffle worn down the front of a dress or shirt
jac·a·ran·da \ˌja-kə-ˈran-də\ *n* **:** any of a genus of pinnate-leaved tropical American trees with clusters of showy blue flowers
1jack \ˈjak\ *n* **1 :** a mechanical device; *esp* **:** one used to raise a heavy body a short distance **2 :** a male donkey **3 :** a small target ball in lawn bowling **4 ♦ :** a small national flag flown by a ship **5 :** a small 6-pointed metal object used in a game (**jacks**) **6 :** a playing card bearing the figure of a soldier or servant **7 :** a socket into which a plug is inserted for connecting electric circuits **8 a :** an adult male human **b :** a member of a ship's crew

♦ banner, colors (*or* colours), ensign, flag, pennant, standard, streamer

2jack *vb* **1 ♦ :** to raise by means of a jack **2 ♦ :** to raise the level of ⟨~ up prices⟩

♦ boost, crane, elevate, heave, heft, heighten, hike, hoist, lift, pick up, raise, up, uphold

jack·al \ˈja-kəl\ *n* **:** any of several mammals of Asia and Africa related to the wolves
jack·a·napes \ˈja-kə-ˌnāps\ *n* **1 :** MONKEY, APE **2 :** an impudent or conceited person
jack·ass \ˈjak-ˌas\ *n* **1 ♦ :** the domestic ass **:** DONKEY; *esp* **:** a male donkey **2 ♦ :** a stupid person

♦ [1] ass, donkey ♦ [2] blockhead, dolt, donkey, dope, dummy, idiot, imbecile, nitwit, numskull, simpleton

jack·boot \-ˌbüt\ *n* **1 :** a heavy military boot of glossy black leather extending above the knee **2 :** a laceless military boot reaching to the calf
jack·daw \ˈjak-ˌdȯ\ *n* **:** a black and gray Old World crowlike bird
jack·et \ˈja-kət\ *n* **1 :** a garment for the upper body usually having a front opening, collar, and sleeves **2 ♦ :** an outer covering or casing ⟨a book ~⟩

♦ armor, capsule, case, casing, cocoon, cover, housing, husk, pod, sheath, shell

Jack Frost *n* **:** frost or frosty weather personified
jack·ham·mer \ˈjak-ˌha-mər\ *n* **:** a pneumatic percussion tool for drilling rock or breaking pavement
jack–in–the–box *n, pl* **jack–in–the–boxes** *or* **jacks–in–the–box :** a toy consisting of a small box out of which a figure springs when the lid is raised
jack–in–the–pulpit *n, pl* **jack–in–the–pulpits** *also* **jacks–in–the–pulpit :** a No. American spring-flowering woodland herb having an upright club-shaped spadix arched over by a green and purple spathe
1jack·knife \ˈjak-ˌnīf\ *n* **1 :** a large pocketknife **2 :** a dive in which the diver bends from the waist and touches the ankles before straightening out
2jackknife *vb* **:** to fold like a jackknife ⟨the trailer truck *jackknifed*⟩
jack·leg \ˈjak-ˌleg\ *adj* **1 :** lacking skill or training **2 :** MAKESHIFT
jack–of–all–trades *n, pl* **jacks–of–all–trades :** one who is able to do passable work at various tasks
jack–o'–lan·tern \ˈja-kə-ˌlan-tərn\ *n* **:** a lantern made of a pumpkin cut to look like a human face

jack•pot \ˈjak-ˌpät\ *n* **1 :** a large sum of money formed by the accumulation of stakes from previous play (as in poker) **2 :** an impressive and often unexpected success or reward
jack•rab•bit \-ˌra-bət\ *n* **:** any of several large hares of western No. America with very long ears and hind legs
Jack Russell terrier \ˈjak-ˈrə-səl-\ *n* **:** any of a breed of small terriers having a white coat with dark markings
jack•straw \-ˌstrȯ\ *n* **1** *pl* **:** a game in which straws or thin sticks are let fall in a heap and each player in turn tries to remove them one at a time without disturbing the rest **2 :** one of the straws or sticks in jackstraws
jack–tar \-ˈtär\ *n, often cap* ♦ **:** a member of a ship's crew **:** SAILOR

♦ gob, jack, mariner, sailor, seaman, swab, tar

Ja•cob's ladder \ˈjā-kəbz-\ *n* **:** any of several perennial herbs related to phlox that have pinnate leaves and blue or white bell-shaped flowers
jac•quard \ˈja-ˌkärd\ *n, often cap* **:** a fabric of intricate variegated weave or pattern
¹jade \ˈjād\ *n* **1 :** a broken-down, vicious, or worthless horse **2 :** a disreputable woman
²jade *vb* **jad•ed; jad•ing 1 :** to wear out by overwork or abuse **2** ♦ **:** to become weary especially through repetition or excess

♦ bore, tire, weary

³jade *n* **:** a usually green gemstone that takes a high polish
jad•ed *adj* ♦ **:** fatigued by overwork; *also* **:** made dull, apathetic, or cynical by experience or by surfeit

♦ beat, bushed, dead, drained, limp, prostrate, spent, tired, weary, worn-out

¹jag \ˈjag\ *n* **:** a sharp projecting part
²jag *n* **:** SPREE
jag•ged \ˈja-gəd\ *adj* ♦ **:** sharply notched

♦ broken, craggy, ragged, scraggly

jag•uar \ˈja-ˌgwär\ *n* **:** a black-spotted tropical American cat that is larger and stockier than the Old World leopard
jai alai \ˈhī-ˌlī\ *n* **:** a court game played by usually two or four players with a ball and a curved wicker basket strapped to the wrist
¹jail \ˈjāl\ *n* ♦ **:** a place of confinement for persons held in lawful custody **:** PRISON; *esp* **:** such a place for the confinement of persons awaiting trial or those convicted of minor crimes

♦ brig, hoosegow, jug, lockup, pen, penitentiary, prison, stockade

²jail *vb* ♦ **:** to confine in or as if in a jail

♦ commit, confine, immure, imprison

jail•bird \-ˌbərd\ *n* **:** an habitual criminal
jail•break \-ˌbrāk\ *n* **:** a forcible escape from jail
jail•er *also* **jail•or** \ˈjā-lər\ *n* **:** a keeper of a jail
jal•ap \ˈja-ləp, ˈjä-\ *n* **:** a powdered purgative drug from the root of a Mexican plant related to the morning glory; *also* **:** this root or plant
ja•la•pe•ño \ˌhä-lə-ˈpān-(ˌ)yō\ *n* **:** a small plump dark green chili pepper
ja•lopy \jə-ˈlä-pē\ *n, pl* **ja•lop•ies :** a dilapidated vehicle (as an automobile)
jal•ou•sie \ˈja-lə-sē\ *n* **:** a blind, window, or door with adjustable horizontal slats or louvers
¹jam \ˈjam\ *vb* **jammed; jam•ming 1** ♦ **:** to press into a close or tight position; *also* **:** to become blocked or wedged **2 :** to cause to become wedged so as to be unworkable; *also* **:** to make or become unworkable through the jamming of a movable part **3 :** to push forcibly ⟨~ on the brakes⟩ **4 :** CRUSH, BRUISE **5 :** to make unintelligible by sending out interfering signals or messages **6 :** to take part in a jam session **7 :** to fill often to excess — **jam•mer** *n*

♦ cram, crowd, ram, sandwich, squeeze, stuff, wedge ♦ block, choke, clog, close (off), congest, dam, obstruct, plug (up), stop (up), stuff

²jam *n* **1** ♦ **:** a crowded mass that impedes or blocks ⟨traffic ~⟩ **2 :** a difficult state of affairs

♦ backup, bottleneck, snarl

³jam *n* **:** a food made by boiling fruit and sugar to a thick consistency
Jam *abbr* Jamaica
Ja•mai•can \jə-ˈmā-kən\ *n* **:** a native or inhabitant of Jamaica — **Jamaican** *adj*
jamb \ˈjam\ *n* **:** an upright piece forming the side of an opening (as of a door)
jam•ba•laya \ˌjəm-bə-ˈlī-ə\ *n* **:** rice cooked with ham, sausage, chicken, shrimp, or oysters and seasoned with herbs
jam•bo•ree \ˌjam-bə-ˈrē\ *n* **:** a large festive gathering
James \ˈjāmz\ *n* **:** a moral lecture addressed to early Christians and included as a book in the New Testament
jam–pack \ˈjam-ˈpak\ *vb* ♦ **:** to pack tightly or to excess

♦ charge, cram, fill, heap, jam, load, pack, stuff

jam session *n* **:** an impromptu performance especially by jazz musicians
Jan *abbr* January
jan•gle \ˈjaŋ-gəl\ *vb* **jan•gled; jan•gling :** to make a harsh or discordant sound — **jangle** *n*
jan•i•tor \ˈja-nə-tər\ *n* **1** ♦ **:** a person who has the care of a building **2 :** a person who tends a door — **jan•i•to•ri•al** \ˌja-nə-ˈtōr-ē-əl\ *adj*

♦ caretaker, custodian, guardian, keeper, warden, watchman

Jan•u•ary \ˈja-nyə-ˌwer-ē\ *n* **:** the 1st month of the year
¹ja•pan \jə-ˈpan\ *n* **:** a varnish giving a hard brilliant finish
²japan *vb* **ja•panned; ja•pan•ning :** to cover with a coat of japan
Jap•a•nese \ˌja-pə-ˈnēz, -ˈnēs\ *n, pl* **Japanese 1 :** a native or inhabitant of Japan **2 :** the language of Japan — **Japanese** *adj*
Japanese beetle *n* **:** a small metallic green and brown scarab beetle introduced from Japan that is a pest on the roots of grasses as a grub and on foliage and fruits as an adult
¹jape \ˈjāp\ *vb* **japed; jap•ing 1 :** JOKE **2 :** MOCK
²jape *n* **:** JEST, GIBE
¹jar \ˈjär\ *vb* **jarred; jar•ring 1 :** to make a harsh or discordant sound **2** ♦ **:** to have a harsh or disagreeable effect **3 :** VIBRATE, SHAKE

♦ clash, collide, conflict

²jar *n* **1 :** a state of conflict **2 :** a harsh discordant sound **3** ♦ **:** a sudden or unexpected shake **:** JOLT **4 :** a painful effect **:** SHOCK

♦ bump, collision, concussion, crash, impact, jolt, shock, smash, strike, wallop

³jar *n* **:** a widemouthed container usually of glass or earthenware
jar•di•niere \ˌjärd-ᵊn-ˈir\ *n* **:** an ornamental stand for plants or flowers
jar•gon \ˈjär-gən\ *n* **1 :** confused unintelligible language **2** ♦ **:** the special vocabulary of a particular group or activity **3 :** obscure and often pretentious language

♦ argot, cant, language, lingo, slang, terminology, vocabulary

Jas *abbr* James
jas•mine \ˈjaz-mən\ *n* **:** any of various climbing shrubs with fragrant flowers
jas•per \ˈjas-pər\ *n* **:** a usually red, yellow, or brown opaque quartz
jaun•dice \ˈjȯn-dəs\ *n* **1 :** yellowish discoloration of skin, tissues, and body fluids by bile pigments; *also* **:** an abnormal condition marked by jaundice **2 :** a state or attitude characterized by satiety, distaste, or hostility
jaun•diced \-dəst\ *adj* **1 :** affected with or as if with jaundice **2** ♦ **:** exhibiting envy, distaste, or hostility

♦ covetous, envious, jealous, resentful ♦ antagonistic, hostile, inhospitable, inimical, negative, unfriendly, unsympathetic

jaunt \ˈjȯnt\ *n* ♦ **:** a short trip usually for pleasure

♦ excursion, junket, outing, sally

jaun•ti•ly \ˈjȯn-tə-lē\ *adv* ♦ **:** in a light or carefree manner

♦ exuberantly, gaily, sprightly

jaun•ty \ˈjȯn-tē\ *adj* **jaun•ti•er; -est** ♦ **:** sprightly in manner or appearance **:** LIVELY — **jaun•ti•ness** \-tē-nəs\ *n*

♦ active, animate, animated, brisk, energetic, lively, snappy, spirited, sprightly, springy

Ja•va•nese \ˌja-və-ˈnēz, ˌjä-, -ˈnēs\ *n* **:** a native or inhabitant of the Indonesian island of Java
jav•e•lin \ˈja-və-lən\ *n* **1 :** a light spear **2 :** a slender shaft thrown for distance in a track-and-field contest
¹jaw \ˈjȯ\ *n* **1 :** either of the bony or cartilaginous structures that support the soft tissues enclosing the mouth and that usually bear teeth **2 :** the parts forming the walls of the mouth and serving to open and close it — usually used in plural **3 :** one of a pair of movable parts for holding or crushing something — **jawed** \ˈjȯd\ *adj*
²jaw *vb* ♦ **:** to talk abusively, indignantly, or at length

♦ admonish, chide, lecture, rail (at *or* against), rate, rebuke, reprimand, scold ♦ chat, converse, gab, palaver, patter, prattle, rattle, talk, visit

¹**jaw•bone** \-ˌbōn\ *n* : JAW 1
²**jawbone** *vb* : to talk forcefully and persuasively
jaw•break•er \-ˌbrā-kər\ *n* **1** : a word difficult to pronounce **2** : a round hard candy
jaw–drop•ping \ˈjȯ-ˌdra-piŋ\ *adj* : causing great surprise or astonishment
jaw•less fish \ˈjȯ-ləs-\ *n* : any of a group of primitive vertebrates (as lampreys) without jaws
jay \ˈjā\ *n* : any of various noisy brightly colored often largely blue birds smaller than the related crows
jay•bird \ˈjā-ˌbərd\ *n* : JAY
jay•vee \ˌjā-ˈvē\ *n* **1** : JUNIOR VARSITY **2** : a member of a junior varsity team
jay•walk \ˈjā-ˌwȯk\ *vb* : to cross a street carelessly without regard for traffic regulations — **jay•walk•er** *n*
¹**jazz** \ˈjaz\ *n* **1** : American music characterized by improvisation, syncopated rhythms, and contrapuntal ensemble playing **2** ♦ : empty talk **3** : similar but unspecified things : STUFF

♦ bunk, claptrap, drivel, gibberish, hogwash, nonsense, piffle, prattle, rot

²**jazz** *vb* ♦ : to increase the appeal or excitement of : ENLIVEN ⟨~ things up⟩

♦ *usu* **jazz up** animate, brace, energize, enliven, fire, invigorate, liven up, pep up, quicken, stimulate, vitalize, vivify, zip (up)

jazzy \ˈja-zē\ *adj* **jazz•i•er; -est** **1** : having the characteristics of jazz **2** ♦ : marked by unrestraint, animation, or flashiness

♦ active, animate, animated, flashy, jaunty, lively, racy, sharp, smart, snappy, spirited, sprightly

JCS *abbr* joint chiefs of staff
jct *abbr* junction
JD *abbr* **1** doctor of jurisprudence; doctor of law **2** doctor of laws **3** justice department **4** juvenile delinquent
jeal•ous \ˈje-ləs\ *adj* **1** : demanding complete devotion **2** ♦ : hostile toward a rival or of one believed to enjoy an advantage **3** : VIGILANT — **jeal•ous•ly** *adv*

♦ covetous, envious, jaundiced, resentful

jeal•ou•sy \-lə-sē\ *n* **1** ♦ : a jealous disposition, attitude, or feeling **2** : zealous vigilance

♦ covetousness, enviousness, envy, resentment

jeans \ˈjēnz\ *n pl* : pants made of durable twilled cotton cloth
jeep \ˈjēp\ *n* : a small four-wheel drive general-purpose motor vehicle used in World War II
¹**jeer** \ˈjir\ *vb* ♦ : to speak or cry out in derision : MOCK

♦ deride, gibe, laugh, mock, ridicule, scout

²**jeer** *n* ♦ : a jeering remark or sound : TAUNT

♦ boo, catcall, hiss, hoot, raspberry, snort, taunt

Je•ho•vah \ji-ˈhō-və\ *n* ♦ : the supreme or ultimate reality

♦ Almighty, deity, Supreme Being

je•hu \ˈjē-hü, -hyü\ *n* : a driver of a coach or cab
je•june \ji-ˈjün\ *adj* : lacking interest or significance : DULL
je•ju•num \ji-ˈjü-nəm\ *n* : the section of the small intestine between the duodenum and the ileum — **je•ju•nal** \-ˈjün-ᵊl\ *adj*
jell \ˈjel\ *vb* **1** ♦ : to come to the consistency of jelly **2** ♦ : to take shape

♦ [1] clot, coagulate, congeal, gel, set ♦ [2] crystallize, form, shape, solidify

¹**jel•ly** \ˈje-lē\ *n, pl* **jellies** **1** : a food with a soft elastic consistency due usually to the presence of gelatin or pectin; *esp* : a fruit product made by boiling sugar and the juice of a fruit **2** : a substance resembling jelly
²**jelly** *vb* : to bring to or come to the consistency of jelly
jelly bean *n* : a bean-shaped candy
jel•ly•fish \ˈje-lē-ˌfish\ *n* : a marine coelenterate with a nearly transparent jellylike body and stinging tentacles
jen•net \ˈje-nət\ *n* **1** : a small Spanish horse **2** : a female donkey
jen•ny \ˈje-nē\ *n, pl* **jennies** : a female bird or donkey
jeop•ar•dize \-ˌdīz\ *vb* ♦ : to expose to danger or risk

♦ adventure, compromise, gamble with, hazard, imperil, menace, risk, venture

jeop•ar•dy \ˈje-pər-dē\ *n* ♦ : exposure to death, loss, or injury

♦ danger, distress, peril, risk, trouble

Jer *abbr* Jeremiah; Jeremias
jer•e•mi•ad \ˌjer-ə-ˈmī-əd, -ˌad\ *n* : a prolonged lamentation or complaint; *also* : a cautionary or angry harangue
Jer•e•mi•ah \ˌjer-ə-ˈmī-ə\ *n* : a book of Jewish and Christian Scripture
Jer•e•mi•as \ˌjer-ə-ˈmī-əs\ *n* : JEREMIAH
¹**jerk** \ˈjərk\ *n* **1** ♦ : a short quick pull or twist : TWITCH **2** ♦ : an annoyingly stupid or foolish person — **jerk•i•ly** \ˈjər-kə-lē\ *adv*

♦ [1] draw, haul, pluck, pull, tug, twitch, wrench ♦ [2] beast, boor, churl, clown, creep, cretin, cur, heel, joker, louse, lout, skunk, slob, snake

²**jerk** *vb* **1** ♦ : to give a sharp quick push, pull, or twist **2** ♦ : to move in short abrupt motions

♦ [1] buck, hitch, jolt, twitch ♦ [2] fiddle, fidget, squirm, twitch, wiggle

jer•kin \ˈjər-kən\ *n* : a close-fitting usually sleeveless jacket
jerk•wa•ter \ˈjərk-ˌwȯ-tər, -ˌwä-\ *adj* : of minor importance : INSIGNIFICANT ⟨~ towns⟩
jerky \ˈjər-kē\ *adj* **1** : moving along with or marked by fits and starts **2** : lacking in sense, judgment, or discretion
jer•ry–built \ˈjer-ē-ˌbilt\ *adj* : built cheaply and flimsily
jer•ry–rigged \-ˌrigd\ *adj* ♦ : organized or constructed in a crude or improvised manner

♦ artless, clumsy, crude, rough, rude, unrefined

jer•sey \ˈjər-zē\ *n, pl* **jerseys** **1** : a plain weft-knitted fabric **2** : a close-fitting knitted shirt **3** *often cap* : any of a breed of small usually fawn-colored dairy cattle
Jersey barrier *n* : a concrete slab that is used with others to block or reroute traffic or to divide a highway
Je•ru•sa•lem artichoke \jə-ˈrü-sə-ləm-\ *n* : a No. American sunflower widely grown for its edible tubers that are used as a vegetable; *also* : its tubers
jess \ˈjes\ *n* : a leg strap by which a captive bird of prey may be controlled
jessamine *var of* JASMINE
¹**jest** \ˈjest\ *n* **1** ♦ : an act intended to provoke laughter **2** ♦ : a witty remark **3** ♦ : a frivolous mood ⟨said in ~⟩

♦ [1, 2] crack, gag, joke, laugh, pleasantry, quip, sally, waggery, wisecrack, witticism ♦ [3] fun, game, play, sport

²**jest** *vb* ♦ : to speak or act without seriousness or in a frivolous manner; *also* : to make a witty remark

♦ banter, fool, fun, jive, joke, josh, kid, quip, wisecrack

jest•er \ˈjes-tər\ *n* ♦ : a retainer formerly kept to provide casual entertainment; *broadly* : one given to jests

♦ card, comedian, comic, humorist, joker, wag, wit

¹**jet** \ˈjet\ *n* : a velvet-black coal that takes a good polish and is often used for jewelry
²**jet** *vb* **jet•ted; jet•ting** ♦ : to spout or emit in a stream

♦ gush, pour, rush, spew, spout, spurt, squirt

³**jet** *n* **1** : a forceful rush (as of liquid or gas) through a narrow opening; *also* : a nozzle for a jet of fluid **2** : a jet-propelled airplane
⁴**jet** *vb* **jet•ted; jet•ting** : to travel by jet
jet lag *n* : a condition that is marked especially by fatigue and irritability and occurs following a long flight through several time zones — **jet–lagged** *adj*
jet•lin•er \ˈjet-ˌlī-nər\ *n* : a jet-propelled airliner
jet•port \-ˌpōrt\ *n* : an airport designed to handle jets
jet–pro•pelled \ˌjet-prə-ˈpeld\ *adj* : driven by an engine (**jet engine**) that produces propulsion (**jet propulsion**) by the rearward discharge of a jet of fluid (as heated air and exhaust gases)
jet•sam \ˈjet-səm\ *n* : jettisoned goods; *esp* : such goods washed ashore
jet set *n* : an international group of wealthy people who frequent fashionable resorts
jet stream *n* : a long narrow high-altitude current of high-speed winds blowing generally from the west
¹**jet•ti•son** \ˈje-tə-sən\ *vb* **1** : to throw (goods) overboard to lighten a ship or aircraft in distress **2** ♦ : to get rid of as superfluous or encumbering : DISCARD

♦ cast, discard, ditch, dump, fling, junk, lose, reject, scrap, shed, shuck, slough, throw away, throw out, unload

²**jettison** *n* : a voluntary sacrifice of cargo to lighten a ship's load in time of distress

jet•ty \ˈje-tē\ *n, pl* **jetties 1 :** a pier built to influence the current or to protect a harbor **2** ♦ **:** a landing wharf

♦ dock, float, landing, levee, pier, quay, wharf

jeu d'es•prit \zhœ̄-des-ˈprē\ *n, pl* **jeux d'esprit** *same*\ **:** a witty comment or composition

Jew \ˈjü\ *n* **1 :** ISRAELITE **2 :** one whose religion is Judaism — **Jew•ish** *adj*

[1]**jew•el** \ˈjü-əl\ *n* **1 :** an ornament of precious metal **2** ♦ **:** a precious stone **:** GEMSTONE **3** ♦ **:** one that is highly esteemed

♦ [2] brilliant, gem, gemstone ♦ [3] boast, credit, glory, honor (*or* honour), pride, treasure ♦ [3] catch, gem, pearl, plum, prize, treasure

[2]**jewel** *vb* **-eled** *or* **-elled; -el•ing** *or* **-el•ling :** to adorn or equip with jewels

jewel box *n* **:** a thin plastic case for a CD or DVD

jew•el•er *or* **jew•el•ler** \ˈjü-ə-lər\ *n* **:** a person who makes or deals in jewelry and related articles

jew•el•ry *or Can and Brit* **jew•el•lery** \ˈjü-əl-rē\ *n* **:** JEWELS; *esp* **:** objects of precious metal set with gems and worn for personal adornment

Jew•ry \ˈju̇r-ē, ˈju̇-ər-ē, ˈjü-rē\ *n* **:** the Jewish people

jg *abbr* junior grade

[1]**jib** \ˈjib\ *n* **:** a triangular sail set on a line running from the bow to the mast

[2]**jib** *vb* **jibbed; jib•bing :** to refuse to proceed further

[1]**jibe** *var of* GIBE

[2]**jibe** \ˈjīb\ *vb* **jibed; jib•ing** ♦ **:** to be in accord **:** AGREE

♦ accord, agree, answer, check, coincide, comport, conform, correspond, dovetail, fit, go, harmonize, square, tally

ji•ca•ma \ˈhē-kə-mə\ *n* **:** an edible starchy tuber of a tropical American vine of the legume family

jif•fy \ˈji-fē\ *n, pl* **jiffies** ♦ **:** a small portion or point of time **:** MOMENT, INSTANT ⟨I'll be ready in a ~⟩

♦ flash, instant, minute, moment, second, shake, trice, twinkle, twinkling, wink

[1]**jig** \ˈjig\ *n* **1 :** a lively dance in triple rhythm **2** ♦ **:** a crafty procedure or practice meant to deceive or defraud **:** TRICK ⟨the ~ is up⟩ **3 :** a device used to hold work during manufacture or assembly

♦ artifice, device, dodge, gimmick, ploy, scheme, sleight, stratagem, trick, wile

[2]**jig** *vb* **jigged; jig•ging :** to dance a jig

jig•ger \ˈji-gər\ *n* **1 :** a measure usually holding 1 to 2 ounces (30 to 60 milliliters) used in mixing drinks **2** ♦ **:** an often small mechanical or electronic device with a practical use but often thought of as a novelty

♦ contraption, contrivance, gadget, gimmick, gizmo

jig•gle \ˈji-gəl\ *vb* **jig•gled; jig•gling** ♦ **:** to move with quick little jerks — **jiggle** *n*

♦ fiddle, fidget, jerk, squirm, twitch, wiggle

jig•saw \ˈjig-ˌsȯ\ *n* **:** a machine saw with a narrow vertically reciprocating blade for cutting curved lines

jigsaw puzzle *n* **:** a puzzle consisting of small irregularly cut pieces to be fitted together to form a picture

ji•had \ji-ˈhäd, -ˈhad\ *n* **1 :** a Muslim holy war **2 :** a reforming enterprise undertaken with zeal

[1]**jilt** \ˈjilt\ *vb* **:** to drop (a lover) capriciously or unfeelingly

[2]**jilt** *n* **:** one who jilts a lover

jim crow \ˈjim-ˈkrō\ *n, often cap J&C* **:** discrimination against blacks especially by legal enforcement or traditional sanctions — **jim crow** *adj, often cap J&C* — **jim crow•ism** \-ˈkrō-ˌi-zəm\ *n, often cap J&C*

[1]**jim–dan•dy** \ˈjim-ˈdan-dē\ *n* ♦ **:** something excellent of its kind

♦ beauty, crackerjack, dandy, knockout, pip

[2]**jim–dandy** *adj* **:** fine or wonderful of its kind

jim•mies \ˈji-mēz\ *n pl* **:** tiny rod-shaped bits of usually chocolate-flavored candy often sprinkled on ice cream

[1]**jim•my** \ˈji-mē\ *n, pl* **jimmies :** a small crowbar

[2]**jimmy** *vb* **jim•mied; jim•my•ing** ♦ **:** to force open with a jimmy

♦ prize, pry

jim•son•weed \ˈjim-sən-ˌwēd\ *n, often cap* **:** a coarse poisonous weed related to the tomato that has large trumpet-shaped white or violet flowers

[1]**jin•gle** \ˈjiŋ-gəl\ *vb* **jin•gled; jin•gling** ♦ **:** to make a light clinking or tinkling sound

♦ chink, tinkle

[2]**jingle** *n* **1 :** a light clinking or tinkling sound **2** ♦ **:** a short verse or song with catchy repetition

♦ lay, lyric, song, vocal

jin•go•ism \ˈjiŋ-gō-ˌi-zəm\ *n* **:** extreme chauvinism or nationalism marked especially by a belligerent foreign policy — **jin•go•ist** \-ist\ *n* — **jin•go•is•tic** \ˌjiŋ-gō-ˈis-tik\ *adj*

jin•rik•sha \jin-ˈrik-ˌshȯ\ *n* **:** RICKSHA

[1]**jinx** \ˈjiŋks\ *n* **:** one that brings bad luck

[2]**jinx** *vb* **:** to foredoom to failure or misfortune

jit•ney \ˈjit-nē\ *n, pl* **jitneys :** a small bus that serves a regular route on a flexible schedule

jit•ter•bug \ˈji-tər-ˌbəg\ *n* **:** a dance in which couples two-step, balance, and twirl vigorously in standardized patterns — **jitterbug** *vb*

jit•ters \ˈji-tərz\ *n pl* ♦ **:** extreme nervousness

♦ shakes, shivers, willies

jit•tery \-tə-rē\ *adj* **1** ♦ **:** suffering from the jitters **2** ♦ **:** marked by jittering movements

♦ excitable, flighty, fluttery, high-strung, jumpy, nervous, skittish, spooky ♦ aflutter, anxious, edgy, jumpy, nervous, nervy, perturbed, tense, troubled, uneasy, upset, worried

[1]**jive** \ˈjīv\ *n* **1 :** swing music or dancing performed to it **2 :** glib, deceptive, or foolish talk **3 :** the jargon of jazz enthusiasts **4** ♦ **:** a special jargon of difficult or slang terms

♦ argot, cant, dialect, jargon, language, lingo, patois, patter, slang, terminology, vocabulary

[2]**jive** *vb* **jived; jiv•ing 1** ♦ **:** to persuade with flattery or gentle urging especially in the face of reluctance **:** TEASE; *also* **:** kid around **2 :** to dance to or play jive

♦ chaff, josh, kid, rally, razz, rib, ride, roast, tease

Jn *or* **Jno** *abbr* John

Jo *abbr* Joel

[1]**job** \ˈjäb\ *n* **1 :** a piece of work **2** ♦ **:** something that has to be done **:** TASK; *also* **:** a specific duty, role, or function **3** ♦ **:** a regular remunerative position — **job•less** *adj*

♦ [2] assignment, chore, duty, stint, task ♦ [2] assignment, charge, mission, operation, post ♦ [3] appointment, billet, capacity, function, place, position, post, situation

[2]**job** *vb* **jobbed; job•bing 1 :** to do occasional pieces of work for hire **2 :** to hire or let by the job

Job \ˈjōb\ *n* **:** a book of Jewish and Christian Scripture

job action *n* **:** a protest action by workers to force compliance with demands

job•ber \ˈjä-bər\ *n* **1 :** a person who buys goods and then sells them to other dealers **:** MIDDLEMAN **2 :** a person who does work by the job

job•hold•er \ˈjäb-ˌhōl-dər\ *n* ♦ **:** one having a regular job

♦ employee, hand, hireling, worker

jock \ˈjäk\ *n* **:** ATHLETE; *esp* **:** a college athlete

[1]**jock•ey** \ˈjä-kē\ *n, pl* **jockeys :** one who rides a horse especially as a professional in a race

[2]**jockey** *vb* **jock•eyed; jock•ey•ing :** to maneuver or manipulate by adroit or devious means

jock•strap \ˈjäk-ˌstrap\ *n* **:** ATHLETIC SUPPORTER

jo•cose \jō-ˈkōs\ *adj* **:** given to joking **:** MERRY; *also* **:** characterized by joking

joc•u•lar \ˈjä-kyə-lər\ *adj* ♦ **:** marked by jesting **:** PLAYFUL — **joc•u•lar•i•ty** \ˌjäk-yə-ˈlar-ə-tē\ *n* — **joc•u•lar•ly** *adv*

♦ clever, facetious, humorous, playful, smart, witty

jo•cund \ˈjä-kənd\ *adj* ♦ **:** marked by mirth or cheerfulness

♦ blithe, boon, festive, gay, gleeful, jolly, jovial, merry, mirthful, sunny

jodh•pur \ˈjäd-pər\ *n* **1** *pl* **:** riding breeches loose above the knee and tight-fitting below **2 :** an ankle-high boot fastened with a strap

Joe Blow \ˈjō-\ *n* **:** an average or ordinary man

Jo•el \ˈjō-əl\ *n* **:** a book of Jewish and Christian Scripture

Joe Six–Pack \ˈjō-\ *n* **:** a blue-collar worker

[1]**jog** \ˈjäg\ *vb* **jogged; jog•ging 1 :** to give a slight shake or push to **2 :** to go at a slow monotonous pace **3 :** to run or ride at a slow trot **4** ♦ **:** to move up and down or about with a short heavy motion — **jog•ger** *n*

♦ bob, bobble, jounce, nod, pump, seesaw

[2]**jog** *n* **1 :** a slight shake **2 :** a jogging movement or pace

3jog *n* **1 :** a projecting or retreating part of a line or surface **2 :** a brief abrupt change in direction

jog•gle \ˈjä-gəl\ *vb* **jog•gled; jog•gling :** to shake slightly — **jog•gle** *n*

john \ˈjän\ *n* **1 :** TOILET **2 :** a prostitute's client

John \ˈjän\ *n* **1 :** the fourth Gospel in the New Testament **2 :** any of three short didactic letters addressed to early Christians and included in the New Testament

john•ny \ˈjä-nē\ *n, pl* **johnnies :** a short-sleeved gown opening in the back that is worn by hospital patients

John•ny–jump–up \ˌjä-nē-ˈjəmp-ˌəp\ *n* **:** any of various small-flowered cultivated pansies

joie de vi•vre \ˌzhwä-də-ˈvēvr^{ə}\ *n* **:** keen enjoyment of life

join \ˈjȯin\ *vb* **1** ♦ **:** to come or bring together so as to form a unit **2 :** to come or bring into close association **3** ♦ **:** to become a member of **4** ♦ **:** to lie next to or in contact with **:** ADJOIN **5** ♦ **:** to take part in a collective activity

♦ [1] associate, coalesce, combine, conjoin, connect, couple, fuse, link, marry, unify, unite ♦ [3] enlist, enroll, enter, sign on, sign up ♦ [4] abut, adjoin, border (on), flank, fringe, skirt, touch, verge (on) ♦ [5] collaborate, concert, cooperate, team

join•er \ˈjȯi-nər\ *n* **1 :** a worker who constructs articles by joining pieces of wood **2 :** a gregarious person who joins many organizations

1joint \ˈjȯint\ *n* **1 :** the point of contact between bones of an animal skeleton with the parts that surround and support it **2 :** a cut of meat suitable for roasting **3** ♦ **:** a place where two things or parts are connected **4 :** a place of business or residence with its furnishings and staff **:** ESTABLISHMENT; *esp* **:** a shabby or disreputable establishment **5 :** a marijuana cigarette — **joint•ed** *adj*

♦ connection, coupling, junction, juncture

2joint *adj* **1** ♦ **:** acting in concert **:** UNITED **2 :** common to two or more — **joint•ly** *adv*

♦ collective, common, communal, concerted, conjoint, mutual, public, united

3joint *vb* **1 :** to unite by or provide with a joint **2 :** to separate the joints of

joist \ˈjȯist\ *n* **:** any of the small beams ranged parallel from wall to wall in a building to support a floor or ceiling

1joke \ˈjōk\ *n* ♦ **:** something said or done to provoke laughter; *esp* **:** a brief narrative with a humorous climax

♦ crack, gag, jest, laugh, pleasantry, quip, sally, waggery, wisecrack, witticism

2joke *vb* **joked; jok•ing** ♦ **:** to make jokes — **jok•ing•ly** *adv*

♦ banter, fool, fun, jest, jive, josh, kid, quip, wisecrack

jok•er \ˈjō-kər\ *n* **1** ♦ **:** a person who jokes **2 :** an extra card used in some card games **3 :** a misleading part of an agreement that works to one party's disadvantage **4 a :** an adult male human **b** ♦ **:** an insignificant, obnoxious, or incompetent person

♦ [1] card, comedian, comic, humorist, jester, wag, wit ♦ [4b] beast, boor, churl, clown, creep, cretin, cur, heel, jerk, louse, lout, skunk, slob, snake

jol•li•fi•ca•tion \ˌjä-li-fə-ˈkā-shən\ *n* ♦ **:** a festive celebration

♦ conviviality, festivity, gaiety, merriment, merrymaking, revelry

jol•li•ty \ˈjä-lə-tē\ *n, pl* **-ties :** the quality or state of being jolly **:** GAIETY, MERRIMENT

jol•ly \ˈjä-lē\ *adj* **jol•li•er; -est** ♦ **:** full of high spirits **:** MERRY

♦ blithe, boon, festive, gay, gleeful, jocund, jovial, merry, mirthful, sunny

1jolt \ˈjōlt\ *vb* **1 :** to give a quick hard knock or blow to **2** ♦ **:** to move with a sudden jerky motion **3** ♦ **:** to disturb the composure of — **jolt•er** *n*

♦ [2] agitate, convulse, jounce, quake, quiver, shake, shudder, vibrate, wobble ♦ [2] buck, hitch, jerk, twitch ♦ [3] appall, bowl, floor, shake up, shock

2jolt *n* **1** ♦ **:** an abrupt jerky blow or movement **2** ♦ **:** a sudden shock

♦ [1] bump, collision, concussion, crash, impact, jar, shock, smash, strike, wallop ♦ [2] bolt, bombshell, jar, surprise

Jon *abbr* Jonah; Jonas

Jo•nah \ˈjō-nə\ *n* **:** a book of Jewish and Christian Scripture

Jo•nas \ˈjō-nəs\ *n* **:** JONAH

1jones \ˈjōnz\ *n* **1** *slang* **:** addiction to heroin **2** *slang* **:** HEROIN **3** *slang* **:** a craving for something

2jones *vb, slang* **:** to have a craving for something

jon•gleur \zhō^{n}-ˈglər\ *n* **:** an itinerant medieval minstrel

jon•quil \ˈjän-kwəl\ *n* **:** a narcissus with fragrant clustered white or yellow flowers

Jor•da•ni•an \jȯr-ˈdā-nē-ən\ *n* **:** a native or inhabitant of Jordan — **Jordanian** *adj*

josh \ˈjäsh\ *vb* ♦ **:** to tease good-naturedly; *also* **:** JOKE

♦ chaff, jive, kid, rally, razz, rib, ride, roast, tease ♦ banter, fool, fun, jest, jive, joke, kid, quip, wisecrack

Josh *abbr* Joshua

Josh•ua \ˈjä-shü-ə\ *n* **:** a book of Jewish and Christian Scripture

Joshua tree *n* **:** a tall branched yucca of the southwestern U.S.

jos•tle \ˈjä-səl\ *vb* **jos•tled; jos•tling 1 :** to come in contact or into collision **2 :** to make one's way by pushing and shoving

Jos•ue \ˈjä-shü-ē\ *n* **:** JOSHUA

1jot \ˈjät\ *n* ♦ **:** the least bit **:** IOTA

♦ hoot, iota, lick, modicum, rap, tittle, whit

2jot *vb* **jot•ted; jot•ting** ♦ **:** to write briefly and hurriedly

♦ *usu* **jot down** log, mark, note, put down, record, register, set down

jot•ting \ˈjä-tiŋ\ *n* **:** a brief note

joule \ˈjül\ *n* **:** a unit of work or energy equal to the work done by a force of one newton acting through a distance of one meter

jounce \ˈjau̇ns\ *vb* **jounced; jounc•ing** ♦ **:** to move or cause to move in an up-and-down manner **:** JOLT — **jounce** *n*

♦ agitate, convulse, jolt, quake, quiver, shake, shudder, vibrate, wobble

jour *abbr* **1** journal **2** journeyman

jour•nal \ˈjərn-^{ə}l\ *n* **1 :** a brief account of daily events **2 :** a record of proceedings (as of a legislative body) **3** ♦ **:** a periodical (as a newspaper) dealing especially with current events **4 :** the part of a rotating axle or spindle that turns in a bearing

♦ magazine, organ, paper, review

jour•nal•ese \ˌjər-nə-ˈlēz, -ˈlēs\ *n* **:** a style of writing held to be characteristic of newspapers

jour•nal•ism \ˈjər-nə-ˌli-zəm\ *n* **1 :** the business of writing for, editing, or publishing periodicals (as newspapers) **2 :** writing designed for or characteristic of newspapers — **jour•nal•ist** \-list\ *n* — **jour•nal•is•tic** \ˌjər-nə-ˈlis-tik\ *adj*

jour•nal•ist \ˈjər-nə-ˌlist\ *n* **1** ♦ **:** a person engaged in journalism **2 :** one who keeps a journal

♦ correspondent, newsman, reporter

1jour•ney \ˈjər-nē\ *n, pl* **journeys** ♦ **:** a traveling from one place to another

♦ expedition, passage, peregrination, trek, trip

2journey *vb* **jour•neyed; jour•ney•ing** ♦ **:** to go on a journey **:** TRAVEL

♦ tour, travel, trek, voyage

jour•ney•man \-mən\ *n* **1 :** a worker who has learned a trade and works for another person **2 :** an experienced reliable worker

1joust \ˈjau̇st\ *vb* **:** to engage in a joust

2joust *n* **:** a combat on horseback between two knights with lances especially as part of a tournament

jo•vial \ˈjō-vē-əl\ *adj* ♦ **:** marked by good humor

♦ blithe, boon, festive, gay, gleeful, jocund, jolly, merry, mirthful, sunny

jo•vi•al•i•ty \ˌjō-vē-ˈa-lə-tē\ *n* ♦ **:** the quality or state of being jovial

♦ cheer, cheerfulness, cheeriness, glee, hilarity, merriment, mirth

jo•vi•al•ly *adv* ♦ **:** in a jovial manner

♦ cheerfully, gaily, happily, heartily, merrily, mirthfully

1jowl \ˈjau̇(-ə)l\ *n* **:** loose flesh about the lower jaw or throat

2jowl *n* **1 :** the lower jaw **2 :** CHEEK

1joy \ˈjȯi\ *n* **1** ♦ **:** a feeling of happiness that comes from success, good fortune, or a sense of well-being **2** ♦ **:** a source of happiness

♦ [1] blessedness, bliss, felicity, gladness, happiness ♦ [2] delectation, delight, kick, manna, pleasure, treat

2joy *vb* **:** to experience great pleasure or delight **:** REJOICE

joy•ful \-fəl\ *adj* ♦ : experiencing, causing, or showing joy — **joy•ful•ly** *adv*

♦ blissful, delighted, glad, happy, pleased

joy•less *adj* **1 :** not experiencing joy **2 :** not inspiring or causing joy

joy•ous \ˈjȯi-əs\ *adj* experiencing, causing, or showing joy : JOYFUL — **joy•ous•ly** *adv* — **joy•ous•ness** *n*

joy•ride \ˈjȯi-ˌrīd\ *n* : a ride for pleasure often marked by reckless driving — **joyride** *vb* — **joy•rid•er** *n* — **joy•rid•ing** *n*

joy•stick \-ˌstik\ *n* : a control device (as for a computer display) consisting of a lever capable of motion in two or more directions

JP *abbr* **1** jet propulsion **2** justice of the peace

JPEG \ˈjā-ˌpeg\ *n* : a computer file format for usually high-quality digital images

Jr *abbr* junior

jt *or* **jnt** *abbr* joint

ju•bi•lant \ˈjü-bə-lənt\ *adj* ♦ : filled with or expressing great joy or triumph : EXULTANT — **ju•bi•lant•ly** *adv*

♦ exultant, rejoicing, triumphant

ju•bi•la•tion \ˌjü-bə-ˈlā-shən\ *n* : EXULTATION

ju•bi•lee \ˈjü-bə-ˌlē, ˌjü-bə-ˈlē\ *n* **1 :** a 50th anniversary **2** ♦ **:** a season or occasion of celebration

♦ carnival, celebration, festival, festivity, fete, fiesta, gala

ju•co \ˈjü-ˌkō\ *n, pl* **jucos** : JUNIOR COLLEGE; *also* : an athlete at a junior college

Jud *abbr* Judith

Ju•da•ic \jü-ˈdā-ik\ *also* **Ju•da•ical** \-ˈdā-ə-kəl\ *adj* : of, relating to, or characteristic of Jews or Judaism

Ju•da•ism \ˈjü-də-ˌi-zəm, -dā-, -dē-\ *n* : a religion developed among the ancient Hebrews and marked by belief in one God and by the moral and ceremonial laws of the Old Testament and the rabbinic tradition

Jude \ˈjüd\ *n* : a short hortatory epistle addressed to early Christians and included as a book in the New Testament

Judg *abbr* Judges

¹judge \ˈjəj\ *vb* **judged; judg•ing** **1 :** to form an authoritative opinion **2** ♦ **:** to decide as a judge **3** ♦ **:** to form an estimate or evaluation about something

♦ [2] adjudicate, arbitrate, decide, determine, referee, rule, settle, umpire ♦ [3] calculate, call, conjecture, estimate, figure, gauge, guess, make, place, put, reckon, suppose ♦ [3] conclude, deduce, extrapolate, gather, infer, reason, understand

²judge *n* **1** ♦ **:** a public official authorized to decide questions brought before a court **2** ♦ **:** one appointed to decide in a contest or competition : UMPIRE **3 :** one who gives an authoritative opinion : CRITIC — **judge•ship** *n*

♦ [1] bench, court, justice, magistrate ♦ [2] arbiter, arbitrator, referee, umpire

Judges *n* : a book of Jewish and Christian Scripture

judg•ment *or* **judge•ment** \ˈjəj-mənt\ *n* **1** ♦ **:** a decision or opinion given after judging; *esp* : a formal decision given by a court **2** *cap* **:** the final judging of mankind by God **3** ♦ **:** the process of forming an opinion by discerning and comparing **4 :** the capacity for judging : DISCERNMENT

♦ [1] appraisal, assessment, estimate, estimation, evaluation ♦ [1] doom, finding, holding, ruling, sentence ♦ [3] belief, conviction, eye, feeling, mind, notion, opinion, persuasion, sentiment, verdict, view ♦ [3] conclusion, decision, determination, diagnosis, resolution

judg•men•tal \ˌjəj-ˈmen-təl\ *adj* **1 :** of, relating to, or involving judgment **2 :** characterized by a tendency to judge harshly — **judg•men•tal•ly** *adv*

judgment call *n* : a subjective decision, ruling, or opinion

Judgment Day *n* : the day of the final judging of all human beings by God

ju•di•ca•ture \ˈjü-di-kə-ˌchu̇r\ *n* **1 :** the administration of justice **2 :** JUDICIARY 1

ju•di•cial \ju̇-ˈdi-shəl\ *adj* **1 :** of or relating to the administration of justice or the judiciary **2 :** ordered or enforced by a court **3 :** CRITICAL — **ju•di•cial•ly** *adv*

ju•di•cia•ry \ju̇-ˈdi-shē-ˌer-ē, -shə-rē\ *n* **1 :** a system of courts of law; *also* : the judges of these courts **2 :** a branch of government in which judicial power is vested — **judiciary** *adj*

ju•di•cious \ju̇-ˈdi-shəs\ *adj* ♦ : having, exercising, or characterized by sound judgment — **ju•di•cious•ly** *adv*

♦ advisable, desirable, expedient, politic, prudent, tactical, wise

Ju•dith \ˈjü-dəth\ *n* : a book of Scripture in the Roman Catholic canon of the Old Testament and in the Protestant Apocrypha

ju•do \ˈjü-dō\ *n* : a sport derived from jujitsu that emphasizes the use of quick movement and leverage to throw an opponent — **ju•do•ist** \-ist\ *n*

ju•do•ka \ˈjü-dō-ˌkä\ *n, pl* **judoka** *or* **judokas** : one who participates in judo

¹jug \ˈjəg\ *n* **1** ♦ **:** a large deep container with a narrow mouth and a handle **2 :** a place of confinement for persons held in lawful custody : JAIL, PRISON

♦ ewer, flagon, pitcher

²jug *vb* **jugged; jug•ging** : to confine in or as if in a jail : JAIL, IMPRISON

jug–eared \ˈjəg-ˌird\ *adj* : having protuberant ears

jug•ger•naut \ˈjə-gər-ˌnȯt\ *n* : a massive inexorable force or object that crushes everything in its path

jug•gle \ˈjə-gəl\ *vb* **jug•gled; jug•gling** **1 :** to keep several objects in motion in the air at the same time **2 :** to manipulate especially in order to achieve a desired and often fraudulent end — **jug•gler** \ˈjə-glər\ *n*

jug•u•lar \ˈjə-gyə-lər\ *adj* : of, relating to, or situated in or on the throat or neck ⟨the ~ veins⟩

juice \ˈjüs\ *n* **1 :** the extractable fluid contents of cells or tissues **2** *pl* **:** the natural fluids of an animal body **3 :** something that supplies power; *esp* : ELECTRICITY 2

juic•er \ˈjü-sər\ *n* : an appliance for extracting juice (as from fruit)

juice up *vb* : to give life, energy, or spirit to

juicy \ˈjü-sē\ *adj* **juic•i•er; -est** **1** ♦ **:** full of juice : SUCCULENT **2 :** rich in interest; *also* : RACY — **juic•i•ly** \-sə-lē\ *adv* — **juic•i•ness** \-sē-nəs\ *n*

♦ fleshy, pulpy, succulent

ju•jit•su *also* **ju•jut•su** \jü-ˈjit-sü\ *n* : an art of fighting employing holds, throws, and paralyzing blows

ju•ju \ˈjü-jü\ *n* : a style of African music characterized by a rapid beat, use of percussion instruments, and vocal harmonies

ju•jube \ˈjü-ˌjüb, ˈjü-ju̇-ˌbē\ *n* : a fruit-flavored gumdrop or lozenge

juke•box \ˈjük-ˌbäks\ *n* : a coin-operated machine that automatically plays selected recordings

Jul *abbr* July

ju•lep \ˈjü-ləp\ *n* : a drink made of bourbon, sugar, and mint served over crushed ice

Ju•ly \ju̇-ˈlī\ *n* : the 7th month of the year

¹jum•ble \ˈjəm-bəl\ *vb* **jum•bled; jum•bling** : to mix in a confused mass

²jumble *n* ♦ : a mass of things mingled together without order or plan; *also* : a state of confusion

♦ chaos, confusion, disarray, disorder, disorganization, havoc, hell, mess, muddle, shambles ♦ assortment, clutter, medley, mélange, miscellany, motley, muddle, variety, welter

¹jum•bo \ˈjəm-bō\ *n, pl* **jumbos** ♦ : a very large specimen of its kind

♦ behemoth, blockbuster, colossus, giant, leviathan, mammoth, monster, titan, whale, whopper

²jumbo *adj* : very large

¹jump \ˈjəmp\ *vb* **1** ♦ **:** to spring into the air : leap over **2** ♦ **:** to give a start **3 :** to rise or increase suddenly or sharply **4** ♦ **:** to make a sudden attack **5 :** ANTICIPATE ⟨~ the gun⟩ **6 :** to leave hurriedly and often furtively ⟨~ town⟩ **7 :** to act or move before (as a signal) — **jump bail** : to abscond after being released from custody on bail — **jump ship** **1 :** to leave the company of a ship without authority **2 :** to desert a cause

♦ [1] bound, hop, leap, spring, vault ♦ [2] bolt, start, startle ♦ *usu* **jump on** [4] abuse, castigate, excoriate, lambaste, slam, vituperate ♦ *usu* **jump on** [4] assail, assault, attack, beset, charge, descend, pounce (on *or* upon), raid, rush, storm, strike

²jump *n* **1** ♦ **:** a spring into the air; *esp* : one made for height or distance in a track meet **2 :** a sharp sudden increase **3** ♦ **:** an initial advantage

♦ [1] bound, hop, leap, spring, vault ♦ [3] advantage, better, drop, edge, upper hand, vantage

¹jump•er \ˈjəm-pər\ *n* : one that jumps

²jumper *n* **1 :** a loose blouse **2 :** a sleeveless one-piece dress worn usually with a blouse **3** *pl* **:** a child's sleeveless coverall

jumping bean *n* : a seed of any of several Mexican shrubs that tumbles about because of the movements of a small moth larva inside it

jump•ing–off place *n* **1 :** a remote or isolated place **2 :** a place from which an enterprise is launched
jump•mas•ter \ˈjəmp-ˌmas-tər\ *n* **:** a person who supervises parachutists
jump–start \ˈjəmp-ˌstärt\ *vb* **:** to start (an engine or vehicle) by connection to an external power source
jump•suit \ˈjəmp-ˌsüt\ *n* **1 :** a coverall worn by parachutists in jumping **2 :** a one-piece garment consisting of a blouse or shirt with attached pants or shorts
jumpy \ˈjəm-pē\ *adj* **jump•i•er; -est** ♦ **:** easily excited or irritated **:** NERVOUS, JITTERY

♦ edgy, excitable, high-strung, jittery, nervous, skittish, spooky

jun *abbr* junior
Jun *abbr* June
junc *abbr* junction
jun•co \ˈjəŋ-kō\ *n, pl* **juncos** *or* **juncoes :** any of a genus of small common pink-billed No. American finches that are largely gray with conspicuous white tail feathers
junc•tion \ˈjəŋk-shən\ *n* **1** ♦ **:** an act of joining **2** ♦ **:** a place or point of meeting

♦ [1] combination, connection, consolidation, coupling, unification, union ♦ [2] connection, coupling, joint, juncture

junc•ture \ˈjeŋk-chər\ *n* **1 :** a place where two things or parts are joined **:** JOINT, CONNECTION **2 :** UNION **3** ♦ **:** a critical time or state of affairs

♦ clutch, crisis, crunch, emergency, head

June \ˈjün\ *n* **:** the 6th month of the year
jun•gle \ˈjəŋ-gəl\ *n* **1 :** a thick tangled mass of tropical vegetation; *also* **:** a tract overgrown with vegetation **2 :** a place of ruthless struggle for survival
¹ju•nior \ˈjü-nyər\ *adj* **1 :** YOUNGER **2** ♦ **:** lower in rank **3 :** of or relating to juniors

♦ inferior, less, lesser, lower, minor, subordinate, under

²junior *n* **1 :** a person who is younger or of lower rank than another **2 :** a student in the next-to-last year before graduating
junior college *n* **:** a school that offers studies corresponding to those of the 1st two years of college
junior high school *n* **:** a school usually including grades 7–9
junior varsity *n* **:** a team whose members lack the experience or qualifications required for the varsity
ju•ni•per \ˈjü-nə-pər\ *n* **:** any of numerous coniferous shrubs or trees with leaves like needles or scales and female cones like berries
¹junk \ˈjəŋk\ *n* **1** ♦ **:** old iron, glass, paper, or waste; *also* **:** discarded articles **2 :** a shoddy product **3** *slang* **:** NARCOTICS; *esp* **:** HEROIN

♦ chaff, deadwood, dust, garbage, litter, refuse, riffraff, rubbish, scrap, trash, waste

²junk *vb* **:** to get rid of as worthless **:** DISCARD, SCRAP

♦ cast, discard, ditch, dump, fling, jettison, lose, reject, scrap, shed, shuck, slough, throw away, throw out, unload

³junk *n* **:** a ship of eastern Asia with a high stern and 4-cornered sails
junk•er \ˈjəŋ-kər\ *n* **:** something (as an old automobile) ready for scrapping
Jun•ker \ˈyüŋ-kər\ *n* **:** a member of the Prussian landed aristocracy
jun•ket \ˈjəŋ-kət\ *n* **1 :** a pudding of sweetened flavored milk set by rennet **2** ♦ **:** a pleasure trip or outing; *esp* **:** a trip made by an official at public expense ostensibly for public business

♦ excursion, jaunt, outing, sally

junk food *n* **:** food that is high in calories but low in nutritional content
junk•ie *also* **junky** \ˈjəŋ-kē\ *n, pl* **junkies 1** *slang* **:** a narcotics peddler or addict **2 :** one that derives inordinate pleasure from or is dependent on something ⟨sugar ~⟩
junky *adj* ♦ **:** having the character of junk **:** constituting junk

♦ chaffy, empty, no-good, null, valueless, worthless

jun•ta \ˈhün-tə, ˈjən-, ˈhən-\ *n* **:** a group of persons controlling a government especially after a revolutionary seizure of power
Ju•pi•ter \ˈjü-pə-tər\ *n* **:** the largest of the planets and the one 5th in order of distance from the sun
Ju•ras•sic \jü-ˈra-sik\ *adj* **:** of, relating to, or being the period of the Mesozoic era between the Triassic and the Cretaceous that is marked especially by the presence of dinosaurs — **Jurassic** *n*
ju•rid•i•cal \jü-ˈri-di-kəl\ *also* **ju•rid•ic** \-dik\ *adj* **1 :** of or relating to the administration of justice **2 :** LEGAL — **ju•rid•i•cal•ly** \-di-k(ə-)lē\ *adv*
ju•ris•dic•tion \ˌju̇r-əs-ˈdik-shən\ *n* **1 :** the power, right, or authority to interpret and apply the law **2** ♦ **:** the authority of a sovereign power **3 :** the limits or territory within which authority may be exercised — **ju•ris•dic•tion•al** \-shə-nəl\ *adj*

♦ administration, authority, government, regime, rule

ju•ris•pru•dence \-ˈprüd-ᵊns\ *n* **1 :** a system of laws **2 :** the science or philosophy of law
ju•rist \ˈju̇r-ist\ *n* ♦ **:** one having a thorough knowledge of law; *esp* **:** JUDGE

♦ arbiter, arbitrator, judge, referee

ju•ris•tic \ju̇-ˈris-tik\ *adj* **1 :** of or relating to a jurist or jurisprudence **2 :** of, relating to, or recognized in law
ju•ror \ˈju̇r-ər, -ˌȯr\ *n* **:** a member of a jury
¹ju•ry \ˈju̇r-ē\ *n, pl* **juries 1 :** a body of persons sworn to inquire into a matter submitted to them and to give their verdict **2 :** a committee for judging and awarding prizes
²jury *adj* **:** improvised for temporary use especially in an emergency ⟨a ~ mast⟩
jury nullification *n* **:** the acquitting of a defendant by a jury in disregard of the judge's instructions and contrary to the jury's findings of fact
jury–rig \ˈju̇r-ē-ˌrig\ *vb* **:** to construct or arrange in a makeshift fashion
¹just \ˈjəst\ *adj* **1** ♦ **:** having a basis in or conforming to fact or reason **:** REASONABLE ⟨~ comment⟩ **2** ♦ **:** conforming to a standard of correctness ⟨~ proportions⟩ **3** ♦ **:** morally or legally right ⟨a ~ title⟩ **4 :** being what is merited ⟨~ punishment⟩ — **just•ly** *adv* — **just•ness** *n*

♦ [1] good, hard, informed, levelheaded, logical, rational, reasonable, reasoned, sensible, sober, solid, valid, well-founded ♦ [2] due, right *Ant* undeserved, undue, unjust, unwarranted ♦ [2] disinterested, dispassionate, equal, equitable, fair, impartial, nonpartisan, objective, square, unbiased, unprejudiced ♦ [3] decent, ethical, good, honest, honorable (*or* honourable), moral, principled, right, righteous, straight, upright, upstanding, virtuous

²just \ˈjəst, ˈjist\ *adv* **1** ♦ **:** in a manner or measure or to a degree or number that strictly conforms to a fact or condition **:** EXACTLY ⟨~ right⟩ **2** ♦ **:** very recently ⟨has ~ left⟩ **3** ♦ **:** by a very small margin **:** BARELY ⟨~ too late⟩ **4 :** DIRECTLY ⟨~ west of here⟩ **5** ♦ **:** to the exclusion of all else **:** ONLY ⟨~ last year⟩ **6 :** QUITE ⟨~ wonderful⟩ **7 :** POSSIBLY ⟨it ~ might work⟩

♦ [1] accurately, exactly, precisely, right, sharp, squarely ♦ [2] freshly, late, lately, new, newly, now, only, recently ♦ [3] barely, hardly, marginally, scarcely, slightly *Ant* considerably, significantly, substantially, well ♦ [5] but, merely, only, simply

jus•tice \ˈjəs-təs\ *n* **1 :** the administration of what is just (as by assigning merited rewards or punishments) **2** ♦ **:** a public official authorized to decide questions brought before a court **:** JUDGE **3 :** the administration of law **4 :** FAIRNESS; *also* **:** RIGHTEOUSNESS

♦ bench, court, judge, magistrate

justice of the peace : a local magistrate empowered chiefly to try minor cases, to administer oaths, and to perform marriages
jus•ti•fi•able *adj* ♦ **:** capable of being justified

♦ defensible, maintainable, supportable, sustainable, tenable

jus•ti•fi•ca•tion \ˌjəs-tə-fə-ˈkā-shən\ *n* ♦ **:** the act or an instance of justifying

♦ alibi, defense (*or* defence), excuse, plea, reason

jus•ti•fy \ˈjəs-tə-ˌfī\ *vb* **-fied; -fy•ing 1** ♦ **:** to prove or show to be just, right, or reasonable **2 :** to pronounce free from guilt or blame **3 :** to adjust spaces in a line of printed text so the margins are even

♦ defend, maintain, support, uphold ♦ account, condone, excuse, explain, rationalize

jut \ˈjət\ *vb* **jut•ted; jut•ting :** to shoot out or forward **:** PROJECT, PROTRUDE
jute \ˈjüt\ *n* **:** a strong glossy fiber from either of two tropical plants used especially for making sacks and twine

juv *abbr* juvenile

1ju·ve·nile \ˈjü-və-ˌnīl, -nəl\ *adj* **1** ♦ **:** showing incomplete development **2** ♦ **:** of, relating to, or characteristic of children or young people

♦ [1] adolescent, immature, young, youthful ♦ [2] adolescent, babyish, childish, immature, infantile, kiddish

2juvenile *n* **1** ♦ **:** a young person; *esp* **:** one below the legally established age of adulthood **2 :** a young animal (as a fish or a bird) or plant **3 :** an actor or actress who plays youthful parts

♦ child, cub, kid, youngster, youth

juvenile delinquency *n* **:** violation of the law or antisocial behavior by a juvenile — **juvenile delinquent** *n*

jux·ta·pose \ˈjək-stə-ˌpōz\ *vb* **-posed; -pos·ing :** to place side by side — **jux·ta·po·si·tion** \ˌjək-stə-pə-ˈzi-shən\ *n*

JV *abbr* junior varsity

K

1k \ˈkā\ *n, pl* **k's** *or* **ks** \ˈkāz\ **1** *often cap* **:** the 11th letter of the English alphabet **2** *cap* **:** STRIKEOUT

2k *abbr* **1** karat **2** kitchen **3** knit **4** kosher — often enclosed in a circle

1K *abbr* Kelvin

2K *symbol* potassium

kab·ba·lah *also* **kab·ba·la** *or* **ka·ba·la** *or* **ca·ba·la** \kə-ˈbä-lə, ˈka-bə-lə\ *n, often cap* **1 :** a medieval Jewish mysticism marked by belief in creation through emanation and a cipher method of interpreting Scripture **2 :** esoteric or mysterious doctrine

kabob *var of* KEBAB

Ka·bu·ki \kə-ˈbü-kē\ *n* **:** traditional Japanese popular drama with highly stylized singing and dancing

kad·dish \ˈkä-dish\ *n, often cap* **:** a Jewish prayer recited in the daily synagogue ritual and by mourners at public services after the death of a close relative

kaf·fee·klatsch \ˈkȯ-fē-ˌklach, ˈkä-\ *n, often cap* **:** an informal social gathering for coffee and conversation

kai·ser \ˈkī-zər\ *n* **:** EMPEROR; *esp* **:** the ruler of Germany from 1871 to 1918

Ka·lash·ni·kov \kə-ˈlash-nə-ˌkȯf\ *n* **:** a Soviet-designed assault rifle

kale \ˈkāl\ *n* **:** a hardy cabbage with curled leaves that do not form a head

ka·lei·do·scope \kə-ˈlī-də-ˌskōp\ *n* **:** a tube containing loose bits of colored material (as glass) and two mirrors at one end that shows many different patterns as it is turned — **ka·lei·do·scop·ic** \-ˌlī-də-ˈskä-pik\ *adj* — **ka·lei·do·scop·i·cal·ly** \-pi-k(ə-)lē\ *adv*

ka·ma·ai·na \ˌkä-mə-ˈī-nə\ *n* **:** one who has lived in Hawaii for a long time

kame \ˈkām\ *n* **:** a short ridge or mound of material deposited by water from a melting glacier

ka·mi·ka·ze \ˌkä-mi-ˈkä-zē\ *n* **:** a member of a corps of Japanese pilots assigned to make a suicidal crash on a target; *also* **:** an airplane flown in such an attack

Kan *or* **Kans** *abbr* Kansas

kan·ga·roo \ˌkaŋ-gə-ˈrü\ *n, pl* **-roos :** any of various large leaping marsupial mammals of Australia and adjacent islands with powerful hind legs and a long thick tail

kangaroo court *n* **:** a court or an illegal self-appointed tribunal characterized by irresponsible, perverted, or irregular procedures

ka·o·lin \ˈkā-ə-lən\ *n* **:** a fine usually white clay used in ceramics and refractories and for the treatment of diarrhea

ka·pok \ˈkā-ˌpäk\ *n* **:** silky fiber from the seeds of a tropical tree used especially as a filling (as for life preservers)

Kap·o·si's sar·co·ma \ˈka-pə-sēz-sär-ˈkō-mə\ *n* **:** a neoplastic disease associated especially with AIDS that affects especially the skin and mucous membranes and is characterized usually by the formation of pink to reddish-brown or bluish plaques

kap·pa \ˈka-pə\ *n* **:** the 10th letter of the Greek alphabet — Κ or κ

ka·put *also* **ka·putt** \kä-ˈpu̇t, kə-, -ˈpüt\ *adj* **1 :** utterly defeated or destroyed **2 :** unable to function **:** USELESS

kar·a·kul \ˈkar-ə-kəl\ *n* **:** the usually curly glossy black coat of a very young lamb of a hardy Asian breed of sheep

kar·a·o·ke \ˌkar-ē-ˈō-kē\ *n* **:** a device that plays instrumental accompaniments for songs to which the user sings along

kar·at \ˈkar-ət\ *n* **:** a unit for expressing proportion of gold in an alloy equal to $\frac{1}{24}$ part of pure gold

ka·ra·te \kə-ˈrä-tē\ *n* **:** an art of self-defense in which an attacker is disabled by crippling kicks and punches

kar·ma \ˈkär-mə\ *n, often cap* **:** the force generated by a person's actions held in Hinduism and Buddhism to perpetuate reincarnation and to determine the nature of the person's next existence — **kar·mic** \-mik\ *adj*

karst \ˈkärst\ *n* **:** an irregular limestone region with sinks, underground streams, and caverns

ka·ty·did \ˈkā-tē-ˌdid\ *n* **:** any of several large green tree-dwelling American grasshoppers with long antennae

kay·ak \ˈkī-ˌak\ *n* **:** an Eskimo canoe made of a skin-covered frame with a small opening and propelled by a double-bladed paddle; *also* **:** a similar portable boat — **kay·ak·er** *n*

kayo \(ˌ)kā-ˈō, ˈkā-ō\ *n* **:** KNOCKOUT — **kayo** *vb*

ka·zoo \kə-ˈzü\ *n, pl* **kazoos :** a toy musical instrument consisting of a tube with a membrane sealing one end and a side hole to sing or hum into

KB *abbr* kilobyte

kc *abbr* kilocycle

KC *abbr* **1** Kansas City **2** King's Counsel **3** Knights of Columbus

kc/s *abbr* kilocycles per second

KD *abbr* knocked down

ke·bab, ke·bob \kə-ˈbäb, ˈkā-ˌbäb\ *n* **:** cubes of meat cooked with vegetables usually on a skewer

kedge \ˈkej\ *n* **:** a small anchor

1keel \ˈkēl\ *n* **1 :** the chief structural member of a ship running lengthwise along the center of its bottom **2 :** something (as a bird's breastbone) like a ship's keel in form or use — **keeled** \ˈkēld\ *adj*

2keel *vb* **:** FAINT, SWOON — usually used with *over*

keel·boat \ˈkēl-ˌbōt\ *n* **:** a shallow covered keeled riverboat for freight that is usually rowed, poled, or towed

keel·haul \-ˌhȯl\ *vb* **1 :** to haul under the keel of a ship as punishment **2** ♦ **:** to rebuke severely

♦ admonish, chide, lecture, rail (at *or* against), rate, rebuke, reprimand, scold

1keen \ˈkēn\ *adj* **1** ♦ **:** having a fine edge or point **:** SHARP 〈a ~ knife〉 **2** ♦ **:** affecting one as if by cutting 〈a ~ wind〉 **3** ♦ **:** showing a quick and ardent responsiveness **:** ENTHUSIASTIC 〈~ about swimming〉 **4** ♦ **:** mentally alert 〈a ~ mind〉 **5** ♦ **:** extremely sensitive in perception **:** STRONG, ACUTE 〈~ eyesight〉 **6 :** unusually good **:** WONDERFUL, EXCELLENT — **keen·ly** *adv*

♦ [1] cutting, edgy, ground, sharp ♦ [2] biting, bitter, cutting, penetrating, piercing, raw, sharp ♦ [3] agog, anxious, ardent, athirst, avid, crazy, eager, enthusiastic, gung ho, hot, hungry, nuts, raring, solicitous, thirsty, voracious ♦ [4] alert, brainy, bright, brilliant, clever, intelligent, nimble, quick, quick-witted, sharp, smart ♦ [5] acute, delicate, perceptive, sensitive, sharp

2keen *n* ♦ **:** a lamentation for the dead uttered in a loud wailing voice or in a wordless cry

♦ groan, howl, lament, moan, plaint, wail

3keen *vb* **1 :** to lament with a keen **2** ♦ **:** to make a sound suggestive of a keen

♦ bay, howl, wail, yowl

keen·ness *n* ♦ **:** the quality or state of being keen

♦ appetite, ardor, avidity, eagerness, enthusiasm, excitement, hunger, impatience, thirst ♦ acuity, acuteness, delicacy, sensitiveness, sensitivity

¹keep \ˈkēp\ *vb* **kept** \ˈkept\; **keep·ing** **1** ♦ **:** to be faithful to especially by appropriate conduct **:** FULFILL, OBSERVE ⟨∼ a promise⟩ ⟨∼ a holiday⟩ **2 :** GUARD ⟨∼ us from harm⟩; *also* **:** to take care of ⟨∼ a neighbor's children⟩ **3 :** MAINTAIN ⟨∼ silence⟩ **4 :** to have in one's service or at one's disposal ⟨∼ a horse⟩ **5 :** to preserve a record in ⟨∼ a diary⟩ **6 :** to have in stock for sale **7** ♦ **:** to retain in one's possession ⟨∼ what you find⟩ **8 :** to carry on (as a business) **:** CONDUCT **9 :** HOLD, DETAIN ⟨∼ him in jail⟩ **10 :** to refrain from revealing ⟨∼ a secret⟩ **11 :** to continue in good condition ⟨meat will ∼ in a freezer⟩ **12** ♦ **:** to resist an impulse or desire **:** ABSTAIN, REFRAIN

♦ [1] answer, comply, fill, fulfill, meet, redeem, satisfy ♦ [1] celebrate, commemorate, observe *Ant* break, transgress, violate ♦ [7] hang on, hold, reserve, retain, withhold *Ant* hand over, relinquish, surrender ♦ *usu* **keep from** [12] abstain (from), forbear, forgo, refrain

²keep *n* **1 :** FORTRESS **2 :** the means or provisions by which one is kept — **for keeps 1 :** with the provision that one keep what one has won ⟨play marbles *for keeps*⟩ **2 :** PERMANENTLY

keep–away \ˈkēp-ə-ˌwā\ *n* **:** a game in which players try to keep an object from one or more other players

keep·er *n* ♦ **:** one that keeps; *esp* **:** one who cares for another or another's property

♦ custodian, guard, guardian, lookout, picket, sentry, warden, warder, watch, watchman ♦ caretaker, custodian, guardian, janitor, warden, watchman

keep·ing *n* **1 :** CONFORMITY ⟨in ∼ with good taste⟩ **2** ♦ **:** the act of one that keeps **:** the care, possession, or observance of something

♦ care, custody, guardianship, safekeeping, trust, ward ♦ control, hands, possession

keeping room *n* **:** a common room used for multiple purposes

keep·sake \ˈkēp-ˌsāk\ *n* ♦ **:** something kept or given to be kept as a memento

♦ memento, memorial, monument, remembrance, souvenir, token

keep up *vb* **1** ♦ **:** to persist or persevere in **2** ♦ **:** to keep in an existing state **:** MAINTAIN **3 :** to keep informed **4** ♦ **:** to continue without interruption

♦ [1, 4] abide, continue, endure, hold, last, persist, run on ♦ [2] conserve, maintain, preserve, save

keg \ˈkeg\ *n* ♦ **:** a small cask or barrel

♦ barrel, cask, hogshead, pipe, puncheon

keg·ger \ˈke-gər\ *n* **:** a party featuring one or more kegs of beer

keg·ler \ˈke-glər\ *n* **:** ¹BOWLER

kelp \ˈkelp\ *n* **:** any of various coarse brown seaweeds; *also* **:** a mass of these or their ashes often used as fertilizer

kel·vin \ˈkel-vən\ *n* **:** a unit of temperature equal to $\frac{1}{273.16}$ of the Kelvin scale temperature of the triple point of water and equal to the Celsius degree

Kelvin *adj* **:** relating to, conforming to, or being a temperature scale according to which absolute zero is 0 K, the equivalent of –273.15°C

ken \ˈken\ *n* **1 :** range of vision **:** SIGHT **2 :** range of understanding

ken·nel \ˈken-ᵊl\ *n* **:** a shelter for a dog or cat; *also* **:** an establishment for the breeding or boarding of dogs or cats — **kennel** *vb*

ke·no \ˈkē-nō\ *n* **:** a game resembling bingo

ke·no·sis \kə-ˈnō-səs\ *n* **:** the relinquishment of divine attributes by Jesus Christ in becoming human — **ke·not·ic** \-ˈnä-tik\ *adj*

ken·te cloth \ˈken-ˌtā-\ *n* **:** colorfully patterned cloth traditionally woven by hand in Ghana

Ken·tucky bluegrass \kən-ˈtə-kē-\ *n* **:** a valuable pasture and meadow grass of both Europe and America

Ken·yan \ˈke-nyən, ˈkē-\ *n* **:** a native or inhabitant of Kenya — **Kenyan** *adj*

Ke·ogh plan \ˈkē-(ˌ)ō-\ *n* **:** an individual retirement account for the self-employed

ke·pi \ˈkā-pē, ˈke-\ *n* **:** a military cap with a round flat top and a visor

ker·a·tin \ˈker-ət-ᵊn\ *n* **:** any of various sulfur-containing proteins that make up hair and horny tissues

kerb \ˈkərb\ *n, Brit* **:** CURB 3

ker·chief \ˈkər-chəf, -ˌchēf\ *n, pl* **kerchiefs** \-chəfs, -ˌchēfs\ *also* **kerchieves** \-ˌchēvz\ **1** ♦ **:** a square of cloth worn by women especially as a head covering **2 :** HANDKERCHIEF

♦ babushka, bandanna, do-rag, mantilla

kerf \ˈkərf\ *n* **:** a slit or notch made by a saw or cutting torch

ker·nel \ˈkərn-ᵊl\ *n* **1 :** the inner softer part of a seed, fruit stone, or nut **2 :** a whole seed of a cereal ⟨a ∼ of corn⟩ **3 :** a central or essential part **:** CORE

ker·o·sene *or* **ker·o·sine** \ˈker-ə-ˌsēn, ˌker-ə-ˈsēn\ *n* **:** a flammable oil produced from petroleum and used for a fuel and as a solvent

kes·trel \ˈkes-trəl\ *n* **:** any of various small falcons that usually hover in the air while searching for prey

ketch \ˈkech\ *n* **:** a large fore-and-aft rigged boat with two masts

ketch·up, catch·up \ˈke-chəp, ˈka-\ *n* **:** a seasoned tomato puree

ket·tle \ˈket-ᵊl\ *n* **:** a metallic vessel for boiling liquids

ket·tle·drum \-ˌdrəm\ *n* **:** a brass, copper, or fiberglass drum with calfskin or plastic stretched across the top

¹key \ˈkē\ *n* **1 :** a usually metal instrument by which the bolt of a lock is turned; *also* **:** a device having the form or function of a key **2 :** a means of gaining or preventing entrance, possession, or control **3 :** EXPLANATION, SOLUTION **4 :** one of the levers pressed by a finger in operating or playing an instrument **5 :** a leading individual or principle **6 :** a system of seven tones based on their relationship to a tonic; *also* **:** the tone or pitch of a voice **7 :** a small switch for opening or closing an electric circuit ⟨a telegraph ∼⟩

²key *vb* **1 :** SECURE, FASTEN **2 :** to regulate the musical pitch of **3** ♦ **:** to bring into harmony or conformity **4 :** to make nervous — usually used with *up*

♦ accommodate, conciliate, conform, coordinate, harmonize, reconcile

³key *adj* ♦ **:** marked by or indicative of significant worth or consequence ⟨∼ issues⟩

♦ arch, cardinal, central, chief, dominant, first, foremost, grand, main, paramount, predominant, preeminent, premier, primary, principal, sovereign, supreme ♦ critical, crucial, pivotal, vital

⁴key *n* ♦ **:** a low island or reef (as off the southern coast of Florida)

♦ cay, island, isle

⁵key *n, slang* **:** a kilogram especially of marijuana or heroin

key·board \-ˌbōrd\ *n* **1 :** a row of keys (as on a piano) **2 :** an assemblage of keys for operating a machine

key club *n* **:** a private club serving liquor and providing entertainment

key·hole \ˈkē-ˌhōl\ *n* **:** a hole for receiving a key

¹key·note \-ˌnōt\ *n* **1 :** the first and harmonically fundamental tone of a scale **2 :** the central fact, idea, or mood

²keynote *vb* **1 :** to set the keynote of **2 :** to deliver the major address (as at a convention) — **key·not·er** *n*

key·punch \ˈkē-ˌpənch\ *n* **:** a machine with a keyboard used to cut holes or notches in punch cards — **keypunch** *vb* — **key·punch·er** *n*

key·stone \-ˌstōn\ *n* **1 :** the wedge-shaped piece at the crown of an arch that locks the other pieces in place **2** ♦ **:** something on which associated things depend for support

♦ base, basis, bedrock, cornerstone, footing, foundation, ground, groundwork, underpinning

key·stroke \-ˌstrōk\ *n* **:** an act or instance of depressing a key on a keyboard

key word *n* **:** a word that is a key; *esp, usu* **key·word :** a significant word from a title or document used especially as an indication of the content

kg *abbr* kilogram

KGB *abbr* (Soviet) State Security Committee

kha·ki \ˈka-kē, ˈkä-\ *n* **1 :** a light yellowish brown color **2 :** a khaki-colored cloth; *also* **:** a military uniform of this cloth

khan \ˈkän, ˈkan\ *n* **:** a Mongol leader; *esp* **:** a successor of Genghis Khan

khe·dive \kə-ˈdēv\ *n* **:** a ruler of Egypt from 1867 to 1914 governing as a viceroy of the sultan of Turkey

kHz *abbr* kilohertz

KIA *abbr* killed in action

kib·ble \ˈki-bəl\ *vb* **kib·bled; kib·bling :** to grind coarsely — **kibble** *n*

kib·butz \ki-ˈbu̇ts, -ˈbüts\ *n, pl* **kib·but·zim** \-ˌbu̇t-ˈsēm, -ˌbüt-\ **:** a communal farm or settlement in Israel

ki·bitz·er \ˈki-bət-sər, kə-ˈbit-\ *n* ♦ **:** one who looks on and usually offers unwanted advice especially at a card game — **kib·itz** \ˈki-bəts\ *vb*

♦ busybody, interloper, intruder, meddler

ki·bosh \ˈkī-ˌbäsh\ *n* **:** something that serves as a check or stop ⟨put the ∼ on his plan⟩

¹kick \ˈkik\ *vb* **1 :** to strike out or hit with the foot; *also* **:** to score by kicking a ball **2** ♦ **:** to object strongly **3 :** to recoil when fired — **kick•er** *n*

♦ beef, bellyache, complain, fuss, gripe, grouse, growl, grumble, moan, object, squawk, wail, whine

[2]**kick** *n* **1 :** a blow or thrust with the foot; *esp* **:** a propelling of a ball with the foot **2 :** the recoil of a gun **3** ♦ **:** a feeling or expression of objection **4** ♦ **:** stimulating effect especially of pleasure

♦ [3] challenge, complaint, demur, expostulation, fuss, objection, protest, question, remonstrance ♦ [4] bang, exhilaration, thrill, titillation

kick•back \ˈkik-ˌbak\ *n* **1 :** a sharp violent reaction **2 :** a secret return of a part of a sum received

kick back *vb* ♦ **:** to assume a relaxed position or attitude

♦ bask, loll, lounge, relax, repose, rest

kick•box•ing \ˈkik-ˌbäk-siŋ\ *n* **:** boxing in which boxers are permitted to kick with bare feet — **kick•box•er** \-sər\ *n*

kick in *vb* **1** ♦ **:** to give or supply in common with others **:** CONTRIBUTE **2** *slang* **:** DIE **3 :** to begin operating or having an effect

♦ chip in, contribute, pitch in

kick•off \ˈkik-ˌȯf\ *n* **1 :** a kick that puts the ball in play (as in football) **2 :** COMMENCEMENT

kick off *vb* **1 :** to start or resume play with a placekick **2 :** to begin proceedings **3** *slang* **:** DIE

kick over *vb* **:** to begin or cause to begin to fire — used of an internal combustion engine

kick•shaw \ˈkik-ˌshȯ\ *n* **1 :** DELICACY **2 :** TRINKET

kick•stand \ˈkik-ˌstand\ *n* **:** a swiveling metal bar attached to a 2-wheeled vehicle for holding it up when not in use

kick–start \ˈkik-ˌstärt\ *vb* **:** JUMP-START

kicky \ˈki-kē\ *adj* **:** providing a kick or thrill **:** EXCITING

[1]**kid** \ˈkid\ *n* **1 :** a young goat **2 :** the flesh, fur, or skin of a young goat; *also* **:** something made of kid **3** ♦ **:** a young person **:** CHILD, YOUNGSTER

♦ child, cub, juvenile, youngster, youth

[2]**kid** *vb* **kid•ded; kid•ding 1** ♦ **:** to deceive as a joke **:** FOOL **2** ♦ **:** to make fun of **:** TEASE — **kid•der** *n* — **kid•ding•ly** *adv*

♦ [1] banter, fool, fun, jest, jive, joke, josh, quip, wisecrack ♦ [2] chaff, jive, josh, rally, razz, rib, ride, roast, tease

kid•dish *adj* ♦ **:** marked by or suggestive of immaturity and lack of poise

♦ adolescent, babyish, childish, immature, infantile, juvenile

kid•do \ˈki-dō\ *n, pl* **kiddos 1** — used as a familiar form of address ⟨you're okay, ~⟩ **2** ♦ **:** a young person who is between infancy and adulthood **:** CHILD, KID

♦ child, cub, juvenile, kid, moppet, whelp, youngster, youth

kid•nap \ˈkid-ˌnap\ *vb* **kid•napped** *also* **kid•naped** \-ˌnapt\; **kid•nap•ping** *also* **kid•nap•ing** \-ˌna-piŋ\ **:** to hold or carry a person away by unlawful force or by fraud and against one's will — **kid•nap•per** *also* **kid•nap•er** \-ˌna-pər\ *n*

kid•ney \ˈkid-nē\ *n, pl* **kidneys :** either of a pair of organs lying near the backbone that excrete waste products of the body in the form of urine

kidney bean *n* **1 :** an edible seed of the common cultivated bean; *esp* **:** one that is large and dark red **2 :** a plant bearing kidney beans

kid•skin \ˈkid-ˌskin\ *n* **:** the skin of a young goat used for leather

kiel•ba•sa \kēl-ˈbä-sə, kil-\ *n, pl* **-basas** *also* **-ba•sy** \-ˈbä-sē\ **:** a smoked sausage of Polish origin

[1]**kill** \ˈkil\ *vb* **1** ♦ **:** to deprive of life **2 :** to put an end to ⟨~ competition⟩; *also* **:** DEFEAT ⟨~ a proposed amendment⟩ **3 :** USE UP ⟨~ time⟩ **4 :** to mark for omission — **kill•er** *n*

♦ destroy, dispatch, do in, fell, slay *Ant* animate

[2]**kill** *n* **1 :** an act of killing **2 :** an animal or animals killed (as in a hunt); *also* **:** an aircraft, ship, or vehicle destroyed by military action

kill•deer \ˈkil-ˌdir\ *n, pl* **killdeers** *or* **killdeer :** an American plover with a plaintive penetrating cry

killer app \-ˈap\ *n* **:** a component (as a computer application) that in itself makes something worth having or using

killer bee *n* **:** AFRICANIZED BEE

killer whale *n* **:** a small gregarious black and white flesh-eating whale with a white oval patch behind each eye

kill•ing *n* **:** a sudden notable gain or profit

killing field *n* **:** a scene of mass killing

kill•joy \ˈkil-ˌjȯi\ *n* **:** one who spoils the pleasures of others

kiln \ˈkil, ˈkiln\ *n* **:** a heated enclosure (as an oven) for processing a substance by burning, firing, or drying — **kiln** *vb*

ki•lo \ˈkē-lō\ *n, pl* **kilos :** KILOGRAM

ki•lo•byte \ˈki-lə-ˌbīt, ˈkē-\ *n* **:** 1024 bytes

kilo•cy•cle \ˈki-lə-ˌsī-kəl\ *n* **:** KILOHERTZ

ki•lo•gram \ˈkē-lə-ˌgram, ˈki-\ *n* **1 :** the basic metric unit of mass that is nearly equal to the mass of 1000 cubic centimeters of water at its maximum density **2 :** the weight of a kilogram mass under earth's gravity

ki•lo•hertz \ˈki-lə-ˌhərts, ˈkē-, -ˌherts\ *n* **:** 1000 hertz

kilo•li•ter \ˈki-lə-ˌlē-tər\ *n* **:** a metric unit of capacity equal to 1000 liters

ki•lo•me•ter \ki-ˈlä-mə-tər, ˈki-lə-ˌmē-\ *or Can and Brit* **ki•lo•me•tre** *n* **:** a metric unit of length equal to 1000 meters

ki•lo•ton \ˈki-lə-ˌtən, ˈkē-lō-\ *n* **1 :** 1000 tons **2 :** an explosive force equivalent to that of 1000 tons of TNT

ki•lo•volt \-ˌvōlt\ *n* **:** 1000 volts

kilo•watt \ˈki-lə-ˌwät\ *n* **:** 1000 watts

kilowatt–hour *n* **:** a unit of energy equal to that expended by one kilowatt in one hour

kilt \ˈkilt\ *n* **:** a knee-length pleated skirt usually of tartan worn by men in Scotland

kil•ter \ˈkil-tər\ *n* ♦ **:** proper condition ⟨out of ~⟩

♦ condition, fettle, form, order, repair, shape, trim

ki•mo•no \kə-ˈmō-nə\ *n, pl* **-nos 1 :** a loose robe with wide sleeves traditionally worn with a wide sash as an outer garment by the Japanese **2 :** a loose dressing gown or jacket

kin \ˈkin\ *n* **1** ♦ **:** an individual's relatives **2** ♦ **:** a person connected with another by blood or marriage **:** KINSMAN

♦ [1] blood, clan, family, folks, house, kindred, kinfolk, line, lineage, people, race, stock, tribe ♦ [2] kinsman, relation, relative

ki•na•ra \kē-ˈnä-rə\ *n* **:** a candelabra with seven candlesticks used during Kwanzaa

[1]**kind** \ˈkīnd\ *n* **1 :** essential quality or character **2** ♦ **:** a group united by common traits or interests; *also* **:** VARIETY **3 :** goods or commodities as distinguished from money

♦ breed, class, description, feather, ilk, like, manner, nature, order, sort, species, type, variety ♦ bracket, category, class, division, family, grade, group, set

[2]**kind** *adj* **1** ♦ **:** of a sympathetic, forbearing, or pleasant nature **2** ♦ **:** arising from sympathy or forbearance ⟨~ deeds⟩

♦ [1] beneficent, benevolent, compassionate, good-hearted, humane, kindly, sympathetic, tender, tenderhearted, warmhearted ♦ [2] attentive, considerate, solicitous, thoughtful

kin•der•gar•ten \ˈkin-dər-ˌgärt-ᵊn\ *n* **:** a school or class for children usually from four to six years old

kin•der•gart•ner \-ˌgärt-nər\ *n* **1 :** a kindergarten pupil **2 :** a kindergarten teacher

kind•heart•ed \ˌkīnd-ˈhär-təd\ *adj* **:** marked by a sympathetic nature

kin•dle \ˈkind-ᵊl\ *vb* **kin•dled; kin•dling 1** ♦ **:** to set on fire **:** start burning **2 :** to stir up **:** AROUSE **3 :** ILLUMINATE, GLOW

♦ burn, fire, ignite, inflame, light

kind•li•ness *n* **1** ♦ **:** the quality or state of being kindly **2 :** a kindly deed

♦ amity, benevolence, cordiality, fellowship, friendliness, friendship, goodwill ♦ charity, commiseration, compassion, feeling, heart, humanity, kindness, mercy, pity, sympathy

kin•dling \ˈkind-liŋ, ˈkin-lən\ *n* **:** easily combustible material for starting a fire

[1]**kind•ly** \ˈkīnd-lē\ *adj* **kind•li•er; -est 1 :** of an agreeable or beneficial nature **2** ♦ **:** of a sympathetic or generous nature

♦ beneficent, benevolent, compassionate, good-hearted, humane, kind, sympathetic, tender, tenderhearted, warmhearted

[2]**kindly** *adv* **1 :** READILY ⟨does not take ~ to criticism⟩ **2 :** SYMPATHETICALLY **3** ♦ **:** in a gracious manner **:** COURTEOUSLY

♦ courteously, nicely, thoughtfully, well

kind•ness *n* **1** ♦ **:** a kind deed **2** ♦ **:** the quality or state of being kind

♦ [1] boon, courtesy, favor (*or* favour), grace, indulgence, mercy, service, turn ♦ [2] charity, commiseration, compassion, feeling, heart, humanity, kindliness, mercy, pity, sympathy

kind of *adv* ♦ **:** to a moderate degree ⟨it's *kind of* late to begin⟩

♦ enough, fairly, moderately, pretty, quite, rather, so-so, somewhat, sort of

¹**kin•dred** \ˈkin-drəd\ *n* **1** ♦ **:** a group of related individuals **2 :** one's relatives

♦ blood, clan, family, folks, house, kin, kinfolk, line, lineage, people, race, stock, tribe

²**kindred** *adj* ♦ **:** of a like nature or character

♦ akin, related

kine \ˈkīn\ *archaic pl of* COW
ki•ne•mat•ics \ˌki-nə-ˈma-tiks\ *n* **:** a science that deals with motion apart from considerations of mass and force — **ki•ne•mat•ic** \-tik\ *or* **ki•ne•mat•i•cal** \-ti-kəl\ *adj*
kin•es•the•sia \ˌki-nəs-ˈthē-zhə, -zhē-ə\ *or* **kin•es•the•sis** \-ˈthē-səs\ *n, pl* **-the•sias** *or* **-the•ses** \-ˌsēz\ **:** a sense that perceives bodily movement, position, and weight and is mediated by nervous receptors in tendons, muscles, and joints; *also* **:** sensory experience derived from this sense — **kin•es•thet•ic** \-ˈthe-tik\ *adj*
ki•net•ic \kə-ˈne-tik\ *adj* **:** of or relating to the motion of material bodies and the forces and energy (**kinetic energy**) associated with them
ki•net•ics \-tiks\ *n sing or pl* **:** a science that deals with the effects of forces upon the motions of material bodies or with changes in a physical or chemical system
kin•folk \ˈkin-ˌfōk\ *or* **kinfolks** *n pl* ♦ **:** persons connected with each other by blood or affinity **:** RELATIVES

♦ blood, clan, family, folks, house, kin, kindred, line, lineage, people, race, stock, tribe

king \ˈkiŋ\ *n* **1 :** a male sovereign **2** ♦ **:** a chief among competitors ⟨home-run ~⟩ **3 :** the principal piece in the game of chess **4 :** a playing card bearing the figure of a king **5 :** a checker that has been crowned — **king•less** *adj* — **king•ship** *n*

♦ baron, czar, magnate, mogul, prince, tycoon

king crab *n* **1 :** HORSESHOE CRAB **2 :** a large crab of the No. Pacific caught commercially for food
king•dom \ˈkiŋ-dəm\ *n* **1 :** a country whose head is a king or queen **2 :** a realm or region in which something or someone is dominant ⟨a cattle ~⟩ **3 :** one of the three primary divisions of lifeless material, plants, and animals into which natural objects are grouped; *also* **:** a biological category that ranks above the phylum
king•fish•er \-ˌfi-shər\ *n* **:** any of numerous usually bright-colored crested birds that feed chiefly on fish
king•ly *adj* **1 :** of, relating to, or befitting a king **2** ♦ **:** of, relating to, suggestive of, or characteristic of a monarch or monarchy

♦ monarchical, princely, queenly, regal, royal

king•pin \ˈkiŋ-ˌpin\ *n* **1 :** HEADPIN **2** ♦ **:** the leader in a group or undertaking

♦ boss, captain, chief, foreman, head, headman, helmsman, leader, master, taskmaster

Kings *n* **:** either of two books of Jewish and Christian Scripture
king–size \ˈkiŋ-ˌsīz\ *or* **king–sized** \-ˌsīzd\ *adj* **1 :** longer than the regular or standard size **2 :** unusually large **3 :** having dimensions of about 76 by 80 inches (1.9 by 2.0 meters) ⟨a ~ bed⟩; *also* **:** of a size that fits a king-size bed
kink \ˈkiŋk\ *n* **1 :** a short tight twist or curl **2 :** a mental peculiarity **:** QUIRK **3 :** CRAMP ⟨a ~ in the back⟩ **4 :** an imperfection likely to cause difficulties in operation
kinky *adj* ♦ **:** strikingly out of the ordinary

♦ bizarre, curious, far-out, funny, odd, outlandish, outré, peculiar, quaint, queer, quirky, remarkable, screwy, strange, wacky, weird, wild

kin•ship \ˈkin-ˌship\ *n* ♦ **:** the quality or state of being kin **:** RELATIONSHIP

♦ association, bearing, connection, liaison, linkage, relation, relationship

kins•man \ˈkinz-mən\ *n* ♦ **:** a person connected with another by blood or marriage **:** RELATIVE; *esp* **:** a male relative

♦ kin, relation, relative

kins•wom•an \-ˌwu̇-mən\ *n* **:** a female relative
ki•osk \ˈkē-ˌäsk\ *n* **1 :** a small structure with one or more open sides **2 :** a stand-alone device providing information and services on a computer screen
Ki•o•wa \ˈkī-ə-ˌwȯ, -ˌwä, -ˌwā\ *n, pl* **Kiowa** *or* **Kiowas :** a member of an American Indian people of Colorado, Kansas, New Mexico, Oklahoma, and Texas
kip•per \ˈki-pər\ *n* **:** a fish (as a herring) preserved by salting and drying or smoking — **kipper** *vb*
kirk \ˈkərk, ˈkirk\ *n, chiefly Scot* **:** CHURCH
kir•tle \ˈkərt-ᵊl\ *n* **:** a long gown or dress worn by women
kis•met \ˈkiz-ˌmet, -mət\ *n, often cap* **:** FATE
¹**kiss** \ˈkis\ *vb* **1 :** to touch or caress with the lips as a mark of affection or greeting **2** ♦ **:** to touch gently or lightly

♦ brush, graze, nick, shave, skim

²**kiss** *n* **1 :** a caress with the lips **2 :** a gentle touch or contact **3 :** a bite-size candy
kiss•er \ˈki-sər\ *n* **1 :** one that kisses **2** *slang* **:** MOUTH **3** *slang* **:** FACE
kit \ˈkit\ *n* **1 :** a set of articles for personal use; *also* **:** a set of tools or implements or of parts to be assembled **2 :** a container (as a case) for a kit
kitch•en \ˈki-chən\ *n* **1 :** a room with cooking facilities **2 :** the staff that prepares, cooks, and serves food
kitch•en•ette \ˌki-chə-ˈnet\ *n* **:** a small kitchen or an alcove containing cooking facilities
kitchen police *n* **1 :** KP **2 :** the work of KPs
kitch•en•ware \ˈki-chən-ˌwar\ *n* **:** utensils and appliances for kitchen use
kite \ˈkīt\ *n* **1 :** any of various long-winged hawks often with deeply forked tails **2 :** a light frame covered with paper or cloth and designed to be flown in the air at the end of a long string
kith \ˈkith\ *n* **:** familiar friends, neighbors, or relatives ⟨~ and kin⟩
kitsch \ˈkich\ *n* **:** something often of poor quality that appeals to popular or lowbrow taste — **kitschy** *adj*
kit•ten \ˈkit-ᵊn\ *n* **:** a young cat
kit•ten•ish *adj* ♦ **:** resembling or suggestive of a kitten; *esp* **:** coyly playful

♦ coquettish, coy, demure

¹**kit•ty** \ˈki-tē\ *n, pl* **kitties** ♦ **:** a carnivorous mammal long domesticated as a pet and for catching rats and mice **:** CAT; *esp* **:** KITTEN

♦ cat, feline, puss

²**kitty** *n, pl* **kitties** ♦ **:** a fund in a poker game made up of contributions from each pot; *also* **:** POOL

♦ account, budget, deposit, fund, nest egg, pool

kit•ty–cor•ner *also* **cat•ty–cor•ner** *or* **cat•er•cor•ner** \ˈki-tē-ˌkȯr-nər, ˈka-; ˈka-tə-\ *or* **kit•ty–cor•nered** *or* **cat•ty–cor•nered** *or* **cat•er•cornered** \-nərd\ *adv or adj* **:** in a diagonal or oblique position
ki•wi \ˈkē-(ˌ)wē\ *n* **1 :** any of a small genus of flightless New Zealand birds **2 :** KIWIFRUIT
ki•wi•fruit \-ˌfrüt\ *n* **:** a brownish hairy egg-shaped fruit of a subtropical vine that has sweet bright green flesh and small edible black seeds
KJV *abbr* King James Version
KKK *abbr* Ku Klux Klan
kl *abbr* kiloliter
klatch *or* **klatsch** \ˈklach\ *n* **:** a gathering marked by informal conversation
klep•toc•ra•cy \klep-ˈtä-krə-sē\ *n, pl* **-cies :** government by those who seek chiefly status and personal gain at the expense of the governed
klep•to•ma•nia \ˌklep-tə-ˈmā-nē-ə\ *n* **:** a persistent neurotic impulse to steal especially without economic motive — **klep•to•ma•ni•ac** \-nē-ˌak\ *n*
klieg light *or* **kleig light** \ˈklēg-\ *n* **:** a very bright lamp used in making motion pictures
klutz \ˈkləts\ *n* **:** a clumsy person — **klutzy** *adj*
km *abbr* kilometer
kn *abbr* knot
knack \ˈnak\ *n* **1 :** a clever way of doing something **2** ♦ **:** natural aptitude

♦ aptitude, endowment, faculty, flair, genius, gift, talent

knap•sack \ˈnap-ˌsak\ *n* **:** a bag (as of canvas) strapped on the back and used especially for carrying supplies
knave \ˈnāv\ *n* **1** ♦ **:** a tricky deceitful fellow **:** ROGUE **2 :** JACK 6

♦ beast, devil, evildoer, fiend, no-good, reprobate, rogue, varlet, villain, wretch

knav•ery \ˈnā-və-rē\ *n* ♦ **:** the character or actions of a rascal; *also* **:** a roguish or mischievous act

♦ devilishness, impishness, mischief, mischievousness, rascality, shenanigans, waggery, wickedness

knav•ish \ˈnā-vish\ *adj* ♦ **:** of, relating to, or characteristic of a knave

♦ devilish, impish, mischievous, rascally, roguish, sly, waggish, wicked

knead \ˈnēd\ *vb* **:** to work and press into a mass with the hands; *also* **:** MASSAGE — **knead•er** *n*
knee \ˈnē\ *n* **:** the joint in the middle part of the leg — **kneed** \ˈnēd\ *adj*
knee•cap \ˈnē-ˌkap\ *n* **:** a thick flat triangular movable bone forming the front of the knee
knee•hole \-ˌhōl\ *n* **:** a space (as under a desk) for the knees
knee–jerk \ˈnē-ˌjərk\ *adj* **:** readily predictable ⟨a ~ reaction⟩
kneel \ˈnēl\ *vb* **knelt** \ˈnelt\ *or* **kneeled; kneel•ing :** to bend the knee **:** fall or rest on the knees
[1]**knell** \ˈnel\ *vb* **1** ♦ **:** to ring especially for a death or disaster **2 :** to summon, announce, or proclaim by a knell

♦ chime, peal, ring, toll

[2]**knell** *n* **1 :** a stroke of a bell especially when tolled (as for a funeral) **2 :** an indication of the end or failure of something
knew *past of* KNOW
knick•ers \ˈni-kərz\ *n pl* **:** loose-fitting short pants gathered at the knee
knick•knack \ˈnik-ˌnak\ *n* ♦ **:** a small trivial article intended for ornament

♦ bauble, curiosity, gewgaw, novelty, trinket

[1]**knife** \ˈnīf\ *n, pl* **knives** \ˈnīvz\ **1 :** a cutting instrument consisting of a sharp blade fastened to a handle **2 :** a sharp cutting tool in a machine
[2]**knife** *vb* **knifed; knif•ing :** to stab, slash, or wound with a knife
[1]**knight** \ˈnīt\ *n* **1 :** a mounted warrior of feudal times serving a king **2 :** a man honored by a sovereign for merit and in Great Britain ranking below a baronet **3 :** a man devoted to the service of a lady **4 :** a member of an order or society **5 :** a chess piece having an L-shaped move — **knight•ly** *adj*
[2]**knight** *vb* **:** to make a knight of
knight•hood \ˈnīt-ˌhu̇d\ *n* **1 :** the rank, dignity, or profession of a knight **2 :** CHIVALRY **3 :** knights as a class or body
knish \kə-ˈnish\ *n* **:** a small round or square of dough stuffed with a filling (as of meat or fruit) and baked or fried
[1]**knit** \ˈnit\ *vb* **knit** *or* **knit•ted; knit•ting 1 :** to link firmly or closely **2 :** WRINKLE ⟨~ her brows⟩ **3 :** to form a fabric by interlacing yarn or thread in connected loops with needles **4 :** to grow together — **knit•ter** *n*
[2]**knit** *n* **1 :** a basic knitting stitch **2 :** a knitted garment or fabric
knit•wear \-ˌwar\ *n* **:** knitted clothing
knob \ˈnäb\ *n* **1 :** a rounded protuberance; *also* **:** a small rounded ornament or handle **2 :** a rounded usually isolated hill — **knobbed** \ˈnäbd\ *adj* — **knob•by** \ˈnä-bē\ *adj*
[1]**knock** \ˈnäk\ *vb* **1 :** to strike with a sharp blow **2** ♦ **:** to collide with something **:** BUMP **3 :** to make a pounding noise; *esp* **:** to have engine knock **4** ♦ **:** to find fault with **5** ♦ **:** to move about without a fixed course, aim, or goal

♦ [2] bang, bash, bump, collide, crash, hit, impact, ram, slam, smash, strike, swipe, thud ♦ [4] blame, censure, condemn, criticize, denounce, fault, pan, reprehend ♦ [5] gad, gallivant, maunder, meander, mope, ramble, range, roam, rove, traipse, wander

[2]**knock** *n* **1 :** a sharp blow **2 :** a pounding noise; *esp* **:** one caused by abnormal ignition in an automobile engine **3** ♦ **:** a severe misfortune or hardship

♦ adversity, misadventure, mischance, misfortune, mishap

knock•down \ˈnäk-ˌdau̇n\ *n* **1 :** the action of knocking down **2 :** something (as a blow) that knocks down **3 :** something that can be easily assembled or disassembled
knock down *vb* **1** ♦ **:** to strike to the ground with or as if with as sharp blow **2** ♦ **:** to take apart **:** DISASSEMBLE **3 :** to receive as income or salary **:** EARN **4 :** to make a reduction in

♦ [1] bowl, down, drop, fell, floor, level ♦ [2] disassemble, dismantle, strike, take down

knock•er \ˈnä-kər\ *n* **:** one that knocks; *esp* **:** a device hinged to a door for use in knocking
knock–knee \ˈnäk-ˌnē\ *n* **:** a condition in which the legs curve inward at the knees — **knock–kneed** \-ˌnēd\ *adj*
knock•off \ˈnäk-ˌȯf\ *n* **:** a copy or imitation of someone or something popular
knock off *vb* **1** ♦ **:** to stop doing something **2 :** to do quickly, carelessly, or routinely **3 :** to deduct from a price **4 :** KILL **5 :** ROB **6 :** COPY, IMITATE

♦ break, break off, cease, cut, desist, discontinue, drop, end, halt, layoff, leave off, quit, shut off, stop

knock•out \ˈnäk-ˌau̇t\ *n* **1 :** a blow that fells and immobilizes an opponent (as in boxing) **2** ♦ **:** something sensationally striking or attractive **3** ♦ **:** the act of knocking out; *also* **:** the condition of being knocked out

♦ [2] beauty, dream, enchantress, fox, goddess, queen ♦ [2] beauty, crackerjack, dandy, jim-dandy, pip ♦ [3] blackout, faint, swoon

knock out *vb* **1 :** to defeat by a knockout **2 :** to make unconscious or inoperative **3 :** to tire out **:** EXHAUST
knock•wurst *also* **knack•wurst** \ˈnäk-ˌwərst, -ˌvu̇rst\ *n* **:** a short thick heavily seasoned sausage
knoll \ˈnōl\ *n* **:** a small round hill
[1]**knot** \ˈnät\ *n* **1 :** an interlacing (as of string) forming a lump or knob and often used for fastening or tying together **2** ♦ **:** something hard to solve **:** PROBLEM **3** ♦ **:** a bond of union; *esp* **:** the marriage bond **4** ♦ **:** a protuberant lump or swelling in tissue **5 :** a rounded cross-grained area in lumber that is a section through the junction of a tree branch with the trunk; *also* **:** the woody tissue forming this junction in a tree **6 :** a cluster of persons or things **:** GROUP **7 :** an ornamental bow of ribbon **8 :** one nautical mile per hour; *also* **:** one nautical mile

♦ [2] case, matter, problem, trouble ♦ [3] bond, cement, ligature, link, tie ♦ [4] bump, lump, nodule, swelling

[2]**knot** *vb* **knot•ted; knot•ting 1 :** to tie in or with a knot **2** ♦ **:** to unite closely or intricately **:** ENTANGLE

♦ entangle, interlace, intertwine, interweave, snarl, tangle

knot•hole \-ˌhōl\ *n* **:** a hole in a board or tree trunk where a knot has come out
knot•ty *adj* ♦ **:** marked by or full of knots; *esp* **:** so full of difficulties and complications as to be likely to defy solution

♦ complex, complicated, convoluted, elaborate, intricate, involved, sophisticated ♦ catchy, delicate, difficult, problematic, spiny, thorny, ticklish, touchy, tough, tricky

knout \ˈnau̇t, ˈnüt\ *n* **:** a whip used for flogging
know \ˈnō\ *vb* **knew** \ˈnü, ˈnyü\; **known** \ˈnōn\; **know•ing 1** ♦ **:** to perceive directly **:** have understanding or direct cognition of; *also* **:** to recognize the nature of **2 :** to be acquainted or familiar with **3 :** to be aware of the truth of **4** ♦ **:** to have a practical understanding of — **know•able** *adj* — **know•er** *n* — **in the know :** possessing confidential information

♦ [1] endure, experience, feel, have, see, suffer, sustain, taste, undergo ♦ [4] comprehend, grasp, understand

know–how \ˈnō-ˌhau̇\ *n* ♦ **:** knowledge of how to do something smoothly and efficiently

♦ experience, expertise, proficiency, savvy

knowing *adj* **1 :** having or reflecting knowledge, intelligence, or information **2** ♦ **:** shrewdly and keenly alert **3 :** DELIBERATE, INTENTIONAL

♦ astute, canny, hardheaded, sharp, shrewd, smart

know•ing•ly *adv* ♦ **:** in a knowing manner; *esp* **:** with awareness, deliberateness, or intention

♦ consciously, deliberately, intentionally, purposely, willfully

knowl•edge \ˈnä-lij\ *n* **1 :** understanding gained by actual experience ⟨a ~ of carpentry⟩ **2 :** range of information ⟨to the best of my ~⟩ **3 :** clear perception of truth **4** ♦ **:** something learned and kept in the mind **5** ♦ **:** acquaintance with or understanding of a science, art, or technique

♦ [4] intelligence, lore, science, wisdom ♦ [5] education, erudition, learning, scholarship, science

knowl•edge•able \ˈnä-li-jə-bəl\ *adj* ♦ **:** having or showing knowledge or intelligence

♦ abreast, conversant, familiar, informed, up, up-to-date, versed ♦ educated, erudite, learned, literate, scholarly, well-read

know–noth•ing \ˈnō-ˌnə-thiŋ\ *n* ♦ **:** an utterly ignorant person **:** IGNORAMUS

♦ blockhead, dope, dummy, idiot, imbecile, jackass, moron, numskull

knuck•le \ˈnə-kəl\ *n* : the rounded knob at a joint and especially at a finger joint
knuckle down *vb* : to apply oneself earnestly
knuckle under *vb* ♦ : to yield under insistence or entreaty : SUBMIT, SURRENDER

♦ bow, budge, capitulate, concede, give in, quit, submit, succumb, surrender, yield

knurl \ˈnərl\ *n* **1 :** KNOB **2 :** one of a series of small ridges on a metal surface to aid in gripping — **knurled** \ˈnərld\ *adj* — **knurly** *adj*
[1]**KO** \(ˌ)kā-ˈō, ˈkā-ō\ *n* : KNOCKOUT
[2]**KO** *vb* **KO'd; KO'•ing** : to knock out in boxing
ko•ala \kō-ˈä-lə\ *n* : a gray furry Australian marsupial that has large hairy ears and feeds on eucalyptus leaves
K of C *abbr* Knights of Columbus
kohl•ra•bi \kōl-ˈrä-bē\ *n, pl* **-bies** : a cabbage that forms no head but has a swollen fleshy edible stem
koi \ˈkȯi\ *n, pl* **koi** : a carp bred for large size and a variety of colors and often stocked in ornamental ponds
ko•lin•sky \kə-ˈlin-skē\ *n, pl* **-skies** : the fur of various Asian minks
Ko•mo•do dragon \kə-ˈmō-dō-\ *n* : a carnivorous lizard of Indonesia that is the largest of all known lizards
kook \ˈkük\ *n* ♦ : one whose ideas or actions are eccentric, fantastic, or insane : SCREWBALL

♦ character, crackpot, crank, eccentric, nut, oddball, screwball, weirdo

kooky *also* **kook•ie** \ˈkü-kē\ *adj* **kook•i•er; -est** ♦ : having the characteristics of a kook : CRAZY — **kook•i•ness** *n*

♦ absurd, crazy, cuckoo, fatuous, foolish, mad, nonsensical, nutty, senseless, silly, stupid

Koo•te•nai *or* **Ku•te•nai** \ˈkü-tə-ˌnā\ *n, pl* **-nai** *or* **-nais** : a member of an American Indian people of the Rocky Mountains in both the U.S. and Canada; *also* : their language
ko•ra \ˈkȯr-ə\ *n* : a 21-stringed African musical instrument
Ko•ran \kə-ˈran, -ˈrän\ *n* : a sacred book of Islam that contains revelations made to Muhammad by Allah
Ko•re•an \kə-ˈrē-ən\ *n* : a native or inhabitant of Korea — **Korean** *adj*
ko•sher \ˈkō-shər\ *adj* **1 :** ritually fit for use according to Jewish law **2 :** selling or serving kosher food
kow•tow \kau̇-ˈtau̇, ˈkau̇-ˌtau̇\ *vb* **1** ♦ **:** to show obsequious deference **2 :** to kneel and touch the forehead to the ground as a sign of homage or deep respect

♦ fawn, fuss, toady

KP \ˌkā-ˈpē\ *n* **1 :** an enlisted man detailed to help the cooks in a military mess **2 :** the work of KPs
kph *abbr* kilometers per hour
Kr *symbol* krypton
kraal \ˈkräl, ˈkrȯl\ *n* **1 :** a native village in southern Africa **2 :** an enclosure for domestic animals in southern Africa
kraut \ˈkrau̇t\ *n* : SAUERKRAUT
Krem•lin \ˈkrem-lən\ *n* : the Russian government
Krem•lin•ol•o•gist \ˌkrem-lə-ˈnä-lə-jist\ *n* : a specialist in the policies and practices of the former Soviet government
Kru•ger•rand \ˈkrü-gər-ˌrand, -ˌränd\ *n* : a 1-ounce gold coin of the Republic of South Africa
kryp•ton \ˈkrip-ˌtän\ *n* : a gaseous chemical element used especially in electric lamps
KS *abbr* Kansas
kt *abbr* **1** karat **2** knight
ku•do \ˈkü-dō, ˈkyü-\ *n, pl* **kudos** **1 :** AWARD, HONOR **2 :** COMPLIMENT, PRAISE
ku•dos \ˈkü-ˌdäs, ˈkyü-\ *n* : fame and renown resulting from achievement
kud•zu \ˈku̇d-zü, ˈkəd-\ *n* : a fast-growing weedy leguminous vine used for forage and erosion control
ku•lak \kü-ˈlak, kyü-, -ˈläk\ *n* **1 :** a wealthy peasant farmer in 19th century Russia **2 :** a farmer characterized by Communists as too wealthy
kum•quat \ˈkəm-ˌkwät\ *n* : any of several small citrus fruits with sweet spongy rind and acid pulp
kung fu \ˌkəŋ-ˈfü, ˌku̇ŋ-\ *n* : a Chinese art of self-defense resembling karate
kung pao \ˈkəŋ-ˈpau̇, ˈküŋ-, ˈku̇ŋ-\ *adj* : being stir-fried or deep-fried and served in a spicy hot sauce usually with peanuts
kur•ta \ˈkər-tə\ *n* : a long loose-fitting collarless shirt
ku•rus \kə-ˈrüsh\ *n, pl* **kurus** : a Turkish piaster equal to $\frac{1}{100}$ lira
Ku•waiti \ku̇-ˈwā-tē\ *n* : a native or inhabitant of Kuwait — **Kuwaiti** *adj*
kV *abbr* kilovolt
kvell \ˈkvel\ *vb* : to be extraordinarily proud
kvetch \ˈkvech, ˈkfech\ *vb* : to complain habitually — **kvetch** *n*
kW *abbr* kilowatt
Kwan•zaa, Kwan•za \ˈkwän-zə\ *n* : an African-American cultural festival held from December 26 to January 1
kwash•i•or•kor \ˌkwä-shē-ˈȯr-kȯr, -ȯr-ˈkȯr\ *n* : a disease of young children caused by deficient intake of protein
kWh *abbr* kilowatt-hour
Ky *or* **KY** *abbr* Kentucky

L

[1]**l** \ˈel\ *n, pl* **l's** *or* **ls** \ˈelz\ *often cap* : the 12th letter of the English alphabet
[2]**l** *abbr, often cap* **1** lake **2** large **3** left **4** pound **5** line **6** liter
[1]**La** *abbr* Louisiana
[2]**La** *symbol* lanthanum
LA *abbr* **1** law agent **2** Los Angeles **3** Louisiana
lab \ˈlab\ *n* : LABORATORY
Lab *n* : LABRADOR RETRIEVER
[1]**la•bel** \ˈlā-bəl\ *n* **1** ♦ **:** a slip attached to something for identification or description **2 :** a descriptive or identifying word or phrase **3 :** BRAND 3

♦ marker, tag, ticket

[2]**label** *vb* **-beled** *or* **-belled; -bel•ing** *or* **-bel•ling** **1** ♦ **:** to affix a label to **2** ♦ **:** to describe or name with a label

♦ [1] mark, tag, ticket ♦ [2] baptize, call, christen, denominate, designate, dub, entitle, name, style, term, title

la•bi•al \ˈlā-bē-əl\ *adj* : of, relating to, or situated near the lips or labia
la•bia ma•jo•ra \ˈlā-bē-ə-mə-ˈjōr-ə\ *n pl* : the outer fatty folds of the vulva
labia mi•no•ra \-mə-ˈnōr-ə\ *n pl* : the inner highly vascular folds of the vulva
la•bile \ˈlā-ˌbī(-ə)l, -bəl\ *adj* **1 :** UNSTABLE **2 :** ADAPTABLE
la•bi•um \ˈlā-bē-əm\ *n, pl* **la•bia** \-ə\ : any of the folds at the margin of the vulva
[1]**la•bor** *or Can and Brit* **la•bour** \ˈlā-bər\ *n* **1** ♦ **:** physical or mental effort; *also* : human activity that provides the goods or services in an economy **2** ♦ **:** the physical efforts of giving birth; *also* : the period of such labor **3** ♦ **:** an act or process requiring labor **4 :** those who do manual labor or work for wages; *also* : labor unions or their officials

♦ [1] effort, exertion, expenditure, pains, sweat, trouble, while, work ♦ [2] childbirth, delivery ♦ [3] drudgery, grind, slavery, sweat, toil, travail

[2]**labor** *or Can and Brit* **labour** *vb* **1** ♦ **:** to exert oneself physically or mentally especially with painful or strenuous effort : WORK **2 :** to move with great effort **3 :** to be in the labor of giving birth **4 :** to suffer from some disadvantage or distress ⟨~ under a delusion⟩ **5 :** to treat or work out laboriously

♦ drudge, endeavor (*or* endeavour), fag, grub, hustle, peg, plod, plug, slave, slog, strain, strive, struggle, sweat, toil, work ***Ant*** dabble, fiddle (around), fool (around), mess (around), putter (around)

lab•o•ra•to•ry \ˈla-brə-ˌtōr-ē, -bə-rə-\ *n, pl* **-ries** : a place equipped for making scientific experiments or tests

Labor Day *or Can* **Labour Day** *n* : the 1st Monday in September observed as a legal holiday in recognition of the working people
la•bored *or Can and Brit* **la•boured** \ˈlā-bərd\ *adj* : not freely or easily done ⟨~ breathing⟩
la•bor•er *or Can and Brit* **la•bour•er** *n* : one that labors; *specif* : a person who does unskilled physical work for wages
la•bo•ri•ous \lə-ˈbōr-ē-əs\ *adj* **1** ♦ : devoted to labor : INDUSTRIOUS **2** ♦ : requiring great effort

♦ [1] active, assiduous, busy, diligent, engaged, industrious, occupied, sedulous, working ♦ [2] arduous, challenging, demanding, difficult, exacting, formidable, grueling, hard, onerous, rough, stiff, strenuous, tall, taxing, toilsome, tough

la•bo•ri•ous•ly *adv* ♦ : in a laborious manner

♦ determinedly, diligently, hard, hardly, mightily, slavishly, strenuously, tirelessly

la•bor•sav•ing *or Can and Brit* **labour–saving** \ˈlā-bər-ˌsā-viŋ\ *adj* ♦ : designed to replace or decrease labor

♦ automatic, robotic, self-acting

labor union *n* : an organization of workers formed to advance its members' interest in respect to wages and working conditions
labour *Can and Brit var of* LABOR
lab•ra•dor•ite \ˈla-brə-ˌdȯr-ˌīt\ *n* : an iridescent feldspar used in jewelry
Lab•ra•dor retriever \ˈla-brə-ˌdȯr-\ *n* : any of a breed of strongly built retrievers having a short dense black, yellow, or chocolate coat
la•bur•num \lə-ˈbər-nəm\ *n* : any of a genus of leguminous shrubs or trees with hanging clusters of yellow flowers
lab•y•rinth \ˈla-bə-ˌrinth\ *n* : a place constructed of or filled with confusing intricate passageways : MAZE
lab•y•rin•thine \ˌla-bə-ˈrin-thən, -ˌthīn, -ˌthēn\ *adj* : INTRICATE, INVOLVED
lac \ˈlak\ *n* : a resinous substance secreted by a scale insect and used chiefly in the form of shellac
¹lace \ˈlās\ *vb* **laced; lac•ing 1** : TIE **2** ♦ : to adorn with or as if with lace ⟨countryside *laced* with small villages⟩ **3** ♦ : to unite by twining one with another : INTERTWINE **4** : to hit repeatedly : BEAT **5** : to add something to impart zest or savor to

♦ interlace, intersperse, intertwine, interweave, thread, weave, wreathe

²lace *n* **1** ♦ : a cord or string used for drawing together two edges **2** ♦ : an ornamental braid **3** : a fine openwork usually figured fabric made of thread — **lacy** \ˈlā-sē\ *adj*

♦ [1] cable, cord, line, rope, string, wire ♦ [2] braid, plait

lac•er•ate \ˈla-sə-ˌrāt\ *vb* **-at•ed; -at•ing** : to tear roughly
lac•er•a•tion \ˌla-sə-ˈrā-shən\ *n* ♦ : a torn and ragged wound

♦ gash, rent, rip, slash, slit, tear

lace•wing \ˈlās-ˌwiŋ\ *n* : any of various insects with delicate wing veins, long antennae, and often brilliant eyes
lach•ry•mal *or* **lac•ri•mal** \ˈla-krə-məl\ *adj* **1** *usu lacrimal* : of, relating to, or being glands that produce tears **2** : of, relating to, or marked by tears
lach•ry•mose \ˈla-krə-ˌmōs\ *adj* **1** : TEARFUL **2** : MOURNFUL
¹lack \ˈlak\ *vb* **1** : to be wanting or missing **2** : to be deficient in
²lack *n* ♦ : the fact or state of being wanting or deficient

♦ dearth, deficiency, deficit, failure, famine, inadequacy, insufficiency, paucity, poverty, scantiness, scarcity, shortage, want ♦ absence, need, want

lack•a•dai•si•cal \ˌla-kə-ˈdā-zi-kəl\ *adj* ♦ : lacking life, spirit, or zest — **lack•a•dai•si•cal•ly** \-k(ə-)lē\ *adv*

♦ enervated, languid, languorous, limp, listless, spiritless

lack•ey \ˈla-kē\ *n, pl* **lackeys 1** ♦ : someone who does tasks or errands for another : FOOTMAN, SERVANT **2** : TOADY

♦ domestic, flunky, menial, retainer, servant, steward

lack•lus•ter *or Can and Brit* **lack•lus•tre** \ˈlak-ˌləs-tər\ *adj* : DULL
la•con•ic \lə-ˈkä-nik\ *adj* ♦ : sparing of words : TERSE

♦ brief, compact, compendious, concise, crisp, epigrammatic, pithy, succinct, summary, terse

la•con•i•cal•ly \-ni-k(ə-)lē\ *adv* ♦ : in a laconic manner

♦ compactly, concisely, crisply, shortly, succinctly, summarily, tersely

lac•quer \ˈla-kər\ *n* : a clear or colored usually glossy and quick-drying surface coating — **lacquer** *vb*

lac•ri•ma•tion \ˌla-krə-ˈmā-shən\ *n* : secretion of tears
la•crosse \lə-ˈkrȯs\ *n* : a goal game in which players use a long-handled triangular-headed stick having a mesh pouch for catching, carrying, and throwing the ball
lac•tate \ˈlak-ˌtāt\ *vb* **lac•tat•ed; lac•tat•ing** : to secrete milk — **lac•ta•tion** \lak-ˈtā-shən\ *n*
lac•tic \ˈlak-tik\ *adj* **1** : of or relating to milk **2** : obtained from sour milk or whey
lactic acid *n* : a syrupy acid present in blood and muscle tissue and used especially in food and medicine
lac•tose \ˈlak-ˌtōs\ *n* : a sugar present in milk
la•cu•na \lə-ˈkü-nə, -ˈkyü-\ *n, pl* **la•cu•nae** \-nē\ *also* **la•cu•nas** : a blank space or missing part : GAP
lad \ˈlad\ *n* ♦ : a male person of any age between early boyhood and maturity : YOUTH; *also* : FELLOW

♦ boy, nipper, shaver, stripling, youth ♦ buck, chap, dude, fellow, gent, gentleman, guy, hombre, jack, joker, male, man

lad•der \ˈla-dər\ *n* **1** : a structure for climbing that consists of two parallel sidepieces joined at intervals by crosspieces **2** ♦ : a series of usually ascending steps or stages

♦ graduation, scale

lad•die \ˈla-dē\ *n* : a young lad
lad•en \ˈlād-ᵊn\ *adj* : LOADED, BURDENED
lad•ing \ˈlā-diŋ\ *n* ♦ : the goods or merchandise conveyed in a ship, airplane, or vehicle : CARGO, FREIGHT

♦ burden, cargo, freight, haul, load, payload, weight

¹la•dle \ˈlād-ᵊl\ *n* : a deep-bowled long-handled spoon used in taking up and conveying liquids
²ladle *vb* ♦ : to take up and convey in or as if in a ladle

♦ dip, scoop, spoon

la•dy \ˈlā-dē\ *n, pl* **ladies 1** ♦ : a woman of property, rank, or authority; *also* : a woman of superior social position or of refinement **2** : WOMAN **3** ♦ : a female partner in a marriage : WIFE

♦ [1] dame, gentlewoman, noblewoman ♦ [3] helpmate, wife

lady beetle *n* : LADYBUG
la•dy•bird \ˈlā-dē-ˌbərd\ *n* : LADYBUG
la•dy•bug \-ˌbəg\ *n* : any of various small nearly hemispherical and usually brightly colored beetles that feed mostly on other insects
la•dy•fin•ger \-ˌfiŋ-gər\ *n* : a small finger-shaped sponge cake
lady–in–waiting *n, pl* **ladies–in–waiting** : a lady appointed to attend or wait on a queen or princess
la•dy•like \ˈlā-dē-ˌlīk\ *adj* : WELL-BRED
la•dy•ship \-ˌship\ *n* : the condition of being a lady : rank of lady
lady's slipper *n* : any of several No. American orchids with slipper-shaped flowers
¹lag \ˈlag\ *n* **1** : a slowing up or falling behind; *also* : the amount by which one lags **2** : INTERVAL
²lag *vb* **lagged; lag•ging 1** ♦ : to fail to keep up : stay behind **2** ♦ : to slacken gradually

♦ [1] crawl, creep, dally, dawdle, delay, dillydally, drag, linger, loiter, poke, tarry ♦ [2] decay, droop, fail, flag, go, languish, sag, waste, weaken, wilt

la•ger \ˈlä-gər\ *n* : a beer brewed by slow fermentation and matured under refrigeration
lag•gard \ˈla-gərd\ *adj* ♦ : tending to lag — **laggard** *n* — **laggard•ly** *adj* — **lag•gard•ness** *n*

♦ creeping, dilatory, languid, poky, slow, sluggish, tardy

lag•gard•ly *adv* ♦ : in a laggard manner

♦ slow, slowly, sluggishly, tardily

la•gniappe \ˈlan-ˌyap\ *n* ♦ : something given free especially with a purchase

♦ bonus, dividend, extra, perquisite, tip ♦ bestowal, donation, freebie, gift, largesse, present

la•goon \lə-ˈgün\ *n* : a shallow sound, channel, or pond near or connected to a larger body of water
laid *past and past part of* LAY
laid–back \ˈlād-ˈbak\ *adj* ♦ : having a relaxed style or character ⟨~ music⟩

♦ affable, breezy, easygoing, happy-go-lucky

lain *past part of* ¹LIE
lair \ˈlar\ *n* **1** ♦ : the resting or living place of a wild animal : DEN **2** ♦ : a refuge or place for hiding

♦ [1] burrow, den, hole, lodge ♦ [2] concealment, covert, den, hideout, nest

laird \ˈlard\ *n, chiefly Scot* : a landed proprietor
lais•ser–faire *chiefly Brit var of* LAISSEZ-FAIRE
lais•sez–faire \ˌle-ˌsā-ˈfar, ˌlā-, -ˌzā-\ *n* : a doctrine opposing governmental control of economic affairs beyond that necessary to maintain peace and property rights
la•ity \ˈlā-ə-tē\ *n* **1** : the people of a religious faith as distinct from its clergy **2** : the mass of people as distinct from those of a particular field
lake \ˈlāk\ *n* : an inland body of standing water of considerable size; *also* : a pool of liquid (as lava or pitch)
La•ko•ta \lə-ˈkō-tə\ *n, pl* **Lakota** *also* **Lakotas** : a member of a western division of the Dakota peoples; *also* : their language
¹lam \ˈlam\ *vb* **lammed; lam•ming** ♦ : to flee hastily

♦ abscond, clear out, escape, flee, fly, get out, run away, run off

²lam *abbr* laminated
³lam *n* ♦ : sudden or hurried flight especially from the law

♦ escape, flight, getaway, slip

Lam *abbr* Lamentations
la•ma \ˈlä-mə\ *n* : a Buddhist monk of Tibet or Mongolia
la•ma•sery \ˈlä-mə-ˌser-ē\ *n, pl* **-ser•ies** : a monastery for lamas
¹lamb \ˈlam\ *n* **1** : a young sheep; *also* : its flesh used as food **2** ♦ : an innocent or gentle person

♦ angel, dove, innocent, sheep ***Ant*** wolf

²lamb *vb* : to bring forth a lamb
lam•baste *or* **lam•bast** \lam-ˈbāst, -ˈbast\ *vb* **1** : to assault violently : BEAT **2** ♦ : to attack verbally : EXCORIATE

♦ abuse, assail, attack, belabor, blast, castigate, excoriate, jump, slam, vituperate ♦ admonish, chide, lecture, rail (at *or* against), rate, rebuke, reprimand, scold

lamb•da \ˈlam-də\ *n* : the 11th letter of the Greek alphabet — Λ or λ
lam•bent \ˈlam-bənt\ *adj* **1** : FLICKERING **2** ♦ : softly radiant ⟨~ eyes⟩ **3** : marked by lightness or brilliance ⟨~ humor⟩ — **lam•ben•cy** \-bən-sē\ *n* — **lam•bent•ly** *adv*

♦ beaming, bright, brilliant, effulgent, glowing, incandescent, lucent, lucid, luminous, lustrous, radiant, refulgent, shiny

lamb•skin \ˈlam-ˌskin\ *n* : a lamb's skin or a small fine-grade sheepskin or the leather made from either
¹lame \ˈlām\ *adj* **lam•er; lam•est** **1** : having a body part and especially a limb so disabled as to impair freedom of movement; *also* : marked by stiffness and soreness **2** : lacking substance : WEAK — **lame•ly** *adv* — **lame•ness** *n*
²lame *vb* **lamed; lam•ing** ♦ : to make lame : CRIPPLE, DISABLE

♦ cripple, disable, maim, mutilate

la•mé \lä-ˈmā, la-\ *n* : a brocaded clothing fabric with tinsel filling threads (as of gold or silver)
lame•brain \ˈlām-ˌbrān\ *n* : DOLT
lame duck *n* : an elected official continuing to hold office between an election and the inauguration of a successor — **lame–duck** *adj*
¹la•ment \lə-ˈment\ *vb* **1** : to mourn aloud : WAIL **2** ♦ : to express sorrow or regret for

♦ bemoan, bewail, deplore, grieve, mourn, wail ***Ant*** exult (in), glory (in), rejoice (in) ♦ bemoan, deplore, regret, repent, rue

²lament *n* **1** ♦ : a crying out in grief : WAIL **2** ♦ : a slow, solemn, and mournful piece of music : DIRGE, ELEGY **3** : COMPLAINT

♦ [1] groan, howl, keen, moan, plaint, wail ***Ant*** exultation, rejoicing ♦ [2] dirge, elegy, requiem, threnody

lam•en•ta•ble \ˈla-mən-tə-bəl, lə-ˈmen-tə-\ *adj* **1** ♦ : that is to be regretted or lamented **2** ♦ : expressing grief — **lam•en•ta•bly** \-blē\ *adv*

♦ [1] deplorable, distressful, grievous, heartbreaking, regrettable, unfortunate, woeful ♦ [2] anguished, dolorous, mournful, plaintive, sorrowful, sorry, woeful

lam•en•ta•tion \ˌla-mən-ˈtā-shən\ *n* : an act or instance of lamenting
Lamentations *n* : a book of Jewish and Christian Scripture
la•mia \ˈlā-mē-ə\ *n* : a female demon
lam•i•na \ˈla-mə-nə\ *n, pl* **-nae** \-ˌnē\ *or* **-nas** : a thin plate or scale
¹lam•i•nate \ˈla-mə-ˌnāt\ *vb* **-nat•ed; -nat•ing** : to make by uniting layers of one or more materials — **lam•i•na•tion** \ˌla-mə-ˈnā-shən\ *n*
²lam•i•nate \-nət\ *n* : a product manufactured by laminating
lamp \ˈlamp\ *n* **1** : a vessel with a wick for burning a flammable liquid (as oil) to produce light **2** : a device for producing light or heat
lamp•black \-ˌblak\ *n* : black soot used especially as a pigment
lamp•light•er \-ˌlī-tər\ *n* : one that lights a lamp
lam•poon \lam-ˈpün\ *n* : SATIRE; *esp* : a harsh satire directed against an individual — **lampoon** *vb*
lam•prey \ˈlam-prē\ *n, pl* **lampreys** : any of a family of eel-shaped jawless fishes that have well-developed eyes and a large disk-shaped sucking mouth armed with horny teeth
LAN \ˈlan, ˌel-ˌā-ˈen\ *n* : LOCAL AREA NETWORK
la•nai \lə-ˈnī\ *n* : PORCH, VERANDA
¹lance \ˈlans\ *n* **1** ♦ : a spear carried by mounted soldiers **2** : any of various sharp-pointed implements; *esp* : LANCET

♦ pike, spear

²lance *vb* **lanced; lanc•ing** ♦ : to pierce or open with a lance ⟨~ a boil⟩

♦ gore, harpoon, impale, pierce, puncture, skewer, spear, spike, stab, stick, transfix

lance corporal *n* : an enlisted man in the marine corps ranking above a private first class and below a corporal
lanc•er \ˈlan-sər\ *n* : a cavalryman of a unit formerly armed with lances
lan•cet \ˈlan-sət\ *n* : a sharp-pointed and usually 2-edged surgical instrument
¹land \ˈland\ *n* **1** ♦ : the solid part of the surface of the earth; *also* : a part of the earth's surface ⟨fenced ~⟩ ⟨marshy ~⟩ **2** ♦ : the people of a country : NATION **3** : REALM, DOMAIN — **land•less** *adj*

♦ [1] belt, region, tract, zone ♦ [1] dirt, dust, earth, ground, soil ♦ [2] commonwealth, country, nation, sovereignty, state

²land *vb* **1** ♦ : to set or put on shore from a ship : DISEMBARK; *also* : to touch at a place on shore **2** ♦ : to alight or cause to alight on a surface **3** ♦ : to bring to or arrive at a destination **4** ♦ : to catch and bring in ⟨~ a fish⟩; *also* : GAIN, SECURE ⟨~ a job⟩

♦ [1] disembark, dock, moor, tie up ♦ [2] alight, light, perch, roost, settle ♦ [3] arrive, come, show up, turn up ♦ [4] acquire, attain, capture, carry, draw, earn, gain, garner, get, make, obtain, procure, realize, secure, win

lan•dau \ˈlan-ˌdau̇\ *n* : a 4-wheeled carriage with a top divided into two sections that can be lowered, thrown back, or removed
land•ed *adj* : having an estate in land ⟨~ gentry⟩
land•er \ˈlan-dər\ *n* : a space vehicle designed to land on a celestial body
land•fall \ˈland-ˌfȯl\ *n* : a sighting or making of land (as after a voyage); *also* : the land first sighted
land•fill \-ˌfil\ *n* : a low-lying area on which refuse is buried between layers of earth
land•form \-ˌfȯrm\ *n* : a natural feature of a land surface
land•hold•er \-ˌhōl-dər\ *n* : a holder or owner of land — **land•hold•ing** \-diŋ\ *adj or n*
land•ing \ˈlan-diŋ\ *n* **1** : the action of one that lands **2** ♦ : a place for discharging or taking on passengers and cargo **3** : a level part of a staircase

♦ dock, float, jetty, levee, pier, quay, wharf

landing gear *n* : the part that supports the weight of an aircraft when it is on the ground
land•la•dy \ˈland-ˌlā-dē\ *n* : a woman who is a landlord
land•locked \-ˌläkt\ *adj* **1** : enclosed or nearly enclosed by land ⟨a ~ country⟩ **2** : confined to fresh water by some barrier ⟨~ salmon⟩
land•lord \-ˌlȯrd\ *n* **1** : the owner of property leased or rented to another **2** : a person who rents lodgings : INNKEEPER
land•lub•ber \-ˌlə-bər\ *n* : one who knows little of the sea or seamanship
land•mark \-ˌmärk\ *n* **1** : an object that marks a course or boundary or serves as a guide **2** : an event that marks a turning point **3** : a structure of unusual historical and usually aesthetic interest
land•mass \-ˌmas\ *n* : a large area of land
land mine *n* **1** : a mine placed on or just below the surface of the ground and designed to be exploded by the weight of someone or something passing over it **2** : a trap for the unwary
land•own•er \-ˌō-nər\ *n* : an owner of land
¹land•scape \-ˌskāp\ *n* **1** : a picture of natural inland scenery **2** : a portion of land that can be seen in one glance
²landscape *vb* **land•scaped; land•scap•ing** : to modify (a natural landscape) by grading, clearing, or decorative planting
land•slide \-ˌslīd\ *n* **1** : the slipping down of a mass of rocks or

earth on a steep slope; *also* **:** the mass of material that slides **2 :** an overwhelming victory especially in a political contest

lands•man \ˈlandz-mən\ *n* **:** a person who lives on land; *esp* **:** LANDLUBBER

land•ward \ˈland-wərd\ *adv or adj* **:** to or toward the land

lane \ˈlān\ *n* **1 :** a narrow passageway (as between fences) **2 :** a relatively narrow way or track ⟨traffic ~⟩

lang *abbr* language

lan•guage \ˈlaŋ-gwij\ *n* **1 ♦ :** the words, their pronunciation, and the methods of combining them used and understood by a community **2 ♦ :** form or style of verbal expression **3 ♦ :** a system of signs and symbols and rules for using them that is used to carry information

♦ [1] argot, cant, jargon, lingo, slang, terminology, vocabulary ♦ [2] diction, phraseology, phrasing, wording ♦ [3] lingo, speech, tongue, vocabulary

lan•guid \ˈlaŋ-gwəd\ *adj* **1 ♦ :** drooping or flagging from or as if from exhaustion **:** WEAK **2 ♦ :** sluggish in character or disposition **:** LISTLESS **3 ♦ :** lacking force or quickness of movement **:** SLOW — **lan•guid•ly** *adv* — **lan•guid•ness** *n*

♦ [1] delicate, effete, enervated, faint, feeble, frail, infirm, low, prostrate, slight, soft, tender, torpid, unsubstantial, wasted, weak, wimpy ♦ [2] enervated, lackadaisical, languorous, limp, listless, spiritless ♦ [3] creeping, dilatory, laggard, poky, slow, sluggish, tardy

lan•guish \ˈlaŋ-gwish\ *vb* **1 ♦ :** to become languid **2 :** to become dispirited **:** PINE **3 :** to appeal for sympathy by assuming an expression of grief

♦ decay, droop, fail, flag, go, lag, sag, waste, weaken, wilt

lan•guor \ˈlaŋ-gər\ *n* **1 ♦ :** a languid feeling **2 ♦ :** listless indolence or inertia

♦ [1, 2] debility, delicacy, enfeeblement, faintness, feebleness, frailty, infirmity, lowness, weakness

lan•guor•ous *adj* **♦ :** full of or characterized by languor — **lan•guor•ous•ly** *adv*

♦ enervated, lackadaisical, languid, limp, listless, spiritless

La Ni•ña \lä-ˈnē-nyə\ *n* **:** an upwelling of unusually cold ocean water along the west coast of So. America that often follows an El Niño

lank \ˈlaŋk\ *adj* **1 :** not well filled out **2 ♦ :** hanging straight and limp

♦ droopy, flaccid, floppy, limp, slack, yielding

lanky \ˈlaŋ-kē\ *adj* **lank•i•er; -est ♦ :** ungracefully tall and thin

♦ gangling, rangy, spindly

lan•o•lin \ˈlan-ᵊl-ən\ *n* **:** the fatty coating of sheep's wool especially when refined for use in ointments and cosmetics

lan•ta•na \lan-ˈtä-nə\ *n* **:** any of a genus of tropical shrubs related to the vervains with showy heads of small bright flowers

lan•tern \ˈlan-tərn\ *n* **1 :** a usually portable light with a protective covering **2 :** the chamber in a lighthouse containing the light **3 :** a projector for slides

lan•tha•num \ˈlan-thə-nəm\ *n* **:** a soft malleable metallic chemical element

lan•yard \ˈlan-yərd\ *n* **:** a piece of rope for fastening something in ships; *also* **:** any of various cords

Lao•tian \lā-ˈō-shən, ˈlau̇-shən\ *n* **:** a native or inhabitant of Laos — **Laotian** *adj*

[1]lap \ˈlap\ *n* **1 :** a loose panel of a garment **2 :** the clothing that lies on the knees, thighs, and lower part of the trunk when one sits; *also* **:** the front part of the lower trunk and thighs of a seated person **3 :** an environment of nurture ⟨the ~ of luxury⟩ **4 :** CHARGE, CONTROL ⟨in the ~ of the gods⟩

[2]lap *vb* **lapped; lap•ping 1 :** FOLD **2 ♦ :** to envelop entirely **:** WRAP **3 ♦ :** to lay over or near so as to partly cover

♦ [2] embrace, enclose, encompass, enfold, enshroud, envelop, invest, mantle, shroud, swathe, veil, wrap ♦ [3] overlap, overlay, overlie, overspread

[3]lap *n* **1 :** the amount by which an object overlaps another; *also* **:** the part of an object that overlaps another **2 ♦ :** an act or instance of going over a course (as a track or swimming pool)

♦ leg, stage, step

[4]lap *vb* **lapped; lap•ping 1 :** to scoop up food or drink with the tip of the tongue; *also* **:** DEVOUR — usually used with *up* **2 ♦ :** to splash gently ⟨*lapping* waves⟩

♦ plash, slosh, splash, swash

[5]lap *n* **1 :** an act or instance of lapping **2 :** a gentle splashing sound

lap•a•ros•co•py \ˌla-pə-ˈräs-kə-pē\ *n, pl* **-pies 1 :** visual examination of the abdomen by means of an endoscope; *also* **:** surgery using laparoscopy — **lap•a•ro•scope** \ˈla-pə-rə-ˌskōp\ *n* — **lap•a•ro•scop•ic** \ˌla-pə-rə-ˈskä-pik\ *adj*

lap•dog \ˈlap-ˌdȯg\ *n* **:** a small dog that may be held in the lap

la•pel \lə-ˈpel\ *n* **:** the fold of the front of a coat that is usually a continuation of the collar

[1]lap•i•dary \ˈla-pə-ˌder-ē\ *n, pl* **-dar•ies :** a person who cuts, polishes, or engraves precious stones

[2]lapidary *adj* **1 :** of, relating to, or suitable for engraved inscriptions **2 :** of or relating to precious stones or the art of cutting them

lap•in \ˈla-pən\ *n* **:** rabbit fur usually sheared and dyed

la•pis la•zu•li \ˌla-pəs-ˈla-zə-lē, -zhə-\ *n* **:** a usually blue semiprecious stone often having sparkling bits of pyrite

lap•pet \ˈla-pət\ *n* **:** a fold or flap on a garment

[1]lapse \ˈlaps\ *n* **1 ♦ :** a slight error **2 ♦ :** a fall from a higher to a lower state **3 :** the termination of a right or privilege through failure to meet requirements **4 :** a gap in the continuity of something **:** INTERRUPTION **5 :** APOSTASY **6 :** a passage of time; *also* **:** INTERVAL

♦ [1] blunder, error, fault, flub, fumble, goof, miscue, misstep, mistake, oversight, slip, stumble ♦ [2] reversal, reverse, setback

[2]lapse *vb* **lapsed; laps•ing 1 :** to commit apostasy **2 :** to sink or slip gradually **:** SUBSIDE **3 ♦ :** to go out of existence **:** CEASE

♦ break off, break up, cease, close, conclude, die, discontinue, elapse, end, expire, finish, halt, leave off, let up, pass, quit, stop, terminate, wind up

lap•top \ˈlap-ˌtäp\ *adj* **:** of a size that can be used conveniently on one's lap ⟨a ~ computer⟩ — **laptop** *n*

lap•wing \ˈlap-ˌwiŋ\ *n* **:** an Old World crested plover

lar•board \ˈlär-bərd\ *n* **:** [5]PORT

lar•ce•ny \ˈlär-sə-nē\ *n, pl* **-nies ♦ :** the unlawful taking of personal property with intent to deprive the rightful owner of it permanently **:** THEFT — **lar•ce•nous** \-nəs\ *adj*

♦ robbery, theft, thievery

larch \ˈlärch\ *n* **:** any of a genus of trees related to the pines that shed their needles in the fall

[1]lard \ˈlärd\ *vb* **1 :** to insert strips of usually pork fat into (meat) before cooking; *also* **:** GREASE **2** *obs* **:** ENRICH

[2]lard *n* **:** a soft white fat obtained by rendering fatty tissue of the hog

lar•der \ˈlär-dər\ *n* **:** a place where foods (as meat) are kept

lar•es and pe•na•tes \ˈlar-ēz . . . pə-ˈnā-tēz\ *n pl* **1 :** household gods **2 :** personal or household effects

large \ˈlärj\ *adj* **larg•er; larg•est 1 :** having more than usual power, capacity, or scope **2 ♦ :** exceeding most other things of like kind in quantity or size — **at large 1 :** UNCONFINED **2 :** as a whole

♦ big, bumper, considerable, goodly, grand, great, handsome, hefty, sizable, substantial, voluminous ***Ant*** little, puny, small, undersized

large•ly \ˈlärj-lē\ *adv* **♦ :** to a large extent **:** for the greatest part

♦ altogether, basically, chiefly, generally, mainly, mostly, overall, predominantly, primarily, principally

large•ness *n* **♦ :** the quality or state of being large

♦ bigness, grandness, greatness ***Ant*** fineness, littleness, smallness

lar•gesse \lär-ˈzhes, -ˈjes\ *n* **1 :** liberal giving **2 ♦ :** a generous gift **3 ♦ :** the quality or fact of being generous

♦ [2] bestowal, donation, freebie, gift, lagniappe, present ♦ [3] bounty, generosity, liberality, philanthropy, unselfishness

[1]lar•go \ˈlär-gō\ *adv or adj* **:** at a very slow tempo — used as a direction in music

[2]largo *n, pl* **largos :** a largo movement

lar•i•at \ˈlar-ē-ət\ *n* **:** a long rope used to catch or tether livestock **:** LASSO

[1]lark \ˈlärk\ *n* **:** any of a family of small songbirds; *esp* **:** SKYLARK

[2]lark *n* **♦ :** something done solely for fun or adventure

♦ binge, fling, frolic, gambol, revel, rollick, romp

[3]lark *vb* **♦ :** to engage in harmless fun or mischief — often used with *about*

♦ caper, cavort, disport, frisk, frolic, gambol, rollick, romp, sport

lark•spur \ˈlärk-ˌspər\ *n* **:** DELPHINIUM; *esp* **:** any of the widely cultivated annual delphiniums

lar•va \ˈlär-və\ *n, pl* **lar•vae** \-(ˌ)vē\ *also* **larvas :** the wingless often wormlike form in which insects hatch from the egg; *also* **:** any young animal (as a tadpole) that is fundamentally unlike its parent — **lar•val** \-vəl\ *adj*

lar•yn•gi•tis \ˌlar-ən-ˈjī-təs\ *n* **:** inflammation of the larynx

lar•ynx \ˈlar-iŋks\ *n, pl* **la•ryn•ges** \lə-ˈrin-ˌjēz\ *or* **lar•ynx•es :** the upper part of the trachea containing the vocal cords — **la•ryn•ge•al** \lə-ˈrin-jəl\ *adj*

la•sa•gna \lə-ˈzän-yə\ *n* **:** boiled broad flat noodles baked with a sauce usually of tomatoes, cheese, and meat

las•car \ˈlas-kər\ *n* **:** an Indian sailor

las•civ•i•ous \lə-ˈsi-vē-əs\ *adj* ♦ **:** sexually unchaste or licentious **:** LEWD

♦ lewd, lustful, passionate, wanton

las•civ•i•ous•ness *n* **:** the quality or state of being lascivious

la•ser \ˈlā-zər\ *n* **:** a device that produces an intense monochromatic beam of light

laser disc *n* **:** OPTICAL DISK; *esp* **:** one containing a video recording

1**lash** \ˈlash\ *vb* **1 :** to move violently or suddenly **2** ♦ **:** to thrash or beat violently **:** WHIP **3 :** to attack verbally

♦ flail, flog, hide, scourge, slash, switch, thrash, whale, whip

2**lash** *n* **1 a :** a stroke especially with a whip **b** ♦ **:** the flexible part of a whip; *also* **:** WHIP **2 :** a stinging rebuke **3 :** EYELASH

♦ scourge, switch, whip

3**lash** *vb* **:** to bind with or as if with a line

lass \ˈlas\ *n* ♦ **:** a young woman **:** GIRL

♦ doll, girl, maid, maiden, miss

lass•ie \ˈla-sē\ *n* **:** a young woman **:** LASS

las•si•tude \ˈla-sə-ˌtüd, -ˌtyüd\ *n* **1** ♦ **:** weakness or weariness of body or mind **:** FATIGUE **2 :** LANGUOR

♦ burnout, collapse, exhaustion, fatigue, prostration, tiredness, weariness

las•so \ˈla-sō, la-ˈsü\ *n, pl* **lassos** *or* **lassoes :** a rope or long leather thong with a noose used for catching livestock — **lasso** *vb*

1**last** \ˈlast\ *vb* **1** ♦ **:** to continue in existence or operation **2 :** to remain fresh or unimpaired **:** ENDURE **3 :** to manage to continue **4** ♦ **:** to be enough for the needs of

♦ [1] abide, continue, endure, hold, keep up, persist, run on ♦ [1, 4] hold, hold out, keep up, prevail, survive

2**last** *n* **:** a foot-shaped form on which a shoe is shaped or repaired

3**last** *vb* **:** to shape with a last

4**last** *adv* **1 :** at the end **2 :** most recently **3 :** in conclusion

5**last** *adj* **1** ♦ **:** following all the rest **:** FINAL **2 :** next before the present **3 :** most up-to-date **4 :** farthest from a specified quality, attitude, or likelihood ⟨the ~ thing we want⟩ **5 :** CONCLUSIVE; *also* **:** SUPREME — **last•ly** *adv*

♦ final, hindmost, latter, terminal, ultimate ***Ant*** beginning, earliest, first, inaugural, initial, maiden, opening, original, primary, starting

6**last** *n* **:** something that is last — **at last :** FINALLY

last–ditch \ˈlast-ˌdich\ *adj* **:** made as a final effort especially to avert disaster

last•ing \ˈlas-tiŋ\ *adj* ♦ **:** existing or continuing a long while **:** ENDURING

♦ abiding, ageless, continuing, dateless, enduring, eternal, everlasting, immortal, imperishable, perennial, perpetual, timeless, undying

last laugh *n* **:** an ultimate satisfaction or triumph despite previous doubt or criticism

Last Supper *n* **:** the supper eaten by Jesus and his disciples on the night of his betrayal

lat *abbr* latitude

Lat *abbr* Latin

1**latch** \ˈlach\ *vb* **:** to catch or get hold

2**latch** *n* **:** a catch that holds a door or gate closed

3**latch** *vb* **:** to make fast with a latch

latch•et \ˈla-chət\ *n* **:** a strap, thong, or lace for fastening a shoe or sandal

latch•key \ˈlach-ˌkē\ *n* **:** a key for opening a door latch especially from the outside

latch•string \-ˌstriŋ\ *n* **:** a string on a latch that may be left hanging outside the door for raising the latch

1**late** \ˈlāt\ *adj* **lat•er; lat•est 1** ♦ **:** coming or remaining after the due, usual, or proper time **2 :** far advanced toward the close or end **3** ♦ **:** recently deceased **4 :** made, appearing, or happening just previous to the present **:** RECENT **5** ♦ **:** being something or holding some position or relationship recently but not now — **late•ness** *n*

♦ [1] behind, belated, delinquent, overdue, tardy ***Ant*** early, premature ♦ [3] breathless, dead, deceased, defunct, gone, lifeless ♦ [5] erstwhile, former, old, onetime, past, sometime, whilom

2**late** *adv* **lat•er; lat•est 1 :** after the usual or proper time; *also* **:** at or to an advanced point in time **2 :** not long before the current time **:** RECENTLY

late•com•er \ˈlāt-ˌkə-mər\ *n* **:** one who arrives late

la•teen \lə-ˈtēn\ *adj* **:** relating to or being a triangular sail extended by a long spar slung to a low mast

late•ly *adv* ♦ **:** of late

♦ freshly, just, late, new, newly, now, only, recently

la•ten•cy \-ᵊn-sē\ *n* ♦ **:** the quality or state of being latent

♦ abeyance, doldrums, dormancy, quiescence, suspension

la•tent \ˈlāt-ᵊnt\ *adj* ♦ **:** present but not visible or active

♦ dead, dormant, fallow, free, idle, inactive, inert, inoperative, off, vacant

later *adv* ♦ **:** at some time subsequent to a given time

♦ after, afterward, subsequently, thereafter

1**lat•er•al** \ˈla-tə-rəl\ *adj* **:** situated on, directed toward, or coming from the side — **lat•er•al•ly** *adv*

2**lateral** *n* **1 :** a branch from the main part **2 :** a football pass thrown parallel to the line of scrimmage or away from the opponent's goal

la•tex \ˈlā-ˌteks\ *n, pl* **la•ti•ces** \ˈlā-tə-ˌsēz, ˈla-\ *or* **la•tex•es 1 :** a milky juice produced by various plant cells (as of milkweeds, poppies, and the rubber tree) **2 :** a water emulsion of a synthetic rubber or plastic used especially in paint

lath \ˈlath, ˈla<u>th</u>\ *n, pl* **laths** *or* **lath :** a thin narrow strip of wood used especially as a base for plaster; *also* **:** a building material in sheets used for the same purpose — **lath** *vb*

lathe \ˈlā<u>th</u>\ *n* **:** a machine in which a piece of material is held and turned while being shaped by a tool

1**lath•er** \ˈla-<u>th</u>ər\ *n* **1** ♦ **:** a foam or froth formed when a detergent is agitated in water; *also* **:** foam from profuse sweating (as by a horse) **2** ♦ **:** an agitated or overwrought state **:** DITHER

♦ [1] foam, froth, head, spume ♦ [2] dither, fluster, fret, fuss, huff, pother, stew, tizzy, twitter

2**lather** *vb* **:** to spread lather over; *also* **:** to form a lather

Lat•in \ˈlat-ᵊn\ *n* **1 :** the language of ancient Rome **2 :** a member of any of the peoples whose languages derive from Latin — **Latin** *adj*

La•ti•na \lə-ˈtē-nə\ *n* **:** a woman or girl who is a native or inhabitant of Latin America; *also* **:** a woman or girl of Latin-American origin living in the U.S.

Latin American *n* **:** a native or inhabitant of any of the countries of No., Central, or So. America whose official language is Spanish or Portuguese — **Latin–American** *adj*

La•ti•no \lə-ˈtē-nō\ *n, pl* **-nos :** a native or inhabitant of Latin America; *also* **:** a person of Latin-American origin living in the U.S. — **Latino** *adj*

lat•i•tude \ˈla-tə-ˌtüd, -ˌtyüd\ *n* **1 :** angular distance north or south from the earth's equator measured in degrees **2 :** a region marked by its latitude **3** ♦ **:** freedom of action or choice

♦ authorization, freedom, license (*or* licence), run

lat•i•tu•di•nar•i•an \ˌla-tə-ˌtü-də-ˈner-ē-ən, -ˌtyü-\ *n* **:** a person who is liberal in religious belief and conduct

la•trine \lə-ˈtrēn\ *n* **:** a room with conveniences for washing and usually with one or more toilets **:** TOILET

lat•ter \ˈla-tər\ *adj* **1** ♦ **:** more recent; *also* **:** FINAL **2 :** of, relating to, or being the second of two things referred to

♦ final, hindmost, last, terminal, ultimate

lat•ter–day *adj* **1 :** of present or recent times **2 :** of a later or subsequent time

Latter–day Saint *n* **:** a member of a religious body founded by Joseph Smith in 1830 and accepting the Book of Mormon as divine revelation **:** MORMON

lat•ter•ly \ˈla-tər-lē\ *adv* **1 :** LATER **2 :** of late **:** RECENTLY

lat•tice \ˈla-təs\ *n* **1 :** a framework of crossed wood or metal strips; *also* **:** a window, door, or gate having a lattice **2 :** a regular geometrical arrangement

lat•tice•work \-ˌwərk\ *n* : LATTICE; *also* : work made of lattices
Lat•vi•an \ˈlat-vē-ən\ *n* **1** : a native or inhabitant of Latvia **2** : the language of the Latvians — **Latvian** *adj*
[1]**laud** \ˈlȯd\ *n* : PRAISE, ACCLAIM
[2]**laud** *vb* ♦ : to express a favorable judgment of : PRAISE — **laud•ably** *adv*

♦ acclaim, applaud, cheer, crack up, hail, praise, salute, tout ♦ bless, extol, glorify, magnify, praise

laud•able *adj* ♦ : worthy of praise

♦ admirable, commendable, creditable, meritorious, praiseworthy

lau•da•num \ˈlȯd-ᵊn-əm\ *n* : a tincture of opium
lau•da•to•ry \ˈlȯ-də-ˌtōr-ē\ *adj* : of, relating to, or expressive of praise
[1]**laugh** \ˈlaf, ˈlȧf\ *vb* ♦ : to show mirth, joy, or scorn with a smile and chuckle or explosive sound; *also* : to become amused or derisive — **laugh•ing•ly** *adv*

♦ *usu* **laugh at** deride, gibe, jeer, mock, ridicule, scout

[2]**laugh** *n* **1** ♦ : the act of laughing **2** ♦ : a cause for derision or merriment : JOKE; *also* : an expression of scorn or mockery : JEER **3** *pl* : SPORT 1

♦ [1] cackle, chortle, laughter, snicker, titter ♦ [2] crack, gag, jeer, jest, joke, pleasantry, quip, sally, waggery, wisecrack, witticism

laugh•able *adj* ♦ : of a kind to provoke laughter or sometimes derision : amusingly ridiculous

♦ antic, comic, comical, droll, farcical, funny, hilarious, humorous, hysterical, ludicrous, ridiculous, riotous, risible, screaming, uproarious ♦ absurd, comical, derisive, farcical, ludicrous, preposterous, ridiculous, risible, silly

laughing gas *n* : NITROUS OXIDE
laugh•ing•stock \ˈla-fiŋ-ˌstäk, ˈlȧ-\ *n* ♦ : an object of ridicule

♦ butt, mark, mock, mockery, target

laugh•ter \ˈlaf-tər, ˈlȧf-\ *n* ♦ : the action or sound of laughing

♦ cackle, chortle, laugh, snicker, titter

[1]**launch** \ˈlȯnch\ *vb* **1** ♦ : to throw forward : HURL; *also* : to send off ⟨~ a rocket⟩ **2** : to set afloat **3** ♦ : to set in operation : START — **launch•er** *n*

♦ [1] cast, catapult, chuck, dash, fire, fling, heave, hurl, hurtle, peg, pelt, pitch, sling, throw, toss ♦ [3] constitute, establish, found, inaugurate, initiate, innovate, institute, introduce, pioneer, set up, start ♦ [3] begin, commence, embark (on *or* upon), enter, get off, open, start, strike

[2]**launch** *n* ♦ : an act or instance of launching

♦ beginning, birth, commencement, dawn, genesis, morning, onset, outset, start, threshold

[3]**launch** *n* : a small open or half-decked motorboat
launch•pad \ˈlȯnch-ˌpad\ *n* : a platform from which a rocket is launched
laun•der \ˈlȯn-dər\ *vb* **1** : to wash or wash and iron clothing and household linens **2** : to transfer (as money of an illegal origin) through an outside party to conceal the true source — **laun•der•er** *n*
laun•dress \ˈlȯn-drəs\ *n* : a woman who is a laundry worker
laun•dry \ˈlȯn-drē\ *n, pl* **laundries** **1** : a place where laundering is done **2** : clothes or linens that have been or are to be laundered — **laun•dry•man** \-mən\ *n*
lau•re•ate \ˈlȯr-ē-ət\ *n* : the recipient of honor for achievement in an art or science — **lau•re•ate•ship** *n*
lau•rel \ˈlȯ-rəl\ *n* **1** : an evergreen tree or shrub of southern Europe that is related to the sassafras and cinnamon and has glossy aromatic leaves; *esp* : a small tree of southern Europe **2** : MOUNTAIN LAUREL **3 a** : a crown of laurel **b** ♦ : a recognition of achievement : HONOR — usually used in plural

♦ *usu* **laurels** acclaim, accolade, credit, distinction, glory, homage, honor (*or* honour)

lav *abbr* lavatory
la•va \ˈlä-və, ˈla-\ *n* : melted rock coming from a volcano; *also* : such rock that has cooled and hardened
la•vage \lə-ˈväzh\ *n* : WASHING; *esp* : the washing out (as of an organ) especially for medicinal reasons
lav•a•to•ry \ˈla-və-ˌtōr-ē\ *n, pl* **-ries** **1** : a fixed washbowl with running water and drainpipe **2** ♦ : a room with conveniences for washing and usually with one or more toilets : BATHROOM

♦ bathroom, toilet

lave \ˈlāv\ *vb* **laved; lav•ing** ♦ : to wash or flow along or against : WASH

♦ lap, splash, wash

lav•en•der \ˈla-vən-dər\ *n* **1** : a Mediterranean mint or its dried leaves and flowers used to perfume clothing and bed linen **2** : a pale purple color
[1]**lav•ish** \ˈla-vish\ *adj* **1** ♦ : expending or bestowing profusely **2** ♦ : expended or produced in abundance **3** ♦ : marked by excess

♦ [1] deluxe, luxuriant, luxurious, opulent, palatial, plush, sumptuous ♦ [2] copious, profuse, riotous ♦ [3] excessive, extravagant, extreme, immoderate, inordinate, overmuch

[2]**lavish** *vb* ♦ : to expend or give with profusion

♦ heap, pour, rain, shower ♦ blow, dissipate, fritter, misspend, run through, spend, squander, throw away, waste

lav•ish•ly *adv* ♦ : in a lavish manner

♦ expensively, extravagantly, grandly, high, luxuriously, opulently, richly

lav•ish•ness *n* ♦ : a lavish quality; *also* : a lavish manner or propensity

♦ extravagance, prodigality, wastefulness

law \ˈlȯ\ *n* **1** ♦ : a rule of conduct or action established by custom or laid down and enforced by a governing authority; *also* : the whole body of such rules **2** : the control brought about by enforcing rules **3** *cap* : the revelation of the divine will set forth in the Old Testament of Christian Scripture; *also* : the first part of the Jewish Scripture **4** : a rule or principle of construction or procedure **5** : the science that deals with laws and their interpretation and application **6** : the profession of a lawyer **7** : a rule or principle stating something that always works in the same way under the same conditions

♦ act, enactment, ordinance, statute

law•break•er \ˈlȯ-ˌbrā-kər\ *n* ♦ : one who violates the law

♦ criminal, crook, culprit, felon, malefactor, offender

law•ful \ˈlȯ-fəl\ *adj* **1** : permitted by law **2** : RIGHTFUL — **law•ful•ly** *adv*
law•giv•er \-ˌgi-vər\ *n* : one that makes laws : LEGISLATOR
law•less \ˈlȯ-ləs\ *adj* **1** : having no laws **2** ♦ : not restrained or controlled by law : UNRULY, DISORDERLY ⟨a ~ mob⟩ — **law•less•ly** *adv* — **law•less•ness** *n*

♦ anarchic, disorderly, unruly ***Ant*** orderly

law•mak•er \-ˌmā-kər\ *n* ♦ : one that makes laws : LEGISLATOR

♦ legislator, solon

law•man \ˈlȯ-mən\ *n* : a law enforcement official (as a sheriff or marshal)
[1]**lawn** \ˈlȯn\ *n* : ground (as around a house) covered with mowed grass
[2]**lawn** *n* : a fine sheer linen or cotton fabric
lawn bowling *n* : a bowling game played on a green with wooden balls which are rolled at a jack
law•ren•ci•um \lȯ-ˈren-sē-əm\ *n* : a short-lived radioactive element
law•suit \ˈlȯ-ˌsüt\ *n* ♦ : a suit in law

♦ action, proceeding, suit

law•yer \ˈlȯ-yər\ *n* ♦ : one who conducts lawsuits for clients or advises as to legal rights and obligations in other matters — **law•yer•ly** *adj*

♦ advocate, attorney, counsel

lax \ˈlaks\ *adj* **1** ♦ : not strict ⟨~ discipline⟩ **2** ♦ : not tense, firm, or rigid — **lax•ly** *adv*

♦ [1] careless, derelict, negligent, remiss, slack ♦ [1] easygoing, flexible, relaxed, unrestrained, unrestricted ♦ [2] insecure, loose, slack

[1]**lax•a•tive** \ˈlak-sə-tiv\ *adj* : relieving constipation
[2]**laxative** *n* : a usually mild laxative drug
lax•i•ty \ˈlak-sə-tē\ *n* ♦ : the quality or state of being lax

♦ delinquency, dereliction, laxness, neglect, negligence, omission, remissness, slackness

lax•ness *n* ♦ : the quality or state of being lax

♦ carelessness, dereliction, heedlessness, negligence, remissness, slackness

[1]lay \ˈlā\ *vb* **laid** \ˈlād\; **lay·ing** **1 :** to beat or strike down **2** ♦ **:** to put on or set down **:** PLACE **3 :** to produce and deposit eggs **4 :** SETTLE; *also* **:** ALLAY **5 :** SPREAD **6** ♦ **:** to make ready beforehand for some purpose, use, or activity **:** PREPARE, CONTRIVE **7** ♦ **:** to stake on the outcome of an issue or the performance of a contestant **:** WAGER **8** ♦ **:** to impose especially as a duty or burden **9** ♦ **:** to set in order or position **10 :** to bring to a specified condition **11 :** to put forward **:** SUBMIT

♦ [2, 9] deposit, dispose, fix, place, position, put, set, set up, stick ♦ [6] contrive, fit, fix, get, prepare, ready ♦ [7] bet, gamble, go, stake, wager ♦ [8] assess, charge, exact, fine, impose, levy, put

[2]lay *n* **:** the way in which something lies or is laid in relation to something else
[3]lay *past of* [1]LIE
[4]lay *n* **1 :** a simple narrative poem **2** ♦ **:** a short musical composition of words and music **:** SONG

♦ air, melody, song, strain, tune, warble

[5]lay *adj* **1 :** of or relating to the laity **2 :** not of a particular profession; *also* **:** lacking extensive knowledge of a particular subject
lay·away \ˈlā-ə-ˌwā\ *n* **:** a purchasing agreement by which a retailer agrees to hold merchandise secured by a deposit until the price is paid in full
lay away *vb* ♦ **:** to put aside for future use or delivery

♦ cache, hoard, lay up, put by, salt away, stash, stockpile, store

lay down *vb* ♦ **:** to institute (as a law) by enactment or agreement; *also* **:** to assert or command dogmatically

♦ define, prescribe, specify ♦ enact, legislate, make, pass

lay·er \ˈlā-ər\ *n* **1 :** one that lays **2 :** one thickness, course, or fold laid or lying over or under another
lay·ette \lā-ˈet\ *n* **:** an outfit of clothing and equipment for a newborn infant
lay·man \ˈlā-mən\ *n* **:** a person who is a member of the laity
lay·off \ˈlā-ˌȯf\ *n* **1 :** a period of inactivity **2** ♦ **:** the act of dismissing an employee usually temporarily

♦ discharge, dismissal

lay off *vb* ♦ **:** to desist from

♦ *usu* **lay off of** discontinue, drop, give up, knock off, quit

lay on *vb* **:** to make an attack
lay·out \ˈlā-ˌau̇t\ *n* ♦ **:** the final arrangement, plan, or design of something

♦ arrangement, composition, configuration, design, form, format, makeup, pattern

lay out *vb* **1** ♦ **:** to use up or pay out **2** ♦ **:** to plan in detail

♦ [1] disburse, expend, give, pay, spend ♦ [2] arrange, blueprint, calculate, chart, design, frame, map, plan, project, scheme

lay·over \-ˌō-vər\ *n* **:** STOPOVER
lay·per·son \-ˌpər-sən\ *n* **:** a member of the laity
lay up *vb* ♦ **:** to store up

♦ cache, hoard, lay away, put by, salt away, stash, stockpile, store

lay·wom·an \ˈlā-ˌwu̇-mən\ *n* **:** a woman who is a member of the laity
la·zar \ˈla-zər, ˈlā-\ *n* **:** LEPER
laze \ˈlāz\ *vb* **lazed; laz·ing :** to pass time in idleness or relaxation
la·zi·ness \-zē-nəs\ *n* ♦ **:** the quality or state of being lazy

♦ idleness, indolence, inertia, sloth *Ant* drive, industriousness, industry

la·zy \ˈlā-zē\ *adj* **la·zi·er; -est** **1** ♦ **:** disliking activity or exertion **2 :** encouraging idleness **3 :** SLUGGISH **4 :** DROOPY, LAX **5 :** not rigorous or strict — **la·zi·ly** \-zə-lē\ *adv*

♦ idle, indolent, shiftless, slothful *Ant* industrious

la·zy·bones \-ˌbōnz\ *n sing or pl* ♦ **:** a lazy individual

♦ idler, loafer, slouch, slug, sluggard *Ant* doer, go-getter, hummer, hustler, rustler, self-starter

lazy Su·san \ˌlā-zē-ˈsüz-ᵊn\ *n* **:** a revolving tray used for serving food
lb *abbr* pound
lc *abbr* lowercase
LC *abbr* Library of Congress
[1]LCD \ˌel-(ˌ)sē-ˈdē\ *n* **:** a display (as of the time in a digital watch) that consists of segments of a liquid crystal whose reflectivity varies with the voltage applied to them
[2]LCD *abbr* least common denominator; lowest common denominator
LCDR *abbr* lieutenant commander
LCM *abbr* least common multiple; lowest common multiple
LCpl *abbr* lance corporal
LCS *abbr* League Championship Series
ld *abbr* **1** load **2** lord
LD *abbr* learning disabled; learning disability
LDC *abbr* less developed country
ldg *abbr* **1** landing **2** loading
LDL \ˌel-(ˌ)dē-ˈel\ *n* **:** a cholesterol-rich protein-poor lipoprotein of blood plasma correlated with increased probability of developing atherosclerosis
L–do·pa \ˈel-ˈdō-pə\ *n* **:** an isomer of dopa used especially in the treatment of Parkinson's disease
LDS *abbr* Latter-day Saints
lea \ˈlē, ˈlā\ *n* **:** farmland having chiefly forage plants and especially grasses **:** PASTURE
leach \ˈlēch\ *vb* **:** to pass a liquid (as water) through to carry off the soluble components; *also* **:** to dissolve out by such means ⟨~ alkali from ashes⟩
[1]lead \ˈlēd\ *vb* **led** \ˈled\; **lead·ing** **1** ♦ **:** to guide on a way **2 :** LIVE ⟨~ a quiet life⟩ **3** ♦ **:** to direct the operations, activity, or performance of ⟨~ an orchestra⟩ **4 :** to go at the head of **:** be first ⟨~ a parade⟩ **5 :** to begin play with; *also* **:** BEGIN, OPEN **6 :** to tend toward a definite result ⟨study ~*ing* to a degree⟩ **7** ♦ **:** to lie, run, or open in a specified place or direction

♦ [1] conduct, direct, guide, marshal, pilot, route, show, steer, usher *Ant* follow, trail ♦ [3] boss, captain, command, dominate, head, spearhead ♦ [7] extend, go, head, lie, run

[2]lead \ˈlēd\ *n* **1 a :** a position at the front **b** ♦ **:** a margin by which one leads **2 :** the privilege of leading in cards; *also* **:** the card or suit led **3 :** EXAMPLE **4 :** one that leads **5 :** a principal role (as in a play); *also* **:** one who plays such a role **6** ♦ **:** something serving as an indication, tip, or clue **7 :** an insulated electrical conductor

♦ [1b] distance, length, remove, spread, stretch, way ♦ [6] clue, cue, hint, indication, inkling, intimation, suggestion, tip

[3]lead \ˈled\ *n* **1 :** a heavy malleable bluish white chemical element **2 :** an article made of lead; *esp* **:** a weight for sounding at sea **3 :** a thin strip of metal used to separate lines of type in printing **4 :** a thin stick of marking substance in or for a pencil
[4]lead \ˈled\ *vb* **1 :** to cover, line, or weight with lead **2 :** to fix (glass) in position with lead **3 :** to treat or mix with lead or a lead compound
lead·en \ˈled-ᵊn\ *adj* **1 a :** made of lead **b** ♦ **:** of the color of lead **2 a :** SLUGGISH **b** ♦ **:** lacking spirit or animation **:** DULL

♦ [1b] gray (*or* grey), pewter, silver, silvery, slate, steely ♦ [2b] drab, dreary, dry, dull, flat, heavy, humdrum, monotonous, ponderous

lead·er *n* **1** ♦ **:** something that leads; *also* **:** a conduit for leading fluid from one place to another **2** ♦ **:** a person who leads — **lead·er·less** *adj* — **lead·er·ship** *n*

♦ [1] channel, conduit, duct, line, penstock, pipe, tube ♦ [2] boss, captain, chief, foreman, head, headman, helmsman, kingpin, master, taskmaster

lead·off \ˈlēd-ˌȯf\ *adj* ♦ **:** of, relating to, or being one that leads off — **leadoff** *n*

♦ first, foremost, inaugural, initial, maiden, original, pioneer, premier

lead off *vb* **:** OPEN, BEGIN; *esp* **:** to bat first in an inning
lead on *vb* ♦ **:** to entice or induce to adopt or continue in a course or belief especially when unwise or mistaken

♦ allure, beguile, decoy, entice, lure, seduce, tempt

[1]leaf \ˈlēf\ *n, pl* **leaves** \ˈlēvz\ **1 :** a usually flat and green outgrowth of a plant stem that is a unit of foliage and functions especially in photosynthesis; *also* **:** FOLIAGE **2 :** something that is suggestive of a leaf — **leaf·less** *adj*
[2]leaf *vb* **1 :** to produce leaves **2 :** to turn the pages of a book
leaf·age \ˈlē-fij\ *n* ♦ **:** all the leaves of one or more plants **:** FOLIAGE

♦ flora, foliage, green, greenery, herbage, vegetation, verdure

leafed \ˈlēft\ *adj* **:** LEAVED
leaf·hop·per \ˈlēf-ˌhä-pər\ *n* **:** any of a family of small leaping insects related to the cicadas that suck the juices of plants
leaf·let \ˈlē-flət\ *n* **1 :** a division of a compound leaf **2** ♦ **:** a usu-

ally folded printed sheet intended for free distribution : PAMPHLET, FOLDER

♦ booklet, brochure, circular, folder, pamphlet

leaf mold *n* : a compost or layer composed chiefly of decayed leaves
leaf•stalk \ˈlēf-ˌstȯk\ *n* : PETIOLE
leafy *adj* **leaf•i•er; -est** ♦ : furnished with or abounding in leaves

♦ green, lush, luxuriant, verdant

¹league \ˈlēg\ *n* : a unit of distance equal to about three miles (five kilometers)
²league *n* **1** ♦ : an association or alliance for a common purpose **2** : CLASS, CATEGORY — **leagu•er** \ˈlē-gər\ *n*

♦ association, brotherhood, club, college, congress, council, fellowship, fraternity, guild, institute, institution, order, organization, society ♦ alliance, bloc, coalition, combination, combine, confederacy, confederation, federation, union

³league *vb* **leagued; leagu•ing** ♦ : to form a league

♦ ally, associate, band, club, confederate, conjoin, cooperate, federate, unite

¹leak \ˈlēk\ *vb* **1** : to enter or escape through a leak **2** : to let a substance in or out through an opening **3** ♦ : to become or make known

♦ *usu* **leak out** come out, get out, out, spread

²leak *n* **1** : a crack or hole that accidentally admits a fluid or light or lets it escape; *also* : something that secretly or accidentally permits the admission or escape of something else **2** : LEAKAGE — **leaky** *adj*
leak•age \ˈlē-kij\ *n* **1** : the act of leaking **2** : the thing or amount that leaks
¹lean \ˈlēn\ *vb* **1** ♦ : to bend from a vertical position : INCLINE **2** : to cast one's weight to one side for support **3** ♦ : to rely for support **4** ♦ : to incline in opinion, taste, or desire

♦ [1] angle, cant, cock, heel, incline, list, slant, slope, tilt, tip ♦ [3] count, depend, reckon, rely ♦ [4] incline, run, tend, trend ♦ *usu* **lean toward** [4] favor (*or* favour), like, prefer

²lean *adj* **1** ♦ : lacking or deficient in flesh and especially in fat **2** : lacking richness or productiveness **3** : low in fuel content — **lean•ness** *n*

♦ skinny, slender, slim, spare, thin

³lean *n* ♦ : the act or an instance of leaning

♦ cant, diagonal, grade, inclination, incline, pitch, slant, slope, tilt, upgrade

leaning *n* ♦ : a definite but not decisive attraction or tendency — often used in plural

♦ affinity, bent, devices, disposition, genius, inclination, partiality, penchant, predilection, predisposition, proclivity, propensity, talent, tendency, turn ♦ current, drift, run, tendency, tide, trend, wind

leant \ˈlent\ *chiefly Brit past of* LEAN
lean–to \ˈlēn-ˌtü\ *n, pl* **lean–tos** \-ˌtüz\ : a wing or extension of a building having a roof of only one slope; *also* : a rough shed or shelter with a similar roof
¹leap \ˈlēp\ *vb* **leapt** \ˈlēpt, ˈlept\ *or* **leaped; leap•ing** ♦ : to spring free from a surface or over an obstacle : JUMP

♦ bound, hop, jump, spring, vault

²leap *n* ♦ : an act of leaping : JUMP

♦ bound, hop, jump, spring, vault

leap•frog \ˈlēp-ˌfrȯg, -ˌfräg\ *n* : a game in which a player bends down and is vaulted over by another — **leapfrog** *vb*
leap year *n* : a year containing 366 days with February 29 as the extra day
learn \ˈlərn\ *vb* **learned** \ˈlərnd, ˈlərnt\ *or Can and Brit* **learnt** \ˈlərnt\; **learn•ing** **1 a** ♦ : to gain knowledge, understanding, or skill by study or experience **b** : to commit to memory : MEMORIZE **2** ♦ : to find out : ASCERTAIN — **learn•er** *n*

♦ [1a] get, master, pick up ***Ant*** unlearn ♦ [2] detect, determine, dig up, discover, ferret out, find, hit on, locate, track down

learn•ed \ˈlər-nəd\ *adj* ♦ : characterized by or associated with learning : ERUDITE — **learn•ed•ly** *adv*

♦ educated, erudite, knowledgeable, literate, scholarly, well-read

learn•ing \ˈlər-niŋ\ *n* ♦ : knowledge or skill acquired by instruction or study : ERUDITION

♦ education, erudition, knowledge, scholarship, science

learning disability *n* : any of various conditions (as dyslexia) that interfere with a person's ability to learn and so result in impaired functioning (as in language) — **learning disabled** *adj*
learnt \ˈlərnt\ *chiefly Can and Brit past and past part of* LEARN
¹lease \ˈlēs\ *n* : a contract transferring real estate for a term of years or at will usually for a specified rent
²lease *vb* **leased; leas•ing** **1** : to grant by lease **2** ♦ : to hold under a lease

♦ engage, hire, let, rent

lease•hold \ˈlēs-ˌhōld\ *n* **1** : a tenure by lease **2** : land held by lease — **lease•hold•er** *n*
leash \ˈlēsh\ *n* : a line for leading or restraining an animal — **leash** *vb*
¹least \ˈlēst\ *adj* **1** : lowest in importance or position **2** ♦ : smallest in size or degree **3** : SLIGHTEST

♦ minimal, minimum

²least *n* : one that is least
³least *adv* : in the smallest or lowest degree
least common denominator *n* : the least common multiple of two or more denominators
least common multiple *n* : the smallest common multiple of two or more numbers
least•wise \ˈlēst-ˌwīz\ *adv* : at least
leath•er \ˈle-t͟hər\ *n* : animal skin dressed for use — **leath•ern** \-t͟hərn\ *adj* — **leath•ery** *adj*
leath•er•back \-ˌbak\ *n* : the largest existing sea turtle with a flexible leathery carapace
leath•er•neck \-ˌnek\ *n* : MARINE
¹leave \ˈlēv\ *vb* **left** \ˈleft\; **leav•ing** **1** ♦ : to allow or cause to remain behind **2** : to have as a remainder **3** ♦ : to give or leave by will : BEQUEATH **4** : to let stay without interference **5** : to go away : depart from **6** ♦ : to give up especially with the intent of never again claiming a right or interest in

♦ [1] abandon, desert, forsake, quit ♦ [3] commend, commit, consign, delegate, deliver, entrust, give, hand over, pass, transfer, transmit, trust, turn over, vest ♦ [6] quit, resign, retire, step down

²leave *n* **1** ♦ : permission to do something; *also* : authorized absence from duty **2** : DEPARTURE

♦ break, recess, vacation ♦ allowance, authorization, clearance, concurrence, consent, license (*or* licence), permission, sanction, sufferance

³leave *vb* **leaved; leav•ing** : LEAF
leaved \ˈlēvd\ *adj* : having leaves
¹leav•en \ˈle-vən\ *n* **1** : a substance (as yeast) used to produce fermentation (as in dough) **2** : something that modifies or lightens
²leaven *vb* : to raise (dough) with a leaven; *also* : to permeate with a modifying or vivifying element
leav•en•ing *n* : LEAVEN
leave off *vb* ♦ : to cause to cease; *also* : to cease activity or operation

♦ break, break off, cease, cut, desist, discontinue, drop, end, halt, knock off, layoff, quit, shut off, stop

leaves *pl of* LEAF
leave–tak•ing \ˈlēv-ˌtā-kiŋ\ *n* ♦ : the act or an instance of departing : FAREWELL

♦ departure, exit, farewell, parting

leav•ings \ˈlē-viŋz\ *n pl* ♦ : a usually small part, member, or trace remaining : REMNANT, RESIDUE

♦ balance, leftovers, odds and ends, remainder, remains, remnant, residue, rest

Leb•a•nese \ˌle-bə-ˈnēz, -ˈnēs\ *n* : a native or inhabitant of Lebanon — **Lebanese** *adj*
lech•ery \ˈle-chə-rē\ *n* : inordinate indulgence in sexual activity — **lech•er** \ˈle-chər\ *n* — **lech•er•ous** \ˈle-chə-rəs\ *adj* — **lech•er•ous•ly** *adv* — **lech•er•ous•ness** *n*
lec•i•thin \ˈle-sə-thən\ *n* : any of several waxy phosphorus-containing substances that are common in animals and plants, form colloidal solutions in water, and have emulsifying and wetting properties
lect *abbr* lecture; lecturer
lec•tern \ˈlek-tərn\ *n* : a stand to support a book for a standing reader

lec•tor \-tər\ *n* **:** one whose chief duty is to read the lessons in a church service
¹lec•ture \ˈlek-chər\ *n* **1 :** a discourse given before an audience especially for instruction **2 :** REPRIMAND — **lec•tur•er** *n* — **lec•ture•ship** *n*
²lec•ture *vb* **lec•tured; lec•tur•ing 1** ♦ **:** to deliver a lecture or a course of lectures **2** ♦ **:** to reprove formally

♦ [1] declaim, descant, discourse, harangue, orate, speak, talk ♦ [2] rebuke, reprimand, reproach, scold

led *past and past part of* LEAD
LED \ˌel-(ˌ)ē-ˈdē\ *n* **:** a semiconductor diode that emits light when a voltage is applied to it and is used especially for electronic displays
le•der•ho•sen \ˈlā-dər-ˌhōz-ᵊn\ *n pl* **:** leather shorts often with suspenders worn especially in Bavaria
ledge \ˈlej\ *n* **1 :** a shelflike projection from a top or an edge **2 :** REEF
led•ger \ˈle-jər\ *n* **:** a book containing accounts to which debits and credits are transferred in final form
lee \ˈlē\ *n* **1 :** a protecting shelter **2 :** the side (as of a ship) that is sheltered from the wind — **lee** *adj*
leech \ˈlēch\ *n* **1 :** any of various bloodsucking segmented usually freshwater worms that are related to the earthworms and have a sucker at each end **2** ♦ **:** a hanger-on who seeks gain

♦ hanger-on, parasite, sponge

leek \ˈlēk\ *n* **:** an onionlike herb grown for its mildly pungent leaves and stalk
leer \ˈlir\ *n* **:** a suggestive, knowing, or malicious look — **leer** *vb*
leery \ˈlir-ē\ *adj* ♦ **:** disposed to suspect **:** SUSPICIOUS

♦ distrustful, incredulous, mistrustful, skeptical, suspicious

lees \ˈlēz\ *n pl* ♦ **:** the sediment of a liquor (as wine) during fermentation and aging **:** DREGS

♦ dregs, grounds, sediment

¹lee•ward \ˈlē-wərd, ˈlü-ərd\ *n* **:** the lee side
²leeward *adj* **:** situated away from the wind
lee•way \ˈlē-ˌwā\ *n* **1 :** lateral movement of a ship when under way **2 :** an allowable margin of freedom or variation
¹left \ˈleft\ *adj* **1 :** of, relating to, or being the side of the body in which the heart is mostly located; *also* **:** located nearer to this side than to the right **2** *often cap* **:** of, adhering to, or constituted by the political left — **left** *adv*
²left *n* **1 :** the left hand; *also* **:** the side or part that is on or toward the left side **2** *often cap* **:** those professing political views marked by desire to reform the established order and usually to give greater freedom to the common people
³left *past and past part of* LEAVE
left–hand *adj* **1 :** situated on the left **2 :** LEFT-HANDED
left–hand•ed \ˈleft-ˈhan-dəd\ *adj* **1 :** using the left hand habitually or more easily than the right **2 :** designed for or done with the left hand **3** ♦ **:** not sincere **:** INSINCERE, BACKHANDED ⟨a ~ compliment⟩ **4 :** COUNTERCLOCKWISE — **left–handed** *adv*

♦ artificial, double-dealing, feigned, hypocritical, insincere, mealy, mealymouthed, two-faced, unctuous

left•ism \ˈlef-ˌti-zəm\ *n* **1 :** the principles and views of the Left **2 :** advocacy of the doctrines of the Left — **left•ist** \-tist\ *n or adj*
left•over \ˈleft-ˌō-vər\ *n* ♦ **:** something that remains unused or unconsumed; *esp* **:** leftover food served at a later meal — usually used in plural

♦ end, fag end, remainder, remnant, scrap ♦ *usu* **leftovers** balance, leavings, odds and ends, remainder, remains, remnant, residue, rest

lefty \ˈlef-tē\ *n, pl* **left•ies 1 :** a left-handed person **2 :** an advocate of leftism
¹leg \ˈleg\ *n* **1 :** a limb of an animal used especially for supporting the body and in walking; *also* **:** the part of the vertebrate leg between knee and foot **2 :** something resembling or analogous to an animal leg ⟨table ~⟩ **3 :** the part of an article of clothing that covers the leg **4** ♦ **:** a portion of a trip **5** *pl* **:** long-term appeal or interest — **leg•ged** \ˈle-gəd\ *adj* — **leg•less** *adj*

♦ lap, stage, step

²leg *vb* **legged; leg•ging** ♦ **:** to use the legs in walking or especially in running

♦ *usu* **leg it** foot, pad, step, traipse, tread, walk

³leg *abbr* **1** legal **2** legislative; legislature
leg•a•cy \ˈle-gə-sē\ *n, pl* **-cies :** something that is or may be inherited **:** INHERITANCE; *also* **:** something that has come from a predecessor or the past
le•gal \ˈlē-gəl\ *adj* **1 :** of or relating to law or lawyers **2 a** ♦ **:** conforming to or permitted by law or established rules **:** LAWFUL **b :** STATUTORY **3 :** enforced in courts of law — **le•gal•i•ty** \li-ˈga-lə-tē\ *n* — **le•gal•ize** \ˈlē-gə-ˌlīz\ *vb* — **le•gal•ly** *adv*

♦ clean, fair, sportsmanlike ♦ allowable, good, innocent, justifiable, permissible, proper, regulation, right ***Ant*** illegal, illegitimate, illicit, unlawful, wrongful

le•gal•ese \ˌlē-gə-ˈlēz\ *n* **:** the specialized language of the legal profession
le•gal•ism \ˈlē-gə-ˌli-zəm\ *n* **1 :** strict, literal, or excessive conformity to the law or to a religious or moral code **2 :** a legal term — **le•gal•is•tic** \ˌlē-gə-ˈlis-tik\ *adj*
leg•ate \ˈle-gət\ *n* ♦ **:** an official representative

♦ ambassador, delegate, emissary, envoy, minister, representative

leg•a•tee \ˌle-gə-ˈtē\ *n* **:** a person to whom a legacy is bequeathed
le•ga•tion \li-ˈgā-shən\ *n* **1 :** a diplomatic mission headed by a minister **2 :** the official residence and office of a minister in a foreign country
le•ga•to \li-ˈgä-tō\ *adv or adj* **:** in a smooth and connected manner (as of music)
leg•end \ˈle-jənd\ *n* **1 a :** a story coming down from the past; *esp* **:** one popularly accepted as historical though not verifiable **b** ♦ **:** a body of popular stories **2 :** an inscription on an object; *also* **:** CAPTION **3 :** an explanatory list of the symbols on a map or chart

♦ folklore, lore, myth, mythology, tradition

leg•end•ary \ˈle-jən-ˌder-ē\ *adj* **1** ♦ **:** of, relating to, or characteristic of a legend **2 :** FAMOUS — **leg•en•dari•ly** \-ˌder-ə-lē\ *adv*

♦ fabled, fabulous, mythical

leg•er•de•main \ˌle-jər-də-ˈmān\ *n* **1 :** SLEIGHT OF HAND **2 a** ♦ **:** skill and dexterity in conjuring tricks **b** ♦ **:** adroitness in deception

♦ [2a] magic, prestidigitation ♦ [2b] artifice, chicanery, hanky-panky, subterfuge, trickery

leg•ging *or* **leg•gin** \ˈle-gən, -giŋ\ *n* **:** a covering for the leg; *also* **:** TIGHTS
leg•gy \ˈle-gē\ *adj* **leg•gi•er; -est 1 :** having unusually long legs **2 :** having long and attractive legs **3 :** SPINDLY — used of a plant
leg•horn \ˈleg-ˌhȯrn, ˈle-gərn\ *n* **1 :** a fine plaited straw; *also* **:** a hat made of this straw **2 :** any of a Mediterranean breed of small hardy chickens
leg•i•ble \ˈle-jə-bəl\ *adj* **:** capable of being read **:** CLEAR — **leg•i•bil•i•ty** \ˌle-jə-ˈbi-lə-tē\ *n* — **leg•i•bly** \ˈle-jə-blē\ *adv*
¹le•gion \ˈlē-jən\ *n* **1 :** a unit of the Roman army comprising 3000 to 6000 soldiers **2** ♦ **:** a very large number **:** MULTITUDE **3 :** an association of ex-servicemen **4** ♦ **:** a large military force

♦ [2] army, crowd, crush, drove, flock, horde, host, mob, multitude, press, swarm, throng ♦ [4] army, battalion, host

²legion *adj* **:** MANY, NUMEROUS
le•gion•ary \-jə-ˌner-ē\ *n* **:** LEGIONNAIRE
le•gion•naire \ˌlē-jə-ˈnar\ *n* ♦ **:** a member of a legion

♦ fighter, man-at-arms, regular, serviceman, soldier, warrior

Legionnaires' disease *also* **Legionnaire's disease** \-ˈnerz-\ *n* **:** a lobar pneumonia caused by a bacterium
legis *abbr* legislation; legislative; legislature
leg•is•late \ˈle-jəs-ˌlāt\ *vb* **-lat•ed; -lat•ing** ♦ **:** to make or enact laws; *also* **:** to bring about by legislation

♦ enact, lay down, make, pass

leg•is•la•tion \ˌle-jəs-ˈlā-shən\ *n* **1 :** the action of legislating **2 :** laws made by a legislative body
leg•is•la•tive \ˈle-jəs-ˌlā-tiv\ *adj* **1 :** having the power of legislating **2 :** of or relating to a legislature or legislation
leg•is•la•tor \-ˌlā-tər\ *n* ♦ **:** one that makes laws especially for a political unit; *esp* **:** a member of a legislative body

♦ lawmaker, solon

leg•is•la•ture \ˈle-jəs-ˌlā-chər\ *n* **:** an organized body of persons having the authority to make laws
le•git \li-ˈjit\ *adj, slang* **:** LEGITIMATE
¹le•git•i•mate \li-ˈji-tə-mət\ *adj* **1 :** lawfully begotten **2 :** GENUINE **3 :** LAWFUL **4 :** conforming to recognized principles or accepted rules or standards — **le•git•i•ma•cy** \-mə-sē\ *n* — **le•git•i•mate•ly** *adv*

2**le·git·i·mate** \-ˌmāt\ *vb* **-mat·ed; -mat·ing :** to make legitimate

le·git·i·mise *chiefly Brit var of* LEGITIMIZE

le·git·i·mize \li-ˈji-tə-ˌmīz\ *vb* **-mized; -miz·ing :** LEGITIMATE

leg·man \ˈleg-ˌman\ *n* **1 :** a reporter assigned usually to gather information **2 :** an assistant who gathers information and runs errands

le·gume \ˈle-ˌgyüm, li-ˈgyüm\ *n* **1 :** any of a large family of plants having fruits that are dry pods and split when ripe and including important food and forage plants (as beans and clover); *also* **:** the part (as seeds or pods) of a legume used as food **2 :** the pod of a legume — **le·gu·mi·nous** \li-ˈgyü-mə-nəs\ *adj*

1**lei** \ˈlā, ˈlā-ˌē\ *n* **:** a wreath or necklace usually of flowers

lei·sure \ˈlē-zhər, ˈle-, ˈlā-\ *n* **1** ♦ **:** freedom provided by the cessation of activities; *also* **:** time free from work or duties **2 :** EASE; *also* **:** CONVENIENCE

♦ ease, relaxation, repose, rest

1**lei·sure·ly** *adj* **:** characterized by slowness

2**leisurely** *adv* **:** without haste

leit·mo·tif *also* **leit·mo·tiv** \ˈlīt-mō-ˌtēf\ *n* **:** a dominant recurring theme

lem·ming \ˈle-miŋ\ *n* **:** any of various short-tailed rodents found mostly in northern regions and noted for recurrent mass migrations

lem·on \ˈle-mən\ *n* **1 :** an acid yellow usually nearly oblong citrus fruit; *also* **:** a citrus tree that bears lemons **2** ♦ **:** something (as an automobile) unsatisfactory or defective — **lem·ony** *adj*

♦ bummer, dud, failure, fizzle, flop, loser, turkey, washout

lem·on·ade \ˌle-mə-ˈnād\ *n* **:** a beverage of lemon juice, sugar, and water

lemon curd *n* **:** a custard made with lemon juice, butter, sugar, and eggs

lem·on·grass \ˈle-mən-ˌgras\ *n* **:** a tropical Asian grass grown for its lemon-scented foliage used as a seasoning

le·mur \ˈlē-mər\ *n* **:** any of various arboreal primates largely of Madagascar that have large eyes, very soft woolly fur, and a long furry tail

Len·a·pe \ˈle-nə-pē, lə-ˈnä-pē\ *n, pl* **Lenape** *or* **Lenapes :** DELAWARE

lend \ˈlend\ *vb* **lent** \ˈlent\; **lend·ing 1 :** to give for temporary use on condition that the same or its equivalent be returned **2 :** AFFORD, FURNISH **3 :** ACCOMMODATE — **lend·er** *n*

lend–lease \-ˈlēs\ *n* **:** the transfer of goods and services to an ally to aid in a common cause with payment made by a return of the items or their use in the cause or by a similar transfer of other goods and services

length \ˈleŋth\ *n* **1 a :** the longer or longest dimension of an object **b** ♦ **:** a measured distance **2 :** duration or extent in time or space **3 :** the length of something taken as a unit of measure **4 :** a single piece of a series of pieces that may be joined together ⟨a ~ of pipe⟩ — **at length 1 :** in full **2 :** FINALLY

♦ distance, lead, remove, spread, stretch, way

length·en \ˈleŋ-thən\ *vb* ♦ **:** to make or become longer

♦ draw out, elongate, extend, prolong, protract, stretch

length·wise \ˈleŋth-ˌwīz\ *adv* **:** in the direction of the length — **lengthwise** *adj*

lengthy \ˈleŋ-thē\ *adj* **length·i·er; -est 1 :** protracted excessively **2** ♦ **:** drawn out in length especially of time **:** EXTENDED, LONG

♦ extended, far, great, long

le·ni·en·cy \ˈlē-nē-ən-sē, -nyən-sē\ *n* ♦ **:** the quality or state of being lenient; *also* **:** a lenient disposition or practice

♦ charity, clemency, mercy, quarter

le·nient \ˈlē-nē-ənt, -nyənt\ *adj* **:** of mild and tolerant disposition or effect — **le·ni·ent·ly** *adv*

len·i·tive \ˈle-nə-tiv\ *adj* **:** alleviating pain or harshness

len·i·ty \ˈle-nə-tē\ *n* **:** the quality or state of being lenient **:** LENIENCY

lens \ˈlenz\ *n* **1 :** a curved piece of glass or plastic used singly or combined in an optical instrument for forming an image; *also* **:** a device for focusing radiation other than light **2 :** a transparent body in the eye that focuses light rays on receptors at the back of the eye

Lent \ˈlent\ *n* **:** a 40-day period of penitence and fasting observed from Ash Wednesday to Easter by many churches — **Lent·en** \-ᵊn\ *adj*

len·til \ˈlent-ᵊl\ *n* **:** a Eurasian annual legume grown for its flat edible seeds and for fodder; *also* **:** its seed

Leo \ˈlē-ō\ *n* **1 :** a zodiacal constellation between Cancer and Virgo usually pictured as a lion **2 :** the 5th sign of the zodiac in astrology; *also* **:** one born under this sign

le·o·nine \ˈlē-ə-ˌnīn\ *adj* **:** of, relating to, or resembling a lion

leop·ard \ˈle-pərd\ *n* **:** a large usually tawny and black-spotted cat of southern Asia and Africa

le·o·tard \ˈlē-ə-ˌtärd\ *n* **:** a close-fitting garment worn especially by dancers and for exercise

lep·er \ˈle-pər\ *n* **1 :** a person affected with leprosy **2 :** OUTCAST

lep·re·chaun \ˈle-prə-ˌkän\ *n* ♦ **:** a mischievous elf of Irish folklore

♦ brownie, dwarf, elf, fairy, fay, gnome, hobgoblin, pixie, puck, troll

lep·ro·sy \ˈle-prə-sē\ *n* **:** a chronic bacterial disease marked especially if not treated by slow-growing swellings with deformity and loss of sensation of affected parts — **lep·rous** \-prəs\ *adj*

lep·tin \ˈlep-tən\ *n* **:** a hormone that is produced by fat-containing cells and plays a role in body weight regulation

les·bi·an \ˈlez-bē-ən\ *n* **:** a woman who is a homosexual — **lesbian** *adj* — **les·bi·an·ism** \-ə-ˌni-zəm\ *n*

lèse ma·jes·té *or* **lese maj·es·ty** \ˈlāz-ˈma-jə-stē, ˈlez-, ˈlēz-\ *n* **:** an offense violating the dignity of a sovereign

le·sion \ˈlē-zhən\ *n* **:** an abnormal structural change in the body due to injury or disease; *esp* **:** one clearly marked off from healthy tissue around it

1**less** \ˈles\ *adj, comparative of* 1LITTLE **1 :** FEWER ⟨~ than six⟩ **2** ♦ **:** of lower rank, degree, or importance **3 :** SMALLER; *also* **:** more limited in quantity

♦ inferior, junior, lesser, lower, minor, subordinate, under

2**less** *adv, comparative of* 2LITTLE **:** to a lesser extent or degree

3**less** *n, pl* **less 1 :** a smaller portion **2 :** something of less importance

4**less** *prep* **:** diminished by **:** MINUS

-less \ləs\ *adj suffix* **1 :** destitute of **:** not having ⟨child*less*⟩ **2 :** unable to be acted on or to act (in a specified way) ⟨daunt*less*⟩

les·see \le-ˈsē\ *n* **:** a tenant under a lease

less·en \ˈles-ᵊn\ *vb* ♦ **:** to make or become less

♦ abate, de-escalate, decline, decrease, die, diminish, dwindle, ebb, fall, let up, lower, moderate, recede, reduce, relent, shrink, subside, taper, wane

less·er \ˈle-sər\ *adj, comparative of* 1LITTLE ♦ **:** of less size, quality, or significance

♦ inferior, junior, less, lower, minor, subordinate, under *Ant* major, more, primary, prime, senior, superior

les·son \ˈles-ᵊn\ *n* **1 :** a passage from sacred writings read in a service of worship **2 :** a reading or exercise to be studied by a pupil; *also* **:** something learned **3 :** a period of instruction **4 :** an instructive example

les·sor \ˈle-ˌsȯr, le-ˈsȯr\ *n* **:** one who conveys property by a lease

lest \ˌlest\ *conj* **:** for fear that

1**let** \ˈlet\ *n* **1 :** something that impedes **:** HINDRANCE, OBSTACLE **2 :** a shot or point in racket games that does not count

2**let** *vb* **let; let·ting 1 :** to cause to **:** MAKE ⟨~ it be known⟩ **2 :** to offer or grant for rent or lease; *also* **:** to assign especially after bids **3** ♦ **:** to give opportunity or permission to **:** ALLOW, PERMIT ⟨~ me go⟩

♦ allow, enable, permit, suffer

-let \lət\ *n suffix* **1 :** small one ⟨book*let*⟩ **2 :** article worn on ⟨wrist*let*⟩

let·down \ˈlet-ˌdau̇n\ *n* **1** ♦ **:** the state or emotion of being disappointed **2 :** a slackening of effort

♦ disappointment, dismay, dissatisfaction, frustration

let down *vb* ♦ **:** to fail to meet the expectation or hope of; *also* **:** to cause disappointment

♦ cheat, disappoint, dissatisfy, fail

le·thal \ˈlē-thəl\ *adj* ♦ **:** of, relating to, or causing death **:** DEADLY, FATAL — **le·thal·ly** *adv*

♦ baleful, deadly, deathly, fatal, fell, mortal, murderous, pestilent, vital

le·thar·gic \li-ˈthär-jik\ *adj* ♦ **:** of, relating to, or characterized by lethargy

♦ dull, inactive, inert, quiescent, sleepy, sluggish, torpid

leth·ar·gy \ˈle-thər-jē\ *n* **1 :** abnormal drowsiness **2 :** the quality or state of being lazy or indifferent

let on *vb* **1 :** REVEAL 1 **2 :** PRETEND

1**let·ter** \ˈle-tər\ *n* **1 :** a symbol that stands for a speech sound and constitutes a unit of an alphabet **2** ♦ **:** a written or printed communication **3** *pl* **:** LITERATURE; *also* **:** LEARNING **4 :** the literal meaning ⟨the ~ of the law⟩ **5 :** a single piece of type

♦ dispatch, memorandum, missive, note

²letter *vb* **:** to mark with letters **:** INSCRIBE — **let•ter•er** *n*

letter bomb *n* **:** an explosive device concealed in an envelope and mailed to the intended victim

let•ter•boxed \ˈle-tər-ˌbäkst\ *adj* **:** being a video recording formatted to display a frame size proportional to a standard theater screen

letter carrier *n* ♦ **:** an individual who delivers mail

♦ mailman, postman

let•ter•head \ˈle-tər-ˌhed\ *n* **:** stationery with a printed or engraved heading; *also* **:** the heading itself

let•ter–per•fect \ˌle-tər-ˈpər-fikt\ *adj* ♦ **:** correct to the smallest detail

♦ absolute, faultless, flawless, ideal, impeccable, perfect, unblemished

let•ter•press \ˈle-tər-ˌpres\ *n* **:** printing done directly by impressing the paper on an inked raised surface

letters of marque \-ˈmärk\ **:** a license granted to a private person by a government to fit out an armed ship to capture enemy shipping

letters patent *n pl* **:** a written grant from a government to a person in a form readily open for inspection by all

let•tuce \ˈle-təs\ *n* **:** a garden composite plant with crisp leaves used especially in salads

let•up \ˈlet-ˌəp\ *n* **:** a lessening of effort

let up *vb* ♦ **:** to diminish or slow down; *also* **:** to come to a stop

♦ cease, end, halt, quit, stop ♦ abate, decrease, die, diminish, dwindle, ebb, fall, lessen, subside, taper, wane

leu•kae•mia *chiefly Brit var of* LEUKEMIA

leu•ke•mia \lü-ˈkē-mē-ə\ *n* **:** a malignant disease characterized by an abnormal increase in the number of white blood cells in the blood-forming tissues — **leu•ke•mic** \-mik\ *adj or n*

leu•ko•cyte \ˈlü-kə-ˌsīt\ *n* **:** WHITE BLOOD CELL

Lev *or* **Levit** *abbr* Leviticus

¹le•vee \ˈle-vē; lə-ˈvē, -ˈvā\ *n* **:** a reception held by or for a person of distinction

²lev•ee \ˈle-vē\ *n* ♦ **:** an embankment to prevent or confine flooding; *also* **:** a river landing place

♦ dam, dike, embankment ♦ dock, landing, pier

¹lev•el \ˈle-vəl\ *n* **1 :** a device for establishing a horizontal line or plane **2 :** horizontal condition **3 :** a horizontal position, line, or surface often taken as an index of altitude; *also* **:** a flat area of ground **4** ♦ **:** height, position, rank, or size in a scale

♦ degree, footing, place, position, rank, situation, standing, station, status

²level *vb* **-eled** *or* **-elled; -el•ing** *or* **-el•ling 1** ♦ **:** to make flat or level; *also* **:** to come to a level **2 :** to direct to or toward a specified object or goal **:** AIM **3** ♦ to bring to a common level or plane **:** EQUALIZE **4 :** RAZE **5** ♦ **:** to knock down — **lev•el•er** *n*

♦ [1] even, plane, smooth ♦ [3] balance, equalize, equate, even ♦ [5] bowl, down, drop, fell, floor, knock

³level *adj* **1** ♦ **:** having a flat even surface **2 :** HORIZONTAL **3 :** of the same height or rank; *also* **:** UNIFORM **4 :** steady and cool in judgment — **lev•el•ly** *adv* — **lev•el•ness** *n*

♦ even, flat, flush, plane, smooth *Ant* bumpy, coarse, lumpy, rough, uneven

lev•el•head•ed \ˌle-vəl-ˈhe-dəd\ *adj* ♦ **:** having sound judgment **:** SENSIBLE

♦ good, hard, informed, just, logical, rational, reasonable, reasoned, sensible, sober, solid, valid, well-founded

le•ver \ˈle-vər, ˈlē-\ *n* **1 :** a bar used for prying or dislodging something; *also* **:** a means for achieving one's purpose **2 :** a rigid piece turning about an axis and used for transmitting and changing force and motion

le•ver•age \ˈle-vrij, ˈlē-, -və-rij\ *n* **:** the action or mechanical effect of a lever

le•vi•a•than \li-ˈvī-ə-thən\ *n* **1 :** a large sea animal **2** ♦ **:** something large or formidable

♦ behemoth, blockbuster, colossus, giant, jumbo, mammoth, monster, titan, whale, whopper

lev•i•tate \ˈle-və-ˌtāt\ *vb* **-tat•ed; -tat•ing :** to rise or cause to rise in the air in seeming defiance of gravitation — **lev•i•ta•tion** \ˌle-və-ˈtā-shən\ *n*

Le•vit•i•cus \li-ˈvi-tə-kəs\ *n* **:** a book of Jewish and Christian Scripture

lev•i•ty \ˈle-və-tē\ *n* ♦ **:** lack of seriousness

♦ facetiousness, flightiness, flippancy, frivolity, lightness

levo•do•pa \ˌle-və-ˈdō-pə\ *n* **:** L-DOPA

¹levy \ˈle-vē\ *n, pl* **lev•ies 1** ♦ **:** the imposition or collection of an assessment; *also* **:** an amount levied **2 :** the enlistment or conscription of men for military service; *also* **:** troops raised by levy

♦ assessment, duty, impost, tax

²levy *vb* **lev•ied; levy•ing 1** ♦ **:** to impose or collect by legal authority **2 :** to enlist for military service **3 :** WAGE ⟨~ war⟩ **4 :** to seize property

♦ assess, charge, exact, fine, impose, lay, put

lewd \ˈlüd\ *adj* **1** ♦ **:** sexually unchaste **2** ♦ **:** abhorrent to morality or virtue **:** OBSCENE, VULGAR — **lewd•ly** *adv*

♦ [1] lascivious, lustful, passionate, wanton ♦ [2] bawdy, coarse, crude, indecent, lascivious, obscene, pornographic, ribald, smutty, unprintable, vulgar, wanton

lewd•ness *n* ♦ **:** the quality or state of being lewd

♦ bawdiness, coarseness, grossness, indecency, nastiness, obscenity, ribaldry, smut, vulgarity

lex•i•cog•ra•phy \ˌlek-sə-ˈkä-grə-fē\ *n* **1 :** the editing or making of a dictionary **2 :** the principles and practices of dictionary making — **lex•i•cog•ra•pher** \-fər\ *n* — **lex•i•co•graph•i•cal** \-kō-ˈgra-fi-kəl\ *or* **lex•i•co•graph•ic** \-fik\ *adj*

lex•i•con \ˈlek-sə-ˌkän\ *n, pl* **lex•i•ca** \-si-kə\ *or* **lexicons 1 :** DICTIONARY **2 :** the vocabulary of a language, speaker, or subject

lg *abbr* **1** large **2** long

LH *abbr* **1** left hand **2** lower half

li *abbr* link

Li *symbol* lithium

LI *abbr* Long Island

li•a•bil•i•ty \ˌlī-ə-ˈbi-lə-tē\ *n, pl* **-ties 1** ♦ **:** the quality or state of being liable **2** *pl* **:** DEBTS **3** ♦ **:** one that acts as a disadvantage **:** DISADVANTAGE

♦ [1] blame, fault, responsibility ♦ [3] disadvantage, drawback, handicap, minus, penalty, strike

li•a•ble \ˈlī-ə-bəl\ *adj* **1** ♦ **:** legally obligated **:** RESPONSIBLE **2 :** LIKELY, APT ⟨~ to fall⟩ **3** ♦ **:** exposed or subject to something usually adverse **:** SUSCEPTIBLE

♦ [1] accountable, answerable, responsible ♦ [3] exposed, open, sensitive, subject, susceptible, vulnerable *Ant* invulnerable, unexposed

li•ai•son \ˈlē-ə-ˌzän, lē-ˈā-\ *n* **1** ♦ **:** a close bond or connection **2 :** an illicit sexual relationship **3 :** communication for mutual understanding (as between parts of an armed force); *also* **:** one that carries on a liaison

♦ affiliation, alliance, association, collaboration, confederation, connection, cooperation, hookup, partnership, relation, relationship, union

li•ar \ˈlī-ər\ *n* ♦ **:** a person who lies

♦ fibber, prevaricator

¹lib \ˈlib\ *n* **:** LIBERATION

²lib *abbr* **1** liberal **2** librarian; library

li•ba•tion \lī-ˈbā-shən\ *n* **1 :** an act of pouring a liquid as a sacrifice (as to a god); *also* **:** the liquid poured **2** ♦ **:** a drinkable liquid **:** DRINK

♦ beverage, drink, quencher

¹li•bel \ˈlī-bəl\ *n* **1 :** a spoken or written statement or a representation that gives an unjustly unfavorable impression of a person or thing **2** ♦ **:** the action or crime of publishing a libel

♦ defamation, slander, vilification

²libel *vb* **-beled** *or* **-belled; -bel•ing** *or* **-bel•ling** ♦ **:** to make or publish a libel — **li•bel•er** *n* — **li•bel•ist** *n*

♦ blacken, defame, malign, slander, smear, traduce, vilify

li•bel•ous *or* **li•bel•lous** \-bə-ləs\ *adj* ♦ **:** constituting or including a libel

♦ defamatory, scandalous, slanderous

¹lib•er•al \ˈli-brəl, -bə-rəl\ *adj* **1 :** of, relating to, or based on the liberal arts **2** ♦ **:** given or provided in a generous and openhanded way **:** GENEROUS, BOUNTIFUL; *also* **:** generous or more than adequate in size, scope, or capacity **3 :** not literal **4 a :** not narrow in opinion or judgment **:** TOLERANT **b** ♦ **:** not orthodox **5 :** not conservative — **lib•er•al•ize** \ˈli-brə-ˌlīz, -bə-rə-\ *vb*

♦ [2] abundant, ample, comfortable, generous, plentiful ♦ [2] bountiful, charitable, free, generous, munificent, openhanded, unselfish, unsparing ♦ [4b] broad-minded, nonorthodox, nontraditional, open-minded, progressive, radical, unconventional, unorthodox *Ant* conservative, conventional, old-fashioned, orthodox, traditional

[2]**liberal** *n* **:** a person who holds liberal views

liberal arts *n pl* **:** the studies (as language, philosophy, history, literature, or abstract science) in a college or university intended to provide chiefly general knowledge and to develop the general intellectual capacities

lib•er•al•ism \ˈli-brə-ˌli-zəm, -bə-rə-\ *n* **:** liberal principles and theories

lib•er•al•i•ty \ˌli-bə-ˈra-lə-tē\ *n* ♦ **:** the quality or state of being liberal; *also* **:** an instance of this

♦ bounty, generosity, largesse, philanthropy, unselfishness *Ant* cheapness, closeness, meanness, miserliness, parsimony, pinching, stinginess, tightness

lib•er•al•ly *adv* ♦ **:** in a liberal manner

♦ bountifully, generously, handsomely, well

lib•er•ate \ˈli-bə-ˌrāt\ *vb* **-at•ed; -at•ing 1** ♦ **:** to free from bondage or restraint; *also* **:** to raise to equal rights and status **2 :** to free (as a gas) from combination — **lib•er•a•tor** \ˈli-bə-ˌrā-tər\ *n*

♦ discharge, emancipate, enfranchise, free, loose, loosen, manumit, release, spring, unbind, unchain, unfetter

lib•er•at•ed *adj* **:** freed from or opposed to traditional social and sexual attitudes or roles ⟨a ~ marriage⟩

lib•er•a•tion \ˌli-bə-ˈrā-shən\ *n* ♦ **:** the act of liberating **:** the state of being liberated

♦ emancipation, enfranchisement, manumission *Ant* enslavement

Li•be•ri•an \lī-ˈbir-ē-ən\ *n* **:** a native or inhabitant of Liberia — **Liberian** *adj*

lib•er•tar•i•an \ˌli-bər-ˈter-ē-ən\ *n* **1 :** an advocate of the doctrine of free will **2 :** one who upholds the principles of unrestricted liberty

lib•er•tine \ˈli-bər-ˌtēn\ *n* ♦ **:** a person who leads a dissolute life

♦ decadent, degenerate, pervert, profligate

lib•er•ty \ˈli-bər-tē\ *n, pl* **-ties 1** ♦ **:** the quality or state of being free **:** FREEDOM **2 :** an action going beyond normal limits; *esp* **:** FAMILIARITY **3 :** a short leave from naval duty

♦ autonomy, freedom, independence, self-government, sovereignty

li•bid•i•nous \lə-ˈbid-ᵊn-əs\ *adj* **1 :** LASCIVIOUS **2 :** LIBIDINAL

li•bi•do \lə-ˈbē-dō, -ˈbī-\ *n, pl* **-dos 1 :** psychic energy derived from basic biological urges **2 :** sexual drive — **li•bid•i•nal** \lə-ˈbid-ᵊn-əl\ *adj*

Li•bra \ˈlē-brə\ *n* **1 :** a zodiacal constellation between Virgo and Scorpio usually pictured as a balance scale **2 :** the 7th sign of the zodiac in astrology; *also* **:** one born under this sign

li•brar•i•an \lī-ˈbrer-ē-ən\ *n* **:** a specialist in the management of a library

li•brary \ˈlī-ˌbrer-ē\ *n, pl* **-brar•ies 1 :** a place in which books and related materials are kept for use but not for sale **2 :** a collection of books

li•bret•to \lə-ˈbre-tō\ *n, pl* **-tos** *or* **-ti** \-tē\ **:** the text especially of an opera — **li•bret•tist** \-tist\ *n*

Lib•y•an \ˈli-bē-ən\ *n* **:** a native or inhabitant of Libya — **Libyan** *adj*

lice *pl of* LOUSE

[1]**li•cense** *or* **li•cence** \ˈlīs-ᵊns\ *n* **1** ♦ **:** permission to act **2** ♦ **:** a permission granted by authority to engage in an activity **3 :** a document, plate, or tag providing proof of a license **4 :** freedom used irresponsibly

♦ [1] authorization, freedom, latitude, run ♦ [2] allowance, authorization, clearance, concurrence, consent, leave, permission, sanction, sufferance

[2]**license** *or chiefly Brit* **licence** *vb* ♦ **:** to issue a license to

♦ accredit, authorize, certify, commission, empower, enable, invest, qualify

licensed practical nurse *n* **:** a specially trained person who is licensed (as by a state) to provide routine care for the sick

li•cens•ee \ˌlīs-ᵊn-ˈsē\ *n* **:** a licensed person

li•cen•ti•ate \lī-ˈsen-chē-ət\ *n* **:** one licensed to practice a profession

li•cen•tious \lī-ˈsen-chəs\ *adj* **:** lacking legal or moral restraints; *also* **:** disregarding sexual restraints **:** LEWD, LASCIVIOUS — **li•cen•tious•ly** *adv*

li•cen•tious•ness *n* ♦ **:** the quality or state of being licentious

♦ corruption, debauchery, depravity, immorality, iniquity, sin, vice

lichee *var of* LITCHI

li•chen \ˈlī-kən\ *n* **:** any of various complex plantlike organisms made up of an alga and a fungus growing as a unit on a solid surface — **li•chen•ous** *adj*

lic•it \ˈli-sət\ *adj* **:** LAWFUL

[1]**lick** \ˈlik\ *vb* **1 :** to draw the tongue over; *also* **:** to flicker over like a tongue **2 :** to beat soundly **:** THRASH; *also* **:** DEFEAT

[2]**lick** *n* **1 :** a stroke of the tongue **2** ♦ **:** a small amount **3 :** a hasty careless effort **4 :** a sharp hit **:** BLOW **5 :** a natural deposit of salt that animals lick

♦ bit, dab, little, particle, shred, touch, trace

lick•e•ty–split \ˌli-kə-tē-ˈsplit\ *adv* **:** at great speed

lick•spit•tle \ˈlik-ˌspit-ᵊl\ *n* **:** a fawning subordinate **:** TOADY

lic•o•rice \ˈli-kə-rish, -rəs\ *n* **1 :** the dried root of a European leguminous plant; *also* **:** an extract from it used especially as a flavoring and in medicine **2 :** a candy flavored with licorice **3 :** a plant yielding licorice

lid \ˈlid\ *n* **1** ♦ **:** a movable cover **2 :** EYELID **3 :** something that confines or suppresses — **lid•ded** \ˈli-dəd\ *adj*

♦ cap, cover, top

li•do \ˈlē-dō\ *n, pl* **lidos :** a fashionable beach resort

[1]**lie** \ˈlī\ *vb* **lay** \ˈlā\; **lain** \ˈlān\; **ly•ing** \ˈlī-iŋ\ **1 :** to be in, stay at rest in, or assume a horizontal position; *also* **:** to be in a helpless or defenseless state **2** ♦ **:** to have direction **:** EXTEND **3** ♦ **:** to occupy a certain relative position **4 :** to have an effect especially through mere presence

♦ [2] extend, go, head, lead, run ♦ [3] be, sit, stand

[2]**lie** *n* **:** the position in which something lies

[3]**lie** *vb* **lied; ly•ing** \ˈlī-iŋ\ ♦ **:** to tell a lie

♦ fabricate, fib, prevaricate

[4]**lie** *n* ♦ **:** an untrue statement made with intent to deceive

♦ fabrication, fairy tale, falsehood, falsity, fib, mendacity, prevarication, story, tale, untruth, whopper *Ant* truth

lied \ˈlēt\ *n, pl* **lie•der** \ˈlē-dər\ **:** a German song especially of the 19th century

lie detector *n* **:** a polygraph for detecting physiological evidence of the tension that accompanies lying

lief \ˈlēv, ˈlēf\ *adv* **:** GLADLY, WILLINGLY

[1]**liege** \ˈlēj\ *adj* **:** LOYAL, FAITHFUL

[2]**liege** *n* **1 :** VASSAL **2 :** a feudal superior

lien \ˈlēn, ˈlē-ən\ *n* **:** a legal claim on the property of another for the satisfaction of a debt or duty

lieu \ˈlü\ *n, archaic* **:** PLACE, STEAD — **in lieu of :** in the place of

lieut *abbr* lieutenant

lieu•ten•ant \lü-ˈte-nənt\ *n* **1 :** a representative of another in the performance of duty **2 :** FIRST LIEUTENANT; *also* **:** SECOND LIEUTENANT **3 :** a commissioned officer in the navy ranking next below a lieutenant commander — **lieu•ten•an•cy** \-nən-sē\ *n*

lieutenant colonel *n* **:** a commissioned officer (as in the army) ranking next below a colonel

lieutenant commander *n* **:** a commissioned officer in the navy ranking next below a commander

lieutenant general *n* **:** a commissioned officer (as in the army) ranking next below a general

lieutenant governor *n* **:** a deputy or subordinate governor

lieutenant junior grade *n, pl* **lieutenants junior grade :** a commissioned officer in the navy ranking next below a lieutenant

life \ˈlīf\ *n, pl* **lives** \ˈlīvz\ **1 :** the quality that distinguishes a vital and functional being from a dead body or inanimate matter; *also* **:** a state of an organism characterized especially by capacity for metabolism, growth, reaction to stimuli, and reproduction **2 :** the physical and mental experiences of an individual **3 :** a written history of a person's life **:** BIOGRAPHY **4** ♦ **:** a specific phase or period ⟨adult ~⟩ **5 :** the period from birth to death; *also* **:** a sentence of imprisonment for the remainder of a person's life **6** ♦ **:** a way of living **7 :** a vital or living being; *specif* **:** PERSON **8** ♦ **:** a lively or brisk quality in a person or a person's actions **9 :** living beings ⟨forest ~⟩ **10 :** animate activity ⟨signs of ~⟩ **11 :** one providing interest and vigor ⟨~ of the party⟩

♦ [4] date, duration, lifetime, run, standing, time ♦ [6] civilization, culture, lifestyle, society ♦ [8] dash, energy, pep, vigor (*or* vigour), vim, vitality

life•blood \ˈlīf-ˌbləd\ *n* : a basic source of strength and vitality
life•boat \-ˌbōt\ *n* : a sturdy boat designed for use in saving lives at sea
life•guard \-ˌgärd\ *n* : a usually expert swimmer employed to safeguard bathers
life•less *adj* ♦ : having no life

♦ breathless, dead, deceased, defunct, gone, late

life•like *adj* ♦ : accurately representing or imitating real life

♦ natural, near, realistic

life•line \-ˌlīn\ *n* **1 :** a line to which persons may cling for safety **2 :** something considered vital for survival
life•long \-ˌlȯŋ\ *adj* : continuing through life
life preserver *n* : a buoyant device designed to save a person from drowning
lif•er \ˈlī-fər\ *n* **1 :** a person sentenced to life imprisonment **2 :** a person who makes a career in the armed forces
life raft *n* : a raft for use by people forced into the water
life•sav•ing \ˈlīf-ˌsā-viŋ\ *n* : the skill or practice of saving or protecting lives especially of drowning persons — **life•sav•er** \-ˌsā-vər\ *n*
life science *n* : a branch of science (as biology, medicine, and sometimes anthropology or sociology) that deals with living organisms and life processes — usually used in plural — **life scientist** *n*
life span *n* : the duration of existence of an individual
life•style \ˈlīf-stīl\ *n* ♦ : a way of living

♦ civilization, culture, life, society

life•time \-ˌtīm\ *n* ♦ : the duration of an individual's existence

♦ date, duration, life, run, standing, time

life•work \-ˈwərk\ *n* : the entire or principal work of one's lifetime; *also* : a work extending over a lifetime
life•world \-ˌwər(-ə)ld\ *n* : the total of an individual's physical surroundings and everyday experiences
LIFO *abbr* last in, first out
1**lift** \ˈlift\ *vb* **1** ♦ : to raise from a lower to a higher position : ELEVATE; *also* : RISE, ASCEND **2 :** to put an end to : STOP **3 :** to pay off ⟨~ a mortgage⟩ — **lift•er** *n*

♦ boost, crane, elevate, heave, heft, heighten, hike, hoist, jack, pick up, raise, up, uphold ♦ arise, ascend, climb, mount, rise, soar, up

2**lift** *n* **1 :** LOAD **2 :** the action or an instance of lifting **3** ♦ : the act of assisting or the help supplied; *also* : a ride along one's way **4 :** RISE, ADVANCE **5** *chiefly Brit* : ELEVATOR **6 :** an elevation of the spirits **7 :** the upward force that is developed by a moving airfoil and that opposes the pull of gravity

♦ aid, assist, assistance, backing, boost, help, support

lift•off \ˈlif-ˌtȯf\ *n* : a vertical takeoff (as by a rocket)
lift truck *n* : a small truck for lifting and transporting loads
lig•a•ment \ˈli-gə-mənt\ *n* : a band of tough fibrous tissue that holds bones together or supports an organ in place
li•gate \ˈlī-ˌgāt\ *vb* **li•gat•ed; li•gat•ing** : to tie with a ligature — **li•ga•tion** \lī-ˈgā-shən\ *n*
lig•a•ture \ˈli-gə-ˌchu̇r, -chər\ *n* **1** ♦ : something that binds or ties; *also* : a thread used in surgery especially for tying blood vessels **2 :** a printed or written character consisting of two or more letters or characters (as æ) united

♦ bond, cement, knot, link, tie

1**light** \ˈlīt\ *n* **1** ♦ : something that makes vision possible : electromagnetic radiation visible to the human eye; *also* : the sensation aroused by stimulation of the visual sense organs **2 :** DAYLIGHT **3** ♦ : a source of light (as a candle) **4 :** ENLIGHTENMENT; *also* : TRUTH **5 :** public knowledge ⟨facts brought to ~⟩ **6 :** a particular aspect presented to view ⟨saw the matter in a different ~⟩ **7 :** WINDOW **8** *pl* : STANDARDS ⟨according to his ~*s*⟩ **9** ♦ : a noteworthy person in a particular place or field : CELEBRITY **10 :** LIGHTHOUSE, BEACON; *also* : TRAFFIC LIGHT **11 :** a flame for lighting something

♦ [1] blaze, flare, fluorescence, glare, gleam, glow, illumination, incandescence, luminescence, radiance, shine ♦ [3] flare ♦ [9] celebrity, figure, luminary, notable, personage, personality, somebody, standout, star, superstar, VIP

2**light** *adj* **1** ♦ : having light : BRIGHT **2 :** not dark, intense, or swarthy in color or coloring : PALE ⟨~ blue⟩

♦ ablaze, alight, bright

3**light** *vb* **lit** \ˈlit\ *or* **light•ed; light•ing 1 :** to make or become light **2** ♦ : to cause to burn : BURN **3 :** to conduct with a light **4** ♦ : to supply or brighten with light : ILLUMINATE

♦ [2] burn, fire, ignite, inflame, kindle ♦ [4] illuminate

4**light** *adj* **1** ♦ : not heavy **2 :** not serious ⟨~ reading⟩ **3 :** not abundant : SCANTY ⟨~ rain⟩ **4 :** easily disturbed ⟨a ~ sleeper⟩ **5 a :** exerting a minimum of force or pressure : GENTLE ⟨a ~ blow⟩ **b** ♦ : requiring minimal effort or energy **6** ♦ : easily endurable ⟨a ~ cold⟩; *also* : requiring little effort ⟨~ exercise⟩ **7** ♦ : capable of moving swiftly or nimbly **8 :** FRIVOLOUS **9 :** DIZZY **10 :** made with lower calorie content or less of some ingredient than usual ⟨~ salad dressing⟩ **11 :** producing goods for direct consumption by the consumer ⟨~ industry⟩

♦ [1] airy, ethereal, feathery, fluffy, weightless ***Ant*** heavy, hefty, leaden, overweight, ponderous, weighty ♦ [5b] easy, effortless, facile, fluent, fluid, painless, ready, simple, smooth, snap, soft ♦ [6] balmy, benign, bland, delicate, gentle, mellow, mild, soft, soothing, tender ♦ [7] agile, graceful, lissome, lithe, nimble, spry

5**light** *adv* **1 :** LIGHTLY **2 :** with little baggage ⟨travel ~⟩
6**light** *vb* **lit** \ˈlit\ *or* **light•ed; light•ing 1** ♦ : to descend from or as if from the air and come to rest : SETTLE, ALIGHT **2 :** to fall unexpectedly **3 :** HAPPEN

♦ alight, land, perch, roost, settle

light bulb *n* **1 :** a lamp in which an electrically heated filament emits light **2 :** FLUORESCENT LAMP
light–emitting diode *n* : LED
1**light•en** \ˈlīt-ᵊn\ *vb* **1 :** to make light or clear : ILLUMINATE **2 :** to give out flashes of lightning
2**lighten** *vb* **1 :** to relieve of a burden **2 :** GLADDEN **3 :** to become lighter
lighten up *vb* : to take things less seriously
1**ligh•ter** \ˈlī-tər\ *n* : a barge used especially in loading or unloading ships
2**light•er** \ˈlī-tər\ *n* : one that lights; *esp* : a device for lighting
light•face \ˈlīt-ˌfās\ *n* : a type having light thin lines — **light-faced** \-ˌfāst\ *adj*
light–head•ed \ˈlīt-ˌhe-dəd\ *adj* **1** ♦ : feeling confused or dizzy **2** ♦ : lacking maturity or seriousness

♦ [1] dizzy, giddy ♦ [2] flighty, frivolous, giddy, goofy, harebrained, scatterbrained, silly

light•heart•ed \-ˌhär-təd\ *adj* ♦ : free from worry — **light-heart•ed•ly** *adv*

♦ carefree, careless, cavalier, easygoing, gay, happy-go-lucky, insouciant, unconcerned

light•heart•ed•ness *n* ♦ : the quality or state of being lighthearted

♦ abandon, abandonment, ease, naturalness, spontaneity, unrestraint

light•house \-ˌhau̇s\ *n* : a structure with a powerful light for guiding sailors
light•ly *adv* ♦ : in a light manner

♦ easily, effortlessly, fluently, freely, handily, painlessly, readily, smoothly

light meter *n* : a usually hand-held device for indicating correct photographic exposure
1**light•ness** *n* ♦ : the quality or state of being illuminated

♦ brilliance, dazzle, effulgence, illumination, lucidity, luminosity, radiance, refulgence, splendor

2**light•ness** *n* **1** ♦ : lack of seriousness and stability of character often accompanied by casual heedlessness **2 :** the quality or state of being light especially in weight

♦ facetiousness, flightiness, flippancy, frivolity, levity

1**light•ning** \ˈlīt-niŋ\ *n* : the flashing of light produced by a discharge of atmospheric electricity; *also* : the discharge itself
2**lightning** *adj* ♦ : extremely fast

♦ breakneck, breathless, brisk, dizzy, fast, fleet, hasty, nippy, quick, rapid, rattling, snappy, speedy, swift

lightning bug *n* : FIREFLY
lightning rod *n* : a grounded metallic rod set up on a structure to protect it from lightning
light out *vb* : to leave in a hurry

light•proof \ˈlīt-ˌprüf\ *adj* : impenetrable by light
lights \ˈlīts\ *n pl* : the lungs especially of a slaughtered animal
light•ship \ˈlīt-ˌship\ *n* : a ship with a powerful light moored at a place dangerous to navigation
light show *n* : a kaleidoscopic display (as of colored lights)
light•some \ˈlīt-səm\ *adj* **1** ♦ : free from care **2** : NIMBLE

♦ blithe, bright, buoyant, cheerful, cheery, chipper, gay, sunny, upbeat

¹light•weight \ˈlīt-ˌwāt\ *n* **1** : one of less than average weight; *esp* : a boxer weighing not over 135 pounds **2** : one of little consequence or ability
²lightweight *adj* **1** : INCONSEQUENTIAL **2** : of less than average weight
light–year \ˈlīt-ˌyir\ *n* **1** : an astronomical unit of distance equal to the distance that light travels in one year in a vacuum or about 5.88 trillion miles (9.46 trillion kilometers) **2** : an extremely large measure of comparison ⟨saw it ∼*s* ago⟩
lig•nin \ˈlig-nən\ *n* : a substance related to cellulose that occurs in the woody cell walls of plants and in the cementing material between them
lig•nite \ˈlig-ˌnīt\ *n* : brownish black soft coal
¹like \ˈlīk\ *vb* **liked; lik•ing** **1** ♦ : to feel attraction toward or take pleasure in : ENJOY ⟨∼*s* baseball⟩ **2** ♦ : to wish to have : WANT **3** ♦ : to feel inclined : CHOOSE ⟨does as she ∼*s*⟩ — **lik•able** *or* **like•able** \ˈlī-kə-bəl\ *adj*

♦ [1] favor (*or* favour), lean, prefer ♦ [1] adore, delight, dig, enjoy, fancy, groove, love, relish, revel ♦ [2, 3] choose, want, will, wish

²like *n* ♦ : favorable regard : PREFERENCE

♦ appetite, fancy, favor (*or* favour), fondness, liking, love, partiality, preference, relish, shine, taste, use

³like *adj* ♦ : the same or nearly the same (as in appearance, character, or quantity) : SIMILAR

♦ akin, alike, analogous, comparable, correspondent, parallel, similar, such

⁴like *prep* **1** : similar or similarly to ⟨it's ∼ when we were kids⟩ **2** : typical of **3** : comparable to **4** : as though there would be ⟨looks ∼ rain⟩ **5** : such as ⟨a subject ∼ physics⟩
⁵like *n* **1 a** : one that is similar **b** ♦ : a group having common traits **2** ♦ : one that is similar to another — **and the like** : ET CETERA

♦ [1b] breed, class, description, feather, ilk, kind, manner, nature, order, sort, species, type ♦ [2] coordinate, counterpart, equal, equivalent, fellow, match, parallel, peer, rival

⁶like *conj* : in the same way that
-like \ˌlīk\ *adj comb form* : resembling or characteristic of ⟨lady*like*⟩ ⟨life*like*⟩
like•li•hood \ˈlī-klē-ˌhu̇d\ *n* : PROBABILITY
¹like•ly \ˈlī-klē\ *adj* **like•li•er; -est** **1** ♦ : very probable **2** ♦ : offering reasonable grounds for being believed : BELIEVABLE **3** ♦ : likely to succeed or to yield good results : PROMISING ⟨a ∼ place to fish⟩

♦ [1] apt, bound, probable ***Ant*** doubtful, dubious, improbable, questionable, unlikely ♦ [2] believable, credible, plausible, probable ♦ [3] auspicious, bright, encouraging, fair, golden, heartening, hopeful, promising, propitious, rosy, upbeat

²likely *adv* ♦ : in all probability

♦ doubtless, presumably, probably

lik•en \ˈlī-kən\ *vb* ♦ : to represent as similar : COMPARE

♦ bracket, compare, equate

like•ness \ˈlīk-nəs\ *n* **1** ♦ : a pictorial representation (as a painting) of a person usually showing the face; *also* : one that resembles or corresponds to another **2** : SEMBLANCE **3** ♦ : the quality or state of being like : RESEMBLANCE

♦ [1] illustration, image, picture ♦ [3] community, correspondence, parallelism, resemblance, similarity, similitude

like•wise \-ˌwīz\ *adv* **1** ♦ : in the same manner **2** ♦ : in addition : ALSO

♦ [1] alike, also, correspondingly, similarly, so ♦ [2] additionally, again, also, besides, further, furthermore, more, moreover, then, too, withal, yet

lik•ing \ˈlī-kiŋ\ *n* ♦ : favorable regard; *also* : TASTE

♦ appetite, fancy, favor (*or* favour), fondness, like, love, partiality, preference, relish, shine, taste, use ***Ant*** aversion, dislike, disfavor, distaste, hatred, loathing

li•lac \ˈlī-lək, -ˌlak, -ˌläk\ *n* **1** : a shrub related to the olive that produces large clusters of fragrant grayish pink, purple, or white flowers **2** : a moderate purple color
lil•li•pu•tian \ˌli-lə-ˈpyü-shən\ *adj, often cap* **1** : SMALL, MINIATURE **2** : PETTY
lilt \ˈlilt\ *n* **1** : a cheerful lively song or tune **2** : a rhythmical swing or flow
lily \ˈli-lē\ *n, pl* **lil•ies** : any of a genus of tall bulbous herbs with leafy stems and usually funnel-shaped flowers; *also* : any of various related plants
lily of the valley : a low perennial herb related to the lilies that produces a raceme of fragrant nodding bell-shaped white flowers
li•ma bean \ˈlī-mə-\ *n* : a bushy or tall-growing bean widely cultivated for its flat edible usually pale green or whitish seeds; *also* : the seed
limb \ˈlim\ *n* **1** : one of the projecting paired appendages (as legs, arms, or wings) used by an animal especially in moving or grasping **2** : a large branch of a tree : BOUGH — **limb•less** *adj*
¹lim•ber \ˈlim-bər\ *adj* **1** ♦ : capable of being shaped : FLEXIBLE, SUPPLE **2** : LITHE, NIMBLE

♦ flexible, lissome, lithe, pliable, supple, willowy

²limber *vb* : to make or become limber
lim•bic \ˈlim-bik\ *adj* : of, relating to, or being a group of structures of the brain (**limbic system**) concerned especially with emotion and motivation
¹lim•bo \ˈlim-bō\ *n, pl* **limbos** **1** *often cap* : an abode of souls barred from heaven through no fault of their own **2** : a place or state of confinement, oblivion, or uncertainty
²limbo *n, pl* **limbos** : an acrobatic dance or contest that involves passing under a horizontal pole
Lim•burg•er \ˈlim-ˌbər-gər\ *n* : a pungent semisoft surface-ripened cheese
¹lime \ˈlīm\ *n* : a caustic powdery white solid that consists of calcium and oxygen, is obtained from limestone or shells, and is used in making cement and in fertilizer — **lime** *vb* — **limy** \ˈlī-mē\ *adj*
²lime *n* : a small yellowish green citrus fruit with juicy acid pulp
lime•ade \ˌlīm-ˈād, ˈlī-ˌmād\ *n* : a beverage of lime juice, sugar, and water
lime•light \ˈlīm-ˌlīt\ *n* **1** : a device in which flame is directed against a cylinder of lime formerly used in the theater to cast a strong white light on the stage **2** : the center of public attention
lim•er•ick \ˈli-mə-rik\ *n* : a light or humorous poem of 5 lines
lime•stone \ˈlīm-ˌstōn\ *n* : a rock that is formed by accumulation of organic remains (as shells), is used in building, and yields lime when burned
¹lim•it \ˈli-mət\ *n* **1** ♦ : something that restrains or confines; *also* : the utmost extent **2** : BOUNDARY; *also, pl* : BOUNDS **3** : a prescribed maximum or minimum — **lim•it•less•ness** *n*

♦ bound, boundary, ceiling, confines, end, extent, limitation, line, termination

²limit *vb* **1 a** ♦ : to set limits to **b** ♦ : to confine within set limits **2** : to reduce in quantity or extent

♦ [1a] bound, circumscribe, define, delimit, demarcate, mark, terminate ♦ [1b] check, circumscribe, confine, control, curb, inhibit, restrain, restrict ***Ant*** exceed

lim•i•ta•tion \ˌli-mə-ˈtā-shən\ *n* **1** : an act or instance of limiting **2** ♦ : something that limits

♦ check, condition, constraint, curb, fetter, restraint, restriction

lim•it•ed *adj* **1** ♦ : confined within limits **2** : offering faster service especially by making fewer stops

♦ definite, determinate, finite, measured, narrow, restricted ***Ant*** boundless, endless, illimitable, immeasurable, indefinite, infinite, limitless, measureless, unbounded, undefined, unlimited, unmeasured

lim•it•less *adj* ♦ : having no limits

♦ boundless, endless, illimitable, immeasurable, indefinite, infinite, measureless, unbounded, unfathomable, unlimited

limn \ˈlim\ *vb* **limned; limn•ing** \ˈli-miŋ, ˈlim-niŋ\ **1** : DRAW; *also* : PAINT **2** : DELINEATE **3** : DESCRIBE
limo \ˈli-(ˌ)mō\ *n, pl* **limos** : LIMOUSINE
li•mo•nite \ˈlī-mə-ˌnīt\ *n* : a ferric oxide that is a major ore of iron — **li•mo•nit•ic** \ˌlī-mə-ˈni-tik\ *adj*
lim•ou•sine \ˈli-mə-ˌzēn, ˌli-mə-ˈzēn\ *n* **1** : a large luxurious often chauffeur-driven sedan **2** : a large vehicle for transporting passengers to and from an airport
¹limp \ˈlimp\ *vb* ♦ : to walk lamely; *also* : to proceed with difficulty

♦ flounder, lumber, plod, stumble

²limp *n* **:** a limping movement or gait
³limp *adj* **1** ♦ **:** having no defined shape; *also* **:** not stiff or rigid **2** ♦ **:** lacking in strength or firmness — **limp·ly** *adv* — **limp·ness** *n*

♦ [1] droopy, flaccid, floppy, lank, slack, yielding *Ant* inflexible, resilient, rigid, stiff, sturdy, tense; firm, hard, indurated, solid, sound, strong ♦ [2] enervated, lackadaisical, languid, languorous, listless, spiritless, weary

lim·pet \ˈlim-pət\ *n* **:** any of numerous gastropod sea mollusks with a conical shell that clings to rocks or timbers
lim·pid \ˈlim-pəd\ *adj* ♦ **:** marked by transparency **:** CLEAR

♦ clear, liquid, lucent, pellucid, transparent

lin *abbr* **1** lineal **2** linear
lin·age \ˈlī-nij\ *n* **:** the number of lines of written or printed matter
linch·pin \ˈlinch-ˌpin\ *n* **:** a locking pin inserted crosswise (as through the end of an axle)
lin·den \ˈlin-dən\ *n* **:** any of a genus of trees with large heart-shaped leaves and clustered yellowish flowers rich in nectar
¹line \ˈlīn\ *n* **1** ♦ **:** a length of cord or cord-like material **:** ROPE, WIRE; *also* **:** a length of material used in measuring and leveling **2** ♦ **:** pipes for conveying a fluid ⟨a gas ~⟩ **3 :** a horizontal row of written or printed characters; *also* **:** VERSE **4 :** NOTE **5 :** the words making up a part in a drama — usually used in plural **6 a :** something distinct, long, and narrow **b** ♦ **:** the course or direction of something in motion **:** ROUTE **7 :** a state of agreement **8** ♦ **:** a course of conduct, action, or thought; *also* **:** a field of activity or interest **:** OCCUPATION **9 :** something that bounds, restrains, or confines **:** LIMIT **10** ♦ **:** an arrangement of persons or objects of one kind in an orderly series ⟨waiting in ~⟩ **11 :** a transportation system **12 :** the football players who are stationed on the line of scrimmage **13 :** a long narrow mark; *also* **:** EQUATOR **14 :** a geometric element that is the path of a moving point **15 :** CONTOUR **16 :** a general plan **17 :** an indication based on insight or investigation **18** ♦ **:** a group of persons of common ancestry

♦ [1] cable, cord, lace, rope, string, wire ♦ [2] channel, conduit, duct, leader, penstock, pipe, tube ♦ [6b] course, path, route, track, way ♦ [8] area, arena, discipline, domain, field, province, realm, specialty, sphere ♦ [8] course, policy, procedure, program ♦ [8] calling, employment, occupation, profession, trade, vocation, work ♦ [10] column, cue, file, queue, range, string, train ♦ [18] ancestry, birth, blood, bloodline, breeding, descent, extraction, family tree, genealogy, lineage, origin, parentage, pedigree, stock, strain

²line *vb* **lined; lin·ing 1 :** to mark with a line **2 :** to place or form a line along **3 :** ALIGN
³line *vb* **lined; lin·ing :** to cover the inner surface of
lin·eage \ˈli-nē-ij\ *n* ♦ **:** lineal descent from a common progenitor; *also* **:** FAMILY

♦ blood, clan, family, folks, house, kin, kindred, kinfolk, line, people, race, stock, tribe ♦ ancestry, birth, bloodline, breeding, descent, extraction, family tree, genealogy, origin, parentage

lin·eal \ˈli-nē-əl\ *adj* **1 :** LINEAR **2 :** consisting of or being in a direct line of ancestry; *also* **:** HEREDITARY
lin·ea·ment \ˈli-nē-ə-mənt\ *n* **:** an outline, feature, or contour of a body and especially of a face — usually used in plural
lin·ear \ˈli-nē-ər\ *adj* **1 :** of, relating to, resembling, or having a graph that is a line and especially a straight line **:** STRAIGHT **2 :** composed of simply drawn lines with little attempt at pictorial representation ⟨~ script⟩ **3 :** being long and uniformly narrow
line·back·er \ˈlīn-ˌba-kər\ *n* **:** a defensive football player who lines up just behind the line of scrimmage
line drive *n* **:** a batted baseball hit in a flatter path than a fly ball
line·man \ˈlīn-mən\ *n* **1 :** a person who sets up or repairs communication or power lines **2 :** a player in the line in football
lin·en \ˈli-nən\ *n* **1 :** cloth made of flax; *also* **:** thread or yarn spun from flax **2 :** clothing or household articles made of linen cloth or similar fabric
line of scrimmage : an imaginary line in football parallel to the goal lines and tangent to the nose of the ball laid on the ground before a play
¹lin·er \ˈlī-nər\ *n* **:** a ship or airplane of a regular transportation line
²liner *n* **:** one that lines or is used as a lining — **lin·er·less** *adj*
line score *n* **:** a score of a baseball game giving the runs, hits, and errors made by each team
lines·man \ˈlīnz-mən\ *n* **1 :** LINEMAN 1 **2 :** an official who assists a referee
line–up \ˈlī-ˌnəp\ *n* **1 :** a list of players taking part in a game (as of baseball) **2 :** a line of persons arranged especially for identification by police
ling \ˈliŋ\ *n* **:** any of various fishes related to the cod
-ling \liŋ\ *n suffix* **1 :** one associated with ⟨nest*ling*⟩ **2 :** young, small, or minor one ⟨duck*ling*⟩
lin·ger \ˈliŋ-gər\ *vb* ♦ **:** to be slow in parting or in quitting something **:** TARRY; *also* **:** to be slow to act — **lin·ger·er** *n*

♦ crawl, creep, dally, dawdle, delay, dillydally, drag, lag, loiter, poke, tarry

lin·ge·rie \ˌlän-jə-ˈrā, ˌlaⁿ-zhə-, -ˈrē\ *n* **:** women's intimate apparel
lin·go \ˈliŋ-gō\ *n, pl* **lingoes** ♦ **:** a usually strange or incomprehensible language

♦ argot, cant, jargon, language, slang, terminology, vocabulary

lin·gua fran·ca \ˌliŋ-gwə-ˈfraŋ-kə\ *n, pl* **lingua francas** *or* **lin·guae fran·cae** \-gwē-ˈfraŋ-ˌkē\ **1** *often cap* **:** a common language consisting of Italian mixed with French, Spanish, Greek, and Arabic that was formerly spoken in Mediterranean ports **2 :** a common or commercial tongue among speakers of different languages
lin·gual \ˈliŋ-gwəl\ *adj* **:** of, relating to, or produced by the tongue
lin·gui·ca \liŋ-ˈgwē-sə\ *n* **:** a spicy Portuguese sausage
lin·guist \ˈliŋ-gwist\ *n* **1 :** a person skilled in languages **2 :** a person who specializes in linguistics
lin·guis·tics \liŋ-ˈgwis-tiks\ *n* **:** the study of human speech including the units, nature, structure, and modification of language — **lin·guis·tic** \-tik\ *adj*
lin·i·ment \ˈli-nə-mənt\ *n* **:** a liquid preparation rubbed on the skin especially to relieve pain
lin·ing \ˈlī-niŋ\ *n* **:** material used to line especially an inner surface
¹link \ˈliŋk\ *n* **1 :** a connecting structure; *esp* **:** a single ring of a chain **2** ♦ **:** a connecting element or factor **:** BOND, TIE

♦ bond, cement, knot, ligature, tie

²link *vb* ♦ **:** to couple or connect by or as if by a link; *also* **:** to become connected by or as if by a link — often used with *up* — **link·er** *n*

♦ chain, compound, connect, couple, hitch, hook, join, yoke ♦ associate, connect, correlate, identify, relate ♦ *usu* **link up** coalesce, combine, conjoin, marry, unify, unite

link·age \ˈliŋ-kij\ *n* **1 :** the manner or style of being united **2** ♦ **:** the quality or state of being linked **3 :** a system of links

♦ association, bearing, connection, kinship, liaison, relation, relationship

linking verb *n* **:** a word or expression (as a form of *be, become, feel,* or *seem*) that links a subject with its predicate
links \ˈliŋks\ *n pl* **:** a golf course
link·up \ˈliŋ-ˌkəp\ *n* **1 :** MEETING **2 :** something that serves as a linking device or factor
lin·net \ˈli-nət\ *n* **:** an Old World finch
li·no·leum \lə-ˈnō-lē-əm\ *n* **:** a floor covering with a canvas back and a surface of hardened linseed oil and a filler
lin·seed \ˈlin-ˌsēd\ *n* **:** the seeds of flax yielding a yellowish oil (**linseed oil**) used especially in paints and linoleum
lin·sey–wool·sey \ˌlin-zē-ˈwu̇l-zē\ *n* **:** a coarse sturdy fabric of wool and linen or cotton
lint \ˈlint\ *n* **1 :** linen made into a soft fleecy substance **2** ♦ **:** fine ravels and short fibers of yarn or fabric **3 :** the fibers that surround cotton seeds and form the cotton staple

♦ down, floss, fluff, fur, fuzz, nap, pile

lin·tel \ˈlint-ᵊl\ *n* **:** a horizontal piece across the top of an opening (as of a door) that carries the weight of the structure above it
linz·er torte \ˈlin-sər-, -zər-\ *n, often cap L* **:** a baked buttery torte made with chopped almonds, sugar, and spices and filled with jam or preserves
li·on \ˈlī-ən\ *n, pl* **lions :** a large heavily-built cat of Africa and southern Asia with a shaggy mane in the male
li·on·ess \ˈlī-ə-nəs\ *n* **:** a female lion
li·on·heart·ed \ˌlī-ən-ˈhär-təd\ *adj* ♦ **:** having or characterized by courage **:** BRAVE

♦ brave, courageous, dauntless, doughty, fearless, gallant, greathearted, heroic, intrepid, manful, stalwart, stout, undaunted, valiant, valorous

li·on·ise *chiefly Brit var of* LIONIZE
li·on·ize \ˈlī-ə-ˌnīz\ *vb* **-ized; -iz·ing :** to treat as an object of great interest or importance — **li·on·i·za·tion** \lī-ə-nə-ˈzā-shən\ *n*
lion's den *n* **:** a place or state of extreme disadvantage, antagonism, or hostility

lip \ˈlip\ *n* **1 :** either of the two fleshy folds that surround the mouth; *also* **:** the margin of the human lip **2 :** a part or projection suggesting a lip **3 :** the edge of a hollow vessel or cavity — **lipped** \ˈlipt\ *adj*
lip•id \ˈli-pəd\ *n* **:** any of various substances (as fats and waxes) that with proteins and carbohydrates make up the principal structural parts of living cells
lip–lock \ˈlip-ˌläk\ *n* **:** a long amorous kiss
li•po•pro•tein \ˌlī-pō-ˈprō-ˌtēn, ˌli-\ *n* **:** a protein that is a complex of protein and lipid
li•po•suc•tion \ˈli-pə-ˌsək-shən, ˈlī-\ *n* **:** surgical removal of local fat deposits (as in the thighs) especially for cosmetic purposes
lip•read•ing \ˈlip-ˌrē-diŋ\ *n* **:** the interpreting of a speaker's words by watching lip and facial movements without hearing the voice
lip service *n* **:** an avowal of allegiance that is not matched by action
lip•stick \ˈlip-ˌstik\ *n* **:** a waxy solid colored cosmetic in stick form for the lips — **lip•sticked** \-ˌstikt\ *adj*
liq *abbr* **1** liquid **2** liquor
liq•ue•fy *also* **liq•ui•fy** \ˈli-kwə-ˌfī\ *vb* **-fied; -fy•ing** ♦ **:** to make or become liquid — **liq•ue•fi•er** \-ˌfī-ər\ *n*

♦ deliquesce, flux, fuse, melt, run, thaw *Ant* harden, set, solidify

li•queur \li-ˈkər\ *n* **:** a distilled alcoholic liquor flavored with aromatic substances and usually sweetened
¹liq•uid \ˈli-kwəd\ *adj* **1** ♦ **:** flowing freely like water **2 :** neither solid nor gaseous **3** ♦ **:** shining and clear ⟨large ~ eyes⟩ **4 :** smooth and musical in tone; *also* **:** smooth and unconstrained in movement **5 :** consisting of or capable of ready conversion into cash ⟨~ assets⟩ — **li•quid•i•ty** \li-ˈkwi-də-tē\ *n*

♦ [1] fluent, fluid, runny ♦ [3] clear, limpid, lucent, pellucid, transparent

²liquid *n* **:** a liquid substance
liq•ui•date \ˈli-kwə-ˌdāt\ *vb* **-dat•ed; -dat•ing 1 :** to settle the accounts and distribute the assets of (as a business) **2** ♦ **:** to pay off ⟨~ a debt⟩ **3** ♦ **:** to get rid of; *esp* **:** to get rid of by force or violence and especially by killing — **liq•ui•da•tion** \ˌli-kwə-ˈdā-shən\ *n*

♦ [2] clear, discharge, foot, pay, pay off, quit, recompense, settle, spring, stand ♦ [3] annihilate, blot out, demolish, eradicate, exterminate, obliterate, root, rub out, snuff, stamp, wipe out ♦ [3] dispatch, do in, execute, murder, slay

liquid crystal *n* **:** an organic liquid that resembles a crystal in having ordered molecular arrays
liquid crystal display *n* **:** LCD
liquid measure *n* **:** a unit or series of units for measuring liquid capacity
li•quor \ˈli-kər\ *n* **1 :** a liquid substance **2** ♦ **:** a distilled alcoholic beverage

♦ alcohol, booze, drink, intoxicant, moonshine, spirits

li•quo•rice *chiefly Brit var of* LICORICE
li•ra \ˈlir-ə, ˈlē-rə\ *n* **:** a basic monetary unit of Malta and Turkey and former monetary unit of Italy
lisle \ˈlīl\ *n* **:** a smooth tightly twisted thread usually made of long-staple cotton
lisp \ˈlisp\ *vb* **:** to pronounce s and z imperfectly especially by turning them into th and th; *also* **:** to speak childishly — **lisp** *n* — **lisp•er** *n*
lis•some *also* **lis•som** \ˈli-səm\ *adj* **1** ♦ **:** easily flexed **2 :** LITHE 2 **3** ♦ **:** quick and light in motion **:** NIMBLE — **lis•some•ly** *adv*

♦ [1] flexible, limber, lithe, pliable, supple, willowy ♦ [3] agile, graceful, light, lithe, nimble, spry

¹list \ˈlist\ *vb, archaic* **:** PLEASE; *also* **:** WISH
²list *vb, archaic* **:** LISTEN
³list *n* **1 :** a simple series of words or numerals; *also* **:** an official roster **2** ♦ **:** a written record containing regular entries of items or details **:** CATALOG, CHECKLIST

♦ catalog, checklist, listing, menu, register, registry, roll, roster, schedule, table

⁴list *vb* ♦ **:** to make a list of; *also* **:** to include on a list — **list•ee** \li-ˈstē\ *n*

♦ enumerate, inventory, itemize, numerate ♦ catalog, enroll, enter, index, inscribe, put down, record, register, schedule, slate

⁵list *vb* ♦ **:** to tilt to one side; *also* **:** to cause to list

♦ angle, cant, cock, heel, incline, lean, slant, slope, tilt, tip

⁶list *n* **:** a leaning to one side **:** TILT
⁷list *n* **:** a band or strip of material
lis•ten \ˈlis-ᵊn\ *vb* **1** ♦ **:** to pay attention in order to hear **2** ♦ **:** give consideration **:** HEED — **lis•ten•er** *n*

♦ [1] attend, hark, hear, heed, mind *Ant* ignore, tune out ♦ [2] follow, heed, mind, note, observe, regard, watch

lis•ten•er•ship \ˈlis-ᵊn-ər-ˌship\ *n* **:** the audience for a radio program or recording
list•ing \ˈlis-tiŋ\ *n* **1 :** an act or instance of making or including in a list **2 :** something that is listed **3** ♦ **:** a simple series of words or numerals (as the names of persons or objects)

♦ catalog, checklist, list, menu, register, registry, roll, roster, schedule, table

list•less \ˈlist-ləs\ *adj* ♦ **:** characterized by lack of interest, energy, or spirit **:** SPIRITLESS, LANGUID — **list•less•ly** *adv*

♦ enervated, lackadaisical, languid, languorous, limp, spiritless *Ant* ambitious, animated, energetic, enterprising, motivated

list•less•ness *n* ♦ **:** the quality or state of being listless

♦ boredom, doldrums, ennui, restlessness, tedium, tiredness, weariness

list price *n* **:** the price of an item as published in a catalog, price list, or advertisement before being discounted
lists \ˈlists\ *n pl* **:** an arena for combat (as jousting)
¹lit \ˈlit\ *past and past part of* LIGHT
²lit *abbr* **1** liter **2** literal; literally **3** literary **4** literature
lit•a•ny \ˈlit-ᵊn-ē\ *n, pl* **-nies 1 :** a prayer consisting of a series of supplications and responses said alternately by a leader and a group **2 :** a lengthy recitation ⟨a ~ of complaints⟩
li•tchi *var of* LYCHEE
lite \ˈlīt\ *adj* **1 :** ⁴LIGHT 10 **2** lacking in substance or seriousness
li•ter *or chiefly Can and Brit* **li•tre** \ˈlē-tər\ *n* **:** the basic metric unit of volume measure
lit•er•al \ˈli-tə-rəl\ *adj* **1** ♦ **:** adhering to fact or to the ordinary or usual meaning (as of a word) **2 :** UNADORNED; *also* **:** PROSAIC **3 :** VERBATIM

♦ documentary, factual, hard, historical, matter-of-fact, nonfictional, objective, true

lit•er•al•ism \-rə-ˌli-zəm\ *n* **1 :** adherence to the explicit substance (as of an idea) **2 :** fidelity to observable fact — **lit•er•al•ist** \-list\ *n* — **lit•er•al•is•tic** \ˌli-tə-rə-ˈlis-tik\ *adj*
lit•er•al•ly \ˈli-tə-rə-lē, ˈli-trə-\ *adv* **1 :** ACTUALLY ⟨was ~ insane⟩ **2 :** VIRTUALLY ⟨~ poured out new ideas⟩
lit•er•ary \ˈli-tə-ˌrer-ē\ *adj* **1 a :** of or relating to literature **b** ♦ **:** having a formal style characteristic of the language of literature **2 :** WELL-READ

♦ bookish, erudite, learned

lit•er•ate \ˈli-trət, -tə-rət\ *adj* **1** ♦ **:** having an education **:** EDUCATED; *also* **:** able to read and write **2 :** LITERARY; *also* **:** POLISHED, LUCID — **lit•er•a•cy** \ˈli-trə-sē, -tə-rə-\ *n* — **literate** *n*

♦ educated, erudite, knowledgeable, learned, scholarly, well-read

li•te•ra•ti \ˌli-tə-ˈrä-tē\ *n pl* **1 :** the educated class **2 :** persons interested in literature or the arts
lit•er•a•ture \ˈli-trə-ˌchu̇r, -tə-rə-, -chər\ *n* **1 :** the production of written works having excellence of form or expression and dealing with ideas of permanent interest **2 :** the written works produced in a particular language, country, or age
lithe \ˈlīth, ˈlīth\ *adj* **1** ♦ **:** easily bent or flexed **:** SUPPLE **2 a** ♦ **:** characterized by effortless grace **b :** athletically slim

♦ [1] flexible, limber, lissome, pliable, supple, willowy ♦ [2a] agile, graceful, light, lissome, nimble, spry

lithe•some \ˈlīth-səm, ˈlīth-\ *adj* **:** quick and light in motion **:** LISSOME
lith•i•um \ˈli-thē-əm\ *n* **:** a light silver-white metallic chemical element
li•thog•ra•phy \li-ˈthä-grə-fē\ *n* **:** the process of printing from a plane surface (as a smooth stone or metal plate) on which the image to be printed is ink-receptive and the blank area ink-repellent — **lith•o•graph** \ˈli-thə-ˌgraf\ *vb* — **lithograph** *n* — **li•thog•ra•pher** \li-ˈthä-grə-fər, ˈli-thə-ˌgra-fər\ *n* — **lith•o•graph•ic** \ˌli-thə-ˈgra-fik\ *adj* — **lith•o•graph•i•cal•ly** \-fi-k(ə-)lē\ *adv*
li•thol•o•gy \li-ˈthä-lə-jē\ *n, pl* **-gies :** the study of rocks — **lith•o•log•ic** \ˌli-thə-ˈlä-jik\ *or* **lith•o•log•i•cal** \-ji-kəl\ *adj*
lith•o•sphere \ˈli-thə-ˌsfir\ *n* **:** the outer part of the solid earth
Lith•u•a•nian \ˌli-thü-ˈwā-nē-ən, -thyü-\ *n* **1 :** a native or inhabitant of Lithuania **2 :** the language of the Lithuanians — **Lithuanian** *adj*
lit•i•gant \ˈli-ti-gənt\ *n* **:** a party to a lawsuit — **litigant** *adj*

lit·i·gate \-ˌgāt\ *vb* **-gat·ed; -gat·ing :** to carry on a legal contest by judicial process; *also* **:** to contest at law — **lit·i·ga·tion** \ˌli-tə-ˈgā-shən\ *n*
li·ti·gious \lə-ˈti-jəs\ *adj* **1 :** CONTENTIOUS **2 :** prone to engage in lawsuits **3 :** of or relating to litigation — **li·ti·gious·ly** *adv* — **li·ti·gious·ness** *n*
lit·mus \ˈlit-məs\ *n* **:** a coloring matter from lichens that turns red in acid solutions and blue in alkaline
litmus test *n* **:** a test in which a single factor (as an attitude) is decisive
Litt D *or* **Lit D** *abbr* **:** doctor of letters; doctor of literature
1lit·ter \ˈli-tər\ *n* **1 :** a covered and curtained couch with shafts that is used to carry a single passenger; *also* **:** a device (as a stretcher) for carrying a sick or injured person **2 :** material used as bedding for animals; *also* **:** material used to absorb the urine and feces of animals **3 :** the offspring of an animal at one birth **4** ♦ **:** trash, wastepaper, or garbage lying scattered about **:** RUBBISH; *also* **:** an untidy accumulation of objects

♦ chaff, deadwood, dust, garbage, junk, refuse, riffraff, rubbish, scrap, trash, waste ♦ assortment, clutter, jumble, medley, mélange, miscellany, motley, muddle, variety, welter

2litter *vb* **1 :** to give birth to young **2 :** to strew or mark with scattered objects
lit·ter·bug \ˈli-tər-ˌbəg\ *n* **:** one who litters a public area
1lit·tle \ˈlit-ᵊl\ *adj* **lit·tler** \ˈlit-ᵊl-ər\ *or* **less** \ˈles\ *or* **less·er** \ˈle-sər\; **lit·tlest** \ˈlit-ᵊl-əst\ *or* **least** \ˈlēst\ **1 a** ♦ **:** not big **b :** YOUNG **2** ♦ **:** not important **3** ♦ **:** illiberal in views or disposition **:** PETTY 3 **4 :** not much **5** ♦ **:** short in duration — **lit·tle·ness** *n*

♦ [1a] dwarf, dwarfish, fine, pocket, pygmy, slight, small, undersized ♦ [2] frivolous, inconsequential, inconsiderable, insignificant, minor, minute, negligible, slight, small, trifling, trivial, unimportant ♦ [3] insular, narrow, parochial, petty, provincial, sectarian, small ♦ [5] brief, short, short-lived

2little *adv* **less** \ˈles\; **least** \ˈlēst\ **1 :** in only a small quantity or degree **:** SLIGHTLY; *also* **:** not at all **2** ♦ **:** in few instances **:** INFREQUENTLY

♦ infrequently, rarely, seldom

3little *n* **1 :** a small amount or quantity **2 :** a short time or distance
Little Dipper *n* **:** the seven bright stars of Ursa Minor arranged in a form resembling a dipper
little finger *n* **:** PINKIE
little theater *n* **:** a small theater for low-cost dramatic productions designed for a limited audience
lit·to·ral \ˈli-tə-rəl; ˌli-tə-ˈral\ *adj* **:** of, relating to, or growing on or near a shore especially of the sea — **littoral** *n*
lit·ur·gy \ˈli-tər-jē\ *n, pl* **-gies :** a rite or body of rites prescribed for public worship — **li·tur·gi·cal** \lə-ˈtər-ji-kəl\ *adj* — **li·tur·gi·cal·ly** \-k(ə-)lē\ *adv* — **lit·ur·gist** \ˈli-tər-jist\ *n*
liv·able *also* **live·able** \ˈli-və-bəl\ *adj* **1 :** suitable for living in or with **2 :** ENDURABLE — **liv·a·bil·i·ty** \ˌli-və-ˈbi-lə-tē\ *n*
1live \ˈliv\ *vb* **lived; liv·ing 1** ♦ **:** to be or continue alive **2 :** SUBSIST **3** ♦ **:** to occupy a home **:** RESIDE **4 :** to conduct one's life **5 :** to remain in human memory or record

♦ [1] be, breathe, exist, subsist ♦ [3] abide, dwell, reside

2live \ˈlīv\ *adj* **1** ♦ **:** having life **2 :** BURNING, GLOWING ⟨a ~ cigar⟩ **3 :** connected to electric power ⟨a ~ wire⟩ **4 :** charged with explosive but not yet exploded ⟨a ~ bomb⟩ **5 :** of continuing interest ⟨a ~ issue⟩ **6 :** of or involving the actual presence of real people ⟨~ audience⟩; *also* **:** broadcast directly at the time of production ⟨a ~ radio program⟩ **7 :** being in play ⟨a ~ ball⟩

♦ alive, animate, living

lived–in \ˈlivd-ˌin\ *adj* **:** of or suggesting long-term human habitation or use
live down *vb* **:** to live so as to wipe out the memory or effects of
live in *vb* **:** to live in one's place of employment — used of a servant — **live–in** \ˈliv-ˌin\ *adj*
live·li·hood \ˈlīv-lē-ˌhu̇d\ *n* **:** means of support or subsistence
live·li·ness *n* ♦ **:** the quality or state of being lively

♦ animation, briskness, exuberance, lustiness, robustness, sprightliness, vibrancy, vitality

live·long \ˈliv-ˌlȯŋ\ *adj* **:** WHOLE, ENTIRE ⟨the ~ day⟩
live·ly \ˈlīv-lē\ *adj* **live·li·er; -est 1** ♦ **:** briskly alert and energetic **:** ANIMATED ⟨~ debate⟩ **2 :** KEEN, VIVID ⟨~ interest⟩ **3 :** showing activity or vigor ⟨a ~ manner⟩ **4 :** quick to rebound ⟨a ~ ball⟩ **5** ♦ **:** full of life — **live·ly** *adv*

♦ [1] active, animate, animated, brisk, energetic, frisky, peppy, perky, pert, spirited, sprightly, springy, vital, vivacious ***Ant*** inactive, inanimate, languid, languorous, limp, listless, spiritless ♦ [5] alive, animated, astir, busy, vibrant

liv·en \ˈlī-vən\ *vb* ♦ **:** to give life, action, or spirit to **:** ENLIVEN — often used with *up*; *also* **:** to become lively

♦ *usu* **liven up** animate, brace, energize, enliven, fire, invigorate, jazz up, pep up, quicken, stimulate, vitalize, vivify, zip (up)

live oak *n* **:** any of several American evergreen oaks; *esp* **:** one of the southeastern U.S. that is often planted as a shade tree
1liv·er \ˈli-vər\ *n* **1 :** a large glandular organ of vertebrates that secretes bile and is a center of metabolic activity **2 :** the liver of an animal (as a calf or chicken) eaten as food
2liver *n* **:** one that lives especially in a specified way ⟨a fast ~⟩
liv·er·ish \ˈli-və-rish\ *adj* **1 :** resembling liver especially in color **2 :** BILIOUS **3 :** PEEVISH — **liv·er·ish·ness** *adj*
liv·er·wort \ˈli-vər-ˌwərt\ *n* **:** any of a class of flowerless plants resembling the related mosses
liv·er·wurst \-ˌwərst, -ˌwu̇rst\ *n* **:** a sausage consisting chiefly of liver
liv·ery \ˈli-və-rē\ *n, pl* **-er·ies 1 :** a servant's uniform; *also* **:** distinctive dress **2 :** the feeding, care, and stabling of horses for pay; *also* **:** an establishment (as a stable or business) keeping horses or vehicles for hire — **liv·er·ied** \-rēd\ *adj*
liv·ery·man \-mən\ *n* **:** the keeper of a livery
lives *pl of* LIFE
live·stock \ˈlīv-ˌstäk\ *n* **:** farm animals kept for use and profit
live wire *n* ♦ **:** an alert, active, or aggressive person

♦ go-getter, hustler, powerhouse, self-starter

liv·id \ˈli-vəd\ *adj* **1 :** discolored by bruising **2** ♦ **:** deadly pale **:** ASHEN, PALLID **3 :** REDDISH **4 :** ENRAGED — **li·vid·i·ty** \li-ˈvi-də-tē\ *n*

♦ ashen, cadaverous, lurid, pale, pasty, peaked

1liv·ing \ˈli-viŋ\ *adj* **1** ♦ **:** having life or existence **2 :** NATURAL **3 :** full of life and vigor; *also* **:** VIVID **4** ♦ **:** marked by present operation, transaction, movement, or use

♦ [1] alive, animate, existent, extant, live ♦ [4] active, alive, functional, on, operational, operative, running, working

2living *n* **1 :** the condition of being alive **2 :** LIVELIHOOD **3 :** manner of life
living room *n* **:** a room in a residence used for the common social activities of the occupants
living wage *n* **:** a wage sufficient to provide an acceptable standard of living
living will *n* **:** a document requesting that the signer not be kept alive by artificial means unless there is a reasonable expectation of recovery
livre \ˈlēvrᵊ\ *n* **:** the pound of Lebanon
liz·ard \ˈli-zərd\ *n* **:** any of a group of 4-legged reptiles with long tapering tails
Lk *abbr* Luke
ll *abbr* lines
lla·ma \ˈlä-mə\ *n* **:** any of a genus of wild or domesticated So. American mammals related to the camels but smaller and without a hump
lla·no \ˈlä-nō\ *n, pl* **llanos :** an open grassy plain especially of Latin America
LLD *abbr* doctor of laws
LNG *abbr* liquefied natural gas
1load \ˈlōd\ *n* **1 a :** PACK **b** ♦ **:** whatever is put in a ship or vehicle or airplane for conveyance **:** CARGO **2 :** a mass of weight supported by something **3 :** something that burdens the mind or spirits **4** ♦ **:** a large quantity — usually used in plural **5 :** a standard, expected, or authorized burden

♦ [1b] burden, cargo, freight, haul, lading, payload, weight ♦ *usu* **loads** [4] abundance, deal, gobs, heap, lot, pile, plenty, quantity, scads

2load *vb* **1 a** ♦ **:** to put a load in or on; *also* **:** to receive a load **b** ♦ **:** to fill with a load **2 :** to encumber with an obligation or something heavy or disheartening **3 :** to increase the weight of by adding something **4 :** to supply abundantly **5 :** to put a charge in (as a firearm)

♦ [1a] burden, encumber, lumber, saddle, weight ***Ant*** disencumber, unburden, unload ♦ [1b] charge, cram, fill, heap, jam, jam-pack, pack, stuff

load·ed *adj* **1** *slang* **:** HIGH 12 **2** ♦ **:** having a large amount of money **3 :** equipped with an abundance of options

♦ affluent, flush, moneyed, opulent, rich, wealthy, well-fixed, well-heeled, well-off, well-to-do

load•stone *var of* LODESTONE
¹loaf \ˈlōf\ *n, pl* **loaves** \ˈlōvz\ : a shaped or molded mass especially of bread
²loaf *vb* ♦ : to spend time in idleness : LOUNGE

♦ dally, dawdle, dillydally, hang around, hang out, idle, loll, lounge

loaf•er *n* **1** ♦ : one that loafs **2** : a low step-in shoe

♦ idler, lazybones, slouch, slug, sluggard

loam \ˈlōm, ˈlüm\ *n* : SOIL; *esp* : a loose soil of mixed clay, sand, and silt — **loamy** *adj*
¹loan \ˈlōn\ *n* **1** : money lent at interest; *also* : something lent for the borrower's temporary use **2** : the grant of temporary use
²loan *vb* : LEND
loan shark *n* : a person who lends money at excessive rates of interest — **loan•shark•ing** \ˈlōn-ˌshär-kiŋ\ *n*
loan•word \ˈlōn-ˌwərd\ *n* : a word taken from another language and at least partly naturalized
loath \ˈlōth, ˈlō<u>th</u>\ *also* **loathe** \lō<u>th</u>, lōth\ *adj* : RELUCTANT
loathe \ˈlō<u>th</u>\ *vb* **loathed; loath•ing** ♦ : to dislike greatly

♦ abhor, abominate, despise, detest, execrate, hate

loath•ing \ˈlō-<u>th</u>iŋ\ *n* ♦ : extreme disgust

♦ disgust, distaste, nausea, repugnance, repulsion, revulsion ♦ abhorrence, abomination, execration, hate, hatred

loath•some \ˈlōth-səm, ˈlō<u>th</u>-\ *adj* : exciting loathing : REPULSIVE
lob \ˈläb\ *vb* **lobbed; lob•bing** : to throw, hit, or propel something in a high arc — **lob** *n*
¹lob•by \ˈlä-bē\ *n, pl* **lobbies** **1** ♦ : a corridor used especially as a passageway or waiting room **2** : a group of persons engaged in lobbying

♦ entry, foyer, hall, vestibule

²lobby *vb* **lob•bied; lob•by•ing** : to try to influence public officials and especially legislators — **lob•by•ist** *n*
lobe \ˈlōb\ *n* : a curved or rounded part especially of a bodily organ — **lo•bar** \ˈlō-bər\ *adj* — **lobed** \ˈlōbd\ *adj*
lo•be•lia \lō-ˈbēl-yə\ *n* : any of a genus of plants often grown for their clusters of showy flowers
lo•bot•o•my \lō-ˈbä-tə-mē\ *n, pl* **-mies** : surgical severance of certain nerve fibers in the brain performed especially formerly to relieve some mental disorders
lob•ster \ˈläb-stər\ *n* : any of a family of edible marine crustaceans with two large pincerlike claws and four other pairs of legs; *also* : SPINY LOBSTER
¹lo•cal \ˈlō-kəl\ *adj* **1** : of, relating to, or occupying a particular place **2** : serving a particular limited district; *also* : making all stops ⟨a ~ train⟩ **3** : affecting a small part of the body ⟨~ infection⟩ — **lo•cal•ly** *adv*
²local *n* ♦ : one that is local; *esp* : a local or particular branch, lodge, or chapter of an organization (as a labor union)

♦ affiliate, branch, chapter

local area network *n* : a network of personal computers in a small area (as an office)
lo•cale \lō-ˈkal\ *n* ♦ : a place that is the setting for a particular event

♦ location, place, point, position, site, spot

lo•cal•ise *chiefly Brit var of* LOCALIZE
lo•cal•i•ty \lō-ˈka-lə-tē\ *n, pl* **-ties** : a particular spot, situation, or location
lo•cal•ize \ˈlō-kə-ˌlīz\ *vb* **-ized; -iz•ing** : to fix in or confine to a definite place or locality — **lo•cal•i•za•tion** \ˌlō-kə-lə-ˈzā-shən\ *n*
lo•cate \ˈlō-ˌkāt, lō-ˈkāt\ *vb* **lo•cat•ed; lo•cat•ing** **1** : STATION, SETTLE **2** ♦ : to determine the site of **3** : to find or fix the place of in a sequence

♦ detect, determine, dig up, discover, ferret out, find, hit on, track down

lo•ca•tion \lō-ˈkā-shən\ *n* **1** ♦ : a position or site occupied or available for occupancy or marked by some distinguishing feature : PLACE **2** : the process of locating **3** : a place outside a studio where a motion picture is filmed

♦ locale, place, point, position, site, spot

loc cit *abbr* in the place cited
loch \ˈläk, ˈläk̲\ *n, Scot* : LAKE; *also* : a bay or arm of the sea especially when nearly landlocked
¹lock \ˈläk\ *n* : a tuft, strand, or ringlet of hair; *also* : a cohering bunch (as of wool or flax)
²lock *n* **1** : a fastening in which a bolt is operated **2** : the mechanism of a firearm by which the charge is exploded **3** : an enclosure (as in a canal) used in raising or lowering boats from level to level **4** : AIR LOCK **5** : a wrestling hold
³lock *vb* **1** : to fasten the lock of; *also* : to make fast with a lock **2** ♦ : to confine or exclude by means of a lock — often used with *in* or *up* **3** : INTERLOCK **4** : to make or become motionless by the interlocking of parts

♦ commit, confine, immure, imprison, jail

lock•er \ˈlä-kər\ *n* **1** ♦ : a drawer, cupboard, or compartment for individual storage use **2** : an insulated compartment for storing frozen food

♦ box, caddy, case, casket, chest, trunk ♦ buffet, cabinet, closet, cupboard, hutch, sideboard

lock•et \ˈlä-kət\ *n* : a small usually metal case for a memento worn suspended from a chain or necklace
lock•jaw \ˈläk-ˌjȯ\ *n* : a symptom of tetanus marked by spasms of the jaw muscles and inability to open the jaws; *also* : TETANUS
lock•nut \-ˌnət\ *n* **1** : a nut screwed tight on another to prevent it from slacking back **2** : a nut designed to lock itself when screwed tight
lock•out \-ˌau̇t\ *n* : the suspension of work by an employer during a labor dispute in order to make employees accept the terms being offered
lock•smith \-ˌsmith\ *n* : one who makes or repairs locks
lock•step \-ˌstep\ *n* : a mode of marching in step by a body of men moving in a very close single file
lock•up \-ˌəp\ *n* : JAIL; *esp* : a local jail where persons are detained prior to court hearing
lo•co \ˈlō-kō\ *adj slang* ♦ : mentally disordered : CRAZY, FRENZIED

♦ balmy, crazy, cuckoo, deranged, frenzied, insane, lunatic, mad, maniacal, nutty, screwy, unsound, wacky

lo•co•mo•tion \ˌlō-kə-ˈmō-shən\ *n* **1** : the act or power of moving from place to place **2** : TRAVEL
¹lo•co•mo•tive \ˌlō-kə-ˈmō-tiv\ *adj* : of or relating to locomotion or a locomotive
²locomotive *n* : a self-propelled vehicle used to move railroad cars
lo•co•mo•tor \ˌlō-kə-ˈmō-tər\ *adj* : of or relating to locomotion or organs used in locomotion
lo•co•weed \ˈlō-kō-ˌwēd\ *n* : any of several leguminous plants of western No. America that are poisonous to livestock
lo•cus \ˈlō-kəs\ *n, pl* **lo•ci** \ˈlō-ˌsī\ **1** : the place where something is situated or occurs : LOCALITY **2** : the set of all points whose location is determined by stated conditions
lo•cust \ˈlō-kəst\ *n* **1** : a usually destructive migratory grasshopper **2** : CICADA **3** : any of various leguminous trees; *also* : the wood of a locust
lo•cu•tion \lō-ˈkyü-shən\ *n* ♦ : a particular form of expression; *also* : PHRASEOLOGY

♦ manner, mode, phraseology, style, tone, vein

lode \ˈlōd\ *n* : an ore deposit
lode•stone \-ˌstōn\ *n* **1** : an iron-containing rock with magnetic properties **2** ♦ : something that strongly attracts

♦ attraction, draw, magnet

¹lodge \ˈläj\ *vb* **lodged; lodg•ing** **1** ♦ : to provide quarters for; *also* : to settle in a place **2** : CONTAIN **3** : to come to a rest and remain **4** : to deposit for safekeeping **5** : to vest (as authority) in an agent **6** : FILE ⟨~ a complaint⟩

♦ ensconce, install, perch, roost, settle ♦ accommodate, billet, domicile, harbor (*or* harbour), house, put up, quarter, roof, shelter, take in

²lodge *n* **1** ♦ : a house set apart for residence in a special season or by an employee on an estate; *also* : INN **2** ♦ : a den or lair especially of gregarious animals **3** : the meeting place of a branch of a fraternal organization; *also* : the members of such a branch

♦ [1] cabin, camp, chalet, cottage ♦ [1] hospice, hotel, inn, public house, tavern ♦ [2] burrow, den, hole, lair

lodg•er \ˈlä-jər\ *n* ♦ : a person who occupies a rented room in another's house

♦ boarder, renter, roomer, tenant

lodg•ing \ˈlä-jiŋ\ *n* **1** : a place to live : DWELLING **2** ♦ : a room or suite of rooms in another's house rented as a dwelling place — usually used in plural

♦ flat, suite

lodg•ment *or* **lodge•ment** \ˈläj-mənt\ *n* **1** ♦ **:** a lodging place **2 :** the act or manner of lodging **3 :** DEPOSIT

♦ accommodation, lodging

loess \ˈles, ˈləs\ *n* **:** a usually yellowish brown loamy deposit believed to be chiefly deposited by the wind

lo–fi \ˈlō-ˌfī\ *n* **:** audio production of rough or unpolished sound quality — **lo–fi** *adj*

1loft \ˈlȯft\ *n* **1 :** ATTIC **2 :** GALLERY ⟨organ ~⟩ **3 :** an upper floor (as in a warehouse or barn) especially when not partitioned **4 :** the thickness of a fabric or insulated material (as of a sleeping bag)

2loft *vb* **:** to strike or throw (a ball) so that it rises high in the air

loft•i•ness \-tē-nəs\ *n* ♦ **:** the quality or state of being lofty

♦ arrogance, haughtiness, pretense, pretension, pretentiousness, self-importance, superiority

lofty \ˈlȯf-tē\ *adj* **loft•i•er; -est** **1** ♦ **:** elevated in character and spirit **:** NOBLE; *also* **:** SUPERIOR **2** ♦ **:** extremely proud; *also* **:** haughty and overbearingly arrogant **3 :** rising to a great height **:** HIGH, TALL — **loft•i•ly** \ˈlȯf-tə-lē\ *adv*

♦ [1] chivalrous, gallant, great, greathearted, high, high-minded, lordly, magnanimous, noble, sublime ♦ [1] eloquent, formal, high-flown, majestic, stately, superior, towering ♦ [2] arrogant, haughty, highfalutin, imperious, peremptory, pompous, presumptuous, pretentious, supercilious

1log \ˈlȯg, ˈläg\ *n* **1 :** a bulky piece of a cut or fallen tree **2 :** an apparatus for measuring a ship's speed **3 :** the daily record of a ship's progress; *also* **:** a regularly kept record of performance or events

2log *vb* **logged; log•ging** **1 :** to cut (trees) for lumber; *also* **:** to clear (land) of trees in lumbering **2** ♦ **:** to enter in a log; *broadly* **:** to make a note or record of **3 :** to sail a ship or fly an airplane for (an indicated distance or period of time) **4 :** to have (an indicated record) to one's credit **:** ACHIEVE — **log•ger** \ˈlȯ-gər, ˈlä-\ *n*

♦ jot, mark, note, put down, record, register, set down

3log *n* **:** LOGARITHM

lo•gan•ber•ry \ˈlō-gən-ˌber-ē\ *n* **:** a red-fruited upright-growing dewberry; *also* **:** its berry

log•a•rithm \ˈlȯ-gə-ˌri-t͟həm, ˈlä-\ *n* **:** the exponent that indicates the power to which a base is raised to produce a given number ⟨the ~ of 100 to base 10 is 2 since $10^2 = 100$⟩ — **log•a•rith•mic** \ˌlȯ-gə-ˈrit͟h-mik, ˌlä-\ *adj*

loge \ˈlōzh\ *n* **1 :** a small compartment; *also* **:** a box in a theater **2 :** a small partitioned area; *also* **:** the forward section of a theater mezzanine

log•ger•head \ˈlȯ-gər-ˌhed, ˈlä-\ *n* **:** a large sea turtle of subtropical and temperate waters — **at loggerheads :** in a state of quarrelsome disagreement

log•gia \ˈlō-jē-ə, ˈlȯ-jä\ *n, pl* **loggias** \ˈlō-jē-əz, ˈlȯ-jäz\ **:** a roofed open gallery

log•ic \ˈlä-jik\ *n* **1 :** a science that deals with the rules and tests of sound thinking and proof by reasoning **2** ♦ **:** sound reasoning **3 :** the arrangement of circuit elements for arithmetical computation in a computer — **log•i•cal•ly** \-jik(ə-)lē\ *adv* — **lo•gi•cian** \lō-ˈji-shən\ *n*

♦ reason, reasoning, sense

log•i•cal \-ji-kəl\ *adj* ♦ **:** of, relating to, involving, or being in accordance with logic

♦ analytic, coherent, good, rational, reasonable, sensible, sober, sound, valid ***Ant*** incoherent, illogical, invalid, irrational, unreasonable, unsound

lo•gis•tics \lō-ˈjis-tiks\ *n sing or pl* **:** the procurement, maintenance, and transportation of matériel, facilities, and personnel — **lo•gis•tic** \-tik\ *or* **lo•gis•ti•cal** \-ti-kəl\ *adj*

log•jam \ˈlȯg-ˌjam, ˈläg-\ *n* **1 :** a deadlocked jumble of logs in a watercourse **2 :** DEADLOCK

logo \ˈlō-gō\ *n, pl* **log•os** \-gōz\ ♦ **:** an identifying symbol (as for advertising)

♦ emblem, hallmark, symbol, trademark

logo•type \ˈlȯ-gə-ˌtīp, ˈlä-\ *n* **:** LOGO

log•roll•ing \-ˌrō-liŋ\ *n* **:** the trading of votes by legislators to secure favorable action on projects of individual interest

lo•gy \ˈlō-gē\ *also* **log•gy** \ˈlȯ-gē, ˈlä-\ *adj* **lo•gi•er; -est :** deficient in vitality **:** SLUGGISH

loin \ˈlȯin\ *n* **1 :** the part of the body on each side of the spinal column and between the hip and the lower ribs; *also* **:** a cut of meat from this part of an animal **2** *pl* **:** the pubic region; *also* **:** the organs of reproduction

loin•cloth \-ˌklȯth\ *n* **:** a cloth worn about the loins often as the sole article of clothing in warm climates

loi•ter \ˈlȯi-tər\ *vb* **1** ♦ **:** to delay an activity with idle stops and pauses **:** LINGER **2 :** to hang around idly — **loi•ter•er** *n*

♦ crawl, creep, dally, dawdle, delay, dillydally, drag, lag, linger, poke, tarry

loll \ˈläl\ *vb* **1** ♦ **:** to hang loosely or laxly **:** DROOP, DANGLE **2** ♦ **:** to act or move in a lax, lazy, or indolent manner **:** LOUNGE

♦ [1] dangle, droop, flag, hang, sag, wilt ♦ [2] bask, lounge, relax, repose, rest

lol•la•pa•loo•za \ˌlä-lə-pə-ˈlü-zə\ *n* **:** something extraordinarily impressive or outstanding

lol•li•pop *or* **lol•ly•pop** \ˈlä-li-ˌpäp\ *n* **:** a lump of hard candy on a stick

lol•ly•gag \ˈlä-lē-ˌgag\ *vb* **-gagged; -gag•ging :** DAWDLE

Lond *abbr* London

lone \ˈlōn\ *adj* **1** ♦ **:** having no company **:** SOLITARY ⟨a ~ sentinel⟩ **2** ♦ **:** alone in a class or category **:** SOLE, ONLY ⟨the ~ theater in town⟩ **3 :** ISOLATED ⟨a ~ tree⟩

♦ alone, only, singular, sole, solitary, special, unique

lone•ly \ˈlōn-lē\ *adj* **lone•li•er; -est** **1** ♦ **:** being without company **2 :** UNFREQUENTED ⟨a ~ spot⟩ **3 :** sad from being alone **:** LONESOME — **lone•li•ness** *n*

♦ alone, lone, lonesome, solitary, unaccompanied

lon•er \ˈlō-nər\ *n* ♦ **:** one that avoids others; *also* **:** one who pursues an independent course of thought or action

♦ bohemian, deviant, individualist, maverick, nonconformist

lone•some \ˈlōn-səm\ *adj* **1** ♦ **:** sad from lack of companionship **2 a :** REMOTE **b :** having no company **:** SOLITARY — **lone•some•ly** *adv* — **lone•some•ness** *n*

♦ desolate, forlorn, lonely

1long \ˈlȯŋ\ *adj* **lon•ger** \ˈlȯŋ-gər\; **lon•gest** \ˈlȯŋ-gəst\ **1** ♦ **:** extending for a considerable distance; *also* **:** having greater height than usual **:** ELONGATED **2 :** having a specified length **3** ♦ **:** extending over a considerable time; *also* **:** TEDIOUS **4 :** containing many items in a series **5 :** being a syllable or speech sound of relatively great duration **6 :** extending far into the future **7 :** well furnished with something — used with *on*

♦ [1] extended, lengthy ***Ant*** brief, short ♦ [3] extended, far, great, lengthy, marathon ***Ant*** brief, short, short-lived, short-term

2long *adv* **:** for or during a long time

3long *n* **:** a long period of time

4long *vb* **longed; long•ing** \ˈlȯŋ-iŋ\ ♦ **:** to feel a strong desire or wish

♦ *usu* **long for** ache for, covet, crave, desire, die for, hanker for, hunger for, lust (for *or* after), pine for, repine for, thirst for, want, wish for, yearn for

5long *abbr* longitude

long•boat \ˈlȯŋ-ˌbōt\ *n* **:** a large boat usually carried by a merchant sailing ship

long•bow \-ˌbō\ *n* **:** a wooden bow drawn by hand and used especially by medieval English archers

lon•gev•i•ty \län-ˈje-və-tē\ *n* **:** a long duration of individual life; *also* **:** length of life

long•hair \ˈlȯŋ-ˌher\ *n* **1 :** a lover of classical music **2 :** HIPPIE **3 :** a domestic cat having long outer fur — **long•haired** \-ˌherd\ *or* **long•hair** *adj*

long•hand \-ˌhand\ *n* **:** writing done by hand **:** HANDWRITING; *also* **:** cursive writing

long•horn \-ˌhȯrn\ *n* **:** any of the cattle with long horns formerly common in the southwestern U.S.

long hundredweight *n, Brit* **:** a unit of weight equal to 112 pounds

long•ing \ˈlȯŋ-iŋ\ *n* ♦ **:** a strong desire especially for something unattainable — **long•ing•ly** *adv*

♦ appetite, craving, desire, drive, hankering, hunger, itch, lust, passion, thirst, urge, yearning, yen

lon•gi•tude \ˈlän-jə-ˌtüd, -ˌtyüd\ *n* **:** angular distance expressed usually in degrees east or west from the prime meridian through Greenwich, England

lon•gi•tu•di•nal \ˌlän-jə-ˈtüd-ᵊn-əl, -ˈtyüd-\ *adj* **1 :** extending lengthwise **2 :** of or relating to length — **lon•gi•tu•di•nal•ly** *adv*

long–range \ˈlȯŋ-ˈrānj\ *adj* **1 :** relating to or fit for long distances **2 :** involving a long period of time
long•shore•man \ˈlȯŋ-ˌshōr-mən\ *n* **:** a laborer at a wharf who loads and unloads cargo
long–suf•fer•ing \-ˈsə-friŋ, -fə-riŋ\ *adj* ♦ **:** patiently enduring lasting offense or hardship

♦ forbearing, patient, stoic, tolerant, uncomplaining

long–term \ˈlȯŋ-ˈtərm\ *adj* **1 :** extending over or involving a long period of time **2 :** constituting a financial obligation based on a term usually of more than 10 years ⟨~ bonds⟩
long•time \ˈlȯŋ-ˈtīm\ *adj* **:** of long duration ⟨~ friends⟩
long ton *n* **:** a British unit of weight equal to 20 long hundredweight
lon•gueur \lōⁿ-ˈgœr\ *n, pl* **longueurs** *same or* -ˈgœrz\ **:** a dull tedious portion (as of a book)
long–wind•ed \ˌlȯŋ-ˈwin-dəd\ *adj* ♦ **:** tediously long in speaking or writing

♦ circuitous, diffuse, prolix, rambling, verbose, windy, wordy

loo•fah \ˈlü-fə\ *n* **:** a sponge consisting of the fibrous skeleton of a gourd
¹look \ˈlu̇k\ *vb* **1 :** to exercise the power of vision **:** SEE **2 :** EXPECT **3 :** to have an appearance that befits ⟨~*s* the part⟩ **4** ♦ **:** to have the appearance or likelihood of being **:** SEEM ⟨~*s* thin⟩ **5 :** to direct one's attention **:** HEED **6** ♦ **:** to have a specified direction **:** POINT, FACE **7 :** to show a tendency **8** ♦ **:** to express by the eyes or facial expression — **look after :** to take care of — **look for :** EXPECT

♦ [4] act, appear, make, seem, sound ♦ *usu* **look toward** [6] face, front, point ♦ [8] air, express, give, sound, state, vent, voice

²look *n* **1** ♦ **:** the action of looking **:** GLANCE **2** ♦ **:** the expression of the countenance; *also* **:** physical appearance — usually used in plural **3** ♦ **:** the state or form in which something appears **:** ASPECT

♦ [1] cast, eye, gander, glance, glimpse, peek, peep, regard, sight, view ♦ [2] cast, countenance, expression, face, visage ♦ *usu* **looks** [2] attractiveness, beauty, comeliness, handsomeness, loveliness, prettiness ♦ [3] appearance, aspect, mien, presence

look down *vb* **:** to regard with contempt — used with *on* or *upon*
looking glass *n* **:** MIRROR
look into *vb* ♦ **:** to investigate, study, or analyze

♦ delve, dig, explore, go, inquire into, investigate, probe, research

look•out \ˈlu̇k-ˌau̇t\ *n* **1** ♦ **:** a person assigned to watch (as on a ship) **2** ♦ **:** a careful watch **3** ♦ **:** a view from a particular place **:** VIEW **4 :** a matter of concern **5 :** an elevated place or structure affording a wide view for observation

♦ [1] custodian, guard, guardian, keeper, picket, sentry, warden, warder, watch, watchman ♦ [2] alertness, attentiveness, vigilance, watch ♦ [3] outlook, panorama, prospect, view, vista

look up *vb* **1 :** IMPROVE ⟨business is *looking up*⟩ **2 :** to search for in or as if in a reference work **3 :** to seek out especially for a brief visit
¹loom \ˈlüm\ *n* **:** a frame or machine for weaving together threads or yarns into cloth
²loom *vb* **1 :** to come into sight in an unnaturally large, indistinct, or distorted form **2 :** to appear in an impressively exaggerated form **3 :** to take shape as an impending occurrence
loon \ˈlün\ *n* **:** any of several web-footed black-and-white fish-eating diving birds
loon•ie \ˈlü-nē\ *n Can* **:** a coin worth one Canadian dollar
loo•ny *also* **loo•ney** \ˈlü-nē\ *adj* **loo•ni•er; -est :** disordered in mind **:** CRAZY, FOOLISH
loony bin *n* **:** a psychiatric hospital
¹loop \ˈlüp\ *n* **1 a :** a fold or doubling of a line through which another line or hook can be passed **b :** a loop-shaped figure or course ⟨a ~ in a river⟩ **2 :** a circular airplane maneuver executed in the vertical plane **3 :** a continuously repeated segment of film, music, or sound
²loop *vb* ♦ **:** to make a loop in, on, or about

♦ circle, circumnavigate, coil, compass, encircle, girdle, orbit, ring, round

loop•er \ˈlü-pər\ *n* **:** any of numerous rather small hairless moth caterpillars that move with a looping motion
loop•hole \ˈlüp-ˌhōl\ *n* **1 :** a small opening in a wall through which firearms may be discharged **2 :** a means of escape; *esp* **:** an ambiguity or omission that allows one to evade the intent of a law or contract
¹loose \ˈlüs\ *adj* **loos•er; loos•est 1** ♦ **:** not rigidly fastened **2** ♦ **:** free from restraint or obligation **3 :** not dense or compact in structure **4 :** not chaste **:** LEWD **5** ♦ **:** not tightly drawn or stretched **:** SLACK **6** ♦ **:** not precise or exact — **loose•ly** *adv* — **loose•ness** *n*

♦ [1, 5] insecure, lax, relaxed, slack *Ant* taut, tense, tight ♦ [2] footloose, free, unbound, unconfined, unrestrained ♦ [6] imprecise, inaccurate, inexact

²loose *vb* **loosed; loos•ing 1** ♦ **:** to let loose **:** RELEASE; *also* **:** to free from restraint **2 :** UNTIE **3 :** DETACH **4** ♦ **:** to let fly **:** DISCHARGE **5 :** RELAX, SLACKEN

♦ [1] discharge, emancipate, enfranchise, free, liberate, loosen, manumit, release, spring, unbind, unchain, unfetter ♦ [4] blast, discharge, fire, shoot

³loose *adv* **:** LOOSELY
loos•en \ˈlüs-ᵊn\ *vb* **1** ♦ **:** to release from restraint **:** FREE **2** ♦ **:** to make or become loose **3 :** to relax the severity of

♦ [1] free, loose, release, uncork, unleash, unlock, unloosen ♦ [2] ease, relax, slack, slacken

loosen up *vb* **:** to become less tense
¹loot \ˈlüt\ *n* ♦ **:** goods taken in war or by robbery **:** PLUNDER — **loot•er** *n*

♦ booty, plunder, spoil, swag

²loot *vb* ♦ **:** to plunder or sack in war

♦ despoil, maraud, pillage, plunder, ransack, sack, strip

¹lop \ˈläp\ *vb* **lopped; lop•ping 1 :** to cut branches or twigs from **2** ♦ **:** to eliminate as unnecessary or undesirable — usually used with *off*

♦ *usu* **lop off** bob, clip, crop, curtail, cut, cut back, dock, nip, prune, shave, shear, trim

²lop *vb* **lopped; lop•ping :** to hang downward; *also* **:** to flop or sway loosely
¹lope \ˈlōp\ *n* **:** an easy bounding gait
²lope *vb* **:** to move or ride at a lope
lop•sid•ed \ˈläp-ˈsī-dəd\ *adj* **1** ♦ **:** leaning to one side **2 :** not symmetrical — **lop•sid•ed•ly** *adv* — **lop•sid•ed•ness** *n*

♦ askew, awry, cockeyed, crooked, listing, slantwise, uneven

lo•qua•cious \lō-ˈkwā-shəs\ *adj* ♦ **:** excessively talkative — **lo•quac•i•ty** \-ˈkwa-sə-tē\ *n*

♦ chatty, conversational, gabby, garrulous, talkative

¹lord \ˈlȯrd\ *n* **1 :** one having power and authority over others; *esp* **:** a person from whom a feudal fee or estate is held **2 :** a man of rank or high position; *esp* **:** a British nobleman **3** *pl, cap* **:** the upper house of the British parliament **4 :** a person of great power in some field **5** *cap* **:** GOD 1
²lord *vb* **:** to act like a lord; *esp* **:** to put on airs — usually used with *it*
lord chancellor *n, pl* **lords chancellor :** a British officer of state who presides over the House of Lords, serves as head of the British judiciary, and is usually a leading member of the cabinet
lord•ly \-lē\ *adj* **lord•li•er; -est 1** ♦ **:** of, relating to, or having the characteristics of a lord **:** DIGNIFIED; *also* **:** possessing or arising from a sense of high moral character **2** ♦ **:** exhibiting the pride and assurance associated with one of the highest birth or rank **:** HAUGHTY

♦ [1] chivalrous, dignified, gallant, great, greathearted, high, high-minded, lofty, magnanimous, noble, sublime ♦ [2] disdainful, haughty, highfalutin, lofty, prideful, proud, superior

lord•ship \-ˌship\ *n* **1 :** the rank or dignity of a lord — used as a title **2 :** the authority or territory of a lord
Lord's Supper *n* **:** COMMUNION
lore \ˈlōr\ *n* **1** ♦ **:** something that has been learned **:** KNOWLEDGE; *esp* **:** traditional knowledge or belief **2** ♦ **:** a particular body of knowledge or tradition

♦ [1] intelligence, knowledge, science, wisdom ♦ [2] folklore, legend, myth, mythology, tradition

lor•gnette \lȯrn-ˈyet\ *n* **:** a pair of eyeglasses or opera glasses with a handle
lorn \ˈlȯrn\ *adj* **:** miserable and forlorn as if deserted **:** DESOLATE
lor•ry \ˈlȯr-ē\ *n, pl* **lorries** *chiefly Brit* **:** MOTORTRUCK
lose \ˈlüz\ *vb* **lost** \ˈlȯst\; **los•ing** \ˈlü-ziŋ\ **1 :** DESTROY **2 :** to miss from a customary place **:** MISLAY **3 :** to suffer deprivation of

4 : to fail to use **:** WASTE **5 :** to fail to win or obtain ⟨~ the game⟩ **6 :** to fail to keep or maintain ⟨~ his balance⟩ **7 :** to wander from ⟨~ her way⟩ **8** ◆ **:** to get rid of

◆ cast, discard, ditch, dump, fling, jettison, junk, reject, scrap, shed, shuck, slough, throw away, throw out, unload

los•er *n* **1 :** a person or thing that loses especially consistently **2 a :** a person who is incompetent or unable to succeed **b** ◆ **:** something doomed to fail or disappoint

◆ bummer, bust, catastrophe, debacle, dud, failure, fiasco, fizzle, flop, lemon, turkey, washout

loss \ˈlȯs\ *n* **1** ◆ **:** the state or fact of being destroyed **:** RUIN **2 :** the harm resulting from losing **3** ◆ **:** something that is lost **4** *pl* **:** killed, wounded, or captured soldiers **5** ◆ **:** failure to win **6 :** an amount by which the cost exceeds the selling price **7** ◆ **:** decrease in amount or degree **8 :** the act of losing possession

◆ [1] annihilation, demolition, desolation, destruction, devastation, havoc, obliteration, ruin, wastage, wreckage ◆ [3] casualty, fatality, victim ◆ [5] defeat, rout, shellacking ◆ [7] abatement, decline, decrease, decrement, diminution, drop, fall, reduction, shrinkage

loss leader *n* **:** an article sold at a loss in order to draw customers

lost \ˈlȯst\ *adj* **1 :** not used, won, or claimed **2** ◆ **:** no longer possessed or known **3 :** ruined or destroyed physically or morally **4 :** DENIED; *also* **:** HARDENED **5 :** unable to find the way; *also* **:** HELPLESS **6 :** ABSORBED, RAPT **7 :** not appreciated or understood ⟨his jokes were ~ on me⟩

◆ gone, missing *Ant* owned, possessed, retained

lot \ˈlät\ *n* **1 :** an object used in deciding something by chance; *also* **:** the use of lots to decide something **2 a :** SHARE, PORTION **b** ◆ **:** one's way of life or worldly fate **:** FORTUNE **3** ◆ **:** a plot of land **4** ◆ **:** a group of individuals **5** ◆ **:** a considerable quantity

◆ [2b] circumstance, destiny, doom, fate, fortune, portion ◆ [3] parcel, plat, plot, property, tract ◆ [4] array, batch, body, bunch, cluster, crop, group, huddle, knot, parcel, party ◆ [5] abundance, barrel, bucket, bushel, chunk, deal, gobs, heap, loads, mass, mess, mountain, much, oodles, pile, plenty, profusion, quantity, reams, scads, stack, wad, wealth *Ant* bit, hint, little, pinch, smidgen, speck, spot, touch, trace

loth *var of* LOATH

lo•tion \ˈlō-shən\ *n* **:** a liquid preparation for cosmetic and external medicinal use

lot•tery \ˈlä-tə-rē\ *n, pl* **-ter•ies 1 :** a drawing of lots in which prizes are given to the winning names or numbers **2 :** a matter determined by chance

lo•tus \ˈlō-təs\ *n* **1 :** a fruit held in Greek legend to cause dreamy contentment and forgetfulness **2 :** any of various water lilies represented especially in ancient Egyptian and Hindu art **3 :** any of several leguminous forage plants

loud \ˈlau̇d\ *adj* **1** ◆ **:** marked by intensity or volume of sound **2 :** CLAMOROUS, NOISY **3** ◆ **:** obtrusive or offensive in color or pattern ⟨a ~ suit⟩ — **loud** *adv* — **loud•ly** *adv* — **loud•ness** *n*

◆ [1] booming, clamorous (*or* clamourous), deafening, ear-splitting, piercing, resounding, ringing, roaring, sonorous, stentorian, thunderous *Ant* gentle, low, soft ◆ [3] flamboyant, flashy, garish, gaudy, glitzy, ostentatious, swank, tawdry

loud•mouthed \-ˌmau̇tht, -ˌmau̇t͟hd\ *adj* **:** given to loud offensive talk

loud•speak•er \-ˌspē-kər\ *n* **:** a device that changes electrical signals into sound

[1]**lounge** \ˈlau̇nj\ *vb* **lounged; loung•ing** ◆ **:** to act or move lazily or listlessly

◆ bask, loll, relax, repose, rest ◆ dally, dawdle, dillydally, hang around, hang out, idle, loaf, loll

[2]**lounge** *n* **1 :** a room with comfortable furniture; *also* **:** a room (as in a theater) with lounging, smoking, and toilet facilities **2** ◆ **:** a long couch

◆ couch, davenport, divan, settee, sofa

lour, loury *var of* LOWER, LOWERY

louse \ˈlau̇s\ *n, pl* **lice** \ˈlīs\ **1 :** any of various small wingless usually flattened insects parasitic on warm-blooded animals **2 :** a plant pest (as an aphid) **3** *pl* **lous•es** ◆ **:** a contemptible person

◆ beast, boor, churl, clown, creep, cretin, cur, heel, jerk, joker, lout, skunk, slob, snake

lousy \ˈlau̇-zē\ *adj* **lous•i•er; -est 1 :** infested with lice **2** ◆ **:** miserably poor or inferior **3 :** amply supplied ⟨~ with money⟩ **4** ◆ **:** totally repulsive — **lous•i•ly** \-zə-lē\ *adv* — **lous•i•ness** \-zē-nəs\ *n*

◆ [2] atrocious, awful, bad, deficient, inferior, off, poor, punk, rotten, substandard, terrible, unacceptable, unsatisfactory, wanting, wretched, wrong ◆ [4] contemptible, despicable, nasty, pitiful, scabby, scurvy, sorry, wretched

lout \ˈlau̇t\ *n* ◆ **:** a stupid awkward fellow

◆ clod, hulk, lubber, lug, oaf

lout•ish *adj* ◆ **:** resembling or befitting a lout — **lout•ish•ly** *adv*

◆ boorish, churlish, clownish, uncouth

lou•ver *or* **lou•vre** \ˈlü-vər\ *n* **1 :** an opening having parallel slanted slats to allow flow of air but to exclude rain or sun or to provide privacy; *also* **:** a slat in such an opening **2 :** a device with movable slats for controlling the flow of air or light

lov•able \ˈlə-və-bəl\ *adj* ◆ **:** having qualities that attract affection

◆ adorable, darling, dear, endearing, precious, sweet, winning *Ant* abhorrent, abominable, detestable, hateful, odious, unlovable

[1]**love** \ˈləv\ *n* **1** ◆ **:** strong affection **2** ◆ **:** warm attachment ⟨~ of the sea⟩ **3 :** attraction based on sexual desire **4** ◆ **:** a beloved person **5 :** unselfish loyal and benevolent concern for others **6 :** a score of zero in tennis — **love•less** *adj*

◆ [1] appetite, fancy, favor (*or* favour), fondness, like, liking, partiality, preference, relish, shine, taste, use ◆ [2] affection, attachment, devotion, fondness, passion *Ant* abomination, hate, hatred, loathing, rancor ◆ [4] beloved, darling, dear, flame, honey, sweet, sweetheart

[2]**love** *vb* **loved; lov•ing 1** ◆ **:** to value highly **:** CHERISH **2** ◆ **:** to feel a lover's passion, devotion, or tenderness for **3** ◆ **:** to touch or stroke lightly in a loving or endearing manner **:** CARESS **4** ◆ **:** to like or desire actively ⟨~*s* to play bridge⟩

◆ [1] appreciate, cherish, prize, treasure, value ◆ [2] adore, cherish, worship *Ant* abhor, abominate, despise, detest, execrate, hate, loathe ◆ [3] caress, fondle, pat, pet, stroke ◆ [4] adore, delight, dig, enjoy, fancy, groove, like, relish, revel

love affair *n* ◆ **:** a romantic attachment or episode between lovers

◆ affair, amour, romance

love•bird \ˈləv-ˌbərd\ *n* **:** any of various small usually gray or green parrots that seem to show caring behavior for their mates

loved *adj* ◆ **:** held dear

◆ beloved, darling, dear, favorite (*or* favourite), pet, precious, special, sweet

love•li•ness *n* ◆ **:** the quality or state of being lovely

◆ attractiveness, beauty, comeliness, handsomeness, looks, prettiness

love•lorn \-ˌlȯrn\ *adj* **:** deprived of love or of a lover

love•ly \ˈləv-lē\ *adj* **love•li•er; -est** ◆ **:** delightful for beauty, harmony, or grace **:** BEAUTIFUL — **love•li•ly** \ˈləv-lə-lē\ *adv* — **lovely** *adv*

◆ attractive, beautiful, cute, fair, gorgeous, handsome, knockout, pretty, ravishing, stunning

love•mak•ing \-ˌmā-kiŋ\ *n* **1 :** COURTSHIP **2 :** sexual activity; *esp* **:** COPULATION

lov•er *n* ◆ **:** a person in love; *also* **:** an ardent follower, supporter, or enthusiast (as of a religion, art form, or sport)

◆ addict, aficionado, buff, bug, devotee, enthusiast, fan, fanatic, fancier, fiend, freak, maniac, nut

love•sick \-ˌsik\ *adj* **1 :** YEARNING **2 :** expressing a lover's longing — **love•sick•ness** *n*

lov•ing \ˈlə-viŋ\ *adj* **1** ◆ **:** having affection or warm regard **:** AFFECTIONATE **2 :** PAINSTAKING — **lov•ing•ly** *adv*

◆ affectionate, devoted, fond, tender, tenderhearted *Ant* unloving

[1]**low** \ˈlō\ *vb* **:** MOO

[2]**low** *n* **:** MOO

[3]**low** *adj* **low•er** \ˈlō-ər\; **low•est** \ˈlō-əst\ **1 :** not high or tall ⟨~ wall⟩; *also* **:** DÉCOLLETÉ **2 :** situated or passing below the normal level or surface ⟨~ ground⟩; *also* **:** marking a nadir **3** ◆ **:** not loud ⟨~ voice⟩ **4 :** being near the equator **5 a** ◆ **:** humble in status **b** ◆ **:** lacking in cultural advancement **c** ◆ **:** lacking in dignity **6** ◆ **:** lacking strength, health, or vitality **:** WEAK; *also* **:** DEPRESSED **7 :** STRICKEN, PROSTRATE **8** ◆ **:** less than usual in

number, amount, or value; *also* **:** of lesser degree than average **9 :** falling short of a standard **10 :** UNFAVORABLE — **low** *adv*

♦ [3] dull, quiet, soft ♦ [5a] common, humble, ignoble, inferior, lowly, mean, plebeian, vulgar ♦ [5b] crude, primitive, rude, rudimentary ♦ [5b] coarse, common, crass, crude, gross, ill-bred, rough, rude, tasteless, uncouth, uncultivated, uncultured, unpolished, unrefined, vulgar ♦ [5c] base, contemptible, despicable, detestable, dirty, dishonorable (*or* dishonourable), ignoble, mean, snide, sordid, vile, wretched ♦ [6] blue, dejected, depressed, down, downcast, glum, melancholy, sad, sorrowful, sorry, unhappy, woeful, wretched ♦ [6] faint, feeble, frail, infirm, unsubstantial, weak ♦ [8] cheap, cut-rate, reasonable

⁴low *n* **1 :** something that is low **2 :** a region of low barometric pressure **3 :** the arrangement of gears in an automobile transmission that gives the slowest speed and greatest power

low•ball \ˈlō-ˌbȯl\ *vb* **:** to give a deceptively low price, cost estimate, or offer to

low beam *n* **:** a vehicle headlight beam with short-range focus

low blow *n* **:** an unprincipled attack

low•brow \ˈlō-ˌbrau̇\ *adj* **:** having little taste or intellectual interest — **lowbrow** *n*

low–density lipoprotein *n* **:** LDL

low•down \-ˌdau̇n\ *n* ♦ **:** pertinent and especially guarded information

♦ dope, scoop, tip

low–down \-ˌdau̇n\ *adj* **1 :** MEAN, CONTEMPTIBLE **2 :** deeply emotional

low–end \-ˌend\ *adj* **:** of, relating to, or being the lowest-priced merchandise in a manufacturer's line

¹low•er \ˈlau̇-ər\ *vb* **1** ♦ **:** to look sullen **:** FROWN **2 :** to become dark, gloomy, and threatening

♦ frown, glare, gloom, glower, scowl

²low•er \ˈlō-ər\ *adj* **1** ♦ **:** relatively low (as in rank) **2 :** situated beneath the earth's surface **3 :** constituting the popular and more representative branch of a bicameral legislative body **4 :** less advanced in the scale of evolutionary development

♦ inferior, junior, less, lesser, minor, subordinate, under

³low•er \ˈlō-ər\ *vb* **1** ♦ **:** to move down **:** DROP; *also* **:** DIMINISH **2 :** to let descend by its own weight; *also* **:** to reduce the height of **3** ♦ **:** to reduce or decline in value, number, or amount **4** ♦ **:** to bring down in quality or character **:** DEGRADE; *also* **:** HUMBLE

♦ [1] decline, descend, diminish, dip, drop, fall, plummet, plunge, sink, tumble ♦ [3] abate, de-escalate, decrease, diminish, downsize, dwindle, lessen, reduce ♦ [4] abase, debase, degrade, demean, discredit, disgrace, dishonor (*or* dishonour), humble, humiliate, shame, smirch, take down

low•er•case \ˌlō-ər-ˈkās\ *adj* **:** being a letter that belongs to or conforms to the series a, b, c, etc., rather than A, B, C, etc. — **lowercase** *n*

lower class *n* **:** a social class occupying a position below the middle class and having the lowest status in a society — **lower–class** \-ˈklas\ *adj*

low•er•most \ˈlō-ər-ˌmōst\ *adj* **:** LOWEST

low•ery \ˈlau̇-ə-rē\ *adj* **:** GLOOMY, LOWERING

lowest common denominator *n* **1 :** LEAST COMMON DENOMINATOR **2 :** something designed to appeal to a lowbrow audience; *also* **:** such an audience

lowest common multiple *n* **:** LEAST COMMON MULTIPLE

low–key \ˈlō-ˈkē\ *also* **low–keyed** \-ˈkēd\ *adj* **:** of low intensity **:** RESTRAINED

low•land \ˈlō-lənd, -ˌland\ *n* **:** low and usually level country

low–lev•el \ˈlō-ˈle-vəl\ *adj* **1 :** being of low importance or rank **2 :** being or relating to nuclear waste of low concentration

low•life \ˈlō-ˌlīf\ *n, pl* **low•lifes** \-ˌlīfs\ *also* **low•lives** \-ˌlīvz\ **:** a person of low social status or moral character

low•li•ness *n* ♦ **:** the quality or state of being lowly

♦ humbleness, humility, meekness, modesty

low•ly \ˈlō-lē\ *adj* **low•li•er; -est 1** ♦ **:** humble in manner or spirit **:** MEEK **2** ♦ **:** ranking low in some hierarchy

♦ [1] demure, humble, meek, modest, retiring, unassuming, unpretentious ♦ [2] common, humble, ignoble, inferior, low, mean, plebeian, vulgar

low•ness *n* ♦ **:** the quality or state of being low

♦ debility, delicacy, enfeeblement, faintness, feebleness, frailty, infirmity, languor, weakness ♦ coarseness, grossness, indelicacy, rudeness, vulgarity

low–rise \ˈlō-ˈrīz\ *adj* **1 :** having few stories and not equipped with elevators ⟨a ~ building⟩ **2 :** of, relating to, or characterized by low-rise buildings

low–slung \ˈlō-ˌsləŋ\ *adj* **:** relatively low to the ground or floor ⟨a ~ building⟩ ⟨~ pants⟩

low–tech \ˈlō-ˈtek\ *adj* **:** technologically simple or unsophisticated

¹lox \ˈläks\ *n* **:** liquid oxygen

²lox *n, pl* **lox** *or* **lox•es :** salmon cured in brine and sometimes smoked

loy•al \ˈlȯi-əl\ *adj* **1 :** faithful in allegiance to one's government **2** ♦ **:** faithful especially to a cause or ideal **:** CONSTANT — **loy•al•ly** \ˈlȯi-ə-lē\ *adv*

♦ constant, devoted, faithful, fast, good, pious, staunch, steadfast, steady, true, true-blue

loy•al•ist \ˈlȯi-ə-list\ *n* **:** one who is or remains loyal to a political party, government, or sovereign

loy•al•ty \ˈlȯi-əl-tē\ *n* ♦ **:** the quality or state or an instance of being loyal

♦ allegiance, constancy, dedication, devotion, faith, faithfulness, fastness, fealty, fidelity, steadfastness

loz•enge \ˈlä-zənj\ *n* **1 :** a diamond-shaped figure **2 :** a small flat often medicated candy

LP *abbr* low pressure

LPG *abbr* liquefied petroleum gas

LPGA *abbr* Ladies Professional Golf Association

LPN \ˈel-ˈpē-ˈen\ *n* **:** LICENSED PRACTICAL NURSE

Lr *symbol* Lawrencium

LSD \ˌel-(ˌ)es-ˈdē\ *n* **:** an illicit and highly potent hallucinogenic drug derived from ergot or produced synthetically

lt *abbr* light

Lt *abbr* lieutenant

LT *abbr* long ton

LTC *or* **Lt Col** *abbr* lieutenant colonel

Lt Comdr *abbr* lieutenant commander

ltd *abbr* limited

LTG *or* **Lt Gen** *abbr* lieutenant general

LTJG *abbr* lieutenant, junior grade

ltr *abbr* letter

Lu *symbol* lutetium

lu•au \ˈlü-ˌau̇\ *n* **:** a Hawaiian feast

lub *abbr* lubricant; lubricating

lub•ber \ˈlə-bər\ *n* **1** ♦ **:** a big clumsy fellow **:** LOUT **2 :** an unskilled seaman

♦ clod, hulk, lout, lug, oaf

lub•ber•ly *adj* ♦ **:** resembling or having the characteristics of a lubber

♦ awkward, clumsy, gawky, graceless, heavy-handed, lumpish, ungainly, unhandy

lube \ˈlüb\ *n* **:** LUBRICANT; *also* **:** an application of a lubricant

lu•bri•cant \ˈlü-bri-kənt\ *n* **:** a material capable of reducing friction when applied between moving parts

lu•bri•cate \ˈlü-brə-ˌkāt\ *vb* **-cat•ed; -cat•ing** ♦ **:** to apply a lubricant to — **lu•bri•ca•tion** \ˌlü-brə-ˈkā-shən\ *n* — **lu•bri•ca•tor** \ˈlü-brə-ˌkā-tər\ *n*

♦ grease, oil, slick, wax

lu•bri•cious \lü-ˈbri-shəs\ *or* **lu•bri•cous** \ˈlü-bri-kəs\ *adj* **1 :** SMOOTH, SLIPPERY **2 :** LECHEROUS; *also* **:** SALACIOUS — **lu•bric•i•ty** \lü-ˈbri-sə-tē\ *n*

lu•cent \ˈlüs-ᵊnt\ *adj* **1** ♦ **:** glowing with light **:** LUMINOUS **2** ♦ **:** marked by clarity or translucence **:** CLEAR — **lu•cent•ly** *adv*

♦ [1] beaming, bright, brilliant, effulgent, glowing, incandescent, lambent, lucid, luminous, lustrous, radiant, refulgent, shiny ♦ [2] clear, limpid, liquid, pellucid, transparent

lu•cerne \lü-ˈsərn\ *n, chiefly Brit* **:** ALFALFA

lu•cid \ˈlü-səd\ *adj* **1 :** suffused with light **:** SHINING **2** ♦ **:** mentally sound **3** ♦ **:** easily understood — **lu•cid•ly** *adv*

♦ [2] balanced, clearheaded, normal, right, sane, stable ♦ [3] apparent, broad, clear, clear-cut, distinct, evident, manifest, obvious, palpable, patent, perspicuous, plain, transparent, unambiguous, unequivocal, unmistakable

lu•cid•i•ty \lü-ˈsi-də-tē\ *n* ♦ **:** clearness of thought or style

♦ clarity, explicitness, perspicuity, simplicity

lu•cid•ness *n* **:** the quality or state of being lucid especially in thought or style

Lu•ci•fer \ˈlü-sə-fər\ *n* **:** DEVIL, SATAN

¹luck \ˈlək\ *n* **1** ♦ **:** a force that brings good fortune or adversity **:** CHANCE **2** ♦ **:** good fortune

♦ [1] accident, chance, circumstance, hazard ♦ [2] chance, fortune *Ant* mischance, misfortune

²luck *vb* **1 :** to prosper or succeed especially through chance or good fortune — usually used with *out* **2 :** to come upon something desirable by chance — usually used with *out, on, onto,* or *into*
luck•i•ly \ˈlə-kə-lē\ *adv* **1 :** in a lucky manner **2 :** FORTUNATELY 2
luck•less *adj* ♦ **:** being without luck

♦ hapless, ill-fated, ill-starred, unfortunate, unhappy, unlucky

lucky \ˈlə-kē\ *adj* **luck•i•er; -est 1** ♦ **:** favored by luck **:** FORTUNATE **2** ♦ **:** happening by chance **:** FORTUITOUS **3 :** seeming to bring good luck — **luck•i•ness** *n*

♦ [1] blessed, fortunate, happy *Ant* hapless, ill-fated, ill-starred, luckless, unfortunate, unlucky ♦ [2] fluky, fortuitous, fortunate, happy, providential

lu•cra•tive \ˈlü-krə-tiv\ *adj* ♦ **:** producing wealth **:** PROFITABLE — **lu•cra•tive•ly** *adv* — **lu•cra•tive•ness** *n*

♦ fat, gainful, profitable, remunerative

lu•cre \ˈlü-kər\ *n* ♦ **:** monetary gain **:** PROFIT; *also* **:** MONEY

♦ earnings, gain, net, payoff, proceeds, profit, return ♦ cash, currency, dough, money, pelf, tender

lu•cu•bra•tion \ˌlü-kyə-ˈbrā-shən, -kə-\ *n* **:** laborious study **:** MEDITATION
Ludd•ite \ˈlə-ˌdīt\ *n* **:** one who is opposed to technological change
lu•di•crous \ˈlü-də-krəs\ *adj* ♦ **:** amusing or laughable through obvious absurdity, incongruity, exaggeration, or eccentricity **:** RIDICULOUS; *also* **:** meriting derisive laughter or scorn as absurdly inept, false, or foolish — **lu•di•crous•ly** *adv* — **lu•di•crous•ness** *n*

♦ antic, comic, droll, funny, hilarious, humorous, hysterical, laughable, riotous, screaming, uproarious ♦ absurd, comical, derisive, farcical, laughable, preposterous, ridiculous, risible, silly

luff \ˈləf\ *vb* **:** to turn the head of a ship toward the wind
¹lug \ˈləg\ *vb* **lugged; lug•ging 1** ♦ **:** to draw slowly or heavily **:** DRAG, PULL **2** ♦ **:** to carry laboriously

♦ [1] drag, draw, hale, haul, pull, tow, tug ♦ [2] bear, carry, cart, convey, ferry, haul, pack, tote, transport

²lug *n* **1 :** a projecting piece (as for fastening, support, or traction) **2 :** a nut securing a wheel on an automobile **3** ♦ **:** a big clumsy fellow

♦ clod, hulk, lout, lubber, oaf

lug•gage \ˈlə-gij\ *n* **:** containers (as suitcases) for carrying personal belongings **:** BAGGAGE
lu•gu•bri•ous \lü-ˈgü-brē-əs\ *adj* ♦ **:** mournful often to an exaggerated degree — **lu•gu•bri•ous•ly** *adv* — **lu•gu•bri•ous•ness** *n*

♦ dolorous, funeral, mournful, plaintive, regretful, rueful, sorrowful, weeping, woeful

Luke \ˈlük\ *n* **:** a book of the New Testament of Christian Scripture
luke•warm \ˈlük-ˈwȯrm\ *adj* **1 :** moderately warm **:** TEPID **2 :** not enthusiastic — **luke•warm•ly** *adv*
¹lull \ˈləl\ *vb* **1** ♦ **:** to make peaceful **:** SOOTHE, CALM **2 :** to cause to relax vigilance

♦ allay, calm, compose, quiet, settle, soothe, still, tranquilize

²lull *n* **1 :** a temporary calm (as during a storm) **2** ♦ **:** a temporary drop in activity

♦ break, breath, breather, interruption, pause

lul•la•by \ˈlə-lə-ˌbī\ *n, pl* **-bies :** a song to lull children to sleep
lum•ba•go \ˌləm-ˈbā-gō\ *n* **:** acute or chronic pain in the lower back
lum•bar \ˈləm-bər, -ˌbär\ *adj* **:** of, relating to, or constituting the loins or the vertebrae between the thoracic vertebrae and sacrum ⟨~ region⟩
¹lum•ber \ˈləm-bər\ *vb* **1** ♦ **:** to move heavily or clumsily **2** ♦ **:** to make a low heavy rolling sound

♦ [1] clump, flounder, lump, plod, scuff, scuffle, shamble, shuffle, stamp, stomp, stumble, tramp, tromp *Ant* breeze, coast, glide, slide, waltz, whisk ♦ [2] growl, grumble, roll, rumble

²lumber *n* **1 :** surplus or disused articles that are stored away **2 :** timber or logs especially when dressed for use
³lumber *vb* **1 :** to cut logs; *also* **:** to saw logs into lumber **2** ♦ **:** to clutter with or as if with lumber — **lum•ber•man** \-mən\ *n*

♦ burden, encumber, load, saddle, weight

lum•ber•jack \-ˌjak\ *n* **:** LOGGER
lum•ber•yard \-ˌyärd\ *n* **:** a place where lumber is kept for sale
lu•mi•nary \ˈlü-mə-ˌner-ē\ *n, pl* **-nar•ies 1** ♦ **:** a very famous person **2 :** a source of light; *esp* **:** a celestial body

♦ celebrity, figure, light, notable, personage, personality, somebody, standout, star, superstar, VIP

lu•mi•nes•cence \ˌlü-mə-ˈnes-ᵊns\ *n* ♦ **:** the low-temperature emission of light (as by a chemical or physiological process); *also* **:** such light — **lu•mi•nes•cent** \-ᵊnt\ *adj*

♦ blaze, flare, fluorescence, glare, gleam, glow, illumination, incandescence, light, radiance, shine

lu•mi•nos•i•ty \ˌlü-mə-ˈnä-sə-tē\ *n* ♦ **:** the quality or state of being luminous

♦ brilliance, dazzle, effulgence, illumination, lightness, lucidity, radiance, refulgence, splendor

lu•mi•nous \ˈlü-mə-nəs\ *adj* **1** ♦ **:** emitting light; *also* **:** LIGHTED **2 :** CLEAR, INTELLIGIBLE **3 :** ILLUSTRIOUS — **lu•mi•nance** \-nəns\ *n* — **lu•mi•nous•ly** *adv*

♦ beaming, bright, brilliant, effulgent, glowing, incandescent, lambent, lucent, lucid, lustrous, radiant, refulgent, shiny

lum•mox \ˈlə-məks\ *n* **:** a clumsy person
¹lump \ˈləmp\ *n* **1** ♦ **:** a piece or mass of indefinite size and shape **2 :** AGGREGATE, TOTALITY **3** ♦ **:** a usually abnormal swelling

♦ [1] blob, chunk, clod, clump, glob, gob, hunk, nub, wad ♦ [3] excrescence, growth, neoplasm, tumor ♦ [3] bump, knot, nodule, swelling

²lump *vb* **1** ♦ **:** to heap together in a lump **2 :** to form into lumps **3 :** to move noisily and clumsily

♦ accumulate, amass, assemble, collect, concentrate, garner, gather, group, pick up, round up, scrape

³lump *adj* **:** not divided into parts ⟨a ~ sum⟩
lump•ec•to•my \ˌləm-ˈpek-tə-mē\ *n, pl* **-mies :** excision of a breast tumor
lump•ish *adj* ♦ **:** lacking ease or grace (as of movement or expression)

♦ awkward, clumsy, gawky, graceless, heavy-handed, lubberly, ungainly, unhandy

lumpy *adj* ♦ **:** filled or covered with lumps

♦ broken, bumpy, coarse, irregular, jagged, pebbly, ragged, rough, rugged, uneven

lu•na•cy \ˈlü-nə-sē\ *n, pl* **-cies 1** ♦ **:** a deranged state of the mind **:** INSANITY **2** ♦ **:** extreme folly; *also* **:** a foolish act

♦ [1] aberration, dementia, derangement, insanity, madness, mania ♦ [2] absurdity, fatuity, folly, foolery, foolishness, idiocy, inanity, madness, stupidity

lu•nar \ˈlü-nər\ *adj* **:** of or relating to the moon
lu•nate \ˈlü-ˌnāt\ *adj* **:** shaped like a crescent
¹lu•na•tic \ˈlü-nə-ˌtik\ *adj* **1 a :** affected with lunacy **:** INSANE **b :** used for insane persons **2** ♦ **:** extremely foolish

♦ absurd, crazy, cuckoo, fatuous, foolish, mad, nonsensical, nutty, senseless, silly, stupid

²lunatic *n* ♦ **:** a person affected with lunacy; *also* **:** one capable of crazy actions or extravagances

♦ maniac, nut, psychotic

¹lunch \ˈlənch\ *n* **1 :** a light meal usually eaten in the middle of the day **2 :** the food prepared for a lunch
²lunch *vb* **:** to eat lunch
lun•cheon \ˈlən-chən\ *n* **:** a usually formal lunch
lun•cheon•ette \ˌlən-chə-ˈnet\ *n* **:** a small restaurant serving light lunches
lunch•room \ˈlənch-ˌrüm, -ˌru̇m\ *n* **1 :** LUNCHEONETTE **2 :** a room (as in a school) where lunches are sold and eaten or lunches brought from home may be eaten
lu•nette \lü-ˈnet\ *n* **:** something shaped like a crescent

lung \ˈləŋ\ *n* **1 :** one of the usually paired baglike breathing organs in the chest of an air-breathing vertebrate **2 :** a mechanical device to promote breathing and make it easier — **lunged** \ˈləŋd\ *adj*
lunge \ˈlənj\ *n* **1 :** a sudden thrust or pass (as with a sword) **2 :** a sudden forward stride or leap — **lunge** *vb*
lu•pine \ˈlü-pən\ *n* **:** any of a genus of leguminous plants with long upright clusters of pealike flowers
lu•pus \ˈlü-pəs\ *n* **:** any of several diseases characterized by skin lesions; *esp* **:** SYSTEMIC LUPUS ERYTHEMATOSUS
¹lurch \ˈlərch\ *n* **:** a sudden swaying or tipping movement
²lurch *vb* ♦ **:** to roll or tip abruptly; *also* **:** to move with a lurch

♦ careen, pitch, rock, roll, seesaw, sway, toss, wobble ♦ careen, dodder, reel, stagger, teeter, totter

¹lure \ˈlu̇r\ *n* **1** ♦ **:** an inducement to pleasure or gain **:** ENTICEMENT; *also* **:** APPEAL **2 :** an artificial bait for catching fish

♦ appeal, attraction, bait, call, decoy, enticement, incentive, inducement, persuasion, seduction, snare, spur, temptation, trap

²lure *vb* **lured; lur•ing** ♦ **:** to draw on with a promise of pleasure or gain

♦ allure, beguile, decoy, entice, lead on, seduce, tempt

lu•rid \ˈlu̇r-əd\ *adj* **1** ♦ **:** wan and ghostly pale in appearance **2 :** shining with the red glow of fire seen through smoke or cloud **3 a** ♦ **:** causing horror or revulsion **:** GRUESOME **b :** SENSATIONAL — **lu•rid•ly** *adv*

♦ [1] ashen, cadaverous, livid, pale, pasty, peaked ♦ [3a] appalling, atrocious, awful, dreadful, frightful, ghastly, grisly, gruesome, hideous, horrible, horrid, macabre, monstrous, nightmarish, shocking, terrible

lurk \ˈlərk\ *vb* **1** ♦ **:** to move furtively **:** SNEAK **2 :** to lie concealed

♦ pussyfoot, skulk, slide, slink, slip, snake, sneak, steal

lus•cious \ˈlə-shəs\ *adj* **1** ♦ **:** having a pleasingly sweet taste or smell **2** ♦ **:** sensually appealing — **lus•cious•ly** *adv*

♦ [1] agreeable, ambrosial, appetizing, delectable, delicious, delightful, enjoyable, flavorful (*or* flavourful), palatable, savory, scrumptious, tasty, toothsome, yummy ♦ [2] carnal, fleshly, sensual, sensuous, voluptuous

lus•cious•ness *n* ♦ **:** the quality or state of being luscious

♦ savor, tastiness

¹lush \ˈləsh\ *adj* ♦ **:** having or covered with abundant growth ⟨~ pastures⟩

♦ green, leafy, luxuriant, verdant ***Ant*** barren, leafless

²lush *n* **:** an habitual heavy drinker
¹lust \ˈləst\ *n* **1 :** usually intense or unbridled sexual desire **:** LASCIVIOUSNESS **2** ♦ **:** an intense longing

♦ appetite, craving, desire, drive, hankering, hunger, itch, longing, passion, thirst, urge, yearning, yen

²lust *vb* ♦ **:** to have an intense desire or need

♦ *usu* **lust for** *or* **lust after** ache for, covet, crave, desire, die for, hanker for, hunger for, long for, pine for, repine for, thirst for, want, wish for, yearn for

lus•ter *or* **lus•tre** \ˈləs-tər\ *n* **1** ♦ **:** a shine or sheen especially from reflected light **2 :** BRIGHTNESS, GLITTER **3 :** GLORY, SPLENDOR

♦ gloss, polish, sheen, shine

lus•ter•less *adj* ♦ **:** lacking luster

♦ dim, dull, flat

lust•ful *adj* ♦ **:** excited by lust

♦ lascivious, lewd, passionate, wanton

lust•i•ness \-tē-nəs\ *n* ♦ **:** the quality or state of being lusty

♦ animation, briskness, exuberance, liveliness, robustness, sprightliness, vibrancy, vitality

lus•tral \ˈləs-trəl\ *adj* **:** serving or intended to purify
lus•trous \-trəs\ *adj* ♦ **:** reflecting light evenly and efficiently without glitter or sparkle

♦ beaming, bright, brilliant, effulgent, glowing, incandescent, lambent, lucent, lucid, luminous, radiant, refulgent, shiny ♦ glossy, polished, satiny, sleek

lusty \ˈləs-tē\ *adj* **lust•i•er; -est 1** ♦ **:** full of vitality **:** ROBUST **2** ♦ **:** full of energy or activity — **lust•i•ly** \ˈləs-tə-lē\ *adv*

♦ [1] dynamic, energetic, flush, peppy, robust, strenuous, vigorous, vital ♦ [2] firm, forceful, hearty, robust, solid, stout, strong, sturdy, vigorous

lute \ˈlüt\ *n* **:** a stringed musical instrument with a large pear-shaped body and a fretted fingerboard — **lu•te•nist** *or* **lu•ta•nist** \ˈlüt-ᵊn-ist\ *n*
lu•te•tium *also* **lu•te•cium** \lü-ˈtē-shē-əm, -shəm\ *n* **:** a metallic chemical element
Lu•ther•an \ˈlü-thə-rən\ *n* **:** a member of a Protestant denomination adhering to the doctrines of Martin Luther — **Lu•ther•an•ism** \-rə-ˌni-zəm\ *n*
lux•u•ri•ant \ˌləg-ˈzhu̇r-ē-ənt, ˌlək-ˈshu̇r-\ *adj* **1** ♦ **:** yielding or growing abundantly **:** LUSH, PRODUCTIVE **2 :** abundantly rich and varied; *also* **:** FLORID **3 :** characterized by luxury — **lux•u•ri•ance** \-ē-əns\ *n* — **lux•u•ri•ant•ly** *adv*

♦ green, leafy, lush, verdant ♦ fat, fecund, fertile, fruitful, productive, prolific, rich

lux•u•ri•ate \-ē-ˌāt\ *vb* **-at•ed; -at•ing 1 :** to grow profusely **2 :** REVEL
lux•u•ri•ous \ˌləg-ˈzhu̇r-ē-əs, ˌlək-ˈshu̇r-\ *adj* ♦ **:** of, relating to, or marked by luxury

♦ deluxe, lavish, luxuriant, opulent, palatial, plush, sumptuous ***Ant*** ascetic, austere, humble

lux•u•ri•ous•ly *adv* ♦ **:** in a luxurious manner

♦ expensively, extravagantly, grandly, high, lavishly, opulently, richly

¹lux•u•ry \ˈlək-shə-rē, ˈləg-zhə-\ *n, pl* **-ries 1 :** great ease and comfort **2** ♦ **:** something adding to pleasure or comfort but not absolutely necessary

♦ amenity, comfort, extra, frill, indulgence, superfluity ***Ant*** basic, essential, fundamental, necessity, requirement

²luxury *adj* ♦ **:** of or relating to luxury or luxuries or catering to luxurious tastes

♦ deluxe, lavish, luxuriant, luxurious, opulent, palatial, plush, sumptuous

lv *abbr* leave
LWV *abbr* League of Women Voters
¹-ly \lē\ *adj suffix* **1 :** like in appearance, manner, or nature ⟨queen*ly*⟩ **2 :** characterized by regular recurrence in (specified) units of time **:** every ⟨hour*ly*⟩
²-ly *adv suffix* **1 :** in a (specified) manner ⟨slow*ly*⟩ **2 :** from a (specified) point of view ⟨grammatical*ly*⟩
ly•ce•um \lī-ˈsē-əm, ˈlī-sē-\ *n* **1 :** a hall for public lectures **2 :** an association providing public lectures, concerts, and entertainments
ly•chee *or* **li•tchi** \ˈlē-chē\ *n* **1 :** an oval fruit with a hard scaly outer covering, a small hard seed, and edible flesh **2 :** an Asian tree bearing lychees
lye \ˈlī\ *n* **:** a corrosive alkaline substance used especially in making soap
ly•ing \ˈlī-iŋ\ *adj* ♦ **:** marked by or containing falsehoods **:** UNTRUTHFUL

♦ dishonest, mendacious

ly•ing–in \ˌlī-iŋ-ˈin\ *n, pl* **lyings–in** *or* **lying–ins :** the state during and consequent to childbirth **:** CONFINEMENT
Lyme disease \ˈlīm-\ *n* **:** an acute inflammatory disease that is caused by a spirochete transmitted by ticks, is characterized usually by chills and fever, and if left untreated may result in joint pain, arthritis, and cardiac and neurological disorders
lymph \ˈlimf\ *n* **:** a usually clear fluid consisting chiefly of blood plasma and white blood cells, circulating in thin-walled tubes (**lymphatic vessels**), and bathing the body tissues — **lym•phat•ic** \lim-ˈfa-tik\ *adj*
lymph•ade•nop•a•thy \ˌlim-ˌfad-ᵊn-ˈä-pə-thē\ *n, pl* **-thies :** abnormal enlargement of the lymph nodes
lymph node *n* **:** any of the rounded masses of lymphoid tissue surrounded by a capsule
lym•pho•cyte \ˈlim-fə-ˌsīt\ *n* **:** any of the white blood cells arising from lymphoid tissue that are typically found in lymph and blood and that include the cellular mediators (as a B cell or a T cell) of immunity — **lym•pho•cyt•ic** \ˌlim-fə-ˈsi-tik\ *adj*
lym•phoid \ˈlim-ˌfȯid\ *adj* **1 :** of, relating to, or being tissue (as of the lymph nodes) containing lymphocytes **2 :** of, relating to, or resembling lymph

lym•pho•ma \lim-ˈfō-mə\ *n, pl* **-mas** *or* **-ma•ta** \-mə-tə\ **:** a usually malignant tumor of lymphoid tissue

lynch \ˈlinch\ *vb* **:** to put to death by mob action without legal sanction or due process of law — **lynch•er** *n*

lynx \ˈliŋks\ *n, pl* **lynx** *or* **lynx•es :** any of several wildcats with a short tail, long legs, and usually tufted ears

lyre \ˈlīr\ *n* **:** a stringed musical instrument of the harp class having a U-shaped frame and used by the ancient Greeks

[1]**lyr•ic** \ˈlir-ik\ *n* **1** ♦ **:** a lyric poem **2 :** the words of a popular song — often used in plural

♦ poem, song, verse

[2]**lyric** *adj* **1** ♦ **:** suitable for singing **:** MELODIC **2** ♦ **:** expressing direct and usually intense personal emotion

♦ [1] euphonious, mellifluous, mellow, melodic, melodious, musical ♦ [2] bardic, lyrical, poetic

lyr•i•cal \-i-kəl\ *adj* ♦ **:** having qualities suggestive of music or poetry **:** LYRIC

♦ bardic, lyric, poetic

ly•ser•gic acid di•eth•yl•am•ide \lə-ˈsər-jik . . . ˌdī-ˌe-thə-ˈla-ˌmīd, lī-, -ˈla-məd\ *n* **:** LSD

LZ *abbr* landing zone

M

[1]**m** \ˈem\ *n, pl* **m's** *or* **ms** \ˈemz\ *often cap* **:** the 13th letter of the English alphabet

[2]**m** *abbr, often cap* **1** Mach **2** male **3** married **4** masculine **5** medium **6** noon **7** meter **8** mile **9** thousand **10** minute **11** month **12** moon

ma \ˈmä, ˈmȯ\ *n* **:** a female parent **:** MOTHER

♦ mom, mommy, mother

MA *abbr* **1** master of arts **2** Massachusetts **3** mental age

ma'am \ˈmam, *after "yes" often* əm\ *n* **:** MADAM

Mac *abbr* Machabees

Mac *or* **Macc** *abbr* Maccabees

ma•ca•bre \mə-ˈkäb; -ˈkä-brə, -bər\ *adj* **1 :** having death as a subject **2 :** dwelling on the gruesome **3** ♦ **:** tending to produce horror in a beholder

♦ appalling, atrocious, awful, dreadful, frightful, ghastly, grisly, gruesome, hideous, horrible, horrid, lurid, monstrous, nightmarish, shocking, terrible

mac•ad•am \mə-ˈka-dəm\ *n* **:** a roadway or pavement of small closely packed broken stone — **mac•ad•am•ize** \-də-ˌmīz\ *vb*

mac•a•da•mia nut \ˌma-kə-ˈdā-mē-ə\ *n* **:** a hard-shelled richly-flavored nut of any of several Australian trees

ma•caque \mə-ˈkak, -ˈkäk\ *n* **:** any of a genus of short-tailed chiefly Asian monkeys; *esp* **:** RHESUS MONKEY

mac•a•ro•ni \ˌma-kə-ˈrō-nē\ *n* **1 :** pasta made chiefly of wheat flour and shaped in the form of slender tubes **2** *pl* **-nis** *or* **-nies :** FOP, DANDY

mac•a•roon \ˌma-kə-ˈrün\ *n* **:** a small cookie made chiefly of egg whites, sugar, and ground almonds or coconut

ma•caw \mə-ˈkȯ\ *n* **:** any of numerous parrots of Central and So. America

Mac•ca•bees \ˈma-kə-ˌbēz\ *n* **:** either of two books of Scripture in the Roman Catholic canon and the Protestant Apocrypha

[1]**mace** \ˈmās\ *n* **:** a spice made from the fibrous coating of the nutmeg

[2]**mace** *n* **1 :** a heavy often spiked club used as a weapon especially in the Middle Ages **2 :** an ornamental staff carried as a symbol of authority

Mac•e•do•nian \ˌma-sə-ˈdō-nyən, -nē-ən\ *n* **:** a native or inhabitant of Macedonia — **Macedonian** *adj*

mac•er•ate \ˈma-sə-ˌrāt\ *vb* **-at•ed; -at•ing 1 :** to cause to waste away **2 :** to soften by steeping or soaking so as to separate the parts — **mac•er•a•tion** \ˌma-sə-ˈrā-shən\ *n*

Mac•Guf•fin *or* **Mc•Guf•fin** \mə-ˈgə-fən\ *n* **:** an object, event, or character whose main purpose is to advance the plot of a motion picture

mach *abbr* machine; machinery; machinist

Mach \ˈmäk\ *n* **:** a speed expressed by a Mach number

Mach•a•bees \ˈma-kə-ˌbēz\ *n* **:** MACCABEES

ma•chete \mə-ˈshe-tē\ *n* **:** a large heavy knife used for cutting sugarcane and underbrush and as a weapon

Ma•chi•a•vel•lian \ˌma-kē-ə-ˈve-lē-ən\ *adj* ♦ **:** characterized by cunning, duplicity, and bad faith — **Ma•chi•a•vel•lian•ism** *n*

♦ cutthroat, immoral, unconscionable, unethical, unprincipled, unscrupulous

mach•i•nate \ˈma-kə-ˌnāt, ˈma-shə-\ *vb* ♦ **:** to plan or plot especially to do harm

♦ conspire, contrive, intrigue, plot, scheme ♦ contrive, finagle, finesse, frame, maneuver (*or* manoeuvre), mastermind, negotiate, wangle

mach•i•na•tion \ˌma-kə-ˈnā-shən, ˌma-shə-\ *n* ♦ **:** an act of planning especially to do harm; *esp* **:** PLOT

♦ conspiracy, design, intrigue, plot, scheme

[1]**ma•chine** \mə-ˈshēn\ *n* **1** ♦ **:** an automotive vehicle not operated on rails; *esp* **:** AUTOMOBILE **2 :** a combination of mechanical parts that transmit forces, motion, and energy one to another **3 :** an instrument (as a lever) for transmitting or modifying force or motion **4 :** an electrical, electronic, or mechanical device for performing a task ⟨a sewing ~⟩ **5 :** a highly organized political group under the leadership of a boss or small clique

♦ automobile, car, motor vehicle

[2]**machine** *vb* **ma•chined; ma•chin•ing :** to shape or finish by machine-operated tools — **ma•chin•able** \-ˈshē-nə-bəl\ *adj*

machine gun *n* **:** an automatic gun capable of rapid continuous firing — **machine–gun** *vb* — **machine gunner** *n*

machine language *n* **:** the set of symbolic instruction codes used to represent operations and data in a machine (as a computer)

machine–readable *adj* **:** directly usable by a computer

ma•chin•ery \mə-ˈshē-nə-rē\ *n, pl* **-er•ies 1 :** MACHINES; *also* **:** the working parts of a machine **2** ♦ **:** the means by which something is done

♦ agency, agent, instrument, instrumentality, means, medium, organ, vehicle

ma•chin•ist \mə-ˈshē-nist\ *n* **:** a person who makes or works on machines

ma•chis•mo \mä-ˈchēz-(ˌ)mō, -ˈchiz-\ *n* **:** a strong or exaggerated pride in one's masculinity

Mach number \ˈmäk-\ *n* **:** a number representing the ratio of the speed of a body (as an aircraft) to the speed of sound in the surrounding atmosphere

ma•cho \ˈmä-chō\ *adj* **:** characterized by machismo

mack•er•el \ˈma-kə-rəl\ *n, pl* **mackerel** *or* **mackerels :** a No. Atlantic food fish greenish above and silvery below

mack•i•naw \ˈma-kə-ˌnȯ\ *n* **:** a short heavy plaid coat

mack•in•tosh *also* **mac•in•tosh** \ˈma-kən-ˌtäsh\ *n* **1** *chiefly Brit* **:** RAINCOAT **2 :** a lightweight waterproof fabric

mac•ra•mé *also* **mac•ra•me** \ˈma-krə-ˌmā\ *n* **:** a coarse lace or fringe made by knotting threads or cords in a geometrical pattern

[1]**mac•ro** \ˈma-(ˌ)krō\ *adj* **:** very large; *also* **:** involving large quantities or being on a large scale

[2]**macro** *n, pl* **macros :** a single computer instruction that stands for a sequence of operations

mac•ro•bi•ot•ic \ˌma-krō-bī-ˈä-tik, -bē-\ *adj* **:** relating to or being a very restricted diet (as one containing chiefly whole cereals or grains)

mac•ro•cosm \ˈma-krə-ˌkä-zəm\ *n* ♦ **:** the great world **:** UNIVERSE

♦ cosmos, creation, nature, universe, world

ma•cron \ˈmā-ˌkrän, ˈma-\ *n* **:** a mark {macr} placed over a vowel (as in māk) to show that the vowel is long

mac•ro•scop•ic \ˌma-krə-ˈskä-pik\ *adj* **:** visible to the naked eye — **mac•ro•scop•i•cal•ly** \-pi-k(ə-)lē\ *adv*

mac•u•la \ˈma-kyə-lə\ *n, pl* **-lae** \-ˌlē, -ˌlī\ *also* **-las :** an anatomical spot distinguishable from surrounding tissues — **mac·u·lar** \-lər\ *adj*

mad \ˈmad\ *adj* **mad·der; mad·dest** **1** ♦ **:** disordered in mind **:** INSANE **2** ♦ **:** being rash and foolish **3** ♦ **:** carried away by intense anger **:** FURIOUS, ENRAGED ⟨~ at myself⟩ ⟨~ about the delay⟩ **4** ♦ **:** carried away by enthusiasm or desire ⟨~ about horses⟩ ⟨~ for the boy next door⟩ **5 :** RABID **6 :** marked by wild gaiety and merriment **7** ♦ **:** intensely excited **:** FRANTIC **8** ♦ **:** marked by intense and often chaotic activity **:** WILD

♦ [1, 2] absurd, crazy, cuckoo, fatuous, foolish, mad, nonsensical, nutty, senseless, silly, stupid ♦ [3] angry, boiling, enraged, furious, irate, rabid, sore, wrathful ♦ *usu* **mad about** [4] crazy, nuts ♦ [7, 8] delirious, feverish, fierce, frantic, frenetic, frenzied, furious, rabid, violent, wild

Mad·a·gas·can \ˌma-də-ˈgas-kən\ *n* **:** a native or inhabitant of Madagascar

mad·am \ˈma-dəm\ *n* **1** *pl* **mes·dames** \mā-ˈdäm\ — used as a form of polite address to a woman **2** *pl* **madams :** the female head of a house of prostitution

ma·dame \mə-ˈdam, *before a surname also* ˈma-dəm\ *n, pl* **mes·dames** \mā-ˈdäm\ **:** MISTRESS — used as a title equivalent to *Mrs.* for a married woman not of English-speaking nationality

[1]**mad·cap** \ˈmad-ˌkap\ *adj* ♦ **:** marked by capriciousness, recklessness, or foolishness — **madcap** *n*

♦ brash, foolhardy, overbold, overconfident, reckless

[2]**madcap** *n* ♦ **:** one who is madcap

♦ daredevil, devil

mad cow disease : a fatal disease of the brain of cattle affecting the nervous system and probably caused by infected tissue in food

mad·den \ˈmad-ᵊn\ *vb* ♦ **:** to make mad

♦ craze, derange, unhinge ♦ anger, antagonize, enrage, incense, inflame, infuriate, outrage, rankle, rile, roil

mad·den·ing *adj* ♦ **:** tending to infuriate or irritate — **mad·den·ing·ly** *adv*

♦ aggravating, annoying, galling, irritating

mad·der \ˈma-dər\ *n* **:** a Eurasian herb with yellow flowers and fleshy red roots; *also* **:** its root or a dye prepared from it

made *past and past part of* MAKE

Ma·dei·ra \mə-ˈdir-ə\ *n* **:** an amber-colored dessert wine

ma·de·moi·selle \ˌma-də-mə-ˈzel, -mwə-, mam-ˈzel\ *n, pl* **ma·de·moi·selles** \-ˈzelz\ *or* **mes·de·moi·selles** \ˌmā-də-me-ˈzel, -mwe-\ **:** an unmarried girl or woman — used as a title for an unmarried woman not of English-speaking nationality

made–to–measure *adj* **:** CUSTOM-MADE

made–up \ˈmā-ˈdəp\ *adj* **1** ♦ **:** fancifully conceived or falsely devised **2 :** marked by the use of makeup

♦ chimerical, fabulous, fanciful, fantastic, fictitious, imaginary, mythical, phantom, pretend, unreal

mad·house \ˈmad-ˌhau̇s\ *n* **1 :** a place for the detention and care of the insane **2** ♦ **:** a place of great uproar

♦ bedlam, circus, hell

mad·ly \ˈmad-lē\ *adv* **1** ♦ **:** in a mad manner **2 :** to an extreme or excessive degree

♦ amok, berserk, frantically, harum-scarum, hectically, helter≈skelter, pell-mell, wild, wildly

mad·man \ˈmad-ˌman, -mən\ *n* **:** LUNATIC

mad·ness \ˈmad-nəs\ *n* **1** ♦ **:** the quality or state of being mad **2** ♦ **:** lack of good sense or judgment

♦ [1] aberration, dementia, derangement, insanity, lunacy, mania ♦ [2] absurdity, asininity, balminess, craziness, daftness, fatuity, folly, foolishness, inanity, insanity, lunacy, silliness, simplicity, zaniness

Ma·don·na \mə-ˈdä-nə\ *n* **:** a representation (as a picture or statue) of the Virgin Mary

ma·dras \ˈma-drəs; ˌmə-ˈdras, -ˈdräs\ *n* **:** a fine usually cotton fabric with various designs (as plaid)

ma·dras·sa *or* **ma·dra·sa** \mə-ˈdra-sə, -ˈdrä-\ *n* **:** a Muslim school, college, or university that is often part of a mosque

mad·ri·gal \ˈma-dri-gəl\ *n* **1 :** a short lyrical poem in a strict poetic form **2 :** an elaborate part-song especially of the 16th and 17th centuries

mad·wom·an \ˈmad-ˌwu̇-mən\ *n* **:** a woman who is insane

mael·strom \ˈmāl-strəm\ *n* **1 :** a violent whirlpool **2 :** TUMULT

mae·stro \ˈmī-strō\ *n, pl* **maestros** *or* **mae·stri** \-ˌstrē\ **1** ♦ **:** a master in an art **2 :** an eminent composer, conductor, or teacher of music

♦ ace, adept, artist, authority, crackerjack, expert, master, scholar, shark, virtuoso, whiz, wizard

Ma·fia \ˈmä-fē-ə\ *n* **:** a secret criminal society of Sicily or Italy; *also* **:** a similar organization elsewhere

ma·fi·o·so \ˌmä-fē-ˈō-(ˌ)sō\ *n, pl* **-si** \-(ˌ)sē\ **:** a member of the Mafia

[1]**mag** \ˈmag\ *n* **:** MAGAZINE

[2]**mag** *abbr* **1** magnetism **2** magneto **3** magnitude

mag·a·zine \ˈma-gə-ˌzēn\ *n* **1** ♦ **:** a storehouse especially for military supplies **2 :** a place for keeping gunpowder in a fort or ship **3 :** a publication usually containing stories, articles, or poems and issued periodically **4 :** a container in a gun for holding cartridges; *also* **:** a chamber (as on a camera) for film

♦ armory, arsenal, depot, dump

ma·gen·ta \mə-ˈjen-tə\ *n* **:** a deep purplish red color

mag·got \ˈma-gət\ *n* **:** the legless wormlike larva of a dipteran fly — **mag·goty** *adj*

ma·gi \ˈmā-jī\ *n pl, often cap* **:** the three wise men from the East who paid homage to the infant Jesus

[1]**mag·ic** \ˈma-jik\ *n* **1 :** the use of means (as charms or spells) believed to have supernatural power over natural forces **2 a** ♦ **:** an extraordinary power or influence seemingly from a supernatural force **b** ♦ **:** something that seems to cast a spell **3** ♦ **:** the art of producing illusions by sleight of hand

♦ [2a] bewitchment, enchantment, necromancy, sorcery, witchcraft, wizardry ♦ [2b] allure, appeal, attractiveness, captivation, charisma, charm, enchantment, fascination, glamour, magnetism ♦ [3] legerdemain, prestidigitation

[2]**magic** *adj* **1 :** of or relating to magic **2** ♦ **:** having unusually distinctive qualities resembling the supernatural

♦ magical, mystic, occult, weird

mag·i·cal \ˈma-ji-kəl\ *adj* **1 :** of or relating to magic **2** ♦ **:** resembling magic; *also* **:** giving a feeling of enchantment — **mag·i·cal·ly** \-ji-k(ə-)lē\ *adv*

♦ miraculous, phenomenal, superhuman, supernatural, uncanny, unearthly

ma·gi·cian \mə-ˈji-shən\ *n* ♦ **:** a person skilled in magic

♦ conjurer, enchanter, necromancer, sorcerer, voodoo, witch, wizard ♦ conjurer, illusionist, trickster

mag·is·te·ri·al \ˌma-jə-ˈstir-ē-əl\ *adj* **1 :** AUTHORITATIVE **2 :** of or relating to a magistrate or a magistrate's office or duties

ma·gis·tral \ˈma-jə-strəl\ *adj* **:** AUTHORITATIVE

mag·is·trate \ˈma-jə-ˌstrāt\ *n* ♦ **:** an official entrusted with administration of the laws — **mag·is·tra·cy** \-strə-sē\ *n*

♦ bench, court, judge, justice

mag·lev \ˈmag-lev\ *n* **1 :** the use of magnetic fields to float an object above a solid surface **2 :** a train using maglev technology

mag·ma \ˈmag-mə\ *n* **:** molten rock material within the earth — **mag·mat·ic** \mag-ˈma-tik\ *adj*

mag·nan·i·mous \mag-ˈna-nə-məs\ *adj* **1 :** showing or suggesting a lofty and courageous spirit **2** ♦ **:** showing or suggesting nobility of feeling and generosity of mind — **mag·na·nim·i·ty** \ˌmag-nə-ˈni-mə-tē\ *n* — **mag·nan·i·mous·ness** *n*

♦ chivalrous, gallant, great, greathearted, high, high-minded, lofty, lordly, noble, sublime

mag·nan·i·mous·ly \-lē\ *adv* ♦ **:** in a magnanimous manner

♦ gallantly, grandly, greatly, heroically, honorably (*or* honourably), nobly

mag·nate \ˈmag-ˌnāt\ *n* ♦ **:** a person of rank, influence, or distinction

♦ baron, czar, king, mogul, prince, tycoon

mag·ne·sia \mag-ˈnē-shə, -zhə\ *n* **:** a light white oxide of magnesium used as a laxative

mag·ne·sium \mag-ˈnē-zē-əm, -zhəm\ *n* **:** a silver-white light malleable metallic chemical element

mag·net \ˈmag-nət\ *n* **1 :** LODESTONE **2 :** a body that is able to attract iron **3** ♦ **:** something that attracts

♦ attraction, draw, lodestone

mag·net·ic \mag-ˈne-tik\ *adj* **1** ♦ **:** having an unusual ability to attract ⟨a ~ leader⟩ **2 :** of or relating to a magnet or magnetism **3 :** magnetized or capable of being magnetized — **mag·net·i·cal·ly** \-ti-k(ə-)lē\ *adv*

♦ alluring, attractive, captivating, charming, elfin, engaging, fascinating, fetching, glamorous, seductive

magnetic disk *n* : DISK 3
magnetic levitation *n* : MAGLEV 1
magnetic north *n* : the northerly direction in the earth's magnetic field indicated by the north-seeking pole of a compass needle
magnetic resonance imaging *n* : a noninvasive diagnostic technique that produces computerized images of internal body tissues based on electromagnetically induced activity of atoms within the body
magnetic tape *n* : a ribbon coated with a magnetic material on which information (as sound) may be stored
mag•ne•tise *chiefly Brit var of* MAGNETIZE
mag•ne•tism \ˈmag-nə-ˌti-zəm\ *n* **1** : the power (as of a magnet) to attract iron **2** : the science that deals with magnetic phenomena **3** ♦ : an ability to attract or charm

♦ allure, appeal, attractiveness, captivation, charisma, charm, enchantment, fascination, glamour, magic

mag•ne•tite \ˈmag-nə-ˌtīt\ *n* : a black mineral that is an important iron ore
mag•ne•tize \ˈmag-nə-ˌtīz\ *vb* **-tized; -tiz•ing** **1** : to induce magnetic properties in **2** : to attract like a magnet : CHARM — **mag•ne•tiz•able** *adj* — **mag•ne•ti•za•tion** \ˌmag-nə-tə-ˈzā-shən\ *n* — **mag•ne•tiz•er** *n*
mag•ne•to \mag-ˈnē-tō\ *n, pl* **-tos** : a generator used to produce sparks in an internal combustion engine
mag•ne•tom•e•ter \ˌmag-nə-ˈtä-mə-tər\ *n* : an instrument for measuring the strength of a magnetic field
mag•ne•to•sphere \mag-ˈnē-tə-ˌsfir, -ˈne-\ *n* : a region around a celestial object (as the earth) in which charged particles are trapped by its magnetic field — **mag•ne•to•spher•ic** \-ˌnē-tə-ˈsfir-ik, -ˈsfer-\ *adj*
mag•ni•fi•ca•tion \ˌmag-nə-fə-ˈkā-shən\ *n* **1** ♦ : the act of magnifying **2** : the amount by which an optical lens or instrument magnifies

♦ caricature, elaboration, embellishment, exaggeration, hyperbole, overstatement, padding

mag•nif•i•cence \mag-ˈni-fə-səns\ *n* **1** ♦ : the quality or state of being magnificent **2** : splendor of surroundings

♦ augustness, brilliance, glory, grandeur, grandness, majesty, nobility, nobleness, resplendence, splendor, stateliness

mag•nif•i•cent \mag-ˈni-fə-sənt\ *adj* **1** ♦ : characterized by grandeur or beauty : SPLENDID **2** : EXALTED, NOBLE — **mag•nif•i•cent•ly** *adv*

♦ august, baronial, gallant, glorious, grand, grandiose, heroic, imposing, majestic, monumental, noble, proud, regal, royal, splendid, stately

mag•nif•i•co \mag-ˈni-fi-ˌkō\ *n, pl* **-coes** *or* **-cos** **1** : a nobleman of Venice **2** : a person of high position
mag•ni•fy \ˈmag-nə-ˌfī\ *vb* **-fied; -fy•ing** **1 a** : to praise highly : EXTOL, LAUD **b** ♦ : to cause to be held in greater esteem **2 a** ♦ : to increase in significance : INTENSIFY **b** ♦ : to enlarge beyond bounds or the truth : EXAGGERATE **3** : to enlarge in fact or in appearance ⟨a microscope *magnifies* an object⟩ — **mag•ni•fi•er** \ˈmag-nə-ˌfī-ər\ *n*

♦ [1b] aggrandize, dignify, ennoble, exalt, glorify ♦ [2a] amplify, beef, boost, consolidate, deepen, enhance, heighten, intensify, redouble, step up, strengthen ♦ [2b] color (*or* colour), elaborate, embellish, embroider, exaggerate, pad, stretch

mag•nil•o•quent \mag-ˈni-lə-kwənt\ *adj* : characterized by an exalted and often bombastic style or manner — **mag•nil•o•quence** \-kwəns\ *n*
mag•ni•tude \ˈmag-nə-ˌtüd, -ˌtyüd\ *n* **1** ♦ : greatness of size or extent **2** ♦ : spatial quality : SIZE **3** : QUANTITY **4** : a number representing the brightness of a celestial body **5** ♦ : the importance, quality, or caliber of something **6** : a number representing the intensity of an earthquake

♦ [1] enormity, hugeness, immensity, massiveness, vastness ♦ [2] dimension, extent, measure, measurement, proportion, size ♦ [5] consequence, import, moment, significance, weight

mag•no•lia \mag-ˈnōl-yə\ *n* : any of a genus of usually spring-flowering shrubs and trees with large often fragrant flowers
mag•num opus \ˈmag-nəm-ˈō-pəs\ *n* : the greatest achievement of an artist or writer
mag•pie \ˈmag-ˌpī\ *n* **1** : any of various long-tailed often black-and-white birds related to the jays **2** ♦ : a person who chatters noisily

♦ chatterbox, jabberer, talker

Mag•yar \ˈmag-ˌyär, ˈmäg-; ˈmä-ˌjär\ *n* : a member of the dominant people of Hungary — **Magyar** *adj*
ma•ha•ra•ja *or* **ma•ha•ra•jah** \ˌmä-hə-ˈrä-jə\ *n* : a Hindu prince ranking above a raja
ma•ha•ra•ni *or* **ma•ha•ra•nee** \-ˈrä-nē\ *n* **1** : the wife of a maharaja **2** : a Hindu princess ranking above a rani
ma•ha•ri•shi \ˌmä-hə-ˈrē-shē\ *n* : a Hindu teacher of mystical knowledge
ma•hat•ma \mə-ˈhät-mə, -ˈhat-\ *n* : a person revered for high-mindedness, wisdom, and selflessness
Ma•hi•can \mə-ˈhē-kən\ *or* **Mo•hi•can** \mō-, mə-\ *n, pl* **-can** *or* **-cans** : a member of an American Indian people of the upper Hudson River valley
ma•hog•a•ny \mə-ˈhä-gə-nē\ *n, pl* **-nies** : the reddish wood of any of various chiefly tropical trees that is used in furniture; *also* : a tree yielding this wood
ma•hout \mə-ˈhau̇t\ *n* : a keeper and driver of an elephant
maid \ˈmād\ *n* **1** : an unmarried girl or young woman **2** ♦ : a female servant : MAIDSERVANT

♦ domestic, girl, housemaid, maidservant

[1]**maid•en** \ˈmād-ᵊn\ *n* ♦ : an unmarried girl or young woman : MAID — **maid•en•ly** *adj*

♦ doll, girl, lass, maid, miss

[2]**maiden** *adj* **1** : UNMARRIED; *also* : VIRGIN **2** : of, relating to, or befitting a maiden **3** ♦ : preceding all others in time or order : FIRST ⟨~ voyage⟩

♦ first, inaugural, initial, original, pioneer, premier

maid•en•hair fern \-ˌhar-\ *n* : any of a genus of ferns with delicate feathery fronds
maid•en•head \ˈmād-ᵊn-ˌhed\ *n* **1** : VIRGINITY **2** : HYMEN
maid•en•hood \-ˌhu̇d\ *n* : the condition or time of being a maiden
maid–in–waiting *n, pl* **maids–in–waiting** : a young woman appointed to attend a queen or princess
maid of honor : a bride's principal unmarried wedding attendant
maid•ser•vant \ˈmād-ˌsər-vənt\ *n* ♦ : a girl or woman who is a servant

♦ domestic, girl, housemaid, maid

[1]**mail** \ˈmāl\ *n* **1** ♦ : something sent or carried in the postal system **2** : a nation's postal system — often used in plural

♦ matter, parcel post, post, snail mail

[2]**mail** *vb* : to send by mail
[3]**mail** *n* : armor made of metal links or plates
mail•box \ˈmāl-ˌbäks\ *n* **1** : a public box for the collection of mail **2** : a private box for the delivery of mail
mail carrier *n* : LETTER CARRIER
mail•man \-ˌman\ *n* ♦ : a man who delivers mail

♦ letter carrier, postman

maim \ˈmām\ *vb* ♦ : to mutilate, disfigure, or wound seriously : CRIPPLE

♦ cripple, disable, lame, mutilate

[1]**main** \ˈmān\ *n* **1** ♦ : physical strength : FORCE ⟨with might and ~⟩ **2** : MAINLAND; *also* : HIGH SEA **3** ♦ : the chief part **4** : a principal pipe, duct, or circuit of a utility system

♦ [1] energy, force, might, muscle, potency, power, sinew, strength, vigor (*or* vigour) ♦ [3] body, bulk, core, generality, mass, staple, weight

[2]**main** *adj* **1** ♦ : of greatest importance or influence : CHIEF, PRINCIPAL **2** : fully exerted ⟨~ force⟩ **3** : expressing the chief predication in a complex sentence ⟨the ~ clause⟩

♦ arch, cardinal, central, chief, dominant, first, foremost, grand, key, paramount, predominant, preeminent, premier, primary, principal, sovereign, supreme

main•frame \ˈmān-ˌfrām\ *n* : a large fast computer
main•land \-ˌland, -lənd\ *n* : a continuous body of land constituting the chief part of a country or continent
main•line \-ˌlīn\ *vb, slang* : to inject a narcotic drug into a vein
main line *n* : a principal highway or railroad line
main•ly \ˈmān-lē\ *adv* ♦ : for the most part : CHIEFLY

♦ altogether, basically, chiefly, generally, largely, mostly, overall, predominantly, primarily, principally

main•mast \ˈmān-ˌmast, -məst\ *n* **:** the principal mast on a sailing ship
main•sail \-ˌsāl, -səl\ *n* **:** the largest sail on the mainmast
main•spring \-ˌspriŋ\ *n* **1 :** the chief spring in a mechanism (as of a watch) **2 :** the chief motive, agent, or cause
main•stay \-ˌstā\ *n* **1 :** a stay running from the head of the mainmast to the foot of the foremast **2** ♦ **:** a chief support

♦ buttress, dependence, pillar, reliance, standby, support

main•stream \-ˌstrēm\ *n* **:** a prevailing current or direction of activity or influence — **mainstream** *adj*
main•tain \mān-ˈtān\ *vb* **1** ♦ **:** to keep in an existing state (as of repair) **2** ♦ **:** to sustain against opposition or danger **3 :** to continue in **:** CARRY ON **4 :** to provide for **:** SUPPORT **5** ♦ **:** to affirm in or as if in argument **:** ASSERT

♦ [1] conserve, keep up, preserve, save ♦ [2] defend, justify, support, uphold ♦ [5] affirm, allege, argue, assert, aver, avouch, avow, claim, contend, declare, insist, profess, protest, warrant

main•tain•able \mān-ˈtā-nə-bəl\ *adj* ♦ **:** capable of being maintained — **main•tain•abil•i•ty** \-ˌtā-nə-ˈbi-lə-tē\ *n*

♦ defensible, justifiable, supportable, sustainable, tenable

main•te•nance \ˈmānt-ᵊn-əns\ *n* ♦ **:** the act of maintaining **:** the state of being maintained

♦ conservation, preservation, upkeep

main•top \ˈmān-ˌtäp\ *n* **:** a platform at the head of the mainmast of a square-rigged ship
mai•son•ette \ˌmāz-ᵊn-ˈet\ *n* **1 :** a small house **2 :** an apartment often on two floors
mai tai \ˈmī-ˌtī\ *n* **:** a cocktail made with liquors and fruit juices
maî•tre d' *or* **mai•tre d'** \ˌmā-trə-ˈdē, ˌme-\ *n, pl* **maître d's** *or* **maitre d's** \-ˈdēz\ **:** MAÎTRE D'HÔTEL
maî•tre d'hô•tel \ˌmā-trə-dō-ˈtel, ˌme-\ *n, pl* **maîtres d'hôtel** *same*\ **1 :** MAJORDOMO **2 :** HEADWAITER
maize \ˈmāz\ *n* **:** INDIAN CORN
Maj *abbr* major
ma•jes•tic \mə-ˈjes-tik\ *adj* ♦ **:** having or exhibiting majesty — **ma•jes•ti•cal•ly** \-ti-k(ə-)lē\ *adv*

♦ august, baronial, gallant, glorious, grand, grandiose, heroic, imposing, magnificent, monumental, noble, proud, regal, royal, splendid, stately

maj•es•ty \ˈma-jə-stē\ *n, pl* **-ties 1 :** sovereign power, authority, or dignity; *also* **:** the person of a sovereign — used as a title **2** ♦ **:** greatness or splendor of quality or character

♦ augustness, brilliance, glory, grandeur, grandness, magnificence, nobility, nobleness, resplendence, splendor, stateliness

Maj Gen *abbr* Major General
ma•jol•i•ca \mə-ˈjä-li-kə\ *also* **ma•iol•i•ca** \-ˈyä-\ *n* **:** any of several faiences; *esp* **:** an Italian tin-glazed pottery
¹ma•jor \ˈmā-jər\ *adj* **1** ♦ **:** greater in number, extent, or importance ⟨a ~ poet⟩ **2 :** notable or conspicuous in effect or scope ⟨a ~ improvement⟩ **3 :** SERIOUS ⟨a ~ illness⟩ **4 :** having half steps between the 3d and 4th and the 7th and 8th degrees ⟨~ scale⟩; *also* **:** based on a major scale ⟨~ key⟩ ⟨~ chord⟩

♦ big, consequential, eventful, important, material, meaningful, momentous, significant, substantial, weighty

²major *n* **1 :** a commissioned officer (as in the army) ranking next below a lieutenant colonel **2 :** an academic subject chosen as a field of specialization; *also* **:** a student specializing in such a field
³major *vb* **:** to pursue an academic major
ma•jor•do•mo \ˌmā-jər-ˈdō-mō\ *n, pl* **-mos 1 :** a head steward **2 :** BUTLER
ma•jor•ette \ˌmā-jə-ˈret\ *n* **:** DRUM MAJORETTE
major general *n* **:** a commissioned officer (as in the army) ranking next below a lieutenant general
ma•jor•i•ty \mə-ˈjȯr-ə-tē\ *n, pl* **-ties 1 :** the age at which full civil rights are accorded; *also* **:** the status of one who has attained this age **2 :** a number greater than half of a total; *also* **:** the excess of this greater number over the remainder **3 :** the rank of a major
ma•jus•cule \ˈma-jəs-ˌkyül, mə-ˈjəs-\ *n* **:** a large letter (as a capital)
Ma•kah \ˈmä-kä\ *n, pl* **Makah** *or* **Makahs :** a member of an American Indian people of the northwest coast of No. America
¹make \ˈmāk\ *vb* **made** \ˈmād\; **mak•ing 1 a** ♦ **:** to cause to exist, occur, or appear **b :** DESTINE ⟨was *made* to be an actor⟩ **2 a** ♦ **:** to bring into being by forming, shaping, or altering material ⟨~ a dress⟩ **b :** COMPOSE **3 :** to formulate in the mind ⟨~ plans⟩ **4** ♦ **:** to put together from components ⟨house *made* of stone⟩ **5** ♦ **:** to compute or estimate to be **6 :** to set in order **:** PREPARE ⟨~ a bed⟩ **7 :** to cause to be or become; *also* **:** APPOINT **8 a :** to establish by legal and authoritative act **:** ENACT **b :** EXECUTE ⟨~ a will⟩ **9 :** CONCLUDE ⟨didn't know what to ~ of it⟩ **10 a** ♦ **:** to carry out (an action indicated or implied by the object) ⟨~ war⟩ **b :** to perform with a bodily movement ⟨~ a gesture⟩ **11** ♦ **:** to cause to act in a certain way **:** COMPEL **12 :** to assure the success of ⟨will ~ us or break us⟩ **13 :** to amount to in significance ⟨~*s* no difference⟩ **14 :** to be capable of developing or being fashioned into **15 :** to reach as an end **:** ATTAIN; *also* **:** GAIN **16 :** to start out **:** GO **17 :** to have weight or effect ⟨courtesy ~*s* for safer driving⟩ **18 :** to act so as to be or to seem to be ⟨~ merry⟩ **19** ♦ **:** to gain (as money) by working, trading, or dealing — **mak•er** *n* — **make believe :** PRETEND — **make do :** to manage with the means at hand — **make fun of :** RIDICULE, MOCK — **make good 1 :** INDEMNIFY ⟨*make good* the loss⟩; *also* **:** to carry out successfully ⟨*make good* his promise⟩ **2 :** SUCCEED — **make way 1 :** to give room for passing, entering, or occupying **2 :** to make progress

♦ [1a] bring about, cause, create, effect, effectuate, generate, induce, produce, prompt, result, work, yield ♦ [2a] fabricate, fashion, form, frame, manufacture, produce ♦ [4] assemble, build, construct, erect, fabricate, make up, piece, put up, raise, rear, set up ♦ [5] calculate, call, conjecture, estimate, figure, gauge, guess, judge, place, put, reckon, suppose ♦ [10a] accomplish, achieve, carry out, commit, compass, do, execute, follow through, fulfill, perform ♦ [11] coerce, compel, constrain, drive, force, muscle, obligate, oblige, press, pressure ♦ [19] acquire, attain, capture, carry, draw, earn, gain, garner, get, land, obtain, procure, realize, secure, win

²make *n* **1 :** the manner or style of construction; *also* **:** BRAND 3 **2 :** MAKEUP **3 :** the action of manufacturing — **on the make :** in search of wealth, social status, or sexual adventure
¹make–be•lieve \ˈmāk-bə-ˌlēv\ *n* **:** a pretending that what is not real is real
²make–believe *adj* **:** existing only in the imagination
make–do \-ˌdü\ *adj* **:** MAKESHIFT
make out *vb* **1 :** to draw up in writing ⟨*make out* a list⟩ **2** ♦ **:** to find or grasp the meaning of ⟨can you *make* that *out*⟩ **3 :** to represent as being **4 :** to pretend to be true **5 :** DISCERN ⟨*make out* a ship in the fog⟩ **6** ♦ **:** to meet one's needs **:** GET ALONG, FARE ⟨*make out* well in life⟩ **7** ♦ **:** to engage in amorous kissing and caressing

♦ [2] appreciate, apprehend, catch, catch on (to), comprehend, get, grasp, make, perceive, see, seize, understand ♦ [6] cope, do, fare, get along, manage, shift ♦ [7] kiss, pet

make over *vb* **1** ♦ **:** to transfer the title of (property) **2** ♦ **:** to make anew or in a different form — **make•over** \ˈmā-ˌkō-vər\ *n*

♦ [1] alienate, assign, cede, deed, transfer ♦ [2] alter, change, convert, modify, recast, redo, refashion, remake, remodel, revamp, revise, rework, vary

¹make•shift \ˈmāk-ˌshift\ *n* **:** a temporary expedient
²makeshift *adj* **:** serving as a temporary expedient
make•up \ˈmā-ˌkəp\ *n* **1** ♦ **:** the way in which something is put together; *also* **:** physical, mental, and moral constitution **2 :** cosmetics especially for the face; *also* **:** materials (as wigs and cosmetics) used in making up

♦ arrangement, composition, configuration, design, form, format, layout, pattern

make up *vb* **1 a :** to form by fitting together or assembling **b** ♦ **:** to form the substance of **:** COMPOSE **2** ♦ **:** to compensate for (as a deficiency or omission) ⟨*make up* for lost time⟩ **3 :** SETTLE ⟨*made up* my mind⟩ **4** ♦ **:** to devise by thinking **:** INVENT, IMPROVISE **5 :** to become reconciled **6 :** to put on makeup (as for a play)

♦ [1b] compose, comprise, constitute, form ♦ *usu* **make up for** [2] annul, cancel, compensate, correct, counteract, counterbalance, neutralize, offset ♦ [4] concoct, contrive, cook up, devise, fabricate, invent, manufacture, think up

make–work \ˈmāk-ˌwərk\ *n* **:** BUSYWORK
mak•ings \ˈmā-kiŋz\ *n pl* **:** the material from which something is made
Mal *abbr* Malachi
Mal•a•chi \ˈma-lə-ˌkī\ *n* **:** a book of Jewish and Christian Scripture
Mal•a•chi•as \ˌma-lə-ˈkī-əs\ *n* **:** MALACHI
mal•a•chite \ˈma-lə-ˌkīt\ *n* **:** a mineral that is a green carbonate of copper used for making ornamental objects
mal•adapt•ed \ˌma-lə-ˈdap-təd\ *adj* **:** poorly suited to a particular use, purpose, or situation

mal•ad•just•ed \ˌma-lə-ˈjəs-təd\ *adj* **:** poorly or inadequately adjusted (as to one's environment) — **mal•ad•just•ment** \-ˈjəst-mənt\ *n*

mal•adroit \ˌma-lə-ˈdrȯit\ *adj* ♦ **:** not adroit **:** INEPT

♦ awkward, clumsy, inept, inexpert

mal•a•dy \ˈma-lə-dē\ *n, pl* **-dies** ♦ **:** a disease or disorder of body or mind

♦ ailment, bug, complaint, condition, disease, disorder, fever, ill, illness, infirmity, sickness, trouble

mal•aise \mə-ˈlāz, ma-\ *n* **:** a hazy feeling of not being well

mal•a•mute \ˈma-lə-ˌmyüt\ *n* **:** a dog often used to draw sleds especially in northern No. America

mal•a•prop•ism \ˈma-lə-ˌprä-ˌpi-zəm\ *n* **:** a usually humorous misuse of a word

mal•ap•ro•pos \ˌma-ˌla-prə-ˈpō, ma-ˈla-prə-ˌpō\ *adv* **:** in an inappropriate or inopportune way — **malapropos** *adj*

ma•lar•ia \mə-ˈler-ē-ə\ *n* **:** a disease marked by recurring chills and fever and caused by a protozoan parasite of the blood that is transmitted by anopheles mosquitoes — **ma•lar•i•al** \-əl\ *adj*

ma•lar•key \mə-ˈlär-kē\ *n* **:** insincere or foolish talk

mal•a•thi•on \ˌma-lə-ˈthī-ən, -ˌän\ *n* **:** an insecticide with a relatively low toxicity for mammals

Ma•la•wi•an \mə-ˈlä-wē-ən\ *n* **:** a native or inhabitant of Malawi — **Malawian** *adj*

Ma•lay \mə-ˈlā, ˈmā-ˌlā\ *n* **1 :** a member of a people of the Malay Peninsula and Archipelago **2 :** the language of the Malays — **Malay** *adj* — **Ma•lay•an** \mə-ˈlā-ən, ˈmā-ˌlā-\ *n or adj*

Ma•lay•sian \mə-ˈlā-zhən, -shən\ *n* **:** a native or inhabitant of Malaysia — **Malaysian** *adj*

mal•con•tent \ˌmal-kən-ˈtent\ *adj* ♦ **:** marked by a dissatisfaction with the existing state of affairs **:** DISCONTENTED — **malcontent** *n*

♦ aggrieved, discontent, discontented, dissatisfied

mal de mer \ˌmal-də-ˈmer\ *n* **:** SEASICKNESS

[1]**male** \ˈmāl\ *adj* **1 :** of, relating to, or being the sex that produces germ cells which fertilize the eggs of a female; *also* **:** STAMINATE **2** ♦ **:** of, relating to, or characteristic of the male sex — **maleness** *n*

♦ man-size, manly, mannish, masculine, virile

[2]**male** *n* ♦ **:** a male individual

♦ buck, chap, dude, fellow, gent, gentleman, guy, hombre, jack, joker, lad, man

male•dic•tion \ˌma-lə-ˈdik-shən\ *n* ♦ **:** a prayer or invocation for harm or injury to come upon one **:** CURSE, EXECRATION

♦ anathema, curse, execration, imprecation

mal•e•fac•tion \ˌma-lə-ˈfak-shən\ *n* ♦ **:** an evil deed

♦ breach, crime, error, misdeed, misdoing, offense, sin, transgression, trespass, violation, wrongdoing

male•fac•tor \ˈma-lə-ˌfak-tər\ *n* ♦ **:** one who does ill toward another; *esp* **:** one who commits an offense against the law

♦ criminal, crook, culprit, felon, lawbreaker, offender

ma•lef•ic \mə-ˈle-fik\ *adj* **1 :** BALEFUL **2 :** MALICIOUS

ma•lef•i•cent \-fə-sənt\ *adj* **:** working or productive of harm or evil

ma•lev•o•lence \mə-ˈle-və-ləns\ *n* **:** the quality or state of being malevolent

ma•lev•o•lent \mə-ˈle-və-lənt\ *adj* ♦ **:** having, showing, or arising from ill will, spite, or hatred

♦ catty, cruel, hateful, malicious, malign, malignant, mean, nasty, spiteful, virulent

mal•fea•sance \mal-ˈfēz-ᵊns\ *n* ♦ **:** wrongful conduct especially by a public official

♦ misbehavior, misconduct, misdoing, wrongdoing

mal•for•ma•tion \ˌmal-fȯr-ˈmā-shən\ *n* **:** irregular or faulty formation or structure; *also* **:** an instance of this

mal•formed \mal-ˈfȯrmd\ *adj* ♦ **:** characterized by malformation

♦ deformed, distorted, misshapen, monstrous, shapeless *Ant* shapely

mal•func•tion \mal-ˈfəŋk-shən\ *vb* **:** to fail to operate normally — **malfunction** *n*

Ma•li•an \ˈmä-lē-ən\ *n* **:** a native or inhabitant of Mali — **Malian** *adj*

mal•ice \ˈma-ləs\ *n* ♦ **:** desire to cause injury or distress to another

♦ cattiness, despite, hatefulness, malignity, meanness, nastiness, spite, spleen, venom, viciousness

ma•li•cious \mə-ˈli-shəs\ *adj* ♦ **:** given to, marked by, or arising from malice

♦ catty, cruel, hateful, malevolent, malign, malignant, mean, nasty, spiteful, virulent

ma•li•cious•ly \-lē\ *adv* ♦ **:** in a malicious manner

♦ hatefully, meanly, nastily, spitefully, viciously, wickedly

[1]**ma•lign** \mə-ˈlīn\ *adj* **1** ♦ **:** evil in nature, influence, or effect; *also* **:** MALIGNANT **2** ♦ **:** moved by ill will

♦ [1, 2] catty, cruel, hateful, malevolent, malicious, malignant, mean, nasty, spiteful, virulent

[2]**malign** *vb* ♦ **:** to speak evil of **:** DEFAME

♦ blacken, defame, libel, slander, smear, traduce, vilify

ma•lig•nan•cy \mə-ˈlig-nən-sē\ *n* **:** the quality or state of being malignant

ma•lig•nant \mə-ˈlig-nənt\ *adj* **1** ♦ **:** passionately and relentlessly malevolent **:** MALIGN **2 :** tending to produce death or deterioration ⟨a ~ tumor⟩

♦ catty, cruel, hateful, malevolent, malicious, malign, mean, nasty, spiteful, virulent

ma•lig•nant•ly \-lē\ *adv* **:** in a malignant manner

ma•lig•ni•ty \mə-ˈlig-nə-tē\ *n* ♦ **:** the quality or state of being malignant

♦ cattiness, despite, hatefulness, malice, meanness, nastiness, spite, spleen, venom, viciousness

ma•lin•ger \mə-ˈliŋ-gər\ *vb* **:** to pretend illness so as to avoid duty — **ma•lin•ger•er** *n*

mal•i•son \ˈma-lə-sən, -zən\ *n* **:** CURSE

mall \ˈmȯl, ˈmal\ *n* **1 :** a shaded walk **:** PROMENADE **2 :** an urban shopping area featuring a variety of shops surrounding a concourse **3 :** a usually large enclosed suburban shopping area containing various shops

mal•lard \ˈma-lərd\ *n, pl* **mallard** *or* **mallards :** a common wild duck that is the source of domestic ducks

mal•lea•ble \ˈma-lē-ə-bəl\ *adj* **1 :** capable of being extended or shaped by beating with a hammer or by the pressure of rollers **2 a** ♦ **:** capable of being altered or controlled by outside forces or influences **b :** having a capacity for adaptive change — **mal•le•a•bil•i•ty** \ˌma-lē-ə-ˈbi-lə-tē\ *n*

♦ adaptable, adjustable, changeable, elastic, flexible, fluid, variable

mal•let \ˈma-lət\ *n* **1 :** a tool with a large head for driving another tool or for striking a surface without marring it **2 :** a long-handled hammerlike implement for striking a ball (as in croquet)

mal•le•us \ˈma-lē-əs\ *n, pl* **mal•lei** \-lē-ˌī, -lē-ˌē\ **:** the outermost of the three small bones of the mammalian middle ear

mal•low \ˈma-lō\ *n* **:** any of a genus of herbs with lobed leaves, usually showy flowers, and a disk-shaped fruit

malm•sey \ˈmälm-zē\ *n, often cap* **:** the sweetest variety of Madeira

mal•nour•ished \mal-ˈnər-isht\ *adj* **:** UNDERNOURISHED

mal•nu•tri•tion \ˌmal-nü-ˈtri-shən, -nyü-\ *n* **:** faulty and especially inadequate nutrition

mal•oc•clu•sion \ˌma-lə-ˈklü-zhən\ *n* **:** faulty coming together of teeth in biting

mal•odor•ous \ma-ˈlō-də-rəs\ *adj* ♦ **:** ill-smelling — **mal•odor•ous•ly** *adv* — **mal•odor•ous•ness** *n*

♦ fetid, foul, fusty, musty, noisome, rank, reeky, smelly, strong *Ant* ambrosial, aromatic, fragrant, perfumed, redolent, savory, scented, sweet

mal•prac•tice \mal-ˈprak-təs\ *n* **:** a dereliction of professional duty or a failure of professional skill that results in injury, loss, or damage

malt \ˈmȯlt\ *n* **1 :** grain and especially barley steeped in water until it has sprouted and used in brewing and distilling **2 :** liquor made with malt — **malty** *adj*

malted milk \ˈmȯl-təd-\ *n* **:** a powder prepared from dried milk and an extract from malt; *also* **:** a beverage of this powder in milk or other liquid

Mal•thu•sian \mal-ˈthü-zhən, -ˈthyü-\ *adj* **:** of or relating to a theory that population unless checked (as by war) tends to increase faster than its means of subsistence — **Malthusian** *n* — **Mal•thu•sian•ism** \-zhə-ˌni-zəm\ *n*

malt•ose \ˈmȯl-ˌtōs\ *n* **:** a sugar formed especially from starch by the action of enzymes

mal•treat \mal-ˈtrēt\ *vb* ♦ **:** to treat cruelly or roughly — **mal•treat•ment** *n*

♦ abuse, ill-treat, manhandle, mishandle, mistreat, misuse

ma•ma *also* **mam•ma** \ˈmä-mə\ *n* **:** a female parent **:** MOTHER
mam•bo \ˈmäm-bō\ *n, pl* **mambos :** a dance of Cuban origin related to the rumba — **mambo** *vb*
mam•mal \ˈma-məl\ *n* **:** any of a class of warm-blooded vertebrates that includes humans and all other animals which nourish their young with milk and have the skin more or less covered with hair — **mam•ma•li•an** \mə-ˈmā-lē-ən, ma-\ *adj or n*
mam•ma•ry \ˈma-mə-rē\ *adj* **:** of, relating to, or being the glands (**mammary glands**) that in female mammals secrete milk
mam•mo•gram \ˈma-mə-ˌgram\ *n* **:** an X-ray photograph of the breasts
mam•mog•ra•phy \ma-ˈmä-grə-fē\ *n* **:** X-ray examination of the breasts (as for early detection of cancer)
mam•mon \ˈma-mən\ *n, often cap* **:** material wealth having a debasing influence
[1]**mam•moth** \ˈma-məth\ *n* **1 :** any of a genus of large hairy extinct elephants **2** ♦ **:** something immense of its kind

♦ behemoth, blockbuster, colossus, giant, jumbo, leviathan, monster, titan, whale, whopper

[2]**mammoth** *adj* **:** of very great size **:** GIGANTIC
[1]**man** \ˈman\ *n, pl* **men** \ˈmen\ **1 a** ♦ **:** a human being **b** ♦ **:** an adult male **2** ♦ **:** the human race **:** MANKIND **3 :** one possessing in high degree the qualities considered distinctive of manhood **4 :** an adult male servant or employee **5 :** the individual who can fulfill one's requirements ⟨he's your ~⟩ **6 :** one of the pieces with which various games (as chess) are played; *also* **:** one of the players on a team **7** *often cap* **:** white society or people ⟨having difficulty coping with the *Man*⟩ **8** ♦ **:** a male lover

♦ [1a] being, body, creature, human, individual, mortal, person ♦ [1b] buck, chap, dude, fellow, gent, gentleman, guy, hombre, jack, joker, lad, male ♦ [2] Homo sapiens, humanity, humankind, mankind ♦ [8] beau, boyfriend, fellow, swain

[2]**man** *vb* **manned; man•ning 1 :** to supply with men ⟨~ a fleet⟩ **2 :** FORTIFY, BRACE
[3]**man** *abbr* manual
Man *abbr* Manitoba
man–about–town *n, pl* **men–about–town :** a worldly and socially active man
man•a•cle \ˈma-ni-kəl\ *n* **1** ♦ **:** a shackle for the hand or wrist **2** ♦ **:** something used as a restraint

♦ band, bond, chain, fetter, irons, ligature, shackle

man•age \ˈma-nij\ *vb* **man•aged; man•ag•ing 1** ♦ **:** to handle or direct with a degree of skill **2 :** to make and keep compliant **3 :** to treat with care **:** HUSBAND **4** ♦ **:** to achieve one's purpose; *also* **:** get on or along — **man•age•abil•i•ty** \ˌma-ni-jə-ˈbi-lə-tē\ *n* — **man•age•able** \ˈma-ni-jə-bəl\ *adj* — **man•age•able•ness** *n* — **man•age•ably** \-blē\ *adv*

♦ [1] contend with, cope with, grapple with, handle, maneuver (*or* manoeuvre), negotiate, swing, treat ♦ [1] administer, carry on, conduct, control, direct, govern, guide, handle, operate, oversee, regulate, run, superintend, supervise ♦ [4] cope, do, fare, get along, make out, shift

managed care *n* **:** a health-care system that controls costs by limiting doctor's fees and by restricting the patient's choice of doctors
man•age•ment \ˈma-nij-mənt\ *n* **1** ♦ **:** the act or art of managing **:** CONTROL **2 :** judicious use of means to accomplish an end **3 :** the group of those who manage or direct an enterprise

♦ administration, conduct, control, direction, government, guidance, operation, oversight, regulation, running, superintendence, supervision

man•ag•er \ˈma-ni-jər\ *n* ♦ **:** one that manages

♦ administrator, director, executive, superintendent, supervisor

man•a•ge•ri•al \ˌma-nə-ˈjir-ē-əl\ *adj* ♦ **:** of, relating to, or characteristic of a manager

♦ directorial, executive, supervisory

ma•ña•na \mən-ˈyä-nə\ *n* **:** an indefinite time in the future
man–at–arms *n, pl* **men–at–arms** ♦ **:** one engaged in military service **:** SOLDIER; *esp* **:** one who is heavily armed and mounted

♦ fighter, legionnaire, regular, serviceman, soldier, warrior

man•a•tee \ˈma-nə-ˌtē\ *n* **:** any of a genus of chiefly tropical plant-eating aquatic mammals having a broad rounded tail

Man•chu•ri•an \man-ˈchu̇r-ē-ən\ *n* **:** a native or inhabitant of Manchuria, China — **Manchurian** *adj*
man•ci•ple \ˈman-sə-pəl\ *n* **:** a steward or purveyor especially for a college or monastery
man•da•mus \man-ˈdā-məs\ *n* **:** a writ issued by a superior court commanding that an official act or duty be performed
man•da•rin \ˈman-də-rən\ *n* **1 :** a public official of high rank under the Chinese Empire **2** *cap* **:** the chief dialect group of China **3 :** a yellow to reddish orange loose-skinned citrus fruit; *also* **:** a tree that bears mandarins
man•date \ˈman-ˌdāt\ *n* **1 :** an authoritative command **2** ♦ **:** an authorization to act given to a representative **3 :** a commission granted by the League of Nations to a member nation for governing conquered territory; *also* **:** a territory so governed

♦ authorization, commission, delegation, license (*or* licence)

man•da•to•ry \ˈman-də-ˌtōr-ē\ *adj* **1** ♦ **:** containing or constituting a command **:** OBLIGATORY **2 :** of or relating to a League of Nations mandate

♦ compulsory, imperative, incumbent, involuntary, necessary, nonelective, obligatory, peremptory *Ant* elective, optional, voluntary

man•di•ble \ˈman-də-bəl\ *n* **1 :** JAW; *esp* **:** a lower jaw **2 :** either segment of a bird's bill — **man•dib•u•lar** \man-ˈdi-byə-lər\ *adj*
man•do•lin \ˌman-də-ˈlin, ˈmand-ᵊl-ən\ *n* **:** a stringed musical instrument with a pear-shaped body and a fretted neck
man•drake \ˈman-ˌdrāk\ *n* **1 :** an Old World herb related to the nightshades or its large forked root formerly credited with magical properties **2 :** MAYAPPLE
man•drel *also* **man•dril** \ˈman-drəl\ *n* **1 :** an axle or spindle inserted into a hole in a piece of work to support it during machining **2 :** a metal bar used as a core around which material may be cast, shaped, or molded
man•drill \ˈman-drəl\ *n* **:** a large baboon of western central Africa
mane \ˈmān\ *n* **:** long heavy hair growing about the neck of some mammals (as a horse) — **maned** \ˈmānd\ *adj*
man–eat•er \ˈman-ˌē-tər\ *n* **:** one (as a shark or cannibal) that has or is thought to have an appetite for human flesh — **man–eat•ing** *adj*
ma•nège \ma-ˈnezh, mə-\ *n* **:** the art of horsemanship or of training horses
ma•nes \ˈmä-ˌnās, ˈmā-ˌnēz\ *n pl, often cap* **:** the spirits of the dead and gods of the lower world in ancient Roman belief
[1]**ma•neu•ver** *or Can and Brit* **ma•noeu•vre** \mə-ˈnü-vər, -ˈnyü-\ *n* **1 :** a military or naval movement; *also* **:** an armed forces training exercise — often used in plural **2 :** a procedure involving expert physical movement **3 :** an evasive movement or shift of tactics; *also* **:** an action taken to gain a tactical end — **maneuver** *vb* — **ma•neu•ver•abil•i•ty** \-ˌnü-və-rə-ˈbi-lə-tē, -ˌnyü-\ *n* — **ma•neu•ver•able** \-ˈnü-və-rə-bəl, -ˈnyü-\ *adj*
[2]**maneuver** *or Can and Brit* **manoeuvre** *vb* **maneuvered** *or* **manoeuvred; maneuvering** *or* **manoeuvring** ♦ **:** to guide with adroitness and design; *also* **:** to use stratagems

♦ contend with, cope with, grapple with, handle, manage, negotiate, swing, treat ♦ contrive, finagle, finesse, frame, machinate, mastermind, negotiate, wangle

man Friday *n* **:** an efficient and devoted aide or employee
man•ful \ˈman-fəl\ *adj* ♦ **:** having or showing courage and resolution — **man•ful•ly** *adv*

♦ brave, courageous, dauntless, doughty, fearless, gallant, greathearted, heroic, intrepid, lionhearted, stalwart, stout, undaunted, valiant, valorous

man•ga•nese \ˈmaŋ-gə-ˌnēz, -ˌnēs\ *n* **:** a metallic chemical element resembling iron but not magnetic
mange \ˈmānj\ *n* **:** any of several contagious itchy skin diseases especially of domestic animals
man•ger \ˈmān-jər\ *n* **:** a trough or open box for livestock feed or fodder
[1]**man•gle** \ˈmaŋ-gəl\ *vb* **man•gled; man•gling 1 :** to cut, bruise, or hack with repeated blows **2** ♦ **:** to spoil, injure or make incoherent especially through ineptitude ⟨a story *mangled* beyond recognition⟩ — **man•gler** *n*

♦ bobble, botch, bungle, butcher, flub, foul up, fumble, mess up, screw up

[2]**mangle** *n* **:** a machine with heated rollers for ironing laundry
man•go \ˈmaŋ-gō\ *n, pl* **mangoes** *also* **mangos :** an edible juicy yellowish-red fruit borne by a tropical evergreen tree related to the sumacs; *also* **:** this tree
man•grove \ˈman-ˌgrōv\ *n* **:** any of a genus of tropical maritime

trees that send out many prop roots and form dense thickets important in coastal land building

mangy \ˈmān-jē\ *adj* **1 :** affected with or resulting from mange **2** ♦ **:** decayed, deteriorated, or fallen into partial ruin especially through neglect or misuse

♦ dilapidated, grungy, mean, neglected, ratty, seedy, shabby

man•han•dle \ˈman-ˌhand-ᵊl\ *vb* ♦ **:** to handle roughly

♦ maltreat, maul, mishandle, rough

man•hat•tan \man-ˈhat-ᵊn\ *n, often cap* **:** a cocktail made of whiskey and vermouth

man•hole \ˈman-ˌhōl\ *n* **:** a hole through which a person may go especially to gain access to an underground or enclosed structure

man•hood \-ˌhu̇d\ *n* **1 :** the condition of being an adult male **2** ♦ **:** qualities associated with men **:** MANLINESS **3 :** MEN ⟨the nation's ~⟩

♦ manliness, masculinity, virility

man–hour \-ˈau̇r\ *n* **:** a unit of one hour's work by one person

man•hunt \-ˌhənt\ *n* **:** an organized hunt for a person and especially for one charged with a crime

ma•nia \ˈmā-nē-ə, -nyə\ *n* **1** ♦ **:** excitement manifested by mental and physical hyperactivity, disorganized behavior, and elevated mood **2 a :** excessive enthusiasm **b** ♦ **:** the object of enthusiasm

♦ [1] aberration, dementia, derangement, insanity, lunacy, madness ♦ [2b] fetish, fixation, obsession, preoccupation, prepossession

ma•ni•ac \ˈmā-nē-ˌak\ *n* **1** ♦ **:** one who is insane **:** LUNATIC **2** ♦ **:** a person characterized by an inordinate or ungovernable enthusiasm for something

♦ [1] lunatic, nut, psychotic ♦ [2] addict, aficionado, buff, bug, devotee, enthusiast, fan, fanatic, fancier, fiend, freak, lover, nut

ma•ni•a•cal \mə-ˈnī-ə-kəl\ *also* **ma•ni•ac** \ˈmā-nē-ak\ *adj* **1** ♦ **:** affected with or suggestive of madness **2 :** FRANTIC

♦ crazy, deranged, insane, loco, lunatic, mad

man•ic \ˈma-nik\ *adj* **:** affected with, relating to, characterized by, or resulting from mania — **manic** *n* — **man•i•cal•ly** \-ni-k(ə-)lē\ *adv*

manic depression *n* **:** BIPOLAR DISORDER

man•ic–de•pres•sive \ˌma-nik-di-ˈpre-siv\ *adj* **:** characterized by or affected with either mania or depression or alternating episodes of mania and depression — **manic–depressive** *n*

¹man•i•cure \ˈma-nə-ˌkyu̇r\ *n* **1 :** MANICURIST **2 :** a treatment for the care of the hands and nails

²manicure *vb* **-cured; -cur•ing 1 :** to do manicure work on **2 :** to trim closely and evenly

man•i•cur•ist \-ˌkyu̇r-ist\ *n* **:** a person who gives manicure treatments

¹man•i•fest \ˈma-nə-ˌfest\ *adj* **1 :** readily perceived by the senses and especially by the sight **2** ♦ **:** easily understood **:** OBVIOUS — **man•i•fest•ly** *adv*

♦ apparent, broad, clear, clear-cut, distinct, evident, lucid, obvious, palpable, patent, perspicuous, plain, transparent, unambiguous, unequivocal, unmistakable

²manifest *vb* ♦ **:** to make evident or certain by showing or displaying

♦ bespeak, betray, demonstrate, display, evince, expose, give away, reveal, show

³manifest *n* **:** a list of passengers or an invoice of cargo for a ship or plane

man•i•fes•ta•tion \ˌma-nə-fə-ˈstā-shən\ *n* **1 :** the act, process, or an instance of manifesting **2** ♦ **:** a perceptible, outward, or visible expression

♦ embodiment, epitome, incarnation, personification

man•i•fes•to \ˌma-nə-ˈfes-tō\ *n, pl* **-tos** *or* **-toes :** a public declaration of intentions, motives, or views

¹man•i•fold \ˈma-nə-ˌfōld\ *adj* **1** ♦ **:** marked by diversity or variety **2 :** consisting of or operating many of one kind combined

♦ multifarious, myriad

²manifold *n* **:** a pipe fitting with several lateral outlets for connecting it with other pipes

³manifold *vb* **1 :** MULTIPLY **2 :** to make a number of copies of (as a letter)

man•i•kin *also* **man•ni•kin** \ˈma-ni-kən\ *n* **1** ♦ **:** a form representing the human figure used especially for displaying clothes **:** MANNEQUIN **2 :** a little man **:** DWARF

♦ dummy, figure, form, mannequin

Ma•nila hemp \mə-ˈni-lə-\ *n* **:** a tough fiber from a Philippine plant related to the banana that is used for cordage

manila paper *n, often cap M* **:** a tough brownish paper made orig. from Manila hemp

man•i•oc \ˈma-nē-ˌäk\ *n* **:** CASSAVA

ma•nip•u•late \mə-ˈni-pyə-ˌlāt\ *vb* **-lat•ed; -lat•ing 1 :** to treat or operate manually or mechanically especially with skill **2 :** to manage or use skillfully **3 :** to influence especially with intent to deceive — **ma•nip•u•la•tion** \mə-ni-pyə-ˈlā-shən\ *n* — **ma•nip•u•la•tive** \-ˈni-pyə-ˌlā-tiv\ *adj* — **ma•nip•u•la•tor** \-ˌlā-tər\ *n*

ma•nip•u•la•tives \mə-ˈni-pyə-ˌlā-tivz\ *n pl* **:** objects that a student is instructed to use in a way that teaches or reinforces a lesson

man•kind *n* **1** \ˈman-ˈkīnd\ ♦ **:** the totality of human beings **2** \-ˌkīnd\ **:** men as distinguished from women

♦ Homo sapiens, humanity, humankind, man

man•li•ness \ˈman-lē-nəs\ *n* ♦ **:** the quality or state of being manly

♦ manhood, masculinity, virility

¹man•ly \ˈman-lē\ *adj* **man•li•er; -est** ♦ **:** having qualities appropriate to or generally associated with a man

♦ male, man-size, mannish, masculine, virile

²manly *adv* **:** in a manly manner

man–made \ˈman-ˈmād\ *adj* **:** made by humans rather than nature ⟨~ systems⟩; *esp* **:** SYNTHETIC ⟨~ fibers⟩

man•na \ˈma-nə\ *n* **1 :** food miraculously supplied to the Israelites in the wilderness **2** ♦ **:** a usually sudden and unexpected source of gratification, pleasure, or gain

♦ benefit, blessing, boon, felicity, godsend, good, windfall

manned \ˈmand\ *adj* **:** carrying or performed by a person ⟨~ spaceflight⟩

man•ne•quin \ˈma-ni-kən\ *n* **1** ♦ **:** a form representing the human figure used especially for displaying clothes **2 :** a person employed to model clothing

♦ dummy, figure, form, manikin

man•ner \ˈma-nər\ *n* **1** ♦ **:** a group united by common traits or interests **:** KIND, SORT **2 a** ♦ **:** a way of acting or proceeding ⟨worked in a brisk ~⟩ **b** ♦ **:** a characteristic or customary mode of acting ⟨spoke bluntly as was his ~⟩ **3 :** a method of artistic execution **4** *pl* **:** social conduct; *also* **:** BEARING **5** *pl* ♦ **:** social conduct or rules of conduct as shown in the prevalent customs ⟨taught the child good ~*s*⟩

♦ [1] breed, class, description, feather, ilk, kind, like, nature, order, sort, species, type ♦ [2a] approach, fashion, form, method, strategy, style, system, tack, tactics, technique, way ♦ [2b] locution, mode, phraseology, style, tone, vein ♦ **manners** *pl* [5] etiquette, mores

man•nered \ˈma-nərd\ *adj* **1 :** having manners of a specified kind ⟨well-*mannered*⟩ **2 :** having an artificial character ⟨a highly ~ style⟩

man•ner•ism \ˈma-nə-ˌri-zəm\ *n* **1 :** ARTIFICIALITY, PRECIOSITY **2** ♦ **:** a peculiarity of action, bearing, or treatment

♦ crotchet, eccentricity, idiosyncrasy, oddity, peculiarity, quirk, singularity, trick

man•ner•li•ness \ˈma-nər-lē-nəs\ *n* ♦ **:** the quality or state of being mannerly

♦ civility, courtesy, gentility, graciousness, politeness

man•ner•ly \ˈma-nər-lē\ *adj* ♦ **:** showing good manners **:** POLITE — **mannerly** *adv*

♦ civil, courteous, genteel, gracious, polite, well-bred

man•nish \ˈma-nish\ *adj* **1** ♦ **:** resembling or suggesting a man rather than a woman **2** ♦ **:** generally associated with or characteristic of a man — **man•nish•ly** *adv* — **man•nish•ness** *n*

♦ male, man-size, manly, masculine, virile

ma•no a ma•no \ˌmä-nō-ä-ˈmä-nō\ *adv or adj* **:** in direct competition or conflict

ma•noeu•vre \mə-ˈnü-vər, -ˈnyü-\ *chiefly Can and Brit var of* MANEUVER

man–of–war \ˌman-əv-ˈwȯr\ *n, pl* **men–of–war** \ˌmen-\ **:** WARSHIP

ma·nom·e·ter \mə-ˈnä-mə-tər\ *n* : an instrument for measuring the pressure of gases and vapors — **mano·met·ric** \ˌma-nə-ˈme-trik\ *adj*

man·or \ˈma-nər\ *n* **1 a** ♦ : the house or hall of an estate **b** : a landed estate **2** : an English estate of a feudal lord — **ma·no·ri·al** \mə-ˈnōr-ē-əl\ *adj* — **ma·no·ri·al·ism** \-ə-ˌli-zəm\ *n*

♦ castle, estate, hall, mansion, palace, villa

man power *n* **1** : power available from or supplied by the physical effort of human beings **2** *usu* **man·pow·er** : the total supply of persons available and fitted for service

man·qué \mä^{n}-ˈkā\ *adj* : short of or frustrated in the fulfillment of one's aspirations or talents ⟨a poet ~⟩

man·sard \ˈman-ˌsärd, -sərd\ *n* : a roof having two slopes on all sides with the lower slope steeper than the upper one

manse \ˈmans\ *n* : the residence especially of a Presbyterian minister

man·ser·vant \ˈman-ˌsər-vənt\ *n, pl* **men·ser·vants** \ˈmen-ˌsər-vənts\ : a male servant

man·sion \ˈman-chən\ *n* **1** ♦ : a large imposing residence **2** : a separate apartment in a large structure

♦ castle, estate, hall, manor, palace, villa

man–size \ˈman-ˌsīz\ *or* **man–sized** \-ˌsīzd\ *adj* ♦ : suitable for or requiring a man

♦ male, manly, mannish, masculine, virile

man·slaugh·ter \-ˌslȯ-tər\ *n* : the unlawful killing of a human being without express or implied malice

man·ta \ˈman-tə\ *n* **1** : a square piece of cloth or blanket used in southwestern U.S. and Latin America as a cloak or shawl **2** : MANTA RAY

manta ray *n* : any of several extremely large rays

man·teau \man-ˈtō\ *n* : a loose cloak, coat, or robe

man·tel \ˈmant-^{ə}l\ *n* : a beam, stone, or arch serving as a lintel to support the masonry above a fireplace; *also* : a shelf above a fireplace

man·tel·piece \ˈmant-^{ə}l-ˌpēs\ *n* : the shelf of a mantel

man·til·la \man-ˈtē-yə, -ˈti-lə\ *n* : a light scarf worn over the head and shoulders especially by Spanish and Latin-American women

♦ babushka, bandanna, do-rag, kerchief

man·tis \ˈman-təs\ *n, pl* **man·tis·es** *also* **man·tes** \-ˌtēz\ : any of a group of large usually green insect-eating insects that hold their prey in forelimbs folded as if in prayer

man·tis·sa \man-ˈti-sə\ *n* : the part of a logarithm to the right of the decimal point

1**man·tle** \ˈmant-^{ə}l\ *n* **1** : a loose sleeveless garment worn over other clothes **2** ♦ : something that covers, enfolds, or envelops **3** : a lacy sheath that gives light by incandescence when placed over a flame **4** : the portion of the earth lying between the crust and the core **5** : MANTEL

♦ cloak, curtain, hood, mask, shroud, veil

2**mantle** *vb* **man·tled; man·tling** **1** ♦ : to cover with or as if with a mantle **2** : BLUSH

♦ embrace, enclose, encompass, enfold, enshroud, envelop, invest, lap, shroud, swathe, veil, wrap

man·tra \ˈman-trə\ *n* : a mystical formula of invocation or incantation (as in Hinduism)

1**man·u·al** \ˈman-yə-wəl\ *adj* **1** : of, relating to, or involving the hands; *also* : worked by hand ⟨a ~ pump⟩ **2** : requiring or using physical skill and energy — **man·u·al·ly** *adv*

2**manual** *n* **1** ♦ : a small book; *esp* : a concise reference book covering a particular subject : HANDBOOK **2** : the prescribed movements in the handling of a military item and especially a weapon during a drill or ceremony ⟨the ~ of arms⟩ **3** : a keyboard especially of an organ

♦ handbook, primer, textbook

man·u·fac·to·ry \ˌman-yə-ˈfak-tə-rē\ *n* : a building or set of buildings with facilities for manufacturing : FACTORY

1**man·u·fac·ture** \ˌman-yə-ˈfak-chər\ *n* **1** : something made from raw materials **2** : the process of making wares by hand or by machinery; *also* : a productive industry using machinery

2**manufacture** *vb* **-tured; -tur·ing** **1** ♦ : to make from raw materials by hand or by machinery; *also* : to engage in manufacture **2** ♦ : to devise by thinking : INVENT, FABRICATE — **man·u·fac·tur·er** *n*

♦ [1] fabricate, fashion, form, frame, make, produce ♦ [2] concoct, contrive, cook up, devise, fabricate, invent, make up, think up

man·u·mis·sion \-ˈmi-shən\ *n* ♦ : the act or process of manumitting

♦ emancipation, enfranchisement, liberation

man·u·mit \ˌman-yə-ˈmit\ *vb* **-mit·ted; -mit·ting** ♦ : to free from slavery

♦ discharge, emancipate, enfranchise, free, liberate, loose, loosen, release, spring, unbind, unchain, unfetter

1**ma·nure** \mə-ˈnu̇r, -ˈnyu̇r\ *vb* **ma·nured; ma·nur·ing** : to fertilize land with manure

2**manure** *n* : FERTILIZER; *esp* : refuse from stables and barnyards — **ma·nu·ri·al** \-ˈnu̇r-ē-əl, -ˈnyu̇r-\ *adj*

man·u·script \ˈman-yə-ˌskript\ *n* **1** : a written or typewritten composition or document; *also* : a document submitted for publication **2** ♦ : writing as opposed to print

♦ handwriting, penmanship, script

Manx \ˈmaŋks\ *n pl* : the people of the Isle of Man — **Manx** *adj*

1**many** \ˈme-nē\ *adj* **more** \ˈmōr\; **most** \ˈmōst\ ♦ : consisting of or amounting to a large but indefinite number ⟨~ years ago⟩

♦ multiple, multitudinous, numerous ***Ant*** few

2**many** *pron* : a large number ⟨~ are called⟩

3**many** *n* : a large but indefinite number ⟨a good ~ of them⟩

many·fold \ˌme-nē-ˈfōld\ *adv* : by many times

many–sid·ed \-ˈsī-dəd\ *adj* **1** : having many sides or aspects **2** : VERSATILE

Mao·ism \ˈmau̇-ˌi-zəm\ *n* : the theory and practice of Communism developed in China chiefly by Mao Zedong — **Mao·ist** \ˈmau̇-ist\ *n or adj*

Mao·ri \ˈmau̇(-ə)r-ē\ *n, pl* **Maori** *or* **Maoris** : a member of a Polynesian people native to New Zealand

1**map** \ˈmap\ *n* **1** : a representation usually on a flat surface of the whole or part of an area **2** : a representation of the celestial sphere or part of it

2**map** *vb* **mapped; map·ping** **1** : to make a map of **2** ♦ : to plan in detail — often used with *out* ⟨~ out a program⟩ — **map·pa·ble** \ˈma-pə-bəl\ *adj* — **map·per** *n*

♦ *usu* **map out** arrange, blueprint, calculate, chart, design, frame, lay out, plan, project, scheme

MAP *abbr* modified American plan

ma·ple \ˈmā-pəl\ *n* : any of a genus of trees or shrubs with 2-winged dry fruit and opposite leaves; *also* : the hard light-colored wood of a maple used especially for floors and furniture

maple sugar *n* : sugar made by boiling maple syrup

maple syrup *n* : syrup made by concentrating the sap of maple trees and especially the sugar maple

mar \ˈmär\ *vb* **marred; mar·ring** ♦ : to detract from the wholeness or perfection of : SPOIL

♦ blemish, poison, spoil, stain, taint, tarnish, touch, vitiate

Mar *abbr* March

ma·ra·ca \mə-ˈrä-kə, -ˈra-\ *n* : a rattle usually made from a gourd and used as a percussion instrument

mar·a·schi·no \ˌmar-ə-ˈskē-nō, -ˈshē-\ *n, often cap* : a cherry preserved in a sweet liqueur made from the juice of a bitter wild cherry

1**mar·a·thon** \ˈmar-ə-ˌthän\ *n* **1** : a long-distance race especially on foot **2** : an endurance contest

2**marathon** *adj* ♦ : belonging to, suggestive of, or suited for a marathon race or competition (as in being marked by unusual length of time)

♦ extended, far, great, lengthy, long

mar·a·thon·er \ˈmar-ə-ˌthä-nər\ *n* : a person who takes part in a marathon — **mar·a·thon·ing** *n*

ma·raud \mə-ˈrȯd\ *vb* ♦ : to roam about and raid in search of plunder : PILLAGE — **ma·raud·er** *n*

♦ despoil, loot, pillage, plunder, ransack, sack, strip

mar·ble \ˈmär-bəl\ *n* **1** : a limestone that can be polished and used in fine building work **2** : something resembling marble (as in coldness) **3** : a small ball (as of glass) used in various games; *also, pl* : a children's game played with these small balls — **mar·ble** *adj*

mar·bling \-bə-liŋ, -bliŋ\ *n* : an intermixture of fat through the lean of a cut of meat

mar·cel \mär-ˈsel\ *n* : a deep soft wave made in the hair by the use of a heated curling iron — **marcel** *vb*

1**march** \ˈmärch\ *n* : a border region : FRONTIER

2**march** *vb* **1** ♦ : to move along in or as if in military formation **2 a** : to walk in a direct purposeful manner **b** ♦ : to make steady progress : ADVANCE **3 :** TRAVERSE ⟨~*ed* 10 miles⟩ — **march•er** *n*

♦ [1] file, pace, parade, stride ♦ [2b] advance, fare, forge, get along, go, proceed, progress

³march *n* **1 :** the action of marching; *also* **:** the distance covered (as by a military unit) in a march **2 :** a regular measured stride or rhythmic step used in marching **3** ♦ **:** forward movement **4 :** a piece of music with marked rhythm suitable for marching to

♦ advance, advancement, furtherance, headway, onrush, passage, process, procession, progress, progression

March *n* **:** the 3d month of the year

mar•chio•ness \ˈmär-shə-nəs\ *n* **1 :** the wife or widow of a marquess **2 :** a woman holding the rank of a marquess in her own right

Mar•di Gras \ˈmär-dē-ˌgrä\ *n* **:** the Tuesday before Ash Wednesday often observed with parades and merrymaking

¹mare \ˈmar\ *n* **:** an adult female of the horse or a related mammal

²ma•re \ˈmär-(ˌ)ā\ *n, pl* **ma•ria** \ˈmär-ē-ə\ **:** any of several large dark areas on the surface of the moon or Mars

mar•ga•rine \ˈmär-jə-rən\ *n* **:** a food product made usually from vegetable oils churned with skimmed milk and used as a substitute for butter

mar•ga•ri•ta \ˌmär-gə-ˈrē-tə\ *n* **:** a cocktail consisting of tequila, lime or lemon juice, and an orange-flavored liqueur

mar•gin \ˈmär-jən\ *n* **1 :** the part of a page outside the main body of printed or written matter **2** ♦ **:** the outside limit and adjoining surface of something **:** EDGE **3 :** a spare amount, measure, or degree allowed for use if needed **4 :** measure or degree of difference ⟨a one-vote ~⟩

♦ border, bound, boundary, circumference, compass, confines, edge, end, fringe, perimeter, periphery, rim, skirt, verge

mar•gin•al \-jə-nəl\ *adj* **1 :** written or printed in the margin **2 :** of, relating to, or situated at a margin or border **3 :** close to the lower limit of quality or acceptability **4 :** excluded from or existing outside the mainstream of society or a group

mar•gi•na•lia \ˌmär-jə-ˈnā-lē-ə\ *n pl* **:** marginal notes or embellishments

mar•gin•al•ize \ˈmär-jə-nᵊl-ˌīz\ *vb* **-ized; -iz•ing :** to relegate to an unimportant position within a society or group

mar•gin•al•ly \ˌmärj-nə-lē, ˈmär-jə-nᵊl-ē\ *adv* ♦ **:** in a marginal manner

♦ barely, hardly, just, scarcely, slightly

mar•grave \ˈmär-ˌgrāv\ *n* **:** the military governor especially of a medieval German border province

ma•ri•a•chi \ˌmär-ē-ˈä-chē, ˌmar-\ *n* **:** a Mexican street band; *also* **:** a member of or the music of such a band

mari•gold \ˈmar-ə-ˌgōld, ˈmer-\ *n* **:** any of a genus of tropical American herbs related to the daisies that are grown for their showy usually yellow, orange, or maroon flower heads

mar•i•jua•na *also* **mar•i•hua•na** \ˌmar-ə-ˈwä-nə, -ˈhwä-\ *n* **:** the dried leaves and flowering tops of the female hemp plant smoked usually illegally for their intoxicating effect; *also* **:** HEMP

ma•rim•ba \mə-ˈrim-bə\ *n* **:** a xylophone of southern Africa and Central America; *also* **:** a modern version of it

ma•ri•na \mə-ˈrē-nə\ *n* **:** a dock or basin providing secure moorings for pleasure boats

mar•i•nade \ˌmer-ə-ˈnād\ *n* **:** a savory usually acidic sauce in which meat, fish, or a vegetable is soaked to enrich its flavor or to tenderize it

mar•i•na•ra \ˌmar-ə-ˈnar-ə\ *adj* **:** made with tomatoes, onions, garlic, and spices; *also* **:** served with marinara sauce

mar•i•nate \ˈmar-ə-ˌnāt\ *vb* **-nat•ed; -nat•ing :** to steep (as meat or fish) in a brine or pickle

¹ma•rine \mə-ˈrēn\ *adj* **1** ♦ **:** of or relating to the sea or its navigation or commerce **2 :** of or relating to marines

♦ maritime, oceanic, pelagic

²marine *n* **1 :** the mercantile and naval shipping of a country **2 :** any of a class of soldiers serving on shipboard or with a naval force

mar•i•ner \ˈmar-ə-nər\ *n* ♦ **:** a person who navigates or assists in navigating a ship **:** SAILOR

♦ gob, jack, jack-tar, sailor, seaman, swab, tar

mar•i•o•nette \ˌmar-ē-ə-ˈnet, ˌmer-\ *n* **:** a puppet moved by strings or by hand

mar•i•tal \ˈmar-ət-ᵊl\ *adj* ♦ **:** of or relating to marriage **:** CONJUGAL

♦ conjugal, connubial, matrimonial, nuptial

mar•i•time \ˈmar-ə-ˌtīm\ *adj* **1** ♦ **:** of, relating to, or bordering on the sea **2** ♦ **:** of or relating to navigation or commerce of the sea

♦ [1] marine, oceanic, pelagic ♦ [2] marine

mar•jo•ram \ˈmär-jə-rəm\ *n* **:** any of various fragrant mints often used as seasoning

¹mark \ˈmärk\ *n* **1 :** something (as a line or fixed object) designed to record position; *also* **:** the starting line or position in a track event **2 a :** TARGET **b :** the end toward which effort is directed **:** GOAL, OBJECT **3** ♦ **:** an object of abuse or ridicule **4 :** the question under discussion **5** ♦ **:** a standard of performance, quality, or condition ⟨not up to the ~⟩ **6 a :** a visible sign **:** INDICATION **b** ♦ **:** a distinguishing trait or quality **:** CHARACTERISTIC **7 :** a written or printed symbol **8 :** GRADE ⟨a ~ of B+⟩ **9 :** IMPORTANCE, DISTINCTION **10 a** ♦ **:** a lasting impression **:** an enduring effect ⟨made his ~ in the world⟩ **b :** a damaging impression (as a scratch, scar, or stain) left on a surface

♦ [3] butt, laughingstock, mock, mockery, target ♦ [5] criterion, grade, measure, par, standard, touchstone, yardstick ♦ [6b] attribute, character, characteristic, feature, peculiarity, point, property, quality, trait ♦ [10a] effect, impact, influence, repercussion, sway

²mark *vb* **1** ♦ **:** to set apart by a line or boundary **2 :** to designate by a mark or make a mark on **3 :** CHARACTERIZE ⟨the vehemence that ~*s* his speeches⟩; *also* **:** SIGNALIZE ⟨this year ~*s* our 50th anniversary⟩ **4 :** to take notice of **:** OBSERVE **5** ♦ **:** to label so as to indicate price or quality **6** ♦ **:** to make note of in writing

♦ [1] bound, circumscribe, define, delimit, demarcate, limit, terminate ♦ [5] label, tag, ticket ♦ [6] jot, log, note, put down, record, register, set down

³mark *n* **:** a former monetary unit of Germany

Mark \ˈmärk\ *n* **:** a book of the New Testament of Christian Scripture

mark•down \ˈmärk-ˌdau̇n\ *n* **1 :** a lowering of price **2 :** the amount by which an original price is reduced

mark down *vb* ♦ **:** to put a lower price on

♦ cheapen, depreciate, depress, write off

marked \ˈmärkt\ *adj* ♦ **:** having a distinctive or emphasized character **:** NOTICEABLE — **mark•ed•ly** \ˈmär-kəd-lē\ *adv*

♦ bold, catchy, conspicuous, emphatic, noticeable, prominent, pronounced, remarkable, striking

mark•er \ˈmär-kər\ *n* ♦ **:** one that marks

♦ label, tag, ticket

¹mar•ket \ˈmär-kət\ *n* **1 :** a meeting together of people for trade by purchase and sale; *also* **:** a public place where such a meeting is held **2 :** the rate or price offered for a commodity or security **3 :** a geographical area of demand for commodities; *also* ♦ **:** extent of demand **4 :** a retail establishment usually of a specific kind

♦ call, demand, request

²market *vb* **1 :** to go to a market to buy or sell **2** ♦ **:** to offer for sale **:** SELL — **mar•ket•able** *adj*

♦ deal, merchandise, put up, retail, sell, vend *Ant* buy, purchase

mar•ket•place \ˈmär-kət-ˌplās\ *n* **1 :** an open square in a town where markets are held **2** ♦ **:** the world of trade or economic activity

♦ business, commerce, trade, traffic

mark•ka \ˈmär-ˌkä\ *n, pl* **mark•kaa** \ˈmär-ˌkä\ *or* **markkas** \-ˌkäz\ **:** the basic monetary unit of Finland from 1917 to 2001

marks•man \ˈmärks-mən\ *n* ♦ **:** a person skillful at hitting a target — **marks•man•ship** *n*

♦ sharpshooter, shooter, shot

mark•up \ˈmär-ˌkəp\ *n* **1 :** a raising of price **2 :** an amount added to the cost price of an article to determine the selling price

mark up *vb* **:** to put a higher price on

markup language *n* **:** a system for marking the components and layout of a computer document

marl \ˈmärl\ *n* **:** an earthy deposit rich in lime used especially as fertilizer — **marly** \ˈmär-lē\ *adj*

mar•lin \ˈmär-lən\ *n* **:** any of several large oceanic sport fishes related to sailfishes

mar•line•spike *also* **mar•lin•spike** \ˈmär-lən-ˌspīk\ *n* **:** a pointed iron tool used to separate strands of rope or wire (as in splicing)

mar•ma•lade \ˈmär-mə-ˌlād\ *n* **:** a clear jelly holding in suspension pieces of fruit and fruit rind
mar•mo•re•al \mär-ˈmōr-ē-əl\ *adj* **:** of, relating to, or suggestive of marble
mar•mo•set \ˈmär-mə-ˌset\ *n* **:** any of numerous small bushy-tailed monkeys of Central and So. America
mar•mot \ˈmär-mət\ *n* **:** any of a genus of stout short-legged burrowing No. American rodents
[1]**ma•roon** \mə-ˈrün\ *vb* **1 :** to put ashore (as on a desolate island) and leave to one's fate **2** ♦ **:** to leave in isolation and without hope of escape

♦ abandon, desert, forsake, quit

[2]**maroon** *n* **:** a dark red color
[1]**mar•quee** \mär-ˈkē\ *n* **1 :** a large tent set up (as for an outdoor party) **2 :** a usually metal and glass canopy over an entrance (as of a theater) **3 :** a sign over the entrance of a theater or arena advertising a performance
[2]**marquee** *adj* **:** having or being a great attraction **:** PREEMINENT ⟨~ athletes⟩
mar•quess \ˈmär-kwəs\ *or* **mar•quis** \ˈmär-kwəs, mär-ˈkē\ *n* **1 :** a nobleman of hereditary rank in Europe and Japan **2 :** a member of the British peerage ranking below a duke and above an earl
mar•que•try \ˈmär-kə-trē\ *n* **:** inlaid work of wood, shell, or ivory (as on a table or cabinet)
mar•quis \ˈmär-kwəs, mär-ˈkē\ *n* **:** MARQUESS
mar•quise \mär-ˈkēz\ *n, pl* **mar•quises** *same or* -ˈkē-zəz\ **:** MARCHIONESS
mar•riage \ˈmar-ij\ *n* **1** ♦ **:** the state of being married **2** ♦ **:** a wedding ceremony and attendant festivities **3 :** a close union — **mar•riage•able** *adj*

♦ [1] match, matrimony ♦ [2] espousal, wedding

married name *n* **:** a woman's surname acquired through marriage
mar•row \ˈmar-ō\ *n* **:** a soft vascular tissue that fills the cavities of most bones
mar•row•bone \ˈmar-ə-ˌbōn, ˈmar-ō-\ *n* **:** a bone (as a shinbone) rich in marrow
mar•ry \ˈmar-ē\ *vb* **mar•ried; mar•ry•ing 1 a :** to join in marriage according to law or custom **b** ♦ **:** to give in marriage ⟨*married* his daughter to his partner's son⟩ **2 :** to take as a spouse **:** WED **3** ♦ **:** to enter into a close union — **mar•ried** *adj or n*

♦ [1b] match ♦ [3] associate, coalesce, combine, conjoin, connect, couple, fuse, join, link, unify, unite

Mars \ˈmärz\ *n* **:** the planet 4th from the sun and conspicuous for its red color
marsh \ˈmärsh\ *n* ♦ **:** a tract of soft wet land — **marshy** *adj*

♦ bog, fen, mire, morass, slough, swamp

[1]**mar•shal** \ˈmär-shəl\ *n* **1 :** a high official in a medieval household; *also* **:** a person in charge of the ceremonial aspects of a gathering **2 :** a general officer of the highest military rank **3 :** an administrative officer (as of a U.S. judicial district) having duties similar to a sheriff's **4 :** the administrative head of a city police or fire department
[2]**marshal** *vb* **mar•shaled** *or* **mar•shalled; mar•shal•ing** *or* **mar•shal•ling 1** ♦ **:** to arrange in order, rank, or position **2** ♦ **:** to bring together and order in an appropriate or effective way **3** ♦ **:** to lead with ceremony **:** USHER

♦ [1] arrange, array, classify, codify, dispose, draw up, order, organize, range, systematize ♦ [2] mobilize, muster, rally ♦ [3] conduct, direct, guide, lead, pilot, route, show, steer, usher

marsh gas *n* **:** METHANE
marsh•mal•low \ˈmärsh-ˌme-lō, -ˌma-\ *n* **:** a light spongy confection made from corn syrup, sugar, albumen, and gelatin
marsh marigold *n* **:** a swamp herb related to the buttercups that has bright yellow flowers
mar•su•pi•al \mär-ˈsü-pē-əl\ *n* **:** any of an order of primitive mammals (as opossums, kangaroos, or wombats) that bear very immature young which are nourished in a pouch on the abdomen of the female — **marsupial** *adj*
mart \ˈmärt\ *n* **:** MARKET
mar•ten \ˈmärt-ᵊn\ *n, pl* **marten** *or* **martens :** a slender mammal that is larger than the related weasels and has soft gray or brown fur; *also* **:** this fur
mar•tial \ˈmär-shəl\ *adj* **1 :** of, relating to, or suited for war or a warrior ⟨~ music⟩ **2 :** of or relating to an army or military life **3 :** WARLIKE
martial law *n* **1 :** the law applied in occupied territory by the occupying military forces **2 :** the established law of a country administered by military forces in an emergency when civilian law enforcement agencies are unable to maintain public order and safety
mar•tian \ˈmär-shən\ *adj, often cap* **:** of or relating to the planet Mars or its hypothetical inhabitants — **martian** *n, often cap*
mar•tin \ˈmärt-ᵊn\ *n* **:** any of several swallows and especially one of No. America with purplish blue plumage
mar•ti•net \ˌmärt-ᵊn-ˈet\ *n* **:** a strict disciplinarian
mar•tin•gale \ˈmärt-ᵊn-ˌgāl\ *n* **:** a strap connecting a horse's girth to the bit or reins so as to hold down its head
mar•ti•ni \mär-ˈtē-nē\ *n* **:** a cocktail made of gin or vodka and dry vermouth
[1]**mar•tyr** \ˈmär-tər\ *n* **1 :** a person who dies rather than renounce a religion; *also* **:** a person who makes a great sacrifice for the sake of principle **2 :** a great or constant sufferer
[2]**martyr** *vb* **1 :** to put to death for adhering to a belief **2** ♦ **:** to inflict agonizing pain on **:** TORTURE

♦ afflict, agonize, bedevil, curse, harrow, persecute, plague, rack, torment, torture

mar•tyr•dom \ˈmär-tər-dəm\ *n* **1 :** the suffering and death of a martyr **2 :** TORTURE
[1]**mar•vel** \ˈmär-vəl\ *n* **1** ♦ **:** one that causes wonder or astonishment **2 :** intense surprise or interest

♦ caution, flash, miracle, phenomenon, portent, prodigy, sensation, wonder

[2]**marvel** *vb* **mar•veled** *or* **mar•velled; mar•vel•ing** *or* **mar•vel•ling :** to feel surprise, wonder, or amazed curiosity
mar•vel•ous *or* **mar•vel•lous** \ˈmär-və-ləs\ *adj* **1** ♦ **:** causing wonder **2** ♦ **:** of the highest kind or quality — **mar•vel•ous•ly** *adv* — **mar•vel•ous•ness** *n*

♦ [1] amazing, astonishing, astounding, awesome, eye-opening, fabulous, miraculous, portentous, prodigious, stunning, stupendous, sublime, surprising, wonderful ♦ [2] excellent, fabulous, fine, grand, great, sensational, splendid, superb, superior, swell, terrific, wonderful

Marx•ism \ˈmärk-ˌsi-zəm\ *n* **:** the political, economic, and social principles and policies advocated by Karl Marx — **Marx•ist** \-sist\ *n or adj*
mar•zi•pan \ˈmärt-sə-ˌpän, -ˌpan; ˈmär-zə-ˌpan\ *n* **:** a confection of almond paste, sugar, and egg whites
masc *abbr* masculine
mas•cara \mas-ˈkar-ə\ *n* **:** a cosmetic especially for darkening the eyelashes
mas•car•po•ne \ˌmas-kär-ˈpō-nā\ *n* **:** an Italian cream cheese
mas•cot \ˈmas-ˌkät, -kət\ *n* ♦ **:** a person, animal, or object adopted usually by a group to bring good luck

♦ amulet, charm, fetish, talisman

[1]**mas•cu•line** \ˈmas-kyə-lən\ *adj* **1 a :** MALE **b** ♦ **:** having qualities appropriate to or usually associated with a man **:** MANLY **2 :** of, relating to, or constituting the gender that includes most words or grammatical forms referring to males

♦ male, man-size, manly, mannish, virile *Ant* effeminate, unmanly, unmasculine

[2]**masculine** *n* **:** a noun, pronoun, adjective, or inflectional form or class of the masculine gender; *also* **:** the masculine gender
mas•cu•lin•i•ty \ˌmas-kyə-ˈli-nə-tē\ *n* ♦ **:** the quality, state, or degree of being masculine

♦ manhood, manliness, virility

[1]**mash** \ˈmash\ *n* **1 :** a mixture of ground feeds for livestock **2 :** crushed malt or grain steeped in hot water to make wort **3 :** a soft pulpy mass
[2]**mash** *vb* **1** ♦ **:** to reduce to a soft pulpy state **2 :** CRUSH, SMASH ⟨~ a finger⟩ — **mash•er** *n*

♦ crush, squash

MASH *abbr* mobile army surgical hospital
[1]**mask** \ˈmask\ *n* **1 :** a cover for the face usually for disguise or protection **2 :** MASQUE **3 :** a figure of a head worn on the stage in antiquity **4 :** a copy of a face made by means of a mold ⟨death ~⟩ **5** ♦ **:** something that conceals or disguises **6 :** the face of an animal

♦ cloak, curtain, hood, mantle, shroud, veil

[2]**mask** *vb* **1** ♦ **:** to conceal from view or perception **2 :** to cover for protection

♦ camouflage, cloak, disguise, dress up ♦ blanket, blot out, cloak, conceal, cover, curtain, enshroud, hide, obscure, occult, screen, shroud, veil

mask•er \ˈmas-kər\ *n* **:** a participant in a masquerade
mas•och•ism \ˈma-sə-ˌki-zəm, ˈma-zə-\ *n* **1 :** a sexual perversion characterized by pleasure in being subjected to pain or humiliation **2 :** pleasure in being abused or dominated — **mas•och•ist** \-kist\ *n* — **mas•och•is•tic** \ˌma-sə-ˈkis-tik, ˌma-zə-\ *adj*
ma•son \ˈmās-ᵊn\ *n* **1 :** a skilled worker who builds with stone, brick, or concrete **2** *cap* **:** FREEMASON
Ma•son•ic \mə-ˈsä-nik\ *adj* **:** of or relating to Freemasons or Freemasonry
ma•son•ry \ˈmās-ᵊn-rē\ *n, pl* **-ries 1 :** something constructed of materials used by masons **2 :** the art, trade, or work of a mason **3** *cap* **:** FREEMASONRY
masque \ˈmask\ *n* **1 :** MASQUERADE **2 :** a short allegorical dramatic performance (as of the 17th century)
[1]**mas•quer•ade** \ˌmas-kə-ˈrād\ *n* **1 :** a social gathering of persons wearing masks; *also* **:** a costume for wear at such a gathering **2 :** DISGUISE **3** ♦ **:** an action or appearance that is mere disguise or show

♦ act, airs, facade, front, guise, pose, pretense, put-on, semblance, show

[2]**masquerade** *vb* **-ad•ed; -ad•ing 1** ♦ **:** to disguise oneself **:** POSE **2 :** to take part in a masquerade — **mas•quer•ad•er** *n*

♦ impersonate, play, pose

[1]**mass** \ˈmas\ *n* **1** *cap* **:** a sequence of prayers and ceremonies forming the eucharistic service of the Roman Catholic Church **2** *often cap* **:** a celebration of the Eucharist **3 :** a musical setting for parts of the Mass
[2]**mass** *n* **1 :** a quantity or aggregate of matter usually of considerable size **2 :** EXPANSE, BULK; *also* **:** MASSIVENESS **3** ♦ **:** the principal part **4 :** AGGREGATE, WHOLE **5 :** the quantity of matter that a body possesses as measured by its inertia **6 :** a large quantity, amount, or number **7** ♦ **:** the great body of people — usually used in plural — **massy** *adj*

♦ [3] body, bulk, core, generality, main, staple, weight ♦ *usu* **masses** *pl* [7] commoners, herd, mob, people, plebeians, populace, rank and file ***Ant*** elite

[3]**mass** *vb* ♦ **:** to form or collect into a mass

♦ accumulate, amass, collect, conglomerate, gather, heap, pile up

Mass *abbr* Massachusetts
[1]**mas•sa•cre** \ˈma-si-kər\ *n* **1** ♦ **:** the killing of many persons under cruel or atrocious circumstances **2 :** a wholesale slaughter

♦ butchery, carnage, slaughter

[2]**massacre** *vb* ♦ **:** to kill by massacre

♦ butcher, slaughter

[1]**mas•sage** \mə-ˈsäzh, -ˈsäj\ *n* **:** manipulation of tissues (as by rubbing and kneading) especially for therapeutic purposes
[2]**massage** *vb* **mas•saged; mas•sag•ing 1 :** to subject to massage **2 :** to treat flatteringly; *also* **:** MANIPULATE, DOCTOR ⟨~ data⟩
mas•seur \ma-ˈsər\ *n* **:** a man who practices massage
mas•seuse \-ˈsərz, -ˈsüz\ *n* **:** a woman who practices massage
mas•sif \ma-ˈsēf\ *n* **:** a principal mountain mass
mas•sive \ˈma-siv\ *adj* **1** ♦ **:** forming or consisting of a large mass **2** ♦ **:** large in structure, scope, or degree

♦ [1] heavy, hefty, ponderous, weighty ♦ [2] colossal, enormous, giant, gigantic, grand, huge, mammoth, monumental, prodigious, titanic, tremendous

mas•sive•ly \-lē\ *adv* ♦ **:** in a massive manner

♦ broadly, considerably, greatly, hugely, largely, monstrously, much, sizably, stupendously, tremendously, utterly, vastly.

mas•sive•ness \-nəs\ *n* ♦ **:** the quality or state of being massive

♦ enormity, hugeness, immensity, magnitude, vastness

mass•less \ˈmas-ləs\ *adj* **:** having no mass ⟨~ particles⟩
mass medium *n, pl* **mass media :** a medium of communication (as the newspapers or television) that is designed to reach the mass of the people
mass–pro•duce \ˌmas-prə-ˈdüs, -ˈdyüs\ *vb* **:** to produce in quantity usually by machinery — **mass production** *n*
[1]**mast** \ˈmast\ *n* **1 :** a long pole or spar rising from the keel or deck of a ship and supporting the yards, booms, and rigging **2 :** a slender vertical structure — **mast•ed** \ˈmas-təd\ *adj*
[2]**mast** *n* **:** nuts (as acorns) accumulated on the forest floor and often serving as food for animals (as hogs)

mas•tec•to•my \ma-ˈstek-tə-mē\ *n, pl* **-mies :** surgical removal of the breast
[1]**mas•ter** \ˈmas-tər\ *n* **1 :** a male teacher; *also* **:** a person holding an academic degree higher than a bachelor's but lower than a doctor's **2** ♦ **:** one highly skilled (as in an art or profession) **3** ♦ **:** one having authority or control **4 :** one that conquers or masters **:** VICTOR **5 :** the commander of a merchant ship **6 :** a youth or boy too young to be called *mister* — used as a title **7 :** an original from which copies are made — **master** *adj*

♦ [2] ace, adept, artist, authority, crackerjack, expert, maestro, scholar, shark, virtuoso, whiz, wizard ♦ [3] boss, captain, chief, foreman, head, headman, helmsman, kingpin, leader, taskmaster

[2]**master** *vb* **1 :** to become master of **:** OVERCOME **2 :** to become skilled or proficient in **3 :** to produce a master recording of (as a musical performance)
master chief petty officer *n* **:** a petty officer of the highest rank in the navy
mas•ter•ful \ˈmas-tər-fəl\ *adj* **1 :** inclined and usually competent to act as a master **2** ♦ **:** having or reflecting the skill of a master **3** ♦ **:** suggestive of a domineering nature

♦ [2] adroit, artful, dexterous, practiced, skillful, virtuoso ♦ [2] accomplished, adept, consummate, crack, crackerjack, good, great, proficient, skilled ♦ [3] authoritarian, autocratic, bossy, despotic, dictatorial, domineering, imperious, overbearing, peremptory, tyrannical, tyrannous

mas•ter•ful•ly \-fə-lē\ *adv* ♦ **:** in a masterful manner

♦ ably, adeptly, capably, expertly, proficiently, skillfully, well

mas•ter•ful•ness \-nəs\ *n* ♦ **:** the quality or state of being masterful

♦ adeptness, adroitness, art, artfulness, artifice, artistry, cleverness, craft, cunning, deftness, skill

master gunnery sergeant *n* **:** a noncommissioned officer in the marine corps ranking above a master sergeant
master key *n* **:** a key designed to open several different locks
mas•ter•ly \ˈmas-tər-lē\ *adj* **1** ♦ **:** indicating thorough knowledge or superior skill ⟨~ performance⟩ **2** ♦ **:** having the power and skill of a master — **mas•ter•ly** *adv*

♦ accomplished, adept, consummate, crack, crackerjack, expert, good, great, master, masterful, proficient, skilled, skillful, virtuoso

[1]**mas•ter•mind** \-ˌmīnd\ *n* **:** a person who provides the directing or creative intelligence for a project
[2]**mastermind** *vb* ♦ **:** to be the mastermind of

♦ contrive, finagle, finesse, frame, machinate, maneuver (*or* manoeuvre), negotiate, wangle

master of ceremonies : a person who acts as host for a special event or a program of entertainment (as on television)
mas•ter•piece \ˈmas-tər-ˌpēs\ *n* **:** a work done with extraordinary skill
master plan *n* **:** an overall plan
mas•ter's \ˈmas-tərz\ *n* **:** a master's degree
master sergeant *n* **1 :** a noncommissioned officer in the army ranking next below a sergeant major **2 :** a noncommissioned officer in the air force ranking next below a senior master sergeant **3 :** a noncommissioned officer in the marine corps ranking next below a master gunnery sergeant
mas•ter•stroke \ˈmas-tər-ˌstrōk\ *n* **:** a masterly performance or move
mas•ter•work \-ˌwərk\ *n* **:** MASTERPIECE
mas•tery \ˈmas-tə-rē\ *n* **1** ♦ **:** the authority of a master **:** DOMINION; *also* **:** SUPERIORITY **2 :** possession or display of great skill or knowledge

♦ arm, authority, clutch, command, control, dominion, grip, hold, power, superiority, sway

mast•head \ˈmast-ˌhed\ *n* **1 :** the top of a mast **2 :** the printed matter in a newspaper or periodical giving the title and details of ownership and rates of subscription or advertising
mas•tic \ˈmas-tik\ *n* **:** a pasty material used as a coating or cement
mas•ti•cate \ˈmas-tə-ˌkāt\ *vb* **-cat•ed; -cat•ing :** to grind or crush (food) with or as if with the teeth **:** CHEW — **mas•ti•ca•tion** \ˌmas-tə-ˈkā-shən\ *n*
mas•tiff \ˈmas-təf\ *n* **:** any of a breed of large smooth-coated dogs used especially as guard dogs
mast•odon \ˈmas-tə-ˌdän\ *n* **:** any of numerous huge extinct mammals related to the mammoths
mas•toid \ˈmas-ˌtȯid\ *n* **:** a bony prominence behind the ear — **mastoid** *adj*

mas•tur•ba•tion \ˌmas-tər-ˈbā-shən\ *n* : stimulation of the genital organs apart from sexual intercourse, usually to orgasm, and especially by use of one's own hand — **mas•tur•bate** \ˈmas-tər-ˌbāt\ *vb* — **mas•tur•ba•to•ry** \ˈmas-tər-bə-ˌtōr-ē\ *adj*

¹mat \ˈmat\ *n* **1** : a piece of coarse woven or plaited fabric **2** : something made up of many intertwined strands **3** : a large thick pad used as a surface for wrestling and gymnastics

²mat *vb* **mat•ted; mat•ting** **1** : to provide with a mat **2** : to form into a tangled mass

³mat *vb* **mat•ted; mat•ting** **1** : to make (as a color) matte **2** : to provide (a picture) with a mat

⁴mat *var of* MATTE

⁵mat *or* **matt** *or* **matte** *n* : a border going around a picture between picture and frame or serving as the frame

mat•a•dor \ˈma-tə-ˌdȯr\ *n* : a bullfighter whose role is to kill the bull in a bullfight

¹match \ˈmach\ *n* **1** ♦ : a person or thing equal or similar to another; *also* : one able to cope with another : RIVAL **2** : a suitable pairing of persons or objects **3** ♦ : a contest or game between two or more individuals **4** : a marriage union; *also* : a prospective marriage partner

♦ [1] coordinate, counterpart, equal, equivalent, fellow, like, parallel, peer, rival ♦ [1] carbon copy, counterpart, double, duplicate, duplication, facsimile, image, likeness, picture, replica, ringer, spit ♦ [3] bout, competition, contest, event, game, meet, tournament

²match *vb* **1** : to meet as an antagonist; *also* : PIT **2** : to provide with a worthy competitor; *also* : to set in comparison with **3** : to join or give in marriage : MARRY **4** : to combine suitably or congenially; *also* : ADAPT, SUIT **5** ♦ : to provide with a counterpart **6** ♦ : to be the counterpart of

♦ [5] equal, meet, tie ♦ [6] correspond, equal, parallel

³match *n* : a short slender piece of flammable material (as wood) tipped with a combustible mixture that ignites through friction

match•book \ˈmach-ˌbu̇k\ *n* : a small folder containing rows of paper matches

match•less \-ləs\ *adj* ♦ : having no equal

♦ incomparable, inimitable, nonpareil, only, peerless, unequaled, unmatched, unparalleled, unrivaled, unsurpassed

match•lock \-ˌläk\ *n* : a musket with a slow-burning cord lowered over a hole in the breech to ignite the charge

match•mak•er \-ˌmā-kər\ *n* : one who arranges a match and especially a marriage

match•wood \-ˌwu̇d\ *n* : small pieces of wood

¹mate \ˈmāt\ *vb* **mat•ed; mat•ing** : CHECKMATE — **mate** *n*

²mate *n* **1 a** ♦ : one that customarily associates with another : ASSOCIATE, COMPANION **b** ♦ : an assistant to a more skilled worker : HELPER **2** : a deck officer on a merchant ship ranking below the captain **3 a** ♦ : one of a pair **b** ♦ : either member of a married couple or a breeding pair of animals

♦ [1a] associate, cohort, companion, comrade, crony, fellow ♦ [1b] aid, apprentice, assistant, deputy, helper, helpmate, sidekick ♦ [3a] companion, half, match, twin ♦ [3b] consort, partner, spouse

³mate *vb* **mat•ed; mat•ing** **1** : to join or fit together **2** : to come or bring together as mates **3** : COPULATE

¹ma•te•ri•al \mə-ˈtir-ē-əl\ *adj* **1** ♦ : having material existence : PHYSICAL ⟨~ world⟩; *also* : of or relating to the body : BODILY ⟨~ needs⟩ **2** : of or relating to matter rather than form ⟨~ cause⟩; *also* : EMPIRICAL ⟨~ knowledge⟩ **3** ♦ : highly important : SIGNIFICANT **4** ♦ : of a physical or worldly nature ⟨~ progress⟩ — **ma•te•ri•al•ly** *adv*

♦ [1] bodily, concrete, physical, substantial ***Ant*** immaterial, nonmaterial, nonphysical ♦ [3] big, consequential, eventful, important, major, meaningful, momentous, significant, substantial, weighty ♦ [3] applicable, apposite, apropos, germane, pertinent, pointed, relative, relevant ♦ [4] carnal, earthly, fleshly, mundane, temporal, terrestrial, worldly

²material *n* **1** ♦ : the elements or substance of which something is composed or made **2** : apparatus necessary for doing or making something

♦ raw material, stuff, substance

ma•te•ri•al•ise *chiefly Brit var of* MATERIALIZE

ma•te•ri•al•ism \mə-ˈtir-ē-ə-ˌli-zəm\ *n* **1** : a theory that everything can be explained as being or coming from matter **2** : a preoccupation with material rather than intellectual or spiritual things — **ma•te•ri•al•ist** \-list\ *n or adj* — **ma•te•ri•al•is•tic** \-ˌtir-ē-ə-ˈlis-tik\ *adj* — **ma•te•ri•al•is•ti•cal•ly** \-ti-k(ə-)lē\ *adv*

ma•te•ri•al•ize \mə-ˈtir-ē-ə-ˌlīz\ *vb* **-ized; -iz•ing** **1** ♦ : to give material form to; *also* : to assume bodily form **2** ♦ : to make an often unexpected appearance **3** ♦ : to come into existence — **ma•te•ri•al•i•za•tion** \mə-ˌtir-ē-ə-lə-ˈzā-shən\ *n*

♦ [1] embody, epitomize, manifest, personify, substantiate ♦ [2] appear, come out, show up, turn up ♦ [2, 3] arise, begin, commence, dawn, form, originate, spring, start

ma•té•ri•el *or* **ma•te•ri•el** \mə-ˌtir-ē-ˈel\ *n* ♦ : equipment, apparatus, and supplies used by an organization

♦ accoutrements (*or* accouterments), apparatus, equipment, gear, outfit, paraphernalia, tackle

ma•ter•nal \mə-ˈtərn-ᵊl\ *adj* **1** : MOTHERLY **2** : related through or inherited or derived from a female parent — **ma•ter•nal•ly** *adv*

¹ma•ter•ni•ty \mə-ˈtər-nə-tē\ *n, pl* **-ties** **1** : the quality or state of being a mother; *also* : MOTHERLINESS **2** : a hospital facility for the care of women before and during childbirth and for newborn babies

²maternity *adj* **1** : designed for wear during pregnancy ⟨a ~ dress⟩ **2** : effective for the period close to and including childbirth ⟨~ leave⟩

¹math \ˈmath\ *n* : MATHEMATICS

²math *abbr* mathematical; mathematician

math•e•mat•i•cal \ˌma-thə-ˈma-ti-kəl\ *adj* **1** : of, relating to, or according with mathematics **2** ♦ : rigorously exact

♦ accurate, close, delicate, exact, fine, pinpoint, precise, rigorous

math•e•mat•ics \ˌma-thə-ˈma-tiks\ *n* : the science of numbers and their properties, operations, and relations and with shapes in space and their structure and measurement — **math•e•mat•i•cal•ly** \-ti-k(ə-)lē\ *adv* — **math•e•ma•ti•cian** \ˌma-thə-mə-ˈti-shən\ *n*

mat•i•nee *or* **mat•i•née** \ˌmat-ᵊn-ˈā\ *n* : a musical or dramatic performance in the daytime and especially the afternoon

mat•ins \ˈmat-ᵊnz\ *n pl, often cap* **1** : special prayers said between midnight and 4 a.m. **2** : a morning service of liturgical prayer in Anglican churches

ma•tri•arch \ˈmā-trē-ˌärk\ *n* ♦ : a woman who rules or dominates a family, group, or state — **ma•tri•ar•chal** \ˌmā-trē-ˈär-kəl\ *adj* — **ma•tri•ar•chy** \ˈmā-trē-ˌär-kē\ *n*

♦ dame, dowager, matron

ma•tri•cide \ˈma-trə-ˌsīd, ˈmā-\ *n* : the murder of a mother by her child — **ma•tri•cid•al** \ˌma-trə-ˈsīd-ᵊl, ˌmā-\ *adj*

ma•tric•u•late \mə-ˈtri-kyə-ˌlāt\ *vb* **-lat•ed; -lat•ing** ♦ : to enroll as a member of a body and especially of a college or university — **ma•tric•u•la•tion** \-ˌtri-kyə-ˈlā-shən\ *n*

♦ enroll, inscribe, list, register

mat•ri•mo•nial \ˌma-trə-ˈmō-nē-əl\ *adj* ♦ : of or relating to matrimony — **mat•ri•mo•nial•ly** *adv*

♦ conjugal, connubial, marital, nuptial

mat•ri•mo•ny \ˈma-trə-ˌmō-nē\ *n* ♦ : the state of being united to another person according to law or custom : MARRIAGE

♦ marriage, match

ma•trix \ˈmā-triks\ *n, pl* **ma•tri•ces** \ˈmā-trə-ˌsēz, ˈma-\ *or* **ma•trix•es** \ˈmā-trik-səz\ **1** : something within or from which something else originates, develops, or takes form **2** : a mold from which a relief surface (as a piece of type) is made

ma•tron \ˈmā-trən\ *n* **1** ♦ : a married woman usually of dignified maturity or social distinction **2** : a woman supervisor (as in a school or police station) — **ma•tron•ly** *adj*

♦ dame, dowager, matriarch

Matt *abbr* Matthew

¹matte *or* **matt** *var of* ³MAT

²matte *also* **mat** *or* **matt** \ˈmat\ *adj* : not shiny : DULL

¹mat•ter \ˈma-tər\ *n* **1** ♦ : a subject of interest or concern **2** *pl* : events or circumstances of a particular situation **3** : the subject of a discourse or writing **4** ♦ : a source of perplexity, distress, or vexation : TROUBLE ⟨what's the ~⟩ **5** : the substance of which a physical object is composed **6** : PUS **7** : an indefinite amount or quantity ⟨a ~ of a few days⟩ **8** : something written or printed **9** ♦ : something sent through the mail

♦ mail, parcel post, post, snail mail

♦ [1] content, motif, question, subject, theme, topic ♦ [1] affair, business, thing ♦ [4] case, knot, problem, trouble

²matter *vb* ♦ : to have significance

♦ count, import, mean, signify, weigh

mat·ter–of–fact \ˌma-tə-rəv-ˈfakt\ *adj* **1** ♦ **:** adhering to fact **2** ♦ **:** being plain, straightforward, or unemotional — **mat·ter–of–fact·ly** *adv* — **mat·ter–of–fact·ness** *n*

♦ [1] documentary, factual, hard, historical, literal, nonfictional, objective, true ♦ [2] down-to-earth, earthy, hardheaded, practical, pragmatic, realistic

Mat·thew \ˈma-thyü\ *n* **:** a book of the New Testament of Christian Scripture

mat·tins *often cap, chiefly Brit var of* MATINS

mat·tock \ˈma-tək\ *n* **:** a digging and grubbing tool with features of an adze and an ax or pick

mat·tress \ˈma-trəs\ *n* **1 :** a fabric case filled with resilient material used as or for a bed **2 :** an inflatable airtight sack for use as a mattress

mat·u·rate \ˈma-chə-ˌrāt\ *vb* **-rat·ed; -rat·ing :** MATURE

mat·u·ra·tion \ˌma-chə-ˈrā-shən\ *n* **1** ♦ **:** the process of maturing **2 :** the emergence of personal and behavioral characteristics through growth processes — **mat·u·ra·tion·al** \-shə-nəl\ *adj*

♦ development, growth

[1]**ma·ture** \mə-ˈtu̇r, -ˈtyu̇r\ *adj* **ma·tur·er; -est** **1 :** based on slow careful consideration **2** ♦ **:** having attained a final or desired state **3 :** of or relating to a condition of full development **4 :** due for payment **5 :** suitable only for adults — **ma·ture·ly** *adv*

♦ adult, full-blown, full-fledged, ripe ***Ant*** green, immature, juvenile, unripened, young, youthful

[2]**mature** *vb* **ma·tured; ma·tur·ing** ♦ **:** to reach or bring to maturity or completion

♦ age, develop, grow, grow up, progress, ripen

ma·tu·ri·ty \mə-ˈtu̇r-ə-tē, -ˈtyu̇r-\ *n* **1 :** the quality or state of being mature; *esp* **:** full development **2 :** the date when a note becomes due for payment

ma·tu·ti·nal \ˌma-chü-ˈtīn-ᵊl; mə-ˈtüt-ᵊn-əl, -ˈtyüt-\ *adj* **:** of, relating to, or occurring in the morning **:** EARLY

mat·zo *or* **mat·zoh** \ˈmät-sə\ *n, pl* **mat·zoth** \-ˌsōt, -ˌsōth, -sōs\ *or* **mat·zos** *or* **mat·zohs :** unleavened bread eaten especially at the Passover

maud·lin \ˈmȯd-lən\ *adj* **1 :** drunk enough to be silly **2** ♦ **:** weakly and effusively sentimental

♦ corny, mawkish, mushy, saccharine, sappy, schmaltzy, sentimental

[1]**maul** \ˈmȯl\ *n* **:** a heavy hammer often with a wooden head used especially for driving wedges

[2]**maul** *vb* **1 a :** to strike repeatedly **:** BEAT **b :** MANGLE **2** ♦ **:** to handle roughly

♦ maltreat, manhandle, mishandle, rough

maun·der \ˈmȯn-dər\ *vb* **1** ♦ **:** to wander slowly and idly **2** ♦ **:** to speak indistinctly or disconnectedly

♦ [1] gad, gallivant, knock, meander, mope, ramble, range, roam, rove, traipse, wander ♦ [2] ramble, rattle, run on

mau·so·le·um \ˌmȯ-sə-ˈlē-əm, ˌmȯ-zə-\ *n, pl* **-leums** *or* **-lea** \-ˈlē-ə\ **:** a large tomb; *esp* **:** a usually stone building for entombment of the dead above ground

mauve \ˈmōv, ˈmȯv\ *n* **:** a moderate purple, violet, or lilac color

ma·ven *also* **ma·vin** \ˈmā-vən\ *n* **:** EXPERT

mav·er·ick \ˈma-vrik, -və-rik\ *n* **1 :** an unbranded range animal **2** ♦ **:** a person who does not conform to a generally accepted pattern of thought or action **:** NONCONFORMIST

♦ bohemian, deviant, individualist, loner, nonconformist

maw \ˈmȯ\ *n* **1 :** STOMACH; *also* **:** the crop of a bird **2 :** the throat, gullet, or jaws especially of a voracious animal

mawk·ish \ˈmȯ-kish\ *adj* ♦ **:** sickly sentimental — **mawk·ish·ly** *adv*

♦ corny, maudlin, mushy, saccharine, sappy, schmaltzy, sentimental

mawk·ish·ness \-nəs\ *n* ♦ **:** the quality or state of being mawkish

♦ mush, sentimentality

max *abbr* maximum

maxi \ˈmak-sē\ *n, pl* **max·is :** a long skirt, dress, or coat

maxi- *comb form* **1 :** extra long ⟨*maxi*-kilt⟩ **2 :** extra large ⟨*maxi*-problems⟩

max·il·la \mak-ˈsi-lə\ *n, pl* **max·il·lae** \-ˈsi-(ˌ)lē\ *or* **maxillas :** JAW 1; *esp* **:** an upper jaw — **max·il·lary** \ˈmak-sə-ˌler-ē\ *adj*

max·im \ˈmak-səm\ *n* ♦ **:** a proverbial saying

♦ adage, aphorism, byword, epigram, proverb, saying

max·i·mal \ˈmak-sə-məl\ *adj* **:** MAXIMUM — **max·i·mal·ly** *adv*

max·i·mise *chiefly Brit var of* MAXIMIZE

max·i·mize \ˈmak-sə-ˌmīz\ *vb* **-mized; -miz·ing** **1 :** to increase to a maximum **2 :** to make the most of — **max·i·mi·za·tion** \ˌmak-sə-mə-ˈzā-shən\ *n*

[1]**max·i·mum** \ˈmak-sə-məm\ *n, pl* **-ma** \-mə\ *or* **-mums** **1 :** the greatest quantity, value, or degree **2 :** an upper limit allowed by authority **3 :** the largest of a set of numbers

[2]**maximum** *adj* ♦ **:** greatest in quantity or highest in degree attainable or attained

♦ consummate, full, most, nth, paramount, supreme, top, ultimate, utmost

max out *vb* **1 :** to push to or reach a limit or an extreme **2 :** to use up all available credit on (a credit card)

may \ˈmā\ *verbal auxiliary, past* **might** \ˈmīt\ *pres sing & pl* **may** **1 :** have permission or liberty to ⟨you ~ go now⟩ **2 :** be in some degree likely to ⟨you ~ be right⟩ **3** — used as an auxiliary to express a wish, purpose, contingency, or concession

May \ˈmā\ *n* **:** the 5th month of the year

Ma·ya \ˈmī-ə\ *n, pl* **Maya** *or* **Mayas :** a member of a group of American Indian peoples of Yucatán, Guatemala, and adjacent areas — **Ma·yan** \ˈmī-ən\ *n or adj*

may·ap·ple \ˈmā-ˌa-pəl\ *n* **:** a No. American woodland herb related to the barberry that has a poisonous root, one or two large leaves, and an edible egg-shaped yellow fruit

may·be \ˈmā-bē, ˈme-\ *adv* ♦ **:** possibly but not certainly **:** PERHAPS

♦ conceivably, perchance, perhaps, possibly

May Day \ˈmā-ˌdā\ *n* **:** May 1 celebrated as a springtime festival and in some countries as Labor Day

may·flow·er \ˈmā-ˌflau̇-ər\ *n* **:** any of several spring blooming herbs (as the trailing arbutus or an anemone)

may·fly \ˈmā-flī\ *n* **:** any of an order of insects with an aquatic nymph and a short-lived fragile adult having membranous wings

may·hem \ˈmā-ˌhem, ˈmā-əm\ *n* **1 :** willful and permanent crippling, mutilation, or disfigurement of a person **2 :** needless or willful damage

may·on·naise \ˈmā-ə-ˌnāz\ *n* **:** a dressing made of egg yolks, vegetable oil, and vinegar or lemon juice

may·or \ˈmā-ər\ *n* **:** an official elected to act as chief executive or nominal head of a city or borough — **may·or·al** \-əl\ *adj* — **may·or·al·ty** \-əl-tē\ *n*

may·pole \ˈmā-ˌpōl\ *n, often cap* **:** a tall flower-wreathed pole forming a center for May Day sports and dances

maze \ˈmāz\ *n* **:** a confusing intricate network of passages — **mazy** *adj*

ma·zur·ka \mə-ˈzər-kə\ *n* **:** a Polish dance in moderate triple measure

MB *abbr* Manitoba

MBA *abbr* master of business administration

mc *abbr* megacycle

[1]**MC** *n* **:** MASTER OF CEREMONIES

[2]**MC** *abbr* member of Congress

Mc- \mək; mə *before forms beginning with* k *or* g\ *prefix* **:** used to indicate a convenient, low-quality version of a specified thing ⟨*Mc*Book⟩

Mc·Coy \mə-ˈkȯi\ *n* **:** something that is neither imitation nor substitute ⟨the real ~⟩

McGuffin *var of* MACGUFFIN

MCPO *abbr* master chief petty officer

[1]**Md** *abbr* Maryland

[2]**Md** *symbol* mendelevium

MD *abbr* **1** doctor of medicine **2** Maryland **3** muscular dystrophy

MDMA \ˌem-ˌdē-ˌem-ˈā\ *n* **:** ECSTASY 2

mdnt *abbr* midnight

mdse *abbr* merchandise

MDT *abbr* mountain daylight (saving) time

me \ˈmē\ *pron, objective case of* I

Me *abbr* Maine

ME *abbr* **1** Maine **2** mechanical engineer **3** medical examiner

[1]**mead** \ˈmēd\ *n* **:** an alcoholic beverage brewed from water and honey, malt, and yeast

[2]**mead** *n, archaic* **:** MEADOW

mead·ow \ˈme-dō\ *n* **:** land in or mainly in grass; *esp* **:** a tract of moist low-lying usually level grassland — **mead·ow·land** \-ˌland\ *n* — **mead·owy** \ˈme-də-wē\ *adj*

mead·ow·lark \ˈme-dō-ˌlärk\ *n* **:** any of several American songbirds related to the orioles that are streaked brown above and in northernmost forms have a yellow breast marked with a black crescent

mead·ow·sweet \-ˌswēt\ *n* **:** a No. American native or naturalized spirea

mea·ger *or* **mea·gre** \ˈmē-gər\ *adj* **1 :** THIN **2 a :** lacking richness, fertility, or strength **b** ♦ **:** deficient in quality or quantity **:** POOR — **mea·ger·ly** *adv* — **mea·ger·ness** *n*

♦ light, niggardly, poor, scant, scanty, scarce, skimpy, slender, slim, spare, sparse, stingy ***Ant*** abundant, ample, bountiful, copious, generous, liberal, plenteous, plentiful

[1]**meal** \ˈmēl\ *n* **1 :** an act or the time of eating a portion of food **2** ♦ **:** the portion of food eaten at a meal

♦ board, chow, feed, mess, repast, table

[2]**meal** *n* **1 :** usually coarsely ground seeds of a cereal **2 :** a product resembling seed meal

meal·time \ˈmēl-ˌtīm\ *n* **:** the usual time at which a meal is served

mealy \ˈmē-lē\ *adj* ♦ **:** not plain and straightforward

♦ artificial, double-dealing, feigned, hypocritical, insincere, left-handed, mealymouthed, two-faced, unctuous

mealy·bug \ˈmē-lē-ˌbəg\ *n* **:** any of a family of scale insects with a white cottony or waxy covering that are destructive pests especially of fruit trees

mealy·mouthed \ˈmē-lē-ˌmau̇thd, -ˌmau̇tht\ *adj* ♦ **:** not plain and straightforward

♦ artificial, double-dealing, feigned, hypocritical, insincere, left-handed, mealy, two-faced, unctuous

[1]**mean** \ˈmēn\ *vb* **meant** \ˈment\; **mean·ing** **1** ♦ **:** to have in the mind as a purpose **2** ♦ **:** to serve to convey, show, or indicate **:** SIGNIFY **3** ♦ **:** to have importance to the degree of **4 :** to direct to a particular individual

♦ [1] aim, aspire, contemplate, design, intend, meditate, plan, propose ♦ [2] denote, express, import, signify, spell ♦ [3] count, import, matter, signify, weigh

[2]**mean** *adj* **1** ♦ **:** lacking distinction or eminence **:** HUMBLE **2 :** lacking acumen **:** DULL **3 a** ♦ **:** of poor shabby inferior quality or status **b** ♦ **:** worthy of little regard **4** ♦ **:** lacking dignity or honor **:** IGNOBLE, BASE **5 :** sparing or scant in using, giving, or spending **:** STINGY **6** ♦ **:** pettily selfish or malicious **7 :** VEXATIOUS **8 :** very good of its kind **:** EXCELLENT

♦ [1] common, humble, ignoble, inferior, low, lowly, plebeian, vulgar ♦ [3a] dilapidated, grungy, neglected, ratty, seedy, shabby ♦ [3b] inferior, minor, second-rate, secondary ♦ [4] base, contemptible, despicable, detestable, dirty, dishonorable (*or* dishonourable), ignoble, low, snide, sordid, vile, wretched ♦ [6] catty, cruel, hateful, malevolent, malicious, malign, malignant, nasty, spiteful, virulent

[3]**mean** *adj* **1 :** occupying a middle position (as in space, order, or time) **2 :** being a mean **:** AVERAGE ⟨a ~ value⟩

[4]**mean** *n* **1** ♦ **:** a middle point between extremes **2** *pl* ♦ **:** something helpful in achieving a desired end **3** *pl* ♦ **:** material resources affording a secure life **4 :** ARITHMETIC MEAN

♦ [1] medium, middle, midpoint ♦ **means** *pl* [2] agency, agent, instrument, instrumentality, machinery, medium, organ, vehicle ♦ **means** *pl* [3] assets, capital, fortune, opulence, riches, substance, wealth, wherewithal

[1]**me·an·der** \mē-ˈan-dər\ *n* **1 :** a winding course **2 :** a winding of a stream — **me·an·drous** \-drəs\ *adj*

[2]**meander** *vb* **1 :** to follow a winding course **2** ♦ **:** to wander aimlessly or casually

♦ gad, gallivant, knock, maunder, mope, ramble, range, roam, rove, traipse, wander

mean·ing *n* **1** ♦ **:** the thing one intends to convey especially by language; *also* **:** the thing that is thus conveyed **2** ♦ **:** something meant or intended **:** AIM **3 :** SIGNIFICANCE; *esp* **:** implication of a hidden significance **4** ♦ **:** the logical connotation of a word or phrase; *also* **:** DENOTATION

♦ [1, 4] denotation, drift, import, intent, purport, sense, significance, signification ♦ [2] aim, ambition, aspiration, design, dream, end, goal, intent, mark, object, objective, plan, pretension, purpose, thing

mean·ing·ful \-fəl\ *adj* ♦ **:** full of meaning **:** SIGNIFICANT — **mean·ing·ful·ly** *adv*

♦ eloquent, expressive, meaning, pregnant, significant, suggestive ♦ big, consequential, eventful, important, major, material, momentous, significant, substantial, weighty

mean·ing·less \-ləs\ *adj* ♦ **:** having no meaning

♦ empty, pointless, senseless ***Ant*** meaningful

mean·ly \ˈmēn-lē\ *adv* ♦ **:** in a mean manner

♦ hatefully, maliciously, nastily, spitefully, viciously, wickedly

mean·ness \ˈmēn-nəs\ *n* ♦ **:** the quality or state of being mean

♦ cattiness, despite, hatefulness, malice, malignity, nastiness, spite, spleen, venom, viciousness

[1]**mean·time** \ˈmēn-ˌtīm\ *n* **:** the intervening time

[2]**meantime** *adv* **:** MEANWHILE

[1]**mean·while** \-ˌhwī(-ə)l\ *n* **:** MEANTIME

[2]**meanwhile** *adv* **1 :** during the intervening time **2 :** at the same time

meas *abbr* measure

mea·sles \ˈmē-zəlz\ *n sing or pl* **:** an acute virus disease marked by fever and an eruption of distinct circular red spots

mea·sly \ˈmēz-lē, -zə-lē\ *adj* **mea·sli·er; -est** ♦ **:** contemptibly small or insignificant

♦ inconsequential, inconsiderable, insignificant, minute, negligible, nominal, paltry, petty, slight, trifling, trivial

[1]**mea·sure** \ˈme-zhər, ˈmā-\ *n* **1 :** an adequate or moderate portion; *also* **:** a suitable limit **2** ♦ **:** the dimensions, capacity, or amount of something ascertained by measuring; *also* **:** an instrument for measuring **3 :** a unit of measurement; *also* **:** a system of such units **4 :** the act or process of measuring **5** ♦ **:** rhythmic structure or movement **6 :** the part of a musical staff between two bars **7** ♦ **:** a basis or standard of comparison **:** CRITERION **8** ♦ **:** a means to an end **9 :** a legislative bill **10** ♦ **:** the total number or quantity

♦ [2] dimension, extent, magnitude, measurement, proportion, size ♦ [5] beat, cadence, meter (*or* metre), rhythm ♦ [7] criterion, grade, mark, par, standard, touchstone, yardstick ♦ [8] expedient, move, shift, step ♦ [10] amount, quantity

[2]**measure** *vb* **mea·sured; mea·sur·ing** **1 :** to mark or fix in multiples of a specific unit ⟨~ off five centimeters⟩ **2** ♦ **:** to ascertain the measurements of **3 :** to bring into comparison or competition **4 :** to serve as a means of measuring **5 :** to have a specified measurement — **mea·sur·able** \ˈme-zhə-rə-bəl, ˈmā-\ *adj* — **mea·sur·ably** \-blē\ *adv* — **mea·sur·er** *n*

♦ gauge, scale, span

measured *adj* **1** ♦ **:** marked by rhythm **2** ♦ **:** confined within limits **3** ♦ **:** characterized by or resulting from careful and thorough consideration **:** DELIBERATE, CALCULATED

♦ [1] cadenced, metrical, rhythmic ♦ [2] definite, determinate, finite, limited, narrow, restricted ♦ [3] advised, calculated, deliberate, reasoned, studied, thoughtful, thought-out

mea·sure·less \-ləs\ *adj* **1** ♦ **:** having no observable limit **2** ♦ **:** very great ⟨had ~ energy⟩

♦ [1, 2] boundless, endless, illimitable, immeasurable, indefinite, infinite, limitless, unbounded, unfathomable, unlimited

mea·sure·ment \ˈme-zhər-mənt, ˈmā-\ *n* **1 :** the act or process of measuring **2** ♦ **:** a figure, extent, or amount obtained by measuring

♦ dimension, extent, magnitude, measure, proportion, size

measure up *vb* **1 :** to have necessary or fitting qualifications — often used with *to* **2** ♦ **:** to equal especially in ability — used with *to*

♦ *usu* **measure up to** approach, approximate, compare, stack up

meat \ˈmēt\ *n* **1** ♦ **:** material taken into an organism and used for growth, repair, and vital processes and as a source of energy **:** FOOD; *esp* **:** solid food as distinguished from drink **2 :** animal and especially mammal flesh considered as food **3 :** the edible part inside a covering (as a shell or rind) — **meaty** *adj*

♦ chow, fare, food, grub, provender, provisions, viands, victuals

meat·ball \-ˌbȯl\ *n* **:** a small ball of chopped or ground meat

meat loaf *n* **:** a dish of ground meat seasoned and baked in the form of a loaf

mec·ca \ˈme-kə\ *n, often cap* ♦ **:** a center of a specified activity or interest

♦ base, center (*or* centre), core, cynosure, eye, focus, heart, hub, nucleus, seat

mech *abbr* mechanical; mechanics

[1]**me·chan·ic** \mi-ˈka-nik\ *adj* **:** of or relating to manual work or skill

[2]**mechanic** *n* **1 :** a manual worker **2 :** MACHINIST; *esp* **:** one who repairs cars

me•chan•i•cal \mi-ˈka-ni-kəl\ *adj* **1 :** of or relating to machinery, to manual operations, or to mechanics **2** ♦ **:** done as if by a machine — **me•chan•i•cal•ly** \-k(ə-)lē\ *adv*

♦ automatic, involuntary, spontaneous

mechanical drawing *n* **:** drawing done with the aid of instruments
me•chan•ics \mi-ˈka-niks\ *n sing or pl* **1 :** a branch of physics that deals with energy and forces and their effect on bodies **2 :** the practical application of mechanics (as to the operation of machines) **3 :** mechanical or functional details
mech•a•nism \ˈme-kə-ˌni-zəm\ *n* **1 :** a piece of machinery; *also* **:** a process or technique for achieving a result **2 :** mechanical operation or action **3 :** the fundamental processes involved in or responsible for a natural phenomenon ⟨the visual ~⟩
mech•a•nis•tic \ˌme-kə-ˈnis-tik\ *adj* **1 :** mechanically determined ⟨~ universe⟩ **2 :** MECHANICAL — **mech•a•nis•ti•cal•ly** \-ti-k(ə-)lē\ *adv*
mech•a•nize \ˈme-kə-ˌnīz\ *vb* **-nized; -niz•ing 1 :** to make mechanical **2 :** to equip with machinery especially in order to replace human or animal labor **3 :** to equip with armed and armored motor vehicles — **mech•a•ni•za•tion** \ˌme-kə-nə-ˈzā-shən\ *n* — **mech•a•niz•er** *n*
med *abbr* **1** medical; medicine **2** medieval **3** medium
MEd *abbr* master of education
med•al \ˈmed-ᵊl\ *n* **1 :** a small usually metal object bearing a religious emblem or picture **2 :** a piece of metal issued to commemorate a person or event or to award excellence or achievement
med•al•ist *or* **med•al•list** \ˈmed-ᵊl-ist\ *n* **1 :** a designer or maker of medals **2 :** a recipient of a medal as an award
me•dal•lion \mə-ˈdal-yən\ *n* **1 :** a large medal **2 :** a tablet or panel bearing a portrait or an ornament
med•dle \ˈmed-ᵊl\ *vb* **med•dled; med•dling** ♦ **:** to interfere without right or propriety

♦ butt in, interfere, intrude, mess, nose, obtrude, poke, pry, snoop

med•dler \ˈmed-ᵊl-ər\ *n* ♦ **:** one that meddles

♦ busybody, interloper, intruder, kibitzer

med•dle•some \ˈmed-ᵊl-səm\ *adj* ♦ **:** inclined to meddle

♦ intrusive, nosy, obtrusive, officious, presumptuous, prying

med•e•vac *also* **med•i•vac** \ˈme-də-ˌvak\ *n* **1 :** emergency evacuation of the sick or wounded **2 :** a helicopter used for medevac
me•dia \ˈmē-dē-ə\ *n, pl* **me•di•as 1 :** MEDIUM 4 **2** *sing or pl in constr* **:** MASS MEDIA
me•di•al \ˈmē-dē-əl\ *adj* **:** occurring in or extending toward the middle
1me•di•an \ˈmē-dē-ən\ *n* **1 :** a value in an ordered set of values below and above which there are an equal number of values **2 :** MEDIAN STRIP
2median *adj* **1** ♦ **:** being in the middle or in an intermediate position **2** ♦ **:** relating to or constituting a statistical median

♦ [1] halfway, intermediary, intermediate, medium, middle, midmost ♦ [2] average, middle, moderate, modest

median strip *n* **:** a strip dividing a highway into lanes according to the direction of travel
me•di•ate \ˈmē-dē-ˌāt\ *vb* **-at•ed; -at•ing 1** ♦ **:** to act as an intermediary; *esp* **:** to work with opposing sides in order to resolve (as a dispute) or bring about (as a settlement) **2 :** to bring about, influence, or transmit (as a physical process or effect) by acting as an intermediate or controlling agent or mechanism — **me•di•a•tion** \ˌmē-dē-ˈā-shən\ *n*

♦ intercede, interpose, intervene

me•di•a•tor \ˈmē-dē-ˌā-tər\ *n* ♦ **:** one that mediates

♦ arbiter, arbitrator, broker, go-between, intercessor, intermediary, middleman, peacemaker

med•ic \ˈme-dik\ *n* **:** one engaged in medical work; *esp* **:** CORPSMAN
med•i•ca•ble \ˈme-di-kə-bəl\ *adj* **:** CURABLE
Med•ic•aid \ˈme-di-ˌkād\ *n, often cap* **:** a program of financial assistance for medical care designed for those unable to afford regular medical service and financed jointly by the state and federal governments
med•i•cal \ˈme-di-kəl\ *adj* **:** of or relating to the science or practice of medicine or the treatment of disease — **med•i•cal•ly** \-k(ə-)lē\ *adv*
medical examiner *n* **:** a public officer who performs autopsies on bodies to find the cause of death
me•di•ca•ment \mi-ˈdi-kə-mənt, ˈme-di-kə-\ *n* **:** a substance used in therapy

Medi•care \ˈme-di-ˌker\ *n, often cap* **:** a government program of financial assistance for medical care especially for the aged
med•i•cate \ˈme-də-ˌkāt\ *vb* **-cat•ed; -cat•ing :** to treat with medicine
med•i•ca•tion \ˌme-də-ˈkā-shən\ *n* **1 :** the act or process of medicating **2 :** a substance or preparation used in treating disease **:** MEDICINE
me•dic•i•nal \mə-ˈdis-ᵊn-əl\ *adj* **:** tending or used to cure disease or relieve pain — **me•dic•i•nal•ly** *adv*
med•i•cine \ˈme-də-sən\ *n* **1** ♦ **:** a substance or preparation used in treating disease **2 :** a science and art dealing with the prevention, alleviation, and cure of disease

♦ cure, drug, pharmaceutical, remedy, specific

medicine ball *n* **:** a heavy stuffed leather ball used for conditioning exercises
medicine man *n* **:** a priestly healer or sorcerer especially among the American Indians **:** SHAMAN
med•i•co \ˈme-di-ˌkō\ *n, pl* **-cos :** a medical practitioner or student
me•di•e•val *or* **me•di•ae•val** \ˌmē-dē-ˈē-vəl, ˌme-, mē-ˈdē-vəl\ *adj* **1 :** of, relating to, or characteristic of the Middle Ages **2 :** extremely outmoded or antiquated — **me•di•e•val•ism** \-və-ˌli-zəm\ *n* — **me•di•e•val•ist** \-list\ *n*
me•di•o•cre \ˌmē-dē-ˈō-kər\ *adj* ♦ **:** of moderate or low quality — **me•di•oc•ri•ty** \-ˈä-krə-tē\ *n*

♦ common, fair, indifferent, medium, middling, ordinary, passable, run-of-the-mill, second-rate, so-so

med•i•tate \ˈme-də-ˌtāt\ *vb* **-tat•ed; -tat•ing 1** ♦ **:** to muse over **:** CONTEMPLATE, PONDER **2 :** to plan or project in the mind **:** INTEND — **med•i•ta•tion** \ˌme-də-ˈtā-shən\ *n*

♦ chew over, cogitate, consider, contemplate, debate, deliberate, entertain, mull, ponder, question, ruminate, study, think, weigh

med•i•ta•tive \ˈme-də-ˌtā-tiv\ *adj* **1** ♦ **:** marked by or conducive to meditation **2** ♦ **:** disposed or given to meditation — **med•i•ta•tive•ly** *adv*

♦ [1, 2] contemplative, melancholy, pensive, reflective, ruminant, thoughtful

Med•i•ter•ra•nean \ˌme-də-tə-ˈrā-nē-ən, -ˈrā-nyən\ *adj* **:** of or relating to the Mediterranean Sea or to the lands or people around it
1me•di•um \ˈmē-dē-əm\ *n, pl* **mediums** *or* **me•dia** \-dē-ə\ **1 a :** something in a middle position **b** ♦ **:** a middle position or degree **2** ♦ **:** a means of effecting or conveying something **3 :** a surrounding or enveloping substance **4 :** a channel or system of communication, information, or entertainment **5 :** a mode of artistic expression **6 :** an individual held to be a channel of communication between the earthly world and a world of spirits **7** ♦ **:** a condition or environment in which something may function or flourish

♦ [1b] mean, middle, midpoint ♦ [2] agency, agent, instrument, instrumentality, machinery, means, organ, vehicle ♦ [7] atmosphere, climate, environment, environs, milieu, setting, surroundings

2medium *adj* ♦ **:** intermediate in amount, quality, position, or degree

♦ average, intermediate, median, middle, moderate, modest ♦ halfway, middle, midmost ♦ common, fair, indifferent, mediocre, middling, ordinary, passable, run-of-the-mill, second-rate, so-so

me•di•um•is•tic \ˌmē-dē-ə-ˈmis-tik\ *adj* **:** of, relating to, or being a spiritualistic medium
medivac *var of* MEDEVAC
med•ley \ˈmed-lē\ *n, pl* **medleys 1** ♦ **:** a diverse assortment or mixture **:** HODGEPODGE **2 :** a musical composition made up especially of a series of songs

♦ assortment, clutter, jumble, mélange, miscellany, motley, muddle, variety, welter

me•dul•la \mə-ˈdə-lə\ *n, pl* **-las** *or* **-lae** \-(ˌ)lē, -ˌlī\ **:** an inner or deep anatomical part; *also* **:** the posterior part (**medulla ob•lon•ga•ta** \-ˌä-ˌblȯŋ-ˈgä-tə\) of the vertebrate brain that is continuous with the spinal cord
meed \ˈmēd\ *n* **:** a fitting return
meek \ˈmēk\ *adj* **1** ♦ **:** characterized by patience and long-suffering **2 :** deficient in spirit and courage **3 :** MODERATE

♦ demure, humble, lowly, modest, retiring, unassuming, unpretentious

meek•ly \-lē\ *adv* ♦ **:** in a meek manner

♦ humbly, lowly, modestly, sheepishly

meek•ness \-nəs\ *n* ♦ : the quality or state of being meek

♦ humbleness, humility, lowliness, modesty

meer•schaum \ˈmir-shəm, -ˌshȯm\ *n* : a tobacco pipe made of a light white clayey mineral

1meet \ˈmēt\ *vb* **met** \ˈmet\; **meet•ing** **1** ♦ : to come upon **2** : JOIN, INTERSECT **3** : to appear to the perception of **4** : OPPOSE, FIGHT **5 a** : to join in conversation or discussion **b** ♦ : to come together : ASSEMBLE **6** : to conform to **7** ♦ : to pay fully or fulfill the obligations of **8 a** : to contend successfully with : cope with **b** ♦ : to produce or provide a counterpart or equal to : MATCH **9** : to provide for **10** : to be introduced to

♦ [1] chance, encounter, happen, stumble ♦ [5b] assemble, cluster, collect, concentrate, conglomerate, congregate, convene, forgather, gather, rendezvous ♦ [7] answer, comply, fill, fulfill, keep, redeem, satisfy ♦ [8b] equal, match, tie

2meet *n* ♦ : an assembling especially for a hunt or for competitive sports

♦ bout, competition, contest, event, game, match, tournament

3meet *adj* ♦ : precisely adapted to a particular situation, need, or circumstance : SUITABLE, PROPER

♦ applicable, appropriate, apt, felicitous, fit, fitting, good, happy, proper, right, suitable

meet•ing \ˈmē-tiŋ\ *n* **1** ♦ : the act or process of coming together : ASSEMBLY **2** ♦ : a point where things come together

♦ [1] assembly, conference, congress, convention, convocation, council, gathering, get-together, huddle, powwow, seminar ♦ [2] confluence, conjunction, convergence

meet•ing•house \-ˌhau̇s\ *n* : a building for public assembly and especially for Protestant worship

meg \ˈmeg\ *n* : MEGABYTE

mega- *or* **meg-** *comb form* **1** : great : large ⟨*mega*hit⟩ **2** : million ⟨*mega*hertz⟩

mega•byte \ˈme-gə-ˌbīt\ *n* : 1024 kilobytes or 1,048,576 bytes; *also* : one million bytes

mega•cy•cle \-ˌsī-kəl\ *n* : MEGAHERTZ

mega•death \-ˌdeth\ *n* : one million deaths — used as a unit in reference to nuclear warfare

mega•hertz \ˈme-gə-ˌhərts, -ˌherts\ *n* : a unit of frequency equal to one million hertz

mega•lith \ˈme-gə-ˌlith\ *n* : a large stone used in prehistoric monuments — **mega•lith•ic** \ˌme-gə-ˈli-thik\ *adj*

meg•a•lo•ma•nia \ˌme-gə-lō-ˈmā-nē-ə, -nyə\ *n* : a mental disorder marked by feelings of personal omnipotence and grandeur — **meg•a•lo•ma•ni•ac** \-ˈmā-nē-ˌak\ *adj or n*

meg•a•lop•o•lis \ˌme-gə-ˈlä-pə-ləs\ *n* : a very large urban unit

mega•phone \ˈme-gə-ˌfōn\ *n* : a cone-shaped device used to intensify or direct the voice — **megaphone** *vb*

mega•pix•el \ˈme-gə-ˌpik-səl\ *n* : one million pixels

mega•plex \-ˌpleks\ *n* : a cineplex having usually at least 16 movie theaters

mega•ton \-ˌtən\ *n* : an explosive force equivalent to that of one million tons of TNT

mega•vi•ta•min \-ˌvī-tə-mən\ *adj* : relating to or consisting of very large doses of vitamins — **mega•vi•ta•mins** *n pl*

mei•o•sis \mī-ˈō-səs\ *n* : a process of cell division in gamete-producing cells in which the number of chromosomes is reduced to one half — **mei•ot•ic** \mī-ˈä-tik\ *adj*

meit•ner•i•um \mīt-ˈnir-ē-əm, -ˈner-\ *n* : an artificially produced radioactive chemical element

mel•an•cho•lia \ˌme-lən-ˈkō-lē-ə\ *n* : a mental condition marked by extreme depression often with delusions

mel•an•chol•ic \ˌme-lən-ˈkä-lik\ *adj* **1** : DEPRESSED **2** : of or relating to melancholia

1mel•an•choly \ˈme-lən-ˌkä-lē\ *n, pl* **-chol•ies** ♦ : depression of spirits : DEJECTION — **melancholy** *adj*

♦ blues, dejection, depression, desolation, despondency, doldrums, dumps, forlornness, gloom, heartsickness, sadness

2melancholy *adj* **1 a** : suggestive or expressive of melancholy **b** ♦ : causing or tending to cause sadness or depression of mind or spirit **2 a** ♦ : depressed in spirits **b** : musingly or dreamily thoughtful

♦ [1b] depressing, dismal, dreary, heartbreaking, pathetic, sad, sorry, tearful ♦ [2a] blue, depressed, down, downcast, glum, low, sad, unhappy

Mel•a•ne•sian \ˌme-lə-ˈnē-zhən\ *n* : a member of the dominant native group of the Pacific island grouping of Melanesia — **Melanesian** *adj*

mé•lange \mā-ˈlä^{n}zh, -ˈlänj\ *n* ♦ : a mixture especially of incongruous elements

♦ assortment, clutter, jumble, medley, miscellany, motley, muddle, variety, welter

mel•a•nin \ˈme-lə-nən\ *n* : any of various dark brown pigments of animal or plant structures (as skin or hair)

mel•a•nism \ˈme-lə-ˌni-zəm\ *n* : an increased amount of black or nearly black pigmentation

mel•a•no•ma \ˌme-lə-ˈnō-mə\ *n, pl* **-mas** *also* **-ma•ta** \-mə-tə\ : a usually malignant tumor containing dark pigment

1meld \ˈmeld\ *vb* : to show or announce for a score in a card game

2meld *n* : a card or combination of cards that is or can be melded

3meld *n* : a product of blending : BLEND, MIXTURE

me•lee \ˈmā-ˌlā, mā-ˈlā\ *n* ♦ : a confused struggle

♦ brawl, fracas, fray, free-for-all, row

me•lio•rate \ˈmēl-yə-ˌrāt, ˈmē-lē-ə-\ *vb* **-rat•ed; -rat•ing** : to make or grow better : AMELIORATE — **me•lio•ra•tion** \ˌmēl-yə-ˈrā-shən, ˌmē-lē-ə-\ *n* — **me•lio•ra•tive** \ˈmēl-yə-ˌrā-tiv, ˈmē-lē-ə-\ *adj*

mel•lif•lu•ous \me-ˈli-flə-wəs, mə-\ *adj* ♦ : sweetly flowing — **mel•lif•lu•ous•ly** *adv* — **mel•lif•lu•ous•ness** *n*

♦ euphonious, lyric, mellow, melodic, melodious, musical

1mel•low \ˈme-lō\ *adj* **1** : soft and sweet because of ripeness; *also* : well aged and pleasingly mild ⟨~ wine⟩ **2** : made gentle by age or experience **3** ♦ : being rich and full but not garish or strident ⟨~ colors⟩ **4** : of soft loamy consistency ⟨~ soil⟩ — **mel•low•ness** *n*

♦ balmy, benign, bland, delicate, gentle, light, mild, soft, soothing, tender

2mellow *vb* : to make or become mellow

me•lod•ic \mə-ˈlä-dik\ *adj* ♦ : relating to, containing, constituting, or made up of melody — **me•lod•i•cal•ly** \-di-k(ə-)lē\ *adv*

♦ euphonious, lyric, mellifluous, mellow, melodious, musical

me•lo•di•ous \mə-ˈlō-dē-əs\ *adj* ♦ : pleasing to the ear — **me•lo•di•ous•ly** *adv* — **me•lo•di•ous•ness** *n*

♦ lyric, mellifluous, mellow, melodic, musical ♦ euphonious, harmonious, musical, symphonic, tuneful

melo•dra•ma \ˈme-lə-ˌdrä-mə, -ˌdra-\ *n* **1** : an extravagantly theatrical play in which action and plot predominate over characterization **2** : something having a sensational or theatrical quality — **melo•dra•ma•tist** \ˌme-lə-ˈdra-mə-tist, -ˈdrä-\ *n*

melo•dra•mat•ic \ˌme-lə-drə-ˈma-tik\ *adj* **1** ♦ : of, relating to, or characteristic of melodrama **2** : appealing to the emotions — **melo•dra•mat•i•cal•ly** \-ti-k(ə-)lē\ *adv*

♦ dramatic, histrionic, theatrical

mel•o•dy \ˈme-lə-dē\ *n, pl* **-dies** **1** : sweet or agreeable sound **2** ♦ : a particular succession of notes : TUNE, AIR

♦ air, lay, song, strain, tune, warble

mel•on \ˈme-lən\ *n* : any of various typically sweet fruits (as a muskmelon or watermelon) of the gourd family usually eaten raw

1melt \ˈmelt\ *vb* **1** ♦ : to change from a solid to a liquid state usually by heat **2 a** : DISSOLVE, DISINTEGRATE **b** ♦ : to disperse or disappear or cause to disperse or disappear as if melting **3** : to make or become tender or gentle

♦ [1] deliquesce, flux, fuse, liquefy, run, thaw ♦ [2b] disappear, dissolve, evaporate, fade, flee, go, vanish

2melt *n* : a melted substance

melt•down \ˈmelt-ˌdau̇n\ *n* **1** : the melting of the core of a nuclear reactor **2** : a rapid or disastrous decline or disaster

melting pot *n* : a place where different races, cultures, or individuals assimilate into a cohesive whole

melt•wa•ter \-ˌwȯ-tər, -ˌwä-\ *n* : water derived from the melting of ice and snow

mem *abbr* **1** member **2** memoir **3** memorial

mem•ber \ˈmem-bər\ *n* **1** : a part (as an arm, leg, leaf, or branch) of an animal or plant **2** : one of the individuals composing a group **3** ♦ : a constituent part of a whole

♦ component, constituent, element, factor, ingredient ♦ part, partition, portion, section, segment

mem•ber•ship \-ˌship\ *n* **1** : the state or status of being a member **2** : the body of members

mem•brane \ˈmem-ˌbrān\ *n* : a thin pliable layer especially of animal or plant origin — **mem•bra•nous** \-brə-nəs\ *adj*
me•men•to \mə-ˈmen-tō\ *n, pl* **-tos** *or* **-toes** ♦ : something that serves to warn or remind; *also* : SOUVENIR

♦ keepsake, memorial, monument, remembrance, souvenir, token

memo \ˈme-mō\ *n, pl* **mem•os** : MEMORANDUM
mem•oir \ˈmem-ˌwär\ *n* **1** : MEMORANDUM **2** : AUTOBIOGRAPHY — usually used in plural **3** : an account of something noteworthy; *also, pl* : the record of the proceedings of a learned society
mem•o•ra•bil•ia \ˌme-mə-rə-ˈbi-lē-ə, -ˈbil-yə\ *n pl* : things worthy of remembrance; *also* : MEMENTOS
mem•o•ra•ble \ˈme-mə-rə-bəl\ *adj* : worth remembering : NOTABLE — **mem•o•ra•bil•i•ty** \ˌme-mə-rə-ˈbi-lə-tē\ *n* — **mem•o•ra•ble•ness** *n* — **mem•o•ra•bly** \-blē\ *adv*
mem•o•ran•dum \ˌme-mə-ˈran-dəm\ *n, pl* **-dums** *or* **-da** \-də\ **1** : an informal record or written reminder **2** ♦ : an informal written note

♦ directive, letter, missive, note, notice

¹me•mo•ri•al \mə-ˈmōr-ē-əl\ *adj* : serving to preserve remembrance
²memorial *n* **1** ♦ : something designed to keep remembrance alive; *esp* : MONUMENT **2** : a statement of facts often accompanied with a petition — **me•mo•ri•al•ize** *vb*

♦ keepsake, memento, monument, remembrance, souvenir, token

Memorial Day *n* : the last Monday in May or formerly May 30 observed as a legal holiday in honor of those who died in war
mem•o•rise *chiefly Brit var of* MEMORIZE
mem•o•rize \ˈme-mə-ˌrīz\ *vb* **-rized; -riz•ing** ♦ : to learn by heart — **mem•o•ri•za•tion** \ˌme-mə-rə-ˈzā-shən\ *n* — **mem•o•riz•er** *n*

♦ learn, study ***Ant*** unlearn

mem•o•ry \ˈme-mə-rē\ *n, pl* **-ries** **1** ♦ : the power or process of remembering **2** : the store of things remembered **3** : COMMEMORATION **4** ♦ : something remembered **5** : the time within which past events are remembered **6** : a device (as in a computer) in which information can be stored

♦ [1, 4] recall, recollection, remembrance, reminiscence

men *pl of* MAN
¹men•ace \ˈme-nəs\ *n* **1** : THREAT **2 a** ♦ : one that represents a threat : DANGER **b** : NUISANCE

♦ danger, hazard, peril, pitfall, risk, threat, trouble

²menace *vb* **men•aced; men•ac•ing** **1** ♦ : to make a show of intention to harm : THREATEN **2** ♦ : to represent or pose a threat to : ENDANGER

♦ [1] hang, hover, overhang, threaten ♦ [2] adventure, compromise, endanger, gamble with, hazard, imperil, jeopardize, risk, venture

men•ac•ing *adj* ♦ : presenting, suggesting, or constituting a menace — **men•ac•ing•ly** *adv*

♦ baleful, dire, foreboding, ominous, portentous, sinister ♦ dangerous, grave, grievous, hazardous, parlous, perilous, risky, serious, unhealthy, unsafe, venturesome

mé•nage \mā-ˈnäzh\ *n* : a domestic establishment : HOUSEHOLD
ménage à trois \-ä-ˈtrwä\ *n* : an arrangement in which three persons share sexual relations especially while living together
me•nag•er•ie \mə-ˈna-jə-rē\ *n* : a collection of wild animals especially for exhibition
¹mend \ˈmend\ *vb* **1** : to improve in manners or morals **2** ♦ : to put into good shape : REPAIR **3** ♦ : to improve in or restore to health : HEAL — **mend•er** *n*

♦ [2] doctor, fix, patch, recondition, renovate, repair, revamp ♦ [3] convalesce, gain, heal, rally, recover, recuperate, snap back

²mend *n* **1** : an act of mending **2** : a mended place
men•da•cious \men-ˈdā-shəs\ *adj* ♦ : given to deception or falsehood : UNTRUTHFUL — **men•da•cious•ly** *adv*

♦ dishonest, lying

men•dac•i•ty \-ˈda-sə-tē\ *n* **1** : the quality or state of being mendacious **2** ♦ : an untrue statement made with intent to deceive : LIE

♦ fabrication, fairy tale, falsehood, falsity, fib, lie, prevarication, story, tale, untruth, whopper

men•de•le•vi•um \ˌmen-də-ˈlē-vē-əm, -ˈlā-\ *n* : a radioactive chemical element artificially produced
men•di•cant \ˈmen-di-kənt\ *n* **1** : BEGGAR **2** *often cap* : FRIAR — **men•di•can•cy** \-kən-sē\ *n* — **mendicant** *adj*
men•folk \ˈmen-ˌfōk\ *or* **men•folks** \-ˌfōks\ *n pl* **1** : men in general **2** : the men of a family or community
men•ha•den \men-ˈhād-ᵊn, mən-\ *n, pl* **-den** *also* **-dens** : a marine fish related to the herring that is abundant along the Atlantic coast of the U.S.
¹me•nial \ˈmē-nē-əl, -nyəl\ *adj* **1** : of or relating to servants **2** : HUMBLE; *also* : SERVILE — **me•ni•al•ly** *adv*
²menial *n* ♦ : a domestic servant

♦ domestic, flunky, lackey, retainer, servant, steward

men•in•gi•tis \ˌme-nən-ˈjī-təs\ *n, pl* **-git•i•des** \-ˈji-tə-ˌdēz\ : inflammation of the membranes enclosing the brain and spinal cord; *also* : a usually bacterial disease marked by this
me•ninx \ˈmē-niŋks, ˈme-\ *n, pl* **me•nin•ges** \mə-ˈnin-(ˌ)jēz\ : any of the three membranes that envelop the brain and spinal cord — **men•in•ge•al** \ˌme-nən-ˈjē-əl\ *adj*
me•nis•cus \mə-ˈnis-kəs\ *n, pl* **me•nis•ci** \-ˈnis-ˌkī, -ˌkē\ *also* **me•nis•cus•es** **1** : CRESCENT **2** : the curved upper surface of a column of liquid
men•o•pause \ˈme-nə-ˌpȯz\ *n* : the period of life when menstruation stops naturally — **men•o•paus•al** \ˌme-nə-ˈpȯ-zəl\ *adj*
me•no•rah \mə-ˈnōr-ə\ *n* : a candelabrum that is used in Jewish worship
men•ses \ˈmen-ˌsēz\ *n sing or pl* : the menstrual flow
menstrual cycle *n* : the complete cycle of physiological changes from the beginning of one menstrual period to the beginning of the next
men•stru•a•tion \ˌmen-strə-ˈwā-shən, men-ˈstrā-\ *n* : a discharging of bloody matter at approximately monthly intervals from the uterus of breeding-age nonpregnant primate females; *also* : PERIOD 6 — **men•stru•al** \ˈmen-strə-wəl\ *adj* — **men•stru•ate** \ˈmen-strə-ˌwāt, -ˌstrāt\ *vb*
men•su•ra•ble \ˈmen-sə-rə-bəl, ˈ-chə-\ *adj* : MEASURABLE
men•su•ra•tion \ˌmen-sə-ˈrā-shən, ˌmen-chə-\ *n* : MEASUREMENT
-ment \mənt\ *n suffix* **1** : concrete result, object, or agent of a (specified) action ⟨embank*ment*⟩ ⟨entangle*ment*⟩ **2** : concrete means or instrument of a (specified) action ⟨entertain*ment*⟩ **3** : action : process ⟨encircle*ment*⟩ ⟨develop*ment*⟩ **4** : place of a (specified) action ⟨encamp*ment*⟩ **5** : state : condition ⟨amaze*ment*⟩
men•tal \ˈment-ᵊl\ *adj* **1** ♦ : of or relating to the mind **2** ♦ : of, relating to, or affected with a disorder of the mind ⟨~ illness⟩ — **men•tal•ly** *adv*

♦ [1] cerebral, inner, intellectual, psychological ♦ [2] crazy, deranged, insane, mad

mental age *n* : a measure of a child's mental development in terms of the number of years it takes an average child to reach the same level
mental deficiency *n* : MENTAL RETARDATION
men•tal•i•ty \men-ˈta-lə-tē\ *n, pl* **-ties** **1** ♦ : mental power or capacity **2** : mode or way of thought

♦ brains, gray matter (*or* grey matter), intellect, intelligence, reason, sense

mental retardation *n* : subaverage intellectual ability present from infancy that is characterized by an IQ of 70 or less and problems in development, learning, and social adjustment — **mentally retarded** *adj*
men•tee \men-ˈtē\ *n* : PROTÉGÉ
men•thol \ˈmen-ˌthȯl, -ˌthōl\ *n* : an alcohol occurring especially in mint oils that has the odor and cooling properties of peppermint — **men•tho•lat•ed** \-thə-ˌlā-təd\ *adj*
¹men•tion \ˈmen-chən\ *n* **1** : a brief or casual reference **2** : a formal citation for outstanding achievement
²mention *vb* **1** ♦ : to refer to : CITE **2** : to cite for superior achievement — **not to mention** : to say nothing of

♦ advert (to), cite, instance, name, note, notice, quote, refer (to), specify, touch (*on* or *upon*)

¹men•tor \ˈmen-ˌtȯr, -tər\ *n* : a trusted counselor or guide; *also* : TUTOR, COACH
²mentor *vb* ♦ : to serve as a mentor for

♦ coach, counsel, guide, lead, pilot, shepherd, show, tutor

menu \ˈmen-yü, ˈmān-\ *n, pl* **menus** **1** : a list of the dishes available (as in a restaurant) for a meal; *also* : the dishes served **2** ♦ : a list of offerings or options

♦ catalog, checklist, list, listing, register, registry, roll, roster, schedule, table

me•ow \mē-ˈau̇\ *vb* **:** to make the characteristic cry of a cat — **meow** *n*

mer *abbr* meridian

mer•can•tile \ˈmər-kən-ˌtēl, -ˌtīl\ *adj* **:** of or relating to merchants or trading

[1]**mer•ce•nary** \ˈmərs-ᵊn-ˌer-ē\ *n, pl* **-nar•ies :** a person who serves merely for wages; *esp* **:** a soldier hired into foreign service

[2]**mercenary** *adj* **1** ♦ **:** serving merely for pay or gain **2 :** hired for service in a foreign army

♦ acquisitive, avaricious, avid, covetous, grasping, greedy, rapacious

mer•cer \ˈmər-sər\ *n, Brit* **:** a dealer in usually expensive fabrics

mer•cer•ise *chiefly Brit var of* MERCERIZE

mer•cer•ize \ˈmər-sə-ˌrīz\ *vb* **-ized; -iz•ing :** to treat cotton yarn or cloth with alkali so that it looks silky or takes a better dye

[1]**mer•chan•dise** \ˈmər-chən-ˌdīz, -ˌdīs\ *n* ♦ **:** the commodities or goods that are bought and sold in business

♦ commodities, wares

[2]**mer•chan•dise** \-ˌdīz\ *vb* **-dised; -dis•ing** ♦ **:** to buy and sell in business

♦ deal, market, put up, retail, sell, vend

mer•chan•dis•er *n* **:** one that buys and sells in business

mer•chant \ˈmər-chənt\ *n* **1** ♦ **:** a buyer and seller of commodities for profit **2 :** STOREKEEPER

♦ dealer, trader, trafficker

mer•chant•able \ˈmər-chən-tə-bəl\ *adj* **:** acceptable to buyers **:** MARKETABLE

mer•chant•man \ˈmər-chənt-mən\ *n* **:** a ship used in commerce

merchant marine *n* **:** the commercial ships of a nation

merchant ship *n* **:** MERCHANTMAN

mer•ci•ful•ly \ˈmər-si-fə-lē\ *adv* **1 :** in a merciful manner **2 :** FORTUNATELY 2

mer•ci•less \ˈmər-si-ləs\ *adj* ♦ **:** having or showing no mercy — **mer•ci•less•ly** *adv*

♦ callous, hard, heartless, inhuman, inhumane, pitiless, soulless, unfeeling, unsympathetic

mer•cu•ri•al \ˌmər-ˈkyu̇r-ē-əl\ *adj* **1** ♦ **:** unpredictably changeable **2 :** MERCURIC — **mer•cu•ri•al•ly** *adv* — **mer•cu•ri•al•ness** *n*

♦ capricious, changeable, fickle, inconstant, unpredictable

mer•cu•ric \ˌmər-ˈkyu̇r-ik\ *adj* **:** of, relating to, or containing mercury

mercuric chloride *n* **:** a poisonous compound of mercury and chlorine used as an antiseptic and fungicide

mer•cu•ry \ˈmər-kyə-rē\ *n, pl* **-ries 1 :** a heavy silver-white liquid metallic chemical element used especially in scientific instruments **2** *cap* **:** the planet nearest the sun

mer•cy \ˈmər-sē\ *n, pl* **mercies 1** ♦ **:** compassion shown to an offender; *also* **:** imprisonment rather than death for first-degree murder **2 :** a blessing resulting from divine favor or compassion; *also* **:** a fortunate circumstance **3** ♦ **:** compassionate treatment of those in distress — **mer•ci•ful** \-si-fəl\ *adj* — **mercy** *adj*

♦ [1] charity, clemency, leniency, quarter ♦ [3] boon, courtesy, favor (*or* favour), grace, indulgence, kindness, service, turn

mercy killing *n* **:** EUTHANASIA

[1]**mere** \ˈmir\ *n* **:** LAKE, POOL

[2]**mere** *adj, superlative* **mer•est 1 :** being nothing more than ⟨a ~ child⟩ **2 :** not diluted **:** PURE

mere•ly \-lē\ *adv* ♦ **:** no more than

♦ but, just, only, simply

mer•e•tri•cious \ˌmer-ə-ˈtri-shəs\ *adj* **:** tawdrily attractive; *also* **:** SPECIOUS — **mer•e•tri•cious•ly** *adv* — **mer•e•tri•cious•ness** *n*

mer•gan•ser \(ˌ)mər-ˈgan-sər\ *n* **:** any of various fish-eating wild ducks with a usually crested head and a slender bill hooked at the end and serrated along the margins

merge \ˈmərj\ *vb* **merged; merg•ing 1 :** to blend gradually **2** ♦ **:** to combine, unite, or coalesce into one

♦ amalgamate, blend, commingle, fuse, incorporate, integrate, intermingle, mingle, mix

merg•er \ˈmər-jər\ *n* **1 :** the act or process of merging **2 :** absorption by a corporation of one or more others

me•rid•i•an \mə-ˈri-dē-ən\ *n* **1** ♦ **:** the highest point **:** CULMINATION **2 :** any of the imaginary circles on the earth's surface passing through the north and south poles — **meridian** *adj*

♦ acme, apex, climax, crown, culmination, head, height, peak, pinnacle, summit, tip-top, top, zenith

me•ringue \mə-ˈraŋ\ *n* **:** a baked dessert topping of stiffly beaten egg whites and powdered sugar

me•ri•no \mə-ˈrē-nō\ *n, pl* **-nos 1 :** any of a breed of sheep noted for fine soft wool **2 :** a fine soft fabric or yarn of wool or wool and cotton

[1]**mer•it** \ˈmer-ət\ *n* **1 :** laudable or blameworthy traits or actions **2** ♦ **:** a praiseworthy quality; *also* **:** character or conduct deserving reward or honor **3** *pl* **:** the intrinsic nature of a legal case; *also* **:** legal significance

♦ distinction, excellence, value, virtue ♦ account, valuation, value, worth

[2]**merit** *vb* ♦ **:** to be worthy of or entitled or liable to **:** EARN, DESERVE

♦ deserve, earn, rate

mer•i•toc•ra•cy \ˌmer-ə-ˈtä-krə-sē\ *n, pl* **-cies :** a system in which the talented are chosen and moved ahead based on their achievement; *also* **:** leadership by the talented

mer•i•to•ri•ous \ˌmer-ə-ˈtōr-ē-əs\ *adj* ♦ **:** deserving honor or esteem — **mer•i•to•ri•ous•ly** *adv* — **mer•i•to•ri•ous•ness** *n*

♦ admirable, commendable, creditable, laudable, praiseworthy ♦ deserving, good, worthy

mer•lin \ˈmər-lən\ *n* **:** a small compact falcon of the northern hemisphere

mer•lot \mer-ˈlō, mər-\ *n* **:** a dry red wine made from a widely grown grape; *also* **:** the grape itself

mer•maid \ˈmər-ˌmād\ *n* **:** a legendary sea creature with a woman's upper body and a fish's tail

mer•man \-ˌman, -mən\ *n* **:** a legendary sea creature with a man's upper body and a fish's tail

mer•ri•ly \ˈmer-ə-lē\ *adv* ♦ **:** in a merry manner

♦ cheerfully, gaily, happily, heartily, jovially, mirthfully

mer•ri•ment \ˈmer-i-mənt\ *n* **1** ♦ **:** lighthearted gaiety or funmaking **:** HILARITY **2** ♦ **:** a lively celebration or party **:** FESTIVITY

♦ [1] cheer, cheerfulness, cheeriness, glee, hilarity, joviality, mirth ♦ [2] conviviality, festivity, gaiety, jollification, merrymaking, revelry

mer•ry \ˈmer-ē\ *adj* **mer•ri•er; -est 1** ♦ **:** full of gaiety or high spirits **2 :** marked by festivity **3 :** BRISK ⟨a ~ pace⟩

♦ blithe, boon, festive, gay, gleeful, jocund, jolly, jovial, mirthful, sunny

merry–go–round \ˈmer-ē-gō-ˌrau̇nd\ *n* **1 :** a circular revolving platform with benches and figures of animals on which people sit for a ride **2 :** a busy round of activities

mer•ry•mak•er \ˈmer-ē-ˌmā-kər\ *n* ♦ **:** one who engages in merrymaking

♦ celebrant, reveler, roisterer

mer•ry•mak•ing \ˈmer-ē-ˌmā-kiŋ\ *n* **1** ♦ **:** gay or festive activity **2 :** a festive occasion

♦ conviviality, festivity, gaiety, jollification, merriment, revelry

me•sa \ˈmā-sə\ *n* ♦ **:** a flat-topped hill with steep sides

♦ plateau, table, tableland

mes•cal \me-ˈskal, mə-\ *n* **1 :** PEYOTE 2 **2 :** a usually colorless liquor distilled from the leaves of an agave; *also* **:** this agave

mes•ca•line \ˈmes-kə-lən, -ˌlēn\ *n* **:** a hallucinatory alkaloid from the peyote cactus

mes•clun \ˈmes-klən\ *n* **:** a mixture of young tender greens; *also* **:** a salad made with mesclun

mesdames *pl of* MADAM *or of* MADAME *or of* MRS.

mesdemoiselles *pl of* MADEMOISELLE

[1]**mesh** \ˈmesh\ *n* **1 :** one of the openings between the threads or cords of a net; *also* **:** one of the similar spaces in a network **2 :** the fabric of a net **3 :** NETWORK **4 :** working contact (as of the teeth of gears) ⟨in ~⟩ **5** ♦ **:** a woven, knit, or knotted material of open texture with evenly spaced holes — **meshed** \ˈmesht\ *adj*

♦ net, network

[2]**mesh** *vb* **1** ♦ **:** to catch in or as if in a mesh **2 :** to be in or come into mesh **:** ENGAGE **3 :** to fit together properly

♦ enmesh, ensnare, entangle, entrap, snare, tangle, trap

mesh•work \ˈmesh-ˌwərk\ *n* **:** NETWORK

me•si•al \ˈmē-zē-əl, -sē-\ *adj* **:** of, relating to, or being the surface of a tooth that is closest to the middle of the front of the jaw

mes•mer•ise *chiefly Brit var of* MESMERIZE

mes•mer•ize \ˈmez-mə-ˌrīz\ *vb* **-ized; -iz•ing** ♦ **:** to dazzle or overcome by or as if by suggestion **:** HYPNOTIZE — **mes•mer•ic** \mez-ˈmer-ik\ *adj* — **mes•mer•ism** \ˈmez-mə-ˌri-zəm\ *n*

♦ arrest, enchant, enthrall, fascinate, grip, hypnotize

Me•so•lith•ic \ˌme-zə-ˈli-thik\ *adj* **:** of, relating to, or being a transitional period of the Stone Age between the Paleolithic and the Neolithic periods

me•so•sphere \ˈme-zə-ˌsfir\ *n* **:** a layer of the atmosphere between the stratosphere and the thermosphere

Me•so•zo•ic \ˌme-zə-ˈzō-ik, ˌmē-\ *adj* **:** of, relating to, or being the era of geologic history between the Paleozoic and the Cenozoic and extending from about 245 million years ago to about 65 million years ago — **Mesozoic** *n*

mes•quite \mə-ˈskēt, me-\ *n* **:** any of several spiny leguminous trees and shrubs chiefly of the southwestern U.S. with sugar-rich pods important as fodder; *also* **:** mesquite wood used especially in grilling food

¹mess \ˈmes\ *n* **1 a** ♦ **:** a quantity of food **b :** enough food of a specified kind for a dish or meal ⟨a ~ of beans⟩ **2** ♦ **:** a group of persons who regularly eat together; *also* **:** a meal eaten by such a group **3 :** a place where meals are regularly served to a group **4** ♦ **:** a confused, dirty, or offensive state

♦ [1a, 2] board, chow, feed, meal, repast, table ♦ [4] chaos, confusion, disarray, disorder, disorganization, eyesore, havoc, hell, jumble, muddle, shambles

²mess *vb* **1 :** to supply with meals; *also* **:** to take meals with a mess **2 a** ♦ **:** to make dirty or untidy — often used with *up* **b** ♦ **:** to become confused or make an error **:** BUNGLE — usually used with *up* **3** ♦ **:** to interest oneself in what is not one's concern **:** INTERFERE, MEDDLE **4 :** PUTTER, TRIFLE **5** ♦ **:** to handle or play with something especially carelessly

♦ *often* **mess up** [2a] confuse, disorder, jumble, mix, muddle, rumple ♦ *usu* **mess up** [2b] bobble, botch, bungle, butcher, flub, foul up, fumble, mangle, screw up ♦ [3] butt in, interfere, intrude, meddle, nose, obtrude, poke, pry, snoop ♦ *usu* **mess with** [5] fiddle, fool, monkey, play, tamper, tinker

mes•sage \ˈme-sij\ *n* **:** a communication sent by one person to another

message board *n* **:** BULLETIN BOARD 2

mess around *vb* ♦ **:** to waste time

♦ fiddle, fool, monkey, play, potter, putter, trifle

messeigneurs *pl of* MONSEIGNEUR

mes•sen•ger \ˈmes-ᵊn-jər\ *n* ♦ **:** one who carries a message or does an errand

♦ courier, go-between, page, runner

messenger RNA *n* **:** an RNA that carries the code for a particular protein from DNA in the nucleus to a ribosome in the cytoplasm and acts as a template for the formation of that protein

Mes•si•ah \mə-ˈsī-ə\ *n* **1 :** the expected king and deliverer of the Jews **2 :** Jesus **3** *not cap* **:** a professed or accepted leader of a cause — **mes•si•an•ic** \ˌme-sē-ˈa-nik\ *adj*

messieurs *pl of* MONSIEUR

mess•i•ness \ˈme-sē-nəs\ *n* ♦ **:** the quality or state of being messy

♦ chaos, confusion, disarray, disorder, disorganization, havoc, hell, jumble, mess, muddle, muss, shambles, tumble, welter

mess•mate \ˈmes-ˌmāt\ *n* **:** a member of a group who eat regularly together

Messrs. \ˈme-sərz\ *pl of* MR.

messy \ˈme-sē\ *adj* ♦ **:** marked by confusion, disorder, or dirt

♦ chaotic, confused, disheveled, disordered, muddled, sloppy, unkempt, untidy ***Ant*** neat, ordered, orderly, tidy

mes•ti•zo \me-ˈstē-zō\ *n, pl* **-zos :** a person of mixed blood

¹met *past and past part of* MEET

²met *abbr* metropolitan

me•tab•o•lism \mə-ˈta-bə-ˌli-zəm\ *n* **:** the processes by which the substance of plants and animals incidental to life is built up and broken down; *also* **:** the processes by which a substance is handled in the living body ⟨~ of sugar⟩ — **met•a•bol•ic** \ˌme-tə-ˈbä-lik\ *adj* — **me•tab•o•lize** \mə-ˈta-bə-ˌlīz\ *vb*

me•tab•o•lite \-ˌlīt\ *n* **1 :** a product of metabolism **2 :** a substance essential to the metabolism of a particular organism or to a metabolic process

meta•car•pal \ˌme-tə-ˈkär-pəl\ *n* **:** any of usually five more or less elongated bones of the part of the hand or forefoot between the wrist and the bones of the digits — **metacarpal** *adj*

meta•car•pus \-ˈkär-pəs\ *n* **:** the part of the hand or forefoot that contains the metacarpals

met•al \ˈmet-ᵊl\ *n* **1 :** any of various opaque, fusible, ductile, and typically lustrous substances that are good conductors of electricity and heat **2 :** METTLE; *also* **:** the material out of which a person or thing is made — **me•tal•lic** \mə-ˈta-lik\ *adj*

met•al•lur•gy \ˈmet-ᵊl-ˌər-jē\ *n* **:** the science and technology of metals — **met•al•lur•gi•cal** \ˌmet-ᵊl-ˈər-ji-kəl\ *adj* — **met•al•lur•gist** \ˈmet-ᵊl-ˌər-jist\ *n*

met•al•ware \ˈmet-ᵊl-ˌwar\ *n* **:** metal utensils for household use

met•al•work \-ˌwərk\ *n* **:** work and especially artistic work made of metal — **met•al•work•er** \-ˌwər-kər\ *n* — **met•al•work•ing** *n*

meta•mor•phism \ˌme-tə-ˈmȯr-ˌfi-zəm\ *n* **:** a change in the structure of rock; *esp* **:** a change to a more compact and more highly crystalline form produced by pressure, heat, and water — **meta•mor•phic** \-ˈmȯr-fik\ *adj*

meta•mor•phose \ˌme-tə-ˈmȯr-ˌfōz, -ˌfōs\ *vb* **1 :** to change into a different physical form especially by supernatural means **2** ♦ **:** to change strikingly the appearance or character of

♦ convert, make over, transfigure, transform

meta•mor•pho•sis \ˌme-tə-ˈmȯr-fə-səs\ *n, pl* **-pho•ses** \-ˌsēz\ **1 a :** a change of physical form, structure, or substance especially by supernatural means **b** ♦ **:** a striking alteration (as in appearance or character) **2 :** a fundamental change in form and often habits of an animal accompanying the transformation of a larva into an adult

♦ changeover, conversion, transfiguration, transformation

met•a•phor \ˈme-tə-ˌfȯr\ *n* **:** a figure of speech in which a word for one idea or thing is used in place of another to suggest a likeness between them (as in "the ship plows the sea") — **met•a•phor•ic** \ˌme-tə-ˈfȯr-ik\ *or* **met•a•phor•i•cal** \ˌme-tə-fȯr-i-kəl\ *adj* — **met•a•phor•i•cal•ly** \-i-k(ə-)lē\ *adv*

meta•phys•i•cal \ˌme-tə-ˈfi-zi-kəl\ *adj* **1 :** of or relating to metaphysics **2** ♦ **:** of or relating to the transcendent or to a reality beyond what is perceptible to the senses

♦ preternatural, superhuman, supernatural, unearthly

meta•phys•ics \ˌme-tə-ˈfi-ziks\ *n* **:** the philosophical study of the ultimate causes and underlying nature of things — **meta•phy•si•cian** \-fə-ˈzi-shən\ *n*

me•tas•ta•sis \mə-ˈtas-tə-səs\ *n, pl* **-ta•ses** \-ˌsēz\ **:** the spread of a health-impairing agency (as cancer cells) from the initial or primary site of disease to another part of the body; *also* **:** a secondary growth of a malignant tumor — **me•tas•ta•size** \-tə-ˌsīz\ *vb* — **met•a•stat•ic** \ˌme-tə-ˈsta-tik\ *adj*

meta•tar•sal \ˌme-tə-ˈtär-səl\ *n* **:** any of the bones of the foot between the tarsus and the bones of the digits that in humans include five elongated bones — **metatarsal** *adj*

meta•tar•sus \-ˈtär-səs\ *n* **:** the part of the human foot or the hind foot in quadrupeds that contains the metatarsals

¹mete \ˈmēt\ *vb* **met•ed; met•ing 1** *archaic* **:** MEASURE **2** ♦ **:** to give out by measure — usually used with *out*

♦ *usu* **mete out** administer, allocate, apportion, deal, dispense, distribute, parcel, portion, prorate

²mete *n* **:** BOUNDARY ⟨~*s* and bounds⟩

me•te•or \ˈmē-tē-ər, -ˌȯr\ *n* **1 :** a small particle of matter in the solar system directly observable only by its glow from frictional heating on falling into the earth's atmosphere **2 :** the streak of light produced by a meteor

me•te•or•ic \ˌmē-tē-ˈȯr-ik\ *adj* **1 :** of, relating to, or resembling a meteor **2 :** transiently brilliant ⟨a ~ career⟩ — **me•te•or•i•cal•ly** \-i-k(ə-)lē\ *adv*

me•te•or•ite \ˈmē-tē-ə-ˌrīt\ *n* **:** a meteor that reaches the surface of the earth

me•te•or•oid \ˈmē-tē-ə-ˌrȯid\ *n* **:** a small particle of matter in the solar system

me•te•o•rol•o•gy \ˌmē-tē-ə-ˈrä-lə-jē\ *n* **:** a science that deals with the atmosphere and its phenomena and especially with weather forecasting — **me•te•o•ro•log•ic** \ˌmē-tē-ˌȯr-ə-ˈlä-jik\ *or* **me•te•o•ro•log•i•cal** \-ˈlä-ji-kəl\ *adj* — **me•te•o•rol•o•gist** \ˌmē-tē-ə-ˈrä-lə-jist\ *n*

¹me•ter *or Can and Brit* **metre** \ˈmē-tər\ *n* ♦ **:** rhythm in verse or music

♦ beat, cadence, measure, rhythm

²meter *or Can and Brit* **metre** *n* **:** the basic metric unit of length

³meter *n* **:** a measuring and sometimes recording instrument

⁴meter *vb* **1 :** to measure by means of a meter **2 :** to print postal indicia on by means of a postage meter ⟨~*ed* mail⟩

meter–kilogram–second *or Can and Brit* **metre–kilogram–**

second *adj* : of, relating to, or being a system of units based on the meter, the kilogram, and the second

meter maid *n* : a woman assigned to write tickets for parking violations

meth•a•done \ˈme-thə-ˌdōn\ *also* **meth•a•don** \-ˌdän\ *n* : a synthetic addictive narcotic drug used especially as a substitute narcotic in the treatment of heroin addiction

meth•am•phet•amine \ˌme-tham-ˈfe-tə-ˌmēn, -thəm-, -mən\ *n* : a drug used medically in the form of its hydrochloride in the treatment of obesity and often illicitly as a stimulant

meth•ane \ˈme-ˌthān\ *n* : a colorless odorless flammable gas produced by decomposition of organic matter or from coal and used especially as a fuel

meth•a•nol \ˈme-thə-ˌnȯl, -ˌnōl\ *n* : a volatile flammable poisonous liquid alcohol used especially as a solvent and as an antifreeze

meth•aqua•lone \me-ˈtha-kwə-ˌlōn\ *n* : a sedative and hypnotic habit-forming drug that is not a barbiturate

meth•od \ˈme-thəd\ *n* **1** ♦ : a procedure or process for achieving an end **2** : orderly arrangement : PLAN

♦ approach, fashion, form, manner, strategy, style, system, tack, tactics, technique, way

me•thod•i•cal \mə-ˈthä-di-kəl\ *adj* **1** ♦ : arranged, characterized by, or performed with method or order ⟨a ~ treatment of the subject⟩ **2** : habitually proceeding according to method ⟨~ in his daily routine⟩ — **me•thod•i•cal•ly** \-k(ə-)lē\ *adv* — **me•thod•i•cal•ness** *n*

♦ orderly, regular, systematic *Ant* disorganized, haphazard, irregular, unsystematic

meth•od•ise *chiefly Brit var of* METHODIZE

Meth•od•ist \ˈme-thə-dist\ *n* : a member of a Protestant denomination adhering to the doctrines of John Wesley — **Meth•od•ism** \-ˌdi-zəm\ *n*

meth•od•ize \ˈme-thə-ˌdīz\ *vb* **-ized; -iz•ing** : SYSTEMATIZE

meth•od•ol•o•gy \ˌme-thə-ˈdä-lə-jē\ *n, pl* **-gies** **1** : a body of methods and rules followed in a science or discipline **2** : the study of the principles or procedures of inquiry in a particular field

meth•yl \ˈme-thəl\ *n* : a chemical radical consisting of carbon and hydrogen

methyl alcohol *n* : METHANOL

meth•yl•mer•cury \ˌme-thəl-ˈmər-kyə-rē\ *n* : any of various toxic compounds of mercury that often occur as pollutants which accumulate in animals especially at the top of a food chain

me•tic•u•lous \mə-ˈti-kyə-ləs\ *adj* ♦ : extremely careful in attending to details — **me•tic•u•lous•ly** *adv* — **me•tic•u•lous•ness** *n*

♦ careful, conscientious, fussy, painstaking

me•tic•u•lous•ness \mə-ˈti-kyə-ləs-nəs\ *n* ♦ : the quality or state of being meticulous

♦ care, carefulness, heed, heedfulness, pains, scrupulousness

mé•tier \ˈme-ˌtyā, me-ˈtyā\ *n* : an area of activity in which one is expert or successful

me•tre \ˈmē-tər\ *Can and Brit var of* 1METER, 2METER

met•ric \ˈme-trik\ *adj* **1** : of or relating to measurement; *esp* : of or relating to the metric system **2** : METRICAL 1

met•ri•cal \ˈme-tri-kəl\ *adj* **1** ♦ : of, relating to, or composed in meter **2** : of or relating to measure and especially the metric system — **met•ri•cal•ly** \-k(ə-)lē\ *adv*

♦ cadenced, measured, rhythmic

met•ri•ca•tion \ˌme-tri-ˈkā-shən\ *n* : the act or process of converting into or expressing in the metric system

met•ri•cize \ˈme-trə-ˌsīz\ *vb* **-cized; -ciz•ing** : to change into or express in the metric system

metric system *n* : a decimal system of weights and measures based on the meter and on the kilogram

metric ton *n* : a metric unit of weight equal to 1,000 kilograms

1**met•ro** \ˈme-trō\ *n, pl* **metros** : SUBWAY

2**metro** *adj* : of, relating to, or characteristic of a metropolis and sometimes including its suburbs

met•ro•nome \ˈme-trə-ˌnōm\ *n* : an instrument for marking exact time by a regularly repeated tick

me•trop•o•lis \mə-ˈträ-pə-ləs\ *n* ♦ : the chief or capital city of a country, state, or region; *also* : a large important city — **met•ro•pol•i•tan** \ˌme-trə-ˈpä-lət-ᵊn\ *adj*

♦ city, municipality

met•tle \ˈmet-ᵊl\ *n* **1** : SPIRIT, COURAGE **2** : quality of temperament

met•tle•some \ˈmet-ᵊl-səm\ *adj* ♦ : full of mettle

♦ fiery, high-spirited, peppery, spirited, spunky

MeV *abbr* million electron volts

1**mew** \ˈmyü\ *vb* : MEOW — **mew** *n*

2**mew** *vb* : CONFINE

mews \ˈmyüz\ *n sing or pl, chiefly Brit* : stables usually with living quarters built around a court; *also* : a narrow street with dwellings converted from stables

Mex *abbr* Mexican; Mexico

Mex•i•can \ˈmek-si-kən\ *n* : a native or inhabitant of Mexico — **Mexican** *adj*

mez•za•nine \ˈmez-ᵊn-ˌēn, ˌmez-ᵊn-ˈēn\ *n* **1** : a low-ceilinged story between two main stories of a building **2** : the lowest balcony in a theater; *also* : the first few rows of such a balcony

mez•zo for•te \ˌmet-(ˌ)sō-ˈfȯr-ˌtā, ˌmed-(ˌ)zō-, -tē\ *adj or adv* : moderately loud — used as a direction in music

mez•zo pia•no \-pē-ˈä-(ˌ)nō\ *adj or adv* : moderately soft — used as a direction in music

mez•zo–so•pra•no \-sə-ˈpra-nō, -ˈprä-\ *n* : a woman's voice having a range between that of the soprano and contralto; *also* : a singer having such a voice

MFA *abbr* master of fine arts

mfr *abbr* manufacture; manufacturer

mg *abbr* milligram

Mg *symbol* magnesium

MG *abbr* **1** machine gun **2** major general **3** military government

mgr *abbr* **1** manager **2** monseigneur **3** monsignor

mgt *or* **mgmt** *abbr* management

MGy Sgt *abbr* master gunnery sergeant

MHz *abbr* megahertz

mi *abbr* **1** mile; mileage **2** mill

MI *abbr* **1** Michigan **2** military intelligence

MIA \ˌem-(ˌ)ī-ˈā\ *n* : a member of the armed forces whose whereabouts following a combat mission are unknown

Mi•ami \mī-ˈa-mē, -mə\ *n, pl* **Mi•ami** *or* **Mi•am•is** : a member of an American Indian people orig. of Wisconsin and Indiana

mi•as•ma \mī-ˈaz-mə, mē-\ *n, pl* **-mas** *also* **-ma•ta** \-mə-tə\ **1** : a vapor from a swamp formerly believed to cause disease **2** : a harmful influence or atmosphere — **mi•as•mal** \-məl\ *adj* — **mi•as•mic** \-mik\ *adj*

mic \ˈmīk\ *n* : MICROPHONE

Mic *abbr* Micah

mi•ca \ˈmī-kə\ *n* : any of various mineral silicates readily separable into thin transparent sheets

Mi•cah \ˈmī-kə\ *n* : a book of Jewish and Christian Scripture

mice *pl of* MOUSE

Mich *abbr* Michigan

Mi•che•as \ˈmī-kē-əs, mī-ˈkē-əs\ *n* : MICAH

Mic•mac \ˈmik-ˌmak\ *n, pl* **Micmac** *or* **Micmacs** : a member of an American Indian people of eastern Canada

micr- *or* **micro-** *comb form* **1** : small : minute ⟨*micro*capsule⟩ **2** : one millionth part of a specified unit ⟨*micro*second⟩

1**mi•cro** \ˈmī-krō\ *adj* **1** : very small; *esp* : MICROSCOPIC **2** : involving minute quantities or variations

2**micro** *n* : MICROCOMPUTER

mi•crobe \ˈmī-ˌkrōb\ *n* : MICROORGANISM; *esp* : one causing disease — **mi•cro•bi•al** \mī-ˈkrō-bē-əl\ *adj*

mi•cro•bi•ol•o•gy \ˌmī-krō-bī-ˈä-lə-jē\ *n* : a branch of biology dealing especially with microscopic forms of life — **mi•cro•bi•o•log•i•cal** \-ˌbī-ə-ˈlä-ji-kəl\ *adj* — **mi•cro•bi•ol•o•gist** \-bī-ˈä-lə-jist\ *n*

mi•cro•brew•ery \ˈmī-krō-ˌbrü-ə-rē\ *n* : a small brewery making specialty beer in limited quantities

mi•cro•burst \-ˌbərst\ *n* : a violent short-lived localized downdraft that creates extreme wind shears at low altitudes

mi•cro•cap•sule \ˈmī-krō-ˌkap-səl, -sül\ *n* : a tiny capsule containing material (as a medicine) released when the capsule is broken, melted, or dissolved

mi•cro•chip \-ˌchip\ *n* : INTEGRATED CIRCUIT

mi•cro•cir•cuit \-ˌsər-kət\ *n* : a compact electronic circuit

mi•cro•com•put•er \-kəm-ˌpyü-tər\ *n* : a small computer that uses a microprocessor; *esp* : PERSONAL COMPUTER

mi•cro•cosm \ˈmī-krə-ˌkä-zəm\ *n* : an individual or community thought of as a miniature world or universe

mi•cro•elec•tron•ics \ˈmī-krō-i-ˌlek-ˈträ-niks\ *n* : a branch of electronics that deals with the miniaturization of electronic circuits and components — **mi•cro•elec•tron•ic** \-nik\ *adj*

mi•cro•en•cap•su•late \ˌmī-krō-in-ˈkap-sə-ˌlāt\ *vb* : to enclose (as a drug) in a microcapsule — **mi•cro•en•cap•su•la•tion** \-in-ˌkap-sə-ˈlā-shən\ *n*

mi•cro•fiche \ˈmī-krō-ˌfēsh, -ˌfish\ *n, pl* **-fiche** *or* **-fiches** *same*

or -ˌfē-shəz, -ˌfi-\ : a sheet of microfilm containing rows of images of pages of printed matter
mi•cro•fiber \ˈmī-krō-ˌfī-bər\ *n* : a fine usually soft polyester fiber; *also* : a fabric made from such fibers
mi•cro•film \-ˌfilm\ *n* : a film bearing a photographic record (as of print) on a reduced scale — **microfilm** *vb*
mi•cro•graph \ˈmī-krə-ˌgraf\ *n* : a graphic reproduction of the image of an object formed by a microscope
mi•cro•man•age \ˌmī-krō-ˈma-nij\ *vb* : to manage especially with excessive control or attention to details — **mi•cro•man•age•ment** \-mənt\ *n* — **mi•cro•man•ag•er** \-ni-jər\ *n*
mi•cro•me•te•or•ite \ˌmī-krō-ˈmē-tē-ə-ˌrīt\ *n* : a very small particle in interplanetary space
mi•crom•e•ter \mī-ˈkrä-mə-tər\ *n* : an instrument used with a telescope or microscope for measuring minute distances
mi•cro•min•ia•tur•iza•tion \ˌmī-kro-ˌmi-nē-ə-ˌchu̇r-ə-ˈzā-shən, -ˌmi-ni-ˌchu̇r-, -chər-\ *n* : the process of producing things in a very small size and especially in a size smaller than one considered miniature — **mi•cro•min•ia•tur•ized** \-ˈmi-nē-ə-chə-ˌrīzd, -ˈmi-ni-chə-\ *adj*
mi•cron \ˈmī-ˌkrän\ *n* : one millionth of a meter
mi•cro•or•gan•ism \ˌmī-krō-ˈȯr-gə-ˌni-zəm\ *n* : an organism (as a bacterium) too tiny to be seen by the unaided eye
mi•cro•phone \ˈmī-krə-ˌfōn\ *n* : an instrument for converting sound waves into variations of an electric current for transmitting or recording sound
mi•cro•pho•to•graph \ˌmī-krə-ˈfō-tə-ˌgraf\ *n* : PHOTOMICROGRAPH
mi•cro•pro•ces•sor \ˌmī-krō-ˈprä-ˌse-sər\ *n* : a computer processor contained on a microchip
mi•cro•scope \ˈmī-krə-ˌskōp\ *n* : an instrument for making magnified images of minute objects usually using light — **mi•cros•co•py** \mī-ˈkräs-kə-pē\ *n*
mi•cro•scop•ic \ˌmī-krə-ˈskä-pik\ *also* **mi•cro•scop•i•cal** \-pi-kəl\ *adj* **1** : of, relating to, or involving the use of the microscope **2 a** : too tiny to be seen without the use of a microscope **b** ♦ : very small — **mi•cro•scop•i•cal•ly** \-pi-k(ə-)lē\ *adv*

♦ atomic, infinitesimal, miniature, minute, teeny, tiny, wee

mi•cro•sec•ond \ˈmī-krō-ˌse-kənd\ *n* : one millionth of a second
mi•cro•sur•gery \ˌmī-krō-ˈsər-jə-rē\ *n* : minute dissection or manipulation (as by a laser beam) of living structures or tissue — **mi•cro•sur•gi•cal** \-ˈsər-ji-kəl\ *adj*
mi•cro•tech•nol•o•gy \-tek-ˈnä-lə-jē\ *n* : technology on a small or microscopic scale
¹mi•cro•wave \ˈmī-krə-ˌwāv\ *n* **1** : a radio wave between one millimeter and one meter in wavelength **2** : MICROWAVE OVEN
²microwave *vb* : to heat or cook in a microwave oven — **mi•cro•wav•able** *or* **mi•cro•wave•able** \ˌmī-krə-ˈwā-və-bəl\ *adj*
microwave oven *n* : an oven in which food is cooked by the absorption of microwave energy by water molecules in the food
¹mid \ˈmid\ *adj* : occupying a middle position : MIDDLE
²mid *abbr* middle
mid•air \ˈmid-ˈar\ *n* : a point or region in the air well above the ground
mid•day \ˈmid-ˌdā, -ˈdā\ *n* ♦ : the middle part of the day

♦ noon, noontime

mid•den \ˈmid-ᵊn\ *n* : a refuse heap
¹mid•dle \ˈmid-ᵊl\ *adj* **1** ♦ : equally distant from the extremes **2** ♦ : being at neither extreme : INTERMEDIATE **3** *cap* : constituting an intermediate period

♦ [1, 2] central, halfway, intermediary, intermediate, median, medium, midmost ***Ant*** extreme, farthest, furthest, outermost ♦ [1, 2] average, intermediate, moderate, modest

²middle *n* **1** ♦ : a middle part, point, or position **2** ♦ : the central portion of the human body : WAIST **3** ♦ : the position of being among or in the midst of something ⟨caught in the ~ of their conflict⟩

♦ [1] mean, medium, midpoint ♦ [2] midriff, waist ♦ [3] deep, depth, height, midst, thick

middle age *n* : the period of life from about 45 to about 64 — **mid•dle–aged** \ˌmid-ᵊl-ˈājd\ *adj*
Middle Ages *n pl* : the period of European history from about A.D. 500 to about 1500
mid•dle•brow \ˈmid-ᵊl-ˌbrau̇\ *n* : a person who is moderately but not highly cultivated — **middlebrow** *adj*
middle class *n* : a social class holding a position between the upper class and the lower class — **middle–class** *adj*
middle ear *n* : a small membrane-lined cavity of the ear through which sound waves are transmitted by a chain of tiny bones
middle finger *n* : the midmost of the five digits of the hand
mid•dle•man \ˈmid-ᵊl-ˌman\ *n* **1** ♦ : an intermediary or agent between two parties **2** : one who is intermediate between the producer of goods and the retailer or consumer

♦ arbiter, arbitrator, go-between, intercessor, intermediary, mediator, peacemaker

middle–of–the–road *adj* : standing for or following a course of action midway between extremes; *esp* : being neither liberal nor conservative in politics — **mid•dle–of–the–road•er** \-ˈrō-dər\ *n* — **mid•dle–of–the–road•ism** \-ˈrō-ˌdi-zəm\ *n*
middle school *n* : a school usually including grades 5 to 8 or 6 to 8
mid•dle•weight \ˈmid-ᵊl-ˌwāt\ *n* : one of average weight; *esp* : a boxer weighing not over 160 pounds
mid•dling \ˈmid-liŋ, -lən\ *adj* **1** : of middle, medium, or moderate size, degree, or quality **2** ♦ : of moderate or low quality, value, ability, or performance : MEDIOCRE

♦ common, fair, indifferent, mediocre, medium, ordinary, passable, run-of-the-mill, second-rate, so-so

mid•dy \ˈmi-dē\ *n, pl* **middies** : MIDSHIPMAN
midge \ˈmij\ *n* : a very small fly : GNAT
midg•et \ˈmi-jət\ *n* **1** *sometimes offensive* : a very small person **2** ♦ : something (as an animal) very small for its kind

♦ dwarf, mite, peewee, pygmy, runt, scrub, shrimp

midi \ˈmi-dē\ *n* : a calf-length dress, coat, or skirt
MIDI \ˈmi-dē\ *n* : a proctocol for the transmission of digitally encoded music
mid•land \ˈmid-lənd, -ˌland\ *n* : the interior or central region of a country
mid•life \ˈmid-ˈlīf\ *n* : MIDDLE AGE
midlife crisis *n* : a period of emotional turmoil in middle age characterized especially by a strong desire for change
mid•most \-ˌmōst\ *adj* ♦ : being in or near the exact middle — **midmost** *adv*

♦ halfway, intermediary, intermediate, median, medium, middle

mid•night \-ˌnīt\ *n* : 12 o'clock at night
mid–ocean ridge \ˈmid-ˈō-shən-\ *n* : an elevation on an ocean floor at the boundary of diverging tectonic plates
mid•point \ˈmid-ˌpȯint, -ˈpȯint\ *n* ♦ : a point at or near the center or middle

♦ mean, medium, middle ♦ center (*or* centre), core, midst

mid•riff \ˈmi-ˌdrif\ *n* **1** : DIAPHRAGM 1 **2** ♦ : the mid-region of the human torso

♦ middle, waist

mid•sec•tion \-ˌsek-shən\ *n* : a section midway between the extremes; *esp* : MIDRIFF 2
mid•ship•man \ˈmid-ˌship-mən, (ˌ)mid-ˈship-\ *n* : a student in a naval academy
mid•ships \-ˌships\ *adv* : AMIDSHIPS
¹midst \ˈmidst\ *n* **1** ♦ : the interior or central part or point **2** : a position of proximity to the members of a group ⟨in our ~⟩ **3** ♦ : the condition of being surrounded or beset

♦ [1] center (*or* centre), core, midpoint ♦ [3] deep, depth, height, middle, thick

²midst *prep* ♦ : in the midst of

♦ amid, among, through

mid•stream \ˈmid-ˈstrēm, -ˌstrēm\ *n* : the middle of a stream
mid•sum•mer \-ˈsə-mər, -ˌsə-\ *n* **1** : the middle of summer **2** : the summer solstice
mid•town \ˈmid-ˌtau̇n, -ˈtau̇n\ *n* : a central section of a city; *esp* : one situated between sections called *downtown* and *uptown* — **midtown** *adj*
¹mid•way \ˈmid-ˌwā, -ˈwā\ *adv* : in the middle of the way or distance
²mid•way \-ˌwā\ *n* : an avenue (as at a carnival) for concessions and amusements
mid•week \-ˌwēk\ *n* : the middle of the week — **mid•week•ly** \-ˌwē-klē, -ˈwē-\ *adj or adv*
mid•wife \ˈmid-ˌwīf\ *n* : a person who helps women in childbirth — **mid•wife•ry** \-ˌwī-fə-rē\ *n*
mid•win•ter \ˈmid-ˈwin-tər, -ˌwin-\ *n* **1** : the winter solstice **2** : the middle of winter
mid•year \-ˌyir\ *n* **1** : the middle of a year **2** : a midyear examination — **midyear** *adj*
mien \ˈmēn\ *n* **1** : air or bearing especially as expressive of mood or personality : DEMEANOR **2** ♦ : outward aspect : APPEARANCE

♦ appearance, aspect, look, presence

miff \ˈmif\ *vb* **:** to put into an ill humor

[1]might \ˈmīt\ *verbal auxiliary, past of* MAY — used as an auxiliary to express permission or possibility in the past, a present condition contrary to fact, less probability or possibility than *may*, or as a polite alternative to *may, ought*, or *should*

[2]might *n* ♦ **:** the power, authority, or resources of an individual or a group

♦ energy, force, main, muscle, potency, power, sinew, strength, vigor (*or* vigour)

might•i•ly \ˈmī-tə-lē\ *adv* **1** ♦ **:** in a mighty manner ⟨applauded ~⟩ **2** ♦ **:** very much ⟨depressed me ~⟩

♦ [1] energetically, firmly, forcefully, forcibly, hard, powerfully, stiffly, stoutly, strenuously, strongly, sturdily, vigorously ♦ [2] especially, extremely, greatly, highly, hugely, mighty, mortally, most, much, real, right, so, very

[1]mighty \ˈmī-tē\ *adj* **might•i•er; -est 1** ♦ **:** very strong **:** POWERFUL **2 :** GREAT, NOTABLE — **might•i•ness** \-tē-nəs\ *n*

♦ important, influential, potent, powerful, significant, strong

[2]mighty *adv* **:** to a high degree

mi•gnon•ette \ˌmin-yə-ˈnet\ *n* **:** an annual garden herb with spikes of tiny fragrant flowers

mi•graine \ˈmī-ˌgrān\ *n* **:** a condition marked by recurrent severe headache and often nausea; *also* **:** an attack of migraine

mi•grant \ˈmī-grənt\ *n* ♦ **:** one that migrates; *esp* **:** a person who moves in order to find work (as picking crops) — **migrant** *adj*

♦ emigrant, émigré, immigrant, settler

mi•grate \ˈmī-ˌgrāt\ *vb* **mi•grat•ed; mi•grat•ing 1 :** to move from one country or place to another **2 :** to pass usually periodically from one region or climate to another for feeding or breeding — **mi•gra•tion** \mī-ˈgrā-shən\ *n* — **mi•gra•to•ry** \ˈmī-grə-ˌtōr-ē\ *adj*

mi•ka•do \mə-ˈkä-dō\ *n, pl* **-dos :** an emperor of Japan

mike \ˈmīk\ *n* **:** MICROPHONE

[1]mil \ˈmil\ *n* **:** a unit of length equal to $\frac{1}{1000}$ inch

[2]mil *abbr* military

milch \ˈmilk, ˈmilch\ *adj* **:** giving milk ⟨~ cow⟩

mild \ˈmī(-ə)ld\ *adj* **1** ♦ **:** gentle in nature or behavior **2 :** moderate in action or effect **3** ♦ **:** not severe **:** TEMPERATE — **mild•ly** *adv* — **mild•ness** *n*

♦ [1] balmy, benign, bland, delicate, gentle, light, mellow, soft, soothing, tender ♦ [3] balmy, clement, equable, gentle, moderate, temperate

mil•dew \ˈmil-ˌdü, -ˌdyü\ *n* **:** a superficial usually whitish growth produced on organic matter and on plants by a fungus; *also* **:** a fungus producing this growth — **mildew** *vb*

mile \ˈmī(-ə)l\ *n* **1 :** a unit of length equal to 5280 ft. **2 :** NAUTICAL MILE

mile•age \ˈmī-lij\ *n* **1 :** an allowance for traveling expenses at a certain rate per mile **2 :** distance in miles traveled (as in a day) **3 :** the amount of service yielded (as by a tire) expressed in terms of miles of travel **4 :** the average number of miles a motor vehicle will travel on a gallon of gasoline

mile•post \ˈmī(-ə)l-ˌpōst\ *n* **:** a post indicating the distance in miles from a given point

mile•stone \-ˌstōn\ *n* **1 :** a stone serving as a milepost **2 :** a significant point in development

mi•lieu \mēl-ˈyər, -ˈyü, -ˈyœ\ *n, pl* **mi•lieus** *or* **mi•lieux** *same or* -ˈyərz, -ˈyüz, -ˈyœz\ ♦ **:** the physical or social setting in which something occurs or develops **:** ENVIRONMENT, SETTING

♦ atmosphere, climate, environment, environs, medium, setting, surroundings

mil•i•tan•cy \ˈmi-lə-tən-sē\ *n* ♦ **:** the quality or state of being militant

♦ aggression, aggressiveness, belligerence, fight, pugnacity, truculence

[1]mil•i•tant \ˈmi-lə-tənt\ *adj* **1 a :** engaged in warfare **b** ♦ **:** prone to fighting **2** ♦ **:** aggressively active especially in a cause — **mil•i•tance** \-təns\ *n* — **mil•i•tant•ly** *adv*

♦ [1b] aggressive, argumentative, bellicose, belligerent, combative, contentious, discordant, disputatious, pugnacious, quarrelsome, scrappy, truculent, warlike ♦ [2] aggressive, ambitious, assertive, enterprising, fierce, go-getting, high-pressure, self-assertive

[2]militant *n* ♦ **:** one who is militant

♦ crusader, fanatic, partisan, zealot

mil•i•ta•rise *chiefly Brit var of* MILITARIZE

mil•i•ta•rism \ˈmi-lə-tə-ˌri-zəm\ *n* **1 :** predominance of the military class or its ideals **2 :** a policy of aggressive military preparedness — **mil•i•ta•rist** \-rist\ *n* — **mil•i•ta•ris•tic** \ˌmi-lə-tə-ˈris-tik\ *adj*

mil•i•ta•rize \ˈmi-lə-tə-ˌrīz\ *vb* **-rized; -riz•ing 1 :** to equip with military forces and defenses **2 :** to give a military character to

[1]mil•i•tary \ˈmi-lə-ˌter-ē\ *adj* **1 :** of or relating to soldiers, arms, war, or the army **2 :** performed by armed forces; *also* **:** supported by armed force — **mil•i•tar•i•ly** \ˌmi-lə-ˈter-ə-lē\ *adv*

[2]military *n, pl* **military** *also* **mil•i•tar•ies 1** ♦ **:** the military, naval, and air forces of a nation **2 :** military persons

♦ armed forces, services, troops

military police *n* **:** a branch of an army that exercises guard and police functions

mil•i•tate \ˈmi-lə-ˌtāt\ *vb* **-tat•ed; -tat•ing :** to have weight or effect

mi•li•tia \mə-ˈli-shə\ *n* **:** a part of the organized armed forces of a country liable to call only in an emergency — **mi•li•tia•man** \-mən\ *n*

[1]milk \ˈmilk\ *n* **1 :** a nutritive usually whitish fluid secreted by female mammals for feeding their young **2 :** a milklike liquid (as a plant juice) — **milk•i•ness** \ˈmil-kē-nəs\ *n* — **milky** *adj*

[2]milk *vb* **1 :** to draw off the milk of ⟨~ a cow⟩ **2 :** to draw something from as if by milking

milk•maid \ˈmilk-ˌmād\ *n* **:** DAIRYMAID

milk•man \-ˌman, -mən\ *n* **:** a person who sells or delivers milk

milk of magnesia : a milk-white mixture of hydroxide of magnesium and water used as an antacid and laxative

milk shake *n* **:** a thoroughly blended drink made of milk, a flavoring syrup, and often ice cream

milk•sop \ˈmilk-ˌsäp\ *n* **:** an unmanly man

milk•weed \-ˌwēd\ *n* **:** any of a genus of herbs with milky juice and clustered flowers

Milky Way *n* **1 :** a broad irregular band of light that stretches across the sky and is caused by the light of a very great number of faint stars **2 :** MILKY WAY GALAXY

Milky Way galaxy *n* **:** the galaxy of which the sun is a member and which includes the stars that create the light of the Milky Way

[1]mill \ˈmil\ *n* **1 :** a building with machinery for grinding grain into flour **2 :** a machine used in processing (as by grinding, stamping, cutting, or finishing) raw material **3** ♦ **:** a building or collection of buildings with machinery for manufacturing **:** FACTORY

♦ factory, plant, shop, works, workshop

[2]mill *vb* **1 :** to process in a mill **2 :** to move in a circle or in an eddying mass

[3]mill *n* **:** one tenth of a cent

mill•age \ˈmi-lij\ *n* **:** a rate (as of taxation) expressed in mills

mil•len•ni•um \mə-ˈle-nē-əm\ *n, pl* **-nia** \-nē-ə\ *or* **-niums 1 :** a period of 1000 years; *also* **:** a 1000th anniversary or its celebration **2 :** the 1000 years mentioned in Revelation 20 when holiness is to prevail and Christ is to reign on earth **3 :** a period of great happiness or human perfection

mill•er \ˈmi-lər\ *n* **1 :** one that operates a mill and especially a flour mill **2 :** any of various moths having powdery wings

mil•let \ˈmi-lət\ *n* **:** any of several small-seeded cereal and forage grasses cultivated for grain or hay; *also* **:** the grain of a millet

milli– *comb form* **:** one thousandth part of

mil•li•am•pere \ˌmi-lē-ˈam-ˌpir\ *n* **:** one thousandth of an ampere

mil•liard \ˈmil-ˌyärd, ˈmi-lē-ˌärd\ *n, Brit* **:** a thousand millions

mil•li•bar \ˈmi-lə-ˌbär\ *n* **:** a unit of atmospheric pressure

mil•li•gram \-ˌgram\ *n* **:** a metric unit of weight equal to $\frac{1}{1000}$ gram

mil•li•li•ter \-ˌlē-tər\ *or Can and Brit* **mil•li•li•tre** *n* **:** a metric unit of volume equal to $\frac{1}{1000}$ liter

mil•li•me•ter \ˈmi-lə-ˌmē-tər\ *or Can and Brit* **mil•li•me•tre** *n* **:** a metric unit of length equal to $\frac{1}{1000}$ meter

mil•li•ner \ˈmi-lə-nər\ *n* **:** a person who designs, makes, trims, or sells women's hats

mil•li•nery \ˈmi-lə-ˌner-ē\ *n* **1 :** women's apparel for the head **2 :** the business or work of a milliner

mill•ing \ˈmi-liŋ\ *n* **:** a corrugated edge on a coin

mil•lion \ˈmil-yən\ *n, pl* **millions** *or* **million :** a thousand thousands — **million** *adj* — **mil•lionth** \-yənth\ *adj or n*

mil•lion•aire \ˌmil-yə-ˈner, ˈmil-yə-ˌner\ *n* **:** one whose wealth is estimated at a million or more (as of dollars or pounds)

mil•li•pede \ˈmi-lə-ˌpēd\ *n* **:** any of a class of arthropods related to the centipedes and having a long segmented body with a hard covering, two pairs of legs on most segments, and no poison fangs

mil•li•sec•ond \-ˌse-kənd\ *n* **:** one thousandth of a second

mil•li•volt \-ˌvōlt\ *n* : one thousandth of a volt
mill•pond \ˈmil-ˌpänd\ *n* : a pond made by damming a stream to produce a fall of water for operating a mill
mill•race \-ˌrās\ *n* : a canal in which water flows to and from a mill wheel
mill•stone \-ˌstōn\ *n* : either of two round flat stones used for grinding grain
mill•stream \-ˌstrēm\ *n* : a stream whose flow is used to run a mill; *also* : the stream in a millrace
mill wheel *n* : a waterwheel that drives a mill
mill•wright \ˈmil-ˌrīt\ *n* : a person who builds mills or sets up or maintains their machinery
milt \ˈmilt\ *n* : the sperm-containing fluid of a male fish
¹mime \ˈmīm\ *n* **1** : MIMIC **2** : a story performed silently and entirely by body movements : PANTOMIME **3** ♦ an actor in a mime

♦ mimic, mummer, pantomime

²mime *vb* ♦ : to imitate closely

♦ ape, copy, emulate, imitate, mimic

mim•eo•graph \ˈmi-mē-ə-ˌgraf\ *n* : a machine for making many copies by means of a stencil through which ink is pressed — **mimeograph** *vb*
mi•me•sis \mə-ˈmē-səs, mī-\ *n* : IMITATION, MIMICRY
mi•met•ic \-ˈme-tik\ *adj* **1** : marked by imitation : IMITATIVE **2** : relating to, characterized by, or exhibiting biological mimicry
¹mim•ic \ˈmi-mik\ *n* **1** ♦ : an actor in a mime **2** ♦ : one that mimics

♦ [1] mime, mummer, pantomime ♦ [2] imitator, impersonator, impressionist

²mimic *vb* **mim•icked** \-mikt\; **mim•ick•ing** **1** ♦ : to imitate closely **2** ♦ : to ridicule by imitation **3** : to resemble by biological mimicry

♦ [1] ape, copy, emulate, imitate, mime ♦ [2] burlesque, caricature, imitate, mock, parody, take off, travesty

mim•ic•ry \ˈmi-mi-krē\ *n, pl* **-ries** **1** : an instance of mimicking **2** : a superficial resemblance of one organism to another or to natural objects among which it lives that gives it an advantage (as protection from predation)
mi•mo•sa \mə-ˈmō-sə, mī-, -zə\ *n* : any of a genus of trees, shrubs, and herbs of the legume family that occur in warm regions and have ball-shaped heads of small white or pink flowers
min *abbr* **1** minim **2** minimum **3** mining **4** minister **5** minor **6** minute
min•a•ret \ˌmi-nə-ˈret\ *n* : a tall slender tower of a mosque from which a muezzin calls the faithful to prayer
mi•na•to•ry \ˈmi-nə-ˌtōr-ē, ˈmī-\ *adj* : THREATENING, MENACING
mince \ˈmins\ *vb* **minced; minc•ing** **1** ♦ : to cut into very small pieces **2** : to restrain (words) within the bounds of decorum **3** : to walk in a prim affected manner

♦ chop, hash

mince•meat \ˈmins-ˌmēt\ *n* : a finely chopped mixture especially of raisins, apples, spices, and often meat used as a filling for a pie
¹mind \ˈmīnd\ *n* **1** ♦ : the power or process of reproducing or recalling what has been learned and retained : MEMORY **2** : the part of an individual that feels, perceives, thinks, wills, and especially reasons **3** : INTENTION, DESIRE **4** ♦ : normal mental condition **5** ♦ : a belief stronger than impression and less strong than positive knowledge : OPINION, VIEW **6** : MOOD **7** : mental qualities of a person or group **8** : intellectual ability **9** : ATTENTION ⟨pay them no ~⟩

♦ [1] memory, recollection, remembrance, reminiscence ♦ [4] head, reason, sanity, wit ***Ant*** derangement, insanity, lunacy, madness, mania ♦ [5] belief, conviction, eye, feeling, judgment (*or* judgement), notion, opinion, persuasion, sentiment, verdict, view

²mind *vb* **1** *chiefly dial* : REMEMBER **2** ♦ : to attend to closely **3** ♦ : to follow the orders or instructions of : OBEY **4** : to be concerned about; *also* : DISLIKE **5** ♦ : to be careful or cautious about **6** ♦ : to take charge of **7** : to regard with attention

♦ [2] attend, hark, hear, heed, listen ♦ [2, 3] comply, follow, heed, listen, note, obey, observe, regard, watch ♦ [5] beware (of), guard (against), watch out (for) ♦ [6] attend, care, oversee, superintend, supervise, tend

mind–bend•ing \ˈmīnd-ˌben-diŋ\ *adj* : MIND-BLOWING
mind–blow•ing \-ˌblō-iŋ\ *adj* : PSYCHEDELIC 1; *also* : MIND-BOGGLING
mind–bog•gling \-ˌbä-gə-liŋ\ *adj* : mentally or emotionally exciting or overwhelming
mind•ed \ˈmīn-dəd\ *adj* **1** ♦ : having inclination, disposition, or tendency : INCLINED, DISPOSED **2** : having a mind of a specified kind or concerned with a specific thing — usually used in combination ⟨narrow-*minded*⟩

♦ amenable, disposed, game, glad, inclined, ready, willing

mind•ful \ˈmīnd-fəl\ *adj* ♦ : bearing in mind : AWARE — **mind•ful•ly** *adv* — **mind•ful•ness** *n*

♦ alive, aware, cognizant, conscious, sensible, sentient, witting

mind•less \-ləs\ *adj* **1 a** : marked by a lack of mind or consciousness **b** ♦ : marked by no use of the intellect **2** ♦ : not mindful : HEEDLESS — **mind•less•ly** *adv*

♦ [1b] dumb, senseless, stupid, witless ♦ [2] careless, heedless, unguarded, unsafe, unwary

mind•less•ness \-nəs\ *n* ♦ : the quality or state of being mindless

♦ dopiness, foolishness, imbecility, stupidity

¹mine \ˈmīn\ *pron* : that which belongs to me
²mine *n* **1** : an excavation in the earth from which minerals are taken; *also* : an ore deposit **2** : an underground passage beneath an enemy position **3** : an explosive device for destroying enemy personnel, vehicles, or ships **4** : a rich source of supply
³mine *vb* **mined; min•ing** **1** : to dig a mine **2** : UNDERMINE **3** : to get ore from the earth **4** : to place military mines in — **min•er** *n*
mine•field \ˈmīn-ˌfēld\ *n* **1** : an area set with mines **2** : something resembling a minefield especially in having many dangers
mine•lay•er \-ˌlā-ər\ *n* : a naval vessel for laying underwater mines
min•er•al \ˈmi-nə-rəl\ *n* **1** : a crystalline substance (as diamond or quartz) of inorganic origin **2** : a naturally occurring substance (as coal, salt, or water) obtained usually from the ground — **mineral** *adj*
min•er•al•ise *chiefly Brit var of* MINERALIZE
min•er•al•ize \ˈmi-nə-rə-ˌlīz\ *vb* **-ized; -iz•ing** **1** : to impregnate or supply with minerals **2** : to change into mineral form — **min•er•al•i•za•tion** \-rə-lə-ˈzā-shən\ *n*
min•er•al•o•gy \ˌmi-nə-ˈrä-lə-jē, -ˈra-\ *n* : a science dealing with minerals — **min•er•al•og•i•cal** \ˌmi-nə-rə-ˈlä-ji-kəl\ *adj* — **min•er•al•o•gist** \ˌmi-nə-ˈrä-lə-jist, -ˈra-\ *n*
mineral oil *n* : an oil of mineral origin; *esp* : a refined petroleum oil used as a laxative
mineral water *n* : water infused with mineral salts or gases
min•e•stro•ne \ˌmi-nə-ˈstrō-nē, -ˈstrōn\ *n* : a rich thick vegetable soup
mine•sweep•er \ˈmīn-ˌswē-pər\ *n* : a warship designed for removing or neutralizing underwater mines
min•gle \ˈmiŋ-gəl\ *vb* **min•gled; min•gling** **1** ♦ : to bring or combine together **2** ♦ : to come into contact : ASSOCIATE; *also* : to move about (as in a group)

♦ [1] amalgamate, blend, combine, commingle, fuse, incorporate, integrate, intermingle, merge, mix ♦ [2] associate, fraternize, hobnob, mix, socialize

ming tree \ˈmiŋ-\ *n* : a dwarfed usually evergreen tree grown as bonsai; *also* : an artificial plant resembling this
mini \ˈmi-nē\ *n, pl* **min•is** : something small of its kind — **mini** *adj*
mini- *comb form* : smaller or briefer than usual, normal, or standard
¹min•ia•ture \ˈmi-nē-ə-ˌchu̇r, ˈmi-ni-ˌchu̇r, -chər\ *n* **1** : a copy on a much reduced scale; *also* : something small of its kind **2** : a small painting (as on ivory or metal) — **min•ia•tur•ist** \-ˌchu̇r-ist, -chər-\ *n*
²miniature *adj* ♦ : being or represented on a small scale

♦ atomic, infinitesimal, microscopic, minute, teeny, tiny, wee

min•ia•tur•ize \ˈmi-nē-ə-chə-ˌrīz, ˈmi-ni-\ *vb* **-ized; -iz•ing** : to design or construct in small size — **min•ia•tur•i•za•tion** \ˌmi-nē-ə-ˌchu̇r-ə-ˈzā-shən, ˌmi-ni-, -chər-\ *n*
mini•bar \ˈmi-nē-ˌbär\ *n* : a small refrigerator in a hotel room that is stocked with beverages and snacks
mini•bike \ˈmi-nē-ˌbīk\ *n* : a small one-passenger motorcycle
mini•bus \-ˌbəs\ *n* : a small bus or van
mini•com•put•er \-kəm-ˌpyü-tər\ *n* : a computer between a mainframe and a microcomputer in size and speed
mini•disc \ˈmi-nē-ˌdisk\ *n* : a miniature optical disk
min•im \ˈmi-nəm\ *n* : a unit of liquid measure equal to $\frac{1}{60}$ fluid dram
min•i•mal \ˈmi-nə-məl\ *adj* **1** ♦ : relating to or being a minimum : LEAST **2** : of or relating to minimalism or minimal art — **min•i•mal•ly** *adv*

♦ least, minimum *Ant* full, largest, maximum, top, topmost, utmost

minimal art *n* **:** abstract art consisting primarily of simple geometric forms executed in an impersonal style — **minimal artist** *n*
min•i•mal•ism \ˈmi-nə-mə-ˌli-zəm\ *n* **:** MINIMAL ART; *also* **:** a style (as in music or literature) marked by extreme spareness or simplicity — **min•i•mal•ist** \-list\ *n*
mini•mart \ˈmi-nē-ˌmärt\ *n* **:** CONVENIENCE STORE
min•i•mise *chiefly Brit var of* MINIMIZE
min•i•mize \ˈmi-nə-ˌmīz\ *vb* **-mized; -miz•ing 1 :** to reduce or keep to a minimum **2 a :** to underestimate intentionally **b ♦ :** to speak slightingly of **:** BELITTLE

♦ belittle, cry down, decry, deprecate, depreciate, diminish, discount, disparage, put down, write off

[1]**min•i•mum** \ˈmi-nə-məm\ *n, pl* **-ma** \-mə\ *or* **-mums 1 :** the least quantity assignable, admissible, or possible **2 :** the least of a set of numbers **3 :** the lowest degree or amount of variation (as of temperature) reached or recorded
[2]**minimum** *adj* **♦ :** of, relating to, or constituting a minimum

♦ least, minimal

min•ion \ˈmin-yən\ *n* **1 :** a servile dependent, follower, or underling **2 ♦ :** one highly favored **3 :** a subordinate official

♦ darling, favorite (*or* favourite), pet, preference

min•is•cule \ˈmi-nəs-ˌkyül\ *var of* MINUSCULE
mini•se•ries \ˈmi-nē-ˌsir-ēz\ *n* **:** a television story presented in sequential episodes
mini•skirt \-ˌskərt\ *n* **:** a skirt with the hemline several inches above the knee
[1]**min•is•ter** \ˈmi-nə-stər\ *n* **1 :** AGENT **2 ♦ :** a member of the clergy especially of a Protestant communion **3 :** a high officer of state who heads a division of governmental activities **4 ♦ :** a diplomatic representative to a foreign state

♦ [2] clergyman, divine, ecclesiastic, father, preacher, priest, reverend ♦ [4] ambassador, delegate, emissary, envoy, legate, representative

[2]**minister** *vb* **1 :** to perform the functions of a minister of religion **2 ♦ :** to give aid or service ⟨~ to the sick⟩ — **min•is•tra•tion** \ˌmi-nə-ˈstrā-shən\ *n*

♦ *usu* **minister to** aid, care, mother, nurse

min•is•te•ri•al \ˌmi-nə-ˈstir-ē-əl\ *adj* **♦ :** of, relating to, or characteristic of a minister or the ministry

♦ clerical, pastoral, priestly, sacerdotal

[1]**min•is•trant** \ˈmi-nə-strənt\ *adj, archaic* **:** performing service as a minister
[2]**ministrant** *n* **:** one that ministers
min•is•try \ˈmi-nə-strē\ *n, pl* **-tries 1 :** MINISTRATION **2 :** the office, duties, or functions of a minister; *also* **:** the period of service or office **3 :** CLERGY **4 :** AGENCY **5** *often cap* **:** the body of ministers governing a nation or state; *also* **:** a government department headed by a minister
mini•tower \ˈmi-nē-ˌtau̇(-ə)r\ *n* **:** a computer tower of intermediate size
mini•van \ˈmi-nē-ˌvan\ *n* **:** a small van
mink \ˈmiŋk\ *n, pl* **mink** *or* **minks :** either of two slender flesh-eating mammals resembling the related weasels; *also* **:** the soft lustrous typically dark brown fur of a mink
min•ke whale \ˈmiŋ-kə-\ *n* **:** a small grayish baleen whale with a whitish underside
Minn *abbr* Minnesota
min•ne•sing•er \ˈmi-ni-ˌsiŋ-ər, -ˌziŋ-\ *n* **:** any of a class of German lyric poets and musicians of the 12th to the 14th centuries
min•now \ˈmi-nō\ *n, pl* **minnows** *also* **minnow :** any of numerous small freshwater fishes
[1]**mi•nor** \ˈmī-nər\ *adj* **1 ♦ :** inferior in importance, size, or degree **2 :** not having reached majority **3 :** having the third, sixth, and sometimes the seventh degrees lowered by a half step ⟨~ scale⟩; *also* **:** based on a minor scale ⟨~ key⟩ **4 :** not serious ⟨~ illness⟩

♦ inferior, junior, less, lesser, lower, subordinate, under ♦ frivolous, inconsequential, inconsiderable, insignificant, little, minute, negligible, slight, small, trifling, trivial, unimportant

[2]**minor** *n* **1 :** a person who has not attained majority **2 :** a subject of academic study chosen as a secondary field of specialization
[3]**minor** *vb* **:** to pursue an academic minor
mi•nor•i•ty \mə-ˈnȯr-ə-tē, mī-\ *n, pl* **-ties 1 :** the period or state of being a minor **2 :** the smaller in number of two groups; *esp* **:** a group having less than the number of votes necessary for control **3 :** a part of a population differing from others (as in race); *also* **:** a member of a minority
mi•nox•i•dil \mə-ˈnäk-sə-ˌdil\ *n* **:** a drug used orally to treat hypertension and topically in solution to promote hair regrowth in some forms of baldness
min•ster \ˈmin-stər\ *n* **:** a large or important church
min•strel \ˈmin-strəl\ *n* **1 :** a medieval singer of verses **2 a :** MUSICIAN **b ♦ :** one who writes poetry **:** POET **2 :** any of a group of performers usually with blackened faces in a program of black American songs, jokes, and impersonations ⟨a ~ show⟩

♦ bard, poet, versifier

min•strel•sy \-sē\ *n* **:** the singing and playing of a minstrel; *also* **:** a body of minstrels
[1]**mint** \ˈmint\ *n* **1 :** any of a large family of aromatic square-stemmed herbs and shrubs; *esp* **:** one (as spearmint) that is fragrant and is the source of a flavoring oil **2 :** a mint-flavored piece of candy — **minty** *adj*
[2]**mint** *n* **1 :** a place where coins are made **2 ♦ :** a vast sum — **mint** *vb* — **mint•age** \-ij\ *n* — **mint•er** *n*

♦ fortune, wad

[3]**mint** *vb* **1 :** to make (as coins) out of metal **2 :** CREATE; *also* **:** to give a certain status to ⟨newly ~*ed* lawyers⟩ — **mint•age** \-ij\ *n* — **mint•er** *n*
[4]**mint** *adj* **:** unmarred as if fresh from a mint ⟨in ~ condition⟩
min•u•end \ˈmin-yə-ˌwend\ *n* **:** a number from which another is to be subtracted
min•u•et \ˌmin-yə-ˈwet\ *n* **:** a slow graceful dance
[1]**mi•nus** \ˈmī-nəs\ *prep* **1 :** diminished by **:** LESS ⟨7 ~ 3 equals 4⟩ **2 ♦ :** deprived of **:** WITHOUT ⟨~ his hat⟩

♦ sans, wanting, without

[2]**minus** *n* **♦ :** a negative quantity or quality

♦ disadvantage, drawback, handicap, liability, penalty, strike

[3]**minus** *adj* **1 :** algebraically negative ⟨~ quantity⟩ **2 :** having negative qualities
[1]**mi•nus•cule** \ˈmi-nəs-ˌkyül\ *n* **:** a lowercase letter
[2]**minuscule** *adj* **♦ :** very small

♦ atomic, infinitesimal, microscopic, miniature, minute, tiny, wee

minus sign *n* **:** a sign – used in mathematics to indicate subtraction or a negative quantity
[1]**min•ute** \ˈmi-nət\ *n* **1 :** a 60th part of an hour or of a degree **:** 60 seconds **2 ♦ :** a short space of time **3** *pl* **:** the official record of the proceedings of a meeting

♦ flash, instant, jiffy, moment, second, shake, trice, twinkle, twinkling, wink

[2]**mi•nute** \mī-ˈnüt, mə-, -ˈnyüt\ *adj* **mi•nut•er; -est 1 ♦ :** very small **2 ♦ :** of little importance **:** TRIFLING **3 ♦ :** marked by close attention to details — **mi•nute•ness** *n*

♦ [1] atomic, infinitesimal, microscopic, miniature, tiny, wee ♦ [2] frivolous, inconsequential, inconsiderable, insignificant, little, minor, negligible, slight, small, trifling, trivial, unimportant ♦ [3] circumstantial, detailed, elaborate, full, thorough

mi•nute•ly \mī-ˈnüt-lē, mə-, -ˈnyüt-\ *adv* **♦ :** in a minute manner or degree

♦ completely, exhaustively, fully, roundly, thoroughly, totally

min•ute•man \ˈmi-nət-ˌman\ *n* **:** a member of a group of armed men pledged to take the field at a minute's notice during and immediately before the American Revolution
mi•nu•tia \mə-ˈnü-shə, -ˈnyü-, -shē-ə\ *n, pl* **-ti•ae** \-shē-ˌē\ **:** a minute or minor detail — usually used in plural
minx \ˈmiŋks\ *n* **:** a pert girl
Mio•cene \ˈmī-ə-ˌsēn\ *adj* **:** of, relating to, or being the epoch of the Tertiary between the Oligocene and the Pliocene — **Miocene** *n*
mir•a•cle \ˈmir-i-kəl\ *n* **1 :** an extraordinary event manifesting divine intervention in human affairs **2 ♦ :** an unusual event, thing, or accomplishment **:** WONDER, MARVEL

♦ caution, flash, marvel, phenomenon, portent, prodigy, sensation, wonder

miracle drug *n* **:** a usually newly discovered drug that elicits a dramatic response in a patient's condition
mi•rac•u•lous \mə-ˈra-kyə-ləs\ *adj* **1 ♦ :** of the nature of a miracle **2 ♦ :** suggesting a miracle **:** MARVELOUS **3 :** working or able to work miracles — **mi•rac•u•lous•ly** *adv*

♦ [1] magical, phenomenal, superhuman, supernatural, uncanny, unearthly ♦ [2] amazing, astonishing, astounding, awesome, fabulous, marvelous (*or* marvellous), stunning, stupendous, sublime, surprising, wonderful

mi•rage \mə-ˈräzh\ *n* **1 :** an illusion that often appears as a pool of water or a mirror in which distant objects are seen inverted, is sometimes seen at sea, in the desert, or over a hot pavement, and results from atmospheric conditions **2 :** something illusory and unattainable

¹mire \ˈmīr\ *n* ♦ **:** heavy and often deep mud or slush

♦ muck, mud, ooze, slime, slop, sludge, slush ♦ bog, fen, marsh, morass, slough, swamp

²mire *vb* **mired; mir•ing 1 :** to stick or sink in or as if in mire **2** ♦ **:** to cover or soil with mire

♦ befoul, begrime, besmirch, blacken, dirty, foul, grime, muddy, smirch, soil, stain

mire•poix \mir-ˈpwä\ *n, pl* **mirepoix :** a mixture of diced vegetables and sometimes meats used in soups, stews, and sauces

¹mir•ror \ˈmir-ər\ *n* **1 :** a polished or smooth surface (as of glass) that forms images by reflection **2 :** a true representation

²mirror *vb* **1 :** to reflect in or as if in a mirror **2 :** RESEMBLE

mirth \ˈmərth\ *n* ♦ **:** gladness or gaiety accompanied with laughter — **mirth•less** *adj*

♦ cheer, cheerfulness, cheeriness, glee, hilarity, joviality, merriment

mirth•ful \-fəl\ *adj* ♦ **:** full of mirth or merriment

♦ blithe, boon, festive, gay, gleeful, jocund, jolly, jovial, merry, sunny

mirth•ful•ly \-fə-lē\ *adv* ♦ **:** in a mirthful manner

♦ cheerfully, gaily, happily, heartily, jovially, merrily

mirth•ful•ness \-nəs\ *n* ♦ **:** the quality or state of being mirthful

♦ cheer, cheerfulness, glee, hilarity, joviality, merriment, mirth

MIRV \ˈmərv\ *n* **:** an ICBM with multiple warheads that have different targets — **MIRV** *vb*

miry \ˈmīr-ē\ *adj* ♦ **:** resembling a mire **:** characterized by swampy ground

♦ mucky, muddy, oozy, slimy, slushy

mis•ad•ven•ture \ˌmi-səd-ˈven-chər\ *n* **1** ♦ **:** bad luck **2** ♦ **:** a piece of bad luck

♦ [1, 2] adversity, knock, mischance, misfortune, mishap

mis•aligned \ˌmi-sə-ˈlīnd\ *adj* **:** not properly aligned — **mis•align•ment** \-ˈlīn-mənt\ *n*

mis•al•li•ance \ˌmi-sə-ˈlī-əns\ *n* **:** an improper or unsuitable marriage

mis•al•lo•ca•tion \ˌmi-ˌsa-lə-ˈkā-shən\ *n* **:** faulty or improper allocation

mis•an•dry \ˈmi-ˌsan-drē\ *n* **:** a hatred of men — **mis•an•drist** \-drist\ *n or adj*

mis•an•thrope \ˈmis-ᵊn-ˌthrōp\ *n* **:** one who hates humankind — **mis•an•throp•ic** \ˌmis-ᵊn-ˈthrä-pik\ *adj* — **mis•an•throp•i•cal•ly** \-pi-k(ə-)lē\ *adv* — **mis•an•thro•py** \mi-ˈsan-thrə-pē\ *n*

mis•ap•pli•ca•tion \ˌmi-ˌsa-plə-ˈkā-shən\ *n* **:** the action of misapplying

mis•ap•ply \ˌmi-sə-ˈplī\ *vb* ♦ **:** to apply wrongly

♦ abuse, misuse, pervert

mis•ap•pre•hend \ˌmi-ˌsa-pri-ˈhend\ *vb* ♦ **:** to fail to understand **:** MISUNDERSTAND

♦ misconstrue, misinterpret, misread, miss, mistake, misunderstand

mis•ap•pre•hen•sion \-ˈhen-chən\ *n* ♦ **:** the act or instance of misapprehending

♦ misjudgment, mistake, misunderstanding ♦ misconstruction, misinterpretation, misunderstanding

mis•ap•pro•pri•ate \ˌmi-sə-ˈprō-prē-ˌāt\ *vb* ♦ **:** to appropriate wrongly (as by embezzlement) — **mis•ap•pro•pri•a•tion** \-ˌprō-prē-ˈā-shən\ *n*

♦ appropriate, filch, hook, nip, pilfer, pocket, purloin, snitch, steal, swipe, thieve

mis•be•got•ten \-bi-ˈgät-ᵊn\ *adj* **:** born of parents not married to each other **:** ILLEGITIMATE; *also* **:** ill-conceived

mis•be•have \ˌmis-bi-ˈhāv\ *vb* **:** to behave improperly — **mis•be•hav•er** *n*

♦ act out, act up, carry on

mis•be•hav•ior \-ˈhā-vyər\ *n* ♦ **:** bad, improper, or rude behavior

♦ malfeasance, misconduct, misdoing, wrongdoing

mis•be•lief \ˌmis-bə-ˈlēf\ *n* ♦ **:** erroneous or false belief

♦ error, fallacy, falsehood, falsity, illusion, misconception, myth, untruth

mis•be•liev•er \-bə-ˈlē-vər\ *n* **:** one who holds a false or unorthodox belief

mis•brand \mis-ˈbrand\ *vb* **:** to brand falsely or in a misleading manner

misc *abbr* miscellaneous

mis•cal•cu•late \mis-ˈkal-kyə-ˌlāt\ *vb* ♦ **:** to calculate wrongly — **mis•cal•cu•la•tion** \ˌmis-ˌkal-kyə-ˈlā-shən\ *n*

♦ misconceive, misjudge, mistake

mis•call \mis-ˈkȯl\ *vb* **:** MISNAME

mis•car•riage \-ˈkar-ij\ *n* **1 :** failure in the administration of justice **2 :** spontaneous expulsion of a fetus before it is capable of independent life

mis•car•ry \-ˈkar-ē\ *vb* **1 :** to have a miscarriage of a fetus **2 :** to go wrong; *also* **:** to be unsuccessful

mis•ce•ge•na•tion \mi-se-jə-ˈnā-shən, ˌmi-si-jə-ˈnā-\ *n* **:** marriage, cohabitation, or sexual intercourse between persons of different races

mis•cel•la•neous \ˌmi-sə-ˈlā-nē-əs\ *adj* **1** ♦ **:** consisting of diverse things or members **2 :** having various traits; *also* **:** dealing with or interested in diverse subjects — **mis•cel•la•neous•ly** *adv* — **mis•cel•la•neous•ness** *n*

♦ assorted, heterogeneous, mixed, motley, varied ***Ant*** homogeneous

mis•cel•la•ny \ˈmi-sə-ˌlā-nē\ *n, pl* **-nies 1** ♦ **:** a collection of writings on various subjects **2** ♦ **:** a mixture of various things **:** HODGEPODGE

♦ [1] album, anthology, compilation ♦ [2] assortment, clutter, hash, hodgepodge, jumble, litter, medley, mélange, motley, muddle, potpourri, rummage, scramble, shuffle, tumble, variety, welter

mis•chance \mis-ˈchans\ *n* **1** ♦ **:** bad luck **2** ♦ **:** a piece of bad luck; *also* **:** an unfortunate accident

♦ adversity, knock, misadventure, misfortune, mishap

mis•chief \ˈmis-chəf\ *n* **1 :** injury caused by a particular agent **2** ♦ **:** a source of harm or irritation; *esp* **:** a person who causes mischief **3 a** ♦ **:** action that annoys **b** ♦ **:** the quality or state of being mischievous **:** MISCHIEVOUSNESS

♦ [2] devil, hellion, imp, monkey, rapscallion, rascal, rogue, scamp, urchin ♦ [3a, b] devilishness, impishness, knavery, mischievousness, rascality, shenanigans, waggery, wickedness

mis•chie•vous \ˈmis-chə-vəs\ *adj* **1** ♦ **:** of a kind likely to be damaging **:** HARMFUL, INJURIOUS **2 :** causing annoyance or minor injury **3** ♦ **:** irresponsibly playful — **mis•chie•vous•ly** *adv*

♦ [1] adverse, damaging, detrimental, harmful, hurtful, injurious, prejudicial ♦ [3] devilish, impish, knavish, naughty, rascally, roguish, sly, waggish, wicked

mis•chie•vous•ness *n* ♦ **:** the quality or state of being mischievous

♦ devilishness, impishness, knavery, mischief, rascality, shenanigans, waggery, wickedness

mis•ci•ble \ˈmi-sə-bəl\ *adj* **:** capable of being mixed

mis•com•mu•ni•ca•tion \ˌmis-kə-ˌmyü-nə-ˈkā-shən\ *n* **:** failure to communicate clearly

mis•con•ceive \ˌmis-kən-ˈsēv\ *vb* ♦ **:** to interpret incorrectly

♦ miscalculate, misjudge, mistake

mis•con•cep•tion \-ˈsep-shən\ *n* ♦ **:** the act or result of misconceiving

♦ error, fallacy, falsehood, falsity, illusion, myth, untruth

mis•con•duct \mis-ˈkän-(ˌ)dəkt\ *n* **1 :** MISMANAGEMENT **2** ♦ **:** intentional wrongdoing **3** ♦ **:** improper behavior

♦ [2, 3] malfeasance, misbehavior, misdoing, wrongdoing

mis•con•struc•tion \-ˈstrək-shən\ *n* ♦ **:** the action of misconstruing

♦ misapprehension, misinterpretation, misunderstanding

mis•con•strue \ˌmis-kən-ˈstrü\ *vb* ♦ **:** to interpret wrongly **:** MISINTERPRET

♦ misapprehend, misinterpret, misread, miss, mistake, misunderstand

mis·count \mis-ˈkau̇nt\ *vb* **:** to count incorrectly **:** MISCALCULATE
mis·cre·ant \ˈmis-krē-ənt\ *n* **:** one who behaves criminally or viciously — **miscreant** *adj*
mis·cue \mis-ˈkyü\ *n* ♦ **:** a wrong action or statement **:** MISTAKE, ERROR — **miscue** *vb*

♦ blunder, error, fault, flub, fumble, goof, lapse, misstep, mistake, oversight, slip, stumble

mis·deed \mis-ˈdēd\ *n* ♦ **:** a wrong deed

♦ breach, crime, error, malefaction, misdoing, offense, sin, transgression, violation, wrongdoing

mis·de·mean·or *or Can and Brit* **mis·de·mean·our** \ˌmis-di-ˈmē-nər\ *n* **1 :** a crime less serious than a felony **2 :** MISDEED
mis·di·rect \ˌmis-də-ˈrekt, -dī-\ *vb* **:** to give a wrong direction to — **mis·di·rec·tion** \-ˈrek-shən\ *n*
mis·do·ing \mis-ˈdü-iŋ\ *n* ♦ **:** the act or an instance of misbehaving **:** WRONGDOING — **mis·do** \-ˈdü\ *vb* — **mis·do·er** \-ˈdü-ər\ *n*

♦ malfeasance, misbehavior, misconduct, wrongdoing

mise–en–scène \ˌmē-ˌzä^{n}-ˈsen, -ˈsān\ *n, pl* **mise–en–scènes** *same or* -ˈsenz, -ˈsānz\ **1 :** the arrangement of the scenery, property, and actors on a stage **2 :** SETTING; *also* **:** ENVIRONMENT
mi·ser \ˈmī-zər\ *n* ♦ **:** a person who hoards and is stingy with money — **mi·ser·ly** *adj*

♦ cheapskate, niggard, skinflint, tightwad

mis·er·a·ble \ˈmi-zə-rə-bəl, ˈmiz-rə-\ *adj* **1 a** ♦ **:** wretchedly deficient, meager, or of poor quality **b** ♦ **:** causing extreme discomfort or unhappiness **2** ♦ **:** being in a state of poverty or distress **3 :** being likely to discredit or shame — **mis·er·a·ble·ness** *n* — **mis·er·a·bly** \-blē\ *adv*

♦ [1a] bad, cheap, inferior, mediocre, poor, rotten, second-rate, shabby, shoddy, sleazy, tacky, terrible, threadbare, wretched ♦ [1b] bleak, dark, dismal, dreary, gloomy, gray (*or* grey), somber (*or* sombre), wretched ♦ [2] heartbreaking, pathetic, piteous, pitiful, poor, rueful, sorry, unhappy, wretched

mi·ser·li·ness \ˈmī-zər-lē-nəs\ *n* ♦ **:** the quality or state of being a miser or like a miser

♦ cheapness, closeness, parsimony, stinginess, tightness

mis·ery \ˈmi-zə-rē\ *n, pl* **-er·ies 1** ♦ **:** suffering and want caused by poverty or affliction **2 :** a cause of suffering or discomfort **3 :** emotional distress

♦ affliction, agony, anguish, distress, pain, torment, torture, tribulation, woe

mis·fea·sance \mis-ˈfēz-^{ə}ns\ *n* **:** the performance of a lawful action in an illegal or improper manner
mis·file \-ˈfī(-ə)l\ *vb* **:** to file in the wrong place
mis·fire \-ˈfī(-ə)r\ *vb* **1 :** to fail to fire **2 :** to miss an intended effect — **misfire** *n*
mis·fit \ˈmis-ˌfit, *sense 1 also* mis-ˈfit\ *n* **1 :** something that fits badly **2 :** a person who is poorly adjusted to a situation or environment
mis·for·tune \mis-ˈfȯr-chən\ *n* **1** ♦ **:** bad luck **2** ♦ **:** an unfortunate condition or event

♦ [1, 2] adversity, knock, misadventure, mischance, mishap *Ant* fortune, luck

mis·giv·ing \-ˈgi-viŋ\ *n* ♦ **:** a feeling of doubt or suspicion especially concerning an action or future event

♦ distrust, doubt, incertitude, mistrust, skepticism, suspicion, uncertainty ♦ compunction, qualm, scruple ♦ alarm, apprehension, dread, foreboding

mis·gov·ern \-ˈgə-vərn\ *vb* ♦ **:** to govern badly — **mis·gov·ern·ment** *n*

♦ misconduct, mishandle, mismanage, misrule

mis·guid·ance \mis-ˈgīd-^{ə}ns\ *n* **:** faulty guidance
mis·guide \mis-ˈgīd\ *vb* **:** to lead astray
mis·guid·ed \-ˈgī-dəd\ *adj* **:** led or prompted by wrong or inappropriate motives or ideals — **mis·guid·ed·ly** *adv*
mis·han·dle \-ˈhand-^{ə}l\ *vb* **1** ♦ **:** to treat roughly **:** MALTREAT **2** ♦ **:** to manage wrongly

♦ [1] abuse, ill-treat, maltreat, manhandle, mistreat, misuse ♦ [2] misconduct, misgovern, mismanage, misrule

mis·hap \ˈmis-ˌhap\ *n* ♦ **:** an unfortunate accident

♦ accident, casualty ♦ adversity, knock, misadventure, mischance, misfortune

mish·mash \ˈmish-ˌmash, -ˌmäsh\ *n* **:** a mass of things mingled together **:** HODGEPODGE, JUMBLE
mis·in·form \ˌmis-^{ə}n-ˈfȯrm\ *vb* ♦ **:** to give false or misleading information to — **mis·in·for·ma·tion** \ˌmi-ˌsin-fər-ˈmā-shən\ *n*

♦ beguile, bluff, cozen, deceive, delude, dupe, fool, gull, have, hoax, hoodwink, humbug, mislead, string along, take in, trick

mis·in·ter·pret \ˌmis-^{ə}n-ˈtər-prət\ *vb* ♦ **:** to understand or explain wrongly

♦ color (*or* colour), distort, falsify, garble, misrepresent, misstate, pervert, twist, warp ♦ misapprehend, misconstrue, misread, miss, mistake, misunderstand

mis·in·ter·pre·ta·tion \ˌmis-^{ə}n-ˌtər-prə-ˈtā- shən\ *n* ♦ **:** incorrect interpretation

♦ misapprehension, misconstruction, misunderstanding

mis·judge \mis-ˈjəj\ *vb* **1** ♦ **:** to estimate wrongly **2 :** to have an unjust opinion of

♦ miscalculate, misconceive, mistake

mis·judg·ment \mis-ˈjəj-mənt\ *n* ♦ **:** incorrect or distorted judgment

♦ misapprehension, mistake, misunderstanding

mis·la·bel \-ˈlā-bəl\ *vb* **:** to label incorrectly or falsely
mis·lay \mis-ˈlā\ *vb* **-laid** \-ˈlād\; **-lay·ing :** MISPLACE, LOSE
mis·lead \mis-ˈlēd\ *vb* **-led** \-ˈled\; **-lead·ing** ♦ **:** to lead in a wrong direction or into a mistaken action or belief — **mis·lead·ing·ly** *adv*

♦ beguile, bluff, cozen, deceive, delude, dupe, fool, gull, have, hoax, hoodwink, humbug, misinform, string along, take in, trick

misleading *adj* ♦ **:** tending to mislead

♦ deceitful, deceptive, delusive, fallacious, false, specious

mis·like \-ˈlīk\ *vb* **:** DISLIKE — **mis·like** *n*
mis·man·age \-ˈma-nij\ *vb* ♦ **:** to manage wrongly or incompetently — **mis·man·age·ment** *n*

♦ misconduct, misgovern, mishandle, misrule

mis·match \-ˈmach\ *vb* **:** to match unsuitably or badly — **mis·match** \mis-ˈmach, ˈmis-ˌmach\ *n*
mis·name \-ˈnām\ *vb* **:** to name incorrectly **:** MISCALL
mis·no·mer \mis-ˈnō-mər\ *n* **:** a wrong or inappropriate name or designation
mi·so \ˈmē-sō\ *n* **:** a high-protein fermented food paste consisting chiefly of soybeans, salt, and usually grain
mi·sog·y·ny \mə-ˈsä-jə-nē\ *n* **:** a hatred of women — **mi·sog·y·nist** \-nist\ *n or adj* — **mi·sog·y·nis·tic** \mə-ˌsä-jə-ˈnis-tik\ *adj*
mis·ori·ent \mi-ˈsōr-ē-ˌent\ *vb* **:** to orient improperly or incorrectly — **mis·ori·en·ta·tion** \mi-ˌsōr-ē-ən-ˈtā-shən\ *n*
mis·place \mis-ˈplās\ *vb* **1 :** to put in a wrong or unremembered place **2 :** to set on a wrong object ⟨∼ trust⟩
mis·play \-ˈplā\ *n* **:** a wrong or unskillful play — **mis·play** \mis-ˈplā, ˈmis-ˌplā\ *vb*
mis·print \ˈmis-ˌprint\ *n* **:** a mistake in printed matter — **mis·print** \mis-ˈprint\ *vb*
mis·pro·nounce \ˌmis-prə-ˈnau̇ns\ *vb* **:** to pronounce incorrectly — **mis·pro·nun·ci·a·tion** \-prə-ˌnən-sē-ˈā-shən\ *n*
mis·quote \mis-ˈkwōt\ *vb* **:** to quote incorrectly — **mis·quo·ta·tion** \ˌmis-kwō-ˈtā-shən\ *n*
mis·read \-ˈrēd\ *vb* **-read** \-ˈred\; **-read·ing** \-ˈrē-diŋ\ ♦ **:** to read or interpret incorrectly

♦ misapprehend, misconstrue, misinterpret, miss, mistake, misunderstand

mis·rep·re·sent \ˌmis-ˌre-pri-ˈzent\ *vb* ♦ **:** to represent falsely or unfairly — **mis·rep·re·sen·ta·tion** \-ˌzen-ˈtā-shən\ *n*

♦ color (*or* colour), distort, falsify, garble, misinterpret, misstate, pervert, twist, warp

[1]**mis·rule** \mis-ˈrül\ *vb* ♦ **:** to rule incompetently **:** MISGOVERN

♦ misconduct, misgovern, mishandle, mismanage

[2]**misrule** *n* **1 :** MISGOVERNMENT **2 :** DISORDER
[1]**miss** \ˈmis\ *vb* **1 :** to fail to hit, reach, or contact **2 :** to feel the absence of **3 :** to fail to obtain **4 :** AVOID ⟨just ∼*ed* hitting the other car⟩ **5 :** OMIT **6** ♦ **:** to fail to understand **7 :** to fail to perform or attend; *also* **:** MISFIRE

♦ misapprehend, misconstrue, misinterpret, misread, mistake, misunderstand

2miss *n* **1** ♦ **:** a failure to hit or to attain a result **2 :** MISFIRE

♦ default, delinquency, dereliction, failure, neglect, negligence, oversight

3miss *n* **1** *cap* — used as a title prefixed to the name of an unmarried woman or girl **2** ♦ **:** a young unmarried woman or girl

♦ doll, girl, lass, maid, maiden

Miss *abbr* Mississippi
mis•sal \ˈmi-səl\ *n* **:** a book containing all that is said or sung at mass during the entire year
mis•send \mis-ˈsend\ *vb* **:** to send incorrectly ⟨*missent* mail⟩
mis•shap•en \-ˈshā-pən\ *adj* ♦ **:** badly shaped **:** having an ugly shape

♦ deformed, distorted, malformed, monstrous, shapeless

mis•sile \ˈmi-səl\ *n* **:** an object (as a stone, bullet, or rocket) thrown or projected usually so as to strike a target
miss•ing \ˈmi-siŋ\ *adj* ♦ **:** not present or available; *also* **:** in an unknown location

♦ absent, away, out ♦ absent, nonexistent, wanting ♦ gone, lost

mis•sion \ˈmi-shən\ *n* **1 :** a group of missionaries; *also* **:** a place where missionaries work **2 :** a group of envoys to a foreign country; *also* **:** a team of specialists or cultural leaders sent to a foreign country **3** ♦ **:** a specific task with which a person or a group is charged

♦ assignment, charge, job, operation, post

1mis•sion•ary \ˈmi-shə-ˌner-ē\ *adj* **:** of, relating to, or engaged in missions
2missionary *n, pl* **-ar•ies :** a person commissioned by a church to spread its faith or carry on humanitarian work
mis•sion•er \ˈmi-shə-nər\ *n* **:** MISSIONARY
Mis•sis•sip•pi•an \ˌmi-sə-ˈsi-pē-ən\ *adj* **:** of, relating to, or being the period of the Paleozoic era between the Devonian and the Pennsylvanian — **Mississippian** *n*
mis•sive \ˈmi-siv\ *n* ♦ **:** a written communication **:** LETTER

♦ dispatch, letter, memorandum, note

mis•speak \mis-ˈspēk\ *vb* **:** to say imperfectly or incorrectly
mis•spell \-ˈspel\ *vb* **:** to spell incorrectly — **mis•spell•ing** *n*
mis•spend \-ˈspend\ *vb* **-spent** \-ˈspent\; **-spend•ing** ♦ **:** to spend wrongly **:** WASTE, SQUANDER ⟨my *misspent* youth⟩

♦ blow, dissipate, fritter, lavish, run through, spend, squander, throw away, waste

mis•state \mis-ˈstāt\ *vb* ♦ **:** to state incorrectly — **mis•state•ment** *n*

♦ color (*or* colour), distort, falsify, garble, misinterpret, misrepresent, pervert, twist, warp

mis•step \-ˈstep\ *n* **1 :** a wrong step **2** ♦ **:** a mistake in judgment or action **:** BLUNDER

♦ blunder, error, fault, flub, fumble, goof, lapse, miscue, mistake, oversight, slip, stumble

1mist \ˈmist\ *n* **1 :** water in the form of particles suspended or falling in the air **2 :** something that obscures understanding
2mist *vb* **1 :** to be or become misty **2 :** to become moist or blurred **3** ♦ **:** to cover with or as if with a mist

♦ becloud, befog, blur, cloud, darken, dim, fog, haze, obscure, overshadow, shroud

mis•tak•able \mə-ˈstā-kə-bəl\ *adj* **:** capable of being misunderstood or mistaken
1mis•take \mi-ˈstāk\ *vb* **-took** \-ˈstu̇k\; **-tak•en** \-ˈstā-kən\; **-tak•ing** **1 :** to blunder in the choice of **2** ♦ **:** to misunderstand the meaning or intention of **:** MISINTERPRET **3** ♦ **:** to make a wrong judgment of the character or ability of **4 :** to confuse with another — **mis•tak•er** *n*

♦ [2] misapprehend, misconstrue, misinterpret, misread, miss, misunderstand ♦ [3] miscalculate, misconceive, misjudge

2mistake *n* **1** ♦ **:** a wrong judgment **:** MISUNDERSTANDING **2** ♦ **:** a wrong action or statement **:** ERROR

♦ [1] misapprehension, misconstruction, misinterpretation, misjudgment, misunderstanding ♦ [2] blunder, error, fault, flub, fumble, goof, lapse, miscue, misstep, oversight, slip, stumble

mis•tak•en•ly \mi-ˈstā-kən-lē\ *adv* ♦ **:** in a way that is wrong in action or thought

♦ amiss, erroneously, faultily, improperly, inaptly, incorrectly, wrongly

1mis•ter \ˈmis-tər\ *n* **1** *cap* — used sometimes instead of *Mr.* **2 :** SIR — used without a name in addressing a man
2mist•er \ˈmis-tər\ *n* **:** a device for spraying mist
mis•tle•toe \ˈmi-səl-ˌtō\ *n* **:** a European parasitic green shrub that grows on trees and has yellowish flowers and waxy white berries
mis•tral \ˈmis-trəl, mi-ˈsträl\ *n* **:** a strong cold dry northerly wind of southern France
mis•treat \mis-ˈtrēt\ *vb* ♦ **:** to treat badly **:** ABUSE — **mis•treat•ment** *n*

♦ abuse, ill-treat, maltreat, manhandle, mishandle, misuse

mis•tress \ˈmis-trəs\ *n* **1 :** a woman who has power, authority, or ownership ⟨~ of the house⟩ **2 :** something personified as female that rules or dominates ⟨when Rome was ~ of the world⟩ **3 :** a woman other than his wife with whom a married man has sexual relations; *also, archaic* **:** SWEETHEART **4** — used archaically as a title prefixed to the name of a married or unmarried woman
mis•tri•al \ˈmis-ˌtrī(-ə)l\ *n* **:** a trial that has no legal effect
1mis•trust \mis-ˈtrəst\ *n* ♦ **:** a lack of confidence **:** DISTRUST

♦ distrust, doubt, incertitude, misgiving, skepticism, suspicion, uncertainty

2mistrust *vb* ♦ **:** to have no trust or confidence in **:** SUSPECT

♦ distrust, doubt, question, suspect

mis•trust•ful \-fəl\ *adj* ♦ **:** marked by mistrust

♦ distrustful, incredulous, leery, skeptical, suspicious

mis•trust•ful•ly \-fə-lē\ *adv* ♦ **:** in a mistrustful manner

♦ askance, distrustfully, dubiously, suspiciously

mis•trust•ful•ness \-nəs\ *n* **:** the quality or state of being mistrustful
misty \ˈmis-tē\ *adj* **mist•i•er; -est** **1** ♦ **:** obscured by or as if by mist **2 :** TEARFUL — **mist•i•ly** \-tə-lē\ *adv* — **mist•i•ness** \-tē-nəs\ *n*

♦ cloudy, foggy, hazy, murky, smoggy, soupy

mis•un•der•stand \ˌmi-ˌsən-dər-ˈstand\ *vb* **-stood** \-ˈstu̇d\; **-stand•ing** **1** ♦ **:** to fail to understand **2** ♦ **:** to interpret incorrectly

♦ [1, 2] misapprehend, misconstrue, misinterpret, misread, miss, mistake *Ant* apprehend, catch, comprehend, conceive, fathom, grasp, know, make out, penetrate, perceive, savvy, see, seize, take in, understand

mis•un•der•stand•ing \-ˈstan-diŋ\ *n* **1** ♦ **:** a failure to understand **:** MISINTERPRETATION **2** ♦ **:** a usually verbal conflict between antagonists **:** DISAGREEMENT, QUARREL

♦ [1] misapprehension, misconstruction, misinterpretation ♦ [2] altercation, argument, bicker, brawl, disagreement, dispute, fight, hassle, quarrel, row, scrap, spat, squabble, wrangle

mis•us•age \mis-ˈyü-sij\ *n* **1 :** bad treatment **:** ABUSE **2 :** wrong or improper use
1mis•use \mis-ˈyüz\ *vb* **1** ♦ **:** to use incorrectly **2** ♦ **:** to treat badly **:** ABUSE, MISTREAT

♦ [1] abuse, misapply, pervert, profane, prostitute ♦ [2] abuse, ill-treat, maltreat, manhandle, mishandle, mistreat

2misuse \-ˈyüs\ *n* ♦ **:** wrong, careless, or improper use

♦ abuse, perversion

1mite \ˈmīt\ *n* **:** any of numerous tiny arthropod animals related to the spiders that often live and feed on animals or plants
2mite *n* **1** ♦ **:** a small coin or sum of money **2** ♦ **:** a small amount **:** BIT **3** ♦ **:** a small object or creature

♦ [1] peanuts, pittance, shoestring, song *Ant* fortune, mint, wad ♦ [2] bit, dab, little, particle, speck, touch, trace ♦ [3] dwarf, midget, peewee, pygmy, runt, scrub, shrimp

1mi•ter *or* **mi•tre** \ˈmī-tər\ *n* **1 :** a headdress worn by bishops and abbots **2 :** MITER JOINT
2miter *or* **mitre** *vb* **mi•tered** *or* **mi•tred; mi•ter•ing** *or* **mi•tring** \ˈmī-tə-riŋ\ **1 :** to match or fit together in a miter joint **2 :** to bevel the ends of for making a miter joint
miter joint *n* **:** a usually perpendicular joint made by fitting together two parts with the ends cut at an angle
mit•i•gate \ˈmi-tə-ˌgāt\ *vb* **-gat•ed; -gat•ing** **1 :** to make less harsh or hostile **2** ♦ **:** to make less severe or painful — **mit•i•ga•tion** \ˌmi-tə-ˈgā-shən\ *n* — **mit•i•ga•tive** \ˈmi-tə-ˌgā-tiv\ *adj*

♦ allay, alleviate, assuage, ease, help, mollify, palliate, relieve, soothe

mi•to•chon•dri•on \ˌmī-tə-ˈkän-drē-ən\ *n, pl* **-dria** \-drē-ə\ : any of various round or long cellular organelles that produce energy for the cell — **mi•to•chon•dri•al** \-drē-əl\ *adj*
mi•to•sis \mī-ˈtō-səs\ *n, pl* **-to•ses** \-ˌsēz\ : a process that takes place in the nucleus of a dividing cell and results in the formation of two new nuclei each of which has the same number of chromosomes as the parent nucleus; *also* : cell division in which mitosis occurs — **mi•tot•ic** \-ˈtä-tik\ *adj*
mitt \ˈmit\ *n* **1** : a baseball catcher's or first baseman's glove **2** *slang* : HAND
mit•ten \ˈmit-ᵊn\ *n* : a covering for the hand having a separate section for the thumb only
[1]**mix** \ˈmiks\ *vb* **1** ♦ : to combine into one mass **2** ♦ : to enter into relations : ASSOCIATE **3** : to form by mingling components **4** : to produce (a recording) by electronically combining sounds from different sources **5** : HYBRIDIZE **6** ♦ : to put in disorder : CONFUSE — often used with *up* ⟨~*es* up the facts⟩ **7** : to become involved — **mix•able** *adj* — **mix•er** *n*

♦ [1] amalgamate, blend, combine, commingle, fuse, incorporate, integrate, intermingle, merge, mingle ***Ant*** segregate, separate, sort (out) ♦ [2] associate, fraternize, hobnob, mingle, socialize ♦ *usu* **mix up** [6] confuse, disorder, jumble, mess, muddle, scramble, shuffle

[2]**mix** *n* ♦ : a product of mixing; *esp* : a commercially prepared mixture of food ingredients

♦ admixture, amalgam, blend, combination, composite, compound, fusion, intermixture, mixture

mixed \ˈmikst\ *adj* **1** ♦ : made up of or involving individuals or items of more than one kind **2** ♦ : deriving from two or more races or breeds

♦ [1] assorted, heterogeneous, miscellaneous, motley, varied ♦ [2] hybrid, mongrel ***Ant*** full-blooded, purebred, thoroughbred

mixed number *n* : a number (as $5\frac{2}{3}$) composed of an integer and a fraction
mixed–up \ˈmikst-ˈəp\ *adj* : CONFUSED
mix•er \ˈmik-sər\ *n* **1** : one that mixes; *esp* : a machine or device for mixing **2** : an event (as a dance) that encourages meeting and socializing **3** : a nonalcoholic beverage used in a cocktail
mixt *abbr* mixture
mix•ture \ˈmiks-chər\ *n* **1** : the act or process of mixing; *also* : the state of being mixed **2** ♦ : a product of mixing

♦ admixture, amalgam, blend, combination, composite, compound, fusion, intermixture, mix

mix–up \ˈmiks-ˌəp\ *n* **1** : an instance of confusion **2** : CONFLICT, FIGHT
miz•zen *also* **miz•en** \ˈmiz-ᵊn\ *n* **1** : a fore-and-aft sail set on the mizzenmast **2** : MIZZENMAST — **mizzen** *also* **mizen** *adj*
miz•zen•mast \-ˌmast, -məst\ *n* : the mast aft or next aft of the mainmast
mk *abbr* **1** mark **2** markka
Mk *abbr* Mark
mks *abbr* meter-kilogram-second
mkt *abbr* market
mktg *abbr* marketing
ml *abbr* milliliter
Mlle *abbr* mademoiselle
Mlles *abbr* mesdemoiselles
mm *abbr* millimeter
MM *abbr* messieurs
Mme *abbr* madame
Mmes *abbr* mesdames
Mn *symbol* manganese
MN *abbr* Minnesota
mne•mon•ic \nə-ˈmä-nik\ *adj* : assisting or designed to assist memory; *also* : of or relating to memory
mo *abbr* month
[1]**Mo** *abbr* **1** Missouri **2** Monday
[2]**Mo** *symbol* molybdenum
MO *abbr* **1** mail order **2** medical officer **3** Missouri **4** modus operandi **5** money order
[1]**moan** \ˈmōn\ *n* ♦ : a low prolonged sound indicative of pain or grief

♦ groan, howl, keen, lament, plaint, wail

[2]**moan** *vb* **1** ♦ : to express grief, pain, or discontent **2** : to make a moan

♦ beef, bellyache, carp, complain, crab, croak, fuss, gripe, grouse, growl, grumble, kick, squawk, wail, whine

moat \ˈmōt\ *n* : a deep wide usually water-filled trench around a castle
[1]**mob** \ˈmäb\ *n* **1** ♦ : the lower classes of a community : MASSES **2** ♦ : a disorderly crowd **3** ♦ : a criminal gang

♦ [1] commoners, herd, masses, people, plebeians, populace, rank and file ♦ [2] army, crowd, crush, drove, flock, horde, host, legion, multitude, press, swarm, throng ♦ [3] cabal, conspiracy, gang, ring, syndicate

[2]**mob** *vb* **mobbed; mob•bing** **1** : to crowd about and attack or annoy **2** ♦ : to crowd into or around ⟨shoppers *mobbed* the stores⟩

♦ crowd, flock, swarm, throng

[1]**mo•bile** \ˈmō-bəl, -ˌbīl, -ˌbēl\ *adj* **1** : capable of moving or being moved **2** : changeable in appearance, mood, or purpose; *also* : ADAPTABLE **3** : having the opportunity for or undergoing a shift in social status **4** : using vehicles for transportation ⟨~ warfare⟩ — **mo•bil•i•ty** \mō-ˈbi-lə-tē\ *n*
[2]**mo•bile** \ˈmō-ˌbēl\ *n* : a construction or sculpture (as of wire and sheet metal) with parts that can be set in motion by air currents; *also* : a similar structure suspended so that it is moved by a current of air
mobile home *n* : a trailer used as a permanent dwelling
mo•bi•lise *chiefly Brit var of* MOBILIZE
mo•bi•li•za•tion \ˌmō-bə-lə-ˈzā-shən\ *n* **1** ♦ : the act of mobilizing **2** : the state of being mobilized

♦ muster, rally

mo•bi•lize \ˈmō-bə-ˌlīz\ *vb* **-lized; -liz•ing** **1** : to put into movement or circulation **2** ♦ : to assemble and make ready for use or action ⟨~ army reserves⟩ — **mo•bi•liz•er** \ˈmō-bə-ˌlī-zər\ *n*

♦ marshal, muster, rally ***Ant*** demobilize

mob•ster \ˈmäb-stər\ *n* ♦ : a member of a criminal gang

♦ bully, gangster, goon, hood, hoodlum, mug, punk, rowdy, ruffian, thug, tough

moc•ca•sin \ˈmä-kə-sən\ *n* **1** : a soft leather heelless shoe **2** : WATER MOCCASIN
mo•cha \ˈmō-kə\ *n* **1** : choice coffee grown in Arabia **2** : a mixture of coffee and chocolate or cocoa **3** : a dark chocolate-brown color
[1]**mock** \ˈmäk, ˈmȯk\ *vb* **1** ♦ : to treat with contempt or ridicule **2** : DELUDE **3** : DEFY **4** ♦ : to mimic in sport or derision — **mock** *n* — **mock•ing•ly** *adv*

♦ [1] deride, gibe, jeer, laugh, ridicule, scout ♦ [4] burlesque, caricature, imitate, mimic, parody, take off, travesty

[2]**mock** *adj* **1** ♦ : of, relating to, or having the character of an imitation **2** ♦ : not real or genuine

♦ [1] artificial, fake, faux, imitation, sham, synthetic ♦ [2] affected, artificial, assumed, contrived, feigned, mechanical, phony, put-on, spurious, unnatural

mock•er *n* ♦ : one that mocks

♦ heckler, quiz, scoffer, taunter, tease

mock•ery \ˈmä-kə-rē, ˈmȯ-\ *n* **1** : insulting or contemptuous action or speech **2** ♦ : a subject of laughter, derision, or sport **3** ♦ : an insincere, contemptible, or impertinent imitation

♦ [2] butt, laughingstock, mark, mock, target ♦ [3] caricature, farce, joke, parody, sham, travesty

mock–he•ro•ic \ˌmäk-hi-ˈrō-ik, ˌmȯk-\ *adj* : ridiculing or burlesquing heroic style, character, or action ⟨a ~ poem⟩
mock•ing•bird \ˈmä-kiŋ-ˌbərd, ˈmȯ-\ *n* : a grayish No. American songbird related to the catbirds and thrashers that mimics the calls of other birds
mock–up \ˈmä-ˌkəp, ˈmȯ-\ *n* : a full-sized structural model built for study, testing, or display ⟨a ~ of a car⟩
[1]**mod** \ˈmäd\ *adj* **1** : of, relating to, or being the style of the 1960s British youth culture **2** ♦ : very fashionable

♦ contemporary, current, hot, modern, new, newfangled, red-hot, space-age, ultramodern, up-to-date

[2]**mod** *abbr* **1** moderate **2** modern **3** modification; modified
[1]**mode** \ˈmōd\ *n* **1 a** : a particular form or variety of something **b** ♦ : a form or manner of expression : STYLE **2** : a manner of doing something **3** : the most frequent value of a set of data **4** ♦ : a conscious state of mind or predominant emotion — **mod•al** \ˈmōd-ᵊl\ *adj*

♦ [1b] locution, manner, phraseology, style, tone, vein ♦ [4] cheer, frame, humor (*or* humour), mood, spirit, temper

2**mode** *n* ♦ **:** a prevailing fashion or style (as of dress or behavior)

♦ craze, fad, rage, style, trend, vogue

1**mod•el** \ˈmäd-ᵊl\ *n* **1 :** structural design **2 :** a miniature representation; *also* **:** a pattern of something to be made **3** ♦ **:** an example for imitation or emulation **4 :** one who poses (as for an artist or to display clothes); *also* **:** MANNEQUIN **5 :** TYPE, DESIGN

♦ beau ideal, classic, exemplar, ideal, nonpareil, paragon

2**model** *vb* **mod•eled** *or* **mod•elled; mod•el•ing** *or* **mod•el•ling** **1 :** SHAPE, FASHION, CONSTRUCT **2 :** to work as a fashion model

3**model** *adj* **1** ♦ **:** serving as or worthy of being a pattern ⟨a ~ student⟩ **2 :** being a miniature representation of something ⟨a ~ airplane⟩

♦ classic, paradigmatic, quintessential

mo•dem \ˈmō-dəm, -ˌdem\ *n* **:** a device that converts signals from one device (as a computer) to a form compatible with another (as a telephone)

1**mod•er•ate** \ˈmä-də-rət\ *adj* **1 a :** avoiding extremes **b** ♦ **:** having a climate that especially lacks extremes in temperature **2** ♦ **:** tending toward the mean or average amount or dimension **3 :** limited in scope or effect **4 :** not expensive — **moderate** *n* — **mod•er•ate•ness** *n*

♦ [1b] balmy, clement, equable, gentle, mild, temperate ♦ [2] average, intermediate, median, medium, middle, modest

2**mod•er•ate** \ˈmä-də-ˌrāt\ *vb* **-at•ed; -at•ing** **1 :** to lessen the intensity of **:** TEMPER **2 :** to act as a moderator **3** ♦ **:** to become less violent, severe, or intense — **mod•er•a•tion** \ˌmä-də-ˈrā-shən\ *n*

♦ abate, de-escalate, decline, decrease, die, diminish, dwindle, ebb, fall, lessen, let up, lower, recede, relent, shrink, subside, taper, wane

mod•er•ate•ly \-lē\ *adv* ♦ **:** in a moderate manner or to a moderate extent

♦ enough, fairly, kind of, pretty, quite, rather, so-so, somewhat, sort of

mod•er•a•tor \ˈmä-də-ˌrā-tər\ *n* **1 :** MEDIATOR **2** ♦ **:** one who presides over an assembly, meeting, or discussion

♦ chair, chairman, president, speaker

mod•ern \ˈmä-dərn\ *adj* ♦ **:** of, relating to, or characteristic of the present or the immediate past **:** CONTEMPORARY — **modern** *n* — **mo•der•ni•ty** \mə-ˈdər-nə-tē\ *n* — **mod•ern•ly** *adv* — **mod•ern•ness** *n*

♦ contemporary, current, hot, mod, new, newfangled, red-hot, space-age, ultramodern, up-to-date ***Ant*** antiquated, archaic, dated, fusty, musty, old-fashioned, old-time, out-of-date, passé

mod•ern•ise, mod•ern•i•sa•tion *chiefly Brit var of* MODERNIZE, MODERNIZATION

mod•ern•ism \ˈmä-dər-ˌni-zəm\ *n* **:** a practice, movement, or belief peculiar to modern times

mod•ern•ize \ˈmä-dər-ˌnīz\ *vb* **-ized; -iz•ing** **:** to make or become modern — **mod•ern•i•za•tion** \ˌmä-dər-nə-ˈzā-shən\ *n* — **mod•ern•iz•er** *n*

mod•est \ˈmä-dəst\ *adj* **1 a** ♦ **:** having a moderate estimate of oneself **b** ♦ **:** neither bold nor self-assertive **:** DIFFIDENT **2** ♦ **:** observing the proprieties of dress and behavior **3** ♦ **:** limited in size, amount, or scope

♦ [1a] demure, humble, lowly, meek, retiring, unassuming, unpretentious ♦ [1b] bashful, coy, demure, diffident, introverted, retiring, sheepish, shy ♦ [2] chaste, clean, decent, immaculate, pure ♦ [3] average, intermediate, median, medium, middle, moderate

mod•est•ly \-lē\ *adv* ♦ **:** in a modest manner or to a modest extent

♦ humbly, lowly, meekly, sheepishly ♦ chastely, purely, righteously, virtuously

mod•es•ty \ˈmä-də-stē\ *n* **1** ♦ **:** freedom from conceit or vanity **2** ♦ **:** propriety in dress, speech, or conduct

♦ [1] humbleness, humility, lowliness, meekness ♦ [2] chastity, purity

mod•i•cum \ˈmä-di-kəm\ *n* ♦ **:** a small amount

♦ hoot, jot, lick, rap, tittle, whit

modif *abbr* modification

mod•i•fi•ca•tion \ˌmä-də-fə-ˈkā-shən\ *n* ♦ **:** the act, process, or result of modifying

♦ alteration, change, difference, revise, revision, variation

mod•i•fy \ˈmä-də-ˌfī\ *vb* **-fied; -fy•ing** **1 :** MODERATE **2 :** to limit the meaning of especially in a grammatical construction **3** ♦ **:** to make changes in **:** ALTER — **mod•i•fi•er** \ˈmä-də-ˌfī-ər\ *n*

♦ alter, change, make over, recast, redo, refashion, remake, remodel, revamp, revise, rework, vary

mod•ish \ˈmō-dish\ *adj* ♦ **:** conforming to the custom, fashion, or established mode **:** FASHIONABLE — **mod•ish•ly** *adv*

♦ à la mode, chic, fashionable, in, popular, sharp, smart, snappy, stylish

mod•ish•ness \-nəs\ *n* ♦ **:** the quality or state of being modish

♦ favor, popularity, vogue

mo•diste \mō-ˈdēst\ *n* **:** a maker of fashionable dresses and hats

mod•u•lar \ˈmä-jə-lər\ *adj* **:** constructed with standardized units

mod•u•lar•ized \ˈmä-jə-lə-ˌrīzd\ *adj* **:** containing or consisting of modules

mod•u•late \ˈmä-jə-ˌlāt\ *vb* **-lat•ed; -lat•ing** **1 :** to tune to a key or pitch **2 :** to keep in proper measure or proportion **:** TEMPER **3 :** to vary the amplitude or frequency of a carrier wave for the transmission of information (as in radio or television) — **mod•u•la•tion** \ˌmä-jə-ˈlā-shən\ *n* — **mod•u•la•tor** \ˈmä-jə-ˌlā-tər\ *n* — **mod•u•la•to•ry** \-lə-ˌtōr-ē\ *adj*

mod•ule \ˈmä-jül\ *n* **1 :** any in a series of standardized units for use together **2 :** an assembly of wired electronic parts for use with other such assemblies **3 :** an independent unit that constitutes a part of the total structure of a space vehicle ⟨a propulsion ~⟩

mo•dus op•er•an•di \ˌmō-dəs-ˌä-pə-ˈran-dē, -ˌdī\ *n, pl* **mo•di operandi** \ˈmō-ˌdē-ˌä-, ˈmō-ˌdī-\ **:** a method of procedure

1**mo•gul** \ˈmō-gəl, mō-ˈgəl\ *n* ♦ **:** an important person **:** MAGNATE

♦ baron, czar, king, magnate, prince, tycoon

2**mogul** \ˈmō-gəl\ *n* **:** a bump in a ski run

mo•hair \ˈmō-ˌhar\ *n* **:** a fabric or yarn made wholly or in part from the long silky hair of the Angora goat; *also* **:** this goat hair

Mo•ham•med•an *also* **Mu•ham•mad•an** \mō-ˈha-mə-dən, -ˈhä-, mü-\ *n* **:** MUSLIM — **Mo•ham•med•an•ism** *also* **Mu•ham•mad•an•ism** \-də-ˌni-zəm\ *n*

Mo•hawk \ˈmō-ˌhȯk\ *n, pl* **Mohawk** *or* **Mohawks :** a member of an American Indian people of the Mohawk River valley, New York; *also* **:** the language of the Mohawk people

Mo•he•gan \mō-ˈhē-gən, mə-\ *or* **Mo•hi•can** \-ˈhē-kən\ *n, pl* **Mohegan** *or* **Mohegans** *or* **Mohican** *or* **Mohicans :** a member of an American Indian people of southeastern Connecticut

mo•hel \ˈmō-(h)el, ˈmȯi(-ə)l\ *n, pl* **mohels** *also* **mo•hal•im** \ˌmō-hä-ˈlēm\ *also* **mo•hel•im** \-(h)e-ˈlēm\ **:** a person who performs Jewish circumcisions

Mohican *var of* MAHICAN

moi•e•ty \ˈmȯi-ə-tē\ *n, pl* **-ties :** one of two equal or approximately equal parts

moil \ˈmȯi(-ə)l\ *vb* **:** to work hard **:** DRUDGE — **moil** *n* — **moil•er** *n*

moi•ré \mȯ-ˈrā, mwä-\ *or* **moire** *same or* ˈmȯir, ˈmwär\ *n* **:** a fabric (as silk) having a watered appearance

moist \ˈmȯist\ *adj* **:** slightly or moderately wet — **moist•ly** *adv* — **moist•ness** *n*

moist•en \ˈmȯis-ᵊn\ *vb* **:** to make or become moist — **moist•en•er** *n*

mois•ture \ˈmȯis-chər\ *n* **:** the small amount of liquid that causes dampness

mois•tur•ise *chiefly Brit var of* MOISTURIZE

mois•tur•ize \ˈmȯis-chə-ˌrīz\ *vb* **-ized; -iz•ing :** to add moisture to — **mois•tur•iz•er** *n*

mol *abbr* molecular; molecule

mo•lar \ˈmō-lər\ *n* **:** any of the broad teeth adapted to grinding food and located in the back of the jaw — **molar** *adj*

mo•las•ses \mə-ˈla-səz\ *n* **:** the thick brown syrup that is separated from raw sugar in sugar manufacture

1**mold** *or Can and Brit* **mould** \ˈmōld\ *n* **:** crumbly soil rich in organic matter

2**mold** *or Can and Brit* **mould** *n* **1 :** distinctive nature or character **2 :** the frame on or around which something is constructed **3 :** a cavity in which something is shaped; *also* **:** an object so shaped **4 :** MOLDING

3**mold** *or Can and Brit* **mould** *vb* **1 :** to shape in or as if in a mold **2 :** to ornament with molding — **mold•er** *n*

4**mold** *or Can and Brit* **mould** *n* **:** a surface growth of fungus especially on damp or decaying matter; *also* **:** a fungus that produces molds — **mold•i•ness** \ˈmōl-dē-nəs\ *n* — **moldy** *adj*

[5]**mold** *or Can and Brit* **mould** *vb* **:** to become moldy

mold•board *or Can and Brit* **mould•board** \ˈmōld-ˌbōrd\ *n* **:** a curved iron plate attached above the plowshare to lift and turn the soil

mold•er *or Can and Brit* **mould•er** \ˈmōl-dər\ *vb* ♦ **:** to crumble into small pieces

♦ break down, corrupt, decay, decompose, disintegrate, putrefy, rot, spoil

mold•ing *or Can and Brit* **mould•ing** \ˈmōl-diŋ\ *n* **1 :** an act or process of shaping in a mold; *also* **:** an object so shaped **2 :** a decorative surface, plane, or curved strip

[1]**mole** \ˈmōl\ *n* **:** a small often pigmented spot or protuberance on the skin

[2]**mole** *n* **:** any of numerous small burrowing insect-eating mammals related to the shrews and hedgehogs

[3]**mole** *n* **:** a massive breakwater or jetty

mo•lec•u•lar \mə-ˈle-kyə-lər\ *adj* **:** of, relating to, or being a molecule

molecular biology *n* **:** a branch of biology dealing with the ultimate physical and chemical organization of living matter and especially with the molecular basis of inheritance and protein synthesis — **molecular biologist** *n*

molecular weight *n* **:** the mass of a molecule that is equal to the sum of the masses of all atoms contained in the molecule's formula

mol•e•cule \ˈmä-li-ˌkyül\ *n* **1 :** the smallest particle of matter that is the same chemically as the whole mass **2** ♦ **:** a tiny bit

♦ atom, bit, crumb, fleck, flyspeck, grain, granule, morsel, mote, particle, patch, scrap, scruple, speck, tittle

mole•hill \ˈmōl-ˌhil\ *n* **:** a little ridge of earth thrown up by a mole

mole•skin \-ˌskin\ *n* **1 :** the skin of the mole used as fur **2 :** a heavy durable cotton fabric

mo•lest \mə-ˈlest\ *vb* **1 :** ANNOY, DISTURB **2 :** to make annoying sexual advances to; *esp* **:** to force physical and usually sexual contact on — **mo•les•ta•tion** \ˌmō-ˌles-ˈtā-shən\ *n* — **mo•lest•er** *n*

moll \ˈmäl\ *n* **:** a gangster's girlfriend

mol•li•fy \ˈmä-lə-ˌfī\ *vb* **-fied; -fy•ing 1** ♦ **:** to soothe in temper **:** APPEASE **2 :** SOFTEN **3** ♦ **:** to reduce in intensity **:** ASSUAGE — **mol•li•fi•ca•tion** \ˌmä-lə-fə-ˈkā-shən\ *n*

♦ [1] appease, conciliate, disarm, pacify, placate, propitiate ♦ [3] allay, alleviate, assuage, ease, help, mitigate, palliate, relieve, soothe

mol•lusk *or* **mol•lusc** \ˈmä-ləsk\ *n* **:** any of a large phylum of usually shelled and aquatic invertebrate animals (as snails, clams, and squids) — **mol•lus•can** *also* **mol•lus•kan** \mə-ˈləs-kən\ *adj*

[1]**mol•ly•cod•dle** \ˈmä-lē-ˌkäd-ᵊl\ *n* **:** a pampered man or boy

[2]**mollycoddle** *vb* **mol•ly•cod•dled; mol•ly•cod•dling** ♦ **:** to treat with an excessive or absurd degree of indulgence and attention **:** PAMPER

♦ baby, coddle, nurse, pamper, spoil

Mo•lo•tov cocktail \ˈmä-lə-ˌtȯf-, ˈmȯ-\ *n* **:** a crude bomb made of a bottle filled usually with gasoline and fitted with a wick (as a saturated rag) that is ignited just prior to hurling

[1]**molt** *or Can and Brit* **moult** \ˈmōlt\ *vb* **:** to shed hair, feathers, outer skin, or horns periodically with the cast-off parts being replaced by new growth — **molt•er** *n*

[2]**molt** *or Can and Brit* **moult** *n* **:** the act or process of molting

mol•ten \ˈmōlt-ᵊn\ *adj* **1 :** fused or liquefied by heat **2 :** GLOWING

mo•ly \ˈmō-lē\ *n* **:** a mythical herb with black root, white flowers, and magic powers

mo•lyb•de•num \mə-ˈlib-də-nəm\ *n* **:** a metallic chemical element used in strengthening and hardening steel

mom \ˈmäm, ˈməm\ *n* **:** a female parent **:** MOTHER

♦ ma, mommy, mother

mom–and–pop *adj* **:** being a small owner-operated business

mo•ment \ˈmō-mənt\ *n* **1** ♦ **:** a minute portion of time **:** INSTANT **2 :** a time of excellence ⟨he has his ∼*s*⟩ **3 :** IMPORTANCE **4** ♦ **:** present time

♦ [1] flash, instant, jiffy, minute, second, shake, trice, twinkle, twinkling, wink ♦ [4] now, present, today

mo•men•tari•ly \ˌmō-mən-ˈter-ə-lē\ *adv* **1 :** for a moment **2** *archaic* **:** INSTANTLY **3** ♦ **:** at any moment **:** SOON

♦ anon, presently, shortly, soon

mo•men•tary \ˈmō-mən-ˌter-ē\ *adj* **1** ♦ **:** continuing only a moment **2 :** recurring at every moment — **mo•men•tar•i•ness** \-ˌter-ē-nəs\ *n*

♦ ephemeral, evanescent, flash, fleeting, fugitive, impermanent, short-lived, transient *Ant* enduring, eternal, everlasting, lasting, permanent, perpetual

mo•men•tous \mō-ˈmen-təs\ *adj* ♦ **:** very important — **mo•men•tous•ly** *adv* — **mo•men•tous•ness** *n*

♦ big, consequential, eventful, important, major, material, meaningful, significant, substantial, weighty

mo•men•tum \mō-ˈmen-təm\ *n, pl* **mo•men•ta** \-ˈmen-tə\ *or* **momentums 1 :** a property that a moving body has due to its mass and motion **2** ♦ **:** something that rouses or incites to activity **:** IMPETUS

♦ boost, encouragement, goad, impetus, impulse, incentive, incitement, instigation, motivation, provocation, spur, stimulus, yeast

mom•my \ˈmä-mē, ˈmə-\ *n, pl* **mom•mies :** MOTHER

♦ ma, mom, mother

Mon *abbr* Monday

mon•arch \ˈmä-nərk, -ˌnärk\ *n* **1** ♦ **:** a person who reigns over a kingdom or an empire **2 :** one holding preeminent position or power **3 :** MONARCH BUTTERFLY

♦ autocrat, ruler, sovereign

monarch butterfly *n* **:** a large orange and black migratory American butterfly whose larva feeds on milkweed

mo•nar•chi•cal \mə-ˈnär-ki-kəl, mä-\ *also* **mon•ar•chic** *adj* ♦ **:** of, relating to, suggestive of, or characteristic of a monarch or monarchy

♦ kingly, princely, queenly, regal, royal

mon•ar•chist \ˈmä-nər-kist\ *n* **:** a believer in monarchical government — **mon•ar•chism** \-ˌki-zəm\ *n*

mon•ar•chy \ˈmä-nər-kē\ *n, pl* **-chies :** a nation or state governed by a monarch

mon•as•tery \ˈmä-nə-ˌster-ē\ *n, pl* **-ter•ies** ♦ **:** a house for persons under religious vows (as monks)

♦ abbey, cloister, friary, priory

mo•nas•tic \mə-ˈnas-tik\ *adj* **:** of or relating to monasteries or to monks or nuns — **monastic** *n* — **mo•nas•ti•cal•ly** \-ti-k(ə-)lē\ *adv* — **mo•nas•ti•cism** \-tə-ˌsi-zəm\ *n*

mon•au•ral \mä-ˈnȯr-əl\ *adj* **:** MONOPHONIC — **mon•au•ral•ly** *adv*

Mon•day \ˈmən-dē, -ˌdā\ *n* **:** the second day of the week

mon•e•tary \ˈmä-nə-ˌter-ē, ˈmə-\ *adj* ♦ **:** of or relating to money or to the mechanisms by which it is supplied and circulated in the economy

♦ financial, fiscal, pecuniary

mon•ey \ˈmə-nē\ *n, pl* **moneys** *or* **mon•ies** \ˈmə-nēz\ **1** ♦ **:** something (as metal currency) accepted as a medium of exchange **2 :** wealth reckoned in monetary terms **3 :** the 1st, 2d, and 3d places in a horse or dog race

♦ cash, currency, dough, lucre, pelf, tender

mon•eyed \ˈmə-nēd\ *adj* **1** ♦ **:** having money **:** WEALTHY **2 :** consisting in or derived from money

♦ affluent, flush, loaded, opulent, rich, wealthy, well-fixed, well-heeled, well-off, well-to-do

mon•ey•lend•er \ˈmə-nē-ˌlen-dər\ *n* **:** one (as a bank or pawnbroker) whose business is lending money

money market *n* **:** the trade in short-term negotiable financial instruments

money of account : a denominator of value or basis of exchange used in keeping accounts

money order *n* **:** an order purchased at a post office, bank, or telegraph office directing another office to pay a sum of money to a party named on it

mon•ger \ˈməŋ-gər, ˈmäŋ-\ *n* **1 :** DEALER **2 :** one who tries to stir up or spread something

Mon•gol \ˈmäŋ-gəl, ˈmän-ˌgōl\ *n* **:** a member of any of several traditionally pastoral peoples of Mongolia — **Mongol** *adj*

Mon•go•lian \män-ˈgōl-yən, mäŋ-, -ˈgō-lē-ən\ *n* **1 :** a native or inhabitant of Mongolia **2 :** a member of the Mongoloid racial stock — **Mongolian** *adj*

Mon•gol•oid \ˈmäŋ-gə-ˌlȯid\ *adj* **:** of or relating to a major racial stock native to Asia that includes peoples of northern and eastern

Asia, Malaysians, Eskimos, and often American Indians — **Mongoloid** *n*
mon•goose \ˈmän-ˌgüs, ˈmäŋ-\ *n, pl* **mon•goos•es** *also* **mongeese** \-ˌgēs\ **:** any of a group of small, agile Old World mammals that are related to the civet cats and feed chiefly on small animals and fruits
mon•grel \ˈmäŋ-grəl, ˈməŋ-\ *n* ♦ **:** an offspring of parents of different breeds; *esp* **:** one of uncertain ancestry

♦ cross, hybrid

mon•i•ker \ˈmä-ni-kər\ *n* **:** NAME, NICKNAME
mo•nism \ˈmō-ˌni-zəm, ˈmä-\ *n* **:** a view that reality is basically one unitary organic whole — **mo•nist** \ˈmō-nist, ˈmä-\ *n*
mo•ni•tion \mō-ˈni-shən, mə-\ *n* **:** WARNING, CAUTION
¹**mon•i•tor** \ˈmä-nə-tər\ *n* **1 :** a student appointed to assist a teacher **2 :** one that monitors; *esp* **:** a video display screen (as for a computer)
²**monitor** *vb* **:** to watch, check, or observe for a special purpose
mon•i•to•ry \ˈmä-nə-ˌtōr-ē\ *adj* **:** giving admonition **:** WARNING
¹**monk** \ˈməŋk\ *n* **:** a man belonging to a religious order and living in a monastery — **monk•ish** *adj*
²**monk** *n* **:** MONKEY
¹**mon•key** \ˈməŋ-kē\ *n, pl* **monkeys 1 :** a nonhuman primate mammal; *esp* **:** one of the smaller, longer-tailed, and usually more arboreal primates as contrasted with the apes **2** ♦ **:** a person resembling a monkey in appearance or behavior

♦ devil, hellion, imp, mischief, rapscallion, rascal, rogue, scamp, urchin

²**monkey** *vb* **mon•keyed; mon•key•ing 1** ♦ **:** to behave foolishly **:** FOOL — often used with *around* **2** ♦ **:** to try foolish or dangerous experiments **:** TAMPER — usually used with *with*

♦ *usu* **monkey around** [1] act up, clown, cut up, fool, show off, skylark ♦ *usu* **monkey around** [1] fiddle, fool, mess, play, potter, putter, trifle ♦ *usu* **monkey with** [2] fiddle, fool, mess, play, tamper, tinker

monkey bars *n pl* **:** a framework of bars on which children can play
mon•key•shine \ˈmən-kē-ˌshīn\ *n* ♦ **:** a mischievous act; *also* **:** mischievous behavior — usually used in plural

♦ *usu* **monkeyshines** *pl* antic, caper, escapade, frolic, practical joke, prank, trick ♦ *usu* **monkeyshines** *pl* foolery, high jinks, horseplay, roughhouse, shenanigans, tomfoolery

monkey wrench *n* **:** a wrench with one fixed and one adjustable jaw at right angles to a handle
monk•fish \ˈməŋk-ˌfish\ *n* **:** either of two marine bony fishes that have a large flattened head and are used for food
monks•hood \ˈməŋks-ˌhu̇d\ *n* **:** any of a genus of poisonous plants related to the buttercups; *esp* **:** a tall Eurasian herb with white or purplish flowers
¹**mono** \ˈmä-nō\ *adj* **:** MONOPHONIC
²**mono** *n* **:** INFECTIOUS MONONUCLEOSIS
mono•chro•mat•ic \ˌmä-nə-krō-ˈma-tik\ *adj* **1 :** having or consisting of one color **2 :** consisting of radiation (as light) of a single wavelength
mono•chrome \ˈmä-nə-ˌkrōm\ *adj* **:** involving or producing visual images in a single color or in varying tones of a single color ⟨∼ television⟩
mon•o•cle \ˈmä-ni-kəl\ *n* **:** an eyeglass for one eye
mono•clo•nal \ˌmä-nə-ˈklō-nəl\ *adj* **:** produced by, being, or composed of cells derived from a single cell ⟨∼ antibodies⟩
mono•cot•y•le•don \ˌmä-nə-ˌkät-ᵊl-ˈēd-ᵊn\ *n* **:** any of a class or subclass of chiefly herbaceous seed plants having an embryo with a single cotyledon and usually parallel-veined leaves
mon•o•dy \ˈmä-nə-dē\ *n, pl* **-dies :** ELEGY, DIRGE — **mo•nod•ic** \mə-ˈnä-dik\ *or* **mo•nod•i•cal** \-di-kəl\ *adj* — **mon•o•dist** \ˈmä-nə-dist\ *n*
mo•nog•a•my \mə-ˈnä-gə-mē\ *n* **1 :** marriage with but one person at a time **2 :** the practice of having a single mate during a period of time — **mo•nog•a•mist** \-mist\ *n* — **mo•nog•a•mous** \-məs\ *adj*
mono•gram \ˈmä-nə-ˌgram\ *n* **:** a sign of identity composed of the combined initials of a name — **monogram** *vb*
mono•graph \ˈmä-nə-ˌgraf\ *n* **:** a learned treatise on a small area of learning
mono•lin•gual \ˌmä-nə-ˈliŋ-gwəl\ *adj* **:** knowing or using only one language
mono•lith \ˈmän-ᵊl-ˌith\ *n* **1 :** a single great stone often in the form of a monument or column **2 :** something large and powerful that acts as a single unified force — **mono•lith•ic** \ˌmän-ᵊl-ˈi-thik\ *adj*
mono•logue *also* **mono•log** \ˈmän-ᵊl-ˌȯg\ *n* **1 :** a dramatic soliloquy; *also* **:** a long speech monopolizing conversation **2 :** the routine of a stand-up comic — **mono•logu•ist** \-ˌȯg-ist\ *or* **mo•no•lo•gist** \mə-ˈnä-lə-jist, ˈmän-ᵊl-ˌȯ-gist\ *n*
mono•ma•nia \ˌmä-nə-ˈmā-nē-ə, -nyə\ *n* **1 :** mental disorder limited in expression to one area of thought **2 :** excessive concentration on a single object or idea — **mono•ma•ni•ac** \-nē-ˌak\ *n or adj*
mono•mer \ˈmä-nə-mər\ *n* **:** a simple chemical compound that can be polymerized
mono•nu•cle•o•sis \ˌmä-nō-ˌnü-klē-ˈō-səs, -ˌnyü-\ *n* **:** INFECTIOUS MONONUCLEOSIS
mono•phon•ic \ˌmä-nə-ˈfä-nik\ *adj* **:** of or relating to sound recording or reproduction involving a single transmission path
mono•plane \ˈmä-nə-ˌplān\ *n* **:** an airplane with only one set of wings
mo•nop•o•ly \mə-ˈnä-pə-lē\ *n, pl* **-lies 1 :** exclusive ownership (as through command of supply) **2 :** a commodity controlled by one party **3 :** one that has a monopoly — **mo•nop•o•list** \-list\ *n* — **mo•nop•o•lis•tic** \mə-ˌnä-pə-ˈlis-tik\ *adj* — **mo•nop•o•li•za•tion** \-lə-ˈzā-shən\ *n* — **mo•nop•o•lize** \mə-ˈnä-pə-ˌlīz\ *vb*
mono•rail \ˈmä-nə-ˌrāl\ *n* **:** a single rail serving as a track for a vehicle; *also* **:** a vehicle traveling on such a track
mono•so•di•um glu•ta•mate \ˌmä-nə-ˌsō-dē-əm-ˈglü-tə-ˌmāt\ *n* **:** a crystalline salt used to enhance the flavor of food
mono•syl•la•ble \ˈmä-nə-ˌsi-lə-bəl\ *n* **:** a word of one syllable — **mono•syl•lab•ic** \ˌmä-nə-sə-ˈla-bik\ *adj* — **mono•syl•lab•i•cal•ly** \-bi-k(ə-)lē\ *adv*
mono•the•ism \ˈmä-nə-(ˌ)thē-ˌi-zəm\ *n* **:** a doctrine or belief that there is only one deity — **mono•the•ist** \-ˌthē-ist\ *n* — **mono•the•is•tic** \-thē-ˈis-tik\ *adj*
mono•tone \ˈmä-nə-ˌtōn\ *n* **:** a succession of syllables, words, or sentences in one unvaried key or pitch
mo•not•o•nous \mə-ˈnät-ᵊn-əs\ *adj* **1 :** uttered or sounded in one unvarying tone **2** ♦ **:** tediously uniform — **mo•not•o•nous•ly** *adv* — **mo•not•o•nous•ness** *n*

♦ drab, dreary, dry, dull, flat, uninteresting, weary

mo•not•o•ny \mə-ˈnät-ᵊn-ē\ *n* **:** tedious sameness or uniformity
mono•un•sat•u•rat•ed \ˌmä-nō-ˌən-ˈsa-chə-ˌrā-təd\ *adj* **:** containing one double or triple bond per molecule — used especially of an oil or fatty acid
mon•ox•ide \mə-ˈnäk-ˌsīd\ *n* **:** an oxide containing one atom of oxygen in a molecule
mon•sei•gneur \ˌmōⁿ-ˌsān-ˈyər\ *n, pl* **mes•sei•gneurs** \ˌmā-ˌsān-ˈyər, -ˈyərz\ **:** a French dignitary — used as a title
mon•sieur \məs-ˈyər, mə-ˈshər, *Fr* mə-ˈsyœ\ *n, pl* **mes•sieurs** *same or* -ˈyərz, -ˈshərz\ **:** a Frenchman of high rank or station — used as a title equivalent to *Mister*
mon•si•gnor \män-ˈsē-nyər\ *n, pl* **monsignors** *or* **mon•si•gno•ri** \ˌmän-ˌsēn-ˈyōr-ē\ **:** a Roman Catholic prelate — used as a title
mon•soon \män-ˈsün\ *n* **1 :** a periodic wind especially in the Indian Ocean and southern Asia **2 :** the season of the southwest monsoon especially in India **3 :** rainfall associated with the monsoon
¹**mon•ster** \ˈmän-stər\ *n* **1 :** an abnormally developed plant or animal **2 a :** an animal of strange or terrifying shape **b** ♦ **:** one unusually large of its kind **3** ♦ **:** an extremely ugly, wicked, or cruel person **4 :** something monstrous

♦ [2b] behemoth, blockbuster, colossus, giant, jumbo, leviathan, mammoth, titan, whale, whopper ♦ [3] beast, brute, devil, fiend, savage, villain

²**monster** *adj* **:** very large **:** ENORMOUS
mon•strance \ˈmän-strəns\ *n* **:** a vessel in which the consecrated Host is exposed for the adoration of the faithful
mon•stros•i•ty \män-ˈsträ-sə-tē\ *n* **1 a :** a malformation of a plant or animal **b** ♦ **:** something deviating from the normal **:** FREAK **2** ♦ **:** the quality or state of being monstrous **3 a :** an object of great and often frightening size, force, or complexity **b** ♦ **:** an excessively bad or shocking example

♦ [1b] abnormality, freak, monster ♦ [2] atrociousness, atrocity, frightfulness, hideousness, horror, repulsiveness ♦ [2] atrociousness, atrocity, depravity, enormity, heinousness, vileness, wickedness ♦ [3b] eyesore, fright, horror, mess, sight

mon•strous \ˈmän-strəs\ *adj* **1** ♦ **:** having extraordinary often overwhelming size **2** ♦ **:** extraordinarily ugly or vicious **3** ♦ **:** deviating greatly from the natural form or character

♦ [1] enormous, giant, gigantic, huge, mammoth, massive, monster, monumental, prodigious, tremendous, whopping ♦ [2] appalling, atrocious, awful, dreadful, frightful, ghastly, grisly, gruesome, hideous, horrible, horrid, lurid, macabre, nightmarish, shocking, terrible ♦ [3] deformed, distorted, malformed, misshapen, shapeless

mon•strous•ly \-lē\ *adv* ♦ **:** in a monstrous manner

♦ devilishly, excessively, inordinately, overly, overmuch, too ♦ broadly, considerably, greatly, hugely, largely, massively, much, sizably, stupendously, tremendously, utterly, vastly

Mont *abbr* Montana
mon•tage \män-ˈtäzh\ *n* **1 :** a composite photograph made by combining several separate pictures **2 :** an artistic composition made up of several different kinds of elements **3 :** a varied mixture **:** JUMBLE
month \ˈmənth\ *n, pl* **months** \ˈməns, ˈmənths\ **:** one of the 12 parts into which the year is divided — **month•ly** *adv or adj or n*
month•long \ˈmənth-ˈlȯŋ\ *adj* **:** lasting a month
mon•u•ment \ˈmän-yə-mənt\ *n* **1** ♦ **:** a lasting reminder; *esp* **:** a structure erected in remembrance of a person or event **2 :** NATIONAL MONUMENT

♦ gravestone, headstone, tombstone ♦ keepsake, memento, memorial, remembrance, souvenir, token

mon•u•men•tal \ˌmän-yə-ˈment-ᵊl\ *adj* **1 :** of or relating to a monument **2 a** ♦ **:** having impressive bulk or size **b :** highly significant **:** OUTSTANDING **3** ♦ **:** very great — **mon•u•men•tal•ly** *adv*

♦ colossal, enormous, giant, gigantic, grand, heroic, huge, mammoth, massive, outsize, oversize, prodigious, titanic, tremendous, vast

moo \ˈmü\ *vb* **:** to make the natural throat noise of a cow — **moo** *n*
mooch•er \ˈmü-chər\ *n* ♦ **:** one that begs or lives off another's expense

♦ hanger-on, leech, parasite, sponge

¹mood \ˈmüd\ *n* **1** ♦ **:** a conscious state of mind or predominant emotion **2 :** a prevailing attitude **:** DISPOSITION **3** ♦ **:** a distinctive atmosphere

♦ [1] cheer, frame, humor (*or* humour), mode, spirit, temper ♦ [3] air, atmosphere, aura, climate, flavor (*or* flavour), note, temper

²mood *n* **:** distinction of form of a verb to express whether its action or state is conceived as fact or in some other manner (as wish)
moody \ˈmü-dē\ *adj* **mood•i•er; -est 1 :** GLOOMY **2** ♦ **:** subject to moods **:** TEMPERAMENTAL — **mood•i•ly** \-də-lē\ *adv* — **mood•i•ness** \-dē-nəs\ *n*

♦ glum, morose, sulky, sullen, surly

¹moon \ˈmün\ *n* **1 :** the earth's natural satellite **2 :** SATELLITE 2 **3** ♦ **:** an indefinite usually extended period of time — often used in plural

♦ aeon (*or* eon), age, cycle, eternity

²moon *vb* **:** to engage in idle reverie
moon•beam \ˈmün-ˌbēm\ *n* **:** a ray of light from the moon
¹moon•light \-ˌlīt\ *n* **:** the light of the moon — **moon•lit** \-ˌlit\ *adj*
²moonlight *vb* **moon•light•ed; moon•light•ing :** to hold a second job in addition to a regular one — **moon•light•er** *n*
moon•roof \-ˌrüf, -ˌru̇f\ *n* **:** a glass sunroof
moon•scape \-ˌskāp\ *n* **:** the surface of the moon as seen or as pictured
moon•shine \-ˌshīn\ *n* **1 :** MOONLIGHT **2 :** empty talk **3** ♦ **:** intoxicating liquor usually illegally distilled

♦ alcohol, booze, drink, intoxicant, liquor, spirits

moon•stone \-ˌstōn\ *n* **:** a transparent or translucent feldspar of pearly luster used as a gem
moon•struck \-ˌstrək\ *adj* **1 :** mentally unbalanced **2 :** romantically sentimental **3 :** lost in fantasy
¹moor \ˈmu̇r\ *n* **1** *chiefly Brit* **:** an expanse of open rolling infertile land **2 :** a boggy area; *esp* **:** one that is peaty and dominated by grasses and sedges
²moor *vb* ♦ **:** to make fast with or as if with cables, lines, or anchors

♦ anchor, catch, clamp, fasten, fix, hitch, secure, set ♦ disembark, dock, land, tie up

Moor \ˈmu̇r\ *n* **:** one of the Arab and Berber conquerors of Spain — **Moor•ish** *adj*
moor•ing \ˈmu̇r-iŋ\ *n* **1 :** a place where or an object to which a craft can be made fast **2 :** an established practice or stabilizing influence — usually used in plural
moor•land \-lənd, -ˌland\ *n* **:** land consisting of moors
moose \ˈmüs\ *n, pl* **moose :** a large heavy-antlered ruminant mammal related to the deer that has humped shoulders and long legs and inhabits northern forested areas
¹moot \ˈmüt\ *vb* **1** ♦ **:** to bring up for discussion **2** ♦ **:** to argue about **:** DEBATE

♦ [1] bring up, broach, introduce, raise ♦ [2] argue, chew over, debate, discuss, dispute, hash, talk over

²moot *adj* **1** ♦ **:** open to question; *also* **:** DISPUTED **2 :** having no practical significance

♦ arguable, debatable, disputable, doubtful, questionable

¹mop \ˈmäp\ *n* **:** an implement made of absorbent material fastened to a handle and used especially for cleaning floors
²mop *vb* **mopped; mop•ping :** to use a mop on **:** clean with a mop
mope \ˈmōp\ *vb* **moped; mop•ing 1 :** to become dull, dejected, or listless **2** ♦ **:** to move slowly or aimlessly

♦ gad, gallivant, knock, maunder, meander, ramble, range, roam, rove, traipse, wander

mo•ped \ˈmō-ˌped\ *n* **:** a light low-powered motorbike that can be pedaled
mop•pet \ˈmä-pət\ *n* ♦ **:** a young person who is between infancy and adulthood **:** CHILD

♦ child, cub, juvenile, kid, kiddo, whelp, youngster, youth

mo•raine \mə-ˈrān\ *n* **:** an accumulation of earth and stones left by a glacier
¹mor•al \ˈmȯr-əl\ *adj* **1 :** of or relating to principles of right and wrong **2** ♦ **:** conforming to a standard of right behavior; *also* **:** capable of right and wrong action **3 :** probable but not proved ⟨a ∼ certainty⟩ **4 :** perceptual or psychological rather than tangible or practical in nature or effect ⟨a ∼ victory⟩

♦ decent, ethical, good, honest, honorable (*or* honourable), just, right, righteous, straight, upright, virtuous

²moral *n* **1 :** the practical meaning (as of a story) **2** *pl* ♦ **:** moral practices or teachings

♦ **morals** *pl* ethics, morality, principles, standards

mo•rale \mə-ˈral\ *n* **1 :** MORALITY **2 :** the mental and emotional attitudes of an individual toward the tasks at hand; *also* **:** ESPRIT DE CORPS
mor•al•ise *chiefly Brit var of* MORALIZE
mor•al•ist \ˈmȯr-ə-list\ *n* **1 :** one who leads a moral life **2 :** a thinker or writer concerned with morals **3 :** one concerned with regulating the morals of others — **mor•al•is•tic** \ˌmȯr-ə-ˈlis-tik\ *adj* — **mor•al•is•ti•cal•ly** \-ti-k(ə-)lē\ *adv*
mo•ral•i•ty \mə-ˈra-lə-tē\ *n, pl* **-ties 1** ♦ **:** a doctrine or system of moral conduct **2** ♦ **:** moral conduct **:** VIRTUE

♦ [1] ethics, morals, principles, standards ♦ [2] character, decency, goodness, honesty, honor (*or* honour), integrity, probity, rectitude, righteousness, uprightness, virtue ***Ant*** badness, evil, immorality, wickedness

mor•al•ize \ˈmȯr-ə-ˌlīz\ *vb* **-ized; -iz•ing :** to make moral reflections — **mor•al•i•za•tion** \ˌmȯr-ə-lə-ˈzā-shən\ *n* — **mor•al•iz•er** \ˈmȯr-ə-ˌlī-zər\ *n*
mor•al•ly \ˈmȯr-əl\ *adv* **:** in accordance with morals **:** in a moral manner
mo•rass \mə-ˈras\ *n* ♦ **:** a tract of soft wet land **:** SWAMP; *also* **:** something that entangles, impedes, or confuses

♦ bog, fen, marsh, mire, slough, swamp

mor•a•to•ri•um \ˌmȯr-ə-ˈtōr-ē-əm\ *n, pl* **-ri•ums** *or* **-ria** \-ē-ə\ ♦ **:** a suspension of activity

♦ abeyance, doldrums, dormancy, holding pattern, latency, quiescence, suspension

mo•ray eel \mə-ˈrā-, ˈmȯr-ˌā-\ *n* **:** any of numerous often brightly colored biting eels of warm seas
mor•bid \ˈmȯr-bəd\ *adj* **1 :** of, relating to, or typical of disease; *also* **:** DISEASED, SICKLY **2 :** characterized by gloomy or unwholesome ideas or feelings **3 :** GRISLY, GRUESOME ⟨∼ details⟩ — **mor•bid•i•ty** \mȯr-ˈbi-də-tē\ *n* — **mor•bid•ly** *adv* — **mor•bid•ness** *n*
mor•dant \ˈmȯrd-ᵊnt\ *adj* **1** ♦ **:** biting or caustic in manner or style **2 :** BURNING, PUNGENT — **mor•dant•ly** *adv*

♦ acrid, biting, caustic, cutting, pungent, sarcastic, satiric, scathing, sharp, tart

¹more \ˈmōr\ *adj* **1 :** GREATER **2 ♦ :** existing by way of addition **:** ADDITIONAL

♦ additional, another, else, farther, further, other

²more *adv* **1 :** in addition **2 :** to a greater or higher degree
³more *n* **1 :** a greater quantity, number, or amount ⟨the ~ the merrier⟩ **2 :** an additional amount ⟨costs a little ~⟩
⁴more *pron* **:** additional persons or things or a greater amount
mo•rel \mə-ˈrel\ *n* **:** any of several pitted edible fungi
more•over \mōr-ˈō-vər\ *adv* **♦ :** in addition **:** FURTHER

♦ additionally, again, also, besides, further, furthermore, likewise, more, then, too, withal, yet

mo•res \ˈmȯr-ˌāz\ *n pl* **1 ♦ :** the fixed morally binding customs of a group **2 :** HABITS, MANNERS

♦ etiquette, manners

Mor•gan \ˈmȯr-gən\ *n* **:** any of an American breed of lightly built horses
morgue \ˈmȯrg\ *n* **:** a place where the bodies of dead persons are kept until released for burial or autopsy
mor•i•bund \ˈmȯr-ə-(ˌ)bənd\ *adj* **:** being in a dying condition
Mor•mon \ˈmȯr-mən\ *n* **:** a member of the Church of Jesus Christ of Latter-day Saints — **Mor•mon•ism** \-mə-ˌni-zəm\ *n*
morn \ˈmȯrn\ *n* **1 :** the first appearance of light in the morning followed by sunrise **2 :** MORNING
morn•ing \ˈmȯr-niŋ\ *n* **1 a ♦ :** the first appearance of light in the morning followed by sunrise **b :** the time from the sunrise to noon **2 ♦ :** a period of first development **:** BEGINNING

♦ [1a] aurora, cockcrow, dawn, sunrise ♦ [2] beginning, birth, commencement, dawn, genesis, launch, onset, outset, start, threshold

morn•ing–after pill \ˌmȯr-niŋ-ˈaf-tər-\ *n* **:** a contraceptive drug taken up to usually three days after sexual intercourse
morning glory *n* **:** any of various twining plants related to the sweet potato that have often showy bell-shaped or funnel-shaped flowers
morning sickness *n* **:** nausea and vomiting that typically occur in the morning especially during early pregnancy
morning star *n* **:** a bright planet (as Venus) seen in the eastern sky before or at sunrise
Mo•roc•can \mə-ˈrä-kən\ *n* **:** a native or inhabitant of Morocco
mo•roc•co \mə-ˈrä-kō\ *n* **:** a fine leather made of goatskins tanned with sumac
mo•ron \ˈmōr-ˌän\ *n* **1** *usu offensive* **:** a mildly mentally retarded person **2 ♦ :** a very stupid person — **mo•ron•ic** \mə-ˈrä-nik\ *adj* — **mo•ron•i•cal•ly** \-ni-k(ə-)lē\ *adv*

♦ blockhead, dolt, dope, dummy, idiot, imbecile, jackass, nitwit, numskull, simpleton

mo•rose \mə-ˈrōs\ *adj* **1 ♦ :** having a sullen disposition **2 :** marked by or expressive of gloom **:** GLOOMY — **mo•rose•ly** *adv* — **mo•rose•ness** *n*

♦ glum, moody, sulky, sullen, surly

morph \ˈmȯrf\ *vb* **:** to change the form or character of **:** TRANSFORM
mor•pheme \ˈmȯr-ˌfēm\ *n* **:** a meaningful linguistic unit that contains no smaller meaningful parts — **mor•phe•mic** \mȯr-ˈfē-mik\ *adj*
mor•phia \ˈmȯr-fē-ə\ *n* **:** MORPHINE
mor•phine \ˈmȯr-ˌfēn\ *n* **:** an addictive drug obtained from opium and used to ease pain or induce sleep
mor•phol•o•gy \mȯr-ˈfä-lə-jē\ *n* **1 :** a branch of biology dealing with the form and structure of organisms **2 :** a study and description of word formation in a language — **mor•pho•log•i•cal** \ˌmȯr-fə-ˈlä-ji-kəl\ *adj* — **mor•phol•o•gist** \mȯr-ˈfä-lə-jist\ *n*
mor•ris \ˈmȯr-əs\ *n* **:** a vigorous English dance traditionally performed by men wearing costumes and bells
mor•row \ˈmär-ō\ *n* **:** the next day
Morse code \ˈmȯrs-\ *n* **:** either of two codes consisting of dots and dashes or long and short sounds used for transmitting messages
mor•sel \ˈmȯr-səl\ *n* **1 ♦ :** a small piece or quantity **2 :** a tasty dish **3 ♦ :** a small piece of food

♦ [1] bit, crumb, grain, granule, particle, scrap ♦ [3] bite, mouthful, nibble, taste, tidbit

¹mor•tal \ˈmȯrt-ᵊl\ *adj* **1 a ♦ :** causing death **:** FATAL **b :** leading to eternal punishment ⟨~ sin⟩ **2 :** subject to death ⟨~ man⟩ **3 :** implacably hostile ⟨~ foe⟩ **4 :** very great **:** EXTREME ⟨~ fear⟩ **5 :** HUMAN ⟨~ limitations⟩ **6 ♦ :** of, relating to, or connected with death — **mor•tal•i•ty** \mȯr-ˈta-lə-tē\ *n*

♦ baleful, deadly, deathly, fatal, fell, lethal, murderous, pestilent, vital

²mortal *n* **♦ :** a human being

♦ being, body, creature, human, individual, man, person

mor•tal•ly \ˈmȯrt-ᵊl-ē\ *adv* **1 :** in a deadly or fatal manner ⟨~ wounded⟩ **2 ♦ :** to an extreme degree ⟨~ afraid⟩

♦ especially, extremely, greatly, highly, hugely, mightily, mighty, most, much, real, right, so, very

¹mor•tar \ˈmȯr-tər\ *n* **1 :** a strong bowl in which substances are pounded or crushed with a pestle **2 :** a short-barreled cannon used to fire shells at high angles
²mortar *n* **:** a building material (as a mixture of lime and cement with sand and water) that is spread between bricks or stones to bind them together as it hardens — **mortar** *vb*
mor•tar•board \ˈmȯr-tər-ˌbōrd\ *n* **1 :** a square board for holding mortar **2 :** an academic cap with a flat square top
mort•gage \ˈmȯr-gij\ *n* **:** a transfer of rights to a piece of property usually as security for the payment of a loan or debt that becomes void when the debt is paid — **mortgage** *vb* — **mort•gag•ee** \ˌmȯr-gi-ˈjē\ *n* — **mort•gag•or** \ˌmȯr-gi-ˈjȯr\ *n*
mor•ti•cian \mȯr-ˈti-shən\ *n* **:** UNDERTAKER
mor•ti•fi•ca•tion \ˌmȯr-tə-fə-ˈkā-shən\ *n* **♦ :** a sense of humiliation and shame caused by something that wounds one's pride or self-respect

♦ abashment, confusion, discomfiture, embarrassment, fluster

mor•ti•fy \ˈmȯr-tə-ˌfī\ *vb* **-fied; -fy•ing** **1 :** to subdue (as the body) especially by abstinence or self-inflicted pain **2 ♦ :** to subject to severe and vexing embarrassment **3 :** to become necrotic or gangrenous

♦ abash, confound, confuse, discomfit, disconcert, discountenance, embarrass, faze, fluster, rattle

mor•tise *also* **mor•tice** \ˈmȯr-təs\ *n* **:** a hole cut in a piece of wood into which another piece fits to form a joint
mor•tu•ary \ˈmȯr-chə-ˌwer-ē\ *n, pl* **-ar•ies :** a place in which dead bodies are kept until burial
mos *abbr* months
mo•sa•ic \mō-ˈzā-ik\ *n* **:** a surface decoration made by inlaying small pieces (as of colored glass or stone) to form figures or patterns; *also* **:** a design made in mosaic — **mosaic** *adj*
mo•sey \ˈmō-zē\ *vb* **mo•seyed; mo•sey•ing :** SAUNTER
mosh \ˈmäsh\ *vb* **:** to engage in rough uninhibited dancing near the stage at a rock concert
mosh pit *n* **:** an area in front of a stage where rough dancing takes place at a rock concert
Mos•lem \ˈmäz-ləm\ *var of* MUSLIM
mosque \ˈmäsk\ *n* **:** a building used for public worship by Muslims
mos•qui•to \mə-ˈskē-tō\ *n, pl* **-toes** *also* **-tos :** any of a family of dipteran flies the female of which sucks the blood of animals
mosquito net *n* **:** a net or screen for keeping out mosquitoes
moss \ˈmȯs\ *n* **:** any of a class of green plants that lack flowers but have small leafy stems and often grow in clumps — **mossy** *adj*
moss•back \ˈmȯs-ˌbak\ *n* **:** an extremely conservative person **:** FOGY
¹most \ˈmōst\ *adj* **1 ♦ :** greatest in quantity, extent, or degree ⟨the ~ ability⟩ **2 :** the majority of ⟨~ people⟩

♦ consummate, maximum, nth, paramount, supreme, top, ultimate, utmost

²most *adv* **1 :** to the greatest or highest degree ⟨~ beautiful⟩ **2 :** to a very great degree ⟨a ~ careful driver⟩
³most *n* **:** the greatest amount ⟨the ~ I can do⟩
⁴most *pron* **:** the greatest number or part ⟨~ became discouraged⟩
⁵most *adv* **♦ :** very nearly but not exactly or entirely **:** ALMOST

♦ about, almost, much, near, nearly, next to, nigh, practically, some, virtually, well-nigh

-most \ˌmōst\ *adj suffix* **:** most ⟨inner*most*⟩ **:** most toward ⟨end*most*⟩
most•ly \ˈmōst-lē\ *adv* **♦ :** for the greatest part **:** MAINLY

♦ altogether, basically, chiefly, generally, largely, mainly, overall, predominantly, primarily, principally

mot \ˈmō\ *n, pl* **mots** *same or* ˈmōz\ **:** a witty saying
mote \ˈmōt\ *n* **♦ :** a small particle

♦ bit, fleck, flyspeck, molecule, particle, speck

mo•tel \mō-ˈtel\ *n* **:** a hotel in which the rooms are accessible from the parking area

mo•tet \mō-ˈtet\ *n* **:** a choral work on a sacred text for several voices usually without instrumental accompaniment
moth \ˈmȯth\ *n, pl* **moths** \ˈmȯt͟hz, ˈmȯths\ **:** any of various insects belonging to the same order as the butterflies but usually night-flying and with a stouter body and smaller wings
moth•ball \ˈmȯth-ˌbȯl\ *n* **1 :** a ball (as of naphthalene) used to keep moths out of clothing **2** *pl* **:** protective storage
[1]**moth•er** \ˈmə-t͟hər\ *n* **1** ♦ **:** a female parent **2 :** the superior of a religious community of women **3 :** SOURCE, ORIGIN — **moth•er•hood** \-ˌhu̇d\ *n* — **moth•er•less** *adj* — **moth•er•li•ness** \-lē-nəs\ *n* — **moth•er•ly** *adj*

♦ ma, mom, mommy

[2]**mother** *vb* **1 :** to give birth to; *also* **:** PRODUCE **2** ♦ **:** to care for or protect like a mother

♦ aid, care, minister, nurse

moth•er•board \ˈmə-t͟hər-ˌbōrd\ *n* **:** the main circuit board especially of a microcomputer
moth•er–in–law \ˈmə-t͟hər-ən-ˌlȯ\ *n, pl* **mothers–in–law** \ˈmə-t͟hərz-\ **:** the mother of one's spouse
moth•er•land \ˈmə-t͟hər-ˌland\ *n* **1 :** the land of origin of something **2** ♦ **:** the native land of one's ancestors

♦ country, fatherland, home, homeland, sod

moth•er–of–pearl \ˌmə-t͟hər-əv-ˈpərl\ *n* **:** the hard pearly matter forming the inner layer of a mollusk shell
mother ship *n* **:** a ship serving smaller craft
mo•tif \mō-ˈtēf\ *n* **1** ♦ **:** a dominant idea or central theme (as in a work of art) **2** ♦ **:** a single or repeated design or color

♦ [1] content, matter, question, subject, theme, topic ♦ [2] design, figure, motive, pattern

mo•tile \ˈmōt-ᵊl, ˈmō-ˌtīl\ *adj* **:** capable of spontaneous movement — **mo•til•i•ty** \mō-ˈti-lə-tē\ *n*
[1]**mo•tion** \ˈmō-shən\ *n* **1** ♦ **:** an act, process, or instance of moving **2 :** a proposal for action (as by a deliberative body) **3** *pl* **:** ACTIVITIES, MOVEMENTS — **mo•tion•less** *adj* — **mo•tion•less•ly** *adv* — **mo•tion•less•ness** *n*

♦ move, movement, moving, shift, stir, stirring

[2]**motion** *vb* ♦ **:** to direct or signal by a movement

♦ flag, gesture, signal, wave

motion picture *n* **1 :** a series of pictures projected on a screen so rapidly that they produce a continuous picture in which persons and objects seem to move **2** ♦ **:** a representation (as of a story) by means of motion pictures

♦ film, movie, picture

motion sickness *n* **:** sickness induced by motion and characterized by nausea
mo•ti•vate \ˈmō-tə-ˌvāt\ *vb* **-vat•ed; -vat•ing :** to provide with a motive **:** IMPEL — **mo•ti•va•tor** \ˈmō-tə-ˌvā-tər\ *n*
mo•ti•va•tion \ˌmō-tə-ˈvā-shən\ *n* **1 a :** the act or process of motivating **b :** the condition of being motivated **2** ♦ **:** a motivating force, stimulus, or influence — **mo•ti•va•tion•al** \-shə-nəl\ *adj*

♦ boost, encouragement, goad, impetus, impulse, incentive, incitement, instigation, momentum, provocation, spur, stimulus, yeast

[1]**mo•tive** \ˈmō-tiv, *2 also* mō-ˈtēv\ *n* **1** ♦ **:** something (as a need or desire) that causes a person to act **2 :** a recurrent theme in a musical composition **3 :** a dominant idea or central theme (as in a work of art) **:** MOTIF **4 :** a single or repeated design or color **:** MOTIF — **mo•tive•less** *adj*

♦ grounds, reason, wherefore, why

[2]**mo•tive** \ˈmō-tiv\ *adj* **1 :** moving to action **2 :** of or relating to motion
[1]**mot•ley** \ˈmät-lē\ *adj* **1** ♦ **:** variegated in color **2** ♦ **:** made up of diverse often incongruous elements

♦ [1] multicolored, variegated ♦ [2] assorted, heterogeneous, miscellaneous, mixed, varied

[2]**motley** *n* **:** a mixture of incongruous elements
[1]**mo•tor** \ˈmō-tər\ *n* **1 :** one that imparts motion **2 :** a machine that produces motion or power for doing work **3 :** a usually 4-wheeled automotive vehicle designed for passenger transportation **:** AUTOMOBILE
[2]**motor** *vb* **:** to travel or transport by automobile **:** DRIVE — **mo•tor•ist** *n*
mo•tor•bike \ˈmō-tər-ˌbīk\ *n* **:** a small lightweight motorcycle
mo•tor•boat \-ˌbōt\ *n* **:** a boat propelled by a motor
mo•tor•cade \-ˌkād\ *n* ♦ **:** a procession of motor vehicles

♦ armada, caravan, cavalcade, fleet, train

mo•tor•car \-ˌkär\ *n* **:** a usually 4-wheeled automotive vehicle designed for passenger transportation **:** AUTOMOBILE
mo•tor•cy•cle \ˈmō-tər-ˌsī-kəl\ *n* **:** a 2-wheeled automotive vehicle — **mo•tor•cy•clist** \-k(ə-)list\ *n*
motor home *n* ♦ **:** a large motor vehicle equipped as living quarters

♦ camper, caravan, trailer

motor inn *n* **:** MOTEL
mo•tor•ise *chiefly Brit var of* MOTORIZE
mo•tor•ize \ˈmō-tə-ˌrīz\ *vb* **-ized; -iz•ing 1 :** to equip with a motor **2 :** to equip with automobiles
mo•tor•man \ˈmō-tər-mən\ *n* **:** an operator of a motor-driven vehicle (as a streetcar or subway train)
motor scooter *n* **:** a low 2- or 3-wheeled automotive vehicle resembling a child's scooter but having a seat
mo•tor•truck \ˈmō-tər-ˌtrək\ *n* **:** an automotive truck
motor vehicle *n* ♦ **:** an automotive vehicle (as an automobile) not operated on rails

♦ automobile, car, machine

mot•tle \ˈmät-ᵊl\ *vb* **mot•tled; mot•tling** ♦ **:** to mark with spots of different color **:** BLOTCH

♦ blotch, dapple, dot, fleck, freckle, pepper, speck, spot, sprinkle, stipple

mot•tled \ˈmä-tᵊld\ *adj* ♦ **:** marked with spots of different colors

♦ dappled, piebald, pied, spotted ♦ dappled, spotted, spotty, variegated

mot•to \ˈmä-tō\ *n, pl* **mottoes** *also* **mottos 1 :** a sentence, phrase, or word inscribed on something to indicate its character or use **2 :** a short expression of a guiding rule of conduct
moue \ˈmü\ *n* **:** a little grimace
mould *chiefly Can and Brit var of* MOLD
moult *chiefly Can and Brit var of* MOLT
[1]**mound** \ˈmau̇nd\ *vb* ♦ **:** to form into a mound

♦ heap, hill, pile, stack

[2]**mound** *n* **1** ♦ **:** an artificial bank or hill of earth or stones **2** ♦ **:** a rounded hill or natural formation **3** ♦ **:** a collection of things thrown one on another **:** HEAP, PILE; *also* **:** a great number or large quantity ⟨~*s* of work⟩ **4 :** a small rounded mass

♦ [1] bank, bar, drift ♦ [2] elevation, eminence, height, highland, hill, prominence, rise ♦ [3] cock, heap, hill, mountain, pile, rick, stack

[1]**mount** \ˈmau̇nt\ *n* ♦ **:** a high hill

♦ mountain, peak

[2]**mount** *vb* **1 a** ♦ **:** to increase in amount or extent **b** ♦ **:** to move upward **:** RISE, ASCEND **2 :** to get up on something; *esp* **:** to seat oneself on (as a horse) for riding **3 :** to put in position ⟨~ artillery⟩ **4 :** to set on something that elevates **5 :** to attach to a support **6** ♦ **:** to prepare especially for examination or display — **mount•able** *adj* — **mount•er** *n*

♦ [1a] accumulate, appreciate, balloon, build, burgeon, enlarge, escalate, expand, increase, multiply, mushroom, proliferate, rise, snowball, swell, wax ♦ [1b] arise, ascend, climb, lift, rise, soar, up ♦ [6] carry, give, offer, present, stage

[3]**mount** *n* **1** ♦ **:** an arrangement of structural parts that gives form or support **:** SUPPORT **2 :** a means of conveyance; *esp* **:** SADDLE HORSE

♦ brace, bulwark, buttress, shore, stay, support, underpinning

moun•tain \ˈmau̇nt-ᵊn\ *n* **1** ♦ **:** a landmass higher than a hill **2 a** ♦ **:** a great mass **b** ♦ **:** a vast number or quantity — **moun•tainy** \-ᵊn-ē\ *adj*

♦ [1] mount, peak ♦ [2a] cock, heap, hill, mound, pile, rick, stack ♦ [2b] abundance, deal, gobs, heap, loads, lot, pile, plenty, quantity, scads

mountain ash *n* **:** any of various trees related to the roses that have pinnate leaves and red or orange-red fruits
mountain bike *n* **:** a bicycle with wide knobby tires, straight handlebars, and 18 or 21 gears that is designed to operate especially over unpaved terrain
moun•tain•eer \ˌmau̇nt-ᵊn-ˈir\ *n* **1 :** a native or inhabitant of a mountainous region **2 :** one who climbs mountains for sport
mountain goat *n* **:** a ruminant mammal of mountainous northwestern No. America that resembles a goat

mountain laurel *n* : a No. American evergreen shrub or small tree of the heath family with glossy leaves and clusters of rose-colored or white flowers

mountain lion *n* ♦ : a large powerful tawny brown wild American cat : COUGAR

♦ cougar, panther

moun•tain•ous \ˈmau̇n-tə-nəs, ˈmau̇nt-nəs\ *adj* **1** : containing many mountains **2** : resembling a mountain : HUGE

moun•tain•side \ˈmau̇nt-ᵊn-ˌsīd\ *n* : the side of a mountain

moun•tain•top \-ˌtäp\ *n* : the summit of a mountain

moun•te•bank \ˈmau̇n-ti-ˌbaŋk\ *n* ♦ : a boastful unscrupulous pretender : QUACK, CHARLATAN

♦ charlatan, fake, fraud, hoaxer, humbug, phony, pretender, quack

Mount•ie \ˈmau̇n-tē\ *n* : a member of the Royal Canadian Mounted Police

mount•ing \ˈmau̇n-tiŋ\ *n* : something that serves as a frame or support

mourn \ˈmōrn\ *vb* ♦ : to feel or express grief or sorrow — **mourn•er** *n*

♦ agonize, bleed, feel, grieve, hurt, sorrow, suffer ♦ *usu* **mourn for** bemoan, bewail, deplore, grieve, lament, wail

mourn•ful \-fəl\ *adj* ♦ : expressing, feeling, or causing sorrow — **mourn•ful•ness** *n*

♦ dolorous, funeral, lugubrious, plaintive, regretful, rueful, sorrowful, weeping, woeful ♦ blue, depressed, despondent, disconsolate, down, downcast, forlorn, gloomy, glum, low, melancholy, miserable, sad, sorrowful, sorry, unhappy

mourn•ful•ly \-fə-lē\ *adv* : in a mournful manner

mourn•ing \ˈmōr-niŋ\ *n* **1** : an outward sign (as black clothes) of grief for a person's death **2** : a period of time during which signs of grief are shown

mouse \ˈmau̇s\ *n, pl* **mice** \ˈmīs\ **1** : any of numerous small rodents with pointed snout, long body, and slender tail **2** : a small manual device that controls cursor movement on a computer display

mouse pad *n* : a thin flat pad on which a computer mouse is used

mous•er \ˈmau̇-sər\ *n* : a cat proficient at catching mice

mouse•trap \ˈmau̇s-ˌtrap\ *n* **1** : a trap for catching mice **2** : a stratagem that lures one to defeat or destruction — **mousetrap** *vb*

mousse \ˈmüs\ *n* **1** : a molded chilled dessert made with sweetened and flavored whipped cream or egg whites and gelatin **2** : a foamy preparation used in styling hair — **mousse** *vb*

moustache *chiefly Can and Brit var of* MUSTACHE

mousy *or* **mous•ey** \ˈmau̇-sē, -zē\ *adj* **mous•i•er; -est** **1** : QUIET, STEALTHY **2** ♦ : lacking in boldness or determination : TIMID **3** : grayish brown — **mous•i•ness** \ˈmau̇-sē-nəs, -zē-\ *n*

♦ fainthearted, fearful, scary, shy, skittish, timid

[1]**mouth** \ˈmau̇th\ *n, pl* **mouths** \ˈmau̇t͟hz, ˈmau̇ths\ **1** : the opening through which an animal takes in food; *also* : the cavity that encloses the tongue, lips, and teeth in the typical vertebrate **2** : something resembling a mouth (as in affording entrance) **3** : a facial expression usually of disgust, disapproval, or pain : GRIMACE — **mouthed** \ˈmau̇t͟hd, ˈmau̇tht\ *adj*

[2]**mouth** \ˈmau̇t͟h\ *vb* **1** : SPEAK; *also* : DECLAIM **2** : to repeat without comprehension or sincerity **3** : to form soundlessly with the lips **4** ♦ : to utter indistinctly **5** ♦ : to talk pompously — often used with *off*

♦ [4] mumble, murmur, mutter ♦ *usu* **mouth off** [5] declaim, discourse, harangue, orate

mouth•ful \ˈmau̇th-fəl\ **1** : as much as a mouth will hold **2** ♦ : the quantity usually taken into the mouth at one time

♦ bite, morsel, nibble, taste, tidbit

mouth harp *n* : HARMONICA

mouth•part \ˈmau̇th-ˌpärt\ *n* : a structure or appendage near the mouth (as of an insect) especially when adapted for eating

mouth•piece \-ˌpēs\ *n* **1** : a part (as of a musical instrument) that goes in the mouth or to which the mouth is applied **2** ♦ : one that expresses or interprets another's views : SPOKESMAN

♦ speaker, spokesman, spokesperson, spokeswoman

mouth-to-mouth *adj* : of, relating to, or being a method of artificial respiration in which air from a rescuer's mouth is forced into a victim's lungs

mouth•wash \-ˌwȯsh, -ˌwäsh\ *n* : a usually antiseptic liquid preparation for cleaning the mouth and teeth

mou•ton \ˈmü-ˌtän\ *n* : processed sheepskin that has been sheared or dyed to resemble beaver or seal

[1]**move** \ˈmüv\ *vb* **moved; mov•ing** **1** ♦ : to change or cause to change position or posture **2** ♦ : to go or cause to go from one point to another; *also* : DEPART **3** ♦ : to take or cause to take action **4** : to show marked activity **5** ♦ : to stir the emotions **6** : to make a formal request, application, or appeal **7** : to change one's residence **8** : EVACUATE 2 **9** ♦ : to cause to operate or function — **mov•able** *or* **move•able** \ˈmü-və-bəl\ *adj*

♦ [1] budge, dislocate, displace, disturb, remove, shift, transfer ♦ [2] clear out, depart, exit, get off, go, pull, quit, sally, shove, take off ♦ [3] affect, impact, impress, influence, strike, sway, tell, touch ♦ [3] argue, convince, get, induce, persuade, prevail, satisfy, talk, win ♦ [5] arouse, encourage, excite, fire, incite, instigate, pique, provoke, stimulate, stir ♦ [9] activate, actuate, crank, drive, propel, run, set off, spark, start, touch off, trigger, turn on

[2]**move** *n* **1** : an act of moving **2** ♦ : a calculated step taken to gain an objective **3** : a change of location **4** : an agile action especially in sports

♦ expedient, measure, shift, step

move•ment \ˈmüv-mənt\ *n* **1** ♦ : the act or process of moving : MOVE **2** ♦ : a series of organized activities working toward an objective **3** : the moving parts of a mechanism (as of a watch) **4** : RHYTHM **5** : a section of an extended musical composition **6** : an act of voiding the bowels; *also* : STOOL 4

♦ [1] motion, move, moving, shift, stir, stirring *Ant* motionlessness ♦ [2] bandwagon, campaign, cause, crusade, drive

mov•er \ˈmü-vər\ *n* : one that moves; *esp* : one that moves the belongings of others from one location to another

mov•ie \ˈmü-vē\ *n* **1** ♦ : a representation (as of a story) by means of motion pictures **2** *pl* : a showing of a motion picture **3** *pl* ♦ : the motion-picture industry

♦ [1] film, motion picture, picture ♦ **movies** *pl* [3] film, screen

moving *adj* ♦ : stirring deeply in a way that evokes a strong emotional response

♦ affecting, emotional, impressive, poignant, stirring, touching *Ant* unemotional, unimpressive

[1]**mow** \ˈmau̇\ *n* : the part of a barn where hay or straw is stored

[2]**mow** \ˈmō\ *vb* **mowed; mowed** *or* **mown** \ˈmōn\; **mow•ing** **1** : to cut (as grass) with a scythe or machine **2** : to cut the standing herbage of ⟨~ the lawn⟩ — **mow•er** *n*

mox•ie \ˈmäk-sē\ *n* **1** : ENERGY, PEP **2** : COURAGE, DETERMINATION

Mo•zam•bi•can \ˌmō-zəm-ˈbē-kən\ *n* : a native or inhabitant of Mozambique

moz•za•rel•la \ˌmät-sə-ˈre-lə\ *n* : a moist white unsalted unripened mild cheese of a smooth rubbery texture

[1]**MP** \ˈem-pē\ *n* **1** : a member of the military police **2** : an elected member of a parliament

[2]**MP** *abbr* **1** melting point **2** metropolitan police

mpg *abbr* miles per gallon

mph *abbr* miles per hour

Mr. \ˈmis-tər\ *n, pl* **Messrs.** \ˈme-sərz\ — used as a conventional title of courtesy before a man's surname or his title of office

MRI \ˌem-ˌär-ˈī\ *n* : MAGNETIC RESONANCE IMAGING

Mr. Right *n* : a man who would make the perfect husband

Mrs. \ˈmi-səz, -səs, *esp Southern* ˈmi-zəz, -zəs\ *n, pl* **Mes•dames** \mā-ˈdäm, -ˈdam\ — used as a conventional title of courtesy before a married woman's surname

Ms. \ˈmiz\ *n, pl* **Mss.** *or* **Mses.** \ˈmi-zez\ — used instead of *Miss* or *Mrs.*

MS *abbr* **1** manuscript **2** master of science **3** military science **4** Mississippi **5** motor ship **6** multiple sclerosis

msec *abbr* millisecond

msg *abbr* message

MSG *abbr* **1** master sergeant **2** monosodium glutamate

msgr *abbr* **1** monseigneur **2** monsignor

MSgt *abbr* master sergeant

MSS *abbr* manuscripts

MST *abbr* mountain standard time

mt *abbr* mount; mountain

Mt *abbr* Matthew

MT *abbr* **1** metric ton **2** Montana **3** mountain time

mtg *abbr* **1** meeting **2** mortgage

mtge *abbr* mortgage

mu \ˈmyü, ˈmü\ *n* : the 12th letter of the Greek alphabet — M or μ

[1]**much** \ˈməch\ *adj* **more** \ˈmōr\; **most** \ˈmōst\ **:** great in quantity, amount, extent, or degree ⟨∼ money⟩
[2]**much** *adv* **more; most 1** ♦ **:** to a great degree or extent ⟨∼ happier⟩ **2** ♦ **:** almost but not quite **:** NEARLY ⟨looks ∼ as he did before⟩

♦ [1] broadly, considerably, greatly, hugely, largely, massively, monstrously, sizably, stupendously, tremendously, utterly, vastly ♦ [2] about, almost, most, near, nearly, next to, nigh, practically, some, virtually, well-nigh

[3]**much** *n* **1** ♦ **:** a great quantity, amount, extent, or degree **2 :** something considerable or impressive

♦ abundance, deal, gobs, heap, loads, lot, pile, plenty, quantity, scads

mu•ci•lage \ˈmyü-sə-lij\ *n* **:** a watery sticky solution (as of a gum) used especially as an adhesive — **mu•ci•lag•i•nous** \ˌmyü-sə-ˈla-jə-nəs\ *adj*
muck \ˈmək\ *n* **1 :** soft moist barnyard manure **2** ♦ **:** slimy dirt or filth **3 a :** a dark richly organic soil **b :** heavy often deep mud or slush **:** MUD, MIRE

♦ dirt, filth, grime, smut, soil

muck•rake \-ˌrāk\ *vb* **:** to expose publicly real or apparent misconduct of a prominent individual or business — **muck•rak•er** *n*
mucky \ˈmə-kē\ *adj* **1** ♦ **:** not clean **2** ♦ **:** consisting of, marked by, or full of muck

♦ [1] dirty, filthy, grubby, grungy, muddy, unclean ♦ [2] miry, muddy, oozy, slimy, slushy

mu•cus \ˈmyü-kəs\ *n* **:** a slimy slippery protective secretion of membranes (**mucous membranes**) lining some body cavities — **mu•cous** \-kəs\ *adj*
mud \ˈməd\ *n* ♦ **:** soft wet earth **:** MIRE

♦ mire, muck, ooze, slime, slop, sludge, slush

[1]**mud•dle** \ˈməd-ᵊl\ *vb* **mud•dled; mud•dling 1 :** to make muddy **2** ♦ **:** to confuse especially with liquor **3** ♦ **:** to mix up or make a mess of **4 :** to think or act in a confused way

♦ [2] addle, baffle, befog, befuddle, bemuse, bewilder, confound, confuse, disorient, muddy, mystify, perplex, puzzle ♦ [3] disarray, dishevel, dislocate, disorder, disrupt, disturb, mess, mix

[2]**muddle** *n* **1** ♦ **:** a state of especially mental confusion **2** ♦ **:** a confused mess

♦ [1] daze, fog, haze, spin ♦ [1] bafflement, bewilderment, confusion, distraction, mystification, perplexity, puzzlement, whirl ♦ [2] chaos, confusion, disarray, disorder, jumble, mess, shambles ♦ [2] assortment, clutter, jumble, medley, mélange, miscellany, motley, variety, welter

muddled *adj* ♦ **:** characterized by a confused state

♦ chaotic, confused, disordered, messy

mud•dle•head•ed \ˌməd-ᵊl-ˈhe-dəd\ *adj* **1 :** mentally confused **2 :** INEPT
[1]**mud•dy** \ˈmə-dē\ *adj* **mud•di•er; -est 1** ♦ **:** full of or covered with mud **2** ♦ **:** turbid with sediment — **mud•di•ness** \-dē-nəs\ *n*

♦ [1] miry, mucky, oozy, slimy, slushy ♦ [2] cloudy, turbid

[2]**muddy** *vb* **1** ♦ **:** to soil or stain with or as if with mud **2 a** ♦ **:** to make indistinct ⟨don't ∼ the issue⟩ **b :** to disturb in mind or purpose **:** CONFUSE — **mud•di•ly** \ˈmə-də-lē\ *adv*

♦ [1] befoul, begrime, besmirch, blacken, dirty, foul, grime, mire, smirch, soil, stain ♦ [2a] becloud, befog, blur, cloud, confuse, fog

mud•flat \ˈməd-ˌflat\ *n* **:** a level tract alternately covered and left bare by the tide
mud•guard \ˈməd-ˌgärd\ *n* **:** a guard over or a flap behind a wheel of a vehicle to catch or deflect mud
mud•room \-ˌrüm, -ˌrům\ *n* **:** a room in a house for removing dirty or wet footwear and clothing
mud•sling•er \-ˌsliŋ-ər\ *n* **:** one who uses invective especially against a political opponent — **mud•sling•ing** \-ˌsliŋ-iŋ\ *n*
Muen•ster \ˈmən-stər, ˈmün-, ˈmůn-\ *n* **:** a semisoft bland cheese
mu•ez•zin \mü-ˈez-ᵊn, myü-\ *n* **:** a Muslim crier who calls the hour of daily prayer
[1]**muff** \ˈməf\ *n* **:** a warm tubular covering for the hands
[2]**muff** *vb* ♦ **:** to act or do (something) stupidly or clumsily

♦ bobble, botch, bungle, butcher, flub, foul up, fumble, mangle, mess up, screw up

[3]**muff** *n* **:** a bungling performance; *esp* **:** a failure to hold a ball in attempting a catch — **muff** *vb*
muf•fin \ˈmə-fən\ *n* **:** a small soft cake baked in a cup-shaped container
muf•fle \ˈmə-fəl\ *vb* **muf•fled; muf•fling 1 :** to wrap up so as to conceal or protect **2 :** to wrap or pad with something to dull the sound of **3 :** to keep down **:** SUPPRESS
muf•fler \ˈmə-flər\ *n* **1 :** a scarf worn around the neck **2 :** a device (as on a car's exhaust) to deaden noise
muf•ti \ˈməf-tē\ *n* **:** civilian clothes
[1]**mug** \ˈməg\ *n* **1 :** a usually metal or earthenware cylindrical drinking cup **2** ♦ **:** the face or mouth of a person **3** ♦ **:** a usually petty gangster, hoodlum, or ruffian

♦ [2] countenance, face, visage ♦ [3] bully, gangster, goon, hood, hoodlum, mobster, punk, rowdy, ruffian, thug, tough

[2]**mug** *vb* **mugged; mug•ging 1 :** to pose or make faces especially to attract attention or for a camera **2 :** to take a photograph of **:** PHOTOGRAPH
[3]**mug** *vb* **mugged; mug•ging :** to assault usually with intent to rob — **mug•ger** *n*
mug•gy \ˈmə-gē\ *adj* **mug•gi•er; -est** ♦ **:** being warm and humid — **mug•gi•ness** \-gē-nəs\ *n*

♦ humid, sticky, sultry

mug•wump \ˈməg-ˌwəmp\ *n* **:** an independent in politics
Mu•ham•mad•an \mō-ˈha-mə-dən, -ˈhä-; mü-\ *n* **:** MUSLIM — **Mu•ham•mad•an•ism** \-də-ˌni-zəm\ *n*
mu•ja•hid•een *or* **mu•ja•hed•in** \mü-ˌja-hi-ˈdēn, -ˌjä-\ *n pl* **:** Islamic guerrilla fighters especially in the Middle East
muk•luk \ˈmək-ˌlək\ *n* **1 :** an Eskimo boot of sealskin or reindeer skin **2 :** a boot with a soft leather sole worn over several pairs of socks
mu•lat•to \mů-ˈla-tō, myů-, -ˈlä-\ *n, pl* **-toes** *or* **-tos :** a first-generation offspring of a black person and a white person; *also* **:** a person of mixed white and black ancestry
mul•ber•ry \ˈməl-ˌber-ē\ *n* **:** any of a genus of trees with edible berrylike fruit and leaves used as food for silkworms; *also* **:** the fruit
mulch \ˈməlch\ *n* **:** a protective covering (as of straw or leaves) spread on the ground especially to reduce evaporation or control weeds — **mulch** *vb*
[1]**mulct** \ˈməlkt\ *n* **:** a sum imposed as punishment for an offense **:** FINE, PENALTY
[2]**mulct** *vb* **1 :** FINE **2** ♦ **:** to defraud especially of money **:** CHEAT

♦ bleed, cheat, chisel, cozen, defraud, fleece, gyp, hustle, rook, shortchange, skin, squeeze, stick, sting, swindle, victimize

[1]**mule** \ˈmyül\ *n* **1 :** a hybrid offspring of a male donkey and a female horse **2 :** a very stubborn person
[2]**mule** *n* **:** a slipper whose upper does not extend around the heel of the foot
mule deer *n* **:** a long-eared deer of western No. America
mu•le•teer \ˌmyü-lə-ˈtir\ *n* **:** one who drives mules
mul•ish \ˈmyü-lish\ *adj* ♦ **:** unreasonably and inflexibly obstinate — **mul•ish•ly** *adv*

♦ dogged, hardheaded, headstrong, obdurate, obstinate, opinionated, peevish, pertinacious, perverse, pigheaded, stubborn, unyielding, willful

mu•lish•ness \-nəs\ *n* ♦ **:** the quality or state of being mulish

♦ hardheadedness, obduracy, obstinacy, peevishness, pertinacity, self-will, stubbornness, tenacity

[1]**mull** \ˈməl\ *vb* ♦ **:** to consider at length **:** PONDER, MEDITATE — often used with *over*

♦ *usu* **mull over** chew over, cogitate, consider, contemplate, debate, deliberate, entertain, meditate, ponder, question, ruminate, study, think, weigh

[2]**mull** *vb* **:** to heat, sweeten, and flavor (as wine) with spices
mul•lein \ˈmə-lən\ *n* **:** a tall herb related to the snapdragons that has coarse woolly leaves and flowers in spikes
mul•let \ˈmə-lət\ *n, pl* **mullet** *or* **mullets :** any of a family of largely gray chiefly marine bony fishes including valuable food fishes
mul•li•gan stew \ˈmə-li-gən-\ *n* **:** a stew made from whatever ingredients are available
mul•li•ga•taw•ny \ˌmə-li-gə-ˈtó-nē\ *n* **:** a soup usually of chicken stock seasoned with curry
mul•lion \ˈməl-yən\ *n* **:** a vertical strip separating windowpanes
multi- *comb form* **1 :** many **:** multiple ⟨*multi*unit⟩ **2 :** many times over ⟨*multi*millionaire⟩

mul·ti·col·ored \ˌməl-ti-ˈkə-lərd\ *adj* ♦ **:** having many colors

♦ colorful (*or* colourful), variegated

mul·ti·cul·tur·al \ˌməl-tē-ˈkəl-chə-rəl, -ˌtī-\ *adj* **:** of, relating to, reflecting, or adapted to diverse cultures ‹a ~ society›
mul·ti·di·men·sion·al \-ti-də-ˈmen-chə-nəl, -ˌtī-, -dī-\ *adj* **:** of, relating to, or having many facets or dimensions ‹a ~ problem› ‹~ space›
mul·ti·eth·nic \-ˈeth-nik\ *adj* **:** including, involving, or made up of people of various ethnic groups
mul·ti·fac·et·ed \-ˈfa-sə-təd\ *adj* **:** having several distinct facets or aspects
mul·ti·fam·i·ly \-ˈfam-lē, -ˈfa-mə-\ *adj* **:** designed for use by several families
mul·ti·far·i·ous \ˌməl-tə-ˈfar-ē-əs\ *adj* ♦ **:** having great variety — **mul·ti·far·i·ous·ness** *n*

♦ manifold, myriad

mul·ti·form \ˈməl-ti-ˌfȯrm\ *adj* **:** having many forms or appearances — **mul·ti·for·mi·ty** \ˌməl-ti-ˈfȯr-mə-tē\ *n*
mul·ti·lat·er·al \ˌməl-ti-ˈla-tə-rəl, -ˌtī-, -ˈla-trəl\ *adj* **:** having many sides or participants ‹~ treaty› — **mul·ti·lat·er·al·ism** \-ˈla-tə-rə-ˌli-zəm\ *n*
multilayered \-ˈlā-ərd, -ˈlerd\ *or* **multilayer** \-ˈlā-ər, ˈler\ *adj* **:** having or involving several distinct layers or levels
mul·ti·lev·el \-ˈle-vəl\ *adj* **:** having several levels
mul·ti·lin·gual \-ˈliŋ-gwəl\ *adj* **:** knowing or using several languages — **mul·ti·lin·gual·ism** \-gwə-ˌli-zəm\ *n*
1**mul·ti·me·dia** \-ˈmē-dē-ə\ *adj* **:** using, involving, or encompassing several media ‹a ~ advertising campaign›
2**multimedia** *n sing or pl* **:** the technique of using several media (as in art); *also* **:** something (as software) that uses or facilitates it
mul·ti·mil·lion·aire \ˌməl-ti-ˌmil-yə-ˈnar, -ˌtī-, -ˈmil-yə-ˌnar\ *n* **:** a person worth several million dollars
mul·ti·na·tion·al \-ˈna-shə-nəl\ *adj* **1 :** of or relating to several nationalities **2 :** relating to or involving several nations **3 :** having divisions in several countries ‹a ~ corporation› — **multinational** *n*
mul·ti·pack \ˈməl-tē-ˌpak\ *n* **:** a package of several individually packed items sold as a unit
1**mul·ti·ple** \ˈməl-tə-pəl\ *adj* **1 a :** more than one **b** ♦ **:** consisting of or amounting to a large but indefinite number **:** MANY **2 :** VARIOUS

♦ many, multitudinous, numerous

2**multiple** *n* **:** the product of a quantity by an integer ‹35 is a ~ of 7›
multiple–choice *adj* **:** having several answers given from which the correct one is to be chosen ‹a ~ question›
multiple personality disorder *n* **:** a neurosis in which the personality becomes separated into two or more parts each of which controls behavior part of the time
multiple sclerosis *n* **:** a disease marked by patches of hardened tissue in the brain or spinal cord and associated especially with partial or complete paralysis and muscular tremor
mul·ti·plex \ˈməl-tə-ˌpleks\ *n* **:** CINEPLEX
mul·ti·pli·cand \ˌməl-tə-pli-ˈkand\ *n* **:** the number that is to be multiplied by another
mul·ti·pli·ca·tion \ˌməl-tə-plə-ˈkā-shən\ *n* **1** ♦ **:** the act or process of multiplying **:** the state of being multiplied **2 :** a short method of finding the result of adding a figure the number of times indicated by another figure

♦ accumulation, addition, increase, proliferation ***Ant*** decrease

multiplication sign *n* **1 :** TIMES SIGN **2 :** a centered dot indicating multiplication
mul·ti·plic·i·ty \ˌməl-tə-ˈpli-sə-tē\ *n, pl* **-ties :** a great number or variety
mul·ti·pli·er \ˈməl-tə-ˌplī-ər\ *n* **:** one that multiplies; *esp* **:** a number by which another number is multiplied
mul·ti·ply \ˈməl-tə-ˌplī\ *vb* **-plied; -ply·ing 1** ♦ **:** to increase in number (as by breeding) **2 :** to find the product of by multiplication; *also* **:** to perform multiplication

♦ accumulate, appreciate, balloon, build, burgeon, enlarge, escalate, expand, increase, mount, mushroom, proliferate, rise, snowball, swell, wax ♦ add, aggrandize, amplify, augment, boost, compound, enlarge, escalate, expand, extend, increase, raise, swell, up ♦ breed, procreate, propagate, reproduce

mul·ti·pur·pose \ˌməl-ti-ˈpər-pəs, -ˌtī-\ *adj* **:** having or serving several purposes
mul·ti·ra·cial \-ˈrā-shəl\ *adj* **:** composed of, involving, or representing various races
mul·ti·sense \-ˌsens\ *adj* **:** having several meanings ‹~ words›
mul·ti·sto·ry \-ˌstōr-ē\ *adj* **:** having several stories ‹~ buildings›
mul·ti·task·ing \ˈməl-tē-ˌtas-kiŋ, -ˌtī-\ *n* **1 :** the concurrent performance of several jobs by a computer **2 :** the performance of multiple tasks at one time — **mul·ti·task** \-ˌtask\ *vb* — **mul·ti·task·er** \-ˌtaskər\ *n*
mul·ti·tude \ˈməl-tə-ˌtüd, -ˌtyüd\ *n* ♦ **:** a great number

♦ army, crowd, crush, drove, flock, horde, host, legion, mob, press, swarm, throng

mul·ti·tu·di·nous \ˌməl-tə-ˈtüd-ᵊn-əs, -ˈtyüd-\ *adj* ♦ **:** existing in a great multitude

♦ many, multiple, numerous

mul·ti·unit \ˌməl-ti-ˈyü-nət, -ˌtī-\ *adj* **:** having several units
mul·ti·vi·ta·min \-ˈvī-tə-mən\ *adj* **:** containing several vitamins and especially all known to be essential to health — **multivitamin** *n*
1**mum** \ˈməm\ *adj* ♦ **:** making no utterance **:** SILENT

♦ dumb, mute, silent, speechless, uncommunicative

2**mum** *n* **:** CHRYSANTHEMUM
3**mum** *chiefly Can and Brit var of* MOM
1**mum·ble** \ˈməm-bəl\ *vb* **mum·bled; mum·bling** ♦ **:** to speak in a low indistinct manner — **mum·bler** *n* — **mum·bly** *adj*

♦ mouth, murmur, mutter ***Ant*** speak out, speak up

2**mumble** *n* ♦ **:** a low confused indistinct utterance

♦ murmur, mutter

mum·ble·ty–peg \ˈməm-bəl-tē-ˌpeg\ *also* **mum·ble–the–peg** \ˈməm-bəl-t͟hə-\ *n* **:** a game in which the players try to flip a knife from various positions so that the blade will stick into the ground
mum·bo jum·bo \ˌməm-bō-ˈjəm-bō\ *n* **1 :** a complicated ritual with elaborate trappings **2 :** unnecessarily involved and incomprehensible language **:** GIBBERISH, NONSENSE
mum·mer \ˈmə-mər\ *n* **1 a** ♦ **:** a performer in a pantomime **b :** ACTOR **2 :** a person who goes merrymaking in disguise during festivals — **mum·mery** *n*

♦ mime, mimic, pantomime

1**mum·my** \ˈmə-mē\ *n, pl* **mummies :** a body embalmed for burial in the manner of the ancient Egyptians — **mum·mi·fi·ca·tion** \ˌmə-mi-fə-ˈkā-shən\ *n* — **mum·mi·fy** \ˈmə-mi-ˌfī\ *vb*
2**mummy** *chiefly Can and Brit var of* MOMMY
mumps \ˈməmps\ *n sing or pl* **:** a virus disease marked by fever and swelling especially of the salivary glands
mun *or* **munic** *abbr* municipal
munch \ˈmənch\ *vb* **:** to eat with a chewing action; *also* **:** to snack on
munch·ies \ˈmən-chēz\ *n pl* **1 :** hunger pangs **2 :** light snack foods
mun·dane \ˌmən-ˈdān, ˈmən-ˌdān\ *adj* **1** ♦ **:** of or relating to the world **2** ♦ **:** concerned with the practical details of everyday life — **mun·dane·ly** *adv*

♦ [1] earthly, temporal, terrestrial, worldly ♦ [2] everyday, prosaic, workaday

mung bean \ˈməŋ-\ *n* **:** an erect bushy bean widely grown in warm regions for its edible seeds and as the chief source of bean sprouts; *also* **:** its seed
mu·nic·i·pal \myu̇-ˈni-sə-pəl\ *adj* **1 :** of, relating to, or characteristic of a municipality **2 :** restricted to one locality — **mu·nic·i·pal·ly** *adv*
mu·nic·i·pal·i·ty \myu̇-ˌni-sə-ˈpa-lə-tē\ *n, pl* **-ties** ♦ **:** an urban political unit with corporate status and usually powers of self-government

♦ city, metropolis

mu·nif·i·cent \myu̇-ˈni-fə-sənt\ *adj* ♦ **:** liberal in giving **:** GENEROUS — **mu·nif·i·cence** \-səns\ *n*

♦ bountiful, charitable, free, generous, liberal, openhanded, unselfish, unsparing

mu·ni·tion \myu̇-ˈni-shən\ *n* **:** ARMAMENT, AMMUNITION
1**mu·ral** \ˈmyu̇r-əl\ *adj* **1 :** of or relating to a wall **2 :** applied to and made part of a wall or ceiling surface
2**mural** *n* **:** a mural painting — **mu·ral·ist** *n*
1**mur·der** \ˈmər-dər\ *n* **1** ♦ **:** the crime of unlawfully killing a person especially with premeditated malice **2** ♦ **:** something unusually difficult or dangerous

♦ [1] homicide ♦ [2] agony, hell, horror, misery, nightmare, torment, torture

²murder *vb* **1 a :** to commit a murder **b ♦ :** to kill (a human being) unlawfully and with premeditated malice; *also* : to kill brutally **2 :** to put an end to **3 ♦ :** to spoil by performing poorly ⟨~ a song⟩ — **mur•der•er** *n*

♦ [1b] dispatch, do in, execute, liquidate, slay ♦ [3] bobble, botch, bungle, butcher, flub, foul up, fumble, mangle, mess up, screw up

mur•der•ess \ˈmər-də-rəs\ *n* : a woman who murders
mur•der•ous \ˈmər-də-rəs\ *adj* **1 ♦ :** having or appearing to have the purpose of murder **2 ♦ :** marked by or causing murder or bloodshed ⟨~ gunfire⟩ **3 ♦ :** having the ability or power to overwhelm ⟨~ heat⟩ **4 ♦ :** characterized by extreme difficulty ⟨the exam was ~⟩ — **mur•der•ous•ly** *adv*

♦ [1] bloodthirsty, bloody, homicidal, sanguinary, sanguine ♦ [2] baleful, deadly, deathly, fatal, fell, lethal, mortal, pestilent, vital ♦ [3] bitter, brutal, burdensome, cruel, excruciating, grievous, grim, hard, harsh, heavy, inhuman, onerous, oppressive, rough, rugged, severe, stiff, tough, trying ♦ [4] arduous, demanding, difficult, exacting, formidable, grueling, hard, herculean, laborious, rough, stiff, strenuous, tall, toilsome, tough

murk \ˈmərk\ *n* **1 ♦ :** partial or total darkness : GLOOM **2 ♦ :** a murky condition of the atmosphere or a substance causing it : FOG — **murk•i•ly** \ˈmər-kə-lē\ *adv*

♦ [1] dark, darkness, dusk, gloaming, gloom, night, semidarkness, shade, shadows, twilight ♦ [2] fog, haze, smog, soup

murk•i•ness \ˈmər-kē-nəs\ *n* **♦ :** the quality or state of being murky

♦ ambiguity, darkness, obscurity, opacity

murky \ˈmər-kē\ *adj* **1 ♦ :** characterized by a heavy dimness or obscurity caused by or like that caused by overhanging fog or smoke **2 ♦ :** characterized by thickness and heaviness of air : FOGGY, MISTY **3 ♦ :** darkly vague or obscure ⟨~ writings⟩

♦ [1] dark, darkling, dim, dusky, gloomy, obscure, somber (*or* sombre) ♦ [2] cloudy, foggy, hazy, misty, smoggy, soupy ♦ [3] ambiguous, cryptic, dark, darkling, deep, enigmatic, equivocal, inscrutable, mysterious, mystic, nebulous, obscure, occult

¹mur•mur \ˈmər-mər\ *n* **1 ♦ :** a muttered complaint **2 a :** a low indistinct often continuous sound **b ♦ :** a soft or gentle utterance — **mur•mur•ous** *adj*

♦ [1] beef, complaint, fuss, grievance, gripe, grumble, plaint, squawk ♦ [2b] mumble, mutter

²murmur *vb* **1 :** to make a murmur ⟨traffic ~*ed* in the distance⟩ **2 :** to express grief, pain, or discontent
mur•mur•er *n* : one that murmurs
mus *abbr* **1** museum **2** music; musical; musician
mus•ca•tel \ˌməs-kə-ˈtel\ *n* : a sweet fortified wine
¹mus•cle \ˈmə-səl\ *n* **1 :** a body tissue consisting of long cells that contract when stimulated and produce motion; *also* : an organ consisting of this tissue and functioning in moving a body part **2 ♦ :** effective strength : BRAWN — **mus•cled** \ˈmə-səld\ *adj*

♦ energy, force, main, might, potency, power, sinew, strength, vigor (*or* vigour)

²muscle *vb* **mus•cled; mus•cling 1 ♦ :** to move or force by or as if by muscular effort **2 ♦ :** to make one's way by brute strength or by force

♦ [1] coerce, compel, constrain, drive, force, make, obligate, oblige, press, pressure ♦ [2] bulldoze, elbow, press, push

mus•cle–bound \ˈmə-səl-ˌbau̇nd\ *adj* : having some of the muscles abnormally enlarged and lacking in elasticity (as from excessive exercise)
mus•cle•man \-ˌman\ *n* : a man with a muscular physique
mus•cu•lar \ˈməs-kyə-lər\ *adj* **1 a :** of, relating to, or constituting muscle **b :** of, relating to, or performed by the muscles **2 ♦ :** having well-developed musculature **3 :** of or relating to physical strength — **mus•cu•lar•i•ty** \ˌməs-kyə-ˈlar-ə-tē\ *n*

♦ brawny, rugged, sinewy, stalwart, stout, strong

muscular dystrophy *n* : any of a group of diseases characterized by progressive wasting of muscles
mus•cu•la•ture \ˈməs-kyə-lə-ˌchu̇r\ *n* : the muscles of the body or its parts
muscu•lo•skel•e•tal \ˌməs-kyə-lō-ˈske-lə-tᵊl\ *adj* : of, relating to, or involving both musculature and skeleton
¹muse \ˈmyüz\ *vb* **mused; mus•ing :** to become absorbed in thought — **mus•ing•ly** *adv*
²muse *n* : a source of inspiration
mu•se•um \myu̇-ˈzē-əm\ *n* : an institution devoted to the procurement, care, and display of objects of lasting interest or value
¹mush \ˈməsh\ *n* **1 :** cornmeal boiled in water **2 :** sentimental drivel **3 ♦ :** mawkish amorousness

♦ mawkishness, sentimentality

²mush *vb* : to travel especially over snow with a sled drawn by dogs
¹mush•room \ˈməsh-ˌrüm, -ˌru̇m\ *n* : the fleshy usually caplike spore-bearing organ of various fungi especially when edible; *also* : such a fungus
²mushroom *vb* **1 :** to collect wild mushrooms **2 ♦ :** to spread out : EXPAND **3 :** to grow rapidly

♦ accumulate, appreciate, balloon, build, burgeon, enlarge, escalate, expand, increase, mount, multiply, proliferate, rise, snowball, swell, wax

mushy \ˈmə-shē\ *adj* **mush•i•er; -est 1 ♦ :** soft like mush **2 ♦ :** excessively sentimental

♦ [1] flabby, pulpy, soft, spongy ♦ [2] corny, maudlin, mawkish, saccharine, sappy, schmaltzy, sentimental

mu•sic \ˈmyü-zik\ *n* **1 :** the science or art of combining tones into a composition having structure and continuity; *also* : vocal or instrumental sounds having rhythm, melody, or harmony **2 :** an agreeable sound
¹mu•si•cal \ˈmyü-zi-kəl\ *adj* **1 :** of or relating to music or musicians **2 ♦ :** having the pleasing tonal qualities of music **3 :** fond of or gifted in music — **mu•si•cal•ly** \-k(ə-)lē\ *adv*

♦ euphonious, lyric, mellifluous, mellow, melodic, melodious ♦ harmonious, symphonic, tuneful

²musical *n* : a film or theatrical production consisting of musical numbers and dialogue based on a unifying plot
mu•si•cale \ˌmyü-zi-ˈkal\ *n* : a usually private social gathering featuring music
mu•si•cian \myu̇-ˈzi-shən\ *n* : a composer, conductor, or performer of music — **mu•si•cian•ly** *adj* — **mu•si•cian•ship** *n*
mu•si•col•o•gy \ˌmyü-zi-ˈkä-lə-jē\ *n* : the study of music as a field of knowledge or research — **mu•si•co•log•i•cal** \-kə-ˈlä-ji-kəl\ *adj* — **mu•si•col•o•gist** \-ˈkä-lə-jist\ *n*
musk \ˈməsk\ *n* : a substance obtained especially from a small Asian deer (**musk deer**) and used as a perfume fixative — **musk•i•ness** \ˈməs-kē-nəs\ *n* — **musky** *adj*
mus•keg \ˈməs-ˌkeg\ *n* : wet spongy ground : BOG; *esp* : a mossy bog in northern No. America
mus•kel•lunge \ˈməs-kə-ˌlənj\ *n, pl* **muskellunge :** a large No. American pike that is a valuable sport fish
mus•ket \ˈməs-kət\ *n* : a heavy large-caliber muzzle-loading shoulder firearm — **mus•ke•teer** \ˌməs-kə-ˈtir\ *n*
mus•ket•ry \ˈməs-kə-trē\ *n* **1 :** MUSKETS **2 :** MUSKETEERS **3 :** musket fire
musk•mel•on \ˈməsk-ˌme-lən\ *n* : a small round to oval melon that has usually a sweet edible green or orange flesh and a musky odor
musk ox *n* : a heavyset shaggy-coated wild ox of Greenland and the arctic tundra of northern No. America
musk•rat \ˈməs-ˌkrat\ *n, pl* **muskrat** *or* **muskrats :** a large No. American aquatic rodent with webbed feet and dark brown fur; *also* : its fur
Mus•lim \ˈməz-ləm\ *n* : an adherent of Islam — **Muslim** *adj*
mus•lin \ˈməz-lən\ *n* : a plain-woven sheer to coarse cotton fabric
¹muss \ˈməs\ *n* **♦ :** a state of disorder

♦ chaos, confusion, disarray, disorder, disorganization, havoc, hell, jumble, mess, messiness, muddle, shambles, tumble, welter

²muss *vb* : to make untidy : DISARRANGE
mus•sel \ˈmə-səl\ *n* **1 :** a dark edible saltwater bivalve mollusk **2 :** any of various freshwater bivalve mollusks of the central U.S. having shells with a pearly lining
mussy \ˈmə-sē\ *adj* : characterized by clutter or muss — **muss•i•ly** \ˈmə-sə-lē\ *adv* — **muss•i•ness** \-sē-nəs\ *n*
¹must \ˈməst\ *vb* **♦** — used as an auxiliary especially to express a command, requirement, obligation, or necessity

♦ have, need, ought, shall, should

²must *n* **1 ♦ :** an imperative duty **2 ♦ :** an indispensable item

♦ [1, 2] condition, demand, essential, necessity, need, requirement, requisite

mus•tache *or chiefly Can and Brit* **mous•tache** \ˈməs-ˌtash,

(ˌ)məs-ˈtash\ *n* **:** the hair growing on the human upper lip — **mus•tached** \-ˌtasht, -ˈtasht\ *adj*
mus•tang \ˈməs-ˌtaŋ\ *n* **:** a small hardy naturalized horse of the western plains of America; *also* **:** BRONC
mus•tard \ˈməs-tərd\ *n* **1 :** a pungent yellow powder of the seeds of an herb related to the cabbage and used as a condiment or in medicine **2 :** a plant that yields mustard; *also* **:** a closely related plant — **mustardy** *adj*
mustard gas *n* **:** a poison gas used in warfare that has violent irritating and blistering effects
¹mus•ter \ˈməs-tər\ *n* **1 a ♦ :** an act of assembling (as for military inspection) **b :** critical examination **2 ♦ :** an assembled group

♦ [1a] mobilization, rally ♦ [2] assemblage, assembly, conference, congregation, convocation, gathering, meeting

²muster *vb* **1 a ♦ :** to gather or cause to gather **b :** to call the roll of **2 :** ACCUMULATE **3 :** to call forth **:** ROUSE **4 :** to amount to **:** COMPRISE

♦ marshal, mobilize, rally ♦ assemble, call, convene, convoke, summon

muster out *vb* **:** to discharge from military service
musty \ˈməs-tē\ *adj* **mus•ti•er; -est 1 :** impaired by damp or mildew **:** MOLDY **2 ♦ :** tasting or smelling of damp or decay **3 ♦ :** tedious from familiarity **:** STALE — **must•i•ly** \-tə-lē\ *adv* — **must•i•ness** \-tē-nəs\ *n*

♦ [2] fetid, foul, fusty, malodorous, noisome, rank, reeky, smelly, strong ♦ [3] banal, commonplace, hackneyed, stale, stereotyped, threadbare, tired, trite

mu•ta•ble \ˈmyü-tə-bəl\ *adj* **1 ♦ :** prone to change **:** FICKLE **2 :** capable of or liable to mutation **:** VARIABLE — **mu•ta•bil•i•ty** \ˌmyü-tə-ˈbi-lə-tē\ *n*

♦ capricious, changeable, fickle, fluid, inconstant, mercurial, temperamental, uncertain, unpredictable, unsettled, unstable, unsteady, variable, volatile

mu•tant \ˈmyüt-ᵊnt\ *adj* **:** of, relating to, or produced by mutation — **mu•tant** *n*
mu•tate \ˈmyü-ˌtāt\ *vb* **mu•tat•ed; mu•tat•ing ♦ :** to undergo or cause to undergo mutation — **mu•ta•tive** \ˈmyü-ˌtā-tiv, -tə-tiv\ *adj*

♦ change, fluctuate, shift, vary

mu•ta•tion \myü-ˈtā-shən\ *n* **1 :** CHANGE **2 :** an inherited physical or biochemical change in genetic material; *also* **:** the process of producing a mutation **3 :** an individual, strain, or trait resulting from mutation — **mu•ta•tion•al** *adj*
¹mute \ˈmyüt\ *adj* **mut•er; mut•est 1 ♦ :** unable to speak **:** DUMB **2 ♦ :** characterized by absence of speech **:** SILENT — **mute•ly** *adv* — **mute•ness** *n*

♦ [1] dumb, inarticulate, speechless, voiceless ♦ [2] dumb, mum, silent, speechless, uncommunicative

²mute *n* **1 :** a person who cannot or does not speak **2 :** a device on a musical instrument that reduces, softens, or muffles the tone
³mute *vb* **mut•ed; mut•ing ♦ :** to muffle, reduce, or eliminate the sound of

♦ hush, quell, settle, silence, still

muted *adj* **1 ♦ :** being mute **:** SILENT **2 ♦ :** toned down **:** SUBDUED

♦ [1] hushed, noiseless, quiet, silent, soundless, still ♦ [2] conservative, quiet, restrained, subdued, unpretentious

mu•ti•late \ˈmyüt-ᵊl-ˌāt\ *vb* **-lat•ed; -lat•ing 1 :** to cut up or alter radically so as to make imperfect **2 ♦ :** to cut off or permanently destroy a limb or essential part of **:** MAIM, CRIPPLE — **mu•ti•la•tion** \ˌmyüt-ᵊl-ˈā-shən\ *n* — **mu•ti•la•tor** \ˈmyüt-ᵊl-ˌā-tər\ *n*

♦ cripple, disable, lame, maim

mu•ti•neer \ˌmyüt-ᵊn-ˈir\ *n* **♦ :** one that mutinies

♦ insurgent, insurrectionist, rebel, red, revolter, revolutionary

mu•ti•nous \ˈmyüt-ᵊn-əs\ *adj* **1 ♦ :** disposed to or being in a state of mutiny **2 :** of, relating to, or constituting mutiny — **mu•ti•nous•ly** *adv*

♦ insurgent, rebellious, revolutionary

mu•ti•ny \ˈmyü-tə-nē\ *n, pl* **-nies ♦ :** willful refusal to obey constituted authority; *esp* **:** revolt against a superior officer — **mutiny** *vb*

♦ insurrection, rebellion, revolt, revolution, uprising

mutt \ˈmət\ *n* **:** MONGREL, CUR

¹mut•ter \ˈmə-tər\ *vb* **1 ♦ :** to speak indistinctly or with a low voice and lips partly closed **2 ♦ :** to murmur complainingly or angrily **:** GRUMBLE

♦ [1] mouth, mumble, murmur ♦ [2] beef, bellyache, carp, complain, crab, croak, fuss, gripe, grouse, growl, grumble, kick, moan, murmur, repine, squawk, wail, whine

²mutter *n* **♦ :** a subdued scarcely audible utterance

♦ mumble, murmur

mut•ton \ˈmət-ᵊn\ *n* **:** the flesh of a mature sheep used for food — **mut•tony** *adj*
mut•ton•chops \ˈmət-ᵊn-ˌchäps\ *n pl* **:** whiskers on the side of the face that are narrow at the temple and broad and round by the lower jaws
mu•tu•al \ˈmyü-chə-wəl\ *adj* **1 :** given and received in equal amount ⟨∼ trust⟩ **2 :** having the same feelings one for the other ⟨∼ enemies⟩ **3 ♦ :** shared in common **:** COMMON, JOINT ⟨a ∼ friend⟩ — **mu•tu•al•ly** *adv*

♦ collective, common, communal, concerted, conjoint, joint, public, united

mutual fund *n* **:** an investment company that invests money of its shareholders in a usually diversified group of securities of other corporations
muu•muu \ˈmü-ˌmü\ *n* **:** a loose dress of Hawaiian origin
¹muz•zle \ˈmə-zəl\ *n* **1 :** the nose and jaws of an animal; *also* **:** a covering for the muzzle to prevent biting or eating **2 :** the mouth of a gun
²muzzle *vb* **muz•zled; muz•zling 1 :** to put a muzzle on **2 :** to restrain from expression **:** GAG
mV *abbr* millivolt
MV *abbr* motor vessel
MVP *abbr* most valuable player
MW *abbr* megawatt
my \ˈmī\ *adj* **1 :** of or relating to me or myself **2** — used interjectionally especially to express surprise
my•col•o•gy \mī-ˈkä-lə-jē\ *n* **:** a branch of biology dealing with fungi — **my•co•log•i•cal** \ˌmī-kə-ˈlä-ji-kəl\ *adj* — **my•col•o•gist** \mī-ˈkä-lə-jist\ *n*
my•elo•ma \ˌmī-ə-ˈlō-mə\ *n, pl* **-mas** *or* **-ma•ta** \-mə-tə\ **:** a primary tumor of the bone marrow
my•nah *or* **my•na** \ˈmī-nə\ *n* **:** any of several Asian starlings; *esp* **:** a dark brown slightly crested bird sometimes taught to mimic speech
my•o•pia \mī-ˈō-pē-ə\ *n* **:** a condition in which visual images come to a focus in front of the retina resulting especially in defective vision of distant objects — **my•o•pic** \-ˈō-pik, -ˈä-\ *adj* — **my•o•pi•cal•ly** \-pi-k(ə-)lē\ *adv*
¹myr•i•ad \ˈmir-ē-əd\ *n* **:** an indefinitely large number
²myriad *adj* **♦ :** consisting of a very great but indefinite number; *also* **:** both numerous and varied

♦ manifold, multifarious

myr•mi•don \ˈmər-mə-ˌdän\ *n* **:** a loyal follower; *esp* **:** one who executes orders without protest or pity
myrrh \ˈmər\ *n* **:** a fragrant aromatic plant gum used in perfumes and formerly for incense
myr•tle \ˈmərt-ᵊl\ *n* **:** an evergreen shrub of southern Europe with shiny leaves, fragrant flowers, and black berries; *also* **:** PERIWINKLE
my•self \mī-ˈself, mə-\ *pron* **:** I, ME — used reflexively, for emphasis, or in absolute constructions ⟨I hurt ∼⟩ ⟨I ∼ did it⟩ ⟨∼ busy, I sent him instead⟩
mys•te•ri•ous \mis-ˈtir-ē-əs\ *adj* **1 ♦ :** of, relating to, or constituting mystery **2 ♦ :** exciting wonder, curiosity, or surprise while baffling efforts to comprehend or identify — **mys•te•ri•ous•ly** *adv* — **mys•te•ri•ous•ness** *n*

♦ [1] ambiguous, equivocal, murky, nebulous, obscure ♦ [2] cryptic, darkling, deep, enigmatic, impenetrable, inscrutable, mystic, occult, uncanny

mys•tery \ˈmis-tə-rē\ *n, pl* **-ter•ies 1 :** a religious truth known by revelation alone **2 ♦ :** something not understood or beyond understanding **3 :** enigmatic quality or character **4 :** a work of fiction dealing with the solution of a mysterious crime

♦ conundrum, enigma, mystification, puzzle, puzzlement, riddle, secret

¹mys•tic \ˈmis-tik\ *adj* **1 :** of or relating to mystics or mysticism **2 a :** exciting wonder, curiosity, or surprise while baffling efforts to comprehend or identify **:** MYSTERIOUS **b :** MYSTIFYING **3 ♦ :** having magical properties

♦ magic, magical, occult, weird

2**mystic** *n* **:** a person who follows, advocates, or experiences mysticism

mys•ti•cal \ˈmis-ti-kəl\ *adj* **1 :** SPIRITUAL, SYMBOLIC **2 :** of or relating to an intimate knowledge of or direct communion with God (as through contemplation or visions)

mys•ti•cism \ˈmis-tə-ˌsi-zəm\ *n* **:** the belief that direct knowledge of God or ultimate reality is attainable through immediate intuition or insight

mys•ti•fi•ca•tion \ˌmis-tə-fə-ˈkā-shən\ *n* **1** ♦ **:** the quality or state of being mystified **2** ♦ **:** something designed to mystify

♦ [1] bafflement, bewilderment, confusion, distraction, muddle, perplexity, puzzlement, whirl ♦ [2] conundrum, enigma, mystery, puzzle, puzzlement, riddle, secret

mys•ti•fy \ˈmis-tə-ˌfī\ *vb* **-fied; -fy•ing 1** ♦ **:** to perplex the mind of **2 :** to make mysterious

♦ addle, baffle, befog, befuddle, bemuse, bewilder, confound, confuse, disorient, muddle, muddy, perplex, puzzle

mys•tique \mi-ˈstēk\ *n* **1 :** an air or attitude of mystery and reverence developing around something or someone **2 :** the special esoteric skill essential in a calling or activity

myth \ˈmith\ *n* **1 :** a usually legendary narrative that presents part of the beliefs of a people or explains a practice or natural phenomenon **2 :** an imaginary or unverifiable person or thing **3** ♦ **:** an unfounded or false notion **4** ♦ **:** the whole body of myths

♦ [3] error, fallacy, falsehood, falsity, illusion, misconception, untruth ♦ [4] folklore, legend, lore, mythology, tradition

myth•i•cal \ˈmi-thi-kəl\ *or* **myth•ic** *adj* **1** ♦ **:** based on or described in a myth especially as contrasted with history **2** *usu mythical* ♦ **:** existing only in the imagination

♦ [1] fabled, fabulous, legendary ♦ [2] chimerical, fabulous, fanciful, fantastic, fictitious, imaginary, made-up, phantom, pretend, unreal

my•thol•o•gy \mi-ˈthä-lə-jē\ *n, pl* **-gies** ♦ **:** a body of myths and especially of those dealing with the gods and heroes of a people — **myth•o•log•i•cal** \ˌmi-thə-ˈlä-ji-kəl\ *adj* — **my•thol•o•gist** \mi-ˈthä-lə-jist\ *n* — **my•thol•o•gize** \-ˌjīz\ *vb*

♦ folklore, legend, lore, myth, tradition

N

1**n** \ˈen\ *n, pl* **n's** *or* **ns** \ˈenz\ *often cap* **1 :** the 14th letter of the English alphabet **2 :** an unspecified quantity

2**n** *abbr, often cap* **1** net **2** neuter **3** noon **4** normal **5** north; northern **6** note **7** noun **8** number

N *symbol* nitrogen

-n — see -EN

Na *symbol* sodium

NA *abbr* **1** no account **2** North America **3** not applicable **4** not available

NAACP \ˌen-ˌdə-bəl-ˌā-ˌsē-ˈpē, ˌen-ˌā-ˌā-ˌsē-\ *abbr* National Association for the Advancement of Colored People

nab \ˈnab\ *vb* **nabbed; nab•bing 1** ♦ **:** to seize suddenly **:** SEIZE **2** ♦ **:** to catch or seize in arrest **:** ARREST

♦ [1] bag, capture, catch, collar, corral, get, grab, grapple, hook, land, seize, snare, trap ♦ [2] apprehend, arrest, pick up, restrain, seize

NAB *abbr* New American Bible

na•bob \ˈnā-ˌbäb\ *n* ♦ **:** a person of great wealth or prominence

♦ big shot, celebrity, eminence, figure, immortal, light, luminary, notable, personage, personality, somebody, standout, star, superstar, VIP

na•celle \nə-ˈsel\ *n* **:** an enclosure (as for an engine) on an aircraft

na•cho \ˈnä-chō\ *n, pl* **nachos :** a tortilla chip topped with melted cheese and often additional savory toppings

na•cre \ˈnā-kər\ *n* **:** MOTHER-OF-PEARL

na•dir \ˈnā-ˌdir, -dər\ *n* **1 :** the point of the celestial sphere that is directly opposite the zenith and directly beneath the observer **2 :** the lowest point

1**nag** \ˈnag\ *n* **:** a horse and especially an old or decrepit horse

2**nag** *vb* **nagged; nag•ging 1 :** to find fault incessantly **:** COMPLAIN **2** ♦ **:** to irritate by constant scolding or urging **3 :** to be a continuing source of annoyance ⟨a *nagging* backache⟩

♦ henpeck, hound, needle

3**nag** *n* **:** one who nags habitually

Nah *abbr* Nahum

Na•huatl \ˈnä-ˌwät-ᵊl\ *n* **:** a group of American Indian languages of central and southern Mexico

Na•hum \ˈnā-həm, -əm\ *n* **:** a book of Jewish and Christian Scripture

NAIA *abbr* National Association of Intercollegiate Athletes

na•iad \ˈnā-əd, ˈnī-, -ˌad\ *n, pl* **naiads** *or* **na•ia•des** \-ə-ˌdēz\ **1 :** one of the nymphs in ancient mythology living in lakes, rivers, springs, and fountains **2 :** an aquatic young of some insects (as a dragonfly)

1**na•ïf** *or* **na•if** \nä-ˈēf\ *adj* **:** NAIVE

2**naïf** *or* **naif** *n* **:** a naive person

1**nail** \ˈnāl\ *n* **1 :** a horny sheath protecting the end of each finger and toe in humans and related primates **2 :** a slender pointed fastener with a head designed to be pounded in

2**nail** *vb* **:** to fasten with or as if with a nail — **nail•er** *n*

nail down *vb* **:** to settle or establish clearly and unmistakably

nain•sook \ˈnān-ˌsu̇k\ *n* **:** a soft lightweight muslin

na•ive *or* **na•ïve** \nä-ˈēv\ *adj* **na•iv•er; -est 1** ♦ **:** marked by unaffected simplicity **:** ARTLESS, INGENUOUS **2** ♦ **:** lacking in worldly wisdom or informed judgment — **na•ive•ness** *n*

♦ [1] artless, genuine, honest, ingenuous, innocent, natural, real, simple, sincere, true, unaffected, unpretentious ♦ [2] green, ingenuous, innocent, simple, unknowing, unsophisticated, unwary, unworldly ***Ant*** cynical, experienced, knowing, sophisticated, worldly, worldly-wise

na•ive•ly *adv* ♦ **:** in a naive manner **:** with naïveté

♦ artlessly, ingenuously, naturally, unaffectedly

na•ïve•té *also* **na•ive•te** *or* **na•ive•té** \ˌnä-ˌē-və-ˈtā, nä-ˈē-və-ˌtā\ *n* **1 :** a naive remark or action **2** ♦ **:** the quality or state of being naive

♦ artlessness, greenness, ingenuousness, innocence, naturalness, simplicity, unworldliness ***Ant*** artfulness, cynicism, sophistication, worldliness

na•ked \ˈnā-kəd\ *adj* **1** ♦ **:** having no clothes on **:** NUDE **2 :** UNSHEATHED ⟨a ~ sword⟩ **3** ♦ **:** lacking a usual or natural covering (as of foliage or feathers) **4** ♦ **:** lacking embellishment **:** PLAIN, UNADORNED ⟨the ~ truth⟩ **5 :** not aided by artificial means ⟨seen by the ~ eye⟩ — **na•ked•ly** *adv* — **na•ked•ness** *n*

♦ [1] bare, nude, unclad, unclothed, undressed ***Ant*** appareled, attired, clad, clothed, invested, robed, suited ♦ [3] bald, bare, exposed, open, uncovered ***Ant*** covered ♦ [4] bald, bare, plain, simple, unadorned, undecorated, unvarnished

nam•by–pam•by \ˌnam-bē-ˈpam-bē\ *adj* **1** ♦ **:** lacking in character or substance **2 :** WEAK, INDECISIVE

♦ bland, flat, wishy-washy

1**name** \ˈnām\ *n* **1** ♦ **:** a word or words by which a person or thing is known **2** ♦ **:** a disparaging epithet ⟨call him ~*s*⟩ **3** ♦ **:** overall quality or character as seen or judged by people in general **:** REPUTATION; *esp* **:** distinguished reputation ⟨made a ~ for herself⟩ **4 :** FAMILY, CLAN ⟨was a disgrace to their ~⟩ **5** ♦ **:** appearance as opposed to reality ⟨a friend in ~ only⟩

♦ [1] appellation, cognomen, denotation, designation, handle, title ♦ [2] affront, barb, dart, dig, indignity, insult, offense, outrage, put-down, sarcasm, slight, slur, wound ♦ [3] character, mark, note, report, reputation ♦ [5] appearance, face, guise, semblance, show

2**name** *vb* **named; nam•ing 1** ♦ **:** to give a name to **:** CALL **2 :** to mention or identify by name **3** ♦ **:** to assign to some purpose **:** APPOINT **4** ♦ **:** to decide on **:** CHOOSE **5** ♦ **:** to mention explicitly **:** SPECIFY ⟨~ a price⟩ — **name•able** *adj*

♦ [1] baptize, call, christen, denominate, designate, dub, entitle, label, style, term, title ♦ [3] appoint, assign, attach, commission, constitute, designate, detail ♦ [4] choose, cull, elect, handpick, opt, pick, prefer, select, single, take ♦ [5] advert (to), cite, instance, mention, note, notice, quote, refer (to), specify, touch (*on* or *upon*)

[3]**name** *adj* **1 :** of, relating to, or bearing a name ⟨~ tag⟩ **2** ♦ **:** having an established reputation ⟨~ brands⟩

♦ prestigious, reputable, reputed, respectable

name day *n* **:** the church feast day of the saint after whom one is named

name•less \ˈnām-ləs\ *adj* **1** ♦ **:** having no name **2 :** not marked with a name ⟨a ~ grave⟩ **3 a** ♦ **:** not known by name ⟨a ~ hero⟩ **b** ♦ **:** relatively unknown **4 a** ♦ **:** impossible to identify precisely or by name **b :** too distressing to be described ⟨~ fears⟩ — **name•less•ly** *adv*

♦ [1, 3a] anonymous, unbaptized, unchristened, unidentified, unnamed, untitled *Ant* baptized, christened, dubbed, named, termed ♦ [3b] anonymous, obscure, unknown, unsung ♦ [4a] indescribable, ineffable, inexpressible, unspeakable, unutterable

name•ly \-lē\ *adv* **:** that is to say **:** AS ⟨the cat family, ~, lions, tigers, and similar animals⟩

name•plate \-ˌplāt\ *n* **:** a plate or plaque bearing a name (as of a resident)

name•sake \-ˌsāk\ *n* **:** one that has the same name as another; *esp* **:** one named after another

Na•mib•ian \nə-ˈmi-bē-ən, -byən\ *n* **:** a native or inhabitant of Namibia — **Namibian** *adj*

nan•keen \nan-ˈkēn\ *n* **:** a durable brownish yellow cotton fabric orig. woven by hand in China

nan•ny \ˈna-nē\ *n* ♦ **:** a child's nurse or caregiver

♦ nurse, nursemaid

nan•ny goat \ˈna-nē-\ *n* **:** a female domestic goat

nano•me•ter \ˈna-nə-ˌmē-tər\ *n* **:** one billionth of a meter

nano•scale \-ˌskāl\ *adj* **:** having dimensions measured in nanometers

nano•sec•ond \-ˌse-kənd\ *n* **:** one billionth of a second

nano•sec•ond \-ˌse-kənd\ *n* **:** one billionth of a second

nano•tech•nol•o•gy \ˌna-nō-tek-ˈnä-lə-jē\ *n* **:** the manipulation of materials on an atomic or molecular scale

[1]**nap** \ˈnap\ *vb* **napped; nap•ping 1** ♦ **:** to sleep briefly especially during the day **:** DOZE **2 :** to be off guard ⟨was caught *napping*⟩

♦ catnap, doze, drowse, slumber, snooze

[2]**nap** *n* ♦ **:** a short sleep especially during the day

♦ catnap, doze, drowse, forty winks, siesta, snooze, wink

[3]**nap** *n* ♦ **:** a soft downy fibrous surface (as on yarn and cloth) — **nap•less** *adj* — **napped** \ˈnapt\ *adj*

♦ down, floss, fluff, fur, fuzz, lint, pile

na•palm \ˈnā-ˌpälm, -ˌpäm\ *n* **1 :** a thickener used in jelling gasoline (as for incendiary bombs) **2 :** fuel jelled with napalm

nape \ˈnāp, ˈnap\ *n* **:** the back of the neck

na•pery \ˈnā-pə-rē\ *n* **:** household linen especially for the table

naph•tha \ˈnaf-thə, ˈnap-\ *n* **:** any of various liquid hydrocarbon mixtures used chiefly as solvents

naph•tha•lene \-ˌlēn\ *n* **:** a crystalline substance used especially in organic synthesis and as a moth repellent

nap•kin \ˈnap-kən\ *n* **1 :** a piece of material (as cloth) used at table to wipe the lips or fingers and protect the clothes **2 :** a small cloth or towel

na•po•leon \nə-ˈpōl-yən, -ˈpō-lē-ən\ *n* **:** an oblong pastry with a filling of cream, custard, or jelly

Na•po•le•on•ic \nə-ˌpō-lē-ˈä-nik\ *adj* **:** of, relating to, or characteristic of Napoleon I or his family

narc *also* **nark** \ˈnärk\ *n, slang* **:** a person (as a government agent) who investigates narcotics violations

nar•cis•sism \ˈnär-sə-ˌsi-zəm\ *n* **1 :** undue dwelling on one's own self or attainments **2 :** love of or sexual desire for one's own body — **nar•cis•sist** \-sist\ *n or adj* — **nar•cis•sis•tic** \ˌnär-sə-ˈsis-tik\ *adj*

nar•cis•sus \när-ˈsi-səs\ *n, pl* **nar•cis•si** \-ˌsī, -ˌsē\ *or* **nar•cis•sus•es** *or* **narcissus :** DAFFODIL; *esp* **:** one with short-tubed flowers usually borne separately

nar•co•lep•sy \ˈnär-kə-ˌlep-sē\ *n, pl* **-sies :** a condition characterized by brief attacks of deep sleep — **nar•co•lep•tic** \ˌnär-kə-ˈlep-tik\ *adj or n*

nar•co•sis \när-ˈkō-səs\ *n, pl* **-co•ses** \-ˌsēz\ **:** a state of stupor, unconsciousness, or arrested activity produced by the influence of chemicals (as narcotics)

nar•co–ter•ror•ism \ˈnär-kō-ˈter-ər-ˌi-zəm\ *n* **:** terrorism financed by profits from illegal drug trafficking

nar•cot•ic \när-ˈkä-tik\ *n* **1 :** a drug (as opium) that dulls the senses, relieves pain, and induces sleep **2 :** an illegal drug (as marijuana or LSD) — **narcotic** *adj*

narcotic *adj* ♦ **:** something that soothes, relieves, or lulls

♦ comforting, dreamy, sedative, soothing

nar•co•tize \ˈnär-kə-ˌtīz\ *vb* **-tized; -tiz•ing 1 :** to treat with or subject to a narcotic; *also* **:** to put into a state of narcosis **2 :** to soothe to unconsciousness or unawareness

nard \ˈnärd\ *n* **:** a fragrant ointment of the ancients

na•res \ˈnar-(ˌ)ēz\ *n pl* **:** the pair of openings of the nose

Nar•ra•gan•sett \ˌnar-ə-ˈgan-sət\ *n, pl* **-sett** *or* **-setts 1 :** a member of an American Indian people of Rhode Island **2 :** the Algonquian language of the Narragansett people

nar•rate \ˈnar-ˌāt\ *vb* **nar•rat•ed; nar•rat•ing** ♦ **:** to recite the details of (as a story) **:** RELATE, TELL — **nar•ra•tor** \ˈnar-ˌā-tər\ *n*

♦ describe, recite, recount, rehearse, relate, report, tell

nar•ra•tion \na-ˈrā-shən\ *n* ♦ **:** an account of incidents or events **:** STORY

♦ account, chronicle, commentary, history, narrative, record, report, story

nar•ra•tive \ˈnar-ə-tiv\ *n* **1 a :** something that is narrated **b** ♦ **:** a fictional narrative shorter than a novel **2** ♦ **:** the art or practice of narrating

♦ [1b] novella, short story, story, tale ♦ [2] account, chronicle, history, record, report, story

[1]**nar•row** \ˈnar-ō\ *adj* **1** ♦ **:** of slender or less than standard width **2** ♦ **:** limited in size or scope **:** RESTRICTED **3** ♦ **:** not liberal in views **4 :** interpreted or interpreting strictly **5** ♦ **:** barely sufficient **:** CLOSE ⟨won by a ~ margin⟩; *also* **:** barely successful ⟨a ~ escape⟩ — **nar•row•ly** *adv* — **nar•row•ness** *n*

♦ [1] fine, skinny, slender, slim, thin *Ant* broad, fat, wide ♦ [2] definite, determinate, finite, limited, measured, restricted ♦ [3] bigoted, intolerant, narrow-minded, prejudiced ♦ [3] insular, little, parochial, petty, provincial, sectarian, small *Ant* broad-minded, catholic, cosmopolitan, liberal, open, open-minded, receptive, tolerant ♦ [5] close, neck and neck, nip and tuck, tight

[2]**narrow** *n* ♦ **:** a narrow passage **:** STRAIT — usually used in plural

♦ channel, sound, strait

[3]**narrow** *vb* **:** to lessen in width or extent

nar•row–mind•ed \ˌnar-ō-ˈmīn-dəd\ *adj* ♦ **:** not liberal or broad-minded

♦ bigoted, intolerant, narrow, prejudiced

nar•whal \ˈnär-ˌhwäl, ˈnär-wəl\ *n* **:** an arctic sea mammal about 20 feet (6 meters) long that is related to the dolphins and in the male has a long twisted ivory tusk

NAS *abbr* naval air station

NASA \ˈna-sə\ *abbr* National Aeronautics and Space Administration

[1]**na•sal** \ˈnā-zəl\ *n* **1 :** a nasal part **2 :** a nasal consonant or vowel

[2]**nasal** *adj* **1 :** of or relating to the nose **2 :** uttered through the nose — **na•sal•ly** *adv*

na•sal•ize \ˈnā-zə-ˌlīz\ *vb* **-ized; -iz•ing :** to make nasal or pronounce as a nasal sound — **na•sal•i•za•tion** \ˌnā-zə-lə-ˈzā-shən\ *n*

na•scent \ˈnas-ᵊnt, ˈnās-\ *adj* **:** coming into existence **:** beginning to grow or develop — **na•scence** \-ᵊns\ *n*

nas•ti•ly \ˈnas-tē-lē\ *n* ♦ **:** in a nasty manner or condition

♦ hatefully, maliciously, meanly, spitefully, viciously, wickedly *Ant* benevolently, kindly

nas•ti•ness \ˈnas-tē-nəs\ *n* ♦ **:** the quality or state of being nasty

♦ cattiness, despite, hatefulness, malice, malignity, meanness, spite, spleen, venom, viciousness ♦ bawdiness, coarseness, dirt, dirtiness, filth, filthiness, foulness, grossness, indecency, lewdness, obscenity, ribaldry, smut, vulgarity ♦ dinginess, dirtiness, filthiness, foulness, grubbiness, uncleanliness

nas•tur•tium \nə-ˈstər-shəm, na-\ *n* **:** either of two widely cultivated watery-stemmed herbs with showy spurred flowers and pungent seeds

nas•ty \ˈnas-tē\ *adj* **nas•ti•er; -est** **1 :** FILTHY **2** ♦ **:** abhorrent to morality or virtue **:** INDECENT, OBSCENE **3 a :** HARMFUL, DANGEROUS ⟨took a ~ fall⟩ **b** ♦ **:** causing severe pain or suffering **4** ♦ **:** sharply unpleasant ⟨~ weather⟩ **5** ♦ **:** characterized by petty selfishness or malice **:** MEAN, ILL-NATURED ⟨a ~ temper⟩ **6 :** DIFFICULT, VEXATIOUS ⟨a ~ problem⟩ **7 :** UNFAIR, DIRTY ⟨a ~ trick⟩

♦ [2] bawdy, coarse, crude, dirty, filthy, foul, gross, indecent, lascivious, lewd, obscene, pornographic, ribald, smutty, unprintable, vulgar, wanton ♦ [3b] achy, painful, sore ♦ [4] bad, bleak, dirty, disagreeable, foul, inclement, raw, rough, squally, stormy, tempestuous, turbulent, unpleasant ♦ [5] catty, cruel, hateful, malevolent, malicious, malign, malignant, mean, spiteful, virulent

nat *abbr* **1** national **2** native **3** natural

na•tal \ˈnāt-ᵊl\ *adj* **1 :** NATIVE **2 :** of, relating to, or present at birth

na•ta•to•ri•um \ˌnā-tə-ˈtōr-ē-əm, ˌna-\ *n* **:** a swimming pool especially indoors

na•tion \ˈnā-shən\ *n* **1 :** NATIONALITY 5; *also* **:** a politically organized nationality **2** ♦ **:** a community of people composed of one or more nationalities with its own territory and government **3 :** the territory of a nation **4 :** a federation of tribes (as of American Indians) — **na•tion•hood** *n*

♦ commonwealth, country, land, sovereignty, state

¹na•tion•al \ˈna-shə-nəl\ *adj* **1** ♦ **:** of or relating to a nation **2 :** comprising or characteristic of a nationality **3 :** FEDERAL 3 — **na•tion•al•ly** *adv*

♦ civil, public, state

²national *n* **1 :** one who owes allegiance to a nation **2 :** a competition that is national in scope — usually used in plural

National Guard *n* **1 :** a militia force recruited by each state of the U.S., equipped by the federal government, and jointly maintained subject to the call of either **2** *often not cap* **:** a military force serving as a national constabulary and defense force

na•tion•al•ise *chiefly Brit var of* NATIONALIZE

na•tion•al•ism \ˈna-shə-nə-ˌli-zəm\ *n* **:** devotion to national interests, unity, and independence

na•tion•al•ist \-list\ *n* **1 :** an advocate of or believer in nationalism **2** *cap* **:** a member of a political party or group advocating national independence or strong national government — **nationalist** *adj, often cap* — **na•tion•al•is•tic** \ˌna-shə-nə-ˈlis-tik\ *adj*

na•tion•al•i•ty \ˌna-shə-ˈna-lə-tē\ *n, pl* **-ties** **1 :** national character **2 :** a legal relationship involving allegiance of an individual and protection on the part of the state **3 :** membership in a particular nation **4 :** political independence or existence as a separate nation **5 :** a people having a common origin, tradition, and language and capable of forming a state **6 :** an ethnic group within a larger unit (as a nation)

na•tion•al•ize \ˈna-shə-nə-ˌlīz\ *vb* **-ized; -iz•ing** **1 :** to make national **:** make a nation of **2 :** to remove from private ownership and place under government control — **na•tion•al•i•za•tion** \ˌna-shə-nə-lə-ˈzā-shən\ *n*

national monument *n* **:** a place of historic, scenic, or scientific interest set aside for preservation usually by presidential proclamation

national park *n* **:** an area of special scenic, historical, or scientific importance set aside and maintained by a national government especially for recreation or study

national seashore *n* **:** a recreational area adjacent to a seacoast and maintained by the federal government

na•tion•wide \ˌnā-shən-ˈwīd\ *adj* **:** extending throughout a nation

¹na•tive \ˈnā-tiv\ *adj* **1 :** INBORN, NATURAL **2** ♦ **:** born in a particular place or country **3 :** belonging to a person because of the place or circumstances of birth ⟨her ~ language⟩ **4** ♦ **:** grown, produced, or originating in a particular place **:** INDIGENOUS **5** ♦ **:** left or remaining in a natural state **:** being without embellishment or artificial change

♦ [2, 4] aboriginal, born, endemic, indigenous ♦ [5] crude, natural, raw, undressed, unprocessed, unrefined, untreated

²native *n* **:** one that is native; *esp* **:** a person who belongs to a particular country by birth

Native American *n* **:** a member of any of the aboriginal peoples of the western hemisphere except often the Eskimos; *esp* **:** an American Indian of North America and especially the U.S. **:** AMERICAN INDIAN

na•tiv•ism \ˈnā-ti-ˌvi-zəm\ *n* **1 :** a policy of favoring native inhabitants over immigrants **2 :** the revival or perpetuation of a native culture especially in opposition to acculturation

na•tiv•i•ty \nə-ˈti-və-tē, nā-\ *n, pl* **-ties** **1 :** the process or circumstances of being born **:** BIRTH **2** *cap* **:** the birth of Christ

natl *abbr* national

NATO \ˈnā-(ˌ)tō\ *abbr* North Atlantic Treaty Organization

nat•ty \ˈna-tē\ *adj* **nat•ti•er; -est** ♦ **:** trimly neat and tidy **:** SMART — **nat•ti•ly** \-tə-lē\ *adv* — **nat•ti•ness** \-tē-nəs\ *n*

♦ dapper, sharp, smart, spruce

¹nat•u•ral \ˈna-chə-rəl\ *adj* **1** ♦ **:** determined by nature **:** INBORN, INNATE ⟨~ ability⟩ **2 :** having a specified character by nature **:** BORN ⟨a ~ fool⟩ **3 :** not recognized as lawful offspring; *specif* **:** born of parents not married to each other **4 :** HUMAN **5** ♦ **:** of or relating to nature **6** ♦ **:** not artificial **7** ♦ **:** being simple and sincere **:** not affected **8** ♦ **:** closely resembling an original **:** true to nature **9 :** being neither sharp nor flat

♦ [1] essential, inborn, ingrained, inherent, innate, integral, intrinsic ♦ [5] uncultivated, untamed, wild ♦ [6] crude, native, raw, undressed, unprocessed, unrefined, untreated ♦ [7] artless, genuine, honest, ingenuous, innocent, naive, real, simple, sincere, true, unaffected, unpretentious ♦ [8] lifelike, near, realistic *Ant* unrealistic

²natural *n* **1 :** IDIOT **2 :** a character ♮ placed on a line or space of the musical staff to nullify the effect of a preceding sharp or flat **3 :** one obviously suitable for a purpose **4 :** AFRO

natural childbirth *n* **:** a system of managing childbirth in which the mother prepares to remain conscious and assist in delivery with little or no use of drugs

natural gas *n* **:** a combustible gaseous mixture of hydrocarbons coming from the earth's crust and used chiefly as a fuel and raw material

natural history *n* **1 :** a treatise on some aspect of nature **2 :** the study of natural objects especially from an amateur or popular point of view

nat•u•ral•ise *chiefly Brit var of* NATURALIZE

nat•u•ral•ism \ˈna-chə-rə-ˌli-zəm\ *n* **1 :** action or thought based only on natural desires and instincts **2 :** a doctrine that denies a supernatural explanation of the origin or development of the universe and holds that scientific laws account for all of nature **3 :** realism in art and literature — **nat•u•ral•is•tic** \ˌna-chə-rə-ˈlis-tik\ *adj*

nat•u•ral•ist \-list\ *n* **1 :** one that advocates or practices naturalism **2 :** a student of animals or plants especially in the field

nat•u•ral•ize \-ˌlīz\ *vb* **-ized; -iz•ing** **1 :** to become or cause to become established as if native ⟨~ new forage crops⟩ **2 :** to confer the rights of a citizen on — **nat•u•ral•i•za•tion** \ˌna-chə-rə-lə-ˈzā-shən\ *n*

nat•u•ral•ly \ˈna-chə-rə-lē, ˈnach-rə-\ *adv* **1** ♦ **:** by nature **:** by natural character or ability **2** ♦ **:** as might be expected **3** ♦ **:** without artificial aid; *also* **:** without affectation **4 :** REALISTICALLY

♦ [1] constitutionally, inherently, innately, intrinsically ♦ [2] commonly, generally, normally, ordinarily, typically, usually *Ant* abnormally, atypically, extraordinarily, uncommonly, unusually ♦ [3] artlessly, ingenuously, naively, unaffectedly *Ant* affectedly, artificially, hypocritically, insincerely, pretentiously, unnaturally

nat•u•ral•ness *n* ♦ **:** the quality or state of being natural

♦ artlessness, greenness, ingenuousness, innocence, naïveté, simplicity, unworldliness

natural science *n* **:** a science (as physics, chemistry, or biology) that deals with matter, energy, and their interrelations and transformations or with objectively measurable phenomena — **natural scientist** *n*

natural selection *n* **:** the natural process that results in the survival of individuals or groups best adjusted to their environment

na•ture \ˈnā-chər\ *n* **1** ♦ **:** the inherent quality or basic constitution of a person or thing **2** ♦ **:** a kind or class usually distinguished by fundamental or essential characteristics **3** ♦ **:** the fundamental character, disposition, or temperament of a living being usually innate and unchangeable **:** TEMPERAMENT, DISPOSITION **4** ♦ **:** the physical universe **5 :** one's natural instincts or way of life ⟨quirks of human ~⟩; *also* **:** primitive state ⟨a return to ~⟩ **6** ♦ **:** natural scenery or environment ⟨beauties of ~⟩

♦ [1] essence, quintessence, soul, stuff, substance ♦ [1] character, complexion, constitution, genius, personality, tone ♦ [2] breed, class, description, feather, ilk, kind, like, manner, order, sort, species, type ♦ [3] disposition, grain, temper, temperament ♦ [4] cosmos, creation, macrocosm, universe, world ♦ [6] open, outdoors, wild, wilderness

naught \'nȯt, 'nät\ *n* **1 :** NOTHING **2** ♦ **:** the arithmetical symbol 0 **:** ZERO

♦ aught, cipher, nil, nothing, zero, zip

naugh•ty \'nȯ-tē, 'nä-\ *adj* **naugh•ti•er; -est 1** ♦ **:** guilty of disobedience or misbehavior **2 :** lacking in taste or propriety — **naugh•ti•ly** \-tə-lē\ *adv* — **naugh•ti•ness** \-tē-nəs\ *n*

♦ bad, contrary, errant, froward, mischievous *Ant* behaved, behaving, nice, orderly

nau•sea \'nȯ-zē-ə, -sē-; 'nȯ-zhə, -shə\ *n* **1** ♦ **:** sickness of the stomach with a desire to vomit **2** ♦ **:** extreme disgust

♦ [1] queasiness, sickness, squeamishness ♦ [2] aversion, disgust, distaste, loathing, repugnance, repulsion, revulsion

nau•se•ate \'nȯ-zē-,āt, -sē-, -zhē-, -shē-\ *vb* **-at•ed; -at•ing** ♦ **:** to affect or become affected with nausea — **nau•se•at•ing•ly** *adv*

♦ disgust, repel, repulse, revolt, sicken, turn off

nauseating *adj* ♦ **:** causing nausea or especially disgust

♦ distasteful, noisome, offensive, repellent, repugnant, repulsive, revolting, ugly

nau•seous \'nȯ-shəs, -zē-əs\ *adj* **1 :** causing nausea or disgust **2** ♦ **:** affected with nausea or disgust

♦ ill, queasy, queer, sick, squeamish

naut *abbr* nautical

nau•ti•cal \'nȯ-ti-kəl\ *adj* **:** of or relating to sailors, navigation, or ships — **nau•ti•cal•ly** \-k(ə-)lē\ *adv*

nautical mile *n* **:** a unit of distance equal to about 6080 feet (1852 meters)

nau•ti•lus \'nȯt-ᵊl-əs\ *n, pl* **-lus•es** *or* **-li** \-ᵊl-,ī, -,ē\ **:** any of a genus of sea mollusks related to the octopuses but having a spiral chambered shell

nav *abbr* **1** naval **2** navigable; navigation

Na•va•jo *also* **Na•va•ho** \'na-və-,hō, 'nä-\ *n, pl* **-jo** *or* **-jos** *also* **-ho** *or* **-hos :** a member of an American Indian people of northern New Mexico and Arizona; *also* **:** their language

na•val \'nā-vəl\ *adj* **:** of, relating to, or possessing a navy

naval stores *n pl* **:** products (as pitch, turpentine, or rosin) obtained from resinous conifers (as pines)

nave \'nāv\ *n* **:** the central part of a church running lengthwise

na•vel \'nā-vəl\ *n* **:** a depression in the middle of the abdomen that marks the point of attachment of fetus and mother

navel–gaz•ing \'nā-vəl-'gā-ziŋ\ *n* **:** useless or excessive self-contemplation

navel orange *n* **:** a seedless orange having a pit at the blossom end where the fruit encloses a small secondary fruit

nav•i•ga•ble \'na-vi-gə-bəl\ *adj* **1 :** capable of being navigated ⟨a ~ river⟩ **2 :** capable of being steered — **nav•i•ga•bil•i•ty** \,na-vi-gə-'bi-lə-tē\ *n*

nav•i•gate \'na-və-,gāt\ *vb* **-gat•ed; -gat•ing 1 :** to sail on or through ⟨~ the Atlantic Ocean⟩ **2 :** to steer or direct the course of a ship or aircraft **3 :** MOVE; *esp* **:** WALK ⟨could hardly ~⟩ **4** ♦ **:** to travel by water **:** SAIL — **nav•i•ga•tion** \,na-və-'gā-shən\ *n*

♦ boat, cruise, sail, voyage

nav•i•ga•tor \'na-və-,gā-tər\ *n* **:** one that navigates or is qualified to navigate

na•vy \'nā-vē\ *n, pl* **navies 1 :** FLEET; *also* **:** the warships belonging to a nation **2** *often cap* **:** a nation's organization for naval warfare

navy yard *n* **:** a yard where naval vessels are built or repaired

na•wab \nə-'wäb\ *n* ♦ **:** a person of great wealth or prominence **:** NABOB

♦ big leaguer, big shot, bigwig, kingpin, nabob, wheel

[1]nay \'nā\ *adv* **:** NO

[2]nay *n* **1 :** a negative vote; *also* **:** a person casting such a vote **2 :** refusal to satisfy a request or desire

[3]nay *conj* ♦ **:** not merely this but also **:** not only so but ⟨he was happy, ~, ecstatic⟩

♦ even, indeed, truly, verily, yea

nay•say•er \'nā-,sā-ər\ *n* **:** one who denies, refuses, or opposes something

Na•zi \'nät-sē, 'nat-\ *n* **:** a member of a German fascist party controlling Germany from 1933 to 1945 under Adolf Hitler — **Nazi** *adj* — **Na•zism** \'nät-,si-zəm, 'nat-\ *also* **Na•zi•ism** \-sē-,i-zəm\ *n*

Nb *symbol* niobium

NB *abbr* **1** New Brunswick **2** nota bene

NBA *abbr* **1** National Basketball Association **2** National Boxing Association

NBC *abbr* National Broadcasting Company

NBS *abbr* National Bureau of Standards

NC *abbr* **1** no charge **2** North Carolina

NCAA *abbr* National Collegiate Athletic Association

NCO \,en-,sē-'ō\ *n* **:** NONCOMMISSIONED OFFICER

nd *abbr* no date

Nd *symbol* neodymium

ND *abbr* North Dakota

N Dak *abbr* North Dakota

Ne *symbol* neon

NE *abbr* **1** Nebraska **2** New England **3** northeast

[1]Ne•an•der•thal \nē-'an-dər-,thȯl, nā-'än-dər-,täl\ *adj* **1** *or* **Ne•an•der•tal** \-,täl\ **:** of, relating to, or being an extinct Old World hominid that lived from about 200,000 to 30,000 years ago **2** ♦ **:** suggestive of a caveman

♦ barbarous, heathen, heathenish, rude, savage, uncivil, uncivilized, uncultivated, wild

[2]Neanderthal *or* **Neandertal** *n* ♦ **:** one who suggests a caveman in appearance, mentality, or behavior

♦ clod, gawk, hulk, lout, lubber, lug, oaf

neap tide \'nēp-\ *n* **:** a tide of minimum range occurring at the first and third quarters of the moon

[1]near \'nir\ *adv* **1** ♦ **:** at, within, or to a short distance or time **2 :** very nearly but not exactly or entirely **:** ALMOST

♦ around, by, close, hard, in, nearby, nigh *Ant* far

[2]near *prep* ♦ **:** close to

♦ about, around, by, next to

[3]near *adj* **1 :** closely related or associated; *also* **:** INTIMATE **2** ♦ **:** not far away; *also* **:** being the closer or left-hand member of a pair **3 :** barely avoided ⟨a ~ accident⟩ **4 :** DIRECT, SHORT ⟨by the ~*est* route⟩ **5 :** STINGY **6** ♦ **:** not real but very like ⟨~ silk⟩ **7 :** being the closer of two

♦ [2] close, immediate, nearby, nigh ♦ [6] lifelike, natural, realistic

[4]near *vb* **1** ♦ **:** to come closer in space or time **:** APPROACH **2 :** to draw near to

♦ advance, approach, close

near beer *n* **:** any of various malt liquors low in alcohol

[1]near•by \nir-'bī, 'nir-,bī\ *adj* ♦ **:** close at hand

♦ close, immediate, near, nigh

[2]near•by \nir-'bī, 'nir-,bī\ *adv* ♦ **:** close at hand

♦ around, by, close, hard, in, near, nigh

near•ly *adv* **1 :** in a close manner or relationship **2** ♦ **:** almost but not quite

♦ about, almost, most, much, near, next to, nigh, practically, some, virtually, well-nigh

near•ness *n* **1** ♦ **:** the quality or state of being near **2** ♦ **:** the state of being in a close personal relationship especially marked by affection or love

♦ [1] closeness, contiguity, immediacy, proximity ♦ [2] closeness, familiarity, intimacy

near•sight•ed \'nir-'sī-təd\ *adj* **:** able to see near things more clearly than distant ones **:** MYOPIC — **near•sight•ed•ly** *adv* — **near•sight•ed•ness** *n*

neat \'nēt\ *adj* **1** ♦ **:** being orderly and clean **2** ♦ **:** not mixed or diluted ⟨~ brandy⟩ **3 :** marked by tasteful simplicity **4 :** PRECISE, SYSTEMATIC **5 :** SKILLFUL, ADROIT **6 :** superior in character, nature, ability, or prospects **:** FINE — **neat** *adv* — **neat•ly** *adv* — **neat•ness** *n*

♦ [1] crisp, orderly, shipshape, snug, tidy, trim, uncluttered *Ant* disheveled, disordered, disorderly, messy, mussed, mussy, slovenly, unkempt, untidy ♦ [2] absolute, fine, plain, pure, refined, straight, unadulterated, undiluted, unmixed

neath \'nēth\ *prep, dial* **:** BENEATH

neat•nik \'nēt-nik\ *n* **:** a person who is compulsively neat

neb \'neb\ *n* **1 :** the beak of a bird or tortoise; *also* **:** NOSE, SNOUT **2 :** NIB

Neb *or* **Nebr** *abbr* Nebraska

NEB *abbr* New English Bible

neb•u•la \'ne-byə-lə\ *n, pl* **-lae** \-,lē, -,lī\ *also* **-las 1 :** any of nu-

merous clouds of gas or dust in interstellar space **2 :** GALAXY — **neb·u·lar** \-lər\ *adj*
neb·u·liz·er \ˈne-byə-ˌlī-zər\ *n* **:** ATOMIZER
neb·u·lous \ˈne-byə-ləs\ *adj* **1 :** of or relating to a nebula **2 a** ♦ **:** lacking clarity of feature or sharpness of outline **:** HAZY, INDISTINCT **b** ♦ **:** vaguely defined **:** dimly realized

♦ bleary, dim, faint, foggy, fuzzy, hazy, indefinite, indistinct, indistinguishable, murky, obscure, opaque, shadowy, unclear, undefined, undetermined, vague

nec·es·sar·i·ly \ˌne-sə-ˈser-ə-lē\ *adv* ♦ **:** of necessity

♦ inevitably, needs, perforce, unavoidably

¹nec·es·sary \ˈne-sə-ˌser-ē\ *n, pl* **-sar·ies :** an indispensable item
²necessary *adj* **1** ♦ **:** of an inevitable nature **:** INEVITABLE, INESCAPABLE; *also* **:** CERTAIN **2 :** PREDETERMINED **3** ♦ **:** containing or constituting a command **:** COMPULSORY **4** ♦ **:** positively needed **:** INDISPENSABLE

♦ [1] certain, inescapable, inevitable, sure, unavoidable ♦ [3] compulsory, imperative, incumbent, involuntary, mandatory, nonelective, obligatory, peremptory ♦ [4] essential, imperative, indispensable, integral, needful, requisite, vital

ne·ces·si·tate \ni-ˈse-sə-ˌtāt\ *vb* **-tat·ed; -tat·ing** ♦ **:** to make necessary

♦ demand, need, require, take, want, warrant

ne·ces·si·tous \ni-ˈse-sə-təs\ *adj* **1 :** NEEDY, IMPOVERISHED **2 :** URGENT **3 :** NECESSARY
ne·ces·si·ty \ni-ˈse-sə-tē\ *n, pl* **-ties 1 :** conditions that cannot be changed **2 :** WANT, POVERTY **3** ♦ **:** something that is necessary **4 :** very great need

♦ condition, demand, essential, must, need, requirement, requisite

¹neck \ˈnek\ *n* **1 :** the part of the body connecting the head and the trunk **2 :** the part of a garment covering or near to the neck **3 :** a relatively narrow part suggestive of a neck ⟨~ of a bottle⟩ ⟨~ of land⟩ **4 :** a narrow margin especially of victory ⟨won by a ~⟩ — **necked** \ˈnekt\ *adj*
²neck *vb* **:** to kiss and caress amorously
neck and neck *adj* ♦ **:** being very close (as in margin or standing)

♦ close, narrow, nip and tuck, tight

neck and neck *adv* **:** very close (as in a race)
neck·er·chief \ˈne-kər-chəf, -ˌchēf\ *n, pl* **-chiefs** \-chəfs, -ˌchēfs\ *also* **-chieves** \-ˌchēvz\ **:** a square of cloth worn folded about the neck like a scarf
neck·lace \ˈne-kləs\ *n* **:** an ornament worn around the neck
neck·line \ˈnek-ˌlīn\ *n* **:** the outline of the neck opening of a garment
neck·tie \-ˌtī\ *n* **:** a strip of cloth worn around the neck and tied in front
ne·crol·o·gy \nə-ˈkrä-lə-jē\ *n, pl* **-gies 1 :** OBITUARY **2 :** a list of the recently dead
nec·ro·man·cer \ˈne-krə-ˌman-sər\ *n* ♦ **:** one that practices necromancy

♦ conjurer, enchanter, magician, sorcerer, voodoo, witch, wizard

nec·ro·man·cy \ˈne-krə-ˌman-sē\ *n* **1 :** the art or practice of conjuring up the spirits of the dead for purposes of magically revealing the future **2** ♦ **:** the use of means (as charms or spells) believed to have supernatural power over natural forces **:** MAGIC, SORCERY

♦ bewitchment, enchantment, magic, sorcery, witchcraft, wizardry

ne·crop·o·lis \nə-ˈkrä-pə-ləs, ne-\ *n, pl* **-lis·es** *or* **-les** \-ˌlēz\ *or* **-leis** \-ˌlās\ *or* **-li** \-ˌlī, -ˌlē\ **:** CEMETERY; *esp* **:** a large elaborate cemetery of an ancient city
ne·cro·sis \nə-ˈkrō-səs, ne-\ *n, pl* **ne·cro·ses** \-ˌsēz\ **:** usually local death of body tissue — **ne·crot·ic** \-ˈkrä-tik\ *adj*
nec·tar \ˈnek-tər\ *n* **1 :** the drink of the Greek and Roman gods; *also* **:** any delicious drink **2 :** a sweet plant secretion that is the raw material of honey
nec·tar·ine \ˌnek-tə-ˈrēn\ *n* **:** a smooth-skinned peach
née *or* **nee** \ˈnā\ *adj* — used to identify a woman by her maiden family name
¹need \ˈnēd\ *n* **1** ♦ **:** necessary duty **:** OBLIGATION ⟨no ~ to hurry⟩ **2** ♦ **:** a lack of something requisite, desirable, or useful **3 :** a condition requiring supply or relief ⟨when the ~ arises⟩ **4** ♦ **:** lack of the means of subsistence **:** POVERTY **5** ♦ **:** a requirement for the well-being of an organism

♦ [1] burden, charge, commitment, duty, obligation, responsibility ♦ [2] absence, lack, want ♦ [4] beggary, destitution, impecuniousness, impoverishment, indigence, pauperism, penury, poverty, want ♦ [5] condition, demand, essential, must, necessity, requirement, requisite

²need *vb* **1 :** to be in want **2** ♦ **:** to have cause or occasion for **:** REQUIRE ⟨he ~*s* advice⟩ **3** ♦ **:** to be under obligation or necessity ⟨we ~ to know the truth⟩

♦ [2] demand, necessitate, require, take, want, warrant ***Ant*** have, hold ♦ **need to** [3] have, must, ought, shall, should

need·ful \ˈnēd-fəl\ *adj* ♦ **:** absolutely needed **:** NECESSARY, REQUISITE

♦ essential, imperative, indispensable, integral, necessary, requisite, vital

¹nee·dle \ˈnēd-ᵊl\ *n* **1 :** a slender pointed usually steel implement used in sewing **2 :** a slender rod (as for knitting, controlling a small opening, or transmitting vibrations to or from a recording) ⟨a phonograph ~⟩ **3** ♦ **:** a slender hollow instrument by which material is introduced into or withdrawn from the body **4** ♦ **:** a slender indicator on a dial **5 :** a needle-shaped leaf (as of a pine)

♦ [3] hypodermic syringe, syringe ♦ [4] hand, index, indicator, pointer

²needle *vb* **nee·dled; nee·dling 1** ♦ **:** to vex by repeated sharp prods or gibes; *esp* **:** to incite to action by repeated gibes **2** ♦ **:** to disturb or annoy by persistent irritating or provoking especially in a petty or mischievous way

♦ [1] henpeck, hound, nag ♦ [2] bait, bug, hassle, heckle, ride, taunt, tease

nee·dle-nose pliers \ˈnē-dᵊl-ˌnōz-\ *n pl* **:** pliers with long slender jaws for grasping small or thin objects
nee·dle·point \ˈnē-dᵊl-ˌpȯint\ *n* **1 :** lace worked with a needle over a paper pattern **2 :** embroidery done on canvas across counted threads — **needlepoint** *adj*
need·less \ˈnēd-ləs\ *adj* **:** not necessary — **need·less·ly** *adv* — **need·less·ness** *n*
nee·dle·wom·an \ˈnēd-ᵊl-ˌwu̇-mən\ *n* **:** a woman who does needlework; *esp* **:** SEAMSTRESS
nee·dle·work \-ˌwərk\ *n* **:** work done with a needle; *esp* **:** work (as embroidery) other than plain sewing
needs \ˈnēdz\ *adv* ♦ **:** of necessity **:** NECESSARILY ⟨must ~ be recognized⟩

♦ inevitably, necessarily, perforce, unavoidably ***Ant*** unnecessarily

needy \ˈnē-dē\ *adj* **need·i·er; -est** ♦ **:** being in want **:** POVERTY-STRICKEN

♦ broke, destitute, impecunious, indigent, penniless, penurious, poor, poverty-stricken

ne'er \ˈner\ *adv* **:** NEVER
ne'er–do–well \ˈner-du̇-ˌwel\ *n* **:** an idle worthless person — **ne'er–do–well** *adj*
ne·far·i·ous \ni-ˈfar-ē-əs\ *adj* ♦ **:** very wicked **:** EVIL — **ne·far·i·ous·ly** *adv*

♦ bad, black, evil, immoral, iniquitous, rotten, sinful, unethical, unsavory, vicious, vile, villainous, wicked, wrong

neg *abbr* negative
ne·gate \ni-ˈgāt\ *vb* **ne·gat·ed; ne·gat·ing 1** ♦ **:** to deny the existence or truth of **2** ♦ **:** to cause to be ineffective or invalid **:** NULLIFY

♦ [1] contradict, deny, disallow, disavow, disclaim, gainsay, negative, reject, repudiate ♦ [2] abolish, abrogate, annul, cancel, dissolve, invalidate, nullify, quash, repeal, rescind, void

ne·ga·tion \ni-ˈgā-shən\ *n* **1** ♦ **:** the action or operation of negating or making negative **2 :** a negative doctrine or statement

♦ contradiction, denial, disallowance, disavowal, disclaimer, rejection, repudiation

¹neg·a·tive \ˈne-gə-tiv\ *adj* **1** ♦ **:** marked by denial, prohibition, or refusal ⟨a ~ reply⟩ **2 :** not positive or constructive; *esp* **:** not affirming the presence of what is sought or suspected to be present ⟨test results were ~⟩ **3 :** less than zero ⟨a ~ number⟩ **4 :** being, relating to, or charged with electricity of which the electron is the elementary unit **5 :** having the light and dark parts opposite to what they were in the original photographic subject — **neg·a·tive·ly** *adv* — **neg·a·tive·ness** *n* — **neg·a·tiv·i·ty** \ˌne-gə-ˈti-və-tē\ *n*

♦ adverse, counter, disadvantageous, hostile, inimical, prejudicial, unfavorable (*or* unfavourable), unfriendly, unsympathetic

[2]negative *n* **1 :** a negative word or statement **2 :** a negative vote or reply; *also* **:** REFUSAL **3** ♦ **:** something that is the opposite or negation of something else **4 :** the side that votes or argues for the opposition (as in a debate) **5 :** a negative number **6 :** a negative photographic image on transparent material

♦ antipode, antithesis, contrary, opposite, reverse

[3]negative *vb* **-tived; -tiv•ing 1 :** to refuse to accept or approve **2** ♦ **:** to vote against **3 :** DISPROVE **4 :** to imply the opposite or a denial of **5** ♦ **:** to deny the truth, reality, or validity of

♦ [2] blackball, kill, veto ***Ant*** confirm, ratify ♦ [5] contradict, deny, disallow, disavow, disclaim, gainsay, negate, reject, repudiate

negative income tax *n* **:** a system of federal subsidy payments to families with incomes below a stipulated level

neg•a•tiv•ism \ˈne-gə-ti-ˌvi-zəm\ *n* **:** an attitude of skepticism and denial of nearly everything affirmed or suggested by others

[1]ne•glect \ni-ˈglekt\ *vb* **1** ♦ **:** to give little attention or respect to **:** DISREGARD **2** ♦ **:** to leave undone or unattended to especially through carelessness

♦ [1] disregard, forget, ignore, overlook, pass over, slight, slur ***Ant*** attend (to), heed, mind, regard, tend (to) ♦ [2] fail, forget, omit

[2]neglect *n* **1** ♦ **:** an act or instance of neglecting something **2** ♦ **:** the condition of being neglected

♦ [1] default, delinquency, dereliction, failure, negligence, oversight ♦ [2] desolation, dilapidation, disrepair ***Ant*** repair

ne•glect•ed \ni-ˈglek-təd\ *adj* ♦ **:** that evidences improper or insufficient attention or care

♦ dilapidated, grungy, mean, ratty, seedy, shabby

ne•glect•ful *adj* **:** given to neglecting

neg•li•gee *also* **neg•li•gé** \ˌne-glə-ˈzhā\ *n* **:** a woman's long flowing dressing gown

neg•li•gence \ˈne-gli-jəns\ *n* **1** ♦ **:** the quality or state of being negligent **2** ♦ **:** an act or instance of being negligent

♦ [1] carelessness, dereliction, heedlessness, laxness, remissness, slackness ***Ant*** care, carefulness, caution, cautiousness, heedfulness ♦ [2] default, delinquency, dereliction, failure, neglect, oversight

neg•li•gent \ˈne-gli-jənt\ *adj* ♦ **:** marked by neglect — **neg•li•gent•ly** *adv*

♦ careless, derelict, lax, remiss, slack ***Ant*** attentive, careful, conscientious

neg•li•gi•ble \ˈne-gli-jə-bəl\ *adj* ♦ **:** so small or unimportant or of so little consequence as to warrant little or no attention

♦ inconsequential, inconsiderable, insignificant, measly, minute, nominal, paltry, petty, slight, trifling, trivial, unimportant ***Ant*** big, consequential, considerable, important, material, significant

ne•go•tiant \ni-ˈgō-shē-ənt\ *n* **:** NEGOTIATOR

ne•go•ti•ate \ni-ˈgō-shē-ˌāt\ *vb* **-at•ed; -at•ing 1** ♦ **:** to confer with another so as to arrive at the settlement of some matter; *also* **:** to arrange for or bring about by such conferences ⟨~ a treaty⟩ **2 :** to transfer to another by delivery or endorsement in return for equivalent value ⟨~ a check⟩ **3 :** to get through, around, or over successfully ⟨~ a turn⟩ **4** ♦ **:** to deal with (some matter or affair that requires ability for its successful handling) — **ne•go•tia•ble** \-shə-bəl, -shē-ə-\ *adj* — **ne•go•ti•a•tor** \-ˈgō-shē-ˌā-tər\ *n*

♦ [1] arrange, concert, conclude ♦ [4] contend with, cope with, grapple with, handle, manage, maneuver (*or* manoeuvre), swing, treat

ne•go•ti•a•tion \ni-ˌgō-sē-ˈā-shən, -shē-\ *n* ♦ **:** the action or process of negotiating or being negotiated

♦ accommodation, compromise, concession, give-and-take

ne•gri•tude \ˈne-grə-ˌtüd, -ˌtyüd, ˈnē-\ *n* **:** a consciousness of and pride in one's African heritage

Ne•gro \ˈnē-grō\ *n, pl* **Negroes** *sometimes offensive* **:** a member of the human race native to Africa and classified according to physical features (as dark skin pigmentation) — **Negro** *adj, sometimes offensive* — **Ne•groid** \ˈnē-ˌgrȯid\ *n or adj, often not cap*

Neh *abbr* Nehemiah

Ne•he•mi•ah \ˌnē-ə-ˈmī-ə\ *n* **:** a book of Jewish and Christian Scripture

neigh \ˈnā\ *n* **:** a loud prolonged cry of a horse — **neigh** *vb*

[1]neigh•bor *or Can and Brit* **neigh•bour** \ˈnā-bər\ *n* **1 :** one living or located near another **2 :** FELLOW MAN

[2]neighbor *or Can and Brit* **neigh•bour** *vb* ♦ **:** to be next to or near to **:** border on

♦ abut, adjoin, border (on), flank, fringe, join, skirt, touch, verge (on)

neigh•bor•hood \ˈnā-bər-ˌhu̇d\ *or Can and Brit* **neigh•bour•hood** \ˈnā-bər-ˌhu̇d\ *n* **1 :** NEARNESS **2 :** a place or region near **:** VICINITY; *also* **:** a number or amount near ⟨costs in the ~ of $10⟩ **3 :** the people living near one another **4** ♦ **:** a section lived in by neighbors and usually having distinguishing characteristics

♦ district, quarter, section

neigh•bor•li•ness *or Can and Brit* **neigh•bour•li•ness** \ˈnā-bər-lē-nəs\ *n* ♦ **:** the quality or state of being neighborly

♦ amity, benevolence, cordiality, fellowship, friendliness, friendship, goodwill, kindliness

neigh•bor•ly *or Can and Brit* **neigh•bour•ly** \ˈnā-bər-lē\ *adj* ♦ **:** befitting congenial neighbors; *esp* **:** FRIENDLY

♦ amicable, companionable, comradely, cordial, friendly, genial, hearty, warm, warmhearted

neighbour *Can and Brit var of* NEIGHBOUR

[1]nei•ther \ˈnē-t͟hər, ˈnī-\ *pron* **:** neither one **:** not the one and not the other ⟨~ of the two⟩

[2]neither *conj* **1 :** not either ⟨~ good nor bad⟩ **2 :** NOR ⟨~ did I⟩

[3]neither *adj* **:** not either ⟨~ hand⟩

nel•son \ˈnel-sən\ *n* **:** a wrestling hold in which one applies leverage against an opponent's arm, neck, and head

nem•a•tode \ˈne-mə-ˌtōd\ *n* **:** any of a phylum of elongated cylindrical worms parasitic in animals or plants or free-living in soil or water

nem•e•sis \ˈne-mə-səs\ *n, pl* **-e•ses** \-ˌsēz\ **1** ♦ **:** one that inflicts retribution or vengeance **2 :** a formidable and usually victorious rival **3** ♦ **:** an act or effect of retribution; *also* **:** CURSE

♦ [1] avenger, castigator, scourge ♦ [3] castigation, chastisement, correction, curse, desert, discipline, penalty, punishment, wrath

neo•clas•sic \ˌnē-ō-ˈkla-sik\ *or* **neo•clas•si•cal** \-si-kəl\ *adj* **:** of or relating to a revival or adaptation of the classical style especially in literature, art, or music

neo•co•lo•nial•ism \ˌnē-ō-kə-ˈlō-nē-ə-ˌli-zəm\ *n* **:** the economic and political policies by which a nation indirectly maintains or extends its influence over other areas or peoples — **neo•co•lo•nial** *adj* — **neo•co•lo•nial•ist** \-list\ *n or adj*

neo•con \ˈnē-ō-ˌkän\ *n* **:** NEOCONSERVATIVE

neo•con•ser•va•tive \-kən-ˈsər-və-tiv\ *n* **:** a former liberal espousing political conservatism — **neo•con•ser•va•tism** \-və-ˌti-zəm\ *n* — **neoconservative** *adj*

neo•dym•i•um \ˌnē-ō-ˈdi-mē-əm\ *n* **:** a silver-white to yellow metallic chemical element

neo–im•pres•sion•ism \ˌnē-ō-im-ˈpre-shə-ˌni-zəm\ *n, often cap N&I* **:** a late 19th century French art movement that attempted to make impressionism more precise and to use a pointillist painting technique

Neo•lith•ic \ˌnē-ə-ˈli-thik\ *adj* **:** of or relating to the latest period of the Stone Age characterized by polished stone implements

ne•ol•o•gism \nē-ˈä-lə-ˌji-zəm\ *n* **:** a new word or expression

ne•on \ˈnē-ˌän\ *n* **1 :** a gaseous colorless chemical element used in electric lamps **2 :** a lamp in which a discharge through neon gives a reddish glow — **neon** *adj*

neo•na•tal \ˌnē-ō-ˈnāt-ᵊl\ *adj* **:** of, relating to, or affecting the newborn — **neo•na•tal•ly** *adv*

ne•o•nate \ˈnē-ə-ˌnāt\ *n* **:** a newborn child

neo–pa•gan \ˌnē-ō-ˈpā-gən\ *n* **:** a person who practices a contemporary form of paganism

neo•phyte \ˈnē-ə-ˌfīt\ *n* **1 :** a new convert **:** PROSELYTE **2 :** NOVICE **3** ♦ **:** one that begins something; *esp* **:** an inexperienced person **:** BEGINNER

♦ beginner, fledgling, freshman, greenhorn, newcomer, novice, recruit, rookie, tenderfoot, tyro

neo•plasm \ˈnē-ə-ˌpla-zəm\ *n* ♦ **:** a new growth of tissue serving no useful purpose in the body **:** TUMOR — **neo•plas•tic** \ˌnē-ə-ˈplas-tik\ *adj*

♦ excrescence, growth, lump, tumor

neo•prene \ˈnē-ə-ˌprēn\ *n* **:** a synthetic rubber used especially for special-purpose clothing (as wet suits)
neo•trop•i•cal \ˌnē-ō-ˈträ-pi-kəl\ *adj, often cap* **:** of or relating to a zoogeographic region of America that extends south from the central plateau of Mexico
Ne•pali \nə-ˈpȯ-lē, -ˈpä-\ *n, pl* **Nepali :** a native or inhabitant of Nepal — **Nepali** *adj*
ne•pen•the \nə-ˈpen-thē\ *n* **1 :** a potion used by the ancients to dull pain and sorrow **2 :** something capable of making one forget grief or suffering
neph•ew \ˈne-fyü, *chiefly Brit* -vyü\ *n* **:** a son of one's brother, sister, brother-in-law, or sister-in-law
ne•phrit•ic \ni-ˈfri-tik\ *adj* **1 :** RENAL **2 :** of, relating to, or affected with nephritis
ne•phri•tis \ni-ˈfrī-təs\ *n, pl* **ne•phrit•i•des** \-ˈfri-tə-ˌdēz\ **:** kidney inflammation
ne plus ul•tra \ˌnē-ˌpləs-ˈəl-trə\ *n* **:** the highest point capable of being attained
nep•o•tism \ˈne-pə-ˌti-zəm\ *n* **:** favoritism shown to a relative (as in the granting of jobs)
Nep•tune \ˈnep-ˌtün, -ˌtyün\ *n* **:** the planet 8th in order from the sun — **Nep•tu•ni•an** \nep-ˈtü-nē-ən, -ˈtyü-\ *adj*
nep•tu•ni•um \nep-ˈtü-nē-əm, -ˈtyü-\ *n* **:** a short-lived radioactive element
nerd \ˈnərd\ *n* **:** an unstylish or socially inept person; *esp* ♦ **:** one slavishly devoted to intellectual pursuits — **nerdy** *adj*

♦ egghead, highbrow, intellectual

Ne•re•id \ˈnir-ē-əd\ *n* **:** a sea nymph in Greek mythology
[1]**nerve** \ˈnərv\ *n* **1 :** SINEW, TENDON ⟨strain every ~⟩ **2 :** any of the strands of nervous tissue that carry nerve impulses between the brain and spinal cord and every part of the body **3 a** ♦ **:** power of endurance or control **:** FORTITUDE **b** ♦ **:** the quality or state of being bold **:** BOLDNESS, DARING **4** *pl* **:** NERVOUSNESS **5 :** a vein of a leaf or insect wing — **nerved** \ˈnərvd\ *adj*

♦ [3a] bravery, courage, daring, fearlessness, fortitude, gallantry, guts, hardihood, heart, heroism, stoutness, valor ♦ [3b] audacity, brass, brazenness, cheek, chutzpah, daring, effrontery, gall, presumption, sauce, sauciness, temerity

[2]**nerve** *vb* **nerved; nerv•ing** ♦ **:** to give strength or courage to

♦ brace, forearm, fortify, psych (up), ready, steel, strengthen

nerve cell *n* **:** NEURON; *also* **:** CELL BODY
nerve gas *n* **:** a chemical weapon damaging especially to the nervous and respiratory systems
nerve impulse *n* **:** a physical and chemical change that moves along a process of a neuron after stimulation and carries a record of sensation or an instruction to act
nerve•less *adj* **1** ♦ **:** destitute of strength or courage **2** ♦ **:** exhibiting control or balance

♦ [1] effete, frail, soft, spineless, weak, wimpy, wishy-washy ♦ [2] imperturbable, unflappable, unshakable

nerve–rack•ing *or* **nerve–wrack•ing** \ˈnərv-ˌra-kiŋ\ *adj* **:** extremely trying on the nerves
ner•vous \ˈnər-vəs\ *adj* **1 :** FORCIBLE, SPIRITED **2 :** of, relating to, or made up of neurons or nerves **3** ♦ **:** easily excited or annoyed **:** JUMPY **4** ♦ **:** viewing the future with anxiety or alarm ⟨a ~ smile⟩ **5** ♦ **:** causing physical or mental discomfort — **nervous•ly** *adv*

♦ [3] excitable, flighty, fluttery, high-strung, jittery, jumpy, skittish, spooky ♦ [4] aflutter, anxious, edgy, jittery, jumpy, nervy, perturbed, tense, troubled, uneasy, upset, worried ***Ant*** calm, easy, collected, cool, nerveless, relaxed ♦ [5] anxious, distressful, restless, tense, unsettling, upsetting, worrisome ***Ant*** calming, comfortable, easy, peaceful, quiet, quieting, tranquil

nervous breakdown *n* **:** an attack of mental or emotional disorder of sufficient severity to be incapacitating especially when requiring hospitalization
ner•vous•ness *n* ♦ **:** the quality or state of being nervous

♦ agitation, anxiety, apprehension, care, concern, disquiet, perturbation, uneasiness, worry

nervous system *n* **:** a bodily system that in vertebrates is made up of the brain and spinal cord, nerves, ganglia, and parts of the sense organs and that receives and interprets stimuli and transmits nerve impulses
nervy \ˈnər-vē\ *adj* **nerv•i•er; -est 1** ♦ **:** showing calm courage **2** ♦ **:** marked by impudence or presumption ⟨a ~ salesperson⟩ **3 :** marked by nervousness **:** NERVOUS

♦ [1] adventurous, audacious, bold, daring, enterprising, gutsy, hardy, venturesome ♦ [2] arch, bold, brash, brazen, cheeky, cocky, fresh, impertinent, impudent, insolent, sassy, saucy ***Ant*** meek, mousy, retiring, shy, timid

-ness \nəs\ *n suffix* **:** state **:** condition **:** quality **:** degree ⟨good*ness*⟩
[1]**nest** \ˈnest\ *n* **1 :** the shelter prepared by a bird for its eggs and young **2 :** a place where eggs (as of insects or fish) are laid and hatched **3** ♦ **:** a place of rest, retreat, or lodging **4 :** DEN, HANGOUT ⟨a ~ of thieves⟩ **5 :** the occupants of a nest **6 :** a series of objects (as bowls or tables) fitting inside or under one another

♦ concealment, covert, den, hideout, lair

[2]**nest** *vb* **1 :** to build or occupy a nest **2 :** to fit compactly together or within one another
nest egg *n* ♦ **:** a fund of money accumulated as a reserve

♦ account, budget, deposit, fund, kitty, pool

nes•tle \ˈne-səl\ *vb* **nes•tled; nes•tling 1** ♦ **:** to settle snugly or comfortably **2** ♦ **:** to press closely and affectionately **:** CUDDLE **3 :** to settle, shelter, or house as if in a nest

♦ cuddle, curl up, snug, snuggle

nest•ling \ˈnest-liŋ\ *n* **:** a bird too young to leave its nest
[1]**net** \ˈnet\ *n* **1** ♦ **:** a meshed fabric twisted, knotted, or woven together at regular intervals **2** ♦ **:** a device made all or partly of net and used especially to catch birds, fish, or insects **3** ♦ **:** something made of net used especially for protecting, confining, carrying, or dividing ⟨a tennis ~⟩ **4 :** an entrapping device or situation **:** SNARE, TRAP **5** *often cap* **:** INTERNET

♦ [1] mesh, network ♦ [2, 3] entanglement, snare, web

[2]**net** *vb* **net•ted; net•ting 1 :** to cover or enclose with or as if with a net **2 :** to catch in or as if in a net
[3]**net** *adj* **:** free from all charges or deductions ⟨~ profit⟩ ⟨~ weight⟩
[4]**net** *vb* **net•ted; net•ting :** to gain or produce as profit **:** CLEAR, YIELD ⟨his business *netted* $50,000 a year⟩
[5]**net** *n* ♦ **:** a net amount, profit, weight, or price

♦ earnings, gain, lucre, payoff, proceeds, profit, return

Neth *abbr* Netherlands
neth•er \ˈne-t͟hər\ *adj* **:** situated down or below ⟨the ~ regions of the earth⟩
Neth•er•land•er \ˈne-t͟hər-ˌlan-dər\ *n* **:** a native or inhabitant of the Netherlands
neth•er•most \-ˌmōst\ *adj* **:** LOWEST
neth•er•world \-ˌwərld\ *n* **1 :** the world of the dead **2 :** UNDERWORLD
net•i•quette \ˈne-ti-kət, -ˌket\ *n* **:** etiquette governing communication on the Internet
net•ting *n* **1 :** a fabric or structure of cords or wires that cross at regular intervals and are knotted or secured at the crossings **:** NETWORK **2 :** the act or process of making a net or network
[1]**net•tle** \ˈnet-ᵊl\ *n* **:** any of a genus of coarse herbs with stinging hairs
[2]**nettle** *vb* **net•tled; net•tling** ♦ **:** to arouse to sharp but transitory annoyance or anger **:** VEX, IRRITATE

♦ aggravate, annoy, bother, bug, chafe, exasperate, gall, get, grate, irk, irritate, peeve, persecute, pique, put out, rasp, rile, vex

net•tle•some \ˈnet-ᵊl-səm\ *adj* **:** causing vexation **:** IRRITATING
net•work \ˈnet-ˌwərk\ *n* **1** ♦ **:** a fabric or structure of cords or wires that cross at regular intervals and are knotted or secured at the crossings **:** NET **2 :** a system of elements (as lines or channels) that cross in the manner of the threads in a net **3 :** a group or system of related or connected parts; *esp* **:** a chain of radio or television stations **4 :** a system of computers that are connected (as by telephone wires)

♦ mesh, net

net•work•ing \ˈnet-ˌwər-kiŋ\ *n* **:** the exchange of information or services among individuals, groups, or institutions
neu•ral \ˈnu̇r-əl, ˈnyu̇r-\ *adj* **:** of, relating to, or involving a nerve or the nervous system
neu•ral•gia \nu̇-ˈral-jə, nyu̇-\ *n* **:** acute pain that follows the course of a nerve — **neu•ral•gic** \-jik\ *adj*
neur•as•then•ia \ˌnu̇r-əs-ˈthē-nē-ə\ *n* **:** a psychological disorder marked especially by fatiguing easily, lack of motivation, feelings of inadequacy, and psychosomatic symptoms — **neur•as•then•ic** \-ˈthe-nik, -ˈthē-\ *adj or n*
neu•ri•tis \-ˈrī-təs\ *n, pl* **-rit•i•des** \-ˈri-tə-ˌdēz\ *or* **-ri•tis•es :** inflammation of a nerve — **neu•rit•ic** \-ˈri-tik\ *adj or n*

neu•ro•bi•ol•o•gy \ˌnu̇r-ō-bī-'ä-lə-jē\ *n* : a branch of biology that deals with the nervous system — **neu•ro•bi•o•log•i•cal** \-ˌbī-ə-'lä-ji-kəl\ *adj* — **neu•ro•bi•ol•o•gist** \-bī-'ä-lə-jist\ *n*

neu•rol•o•gy \nu̇-'rä-lə-jē, nyu̇-\ *n* : the scientific study of the nervous system — **neu•ro•log•i•cal** \ˌnu̇r-ə-'lä-ji-kəl, ˌnyu̇r-\ *or* **neu•ro•log•ic** \-jik\ *adj* — **neu•ro•log•i•cal•ly** \-ji-k(ə-)lē\ *adv* — **neu•rol•o•gist** \nu̇-'rä-lə-jist, nyu̇-\ *n*

neu•ro•mus•cu•lar \ˌnu̇r-ō-'məs-kyə-lər, ˌnyu̇r-\ *adj* : of, relating to, or affecting nerves and muscles ⟨a ~ disease⟩

neu•ron \'nü-ˌrän, 'nyü-\ *n* : a cell with specialized processes that is the fundamental functional unit of nervous tissue — **neu•ro•nal** \'nu̇r-ə-nᵊl, 'nyu̇r-\ *adj*

neu•rone \-ˌrōn\ *chiefly Brit var of* NEURON

neu•ro•sci•ence \ˌnu̇r-ō-'sī-əns, ˌnyu̇r-\ *n* : a branch of the life sciences that deals with the anatomy, physiology, biochemistry, or molecular biology of nerves and nervous tissue and especially with their relation to behavior and learning — **neu•ro•sci•en•tist** \-ən-tist\ *n*

neu•ro•sis \nu̇-'rō-səs, nyu̇-\ *n, pl* **-ro•ses** \-ˌsēz\ : a mental and emotional disorder that is less serious than a psychosis, is not characterized by disturbance of the use of language, and is accompanied by various bodily and mental disturbances (as visceral symptoms, anxieties, or phobias)

neu•ro•sur•gery \nu̇r-ō-'sər-jə-rē, ˌnyu̇r-\ *n* : surgery of nervous structures (as nerves, the brain, or the spinal cord) — **neu•ro•sur•geon** \-'sər-jən\ *n*

[1]**neu•rot•ic** \nu̇-'rä-tik, nyu̇-\ *adj* : of, relating to, being, or affected with a neurosis; *also* : NERVOUS — **neu•rot•i•cal•ly** \-ti-k(ə-)lē\ *adv*

[2]**neurotic** *n* : an emotionally unstable or neurotic person

neu•ro•trans•mit•ter \ˌnu̇r-ō-trans-'mi-tər, ˌnyu̇r-, -tranz-\ *n* : a substance (as acetylcholine) that transmits nerve impulses across a synapse

neut *abbr* neuter

[1]**neu•ter** \'nü-tər, 'nyü-\ *adj* **1** : of, relating to, or constituting the gender that includes most words or grammatical forms referring to things classed as neither masculine nor feminine **2** : lacking or having imperfectly developed sex organs

[2]**neuter** *n* **1** : a noun, pronoun, adjective, or inflectional form or class of the neuter gender; *also* : the neuter gender **2** : WORKER 2; *also* : a spayed or castrated animal

[3]**neuter** *vb* : to remove the sex organs of : CASTRATE, SPAY

[1]**neu•tral** \'nü-trəl, 'nyü-\ *n* **1** : one that is neutral **2** : a neutral color **3** : a position of disengagement (as of gears)

[2]**neutral** *adj* **1** ♦ : not favoring either side in a quarrel, contest, or war **2** : of or relating to a neutral state or power **3** : MIDDLING, INDIFFERENT **4** : having no hue : GRAY; *also* : not decided in color **5** : neither acid nor basic ⟨a ~ solution⟩ **6** : not electrically charged

♦ disinterested, impartial, nonpartisan, unbiased *Ant* allied, confederate

neu•tral•ise *chiefly Brit var of* NEUTRALIZE

neu•tral•ism \'nü-trə-ˌli-zəm, 'nyü-\ *n* : a policy or the advocacy of neutrality especially in international affairs

neu•tral•i•ty \nü-'tra-lə-tē, nyü-\ *n* ♦ : the quality or state of being neutral; *esp* : refusal to take part in a war between other powers

♦ detachment, disinterestedness, impartiality, objectivity

neu•tral•ize \'nü-trə-ˌlīz, 'nyü-\ *vb* **-ized; -iz•ing** ♦ : to make neutral; *esp* : to counteract the activity or effect of : COUNTERACT — **neu•tral•i•za•tion** \ˌnü-trə-lə-'zā-shən, ˌnyü-\ *n*

♦ annul, cancel, compensate, correct, counteract, counterbalance, make up, offset

neu•tri•no \nü-'trē-nō, nyü-\ *n, pl* **-nos** : an uncharged elementary particle held to be massless or very light

neu•tron \'nü-ˌträn, 'nyü-\ *n* : an uncharged atomic particle that is nearly equal in mass to the proton

neutron bomb *n* : a nuclear bomb designed to produce lethal neutrons but less blast and fire damage than other nuclear bombs

neutron star *n* : a dense celestial object that results from the collapse of a large star

Nev *abbr* Nevada

nev•er \'ne-vər\ *adv* **1** : not ever **2** ♦ : not in any degree, way, or condition

♦ no, none, nothing, nowise *Ant* anyhow, anyway, anywise, at all, ever, half, however

nev•er•more \ˌne-vər-'mōr\ *adv* : never again

nev•er–nev•er land \ˌne-vər-'ne-vər-\ *n* : an ideal or imaginary place

nev•er•the•less \ˌne-vər-t͟hə-'les\ *adv* ♦ : in spite of that : HOWEVER

♦ but, howbeit, however, nonetheless, notwithstanding, still, though, withal, yet

ne•vus \'nē-vəs\ *n, pl* **ne•vi** \-ˌvī\ : a usually pigmented area on the skin : MOLE

[1]**new** \'nü, 'nyü\ *adj* **1** ♦ : having recently come into existence or occurred; *also* : of or characteristic of the present time : MODERN **2** ♦ : recently discovered, recognized, or learned about ⟨~ drugs⟩ **3** : not familiar : UNFAMILIAR **4** ♦ : different from the former **5** : not accustomed ⟨~ to the work⟩ **6** : beginning as a repetition of a previous act or thing ⟨a ~ year⟩ **7** : made or become fresh : REFRESHED, REGENERATED ⟨rest made a ~ man of him⟩ **8** : being in a position or place for the first time ⟨a ~ member⟩ **9** *cap* : having been in use after medieval times : MODERN ⟨*New* Latin⟩ — **new•ish** *adj*

♦ [1] contemporary, current, hot, mod, modern, newfangled, red-hot, space-age, ultramodern, up-to-date ♦ [1] brand-new, spick-and-span, unused *Ant* hand-me-down, second hand, used ♦ [2] fresh, novel, original, strange, unfamiliar, unknown *Ant* familiar, old, time-honored, tired ♦ [4] backup, substitute *Ant* original

[2]**new** *adv* ♦ : not long ago : NEWLY ⟨*new*-mown hay⟩

♦ freshly, just, late, lately, newly, now, only, recently

new age *adj, often cap N&A* **1** : of, relating to, or being New Age **2** : CONTEMPORARY, MODERN

New Age *n* **1** : a group of late 20th century social attitudes adapted from a variety of ancient and modern beliefs relating to spirituality, right living, and health **2** : a soft soothing form of instrumental music

new•bie \'nü-bē, 'nyü-\ *n* ♦ : one that begins something without prior experience : NEWCOMER; *esp* : a newcomer to cyberspace

♦ beginner, fledgling, freshman, greenhorn, neophyte, newcomer, novice, recruit, rookie, tenderfoot, tyro

[1]**new•born** \-ˌbȯrn\ *adj* **1** : recently born **2** : born anew ⟨~ hope⟩

[2]**newborn** *n, pl* **newborn** *or* **newborns** ♦ : a newborn individual

♦ baby, child, infant

new•com•er \-ˌkə-mər\ *n* **1** : one recently arrived **2** ♦ : one that begins something without prior experience : BEGINNER

♦ beginner, fledgling, freshman, greenhorn, neophyte, novice, recruit, rookie, tenderfoot, tyro

New Deal *n* : the legislative and administrative program of President F. D. Roosevelt to promote economic recovery and social reform during the 1930s — **New Dealer** *n*

new•el \'nü-əl, 'nyü-\ *n* : a post about which the steps of a circular staircase wind; *also* : a post at the foot of a stairway or one at a landing

new•fan•gled \'nü-'faŋ-gəld, 'nyü-\ *adj* **1** : attracted to novelty **2** ♦ : of the newest style : NOVEL

♦ contemporary, current, hot, mod, modern, new, novel, red-hot, space-age, ultramodern, up-to-date

new–fash•ioned \-'fa-shənd\ *adj* **1** : made in a new fashion or form **2** : abreast of the times : UP-TO-DATE

new•found \-'fau̇nd\ *adj* : newly found

New Left *n* : a radical political movement originating in the 1960s

new•ly \'nü-lē, 'nyü-\ *adv* **1** ♦ : not long ago : LATELY, RECENTLY **2** : ANEW, AFRESH

♦ freshly, just, late, lately, new, now, only, recently

new•ly•wed \-ˌwed\ *n* : a person recently married

new moon *n* : the phase of the moon with its dark side toward the earth; *also* : the thin crescent moon seen for a few days after the new moon phase

new•ness *n* ♦ : the quality or state of being new

♦ freshness, novelty, originality

news \'nüz, 'nyüz\ *n* **1** ♦ : a report of recent events : TIDINGS **2** : material reported in a newspaper or news periodical or on a newscast

♦ intelligence, item, story, tidings, word

news•boy \'nüz-ˌbȯi, 'nyüz-\ *n* : one who delivers or sells newspapers

news•cast \-ˌkast\ *n* : a radio or television broadcast of news — **news•cast•er** \-ˌkas-tər\ *n*

news•group \-ˌgrüp\ : an Internet bulletin devoted to a certain topic

news•let•ter \-ˌle-tər\ *n* **:** a small newspaper containing news or information of interest chiefly to a special group
news•mag•a•zine \-ˌma-gə-ˌzēn\ *n* **:** a usually weekly magazine devoted chiefly to summarizing and analyzing news
news•man \-mən, -ˌman\ *n* ♦ **:** a person who gathers, reports, or comments on the news **:** REPORTER

♦ correspondent, journalist, reporter

news•pa•per \-ˌpā-pər\ *n* **:** a paper that is published at regular intervals and contains news, articles of opinion, features, and advertising
news•pa•per•man \-ˌpā-pər-ˌman\ *n* **:** a person who owns or is employed by a newspaper
news•print \-ˌprint\ *n* **:** paper made chiefly from wood pulp and used mostly for newspapers
news•reel \-ˌrēl\ *n* **:** a short motion picture portraying current events
news•stand \-ˌstand\ *n* **:** a place where newspapers and periodicals are sold
news•week•ly \-ˌwēk-lē\ *n* **:** a weekly newspaper or newsmagazine
news•wire \-ˌwī(-ə)r\ *n* **:** WIRE SERVICE
news•wom•an \-ˌwu̇-mən\ *n* **:** a woman who is a reporter
news•wor•thy \-ˌwər-t͟hē\ *adj* **:** sufficiently interesting to the general public to warrant reporting (as in a newspaper)
newsy \ˈnü-zē, ˈnyü-\ *adj* **news•i•er; -est 1 :** filled with news; *esp* **:** TALKATIVE **2** ♦ **:** given to gossip

♦ chatty, colloquial, conversational

newt \ˈnüt, ˈnyüt\ *n* **:** any of various small chiefly aquatic salamanders
New Testament *n* **:** the second of the two chief divisions of the Christian Scripture
new•ton \ˈnüt-ᵊn, ˈnyüt-\ *n* **:** the unit of force in the metric system equal to the force required to impart an acceleration of one meter per second per second to a mass of one kilogram
new wave *n, often cap N&W* **:** the latest and especially the most outrageous style — **new–wave** *adj*
New World *n* **:** the western hemisphere; *esp* **:** the continental landmass of No. and So. America
New Year *n* **1 :** NEW YEAR'S DAY; *also* **:** the first days of the year **2 :** ROSH HASHANAH
New Year's Day *n* **:** January 1 observed as a legal holiday
New Zea•land•er \nü-ˈzē-lən-dər, nyü-\ *n* **:** a native or inhabitant of New Zealand
¹**next** \ˈnekst\ *adj* **1 :** immediately preceding or following **2** ♦ **:** following that approaching or in progress

♦ coming, following, succeeding ***Ant*** antecedent, foregoing, precedent, preceding, previous, prior

²**next** *prep* **:** nearest or adjacent to
³**next** *adv* **1 :** in the time, place, or order nearest or immediately succeeding **2 :** on the first occasion to come
¹**next to** *prep* **1** ♦ **:** immediately following or adjacent to **2 :** in comparison to ⟨*next to* you I'm wealthy⟩

♦ about, around, by, near

²**next to** *adv* ♦ **:** very nearly ⟨*next to* impossible to win⟩

♦ about, almost, most, much, near, nearly, nigh, practically, some, virtually, well-nigh

Nez Percé \ˈnez-ˈpərs, *F* nā-per-sā\ *n* **:** a member of an American Indian people of Idaho, Washington, and Oregon; *also* **:** the language of the Nez Percé
NF *abbr* Newfoundland
NFC *abbr* National Football Conference
NFL *abbr* National Football League
Nfld *abbr* Newfoundland
NG *abbr* **1** National Guard **2** no good
NH *abbr* New Hampshire
NHL *abbr* National Hockey League
Ni *symbol* nickel
ni•a•cin \ˈnī-ə-sən\ *n* **:** an organic acid of the vitamin B complex found widely in plants and animals and used especially against pellagra
nib \ˈnib\ *n* **1 :** POINT; *esp* **:** a pen point **2 :** the jaws of a bird together with their horny covering
¹**nib•ble** \ˈni-bəl\ *vb* **nib•bled; nib•bling :** to bite gently or bit by bit; *also* **:** eat in small pieces
²**nibble** *n* ♦ **:** a small or cautious bite; *also* **:** an amount of food taken with a small bite

♦ bite, morsel, mouthful, taste, tidbit

ni•cad \ˈnī-ˌkad\ *n* **:** a rechargeable dry cell that has a nickel cathode and a cadmium anode
Nic•a•ra•guan \ˌni-kə-ˈrä-gwən\ *n* **:** a native or inhabitant of Nicaragua — **Nicaraguan** *adj*
nice \ˈnīs\ *adj* **nic•er; nic•est 1** ♦ **:** showing fastidious or finicky tastes **:** FASTIDIOUS **2** ♦ **:** marked by delicate discrimination or treatment **3 a** ♦ **:** giving pleasure **:** PLEASING, AGREEABLE **b :** well-executed **4 :** WELL-BRED ⟨~ people⟩ **5** ♦ **:** decent or correct in character or behavior **:** RESPECTABLE **6** ♦ **:** of a sympathetic or helpful nature

♦ [1] choosy, dainty, delicate, demanding, exacting, fastidious, finicky, fussy, old-maidish, particular, picky ♦ [2] delicate, exact, fine, minute, refined, subtle ♦ [3a] agreeable, congenial, delectable, delicious, delightful, dreamy, felicitous, good, grateful, gratifying, palatable, pleasant, pleasurable, satisfying ♦ [5] correct, decent, decorous, genteel, polite, proper, respectable, seemly ♦ [6] affable, agreeable, amiable, genial, good-natured, gracious, sweet, well-disposed

nice•ly *adv* ♦ **:** in a pleasing, satisfactory, courteous, or reasonable manner

♦ agreeably, favorably (*or* favourably), pleasantly, pleasingly, satisfyingly, well ♦ courteously, kindly, thoughtfully, well

nice–nel•ly \ˈnīs-ˈne-lē\ *adj, often cap 2d N* **1 :** marked by euphemism **2 :** PRUDISH — **nice nelly** *n, often cap 2d N* — **nice–nel•ly•ism** \-ˌi-zəm\ *n, often cap 2d N*
nice•ness *n* ♦ **:** the quality or state of being nice

♦ agreeableness, amenity, amiability, geniality, graciousness, pleasantness, sweetness

nice•ty \ˈnī-sə-tē\ *n, pl* **-ties 1 :** a dainty, delicate, or elegant thing ⟨enjoy the *niceties* of life⟩ **2 :** a fine point or distinction ⟨*niceties* of workmanship⟩ **3 :** EXACTNESS, PRECISION, ACCURACY
niche \ˈnich\ *n* **1** ♦ **:** a recess in a wall especially for a statue **2 :** a place, employment, or activity for which a person or thing is best fitted **3** ♦ **:** the living space or role of an organism in an ecological community especially with regard to food consumption

♦ [1] alcove, nook, recess ♦ [3] habitat, home, range, territory

¹**nick** \ˈnik\ *n* **1** ♦ **:** a small notch, groove, or chip **2 :** the final critical moment ⟨in the ~ of time⟩

♦ chip, hack, indentation, notch

²**nick** *vb* **:** NOTCH, CHIP
nick•el \ˈni-kəl\ *n* **1 :** a hard silver-white metallic chemical element capable of a high polish and used in alloys **2 :** the U.S. 5-cent piece made of copper and nickel; *also* **:** the Canadian 5-cent piece
nick•el•ode•on \ˌni-kə-ˈlō-dē-ən\ *n* **1 :** an early movie theater to which admission cost five cents **2 :** JUKEBOX
nick•er \ˈni-kər\ *vb* **:** to neigh gently **:** NEIGH, WHINNY — **nicker** *n*
nick•name \ˈnik-ˌnām\ *n* **1** ♦ **:** a usually descriptive name given instead of or in addition to the one belonging to a person, place, or thing **2 :** a familiar form of a proper name — **nickname** *vb*

♦ alias, cognomen

nic•o•tine \ˈni-kə-ˌtēn\ *n* **:** a poisonous and addictive substance in tobacco that is used as an insecticide
nic•o•tin•ic acid \ˌni-kə-ˈtē-nik-, -ˈti-\ *n* **:** an organic acid of the vitamin B complex found in plants and animals and used against pellagra
niece \ˈnēs\ *n* **:** a daughter of one's brother, sister, brother-in-law, or sister-in-law
nif•ty \ˈnif-tē\ *adj* **nif•ti•er; -est :** very good **:** very attractive
Ni•ge•ri•an \nī-ˈjir-ē-ən\ *n* **:** a native or inhabitant of Nigeria — **Nigerian** *adj*
nig•gard \ˈni-gərd\ *n* ♦ **:** a stingy person **:** MISER

♦ cheapskate, miser, skinflint, tightwad

nig•gard•ly *adj* **1** ♦ **:** grudgingly mean about spending or granting **2** ♦ **:** provided in meanly limited supply — **nig•gard•li•ness** \-lē-nəs\ *n* — **nig•gard•ly** *adv*

♦ [1] cheap, close, mean, parsimonious, penurious, spare, sparing, stingy, tight, tightfisted, uncharitable ♦ [2] light, meager (*or* meagre), poor, scant, scanty, scarce, skimpy, slender, slim, spare, sparse, stingy

nig•gling \ˈni-gə-liŋ\ *adj* **1 :** PETTY **2 :** bothersome in a petty way
¹**nigh** \ˈnī\ *adv* **1** ♦ **:** near in place, time, or relationship **2** ♦ **:** almost but not quite **:** NEARLY, ALMOST

♦ [1] around, by, close, hard, in, near, nearby ♦ [2] about, almost, most, much, near, nearly, next to, practically, some, virtually, well-nigh

[2]**nigh** *adj* : being near in time, space, effect, or degree : CLOSE, NEAR
[3]**nigh** *prep* : NEAR
night \ˈnīt\ *n* **1** ♦ : the period between dusk and dawn **2** ♦ : the darkness of night **3** : a period of misery or unhappiness **4** : NIGHTFALL

♦ [1] dark, darkness, nighttime *Ant* day, daytime ♦ [2] dark, darkness, dusk, gloaming, gloom, murk, semidarkness, shade, shadows, twilight

night *adj* ♦ : of, relating to, or associated with the night

♦ nighttime, nocturnal

night blindness *n* : reduced visual capacity in faint light (as at night)
night•cap \ˈnīt-ˌkap\ *n* **1** : a cloth cap worn with nightclothes **2** : a usually alcoholic drink taken at bedtime
night•clothes \-ˌklōthz, -ˌklōz\ *n pl* : garments worn in bed
night•club \-ˌkləb\ *n* ♦ : a place of entertainment open at night usually serving food and liquor and providing music for dancing

♦ café, disco, discotheque

night crawl•er \-ˌkrȯ-lər\ *n* : EARTHWORM; *esp* : a large earthworm found on the soil surface at night
night•dress \ˈnīt-ˌdres\ *n* : a loose garment for wear in bed : NIGHTGOWN
night•fall \-ˌfȯl\ *n* ♦ : the coming of night

♦ dusk, evening, gloaming, sundown, sunset, twilight

night•gown \-ˌgau̇n\ *n* : a loose garment for wear in bed
night•hawk \-ˌhȯk\ *n* : any of a genus of American birds related to and resembling the whip-poor-will
night•in•gale \ˈnīt-ᵊn-ˌgāl, ˈnī-tiŋ-\ *n* : any of several Old World thrushes noted for the sweet usually nocturnal song of the male
night•life \ˈnīt-ˌlīf\ *n* : the activity of pleasure-seekers at night
night•ly \ˈnīt-lē\ *adj* **1** : happening, done, or produced by night or every night **2** : of or relating to the night or every night — **nightly** *adv*
night•mare \ˈnīt-ˌmar\ *n* **1** : a frightening dream **2** ♦ : a frightening or horrible experience — **nightmare** *adj*

♦ agony, hell, horror, misery, murder, torment, torture

night•mar•ish *adj* ♦ : resembling or suggestive of a nightmare

♦ appalling, atrocious, awful, dreadful, frightful, ghastly, grisly, gruesome, hideous, horrible, horrid, lurid, macabre, monstrous, shocking, terrible

night rider *n* : a member of a secret band who ride masked at night doing violence to punish or terrorize
night•shade \ˈnīt-ˌshād\ *n* : any of a large genus of herbs, shrubs, and trees that includes poisonous forms (as the belladonna), ornamentals (as the petunias), and important food plants (as the potato and eggplant)
night•shirt \-ˌshərt\ *n* : a nightgown resembling a shirt
night soil *n* : human feces used especially for fertilizing the soil
night•stick \ˈnīt-ˌstik\ *n* ♦ : a police officer's club

♦ bat, billy club, bludgeon, cudgel, truncheon

night•time \-ˌtīm\ *n* ♦ : the time from dusk to dawn

♦ dark, darkness, night

night•walk•er \-ˌwȯ-kər\ *n* : a person who roves about at night especially with criminal or immoral intent
ni•hil•ism \ˈnī-ə-ˌli-zəm, ˈnē-hə-\ *n* **1** : a viewpoint that traditional values and beliefs are unfounded and that existence is senseless and useless **2** : ANARCHISM — **ni•hil•ist** \-list\ *n or adj* — **ni•hil•is•tic** \ˌnī-ə-ˈlis-tik, ˌnē-hə-\ *adj*
nil \ˈnil\ *n* ♦ : the arithmetical symbol 0 denoting the absence of all magnitude or quantity : ZERO, NOTHING

♦ aught, cipher, naught, nothing, zero, zip

nim•ble \ˈnim-bəl\ *adj* **nim•bler; nim•blest** **1** ♦ : quick and light in motion : AGILE ⟨a ~ dancer⟩ **2** ♦ : quick in understanding and learning : CLEVER ⟨a ~ mind⟩ — **nim•bly** \-blē\ *adv*

♦ [1] agile, graceful, light, lissome, lithe, spry ♦ [2] alert, brainy, bright, brilliant, clever, intelligent, keen, quick, quick-witted, sharp, smart

nim•ble•ness *n* ♦ : the quality or state of being nimble

♦ agility, deftness, dexterity, sleight

nim•bus \ˈnim-bəs\ *n, pl* **nim•bi** \-ˌbī, -bē\ *or* **nim•bus•es** **1** : a figure (as a disk) in an art work suggesting radiant light about the head of a divinity, saint, or sovereign **2** : a rain cloud; *also* : THUNDERHEAD

NIMBY \ˈnim-bē\ *n* : opposition to the placement of something undesirable (as a prison) in one's neighborhood
nim•rod \ˈnim-ˌräd\ *n* **1** : HUNTER **2** : IDIOT, JERK
nin•com•poop \ˈnin-kəm-ˌpüp\ *n* **1** : a person lacking in judgment or prudence : FOOL, SIMPLETON **2** : an unsophisticated person
nine \ˈnīn\ *n* **1** : one more than eight **2** : the 9th in a set or series **3** : something having nine units; *esp* : a baseball team — **nine** *adj or pron* — **ninth** \ˈnīnth\ *adj or adv or n*
nine days' wonder *n* : something that creates a short-lived sensation
nine•pins \ˈnīn-ˌpinz\ *n* : a bowling game using nine pins arranged usually in a diamond-shaped configuration
nine•teen \ˈnīn-ˈtēn\ *n* : one more than 18 — **nineteen** *adj or pron* — **nine•teenth** \-ˈtēnth\ *adj or n*
nine•ty \ˈnīn-tē\ *n, pl* **nineties** : nine times 10 — **nine•ti•eth** \-tē-əth\ *adj or n* — **ninety** *adj or pron*
nin•ja \ˈnin-jə, -(ˌ)jä\ *n, pl* **ninja** *or* **ninjas** : a person trained in ancient Japanese martial arts and employed especially for espionage and assassinations
nin•ny \ˈni-nē\ *n, pl* **ninnies** **1** : a person lacking in judgment or prudence : FOOL **2** : an unsophisticated person
ni•o•bi•um \nī-ˈō-bē-əm\ *n* : a gray metallic chemical element used in alloys
[1]**nip** \ˈnip\ *vb* **nipped; nip•ping** **1** : to catch hold of and squeeze tightly between two surfaces, edges, or points **2** : to sever by or as if by pinching sharply; *also* : to remove by cutting or pinching **3** : to destroy the growth, progress, or fulfillment of ⟨*nipped* in the bud⟩ **4** : to injure or make numb with cold : CHILL **5** : to take or appropriate without right or leave and with intent to keep or make use of wrongfully : STEAL
[2]**nip** *n* **1** ♦ : a sharp stinging cold **2** : a biting or pungent flavor **3** : PINCH, BITE **4** : a small portion : BIT

♦ bite, bitterness, bleakness, chill, rawness, sharpness

[3]**nip** *n* : a small quantity of liquor : SIP
[4]**nip** *vb* **nipped; nip•ping** : to take liquor in nips : TIPPLE
nip and tuck *adj or adv* ♦ : so close that the lead shifts rapidly from one contestant to another

♦ close, narrow, neck and neck, tight

nip•per \ˈni-pər\ *n* **1** : one that nips **2** *pl* : a gripping instrument with two handles and two jaws : PINCERS **3** ♦ : a young person especially between infancy and youth : CHILD; *esp* : a small boy

♦ boy, child, lad, shaver, stripling, youth

nip•ple \ˈni-pəl\ *n* : the protuberance of a mammary gland through which milk is drawn off : TEAT; *also* : something resembling a nipple
nip•py \ˈni-pē\ *adj* **nip•pi•er; -est** **1** : having an intense flavor or odor : PUNGENT, SHARP **2** ♦ : noticeably cold : CHILLY **3** : brisk, quick, or nimble in movement

♦ bitter, chill, chilly, cold, cool, frosty, raw, sharp, snappy, wintry

nir•va•na \nir-ˈvä-nə\ *n, often cap* **1** : the final freeing of a soul from all that enslaves it; *esp* : the supreme happiness that according to Buddhism comes when all passion, hatred, and delusion die out and the soul is released from the necessity of further purification **2** : OBLIVION; *also* : PARADISE
ni•sei \nē-ˈsā, ˈnē-ˌsā\ *n, pl* **nisei** *often cap* : a son or daughter of immigrant Japanese parents who is born and educated in America
ni•si \ˈnī-ˌsī\ *adj* : taking effect at a specified time unless previously modified or voided ⟨a divorce decree ~⟩
nit \ˈnit\ *n* **1** : the egg of a parasitic insect (as a louse); *also* : the young insect **2** : a minor shortcoming
nite *var of* NIGHT
ni•ter *or Can and Brit* **ni•tre** \ˈnī-tər\ *n* : POTASSIUM NITRATE
nit•pick•er *n* ♦ : one who engages in nitpicking

♦ carper, castigator, caviler, censurer, critic, faultfinder, railer, scold

nit–pick•ing \ˈnit-ˌpi-kiŋ\ *n* : minute and usually unjustified criticism
[1]**ni•trate** \ˈnī-ˌtrāt, -trət\ *n* **1** : a salt or ester of nitric acid **2** : sodium nitrate or potassium nitrate used as a fertilizer
[2]**ni•trate** \-ˌtrāt\ *vb* **ni•trat•ed; ni•trat•ing** : to treat or combine with nitric acid or a nitrate — **ni•tra•tion** \nī-ˈtrā-shən\ *n*
ni•tre *Can and Brit var of* NITER
ni•tric acid \ˈnī-trik-\ *n* : a corrosive liquid acid used especially in making dyes, explosives, and fertilizers
ni•tri•fi•ca•tion \ˌnī-trə-fə-ˈkā-shən\ *n* : the oxidation (as by

bacteria) of ammonium salts to nitrites and then to nitrates — **ni·tri·fy·ing** \ˈnī-trə-ˌfī-iŋ\ *adj*
ni·trite \ˈnī-ˌtrīt\ *n* **:** a salt of nitrous acid
ni·tro \ˈnī-trō\ *n, pl* **nitros :** any of various nitrated products; *esp* **:** NITROGLYCERIN
ni·tro·gen \ˈnī-trə-jən\ *n* **:** a tasteless odorless gaseous chemical element constituting 78 percent of the atmosphere by volume — **ni·trog·e·nous** \nī-ˈträ-jə-nəs\ *adj*
nitrogen narcosis *n* **:** a state of euphoria and confusion caused by nitrogen forced into a diver's bloodstream from atmospheric air under pressure
ni·tro·glyc·er·in *or* **ni·tro·glyc·er·ine** \ˌnī-trə-ˈgli-sə-rən\ *n* **:** an oily explosive liquid used to make dynamite and in medicine to dilate blood vessels
ni·trous acid \ˈnī-trəs-\ *n* **:** an unstable nitrogen-containing acid known only in solution or in the form of its salts
nitrous oxide *n* **:** a colorless gas used especially as an anesthetic in dentistry
nit·ty–grit·ty \ˈni-tē-ˌgri-tē, ˌni-tē-ˈgri-tē\ *n* **:** what is essential and basic **:** specific practical details
nit·wit \ˈnit-ˌwit\ *n* ♦ **:** a scatterbrained or stupid person

♦ booby, fool, goose, half-wit, jackass, lunatic, nut, simpleton, turkey ♦ blockhead, dope, dummy, idiot, imbecile, jackass, moron, numskull

1nix \ˈniks\ *n* **:** NOTHING
2nix *vb* **:** VETO, REJECT
3nix *adv* **:** NO
NJ *abbr* New Jersey
NL *abbr* National League
NLRB *abbr* National Labor Relations Board
NM *abbr* **1** nautical mile **2** New Mexico
N Mex *abbr* New Mexico
NMI *abbr* no middle initial
NNE *abbr* north-northeast
NNW *abbr* north-northwest
1no \ˈnō\ *adv* **1** — used to express the negative of an alternative ⟨shall we continue or ~⟩ **2** ♦ **:** in no respect or degree ⟨he is ~ better than the others⟩ **3 :** not so ⟨~, I'm not ready⟩ **4** — used with an adjective to imply a meaning opposite to the positive statement ⟨in ~ uncertain terms⟩ **5** — used to introduce a more emphatic or explicit statement ⟨has the right, ~, the duty to continue⟩ **6** ♦ — used as an interjection to express surprise or doubt ⟨~ — you don't say⟩ **7** — used in combination with a verb to form a compound adjective ⟨*no*-bake pie⟩

♦ [2] never, none, nothing, nowise ♦ [6] indeed, well, why

2no *adj* **1 :** not any; *also* **:** hardly any **2 :** not a ⟨she's ~ expert⟩
3no \ˈnō\ *n, pl* **noes** *or* **nos** \ˈnōz\ **1** ♦ **:** an act or instance of refusing or denying by the use of the word no **:** REFUSAL, DENIAL **2** ♦ **:** a negative vote or decision; *also, pl* **:** persons voting in the negative

♦ blackball, denial, nay, negation, negative, refusal, veto *Ant* positive, yea, yes

4no *abbr* **1** north; northern **2** number
1No *var of* NOH
2No *symbol* nobelium
No·bel·ist \nō-ˈbe-list\ *n* **:** a winner of a Nobel prize
no·bel·i·um \nō-ˈbe-lē-əm\ *n* **:** a radioactive metallic chemical element produced artificially
No·bel prize \nō-ˈbel-, ˈnō-ˌbel-\ *n* **:** any of various annual prizes (as in peace, literature, or medicine) established by the will of Alfred Nobel for the encouragement of persons who work for the interests of humanity
no·bil·i·ty \nō-ˈbi-lə-tē\ *n* **1** ♦ **:** the quality or state of being noble in character, quality, or rank **2 :** nobles considered as forming a class

♦ augustness, brilliance, glory, grandeur, grandness, magnificence, majesty, nobleness, resplendence, splendor, stateliness

1no·ble \ˈnō-bəl\ *adj* **no·bler; no·blest 1** ♦ **:** possessing outstanding qualities **:** ILLUSTRIOUS; *also* **:** FAMOUS, NOTABLE **2** ♦ **:** of high birth, rank, or station **:** ARISTOCRATIC **3 :** possessing very high or excellent qualities or properties **:** EXCELLENT **4** ♦ **:** grand or impressive especially in appearance **:** STATELY, IMPOSING ⟨a ~ edifice⟩ **5** ♦ **:** of a superior nature especially in character

♦ [1] distinguished, eminent, famous, illustrious, notable, noteworthy, outstanding, preeminent, prestigious, signal, star, superior ♦ [2] aristocratic, genteel, gentle, grand, highborn, patrician, wellborn *Ant* baseborn, common, humble, ignoble, low, lowly, mean, plebeian ♦ [4] august, baronial, gallant, glorious, grand, grandiose, heroic, imposing, magnificent, majestic, monumental, proud, regal, royal, splendid, stately ♦ [5] decent, ethical, honest, honorable, just, principled, respectable, righteous, upright, upstanding ♦ [5] chivalrous, gallant, great, greathearted, high, high-minded, lofty, lordly, magnanimous, sublime *Ant* base, debased, degenerate, degraded, ignoble, low

2noble *n* ♦ **:** a person of noble rank or birth

♦ aristocrat, gentleman, grandee, patrician

no·ble·man \ˈnō-bəl-mən\ *n* **:** a member of the nobility
no·ble·ness *n* ♦ **:** the quality or state of being noble

♦ augustness, brilliance, glory, grandeur, grandness, magnificence, majesty, nobility, resplendence, splendor, stateliness

no·blesse oblige \nō-ˌbles-ə-ˈblēzh\ *n* **:** the obligation of honorable, generous, and responsible behavior associated with high rank or birth
no·ble·wom·an \ˈnō-bəl-ˌwu̇-mən\ *n* ♦ **:** a woman of noble rank

♦ dame, gentlewoman, lady

no·bly \-blē\ *adv* ♦ **:** with greatness of soul

♦ gallantly, grandly, greatly, heroically, honorably (*or* honourably), magnanimously

1no·body \ˈnō-ˌbä-dē, -bə-\ *pron* **:** no person
2nobody *n, pl* **no·bod·ies** ♦ **:** a person of no influence or importance

♦ nonentity, nothing, whippersnapper, zero *Ant* big shot, bigwig, eminence, figure, magnate, nabob, personage, somebody, VIP

no–brain·er \ˈnō-ˈbrā-nər\ *n* **:** something that requires a minimum of thought
noc·tur·nal \näk-ˈtərn-ᵊl\ *adj* **1** ♦ **:** of, relating to, or occurring in the night **2 :** active at night ⟨a ~ bird⟩

♦ night, nighttime *Ant* daily, diurnal

noc·turne \ˈnäk-ˌtərn\ *n* **:** a work of art dealing with night; *esp* **:** a dreamy pensive composition for the piano
noc·u·ous \ˈnä-kyə-wəs\ *adj* **:** HARMFUL — **noc·u·ous·ly** *adv*
nod \ˈnäd\ *vb* **nod·ded; nod·ding 1 :** to bend the head downward or forward (as in bowing, going to sleep, or giving assent) **2** ♦ **:** to move up and down ⟨tulips *nodding* in the breeze⟩ **3 :** to show by a nod of the head ⟨~ agreement⟩ **4 :** to make a slip or error in a moment of abstraction — **nod** *n*

♦ bob, bobble, jog, jounce, pump, seesaw

nod·dle \ˈnäd-ᵊl\ *n* **:** a person's head especially as the seat of intellect **:** HEAD
nod·dy \ˈnä-dē\ *n, pl* **noddies 1 :** FOOL **2 :** a stout-bodied tropical tern
node \ˈnōd\ *n* **:** a thickened, swollen, or differentiated area (as of tissue); *esp* **:** the part of a stem from which a leaf arises — **nod·al** \-ᵊl\ *adj*
nod·ule \ˈnä-jül\ *n* ♦ **:** a small lump or swelling — **nod·u·lar** \ˈnä-jə-lər\ *adj*

♦ bump, knot, lump, swelling

no·el \nō-ˈel\ *n* **1 :** a Christmas carol **2** *cap* **:** the Christmas season

♦ Christmastide, Christmastime, yuletide

noes *pl of* NO
no–fault \ˈnō-ˈfȯlt\ *adj* **1 :** of, relating to, or being a motor vehicle insurance plan under which someone involved in an accident is compensated usually up to a stipulated limit for actual losses by that person's own insurance company regardless of who is responsible **2 :** of, relating to, or being a divorce law under which neither party is held responsible for the breakup of the marriage
nog·gin \ˈnä-gən\ *n* **1 :** a small mug or cup; *also* **:** a small quantity of drink **2** ♦ **:** a person's head

♦ head, pate, poll

no–good \ˈnō-ˈgu̇d\ *adj* ♦ **:** having no worth, virtue, use, or chance of success — **no–good** \ˈnō-ˌgu̇d\ *n*

♦ chaffy, empty, junky, null, valueless, worthless

Noh *also* **No** \ˈnō\ *n, pl* **Noh** *also* **No :** classic Japanese dance-drama having a heroic theme, a chorus, and highly stylized action, costuming, and scenery
no–hit·ter \(ˌ)nō-ˈhi-tər\ *n* **:** a baseball game or part of a game in which a pitcher allows no base hits
no·how \ˈnō-ˌhau̇\ *adv* **:** in no manner
1noise \ˈnȯiz\ *n* **1** ♦ **:** loud, confused, or senseless shouting or outcry **2** ♦ **:** sound or a sound that lacks agreeable musical quality or is noticeably loud, harsh, or discordant **3 :** unwanted electronic signal or disturbance — **noise·less·ly** *adv*

◆ [1] clamor (*or* clamour), howl, hubbub, hue and cry, hullabaloo, outcry, roar, tumult, uproar ◆ [2] bluster, cacophony, clamor, din, racket, roar ***Ant*** quiet, silence, still, stillness

²noise *vb* **noised; nois•ing** ◆ : to spread by rumor or report ⟨the story was *noised* about⟩

◆ *usu* **noise about** circulate, rumor, whisper

noise•less *adj* ◆ : making or causing no noise or stir : free from noise

◆ hushed, muted, quiet, silent, soundless, still

noise•mak•er \ˈnȯiz-ˌmā-kər\ *n* : one that makes noise; *esp* : a device used to make noise at parties

noise pollution *n* : annoying or harmful noise in an environment

noi•some \ˈnȯi-səm\ *adj* **1** ◆ : physically harmful or destructive to living beings : UNWHOLESOME **2** ◆ : offensive to the senses (as smell); *also* : highly objectionable

◆ [1] noxious, unhealthy, unwholesome ◆ [2] fetid, foul, fusty, malodorous, musty, rank, reeky, smelly, strong

noisy \ˈnȯi-zē\ *adj* **nois•i•er; -est** **1** : making loud noises **2** ◆ : full of noises : LOUD — **nois•i•ly** \-zə-lē\ *adv* — **nois•i•ness** \-zē-nəs\ *n*

◆ boisterous, clamorous, loud, raucous, resounding, uproarious ***Ant*** hushed, noiseless, quiet, silent, soundless, stilled

nol•le pro•se•qui \ˌnä-lē-ˈprä-sə-ˌkwī\ *n* : an entry on the record of a legal action that the prosecutor or plaintiff will proceed no further in an action or suit or in some aspect of it

no•lo con•ten•de•re \ˌnō-lō-kən-ˈten-də-rē\ *n* : a plea in a criminal prosecution that subjects the defendant to conviction but does not admit guilt or preclude denying the charges in another proceeding

nol–pros \ˈnäl-ˈpräs\ *vb* **nol–prossed; nol–pros•sing** : to discontinue by entering a nolle prosequi

nom *abbr* nominative

no•mad \ˈnō-ˌmad\ *n* **1** : a member of a people who have no fixed residence but move from place to place **2** ◆ : an individual who roams about aimlessly

◆ drifter, rambler, rover, vagabond, wanderer

nomad *adj* ◆ : traversing a random course

◆ errant, itinerant, peripatetic, roaming, vagabond, vagrant

no•mad•ic \nō-ˈma-dik\ *adj* : NOMAD

no–man's–land \ˈnō-ˌmanz-ˌland\ *n* **1** : an area of unowned, unclaimed, or uninhabited land **2** : an unoccupied area between opposing troops

nom de guerre \ˌnäm-di-ˈger\ *n, pl* **noms de guerre** *same or* ˌnämz-\ : PSEUDONYM

nom de plume \-ˈplüm\ *n, pl* **noms de plume** *same or* ˌnämz-\ : PEN NAME

no•men•cla•ture \ˈnō-mən-ˌklā-chər\ *n* **1** : NAME, DESIGNATION **2** : a system of terms used in a science or art

nom•i•nal \ˈnä-mən-ᵊl\ *adj* **1** ◆ : being something in name or form only ⟨~ head of a party⟩ **2** ◆ : lacking in significance or solid worth : TRIFLING ⟨a ~ price⟩ — **nom•i•nal•ly** *adv*

◆ [1] formal, paper, titular ◆ [2] inconsequential, inconsiderable, insignificant, measly, minute, negligible, paltry, petty, slight, trifling, trivial

nom•i•nate \ˈnä-mə-ˌnāt\ *vb* **-nat•ed; -nat•ing** : to choose as a candidate for election, appointment, or honor — **nom•i•na•tion** \ˌnä-mə-ˈnā-shən\ *n*

nom•i•na•tive \ˈnä-mə-nə-tiv\ *adj* : of, relating to, or constituting a grammatical case marking typically the subject of a verb — **nominative** *n*

nom•i•nee \ˌnä-mə-ˈnē\ *n* : a person nominated for an office, duty, or position

non- \(ˈ)nän *or* ˌnän *before stressed syllables*; ˌnän *elsewhere*\ *prefix* **1** : not : reverse of : absence of **2** : having no importance

nonabrasive
nonabsorbent
nonacademic
nonacceptance
nonacid
nonactivated
nonadaptive
nonaddictive
nonadhesive
nonadjacent
nonadjustable
nonaggression
nonalcoholic
nonappearance
nonaromatic
nonathletic
nonattendance
nonbeliever
nonbelligerent
nonbreakable
noncancerous
noncandidate
noncellular
nonclerical
noncoital
noncombat
noncommercial
noncommunist
noncompeting
noncompetitive
noncompliance
noncomplying
nonconducting
nonconflicting
nonconformance
nonconstructive
noncontagious
noncontinuous
noncorroding
noncorrosive
noncritical
noncrystalline
nondeductible
nondelivery
nondemocratic
nondenominational
nondepartmental
nondestructive
nondevelopment
nondiscrimination
nondiscriminatory
nondistinctive
nondurable
noneconomic
noneducational
nonelastic
nonelection
nonelectric
nonelectrical
nonemotional
nonenforcement
nonessential
nonethical
non–euclidean
nonexclusive
nonexempt
nonexistence
nonexplosive
nonfarm
nonfatal
nonfattening
nonfederated
nonferrous
nonfiction
nonfilamentous
nonfilterable
nonflowering
nonfood
nonfreezing
nonfulfillment
nongraded
nonhereditary
nonhomogeneous
nonhomologous
nonhuman
nonidentical
nonimportation
nonindustrial
noninfectious
nonintellectual
nonintercourse
noninterference
nonintoxicant
nonintoxicating
noninvasive
nonionizing
nonirritating
nonlegal
nonlethal
nonlife
nonlinear
nonliving
nonlogical
nonmagnetic
nonmalignant
nonmember
nonmembership
nonmigratory
nonmilitary
nonmoral
nonmoving
nonnegotiable
nonobservance
nonoccurrence
nonofficial
nonoily
nonparallel
nonparasitic
nonparticipant
nonparticipating
nonpathogenic
nonpaying
nonpayment
nonperformance
nonperishable
nonpoisonous
nonpolar
nonpolitical
nonporous
nonpregnant
nonproductive
nonprotein
nonradioactive
nonrandom
nonreactive
nonreciprocal
nonrecognition
nonrecurrent
nonrecurring
nonrefillable
nonrenewable
nonresidential
nonrestricted
nonreturnable
nonreversible
nonruminant
nonsalable
nonscientific
nonscientist
nonseasonal
nonsectarian
nonsegregated
nonselective
non–self–governing
nonsexist
nonsexual
nonshrinkable
nonsinkable
nonsmoker
nonsmoking
nonsocial
nonspeaking
nonspecialist
nonsteroidal
nonsurgical
nontaxable
nonteaching
nontechnical
nontemporal
nontenured
nontheistic
nonthreatening
nontoxic
nontransferable
nontypical
nonuniform
nonvascular
nonvenomous
nonverbal
nonviable
nonvisual
nonvocal
nonvolatile
nonvoter
nonvoting
nonworker
nonworking
nonzero

non•age \ˈnä-nij, ˈnō-\ *n* **1 :** legal minority **2 :** a period of youth **3 :** IMMATURITY
no•na•ge•nar•i•an \ˌnō-nə-jə-ˈner-ē-ən, ˌnä-\ *n* **:** a person whose age is in the nineties
non•aligned \ˌnän-ə-ˈlīnd\ *adj* **:** not allied with other nations
no–name \ˈnō-ˌnām\ *adj* **:** not having a readily recognizable name ⟨~ brands⟩
non•book \ˈnän-ˌbu̇k\ *n* **:** a book of little literary merit that is often a compilation (as of pictures or speeches)
[1]**nonce** \ˈnäns\ *n* **:** the one, particular, or present occasion or purpose ⟨for the ~⟩
[2]**nonce** *adj* **:** occurring, used, or made only once or for a special occasion ⟨a ~ word⟩
non•cha•lance \ˌnän-shə-ˈläns\ *n* ♦ **:** the quality or state of being nonchalant

♦ disinterestedness, disregard, indifference, insouciance

non•cha•lant \ˌnän-shə-ˈlänt\ *adj* ♦ **:** giving an effect of unconcern or indifference — **non•cha•lant•ly** *adv*

♦ casual, disinterested, indifferent, insouciant, unconcerned

non•com \ˈnän-ˌkäm\ *n* **:** NONCOMMISSIONED OFFICER
non•com•ba•tant \ˌnän-kəm-ˈbat-ᵊnt, nän-ˈkäm-bə-tənt\ *n* **:** a member (as a chaplain) of the armed forces whose duties do not include fighting; *also* **:** CIVILIAN — **noncombatant** *adj*
non•com•bus•ti•ble \ˌnän-kəm-ˈbəs-tə-bəl\ *adj* ♦ **:** not combustible **:** incapable of catching fire and burning when subjected to fire

♦ fireproof, nonflammable, noninflammable

non•com•mis•sioned officer \ˌnän-kə-ˈmi-shənd-\ *n* **:** a subordinate officer in the armed forces appointed from enlisted personnel
non•com•mit•tal \ˌnän-kə-ˈmit-ᵊl\ *adj* **:** indicating neither consent nor dissent
non com•pos men•tis \ˌnän-ˌkäm-pəs-ˈmen-təs\ *adj* **:** not of sound mind
non•con•duc•tor \ˌnän-kən-ˈdək-tər\ *n* **:** a substance that is a very poor conductor of heat, electricity, or sound
non•con•form•ing \ˌnän-kən-ˈfȯr-miŋ\ *adj* ♦ **:** not conforming **:** declining conformity

♦ dissident, heretical, heterodox, nonconformist, nonorthodox, unconventional, unorthodox

non•con•form•ist \-kən-ˈfȯr-mist\ *n* **1** *often cap* **:** a person who does not conform to an established church and especially the Church of England **2** ♦ **:** a person who does not conform to a generally accepted pattern of thought or action — **nonconformist** *adj*

♦ dissenter, dissident, heretic ♦ bohemian, deviant, individualist, loner, maverick

non•con•for•mi•ty \-ˈfȯr-mə-tē\ *n* ♦ **:** refusal to conform to an established or conventional creed, rule, or practice

♦ dissent, heresy, heterodoxy

non•co•op•er•a•tion \ˌnän-kō-ˌä-pə-ˈrā-shən\ *n* **:** failure or refusal to cooperate; *esp* **:** refusal through civil disobedience of a people to cooperate with the government of a country
non•cred•it \(ˌ)nän-ˈkre-dət\ *adj* **:** not offering credit toward a degree
non•cus•to•di•al \ˌnän-kə-ˈstō-dē-əl\ *adj* **:** of or being a parent who does not have legal custody of a child
non•dairy \ˈnän-ˈder-ē\ *adj* **:** containing no milk or milk products
non•de•script \ˌnän-di-ˈskript\ *adj* **1 :** not belonging to any particular class or kind **2 :** lacking distinctive qualities
non•drink•er \-ˈdriŋ-kər\ *n* **:** a person who abstains from alcohol
[1]**none** \ˈnən\ *pron* **1 :** not any ⟨~ of them went⟩ **2 :** not one ⟨~ of the family⟩ **3 a :** not any such thing ⟨half a loaf is better than ~⟩ **b :** not any such person
[2]**none** *adj, archaic* **:** not any **:** NO
[3]**none** *adv* **1 :** by no means **:** not at all ⟨he got there ~ too soon⟩ **2** ♦ **:** in no way **:** to no extent ⟨~ the worse for wear⟩

♦ hardly, no, scarcely ♦ never, no, nothing, nowise

non•elec•tive \nän-ˌi-ˈlek-tiv\ *adj* ♦ **:** not permitting a choice

♦ compulsory, imperative, incumbent, involuntary, mandatory, necessary, obligatory, peremptory

non•en•ti•ty \ˌnän-ˈen-tə-tē\ *n* **1 :** something that does not exist or exists only in the imagination **2** ♦ **:** one of no consequence or significance

♦ nobody, nothing, shrimp, whippersnapper, zero

nones \ˈnōnz\ *n sing or pl* **:** the 7th day of March, May, July, or October or the 5th day of any other month in the ancient Roman calendar
non•es•sen•tial \ˌnän-i-ˈsen-shəl\ *adj* **1 :** not essential **2 :** being a substance synthesized by the body in sufficient quantity to satisfy dietary needs
none•such \ˈnən-ˌsəch\ *n* **:** one without an equal — **nonesuch** *adj*
none•the•less \ˌnən-t͟hə-ˈles\ *adv* ♦ **:** in spite of that **:** NEVERTHELESS

♦ but, howbeit, however, nevertheless, notwithstanding, still, though, withal, yet

non•event \ˈnän-i-ˌvent\ *n* **1 :** an event that fails to take place or to satisfy expectations **2 :** a highly promoted event of little intrinsic interest
non•ex•is•tent \nän-ig-ˈzis-tənt\ *adj* ♦ **:** not having existence

♦ absent, missing, wanting

non•fat \-ˈfat\ *adj* **:** lacking fat solids **:** having fat solids removed ⟨~ milk⟩
non•fic•tion•al \-ˈfik-shə-nəl\ *adj* ♦ **:** not fictional

♦ documentary, factual, hard, historical, literal, matter-of-fact, objective, true

non•fig•u•ra•tive \ˈnän-ˈfi-gyə-rə-tiv, -ˈfi-gə-\ *adj* ♦ **:** representing or intended to represent no natural or actual object, figure, or scene

♦ abstract, metaphysical, theoretical

non•flam•ma•ble \-ˈfla-mə-bəl\ *adj* ♦ **:** not flammable

♦ fireproof, noncombustible, noninflammable

non•func•tion•al \-ˈfəŋk-shə-nəl\ *adj* ♦ **:** not performing or able to perform its regular function

♦ inoperable, inoperative

non•gono•coc•cal \ˌnän-ˌgä-nə-ˈkä-kəl\ *adj* **:** not caused by a gonococcus
non•he•ro \ˈnän-ˈhē-rō\ *n* **:** ANTIHERO
non–Hodg•kin's lymphoma \ˈnän-ˈhäj-kənz-\ *n* **:** any of numerous malignant lymphomas not classified as Hodgkin's disease
non•in•flam•ma•ble \ˌnän-in-ˈfla-mə-bəl\ *adj* ♦ **:** incapable of being easily ignited and of burning very quickly

♦ fireproof, noncombustible, nonflammable

non•in•ter•ven•tion \ˌnän-ˌin-tər-ˈven-chən\ *n* **:** refusal or failure to intervene (as in the affairs of other countries)
non•is•sue \ˈnän-ˈi-shü\ *n* **:** an issue of little importance or concern
non•lit•er•ary \ˌnän-ˈli-tə-ˌrer-ē\ *adj* ♦ **:** colloquial and informal as opposed to literary and formal

♦ colloquial, conversational, informal, vernacular, vulgar

non•ma•te•ri•al \ˌnän-mə-ˈtir-ē-əl\ *adj* ♦ **:** not consisting of matter

♦ bodiless, immaterial, incorporeal, insubstantial, nonphysical, spiritual, unsubstantial

non•met•al \ˈnän-ˈmet-ᵊl\ *n* **:** a chemical element (as carbon) that lacks the characteristics of a metal — **non•me•tal•lic** \ˌnän-mə-ˈta-lik\ *adj*
non•mo•tile \ˌnän-ˈmō-ˌtī(-əl\ *adj* ♦ **:** not exhibiting or capable of movement

♦ immobile, immovable, unbudging, unmovable

non•neg•a•tive \-ˈne-gə-tiv\ *adj* **:** not negative **:** being either positive or zero
non•nu•cle•ar \ˈnän-ˈnü-klē-ər\ *adj* **1 :** not nuclear **2 :** not having, using, or involving nuclear weapons
non•ob•jec•tive \ˌnän-əb-ˈjek-tiv\ *adj* **1 :** not objective **2 :** representing no natural or actual object, figure, or scene ⟨~ art⟩
non•or•tho•dox \ˌnän-ˈȯr-thə-ˌdäks\ *adj* **1** ♦ **:** not conforming to established doctrine especially in religion **2** ♦ **:** not according with, sanctioned by, or based on convention

♦ [1] dissident, heretical, heterodox, nonconforming, nonconformist, unconventional, unorthodox ♦ [2] broad-minded, liberal, nontraditional, open-minded, progressive, radical, unconventional, unorthodox

[1]**non•pa•reil** \ˌnän-pə-ˈrel\ *adj* ♦ **:** having no equal **:** PEERLESS

♦ incomparable, inimitable, matchless, only, peerless, unequaled, unmatched, unparalleled, unrivaled, unsurpassed

[2]**nonpareil** *n* **1** ♦ **:** an individual of unequaled excellence **:** PARAGON **2 :** a small flat disk of chocolate covered with white sugar pellets

♦ beau ideal, classic, exemplar, ideal, model, paragon

non·par·ti·san \ˈnän-ˈpär-tə-zən\ *adj* ♦ **:** not partisan; *esp* **:** not influenced by political party spirit or interests

♦ disinterested, dispassionate, equal, equitable, fair, impartial, just, objective, square, unbiased, unprejudiced

non·per·son \-ˈpərs-ᵊn\ *n* **1 :** UNPERSON **2 :** a person having no social or legal status

non·phys·i·cal \ˈnän-ˈfi-zi-kəl\ *adj* ♦ **:** not physical **:** incapable of being touched or perceived by touch

♦ bodiless, immaterial, incorporeal, insubstantial, nonmaterial, spiritual, unsubstantial

non·plus \ˈnän-ˈpləs\ *vb* **-plussed** *also* **-plused** \-ˈpləst\; **-plus·sing** *also* **-plus·ing :** to cause to be at a loss as to what to say, think, or do **:** PUZZLE, PERPLEX

non·pre·scrip·tion \ˌnän-pri-ˈskrip-shən\ *adj* **:** available for sale legally without a doctor's prescription

non·pro·fes·sion·al \ˈnän-prə-ˈfe-shə-nəl\ *adj* ♦ **:** not characterized by or conforming to the technical or ethical standards of a profession; *also* **:** not having the training or experience of a professional

♦ amateur, amateurish, inexperienced, inexpert, unprofessional, unskilled, unskillful

non·prof·it \ˈnän-ˈprä-fət\ *adj* **:** not conducted or maintained for the purpose of making a profit ⟨a ∼ organization⟩

non·pro·lif·er·a·tion \ˌnän-prə-ˌli-fə-ˈrā-shən\ *adj* **:** providing for the stoppage of proliferation (as of nuclear arms) ⟨a ∼ treaty⟩

non·read·er \ˈnän-ˈrē-dər\ *n* **:** one who does not read or has difficulty reading

non·re·li·gious \ˌnän-ri-ˈli-jəs\ *adj* **1** ♦ **:** not religious **:** not having a religious character **2 :** having no religion

♦ profane, secular, temporal

non·rep·re·sen·ta·tion·al \ˌnän-ˌre-pri-ˌzen-ˈtā-shə-nəl\ *adj* **:** NONOBJECTIVE 2

non·res·i·dent \ˈnän-ˈre-zə-dənt\ *adj* **:** not living in a particular place — **non·res·i·dence** \-dəns\ *n* — **nonresident** *n*

non·re·sis·tance \ˌnän-ri-ˈzis-təns\ *n* **:** the principles or practice of passive submission to authority even when unjust or oppressive

non·re·stric·tive \-ri-ˈstrik-tiv\ *adj* **1 :** not serving or tending to restrict **2 :** not limiting the reference of the word or phrase modified ⟨a ∼ clause⟩

non·rig·id \nän-ˈri-jəd\ *adj* **:** maintaining form by pressure of contained gas ⟨a ∼ airship⟩

non·sched·uled \ˈnän-ˈske-jüld\ *adj* **:** licensed to carry passengers or freight by air without a regular schedule

non·sense \ˈnän-ˌsens, -səns\ *n* **1** ♦ **:** foolish or meaningless words or actions **2 :** things of no importance or value

♦ bunk, claptrap, drivel, fiddlesticks, folly, foolishness, fudge, hogwash, humbug, piffle, rot, silliness, slush, stupidity, trash

non·sen·si·cal \nän-ˈsen-si-kəl\ *adj* ♦ **:** being nonsense or full of nonsense — **non·sen·si·cal·ly** \-k(ə-)lē\ *adv*

♦ absurd, crazy, cuckoo, fatuous, foolish, mad, nonsensical, nutty, senseless, silly, stupid

non se·qui·tur \nän-ˈse-kwə-tər\ *n* **:** an inference that does not follow from the premises

non·skid \ˈnän-ˈskid\ *adj* **:** designed to prevent skidding

non·slip \-ˈslip\ *adj* **:** designed to prevent slipping

non·spe·cif·ic \-spi-ˈsi-fik\ *adj* ♦ **:** not specific

♦ all-around, bird's-eye, broad, general, overall

non·stan·dard \ˌnän-ˈstan-dərd\ *adj* **1 :** not standard **2 :** not conforming to the usage characteristic of educated native speakers of a language

non·start·er \ˈnän-ˈstär-tər\ *n* **1 :** one that does not start **2 :** one that is not productive or effective

non·stick \-ˈstik\ *adj* **:** allowing easy removal of cooked food particles

non·stop \-ˈstäp\ *adj* **:** done or made without a stop — **nonstop** *adv*

non·suc·cess \-sək-ˈses\ *n* ♦ **:** the failure to attain wealth, favor, or eminence

♦ collapse, crash, cropper, defeat, failure, fizzle

non·sup·port \ˌnän-sə-ˈpōrt\ *n* **:** failure to support; *esp* **:** failure on the part of one under obligation to provide maintenance

non·threat·en·ing \-ˈthret-niŋ, -ˈthre-tᵊn-iŋ\ *adj* **:** not likely to cause danger or anxiety ⟨a ∼ illness⟩ ⟨a ∼ environment⟩

non·tra·di·tion·al \-trə-ˈdi-shə-nəl\ *adj* ♦ **:** not traditional **:** not conforming to tradition

♦ broad-minded, liberal, nonorthodox, open-minded, progressive, radical, unconventional, unorthodox

non–U \ˈnän-ˈyü\ *adj* **:** not characteristic of the upper classes

non·union \-ˈyü-nyən\ *adj* **1 :** not belonging to a trade union ⟨∼ carpenters⟩ **2 :** not recognizing or favoring trade unions or their members ⟨∼ employers⟩

non·us·er \-ˈyü-zər\ *n* **:** one who does not make use of something (as drugs)

non·vi·o·lence \ˈnän-ˈvī-ə-ləns\ *n* **1 :** abstention from violence as a matter of principle **2 :** avoidance of violence **3 :** nonviolent political demonstrations — **non·vi·o·lent** \-lənt\ *adj*

non·white \ˌnän-ˈhwīt, -ˈwīt\ *n* **:** a person whose features and especially skin color are different from those of peoples of northwestern Europe — **nonwhite** *adj*

non·wo·ven \ˈnän-ˈwō-vən\ *adj* **:** made of fibers held together by interlocking or bonding (as by chemical or thermal means) — **nonwoven** *n*

noo·dle \ˈnüd-ᵊl\ *n* **:** a food paste made usually with egg and shaped typically in ribbon form

nook \ˈnu̇k\ *n* **1 :** an interior angle or corner formed usually by two walls ⟨a chimney ∼⟩ **2 :** a sheltered or hidden place ⟨searched every ∼ and cranny⟩ **3** ♦ **:** a small often recessed section of a larger room ⟨a breakfast ∼⟩

♦ alcove, niche, recess

noon \ˈnün\ *n* ♦ **:** the middle of the day **:** 12 o'clock in the daytime — **noon** *adj*

♦ midday, noontime

noon·day \ˈnün-ˌdā\ *n* **:** the middle of the day **:** NOON, MIDDAY

no one *pron* **:** no person **:** NOBODY

noon·tide \ˈnün-ˌtīd\ *n* **:** the middle of the day **:** NOON

noon·time \-ˌtīm\ *n* ♦ **:** the middle of the day **:** NOON

♦ midday, noon

noose \ˈnüs\ *n* **:** a loop with a slipknot that binds closer the more it is drawn

nope \ˈnōp\ *adv* **:** NO

nor \ˈnȯr\ *conj* **:** and not ⟨not for you ∼ for me⟩ — used especially to introduce and negate the second member and each later member of a series of items preceded by *neither* ⟨neither here ∼ there⟩

Nor·dic \ˈnȯr-dik\ *adj* **1 :** of or relating to the Germanic peoples of northern Europe and especially of Scandinavia **2 :** of or relating to competitive ski events involving cross-country racing, ski jumping, or biathlon — **Nordic** *n*

nor·epi·neph·rine \ˈnȯr-ˌe-pə-ˈne-frən\ *n* **:** a nitrogen-containing neurotransmitter in parts of the sympathetic and central nervous systems

norm \ˈnȯrm\ *n* **1** ♦ **:** an authoritative standard or model; *esp* **:** a set standard of development or achievement usually derived from the average or median achievement of a large group **2 :** a typical or widespread practice, procedure, or custom

♦ average, normal, par, standard

[1]**nor·mal** \ˈnȯr-məl\ *adj* **1** ♦ **:** conforming to a type, standard, or regular pattern **:** STANDARD **2 a :** of average intelligence **b** ♦ **:** sound in mind and body

♦ [1] average, common, commonplace, everyday, ordinary, prosaic, regular, routine, run-of-the-mill, standard, typical, unexceptional, unremarkable, usual, workaday ♦ [2b] balanced, clearheaded, lucid, right, sane, stable

[2]**normal** *n* **1 :** one that is normal **2 :** the usual condition, level, or quantity — **nor·mal·cy** \-sē\ *n* — **nor·mal·i·ty** \nȯr-ˈma-lə-tē\ *n*

nor·mal·ise *chiefly Brit var of* NORMALIZE

nor·mal·ize \ˈnȯr-mə-ˌlīz\ *vb* **-ized; -iz·ing** ♦ **:** to make or restore to normal — **nor·mal·i·za·tion** \ˌnȯr-mə-lə-ˈzā-shən\ *n*

♦ formalize, homogenize, regularize, standardize

nor·mal·ly *adv* ♦ **:** as a general thing **:** often in the usual course of events

♦ commonly, generally, naturally, ordinarily, typically, usually

Nor·man \ˈnȯr-mən\ *n* **1 :** a native or inhabitant of Normandy **2 :** one of the 10th century Scandinavian conquerors of Normandy **3 :** one of the Norman-French conquerors of England in 1066 — **Norman** *adj*

nor•ma•tive \ˈnȯr-mə-tiv\ *adj* **:** of, relating to, or determining norms — **nor•ma•tive•ly** *adv* — **nor•ma•tive•ness** *n*

Norse \ˈnȯrs\ *n, pl* **Norse 1 :** NORWEGIAN; *also* **:** any of the western Scandinavian dialects or languages **2** *pl* **:** SCANDINAVIANS; *also* **:** NORWEGIANS

Norse•man \-mən\ *n* **:** any of the ancient Scandinavians

1**north** \ˈnȯrth\ *adv* **:** to, toward, or in the north

2**north** *adj* **1 :** situated toward or at the north **2 :** coming from the north

3**north** *n* **1 :** the direction to the left of one facing east **2 :** the compass point directly opposite to south **3** *cap* **:** regions or countries north of a specified or implied point — **north•er•ly** \ˈnȯr-t͟hər-lē\ *adv or adj* — **north•ern** \-t͟hərn\ *adj* — **North•ern•er** \-t͟hər-nər\ *n* — **north•ern•most** \-t͟hərn-ˌmōst\ *adj* — **north•ward** \ˈnȯrth-wərd\ *adv or adj* — **north•wards** \-wərdz\ *adv*

north•east \nȯr-ˈthēst\ *n* **1 :** the general direction between north and east **2 :** the compass point midway between north and east **3** *cap* **:** regions or countries northeast of a specified or implied point — **northeast** *adj or adv* — **north•east•er•ly** \-ˈthē-stər-lē\ *adv or adj* — **north•east•ern** \-stərn\ *adj*

north•east•er \-ˈthēs-tər\ *n* **1 :** a strong northeast wind **2 :** a storm with northeast winds

north•er \ˈnȯr-t͟hər\ *n* **1 :** a strong north wind **2 :** a storm with north winds

northern lights *n pl* **:** AURORA BOREALIS

north pole *n, often cap N&P* **:** the northernmost point of the earth

North Star *n* **:** the star toward which the northern end of the earth's axis points

north•west \nȯrth-ˈwest\ *n* **1 :** the general direction between north and west **2 :** the compass point midway between north and west **3** *cap* **:** regions or countries northwest of a specified or implied point — **northwest** *adj or adv* — **north•west•er•ly** \-ˈwe-stər-lē\ *adv or adj* — **north•west•ern** \-ˈwe-stərn\ *adj*

Norw *abbr* Norway; Norwegian

Nor•we•gian \nȯr-ˈwē-jən\ *n* **1 :** a native or inhabitant of Norway **2 :** the language of Norway — **Norwegian** *adj*

nos *abbr* numbers

1**nose** \ˈnōz\ *n* **1 :** the part of the face or head containing the nostrils and covering the front of the nasal cavity **2 :** the sense of smell **3 :** something (as a point, edge, or projecting front part) that resembles a nose ⟨the ~ of a plane⟩ — **nosed** \ˈnōzd\ *adj*

2**nose** *vb* **nosed; nos•ing 1** ♦ **:** to detect by or as if by smell **:** SCENT **2 :** to push or move with the nose **3 :** to touch or rub with the nose **:** NUZZLE **4** ♦ **:** to search impertinently **:** PRY **5 :** to move ahead slowly ⟨the ship *nosed* into her berth⟩

♦ [1] scent, smell, whiff ♦ [4] butt in, interfere, intrude, meddle, mess, obtrude, poke, pry, snoop

nose•bleed \ˈnōz-ˌblēd\ *n* **:** a bleeding from the nose

nose cone *n* **:** a protective cone constituting the forward end of an aerospace vehicle

nose•dive \ˈnōz-ˌdīv\ *n* **1 :** a downward nose-first plunge (as of an airplane) **2 :** a sudden extreme drop (as in prices)

nose•gay \ˈnōz-ˌgā\ *n* **:** a small bunch of flowers **:** POSY

nose out *vb* **1 :** to discover often by prying **2 :** to defeat by a narrow margin

nose•piece \-ˌpēs\ *n* **1 :** a fitting at the lower end of a microscope tube to which the objectives are attached **2 :** the bridge of a pair of eyeglasses

no–show \ˈnō-ˈshō\ *n* **:** a person who does not show up for an event as expected

nos•tal•gia \nä-ˈstal-jə\ *n* **1 :** HOMESICKNESS **2 :** a wistful yearning for something past or irrecoverable — **nos•tal•gic** \-jik\ *adj*

nos•tril \ˈnäs-trəl\ *n* **1 :** either of the nares usually with the adjoining nasal wall and passage **2 :** either fleshy lateral wall of the nose

nos•trum \ˈnäs-trəm\ *n* **:** a questionable medicine or remedy

nosy *or* **nos•ey** \ˈnō-zē\ *adj* **nos•i•er; -est** ♦ **:** of prying or inquisitive disposition or quality **:** PRYING

♦ inquisitive, intrusive, meddlesome, obtrusive, officious, presumptuous, prying

not \ˈnät\ *adv* **1** — used to make negative a group of words or a word ⟨the boys are ~ here⟩ **2** — used to stand for the negative of a preceding group of words ⟨sometimes hard to see and sometimes ~⟩

no•ta be•ne \ˌnō-tə-ˈbē-nē, -ˈbe-\ — used to call attention to something important

no•ta•bil•i•ty \ˌnō-tə-ˈbi-lə-tē\ *n, pl* **-ties 1 :** the quality or state of being notable **2 :** NOTABLE

1**no•ta•ble** \ˈnō-tə-bəl\ *adj* **1 :** NOTEWORTHY, REMARKABLE ⟨a ~ achievement⟩ **2** ♦ **:** marked by eminence, distinction, or excellence **:** DISTINGUISHED ⟨two ~ politicians made speeches⟩

♦ distinguished, eminent, illustrious, noble, noteworthy, outstanding, preeminent, prestigious, signal, star, superior

2**notable** *n* ♦ **:** a person of note

♦ celebrity, eminence, figure, light, luminary, personage, personality, somebody, standout, star, superstar, VIP

no•ta•bly \ˈnō-tə-blē\ *adv* **1 :** in a notable manner **2 :** ESPECIALLY, PARTICULARLY

no•tar•i•al \nō-ˈter-ē-əl\ *adj* **:** of, relating to, or done by a notary public

no•ta•rize \ˈnō-tə-ˌrīz\ *vb* **-rized; -riz•ing :** to acknowledge or make legally authentic as a notary public

no•ta•ry public \ˈnō-tə-rē-\ *n, pl* **notaries public** *or* **notary publics :** a public official who attests or certifies writings (as deeds) to make them legally authentic

no•ta•tion \nō-ˈtā-shən\ *n* **1 :** a written reminder **:** NOTE **2 :** the act, process, or method of representing data by marks, signs, figures, or characters; *also* **:** a system of symbols (as letters, numerals, or musical notes) used in such notation

1**notch** \ˈnäch\ *n* **1** ♦ **:** a V-shaped hollow in an edge or surface **2** ♦ **:** a narrow pass between two mountains **3** ♦ **:** a step or stage in a process, course, or order of classification

♦ [1] chip, hack, indentation, nick ♦ [2] canyon, defile, flume, gap, gorge, gulch, gulf, pass, ravine ♦ [3] cut, degree, grade, inch, peg, phase, point, stage, step

2**notch** *vb* **1 :** to cut or make notches in **2** ♦ **:** to score or record by or as if by cutting a series of notches ⟨~*ed* 20 points for the team⟩

♦ achieve, attain, gain, hit, make, score, win

notch•back \ˈnäch-ˌbak\ *n* **:** an automobile with a trunk whose lid forms a distinct deck

1**note** \ˈnōt\ *vb* **not•ed; not•ing 1** ♦ **:** to notice or observe with care; *also* **:** to record or preserve in writing **2** ♦ **:** to make special mention of

♦ [1] jot, log, mark, put down, record, register, set down ♦ [1] behold, descry, discern, distinguish, espy, eye, look, notice, observe, perceive, regard, remark, see, sight, spy, view, witness ♦ [2] advert (to), cite, instance, mention, name, notice, quote, refer (to), remark, specify, touch (*on* or *upon*)

2**note** *n* **1 :** a musical sound **2 :** a cry, call, or sound especially of a bird **3 :** a special tone in a person's words or voice ⟨a ~ of fear⟩ **4 :** a character in music used to indicate duration of a tone by its shape and pitch by its position on the staff **5** ♦ **:** a characteristic feature **:** MOOD ⟨a ~ of optimism⟩ **6** ♦ **:** a written reminder **:** MEMORANDUM **7 :** a brief and informal record; *also* **:** a written or printed comment or explanation **8 :** a written promise to pay a debt **9 :** a piece of paper money **10** ♦ **:** a short informal letter **11 :** a formal diplomatic or official communication **12** ♦ **:** overall quality or character as seen or judged by people in general **:** REPUTATION ⟨an artist of ~⟩ **13 :** OBSERVATION, NOTICE, HEED ⟨take ~ of the time⟩

♦ [5] air, atmosphere, aura, climate, flavor (*or* flavour), mood, temper ♦ [6, 10] dispatch, letter, memorandum, missive ♦ [12] character, mark, name, report, reputation

note•book \ˈnōt-ˌbu̇k\ *n* **:** a book for notes or memoranda

not•ed \ˈnō-təd\ *adj* ♦ **:** well known by reputation **:** EMINENT, CELEBRATED

♦ celebrated, eminent, famed, famous, notorious, prominent, renowned, star, well-known

note•wor•thy \ˈnōt-ˌwər-t͟hē\ *adj* ♦ **:** worthy of note

♦ distinguished, eminent, illustrious, noble, notable, outstanding, preeminent, prestigious, signal, star, superior

1**noth•ing** \ˈnə-thiŋ\ *pron* **1 :** no thing ⟨leaves ~ to the imagination⟩ **2 :** no part **3 :** one of no interest, value, or importance ⟨she's ~ to me⟩

2**nothing** *adv* ♦ **:** not at all **:** in no degree

♦ never, no, none, nowise

3**nothing** *n* **1 :** something that does not exist **2** ♦ **:** the arithmetical symbol 0 denoting the absence of all magnitude or quantity **:** ZERO **3** ♦ **:** a person or thing of little or no value or importance

♦ [2] aught, cipher, naught, nil, zero, zip ♦ [3] nobody, nonentity, whippersnapper, zero

4**nothing** *adj* **:** of no account **:** WORTHLESS

noth•ing•ness \ˈnə-thiŋ-nəs\ *n* **1** : the quality or state of being nothing **2 a** : the state or fact of having no existence **b** : utter insignificance **3** : something insignificant or valueless

¹no•tice \ˈnō-təs\ *n* **1** ♦ : warning or intimation of something : WARNING **2** : notification of the termination of an agreement or contract at a specified time **3** ♦ : consideration with a view to action : ATTENTION, HEED ⟨bring the matter to my ~⟩ **4** ♦ : a written or printed announcement **5** : a short critical account or examination (as of a play) : REVIEW

♦ [1] admonition, alarm, alert, caution, warning ♦ [3] attention, awareness, cognizance, ear, eye, heed, observance, observation ♦ [4] announcement, directive, memorandum, notification

²notice *vb* **no•ticed; no•tic•ing** **1** ♦ : to make mention of : remark on **2** ♦ : to take notice of : OBSERVE

♦ [1] advert (to), cite, instance, mention, name, note, quote, refer (to), specify, touch (*on* or *upon*) ♦ [2] behold, descry, discern, distinguish, espy, eye, look, note, observe, perceive, regard, remark, see, sight, spy, view, witness

no•tice•able \ˈnō-tə-sə-bəl\ *adj* **1** : worthy of notice **2** ♦ : capable of being or likely to be noticed — **no•tice•ably** \-blē\ *adv*

♦ bold, catchy, conspicuous, emphatic, marked, prominent, pronounced, remarkable, striking ***Ant*** inconspicuous, unemphatic, unnoticeable, unobtrusive, unremarkable

no•ti•fi•ca•tion \ˌnō-tə-fə-ˈkā-shən\ *n* ♦ : the act or an instance of notifying

♦ advertisement, announcement, bulletin, notice, release

no•ti•fy \ˈnō-tə-ˌfī\ *vb* **-fied; -fy•ing** **1** : to give notice of : report the occurrence of **2** : to give notice to

no•tion \ˈnō-shən\ *n* **1** ♦ : an individual's conception or impression of something known, experienced, or imagined : IDEA, CONCEPTION ⟨have a ~ of what he means⟩ **2** ♦ : a belief held : OPINION, VIEW **3** ♦ : a personal inclination : WHIM, FANCY ⟨a sudden ~ to go⟩ **4** *pl* ♦ : small useful articles (as pins, needles, or thread)

♦ [1] concept, idea, image, impression, picture, thought ♦ [2] belief, conviction, eye, feeling, judgment (*or* judgement), mind, opinion, persuasion, sentiment, verdict, view ♦ [3] caprice, fancy, freak, vagary, whim ♦ **notions** [4] novelties, odds and ends, sundries

no•tion•al \ˈnō-shə-nəl\ *adj* **1** : existing in the mind only : IMAGINARY, UNREAL **2** : given to foolish or fanciful moods or ideas : WHIMSICAL

no•to•ri•ety \ˌnō-tə-ˈrī-ə-tē\ *n* ♦ : the quality or state of being notorious

♦ celebrity, fame, renown

no•to•ri•ous \nō-ˈtōr-ē-əs\ *adj* ♦ : generally known and talked of; *esp* : widely and unfavorably known — **no•to•ri•ous•ly** \nō-ˈtōr-ē-əs-lē\ *adv*

♦ celebrated, famed, famous, noted, prominent, renowned, star, well-known ♦ discreditable, disgraceful, dishonorable (*or* dishonourable), disreputable, ignominious, infamous, shameful

¹not•with•stand•ing \ˌnät-with-ˈstan-diŋ, -with-\ *prep* ♦ : in spite of

♦ despite, regardless of, with

²notwithstanding *adv* ♦ : in spite of that : NEVERTHELESS

♦ but, howbeit, however, nevertheless, nonetheless, still, though, withal, yet

³notwithstanding *conj* : ALTHOUGH

nou•gat \ˈnü-gət\ *n* : a confection of nuts or fruit pieces in a sugar paste

nought *var of* NAUGHT

noun \ˈnau̇n\ *n* : a word that is the name of a subject of discourse (as a person or place)

nour•ish \ˈnər-ish\ *vb* ♦ : to promote the growth or development of

♦ advance, cultivate, encourage, forward, foster, further, nurture, promote

nour•ish•ing *adj* ♦ : giving nourishment

♦ nutritious

nour•ish•ment \ˈnər-ish-mənt\ *n* **1** : FOOD, NUTRIENT **2** : the action or process of nourishing

nou•veau riche \ˌnü-ˌvō-ˈrēsh\ *n, pl* **nou•veaux riches** *same*\ : a person newly rich : PARVENU

Nov *abbr* November

no•va \ˈnō-və\ *n, pl* **novas** *or* **no•vae** \-(ˌ)vē, -ˌvī\ : a star that suddenly increases greatly in brightness and then within a few months or years grows dim again

¹nov•el \ˈnä-vəl\ *adj* **1** ♦ : having no precedent : NEW **2** : STRANGE, UNUSUAL

♦ fresh, new, original, strange, unfamiliar, unknown

²novel *n* : a long invented prose narrative dealing with human experience through a connected sequence of events — **nov•el•ist** \-və-list\ *n*

nov•el•ette \ˌnä-və-ˈlet\ *n* : a brief novel or long short story

nov•el•ize \ˈnä-və-ˌlīz\ *vb* **-ized; -iz•ing** : to convert into the form of a novel — **nov•el•i•za•tion** \ˌnä-və-lə-ˈzā-shən\ *n*

no•vel•la \nō-ˈve-lə\ *n, pl* **novellas** *or* **no•vel•le** \-ˈve-lē\ ♦ : a work of fiction between a short story and a novel in length and complexity : NOVELETTE

♦ narrative, short story, story, tale

nov•el•ty \ˈnä-vəl-tē\ *n, pl* **-ties** **1** : something new or unusual **2** ♦ : the quality or state of being new : NEWNESS **3** ♦ : a small manufactured article intended mainly for personal or household adornment — usually used in plural

♦ [2] freshness, newness, originality ♦ [3] bauble, curiosity, gewgaw, knickknack, trinket ♦ *usu* **novelties** [3] notions, odds and ends, sundries

No•vem•ber \nō-ˈvem-bər\ *n* : the 11th month of the year

no•ve•na \nō-ˈvē-nə\ *n* : a Roman Catholic nine-day period of prayer

nov•ice \ˈnä-vəs\ *n* **1** : a new member of a religious order who is preparing to take the vows of religion **2** ♦ : one who is inexperienced or untrained

♦ beginner, fledgling, freshman, greenhorn, neophyte, newcomer, recruit, rookie, tenderfoot, tyro

no•vi•tiate \nō-ˈvi-shət\ *n* **1** : the period or state of being a novice **2** : a house where novices are trained **3** : NOVICE

¹now \ˈnau̇\ *adv* **1** ♦ : at the present time or moment **2** ♦ : in the time immediately before the present **3** ♦ : in the time immediately to follow : IMMEDIATELY, FORTHWITH **4** — used with the sense of present time weakened or lost (as to express command, introduce an important point, or indicate a transition) ⟨~ hear this⟩ **5** : at times : SOMETIMES ⟨~ one and ~ another⟩ **6** : under the present circumstances **7** : at the time referred to

♦ [1] anymore, nowadays, presently, right now, today ***Ant*** before, formerly, long, once, then ♦ [2] freshly, just, late, lately, new, newly, only, recently ♦ [3] directly, forthwith, immediately, instantly, promptly, pronto, right away, right now

²now *conj* ♦ : in view of the fact ⟨~ that you're here, we'll start⟩

♦ because, for, since, whereas

³now *n* ♦ : the present time or moment : PRESENT

♦ moment, present, today

⁴now *adj* **1** : of or relating to the present time ⟨the ~ president⟩ **2** : excitingly new ⟨~ clothes⟩; *also* : constantly aware of what is new ⟨~ people⟩

NOW *abbr* **1** National Organization for Women **2** negotiable order of withdrawal

now•a•days \ˈnau̇-ə-ˌdāz\ *adv* ♦ : at the present time

♦ anymore, now, presently, right now, today

no•way \ˈnō-ˌwā\ *or* **no•ways** \-ˌwāz\ *adv* : NOWISE

no•where \-ˌhwer\ *adv* : not anywhere — **nowhere** *n*

nowhere near *adv* : not nearly

no•wise \ˈnō-ˌwīz\ *adv* ♦ : in no way

♦ never, no, none, nothing

nox•ious \ˈnäk-shəs\ *adj* ♦ : harmful especially to health or morals

♦ noisome, unhealthy, unwholesome ♦ adverse, bad, baleful, baneful, damaging, deleterious, detrimental, evil, harmful, hurtful, ill, injurious, mischievous, pernicious, prejudicial

noz•zle \ˈnä-zəl\ *n* : a short tube constricted in the middle or at one end and used (as on a hose) to speed up or direct a flow of fluid

np *abbr* **1** no pagination **2** no place (of publication)

Np *symbol* neptunium

NP *abbr* notary public

NR *abbr* not rated

NRA *abbr* National Rifle Association

NS *abbr* **1** not specified **2** Nova Scotia
NSA *abbr* National Security Agency
NSC *abbr* National Security Council
NSF *abbr* **1** National Science Foundation **2** not sufficient funds
NSW *abbr* New South Wales
NT *abbr* **1** New Testament **2** Northern Territory **3** Northwest Territories
nth \ˈenth\ *adj* **1 :** numbered with an unspecified or indefinitely large ordinal number ⟨for the ~ time⟩ **2** ♦ **:** of the greatest or highest degree, quantity, number, or amount **:** UTMOST ⟨to the ~ degree⟩

♦ consummate, maximum, most, paramount, supreme, top, ultimate, utmost

NTP *abbr* normal temperature and pressure
nt wt *or* **n wt** *abbr* net weight
nu \ˈnü, ˈnyü\ *n* **:** the 13th letter of the Greek alphabet — **N** or *ν*
NU *abbr* name unknown
nu•ance \ˈnü-ˌäns; ˈnyü-, nu̇-ˈäns, nyu̇-\ *n* **:** a shade of difference **:** a delicate variation (as in tone or meaning)
nub \ˈnəb\ *n* **1 :** a piece or mass of indefinite size and shape **:** KNOB, LUMP **2** ♦ **:** the main point or part **:** GIST ⟨the ~ of the story⟩

♦ core, crux, gist, heart, pith, pivot

nub•bin \ˈnə-bən\ *n* **1 :** something (as an ear of Indian corn) that is small for its kind, stunted, undeveloped, or imperfect **2 :** a small usually projecting part or bit
nu•bile \ˈnü-ˌbīl, ˈnyü-, -bəl\ *adj* **1 :** of marriageable condition or age **:** sexually mature **2 :** sexually attractive ⟨~ young women⟩
nu•cle•ar \ˈnü-klē-ər, ˈnyü-\ *adj* **1 :** of, relating to, or constituting a nucleus **2 :** of, relating to, or using the atomic nucleus or energy derived from it **3 :** of, relating to, or being a weapon whose destructive power results from an uncontrolled nuclear reaction
nu•cle•ate \ˈnü-klē-ˌāt, ˈnyü-\ *vb* **-at•ed; -at•ing :** to form, act as, or have a nucleus — **nu•cle•ation** \ˌnü-klē-ˈā-shən, ˌnyü-\ *n*
nu•cle•ic acid \nu̇-ˈklē-ik-, nyu̇-, -ˈklā-\ *n* **:** any of various complex organic acids (as DNA or RNA) found especially in cell nuclei
nu•cle•o•tide \ˈnü-klē-ə-ˌtīd, ˈnyü-\ *n* **:** any of several compounds that are the basic structural units of nucleic acids
nu•cle•us \ˈnü-klē-əs, ˈnyü-\ *n, pl* **nu•clei** \-klē-ˌī\ *also* **nu•cle•us•es** **1 :** a central mass or part about which matter gathers or is collected **:** CORE **2 :** a cell part that is characteristic of all living things except viruses, bacteria, and certain algae, that is necessary for heredity and for making proteins, that contains the chromosomes with their genes, and that is enclosed in a membrane **3 :** a mass of gray matter or group of cell bodies of neurons in the central nervous system **4 :** the central part of an atom that comprises nearly all of the atomic mass **5** ♦ **:** a basic or essential part

♦ base, center (*or* centre), core, cynosure, eye, focus, heart, hub, mecca, seat

[1]**nude** \ˈnüd, ˈnyüd\ *adj* **nud•er; nud•est** **1** ♦ **:** devoid of a natural or conventional covering **:** BARE, NAKED **2 :** featuring or catering to naked people — **nu•di•ty** \ˈnü-də-tē, ˈnyü-\ *n*

♦ bare, naked, unclad, unclothed, undressed

[2]**nude** *n* **1 :** a nude human figure especially as depicted in art **2 :** the condition of being nude ⟨in the ~⟩
nudge \ˈnəj\ *vb* **nudged; nudg•ing :** to touch or push gently (as with the elbow) usually in order to seek attention — **nudge** *n*
nud•ism \ˈnü-ˌdi-zəm, ˈnyü-\ *n* **:** the practice of going nude especially in mixed groups at specially secluded places — **nud•ist** \-dist\ *n*
nu•ga•to•ry \-gə-ˌtōr-ē\ *adj* **1 :** INCONSEQUENTIAL, WORTHLESS **2 :** having no force **:** INEFFECTUAL
nug•get \ˈnə-gət\ *n* **1 :** a solid lump; *esp* **:** a lump of precious metal (as gold) **2 :** TIDBIT
nui•sance \ˈnüs-ᵊns, ˈnyüs-\ *n* ♦ **:** an annoying or troublesome person or thing

♦ annoyance, bother, gadfly, persecutor, pest, tease ♦ aggravation, annoyance, bother, exasperation, frustration, hassle, headache, inconvenience, irritant, peeve, pest, problem, thorn

nuisance tax *n* **:** an excise tax collected in small amounts directly from the consumer
[1]**nuke** \ˈnük, ˈnyük\ *n* **1 :** a nuclear weapon **2 :** a nuclear power plant
[2]**nuke** *vb* **nuked; nuk•ing** **1 :** to attack with nuclear weapons **2 :** MICROWAVE
null \ˈnəl\ *adj* **1** ♦ **:** having no legal or binding force **:** INVALID, VOID **2** ♦ **:** amounting to nothing **3 :** INSIGNIFICANT — **nul•li•ty** \ˈnə-lə-tē\ *n*

♦ [1] invalid, void *Ant* binding, good, valid ♦ [2] chaffy, empty, junky, no-good, valueless, worthless

null and void *adj* **:** having no force, binding power, or validity
nul•li•fy \ˈnə-lə-ˌfī\ *vb* **-fied; -fy•ing** ♦ **:** to make null or valueless; *also* **:** to declare or make legally invalid or void — **nul•li•fi•ca•tion** \ˌnə-lə-fə-ˈkā-shən\ *n*

♦ abolish, abrogate, annul, cancel, dissolve, invalidate, negate, quash, repeal, rescind, void

num *abbr* numeral
Num *or* **Numb** *abbr* Numbers
numb \ˈnəm\ *adj* ♦ **:** lacking sensation or emotion — **numb•ly** *adv*

♦ asleep, dead, unfeeling *Ant* feeling, sensitive

numb *vb* ♦ **:** to make as if dead **:** impair in vigor, force, activity, or sensation

♦ blunt, dampen, deaden, dull

[1]**num•ber** \ˈnəm-bər\ *n* **1 :** the total of individuals or units taken together **2 :** an indefinite total ⟨a small ~ of tickets remain unsold⟩ **3 :** an ascertainable total ⟨the sands of the desert are without ~⟩ **4 :** a distinction of word form to denote reference to one or more than one **5 :** a unit belonging to a mathematical system and subject to its laws; *also, pl* **:** ARITHMETIC **6** ♦ **:** a symbol used to represent a mathematical number; *also* **:** such a number used to identify or designate ⟨a phone ~⟩ **7 :** one in a series of musical or theatrical performances ⟨the best ~ on the program⟩

♦ digit, figure, integer, numeral, whole number

[2]**number** *vb* **1 :** to indicate or name by units or groups so as to find the total number of units involved **:** COUNT, ENUMERATE **2** ♦ **:** to include with or be one of a group **3 :** to restrict to a small or definite number **4 :** to assign a number to **5** ♦ **:** to comprise in number **:** TOTAL

♦ [2] carry, comprehend, contain, embrace, encompass, entail, include, involve, take in ♦ [5] add up, amount, come, sum, total

number crunching *n* ♦ **:** the performance of long complex often repetitive mathematical calculations; *also* **:** statistical analysis

♦ arithmetic, calculation, computation, reckoning

num•ber•less \-ləs\ *adj* ♦ **:** too many to be numbered **:** INNUMERABLE, COUNTLESS

♦ countless, innumerable, uncountable, unnumbered, untold

Numbers *n* **:** a book of Jewish and Christian Scripture
numb•ing \ˈnə-miŋ\ *adj* **:** tending to make numb ⟨a ~ lecture⟩ ⟨a ~ realization⟩
numb•ness *n* ♦ **:** reduced sensitivity to perception or emotion

♦ apathy, impassivity, phlegm, stupor

numbskull *var of* NUMSKULL
nu•mer•acy \ˈnü-mə-rə-sē, ˈnyü-\ *n* **:** the capacity for quantitative thought or expression
nu•mer•al \ˈnü-mə-rəl, ˈnyü-\ *n* ♦ **:** a conventional symbol representing a number — **numeral** *adj*

♦ digit, figure, integer, number, whole number

nu•mer•ate \ˈnü-mə-ˌrāt, ˈnyü-\ *vb* **-at•ed; -at•ing** **1 :** to ascertain the number of **2** ♦ **:** to specify one after another

♦ detail, enumerate, itemize, list, rehearse, tick (off)

nu•mer•a•tor \-ˌrā-tər\ *n* **:** the part of a fraction above the line
nu•mer•ic \nu̇-ˈmer-ik, nyu̇-\ *adj* **:** NUMERICAL; *esp* **:** denoting a number or a system of numbers
nu•mer•i•cal \-ˈmer-i-kəl\ *adj* **1 :** of or relating to numbers **2 :** expressed in or involving numbers — **nu•mer•i•cal•ly** \-k(ə-)lē\ *adv*
nu•mer•ol•o•gy \ˌnü-mə-ˈrä-lə-jē, ˌnyü-\ *n* **:** the study of the occult significance of numbers — **nu•mer•ol•o•gist** \-jist\ *n*
nu•mer•ous \ˈnü-mə-rəs, ˈnyü-\ *adj* ♦ **:** consisting of, including, or relating to a great number **:** MANY

♦ many, multiple, multitudinous

nu•mis•mat•ics \ˌnü-məz-ˈma-tiks, ˌnyü-\ *n* **:** the study or collection of monetary objects — **nu•mis•mat•ic** \-tik\ *adj* — **nu•mis•ma•tist** \nü-ˈmiz-mə-tist, nyü-\ *n*
num•skull \ˈnəm-ˌskəl\ *n* ♦ **:** a stupid person **:** DUNCE

♦ blockhead, dope, dummy, idiot, imbecile, jackass, moron

nun \ˈnən\ *n* **:** a woman belonging to a religious order; *esp* **:** one under solemn vows of poverty, chastity, and obedience
nun·cio \ˈnən-sē-ˌō, ˈnu̇n-\ *n, pl* **-ci·os :** a permanent high-ranking papal representative to a civil government
nun·nery \ˈnə-nə-rē\ *n, pl* **-ner·ies :** a convent of nuns
[1]nup·tial \ˈnəp-shəl\ *adj* ♦ **:** of or relating to marriage or a wedding

♦ conjugal, connubial, marital, matrimonial

[2]nuptial *n* **:** MARRIAGE, WEDDING — usually used in plural
[1]nurse \ˈnərs\ *n* **1** ♦ **:** a girl or woman employed to take care of children **2 :** a person trained to care for sick people

♦ nanny, nursemaid

[2]nurse *vb* **nursed; nurs·ing 1 :** SUCKLE **2** ♦ **:** to take charge of and watch over **3 :** TEND ⟨~ an invalid⟩ **4** ♦ **:** to treat with special care ⟨~ a headache⟩ **5** ♦ **:** to hold in one's mind or consideration ⟨~ a grudge⟩ **6 :** to act or serve as a nurse

♦ [2] aid, care, minister, mother ♦ [4] baby, coddle, mollycoddle, pamper, spoil ♦ [5] bear, cherish, entertain, harbor (*or* harbour), have, hold

nurse·maid \ˈnərs-ˌmād\ *n* ♦ **:** a girl or woman who is regularly employed to look after children **:** NURSE 1

♦ nanny, nurse

nurse–prac·ti·tion·er \-prak-ˈti-shə-nər\ *n* **:** a registered nurse who is qualified to assume some of the duties formerly assumed only by a physician
nurs·ery \ˈnər-sə-rē\ *n, pl* **-er·ies 1 :** a room for children **2 :** a place where children are temporarily cared for in their parents' absence **3 :** a place where young plants are grown usually for transplanting
nurs·ery·man \-mən\ *n* **:** a man who keeps or works in a plant nursery
nursery school *n* **:** a school for children under kindergarten age
nursing home *n* **:** a private establishment providing care for persons (as the aged or the chronically ill) who are unable to care for themselves
nurs·ling \ˈnərs-liŋ\ *n* **1 :** one that is solicitously cared for **2 :** a nursing child
[1]nur·ture \ˈnər-chər\ *n* **1 :** TRAINING, UPBRINGING; *also* **:** the influences that modify the expression of an individual's heredity **2 :** FOOD, NOURISHMENT
[2]nurture *vb* **nur·tured; nur·tur·ing 1 :** to care for **:** FEED, NOURISH **2** ♦ **:** to develop mentally, morally, or aesthetically especially by instruction **:** EDUCATE **3** ♦ **:** to further the development of **:** FOSTER

♦ [2] edify, educate, enlighten ♦ [3] advance, cultivate, encourage, forward, foster, further, nourish, promote

nut \ˈnət\ *n* **1 :** a dry fruit or seed with a hard shell and a firm inner kernel; *also* **:** its kernel **2 :** a metal block with a hole through it that is fastened to a bolt or screw by means of a screw thread within the hole **3 :** the ridge on the upper end of the fingerboard in a stringed musical instrument over which the strings pass **4** ♦ **:** a foolish, eccentric, or crazy person **5** ♦ **:** one who is ardently attached to a cause, object, or pursuit **:** ENTHUSIAST

♦ [4] character, crackpot, crank, eccentric, kook, oddball, screwball, weirdo ♦ [4] booby, fool, goose, half-wit, jackass, lunatic, nitwit, simpleton, turkey ♦ [5] addict, aficionado, buff, bug, devotee, enthusiast, fan, fanatic, fancier, fiend, freak, lover, maniac

nut·crack·er \ˈnət-ˌkra-kər\ *n* **:** an instrument for cracking nuts
nut·hatch \-ˌhach\ *n* **:** any of various small tree-climbing chiefly insect-eating birds
nut·meg \-ˌmeg, -ˌmāg\ *n* **:** a spice made by grinding the nutlike aromatic seed of a tropical tree; *also* **:** the seed or tree
nu·tria \ˈnü-trē-ə, ˈnyü-\ *n* **1 :** the durable usually light brown fur of a nutria **2 :** a large So. American aquatic rodent with webbed hind feet
[1]nu·tri·ent \ˈnü-trē-ənt, ˈnyü-\ *adj* **:** furnishing nourishment **:** NOURISHING
[2]nutrient *n* **:** a nutritive substance or ingredient
nu·tri·ment \-trə-mənt\ *n* **:** NUTRIENT
nu·tri·tion \nu̇-ˈtri-shən, nyu̇-\ *n* **:** the act or process of nourishing; *esp* **:** the processes by which an individual takes in and utilizes food material
nu·tri·tion·al \-shə-nəl\ *adj* **:** of, relating to, or functioning in nutrition
nu·tri·tious \-shəs\ *adj* ♦ **:** giving nourishment

♦ nourishing

nu·tri·tive \ˈnü-trə-tiv, ˈnyü-\ *adj* **:** of or relating to nutrition
nuts \ˈnəts\ *adj* **1** ♦ filled with or marked by enthusiasm **2 :** mentally disordered **:** CRAZY, DEMENTED

♦ ardent, eager, enthusiastic, gung ho, keen ♦ *usu* **nuts about** crazy, mad

nut·shell \ˈnət-ˌshel\ *n* **:** the shell of a nut — **in a nutshell :** in a few words ⟨that's the story *in a nutshell*⟩
nut·ty \ˈnə-tē\ *adj* **nut·ti·er; -est 1 :** containing or suggesting nuts ⟨a ~ flavor⟩ **2** ♦ **:** mentally unbalanced; *also* **:** lacking in seriousness **:** SILLY

♦ absurd, crazy, cuckoo, fatuous, foolish, mad, nonsensical, nutty, senseless, silly, stupid

nuz·zle \ˈnə-zəl\ *vb* **nuz·zled; nuz·zling 1 :** to root around, push, or touch with or as if with the nose **2** ♦ **:** to press closely and affectionately **:** SNUGGLE

♦ cuddle, nestle, snug, snuggle

NV *abbr* Nevada
NW *abbr* northwest
NWT *abbr* Northwest Territories
NY *abbr* New York
NYC *abbr* New York City
ny·lon \ˈnī-ˌlän\ *n* **1 :** any of numerous strong tough elastic synthetic materials used especially in textiles and plastics **2** *pl* **:** stockings made of nylon
nymph \ˈnimf\ *n* **1 :** any of the lesser goddesses in ancient mythology represented as maidens living in the mountains, forests, meadows, and waters **2 :** GIRL **3 :** an immature insect resembling the adult but smaller, less differentiated, and usually lacking wings
nym·pho·ma·nia \ˌnim-fə-ˈmā-nē-ə, -nyə\ *n* **:** excessive sexual desire by a female — **nym·pho·ma·ni·ac** \-nē-ˌak\ *n or adj*
NZ *abbr* New Zealand

O

[1]o \ˈō\ *n, pl* **o's** *or* **os** \ˈōz\ *often cap* **1 :** the 15th letter of the English alphabet **2 :** ZERO
[2]o *abbr, often cap* **1** ocean **2** Ohio **3** ohm
[1]O *var of* OH
[2]O *abbr* Ohio
[3]O *symbol* oxygen
o/a *abbr* on or about
oaf \ˈōf\ *n* ♦ **:** a stupid or awkward person

♦ clod, gawk, hulk, lout, lubber, lug

oaf·ish *adj* **:** having the qualities typical of an oaf
oak \ˈōk\ *n, pl* **oaks** *or* **oak :** any of a genus of trees or shrubs related to the beech and chestnut and bearing a rounded thin-shelled nut surrounded at the base by a hardened cup; *also* **:** the usually tough hard durable wood of an oak — **oak·en** \ˈō-kən\ *adj*
oa·kum \ˈō-kəm\ *n* **:** loosely twisted hemp or jute fiber impregnated with tar and used especially in caulking ships
oar \ˈōr\ *n* **:** a long pole with a broad blade at one end used for propelling or steering a boat
oar·lock \ˈōr-ˌläk\ *n* **:** a U-shaped device for holding an oar in place
oars·man \ˈōrz-mən\ *n* **:** one who rows especially in a racing crew
OAS *abbr* Organization of American States
oa·sis \ō-ˈā-səs\ *n, pl* **oa·ses** \-ˌsēz\ **:** a fertile or green area in an arid region

oat \ˈōt\ *n* **:** a cereal grass widely grown for its edible seed; *also* **:** this seed — **oat•en** \-ᵊn\ *adj*
oat•cake \ˈōt-ˌkāk\ *n* **:** a thin flat oatmeal cake
oath \ˈōth\ *n, pl* **oaths** \ˈōt͟hz, ˈōths\ **1** ♦ **:** a solemn appeal to God to witness to the truth of a statement or the sacredness of a promise **2 :** an irreverent or careless use of a sacred name

♦ pledge, promise, troth, vow, word

oat•meal \ˈōt-ˌmēl\ *n* **1 :** ground or rolled oats **2 :** porridge made from ground or rolled oats
Ob *or* **Obad** *abbr* Obadiah
Oba•di•ah \ˌō-bə-ˈdī-ə\ *n* **:** a book of canonical Jewish and Christian Scripture
ob•bli•ga•to \ˌä-blə-ˈgä-tō\ *n, pl* **-tos** *also* **-ti** \-ˈgä-tē\ **:** an accompanying part usually played by a solo instrument
ob•du•ra•cy \ˈäb-də-rə-sē, -dyə-\ *n* ♦ **:** the quality or state of being obdurate

♦ hardheadedness, mulishness, obstinacy, peevishness, pertinacity, self-will, stubbornness, tenacity

ob•du•rate \ˈäb-də-rət, -dyə-\ *adj* **1** ♦ **:** stubbornly resistant **:** UNYIELDING **2** ♦ **:** hardened in feelings

♦ [1] dogged, hardheaded, headstrong, mulish, obstinate, opinionated, peevish, pertinacious, perverse, pigheaded, stubborn, unyielding, willful ♦ [2] callous, hard, heartless, inhuman, inhumane, pitiless, soulless, unfeeling, unsympathetic

obe•di•ence \ō-ˈbē-dē-əns\ *n* ♦ **:** an act or instance of obeying

♦ compliance, conformity, observance, submission, subordination *Ant* disobedience, insubordination, noncompliance, rebelling, rebellion

obe•di•ent \ō-ˈbē-dē-ənt\ *adj* ♦ **:** submissive to the restraint or command of authority — **obe•di•ent•ly** *adv*

♦ amenable, compliant, conformable, docile, submissive, tractable *Ant* contrary, disobedient, froward, insubordinate, intractable, rebellious, recalcitrant, refractory, unruly

obei•sance \ō-ˈbē-səns, -ˈbā-\ *n* **:** a bow made to show respect or submission; *also* **:** DEFERENCE, HOMAGE
obe•lisk \ˈä-bə-ˌlisk\ *n* **:** a 4-sided pillar that tapers toward the top and ends in a pyramid
obese \ō-ˈbēs\ *adj* ♦ **:** excessively fat

♦ chubby, corpulent, fat, fleshy, full, gross, overweight, plump, portly, rotund, round

obe•si•ty \-ˈbē-sə-tē\ *n* ♦ **:** a condition characterized by the excessive accumulation and storage of fat in the body

♦ corpulence, fatness, grossness, plumpness

obey \ō-ˈbā\ *vb* **obeyed; obey•ing 1 :** to follow the commands or guidance of **:** behave obediently **2** ♦ **:** to comply with ⟨~ orders⟩

♦ comply, conform, follow, mind, observe *Ant* disobey

ob•fus•cate \ˈäb-fə-ˌskāt\ *vb* **-cat•ed; -cat•ing 1 :** to make dark or obscure **2 :** CONFUSE — **ob•fus•ca•tion** \ˌäb-fəs-ˈkā-shən\ *n*
OB–GYN *abbr* obstetrician gynecologist; obstetrics gynecology
obi \ˈō-bē\ *n* **:** a broad sash worn especially with a Japanese kimono
obit \ō-ˈbit, ˈō-bət\ *n* **:** OBITUARY
obi•ter dic•tum \ˌō-bə-tər-ˈdik-təm\ *n, pl* **obiter dic•ta** \-tə\ **:** an incidental remark or observation
obit•u•ary \ə-ˈbi-chə-ˌwer-ē\ *n, pl* **-ar•ies :** a notice of a person's death usually with a short biographical account
obj *abbr* object; objective
¹ob•ject \ˈäb-jikt\ *n* **1** ♦ **:** something that may be seen or felt; *also* **:** something that may be perceived or examined mentally **2 :** something that arouses an emotional response (as of affection or pity) **3** ♦ **:** the goal or end of an effort or activity **:** AIM, PURPOSE **4 :** a word or word group denoting that on or toward which the action of a verb is directed; *also* **:** a noun or noun equivalent in a prepositional phrase

♦ [1] being, entity, individual, substance, thing ♦ [3] aim, ambition, aspiration, design, dream, end, goal, intent, mark, meaning, objective, plan, pretension, purpose, thing

²ob•ject \əb-ˈjekt\ *vb* **1** ♦ **:** to offer in opposition **2** ♦ **:** to oppose something; *also* **:** DISAPPROVE — **ob•jec•tor** \-ˈjek-tər\ *n*

♦ [1, 2] challenge, complain, criticize, demur, disapprove, dispute, kick, protest, quarrel, remonstrate

object code *n* **:** a computer program after translation from source code

ob•jec•ti•fy \əb-ˈjek-tə-ˌfī\ *vb* **-fied; -fy•ing :** to make objective
ob•jec•tion \əb-ˈjek-shən\ *n* **1** ♦ **:** the act of objecting **2 :** a reason for or a feeling of disapproval

♦ challenge, complaint, demur, expostulation, fuss, kick, protest, question, remonstrance

ob•jec•tion•able \əb-ˈjek-shə-nə-bəl\ *adj* ♦ **:** arousing objection **:** UNDESIRABLE, OFFENSIVE — **ob•jec•tion•ably** \-blē\ *adv*

♦ censurable, obnoxious, offensive, reprehensible *Ant* inoffensive, unobjectionable

¹ob•jec•tive \əb-ˈjek-tiv\ *adj* **1 :** of or relating to an object or end **2 :** existing outside and independent of the mind **3 :** of, relating to, or constituting a grammatical case marking typically the object of a verb or preposition **4** ♦ **:** treating or dealing with facts without distortion by personal feelings or prejudices — **ob•jec•tive•ly** *adv* — **ob•jec•tive•ness** *n*

♦ disinterested, dispassionate, equal, equitable, fair, impartial, just, nonpartisan, square, unbiased, unprejudiced

²objective *n* **1 :** the lens (as in a microscope) nearest the object and forming an image of it **2** ♦ **:** an aim, goal, or end of action

♦ aim, ambition, aspiration, design, dream, end, goal, intent, mark, meaning, object, plan, pretension, purpose, thing

ob•jec•tiv•i•ty \ˌäb-ˌjek-ˈti-və-tē\ *n* ♦ **:** the quality, state, or relation of being objective

♦ detachment, disinterestedness, impartiality, neutrality

ob•jet d'art \ˌȯb-ˌzhā-ˈdär\ *n, pl* **ob•jets d'art** *same*\ **:** an article of artistic worth; *also* **:** CURIO
ob•jet trou•vé \ˈȯb-ˌzhā-trü-ˈvā\ *n, pl* **objets trouvés** *same*\ **:** a found natural or discarded object (as a piece of driftwood) held to have aesthetic value
ob•jur•ga•tion \ˌäb-jər-ˈgā-shən\ *n* **:** a harsh rebuke — **ob•jur•gate** \ˈäb-jər-ˌgāt\ *vb*
obl *abbr* **1** oblique **2** oblong
ob•late \ä-ˈblāt\ *adj* **:** flattened or depressed at the poles ⟨an ~ spheroid⟩
ob•la•tion \ə-ˈblā-shən\ *n* **:** a religious offering
ob•li•gate \ˈä-blə-ˌgāt\ *vb* **-gat•ed; -gat•ing** ♦ **:** to bind legally or morally

♦ coerce, compel, constrain, drive, force, make, muscle, oblige, press, pressure

ob•li•gat•ed \ˈä-blə-ˌgā-təd\ *adj* ♦ **:** bound legally or morally

♦ beholden, indebted, obliged

ob•li•ga•tion \ˌä-blə-ˈgā-shən\ *n* **1 :** an act of obligating oneself to a course of action **2** ♦ **:** something (as a promise or a contract) that binds one to a course of action **3 :** INDEBTEDNESS; *also* **:** LIABILITY **4 :** DUTY

♦ burden, charge, commitment, duty, need, responsibility

oblig•a•to•ry \ə-ˈbli-gə-ˌtōr-ē\ *adj* ♦ **:** binding in law or conscience

♦ compulsory, imperative, incumbent, involuntary, mandatory, necessary, nonelective, peremptory

oblige \ə-ˈblīj\ *vb* **obliged; oblig•ing 1** ♦ **:** to constrain by physical, moral, or legal force or by the requirements of circumstance **:** FORCE, COMPEL **2 :** to bind by a favor; *also* **:** to do a favor for or do something as a favor

♦ coerce, compel, constrain, drive, force, make, muscle, obligate, press, pressure

obliged \ə-ˈblījd\ *adj* **1** ♦ **:** full of appreciation **2** ♦ **:** in someone's debt by a favor or service

♦ [1] appreciative, grateful, thankful ♦ [2] beholden, indebted, obligated

oblig•ing *adj* ♦ **:** willing to do favors — **oblig•ing•ly** *adv*

♦ accommodating, friendly, indulgent

oblique \ō-ˈblēk\ *adj* **1** ♦ **:** neither perpendicular nor parallel **:** having a slant **2 :** not straightforward **:** INDIRECT — **oblique•ness** *n* — **obliq•ui•ty** \-ˈbli-kwə-tē\ *n*

♦ canted, diagonal, inclined, leaning, listing, slantwise

oblique case *n* **:** a grammatical case other than the nominative or vocative
oblique•ly *adv* ♦ **:** in an oblique way or direction

♦ athwart, crosswise, transversely

oblit•er•ate \ə-ˈbli-tə-ˌrāt\ *vb* **-at•ed; -at•ing 1 :** to make undecipherable by wiping out or covering over **2 :** to remove from recognition or memory **3 :** CANCEL **4** ♦ **:** to remove from existence

♦ annihilate, blot out, demolish, eradicate, exterminate, liquidate, root, rub out, snuff, stamp, wipe out

oblit•er•a•tion \ə-ˌbli-tə-ˈrā-shən\ *n* ♦ **:** the state of being obliterated

♦ annihilation, demolition, desolation, destruction, devastation, havoc, loss, ruin, wastage, wreckage

obliv•i•on \ə-ˈbli-vē-ən\ *n* **1 :** the condition of being oblivious **2 :** the condition or state of being forgotten

obliv•i•ous \ə-ˈbli-ve-əs\ *adj* **1 :** lacking memory or mindful attention **2** ♦ **:** lacking active conscious knowledge or awareness **:** UNAWARE — **obliv•i•ous•ly** *adv*

♦ ignorant, unaware, unconscious, uninformed, unknowing, unwitting

obliv•i•ous•ness *n* ♦ **:** the quality or state of being oblivious

♦ ignorance, unawareness

ob•long \ˈä-ˌblȯŋ\ *adj* **:** deviating from a square, circular, or spherical form by elongation in one dimension — **oblong** *n*

ob•lo•quy \ˈä-blə-kwē\ *n, pl* **-quies 1 :** strongly condemnatory utterance or language **2 :** bad repute **:** DISGRACE

ob•nox•ious \äb-ˈnäk-shəs\ *adj* **1** ♦ **:** odiously or disgustingly objectionable **:** highly offensive **:** REPUGNANT, OFFENSIVE **2** *archaic* **:** deserving of censure — **ob•nox•ious•ly** *adv* — **ob•nox•ious•ness** *n*

♦ abhorrent, abominable, appalling, awful, distasteful, dreadful, foul, nauseating, noisome, odious, offensive, repellent, repugnant, repulsive, revolting

oboe \ˈō-bō\ *n* **:** a woodwind instrument with a slender conical tube and a double reed mouthpiece — **obo•ist** \ˈō-ˌbō-ist\ *n*

ob•scene \äb-ˈsēn\ *adj* **1 :** disgusting to the senses **:** REPULSIVE **2** ♦ **:** deeply offensive to morality or decency; *esp* **:** designed to incite to lust or depravity — **ob•scene•ly** *adv*

♦ bawdy, coarse, crude, dirty, filthy, foul, gross, indecent, lascivious, lewd, nasty, pornographic, ribald, smutty, unprintable, vulgar, wanton *Ant* clean, decent

ob•scen•i•ty \-ˈse-nə-tē\ *n* ♦ **:** the quality or state of being obscene

♦ bawdiness, coarseness, dirt, dirtiness, filth, filthiness, foulness, grossness, indecency, lewdness, nastiness, ribaldry, smut, vulgarity

ob•scu•ran•tism \äb-ˈskyu̇r-ən-ˌti-zəm, ˌäb-skyu̇-ˈran-\ *n* **1 :** opposition to the spread of knowledge **2 :** deliberate vagueness or abstruseness — **ob•scu•ran•tist** \-tist\ *n or adj*

¹ob•scure \äb-ˈskyu̇r\ *adj* **1** ♦ **:** emitting or having a limited or insufficient amount of light **:** DIM, GLOOMY **2** ♦ **:** not readily understood **3** ♦ **:** relatively unknown; *also* **:** HUMBLE — **ob•scure•ly** *adv*

♦ [1] dark, darkling, dim, dusky, gloomy, murky, somber (*or* sombre) ♦ [2] ambiguous, cryptic, dark, darkling, deep, enigmatic, equivocal, inscrutable, murky, mysterious, mystic, nebulous, occult, unclear, vague *Ant* clear, obvious, plain, unambiguous, unequivocal ♦ [3] anonymous, humble, nameless, unknown, unsung *Ant* celebrated, famed, famous, noted, notorious, prominent, renowned, well-known

²obscure *vb* **ob•scured; ob•scur•ing 1** ♦ **:** to make dark, dim, or indistinct **2** ♦ **:** to conceal or hide by or as if by covering

♦ [1] becloud, befog, blur, cloud, darken, dim, fog, haze, mist, overcast, overshadow, shroud ♦ [2] blanket, blot out, cloak, conceal, cover, curtain, enshroud, hide, mask, occult, screen, shroud, veil

ob•scu•ri•ty \-ˈskyu̇r-ə-tē\ *n* ♦ **:** the quality or state of being obscure

♦ ambiguity, darkness, murkiness, opacity *Ant* clarity, clearness, obviousness, plainness

ob•se•qui•ous \əb-ˈsē-kwē-əs\ *adj* **:** humbly or excessively attentive (as to a person in authority) **:** FAWNING, SYCOPHANTIC — **ob•se•qui•ous•ly** *adv* — **ob•se•qui•ous•ness** *n*

ob•se•quy \ˈäb-sə-kwē\ *n, pl* **-quies :** a funeral or burial rite — usually used in plural

ob•serv•able \əb-ˈzər-və-bəl\ *adj* **1 :** NOTEWORTHY **2** ♦ **:** capable of being observed — **ob•serv•abil•ity** \-ˈbi-lə-tē\ *n*

♦ apparent, visible, visual

ob•ser•vance \əb-ˈzər-vəns\ *n* **1** ♦ **:** a customary practice or ceremony **2** ♦ **:** an act or instance of following a custom, rule, or law **3** ♦ **:** an act or instance of watching **:** OBSERVATION

♦ [1] ceremonial, ceremony, form, formality, rite, ritual, solemnity ♦ [2] compliance, conformity, obedience, submission, subordination ♦ [3] attention, awareness, cognizance, ear, eye, heed, notice, observation

ob•ser•vant \-vənt\ *adj* **1** ♦ **:** paying strict attention ⟨~ spectators⟩ **2 :** KEEN, PERCEPTIVE **3 :** MINDFUL ⟨~ of the amenities⟩

♦ absorbed, attentive, engrossed, intent, rapt

ob•ser•va•tion \ˌäb-sər-ˈvā-shən, -zər-\ *n* **1** ♦ **:** an act or instance of observing **2 :** the gathering of information (as for scientific studies) by noting facts or occurrences **3** ♦ **:** a conclusion drawn from observing; *also* **:** REMARK **4 :** the fact of being observed — **ob•ser•va•tion•al** \-shə-nəl\ *adj*

♦ [1] attention, awareness, cognizance, ear, eye, heed, notice, observance ♦ [3] comment, note, reflection, remark

ob•ser•va•to•ry \əb-ˈzər-və-ˌtōr-ē\ *n, pl* **-ries :** a place or institution equipped for observation of natural phenomena (as in astronomy)

ob•serve \əb-ˈzərv\ *vb* **ob•served; ob•serv•ing 1** ♦ **:** to conform one's action or practice to **2** ♦ **:** to celebrate or solemnize (as a ceremony or festival) in a customary or accepted way **:** CELEBRATE **3 :** to make a scientific observation of **4** ♦ **:** to see or sense especially through careful attention **5 :** to come to realize especially through consideration of noted facts **6** ♦ **:** to utter as a remark **:** REMARK — **ob•serv•er** *n*

♦ [1] comply, conform, follow, mind, obey ♦ [2] celebrate, commemorate, keep ♦ [4] behold, descry, discern, distinguish, espy, eye, look, note, notice, perceive, regard, remark, see, sight, spy, view, witness ♦ [6] comment, note, opine, remark

ob•sess \əb-ˈses\ *vb* **:** to preoccupy intensely or abnormally

ob•ses•sion \äb-ˈse-shən\ *n* ♦ **:** a persistent disturbing preoccupation with an idea or feeling; *also* **:** an emotion or idea causing such a preoccupation — **ob•ses•sive** \-ˈse-siv\ *adj or n* — **ob•ses•sive•ly** *adv*

♦ fetish, fixation, mania, preoccupation, prepossession

obsessive–compulsive *adj* **:** relating to, characterized by, or affected with recurring obsessions and compulsions especially as symptoms of a neurotic state

ob•sid•i•an \əb-ˈsi-dē-ən\ *n* **:** a dark natural glass formed by the cooling of molten lava

ob•so•les•cent \ˌäb-sə-ˈles-ᵊnt\ *adj* **:** going out of use **:** becoming obsolete — **ob•so•les•cence** \-ᵊns\ *n*

ob•so•lete \ˌäb-sə-ˈlēt, ˈäb-sə-ˌlēt\ *adj* ♦ **:** no longer in use; *also* **:** OLD-FASHIONED

♦ antiquated, archaic, dated, old-fashioned, outdated, outmoded, outworn, passé

ob•sta•cle \ˈäb-sti-kəl\ *n* ♦ **:** something that stands in the way or opposes

♦ bar, block, clog, crimp, drag, embarrassment, encumbrance, fetter, handicap, hindrance, let, stop, stumbling block

ob•stet•rics \əb-ˈste-triks\ *n sing or pl* **:** a branch of medicine that deals with birth and with its antecedents and sequels — **ob•stet•ric** \-trik\ *or* **ob•stet•ri•cal** \-tri-kəl\ *adj* — **ob•ste•tri•cian** \ˌäb-stə-ˈtri-shən\ *n*

ob•sti•na•cy \ˈäb-stə-nə-sē\ *n* ♦ **:** the quality or state of being obstinate

♦ hardheadedness, mulishness, obduracy, peevishness, pertinacity, self will, stubbornness, tenacity

ob•sti•nate \ˈäb-stə-nət\ *adj* ♦ **:** fixed and unyielding (as in an opinion or course) despite reason or persuasion **:** STUBBORN — **ob•sti•nate•ly** *adv*

♦ dogged, hardheaded, headstrong, mulish, obdurate, opinionated, peevish, pertinacious, perverse, pigheaded, stubborn, unyielding, willful

ob•strep•er•ous \əb-ˈstre-pə-rəs\ *adj* **1** ♦ **:** uncontrollably noisy **2 :** stubbornly resistant to control **:** UNRULY — **ob•strep•er•ous•ness** *n*

♦ blatant, clamorous, vociferous

ob•struct \əb-ˈstrəkt\ *vb* **1** ♦ **:** to block by an obstacle **2** ♦ **:** to impede the passage, action, or operation of **3 :** to cut off from sight — **ob•struc•tive** \-ˈstrək-tiv\ *adj* — **ob•struc•tor** \-tər\ *n*

♦ [1] block, choke, clog, close (off), congest, dam, jam, plug (up), stop (up), stuff ♦ [2] delay, hamper, hinder, hold back, hold up, impede, inhibit, interfere with

ob•struc•tion \əb-ˈstrək-shən\ *n* **1 :** an act of obstructing **:** the

state of being obstructed **2** : something that obstructs : HINDRANCE
ob•struc•tion•ist \-shə-nist\ *n* : a person who hinders progress or business especially in a legislative body — **ob•struc•tion•ism** \-shə-ˌni-zəm\ *n*
ob•tain \əb-ˈtān\ *vb* **1** ♦ : to gain or attain usually by planning or effort **2** : to be generally recognized or established

♦ acquire, attain, capture, carry, draw, earn, gain, garner, get, land, make, procure, realize, secure, win

ob•tain•able *adj* ♦ : capable of being obtained

♦ accessible, acquirable, attainable, available, procurable

ob•trude \əb-ˈtrüd\ *vb* **ob•trud•ed; ob•trud•ing** **1** : to thrust out **2** : to thrust forward without warrant or request **3** ♦ : to become unduly prominent or interfering : INTRUDE — **ob•tru•sion** \-ˈtrü-zhən\ *n* — **ob•tru•sive•ly** *adv* — **ob•tru•sive•ness** *n*

♦ butt in, interfere, intrude, meddle, mess, nose, poke, pry, snoop

ob•tru•sive \-ˈtrü-siv\ *adj* ♦ : forward in manner or conduct

♦ intrusive, meddlesome, nosy, officious, presumptuous, prying

ob•tuse \äb-ˈtüs, -ˈtyüs\ *adj* **ob•tus•er; -est** **1** : exceeding 90 degrees but less than 180 degrees ⟨∼ angle⟩ **2** ♦ : not pointed or acute : BLUNT **3** ♦ : not sharp or quick of wit — **ob•tuse•ly** *adv*

♦ [2] blunt, dull ♦ [3] dense, dull, dumb, slow, stupid, thick, unintelligent

ob•tuse•ness *n* ♦ : the quality or state of being obtuse

♦ denseness, stupidity

obv *abbr* obverse
¹**ob•verse** \äb-ˈvərs, ˈäb-ˌvərs\ *adj* **1** : facing the observer or opponent **2** : being a counterpart or complement — **ob•verse•ly** *adv*
²**ob•verse** \ˈäb-ˌvərs, äb-ˈvərs\ *n* **1** : the side (as of a coin) bearing the principal design and lettering **2** : a front or principal surface **3** : a counterpart having the opposite orientation or force
ob•vi•ate \ˈäb-vē-ˌāt\ *vb* **-at•ed; -at•ing** ♦ : to anticipate and prevent (as a situation) or make unnecessary (as an action) — **ob•vi•a•tion** \ˌäb-vē-ˈā-shən\ *n*

♦ avert, forestall, help, preclude, prevent

ob•vi•ous \ˈäb-vē-əs\ *adj* ♦ : easily found, seen, or understood — **ob•vi•ous•ly** *adv* — **ob•vi•ous•ness** *n*

♦ apparent, broad, clear, clear-cut, distinct, evident, lucid, manifest, palpable, patent, perspicuous, plain, transparent, unambiguous, unequivocal, unmistakable ♦ blatant, conspicuous, egregious, flagrant, glaring, gross, patent, prominent, pronounced, rank, striking

OC *abbr* officer candidate
oc•a•ri•na \ˌä-kə-ˈrē-nə\ *n* : a wind instrument typically having an oval body with finger holes and a projecting mouthpiece
occas *abbr* occasionally
¹**oc•ca•sion** \ə-ˈkā-zhən\ *n* **1** ♦ : a favorable opportunity **2** ♦ : a direct or indirect cause **3** : the time of an event **4** : EXIGENCY **5** *pl* : AFFAIRS, BUSINESS **6** : a special event : CELEBRATION **7** ♦ : something that happens

♦ [1] chance, opening, opportunity, room ♦ [2] antecedent, cause, reason ♦ [7] affair, circumstance, episode, event, happening, incident, occurrence, thing

²**occasion** *vb* : BRING ABOUT, CAUSE
oc•ca•sion•al \ə-ˈkā-zhə-nəl\ *adj* **1** ♦ : happening or met with now and then ⟨∼ visits⟩ **2** : used or designed for a special occasion ⟨∼ verse⟩ — **oc•ca•sion•al•ly** *adv*

♦ casual, choppy, discontinuous, erratic, fitful, intermittent, irregular, spasmodic, sporadic, spotty, unsteady ♦ infrequent, rare, sporadic

oc•ci•den•tal \ˌäk-sə-ˈdent-ᵊl\ *adj, often cap* : WESTERN — **Occidental** *n*
Oc•ci•tan \ˈäk-sə-ˌtan\ *n* : a Romance language spoken in southern France
oc•clude \ə-ˈklüd\ *vb* **oc•clud•ed; oc•clud•ing** **1** ♦ : to block by an obstacle : OBSTRUCT ⟨an *occluded* artery⟩ **2** : to come together with opposing surfaces in contact — used of teeth — **oc•clu•sion** \-ˈklü-zhən\ *n* — **oc•clu•sive** \-ˈklü-siv\ *adj*

♦ block, choke, clog, close (off), congest, dam, jam, obstruct, plug (up), stop (up), stuff

¹**oc•cult** \ə-ˈkəlt\ *adj* **1** : not revealed : SECRET **2** ♦ : not easily apprehended or understood : MYSTERIOUS **3** ♦ : of or relating to supernatural agencies, their effects, or knowledge of them — **oc•cult•ism** \-ˈkəl-ˌti-zəm\ *n* — **oc•cult•ist** \-tist\ *n*

♦ [2] cryptic, darkling, deep, enigmatic, impenetrable, inscrutable, mysterious, mystic, uncanny ♦ [3] magic, magical, mystic, weird

²**occult** *n* : occult matters — used with *the*
oc•cu•pan•cy \ˈä-kyə-pən-sē\ *n, pl* **-cies** **1** : the act of occupying : the state of being occupied **2** : an occupied building or part of a building
oc•cu•pant \-pənt\ *n* ♦ : one who occupies something; *esp* : RESIDENT

♦ denizen, dweller, inhabitant, resident

oc•cu•pa•tion \ˌä-kyə-ˈpā-shən\ *n* **1** ♦ : an activity in which one engages; *esp* : VOCATION **2** : the taking possession of property; *also* : the taking possession of an area by a foreign military force — **oc•cu•pa•tion•al** \-shə-nəl\ *adj* — **oc•cu•pa•tion•al•ly** *adv*

♦ calling, employment, line, profession, trade, vocation, work

occupational therapy *n* : therapy by means of activity; *esp* : creative activity prescribed for its effect in promoting recovery or rehabilitation — **occupational therapist** *n*
oc•cu•pied \ˈä-kyə-ˌpīd\ *adj* ♦ : engaged in activity

♦ active, assiduous, busy, diligent, engaged, laborious, sedulous, working

oc•cu•py \ˈä-kyə-ˌpī\ *vb* **-py•ing** **1** ♦ : to engage the attention or energies of **2** : to fill up (an extent in space or time) **3** ♦ : to take or hold possession of **4** : to reside in as owner or tenant — **oc•cu•pi•er** *n*

♦ [1] absorb, busy, engage, engross, enthrall, fascinate, grip, immerse, interest, intrigue, involve ♦ [3] command, enjoy, have, hold, own, possess, retain

oc•cur \ə-ˈkər\ *vb* **oc•curred; oc•cur•ring** **1** : to be found or met with : APPEAR **2** ♦ : to come into existence : HAPPEN **3** : to come to mind ⟨it *occurred* to her⟩

♦ be, befall, betide, chance, come, go, happen, pass, transpire

oc•cur•rence \ə-ˈkər-əns\ *n* **1** ♦ : something that takes place **2** : the action or process of occurring

♦ affair, circumstance, episode, event, happening, incident, occasion, thing

ocean \ˈō-shən\ *n* **1** ♦ : the whole body of salt water that covers nearly three fourths of the surface of the earth **2** : any of the large bodies of water into which the great ocean is divided

♦ blue, brine, deep, sea

ocean•ar•i•um \ˌō-shə-ˈnar-ē-əm\ *n, pl* **-iums** *or* **-ia** \-ē-ə\ : a large marine aquarium
ocean•front \ˈō-shən-ˌfrənt\ *n* : a shore area on the ocean
ocean•go•ing \-ˌgō-iŋ\ *adj* : of, relating to, or suitable for travel on the ocean
oce•an•ic \ˌō-shē-ˈa-nik\ *adj* ♦ : of or relating to the ocean

♦ marine, maritime, pelagic

ocean•og•ra•phy \ˌō-shə-ˈnä-grə-fē\ *n* : a science dealing with the ocean and its phenomena — **ocean•og•ra•pher** \-fər\ *n* — **ocean•o•graph•ic** \-nə-ˈgra-fik\ *adj*
oce•lot \ˈä-sə-ˌlät, ˈō-\ *n* : a medium-sized American wildcat ranging southward from Texas to northern Argentina and having a tawny yellow or gray coat with black markings
ocher *or* **ochre** \ˈō-kər\ *n* : an earthy usually red or yellow iron ore used as a pigment; *also* : the color especially of yellow ocher
o'•clock \ə-ˈkläk\ *adv* : according to the clock
OCR *abbr* optical character reader; optical character recognition
OCS *abbr* officer candidate school
oct *abbr* octavo
Oct *abbr* October
oc•ta•gon \ˈäk-tə-ˌgän\ *n* : a polygon of eight angles and eight sides — **oc•tag•o•nal** \äk-ˈta-gən-ᵊl\ *adj*
oc•tane \ˈäk-ˌtān\ *n* : OCTANE NUMBER
octane number *n* : a number used to measure the antiknock properties of gasoline that increases as the likelihood of knocking decreases
oc•tave \ˈäk-tiv\ *n* **1** : a musical interval embracing eight degrees; *also* : a tone or note at this interval or the whole series of notes, tones, or keys within this interval **2** : a group of eight
oc•ta•vo \äk-ˈtā-vō, -ˈtä-\ *n, pl* **-vos** **1** : the size of a piece of paper cut eight from a sheet **2** : a book printed on octavo pages

oc•tet \äk-ˈtet\ *n* **1 :** a musical composition for eight voices or eight instruments; *also* **:** the performers of such a composition **2 :** a group or set of eight

Oc•to•ber \äk-ˈtō-bər\ *n* **:** the 10th month of the year

oc•to•ge•nar•i•an \ˌäk-tə-jə-ˈner-ē-ən\ *n* **:** a person whose age is in the eighties

oc•to•pus \ˈäk-tə-pəs\ *n, pl* **-pus•es** *or* **-pi** \-ˌpī\ **:** any of various sea mollusks with eight long muscular arms furnished with suckers

oc•to•syl•lab•ic \ˌäk-tə-sə-ˈla-bik\ *adj* **:** composed of verses having eight syllables — **octosyllabic** *n*

1**oc•u•lar** \ˈä-kyə-lər\ *adj* **1** ♦ **:** based on what has been seen **:** VISUAL **2 :** of or relating to the eye or the eyesight

♦ optical, visual

2**ocular** *n* **:** EYEPIECE

oc•u•list \ˈä-kyə-list\ *n* **1 :** OPHTHALMOLOGIST **2 :** OPTOMETRIST

1**OD** \ˌō-ˈdē\ *n* **:** an overdose of a drug and especially a narcotic

2**OD** *vb* **OD'd** *or* **ODed; OD'•ing; OD's :** to become ill or die from an OD

3**OD** *abbr* **1** doctor of optometry **2** right eye **3** officer of the day **4** olive drab **5** overdraft **6** overdrawn

odd \ˈäd\ *adj* **1 :** being only one of a pair or set ⟨an ~ shoe⟩ **2 :** somewhat more than the number mentioned ⟨forty ~ years ago⟩ **3 :** being an integer (as 1, 3, or 5) not divisible by two without leaving a remainder **4 :** additional to what is usual ⟨~ jobs⟩ **5** ♦ **:** differing markedly from the usual or ordinary or accepted **:** STRANGE ⟨an ~ way of behaving⟩ — **odd•ness** *n*

♦ bizarre, curious, far-out, funny, kinky, outlandish, outré, peculiar, quaint, queer, quirky, remarkable, screwy, strange, wacky, weird, wild ♦ aberrant, abnormal, atypical, exceptional, extraordinary, freak, peculiar, phenomenal, rare, singular, uncommon, uncustomary, unique, unusual, unwonted

odd•ball \ˈäd-ˌbȯl\ *n* ♦ **:** one that is eccentric — **oddball** *adj*

♦ character, crackpot, crank, eccentric, kook, nut, screwball, weirdo

odd•i•ty \ˈä-də-tē\ *n, pl* **-ties 1** ♦ **:** one that is odd **2** ♦ **:** the quality or state of being odd

♦ [1] crotchet, eccentricity, idiosyncrasy, mannerism, peculiarity, quirk, singularity, trick ♦ [1, 2] curiosity, exotic, rarity

odd•ly \ˈäd-lē\ *adv* **1 :** in an odd manner **2 :** as is odd ⟨~ enough, I agree⟩

odd•ment \ˈäd-mənt\ *n* **:** something left over **:** REMNANT

odds \ˈädz\ *n pl* **1** ♦ **:** a difference by which one thing is favored over another **2 :** DISAGREEMENT — usually used with *at* **3 :** the ratio between the amount to be paid for a winning bet and the amount of the bet ⟨the horse went off at ~ of 6–1⟩

♦ chance, percentage, probability

odds and ends *n pl* **1** ♦ **:** miscellaneous things or matters **2** ♦ **:** miscellaneous remnants or leftovers

♦ [1] notions, novelties, sundries ♦ [2] balance, leavings, leftovers, remainder, remains, remnant, residue, rest

odds–on \ˈädz-ˈȯn, -ˈän\ *adj* **:** having a better than even chance to win

ode \ˈōd\ *n* **:** a lyric poem that expresses a noble feeling with dignity

odi•ous \ˈō-dē-əs\ *adj* ♦ **:** causing or deserving hatred or repugnance — **odi•ous•ly** *adv* — **odi•ous•ness** *n*

♦ abhorrent, abominable, appalling, awful, distasteful, nauseating, noisome, obnoxious, offensive, repellent, repugnant, repulsive, revolting

odi•um \ˈō-dē-əm\ *n* **1 :** merited loathing **:** HATRED **2** ♦ **:** disrepute or infamy attached to something **:** DISGRACE

♦ discredit, disgrace, dishonor (*or* dishonour), disrepute, ignominy, infamy, opprobrium, reproach, shame

odom•e•ter \ō-ˈdä-mə-tər\ *n* **:** an instrument for measuring distance traveled (as by a vehicle)

odor *or Can and Brit* **odour** \ˈō-dər\ *n* **1** ♦ **:** the quality of something that stimulates the sense of smell; *also* **:** a sensation resulting from such stimulation **2 :** REPUTE, ESTIMATION — **odored** \ˈō-dərd\ *adj* — **odor•less** *adj* — **odor•ous** *adj*

♦ redolence, scent, smell

odor•if•er•ous \ˌō-də-ˈri-fə-rəs\ *adj* **:** having or yielding an odor

odour *Can and Brit var of* ODOR

od•ys•sey \ˈä-də-sē\ *n, pl* **-seys :** a long wandering marked usually by many changes of fortune

oe•cu•men•i•cal \ˌē-\ *chiefly Brit var of* ECUMENICAL

OED *abbr* Oxford English Dictionary

oe•de•ma *chiefly Brit var of* EDEMA

oe•di•pal \ˈe-də-pəl, ˈē-\ *adj, often cap* **:** of, relating to, or resulting from the Oedipus complex

Oe•di•pus complex \-pəs-\ *n* **:** the positive sexual feelings of a child toward the parent of the opposite sex and hostile or jealous feelings toward the parent of the same sex that may be a source of adult personality disorder when unresolved

OEO *abbr* Office of Economic Opportunity

o'er \ˈōr\ *adv or prep* **1 :** across a barrier or intervening space **:** OVER **2 :** once more **3 :** in or to a higher place

OES *abbr* Order of the Eastern Star

oe•soph•a•gus *chiefly Brit var of* ESOPHAGUS

oeu•vre \ˈər-vrə\ *n, pl* **oeuvres** *same*\ **:** a substantial body of work constituting the lifework of a writer, an artist, or a composer

of \ˈəv, ˈäv\ *prep* **1 :** FROM ⟨a man ~ the West⟩ **2 :** having as a significant background or character element ⟨a man ~ noble birth⟩ ⟨a woman ~ ability⟩ **3 :** owing to ⟨died ~ flu⟩ **4 :** BY ⟨the plays ~ Shakespeare⟩ **5 :** having as component parts or material, contents, or members ⟨a house ~ brick⟩ ⟨a glass ~ water⟩ ⟨a pack ~ fools⟩ **6 :** belonging to or included by ⟨the front ~ the house⟩ ⟨a time ~ life⟩ ⟨one ~ you⟩ ⟨the best ~ its kind⟩ ⟨the son ~ a doctor⟩ **7** ♦ **:** relating to **:** ABOUT ⟨tales ~ the West⟩ **8 :** connected with **:** OVER ⟨the queen ~ England⟩ **9 :** that is **:** signified as ⟨the city ~ Rome⟩ **10** — used to indicate apposition of the words it joins ⟨that fool ~ a husband⟩ **11 :** as concerns **:** FOR ⟨love ~ nature⟩ **12** — used to indicate the application of an adjective ⟨fond ~ candy⟩ **13** ♦ **:** preceding in time **:** BEFORE ⟨quarter ~ ten⟩

♦ [7] about, apropos of, concerning, on, regarding, respecting, toward ♦ [13] ahead of, before, ere, previous to, prior to, to

OF *abbr* outfield

1**off** \ˈȯf\ *adv* **1 :** from a place or position ⟨drove ~ in a new car⟩; *also* **:** ASIDE ⟨turned ~ into a side road⟩ **2 :** at a distance in time or space ⟨stood ~ a few yards⟩ ⟨several years ~⟩ **3 :** so as to be unattached or removed ⟨the lid blew ~⟩ **4 :** to a state of discontinuance, exhaustion, or completion ⟨shut the radio ~⟩ **5 :** away from regular work ⟨took time ~ for lunch⟩

2**off** *prep* **1 :** away from ⟨just ~ the highway⟩ ⟨take it ~ the table⟩ **2 :** to seaward of ⟨two miles ~ the coast⟩ **3 :** FROM ⟨borrowed a dollar ~ me⟩ **4 :** at the expense of ⟨lives ~ his parents⟩ **5 :** not now engaged in ⟨~ duty⟩ **6 :** abstaining from ⟨~ liquor⟩ **7 :** below the usual level of ⟨~ his game⟩

3**off** *adj* **1 :** more removed or distant **2 :** started on the way **3** ♦ **:** not operating **4** ♦ **:** not correct **5 :** small in degree **:** REMOTE, SLIGHT **6 :** of poor quality **:** INFERIOR **7 :** provided for ⟨well ~⟩

♦ [3] dead, dormant, fallow, free, idle, inactive, inert, inoperative, latent, vacant ♦ [4] erroneous, false, inaccurate, incorrect, inexact, invalid, unsound, untrue, wrong

4**off** *abbr* office; officer; official

of•fal \ˈȯ-fəl\ *n* **:** the waste or by-product of a process; *esp* **:** the viscera and trimmings of a butchered animal removed in dressing

off and on *adv* **:** INTERMITTENTLY

1**off•beat** \ˈȯf-ˌbēt\ *n* **:** the unaccented part of a musical measure

2**offbeat** *adj* ♦ **:** deviating from conventional or accepted usage or conduct especially in odd or whimsical ways

♦ curious, extraordinary, funny, odd, peculiar, queer, rare, strange, unaccustomed, uncommon, unique, unusual, weird

off–col•or \ˈȯf-ˈkə-lər\ *or* **off–col•ored** \-lərd\ *adj* **1 :** not having the right or standard color **2 :** of doubtful propriety **:** verging on indecency ⟨~ stories⟩

of•fend \ə-ˈfend\ *vb* **1** ♦ **:** to violate a law or rule **:** SIN, TRANSGRESS **2 :** to cause discomfort or pain **:** HURT **3** ♦ **:** to cause dislike or vexation

♦ [1] err, sin, transgress, trespass ♦ [3] affront, insult, outrage, slight, wound

of•fend•er *n* ♦ **:** one that offends

♦ criminal, crook, culprit, felon, lawbreaker, malefactor

of•fense *or* **of•fence** \ə-ˈfens, *esp for 2 & 3* ˈä-ˌfens\ *n* **1 :** something that outrages the senses **2** ♦ **:** the act of attacking **:** ATTACK, ASSAULT **3 :** the offensive team or members of a team playing offensive positions **4 a** ♦ **:** the act of displeasing or affronting **b** ♦ **:** the state of being insulted or morally outraged **5** ♦ **:** a breach of a moral or social code **:** SIN, MISDEED **6** ♦ **:** an infraction of law **:** CRIME

♦ [2] aggression, assault, attack, charge, descent, offensive, onset, onslaught, raid, rush, strike ♦ [4a] affront, barb, dart, dig, indignity, insult, name, outrage, put-down, sarcasm, slight, slur, wound ♦ [4b] dudgeon, huff, peeve, pique, resentment, umbrage ♦ [5, 6] breach, crime, error, malefaction, misdeed, misdoing, sin, transgression, trespass, violation, wrongdoing

¹of•fen•sive \ə-ˈfen-siv, *esp for 1 & 2* ˈä-ˌfen-\ *adj* **1 :** AGGRESSIVE **2 :** of or relating to an attempt to score in a game; *also* : of or relating to a team in possession of the ball or puck **3** ♦ **:** giving painful or unpleasant sensations : OBNOXIOUS **4 :** INSULTING — **of•fen•sive•ly** *adv* — **of•fen•sive•ness** *n*

♦ awful, distasteful, foul, horrible, horrid, nauseating, noisome, objectionable, obnoxious, odious, repellent, repugnant, repulsive, shocking, ugly ***Ant*** inoffensive

²offensive *n* : the act of attacking with physical force or unfriendly words : ATTACK
¹of•fer \ˈȯ-fər\ *vb* **of•fered; of•fer•ing 1 :** SACRIFICE **2** ♦ **:** to present for acceptance : TENDER; *also* : to propose as payment **3** ♦ **:** to set before the mind (as for discussion, imitation, or action) : PROPOSE, SUGGEST; *also* : to declare one's readiness **4 :** to try or begin to exert ⟨~ resistance⟩ **5 :** to place on sale **6** ♦ **:** to present in performance or exhibition

♦ [2] extend, give, proffer, tender ♦ [3] advance, pose, proffer, propose, propound, suggest, vote ♦ [6] carry, give, mount, present, stage

²offer *n* **1** ♦ **:** a presenting of something for acceptance : PROPOSAL **2 :** BID **3 :** TRY

♦ proffer, proposal, proposition, suggestion

of•fer•ing *n* : a sacrifice ceremonially offered as a part of worship
of•fer•to•ry \ˈȯ-fər-ˌtōr-ē\ *n, pl* **-ries :** the presentation of offerings at a church service; *also* : the musical accompaniment during it
off–gas•sing \ˈȯf-ˌga-siŋ\ *n* : the emission of especially noxious gases (as from a building material)
off•hand \ˈȯf-ˈhand\ *adj* ♦ **:** done or made without previous thought or preparation — **offhand** *adv*

♦ ad-lib, extemporaneous, impromptu, snap, unplanned, unpremeditated, unprepared, unrehearsed

off–hour \-ˌau̇(-ə)r\ *n* : a period of time other than a rush hour; *also* : a period of time other than business hours
of•fice \ˈȯ-fəs\ *n* **1 :** a special duty or position; *esp* : a position of authority in government ⟨run for ~⟩ **2 :** a prescribed form or service of worship; *also* : RITE **3 :** an assigned or assumed duty or role **4 :** a place where a business is transacted or a service is supplied **5** ♦ **:** a major administrative unit in some governments

♦ bureau, department, desk, division

of•fice•hold•er \ˈȯ-fəs-ˌhōl-dər\ *n* ♦ **:** one holding a public office

♦ functionary, officer, official, public servant

of•fi•cer \ˈȯ-fə-sər\ *n* **1** ♦ **:** one charged with the enforcement of law **2 :** one who holds an office of trust or authority **3 :** a person who holds a position of authority or command in the armed forces; *esp* : COMMISSIONED OFFICER

♦ constable, cop, police officer

¹of•fi•cial \ə-ˈfi-shəl\ *n* ♦ **:** one who holds or is invested with an office : OFFICER

♦ functionary, officeholder, officer, public servant

²official *adj* **1 :** of or relating to an office or to officers **2 :** AUTHORIZED, AUTHORITATIVE **3 :** befitting or characteristic of a person in office — **of•fi•cial•ly** *adv*
of•fi•cial•dom \ə-ˈfi-shəl-dəm\ *n* : officials as a class
of•fi•cial•ism \ə-ˈfi-shə-ˌli-zəm\ *n* : lack of flexibility and initiative combined with excessive adherence to regulations
of•fi•ci•ant \ə-ˈfi-shē-ənt\ *n* : one (as a priest) who officiates at a religious rite
of•fi•ci•ate \ə-ˈfi-shē-ˌāt\ *vb* **-at•ed; -at•ing 1 :** to perform a ceremony, function, or duty **2 :** to act in an official capacity
of•fi•cious \ə-ˈfi-shəs\ *adj* ♦ **:** volunteering one's services where they are neither asked for nor needed — **of•fi•cious•ly** *adv* — **of•fi•cious•ness** *n*

♦ intrusive, meddlesome, nosy, obtrusive, presumptuous, prying

off•ing \ˈȯ-fiŋ\ *n* : the near or foreseeable future
off–line \ˈȯf-ˈlīn\ *adj or adv* : not connected to or controlled directly by a computer
off of *prep* : OFF
off•print \ˈȯf-ˌprint\ *n* : a separately printed excerpt (as from a magazine)
off–road \-ˈrōd\ *adj* : of, relating to, or being a vehicle designed for use away from public roads
off–sea•son \-ˌsēz-ᵊn\ *n* : a time of suspended or reduced activity
¹off•set \-ˌset\ *n* **1 :** a sharp bend (as in a pipe) by which one part is turned aside out of line **2 :** a printing process in which an inked impression is first made on a rubber-blanketed cylinder and then transferred to the paper **3** ♦ **:** something that serves to counterbalance or to compensate for something else

♦ balance, canceler, counterbalance, counterweight, equipoise

²off•set *vb* **off•set; off•set•ting 1 :** to place over against : BALANCE **2** ♦ **:** to compensate for **3 :** to form an offset in (as a wall)

♦ annul, cancel, compensate, correct, counteract, counterbalance, make up, neutralize

off•shoot \ˈȯf-ˌshüt\ *n* **1** ♦ **:** a collateral or derived branch, descendant, or member **2 :** a branch of a main stem (as of a plant)

♦ derivative, outgrowth, spin-off

¹off•shore \ˈȯf-ˈshōr\ *adv* **1 :** at a distance from the shore **2 :** outside the country : ABROAD
²off•shore \ˈȯf-ˌshōr\ *adj* **1 :** moving away from the shore **2 :** situated off the shore but within waters under a country's control
off•side \-ˈsīd\ *adv or adj* : illegally in advance of the ball or puck
off•spring \-ˌspriŋ\ *n, pl* **offspring** *also* **offsprings** ♦ **:** the product of the reproductive processes of an animal or plant : PROGENY

♦ issue, posterity, progeny, seed, spawn

off•stage \ˈȯf-ˈstāj, -ˌstāj\ *adv or adj* **1 :** off or away from the stage **2 :** out of the public view ⟨deals made ~⟩
off–the–record *adj* : given or made in confidence and not for publication
off–the–shelf *adj* : available as a stock item : not specially designed or made
off–the–wall *adj* : highly unusual : BIZARRE
off•track \ˈȯf-ˈtrak\ *adv or adj* : away from a racetrack
off–white \ˈȯf-ˈhwīt\ *n* : a yellowish or grayish white color
off year *n* **1 :** a year in which no major election is held **2 :** a year of diminished activity or production
oft \ˈȯft\ *adv* : OFTEN
of•ten \ˈȯ-fən\ *adv* ♦ **:** many times : FREQUENTLY

♦ constantly, continually, frequently, repeatedly ***Ant*** infrequently, rarely, seldom

of•ten•times \-ˌtīmz\ *or* **oft•times** \ˈȯf-ˌtīmz, ˈȯft-\ *adv* : OFTEN
ogle \ˈō-gəl\ *vb* **ogled; ogling :** to look at in a flirtatious way — **ogle** *n* — **ogler** *n*
ogre \ˈō-gər\ *n* **1 :** a monster of fairy tales and folklore that eats people **2** ♦ **:** a dreaded person or object

♦ bête noire, bogey, bugbear, hobgoblin

ogress \ˈō-grəs\ *n* : a female ogre
oh \ˈō\ *interj* **1** — used to express an emotion or in response to physical stimuli **2** — used in direct address
OH *abbr* Ohio
ohm \ˈōm\ *n* : a unit of electrical resistance equal to the resistance of a circuit in which a potential difference of one volt produces a current of one ampere — **ohm•ic** \ˈō-mik\ *adj*
ohm•me•ter \ˈōm-ˌmē-tər\ *n* : an instrument for indicating resistance in ohms directly
¹oil \ˈȯil\ *n* **1 :** any of numerous fatty or greasy liquid substances obtained from plants, animals, or minerals and used for fuel, food, medicines, and manufacturing **2 :** PETROLEUM **3 a :** artists' colors made with oil **b :** a painting in oil artist's colors — **oil•i•ness** \ˈȯi-lē-nəs\ *n* — **oily** \ˈȯi-lē\ *adj*
²oil *vb* ♦ **:** to put oil in or on — **oil•er** *n*

♦ grease, lubricate, slick, wax

oil•cloth \ˈȯi(-ə)l-ˌklȯth\ *n* : cloth treated with oil or paint and used for table and shelf coverings
oil pan *n* : the lower section of a crankcase used as an oil reservoir
oil shale *n* : a rock (as shale) from which oil can be recovered
oil•skin \ˈȯi(-ə)l-ˌskin\ *n* **1 :** an oiled waterproof cloth **2 :** an oilskin raincoat **3** *pl* : an oilskin coat and pants
oink \ˈȯiŋk\ *n* : the natural noise of a hog — **oink** *vb*
oint•ment \ˈȯint-mənt\ *n* : a salve for use on the skin
OJ *abbr* orange juice
Ojib•wa *or* **Ojib•way** \ō-ˈjib-ˌwā\ *n, pl* **Ojibwa** *or* **Ojibwas** *or* **Ojibway** *or* **Ojibways 1 :** a member of an American Indian people of the region around Lake Superior and westward **2 :** the Algonquian language of the Ojibwa people
OJT *abbr* on-the-job training
¹OK *or* **okay** \ō-ˈkā\ *adv* ♦ **:** ALL RIGHT

♦ all right, alright, yea, yes ♦ adequately, all right, fine, good, nicely, passably, satisfactorily, so-so, tolerably, well

[2]**OK** *or* **okay** *adj* ♦ : ALL RIGHT

♦ acceptable, adequate, all right, decent, fine, passable, respectable, satisfactory, tolerable ♦ agreeable, all right, alright, fine, good, palatable, satisfactory

[3]**OK** *or* **okay** *vb* **OK'd** *or* **okayed; OK'•ing** *or* **okay•ing** **1** ♦ : to give formal or official sanction to : APPROVE, AUTHORIZE **2** ♦ : to have or express a favorable opinion of

♦ [1] approve, authorize, clear, ratify, sanction, warrant ♦ [2] accept, approve, care, countenance, favor (*or* favour), subscribe

[4]**OK** *or* **okay** *n* ♦ : an act or instance of approving

♦ approbation, approval, blessing, favor (*or* favour), imprimatur

[5]**OK** *abbr* Oklahoma
Okla *abbr* Oklahoma
okra \ˈō-krə\ *n* : a tall annual plant related to the mallows that has edible green pods; *also* : these pods
[1]**old** \ˈōld\ *adj* **1** : ANCIENT; *also* : of long standing **2** *cap* : belonging to an early period ⟨*Old* Irish⟩ **3** : having existed for a specified period of time **4** ♦ : of or relating to a past era **5** ♦ : advanced in years **6** : showing the effects of age or use **7** : no longer in use **8** ♦ : having been previously — **old•ish** \ˈōl-dish\ *adj*

♦ [4] age-old, ancient, antediluvian, antique, dateless, hoary, venerable ♦ [5] ancient, elderly, geriatric, senior ♦ [8] erstwhile, former, late, onetime, past, sometime, whilom

[2]**old** *n* : old or earlier time ⟨days of ~⟩
old•en \ˈōl-dən\ *adj* : of or relating to a bygone era
[1]**old–fash•ioned** \ˈōld-ˈfa-shənd\ *adj* **1** ♦ : of, relating to, or characteristic of a past era **2** ♦ : adhering to customs of a past era : CONSERVATIVE

♦ [1] antique, old-time, quaint ***Ant*** contemporary, hot, mod, modern, newfangled, new-fashioned, ultramodern ♦ [2] conservative, orthodox, reactionary, traditional

[2]**old–fashioned** *n* : a cocktail usually made with whiskey, bitters, sugar, a twist of lemon peel, and water or soda water
old–growth \ˈōld-ˈgrōth\ *adj* : of, relating to, or being a forest with large old trees, numerous snags and woody debris, and a multilayered canopy
old guard *n, often cap O&G* : the conservative members of an organization
old hat *adj* **1** : OLD-FASHIONED **2** : STALE, TRITE
old•ie \ˈōl-dē\ *n* : something old; *esp* : a popular song from the past
old lady *n* ♦ : a female partner in a marriage

♦ helpmate, lady, wife

old–line \ˈōld-ˈlīn\ *adj* **1** : ORIGINAL, ESTABLISHED ⟨an ~ business⟩ **2** : adhering to old policies or practices
old maid *n* **1** : SPINSTER **2** : a prim fussy person
old–maid•ish \ˈōld-ˈmā-dish\ *adj* ♦ : characteristic of an old maid

♦ choosy, dainty, delicate, demanding, exacting, fastidious, finicky, fussy, nice, particular, picky

old man *n* **1** : HUSBAND **2** : a male parent : FATHER
old–school *adj* : adhering to traditional policies or practices
old•ster \ˈōld-stər\ *n* ♦ : an old or elderly person

♦ ancient, elder, golden-ager, senior citizen

Old Testament *n* : the first of the two chief divisions of the Christian Scripture
old–time \ˈōld-ˈtīm\ *adj* **1** ♦ : of, relating to, or characteristic of an earlier period **2** : of long standing

♦ antique, old-fashioned, quaint

old–tim•er \-ˈtī-mər\ *n* **1** : veteran **2** : an aging or elderly person : OLDSTER
old wives' tale *n* ♦ : an often traditional belief that is not based on fact

♦ error, fallacy, falsehood, falsity, illusion, misconception, myth, untruth

old–world \-ˈwərld\ *adj* : having old-fashioned charm
Old World *n* : the eastern hemisphere exclusive of Australia; *esp* : continental Europe
ole•ag•i•nous \ˌō-lē-ˈa-jə-nəs\ *adj* : OILY
ole•an•der \ˈō-lē-ˌan-dər\ *n* : a poisonous evergreen shrub often grown for its fragrant white to red flowers
oleo \ˈō-lē-ˌō\ *n, pl* **ole•os** : MARGARINE
oleo•mar•ga•rine \ˌō-lē-ō-ˈmär-jə-rən\ *n* : MARGARINE
ol•fac•to•ry \äl-ˈfak-tə-rē, ōl-\ *adj* : of or relating to the sense of smell
oli•gar•chy \ˈä-lə-ˌgär-kē, ˈō-\ *n, pl* **-chies** **1** : a government in which power is in the hands of a few **2** : a state having an oligarchy; *also* : the group holding power in such a state — **oli•garch** \-ˌgärk\ *n* — **oli•gar•chic** \ˌä-lə-ˈgär-kik, ˌō-\ *or* **oli•gar•chi•cal** \-ki-kəl\ *adj*
Oli•go•cene \ˈä-li-gō-ˌsēn, ə-ˈli-gə-ˌsēn\ *adj* : of, relating to, or being the epoch of the Tertiary between the Eocene and the Miocene — **Oligocene** *n*
olio \ˈō-lē-ˌō\ *n, pl* **oli•os** : HODGEPODGE, MEDLEY
ol•ive \ˈä-liv\ *n* **1** : an Old World evergreen tree grown in warm regions for its fruit that is a food and the source of an edible oil (**olive oil**) **2** : a dull yellowish green color
olive drab *n* **1** : a grayish olive color **2** : an olive drab wool or cotton fabric; *also* : a uniform of this fabric
ol•iv•ine \ˈä-lə-ˌvēn\ *n* : a usually greenish mineral that is a complex silicate of magnesium and iron
Olym•pic Games \ō-ˈlim-pik-\ *n pl* : a modified revival of an ancient Greek festival consisting of international athletic contests that are held at separate winter and summer gatherings at four-year intervals
om \ˈōm\ *n* : a mantra consisting of the sound "om" used in contemplating ultimate reality
Oma•ha \ˈō-mə-ˌhä, -ˌhȯ\ *n, pl* **Omaha** *or* **Omahas** : a member of an American Indian people of northeastern Nebraska
om•buds•man \ˈäm-ˌbu̇dz-mən, äm-ˈbu̇dz-\ *n, pl* **-men** \-mən\ **1** : a government official appointed to investigate complaints made by individuals against abuses or capricious acts of public officials **2** : one that investigates reported complaints (as from students or consumers)
ome•ga \ō-ˈmā-gə\ *n* : the 24th and last letter of the Greek alphabet — Ω or *ω*
om•elet *or* **om•elette** \ˈäm-lət, ˈä-mə-\ *n* : eggs beaten with milk or water, cooked without stirring until set, and folded over
omen \ˈō-mən\ *n* ♦ : an event or phenomenon believed to be a sign or warning of a future occurrence

♦ augury, auspice, foreboding, portent, presage

om•i•cron \ˈä-mə-ˌkrän, ˈō-\ *n* : the 15th letter of the Greek alphabet — O or *o*
om•i•nous \ˈä-mə-nəs\ *adj* **1** ♦ : foretelling evil : THREATENING **2** : being or exhibiting an omen — **om•i•nous•ly** *adv* — **om•i•nous•ness** *n*

♦ baleful, dire, foreboding, menacing, portentous, sinister

omis•si•ble \ō-ˈmi-sə-bəl\ *adj* : that may be omitted
omis•sion \ō-ˈmi-shən\ *n* **1** : something neglected or left undone **2** : the act of omitting : the state of being omitted **3** ♦ : apathy toward or neglect of duty : lack of action

♦ delinquency, dereliction, laxity, laxness, neglect, negligence, remissness, slackness

omit \ō-ˈmit\ *vb* **omit•ted; omit•ting** **1** : to leave out or leave unmentioned **2** ♦ : to fail to perform : NEGLECT

♦ fail, forget, neglect

[1]**om•ni•bus** \ˈäm-ni-(ˌ)bəs\ *n* : BUS
[2]**omnibus** *adj* ♦ : of, relating to, or providing for many things at once ⟨an ~ bill⟩

♦ compendious, complete, comprehensive, encyclopedic, full, global, inclusive, panoramic, universal

om•nip•o•tent \äm-ˈni-pə-tənt\ *adj* : having unlimited authority or influence : ALMIGHTY — **om•nip•o•tence** \-tən(t)s\ *n* — **om•nip•o•tent•ly** *adv*
om•ni•pres•ent \ˌäm-ni-ˈprez-ᵊnt\ *adj* : present in all places at all times — **om•ni•pres•ence** \-ᵊns\ *n*
om•ni•scient \äm-ˈni-shənt\ *adj* : having infinite awareness, understanding, and insight — **om•ni•science** \-shəns\ *n* — **om•ni•scient•ly** *adv*
om•ni•um–gath•er•um \ˌäm-nē-əm-ˈga-t͟hə-rəm\ *n, pl* **omnium–gatherums** : a miscellaneous collection
om•niv•o•rous \äm-ˈni-və-rəs\ *adj* **1** : feeding on both animal and vegetable substances **2** : AVID ⟨an ~ reader⟩ — **om•niv•o•rous•ly** *adv*
[1]**on** \ˈȯn, ˈän\ *prep* **1** : in or to a position over and in contact with ⟨jumped ~ his horse⟩ **2** : touching the surface of ⟨shadows ~ the wall⟩ **3** : AT, TO ⟨~ the right were the mountains⟩ **4** : IN,

ABOARD ⟨went ~ the train⟩ **5 :** during or at the time of ⟨came ~ Monday⟩ ⟨every hour ~ the hour⟩ **6 :** through the agency of ⟨was cut ~ a tin can⟩ **7 :** in a state or process of ⟨~ fire⟩ ⟨~ the wane⟩ **8 :** connected with as a member or participant ⟨~ a committee⟩ ⟨~ tour⟩ **9** — used to indicate a basis, source, or standard of computation ⟨has it ~ good authority⟩ ⟨10 cents ~ the dollar⟩ **10 :** with regard to ⟨a monopoly ~ wheat⟩ **11 :** at or toward as an object ⟨crept up ~ her⟩ **12 :** used as a function word to indicate the subject of study, discussion, or consideration **:** ABOUT, CONCERNING ⟨a book ~ minerals⟩

[2]**on** *adv* **1 :** in or into a position of contact with or attachment to a surface **2** ♦ **:** forward or at a more advanced point in space or time **:** FORWARD **3 :** into operation

♦ ahead, along, forth, forward, onward

[3]**on** *adj* ♦ **:** being in operation or in progress

♦ active, alive, functional, living, operational, operative, running, working

ON *abbr* Ontario

[1]**once** \ˈwəns\ *adv* **1 :** one time only **2 :** at any one time **3 :** FORMERLY **4 :** by one degree of relationship

[2]**once** *n* **:** one single time — **at once 1 :** at the same time **2 :** IMMEDIATELY

[3]**once** *adj* **:** FORMER

[4]**once** *conj* **:** AS SOON AS

once–over \ˈwəns-ˌō-vər\ *n* **:** a swift examination or survey

on•co•gene \ˈäŋ-kō-ˌjēn\ *n* **:** a gene having the potential to casue a normal cell to become cancerous

on•col•o•gy \än-ˈkä-lə-jē\ *n* **:** the study of tumors — **on•co•log•i•cal** \ˌäŋ-kə-ˈlä-ji-kəl\ *also* **on•co•log•ic** \-jik\ *adj* — **on•col•o•gist** \än-ˈkä-lə-jist\ *n*

on•com•ing \ˈȯn-ˌkə-miŋ, ˈän-\ *adj* ♦ **:** coming nearer in time or space ⟨~ traffic⟩

♦ coming, forthcoming, imminent, impending, pending

[1]**one** \ˈwən\ *adj* **1 :** being a single unit or thing ⟨~ person went⟩ **2 :** being one in particular ⟨early ~ morning⟩ **3 :** being the same in kind or quality ⟨members of ~ race⟩; *also* **:** UNITED **4** ♦ **:** being not specified or fixed ⟨~ day soon⟩

♦ anonymous, certain, some, unidentified, unnamed, unspecified

[2]**one** *n* **1 :** the number denoting unity **2 :** the 1st in a set or series **3 :** a single person or thing — **one•ness** \ˈwən-nəs\ *n*

[3]**one** *pron* **1 :** a certain indefinitely indicated person or thing ⟨saw ~ of his friends⟩ **2 :** a person in general ⟨~ never knows⟩ **3** — used in place of a first-person pronoun

Onei•da \ō-ˈnī-də\ *n, pl* **Oneida** *or* **Oneidas :** a member of an American Indian people orig. of New York

one–man band *n* **1 :** a musician who plays several instruments during a solo performance **2 :** a person who alone undertakes or is responsible for several tasks

oner•ous \ˈä-nə-rəs, ˈō-\ *adj* ♦ **:** imposing or constituting a burden

♦ arduous, burdensome, challenging, demanding, exacting, grueling, laborious, taxing, toilsome

one•self \(ˌ)wən-ˈself\ *also* **one's self** *pron* **:** one's own self — usually used reflexively or for emphasis

one–sid•ed \ˈwən-ˈsī-dəd\ *adj* **1 :** having or occurring on one side only; *also* **:** having one side prominent or more developed **2** ♦ **:** of, relating to, or affecting one side of a subject **:** PARTIAL ⟨a ~ interpretation⟩

♦ biased, partial, partisan, prejudiced

one•time \-ˌtīm\ *adj* ♦ **:** of, relating to, or occurring in the past **:** FORMER

♦ erstwhile, former, late, old, past, sometime, whilom

one–to–one \ˌwən-tə-ˈwən\ *adj* **:** pairing each element of a set uniquely with an element of another set

one up *adj* **:** being in a position of advantage ⟨was *one up* on the others⟩

one–way *adj* **:** moving, allowing movement, or functioning in only one direction ⟨~ streets⟩

on•go•ing \ˈȯn-ˌgō-iŋ, ˈän-\ *adj* **1** ♦ **:** continuously moving forward **2** ♦ **:** being actually in process

♦ [1] afoot, proceeding ***Ant*** arrested, halted, stalled, stopped
♦ [2] current, extant, present

on•ion \ˈən-yən\ *n* **:** the pungent edible bulb of a widely cultivated plant related to the lilies; *also* **:** this plant

on•ion•skin \-ˌskin\ *n* **:** a thin strong translucent paper of very light weight

on•line \ˈȯn-ˈlīn, ˈän-\ *adj or adv* **:** connected to, served by, or available through a computer network (as the Internet); *also* **:** done while online

on•look•er \ˈȯn-ˌlu̇-kər, ˈän-\ *n* **:** SPECTATOR

[1]**on•ly** \ˈōn-lē\ *adj* **1** ♦ **:** unquestionably the best **2** ♦ **:** alone in a class or category **:** SOLE

♦ [1] incomparable, inimitable, matchless, nonpareil, peerless, unequaled, unmatched, unparalleled, unrivaled, unsurpassed
♦ [2] alone, lone, singular, sole, solitary, special, unique

[2]**only** *adv* **1 :** as a single fact or instance and nothing more or different **:** MERELY, JUST ⟨~ $2⟩ **2** ♦ **:** to the exclusion of all else **:** SOLELY ⟨known ~ to me⟩ **3 :** at the very least ⟨was ~ too true⟩ **4 :** as a final result ⟨will ~ make you sick⟩ **5** ♦ **:** in the immediate past

♦ [2] alone, exclusively, just, simply, solely ♦ [5] freshly, just, late, lately, new, newly, now, recently

[3]**only** *conj* ♦ **:** except that

♦ but, except, yet

on•o•mato•poe•ia \ˌä-nə-ˌmä-tə-ˈpē-ə\ *n* **1 :** formation of words in imitation of natural sounds (as *buzz* or *hiss*) **2 :** the use of words whose sound suggests the sense — **on•o•mato•poe•ic** \-ˈpē-ik\ *or* **on•o•mato•po•et•ic** \-pō-ˈe-tik\ *adj* — **on•o•mato•poe•i•cal•ly** \-ˈpē-ə-k(ə-)lē\ *or* **on•o•mato•po•et•i•cal•ly** \-pō-ˈe-ti-k(ə-)lē\ *adv*

On•on•da•ga \ˌä-nən-ˈdȯ-gə, -ˈdā-, -ˈdä-\ *n, pl* **-ga** *or* **-gas :** a member of an American Indian people of New York and Canada

on•rush \ˈȯn-ˌrəsh, ˈän-\ *n* ♦ **:** a rushing onward — **on•rush•ing** *adj*

♦ advance, advancement, furtherance, headway, march, passage, process, procession, progress, progression

on–screen \ˈȯn-ˈskrēn, ˈän-\ *adv or adj* **:** on a screen (as of a computer or television)

on•set \-ˌset\ *n* **1 :** the act of attacking with physical force or unfriendly words **:** ATTACK **2** ♦ **:** the point at which something begins **:** BEGINNING

♦ beginning, birth, commencement, dawn, genesis, launch, morning, outset, start, threshold

on•shore \-ˌshōr\ *adj* **1 :** moving toward the shore **2 :** situated on or near the shore — **on•shore** \-ˈshōr\ *adv*

on•slaught \ˈȯn-ˌslȯt, ˈän-\ *n* ♦ **:** a fierce attack; *also* **:** something resembling such an attack ⟨an ~ of questions⟩

♦ aggression, assault, attack, charge, descent, offense (*or* offence), offensive, onset, raid, rush, strike

Ont *abbr* Ontario

on•to \ˈȯn-tü, ˈän-\ *prep* **:** to a position or point on

onus \ˈō-nəs\ *n* **1 :** BURDEN **2 :** OBLIGATION **3 :** BLAME

[1]**on•ward** \ˈȯn-wərd, ˈän-\ *also* **on•wards** \-wərdz\ *adv* ♦ **:** toward or at a point lying ahead in space or time **:** FORWARD

♦ ahead, along, forth, forward, on

[2]**onward** *adj* **:** directed or moving onward **:** FORWARD

on•yx \ˈä-niks\ *n* **:** a translucent chalcedony in parallel layers of different colors

oo•dles \ˈüd-ᵊlz\ *n pl* ♦ **:** a great quantity **:** LOT

♦ abundance, deal, gobs, heap, loads, lot, pile, plenty, quantity, scads

oo•lite \ˈō-ə-ˌlīt\ *n* **:** a rock consisting of small round grains cemented together — **oo•lit•ic** \ˌō-ə-ˈli-tik\ *adj*

[1]**ooze** \ˈüz\ *n* **1 :** a soft deposit (as of mud) on the bottom of a body of water **2** ♦ **:** soft wet ground **:** MUD

♦ mire, muck, mud, slime, slop, sludge, slush

[2]**ooze** *vb* **oozed; ooz•ing 1** ♦ **:** to flow or leak out slowly or imperceptibly **2** ♦ **:** EXUDE

♦ [1, 2] bleed, exude, percolate, seep, strain, sweat, weep

[3]**ooze** *n* **:** something that oozes

oozy \ˈü-zē\ *adj* ♦ **:** containing or composed of ooze

♦ miry, mucky, muddy, slimy, slushy

op *abbr* **1** operation; operative; operator **2** opportunity **3** opus

OP *abbr* **1** observation post **2** out of print

opac•i•ty \ō-ˈpa-sə-tē\ *n, pl* **-ties 1 :** the quality or state of being opaque **2** ♦ **:** obscurity of meaning **3 :** mental dullness **4 :** an opaque spot in a normally transparent structure

♦ ambiguity, darkness, murkiness, obscurity

opal \ˈō-pəl\ *n* : a mineral with iridescent colors that is used as a gem

opal•es•cent \ˌō-pə-ˈles-ᵊnt\ *adj* : IRIDESCENT — **opal•es•cence** \-ᵊns\ *n*

opaque \ō-ˈpāk\ *adj* **1** : blocking the passage of radiant energy and especially light **2** ♦ : not easily understood **3** : OBTUSE — **opaque•ly** *adv* — **opaque•ness** *n*

♦ bleary, dim, faint, foggy, fuzzy, hazy, indefinite, indistinct, indistinguishable, murky, nebulous, obscure, shadowy, unclear, undefined, undetermined, vague

op art \ˈäp-\ *n* : OPTICAL ART — **op artist** *n*

op cit *abbr* in the work cited

ope \ˈōp\ *vb* **oped; op•ing** *archaic* : OPEN

OPEC *abbr* Organization of Petroleum Exporting Countries

op–ed \ˈäp-ˈed\ *n, often cap O&E* : a page of special features usually opposite the editorial page of a newspaper

[1]open \ˈō-pən\ *adj* **open•er; open•est** **1** : not shut or shut up ⟨an ~ door⟩ **2 a** : not secret or hidden **b** ♦ : free from reserve or pretense : FRANK **3 a** : not enclosed or covered ⟨an ~ fire⟩ **b** ♦ : not protected or covered **4** ♦ : free to be entered or used ⟨an ~ tournament⟩ **5** ♦ : easy to get through or see ⟨~ country⟩ **6** : spread out : EXTENDED **7** ♦ : not decided ⟨an ~ question⟩ **8 a** : readily accessible and cooperative; *also* : GENEROUS **b** : willing to hear and consider or to accept and deal with **9** : having components separated by a space in writing and printing ⟨the name *Spanish moss* is an ~ compound⟩ **10** : having openings, interruptions, or spaces ⟨an ~ mesh⟩ **11** : ready to operate ⟨stores are ~⟩ **12** : free from restraints or controls ⟨~ season⟩ — **open•ly** *adv*

♦ [2b] candid, direct, forthright, foursquare, frank, honest, outspoken, plain, straight, straightforward, unguarded, unreserved ♦ [3b] bald, bare, exposed, naked, uncovered ♦ [4] free-for-all, public, unrestricted ***Ant*** closed, exclusive, private, restricted ♦ [5] clear, free, unobstructed ***Ant*** blocked, closed, obstructed, uncleared ♦ [7] pending, undecided, undetermined, unresolved, unsettled

[2]open \ˈō-pən\ *vb* **opened; open•ing** **1 a** : to change or move from a shut position **b** ♦ : to make open by clearing away obstacles **2** : to make accessible **3** : to make openings in **4** : to make or become functional ⟨~ a store⟩ **5** : REVEAL; *also* : ENLIGHTEN **6** ♦ : to enter upon : BEGIN — **open•er** *n*

♦ [1b] clear, free, unblock ♦ [6] begin, commence, embark (on *or* upon), enter, get off, launch, start, strike

[3]open *n* **1** ♦ : open and unobstructed space : OUTDOORS **2** : a contest or tournament open to all

♦ nature, outdoors, wild, wilderness

open–air *adj* : of or relating to the outdoors : OUTDOOR ⟨~ theaters⟩

open arms *n pl* : an eager or warm welcome

open•hand•ed \ˌō-pən-ˈhan-dəd\ *adj* ♦ : liberal in giving : GENEROUS — **open•hand•ed•ly** *adv*

♦ bountiful, charitable, free, generous, liberal, munificent, unselfish, unsparing

open–heart *adj* : of, relating to, or performed on a heart temporarily relieved of circulatory function and laid open for repair of defects or damage

open–hearth *adj* : of, relating to, or being a process of making steel in a furnace that reflects the heat from the roof onto the material

open•ing *n* **1** : an act or instance of making or becoming open **2** : BEGINNING **3** ♦ : something that is open **4** ♦ : a favorable opportunity or circumstance : OCCASION; *also* : an opportunity for employment

♦ [3] breach, break, discontinuity, gap, gulf, hole, interval, rent, rift, separation ♦ [4] chance, occasion, opportunity, room

open mike *n* : an event in which amateurs may perform

open–mind•ed \ˌō-pən-ˈmīn-dəd\ *adj* ♦ : free from rigidly fixed preconceptions — **open–mind•ed•ness** *n*

♦ broad-minded, liberal, nonorthodox, nontraditional, progressive, radical, unconventional, unorthodox ♦ broad-minded, open, receptive ***Ant*** narrow-minded

open•ness *n* ♦ : the quality or state of being open

♦ candor (*or* candour), directness, forthrightness, frankness, plainness

open sentence *n* : a statement (as in mathematics) containing at least one blank or unknown so that when the blank is filled or a quantity substituted for the unknown the statement becomes a complete statement that is either true or false

open shop *n* : an establishment having members and nonmembers of a labor union on the payroll

open•work \ˈō-pən-ˌwərk\ *n* : work so made as to show openings through its substance ⟨a railing of wrought-iron ~⟩ — **open–worked** \-ˌwərkt\ *adj*

[1]opera *pl of* OPUS

[2]op•era \ˈä-prə, -pə-rə\ *n* : a drama set to music — **op•er•at•ic** \ˌä-pə-ˈra-tik\ *adj*

op•er•a•ble \ˈä-pə-rə-bəl\ *adj* **1** ♦ : fit, possible, or desirable to use **2** : likely to result in a favorable outcome upon surgical treatment

♦ available, fit, functional, practicable, serviceable, usable, useful

opera glasses *n pl* : small binoculars for use in a theater

op•er•ate \ˈä-pə-ˌrāt\ *vb* **-at•ed; -at•ing** **1** ♦ : to perform work : FUNCTION **2** ♦ : to produce an effect **3** ♦ : to put or keep in operation; *also* : to manage the operation of **4** : to perform or subject to an operation — **op•er•a•tor** \-ˌrā-tər\ *n*

♦ [1, 2] act, function, perform, take, work ♦ [3] command, control, direct, drive, guide, handle, maneuver, pilot, run, steer, use, wield, work ♦ [3] administer, carry on, conduct, govern, guide, handle, manage, oversee, regulate, run, superintend, supervise

operating system *n* : software that controls the operation of a computer

op•er•a•tion \ˌä-pə-ˈrā-shən\ *n* **1** : a doing or performing of practical work **2 a** ♦ : an exertion of power or influence **b** ♦ : method or manner of functioning **3** : a surgical procedure **4 a** : a process of deriving one mathematical expression from others according to a rule **b** : a function or correlation when conceived as a process of proceeding from one or more entities to another according to a definite rule **5** : a usually military action or mission **6** : a usually small business

♦ [2a] administration, conduct, control, direction, government, guidance, management, oversight, regulation, running, superintendence, supervision ♦ [2b] course, procedure, proceeding, process ♦ [2b] application, employment, exercise, play, use

op•er•a•tion•al \-shə-nəl\ *adj* ♦ : of or relating to operation or an operation

♦ active, alive, functional, living, on, operative, running, working

[1]op•er•a•tive \ˈä-pə-rə-tiv, -ˌrā-\ *adj* **1** : producing an appropriate effect **2** : engaged in some form of operation : OPERATING ⟨an ~ force⟩ **3** : having to do with physical operations; *also* : WORKING ⟨an ~ craftsman⟩ **4** : based on or consisting of an operation ⟨~ dentistry⟩

[2]operative *n* **1** : OPERATOR **2 a** : a secret agent **b** ♦ : a person not a member of a police force who is licensed to do detective work

♦ detective, investigator, shadow, sleuth, tail

op•er•et•ta \ˌä-pə-ˈre-tə\ *n* : a light musical-dramatic work with a romantic plot, spoken dialogue, and dancing scenes

oph•thal•mic \äf-ˈthal-mik, äp-\ *adj* : of, relating to, or located near the eye

oph•thal•mol•o•gy \ˌäf-ˌthal-ˈmä-lə-jē, ˌäp-\ *n* : a branch of medicine dealing with the structure, functions, and diseases of the eye — **oph•thal•mol•o•gist** \-jist\ *n*

oph•thal•mo•scope \äf-ˈthal-mə-ˌskōp, äp-\ *n* : an instrument for use in viewing the interior of the eye and especially the retina

[1]opi•ate \ˈō-pē-ət, -pē-ˌāt\ *n* **1** : a preparation or derivative of opium **2** : a narcotic or a substance with similar activity

[2]opiate *adj* : inducing sleep : NARCOTIC

♦ drowsy, hypnotic, narcotic, slumberous

opine \ō-ˈpīn\ *vb* **opined; opin•ing** ♦ : to express an opinion

♦ comment, note, observe, remark

opin•ion \ə-ˈpin-yən\ *n* **1** ♦ : a belief stronger than impression and less strong than positive knowledge **2** : JUDGMENT **3** ♦ : a formal statement by an expert after careful study

♦ [1] belief, conviction, eye, feeling, judgment (*or* judgement), mind, notion, persuasion, sentiment, verdict, view ♦ [3] conclusion, decision, deliverance, determination, diagnosis, judgment (*or* judgement), resolution, verdict

opin•ion•at•ed \ə-ˈpin-yə-ˌnā-təd\ *adj* ♦ : obstinately adhering to personal opinions

♦ dogged, hardheaded, headstrong, mulish, obdurate, obstinate, peevish, pertinacious, perverse, pigheaded, stubborn, unyielding, willful

opi•um \ˈō-pē-əm\ *n* : an addictive narcotic drug that is the dried latex of a Eurasian poppy

opos•sum \ə-ˈpä-səm\ *n, pl* **opossums** *also* **opossum** : an omnivorous tree-dwelling No. American marsupial that is active chiefly at night and has a pointed snout and a prehensile tail

opp *abbr* opposite

op•po•nent \ə-ˈpō-nənt\ *n* ♦ : one that opposes : ADVERSARY

♦ adversary, antagonist, rival

op•por•tune \ˌä-pər-ˈtün, -ˈtyün\ *adj* : SUITABLE — **op•por•tune•ly** *adv*

op•por•tun•ism \ˌä-pər-ˈtü-ˌni-zəm, -ˈtyü-\ *n* : a taking advantage of opportunities or circumstances especially with little regard for principles or ultimate consequences — **op•por•tun•ist** \-nist\ *n* — **op•por•tu•nis•tic** \-tü-ˈnis-tik, -tyü-\ *adj*

op•por•tu•ni•ty \ˌä-pər-ˈtü-nə-tē, -ˈtyü-\ *n, pl* **-ties** **1** ♦ : a favorable combination of circumstances, time, and place **2** : a chance for advancement

♦ chance, occasion, opening, room

op•pose \ə-ˈpōz\ *vb* **op•posed; op•pos•ing** **1** : to place opposite or against something (as to provide resistance or contrast) **2** ♦ : to strive against : offer resistance to — **op•po•si•tion** \ˌä-pə-ˈzi-shən\ *n*

♦ buck, defy, fight, repel, resist, withstand ♦ battle, combat, contend, counter, fight

¹op•po•site \ˈä-pə-zət\ *adj* **1** : set over against something that is at the other end or side **2** : OPPOSED, HOSTILE; *also* : CONTRARY **3** : contrarily turned or moving **4** ♦ : diametrically different **5** : being the other of a matching or contrasting pair — **op•po•site•ly** *adv* — **op•po•site•ness** *n*

♦ antipodal, antithetical, contradictory, contrary, diametric, polar

²opposite *n* ♦ : one that is opposed or contrary

♦ antipode, antithesis, contrary, negative, reverse

³opposite *adv* : on or to an opposite side

⁴opposite *prep* : across from and usually facing ⟨the house ~ ours⟩

op•press \ə-ˈpres\ *vb* **1** : to crush by abuse of power or authority **2** ♦ : to be a burden to mentally or spiritually

♦ burden, depress, sadden ♦ carry away, crush, devastate, floor, overcome, overpower, overwhelm, prostrate, snow under, swamp

op•pres•sion \ə-ˈpre-shən\ *n* **1** : unjust or cruel exercise of power or authority **2** : a sense of being affected as if with a heavy weight in body or mind : DEPRESSION

op•pres•sive \-ˈpre-siv\ *adj* ♦ : unreasonably burdensome or severe

♦ burdensome, grim, hard, harsh, heavy, onerous, rough, rugged, severe, stiff, tough, trying

op•pres•sive•ly *adv* ♦ : in an oppressive manner

♦ hard, hardly, harshly, ill, roughly, severely, sternly, stiffly

op•pres•sor \-ˈpre-sər\ *n* ♦ : one that oppresses especially when in a position of public authority

♦ autocrat, despot, dictator, tyrant

op•pro•bri•ous \ə-ˈprō-brē-əs\ *adj* ♦ : expressing or deserving opprobrium — **op•pro•bri•ous•ly** *adv*

♦ abusive, scurrilous

op•pro•bri•um \-brē-əm\ *n* **1** : something that brings disgrace **2** ♦ : public disgrace or ill fame that follows from conduct considered grossly wrong or vicious : INFAMY

♦ discredit, disgrace, dishonor (*or* dishonour), disrepute, ignominy, infamy, odium, reproach, shame

¹opt \ˈäpt\ *vb* **1** ♦ : to make a choice **2** ♦ : to decide in favor of something — usually used with *for*

♦ [1] choose, conclude, decide, determine, figure, resolve ♦ *usu* **opt for** [2] choose, cull, elect, handpick, name, pick, prefer, select, single, take

²opt *abbr* **1** optical; optician; optics **2** option; optional

op•tic \ˈäp-tik\ *adj* : of or relating to vision or the eye

op•ti•cal \ˈäp-ti-kəl\ *adj* **1** : relating to optics **2** ♦ : of or relating to vision : OPTIC **3** : of, relating to, or using light

♦ ocular, visual

optical art *n* : nonobjective art characterized by the use of geometric patterns often for an illusory effect

optical disk *n* : a disk on which information has been recorded digitally and which is read using a laser

optical fiber *n* : a single fiber-optic strand

op•ti•cian \äp-ˈti-shən\ *n* **1** : a maker of or dealer in optical items and instruments **2** : a person who makes or orders eyeglass and contact lenses to prescription and sells glasses

op•tics \ˈäp-tiks\ *n pl* : a science that deals with the nature and properties of light

op•ti•mal \ˈäp-tə-məl\ *adj* : most desirable or satisfactory — **op•ti•mal•ly** *adv*

op•ti•mism \ˈäp-tə-ˌmi-zəm\ *n* **1** : a doctrine that this world is the best possible world **2** : an inclination to anticipate the best possible outcome of actions — **op•ti•mist** \-ˌmist\ *n* — **op•ti•mis•tic** \-ˌmis-tik\ *adj*

op•ti•mize \ˈäp-tə-ˌmīz\ *vb* **-mized; -miz•ing** : to make as perfect, effective, or functional as possible — **op•ti•mi•za•tion** \ˌäp-tə-mə-ˈzā-shən\ *n*

op•ti•mum \ˈäp-tə-məm\ *n, pl* **-ma** \-mə\ *also* **-mums** : the amount or degree of something most favorable to an end; *also* : greatest degree attained under implied or specified conditions

op•tion \ˈäp-shən\ *n* **1** ♦ : the power or right to choose **2** : a right to buy or sell something at a specified price during a specified period **3** : something offered for choice **4** ♦ : an act of choosing

♦ [1] accord, choice, free will, self-determination, volition, will ♦ [4] alternative, choice, discretion, pick, preference, way

op•tion•al \-shə-nəl\ *adj* ♦ : involving an option : not compulsory

♦ discretionary, elective, voluntary ***Ant*** compulsory, mandatory, nonelective, obligatory, required

op•tom•e•try \äp-ˈtä-mə-trē\ *n* : the health-care profession concerned especially with examining the eyes for defects of vision and with prescribing corrective lenses or eye exercises — **op•tom•e•trist** \-trist\ *n*

opt out *vb* : to choose not to participate

op•u•lence \ˈä-pyə-ləns\ *n* **1** ♦ : abundance of valuable material possessions or resources : WEALTH **2** : ABUNDANCE

♦ assets, capital, fortune, means, riches, substance, wealth, wherewithal

op•u•lent \ˈä-pyə-lənt\ *adj* **1** ♦ : exhibiting or characterized by opulence **2** : richly abundant

♦ deluxe, lavish, luxuriant, luxurious, palatial, plush, sumptuous ♦ affluent, flush, loaded, moneyed, rich, wealthy, well-fixed, well-heeled, well-off, well-to-do

op•u•lent•ly *adv* ♦ : with opulence : in an opulent manner

♦ expensively, extravagantly, grandly, high, lavishly, luxuriously, richly

opus \ˈō-pəs\ *n, pl* **opera** \ˈō-pə-rə, ˈä-\ *also* **opus•es** \ˈō-pə-səz\ ♦ : something produced by the exercise of creative talent or expenditure of creative effort; *esp* : a musical composition

♦ composition, piece, work

or \ˈȯr\ *conj* — used as a function word to indicate an alternative ⟨sink ~ swim⟩

OR *abbr* **1** operating room **2** Oregon

-or \ər\ *n suffix* : one that does a (specified) thing ⟨calculat*or*⟩

or•a•cle \ˈȯr-ə-kəl\ *n* **1** : one held to give divinely inspired answers or revelations **2** : an authoritative or wise utterance; *also* : a person of great authority or wisdom — **orac•u•lar** \ȯ-ˈra-kyə-lər\ *adj*

¹oral \ˈōr-əl\ *adj* **1** ♦ : uttered by the mouth or in words **2** : of, given through, or involving the mouth **3** : of, relating to, or characterized by the first stage of psychosexual development in psychoanalytic theory in which libidinal gratification is derived from intake (as of food), by sucking, and later by biting **4** : relating to or characterized by personality traits of passive dependency and aggressiveness — **oral•ly** *adv*

♦ vocal, voiced ♦ spoken, unwritten, verbal

²oral *n* : an oral examination — usually used in plural

oral sex *n* : oral stimulation of the genitals : CUNNILINGUS, FELLATIO

orang \ə-ˈraŋ\ *n* : ORANGUTAN

or•ange \ˈȯr-inj\ *n* **1** : a juicy citrus fruit with reddish yellow rind; *also* : an evergreen tree with fragrant white flowers that bears this fruit **2** : a color between red and yellow

or•ange•ade \ˌȯr-in-ˈjād\ *n* : a beverage of orange juice, sugar, and water

orange hawkweed *n* : a weedy herb related to the daisies with bright orange-red flower heads

or•ange•ry \'ȯr-inj-rē\ *n, pl* **-ries :** a protected place (as a greenhouse) for raising oranges in cool climates
orang•utan \ə-'raŋ-ə-ˌtaŋ, -ˌtan\ *n* **:** a large reddish brown tree-living anthropoid ape of Borneo and Sumatra
orate \ȯ-'rāt\ *vb* **orat•ed; orat•ing** ♦ **:** to speak in a declamatory manner

♦ declaim, discourse, harangue, lecture, mouth, speak, talk

ora•tion \ə-'rā-shən\ *n* ♦ **:** an elaborate discourse delivered in a formal and dignified manner

♦ address, declamation, harangue, speech, talk

or•a•tor \'ȯr-ə-tər\ *n* **:** one noted for skill and power as a public speaker
or•a•tor•i•cal \ˌȯr-ə-'tȯr-i-kəl\ *adj* ♦ **:** of, relating to, or characteristic of an orator or oratory; *also* **:** of or relating to an inflated style of speech or writing — **or•a•tor•i•cal•ly** \-'tȯr-i-k(ə-)lē\ *adv*

♦ bombastic, gaseous, grandiloquent, rhetorical, windy

or•a•to•rio \ˌȯr-ə-'tōr-ē-ˌō\ *n, pl* **-rios :** a lengthy choral work usually on a scriptural subject
¹or•a•to•ry \'ȯr-ə-ˌtōr-ē\ *n, pl* **-ries :** a private or institutional chapel
²oratory *n* **1 :** the art of speaking eloquently and effectively in public **2 :** the substance of oratorical speech
orb \'ȯrb\ *n* ♦ **:** a spherical body; *also* **:** EYE

♦ ball, sphere

¹or•bit \'ȯr-bət\ *n* **1 :** a path described by one body in its revolution about another **2 :** range or sphere of activity — **or•bit•al** \-ᵊl\ *adj*
²orbit *vb* **1** ♦ **:** to revolve in an orbit around **:** CIRCLE **2 :** to send up and make revolve in an orbit ⟨~ a satellite⟩ — **or•bit•er** *n*

♦ circle, circumnavigate, coil, compass, encircle, girdle, loop, ring, round

or•ca \'ȯr-kə\ *n* **:** KILLER WHALE
orch *abbr* orchestra
or•chard \'ȯr-chərd\ *n* **:** a place where fruit trees, sugar maples, or nut trees are grown; *also* **:** the trees of such a place — **or•chard•ist** \-chər-dist\ *n*
or•ches•tra \'ȯr-kə-strə\ *n* **1 :** the front section of seats on the main floor of a theater **2 :** a group of instrumentalists organized to perform ensemble music — **or•ches•tral** \ȯr-'kes-trəl\ *adj* — **or•ches•tral•ly** *adv*
or•ches•trate \'ȯr-kə-ˌstrāt\ *vb* **-trat•ed; -trat•ing 1 :** to compose or arrange for an orchestra **2 :** to arrange so as to achieve a desired effect — **or•ches•tra•tion** \ˌȯr-kə-'strā-shən\ *n*
or•chid \'ȯr-kəd\ *n* **:** any of a large family of plants having often showy flowers with three petals of which the middle one is enlarged into a lip; *also* **:** a flower of an orchid
ord *abbr* **1** order **2** ordnance
or•dain \ȯr-'dān\ *vb* **1 :** to admit to the ministry or priesthood by the ritual of a church **2 a** ♦ **:** to order by fiat or by virtue of great or supreme authority **:** DECREE **b** ♦ **:** to predestine or destine **:** DESTINE — **or•dain•ment** *n*

♦ [2a] command, decree, dictate, direct, order ♦ [2b] destine, doom, fate, foredoom, foreordain, predestine

or•deal \ȯr-'dēl, 'ȯr-ˌdel\ *n* ♦ **:** a severe trial or experience

♦ cross, gauntlet, trial

¹or•der \'ȯr-dər\ *vb* **1** ♦ **:** to arrange according to a particular plan **2** ♦ **:** to give an order to **:** COMMAND **3** ♦ **:** to place an order **4** ♦ **:** to issue orders

♦ [1] arrange, array, classify, codify, dispose, draw up, marshal, organize, range, systematize *Ant* derange, disarrange, disarray, disorder, mess (up), muss (up), rumple, upset ♦ [2] command, decree, dictate, direct, ordain ♦ [3] ask, request, requisition ♦ [4] bid, boss, charge, command, direct, enjoin, instruct, tell

²order *n* **1 a :** a group of people formally united **b :** a badge or medal of such a group **2 :** any of the several grades of the Christian ministry; *also, pl* **:** ORDINATION **3 a** ♦ **:** a rank, class, or special group of persons or things **b** ♦ **:** a division within a system of classification **4 :** a category of biological classification ranking above the family and below the class **5** ♦ **:** the arrangement or sequence of objects or of events in time **:** ARRANGEMENT, SEQUENCE; *also* **:** the prevailing state of things **6 :** a customary mode of procedure; *also* **:** the rule of law or proper authority **7** ♦ **:** a specific rule, regulation, or authoritative direction **8 :** a style of building; *also* **:** an architectural column forming the unit of a style **9** ♦ **:** condition especially with regard to repair **10 :** a written direction to pay money or to buy or sell goods; *also* **:** goods bought or sold **11** ♦ **:** a particular sphere or aspect of a sociopolitical system

♦ [3a, 11] caste, class, estate, folk, stratum ♦ [3b] bracket, category, class, division, family, grade, group, kind, set, species, type ♦ [5] arrangement, array, disposal, disposition, distribution, sequence, setup ♦ [7] behest, charge, command, commandment, decree, dictate, direction, directive, edict, instruction, word ♦ [9] condition, estate, fettle, form, repair, shape, trim

¹or•der•ly \'ȯr-dər-lē\ *adj* **1 a** ♦ **:** arranged according to some order **b** ♦ **:** marked by order **:** NEAT, TIDY **2 :** well behaved ⟨an ~ crowd⟩ — **or•der•li•ness** *n*

♦ [1a] methodical, regular, systematic ♦ [1b] crisp, neat, shipshape, snug, tidy, trim, uncluttered

²orderly *n, pl* **-lies 1 :** a soldier who attends a superior officer **2 :** a hospital attendant who does general work
or•di•nal \'ȯrd-ᵊn-əl\ *adj* **:** indicating order or rank (as sixth) in a series
ordinal number *n* **:** a number (as first, second, or third) that designates the place of an item in an ordered sequence — compare CARDINAL NUMBER
or•di•nance \'ȯrd-ᵊn-əns\ *n* ♦ **:** an authoritative decree or law; *esp* **:** a municipal regulation

♦ act, enactment, law, statute

or•di•nar•i•ly \ˌȯrd-ᵊn-'er-ə-lē\ *adv* ♦ **:** in an ordinary manner

♦ commonly, generally, naturally, normally, typically, usually

or•di•nary \'ȯrd-ᵊn-ˌer-ē\ *adj* **1** ♦ **:** to be expected **:** USUAL **2** ♦ **:** of common quality, rank, or ability; *also* **:** POOR, INFERIOR — **or•di•nar•i•ness** \'ȯrd-ᵊn-ˌer-ē-nəs\ *n*

♦ [1] average, common, commonplace, everyday, normal, prosaic, routine, run-of-the-mill, standard, unexceptional, unremarkable, usual, workaday *Ant* abnormal, exceptional, extraordinary, odd, out-of-the-way, strange, unusual ♦ [2] common, fair, indifferent, inferior, mediocre, medium, middling, passable, poor, run-of-the-mill, second-rate, so-so

or•di•nate \'ȯrd-ᵊn-ət, -ˌāt\ *n* **:** the vertical coordinate of a point in a plane coordinate system obtained by measuring parallel to the y-axis
or•di•na•tion \ˌȯrd-ᵊn-'ā-shən\ *n* **:** the act or ceremony by which a person is ordained
ord•nance \'ȯrd-nəns\ *n* **1 :** military supplies **2 :** CANNON, ARTILLERY
Or•do•vi•cian \ˌȯr-də-'vi-shən\ *adj* **:** of, relating to, or being the period of the Paleozoic era between the Cambrian and the Silurian — **Ordovician** *n*
or•dure \'ȯr-jər\ *n* **:** EXCREMENT
ore \'ōr\ *n* **:** a naturally occurring mineral mined to obtain a substance that it contains
Ore *or* **Oreg** *abbr* Oregon
oreg•a•no \ə-'re-gə-ˌnō\ *n* **:** a bushy perennial mint used as a seasoning and a source of oil
org *abbr* organization; organized
or•gan \'ȯr-gən\ *n* **1 :** a musical instrument having sets of pipes sounded by compressed air and controlled by keyboards; *also* **:** an electronic keyboard instrument that approximates the sounds of the pipe organ by electronic devices **2 :** a differentiated animal or plant structure (as a heart or a leaf) made up of cells and tissues and performing some bodily function **3 :** a group that performs a specialized function ⟨the various ~s of government⟩ **4 :** PERIODICAL **5** ♦ **:** a means exercising some function or accomplishing some end

♦ agency, agent, instrument, instrumentality, machinery, means, medium, vehicle

or•gan•dy *also* **or•gan•die** \'ȯr-gən-dē\ *n, pl* **-dies :** a fine transparent muslin with a stiff finish
or•gan•elle \ˌȯr-gə-'nel\ *n* **:** a specialized cell part that resembles an organ in having a special function
or•gan•ic \ȯr-'ga-nik\ *adj* **1 :** of, relating to, or arising in a bodily organ **2 :** of, relating to, or derived from living things **3 :** of, relating to, or containing carbon compounds **4 :** of or relating to a branch of chemistry dealing with carbon compounds **5 :** involving, producing, or dealing in foods produced without the use of laboratory-made fertilizers, growth substances, antibiotics, or pesticides **6 :** ORGANIZED ⟨an ~ whole⟩ — **or•gan•i•cal•ly** \-ni-k(ə-)lē\ *adv*
or•ga•ni•sa•tion, or•ga•nise *chiefly Brit var of* ORGANIZATION, ORGANIZE

or•gan•ism \ˈȯr-gə-ˌni-zəm\ *n* : an individual living thing (as a person, animal, or plant) — **or•gan•is•mic** \ˌȯr-gə-ˈniz-mik\ *adj*
or•gan•ist \ˈȯr-gə-nist\ *n* : a person who plays an organ
or•ga•ni•za•tion \ˌȯr-gə-nə-ˈzā-shən\ *n* **1** : the act or process of organizing or of being organized; *also* : the condition or manner of being organized **2** ♦ : an association of persons having a common interest : SOCIETY **3** : an administrative structure (as a business or a political party) — **or•ga•ni•za•tion•al** \-shə-nəl\ *adj*

♦ association, brotherhood, club, college, congress, council, fellowship, fraternity, guild, institute, institution, league, order, society

or•ga•nize \ˈȯr-gə-ˌnīz\ *vb* **-nized; -niz•ing** **1** : to develop an organic structure **2** : to form into a complete and functioning whole **3** : to set up an administrative structure for **4** ♦ : to arrange by systematic planning and united effort **5** : to join in a union; *also* : UNIONIZE — **or•ga•niz•er** *n*

♦ arrange, array, classify, codify, dispose, draw up, marshal, order, range, systematize

or•gano•chlo•rine \ȯr-ˌga-nə-ˈklōr-ˌēn\ *adj* : of, relating to, or being a chlorinated hydrocarbon pesticide (as DDT) — **organochlorine** *n*
or•gano•phos•phate \-ˈfäs-ˌfāt\ *n* : an organophosphorus pesticide — **organophosphate** *adj*
or•gano•phos•pho•rus \-ˈfäs-fə-rəs\ *also* **or•gano•phos•pho•rous** \-fäs-ˈfōr-əs\ *adj* : of, relating to, or being a phosphorus-containing organic pesticide (as malathion)
or•gan•za \ȯr-ˈgan-zə\ *n* : a sheer dress fabric resembling organdy and usually made of silk, rayon, or nylon
or•gasm \ˈȯr-ˌga-zəm\ *n* : the climax of sexual excitement — **or•gas•mic** \ȯr-ˈgaz-mik\ *adj*
or•gi•as•tic \ˌȯr-jē-ˈas-tik\ *adj* : of, relating to, or marked by orgies
or•gu•lous \ˈȯr-gyə-ləs, -gə-\ *adj* : PROUD
or•gy \ˈȯr-jē\ *n, pl* **orgies** : a gathering marked by unrestrained indulgence (as in sexual activity, alcohol, or drugs)
ori•el \ˈōr-ē-əl\ *n* : a window built out from a wall and usually supported by a bracket
ori•ent \ˈōr-ē-ˌent\ *vb* **1** : to set in a definite position especially in relation to the points of the compass **2** ♦ : to acquaint with an existing situation or environment **3** : to direct toward the interests of a particular group

♦ acquaint, familiarize, initiate, introduce

Orient *n* : EAST 3; *esp* : the countries of eastern Asia
ori•en•tal \ˌōr-ē-ˈent-ᵊl\ *adj, often cap* : of or situated in the Orient — **Oriental** *n*
ori•en•tate \ˈōr-ē-ən-ˌtāt\ *vb* **-tat•ed; -tat•ing** **1** : to acquaint with the existing situation or environment : ORIENT **2** : to face east
ori•en•ta•tion \ˌōr-ē-ən-tā-shən\ *n* **1** : the act or state of being oriented **2** : a person's identity based on sexual tendencies
or•i•fice \ˈȯr-ə-fəs\ *n* ♦ : an opening (as a vent, mouth, or hole) through which something may pass : OPENING

♦ aperture, hole, opening, perforation

ori•flamme \ˈȯr-ə-ˌflam\ *n* : a brightly colored banner used as a standard or ensign in battle
orig *abbr* original; originally
ori•ga•mi \ˌȯr-ə-ˈgä-mē\ *n* : the art or process of Japanese paper folding
or•i•gin \ˈȯr-ə-jən\ *n* **1** ♦ : line of descent : ANCESTRY **2** : rise, beginning, or derivation from a source; *also* : CAUSE **3** : the intersection of coordinate axes

♦ ancestry, birth, blood, bloodline, breeding, descent, extraction, family tree, genealogy, line, lineage, parentage, pedigree, stock, strain

¹orig•i•nal \ə-ˈri-jə-nəl\ *n* : something from which a copy, reproduction, or translation is made : PROTOTYPE
²original *adj* **1** ♦ : existing from the start : FIRST, INITIAL **2** ♦ : not copied from something else : FRESH **3** ♦ : gifted with powers of independent thought, direct insight, or constructive imagination : INVENTIVE

♦ [1] first, inaugural, initial, maiden, pioneer, premier ♦ [2] fresh, new, novel, strange, unfamiliar, unknown ♦ [3] creative, imaginative, ingenious, innovative, inventive

orig•i•nal•i•ty \-ˌri-jə-ˈna-lə-tē\ *n* **1** ♦ : freshness of aspect, design, or style **2** ♦ : the power of independent thought or constructive imagination

♦ [1] freshness, newness, novelty ♦ [2] creativity, ingenuity, invention, inventiveness

orig•i•nal•ly \-ˈri-jən-ᵊl-ē\ *adv* ♦ : in the beginning : in the first place

♦ firstly, initially, primarily

orig•i•nate \ə-ˈri-jə-ˌnāt\ *vb* **-nat•ed; -nat•ing** **1** : to give rise to : INITIATE **2** ♦ : to come into existence : BEGIN

♦ arise, begin, commence, dawn, form, materialize, spring, start

orig•i•na•tor \-ˌnā-tər\ *n* ♦ : one that originates

♦ author, creator, father, founder ♦ designer, developer, innovator, inventor

ori•ole \ˈōr-ē-ˌōl\ *n* : any of various New World birds of which the males are usually black and yellow or black and orange
or•i•son \ˈȯr-ə-sən\ *n* : PRAYER
or•mo•lu \ˈȯr-mə-ˌlü\ *n* : a golden or gilded brass used for decorative purposes
¹or•na•ment \ˈȯr-nə-mənt\ *n* ♦ : something that lends grace or beauty — **or•na•men•ta•tion** \ˌȯr-nə-mən-ˈtā-shən\ *n*

♦ adornment, caparison, decoration, embellishment, frill, garnish, trim

²or•na•ment \-ˌment\ *vb* ♦ : to provide with ornament : ADORN

♦ adorn, array, beautify, bedeck, deck, decorate, do, dress, embellish, enrich, garnish, grace, trim

or•na•men•tal \ˌȯr-nə-ˈment-ᵊl\ *adj* : DECORATIVE : of, relating to, or serving as ornament
or•nate \ȯr-ˈnāt\ *adj* ♦ : elaborately decorated — **or•nate•ly** *adv* — **or•nate•ness** *n*

♦ florid, overwrought *Ant* austere, plain, severe, stark, unadorned

or•nery \ˈȯr-nə-rē, ˈä-nə-\ *adj* ♦ : having an irritable disposition

♦ bearish, bilious, cantankerous, disagreeable, dyspeptic, ill-humored, ill-tempered, splenetic, surly

or•ni•thol•o•gy \ˌȯr-nə-ˈthä-lə-jē\ *n, pl* **-gies** : a branch of zoology dealing with birds — **or•ni•tho•log•i•cal** \-thə-ˈlä-ji-kəl\ *adj* — **or•ni•thol•o•gist** \-ˈthä-lə-jist\ *n*
oro•tund \ˈȯr-ə-ˌtənd\ *adj* **1** : SONOROUS **2** : POMPOUS — **oro•tun•di•ty** \ȯr-ə-ˈtən-di-tē\ *n*
or•phan \ˈȯr-fən\ *n* : a child deprived by death of one or usually both parents — **orphan** *vb*
or•phan•age \ˈȯr-fə-nij\ *n* : an institution for the care of orphans
or•tho•don•tia \ˌȯr-thə-ˈdän-chə, -chē-ə\ *n* : ORTHODONTICS
or•tho•don•tics \ˌȯr-thə-ˈdän-tiks\ *n* : a branch of dentistry concerned with the correction of faults in the arrangement and placing of the teeth — **or•tho•don•tist** \-ˈdän-tist\ *n*
or•tho•dox \ˈȯr-thə-ˌdäks\ *adj* **1** ♦ : conforming to established doctrine especially in religion **2** ♦ : according with, sanctioned by, or based on convention : CONVENTIONAL **3** *cap* : of or relating to a Christian church originating in the church of the Eastern Roman Empire — **or•tho•doxy** \-ˌdäk-sē\ *n*

♦ [1] conservative, old-fashioned, reactionary, traditional ♦ [2] ceremonial, ceremonious, conventional, formal, regular, routine

or•thog•ra•phy \ȯr-ˈthä-grə-fē\ *n* : SPELLING — **or•tho•graph•ic** \ˌȯr-thə-ˈgra-fik\ *adj*
or•tho•pe•dics \ˌȯr-thə-ˈpē-diks\ *n sing or pl* : a branch of medicine concerned with the correction or prevention of skeletal injuries or disorders — **or•tho•pe•dic** \-dik\ *adj* — **or•tho•pe•dist** \-dist\ *n*
-ory \ˌōr-ē, ə-rē\ *adj suffix* **1** : of, relating to, or characterized by ⟨anticipat*ory*⟩ **2** : serving for, producing, or maintaining ⟨illus*ory*⟩
Os *symbol* osmium
OS *abbr* **1** left eye **2** ordinary seaman **3** out of stock
Osage \ō-ˈsāj\ *n, pl* **Osag•es** *or* **Osage** : a member of an American Indian people orig. of Missouri
os•cil•late \ˈä-sə-ˌlāt\ *vb* **-lat•ed; -lat•ing** **1** : to swing backward and forward like a pendulum **2** : to move or travel back and forth between two points **3** : VARY, FLUCTUATE — **os•cil•la•tor** \ˈä-sə-ˌlā-tər\ *n* — **os•cil•la•to•ry** \ˈä-sə-lə-ˌtōr-ē\ *adj*
os•cil•la•tion \ˌä-sə-ˈlā-shən\ *n* : the action or state of oscillating

♦ quivering, vibration

os•cil•lo•scope \ä-ˈsi-lə-ˌskōp\ *n* : an instrument in which variations in current or voltage appear as a visible wave form on a fluorescent screen
os•cu•late \ˈäs-kyə-ˌlāt\ *vb* **-lat•ed; -lat•ing** : KISS — **os•cu•la•tion** \ˌäs-kyə-ˈlā-shən\ *n* — **os•cu•la•to•ry** \ˈäs-kyə-lə-ˌtōr-ē\ *adj*

Osee \ˈō-ˌzē, ō-ˈzā-ə\ *n* : HOSEA
OSHA \ˈō-shə\ *abbr* Occupational Safety and Health Administration
osier \ˈō-zhər\ *n* : any of various willows with pliable twigs used especially in making baskets and furniture; *also* : a twig from an osier
os•mi•um \ˈäz-mē-əm\ *n* : a heavy hard brittle metallic chemical element used especially as a catalyst and in alloys
os•mo•sis \äz-ˈmō-səs, äs-\ *n* : movement of a solvent through a semipermeable membrane into a solution of higher concentration that tends to equalize the concentrations of the solutions on either side of the membrane — **os•mot•ic** \-ˈmä-tik\ *adj*
os•prey \ˈäs-prē, -ˌprā\ *n, pl* **ospreys** : a large dark brown and white fish-eating hawk
os•si•fy \ˈä-sə-ˌfī\ *vb* **-fied; -fy•ing** : to make or become hardened or set in one's ways — **os•si•fi•ca•tion** \ˌä-sə-fə-ˈkā-shən\ *n*
os•su•ary \ˈä-shə-ˌwer-ē, -syə-\ *n, pl* **-ar•ies** : a depository for the bones of the dead
os•ten•si•ble \ä-ˈsten-sə-bəl\ *adj* ♦ : shown outwardly : APPARENT

♦ apparent, assumed, evident, reputed, seeming, supposed

os•ten•si•bly \-blē\ *adv* **1** : in an ostensible manner **2** ♦ : to all outward appearances

♦ apparently, evidently, presumably, seemingly, supposedly

os•ten•ta•tion \ˌäs-tən-ˈtā-shən\ *n* ♦ : pretentious or excessive display — **os•ten•ta•tious•ly** *adv*

♦ flamboyance, flashiness, gaudiness, glitz, pretentiousness, showiness, swank *Ant* austerity, plainness, severity

os•ten•ta•tious \-shəs\ *adj* ♦ : marked by or fond of conspicuous or sometimes pretentious display

♦ flamboyant, flashy, garish, gaudy, glitzy, loud, swank, tawdry ♦ affected, grandiose, highfalutin, pompous, pretentious

os•teo•path \ˈäs-tē-ə-ˌpath\ *n* : a practitioner of osteopathy
os•te•op•a•thy \ˌäs-tē-ˈä-pə-thē\ *n* : a system of treating diseases emphasizing manipulation (as of joints) but not excluding other agencies (as the use of medicine and surgery) — **os•teo•path•ic** \ˌäs-tē-ə-ˈpa-thik\ *adj*
os•teo•po•ro•sis \ˌäs-tē-ō-pə-ˈrō-səs\ *n, pl* **-ro•ses** \-ˌsēz\ : a condition affecting especially older women and characterized by fragile and porous bones
os•tra•cise *chiefly Brit var of* OSTRACIZE
os•tra•cize \ˈäs-trə-ˌsīz\ *vb* **-cized; -ciz•ing** : to exclude from a group by common consent — **os•tra•cism** \-ˌsi-zəm\ *n*
os•trich \ˈäs-trich, ˈȯs-\ *n* : a very large swift-footed flightless bird of Africa and Arabia
Os•we•go tea \ä-ˈswē-gō-\ *n* : a No. American mint with showy scarlet flowers
OT *abbr* **1** occupational therapy **2** Old Testament **3** overtime
¹oth•er \ˈə-t͟hər\ *adj* **1** : being the one left; *also* : being the ones distinct from those first mentioned **2** : ALTERNATE ⟨every ~ day⟩ **3** ♦ : not the same : DIFFERENT **4** ♦ : existing by way of addition : ADDITIONAL **5** : recently past ⟨the ~ night⟩

♦ [3] different, disparate, dissimilar, distinct, distinctive, distinguishable, diverse, unalike, unlike ♦ [4] additional, another, else, farther, further, more

²other *pron* **1** : remaining one or ones **2** : a different or additional one ⟨something or ~⟩
other than *prep* ♦ : with the exception of : BESIDES

♦ aside from, bar, barring, besides, but, except, except for, exclusive of, outside (of), save

oth•er•wise \ˈə-t͟hər-ˌwīz\ *adv* **1** ♦ : in a different way **2** : in different circumstances **3** : in other respects **4** : if not **5** : NOT — **otherwise** *adj*

♦ differently, else, other *Ant* likewise

oth•er•world \-ˌwərld\ *n* : a world beyond death or beyond present reality
oth•er•world•ly \ˌə-t͟hər-ˈwərld-lē\ *adj* : not worldly : concerned with spiritual, intellectual, or imaginative matters
oti•ose \ˈō-shē-ˌōs, ˈō-tē-\ *adj* **1** : FUTILE **2** : IDLE **3** : USELESS
oto•lar•yn•gol•o•gy \ˌō-tō-ˌlar-ən-ˈgä-lə-jē\ *n* : a medical specialty concerned especially with the ear, nose, and throat — **oto•lar•yn•gol•o•gist** \-jist\ *n*
oto•rhi•no•lar•yn•gol•o•gy \ˌō-tō-ˌrī-nō-ˌlar-ən-ˈgä-lə-jē\ *n* : OTOLARYNGOLOGY — **oto•rhi•no•lar•yn•gol•o•gist** \-jist\ *n*
OTS *abbr* officers' training school
Ot•ta•wa \ˈä-tə-wə, -ˌwä, -ˌwȯ\ *n, pl* **Ottawas** *or* **Ottawa** : a member of an American Indian people of Michigan and southern Ontario
ot•ter \ˈä-tər\ *n, pl* **otters** *also* **otter** : any of various web-footed fish-eating mammals with dark brown fur that are related to the weasels; *also* : the fur
ot•to•man \ˈä-tə-mən\ *n* : an upholstered seat or couch usually without a back; *also* : an overstuffed footstool
ou•bli•ette \ˌü-blē-ˈet\ *n* : a dungeon with an opening at the top
ought \ˈȯt\ *verbal auxiliary* ♦ — used to express moral obligation, advisability, natural expectation, or logical consequence

♦ *usu* **ought to** have, must, need, shall, should

ounce \ˈau̇ns\ *n* **1 a** : a unit of avoirdupois, troy, and apothecaries' weight; *specif* : a unit of weight equal to $\frac{1}{16}$ pound **b** ♦ : a small amount **2** : FLUID OUNCE

♦ bit, little, particle, shred, speck, touch, trace

our \är, ˈau̇r\ *adj* : of or relating to us or ourselves
ours \ˈau̇rz, ˈärz\ *pron* : that which belongs to us
our•selves \är-ˈselvz, au̇r-\ *pron* : our own selves — used reflexively, for emphasis, or in absolute constructions ⟨we pleased ~⟩ ⟨we'll do it ~⟩ ⟨we were tourists ~⟩
-ous \əs\ *adj suffix* : full of : abounding in : having : possessing the qualities of ⟨clamor*ous*⟩ ⟨poison*ous*⟩
oust \ˈau̇st\ *vb* ♦ : to eject from or deprive of property or position

♦ banish, boot (out), bounce, cast, chase, dismiss, drum, eject, expel, rout, run off, throw out ♦ depose

oust•er \ˈau̇s-tər\ *n* : EXPULSION
¹out \ˈau̇t\ *adv* **1** : in a direction away from the inside or center **2** : beyond control **3** : to extinction, exhaustion, or completion **4** : in or into the open **5** : so as to retire a batter or base runner; *also* : so as to be retired
²out *vb* ♦ : to become known ⟨the truth will ~⟩

♦ come out, get out, leak out, spread

³out *prep* **1** : out through ⟨looked ~ the window⟩ **2** : outward on or along ⟨drive ~ the river road⟩
⁴out *adj* **1** : situated outside or at a distance **2** ♦ : not in : ABSENT; *also* : not being in power **3** : removed from play as a batter or base runner **4** : not being in vogue or fashion : not up-to-date

♦ absent, away, missing

⁵out *n* **1** : one who is out of office **2** : the retiring of a batter or base runner **3** ♦ : a way of escaping from an embarrassing or difficult situation

♦ avoidance, cop-out, escape, evasion

out•age \ˈau̇-tij\ *n* : a period or instance of interruption especially of electricity
out–and–out *adj* ♦ : being such completely at all times, in every way, or from every point of view : COMPLETE, THOROUGHGOING ⟨an ~ fraud⟩

♦ absolute, all-out, complete, consummate, outright, thorough, thoroughgoing, total, unqualified, utter

out•bid \ˌau̇t-ˈbid\ *vb* : to make a higher bid than
¹out•board \ˈau̇t-ˌbōrd\ *adj* **1** : situated outboard **2** : having or using an outboard motor
²outboard *adv* **1** : outside a ship's hull : away from the long axis of a ship **2** : in a position closer to the wing tip of an airplane
outboard motor *n* : a small internal combustion engine with propeller attached for mounting at the stern of a small boat
out•bound \ˈau̇t-ˌbau̇nd\ *adj* : outward bound ⟨~ traffic⟩
out•break \-ˌbrāk\ *n* **1** ♦ : a sudden increase in activity, incidence, or numbers **2** : INSURRECTION, REVOLT

♦ burst, flare, flare-up, flash, flurry, flutter, outburst, spurt

out•build•ing \-ˌbil-diŋ\ *n* : a building separate from but accessory to a main house
out•burst \-ˌbərst\ *n* **1 a** : ERUPTION **b** ♦ : a violent expression of feeling **2** : a surge of activity or growth

♦ agony, burst, eruption, explosion, fit, flare, flare-up, flash, flush, gale, gush, gust, paroxysm, spasm, storm

out•cast \-ˌkast\ *n* ♦ : one that is cast out by society

♦ castaway, reject

out•class \au̇t-ˈklas\ *vb* ♦ : to be superior to in quality, degree, or performance : SURPASS

♦ beat, better, eclipse, excel, outdistance, outdo, outshine, outstrip, surpass, top, transcend

out•come \ˈau̇t-ˌkəm\ *n* ♦ : a final consequence : RESULT

♦ aftermath, conclusion, consequence, corollary, development, effect, issue, outgrowth, product, result, resultant, sequence, upshot

out•crop \-ˌkräp\ *n* : a coming out of bedrock to the surface of the ground; *also* : the part of a rock formation that thus appears — **outcrop** *vb*
out•cry \-ˌkrī\ *n* ♦ : a loud cry : CLAMOR

♦ clamor (*or* clamour), howl, hubbub, hue and cry, hullabaloo, noise, roar, tumult, uproar

out•dat•ed \au̇t-ˈdā-təd\ *adj* ♦ : no longer current : OUTMODED

♦ antiquated, archaic, dated, obsolete, outmoded, outworn, passé

out•dis•tance \-ˈdis-təns\ *vb* ♦ : to leave behind : go ahead of

♦ beat, better, eclipse, excel, outdo, outshine, outstrip, surpass, top, transcend

out•do \-ˈdü\ *vb* **-did** \-ˈdid\; **-done** \-ˈdən\; **-do•ing; -does** \-ˈdəz\ ♦ : to go beyond in action or performance

♦ beat, better, eclipse, excel, outdistance, outshine, outstrip, surpass, top, transcend

out•door \ˈau̇t-ˌdōr, -ˈdōr\ *also* **out•doors** \-ˌdōrz, -ˈdōrz\ *adj* **1** : of or relating to the outdoors **2** : performed outdoors **3** : not enclosed (as by a roof)
¹out•doors \ˈau̇t-ˌdōrz, -ˈdōrz\ *adv* : in or into the open air
²outdoors *n* **1** : the open air **2** ♦ : the world away from human habitation — **out•doorsy** \ˌau̇t-ˈdȯr-zē\ *adj*

♦ nature, open, wild, wilderness

out•draw \au̇t-ˈdrȯ\ *vb* **-drew** \-ˈdrü\; **-drawn** \-ˈdrȯn\; **-draw•ing** **1** : to attract a larger audience than **2** : to draw a handgun more quickly than
out•er \ˈau̇-tər\ *adj* **1** ♦ : of, relating to, or connected with the outside or an outer part : EXTERNAL **2** ♦ : situated farther out; *also* : being away from a center

♦ [1, 2] exterior, external, outside, outward ***Ant*** inner, inside, interior, internal, inward

outer ear *n* : the outer visible portion of the ear that collects and directs sound waves toward the eardrum
out•er•most \-ˌmōst\ *adj* ♦ : farthest out

♦ extreme, farthest, furthest, ultimate, utmost

outer space *n* : SPACE 5
out•er•wear \ˈau̇-tər-ˌwer\ *n* **1** : clothing for outdoor wear **2** : outer clothing as opposed to underwear
out•face \au̇t-ˈfās\ *vb* **1** : to cause to waver or submit **2** : DEFY
out•field \ˈau̇t-ˌfēld\ *n* : the part of a baseball field beyond the infield and within the foul lines; *also* : players in the outfield — **out•field•er** \-ˌfēl-dər\ *n*
out•fight \au̇t-ˈfīt\ *vb* : to surpass in fighting : DEFEAT
¹out•fit \ˈau̇t-ˌfit\ *n* **1** ♦ : the equipment or apparel for a special purpose or occasion **2** ♦ : a group that works as a team **3** ♦ : an organization engaged in a particular industry or activity

♦ [1] dress, garb, getup, guise ♦ [1] accoutrements (*or* accouterments), apparatus, equipment, gear, matériel, paraphernalia, tackle ♦ [2] band, company, crew, gang, party, squad, team ♦ [3] business, company, concern, enterprise, establishment, firm, house

²outfit *vb* **out•fit•ted; out•fit•ting** ♦ : to provide or supply with what is needed, useful, or desirable : EQUIP — **out•fit•ter** *n*

♦ accoutre, equip, fit, furnish, rig, supply

out•flank \au̇t-ˈflaŋk\ *vb* : to get around the flank of (an opposing force)
out•flow \ˈau̇t-ˌflō\ *n* **1** ♦ : a flowing out **2** : something that flows out

♦ gush, outpouring ***Ant*** flux, inflow, influx, inrush

out•fox \au̇t-ˈfäks\ *vb* ♦ : to outdo in trickery : OUTWIT

♦ fox, outmaneuver, outsmart, outwit, overreach

out•go \ˈau̇t-ˌgō\ *n, pl* **outgoes** ♦ : something that goes out : OUTLAY

♦ cost, disbursement, expenditure, expense, outlay

out•go•ing \-ˌgō-iŋ\ *adj* **1** : going out ⟨~ tide⟩ **2** : retiring from a place or position **3** ♦ : openly friendly and responsive

♦ boon, companionable, convivial, extroverted, gregarious, sociable, social

out•grow \au̇t-ˈgrō\ *vb* **-grew** \-ˈgrü\; **-grown** \-ˈgrōn\; **-grow•ing** **1** : to grow faster than **2** : to grow too large for
out•growth \ˈau̇t-ˌgrōth\ *n* **1** ♦ : a product of growing out : OFFSHOOT **2** : something produced by a cause or necessarily following from a set of conditions : CONSEQUENCE, RESULT

♦ derivative, offshoot, spin-off

out•guess \au̇t-ˈges\ *vb* : OUTWIT
out•gun \-ˈgən\ *vb* : to surpass in firepower
out•house \ˈau̇t-ˌhau̇s\ *n* : OUTBUILDING; *esp* : an outdoor toilet
out•ing \ˈau̇-tiŋ\ *n* ♦ : a brief stay or trip in the open

♦ excursion, jaunt, junket, sally

out•land•ish \au̇t-ˈlan-dish\ *adj* **1 a** ♦ : of foreign appearance or manner **b** ♦ : strikingly out of the ordinary **2** : remote from civilization — **out•land•ish•ly** *adv*

♦ bizarre, curious, exotic, far-out, funny, kinky, odd, outré, peculiar, quaint, queer, quirky, remarkable, screwy, strange, wacky, weird, wild

out•last \-ˈlast\ *vb* : to last longer than
¹out•law \ˈau̇t-ˌlȯ\ *n* **1** : a person excluded from the protection of the law **2** : a lawless person
²outlaw *vb* **1** : to deprive of the protection of the law **2** : to make illegal **3** ♦ : to place under a ban or restriction — **out•law•ry** \ˈau̇t-ˌlȯr-ē\ *n*

♦ ban, bar, enjoin, forbid, interdict, prohibit, proscribe

out•lay \ˈau̇t-ˌlā\ *n* **1** : the act of spending **2** ♦ : something expended : EXPENDITURE

♦ cost, disbursement, expenditure, expense, outgo

out•let \ˈau̇t-ˌlet, -lət\ *n* **1** ♦ : a place or opening through which something is let out : EXIT **2** : a means of release (as for an emotion) **3** : a market for a commodity **4** : a receptacle for the plug of an electrical device

♦ egress, exit, issue

¹out•line \ˈau̇t-ˌlīn\ *n* **1** ♦ : a line marking the outer limits of an object or figure **2** : a drawing in which only contours are marked **3** ♦ : a condensed treatment of a particular subject : a summary of a written work : SUMMARY, SYNOPSIS **4** : PLAN

♦ [1] contour, figure, silhouette ♦ [3] abstract, digest, encapsulation, epitome, précis, recapitulation, roundup, résumé (*or* resume), sum, summary, synopsis, wrap-up

²outline *vb* **1** ♦ : to draw the outline of **2** : to indicate the chief features or parts of

♦ define, delineate, silhouette, sketch, trace

out•live \au̇t-ˈliv\ *vb* : to live longer than
out•look \ˈau̇t-ˌlu̇k\ *n* **1 a** : a place offering a view **b** ♦ : a view from a particular place : VIEW **2** ♦ : a position from which something is considered or evaluated : STANDPOINT **3** : the prospect for the future

♦ [1b] lookout, panorama, prospect, view, vista ♦ [2] angle, perspective, point of view, slant, standpoint, viewpoint

out•ly•ing \-ˌlī-iŋ\ *adj* : distant from a center or main body
out•ma•neu•ver \ˌau̇t-mə-ˈnü-vər, -ˈnyü-\ *vb* ♦ : to defeat by more skillful maneuvering

♦ fox, outfox, outsmart, outwit, overreach

out•mod•ed \au̇t-ˈmō-dəd\ *adj* **1** ♦ : no longer in style **2** ♦ : no longer acceptable, current, or usable

♦ [1, 2] antiquated, archaic, dated, obsolete, outdated, outworn, passé

out•num•ber \-ˈnəm-bər\ *vb* : to exceed in number
out of *prep* **1** : out from within or behind ⟨walk *out of* the room⟩ ⟨look *out of* the window⟩ **2** : from a state of ⟨wake up *out of* a deep sleep⟩ **3** : beyond the limits of ⟨*out of* sight⟩ **4** : BECAUSE OF ⟨asked *out of* curiosity⟩ **5** : FROM, WITH ⟨built it *out of* scrap⟩ **6** : in or into a state of loss or not having ⟨cheated him *out of* $5000⟩ ⟨we're *out of* matches⟩ **7** : from among ⟨one *out of* four⟩ — **out of it** : SQUARE, OLD-FASHIONED
out–of–bounds *adv or adj* : outside the prescribed boundaries or limits
out–of–date *adj* : no longer in fashion or in use : OUTMODED
out–of–door *or* **out–of–doors** *adj* : of or relating to the outdoors : OUTDOOR
out–of–the–way *adj* **1** : UNUSUAL **2** : being off the beaten track
out•pa•tient \ˈau̇t-ˌpā-shənt\ *n* : a patient who visits a hospital or clinic for diagnosis or treatment without staying overnight
out•per•form \ˌau̇t-pər-ˈfȯrm\ *vb* : to perform better than

out•play \au̇t-ˈplā\ *vb* **:** to play more skillfully than
out•point \-ˈpȯint\ *vb* **:** to win more points than
out•post \ˈau̇t-ˌpōst\ *n* **1 :** a security detachment dispatched by a main body of troops to protect it from enemy surprise; *also* **:** a military base established (as by treaty) in a foreign country **2 :** an outlying or frontier settlement
out•pour•ing \-ˌpōr-iŋ\ *n* ♦ **:** something that pours out or is poured out

♦ gush, outflow

out•pull \au̇t-ˈpu̇l\ *vb* **:** OUTDRAW 1
¹out•put \ˈau̇t-ˌpu̇t\ *n* **1 a** ♦ **:** the amount produced (as by a machine or factory) **:** PRODUCTION **b** ♦ **:** mental or artistic production **2 :** the information produced by a computer

♦ [1a, b] affair, handiwork, produce, product, thing, work, yield

²output *vb* **out•put•ted** *or* **output; out•put•ting :** to produce as output
¹out•rage \ˈau̇t-ˌrāj\ *n* **1 :** a violent or shameful act **2** ♦ **:** a gross indignity **:** INSULT **3** ♦ **:** the anger or resentment aroused by an outrage

♦ [2] affront, barb, dart, dig, indignity, insult, name, offense, put-down, sarcasm, slight, slur, wound ♦ [3] anger, furor, fury, indignation, ire, rage, spleen, wrath, wrathfulness

²outrage *vb* **out•raged; out•rag•ing 1 :** RAPE **2** ♦ **:** to subject to violent injury or gross insult **3** ♦ **:** to arouse to extreme resentment

♦ [2] affront, insult, offend, slight, wound ♦ [3] anger, antagonize, enrage, incense, inflame, infuriate, madden, rankle, rile, roil

out•ra•geous \au̇t-ˈrā-jəs\ *adj* **:** extremely offensive, insulting, or shameful **:** SHOCKING — **out•ra•geous•ly** *adv*
out•rank \-ˈraŋk\ *vb* **:** to rank higher than
ou•tré \ü-ˈtrā\ *adj* ♦ **:** violating convention or propriety **:** BIZARRE

♦ bizarre, curious, far-out, funny, kinky, odd, outlandish, peculiar, quaint, queer, quirky, remarkable, screwy, strange, wacky, weird, wild

¹out•reach \au̇t-ˈrēch\ *vb* **1 :** to surpass in reach **2 :** to get the better of by trickery
²out•reach \ˈau̇t-ˌrēch\ *n* **1 :** the act of reaching out **2 :** the extent of reach **3 :** the extending of services beyond usual limits
out•rid•er \-ˌrī-dər\ *n* **:** a mounted attendant
out•rig•ger \-ˌri-gər\ *n* **1 :** a frame attached to the side of a boat to prevent capsizing **2 :** a craft equipped with an outrigger
¹out•right \au̇t-ˈrīt\ *adv* **1 :** COMPLETELY **2 :** INSTANTANEOUSLY
²out•right \ˈau̇t-ˌrīt\ *adj* **1 :** being exactly what is stated 〈an ~ lie〉 **2** ♦ **:** given or made without reservation or encumbrance 〈an ~ sale〉

♦ absolute, all-out, complete, consummate, out-and-out, perfect, pure, sheer, thorough, thoroughgoing, total, utter

out•run \au̇t-ˈrən\ *vb* **-ran** \-ˈran\; **-run; -run•ning 1 :** to run faster than **2** ♦ **:** to go or be beyond the limit of **:** EXCEED

♦ exceed, overreach, overrun, overshoot, overstep, surpass, transcend

out•sell \-ˈsel\ *vb* **-sold** \-ˈsōld\; **-sell•ing :** to exceed in sales
out•set \ˈau̇t-ˌset\ *n* ♦ **:** a setting out **:** BEGINNING, START

♦ beginning, birth, commencement, dawn, genesis, launch, morning, onset, start, threshold

out•shine \au̇t-ˈshīn\ *vb* **-shone** \-ˈshōn\ *or* **-shined; -shin•ing 1 :** to shine brighter than **2** ♦ **:** to go beyond in action or performance **:** SURPASS

♦ beat, better, eclipse, excel, outdistance, outdo, outstrip, surpass, top, transcend

¹out•side \au̇t-ˈsīd, ˈau̇t-ˌsīd\ *n* **1 :** a place or region beyond an enclosure or boundary **2** ♦ **:** an outer side or surface **:** EXTERIOR **3 :** the utmost limit or extent

♦ exterior, face, skin, surface, veneer

²outside *adj* **1** ♦ **:** of, relating to, or being on or toward the outer side or surface **:** OUTER **2 :** coming from without 〈~ influences〉 **3 :** being apart from one's regular duties 〈~ activities〉 **4** ♦ **:** barely possible **:** REMOTE 〈an ~ chance〉

♦ [1] exterior, external, outer, outward ♦ [4] negligible, off, remote, slight, slim, small

³outside *adv* **:** on or to the outside

⁴outside *prep* **1 :** on or to the outside of **2** ♦ **:** beyond the limits of **3** ♦ **:** with the exclusion or exception of **:** EXCEPT

♦ [2] beyond, without ♦ *usu* **outside of** [3] aside from, bar, barring, besides, but, except, save

outside of *prep* **1 :** with the exclusion or exception of **:** OUTSIDE **2 :** BESIDES **3 :** beyond the limits or compass of
out•sid•er \au̇t-ˈsī-dər\ *n* **:** a person who does not belong to a group
out•size \ˈau̇t-ˌsīz\ *also* **out•sized** \-ˌsīzd\ *adj* ♦ **:** unusually large **:** extravagant in size or degree

♦ astronomical, enormous, giant, gigantic, grand, huge, jumbo, mammoth, massive, monumental, oversize, prodigious, titanic, tremendous, vast

out•skirts \-ˌskərts\ *n pl* ♦ **:** the outlying parts (as of a city)

♦ environs, exurbia, suburbia

out•smart \au̇t-ˈsmärt\ *vb* ♦ **:** to get the better of **:** OUTWIT

♦ fox, outfox, outmaneuver, outwit, overreach

out•source \ˈau̇t-ˌsȯrs\ *vb* **-sourced; -sourc•ing :** to obtain (goods or services) from an outside supplier
out•spend \-ˈspend\ *vb* **1 :** to exceed the limits of in spending 〈~*s* his income〉 **2 :** to spend more than
out•spo•ken \au̇t-ˈspō-kən\ *adj* ♦ **:** direct and open in speech or expression — **out•spo•ken•ly** *adv*

♦ candid, direct, forthright, foursquare, frank, honest, open, plain, straight, straightforward, unguarded, unreserved

out•spo•ken•ness \au̇t-ˈspō-kən-nəs\ *n* ♦ **:** the quality or state of being outspoken

♦ candidness, candor, directness, forthrightness, frankness, openness, plainness

out•spread \-ˈspred\ *vb* **-spread; -spread•ing :** to spread out
out•stand•ing \-ˈstan-diŋ\ *adj* **1 :** PROJECTING **2 a** ♦ **:** not paid **:** UNPAID **b :** UNRESOLVED **3 :** publicly issued and sold **4 a :** CONSPICUOUS **b** ♦ **:** marked by eminence and distinction **:** DISTINGUISHED — **out•stand•ing•ly** *adv*

♦ [2a] overdue, payable, unpaid, unsettled ***Ant*** cleared, liquidated, paid (off *or* up), repaid, settled ♦ [4b] distinguished, eminent, illustrious, noble, notable, noteworthy, preeminent, prestigious, signal, star, superior

out•stay \-ˈstā\ *vb* **1 :** OVERSTAY **2 :** to surpass in endurance
out•stretch \ˌau̇t-ˈstrech\ *vb* **:** to stretch out **:** EXTEND
out•strip \-ˈstrip\ *vb* **1 :** to go faster than **2** ♦ **:** to get ahead of **:** EXCEL, SURPASS

♦ beat, better, eclipse, excel, outdistance, outdo, outshine, surpass, top, transcend

out•take \ˈau̇t-ˌtāk\ *n* **:** something taken out; *esp* **:** a take that is not used in an edited version of a film or videotape
out•vote \-ˈvōt\ *vb* **:** to defeat by a majority of votes
¹out•ward \ˈau̇t-wərd\ *adj* **1 :** moving or directed toward the outside **2 :** showing outwardly **3** ♦ **:** situated or lying on the outside of an enclosure or surface

♦ exterior, external, outer, outside

²outward *or* **out•wards** \-wərdz\ *adv* **:** toward the outside
out•ward•ly \-wərd-lē\ *adv* **:** on the outside **:** EXTERNALLY
out•wear \au̇t-ˈwar\ *vb* **-wore** \-ˈwōr\; **-worn** \-ˈwōrn\; **-wear•ing :** to wear longer than **:** OUTLAST
out•weigh \-ˈwā\ *vb* ♦ **:** to exceed in weight, value, or importance

♦ overshadow

out•wit \-ˈwit\ *vb* ♦ **:** to get the better of by superior cleverness

♦ fox, outfox, outmaneuver, outsmart, overreach

¹out•work \-ˈwərk\ *vb* **:** to outdo in working
²out•work \ˈau̇t-ˌwərk\ *n* **:** a minor defensive position outside a fortified area
out•worn \au̇t-ˈwōrn\ *adj* ♦ **:** no longer useful or accepted **:** OUTMODED

♦ antiquated, archaic, dated, obsolete, outdated, outmoded, passé

ou•zo \ˈü-(ˌ)zō\ *n* **:** a colorless anise-flavored unsweetened Greek liqueur
ova *pl of* OVUM
oval \ˈō-vəl\ *adj* **:** egg-shaped; *also* **:** broadly elliptical — **oval** *n*
ova•ry \ˈō-və-rē\ *n, pl* **-ries 1 :** one of the usually paired female reproductive organs producing eggs and in vertebrates sex hor-

mones **2 :** the part of a flower in which seeds are produced — **ovar•i•an** \ō-ˈvar-ē-ən, -ˈver-\ *adj*
ovate \ˈō-ˌvāt\ *adj* **:** egg-shaped
ova•tion \ō-ˈvā-shən\ *n* ♦ **:** an enthusiastic popular tribute

♦ acclamation, applause

ov•en \ˈə-vən\ *n* **:** a chamber (as in a stove) for baking, heating, or drying
oven•bird \-ˌbərd\ *n* **:** a large olive-green American warbler that builds its dome-shaped nest on the ground
¹**over** \ˈō-vər\ *adv* **1 :** across a barrier or intervening space **2 :** across the brim ⟨boil ~⟩ **3** ♦ **:** so as to bring the underside up or the upperside down **4 :** out of a vertical position **5 :** beyond some quantity, limit, or norm **6** ♦ **:** in or to a higher place **:** ABOVE **7 :** at an end **8** ♦ **:** from beginning to end **:** THROUGH; *also* **:** THOROUGHLY **9** ♦ **:** for a second or successive time **:** AGAIN ⟨do it ~⟩

♦ [3] below, down, downward ♦ [6] above, aloft, overhead, skyward ♦ [8] around, round, thoroughly, through, throughout ♦ [9] again, anew

²**over** *prep* **1 :** above in position, authority, or scope ⟨towered ~ her⟩ ⟨obeyed those ~ him⟩ **2 :** more than ⟨cost ~ $100⟩ **3 :** ON, UPON ⟨a cape ~ her shoulders⟩ **4 :** along the length of ⟨~ the road⟩ **5 :** through the medium of **:** ON ⟨spoke ~ TV⟩ **6** ♦ **:** all through ⟨showed me ~ the house⟩ **7** ♦ **:** on or to the other side or beyond ⟨jump ~ a ditch⟩ **8 :** throughout the duration of **:** DURING ⟨~ the past 25 years⟩ **9 :** on account of ⟨trouble ~ money⟩

♦ [6] about, around, round, through, throughout ♦ [7] across, athwart, through

³**over** *adj* **1 :** being higher or in a superior position **2 :** REMAINING **3** ♦ **:** being at an end **:** ENDED

♦ complete, done, down, through, up

over- *prefix* **1 :** so as to exceed or surpass **2 :** excessive; excessively

overabundant
overachiever
overaggressive
overambitious
overanxious
overbid
overbuild
overbuy
overcapacity
overcapitalize
overcareful
overcautious
overcompensation
overconfidence
overconscientious
overcook
overcrowd
overdecorated
overdependence
overdetermined
overdevelop
overdress
overeager
overeat
overeducated
overemphasis
overemphasize
overenthusiastic
overestimate
overexcite
overexcited
overexert
overexertion
overextend
overfatigued
overfeed
overgeneralization
overgeneralize
overgenerous
overgraze
overhasty
overheat
overindulge
overindulgence
overindulgent
overlarge
overlearn
overlong
overmodest
overnice
overoptimism
overoptimistic
overpay
overproduce
overproduction
overprotect
overprotective
overrate
overreact
overreaction
overrefinement
overrepresented
oversensitive
oversensitiveness
oversimple
oversimplification
oversimplify
overspecialization
overspecialize
overspend
overstimulation
overstock
oversubtle
oversupply
overtax
overtired
overtrain
overuse
overvalue
overzealous

over•abun•dance \ō-vər-ə-ˈbən-dən(t)s\ *n* ♦ **:** an excessive abundance

♦ excess, fat, overflow, overkill, overmuch, superabundance, superfluity, surfeit, surplus

over•act \ˌō-vər-ˈakt\ *vb* **:** to exaggerate in acting
over•ac•tive \-ˈak-tiv\ *adj* ♦ **:** excessively or abnormally active ⟨~ glands⟩ ⟨an ~ imagination⟩ — **over•ac•tiv•i•ty** \-ak-ˈti-və-tē\ *n*

♦ agitated, feverish, frenzied, heated, hectic, overwrought

¹**over•age** \ˌō-vər-ˈāj\ *adj* **1 :** too old to be useful **2 :** older than is normal for one's position, function, or grade
²**over•age** \ˈō-və-rij\ *n* **:** SURPLUS
¹**over•all** \ˌō-vər-ˈȯl\ *adj* **1** ♦ **:** including everything ⟨~ expenses⟩ **2** ♦ **:** viewed as a whole

♦ [1] blanket, common, general, generic, global, universal ♦ [1] all around, altogether, collectively, together ♦ [1, 2] all-around, bird's-eye, broad, general, nonspecific

²**over•all** \ˌō-vər-ˈȯl\ *adv* ♦ **:** as a whole

♦ altogether, basically, chiefly, generally, largely, mainly, mostly, predominantly, primarily, principally

over•alls \ˈō-vər-ˌȯlz\ *n pl* **:** pants of strong material usually with a piece extending up to cover the chest
over•arm \-ˌärm\ *adj* **:** done with the arm raised above the shoulder
over•awe \ˌō-vər-ˈȯ\ *vb* **:** to restrain or subdue by awe
over•bal•ance \-ˈba-ləns\ *vb* **1 :** to exceed in weight, value, or importance **:** OUTWEIGH **2 :** to cause to lose balance
over•bear•ing \-ˈbar-iŋ\ *adj* ♦ **:** decisively important **:** DOMINEERING

♦ authoritarian, autocratic, bossy, despotic, dictatorial, domineering, imperious, masterful, peremptory, tyrannical, tyrannous

over•bite \ˈō-vər-ˌbīt\ *n* **:** the projection of the upper front teeth over the lower
over•blown \-ˈblōn\ *adj* **1 :** PORTLY **2 :** INFLATED, PRETENTIOUS
over•board \ˈō-vər-ˌbōrd\ *adv* **1 :** over the side of a ship into the water **2 :** to extremes of enthusiasm
over•bold \-ˈbōld\ *adj* ♦ **:** excessively bold or forward

♦ brash, foolhardy, madcap, overconfident, reckless

over•bur•den \-ˈbər-dᵊn\ *vb* ♦ **:** to place an excessive burden on

♦ overcharge, overload

¹**over•cast** \ˈō-vər-ˌkast\ *adj* ♦ **:** clouded over **:** GLOOMY

♦ cloudy, dull, gloomy, hazy, heavy ***Ant*** clear, cloudless

²**overcast** *n* **:** COVERING; *esp* **:** a covering of clouds
over•charge \ˌō-vər-ˈchärj\ *vb* **1** ♦ **:** to charge too much **2 :** to fill or load too full — **over•charge** \ˈō-vər-ˌchärj\ *n*

♦ gouge, soak, sting ***Ant*** undercharge

over•coat \ˈō-vər-ˌkōt\ *n* **:** a warm coat worn over indoor clothing
over•come \ˌō-vər-ˈkəm\ *vb* **-came** \-ˈkām\; **-come; -com•ing** **1** ♦ **:** to get the better of **:** CONQUER **2** ♦ **:** to make helpless or exhausted

♦ [1] beat, best, clobber, conquer, crush, defeat, drub, lick, master, prevail, rout, skunk, subdue, surmount, thrash, trim, triumph, trounce, wallop, whip, win ♦ [2] carry away, crush, devastate, floor, oppress, overpower, overwhelm, prostrate, snow under, swamp

over•con•fi•dent \-ˈkän-fə-dənt, -ˌdent\ *adj* ♦ **:** marked by or reflecting overconfidence

♦ brash, foolhardy, madcap, overbold, reckless

over•crit•i•cal \-ˈkri-ti-kəl\ *adj* ♦ **:** meticulously or excessively critical

♦ captious, carping, critical, hypercritical

over•do \ˌō-vər-ˈdü\ *vb* **-did** \-ˈdid\; **-done** \-ˈdən\; **-do•ing; -does** \-ˈdəz\ **1 :** to do too much; *also* **:** to tire oneself **2** ♦ **:** to do in excess **:** EXAGGERATE **3 :** to cook too long

♦ exaggerate, overstate, put on

over•dose \ˈō-vər-ˌdōs\ *n* **:** too great a dose (as of medicine); *also* **:** a lethal or toxic amount (as of a drug) — **over•dose** \ˌō-vər-ˈdōs\ *vb*
over•draft \ˈō-vər-ˌdraft, -ˌdråft\ *n* **:** an overdrawing of a bank account; *also* **:** the sum overdrawn
over•draw \ˌō-vər-ˈdrȯ\ *vb* **-drew** \-ˈdrü\; **-drawn** \-ˈdrȯn\; **-draw•ing** **1 :** to draw checks on a bank account for more than the balance **2 :** to do in excess **:** EXAGGERATE
over•drive \ˈō-vər-ˌdrīv\ *n* **:** an automotive transmission gear that transmits to the driveshaft a speed greater than the engine speed
over•dub \ˌō-vər-ˈdəb\ *vb* **:** to transfer (recorded sound) onto an earlier recording for a combined effect — **over•dub** \ˈō-vər-ˌdəb\ *n*

over•due \-ˈdü, -ˈdyü\ *adj* **1 a** ♦ **:** unpaid when due **b** ♦ **:** not appearing or presented on time **2 :** more than ready

♦ [1a] outstanding, payable, unpaid, unsettled ♦ [1b] behind, belated, delinquent, late, tardy

over•ex•pose \ˌō-vər-ik-ˈspōz\ *vb* **:** to expose (as film) for more time than is needed — **over•ex•po•sure** \-ˈspō-zhər\ *n*
over•fill \-ˈfil\ *vt* **:** to fill to overflowing
¹over•flow \-ˈflō\ *vb* **1** ♦ **:** to cover with or as if with water **:** INUNDATE; *also* **:** to pour forth in a flood **2 :** to flow over the brim or top of

♦ deluge, drown, engulf, flood, inundate, overwhelm, submerge, swamp

²over•flow \ˈō-vər-ˌflō\ *n* **1 a** ♦ **:** a flowing over **:** FLOOD **b** ♦ **:** a flowing over **:** SURPLUS **2 :** an outlet for surplus liquid

♦ [1a] cataclysm, cataract, deluge, flood, inundation, spate, torrent ♦ [1b] excess, fat, overabundance, overkill, overmuch, superabundance, superfluity, surfeit, surplus

over•fly \ˌō-vər-ˈflī\ *vb* **-flew** \-ˈflü\; **-flown** \-ˈflōn\; **-fly•ing :** to fly over in an aircraft or spacecraft — **over•flight** \ˈō-vər-ˌflīt\ *n*
over•grow \ˌō-vər-ˈgrō\ *vb* **-grew** \-ˈgrü\; **-grow•ing 1 :** to grow over so as to cover **2 :** OUTGROW **3 :** to grow excessively
over•grown \-ˈgrōn\ *adj* **:** covered with overgrowth
over•hand \ˈō-vər-ˌhand\ *adj* **:** made with the hand brought down from above — **overhand** *adv* — **over•hand•ed** \-ˌhan-dəd\ *adv or adj*
¹over•hang \ˈō-vər-ˌhaŋ, ˌō-vər-ˈhaŋ\ *vb* **-hung** \-ˌhəŋ, -ˈhəŋ\; **-hang•ing 1 :** to project over **:** jut out **2** ♦ **:** to hang over threateningly

♦ hang, hover, menace, threaten

²over•hang \ˈō-vər-ˌhaŋ\ *n* ♦ **:** a part (as of a roof) that overhangs

♦ bulge, projection, protrusion

¹over•head \ˌō-vər-ˈhed\ *adv* ♦ **:** above one's head **:** ALOFT

♦ above, aloft, over, skyward

²over•head \ˈō-vər-ˌhed\ *adj* **:** operating or lying above ⟨~ door⟩
³over•head \ˈō-vər-ˌhed\ *n* **:** business expenses not chargeable to a particular part of the work
over•hear \ˌō-vər-ˈhir\ *vb* **-heard** \-ˈhərd\; **-hear•ing :** to hear without the speaker's knowledge or intention
over•joyed \ˌō-vər-ˈjȯid\ *adj* **:** filled with great joy
over•kill \ˈō-vər-ˌkil\ *n* **1 :** destructive capacity greatly exceeding that required for a target **2** ♦ **:** a large excess

♦ excess, fat, overabundance, overflow, overmuch, superabundance, superfluity, surfeit, surplus

over•land \ˈō-vər-ˌland, -lənd\ *adv or adj* **:** by, on, or across land
¹over•lap \ˌō-vər-ˈlap\ *vb* **1** ♦ **:** to lap over **2 :** to have something in common

♦ lap, overlay, overlie, overspread

²over•lap \ˈō-vər-ˌlap\ *n* **:** the condition or relationship of things that overlap
over•lay \ˌō-vər-ˈlā\ *vb* **-laid** \-ˈlād\; **-lay•ing** ♦ **:** to lay or spread over or across — **over•lay** \ˈō-vər-ˌlā\ *n*

♦ blanket, carpet, coat, cover, overlie, overspread

over•leap \ˌō-vər-ˈlēp\ *vb* **-leaped** *or* **-leapt** \-ˈlēpt, -ˈlept\; **-leap•ing 1 :** to leap over or across **2 :** to defeat (oneself) by going too far
over•lie \ˌō-vər-ˈlī\ *vb* **-lay** \-ˈlā\; **-lain** \-ˈlān\; **-ly•ing** ♦ **:** to lie over or upon

♦ lap, overlap, overlay, overspread

over•load \-ˈlōd\ *vb* ♦ **:** to load to excess

♦ overburden, overcharge

¹over•look \ˌō-vər-ˈlu̇k\ *vb* **1 :** INSPECT **2 :** to look down on from above **3 :** to fail to see **4** ♦ **:** to refuse to take notice of **:** IGNORE; *also* **:** EXCUSE **5 :** SUPERINTEND

♦ disregard, excuse, forget, ignore, neglect, pass over, slight, slur

²over•look \ˈō-vər-ˌlu̇k\ *n* **:** a place from which to look upon a scene below
over•lord \-ˌlȯrd\ *n* **:** a lord who has supremacy over other lords
over•ly \ˈō-vər-lē\ *adv* ♦ **:** to an excessive degree **:** EXCESSIVELY

♦ devilishly, excessively, inordinately, monstrously, overmuch, too

over•match \ˌō-vər-ˈmach\ *vb* **:** to be more than a match for **:** DEFEAT
¹over•much \-ˈməch\ *adj* ♦ **:** too much

♦ devilish, excessive, exorbitant, extravagant, extreme, immoderate, inordinate, lavish, overweening, steep, stiff, towering, unconscionable

²overmuch *adv* ♦ **:** in too great a degree

♦ devilishly, excessively, inordinately, monstrously, overly, too

¹over•night \-ˈnīt\ *adv* **1 :** on or during the night **2 :** SUDDENLY ⟨became famous ~⟩
²overnight *adj* **:** of, lasting, or staying the night ⟨~ guests⟩
over•pass \ˈō-vər-ˌpas\ *n* **1 :** a crossing (as of two highways) at different levels by means of a bridge **2 :** the upper level of an overpass
over•play \ˌō-vər-ˈplā\ *vb* **1 :** EXAGGERATE; *also* **:** to put undue emphasis on **2 :** to rely too much on the strength of
over•pop•u•la•tion \ˌō-vər-ˌpä-pyə-ˈlā-shən\ *n* **:** the condition of having a population so dense as to cause a decline in population or in living conditions — **over•pop•u•la•ted** \-ˈpä-pyə-ˌlā-təd\ *adj*
over•pow•er \-ˈpau̇-ər\ *vb* **1** ♦ **:** to overcome by superior force **2** ♦ **:** to affect with overwhelming intensity

♦ [1] conquer, dominate, subdue, subject, vanquish ♦ [2] carry away, crush, devastate, floor, oppress, overcome, overwhelm, prostrate, snow under, swamp

over•praise \-ˈprāz\ *vb* ♦ **:** to praise excessively

♦ blarney, flatter

over•price \ˌō-vər-ˈprīs\ *vb* **:** to price too high
over•print \-ˈprint\ *vb* **:** to print over with something additional — **over•print** \ˈō-vər-ˌprint\ *n*
over•qual•i•fied \-ˈkwä-lə-ˌfīd\ *adj* **:** having more education, training, or experience than a job calls for
over•reach \ˌō-vər-ˈrēch\ *vb* **1 :** to defeat (oneself) by too great an effort **2** ♦ **:** to get the better of especially in dealing and bargaining and typically by unscrupulous or crafty methods **3** ♦ **:** to reach above or beyond

♦ [2] fox, outfox, outmaneuver, outsmart, outwit ♦ [3] exceed, overrun, overshoot, overstep, surpass

over•ride \-ˈrīd\ *vb* **-rode** \-ˈrōd\; **-rid•den** \-ˈrid-ᵊn\; **-rid•ing 1 :** to ride over or across **2 :** to prevail over; *also* **:** to set aside ⟨~ a veto⟩
over•ripe \ˌō-və(r)-ˈrīp\ *adj* ♦ **:** marked by decay or decline **:** DECADENT — **over–ripe•ness** \-nəs\ *n*

♦ decadent, degenerate, effete

over•rule \-ˈrül\ *vb* **1 :** to prevail over **2 :** to rule against **3 :** to set aside
¹over•run \-ˈrən\ *vb* **-ran** \-ˈran\; **-run•ning 1** ♦ **:** to defeat and occupy the positions of **2 :** OVERSPREAD; *also* **:** INFEST **3 :** to go beyond **4 :** to flow over

♦ foray, invade, raid

²over•run \ˈō-vər-ˌrən\ *n* **1 :** an act or instance of overrunning; *esp* **:** an exceeding of estimated costs **2 :** the amount by which something overruns
over•sea \ˌō-vər-ˈsē, ˈō-vər-ˌsē\ *adj or adv* **:** OVERSEAS
over•seas \ˌō-vər-ˈsēz, -ˌsēz\ *adv or adj* **:** beyond or across the sea **:** ABROAD
over•see \ˌō-vər-ˈsē\ *vb* **-saw** \-ˈsȯ\; **-seen** \-ˈsēn\; **-see•ing 1 :** OVERLOOK **2 a :** INSPECT **b** ♦ **:** to have or exercise the charge and oversight of **:** SUPERVISE — **over•seer** \ˈō-vər-ˌsir\ *n*

♦ administer, carry on, conduct, control, direct, govern, guide, handle, manage, operate, regulate, run, superintend, supervise

over•sell \ˌō-vər-ˈsel\ *vb* **-sold; -sel•ling :** to sell too much to or too much of
over•sexed \ˌō-vər-ˈsekst\ *adj* **:** exhibiting excessive sexual drive or interest
over•shad•ow \-ˈsha-dō\ *vb* **1** ♦ **:** to cast a shadow over **2** ♦ **:** to exceed in importance

♦ [1] becloud, befog, blur, cloud, darken, dim, fog, haze, mist, obscure, overcast, shroud ♦ [2] outweigh

over•shoe \ˈō-vər-ˌshü\ *n* **:** a protective outer shoe; *esp* **:** GALOSH
over•shoot \ˌō-vər-ˈshüt\ *vb* **-shot** \-ˈshät\; **-shoot•ing 1 :** to pass swiftly beyond **2** ♦ **:** to shoot over or beyond **3** ♦ **:** to overreach (oneself) or cause (oneself) to go astray

♦ [2, 3] exceed, overreach, overrun, overstep, surpass

over•sight \ˌō-vər-ˈsīt\ *n* **1** ♦ **:** watchful and responsible care **:** SUPERVISION **2** ♦ **:** an inadvertent omission or error

♦ [1] administration, care, charge, conduct, control, direction, government, guidance, management, operation, regulation, running, superintendence, supervision ♦ [2] blunder, error, fault, flub, fumble, goof, lapse, miscue, misstep, mistake, slip, stumble

over•size \ˌō-vər-ˈsīz\ *or* **over•sized** \-ˈsīzd\ *adj* ♦ **:** of more than ordinary size

♦ big, considerable, goodly, grand, great, hefty, large, outsize, sizable, substantial

over•sleep \ˌō-vər-ˈslēp\ *vb* **-slept** \-ˈslept\; **-sleep•ing :** to sleep beyond the time for waking

over•spread \-ˈspred\ *vb* **-spread; -spread•ing** ♦ **:** to spread over or above

♦ blanket, carpet, coat, cover, overlay, overlie

over•state \-ˈstāt\ *vb* ♦ **:** to state in too strong terms **:** EXAGGERATE

♦ exaggerate, overdo, put on ***Ant*** understate

over•state•ment *n* ♦ **:** the act of overstating

♦ caricature, elaboration, embellishment, exaggeration, hyperbole, magnification, padding

over•stay \-ˈstā\ *vb* **:** to stay beyond the time or limits of

over•step \-ˈstep\ *vb* ♦ **:** to step over or beyond **:** EXCEED

♦ exceed, overreach, overrun, overshoot, surpass

over•sub•scribe \-səb-ˈskrīb\ *vb* **:** to subscribe for more of than is available, asked for, or offered for sale

overt \ō-ˈvərt, ˈō-ˌvərt\ *adj* **:** not secret — **overt•ly** *adv*

over•take \ˌō-vər-ˈtāk\ *vb* **-took** \-ˈtu̇k\; **-tak•en** \-ˈtā-kən\; **-tak•ing :** to catch up with; *also* **:** to catch up with and pass by

over–the–counter *adj* **:** sold lawfully without a prescription ⟨~ drugs⟩

over–the–hill *adj* **1 :** past one's prime **2 :** advanced in age

over–the–top *adj* extremely flamboyant or outrageous

[1]**over•throw** \ˌō-vər-ˈthrō\ *vb* **-threw** \-ˈthrü\; **-thrown** \-ˈthrōn\; **-throw•ing 1 :** UPSET **2 :** to bring down **:** DEFEAT ⟨~ a government⟩ **3 :** to throw over or past

[2]**over•throw** \ˈō-vər-ˌthrō\ *n* **:** an act of overthrowing or the state of being overthrown

over•time \ˈō-vər-ˌtīm\ *n* **:** time beyond a set limit; *esp* **:** working time in excess of a standard day or week — **overtime** *adv*

over•tone \-ˌtōn\ *n* **1 :** one of the higher tones in a complex musical tone **2 :** IMPLICATION, SUGGESTION

over•trick \ˈō-vər-ˌtrik\ *n* **:** a card trick won in excess of the number bid

over•ture \ˈō-vər-ˌchu̇r, -chər\ *n* **1 :** an opening offer **2 :** an orchestral introduction to a musical dramatic work

over•turn \ˌō-vər-ˈtərn\ *vb* **1 :** to turn over **:** UPSET **2 :** INVALIDATE

over•view \ˈō-vər-ˌvyü\ *n* **:** a general survey **:** SUMMARY

over•ween•ing \ˌō-vər-ˈwē-niŋ\ *adj* **1** ♦ **:** unduly confident **2** ♦ **:** exceeding what is usual, proper, necessary, or normal **:** IMMODERATE

♦ [1] complacent, conceited, egotistic, important, pompous, prideful, proud, self-important, self-satisfied, smug, stuck-up, vain ♦ [2] devilish, excessive, exorbitant, extravagant, extreme, immoderate, inordinate, lavish, overmuch, steep, stiff, towering, unconscionable

over•weight \ˈō-vər-ˌwāt\ *adj* **1 :** having weight above what is required or allowed **2** ♦ **:** having bodily weight greater than normal — **overweight** *n*

♦ chubby, corpulent, fat, fleshy, full, gross, obese, plump, portly, rotund, round

over•whelm \ˌō-vər-ˈhwelm\ *vb* **1 :** OVERTHROW **2** ♦ **:** to cover over completely (as by a great wave) **:** SUBMERGE **3** ♦ **:** to overcome completely (as in thought or feeling)

♦ [2] deluge, drown, engulf, flood, inundate, overflow, submerge, swamp ♦ [3] carry away, crush, devastate, floor, oppress, overcome, overpower, prostrate, snow under, swamp

over•whelm•ing *adj* **:** EXTREME, GREAT ⟨~ joy⟩ — **over•whelm•ing•ly** *adv*

over•win•ter \-ˈwin-tər\ *vb* **:** to survive or pass the winter

over•work \-ˈwərk\ *vb* **1 :** to work or cause to work too hard or long **2 :** to use too much — **overwork** *n*

over•wrought \ˌō-vər-ˈrȯt\ *adj* **1** ♦ **:** extremely excited **2** ♦ **:** elaborated to excess

♦ [1] agitated, feverish, frenzied, heated, hectic, overactive ♦ [2] florid, ornate

ovi•duct \ˈō-və-ˌdəkt\ *n* **:** a tube that serves for the passage of eggs from an ovary

ovip•a•rous \ō-ˈvi-pə-rəs\ *adj* **:** reproducing by eggs that hatch outside the parent's body

ovoid \ˈō-ˌvȯid\ *or* **ovoi•dal** \ō-ˈvȯid-ᵊl\ *adj* **:** egg-shaped **:** OVAL

ovu•la•tion \ˌäv-yə-ˈlā-shən, ˌōv-\ *n* **:** the discharge of a mature egg from the ovary — **ovu•late** \ˈäv-yə-ˌlāt, ˈōv-\ *vb*

ovule \ˈäv-yül, ˈōv-\ *n* **:** any of the bodies in a plant ovary that after fertilization become seeds

ovum \ˈō-vəm\ *n, pl* **ova** \-və\ **:** EGG 2

ow \ˈau̇\ *interj* — used especially to express sudden pain

owe \ˈō\ *vb* **owed; ow•ing 1 :** to be under obligation to pay or render **2 :** to be indebted to or for; *also* **:** to be in debt

owing to *prep* ♦ **:** because of

♦ because of, due to, through, with

owl \ˈau̇(-ə)l\ *n* **:** any of an order of chiefly nocturnal birds of prey with a large head and eyes and strong talons — **owl•ish** *adj* — **owl•ish•ly** *adv*

owl•et \ˈau̇-lət\ *n* **:** a young or small owl

[1]**own** \ˈōn\ *adj* **:** belonging to oneself — used as an intensive after a possessive adjective ⟨her ~ car⟩

[2]**own** *vb* **1** ♦ **:** to have or hold as property **2** ♦ **:** to admit or confess frankly and fully **:** ACKNOWLEDGE; *also* **:** CONFESS — **own•er•ship** *n*

♦ [1] command, enjoy, have, hold, occupy, possess, retain ♦ *usu* **own up** [2] acknowledge, admit, agree, allow, concede, confess, grant

[3]**own** *pron* **:** one or ones belonging to oneself

own•er *n* ♦ **:** one that owns **:** one that has the legal or rightful title whether the possessor or not

♦ holder, possessor, proprietor

ox \ˈäks\ *n, pl* **ox•en** \ˈäk-sən\ *also* **ox :** any of the large domestic bovine mammals kept for milk, draft, and meat; *esp* **:** an adult castrated male ox

ox•blood \ˈäks-ˌbləd\ *n* **:** a moderate reddish brown

ox•bow \-ˌbō\ *n* **1 :** a U-shaped collar worn by a draft ox **2 :** a U-shaped bend in a river — **oxbow** *adj*

ox•ford \ˈäks-fərd\ *n* **:** a low shoe laced or tied over the instep

ox•i•dant \ˈäk-sə-dənt\ *n* **:** OXIDIZING AGENT — **oxidant** *adj*

ox•i•da•tion \ˌäk-sə-ˈdā-shən\ *n* **:** the act or process of oxidizing; *also* **:** the condition of being oxidized — **ox•i•da•tive** \ˈäk-sə-ˌdā-tiv\ *adj*

ox•ide \ˈäk-ˌsīd\ *n* **:** a compound of oxygen with another element or group

ox•i•dize \ˈäk-sə-ˌdīz\ *vb* **-dized; -diz•ing :** to combine with oxygen ⟨iron rusts because it is *oxidized* by exposure to the air⟩ — **ox•i•diz•er** *n*

oxidizing agent *n* **:** a substance (as oxygen or nitric acid) that oxidizes by taking up electrons

ox•y•gen \ˈäk-si-jən\ *n* **:** a colorless odorless gaseous chemical element that is found in the air, is essential to life, and is involved in combustion

ox•y•gen•ate \ˈäk-si-jə-ˌnāt\ *vb* **-at•ed; -at•ing :** to impregnate, combine, or supply with oxygen — **ox•y•gen•a•tion** \ˌäk-si-jə-ˈnā-shən\ *n*

oxygen mask *n* **:** a device worn over the nose and mouth through which oxygen is supplied

oxygen tent *n* **:** a canopy which can be placed over a bedridden person and within which a flow of oxygen can be maintained

ox•y•mo•ron \ˌäk-sē-ˈmōr-ˌän\ *n* **:** a combination of contradictory words (as *cruel kindness*)

oys•ter \ˈȯi-stər\ *n* **:** any of various marine mollusks with an irregular 2-valved shell that include commercially important edible shellfish and pearl producers — **oys•ter•ing** *n* — **oys•ter•man** \ˈȯi-stər-mən\ *n*

oz *abbr* ounce; ounces

ozone \ˈō-ˌzōn\ *n* **1 :** a bluish gaseous reactive form of oxygen that is formed naturally in the atmosphere and is used for disinfecting, deodorizing, and bleaching **2 :** pure and refreshing air

ozone layer *n* **:** an atmospheric layer at heights of about 25 miles (40 kilometers) with high ozone content which blocks most solar ultraviolet radiation

P

1p \ˈpē\ *n, pl* **p's** *or* **ps** \ˈpēz\ *often cap* : the 16th letter of the English alphabet

2p *abbr, often cap* **1** page **2** participle **3** past **4** pawn **5** pence; penny **6** per **7** petite **8** pint **9** pressure **10** purl

P *symbol* phosphorus

pa \ˈpä, ˈpȯ\ *n* : a man who has begotten a child : FATHER

1Pa *abbr* **1** pascal **2** Pennsylvania

2Pa *symbol* protactinium

1PA \(ˌ)pē-ˈā\ *n* : PHYSICIAN'S ASSISTANT

2PA *abbr* **1** Pennsylvania **2** per annum **3** power of attorney **4** press agent **5** private account **6** professional association **7** public address **8** purchasing agent

pab•u•lum \ˈpa-byə-ləm\ *n* : usually soft digestible food

Pac *abbr* Pacific

PAC *abbr* political action committee

1pace \ˈpās\ *n* **1** : rate of movement or progress (as in walking or working) **2** : a step in walking; *also* : a measure of length based on such a step **3** : GAIT; *esp* : a horse's gait in which the legs on the same side move together

2pace *vb* **paced; pac•ing** **1** ♦ : to go or cover at a pace or with slow steps **2** : to measure off by paces **3** : to set or regulate the pace of

♦ file, march, parade, stride

3pace \ˈpā-sē; ˈpä-ˌkā, -ˌchā\ *prep* : contrary to the opinion of

pace•mak•er \ˈpās-ˌmā-kər\ *n* **1** : one that sets the pace for another **2** : a body part (as of the heart) that serves to establish and maintain a rhythmic activity **3** : an electrical device for stimulating or steadying the heartbeat

pac•er \ˈpā-sər\ *n* **1** : a horse that paces **2** : PACEMAKER

pachy•derm \ˈpa-ki-ˌdərm\ *n* : any of various thick-skinned hoofed mammals (as an elephant)

pach•ys•an•dra \ˌpa-ki-ˈsan-drə\ *n* : any of a genus of low perennial evergreen plants used as a ground cover

pa•cif•ic \pə-ˈsi-fik\ *adj* **1** ♦ : tending to lessen conflict **2** : CALM, PEACEFUL

♦ conciliatory, propitiatory *Ant* antagonizing

pac•i•fi•er \ˈpa-sə-ˌfī-ər\ *n* : one that pacifies; *esp* : a device for a baby to chew or suck on

pac•i•fism \ˈpa-sə-ˌfi-zəm\ *n* : opposition to war or violence as a means of settling disputes — **pac•i•fist** \-fist\ *n or adj* — **pac•i•fis•tic** \ˌpa-sə-ˈfis-tik\ *adj*

pac•i•fy \ˈpa-sə-ˌfī\ *vb* **-fied; -fy•ing** **1** ♦ : to allay anger or agitation in **2** : SETTLE; *also* : SUBDUE — **pac•i•fi•ca•tion** \ˌpa-sə-fə-ˈkā-shən\ *n*

♦ appease, conciliate, disarm, mollify, placate, propitiate *Ant* anger, enrage, incense, infuriate, madden, outrage

1pack \ˈpak\ *n* **1** : a compact bundle; *also* : a flexible container for carrying a bundle especially on the back **2** : a large amount : HEAP **3** : a set of playing cards **4** : a group or band of people or animals **5** : wet absorbent material for application to the body

2pack *vb* **1** : to stow goods in for transportation **2** ♦ : to fill in or surround so as to prevent passage of air, steam, or water **3** : to put into a protective container **4** : to load with a pack ⟨~ a mule⟩ **5** : to crowd in **6** : to make into a pack **7** : to cause to go without ceremony ⟨~ them off to school⟩ **8** ♦ : to wear or carry as equipment ⟨~ a gun⟩

♦ [2] charge, cram, fill, heap, jam, jam-pack, load ♦ [8] bear, carry, cart, convey, ferry, haul, lug, tote, transport

3pack *vb* : to make up fraudulently so as to secure a desired result ⟨~ a jury⟩

1pack•age \ˈpa-kij\ *n* **1** ♦ : a wrapped bundle : PARCEL **2** ♦ : a group of related things offered as a whole

♦ [1] bundle, pack, parcel ♦ [2] array, assemblage, bank, batch, block, bunch, clump, cluster, collection, group, huddle, knot, lot, parcel, set, suite

2package *vb* **pack•aged; pack•ag•ing** : to make into or enclose in a package

package deal *n* : an offer containing several items all or none of which must be accepted

package store *n* : a store that sells alcoholic beverages in sealed containers for consumption off the premises

packed \ˈpakt\ *adj* **1 a** : COMPRESSED **b** ♦ : having elements crowded or stuffed **2** ♦ : filled to capacity

♦ [1b] close, compact, crowded, dense, serried, thick, tight ♦ [2] brimful, chock-full, crowded, fat, fraught, full, loaded, replete

pack•er \ˈpa-kər\ *n* : one that packs; *esp* : a wholesale food dealer

pack•et \ˈpa-kət\ *n* **1** : a small bundle or package **2** : a passenger boat carrying mail and cargo on a regular schedule

pack•horse \ˈpak-ˌhȯrs\ *n* : a horse used to carry goods or supplies

pack•ing \ˈpa-kiŋ\ *n* : material used to pack something

pack•ing•house \-ˌhau̇s\ *n* : an establishment for processing and packing food and especially meat and its by-products

pack rat *n* **1** : a bushy-tailed rodent of western No. America that hoards food and miscellaneous objects **2** a person who collects or saves many especially unneeded items

pack•sad•dle \ˈpak-ˌsad-ᵊl\ *n* : a saddle for supporting loads on the back of an animal

pack•thread \-ˌthred\ *n* : strong thread for tying

pact \ˈpakt\ *n* ♦ : an agreement or covenant between two or more parties

♦ accord, agreement, bargain, compact, contract, convention, covenant, deal, settlement, understanding

1pad \ˈpad\ *vb* ♦ : to traverse or go on foot

♦ foot, leg, step, traipse, tread, walk

2pad *n* **1** ♦ : a cushioning part or thing : CUSHION **2** : the cushioned underside of the foot or toes of some mammals **3** : the floating leaf of a water plant **4** : a writing tablet **5** : LAUNCHPAD **6 a** : living quarters **b** : a piece of furniture on or in which to lie and sleep : BED

♦ buffer, bumper, cushion, fender

3pad *vb* **pad•ded; pad•ding** **1** : to furnish with a pad or padding **2** ♦ : to expand with needless or fraudulent matter

♦ color (*or* colour), elaborate, embellish, embroider, exaggerate, magnify, stretch

pad•ding *n* ♦ : the material with which something is padded

♦ fill, filler, filling, stuffing ♦ caricature, elaboration, embellishment, exaggeration, hyperbole, magnification, overstatement

1pad•dle \ˈpad-ᵊl\ *vb* **pad•dled; pad•dling** : to move the hands and feet about in shallow water

2paddle *n* **1** : an implement with a flat blade used in propelling and steering a small craft (as a canoe) **2** : an implement used for stirring, mixing, or beating **3** : a broad board on the outer rim of a waterwheel or a paddle wheel

3paddle *vb* **pad•dled; pad•dling** **1** : to move on or through water by or as if by using a paddle **2** : to beat or stir with a paddle

paddle wheel *n* : a wheel with paddles around its outer edge used to move a boat

paddle wheeler *n* : a steam-driven vessel propelled by a paddle wheel

pad•dock \ˈpa-dək\ *n* **1** : a usually enclosed area for pasturing or exercising animals; *esp* : one where racehorses are saddled and paraded before a race **2** : an area at a racecourse where racing cars are parked

pad•dy \ˈpa-dē\ *n, pl* **paddies** : wet land where rice is grown

paddy wagon *n* : an enclosed motortruck for carrying prisoners

pad•lock \ˈpad-ˌläk\ *n* : a removable lock with a curved piece that snaps into a catch — **padlock** *vb*

pa•dre \ˈpä-drā\ *n* **1** : a Christian clergyman; *esp* : PRIEST **2** : a military chaplain

pad thai \ˈpäd-ˈtī\ *n, often cap T* : a Thai dish of rice noodles stir-fried with additional ingredients

pae•an \ˈpē-ən\ *n* ♦ : an exultant song of praise or thanksgiving

♦ accolade, citation, commendation, encomium, eulogy, homage, panegyric, salutation, tribute

pae·di·at·ric, pae·di·a·tri·cian, pae·di·at·rics *chiefly Brit var of* PEDIATRIC, PEDIATRICIAN, PEDIATRICS
pa·el·la \pä-ˈe-lə; -ˈāl-yə, -ˈā-yə\ *n* **:** a saffron-flavored dish of rice, meat, seafood, and vegetables
pa·gan \ˈpā-gən\ *n* **:** an unconverted member of a people or nation that does not acknowledge the God of the Bible **:** HEATHEN — **pagan** *adj* — **pa·gan·ism** \-gə-ˌni-zəm\ *n*
[1]**page** \ˈpāj\ *n* ♦ **:** one employed to deliver messages, assist patrons, serve as a guide, or attend to similar duties

♦ courier, go-between, messenger, runner

[2]**page** *vb* **paged; pag·ing 1 :** to summon by repeatedly calling out the name of **2 :** to send a message to via a pager
[3]**page** *n* **1 :** a single leaf (as of a book); *also* **:** a single side of such a leaf **2 :** the information at a single World Wide Web address
[4]**page** *vb* **paged; pag·ing :** to mark or number the pages of
pag·eant \ˈpa-jənt\ *n* **:** an elaborate spectacle, show, or procession especially with tableaux or floats — **pag·eant·ry** \-jən-trē\ *n*
page·boy \ˈpāj-ˌbȯi\ *n* **:** an often shoulder-length hairdo with the ends of the hair turned smoothly under
pag·er \ˈpā-jər\ *n* **:** one that pages; *esp* **:** a small radio receiver that alerts its user to incoming messages
pag·i·nate \ˈpa-jə-ˌnāt\ *vb* **-nat·ed; -nat·ing :** [4]PAGE
pag·i·na·tion \ˌpa-jə-ˈnā-shən\ *n* **1 :** the paging of written or printed matter **2 :** the number and arrangement of pages (as of a book)
pa·go·da \pə-ˈgō-də\ *n* **:** a tower with roofs curving upward at the division of each of several stories
paid *past and past part of* PAY
pail \ˈpāl\ *n* **:** a usually cylindrical vessel with a handle — **pail·ful** \-ˌfu̇l\ *n*
[1]**pain** \ˈpān\ *n* **1 :** PUNISHMENT, PENALTY **2 a** ♦ **:** suffering or distress of body or mind **b** ♦ **:** a basic bodily sensation marked by discomfort (as throbbing or aching) **3** *pl* ♦ **:** great care **4 :** one that irks or annoys

♦ [2a] affliction, agony, anguish, distress, misery, torment, torture, tribulation, woe ♦ [2b] ache, pang, prick, smart, sting, stitch, tingle, twinge ♦ **pains** [3] care, carefulness, heed, heedfulness, scrupulousness ♦ **pains** [3] effort, exertion, expenditure, labor (*or* labour), sweat, trouble, while, work

[2]**pain** *vb* ♦ **:** to cause or experience pain

♦ ache, hurt, smart

pain·ful \-fəl\ *adj* ♦ **:** feeling or giving pain

♦ achy, nasty, sore *Ant* painless

pain·ful·ly \-f(ə-)lē\ *adv* **:** in a painful manner
pain·kill·er \ˈpān-ˌki-lər\ *n* **:** something (as a drug) that relieves pain — **pain·kill·ing** *adj*
pain·less \-ləs\ *adj* ♦ **:** not causing pain

♦ easy, effortless, facile, fluent, fluid, light, ready, simple, smooth, snap, soft

pain·less·ly \-ləs-lē\ *adv* ♦ **:** in a painless manner

♦ easily, effortlessly, fluently, freely, handily, lightly, readily, smoothly

pains·tak·ing \ˈpānz-ˌstā-kiŋ\ *adj* ♦ **:** taking pains **:** showing care — **pains·taking** *n* — **pains·tak·ing·ly** *adv*

♦ careful, conscientious, fussy, meticulous *Ant* careless

[1]**paint** \ˈpānt\ *vb* **1** ♦ **:** to apply color, pigment, or paint to **2 :** to produce or portray in lines or colors on a surface; *also* **:** to practice the art of painting **3 :** to decorate with colors **4 :** to use cosmetics **5** ♦ **:** to describe vividly **6 :** SWAB — **paint·er** *n*

♦ [1] color (*or* colour), dye, stain, tinge, tint ♦ [5] delineate, depict, describe, draw, image, picture, portray, sketch

[2]**paint** *n* **1 :** something produced by painting **2 :** MAKEUP **3 :** a mixture of a pigment and a liquid that forms a thin adherent coating when spread on a surface; *also* **:** the dry pigment used in making this mixture **4 :** an applied coating of paint
paint·ball \ˈpānt-ˌbȯl\ *n* **:** a game in which two teams try to capture each other's flag using guns that shoot paint-filled pellets
paint·brush \ˈpānt-ˌbrəsh\ *n* **:** a brush for applying paint
painted lady *n* **:** a migratory butterfly with wings mottled in brown, orange, black, and white
paint·ing \ˈpān-tiŋ\ *n* **1** ♦ **:** a work (as a picture) produced by painting **2 :** the art or occupation of painting

♦ oil

[1]**pair** \ˈpar\ *n, pl* **pairs** *also* **pair 1** ♦ **:** two things of a kind designed for use together **2 :** something made up of two corresponding pieces ⟨a ~ of pants⟩ **3 :** a set of two people or animals

♦ brace, couple, duo, twain, twosome

[2]**pair** *vb* **1 :** to arrange in pairs **2 :** to form a pair **:** MATCH **3 :** to become associated with another
pais·ley \ˈpāz-lē\ *adj, often cap* **:** decorated with colorful curved abstract figures ⟨a ~ shawl⟩
Pai·ute \ˈpī-ˌüt, -ˌyüt\ *n* **:** a member of an American Indian people orig. of Utah, Arizona, Nevada, and California
pa·ja·mas *chiefly Can and Brit* **py·ja·mas** \pə-ˈjä-məz, -ˈja-\ *n pl* **:** a loose suit for sleeping or lounging
Pak·i·stani \ˌpa-ki-ˈsta-nē, ˌpä-ki-ˈstä-nē\ *n* **:** a native or inhabitant of Pakistan — **Pak·i·stani** *adj*
pal \ˈpal\ *n* ♦ **:** a close friend

♦ buddy, chum, comrade, crony, familiar, friend, intimate

pal·ace \ˈpa-ləs\ *n* **1 :** the official residence of a chief of state **2** ♦ **:** a large stately house **:** MANSION

♦ castle, estate, hall, manor, mansion, villa

pal·a·din \ˈpa-lə-dən\ *n* **1 :** a trusted military leader (as for a medieval prince) **2** ♦ **:** a leading champion of a cause

♦ advocate, apostle, backer, booster, champion, exponent, friend, promoter, proponent, supporter

pa·laes·tra \pə-ˈles-trə\ *n, pl* **-trae** \-(ˌ)trē\ **:** a school in ancient Greece or Rome for sports (as wrestling)
pa·lan·quin \ˌpa-lən-ˈkēn\ *n* **:** an enclosed couch for one person borne on the shoulders of men by means of poles
pal·at·abil·i·ty \ˌpa-lə-tə-ˈbi-lə-tē\ *n* ♦ **:** the quality or state of being palatable

♦ deliciousness, lusciousness, savor, tastiness

pal·at·able \ˈpa-lə-tə-bəl\ *adj* **1** ♦ **:** agreeable to the taste **2** ♦ **:** agreeable or acceptable to the mind

♦ [1, 2] agreeable, all right, alright, fine, good, OK, satisfactory ♦ [2] agreeable, congenial, felicitous, good, grateful, gratifying, nice, pleasant, pleasurable, satisfying

pal·a·tal \ˈpa-lət-ᵊl\ *adj* **1 :** of or relating to the palate **2 :** pronounced with some part of the tongue near or touching the hard palate ⟨the y in *yeast* and the sh in *she* are ~ sounds⟩
pal·a·tal·ize \ˈpa-lət-ᵊl-ˌīz\ *vb* **-ized; -iz·ing :** to pronounce as or change into a palatal sound — **pal·a·tal·i·za·tion** \ˌpa-lət-ᵊl-ə-ˈzā-shən\ *n*
pal·ate \ˈpa-lət\ *n* **1 :** the roof of the mouth separating the mouth from the nasal cavity **2 :** TASTE
pa·la·tial \pə-ˈlā-shəl\ *adj* **1 :** of, relating to, or being a palace **2** ♦ **:** suitable to a palace

♦ deluxe, lavish, luxuriant, luxurious, opulent, plush, sumptuous

pa·lat·i·nate \pə-ˈlat-ᵊn-ət\ *n* **:** the territory of a palatine
[1]**pal·a·tine** \ˈpa-lə-ˌtīn\ *adj* **1 :** possessing royal privileges; *also* **:** of or relating to a palatine or a palatinate **2 :** of or relating to a palace **:** PALATIAL
[2]**palatine** *n* **1 :** a feudal lord having sovereign power within his domains **2 :** a high officer of an imperial palace
[1]**pa·la·ver** \pə-ˈla-vər, -ˈlä-\ *n* **1 :** a long parley **2** ♦ **:** idle talk — **palaver** *vb*

♦ chat, chatter, chitchat, gabfest, gossip, rap, talk

[2]**palaver** *vb* **:** to talk profusely or idly
[1]**pale** \ˈpāl\ *n* **1 :** a stake or picket of a fence **2 :** an enclosed place; *also* **:** a district or territory within certain bounds or under a particular jurisdiction **3 :** LIMITS, BOUNDS ⟨conduct beyond the ~⟩
[2]**pale** *vb* **paled; pal·ing :** to enclose with or as if with pales **:** FENCE
[3]**pale** *adj* **pal·er; pal·est 1** ♦ **:** deficient in color or intensity **:** WAN ⟨a ~ face⟩ **2 :** lacking in brightness **:** DIM ⟨a ~ star⟩ **3** ♦ **:** not dark or intense in hue ⟨a ~ blue⟩ — **pale·ness** *n*

♦ [1] ashen, cadaverous, livid, lurid, pasty, peaked *Ant* florid, flush, rubicund, ruddy, sanguine ♦ [3] dull, light, pastel, washed-out *Ant* dark, deep, gay, rich

[4]**pale** *vb* **paled; pal·ing** ♦ **:** to make or become pale

♦ blanch, bleach, blench, dull, fade, wash out, whiten *Ant* darken, deepen

pale ale *n* **:** a medium-colored very dry ale
pale·face \ˈpāl-ˌfās\ *n* **:** a white person
Pa·leo·cene \ˈpā-lē-ə-ˌsēn\ *adj* **:** of, relating to, or being the earliest epoch of the Tertiary — **Paleocene** *n*

pa•leo•con•ser•va•tive \ˌpā-lē-ō-kən-ˈsər-və-tiv\ *n* **:** a conservative espousing traditional principles and policies
pa•le•og•ra•phy \ˌpā-lē-ˈä-grə-fē\ *n* **:** the study of ancient writings and inscriptions — **pa•le•og•ra•pher** *n*
Pa•leo•lith•ic \ˌpā-lē-ə-ˈli-thik\ *adj* **:** of or relating to the earliest period of the Stone Age characterized by rough or chipped stone implements
pa•le•on•tol•o•gy \ˌpā-lē-ˌän-ˈtä-lə-jē\ *n* **:** a science dealing with the life of past geologic periods as known from fossil remains — **pa•le•on•tol•o•gist** \-ˌän-ˈtä-lə-jist, -ən-\ *n*
Pa•leo•zo•ic \ˌpā-lē-ə-ˈzō-ik\ *adj* **:** of, relating to, or being the era of geologic history extending from about 570 million years ago to about 245 million years ago — **Paleozoic** *n*
pal•ette \ˈpa-lət\ *n* **:** a thin often oval board that a painter holds and mixes colors on; *also* **:** the colors on a palette
pal•frey \ˈpȯl-frē\ *n, pl* **palfreys** *archaic* **:** a saddle horse that is not a warhorse; *esp* **:** one suitable for a woman
pa•limp•sest \ˈpa-ləmp-ˌsest\ *n* **:** writing material (as a parchment) used after the erasure of earlier writing
pal•in•drome \ˈpa-lən-ˌdrōm\ *n* **:** a word, verse, or sentence (as "Able was I ere I saw Elba") or a number (as 1881) that reads the same backward or forward
pal•ing \ˈpā-liŋ\ *n* **1 :** a fence of pales **2 :** material for pales **3 :** PALE, PICKET
pal•i•sade \ˌpa-lə-ˈsād\ *n* **1 :** a high fence of stakes especially for defense **2** ♦ **:** a line of steep cliffs

♦ bluff, cliff, crag, escarpment, precipice, scarp

¹pall \ˈpȯl\ *vb* **1 :** to lose in interest or attraction **2 :** SATIATE, CLOY
²pall *n* **1 :** a heavy cloth draped over a coffin **2 :** something that produces a gloomy atmosphere
pal•la•di•um \pə-ˈlā-dē-əm\ *n* **:** a silver-white metallic chemical element used especially as a catalyst and in alloys
pall•bear•er \ˈpȯl-ˌbar-ər\ *n* **:** a person who attends the coffin at a funeral
¹pal•let \ˈpa-lət\ *n* **:** a small, hard, or makeshift bed
²pallet *n* **:** a portable platform for transporting and storing materials
pal•li•ate \ˈpa-lē-ˌāt\ *vb* **-at•ed; -at•ing** **1** ♦ **:** to ease (as a disease) without curing **2** ♦ **:** to cover by excuses and apologies — **pal•li•a•tion** \ˌpa-lē-ˈā-shən\ *n* — **pal•li•a•tive** \ˈpa-lē-ˌā-tiv\ *adj or n*

♦ [1] allay, alleviate, assuage, ease, help, mitigate, mollify, relieve, soothe ♦ [2] excuse, gloss, whitewash

pal•lid \ˈpa-ləd\ *adj* **:** deficient in color **:** PALE, WAN
pal•lor \ˈpa-lər\ *n* **:** PALENESS
¹palm \ˈpäm, ˈpälm\ *n* **1 :** any of a family of mostly tropical trees, shrubs, or vines usually with a tall unbranched stem topped by a crown of large leaves **2 :** a symbol of victory; *also* **:** VICTORY
²palm *n* **:** the underpart of the hand between the fingers and the wrist
³palm *vb* **1 :** to conceal in or with the hand ⟨∼ a card⟩ **2 :** to impose by fraud
pal•mate \ˈpal-ˌmāt, ˈpäl-\ *also* **pal•mat•ed** \-ˌmā-təd\ *adj* **:** resembling a hand with the fingers spread
pal•met•to \pal-ˈme-tō\ *n, pl* **-tos** *or* **-toes** **:** any of several usually small palms with fan-shaped leaves
palm•ist•ry \ˈpä-mə-strē, ˈpäl-\ *n* **:** the practice of reading a person's character or future from the markings on the palms — **palm•ist** \ˈpä-mist, ˈpäl-\ *n*
Palm Sunday *n* **:** the Sunday preceding Easter and commemorating Christ's triumphal entry into Jerusalem
palm•top \ˈpäm-ˌtäp, ˈpälm-\ *n* **:** a portable computer small enough to hold in the hand
palmy \ˈpä-mē, ˈpäl-\ *adj* **palm•i•er; -est** **1 :** abounding in or bearing palms **2** ♦ **:** marked by prosperity **:** PROSPEROUS

♦ booming, golden, prosperous, roaring, successful

pal•o•mi•no \ˌpa-lə-ˈmē-nō\ *n, pl* **-nos** **:** a horse with a pale cream to golden coat and cream or white mane and tail
pal•pa•ble \ˈpal-pə-bəl\ *adj* **1** ♦ **:** capable of being touched or felt **2** ♦ **:** easily perceptible by the mind — **pal•pa•bly** \-blē\ *adv*

♦ [1, 2] appreciable, detectable, discernible, distinguishable, perceptible, sensible ♦ [2] apparent, broad, clear, clear-cut, distinct, evident, lucid, manifest, obvious, patent, perspicuous, plain, transparent, unambiguous, unequivocal, unmistakable

pal•pate \ˈpal-ˌpāt\ *vb* **pal•pat•ed; pal•pat•ing** **:** to examine by touch especially medically — **pal•pa•tion** \pal-ˈpā-shən\ *n*
pal•pi•tate \ˈpal-pə-ˌtāt\ *vb* **-tat•ed; -tat•ing** ♦ **:** to beat rapidly and strongly **:** THROB

♦ beat, pitter-patter, pulsate, pulse, throb

pal•pi•ta•tion \ˌpal-pə-ˈtā-shən\ *n* ♦ **:** a rapid pulsation

♦ beat, pulsation, pulse, throb

pal•sy \ˈpȯl-zē\ *n, pl* **palsies** **1 :** PARALYSIS **2 :** a condition marked by tremor — **pal•sied** \-zēd\ *adj*
pal•ter \ˈpȯl-tər\ *vb* **pal•tered; pal•ter•ing** **1 :** to act insincerely **:** EQUIVOCATE **2** ♦ **:** to negotiate over the terms of a purchase, agreement, or contract **:** HAGGLE

♦ bargain, chaffer, deal, dicker, haggle, negotiate

pal•try \ˈpȯl-trē\ *adj* **pal•tri•er; -est** **1 :** TRASHY ⟨a ∼ pamphlet⟩ **2 :** MEAN, DESPICABLE ⟨a ∼ trick⟩ **3** ♦ **:** of little worth or importance **:** TRIVIAL ⟨∼ excuses⟩ **4 :** MEAGER, MEASLY ⟨a ∼ sum⟩

♦ inconsequential, inconsiderable, insignificant, measly, minute, negligible, nominal, petty, slight, trifling, trivial

pam *abbr* pamphlet
pam•pas \ˈpam-pəz, ˈpäm-, -pəs\ *n pl* **:** wide grassy So. American plains
pam•per \ˈpam-pər\ *vb* ♦ **:** to treat with excessive attention

♦ baby, coddle, mollycoddle, nurse, spoil

pam•phlet \ˈpam-flət\ *n* ♦ **:** an unbound printed publication

♦ booklet, brochure, circular, folder, leaflet

pam•phle•teer \ˌpam-flə-ˈtir\ *n* **:** a writer of pamphlets attacking something or urging a cause
¹pan \ˈpan\ *n* **1 :** a usually broad, shallow, and open container for domestic use; *also* **:** something resembling such a container **2 :** a basin or depression in land **3 :** HARDPAN
²pan *vb* **panned; pan•ning** **1 :** to wash earth or gravel in a pan in searching for gold **2** ♦ **:** to criticize severely

♦ blame, censure, condemn, criticize, denounce, fault, knock, reprehend

Pan *abbr* Panama
pan•a•cea \ˌpa-nə-ˈsē-ə\ *n* **:** a remedy for all ills or difficulties **:** CURE-ALL
pa•nache \pə-ˈnash, -ˈnäsh\ *n* **1 :** an ornamental tuft (as of feathers) especially on a helmet **2 :** dash or flamboyance in style and action
pan•a•ma \ˈpa-nə-ˌmä, -ˌmȯ\ *n, often cap* **:** a handmade hat braided from strips of the leaves from a tropical American tree
Pan•a•ma•ni•an \ˌpa-nə-ˈmā-nē-ən\ *n* **:** a native or inhabitant of Panama — **Panamanian** *adj*
pan•a•tela \ˌpa-nə-ˈte-lə\ *n* **:** a long slender cigar with straight sides
pan•cake \ˈpan-ˌkāk\ *n* ♦ **:** a flat cake made of thin batter and fried on both sides

♦ flapjack, griddle cake

pan•chro•mat•ic \ˌpan-krō-ˈma-tik\ *adj* **:** sensitive to all colors of visible light ⟨∼ film⟩
pan•cre•as \ˈpaŋ-krē-əs, ˈpan-\ *n* **:** a large compound gland of vertebrates that produces insulin and discharges enzymes into the intestine — **pan•cre•at•ic** \ˌpaŋ-krē-ˈa-tik, ˌpan-\ *adj*
pan•da \ˈpan-də\ *n* **1 :** a long-tailed reddish brown Himalayan mammal related to and resembling the racoon **2 :** a large black-and-white mammal of China usually classified with the bears
pan•dem•ic \pan-ˈde-mik\ *n* **:** a widespread outbreak of disease — **pandemic** *adj*
pan•de•mo•ni•um \ˌpan-də-ˈmō-nē-əm\ *n* ♦ **:** a wild uproar **:** TUMULT

♦ commotion, disturbance, furor, hubbub, hullabaloo, row, tumult, turmoil, uproar

¹pan•der \ˈpan-dər\ *n* **1 :** a go-between in love intrigues **2 :** PIMP **3 :** a person who caters to or exploits others' desires or weaknesses
²pander *vb* **:** to act as a pander
P & I *abbr* principal and interest
P & L *abbr* profit and loss
Pan•do•ra's box \pan-ˈdȯr-əz-\ *n* **:** a prolific source of troubles
pan•dow•dy \pan-ˈdau̇-dē\ *n, pl* **-dies** **:** a deep-dish apple dessert spiced, sweetened, and covered with a crust
pane \ˈpān\ *n* **:** a sheet of glass (as in a door or window)
pan•e•gy•ric \ˌpa-nə-ˈjir-ik\ *n* ♦ **:** a eulogistic oration or writing — **pan•e•gyr•ist** \-ˈjir-ist\ *n*

♦ accolade, citation, commendation, encomium, eulogy, homage, paean, salutation, tribute

¹pan•el \ˈpan-ᵊl\ *n* **1 a :** a list of persons appointed for special duty ⟨a jury ∼⟩ **b :** a group of people taking part in a discussion or quiz program **c** ♦ **:** a formal discussion by a panel **2 :** a section of something (as a wall or door) often sunk below the level of the frame; *also* **:** a flat piece of construction material **3 :** a flat piece of wood on which a picture is painted **4 :** a mount for controls or dials

♦ colloquy, conference, council, forum, parley, powwow, seminar, symposium

²panel *vb* **-eled** *or* **-elled; -el•ing** *or* **-el•ling :** to decorate with panels

paneling *n* **:** decorative panels

pan•el•ist \ˈpan-ᵊl-ist\ *n* **:** a member of a discussion or quiz panel

panel truck *n* **:** a small motortruck with a fully enclosed body

pang \ˈpaŋ\ *n* ♦ **:** a sudden sharp spasm (as of pain) or attack (as of remorse)

♦ ache, pain, prick, smart, sting, stitch, tingle, twinge

¹pan•han•dle \ˈpan-ˌhand-ᵊl\ *n* **:** a narrow projection of a larger territory (as a state) ⟨the Texas ~⟩

²panhandle *vb* **-dled; -dling :** to ask for money on the street — **pan•han•dler** *n*

¹pan•ic \ˈpa-nik\ *n* ♦ **:** a sudden overpowering fright — **pan•icky** \-ni-kē\ *adj*

♦ alarm, anxiety, apprehension, dread, fear, fright, horror, terror, trepidation

²panic *vb* **pan•icked** \-nikt\; **pan•ick•ing** ♦ **:** to affect or be affected with panic

♦ alarm, frighten, horrify, scare, shock, spook, startle, terrify, terrorize

pan•i•cle \ˈpa-ni-kəl\ *n* **:** a branched flower cluster (as of a lilac) in which each branch from the main stem has one or more flowers

pan•jan•drum \pan-ˈjan-drəm\ *n, pl* **-drums** *also* **-dra** \-drə\ **:** a powerful personage or pretentious official

pan•nier *also* **pan•ier** \ˈpan-yər\ *n* **:** a large basket especially for bearing on the back

pan•o•ply \ˈpa-nə-plē\ *n, pl* **-plies 1 :** a full suit of armor **2 :** a protective covering **3 :** an impressive array

pan•ora•ma \ˌpa-nə-ˈra-mə, -ˈrä-\ *n* **1 :** a picture unrolled before one's eyes **2** ♦ **:** a complete view in every direction

♦ lookout, outlook, prospect, view, vista

pan•oram•ic \ˌpa-nə-ˈra-mik\ *adj* ♦ **:** of, relating to, or resembling a panorama

♦ compendious, complete, comprehensive, encyclopedic, full, global, inclusive, omnibus, universal

pan out *vb* **1** ♦ **:** to become in maturity **:** TURN OUT **2** ♦ **:** to turn out well **:** SUCCEED

♦ [1] come out, prove, turn out ♦ [2] click, deliver, go over, succeed, work out

pan•sy \ˈpan-zē\ *n, pl* **pansies :** a low-growing garden herb related to the violet; *also* **:** its showy flower

¹pant \ˈpant\ *vb* **1** ♦ **:** to breathe in a labored manner **2 :** to long eagerly **:** YEARN **3 :** THROB

♦ blow, gasp, puff, wheeze

²pant *n* **:** a panting breath or sound

³pant *n* **1** ♦ **:** an outer garment covering each leg separately and usually extending from the waist to the ankle — usually used in plural **2** *pl* **:** PANTIE

♦ **pants** britches, pantaloons, slacks, trousers

pan•ta•loons \ˌpan-tə-ˈlünz\ *n pl* **1 :** close-fitting pants of the 19th century usually having straps passing under the instep **2** ♦ **:** loose-fitting usually shorter than ankle-length trousers

♦ britches, pants, slacks, trousers

pan•the•ism \ˈpan-thē-ˌi-zəm\ *n* **:** a doctrine that equates God with the forces and laws of the universe — **pan•the•ist** \-ist\ *n* — **pan•the•is•tic** \ˌpan-thē-ˈis-tik\ *adj*

pan•the•on \ˈpan-thē-ˌän, -ən\ *n* **1 :** a temple dedicated to all the gods; *also* **:** the gods of a people **2 :** a group of illustrious people

pan•ther \ˈpan-thər\ *n, pl* **panthers** *also* **panther 1 :** LEOPARD; *esp* **:** a black one **2** ♦ **:** a large powerful tawny brown wild American cat **:** COUGAR **3 :** JAGUAR

♦ cougar, mountain lion

pant•ie *or* **panty** \ˈpan-tē\ *n, pl* **pant•ies :** a woman's or child's short underpants — usually used in plural

pan•to•mime \ˈpan-tə-ˌmīm\ *n* **1 :** a play in which the actors use no words **2 :** expression of something by bodily or facial movements only **3** ♦ **:** an actor or dancer in pantomimes — **pantomime** *vb* — **pan•to•mim•ic** \ˌpan-tə-ˈmi-mik\ *adj*

♦ mime, mimic, mummer

pan•try \ˈpan-trē\ *n, pl* **pantries :** a storage room for food or dishes

pant•suit \ˈpant-ˌsüt\ *n* **:** a woman's outfit consisting usually of a long jacket and pants of the same material

panty hose *n pl* **:** a one-piece undergarment for women consisting of hosiery combined with a pantie

panty•waist \ˈpan-tē-ˌwāst\ *n* **:** SISSY

pap \ˈpap\ *n* **:** soft food for infants or invalids

pa•pa \ˈpä-pə\ *n* ♦ **:** a man who has begotten a child **:** FATHER

♦ daddy, father, pop

pa•pa•cy \ˈpā-pə-sē\ *n, pl* **-cies 1 :** the office of pope **2 :** a succession of popes **3 :** the term of a pope's reign **4** *cap* **:** the system of government of the Roman Catholic Church

pa•pa•in \pə-ˈpā-ən, -ˈpī-ən\ *n* **:** an enzyme in papaya juice used especially as a meat tenderizer and in medicine

pa•pal \ˈpā-pəl\ *adj* **:** of or relating to the pope or to the Roman Catholic Church

papaw *var of* PAWPAW

pa•pa•ya \pə-ˈpī-ə\ *n* **:** a tropical American tree with large yellow black-seeded edible fruit; *also* **:** its fruit

¹pa•per \ˈpā-pər\ *n* **1 :** a pliable substance made usually of vegetable matter and used to write or print on, to wrap things in, or to cover walls; *also* **:** a single sheet of this substance **2** ♦ **:** a printed or written document **3 :** NEWSPAPER **4 :** WALLPAPER **5** ♦ **:** a formal written composition often designed for publication and often intended to be read aloud — **paper** *vb* — **pa•pery** \ˈpā-pə-rē\ *adj*

♦ [2] blank, document, form ♦ [5] article, composition, essay, theme

²paper *adj* **1 :** made of paper, cardboard, or papier-mâché **2 :** of or relating to clerical work or written communication **3 :** existing only in theory **:** NOMINAL

pa•per•back \-ˌbak\ *n* **:** a paper-covered book

pa•per•board \-ˌbōrd\ *n* **:** CARDBOARD

pa•per•hang•er \ˈpā-pər-ˌhaŋ-ər\ *n* **:** one that applies wallpaper — **pa•per•hang•ing** *n*

pa•per•weight \-ˌwāt\ *n* **:** an object used to hold down loose papers by its weight

pa•pier–mâ•ché \ˌpā-pər-mə-ˈshā, ˌpa-ˌpyā-mə-, -ma-\ *n* **:** a molding material of wastepaper and additives (as glue) — **papier–mâché** *adj*

pa•pil•la \pə-ˈpi-lə\ *n, pl* **-lae** \-(ˌ)lē, -ˌlī\ **:** a small projecting bodily part (as one of the nubs on the surface of the tongue) that resembles a tiny nipple in form — **pap•il•lary** \ˈpa-pə-ˌler-ē, pə-ˈpi-lə-rē\ *adj*

pa•poose \pa-ˈpüs, pə-\ *n* **:** a young child of No. American Indian parents

pa•pri•ka \pə-ˈprē-kə, pa-\ *n* **:** a mild red spice made from the fruit of various cultivated sweet peppers

Pap smear \ˈpap-\ *n* **:** a method for the early detection of cancer especially of the uterine cervix

Pap test *n* **:** PAP SMEAR

pap•ule \ˈpa-pyül\ *n* **:** a small solid usually conical elevation of the skin — **pap•u•lar** \-pyə-lər\ *adj*

pa•py•rus \pə-ˈpī-rəs\ *n, pl* **-rus•es** *or* **-ri** \-(ˌ)rē, -ˌrī\ **1 :** a tall grassy sedge of the Nile valley **2 :** paper made from papyrus pith

¹par \ˈpär\ *n* **1 :** a stated value (as of a security) **2** ♦ **:** a common level **:** EQUALITY **3** ♦ **:** an accepted standard or normal condition **4 :** the score standard set for each hole of a golf course — **par** *adj*

♦ [2] equality, equivalence, parity, sameness ♦ [3] criterion, grade, mark, measure, standard, touchstone, yardstick ♦ [3] average, norm, normal, standard

²par *abbr* **1** paragraph **2** parallel **3** parish

par•a•ble \ˈpar-ə-bəl\ *n* **:** a simple story told to illustrate a moral truth

pa•rab•o•la \pə-ˈra-bə-lə\ *n* **:** a plane curve formed by a point moving so that its distance from a fixed point is equal to its distance from a fixed line — **par•a•bol•ic** \ˌpar-ə-ˈbä-lik\ *adj*

para•chute \ˈpar-ə-ˌshüt\ *n* **:** a device for slowing the descent of a person or object through the air that consists of a usually hemispherical canopy beneath which the person or object is suspended — **parachute** *vb* — **para•chut•ist** \-ˈshü-tist\ *n*

parachute pants *n pl* **:** baggy casual pants of lightweight fabric

¹pa•rade \pə-ˈrād\ *n* **1 :** a pompous display **:** EXHIBITION **2 :** MARCH, PROCESSION; *esp* **:** a ceremonial formation and march **3 :** a place for strolling

²parade *vb* **pa•rad•ed; pa•rad•ing 1** ♦ **:** to march in a parade **2 :** PROMENADE **3** ♦ **:** to exhibit ostentatiously **:** SHOW OFF **4 :** MASQUERADE

♦ [1] file, march, pace, stride ♦ [3] display, disport, exhibit, expose, flash, flaunt, show, show off, sport, strut, unveil

par•a•digm \ˈpar-ə-ˌdīm, -ˌdim\ *n* **1 :** MODEL, PATTERN **2 :** a systematic inflection of a verb or noun showing a complete conjugation or declension

par•a•dig•mat•ic \ˌpar-ə-dig-ˈma-tik\ *adj* ♦ **:** serving as a pattern; *also* **:** deserving imitation

♦ classic, model, quintessential

par•a•dise \ˈpar-ə-ˌdīs, -ˌdīz\ *n* **1 :** HEAVEN **2** ♦ **:** a place or state of bliss

♦ Eden, Elysium, heaven, utopia *Ant* hell ♦ ecstasy, elation, euphoria, exhilaration, heaven, intoxication, rapture, rhapsody, transport

par•a•di•si•a•cal \ˌpar-ə-də-ˈsī-ə-kəl\ *or* **par•a•dis•i•ac** \-ˈdi-zē-ˌak, -sē-\ *adj* **:** of, relating to, or resembling paradise

par•a•dox \ˈpar-ə-ˌdäks\ *n* **:** a statement that seems contrary to common sense and yet is perhaps true — **par•a•dox•i•cal** \ˌpar-ə-ˈdäk-si-kəl\ *adj* — **par•a•dox•i•cal•ly** \-k(ə-)lē\ *adv*

par•af•fin \ˈpar-ə-fən\ *n* **:** a waxy substance used especially for making candles and sealing foods

para•glid•ing \ˈpa-rə-ˌglī-diŋ\ *n* **:** the sport of soaring from a slope or cliff using a modified parachute

par•a•gon \ˈpar-ə-ˌgän, -gən\ *n* ♦ **:** a model of perfection

♦ beau ideal, classic, exemplar, ideal, model, nonpareil

¹para•graph \ˈpar-ə-ˌgraf\ *n* **:** a subdivision of a written composition that deals with one point or gives the words of one speaker; *also* **:** a character (as ¶) marking the beginning of a paragraph

²paragraph *vb* **:** to divide into paragraphs

Par•a•guay•an \ˌpar-ə-ˈgwī-ən, -ˈgwā-\ *n* **:** a native or inhabitant of Paraguay — **Paraguayan** *adj*

par•a•keet \ˈpar-ə-ˌkēt\ *n* **:** any of numerous usually small slender parrots with a long graduated tail

para•le•gal \ˌpar-ə-ˈlē-gəl\ *adj* **:** of, relating to, or being a paraprofessional who assists a lawyer — **paralegal** *n*

Par•a•li•pom•e•non \ˌpar-ə-lə-ˈpä-mə-ˌnän\ *n* **:** CHRONICLES

par•al•lax \ˈpar-ə-ˌlaks\ *n* **:** the difference in apparent direction of an object as seen from two different points

¹par•al•lel \ˈpar-ə-ˌlel\ *adj* **1 :** lying or moving in the same direction but always the same distance apart **2** ♦ **:** similar in essential parts

♦ akin, alike, analogous, comparable, correspondent, like, similar, such

²parallel *n* **1 :** a parallel line, curve, or surface **2 :** one of the imaginary circles on the earth's surface that parallel the equator and mark the latitude **3** ♦ **:** something essentially similar to another **4** ♦ **:** a comparable aspect **:** SIMILARITY

♦ [3] coordinate, counterpart, equal, equivalent, fellow, like, match, peer, rival ♦ [4] correspondence, resemblance, similarity, similitude

³parallel *vb* **1 :** COMPARE **2** ♦ **:** to correspond to **3 :** to extend in a parallel direction with

♦ correspond, equal, match

par•al•lel•ism \ˈpar-ə-ˌle-ˌli-zəm\ *n* **1 :** the quality or state of being parallel **2** ♦ **:** the quality or state of being similar in essential parts

♦ community, correspondence, likeness, resemblance, similarity, similitude

par•al•lel•o•gram \ˌpar-ə-ˈle-lə-ˌgram\ *n* **:** a 4-sided geometric figure with opposite sides equal and parallel

par•a•lyse *chiefly Brit var of* PARALYZE

pa•ral•y•sis \pə-ˈra-lə-səs\ *n, pl* **-y•ses** \-ˌsēz\ **:** complete or partial loss of function especially when involving the motion or sensation in a part of the body — **par•a•lyt•ic** \ˌpar-ə-ˈli-tik\ *adj or n*

par•a•lyze \ˈpar-ə-ˌlīz\ *vb* **-lyzed; -lyz•ing 1 :** to affect with paralysis **2** ♦ **:** to make powerless or inactive — **par•a•lyz•ing•ly** *adv*

♦ cripple, disable, hamstring, immobilize, incapacitate, prostrate

par•a•me•cium \ˌpar-ə-ˈmē-shəm, -shē-əm, -sē-əm\ *n, pl* **-cia** \-shə, -shē-ə, -sē-ə\ *also* **-ciums :** any of a genus of slipper-shaped protozoans that move by cilia

para•med•ic \ˌpar-ə-ˈme-dik\ *also* **para•med•i•cal** \-di-kəl\ *n* **1 :** a person who assists a physician in a paramedical capacity **2 :** a specially trained medical technician licensed to provide a wide range of emergency services before or during transportation to a hospital

para•med•i•cal \ˌpar-ə-ˈme-di-kəl\ *also* **para•med•ic** \-ˈme-dik\ *adj* **:** concerned with supplementing the work of trained medical professionals

pa•ram•e•ter \pə-ˈra-mə-tər\ *n* **1 :** a quantity whose value characterizes a statistical population or a member of a system (as a family of curves) **2 :** a physical property whose value determines the characteristics or behavior of a system **3 :** a characteristic element **:** FACTOR — **para•met•ric** \ˌpar-ə-ˈme-trik\ *adj*

para•mil•i•tary \ˌpar-ə-ˈmi-lə-ˌter-ē\ *adj* **:** formed on a military pattern especially as an auxiliary military force

par•a•mount \ˈpar-ə-ˌmau̇nt\ *adj* ♦ **:** superior to all others **:** SUPREME

♦ arch, cardinal, central, chief, dominant, first, foremost, grand, key, main, predominant, preeminent, premier, primary, principal, sovereign, supreme ♦ consummate, maximum, most, nth, supreme, top, ultimate, utmost

par•amour \ˈpar-ə-ˌmu̇r\ *n* **:** an illicit lover

para•noia \ˌpar-ə-ˈnȯi-ə\ *n* **:** a psychosis marked by delusions and irrational suspicion usually without hallucinations — **par•a•noid** \ˈpar-ə-ˌnȯid\ *adj or n*

para•nor•mal \ˌpa-rə-ˈnȯr-məl\ *adj* **:** not scientifically explainable **:** SUPERNATURAL

par•a•pet \ˈpar-ə-pət, -ˌpet\ *n* **1 :** a protecting rampart **2 :** a low wall or railing (as at the edge of a bridge)

par•a•pher•na•lia \ˌpar-ə-fə-ˈnāl-yə, -fər-\ *n sing or pl* **1** ♦ **:** personal belongings **2** ♦ **:** articles of equipment **:** APPARATUS

♦ [1] belongings, chattels, effects, holdings, possessions, things ♦ [2] accoutrements (*or* accouterments), apparatus, equipment, gear, matériel, outfit, tackle

¹para•phrase \ˈpar-ə-ˌfrāz\ *n* ♦ **:** a restatement of a text giving the meaning in different words

♦ translation *Ant* quotation, quote

²paraphrase *vb* ♦ **:** to make a paraphrase

♦ rephrase, restate, translate *Ant* quote

para•ple•gia \ˌpar-ə-ˈplē-jə, -jē-ə\ *n* **:** paralysis of the lower trunk and legs — **para•ple•gic** \-jik\ *adj or n*

para•pro•fes•sion•al \-prə-ˈfe-shə-nəl\ *n* **:** a trained aide who assists a professional — **paraprofessional** *adj*

para•psy•chol•o•gy \ˌpar-ə-sī-ˈkä-lə-jē\ *n* **:** a field of study concerned with investigating paranormal psychological phenomena (as extrasensory perception) — **para•psy•chol•o•gist** \-jist\ *n*

par•a•site \ˈpar-ə-ˌsīt\ *n* **1 :** a plant or animal living in, with, or on another organism usually to its harm **2** ♦ **:** one depending on another and not making adequate return — **par•a•sit•ic** \ˌpar-ə-ˈsi-tik\ *adj* — **par•a•sit•ism** \ˈpar-ə-sə-ˌti-zəm, -ˌsī-ˌti-\ *n* — **par•a•sit•ize** \-sə-ˌtīz\ *vb*

♦ hanger-on, leech, sponge

par•a•si•tol•o•gy \ˌpar-ə-sə-ˈtä-lə-jē\ *n* **:** a branch of biology dealing with parasites and parasitism especially among animals — **par•a•si•tol•o•gist** \-jist\ *n*

para•sol \ˈpar-ə-ˌsȯl\ *n* **:** a lightweight umbrella used as a shield against the sun

para•sym•pa•thet•ic nervous system \ˌpar-ə-ˌsim-pə-ˈthe-tik-\ *n* **:** the part of the autonomic nervous system that tends to induce secretion, to increase the tone and contractility of smooth muscle, and to slow heart rate

para•thi•on \ˌpar-ə-ˈthī-ən, -ˌän\ *n* **:** an extremely toxic insecticide

para•thy•roid \-ˈthī-ˌrȯid\ *n* **:** PARATHYROID GLAND — **parathyroid** *adj*

parathyroid gland *n* **:** any of usually four small endocrine glands adjacent to or embedded in the thyroid gland that produce a hormone (**parathyroid hormone**) concerned with calcium and phosphorus metabolism

para•tran•sit \ˌpa-rə-ˈtran-sət, -zət\ *n* **:** transportation service that provides individualized rules without fixed routes or timetables

para•troop•er \ˈpar-ə-ˌtrü-pər\ *n* **:** a member of the paratroops

para•troops \-ˌtrüps\ *n pl* **:** troops trained to parachute from an airplane

para•ty•phoid \ˌpar-ə-ˈtī-ˌfȯid\ *n* **:** a bacterial food poisoning resembling typhoid fever

par•boil \'pär-ˌbȯil\ *vb* **:** to boil briefly

¹par•cel \'pär-səl\ *n* **1** ♦ **:** a tract or plot of land **2** ♦ **:** a company, collection, or group of persons, animals, or things **:** LOT **3 :** a wrapped bundle **:** PACKAGE

♦ [1] field, ground, lot, plat, plot, tract ♦ [2] array, assemblage, bank, batch, block, bunch, clump, cluster, collection, group, huddle, knot, lot, package, set, suite

²parcel *vb* **-celed** *or* **-celled; -cel•ing** *or* **-cel•ling** ♦ **:** to divide into portions — often used with *out*

♦ *usu* **parcel out** administer, allocate, apportion, deal, dispense, distribute, mete, portion, prorate

parcel post *n* **1 :** a mail service handling parcels **2 :** packages handled by parcel post

♦ mail, matter, post, snail mail

parch \'pärch\ *vb* **1 :** to toast under dry heat **2** ♦ **:** to shrivel with heat

♦ dehydrate, dry, sear

parch•ment \'pärch-mənt\ *n* **:** the skin of an animal prepared for writing on; *also* **:** a writing on such material

pard \'pärd\ *n* **:** LEOPARD

¹par•don \'pärd-ᵊn\ *n* ♦ **:** excuse of an offense without penalty; *esp* **:** an official release from legal punishment

♦ absolution, amnesty, forgiveness, remission ***Ant*** penalty, punishment, retribution

²pardon *vb* ♦ **:** to free from penalty **:** EXCUSE, FORGIVE

♦ condone, disregard, excuse, forgive, gloss over, ignore, pass over, shrug off, wink at

par•don•able \'pärd-ᵊn-ə-bəl\ *adj* ♦ **:** worthy of or subject to being pardoned **:** EXCUSABLE

♦ excusable, forgivable, venial

par•don•er \'pärd-ᵊn-ər\ *n* **1 :** a medieval preacher delegated to raise money for religious works by soliciting offerings and granting indulgences **2 :** one that pardons

pare \'par\ *vb* **pared; par•ing 1 :** to trim off an outside, excess, or irregular part of **2 :** to reduce as if by paring ⟨~ expenses⟩ — **par•er** *n*

par•e•go•ric \ˌpar-ə-'gȯr-ik\ *n* **:** an alcoholic preparation of opium and camphor used especially to relieve pain

par•ent \'par-ənt\ *n* **1 :** one that begets or brings forth offspring **:** FATHER, MOTHER **2 :** one who brings up and cares for another **3 :** SOURCE, ORIGIN — **pa•ren•tal** \pə-'rent-ᵊl\ *adj* — **par•ent•hood** *n*

par•ent•age \-ən-tij\ *n* ♦ **:** descent from parents or ancestors

♦ ancestry, birth, blood, bloodline, breeding, descent, extraction, family tree, genealogy, line, lineage, origin, pedigree, stock, strain

pa•ren•the•sis \pə-'ren-thə-səs\ *n, pl* **-the•ses** \-ˌsēz\ **1 :** a word, phrase, or sentence inserted in a passage to explain or modify the thought **2 :** one of a pair of punctuation marks ( ) used especially to enclose parenthetic matter — **par•en•thet•ic** \ˌpar-ən-'the-tik\ *or* **par•en•thet•i•cal** \-ti-kəl\ *adj* — **par•en•thet•i•cal•ly** \-k(ə-)lē\ *adv*

pa•ren•the•size \pə-'ren-thə-ˌsīz\ *vb* **-sized; -siz•ing :** to make a parenthesis of

par•ent•ing \'par-ən-tiŋ, 'per-\ *n* **:** the raising of a child by its parents

pa•re•sis \pə-'rē-səs, 'par-ə-\ *n, pl* **pa•re•ses** \-ˌsēz\ **:** a usually incomplete paralysis; *also* **:** insanity caused by syphilitic alteration of the brain that leads to dementia and paralysis

par ex•cel•lence \ˌpär-ˌek-sə-'läⁿs\ *adj* **:** being the best of a kind **:** PREEMINENT

par•fait \pär-'fā\ *n* **:** a cold dessert made of layers of fruit, syrup, ice cream, and whipped cream

pa•ri•ah \pə-'rī-ə\ *n* **:** one that is despised or rejected **:** OUTCAST

pa•ri•etal \pə-'rī-ət-ᵊl\ *adj* **1 :** of, relating to, or forming the walls of an anatomical structure **2 :** of or relating to college living or its regulation

pari–mu•tu•el \ˌpar-i-'myü-chə-wəl\ *n* **:** a betting system in which winners share the total stakes minus a percentage for the management

par•ing \'par-iŋ\ *n* **:** a pared-off piece

pa•ri pas•su \ˌpar-i-'pa-sü\ *adv or adj* **:** at an equal rate or pace

par•ish \'par-ish\ *n* **1 :** a church district in the care of one pastor; *also* **:** the residents of such an area **2 :** a local church community **3 :** a civil division of the state of Louisiana **:** COUNTY

pa•rish•io•ner \pə-'ri-shə-nər\ *n* **:** a member or resident of a parish

par•i•ty \'par-ə-tē\ *n, pl* **-ties** ♦ **:** the quality or state of being equal or equivalent

♦ equality, equivalence, par, sameness

¹park \'pärk\ *n* **1 :** a tract of ground kept as a game preserve or recreation area **2 :** a place where vehicles (as automobiles) are parked **3 :** an enclosed stadium used especially for ball games **4** ♦ **:** a tract of land attached to a country house

♦ demesne, grounds, premises, yard

²park *vb* **1 :** to leave a vehicle temporarily (as in a parking lot or garage) **2 :** to set and leave temporarily

par•ka \'pär-kə\ *n* **:** a very warm jacket with a hood

Par•kin•son's disease \'pär-kən-sənz-\ *n* **:** a chronic progressive neurological disease chiefly of later life marked especially by tremor and weakness of resting muscles and by a shuffling gait

Parkinson's Law *n* **:** an observation in office organization: work expands so as to fill the time available for its completion

park•way \'pärk-ˌwā\ *n* **:** a broad landscaped thoroughfare

par•lance \'pär-ləns\ *n* **1 :** SPEECH **2 :** manner of speaking ⟨military ~⟩

¹par•lay \'pär-ˌlā, -lē\ *vb* **:** to increase or change into something of much greater value

²parlay *n* **:** a series of bets in which the original stake plus its winnings are risked on successive wagers

¹par•ley \'pär-lē\ *vb* **:** to speak with another **:** CONFER

²parley *n, pl* **parleys** ♦ **:** a conference usually over matters in dispute

♦ argument, colloquy, conference, deliberation, discourse, discussion, give-and-take, talk

par•lia•ment \'pär-lə-mənt\ *n* **1 :** a formal governmental conference **2** *cap* **:** an assembly that constitutes the supreme legislative body of a country (as the United Kingdom) — **par•lia•men•ta•ry** \ˌpär-lə-'men-tə-rē\ *adj*

par•lia•men•tar•i•an \ˌpär-lə-ˌmen-'ter-ē-ən\ *n* **1** *often cap* **:** an adherent of the parliament during the English Civil War **2 :** an expert in parliamentary procedure

par•lor *or Can and Brit* **par•lour** \'pär-lər\ *n* **1 :** a room for conversation or the reception of guests **2 :** a place of business ⟨beauty ~⟩

par•lous \'pär-ləs\ *adj* ♦ **:** full of danger or risk — **par•lous•ly** *adv*

♦ dangerous, grave, grievous, hazardous, menacing, perilous, risky, serious, unhealthy, unsafe, venturesome

Par•me•san \'pär-mə-ˌzän, -ˌzhän, -ˌzan\ *n* **:** a hard dry cheese with a sharp flavor

par•mi•gia•na \ˌpär-mi-'jä-nə, ˌpär-mi-'zhän\ *or* **par•mi•gia•no** \-'jä-(ˌ)nō\ *adj* **:** made or covered with Parmesan cheese ⟨veal ~⟩

pa•ro•chi•al \pə-'rō-kē-əl\ *adj* **1 :** of or relating to a church parish **2** ♦ **:** limited in scope **:** NARROW, PROVINCIAL — **pa•ro•chi•al•ism** \-ə-ˌli-zəm\ *n*

♦ insular, little, narrow, petty, provincial, sectarian, small

parochial school *n* **:** a school maintained by a religious body

¹par•o•dy \'par-ə-dē\ *n, pl* **-dies 1** ♦ **:** a humorous or satirical imitation **2** ♦ **:** a feeble or ridiculous imitation — **parody** *vb*

♦ [1] burlesque, caricature, spoof, takeoff ♦ [2] caricature, farce, joke, mockery, sham, travesty

²parody *vb* **1 :** to compose a parody on **2** ♦ **:** to imitate in the manner of a parody

♦ burlesque, caricature, imitate, mimic, mock, take off, travesty

pa•role \pə-'rōl\ *n* **:** a conditional release of a prisoner whose sentence has not expired — **parole** *vb* — **pa•rol•ee** \-ˌrō-'lē, -'rō-ˌlē\ *n*

par•ox•ysm \'par-ək-ˌsi-zəm, pə-'räk-\ *n* **1 :** a sudden sharp attack (as of pain or coughing) **:** CONVULSION **2** ♦ **:** a sudden violent emotion or action — **par•ox•ys•mal** \ˌpar-ək-'siz-məl, pə-ˌräk-\ *adj*

♦ agony, burst, eruption, explosion, fit, flare, flare-up, flash, flush, gale, gush, gust, outburst, spasm, storm

par•quet \'pär-ˌkā, pär-'kā\ *n* **1 :** a flooring of parquetry **2 :** the lower floor of a theater; *esp* **:** the forward part of the orchestra

par•que•try \'pär-kə-trē\ *n, pl* **-tries :** fine woodwork inlaid in patterns

par•ri•cide \'par-ə-ˌsīd\ *n* **1 :** one that murders a parent or a close relative **2 :** the act of a parricide

par•rot \ˈpar-ət\ *n* : any of numerous bright-colored tropical birds that have a stout hooked bill
parrot fever *n* : PSITTACOSIS
par•ry \ˈpar-ē\ *vb* **par•ried; par•ry•ing** **1** : to ward off a weapon or blow **2** : to evade especially by an adroit answer — **parry** *n*
parse \ˈpärs *also* ˈpärz\ *vb* **parsed; pars•ing** : to give a grammatical description of a word or a group of words
par•sec \ˈpär-ˌsek\ *n* : a unit of measure for interstellar space equal to 3.26 light-years
par•si•mo•ni•ous \ˌpär-sə-ˈmō-nē-əs\ *adj* ♦ : exhibiting or marked by parsimony — **par•si•mo•ni•ous•ly** *adv*

♦ cheap, close, mean, niggardly, penurious, spare, sparing, stingy, tight, tightfisted, uncharitable

par•si•mo•ny \ˈpär-sə-ˌmō-nē\ *n* ♦ : extreme or excessive frugality

♦ cheapness, closeness, miserliness, stinginess, tightness ***Ant*** generosity, liberality, philanthropy

pars•ley \ˈpär-slē\ *n* : a garden plant related to the carrot that has finely divided leaves used as a seasoning or garnish; *also* : the leaves
pars•nip \ˈpär-snəp\ *n* : a garden plant related to the carrot that has a long edible usually whitish root which is cooked as a vegetable; *also* : the root
par•son \ˈpärs-ᵊn\ *n* : a member of the clergy : MINISTER
par•son•age \ˈpärs-ᵊn-ij\ *n* : a house provided by a church for its pastor
¹part \ˈpärt\ *n* **1** ♦ : a division or portion of a whole **2** : the melody or score for a particular voice or instrument **3** : a spare piece for a machine **4** : DUTY, FUNCTION **5** : one of the sides in a dispute **6** : ROLE; *also* : an actor's lines in a play **7** *pl* : TALENTS, ABILITY **8** : the line where one's hair divides (as in combing) **9** ♦ : something falling to one in a division or apportionment **10** ♦ : a function or course of action performed

♦ [1] member, partition, portion, section, segment ♦ [9] allotment, allowance, cut, portion, proportion, quota, share ♦ [10] capacity, function, job, place, position, purpose, role, task, work

²part *vb* **1** : to take leave of someone **2** ♦ : to divide or break into parts : SEPARATE **3** : to go away : DEPART; *also* : DIE **4** : to give up possession ⟨~*ed* with her jewels⟩ **5** : APPORTION, SHARE

♦ break up, disconnect, disjoint, dissever, dissociate, disunite, divide, divorce, resolve, separate, sever, split, sunder, unyoke

³part *abbr* **1** participial; participle **2** particular
par•take \pär-ˈtāk\ *vb* **-took** \-ˈtu̇k\; **-tak•en** \-ˈtā-kən\; **-tak•ing** **1** : to have a share or part **2** : to take a portion (as of food)
par•tak•er \-ˈtā-kər\ *n* ♦ : one that partakes

♦ participant, party, sharer

par•terre \pär-ˈter\ *n* **1** : an ornamental garden with paths between the flower beds **2** : the part of a theater floor behind the orchestra
par•the•no•gen•e•sis \ˌpär-thə-nō-ˈje-nə-səs\ *n* : development of a new individual from an unfertilized usually female sex cell — **par•the•no•ge•net•ic** \-jə-ˈne-tik\ *adj*
par•tial \ˈpär-shəl\ *adj* **1** ♦ : of or relating to a part rather than the whole **2** ♦ : favoring one party over the other : BIASED **3** ♦ : markedly fond — used with *to*

♦ [1] deficient, fragmentary, halfway, incomplete ♦ [2] biased, one-sided, partisan, prejudiced ***Ant*** evenhanded, impartial, neutral, nonpartisan, unbiased, unprejudiced ♦ [3] fond, inclined

par•tial•i•ty \ˌpär-shē-ˈa-lə-tē\ *n* **1** ♦ : the quality or state of being partial **2** ♦ : a special taste or liking

♦ [1] bias, favor (*or* favour), partisanship, prejudice ♦ [2] bent, devices, disposition, genius, inclination, leaning, penchant, predilection, proclivity, propensity, tendency, turn ♦ [2] appetite, fancy, favor (*or* favour), fondness, like, liking, love, preference, relish, shine, taste, use

par•tial•ly \ˈpär-sh(ə-)lē\ *adv* ♦ : to some extent : in some degree

♦ part, partly

par•tic•i•pant \pär-ˈti-sə-pənt\ *n* ♦ : one that participates — **participant** *adj*

♦ partaker, party, sharer ***Ant*** nonparticipant

par•tic•i•pate \pär-ˈti-sə-ˌpāt\ *vb* **-pat•ed; -pat•ing** **1** : to take part in something ⟨~ in a game⟩ **2** : SHARE — **par•tic•i•pa•tion** \-ˌti-sə-ˈpā-shən\ *n* — **par•tic•i•pa•to•ry** \-ˈti-sə-pə-ˌtōr-ē\ *adj*
par•tic•i•pa•tor \pär-ˈti-sə-ˈti-sə-ˌpā-tər\ *n* : one that participates
par•ti•ci•ple \ˈpär-tə-ˌsi-pəl\ *n* : a word having the characteristics of both verb and adjective — **par•ti•cip•i•al** \ˌpär-tə-ˈsi-pē-əl\ *adj*
par•ti•cle \ˈpär-ti-kəl\ *n* **1** ♦ : a very small quantity or fragment **2** : a unit of speech (as an article, preposition, or conjunction) expressing some general aspect of meaning or some connective or limiting relation

♦ atom, fleck, grain, granule, molecule, morsel, scrap ♦ bit, crumb, dab, glimmer, hint, lick, little, mite, nip, ounce, shred, speck, spot, suspicion, touch, trace

par•ti•cle•board \-ˌbōrd\ *n* : a board made of very small pieces of wood bonded together
par•ti–col•or \ˌpär-tē-ˈkə-lər\ *or* **par•ti–col•ored** \-lərd\ *adj* : showing different colors or tints; *esp* : having one main color broken by patches of one or more other colors
¹par•tic•u•lar \pər-ˈti-kyə-lər\ *adj* **1** ♦ : of or relating to a specific person or thing ⟨the laws of a ~ state⟩ **2** : DISTINCTIVE, SPECIAL ⟨the ~ point of his talk⟩ **3** : SEPARATE, INDIVIDUAL ⟨each ~ hair⟩ **4** : attentive to details **5** ♦ : hard to please

♦ [1] individual, peculiar, personal, private, separate, singular, unique ♦ [5] choosy, dainty, delicate, demanding, exacting, fastidious, finicky, fussy, nice, old-maidish, picky

²particular *n* ♦ : an individual fact or detail

♦ detail, fact, item, point

par•tic•u•lar•ise *chiefly Brit var of* PARTICULARIZE
par•tic•u•lar•i•ty \pər-ˌti-kyə-ˈlar-ə-tē\ *n* : a minute detail
par•tic•u•lar•ize \pər-ˈti-kyə-lə-ˌrīz\ *vb* **-ized; -iz•ing** **1** : to state in detail : SPECIFY **2** : to go into details
par•tic•u•lar•ly \-lē\ *adv* **1** : to an unusual degree **2** : in particular : SPECIFICALLY
par•tic•u•late \pər-ˈti-kyə-lət, pär-, -ˌlāt\ *adj* : relating to or existing as minute separate particles — **particulate** *n*
¹part•ing *n* **1** : a place or point of separation or divergence **2** ♦ : a mutual separation of two or more persons

♦ farewell, leave-taking, separation

²parting *adj* : given, taken, or done at parting ⟨a ~ kiss⟩
¹par•ti•san *also* **par•ti•zan** \ˈpär-tə-zən, -sən\ *n* **1** ♦ : one that takes the part of another : ADHERENT **2** : GUERRILLA **3** ♦ : a strong or devoted supporter

♦ [1] adherent, convert, disciple, follower, pupil, votary ♦ [3] crusader, fanatic, militant, zealot

²partisan *adj* ♦ : exhibiting, characterized by, or resulting from partisanship

♦ biased, one-sided, partial, prejudiced

par•ti•san•ship \-ship\ *n* ♦ : the quality or state of being a partisan

♦ bias, favor (*or* favour), partiality, prejudice

par•tite \ˈpär-ˌtīt\ *adj* : divided into a usually specified number of parts
par•ti•tion \pär-ˈti-shən\ *n* **1** ♦ : the action of parting : the state of being parted **2** : something that divides or separates; *esp* : an interior dividing wall **3** ♦ : one of the parts or sections of a whole — **partition** *vb*

♦ [1] breakup, dissolution, division, schism, separation, split ♦ [3] member, part, portion, section, segment

par•ti•tive \ˈpär-tə-tiv\ *adj* : of, relating to, or denoting a part
part•ly \ˈpärt-lē\ *adv* ♦ : in part : in some measure or degree

♦ part, partially ***Ant*** completely, entirely, totally, wholly

part•ner \ˈpärt-nər\ *n* **1** : ASSOCIATE, COLLEAGUE **2** : either of two persons who dance together **3** : one who plays on the same team with another **4** ♦ : married person : SPOUSE **5** : one of two or more persons contractually associated as joint principals in a business

♦ consort, mate, spouse

part•ner•ship \-ship\ *n* ♦ : a relationship usually involving close cooperation between parties having specified and joint rights and responsibilities

♦ affiliation, alliance, association, collaboration, confederation, connection, cooperation, hookup, liaison, relation, relationship, union

part of speech : a class of words (as nouns or verbs) distinguished according to the kind of idea denoted and the function performed in a sentence

par•tridge \ˈpär-trij\ *n, pl* **partridge** *or* **par•tridg•es** : any of various stout-bodied Old World game birds
part–song \ˈpärt-ˌsȯŋ\ *n* : a song with two or more voice parts
part–time \-ˈtīm\ *adj or adv* : involving or working less than a full or regular schedule — **part–tim•er** \-ˌtī-mər\ *n*
par•tu•ri•tion \ˌpär-tə-ˈri-shən, ˌpär-chə-, ˌpär-tyu̇-\ *n* : the action or process of giving birth to offspring : CHILDBIRTH
part•way \ˈpärt-ˈwā\ *adv* : to some extent : PARTLY
par•ty \ˈpär-tē\ *n, pl* **parties** **1** : a person or group taking one side of a question; *esp* : a group of persons organized for the purpose of directing the policies of a government **2** ♦ : a person or group concerned in an action or affair : PARTICIPANT **3** ♦ : a group of persons detailed for a common task **4** ♦ : a social gathering **5** : a particular individual

♦ [2] partaker, participant, sharer ♦ [3] band, company, crew, gang, group, outfit, squad, team ♦ [4] affair, blowout, event, fete, function, get-together

party animal *n* : a person known for frequent attendance at parties
par•ty•go•er \ˈpär-tē-ˌgō-ər\ *n* : a person who attends a party or who attends parties frequently
par•ve•nu \ˈpär-və-ˌnü, -ˌnyü\ *n* : one who has recently or suddenly risen to wealth or power but has not yet secured the social position associated with it
pas \ˈpä\ *n, pl* **pas** *same or* ˈpäz\ : a dance step or combination of steps
pas•cal \pas-ˈkal\ *n* : a unit of pressure in the metric system equal to one newton per square meter
pas•chal \ˈpas-kəl\ *adj* : of, relating to, appropriate for, or used during Passover or Easter ceremonies
pa•sha \ˈpä-shə, ˈpa-; pə-ˈshä\ *n* : a man (as formerly a governor in Turkey) of high rank
pash•mi•na \ˌpəsh-ˈmē-nə\ *n* : a fine wool from the undercoat of domestic Himalayan goats; *also* : a shawl made from this wool
¹**pass** \ˈpas\ *vb* **1** : MOVE, PROCEED **2 a** : to go away **b** ♦ : to stop existing or functioning : DIE — often used with *on* **3** : to move past, beyond, or over **4** : to allow to elapse : SPEND **5** ♦ : to go or make way through **6** : to go or allow to go unchallenged **7 a** : to undergo transfer **b** ♦ : to transfer or transmit from one to another **8** : to render a legal judgment **9** ♦ : to come into existence : OCCUR **10** ♦ : to become approved by a legislature or body empowered to sanction or reject **11** : to go or cause to go through an inspection, test, or course of study successfully **12** : to be regarded **13** : CIRCULATE **14** : VOID 2 **15** : to transfer the ball or puck to another player **16** : to decline to bid or bet on one's hand in a card game **17** : to give a base on balls to — **pass•er** *n*

♦ *usu* **pass on** [2b] decease, depart, die, expire, pass away, perish, succumb ♦ *usu* **pass over** [5] cover, crisscross, cross, cut, follow, go, proceed, travel, traverse ♦ [7b] hand, hand over, reach, transfer ♦ [9] be, befall, betide, chance, come, go, happen, occur, transpire ♦ [10] enact, lay down, legislate, make

²**pass** *n* ♦ : a gap in a mountain range

♦ canyon, defile, flume, gap, gorge, gulch, gulf, notch, ravine

³**pass** *n* **1** : the act or an instance of passing **2** ♦ : the state of being realized or accomplished : REALIZATION, ACCOMPLISHMENT **3** : a state of affairs **4** ♦ : a written authorization to leave, enter, or move about freely **5** : a transfer of a ball or puck from one player to another **6** : BASE ON BALLS **7** ♦ : a serious attempt : TRY **8** : a sexually inviting gesture or approach

♦ [2] accomplishment, achievement, actuality, attainment, consummation, fruition, fulfillment, realization ♦ [4] check, ticket ♦ [7] attempt, bid, crack, endeavor (*or* endeavour), essay, fling, go, shot, stab, trial, try, whack

⁴**pass** *abbr* **1** passenger **2** passive
pass•able \ˈpa-sə-bəl\ *adj* **1** ♦ : capable of being passed or traveled on **2** ♦ : just good enough

♦ [1, 2] acceptable, adequate, all right, decent, fine, OK, respectable, satisfactory, tolerable ♦ [2] common, fair, indifferent, mediocre, medium, middling, ordinary, run-of-the-mill, second-rate, so-so

pass•ably \-blē\ *adv* ♦ : in a passable manner or to a passable extent

♦ adequately, all right, fine, good, nicely, OK, satisfactorily, so-so, tolerably, well

pas•sage \ˈpa-sij\ *n* **1** ♦ : a means (as a road or corridor) of passing **2** ♦ : the action or process of passing **3** ♦ : a voyage especially by sea or air **4** : a right or permission to pass **5** : ENACTMENT **6** : a usually brief portion or section (as of a book) **7** : a continuous movement or flow

♦ [1] approach, avenue, path, route, way ♦ [2] expedition, journey, peregrination, trek, trip ♦ [3] crossing, cruise, sail, voyage

pas•sage•way \-ˌwā\ *n* : a way that allows passage
pass away *vb* **1** : to go out of existence **2** ♦ : to pass from physical life

♦ decease, depart, die, expire, pass, perish, succumb

pass•book \ˈpas-ˌbu̇k\ *n* : BANKBOOK
pas•sé \pa-ˈsā\ *adj* **1** : past one's prime **2** ♦ : not up-to-date : OUTMODED

♦ antiquated, archaic, dated, obsolete, outdated, outmoded, outworn

pas•sel \ˈpa-səl\ *n* : a large number
pas•sen•ger \ˈpas-ᵊn-jər\ *n* : a traveler in a public or private conveyance
pass•er•by \ˈpa-sər-ˌbī\ *n, pl* **pass•ers•by** : one who passes by
pas•ser•ine \ˈpa-sə-ˌrīn\ *adj* : of or relating to the large order of birds comprising singing birds that perch
pas•sim \ˈpa-səm\ *adv* : here and there : THROUGHOUT
pass•ing *n* ♦ : the act of one that passes or causes to pass; *esp* : DEATH

♦ death, decease, demise, doom, end, quietus

pas•sion \ˈpa-shən\ *n* **1** *often cap* : the sufferings of Christ between the night of the Last Supper and his death **2** ♦ : strong feeling; *also, pl* : the emotions as distinguished from reason **3** : RAGE, ANGER **4** ♦ : ardent affection : LOVE; *also* : an object of affection or enthusiasm **5** : sexual desire **6** ♦ : a strong liking or desire for or devotion to some activity, object, or concept — **pas•sion•less** *adj*

♦ [2] ardor, emotion, fervency, fervor, heat, intensity, vehemence, warmth ♦ [4] affection, attachment, devotion, fondness, love ♦ [6] appetite, craving, desire, drive, hankering, hunger, itch, longing, lust, thirst, urge, yearning, yen

pas•sion•ate \ˈpa-shə-nət\ *adj* **1 a** ♦ : capable of, affected by, or expressing intense feeling **b** : ENTHUSIASTIC **2** ♦ : swayed by or affected with sexual desire — **pas•sion•ate•ly** *adv*

♦ [1a] ardent, burning, charged, emotional, fervent, fiery, hot-blooded, impassioned, red-hot, vehement ♦ [2] lascivious, lewd, lustful, wanton

pas•sion•flow•er \ˈpa-shən-ˌflau̇-ər\ *n* : any of a genus of chiefly tropical woody climbing vines or erect herbs with showy flowers and pulpy often edible berries (**passion fruit**)
pas•sive \ˈpa-siv\ *adj* **1** : not active : acted upon **2** : asserting that the grammatical subject is subjected to or affected by the action represented by the verb ⟨~ voice⟩ **3** : making use of the sun's heat usually without the aid of mechanical devices **4** ♦ : receiving or enduring without resistance — **passive** *n* — **pas•sive•ly** *adv* — **pas•siv•i•ty** \pa-ˈsi-və-tē\ *n*

♦ acquiescent, resigned, tolerant, unresistant, unresisting, yielding *Ant* protesting, resistant, resisting, unyielding

pas•sive–ma•trix \-ˈmā-triks\ *adj* : of, relating to, or being on LCD in which pixels are controlled in groups
pass•key \ˈpas-ˌkē\ *n* : a key for opening two or more locks
pass out *vb* ♦ : to lose consciousness

♦ black out, faint, swoon

Pass•over \ˈpas-ˌō-vər\ *n* : a Jewish holiday celebrated in March or April in commemoration of the Hebrews' liberation from slavery in Egypt
pass over *vb* **1** ♦ : to ignore in passing **2** ♦ : to pay no attention to the claims of

♦ [1] disregard, forget, ignore, neglect, overlook, slight, slur ♦ [1, 2] condone, disregard, excuse, gloss over, ignore, pardon, shrug off, wink at

pass•port \ˈpas-ˌpōrt\ *n* **1** : an official document issued by a country upon request to a citizen requesting protection during travel abroad **2** ♦ : something that secures admission, acceptance, or attainment

♦ gateway, key

pass up *vb* : DECLINE, REJECT
pass•word \ˈpas-ˌwərd\ *n* **1** : a word or phrase that must be spoken by a person before being allowed to pass a guard **2** : a sequence of characters required for access to a computer system
¹**past** \ˈpast\ *adj* **1** : AGO ⟨10 years ~⟩ **2** : just gone or elapsed ⟨the ~ month⟩ **3** ♦ : having existed or taken place in a period

before the present **4 :** of, relating to, or constituting a verb tense that expresses time gone by

♦ erstwhile, former, late, old, onetime, sometime, whilom

²past *prep or adv* **:** BEYOND

³past *n* **1 :** time gone by **2** ♦ **:** something that happened or was done in a former time **3 :** the past tense; *also* **:** a verb form in it **4 :** a secret past life

♦ history, yesteryear, yore

pas•ta \ˈpäs-tə\ *n* **1 :** a paste in processed form (as macaroni) or in the form of fresh dough (as ravioli) **2 :** a dish of cooked pasta

¹paste \ˈpāst\ *n* **1 :** DOUGH **2 :** a smooth food product made by evaporation or grinding ⟨tomato ~⟩ **3 :** a shaped dough (as spaghetti or ravioli) **4 :** a preparation (as of flour and water) for sticking things together **5 :** a brilliant glass used for artificial gems

²paste *vb* **past•ed; past•ing :** to cause to adhere by paste **:** STICK

³paste *vb* **past•ed; past•ing :** to strike hard at

paste•board \ˈpāst-ˌbōrd\ *n* **:** CARDBOARD

¹pas•tel \pas-ˈtel\ *n* **1 :** a paste made of powdered pigment; *also* **:** a crayon of such paste **2 :** a drawing in pastel **3 :** a pale or light color

²pastel *adj* **1 :** of or relating to a pastel **2** ♦ **:** pale in color

♦ dull, light, pale, washed-out

pas•tern \ˈpas-tərn\ *n* **:** the part of a horse's foot extending from the fetlock to the top of the hoof

pas•teur•i•za•tion \ˌpas-chə-rə-ˈzā-shən, ˌpas-tə-\ *n* **:** partial sterilization of a substance (as milk) by heat or radiation — **pas•teur•ize** \ˈpas-chə-ˌrīz, ˈpas-tə-\ *vb* — **pas•teur•iz•er** *n*

pas•tiche \pas-ˈtēsh\ *n* **:** a composition (as in literature or music) made up of selections from different works

pas•tille \pas-ˈtēl\ *n* **:** LOZENGE 2

pas•time \ˈpas-ˌtīm\ *n* **:** DIVERSION; *esp* **:** something that serves to make time pass agreeably

pas•tor \ˈpas-tər\ *n* **:** a minister or priest serving a local church or parish — **pas•tor•ate** \-tə-rət\ *n*

¹pas•to•ral \ˈpas-tə-rəl\ *adj* **1** ♦ **:** of or relating to shepherds or to rural life **2 :** of or relating to spiritual guidance especially of a congregation **3** ♦ **:** of or relating to the pastor of a church

♦ [1] bucolic, country, rural, rustic ♦ [3] clerical, ministerial, priestly, sacerdotal

²pastoral *n* **:** a literary work dealing with shepherds or rural life

pas•to•rale \ˌpas-tə-ˈräl, -ˈral\ *n* **:** a musical composition having a pastoral theme

past participle *n* **:** a participle that typically expresses completed action, that is one of the principal parts of the verb, and that is used in the formation of perfect tenses in the active voice and of all tenses in the passive voice

pas•tra•mi \pə-ˈsträ-mē\ *n* **:** a highly seasoned smoked beef prepared especially from shoulder cuts

pas•try \ˈpā-strē\ *n, pl* **pastries :** sweet baked goods made of dough or with a crust made of enriched dough

pas•tur•age \ˈpas-chə-rij\ *n* **:** PASTURE

¹pas•ture \ˈpas-chər\ *n* **1 :** plants (as grass) for the feeding especially of grazing livestock **2** ♦ **:** land or a plot of land used for grazing

♦ range

²pasture *vb* **pas•tured; pas•tur•ing 1** ♦ **:** to feed on growing herbage **:** GRAZE **2 :** to use as pasture

♦ browse, forage, graze

pasty \ˈpā-stē\ *adj* **past•i•er; -est 1 :** resembling paste **2** ♦ **:** pallid and unhealthy in appearance

♦ ashen, cadaverous, livid, lurid, pale, peaked, sallow

¹pat \ˈpat\ *n* **1 :** a light tap especially with the hand or a flat instrument; *also* **:** the sound made by it **2 :** something (as butter) shaped into a small flat usually square individual portion

²pat *adv* **:** in a pat manner **:** PERFECTLY

³pat *vb* **pat•ted; pat•ting 1 :** to strike lightly with a flat instrument **2 :** to flatten, smooth, or put into place or shape with a pat **3 :** to tap gently or lovingly with the hand

⁴pat *adj* **1 :** exactly suited to the occasion **:** APT **2 :** memorized exactly **3** ♦ **:** characterized by firmness or obduracy **:** UNYIELDING

♦ adamant, hard, immovable, implacable, inflexible, rigid, unbending, uncompromising, unrelenting, unyielding

PAT *abbr* point after touchdown

¹patch \ˈpach\ *n* **1 :** a piece used to cover a torn or worn place; *also* **:** one worn on a garment as an ornament or insignia **2 :** a small area distinct from that about it **3 :** a shield worn over the socket of an injured or missing eye **4 :** a small piece **:** SCRAP

²patch *vb* **1 :** to mend or cover with a patch **2 :** to make of fragments **3** ♦ **:** to repair usually in hasty fashion

♦ doctor, fix, mend, recondition, renovate, repair, revamp

patch•ou•li \ˈpa-chə-lē, pə-ˈchü-lē\ *n* **:** a heavy perfume made from the fragrant essential oil of an Asian mint; *also* **:** the plant itself

patch test *n* **:** a test for allergic sensitivity made by applying to the unbroken skin small pads soaked with the allergen to be tested

patch•work \ˈpach-ˌwərk\ *n* **:** something made of pieces of different materials, shapes, or colors

patchy \ˈpa-chē\ *adj* **patch•i•er; -est :** marked by or consisting of patches; *also* **:** irregular in appearance or quality — **patch•i•ness** \-chē-nəs\ *n*

pate \ˈpāt\ *n* ♦ **:** a person's head; *esp* **:** the crown of the head

♦ head, noggin, poll

pâ•té *also* **pate** \pä-ˈtā\ *n* **1 :** a meat or fish pie or patty **2 :** a spread of finely chopped or pureed seasoned meat

pa•tel•la \pə-ˈte-lə\ *n, pl* **-lae** \-ˈte-(ˌ)lē, -ˌlī\ *or* **-las :** KNEECAP

pat•en \ˈpat-ᵊn\ *n* **1 :** PLATE; *esp* **:** one of precious metal for the eucharistic bread **2 :** a thin disk

¹pa•tent *1 & 4 are* ˈpat-ᵊnt, *Brit also* ˈpāt-, *2 & 3 are* ˈpat-ᵊnt, ˈpāt-\ *adj* **1 :** open to public inspection — used chiefly in the phrase *letters patent* **2 :** free from obstruction **3** ♦ **:** readily visible or intelligible **:** OBVIOUS **4 :** protected by a patent — **pat•ent•ly** *adv*

♦ apparent, broad, clear, clear-cut, distinct, evident, lucid, manifest, obvious, palpable, perspicuous, plain, transparent, unambiguous, unequivocal, unmistakable

²pat•ent \ˈpat-ᵊnt, *Brit also* ˈpāt-\ *n* **1 :** an official document conferring a right or privilege **2 :** a document securing to an inventor for a term of years exclusive right to his or her invention **3 :** something patented

³pat•ent *vb* **:** to secure by patent

pat•en•tee \ˌpat-ᵊn-ˈtē, *Brit also* ˌpāt-\ *n* **:** one to whom a grant is made or a privilege secured by patent

pat•ent medicine \ˈpat-ᵊnt-\ *n* **:** a packaged nonprescription drug protected by a trademark; *also* **:** any proprietary drug

pa•ter•fa•mil•i•as \ˌpā-tər-fə-ˈmi-lē-əs\ *n, pl* **pa•tres•fa•mil•i•as** \ˌpā-ˌtrēz-\ **:** the father of a family **:** the male head of a household

pa•ter•nal \pə-ˈtərn-ᵊl\ *adj* **1 :** FATHERLY **2 :** related through or inherited or derived from a father — **pa•ter•nal•ly** *adv*

pa•ter•nal•ism \-ˌi-zəm\ *n* **:** a system under which an authority treats those under its control paternally (as by regulating their conduct and supplying their needs)

pa•ter•ni•ty \pə-ˈtər-nə-tē\ *n* **1 :** FATHERHOOD **2 :** descent from a father

¹path \ˈpath, ˈpȧth\ *n, pl* **paths** \ˈpathz, ˈpaths, ˈpȧthz, ˈpȧths\ **1** ♦ **:** a trodden way **2** ♦ **:** a line of travel **:** ROUTE — **path•less** *adj*

♦ [1] footpath, trace, track, trail ♦ [2] course, line, route, track, way

²path *or* **pathol** *abbr* pathology

path•break•ing \ˈpath-ˌbrā-kiŋ\ *adj* **:** TRAILBLAZING

pa•thet•ic \pə-ˈthe-tik\ *adj* **1** ♦ **:** evoking tenderness, pity, or sorrow **2 :** pitifully inadequate — **pa•thet•i•cal•ly** \-ti-k(ə-)lē\ *adv*

♦ depressing, dismal, dreary, heartbreaking, melancholy, sad, sorry, tearful

path•find•er \ˈpath-ˌfīn-dər, ˈpȧth-\ *n* **:** one that discovers a way; *esp* **:** one that explores untraveled regions to mark out a new route

patho•gen \ˈpa-thə-jən\ *n* **:** a specific agent (as a bacterium) causing disease — **patho•gen•ic** \ˌpa-thə-ˈje-nik\ *adj* — **patho•ge•nic•i•ty** \-jə-ˈni-sə-tē\ *n*

pa•thog•ra•phy \pə-ˈthä-grə-fē\ *n* **:** biography focusing on a person's flaws and misfortunes

pa•thol•o•gy \pə-ˈthä-lə-jē\ *n, pl* **-gies 1 :** the study of the essential nature of disease **2 :** the abnormality of structure and function characteristic of a disease — **path•o•log•i•cal** \ˌpa-thə-ˈlä-ji-kəl\ *adj* — **pa•thol•o•gist** \pə-ˈthä-lə-jist\ *n*

pa•thos \ˈpā-ˌthäs, -ˌthōs\ *n* **:** an element in experience or artistic representation evoking pity or compassion

path•way \ˈpath-ˌwā, ˈpȧth-\ *n* **:** PATH

pa•tience \ˈpā-shəns\ *n* **1** ♦ **:** the capacity, habit, or fact of being patient **2** *chiefly Brit* **:** SOLITAIRE 2

♦ forbearance, long-suffering, sufferance, tolerance ***Ant*** impatience

¹pa•tient \ˈpā-shənt\ *adj* **1** ♦ **:** bearing pain or trials without complaint **2 :** showing self-control : CALM **3** ♦ **:** steadfast despite opposition, difficulty, or adversity : PERSEVERING — **pa·tient·ly** *adv*

♦ [1] forbearing, long-suffering, stoic, tolerant, uncomplaining *Ant* complaining, fed up, impatient, protesting ♦ [3] dogged, insistent, persevering, persistent, pertinacious, tenacious

²patient *n* **:** one under medical care

pa·ti·na \ˈpa-tə-nə, pə-ˈtē-\ *n, pl* **pa·ti·nas** \-nəz\ *or* **pa·ti·nae** \ˈpa-tə-ˌnē, -ˌnī\ **1 :** a green film formed on copper and bronze by exposure to moist air **2 :** a superficial covering or exterior

pa·tio \ˈpa-tē-ˌō, ˈpä-\ *n, pl* **pa·ti·os** **1 :** a court or enclosure adjacent to a building : COURTYARD **2 :** an often paved area near a dwelling used especially for outdoor dining

pa·tois \ˈpa-ˌtwä\ *n, pl* **pa·tois** \-ˌtwäz\ **1 :** a dialect other than the standard dialect; *esp* **:** uneducated or provincial speech **2** ♦ **:** the characteristic special language of an occupational or social group : JARGON

♦ argot, cant, dialect, jargon, language, lingo, patter, slang, vocabulary

pa·tri·arch \ˈpā-trē-ˌärk\ *n* **1 :** a man revered as father or founder (as of a tribe) **2 :** a venerable old man **3 :** an ecclesiastical dignitary (as the bishop of an Eastern Orthodox see) — **pa·tri·ar·chal** \ˌpā-trē-ˈär-kəl\ *adj* — **pa·tri·arch·ate** \ˈpā-trē-ˌär-kət, -ˌkāt\ *n* — **pa·tri·ar·chy** \-ˌär-kē\ *n*

¹pa·tri·cian \pə-ˈtri-shən\ *n* **:** a person of high birth : ARISTOCRAT

²patrician *adj* ♦ **:** of, relating to, or characteristic of patricians

♦ aristocratic, genteel, gentle, grand, highborn, noble, wellborn

pat·ri·cide \ˈpa-tre-ˌsīd\ *n* **1 :** one who murders his or her own father **2 :** the murder of one's own father

pat·ri·mo·ny \ˈpa-trə-ˌmō-nē\ *n* **:** something (as an estate) inherited or derived especially from one's father : HERITAGE — **pat·ri·mo·ni·al** \ˌpa-trə-ˈmō-nē-əl\ *adj*

pa·tri·ot \ˈpā-trē-ət, -ˌät\ *n* **:** one who loves his or her country — **pa·tri·ot·ic** \ˌpā-trē-ˈä-tik\ *adj* — **pa·tri·ot·i·cal·ly** \-ti-k(ə-)lē\ *adv* — **pa·tri·o·tism** \ˈpā-trē-ə-ˌti-zəm\ *n*

pa·tris·tic \pə-ˈtris-tik\ *adj* **:** of or relating to the church fathers or their writings

¹pa·trol \pə-ˈtrōl\ *n* **:** the action of going the rounds (as of an area) for observation or the maintenance of security; *also* **:** a person or group performing such an action

²patrol *vb* **pa·trolled; pa·trol·ling :** to carry out a patrol

pa·trol·man \pə-ˈtrōl-mən\ *n* **:** a police officer assigned to a beat

patrol wagon *n* **:** PADDY WAGON

pa·tron \ˈpā-trən\ *n* **1 :** a person chosen or named as special protector **2** ♦ **:** a wealthy or influential supporter ⟨~ of poets⟩; *also* **:** BENEFACTOR **3** ♦ **:** a regular client or customer

♦ [2] backer, guarantor, sponsor, surety ♦ [3] customer, guest

pa·tron·age \ˈpa-trə-nij, ˈpā-\ *n* **1 :** the support or influence of a patron **2 :** the trade of customers **3 :** control of appointment to government jobs

pa·tron·ess \ˈpā-trə-nəs\ *n* **:** a woman who is a patron

pa·tron·ise *chiefly Brit var of* PATRONIZE

pa·tron·ize \ˈpā-trə-ˌnīz, ˈpa-\ *vb* **-ized; -iz·ing** **1 :** to be a customer of **2 :** to treat condescendingly, haughtily, or coolly **3** ♦ **:** to act as patron of : provide aid or support for

♦ advocate, back, champion, endorse, support

pat·ro·nym·ic \ˌpa-trə-ˈni-mik\ *n* **:** a name derived from the name of one's father or a paternal ancestor usually by the addition of an affix

pa·troon \pə-ˈtrün\ *n* **:** the proprietor of a manorial estate especially in New York under Dutch rule

pat·sy \ˈpat-sē\ *n, pl* **pat·sies :** a person who is easily duped or victimized

¹pat·ter \ˈpa-tər\ *vb* **:** to talk glibly or mechanically

²patter *n* **1** ♦ **:** a specialized lingo **2 :** extremely rapid talk ⟨a comedian's ~⟩

♦ argot, cant, dialect, jargon, language, lingo, patois, slang, vocabulary

³patter *vb* **:** to strike, pat, or tap rapidly

⁴patter *n* **:** a quick succession of taps or pats ⟨the ~ of rain⟩

¹pat·tern \ˈpa-tərn\ *n* **1 :** an ideal model **2 :** something used as a model for making things ⟨a dressmaker's ~⟩ **3 :** SAMPLE **4** ♦ **:** an artistic design **5 :** CONFIGURATION **6** ♦ **:** an established mode of behavior or set of beliefs or attitudes

♦ [4] design, figure, motif, motive ♦ [6] custom, fashion, groove, habit, practice, routine, rut, treadmill, way, wont

²pattern *vb* **:** to form according to a pattern

pat·ty *also* **pat·tie** \ˈpa-tē\ *n, pl* **patties** **1 :** a little pie **2** ♦ **:** a small flat cake especially of chopped food

♦ cutlet, fritter

pau·ci·ty \ˈpȯ-sə-tē\ *n* ♦ **:** smallness of number or quantity

♦ dearth, deficiency, deficit, failure, famine, inadequacy, insufficiency, lack, poverty, scantiness, scarcity, shortage, want

paunch \ˈpȯnch\ *n* **:** a usually large belly : POTBELLY — **paunchy** *adj*

pau·per \ˈpȯ-pər\ *n* **:** a person without means of support except from charity — **pau·per·ize** \-pə-ˌrīz\ *vb*

pau·per·ism \ˈpȯ-pə-ˌri-zəm\ *n* ♦ **:** the quality or state of being a pauper

♦ beggary, destitution, impecuniousness, impoverishment, indigence, need, penury, poverty, want

¹pause \ˈpȯz\ *n* **1** ♦ **:** a temporary stop; *also* **:** a period of inaction **2 :** a brief suspension of the voice **3 :** a sign (as 𝄐) above or below a musical note or rest to show it is to be prolonged **4 :** a reason for pausing **5 :** a function of an electronic device that pauses a recording

♦ break, breath, breathe, interruption, lull

²pause *vb* **paused; paus·ing :** to stop, rest, or linger for a time

pave \ˈpāv\ *vb* **paved; pav·ing :** to cover (as a road) with hard material in order to smooth or firm the surface

pave·ment \ˈpāv-mənt\ *n* **1 :** a paved surface **2 :** the material with which something is paved

pa·vil·ion \pə-ˈvil-yən\ *n* **1 :** a large tent **2 :** a light structure (as in a park) used for entertainment or shelter

pav·ing \ˈpā-viŋ\ *n* **:** PAVEMENT

¹paw \ˈpȯ\ *n* **:** the foot of a quadruped (as a dog or lion) having claws

²paw *vb* **1 :** to touch or strike with a paw; *also* **:** to scrape with a hoof **2 :** to feel or handle clumsily or rudely **3 :** to flail about or grab for with the hands

pawl \ˈpȯl\ *n* **:** a pivoted tongue or sliding bolt designed to fall into notches on another machine part to permit motion in one direction only

¹pawn \ˈpȯn\ *n* **:** a chess piece of the least value

²pawn *n* **1** ♦ **:** something deposited as security for a loan; *also* **:** HOSTAGE **2 :** the state of being pledged

♦ gage, guarantee, guaranty, pledge, security

³pawn *vb* **:** to deposit as a pledge

pawn·bro·ker \ˈpȯn-ˌbrō-kər\ *n* **:** one who lends money on goods pledged

Paw·nee \pȯ-ˈnē\ *n, pl* **Pawnee** *or* **Pawnees :** a member of an American Indian people orig. of Kansas and Nebraska

pawn·shop \ˈpȯn-ˌshäp\ *n* **:** a pawnbroker's place of business

paw·paw *also* **pa·paw** **1** \pə-ˈpȯ\ **:** PAPAYA **2** \ˈpä-pȯ, ˈpȯ-\ **:** a No. American tree with green-skinned edible fruit; *also* **:** its fruit

¹pay \ˈpā\ *vb* **paid** \ˈpād\ *also in sense 7* **payed; pay·ing** **1** ♦ **:** to make due return to for goods or services ⟨~ the grocer⟩ **2** ♦ **:** to discharge indebtedness for : SETTLE ⟨~ a bill⟩ **3 :** to give in forfeit ⟨~ the penalty⟩ **4 :** REQUITE **5 :** to give, offer, or make freely or as fitting ⟨~ attention⟩ **6** ♦ **:** to be profitable to : RETURN **7 :** to make slack and allow to run out ⟨~ out a rope⟩ **8** ♦ **:** to give in return for goods or service ⟨~ good money⟩ — **pay·ee** \pā-ˈē\ *n* — **pay·er** *n*

♦ [1] compensate, recompense, remunerate ♦ [2] clear, discharge, foot, liquidate, pay off, quit, recompense, settle, spring, stand *Ant* repudiate ♦ [6] give, return, yield ♦ [8] disburse, expend, give, lay out, spend

²pay *n* **1** ♦ **:** something paid for a purpose and especially as a salary or wage **2 :** the status of being paid by an employer : EMPLOY

♦ compensation, consideration, payment, recompense, remittance, remuneration, requital ♦ emolument, hire, payment, salary, stipend, wage

³pay *adj* **1 :** containing something valuable (as gold) ⟨~ dirt⟩ **2 :** equipped to receive a fee for use ⟨~ telephone⟩ **3 :** requiring payment

pay·able \ˈpā-ə-bəl\ *adj* ♦ **:** that may, can, or must be paid

♦ outstanding, overdue, unpaid, unsettled

pay·back \ˈpā-ˌbak\ *n* **1 :** a return on an investment equal to the original capital outlay **2 :** something given in return, compensation, or retaliation

pay·check \ˈpā-ˌchek\ *n* **1 :** a check in payment of wages or salary **2 :** WAGES, SALARY

pay·load \-ˌlōd\ *n* ♦ **:** the load carried by a vehicle in addition to what is necessary for its operation; *also* **:** the weight of such a load

♦ burden, cargo, draft, freight, haul, lading, load, weight

pay·mas·ter \-ˌmas-tər\ *n* **:** one who distributes the payroll
pay·ment \ˈpā-mənt\ *n* **1** ♦ **:** the act of paying **2** ♦ **:** something paid

♦ [1] compensation, disbursement, remittance, remuneration *Ant* nonpayment, repudiation ♦ [2] compensation, consideration, deposit, disbursement, expenditure, indemnity, outlay, pay, recompense, redress, remittance, remuneration, rent, reparation, requital, restitution, salary, settlement, stipend, wage

pay·off \-ˌȯf\ *n* **1** ♦ **:** a valuable return **:** PROFIT; *also* **:** RETRIBUTION **2 :** the climax of an incident or enterprise ⟨the ~ of a story⟩

♦ earnings, gain, lucre, net, proceeds, profit, return

pay off *vb* ♦ **:** to pay (a debt or a creditor) in full

♦ clear, discharge, foot, liquidate, pay, quit, recompense, settle, spring, stand

pay–per–view *n* **:** a cable television service by which customers can order access to a single airing of a TV feature
pay·roll \-ˌrōl\ *n* **:** a list of persons entitled to receive pay; *also* **:** the money to pay those on such a list
payt *abbr* payment
pay up *vb* **:** to pay what is due; *also* **:** to pay in full
Pb *symbol* lead
PBS *abbr* Public Broadcasting Service
PBX \ˌpē-(ˌ)bē-ˈeks\ *n* **:** a private telephone switchboard
¹**PC** \ˌpē-ˈsē\ *n, pl* **PCs** *or* **PC's :** MICROCOMPUTER
²**PC** *abbr* **1** Peace Corps **2** percent; percentage **3** politically correct **4** postcard **5** after meals **6** professional corporation
PCB \ˌpē-ˌsē-ˈbē\ *n* **:** POLYCHLORINATED BIPHENYL
PCP \ˌpē-ˌsē-ˈpē\ *n* **:** PHENCYCLIDINE
pct *abbr* percent; percentage
pd *abbr* paid
Pd *symbol* palladium
PD *abbr* **1** per diem **2** police department **3** potential difference
PDA \ˌpē-ˌdē-ˈā\ *n* **:** a small microprocessor device for storing and organizing personal information
PDQ \ˌpē-ˌdē-ˈkyü\ *adv, often not cap* **:** IMMEDIATELY
PDT *abbr* Pacific daylight (saving) time
PE *abbr* **1** physical education **2** printer's error **3** professional engineer
pea \ˈpē\ *n, pl* **peas** *also* **pease** \ˈpēz\ **1 :** the round edible protein-rich seed borne in the pod of a widely grown leguminous vine; *also* **:** this vine **2 :** any of various plants resembling or related to the pea
peace \ˈpēs\ *n* **1** ♦ **:** a state of calm and quiet; *esp* **:** public security under law **2 :** freedom from disturbing thoughts or emotions **3** ♦ **:** a state of concord (as between persons or governments); *also* **:** an agreement to end hostilities — **peace·able** \ˈpē-sə-bəl\ *adj* — **peace·ably** \-blē\ *adv*

♦ [1] calm, calmness, hush, placidity, quiet, quietness, repose, serenity, still, stillness, tranquillity ♦ [3] compatibility, concord, harmony

peace·ful \ˈpēs-fəl\ *adj* ♦ **:** untroubled by conflict, agitation, or commotion — **peace·ful·ly** *adv*

♦ calm, halcyon, hushed, placid, quiet, serene, still, tranquil, untroubled

peace·keep·ing \ˈpēs-ˌkē-piŋ\ *n* **:** the preserving of peace; *esp* **:** international enforcement and supervision of a truce — **peace·keep·er** *n*
peace·mak·er \-ˌmā-kər\ *n* ♦ **:** one who settles an argument or stops a fight

♦ arbiter, arbitrator, go-between, intercessor, intermediary, mediator, middleman

peace·time \-ˌtīm\ *n* **:** a time when a nation is not at war
peach \ˈpēch\ *n* **:** a sweet juicy fuzzy-skinned fruit of a small usually pink-flowered tree related to the cherry and plums; *also* **:** this tree — **peachy** *adj*
pea·cock \ˈpē-ˌkäk\ *n* **:** the male peafowl that can spread its long tail feathers to make a colorful display
pea·fowl \-ˌfau̇(-ə)l\ *n* **:** either of two large domesticated Asian pheasants
pea·hen \-ˌhen\ *n* **:** the female peafowl
¹**peak** \ˈpēk\ *n* **1 :** a pointed or projecting part **2 a :** the top of a hill or mountain **b** ♦ **:** a prominent mountain usually having a well-defined summit **:** MOUNTAIN **3** ♦ **:** the front projecting part of a cap **4 :** the narrow part of a ship's bow or stern **5** ♦ **:** the highest level or greatest degree — **peak** *adj*

♦ [2b] mount, mountain ♦ [3] bill, visor ♦ [5] acme, apex, climax, crown, culmination, head, height, meridian, pinnacle, summit, tip-top, top, zenith

²**peak** *vb* **:** to bring to or reach a maximum
¹**peak·ed** \ˈpēkt\ *adj* **:** having a peak **:** POINTED
²**peaked** \ˈpē-kəd\ *adj* ♦ **:** being pale and wan or emaciated; *also* **:** somewhat unwell

♦ ashen, cadaverous, livid, lurid, pale, pasty ♦ bad, down, ill, indisposed, punk, sick, unhealthy, unsound, unwell

¹**peal** \ˈpēl\ *n* **1 :** the loud ringing of bells **2 :** a set of tuned bells **3 :** a loud sound or succession of sounds
²**peal** *vb* ♦ **:** to give out peals **:** RESOUND

♦ chime, knell, ring, toll

pea·nut \ˈpē-(ˌ)nət\ *n* **1 :** an annual herb related to the pea but having pods that ripen underground; *also* **:** this pod or one of the edible seeds it bears **2** *pl* ♦ **:** a very small amount

♦ mite, pittance, shoestring, song

pear \ˈpar\ *n* **:** the fleshy fruit of a tree related to the apple; *also* **:** this tree
pearl \ˈpərl\ *n* **1 :** a small hard often lustrous body formed within the shell of some mollusks and used as a gem **2** ♦ **:** one that is choice or precious ⟨~*s* of wisdom⟩ **3 :** a slightly bluish medium gray color — **pearly** \ˈpər-lē\ *adj*

♦ catch, gem, jewel, plum, prize, treasure

peas·ant \ˈpez-ᵊnt\ *n* **1 :** any of a class of small landowners or laborers tilling the soil **2 :** a usually uneducated person of low social status — **peas·ant·ry** \-ᵊn-trē\ *n*
pea·shoot·er \ˈpē-ˌshü-tər\ *n* **:** a toy blowgun for shooting peas
peat \ˈpēt\ *n* **:** a dark substance formed by partial decay of plants (as mosses) in water — **peaty** *adj*
peat moss *n* **:** SPHAGNUM
¹**peb·ble** \ˈpe-bəl\ *n* **:** a small usually round stone
²**pebble** *vb* **peb·bled; peb·bling :** to produce a rough surface texture in ⟨~ leather⟩
peb·bly \ˈpe-b(ə-)lē\ *adj* ♦ **:** containing or resembling pebbles

♦ broken, bumpy, coarse, irregular, jagged, lumpy, ragged, rough, rugged, uneven

pec \ˈpek\ *n* **:** PECTORAL MUSCLE
pe·can \pi-ˈkän, -ˈkan; ˈpē-ˌkan\ *n* **:** the smooth thin-shelled edible nut of a large American hickory; *also* **:** this tree
pec·ca·dil·lo \ˌpe-kə-ˈdi-lō\ *n, pl* **-loes** *or* **-los :** a slight offense
pec·ca·ry \ˈpe-kə-rē\ *n, pl* **-ries :** any of several American chiefly tropical mammals resembling but smaller than the related pigs
pec·ca·vi \pe-ˈkä-ˌvē\ *n* **:** an acknowledgment of sin
¹**peck** \ˈpek\ *n* **1 :** a unit of dry capacity equal to ¼ bushel **2 :** a large amount
²**peck** *vb* **1 :** to strike or pierce with or as if with the bill **2 :** to make (as a hole) by pecking **3 :** to pick up with or as if with the bill
³**peck** *n* **1 :** an impression made by pecking **2 :** a quick sharp stroke
pecking order *also* **peck order** *n* **:** a basic pattern of social organization within a flock of poultry in which each bird pecks another lower in the scale without being pecked in return and submits to pecking by one of higher rank; *also* **:** a social hierarchy
pec·tin \ˈpek-tən\ *n* **:** any of various water-soluble plant substances that cause fruit jellies to set — **pec·tic** \-tik\ *adj*
pec·to·ral \ˈpek-tə-rəl\ *adj* **:** of or relating to the breast or chest
pectoral muscle *n* **:** either of two muscles on each side of the body which connect the front walls of the chest with the bones of the upper arm and shoulder
pe·cu·liar \pi-ˈkyül-yər\ *adj* **1** ♦ **:** belonging exclusively to one person or group **2** ♦ **:** characteristic of only one person, group, or thing **:** DISTINCTIVE **3** ♦ **:** differing markedly from the usual or ordinary or accepted **:** ODD — **pe·cu·liar·ly** *adv*

♦ [1] individual, particular, personal, private, separate, singular, unique ♦ [2] characteristic, classic, distinct, distinctive, individual, proper, symptomatic, typical ♦ [3] curious, extraordinary, funny, odd, queer, rare, strange, unaccustomed, uncommon, unique, unusual, weird

pe·cu·liar·i·ty \pi-ˌkyül-ˈyar-ə-tē, -ˌkyü-lē-ˈar-\ *n* **1 :** the quality or state of being peculiar **2** ♦ **:** a distinguishing characteristic **3** ♦ **:** an odd person, thing, event, or trait

♦ [2] attribute, character, characteristic, feature, mark, point, property, quality, trait ♦ [3] crotchet, eccentricity, idiosyncrasy, mannerism, oddity, quirk, singularity, trick

pe•cu•ni•ary \pi-ˈkyü-nē-ˌer-ē\ *adj* ♦ : of or relating to money : MONETARY

♦ financial, fiscal, monetary

ped•a•gogue *also* **ped•a•gog** \ˈpe-də-ˌgäg\ *n* ♦ : one that teaches : TEACHER

♦ educator, instructor, schoolteacher, teacher

ped•a•go•gy \ˈpe-də-ˌgō-jē, -ˌgä-\ *n* : the art or profession of teaching; *esp* : EDUCATION 2 — **ped•a•gog•ic** \ˌpe-də-ˈgä-jik, -ˈgō-\ *or* **ped•a•gog•i•cal** \-ji-kəl\ *adj*

¹ped•al \ˈped-ᵊl\ *n* : a lever worked by the foot

²pedal *adj* : of or relating to the foot

³ped•al \ˈped-ᵊl\ *vb* **ped•aled** *also* **ped•alled; ped•al•ing** *also* **ped•al•ling** **1** : to use or work a pedal (as of a piano or bicycle) **2** : to ride a bicycle

ped•ant \ˈped-ᵊnt\ *n* **1** : a person who makes a show of knowledge **2** : a formal uninspired teacher — **pe•dan•tic** \pi-ˈdan-tik\ *adj* — **ped•ant•ry** \ˈped-ᵊn-trē\ *n*

ped•dle \ˈped-ᵊl\ *vb* **ped•dled; ped•dling** : to sell or offer for sale from place to place — **ped•dler** *also* **ped•lar** \ˈped-lər\ *n*

ped•er•ast \ˈpe-də-ˌrast\ *n* : one who practices anal intercourse especially with a boy — **ped•er•as•ty** \ˈpe-də-ˌras-tē\ *n*

ped•es•tal \ˈpe-dəst-ᵊl\ *n* **1** : the support or foot of something (as a column, statue, or vase) that is upright **2** : a position of high regard

¹pe•des•tri•an \pə-ˈdes-trē-ən\ *adj* **1** : marked by dullness or ordinariness : ORDINARY **2** : going on foot

²pedestrian *n* : WALKER

pe•di•at•rics \ˌpē-dē-ˈa-triks\ *n* : a branch of medicine dealing with the development, care, and diseases of children — **pe•di•at•ric** \-trik\ *adj* — **pe•di•a•tri•cian** \ˌpē-dē-ə-ˈtri-shən\ *n*

pedi•cab \ˈpe-di-ˌkab\ *n* : a pedal-driven tricycle with seats for a driver and two passengers

pedi•cure \ˈpe-di-ˌkyu̇r\ *n* : care of the feet, toes, and nails; *also* : a single treatment of these parts — **pedi•cur•ist** \-ˌkyu̇r-ist\ *n*

ped•i•gree \ˈpe-də-ˌgrē\ *n* **1** : a record of a line of ancestors **2** ♦ : an ancestral line — **ped•i•greed** \-grēd\ *adj*

♦ ancestry, birth, blood, bloodline, breeding, descent, extraction, family tree, genealogy, line, lineage, origin, parentage, stock, strain

ped•i•ment \ˈpe-də-mənt\ *n* : a low triangular gablelike decoration (as over a door or window) on a building

pe•dom•e•ter \pi-ˈdä-mə-tər\ *n* : an instrument that measures the distance one walks

pe•do•phile \ˈpe-də-ˌfī(-ə)l, ˈpē\ *n* : one affected with pedophilia

pe•do•phil•ia \ˌpe-də-ˈfi-lē-ə, ˌpē\ *n* : sexual perversion in which children are the preferred sexual object

pe•dun•cle \ˈpē-ˌdəŋ-kəl\ *n* : a narrow supporting stalk

¹peek \ˈpēk\ *vb* **1** : to look furtively **2** : to peer from a place of concealment **3** : to take a brief look : GLANCE

²peek *n* **1** : a furtive look **2** ♦ : a brief look : GLANCE

♦ cast, eye, gander, glance, glimpse, look, peep, regard, sight, view

¹peel \ˈpēl\ *vb* **1** ♦ : to strip the skin, bark, or rind from **2 a** ♦ : to strip off (as a coat) — often used with *off* **b** : to come off **3** : to lose the skin, bark, or rind

♦ [1] bark, flay, hull, husk, shell, skin ♦ *usu* **peel off** [2a] doff, put off, remove, take off

²peel *n* : a skin or rind especially of a fruit

peel•ing \ˈpē-liŋ\ *n* : a peeled-off piece or strip (as of skin or rind)

peen \ˈpēn\ *n* : the usually hemispherical or wedge-shaped end of the head of a hammer opposite the face

¹peep \ˈpēp\ *vb* ♦ : to utter a feeble shrill sound or the slightest sound

♦ cheep, chirp, pipe, tweet, twitter

²peep *n* : a feeble shrill sound

³peep *vb* **1** : to look slyly especially through an aperture : PEEK **2** : to begin to emerge **3** : to look at : WATCH — **peep•er** *n*

⁴peep *n* **1** : a first faint appearance **2** ♦ : a brief or furtive look

♦ cast, eye, gander, glance, glimpse, look, peek, regard, sight, view

peep•hole \ˈpēp-ˌhōl\ *n* : a hole to peep through

¹peer \ˈpir\ *n* **1** ♦ : one of equal standing with another : EQUAL **2** : NOBLE — **peer•age** \-ij\ *n*

♦ coordinate, counterpart, equal, equivalent, fellow, like, match, parallel, rival

²peer *vb* **1** : to look intently or curiously **2** : to come slightly into view

peer•ess \ˈpir-əs\ *n* : a woman who is a peer

peer•less \ˈpir-ləs\ *adj* ♦ : having no equal : MATCHLESS

♦ incomparable, inimitable, matchless, unequaled, unmatched, unparalleled, unrivaled, unsurpassed

¹peeve \ˈpēv\ *vb* **peeved; peev•ing** ♦ : to make resentful : ANNOY

♦ aggravate, annoy, bother, bug, chafe, exasperate, gall, get, grate, irk, irritate, nettle, persecute, pique, put out, rasp, rile, vex

²peeve *n* **1** ♦ : a feeling or mood of resentment **2** ♦ : a particular grievance

♦ [1] dudgeon, huff, offense, pique, resentment, umbrage ♦ [2] aggravation, annoyance, bother, exasperation, frustration, hassle, headache, inconvenience, irritant, nuisance, pest, problem, thorn

pee•vish \ˈpē-vish\ *adj* **1** : querulous in temperament : FRETFUL **2** ♦ : perversely obstinate **3** ♦ : marked by ill temper — **pee•vish•ly** *adv*

♦ [2] dogged, hardheaded, headstrong, mulish, obdurate, obstinate, opinionated, pertinacious, perverse, pigheaded, stubborn, unyielding, willful ♦ [3] crabby, cranky, cross, crotchety, grouchy, grumpy, irritable, short-tempered, snappish, snappy, snippy, testy, waspish

pee•vish•ness \-nəs\ *n* ♦ : the quality or state of being peevish

♦ hardheadedness, mulishness, obduracy, obstinacy, pertinacity, self-will, stubbornness, tenacity ♦ biliousness, grumpiness, irritability, perverseness, perversity

pee•wee \ˈpē-(ˌ)wē\ *n* ♦ : one that is diminutive or tiny

♦ dwarf, midget, mite, pygmy, runt, scrub, shrimp

¹peg \ˈpeg\ *n* **1** : a small pointed piece (as of wood) used to pin down or fasten things or to fit into holes **2** : a projecting piece used as a support or boundary marker **3** : SUPPORT, PRETEXT **4** ♦ : a step or degree especially in estimation ⟨set him down a ~⟩ **5** : THROW

♦ cut, degree, grade, inch, notch, phase, point, stage, step

²peg *vb* **pegged; peg•ging** **1** : to put a peg into : fasten, pin down, or attach with or as if with pegs **2** : to work hard and steadily : PLUG **3** : HUSTLE **4** : to mark by pegs **5** : to hold (as prices) at a set level or rate **6** ♦ : to place in a definite category **7** : to propel through the air by a forward motion of the hand and arm : THROW **8** ♦ : to work steadily and diligently — often used with *away*

♦ [6] assort, break down, categorize, class, classify, grade, group, place, range, rank, separate, sort ♦ *usu* **peg away** [8] drudge, endeavor (*or* endeavour), fag, grub, hustle, labor (*or* labour), plod, plug, slave, slog, strain, strive, struggle, sweat, toil, work

PEI *abbr* Prince Edward Island

pei•gnoir \pān-ˈwär, pen-\ *n* : NEGLIGEE

¹pe•jo•ra•tive \pi-ˈjȯr-ə-tiv\ *n* : a pejorative word or phrase

²pejorative *adj* : having negative connotations : DISPARAGING — **pe•jo•ra•tive•ly** *adv*

peke \ˈpēk\ *n, often cap* : PEKINGESE

Pe•king•ese *or* **Pe•kin•ese** \ˌpē-kə-ˈnēz, -ˈnēs; -kiŋ-ˈēz, -ˈēs\ *n, pl* **Pekingese** *or* **Pekinese** : any of a breed of Chinese origin of small short-legged long-haired dogs

pe•koe \ˈpē-(ˌ)kō\ *n* : a black tea made from young tea leaves

pel•age \ˈpe-lij\ *n* ♦ : the hairy covering of a mammal

♦ coat, fleece, fur, hair, pile, wool

pe•lag•ic \pə-ˈla-jik\ *adj* ♦ : of, relating to, or living or occurring in the open sea : OCEANIC

♦ marine, maritime, oceanic

pelf \ˈpelf\ *n* ♦ : something generally accepted as a medium of exchange : MONEY

♦ cash, currency, dough, lucre, money, tender

pel•i•can \ˈpe-li-kən\ *n* : any of a genus of large web-footed birds having a pouched lower bill used to scoop in fish

pel•la•gra \pə-ˈla-grə, -ˈlā-\ *n* : a disease caused by a diet with too little niacin and protein and marked by a skin rash, disease of the digestive system, and mental disturbances

pel•let \ˈpe-lət\ *n* **1** : a little ball (as of medicine) **2** : BULLET — **pel•let•al** \-lə-təl\ *adj* — **pel•let•ize** \-ˌtīz\ *vb*

pell–mell \ˌpel-ˈmel\ *adv* **1** ◆ **:** in mingled confusion **2** ◆ **:** in confused haste **:** HEADLONG

◆ [1] amok, berserk, frantically, harum-scarum, hectically, helter-skelter, madly, wild, wildly ◆ [2] cursorily, hastily, headlong, hurriedly, precipitately, rashly

pel•lu•cid \pə-ˈlü-səd\ *adj* ◆ **:** extremely clear **:** LIMPID, TRANSPARENT

◆ clear, limpid, liquid, lucent, transparent

pe•lo•ton \ˌpe-lə-ˈtän\ *n* **:** the main body of riders in a bicycle race

1**pelt** \ˈpelt\ *n* ◆ **:** a skin especially of a fur-bearing animal

◆ fur, hide, skin

2**pelt** *vb* **1** ◆ **:** to strike with a succession of blows or missiles **2 :** to propel through the air by a forward motion of the hand and arm **:** THROW **3** ◆ **:** to move rapidly and vigorously

◆ [1] bash, bat, batter, beat, hammer, pound, thrash, thump ◆ [3] dash, fly, hasten, hurry, hustle, race, rocket, run, rush, shoot, speed, tear, zip, zoom

pel•vis \ˈpel-vəs\ *n, pl* **pel•vis•es** \-və-səz\ *or* **pel•ves** \-ˌvēz\ **:** a basin-shaped part of the vertebrate skeleton consisting of the large bone of each hip and the nearby bones of the spine — **pelvic** \-vik\ *adj*

pem•mi•can *also* **pem•i•can** \ˈpe-mi-kən\ *n* **:** dried meat pounded fine and mixed with melted fat

1**pen** \ˈpen\ *vb* **penned; pen•ning** ◆ **:** to shut in or as if in a pen

◆ cage, closet, coop up, corral, encase, enclose, envelop, fence, hedge, hem, house, immure, wall

2**pen** *n* **1** ◆ **:** a small enclosure for animals **2 :** a small place of confinement or storage

◆ cage, coop, corral, pound

3**pen** *n* **1 :** an implement for writing or drawing with ink or a similar fluid **2 :** a writing instrument regarded as a means of expression **3 :** STYLUS 3

4**pen** *vb* **penned; pen•ning** ◆ **:** to set down in writing as the author of **:** WRITE

◆ author, scribble, write

5**pen** *n* ◆ **:** a state or federal prison **:** PENITENTIARY

◆ brig, hoosegow, jail, jug, lockup, penitentiary, prison, stockade

6**pen** *abbr* peninsula

PEN *abbr* International Association of Poets, Playwrights, Editors, Essayists and Novelists

pe•nal \ˈpēn-ᵊl\ *adj* ◆ **:** of or relating to punishment

◆ corrective, disciplinary, punitive

pe•nal•ise *chiefly Brit var of* PENALIZE

pe•nal•ize \ˈpēn-ᵊl-ˌīz, ˈpen-\ *vb* **-ized; -iz•ing** ◆ **:** to put a penalty on

◆ castigate, chasten, chastise, correct, discipline, punish

pen•al•ty \ˈpen-ᵊl-tē\ *n, pl* **-ties 1** ◆ **:** punishment for crime or offense **2** ◆ **:** something forfeited when a person fails to do something agreed to **3 :** disadvantage, loss, or hardship due to some action

◆ [1] castigation, chastisement, correction, desert, discipline, nemesis, punishment, wrath ◆ [2] damages, fine, forfeit, mulct

pen•ance \ˈpe-nəns\ *n* **1 :** an act performed to show sorrow or repentance for sin **2 :** a sacrament (as in the Roman Catholic Church) consisting of confession, absolution, and a penance directed by the confessor

pence \ˈpens\ *pl of* PENNY

pen•chant \ˈpen-chənt\ *n* ◆ **:** a strong inclination

◆ bent, devices, disposition, genius, inclination, leaning, partiality, predilection, proclivity, propensity, tendency, turn

1**pen•cil** \ˈpen-səl\ *n* **:** a writing or drawing tool consisting of or containing a slender cylinder of a solid marking substance

2**pencil** *vb* **-ciled** *or* **-cilled; -cil•ing** *or* **-cil•ling :** to draw or write with a pencil

pen•dant *also* **pen•dent** \ˈpen-dənt\ *n* ◆ **:** a hanging ornament

◆ charm

pen•dent *or* **pen•dant** \ˈpen-dənt\ *adj* **:** supported from above **:** SUSPENDED, OVERHANGING

1**pend•ing** \ˈpen-diŋ\ *prep* **1 :** DURING **2 :** while awaiting

2**pending** *adj* **1** ◆ **:** not yet decided **2** ◆ **:** ready to take place **:** IMMINENT

◆ [1] open, undecided, undetermined, unresolved, unsettled *Ant* decided, determined, resolved, settled ◆ [2] coming, forthcoming, imminent, impending, oncoming

pen•du•lous \ˈpen-jə-ləs, -də-\ *adj* ◆ **:** hanging loosely

◆ droopy ◆ dependent

pen•du•lum \-ləm\ *n* **:** a body that swings freely from a fixed point

pe•ne•plain *also* **pe•ne•plane** \ˈpē-ni-ˌplān\ *n* **:** a large almost flat land surface shaped by erosion

pen•e•tra•ble \ˈpe-nə-trə-bəl\ *adj* ◆ **:** capable of being penetrated

◆ passable, permeable, porous *Ant* impassable, impenetrable, impermeable, impervious, nonporous

pen•e•trate \ˈpe-nə-ˌtrāt\ *vb* **-trat•ed; -trat•ing 1** ◆ **:** to enter into **:** PIERCE **2 :** PERMEATE **3 :** to see into **:** UNDERSTAND **4 :** to affect deeply — **pen•e•tra•tion** \ˌpe-nə-ˈtrā-shən\ *n* — **pen•e•tra•tive** \ˈpe-nə-ˌtrā-tiv\ *adj*

◆ access, enter, pierce, probe

pen•e•trat•ing *adj* **1** ◆ **:** having the power of entering, piercing, or pervading ⟨a ∼ shriek⟩ ⟨a ∼ wind⟩ **2 :** ACUTE, DISCERNING ⟨a ∼ look⟩

◆ biting, bitter, cutting, keen, piercing, raw, sharp

pen•guin \ˈpen-gwən, ˈpeŋ-\ *n* **:** any of various erect short-legged flightless seabirds of the southern hemisphere

pen•i•cil•lin \ˌpe-nə-ˈsi-lən\ *n* **:** any of several antibiotics produced by molds or synthetically and used against various bacteria

pen•in•su•la \pə-ˈnin-sə-lə\ *n* ◆ **:** a long narrow portion of land extending out into the water — **pen•in•su•lar** \-lər\ *adj*

◆ arm, cape, headland, point, promontory, spit

pe•nis \ˈpē-nəs\ *n, pl* **pe•nis•es** *also* **pe•nes** \-ˌnēz\ **:** a male organ of copulation that in the human male also functions as the channel by which urine leaves the body

pen•i•tence \ˈpe-nə-təns\ *n* ◆ **:** the quality or state of being penitent

◆ contrition, guilt, remorse, repentance, self-reproach, shame

1**pen•i•tent** \ˈpe-nə-tənt\ *adj* ◆ **:** feeling sorrow for sins or offenses **:** REPENTANT — **pen•i•ten•tial** \ˌpe-nə-ˈten-chəl\ *adj*

◆ apologetic, contrite, regretful, remorseful, repentant, rueful, sorry

2**penitent** *n* **:** a penitent person

1**pen•i•ten•tia•ry** \ˌpe-nə-ˈten-chə-rē\ *n, pl* **-ries** ◆ **:** a state or federal prison

◆ brig, hoosegow, jail, jug, lockup, pen, prison

2**penitentiary** *adj* **:** of, relating to, or incurring confinement in a penitentiary

pen•knife \ˈpen-ˌnīf\ *n* **:** a small pocketknife

pen•light *also* **pen•lite** \-ˌlīt\ *n* **:** a small flashlight resembling a fountain pen in size or shape

pen•man \ˈpen-mən\ *n* **1 :** COPYIST **2 :** one skilled in penmanship **3 :** AUTHOR

pen•man•ship \-ˌship\ *n* **1** ◆ **:** the art or practice of writing with the pen **2** ◆ **:** quality or style of handwriting

◆ handwriting, manuscript, script

Penn *or* **Penna** *abbr* Pennsylvania

pen name *n* **:** an author's pseudonym

pen•nant \ˈpe-nənt\ *n* **1** ◆ **:** a tapering flag used especially for signaling **2 :** a flag symbolic of championship

◆ banner, colors (*or* colours), ensign, flag, jack, standard, streamer

pen•ne \ˈpe-nā\ *n* **:** short diagonally cut tubular pasta

pen•ni•less \ˈpe-ni-ləs\ *adj* ◆ **:** destitute of money

◆ broke, destitute, impecunious, indigent, needy, penurious, poor, poverty-stricken

pen•non \ˈpe-nən\ *n* **1 :** a long narrow ribbonlike flag borne on a lance **2 :** WING

Penn•syl•va•nian \ˌpen-səl-ˈvā-nyən\ *adj* **1 :** of or relating to Pennsylvania or its people **2 :** of, relating to, or being the period of the Paleozoic era between the Mississippian and the Permian — **Pennsylvanian** *n*

pen•ny \ˈpe-nē\ *n, pl* **pennies** \-nēz\ *or* **pence** \ˈpens\ **1 :** a British monetary unit formerly equal to $^1/_{12}$ shilling but now equal to $^1/_{100}$ pound; *also* **:** a coin of this value **2** *pl* **pennies :** a cent of the U.S. or Canada

pen•ny–pinch•ing \ˈpe-nē-ˌpin-chiŋ\ *n* : PARSIMONY — **pen•ny–pinch•er** *n* — **penny–pinching** *adj*
pen•ny•weight \-ˌwāt\ *n* : a unit of troy weight equal to 1/20 troy ounce
pen•ny–wise \-ˌwīz\ *adj* : wise or prudent only in small matters
pe•nol•o•gy \pi-ˈnä-lə-jē\ *n* : a branch of criminology dealing with prisons and the treatment of offenders
¹pen•sion \ˈpen-chən\ *n* : a fixed sum paid regularly especially to a person retired from service
²pension *vb* : to pay a pension to — **pen•sion•er** *n*
pen•sive \ˈpen-siv\ *adj* ♦ : musingly, dreamily, or sadly thoughtful — **pen•sive•ly** *adv*

♦ contemplative, meditative, melancholy, reflective, ruminant, thoughtful

pen•stock \ˈpen-ˌstäk\ *n* **1** : a sluice or gate for regulating a flow **2** ♦ : a pipe for carrying water

♦ channel, conduit, duct, leader, line, pipe, tube

pent \ˈpent\ *adj* : shut up : CONFINED
pen•ta•gon \ˈpen-tə-ˌgän\ *n* : a polygon of five angles and five sides — **pen•tag•o•nal** \pen-ˈta-gən-ᵊl\ *adj*
pen•tam•e•ter \pen-ˈta-mə-tər\ *n* : a line of verse containing five metrical feet
pen•tath•lon \pen-ˈtath-lən\ *n* : a composite athletic contest consisting of five events
Pen•te•cost \ˈpen-ti-ˌkȯst\ *n* : the 7th Sunday after Easter observed as a church festival commemorating the descent of the Holy Spirit on the apostles — **Pen•te•cos•tal** \ˌpen-ti-ˈkäst-ᵊl\ *adj*
Pentecostal *n* : a member of a Christian religious body that stresses expressive worship, evangelism, and spiritual gifts — **Pen•te•cos•tal•ism** \ˌpen-ti-ˈkäst-ᵊl-ˌi-zəm\ *n*
pent•house \ˈpent-ˌhau̇s\ *n* **1** : a shed or sloping roof attached to a wall or building **2** : an apartment built on the roof of a building **3** ♦ : a smaller structure joined to a building

♦ addition, annex, extension

pen•ul•ti•mate \pi-ˈnəl-tə-mət\ *adj* : next to the last ⟨∼ syllable⟩
pen•um•bra \pə-ˈnəm-brə\ *n, pl* **-brae** \-(ˌ)brē\ *or* **-bras** : the partial shadow surrounding a complete shadow (as in an eclipse)
pe•nu•ri•ous \pə-ˈnu̇r-ē-əs, -ˈnyu̇r-\ *adj* **1** ♦ : marked by or suffering from penury **2** ♦ : given to or marked by extreme stinting frugality

♦ [1] broke, destitute, impecunious, indigent, needy, penniless, poor, poverty-stricken ♦ [2] cheap, close, mean, niggardly, parsimonious, spare, sparing, stingy, tight, tightfisted, uncharitable

pen•u•ry \ˈpe-nyə-rē\ *n* **1** ♦ : extreme poverty **2** : extreme frugality

♦ beggary, destitution, impecuniousness, impoverishment, indigence, need, pauperism, poverty, want

pe•on \ˈpē-ˌän, -ən\ *n, pl* **peons** *or* **pe•o•nes** \pā-ˈō-nēz\ **1** : a member of the landless laboring class in Spanish America **2** : one bound to service for payment of a debt **3** ♦ : one who does menial or tedious labor — **pe•on•age** \-ə-nij\ *n*

♦ drudge, fag, slave, toiler, worker

pe•o•ny \ˈpē-ə-nē\ *n, pl* **-nies** : any of a genus of chiefly Eurasian plants with large often double red, pink, or white flowers; *also* : the flower
¹peo•ple \ˈpē-pəl\ *n, pl* **people** **1** *pl* : human beings making up a group or linked by a common characteristic or interest **2** *pl* ♦ : human beings — often used in compounds instead of *persons* ⟨sales*people*⟩ **3** *pl* ♦ : the mass of persons in a community : POPULACE; *also* : ELECTORATE ⟨the ∼'*s* choice⟩ **4** *pl* **peoples** ♦ : a body of persons (as a tribe, nation, or race) united by a common culture, sense of kinship, or political organization

♦ [2] folks, humanity, humankind, persons, public, society, world ♦ [3] commoners, herd, masses, mob, masses, plebeians, populace, rank and file ♦ [4] blood, clan, family, folks, house, kin, kindred, kinfolk, line, lineage, race, stock, tribe

²people *vb* **peo•pled; peo•pling** : to supply or fill with or as if with people
¹pep \ˈpep\ *n* ♦ : brisk energy or initiative

♦ dash, energy, life, vigor (*or* vigour), vim, vitality

²pep *vb* **pepped; pep•ping** ♦ : to put pep into : STIMULATE

♦ *usu* **pep up** animate, brace, energize, enliven, fire, invigorate, jazz up, liven up, quicken, stimulate, vitalize, vivify, zip (up)

¹pep•per \ˈpe-pər\ *n* **1** : either of two pungent condiments from the berry (**pep•per•corn** \-ˌkȯrn\) of an Indian climbing plant; *also* : this plant **2** : a plant related to the tomato and widely grown for its hot or mild sweet fruit; *also* : this fruit
²pepper *vb* **pep•pered; pep•per•ing** **1** ♦ : to sprinkle or season with or as if with pepper **2** : to shower with missiles or rapid blows

♦ dot, scatter, sow, spray, sprinkle, strew

pep•per•mint \-ˌmint, -mənt\ *n* : a pungent aromatic mint; *also* : candy flavored with its oil
pep•per•o•ni \ˌpe-pə-ˈrō-nē\ *n* : a highly seasoned beef and pork sausage
pepper spray *n* : a temporarily disabling aerosol that causes irritation and blinding of the eyes and inflammation of the nose, throat, and skin
pep•pery \ˈpe-pə-rē\ *adj* **1** : having the qualities of pepper : PUNGENT, HOT **2** : having a hot temper **3** ♦ : full of or exuding emotion or spirit : FIERY

♦ fiery, high-spirited, mettlesome, spirited, spunky

pep•py \ˈpe-pē\ *adj* ♦ : full of pep

♦ active, animate, animated, brisk, energetic, frisky, gay, jaunty, jazzy, lively, perky, pert, racy, snappy, spirited, sprightly, springy, vital, vivacious

pep•sin \ˈpep-sən\ *n* : an enzyme of the stomach that promotes digestion by breaking down proteins; *also* : a preparation of this used medicinally
pep•tic \ˈpep-tik\ *adj* **1** : relating to or promoting digestion **2** : caused by digestive juices ⟨a ∼ ulcer⟩
Pe•quot \ˈpē-ˌkwät\ *n* : a member of an American Indian people of eastern Connecticut
¹per \ˈpər\ *prep* **1** ♦ : by means of **2** : to or for each **3** : ACCORDING TO

♦ by, through, with

²per *adv* : for each : APIECE
³per *abbr* **1** period **2** person
¹per•ad•ven•ture \ˈpər-əd-ˌven-chər\ *adv, archaic* : PERHAPS
²peradventure *n* **1** : DOUBT **2** : CHANCE 4
per•am•bu•late \pə-ˈram-byə-ˌlāt\ *vb* **-lat•ed; -lat•ing** : to travel over especially on foot
per•am•bu•la•tion \pə-ˌram-byə-ˈlā-shən\ *n* ♦ : an act of walking about : STROLL

♦ ramble, stroll, turn, walk

per•am•bu•la•tor \pə-ˈram-byə-ˌlā-tər\ *n, chiefly Brit* : a baby carriage
per an•num \(ˌ)pər-ˈa-nəm\ *adv* : in or for each year : ANNUALLY
per•cale \(ˌ)pər-ˈkāl, ˈpər-ˌ; (ˌ)pər-ˈkal\ *n* : a fine woven cotton cloth
per cap•i•ta \(ˌ)pər-ˈka-pə-tə\ *adv or adj* : by or for each person
per•ceive \pər-ˈsēv\ *vb* **per•ceived; per•ceiv•ing** **1** ♦ : to attain awareness or understanding of **2** ♦ : to become aware of through the senses — **per•ceiv•able** *adj*

♦ [1] appreciate, apprehend, catch, catch on (to), comprehend, get, grasp, make, make out, notice, see, seize, understand ♦ [2] feel, scent, see, sense, smell, taste

¹per•cent \pər-ˈsent\ *adv* : in each hundred
²percent *n, pl* **percent** *or* **percents** **1** : one part in a hundred : HUNDREDTH **2** : PERCENTAGE
per•cent•age \pər-ˈsen-tij\ *n* **1** : a part of a whole expressed in hundredths **2** : the result obtained by multiplying a number by a percent **3** : ADVANTAGE, PROFIT **4** ♦ : a likelihood based on cumulative statistics : PROBABILITY; *also* : favorable odds

♦ chance, odds, probability

percentage point *n* : one hundredth of a whole ⟨rates rose one *percentage point* from 6.5 to 7.5 percent⟩
per•cen•tile \pər-ˈsen-ˌtīl\ *n* : a value on a scale of one hundred indicating the standing of a score or grade in terms of the percentage of scores or grades falling with or below it
per•cept \ˈpər-ˌsept\ *n* : an impression of an object obtained by use of the senses
per•cep•ti•ble \pər-ˈsep-tə-bəl\ *adj* ♦ : capable of being perceived — **per•cep•ti•bly** \-blē\ *adv*

♦ appreciable, detectable, discernible, distinguishable, palpable, sensible *Ant* impalpable, imperceptible, inappreciable, indistinguishable, insensible

per•cep•tion \pər-ˈsep-shən\ *n* **1** ♦ : an act or result of perceiving **2** : awareness of one's environment through physical sensation **3** ♦ : ability to understand

♦ [1] appreciation, apprehension, comprehension, grasp, grip, understanding ♦ [3] discernment, insight, sagacity, sapience, wisdom

per•cep•tive \pər-ˈsep-tiv\ *adj* ♦ : capable of or exhibiting keen perception — **per•cep•tive•ly** *adv*

♦ acute, delicate, keen, sensitive, sharp ♦ discerning, insightful, sagacious, sage, sapient, wise

per•cep•tu•al \pər-ˈsep-chə-wəl\ *adj* : of, relating to, or involving sensory stimulus as opposed to abstract concept — **per•cep•tu•al•ly** *adv*

¹perch \ˈpərch\ *n* **1** : a roost for a bird **2** : a resting place or vantage point

²perch *vb* **1** ♦ : to alight, settle, or rest on a perch, a height, or a precarious spot **2** ♦ : to place on a perch, a height, or a precarious spot

♦ [1, 2] alight, land, light, roost, settle

³perch *n, pl* **perch** *or* **perch•es** : either of two small freshwater bony fishes used for food; *also* : any of various fishes resembling or related to these

per•chance \pər-ˈchans\ *adv* ♦ : possibly but not certainly : PERHAPS

♦ conceivably, maybe, perhaps, possibly

per•cip•i•ent \pər-ˈsi-pē-ənt\ *adj* : capable of or characterized by perception — **per•cip•i•ence** \-əns\ *n*

per•co•late \ˈpər-kə-ˌlāt\ *vb* **-lat•ed; -lat•ing 1** ♦ : to trickle or filter through a permeable substance **2** : to filter hot water through to extract the essence ⟨~ coffee⟩ **3** ♦ : to spread gradually — **per•co•la•tor** \-ˌlā-tər\ *n*

♦ [1] bleed, exude, ooze, seep, strain, sweat, weep ♦ *usu* **percolate into** [3] permeate, suffuse, transfuse

per con•tra \(ˌ)pər-ˈkän-trə\ *adv* **1** : on the contrary **2** : by way of contrast

per•cus•sion \pər-ˈkə-shən\ *n* **1** : a sharp blow : IMPACT; *esp* : a blow upon a cap (**percussion cap**) designed to explode the charge in a firearm **2** : the beating or striking of a musical instrument; *also* : instruments sounded by striking, shaking, or scraping

per di•em \pər-ˈdē-əm, -ˈdī-\ *adv* : by the day — **per diem** *adj or n*

per•di•tion \pər-ˈdi-shən\ *n* **1** : eternal damnation **2** : HELL

per•du•ra•ble \(ˌ)pər-ˈdu̇r-ə-bəl, -ˈdyu̇r-\ *adj* : very durable — **per•du•ra•bil•i•ty** \-ˌdu̇r-ə-ˈbi-lə-tē, -ˌdyu̇r-\ *n*

per•e•gri•na•tion \ˌper-ə-grə-ˈnā-shən\ *n* ♦ : a traveling about especially on foot

♦ expedition, journey, passage, trek, trip

per•e•grine falcon \ˈper-ə-grən, -grēn\ *n* : a swift nearly cosmopolitan falcon that often nests in cities and is often used in falconry

pe•remp•to•ry \pə-ˈremp-tə-rē\ *adj* **1** : barring a right of action or delay **2** ♦ : expressive of urgency or command : IMPERATIVE **3** ♦ : marked by arrogant self-assurance — **pe•remp•to•ri•ly** \-tə-rə-lē\ *adv*

♦ [2] compulsory, imperative, incumbent, involuntary, mandatory, necessary, nonelective, obligatory ♦ [3] arrogant, cavalier, domineering, haughty, high-handed, high-hat, imperious, important, lofty, lordly, masterful, overbearing, overweening, pompous, presumptuous, pretentious, supercilious, superior

¹pe•ren•ni•al \pə-ˈre-nē-əl\ *adj* **1** : present at all seasons of the year ⟨~ streams⟩ **2** : continuing to live from year to year ⟨~ plants⟩ **3** ♦ : existing or continuing a long while : ENDURING **4** : recurring regularly : PERMANENT ⟨~ problems⟩ — **pe•ren•ni•al•ly** *adv*

♦ abiding, ageless, continuing, dateless, enduring, eternal, everlasting, immortal, imperishable, perennial, perpetual, timeless, undying

²perennial *n* : a perennial plant

perf *abbr* **1** perfect **2** perforated

¹per•fect \ˈpər-fikt\ *adj* **1** ♦ : being without fault or defect **2** : EXACT, PRECISE **3** ♦ : lacking in no essential detail : COMPLETE **4** : relating to or being a verb tense that expresses an action or state completed at the time of speaking or at a time spoken of **5** : being completely or exactly what is stated — **per•fect•ness** *n*

♦ [1] absolute, faultless, flawless, ideal, impeccable, letter-perfect, unblemished *Ant* bad, defective, faulty, imperfect ♦ [3] complete, comprehensive, entire, full, grand, intact, integral, plenary, total, whole

²per•fect \pər-ˈfekt\ *vb* **1** ♦ : to bring to final form **2** ♦ : to make perfect : IMPROVE

♦ [1] complete, consummate, finalize, finish ♦ [2] ameliorate, amend, better, enhance, enrich, improve, refine

³per•fect \ˈpər-fikt\ *n* : the perfect tense; *also* : a verb form in it

per•fect•ible \pər-ˈfek-tə-bəl, ˈpər-fik-\ *adj* : capable of improvement or perfection — **per•fect•ibil•i•ty** \pər-ˌfek-tə-ˈbi-lə-tē, ˌpər-fik-\ *n*

per•fec•tion \pər-ˈfek-shən\ *n* **1** : the quality or state of being perfect **2** : the highest degree of excellence **3** : the act or process of perfecting **4** ♦ : an exemplification of supreme excellence

♦ beau ideal, classic, epitome, exemplar, ideal, quintessence

per•fec•tion•ist \-shə-nist\ *n* : a person who will not accept or be content with anything less than perfection

per•fect•ly \ˈpər-fik(t)-lē\ *adv* **1** ♦ : in a perfect manner **2** ♦ : to a complete or adequate extent

♦ [1] faultlessly, flawlessly, ideally, impeccably *Ant* badly, faultily, imperfectly ♦ [2] altogether, completely, dead, entirely, fast, flat, full, fully, quite, thoroughly, well, wholly

per•fec•to \pər-ˈfek-tō\ *n, pl* **-tos** : a cigar that is thick in the middle and tapers almost to a point at each end

per•fid•i•ous \pər-ˈfi-dē-əs\ *adj* ♦ : of, relating to, or characterized by perfidy — **per•fid•i•ous•ly** *adv*

♦ disloyal, faithless, false, fickle, inconstant, loose, recreant, traitorous, treacherous, unfaithful, untrue

per•fi•dy \ˈpər-fə-dē\ *n, pl* **-dies** ♦ : violation of faith or loyalty

♦ betrayal, disloyalty, faithlessness, falseness, falsity, inconstancy, infidelity, treachery, unfaithfulness

per•fo•rate \ˈpər-fə-ˌrāt\ *vb* **-rat•ed; -rat•ing** ♦ : to bore through : PIERCE; *esp* : to make a line of holes in to facilitate separation

♦ bore, drill, hole, pierce, punch, puncture

per•fo•ra•tion \ˌpər-fə-ˈrā-shən\ *n* **1** : the act or process of perforating **2 a** ♦ : a hole or pattern made by or as if by piercing or boring **b** : one of the series of holes (as between rows of postage stamps) in a sheet that serve as an aid in separation

♦ hole, pinhole, prick, punch, puncture, stab

per•force \pər-ˈfōrs\ *adv* ♦ : of necessity

♦ inevitably, necessarily, needs, unavoidably

per•form \pər-ˈfȯrm\ *vb* **1** : to adhere to the terms of : FULFILL **2** ♦ : to bring to a successful issue : CARRY OUT **3** ♦ : to carry out an action or pattern of behavior : FUNCTION **4** : to do in a set manner **5** ♦ : to give a performance (of) — **per•form•er** *n*

♦ [2] accomplish, achieve, carry out, commit, compass, do, execute, follow through, fulfill, make ♦ [3] act, function, operate, take, work ♦ [5] act, impersonate, play, portray

per•for•mance \pər-ˈfȯr-ˌməns\ *n* **1** ♦ : the act or process of performing **2** : DEED, FEAT **3** : a public presentation

♦ accomplishment, achievement, commission, discharge, enactment, execution, fulfillment, implementation, perpetration

¹per•fume \pər-ˈfyüm, ˈpər-ˌfyüm\ *n* **1** ♦ : a usually pleasant odor : FRAGRANCE **2** : a preparation used for scenting

♦ aroma, bouquet, fragrance, incense, redolence, scent, spice

²per•fume \pər-ˈfyüm, ˈpər-ˌfyüm\ *vb* **per•fumed; per•fum•ing** : SCENT

per•fum•ery \ˌpər-ˈfyü-mə-rē\ *n, pl* **-er•ies 1** : the art or process of making perfume **2** : PERFUMES **3** : an establishment where perfumes are made

per•func•to•ry \pər-ˈfəŋk-tə-rē\ *adj* **1** : done merely as a duty **2** ♦ : lacking in interest or enthusiasm — **per•func•to•ri•ly** *adv*

♦ apathetic, casual, disinterested, indifferent, insouciant, nonchalant, unconcerned, uncurious, uninterested

per•go•la \ˈpər-gə-lə\ *n* : a structure consisting of posts supporting an open roof in the form of a trellis

perh *abbr* perhaps

per•haps \pər-ˈhaps\ *adv* ♦ : possibly but not certainly

♦ conceivably, maybe, perchance, possibly

per•i•gee \ˈper-ə-ˌjē\ *n* : the point at which an orbiting object is nearest the body (as the earth) being orbited

peri•he•lion \ˌper-ə-ˈhēl-yən\ *n, pl* **-he•lia** \-ˈhēl-yə\ : the point in the path of a celestial body (as a planet) that is nearest to the sun

per·il \ˈper-əl\ *n* **1** ♦ **:** exposure to the risk of being injured, destroyed, or lost **2** ♦ **:** something that imperils

♦ danger, hazard, menace, pitfall, risk, threat, trouble

per·il·ous \ˈpər-ə-ləs\ *adj* ♦ **:** full of or involving peril — **per·il·ous·ly** *adv*

♦ dangerous, grave, grievous, hazardous, menacing, parlous, risky, serious, unhealthy, unsafe, venturesome

pe·rim·e·ter \pə-ˈri-mə-tər\ *n* **1 :** the boundary of a closed plane figure; *also* **:** its length **2** ♦ **:** a line bounding or protecting an area

♦ border, bound, boundary, confines, edge, periphery

peri·na·tal \ˌper-ə-ˈnā-tᵊl\ *adj* **:** occurring in, concerned with, or being in the period around the time of birth ⟨∼ care⟩

1pe·ri·od \ˈpir-ē-əd\ *n* **1 :** SENTENCE; *also* **:** the full pause closing the utterance of a sentence **2 :** END, STOP **3 :** a punctuation mark . used especially to mark the end of a declarative sentence or an abbreviation **4** ♦ **:** an extent of time; *esp* **:** one regarded as a stage or division in a process or development **5 :** a portion of time in which a recurring phenomenon completes one cycle and is ready to begin again **6 :** a single cyclic occurrence of menstruation

♦ age, epoch, era, time

2period *adj* **:** of or relating to a particular historical period ⟨∼ furniture⟩

pe·ri·od·ic \ˌpir-ē-ˈä-dik\ *adj* **1** ♦ **:** occurring at regular intervals of time **2** ♦ **:** happening repeatedly from time to time **3 :** of or relating to a sentence that has no trailing elements following full grammatical statement of the essential idea

♦ [1] constant, frequent, habitual, regular, repeated, steady ♦ [2] continual, intermittent, recurrent

1pe·ri·od·i·cal \ˌpir-ē-ˈä-di-kəl\ *adj* **1 :** ocurring or recurring at regular intervals or from time to time **:** PERIODIC **2 :** published with a fixed interval between the issues or numbers **3 :** of or relating to a periodical — **pe·ri·od·i·cal·ly** \-k(ə-)lē\ *adv*

2periodical *n* **:** a periodical publication

periodic table *n* **:** an arrangement of chemical elements based on their atomic structure and on their properties

peri·odon·tal \ˌper-ē-ō-ˈdänt-ᵊl\ *adj* **1 :** surrounding a tooth **2 :** of or affecting periodontal tissues or regions

per·i·pa·tet·ic \ˌper-ə-pə-ˈte-tik\ *adj* ♦ **:** performed or performing while moving about **:** ITINERANT

♦ errant, itinerant, nomad, roaming, vagabond, vagrant

1pe·riph·er·al \pə-ˈri-fə-rəl\ *adj* **1 :** of, relating to, involving, or forming a periphery or surface part **2** ♦ **:** added or serving as a supplement

♦ accessory, auxiliary, supplementary

2pe·riph·er·al *n* **:** a device connected to a computer to provide communication or auxiliary functions

peripheral nervous system *n* **:** the part of the nervous system that is outside the central nervous system and comprises the spinal nerves, the cranial nerves except the one supplying the retina, and the autonomic nervous system

pe·riph·ery \pə-ˈri-fə-rē\ *n, pl* **-er·ies 1 :** the boundary of a rounded figure **2** ♦ **:** outward bounds **:** border area

♦ border, bound, boundary, circumference, compass, confines, edge, end, fringe, margin, perimeter, rim, skirt, verge

pe·riph·ra·sis \pə-ˈri-frə-səs\ *n, pl* **-ra·ses** \-ˌsēz\ **:** CIRCUMLOCUTION

peri·scope \ˈper-ə-ˌskōp\ *n* **:** a tubular optical instrument enabling an observer to see an otherwise blocked field of view

per·ish \ˈper-ish\ *vb* ♦ **:** to become destroyed or ruined; *esp* **:** to have one's life come to an end

♦ decease, depart, die, expire, pass, pass away, succumb

per·ish·able \ˈper-i-shə-bəl\ *adj* **:** easily spoiled ⟨∼ foods⟩ — **perishable** *n*

peri·stal·sis \ˌper-ə-ˈstȯl-səs, -ˈstal-\ *n, pl* **-stal·ses :** waves of contraction passing along the walls of a hollow muscular organ (as the intestine) and forcing its contents onward — **per·i·stal·tic** \-ˈstȯl-tik, -ˈstal-\ *adj*

peri·style \ˈper-ə-ˌstīl\ *n* **:** a row of columns surrounding a building or court

peri·to·ne·um \ˌper-ə-tə-ˈnē-əm\ *n, pl* **-ne·ums** *or* **-nea :** the smooth transparent serous membrane that lines the cavity of the abdomen — **peri·to·ne·al** \-ˈnē-əl\ *adj*

peri·to·ni·tis \ˌper-ə-tə-ˈnī-təs\ *n* **:** inflammation of the peritoneum

peri·wig \ˈper-i-ˌwig\ *n* **:** WIG

1per·i·win·kle \ˈper-i-ˌwiŋ-kəl\ *n* **:** a usually blue-flowered creeping plant cultivated as a ground cover

2periwinkle *n* **:** any of various small edible seashore snails

per·ju·ry \ˈpər-jə-rē\ *n* **:** the voluntary violation of an oath to tell the truth **:** lying under oath — **per·jure** \ˈpər-jər\ *vb* — **per·jur·er** *n*

1perk \ˈpərk\ *vb* **1 :** to thrust (as the head) up impudently or jauntily **2 :** to regain vigor or spirit **3 :** to make trim or brisk **:** FRESHEN

2perk *vb* **:** PERCOLATE

3perk *n* **:** PERQUISITE — usually used in plural

perky \ˈpər-kē\ *adj* ♦ **:** sprightly in manner or appearance

♦ active, animate, animated, brisk, energetic, frisky, gay, jaunty, lively, peppy, spirited, sprightly, springy

per·lite \ˈpər-ˌlīt\ *n* **:** volcanic glass that when expanded by heat forms a lightweight material used especially in concrete and plaster and for potting plants

1perm \ˈpərm\ *n* **:** PERMANENT

2perm *vb* **:** to give (hair) a permanent

3perm *abbr* permanent

per·ma·frost \ˈpər-mə-ˌfrȯst\ *n* **:** a permanently frozen layer below the surface in frigid regions of a planet

1per·ma·nent \ˈpər-mə-nənt\ *adj* ♦ **:** continuing or enduring without fundamental or marked change — **per·ma·nence** \-nəns\ *n* — **per·ma·nen·cy** \-nən-sē\ *n*

♦ ceaseless, dateless, deathless, endless, eternal, everlasting, immortal, perpetual, undying, unending

2permanent *n* **:** a long-lasting hair wave or straightening

per·ma·nent·ly \-lē\ *adv* ♦ **:** in a permanent manner

♦ always, eternally, ever, everlastingly, forever, perpetually

permanent press *n* **:** the process of treating fabrics with chemicals (as resin) and heat for setting the shape and for aiding wrinkle resistance

per·me·able \ˈpər-mē-ə-bəl\ *adj* ♦ **:** having small openings that permit liquids or gases to seep through — **per·me·a·bil·i·ty** \ˌpər-mē-ə-ˈbi-lə-tē\ *n*

♦ passable, penetrable, porous

per·me·ate \ˈpər-mē-ˌāt\ *vb* **-at·ed; -at·ing 1** ♦ **:** to spread or diffuse through **:** PERVADE **2 :** to seep through the pores of **:** PENETRATE — **per·me·ation** \ˌpər-mē-ˈā-shən\ *n*

♦ percolate, suffuse, transfuse

Perm·ian \ˈpər-mē-ən\ *adj* **:** of, relating to, or being the latest period of the Paleozoic era — **Permian** *n*

per·mis·si·ble \pər-ˈmi-sə-bəl\ *adj* ♦ **:** that may be permitted **:** ALLOWABLE

♦ admissible, allowable, sufferable ***Ant*** banned, barred, forbidden, impermissible, interdicted, prohibited, proscribed

per·mis·sion \pər-ˈmi-shən\ *n* ♦ **:** formal consent **:** AUTHORIZATION

♦ allowance, authorization, clearance, concurrence, consent, leave, license (*or* licence), sanction, sufferance ***Ant*** interdiction, prohibition, proscription

per·mis·sive \pər-ˈmi-siv\ *adj* **:** granting permission; *esp* **:** INDULGENT — **per·mis·sive·ly** *adv* — **per·mis·sive·ness** *n*

1per·mit \pər-ˈmit\ *vb* **per·mit·ted; per·mit·ting 1** ♦ **:** to consent to **:** ALLOW ⟨∼ access⟩ **2** ♦ **:** to make possible **3** ♦ **:** to give leave ⟨∼ him to go⟩

♦ allow, have, let, suffer

2per·mit \ˈpər-ˌmit, pər-ˈmit\ *n* **:** a written permission **:** LICENSE

per·mu·ta·tion \ˌpər-myu̇-ˈtā-shən\ *n* **1 :** a major or fundamental change **2 :** the act or process of changing the order of an ordered set of objects

per·ni·cious \pər-ˈni-shəs\ *adj* ♦ **:** very destructive or injurious — **per·ni·cious·ly** *adv*

♦ adverse, bad, baleful, baneful, damaging, deleterious, detrimental, evil, harmful, hurtful, ill, injurious, mischievous, noxious, prejudicial

per·ora·tion \ˈper-ə-ˌrā-shən, ˈpər-\ *n* **:** the concluding part of a speech

1per·ox·ide \pə-ˈräk-ˌsīd\ *n* **:** an oxide containing a large proportion of oxygen; *esp* **:** HYDROGEN PEROXIDE

2peroxide *vb* **-id·ed; -id·ing :** to bleach with hydrogen peroxide

perp *abbr* **1** perpendicular **2** perpetrator

per•pen•dic•u•lar \ˌpər-pən-ˈdi-kyə-lər\ *adj* **1** ♦ **:** standing at right angles to the plane of the horizon **2 :** forming a right angle with each other or with a given line or plane — **perpendicular** *n* — **per•pen•dic•u•lar•i•ty** \-ˌdi-kyə-ˈlar-ə-tē\ *n* — **per•pen•dic•u•lar•ly** *adv*

♦ erect, standing, upright, upstanding, vertical

per•pe•trate \ˈpər-pə-ˌtrāt\ *vb* **-trat•ed; -trat•ing :** to carry out (as a crime) **:** COMMIT — **per•pe•tra•tor** \ˈpər-pə-ˌtrā-tər\ *n*
per•pe•tra•tion \ˌpər-pə-ˈtrā-shən\ *n* ♦ **:** the act or process of perpetrating

♦ accomplishment, achievement, commission, discharge, enactment, execution, fulfillment, implementation, performance

per•pet•u•al \pər-ˈpe-chə-wəl\ *adj* **1** ♦ **:** continuing forever **:** EVERLASTING **2 :** occurring continually **:** CONSTANT ⟨~ annoyance⟩

♦ ceaseless, dateless, deathless, endless, eternal, everlasting, immortal, permanent, undying, unending

per•pet•u•al•ly \pər-ˈpe-chə-wə-lē\ *adv* **1** ♦ **:** for a limitless time **2** ♦ **:** at all times **:** CONTINUALLY

♦ [1] always, eternally, ever, everlastingly, forever, permanently ♦ [2] always, constantly, continually, ever, forever, incessantly, invariably, unfailingly

per•pet•u•ate \pər-ˈpe-chə-ˌwāt\ *vb* **-at•ed; -at•ing :** to make perpetual **:** cause to last indefinitely — **per•pet•u•a•tion** \-ˌpe-chə-ˈwā-shən\ *n*
per•pe•tu•i•ty \ˌpər-pə-ˈtü-ə-tē, -ˈtyü-\ *n, pl* **-ties 1 :** ETERNITY 1 **2 :** the quality or state of being perpetual
per•plex \pər-ˈpleks\ *vb* ♦ **:** to disturb mentally; *esp* **:** CONFUSE

♦ addle, baffle, befog, befuddle, bemuse, bewilder, confound, confuse, disorient, muddle, muddy, mystify, puzzle

per•plexed \-ˈplekst\ *adj* **1 :** filled with uncertainty **:** PUZZLED **2 :** full of difficulty **:** COMPLICATED — **per•plexed•ly** \-ˈplek-səd-lē\ *adv*
per•plex•i•ty \pər-ˈplek-sə-tē\ *n* ♦ **:** the state of being perplexed

♦ bafflement, bewilderment, confusion, distraction, muddle, mystification, puzzlement, whirl

per•qui•site \ˈpər-kwə-zət\ *n* ♦ **:** a privilege or profit beyond regular pay

♦ bonus, dividend, extra, lagniappe, tip

pers *abbr* person; personal
¹per se \(ˌ)pər-ˈsā\ *adv* **:** by, of, or in itself **:** as such
²per se *adj* **:** being such inherently, clearly, or as a matter of law
per•se•cute \ˈpər-si-ˌkyüt\ *vb* **-cut•ed; -cut•ing** ♦ **:** to pursue in such a way as to injure or afflict **:** HARASS; *esp* **:** to cause to suffer because of belief — **per•se•cu•tion** \ˌpər-si-ˈkyü-shən\ *n*

♦ afflict, agonize, bedevil, curse, harrow, martyr, plague, rack, torment, torture ♦ aggravate, annoy, bother, bug, chafe, exasperate, gall, get, grate, irk, irritate, nettle, peeve, pique, put out, rasp, rile, vex

per•se•cu•tor \ˈpər-si-ˌkyü-tər\ *n* ♦ **:** one that persecutes

♦ heckler, oppressor, taunter, tormentor, torturer ♦ annoyance, bother, gadfly, nuisance, pest, tease

per•se•vere \ˌpər-sə-ˈvir\ *vb* **-vered; -ver•ing :** to persist (as in an undertaking) in spite of difficulties — **per•se•ver•ance** \-ˈvir-əns\ *n*
persevering *adj* ♦ **:** of or characterized by perseverance

♦ dogged, insistent, patient, persistent, pertinacious, tenacious

Per•sian \ˈpər-zhən\ *n* **1 :** a native or inhabitant of ancient Persia **2 :** a member of one of the peoples of modern Iran **3 :** the language of the Persians
Persian cat *n* **:** any of a breed of stocky round-headed domestic cats that have a long silky coat
Persian lamb *n* **:** a pelt with very silky tightly curled fur that is obtained from newborn lambs which are older than those yielding broadtail
per•si•flage \ˈpər-si-ˌfläzh, ˈper-\ *n* ♦ **:** lightly jesting or mocking talk

♦ banter, chaff, raillery, repartee

per•sim•mon \pər-ˈsi-mən\ *n* **:** either of two trees related to the ebony; *also* **:** the edible usually orange or red plumlike fruit of a persimmon
per•sist \pər-ˈsist, -ˈzist\ *vb* **1 :** to go on resolutely or stubbornly in spite of difficulties **2** ♦ **:** to continue to exist

♦ abide, continue, endure, hold, keep up, last, run on

per•sis•tence \pər-ˈsis-təns, -ˈzis-\ *n* **1** ♦ **:** the action or fact of persisting **2 :** the quality or state of being persistent — **per•sis•ten•cy** \-tən-sē\ *n*

♦ continuance, continuation, duration, endurance, subsistence

per•sis•tent \pər-ˈsis-tənt\ *adj* **1** ♦ **:** continuing or inclined to persist in a course **2 :** continuing to exist in spite of interference or treatment ⟨a ~ cough⟩ — **per•sis•tent•ly** *adv*

♦ dogged, insistent, patient, persevering, pertinacious, tenacious

per•snick•e•ty \pər-ˈsni-kə-tē\ *adj* **:** fussy about small details
per•son \ˈpər-sən\ *n* **1** ♦ **:** a human being **:** INDIVIDUAL — used in combination especially by those who prefer to avoid *man* in compounds applicable to both sexes ⟨chair*person*⟩ **2 :** one of the three modes of being in the Godhead as understood by Trinitarians **3 :** the body of a human being **4 :** the individual personality of a human being **:** SELF **5 :** reference of a segment of discourse to the speaker, to one spoken to, or to one spoken of especially as indicated by certain pronouns

♦ being, body, creature, human, individual, man, mortal ♦ **persons** folks, humanity, humankind, people, public, society, world

per•so•na \pər-ˈsō-nə\ *n, pl* **-nae** \-nē\ *or* **-nas :** the personality that a person projects in public
per•son•able \ˈpər-sə-nə-bəl\ *adj* **:** pleasant in person **:** ATTRACTIVE
per•son•age \ˈpər-sə-nij\ *n* ♦ **:** a person of rank, note, or distinction

♦ celebrity, figure, light, luminary, notable, personality, somebody, standout, star, superstar, VIP

¹per•son•al \ˈpər-sə-nəl\ *adj* **1** ♦ **:** of, relating to, or affecting a person **:** PRIVATE ⟨~ correspondence⟩ **2 :** done in person ⟨a ~ inquiry⟩ **3 :** relating to the person or body ⟨~ injuries⟩ **4 :** relating to an individual especially in an offensive way ⟨resented such ~ remarks⟩ **5 :** of or relating to temporary or movable property as distinguished from real estate **6 :** denoting grammatical person **7 :** intended for use by one person

♦ individual, particular, peculiar, private, separate, singular, unique

²personal *n* **1 :** a short newspaper paragraph relating to a person or group or to personal matters **2 :** a short personal or private communication in the classified ads section of a newspaper
personal computer *n* **:** a computer with a microprocessor designed for an individual user to run especially commercial software
personal digital assistant *n* **:** PDA
per•son•al•ise *chiefly Brit var of* PERSONALIZE
per•son•al•i•ty \ˌpər-sə-ˈna-lə-tē\ *n, pl* **-ties 1 :** an offensively personal remark ⟨indulges in *personalities*⟩ **2** ♦ **:** the collection of emotional and behavioral traits that characterize a person **3 :** distinction of personal and social traits **4** ♦ **:** a well-known person ⟨a TV ~⟩

♦ [2] character, identity, individuality, self-identity ♦ [4] celebrity, figure, light, luminary, notable, personage, somebody, standout, star, superstar, VIP

per•son•al•ize \ˈpər-sə-nə-ˌlīz\ *vb* **-ized; -iz•ing 1 :** to conceive of or represent as a person or as having human qualities or powers **2 :** to make personal or individual; *esp* **:** to mark as belonging to a particular person
per•son•al•ly \-nə-lē\ *adv* **1 :** in person **2 :** as a person **3 :** as far as oneself is concerned
per•son•al•ty \ˈpər-sə-nəl-tē\ *n, pl* **-ties** ♦ **:** personal property

♦ belongings, chattels, effects, holdings, paraphernalia, possessions, things

per•so•na non gra•ta \pər-ˈsō-nə-ˌnän-ˈgra-tə, -ˈgrä-\ *adj* **:** being personally unacceptable or unwelcome
per•son•ate \ˈpər-sə-ˌnāt\ *vb* **-at•ed; -at•ing :** IMPERSONATE, REPRESENT
per•son•i•fi•ca•tion \pər-ˌsä-nə-fə-ˈkā-shən\ *n* ♦ **:** a visible representation of something abstract (as a quality)

♦ embodiment, epitome, incarnation, manifestation

per•son•i•fy \pər-ˈsä-nə-ˌfī\ *vb* **-fied; -fy•ing 1** ♦ **:** to think of or represent as a person **2** ♦ **:** to be the embodiment of **:** INCARNATE ⟨~ the law⟩

♦ [1, 2] embody, epitomize, manifest, materialize, substantiate

per•son•nel \ˌpər-sə-ˈnel\ *n* ♦ **:** a body of persons employed

♦ force, help, pool, staff

per•spec•tive \pər-ˈspek-tiv\ *n* **1 :** the science of painting and drawing so that objects represented have apparent depth and distance **2** ♦ **:** the aspect in which a subject or its parts are mentally viewed; *esp* **:** a view of things (as objects or events) in their true relationship or relative importance

♦ angle, outlook, point of view, slant, standpoint, viewpoint

per•spi•ca•cious \ˌpər-spə-ˈkā-shəs\ *adj* **:** having or showing keen understanding or discernment — **per•spi•cac•i•ty** \-ˈka-sə-tē\ *n*

per•spi•cu•i•ty \ˌpər-spə-ˈkyü-ə-tē\ *n* ♦ **:** the quality or state of being clear to the understanding

♦ clarity, explicitness, lucidity, simplicity

per•spic•u•ous \pər-ˈspi-kyə-wəs\ *adj* ♦ **:** plain to the understanding

♦ apparent, broad, clear, clear-cut, distinct, evident, lucid, manifest, obvious, palpable, patent, plain, transparent, unambiguous, unequivocal, unmistakable

per•spire \pər-ˈspīr\ *vb* **per•spired; per•spir•ing :** SWEAT — **per•spi•ra•tion** \ˌpər-spə-ˈrā-shən\ *n*

per•suade \pər-ˈswād\ *vb* **per•suad•ed; per•suad•ing** ♦ **:** to win over to a belief or course of action by argument or entreaty

♦ argue, convince, get, induce, move, prevail, satisfy, talk, win

per•sua•sion \pər-ˈswā-zhən\ *n* **1** ♦ **:** the act or process of persuading **2** ♦ **:** a system of religious beliefs; *also* **:** a group holding such beliefs **3** ♦ **:** an opinion held with complete assurance

♦ [1] convincing, inducement ♦ [2] creed, cult, faith, religion ♦ [3] belief, conviction, eye, feeling, judgment (*or* judgement), mind, notion, opinion, sentiment, verdict, view

per•sua•sive \pər-ˈswā-siv, -ziv\ *adj* ♦ **:** tending to persuade — **per•sua•sive•ly** *adv*

♦ cogent, compelling, conclusive, convincing, decisive, effective, forceful, satisfying, strong, telling

per•sua•sive•ness \-nəs\ *n* ♦ **:** the quality or state of being persuasive

♦ cogency, effectiveness, force

pert \ˈpərt\ *adj* **1** ♦ **:** saucily free and forward **2 :** stylishly trim **:** JAUNTY **3 :** briskly alert and energetic **:** LIVELY

♦ facetious, flip, flippant, smart

per•tain \pər-ˈtān\ *vb* **1 :** to belong to as a part, quality, or function ⟨duties ∼*ing* to the office⟩ **2** ♦ **:** to have reference **:** RELATE ⟨books ∼*ing* to birds⟩

♦ appertain, apply, bear, refer, relate ♦ *usu* **pertain to** concern, cover, deal, treat

per•ti•na•cious \ˌpər-tə-ˈnā-shəs\ *adj* **1** ♦ **:** holding resolutely to an opinion or purpose **2** ♦ **:** obstinately persistent ⟨a ∼ bill collector⟩

♦ [1] dogged, hardheaded, headstrong, mulish, obdurate, obstinate, opinionated, peevish, perverse, pigheaded, stubborn, unyielding, willful ♦ [2] dogged, insistent, patient, persevering, persistent, tenacious

per•ti•nac•i•ty \ˌpər-tə-ˈna-sə-tē\ *n* ♦ **:** the quality or state of being pertinacious

♦ hardheadedness, mulishness, obduracy, obstinacy, peevishness, self-will, stubbornness, tenacity

per•ti•nence \ˈpərt-ᵊn-əns\ *n* ♦ **:** the quality or state of being pertinent

♦ applicability, bearing, connection, relevance *Ant* irrelevance

per•ti•nent \ˈpərt-ᵊn-ənt\ *adj* ♦ **:** relating to the matter under consideration

♦ applicable, apposite, apropos, germane, material, pointed, relative, relevant *Ant* extraneous, immaterial, inapplicable, irrelevant, pointless

per•turb \pər-ˈtərb\ *vb* ♦ **:** to disturb greatly especially in mind **:** UPSET

♦ agitate, bother, concern, discompose, disquiet, distress, disturb, exercise, freak out, undo, unhinge, unsettle, upset, worry

per•tur•ba•tion \ˌpər-tər-ˈbā-shən\ *n* ♦ **:** the action of perturbing **:** the state of being perturbed

♦ agitation, anxiety, apprehension, care, concern, disquiet, nervousness, uneasiness, worry

perturbed \pər-ˈtərbd\ *adj* ♦ **:** emotionally disturbed or agitated

♦ aflutter, anxious, edgy, jittery, jumpy, nervous, nervy, tense, troubled, uneasy, upset, worried

per•tus•sis \pər-ˈtə-səs\ *n* **:** WHOOPING COUGH

pe•ruke \pə-ˈrük\ *n* **:** WIG

pe•ruse \pə-ˈrüz\ *vb* **pe•rused; pe•rus•ing :** READ; *esp* **:** to read over attentively or leisurely — **pe•rus•al** \-ˈrü-zəl\ *n*

Pe•ru•vi•an \pə-ˈrü-vē-ən\ *n* **:** a native or inhabitant of Peru

per•vade \pər-ˈvād\ *vb* **per•vad•ed; per•vad•ing :** to spread through every part of **:** PERMEATE — **per•va•sive** \-ˈvā-siv, -ziv\ *adj*

per•verse \pər-ˈvərs\ *adj* **1** ♦ **:** turned away from what is right or good **:** CORRUPT **2** ♦ **:** obstinate in opposing what is reasonable or accepted **3** ♦ **:** marked by peevishness or petulance — **per•verse•ly** *adv*

♦ [1] corrupt, debauched, decadent, degenerate, dissolute, perverted, reprobate ♦ [2] dogged, hardheaded, headstrong, mulish, obdurate, obstinate, opinionated, peevish, pertinacious, pigheaded, stubborn, unyielding, willful ♦ [3] choleric, crabby, cranky, cross, crotchety, grouchy, grumpy, irascible, irritable, peevish, petulant, short-tempered, snappish, snappy, snippy, testy, waspish

per•verse•ness \-nəs\ *n* ♦ **:** the quality or state of being perverse

♦ biliousness, grumpiness, irritability, peevishness, perversity

per•ver•sion \pər-ˈvər-zhən\ *n* **1** ♦ **:** the action of perverting **:** the condition of being perverted **2** ♦ **:** a perverted form of something; *esp* **:** aberrant sexual behavior

♦ corruption, debasement, debauchery, decadence, degeneracy, degeneration, degradation, demoralization, depravity, dissipation, dissoluteness

per•ver•si•ty \pər-ˈvər-sə-tē\ *n* ♦ **:** the quality or state of being perverse

♦ biliousness, grumpiness, irritability, peevishness, perverseness

¹per•vert \pər-ˈvərt\ *vb* **1** ♦ **:** to lead astray **:** CORRUPT ⟨∼ the young⟩ **2** ♦ **:** to divert to a wrong purpose **:** MISAPPLY ⟨∼ evidence⟩ **3** ♦ **:** to twist the meaning or sense of — **per•vert•er** *n*

♦ [1] debase, degrade, demean, demoralize, humble, subvert, warp ♦ [2] abuse, misapply, misuse, profane, prostitute ♦ [3] color (*or* colour), distort, falsify, garble, misinterpret, misrepresent, misstate, twist, warp

²per•vert \ˈpər-ˌvərt\ *n* **:** one that is perverted; *esp* **:** one given to sexual perversion

♦ decadent, degenerate, libertine, profligate

per•vert•ed \pər-ˈvər-təd\ *adj* ♦ **:** morally degenerate **:** DEPRAVED

♦ corrupt, debauched, decadent, degenerate, dissolute, perverse, reprobate

pes•ky \ˈpes-kē\ *adj* **pes•ki•er; -est :** causing annoyance **:** TROUBLESOME

pe•so \ˈpā-sō\ *n, pl* **pesos :** the basic monetary unit in many Latin American countries (as Mexico or Chile)

pes•si•mism \ˈpe-sə-ˌmi-zəm\ *n* **:** an inclination to take the least favorable view (as of events) or to expect the worst — **pes•si•mist** \-mist\ *n*

pes•si•mis•tic \ˌpe-sə-ˈmis-tik\ *adj* ♦ **:** of, relating to, or characterized by pessimism

♦ defeatist, despairing, hopeless *Ant* hopeful, rosy, upbeat

pest \ˈpest\ *n* **1 :** a destructive epidemic disease **:** PLAGUE **2 :** a plant or animal detrimental to humans **3** ♦ **:** one that pesters **:** NUISANCE

♦ aggravation, annoyance, bother, exasperation, frustration, hassle, headache, inconvenience, irritant, nuisance, peeve, problem, thorn

pes•ter \ˈpes-tər\ *vb* ♦ **:** to harass with petty irritations

♦ bother, bug, disturb, intrude

pes•ti•cide \ˈpes-tə-ˌsīd\ *n* **:** an agent used to destroy pests

pes•tif•er•ous \pes-ˈti-fə-rəs\ *adj* **1 :** PESTILENT **2** ♦ **:** causing vexation **:** ANNOYING

♦ aggravating, annoying, frustrating, galling, irksome, irritating, pesty, vexatious

pes•ti•lence \ˈpes-tə-ləns\ *n* **:** a destructive infectious swiftly spreading disease; *esp* **:** BUBONIC PLAGUE

pes•ti•lent \-lənt\ *adj* **1** ♦ **:** dangerous to life **:** DEADLY **2 :** PERNICIOUS, HARMFUL **3 :** TROUBLESOME **4 :** INFECTIOUS, CONTAGIOUS

♦ baleful, deadly, deathly, fatal, fell, lethal, mortal, murderous, vital

pes•ti•len•tial \ˌpes-tə-ˈlen-chəl\ *adj* **1 :** causing or tending to cause pestilence **:** DEADLY **2 :** morally harmful
pes•tle \ˈpes-əl, ˈpest-ᵊl\ *n* **:** an implement for grinding substances in a mortar — **pestle** *vb*
pesty \ˈpes-tē\ *adj* ♦ **:** causing trouble or annoyance

♦ aggravating, annoying, bothersome, frustrating, galling, irksome, irritating, vexatious

1pet \ˈpet\ *n* **1** ♦ **:** a person who is treated with unusual kindness or consideration **:** FAVORITE, DARLING **2 :** a domesticated animal kept for pleasure rather than utility

♦ darling, favorite (*or* favourite), minion, preference

2pet *adj* **1 :** kept or treated as a pet ⟨~ dog⟩ **2 :** expressing fondness ⟨~ name⟩ **3** ♦ **:** particularly liked or favored

♦ beloved, darling, dear, favorite (*or* favourite), loved, precious, special, sweet

3pet *vb* **pet•ted; pet•ting 1** ♦ **:** to stroke gently or lovingly **2 :** to make a pet of **:** PAMPER **3** ♦ **:** to engage in amorous kissing and caressing

♦ [1] caress, fondle, love, pat, stroke ♦ [3] kiss, make out

4pet *n* ♦ **:** a fit of peevishness, sulkiness, or anger

♦ pout, sulk, sullenness

Pet *abbr* Peter
pet•al \ˈpet-ᵊl\ *n* **:** one of the modified leaves of a flower's corolla
pe•tard \pə-ˈtärd, -ˈtär\ *n* **:** a case containing an explosive to break down a door or gate or breach a wall
pe•ter \ˈpē-tər\ *vb* **:** to diminish gradually and come to an end ⟨his energy ~*ed* out⟩
Pe•ter \ˈpē-tər\ *n* **:** either of two books of the New Testament of the Christian Scripture
pet•i•ole \ˈpe-tē-ˌōl\ *n* **:** a slender stem that supports a leaf
pe•tite \pə-ˈtēt\ *adj* **:** small and trim of figure ⟨a ~ woman⟩ — **petite** *n*
pe•tit four \ˌpe-tē-ˈfōr\ *n, pl* **petits fours** *or* **petit fours** \-ˈfōrz\ **:** a small cake cut from pound or sponge cake and frosted
1pe•ti•tion \pə-ˈti-shən\ *n* ♦ **:** an earnest request **:** ENTREATY; *esp* **:** a formal written request made to an authority

♦ appeal, cry, entreaty, plea, prayer, solicitation, suit, supplication

2petition *vb* **:** to make a request to or for
pe•ti•tion•er \-sh(ə-)nər\ *n* **:** one that petitions
pe•trel \ˈpe-trəl\ *n* **:** any of numerous seabirds that fly far from land
pe•tri dish \ˈpē-trē-\ *n* **1 :** a small shallow dish used especially for growing bacteria **2 :** something fosterng development or innovation
pet•ri•fy \ˈpe-trə-ˌfī\ *vb* **-fied; -fy•ing 1 :** to convert (organic matter) into stone or stony material **2 :** to make rigid or inactive (as from fear or awe) — **pet•ri•fac•tion** \ˌpe-trə-ˈfak-shən\ *n*
pet•ro•chem•i•cal \ˌpe-trō-ˈke-mi-kəl\ *n* **:** a chemical isolated or derived from petroleum or natural gas — **pet•ro•chem•is•try** \-ˈke-mə-strē\ *n*
pet•rol \ˈpe-trəl\ *n, chiefly Brit* **:** GASOLINE
pet•ro•la•tum \ˌpe-trə-ˈlā-təm\ *n* **:** PETROLEUM JELLY
pe•tro•leum \pə-ˈtrō-lē-əm\ *n* **:** an oily flammable liquid obtained from wells drilled in the ground and refined into gasoline, fuel oils, and other products
petroleum jelly *n* **:** a tasteless, odorless, and oily or greasy substance from petroleum that is used especially in ointments and dressings
1pet•ti•coat \ˈpe-tē-ˌkōt\ *n* **1 :** a skirt worn under a dress **2 :** an outer skirt
2petticoat *adj* **:** of, relating to, or exercised by women **:** FEMALE
pet•ti•fog \ˈpe-tē-ˌfòg, -ˌfäg\ *vb* **-fogged; -fog•ging 1 :** to engage in legal trickery **2 :** to quibble over insignificant details — **pet•ti•fog•ger** *n*
pet•ti•fog•ger \ˈpe-tē-ˌfò-gər, -ˌfä-\ *n* **1 :** a lawyer whose methods are petty, underhanded, or disreputable **2 :** one given to quibbling over trifles — **pet•ti•fog•ging** \-giŋ\ *adj or n*
pet•tish \ˈpe-tish\ *adj* **:** querulous in temperament or mood **:** PEEVISH
pet•ty \ˈpe-tē\ *adj* **pet•ti•er; -est 1 :** having secondary rank **:** MINOR ⟨~ prince⟩ **2** ♦ **:** of little importance **:** TRIFLING ⟨~ faults⟩ **3** ♦ **:** marked by or reflective of narrow interests and sympathies — **pet•ti•ly** \ˈpe-tə-lē\ *adv* — **pet•ti•ness** \-tē-nəs\ *n*

♦ [2] inconsequential, inconsiderable, insignificant, measly, minute, negligible, nominal, paltry, slight, trifling, trivial ♦ [3] insular, little, narrow, parochial, provincial, sectarian, small

petty officer *n* **:** a subordinate officer in the navy or coast guard appointed from among the enlisted men
petty officer first class *n* **:** a petty officer ranking below a chief petty officer
petty officer second class *n* **:** a petty officer ranking below a petty officer first class
petty officer third class *n* **:** a petty officer ranking below a petty officer second class
pet•u•lance \ˈpe-chə-ləns\ *n* **:** the quality or state of being petulant
pet•u•lant \ˈpe-chə-lənt\ *adj* ♦ **:** marked by capricious ill humor — **pet•u•lant•ly** *adv*

♦ choleric, crabby, cranky, cross, crotchety, grouchy, grumpy, irascible, irritable, peevish, perverse, short-tempered, snappish, snappy, snippy, testy, waspish

pe•tu•nia \pi-ˈtün-yə, -ˈtyün-\ *n* **:** any of a genus of tropical American herbs related to the potato and having bright funnel-shaped flowers
pew \ˈpyü\ *n* **:** any of the benches with backs fixed in rows in a church
pe•wee \ˈpē-(ˌ)wē\ *n* **:** any of various small American flycatchers
pew•ter \ˈpyü-tər\ *n* **1 :** an alloy of tin used especially for household utensils **2** ♦ **:** a bluish gray color — **pewter** *adj* — **pew•ter•er** *n*

♦ gray (*or* grey), leaden, silver, silvery, slate, steely

pey•o•te \pā-ˈō-tē\ *also* **pey•otl** \-ˈōt-ᵊl\ *n* **1 :** a hallucinogenic drug derived from the peyote cactus and containing mescaline **2 :** a small cactus of the southwestern U.S. and Mexico
pf *abbr* **1** pfennig **2** preferred
PFC *or* **Pfc** *abbr* private first class
pfd *abbr* preferred
pg *abbr* page
PG *abbr* postgraduate
PGA *abbr* Professional Golfers' Association
pH \(ˌ)pē-ˈāch\ *n* **:** a value used to express acidity and alkalinity; *also* **:** the condition represented by such a value
PH *abbr* **1** pinch hit **2** public health
pha•eton \ˈfā-ət-ᵊn\ *n* **1 :** a light 4-wheeled horse-drawn vehicle **2 :** an open automobile with two cross seats
phage \ˈfāj\ *n* **:** BACTERIOPHAGE
pha•lanx \ˈfā-ˌlaŋks\ *n, pl* **pha•lanx•es** *or* **pha•lan•ges** \fə-ˈlan-ˌjēz\ **1 :** a group or body (as of troops) in compact formation **2** *pl* *phalanges* **:** one of the digital bones of the hand or foot of a vertebrate
phal•a•rope \ˈfa-lə-ˌrōp\ *n, pl* **-ropes** *also* **-rope :** any of a genus of small shorebirds related to sandpipers
phal•lic \ˈfa-lik\ *adj* **1 :** of, relating to, or resembling a phallus **2 :** relating to or being the stage of psychosexual development in psychoanalytic theory during which children become interested in their own sexual organs
phal•lus \ˈfa-ləs\ *n, pl* **phal•li** \ˈfa-ˌlī\ *or* **phal•lus•es :** PENIS; *also* **:** a symbolic representation of the penis
Phan•er•o•zo•ic \ˌfa-nə-rə-ˈzō-ik\ *adj* **:** of, relating to, or being an eon of geologic history comprising the Paleozoic, Mesozoic, and Cenozoic
phan•tasm \ˈfan-ˌta-zəm\ *n* **1** ♦ **:** a product of the imagination **:** ILLUSION **2** ♦ **:** a visible disembodied spirit **:** GHOST

♦ [1] chimera, conceit, daydream, delusion, dream, fancy, fantasy, figment, hallucination, illusion, pipe dream, unreality, vision ♦ [2] apparition, bogey, ghost, phantom, poltergeist, shade, shadow, specter, spirit, spook, vision, wraith

phan•tas•ma•go•ria \fan-ˌtaz-mə-ˈgōr-ē-ə\ *n* **:** a constantly shifting complex succession of things seen or imagined; *also* **:** a scene that constantly changes or fluctuates
phan•tas•mal \ˌfan-ˈtaz-məl\ *adj* **:** of, relating to, or like a phantasm
phantasy *var of* FANTASY
1phan•tom \ˈfan-təm\ *n* **1** ♦ **:** something (as a specter) that is apparent to sense but has no substantial existence **2 :** one that is something in appearance but not in reality **:** a mere show

♦ apparition, bogey, ghost, phantasm, poltergeist, shade, shadow, specter, spirit, spook, vision, wraith

²phantom *adj* ♦ **:** of the nature of, suggesting, or being a phantom

♦ chimerical, fabulous, fanciful, fantastic, fictitious, imaginary, made-up, mythical, pretend, unreal

pha•raoh \ˈfer-ō, ˈfā-rō\ *n, often cap* **:** a ruler of ancient Egypt
phar•i•sa•ical \ˌfar-ə-ˈsā-ə-kəl\ *adj* **:** hypocritically self-righteous
phar•i•see \ˈfar-ə-ˌsē\ *n* **1** *cap* **:** a member of an ancient Jewish sect noted for strict observance of rites and ceremonies of the traditional law **2 :** a self-righteous or hypocritical person — **phar•i•sa•ic** \ˌfar-ə-ˈsā-ik\ *adj*
pharm *abbr* pharmaceutical; pharmacist; pharmacy
¹phar•ma•ceu•ti•cal \ˌfär-mə-ˈsü-ti-kəl\ *adj* **:** of, relating to, or engaged in pharmacy or the manufacture and sale of medicinal drugs
²pharmaceutical *n* ♦ **:** a medicinal drug

♦ cure, drug, medicine, remedy, specific

phar•ma•col•o•gy \ˌfär-mə-ˈkä-lə-jē\ *n* **1 :** the science of drugs especially as related to medicinal uses **2 :** the reactions and properties of one or more drugs — **phar•ma•co•log•i•cal** \-kə-ˈlä-ji-kəl\ *also* **phar•ma•co•log•ic** \-kə-ˈlä-jik\ *adj* — **phar•ma•col•o•gist** \-ˈkä-lə-jist\ *n*
phar•ma•co•poe•ia *also* **phar•ma•co•pe•ia** \-kə-ˈpē-ə\ *n* **1 :** a book describing drugs and medicinal preparations **2 :** a stock of drugs
phar•ma•cy \ˈfär-mə-sē\ *n, pl* **-cies 1 :** the art, practice, or profession of preparing and dispensing medical drugs **2 :** DRUGSTORE — **phar•ma•cist** \-sist\ *n*
phar•ynx \ˈfar-iŋks\ *n, pl* **pha•ryn•ges** \fə-ˈrin-ˌjēz\ *also* **phar•ynx•es :** the muscular tubular passage extending from the back of the nasal cavity and mouth to the esophagus — **pha•ryn•ge•al** \fə-ˈrin-jəl, ˌfar-ən-ˈjē-əl\ *adj*
phase \ˈfāz\ *n* **1 :** a particular appearance in a recurring series of changes ⟨~*s* of the moon⟩ **2** ♦ **:** a stage or interval in a process or cycle ⟨first ~ of an experiment⟩ **3** ♦ **:** an aspect or part under consideration — **pha•sic** \ˈfā-zik\ *adj*

♦ [2] cut, degree, grade, inch, notch, peg, point, stage, step
♦ [3] angle, aspect, facet, hand, side

phase down *vb* **:** to reduce the size or amount of by phases
phase in *vb* **:** to introduce in stages
phase•out \ˈfā-ˌzau̇t\ *n* **:** a gradual stopping of operations or production
phase out *vb* **:** to stop production or use of in stages
PhD *abbr* doctor of philosophy
pheas•ant \ˈfez-ᵊnt\ *n, pl* **pheasant** *or* **pheasants :** any of numerous long-tailed brilliantly colored game birds related to the domestic chicken
phen•cy•cli•dine \ˌfen-ˈsī-klə-ˌdēn\ *n* **:** a drug used especially as a veterinary anesthetic and sometimes illicitly as a hallucinogenic drug
phe•no•bar•bi•tal \ˌfē-nō-ˈbär-bə-ˌtȯl\ *n* **:** a crystalline drug used as a hypnotic and sedative
phe•nol \ˈfē-ˌnȯl\ *n* **:** a corrosive poisonous acidic compound present in coal and wood tars and used in solution as a disinfectant
phe•nom•e•nal \fi-ˈnä-mən-ᵊl\ *adj* ♦ **:** relating to or being a phenomenon; *also* **:** so unusual as to be remarkable — **phe•nom•e•nal•ly** *adv*

♦ aberrant, abnormal, atypical, exceptional, extraordinary, freak, odd, peculiar, rare, singular, uncommon, uncustomary, unique, unusual, unwonted ♦ magical, miraculous, superhuman, supernatural, uncanny, unearthly

phe•nom•e•non \fi-ˈnä-mə-ˌnän, -nən\ *n, pl* **-na** \-nə\ *or* **-nons 1** *pl -na* **:** an observable fact or event **2 :** an outward sign of the working of a law of nature **3** *pl -nons* ♦ **:** an extraordinary person or thing **:** PRODIGY

♦ caution, flash, marvel, miracle, portent, prodigy, sensation, wonder

pher•o•mone \ˈfer-ə-ˌmōn\ *n* **:** a chemical substance that is produced by an animal and serves to stimulate a behavioral response in other individuals of the same species — **pher•o•mon•al** \ˌfer-ə-ˈmōn-ᵊl\ *adj*
phi \ˈfī\ *n* **:** the 21st letter of the Greek alphabet — Φ or ϕ
phi•al \ˈfī-əl\ *n* **:** VIAL
Phil *abbr* Philippians
phi•lan•der \fə-ˈlan-dər\ *vb* **:** to have casual or illicit sexual relations with many women — **phi•lan•der•er** *n*
phil•an•throp•ic \ˌfi-lən-ˈthrä-pik\ *adj* ♦ **:** of, relating to, or characterized by philanthropy — **phil•an•throp•i•cal•ly** \-pi-k(ə-)lē\ *adv*

♦ altruistic, beneficent, benevolent, charitable, humanitarian

phi•lan•thro•py \fə-ˈlan-thrə-pē\ *n, pl* **-pies 1 :** goodwill toward all people; *esp* **:** effort to promote human welfare **2** ♦ **:** a charitable act or gift; *also* **:** an organization that distributes or is supported by donated funds — **phi•lan•thro•pist** \fə-ˈlan-thrə-pist\ *n*

♦ alms, benefaction, beneficence, charity, contribution, donation

phi•lat•e•ly \fə-ˈlat-ᵊl-ē\ *n* **:** the collection and study of postage and imprinted stamps — **phil•a•tel•ic** \ˌfi-lə-ˈte-lik\ *adj* — **phi•lat•e•list** \fə-ˈlat-ᵊl-ist\ *n*
Phi•le•mon \fə-ˈlē-mən, fī-\ *n* **:** a book of the New Testament of the Christian Scripture
Phi•lip•pi•ans \fə-ˈli-pē-ənz\ *n* **:** a book of the New Testament of the Christian Scripture
phi•lip•pic \fə-ˈli-pik\ *n* **:** TIRADE
phi•lis•tine \ˈfi-lə-ˌstēn; fə-ˈlis-tən\ *n, often cap* **:** a person who is smugly insensitive or indifferent to intellectual or artistic values — **philistine** *adj, often cap*
Phil•lips \ˈfi-ləps\ *adj* **:** of, relating to, or being a screw having a head with a cross slot or its corresponding screwdriver
philo•den•dron \ˌfi-lə-ˈden-drən\ *n, pl* **-drons** *also* **-dra** \-drə\ **:** any of various plants of the arum family grown for their showy foliage
phi•lol•o•gy \fə-ˈlä-lə-jē\ *n* **1 :** the study of literature and relevant fields **2 :** LINGUISTICS; *esp* **:** historical and comparative linguistics — **phil•o•log•i•cal** \ˌfi-lə-ˈlä-ji-kəl\ *adj* — **phi•lol•o•gist** \fə-ˈlä-lə-jist\ *n*
philos *abbr* philosopher; philosophy
phi•los•o•pher \fə-ˈlä-sə-fər\ *n* **1 :** a reflective thinker **:** SCHOLAR **2 :** a student of or specialist in philosophy **3 :** a person whose philosophical perspective makes it possible to meet trouble calmly
phi•los•o•phise *chiefly Brit var of* PHILOSOPHIZE
phi•los•o•phize \fə-ˈlä-sə-ˌfīz\ *vb* **-phized; -phiz•ing 1 :** to reason like a philosopher **:** THEORIZE **2 :** to expound a philosophy especially superficially
phi•los•o•phy \fə-ˈlä-sə-fē\ *n, pl* **-phies 1 :** sciences and liberal arts exclusive of medicine, law, and theology ⟨doctor of ~⟩ **2 :** a critical study of fundamental beliefs and the grounds for them **3 :** a system of philosophical concepts ⟨Aristotelian ~⟩ **4 :** a basic theory concerning a particular subject or sphere of activity **5** ♦ **:** the sum of the ideas and convictions of an individual or group ⟨her ~ of life⟩ **6 :** calmness of temper and judgment — **phil•o•soph•i•cal** \ˌfi-lə-ˈsä-fi-kəl\ *also* **phil•o•soph•ic** \-fik\ *adj* — **phil•o•soph•i•cal•ly** \-k(ə-)lē\ *adv*

♦ creed, doctrine, gospel, ideology

phil•ter *or Can and Brit* **phil•tre** \ˈfil-tər\ *n* **1 :** a potion, drug, or charm held to arouse sexual passion **2 :** a magic potion
phle•bi•tis \fli-ˈbī-təs\ *n* **:** inflammation of a vein
phle•bot•o•my \fli-ˈbä-tə-mē\ *n, pl* **-mies :** the opening of a vein especially for removing or releasing blood
phlegm \ˈflem\ *n* **1 :** thick mucus secreted in abnormal quantity especially in the nose and throat **2** ♦ **:** dull or apathetic coldness or indifference

♦ apathy, impassivity, numbness, stupor

phleg•mat•ic \fleg-ˈma-tik\ *adj* ♦ **:** having or showing a slow and stolid temperament

♦ apathetic, cold-blooded, impassive, stoic, stolid, unemotional

phlo•em \ˈflō-ˌem\ *n* **:** a vascular plant tissue external to the xylem that carries dissolved food material and functions in support and storage
phlox \ˈfläks\ *n, pl* **phlox** *or* **phlox•es :** any of a genus of American herbs that have tall stalks with showy spreading terminal clusters of flowers
pho•bia \ˈfō-bē-ə\ *n* **:** an irrational persistent fear or dread — **pho•bic** \ˈfō-bik\ *adj*
phoe•be \ˈfē-(ˌ)bē\ *n* **:** a flycatcher of the eastern U.S. that has a slight crest and is grayish brown above and yellowish white below
phoe•nix \ˈfē-niks\ *n* **:** a legendary bird held to live for centuries and then to burn itself to death and rise fresh and young from its ashes
¹phone \ˈfōn\ *n* **1 :** TELEPHONE **2 :** EARPHONE
²phone *vb* **phoned; phon•ing :** to speak to or attempt to reach by telephone **:** TELEPHONE

phone card *n* : a prepaid card used in paying for telephone calls
pho•neme \ˈfō-ˌnēm\ *n* : one of the elementary units of speech that distinguish one utterance from another — **pho•ne•mic** \fō-ˈnē-mik\ *adj*
pho•net•ics \fə-ˈne-tiks\ *n* : the study and systematic classification of the sounds made in spoken utterance — **pho•net•ic** \-tik\ *adj* — **pho•ne•ti•cian** \ˌfō-nə-ˈti-shən\ *n*
pho•nic \ˈfä-nik\ *adj* **1** : of, relating to, or producing sound **2** : of or relating to the sounds of speech or to phonics — **pho•ni•cal•ly** \-ni-k(ə-)lē\ *adv*
pho•nics \ˈfä-niks\ *n* : a method of teaching people to read and pronounce words by learning the phonetic value of letters, letter groups, and especially syllables
pho•no•graph \ˈfō-nə-ˌgraf\ *n* : an instrument for reproducing sounds by means of the vibration of a needle following a spiral groove on a revolving disc
pho•nol•o•gy \fə-ˈnä-lə-jē\ *n* : a study and description of the sound changes in a language — **pho•no•log•i•cal** \ˌfō-nə-ˈlä-ji-kəl\ *adj* — **pho•nol•o•gist** \fə-ˈnä-lə-jist\ *n*
[1]**pho•ny** *also* **pho•ney** \ˈfō-nē\ *adj* **pho•ni•er; -est** ♦ : not genuine or real : claiming or claimed to be what one is not

♦ bogus, counterfeit, fake, false, inauthentic, sham, spurious, unauthentic ♦ affected, artificial, assumed, contrived, feigned, put-on, unnatural

[2]**phony** *n* ♦ : one that is phony

♦ counterfeit, fake, forgery, hoax, humbug, sham ♦ charlatan, fake, fraud, hoaxer, humbug, mountebank, pretender, quack

phos•phate \ˈfäs-ˌfāt\ *n* : a salt of a phosphoric acid — **phos•phat•ic** \fäs-ˈfa-tik\ *adj*
phos•phor \ˈfäs-fər\ *n* : a phosphorescent substance
phos•pho•res•cence \ˌfäs-fə-ˈres-ᵊns\ *n* **1** : luminescence caused by the absorption of radiations (as light or electrons) and continuing after these radiations stop **2** : an enduring luminescence without sensible heat — **phos•pho•res•cent** \-ᵊnt\ *adj* — **phos•pho•res•cent•ly** *adv*
phosphoric acid \ˌfäs-ˈfór-ik-, -ˈfär-\ *n* : any of several oxygen-containing acids of phosphorus
phos•pho•rus \ˈfäs-fə-rəs\ *n* : a nonmetallic chemical element that has characteristics similar to nitrogen and occurs widely especially as phosphates — **phos•pho•ric** \fäs-ˈfór-ik, -ˈfär-\ *adj* — **phos•pho•rous** \ˈfäs-fə-rəs; fäs-ˈfōr-əs, -ˈfór-\ *adj*
phot- *or* **photo-** *comb form* **1** : light ⟨*photo*graphy⟩ **2** : photograph : photographic ⟨*photo*engraving⟩ **3** : photoelectric ⟨*photo*cell⟩
[1]**pho•to** \ˈfō-tō\ *n, pl* **photos** : a picture or likeness obtained by photography : PHOTOGRAPH — **photo** *adj*
[2]**photo** *vb* : to take a photograph of
pho•to•cell \ˈfō-tə-ˌsel\ *n* : PHOTOELECTRIC CELL
pho•to•chem•i•cal \ˌfō-tō-ˈke-mi-kəl\ *adj* : of, relating to, or resulting from the chemical action of radiant energy
pho•to•com•pose \-kəm-ˈpōz\ *vb* : to compose reading matter for reproduction by means of characters photographed on film — **pho•to•com•po•si•tion** \-ˌkäm-pə-ˈzi-shən\ *n*
pho•to•copy \ˈfō-tə-ˌkä-pē\ *n* : a photographic reproduction of graphic matter — **photocopy** *vb*
pho•to•elec•tric \ˌfō-tō-i-ˈlek-trik\ *adj* : relating to an electrical effect due to the interaction of light with matter — **pho•to•elec•tri•cal•ly** \-tri-k(ə-)lē\ *adv*
photoelectric cell *n* : a device whose electrical properties are modified by the action of light
pho•to•en•grave \ˌfō-tō-in-ˈgrāv\ *vb* : to make a photoengraving of
pho•to•en•grav•ing *n* : a process by which an etched printing plate is made from a photograph or drawing; *also* : a print made from such a plate
photo finish *n* : a race finish so close that a photograph of the finish is used to determine the winner
pho•tog \fə-ˈtäg\ *n* : PHOTOGRAPHER
pho•to•ge•nic \ˌfō-tə-ˈje-nik\ *adj* : eminently suitable especially aesthetically for being photographed
[1]**pho•to•graph** \ˈfō-tə-ˌgraf\ *n* ♦ : a picture taken by photography — **pho•tog•ra•pher** \fə-ˈtä-grə-fər\ *n*

♦ print, shot, snap, snapshot

[2]**photograph** *vb* ♦ : to take a photograph of

♦ mug, shoot, snap

pho•tog•ra•phy \fə-ˈtä-grə-fē\ *n* : the art or process of producing images on a sensitive surface (as film or a CCD chip) by the action of light — **pho•to•graph•ic** \ˌfō-tə-ˈgra-fik\ *adj* — **pho•to•graph•i•cal•ly** \-fi-k(ə-)lē\ *adv*
pho•to•gra•vure \ˌfō-tə-grə-ˈvyu̇r\ *n* : a process for making prints from an intaglio plate prepared by photographic methods
pho•to•li•thog•ra•phy \ˌfō-tō-li-ˈthä-grə-fē\ *n* : the process of photographically transferring a pattern to a surface for etching (as in making an integrated circuit)
pho•tom•e•ter \fō-ˈtä-mə-tər\ *n* : an instrument for measuring the intensity of light — **pho•to•met•ric** \ˌfō-tə-ˈme-trik\ *adj* — **pho•tom•e•try** \fō-ˈtä-mə-trē\ *n*
pho•to•mi•cro•graph \ˌfō-tə-ˈmī-krə-ˌgraf\ *n* : a photograph of a microscope image — **pho•to•mi•crog•ra•phy** \-mī-ˈkrä-grə-fē\ *n*
pho•ton \ˈfō-ˌtän\ *n* : a quantum of electromagnetic radiation
photo op *n* : a situation or event that lends itself to the taking of pictures which favor the individuals photographed
pho•to•play \ˈfō-tō-ˌplā\ *n* : MOTION PICTURE
pho•to•sen•si•tive \ˌfō-tə-ˈsen-sə-tiv\ *adj* : sensitive or sensitized to the action of radiant energy
pho•to•sphere \ˈfō-tə-ˌsfir\ *n* : the luminous surface of a star — **pho•to•spher•ic** \ˌfō-tə-ˈsfir-ik, -ˈsfer-\ *adj*
pho•to•syn•the•sis \ˌfō-tō-ˈsin-thə-səs\ *n* : the process by which chlorophyll-containing plants make carbohydrates from water and from carbon dioxide in the air in the presence of light — **pho•to•syn•the•size** \-ˌsīz\ *vb* — **pho•to•syn•thet•ic** \-sin-ˈthe-tik\ *adj*
phr *abbr* phrase
[1]**phrase** \ˈfrāz\ *n* **1** : a brief expression **2** : a group of two or more grammatically related words that form a sense unit expressing a thought
[2]**phrase** *vb* **phrased; phras•ing** ♦ : to express in words

♦ articulate, clothe, couch, express, formulate, put, say, state, word

phrase•ol•o•gy \ˌfrā-zē-ˈä-lə-jē\ *n, pl* **-gies** ♦ : a manner of phrasing : STYLE

♦ fashion, locution, manner, mode, style, tone, vein

phras•ing *n* ♦ : style of expression

♦ diction, language, phraseology, wording

phren•ic \ˈfre-nik\ *adj* : of or relating to the diaphragm ⟨~ nerves⟩
phre•nol•o•gy \fri-ˈnä-lə-jē\ *n* : the study of the conformation of the skull based on the belief that it indicates mental faculties and character traits
phy•lac•tery \fə-ˈlak-tə-rē\ *n, pl* **-ter•ies** **1** : one of two small square leather boxes containing slips inscribed with scripture passages and traditionally worn on the left arm and forehead by Jewish men during morning weekday prayers **2** : an ornament worn as a charm against evil : AMULET
phy•lum \ˈfī-ləm\ *n, pl* **phy•la** \-lə\ : a major category in biological classification especially of animals that ranks above the class and below the kingdom; *also* : a group (as of people) apparently of common origin
phys *abbr* **1** physical **2** physics
[1]**phys•ic** \ˈfi-zik\ *n* **1** : the profession of medicine **2** : a substance or preparation used in treating disease : MEDICINE; *esp* : PURGATIVE
[2]**physic** *vb* **phys•icked; phys•ick•ing** : PURGE 2
[1]**phys•i•cal** \ˈfi-zi-kəl\ *adj* **1** : of or relating to nature or the laws of nature **2** ♦ : material as opposed to mental or spiritual **3** : of, relating to, or produced by the forces and operations of physics **4** ♦ : of or relating to the body — **phys•i•cal•ly** \-k(ə-)lē\ *adv*

♦ [2] concrete, material, substantial ♦ [4] animal, bodily, carnal, corporal, fleshly, material, somatic *Ant* nonmaterial, nonphysical

[2]**physical** *n* : PHYSICAL EXAMINATION
physical education *n* : instruction in the development and care of the body ranging from simple calisthenics to training in hygiene, gymnastics, and the performance and management of athletic games
physical examination *n* : an examination of the bodily functions and condition of an individual
phys•i•cal•ize \ˈfi-zə-kə-ˌlīz\ *vb* **-ized; -iz•ing** : to give physical form or expression to
physical science *n* : any of the sciences (as physics and astronomy) that deal primarily with nonliving materials — **physical scientist** *n*
physical therapy *n* : the treatment of disease by physical and mechanical means (as massage, exercise, water, or heat) — **physical therapist** *n*
phy•si•cian \fə-ˈzi-shən\ *n* : a doctor of medicine

physician's assistant *n* : a person certified to provide basic medical care usually under a licensed physician's supervision
phys•i•cist \ˈfi-zə-sist\ *n* : a scientist who specializes in physics
phys•ics \ˈfi-ziks\ *n* **1** : the science of matter and energy and their interactions **2** : the physical properties and composition of something
phys•i•og•no•my \ˌfi-zē-ˈäg-nə-mē\ *n, pl* **-mies** : facial appearance especially as a reflection of inner character
phys•i•og•ra•phy \ˌfi-zē-ˈä-grə-fē\ *n* : geography dealing with physical features of the earth — **phys•io•graph•ic** \ˌfi-zē-ō-ˈgra-fik\ *adj*
phys•i•ol•o•gy \ˌfi-zē-ˈä-lə-jē\ *n* **1** : a branch of biology dealing with the functions and functioning of living matter and organisms **2** : functional processes in an organism or any of its parts — **phys•i•o•log•i•cal** \-zē-ə-ˈlä-ji-kəl\ *or* **phys•i•o•log•ic** \-jik\ *adj* — **phys•i•o•log•i•cal•ly** \-ji-k(ə-)lē\ *adv* — **phys•i•ol•o•gist** \-zē-ˈä-lə-jist\ *n*
phys•io•ther•a•py \ˌfi-zē-ō-ˈther-ə-pē\ *n* : PHYSICAL THERAPY — **phys•io•ther•a•pist** \-pist\ *n*
phy•sique \fə-ˈzēk\ *n* ♦ : the build of a person's body : bodily constitution

♦ build, constitution, figure, form, frame, shape

phy•to•chem•i•cal \ˌfī-tō-ˈke-mi-kəl\ *n* : a chemical compound occurring naturally in plants
phy•to•plank•ton \ˈfī-tō-ˌplaŋk-tən\ *n* : plant life of the plankton
pi \ˈpī\ *n, pl* **pis** \ˈpīz\ **1** : the 16th letter of the Greek alphabet — Π or π **2** : the symbol π denoting the ratio of the circumference of a circle to its diameter; *also* : the ratio itself equal to approximately 3.1416
PI *abbr* private investigator
pi•a•nis•si•mo \ˌpē-ə-ˈni-sə-ˌmō\ *adv or adj* : very softly — used as a direction in music
pi•a•nist \pē-ˈa-nist, ˈpē-ə-\ *n* : a person who plays the piano
¹pi•a•no \pē-ˈä-nō\ *adv or adj* : SOFTLY — used as a direction in music
²piano \pē-ˈa-nō\ *n, pl* **pianos** : a musical instrument having steel strings sounded by felt-covered hammers operated from a keyboard
pi•ano•forte \pē-ˌa-nō-ˈfȯr-ˌtā, -tē; pē-ˈa-nə-ˌfȯrt\ *n* : PIANO
pi•az•za \pē-ˈa-zə, *esp for 1* -ˈat-sə\ *n, pl* **piazzas** *or* **pi•az•ze** \-ˈat-(ˌ)sā, -ˈät-\ **1** : an open square especially in an Italian town **2** : a long hall with an arched roof **3** *dial* : VERANDA, PORCH
pi•broch \ˈpē-ˌbräk\ *n* : a set of variations for the bagpipe
pic \ˈpik\ *n, pl* **pics** *or* **pix** \ˈpiks\ **1** : PHOTOGRAPH **2** : MOTION PICTURE
pi•ca \ˈpī-kə\ *n* : a typewriter type with 10 characters to the inch
pi•ca•resque \ˌpi-kə-ˈresk, ˌpē-\ *adj* : of or relating to rogues ⟨~ fiction⟩
pic•a•yune \ˌpi-kē-ˈyün\ *adj* : of little value : TRIVIAL; *also* : PETTY
pic•ca•lil•li \ˌpi-kə-ˈli-lē\ *n* : a relish of chopped vegetables and spices
pic•co•lo \ˈpi-kə-ˌlō\ *n, pl* **-los** : a small shrill flute pitched an octave higher than the ordinary flute
¹pick \ˈpik\ *vb* **1** : to pierce or break up with a pointed instrument **2** : to remove bit by bit; *also* : to remove covering matter from **3** ♦ : to gather by plucking ⟨~ apples⟩ **4** ♦ : to select from a group : CULL, SELECT **5** : ROB ⟨~ a pocket⟩ **6** : PROVOKE ⟨~ a quarrel⟩ **7** : to dig into or pull lightly at **8** : to pluck with fingers or a pick **9** : to loosen or pull apart with a sharp point ⟨~ wool⟩ **10** : to unlock with a wire **11** : to eat sparingly — **pick•er** *n*

♦ [3] gather, harvest, reap ♦ [4] choose, cull, elect, handpick, name, opt, prefer, select, single, take

²pick *n* **1** ♦ : the act or privilege of choosing **2** ♦ : the best or choicest one **3** : the part of a crop gathered at one time

♦ [1] alternative, choice, discretion, option, preference, way ♦ [2] best, choice, cream, elect, elite, fat, flower, prime

³pick *n* **1** : a heavy wooden-handled tool pointed at one or both ends **2** : a pointed implement used for picking **3** : a small thin piece (as of plastic) used to pluck the strings of a stringed instrument
pick•a•back \ˈpi-gē-ˌbak, ˈpi-kə-\ *var of* PIGGYBACK
pick•ax \ˈpik-ˌaks\ *n* : ³PICK 1
pick•er•el \ˈpi-kə-rəl\ *n, pl* **pickerel** *or* **pickerels** : either of two bony fishes related to the pikes; *also* : WALLEYE 2
pick•er•el•weed \-ˌwēd\ *n* : a No. American shallow-water herb that bears spikes of purplish blue flowers
¹pick•et \ˈpi-kət\ *n* **1** : a pointed stake (as for a fence) **2 a** : a detached body of soldiers on outpost duty **b** ♦ : one that watches or guards : SENTINEL **3** : a person posted by a labor union where workers are on strike; *also* : a person posted for a protest

♦ [2a, 2b] custodian, guard, guardian, keeper, lookout, sentinal, sentry, warden, warder, watch, watchman

²picket *vb* **1** : to guard with pickets **2** : TETHER **3** : to post pickets at ⟨~ a factory⟩ **4** : to serve as a picket
pick•ings \ˈpi-kiŋz, -kənz\ *n pl* **1** : gleanable or eatable fragments : SCRAPS **2** : yield for effort expended : RETURN
pick•le \ˈpi-kəl\ *n* **1** : a brine or vinegar solution for preserving foods; *also* : a food (as a cucumber) preserved in a pickle **2** ♦ : a difficult situation — **pickle** *vb*

♦ corner, fix, hole, jam, predicament, spot

pick•lock \ˈpik-ˌläk\ *n* **1** : BURGLAR, THIEF **2** : a tool for picking locks
pick•pock•et \ˈpik-ˌpä-kət\ *n* : one who steals from pockets
pick•up \ˈpik-ˌəp\ *n* **1** : a hitchhiker who is given a ride **2** : a temporary chance acquaintance **3** : a picking up **4** : revival of business activity **5** : ACCELERATION **6** : the conversion of mechanical movements into electrical impulses in the reproduction of sound; *also* : a device for making such conversion **7** : a light truck having an enclosed cab and an open body with low sides and a tailgate
pick up *vb* **1** ♦ : to take hold of and lift **2** : IMPROVE **3** : to put in order **4** : to gather together : COLLECT **5** ♦ : to acquire by study or experience : LEARN **6** ♦ : to obtain especially by payment **7** ♦ : to become progressively greater (as in size, amount, number, or intensity) **8** ♦ : to take into custody

♦ [1] boost, crane, elevate, heave, heft, heighten, hike, hoist, jack, lift, raise, up, uphold ♦ [5] get, learn, master ♦ [6] buy, purchase, take ♦ [7] build, gain, gather, grow ♦ [8] apprehend, arrest, nab, restrain, seize

picky \ˈpi-kē\ *adj* **pick•i•er; -est** ♦ : fastidiously selective

♦ choosy, dainty, delicate, demanding, exacting, fastidious, finicky, fussy, nice, old-maidish, particular, selective

¹pic•nic \ˈpik-ˌnik\ *n* **1** : an outing with food usually provided by members of the group and eaten in the open **2** ♦ : an easy task or feat

♦ breeze, child's play, cinch, pushover, snap

²picnic *vb* **pic•nicked; pic•nick•ing** : to go on a picnic : eat in picnic fashion
pi•cot \ˈpē-ˌkō\ *n* : one of a series of small loops forming an edging on ribbon or lace
pic•to•ri•al \pik-ˈtōr-ē-əl\ *adj* **1** : of, relating to, or consisting of pictures **2** : suggesting or conveying visual images ⟨~ poetry⟩
¹pic•ture \ˈpik-chər\ *n* **1** ♦ : a representation made by painting, drawing, or photography **2** ♦ : a vivid description in words **3** : something that by its likeness vividly suggests some other thing : IMAGE **4** : a transitory visual image (as on a TV screen) **5** : a representation (as of a story) by means of motion pictures : MOVIE **6** : position with respect to conditions and circumstances : SITUATION **7** ♦ : a mental image

♦ [1] illustration, image, likeness ♦ [2] delineation, depiction, description, portrait, portrayal, sketch ♦ [7] concept, idea, image, impression, notion, thought

²picture *vb* **pic•tured; pic•tur•ing** **1** ♦ : to paint or draw a picture of **2** ♦ : to describe vividly in words **3** ♦ : to form a mental image of

♦ [1] depict, image, portray, represent ♦ [2] delineate, depict, describe, draw, image, paint, portray, sketch ♦ [3] conceive, dream, envisage, fancy, imagine, vision, visualize

picture–perfect *adj* ♦ : completely flawless : PERFECT

♦ absolute, faultless, flawless, ideal, immaculate, impeccable, irreproachable, letter-perfect, perfect, unblemished

pic•tur•esque \ˌpik-chə-ˈresk\ *adj* **1** : resembling a picture ⟨a ~ landscape⟩ **2** : CHARMING, QUAINT ⟨a ~ character⟩ **3** : evoking mental images : GRAPHIC, VIVID ⟨a ~ account⟩ — **pic•tur•esque•ness** *n*
picture tube *n* : a cathode-ray tube on which the picture in a television set appears
pid•dle \ˈpid-ᵊl\ *vb* **pid•dled; pid•dling** : to act or work idly : DAWDLE
pid•dling \ˈpid-ᵊl-ən, -iŋ\ *adj* : of little worth or importance : TRIVIAL, PALTRY
pid•dly \ˈpid-lē\ *adj* : TRIVIAL, PIDDLING
pid•gin \ˈpi-jən\ *n* : a simplified speech used for communication between people with different languages

pie \ˈpī\ *n* **:** a dish consisting of a pastry crust and a filling (as of fruit or meat)

[1]**pie·bald** \ˈpī-ˌbȯld\ *adj* ♦ **:** of different colors; *esp* **:** blotched with white and black ⟨a ∼ horse⟩

♦ dappled, mottled, pied, spotted

[2]**piebald** *n* **:** a piebald animal

[1]**piece** \ˈpēs\ *n* **1** ♦ **:** a part of a whole **:** FRAGMENT **2 :** one of a group, set, or mass; *also* **:** a single item ⟨a ∼ of news⟩ **3 :** a length, weight, or size in which something is made or sold **4 :** a product (as an essay) of creative work **5 :** a weapon from which a shot is discharged by gunpowder **:** FIREARM **6 :** COIN **7** ♦ **:** a literary, journalistic, artistic, dramatic, or musical composition

♦ [1] bit, fragment, scrap ♦ [7] composition, opus, work

[2]**piece** *vb* **pieced; piec·ing 1 :** to repair or complete by adding pieces **:** PATCH **2** ♦ **:** to join into a whole

♦ assemble, build, construct, erect, fabricate, make, make up, put up, raise, rear, set up

pièce de ré·sis·tance \pē-ˌes-də-rā-ˌzē-ˈstäns\ *n, pl* **pièces de ré·sis·tance** *same*\ **1 :** the chief dish of a meal **2 :** an outstanding item

piece·meal \ˈpēs-ˌmēl\ *adv or adj* **:** one piece at a time **:** GRADUALLY

piece·work \-ˌwərk\ *n* **:** work done and paid for by the piece — **piece·work·er** *n*

pie chart *n* **:** a circular chart that shows quantities or frequencies by parts of a circle shaped like pieces of pie

pied \ˈpīd\ *adj* ♦ **:** of two or more colors in blotches

♦ dappled, mottled, piebald, spotted

pied–à–terre \pē-ˌā-də-ˈter\ *n, pl* **pieds–à–terre** *same*\ **:** a temporary or second lodging

pier \ˈpir\ *n* **1 :** a support for a bridge span **2** ♦ **:** a structure built out into the water for use as a landing place or a promenade or to protect or form a harbor **3** ♦ **:** an upright supporting part (as a pillar) of a building or structure

♦ [2] dock, float, jetty, landing, levee, quay, wharf ♦ [3] column, pillar, post, stanchion

pierce \ˈpirs\ *vb* **pierced; pierc·ing 1** ♦ **:** to enter or thrust into sharply or painfully **:** STAB **2** ♦ **:** to make a hole in or through **:** PERFORATE **3** ♦ **:** to force or make a way into or through **:** PENETRATE **4 :** to see through **:** DISCERN

♦ [1] gore, harpoon, impale, lance, puncture, skewer, spear, spike, stab, stick, transfix ♦ [2] bore, drill, hole, perforate, punch, puncture ♦ [3] access, enter, penetrate, probe

piercing *adj* **1** ♦ **:** marked by intensity or volume of sound **2 :** PERCEPTIVE ⟨∼ eyes⟩ **3** ♦ **:** penetratingly cold **4 :** CUTTING, INCISIVE ⟨∼ sarcasm⟩

♦ [1] booming, clamorous (*or* clamourous), deafening, earsplitting, loud, resounding, ringing, roaring, sonorous, stentorian, thunderous ♦ [3] biting, bitter, cutting, keen, penetrating, raw, sharp

pies *pl of* PIE

pi·ety \ˈpī-ə-tē\ *n, pl* **pi·et·ies 1 :** fidelity to natural obligations (as to parents) **2** ♦ **:** dutifulness in religion **3 :** a pious act

♦ devotion, faith, religion ♦ blessedness, devoutness, godliness, holiness, sainthood, sanctity

pif·fle \ˈpi-fəl\ *n* ♦ **:** trivial nonsense

♦ bunk, claptrap, drivel, foolishness, hogwash, nonsense

pig \ˈpig\ *n* **1 :** SWINE; *esp* **:** a young domesticated swine **2 :** PORK **3 :** a dirty, gluttonous, or repulsive person **4 :** a crude casting of metal (as iron)

pi·geon \ˈpi-jən\ *n* **1 :** any of numerous stout-bodied short-legged birds with smooth thick plumage **2** ♦ **:** an easy mark **:** DUPE

♦ dupe, gull, sap, sucker, tool

[1]**pi·geon·hole** \ˈpi-jən-ˌhōl\ *n* **:** a small open compartment (as in a desk) for keeping letters or documents

[2]**pigeonhole** *vb* **1 :** to place in or as if in a pigeonhole **:** FILE **2 :** to lay aside **3 :** to assign to a usually restrictive category

pi·geon–toed \-ˌtōd\ *adj* **:** having the toes turned in

pig·gish \ˈpi-gish\ *adj* **1** ♦ **:** having a strong desire for food or drink **:** GREEDY **2 :** STUBBORN

♦ gluttonous, greedy, hoggish, rapacious, ravenous, voracious

pig·gy·back \ˈpi-gē-ˌbak\ *adv or adj* **1 :** up on the back and shoulders **2 :** on a railroad flatcar

pig·head·ed \ˈpig-ˈhe-dəd\ *adj* ♦ **:** willfully or perversely unyielding **:** OBSTINATE, STUBBORN

♦ dogged, hardheaded, headstrong, mulish, obdurate, obstinate, opinionated, peevish, pertinacious, perverse, stubborn, unyielding, willful

pig latin *n, often cap L* **:** a jargon that is made by systematic alteration of English

pig·let \ˈpi-glət\ *n* **:** a small usually young swine

pig·ment \ˈpig-mənt\ *n* **1** ♦ **:** coloring matter **2 :** a powder mixed with a liquid to give color (as in paints) — **pig·ment·ed** \-mən-təd\ *adj*

♦ color (*or* colour), dye, stain

pig·men·ta·tion \ˌpig-mən-ˈtā-shən\ *n* **:** coloration with or deposition of pigment; *esp* **:** an excessive deposition of bodily pigment

pigmy *var of* PYGMY

pig·nut \ˈpig-ˌnət\ *n* **:** the bitter nut of any of several hickory trees; *also* **:** any of these trees

pig·pen \-ˌpen\ *n* **1 :** a pen for pigs **2** ♦ **:** a dirty place

♦ hole, pigsty, shambles

pig·skin \-ˌskin\ *n* **1 :** the skin of a swine or leather made of it **2 :** FOOTBALL 2

pig·sty \-ˌstī\ *n* **1 :** a pen for pigs **2** ♦ **:** a dirty place

♦ [2] hole, pigpen, shambles

pig·tail \-ˌtāl\ *n* **:** a tight braid of hair

pi·ka \ˈpī-kə\ *n* **:** any of various small short-eared mammals related to the rabbits and occurring in rocky uplands of Asia and western No. America

[1]**pike** \ˈpīk\ *n* **:** a sharp point or spike

[2]**pike** *n, pl* **pike** *or* **pikes :** a large slender long-snouted freshwater bony fish valued for food; *also* **:** any of various related fishes

[3]**pike** *n* ♦ **:** a long wooden shaft with a pointed steel head formerly used as a foot soldier's weapon

♦ lance, spear

[4]**pike** *n* **:** a main road; *esp* **:** a paved highway with a rounded surface **:** TURNPIKE

pik·er \ˈpī-kər\ *n* **1 :** one who does things in a small way or on a small scale **2 :** a close or miserly person **:** TIGHTWAD, CHEAPSKATE

pike·staff \ˈpīk-ˌstaf\ *n* **:** the staff of a foot soldier's pike

pi·laf *also* **pi·laff** \pi-ˈläf, ˈpē-ˌläf\ *or* **pi·lau** \pi-ˈlō, -ˈlȯ, ˈpē-lō, -lȯ\ *n* **:** a dish made of seasoned rice often with meat

pi·las·ter \pi-ˈlas-tər, ˈpī-ˌlas-tər\ *n* **:** an architectural support that looks like a rectangular column and projects slightly from a wall

pil·chard \ˈpil-chərd\ *n* **:** a small European marine fish related to the herrings and often packed as a sardine

[1]**pile** \ˈpīl\ *n* **:** a long slender column (as of wood or steel) driven into the ground to support a vertical load

[2]**pile** *n* **1** ♦ **:** a quantity of things heaped together **2 :** PYRE **3** ♦ **:** a great number or quantity **:** LOT

♦ [1] cock, heap, hill, mound, mountain, rick, stack ♦ [3] abundance, deal, gobs, heap, loads, lot, plenty, quantity

[3]**pile** *vb* **piled; pil·ing 1** ♦ **:** to lay in a pile **:** STACK **2** ♦ **:** to heap up **:** ACCUMULATE — usually used with *up* **3 :** to press forward in a mass **:** CROWD

♦ [1] heap, hill, mound, stack ***Ant*** unpile ♦ *usu* **pile up** [2] accumulate, collect, conglomerate, gather, heap

[4]**pile** *n* **1** ♦ **:** a coat or surface of usually short close fine furry hairs **2** ♦ **:** a velvety surface produced by an extra set of filling yarns that form raised loops which are cut and sheared — **piled** \ˈpīld\ *adj* — **pile·less** *adj*

♦ [1] coat, fleece, fur, hair, pelage, wool ♦ [2] down, floss, fluff, fur, fuzz, lint, nap

piles \ˈpīlz\ *n pl* **:** HEMORRHOIDS

pil·fer \ˈpil-fər\ *vb* ♦ **:** to steal in small quantities

♦ appropriate, filch, hook, misappropriate, nip, pocket, purloin, snitch, steal, swipe, thieve

pil·grim \ˈpil-grəm\ *n* **1 :** one who journeys in foreign lands **:** WAYFARER **2 :** one who travels to a shrine or holy place as an act of devotion **3** *cap* **:** one of the English settlers founding Plymouth colony in 1620

pil·grim·age \-grə-mij\ *n* **:** a journey of a pilgrim especially to a shrine or holy place

pil·ing \ˈpī-liŋ\ *n* **:** a structure of piles

pill \ˈpil\ *n* **1** ♦ **:** a medicine in a small rounded mass to be swallowed whole **2 :** a disagreeable or tiresome person **3** *often cap* **:** an oral contraceptive — usually used with *the*

♦ capsule, tablet

pil·lage \ˈpi-lij\ *vb* **pil·laged; pil·lag·ing ♦ :** to take booty **:** LOOT — **pillage** *n* — **pil·lag·er** *n*

♦ despoil, loot, maraud, plunder, ransack, sack, strip

pil·lar \ˈpi-lər\ *n* **1 ♦ :** a strong upright support (as for a roof) **2 :** a column or shaft standing alone especially as a monument **3 ♦ :** a supporting, integral, or upstanding member or part — **pil·lared** \-lərd\ *adj*

♦ [1] column, pier, post, stanchion ♦ [3] buttress, dependence, mainstay, reliance, standby, support

pill·box \ˈpil-ˌbäks\ *n* **1 :** a shallow round box for pills **2 :** a low concrete emplacement especially for machine guns

pil·lion \ˈpil-yən\ *n* **1 :** a pad or cushion placed behind a saddle for an extra rider **2** *chiefly Brit* **:** a motorcycle or bicycle saddle for a passenger

[1]**pil·lo·ry** \ˈpi-lə-rē\ *n, pl* **-ries :** a wooden frame for public punishment having holes in which the head and hands can be locked

[2]**pillory** *vb* **-ried; -ry·ing 1 :** to set in a pillory **2 :** to expose to public scorn

[1]**pil·low** \ˈpi-lō\ *n* **:** a case filled with springy material (as feathers) and used to support the head of a resting person

[2]**pillow** *vb* **:** to rest or place on or as if on a pillow; *also* **:** to serve as a pillow for

pil·low·case \-ˌkās\ *n* **:** a removable covering for a pillow

[1]**pi·lot** \ˈpī-lət\ *n* **1 :** HELMSMAN, STEERSMAN **2 :** a person qualified and licensed to take ships into and out of a port **3 :** GUIDE, LEADER **4 ♦ :** one that flies an aircraft or spacecraft **5 :** a television show filmed or taped as a sample of a proposed series — **pi·lot·less** *adj*

♦ airman, aviator, flier

[2]**pilot** *vb* **♦ :** to act as a guide to **:** lead or conduct over a usually difficult course

♦ coach, counsel, guide, lead, mentor, shepherd, show, tutor ♦ conduct, direct, guide, lead, marshal, route, show, steer, usher

[3]**pilot** *adj* **:** serving as a guiding or activating device or as a testing or trial unit ⟨a ~ light⟩ ⟨a ~ factory⟩

pi·lot·house \ˈpī-lət-ˌhau̇s\ *n* **:** a shelter on the upper deck of a ship for the steering gear and the helmsman

pilot whale *n* **:** either of two mostly black medium-sized whales

pil·sner *also* **pil·sen·er** \ˈpilz-nər, ˈpil-zə-\ *n* **1 :** a light beer with a strong flavor of hops **2 :** a tall slender footed glass for beer

pi·men·to \pə-ˈmen-tō\ *n, pl* **pimentos** *or* **pimento 1 :** ALLSPICE **2 :** PIMIENTO

pi·mien·to \pə-ˈmen-tō\ *n, pl* **-tos :** any of various mild red sweet pepper fruits used especially to stuff olives and to make paprika

pimp \ˈpimp\ *n* **:** a man who solicits clients for a prostitute — **pimp** *vb*

pim·per·nel \ˈpim-pər-ˌnel, -nəl\ *n* **:** any of a genus of herbs related to the primroses

pim·ple \ˈpim-pəl\ *n* **:** a small inflamed swelling on the skin often containing pus — **pim·ply** \-p(ə-)lē\ *adj*

[1]**pin** \ˈpin\ *n* **1 :** a piece of wood or metal used especially for fastening things together or as a support by which one thing may be suspended from another; *esp* **:** a small pointed piece of wire with a head used for fastening clothes or attaching papers **2 :** an ornament or emblem fastened to clothing with a pin **3 :** one of the wooden pieces constituting the target (as in bowling); *also* **:** the staff of the flag marking a hole on a golf course **4 :** LEG

[2]**pin** *vb* **pinned; pin·ning 1 :** to fasten, join, or secure with a pin **2 :** to hold fast or immobile **3 :** ATTACH, HANG ⟨*pinned* their hopes on one man⟩ **4 :** to assign the blame for ⟨~ a crime on someone⟩ **5 :** to define clearly **:** ESTABLISH ⟨~ down an idea⟩

PIN *abbr* personal identification number

pi·ña co·la·da \ˌpēn-yə-kō-ˈlä-də, ˌpē-nə-\ *n* **:** a tall drink made of rum, cream of coconut, and pineapple juice mixed with ice

pin·afore \ˈpi-nə-ˌfōr\ *n* **:** a sleeveless dress or apron fastened at the back

pin·ball machine \ˈpin-ˌbȯl-\ *n* **:** an amusement device in which a ball is maneuvered along a slanted surface among a series of targets for points

pince–nez \paⁿs-ˈnā\ *n, pl* **pince–nez** *same or* -ˈnāz\ **:** eyeglasses clipped to the nose by a spring

pin·cer \ˈpin-sər\ *n* **1** *pl* **:** a gripping instrument with two handles and two grasping jaws **2 :** a claw (as of a lobster) resembling pincers

[1]**pinch** \ˈpinch\ *vb* **1 :** to squeeze between the finger and thumb or between the jaws of an instrument **2 :** to compress painfully **3 :** CONTRACT, SHRIVEL **4 :** to be miserly; *also* **:** to subject to strict economy **5 :** to confine or limit narrowly **6 :** to take (the property of another) wrongfully **:** STEAL **7 :** to take or keep in custody by authority of law **:** ARREST

[2]**pinch** *n* **1 :** a critical point **:** EMERGENCY **2 :** painful effect **3 :** an act of pinching **4 :** a very small quantity **5 :** ARREST

[3]**pinch** *adj* **:** SUBSTITUTE ⟨a ~ runner⟩

pinch–hit \ˌpinch-ˈhit\ *vb* **1 :** to bat in the place of another player especially when a hit is particularly needed **2 ♦ :** to act or serve in place of another — **pinch hit** *n*

♦ cover, fill in, stand in, sub, substitute, take over

pinch hitter *n* **♦ :** one that pinch-hits

♦ backup, relief, replacement, reserve, stand-in, sub, substitute

pin curl *n* **:** a curl made usually by dampening a strand of hair, coiling it, and securing it by a hairpin or clip

pin·cush·ion \ˈpin-ˌku̇-shən\ *n* **:** a cushion for pins not in use

[1]**pine** \ˈpīn\ *n* **:** any of a genus of evergreen cone-bearing trees; *also* **:** the light durable resinous wood of a pine

[2]**pine** *vb* **pined; pin·ing 1 :** to lose vigor or health through distress **2 ♦ :** to long for something intensely

♦ *usu* **pine for** ache for, covet, crave, desire, die (to *or* for), hanker for, hunger for, long for, lust (for *or* after), repine for, thirst for, want, wish for, yearn for

pi·ne·al \ˈpī-nē-əl, pī-ˈnē-əl\ *n* **:** PINEAL GLAND — **pineal** *adj*

pineal gland *n* **:** a small usually conical appendage of the brain of all vertebrates with a cranium that functions primarily as an endocrine organ

pine·ap·ple \ˈpīn-ˌa-pəl\ *n* **:** a tropical plant bearing a large edible juicy fruit; *also* **:** its fruit

pin·feath·er \ˈpin-ˌfe-t͟hər\ *n* **:** a new feather just coming through the skin

ping \ˈpiŋ\ *n* **1 :** a sharp sound like that of a bullet striking **2 :** engine knock

pin·hole \ˈpin-ˌhōl\ *n* **♦ :** a small hole made by, for, or as if by a pin

♦ perforation, prick, punch, puncture, stab

[1]**pin·ion** \ˈpin-yən\ *n* **:** the end section of a bird's wing; *also* **:** WING

[2]**pinion** *vb* **:** to restrain by binding the arms; *also* **:** SHACKLE

[3]**pinion** *n* **:** a gear with a small number of teeth designed to mesh with a larger wheel or rack

[1]**pink** \ˈpiŋk\ *n* **1 :** any of a genus of plants with narrow leaves often grown for their showy flowers **2 :** the highest degree **:** HEIGHT ⟨the ~ of condition⟩

[2]**pink** *n* **:** a light tint of red

[3]**pink** *adj* **1 :** of the color pink **2 :** holding socialistic views — **pink·ish** *adj*

[4]**pink** *vb* **1 :** to perforate in an ornamental pattern **2 :** PIERCE, STAB **3 :** to cut a saw-toothed edge on

pink·eye \ˈpiŋk-ˌī\ *n* **:** an acute contagious eye inflammation

pin·kie *or* **pin·ky** \ˈpiŋ-kē\ *n, pl* **pinkies :** the smallest finger of the hand

pin·nace \ˈpi-nəs\ *n* **1 :** a light sailing ship **2 :** a ship's boat

pin·na·cle \ˈpi-ni-kəl\ *n* **1 :** a turret ending in a small spire **2 :** a lofty peak **3 ♦ :** the highest point of development or achievement **:** ACME

♦ acme, apex, climax, crown, culmination, head, height, meridian, peak, summit, tip-top, top, zenith

pin·nate \ˈpi-ˌnāt\ *adj* **:** resembling a feather especially in having similar parts arranged on each side of an axis ⟨a ~ leaf⟩ — **pin·nate·ly** *adv*

pi·noch·le \ˈpē-ˌnə-kəl\ *n* **:** a card game played with a 48-card deck

pi·ñon *or* **pin·yon** \ˈpin-ˌyōn, -ˌyän\ *n, pl* **pi·ñons** *or* **pi·ño·nes** \pin-ˈyō-nēz\ *or* **pin·yons :** any of various small pines of western No. America with edible seeds; *also* **:** the edible seed of a piñon

pin·point \ˈpin-ˌpȯint\ *vb* **♦ :** to locate, hit, or aim with great precision

♦ distinguish, identify, single

pin·prick \-ˌprik\ *n* **1 :** a small puncture made by or as if by a pin **2 :** a petty irritation or annoyance

pins and needles *n pl* **:** a pricking tingling sensation in a limb growing numb or recovering from numbness — **on pins and needles :** in a nervous or jumpy state of anticipation

pin·stripe \ˈpin-ˌstrīp\ *n* **:** a narrow stripe on a fabric; *also* **:** a suit with such stripes — **pin–striped** \-ˌstrīpt\ *adj*

pint \ˈpīnt\ *n* : a unit of capacity equal to ½ quart
pin·to \ˈpin-ˌtō\ *n, pl* **pintos** *also* **pintoes** : a spotted horse or pony
pinto bean *n* : a spotted seed produced by a kind of kidney bean and used for food
pint–size \ˈpīnt-ˌsīz\ *or* **pint–sized** \-ˌsīzd\ *adj* : having comparatively little size or slight dimensions : SMALL
pin·up \ˈpin-ˌəp\ *adj* : suitable or designed for hanging on a wall; *also* : suited (as by beauty) to be the subject of a pinup photograph
pin·wheel \-ˌhwēl, -ˌwēl\ *n* **1** : a fireworks device in the form of a revolving wheel of colored fire **2** : a toy consisting of lightweight vanes that revolve at the end of a stick
pin·worm \-ˌwərm\ *n* : a nematode worm parasitic in the human intestine
pin·yin \ˈpin-ˈyin\ *n, often cap* : a system for writing Chinese ideograms by using Roman letters to represent the sounds
¹pi·o·neer \ˌpī-ə-ˈnir\ *n* **1** : one that originates or helps open up a new line of thought or activity **2** ♦ : an early settler in a territory

♦ colonist, frontiersman, homesteader, settler

²pioneer *vb* **1** : to act as a pioneer **2** : to open or prepare for others to follow; *also* : SETTLE **3** ♦ : to originate or take part in the development of

♦ constitute, establish, found, inaugurate, initiate, innovate, institute, introduce, launch, set up, start

pi·ous \ˈpī-əs\ *adj* **1** ♦ : marked by reverence for deity : DEVOUT **2** : excessively or affectedly religious **3** : SACRED, DEVOTIONAL **4** ♦ : showing loyal reverence for a person or thing **5** : marked by sham or hypocrisy — **pi·ous·ly** *adv*

♦ [1] devout, faithful, godly, holy, religious, sainted, saintly ♦ [4] constant, devoted, faithful, fast, good, loyal, staunch, steadfast, steady, true, true-blue

¹pip \ˈpip\ *n* : one of the dots used on dice and dominoes to indicate numerical value
²pip *n* **1** : a small fruit seed (as of an apple) **2** ♦ : one extraordinary of its kind

♦ beauty, crackerjack, dandy, jim-dandy, knockout

¹pipe \ˈpīp\ *n* **1** : a tubular musical instrument played by forcing air through it **2** : BAGPIPE **3** ♦ : a tube designed to conduct something (as water, steam, or oil) **4** : a device for smoking having a tube with a bowl at one end and a mouthpiece at the other **5** : a large cask of varying capacity used especially for wine and oil

♦ channel, conduit, duct, leader, line, penstock, tube

²pipe *vb* **piped; pip·ing** **1** : to play on a pipe **2 a** : to speak in a high or shrill voice **b** : to emit a shrill sound **3** ♦ : to convey by or as if by pipes — **pip·er** *n*

♦ channel, conduct, direct, funnel, siphon

pipe down *vb* ♦ : to stop talking or making noise

♦ calm (down), cool (off *or* down), hush, quiet, settle (down) ♦ clam up, hush, quiet (down), shut up

pipe dream *n* ♦ : an illusory or fantastic hope

♦ chimera, conceit, daydream, delusion, dream, fancy, fantasy, figment, hallucination, illusion, phantasm, unreality, vision

pipe·line \ˈpīp-ˌlīn\ *n* **1** : a line of pipe with pumps, valves, and control devices for conveying fluids **2** : a channel for information
pi·pette *or* **pi·pet** \pī-ˈpet\ *n* : a device for measuring and transferring small volumes of liquid
pipe up *vb* : to speak loudly and distinctly; *also* : to express an opinion freely
pip·ing \ˈpī-piŋ\ *n* **1** : the music of pipes **2** : a narrow fold of material used to decorate edges or seams
piping hot *adj* : very hot
pip·pin \ˈpi-pən\ *n* : a crisp tart usually yellowish apple
pip–squeak \ˈpip-ˌskwēk\ *n* ♦ : one that is small or insignificant

♦ nobody, nonentity, nothing, whippersnapper, zero

pi·quant \ˈpē-kənt\ *adj* **1** : pleasantly savory : PUNGENT **2** : engagingly provocative; *also* : having a lively charm — **pi·quan·cy** \-kən-sē\ *n*
¹pique \ˈpēk\ *n* ♦ : a passing feeling of wounded vanity : RESENTMENT

♦ dudgeon, huff, offense, peeve, resentment, umbrage

²pique *vb* **piqued; piqu·ing** **1** ♦ : to arouse anger or resentment in : IRRITATE **2** ♦ : to arouse by a provocation or challenge

♦ [1] aggravate, annoy, bother, bug, chafe, exasperate, gall, get, grate, irk, irritate, nettle, peeve, persecute, put out, rasp, rile, vex ♦ [2] arouse, encourage, excite, fire, incite, instigate, move, provoke, stimulate, stir

pi·qué *or* **pi·que** \pi-ˈkā\ *n* : a durable ribbed clothing fabric
pi·quet \pi-ˈkā\ *n* : a 2-handed card game played with 32 cards
pi·ra·cy \ˈpī-rə-sē\ *n, pl* **-cies** **1** : robbery on the high seas; *also* : an act resembling such robbery **2** : the unauthorized use of another's production or invention
pi·ra·nha \pə-ˈrä-nə, -ˈrän-yə\ *n* : any of various usually small So. American fishes with sharp teeth that include some known to attack humans and large animals
pi·rate \ˈpī-rət\ *n* ♦ : one who commits piracy — **pirate** *vb* — **pi·rat·i·cal** \pə-ˈra-ti-kəl, pī-\ *adj*

♦ buccaneer, corsair, freebooter, rover

¹pir·ou·ette \ˌpir-ə-ˈwet\ *n* : a rapid whirling about of the body; *esp* : a full turn on the toe or ball of one foot in ballet
²pirouette *vb* ♦ : to turn in or as if in a pirouette

♦ gyrate, revolve, roll, rotate, spin, turn, twirl, wheel, whirl

pis *pl of* PI
pis·ca·to·ri·al \ˌpis-kə-ˈtōr-ē-əl\ *adj* : of or relating to fishing
Pi·sces \ˈpī-sēz\ *n* **1** : a zodiacal constellation between Aquarius and Aries usually pictured as a fish **2** : the 12th sign of the zodiac in astrology; *also* : one born under this sign
pis·mire \ˈpis-ˌmīr\ *n* : ANT
pis·ta·chio \pə-ˈsta-shē-ˌō, -ˈstä-\ *n, pl* **-chios** : the greenish edible seed of a small Asian tree related to the sumacs; *also* : the tree
pis·til \ˈpist-ᵊl\ *n* : the female reproductive organ in a flower — **pis·til·late** \ˈpis-tə-ˌlāt\ *adj*
pis·tol \ˈpist-ᵊl\ *n* : a handgun whose chamber is integral with the barrel
pis·tol–whip \-ˌhwip\ *vb* : to beat with a pistol
pis·ton \ˈpis-tən\ *n* : a sliding piece that receives and transmits motion and that usually consists of a short cylinder inside a large cylinder
¹pit \ˈpit\ *n* **1** ♦ : a hole, shaft, or cavity in the ground **2** : an often sunken area designed for a particular use; *also* : an enclosed place (as for cockfights) **3** : HELL; *also, pl* : WORST ⟨it's the ~*s*⟩ **4** ♦ : a natural hollow or indentation in a surface **5** : a small indented mark or scar (as from disease or corrosion) **6** : an area beside a racecourse where cars are fueled and repaired during a race

♦ [1, 4] cavity, concavity, dent, depression, hole, hollow, indentation, recess

²pit *vb* **pit·ted; pit·ting** **1** : to form pits in or become marred with pits **2** : to match for fighting
³pit *n* : the stony seed of some fruits (as the cherry, peach, and date)
⁴pit *vb* **pit·ted; pit·ting** : to remove the pit from
pi·ta \ˈpē-tə\ *n* : a thin flat bread
pit–a–pat \ˌpi-ti-ˈpat\ *n* : PITTER-PATTER — **pit–a–pat** *adv or adj*
pit bull *n* : a powerful compact short-haired dog developed for fighting
¹pitch \ˈpich\ *n* **1** : a dark sticky substance left over especially from distilling tar or petroleum **2** : resin from various conifers
²pitch *vb* **1** ♦ : to erect and fix firmly in place ⟨~ a tent⟩ **2** ♦ : to throw usually with a particular objective or toward a particular point **3** : to deliver a baseball to a batter **4** : to toss (as coins) toward a mark **5** : to set at a particular level ⟨~ the voice low⟩ **6** : to fall headlong **7** : to have the front end (as of a ship) alternately plunge and rise **8** : to incline downward : SLOPE

♦ [1] erect, put up, raise, rear, set up ♦ [2] cast, catapult, chuck, dash, fire, fling, heave, hurl, hurtle, launch, peg, pelt, sling, throw, toss

³pitch *n* **1** : the action or a manner of pitching **2** ♦ : degree of slope ⟨~ of a roof⟩ **3** : the relative level of some quality or state ⟨a high ~ of excitement⟩ **4** : highness or lowness of sound; *also* : a standard frequency for tuning instruments **5** : a presentation delivered to sell or promote something **6** : the delivery of a baseball to a batter; *also* : the baseball delivered

♦ cant, diagonal, grade, inclination, incline, lean, slant, slope, tilt, upgrade

pitch·blende \ˈpich-ˌblend\ *n* : a dark mineral that is the chief source of uranium
¹pitch·er \ˈpi-chər\ *n* ♦ : a container for liquids that usually has a lip and a handle

♦ ewer, flagon, jug

²pitcher *n* : one that pitches especially in a baseball game
pitcher plant *n* : any of various plants with leaves modified to resemble pitchers in which insects are trapped and digested

pitch•fork \ˈpich-ˌfȯrk\ *n* : a long-handled fork used especially in pitching hay
pitch in *vb* **1** : to begin to work **2** ♦ : to contribute to a common effort

♦ chip in, contribute, kick in

pitch•man \ˈpich-mən\ *n* : SALESMAN; *esp* : one who sells merchandise on the streets or from a concession
pitch–per•fect \ˈpich-ˈpər-fikt\ *adj* : having just the right tone or style ⟨a ~ translation⟩
pitchy \ˈpi-chē\ *adj* **1 a** : full of pitch **b** : of, relating to, or having the qualities of pitch **2** : extremely dark or black
pit•e•ous \ˈpi-tē-əs\ *adj* ♦ : arousing pity : PITIFUL — **pit•e•ous•ly** *adv*

♦ heartbreaking, miserable, pathetic, pitiful, poor, rueful, sorry, wretched

pit•fall \ˈpit-ˌfȯl\ *n* **1** : TRAP, SNARE; *esp* : a covered pit used for capturing animals **2** ♦ : a hidden danger or difficulty

♦ booby trap, catch, snag ♦ danger, hazard, menace, peril, risk, threat, trouble

pith \ˈpith\ *n* **1** : loose spongy tissue especially in the center of the stem of vascular plants **2** ♦ : the essential part : CORE

♦ core, crux, gist, heart, nub, pivot

pithy \ˈpi-thē\ *adj* **pith•i•er; -est** **1** : consisting of or filled with pith **2** ♦ : having substance and point : CONCISE

♦ brief, compact, compendious, concise, crisp, epigrammatic, laconic, succinct, summary, terse

piti•able \ˈpi-tē-ə-bəl\ *adj* **1** : arousing or deserving pity : PITIFUL **2** : of a kind to evoke mingled pity and contempt especially because of inadequacy
piti•ful \ˈpi-ti-fəl\ *adj* **1** ♦ : arousing or deserving pity ⟨a ~ sight⟩ **2** ♦ : arousing pitying contempt (as by meanness or inadequacy) — **piti•ful•ly** *adv*

♦ [1] heartbreaking, miserable, pathetic, piteous, poor, rueful, sorry, wretched ♦ [2] contemptible, despicable, lousy, nasty, scabby, scurvy, sorry, wretched

piti•less \ˈpi-ti-ləs\ *adj* ♦ : devoid of pity : MERCILESS — **pit•i•less•ly** *adv*

♦ callous, hard, heartless, inhuman, inhumane, soulless, unfeeling, unsympathetic

pi•ton \ˈpē-ˌtän\ *n* : a spike, wedge, or peg that can be driven into a rock or ice surface as a support
pit•tance \ˈpit-ᵊns\ *n* ♦ : a small portion, amount, or allowance

♦ mite, peanuts, shoestring, song

pit•ted \ˈpi-təd\ *adj* : marked with pits
¹pit•ter–pat•ter \ˈpi-tər-ˌpa-tər, ˈpi-tē-\ *n* : a rapid succession of light taps or sounds — **pitter–patter** \ˌpi-tər-ˈpa-tər, ˌpi-tē-\ *adv or adj*
²pitter–patter \ˌpi-tər-ˈpa-tər, ˌpi-tē-\ *vb* ♦ : to go pitter-patter

♦ beat, palpitate, pulsate, pulse, throb

pi•tu•i•tary \pə-ˈtü-ə-ˌter-ē, -ˈtyü-\ *n, pl* **-i•tar•ies** : PITUITARY GLAND — **pituitary** *adj*
pituitary gland *n* : a small oval endocrine gland located at the base of the brain that produces various hormones that affect most basic bodily functions (as growth and reproduction)
pit viper *n* : any of various mostly New World venomous snakes with a sensory pit on each side of the head and hollow perforated fangs
¹pity \ˈpi-tē\ *n, pl* **pit•ies** **1** ♦ : sympathetic sorrow : COMPASSION **2** : something to be regretted

♦ charity, commiseration, compassion, feeling, heart, humanity, kindliness, kindness, mercy, sympathy

²pity *vb* **pit•ied; pity•ing** ♦ : to feel pity for

♦ bleed, commiserate, feel, sympathize

¹piv•ot \ˈpi-vət\ *n* **1** : a fixed pin on which something turns **2** ♦ : a person, thing, or factor having a major or central role, function, or effect — **pivot** *adj*

♦ core, crux, gist, heart, nub, pith

²pivot *vb* ♦ : to turn on or as if on a pivot

♦ revolve, roll, rotate, spin, swing, swirl, turn, twirl, twist, wheel, whirl

piv•ot•al \ˈpi-vət-ᵊl\ *adj* ♦ : vitally important : CRITICAL

♦ critical, crucial, key, vital

pix *pl of* PIC
pix•el \ˈpik-səl, -ˌsel\ *n* : any of the small elements that together make up an image (as on a television screen)
pix•ie *also* **pixy** \ˈpik-sē\ *n, pl* **pix•ies** : FAIRY; *esp* ♦ : a mischievous sprite

♦ brownie, dwarf, elf, fairy, fay, gnome, hobgoblin, leprechaun, puck, troll

piz•za \ˈpēt-sə\ *n* : an open pie made of rolled bread dough spread with a spiced mixture (as of tomatoes, cheese, and ground meat) and baked
piz•zazz *or* **pi•zazz** \pə-ˈzaz\ *n* **1** : GLAMOUR **2** : VITALITY
piz•ze•ria \ˌpēt-sə-ˈrē-ə\ *n* : an establishment where pizzas are made and sold
piz•zi•ca•to \ˌpit-si-ˈkä-tō\ *adv or adj* : by means of plucking instead of bowing — used as a direction in music
pj's \ˈpē-ˌjāz\ *n pl* : PAJAMAS
pk *abbr* **1** park **2** peak **3** peck **4** pike
pkg *abbr* package
pkt *abbr* **1** packet **2** pocket
pkwy *abbr* parkway
pl *abbr* **1** place **2** plate **3** plural
¹plac•ard \ˈpla-kərd, -ˌkärd\ *n* ♦ : a notice posted in a public place : POSTER

♦ bill, poster

²plac•ard \-ˌkärd, -kərd\ *vb* **1** : to cover with or as if with placards **2** ♦ : to announce by or as if by posting

♦ advertise, announce, blaze, broadcast, declare, enunciate, post, proclaim, promulgate, publicize, publish, sound

pla•cate \ˈplā-ˌkāt, ˈpla-\ *vb* **pla•cat•ed; pla•cat•ing** ♦ : to soothe especially by concessions : APPEASE — **pla•ca•ble** \ˈpla-kə-bəl, ˈplā-\ *adj*

♦ appease, conciliate, disarm, mollify, pacify, propitiate

¹place \ˈplās\ *n* **1** : physical environment : SPACE **2** : an indefinite region : AREA **3** ♦ : a building or locality used for a special purpose **4** : a center of population **5** : a particular part of a surface : SPOT **6** ♦ : relative position in a scale or sequence; *also* : position at the end of a competition ⟨last ~⟩ **7** : ACCOMMODATION; *esp* : SEAT **8** : the position of a figure within a numeral ⟨12 is a two ~ number⟩ **9** ♦ : paid employment : JOB; *esp* : public office **10** : a public square **11** : 2d place at the finish (as of a horse race) **12** ♦ : a proper or designated niche **13** ♦ : a building, part of a building, or area occupied as a home

♦ [3] establishment, joint, salon ♦ [3, 12] locale, location, point, position, site, spot *Ant* scene, region, section, sector ♦ [6] degree, footing, level, position, rank, situation, standing, station, status ♦ [9] appointment, billet, capacity, function, job, position, post, situation ♦ [12] part, purpose, role, task, work ♦ [13] abode, domicile, dwelling, home, house, lodging, quarters, residence

²place *vb* **placed; plac•ing** **1** ♦ : to put in a particular place : SET **2** ♦ : to distribute in an orderly manner **3** : IDENTIFY **4** : to give an order for ⟨~ a bet⟩ **5** ♦ : to earn a given spot in a competition; *esp* : to come in 2d **6** ♦ : to judge tentatively or approximately the value, worth, or significance of : ESTIMATE

♦ [1] deposit, dispose, fix, lay, position, put, set, set up, stick ♦ [2] assort, break down, categorize, class, classify, grade, group, peg, range, rank, separate, sort ♦ [5] be, grade, rank, rate ♦ [6] calculate, call, conjecture, estimate, figure, gauge, guess, judge, make, put, reckon, suppose

pla•ce•bo \plə-ˈsē-bō\ *n, pl* **-bos** : an inert medication used for its psychological effect or for purposes of comparison in an experiment
place•hold•er \ˈplās-ˌhōl-dər\ *n* : a symbol in a mathematical or logical expression that may be replaced by the name of any element of a set
place•kick \-ˌkik\ *n* : the kicking of a ball placed or held on the ground — **placekick** *vb* — **place•kick•er** *n*
place•ment \ˈplās-mənt\ *n* : an act or instance of placing
place–name \-ˌnām\ *n* : the name of a geographical locality
pla•cen•ta \plə-ˈsen-tə\ *n, pl* **-tas** *or* **-tae** \-(ˌ)tē\ : the organ in most mammals by which the fetus is joined to the maternal uterus and is nourished — **pla•cen•tal** \-ˈsent-ᵊl\ *adj*
plac•er \ˈpla-sər\ *n* : a deposit of sand or gravel containing particles of valuable mineral (as gold)
plac•id \ˈpla-səd\ *adj* ♦ : serenely free of interruption or disturbance — **plac•id•ly** *adv*

◆ calm, collected, composed, cool, self-possessed, serene, tranquil, undisturbed, unperturbed, unshaken, untroubled, unworried ◆ calm, halcyon, hushed, peaceful, quiet, still

pla•cid•i•ty \pla-ˈsi-də-tē\ *n* ◆ **:** the quality or state of being placid

◆ calm, calmness, hush, peace, quiet, quietness, repose, serenity, still, stillness, tranquillity

plack•et \ˈpla-kət\ *n* **:** a slit in a garment
pla•gia•rise *chiefly Brit var of* PLAGIARIZE
pla•gia•rize \ˈplā-jə-ˌrīz\ *vb* **-rized; -riz•ing :** to present the ideas or words of another as one's own — **pla•gia•rism** \-ˌri-zəm\ *n* — **pla•gia•rist** \-rist\ *n*
¹plague \ˈplāg\ *n* **1 :** a disastrous evil or influx; *also* **:** NUISANCE **2 :** PESTILENCE; *esp* **:** a destructive contagious bacterial disease (as bubonic plague)
²plague *vb* **plagued; plagu•ing 1** ◆ **:** to afflict with or as if with disease or disaster **2 a :** to cause worry or distress to **b** ◆ **:** to disturb or annoy persistently

◆ [1, 2b] afflict, agonize, bedevil, curse, harrow, martyr, persecute, rack, torment, torture

plaid \ˈplad\ *n* **1 :** a rectangular length of tartan worn especially over the left shoulder as part of the Scottish national costume **2 :** a twilled woolen fabric with a tartan pattern **3 :** a pattern of unevenly spaced repeated stripes crossing at right angles — **plaid** *adj*
¹plain \ˈplān\ *n* ◆ **:** an extensive area of level or rolling treeless country

◆ down, grassland, prairie, savanna, steppe, veld

²plain *adj* **1** ◆ **:** lacking ornament ⟨a ~ dress⟩ **2** ◆ **:** free of extraneous matter **3 :** OPEN, UNOBSTRUCTED ⟨~ view⟩ **4 :** EVIDENT, OBVIOUS **5 a** ◆ **:** easily understood **:** CLEAR **b** ◆ **:** expressing oneself free of any attempt at deception or subterfuge **6** ◆ **:** marked by outspoken candor **:** CANDID, BLUNT **7 :** SIMPLE ⟨~ cooking⟩ **8 :** lacking beauty or ugliness

◆ [1] bald, bare, naked, simple, unadorned, undecorated, unvarnished ***Ant*** adorned, decorated, embellished, fancy, ornamented ◆ [2] absolute, fine, neat, pure, refined, straight, unadulterated, undiluted, unmixed ◆ [5a] apparent, broad, clear, clear cut, distinct, evident, lucid, manifest, obvious, palpable, patent, perspicuous, transparent, unambiguous, unequivocal, unmistakable ◆ [5b, 6] blunt, candid, direct, forthright, foursquare, frank, honest, open, outspoken, straight, straightforward, unguarded, unreserved

plain•clothes•man \ˈplān-ˈklōthz-mən, -ˈklōz-, -ˌman\ *n* **:** a police officer who wears civilian clothes instead of a uniform while on duty **:** DETECTIVE
plain•ly \ˈplān-lē\ *adv* ◆ **:** in a plain manner

◆ directly, forthrightly, foursquare, plain, straight, straightforward

plain•ness \ˈplān-nəs\ *n* ◆ **:** the quality or state of being plain

◆ candor (*or* candour), directness, forthrightness, frankness, openness

plain•spo•ken \-ˈspō-kən\ *adj* **:** marked by honest sincere expression **:** FRANK
plaint \ˈplānt\ *n* **1** ◆ **:** an act or instance of lamenting **:** LAMENTATION, WAIL **2** ◆ **:** a critical protest **:** COMPLAINT

◆ [1] groan, howl, keen, lament, lamentation, moan, wail ◆ [2] beef, complaint, fuss, grievance, gripe, grumble, murmur, squawk

plain•tiff \ˈplān-təf\ *n* **:** the complaining party in a lawsuit
plain•tive \ˈplān-tiv\ *adj* ◆ **:** expressive of suffering or woe — **plain•tive•ly** *adv*

◆ dolorous, funeral, lugubrious, mournful, regretful, rueful, sorrowful, weeping, woeful

¹plait \ˈplāt, ˈplat\ *n* **1 :** PLEAT **2** ◆ **:** a braid especially of hair or straw — **plait** *vb*

◆ braid, lace

¹plan \ˈplan\ *n* **1 :** a drawing or diagram showing the parts or details of something **2 a** ◆ **:** a method for accomplishing an objective **b** ◆ **:** the end toward which effort is directed **:** GOAL, AIM

◆ [2a] arrangement, blueprint, design, game, project, scheme, strategy, system ◆ [2b] aim, ambition, aspiration, design, dream, end, goal, intent, mark, meaning, object, objective, pretension, purpose, thing

²plan *vb* **planned; plan•ning 1** ◆ **:** to form a plan of ⟨~ a new city⟩ **2** ◆ **:** to have in mind **:** INTEND ⟨*planned* to go⟩ — **planner** *n*

◆ [1] arrange, blueprint, calculate, chart, design, frame, lay out, map, project, scheme ◆ [2] aim, aspire, contemplate, design, intend, mean, meditate, propose

¹plane \ˈplān\ *vb* **planed; plan•ing** ◆ **:** to smooth or level off with or as if with a plane — **plan•er** *n*

◆ even, level, smooth

²plane *n* **:** PLANE TREE
³plane *n* **:** a tool for smoothing or shaping a wood surface
⁴plane *n* **1 :** a level or flat surface **2 :** a level of existence, consciousness, or development **3 :** AIRPLANE
⁵plane *adj* **1** ◆ **:** having no elevations or depressions **:** FLAT, LEVEL **2 :** dealing with flat surfaces or figures ⟨~ geometry⟩

◆ even, flat, flush, level, smooth

⁶plane *vb* ◆ **:** to fly while keeping the wings motionless

◆ fly, glide, soar, wing

plane•load \ˈplān-ˌlōd\ *n* **:** a load that fills an airplane
plan•et \ˈpla-nət\ *n* **1 :** any of the large bodies in the solar system that revolve around the sun **2** ◆ **:** the celestial body on which we live that is third in order from the sun — **plan•e•tary** \-nə-ˌter-ē\ *adj*

◆ earth, world

plan•e•tar•i•um \ˌpla-nə-ˈter-ē-əm\ *n, pl* **-i•ums** *or* **-ia** \-ē-ə\ **:** a building or room housing a device to project images of celestial bodies
plan•e•tes•i•mal \ˌpla-nə-ˈtes-ə-məl\ *n* **:** any of numerous small solid celestial bodies which may have existed during the formation of the solar system
plan•e•toid \ˈpla-nə-ˌtȯid\ *n* **:** a body resembling a planet; *esp* **:** ASTEROID
plane tree *n* **:** any of a genus of trees (as a sycamore) with large lobed leaves and globe-shaped fruit
plan•gent \ˈplan-jənt\ *adj* **1 :** having a loud reverberating sound **2 :** having an expressive especially plaintive quality — **plan•gen•cy** \-jən-sē\ *n*
¹plank \ˈplaŋk\ *n* **1 :** a heavy thick board **2 :** an article in the platform of a political party
²plank *vb* **1 :** to cover with planks **2 :** to set or lay down forcibly **3 :** to cook and serve on a board
plank•ing \ˈplaŋ-kiŋ\ *n* **:** a quantity or covering of planks
plank•ton \ˈplaŋk-tən\ *n* **:** the passively floating or weakly swimming animal and plant life of a body of water — **plank•ton•ic** \plaŋk-ˈtä-nik\ *adj*
¹plant \ˈplant\ *vb* **1** ◆ **:** to set in the ground to grow **2 :** ESTABLISH, SETTLE **3 :** to stock or provide with something **4 :** to place firmly or forcibly **5 :** to hide or arrange with intent to deceive

◆ drill, seed, sow

²plant *n* **1 :** any of a kingdom of living things that usually have no locomotor ability or obvious sense organs and have cellulose cell walls and usually capacity for indefinite growth **2 a :** the land, buildings, and machinery used in carrying on a trade or business **b** ◆ **:** a factory or workshop for the manufacture of a particular product

◆ factory, mill, shop, works, workshop

¹plan•tain \ˈplant-ᵊn\ *n* **:** any of a genus of weedy herbs with spikes of tiny greenish flowers
²plantain *n* **:** a banana plant with starchy greenish fruit that is eaten cooked; *also* **:** its fruit
plan•tar \ˈplan-tər, -ˌtär\ *adj* **:** of or relating to the sole of the foot
plan•ta•tion \plan-ˈtā-shən\ *n* **1 :** a large group of plants and especially trees under cultivation **2 :** an agricultural estate usually worked by resident laborers
plant•er \ˈplan-tər\ *n* **1** ◆ **:** one that plants or sows; *esp* **:** an owner or operator of a plantation **2 :** a container for plants

◆ agriculturist, cultivator, farmer, grower, tiller

plant louse *n* **:** APHID
plaque \ˈplak\ *n* **1 :** an ornamental brooch **2 :** a flat thin piece (as of metal) used for decoration; *also* **:** a commemorative tablet **3 :** a bacteria-containing film on a tooth
¹plash \ˈplash\ *n* **:** SPLASH — **plash** *vb*
²plash *vb* **1** ◆ **:** to cause a splashing or spattering effect **2** ◆ **:** to splash with a liquid or with any wet substance

◆ [1] lap, slosh, splash, swash ◆ [2] dash, spatter, splash

plas•ma \ˈplaz-mə\ *n* **1 :** the fluid part of blood, lymph, or milk **2 :** a gas composed of ionized particles — **plas•mat•ic** \plaz-ˈma-tik\ *adj*

[1]**plas•ter** \ˈplas-tər\ *n* **1 :** a dressing consisting of a backing spread with an often medicated substance that clings to the skin ⟨adhesive ~⟩ **2 :** a paste that hardens as it dries and is used for coating walls and ceilings

[2]**plaster** *vb* **:** to cover with or as if with plaster — **plas•ter•er** *n*

plas•ter•board \ˈplas-tər-ˌbōrd\ *n* **:** DRYWALL

plaster of par•is \-ˈpa-rəs\ *often cap 2d P* **:** a white powder made from gypsum and used as a quick-setting paste with water for casts and molds

[1]**plas•tic** \ˈplas-tik\ *adj* **1 :** capable of being molded ⟨~ clay⟩ **2 :** characterized by or using modeling ⟨~ arts⟩ **3 :** made or consisting of a plastic — **plas•tic•i•ty** \plas-ˈti-sə-tē\ *n*

[2]**plastic** *n* **:** a plastic substance; *esp* **:** a synthetic or processed material that can be formed into rigid objects or into films or filaments

plastic surgery *n* **:** surgery to repair, restore, or improve lost, injured, defective, or misshapen body parts — **plastic surgeon** *n*

[1]**plat** \ˈplat\ *n* **1** ♦ **:** a small plot of ground **2** ♦ **:** a plan of a piece of land with actual or proposed features (as lots)

♦ [1, 2] lot, parcel, plot, property, tract

[2]**plat** *vb* **plat•ted; plat•ting :** to make a plat of

[1]**plate** \ˈplāt\ *n* **1 :** a flat thin piece of material **2 :** domestic hollowware made of or plated with gold, silver, or base metals **3 :** DISH **4 :** HOME PLATE **5 :** the molded metal or plastic cast of a page of type to be printed from **6 :** a sheet of glass or plastic coated with a chemical sensitive to light and used in photography **7 :** the part of a denture that fits to the mouth; *also* **:** DENTURE **8 :** something printed from an engraving **9 :** a huge mobile segment of the earth's crust **10** ♦ **:** a full-page illustration often on different paper from the text pages

♦ diagram, figure, graphic, illustration

[2]**plate** *vb* **plat•ed; plat•ing 1 :** to overlay with metal (as gold or silver) **2 :** to make a printing plate of

pla•teau \pla-ˈtō\ *n, pl* **plateaus** *or* **pla•teaux** \-ˈtōz\ ♦ **:** a large level area of high land

♦ mesa, table, tableland

plate glass *n* **:** rolled, ground, and polished sheet glass

plate•let \ˈplāt-lət\ *n* **:** a minute flattened body; *esp* **:** a minute colorless disklike body of mammalian blood that assists in blood clotting

plat•en \ˈplat-ᵊn\ *n* **1 :** a flat plate; *esp* **:** one that exerts or receives pressure (as in a printing press) **2 :** the roller of a typewriter or printer

plate tectonics *n* **1 :** a theory in geology that the lithosphere is divided into plates at the boundaries of which much of earth's seismic activity occurs **2 :** the process and dynamics of tectonic plate movement

plat•form \ˈplat-ˌfȯrm\ *n* **1** ♦ **:** a raised flooring or stage for speakers, performers, or workers **2 :** a declaration of the principles on which a group of persons (as a political party) stands

♦ dais, podium, rostrum, stage, stand

plat•ing \ˈplā-tiŋ\ *n* **:** a coating of metal plates or plate ⟨the ~ of a ship⟩

plat•i•num \ˈplat-ᵊn-əm\ *n* **:** a heavy grayish white metallic chemical element

plat•i•tude \ˈpla-tə-ˌtüd, -ˌtyüd\ *n* ♦ **:** a flat or trite remark — **plat•i•tu•di•nous** \-ˈtüd-ᵊn-əs, -ˈtyüd-\ *adj*

♦ banality, cliché, commonplace, shibboleth

pla•ton•ic love \plə-ˈtä-nik-, plā-\ *n, often cap P* **:** a close relationship between two persons without sexual desire

pla•toon \plə-ˈtün\ *n* **1 :** a subdivision of a company-size military unit usually consisting of two or more squads or sections **2 :** a group of football players trained either for offense or for defense and sent into the game as a body

platoon sergeant *n* **:** a noncommissioned officer in the army ranking below a first sergeant

plat•ter \ˈpla-tər\ *n* **1 :** a large serving plate **2 :** a phonograph record

platy \ˈpla-tē\ *n, pl* **platy** *or* **plat•ys** *or* **plat•ies :** either of two small stocky usually brilliantly colored bony fishes often kept in tropical aquariums

platy•pus \ˈpla-ti-pəs\ *n, pl* **platy•pus•es** *also* **platy•pi** \-ˌpī\ **:** a small aquatic egg-laying marsupial mammal of Australia with webbed feet and a fleshy bill like a duck's

plau•dit \ˈplȯ-dət\ *n* **:** an act of applause

plau•si•ble \ˈplȯ-zə-bəl\ *adj* ♦ **:** seemingly worthy of belief — **plau•si•bil•i•ty** \ˌplȯ-zə-ˈbi-lə-tē\ *n* — **plau•si•bly** \ˈplȯ-zə-blē\ *adv*

♦ believable, credible, likely, probable

[1]**play** \ˈplā\ *n* **1 :** brisk handling of something (as a weapon) **2 :** the course of a game; *also* **:** a particular act or maneuver in a game **3** ♦ **:** recreational activity; *esp* **:** the spontaneous activity of children **4 :** absence of serious or harmful intent **:** JEST ⟨said in ~⟩ **5 :** the act or an instance of punning **6 :** GAMBLING **7** ♦ **:** the state of being active, operative, or relevant **:** OPERATION ⟨bring extra force into ~⟩ **8 :** a brisk or light movement **9 :** free motion (as of part of a machine) **10 :** scope for action **11 :** PUBLICITY **12 :** an effort to arouse liking ⟨made a ~ for her⟩ **13 :** a stage representation of a drama; *also* **:** a dramatic composition **14 :** a function of an electronic device that causes a recording to play — **in play :** in condition or position to be played

♦ [3] dalliance, frolic, fun, relaxation, sport ♦ [7] application, employment, exercise, operation, use

[2]**play** *vb* **1** ♦ **:** to engage in recreation **:** FROLIC **2** ♦ **:** to handle or behave lightly or absentmindedly **3 :** to make a pun ⟨~ on words⟩ **4** ♦ **:** to take advantage ⟨~ on fears⟩ **5 :** to move or operate in a brisk or irregular manner ⟨a flashlight *~ed* over the wall⟩ **6 :** to perform music ⟨~ on a violin⟩; *also* **:** to perform (music) on an instrument ⟨~ a waltz⟩ **7 :** to perform music upon ⟨~ the piano⟩; *also* **:** to sound in performance ⟨the organ is *~ing*⟩ **8 :** to cause to emit sounds ⟨~ a radio⟩; *also* **:** to cause to reproduce recorded material ⟨~ a DVD⟩ **9 a :** to act in a dramatic medium **b** ♦ **:** to act in the character of ⟨~ the hero⟩ **10 :** GAMBLE **11 a :** to behave in a specified way ⟨~ safe⟩ **b** ♦ **:** to feign a specified state or quality **c :** COOPERATE ⟨~ along with him⟩ **12 :** to deal with; *also* **:** EMPHASIZE ⟨~ up her good qualities⟩ **13 :** to perform for amusement ⟨~ a trick⟩ **14 :** WREAK **15 :** to contend with in a game; *also* **:** to fill (a certain position) on a team **16 :** to make wagers on ⟨~ the races⟩ **17 :** WIELD, PLY **18 :** to keep in action

♦ [1] dally, disport, frolic, recreate, rollick, sport ♦ [2] fiddle, fool, mess, monkey, potter, putter, trifle ♦ *usu* **play with** [2] fiddle, fool, mess, monkey, tamper, tinker ♦ *usu* **play on** *or* **play upon** [4] abuse, capitalize, cash in, exploit, impose, use ♦ [9b] act, impersonate, perform, portray ♦ [11b] impersonate, masquerade, pose

play•act•ing \ˈplā-ˌak-tiŋ\ *n* **1 :** performance in theatrical productions **2 :** insincere or artificial behavior

play•back \-ˌbak\ *n* **:** an act of reproducing recorded sound or pictures — **play back** *vb*

play•bill \-ˌbil\ *n* **:** a poster advertising the performance of a play

play•book \-ˌbu̇k\ *n* **:** a notebook containing diagrammed football plays

play•boy \-ˌbȯi\ *n* **:** a man whose chief interest is the pursuit of pleasure

play•date \-ˌdāt\ *n* **:** a usually prearranged play session for small children

play•er \ˈplā-ər\ *n* ♦ **:** one that plays

♦ actor, impersonator, mummer, trouper

play•ful \-fəl\ *adj* ♦ **:** full of play **:** FROLICSOME — **play•ful•ly** *adv*

♦ antic, coltish, elfish, fay, frisky, frolicsome, sportive *Ant* earnest, sober

play•ful•ness \-nəs\ *n* ♦ **:** the quality or state of being playful

♦ friskiness, impishness, mischief, mischievousness *Ant* earnestness, soberness

play•go•er \-ˌgō-ər\ *n* **:** a person who frequently attends plays

play•ground \-ˌgrau̇nd\ *n* **:** an area used for games and play especially by children

play•house \-ˌhau̇s\ *n* **1 :** THEATER **2 :** a small house for children to play in

playing card *n* **:** any of a set of 24 to 78 cards marked to show its rank and suit and used to play a game of cards

play•let \ˈplā-lət\ *n* **:** a short play

play•mate \-ˌmāt\ *n* **:** a companion in play

play–off \-ˌȯf\ *n* **:** a contest or series of contests to break a tie or determine a championship

play out *vb* **:** DEVELOP, UNFOLD ⟨see how things *play out*⟩

play•pen \-ˌpen\ *n* **:** a portable enclosure in which a young child may play

play•suit \-ˌsüt\ *n* **:** a sports and play outfit for women and children

play•thing \-ˌthiŋ\ *n* **:** TOY

play up *vb* ♦ **:** to place emphasis on

♦ accent, accentuate, emphasize, feature, highlight, point, stress, underline, underscore

play•wright \-ˌrīt\ *n* **:** a writer of plays
pla•za \ˈpla-zə, ˈplä-\ *n* **1 :** a public square in a city or town **2 :** a shopping center
PLC *abbr, Brit* public limited company
plea \ˈplē\ *n* **1 :** a defendant's answer in law to a charge or indictment **2** ♦ **:** something alleged as an excuse **3** ♦ **:** an earnest entreaty **:** APPEAL

♦ [2] alibi, defense (*or* defence), excuse, justification, reason ♦ [3] appeal, cry, entreaty, petition, prayer, solicitation, suit, supplication

plead \ˈplēd\ *vb* **plead•ed** *or* **pled** \ˈpled\; **plead•ing 1 :** to argue before a court or authority ⟨∼ a case⟩ **2 :** to answer to a charge or indictment ⟨∼ guilty⟩ **3** ♦ **:** to argue for or against something ⟨∼ for acquittal⟩ **4** ♦ **:** to appeal earnestly ⟨∼*s* for help⟩ ⟨∼*s* to the judge⟩ **5 :** to offer as a plea (as in defense) ⟨∼*ed* illness⟩

♦ [3] argue, assert, contend, maintain, reason ♦ *usu* **plead for** [4] ask, call, quest, request, seek, solicit, sue ♦ *usu* **plead to** [4] appeal, beg, beseech, entreat, implore, importune, petition, pray, solicit, supplicate

plead•er \ˈplē-dər\ *n* ♦ **:** one who pleads

♦ solicitor, suitor

pleas•ant \ˈplez-ᵊnt\ *adj* **1** ♦ **:** giving pleasure **:** AGREEABLE ⟨a ∼ experience⟩ **2 :** marked by pleasing behavior or appearance ⟨a ∼ person⟩

♦ agreeable, congenial, delicious, delightful, felicitous, good, grateful, gratifying, nice, palatable, pleasurable, satisfying *Ant* disagreeable, unpalatable, unpleasant, unwelcome

pleas•ant•ly \-lē\ *adv* ♦ **:** in a pleasant manner

♦ agreeably, delightfully, favorably (*or* favourably), felicitously, nicely, pleasingly, satisfyingly, splendidly, well

pleas•ant•ness \-nəs\ *n* ♦ **:** the quality or state of being pleasant

♦ agreeableness, amenity, amiability, geniality, graciousness, niceness, sweetness

pleas•ant•ry \-ᵊn-trē\ *n, pl* **-ries** ♦ **:** a pleasant and casual act or speech

♦ crack, gag, jest, joke, laugh, quip, sally, waggery, wisecrack, witticism

¹please \ˈplēz\ *vb* **pleased; pleas•ing 1** ♦ **:** to give pleasure or satisfaction to **2 :** LIKE ⟨do as you ∼⟩ **3 :** to be the will or pleasure of ⟨may it ∼ his Majesty⟩

♦ content, delight, gladden, gratify, rejoice, satisfy, suit, warm *Ant* displease

²please *adv* — used as a function word to express politeness or emphasis in a request ⟨∼ come in⟩
pleased \ˈplēzd\ *adj* ♦ **:** affected with or manifesting pleasure

♦ content, contented, glad, happy

pleas•ing *adj* **:** giving pleasure
pleas•ing•ly \-lē\ *adv* ♦ **:** in a pleasing manner

♦ agreeably, delightfully, favorably (*or* favourably), felicitously, gloriously, nicely, pleasantly, satisfyingly, splendidly, well

plea•sur•able \ˈple-zhə-rə-bəl\ *adj* ♦ **:** giving pleasure **:** PLEASANT — **plea•sur•ably** \-blē\ *adv*

♦ amusing, delightful, diverting, enjoyable, entertaining, fun, pleasant

plea•sure \ˈple-zhər\ *n* **1 :** DESIRE, INCLINATION ⟨await your ∼⟩ **2** ♦ **:** a state of gratification **3** ♦ **:** a source of delight or joy

♦ [2] contentment, delectation, delight, enjoyment, gladness, gratification, relish, satisfaction *Ant* discontent, displeasure, dissatisfaction ♦ [3] delight, diversion, entertainment, fun

¹pleat \ˈplēt\ *vb* **1 :** FOLD; *esp* **:** to arrange in pleats **2 :** BRAID
²pleat *n* **:** a fold (as in cloth) made by doubling material over on itself
plebe \ˈplēb\ *n* **:** a freshman at a military or naval academy
¹ple•be•ian \pli-ˈbē-ən\ *n* **1 :** a member of the Roman plebs **2** ♦ **:** one of the common people

♦ *usu* **plebians** commoners, herd, masses, mob, people, populace, rank and file

²plebeian *adj* **1 :** of or relating to plebeians **2** ♦ **:** crude or coarse in manner or style **:** COMMON, VULGAR

♦ common, humble, ignoble, inferior, low, lowly, mean, vulgar

pleb•i•scite \ˈple-bə-ˌsīt, -sət\ *n* **:** a vote of the people (as of a country) on a proposal submitted to them
plebs \ˈplebz\ *n, pl* **ple•bes** \ˈplē-bēz\ **1 :** the general populace **2 :** the common people of ancient Rome
plec•trum \ˈplek-trəm\ *n, pl* **plec•tra** \-trə\ *or* **plec•trums :** ³PICK 3
¹pledge \ˈplej\ *n* **1** ♦ **:** something given as security for the performance of an act **2 :** the state of being held as a security or guaranty **3 :** TOAST 3 **4** ♦ **:** a binding promise or agreement to do or forbear **:** VOW

♦ [1] gage, guarantee, guaranty, pawn, security ♦ [4] oath, promise, troth, vow, word

²pledge *vb* **pledged; pledg•ing 1 :** to deposit as a pledge **2 :** TOAST **3** ♦ **:** to bind by a pledge **4** ♦ **:** to promise the performance of by a pledge **:** PROMISE

♦ [3] commit, engage, troth ♦ [4] covenant, promise, swear, vow

Pleis•to•cene \ˈplī-stə-ˌsēn\ *adj* **:** of, relating to, or being the earlier epoch of the Quaternary — **Pleistocene** *n*
ple•na•ry \ˈplē-nə-rē, ˈple-\ *adj* **1** ♦ **:** complete in every respect **:** FULL ⟨∼ power⟩ **2 :** including all entitled to attend ⟨∼ session⟩

♦ complete, comprehensive, entire, full, grand, intact, integral, perfect, total, whole

pleni•po•ten•tia•ry \ˌple-nə-pə-ˈten-chə-rē, -ˈten-chē-ˌer-ē\ *n, pl* **-ries :** a diplomatic agent having full authority — **plenipotentiary** *adj*
plen•i•tude \ˈple-nə-ˌtüd, -ˌtyüd\ *n* **1 :** COMPLETENESS **2 :** a great sufficiency **:** ABUNDANCE
plen•te•ous \ˈplen-tē-əs\ *adj* **1 :** FRUITFUL **2 :** existing in plenty
plen•ti•ful \ˈplen-ti-fəl\ *adj* **1 :** containing or yielding plenty **2** ♦ **:** characterized by, constituting, or existing in plenty **:** ABUNDANT — **plen•ti•ful•ly** *adv*

♦ abundant, ample, bountiful, comfortable, generous, liberal *Ant* bare, minimal, scant

plen•ty \ˈplen-tē\ *n* ♦ **:** a more than adequate number or amount

♦ abundance, superabundance, wealth *Ant* deficiency, inadequacy, insufficiency ♦ abundance, deal, gobs, heap, loads, lot, pile, quantity

ple•num \ˈple-nəm, ˈplē-\ *n, pl* **-nums** *or* **-na** \-nə\ **:** a general assembly of all members especially of a legislative body
pleth•o•ra \ˈple-thə-rə\ *n* **:** an excessive quantity or fullness; *also* **:** PROFUSION
pleu•ri•sy \ˈplu̇r-ə-sē\ *n* **:** inflammation of the membrane that lines the chest and covers the lungs
plex•us \ˈplek-səs\ *n, pl* **plex•us•es** \-sə-səz\ **:** an interlacing network especially of blood vessels or nerves
pli•able \ˈplī-ə-bəl\ *adj* **1** ♦ **:** supple enough to bend freely or repeatedly without breaking **:** FLEXIBLE **2 :** yielding easily to others — **pli•abil•i•ty** \ˌplī-ə-ˈbi-lə-tē\ *n*

♦ flexible, limber, lissome, lithe, supple, willowy

pli•ant \ˈplī-ənt\ *adj* **1 :** supple enough to bend freely or repeatedly without breaking **:** FLEXIBLE **2 :** easily influenced — **pli•an•cy** \-ən-sē\ *n*
pli•ers \ˈplī-ərz\ *n pl* **:** small pincers for bending or cutting wire or handling small objects
¹plight \ˈplīt\ *vb* **:** to put or give in pledge **:** ENGAGE
²plight *n* **:** an unfortunate, difficult, or precarious situation
plinth \ˈplinth\ *n* **:** the lowest part of the base of an architectural column
Plio•cene \ˈplī-ə-ˌsēn\ *adj* **:** of, relating to, or being the latest epoch of the Tertiary — **Pliocene** *n*
PLO *abbr* Palestine Liberation Organization
plod \ˈpläd\ *vb* **plod•ded; plod•ding 1** ♦ **:** to walk heavily or slowly **2** ♦ **:** to work laboriously and monotonously **:** DRUDGE — **plod•der** *n* — **plod•ding•ly** *adv*

♦ [1] flounder, limp, lumber, stumble ♦ [2] drudge, endeavor (*or* endeavour), fag, grub, hustle, labor (*or* labour), peg, plug, slave, slog, strain, strive, struggle, sweat, toil, work

plonk *var of* PLUNK
plop \ˈpläp\ *vb* **plopped; plop•ping 1 :** to fall or move with a sound like that of something dropping into water **2** ♦ **:** to set, drop, or throw heavily — **plop** *n*

♦ flop, plump, plunk

¹plot \ˈplät\ *n* **1** ♦ **:** a small area of ground **2 :** a ground plan (as of an area) **3 :** the main story (as of a book or movie) **4** ♦ **:** a secret scheme **:** INTRIGUE

♦ [1] lot, parcel, plat, property, tract ♦ [4] conspiracy, design, intrigue, machination, scheme

²plot *vb* **plot•ted; plot•ting 1 :** to make a plot or plan of **2 :** to mark on or as if on a chart **3** ♦ **:** to plan or contrive especially secretly — **plot•ter** *n*

♦ conspire, contrive, intrigue, machinate, scheme

plo•ver \ˈplə-vər, ˈplō-\ *n, pl* **plover** *or* **plovers :** any of a family of shorebirds that differ from the sandpipers in having shorter stouter bills

¹plow *or chiefly Can and Brit* **plough** \ˈplau̇\ *n* **1 :** an implement used to cut, lift, turn over, and partly break up soil **2 :** a device (as a snowplow) operating like a plow

²plow *or chiefly Can and Brit* **plough** *vb* **1 :** to open, break up, or work with a plow **2 :** to move through like a plow ⟨a ship ~*ing* the waves⟩ **3 :** to proceed laboriously — **plow•able** *adj* — **plow•er** *n*

plow•boy *or chiefly Can and Brit* **plough•boy** \ˈplau̇-ˌbȯi\ *n* **:** a boy who leads the horse drawing a plow

plow•man *or chiefly Can and Brit* **plough•man** \-mən, -ˌman\ *n* **1 :** a man who guides a plow **2 :** a farm laborer

plow•share *or chiefly Can and Brit* **plough•share** \-ˌsher\ *n* **:** a part of a plow that cuts the earth

ploy \ˈplȯi\ *n* ♦ **:** a tactic intended to embarrass or frustrate an opponent

♦ artifice, device, dodge, gimmick, jig, scheme, sleight, stratagem, trick, wile

¹pluck \ˈplək\ *vb* **1 :** to pull off or out **:** PICK; *also* **:** to pull something from **2 :** to play (an instrument) by pulling the strings **3 :** TUG, TWITCH

²pluck *n* **1** ♦ **:** an act or instance of plucking **2** ♦ **:** courageous readiness to fight or continue against odds **:** SPIRIT, COURAGE

♦ [1] draw, haul, jerk, pull, tug, wrench ♦ [2] backbone, courage, fiber (*or* fibre), fortitude, grit, guts, spirit, spunk

plucky \ˈplə-kē\ *adj* **pluck•i•er; -est :** COURAGEOUS, SPIRITED

¹plug \ˈpləg\ *n* **1 :** STOPPER; *also* **:** an obstructing mass **2 :** a cake of tobacco **3 :** a poor or worn-out horse **4 :** SPARK PLUG **5 :** a lure with several hooks used in fishing **6 :** a device on the end of a cord for making an electrical connection **7 :** a piece of favorable publicity

²plug *vb* **plugged; plug•ging 1** ♦ **:** to stop, make tight, or secure by inserting a plug **2 :** to hit with a bullet **:** HIT, SHOOT **3** ♦ **:** to publicize insistently **4** ♦ **:** to work doggedly and persistently **:** PLOD, DRUDGE — often used with *away*

♦ [1] block, dam, fill, pack, stop, stuff ♦ *usu* **plug up** [1] block, choke, clog, close (off), congest, dam, jam, obstruct, stop (up), stuff ♦ [3] ballyhoo, boast, promote, publicize, tout ♦ *often* **plug away** [4] drudge, endeavor (*or* endeavour), fag, grub, hustle, labor (*or* labour), peg, plod, slave, slog, strain, strive, struggle, sweat, toil, work

plug and play *n* **:** a computer feature enabling the operating system to automatically detect and configure peripherals — **plug–and-play** *adj*

plugged–in \ˈpləgd-ˈin\ *adj* **:** technologically or socially informed and connected

plug–in \ˈpləg-ˌin\ *n* **:** a small piece of software that supplements a larger program

plum \ˈpləm\ *n* **1 :** a smooth-skinned juicy fruit borne by trees related to the peach and cherry; *also* **:** a tree bearing plums **2 :** a raisin when used in desserts (as puddings) **3** ♦ **:** something excellent; *esp* **:** something desirable given in return for a favor

♦ catch, gem, jewel, pearl, prize, treasure

plum•age \ˈplü-mij\ *n* **:** the feathers of a bird — **plum•aged** \-mijd\ *adj*

¹plumb \ˈpləm\ *n* **:** a weight on the end of a line (**plumb line**) used especially by builders to show vertical direction

²plumb *adv* **1 :** straight down or up **:** VERTICALLY **2 :** COMPLETELY **3 :** EXACTLY; *also* **:** IMMEDIATELY

³plumb *vb* **:** to sound, adjust, or test with a plumb ⟨~ the depth of a well⟩

⁴plumb *adj* **1 :** exactly vertical or true **:** VERTICAL **2 :** COMPLETE

plumb•er \ˈplə-mər\ *n* **:** a worker who fits or repairs pipes and fixtures

plumb•ing \ˈplə-miŋ\ *n* **:** a system of pipes in a building for supplying and carrying off water

¹plume \ˈplüm\ *n* **1 :** FEATHER; *esp* **:** a large, conspicuous, or showy feather **2** ♦ **:** a token of honor or prowess — **plumed** \ˈplümd\ *adj* — **plumy** \ˈplü-mē\ *adj*

♦ award, decoration, distinction, honor (*or* honour), prize

²plume *vb* **plumed; plum•ing 1 :** to provide or deck with feathers **2** ♦ **:** to indulge (oneself) in pride

♦ boast, brag, crow, swagger

¹plum•met \ˈplə-mət\ *n* **:** PLUMB; *also* **:** PLUMB LINE

²plummet *vb* ♦ **:** to drop or plunge straight down

♦ decline, descend, dip, drop, fall, lower, plunge, sink, tumble

¹plump \ˈpləmp\ *vb* **1** ♦ **:** to drop or fall suddenly or heavily **2 :** to favor something strongly ⟨~*ing* for change⟩

♦ flop, plop, plunk

²plump *n* **:** a sudden heavy fall or blow; *also* **:** the sound made by it

³plump *adv* **1 :** straight down; *also* **:** straight ahead **2 :** UNQUALIFIEDLY

⁴plump *adj* ♦ **:** having a full rounded usually pleasing form

♦ chubby, fat, fleshy, full, overweight, portly, rotund, round

plump•ness \-nəs\ *n* ♦ **:** the quality or state of being plump

♦ fatness

¹plun•der \ˈplən-dər\ *vb* ♦ **:** to take the goods of by force or wrongfully **:** PILLAGE — **plun•der•er** *n*

♦ despoil, loot, maraud, pillage, ransack, sack, strip

²plunder *n* ♦ **:** something taken by force or theft **:** LOOT

♦ booty, loot, spoil, swag

¹plunge \ˈplənj\ *vb* **plunged; plung•ing 1 :** IMMERSE, SUBMERGE **2 :** to enter or cause to enter a state or course of action suddenly or violently ⟨~ into war⟩ **3** ♦ **:** to cast oneself into or as if into water **4 :** to gamble heavily and recklessly **5** ♦ **:** to descend suddenly

♦ [3] dive, pitch, sound ♦ [5] decline, descend, dip, drop, fall, lower, plummet, sink, tumble

²plunge *n* ♦ **:** a sudden dive, leap, or rush

♦ descent, dip, dive, down, drop, fall

plung•er \ˈplən-jər\ *n* **1 :** one that plunges **2 :** a sliding piece driven by or against fluid pressure **:** PISTON **3 :** a rubber cup on a handle pushed against an opening to free a waste outlet of an obstruction

plunk \ˈpləŋk\ *vb* **1 :** to make or cause to make a hollow metallic sound **2** ♦ **:** to drop heavily or suddenly — **plunk** *n*

♦ flop, plop, plump

plu•per•fect \(ˌ)plü-ˈpər-fikt\ *adj* **:** of, relating to, or constituting a verb tense that denotes an action or state as completed at or before a past time spoken of — **pluperfect** *n*

plu•ral \ˈplu̇r-əl\ *adj* **:** of, relating to, or constituting a word form used to denote more than one — **plural** *n*

plu•ral•i•ty \plu̇-ˈra-lə-tē\ *n, pl* **-ties 1 :** the state of being plural **2 :** an excess of votes over those cast for an opposing candidate **3 :** the greatest number of votes cast when not a majority

plu•ral•ize \ˈplu̇r-ə-ˌlīz\ *vb* **-ized; -iz•ing :** to make plural or express in the plural form — **plu•ral•i•za•tion** \ˌplu̇r-ə-lə-ˈzā-shən\ *n*

¹plus \ˈpləs\ *adj* **1 :** mathematically positive **2 :** having or being in addition to what is anticipated **3 :** falling high in a specified range ⟨a grade of B ~⟩

²plus *n, pl* **plus•es** \ˈplə-səz\ *also* **plus•ses 1 :** a sign + (**plus sign**) used in mathematics to indicate addition or a positive quantity **2** ♦ **:** an added quantity; *also* **:** a positive quality **3 :** SURPLUS

♦ accretion, addition, augmentation, boost, expansion, gain, increase, increment, proliferation, raise, rise, supplement

³plus *prep* **1 :** increased by **:** with the addition of ⟨3 ~ 4⟩ **2 :** BESIDES

⁴plus *conj* **:** AND ⟨soup ~ salad and bread⟩

¹plush \ˈpləsh\ *n* **:** a fabric with a pile longer and less dense than velvet pile — **plushy** *adj*

²plush *adj* ♦ **:** notably luxurious — **plush•ly** *adv* — **plush•ness** *n*

♦ deluxe, lavish, luxuriant, luxurious, opulent, palatial, sumptuous

plus/minus sign *n* **:** the sign ± used to indicate a quantity taking on both a positive value and its negative or to indicate a plus or minus quantity

plus or minus *adj* **:** indicating a quantity whose positive and negative values bracket a range of values ⟨*plus or minus* 3 inches⟩
Plu•to \ˈplü-tō\ *n* **:** the planet farthest from the sun
plu•toc•ra•cy \plü-ˈtä-krə-sē\ *n, pl* **-cies** **1 :** government by the wealthy **2 :** a controlling class of the wealthy — **plu•to•crat** \ˈplü-tə-ˌkrat\ *n* — **plu•to•crat•ic** \ˌplü-tə-ˈkra-tik\ *adj*
plu•to•ni•um \plü-ˈtō-nē-əm\ *n* **:** a radioactive chemical element formed by the decay of neptunium
plu•vi•al \ˈplü-vē-əl\ *adj* **1 :** of or relating to rain **2 :** characterized by abundant rain
[1]**ply** \ˈplī\ *vb* **plied; ply•ing** **1 :** to use, practice, or work diligently ⟨∼ a trade⟩ **2 :** to keep supplying something to ⟨*plied* them with liquor⟩ **3 :** to go or travel regularly especially by sea
[2]**ply** *n, pl* **plies :** one of the folds, thicknesses, or strands of which something (as plywood or yarn) is made
[3]**ply** *vb* **plied; ply•ing :** to twist together ⟨∼ yarns⟩
ply•wood \ˈplī-ˌwu̇d\ *n* **:** material made of thin sheets of wood glued and pressed together
pm *abbr* premium
Pm *symbol* promethium
PM *abbr* **1** paymaster **2** police magistrate **3** postmaster **4** post meridiem — often not cap. and often punctuated **5** postmortem **6** prime minister **7** provost marshal
pmk *abbr* postmark
PMS \ˌpē-ˌem-ˈes\ *n* **:** PREMENSTRUAL SYNDROME
pmt *abbr* payment
pneu•mat•ic \nu̇-ˈma-tik, nyu̇-\ *adj* **1 :** of, relating to, or using air or wind **2 :** moved by air pressure **3 :** filled with compressed air — **pneu•mat•i•cal•ly** \-ti-k(ə-)lē\ *adv*
pneu•mo•coc•cus \ˌnü-mə-ˈkä-kəs, ˌnyü-\ *n, pl* **-coc•ci** \-ˈkäk-ˌsī, -ˌsē; -ˈkä-ˌkī, -ˌkē\ **:** a bacterium that causes pneumonia — **pneu•mo•coc•cal** \-ˈkä-kəl\ *adj*
pneu•mo•co•ni•o•sis \ˌnü-mō-ˌkō-nē-ˈō-səs, ˌnyü-\ *n* **:** a disease of the lungs caused by habitual inhalation of irritant mineral or metallic particles
pneu•mo•nia \nu̇-ˈmō-nyə, nyu̇-\ *n* **:** an inflammatory disease of the lungs
Po *symbol* polonium
PO *abbr* **1** petty officer **2** post office
[1]**poach** \ˈpōch\ *vb* **:** to cook (as an egg or fish) in simmering liquid
[2]**poach** *vb* **:** to hunt or fish unlawfully — **poach•er** *n*
POB *abbr* post office box
po•bla•no \pō-ˈblä-nō\ *n, pl* **-nos :** a heart-shaped usually mild chili pepper especially when fresh and dark green
po'boy *var of* POOR BOY
pock \ˈpäk\ *n* **:** a small swelling on the skin (as in smallpox); *also* **:** a spot suggesting this
[1]**pock•et** \ˈpä-kət\ *n* **1 :** a small bag open at the top or side inserted in a garment **2** ♦ **:** supply of money **3 :** RECEPTACLE, CONTAINER **4 :** a small isolated area or group **5 :** a small body of ore — **pock•et•ful** *n*

♦ finances, funds, resources, wherewithal

[2]**pocket** *vb* **1 :** to put in or as if in a pocket **2** ♦ **:** to take or appropriate without right or leave and with intent to keep or make use of wrongfully **:** STEAL **3** ♦ **:** to set aside **:** SUPPRESS

♦ [2] appropriate, filch, hook, misappropriate, nip, pilfer, purloin, snitch, steal, swipe, thieve ♦ [3] choke, repress, smother, stifle, strangle, suppress, swallow

[3]**pocket** *adj* **1 a :** small enough to fit in a pocket **b** ♦ **:** having comparatively little size or slight dimensions **:** SMALL **2 :** carried in or paid from one's own pocket

♦ dwarf, dwarfish, fine, little, pygmy, slight, small, undersized

[1]**pock•et•book** \-ˌbu̇k\ *n* **1** ♦ **:** a receptacle for carrying money and often other small objects **2 :** financial resources

♦ bag, handbag, purse

[2]**pocketbook** *adj* **:** relating to money
pocket gopher *n* **:** GOPHER 2
pock•et•knife \ˈpä-kət-ˌnīf\ *n* **:** a knife with a folding blade to be carried in the pocket
pocket veto *n* **:** an indirect veto of a legislative bill by an executive through retention of the bill unsigned until after adjournment of the legislature
pock•mark \ˈpäk-ˌmärk\ *n* ♦ **:** a pit or scar caused by smallpox or acne; *also* **:** an imperfection or depression like a pockmark — **pock•marked** \-ˌmärkt\ *adj*

♦ blemish, defect, deformity, disfigurement, fault, flaw, imperfection, mark, scar

po•co \ˈpō-kō, ˌpȯ-\ *adv* **:** SOMEWHAT — used to qualify a direction in music ⟨∼ allegro⟩
po•co a po•co \ˌpō-kō-ä-ˈpō-kō, ˌpȯ-kō-ä-ˈpȯ-\ *adv* **:** little by little **:** GRADUALLY — used as a direction in music
pod \ˈpäd\ *n* **1** ♦ **:** a dry fruit (as of a pea) that splits open when ripe **2** ♦ **:** an external streamlined compartment (as for a jet engine) on an airplane **3** ♦ **:** a compartment (as for personnel, a power unit, or an instrument) on a ship or craft

♦ [1, 2, 3] armor, capsule, case, casing, cocoon, cover, housing, husk, jacket, sheath, shell

POD *abbr* pay on delivery
po•di•a•try \pə-ˈdī-ə-trē, pō-\ *n* **:** the medical care and treatment of the human foot — **po•di•a•trist** \pə-ˈdī-ə-trist, pō-\ *n*
po•di•um \ˈpō-dē-əm\ *n, pl* **podiums** *or* **po•dia** \-dē-ə\ **1** ♦ **:** a dais especially for an orchestral conductor **2 :** LECTERN

♦ dais, platform, rostrum, stage, stand

POE *abbr* port of entry
po•em \ˈpō-əm\ *n* ♦ **:** a composition in verse

♦ lyric, song, verse

po•esy \ˈpō-ə-zē\ *n* **:** POETRY
po•et \ˈpō-ət\ *n* ♦ **:** a writer of poetry; *also* **:** a creative artist of great sensitivity

♦ bard, minstrel, versifier

po•et•as•ter \ˈpō-ə-ˌtas-tər\ *n* **:** an inferior poet
po•et•ess \ˈpō-ə-təs\ *n* **:** a girl or woman who is a poet
po•et•ic \pō-ˈe-tik\ *or* **po•et•i•cal** \-ti-kəl\ *adj* ♦ **:** having or expressing the qualities of poetry

♦ bardic, lyric, lyrical ***Ant*** prosaic, prose, unpoetic

poetic justice *n* **:** an outcome in which vice is punished and virtue rewarded usually in a manner peculiarly or ironically appropriate
po•et•ry \ˈpō-ə-trē\ *n* **1 :** metrical writing **2 :** POEMS **3** ♦ **:** writing that formulates a concentrated imaginative awareness of experience in language chosen and arranged to create a specific emotional response through meaning, sound, and rhythm

♦ song, verse ***Ant*** prose

po•grom \ˈpō-grəm, pō-ˈgräm\ *n* **:** an organized massacre of helpless people and especially of Jews
poi \ˈpȯi\ *n, pl* **poi** *or* **pois :** a Hawaiian food of taro root cooked, pounded, and kneaded to a paste and often allowed to ferment
poi•gnan•cy \ˈpȯi-nyən-sē\ *n* **:** the quality or state of being poignant
poi•gnant \ˈpȯi-nyənt\ *adj* **1** ♦ **:** painfully affecting the feelings ⟨∼ grief⟩ **2** ♦ **:** deeply moving ⟨∼ scene⟩

♦ [1, 2] affecting, emotional, impressive, moving, stirring, touching

poin•ci•ana \ˌpȯin-sē-ˈa-nə\ *n* **:** any of several ornamental tropical leguminous trees or shrubs with bright orange or red flowers
poin•set•tia \pȯin-ˈse-tē-ə\ *n* **:** a showy tropical American spurge with usually scarlet bracts that suggest petals and surround small yellow flowers
[1]**point** \ˈpȯint\ *n* **1** ♦ **:** an individual detail **:** ITEM; *also* **:** the most important essential **2 :** PURPOSE **3 :** a geometric element that has position but no size **4** ♦ **:** a particular place **:** LOCALITY **5** ♦ **:** a particular stage or degree **6** ♦ **:** a sharp end **:** TIP **7** ♦ **:** a projecting piece of land **8 :** a punctuation mark; *esp* **:** PERIOD **9 :** DECIMAL POINT **10 :** one of the divisions of the compass **11 :** a unit of counting (as in a game score) **12 :** a very small mark **13** ♦ **:** a distinguishing detail **14 :** the quality of something spoken or written of being able to arouse interest and of being generally effective — **pointy** \ˈpȯin-tē\ *adj* — **beside the point :** IRRELEVANT — **to the point :** RELEVANT, PERTINENT

♦ [1] detail, fact, item, particular ♦ [4] locale, location, place, position, site, spot ♦ [5] cut, degree, grade, inch, notch, peg, phase, stage, step ♦ [6] apex, cusp, end, pike, tip ♦ [7] arm, cape, headland, peninsula, promontory, spit ♦ [13] attribute, character, characteristic, feature, mark, peculiarity, property, quality, trait

[2]**point** *vb* **1 :** to furnish with a point **:** SHARPEN **2 :** PUNCTUATE **3 :** to separate (a decimal fraction) from an integer by a decimal point — usually used with *off* **4 :** to indicate the position of especially by extending a finger **5** ♦ **:** to direct attention to ⟨∼ out an error⟩ — usually used with *out* or *up* **6 :** AIM, DIRECT **7** ♦ **:** to lie extended, aimed, or turned in a particular direction **:** FACE, LOOK

♦ *usu* **point up** [5] accent, accentuate, emphasize, feature, highlight, play, stress, underline, underscore ♦ *usu* **point toward** [7] face, front, look

point–and–click *adj* : relating to or being a computer interface that allows the activation of a file by selection with a pointing device (as a mouse)
point–and–shoot *adj* : having or using preset or automatically adjusted controls ⟨a ~ camera⟩
point–blank \ˈpȯint-ˈblaŋk\ *adj* **1** : so close to the target that a missile fired will travel in a straight line to the mark **2** : DIRECT, BLUNT — **point–blank** *adv*
point•ed \ˈpȯin-təd\ *adj* **1** ♦ : having a point **2** ♦ : being to the point : PERTINENT **3** : aimed at a particular person or group; *also* : CONSPICUOUS, MARKED — **point•ed•ly** *adv*

♦ [1] peaked, sharp *Ant* blunt ♦ [2] applicable, apposite, apropos, germane, material, pertinent, relative, relevant

point•er \ˈpȯin-tər\ *n* **1** ♦ : one that points out : INDICATOR **2** : a large short-haired hunting dog **3** ♦ : a useful suggestion or hint : TIP

♦ [1] hand, index, indicator, needle ♦ [3] hint, lead, tip

poin•til•lism \ˈpwan-tē-ˌyi-zəm, ˈpȯint-ᵊl-ˌi-zəm\ *n* : the theory or practice in painting of applying small strokes or dots of color to a surface so that from a distance they blend together — **poin•til•list** \ˌpwan-tē-ˈyēst, ˈpȯint-ᵊl-ist\ *n or adj*
point•less \-ləs\ *adj* ♦ : devoid of meaning

♦ empty, meaningless, senseless

point man *n* : a principal spokesman or advocate
point of no return : a critical point at which turning back or reversal is not possible
point of view ♦ : a position or perspective from which something is considered or evaluated

♦ angle, outlook, perspective, slant, standpoint, viewpoint

point spread *n* : the number of points by which a favorite is expected to defeat an underdog
¹poise \ˈpȯiz\ *n* **1** ♦ : a stably balanced state **2** : self-possessed calmness; *also* : a particular way of carrying oneself

♦ balance, equilibrium, equipoise

²poise *vb* **poised; pois•ing** **1** : BALANCE **2** ♦ : to remain suspended over a place or object

♦ drift, float, glide, hang, hover, ride, sail, waft

poi•sha \ˈpȯi-shə\ *n, pl* **poisha** : the paisa of Bangladesh
¹poi•son \ˈpȯiz-ᵊn\ *n* ♦ : a substance that through its chemical action can injure or kill — **poison** *adj*

♦ bane, toxin, venom

²poison *vb* **1** : to injure or kill with poison **2** ♦ : to treat or taint with poison **3** ♦ : to affect destructively ⟨~*ed* her mind⟩ — **poi•son•er** *n*

♦ [2] befoul, contaminate, defile, foul, pollute, taint ♦ [3] blemish, mar, spoil, stain, taint, tarnish, touch, vitiate

poison hemlock *n* : a large branching poisonous herb with finely divided leaves and white flowers that is related to the carrot
poison ivy *n* **1** : a usually climbing plant related to the sumacs that has leaves composed of three shiny leaflets and produces an irritating oil causing a usually intensely itching skin rash; *also* : any of several related plants **2** : a skin rash caused by poison ivy
poison oak *n* : any of several shrubby plants closely related to poison ivy and having similar properties
poi•son•ous \ˈpȯiz-ᵊn-əs\ *adj* ♦ : having the properties or effects of poison

♦ poison, venomous *Ant* nonpoisonous, nontoxic, nonvenomous

poison sumac *n* : a No. American swamp shrub with pinnate leaves, greenish flowers, greenish white berries, and irritating properties
¹poke \ˈpōk\ *n chiefly Southern & Midland* : BAG, SACK
²poke *vb* **poked; pok•ing** **1** : PROD; *also* : to stir up by prodding **2** : to make a prodding or jabbing movement especially repeatedly **3** : HIT, PUNCH **4** ♦ : to thrust forward obtrusively **5** : RUMMAGE **6** ♦ : to interest oneself in what is not one's concern : MEDDLE, PRY **7** ♦ : to move or act slowly or aimlessly : DAWDLE — **poke fun at** : RIDICULE, MOCK

♦ [4] bag, balloon, beetle, belly, billow, bulge, overhang, project, protrude, start, stick out ♦ [6] butt in, interfere, intrude, meddle, mess, nose, obtrude, pry, snoop ♦ [7] crawl, creep, dally, dawdle, delay, dillydally, drag, lag, linger, loiter, tarry

³poke *n* ♦ : a quick thrust; *also* : PUNCH

♦ dab, dig, jab

¹pok•er \ˈpō-kər\ *n* : a metal rod for stirring a fire
²po•ker \ˈpō-kər\ *n* : any of several card games in which the player with the highest hand at the end of the betting wins
poke•weed \ˈpōk-ˌwēd\ *n* : a coarse American perennial herb with clusters of white flowers and dark purple juicy berries
poky *or* **pok•ey** \ˈpō-kē\ *adj* **pok•i•er; -est** **1** : small and cramped **2** : SHABBY, DULL **3** ♦ : annoyingly slow

♦ creeping, dilatory, laggard, languid, slow, sluggish, tardy

pol \ˈpäl\ *n* : POLITICIAN
po•lar \ˈpō-lər\ *adj* **1 a** : of or relating to a geographical pole **b** ♦ : coming from or having the characteristics (as cold) of such a region **2** : of or relating to a pole (as of a magnet) **3** ♦ : diametrically opposite

♦ [1b] arctic, bitter, chill, chilly, cold, cool, freezing, frigid, frosty, glacial, icy, nippy, raw, snappy, wintry ♦ [3] antipodal, antithetical, contradictory, contrary, diametric, opposite

polar bear *n* : a large creamy-white bear that inhabits arctic regions
Po•lar•is \pə-ˈlar-əs\ *n* : NORTH STAR
po•lar•ise *chiefly Brit var of* POLARIZE
po•lar•i•ty \pō-ˈlar-ə-tē\ *n, pl* **-ties** : the condition of having poles and especially magnetic or electrical poles
po•lar•i•za•tion \ˌpō-lə-rə-ˈzā-shən\ *n* **1** : the action of polarizing : the state of being polarized **2** : concentration about opposing extremes
po•lar•ize \ˈpō-lə-ˌrīz\ *vb* **-ized; -iz•ing** **1** : to cause (light waves) to vibrate in a definite way **2** : to give physical polarity to **3** : to break up into opposing groups
pol•der \ˈpōl-dər, ˈpäl-\ *n* : a tract of low land reclaimed from the sea
¹pole \ˈpōl\ *n* : a long slender piece of wood or metal ⟨telephone ~⟩
²pole *vb* **poled; pol•ing** : to impel or push with a pole
³pole *n* **1** : either end of an axis especially of the earth **2** : either of the terminals of an electric device (as a battery or generator) **3** : one of two or more regions in a magnetized body at which the magnetism is concentrated — **pole•ward** \ˈpōl-wərd\ *adj or adv*
Pole \ˈpōl\ *n* : a native or inhabitant of Poland
¹pole•ax \ˈpō-ˌlaks\ *n* : a battle-ax with a short handle
²poleax *vb* : to attack or fell with or as if with a poleax
pole•cat \ˈpōl-ˌkat\ *n, pl* **polecats** *or* **polecat** **1** : a European carnivorous mammal of which the ferret is considered a domesticated variety **2** : SKUNK
po•lem•ic \pə-ˈle-mik\ *n* : the art or practice of disputation — usually used in plural — **po•lem•i•cal** \-mi-kəl\ *also* **po•lem•ic** \-mik\ *adj* — **po•lem•i•cist** \-sist\ *n*
pole•star \ˈpōl-ˌstär\ *n* **1** : NORTH STAR **2** : a directing principle : GUIDE
pole vault *n* : a field contest in which each contestant uses a pole to vault for height over a crossbar — **pole–vault** *vb* — **pole–vault•er** *n*
¹po•lice \pə-ˈlēs\ *vb* **po•liced; po•lic•ing** **1** : to control, regulate, or keep in order especially by use of police ⟨~ a highway⟩ **2** : to make clean and put in order
²police *n, pl* **police** **1** : the department of government that keeps public order and safety and enforces the laws; *also* : the members of this department **2** : a private organization resembling a police force; *also* : its members **3** : military personnel detailed to clean and put in order
po•lice•man \-mən\ *n* : a member of a police force : POLICE OFFICER
police officer *n* ♦ : a member of a police force

♦ constable, cop, officer

police state *n* : a state characterized by repressive, arbitrary, totalitarian rule by means of secret police
po•lice•wom•an \pə-ˈlēs-ˌwu̇-mən\ *n* : a woman who is a police officer
¹pol•i•cy \ˈpä-lə-sē\ *n, pl* **-cies** ♦ : a definite course or method of action selected to guide and determine present and future decisions

♦ course, line, procedure, program

²policy *n, pl* **-cies** : a writing whereby a contract of insurance is made
pol•i•cy•hold•er \ˈpä-lə-sē-ˌhōl-dər\ *n* : one granted an insurance policy
po•lio \ˈpō-lē-ˌō\ *n* : POLIOMYELITIS — **polio** *adj*
po•lio•my•eli•tis \-ˌmī-ə-ˈlī-təs\ *n* : an acute virus disease marked by inflammation of the gray matter of the spinal cord leading usually to paralysis

¹pol•ish \ˈpä-lish\ *vb* **1** ♦ **:** to make smooth and glossy usually by rubbing **2 :** to refine or improve in manners, condition, or style

♦ buff, burnish, dress, gloss, grind, rub, shine, smooth

²polish *n* **1** ♦ **:** a smooth glossy surface appearance or finish **2** ♦ **:** enlightenment and excellence of taste acquired by intellectual and aesthetic training **:** CULTURE **3 :** the action or process of polishing **4 :** a preparation used to produce a gloss

♦ [1] gloss, luster (*or* lustre), sheen, shine ♦ [2] civilization, cultivation, culture, refinement

Pol•ish \ˈpō-lish\ *n* **:** the Slavic language of the Poles — **Polish** *adj*

polished \ˈpä-lisht\ *adj* **1** ♦ **:** having a smooth and glossy surface produced by or as if by polishing **2** ♦ **:** characterized by elegance and refinement

♦ [1] glossy, lustrous, satiny, sleek ♦ [2] civilized, cultivated, cultured, genteel, refined

polit *abbr* political; politician

po•lit•bu•ro \ˈpä-lət-ˌbyu̇r-ō, ˈpō-, pə-ˈlit-\ *n* **:** the principal policy-making committee of a Communist party

po•lite \pə-ˈlīt\ *adj* **po•lit•er; -est 1** ♦ **:** of, relating to, or having the characteristics of advanced culture ⟨∼ society⟩ **2** ♦ **:** marked by correct social conduct **:** COURTEOUS; *also* **:** CONSIDERATE, TACTFUL — **po•lite•ly** *adv*

♦ [1] correct, decent, decorous, genteel, nice, proper, respectable, seemly ♦ [2] civil, considerate, courteous, genteel, gracious, mannerly, well-bred *Ant* discourteous, impolite, inconsiderate, rude, ungracious, unmannerly

po•lite•ness \-nəs\ *n* ♦ **:** the quality or state of being polite

♦ civility, courtesy, gentility, graciousness, mannerliness *Ant* discourtesy, incivility, rudeness

po•li•tesse \ˌpä-li-ˈtes\ *n* **:** formal politeness

pol•i•tic \ˈpä-lə-ˌtik\ *adj* **1 :** wise in promoting a policy ⟨a ∼ statesman⟩ **2 :** shrewdly tactful ⟨a ∼ move⟩ **3** ♦ **:** suitable to the situation or circumstances

♦ advisable, desirable, expedient, judicious, prudent, tactical, wise

po•lit•i•cal \pə-ˈli-ti-kəl\ *adj* **1 :** of or relating to government or politics **2 :** involving or charged or concerned with acts against a government or a political system ⟨∼ prisoners⟩ — **po•lit•i•cal•ly** \-k(ə-)lē\ *adv*

politically correct *adj* **:** conforming to a belief that language and practices which could offend sensibilities (as in matters of sex or race) should be eliminated

pol•i•ti•cian \ˌpä-lə-ˈti-shən\ *n* **:** a person actively engaged in government or politics

pol•i•tick \ˈpä-lə-ˌtik\ *vb* **:** to engage in political discussion or activity

po•lit•i•co \pə-ˈli-ti-ˌkō\ *n, pl* **-cos** *also* **-coes :** POLITICIAN

pol•i•tics \ˈpä-lə-ˌtiks\ *n sing or pl* **1 :** the art or science of government, of guiding or influencing governmental policy, or of winning and holding control over a government **2 :** political affairs or business; *esp* **:** competition between groups or individuals for power and leadership **3 :** political opinions

pol•i•ty \ˈpä-lə-tē\ *n, pl* **-ties :** a politically organized unit; *also* **:** the form or constitution of such a unit

pol•ka \ˈpōl-kə, ˈpō-kə\ *n* **:** a lively couple dance of Bohemian origin; *also* **:** music for this dance — **polka** *vb*

pol•ka dot \ˈpō-kə-ˌdät\ *n* **:** a dot in a pattern of regularly distributed dots — **polka–dot** *or* **polka–dot•ted** \-ˌdä-təd\ *adj*

¹poll \ˈpōl\ *n* **1** ♦ **:** a person's head **2 :** the casting and recording of votes; *also* **:** the total vote cast **3 :** the place where votes are cast — usually used in plural **4 :** a questioning of persons to obtain information or opinions to be analyzed

♦ head, noggin, pate

²poll *vb* **1 :** to cut off or shorten a growth or part of **:** CLIP, SHEAR **2 :** to receive and record the votes of **3 :** to receive (as votes) in an election **4** ♦ **:** to question in a poll

♦ canvass, solicit, survey

pol•lack *or* **pol•lock** \ˈpä-lək\ *n, pl* **pollack** *or* **pollock :** an important No. Atlantic food fish that is related to the cods; *also* **:** a related food fish of the No. Pacific

pol•len \ˈpä-lən\ *n* **:** a mass of male spores of a seed plant usually appearing as a yellow dust

pol•li•na•tion \ˌpä-lə-ˈnā-shən\ *n* **:** the carrying of pollen to the female part of a plant to fertilize the seed — **pol•li•nate** \ˈpä-lə-ˌnāt\ *vb* — **pol•li•na•tor** \-ˌnā-tər\ *n*

poll•ster \ˈpōl-stər\ *n* **:** one that conducts a poll or compiles data obtained by a poll

poll tax *n* **:** a tax of a fixed amount per person levied on adults and often linked to the right to vote

pol•lut•ant \pə-ˈlüt-ᵊnt\ *n* ♦ **:** something that pollutes

♦ adulterant, contaminant, defilement, impurity

pol•lute \pə-ˈlüt\ *vb* **pol•lut•ed; pol•lut•ing** ♦ **:** to make impure; *esp* **:** to contaminate (an environment) especially with man-made waste — **pol•lut•er** *n* — **pol•lu•tion** \-ˈlü-shən\ *n*

♦ befoul, contaminate, defile, foul, poison, taint

polluted *adj* ♦ **:** made unclean or impure

♦ dilute, impure

pol•ly•wog *or* **pol•li•wog** \ˈpä-lē-ˌwäg\ *n* **:** TADPOLE

po•lo \ˈpō-lō\ *n* **:** a game played by two teams on horseback using long-handled mallets to drive a wooden ball

po•lo•ni•um \pə-ˈlō-nē-əm\ *n* **:** a radioactive metallic chemical element

pol•ter•geist \ˈpōl-tər-ˌgīst\ *n* ♦ **:** a noisy usually mischievous ghost held to be responsible for unexplained noises

♦ apparition, bogey, ghost, phantasm, phantom, shade, shadow, specter, spirit, spook, vision, wraith

pol•troon \päl-ˈtrün\ *n* ♦ **:** a spiritless coward

♦ chicken, coward, craven, dastard, recreant, sissy

poly- *comb form* **1 :** many **:** several ⟨*poly*syllabic⟩ **2 :** polymeric ⟨*poly*ester⟩

poly•chlo•ri•nat•ed bi•phe•nyl \ˌpä-li-ˈklōr-ə-ˌnā-təd-ˌbī-ˈfen-ᵊl, -ˈfēn-\ *n* **:** any of several industrial compounds that are toxic environmental pollutants

poly•clin•ic \ˌpä-li-ˈkli-nik\ *n* **:** a clinic or hospital treating diseases of many sorts

poly•es•ter \ˈpä-lē-ˌes-tər\ *n* **:** a polymer composed of ester groups used especially in making fibers or plastics

poly•eth•yl•ene \ˌpä-lē-ˈe-thə-ˌlēn\ *n* **:** a lightweight plastic resistant to chemicals and moisture and used chiefly in packaging

po•lyg•a•my \pə-ˈli-gə-mē\ *n* **:** the practice of having more than one wife or husband at one time — **po•lyg•a•mist** \-mist\ *n* — **po•lyg•a•mous** \-məs\ *adj*

poly•glot \ˈpä-li-ˌglät\ *adj* **1 :** speaking or writing several languages **2 :** containing or made up of several languages — **poly•glot** *n*

poly•gon \ˈpä-li-ˌgän\ *n* **:** a closed plane figure bounded by straight lines — **po•lyg•o•nal** \pə-ˈli-gən-ᵊl\ *adj*

poly•graph \ˈpä-li-ˌgraf\ *n* **:** an instrument (as a lie detector) for recording variations of several bodily functions (as blood pressure) simultaneously — **po•lyg•ra•pher** \pə-ˈli-grə-fər, ˈpä-li-ˌgra-fər\ *n*

poly•he•dron \ˌpä-li-ˈhē-drən\ *n* **:** a solid formed by plane faces that are polygons — **poly•he•dral** \-drəl\ *adj*

poly•math \ˈpä-li-ˌmath\ *n* **:** a person of encyclopedic learning

poly•mer \ˈpä-lə-mər\ *n* **:** a chemical compound formed by union of small molecules and usually consisting of repeating structural units — **poly•mer•ic** \ˌpä-lə-ˈmer-ik\ *adj*

po•lym•er•i•za•tion \pə-ˌli-mə-rə-ˈzā-shən\ *n* **:** a chemical reaction in which two or more small molecules combine to form polymers — **po•lym•er•ize** \pə-ˈli-mə-ˌrīz\ *vb*

Poly•ne•sian \ˌpä-lə-ˈnē-zhən\ *n* **1 :** a member of any of the indigenous peoples of Polynesia **2 :** a group of Austronesian languages spoken in Polynesia — **Polynesian** *adj*

poly•no•mi•al \ˌpä-lə-ˈnō-mē-əl\ *n* **:** an algebraic expression having one or more terms each of which consists of a constant multiplied by one or more variables raised to a nonnegative integral power — **polynomial** *adj*

pol•yp \ˈpä-ləp\ *n* **1 :** an invertebrate animal (as a coral) that is a coelenterate having a hollow cylindrical body closed at one end **2 :** a growth projecting from a mucous membrane (as of the colon or vocal cords)

po•lyph•o•ny \pə-ˈli-fə-nē\ *n* **:** music consisting of two or more melodically independent but harmonizing voice parts — **poly•phon•ic** \ˌpä-li-ˈfä-nik\ *adj*

poly•pro•pyl•ene \ˌpä-lē-ˈprō-pə-ˌlēn\ *n* **:** any of various polymer plastics or fibers

poly•sty•rene \ˌpä-li-ˈstīr-ˌēn\ *n* **:** a rigid transparent nonconducting thermoplastic used especially in molded products and foams

poly•syl•lab•ic \-sə-ˈla-bik\ *adj* **1 :** having more than three syllables **2 :** characterized by polysyllabic words

poly•syl•la•ble \ˈpä-li-ˌsi-lə-bəl\ *n* **:** a polysyllabic word

poly•tech•nic \ˌpä-li-ˈtek-nik\ *adj* : of, relating to, or instructing in many technical arts or applied sciences
poly•the•ism \ˈpä-li-thē-ˌi-zəm\ *n* : belief in or worship of many gods — **poly•the•ist** \-ˌthē-ist\ *adj or n* — **poly•the•is•tic** \ˌpä-li-thē-ˈis-tik\ *adj*
poly•un•sat•u•rat•ed \ˌpä-lē-ˌən-ˈsa-chə-ˌrā-təd\ *adj* : having many double or triple bonds in a molecule — used especially of an oil or fatty acid
poly•ure•thane \ˌpä-lē-ˈyu̇r-ə-ˌthān\ *n* : any of various polymers used especially in foams and in resins (as for coatings)
poly•vi•nyl \ˌpä-li-ˈvīn-ᵊl\ *adj* : of, relating to, or being a polymerized vinyl compound, resin, or plastic — often used in combination
pome•gran•ate \ˈpä-mə-ˌgra-nət\ *n* : a many-seeded reddish fruit that has an edible crimson pulp and is borne by a tropical Asian tree; *also* : the tree
[1]**pom•mel** \ˈpə-məl, ˈpä-\ *n* **1** : the knob on the hilt of a sword **2** : the knoblike bulge at the front and top of a saddlebow
[2]**pom•mel** \ˈpə-məl\ *vb* **-meled** *or* **-melled; -mel•ing** *or* **-mel•ling** : to strike repeatedly : PUMMEL
pomp \ˈpämp\ *n* **1** : brilliant display : SPLENDOR **2** : OSTENTATION
pom•pa•dour \ˈpäm-pə-ˌdōr\ *n* : a style of dressing the hair high over the forehead
pom•pa•no \ˈpäm-pə-ˌnō, ˈpəm-\ *n, pl* **-no** *or* **-nos** : a narrow silvery fish of coastal waters of the western Atlantic
pom–pom \ˈpäm-ˌpäm\ *n* **1** : an ornamental ball or tuft used on a cap or costume **2** : a fluffy ball flourished by cheerleaders
pom•pon \ˈpäm-ˌpän\ *n* **1** : POM-POM **2** : a chrysanthemum or dahlia with small rounded flower heads
pomp•ous \ˈpäm-pəs\ *adj* **1** ♦ : suggestive of pomp; *esp* : OSTENTATIOUS **2** ♦ : having or exhibiting self-importance **3** : excessively elevated or ornate — **pom•pos•i•ty** \päm-ˈpä-sə-tē\ *n* — **pomp•ous•ly** *adv*

♦ [1] affected, grandiose, highfalutin, ostentatious, pretentious ♦ [2] arrogant, complacent, conceited, egotistic, important, overweening, prideful, proud, self-important, self-satisfied, smug, stuck-up, vain

pon•cho \ˈpän-chō\ *n, pl* **ponchos** **1** : a blanket with a slit in the middle for the head so that it can be worn as a garment **2** : a waterproof garment resembling a poncho
pond \ˈpänd\ *n* : a small body of water
pon•der \ˈpän-dər\ *vb* **pon•dered; pon•der•ing** **1** ♦ : to weigh in the mind **2** ♦ : to consider carefully

♦ [1, 2] chew over, cogitate, consider, contemplate, debate, deliberate, entertain, meditate, mull, question, ruminate, study, think, weigh

pon•der•o•sa pine \ˈpän-də-ˌrō-sə-, -zə-\ *n* : a tall pine of western No. America with long needles; *also* : its strong reddish wood
pon•der•ous \ˈpän-də-rəs\ *adj* **1** ♦ : of very great weight **2** : UNWIELDY, CLUMSY ⟨a ~ weapon⟩ **3** ♦ : oppressively dull ⟨a ~ speech⟩

♦ [1] heavy, hefty, massive, weighty ♦ [3] dull, flat, heavy, leaden, weary

pone \ˈpōn\ *n, Southern & Midland* : an oval-shaped cornmeal cake; *also* : corn bread in the form of pones
pon•iard \ˈpän-yərd\ *n* : DAGGER
pon•tiff \ˈpän-təf\ *n* : POPE — **pon•tif•i•cal** \pän-ˈti-fi-kəl\ *adj*
[1]**pon•tif•i•cate** \pän-ˈti-fi-kət, -fə-ˌkāt\ *n* : the state, office, or term of office of a pontiff
[2]**pon•tif•i•cate** \pän-ˈti-fə-ˌkāt\ *vb* **-cat•ed; -cat•ing** : to deliver dogmatic opinions
pon•toon \pän-ˈtün\ *n* **1** : a flat-bottomed boat **2** : a boat or float used in building a floating temporary bridge **3** : a float of a seaplane
po•ny \ˈpō-nē\ *n, pl* **ponies** : a small horse
po•ny•tail \-ˌtāl\ *n* : a style of arranging hair to resemble the tail of a pony
pooch \ˈpüch\ *n* : a flesh-eating domestic mammal related to the wolves : DOG
poo•dle \ˈpüd-ᵊl\ *n* : any of a breed of active intelligent dogs with a dense curly solid-colored coat
pooh–pooh \ˈpü-ˈpü\ *also* **pooh** \ˈpü\ *vb* **1** : to express contempt or impatience **2** : DERIDE, SCORN
[1]**pool** \ˈpül\ *n* **1** : a small deep body of usually fresh water **2** : a small body of standing liquid **3** : SWIMMING POOL
[2]**pool** *vb* : to form a pool
[3]**pool** *n* **1** : all the money bet on the result of a particular event **2** : any of several games of billiards played on a table having six pockets **3** : the amount contributed by the participants in a joint venture **4** : a combination between competing firms for mutual profit **5** ♦ : a readily available supply (as of resources or workers)

♦ force, help, personnel, staff ♦ budget, fund, supply

[4]**pool** *vb* : to combine (as resources) in a common fund or effort
[1]**poop** \ˈpüp\ *n* : an enclosed superstructure at the stern of a ship
[2]**poop** *n, slang* : INFORMATION
poop deck *n* : a partial deck above a ship's main afterdeck
poor \ˈpu̇r\ *adj* **1** ♦ : lacking material possessions ⟨~ people⟩ **2** : less than adequate : MEAGER ⟨a ~ crop⟩ **3** : arousing pity ⟨you ~ thing⟩ **4** ♦ : inferior in quality or value **5** : producing inferior or little vegetation : UNPRODUCTIVE, BARREN ⟨~ soil⟩ **6** : fairly unsatisfactory ⟨~ prospects⟩; *also* : UNFAVORABLE ⟨a ~ opinion⟩ — **poor•ly** *adv*

♦ [1] broke, destitute, impecunious, indigent, needy, penniless, penurious, poverty-stricken ***Ant*** affluent, flush, moneyed, opulent, rich, wealthy, well-heeled, well-off, well-to-do ♦ [4] cheap, inferior, junky, lousy, mediocre, second-rate, shoddy, sleazy

poor boy \ˈpō-ˌbȯi, ˈpōr-\ *n* ♦ : a large sandwich on a long split roll : SUBMARINE

♦ grinder, hoagie, sub, submarine

poor•house \ˈpu̇r-ˌhau̇s\ *n* : a publicly supported home for needy or dependent persons
poor–mouth \-ˌmau̇th, -ˌmau̇th\ *vb* : to plead poverty as a defense or excuse
[1]**pop** \ˈpäp\ *vb* **popped; pop•ping** **1** ♦ : to go, come, enter, or issue forth suddenly, quickly, or unexpectedly ⟨~ into bed⟩ ⟨~ in for a visit⟩ **2** : to put or thrust suddenly ⟨~ questions⟩ **3** ♦ : to burst or cause to burst with a sharp sound; *also* : to make a sharp sound **4** : to protrude from the sockets **5** : to fire at : SHOOT **6** : to hit a pop-up

♦ *usu* **pop in** [1] call, drop (by *or* in), stop (by *or* in), visit ♦ [3] blow up, burst, detonate, explode, go off

[2]**pop** *n* **1** ♦ : a sharp explosive sound **2** : SHOT **3** : SODA POP

♦ bang, blast, boom, clap, crack, crash, report, slam, smash, snap, thwack, whack

[3]**pop** *n* ♦ : a male parent : FATHER

♦ daddy, father, papa

[4]**pop** *adj* **1** : POPULAR ⟨~ music⟩ **2** : of or relating to pop music ⟨a ~ singer⟩ **3** : of or relating to the popular culture disseminated through the mass media ⟨~ psychology⟩ **4** : of, relating to, or imitating pop art ⟨a ~ painter⟩
[5]**pop** *n* : pop music or culture; *also* : POP ART
[6]**pop** *abbr* population
pop art *n, often cap P & A* : art in which commonplace objects (as comic strips or soup cans) are used as subject matter — **pop artist** *n*
pop•corn \ˈpäp-ˌkȯrn\ *n* : an Indian corn whose kernels burst open into a white starchy mass when heated; *also* : the burst kernels
pope \ˈpōp\ *n, often cap* : the head of the Roman Catholic Church
pop–eyed \ˈpäp-ˌīd\ *adj* : having eyes that bulge (as from disease)
pop fly *n* : POP-UP
pop•gun \ˈpäp-ˌgən\ *n* : a toy gun for shooting pellets with compressed air
pop•in•jay \ˈpä-pən-ˌjā\ *n* : a strutting supercilious person
pop•lar \ˈpä-plər\ *n* **1** : any of a genus of slender quick-growing trees (as a cottonwood) related to the willows **2** : the wood of a poplar
pop•lin \ˈpä-plən\ *n* : a strong plain-woven fabric with crosswise ribs
pop•over \ˈpäp-ˌō-vər\ *n* : a hollow muffin made from a thin batter rich in egg
pop•per \ˈpä-pər\ *n* : a utensil for popping corn
pop•py \ˈpä-pē\ *n, pl* **poppies** : any of a genus of herbs with showy flowers including one that yields opium
pop•py•cock \-ˌkäk\ *n* : empty talk or writing : NONSENSE
pop•u•lace \ˈpä-pyə-ləs\ *n* **1** ♦ : the common people **2** : POPULATION

♦ commoners, herd, masses, mob, people, plebeians, rank and file

pop•u•lar \ˈpä-pyə-lər\ *adj* **1 a** ♦ : of or relating to the general public **b** ♦ : involving participation of all the people ⟨~ government⟩ **2** ♦ : suited to the tastes of the general public ⟨~ style⟩ **3** : INEXPENSIVE ⟨~ rates⟩ **4** ♦ : frequently encountered or widely accepted ⟨~ notion⟩ **5** ♦ : commonly liked or approved ⟨a ~ teacher⟩ — **pop•u•lar•ize** \ˈpä-pyə-lə-ˌrīz\ *vb* — **pop•u•lar•ly** *adv*

♦ [1a] common, general, public, vulgar ♦ [1b] democratic, republican, self-governing ♦ [2, 5] fashionable, in, modish, vogue ***Ant*** out, unpopular ♦ [4] conventional, current, customary, standard, stock, usual

pop•u•lar•i•ty \ˌpä-pyə-ˈlar-ə-tē\ *n* ♦ **:** the quality or state of being popular

♦ favor, modishness, vogue ***Ant*** disfavor, unpopularity

pop•u•late \ˈpä-pyə-ˌlāt\ *vb* **-lat•ed; -lat•ing 1 :** to have a place in **:** INHABIT **2 :** PEOPLE

pop•u•la•tion \ˌpä-pyə-ˈlā-shən\ *n* **1 :** the people or number of people in an area **2 :** the organisms inhabiting a particular locality **3 :** a group of individuals or items from which samples are taken for statistical measurement

population explosion *n* **:** a pyramiding of numbers of a biological population; *esp* **:** the recent great increase in human numbers resulting from increased survival and exponential population growth

pop•u•list \ˈpä-pyə-list\ *n* **:** a believer in or advocate of the rights, wisdom, or virtues of the common people — **pop•u•lism** \-ˌli-zəm\ *n*

pop•u•lous \ˈpä-pyə-ləs\ *adj* **1 :** densely populated; *also* **:** having a large population **2 :** CROWDED — **pop•u•lous•ness** *n*

¹**pop–up** \ˈpäp-ˌəp\ *n* **:** a short high fly in baseball

²**pop–up** *adj* **:** of, relating to, or having a component or device that pops up

por•ce•lain \ˈpōr-sə-lən\ *n* **:** a fine-grained translucent ceramic ware

porch \ˈpōrch\ *n* **:** a covered entrance usually with a separate roof

por•cine \ˈpȯr-ˌsīn\ *adj* **:** of, relating to, or suggesting swine

por•ci•ni \pȯr-ˈchē-nē\ *n, pl* **porcini :** a large edible brownish mushroom

por•ci•no \pȯr-ˈchē-nō\ *n, pl* **-ni :** PORCINI

por•cu•pine \ˈpȯr-kyə-ˌpīn\ *n* **:** any of various mammals having stiff sharp spines mingled with their hair

¹**pore** \ˈpōr\ *vb* **pored; por•ing 1 :** to read studiously or attentively ⟨~ over a book⟩ **2 :** PONDER, REFLECT

²**pore** *n* **:** a tiny hole or space (as in the skin or soil) — **pored** \ˈpōrd\ *adj*

pork \ˈpōrk\ *n* **:** the flesh of swine dressed for use as food

pork barrel *n* **:** government projects or appropriations yielding rich patronage benefits

pork•er \ˈpōr-kər\ *n* **:** HOG; *esp* **:** a young pig suitable for use as fresh pork

por•no•graph•ic \ˌpȯr-nə-ˈgra-fik\ *adj* ♦ **:** of or relating to pornography

♦ bawdy, coarse, crude, dirty, filthy, foul, gross, indecent, lascivious, lewd, nasty, obscene, ribald, smutty, unprintable, vulgar, wanton

por•nog•ra•phy \pȯr-ˈnä-grə-fē\ *n* **:** the depiction of erotic behavior intended to cause sexual excitement

po•rous \ˈpōr-əs\ *adj* **1 :** full of pores **2** ♦ **:** permeable to fluids — **po•ros•i•ty** \pə-ˈrä-sə-tē\ *n*

♦ passable, penetrable, permeable

por•phy•ry \ˈpȯr-fə-rē\ *n, pl* **-ries :** a rock consisting of feldspar crystals embedded in a compact fine-grained base material — **por•phy•rit•ic** \ˌpȯr-fə-ˈri-tik\ *adj*

por•poise \ˈpȯr-pəs\ *n* **:** any of a family of small gregarious blunt-snouted whales with spadelike teeth; *also* **:** DOLPHIN 1

por•ridge \ˈpȯr-ij\ *n* **:** a soft food made by boiling meal of grains or legumes in milk or water

por•rin•ger \ˈpȯr-ən-jər\ *n* **:** a low one-handled metal bowl or cup

¹**port** \ˈpōrt\ *n* **1** ♦ **:** a place where ships may ride secure from storms **:** HARBOR **2 :** a city with a harbor **3 :** AIRPORT

♦ anchorage, harbor (*or* harbour), haven

²**port** *n* **1 :** an inlet or outlet (as in an engine) for a fluid **2 :** PORTHOLE

³**port** *vb* **:** to turn or put a helm to the left

⁴**port** *n* **:** the left side of a ship or airplane looking forward — **port** *adj*

⁵**port** *n* **:** a sweet fortified wine

portabella *or* **portabello** *var of* PORTOBELLO

por•ta•bil•i•ty \ˌpȯr-tə-ˈbil-ə-tē\ *n, pl* **-ties 1 :** the quality or state of being portable **2 :** the ability to transfer benefits from one pension fund to another when a worker changes jobs

por•ta•ble \ˈpōr-tə-bəl\ *adj* **:** capable of being carried — **portable** *n*

¹**por•tage** \ˈpōr-tij, pȯr-ˈtäzh\ *n* **:** the carrying of boats and goods overland between navigable bodies of water; *also* **:** a route for such carrying

²**portage** *vb* **por•taged; por•tag•ing :** to carry gear over a portage

por•tal \ˈpōrt-ᵊl\ *n* ♦ **:** the means or place of entry **:** DOOR; *esp* **:** a grand or imposing one

♦ door, gate, hatch

portal–to–portal *adj* **:** of or relating to the time spent by a worker in traveling from the entrance to an employer's property to the worker's actual job site (as in a mine)

port•cul•lis \pōrt-ˈkə-ləs\ *n* **:** a grating at the gateway of a castle or fortress that can be let down to stop entrance

porte co•chere \ˌpōrt-kō-ˈsher\ *n* **:** a roofed structure extending from the entrance of a building over an adjacent driveway and sheltering those getting in or out of vehicles

por•tend \pȯr-ˈtend\ *vb* **1 :** to give a sign or warning of beforehand **2 :** INDICATE, SIGNIFY

por•tent \ˈpȯr-ˌtent\ *n* **1** ♦ **:** something that foreshadows a coming event **:** OMEN **2 :** one that causes wonder or astonishment **:** MARVEL, PRODIGY

♦ augury, auspice, foreboding, omen, presage

por•ten•tous \pȯr-ˈten-təs\ *adj* **1** ♦ **:** of, relating to, or constituting a portent **2** ♦ **:** eliciting amazement or wonder **:** PRODIGIOUS **3 :** self-consciously solemn **:** POMPOUS

♦ [1] baleful, dire, foreboding, menacing, ominous, sinister ♦ [2] amazing, astonishing, astounding, awesome, fabulous, marvelous (*or* marvellous), prodigious, stunning, surprising, wonderful

¹**por•ter** \ˈpōr-tər\ *n, chiefly Brit* **:** DOORKEEPER

²**porter** *n* **1 :** a person who carries burdens; *esp* **:** one employed (as at a terminal) to carry baggage **2 :** an attendant in a railroad car **3 :** a dark heavy ale

por•ter•house \ˈpōr-tər-ˌhaůs\ *n* **:** a choice beefsteak with a large tenderloin

port•fo•lio \pōrt-ˈfō-lē-ˌō\ *n, pl* **-li•os 1 :** a portable case for papers or drawings **2 :** the office and functions of a minister of state **3 :** the securities held by an investor

port•hole \ˈpōrt-ˌhōl\ *n* **:** an opening (as a window) in the side of a ship or aircraft

por•ti•co \ˈpōr-ti-ˌkō\ *n, pl* **-coes** *or* **-cos :** a row of columns supporting a roof around or at the entrance of a building

¹**por•tion** \ˈpōr-shən\ *n* **1** ♦ **:** one's part or share ⟨a ~ of food⟩ **2 :** DOWRY **3** ♦ **:** an individual's lot, fate, or fortune **4** ♦ **:** a part of a whole ⟨a ~ of the sky⟩

♦ [1] allotment, allowance, cut, part, proportion, quota, share ♦ [3] circumstance, destiny, doom, fate, fortune, lot ♦ [4] member, part, partition, section, segment

²**portion** *vb* **1 :** to divide into portions **2** ♦ **:** to allot to as a portion

♦ administer, allocate, apportion, deal, dispense, distribute, mete, parcel, prorate

port•land cement \ˈpōrt-lənd-\ *n* **:** a cement made by calcining and grinding a mixture of clay and limestone

port•ly \ˈpōrt-lē\ *adj* **port•li•er; -est** ♦ **:** somewhat stout

♦ chubby, fat, fleshy, full, plump, rotund, round

port•man•teau \pōrt-ˈman-ˌtō\ *n, pl* **-teaus** *or* **-teaux** \-ˌtōz\ ♦ **:** a large traveling bag

♦ carryall, grip, handbag, suitcase, traveling bag

por•to•bel•lo \pȯr-tə-ˈbe-lō\ *also* **por•ta•bel•la** \-lə\ *or* **por•ta•bel•lo** \-lō\ *n, pl* **-los** *also* **-las :** a large dark mature mushroom noted for its meaty texture

port of call : an intermediate port where ships customarily stop for supplies, repairs, or transshipment of cargo

port of entry 1 : a place where foreign goods may be cleared through a customhouse **2 :** a place where an alien may enter a country

por•trait \ˈpōr-trət, -ˌtrāt\ *n* **1 :** a picture (as a painting or photograph) of a person usually showing the face **2** ♦ **:** a graphic portrayal in words

♦ delineation, depiction, description, picture, portrayal, sketch

por•trait•ist \-trə-tist\ *n* **:** a maker of portraits

por•trai•ture \ˈpōr-trə-ˌchůr\ *n* **:** the practice or art of making portraits

por•tray \pōr-ˈtrā\ *vb* **1** ♦ **:** to make a picture of **:** DEPICT **2** ♦ **:** to describe in words **3** ♦ **:** to play the role of

♦ [1] depict, image, picture, represent ♦ [2] characterize, delineate, depict, describe, draw, image, paint, picture, sketch ♦ [3] act, impersonate, perform, play

por•tray•al \pōr-ˈtrā(-ə)l\ *n* ♦ : the act or process or an instance of portraying

♦ delineation, depiction, description, picture, portrait, sketch

Por•tu•guese \ˈpōr-chə-ˌgēz, -ˌgēs; ˌpōr-chə-ˈgēz, -ˈgēs\ *n, pl* **Portuguese** **1 :** a native or inhabitant of Portugal **2 :** the language of Portugal and Brazil — **Portuguese** *adj*

Portuguese man–of–war *n* : any of several large colonial marine invertebrate animals related to the jellyfishes and having a large sac by which the colony floats at the surface

por•tu•laca \ˌpōr-chə-ˈla-kə\ *n* : any of a genus of succulent herbs cultivated for their showy flowers

pos *abbr* **1** position **2** positive

¹pose \ˈpōz\ *vb* **posed; pos•ing** **1 :** to assume or cause to assume a posture usually for artistic purposes **2** ♦ **:** to set forth : PROPOSE ⟨~ a question⟩ **3** ♦ **:** to affect an attitude or character

♦ [2] advance, offer, proffer, propose, propound, suggest, vote ♦ *usu* **pose as** [3] impersonate, masquerade, play

²pose *n* **1 :** a sustained posture; *esp* : one assumed by a model **2** ♦ **:** an attitude assumed for effect : PRETENSE

♦ act, airs, facade, front, guise, masquerade, pretense, put-on, semblance, show

¹pos•er \ˈpō-zər\ *n* : a puzzling question

²poser *n* : a person who poses

po•seur \pō-ˈzər\ *n* : an affected or insincere person

posh \ˈpäsh\ *adj* : FASHIONABLE

pos•it \ˈpä-zət\ *vb* : to assume the existence of : POSTULATE

¹po•si•tion \pə-ˈzi-shən\ *n* **1 :** an arranging in order **2 :** the stand taken on a question **3** ♦ **:** the point or area occupied by something or someone **4 :** a certain arrangement of bodily parts ⟨exercise in a sitting ~⟩ **5** ♦ **:** social or official rank or status **6** ♦ **:** an employment for which one has been hired : JOB

♦ [3] locale, location, place, point, site, spot ♦ [5] degree, footing, level, place, rank, situation, standing, station, status ♦ [6] appointment, billet, capacity, function, job, place, post, situation

²position *vb* ♦ **:** to put in a certain position

♦ deposit, dispose, fix, lay, place, put, set, set up, stick

¹pos•i•tive \ˈpä-zə-tiv\ *adj* **1 :** expressed definitely ⟨her answer was a ~ *no*⟩ **2** ♦ **:** fully assured : CONFIDENT, CERTAIN **3 :** of, relating to, or constituting the degree of grammatical comparison that denotes no increase in quality, quantity, or relation **4 :** not fictitious : REAL **5 :** active and effective in function ⟨~ leadership⟩ **6 :** having the light and shade as existing in the original subject ⟨a ~ photograph⟩ **7 :** numerically greater than zero ⟨a ~ number⟩ **8 :** being, relating to, or charged with electricity of which the proton is the elementary unit **9** ♦ **:** marked by or indicating acceptance, approval, or affirmation ⟨a ~ response⟩ — **pos•i•tive•ly** *adv*

♦ [2] assured, certain, clear, cocksure, confident, doubtless, sanguine, sure ♦ [9] appreciative, complimentary, favorable (*or* favourable), friendly, good

²positive *n* **1 :** the positive degree or a positive form in a language **2 :** a positive photograph

pos•i•tive•ness \-nəs\ *n* ♦ **:** the quality or state of being positive

♦ assurance, certainty, certitude, confidence, conviction, sureness

pos•i•tron \ˈpä-zə-ˌträn\ *n* : a positively charged particle having the same mass and magnitude of charge as the electron

po•so•le *or* **po•zo•le** \pō-ˈsō-lā\ *n* : a thick Mexican soup made with pork, hominy, garlic, and chili

poss *abbr* possessive

pos•se \ˈpä-sē\ *n* : a body of persons organized to assist a sheriff in an emergency

pos•sess \pə-ˈzes\ *vb* **1** ♦ **:** to have as property : OWN **2 :** to have as an attribute, knowledge, or skill **3 :** to enter into and control firmly ⟨~*ed* by a devil⟩

♦ command, enjoy, have, hold, occupy, own, retain

pos•ses•sion \-ˈze-shən\ *n* **1** ♦ **:** control or occupancy of property without regard to ownership **2 :** OWNERSHIP **3** ♦ **:** something owned : PROPERTY **4 :** domination by something (as an evil spirit, a passion, or an idea) **5 :** SELF-CONTROL

♦ [1] control, hands, keeping ♦ **possessions** [3] belongings, chattels, effects, holdings, paraphernalia, property, things

pos•ses•sive \pə-ˈze-siv\ *adj* **1 :** of, relating to, or constituting a grammatical case denoting ownership **2 :** showing the desire to possess ⟨a ~ nature⟩ — **possessive** *n* — **pos•ses•sive•ness** *n*

pos•ses•sor \-ˈze-sər\ *n* ♦ **:** one that possesses

♦ holder, owner, proprietor

pos•si•bil•i•ty \ˌpä-sə-ˈbi-lə-tē\ *n* ♦ **:** something that is possible

♦ case, contingency, event, eventuality

pos•si•ble \ˈpä-sə-bəl\ *adj* **1** ♦ **:** being within the limits of ability, capacity, or realization **2 :** being something that may or may not occur ⟨~ dangers⟩ **3 :** able or fitted to become ⟨a ~ site for a bridge⟩

♦ achievable, attainable, doable, feasible, practicable, realizable, viable, workable *Ant* hopeless, impossible, impracticable, unattainable, unworkable

pos•si•bly \ˈpä-sə-blē\ *adv* **1 :** in a possible manner : by any possibility ⟨it's all I can ~ do⟩ **2** ♦ **:** it is possible or imaginable

♦ conceivably, maybe, perchance, perhaps

pos•sum \ˈpä-səm\ *n* : OPOSSUM

¹post \ˈpōst\ *n* **1** ♦ **:** an upright piece of timber or metal serving especially as a support : PILLAR **2 :** a pole or stake set up as a mark or indicator

♦ column, pier, pillar, stanchion

²post *vb* **1 :** to affix to a usual place (as a wall) for public notices **2** ♦ **:** to publish or announce by or as if by a public notice ⟨~ grades⟩ **3 :** to forbid (property) to trespassers by putting up a notice **4 :** SCORE 4 **5 :** to publish in an online forum

♦ advertise, announce, blaze, broadcast, declare, enunciate, placard, proclaim, promulgate, publicize, publish, sound

³post *n* **1** *obs* : COURIER **2** *chiefly Brit* ♦ **:** something sent through the mail; *also* : POST OFFICE

♦ mail, matter, parcel post, snail mail

⁴post *vb* **1 :** to ride or travel with haste : HURRY **2 :** MAIL ⟨~ a letter⟩ **3 :** to enter in a ledger **4 :** INFORM ⟨kept him ~*ed* on new developments⟩

⁵post *n* **1** ♦ **:** the place at which a soldier is stationed; *esp* : a sentry's beat or station **2** ♦ **:** a station or task to which a person is assigned **3 :** the place at which a body of troops is stationed : CAMP **4** ♦ **:** an office or position to which a person is appointed **5 :** a trading settlement or station

♦ [1] position, quarter, station ♦ [2] assignment, charge, job, mission, operation ♦ [4] appointment, billet, capacity, function, job, place, position, situation

⁶post *vb* **1 :** to station in a given place **2 :** to put up (as bond)

post•age \ˈpōs-tij\ *n* : the fee for postal service; *also* : stamps representing this fee

post•al \ˈpōst-ᵊl\ *adj* : of or relating to the mails or the post office

postal card *n* : POSTCARD

postal service *n* : a government agency or department handling the transmission of mail

post•card \ˈpōst-ˌkärd\ *n* : a card on which a message may be written for mailing without an envelope

post chaise *n* : a 4-wheeled closed carriage for two to four persons

post•con•sum•er \ˌpōst-kən-ˈsü-mər\ *adj* **1 :** discarded by a consumer **2 :** having been used and recycled for reuse in another product

post•date \ˌpōst-ˈdāt\ *vb* **1 :** to date with a date later than that of execution ⟨~ a check⟩ **2 :** to follow in time

post•doc•tor•al \-ˈdäk-tə-rəl\ *also* **post•doc•tor•ate** \-tə-rət\ *adj* : of, relating to, or engaged in advanced academic or professional work beyond a doctor's degree

post•er \ˈpō-stər\ *n* ♦ **:** a bill or placard for posting often in a public place

♦ bill, placard

¹pos•te•ri•or \pō-ˈstir-ē-ər, pä-\ *adj* **1** ♦ **:** later in time **2** ♦ **:** situated behind

♦ [1] after, later, subsequent ♦ [2] back, hind, hindmost, rear

²pos•te•ri•or \pä-ˈstir-ē-ər, pō-\ *n* ♦ **:** the hinder bodily parts; *esp* : BUTTOCKS

♦ backside, bottom, butt, buttocks, rear, rump, seat

pos•ter•i•ty \pä-ˈster-ə-tē\ *n* **1** ♦ **:** the descendants from one ancestor **2 :** all future generations

♦ issue, offspring, progeny, seed, spawn

pos•tern \ˈpōs-tərn, ˈpäs-\ *n* **1 :** a back door or gate **2 :** a private or side entrance
post exchange *n* **:** a store at a military post that sells to military personnel and authorized civilians
post•grad \ˈpōst-ˌgrad\ *adj* **:** POSTGRADUATE
post•grad•u•ate \(ˌ)pōst-ˈgra-jə-wət\ *adj* **:** of or relating to studies beyond the bachelor's degree — **postgraduate** *n*
post•haste \ˈpōst-ˈhāst\ *adv* ♦ **:** with all possible speed

♦ apace, briskly, fast, full tilt, hastily, presto, pronto, quick, quickly, rapidly, soon, speedily, swift, swiftly

post•hole \-ˌhōl\ *n* **:** a hole for a post and especially a fence post
post•hu•mous \ˈpäs-chə-məs\ *adj* **1 :** born after the death of the father **2 :** published after the death of the author — **post•hu•mous•ly** *adv*
post•hyp•not•ic \ˌpōst-hip-ˈnä-tik\ *adj* **:** of, relating to, or characteristic of the period following a hypnotic trance
pos•til•ion *or* **pos•til•lion** \pō-ˈstil-yən\ *n* **:** a rider on the left-hand horse of a pair drawing a coach
Post•im•pres•sion•ism \ˌpōst-im-ˈpre-shə-ˌni-zəm\ *n* **:** a late 19th century French theory or practice of art that stresses variously volume, picture structure, or expressionism
post•lude \ˈpōst-ˌlüd\ *n* **:** an organ solo played at the end of a church service
post•man \-mən, -ˌman\ *n* ♦ **:** a man who delivers mail **:** MAILMAN

♦ letter carrier, mailman

post•mark \-ˌmärk\ *n* **:** an official postal marking on a piece of mail; *esp* **:** the mark canceling the postage stamp — **postmark** *vb*
post•mas•ter \-ˌmas-tər\ *n* **:** a person who has charge of a post office
postmaster general *n, pl* **postmasters general :** an official in charge of a national postal service
post•men•o•paus•al \ˌpōst-ˌme-nə-ˈpȯ-zəl\ *adj* **1 :** having undergone menopause **2 :** occurring or administered after menopause
post me•ri•di•em \ˌpōst-mə-ˈri-dē-əm\ *adj* **:** being after noon
post•mis•tress \ˈpōst-ˌmis-trəs\ *n* **:** a woman in charge of a post office
post•mod•ern \ˌpōst-ˈmä-dərn\ *adj* **:** of, relating to, or being any of various movements in reaction to modernism
¹**post•mor•tem** \ˌpōst-ˈmȯr-təm\ *adj* **1 :** done, occurring, or collected after death **2 :** following the event
²**postmortem** *n* **1 :** an analysis or discussion of an event after it is over **2 :** AUTOPSY
post•na•sal drip \ˈpōst-ˌnā-zəl-\ *n* **:** flow of mucous secretion from the posterior part of the nasal cavity onto the wall of the pharynx
post•na•tal \(ˌ)pōst-ˈnāt-ᵊl\ *adj* **:** occurring or being after birth; *esp* **:** of or relating to a newborn infant
post office *n* **1 :** POSTAL SERVICE **2 :** a local branch of a post office department
post•op•er•a•tive \(ˌ)pōst-ˈä-prə-tiv, -pə-ˌrā-\ *adj* **:** following or having undergone a surgical operation 〈∼ care〉
post•paid \ˈpōst-ˈpād\ *adj* **:** having the postage paid by the sender and not chargeable to the receiver
post•par•tum \(ˌ)pōst-ˈpär-təm\ *adj* **:** following parturition — **postpartum** *adv*
post•pone \pōst-ˈpōn\ *vb* **post•poned; post•pon•ing** ♦ **:** to put off to a later time — **post•pone•ment** *n*

♦ defer, delay, hold up, put off, shelve

post road *n* **:** a road over which mail is carried
post•script \ˈpōst-ˌskript\ *n* **:** a note added especially to a completed letter
post time *n* **:** the designated time for the start of a horse race
post–traumatic *adj* **:** occurring after or as a result of trauma 〈∼ stress〉
pos•tu•lant \ˈpäs-chə-lənt\ *n* **:** a probationary candidate for membership in a religious order
¹**pos•tu•late** \ˈpäs-chə-ˌlāt\ *vb* **-lat•ed; -lat•ing** ♦ **:** to assume as true

♦ assume, premise, presume, presuppose, suppose

²**pos•tu•late** \ˈpäs-chə-lət, -ˌlāt\ *n* ♦ **:** a proposition taken for granted as true especially as a basis for a chain of reasoning

♦ assumption, premise, presumption, supposition

¹**pos•ture** \ˈpäs-chər\ *n* **1 :** the position or bearing of the body or one of its parts **2** ♦ **:** state or condition at a given time especially with respect to capability in particular circumstances **3 :** ATTITUDE

♦ footing, picture, scene, situation, status

²**posture** *vb* **pos•tured; pos•tur•ing :** to strike a pose especially for effect
post•war \ˈpōst-ˈwȯr\ *adj* **:** occurring or existing after a war
po•sy \ˈpō-zē\ *n, pl* **posies 1 :** a brief sentiment **:** MOTTO **2 :** a bunch of flowers; *also* **:** FLOWER
¹**pot** \ˈpät\ *n* **1 :** a rounded container used chiefly for domestic purposes **2 :** the total of the bets at stake at one time **3 :** RUIN 〈go to ∼〉 **4 :** a large amount (as of money) — **pot•ful** *n*
²**pot** *vb* **pot•ted; pot•ting 1 :** to preserve or place in a pot **2 :** SHOOT
³**pot** *n* **:** MARIJUANA
po•ta•ble \ˈpō-tə-bəl\ *adj* **:** suitable for drinking — **po•ta•bil•i•ty** \ˌpō-tə-ˈbi-lə-tē\ *n*
po•tage \pȯ-ˈtäzh\ *n* **:** a thick soup
pot•ash \ˈpät-ˌash\ *n* **:** potassium or any of its various compounds especially as used in agriculture
po•tas•si•um \pə-ˈta-sē-əm\ *n* **:** a silver-white soft metallic chemical element that occurs abundantly in nature
potassium bromide *n* **:** a crystalline salt used as a sedative and in photography
potassium carbonate *n* **:** a white salt used in making glass and soap
potassium nitrate *n* **:** a soluble salt used in making gunpowder, as a fertilizer, and in medicine
po•ta•tion \pō-ˈtā-shən\ *n* **:** a usually alcoholic drink; *also* **:** the act of drinking
po•ta•to \pə-ˈtā-tō\ *n, pl* **-toes :** the edible starchy tuber of a plant related to the tomato; *also* **:** this plant
potato beetle *n* **:** COLORADO POTATO BEETLE
potato bug *n* **:** COLORADO POTATO BEETLE
potbellied pig *n* **:** any of an Asian breed of small pigs having a straight tail, potbelly, and black, white, or black and white coat
pot•bel•ly \ˈpät-ˌbe-lē\ *n* **:** a protruding abdomen — **pot•bel•lied** \-lēd\ *adj*
pot•boil•er \-ˌbȯi-lər\ *n* **:** a usually inferior work of art or literature produced chiefly for profit
po•ten•cy \ˈpōt-ᵊn-sē\ *n* **1** ♦ **:** ability to act or produce an effect **:** POWER **2** ♦ **:** the quality or state of being potent

♦ [1, 2] energy, force, main, might, muscle, power, sinew, strength, vigor (*or* vigour)

po•tent \ˈpōt-ᵊnt\ *adj* **1** ♦ **:** having authority or influence **:** POWERFUL **2 :** chemically or medicinally effective **3 :** able to copulate — used especially of the male **4** ♦ **:** rich in a characteristic constituent **5** ♦ **:** achieving or bringing about a particular result **:** EFFECTIVE

♦ [1] important, influential, mighty, powerful, significant, strong
♦ [4] concentrated, full, full-bodied, rich, robust, strong
♦ [5] effective, effectual, efficacious, efficient, fruitful, productive

po•ten•tate \ˈpōt-ᵊn-ˌtāt\ *n* **:** one who wields controlling power **:** RULER
¹**po•ten•tial** \pə-ˈten-chəl\ *adj* **:** existing in possibility **:** capable of becoming actual 〈a ∼ champion〉 — **po•ten•tial•ly** \-ˈten-chə-lē\ *adv*
²**potential** *n* **1** ♦ **:** something that can develop or become actual 〈a ∼ for violence〉 **2 :** the work required to move a unit positive charge from infinity to a point in question; *also* **:** POTENTIAL DIFFERENCE

♦ eventuality, possibility

potential difference *n* **:** the difference in potential between two points that represents the work involved in the transfer of a unit quantity of electricity from one point to the other
potential energy *n* **:** the energy an object has because of its position or nature or the arrangement of its parts
po•ten•ti•al•i•ty \pə-ˌten-chē-ˈa-lə-tē\ *n* **1 :** the ability to develop or come into existence **2 :** something that can develop or become actual
po•ten•ti•ate \pə-ˈten-chē-ˌāt\ *vb* **-at•ed; -at•ing :** to make potent; *esp* **:** to augment the activity of (as a drug) synergistically — **po•ten•ti•a•tion** \-ˌten-chē-ˈā-shən\ *n*
pot•head \ˈpät-ˌhed\ *n* **:** a person who frequently smokes marijuana
poth•er \ˈpä-t͟hər\ *n* **1** ♦ **:** a noisy disturbance **2** ♦ **:** mental turmoil

♦ [1] commotion, disturbance, furor, hubbub, turmoil
♦ [2] dither, fluster, fret, fuss, huff, lather, stew, tizzy, twitter

pot•herb \ˈpät-ˌərb, -ˌhərb\ *n* **:** an herb whose leaves or stems are boiled for greens or used to season food
pot•hole \ˈpät-ˌhōl\ *n* **:** a large pit or hole (as in a road surface)
pot•hook \-ˌhu̇k\ *n* **:** an S-shaped hook for hanging pots and kettles over an open fire

po•tion \ˈpō-shən\ *n* **:** a mixture of liquids (as liquor or medicine)
pot•luck \ˈpät-ˈlək\ *n* **:** the regular meal available to a guest for whom no special preparations have been made
pot•pie \-ˈpī\ *n* **:** pastry-covered meat and vegetables cooked in a deep dish
pot•pour•ri \ˌpō-pu̇-ˈrē\ *n* **1 :** a mixture of flowers, herbs, and spices used for scent **2** ♦ **:** a miscellaneous collection

♦ assortment, clutter, jumble, medley, mélange, miscellany, motley, muddle, variety, welter

pot•sherd \ˈpät-ˌshərd\ *n* **:** a pottery fragment
pot•shot \-ˌshät\ *n* **1 :** a shot taken from ambush or at a random or easy target **2 :** a critical remark made in a random or sporadic manner
pot sticker *n* **:** a crescent-shaped dumpling that is steamed and fried
pot•tage \ˈpä-tij\ *n* **:** a thick soup of vegetables and often meat
[1]pot•ter \ˈpä-tər\ *n* **:** one that makes pottery
[2]potter *vb* ♦ **:** to move or act aimlessly or idly **:** PUTTER

♦ *usu* **potter around** fiddle, fool, mess, monkey, play, putter, trifle

pot•tery \ˈpä-tə-rē\ *n, pl* **-ter•ies 1 :** a place where earthen pots and dishes are made **2 :** the art of the potter **3 :** dishes, pots, and vases made from clay
pot•ty–mouthed \ˈpä-tē-ˌmau̇t͟hd, -ˌmau̇tht\ *adj* **:** given to the use of vulgar language
[1]pouch \ˈpau̇ch\ *n* **1 :** a small bag (as for tobacco) carried on the person **2 :** a bag for storing or transporting goods ⟨mail ∼⟩ ⟨diplomatic ∼⟩ **3 :** an anatomical sac; *esp* **:** one for carrying the young on the abdomen of a female marsupial (as a kangaroo)
[2]pouch *vb* **:** to put or form into or as if into a pouch
poult \ˈpōlt\ *n* **:** a young fowl; *esp* **:** a young turkey
poul•ter•er \ˈpōl-tər-ər\ *n* **:** one that deals in poultry
poul•tice \ˈpōl-təs\ *n* **:** a soft usually heated and medicated mass spread on cloth and applied to a sore or injury — **poultice** *vb*
poul•try \ˈpōl-trē\ *n* **:** domesticated birds kept for eggs or meat — **poul•try•man** \-mən\ *n*
pounce \ˈpau̇ns\ *vb* **pounced; pounc•ing 1 :** to spring or swoop upon and seize something **2** ♦ **:** to make a sudden assault or approach

♦ *usu* **pounce on** *or* **pounce upon** assail, assault, attack, beset, charge, descend, jump, raid, rush, storm, strike

[1]pound \ˈpau̇nd\ *n, pl* **pounds** *also* **pound 1 :** a unit of avoirdupois, troy, and apothecaries' weight **2 :** a unit of weight equal to 16 ounces **3 :** the basic monetary unit of any of several countries including Egypt and the United Kingdom
[2]pound *n* ♦ **:** a public enclosure where stray animals are kept

♦ cage, coop, corral, pen

[3]pound *vb* **1 :** to crush to a powder or pulp by beating **2 a** ♦ **:** to strike or beat heavily or repeatedly **b** ♦ **:** to produce by repeated blows **3 :** DRILL 1 **4 :** to move or move along heavily

♦ [2a] bash, bat, batter, beat, belt, bludgeon, club, hammer, hit, thrash, thump, wallop ♦ [2b] beat, forge, hammer

[4]pound *n* **:** an act or sound of pounding
pound•age \ˈpau̇n-dij\ *n* **:** POUNDS; *also* **:** weight in pounds
pound cake *n* **:** a rich cake made with a large proportion of eggs and shortening
pound–fool•ish \ˈpau̇nd-ˈfü-lish\ *adj* **:** imprudent in dealing with large sums or large matters
pour \ˈpōr\ *vb* **1** ♦ **:** to flow or cause to flow in a stream or flood **2** ♦ **:** to rain hard **3** ♦ **:** to supply freely and copiously

♦ [1] gush, jet, rush, spew, spout, spurt, squirt ♦ [1] flow, roll, run, stream ♦ [2] precipitate, rain, storm ♦ [3] heap, lavish, rain, shower

pour•boire \pu̇r-ˈbwär\ *n* **:** TIP, GRATUITY
[1]pout \ˈpau̇t\ *vb* **:** to show displeasure by thrusting out the lips; *also* **:** to look sullen
[2]pout *n* **1** ♦ **:** a protrusion of the lips expressive of displeasure **2** ♦ **:** a fit of pique

♦ [1] face, frown, grimace, lower, mouth, scowl ♦ [2] pet, sulk, sullenness

pov•er•ty \ˈpä-vər-tē\ *n* **1** ♦ **:** lack of money or material possessions **:** WANT **2 :** poor quality (as of soil) **3** ♦ **:** meagerness of supply

♦ [1] beggary, destitution, impecuniousness, impoverishment, indigence, need, pauperism, penury, want ***Ant*** affluence, opulence, richness ♦ [3] dearth, deficiency, deficit, failure, famine, inadequacy, insufficiency, lack, paucity, scantiness, scarcity, shortage, want

poverty line *n* **:** a level of personal or family income below which one is classified as poor according to government standards
pov•er•ty–strick•en \ˈpä-vər-tē-ˌstri-kən\ *adj* ♦ **:** very poor **:** DESTITUTE

♦ broke, destitute, impecunious, indigent, needy, penniless, penurious, poor

POW \ˌpē-(ˌ)ō-ˈdə-bəl-(ˌ)yü\ *n* **:** PRISONER OF WAR
[1]pow•der \ˈpau̇-dər\ *n* **1 :** dry material made up of fine particles; *also* **:** a usually medicinal or cosmetic preparation in this form **2 :** a solid explosive (as gunpowder)
[2]powder *vb* **1 :** to sprinkle or cover with or as if with powder **2** ♦ **:** to reduce to powder

♦ atomize, crush, grind, pulverize

powder room *n* **:** a rest room for women
pow•dery \ˈpau̇-də-rē\ *adj* ♦ **:** resembling or consisting of powder

♦ dusty, fine, floury

[1]pow•er \ˈpau̇-ər\ *n* **1** ♦ **:** the ability to act or produce an effect **2** ♦ **:** a position of ascendancy over others **:** AUTHORITY **3 :** one that has control or authority; *esp* **:** a sovereign state **4 :** physical might; *also* **:** mental or moral vigor **5 :** the number of times as indicated by an exponent a number is to be multiplied by itself; *also* **:** the resulting product **6 :** force or energy used to do work; *also* **:** the rate at which work is done or energy transferred **7 :** MAGNIFICATION 2

♦ [1] energy, force, main, might, muscle, potency, sinew, strength, vigor (*or* vigour) ***Ant*** impotence, weakness ♦ [2] arm, authority, clutch, command, control, dominion, grip, hold, mastery, sway ***Ant*** impotence

[2]power *vb* **:** to supply with power and especially motive power
[3]power *adj* **:** operated mechanically or electrically rather than manually
pow•er•boat \-ˌbōt\ *n* **:** MOTORBOAT
pow•er•ful \ˈpau̇-ər-fəl\ *adj* ♦ **:** having great power, prestige, or influence

♦ important, influential, mighty, potent, significant, strong

pow•er•ful•ly \-fə-lē\ *adv* ♦ **:** in a powerful manner

♦ energetically, firmly, forcefully, forcibly, hard, mightily, stiffly, stoutly, strenuously, strongly, sturdily, vigorously

pow•er•house \ˈpau̇-ər-ˌhau̇s\ *n* **1 :** POWER PLANT 1 **2** ♦ **:** one having great drive, energy, or ability

♦ go-getter, hustler, live wire, self-starter

pow•er•less \-ləs\ *adj* **1** ♦ **:** devoid of strength or resources **2** ♦ **:** lacking the authority or capacity to act

♦ [1, 2] helpless, impotent, weak ***Ant*** mighty, potent, powerful, puissant, strong

power plant *n* **1 :** a building in which electric power is generated **2 :** an engine and related parts supplying the motive power of a self-propelled vehicle
pow•wow \ˈpau̇-ˌwau̇\ *n* **1 :** a No. American Indian ceremony (as for victory in war) **2** ♦ **:** a meeting for discussion **:** CONFERENCE

♦ assembly, conference, congress, convention, convocation, council, gathering, get-together, huddle, meeting, seminar

pox \ˈpäks\ *n, pl* **pox** *or* **pox•es :** any of various diseases (as smallpox or syphilis) marked by a rash on the skin
pozole *var of* POSOLE
pp *abbr* **1** pages **2** pianissimo
PP *abbr* **1** parcel post **2** past participle **3** postpaid **4** prepaid
ppd *abbr* **1** postpaid **2** prepaid
PPO \ˌpē-ˌpē-ˈō\ *n, pl* **PPOs :** a health-care organization that gives economic incentives to enrolled individuals who use certain health-care providers
PPS *abbr* an additional postscript
ppt *abbr* precipitate
PQ *abbr* Province of Quebec
pr *abbr* **1** pair **2** price
Pr *symbol* praseodymium
[1]PR *or* **p.r.** \ˈpē-ˈär\ *n* **:** PUBLIC RELATIONS
[2]PR *abbr* **1** payroll **2** public relations **3** Puerto Rico
prac•ti•ca•ble \ˈprak-ti-kə-bəl\ *adj* **1** ♦ **:** capable of being put into practice, done, or accomplished **2** ♦ **:** capable of being used — **prac•ti•ca•bil•i•ty** \ˌprak-ti-kə-ˈbi-lə-tē\ *n*

♦ [1] achievable, attainable, doable, feasible, possible, realizable, viable, workable ♦ [2] available, fit, functional, operable, serviceable, usable, useful

prac•ti•cal \ˈprak-ti-kəl\ *adj* **1 :** of, relating to, or shown in practice ⟨~ questions⟩ **2 :** VIRTUAL ⟨~ control⟩ **3** ♦ **:** capable of being put to use ⟨a ~ knowledge of French⟩ **4** ♦ **:** inclined to action as opposed to speculation or abstraction ⟨a ~ person⟩ **5 :** qualified by practice ⟨a good ~ mechanic⟩ — **prac•ti•cal•i•ty** \ˌprak-ti-ˈka-lə-tē\ *n*

♦ [3] applicable, functional, practicable, serviceable, usable, useful, workable, working *Ant* impracticable, impractical, unusable, unworkable, useless ♦ [4] down-to-earth, earthy, hardheaded, matter-of-fact, pragmatic, realistic

practical joke *n* ♦ **:** a prank intended to trick or embarrass someone or cause physical discomfort

♦ antic, caper, escapade, frolic, monkeyshine, prank, trick

prac•ti•cal•ly \ˈprak-ti-k(ə-)lē\ *adv* **1 :** in a practical manner **2** ♦ **:** very nearly but not exactly or entirely **:** ALMOST

♦ about, almost, most, much, near, nearly, next to, nigh, some, virtually, well-nigh

practical nurse *n* **:** a professional nurse without all of the qualifications of a registered nurse; *esp* **:** LICENSED PRACTICAL NURSE

[1]**prac•tice** *chiefly Can and Brit* **prac•tise** \ˈprak-təs\ *vb* **prac•ticed** *also* **prac•tised; prac•tic•ing** *also* **prac•tis•ing 1 :** CARRY OUT, APPLY ⟨~ what you preach⟩ **2 :** to perform or work at repeatedly so as to become proficient ⟨~ tennis strokes⟩ **3 :** to do or perform customarily ⟨~ politeness⟩ **4 :** to be professionally engaged in ⟨~ law⟩

[2]**practice** *n* **1 :** actual performance or application **2** ♦ **:** customary action **:** HABIT **3** ♦ **:** systematic exercise for proficiency **4 :** the exercise of a profession; *also* **:** a professional business

♦ [2] custom, fashion, habit, pattern, way, wont ♦ [3] dry run, rehearsal, trial ♦ [3] drill, exercise, routine, training, workout

practiced *chiefly Can and Brit* **practised** *adj* **1** ♦ **:** made skillful or wise through experience **2 :** learned by practice

♦ adroit, artful, delicate, dexterous, expert, masterful, masterly, skillful, virtuoso

prac•ti•tion•er \prak-ˈti-shə-nər\ *n* **:** one who practices a profession

prae•tor \ˈprē-tər\ *n* **:** an ancient Roman magistrate ranking below a consul — **prae•to•ri•an** \prē-ˈtōr-ē-ən, -ˈtȯr-\ *adj*

prag•mat•ic \prag-ˈma-tik\ *also* **prag•mat•i•cal** \-ti-kəl\ *adj* **1** ♦ **:** of or relating to practical affairs **2 :** concerned with the practical consequences of actions or beliefs — **pragmatic** *n* — **prag•mat•i•cal•ly** \-ti-k(ə-)lē\ *adv*

♦ down-to-earth, earthy, hardheaded, matter-of-fact, practical, realistic

prag•ma•tism \ˈprag-mə-ˌti-zəm\ *n* **:** a practical approach to problems and affairs

prai•rie \ˈprer-ē\ *n* ♦ **:** a broad tract of level or rolling grassland

♦ down, grassland, plain, savanna, steppe, veld

prairie dog *n* **:** an American burrowing black-tailed rodent related to the squirrels and living in colonies

prairie schooner *n* **:** a covered wagon used by pioneers in cross-country travel

praise \ˈprāz\ *vb* **praised; prais•ing 1** ♦ **:** to express approval of **2** ♦ **:** to glorify (a divinity or a saint) especially in song — **praise** *n*

♦ [1] acclaim, applaud, cheer, crack up, hail, laud, salute, tout ♦ [2] bless, extol, glorify, laud, magnify

praise•wor•thy \-ˌwər-t͟hē\ *adj* ♦ **:** worthy of praise **:** LAUDABLE

♦ admirable, commendable, creditable, laudable, meritorious

pra•line \ˈprä-ˌlēn, ˈprā-\ *n* **:** a confection of nuts and sugar

pram \ˈpram\ *n, chiefly Brit* **:** PERAMBULATOR

prance \ˈprans\ *vb* **pranced; pranc•ing 1 :** to spring from the hind legs ⟨a *prancing* horse⟩ **2 :** to walk or move in a spirited manner **:** SWAGGER; *also* **:** CAPER — **prance** *n* — **pranc•er** *n*

prank \ˈpraŋk\ *n* ♦ **:** a playful or mildly mischievous act **:** TRICK

♦ antic, caper, escapade, frolic, monkeyshine, practical joke, trick

prank•ster \ˈpraŋk-stər\ *n* **:** a person who plays pranks

pra•seo•dym•i•um \ˌprā-zē-ō-ˈdi-mē-əm\ *n* **:** a yellowish white metallic chemical element

prate \ˈprāt\ *vb* **prat•ed; prat•ing :** to talk long and idly **:** chatter foolishly

prat•fall \ˈprat-ˌfȯl\ *n* **1 :** a fall on the buttocks **2 :** a humiliating blunder

[1]**prat•tle** \ˈprat-ᵊl\ *vb* **prat•tled; prat•tling 1 :** to talk long and idly **:** PRATE, BABBLE **2** ♦ **:** to utter or make meaningless sounds suggestive of the chatter of children

♦ babble, chatter, drivel, gabble, gibber, jabber, sputter

[2]**prattle** *n* ♦ **:** trifling or childish talk

♦ babble, gabble, gibberish, gobbledygook, nonsense, piffle, rot

prawn \ˈprȯn\ *n* **:** any of various edible shrimplike crustaceans, *also* **:** SHRIMP 1

pray \ˈprā\ *vb* **1** ♦ **:** to make a request to (someone) in an earnest manner **:** ENTREAT, IMPLORE **2 :** to ask earnestly for something **3 :** to address God or a god especially with supplication

♦ appeal, beg, beseech, entreat, implore, importune, petition, plead, solicit, supplicate

prayer \ˈprar\ *n* **1 :** a supplication or expression addressed to God or a god; *also* **:** a set order of words used in praying **2** ♦ **:** an earnest request or wish **3 :** the act or practice of praying to God or a god **4 :** a religious service consisting chiefly of prayers — often used in plural **5 :** something prayed for **6 :** a slight chance

♦ appeal, cry, entreaty, petition, plea, solicitation, suit, supplication

prayer book *n* **:** a book containing prayers and often directions for worship

prayer•ful \ˈprar-fəl\ *adj* **1 :** DEVOUT **2 :** characterized by or proceeding from an intense and serious state of mind **:** EARNEST — **prayer•ful•ly** *adv*

praying mantis *n* **:** MANTIS

PRC *abbr* People's Republic of China

preach \ˈprēch\ *vb* **1 :** to deliver a sermon **2 :** to set forth in a sermon **3 :** to advocate earnestly — **preach•ment** *n*

preach•er \ˈprē-chər\ *n* ♦ **:** one that preaches

♦ clergyman, divine, ecclesiastic, father, minister, priest, reverend

pre•ad•o•les•cence \ˈprē-ˌad-ᵊl-ˈes-ᵊns\ *n* **:** the period of human development just preceding adolescence — **pre•ad•o•les•cent** \-ᵊnt\ *adj or n*

pre•am•ble \ˈprē-ˌam-bəl\ *n* ♦ **:** an introductory part ⟨the ~ to a constitution⟩

♦ foreword, introduction, preface, prologue

pre•ar•range \ˌprē-ə-ˈrānj\ *vb* **:** to arrange beforehand — **pre•ar•range•ment** *n*

pre•as•sign \ˌprē-ə-ˈsīn\ *vb* **:** to assign beforehand

prec *abbr* preceding

Pre•cam•bri•an \ˈprē-ˈkam-brē-ən, -ˈkām-\ *adj* **:** of, relating to, or being the era that is earliest in geologic history and is characterized especially by the appearance of single-celled organisms — **Precambrian** *n*

pre•can•cel \(ˌ)prē-ˈkan-səl\ *vb* **:** to cancel (a postage stamp) in advance of use — **precancel** *n* — **pre•can•cel•la•tion** \ˌprē-ˌkan-sə-ˈlā-shən\ *n*

pre•can•cer•ous \(ˌ)prē-ˈkan-sə-rəs\ *adj* **:** likely to become cancerous

pre•car•i•ous \pri-ˈkar-ē-əs\ *adj* **:** dependent on uncertain conditions **:** dangerously insecure **:** UNSTABLE ⟨a ~ foothold⟩ ⟨~ prosperity⟩ — **pre•car•i•ous•ly** *adv*

pre•car•i•ous•ness \-nəs\ *n* ♦ **:** the quality or state of being precarious

♦ insecurity, instability, shakiness, unsteadiness

pre•cau•tion \pri-ˈkȯ-shən\ *n* **:** a measure taken beforehand to prevent harm or secure good — **pre•cau•tion•ary** \-shə-ˌner-ē\ *adj*

pre•cede \pri-ˈsēd\ *vb* **pre•ced•ed; pre•ced•ing** ♦ **:** to be, go, or come ahead or in front of (as in rank or time)

♦ antedate, forego *Ant* follow, succeed

pre•ce•dence \ˈpre-sə-dəns, pri-ˈsēd-ᵊns\ *n* **1 :** the act or fact of preceding **2 :** consideration based on order of importance **:** PRIORITY

[1]**pre•ce•dent** \pri-ˈsēd-ᵊnt, ˈpre-sə-dənt\ *adj* **:** prior in time, order, or significance

[2]**prec•e•dent** \ˈpre-sə-dənt\ *n* **:** something said or done that may serve to authorize or justify further words or acts of the same or a similar kind

pre•ced•ing \pri-ˈsē-diŋ\ *adj* ♦ **:** that precedes

♦ antecedent, anterior, foregoing, previous, prior

pre•cen•tor \pri-ˈsen-tər\ *n* : a leader of the singing of a choir or congregation

pre•cept \ˈprē-ˌsept\ *n* : a command or principle intended as a general rule of action or conduct

pre•cep•tor \pri-ˈsep-tər, ˈprē-ˌsep-\ *n* : a person charged with the instruction and guidance of another : TUTOR

pre•ces•sion \prē-ˈse-shən\ *n* : a slow gyration of the rotation axis of a spinning body (as the earth) — **pre•cess** \prē-ˈses\ *vb* — **pre•ces•sion•al** \-ˈsə-shə-nəl\ *adj*

pre•cinct \ˈprē-ˌsiŋkt\ *n* **1** : an administrative subdivision (as of a city) : DISTRICT ⟨police ~⟩ ⟨electoral ~⟩ **2** : an enclosure bounded by the limits of a building or place — often used in plural **3** *pl* : ENVIRONS

pre•ci•os•i•ty \ˌpre-shē-ˈä-sə-tē\ *n, pl* **-ties** : fastidious refinement

pre•cious \ˈpre-shəs\ *adj* **1** ♦ : of great value ⟨~ jewels⟩ **2** ♦ : greatly cherished : DEAR ⟨~ memories⟩ **3** : AFFECTED ⟨~ language⟩

♦ [1] costly, dear, expensive, high, valuable ♦ [2] beloved, darling, dear, favorite (*or* favourite), loved, pet, special, sweet ♦ [2] adorable, darling, dear, endearing, lovable, sweet, winning

prec•i•pice \ˈpre-sə-pəs\ *n* ♦ : a steep cliff

♦ bluff, cliff, crag, escarpment, palisade, scarp

pre•cip•i•tan•cy \pri-ˈsi-pə-tən-sē\ *n* : undue hastiness or suddenness

[1]**pre•cip•i•tate** \pri-ˈsi-pə-ˌtāt\ *vb* **-tat•ed; -tat•ing 1** : to throw violently **2** : to throw down **3** : to cause to happen quickly or abruptly ⟨~ a quarrel⟩ **4** : to cause to separate from solution or suspension **5** : to fall as rain, snow, or hail

[2]**pre•cip•i•tate** \pri-ˈsi-pə-tət, -ˌtāt\ *n* ♦ : the solid matter that separates from a solution or suspension

♦ deposit, dregs, grounds, sediment

[3]**pre•cip•i•tate** \pri-ˈsi-pə-tət\ *adj* **1** ♦ : showing extreme or unwise haste : RASH **2** : falling with steep descent; *also* : PRECIPITOUS — **pre•cip•i•tate•ness** *n*

♦ cursory, hasty, headlong, pell-mell, precipitous, rash

pre•cip•i•tate•ly \-lē\ *adv* ♦ : in a precipitate manner

♦ cursorily, hastily, headlong, hurriedly, pell-mell, rashly

pre•cip•i•ta•tion \pri-ˌsi-pə-ˈtā-shən\ *n* **1** ♦ : rash haste **2** : the process of precipitating or forming a precipitate **3** : water that falls to earth especially as rain or snow; *also* : the quantity of this water

♦ haste, hurry, hustle, rush

pre•cip•i•tous \pri-ˈsi-pə-təs\ *adj* **1** : showing extreme or unwise haste : PRECIPITATE **2** ♦ : having the character of a precipice : very steep ⟨a ~ slope⟩; *also* : containing precipices ⟨~ trails⟩

♦ abrupt, bold, sheer, steep

pre•cip•i•tous•ly \-lē\ *adv* : in a precipitous manner

pré•cis \prā-ˈsē\ *n, pl* **pré•cis** \-ˈsēz\ ♦ : a concise summary of essentials

♦ abstract, digest, encapsulation, epitome, outline, recapitulation, résumé (*or* resume), roundup, sum, summary, synopsis, wrap-up

pre•cise \pri-ˈsīs\ *adj* **1** ♦ : exactly defined or stated **2** ♦ : highly accurate : EXACT **3** ♦ : conforming strictly to a standard : SCRUPULOUS

♦ [1] distinct, especial, express, set, special, specific ♦ [2] accurate, correct, exact, proper, right, so, true ♦ [2, 3] accurate, close, delicate, exact, fine, mathematical, pinpoint, rigorous, scrupulous ***Ant*** coarse, imprecise, inaccurate, inexact, rough

pre•cise•ly \-lē\ ♦ : in a precise manner

♦ accurately, exactly, just, right, sharp, squarely, strictly

pre•cise•ness \-nəs\ *n* : the quality or state of being precise

pre•ci•sion \pri-ˈsi-zhən\ *n* ♦ : the quality or state of being precise

♦ accuracy, closeness, delicacy, exactness, fineness, veracity ***Ant*** coarseness, impreciseness, imprecision, inaccuracy, inexactness, roughness

pre•clude \pri-ˈklüd\ *vb* **pre•clud•ed; pre•clud•ing** ♦ : to make impossible : PREVENT

♦ avert, forestall, help, obviate, prevent

pre•co•cious \pri-ˈkō-shəs\ *adj* **1** ♦ : exceptionally early in development or occurrence **2** : exhibiting mature qualities at an unusually early age — **pre•coc•i•ty** \pri-ˈkä-sə-tē\ *n*

♦ early, premature, unseasonable, untimely

pre•co•cious•ly \-lē\ *adv* ♦ : in a precocious manner

♦ beforehand, early, prematurely, unseasonably

pre•con•ceive \ˌprē-kən-ˈsēv\ *vb* : to form an opinion of beforehand — **pre•con•cep•tion** \-ˈsep-shən\ *n*

pre•con•di•tion \-ˈdi-shən\ *vb* : to put in proper or desired condition or frame of mind in advance

pre•cook \ˌprē-ˈku̇k\ *vb* : to cook partially or entirely before final cooking or reheating

pre•cur•sor \pri-ˈkər-sər\ *n* **1** ♦ : one that precedes and indicates the approach of another : FORERUNNER **2** ♦ : one that precedes another in an office or process

♦ [1] angel, forerunner, harbinger, herald ♦ [2] ancestor, antecedent, forerunner

pred *abbr* predicate

pre•da•ceous *or* **pre•da•cious** \pri-ˈdā-shəs\ *adj* : living by preying on others : PREDATORY

pre•date \ˈprē-ˈdāt\ *vb* : to precede in time : ANTEDATE

pre•da•tion \pri-ˈdā-shən\ *n* **1** : the act of preying or plundering **2** : a mode of life in which food is primarily obtained by killing and consuming animals

pred•a•tor \ˈpre-də-tər\ *n* : an animal that lives by predation

pred•a•to•ry \ˈpre-də-ˌtōr-ē\ *adj* **1** : of or relating to plunder ⟨~ warfare⟩ **2** : disposed to exploit others **3** : preying upon other animals

pre•dawn \(ˈ)prē-ˈdȯn\ *adj* : of or relating to the time just before dawn

pre•de•cease \ˌprē-di-ˈsēs\ *vb* **-ceased; -ceas•ing** : to die before another person

pre•de•ces•sor \ˈpre-də-ˌse-sər, ˈprē-\ *n* **1** : a previous holder of a position to which another has succeeded **2** : something that has been followed or displaced by another

pre•des•ig•nate \(ˌ)prē-ˈde-zig-ˌnāt\ *vb* : to designate beforehand

pre•des•ti•na•tion \ˌprē-ˌdes-tə-ˈnā-shən\ *n* : the act of foreordaining to an earthly lot or eternal destiny by divine decree; *also* : the state of being so foreordained — **pre•des•ti•nate** \prē-ˈdes-tə-ˌnāt\ *vb*

pre•des•tine \prē-ˈdes-tən\ *vb* ♦ : to settle beforehand : FOREORDAIN

♦ destine, doom, fate, foredoom, foreordain, ordain

pre•de•ter•mine \ˌprē-di-ˈtər-mən\ *vb* : to determine beforehand

pred•i•ca•ble \ˈpre-di-kə-bəl\ *adj* : capable of being predicated or affirmed

pre•dic•a•ment \pri-ˈdi-kə-mənt\ *n* ♦ : a difficult or trying situation

♦ corner, fix, hole, jam, pickle, spot

[1]**pred•i•cate** \ˈpre-di-kət\ *n* : the part of a sentence or clause that expresses what is said of the subject

[2]**pred•i•cate** \ˈpre-də-ˌkāt\ *vb* **-cat•ed; -cat•ing 1** : AFFIRM **2** : to assert to be a quality or attribute **3** : to set or ground on something : BASE — **pred•i•ca•tion** \ˌpre-də-ˈkā-shən\ *n*

pre•dict \pri-ˈdikt\ *vb* ♦ : to declare in advance — **pre•dict•abil•i•ty** \-ˌdik-tə-ˈbi-lə-tē\ *n* — **pre•dict•able** \-ˈdik-tə-bəl\ *adj* — **pre•dict•ably** \-blē\ *adv*

♦ augur, forecast, foretell, presage, prognosticate, prophesy

pre•dic•tion \pri-ˈdik-shən\ *n* **1** ♦ : an act of predicting **2** : something that is predicted

♦ cast, forecast, prognostication, prophecy, soothsaying

pre•di•gest \ˌprē-dī-ˈjest\ *vb* : to simplify for easy use; *also* : to subject to artificial or natural partial digestion

pre•di•lec•tion \ˌpre-də-ˈlek-shən, ˌprē-\ *n* ♦ : an established preference for something

♦ bent, devices, disposition, genius, inclination, leaning, partiality, penchant, proclivity, propensity, tendency, turn

pre•dis•pose \ˌprē-di-ˈspōz\ *vb* : to incline in advance : make susceptible

pre•dis•po•si•tion \ˌprē-ˌdis-pə-ˈzi-shən\ *n* ♦ : a condition of being predisposed

♦ affinity, bent, devices, disposition, genius, inclination, leaning, partiality, penchant, predilection, proclivity, propensity, talent, tendency, turn

pre•dom•i•nance \pri-ˈdä-mə-nəns\ *n* ♦ **:** the quality or state of being predominant

♦ ascendancy, dominance, dominion, preeminence, supremacy

pre•dom•i•nant \pri-ˈdä-mə-nənt\ *adj* ♦ **:** greater in importance, strength, influence, or authority

♦ arch, cardinal, central, chief, dominant, first, foremost, grand, key, main, paramount, preeminent, premier, primary, principal, sovereign, supreme

pre•dom•i•nant•ly \-nənt-lē\ *adv* ♦ **:** for the most part **:** MAINLY

♦ altogether, basically, chiefly, generally, largely, mainly, mostly, overall, primarily, principally

pre•dom•i•nate \pri-ˈdä-mə-ˌnāt\ *vb* **:** to be superior especially in power or numbers **:** PREVAIL

pre•dom•i•nate•ly \pri-ˈdä-mə-nət-lē\ *adv* **:** PREDOMINANTLY

pree•mie \ˈprē-mē\ *n* **:** a premature baby

pre•em•i•nence \prē-ˈe-mə-nəns\ *n* ♦ **:** the quality or state of being preeminent

♦ distinction, dominance, excellence, greatness, superiority, supremacy

pre•em•i•nent \prē-ˈe-mə-nənt\ *adj* ♦ **:** having highest rank — **pre•em•i•nent•ly** *adv*

♦ arch, cardinal, central, chief, dominant, first, foremost, grand, key, main, paramount, predominant, premier, primary, principal, sovereign, supreme ♦ distinguished, eminent, illustrious, noble, notable, noteworthy, outstanding, prestigious, signal, star, superior

pre•empt \prē-ˈempt\ *vb* **1 :** to settle upon (public land) with the right to purchase before others; *also* **:** to take by such right **2** ♦ **:** to seize upon before someone else can **3 :** to take the place of — **pre•emp•tion** \-ˈemp-shən\ *n*

♦ appropriate, arrogate, commandeer, usurp

pre•emp•tive \prē-ˈemp-tiv\ *adj* **:** marked by the seizing of the initiative **:** initiated by oneself ⟨~ attack⟩

preen \ˈprēn\ *vb* **1 :** to dress or smooth up **:** PRIMP **2 :** to groom with the bill — used of a bird **3 :** to pride (oneself) for achievement

pre•ex•ist \ˌprē-ig-ˈzist\ *vb* **:** to exist before — **pre•ex•is•tence** \-ˈzis-təns\ *n* — **pre•ex•is•tent** \-tənt\ *adj*

pref *abbr* **1** preface **2** preference **3** preferred **4** prefix

¹pre•fab \(ˌ)prē-ˈfab, ˈprē-ˌfab\ *n* **:** a prefabricated structure

²pre•fab *adj* **:** produced by prefabrication

pre•fab•ri•cate \(ˌ)prē-ˈfa-brə-ˌkāt\ *vb* **:** to manufacture the parts of (a structure) beforehand for later assembly — **pre•fab•ri•ca•tion** \ˌprē-ˌfa-bri-ˈkā-shən\ *n*

¹pref•ace \ˈpre-fəs\ *n* ♦ **:** the introductory remarks of a speaker or writer — **pref•a•to•ry** \ˈpre-fə-ˌtōr-ē\ *adj*

♦ foreword, introduction, preamble, prologue

²preface *vb* **pref•aced; pref•ac•ing :** to introduce with a preface

pre•fect \ˈprē-ˌfekt\ *n* **1 :** a high official; *esp* **:** a chief officer or magistrate **2 :** a student monitor

pre•fec•ture \ˈprē-ˌfek-chər\ *n* **:** the office, term, or residence of a prefect

pre•fer \pri-ˈfər\ *vb* **pre•ferred; pre•fer•ring 1 :** PROMOTE **2** ♦ **:** to like better **3 :** to bring (as a charge) against a person — **pref•er•a•ble** \ˈpre-fə-rə-bəl\ *adj*

♦ choose, cull, elect, handpick, name, opt, pick, select, single, take ♦ favor (*or* favour), lean, like

pref•er•a•bly \ˈpre-fə-rə-blē\ *adv* ♦ **:** it is preferred

♦ first, rather, readily, soon

pref•er•ence \ˈpre-frəns, -fə-rəns\ *n* **1** ♦ **:** a special liking for one thing over another **2** ♦ **:** the power or opportunity of choosing **:** CHOICE **3** ♦ **:** one that is preferred — **pref•er•en•tial** \ˌpre-fə-ˈren-chəl\ *adj*

♦ [1] appetite, fancy, favor (*or* favour), fondness, like, liking, love, partiality, relish, shine, taste, use ♦ [2] alternative, choice, discretion, option, pick, way ♦ [3] darling, favorite (*or* favourite), pet, prize, treasure

pre•fer•ment \pri-ˈfər-mənt\ *n* **:** advancement or promotion in dignity, office, or station **:** PROMOTION, ADVANCEMENT

preferred provider organization *n* **:** PPO

pre•fig•ure \prē-ˈfi-gyər\ *vb* **1** ♦ **:** to show, suggest, or announce beforehand **:** FORESHADOW **2** ♦ **:** to imagine beforehand

♦ foreshadow, harbinger

¹pre•fix \ˈprē-ˌfiks, prē-ˈfiks\ *vb* **:** to place before ⟨~ a title to a name⟩

²pre•fix \ˈprē-ˌfiks\ *n* **:** an affix occurring at the beginning of a word

pre•flight \ˌprē-ˈflīt\ *adj* **:** preparing for or preliminary to flight

pre•form \(ˌ)prē-ˈfȯrm, ˈprē-ˌfȯrm\ *vb* **:** to form or shape beforehand

preg•na•ble \ˈpreg-nə-bəl\ *adj* **:** vulnerable to capture ⟨a ~ fort⟩

preg•nant \ˈpreg-nənt\ *adj* **1 :** containing unborn offspring within the body **2** ♦ **:** rich in significance **:** MEANINGFUL — **preg•nan•cy** \-nən-sē\ *n*

♦ eloquent, expressive, meaning, meaningful, significant, suggestive

pre•heat \ˌprē-ˈhēt\ *vb* **:** to heat beforehand; *esp* **:** to heat (an oven) to a designated temperature before using

pre•hen•sile \prē-ˈhen-səl, -ˌsīl\ *adj* **:** adapted for grasping especially by wrapping around ⟨a monkey with a ~ tail⟩

pre•his•tor•ic \ˌprē-his-ˈtȯr-ik\ *also* **pre•his•tor•i•cal** \-i-kəl\ *adj* **:** of, relating to, or existing in the period before written history began

pre•judge \(ˌ)prē-ˈjəj\ *vb* **:** to judge before full hearing or examination

¹prej•u•dice \ˈpre-jə-dəs\ *n* **1 :** DAMAGE; *esp* **:** detriment to one's rights or claims **2** ♦ **:** an opinion made without adequate basis

♦ bias, favor (*or* favour), partiality, partisanship

²prejudice *vb* **-diced; -dic•ing 1 :** to damage by a judgment or action especially at law **2 :** to cause to have prejudice

prejudiced *adj* ♦ **:** resulting from or having a prejudice or bias for or especially against

♦ biased, one-sided, partial, partisan ♦ bigoted, intolerant, narrow, narrow-minded

prej•u•di•cial \ˌpre-jə-ˈdi-shəl\ *adj* **1** ♦ **:** tending to injure or impair **2 :** leading to premature judgment or unwarranted opinion

♦ adverse, counter, disadvantageous, harmful, hostile, inimical, negative, unfavorable (*or* unfavourable), unfriendly, unsympathetic

pre•kin•der•gar•ten \(ˈ)prē-ˈkin-dər-ˌgär-tᵊn\ *n* **1 :** NURSERY SCHOOL **2 :** a class or program preceding kindergarten

prel•ate \ˈpre-lət\ *n* **:** an ecclesiastic (as a bishop) of high rank — **prel•a•cy** \-lə-sē\ *n*

pre•launch \ˈprē-ˈlȯnch\ *adj* **:** preparing for or preliminary to launch

pre•lim \ˈprē-ˌlim, pri-ˈlim\ *n or adj* **:** PRELIMINARY

¹pre•lim•i•nary \pri-ˈli-mə-ˌner-ē\ *n, pl* **-nar•ies :** something that precedes or introduces the main business or event

²preliminary *adj* **:** preceding the main discourse or business

pre•lude \ˈprel-ˌyüd; ˈpre-ˌlüd, ˈprā-\ *n* **1 :** an introductory performance or event **2 :** a musical section or movement introducing the main theme; *also* **:** an organ solo played at the beginning of a church service

prem *abbr* premium

pre•mar•i•tal \(ˌ)prē-ˈmar-ət-ᵊl\ *adj* **:** existing or occurring before marriage

pre•ma•ture \ˌprē-mə-ˈtu̇r, -ˈtyu̇r, -ˈchu̇r\ *adj* ♦ **:** happening, coming, born, or done before the usual or proper time

♦ early, precocious, unseasonable, untimely

pre•ma•ture•ly \-lē\ *adv* ♦ **:** in a premature manner **:** too soon

♦ beforehand, early, precociously, unseasonably

¹pre•med \ˌprē-ˈmed\ *n* **:** a premedical student or course of study

²premed *adj* **:** PREMEDICAL

pre•med•i•cal \(ˌ)prē-ˈme-di-kəl\ *adj* **:** preceding and preparing for the professional study of medicine

pre•med•i•tate \pri-ˈme-də-ˌtāt\ *vb* **:** to consider and plan beforehand — **pre•med•i•ta•tion** \-ˌme-də-ˈtā-shən\ *n*

pre•men•o•paus•al \(ˌ)prē-ˌme-nə-ˈpȯ-zəl\ *adj* **:** of, relating to, or being in the period preceding menopause

pre•men•stru•al \(ˌ)prē-ˈmen-strə-wəl\ *adj* **:** of, relating to, or occurring in the period just before menstruation

premenstrual syndrome *n* **:** a varying group of symptoms manifested by some women prior to menstruation

premie *var of* PREEMIE

¹pre•mier \pri-ˈmir, -ˈmyir, ˈprē-mē-ər\ *adj* **1** ♦ **:** first in rank or importance **:** CHIEF **2** ♦ **:** earliest in time

♦ [1] chief, first, foremost, head, high, lead, preeminent, primary, prime, principal, supreme ♦ [2] first, inaugural, initial, maiden, original, pioneer

[2]**premier** *n* : PRIME MINISTER — **pre•mier•ship** *n*
[1]**pre•miere** \pri-ˈmyer, -ˈmir\ *n* : a first performance
[2]**premiere** *also* **premier** *same as* [1]PREMIERE\ *vb* **pre•miered; pre•mier•ing** : to give or receive a first public performance
prem•ise \ˈpre-məs\ *n* **1** ♦ : a statement of fact or a supposition made or implied as a basis of argument **2** *pl* ♦ : a piece of land with the structures on it; *also* : the place of business of an enterprise

♦ [1] assumption, postulate, presumption, supposition ♦ **premises** [2] demesne, grounds, park, yard

pre•mi•um \ˈprē-mē-əm\ *n* **1** : a reward or recompense for a particular act : REWARD, PRIZE **2** : a sum over and above the stated value **3** : something paid over and above a fixed wage or price **4** : something given with a purchase **5** : the sum paid for a contract of insurance **6** : an unusually high value
pre•mix \ˌprē-ˈmiks\ *vb* : to mix before use
pre•mo•lar \(ˌ)prē-ˈmō-lər\ *adj* : situated in front of or preceding the molar teeth; *esp* : being or relating to those teeth of a mammal in front of the true molars and behind the canines — **premolar** *n*
pre•mo•ni•tion \ˌprē-mə-ˈni-shən, ˌpre-\ *n* **1** : previous warning **2** ♦ : anticipation of an event without conscious reason : PRESENTIMENT — **pre•mon•i•to•ry** \pri-ˈmä-nə-ˌtōr-ē\ *adj*

♦ foreboding, presage, presentiment

pre•na•tal \ˈprē-ˈnāt-ᵊl\ *adj* : occurring, existing, or taking place before birth
pre•nup•tial \prē-ˈnəp-shəl\ *adj* : made or occurring before marriage
prenuptial agreement *n* : an agreement between a man and woman before marrying in which they give up future rights to each other's property in the event of divorce or death
pre•oc•cu•pa•tion \prē-ˌä-kyə-ˈpā-shən\ *n* **1** : complete absorption of the mind or interests **2** ♦ : something that causes complete absorption of the mind or interests

♦ fetish, fixation, mania, obsession, prepossession

pre•oc•cu•pied \prē-ˈä-kyə-ˌpīd\ *adj* **1** ♦ : lost in thought; *also* : absorbed in some preoccupation **2** : already occupied

♦ absent, absentminded, abstracted

pre•oc•cu•py \-ˌpī\ *vb* **1** : to occupy the attention of beforehand **2** : to take possession of before another
pre•op•er•a•tive \(ˌ)prē-ˈä-prə-tiv, -pə-ˌrā-\ *adj* : occurring before a surgical operation
pre•or•dain \ˌprē-ȯr-ˈdān\ *vb* : FOREORDAIN
pre–owned \(ˌ)prē-ˈōnd\ *adj* : SECONDHAND
prep *abbr* **1** preparatory **2** preposition
pre•pack•age \(ˌ)prē-ˈpa-kij\ *vb* : to package (as food) before offering for sale to the customer
preparatory school *n* **1** : a usually private school preparing students primarily for college **2** *Brit* : a private elementary school preparing students primarily for British public schools
pre•pare \pri-ˈpar\ *vb* **pre•pared; pre•par•ing** **1** ♦ : to make or get ready 〈~ dinner〉 〈~ a student for college〉 **2** ♦ : to get ready beforehand **3** : to put together : COMPOUND 〈~ a prescription〉 **4** ♦ : to put into written form — **prep•a•ra•tion** \ˌpre-pə-ˈrā-shən\ *n* — **pre•pa•ra•to•ry** \pri-ˈpar-ə-ˌtōr-ē\ *adj*

♦ [1] equip, fit, qualify, ready, season ♦ [2] fit, fix, get, lay, ready ♦ [4] cast, compose, craft, draft, draw, formulate, frame

prepared *adj* **1** : made ready, fit, or suitable beforehand **2** : subjected to a special process or treatment
pre•pared•ness \pri-ˈpar-əd-nəs\ *n* : a state of adequate preparation
pre•pay \(ˌ)prē-ˈpā\ *vb* **-paid** \-ˈpād\; **-pay•ing** : to pay or pay the charge on in advance
pre•pon•der•ant \pri-ˈpän-də-rənt\ *adj* : having greater weight, force, influence, or frequency — **pre•pon•der•ance** \-rəns\ *n* — **pre•pon•der•ant•ly** *adv*
pre•pon•der•ate \pri-ˈpän-də-ˌrāt\ *vb* **-at•ed; -at•ing** : to exceed in weight, force, influence, or frequency : PREDOMINATE
prep•o•si•tion \ˌpre-pə-ˈzi-shən\ *n* : a word that combines with a noun or pronoun to form a phrase — **prep•o•si•tion•al** \-ˈzi-shə-nəl\ *adj*
pre•pos•sess \ˌprē-pə-ˈzes\ *vb* **1** : to cause to be preoccupied **2** : to influence beforehand especially favorably
pre•pos•sess•ing *adj* : tending to create a favorable impression 〈a ~ manner〉
pre•pos•ses•sion \-ˈze-shən\ *n* **1** : PREJUDICE **2** ♦ : an exclusive concern with one idea or object

♦ fetish, fixation, mania, obsession, preoccupation

pre•pos•ter•ous \pri-ˈpäs-tə-rəs\ *adj* ♦ : contrary to nature or reason : ABSURD

♦ absurd, bizarre, crazy, fanciful, fantastic, foolish, insane, nonsensical, unreal, wild ♦ absurd, comical, derisive, farcical, laughable, ludicrous, ridiculous, risible, silly

prep•py *or* **prep•pie** \ˈpre-pē\ *n, pl* **preppies** **1** : a student at or a graduate of a preparatory school **2** : a person deemed to dress or behave like a preppy
pre•puce \ˈprē-ˌpyüs\ *n* : FORESKIN
pre•quel \ˈprē-kwəl\ *n* : a literary or dramatic work whose story precedes that of an earlier work
pre•re•cord•ed \(ˌ)prē-ri-ˈkȯr-dəd\ *adj* : recorded for later broadcast or play
pre•req•ui•site \prē-ˈre-kwə-zət\ *n* : something required beforehand or for the end in view — **prerequisite** *adj*
pre•rog•a•tive \pri-ˈrä-gə-tiv\ *n* ♦ : an exclusive or special right, power, or privilege

♦ birthright, right

pres *abbr* **1** present **2** president
[1]**pres•age** \ˈpre-sij\ *n* **1** ♦ : something that foreshadows a future event : OMEN **2** ♦ : an intuition or feeling of what is going to happen in the future : FOREBODING

♦ [1] augury, auspice, foreboding, omen, portent ♦ [2] foreboding, premonition, presentiment

[2]**pre•sage** \ˈpre-sij, pri-ˈsāj\ *vb* **pre•saged; pre•sag•ing** **1** : to give an omen or warning of : FORESHADOW **2** ♦ : to tell beforehand : FORETELL, PREDICT

♦ augur, forecast, foretell, predict, prognosticate, prophesy

pres•by•o•pia \ˌprez-bē-ˈō-pē-ə\ *n* : a visual condition in which loss of elasticity of the lens of the eye causes defective accommodation and inability to focus sharply for near vision — **pres•by•o•pic** \-ˈō-pik, -ˈä-\ *adj or n*
pres•by•ter \ˈprez-bə-tər\ *n* **1** : PRIEST, MINISTER **2** : an elder in a Presbyterian church
[1]**Pres•by•te•ri•an** \ˌprez-bə-ˈtir-ē-ən\ *n* : a member of a Presbyterian church
[2]**Presbyterian** *adj* **1** *often not cap* : characterized by a graded system of representative ecclesiastical bodies (as presbyteries) exercising legislative and judicial powers **2** : of or relating to a group of Protestant Christian bodies that are presbyterian in government — **Pres•by•te•ri•an•ism** \-ə-ˌni-zəm\ *n*
pres•by•tery \ˈprez-bə-ˌter-ē\ *n, pl* **-ter•ies** **1** : the part of a church reserved for the officiating clergy **2** : a ruling body in Presbyterian churches consisting of the ministers and representative elders of a district
[1]**pre•school** \ˈprē-ˌskül\ *adj* : of or relating to the period in a child's life from infancy to the age of five or six — **pre•school•er** \-ˌskü-lər\ *n*
[2]**preschool** *n* : NURSERY SCHOOL
pre•science \ˈpre-shəns, ˈprē-\ *n* **1** : foreknowledge of events **2** ♦ : the act or fact of being concerned for and making preparations for the future

♦ foresight, forethought, providence

pre•scient \-shənt, -shē-ənt\ *adj* ♦ : having or marked by prescience : characterized by foresight

♦ farsighted, foresighted, provident

pre•scribe \pri-ˈskrīb\ *vb* **pre•scribed; pre•scrib•ing** **1** ♦ : to lay down as a guide or rule of action **2** : to direct the use of (as a medicine) as a remedy

♦ define, lay down, specify

pre•scrip•tion \pri-ˈskrip-shən\ *n* **1** : the action of prescribing rules or directions **2** : a written direction for the preparation and use of a medicine; *also* : a medicine prescribed
pre•scrip•tive \pri-ˈskrip-tiv\ *adj* **1** : serving to prescribe 〈~ rules〉 **2** : acquired by, based on, or determined by prescription or by custom
pres•ence \ˈprez-ᵊns\ *n* **1** : the fact or condition of being present **2** : the space immediately around a person **3** : one that is present **4** ♦ : the bearing, carriage, or air of a person; *esp* : stately bearing

♦ appearance, aspect, look, mien

[1]**pres•ent** \ˈprez-ᵊnt\ *n* ♦ : something presented : GIFT

♦ bestowal, donation, freebie, gift, lagniappe, largesse

[2]**pre•sent** \pri-ˈzent\ *vb* **1** : to bring into the presence or acquaintance of : INTRODUCE **2** ♦ : to bring before the public 〈~ a play〉 **3** : to make a gift to **4** ♦ : to give formally **5** : to lay (as a charge)

before a court for inquiry **6 :** to aim or direct (as a weapon) so as to face in a particular direction — **pre·sent·able** *adj* — **pre·sent·ment** \pri-ˈzent-mənt\ *n*

♦ [2] carry, give, mount, offer, stage ♦ [4] bestow, contribute, donate, give

³pres·ent \ˈprez-ᵊnt\ *adj* **1** ♦ **:** now existing or in progress ⟨~ conditions⟩ **2 :** being in view or at hand ⟨~ at the meeting⟩ **3 :** under consideration ⟨the ~ problem⟩ **4 :** of, relating to, or constituting a verb tense that expresses present time or the time of speaking

♦ current, extant, ongoing *Ant* ago, past; future

⁴pres·ent \ˈprez-ᵊnt\ *n* **1** *pl* **:** the present legal document **2 :** the present tense; *also* **:** a verb form in it **3** ♦ **:** the present time

♦ moment, now, today *Ant* past; future

pre·sen·ta·tion \ˌprē-ˌzen-ˈtā-shən, ˌprez-ᵊn-\ *n* **1 :** the act of presenting **2 :** something presented

pres·ent–day \ˈprez-ᵊnt-ˈdā\ *adj* **:** now existing or occurring **:** CURRENT

pre·sen·ti·ment \pri-ˈzen-tə-mənt\ *n* ♦ **:** a feeling that something is about to happen **:** PREMONITION

♦ foreboding, premonition, presage

pres·ent·ly \ˈprez-ᵊnt-lē\ *adv* **1** ♦ **:** in the near future **:** SOON **2** ♦ **:** at the present time **:** NOW

♦ [1] anon, momentarily, shortly, soon ♦ [2] anymore, now, nowadays, right now, today

present participle *n* **:** a participle that typically expresses present action and that in English is formed with the suffix *-ing* and is used in the formation of the progressive tenses

pres·er·va·tion \ˌpre-zər-ˈvā-shən\ *n* ♦ **:** the act of preserving or the state of being preserved

♦ conservation, maintenance, upkeep

¹pre·serve \pri-ˈzərv\ *vb* **pre·served; pre·serv·ing 1 :** to keep safe **:** GUARD, PROTECT **2 :** to keep from decaying; *esp* **:** to process food (as by canning or pickling) to prevent spoilage **3 :** MAINTAIN ⟨~ silence⟩ **4** ♦ **:** to keep alive, intact, in existence, or from decay — **pre·ser·va·tive** \pri-ˈzər-və-tiv\ *adj or n* — **pre·serv·er** *n*

♦ conserve, keep up, maintain, save

²preserve *n* **1 :** preserved fruit — often used in plural **2 :** an area for the protection of natural resources (as animals)

pre·set \(ˌ)prē-ˈset\ *vb* **-set; -set·ting :** to set beforehand

pre·shrink \prē-ˈshriŋk\ *vb* **-shrank** \-ˈshraŋk\; **-shrunk** \-ˈshrəŋk\; **-shrink·ing :** to shrink (as a fabric) before making into a garment

pre·side \pri-ˈzīd\ *vb* **pre·sid·ed; pre·sid·ing 1** ♦ **:** to exercise guidance or control **2 :** to occupy the place of authority; *esp* **:** to act as chairman

♦ *usu* **preside over** boss, captain, command, control, govern, rule

pres·i·dent \ˈpre-zə-dənt\ *n* **1** ♦ **:** one chosen to preside ⟨~ of the assembly⟩ **2 :** the chief officer of an organization (as a corporation or society) **3 :** an elected official serving as both chief of state and chief political executive; *also* **:** a chief of state often with only minimal political powers — **pres·i·den·cy** \-dən-sē\ *n* — **pres·i·den·tial** \ˌpre-zə-ˈden-chəl\ *adj*

♦ chair, chairman, moderator, speaker

pre·si·dio \pri-ˈsē-dē-ˌō, -ˈsi-\ *n, pl* **-di·os :** a military post or fortified settlement in an area currently or orig. under Spanish control

pre·sid·i·um \pri-ˈsi-dē-əm\ *n, pl* **-ia** \-dē-ə\ *or* **-iums :** a permanent executive committee that acts for a larger body in a Communist country

¹pre·soak \(ˌ)prē-ˈsōk\ *vb* **:** to soak beforehand

²pre·soak \ˈprē-ˌsōk\ *n* **1 :** an instance of presoaking **2 :** a preparation used in presoaking clothes

pre·sort \(ˌ)prē-ˈsȯrt\ *vb* **:** to sort (mail) by zip code usually before delivery to a post office

¹press \ˈpres\ *n* **1** ♦ **:** a crowd or crowded condition **:** THRONG **2 :** a machine for exerting pressure **3 :** CLOSET, CUPBOARD **4 :** PRESSURE **5 :** the properly creased condition of a freshly pressed garment **6 :** PRINTING PRESS; *also* **:** the act or the process of printing **7 :** a printing or publishing establishment **8 :** the media (as newspapers and magazines) of public news and comment; *also* **:** persons (as reporters) employed in these media **9 :** comment in newspapers and periodicals

♦ army, crowd, crush, drove, flock, horde, host, legion, mob, multitude, swarm, throng

²press *vb* **1** ♦ **:** to bear down upon **:** push steadily against **2 :** ASSAIL, COMPEL **3** ♦ **:** to squeeze out the juice or contents of ⟨~ grapes⟩ **4 :** to squeeze to a desired density, shape, or smoothness; *esp* **:** IRON **5 a :** to try hard to persuade **:** URGE **b** ♦ **:** to move to action or reaction through pressure **6 :** to follow through **:** PROSECUTE **7** ♦ **:** to crowd closely **8** ♦ **:** to force one's way **9 :** to require haste or speed in action **10** ♦ **:** to insist on or request urgently — **press·er** *n*

♦ [1] bear, depress, shove, weigh ♦ [3] crush, express, mash, squeeze ♦ [5b] coerce, compel, constrain, drive, force, make, muscle, obligate, oblige, pressure, urge ♦ [7] bunch, cluster, crowd, huddle ♦ [8] bulldoze, elbow, muscle, push ♦ *often* **press for** [10] call, claim, clamor (*or* clamour), command, demand, enjoin, exact, insist, quest, stipulate (for)

press agent *n* **:** an agent employed to establish and maintain good public relations through publicity

press·ing *adj* ♦ **:** urgently important

♦ acute, critical, dire, imperative, imperious, instant, urgent

press·man \ˈpres-mən, -ˌman\ *n* **:** the operator of a press and especially a printing press

press·room \-rüm, -ˌru̇m\ *n* **1 :** a room in a printing plant containing the printing presses **2 :** a room for the use of reporters

¹pres·sure \ˈpre-shər\ *n* **1 :** the burden of physical or mental distress **2 :** the action of pressing; *esp* **:** the application of force to something by something else in direct contact with it **3 :** the force exerted over a surface divided by its area **4** ♦ **:** the stress or urgency of matters demanding attention

♦ strain, stress, tension ♦ coercion, compulsion, constraint, duress, force

²pressure *vb* **pres·sured; pres·sur·ing 1 :** to apply pressure to **2** ♦ **:** to cause an action or reaction as a result of applied pressure

♦ coerce, compel, constrain, drive, force, make, muscle, obligate, oblige, press

pressure group *n* **:** a group that seeks to influence governmental policy but not to elect candidates to office

pressure suit *n* **:** an inflatable suit for high-altitude flight or spaceflight to protect the body from low pressure

pres·sur·ise *chiefly Brit var of* PRESSURIZE

pres·sur·ize \ˈpre-shə-ˌrīz\ *vb* **-ized; -iz·ing 1 :** to maintain higher pressure within than without; *esp* **:** to maintain normal atmospheric pressure within (as an airplane cabin) during high-altitude flight or spaceflight **2 :** to apply pressure to **3 :** to design to withstand pressure — **pres·sur·i·za·tion** \ˌpre-shə-rə-ˈzā-shən\ *n*

pres·ti·dig·i·ta·tion \ˌpres-tə-ˌdi-jə-ˈtā-shən\ *n* ♦ **:** skill and dexterity in executing tricks or deception **:** SLEIGHT OF HAND

♦ legerdemain, magic

pres·tige \pres-ˈtēzh, -ˈtēj\ *n* **:** standing or estimation in the eyes of people **:** REPUTATION

pres·ti·gious \pres-ˈti-jəs, -ˈtē-\ *adj* ♦ **:** having prestige

♦ name, reputable, reputed, respectable ♦ distinguished, eminent, illustrious, noble, notable, noteworthy, outstanding, preeminent, signal, star, superior

pres·to \ˈpres-tō\ *adv or adj* **1** ♦ **:** suddenly as if by magic **:** IMMEDIATELY **2 :** at a rapid tempo — used as a direction in music

♦ apace, briskly, fast, full tilt, hastily, immediately, posthaste, pronto, quick, quickly, rapidly, soon, speedily, swift, swiftly

pre·stress \(ˌ)prē-ˈstres\ *vb* **:** to introduce internal stresses into (as a structural beam) to counteract later load stresses

pre·sum·ably \pri-ˈzü-mə-blē\ *adv* ♦ **:** by reasonable assumption

♦ apparently, evidently, ostensibly, seemingly, supposedly ♦ doubtless, likely, probably

pre·sume \pri-ˈzüm\ *vb* **pre·sumed; pre·sum·ing 1 :** to take upon oneself without leave or warrant **:** DARE **2** ♦ **:** to take for granted **:** ASSUME **3 :** to act or behave with undue boldness — **pre·sum·able** \-ˈzü-mə-bəl\ *adj*

♦ assume, postulate, premise, presuppose, suppose

pre·sump·tion \pri-ˈzəmp-shən\ *n* **1** ♦ **:** presumptuous attitude or conduct **:** AUDACITY **2** ♦ **:** an attitude or belief dictated by probability; *also* **:** the grounds lending probability to a belief — **pre·sump·tive** \-tiv\ *adj*

♦ [1] audacity, brass, brazenness, cheek, chutzpah, effrontery, gall, nerve, sauce, sauciness, temerity ♦ [2] assumption, postulate, premise, supposition

pre·sump·tu·ous \pri-ˈzəmp-chə-wəs\ *adj* ♦ **:** overstepping due bounds (as of propriety or courtesy) **:** taking liberties — **pre·sump·tu·ous·ly** *adv*

♦ arrogant, cavalier, haughty, high-handed, imperious, important, overweening, pompous, pretentious, supercilious, superior ♦ bold, familiar, forward, free, immodest *Ant* modest, unassuming ♦ intrusive, meddlesome, nosy, obtrusive, officious, prying

pre·sup·pose \ˌprē-sə-ˈpōz\ *vb* **1** ♦ **:** to suppose beforehand **2 :** to require beforehand as a necessary condition

♦ assume, postulate, premise, presume, suppose

pre·sup·po·si·tion \(ˌ)prē-ˌsə-pə-ˈzi-shən\ *n* **:** an act of presupposing or an assumption made in advance

pre·teen \ˈprē-ˈtēn\ *n* **:** a boy or girl not yet 13 years old — **preteen** *adj*

pre·tend \pri-ˈtend\ *vb* **1 :** PROFESS ⟨doesn't ~ to be scientific⟩ **2** ♦ **:** to make believe **:** FEIGN ⟨~ to be angry⟩ **3 :** to lay claim ⟨~ to a throne⟩

♦ affect, assume, counterfeit, fake, feign, profess, put on, sham, simulate ♦ dissemble, dissimulate, let on

pre·tend·er \pri-ˈten-dər\ *n* ♦ **:** one that pretends

♦ charlatan, fake, fraud, hoaxer, humbug, mountebank, phony, quack

pre·tense *or* **pre·tence** \ˈprē-ˌtens, pri-ˈtens\ *n* **1 :** a claim made or implied; *esp* **:** one not supported by fact **2** ♦ **:** an assumed display or attitude of superiority or dignity **3 :** an inadequate or insincere attempt to attain a certain condition ⟨made a ~ at discipline⟩ **4 :** false show **:** PRETEXT **5** ♦ **:** excessive display **:** PRETENTIOUSNESS

♦ [2] act, airs, facade, front, guise, masquerade, pose, put-on, semblance, show ♦ [5] affectation, pretension, pretentiousness

pre·ten·sion \pri-ˈten-chən\ *n* **1 :** an allegation of doubtful value **:** PRETEXT **2** ♦ **:** claim or an effort to establish a claim **3 :** a claim or right to attention or honor because of merit **4** ♦ **:** an aspiration or intention that may or may not reach fulfillment **5 :** the quality or act of making usually unjustified claims (as to excellence) **6 :** an exaggerated sense of self-importance

♦ [2] call, claim, pretense, right ♦ [4] aim, ambition, aspiration, design, dream, end, goal, intent, mark, meaning, object, objective, plan, purpose, thing

pre·ten·tious \pri-ˈten-chəs\ *adj* **1** ♦ **:** making or possessing usually unjustified claims (as to excellence) ⟨a ~ literary style⟩ **2 :** making demands on one's ability or means **:** AMBITIOUS ⟨too ~ an undertaking⟩ — **pre·ten·tious·ly** *adv*

♦ affected, grandiose, highfalutin, ostentatious, pompous *Ant* modest, unpretentious

pre·ten·tious·ness \-nəs\ *n* ♦ **:** the quality or state of being pretentious

♦ affectation, arrogance, haughtiness, loftiness, pretense, pretension, self-importance, superiority

pret·er·it *or* **pret·er·ite** \ˈpre-tə-rət\ *n* **:** a verb form expressing action in the past

pre·term \(ˌ)prē-ˈtərm, ˈprē-ˌ\ *adj* **:** of, relating to, being, or brought forth by premature birth ⟨a ~ infant⟩

pre·ter·nat·u·ral \ˌprē-tər-ˈna-chə-rəl\ *adj* **1 :** exceeding what is natural **2** ♦ **:** inexplicable by ordinary means — **pre·ter·nat·u·ral·ly** *adv*

♦ metaphysical, superhuman, supernatural, unearthly

pre·text \ˈprē-ˌtekst\ *n* **:** a purpose stated or assumed to cloak the real intention or state of affairs

pret·ti·fy \ˈpri-ti-ˌfī\ *vb* **-fied; -fy·ing :** to make pretty — **pret·ti·fi·ca·tion** \ˌpri-ti-fə-ˈkā-shən\ *n*

pret·ti·ness \ˈpri-tē-nəs\ *n* ♦ **:** the quality or state of being pretty

♦ attractiveness, beauty, comeliness, handsomeness, looks, loveliness

1**pret·ty** \ˈpri-tē\ *adj* **pret·ti·er; -est 1** ♦ **:** pleasing by delicacy or grace **:** having conventionally accepted elements of beauty ⟨~ flowers⟩ **2 :** MISERABLE, TERRIBLE ⟨a ~ state of affairs⟩ **3 :** moderately large ⟨a ~ profit⟩ **4 :** PLEASANT — **pret·ti·ly** \-tə-lē\ *adv*

♦ attractive, beautiful, cute, fair, handsome, lovely

2**pretty** *adv* ♦ **:** in some degree **:** MODERATELY

♦ enough, fairly, kind of, moderately, quite, rather, so-so, somewhat, sort of

3**pretty** *vb* **pret·tied; pret·ty·ing :** to make pretty

pretty boy *n* **:** a man who is notably good-looking

pret·zel \ˈpret-səl\ *n* **:** a brittle or chewy glazed usually salted slender bread often shaped like a loose knot

prev *abbr* previous; previously

pre·vail \pri-ˈvāl\ *vb* **1** ♦ **:** to win mastery **:** TRIUMPH **2 :** to be or become effective **:** SUCCEED **3** ♦ **:** to urge successfully ⟨~*ed* upon her to sing⟩ **4 :** to be frequent **:** PREDOMINATE **5** ♦ **:** to be or continue in use or fashion — **pre·vail·ing·ly** *adv*

♦ [1] conquer, triumph, win ♦ *usu* **prevail over** [1] beat, defeat, master, triumph, win ♦ *usu* **prevail on** *or* **prevail upon** [3] argue, convince, get, induce, move, persuade, satisfy, talk, win ♦ [5] hold, hold out, keep up, last, survive

prev·a·lent \ˈpre-və-lənt\ *adj* **:** generally or widely existent **:** WIDESPREAD — **prev·a·lence** \-ləns\ *n*

pre·var·i·cate \pri-ˈvar-ə-ˌkāt\ *vb* **-cat·ed; -cat·ing** ♦ **:** to deviate from the truth

♦ fabricate, fib, lie

pre·var·i·ca·tion \pri-ˌvar-ə-ˈkā-shən\ *n* **1 :** the act or an instance of prevaricating **2** ♦ **:** a statement that deviates from or perverts the truth

♦ fabrication, fairy tale, falsehood, falsity, fib, lie, mendacity, story, tale, untruth, whopper

pre·var·i·ca·tor \pri-ˈvar-ə-ˌkā-tər\ *n* ♦ **:** one who evades or perverts the truth

♦ fibber, liar

pre·vent \pri-ˈvent\ *vb* **1** ♦ **:** to keep from happening or existing ⟨steps to ~ war⟩ **2 :** to hold back **:** HINDER, STOP ⟨~ us from going⟩ — **pre·vent·able** *also* **pre·vent·ible** \-ˈven-tə-bəl\ *adj* — **pre·ven·tive** \-ˈven-tiv\ *adj or n* — **pre·ven·ta·tive** \-ˈven-tə-tiv\ *adj or n*

♦ avert, forestall, help, obviate, preclude

pre·ven·tion \pri-ˈven-chən\ *n* **:** the act of preventing or hindering

pre·ver·bal \ˌprē-ˈvər-bəl\ *adj* **:** having not yet acquired the faculty of speech

1**pre·view** \ˈprē-ˌvyü\ *vb* **:** to see or discuss beforehand; *esp* **:** to view or show in advance of public presentation

2**preview** *n* **1 :** an advance showing or viewing **2** *also* **pre·vue** \-ˌvyü\ **:** a showing of snatches from a motion picture advertised for future appearance **3 :** FORETASTE

pre·vi·ous \ˈprē-vē-əs\ *adj* ♦ **:** going before

♦ antecedent, anterior, foregoing, preceding, prior *Ant* after, ensuing, following, subsequent, succeeding

pre·vi·ous·ly \-lē\ *adv* ♦ **:** in time past

♦ ahead, before, beforehand

previous to *prep* ♦ **:** in advance of **:** BEFORE

♦ ahead of, before, ere, of, prior to, to

pre·vi·sion \prē-ˈvi-zhən\ *n* **1 :** FORESIGHT, PRESCIENCE **2 :** FORECAST, PREDICTION

pre·war \ˈprē-ˈwȯr\ *adj* **:** occurring or existing before a war

1**prey** \ˈprā\ *n, pl* **prey** *also* **preys 1 :** an animal taken for food by a predator; *also* **:** VICTIM **2 :** the act or habit of preying

2**prey** *vb* **1 :** to raid for booty **2 :** to seize and devour prey **3 :** to have a harmful or wearing effect

prf *abbr* proof

1**price** \ˈprīs\ *n* **1** *archaic* **:** VALUE **2** ♦ **:** the amount of money paid or asked for the sale of a specified thing; *also* **:** the cost at which something is obtained

♦ charge, cost, fee, figure

2**price** *vb* **priced; pric·ing 1 :** to set a price on **2 :** to ask the price of **3 :** to drive by raising prices ⟨*priced* themselves out of the market⟩

price–fix·ing \ˈprīs-ˌfik-siŋ\ *n* **:** the setting of prices artificially (as by producers or government)

price·less \-ləs\ *adj* **:** having a value beyond any price **:** INVALUABLE

price support *n* **:** artificial maintenance of prices of a commodity at a level usually fixed through government action

price war *n* **:** a period of commercial competition in which prices are repeatedly cut by the competitors

pric·ey *also* **pricy** \ˈprī-sē\ *adj* **pric·i·er; -est :** EXPENSIVE

[1]prick \ˈprik\ *n* **1** ♦ **:** a mark or small wound made by a pointed instrument **2 :** something sharp or pointed **3 a :** an instance of pricking **b** ♦ **:** a sensation of being pricked

♦ [1] perforation, pinhole, punch, puncture, stab ♦ [3b] ache, pain, pang, smart, sting, stitch, tingle, twinge

[2]prick *vb* **1 :** to pierce slightly with a sharp point; *also* **:** to have or cause a pricking sensation **2 :** to affect with anguish or remorse ⟨∼*s* his conscience⟩ **3 :** to outline with punctures ⟨∼ out a pattern⟩ **4 :** to stand or cause to stand erect ⟨the dog's ears ∼*ed* up at the sound⟩

prick·er \ˈpri-kər\ *n* **:** BRIAR; *also* **:** THORN

[1]prick·le \ˈpri-kəl\ *n* **1 :** a small sharp process (as on a plant) **2 :** a slight stinging pain

[2]prickle *vb* **prick·led; prick·ling 1 :** to prick lightly **2 :** TINGLE

prick·ly \ˈpri-klē\ *adj* ♦ **:** full of or covered with prickles

♦ brambly, scratchy, thorny

prickly heat *n* **:** a red cutaneous eruption with intense itching and tingling caused by inflammation around the ducts of the sweat glands

prickly pear *n* **:** any of numerous cacti with usually yellow flowers and prickly flat or rounded joints; *also* **:** the sweet pulpy pear-shaped edible fruit of various prickly pears

[1]pride \ˈprīd\ *n* **1** ♦ **:** inordinate self-esteem **:** CONCEIT **2** ♦ **:** justifiable self-respect **3 :** elation over an act or possession **4 :** haughty behavior **:** DISDAIN **5 :** ostentatious display **6** ♦ **:** a source of pride

♦ [1] complacence, conceit, ego, egotism, self-conceit, self-esteem, self-importance, self-satisfaction, smugness, vainglory, vanity ♦ [2] ego, self-esteem, self-regard, self-respect ♦ [6] boast, credit, glory, honor (*or* honour), jewel, treasure

[2]pride *vb* **prid·ed; prid·ing :** to indulge (as oneself) in pride

pride·ful \ˈprīd-fəl\ *adj* ♦ **:** full of pride

♦ disdainful, haughty, highfalutin, lofty, lordly, proud, superior

priest \ˈprēst\ *n* **:** a person having authority to perform the sacred rites of a religion; *esp* ♦ **:** a member of the Anglican, Eastern, or Roman Catholic clergy ranking below a bishop and above a deacon — **priest·hood** *n* — **priest·li·ness** *n*

♦ clergyman, divine, ecclesiastic, father, minister, preacher, reverend

priest·ess \ˈprēs-təs\ *n* **:** a woman authorized to perform the sacred rites of a religion

priest·ly \ˈprēst-lē\ *adj* ♦ **:** of, relating to, or characteristic of a priest or the priesthood

♦ clerical, ministerial, pastoral, sacerdotal

prig \ˈprig\ *n* **:** one who irritates by rigid or pointed observance of proprieties — **prig·gish** \ˈpri-gish\ *adj* — **prig·gish·ly** *adv*

[1]prim \ˈprim\ *adj* **prim·mer; prim·mest** ♦ **:** stiffly formal and precise — **prim·ly** *adv* — **prim·ness** *n*

♦ prudish, puritanical, straitlaced

[2]prim *abbr* **1** primary **2** primitive

pri·ma·cy \ˈprī-mə-sē\ *n* **1** ♦ **:** the state of being first (as in rank) **2 :** the office, rank, or character of an ecclesiastical primate

♦ distinction, dominance, eminence, preeminence, superiority, supremacy, transcendence

pri·ma don·na \ˌpri-mə-ˈdä-nə\ *n, pl* **prima donnas 1 :** a principal female singer (as in an opera company) **2 :** a vain undisciplined usually uncooperative person

pri·ma fa·cie \ˈprī-mə-ˈfā-shə, -sē, -shē\ *adj or adv* **1 :** based on immediate impression **:** APPARENT **2 :** SELF-EVIDENT

pri·mal \ˈprī-məl\ *adj* **1** ♦ **:** of or relating to the first period or state **:** PRIMITIVE **2 :** first in importance

♦ ancient, early, primeval, primitive

pri·mar·i·ly \prī-ˈmer-ə-lē\ *adv* **1** ♦ **:** for the most part **2** ♦ **:** in the first place **:** ORIGINALLY

♦ [1] altogether, basically, chiefly, generally, largely, mainly, mostly, overall, predominantly, principally ♦ [2] firstly, initially, originally

[1]pri·ma·ry \ˈprī-ˌmer-ē, -mə-rē\ *adj* **1 :** first in order of time or development; *also* **:** PREPARATORY **2** ♦ **:** of first rank or importance; *also* **:** FUNDAMENTAL **3** ♦ **:** not derived from or dependent on something else ⟨∼ sources⟩

♦ [2] arch, cardinal, central, chief, dominant, first, foremost, fundamental, grand, key, main, paramount, predominant, preeminent, premier, principal, sovereign, supreme ♦ [3] direct, firsthand, immediate

[2]primary *n, pl* **-ries :** a preliminary election in which voters nominate or express a preference among candidates usually of their own party

primary care *n* **:** health care provided by a medical professional with whom a patient has initial contact

primary color *n* **:** any of a set of colors from which all other colors may be derived

primary school *n* **1 :** a school usually including grades 1–3 and sometimes kindergarten **2 :** ELEMENTARY SCHOOL

pri·mate \ˈprī-ˌmāt *or esp for 1* -mət\ *n* **1** *often cap* **:** the highest-ranking bishop of a province or nation **2 :** any of an order of mammals including humans, apes, and monkeys

[1]prime \ˈprīm\ *n* **1 :** the earliest stage of something; *esp* **:** SPRINGTIME **2** ♦ **:** the most active, thriving, or successful stage or period (as of one's life) **3** ♦ **:** the best individual or part **4 :** any integer other than 0, +1, or –1 that is not divisible without remainder by any integer except +1, –1, and plus or minus itself; *esp* **:** any such integer that is positive

♦ [2] bloom, blossom, flower, flush, heyday ♦ [3] best, choice, cream, elect, elite, fat, flower, pick

[2]prime *adj* **1** ♦ **:** standing first (as in time, rank, significance, or quality) ⟨∼ requisite⟩ **2 :** of, relating to, or being a number that is prime

♦ chief, first, foremost, head, high, lead, preeminent, premier, primary, principal, supreme

[3]prime *vb* **primed; prim·ing 1 :** FILL, LOAD **2 :** to lay a preparatory coating upon (as in painting) **3 :** to put in working condition **4 :** to instruct beforehand **:** COACH

prime meridian *n* **:** the meridian of 0° longitude which runs through Greenwich, England, and from which other longitudes are reckoned east and west

prime minister *n* **1 :** the chief minister of a ruler or state **2 :** the chief executive of a parliamentary government

[1]prim·er \ˈpri-mər\ *n* **1 :** a small book for teaching children to read **2** ♦ **:** a small introductory book on a subject

♦ handbook, manual, textbook

[2]prim·er \ˈprī-mər\ *n* **1 :** one that primes **2 :** a device for igniting an explosive **3 :** material for priming a surface

prime rate *n* **:** an interest rate announced by a bank to be the lowest available to its most credit-worthy customers

prime time *n* **1 :** the time period when the television or radio audience is largest; *also* **:** television shows aired in prime time **2 :** the choicest or busiest time

pri·me·val \prī-ˈmē-vəl\ *adj* ♦ **:** of or relating to the earliest ages **:** PRIMITIVE

♦ ancient, early, primal, primitive

[1]prim·i·tive \ˈpri-mə-tiv\ *adj* **1 :** ORIGINAL, PRIMARY **2** ♦ **:** of, relating to, or characteristic of an early stage of development **3 :** ELEMENTAL, NATURAL **4 :** of, relating to, or produced by a tribal people or culture **5 :** SELF-TAUGHT; *also* **:** produced by a self-taught artist — **prim·i·tive·ly** *adv* — **prim·i·tive·ness** *n* — **prim·i·tiv·i·ty** \ˌpri-mə-ˈti-və-tē\ *n*

♦ crude, low, rude, rudimentary ***Ant*** advanced, developed, evolved ♦ ancient, early, primal, primeval

[2]primitive *n* **1 :** something primitive **2 :** a primitive artist **3 :** a member of a primitive people

prim·i·tiv·ism \ˈpri-mə-ti-ˌvi-zəm\ *n* **1 :** belief in the superiority of a simple way of life close to nature **2 :** the style of art of primitive peoples or primitive artists

pri·mo·gen·i·tor \ˌprī-mō-ˈje-nə-tər\ *n* **:** ANCESTOR, FOREFATHER

pri·mo·gen·i·ture \-ˈje-nə-ˌchu̇r\ *n* **1 :** the state of being the firstborn of a family **2 :** an exclusive right of inheritance belonging to the eldest son

pri·mor·di·al \prī-ˈmȯr-dē-əl\ *adj* **:** first created or developed **:** existing in its original state **:** PRIMEVAL

primp \ˈprimp\ *vb* **:** to dress in a careful or finicky manner

prim·rose \ˈprim-ˌrōz\ *n* **:** any of a genus of perennial herbs with large leaves arranged at the base of the stem and clusters of showy flowers

prin *abbr* **1** principal **2** principle

prince \ˈprins\ *n* **1 :** MONARCH, KING **2 :** a male member of a royal family; *esp* **:** a son of the monarch **3** ♦ **:** a person of high standing (as in a class) — **prince·dom** \-dəm\ *n*

♦ baron, czar, king, magnate, mogul, tycoon

prince·ling \-liŋ\ *n* **:** a petty prince

prince•ly \ˈprin(t)s-lē\ *adj* ♦ **:** of, relating to, or befitting a prince

♦ kingly, monarchical, queenly, regal, royal

prin•cess \ˈprin-səs, -ˌses\ *n* **1 :** a female member of a royal family **2 :** the consort of a prince
[1]prin•ci•pal \ˈprin-sə-pəl\ *adj* ♦ **:** most important

♦ arch, cardinal, central, chief, dominant, first, foremost, grand, key, main, paramount, predominant, preeminent, premier, primary, sovereign, supreme

[2]principal *n* **1 :** a leading person (as in a play) **2 :** the chief officer of an educational institution **3 :** the person from whom an agent's authority derives **4 :** a capital sum earning interest or used as a fund
prin•ci•pal•i•ty \ˌprin-sə-ˈpa-lə-tē\ *n, pl* **-ties :** the position, territory, or jurisdiction of a prince
prin•ci•pal•ly \ˈprin-sə-p(ə-)lē\ *adv* ♦ **:** in the chief place or degree **:** CHIEFLY

♦ altogether, basically, chiefly, generally, largely, mainly, mostly, overall, predominantly, primarily

principal parts *n pl* **:** the inflected forms of a verb
prin•ci•ple \ˈprin-sə-pəl\ *n* **1** ♦ **:** a general or fundamental law, doctrine, or assumption **2** ♦ **:** a rule or code of conduct; *also* **:** devotion to such a code **3 :** the laws or facts of nature underlying the working of an artificial device **4 :** a primary source **:** ORIGIN; *also* **:** an underlying faculty or endowment **5 :** the active part (as of a drug)

♦ **principles** [1] elements, essentials, rudiments ♦ **principles** [2] ethics, morality, morals, standards

prin•ci•pled \-pəld\ *adj* ♦ **:** exhibiting, based on, or characterized by principle ⟨high-*principled*⟩

♦ decent, ethical, honest, honorable, just, moral, noble, respectable, righteous, upright, upstanding

prink \ˈpriŋk\ *vb* **:** PRIMP
[1]print \ˈprint\ *n* **1** ♦ **:** a mark made by pressure **2 :** something stamped with an impression **3 :** printed state or form **4 :** printed matter **5** ♦ **:** a copy made by printing **6 :** cloth with a pattern applied by printing

♦ [1] impress, impression, imprint, stamp ♦ [5] photograph, shot, snap, snapshot

[2]print *vb* **1 :** to stamp (as a mark) in or on something **2 :** to produce impressions of (as from type) **3 :** to write in letters like those of printer's type **4 :** to make (a positive picture) from a photographic negative **5** ♦ **:** to publish in print

♦ get out, issue, publish

print•able \ˈprin-tə-bəl\ *adj* **1 :** capable of being printed or of being printed from **2 :** worthy or fit to be published
print•er \ˈprin-tər\ *n* **:** one that prints; *esp* **:** a device that produces printout
print•ing *n* **1 :** reproduction in printed form **2 :** the art, practice, or business of a printer **3 :** IMPRESSION 5
printing press *n* **:** a machine that produces printed copies
print•out \ˈprint-ˌau̇t\ *n* **:** a printed output produced by a computer — **print out** *vb*
[1]pri•or \ˈprī-ər\ *n* **:** the superior ranking next to the abbot or abbess of a religious house
[2]prior *adj* **1** ♦ **:** earlier in time or order **2 :** taking precedence logically or in importance — **pri•or•i•ty** \prī-ˈȯr-ə-tē\ *n*

♦ antecedent, anterior, foregoing, preceding, previous

pri•or•ess \ˈprī-ə-rəs\ *n* **:** a nun corresponding in rank to a prior
pri•or•i•tize \prī-ˈȯr-ə-ˌtīz, ˈprī-ə-rə-ˌtīz\ *vb* **-tized; -tiz•ing :** to list or rate in order of priority
prior to *prep* ♦ **:** in advance of **:** BEFORE

♦ ahead of, before, ere, of, previous to, to

pri•o•ry \ˈprī-ə-rē\ *n, pl* **-ries** ♦ **:** a religious house under a prior or prioress

♦ abbey, cloister, friary, monastery

prise *chiefly Brit var of* [5]PRIZE
prism \ˈpri-zəm\ *n* **1 :** a solid whose sides are parallelograms and whose ends are parallel and alike in shape and size **2 :** a usually 3-sided transparent object that refracts light so that it breaks up into rainbow colors — **pris•mat•ic** \priz-ˈma-tik\ *adj*
pris•on \ˈpriz-ᵊn\ *n* ♦ **:** a place or state of confinement especially for criminals

♦ brig, jail, lockup, pen, penitentiary

pris•on•er \ˈpriz-ᵊn-ər\ *n* ♦ **:** a person deprived of liberty; *esp* **:** one on trial or in prison

♦ captive, capture, internee

prisoner of war : a person and especially a member of the armed forces of a nation captured in war
pris•sy \ˈpri-sē\ *adj* **pris•si•er; -est :** being overly prim and precise **:** PRIGGISH — **pris•si•ness** \-sē-nəs\ *n*
pris•tine \ˈpris-ˌtēn, pri-ˈstēn\ *adj* **1 :** PRIMITIVE **2** ♦ **:** having the purity of its original state

♦ brand-new, fresh, virgin

prith•ee \ˈpri-t͟hē\ *interj, archaic* — used to express a wish or request
pri•va•cy \ˈprī-və-sē\ *n, pl* **-cies 1 :** the quality or state of being apart from others **2 :** SECRECY
[1]pri•vate \ˈprī-vət\ *adj* **1 :** belonging to or intended for a particular individual or group ⟨~ property⟩ **2** ♦ **:** restricted to the individual **:** PERSONAL ⟨~ opinion⟩ **3 :** carried on by the individual independently ⟨~ study⟩ **4 :** not holding public office ⟨a ~ citizen⟩ **5 :** withdrawn from company or observation ⟨a ~ place⟩ **6** ♦ **:** not known publicly — **pri•vate•ly** *adv*

♦ [2] individual, particular, peculiar, personal, separate, singular, unique ♦ [6] confidential, hushed, inside, intimate, secret *Ant* common, open, public

[2]private *n* **:** an enlisted man of the lowest rank in the marine corps or of one of the two lowest ranks in the army — **in private :** not openly or in public
pri•va•teer \ˌprī-və-ˈtir\ *n* **:** an armed private ship licensed to attack enemy shipping; *also* **:** a sailor on such a ship
private first class *n* **:** an enlisted man ranking next below a corporal in the army and next below a lance corporal in the marine corps
pri•va•tion \prī-ˈvā-shən\ *n* **1 :** the act of depriving **2 :** the state of being deprived; *esp* **:** lack of what is needed for existence
priv•et \ˈpri-vət\ *n* **:** a nearly evergreen shrub related to the olive and widely used for hedges
[1]priv•i•lege \ˈpriv-lij, ˈpri-və-\ *n* ♦ **:** a right or immunity granted as an advantage or favor especially to some and not others

♦ boon, concession, honor (*or* honour)

[2]privilege *vb* **-leged; -leg•ing** ♦ **:** to grant a privilege to

♦ authorize, entitle, qualify

priv•i•leged *adj* **1 :** having or enjoying one or more privileges ⟨~ classes⟩ **2 :** not subject to disclosure in a court of law ⟨a ~ communication⟩
[1]privy \ˈpri-vē\ *adj* **1 :** of, relating to, or affecting a particular person exclusively **:** PERSONAL, PRIVATE **2 :** kept from knowledge or view **:** SECRET **3 :** admitted as one sharing in a secret ⟨~ to the conspiracy⟩ — **priv•i•ly** \ˈpri-və-lē\ *adv*
[2]privy *n, pl* **priv•ies :** TOILET; *esp* **:** OUTHOUSE
[1]prize \ˈprīz\ *n* **1** ♦ **:** something offered or striven for in competition or in contests of chance **2** ♦ **:** something exceptionally desirable

♦ [1] award, decoration, distinction, honor (*or* honour), plume ♦ [2] catch, gem, jewel, pearl, plum, treasure

[2]prize *adj* **1 :** awarded or worthy of a prize ⟨a ~ essay⟩; *also* **:** awarded as a prize ⟨a ~ medal⟩ **2 :** OUTSTANDING
[3]prize *vb* **prized; priz•ing** ♦ **:** to value highly **:** ESTEEM

♦ appreciate, cherish, love, treasure, value

[4]prize *n* **:** property (as a ship) lawfully captured in time of war
[5]prize *or Can and Brit* **prise** *vb* **prized** *or* **prised; priz•ing** *or* **prising** ♦ **:** to press, force, or move with or as if with a lever **:** PRY

♦ jimmy, pry

prize•fight \ˈprīz-ˌfīt\ *n* **:** a professional boxing match — **prize•fight•ing** *n*
prize•fight•er \-ˈfī-tər\ *n* ♦ **:** one who particpates in a prizefight

♦ boxer, fighter, pugilist

prize•win•ner \-ˌwi-nər\ *n* **:** a winner of a prize — **prize•win•ning** *adj*
[1]pro \ˈprō\ *n, pl* **pros :** a favorable argument, person, or position
[2]pro *adv* **:** in favor **:** FOR
[3]pro *n or adj* **:** PROFESSIONAL
PRO *abbr* public relations officer
pro•ac•tive \prō-ˈak-tiv\ *adj* ♦ **:** acting in anticipation of future problems or needs — **pro•ac•tive•ly** *adv*

♦ farsighted, foresighted, prescient, provident, visionary

pro–am \ˈprō-ˈam\ *adj* **:** involving professionals competing alongside or against amateurs ⟨a ~ tournament⟩ — **pro–am** *n*
prob *abbr* **1** probable; probably **2** problem
prob·a·bil·i·ty \ˌprä-bə-ˈbi-lə-tē\ *n, pl* **-ties** **1 :** the quality or state of being probable **2 :** something probable **3** ♦ **:** a measure of how often a particular event will occur if something (as tossing a coin) is done repeatedly which results in any of a number of possible events

♦ chance, odds, percentage

prob·a·ble \ˈprä-bə-bəl\ *adj* **1** ♦ **:** apparently or presumably true ⟨a ~ hypothesis⟩ **2 :** likely to be or become true or real ⟨a ~ result⟩

♦ believable, credible, likely, plausible

prob·a·bly \ˈprä-bə-blē\ *adv* ♦ **:** without much doubt

♦ doubtless, likely, presumably *Ant* improbably

¹pro·bate \ˈprō-ˌbāt\ *n* **:** the judicial determination of the validity of a will
²pro·bate *vb* **pro·bat·ed; pro·bat·ing :** to establish (a will) by probate as genuine and valid
pro·ba·tion \prō-ˈbā-shən\ *n* **1 :** subjection of an individual to a period of testing and trial to ascertain fitness (as for a job) **2 :** the action of giving a convicted offender freedom during good behavior under the supervision of a probation officer — **pro·ba·tion·ary** \-shə-ˌner-ē\ *adj*
pro·ba·tion·er \-shə-nər\ *n* **1 :** a person (as a newly admitted student nurse) whose fitness is being tested during a trial period **2 :** a convicted offender on probation
pro·ba·tive \ˈprō-bə-tiv\ *adj* **1 :** serving to test or try **2 :** serving to prove
¹probe \ˈprōb\ *n* **1 :** a slender instrument for examining a cavity (as a wound) **2 :** an information-gathering device sent into outer space **3** ♦ **:** a penetrating investigation

♦ examination, exploration, inquiry, investigation, research, study

²probe *vb* **probed; prob·ing** **1 :** to examine with a probe **2** ♦ **:** to search into and investigate thoroughly

♦ delve, dig, explore, go, inquire into, investigate, look, research

pro·bi·ty \ˈprō-bə-tē\ *n* ♦ **:** adherence to the highest principles and ideals **:** HONESTY

♦ character, decency, goodness, honesty, integrity, morality, rectitude, righteousness, uprightness, virtue

prob·lem \ˈprä-bləm\ *n* **1 :** a question raised for consideration or solution **2** ♦ **:** an intricate unsettled question **3** ♦ **:** a source of perplexity or vexation — **problem** *adj*

♦ [2] case, knot, matter, trouble *Ant* answer, solution ♦ [3] aggravation, annoyance, bother, exasperation, frustration, hassle, headache, inconvenience, irritant, nuisance, peeve, pest, thorn

prob·lem·at·ic \ˌprä-blə-ˈma-tik\ *also* **prob·lem·at·i·cal** \-ti-kəl\ *adj* **1** ♦ **:** difficult to solve or decide **2** ♦ **:** open to question or debate **:** QUESTIONABLE

♦ [1] catchy, delicate, difficult, knotty, spiny, thorny, ticklish, touchy, tough, tricky ♦ [2] debatable, disputable, doubtful, dubious, equivocal, fishy, questionable, shady, shaky, suspect, suspicious

pro·bos·cis \prə-ˈbä-səs, -ˈbäs-kəs\ *n, pl* **-bos·cis·es** *also* **-bos·ci·des** \-ˈbä-sə-ˌdēz\ **:** a long flexible snout (as the trunk of an elephant)
proc *abbr* proceedings
pro·caine \ˈprō-ˌkān\ *n* **:** a drug used especially as a local anesthetic
pro·ce·dure \prə-ˈsē-jər\ *n* **1** ♦ **:** a particular way of doing something ⟨democratic ~⟩ **2** ♦ **:** a series of steps followed in a regular order ⟨a surgical ~⟩ — **pro·ce·dur·al** \-ˈsē-jə-rəl\ *adj*

♦ [1] course, line, policy, program ♦ [2] course, operation, proceeding, process

pro·ceed \prō-ˈsēd\ *vb* **1 :** to come forth **:** ISSUE **2 :** to go on in an orderly way; *also* **:** CONTINUE **3 :** to begin and carry on an action **4 :** to take legal action **5** ♦ **:** to move along a course

♦ advance, fare, forge, get along, go, march, progress ♦ *usu* **proceed along** cover, crisscross, cross, cut, follow, go, pass, travel, traverse

pro·ceed·ing *n* **1 :** a series of steps followed in a regular definite order **:** PROCEDURE **2** *pl* **:** DOINGS **3** *pl* ♦ **:** legal action **4 :** TRANSACTION **5** *pl* **:** an official record of things said or done

♦ action, lawsuit, suit

pro·ceeds \ˈprō-ˌsēdz\ *n pl* ♦ **:** the total amount or the profit arising from a business deal

♦ earnings, income, profit, return, revenue, yield

¹pro·cess \ˈprä-ˌses, ˈprō-\ *n, pl* **pro·cess·es** \-ˌse-səz, -sə-səz, -sə-ˌsēz\ **1 :** a forward or onward movement (as to an objective or to a goal) **:** ADVANCE **2 :** something going on **:** PROCEEDING **3 :** a natural phenomenon marked by gradual changes that lead toward a particular result ⟨the ~ of growth⟩ **4** ♦ **:** a series of actions or operations directed toward a particular result ⟨a manufacturing ~⟩ **5 :** legal action **6 :** a mandate issued by a court; *esp* **:** SUMMONS **7 :** a projecting part of an organism or organic structure

♦ course, operation, procedure, proceeding

²process *vb* **:** to subject to a special process
pro·ces·sion \prə-ˈse-shən\ *n* **1 :** a group of individuals moving along in an orderly often ceremonial way **2** ♦ **:** continuous forward movement

♦ advance, advancement, furtherance, headway, march, onrush, passage, process, progress, progression

pro·ces·sion·al \-ˈse-shə-nəl\ *n* **1 :** music for a procession **2 :** a ceremonial procession
pro·ces·sor \ˈprä-ˌse-sər, ˈprō-\ *n* **1 :** one that processes **2 :** CPU
pro–choice \(ˌ)prō-ˈchȯis\ *adj* **:** favoring the legalization of abortion
pro·claim \prō-ˈklām\ *vb* ♦ **:** to make known publicly **:** DECLARE

♦ advertise, announce, blaze, broadcast, declare, enunciate, placard, post, promulgate, publicize, publish, sound

proc·la·ma·tion \ˌprä-klə-ˈmā-shən\ *n* **:** an official public announcement
pro·cliv·i·ty \prō-ˈkli-və-tē\ *n, pl* **-ties** ♦ **:** an inherent inclination especially toward something objectionable

♦ bent, devices, disposition, genius, inclination, leaning, partiality, penchant, predilection, propensity, tendency, turn

pro·con·sul \-ˈkän-səl\ *n* **1 :** a governor or military commander of an ancient Roman province **2 :** an administrator in a modern colony or occupied area — **pro·con·su·lar** \-sə-lər\ *adj*
pro·cras·ti·nate \prə-ˈkras-tə-ˌnāt, prō-\ *vb* **-nat·ed; -nat·ing** **:** to put off usually habitually doing something that should be done — **pro·cras·ti·na·tion** \-ˌkras-tə-ˈnā-shən\ *n* — **pro·cras·ti·na·tor** \-ˈkras-tə-ˌnā-tər\ *n*
pro·cre·ate \ˈprō-krē-ˌāt\ *vb* **-at·ed; -at·ing** ♦ **:** to beget or bring forth offspring — **pro·cre·ation** \ˌprō-krē-ˈā-shən\ *n* — **pro·cre·ative** \ˈprō-krē-ˌā-tiv\ *adj* — **pro·cre·ator** \-ˌā-tər\ *n*

♦ breed, multiply, propagate, reproduce

pro·crus·te·an \prə-ˈkrəs-tē-ən\ *adj, often cap* **:** marked by arbitrary often ruthless disregard of individual differences or special circumstances
proc·tor \ˈpräk-tər\ *n* **:** one appointed to supervise students (as at an examination) — **proctor** *vb* — **proc·to·ri·al** \präk-ˈtōr-ē-əl\ *adj*
pro·cur·able \prə-ˈkyu̇r-ə-bəl\ *adj* ♦ **:** capable of being procured

♦ accessible, acquirable, attainable, available, obtainable

proc·u·ra·tor \ˈprä-kyə-ˌrā-tər\ *n* **1 :** one that manages another's affairs **2 :** a Roman provincial administrator
pro·cure \-ˈkyu̇r\ *vb* **pro·cured; pro·cur·ing** **1** ♦ **:** to get possession of **:** obtain by particular care and effort **2 :** to make women available for promiscuous sexual intercourse **3 :** ACHIEVE — **pro·cure·ment** *n* — **pro·cur·er** *n*

♦ acquire, attain, capture, carry, draw, earn, gain, garner, get, land, make, obtain, realize, secure, win

¹prod \ˈpräd\ *vb* **prod·ded; prod·ding** **1 :** to thrust a pointed instrument into **:** GOAD **2** ♦ **:** to incite to action — **prod** *n*

♦ egg on, encourage, exhort, goad, press, prompt, urge

²prod *abbr* product; production
¹prod·i·gal \ˈprä-di-gəl\ *adj* **1 :** recklessly extravagant; *also* **:** LUXURIANT **2** ♦ **:** recklessly spendthrift **:** WASTEFUL ⟨the ~ prince⟩

♦ extravagant, profligate, spendthrift, thriftless, unthrifty, wasteful *Ant* conserving, economical, economizing, frugal, scrimping, skimping, thrifty

²prodigal *n* ♦ **:** one who spends or gives lavishly and foolishly

♦ profligate, spendthrift, wastrel *Ant* economizer

prod·i·gal·i·ty \ˌprä-də-ˈga-lə-tē\ *n* ♦ **:** reckless spending of resources

♦ extravagance, lavishness, wastefulness

pro•di•gious \prə-ˈdi-jəs\ *adj* **1** ♦ **:** exciting wonder **2** ♦ **:** extraordinary in size or degree **:** ENORMOUS — **pro•di•gious•ly** *adv*

♦ [1] amazing, astonishing, astounding, awesome, marvelous (*or* marvellous), stunning, stupendous, surprising, wonderful ♦ [2] colossal, enormous, giant, gigantic, huge, mammoth, massive, tremendous, vast

prod•i•gy \ˈprä-də-jē\ *n, pl* **-gies** **1** ♦ **:** something extraordinary **:** WONDER **2 :** a highly talented child

♦ caution, flash, marvel, miracle, phenomenon, portent, sensation, wonder

¹pro•duce \prə-ˈdüs, -ˈdyüs\ *vb* **pro•duced; pro•duc•ing** **1 :** to present to view **:** EXHIBIT **2a** ♦ **:** to give birth or rise to **b** ♦ **:** to become the father of **3 :** EXTEND, PROLONG **4** ♦ **:** to give being or form to **:** MAKE; *esp* **:** MANUFACTURE **5 :** to cause to accrue ⟨∼ a profit⟩ — **pro•duc•er** *n*

♦ [2a, 4] bear, bring about, cause, create, effect, effectuate, generate, induce, make, prompt, result, work, yield ♦ [2b] beget, father, get, sire ♦ [4] fabricate, fashion, form, frame, make, manufacture

²pro•duce \ˈprä-(ˌ)düs, ˈprō- *also* -(ˌ)dyüs\ *n* **1 :** something produced **:** PRODUCT **2 :** agricultural products and especially fresh fruits and vegetables

prod•uct \ˈprä-(ˌ)dəkt\ *n* **1 :** the number resulting from multiplication **2** ♦ **:** something produced **3** ♦ **:** something resulting from or necessarily following from a set of conditions

♦ [2] affair, fruit, handiwork, output, produce, thing, work, yield ♦ [3] aftermath, conclusion, consequence, corollary, development, effect, issue, outcome, outgrowth, result, resultant, sequence, upshot

pro•duc•tion \prə-ˈdək-shən\ *n* **1 :** something produced **:** PRODUCT **2 :** the act or process of producing

pro•duc•tive \prə-ˈdək-tiv\ *adj* **1** ♦ **:** having the quality or power of producing especially in abundance **2** ♦ **:** effective in bringing about — **pro•duc•tiv•i•ty** \(ˌ)prō-ˌdək-ˈti-və-tē, ˌprä-(ˌ)dək-\ *n*

♦ [1] fat, fecund, fertile, fruitful, luxuriant, prolific, rich ♦ [2] effective, effectual, efficacious, efficient, fruitful, potent

pro•duc•tive•ness \-nəs\ *n* ♦ **:** the quality or state of being productive

♦ effectiveness, efficacy, efficiency

product placement *n* **:** the inclusion of a product in a television program or film as a means of advertising

pro•em \ˈprō-ˌem\ *n* **1 :** preliminary comment **:** PREFACE **2 :** PRELUDE

¹prof \ˈpräf\ *n* **:** PROFESSOR

²prof *abbr* professional

¹pro•fane \prō-ˈfān\ *vb* **pro•faned; pro•fan•ing** **1** ♦ **:** to treat (something sacred) with irreverence or contempt **2** ♦ **:** to debase by an unworthy use — **prof•a•na•tion** \ˌprä-fə-ˈnā-shən\ *n*

♦ [1] defile, desecrate, violate ♦ [2] debase, degrade, demean, demoralize, humble, subvert, warp

²profane *adj* **1** ♦ **:** not concerned with religion **:** SECULAR **2 :** not holy because unconsecrated, impure, or defiled **3** ♦ **:** serving to debase what is holy **:** IRREVERENT ⟨∼ language⟩ **4 :** OBSCENE, VULGAR — **pro•fane•ly** *adv* — **pro•fane•ness** *n*

♦ [1] nonreligious, secular, temporal *Ant* religious, sacred ♦ [3] blasphemous, irreverent, sacrilegious

pro•fan•i•ty \prō-ˈfa-nə-tē\ *n, pl* **-ties** **1 :** the quality or state of being profane **2 :** the use of profane language **3 :** profane language

pro•fess \prə-ˈfes\ *vb* **1** ♦ **:** to declare or admit openly **:** AFFIRM **2** ♦ **:** to declare in words only **:** PRETEND **3 :** to confess one's faith in **4 :** to practice or claim to be versed in (a calling or occupation) — **pro•fess•ed•ly** \-ˈfe-səd-lē\ *adv*

♦ [1] affirm, allege, assert, aver, avouch, avow, claim, contend, declare, insist, maintain, protest, warrant ♦ [2] affect, assume, counterfeit, fake, feign, pretend, put on, sham, simulate

pro•fes•sion \prə-ˈfe-shən\ *n* **1** ♦ **:** an open declaration or avowal of a belief or opinion **2** ♦ **:** a calling requiring specialized knowledge and often long academic preparation **3 :** the whole body of persons engaged in a calling

♦ [1] affirmation, assertion, avowal, claim, declaration, protestation ♦ [2] calling, employment, line, occupation, trade, vocation, work

¹pro•fes•sion•al \prə-ˈfe-shə-nəl\ *adj* **1 :** of, relating to, or characteristic of a profession **2 :** engaged in one of the professions **3 :** participating for gain in an activity often engaged in by amateurs — **pro•fes•sion•al•ly** *adv*

²professional *n* **:** one that engages in an activity professionally

pro•fes•sion•al•ism \-nə-ˌli-zəm\ *n* **1 :** the conduct, aims, or qualities that characterize or mark a profession or a professional person **2 :** the following of a profession (as athletics) for gain or livelihood

pro•fes•sion•al•ize \-nə-ˌlīz\ *vb* **-ized; -iz•ing** **:** to give a professional nature to

pro•fes•sor \prə-ˈfe-sər\ *n* **:** a teacher at a university or college; *esp* **:** a faculty member of the highest academic rank — **pro•fes•so•ri•al** \ˌprō-fə-ˈsōr-ē-əl, ˌprä-\ *adj* — **pro•fes•sor•ship** *n*

¹prof•fer \ˈprä-fər\ *vb* **prof•fered; prof•fer•ing** ♦ **:** to present for acceptance **:** OFFER

♦ advance, offer, pose, propose, propound, suggest, vote

²proffer *n* ♦ **:** something proposed for acceptance

♦ offer, proposal, proposition, suggestion

pro•fi•cien•cy \prə-ˈfi-shən-sē\ *n* ♦ **:** the quality or state of being proficient

♦ experience, expertise, know-how, savvy

pro•fi•cient \prə-ˈfi-shənt\ *adj* ♦ **:** well advanced in an art, occupation, or branch of knowledge — **proficient** *n*

♦ accomplished, adept, consummate, crack, crackerjack, expert, good, great, master, masterful, masterly, skilled, skillful, virtuoso *Ant* amateur, amateurish, inexpert, unpolished, unprofessional, unskilled, unskillful

pro•fi•cient•ly \-lē\ *adv* ♦ **:** in a proficient manner

♦ ably, adeptly, capably, expertly, masterfully, skillfully, well

¹pro•file \ˈprō-ˌfīl\ *n* **1 :** a representation of something in outline; *esp* **:** a human head seen in side view **2 :** a concise biographical sketch **3 :** degree or level of public exposure ⟨keep a low ∼⟩

²profile *vb* **pro•filed; pro•fil•ing** **:** to write or draw a profile of

profiling *n* **:** the act of suspecting or targeting a person solely on the basis of observed characteristics or behavior ⟨racial ∼⟩

¹prof•it \ˈprä-fət\ *n* **1** ♦ **:** a valuable return **2** ♦ **:** the excess of the selling price of goods over their cost

♦ [1] earnings, income, proceeds, return, revenue, yield ♦ [2] earnings, gain, lucre, net, payoff, proceeds, return

²profit *vb* **1** ♦ **:** to be of use **:** BENEFIT **2 :** to derive benefit **:** GAIN

♦ avail, benefit, serve

prof•it•able \ˈprä-fə-tə-bəl\ *adj* ♦ **:** affording profits **:** yielding advantageous returns or results — **prof•it•ably** \-blē\ *adv*

♦ advantageous, beneficial, favorable (*or* favourable), helpful, salutary ♦ fat, gainful, lucrative, remunerative *Ant* unprofitable

prof•i•teer \ˌprä-fə-ˈtir\ *n* **:** one who makes what is considered an unreasonable profit — **profiteer** *vb*

prof•it•less \ˈprä-fət-ləs\ *adj* ♦ **:** having no profit

♦ fruitless, futile, ineffective, unproductive, unsuccessful

prof•li•ga•cy \ˈprä-fli-gə-sē\ *n* ♦ **:** the quality or state of being profligate

♦ corruption, debauchery, depravity, immorality, iniquity, licentiousness, sin, vice

¹prof•li•gate \ˈprä-fli-gət, -flə-ˌgāt\ *adj* **1 :** completely given up to dissipation and licentiousness **2** ♦ **:** wildly extravagant — **prof•li•gate•ly** *adv*

♦ extravagant, prodigal, spendthrift, thriftless, unthrifty, wasteful

²profligate *n* ♦ **:** a profligate person

♦ decadent, degenerate, libertine, pervert ♦ prodigal, spendthrift, wastrel

pro for•ma \(ˌ)prō-ˈfȯr-mə\ *adj* **:** done or existing as a matter of form

pro•found \prə-ˈfau̇nd, prō-\ *adj* **1** ♦ **:** marked by intellectual depth or insight ⟨a ∼ thought⟩ **2 :** coming from or reaching to a depth ⟨a ∼ sigh⟩ **3 :** deeply felt **:** INTENSE ⟨∼ sympathy⟩ **4** ♦ **:** all encompassing **:** THOROUGH — **pro•found•ly** *adv* — **pro•fun•di•ty** \-ˈfən-də-tē\ *n*

♦ [1] abstruse, deep, esoteric *Ant* shallow ♦ [4] absolute, complete, thorough, thoroughgoing, total, utter

pro•fuse \-ˈfyüs, prō-\ *adj* ♦ : pouring forth liberally — **pro•fuse•ly** *adv*

♦ copious, extravagant, lavish, luxuriant, riotous *Ant* dribbling, trickling

pro•fu•sion \prə-ˈfyü-zhən\ *n* ♦ : great quantity

♦ abundance, deal, gobs, heap, loads, lot, pile, plenty, quantity, scads

prog *abbr* program

pro•gen•i•tor \prō-ˈje-nə-tər\ *n* **1** : a direct ancestor : FOREFATHER **2** : ORIGINATOR, PRECURSOR

prog•e•ny \ˈprä-jə-nē\ *n, pl* **-nies** ♦ : offspring of a person, animal, or plant

♦ issue, offspring, posterity, seed, spawn

pro•ges•ter•one \prō-ˈjes-tə-ˌrōn\ *n* : a female hormone that causes the uterus to undergo changes so as to provide a suitable environment for a fertilized egg

prog•na•thous \ˈpräg-nə-thəs\ *adj* : having the lower jaw projecting beyond the upper part of the face

prog•no•sis \präg-ˈnō-səs\ *n, pl* **-no•ses** \-ˌsēz\ **1** : the prospect of recovery from disease **2** : a prophecy, estimate, or prediction of a future happening or condition : FORECAST

¹**prog•nos•tic** \präg-ˈnäs-tik\ *n* **1** : PORTENT **2** : PROPHECY

²**prognostic** *adj* : of, relating to, or serving as ground for prognostication or a prognosis

prog•nos•ti•cate \präg-ˈnäs-tə-ˌkāt\ *vb* **-cat•ed; -cat•ing** ♦ : to foretell from signs or symptoms

♦ augur, forecast, foretell, predict, presage, prophesy

prog•nos•ti•ca•tion \präg-ˌnäs-tə-ˈkā-shən\ *n* ♦ : an act, the fact, or the power of prognosticating

♦ cast, forecast, prediction, prophecy, soothsaying

prog•nos•ti•ca•tor \präg-ˈnäs-tə-ˌkā-tər\ *n* ♦ : one that prognosticates

♦ augur, diviner, forecaster, fortune-teller, futurist, prophet, seer, soothsayer

¹**pro•gram** \ˈprō-ˌgram, -grəm\ *n* **1** ♦ : a brief outline of the order to be pursued or the subjects included (as in a public entertainment); *also* : PERFORMANCE **2** ♦ : a plan of procedure **3** : coded instructions for a computer — **pro•gram•mat•ic** \ˌprō-grə-ˈma-tik\ *adj*

♦ [1] agenda, calendar, docket, schedule, timetable ♦ [2] course, line, policy, procedure ♦ [2] blueprint, scheme, strategy, system

²**program** *also* **programme** *vb* **-grammed** *or* **-gramed; -gram•ming** *or* **-gram•ing** **1** : to arrange or furnish a program of or for **2** : to enter in a program **3** : to provide (as a computer) with a program — **pro•gram•ma•bil•i•ty** \(ˌ)prō-ˌgra-mə-ˈbi-lə-tē\ *n* — **pro•gram•ma•ble** \ˈprō-ˌgra-mə-bəl\ *adj* — **pro•gram•mer** *also* **pro•gram•er** \ˈprō-ˌgra-mər, -grə-\ *n*

programmed instruction *n* : instruction through information given in small steps with each requiring a correct response by the learner before going on to the next step

pro•gram•ming *also* **pro•gram•ing** *n* **1** : the planning, scheduling, or performing of a program **2** : the process of instructing or learning by means of an instruction program **3** : the process of preparing an instruction program

¹**prog•ress** \ˈprä-grəs, -ˌgres\ *n* **1** ♦ : a forward movement : ADVANCE **2** ♦ : the action or process of advancing or improving by marked stages or degrees

♦ [1] advance, advancement, furtherance, headway, march, onrush, passage, process, procession, progression ♦ [2] development, elaboration, evolution, expansion, growth, progression

²**pro•gress** \prə-ˈgres\ *vb* **1** ♦ : to move forward : PROCEED **2** ♦ : to develop to a higher, better, or more advanced stage

♦ [1] advance, fare, forge, get along, go, march, proceed ♦ [2] age, develop, grow, grow up, mature, ripen

pro•gres•sion \prə-ˈgre-shən\ *n* **1** ♦ : an act of progressing **2** ♦ : a continuous and connected series

♦ [1] advance, advancement, furtherance, headway, march, onrush, passage, process, procession, progress ♦ [2] chain, sequence, string, train

¹**pro•gres•sive** \prə-ˈgre-siv\ *adj* **1** ♦ : of, relating to, or characterized by progress ⟨a ~ city⟩ **2** : moving forward or onward : ADVANCING **3** : increasing in extent or severity ⟨a ~ disease⟩ **4** *often cap* : of or relating to political Progressives **5** : of, relating to, or constituting a verb form that expresses action in progress at the time of speaking or a time spoken of **6** ♦ : making use of or interested in new ideas, findings, or opportunities — **pro•gres•sive•ly** *adv*

♦ [1] advanced, high, refined ♦ [6] broad-minded, liberal, nonorthodox, nontraditional, open-minded, radical, unconventional, unorthodox

²**progressive** *n* **1** : one that is progressive **2** : a person believing in moderate political change and social improvement by government action; *esp, cap* : a member of a Progressive Party in the U.S.

pro•hib•it \prō-ˈhi-bət\ *vb* **1** ♦ : to forbid by authority **2** : to prevent from doing something

♦ ban, bar, enjoin, forbid, interdict, outlaw, proscribe

pro•hi•bi•tion \ˌprō-ə-ˈbi-shən\ *n* **1** ♦ : the act of prohibiting **2** : the forbidding by law of the sale or manufacture of alcoholic beverages **3** ♦ : an order to restrain or stop — **pro•hi•bi•tion•ist** \-ˈbi-shə-nist\ *n* — **pro•hib•i•tive** \prō-ˈhi-bə-tiv\ *adj* — **pro•hib•i•tive•ly** *adv* — **pro•hib•i•to•ry** \-ˈhi-bə-ˌtōr-ē\ *adj*

♦ [1] barring, forbidding, interdiction, proscription ♦ [3] ban, embargo, interdict, interdiction, proscription, veto *Ant* prescription

¹**proj•ect** \ˈprä-ˌjekt, -jikt\ *n* **1** ♦ : a specific plan or design : SCHEME **2** : a planned undertaking ⟨a research ~⟩

♦ arrangement, blueprint, design, game, plan, scheme, strategy, system

²**pro•ject** \prə-ˈjekt\ *vb* **1** ♦ : to devise in the mind : DESIGN **2** : to throw forward **3** : to jut out : PROTRUDE **4** : to cause (light or shadow) to fall into space or (an image) to fall on a surface ⟨~ a beam of light⟩ **5** : to attribute (a thought, feeling, or personal characteristic) to a person, group, or object

♦ arrange, blueprint, calculate, chart, design, frame, lay out, map, plan, scheme

pro•jec•tile \prə-ˈjekt-ᵊl, -ˈjek-tīl\ *n* **1** : a body hurled or projected by external force; *esp* : a missile for a firearm **2** : a self-propelling weapon

pro•jec•tion \prə-ˈjek-shən\ *n* ♦ : a part that juts out

♦ bulge, overhang, protrusion

pro•jec•tion•ist \prə-ˈjek-shə-nist\ *n* : one that operates a motion-picture projector or television equipment

pro•jec•tor \-ˈjek-tər\ *n* : one that projects; *esp* : a device for projecting pictures on a screen

pro•lapse \prō-ˈlaps, ˈprō-ˌ\ *n* : the falling down or slipping of a body part from its usual position

pro•le•gom•e•non \ˌprō-li-ˈgä-mə-ˌnän, -nən\ *n, pl* **-e•na** \-nə\ : prefatory remarks

pro•le•tar•i•an \ˌprō-lə-ˈter-ē-ən\ *n* : a member of the proletariat — **proletarian** *adj*

pro•le•tar•i•at \-ē-ət\ *n* : the laboring class; *esp* : industrial workers who sell their labor to live

pro–life \(ˌ)prō-ˈlīf\ *n* : ANTIABORTION

pro•lif•er•ate \prə-ˈli-fə-ˌrāt\ *vb* **-at•ed; -at•ing** ♦ : to grow or increase by rapid production of new units (as cells or offspring)

♦ accumulate, appreciate, balloon, build, burgeon, enlarge, escalate, expand, increase, mount, multiply, mushroom, rise, snowball, swell, wax

pro•lif•er•a•tion \prə-ˌli-fə-ˈrā-shən\ *n* **1** : rapid and repeated production of new parts or of buds or offspring **2** ♦ : the act, process, or result of increasing by or as if by proliferation

♦ accretion, addition, augmentation, boost, expansion, gain, increase, increment, plus, raise, rise, supplement ♦ accumulation, multiplication

pro•lif•ic \prə-ˈli-fik\ *adj* **1** ♦ : producing young or fruit abundantly **2** ♦ : marked by abundant inventiveness or productivity ⟨a ~ writer⟩ — **pro•lif•i•cal•ly** \-fik(ə-)lē\ *adv*

♦ [1, 2] fecund, fertile, fruitful, luxuriant, productive, rich

pro•lix \prō-ˈliks, ˈprō-ˌliks\ *adj* ♦ : marked by or using an excess of words : VERBOSE

♦ circuitous, diffuse, long-winded, rambling, verbose, windy, wordy

pro•lix•i•ty \prō-ˈlik-sə-tē\ *n* ♦ : the quality or state of being prolix

♦ circumlocution, redundancy, verbiage, wordiness

pro•logue *also* **pro•log** \ˈprō-ˌlȯg, -ˌläg\ *n* ♦ : the preface or introduction to a literary or dramatic work : PREFACE

♦ foreword, introduction, preamble, preface

pro•long \prə-ˈlȯŋ\ *vb* **1** ♦ : to lengthen in time ⟨~ a meeting⟩ **2** ♦ : to lengthen in extent or range

♦ [1, 2] draw out, elongate, extend, lengthen, protract, stretch

pro•lon•ga•tion \ˌprō-ˌlȯŋ-ˈgā-shən\ *n* ♦ : an act or instance of prolonging

♦ elongation, extension

prom \ˈpräm\ *n* ♦ : a formal dance given by a high school or college class

♦ ball, dance, formal

¹prom•e•nade \ˌprä-mə-ˈnād, -ˈnäd\ *vb* **-nad•ed; -nad•ing** **1 :** to take a promenade **2 :** to walk about in or on
²promenade *n* **1 :** a place for strolling **2 :** a leisurely walk for pleasure or display **3 :** an opening grand march at a formal ball
pro•me•thi•um \prə-ˈmē-thē-əm\ *n* : a metallic chemical element obtained from uranium or neodymium
prom•i•nence \ˈprä-mə-nəns\ *n* **1** ♦ : something prominent **2 :** the quality, state, or fact of being prominent or conspicuous **3 :** a mass of cloudlike gas that arises from the sun's chromosphere

♦ elevation, eminence, height, highland, hill, mound, rise

prom•i•nent \-nənt\ *adj* **1 :** jutting out : PROJECTING **2** ♦ : readily noticeable : CONSPICUOUS **3** ♦ : widely and popularly known — **prom•i•nent•ly** *adv*

♦ [2] bold, catchy, conspicuous, emphatic, marked, noticeable, pronounced, remarkable, striking ♦ [3] celebrated, famed, famous, noted, notorious, renowned, star, well-known

pro•mis•cu•ous \prə-ˈmis-kyə-wəs\ *adj* **1 :** consisting of various sorts and kinds : MIXED **2 :** not restricted to one class or person **3 :** having a number of sexual partners — **pro•mis•cu•i•ty** \ˌprä-mis-ˈkyü-ə-tē, ˌprō-ˌmis-\ *n* — **pro•mis•cu•ous•ly** *adv* — **pro•mis•cu•ous•ness** *n*
¹prom•ise \ˈprä-məs\ *n* **1** ♦ : a pledge to do or not to do something specified **2 :** ground for expectation of success or improvement **3 :** something promised

♦ oath, pledge, troth, vow, word

²promise *vb* **prom•ised; prom•is•ing** **1** ♦ : to engage to do, bring about, or provide ⟨~ help⟩ **2 :** to suggest beforehand ⟨dark clouds ~ rain⟩ **3** ♦ : to give ground for expectation ⟨it ~*s* to be a good game⟩

♦ [1] covenant, pledge, swear, vow ♦ [3] augur, bode

promised land *n* ♦ : something and especially a place or condition believed to promise final satisfaction or realization of hopes

♦ Eden, Elysium, heaven, paradise, utopia

promising *adj* ♦ : likely to succeed or yield good results — **prom•is•ing•ly** *adv*

♦ auspicious, bright, encouraging, fair, golden, heartening, hopeful, likely, propitious, rosy, upbeat ♦ auspicious, bright, encouraging, favorable (*or* favourable), hopeful, propitious

prom•is•so•ry \ˈprä-mə-ˌsōr-ē\ *adj* : containing a promise
prom•on•to•ry \ˈprä-mən-ˌtōr-ē\ *n, pl* **-ries** ♦ : a point of land jutting into the sea : HEADLAND

♦ arm, cape, headland, peninsula, point, spit

pro•mote \prə-ˈmōt\ *vb* **pro•mot•ed; pro•mot•ing** **1** ♦ : to advance in station, rank, or honor **2** ♦ : to contribute to the growth or prosperity of **3 :** LAUNCH **4** ♦ : to present (merchandise) for buyer acceptance through advertising, publicity, or discounting — **pro•mo•tion•al** \-shə-nəl\ *adj*

♦ [1] advance, elevate, raise, upgrade ***Ant*** abase, degrade, demote, downgrade, lower, reduce ♦ [2] advance, cultivate, encourage, forward, foster, further, nourish, nurture ♦ [4] ballyhoo, boast, plug, publicize, tout

pro•mot•er \-ˈmō-tər\ *n* ♦ : one that promotes; *esp* : one that assumes the financial responsibilities of a sports event

♦ advocate, apostle, backer, booster, champion, exponent, friend, proponent, supporter

pro•mo•tion \prə-ˈmō-shən\ *n* ♦ : the act or fact of being raised in position or rank

♦ advancement, ascent, elevation, rise, upgrade

¹prompt \ˈprämpt\ *vb* **1** ♦ : to move to action **2 :** to assist (one acting or reciting) by suggesting the next words **3** ♦ : to serve as the inciting cause of — **prompt•er** *n*

♦ [1] egg on, encourage, exhort, goad, press, prod, urge ♦ [3] bring about, cause, create, effect, effectuate, generate, induce, make, produce, result, work, yield

²prompt *adj* **1** ♦ : being ready and quick to act; *also* : being on time **2** ♦ : performed readily or immediately ⟨~ service⟩

♦ [1, 2] immediate, punctual, quick, ready, timely ***Ant*** belated, late, tardy

prompt•book \-ˌbu̇k\ *n* : a copy of a play with directions for performance used by a theater prompter
promp•ti•tude \ˈprämp-tə-ˌtüd, -ˌtyüd\ *n* ♦ : the quality or habit of being prompt : PROMPTNESS

♦ punctuality, timeliness ***Ant*** tardiness

prompt•ly \ˈpräm(p)t-lē, ˈpräm-plē\ *adv* ♦ : in a prompt manner

♦ directly, forthwith, immediately, instantly, now, pronto, right away, right now

prompt•ness \-nəs\ *n* : the quality or habit of being prompt
pro•mul•gate \ˈprä-məl-ˌgāt; prō-ˈməl-\ *vb* **-gat•ed; -gat•ing** ♦ : to make known or put into force by open declaration — **prom•ul•ga•tion** \ˌprä-məl-ˈgā-shən, ˌprō-(ˌ)məl-\ *n*

♦ advertise, announce, blaze, broadcast, declare, enunciate, placard, post, proclaim, publicize, publish, sound

pron *abbr* **1** pronoun **2** pronounced **3** pronunciation
prone \ˈprōn\ *adj* **1** ♦ : having a tendency or inclination **2 :** lying face downward; *also* : lying flat or prostrate

♦ apt, given, inclined

prone•ness \ˈprōn-nəs\ *n* ♦ : the condition or fact of being prone

♦ aptness, propensity, tendency, way

prong \ˈprȯŋ\ *n* : one of the sharp points of a fork : TINE; *also* : a slender projecting part (as of an antler) — **pronged** \ˈprȯŋd\ *adj*
prong•horn \ˈprȯŋ-ˌhȯrn\ *n, pl* **pronghorn** *or* **pronghorns** : a swift horned ruminant mammal chiefly of grasslands of western No. America that resembles an antelope
pro•noun \ˈprō-ˌnau̇n\ *n* : a word used as a substitute for a noun
pro•nounce \prə-ˈnau̇ns\ *vb* **pro•nounced; pro•nounc•ing** **1 :** to utter officially or as an opinion ⟨~ sentence⟩ **2 :** to employ the organs of speech in order to produce ⟨~ a word⟩; *esp* : to say or speak correctly ⟨she can't ~ his name⟩ — **pronounce•able** *adj* — **pro•nun•ci•a•tion** \-ˌnən-sē-ˈā-shən\ *n*
pro•nounced *adj* ♦ : strongly marked : easily recognizable

♦ bold, catchy, conspicuous, emphatic, marked, noticeable, prominent, remarkable, striking

pro•nounce•ment \prə-ˈnau̇ns-mənt\ *n* : a formal declaration of opinion; *also* : ANNOUNCEMENT
pron•to \ˈprän-ˌtō\ *adv* ♦ : without delay; *also* : very quickly

♦ directly, forthwith, immediately, instantly, now, promptly, right away, right now ♦ apace, briskly, fast, full tilt, hastily, posthaste, presto, quick, quickly, rapidly, soon, speedily, swift, swiftly

pro•nu•clear \ˈprō-ˈnü-klē-ər, -ˈnyü-\ *adj* : supporting the use of nuclear-powered electric generating stations
pro•nun•ci•a•men•to \prō-ˌnən-sē-ə-ˈmen-tō\ *n, pl* **-tos** *or* **-toes** : PROCLAMATION, MANIFESTO
¹proof \ˈprüf\ *n* **1** ♦ : the evidence that compels acceptance by the mind of a truth or fact **2 :** a process or operation that establishes validity or truth : TEST **3 :** a trial impression (as from type) **4 :** a trial print from a photographic negative **5 :** alcoholic content (as of a beverage) indicated by a number that is twice the percent by volume of alcohol present ⟨whiskey of 90 ~ is 45% alcohol⟩

♦ attestation, confirmation, corroboration, documentation, evidence, substantiation, testament, testimony, validation, witness ***Ant*** disproof

²proof *adj* **1 :** successful in resisting or repelling ⟨~ against tampering⟩ ⟨water*proof*⟩ **2 :** of standard strength or quality or alcoholic content
proof•read \-ˌrēd\ *vb* : to read and mark corrections in — **proof•read•er** *n*
¹prop \ˈpräp\ *n* : something that props
²prop *vb* **propped; prop•ping** **1** ♦ : to support by placing something under or against — often used with *up* **2** ♦ : to give support

or relief to — often used with *up* **3 :** to support by placing against something

♦ *usu* **prop up** [1] bear, bolster, brace, buttress, carry, shore, stay, support, uphold ♦ *usu* **prop up** [2] abet, aid, assist, back, help, support

³prop *n* **:** PROPERTY 4
⁴prop *n* **:** PROPELLER
⁵prop *abbr* **1** property **2** proposition **3** proprietor
pro•pa•gan•da \ˌprä-pə-ˈgan-də, ˌprō-\ *n* **:** the spreading of ideas or information to further or damage a cause; *also* **:** ideas or allegations spread for such a purpose — **pro•pa•gan•dist** \-dist\ *n*
pro•pa•gan•dize \-ˌdīz\ *vb* **-dized; -diz•ing :** to subject to or carry on propaganda
prop•a•gate \ˈprä-pə-ˌgāt\ *vb* **-gat•ed; -gat•ing 1** ♦ **:** to reproduce or cause to reproduce biologically **2** ♦ **:** to cause to spread — **prop•a•ga•tion** \ˌprä-pə-ˈgā-shən\ *n*

♦ [1] breed, multiply, procreate, reproduce ♦ [2] broadcast, circulate, disseminate, spread, strew

pro•pane \ˈprō-ˌpān\ *n* **:** a heavy flammable gas found in petroleum and natural gas and used especially as a fuel
pro•pel \prə-ˈpel\ *vb* **pro•pelled; pro•pel•ling** ♦ **:** to drive forward or onward

♦ drive, push, shove, thrust ♦ actuate, drive, impel, move, work

pro•pel•lant *also* **pro•pel•lent** \-ˈpe-lənt\ *n* **:** something (as a fuel) that propels — **propellant** *also* **propellent** *adj*
pro•pel•ler \prə-ˈpe-lər\ *n* **:** a device consisting of a hub fitted with blades that is used to propel a vehicle (as a motorboat or an airplane)
pro•pen•si•ty \prə-ˈpen-sə-tē\ *n, pl* **-ties** ♦ **:** an often intense natural inclination or preference

♦ bent, devices, disposition, genius, inclination, leaning, partiality, penchant, predilection, proclivity, tendency, turn

¹prop•er \ˈprä-pər\ *adj* **1 :** referring to one individual only ⟨~ noun⟩ **2 :** belonging characteristically to a species or individual **:** PECULIAR **3 :** very satisfactory **:** EXCELLENT **4 :** strictly limited to a specified thing ⟨the city ~⟩ **5** ♦ **:** strictly accurate **:** CORRECT ⟨the ~ way to proceed⟩ **6** ♦ **:** strictly decorous **7** ♦ **:** marked by suitability or rightness ⟨~ punishment⟩

♦ [5] accurate, correct, exact, precise, right, so, true ♦ [6] correct, decent, decorous, formal, genteel, nice, polite, respectable, seemly *Ant* improper, incorrect, indecent, indecorous, unbecoming, unseemly ♦ [7] applicable, appropriate, apt, felicitous, fit, fitting, good, happy, meet, right, suitable

²proper *n* **:** the parts of the Mass that vary according to the liturgical calendar
prop•er•ly \-lē\ *adv* ♦ **:** in a proper manner

♦ appropriately, correctly, fittingly, happily, rightly, suitably *Ant* improperly, incongruously, incorrectly, wrongly

prop•er•tied \ˈprä-pər-tēd\ *adj* **:** owning property and especially much property
prop•er•ty \ˈprä-pər-tē\ *n, pl* **-ties 1** ♦ **:** a quality peculiar to an individual or thing **2** ♦ **:** something owned; *esp* **:** a piece of real estate **3 :** OWNERSHIP **4 :** an article or object used in a play or motion picture other than painted scenery and actor's costumes

♦ [1] attribute, character, characteristic, feature, mark, peculiarity, point, quality, trait ♦ [2] lot, parcel, plat, plot, tract

proph•e•cy *also* **proph•e•sy** \ˈprä-fə-sē\ *n, pl* **-cies** *also* **-sies 1 :** an inspired utterance of a prophet **2** ♦ **:** a prediction of something to come

♦ cast, forecast, prediction, prognostication, soothsaying

proph•e•si•er \ˈprä-fə-ˌsī(-ə)r\ *n* **:** one that prophesies
proph•e•sy \-ˌsī\ *vb* **-sied; -sy•ing 1 :** to speak or utter by divine inspiration **2** ♦ **:** to predict with assurance

♦ augur, forecast, foretell, predict, presage, prognosticate

proph•et \ˈprä-fət\ *n* **1 :** one who utters divinely inspired revelations **2** ♦ **:** one who foretells future events

♦ augur, diviner, forecaster, fortune-teller, futurist, prognosticator, seer, soothsayer

proph•et•ess \ˈprä-fə-təs\ *n* **:** a woman who is a prophet
pro•phet•ic \prə-ˈfe-tik\ *or* **pro•phet•i•cal** \-ti-kəl\ *adj* ♦ **:** of, relating to, or characteristic of a prophet or prophecy — **pro•phet•i•cal•ly** \-ti-k(ə-)lē\ *adv*

♦ foreboding, inauspicious, ominous, portentous *Ant* auspicious, promising, propitious, rosy

Proph•ets \ˈprä-fəts\ *n pl* **:** the second part of the canonical Jewish Scripture
¹pro•phy•lac•tic \ˌprō-fə-ˈlak-tik, ˌprä-\ *adj* **1 :** preventing or guarding from the spread or occurrence of disease or infection **2 :** PREVENTIVE
²prophylactic *n* **:** something prophylactic; *esp* **:** a device (as a condom) for preventing venereal infection or conception
pro•phy•lax•is \-ˈlak-səs\ *n, pl* **-lax•es** \-ˈlak-ˌsēz\ **:** measures designed to preserve health and prevent the spread of disease
pro•pin•qui•ty \prə-ˈpiŋ-kwə-tē\ *n* **1 :** KINSHIP **2 :** nearness in place or time **:** PROXIMITY
pro•pi•ti•ate \prō-ˈpi-shē-ˌāt\ *vb* **-at•ed; -at•ing** ♦ **:** to gain or regain the favor of **:** APPEASE — **pro•pi•ti•a•tion** \-ˌpi-shē-ˈā-shən\ *n*

♦ appease, conciliate, disarm, mollify, pacify, placate

pro•pi•tia•to•ry \prō-ˈpi-shē-ə-ˌtōr-ē\ *adj* **1** ♦ **:** intended to propitiate **2 :** of or relating to propitiation

♦ conciliatory, pacific

pro•pi•tious \prə-ˈpi-shəs\ *adj* **1 :** favorably disposed ⟨~ deities⟩ **2** ♦ **:** being of good omen ⟨~ circumstances⟩

♦ auspicious, bright, encouraging, fair, golden, heartening, hopeful, likely, promising, rosy, upbeat

prop•man \ˈpräp-ˌman\ *n* **:** one who is in charge of stage properties
pro•po•nent \prə-ˈpō-nənt\ *n* ♦ **:** one who argues in favor of something

♦ advocate, apostle, backer, booster, champion, exponent, friend, promoter, supporter

¹pro•por•tion \prə-ˈpōr-shən\ *n* **1** ♦ **:** harmonious relation of parts to each other or to the whole **:** BALANCE, SYMMETRY **2** ♦ **:** proper or equal share **3 :** the relation of one part to another or to the whole with respect to magnitude, quantity, or degree **:** RATIO **4 :** physical magnitude, extent, or bulk **:** SIZE — **in proportion :** PROPORTIONAL

♦ [1] balance, coherence, consonance, harmony, symmetry, symphony, unity ♦ [2] allotment, allowance, cut, part, portion, quota, share

²proportion *vb* **-tioned; -tion•ing 1 :** to adjust (a part or thing) in size relative to other parts or things **2 :** to make the parts of harmonious
pro•por•tion•al \prə-ˈpȯr-shə-nəl\ *adj* **:** corresponding in size, degree, or intensity; *also* **:** having the same or a constant ratio — **pro•por•tion•al•ly** *adv*
pro•por•tion•ate \prə-ˈpȯr-shə-nət\ *adj* **:** PROPORTIONAL — **pro•por•tion•ate•ly** *adv*
pro•pos•al \prə-ˈpō-zəl\ *n* **1 :** an act of putting forward or stating something for consideration **2** ♦ **:** something that is proposed

♦ offer, proffer, proposition, suggestion

pro•pose \prə-ˈpōz\ *vb* **pro•posed; pro•pos•ing 1** ♦ **:** to form or put forward a plan or intention ⟨~*s* to buy a house⟩ **2 :** to make an offer of marriage **3** ♦ **:** to offer for consideration **:** SUGGEST ⟨~ a policy⟩ — **pro•pos•er** *n*

♦ [1] aim, aspire, contemplate, design, intend, mean, meditate, plan ♦ [3] advance, offer, pose, proffer, propound, suggest, vote

¹prop•o•si•tion \ˌprä-pə-ˈzi-shən\ *n* **1 :** something proposed for consideration **:** PROPOSAL **2 :** a request for sexual intercourse **3** ♦ **:** a statement of something to be discussed, proved, or explained **4 :** SITUATION, AFFAIR ⟨a tough ~⟩ — **prop•o•si•tion•al** \-ˈzi-shə-nəl\ *adj*

♦ conjecture, hypothesis, supposition, theory

²proposition *vb* **-tioned; -tion•ing :** to make a proposal to; *esp* **:** to suggest sexual intercourse to
pro•pound \prə-ˈpau̇nd\ *vb* ♦ **:** to set forth for consideration ⟨~ a doctrine⟩

♦ advance, offer, pose, proffer, propose, suggest, vote

pro•pri•e•tary \prə-ˈprī-ə-ˌter-ē\ *adj* **1 :** of, relating to, or characteristic of a proprietor ⟨~ rights⟩ **2 :** made and sold by one with the sole right to do so ⟨~ medicines⟩
pro•pri•e•tor \prə-ˈprī-ə-tər\ *n* ♦ **:** a person who has the legal right or exclusive title to something **:** OWNER — **pro•pri•e•tor•ship** *n*

♦ holder, owner, possessor

pro·pri·e·tress \-ˈprī-ə-trəs\ *n* : a woman who is a proprietor
pro·pri·e·ty \prə-ˈprī-ə-tē\ *n, pl* **-ties** **1** ♦ : conformity to what is socially acceptable in conduct or speech **2** *pl* : the customs of polite society

♦ decency, decorum, form

props \ˈpräps\ *n sing or pl* **1** *slang* : DUE 1 ⟨gave him his ~⟩ **2** *slang* : RESPECT 2 ⟨earned the ~ of his peers⟩ **3** *slang* : ACKNOWLEDGMENT ⟨deserves ~ for the effort⟩
pro·pul·sion \prə-ˈpəl-shən\ *n* **1** : the action or process of propelling **2** : something that propels — **pro·pul·sive** \-siv\ *adj*
pro ra·ta \(ˌ)prō-ˈrā-tə, -ˈrä-\ *adv* : in proportion to the share of each : PROPORTIONATELY
pro·rate \(ˌ)prō-ˈrāt\ *vb* **pro·rat·ed; pro·rat·ing** ♦ : to divide, distribute, or assess proportionately

♦ administer, allocate, apportion, deal, dispense, distribute, mete, parcel, portion

pro·rogue \prə-ˈrōg\ *vb* **pro·rogued; pro·rogu·ing** : to suspend or end a session of (a legislative body) — **pro·ro·ga·tion** \ˌprō-rō-ˈgā-shən\ *n*
pros *pl of* PRO
pro·sa·ic \prō-ˈzā-ik\ *adj* **1** : lacking imagination or excitement : DULL **2** ♦ : of a kind to be expected in the normal order of events : EVERYDAY

♦ average, common, commonplace, everyday, normal, ordinary, routine, run-of-the-mill, standard, unexceptional, unremarkable, usual, workaday

pro·sce·ni·um \prō-ˈsē-nē-əm\ *n* **1** : the part of a stage in front of the curtain **2** : the wall containing the arch that frames the stage
pro·scribe \prō-ˈskrīb\ *vb* **pro·scribed; pro·scrib·ing** **1** : to publish the name of as condemned to death with the property of the condemned forfeited to the state **2** ♦ : to condemn or forbid as harmful or unlawful

♦ ban, bar, enjoin, forbid, interdict, outlaw, prohibit

pro·scrip·tion \prō-ˈskrip-shən\ *n* **1** ♦ : the act of proscribing : the state of being proscribed **2** ♦ : an imposed restraint or restriction

♦ [1, 2] ban, barring, embargo, forbidding, interdiction, prohibition

prose \ˈprōz\ *n* : the ordinary language people use in speaking or writing
pros·e·cute \ˈprä-si-ˌkyüt\ *vb* **-cut·ed; -cut·ing** **1** : to follow to the end ⟨~ an investigation⟩ **2** : to seek legal punishment of ⟨~ a forger⟩ — **pros·e·cu·tion** \ˌprä-si-ˈkyü-shən\ *n* — **pros·e·cu·tor** \ˈprä-si-ˌkyü-tər\ *n*
¹pros·e·lyte \ˈprä-sə-ˌlīt\ *n* : a new convert to a religion, belief, or party — **pros·e·ly·tism** \-ˌlī-ˌti-zəm\ *n*
²proselyte *vb* **-lyt·ed; -lyt·ing** : PROSELYTIZE
pros·e·ly·tise *chiefly Brit var of* PROSELYTIZE
pros·e·ly·tize \ˈprä-sə-lə-ˌtīz\ *vb* **-tized; -tiz·ing** **1** : to induce someone to convert to one's faith **2** : to recruit someone to join one's party, institution, or cause
pros·o·dy \ˈprä-sə-dē, -zə-\ *n, pl* **-dies** : the study of versification and especially of metrical structure
¹pros·pect \ˈprä-ˌspekt\ *n* **1** ♦ : an extensive view; *also* : OUTLOOK **2** : the act of looking forward **3** : a mental vision of something to come **4** : something that is awaited or expected : POSSIBILITY **5 a** : a potential buyer or customer **b** ♦ : a likely candidate — **pro·spec·tive** \prə-ˈspek-tiv, ˈprä-ˌspek-\ *adj* — **pro·spec·tive·ly** *adv*

♦ [1] lookout, outlook, panorama, view, vista ♦ [5b] applicant, aspirant, campaigner, candidate, contender, hopeful, seeker

²pros·pect \ˈprä-ˌspekt\ *vb* ♦ : to explore especially for mineral deposits — **pros·pec·tor** \-ˌspek-tər, prä-ˈspek-\ *n*

♦ explore, hunt, probe, search

pro·spec·tus \prə-ˈspek-təs\ *n* : a preliminary statement that describes an enterprise and is distributed to prospective buyers or participants
pros·per \ˈpräs-pər\ *vb* **pros·pered; pros·per·ing** **1** ♦ : to succeed in an enterprise or activity; *esp* : to achieve economic success **2** ♦ : to become strong and flourishing

♦ [1, 2] flourish, succeed, thrive

pros·per·i·ty \präs-ˈper-ə-tē\ *n* : thriving condition : SUCCESS; *esp* : economic well-being
pros·per·ous \ˈpräs-pə-rəs\ *adj* **1** : FAVORABLE ⟨~ winds⟩ **2** ♦ : marked by success or economic well-being ⟨a ~ business⟩ **3** ♦ : enjoying vigorous and healthy growth

♦ [2] palmy, successful, triumphant ♦ [3] booming, golden, palmy, roaring, successful *Ant* unsuccessful

pros·ta·glan·din \ˌpräs-tə-ˈglan-dən\ *n* : any of various oxygenated unsaturated fatty acids of animals that perform a variety of hormonelike actions
pros·tate \ˈpräs-ˌtāt\ *n* : PROSTATE GLAND — **pros·tat·ic** \prä-ˈsta-tik\ *adj*
prostate gland *n* : a glandular body about the base of the male urethra that produces a secretion which is a major part of the fluid ejaculated during an orgasm
pros·ta·ti·tis \ˌpräs-tə-ˈtī-təs\ *n* : inflammation of the prostate gland
pros·the·sis \präs-ˈthē-səs, ˈpräs-thə-\ *n, pl* **-the·ses** \-ˌsēz\ : an artificial replacement for a missing body part — **pros·thet·ic** \präs-ˈthe-tik\ *adj*
pros·thet·ics \-ˈthe-tiks\ *n pl* : the surgical or dental specialty concerned with the design, construction, and fitting of prostheses
¹pros·ti·tute \ˈpräs-tə-ˌtüt, -ˌtyüt\ *vb* **-tut·ed; -tut·ing** **1** : to offer indiscriminately for sexual activity especially for money **2** ♦ : to devote to corrupt or unworthy purposes — **pros·ti·tu·tion** \ˌpräs-tə-ˈtü-shən, -ˈtyü-\ *n*

♦ debase, degrade, demean, demoralize, humble, subvert, warp

²prostitute *n* : one who engages in sexual activities for money
¹pros·trate \ˈprä-ˌstrāt\ *adj* **1** : stretched out with face on the ground in adoration or submission **2** : lying flat **3** ♦ : completely overcome and lacking vitality ⟨~ with a cold⟩

♦ beat, bushed, dead, drained, effete, jaded, limp, spent, tired, weak, weary, worn-out

²prostrate *vb* **pros·trat·ed; pros·trat·ing** **1** : to throw or put into a prostrate position **2** ♦ : to reduce to a weak or powerless condition

♦ debilitate, enervate, enfeeble, sap, soften, tire, waste, weaken ♦ carry away, crush, devastate, floor, oppress, overcome, overpower, overwhelm, snow under, swamp

pros·tra·tion \prä-ˈstrā-shən\ *n* ♦ : complete physical or mental exhaustion

♦ burnout, collapse, exhaustion, fatigue, lassitude, tiredness, weariness

prosy \ˈprō-zē\ *adj* **pros·i·er; -est** **1** : PROSAIC, ORDINARY **2** : TEDIOUS
Prot *abbr* Protestant
prot·ac·tin·i·um \ˌprō-ˌtak-ˈti-nē-əm\ *n* : a metallic radioactive chemical element of relatively short life
pro·tag·o·nist \prō-ˈta-gə-nist\ *n* **1** : the principal character in a drama or story **2** : a leader or supporter of a cause
pro·te·an \ˈprō-tē-ən\ *adj* ♦ : able to assume different shapes or roles

♦ adaptable, all-around, universal, versatile

pro·tect \prə-ˈtekt\ *vb* ♦ : to shield from injury : GUARD

♦ cover, defend, guard, safeguard, screen, secure, shield, ward

pro·tec·tion \prə-ˈtek-shən\ *n* **1** : the act of protecting : the state of being protected **2** ♦ : one that protects ⟨wear a helmet as a ~⟩ **3** : the supervision or support of one that is smaller and weaker **4** : the freeing of producers from foreign competition in their home market by high duties on foreign competitive goods — **pro·tec·tive** \-ˈtek-tiv\ *adj*

♦ aegis, armor, cover, defense (*or* defence), guard, safeguard, screen, security, shield, wall, ward

pro·tec·tion·ist \-shə-nist\ *n* : an advocate of government economic protection for domestic producers through restrictions on foreign competitors — **pro·tec·tion·ism** \-shə-ˌni-zəm\ *n*
pro·tec·tor \prə-ˈtek-tər\ *n* **1** ♦ : one that protects **2** : a device used to prevent injury : GUARD **3** : REGENT 1

♦ custodian, defender, defense (*or* defence), guard, protection

pro·tec·tor·ate \-tə-rət\ *n* **1** : government by a protector **2** : the relationship of superior authority assumed by one state over a dependent one; *also* : the dependent political unit in such a relationship
pro·té·gé \ˈprō-tə-ˌzhā\ *n* : one who is protected, trained, or guided by an influential person
pro·tein \ˈprō-ˌtēn\ *n* : any of various complex nitrogen-containing substances that consist of chains of amino acids, are present in all living cells, and are an essential part of the human diet
pro tem \prō-ˈtem\ *adv* : PRO TEMPORE
pro tem·po·re \prō-ˈtem-pə-rē\ *adv* : for the time being
Pro·te·ro·zo·ic \ˌprä-tə-rə-ˈzō-ik, ˌprō-\ *adj* : of, relating to, or

being the eon of geologic history between the Archean and the Phanerozoic — **Proterozoic** *n*

[1]**pro•test** \ˈprō-ˌtest\ *n* **1 :** the act of protesting; *esp* **:** an organized public demonstration of disapproval **2** ◆ **:** a complaint or objection against an idea, an act, or a course of action

◆ challenge, complaint, demur, expostulation, fuss, kick, objection, question, remonstrance

[2]**pro•test** \prō-ˈtest\ *vb* **1** ◆ **:** to assert positively **:** make solemn declaration of ⟨~*s* his innocence⟩ **2** ◆ **:** to object strongly **:** make a protest against ⟨~ a ruling⟩ — **pro•test•er** *or* **pro•tes•tor** \-tər\ *n*

◆ [1] affirm, allege, assert, aver, avouch, avow, claim, contend, declare, insist, maintain, profess, warrant ◆ [2] demur, kick, object, remonstrate

Prot•es•tant \ˈprä-təs-tənt, *3 also* prə-ˈtes-\ *n* **1 :** a member or adherent of one of the Christian churches deriving from the Reformation **2 :** a Christian not of a Catholic or Orthodox church **3** *not cap* **:** one who makes a protest — **Prot•es•tant•ism** \ˈprä-təs-tən-ˌti-zəm\ *n*

pro•tes•ta•tion \ˌprä-təs-ˈtā-shən\ *n* **1 :** the act or fact of protesting **2** ◆ **:** a formal declaration of dissent to or support of something

◆ affirmation, assertion, avowal, claim, declaration, profession *Ant* disavowal

pro•tha•la•mi•on \ˌprō-thə-ˈlā-mē-ən\ *or* **pro•tha•la•mi•um** \-mē-əm\ *n, pl* **-mia** \-mē-ə\ **:** a song in celebration of a marriage

pro•to•col \ˈprō-tə-ˌkȯl\ *n* **1 :** an original draft or record **2 :** a preliminary memorandum of diplomatic negotiation **3 :** a code of diplomatic or military etiquette **4 :** a set of conventions for formatting data in an electronic communications system

pro•ton \ˈprō-ˌtän\ *n* **:** a positively charged atomic particle present in all atomic nuclei — **pro•ton•ic** \-ˈtä-nik\ *adj*

pro•to•plasm \ˈprō-tə-ˌpla-zəm\ *n* **:** the complex colloidal largely protein substance of living plant and animal cells — **pro•to•plas•mic** \ˌprō-tə-ˈplaz-mik\ *adj*

pro•to•type \ˈprō-tə-ˌtīp\ *n* **:** an original model **:** ARCHETYPE

pro•to•zo•an \ˌprō-tə-ˈzō-ən\ *n* **:** any of a phylum or subkingdom of unicellular lower invertebrate animals that include some pathogenic parasites of humans and domestic animals — **protozoan** *adj*

pro•tract \prō-ˈtrakt\ *vb* ◆ **:** to prolong in time or space

◆ draw out, elongate, extend, lengthen, prolong, stretch

pro•trac•tor \-ˈtrak-tər\ *n* **:** an instrument for drawing and measuring angles

pro•trude \prō-ˈtrüd\ *vb* **pro•trud•ed; pro•trud•ing** ◆ **:** to stick out or cause to stick out **:** jut out

◆ bag, balloon, beetle, belly, billow, bulge, overhang, poke, project, start, stick out

pro•tru•sion \prō-ˈtrü-zhən\ *n* **1 :** the act of protruding **:** the state of being protruded **2** ◆ **:** something that protrudes

◆ bulge, overhang, projection

pro•tu•ber•ance \prō-ˈtü-bə-rəns, -ˈtyü-\ *n* **:** something that protrudes

pro•tu•ber•ant \-rənt\ *adj* **:** extending beyond the surrounding surface in a bulge

proud \ˈprau̇d\ *adj* **1** ◆ **:** having or showing excessive self-esteem **:** HAUGHTY **2 :** highly pleased **:** EXULTANT **3 :** having proper self-respect ⟨too ~ to beg⟩ **4** ◆ **:** giving reason for pride **:** GLORIOUS ⟨a ~ occasion⟩ **5 :** SPIRITED ⟨a ~ steed⟩ — **proud•ly** *adv*

◆ [1] arrogant, disdainful, haughty, highfalutin, lofty, lordly, prideful, superior *Ant* humble, lowly, modest ◆ [4] august, baronial, gallant, glorious, grand, grandiose, heroic, imposing, magnificent, majestic, monumental, noble, regal, royal, splendid, stately

prov *abbr* **1** province; provincial **2** provisional

Prov *abbr* Proverbs

prov•able \ˈprü-və-bəl\ *adj* ◆ **:** capable of being proved

◆ demonstrable, supportable, sustainable, verifiable

prove \ˈprüv\ *vb* **proved; proved** *or* **prov•en** \ˈprü-vən\; **prov•ing** **1 :** to test by experiment or by a standard **2** ◆ **:** to establish the truth of by argument or evidence **3 :** to show to be correct, valid, or genuine **4** ◆ **:** to turn out especially after trial or test ⟨the car *proved* to be a good choice⟩

◆ [2] demonstrate, document, establish, show, substantiate, validate *Ant* disprove, rebut, refute ◆ [4] come out, pan out, turn out

prov•e•nance \ˈprä-və-nəns\ *n* **:** ORIGIN, SOURCE

Pro•ven•çal \ˌprō-ˌvän-ˈsäl, ˌprä-vən-\ *n* **1 :** a native or inhabitant of Provence **2 :** OCCITAN — **Provençal** *adj*

prov•en•der \ˈprä-vən-dər\ *n* **1 :** dry food for domestic animals **:** FEED **2** ◆ **:** food usable by people **:** VICTUALS

◆ chow, fare, food, grub, meat, provisions, viands, victuals

pro•ve•nience \prə-ˈvē-nyəns\ *n* **:** ORIGIN, SOURCE

prov•erb \ˈprä-ˌvərb\ *n* ◆ **:** a pithy popular saying **:** ADAGE

◆ adage, aphorism, byword, epigram, maxim, saying

pro•ver•bi•al \prə-ˈver-bē-əl\ *adj* **1 :** of, relating to, or resembling a proverb **2 :** commonly spoken of

Proverbs *n* **:** a book of moral sayings in the canonical Jewish and Christian Scripture

pro•vide \prə-ˈvīd\ *vb* **pro•vid•ed; pro•vid•ing** **1 :** to take measures beforehand ⟨~ against inflation⟩ **2 :** to make a proviso or stipulation **3 :** to supply what is needed ⟨~ for a family⟩ **4 :** EQUIP **5** ◆ **:** to supply for use — **pro•vid•er** *n*

◆ deliver, feed, furnish, give, hand, hand over, supply

pro•vid•ed *conj* **:** on condition that **:** IF

prov•i•dence \ˈprä-və-dəns\ *n* **1** *often cap* **:** divine guidance or care **2** *cap* **:** GOD 1 **3** ◆ **:** the quality or state of being provident

◆ foresight, forethought, prescience ◆ economy, frugality, husbandry, thrift

prov•i•dent \-dənt\ *adj* **1** ◆ **:** making provision for the future **2** ◆ **:** characterized by or reflecting economy in the use of resources **:** FRUGAL — **prov•i•dent•ly** *adv*

◆ [1] farsighted, forehanded, foresighted, prescient ◆ [2] economical, frugal, sparing, thrifty

prov•i•den•tial \ˌprä-və-ˈden-chəl\ *adj* **1 :** of, relating to, or determined by Providence **2** ◆ **:** occurring by or as if by an intervention of Providence **:** LUCKY

◆ fluky, fortuitous, fortunate, happy, lucky

pro•vid•ing *conj* **:** PROVIDED

prov•ince \ˈprä-vəns\ *n* **1 :** an administrative district or division of a country **2** *pl* **:** all of a country except the metropolises **3** ◆ **:** proper business or scope **:** SPHERE

◆ area, arena, demesne, department, discipline, domain, field, line, realm, specialty, sphere

pro•vin•cial \prə-ˈvin-chəl\ *adj* **1 :** of or relating to a province **2** ◆ **:** limited in outlook **:** NARROW ⟨~ ideas⟩ — **pro•vin•cial•ism** \-chə-ˌli-zəm\ *n*

◆ insular, little, narrow, parochial, petty, sectarian, small

proving ground *n* **:** a place for scientific experimentation or testing

[1]**pro•vi•sion** \prə-ˈvi-zhən\ *n* **1 :** the act or process of providing; *also* **:** a measure taken beforehand **2** ◆ **:** a stock of needed supplies; *esp* **:** a stock of food — usually used in plural **3 :** a conditional stipulation **:** PROVISO

◆ **provisions** chow, fare, food, grub, meat, provender, viands, victuals

[2]**provision** *vb* ◆ **:** to supply with provisions

◆ board, cater, feed

pro•vi•sion•al \-ˈvi-zhə-nəl\ *adj* ◆ **:** provided for a temporary need — **pro•vi•sion•al•ly** *adv*

◆ impermanent, interim, short-term, temporary

pro•vi•so \prə-ˈvī-zō\ *n, pl* **-sos** *also* **-soes** **1 :** an article or clause that introduces a condition **2** ◆ **:** a conditional stipulation

◆ condition, provision, qualification, reservation, stipulation

pro•vo•ca•teur \prō-ˌvä-kə-ˈtər\ *n* **:** one who provokes

prov•o•ca•tion \ˌprä-və-ˈkā-shən\ *n* **1 :** the act of provoking **2** ◆ **:** something that provokes

◆ boost, encouragement, goad, impetus, impulse, incentive, momentum, motivation, spur, yeast ◆ excitement, incitement, instigation, stimulus

pro•voc•a•tive \prə-ˈvä-kə-tiv\ *adj* ◆ **:** serving to provoke or excite

◆ exciting

pro•voke \prə-ˈvōk\ *vb* **pro•voked; pro•vok•ing** **1 :** to incite to anger **:** INCENSE **2 :** to call forth **:** EVOKE ⟨a remark that *provoked* laughter⟩ **3** ◆ **:** to stir up on purpose ⟨~ an argument⟩ — **pro•vok•er** *n*

◆ abet, ferment, foment, incite, instigate, raise, stir, whip

pro•vo•lo•ne \ˌprō-və-ˈlō-nē\ *n* **:** a usually firm pliant often smoked Italian cheese
pro•vost \ˈprō-ˌvōst, ˈprä-vəst\ *n* **:** a high official **:** DIGNITARY; *esp* **:** a high-ranking university administrative officer
pro•vost mar•shal \ˈprō-ˌvō-ˈmär-shəl\ *n* **:** an officer who supervises the military police of a command
prow \ˈprau̇\ *n* **:** the bow of a ship
prow•ess \ˈprau̇-əs\ *n* **1 :** military valor and skill **2 :** extraordinary ability
prowl \ˈprau̇(-ə)l\ *vb* **:** to roam about stealthily — **prowl** *n* — **prowl•er** *n*
prox•i•mal \ˈpräk-sə-məl\ *adj* **1 :** next to or nearest the point of attachment or origin; *esp* **:** located toward the center of the body **2 :** of, relating to, or being the mesial and distal surfaces of a tooth — **prox•i•mal•ly** *adv*
prox•i•mate \ˈpräk-sə-mət\ *adj* **1 :** DIRECT ⟨the ~ cause⟩ **2 :** very near
prox•im•i•ty \präk-ˈsi-mə-tē\ *n* ♦ **:** the quality or state of being proximate **:** NEARNESS

♦ closeness, contiguity, immediacy, nearness *Ant* distance, remoteness

prox•i•mo \ˈpräk-sə-ˌmō\ *adj* **:** of or occurring in the next month after the present
proxy \ˈpräk-sē\ *n, pl* **prox•ies** **1 :** the authority or power to act for another; *also* **:** a document giving such authorization **2** ♦ **:** a person authorized to act for another — **proxy** *adj*

♦ agent, attorney, commissary, delegate, deputy, envoy, factor, representative

prude \ˈprüd\ *n* **:** a person who shows or affects extreme modesty — **prud•ery** \ˈprü-də-rē\ *n*
pru•dence \ˈprüd-ᵊns\ *n* ♦ **:** sagacity or shrewdness in the management of affairs

♦ common sense, discretion, horse sense, sagacity *Ant* imprudence, indiscretion

pru•dent \ˈprüd-ᵊnt\ *adj* **1 :** shrewd in the management of practical affairs **2 :** CAUTIOUS, DISCREET **3 :** PROVIDENT, FRUGAL **4** ♦ **:** marked by wisdom or judiciousness — **pru•den•tial** \prü-ˈden-chəl\ *adj* — **pru•dent•ly** *adv*

♦ advisable, desirable, expedient, judicious, politic, tactical, wise

prud•ish \ˈprü-dish\ *adj* ♦ **:** marked by prudery — **prud•ish•ly** *adv*

♦ prim, puritanical, straitlaced

1prune \ˈprün\ *n* **:** a dried plum
2prune *vb* **pruned; prun•ing** ♦ **:** to cut off unwanted parts (as of a tree)

♦ bob, clip, crop, curtail, cut, cut back, dock, lop, nip, shave, shear, trim

pru•ri•ent \ˈpru̇r-ē-ənt\ *adj* **:** LASCIVIOUS; *also* **:** exciting to lasciviousness — **pru•ri•ence** \-ē-əns\ *n*
1pry \ˈprī\ *vb* **pried; pry•ing** **1 :** to look closely or inquisitively **2** ♦ **:** to make a nosy or presumptuous inquiry

♦ butt in, interfere, intrude, meddle, mess, nose, obtrude, poke, snoop

2pry *vb* **pried; pry•ing** **1** ♦ **:** to raise, move, or pull apart with a pry or lever **2** ♦ **:** to extract, detach, or open with difficulty

♦ [1] jimmy, prize ♦ [2] extract, prize, pull, root, tear, uproot, wrest

3pry *n* **:** a tool for prying
prying ♦ **:** inquisitive in an annoying, officious, or meddlesome way

♦ curious, inquisitive, nosy ♦ intrusive, meddlesome, nosy, obtrusive, officious, presumptuous

Ps *or* **Psa** *abbr* Psalms
PS *abbr* **1** postscript **2** public school
PSA *abbr* public service announcement
psalm \ˈsäm, ˈsälm\ *n, often cap* ♦ **:** a sacred song or poem; *esp* **:** one of the hymns collected in the Book of Psalms — **psalm•ist** *n*

♦ anthem, canticle, carol, chorale, hymn, spiritual

psalm•o•dy \ˈsä-mə-dē, ˈsäl-\ *n* **:** the singing of psalms in worship
Psalms *n* **:** a book of sacred poems in canonical Jewish and Christian Scripture
Psal•ter \ˈsȯl-tər\ *n* **:** the Book of Psalms; *also* **:** a collection of the Psalms arranged for devotional use
pseud *abbr* pseudonym; pseudonymous
pseu•do \ˈsü-dō\ *adj* **:** being apparently rather than actually as stated **:** SPURIOUS, SHAM
pseu•do•nym \ˈsü-də-ˌnim\ *n* **:** a fictitious name — **pseu•don•y•mous** \sü-ˈdä-nə-məs\ *adj*
pseu•do•sci•ence \ˌsü-dō-ˈsī-əns\ *n* **:** a system of theories, assumptions, and methods erroneously regarded as scientific — **pseu•do•sci•en•tif•ic** \-ˌsī-ən-ˈti-fik\ *adj*
PSG *abbr* platoon sergeant
1psi \ˈsī, ˈpsī\ *n* **:** the 23d letter of the Greek alphabet — Ψ or ψ
2psi *abbr* pounds per square inch
psit•ta•co•sis \ˌsi-tə-ˈkō-səs\ *n* **:** an infectious disease of birds marked by diarrhea and wasting and transmissible to humans
pso•ri•a•sis \sə-ˈrī-ə-səs\ *n* **:** a chronic skin disease characterized by red patches covered with white scales
PST *abbr* Pacific standard time
1psych *or* **psyche** \ˈsīk\ *vb* **psyched; psych•ing** **1 :** OUTWIT, OUTGUESS; *also* **:** to analyze beforehand **2 :** INTIMIDATE **3** ♦ **:** to prepare oneself psychologically ⟨get *psyched* up for the game⟩ — often used with *up*

♦ *sometimes* **psych up** brace, encourage, forearm, fortify, nerve, ready, steel, strengthen

2psych *abbr* psychology
psy•che \ˈsī-kē\ *n* **:** SOUL, PERSONALITY; *also* **:** MIND
psy•che•del•ic \ˌsī-kə-ˈde-lik\ *adj* **1 :** of, relating to, or causing abnormal psychic effects ⟨~ drugs⟩ **2 :** relating to the taking of psychedelic drugs ⟨~ experience⟩ **3 :** imitating, suggestive of, or reproducing the effects of psychedelic drugs ⟨~ art⟩ ⟨~ colors⟩ — **psychedelic** *n* — **psy•che•del•i•cal•ly** \-li-k(ə-)lē\ *adv*
psy•chi•a•try \sə-ˈkī-ə-trē, sī-\ *n* **:** a branch of medicine dealing with mental, emotional, and behavioral disorders — **psy•chi•at•ric** \ˌsī-kē-ˈa-trik\ *adj* — **psy•chi•a•trist** \sə-ˈkī-ə-trist, sī-\ *n*
1psy•chic \ˈsī-kik\ *also* **psy•chi•cal** \-ki-kəl\ *adj* **1 :** of or relating to the psyche **2 :** lying outside the sphere of physical science **3 :** sensitive to nonphysical or supernatural forces — **psy•chi•cal•ly** \-k(ə-)lē\ *adv*
2psychic *n* **:** a person apparently sensitive to nonphysical forces; *also* **:** MEDIUM 6
psy•cho \ˈsī-kō\ *n, pl* **psychos** ♦ **:** a mentally disturbed person — **psycho** *adj*

♦ lunatic, maniac, nut, psychotic

psy•cho•ac•tive \ˌsī-kō-ˈak-tiv\ *adj* **:** affecting the mind or behavior
psy•cho•anal•y•sis \ˌsī-kō-ə-ˈna-lə-səs\ *n* **:** a method of dealing with psychic disorders by having the patient talk freely about personal experiences and especially about early childhood and dreams — **psy•cho•an•a•lyst** \-ˈan-ᵊl-ist\ *n* — **psy•cho•an•a•lyt•ic** \-ˌan-ᵊl-ˈi-tik\ *adj* — **psy•cho•an•a•lyze** \-ˈan-ᵊl-ˌīz\ *vb*
psy•cho•bab•ble \ˈsī-kō-ˌba-bəl\ *n* **:** psychological jargon especially when used in a trite or simplistic manner
psy•cho•dra•ma \ˌsī-kə-ˈdrä-mə, -ˈdra-\ *n* **1 :** an extemporized dramatization designed to afford catharsis for one or more of the participants from whose life the plot is taken **2 :** a dramatic event or story with psychological overtones
psy•cho•gen•ic \-ˈje-nik\ *adj* **:** originating in the mind or in mental or emotional conflict
psy•cho•graph•ics \ˌsī-kə-ˈgra-fiks\ *n sing or pl* **:** market research or statistics classifying population groups according to psychological variables
psychol *abbr* psychologist; psychology
psy•cho•log•i•cal \ˌsī-kə-ˈlä-ji-kəl\ *adj* **1 :** of or relating to psychology **2** ♦ **:** of or relating to the mind — **psy•cho•log•i•cal•ly** \-ji-k(ə-)lē\ *adv*

♦ cerebral, inner, intellectual, mental

psy•chol•o•gy \sī-ˈkä-lə-jē\ *n, pl* **-gies** **1 :** the science of mind and behavior **2 :** the mental and behavioral characteristics of an individual or group — **psy•chol•o•gist** \sī-ˈkä-lə-jist\ *n*
psy•cho•path \ˈsī-kō-ˌpath\ *n* **:** a mentally ill or unstable person; *esp* **:** a person who engages in antisocial behavior and exhibits a pervasive disregard for the rights, feelings, and safety of others — **psy•cho•path•ic** \ˌsī-kə-ˈpa-thik\ *adj*
psy•cho•sex•u•al \ˌsī-kō-ˈsek-shə-wəl\ *adj* **1 :** of or relating to the mental, emotional, and behavioral aspects of sexual development **2 :** of or relating to the physiological psychology of sex
psy•cho•sis \sī-ˈkō-səs\ *n, pl* **-cho•ses** \-ˌsēz\ **:** a serious mental illness (as schizophrenia) marked by loss of or greatly lessened ability to test whether what one is thinking and feeling about the real world is really true

psy•cho•so•cial \ˌsī-kō-ˈsō-shəl\ *adj* **1 :** involving both psychological and social aspects **2 :** relating social conditions to mental health

psy•cho•so•mat•ic \ˌsī-kō-sə-ˈma-tik\ *adj* **:** of, relating to, involving, or concerned with bodily symptoms caused by mental or emotional disturbance

psy•cho•ther•a•py \ˌsī-kō-ˈther-ə-pē\ *n* **:** treatment of mental or emotional disorder or of related bodily ills by psychological means — **psy•cho•ther•a•pist** \-pist\ *n*

[1]**psy•chot•ic** \sī-ˈkä-tik\ *adj* **:** of, relating to, marked by, or affected with psychosis ⟨∼ behavior⟩

[2]**psychotic** *n* ♦ **:** an individual who is psychotic

♦ lunatic, maniac, nut

psy•cho•tro•pic \ˌsī-kə-ˈtrō-pik\ *adj* **:** acting on the mind ⟨∼ drugs⟩

pt *abbr* **1** part **2** payment **3** pint **4** point **5** port

Pt *symbol* platinum

PT *abbr* **1** Pacific time **2** part-time **3** physical therapy **4** physical training

PTA *abbr* Parent-Teacher Association

ptar•mi•gan \ˈtär-mi-gən\ *n, pl* **-gan** *or* **-gans :** any of various grouses of northern regions with completely feathered feet

PT boat \(ˌ)pē-ˈtē-\ *n* **:** a small fast patrol craft usually armed with torpedos

pte *abbr, Brit* private

ptg *abbr* printing

PTO *abbr* **1** Parent-Teacher Organization **2** please turn over

pto•maine \ˈtō-ˌmān\ *n* **:** any of various chemical substances formed by bacteria in decaying matter (as meat) and including a few poisonous ones

PTV *abbr* public television

Pu *symbol* plutonium

[1]**pub** \ˈpəb\ *n* ♦ **:** an establishment where alcoholic beverages are sold and consumed **:** TAVERN

♦ bar, barroom, café, saloon, tavern

[2]**pub** *abbr* **1** public **2** publication **3** published; publisher; publishing

pu•ber•ty \ˈpyü-bər-tē\ *n* **:** the condition of being or period of becoming first capable of reproducing sexually — **pu•ber•tal** \-bərt-ᵊl\ *adj*

pu•bes \ˈpyü-bēz\ *n, pl* **pubes 1 :** the hair that appears upon the lower middle region of the abdomen at puberty **2 :** the pubic region

pu•bes•cence \pyü-ˈbes-ᵊns\ *n* **1 :** the quality or state of being pubescent **2 :** a pubescent covering or surface

pu•bes•cent \-ᵊnt\ *adj* **1 :** arriving at or having reached puberty **2 :** covered with fine soft short hairs

pu•bic \ˈpyü-bik\ *adj* **:** of, relating to, or situated near the pubes or the pubis

pu•bis \ˈpyü-bəs\ *n, pl* **pu•bes** \-bēz\ **:** the ventral and anterior of the three principal bones composing either half of the pelvis

publ *abbr* **1** publication **2** published; publisher

[1]**pub•lic** \ˈpə-blik\ *adj* **1 :** exposed to general view ⟨the story became ∼⟩ **2** ♦ **:** of, relating to, or affecting the people as a whole ⟨∼ opinion⟩ **3 :** CIVIC, GOVERNMENTAL ⟨∼ expenditures⟩ **4 :** of, relating to, or serving the community ⟨∼ officials⟩ **5 :** not private **:** SOCIAL ⟨∼ morality⟩ **6** ♦ **:** accessible to or shared by all members of the community ⟨∼ library⟩ **7 :** well known **:** PROMINENT ⟨∼ figures⟩ **8** ♦ **:** of, relating to, or affecting all the people or the whole area of a nation or state — **pub•lic•ly** *adv*

♦ [2] common, general, popular, vulgar ♦ [6] free-for-all, open, unrestricted ♦ [6] collective, common, communal, concerted, conjoint, joint, mutual, united ♦ [8] civil, national, state

[2]**public** *n* **1** ♦ **:** the people as a whole **2 :** a group of people having common interests

♦ folks, humanity, humankind, people, persons, society, world

pub•li•can \ˈpə-bli-kən\ *n* **1 :** a Jewish tax collector for the ancient Romans **2** *chiefly Brit* **:** the licensee of a pub

pub•li•ca•tion \ˌpə-blə-ˈkā-shən\ *n* **1 :** the act or process of publishing **2 :** a published work

public house *n* **1** ♦ **:** an establishment for the lodging and entertaining of travelers **:** INN **2** *chiefly Brit* **:** a licensed saloon or bar

♦ hospice, hotel, inn, lodge, tavern

pub•li•cise *chiefly Brit var of* PUBLICIZE

pub•li•cist \ˈpə-blə-sist\ *n* **:** one that publicizes; *esp* **:** PRESS AGENT

pub•lic•i•ty \(ˌ)pə-ˈbli-sə-tē\ *n* **1 :** information with news value issued to gain public attention or support **2 :** public attention or acclaim

pub•li•cize \ˈpə-blə-ˌsīz\ *vb* **-cized; -ciz•ing** ♦ **:** to bring to public attention

♦ advertise, announce, blaze, broadcast, declare, enunciate, placard, post, proclaim, promulgate, publish, sound ♦ ballyhoo, boast, plug, promote, tout

pub•lic–key \ˈpə-blik-ˈkē\ *n* **:** the publicly shared element of a code usable only to encode messages

public relations *n sing or pl* **:** the business of fostering public goodwill toward a person, firm, or institution; *also* **:** the degree of goodwill and understanding achieved

public school *n* **1 :** an endowed secondary boarding school in Great Britain offering a classical curriculum and preparation for the universities or public service **2 :** a free tax-supported school controlled by a local governmental authority

public servant *n* ♦ **:** a government official or employee

♦ functionary, officeholder, officer, official

public–spirited *adj* **:** motivated by devotion to the general or national welfare

public television *n* **:** television supported by public funds and private contributions rather than by commercials

public works *n pl* **:** works (as schools or highways) constructed with public funds for public use

pub•lish \ˈpə-blish\ *vb* **1** ♦ **:** to make generally known **:** announce publicly **2** ♦ **:** to produce or release literature, information, musical scores or sometimes recordings, or art for sale to the public — **pub•lish•er** *n*

♦ [1] advertise, announce, blaze, broadcast, declare, enunciate, placard, post, proclaim, promulgate, publicize, sound ♦ [2] get out, issue, print

[1]**puck** \ˈpək\ *n* ♦ **:** a mischievous sprite — **puck•ish** *adj* — **puck•ish•ly** *adv*

♦ brownie, dwarf, elf, fairy, fay, gnome, hobgoblin, leprechaun, pixie, troll

[2]**puck** *n* **:** a disk used in ice hockey

[1]**puck•er** \ˈpə-kər\ *vb* **:** to contract into folds or wrinkles

[2]**pucker** *n* **:** FOLD, WRINKLE

pud•ding \ˈpu̇-diŋ\ *n* **:** a soft, spongy, or thick creamy dessert

pud•dle \ˈpəd-ᵊl\ *n* **:** a very small pool of usually dirty or muddy water

pu•den•dum \pyu̇-ˈden-dəm\ *n, pl* **-da** \-də\ **:** the human external genital organs especially of a woman

pudgy \ˈpə-jē\ *adj* **pudg•i•er; -est :** being short and plump **:** CHUBBY

pueb•lo \ˈpwe-blō, pü-ˈe-\ *n, pl* **-los 1 :** an American Indian village of Arizona or New Mexico that consists of flat-roofed stone or adobe houses joined in groups sometimes several stories high **2** *cap* **:** a member of a group of American Indian peoples of the southwestern U.S.

pu•er•ile \ˈpyu̇-ə-rəl\ *adj* **:** marked by or suggestive of immaturity and lack of poise **:** CHILDISH, SILLY — **pu•er•il•i•ty** \ˌpyü-ə-ˈri-lə-tē\ *n*

pu•er•per•al \pyü-ˈər-pə-rəl\ *adj* **:** of, relating to, or occurring during childbirth or the period immediately following ⟨∼ infection⟩ ⟨∼ depression⟩

puerperal fever *n* **:** an abnormal condition that results from infection of the placental site following childbirth or abortion

Puer•to Ri•can \ˌpōr-tə-ˈrē-kən, ˌpwer-\ *n* **:** a native or inhabitant of Puerto Rico — **Puerto Rican** *adj*

[1]**puff** \ˈpəf\ *vb* **1 :** to blow in short gusts **2** ♦ **:** to breathe hard **:** PANT **3 :** to emit small whiffs or clouds **4 :** BLUSTER, BRAG **5 :** INFLATE, SWELL **6 :** to make proud or conceited **7 :** to praise extravagantly

♦ blow, gasp, pant, wheeze

[2]**puff** *n* **1** ♦ **:** a short discharge (as of air or smoke); *also* **:** a slight explosive sound accompanying it **2 :** a light fluffy pastry **3 :** a slight swelling **4 :** a fluffy mass; *also* **:** a small pad for applying cosmetic powder **5 :** a laudatory notice or review — **puffy** *adj*

♦ air, breath, breeze, waft, zephyr

puff•ball \ˈpəf-ˌbȯl\ *n* **:** any of various globe-shaped and often edible fungi

puf•fin \ˈpə-fən\ *n* **:** any of several seabirds having a short neck and a deep grooved parti-colored bill

[1]**pug** \ˈpəg\ *n* **1 :** any of a breed of small stocky short-haired dogs with a wrinkled face **2 :** a close coil of hair

[2]**pug** *n* **:** [1] BOXER

pu•gi•lism \ˈpyü-jə-ˌli-zəm\ *n* **:** BOXING

pu•gi•list \ˈpyü-jə-list\ *n* ♦ : one that fights; *esp* : a professional boxer — **pu•gi•lis•tic** \ˌpyü-jə-ˈlis-tik\ *adj*

♦ boxer, fighter, prizefighter

pug•na•cious \ˌpəg-ˈnā-shəs\ *adj* ♦ : having a quarrelsome or combative nature

♦ aggressive, argumentative, bellicose, belligerent, combative, contentious, discordant, disputatious, quarrelsome, scrappy, truculent

pug•nac•i•ty \ˌpəg-ˈna-sə-tē\ *n* ♦ : a readiness or inclination to fight

♦ aggression, aggressiveness, belligerence, fight, truculence

puis•sance \ˈpwi-səns, ˈpyü-ə-\ *n* : capacity for exertion or endurance : POWER, STRENGTH
puis•sant \ˈpwi-sənt, ˈpyü-ə-\ *adj* : having puissance : POWERFUL
puke \ˈpyük\ *vb* **puked; puk•ing** ♦ : to discharge the contents of the stomach through the mouth : VOMIT — **puke** *n*

♦ barf, gag, heave, hurl, retch, spit up, throw up, vomit

puk•ka \ˈpə-kə\ *adj* : GENUINE, AUTHENTIC; *also* : FIRST-CLASS, COMPLETE
pul•chri•tude \ˈpəl-krə-ˌtüd, -ˌtyüd\ *n* : BEAUTY — **pul•chri•tu•di•nous** \ˌpəl-krə-ˈtüd-ᵊn-əs, -ˈtyüd-\ *adj*
pule \ˈpyül\ *vb* **puled; pul•ing** : WHINE, WHIMPER
1**pull** \ˈpu̇l\ *vb* **1** ♦ : to exert force so as to draw (something) toward the force; *also* : MOVE ⟨~ out of a driveway⟩ **2 a** : PLUCK **b** ♦ : to take out forcibly : EXTRACT ⟨~ a tooth⟩ **3** ♦ : to strain abnormally ⟨~ a tendon⟩ **4** : to draw apart : TEAR **5** : to make (as a proof) by printing **6** : REMOVE **7** : DRAW ⟨~ a gun⟩ **8** : to carry out especially with daring ⟨~ a robbery⟩ **9** : PERPETRATE, COMMIT **10** : ATTRACT **11** : to express strong sympathy — **pull•er** *n*

♦ [1] drag, draw, hale, haul, lug, move, tow, tug ***Ant*** drive, propel, push ♦ [2b] extract, prize, pry, root, tear, uproot, wrest ♦ [3] rack, strain, stretch, wrench

2**pull** *n* **1** ♦ : the act or an instance of pulling **2** : the effort expended in moving **3 a** : ADVANTAGE **b** ♦ : special influence **4** : a device for pulling something or for operating by pulling **5** ♦ : a force that attracts or compels **6** : an injury from abnormal straining or stretching ⟨a muscle ~⟩

♦ [1] draw, haul, jerk, pluck, tug, wrench ***Ant*** push ♦ [3b, 5] authority, clout, influence, sway, weight

pull•back \ˈpu̇l-ˌbak\ *n* : an orderly withdrawal of troops
pull–down *adj* : appearing below a selected item (as a menu title) on a computer display ⟨a ~ menu⟩
pul•let \ˈpu̇-lət\ *n* : a young hen especially of the domestic chicken when less than a year old
pul•ley \ˈpu̇-lē\ *n, pl* **pulleys** : a wheel used to transmit power by means of a belt, rope, or chain; *esp* : one with a grooved rim that forms part of a tackle for hoisting or for changing the direction of a force
Pull•man \ˈpu̇l-mən\ *n* : a railroad passenger car with comfortable furnishings especially for night travel
pull off *vb* : to accomplish successfully
pull•out \ˈpu̇l-ˌau̇t\ *n* : PULLBACK
pull out *vb* **1** ♦ : to go away from : DEPART **2** : to take back or away : REMOVE

♦ clear out, depart, exit, get off, go, move, quit, sally, shove, take off

pull•over \ˈpu̇l-ˌō-vər\ *adj* : put on by being pulled over the head ⟨~ sweater⟩ — **pull•over** *n*
pull–up \ˈpu̇l-ˌəp\ *n* : CHIN-UP
pull up *vb* : to bring or come to an often abrupt halt : STOP
pul•mo•nary \ˈpu̇l-mə-ˌner-ē, ˈpəl-\ *adj* : of, relating to, or carried on by the lungs ⟨the ~ circulation⟩
pulp \ˈpəlp\ *n* **1** : the soft juicy or fleshy part of a fruit or vegetable **2** : a soft moist mass **3** : the soft sensitive tissue that fills the central cavity of a tooth **4** : a material (as from wood) used in making paper **5** : a magazine using cheap paper and often dealing with sensational material
pul•pit \ˈpu̇l-ˌpit\ *n* : a raised platform or high reading desk used in preaching or conducting a worship service
pulp•wood \ˈpəlp-ˌwu̇d\ *n* : wood used in making pulp for paper
pulpy \ˈpəl-pē\ *adj* ♦ : resembling or consisting of pulp

♦ fleshy, juicy, succulent ♦ flabby, mushy, soft, spongy

pul•sar \ˈpəl-ˌsär\ *n* : a celestial source of pulsating electromagnetic radiation (as radio waves)

pul•sate \ˈpəl-ˌsāt\ *vb* **pul•sat•ed; pul•sat•ing** ♦ : to expand and contract rhythmically : BEAT

♦ beat, palpitate, pitter-patter, pulse, throb

pul•sa•tion \ˌpəl-ˈsā-shən\ *n* ♦ : rhythmical throbbing or vibrating

♦ beat, palpitation, pulse, throb

1**pulse** \ˈpəls\ *n* **1** : the regular throbbing in the arteries caused by the contractions of the heart **2** : rhythmical beating, vibrating, or sounding **3** : a brief change in electrical current or voltage
2**pulse** *vb* ♦ : to exhibit a pulse or pulsation

♦ beat, palpitate, pitter-patter, pulsate, throb

pul•ver•ise *chiefly Brit var of* PULVERIZE
pul•ver•ize \ˈpəl-və-ˌrīz\ *vb* **-ized; -iz•ing** **1** ♦ : to reduce (as by crushing or grinding) or be reduced to very small particles **2** ♦ : to destroy by or as if by smashing into fragments : DEMOLISH

♦ [1] atomize, crush, grind, powder ♦ [2] annihilate, blot out, demolish, desolate, destroy, devastate, do in, exterminate, extinguish, obliterate, ruin, shatter, smash, tear down, waste, wipe out, wreck

pu•ma \ˈpü-mə, ˈpyü-\ *n, pl* **pumas** *also* **puma** : a large powerful tawny brown wild American cat : COUGAR
pum•ice \ˈpə-məs\ *n* : a light porous volcanic glass used especially for smoothing and polishing
pum•mel \ˈpə-məl\ *vb* **-meled** *also* **-melled; -mel•ing** *also* **-mel•ling** : to strike repeatedly : BEAT
1**pump** \ˈpəmp\ *n* : a device for raising, transferring, or compressing fluids especially by suction or pressure
2**pump** *vb* **1** : to raise (as water) with a pump **2** : to draw fluid from with a pump; *also* : to fill by means of a pump ⟨~ up a tire⟩ **3** : to force or propel in the manner of a pump **4** ♦ : to move in a manner that resembles the action of a pump handle **5** ♦ : to question persistently — **pump•er** *n*

♦ [4] bob, bobble, jog, jounce, nod, seesaw ♦ [5] examine, grill, interrogate, query, question, quiz

3**pump** *n* : a low shoe that grips the foot chiefly at the toe and heel
pumped \ˈpəmpt\ *adj* : filled with energetic excitement and enthusiasm
pum•per•nick•el \ˈpəm-pər-ˌni-kəl\ *n* : a dark rye bread
pump•kin \ˈpəmp-kən, ˈpəŋ-kən\ *n* : the large usually orange fruit of a vine of the gourd family that is widely used as food; *also* : this vine
pun \ˈpən\ *n* : the humorous use of a word in a way that suggests two or more interpretations — **pun** *vb*
1**punch** \ˈpənch\ *vb* **1 a** : PROD, POKE **b** : to frighten or prod (as game or cattle) into moving in a desired direction : DRIVE, HERD ⟨~*ing* cattle⟩ **2** ♦ : to strike with the fist **3** ♦ : to emboss, perforate, or make with a punch **4** : to operate, produce, or enter (as data) by or as if by punching — **punch•er** *n*

♦ [2] bang, bash, belt, clout, hit, knock, slug, strike, thump, wallop, whack ♦ [3] bore, drill, hole, perforate, pierce, puncture

2**punch** *n* **1** ♦ : a quick blow with or as if with the fist **2** ♦ : effective energy or forcefulness

♦ [1] belt, blow, box, clout, hit, slug, smash, wallop, whack ♦ [2] bounce, dash, drive, esprit, pep, snap, spirit, verve, vim, zing, zip ♦ [2] cogency, effectiveness, force, impact, point

3**punch** *n* **1** : a tool for piercing, stamping, cutting, or forming **2** ♦ : a hole or notch from a perforating operation

♦ perforation, pinhole, prick, puncture, stab

4**punch** *n* : a drink usually composed of wine or alcoholic liquor and nonalcoholic beverages; *also* : a drink composed of nonalcoholic beverages
punch card \ˈpənch-\ *n* : a card with holes punched in particular positions to represent data
punch–drunk \ˈpənch-ˌdrəŋk\ *adj* **1** : suffering from brain injury resulting from repeated head blows received in boxing **2** : DAZED, CONFUSED
pun•cheon \ˈpən-chən\ *n* ♦ : a large cask

♦ barrel, cask, hogshead, keg, pipe

punch line *n* : the sentence or phrase in a joke that makes the point
punch list *n* : a list of tasks to be completed at the end of a project

punchy \ˈpən-chē\ *adj* **punch•i•er; -est** **1 :** having punch **:** FORCEFUL **2 :** DAZED, CONFUSED **3 :** VIVID, VIBRANT
punc•til•io \ˌpəŋk-ˈti-lē-ˌō\ *n, pl* **-i•os** **1 :** a nice detail of conduct in a ceremony or in observance of a code **2 :** careful observance of forms (as in social conduct)
punc•til•i•ous \ˌpəŋk-ˈti-lē-əs\ *adj* ♦ **:** marked by precise accordance with codes or conventions

♦ ceremonious, correct, decorous, formal, proper, starchy

punc•tu•al \ˈpəŋk-chə-wəl\ *adj* ♦ **:** being on time **:** PROMPT — **punc•tu•al•ly** *adv*

♦ immediate, prompt, timely

punc•tu•al•i•ty \ˌpəŋk-chə-ˈwa-lə-tē\ *n* ♦ **:** the quality, state, or habit of being punctual

♦ promptitude, timeliness

punc•tu•ate \ˈpəŋk-chə-ˌwāt\ *vb* **-at•ed; -at•ing** **1 :** to mark or divide (written matter) with punctuation marks **2 :** to break into at intervals **3 :** EMPHASIZE
punc•tu•a•tion \ˌpəŋk-chə-ˈwā-shən\ *n* **:** the act, practice, or system of inserting standardized marks in written matter to clarify the meaning and separate structural units
[1]**punc•ture** \ˈpəŋk-chər\ *n* **1 :** an act of puncturing **2** ♦ **:** a small hole or wound made by puncturing

♦ perforation, pinhole, prick, punch, stab

[2]**puncture** *vb* **punc•tured; punc•tur•ing** **1** ♦ **:** to pierce with or as if with a pointed instrument or object **2 :** to make useless as if by a puncture

♦ bore, drill, hole, perforate, pierce, punch

pun•dit \ˈpən-dət\ *n* **1 :** a learned person **:** TEACHER **2 :** AUTHORITY, CRITIC
pun•dit•oc•ra•cy \ˌpən-dət-ˈä-krə-sē\ *n, pl* **-cies** **:** a group of powerful and influential political commentators
pun•gen•cy \ˈpən-jən-sē\ *n* ♦ **:** the quality or state of being pungent

♦ acidity, acrimony, asperity, bite, bitterness, edge, harshness, keenness, sharpness, tartness

pun•gent \ˈpən-jənt\ *adj* **1** ♦ **:** having a sharp incisive quality **:** CAUSTIC ⟨a ~ editorial⟩ **2 a :** causing a sharp or irritating sensation; *esp* **:** ACRID ⟨~ smell of burning leaves⟩ **b** ♦ **:** having an intense flavor or odor — **pun•gent•ly** *adv*

♦ [1] acrid, biting, caustic, cutting, mordant, sarcastic, satiric, scathing, sharp, tart ♦ [2b] nippy, sharp, strong

pun•ish \ˈpə-nish\ *vb* **1 :** to impose a penalty on for a fault or crime ⟨~ an offender⟩ **2** ♦ **:** to inflict a penalty for ⟨~ treason with death⟩ **3 :** to inflict injury on **:** HURT — **pun•ish•able** *adj*

♦ castigate, chasten, chastise, correct, discipline, penalize *Ant* excuse, pardon, spare

pun•ish•ment *n* **1** ♦ **:** retributive suffering, pain, or loss **:** PENALTY **2 :** rough treatment

♦ castigation, chastisement, correction, desert, discipline, nemesis, penalty, wrath

pu•ni•tive \ˈpyü-nə-tiv\ *adj* ♦ **:** inflicting, involving, or aiming at punishment

♦ corrective, disciplinary, penal

[1]**punk** \ˈpəŋk\ *n* **1 :** a young inexperienced person **2** ♦ **:** a petty hoodlum

♦ bully, gangster, goon, hood, hoodlum, mobster, mug, rowdy, ruffian, thug, tough

[2]**punk** *adj* **1** ♦ **:** very poor **2** ♦ **:** being in poor health

♦ [1] bad, deficient, inferior, lousy, off, poor, rotten, substandard, unacceptable, unsatisfactory, wanting, wretched, wrong ♦ [2] bad, down, ill, indisposed, peaked, sick, unhealthy, unsound, unwell

[3]**punk** *n* **:** dry crumbly wood useful for tinder; *also* **:** a substance made from fungi for use as tinder
pun•ster \ˈpən-stər\ *n* **:** one who is given to punning
[1]**punt** \ˈpənt\ *n* **:** a long narrow flat-bottomed boat with square ends
[2]**punt** *vb* **:** to propel (as a punt) with a pole
[3]**punt** *vb* **:** to kick a football or soccer ball dropped from the hands before it touches the ground
[4]**punt** *n* **:** the act or an instance of punting a ball
pu•ny \ˈpyü-nē\ *adj* **pu•ni•er; -est** **:** slight in power, size, or importance

pup \ˈpəp\ *n* **:** a young dog; *also* **:** one of the young of some other animals
pu•pa \ˈpyü-pə\ *n, pl* **pu•pae** \-(ˌ)pē\ *or* **pupas** **:** a form of some insects (as a bee, moth, or beetle) between the larva and the adult that usually has a protective covering (as a cocoon) — **pu•pal** \-pəl\ *adj*
[1]**pu•pil** \ˈpyü-pəl\ *n* **1 :** a child or young person in school or in the charge of a tutor **2** ♦ **:** one who has been taught or influenced by a famous or distinguished person **:** DISCIPLE

♦ adherent, convert, disciple, follower, partisan, votary

[2]**pupil** *n* **:** the dark central opening of the iris of the eye
pup•pet \ˈpə-pət\ *n* **1 :** a small figure of a person or animal moved by hand or by strings or wires **2 :** DOLL **3 :** one whose acts are controlled by an outside force or influence
pup•pe•teer \ˌpə-pə-ˈtir\ *n* **:** one who manipulates puppets
pup•py \ˈpə-pē\ *n, pl* **puppies** **:** a young domestic dog
pu•pu \ˈpü-ˌpü\ *n* **:** an Asian dish consisting of a variety of foods
pur•blind \ˈpər-ˌblīnd\ *adj* **1 :** partly blind **2 :** lacking in insight **:** OBTUSE
pur•chas•able \ˈpər-chə-sə-bəl\ *adj* **1 :** capable of being purchased **2** ♦ **:** open to corrupt influence and especially bribery

♦ bribable, corruptible, venal

[1]**pur•chase** \ˈpər-chəs\ *vb* **pur•chased; pur•chas•ing** ♦ **:** to obtain by paying money or its equivalent **:** BUY — **pur•chas•er** *n*

♦ buy, pick up, take

[2]**purchase** *n* **1 :** an act or instance of purchasing **2 :** something purchased **3 :** a secure hold or grasp; *also* **:** advantageous leverage
pur•dah \ˈpər-də\ *n* **:** seclusion of women from public observation among Muslims and some Hindus especially in India; *also* **:** a state of seclusion
pure \ˈpyu̇r\ *adj* **pur•er; pur•est** **1** ♦ **:** unmixed with any other matter **:** free from taint ⟨~ gold⟩ ⟨~ water⟩ **2 :** being thus and no other **:** ABSOLUTE ⟨~ nonsense⟩ **3 :** ABSTRACT, THEORETICAL ⟨~ mathematics⟩ **4 :** free from what vitiates, weakens, or pollutes ⟨speaks a ~ French⟩ **5 :** free from moral fault **:** INNOCENT **6** ♦ **:** marked by chastity **:** CHASTE

♦ [1] absolute, fine, neat, plain, refined, straight, unadulterated, undiluted, unmixed *Ant* adulterated, diluted, impure, mixed ♦ [6] chaste, clean, decent, immaculate, modest

pure–blood•ed \-ˌblə-dəd\ *or* **pure–blood** \-ˌbləd\ *adj* **:** FULL-BLOODED — **pure•blood** *n*
pure•bred \-ˈbred\ *adj* ♦ **:** bred from members of a recognized breed, strain, or kind without crossbreeding over many generations — **pure•bred** \-ˌbred\ *n*

♦ full-blooded, thoroughbred *Ant* hybrid, mixed, mongrel

[1]**pu•ree** \pyu̇-ˈrā, -ˈrē\ *n* **:** a paste or thick liquid suspension usually made from finely ground cooked food; *also* **:** a thick soup made of pureed vegetables
[2]**puree** *vb* **pu•reed; pu•ree•ing** **:** to make a puree of
pure•ly \ˈpyu̇r-lē\ *adv* **1 a :** to a full extent **:** TOTALLY ⟨~ by accident⟩ **b :** WHOLLY, EXCLUSIVELY ⟨a selection based ~ on merit⟩ **2 :** without admixture of anything injurious or foreign **3 :** SIMPLY, MERELY ⟨read ~ for relaxation⟩ **4** ♦ **:** in a chaste or innocent manner

♦ chastely, modestly, righteously, virtuously *Ant* evilly, immorally, sinfully, wickedly

pur•ga•tion \ˌpər-ˈgā-shən\ *n* **:** the act or result of purging
[1]**pur•ga•tive** \ˈpər-gə-tiv\ *adj* **:** purging or tending to purge
[2]**purgative** *n* **:** a strong laxative **:** CATHARTIC
pur•ga•to•ry \ˈpər-gə-ˌtōr-ē\ *n, pl* **-ries** **1 :** an intermediate state after death for expiatory purification **2 :** a place or state of temporary punishment — **pur•ga•tor•i•al** \ˌpər-gə-ˈtōr-ē-əl\ *adj*
[1]**purge** \ˈpərj\ *vb* **purged; purg•ing** **1 :** to cleanse or purify especially from sin **2 :** to have or cause strong and usually repeated emptying of the bowels **3 :** to get rid of ⟨the leaders had been *purged*⟩
[2]**purge** *n* **1 :** something that purges; *esp* **:** PURGATIVE **2 :** an act or result of purging; *esp* **:** a ridding of persons regarded as treacherous or disloyal
pu•ri•fy \ˈpyu̇r-ə-ˌfī\ *vb* **-fied; -fy•ing** ♦ **:** to make or become pure — **pu•ri•fi•ca•tion** \ˌpyu̇r-ə-fə-ˈkā-shən\ *n* — **pu•ri•fi•ca•to•ry** \pyu̇-ˈri-fi-kə-ˌtōr-ē\ *adj* — **pu•ri•fi•er** *n*

♦ sanctify ♦ clarify, clear, distill, filter

Pu•rim \ˈpu̇r-(ˌ)im\ *n* **:** a Jewish holiday celebrated in February or March in commemoration of the deliverance of the Jews from the massacre plotted by Haman

pu·rine \ˈpyu̇r-ˌēn\ *n* **:** any of a group of bases including several (as adenine or guanine) that are constituents of DNA or RNA

pur·ism \ˈpyu̇r-ˌi-zəm\ *n* **:** rigid adherence to or insistence on purity or nicety especially in use of words — **pur·ist** \-ist\ *n* — **pu·ris·tic** \pyu̇-ˈris-tik\ *adj*

pu·ri·tan \ˈpyu̇r-ət-ᵊn\ *n* **1** *cap* **:** a member of a 16th and 17th century Protestant group in England and New England opposing the ceremonies and government of the Church of England **2 :** one who practices or preaches a stricter or professedly purer moral code than that which prevails

pu·ri·tan·i·cal \ˌpyu̇r-ə-ˈta-ni-kəl\ *adj* **1** ◆ **:** of, relating to, or characterized by a rigid morality **2 :** of or relating to puritans, the Puritans, or puritanism — **pu·ri·tan·i·cal·ly** *adv*

◆ prim, prudish, straitlaced

pu·ri·ty \ˈpyu̇r-ə-tē\ *n* ◆ **:** the quality or state of being pure

◆ chastity, modesty

[1]**purl** \ˈpərl\ *vb* **:** to knit in purl stitch

[2]**purl** *n* **:** a stitch in knitting

[3]**purl** *n* **:** a gentle murmur or movement (as of purling water)

[4]**purl** *vb* **1 :** EDDY, SWIRL **2 :** to make a soft murmuring sound

pur·lieu \ˈpər-lü, ˈpərl-yü\ *n* **1 :** an outlying district **:** SUBURB **2** *pl* **:** the districts around a city **:** ENVIRONS

pur·loin \(ˌ)pər-ˈlȯin, ˈpər-ˌlȯin\ *vb* ◆ **:** to take or make use of wrongfully and often by a breach of trust **:** STEAL

◆ appropriate, filch, hook, misappropriate, nip, pilfer, pocket, snitch, steal, swipe, thieve

[1]**pur·ple** \ˈpər-pəl\ *adj* **pur·pler; pur·plest 1 :** of the color purple **2 :** highly rhetorical ⟨a ~ passage⟩ **3 :** PROFANE ⟨~ language⟩ — **pur·plish** *adj*

[2]**purple** *n* **1 :** a bluish red color **2 :** a purple robe emblematic especially of regal rank or authority

[1]**pur·port** \ˈpər-ˌpōrt\ *n* ◆ **:** meaning conveyed or implied; *also* **:** GIST

◆ denotation, drift, gist, import, intent, meaning, sense, signification, signification

[2]**pur·port** \(ˌ)pər-ˈpōrt\ *vb* **:** to convey or profess outwardly as the meaning or intention **:** CLAIM — **pur·port·ed·ly** \-ˈpōr-təd-lē\ *adv*

[1]**pur·pose** \ˈpər-pəs\ *n* **1** ◆ **:** something set up as an object or end to be attained **2 :** RESOLUTION, DETERMINATION — **pur·pose·less** *adj*

◆ aim, ambition, aspiration, design, dream, end, goal, intent, mark, meaning, object, objective, plan, pretension, thing ◆ capacity, function, job, part, place, position, role, task, work

[2]**purpose** *vb* **pur·posed; pur·pos·ing :** to propose as an aim to oneself

pur·pose·ful \ˈpər-pəs-fəl\ *adj* **1 :** having a purpose: as **a :** MEANINGFUL ⟨~ activities⟩ **b** ◆ **:** done by intention or design **:** INTENTIONAL ⟨~ ambiguity⟩ **2** ◆ **:** full of determination

◆ [1b] deliberate, freewill, intentional, voluntary, willful, willing ◆ [2] bound, decisive, determined, firm, intent, resolute, set, single-minded

pur·pose·ful·ly \-fə-lē\ *adv* **:** in a purposeful manner

pur·pose·ly *adv* ◆ **:** with a deliberate or express purpose

◆ consciously, deliberately, intentionally, knowingly, willfully

purr \ˈpər\ *n* ◆ **:** a low murmur typical of a contented cat — **purr** *vb*

◆ buzz, drone, hum, whir, whiz, zoom

[1]**purse** \ˈpərs\ *n* **1** ◆ **:** a receptacle (as a pouch) to carry money and often other small objects **2 :** RESOURCES **3 :** a sum of money offered as a prize or present

◆ bag, handbag, pocketbook

[2]**purse** *vb* **pursed; purs·ing :** PUCKER

purs·er \ˈpər-sər\ *n* **:** an official on a ship who keeps accounts and attends to the comfort of passengers

purs·lane \ˈpər-slən, -ˌslān\ *n* **:** a fleshy-leaved weedy trailing plant with tiny yellow flowers that is sometimes used in salads

pur·su·ance \pər-ˈsü-əns\ *n* ◆ **:** the act of carrying out or into effect

◆ accomplishment, achievement, commission, discharge, enactment, execution, fulfillment, implementation, performance, perpetration

pur·su·ant to \-ˈsü-ənt-\ *prep* **:** in carrying out **:** ACCORDING TO

pur·sue \pər-ˈsü\ *vb* **pur·sued; pur·su·ing 1** ◆ **:** to follow in order to overtake or overcome **2 :** to seek to accomplish ⟨~ a goal⟩ **3 :** to proceed along ⟨~ a course⟩ **4 :** to engage in ⟨~ a career⟩ — **pur·su·er** *n*

◆ chase, dog, follow, hound, shadow, tag, tail, trace, track, trail

pur·suit \pər-ˈsüt\ *n* **1** ◆ **:** the act of pursuing **2 :** OCCUPATION, BUSINESS

◆ chase, following, tracing

pu·ru·lent \ˈpyu̇r-ə-lənt, -yə-\ *adj* **:** containing or accompanied by pus ⟨a ~ discharge⟩ — **pu·ru·lence** \-ləns\ *n*

pur·vey \(ˌ)pər-ˈvā\ *vb* **pur·veyed; pur·vey·ing :** to supply (as provisions) usually as a business — **pur·vey·ance** \-əns\ *n* — **pur·vey·or** \-ər\ *n*

pur·view \ˈpər-ˌvyü\ *n* **1 :** the range or limit especially of authority, responsibility, or intention **2 :** range of vision, understanding, or cognizance

pus \ˈpəs\ *n* **:** thick yellowish white fluid matter (as in a boil) formed at a place of inflammation and infection (as an abscess) and containing germs, white blood cells, and tissue debris

[1]**push** \ˈpu̇sh\ *vb* **1** ◆ **:** to press against with force in order to drive or impel **2** ◆ **:** to thrust forward, downward, or outward **3 :** to urge on **:** press forward **4 :** to cause to increase ⟨~ prices to record levels⟩ **5 :** to urge or press the advancement, adoption, or practice of; *esp* **:** to make aggressive efforts to sell **6 :** to engage in the illicit sale of narcotics

◆ [1, 2] drive, propel, shove, thrust ◆ [2] bulldoze, elbow, muscle, press

[2]**push** *n* **1 :** a vigorous effort **:** DRIVE **2 :** an act of pushing **:** SHOVE **3 :** vigorous enterprise **:** ENERGY

push–button *adj* **1 :** operated or done by means of push buttons **2 :** using or dependent on complex and more or less automatic mechanisms ⟨~ warfare⟩

push button *n* **:** a small button or knob that when pushed operates something especially by closing an electric circuit

push·cart \ˈpu̇sh-ˌkärt\ *n* **:** a cart or barrow pushed by hand

push·er \ˈpu̇-shər\ *n* **:** one that pushes; *esp* **:** one that pushes illegal drugs

push·over \-ˌō-vər\ *n* **1 :** an opponent easy to defeat **2 :** SUCKER **3** ◆ **:** something easily accomplished

◆ breeze, child's play, cinch, picnic, snap

push–up \-ˌəp\ *n* **:** a conditioning exercise performed in a prone position by raising and lowering the body with the straightening and bending of the arms while keeping the back straight and supporting the body on the hands and toes

pushy \ˈpu̇-shē\ *adj* **push·i·er; -est :** aggressive often to an objectionable degree

pu·sil·lan·i·mous \ˌpyü-sə-ˈla-nə-məs\ *adj* ◆ **:** contemptibly timid **:** COWARDLY — **pu·sil·la·nim·i·ty** \ˌpyü-sə-lə-ˈni-mə-tē\ *n*

◆ chicken, cowardly, craven, dastardly, recreant, spineless, yellow

[1]**puss** \ˈpu̇s\ *n* ◆ **:** a domestic cat

◆ cat, feline, kitty

[2]**puss** *n, slang* **:** FACE

[1]**pussy** \ˈpu̇-sē\ *n, pl* **puss·ies :** PUSS

[2]**pus·sy** \ˈpə-sē\ *adj* **pus·si·er; -est :** full of or resembling pus

pussy·cat \ˈpu̇-sē-ˌkat\ *n* **:** CAT

pussy·foot \-ˌfu̇t\ *vb* **1** ◆ **:** to tread or move warily or stealthily **2** ◆ **:** to refrain from committing oneself

◆ [1] lurk, skulk, slide, slink, slip, snake, sneak, steal ◆ [2] equivocate, fudge, hedge

pussy willow \ˈpu̇-sē-\ *n* **:** a willow having large silky catkins

pus·tule \ˈpəs-chül\ *n* **:** a pus-filled pimple

put \ˈpu̇t\ *vb* **put; put·ting 1** ◆ **:** to bring into a specified position **:** PLACE ⟨~ the book on the table⟩ **2 :** SEND, THRUST **3 :** to throw with an upward pushing motion ⟨~ the shot⟩ **4 :** to bring into a specified state ⟨~ the plan into effect⟩ **5 :** SUBJECT ⟨~ traitors to death⟩ **6** ◆ **:** to establish or apply by authority **:** IMPOSE **7 :** to set before one for decision ⟨~ the question⟩ **8** ◆ **:** to represent in words **:** EXPRESS **9 :** TRANSLATE, ADAPT **10 :** APPLY, ASSIGN ⟨~ them to work⟩ **11** ◆ **:** to give as an estimate ⟨~ the number at 20⟩ **12 :** ATTACH, ATTRIBUTE ⟨~ a high value on it⟩ **13 :** to take a specified course ⟨the ship ~ out to sea⟩

◆ [1] deposit, dispose, fix, lay, place, position, set, set up, stick ◆ [6] assess, charge, exact, fine, impose, lay, levy ◆ [8] articulate, clothe, couch, express, formulate, phrase, say, state, word ◆ [11] calculate, call, conjecture, estimate, figure, gauge, guess, judge, make, place, reckon, suppose

pu·ta·tive \ˈpyü-tə-tiv\ *adj* **1 :** commonly accepted **2 :** assumed to exist or to have existed

put by *vb* ♦ : to lay aside

♦ cache, hoard, lay away, lay up, salt away, stash, stockpile, store

put–down \ˈpu̇t-ˌdau̇n\ *n* ♦ : an act or instance of putting down; *esp* : a humiliating remark

♦ affront, barb, dart, dig, indignity, insult, name, offense, outrage, sarcasm, slight, slur, wound ♦ deprecation, depreciation, detraction, disparagement

put down *vb* **1** ♦ : to bring to an end **2** ♦ : to speak slightingly of : DISPARAGE, BELITTLE **3 a** ♦ : to put in writing **b** ♦ : to enter in a list

♦ [1] clamp down, crack down, crush, quash, quell, repress, silence, snuff, squash, squelch, subdue, suppress ♦ [2] belittle, cry down, decry, deprecate, depreciate, diminish, discount, disparage, minimize, write off ♦ [3a] jot, log, mark, note, record, register, set down ♦ [3b] catalog, enroll, enter, index, inscribe, list, record, register, schedule, slate

put in *vb* **1** : to come in with : INTERPOSE ⟨*put in* a good word for me⟩ **2** : to spend time at some occupation or job ⟨*put in* eight hours at the office⟩ **3** : to put or set in the ground for growth : PLANT

put off *vb* **1** ♦ : to hold back to a later time : POSTPONE, DELAY **2** : to rid oneself of : TAKE OFF

♦ defer, delay, hold up, postpone, shelve

¹put–on \ˈpu̇t-ˌȯn, -ˌän\ *adj* : professed or avowed but not genuine : ASSUMED

²put–on *n* **1** ♦ : a deliberate act of misleading someone **2** : PARODY, SPOOF

♦ act, airs, facade, front, guise, masquerade, pose, pretense, semblance, show

put on *vb* **1 a** ♦ : to dress oneself in **b** ♦ : to give a false appearance of : FEIGN **2** ♦ : to enlarge beyond bounds or the truth

♦ [1a] don, slip, throw *Ant* doff, remove, take off ♦ [1b] affect, assume, counterfeit, fake, feign, pretend, profess, sham, simulate ♦ [2] exaggerate, overdo, overstate

put out *vb* **1** ♦ : to cause to cease burning : EXTINGUISH **2** : to disturb or irritate especially by repeated acts : ANNOY; *also* : INCONVENIENCE **3** : to cause to be out (as in baseball) **4** ♦ : to bring to bear especially with sustained effort or lasting effect : EXERT

♦ [1] douse, extinguish, quench, snuff ♦ [4] apply, exercise, exert, wield

pu•tre•fac•tion \ˌpyü-trə-ˈfak-shən\ *n* ♦ : the decomposition of organic matter — **pu•tre•fac•tive** \-tiv\ *adj*

♦ breakdown, corruption, decay, decomposition, rot, spoilage

pu•tre•fy \ˈpyü-trə-ˌfī\ *vb* **-fied; -fy•ing** ♦ : to make or become putrid : ROT

♦ break down, corrupt, decay, decompose, disintegrate, molder, rot, spoil

pu•tres•cent \pyü-ˈtres-ᵊnt\ *adj* : becoming putrid : ROTTING — **pu•tres•cence** \-ᵊns\ *n*

pu•trid \ˈpyü-trəd\ *adj* **1** ♦ : being in a state of putrefaction : ROTTEN **2** : VILE, CORRUPT — **pu•trid•i•ty** \pyü-ˈtri-də-tē\ *n*

♦ bad, rotten

putsch \ˈpu̇ch\ *n* : a secretly plotted and suddenly executed attempt to overthrow a government

putt \ˈpət\ *n* : a golf stroke made on the green to cause the ball to roll into the hole — **putt** *vb*

put•ta•nes•ca \ˌpü-tä-ˈnes-kä\ *adj* : served with or being a pungent tomato sauce

put•tee \ˌpə-ˈtē, ˈpə-tē\ *n* **1** : a cloth strip wrapped around the lower leg **2** : a leather legging

¹put•ter \ˈpu̇-tər\ *n* : one that puts

²putt•er \ˈpə-tər\ *n* **1** : a golf club used in putting **2** : one that putts

³put•ter \ˈpə-tər\ *vb* **1** ♦ : to move or act aimlessly or idly **2** : TINKER

♦ *usu* **putter around** fiddle, fool, mess, monkey, play, potter, trifle

put•ty \ˈpə-tē\ *n, pl* **putties** **1** : a doughlike cement used especially to fasten glass in sashes **2** : one who is easily manipulated — **putty** *vb*

put up *vb* **1** : SHEATHE **2** : to prepare so as to preserve for later use **3** ♦ : to offer for public sale ⟨*put* the house *up* for auction⟩ **4** ♦ : to give food and shelter to : ACCOMMODATE **5** ♦ : to form by the fitting together of materials or parts : BUILD **6** : to engage in ⟨*put up* a struggle⟩ **7** : CONTRIBUTE, PAY — **put up with** : TOLERATE 2

♦ [3] deal, market, merchandise, retail, sell, vend ♦ [4] accommodate, billet, chamber, domicile, harbor (*or* harbour), house, lodge, quarter, roof, shelter, take in ♦ [5] assemble, build, construct, erect, fabricate, make, make up, piece, raise, rear, set up

¹puz•zle \ˈpə-zəl\ *vb* **puz•zled; puz•zling** **1** ♦ : to bewilder mentally : PERPLEX **2** ♦ : to solve with difficulty or ingenuity ⟨∼ out a riddle⟩ **3** : to be in a quandary ⟨∼ over what to do⟩ **4** : to attempt a solution of a puzzle ⟨∼ over a person's words⟩ — **puzzler** *n*

♦ [1] addle, baffle, befog, befuddle, bemuse, bewilder, confound, confuse, disorient, muddle, muddy, mystify, perplex ♦ *usu* **puzzle out** [2] answer, break, crack, dope, figure out, resolve, riddle, solve, unravel, work, work out

²puzzle *n* **1** ♦ : something that puzzles **2** : a question, problem, or contrivance designed for testing ingenuity

♦ conundrum, enigma, mystery, mystification, puzzlement, riddle, secret

puz•zle•ment \ˈpə-zəl-mənt\ *n* **1** ♦ : the state of being puzzled **2** : something that puzzles

♦ bafflement, bewilderment, confusion, distraction, muddle, mystification, perplexity, whirl

PVC *abbr* polyvinyl chloride

pvt *abbr* private

PW *abbr* prisoner of war

pwt *abbr* pennyweight

PX *abbr* post exchange

¹pyg•my *also* **pig•my** \ˈpig-mē\ *n, pl* **-mies** **1** *cap* : any of a small people of equatorial Africa **2** ♦ : an unusually small person : DWARF **3** ♦ : something very small of its kind

♦ [2, 3] dwarf, midget, mite, peewee, runt, scrub, shrimp

²pygmy *adj* **1** : of or relating to the Pygmies or a pygmy **2** ♦ : very small

♦ dwarf, dwarfish, fine, little, pocket, slight, small, undersized

py•ja•mas \pə-ˈjä-məz\ *chiefly Can and Brit var of* PAJAMAS

py•lon \ˈpī-ˌlän, -lən\ *n* **1** : a usually massive gateway; *esp* : an Egyptian one flanked by flat-topped pyramids **2** : a tower that supports wires over a long span **3** : a post or tower marking the course in an airplane race

py•or•rhea \ˌpī-ə-ˈrē-ə\ *n* : an inflammation with pus of the sockets of the teeth

¹pyr•a•mid \ˈpir-ə-ˌmid\ *n* **1** : a massive structure with a square base and four triangular faces meeting at a point **2** : a geometrical solid having a polygon for its base and three or more triangles for its sides that meet at a point to form the top — **py•ra•mi•dal** \pə-ˈra-məd-ᵊl, ˌpir-ə-ˈmid-\ *adj*

²pyramid *vb* **1** : to build up in the form of a pyramid : heap up **2** : to increase rapidly on a broadening base

pyramid scheme *n* : a usually illegal operation in which participants pay to join and profit from payments made by subsequent participants

pyre \ˈpī(-ə)r\ *n* : a combustible heap for burning a dead body as a funeral rite

py•re•thrum \pī-ˈrē-thrəm\ *n* : an insecticide made from the dried heads of any of several Old World chrysanthemums

py•rim•i•dine \pī-ˈri-mə-ˌdēn\ *n* : any of a group of bases including several (as cytosine, thymine, or uracil) that are constituents of DNA or RNA

py•rite \ˈpī-ˌrīt\ *n* : a mineral containing sulfur and iron that is brass-yellow in color

py•rol•y•sis \pī-ˈrä-lə-səs\ *n* : chemical change caused by the action of heat

py•ro•ma•nia \ˌpī-rō-ˈmā-nē-ə\ *n* : an irresistible impulse to start fires — **py•ro•ma•ni•ac** \-nē-ˌak\ *n*

py•ro•tech•nics \ˌpī-rə-ˈtek-niks\ *n pl* **1** : a display of fireworks **2** : a spectacular display (as of extreme virtuosity) — **py•ro•tech•nic** \-nik\ *also* **py•ro•tech•ni•cal** \-ni-kəl\ *adj*

Pyr•rhic \ˈpir-ik\ *adj* : achieved at excessive cost ⟨a ∼ victory⟩; *also* : costly to the point of outweighing expected benefits

Py•thag•o•re•an theorem \pī-ˌtha-gə-ˈrē-ən-\ *n* : a theorem in geometry: the square of the length of the hypotenuse of a right triangle equals the sum of the squares of the lengths of the other two sides

py•thon \ˈpī-ˌthän, -thən\ *n* : a large snake (as a boa) that squeezes and suffocates its prey; *esp* : any of the large Old World snakes that include the largest snakes living at the present time

pyx \ˈpiks\ *n* : a small case used to carry the Eucharist to the sick

Q

¹q \ˈkyü\ *n, pl* **q's** *or* **qs** \ˈkyüz\ *often cap* **:** the 17th letter of the English alphabet
²q *abbr, often cap* **1** quart **2** quarto **3** queen **4** query **5** question
QB *abbr* quarterback
QED *abbr* which was to be demonstrated
qi•vi•ut \ˈkē-vē-ˌüt\ *n* **:** the wool of the undercoat of the musk ox
Qld *abbr* Queensland
QM *abbr* quartermaster
QMC *abbr* quartermaster corps
QMG *abbr* quartermaster general
qq v *abbr* which (*pl*) see
qr *abbr* quarter
Q rating *n* **:** a scale measuring popularity based on dividing an assessment of familiarity or recognition by an assessment of favorable opinion; *also* **:** position on such a scale
qt *abbr* **1** quantity **2** quart
q.t. \ˌkyü-ˈtē\ *n, often cap Q&T* **:** QUIET — usually used in the phrase *on the q.t.*
qto *abbr* quarto
qty *abbr* quantity
qu *or* **ques** *abbr* question
¹quack \ˈkwak\ *vb* **:** to make the characteristic cry of a duck
²quack *n* **:** a sound made by quacking
³quack *n* **1** ♦ **:** one making usually showy pretenses to knowledge or ability **:** CHARLATAN **2 :** a pretender to medical skill — **quack** *adj* — **quack•ery** \ˈkwa-kə-rē\ *n* — **quack•ish** *adj*

♦ charlatan, fake, fraud, hoaxer, humbug, mountebank, phony, pretender

¹quad \ˈkwäd\ *n* **:** QUADRANGLE
²quad *n* **:** QUADRUPLET
³quad *abbr* quadrant
quad•ran•gle \ˈkwä-ˌdraŋ-gəl\ *n* **1 :** QUADRILATERAL **2** ♦ **:** a 4-sided courtyard or enclosure — **quad•ran•gu•lar** \kwä-ˈdraŋ-gyə-lər\ *adj*

♦ close, court, courtyard, yard

quad•rant \ˈkwä-drənt\ *n* **1 :** one quarter of a circle **:** an arc of 90° **2 :** any of the four quarters into which something is divided by two lines intersecting each other at right angles
qua•drat•ic \kwä-ˈdra-tik\ *adj* **:** having or being a term in which the variable (as *x*) is squared but containing no term in which the variable is raised to a higher power than a square ⟨a ∼ equation⟩ — **quadratic** *n*
qua•dren•ni•al \kwä-ˈdre-nē-əl\ *adj* **1 :** consisting of or lasting for four years **2 :** occurring every four years
qua•dren•ni•um \-nē-əm\ *n, pl* **-ni•ums** *or* **-nia** \-nē-ə\ **:** a period of four years
quad•ri•ceps \ˈkwä-drə-ˌseps\ *n* **:** a muscle of the front of the thigh that is divided into four parts
¹quad•ri•lat•er•al \ˌkwä-drə-ˈla-tə-rəl\ *n* **:** a polygon of four sides
²quadrilateral *adj* **:** having four sides
qua•drille \kwä-ˈdril, kə-\ *n* **:** a square dance made up of five or six figures in various rhythms
quad•ri•par•tite \ˌkwä-drə-ˈpär-ˌtīt\ *adj* **1 :** consisting of four parts **2 :** shared by four parties or persons
quad•ri•ple•gia \ˌkwä-drə-ˈplē-jə, -jē-ə\ *n* **:** paralysis of both arms and both legs — **quad•ri•ple•gic** \-jik\ *adj or n*
qua•driv•i•um \kwä-ˈdri-vē-əm\ *n* **:** the four liberal arts of arithmetic, music, geometry, and astronomy in a medieval university
quad•ru•ped \ˈkwä-drə-ˌped\ *n* **:** an animal having four feet — **qua•dru•pe•dal** \kwä-ˈdrü-pəd-ᵊl, ˌkwä-drə-ˈped-\ *adj*
¹qua•dru•ple \kwä-ˈdrü-pəl, -ˈdrə-; ˈkwä-drə-\ *vb* **qua•dru•pled; qua•dru•pling :** to make or become four times as great or as many
²quadruple *adj* **:** FOURFOLD
qua•dru•plet \kwä-ˈdrə-plət, -ˈdrü-; ˈkwä-drə-\ *n* **1 :** one of four offspring born at one birth **2 :** a group of four of a kind
¹qua•dru•pli•cate \kwä-ˈdrü-pli-kət\ *adj* **1 :** repeated four times **2 :** FOURTH
²qua•dru•pli•cate \-plə-ˌkāt\ *vb* **-cat•ed; -cat•ing 1 :** QUADRUPLE **2 :** to prepare in quadruplicate — **qua•dru•pli•ca•tion** \-ˌdrü-plə-ˈkā-shən\ *n*
³qua•dru•pli•cate \-ˈdrü-pli-kət\ *n* **1 :** four copies all alike ⟨typed in ∼⟩ **2 :** one of four like things
¹quaff \ˈkwäf, ˈkwaf\ *vb* ♦ **:** to drink deeply or repeatedly

♦ drink, guzzle, imbibe, sup, swig, toss

²quaff *n* ♦ **:** a drink quaffed

♦ draft, drag, drink, nip, shot, slug, snort, swallow, swig

quag•mire \ˈkwag-ˌmī(-ə)r, ˈkwäg-\ *n* **1 :** soft miry land that yields under the foot **2** ♦ **:** a difficult or trying situation **:** PREDICAMENT

♦ corner, fix, hole, jam, morass, pickle, predicament, spot

qua•hog \ˈkō-ˌhȯg, ˈkwȯ-, ˈkwō-, -ˌhäg\ *n* **:** a round thick-shelled edible No. American clam
quai \ˈkā\ *n* **:** QUAY
¹quail \ˈkwāl\ *n, pl* **quail** *or* **quails :** any of numerous small short-winged plump game birds (as a bobwhite) related to the domestic chicken
²quail *vb* **1** ♦ **:** to lose heart **:** COWER **2** ♦ **:** to recoil in dread or terror

♦ [1, 2] blench, cower, cringe, flinch, recoil, shrink, wince

quaint \ˈkwānt\ *adj* **1** ♦ **:** unusual or different in character or appearance **2** ♦ **:** pleasingly old-fashioned or unfamiliar — **quaint•ly** *adv* — **quaint•ness** *n*

♦ [1] bizarre, curious, odd, outré, peculiar, queer, quirky, remarkable, screwy, strange ♦ [2] antique, old-fashioned, old-time

¹quake \ˈkwāk\ *vb* **quaked; quak•ing 1** ♦ **:** to shake usually from shock or instability **2** ♦ **:** to tremble usually from cold or fear

♦ [1, 2] agitate, convulse, jolt, jounce, quiver, shake, shudder, vibrate, wobble

²quake *n* **:** a shaking or trembling; *esp* **:** EARTHQUAKE
Quak•er \ˈkwā-kər\ *n* **:** FRIEND 5
qual *abbr* quality
qual•i•fi•ca•tion \ˌkwä-lə-fə-ˈkā-shən\ *n* **1 :** LIMITATION, MODIFICATION **2** ♦ **:** a special skill that fits a person for some work or position **3** ♦ **:** a condition or standard that must be complied with

♦ [2] capability, command, credentials, expertise, mastery, proficiency ♦ [3] condition, provision, proviso, reservation, stipulation

qual•i•fied \ˈkwä-lə-ˌfīd\ *adj* **1** ♦ **:** fitted for a given purpose or job **2 :** limited in some way

♦ able, capable, competent, fit, good, suitable

qual•i•fi•er \ˈkwä-lə-ˌfī(-ə)r\ *n* **1 :** one that satisfies requirements **2 :** a word or word group that limits the meaning of another word or word group
qual•i•fy \ˈkwä-lə-ˌfī\ *vb* **-fied; -fy•ing 1 :** to reduce from a general to a particular form **:** MODIFY **2 :** to make less harsh **3 :** to limit the meaning of (as a noun) **4** ♦ **:** to fit by skill or training for some purpose **5** ♦ **:** to give or have a legal right to do something **6 :** to demonstrate the necessary ability ⟨∼ for the finals⟩

♦ [4] equip, fit, prepare, ready, season ♦ [5] accredit, authorize, certify, commission, empower, enable, invest, license

qual•i•ta•tive \ˈkwä-lə-ˌtā-tiv\ *adj* **:** of, relating to, or involving quality — **qual•i•ta•tive•ly** *adv*
¹qual•i•ty \ˈkwä-lə-tē\ *n, pl* **-ties 1 :** peculiar and essential character **:** NATURE **2** ♦ **:** degree of excellence **3** ♦ **:** high social status **4** ♦ **:** a distinguishing attribute

♦ [2] caliber (*or* calibre), class, grade, rate ♦ [3] class, rank, standing ♦ [4] attribute, character, characteristic, feature, mark, peculiarity, point, property, trait

²quality *adj* **:** being of high quality
qualm \ˈkwäm, ˈkwälm\ *n* **1 :** a sudden attack (as of nausea) **2** ♦ **:** a sudden feeling of doubt, fear, or uneasiness especially in not following one's conscience or better judgment

♦ compunction, doubt, misgiving, scruple, uneasiness

qualm•ish \ˈkwä-mish, ˈkwäl-\ *adj* **1 :** feeling qualms **:** NAUSEATED **2 :** overly scrupulous **:** SQUEAMISH **3 :** of, relating to, or producing qualms

quan•da•ry \ˈkwän-drē\ *n, pl* **-ries** : a state of perplexity or doubt
quan•ti•fy \ˈkwän-tə-ˌfī\ *vb* **-fied; -fy•ing** : to determine, express, or measure the quantity of — **quan•ti•fi•able** \ˌkwän-tə-ˈfī-ə-bəl\ *adj*
quan•ti•ta•tive \ˈkwän-tə-ˌtā-tiv\ *adj* : of, relating to, or involving quantity — **quan•ti•ta•tive•ly** *adv*
quan•ti•ty \ˈkwän-tə-tē\ *n, pl* **-ties** **1** : a determinate or estimated amount : AMOUNT, NUMBER **2** ♦ : a considerable amount

♦ abundance, deal, gobs, heap, loads, lot, pile, plenty, scads

quan•tize \ˈkwän-ˌtīz\ *vb* **quan•tized; quan•tiz•ing** : to subdivide (as energy) into small units
quan•tum \ˈkwän-təm\ *n, pl* **quan•ta** \-tə\ **1** : QUANTITY, AMOUNT **2** : an elemental unit of energy
[2]quantum *adj* **1** : LARGE, SIGNIFICANT **2** : relating to or employing the principles of quantum mechanics
quantum mechanics *n sing or pl* : a theory of matter based on the concept of possession of wave properties by elementary particles — **quantum mechanical** *adj* — **quantum mechanically** *adv*
quantum mechanics *n sing or pl* : a theory of matter based on the concept of possession of wave properties by elementary particles — **quantum mechanical** *adj* — **quantum mechanically** *adv*
quantum theory *n* : a theory in physics based on the idea that radiant energy (as light) is composed of small separate packets of energy
quar *abbr* quarterly
quar•an•tine \ˈkwȯr-ən-ˌtēn\ *n* **1** : a period during which a ship suspected of carrying contagious disease is forbidden contact with the shore **2** : a restraint on the movements of persons or goods to prevent the spread of pests or disease **3** : a place or period of quarantine **4** : a state of enforced isolation — **quarantine** *vb*
quark \ˈkwȯrk, ˈkwärk\ *n* : a hypothetical elementary particle that carries a fractional charge and is held to be a constituent of heavier particles (as protons and neutrons)
[1]quar•rel \ˈkwȯr-əl\ *n* **1** : a ground of dispute **2** ♦ : a verbal clash

♦ altercation, argument, bicker, brawl, disagreement, dispute, fight, hassle, misunderstanding, row, scrap, spat, squabble, wrangle

[2]quarrel *vb* **-reled** *or* **-relled; -rel•ing** *or* **-rel•ling** **1** : to find fault **2** ♦ : to dispute angrily : WRANGLE

♦ argue, bicker, brawl, dispute, fall out, fight, hassle, row, scrap, spat, squabble, wrangle

quar•rel•some \-səm\ *adj* ♦ : apt or disposed to quarrel in an often petty manner

♦ aggressive, argumentative, bellicose, belligerent, combative, contentious, discordant, disputatious, pugnacious, scrappy, truculent

[1]quar•ry \ˈkwȯr-ē\ *n, pl* **quarries** **1** : game hunted with hawks **2** : PREY
[2]quarry *n, pl* **quarries** : an open excavation usually for obtaining building stone or limestone — **quarry** *vb*
quart \ˈkwȯrt\ *n* **1** : a unit of liquid capacity equal to 1/4 gallon **2** : a unit of dry capacity equal to 1/32 bushel
[1]quar•ter \ˈkwȯr-tər\ *n* **1** : one of four equal parts **2** : a fourth of a dollar; *also* : a coin of this value **3** ♦ : a district of a city **4** *pl* ♦ : living accommodations ⟨moved into new ∼*s*⟩ **5** ♦ : merciful consideration of an opponent : MERCY ⟨gave no ∼⟩ **6** : a fourth part of the moon's period **7** ♦ : an assigned station or post

♦ [3] district, neighborhood (*or* neighbourhood), section ♦ **quarters** [4] abode, domicile, dwelling, home, house, lodging, place, residence ♦ [5] charity, clemency, leniency, mercy ♦ [7] position, post, station

[2]quarter *vb* **1** : to divide into four equal parts **2** ♦ : to provide with shelter

♦ accommodate, billet, chamber, domicile, harbor (*or* harbour), house, lodge, put up, roof, shelter, take in

[1]quar•ter•back \-ˌbak\ *n* : a football player who calls the signals and directs the offensive play for the team
[2]quarterback *vb* **1** : to direct the offensive play of a football team **2** : LEAD, BOSS
quar•ter•deck \-ˌdek\ *n* : the stern area of a ship's upper deck
quarter horse *n* : any of a breed of compact muscular saddle horses characterized by great endurance and by high speed for short distances
[1]quar•ter•ly \ˈkwȯr-tər-lē\ *adv* : at 3-month intervals
[2]quarterly *adj* : occurring, issued, or payable at 3-month intervals
[3]quarterly *n, pl* **-lies** : a periodical published four times a year
quar•ter•mas•ter \-ˌmas-tər\ *n* **1** : a petty officer who attends to a ship's helm, binnacle, and signals **2** : an army officer who provides clothing and subsistence for troops
quar•ter•staff \-ˌstaf\ *n, pl* **-staves** \-ˌstavz, -ˌstāvz\ : a long stout staff formerly used as a weapon
quar•tet *also* **quar•tette** \kwȯr-ˈtet\ *n* **1** : a musical composition for four instruments or voices **2** : a group of four and especially of four musicians
quar•to \ˈkwȯr-tō\ *n, pl* **quartos** **1** : the size of a piece of paper cut four from a sheet **2** : a book printed on quarto pages
quartz \ˈkwȯrts\ *n* : a common often transparent crystalline mineral that is a form of silica
quartz•ite \ˈkwȯrt-ˌsīt\ *n* : a compact granular rock composed of quartz and derived from sandstone
qua•sar \ˈkwā-ˌzär, -ˌsär\ *n* : any of a class of extremely distant starlike celestial objects
[1]quash \ˈkwäsh, ˈkwȯsh\ *vb* ♦ : to suppress or extinguish summarily and completely : QUELL

♦ clamp down, crack down, crush, put down, quell, repress, silence, snuff, squash, squelch, subdue, suppress

[2]quash *vb* ♦ : to set aside by judicial action

♦ abolish, abrogate, annul, cancel, dissolve, invalidate, negate, nullify, repeal, rescind, void

qua•si \ˈkwā-ˌzī, -ˌsī; ˈkwä-zē, -sē\ *adj* : being in some sense or degree ⟨a ∼ corporation⟩
quasi- *comb form* : in some sense or degree ⟨*quasi*-historical⟩
qua•si–gov•ern•men•tal \-gə-vərn-ˈmen-tᵊl\ *adj* : supported by the government but managed privately
Qua•ter•na•ry \ˈkwä-tər-ˌner-ē, kwə-ˈtər-nə-rē\ *adj* : of, relating to, or being the geologic period from the end of the Tertiary to the present — **Quaternary** *n*
Qua•ter•na•ry \ˈkwä-tər-ˌner-ē, kwə-ˈtər-nə-rē\ *adj* : of, relating to, or being the geologic period from the end of the Tertiary to the present — **Quaternary** *n*
qua•train \ˈkwä-ˌtrān\ *n* : a unit of four lines of verse
qua•tre•foil \ˈka-tər-ˌfȯil, ˈka-trə-\ *n* : a stylized figure often of a flower with four petals
qua•ver \ˈkwā-vər\ *vb* **1** : TREMBLE, SHAKE **2** : TRILL **3** : to speak in tremulous tones — **quaver** *n*
quay \ˈkē, ˈkwā, ˈkā\ *n* ♦ : a structure built parallel to the bank of a waterway for use as a landing place : WHARF

♦ dock, float, jetty, landing, levee, pier, wharf

Que *abbr* Quebec
quean \ˈkwēn\ *n* : PROSTITUTE
quea•si•ness \ˈkwē-zē-nəs\ *n* ♦ : the quality or state of being queasy

♦ nausea, sickness, squeamishness

quea•sy \ˈkwē-zē\ *adj* **quea•si•er; -est** ♦ : suffering from nausea : NAUSEATED — **quea•si•ly** \-zə-lē\ *adv*

♦ ill, nauseous, queer, sick, squeamish

Que•chua \ˈke-chə-wə, ˈkech-wə\ *n* : a family of languages spoken in Peru and adjacent countries of the So. American Andes
queen \ˈkwēn\ *n* **1** : the wife or widow of a king **2** : a female monarch **3** ♦ : a woman notable for rank, power, or attractiveness **4** : the most powerful piece in the game of chess **5** : a playing card bearing the figure of a queen **6** : a fertile female of a social insect (as a bee or termite)

♦ beauty, enchantress, fox, goddess, knockout

Queen Anne's lace \-ˈanz-\ *n* : a widely naturalized Eurasian herb from which the cultivated carrot originated
queen consort *n, pl* **queens consort** : the wife of a reigning king
queen•ly *adj* ♦ : of, relating to, suggestive of, or characteristic of a monarch or monarchy

♦ monarchical, regal, royal

queen mother *n* : a dowager queen who is mother of the reigning sovereign
queen–size *adj* : having dimensions of approximately 60 inches by 80 inches ⟨∼ bed⟩; *also* : of a size that fits a queen-size bed
[1]queer \ˈkwir\ *adj* **1** ♦ : differing from the usual or normal : PECULIAR, STRANGE **2** : COUNTERFEIT **3** ♦ : not quite well — **queer** *n* — **queer•ly** *adv* — **queer•ness** *n*

♦ [1] curious, extraordinary, funny, odd, peculiar, rare, strange, unaccustomed, uncommon, unique, unusual, weird ♦ [3] ill, nauseous, queasy, sick, squeamish

[2]queer *vb* : to spoil the effect of : DISRUPT ⟨∼*ed* our plans⟩

queer theory *n* : an approach to literary and cultural study that rejects traditional categories of gender and sexuality
quell \ˈkwel\ *vb* **1** ♦ : to put an end to by force ⟨~ a riot⟩ **2** ♦ : to cause to be quiet

♦ [1] clamp down, crack down, crush, put down, quash, repress, silence, snuff, squash, squelch, subdue, suppress ♦ [2] hush, mute, settle, silence, still

quench \ˈkwench\ *vb* **1** ♦ : to put out the light or fire of : PUT OUT, EXTINGUISH **2** : SUBDUE **3** ♦ : to bring (something immaterial) to an end typically by satisfying, damping, cooling, or decreasing : SATISFY ⟨~*ed* his thirst⟩ — **quench•able** *adj* — **quench•less** *adj*

♦ [1] douse, extinguish, put out, snuff ♦ [3] assuage, sate, satiate, satisfy

quench•er *n* ♦ : a satisfying drink

♦ beverage, drink, libation

quer•u•lous \ˈkwer-ə-ləs, -yə-\ *adj* **1** ♦ : constantly complaining **2** : FRETFUL, WHINING — **quer•u•lous•ly** *adv* — **quer•u•lous•ness** *n*

♦ crabby, cranky, fussy, grouchy, grumpy, peevish, petulant

[1]**que•ry** \ˈkwir-ē, ˈkwer-\ *n, pl* **queries** ♦ : the action or an instance of asking : QUESTION

♦ call, inquiry, question, request

[2]**query** *vb* **1** ♦ : to ask questions about especially in order to resolve a doubt **2** ♦ : to ask questions of especially with a desire for authoritative information

♦ [1] challenge, contest, dispute, question ♦ [2] ask, examine, grill, inquire of, interrogate, pump, question, quiz

que•sa•dil•la \ˌkā-sə-ˈdē-ə\ *n* : a tortilla filled with a savory mixture, folded, and usually fried
[1]**quest** \ˈkwest\ *n* : SEARCH
[2]**quest** *vb* **1** ♦ : to search for **2** ♦ : to ask for

♦ [1] cast about, forage, hunt, pursue, search (for *or* out), seek ♦ [2] ask, call, plead, request, seek, solicit, sue

[1]**ques•tion** \ˈkwes-chən\ *n* **1** : an interrogative expression : QUERY **2** : a subject for debate; *also* : a proposition to be voted on **3** ♦ : an act or instance of asking : INQUIRY **4** ♦ : a subject or aspect in dispute or open for discussion **5** ♦ : a reason or argument presented in opposition : a feeling or expression of disapproval

♦ [3] call, inquiry, query, request ♦ [4] content, matter, motif, motive, subject, theme, topic ♦ [5] challenge, complaint, demur, expostulation, fuss, kick, objection, protest, remonstrance

[2]**question** *vb* **1** ♦ : to ask questions **2** ♦ : to engage in argument : DISPUTE **3** ♦ : to subject to analysis **4** ♦ : to lack confidence in

♦ [1] ask, examine, grill, inquire of, interrogate, pump, query, quiz ♦ [2] challenge, contest, dispute, query ♦ [3] chew over, cogitate, consider, contemplate, debate, deliberate, entertain, meditate, mull, ponder, ruminate, study, think, weigh ♦ [4] distrust, doubt, mistrust, suspect

ques•tion•able \ˈkwes-chə-nə-bəl\ *adj* **1** ♦ : not certain or exact : DOUBTFUL **2** ♦ : not believed to be true, sound, or moral — **ques•tion•ably** \-blē\ *adv*

♦ [1] arguable, debatable, disputable, doubtful, dubious, equivocal, fishy, problematic, shady, shaky, suspect, suspicious ♦ [2] doubtful, dubious, flimsy, improbable, unlikely

ques•tion•er *n* ♦ : one that questions

♦ disbeliever, doubter, skeptic, unbeliever

question mark *n* : a punctuation mark ? used especially at the end of a sentence to indicate a direct question
ques•tion•naire \ˌkwes-chə-ˈnar\ *n* : a set of questions for obtaining information
quet•zal \ket-ˈsäl, -ˈsal\ *n, pl* **quetzals** *or* **quet•za•les** \-ˈsä-lās, -ˈsa-\ : a Central American bird with brilliant plumage
[1]**queue** \ˈkyü\ *n* **1** : a braid of hair usually worn hanging at the back of the head **2** ♦ : a waiting line (as of persons)

♦ column, cue, file, line, range, string, train

[2]**queue** *vb* **queued; queu•ing** *or* **queue•ing** : to line up in a queue
[1]**quib•ble** \ˈkwi-bəl\ *n* **1** : an evasion of or shifting from the point at issue **2** : a minor objection or criticism — **quib•bler** *n*
[2]**quibble** *vb* ♦ : to criticize or object to something on trivial grounds

♦ carp, cavil, fuss

[1]**quick** \ˈkwik\ *adj* **1** : LIVING **2** ♦ : acting or capable of acting with speed ⟨~ steps⟩ **3** ♦ : prompt to understand, think, or perceive : ALERT **4** : easily aroused ⟨a ~ temper⟩ **5** : turning or bending sharply ⟨a ~ turn in the road⟩

♦ [2] alert, expeditious, prompt, ready, willing ♦ [2] brisk, fast, fleet, hasty, rapid, snappy, speedy, swift ♦ [3] alert, brainy, bright, brilliant, clever, intelligent, keen, nimble, quick-witted, sharp, smart

[2]**quick** *adv* ♦ : in a quick manner

♦ apace, briskly, fast, full tilt, hastily, posthaste, presto, pronto, quickly, rapidly, soon, speedily, swift, swiftly

[3]**quick** *n* **1** : a sensitive area of living flesh **2** : a vital part : HEART **3** ♦ : the inmost sensibilities

♦ core, heart, soul

quick bread *n* : a bread made with a leavening agent that permits immediate baking of the dough or batter
quick•en \ˈkwi-kən\ *vb* **1** : to come to life : REVIVE **2** ♦ : to cause to be enlivened : STIMULATE **3** ♦ : to increase in speed : HASTEN **4** : to show vitality (as by growing or moving)

♦ [2] animate, brace, energize, enliven, fire, invigorate, jazz up, liven up, pep up, stimulate, vitalize, vivify, zip (up) ♦ [3] accelerate, hasten, hurry, rush, speed (up), step up, whisk

quick–freeze \ˈkwik-ˈfrēz\ *vb* **-froze** \-ˈfrōz\; **-fro•zen** \-ˈfrōz-ᵊn\; **-freez•ing** : to freeze (food) for preservation so rapidly that the natural juices and flavor are not lost
quick•ie \ˈkwi-kē\ *n* : something hurriedly done or made
quick•lime \ˈkwik-ˌlīm\ *n* : [1]LIME
quick•ly *adv* ♦ : in a quick manner

♦ apace, briskly, fast, full tilt, hastily, posthaste, presto, pronto, quick, rapidly, soon, speedily, swift, swiftly

quick•ness *n* ♦ : the quality or state of being quick

♦ celerity, fastness, fleetness, haste, hurry, rapidity, speed, swiftness, velocity

quick•sand \-ˌsand\ *n* : a deep mass of loose sand mixed with water
quick•sil•ver \-ˌsil-vər\ *n* : MERCURY 1
quick•step \-ˌstep\ *n* : a spirited march tune or dance
quick–wit•ted \ˈkwik-ˈwi-təd\ *adj* ♦ : mentally alert

♦ alert, brainy, bright, brilliant, clever, intelligent, keen, nimble, quick, sharp, smart

quid \ˈkwid\ *n* : a lump of something chewable ⟨a ~ of tobacco⟩
quid pro quo \ˌkwid-ˌprō-ˈkwō\ *n* : something given or received for something else
qui•es•cence \kwī-ˈes-ᵊns\ *n* ♦ : the quality or state of being quiescent

♦ abeyance, doldrums, dormancy, latency, suspension ♦ dormancy, idleness, inaction, inactivity, inertness

qui•es•cent \kwī-ˈes-ᵊnt\ *adj* ♦ : being at rest : QUIET

♦ dull, inactive, inert, lethargic, quiet, sleepy, sluggish, torpid

[1]**qui•et** \ˈkwī-ət\ *n* ♦ : the quality or state of being quiet : REPOSE

♦ calm, calmness, hush, peace, placidity, quietness, repose, serenity, silence, still, stillness, tranquillity

[2]**quiet** *adj* **1** ♦ : marked by little motion or activity : CALM **2** : GENTLE, MILD ⟨a ~ disposition⟩ **3** : enjoyed in peace and relaxation ⟨a ~ cup of tea⟩ **4** ♦ : free from noise or uproar **5** ♦ : not showy : MODEST ⟨~ clothes⟩ **6** ♦ : screened or hidden from view : SECLUDED ⟨a ~ nook⟩

♦ [1, 4] calm, hushed, noiseless, peaceful, restful, serene, silent, soundless, still, tranquil ***Ant*** boisterous, clamorous, deafening, loud, noisy, raucous, roistering, romping, rowdy, tumultuous, uproarious, woolly ♦ [5] conservative, muted, restrained, subdued, unpretentious ***Ant*** flamboyant, flashy, garish, gaudy, glitzy, loud, ostentatious, swank, tawdry ♦ [6] cloistered, covert, isolated, remote, secluded, secret

[3]**quiet** *adv* : QUIETLY
[4]**quiet** *vb* **1** ♦ : to cause to be quiet : CALM **2** ♦ : to become quiet — often used with *down* ⟨~ down⟩

♦ [1] allay, calm, compose, settle, soothe, still, tranquilize ♦ *often* **quite down** [2] calm (down), cool (off *or* down), hush, settle (down) ***Ant*** act up, carry on, cut up

qui•et•ly *adv* ♦ : in a quiet manner

♦ calmly, quiet, still

qui•et•ness *n* ♦ : the quality or state of being quiet

♦ calm, calmness, hush, peace, placidity, quiet, repose, serenity, silence, still, stillness, tranquillity

qui•etude \ˈkwī-ə-ˌtüd, -ˌtyüd\ *n* : a quiet state : QUIETNESS, REPOSE

qui•etus \kwī-ˈē-təs\ *n* **1** ♦ : final settlement (as of a debt) **2** ♦ : removal from activity : DEATH

♦ [1] delivery, discharge, quittance, release ♦ [2] death, decease, demise, doom, end, passing

quill \ˈkwil\ *n* **1** : a large stiff feather; *also* : the hollow tubular part of a feather **2** : one of the hollow sharp spines of a hedgehog or porcupine **3** : a pen made from a feather

¹quilt \ˈkwilt\ *n* : a padded bed coverlet

²quilt *vb* **1** : to fill, pad, or line like a quilt **2** : to stitch or sew in layers with padding in between **3** : to make quilts

quince \ˈkwins\ *n* : a hard yellow applelike fruit; *also* : a tree related to the roses that bears this fruit

qui•nine \ˈkwī-ˌnīn\ *n* : a bitter white drug obtained from cinchona bark and used especially in treating malaria

qui•noa \ˈkēn-ˌwä, kē-ˈnō-ə\ *n* : the starchy seeds of an annual herb related to spinach which are used as food and ground into flour; *also* : this herb

quint \ˈkwint\ *n* : QUINTUPLET

quin•tal \ˈkwint-ᵊl, ˈkant-\ *n* : HUNDREDWEIGHT

quin•tes•sence \kwin-ˈtes-ᵊns\ *n* **1** ♦ : the purest essence of something **2** ♦ : the most typical example — **quin•tes•sen•tial•ly** *adv*

♦ [1] essence, nature, soul, stuff, substance ♦ [2] beau ideal, classic, epitome, exemplar, ideal, perfection

quint•es•sen•tial \ˌkwin-tə-ˈsen-chəl\ *adj* ♦ : being a quintessence

♦ classic, model, paradigmatic

quin•tet *also* **quin•tette** \kwin-ˈtet\ *n* **1** : a musical composition for five instruments or voices **2** : a group of five and especially of five musicians

¹quin•tu•ple \kwin-ˈtü-pəl, -ˈtyü-, -ˈtə-\ *adj* **1** : having five units or members **2** : being five times as great or as many — **quintuple** *n*

²quintuple *vb* **quin•tu•pled; quin•tu•pling** : to make or become five times as great or as many

quin•tu•plet \kwin-ˈtə-plət, -ˈtü-, -ˈtyü-\ *n* **1** : a group of five of a kind **2** : one of five offspring born at one birth

¹quin•tu•pli•cate \kwin-ˈtü-pli-kət, -ˈtyü-\ *adj* **1** : repeated five times **2** : FIFTH

²quintuplicate *n* **1** : one of five like things **2** : five copies all alike ⟨typed in ~⟩

³quin•tu•pli•cate \-plə-ˌkāt\ *vb* **-cat•ed; -cat•ing** **1** : QUINTUPLE **2** : to provide in quintuplicate

¹quip \ˈkwip\ *n* ♦ : a clever remark

♦ crack, gag, jest, joke, laugh, pleasantry, sally, waggery, wisecrack, witticism

²quip *vb* **quipped; quip•ping** **1** ♦ : to make quips : GIBE **2** ♦ : to jest or gibe at

♦ [1, 2] banter, fool, fun, gibe, jest, jive, joke, josh, kid, wisecrack

quire \ˈkwī(-ə)r\ *n* : a set of 24 or sometimes 25 sheets of paper of the same size and quality

quirk \ˈkwərk\ *n* ♦ : a peculiarity of action or behavior

♦ crotchet, eccentricity, idiosyncrasy, mannerism, oddity, peculiarity, singularity, trick

quirky *adj* ♦ : full of quirks

♦ bizarre, curious, far-out, funny, kinky, odd, outlandish, outré, peculiar, quaint, queer, remarkable, screwy, strange, wacky, weird, wild

quirt \ˈkwərt\ *n* : a riding whip with a short handle and a rawhide lash

quis•ling \ˈkwiz-liŋ\ *n* ♦ : one who helps the invaders of one's own country : one who commits treason

♦ apostate, betrayer, double-crosser, recreant, traitor, turncoat

quit \ˈkwit\ *vb* **quit** *also* **quit•ted; quit•ting** **1** : to conduct (oneself) usually satisfactorily especially under stress : CONDUCT, BEHAVE ⟨~ themselves well⟩ **2 a** : to depart from : LEAVE **b** ♦ : to bring to an end **3** ♦ : to give up for good ⟨~ smoking⟩ ⟨~ my job⟩ **4** : to leave the company of **5** ♦ : to admit defeat **6** : to make full payment of — **quit•ter** *n*

♦ [2b] break, break off, cease, cut, desist, discontinue, drop, end, halt, knock off, layoff, leave off, shut off, stop ♦ [3] leave, resign, retire, step down *Ant* stay (at) ♦ [3] discontinue, drop, give up, knock off, lay off *Ant* carry on, continue, keep, keep up, maintain ♦ [5] bow, budge, capitulate, concede, give in, knuckle under, submit, succumb, surrender, yield

quite \ˈkwīt\ *adv* **1** ♦ : to a complete degree : COMPLETELY **2** : to an extreme : POSITIVELY **3** ♦ : to a considerable extent : RATHER

♦ [1] altogether, completely, dead, entirely, fast, flat, full, fully, perfectly, thoroughly, well, wholly ♦ [3] enough, fairly, kind of, moderately, pretty, rather, so-so, somewhat, sort of

quits \ˈkwits\ *adj* : even or equal with another ⟨call it ~⟩

quit•tance \ˈkwit-ᵊns\ *n* **1** ♦ : something given in return, compensation, or retaliation : REQUITAL **2** ♦ : discharge from a debt or an obligation

♦ [1] compensation, damages, indemnity, recompense, redress, remuneration, reparation, requital, restitution, satisfaction ♦ [2] delivery, discharge, quietus, release

¹quiv•er \ˈkwi-vər\ *n* : a case for carrying arrows

²quiver *vb* **quiv•ered; quiv•er•ing** ♦ : to shake with a slight trembling motion — **quiv•er•ing•ly** *adv*

♦ agitate, convulse, jolt, jounce, quake, shake, shudder, vibrate, wobble

³quiver *n* : the act or action of quivering : TREMOR

quiv•er•ing \ˈkwi-v(ə-)riŋ\ *n* ♦ : the action or condition of one that trembles

♦ oscillation, vibration

qui vive \kē-ˈvēv\ *n* : ALERT ⟨on the *qui vive* for prowlers⟩

quix•ot•ic \kwik-ˈsä-tik\ *adj* : foolishly impractical especially in the pursuit of ideals — **quix•ot•i•cal•ly** \-ti-kə-lē\ *adv*

¹quiz \ˈkwiz\ *n, pl* **quiz•zes** **1** : an eccentric person **2** : PRACTICAL JOKE **3** ♦ : a short oral or written test **4** ♦ : a person who ridicules or mocks

♦ [3] examination, test ♦ [4] heckler, mocker, scoffer, taunter, tease

²quiz *vb* **quizzed; quiz•zing** **1** : MOCK **2** : to look at inquisitively **3** ♦ : to question closely

♦ ask, examine, grill, inquire of, interrogate, pump, query, question

quiz•zi•cal \ˈkwi-zi-kəl\ *adj* **1** : comically quaint **2** : mildly teasing or mocking **3** : expressive of puzzlement, curiosity, or disbelief

quoit \ˈkwāt, ˈkwȯit, ˈkȯit\ *n* **1** : a flattened ring of iron or circle of rope used in a throwing game **2** *pl* : a game in which quoits are thrown at an upright pin in an attempt to ring the pin

quon•dam \ˈkwän-dəm, -ˌdam\ *adj* : FORMER

quo•rum \ˈkwōr-əm\ *n* : the number of members required to be present for business to be legally transacted

quot *abbr* quotation

quo•ta \ˈkwō-tə\ *n* ♦ : a proportional part especially when assigned : SHARE

♦ allotment, allowance, cut, part, portion, proportion, share

quot•able \ˈkwō-tə-bəl\ *adj* : fit for or worth quoting — **quot•abil•i•ty** \-ˈbi-lə-tē\ *n*

quo•ta•tion \kwō-ˈtā-shən\ *n* **1** : the act or process of quoting **2** : the price currently bid or offered for something **3** : something that is quoted

quotation mark *n* : one of a pair of punctuation marks " " or ' ' used especially to indicate the beginning and end of a quotation in which exact phraseology is directly cited

quote \ˈkwōt\ *vb* **quot•ed; quot•ing** **1 a** ♦ : to speak or write a passage from another usually with acknowledgment **b** ♦ : to repeat a passage in substantiation or illustration **2** : to state the market price of a commodity, stock, or bond **3** : to inform a hearer or reader that matter following is quoted — **quote** *n*

♦ [1a] advert (to), cite, instance, mention, name, note, notice, refer (to), specify, touch (*on* or *upon*) ♦ [1b] adduce, cite, instance, mention

quoth \ˈkwōth\ *vb past, archaic* : SAID — usually used in the 1st and 3d persons with the subject following

quo•tid•i•an \kwō-ˈti-dē-ən\ *adj* **1** : DAILY **2** : COMMONPLACE, ORDINARY

quo•tient \ˈkwō-shənt\ *n* : the number obtained by dividing one number by another

qv *abbr* which see

qy *abbr* query

R

[1]**r** \ˈär\ *n, pl* **r's** *or* **rs** \ˈärz\ *often cap* **:** the 18th letter of the English alphabet
[2]**r** *abbr, often cap* **1** rabbi **2** radius **3** rare **4** Republican **5** rerun **6** resistance **7** right **8** river **9** roentgen **10** rook **11** run
Ra *symbol* radium
RA *abbr* **1** regular army **2** Royal Academy
[1]**rab•bet** \ˈra-bət\ *n* **:** a groove in the edge or face of a surface (as a board) especially to receive another piece
[2]**rabbet** *vb* **:** to cut a rabbet in; *also* **:** to join by means of a rabbet
rab•bi \ˈra-ˌbī\ *n* **1 :** MASTER, TEACHER — used by Jews as a term of address **2 :** a Jew trained and ordained for professional religious leadership — **rab•bin•ic** \rə-ˈbi-nik\ *or* **rab•bin•i•cal** \-ni-kəl\ *adj*
rab•bin•ate \ˈra-bə-nət, -ˌnāt\ *n* **1 :** the office of a rabbi **2 :** the whole body of rabbis
rab•bit \ˈra-bət\ *n, pl* **rabbit** *or* **rabbits :** any of various long-eared short-tailed burrowing mammals distinguished from the related hares by being blind, furless, and helpless at birth; *also* **:** the pelt of a rabbit
rabbit ears *n pl* **:** an indoor V-shaped television antenna
rabble \ˈra-bəl\ *n* **1 :** MOB 2 **2** ◆ **:** the lowest class of people

◆ riffraff, scum, trash *Ant* aristocracy, elite, gentry, society, upper class, upper crust

rab•ble–rous•er \ˈra-bəl-ˌrau̇-zər\ *n* ◆ **:** one that stirs up (as to hatred or violence) the masses of the people

◆ agitator, demagogue, firebrand, incendiary, inciter

ra•bid \ˈra-bəd\ *adj* **1** ◆ **:** extremely violent **:** FURIOUS **2** ◆ **:** being fanatical or extreme **3 :** affected with rabies — **ra•bid•ly** *adv*

◆ [1] angry, boiling, enraged, fierce, frenzied, furious, irate, mad, sore, violent ◆ [2] extreme, extremist, fanatic, radical, revolutionary, ultra

ra•bies \ˈrā-bēz\ *n, pl* **rabies :** an acute deadly virus disease of the nervous system transmitted by the bite of an affected animal
rac•coon \ra-ˈkün\ *n, pl* **raccoon** *or* **raccoons :** a gray No. American chiefly tree-dwelling mammal with a black mask, a bushy ringed tail, and nocturnal habits; *also* **:** its pelt
[1]**race** \ˈrās\ *n* **1 :** a strong current of running water; *also* **:** its channel **2 :** an onward course (as of time or life) **3 :** a contest of speed **4 :** a contest for a desired end (as election to office)
[2]**race** *vb* **raced; rac•ing 1 :** to run in a race **2** ◆ **:** to run swiftly **:** RUSH **3** ◆ **:** to engage in a race with **4 :** to drive or ride at high speed — **rac•er** *n*

◆ [1] barrel, career, course, dash, fly, hasten, hurry, hurtle, hustle, pelt, rip, rocket, run, rush, shoot, speed, tear, whirl, whisk, zip, zoom ◆ [3] battle, compete, contend, fight, vie

[3]**race** *n* **1** ◆ **:** a family, tribe, people, or nation of the same stock **2 :** a group of individuals within a biological species able to breed together **3 :** a category of humankind that shares certain distinctive physical traits — **ra•cial** \ˈrā-shəl\ *adj* — **ra•cial•ly** *adv*

◆ blood, clan, family, folks, house, kin, kindred, kinfolk, line, lineage, people, stock, tribe

race•course \ˈrās-ˌkōrs\ *n* **:** a course for racing
race•horse \-ˌhȯrs\ *n* **:** a horse bred or kept for racing
ra•ceme \rā-ˈsēm\ *n* **:** a flower cluster with flowers borne along a stem and blooming from the base toward the tip — **rac•e•mose** \ˈra-sə-ˌmōs\ *adj*
race•track \ˈrās-ˌtrak\ *n* **:** a usually oval course on which races are run
race•way \-ˌwā\ *n* **1** ◆ **:** a channel for a current of water **2 :** RACECOURSE

◆ aqueduct, canal, channel, conduit, flume, watercourse

ra•cial \ˈrā-shəl\ *adj* **1 :** of, relating to, or based on a race ⟨a ~ minority⟩ **2 :** existing or occurring between races ⟨~ equality⟩ — **ra•cial•ly** \-shə-lē\ *adv*
ra•cial•ism \ˈrā-shə-ˌli-zəm\ *n* **:** a theory that race determines human traits and capacities; *also* **:** RACISM — **ra•cial•ist** \-list\ *n* — **ra•cial•is•tic** \ˌrā-shə-ˈlis-tik\ *adj*
ra•cial•ize \ˈrā-shə-ˌlīz\ *vb* **–ized; -iz•ing :** to give a racial character to
racing form *n* **:** a paper giving data about racehorses for use by bettors
rac•ism \ˈrā-ˌsi-zəm\ *n* **:** a belief that some races are by nature superior to others; *also* **:** discrimination based on such belief — **rac•ist** \-sist\ *n*
[1]**rack** \ˈrak\ *n* **1 :** an instrument of torture on which a body is stretched **2 :** a framework on or in which something may be placed (as for display or storage) **3 :** a bar with teeth on one side to mesh with a pinion or worm gear
[2]**rack** *vb* **1 :** to torture on or as if on a rack **2** ◆ **:** to stretch or strain by force **3** ◆ **:** to cause to suffer torture, pain, anguish, or ruin **:** TORMENT **4 :** to place on or in a rack

◆ [2] pull, strain, stretch, wrench ◆ [3] afflict, agonize, bedevil, curse, harrow, martyr, persecute, plague, torment, torture

[1]**rack•et** *or* **rac•quet** \ˈra-kət\ *n* **:** a light bat made of netting stretched in an oval open frame having a handle and used for striking a ball or shuttlecock
[2]**racket** *n* **1** ◆ **:** confused noise **:** DIN **2** ◆ **:** a fraudulent or dishonest scheme or activity

◆ [1] bluster, cacophony, clamor (*or* clamour), din, noise, roar ◆ [2] hustle, swindle

[3]**racket** *vb* **:** to make a racket
rack•e•teer \ˌra-kə-ˈtir\ *n* ◆ **:** a person who obtains money by an illegal enterprise usually involving intimidation — **rack•e•teer•ing** *n*

◆ extortionist

rack up *vb* **:** ACCUMULATE, GAIN
ra•con•teur \ˌra-ˌkän-ˈtər\ *n* **:** one good at telling anecdotes
rac•quet•ball \ˈra-kət-ˌbȯl\ *n* **:** a game similar to handball that is played on a 4-walled court with a short-handled racket
racy \ˈrā-sē\ *adj* **rac•i•er; -est 1** ◆ **:** full of zest **2 :** PUNGENT, SPICY **3** ◆ **:** verging on impropriety or indecency **:** RISQUÉ, SUGGESTIVE — **rac•i•ly** \ˈrā-sə-lē\ *adv* — **rac•i•ness** \-sē-nəs\ *n*

◆ [1] active, animate, animated, brisk, energetic, frisky, gay, jaunty, jazzy, lively, peppy, perky, pert, snappy, spirited, sprightly, springy, vital, vivacious ◆ [3] bawdy, lewd, ribald, risqué, spicy, suggestive

rad *abbr* **1** radical **2** radio **3** radius
ra•dar \ˈrā-ˌdär\ *n* **:** a device that emits radio waves for detecting and locating an object by the reflection of the radio waves and that may use this reflection to determine the object's direction and speed
radar gun *n* **:** a handheld device that uses radar to measure the speed of a moving object
ra•dar•scope \ˈrā-ˌdär-ˌskōp\ *n* **:** a visual display for a radar receiver
[1]**ra•di•al** \ˈrā-dē-əl\ *adj* **:** arranged or having parts arranged like rays around a common center ⟨the ~ form of a starfish⟩ — **ra•di•al•ly** *adv*
[2]**radial** *n* **:** a pneumatic tire with cords laid perpendicular to the center line
radial engine *n* **:** an internal combustion engine with cylinders arranged radially like the spokes of a wheel
ra•di•an \ˈrā-dē-ən\ *n* **:** a unit of measure for angles that is equal to approximately 57.3 degrees
ra•di•ance \-əns\ *n* ◆ **:** the quality or state of being radiant

◆ brilliance, dazzle, effulgence, illumination, lightness, lucidity, luminosity, refulgence, splendor ◆ blaze, flare, fluorescence, glare, gleam, glow, illumination, incandescence, light, luminescence, shine

ra•di•ant \ˈrā-dē-ənt\ *adj* **1** ◆ **:** vividly bright and shining **:** GLOWING **2** ◆ **:** beaming with happiness **3 :** transmitted by radiation — **ra•di•ant•ly** *adv*

◆ [1] beaming, bright, brilliant, effulgent, glowing, incandescent, lambent, lucent, lucid, luminous, lustrous, refulgent, shiny ◆ [2] aglow, beaming, glowing, sunny

radiant energy *n* **:** energy traveling as electromagnetic waves
ra•di•ate \ˈrā-dē-ˌāt\ *vb* **-at•ed; -at•ing 1 :** to send out rays

: SHINE, GLOW **2 :** to issue in or as if in rays ⟨light ~*s*⟩ **3** ♦ **:** to spread around as from a center

♦ branch, diverge, fan *Ant* concentrate, converge, focus, funnel, meet

ra•di•a•tion \ˌrā-dē-ˈā-shən\ *n* **1 :** the action or process of radiating **2 :** the process of emitting radiant energy in the form of waves or particles; *also* **:** something (as an X-ray beam) that is radiated

radiation sickness *n* **:** sickness that results from exposure to radiation and is commonly marked by fatigue, nausea, vomiting, loss of teeth and hair, and in more severe cases by damage to blood-forming tissue

radiation therapy *n* **:** RADIOTHERAPY

ra•di•a•tor \ˈrā-dē-ˌā-tər\ *n* **:** any of various devices (as a set of pipes or tubes) for transferring heat from a fluid within to an area or object outside

¹rad•i•cal \ˈra-di-kəl\ *adj* **1 :** FUNDAMENTAL, EXTREME, THOROUGHGOING **2 :** of or relating to radicals in politics **3** ♦ **:** marked by a considerable departure from the usual or traditional — **rad•i•cal•ism** \-kə-ˌli-zəm\ *n* — **rad•i•cal•ly** *adv*

♦ extreme, extremist, fanatic, rabid, revolutionary, ultra ♦ broad-minded, liberal, nonorthodox, nontraditional, open-minded, progressive, unconventional, unorthodox

²radical *n* **1** ♦ **:** a person who favors rapid and sweeping changes in laws and methods of government **2 :** FREE RADICAL; *also* **:** a group of atoms considered as a unit in certain reactions or as a subunit of a larger molecule **3 :** a mathematical expression indicating a root by means of a radical sign; *also* **:** RADICAL SIGN

♦ extremist, revolutionary *Ant* moderate

rad•i•cal•ise *chiefly Brit var of* RADICALIZE

rad•i•cal•ize \-kə-ˌlīz\ *vb* **-ized; -iz•ing :** to make radical especially in politics — **rad•i•cal•i•za•tion** \ˌra-di-kə-lə-ˈzā- shən\ *n*

radical sign *n* **:** the sign √ placed before a mathematical expression to indicate that its root is to be taken

ra•dic•chio \ra-ˈdi-kē-ō\ *n, pl* **–chios :** a chicory with reddish variegated leaves

radii *pl of* RADIUS

¹ra•dio \ˈrā-dē-ˌō\ *n, pl* **ra•di•os 1 :** the wireless transmission or reception of signals using electromagnetic waves **2 :** a radio receiving set **3 :** the radio broadcasting industry — **radio** *adj*

²radio *vb* **:** to communicate or send a message to by radio

ra•dio•ac•tiv•i•ty \ˌrā-dē-ō-ˌak-ˈti-və-tē\ *n* **:** the property that some elements or isotopes have of spontaneously emitting energetic particles by the disintegration of their atomic nuclei — **ra•dio•ac•tive** \-ˈak-tiv\ *adj*

radio astronomy *n* **:** astronomy dealing with radio waves received from outside the earth's atmosphere

ra•dio•car•bon \ˌrā-dē-ō-ˈkär-bən\ *n* **:** CARBON 14

radio frequency *n* **:** an electromagnetic wave frequency intermediate between audio frequencies and infrared frequencies used especially for communication and radar signals

ra•dio•gram \ˈrā-dē-ō-ˌgram\ *n* **:** a message transmitted by radio

ra•dio•graph \-ˌgraf\ *n* **:** a photograph made by some form of radiation other than light; *esp* **:** an X-ray photograph — **radi•ograph** *vb* — **ra•dio•graph•ic** \ˌrā-dē-ō-ˈgra-fik\ *adj* — **ra•dio•graph•i•cal•ly** \-fi-k(ə-)lē\ *adv* — **ra•di•og•ra•phy** \ˌrā-dē-ˈä-grə-fē\ *n*

ra•dio•iso•tope \ˌrā-dē-ō-ˈī-sə-ˌtōp\ *n* **:** a radioactive isotope

ra•di•ol•o•gy \ˌrā-dē-ˈä-lə-jē\ *n* **:** the use of radiant energy (as X-rays and radium radiations) in medicine — **ra•di•ol•o•gist** \-jist\ *n*

ra•dio•man \ˈrā-dē-ō-ˌman\ *n* **:** a radio operator or technician

ra•di•om•e•ter \ˌrā-dē-ˈä-mə-tər\ *n* **:** an instrument for measuring the intensity of radiant energy — **ra•dio•met•ric** \ˌrā-dē-ō-ˈme-trik\ *adj* — **ra•di•om•e•try** \-ˈä-mə-trē\ *n*

ra•dio•phone \ˈrā-dē-ə-ˌfōn\ *n* **:** RADIOTELEPHONE

ra•dio•sonde \ˈrā-dē-ō-ˌsänd\ *n* **:** a small radio transmitter carried aloft (as by balloon) and used to transmit meteorological data

ra•dio•tele•phone \ˌrā-dē-ō-ˈte-lə-ˌfōn\ *n* **:** a telephone that uses radio waves wholly or partly instead of connecting wires — **ra•dio•te•le•pho•ny** \-tə-ˈle-fə-nē, -ˈte-lə-ˌfō-nē\ *n*

radio telescope *n* **:** a radio receiver-antenna combination used for observation in radio astronomy

ra•dio•ther•a•py \ˌrā-dē-ō-ˈther-ə-pē\ *n* **:** the treatment of disease by means of radiation (as X-rays) — **ra•dio•ther•a•pist** \-pist\ *n*

rad•ish \ˈra-dish\ *n* **:** a pungent fleshy root usually eaten raw; *also* **:** a plant related to the mustards that produces this root

ra•di•um \ˈrā-dē-əm\ *n* **:** a very radioactive metallic chemical element that is used in the treatment of cancer

ra•di•us \ˈrā-dē-əs\ *n, pl* **ra•dii** \-ē-ˌī\ *also* **ra•di•us•es 1 :** a straight line extending from the center of a circle or a sphere to the circumference or surface; *also* **:** the length of a radius **2 :** the bone on the thumb side of the human forearm **3 :** a circular area defined by the length of its radius

RADM *abbr* rear admiral

ra•don \ˈrā-ˌdän\ *n* **:** a heavy radioactive gaseous chemical element

RAF *abbr* Royal Air Force

raf•fia \ˈra-fē-ə\ *n* **:** fiber used especially for making baskets and hats that is obtained from the stalks of the leaves of a tropical African palm (**raffia palm**)

raff•ish \ˈra-fish\ *adj* **:** jaunty or sporty especially in a flashy or vulgar manner — **raff•ish•ly** *adv*

raff•ish•ness *n* **:** marked by or suggestive of flashy vulgarity or crudeness

¹raf•fle \ˈra-fəl\ *vb* **raf•fled; raf•fling :** to dispose of by a raffle

²raffle *n* **:** a lottery in which the prize is won by one of a number of persons buying chances

¹raft \ˈraft\ *n* **1 :** a number of logs or timbers fastened together to form a float **2 :** a flat structure for support or transportation on water

²raft *vb* **1 :** to travel or transport by raft **2 :** to make into a raft

³raft *n* **:** a large amount or number **:** LOT

raf•ter \ˈraf-tər\ *n* **:** any of the parallel beams that support a roof

¹rag \ˈrag\ *n* **1 a :** a waste piece of cloth **b** *pl* **:** clothes usually in poor or ragged condition **2 :** a sleazy newspaper

²rag *n* **:** a composition in ragtime

ra•ga \ˈrä-gə\ *n* **1 :** a traditional melodic pattern or mode in Indian music **2 :** an improvisation based on a raga

rag•a•muf•fin \ˈra-gə-ˌmə-fən\ *n* **:** a ragged dirty person

rag•bag \ˈrag-ˌbag\ *n* ♦ **:** a miscellaneous collection

♦ assortment, clutter, jumble, medley, mélange, miscellany, motley, muddle, variety, welter

¹rage \ˈrāj\ *n* **1** ♦ **:** violent and uncontrolled anger **2** ♦ **:** a fad pursued with intense enthusiasm **:** VOGUE, FASHION **3 :** an intense feeling

♦ [1] anger, furor, fury, indignation, ire, outrage, spleen, wrath, wrathfulness ♦ [2] craze, enthusiasm, fad, fashion, go, mode, sensation, style, trend, vogue

²rage *vb* **raged; rag•ing 1** ♦ **:** to be furiously angry **2 :** to continue out of control ⟨the fire *raged*⟩ **3** ♦ **:** to go on a rampage

♦ [1] boil, burn, fume, seethe, steam ♦ [3] fume, storm

rag•ged \ˈra-gəd\ *adj* **1** ♦ **:** torn or worn to tatters; *also* **:** wearing tattered clothes **2 :** done in an uneven way ⟨a ~ performance⟩ **3** ♦ **:** having an irregular edge or outline — **rag•ged•ly** *adv* — **rag•ged•ness** *n*

♦ [1] ratty, seedy, shabby, tattered, threadbare, worn-out ♦ [3] broken, craggy, jagged, scraggly *Ant* clean, even, smooth, unbroken

rag•lan \ˈra-glən\ *n* **:** an overcoat with sleeves (**raglan sleeves**) sewn in with seams slanting from neck to underarm

ra•gout \ra-ˈgü\ *n* **:** a highly seasoned meat stew with vegetables

rag•pick•er \ˈrag-ˌpi-kər\ *n* **:** one who collects rags and refuse for a living

rag•time \-ˌtīm\ *n* **:** music in which there is more or less continuous syncopation in the melody

rag•top \ˈrag-ˌtäp\ *n* **:** CONVERTIBLE

rag•weed \-ˌwēd\ *n* **:** any of several chiefly No. American weedy composite herbs with allergenic pollen

¹raid \ˈrād\ *n* ♦ **:** a sudden usually surprise attack or invasion

♦ descent, foray, incursion, invasion, irruption ♦ aggression, assault, attack, charge, descent, offense (*or* offence), offensive, onset, onslaught, rush, strike

²raid *vb* ♦ **:** to make a raid on — **raid•er** *n*

♦ foray, invade, overrun ♦ assail, assault, attack, beset, charge, descend, jump, pounce (on *or* upon), rush, storm, strike

¹rail \ˈrāl\ *n* **1 :** a bar extending from one support to another as a guard or barrier **2 :** a bar of steel forming a track for wheeled vehicles **3 :** RAILROAD

²rail *vb* **:** to provide with a railing

³rail *n, pl* **rail** *or* **rails :** any of numerous small wading birds often hunted as game birds

⁴rail *vb* ♦ **:** to revile or scold in harsh, insolent, or abusive language **:** SCOLD

♦ *usu* **rail at** *or* **rail against** admonish, chide, lecture, rate, rebuke, reprimand, scold

rail•er *n* ♦ : one that rails

♦ carper, castigator, caviler, censurer, critic, faultfinder, nitpicker, scold

rail•ing \ˈrā-liŋ\ *n* ♦ : a barrier of rails

♦ rail

rail•lery \ˈrā-lə-rē\ *n, pl* **-ler•ies** ♦ : good-natured ridicule : BANTER

♦ banter, chaff, persiflage, repartee

1rail•road \ˈrāl-ˌrōd\ *n* ♦ : a permanent road with rails fixed to ties providing a track for cars; *also* : such a road and its assets constituting a property

♦ rail, road

2railroad *vb* **1** : to put through (as a law) too hastily **2** : to convict hastily or with insufficient or improper evidence **3** : to send by rail **4** : to work on a railroad — **rail•road•er** *n* — **rail•road•ing** *n*
rail•way \-ˌwā\ *n* : a permanent road with rails fixed to ties providing a track for cars : RAILROAD
rai•ment \ˈrā-mənt\ *n* ♦ : garments in general : CLOTHING

♦ apparel, attire, clothing, dress, duds, wear

1rain \ˈrān\ *n* **1** ♦ : water falling in drops from the clouds **2** ♦ : a shower of objects ⟨a ∼ of bullets⟩

♦ [1] cloudburst, deluge, downpour, rainstorm, storm, wet ♦ [2] hail, shower, storm

2rain *vb* **1** : to send down rain **2** ♦ : to fall as or like rain **3** ♦ : to pour down

♦ [2] heap, lavish, pour, shower ♦ [3] pour, precipitate, storm

rain•bow \-ˌbō\ *n* : an arc or circle of colors formed by the refraction and reflection of the sun's rays in rain, spray, or mist
rainbow trout *n* : a large stout-bodied fish of western No. America closely related to the salmons of the Pacific and usually having red or pink stripes with black dots along its sides
rain check *n* **1** : a ticket stub good for a later performance when the scheduled one is rained out **2** : an assurance of a deferred extension of an offer
rain•coat \ˈrān-ˌkōt\ *n* : a waterproof or water-repellent coat
rain date *n* : an alternative date for an event postponed due to rain
rain•drop \-ˌdräp\ *n* : a drop of rain
rain•fall \-ˌfȯl\ *n* **1** : amount of precipitation measured by depth **2** : a fall of rain
rain forest *n* : a tropical woodland having an annual rainfall of at least 100 inches (254 centimeters) and marked by lofty broad-leaved evergreen trees forming a continuous canopy
rain•mak•ing \ˈrān-ˌmā-kiŋ\ *n* : the action or process of producing or attempting to produce rain by artificial means — **rain•mak•er** *n*
rain out *vb* : to interrupt or prevent by rain
rain•storm \ˈrān-ˌstȯrm\ *n* ♦ : a storm of or with rain

♦ cloudburst, deluge, downpour, rain, storm, wet

rain•wa•ter \-ˌwȯ-tər, -ˌwä-\ *n* : water fallen as rain
rainy *adj* ♦ : marked by, abounding with, or bringing rain

♦ stormy, wet

1raise \ˈrāz\ *vb* **raised; rais•ing** **1** ♦ : to cause or help to rise : LIFT ⟨∼ a window⟩ **2** : AWAKEN, AROUSE ⟨enough to ∼ the dead⟩ **3** ♦ : to set upright by lifting or building : ERECT ⟨∼ a monument⟩ **4** : to place higher in rank or dignity : PROMOTE ⟨was *raised* to captain⟩ **5** : END ⟨∼ a siege⟩ **6** : COLLECT ⟨∼ money⟩ **7 a** ♦ : to cause to grow : GROW ⟨∼ cattle⟩ ⟨∼ corn⟩ **b** ♦ : to bring to maturity : BRING UP ⟨∼ a family⟩ **8** ♦ : to cause to arise or appear : stimulate the appearance of ⟨∼ a laugh⟩ **9** ♦ : to bring to notice ⟨∼ an objection⟩ **10** ♦ : to cause to rise in level or amount : INCREASE ⟨∼ prices⟩; *also* : to bet more than **11** : to make light and spongy ⟨∼ dough⟩ **12** : to multiply a quantity by itself a specified number of times **13** : to cause to form ⟨∼ a blister⟩ — **rais•er** *n*

♦ [1] boost, crane, elevate, heave, heft, heighten, hike, hoist, jack, lift, pick up, up, uphold ***Ant*** drop, lower ♦ [3] assemble, build, construct, erect, fabricate, make, make up, piece, put up, rear, set up ♦ [7a] crop, cultivate, culture, grow, promote, rear, tend ♦ [7b] breed, bring up, foster, rear ♦ [8] elicit, evoke ♦ [9] bring up, broach, introduce, moot ♦ [10] add, aggrandize, amplify, augment, boost, compound, enlarge, escalate, expand, extend, increase, multiply, swell, up

2raise *n* ♦ : an increase in amount (as of a bid or bet or one's pay)

♦ accretion, addition, augmentation, boost, expansion, gain, increase, increment, plus, proliferation, rise, supplement

rai•sin \ˈrāz-ᵊn\ *n* : a grape dried for food
rai•son d'être \ˌrā-ˌzōⁿ-ˈdetrᵊ\ *n, pl* **rai•sons d'être** \-ˌzōⁿz-\ : reason or justification for existence
ra•ja *or* **ra•jah** \ˈrä-jə\ *n* : an Indian prince
1rake \ˈrāk\ *n* : a long-handled garden tool having a crossbar with prongs
2rake *vb* **raked; rak•ing** **1** : to gather, loosen, or smooth with or as if with a rake **2** : to sweep the length of (as a trench or ship) with gunfire **3** ♦ : to search through

♦ dig, dredge, hunt, ransack, rifle, rummage, scour, search

3rake *n* : inclination from either perpendicular or horizontal : SLANT
4rake *n* : a dissolute man : LIBERTINE
rake–off \ˈrāk-ˌȯf\ *n* : a percentage or cut taken
1rak•ish \ˈrā-kish\ *adj* : DISSOLUTE — **rak•ish•ness** *n*
2rakish *adj* **1** : having a trim appearance indicative of speed ⟨a ∼ sloop⟩ **2** : JAUNTY, SPORTY ⟨∼ clothes⟩ — **rak•ish•ness** *n*
rak•ish•ly *adv* ♦ : in a rakish manner

♦ flamboyantly, flashily, gaily, jauntily

1ral•ly \ˈra-lē\ *vb* **ral•lied; ral•ly•ing** **1** ♦ : to bring together for a common purpose; *also* : to bring back to order ⟨a leader ∼*ing* his forces⟩ **2** : to arouse to activity or from depression or weakness **3** ♦ : to make a comeback

♦ [1] marshal, mobilize, muster ♦ [3] rebound, recover, snap back

2rally *n, pl* **rallies** **1** ♦ : an act of rallying **2** ♦ : a mass meeting to arouse enthusiasm **3** : a competitive automobile event run over public roads

♦ [1] comeback, convalescence, recovery, recuperation, rehabilitation ♦ [2] mobilization, muster

3rally *vb* **ral•lied; ral•ly•ing** : BANTER
rallying cry *n* : WAR CRY 2
1ram \ˈram\ *n* **1** : a male sheep **2** : BATTERING RAM
2ram *vb* **rammed; ram•ming** **1** : to force or drive in or through **2** ♦ : to make compact : CRAM, CROWD **3** ♦ : to strike against violently

♦ [2] cram, crowd, jam, sandwich, squeeze, stuff, wedge ♦ [3] bang, bash, bump, collide, crash, hit, impact, knock, slam, smash, strike, swipe, thud

RAM \ˈram\ *n* : a computer memory that provides the main internal storage for programs and data
1ram•ble \ˈram-bəl\ *vb* **ram•bled; ram•bling** **1** ♦ : to go about aimlessly : ROAM, WANDER **2** ♦ : to talk or write in a long-winded wandering fashion

♦ gad, gallivant, knock, maunder, meander, mope, range, roam, rove, traipse, wander ♦ maunder, rattle, run on

2ramble *n* ♦ : a leisurely excursion; *esp* : an aimless walk

♦ perambulation, stroll, turn, walk

ram•bler \ˈram-blər\ *n* **1** ♦ : a person who rambles **2** : any of various climbing roses with large clusters of small often double flowers

♦ drifter, nomad, rover, stroller, vagabond, wanderer

ram•bling \ˈram-b(ə-)liŋ\ *adj* ♦ : straying from subject to subject

♦ desultory, digressive, discursive ♦ circuitous, diffuse, long-winded, prolix, verbose, windy, wordy

ram•bunc•tious \ram-ˈbəŋk-shəs\ *adj* ♦ : marked by uncontrollable exuberance

♦ boisterous, raucous, rowdy

ra•mie \ˈrā-mē, ˈra-\ *n* : a strong lustrous bast fiber from an Asian nettle
ram•i•fi•ca•tion \ˌra-mə-fə-ˈkā-shən\ *n* **1** : the act or process of branching **2** : CONSEQUENCE, OUTGROWTH
ram•i•fy \ˈra-mə-ˌfī\ *vb* **-fied; -fy•ing** **1** : to branch out **2** : to separate into divisions
ramp \ˈramp\ *n* : a sloping passage or roadway connecting different levels
1ram•page \ˈram-ˌpāj, (ˌ)ram-ˈpāj\ *vb* **ram•paged; ram•pag•ing** : to rush about wildly
2ram•page \ˈram-ˌpāj\ *n* ♦ : a course of violent or riotous action or behavior — **ram•pa•geous** \ram-ˈpā-jəs\ *adj*

♦ agitation, delirium, distraction, frenzy, furor, fury, hysteria, rage, uproar

ram•pant \ˈram-pənt\ *adj* ♦ **:** unchecked in growth or spread ⟨~ weeds⟩ ⟨fear was ~ in the town⟩ — **ram•pan•cy** \-pən-sē\ *n* — **ram•pant•ly** *adv*

♦ intemperate, unbridled, unchecked, uncontrolled, ungoverned, unhampered, unhindered, unrestrained *Ant* checked, controlled, curbed, hampered, hindered, restrained, temperate

ram•part \ˈram-ˌpärt\ *n* **1 :** a protective barrier **2 :** a broad embankment raised as a fortification

¹ram•rod \ˈram-ˌräd\ *n* **1 :** a rod used to ram a charge into a muzzle-loading gun **2 :** a cleaning rod for small arms **3 :** BOSS, OVERSEER

²ramrod *adj* ♦ **:** marked by rigidity or severity

♦ austere, authoritarian, flinty, hard, harsh, heavy-handed, rigid, rigorous, severe, stern, strict

³ramrod *vb* **:** to direct, supervise, and control

ram•shack•le \ˈram-ˌsha-kəl\ *adj* **:** RICKETY, TUMBLEDOWN

ran *past of* RUN

¹ranch \ˈranch\ *n* **1 :** an establishment for the raising and grazing of livestock (as cattle, sheep, or horses) **2 :** a large farm devoted to a specialty **3 :** RANCH HOUSE 2

²ranch *vb* **:** to live or work on a ranch — **ranch•er** *n*

ranch house *n* **1 :** the main house on a ranch **2 :** a one-story house typically with a low-pitched roof

ran•cho \ˈran-chō, ˈrän-\ *n, pl* **ranchos :** RANCH 1

ran•cid \ˈran-səd\ *adj* **1 :** having a rank smell or taste **2 :** OBNOXIOUS — **ran•cid•i•ty** \ran-ˈsi-də-tē\ *n*

ran•cor *or Can and Brit* **ran•cour** \ˈraŋ-kər\ *n* ♦ **:** bitter deep-seated ill will

♦ animosity, antagonism, antipathy, bitterness, enmity, gall, grudge, hostility

ran•cor•ous *adj* ♦ **:** deeply malevolent

♦ acrid, acrimonious, bitter, hard, resentful, sore

rand \ˈrand, ˈränd, ˈränt\ *n, pl* **rand :** the basic monetary unit of the Republic of South Africa

R & B *abbr* rhythm and blues

R & D *abbr* research and development

ran•dom \ˈran-dəm\ *adj* ♦ **:** lacking a definite plan, purpose, or pattern **:** HAPHAZARD — **ran•dom•ly** *adv* — **ran•dom•ness** *n*

♦ aimless, arbitrary, desultory, erratic, haphazard, scattered, stray *Ant* methodical, nonrandom, orderly, systematic

random–access *adj* **:** allowing access to stored data in any order the user desires

random–access memory *n* **:** RAM

ran•dom•ize \ˈran-də-ˌmīz\ *vb* **-ized; -iz•ing :** to select, assign, or arrange in a random way — **ran•dom•i•za•tion** \ˌran-də-mə-ˈzā-shən\ *n*

R and R *abbr* rest and recreation; rest and recuperation

rang *past of* RING

¹range \ˈrānj\ *n* **1** ♦ **:** a series of things in a row **2 :** a cooking stove having an oven and a flat top with burners **3 a** ♦ **:** open land where animals (as livestock) may roam and graze **b** ♦ **:** the region throughout which a kind of organism or ecological community naturally lives or occurs **4 :** the act of ranging about **:** STROLL **5 :** the distance a weapon will shoot or is to be shot **6 :** a place where shooting is practiced **7** ♦ **:** the space or extent included, covered, or used **:** SCOPE **8** ♦ **:** a variation within limits

♦ [1] column, cue, file, line, queue, string, train ♦ [3a] pasture ♦ [3b] habitat, home, niche, territory ♦ [7] amplitude, breadth, compass, extent, reach, realm, scope, sweep, width ♦ [8] gamut, scale, spectrum, spread, stretch

²range *vb* **ranged; rang•ing 1** ♦ **:** to set in a row or in proper order **2** ♦ **:** to set in place among others of the same kind **3 :** to roam over or through **:** EXPLORE **4** ♦ **:** to roam at large or freely **5 :** to correspond in direction or line **6** ♦ **:** to vary within limits **7 :** to find the range of an object by instrument (as radar)

♦ [1] arrange, array, classify, codify, dispose, draw up, marshal, order, organize, systematize ♦ [2] assort, break down, categorize, class, classify, grade, group, peg, place, rank, separate, sort ♦ [4] gad, gallivant, knock, maunder, meander, mope, ramble, roam, rove, traipse, wander ♦ [6] go, run, vary

rang•er \ˈrān-jər\ *n* **1 :** FOREST RANGER **2 :** a member of a body of troops who range over a region **3 :** an expert in close-range fighting and raiding tactics

rangy \ˈrān-jē\ *adj* **rang•i•er; -est** ♦ **:** being long-limbed and slender — **rang•i•ness** \ˈrān-jē-nəs\ *n*

♦ gangling, lanky, spindly

ra•ni *or* **ra•nee** \rä-ˈnē, ˈrä-ˌnē\ *n* **:** a raja's wife

¹rank \ˈraŋk\ *adj* **1** ♦ **:** strong and vigorous and usually coarse in growth ⟨~ weeds⟩ **2** ♦ **:** unpleasantly strong-smelling **3** ♦ **:** shockingly conspicuous — **rank•ly** *adv* — **rank•ness** *n*

♦ [1] lush, luxuriant, prosperous, rampant, weedy *Ant* sparse ♦ [2] fetid, foul, fusty, malodorous, musty, noisome, reeky, smelly, strong ♦ [3] blatant, conspicuous, egregious, flagrant, glaring, gross, obvious, patent, prominent, pronounced, striking

²rank *n* **1 :** ROW **2 :** a line of soldiers ranged side by side **3** *pl* **:** the body of enlisted personnel ⟨rose from the ~*s*⟩ **4 :** an orderly arrangement **5 :** CLASS, DIVISION **6** ♦ **:** a grade of official standing (as in an army) **7 :** position in a group **8** ♦ **:** superior position

♦ [6] degree, footing, level, place, position, situation, standing, station, status ♦ [8] class, quality, standing

³rank *vb* **1 :** to arrange in lines or in regular formation **2** ♦ **:** to determine the relative position of **3 :** to rate above (as in official standing) **4** ♦ **:** to take or have a relative position

♦ [2] assort, break down, categorize, class, classify, grade, group, peg, place, range, separate, sort ♦ [4] be, grade, place, rate

rank and file *n* ♦ **:** the general membership of a body as contrasted with its leaders

♦ commoners, herd, masses, mob, people, plebeians, populace

rank•ing \ˈraŋ-kiŋ\ *adj* **1 :** having a high position **:** of the highest rank **2 :** being next to the chairman in seniority

ran•kle \ˈraŋ-kəl\ *vb* **ran•kled; ran•kling** ♦ **:** to cause anger, irritation, or bitterness

♦ anger, antagonize, enrage, incense, inflame, infuriate, madden, outrage, rile, roil

ran•sack \ˈran-ˌsak\ *vb* **1** ♦ **:** to search thoroughly **2** ♦ **:** to search through and rob

♦ [1] dig, dredge, hunt, rake, rifle, rummage, scour, search ♦ [2] despoil, loot, maraud, pillage, plunder, sack, strip

¹ran•som \ˈran-səm\ *n* **1 :** something paid or demanded for the freedom of a captive **2 :** the act of ransoming

²ransom *vb* **:** to free from captivity or punishment by paying a price — **ran•som•er** *n*

¹rant \ˈrant\ *vb* **1** ♦ **:** to talk in a noisy, excited, or bombastic manner **2 :** to scold violently — **rant•er** *n* — **rant•ing•ly** *adv*

♦ bluster, fulminate, rave, spout

²rant *n* ♦ **:** a bombastic extravagant speech; *also* **:** the act of ranting

♦ diatribe, harangue, tirade ♦ bluster, bombast, brag, gas, grandiloquence

¹rap \ˈrap\ *n* **1 :** a sharp blow **2 :** a sharp rebuke **3 :** a negative often undeserved reputation ⟨a bum ~⟩ **4** ♦ **:** responsibility for or consequences of an action ⟨take the ~⟩ **5** ♦ **:** a criminal charge

♦ [4] blame, culpability, fault, guilt ♦ [5] charge, complaint, count, indictment

²rap *vb* **rapped; rap•ping 1 :** to strike sharply **:** KNOCK **2 :** to utter sharply **3 :** to criticize sharply

³rap *vb* **rapped; rap•ping 1 :** to talk freely and frankly **2 :** to perform rap music — **rap•per** *n*

⁴rap *n* **1 :** an instance or period of speech or conversation **:** TALK, CONVERSATION **2 :** a rhythmic chanting of usually rhymed couplets to a musical accompaniment; *also* **:** a piece so performed

⁵rap *n* ♦ **:** a minimum amount or degree

♦ hoot, jot, lick, modicum, tittle, whit

ra•pa•cious \rə-ˈpā-shəs\ *adj* **1** ♦ **:** excessively greedy or covetous **2 :** living on prey **3** ♦ **:** having a huge appetite **:** RAVENOUS 2 — **ra•pa•cious•ly** *adv*

♦ [1] acquisitive, avaricious, avid, covetous, grasping, greedy, mercenary ♦ [3] gluttonous, greedy, hoggish, piggish, ravenous, voracious

ra•pa•cious•ness *n* ♦ **:** the quality or state of being rapacious

♦ acquisitiveness, avarice, avidity, covetousness, cupidity, greed

ra•pac•i•ty \-ˈpa-sə-tē\ *n* **:** RAPACIOUSNESS

¹rape \ˈrāp\ *n* **:** a European herb related to the mustards that is grown as a forage crop and for its seeds (**rapeseed** \-ˌsēd\)

²rape *vb* **raped; rap•ing :** to commit rape on — **rap•er** *n* — **rap•ist** \ˈrā-pist\ *n*

³rape *n* **1 :** a carrying away by force **2 :** unlawful sexual activity and usually sexual intercourse carried out forcibly or under threat of injury

[1]**rap•id** \ˈra-pəd\ *adj* ♦ : very fast : SWIFT
♦ fast, fleet, quick, speedy, swift

[2]**rapid** *n* : a place in a stream where the current flows very fast usually over obstructions — usually used in plural
rapid eye movement *n* : rapid conjugate movement of the eyes associated with REM sleep
ra•pid•i•ty \rə-ˈpi-də-tē, ra-\ *n* ♦ : the quality or state of being rapid
♦ celerity, fastness, fleetness, haste, hurry, quickness, speed, swiftness, velocity

rap•id•ly \ˈra-pəd-lē\ *adv* ♦ : in a rapid manner : at a rapid rate
♦ apace, briskly, fast, full tilt, hastily, posthaste, presto, pronto, quick, quickly, soon, speedily, swift, swiftly

rapid transit *n* : fast passenger transportation (as by subway) in cities
[1]**ra•pi•er** \ˈrā-pē-ər\ *n* : a straight 2-edged sword with a narrow pointed blade
[2]**rapier** *adj* : extremely sharp or keen ⟨~ wit⟩
rap•ine \ˈra-pən, -ˌpīn\ *n* : PILLAGE, PLUNDER
rap•pel \rə-ˈpel, ra-\ *vb* **-pelled; -pel•ling** : to descend (as from a cliff) by sliding down a rope
rap•port \ra-ˈpōr\ *n* **1** : RELATION **2** : relation characterized by harmony
rap•proche•ment \ˌra-ˌprōsh-ˈmä^{n}, ra-ˈprōsh-ˌmä^{n}\ *n* : the establishment of or a state of having cordial relations
rap•scal•lion \rap-ˈskal-yən\ *n* **1** : RASCAL **2** ♦ : a mischievous person or animal : SCAMP
♦ devil, hellion, imp, mischief, monkey, rascal, rogue, scamp, urchin

rapt \ˈrapt\ *adj* **1** : carried away with emotion **2** ♦ : wholly absorbed : ENGROSSED — **rapt•ly** \ˈrapt-lē\ *adv* — **rapt•ness** *n*
♦ absorbed, attentive, engrossed, intent, observant

rap•tor \ˈrap-tər, -ˌtȯr\ *n* **1** : BIRD OF PREY **2** : a usually small-to-medium-sized predatory dinosaur
rap•ture \ˈrap-chər\ *n* ♦ : spiritual or emotional ecstasy — **rap•tur•ous•ly** *adv*
♦ ecstasy, elation, euphoria, exhilaration, heaven, intoxication, paradise, rhapsody, transport

rapture of the deep : NITROGEN NARCOSIS
rap•tur•ous \-chə-rəs\ *adj* ♦ : feeling, expressing, or marked by rapture
♦ ecstatic, elated, euphoric, intoxicated, rhapsodic

ra•ra avis \ˌrar-ə-ˈā-vəs\ *n, pl* **ra•ra avis•es** \-ˈā-və-səz\ *or* **ra•rae aves** \ˌrär-ˌī-ˈä-ˌwās\ : a rare person or thing : RARITY
[1]**rare** \ˈrar\ *adj* **rar•er; rar•est** **1** : not thick or dense : THIN ⟨~ air⟩ **2** ♦ : unusually fine **3** ♦ : seldom seen, encountered, or experienced — **rare•ness** *n*
♦ [2] choice, dainty, delicate, elegant, exquisite, select ♦ [3] aberrant, abnormal, atypical, exceptional, extraordinary, freak, odd, peculiar, phenomenal, singular, uncommon, uncustomary, unique, unusual, unwonted ♦ [3] infrequent, occasional, sporadic

[2]**rare** *adj* **rar•er; rar•est** : cooked so that the inside is still red ⟨~ beef⟩
rare•bit \ˈrar-bət\ *n* : WELSH RABBIT
rar•efac•tion \ˌrar-ə-ˈfak-shən\ *n* **1** : the action or process of rarefying **2** : the state of being rarefied
rar•e•fy *also* **rar•i•fy** \ˈrar-ə-ˌfī\ *vb* **-fied; -fy•ing** : to make or become rare, thin, or less dense
rare•ly *adv* ♦ : not often
♦ infrequently, little, seldom

rar•ing \ˈrar-ən, -iŋ\ *adj* ♦ : full of enthusiasm or eagerness ⟨~ to go⟩
♦ agog, anxious, ardent, athirst, avid, crazy, eager, enthusiastic, gung ho, hot, hungry, keen, nuts, solicitous, thirsty, voracious

rar•i•ty \ˈrar-ə-tē\ *n* ♦ : something rare
♦ curiosity, exotic, oddity

ras•cal \ˈras-kəl\ *n* **1** ♦ : a mean or dishonest person **2** ♦ : a mischievous person
♦ [1] beast, evildoer, fiend, no-good, reprobate, rogue, varlet, villain, wretch ♦ [2] devil, hellion, imp, mischief, monkey, rapscallion, rogue, scamp, urchin

ras•cal•i•ty \ras-ˈka-lə-tē\ *n* ♦ : the character or actions of a rascal
♦ devilishness, impishness, knavery, mischief, mischievousness, shenanigans, waggery, wickedness

ras•cal•ly \ˈras-kə-lē\ *adj* ♦ : of or characteristic of a rascal
♦ devilish, impish, knavish, mischievous, roguish, sly, waggish, wicked

[1]**rash** \ˈrash\ *adj* ♦ : having or showing little regard for consequences : too hasty in decision, action, or speech — **rash•ness** *n*
♦ cursory, hasty, headlong, pell-mell, precipitate, precipitous

[2]**rash** *n* : an eruption on the body
rash•er \ˈra-shər\ *n* : a thin slice of bacon or ham broiled or fried; *also* : a portion consisting of several such slices
rash•ly \ˈrash-lē\ *adv* ♦ : in a rash manner
♦ cursorily, hastily, headlong, hurriedly, pell-mell, precipitately

[1]**rasp** \ˈrasp\ *vb* **1** ♦ : to rub with or as if with a rough file **2** ♦ : to grate harshly on (as one's nerves) **3** : to speak in a grating tone
♦ [1] grate, grind, scrape, scratch ♦ [2] aggravate, annoy, bother, bug, chafe, exasperate, gall, get, grate, irk, irritate, nettle, peeve, persecute, pique, put out, rile, vex

[2]**rasp** *n* **1** : a coarse file with cutting points instead of ridges **2** ♦ : a rasping sound, sensation, or effect
♦ grind, scrape, scratch

rasp•ber•ry \ˈraz-ˌber-ē, -bə-rē\ *n* **1** : any of various edible usually black or red berries produced by some brambles; *also* : such a bramble **2** ♦ : a sound of contempt made by protruding the tongue through the lips and expelling air forcibly
♦ boo, catcall, hiss, hoot, jeer, snort

[1]**rat** \ˈrat\ *n* **1** : any of numerous rodents larger than the related mice **2** : a contemptible person; *esp* ♦ : one that betrays friends or associates
♦ betrayer, blabbermouth, informer, snitch, stool pigeon, tattler, tattletale

[2]**rat** *vb* **rat•ted; rat•ting** **1** : to betray or inform on one's associates **2** : to hunt or catch rats
rat cheese *n* : CHEDDAR
ratch•et \ˈra-chət\ *n* : a device that consists of a bar or wheel having slanted teeth into which a pawl drops so as to allow motion in only one direction
[1]**rate** \ˈrāt\ *vb* **rat•ed; rat•ing** ♦ : to scold violently
♦ admonish, chide, lecture, rail (at *or* against), rebuke, reprimand, scold

[2]**rate** *n* **1** : quantity, amount, or degree measured by some standard **2** : an amount (as of payment) measured by its relation to some other amount (as of time) **3** : a charge, payment, or price fixed according to a ratio, scale, or standard ⟨tax ~⟩ **4** ♦ : relative condition or quality : CLASS
♦ caliber (*or* calibre), class, grade, quality

[3]**rate** *vb* **rat•ed; rat•ing** **1** ♦ : to set an estimate on **2** ♦ : to show respect or consideration for : CONSIDER, REGARD **3** : to settle the relative rank or class of **4** ♦ : to be classed : RANK **5** ♦ : to have a right to : DESERVE **6** : to be of consequence — **rat•er** *n*
♦ [1] appraise, assess, estimate, evaluate, set, value ♦ [2] account, call, consider, count, esteem, hold, reckon, regard, take ♦ [4] be, grade, place, rank ♦ [5] deserve, earn, merit

rath•er \ˈra-t͟hər, ˈrä-, ˈrə-\ *adv* **1** : more properly **2** ♦ : more readily or willingly : PREFERABLY **3** : more correctly speaking **4** : to the contrary : INSTEAD **5** ♦ : in some degree : SOMEWHAT
♦ [2] first, preferably, readily, soon ***Ant*** involuntarily, unwillingly ♦ [5] enough, fairly, kind of, moderately, pretty, quite, so-so, somewhat, sort of

rather than *prep* : INSTEAD OF
raths•kel•ler \ˈrät-ˌske-lər, ˈrat-\ *n* : a usually basement tavern or restaurant
rat•i•fy \ˈra-tə-ˌfī\ *vb* **-fied; -fy•ing** ♦ : to approve and accept formally — **rat•i•fi•ca•tion** \ˌra-tə-fə-ˈkā-shən\ *n*
♦ approve, authorize, clear, OK, sanction, warrant

rat•ing \ˈrā-tiŋ\ *n* **1** : a classification according to grade : RANK **2** *Brit* : a naval enlisted man **3** : an estimate of the credit standing and business responsibility of a person or firm
ra•tio \ˈrā-shō, -shē-ˌō\ *n, pl* **ra•tios** **1** : the indicated quotient of two numbers or mathematical expressions **2** : the relationship in number, quantity, or degree between two or more things
ra•ti•o•ci•na•tion \ˌra-tē-ˌōs-^{ə}n-ˈā-shən, -shē-, -ˌäs-\ *n* : exact

thinking : REASONING — **ra•ti•o•ci•nate** \-ˈōs-ᵊn-ˌāt, -ˈäs-\ *vb* — **ra•ti•o•ci•na•tive** \-ˈōs-ᵊn-ˌā-tiv, -ˈäs-\ *adj* — **ra•ti•o•ci•na•tor** \-ˈōs-ᵊn-ˌā-tər, -ˈäs-\ *n*

[1]**ra•tion** \ˈra-shən, ˈrā-\ *n* **1 :** a food allowance for one day **2 :** FOOD, PROVISIONS, DIET — usually used in plural **3 :** SHARE, ALLOTMENT

[2]**ration** *vb* **1** ♦ **:** to supply with or allot as rations **2 :** to use or allot sparingly

♦ allocate, allot, allow, apportion, assign

[1]**ra•tio•nal** \ˈra-shə-nəl\ *adj* **1** ♦ **:** having reason or understanding **2** ♦ **:** of or relating to reason **3 :** relating to, consisting of, or being one or more rational numbers **4** ♦ **:** of, relating to, or in accordance with the principles of rationalism — **ra•tio•nal•ly** *adv*

♦ [1] intelligent, reasonable, reasoning ***Ant*** irrational, unintelligent, unreasonable, unreasoning, unthinking ♦ [2, 4] good, hard, informed, just, levelheaded, logical, reasonable, reasoned, sensible, sober, solid, valid, well-founded

[2]**rational** *n* : RATIONAL NUMBER

ra•tio•nale \ˌra-shə-ˈnal\ *n* **1** ♦ **:** an explanation of principles controlling belief or practice **2 :** an underlying reason

♦ argument, case, defense (*or* defence), explanation, reason

ra•tio•nal•ise *chiefly Brit var of* RATIONALIZE

ra•tio•nal•ism \ˈra-shə-nə-ˌli-zəm\ *n* **:** the practice of guiding one's actions and opinions solely by what seems reasonable — **ra•tio•nal•ist** \-list\ *n* — **rationalist** *or* **ra•tio•nal•is•tic** \ˌra-shə-nə-ˈlis-tik\ *adj*

ra•tio•nal•i•ty \ˌra-shə-ˈna-lə-tē\ *n, pl* **-ties :** the quality or state of being rational

ra•tio•nal•ize \ˈra-shə-nə-ˌlīz\ *vb* **-ized; -iz•ing 1** ♦ **:** to make (something irrational) appear rational or reasonable **2 :** to provide a natural explanation of (as a myth) **3** ♦ **:** to justify (as one's behavior or weaknesses) especially to oneself **4 :** to find plausible but untrue reasons for conduct — **ra•tio•nal•i•za•tion** \ˌra-shə-nə-lə-ˈzā-shən\ *n*

♦ [1, 3] account, explain

rational number *n* **:** a number that can be expressed as an integer or the quotient of an integer divided by a nonzero integer

rat race *n* **:** strenuous, tiresome, and usually competitive activity or rush

rat•tan \ra-ˈtan, rə-\ *n* **:** a cane or switch made from one of the long stems of an Asian climbing palm; *also* **:** this palm

rat•ter \ˈra-tər\ *n* **:** a rat-catching dog or cat

[1]**rat•tle** \ˈrat-ᵊl\ *vb* **rat•tled; rat•tling 1 :** to make or cause to make a series of clattering sounds **2 :** to move with a clattering sound **3 :** to say or do in a brisk lively fashion ⟨~ off the answers⟩ **4** ♦ **:** to upset especially to the point of loss of poise and composure **:** CONFUSE ⟨~ a witness⟩ **5** ♦ **:** to chatter incessantly and aimlessly

♦ [4] abash, confound, confuse, discomfit, disconcert, discountenance, embarrass, faze, fluster, mortify ♦ [5] maunder, ramble, run on

[2]**rattle** *n* **1 :** a toy that produces a rattle when shaken **2 :** a series of clattering and knocking sounds **3 :** a rattling organ at the end of a rattlesnake's tail

rat•tler \ˈrat-lər\ *n* **:** RATTLESNAKE

rat•tle•snake \ˈrat-ᵊl-ˌsnāk\ *n* **:** any of various American pit vipers with a rattle at the end of the tail

rat•tle•trap \ˈrat-ᵊl-ˌtrap\ *n* **:** something (as an old car) rickety and full of rattles

rat•tling \ˈrat-liŋ\ *adj* **1** ♦ **:** acting or capable of acting with speed **:** BRISK **2 :** FIRST-RATE, SPLENDID

♦ breakneck, breathless, brisk, dizzy, fast, fleet, hasty, lightning, nippy, quick, rapid, snappy, speedy, swift

rat•trap \ˈrat-ˌtrap\ *n* **1 :** a trap for rats **2 :** a dilapidated building

rat•ty \ˈra-tē\ *adj* **rat•ti•er; -est 1 :** infested with rats **2 :** of, relating to, or suggestive of rats **3** ♦ **:** threadbare and faded from wear **:** SHABBY

♦ dilapidated, grungy, mean, neglected, seedy, shabby

rau•cous \ˈrȯ-kəs\ *adj* **1 :** HARSH, HOARSE, STRIDENT **2** ♦ **:** boisterously disorderly — **rau•cous•ly** *adv* — **rau•cous•ness** *n*

♦ boisterous, rambunctious, rowdy

raun•chy \ˈrȯn-chē, ˈrän-\ *adj* **raun•chi•er; -est 1 :** SLOVENLY, DIRTY **2 :** OBSCENE, SMUTTY — **raun•chi•ness** \-chē-nəs\ *n*

[1]**rav•age** \ˈra-vij\ *n* **:** an act or result of ravaging **:** DEVASTATION

[2]**ravage** *vb* **rav•aged; rav•ag•ing** ♦ **:** to lay waste **:** DEVASTATE — **rav•ag•er** *n*

♦ destroy, devastate, ruin, scourge

[1]**rave** \ˈrāv\ *vb* **raved; rav•ing 1 :** to talk wildly in or as if in delirium **:** STORM, RAGE **2** ♦ **:** to talk with extreme enthusiasm **3** ♦ **:** to speak out wildly

♦ [2] enthuse, fuss, gush, rhapsodize, slobber ♦ [3] bluster, fulminate, rant, spout

[2]**rave** *n* **1 :** an act or instance of raving **2 :** an extravagantly favorable criticism

[1]**rav•el** \ˈra-vəl\ *vb* **-eled** *or* **-elled; -el•ing** *or* **-el•ling 1 :** to undo the intricacies of **:** UNRAVEL **2 :** TANGLE, CONFUSE

[2]**ravel** *n* **1 :** something tangled **2 :** something raveled out; *esp* **:** a loose thread

[1]**ra•ven** \ˈrā-vən\ *n* **:** a large black bird related to the crow

[2]**raven** *adj* ♦ **:** black and glossy like a raven's feathers

♦ black, ebony

[3]**rav•en** \ˈra-vən\ *vb* **1 :** to devour greedily **2 :** DESPOIL, PLUNDER **3 :** PREY

rav•en•ous \ˈra-və-nəs\ *adj* **1** ♦ **:** having a huge appetite **:** VORACIOUS **2 :** eager for food **:** very hungry — **rav•en•ous•ly** *adv* — **rav•en•ous•ness** *n*

♦ gluttonous, greedy, hoggish, piggish, rapacious, voracious

ra•vine \rə-ˈvēn\ *n* ♦ **:** a small narrow steep-sided valley larger than a gully

♦ canyon, defile, flume, gap, gorge, gulch, gulf, notch, pass

rav•i•o•li \ˌra-vē-ˈō-lē\ *n, pl* **ravioli** *also* **raviolis :** small cases of dough with a savory filling (as of meat or cheese)

rav•ish \ˈra-vish\ *vb* **1 :** to seize and take away by violence **2** ♦ **:** to overcome with emotion and especially with joy or delight **3 :** RAPE — **rav•ish•er** *n* — **rav•ish•ment** *n*

♦ carry away, enrapture, enthrall, entrance, transport

rav•ish•ing \ˈra-vi-shiŋ\ *adj* ♦ **:** unusually attractive, pleasing, or striking

♦ attractive, beautiful, fair, gorgeous, handsome, knockout, lovely, pretty, stunning

[1]**raw** \ˈrȯ\ *adj* **raw•er** \ˈrȯ-ər\; **raw•est** \ˈrȯ-əst\ **1 :** not cooked **2** ♦ **:** changed little from the original form **:** not processed ⟨~ materials⟩ **3 :** having the surface abraded or irritated ⟨a ~ sore⟩ **4** ♦ **:** not trained or experienced ⟨~ recruits⟩ **5 :** VULGAR, COARSE **6** ♦ **:** disagreeably cold and damp ⟨a ~ day⟩ **7 :** UNFAIR ⟨~ deal⟩

♦ [2] crude, native, natural, undressed, unprocessed, unrefined, untreated ♦ [4] adolescent, callow, green, immature, inexperienced, juvenile ♦ [6] bitter, bleak, chill, chilly, nippy, sharp

[2]**raw** *n* **:** a raw place or state; *esp* **:** NUDITY

raw•boned \ˈrȯ-ˌbōnd\ *adj* **1 :** LEAN, GAUNT **2 :** having a heavy frame that seems to have little flesh

raw deal *n* ♦ **:** an instance of unfair treatment

♦ disservice, injury, injustice, wrong

raw•hide \ˈrȯ-ˌhīd\ *n* **:** the untanned skin of cattle; *also* **:** a whip made of this

raw material *n* ♦ **:** something with a potential for improvement, development, or elaboration

♦ material, stuff, substance

raw•ness *n* ♦ **:** the quality or state of being raw

♦ bite, bitterness, bleakness, chill, nip, sharpness

[1]**ray** \ˈrā\ *n* **:** any of an order of large flat cartilaginous fishes that have the eyes on the upper surface and the hind end of the body slender and taillike

[2]**ray** *n* **1 :** any of the lines of light that appear to radiate from a bright object **2 :** a thin beam of radiant energy (as light) **3 :** light from a beam **4 :** a thin line like a beam of light **5 :** an animal or plant structure resembling a ray **6 :** a tiny bit **:** PARTICLE ⟨a ~ of hope⟩

ray•on \ˈrā-ˌän\ *n* **:** a fiber made from cellulose; *also* **:** a yarn, thread, or fabric made from such fibers

raze \ˈrāz\ *vb* **razed; raz•ing 1 :** to scrape, cut, or shave off **2 :** to destroy to the ground **:** DEMOLISH

ra•zor \ˈrā-zər\ *n* **:** a sharp cutting instrument used to shave off hair

ra•zor–backed \ˈrā-zər-ˌbakt\ *or* **ra•zor•back** \-ˌbak\ *adj* **:** having a sharp narrow back ⟨~ horse⟩

razor clam *n* **:** any of a family of marine bivalve mollusks having a long narrow curved thin shell

razor wire *n* **:** coiled wire fitted with sharp edges and used as an obstacle or barrier

¹razz \ˈraz\ *n* : RASPBERRY 2

²razz *vb* ♦ **:** to harass and try to disconcert with questions, challenges, or gibes **:** TEASE

♦ chaff, jive, josh, kid, rally, rib, ride, roast, tease

Rb *symbol* rubidium

RBC *abbr* red blood cells

RBI \ˌär-(ˌ)bē-ˈī, ˈri-bē\ *n, pl* **RBIs** *or* **RBI :** a run in baseball that is driven in by a batter

RC *abbr* **1** Red Cross **2** Roman Catholic

RCAF *abbr* Royal Canadian Air Force

RCMP *abbr* Royal Canadian Mounted Police

RCN *abbr* Royal Canadian Navy

rct *abbr* recruit

rd *abbr* **1** road **2** rod **3** round

RD *abbr* rural delivery

RDA *abbr* recommended daily allowance; recommended dietary allowance

re \ˈrā, ˈrē\ *prep* **:** with regard to

Re *symbol* rhenium

re- \rē, ˌrē, ˈrē\ *prefix* **1 :** again **:** for a second time **2 :** anew **:** in a new or different form **3 :** back **:** backward

reabsorb
reacquire
reactivate
reactivation
readjust
readjustment
readmission
readmit
reaffirm
reaffirmation
realign
realignment
reallocate
reallocation
reanalysis
reanimation
reannex
reannexation
reappear
reappearance
reapplication
reapply
reappoint
reappointment
reapportion
reapportionment
reappraise
rearm
rearmament
rearouse
rearrange
rearrangement
rearrest
reascend
reassemble
reassembly
reassert
reassess
reassessment
reassign
reassignment
reassume
reattach
reattachment
reattain
reattempt
reauthorization
reauthorize
reawaken
rebaptism
rebaptize
rebid
rebind
reboil
rebroadcast
reburial
rebury
recalculate
recalculation
rechannel
recharge
rechargeable
recharter
recheck
rechristen
reclassification
reclassify
recoin
recolonization
recolonize
recolor
recombine
recommence
recommission
recommit
recompile
recompose
recomputation
recompute
reconcentrate
reconception
recondensation
recondense
reconfirm
reconfirmation
reconnect
reconquer
reconquest
reconsecrate
reconsecration
recontact
recontaminate
recontamination
reconvene
reconvert
recook
recopy
recross
recrystallize
recut
redecorate
redecoration
rededicate
rededication
redefine
redefinition
redeposit
redesign
redetermination
redetermine
redevelop
redevelopment
redirect
rediscount
rediscover
rediscovery
redissolve
redistill
redistillation
redraw
reedit
reelect
reelection
reemerge
reemergence
reemphasis
reemphasize
reemploy
reemployment
reenact
reenactment
reenergize
reenlist
reenlistment
reenter
reequip
reestablish
reestablishment
reevaluation
reexport
refight
refigure
refinish
refit
refix
refloat
refold
reforge
reformulate
reformulation
refortify
refound
refreeze
refuel
refurnish
regather
regild
regive
regrade
regrind
regrow
regrowth
rehandle
rehear
rehouse
reimpose
reimposition
reincorporate
reinsert
reinsertion
reintegrate
reinterpret
reinterpretation
reintroduce
reintroduction
reinvention
reinvest
reinvestment
reinvigoration
reissue
rejudge
reknit
relaunch
relearn
relight
reline
reload
remanufacture
remap
remarriage
remarry
rematch
remelt
remigration
remix
remold
rename
renegotiate
renegotiation
renominate
renomination
renumber
reoccupy
reoccur
reorder
reorganization
reorganize
reorient
reorientation
repack
repaint
repass
repeople
rephotograph
replant
repopulate
reprice
reprocess
reprogram
republication
republish
repurchase
reradiate
reread
rereading
rerecord
reroute
reschedule
rescore
rescreen
reseal
reseed
resell
reset
resettle
resettlement
resew
reshow
resocialization
resow
respell
restaff
restatement
restock
restrengthen
restructure
restudy
restuff
restyle
resubmit
resummon
resupply
resurface
resurvey
resynthesis
resynthesize
retaste
retell
retest
retool
retrain
retransmission
retransmit
retrial
reunification
reunify
reunite
reusable
reuse
revaluate
revaluation
revalue
revisit
rewarm
rewash
reweave
rewed
reweigh
rewire
rezone

¹reach \ˈrēch\ *vb* **1 :** to stretch out **2 :** to touch or attempt to touch or seize **3 :** to extend to **4 :** to communicate with **5 :** to arrive at **6** ♦ **:** to hand over — **reach•er** *n*

♦ hand, hand over, pass, transfer

²**reach** *n* **1 :** an unbroken stretch of a river **2 :** the act of reaching **3 :** a reachable distance; *also* **:** ability to reach **4** ♦ **:** a range of knowledge or comprehension **5** ♦ **:** a continuous stretch or expanse

♦ [4] amplitude, breadth, compass, extent, range, realm, scope, sweep, width ♦ [5] breadth, expanse, extent, spread, stretch

reach•able *adj* ♦ **:** capable of being reached

♦ accessible, convenient, handy

re•act \rē-ˈakt\ *vb* **1 :** to exert a return or counteracting influence **2 :** to have or show a reaction **3 :** to act in opposition to a force or influence **4 :** to move or tend in a reverse direction **5 :** to undergo chemical reaction

re•ac•tant \rē-ˈak-tənt\ *n* **:** a chemically reacting substance

re•ac•tion \rē-ˈak-shən\ *n* **1 :** the act or process of reacting **2 :** a counter tendency; *esp* **:** a tendency toward a former especially outmoded political or social order or policy **3** ♦ **:** bodily, mental, or emotional response to a stimulus **4 :** chemical change **5 :** a process involving change in atomic nuclei

♦ reply, response, take

¹**re•ac•tion•ary** \rē-ˈak-shə-ˌner-ē\ *adj* **1 :** relating to, marked by, or favoring especially political reaction **2** ♦ **:** relating to, marked by, or favoring reaction

♦ conservative, old-fashioned, orthodox, traditional

²**reactionary** *n* **:** one that is reactionary; *esp* ♦ **:** one tending to favor established ideas, conditions, or institutions

♦ conservative, rightist, Tory

re•ac•tive \rē-ˈak-tiv\ *adj* **:** reacting or tending to react

re•ac•tor \rē-ˈak-tər\ *n* **1 :** one that reacts **2 :** a device for the controlled release of nuclear energy

¹**read** \ˈrēd\ *vb* **read** \ˈred\; **read•ing** **1 :** to understand language by interpreting written symbols for speech sounds **2 :** to utter aloud written or printed words **3 :** to learn by observing ⟨~ nature's signs⟩ **4 :** to study by a course of reading ⟨~*s* law⟩ **5 :** to discover the meaning of ⟨~ the clues⟩ **6 :** to recognize or interpret as if by reading **7 :** to attribute (a meaning) to something ⟨~ guilt in his manner⟩ **8 :** INDICATE ⟨thermometer ~*s* 10°⟩ **9 :** to consist in phrasing or meaning ⟨the two versions ~ differently⟩ — **read•abil•i•ty** \ˌrē-də-ˈbi-lə-tē\ *n* — **read•able** \ˈrē-də-bəl\ *adj* — **read•ably** \-blē\ *adv* — **read•er** *n*

²**read** \ˈred\ *adj* **:** informed by reading ⟨widely ~⟩

re•ad•dress \rē-ə-ˈdres\ *vb* ♦ **:** to deal with again

♦ reanalyze, reconceive, reconsider, reexamine, rethink, review

read•er•ship \ˈrē-dər-ˌship\ *n* **:** the mass or a particular group of readers

read•i•ly \ˈre-də-lē\ *adv* **1 :** in a ready manner **2** ♦ **:** without much difficulty

♦ easily, effortlessly, fluently, freely, handily, lightly, painlessly, smoothly

read•ing \ˈrēd-iŋ\ *n* **1 :** something read or for reading **2 :** a particular version **3 :** data indicated by an instrument ⟨thermometer ~⟩ **4 :** a particular interpretation (as of a law) **5 :** a particular performance (as of a musical work) **6 :** an indication of a certain state of affairs

read–only memory *n* **:** ROM

read•out \ˈrēd-ˌau̇t\ *n* **1 :** the process of removing information from an automatic device (as a computer) and displaying it in an understandable form; *also* **:** the information removed from such a device **2 :** an electronic device that presents information in visual form

read out *vb* **1 :** to read aloud **2 :** to expel from an organization

¹**ready** \ˈre-dē\ *adj* **read•i•er; -est** **1** ♦ **:** prepared for use or action **2 a :** likely to do something indicated **b** ♦ **:** willingly inclined toward **:** prepared to do **3** ♦ **:** spontaneously prompt ⟨her ~ wit⟩ **4 :** immediately available ⟨~ cash⟩ — **read•i•ness** \-dē-nəs\ *n* — **at the ready :** ready for immediate use

♦ [1] fit, go, set ***Ant*** unprepared, unready ♦ [2b] amenable, disposed, game, glad, inclined, willing ♦ [3] alert, expeditious, prompt, quick, willing

²**ready** *vb* **read•ied; ready•ing** ♦ **:** to make ready

♦ equip, fit, prepare, qualify, season ♦ brace, forearm, fortify, nerve, psych (up), steel, strengthen

ready–made \ˌre-dē-ˈmād\ *adj* **:** already made up for general sale **:** not specially made — **ready–made** *n*

ready room *n* **:** a room in which pilots are briefed and await orders

re•agent \rē-ˈā-jənt\ *n* **:** a substance that takes part in or brings about a particular chemical reaction

¹**re•al** \ˈrēl\ *adj* **1 :** of or relating to fixed or immovable things (as land) ⟨~ property⟩ **2** ♦ **:** not artificial, fraudulent, or illusory **:** GENUINE **3** ♦ **:** occurring or existing in actuality — **re•al•ness** *n* — **for real** **1 :** in earnest **2 :** GENUINE

♦ [2] artless, authentic, bona fide, genuine, honest, ingenuous, innocent, naive, natural, simple, sincere, true, unaffected, unpretentious ♦ [3] actual, concrete, existent, factual, true, very

²**real** *adv* **:** to a high degree **:** VERY

real estate *n* **:** property in buildings and land

re•al•ism \ˈrē-ə-ˌli-zəm\ *n* **1 :** the disposition to face facts and to deal with them practically **2 :** true and faithful portrayal of nature and of people in art or literature — **re•al•ist** \-list\ *adj or n* — **re•al•is•ti•cal•ly** \-ti-k(ə-)lē\ *adv*

re•al•is•tic \ˌrē-ə-ˈlis-tik\ *adj* **1** ♦ **:** of, relating to, or marked by literary or artistic realism **2** ♦ **:** facing reality squarely **:** not impractical or visionary

♦ [1] lifelike, natural, near ♦ [2] down-to-earth, earthy, hardheaded, matter-of-fact, practical, pragmatic ***Ant*** idealistic, impractical, unrealistic, utopian, visionary

re•al•i•ty \rē-ˈa-lə-tē\ *n, pl* **-ties** **1** ♦ **:** the quality or state of being real **2 :** something real **3 :** the totality of real things and events

♦ actuality, existence, subsistence

re•al•iz•able \ˈrē-ə-ˌlī-zə-bəl\ *adj* ♦ **:** capable of being realized

♦ achievable, attainable, doable, feasible, possible, practicable, viable, workable

re•al•i•za•tion \ˌrē-ə-lə-ˈzā-shən\ *n* ♦ **:** the action of realizing **:** the state of being realized

♦ accomplishment, achievement, actuality, attainment, consummation, fruition, fulfillment

re•al•ize \ˈrē-ə-ˌlīz\ *vb* **-ized; -iz•ing** **1 :** to make actual **:** ACCOMPLISH **2 :** to convert into money ⟨~ assets⟩ **3 :** to bring or get by sale, investment, or effort **:** OBTAIN, GAIN ⟨~ a profit⟩ **4** ♦ **:** to be aware of

♦ ascertain, catch on, discover, find out, hear, learn, see

re•al•ly \ˈrē-lē, ˈri-\ *adv* **1** ♦ **:** in truth **:** in fact **2** ♦ **:** without any question — used as an intensifier ⟨a ~ beautiful day⟩

♦ [1] actually, frankly, genuinely, honestly, truly, truthfully, verily ♦ [2] certainly, definitely, doubtless, incontestably, indeed, indisputably, surely, truly, undeniably, undoubtedly, unquestionably

realm \ˈrelm\ *n* **1 :** KINGDOM **2** ♦ **:** an area or range over or within which someone or something acts, exists, or has influence or significance **:** SPHERE, DOMAIN

♦ area, arena, demesne, department, discipline, domain, field, line, province, specialty, sphere

real number *n* **:** a number that has no imaginary part ⟨the set of all *real numbers* comprises the rationals and the irrationals⟩

re•al•po•li•tik \rā-ˈäl-ˌpō-li-ˌtēk\ *n, often cap* **:** politics based on practical and material factors rather than on theoretical or ethical objectives

real time *n* **:** the actual time during which something takes place — **real–time** *adj*

re•al•ty \ˈrēl-tē\ *n* **:** REAL ESTATE

¹**ream** \ˈrēm\ *n* **1 :** a quantity of paper that is variously 480, 500, or 516 sheets **2** ♦ **:** a great amount — usually used in the plural ⟨~*s* of information⟩

♦ **reams** abundance, deal, gobs, heap, loads, lot, pile, plenty, quantity, scads

²**ream** *vb* **:** to enlarge, shape, or clear with a reamer

ream•er \ˈrē-mər\ *n* **:** a tool with cutting edges that is used to enlarge or shape a hole

re•an•a•lyze \rē-ˈan-ᵊl-ˌīz\ *vb* ♦ **:** to analyze again

♦ readdress, reconceive, reconsider, reexamine, rethink, review

re•an•i•mate \rē-ˈa-nə-mət\ *vb* ♦ **:** to give renewed spirit and support to

♦ regenerate, reinvigorate, rejuvenate, renew, resuscitate, revitalize, revive

reap \ˈrēp\ *vb* **1 :** to cut or clear with a scythe, sickle, or machine **2** ♦ **:** to gather by or as if by cutting **:** HARVEST ⟨~ a reward⟩ — **reap•er** *n*

♦ gather, harvest, pick

re•ap•prais•al \rē-ə-ˈprā-zəl\ *n* ♦ **:** a second or fresh appraisal

♦ reexamination, retrospection, review

[1]**rear** \ˈrir\ *vb* **1** ♦ **:** to erect by building **2 :** to set or raise upright **3** ♦ **:** to breed and raise for use or market ⟨∼ livestock⟩ **4** ♦ **:** to bring to maturity or self-sufficiency usually through nurturing care **5 :** to lift or rise up; *esp* **:** to rise on the hind legs

♦ [1] assemble, build, construct, erect, fabricate, make, make up, piece, put up, raise, set up ♦ [3] crop, cultivate, culture, grow, promote, raise, tend ♦ [4] breed, bring up, foster, raise

[2]**rear** *n* **1 :** the unit (as of an army) or area farthest from the enemy **2 :** BACK; *also* **:** the position at the back of something **3** ♦ **:** the seat of the body

♦ backside, bottom, butt, buttocks, posterior, rump, seat

[3]**rear** *adj* ♦ **:** being at the back

♦ back, hind, hindmost, posterior

rear admiral *n* **:** a commissioned officer in the navy or coast guard ranking next below a vice admiral

[1]**rear•ward** \ˈrir-wərd\ *adj* **1 :** being at or toward the rear **2 :** directed toward the rear

[2]**rear•ward** *also* **rear•wards** \-wərdz\ *adv* **:** at or toward the rear

reas *abbr* reasonable

[1]**rea•son** \ˈrēz-ᵊn\ *n* **1** ♦ **:** a statement offered in explanation or justification **2** ♦ **:** a person or thing that is the occasion of an action or state **:** CAUSE **3 :** the power to think **:** INTELLECT **4** ♦ **:** a sane or sound mind **5** ♦ **:** due exercise of the faculty of logical thought

♦ [1] alibi, argument, case, defense (*or* defence), excuse, explanation, justification, rationale ♦ [2] antecedent, cause, grounds, motive, occasion, wherefore, why ♦ [4] head, mind, sanity, wit ♦ [5] logic, reasoning, sense

[2]**reason** *vb* **1 :** to talk with another to cause a change of mind **2 :** to use the faculty of reason **:** THINK **3** ♦ **:** to discover or formulate by the use of reason **4** ♦ **:** to persuade or influence by the use of reason — **rea•son•er** *n*

♦ [3] conclude, deduce, extrapolate, gather, infer, judge, understand ♦ [4] argue, assert, contend, maintain, plead

rea•son•able \ˈrēz-ᵊn-ə-bəl\ *adj* **1 :** being within the bounds of reason **:** not extreme **2 :** reasonable in price **:** INEXPENSIVE **3** ♦ **:** able to reason **:** RATIONAL **4** ♦ **:** being in accordance with reason — **rea•son•able•ness** *n*

♦ [3] intelligent, rational, reasoning ♦ [4] good, hard, informed, just, levelheaded, logical, rational, reasoned, sensible, sober, solid, valid, well-founded

rea•son•ably \-blē\ *adv* **:** in a reasonable manner

rea•soned *adj* ♦ **:** based on or marked by reasoning

♦ advised, calculated, deliberate, measured, studied, thoughtful, thought-out

rea•son•ing *n* ♦ **:** the use of reason

♦ logic, reason, sense

re•as•sure \ˌrē-ə-ˈshu̇r\ *vb* **1 :** to assure again **2** ♦ **:** to restore confidence to **:** free from fear — **re•as•sur•ance** \-ˈshu̇r-əns\ *n* — **re•as•sur•ing•ly** *adv*

♦ assure, cheer, comfort, console, solace, soothe

[1]**re•bate** \ˈrē-ˌbāt\ *vb* **re•bat•ed; re•bat•ing :** to make or give a rebate

[2]**rebate** *n* **:** a return of part of a payment

[1]**reb•el** \ˈre-bəl\ *adj* **:** of or relating to rebels

[2]**rebel** *n* ♦ **:** one that rebels against authority

♦ insurgent, insurrectionist, mutineer, red, revolter, revolutionary

[3]**re•bel** \ri-ˈbel\ *vb* **re•belled; re•bel•ling 1 :** to resist the authority of one's government **2 :** to act in or show disobedience **3 :** to feel or exhibit anger or revulsion

re•bel•lion \ri-ˈbel-yən\ *n* ♦ **:** resistance to authority; *esp* **:** defiance against a government through uprising or revolt

♦ insurrection, mutiny, revolt, revolution, uprising

re•bel•lious \-yəs\ *adj* **1** ♦ **:** given to or engaged in rebellion **2** ♦ **:** inclined to resist authority — **re•bel•lious•ly** *adv*

♦ [1] insurgent, mutinous, revolutionary ♦ [1, 2] contrary, defiant, disobedient, froward, intractable, recalcitrant, refractory, unruly, untoward, wayward, willful

re•bel•lious•ness *n* ♦ **:** the quality or state of being rebellious

♦ defiance, disobedience, insubordination, recalcitrance, refractoriness, unruliness

re•birth \ˌrē-ˈbərth\ *n* **1 :** a new or second birth **2** ♦ **:** a return or renewal of vigor, freshness, or productivity **:** REVIVAL

♦ regeneration, rejuvenation, renewal, resurgence, resurrection, resuscitation, revival

re•born \-ˈbȯrn\ *adj* **:** born again **:** REGENERATED, REVIVED

[1]**re•bound** \ˌrē-ˈbau̇nd, ˈrē-ˌbau̇nd\ *vb* **1** ♦ **:** to spring back on or as if on striking another body **2** ♦ **:** to recover from a setback or frustration

♦ [1] bounce, carom, glance, ricochet, skim, skip ♦ [2] rally, recover, snap back

[2]**re•bound** \ˈrē-ˌbau̇nd\ *n* **1 :** the action of rebounding **2 :** a rebounding ball **3 :** a reaction to setback or frustration

[1]**re•buff** \ri-ˈbəf\ *vb* **:** to reject or criticize sharply

[2]**rebuff** *n* ♦ **:** an abrupt rejection of an offer or advance

♦ brush-off, cold shoulder, repulse, snub

re•build \(ˌ)rē-ˈbild\ *vb* **-built** \-ˈbilt\; **-build•ing 1 :** REPAIR, RECONSTRUCT; *also* **:** REMODEL **2 :** to build again

[1]**re•buke** \ri-ˈbyük\ *vb* **re•buked; re•buk•ing** ♦ **:** to reprimand sharply

♦ censure, condemn, denounce, reprimand, reproach, reprove ♦ admonish, chide, lecture, rail (at *or* against), rate, reprimand, scold

[2]**rebuke** *n* ♦ **:** a sharp reprimand

♦ censure, denunciation, reprimand, reproach, reproof, stricture

re•bus \ˈrē-bəs\ *n* **:** a representation of syllables or words by means of pictures; *also* **:** a riddle composed of such pictures

re•but \ri-ˈbət\ *vb* **re•but•ted; re•but•ting** ♦ **:** to refute especially formally (as in debate) by evidence and arguments — **re•but•ter** *n*

♦ belie, confute, disprove, refute

re•but•tal \ri-ˈbət-ᵊl\ *n* **:** the act of rebutting; *also* ♦ **:** argument or proof that rebuts

♦ confutation, refutation

rec *abbr* **1** receipt **2** record; recording **3** recreation

re•cal•ci•trance \ri-ˈkal-sə-trəns\ *n* ♦ **:** the state of being recalcitrant

♦ defiance, disobedience, insubordination, rebelliousness, refractoriness, unruliness

re•cal•ci•trant \ri-ˈkal-sə-trənt\ *adj* **1** ♦ **:** stubbornly resisting authority **2 :** resistant to handling or treatment

♦ contrary, defiant, disobedient, froward, intractable, rebellious, refractory, unruly, untoward, wayward, willful

[1]**re•call** \ri-ˈkȯl\ *vb* **1 :** to call back **2** ♦ **:** to bring back to mind **:** REMEMBER, RECOLLECT **3** ♦ **:** to call off usually without expectation of conducting or performing at a later time **:** REVOKE, CANCEL

♦ [2] recollect, remember, reminisce, think ♦ [3] abort, call, call off, cancel, drop, repeal, rescind, revoke

[2]**re•call** \ri-ˈkȯl, ˈrē-ˌkȯl\ *n* **1 :** a summons to return **2 :** the procedure of removing an official by popular vote **3** ♦ **:** remembrance of things learned or experienced **4** ♦ **:** the act of revoking **5 :** a call by a manufacturer for the return of a product that may be defective or contaminated

♦ [3] memory, recollection, remembrance, reminiscence ♦ [4] abortion, calling, cancellation, repeal, rescission, revocation

re•cant \ri-ˈkant\ *vb* ♦ **:** to take back (something one has said) publicly **:** make an open confession of error — **re•can•ta•tion** \ˌrē-ˌkan-ˈtā-shən\ *n*

♦ abjure, renounce, retract, take back, unsay, withdraw

[1]**re•cap** \ˈrē-ˌkap, rē-ˈkap\ *vb* **re•capped; re•cap•ping :** to repeat the principal stages or phases of **:** RECAPITULATE

[2]**recap** *vb* **re•capped; re•cap•ping :** RETREAD — **re•cap** \ˈrē-ˌkap\ *n*

[3]**re•cap** \ˈrē-ˌkap\ *n* **:** RECAPITULATION

re•ca•pit•u•late \ˌrē-kə-ˈpi-chə-ˌlāt\ *vb* **-lat•ed; -lat•ing** ♦ **:** to restate briefly **:** SUMMARIZE

♦ abstract, digest, encapsulate, epitomize, outline, sum up, summarize, wrap up

re•ca•pit•u•la•tion \-ˌpi-chə-ˈlā-shən\ *n* ♦ : a concise summary

♦ abstract, digest, encapsulation, epitome, outline, précis, résumé (*or* resume), roundup, sum, summary, synopsis, wrap-up

re•cap•ture \(ˌ)rē-ˈkap-chər\ *vb* **1** ♦ : to capture again **2** : to experience again ⟨~ happy times⟩

♦ reclaim, recoup, recover, regain, repossess, retake, retrieve

re•cast \(ˌ)rē-ˈkast\ *vb* **1** : to cast again **2** ♦ : to alter the structure of : REVISE, REMODEL ⟨~ a sentence⟩

♦ alter, change, make over, modify, redo, refashion, remake, remodel, revamp, revise, rework, vary

recd *abbr* received

re•cede \ri-ˈsēd\ *vb* **re•ced•ed; re•ced•ing 1** ♦ : to move back or away **2** : to slant backward **3** ♦ : to grow less or smaller : DIMINISH

♦ [1] back, fall back, retire, retreat, withdraw ♦ [3] abate, deescalate, decline, decrease, die, diminish, dwindle, ebb, fall, lessen, let up, lower, moderate, relent, shrink, subside, taper, wane

¹re•ceipt \ri-ˈsēt\ *n* **1** : RECIPE **2** : the act of receiving **3** : something received — usually used in plural **4** : a written acknowledgment of something received

²receipt *vb* **1** : to give a receipt for **2** : to mark as paid

re•ceiv•able \ri-ˈsē-və-bəl\ *adj* **1** : capable of being received; *esp* : acceptable as legal ⟨~ certificates⟩ **2** : subject to call for payment ⟨notes ~⟩

re•ceive \ri-ˈsēv\ *vb* **re•ceived; re•ceiv•ing 1** : to take in or accept (as something sent or paid) : come into possession of : GET **2** : CONTAIN, HOLD **3** : to permit to enter : GREET, WELCOME **4** : to be at home to visitors **5** : to accept as true or authoritative **6** : to be the subject of : UNDERGO, EXPERIENCE ⟨~ a shock⟩ **7** : to change incoming radio waves into sounds or pictures

re•ceiv•er \ri-ˈsē-vər\ *n* **1** : one that receives **2** : a person legally appointed to receive and have charge of property or money involved in a lawsuit **3** : a device for converting electromagnetic waves or signals into audio or visual form ⟨telephone ~⟩

re•ceiv•er•ship \-ˌship\ *n* **1** : the office or function of a receiver **2** : the condition of being in the hands of a receiver

re•cen•cy \ˈrēs-ᵊn-sē\ *n* : RECENTNESS

re•cent \ˈrēs-ᵊnt\ *adj* **1** : of the present time or time just past ⟨~ history⟩ **2** : having lately come into existence : NEW, FRESH **3** *cap* : HOLOCENE — **re•cent•ness** *n*

re•cent•ly *adv* ♦ : during a recent period of time

♦ freshly, just, late, lately, new, newly, now, only

re•cep•ta•cle \ri-ˈsep-ti-kəl\ *n* **1** ♦ : something used to receive and hold something else : CONTAINER **2** : the enlarged end of a flower stalk upon which the parts of the flower grow **3** : an electrical fitting containing the live parts of a circuit

♦ container, holder, vessel

re•cep•tion \ri-ˈsep-shən\ *n* **1** : the act of receiving **2** : a social gathering at which guests are formally welcomed

re•cep•tion•ist \ri-ˈsep-shə-nist\ *n* : a person employed to greet callers

re•cep•tive \ri-ˈsep-tiv\ *adj* **1** : able or inclined to receive **2** ♦ : open and responsive to ideas, impressions, or suggestions — **re•cep•tive•ly** *adv* — **re•cep•tive•ness** *n* — **re•cep•tiv•i•ty** \ˌrē-ˌsep-ˈti-və-tē\ *n*

♦ broad-minded, open, open-minded

re•cep•tor \ri-ˈsep-tər\ *n* **1** : one that receives stimuli : SENSE ORGAN **2** : a chemical group or molecule in the outer cell membrane or in the cell interior that has an affinity for a specific chemical group, molecule, or virus

¹re•cess \ˈrē-ˌses, ri-ˈses\ *n* **1** : a secret or secluded place **2** ♦ : an indentation in a line or surface (as an alcove in a room) **3** ♦ : a suspension of business or procedure for rest or relaxation

♦ [2] alcove, niche, nook ♦ [3] break, leave, vacation ♦ [3] break, breath, breather, respite

²recess *vb* **1** : to put into a recess **2** : to make a recess in **3** : to interrupt for a recess **4** : to take a recess

re•ces•sion \ri-ˈse-shən\ *n* **1** : the act of receding : WITHDRAWAL **2** : a departing procession (as at the end of a church service) **3** : a period of reduced economic activity

re•ces•sion•al \ri-ˈse-shə-nəl\ *n* **1** : a hymn or musical piece at the conclusion of a service or program **2** : RECESSION 2

¹re•ces•sive \ri-ˈse-siv\ *adj* **1** : tending to recede **2** : producing or being a bodily characteristic that is masked or not expressed when a contrasting dominant gene or trait is present ⟨~ genes⟩ ⟨~ traits⟩

²recessive *n* : a recessive characteristic or gene; *also* : an individual that has one or more recessive characteristics

re•cher•ché \rə-ˌsher-ˈshā, -ˈsher-ˌshā\ *adj* **1** : CHOICE, RARE **2** : excessively refined

re•cid•i•vism \ri-ˈsi-də-ˌvi-zəm\ *n* : a tendency to relapse into a previous condition; *esp* : relapse into criminal behavior — **re•cid•i•vist** \-vist\ *n*

rec•i•pe \ˈre-sə-(ˌ)pē\ *n* **1** : a set of instructions for making something from various ingredients **2** : a method of procedure : FORMULA

re•cip•i•ent \ri-ˈsi-pē-ənt\ *n* : one that receives

¹re•cip•ro•cal \ri-ˈsi-prə-kəl\ *adj* **1** : inversely related **2** : MUTUAL, SHARED **3** : serving to reciprocate **4** : mutually corresponding — **re•cip•ro•cal•ly** *adv*

²reciprocal *n* **1** : something in a reciprocal relationship to another **2** : one of a pair of numbers (as ⅔ and $3/2$) whose product is one

re•cip•ro•cate \-ˌkāt\ *vb* **-cat•ed; -cat•ing 1** : to move backward and forward alternately **2** : to give and take mutually **3** : to make a return for something done or given — **re•cip•ro•ca•tion** \-ˌsi-prə-ˈkā-shən\ *n*

rec•i•proc•i•ty \ˌre-sə-ˈprä-sə-tē\ *n, pl* **-ties 1** : the quality or state of being reciprocal **2** : mutual exchange of privileges (as trade advantages between countries)

re•cit•al \ri-ˈsīt-ᵊl\ *n* **1** : an act or instance of reciting : ACCOUNT **2** : a public reading or recitation ⟨a poetry ~⟩ **3** : a concert given by a musician, dancer, or dance troupe **4** : a public exhibition of skill given by music or dance pupils — **re•cit•al•ist** \-ᵊl-ist\ *n*

rec•i•ta•tion \ˌre-sə-ˈtā-shən\ *n* **1** : RECITING, RECITAL **2** : delivery before an audience usually of something memorized **3** : a classroom exercise in which pupils answer questions on a lesson they have studied

re•cite \ri-ˈsīt\ *vb* **re•cit•ed; re•cit•ing 1** : to repeat verbatim (as something memorized) **2** ♦ : to recount in some detail : RELATE **3** : to reply to a teacher's questions on a lesson — **re•cit•er** *n*

♦ describe, narrate, recount, rehearse, relate, report, tell

reck•less \ˈre-kləs\ *adj* ♦ : lacking caution — **reck•less•ly** *adv* — **reck•less•ness** *n*

♦ brash, foolhardy, irresponsible ***Ant*** responsible

reck•on \ˈre-kən\ *vb* **1** ♦ : to arrive at or estimate by calculation : CALCULATE **2** ♦ : to regard or think of as : CONSIDER **3** *chiefly dial* : THINK, SUPPOSE, GUESS **4** ♦ : to accept something as certain : place reliance ⟨I ~ on your promise to help⟩

♦ [1] calculate, call, conjecture, estimate, figure, gauge, guess, judge, make, place, put, suppose ♦ [2] account, call, consider, count, esteem, hold, rate, regard, take ♦ [4] count, depend, lean, rely

reck•on•ing *n* **1** ♦ : an act or instance of reckoning **2** : a settling of accounts ⟨day of ~⟩

♦ appraisal, assessment, estimate, estimation, evaluation, valuation ♦ arithmetic, calculation, computation

re•claim \ri-ˈklām\ *vb* **1** ♦ : to correct or change from a pattern of wrong conduct : REFORM **2** : to change from an undesirable to a desired condition ⟨~ marshy land⟩ **3** : to obtain from a waste product or by-product **4** ♦ : to demand or obtain the return of — **re•claim•able** *adj*

♦ [1] redeem, reform, rehabilitate ♦ [4] recapture, recoup, recover, regain, repossess, retake, retrieve

rec•la•ma•tion \ˌre-klə-ˈmā-shən\ *n* ♦ : the act or process of reclaiming

♦ recovery, repossession, retrieval

re•cline \ri-ˈklīn\ *vb* **re•clined; re•clin•ing 1** : to lean or incline backward **2** : to lie down : REST

re•clin•er \ri-ˈklī-nər\ *n* : a chair with an adjustable back and footrest

re•cluse \ˈre-ˌklüs, ri-ˈklüs\ *n* ♦ : a person who leads a secluded or solitary life : HERMIT — **re•clu•sive** \ri-ˈklü-siv\ *adj*

♦ anchorite, hermit, solitary

rec•og•nise *chiefly Brit var of* RECOGNIZE

rec•og•ni•tion \ˌre-kəg-ˈni-shən\ *n* **1** : the act of recognizing : the state of being recognized : ACKNOWLEDGMENT **2** : special notice or attention

re•cog•ni•zance \ri-ˈkäg-nə-zəns\ *n* : a promise recorded before a court or magistrate to do something (as to appear in court or to keep the peace) usually under penalty of a money forfeiture

rec•og•nize \ˈre-kəg-ˌnīz\ *vb* **-nized; -niz•ing 1** : to acknowledge (as a speaker in a meeting) as one entitled to be heard at the time **2 :** to acknowledge the existence or the independence of (a country or government) **3 :** to take notice of **4 :** to acknowledge with appreciation **5 :** to acknowledge acquaintance with **6 :** to identify as previously known **7 :** to perceive clearly **:** REALIZE — **rec•og•niz•able** \ˈre-kəg-ˌnī-zə-bəl\ *adj* — **rec•og•niz•ably** \-blē\ *adv*

¹re•coil \ri-ˈkȯi(-ə)l\ *vb* **1** ♦ **:** to draw back **2 :** to spring back to or as if to a starting point

♦ blench, flinch, quail, shrink, wince

²re•coil \ˈrē-ˌkȯil, ri-ˈkȯil\ *n* **:** the action of recoiling (as by a gun or spring)

re•coil•less \-ˌkȯil-ləs, -ˈkȯil-\ *adj* **:** venting expanding propellant gas before recoil is produced ⟨~ gun⟩

rec•ol•lect \ˌre-kə-ˈlekt\ *vb* ♦ **:** to recall to mind **:** REMEMBER

♦ recall, remember, reminisce, think

rec•ol•lec•tion \ˌre-kə-ˈlek-shən\ *n* **1** ♦ **:** the act or power of recollecting **2 :** something recollected

♦ memory, recall, remembrance, reminiscence

re•com•bi•nant \(ˌ)rē-ˈkäm-bə-nənt\ *adj* **1 :** relating to genetic recombination **2 :** containing or produced by recombinant DNA ⟨~ vaccines⟩

re•com•bi•nant DNA \(ˌ)rē-ˈkäm-bə-nənt-\ *n* **:** genetically engineered DNA prepared in vitro by joining together DNA usually from more than one species of organism

re•com•bi•na•tion \ˌrē-ˌkäm-bə-ˈnā-shən\ *n* **:** the formation of new combinations of genes

rec•om•mend \ˌre-kə-ˈmend\ *vb* **1 :** to present as deserving of acceptance or trial **2 :** to give in charge **:** COMMIT **3 :** to make acceptable **4 :** to give advice to **:** ADVISE, COUNSEL — **rec•om•mend•able** \-ˈmen-də-bəl\ *adj*

rec•om•men•da•tion \ˌre-kə-mən-ˈdā-shən\ *n* **1 :** the act of recommending **2 :** something recommended **3 :** something that recommends

¹rec•om•pense \ˈre-kəm-ˌpens\ *vb* **-pensed; -pens•ing** **1** ♦ **:** to give compensation to **:** pay for **2** ♦ **:** to return in kind **:** REQUITE

♦ [1] clear, discharge, foot, liquidate, pay, pay off, quit, settle, spring, stand ♦ [2] compensate, indemnify, recoup, remunerate, requite

²recompense *n* ♦ **:** an equivalent or a return for something done, suffered, or given **:** COMPENSATION

♦ compensation, damages, indemnity, payment, quittance, redress, remuneration, reparation, requital, restitution, satisfaction

re•con•ceive \rē-kən-ˈsēv\ *vb* ♦ **:** to form again a conception of

♦ readdress, reanalyze, reconsider, reexamine, rethink, review

rec•on•cile \ˈre-kən-ˌsīl\ *vb* **-ciled; -cil•ing** **1** ♦ **:** to cause to be friendly or harmonious again **2 :** ADJUST, SETTLE ⟨~ differences⟩ **3 :** to bring to submission or acceptance — **rec•on•cil•able** *adj* — **rec•on•cile•ment** *n* — **rec•on•cil•er** *n*

♦ accommodate, conciliate, conform, coordinate, harmonize, key

rec•on•cil•i•a•tion \ˌre-kən-ˌsi-lē-ˈā-shən\ *n* **1 :** the action of reconciling **2 :** the Roman Catholic sacrament of penance

re•con•dite \ˈre-kən-ˌdīt\ *adj* **1 :** hard to understand **:** PROFOUND, ABSTRUSE **2 :** little known **:** OBSCURE

re•con•di•tion \ˌrē-kən-ˈdi-shən\ *vb* **1** ♦ **:** to restore to good condition (as by replacing parts) **2 :** to condition anew

♦ doctor, fix, mend, patch, renovate, repair, revamp

re•con•nais•sance \ri-ˈkä-nə-zəns, -səns\ *n* **:** a preliminary survey of an area; *esp* **:** an exploratory military survey of enemy territory

re•con•noi•ter *or* **re•con•noi•tre** \ˌrē-kə-ˈnȯi-tər, ˌre-\ *vb* **-noi•tered** *or* **-noi•tred; -noi•ter•ing** *or* **-noi•tring** **:** to make a reconnaissance of **:** engage in reconnaissance

re•con•sid•er \ˌrē-kən-ˈsi-dər\ *vb* ♦ **:** to consider again with a view to changing or reversing

♦ readdress, reanalyze, reconceive, reexamine, rethink, review

re•con•sid•er•a•tion \-ˌsi-də-ˈrā-shən\ *n* **:** the action of reconsidering or state of being reconsidered

re•con•sti•tute \ˌrē-ˈkän-stə-ˌtüt, -ˌtyüt\ *vb* **:** to restore to a former condition by adding water ⟨~ powdered milk⟩

re•con•struct \ˌrē-kən-ˈstrəkt\ *vb* **:** to construct again **:** REBUILD

re•con•struc•tion \ˌrē-kən-ˈstrək-shən\ *n* **1 :** the action of reconstructing **:** the state of being reconstructed **2** *often cap* **:** the reorganization and reestablishment of the seceded states in the Union after the American Civil War **3 :** something reconstructed

¹re•cord \ri-ˈkȯrd\ *vb* **1** ♦ **:** to set down in writing **2 :** to register permanently **3 :** INDICATE, READ **4 :** to give evidence of **5 :** to cause (as sound or visual images) to be registered (as on a disc or a magnetic tape) in a form that permits reproduction

♦ jot, log, mark, note, set down ♦ catalog, enroll, enter, index, inscribe, list, schedule, slate

²rec•ord \ˈre-kərd\ *n* **1 :** the act of being recorded **2** ♦ **:** a written account of proceedings **3 :** known facts about a person; *also* **:** a collection of items of information (as in a database) treated as a unit **4 :** an attested top performance **5 :** something on which sound or visual images have been recorded

♦ account, chronicle, history, narrative, report, story

³re•cord \ri-ˈkȯrd\ *n* **:** a function of an electronic device that causes it to record

re•cord•er \ri-ˈkȯr-dər\ *n* **1 :** a judge in some city courts **2 :** one who records transactions officially **3 :** a recording device **4 :** a wind instrument with a whistle mouthpiece and eight fingerholes

re•cord•ing *n* **:** RECORD 5

re•cord•ist \ri-ˈkȯr-dist\ *n* **:** one who records sound especially on film

¹re•count \ri-ˈkau̇nt\ *vb* ♦ **:** to relate in detail **:** TELL

♦ describe, narrate, recite, rehearse, relate, report, tell

²re•count \ˈrē-ˌkau̇nt, (ˌ)rē-ˈkau̇nt\ *vb* **:** to count again

³recount *n* **:** a second or fresh count

re•coup \ri-ˈküp\ *vb* **1** ♦ **:** to get an equivalent or compensation for **:** make up for something lost **2** ♦ **:** to gain anew **:** get again

♦ [1] compensate, indemnify, recompense, remunerate, requite ♦ [2] recapture, reclaim, recover, regain, repossess, retake, retrieve

re•course \ˈrē-ˌkōrs, ri-ˈkōrs\ *n* **1 :** a turning to someone or something for assistance or protection **2** ♦ **:** a source of aid **:** RESORT

♦ expedient, resort, resource

re•cov•er \ri-ˈkə-vər\ *vb* **1** ♦ **:** to get back again **:** REGAIN **2** ♦ **:** to regain normal health, poise, or status **3 :** to make up for **:** RECOUP ⟨~*ed* all his losses⟩ **4 :** RECLAIM ⟨~ land from the sea⟩ **5 :** to obtain a legal judgment in one's favor — **re•cov•er•able** *adj*

♦ [1] recapture, reclaim, recoup, regain, repossess, retake, retrieve ♦ [2] convalesce, gain, heal, mend, recuperate ♦ [2] rally, rebound, snap back

re–cov•er \ˌrē-ˈkə-vər\ *vb* **:** to cover again

recovering *adj* **:** being in the process of overcoming a shortcoming or problem ⟨a ~ alcoholic⟩

re•cov•ery \ri-ˈkə-və-rē\ *n* **1** ♦ **:** the act, process, or an instance of recovering **2** ♦ **:** the process of combating a disorder (as alcoholism) or a real or perceived problem

♦ [1] reclamation, repossession, retrieval ♦ [2] comeback, convalescence, rally, recuperation, rehabilitation

¹rec•re•ant \ˈre-krē-ənt\ *adj* **1** ♦ **:** crying for mercy or yielding in a cowardly manner **2** ♦ **:** unfaithful to duty or allegiance

♦ [1] chicken, cowardly, craven, dastardly, pusillanimous, spineless, yellow ♦ [2] disloyal, faithless, false, fickle, inconstant, loose, perfidious, traitorous, treacherous, unfaithful, untrue

²recreant *n* **1 :** a cowardly wretch **:** COWARD **2** ♦ **:** one who forsakes a duty, a cause, or anyone to whom he owes service **:** DESERTER **3** ♦ **:** one that is unfaithful

♦ [2] defector, deserter, renegade ♦ [3] apostate, betrayer, double-crosser, quisling, traitor, turncoat

rec•re•ate \ˈre-krē-ˌāt\ *vb* **-at•ed; -at•ing** **1** ♦ **:** to give new life or freshness to **2** ♦ **:** to take recreation — **rec•re•ative** \-ˌā-tiv\ *adj*

♦ [1] freshen, refresh, regenerate, rejuvenate, renew, restore, revitalize, revive ♦ [2] dally, disport, frolic, play, rollick, sport

re–cre•ate \ˌrē-krē-ˈāt\ *vb* **:** to create again — **re–cre•ation** \-ˈā-shən\ *n* — **re–cre•ative** \-ˈā-tiv\ *adj*

rec•re•ation \ˌre-krē-ˈā-shən\ *n* **:** a refreshing of strength or spirits after work; *also* **:** a means of refreshment — **rec•re•ation•al** \-shə-nəl\ *adj*

recreational vehicle *n* ♦ **:** a vehicle designed for recreational use (as camping)

♦ camper, caravan, motor home, RV, trailer

re•crim•i•na•tion \ri-ˌkri-mə-ˈnā-shən\ *n* **:** a retaliatory accusation — **re•crim•i•nate** \-ˈkri-mə-nāt\ *vb* — **re•crim•i•na•tory** \-ˈkri-mə-nə-ˌtōr-ē\ *adj*

re•cru•des•cence \ˌrē-krü-ˈdes-ᵊns\ *n* **:** a renewal or breaking out again especially of something unhealthful or dangerous

¹re•cruit \ri-ˈkrüt\ *vb* **1 :** to form or strengthen with new members ⟨~ an army⟩ **2 :** to enlist as a member of an armed service **3 :** to secure the services of **4 :** to seek to enroll **5 :** to restore or increase in health or vigor ⟨resting to ~ his strength⟩ — **re•cruit•er** *n* — **re•cruit•ment** *n*

²recruit *n* ♦ **:** a newcomer to an activity or field; *esp* **:** a newly enlisted member of the armed forces

♦ beginner, fledgling, freshman, greenhorn, neophyte, newcomer, novice, rookie, tenderfoot, tyro

rec•tal \ˈrekt-ᵊl\ *adj* **:** of or relating to the rectum — **rec•tal•ly** *adv*

rect•an•gle \ˈrek-ˌtaŋ-gəl\ *n* **:** a 4-sided figure with four right angles; *esp* **:** one with adjacent sides of unequal length — **rect•an•gu•lar** \rek-ˈtaŋ-gyə-lər\ *adj*

rec•ti•fi•er \ˈrek-tə-ˌfī-ər\ *n* **:** one that rectifies; *esp* **:** a device for converting alternating current into direct current

rec•ti•fy \ˈrek-tə-ˌfī\ *vb* **-fied; -fy•ing** ♦ **:** to make or set right **:** CORRECT — **rec•ti•fi•ca•tion** \ˌrek-tə-fə-ˈkā-shən\ *n*

♦ amend, correct, debug, emend, reform, remedy

rec•ti•lin•ear \ˌrek-tə-ˈli-nē-ər\ *adj* **1 :** moving in a straight line ⟨~ motion⟩ **2 :** characterized by straight lines

rec•ti•tude \ˈrek-tə-ˌtüd, -ˌtyüd\ *n* **1** ♦ **:** moral integrity **2 :** correctness of procedure

♦ character, decency, goodness, honesty, honor (*or* honour), integrity, morality, probity, righteousness, uprightness, virtue

rec•to \ˈrek-tō\ *n, pl* **rectos :** a right-hand page

rec•tor \ˈrek-tər\ *n* **1 :** a priest or minister in charge of a parish **2 :** the head of a university or school — **rec•to•ri•al** \rek-ˈtōr-ē-əl\ *adj*

rec•to•ry \ˈrek-tə-rē\ *n, pl* **-ries :** the residence of a rector or a parish priest

rec•tum \ˈrek-təm\ *n, pl* **rectums** *or* **rec•ta** \-tə\ **:** the last part of the intestine joining the colon and anus

re•cum•bent \ri-ˈkəm-bənt\ *adj* **:** lying down **:** RECLINING

re•cu•per•ate \ri-ˈkü-pə-ˌrāt-, -ˈkyü-\ *vb* **-at•ed; -at•ing** ♦ **:** to get back (as health or strength) **:** RECOVER — **re•cu•per•a•tive** \-ˈkü-pə-ˌrā-tiv, -ˈkyü-\ *adj*

♦ convalesce, gain, heal, mend, rally, recover, snap back

re•cu•per•a•tion \-ˌkü-pə-ˈrā-shən, -ˌkyü-\ *n* ♦ **:** restoration to health or strength

♦ comeback, convalescence, rally, recovery, rehabilitation

re•cur \ri-ˈkər\ *vb* **re•curred; re•cur•ring 1 :** to go or come back in thought or discussion **2 :** to occur or appear again especially after an interval **:** occur time after time — **re•cur•rence** \-ˈkər-əns\ *n*

re•cur•rent \-ənt\ *adj* ♦ **:** returning or happening time after time

♦ continual, intermittent, periodic

re•cur•ring \ri-ˈkə-riŋ\ *adj* **:** coming or happening again

re•cy•cle \rē-ˈsī-kəl\ *vb* **1 :** to pass again through a cycle of changes or treatment **2 :** to process (as liquid body waste, glass, or cans) in order to regain materials for human use — **re•cy•cla•ble** \-k(ə-)lə-bəl\ *adj or n* — **recycle** *n*

¹red \ˈred\ *adj* **red•der; red•dest 1 :** of the color red **2 :** endorsing radical social or political change especially by force **3** *often cap* **:** of or relating to the former U.S.S.R. or its allies — **red•ly** *adv* — **red•ness** *n*

²red *n* **1 :** the color of blood or of the ruby **2** ♦ **:** a revolutionary in politics **3** *cap* **:** COMMUNIST **4 :** the condition of showing a loss ⟨in the ~⟩

♦ insurgent, insurrectionist, mutineer, rebel, revolter, revolutionary

re•dact \ri-ˈdakt\ *vb* **1 :** to put in writing **:** FRAME **2 :** EDIT — **re•dac•tor** \-ˈdak-tər\ *n*

re•dac•tion \-ˈdak-shən\ *n* **1 :** an act or instance of redacting **2 :** EDITION

red alga *n* **:** any of a group of reddish usually marine algae

red blood cell *n* **:** any of the hemoglobin-containing cells that carry oxygen from the lungs to the tissues and are responsible for the red color of vertebrate blood

red•breast \ˈred-ˌbrest\ *n* **:** ROBIN

red–carpet *adj* **:** marked by ceremonial courtesy

red cedar *n* **:** an American juniper with scalelike leaves and fragrant close-grained red wood; *also* **:** its wood

red clover *n* **:** a European clover that has globe-shaped heads of reddish flowers and is widely cultivated for hay and forage

red•coat \ˈred-ˌkōt\ *n* **:** a British soldier especially during the Revolutionary War

red•den \ˈred-ᵊn\ *vb* ♦ **:** to make or become red or reddish **:** BLUSH

♦ bloom, blush, color (*or* colour), crimson, flush, glow

red•dish \ˈre-dish\ *adj* **:** tinged with red — **red•dish•ness** *n*

red dwarf *n* **:** a star with lower temperature and less mass than the sun

re•deem \ri-ˈdēm\ *vb* **1 :** to recover (property) by discharging an obligation **2 :** to ransom, free, or rescue by paying a price **3 :** to free from the consequences of sin **4 :** to remove the obligation of by payment ⟨the government ~*s* savings bonds⟩; *also* **:** to convert into something of value **5** ♦ **:** to make good (a promise) by performing **:** FULFILL **6 :** to atone for **7** ♦ **:** to change for the better — **re•deem•able** *adj*

♦ [5] answer, comply, fill, fulfill, keep, meet, satisfy ♦ [7] reclaim, reform, rehabilitate

re•deem•er *n* ♦ **:** a person who redeems

♦ deliverer, rescuer, savior

re•demp•tion \ri-ˈdemp-shən\ *n* **:** the act of redeeming **:** the state of being redeemed — **re•demp•tive** \-tiv\ *adj* — **re•demp•to•ry** \-tə-rē\ *adj*

re•de•ploy \ˌrē-di-ˈplȯi\ *vb* **1 :** to transfer from one area or activity to another **2 :** to relocate men or equipment — **re•de•ploy•ment** *n*

red–eye \ˈred-ˌī\ *n* **1 :** cheap whiskey **2 :** a late night or overnight flight

red•fish \ˈred-ˌfish\ *n* **:** any of various reddish marine fishes of the Atlantic including some used for food

red fox *n* **:** a fox with orange-red to reddish brown fur

red giant *n* **:** a very large star with a relatively low surface temperature

red–hand•ed \ˈred-ˈhan-dəd\ *adv or adj* **:** in the act of committing a misdeed

red•head \-ˌhed\ *n* **:** a person having red hair — **red•head•ed** \-ˌhe-dəd\ *adj*

red herring *n* **:** a diversion intended to distract attention from the real issue

red–hot \ˈred-ˈhät\ *adj* **1** ♦ **:** extremely hot; *esp* **:** glowing with heat **2** ♦ **:** exhibiting or marked by intense emotion, enthusiasm, or violence **3 :** very new ⟨~ news⟩

♦ [1] broiling, burning, fiery, hot, scorching, sultry, torrid ♦ [2] ardent, burning, charged, emotional, fervent, fiery, hot-blooded, impassioned, passionate, vehement

re•dial \ˈrē-ˌdī(-ə)l\ *n* **:** a telephone function that automatically repeats the dialing of the last number called — **redial** *vb*

re•dis•trib•ute \ˌrē-də-ˈstri-byüt\ *vb* **1 :** to alter the distribution of **2 :** to spread to other areas — **re•dis•tri•bu•tion** \(ˌ)rē-ˌdis-trə-ˈbyü-shən\ *n*

re•dis•trict \ˌrē-ˈdis-(ˌ)trikt\ *vb* **:** to organize into new territorial and especially political divisions

red–let•ter \ˈred ˌle-tər\ *adj* **:** of special significance **:** MEMORABLE

red–light district *n* **:** a district with many houses of prostitution

re•do \(ˌ)rē-ˈdü\ *vb* **1** ♦ **:** to do over or again **2 :** to freshen or change a decorative scheme **:** REDECORATE

♦ alter, change, make over, modify, recast, refashion, remake, remodel, revamp, revise, rework, vary ♦ duplicate, reiterate, remake, repeat, replicate

red oak *n* **:** any of various No. American oaks with leaves usually having spiny-tipped lobes and acorns that take two years to mature; *also* **:** the wood of a red oak

red•o•lence \ˈred-ᵊl-əns\ *n* **1** ♦ **:** the quality or state of being redolent **2** ♦ **:** an often pungent or agreeable odor

♦ [1] odor (*or* odour), scent, smell ♦ [2] aroma, bouquet, fragrance, incense, perfume, scent, spice

red•o•lent \ˈred-ᵊl-ənt\ *adj* **1** ♦ **:** exuding fragrance **:** FRAGRANT **2 :** having a specified fragrance ⟨a room ~ of cooked cabbage⟩ **3 :** REMINISCENT, SUGGESTIVE — **red•o•lent•ly** *adv*

♦ ambrosial, aromatic, fragrant, savory, scented, sweet

re•dou•ble \(ˌ)rē-ˈdə-bəl\ *vb* **1 :** to make twice as great in size or amount **2** ♦ **:** to make intense or more intensive **:** INTENSIFY

♦ amplify, beef, boost, consolidate, deepen, enhance, heighten, intensify, magnify, step up, strengthen

re•doubt \ri-ˈdau̇t\ *n* **:** a small usually temporary fortification
re•doubt•able \ri-ˈdau̇-tə-bəl\ *adj* ♦ **:** arousing dread or fear **:** FORMIDABLE

♦ dire, dreadful, fearful, fearsome, forbidding, formidable, frightful, hair-raising, scary

re•dound \ri-ˈdau̇nd\ *vb* **1 :** to have an effect **2 :** to become added or transferred **:** ACCRUE
red pepper *n* **1 :** CAYENNE PEPPER **2 :** a mature red hot pepper or sweet pepper
re•draft \rē-ˈdraft\ *vb* ♦ **:** to prepare a revised copy or a new version of

♦ edit, revamp, revise, rework

¹re•dress \ri-ˈdres\ *vb* **1 :** to set right **:** REMEDY **2 :** COMPENSATE **3 :** to remove the cause of (a grievance) **4 :** AVENGE
²redress *n* **1 :** relief from distress **2 :** means or possibility of seeking a remedy **3** ♦ **:** compensation for loss or injury **4 :** an act or instance of redressing

♦ compensation, damages, indemnity, quittance, recompense, remuneration, reparation, requital, restitution, satisfaction

red•shift \ˈred-ˈshift\ *n* **:** displacement of the spectrum of a heavenly body toward longer wavelength; *also* **:** a measure of this displacement
red snapper *n* **:** any of various reddish fishes including several food fishes
red spider *n* **:** SPIDER MITE
red squirrel *n* **:** a common American squirrel with the upper parts chiefly red
red–tailed hawk \ˈred-ˌtāld-\ *n* **:** a rodent-eating No. American hawk with a rather short tyically reddish tail
red tape *n* **:** official routine or procedure marked by excessive complexity which results in delay or inaction
red tide *n* **:** seawater discolored by the presence of large numbers of dinoflagellates which produce a toxin that renders infected shellfish poisonous
re•duce \ri-ˈdüs, -ˈdyüs\ *vb* **re•duced; re•duc•ing 1** ♦ **:** to diminish in size, amount, extent, or number **:** LESSEN **2 :** to bring to a specified state or condition ⟨*reduced* them to tears⟩ **3** ♦ **:** to put in a lower rank or grade **4 :** CONQUER ⟨∼ a fort⟩ **5 :** to bring into a certain order or classification **6 :** to correct (as a fracture) by restoration of displaced parts **7 :** to lessen one's weight — **re•duc•er** *n* — **re•duc•ible** \-ˈdü-sə-bəl, -ˈdyü-\ *adj*

♦ [1] abate, de-escalate, decrease, diminish, downsize, dwindle, lessen, lower ♦ [3] break, bust, degrade, demote, downgrade

re•duc•tion \ri-ˈdək-shən\ *n* **1** ♦ **:** the act of reducing **:** the state of being reduced **2 :** something made by reducing **3** ♦ **:** the amount taken off in reducing something

♦ [1, 3] abatement, decline, decrease, decrement, diminution, drop, fall, loss, shrinkage ♦ [3] abatement, deduction, discount

re•dun•dan•cy \ri-ˈdən-dən-sē\ *n, pl* **-cies 1 :** the quality or state of being redundant **:** SUPERFLUITY **2 :** something redundant or in excess **3** ♦ **:** the use of surplus words

♦ circumlocution, prolixity, verbiage, wordiness

re•dun•dant \-dənt\ *adj* ♦ **:** exceeding what is needed or normal **:** SUPERFLUOUS; *esp* **:** using more words than necessary — **re•dun•dant•ly** *adv*

♦ excess, extra, spare, superfluous, supernumerary, surplus

red–winged blackbird \ˈred-ˌwiŋd-\ *n* **:** a No. American blackbird of which the adult male is black with a patch of bright scarlet on the wings
red•wood \ˈred-ˌwu̇d\ *n* **:** a tall coniferous timber tree especially of coastal California; *also* **:** its durable wood
re•echo \rē-ˈe-kō\ *vb* ♦ **:** to continue to resound with echoes

♦ echo, resonate, resound, reverberate, sound

reed \ˈrēd\ *n* **1 :** any of various tall slender grasses of wet areas; *also* **:** a stem or growth of reed **2 :** a musical instrument made from the hollow stem of a reed **3 :** an elastic tongue of cane, wood, or metal by which tones are produced in organ pipes and certain other wind instruments — **reedy** *adj*
re•ed•u•cate \(ˌ)rē-ˈe-jə-ˌkāt\ *vb* **:** to train again; *esp* **:** to rehabilitate through education — **re•ed•u•ca•tion** *n*
¹reef \ˈrēf\ *n* **1 :** a part of a sail taken in or let out in regulating the sail's size **2 :** reduction in sail area by reefing
²reef *vb* **:** to reduce the area of a sail by rolling or folding part of it
³reef *n* **:** a ridge of rocks, sand or coral at or near the surface of the water
reef•er \ˈrē-fər\ *n* **:** a marijuana cigarette
¹reek \ˈrēk\ *n* **1 :** a strong or disagreeable fume or odor **2 :** a murky condition of the atmosphere or a substance causing it
²reek *vb* **1 :** to give off or become permeated with a strong or offensive odor **2 :** to give a strong impression of some constituent quality ⟨an excuse that ∼*ed* of falsehood⟩ — **reek•er** *n*
reeky \ˈrē-kē\ *adj* ♦ **:** emitting or permeated with a reek

♦ fetid, foul, fusty, malodorous, musty, noisome, rank, smelly, strong

¹reel \ˈrēl\ *n* **:** a revolvable device on which something flexible (as film or tape) is wound; *also* **:** a quantity of something wound on such a device
²reel *vb* **1 :** to wind on or as if on a reel **2 :** to pull or draw (as a fish) by reeling a line — **reel•able** *adj* — **reel•er** *n*
³reel *vb* **1** ♦ **:** to be in a whirl **:** WHIRL; *also* **:** to be giddy **2 :** to waver or fall back (as from a blow) **3** ♦ **:** to walk or move unsteadily

♦ [1] spin, swim, whirl ♦ [3] careen, dodder, lurch, stagger, teeter, totter

⁴reel *n* ♦ **:** a reeling motion

♦ gyration, pirouette, revolution, roll, rotation, spin, twirl, wheel, whirl

⁵reel *n* **:** a lively Scottish dance or its music
reel off *vb* ♦ **:** to tell or recite rapidly and easily ⟨*reeled off* the right answers⟩

♦ detail, enumerate, itemize, list, numerate, recite, rehearse, tick (off)

re•en•try \rē-ˈen-trē\ *n* **1 :** a second or new entry **2 :** the action of reentering the earth's atmosphere from space
re•eval•u•ate \rē-i-ˈval-yu̇-ˌwāt\ *vb* **:** to determine again the significance, worth, or condition of usually by careful appraisal and study
reeve \ˈrēv\ *vb* **rove** \ˈrōv\ *or* **reeved; reev•ing :** to pass (as a rope) through a hole in a block or cleat
re•ex•am•i•na•tion \rē-ig-ˌza-mə-ˈnā-shən\ *n* ♦ **:** a second or new examination

♦ reappraisal, retrospection, review

re•ex•am•ine \-ig-ˈza-mən\ *vb* ♦ **:** to subject to reexamination

♦ readdress, reanalyze, reconceive, reconsider, rethink, review

¹ref \ˈref\ *n* **:** REFEREE 2
²ref *abbr* **1** reference **2** referred **3** reformed **4** refunding
re•fash•ion \rē-ˈfa-shən\ *vb* ♦ **:** to make again **:** make over

♦ alter, change, make over, modify, recast, redo, remake, remodel, revamp, revise, rework, vary

re•fec•tion \ri-ˈfek-shən\ *n* **1 :** refreshment especially after hunger or fatigue **2 :** food and drink together **:** REPAST
re•fec•to•ry \ri-ˈfek-tə-rē\ *n, pl* **-ries :** a dining hall (as in a monastery or college)
re•fer \ri-ˈfər\ *vb* **re•ferred; re•fer•ring 1 :** to assign to a certain source, cause, or relationship **2 :** to direct or send to some person or place (as for information or help) **3 :** to submit to someone else for consideration or action **4** ♦ **:** to have recourse (as for information or aid) **5** ♦ **:** to have connection **:** RELATE **6** ♦ **:** to direct attention to or speak of **:** MENTION — **re•fer•able** \ˈre-fə-rə-bəl, ri-ˈfər-ə-\ *adj*

♦ *usu* **refer to** [4] go, resort, turn ♦ [5] appertain, apply, bear, pertain, relate ♦ *usu* **refer to** [6] advert (to), cite, instance, mention, name, note, notice, quote, specify, touch (*on* or *upon*)

¹ref•er•ee \ˌre-fə-ˈrē\ *n* **1** ♦ **:** a person to whom an issue especially in law is referred for investigation or settlement **2 :** an umpire in certain games

♦ arbiter, arbitrator, judge, umpire

²referee *vb* **-eed; -ee•ing** ♦ **:** to act as referee

♦ adjudicate, arbitrate, decide, determine, judge, rule, settle, umpire

ref•er•ence \ˈre-frəns, -fə-rəns\ *n* **1 :** the act of referring **2 :** RELATION, RESPECT **3 :** ALLUSION, MENTION **4 :** something that refers a reader to another passage or book **5 :** consultation especially for obtaining information ⟨books for ∼⟩ **6 :** a person of whom inquiries as to character or ability can be made **7 :** a written recommendation of a person for employment
ref•er•en•dum \ˌre-fə-ˈren-dəm\ *n, pl* **-da** \-də\ *or* **-dums :** the

submitting of legislative measures to the voters for approval or rejection; *also* : a vote on a measure so submitted

ref·er·ent \ˈre-frənt, -fə-rənt\ *n* : one that refers or is referred to; *esp* : the thing a word stands for — **referent** *adj*

re·fer·ral \ri-ˈfər-əl\ *n* **1** : the act or an instance of referring **2** : one that is referred

1**re·fill** \ˌrē-ˈfil\ *vb* : to fill again : REPLENISH — **re·fill·able** *adj*

2**re·fill** \ˈrē-ˌfil\ *n* : a new or fresh supply of something

re·fi·nance \ˌrē-fə-ˈnans, (ˌ)rē-ˈfī-nans\ *vb* : to renew or reorganize the financing of

re·fine \ri-ˈfīn\ *vb* **re·fined; re·fin·ing** **1** : to free from impurities or waste matter **2** ♦ : to improve or perfect by pruning or polishing : IMPROVE **3** : to free or become free of what is coarse or uncouth **4** : to make improvements by introducing subtle changes — **re·fin·er** *n*

♦ ameliorate, amend, better, enhance, enrich, improve, perfect

re·fined \ri-ˈfīnd\ *adj* **1** ♦ : freed from impurities **2** ♦ : reflecting a meticulous, sensitive, or demanding attitude **3** ♦ : marked by subtlety of discrimination or precision of method or technique : SUBTLE

♦ [1] absolute, fine, neat, plain, pure, straight, unadulterated, undiluted, unmixed ♦ [2] civilized, cultivated, cultured, genteel, polished ♦ [3] delicate, exact, fine, minute, nice, subtle

re·fine·ment \ri-ˈfīn-mənt\ *n* **1** : the action of refining **2** ♦ : the quality or state of being refined **3** : a refined feature or method **4** ♦ : something intended to improve or perfect

♦ [2] civilization, cultivation, culture, polish ♦ [4] advance, advancement, breakthrough, enhancement, improvement

re·fin·ery \ri-ˈfī-nə-rē\ *n, pl* **-er·ies** : a building and equipment for refining metals, oil, or sugar

re·flect \ri-ˈflekt\ *vb* **1** : to bend or cast back (as light, heat, or sound) **2** : to give back a likeness or image of as a mirror does **3** : to bring as a result ⟨~*ed* credit on him⟩ **4** : to cast reproach or blame ⟨their bad conduct ~*ed* on their training⟩ **5** : PONDER, MEDITATE — **re·flec·tiv·i·ty** \(ˌ)rē-ˌflek-ˈti-və-tē\ *n*

re·flec·tion \-ˈflek-shən\ *n* ♦ : a thought, idea, or opinion formed or a remark made as a result of meditation

♦ comment, note, observation, remark

re·flec·tive \-tiv\ *adj* ♦ : marked by reflection

♦ contemplative, meditative, melancholy, pensive, ruminant, thoughtful

re·flec·tor \ri-ˈflek-tər\ *n* : one that reflects; *esp* : a polished surface for reflecting radiation (as light)

1**re·flex** \ˈrē-ˌfleks\ *n* **1** : an automatic and usually inborn response to a stimulus not involving higher mental centers **2** *pl* : the power of acting or responding with enough speed ⟨an athlete with great ~*es*⟩

2**reflex** *adj* **1** : bent or directed back **2** : of, relating to, or produced by a reflex — **re·flex·ly** *adv*

1**re·flex·ive** \ri-ˈflek-siv\ *adj* : of or relating to an action directed back upon the doer or the grammatical subject ⟨a ~ verb⟩ ⟨the ~ pronoun *himself*⟩ — **re·flex·ive·ly** *adv* — **re·flex·ive·ness** *n*

2**reflexive** *n* : a reflexive verb or pronoun

re·flex·ol·o·gy \ˌrē-ˌflek-ˈsä-lə-jē\ *n* : massage in which pressure is applied to specific points on the hands or feet

re·flux \ˈrē-ˌfləks\ *n* : a flowing back

re·fo·cus \(ˌ)rē-ˈfō-kəs\ *vb* **1** : to focus again **2** : to change the emphasis or direction of ⟨~*ed* her life⟩

re·for·es·ta·tion \ˌrē-ˌfȯr-ə-ˈstā-shən\ *n* : the action of renewing forest cover by planting seeds or young trees — **re·for·est** \rē-ˈfȯr-əst\ *vb*

1**re·form** \ri-ˈfȯrm\ *vb* **1** ♦ : to make better or improve by removal of faults **2** ♦ : to correct or improve one's own character or habits — **re·form·able** *adj*

♦ [1] amend, correct, debug, emend, rectify, remedy ♦ [2] reclaim, redeem, rehabilitate

2**reform** *n* : improvement or correction of what is corrupt or defective

re–form \ˌrē-ˈfȯrm\ *vb* : to form again

ref·or·ma·tion \ˌre-fər-ˈmā-shən\ *n* **1** : the act of reforming : the state of being reformed **2** *cap* : a 16th-century religious movement marked by the establishment of the Protestant churches

re·for·ma·tive \-ˈfȯr-mə-tiv\ *adj* ♦ : intended or tending to reform

♦ corrective, remedial

1**re·for·ma·to·ry** \ri-ˈfȯr-mə-ˌtȯr-ē\ *adj* : aiming at or tending toward reformation : REFORMATIVE

2**reformatory** *n, pl* **-ries** : a penal institution for reforming especially young or first offenders

re·form·er \ri-ˈfȯr-mər\ *n* **1** : one that works for or urges reform **2** *cap* : a leader of the Protestant Reformation

refr *abbr* refraction

re·fract \ri-ˈfrakt\ *vb* : to subject to refraction

re·frac·tion \ri-ˈfrak-shən\ *n* : the bending of a ray (as of light) when it passes obliquely from one medium into another in which its speed is different — **re·frac·tive** \-tiv\ *adj*

refractive index *n* : the ratio of the speed of radiation in one medium to that in another medium

re·frac·to·ri·ness \ri-ˈfrak-tə-rē-nəs\ *n* ♦ : the quality or state of being refractory

♦ defiance, disobedience, insubordination, rebelliousness, recalcitrance, unruliness

re·frac·to·ry \ri-ˈfrak-tə-rē\ *adj* **1** ♦ : resisting control or authority **2** : capable of enduring high temperature ⟨~ bricks⟩ — **refractory** *n*

♦ contrary, defiant, disobedient, froward, headstrong, intractable, rebellious, recalcitrant, uncontrollable, unruly, untoward, wayward, willful

1**re·frain** \ri-ˈfrān\ *vb* ♦ : to hold oneself back : FORBEAR — **re·frain·ment** *n*

♦ *usu* **refrain from** abstain (from), forbear, forgo, keep

2**refrain** *n* : a phrase or verse recurring regularly in a poem or song

re·fresh \ri-ˈfresh\ *vb* **1** ♦ : to make or become fresh or fresher **2** ♦ : to revive by or as if by renewal of supplies ⟨~ one's memory⟩ **3** ♦ : to freshen up : restore to a state of newness or vitality **4** : to supply or take refreshment — **re·fresh·er** *n* — **re·fresh·ing·ly** *adv*

♦ [1, 2, 3] freshen, recreate, regenerate, rejuvenate, renew, restore, revitalize, revive

re·fresh·ing *adj* ♦ : serving to refresh

♦ bracing, invigorating, restorative, stimulative, tonic

re·fresh·ment \-mənt\ *n* **1** : the act of refreshing : the state of being refreshed **2** : something that refreshes **3** *pl* : a light meal; *also* : assorted light foods

re·fried beans \ˈrē-ˌfrīd-\ *n pl* : beans cooked with seasonings, fried, then mashed and fried again

refrig *abbr* refrigerating; refrigeration

re·frig·er·ate \ri-ˈfri-jə-ˌrāt\ *vb* **-at·ed; -at·ing** : to make cool; *esp* : to chill or freeze (food) for preservation — **re·frig·er·ant** \-jə-rənt\ *adj or n* — **re·frig·er·a·tion** \-ˌfri-jə-ˈrā-shən\ *n* — **re·frig·er·a·tor** \-ˈfri-jə-ˌrā-tər\ *n*

ref·uge \ˈre-ˌfyüj\ *n* **1** ♦ : shelter or protection from danger or distress **2** ♦ : a place that provides protection

♦ [1, 2] asylum, haven, retreat, sanctuary, shelter

ref·u·gee \ˌre-fyu̇-ˈjē\ *n* ♦ : one who flees for safety especially to a foreign country

♦ émigré, evacuee, exile, expatriate

re·ful·gence \ri-ˈfu̇l-jəns, -ˈfəl-\ *n* ♦ : a radiant or resplendent quality or state

♦ brilliance, dazzle, effulgence, illumination, lightness, lucidity, luminosity, radiance, splendor

re·ful·gent \-jənt\ *adj* ♦ : giving out a bright light : richly radiant

♦ beaming, bright, brilliant, effulgent, glowing, incandescent, lambent, lucent, lucid, luminous, lustrous, radiant, shiny

1**re·fund** \ri-ˈfənd, ˈrē-ˌfənd\ *vb* : to give or put back (money) : REPAY — **re·fund·able** *adj*

2**re·fund** \ˈrē-ˌfənd\ *n* **1** : the act of refunding **2** : a sum refunded

re·fur·bish \ri-ˈfər-bish\ *vb* : to brighten or freshen up : RENOVATE

re·fus·al \ri-ˈfyü-zəl\ *n* ♦ : the act of refusing or denying

♦ denial, disallowance, nay, no, rejection

1**re·fuse** \ri-ˈfyüz\ *vb* **re·fused; re·fus·ing** **1** ♦ : to decline to accept : REJECT **2** ♦ : to decline to do, give, or grant

♦ [1] decline, disallow, disapprove, negative, reject, repudiate, spurn, turn down ♦ [2] decline, deny, disallow, reject, withhold

2**ref·use** \ˈre-ˌfyüs, -ˌfyüz\ *n* ♦ : rejected or worthless matter : RUBBISH, TRASH

♦ chaff, deadwood, dust, garbage, junk, litter, riffraff, rubbish, scrap, trash, waste

ref·u·ta·tion \ˌre-fyu̇-ˈtā-shən\ *n* ♦ : the act or process of refuting; *also* : proof of falsehood or error

♦ confutation, rebuttal

re•fute \ri-ˈfyüt\ *vb* **re•fut•ed; re•fut•ing** ♦ : to prove to be false by argument or evidence — **re•fut•er** *n*

♦ belie, confute, disprove, rebut

¹reg \ˈreg\ *n* : REGULATION

²reg *abbr* **1** region **2** register; registered; registration **3** regular

re•gain \rē-ˈgān\ *vb* ♦ : to acquire or get possession of again

♦ recapture, reclaim, recoup, recover, repossess, retake, retrieve

re•gal \ˈrē-gəl\ *adj* **1** ♦ : of, relating to, or befitting a king : ROYAL **2** ♦ : of notable excellence or magnificence : STATELY, SPLENDID — **re•gal•ly** *adv*

♦ [1] kingly, monarchical, royal ♦ [2] august, baronial, gallant, glorious, grand, grandiose, heroic, imposing, magnificent, majestic, monumental, noble, proud, royal, splendid, stately

re•gale \ri-ˈgāl\ *vb* **re•galed; re•gal•ing** **1** ♦ : to entertain richly or agreeably especially with fine food and drink **2** ♦ : to give pleasure or amusement to

♦ [1] banquet, dine, feast, junket ♦ [2] amuse, disport, divert, entertain

re•ga•lia \ri-ˈgāl-yə\ *n pl* **1** : the emblems, symbols, or paraphernalia of royalty (as the crown and scepter) **2** : the insignia of an office or order **3** ♦ : special costume : FINERY

♦ array, best, bravery, caparison, feather, finery, frippery, full dress, gaiety

¹re•gard \ri-ˈgärd\ *n* **1** : CONSIDERATION, HEED; *also* : CARE, CONCERN **2** ♦ : a quick or cursory look : GLANCE, LOOK **3** ♦ : a feeling of respect and affection : RESPECT, ESTEEM **4** *pl* ♦ : friendly greetings implying respect and esteem **5** : an aspect to be considered : PARTICULAR — **re•gard•less** *adj*

♦ [2] cast, eye, gander, glance, glimpse, look, peek, peep, sight, view ♦ [3] admiration, appreciation, esteem, estimation, favor (*or* favour), respect ♦ **regards** [4] compliments, greetings, respects

²regard *vb* **1** ♦ : to think of : CONSIDER **2** : to pay attention to **3** ♦ : to show respect for : HEED **4** ♦ : to hold in high esteem : care for **5** : to look at : gaze upon **6** *archaic* : to relate to

♦ [1] account, call, consider, count, esteem, hold, rate, reckon, take ♦ [3] follow, heed, listen, mind, note, observe, watch ♦ [4] admire, appreciate, esteem, respect

re•gard•ful *adj* ♦ : full or expressive of regard or respect

♦ deferential, dutiful, respectful

re•gard•ing *prep* ♦ : with respect to : CONCERNING

♦ about, apropos of, concerning, of, on, respecting, toward

regardless of \ri-ˈgärd-ləs-\ *prep* ♦ : in spite of

♦ despite, notwithstanding, with

re•gat•ta \ri-ˈgä-tə, -ˈga-\ *n* : a boat race or a series of boat races

re•gen•cy \ˈrē-jən-sē\ *n, pl* **-cies** **1** : the office or government of a regent or body of regents **2** : a body of regents **3** : the period during which a regent governs

re•gen•er•a•cy \ri-ˈje-nə-rə-sē\ *n* : the state of being regenerated

¹re•gen•er•ate \ri-ˈje-nə-rət\ *adj* **1** : formed or created again **2** : spiritually reborn or converted

²re•gen•er•ate \ri-ˈje-nə-ˌrāt\ *vb* **1** : to subject to spiritual renewal **2** : to reform completely **3** : to replace (a body part) by a new growth of tissue **4** ♦ : to give new life to : REVIVE **5** ♦ : to restore to original strength or properties — **re•gen•er•a•tive** \-ˈje-nə-ˌrā-tiv\ *adj* — **re•gen•er•a•tor** \-ˌrā-tər\ *n*

♦ [4] reanimate, reinvigorate, rejuvenate, renew, resuscitate, revitalize, revive ♦ [5] freshen, recreate, refresh, renew, restore

re•gen•er•a•tion \-ˌje-nə-ˈrā-shən\ *n* ♦ : an act or the process of regenerating

♦ rebirth, rejuvenation, renewal, resurgence, resurrection, resuscitation, revival

re•gent \ˈrē-jənt\ *n* **1** : a person who rules during the childhood, absence, or incapacity of the sovereign **2** : a member of a governing board (as of a state university) — **regent** *adj*

reg•gae \ˈre-ˌgā\ *n* : popular music of Jamaican origin that combines native styles with elements of rock and soul music

reg•i•cide \ˈre-jə-ˌsīd\ *n* **1** : one who murders a king **2** : murder of a king

re•gime *also* **ré•gime** \rā-ˈzhēm, ri-\ *n* **1** : REGIMEN **2** : a form or system of government **3** ♦ : a government in power; *also* : a period of rule

♦ administration, authority, government, jurisdiction, rule

reg•i•men \ˈre-jə-mən\ *n* **1** : a systematic course of treatment or training ⟨a strict dietary ~⟩ **2** : the continuous exercise of authority over and the performance of functions for a political unit : GOVERNMENT

¹reg•i•ment \ˈre-jə-mənt\ *n* : a military unit consisting usually of a number of battalions — **reg•i•men•tal** \ˌre-jə-ˈment-təl\ *adj*

²reg•i•ment \ˈre-jə-ˌment\ *vb* : to organize rigidly especially for regulation or central control; *also* : to subject to order or uniformity — **reg•i•men•ta•tion** \ˌre-jə-mən-ˈtā-shən\ *n*

reg•i•men•tals \ˌre-jə-ˈmen-təlz\ *n pl* **1** : a regimental uniform **2** : military dress

re•gion \ˈrē-jən\ *n* ♦ : an often indefinitely defined part or area

♦ area, demesne, field, zone ♦ belt, land, tract, zone

re•gion•al \ˈrē-jə-nəl\ *adj* **1** : affecting a particular region : LOCALIZED **2** : of, relating to, characteristic of, or serving a region — **re•gion•al•ly** *adv*

¹reg•is•ter \ˈre-jə-stər\ *n* **1** ♦ : a record of items or details; *also* : a book or system for keeping such a record **2** : the range of a voice or instrument **3** : a device to regulate ventilation or heating **4** : an automatic device recording a number or quantity **5** : CASH REGISTER

♦ catalog, checklist, list, listing, menu, registry, roll, roster, schedule, table

²register *vb* **-tered; -ter•ing** **1** ♦ : to enter in a register (as in a list of guests) **2** : to record automatically **3** : to secure special care for (mail matter) by paying additional postage **4** : to convey an impression of : EXPRESS **5** : to make or adjust so as to correspond exactly **6** ♦ : to make a record of

♦ [1] catalog, enroll, enter, index, inscribe, list, put down, record, schedule, slate ♦ [6] jot, log, mark, note, put down, record, set down

³register *n* : one who registers or records

registered nurse *n* : a graduate trained nurse who has been licensed to practice by a state authority after passing qualifying examinations

reg•is•trant \ˈre-jə-strənt\ *n* : one that registers or is registered

reg•is•trar \-ˌsträr\ *n* ♦ : an official recorder or keeper of records (as at an educational institution)

♦ clerk, register, scribe

reg•is•tra•tion \ˌre-jə-ˈstrā-shən\ *n* **1** : the act of registering **2** : an entry in a register **3** : the number of persons registered : ENROLLMENT **4** : a document certifying an act of registering

reg•is•try \ˈre-jə-strē\ *n, pl* **-tries** **1** : ENROLLMENT, REGISTRATION **2** : a place of registration **3** ♦ : an official record book or an entry in one

♦ catalog, checklist, list, listing, menu, register, roll, roster, schedule, table

reg•nant \ˈreg-nənt\ *adj* **1** : REIGNING **2** : DOMINANT **3** : of common or widespread occurrence

¹re•gress \ˈrē-ˌgres\ *n* **1** : an act or the privilege of going or coming back **2** : RETROGRESSION

²re•gress \ri-ˈgres\ *vb* : to go or cause to go back or to a lower level — **re•gres•sive** *adj* — **re•gres•sor** \-ˈgre-sər\ *n*

re•gres•sion \ri-ˈgre-shən\ *n* : the act or an instance of regressing; *esp* : reversion to an earlier mental or behavioral level

¹re•gret \ri-ˈgret\ *vb* **re•gret•ted; re•gret•ting** **1** : to mourn the loss or death of **2** ♦ : to be very sorry for **3** : to experience regret — **re•gret•ter** *n*

♦ bemoan, deplore, lament, repent, rue

²regret *n* **1** ♦ : sorrow caused by something beyond one's power to remedy **2** : an expression of sorrow **3** *pl* : a note politely declining an invitation

♦ contrition, penitence, remorse, repentance, rue

re•gret•ful \-fəl\ *adj* ♦ : full of regret

♦ apologetic, contrite, penitent, remorseful, repentant, rueful, sorry

re•gret•ful•ly *adv* : with regret

re•gret•ta•ble \-ˈgre-tə-bəl\ *adj* ♦ : deserving regret

♦ deplorable, distressful, grievous, heartbreaking, lamentable, unfortunate, woeful

re•gret•ta•bly \-ˈgre-tə-blē\ *adv* **1 :** to a regrettable extent **2 :** it is to be regretted
re•group \(ˌ)rē-ˈgrüp\ *vb* **:** to form into a new grouping
regt *abbr* regiment
[1]**reg•u•lar** \ˈre-gyə-lər\ *adj* **1 :** belonging to a religious order **2** ♦ **:** made, built, or arranged according to a rule, standard, or type; *also* **:** even or symmetrical in form or structure **3 a :** ORDERLY, METHODICAL ⟨~ habits⟩ **b** ♦ **:** recurring, attending, or functioning at fixed, uniform, or normal intervals **:** not varying ⟨a ~ pace⟩ **4 :** made, selected, or conducted according to rule or custom **5 :** properly qualified ⟨not a ~ lawyer⟩ **6 :** conforming to the normal or usual manner of inflection **7 :** of, relating to, or constituting the permanent standing military force of a state **8 :** having no restriction, exception, or qualification **9** ♦ **:** conforming to a type, standard, or regular pattern — **reg•u•lar•i•ty** \ˌre-gyə-ˈlar-ə-tē\ *n* — **reg•u•lar•ly** *adv*

♦ [2] methodical, orderly, systematic ♦ [3b] constant, frequent, habitual, periodic, repeated, steady ***Ant*** inconstant, infrequent, irregular ♦ [9] average, characteristic, normal, representative, standard, typical

[2]**regular** *n* **1 :** one that is regular (as in attendance) **2 :** a member of the regular clergy **3 :** a soldier in a regular army **4 :** a player on an athletic team who is usually in the starting lineup
reg•u•lar•ize \ˈre-gyə-lə-ˌrīz\ *vb* ♦ **:** to make regular by conformance to law, rules, or custom

♦ formalize, homogenize, normalize, standardize

reg•u•late \ˈre-gyə-ˌlāt\ *vb* **-lat•ed; -lat•ing 1** ♦ **:** to govern or direct according to rule **:** CONTROL **2 :** to bring under the control of law or authority **3 :** to put in good order **4 :** to fix or adjust the time, amount, degree, or rate of — **reg•u•la•tive** \-ˌlā-tiv\ *adj* — **reg•u•la•tor** \-ˌlā-tər\ *n* — **reg•u•la•to•ry** \-lə-ˌtōr-ē\ *adj*

♦ administer, carry on, conduct, control, direct, govern, guide, handle, manage, operate, oversee, run, superintend, supervise

reg•u•la•tion \ˌre-gyə-ˈlā-shən\ *n* **1** ♦ **:** the act of regulating **:** the state of being regulated **2 :** a rule dealing with details of procedure **3 :** an order issued by an executive authority of a government and having the force of law

♦ administration, conduct, control, direction, government, guidance, management, operation, oversight, running, superintendence, supervision

re•gur•gi•tate \rē-ˈgər-jə-ˌtāt\ *vb* **-tat•ed; -tat•ing :** to throw or be thrown back, up, or out ⟨~ food⟩ — **re•gur•gi•ta•tion** \-ˌgər-jə-ˈtā-shən\ *n*
re•hab \ˈrē-ˌhab\ *n* **1 :** REHABILITATION **2 :** a rehabilitated building — **rehab** *vb*
re•ha•bil•i•tate \ˌrē-hə-ˈbi-lə-ˌtāt, ˌrē-ə-\ *vb* **-tat•ed; -tat•ing 1 :** to restore to a former capacity, rank, or right **:** REINSTATE **2** ♦ **:** to restore to good condition or health — **re•ha•bil•i•ta•tive** \-ˌtā-tiv\ *adj*

♦ cure, heal, mend

re•ha•bil•i•ta•tion \-ˌbi-lə-ˈtā-shən\ *n* ♦ **:** the action or process of rehabilitating or of being rehabilitated

♦ comeback, convalescence, rally, recovery, recuperation

re•hash \ˌrē-ˈhash\ *vb* **:** to present again in another form without real change or improvement — **rehash** *n*
re•hear•ing \ˌrē-ˈhir-iŋ\ *n* **:** a second or new hearing by the same tribunal
re•hears•al \ri-ˈhər-səl\ *n* **1 :** something told again **:** RECITAL **2** ♦ **:** a private performance or practice session preparatory to a public appearance

♦ dry run, practice, trial

re•hearse \ri-ˈhərs\ *vb* **re•hearsed; re•hears•ing 1 :** to say again **:** REPEAT **2 a** ♦ **:** to recount in order **:** ENUMERATE **b** ♦ **:** to present an account of **:** RELATE **3 :** to give a rehearsal of **4 :** to train by rehearsal **5 :** to engage in a rehearsal — **re•hears•er** *n*

♦ [2a] detail, enumerate, itemize, list, numerate, tick (off) ♦ [2b] describe, narrate, recite, recount, relate, report, tell

re•heat \ˌrē-ˈhēt\ *vb* **:** to heat again
[1]**reign** \ˈrān\ *n* **1 :** the authority or rule of a sovereign **2 :** the time during which a sovereign rules
[2]**reign** *vb* **1 :** to rule as a sovereign **2 :** to be predominant or prevalent
re•im•burse \ˌrē-əm-ˈbərs\ *vb* **-bursed; -burs•ing :** to pay back **:** make restitution — **re•im•burs•able** *adj* — **re•im•burse•ment** *n*
[1]**rein** \ˈrān\ *n* **1 :** a strap fastened to a bit by which a rider or driver controls an animal **2 :** a restraining influence **:** CHECK **3** ♦ **:** controlling or guiding power **4 :** complete freedom — usually used in the phrase *give rein to*

♦ chair, head, headship, helm

[2]**rein** *vb* ♦ **:** to check or direct by reins

♦ *usu* **rein in** bridle, check, constrain, contain, control, curb, govern, inhibit, regulate, restrain, tame

re•in•car•na•tion \ˌrē-(ˌ)in-(ˌ)kär-ˈnā-shən\ *n* **:** rebirth of the soul in a new body — **re•in•car•nate** \ˌrē-in-ˈkär-ˌnāt\ *vb*
rein•deer \ˈrān-ˌdir\ *n* **:** CARIBOU — used especially for one of the Old World
reindeer moss *n* **:** a gray, erect, tufted, and much-branched edible lichen of northern regions that is an important food of reindeer
re•in•fec•tion \ˌrē-in-ˈfek-shən\ *n* **:** infection following another infection of the same type
re•in•force \ˌrē-ən-ˈfōrs\ *vb* **1 :** to strengthen with additional forces ⟨~ our troops⟩ **2 :** to strengthen with new force, aid, material, or support — **re•in•force•ment** *n* — **re•in•forc•er** *n*
re•in•scribe \ˌrē-ən-ˈskrīb\ *vb* **:** to reestablish or rename in a new and especially stronger form or context
re•in•state \ˌrē-in-ˈstāt\ *vb* **-stat•ed; -stat•ing :** to restore to a former position, condition, or capacity — **re•in•state•ment** *n*
re•in•vent \ˌrē-in-ˈvent\ *vb* **1 :** to make as if for the first time something already invented ⟨~ the wheel⟩ **2 :** to remake completely
re•in•vig•o•rate \rē-in-ˈvi-gə-ˌrāt\ *vb* ♦ **:** to give life and energy to again

♦ reanimate, regenerate, rejuvenate, renew, resuscitate, revitalize, revive

re•it•er•ate \rē-ˈi-tə-ˌrāt\ *vb* **-at•ed; -at•ing** ♦ **:** to state or do over again or repeatedly

♦ duplicate, redo, remake, repeat, replicate

re•it•er•a•tion \-ˌi-tə-ˈrā-shən\ *n* ♦ **:** the action of reiterating

♦ duplication, repeat, repetition, replication

[1]**re•ject** \ri-ˈjekt\ *vb* **1** ♦ **:** to refuse to accept, consider, use, or submit to **2** ♦ **:** to refuse to hear, receive, or admit **3 :** to rebuff or withhold love from **4** ♦ **:** to throw out especially as useless or unsatisfactory **5 :** to subject (a transplanted tissue) to an attack by immune system components of the recipient organism

♦ [1] decline, disallow, disapprove, negative, refuse, repudiate, spurn, turn down ♦ [2] contradict, deny, disallow, disavow, disclaim, gainsay, negate, negative, repudiate ♦ [4] cast, discard, ditch, dump, fling, jettison, junk, lose, scrap, shed, shuck, slough, throw away, throw out, unload

[2]**re•ject** \ˈrē-ˌjekt\ *n* ♦ **:** a rejected person or thing

♦ castaway, outcast ♦ cull, discard, rejection

re•jec•tion \ri-ˈjek-shən\ *n* **1** ♦ **:** the action of rejecting **:** the state of being rejected **2 :** something rejected

♦ contradiction, denial, disallowance, disavowal, disclaimer, negation, refusal, repudiation

re•joice \ri-ˈjȯis\ *vb* **re•joiced; re•joic•ing 1** ♦ **:** to give joy to **:** GLADDEN **2** ♦ **:** to feel joy or great delight — **re•joic•er** *n*

♦ [1] content, delight, gladden, gratify, please, satisfy, suit, warm ♦ [2] crow, delight, exult, glory, joy, triumph

re•joic•ing \ri-ˈjȯi-siŋ\ *adj* ♦ **:** having or expressing feelings of joy or triumph

♦ exultant, jubilant, triumphant

re•join \(ˌ)rē-ˈjȯin *for 1*, ri- *for 2*\ *vb* **1 :** to join again **2** ♦ **:** to say in answer (as to a plaintiff's plea in court) **:** REPLY

♦ answer, reply, respond, retort, return

re•join•der \ri-ˈjȯin-dər\ *n* **:** something said, written, or done in answer or response **:** REPLY; *esp* **:** an answer to a reply
re•ju•ve•nate \ri-ˈjü-və-ˌnāt\ *vb* **-nat•ed; -nat•ing 1** ♦ **:** to make young or youthful again **:** give new vigor to **2** ♦ **:** to restore to an original or new state

♦ [1] reanimate, regenerate, reinvigorate, renew, resuscitate, revitalize, revive ♦ [2] freshen, recreate, refresh, renew, restore, revive

re•ju•ve•na•tion \-ˌjü-və-ˈnā-shən\ *n* ♦ **:** the action of rejuvenating or the state of being rejuvenated

♦ rebirth, regeneration, renewal, resurgence, resurrection, resuscitation, revival

re•kin•dle \rē-ˈkin-dᵊl\ *vb* **:** to kindle again **:** arouse again

rel *abbr* **1** relating; relative **2** religion; religious
¹re·lapse \ri-ˈlaps, ˈrē-ˌlaps\ *n* **1 :** the act or process of backsliding or worsening **2 :** a recurrence of illness after a period of improvement
²re·lapse \ri-ˈlaps\ *vb* **re·lapsed; re·laps·ing :** to slip or fall back into a former worse state (as of illness)
re·late \ri-ˈlāt\ *vb* **re·lat·ed; re·lat·ing** **1** ♦ **:** to give an account of **:** TELL **2** ♦ **:** to show or establish logical or causal connection between **3** ♦ **:** to have relationship or connection **4 :** to have or establish relationship ⟨the way a child ∼*s* to a teacher⟩ **5 :** to respond favorably — **re·lat·able** *adj* — **re·lat·er** *or* **re·la·tor** \-ˈlā-tər\ *n*

♦ [1] describe, narrate, recite, recount, rehearse, report, tell ♦ [2] associate, connect, correlate, identify, link ♦ [3] appertain, apply, bear, pertain, refer

re·lat·ed *adj* **1** ♦ **:** connected by some understood relationship **2 :** connected through membership in the same family — **re·lat·ed·ness** *n*

♦ akin, kindred *Ant* unrelated

re·la·tion \ri-ˈlā-shən\ *n* **1 :** NARRATION, ACCOUNT **2** ♦ **:** an aspect or quality (as resemblance) that connects two or more things or parts as being or belonging or working together or as being of the same kind **:** CONNECTION, RELATIONSHIP **3 :** connection by blood or marriage **:** KINSHIP; *also* **:** RELATIVE **4 :** REFERENCE, RESPECT ⟨in ∼ to⟩ **5 :** the state of being mutually interested or involved (as in social or commercial matters) **6** *pl* ♦ **:** commercial, professional, public, or personal business **:** DEALINGS **7** *pl* **:** SEXUAL INTERCOURSE — **re·la·tion·al** \-shə-nəl\ *adj*

♦ [2] association, bearing, connection, kinship, liaison, linkage, relationship ♦ **relations** [6] dealings, intercourse

re·la·tion·ship \-ˌship\ *n* ♦ **:** the state of being related or interrelated

♦ association, bearing, connection, kinship, liaison, linkage, relation ♦ affiliation, alliance, association, collaboration, confederation, connection, cooperation, hookup, liaison, partnership, relation, union

¹rel·a·tive \ˈre-lə-tiv\ *n* **1 :** a word referring grammatically to an antecedent **2 :** a thing having a relation to or a dependence upon another thing **3** ♦ **:** a person connected with another by blood or marriage

♦ kin, kinsman, relation

²relative *adj* **1 :** introducing a subordinate clause qualifying an expressed or implied antecedent ⟨∼ pronoun⟩; *also* **:** introduced by such a connective ⟨∼ clause⟩ **2** ♦ **:** having significant and demonstrable bearing on the matter at hand **:** PERTINENT **3** ♦ **:** not absolute or independent **:** COMPARATIVE **4 :** expressed as the ratio of the specified quantity to the total magnitude or to the mean of all quantities involved — **rel·a·tive·ness** *n*

♦ [2] applicable, apposite, apropos, germane, material, pertinent, pointed, relevant ♦ [3] approximate, comparative, near

relative humidity *n* **:** the ratio of the amount of water vapor actually present in the air to the greatest amount possible at the same temperature
rel·a·tive·ly *adv* ♦ **:** to a relative degree or extent

♦ fairly, kind of, like, pretty, quite, rather, somewhat, sort of

rel·a·tiv·is·tic \ˌre-lə-ti-ˈvis-tik\ *adj* **1 :** of, relating to, or characterized by relativity **2 :** moving at a velocity that is a significant fraction of the speed of light so that effects predicted by the theory of relativity become evident ⟨a ∼ electron⟩ — **rel·a·tiv·is·ti·cal·ly** \-ti-k(ə-)lē\ *adv*
rel·a·tiv·i·ty \ˌre-lə-ˈti-və-tē\ *n, pl* **-ties** **1 :** the quality or state of being relative **2 :** a theory in physics that considers mass and energy to be equivalent and that predicts changes in mass, dimension, and time which are related to speed but are noticeable especially at speeds approaching that of light
re·lax \ri-ˈlaks\ *vb* **1** ♦ **:** to make or become less firm, tense, or rigid **2 :** to make less severe or strict **3** ♦ **:** to seek rest or recreation — **re·lax·er** *n*

♦ [1] ease, loosen, slack, slacken ♦ [3] bask, loll, lounge, repose, rest ♦ [3] chill out, de-stress, unwind *Ant* tense (up)

¹re·lax·ant \ri-ˈlak-sənt\ *adj* **:** of, relating to, or producing relaxation
²relaxant *n* **:** a relaxing agent; *esp* **:** a drug that induces muscular relaxation
re·lax·ation \ˌrē-ˌlak-ˈsā-shən\ *n* **1** ♦ **:** the act of relaxing or state of being relaxed **:** a lessening of tension **2** ♦ **:** a relaxing or recreative state, activity, or pastime

♦ [1] ease, leisure, repose, rest ♦ [2] dalliance, frolic, fun, play, sport

re·laxed \ri-ˈlakst\ **1** ♦ **:** freed from or lacking in precision or stringency **2** ♦ **:** set or being at rest or at ease **3 :** easy of manner

♦ [1] easygoing, flexible, lax, loose, slack, unrestrained, unrestricted ♦ [2] comfortable, snug

¹re·lay \ˈrē-ˌlā\ *n* **1 :** a fresh supply (as of horses or men) arranged beforehand to relieve others **2 :** a race between teams in which each team member covers a specified part of a course **3 :** an electromagnetic device in which the opening or closing of one circuit activates another device (as a switch in another circuit) **4 :** the act of passing along by stages
²re·lay \ˈrē-ˌlā, ri-ˈlā\ *vb* **re·layed; re·lay·ing** **1 :** to place in or provide with relays **2 :** to pass along by relays **3 :** to control or operate by a relay
³re·lay \(ˌ)rē-ˈlā\ *vb* **-laid** \-ˈlād\; **-lay·ing :** to lay again
¹re·lease \ri-ˈlēs\ *vb* **re·leased; re·leas·ing** **1 a** ♦ **:** to set free from confinement or restraint **b :** DISMISS **2 :** to relieve from something that oppresses, confines, or burdens **3 :** RELINQUISH ⟨∼ a claim⟩ **4 :** to permit publication, performance, exhibition, or sale of; *also* **:** to make available to the public

♦ discharge, emancipate, enfranchise, free, liberate, loose, loosen, manumit, spring, unbind, unchain, unfetter ♦ loose, loosen, uncork, unleash, unlock, unloosen *Ant* bridle, check, constrain, contain, control, curb, govern, hold in, inhibit, regulate, rein (in), restrain, tame

²release *n* **1 :** relief or deliverance from sorrow, suffering, or trouble **2** ♦ **:** discharge from an obligation or responsibility **3 :** an act of setting free **:** the state of being freed **4 :** a document effecting a legal release **5** ♦ **:** a releasing for performance or publication; *also* **:** the matter released (as to the press) **6 :** a device for holding or releasing a mechanism as required

♦ [2] delivery, discharge, quietus, quittance ♦ [5] advertisement, announcement, bulletin, notice, notification

rel·e·gate \ˈre-lə-ˌgāt\ *vb* **-gat·ed; -gat·ing** **1 :** to send into exile **:** BANISH **2 :** to remove or dismiss to some less prominent position **3 :** to assign to a particular class or sphere **4 :** to submit to someone or something for appropriate action **:** DELEGATE — **rel·e·ga·tion** \ˌre-lə-ˈgā-shən\ *n*
re·lent \ri-ˈlent\ *vb* **1** ♦ **:** to become less stern, severe, or harsh **2 :** to make slack (as by lessening tension or firmness) **:** SLACKEN

♦ abate, de-escalate, decline, decrease, die, diminish, dwindle, ebb, fall, lessen, let up, lower, moderate, recede, shrink, subside, taper, wane

re·lent·less \-ləs\ *adj* ♦ **:** showing or promising no abatement of severity, intensity, or pace ⟨∼ pressure⟩ — **re·lent·less·ly** *adv* — **re·lent·less·ness** *n*

♦ determined, dogged, grim, implacable, unflinching, unrelenting, unyielding

rel·e·vance \ˈre-lə-vəns\ *n* ♦ **:** relation to the matter at hand; *also* **:** practical and especially social applicability

♦ applicability, bearing, connection, pertinence

rel·e·van·cy \-vən-sē\ *n* **:** RELEVANCE
rel·e·vant \ˈre-lə-vənt\ *adj* ♦ **:** bearing on the matter at hand **:** PERTINENT — **rel·e·vant·ly** *adv*

♦ applicable, apposite, apropos, germane, material, pertinent, pointed, relative

re·li·abil·i·ty \ri-ˌlī-ə-ˈbi-lə-tē\ *n* ♦ **:** the quality or state of being reliable

♦ dependability, solidity, sureness, trustworthiness

re·li·able \ri-ˈlī-ə-bəl\ *adj* ♦ **:** fit to be trusted or relied on **:** DEPENDABLE, TRUSTWORTHY — **re·li·ably** \-ˈlī-ə-blē\ *adv*

♦ dependable, good, responsible, safe, solid, steady, sure, tried, true, trustworthy

re·li·able·ness *n* **:** the quality or state of being reliable
re·li·ance \ri-ˈlī-əns\ *n* **1 :** the act of relying **2 :** the state of being reliant **3** ♦ **:** one relied on

♦ buttress, dependence, mainstay, pillar, standby, support

re·li·ant \ri-ˈlī-ənt\ *adj* **:** having reliance on someone or something **:** DEPENDENT
rel·ic \ˈre-lik\ *n* **1 :** an object venerated because of its association

with a saint or martyr **2 :** SOUVENIR, MEMENTO **3** *pl* **:** REMAINS, RUINS **4** ♦ **:** a remaining trace **:** VESTIGE

♦ shadow, trace, vestige

rel•ict \'re-likt\ *n* **:** WIDOW
re•lief \ri-'lēf\ *n* **1** ♦ **:** removal or lightening of something oppressive, painful, or distressing **2 :** WELFARE 2 **3 :** military assistance to an endangered post or force **4 a :** release from a post or from performance of a duty **b** ♦ **:** one that takes the place of another on duty **5 :** legal remedy or redress **6 :** projection of figures or ornaments from the background (as in sculpture) **7 :** the elevations of a land surface

♦ [1] alleviation, comfort, ease ♦ [4b] backup, pinch hitter, replacement, reserve, stand-in, sub, substitute

relief pitcher *n* **:** a baseball pitcher who takes over for another during a game
re•lieve \ri-'lēv\ *vb* **re•lieved; re•liev•ing** **1** ♦ **:** to free partly or wholly from a burden or from distress **2** ♦ **:** to bring about the removal or alleviation of **:** MITIGATE **3 :** to release from a post or duty; *also* **:** to take the place of **4 :** to break the monotony of **5 :** to discharge the bladder or bowels of (oneself) — **re•liev•er** *n*

♦ [1] clear, disburden, disencumber, free, rid, unburden ♦ [2] allay, alleviate, assuage, ease, help, mitigate, mollify, palliate, soothe

relig *abbr* religion
re•li•gion \ri-'li-jən\ *n* **1** ♦ **:** the service and worship of God or the supernatural **2 :** devotion to a religious faith **3** ♦ **:** a personal set or institutionalized system of religious beliefs, attitudes, and practices **4 :** a cause, principle, or belief held to with faith and ardor — **re•li•gion•ist** *n*

♦ [1] devotion, faith, piety ♦ [3] creed, cult, faith, persuasion

¹re•li•gious \ri-'li-jəs\ *adj* **1 :** relating or devoted to an acknowledged ultimate reality or deity **2** ♦ **:** of or relating to religious beliefs or observances **3** ♦ **:** scrupulously and conscientiously faithful **4 :** FERVENT, ZEALOUS — **re•li•gious•ly** *adv*

♦ [2] devotional, sacred, spiritual *Ant* nonreligious, profane, secular ♦ [3] devout, faithful, godly, holy, pious, sainted, saintly

²religious *n, pl* **religious :** a member of a religious order under monastic vows
re•lin•quish \ri-'liŋ-kwish, -'lin-\ *vb* **1 :** to withdraw or retreat from **:** ABANDON, QUIT **2** ♦ **:** to yield control or possession of ⟨~ a title⟩ **3 :** to let go of **:** RELEASE

♦ cede, deliver, give up, hand over, leave, render, surrender, turn over, yield ♦ abdicate, abnegate, cede, renounce, resign, step down, surrender

re•lin•quish•ment *n* ♦ **:** the act of relinquishing **:** a giving up

♦ capitulation, submission, surrender

rel•i•quary \'re-lə-ˌkwer-ē\ *n, pl* **-quar•ies :** a container for religious relics
¹rel•ish \'re-lish\ *n* **1 :** characteristic flavor **:** SAVOR **2** ♦ **:** keen enjoyment or delight in something **3** ♦ **:** a strong liking **:** APPETITE **4 :** a highly seasoned sauce (as of pickles) eaten with other food to add flavor

♦ [2] contentment, delectation, delight, enjoyment, gladness, gratification, pleasure, satisfaction ♦ [3] appetite, fancy, favor (*or* favour), fondness, like, liking, love, partiality, preference, shine, taste, use

²relish *vb* **1 :** to add relish to **2** ♦ **:** to be pleased or gratified by **:** ENJOY **3 :** to eat with pleasure — **rel•ish•able** *adj*

♦ adore, delight, dig, enjoy, fancy, groove, like, love, revel

re•live \(ˌ)rē-'liv\ *vb* **:** to live again or over again; *esp* **:** to experience again in the imagination
re•lo•cate \(ˌ)rē-'lō-ˌkāt, ˌrē-lō-'kāt\ *vb* **1 :** to locate again **2 :** to move to a new location — **re•lo•ca•tion** \ˌrē-lō-'kā-shən\ *n*
re•luc•tance \ri-'lək-tən(t)s\ *n* ♦ **:** the quality or state of being reluctant

♦ disinclination, hesitancy, reticence *Ant* inclination, willingness

re•luc•tant \ri-'lək-tənt\ *adj* ♦ **:** feeling or showing aversion, hesitation or unwillingness ⟨~ to get involved⟩ — **re•luc•tant•ly** *adv*

♦ afraid, dubious, hesitant, indisposed

re•ly \ri-'lī\ *vb* **re•lied; re•ly•ing** ♦ **:** to place faith or confidence **:** DEPEND

♦ count, depend, lean, reckon

REM \'rem\ *n* **:** RAPID EYE MOVEMENT
re•main \ri-'mān\ *vb* **1 :** to be left after others have been removed, subtracted, or destroyed **2 :** to be something yet to be shown, done, or treated ⟨it ~*s* to be seen⟩ **3 :** to stay after others have gone **4 :** to continue unchanged **5** ♦ **:** to stay in the same place or with the same person or group

♦ abide, dwell, hang around, stay, stick around, tarry

re•main•der \ri-'mān-dər\ *n* **1** ♦ **:** that which is left over **:** a remaining group, part, or trace **2 :** the number left after a subtraction **3 :** the number that is left over from the dividend after division and that is less than the divisor **4 :** a book sold at a reduced price by the publisher after sales have slowed

♦ end, fag end, leftover, remnant, scrap ♦ balance, leavings, leftovers, odds and ends, remains, remnant, residue, rest

re•mains \-'mānz\ *n pl* **1** ♦ **:** a remaining part or trace ⟨the ~ of a meal⟩ **2 :** a dead body

♦ debris, rubble, ruins, wreck, wreckage

¹re•make \(ˌ)rē-'māk\ *vb* **-made** \-'mād\; **-mak•ing** ♦ **:** to make anew or in a different form

♦ alter, change, make over, modify, recast, redo, refashion, remodel, revamp, revise, rework, vary ♦ duplicate, redo, reiterate, repeat, replicate

²re•make \'rē-ˌmāk\ *n* **:** one that is remade; *esp* **:** a new version of a motion picture
re•mand \ri-'mand\ *vb* **:** to order back; *esp* **:** to return to custody pending trial or for further detention
¹re•mark \ri-'märk\ *n* **1 :** the act of remarking **:** OBSERVATION, NOTICE **2** ♦ **:** a passing observation or comment

♦ comment, note, observation, reflection

²remark *vb* **1** ♦ **:** to take notice of **:** OBSERVE **2** ♦ **:** to express as an observation or comment

♦ [1] behold, descry, discern, distinguish, espy, eye, look, note, notice, observe, perceive, regard, see, sight, spy, view, witness ♦ [2] comment, note, observe, opine, say

re•mark•able \ri-'mär-kə-bəl\ *adj* ♦ **:** worthy of being or likely to be noticed especially as being uncommon or extraordinary **:** NOTEWORTHY — **re•mark•able•ness** *n*

♦ bold, catchy, conspicuous, emphatic, marked, noteworthy, noticeable, prominent, pronounced, striking

re•mark•ably \ri-'mär-kə-blē\ *adv* **1 :** in a remarkable manner **2 :** as is remarkable
re•me•di•a•ble \ri-'mē-dē-ə-bəl\ *adj* **:** capable of being remedied
re•me•di•al \ri-'mē-dē-əl\ *adj* ♦ **:** intended to remedy or improve

♦ corrective, reformative

¹rem•e•dy \'re-mə-dē\ *n, pl* **-dies** **1** ♦ **:** a medicine or treatment that cures or relieves a disease or condition **2 :** something that corrects or counteracts an evil or compensates for a loss

♦ cure, drug, medicine, pharmaceutical, specific

²remedy *vb* **-died; -dy•ing** ♦ **:** to provide or serve as a remedy for

♦ amend, correct, debug, emend, rectify, reform

re•mem•ber \ri-'mem-bər\ *vb* **-bered; -ber•ing** **1** ♦ **:** to bring to mind or think of again **:** RECOLLECT **2 :** to keep from forgetting **:** keep in mind **3 :** to convey greetings from **4 :** COMMEMORATE

♦ recall, recollect, reminisce, think *Ant* forget, unlearn

re•mem•brance \-brəns\ *n* **1** ♦ **:** an act of remembering **:** RECOLLECTION **2** ♦ **:** the ability to remember **:** MEMORY **3 :** the period over which one's memory extends **4 :** a memory of a person, thing, or event **5** ♦ **:** something that serves to bring to mind **:** REMINDER **6 :** a greeting or gift recalling or expressing friendship or affection

♦ [1, 2] memory, recall, recollection, reminiscence ♦ [5] keepsake, memento, memorial, monument, souvenir, token

Remembrance Day *n* **:** November 11 set aside in commemoration of the end of hostilities in 1918 and 1945 and observed as a legal holiday in Canada; *also* **:** REMEMBRANCE SUNDAY
Remembrance Sunday *n* **:** a Sunday that is usually closest to November 11 and that in Great Britain is set aside in commemoration of the end of hostilities in 1918 and 1945
re•mind \ri-'mīnd\ *vb* **:** to put in mind of something **:** cause to remember
re•mind•er *n* **:** something that reminds by association
rem•i•nisce \ˌre-mə-'nis\ *vb* **-nisced; -nisc•ing** ♦ **:** to indulge in reminiscence

♦ *usu* **reminisce about** recall, recollect, remember, think

rem•i•nis•cence \-ˈnis-ᵊns\ *n* **1** ♦ **:** a recalling or telling of a past experience **2 :** an account of a memorable experience

♦ memory, recall, recollection, remembrance

rem•i•nis•cent \-ᵊnt\ *adj* **1 :** of or relating to reminiscence **2 :** marked by or given to reminiscence **3 :** serving to remind **:** SUGGESTIVE — **rem•i•nis•cent•ly** *adv*

re•miss \ri-ˈmis\ *adj* **1 :** negligent or careless in the performance of work or duty **2** ♦ **:** showing neglect or inattention — **re•miss•ly** *adv*

♦ careless, derelict, lax, negligent, slack

re•mis•si•ble \ri-ˈmi-sə-bəl\ *adj* ♦ **:** capable of being forgiven

♦ excusable, forgivable, pardonable, venial

re•mis•sion \ri-ˈmi-shən\ *n* **1** ♦ **:** the act or process of remitting **2 :** a state or period during which something is remitted

♦ absolution, amnesty, forgiveness, pardon

re•miss•ness *n* ♦ **:** the quality or state of being remiss

♦ carelessness, dereliction, heedlessness, laxness, neglect, negligence, slackness

re•mit \ri-ˈmit\ *vb* **re•mit•ted; re•mit•ting 1 :** FORGIVE, PARDON **2 :** to give or gain relief from (as pain) **3 :** to refer for consideration, report, or decision **4 :** to refrain from exacting or enforcing (as a penalty) **5 :** to send (money) in payment of a bill **6 :** to abate in force or intensity **7 :** to place later in order of precedence, preference, or importance

re•mit•tal \ri-ˈmit-ᵊl\ *n* **:** the act or process of remitting **:** REMISSION

re•mit•tance \ri-ˈmit-ᵊns\ *n* **1** ♦ **:** a sum of money remitted **2** ♦ **:** transmittal of money (as to a distant place)

♦ [1, 2] compensation, consideration, disbursement, pay, payment, recompense, remuneration, requital

rem•nant \ˈrem-nənt\ *n* **1** ♦ **:** a usually small part or trace remaining **2 :** an unsold or unused end of a fabric that is sold by the yard

♦ end, fag end, leftover, remainder, scrap

re•mod•el \ˌrē-ˈmäd-ᵊl\ *vb* ♦ **:** to alter the structure of **:** MAKE OVER

♦ alter, change, make over, modify, recast, redo, refashion, remake, revamp, revise, rework, vary

re•mon•strance \ri-ˈmän-strəns\ *n* ♦ **:** an act or instance of remonstrating

♦ challenge, complaint, demur, expostulation, fuss, kick, objection, protest, question

re•mon•strant \-strənt\ *adj* **:** vigorously objecting or opposing — **remonstrant** *n* — **re•mon•strant•ly** *adv*

re•mon•strate \ri-ˈmän-ˌstrāt\ *vb* **-strat•ed; -strat•ing** ♦ **:** to plead in opposition to something **:** speak in protest or reproof — usually used with *with* — **re•mon•stra•tion** \ri-ˌmän-ˈstrā-shən, ˌre-mən-\ *n* — **re•mon•stra•tor** \ri-ˈmän-ˌstrā-tər\ *n*

♦ *usu* **remonstrate with** demur, kick, object, protest

rem•o•ra \ˈre-mə-rə\ *n* **:** any of a family of marine bony fishes with sucking organs on the head by which they cling especially to other fishes

re•morse \ri-ˈmȯrs\ *n* ♦ **:** a gnawing distress arising from a sense of guilt for past wrongs

♦ contrition, guilt, penitence, repentance, self-reproach, shame

re•morse•ful *adj* ♦ **:** motivated or marked by remorse

♦ apologetic, contrite, guilty, penitent, regretful, repentant, rueful, sorry

re•morse•less \-ləs\ *adj* **1 :** MERCILESS **2 :** PERSISTENT, RELENTLESS

¹re•mote \ri-ˈmōt\ *adj* **re•mot•er; -est 1** ♦ **:** far off in place or time **:** not near **2 :** not closely related **:** DISTANT **3** ♦ **:** located out of the way **:** SECLUDED **4 :** acting, acted on, or controlled indirectly or from a distance **5** ♦ **:** small in degree **:** SLIGHT ⟨a ~ chance⟩ **6** ♦ **:** distant or aloof in manner — **re•mote•ly** *adv* — **re•mote•ness** *n*

♦ [1] away, distant, far, far-off ♦ [3] cloistered, covert, isolated, quiet, secluded, secret ♦ [5] negligible, off, outside, slight, slim, small ***Ant*** good ♦ [6] aloof, antisocial, cold, cool, detached, distant, frosty, standoffish, unsociable

²remote *n* **1 :** a radio or television program or a portion of a program originating outside the studio **2 :** REMOTE CONTROL 2

remote control *n* **1 :** control (as by radio signal) of operation from a point at some distance removed **2 :** a device or mechanism for controlling something from a distance

¹re•mount \(ˌ)rē-ˈmau̇nt\ *vb* **1 :** to mount again **2 :** to furnish remounts to

²re•mount \ˈrē-ˌmau̇nt\ *n* **:** a fresh horse to replace one no longer available

re•mov•al \ri-ˈmü-vəl\ *n* ♦ **:** the act or process of removing

♦ disposal, disposition, dumping, jettison, riddance

¹re•move \ri-ˈmüv\ *vb* **re•moved; re•mov•ing 1** ♦ **:** to move from one place to another **:** TRANSFER **2** ♦ **:** to move by lifting or taking off or away **3** ♦ **:** to dismiss from office **4 :** to get rid of **:** ELIMINATE ⟨~ a fire hazard⟩ **5 :** to change one's residence or location **6 :** to go away **:** DEPART **7 :** to be capable of being removed — **re•mov•able** *adj* — **re•mov•er** *n*

♦ [1] budge, dislocate, displace, disturb, move, shift, transfer ♦ [2] doff, peel, put off, take off ***Ant*** don, put on, slip (into) ♦ [2] clear, draw, withdraw ***Ant*** place, put ♦ [3] cashier, dismiss, fire, retire, sack

²remove *n* **1 :** a transfer from one location to another **:** MOVE **2** ♦ **:** a degree or stage of separation

♦ distance, lead, length, spread, stretch, way

REM sleep *n* **:** a state of sleep that recurs cyclically several times during normal sleep and is associated with rapid eye movements and dreaming

re•mu•ner•ate \ri-ˈmyü-nə-ˌrāt\ *vb* **-at•ed; -at•ing** ♦ **:** to pay an equivalent for or to **:** RECOMPENSE — **re•mu•ner•a•tor** \-ˌrā-tər\ *n*

♦ compensate, indemnify, pay, recompense, recoup, requite

re•mu•ner•a•tion \ri-ˌmyü-nə-ˈrā-shən\ *n* **1** ♦ **:** something that remunerates **:** COMPENSATION, PAYMENT **2** ♦ **:** an act or fact of remunerating

♦ [1] compensation, consideration, disbursement, pay, payment, recompense, remittance, requital ♦ [2] compensation, damages, indemnity, quittance, recompense, redress, reparation, requital, restitution, satisfaction

re•mu•ner•a•tive \ri-ˈmyü-nə-rə-tiv, -ˌrā-\ *adj* ♦ **:** serving to remunerate **:** GAINFUL

♦ fat, gainful, lucrative, profitable

re•nais•sance \ˌre-nə-ˈsäns, -ˈzäns\ *n* **1** *cap* **:** the cultural revival and beginnings of modern science in Europe in the 14th–17th centuries; *also* **:** the period of the Renaissance **2** *often cap* **:** a movement or period of vigorous artistic and intellectual activity **3 :** REBIRTH, REVIVAL

re•nal \ˈrēn-ᵊl\ *adj* **:** of, relating to, or located in or near the kidneys

re•na•scence \ri-ˈnas-ᵊns, -ˈnās-\ *n, often cap* **:** RENAISSANCE

rend \ˈrend\ *vb* **rent** \ˈrent\; **rend•ing 1 :** to remove by violence **:** WREST **2** ♦ **:** to tear forcibly apart

♦ rip, rive, shred, tatter, tear

ren•der \ˈren-dər\ *vb* **1 :** to extract (as lard) by heating **2** ♦ **:** to give to another; *also* **:** YIELD **3 :** to give in return **4 :** to do (a service) for another ⟨~ aid⟩ **5 :** to cause to be or become **:** MAKE **6 :** to reproduce or represent by artistic or verbal means **7 :** TRANSLATE ⟨~ into English⟩

♦ cede, deliver, give up, hand over, leave, relinquish, surrender, turn over, yield

¹ren•dez•vous \ˈrän-di-ˌvü, -dā-\ *n, pl* **ren•dez•vous** \-ˌvüz\ **1 a :** a place appointed for a meeting; *also* **:** a meeting at an appointed place **b** ♦ **:** an agreement to meet each other or with another person or thing **2** ♦ **:** a place of popular resort **3 :** the process of bringing two spacecraft together

♦ [1b] appointment, date, engagement, tryst ♦ [2] hangout, haunt, resort

²rendezvous *vb* **-voused** \-ˌvüd\; **-vous•ing** \-ˌvü-iŋ\; **-vouses** \-ˌvüz\ ♦ **:** to come or bring together at a rendezvous

♦ assemble, cluster, collect, concentrate, conglomerate, congregate, convene, forgather, gather, meet

ren•di•tion \ren-ˈdi-shən\ *n* **:** an act or a result of rendering ⟨first ~ of the work into English⟩

ren•e•gade \ˈre-ni-ˌgād\ *n* ♦ **:** a deserter from one faith, cause, principle, or party for another

♦ defector, deserter, recreant ***Ant*** loyalist

re•nege \ri-ˈnig, -ˈneg, -ˈnāg\ *vb* **re•neged; re•neg•ing 1** ♦ **:** to go back on a promise or commitment **2 :** to fail to follow suit when able in a card game in violation of the rules — **re•neg•er** *n*

♦ back down, cop out

re•new \ri-ˈnü, -ˈnyü\ *vb* **1** ♦ **:** to make or become new, fresh, or strong again **2** ♦ **:** to restore to existence **:** REVIVE **3 :** to make or do again **:** REPEAT ⟨~ a complaint⟩ **4** ♦ **:** to begin again **:** RESUME ⟨~*ed* his efforts⟩ **5 :** REPLACE ⟨~ the lining of a coat⟩ **6 :** to grant or obtain an extension of or on ⟨~ a lease⟩ ⟨~ a subscription⟩ — **re•new•er** *n*

♦ [1] freshen, recreate, refresh, regenerate, rejuvenate, restore, revitalize, revive ♦ [1, 2] reanimate, reinvigorate, resuscitate, revive ♦ [4] continue, reopen, restart, resume

re•new•able \ri-ˈnü-ə-bəl, -ˈnyü-\ *adj* **1 :** capable of being renewed **2 :** capable of being replaced by natural ecological cycles or sound management procedures ⟨~ resources⟩

re•new•al \ri-ˈnü-əl, -ˈnyü-\ *n* **1** ♦ **:** the act of renewing **:** the state of being renewed **2 :** something renewed

♦ rebirth, regeneration, rejuvenation, resurgence, resurrection, resuscitation, revival

ren•net \ˈre-nət\ *n* **1 :** the contents of the stomach of an unweaned animal (as a calf) or the lining membrane of the stomach used for curdling milk **2 :** rennin or a substitute used to curdle milk

ren•nin \ˈre-nən\ *n* **:** a stomach enzyme that coagulates casein and is used commercially to curdle milk in the making of cheese

re•nounce \ri-ˈnau̇ns\ *vb* **re•nounced; re•nounc•ing 1** ♦ **:** to give up, refuse, or resign usually by formal declaration **2** ♦ **:** to refuse further to follow, obey, or recognize

♦ [1] abdicate, abnegate, cede, relinquish, resign, step down, surrender ♦ [2] abjure, recant, retract, take back, unsay, withdraw

re•nounce•ment *n* ♦ **:** the act or practice of renouncing

♦ abnegation, renunciation, repudiation, self-denial

ren•o•vate \ˈre-nə-ˌvāt\ *vb* **-vat•ed; -vat•ing 1** ♦ **:** to make like new again **:** put in good condition **2 :** to restore to vigor or activity — **ren•o•va•tion** \ˌre-nə-ˈvā-shən\ *n* — **ren•o•va•tor** \ˈre-nə-ˌvā-tər\ *n*

♦ doctor, fix, mend, patch, recondition, repair, revamp

re•nown \ri-ˈnau̇n\ *n* ♦ **:** a state of being widely acclaimed and honored

♦ celebrity, fame, notoriety

re•nowned \-ˈnau̇nd\ *adj* ♦ **:** having renown

♦ celebrated, famed, famous, noted, notorious, prominent, star, well-known

1rent \ˈrent\ *n* **1 :** money or the amount of money paid or due at intervals for the use of another's property **2 :** property rented or for rent

2rent *vb* **1 :** to give possession and use of in return for rent **2** ♦ **:** to take and hold under an agreement to pay rent **3 :** to be for rent ⟨~*s* for $100 a month⟩

♦ engage, hire, lease, let

3rent *n* **1** ♦ **:** an act or instance of rending **2 :** a split in a party or organized group **:** SCHISM **3** ♦ **:** an opening made by or as if by rending

♦ [1] gash, laceration, rip, slash, slit, tear ♦ [3] breach, break, discontinuity, gap, gulf, hole, interval, opening, rift, separation

1rent•al \ˈren-təl\ *n* **1 :** an amount paid or collected as rent **2 :** something that is rented **3 :** an act of renting

2rental *adj* **:** of or relating to rent

rent•er *n* ♦ **:** one that rents

♦ boarder, lodger, roomer, tenant

re•nun•ci•a•tion \ri-ˌnən-sē-ˈā-shən\ *n* ♦ **:** the act of renouncing **:** REPUDIATION

♦ abnegation, renouncement, repudiation, self-denial ***Ant*** indulgence, self-indulgence

re•open \ˌrē-ˈō-pən\ *vb* ♦ **:** to enter upon again

♦ continue, renew, restart, resume

1rep \ˈrep\ *n* ♦ **:** one that represents another **:** REPRESENTATIVE ⟨sales ~*s*⟩

♦ agent, attorney, commissary, delegate, deputy, envoy, factor, proxy, representative

2rep *abbr* **1** repair **2** repeat **3** report; reporter **4** republic

Rep *abbr* Republican

re•pack•age \(ˌ)rē-ˈpa-kij\ *vb* **:** to package again or anew; *esp* **:** to put into a more attractive form

1re•pair \ri-ˈpar\ *vb* **:** to make one's way **:** GO ⟨~*ed* to the drawing room⟩

2repair *vb* **1** ♦ **:** to restore to good condition **:** FIX **2 :** to restore to a healthy state **3 :** REMEDY ⟨~ a wrong⟩ — **re•pair•er** *n* — **re•pair•man** \-ˌman\ *n*

♦ doctor, fix, mend, patch, recondition, renovate, revamp

3repair *n* **1 :** a result of repairing **2 :** an act of repairing **3 :** condition with respect to need of repairing ⟨in bad ~⟩ **4** ♦ **:** the state of being in good or sound condition

♦ condition, estate, fettle, form, order, shape, trim

rep•a•ra•tion \ˌre-pə-ˈrā-shən\ *n* **1 :** the act of making amends for a wrong **2** ♦ **:** amends made for a wrong or injury; *esp* **:** money paid by a defeated nation in compensation for damages caused during hostilities — usually used in plural

♦ compensation, damages, indemnity, quittance, recompense, redress, remuneration, requital, restitution, satisfaction

re•par•a•tive \ri-ˈpar-ə-tiv\ *adj* **1 :** of, relating to, or effecting repairs **2 :** serving to make amends

rep•ar•tee \ˌre-pər-ˈtē\ *n* **1** ♦ **:** a witty reply **2 a** ♦ **:** a succession of clever replies **b :** skill in making such replies

♦ [1] comeback, retort, riposte ♦ [2a] banter, chaff, persiflage, raillery

re•past \ri-ˈpast, ˈrē-ˌpast\ *n* ♦ **:** a supply of food and drink served as a meal

♦ board, chow, feed, meal, mess, table

re•pa•tri•ate \rē-ˈpā-trē-ˌāt\ *vb* **-at•ed; -at•ing :** to send or bring back to the country of origin or citizenship ⟨~ prisoners of war⟩ — **re•pa•tri•ate** \-trē-ət, -trē-ˌāt\ *n* — **re•pa•tri•a•tion** \-ˌpā-trē-ˈā-shən\ *n*

re•pay \rē-ˈpā\ *vb* **-paid** \-ˈpād\; **-pay•ing 1 :** to pay back **:** REFUND **2 :** to give or do in return or requital **3 :** to make a return payment to **:** RECOMPENSE, REQUITE — **re•pay•able** *adj* — **re•pay•ment** *n*

1re•peal \ri-ˈpēl\ *vb* ♦ **:** to annul by authoritative and especially legislative action — **re•peal•er** *n*

♦ abolish, abrogate, annul, cancel, dissolve, invalidate, negate, nullify, quash, rescind, void

2repeal *n* **:** the act or an instance of repealing

1re•peat \ri-ˈpēt\ *vb* **1 :** to say again **2** ♦ **:** to do again **3 :** to say over from memory **4** ♦ **:** to say after another — **re•peat•able** *adj* — **re•peat•er** *n*

♦ [2] duplicate, redo, reiterate, remake, replicate ♦ [4] echo, quote

2re•peat \ri-ˈpēt, ˈrē-ˌpēt\ *n* **1** ♦ **:** the act of repeating **2 :** something repeated or to be repeated (as a radio or television program)

3re•peat \ri-ˈpēt\ *adj* **:** of, relating to, or being one that repeats an offense, achievement, or action

♦ duplication, reiteration, repetition, replication

re•peat•ed \ri-ˈpē-təd\ *adj* ♦ **:** done or recurring again and again **:** FREQUENT

♦ constant, frequent, habitual, periodic, regular, steady

re•peat•ed•ly *adv* ♦ **:** renewed or recurring again and again

♦ constantly, continually, frequently, often

re•pel \ri-ˈpel\ *vb* **re•pelled; re•pel•ling 1** ♦ **:** to drive away **:** REPULSE **2** ♦ **:** to fight against **:** RESIST **3 :** to turn away **:** REJECT **4** ♦ **:** to cause aversion in **:** DISGUST

♦ [1] fend, repulse, stave off ♦ [2] buck, defy, fight, oppose, resist, withstand ♦ [4] disgust, nauseate, repulse, revolt, sicken, turn off

1re•pel•lent *also* **re•pel•lant** \ri-ˈpe-lənt\ *adj* **1 :** tending to drive away ⟨a mosquito-*repellent* spray⟩ **2** ♦ **:** causing disgust

♦ abhorrent, awful, distasteful, foul, nasty, nauseating, noisome, obnoxious, obscene, odious, offensive, repugnant, repulsive, revolting

2repellent *also* **repellant** *n* **:** something that repels; *esp* **:** a substance that repels insects

re•pent \ri-ˈpent\ *vb* **1 :** to turn from sin and resolve to reform one's life **2** ♦ **:** to feel sorry for (something done) **:** REGRET

♦ bemoan, deplore, lament, regret, rue

re•pen•tance \ri-ˈpent-ᵊns\ *n* ♦ : the action or process of repenting especially for misdeeds or moral shortcomings

♦ contrition, guilt, penitence, remorse, self-reproach, shame

re•pen•tant \-ᵊnt\ *adj* ♦ : experiencing repentance

♦ apologetic, contrite, guilty, penitent, regretful, remorseful, rueful, sorry

re•per•cus•sion \ˌrē-pər-ˈkə-shən, ˌre-\ *n* **1** : REVERBERATION **2** : a reciprocal action or effect **3** ♦ : a widespread, indirect, or unforeseen effect of something done or said

♦ effect, impact, influence, mark, sway

rep•er•toire \ˈre-pər-ˌtwär\ *n* **1** : a list of plays, operas, pieces, or parts which a company or performer is prepared to present **2** : a list of the skills or devices possessed by a person or needed in a person's occupation

rep•er•to•ry \ˈre-pər-ˌtōr-ē\ *n, pl* **-ries** **1** : REPOSITORY **2** : REPERTOIRE **3** : a company that presents its repertoire in the course of one season at one theater

rep•e•ti•tion \ˌre-pə-ˈti-shən\ *n* **1** ♦ : the act or an instance of repeating **2** : the fact of being repeated

♦ duplication, reiteration, repeat, replication

rep•e•ti•tious \-ˈti-shəs\ *adj* : marked by repetition; *esp* : tediously repeating — **rep•e•ti•tious•ly** *adv* — **rep•e•ti•tious•ness** *n*

re•pet•i•tive \ri-ˈpe-ti-tiv\ *adj* : REPETITIOUS — **re•pet•i•tive•ly** *adv* — **re•pet•i•tive•ness** *n*

re•phrase \-ˈfrāz\ *vb* ♦ : to express again in words or in appropriate or telling terms

♦ paraphrase, restate, translate

re•pine \ri-ˈpīn\ *vb* **re•pined; re•pin•ing** **1** ♦ : to feel or express discontent or dejection **2** ♦ : to long for something

♦ [1] beef, bellyache, complain, fuss, gripe, grouse, grumble ♦ *usu* **repine for** [2] ache for, covet, crave, desire, die (to *or* for), hanker for, hunger for, long for, lust (for *or* after), pine for, thirst for, want, wish for, yearn for

repl *abbr* replace; replacement

re•place \ri-ˈplās\ *vb* **1** : to restore to a former place or position **2** ♦ : to take the place of : SUPPLANT **3** : to put something new in the place of — **re•place•able** *adj* — **re•plac•er** *n*

♦ displace, substitute, supersede, supplant

re•place•ment \ri-ˈplās-mənt\ *n* **1** : the act of replacing : the state of being replaced **2** ♦ : one that replaces another especially in a job or function

♦ backup, pinch hitter, relief, reserve, stand-in, sub, substitute

¹**re•play** \(ˌ)rē-ˈplā\ *vb* : to play again or over

²**re•play** \ˈrē-ˌplā\ *n* **1** : an act or instance of replaying **2** : the playing of a tape (as a videotape)

re•plen•ish \ri-ˈple-nish\ *vb* : to fill or build up again : stock or supply anew — **re•plen•ish•ment** *n*

re•plete \ri-ˈplēt\ *adj* **1** : fully provided **2** ♦ : fully or abundantly provided or filled : FULL; *esp* : full of food — **re•plete•ness** *n*

♦ flush, fraught, full, rife, thick

re•ple•tion \ri-ˈplē-shən\ *n* : the state of being replete

rep•li•ca \ˈre-pli-kə\ *n* **1** : an exact reproduction (as of a painting) executed by the original artist **2** ♦ : a copy exact in all details : DUPLICATE

♦ carbon copy, counterpart, double, duplicate, duplication, facsimile, image, likeness, match, picture, ringer, spit

¹**rep•li•cate** \ˈre-plə-ˌkāt\ *vb* **-cat•ed; -cat•ing** **1** ♦ : to make a copy of : DUPLICATE **2** ♦ : to do over or again : REPEAT

♦ [1] copy, duplicate, imitate, reproduce ♦ [2] duplicate, redo, reiterate, remake, repeat

²**rep•li•cate** \-pli-kət\ *n* : one of several identical experiments or procedures

rep•li•ca•tion \ˌre-plə-ˈkā-shən\ *n* **1** : ANSWER, REPLY **2** ♦ : precise copying or reproduction; *also* : an act or process of this **3** ♦ : an imitation, transcript, or reproduction of an original work

♦ [2] duplication, reiteration, repeat, repetition ♦ [3] carbon copy, copy, duplicate, duplication, facsimile, imitation, replica, reproduction

¹**re•ply** \ri-ˈplī\ *vb* **re•plied; re•ply•ing** ♦ : to say or do in answer : RESPOND

♦ answer, rejoin, respond, retort, return

²**reply** *n, pl* **replies** ♦ : something said, written, or done in answer or response : RESPONSE

♦ answer, comeback, response, retort, return

repo \ˈrē-ˌpō\ *adj* : of, relating to, or being in the business of repossessing property (as a car)

¹**re•port** \ri-ˈpōrt\ *n* **1** : common talk : RUMOR **2** ♦ : quality of reputation **3** ♦ : a usually detailed account or statement **4** ♦ : an explosive noise

♦ [2] character, mark, name, note, reputation ♦ [3] account, chronicle, history, narrative, record, story ♦ [4] bang, blast, boom, clap, crack, crash, pop, slam, smash, snap, thwack, whack

²**report** *vb* **1** ♦ : to give an account of : RELATE, TELL **2** : to serve as carrier of (a message) **3** : to prepare or present (as an account of an event) for a newspaper or a broadcast **4** : to make a charge of misconduct against **5** : to present oneself (as for work) **6** : to make known to the authorities ⟨~ a fire⟩ **7** : to return or present (as a matter referred to a committee) with conclusions and recommendations — **re•port•able** *adj*

♦ describe, narrate, recite, recount, rehearse, relate, tell

re•port•age \ri-ˈpōr-tij, *esp for 2* ˌre-pər-ˈtäzh, ˌre-ˌpȯr-ˈ\ *n* **1** : the act or process of reporting news **2** : writing intended to give an account of observed or documented events

report card *n* : a periodic report on a student's grades

re•port•ed•ly \ri-ˈpōr-təd-lē\ *adv* : according to report

re•port•er \ri-ˈpōr-tər\ *n* : one that reports; *esp* : a person who gathers and reports news for a news medium — **re•por•to•ri•al** \ˌre-pər-ˈtōr-ē-əl\ *adj*

¹**re•pose** \ri-ˈpōz\ *vb* **re•posed; re•pos•ing** **1** : to lay at rest **2** : to lie at rest **3** : to lie dead **4** ♦ : to take a rest **5** : to have as a basis or support — usually used with *on*

♦ bask, loll, lounge, relax, rest

²**repose** *n* **1** ♦ : a state of resting (as after exertion); *esp* : SLEEP **2** : eternal or heavenly rest **3** ♦ : freedom from something that disturbs or excites : CALM, PEACE **4** ♦ : cessation or absence of activity, movement, or animation **5** : composure of manner : POISE — **re•pose•ful** *adj*

♦ [1] rest, sleep, slumber ♦ [3] calm, calmness, hush, peace, placidity, quiet, quietness, serenity, still, stillness, tranquillity ♦ [4] ease, leisure, relaxation, rest

³**repose** *vb* **re•posed; re•pos•ing** **1** : to place (as trust) in someone or something **2** : to place for control, management, or use

re•pos•i•to•ry \ri-ˈpä-zə-ˌtōr-ē\ *n, pl* **-ries** **1** ♦ : a place where something is deposited or stored **2** : a person to whom something is entrusted

♦ depository, depot, magazine, storage, storehouse, warehouse

re•pos•sess \ˌrē-pə-ˈzes\ *vb* **1** ♦ : to regain possession of **2** : to take possession of in default of the payment of installments due

♦ recapture, reclaim, recoup, recover, regain, retake, retrieve

re•pos•ses•sion \-ˈze-shən\ *n* ♦ : the act or state of possessing again

♦ reclamation, recovery, retrieval

rep•re•hend \ˌre-pri-ˈhend\ *vb* ♦ : to express disapproval of : CENSURE — **rep•re•hen•sion** \-ˈhen-chən\ *n*

♦ blame, censure, condemn, criticize, denounce, fault, knock, pan

rep•re•hen•si•ble \-ˈhen-sə-bəl\ *adj* ♦ : deserving blame or censure : CULPABLE — **rep•re•hen•si•bly** \-blē\ *adv*

♦ blamable, blameworthy, censurable, culpable ♦ censurable, objectionable, obnoxious, offensive

rep•re•sent \ˌre-pri-ˈzent\ *vb* **1** ♦ : to present a picture or a likeness of : DEPICT **2** : to serve as a sign or symbol of **3** : to act the role of **4** : to stand in the place of : act or speak for; *also* : to manage the legal or business affairs of **5** : to be a member or example of : TYPIFY **6** : to serve as an elected representative of **7** ♦ : to describe as having a specified quality or character **8** : to state with the purpose of affecting judgment or action

♦ [1] depict, image, picture, portray ♦ [7] characterize, define, depict, describe, portray

rep•re•sen•ta•tion \ˌre-pri-ˌzen-ˈtā-shən\ *n* **1** : the act of representing **2** : one (as a picture or image) that represents something else **3** : the state of being represented in a legislative body; *also* : the body of persons representing a constituency **4** : a usually formal statement made to effect a change

¹rep•re•sen•ta•tive \ˌre-pri-ˈzen-tə-tiv\ *adj* **1** ♦ **:** serving to represent **2 :** standing or acting for another **3 :** founded on the principle of representation **:** carried on by elected representatives ⟨~ government⟩ — **rep•re•sen•ta•tive•ly** *adv* — **rep•re•sen•ta•tive•ness** *n*

♦ average, characteristic, normal, regular, standard, typical

²representative *n* **1** ♦ **:** a typical example of a group, class, or quality **2** ♦ **:** one that represents another; *esp* **:** one representing a district in a legislative body usually as a member of a lower house

♦ [1] case, example, exemplar, illustration, instance, sample, specimen ♦ [2] ambassador, delegate, emissary, envoy, legate, minister ♦ [2] agent, attorney, commissary, delegate, deputy, envoy, factor, proxy

re•press \ri-ˈpres\ *vb* **1 a :** to check by or as if by pressure **:** CURB **b** ♦ **:** to put down by force **:** SUBDUE **2** ♦ **:** to prevent the natural or normal expression, activity, or development of **:** SUPPRESS **3 :** to exclude from consciousness — **re•pres•sive** \-ˈpre-siv\ *adj*

♦ [1b] clamp down, crack down, crush, put down, quash, quell, silence, snuff, squash, squelch, subdue, suppress ♦ [2] choke, pocket, smother, stifle, strangle, suppress, swallow

re•pres•sion \-ˈpre-shən\ *n* ♦ **:** the action or process of repressing

♦ constraint, inhibition, restraint, self-control, self-restraint, suppression

¹re•prieve \ri-ˈprēv\ *vb* **re•prieved; re•priev•ing** **1 :** to delay the punishment or execution of **2 :** to give temporary relief to

²reprieve *n* **1 :** the act of reprieving **:** the state of being reprieved **2 :** a formal temporary suspension of a sentence especially of death **3 :** a temporary respite

¹rep•ri•mand \ˈre-prə-ˌmand\ *n* ♦ **:** a severe or formal reproof

♦ censure, denunciation, rebuke, reproach, reproof, stricture

²reprimand *vb* **1** ♦ **:** to reprove severely or formally **2 :** chide for a fault

♦ censure, condemn, denounce, rebuke, reproach, reprove ♦ admonish, chide, lecture, rail (at *or* against), rate, rebuke, scold

¹re•print \(ˌ)rē-ˈprint\ *vb* **:** to print again

²re•print \ˈrē-ˌprint\ *n* **:** a reproduction of printed matter

re•pri•sal \ri-ˈprī-zəl\ *n* ♦ **:** an act in retaliation for something done by another

♦ requital, retaliation, retribution, revenge, vengeance

re•prise \ri-ˈprēz\ *n* **:** a recurrence, renewal, or resumption of an action; *also* **:** a musical repetition

¹re•proach \ri-ˈprōch\ *n* **1** ♦ **:** an expression of disapproval **2 :** the condition of one fallen from grace or honor **:** DISGRACE **3 :** the act of reproaching **:** REBUKE **4 :** a cause or occasion of blame or disgrace — **re•proach•ful** \-fəl\ *adj* — **re•proach•ful•ly** *adv* — **re•proach•ful•ness** *n*

♦ censure, denunciation, rebuke, reprimand, reproof, stricture

²reproach *vb* **1** ♦ **:** to express disappointment in or displeasure with (a person) for conduct that is blameworthy or in need of amendment **:** REBUKE **2 :** to cast discredit on — **re•proach•able** *adj*

♦ admonish, chide, lecture, rail (at *or* against), rate, rebuke, reprimand, scold ♦ censure, condemn, denounce, rebuke, reprimand, reprove

¹rep•ro•bate \ˈre-prə-ˌbāt\ *n* **1 :** a person foreordained to damnation **2 :** a thoroughly bad person **:** SCOUNDREL

²reprobate *adj* ♦ **:** of, relating to, or having the characteristics of a reprobate

♦ corrupt, debauched, decadent, degenerate, dissolute, perverse, perverted

rep•ro•ba•tion \ˌre-prə-ˈbā-shən\ *n* **:** strong disapproval **:** CONDEMNATION

re•pro•duce \ˌrē-prə-ˈdüs, -ˈdyüs\ *vb* **1** ♦ **:** to produce again or anew **2** ♦ **:** to produce offspring — **re•pro•duc•ible** \-ˈdü-sə-bəl, -ˈdyü-\ *adj* — **re•pro•duc•tive** \-ˈdək-tiv\ *adj*

♦ [1] copy, duplicate, imitate, replicate ♦ [2] breed, multiply, procreate, propagate

re•pro•duc•tion \-ˈdək-shən\ *n* ♦ **:** something reproduced

♦ carbon copy, copy, duplicate, duplication, facsimile, imitation, replica, replication

re•proof \ri-ˈprüf\ *n* ♦ **:** blame or censure for a fault

♦ censure, denunciation, rebuke, reprimand, reproach, stricture

re•prove \ri-ˈprüv\ *vb* **re•proved; re•prov•ing** **1** ♦ **:** to administer a rebuke to **2** ♦ **:** to express disapproval of — **re•prov•er** *n*

♦ [1] admonish, chide, rebuke, reprimand, reproach ♦ [2] censure, condemn, denounce

rept *abbr* report

rep•tile \ˈrep-təl, -ˌtīl\ *n* **:** any of a large class of air-breathing scaly vertebrates including snakes, lizards, alligators, turtles, and extinct related forms (as dinosaurs) — **rep•til•i•an** \rep-ˈti-lē-ən\ *adj or n*

re•pub•lic \ri-ˈpə-blik\ *n* **1 :** a government having a chief of state who is not a monarch and is usually a president; *also* **:** a nation or other political unit having such a government **2 :** a government in which supreme power is held by the citizens entitled to vote and is exercised by elected officers and representatives governing according to law; *also* **:** a nation or other political unit having such a form of government **3 :** a constituent political and territorial unit of the former nations of Czechoslovakia, the U.S.S.R., or Yugoslavia

¹re•pub•li•can \-bli-kən\ *adj* **1** ♦ **:** of, relating to, or resembling a republic **2 :** favoring or supporting a republic **3** *cap* **:** of, relating to, or constituting one of the two major political parties in the U.S. evolving in the mid-19th century — **re•pub•li•can•ism** *n, often cap*

♦ democratic, popular, self-governing

²republican *n* **1 :** one that favors or supports a republican form of government **2** *cap* **:** a member of a republican party and especially of the Republican party of the U.S.

re•pu•di•ate \ri-ˈpyü-dē-ˌāt\ *vb* **-at•ed; -at•ing** **1** ♦ **:** to give up or renounce as one's own **:** DISOWN **2** ♦ **:** to refuse to have anything to do with **:** refuse to acknowledge, accept, or pay ⟨~ a charge⟩ ⟨~ a debt⟩ **3** ♦ **:** to reject as untrue or unjust — **re•pu•di•a•tor** \-ˈpyü-dē-ˌā-tər\ *n*

♦ [1, 2] disavow, disclaim, disown ♦ [2, 3] decline, deny, disallow, disapprove, negative, refuse, reject, spurn, turn down

re•pu•di•a•tion \-ˌpyü-dē-ˈā-shən\ *n* ♦ **:** the act of repudiating **:** the state of being repudiated

♦ contradiction, denial, disallowance, disavowal, disclaimer, negation, rejection

re•pug•nance \ri-ˈpəg-nəns\ *n* **1 :** the quality or fact of being contradictory or inconsistent **2** ♦ **:** strong dislike, distaste, or antagonism

♦ aversion, disgust, distaste, loathing, nausea, repulsion, revulsion

re•pug•nant \-nənt\ *adj* **1 :** marked by repugnance **2** ♦ **:** contrary to a person's tastes or principles **:** exciting distaste or aversion — **re•pug•nant•ly** *adv*

♦ distasteful, foul, nasty, nauseating, noisome, obnoxious, obscene, odious, offensive, repellent, repulsive, revolting

¹re•pulse \ri-ˈpəls\ *vb* **re•pulsed; re•puls•ing** **1** ♦ **:** to drive or beat back **:** REPEL **2 :** to repel by discourtesy or denial **:** REBUFF **3** ♦ **:** to cause a feeling of repulsion in **:** DISGUST

♦ [1] fend, repel, stave off ♦ [3] disgust, nauseate, repel, revolt, sicken, turn off

²repulse *n* **1** ♦ **:** an abrupt rejection of an offer or advance **:** REBUFF **2 :** the action of repelling an attacker **:** the fact of being repelled

♦ brush-off, cold shoulder, rebuff, snub

re•pul•sion \ri-ˈpəl-shən\ *n* **1 :** the action of repulsing **:** the state of being repulsed **2 :** the force with which bodies, particles, or like forces repel one another **3** ♦ **:** a feeling of aversion

♦ aversion, disgust, distaste, loathing, nausea, repugnance, revulsion

re•pul•sive \-siv\ *adj* **1 :** serving or tending to repel or reject **2** ♦ **:** arousing aversion or disgust — **re•pul•sive•ly** *adv*

♦ abhorrent, distasteful, horrible, horrid, nasty, nauseating, noisome, obnoxious, offensive, repellent, repugnant, revolting

re•pul•sive•ness *n* ♦ **:** the quality or state of being repulsive

♦ atrociousness, atrocity, frightfulness, hideousness, horror, monstrosity

re•pur•pose \(ˌ)rē-ˈpər-pəs\ *vb* **:** to give a new purpose or use to

rep•u•ta•ble \ˈre-pyə-tə-bəl\ *adj* ♦ : having a good reputation — **rep•u•ta•bly** \-blē\ *adv*

♦ name, prestigious, reputed, respectable

rep•u•ta•tion \ˌre-pyu̇-ˈtā-shən\ *n* **1** ♦ : overall quality or character as seen or judged by people in general **2** : place in public esteem or regard

♦ character, mark, name, note, report

¹re•pute \ri-ˈpyüt\ *vb* **re•put•ed; re•put•ing** : BELIEVE,CONSIDER
²repute *n* **1** : the character or status commonly ascribed to one : REPUTATION **2** : the state of being favorably known or spoken of
re•put•ed \ri-ˈpyü-təd\ *adj* **1** ♦ : having a good repute : REPUTABLE **2** ♦ : according to reputation : SUPPOSED — **re•put•ed•ly** *adv*

♦ [1] name, prestigious, reputable, respectable ♦ [2] apparent, assumed, evident, ostensible, seeming, supposed

req *abbr* **1** request **2** require; required **3** requisition
¹re•quest \ri-ˈkwest\ *n* **1** ♦ : an act or instance of asking for something **2** : a thing asked for **3** : the condition of being asked for ⟨available on ~⟩

♦ call, inquiry, query, question

²request *vb* **1** : to make a request to or of **2** ♦ : to ask for — **re•quest•er** *n*

♦ ask, call, order, requisition

re•qui•em \ˈre-kwē-əm, ˈrā-\ *n* **1** : a mass for a dead person; *also* : a musical setting for this **2** ♦ : a musical service or hymn in honor of the dead **3** : something that resembles a solemn chant in honor of the dead

♦ dirge, elegy, lament, threnody

re•quire \ri-ˈkwīr\ *vb* **re•quired; re•quir•ing** **1** ♦ : to demand as necessary or essential **2** : COMMAND, ORDER

♦ demand, necessitate, need, take, want, warrant

re•quire•ment \-mənt\ *n* **1** : something (as a condition or quality) required ⟨entrance ~*s*⟩ **2** ♦ : something wanted or needed : NECESSITY

♦ condition, demand, essential, must, necessity, need, requisite

¹req•ui•site \ˈre-kwə-zət\ *adj* ♦ : of the utmost importance : NECESSARY

♦ essential, imperative, indispensable, integral, necessary, needful, vital

²requisite *n* : something that is required or necessary
¹req•ui•si•tion \ˌre-kwə-ˈzi-shən\ *n* **1** : formal application or demand (as for supplies) **2** : the state of being in demand or use
²requisition *vb* ♦ : to make a requisition for

♦ ask, order, request

re•quit•al \ri-ˈkwīt-ᵊl\ *n* **1** ♦ : something given in return, compensation, or retaliation **2** ♦ : the act or action of requiting : the state of being requited

♦ [1] compensation, damages, indemnity, payment, quittance, recompense, redress, remuneration, reparation, restitution, satisfaction ♦ [2] reprisal, retaliation, retribution, revenge, vengeance

re•quite \ri-ˈkwīt\ *vb* **re•quit•ed; re•quit•ing** **1** : to make return for : REPAY **2** ♦ : to make retaliation for : AVENGE **3** ♦ : to make return to

♦ [2] avenge, retaliate, revenge ♦ [3] compensate, indemnify, recompense, recoup, remunerate

rere•dos \ˈrer-ə-ˌdäs\ *n* : a usually ornamental wood or stone screen or partition wall behind an altar
re•run \ˈrē-ˌrən, (ˌ)rē-ˈrən\ *n* : the act or an instance of running again or anew; *esp* : a showing of a motion picture or television program after its first run — **re•run** \(ˌ)rē-ˈrən\ *vb*
res *abbr* **1** research **2** reservation; reserve **3** reservoir **4** residence; resident **5** resolution
re•sale \ˈrē-ˌsāl, (ˌ)rē-ˈsāl\ *n* : the act of selling again usually to a new party — **re•sal•able** \(ˌ)rē-ˈsā-lə-bəl\ *adj*
re•scind \ri-ˈsind\ *vb* ♦ : to destroy the force, effectiveness, or validity of : REPEAL

♦ abolish, abrogate, annul, cancel, dissolve, invalidate, negate, nullify, quash, repeal, void

re•scis•sion \-ˈsi-zhən\ *n* ♦ : an act of rescinding

♦ abortion, calling, cancellation, recall, repeal, revocation

re•script \ˈrē-ˌskript\ *n* : an official or authoritative order or decree
¹res•cue \ˈres-kyü\ *vb* **res•cued; res•cu•ing** ♦ : to free from danger, harm, or confinement

♦ deliver, save

²rescue *n* ♦ : an act of rescuing

♦ deliverance, salvation

res•cu•er *n* ♦ : one that rescues

♦ deliverer, redeemer, savior

¹re•search \ri-ˈsərch, ˈrē-ˌsərch\ *n* **1** : careful or diligent search **2** ♦ : studious inquiry or examination aimed at the discovery and interpretation of new knowledge **3** : the collecting of information about a particular subject — **re•search•er** *n*

♦ examination, exploration, inquiry, investigation, probe, study

²research *vb* ♦ : to search or investigate exhaustively

♦ delve, dig, explore, go, inquire into, investigate, look, probe

re•sec•tion \ri-ˈsek-shən\ *n* : the surgical removal of part of an organ or structure
re•sem•blance \ri-ˈzem-bləns\ *n* ♦ : the quality or state of resembling; *also* : a point of likeness

♦ community, correspondence, likeness, parallelism, similarity, similitude

re•sem•ble \ri-ˈzem-bəl\ *vb* **-bled; -bling** : to be like or similar to
re•sent \ri-ˈzent\ *vb* : to feel or exhibit annoyance or indignation at
re•sent•ful \-fəl\ *adj* ♦ : full of resentment : inclined to resent — **re•sent•ful•ly** *adv*

♦ acrid, acrimonious, bitter, hard, rancorous, sore ♦ covetous, envious, jaundiced, jealous

re•sent•ment *n* ♦ : a feeling of indignant displeasure or ill will at something regarded as a wrong, insult, or injury

♦ dudgeon, huff, offense, peeve, pique, umbrage

re•ser•pine \ri-ˈsər-ˌpēn, -pən\ *n* : a drug used in treating high blood pressure and nervous tension
res•er•va•tion \ˌre-zər-ˈvā-shən\ *n* **1** : an act of reserving **2** : something (as a room in a hotel) arranged for in advance **3** : something reserved; *esp* : a tract of public land set aside for special use **4** ♦ : a limiting condition

♦ condition, provision, proviso, qualification, stipulation

¹re•serve \ri-ˈzərv\ *vb* **re•served; re•serv•ing** **1** ♦ : to store for future or special use **2** ♦ : to hold back for oneself **3** ♦ : to set aside or arrange to have set aside or held for special use

♦ [1] accumulate, cache, garner, hoard, lay up, stash, stockpile, store ♦ [2] hang on, hold, keep, retain, withhold ♦ [3] allocate, consecrate, dedicate, devote, earmark, save

²reserve *n* **1** ♦ : something reserved : STORE **2** : a military force withheld from action for later use — usually used in plural **3** : the military forces of a country not part of the regular services; *also* : RESERVIST **4** : a tract set apart : RESERVATION **5** : an act of reserving **6** ♦ : restraint or caution in one's words or bearing **7** : money or its equivalent kept in hand or set apart to meet liabilities **8** ♦ : a person or thing that takes the place or function of another

♦ [1] cache, deposit, hoard, store ♦ [6] constraint, restraint, self-control ♦ [8] backup, pinch hitter, relief, replacement, stand-in, sub, substitute

re•served \ri-ˈzərvd\ *adj* **1** ♦ : restrained in words and actions **2** : set aside for future or special use — **re•serv•ed•ly** \-ˈzər-vəd-lē\ *adv* — **re•serv•ed•ness** \-vəd-nəs\ *n*

♦ closemouthed, laconic, reticent, silent, taciturn, uncommunicative

re•serv•ist \ri-ˈzər-vist\ *n* : a member of a military reserve
res•er•voir \ˈre-zə-ˌvwär, -zər-, -ˌvwȯr\ *n* : a place where something is kept in store; *esp* : an artificial lake where water is collected and kept for use
re•shuf•fle \rē-ˈshə-fəl\ *vb* **1** : to shuffle again **2** : to reorganize usually by redistribution of existing elements — **reshuffle** *n*
re•side \ri-ˈzīd\ *vb* **re•sid•ed; re•sid•ing** **1** ♦ : to make one's home : DWELL **2** : to be present as a quality or vested as a right

♦ abide, dwell, live

res•i•dence \ˈre-zə-dəns\ *n* **1** : the act or fact of residing in a place as a dweller or in discharge of a duty or an obligation

2 ♦ : the place where one actually lives 3 : a building used as a home : DWELLING 4 : the period of living in a place

♦ abode, domicile, dwelling, home, house, lodging, quarters

res•i•den•cy \ˈre-zə-dən-sē\ *n, pl* **-cies** 1 : the residence of or the territory under a diplomatic resident 2 : a period of advanced training in a medical specialty

[1]**res•i•dent** \-dənt\ *adj* 1 : RESIDING 2 : being in residence 3 : not migratory

[2]**resident** *n* 1 ♦ : one who resides in a place 2 : a diplomatic representative with governing powers (as in a protectorate) 3 : a physician serving a residency

♦ denizen, dweller, inhabitant, occupant

res•i•den•tial \ˌre-zə-ˈden-chəl\ *adj* 1 : used as a residence or by residents 2 : occupied by or restricted to residences — **res•i•den•tial•ly** *adv*

[1]**re•sid•u•al** \ri-ˈzi-jə-wəl\ *adj* : being a residue or remainder

[2]**residual** *n* 1 : a residual product or substance 2 : a payment (as to an actor or writer) for each rerun after an initial showing (as of a taped TV show)

re•sid•u•ary \ri-ˈzi-jə-ˌwer-ē\ *adj* : of, relating to, or constituting a residue especially of an estate

res•i•due \ˈre-zə-ˌdü, -ˌdyü\ *n* ♦ : a part remaining after another part has been taken away

♦ balance, leavings, leftovers, odds and ends, remainder, remains, remnant, rest

re•sid•u•um \ri-ˈzi-jə-wəm\ *n, pl* **re•sid•ua** \-jə-wə\ 1 : something remaining or residual after certain deductions are made 2 : a residual product

re•sign \ri-ˈzīn\ *vb* 1 ♦ : to give up deliberately (as one's position) especially by a formal act 2 : to give (oneself) over (as to grief or despair) without resistance — **re•sign•ed•ly** \-ˈzī-nəd-lē\ *adv*

♦ abdicate, abnegate, cede, relinquish, renounce, step down, surrender ♦ *usu* **resign from** leave, quit, retire, step down

re–sign \(ˌ)rē-ˈsīn\ *vb* : to sign again

res•ig•na•tion \ˌre-zig-ˈnā-shən\ *n* 1 : an act or instance of resigning; *also* : a formal notification of such an act 2 : the quality or state of being resigned

re•signed \ri-ˈzīnd\ *adj* ♦ : being resigned to something : characterized by resignation

♦ acquiescent, passive, tolerant, unresistant, unresisting, yielding

re•sil•ience \ri-ˈzil-yəns\ *n* 1 : the ability of a body to regain its original size and shape after being compressed, bent, or stretched 2 : an ability to recover from or adjust easily to change or misfortune

re•sil•ien•cy \-yən-sē\ *n* : RESILIENCE

re•sil•ient \-yənt\ *adj* ♦ : marked by resilience

♦ elastic, flexible, rubbery, springy, stretch, supple

res•in \ˈrez-ᵊn\ *n* : any of various substances obtained from the gum or sap of some trees and used especially in varnishes, plastics, and medicine; *also* : a comparable synthetic product — **res•in•ous** *adj*

[1]**re•sist** \ri-ˈzist\ *vb* 1 ♦ : to fight against : OPPOSE ⟨~ aggression⟩ 2 : to withstand the force or effect of ⟨~ disease⟩ — **re•sist•ible** \-ˈzis-tə-bəl\ *adj* — **re•sist•less** *adj*

♦ buck, defy, fight, oppose, repel, withstand ***Ant*** bow (to), capitulate (to), give in (to), submit (to), succumb (to), surrender (to), yield (to)

[2]**resist** *n* : something (as a coating) that resists or prevents a particular action

re•sis•tance \ri-ˈzis-təns\ *n* 1 : the act or an instance of resisting : OPPOSITION 2 : the power or capacity to resist; *esp* : the inherent ability of an organism to resist harmful influences (as disease or infection) 3 : the opposition offered by a body to the passage through it of a steady electric current

re•sis•tant \-tənt\ *adj* : giving or capable of resistance

re•sis•tor \ri-ˈzis-tər\ *n* : a device used to provide resistance to the flow of an electric current in a circuit

res•o•lute \ˈre-zə-ˌlüt\ *adj* ♦ : firmly determined in purpose — **res•o•lute•ly** *adv*

♦ bound, decisive, determined, firm, intent, purposeful, set, single-minded

res•o•lute•ness *n* : the quality or state of being resolute

res•o•lu•tion \ˌre-zə-ˈlü-shən\ *n* 1 : the act or process of resolving 2 : the action of solving; *also* : SOLUTION 3 ♦ : the quality of being resolute : DETERMINATION 4 ♦ : a formal statement expressing the opinion, will, or intent of a body of persons 5 : a measure of the sharpness of an image or of the fineness with which a device can produce or record such an image

♦ [3] decision, decisiveness, determination, firmness, granite, resolve ♦ [4] conclusion, decision, judgment (*or* judgement), opinion, verdict

re•solv•able *adj* ♦ : capable of being resolved

♦ answerable, explicable, soluble, solvable

[1]**re•solve** \ri-ˈzälv\ *vb* **re•solved; re•solv•ing** 1 : to break up into constituent parts 2 : to distinguish between or make visible adjacent parts of 3 ♦ : to find an answer to : SOLVE 4 ♦ : to reach a firm decision about : DECIDE 5 : to make or pass a formal resolution

♦ [3] answer, break, crack, dope, figure out, puzzle, riddle, solve, unravel, work, work out ♦ [4] choose, conclude, decide, determine, figure, opt

[2]**resolve** *n* 1 ♦ : fixity of purpose 2 : something resolved

♦ decision, decisiveness, determination, firmness, granite, resolution

res•o•nance \ˈre-zə-nəns\ *n* 1 : the quality or state of being resonant 2 : a reinforcement of sound in a vibrating body caused by waves from another body vibrating at nearly the same rate

res•o•nant \-nənt\ *adj* 1 : continuing to sound : RESOUNDING 2 : relating to or exhibiting resonance 3 ♦ : intensified and enriched by or as if by resonance — **res•o•nant•ly** *adv*

♦ golden, resounding, ringing, round, sonorous, vibrant

res•o•nate \-ˌnāt\ *vb* **-nat•ed; -nat•ing** 1 : to produce or exhibit resonance 2 ♦ : to produce or exhibit resonance : REVERBERATE

♦ echo, reecho, resound, reverberate, sound

res•o•na•tor \-ˌnā-tər\ *n* : something that resounds or exhibits resonance

re•sorp•tion \rē-ˈsȯrp-shən, -ˈzȯrp-\ *n* : the action or process of breaking down and assimilating something (as a tooth or an embryo)

[1]**re•sort** \ri-ˈzȯrt\ *n* 1 : one looked to for help : REFUGE 2 ♦ : a turning to someone or something for help or protection : RECOURSE 3 : frequent or general visiting ⟨place of ~⟩ 4 ♦ : a frequently visited place : HAUNT 5 : a place providing recreation especially to vacationers

♦ [2] expedient, recourse, resource ♦ [4] hangout, haunt, rendezvous

[2]**resort** *vb* 1 ♦ : to go often or habitually 2 ♦ : to have recourse ⟨~*ed* to violence⟩

♦ *usu* **resort to** [1] frequent, hang around, hang out, haunt, visit ♦ *usu* **resort to** [2] go, refer, turn

re•sound \ri-ˈzau̇nd\ *vb* 1 ♦ : to become filled with sound : REVERBERATE 2 : to sound loudly

♦ echo, reecho, resonate, reverberate, sound

re•sound•ing *adj* 1 ♦ : producing or characterized by resonant sound : RESONANT 2 ♦ : impressively sonorous ⟨~ name⟩ 3 ♦ : uttered with or marked by emphasis : EMPHATIC ⟨a ~ success⟩ — **re•sound•ing•ly** *adv*

♦ [1, 2] golden, resonant, ringing, round, sonorous, vibrant ♦ [3] aggressive, assertive, dynamic, emphatic, energetic, forceful, strenuous, vehement, vigorous

re•source \ˈrē-ˌsȯrs, ri-ˈsȯrs\ *n* 1 : a source of supply or support — usually used in plural 2 *pl* ♦ : available funds 3 : a possibility of relief or recovery 4 : a means of spending leisure time 5 : ability to meet and handle situations 6 ♦ : something to which one has recourse in difficulty — **re•source•ful** \ri-ˈsȯrs-fəl\ *adj* — **re•source•ful•ness** *n*

♦ **resources** [2] finances, funds, pocket, wherewithal ♦ [6] expedient, recourse, resort

[1]**re•spect** \ri-ˈspekt\ *n* 1 : relation to something usually specified : REGARD ⟨in ~ to⟩ 2 ♦ : high or special regard : ESTEEM 3 *pl* ♦ : an expression of respect or deference 4 : DETAIL, PARTICULAR — **re•spect•ful•ly** *adv* — **re•spect•ful•ness** *n*

♦ [2] admiration, appreciation, esteem, estimation, favor (*or* favour), regard ♦ **respects** [3] compliments, greetings, regards

[2]**respect** *vb* 1 ♦ : to consider deserving of high regard : ESTEEM 2 : to refrain from interfering with ⟨~ another's privacy⟩ 3 : to have reference to : CONCERN — **re•spect•er** *n*

♦ admire, appreciate, esteem, regard

re•spect•able \ri-ˈspek-tə-bəl\ *adj* **1** ♦ : worthy of respect **2** ♦ : decent or correct in conduct **3** ♦ : fair in size, quantity, or quality : TOLERABLE **4** : fit to be seen : PRESENTABLE — **re•spect•a•bil•i•ty** \-ˌspek-tə-ˈbi-lə-tē\ *n* — **re•spect•ably** \-ˈspek-tə-blē\ *adv*

♦ [1] name, prestigious, reputable, reputed *Ant* disreputable, loose ♦ [2] correct, decent, decorous, genteel, nice, polite, proper, seemly ♦ [3] acceptable, adequate, all right, decent, fine, OK, passable, satisfactory, tolerable

re•spect•ful \-fəl\ *adj* ♦ : marked by or showing respect or deference

♦ deferential, dutiful, regardful *Ant* disrespectful

re•spect•ing *prep* ♦ : with regard to

♦ about, apropos of, concerning, of, on, regarding, toward

re•spec•tive \-tiv\ *adj* ♦ : not shared with another : SEPARATE ⟨returned to their ~ homes⟩

♦ different, individual, separate

re•spec•tive•ly \-lē\ *adv* **1** : as relating to each **2** : each in the order given

res•pi•ra•tion \ˌres-pə-ˈrā-shən\ *n* **1** : an act or the process of breathing **2** : the physical and chemical processes (as breathing and oxidation) by which a living thing obtains oxygen and eliminates waste gases (as carbon dioxide) — **re•spi•ra•to•ry** \ˈres-pə-rə-ˌtōr-ē, ri-ˈspī-rə-\ *adj* — **re•spire** \ri-ˈspīr\ *vb*

res•pi•ra•tor \ˈres-pə-ˌrā-tər\ *n* **1** : a device covering the mouth and nose especially to prevent inhaling harmful vapors **2** : a device for artificial respiration

re•spite \ˈres-pət\ *n* **1** : a temporary delay **2** ♦ : an interval of rest or relief

♦ break, breath, breather, recess

re•splen•dence \-dəns\ *n* ♦ : the quality or state of being resplendent

♦ augustness, brilliance, glory, grandeur, grandness, magnificence, majesty, nobility, nobleness, splendor, stateliness

re•splen•dent \ri-ˈsplen-dənt\ *adj* : SPLENDID — **re•splen•dent•ly** *adv*

re•spond \ri-ˈspänd\ *vb* **1** ♦ : to say something in return : ANSWER, REPLY **2** : REACT ⟨~*ed* to a call for help⟩ **3** : to show favorable reaction ⟨~ to medication⟩ — **re•spond•er** *n*

♦ answer, rejoin, reply, retort, return

re•spon•dent \ri-ˈspän-dənt\ *n* : one who responds; *esp* : one who answers in various legal proceedings — **respondent** *adj*

re•sponse \ri-ˈspäns\ *n* **1** ♦ : an act of responding **2** ♦ : something constituting a reply or a reaction

♦ [1] reaction, reply, take ♦ [2] answer, comeback, reply, retort, return

re•spon•si•bil•i•ty \ri-ˌspän-sə-ˈbi-lə-tē\ *n, pl* **-ties** **1** ♦ : the quality or state of being responsible **2** ♦ : something for which one is responsible

♦ [1] blame, fault, liability ♦ [2] burden, charge, commitment, duty, need, obligation

re•spon•si•ble \ri-ˈspän-sə-bəl\ *adj* **1** ♦ : liable to be called upon to answer for one's acts or decisions : ANSWERABLE **2** ♦ : able to fulfill one's obligations : TRUSTWORTHY **3** : able to choose for oneself between right and wrong **4** : involving accountability or important duties ⟨~ position⟩ — **re•spon•si•ble•ness** *n* — **re•spon•si•bly** \-blē\ *adv*

♦ [1] accountable, answerable, liable *Ant* irresponsible, unaccountable ♦ [2] dependable, good, reliable, safe, solid, steady, sure, tried, true, trustworthy

re•spon•sive \-siv\ *adj* **1** : RESPONDING **2** : quick to respond **3** : using responses ⟨~ readings⟩ — **re•spon•sive•ly** *adv* — **re•spon•sive•ness** *n*

[1]**rest** \ˈrest\ *n* **1** ♦ : a bodily state characterized by minimal functional and metabolic activities : SLEEP **2** ♦ : freedom from work or activity **3** : a state of motionlessness or inactivity **4** : a place of shelter or lodging **5** : a silence in music equivalent in duration to a note of the same value; *also* : a character indicating this **6** : something used as a support — **rest•ful•ly** *adv*

♦ [1] repose, sleep, slumber ♦ [2] ease, leisure, relaxation, repose *Ant* exertion, labor, toil, work

[2]**rest** *vb* **1** ♦ : to get rest by lying down; *esp* : SLEEP **2** ♦ : to cease from action or motion **3** : to give rest to : set at rest **4** : to sit or lie fixed or supported **5** : to place on or against a support **6** : to remain based or founded **7** ♦ : to cause to be firmly fixed : GROUND **8** : to remain for action : DEPEND

♦ [1] catnap, doze, nap, sleep, slumber, snooze ♦ [2] bask, loll, lounge, relax, repose ♦ [7] base, ground

[3]**rest** *n* ♦ : something left over

♦ balance, leavings, leftovers, odds and ends, remainder, remains, remnant, residue

re•start \(ˈ)rē-ˈstärt\ *vb* ♦ : to begin again an activity or undertaking

♦ continue, renew, reopen, resume

re•state \(ˈ)rē-ˈstāt\ *vb* ♦ : to express again in words

♦ paraphrase, rephrase, translate

res•tau•rant \ˈres-trənt, -tə-ˌränt\ *n* ♦ : a public eating place

♦ café, diner, grill

res•tau•ra•teur \ˌres-tə-rə-ˈtər\ *also* **res•tau•ran•teur** \-ˌrän-\ *n* : the operator or proprietor of a restaurant

rest•ful \ˈrest-fəl\ *adj* ♦ : marked by, affording, or suggesting rest and repose

♦ calm, hushed, peaceful, quiet, serene, still, tranquil

rest home *n* : an establishment that gives care for the aged or convalescent

res•ti•tu•tion \ˌres-tə-ˈtü-shən, -ˈtyü-\ *n* **1** : the act of restoring : the state of being restored; *esp* : restoration of something to its rightful owner **2** ♦ : a compensating, repaying, or giving an equivalent for some injury

♦ compensation, damages, indemnity, quittance, recompense, redress, remuneration, reparation, requital, satisfaction

res•tive \ˈres-tiv\ *adj* **1** : stubbornly resisting control : BALKY **2** : marked by impatience or uneasiness : UNEASY — **res•tive•ly** *adv*

res•tive•ness *n* : the quality or state of being restive

rest•less \ˈrest-ləs\ *adj* **1** ♦ : lacking or denying rest ⟨a ~ night⟩ **2** : never resting or settled : always moving ⟨the ~ sea⟩ **3** ♦ : marked by or showing unrest especially of mind ⟨~ pacing back and forth⟩ — **rest•less•ly** *adv*

♦ [1] uneasy *Ant* restful ♦ [3] anxious, distressful, nervous, tense, unsettling, upsetting, worrisome

rest•less•ness *n* ♦ : the quality or state of being restless

♦ disquiet, ferment, turmoil, uneasiness, unrest

re•stor•able \ri-ˈstōr-ə-bəl\ *adj* : fit for restoring or reclaiming

res•to•ra•tion \ˌres-tə-ˈrā-shən\ *n* **1** : an act of restoring : the state of being restored **2** : something (as a building) that has been restored

[1]**re•stor•ative** \ri-ˈstōr-ə-tiv\ *n* : something that restores especially to consciousness or health

[2]**restorative** *adj* ♦ : of or relating to restoration; *esp* : having power to restore

♦ healthful, healthy, salubrious, salutary, wholesome ♦ bracing, invigorating, refreshing, stimulative, tonic

re•store \ri-ˈstōr\ *vb* **re•stored; re•stor•ing** **1** : to give back : RETURN **2** : to put back into use or service **3** ♦ : to put or bring back into a former or original state **4** : to put again in possession of something — **re•stor•er** *n*

♦ freshen, recreate, refresh, regenerate, rejuvenate, renew, revitalize, revive

re•strain \ri-ˈstrān\ *vb* **1** : to prevent from doing something **2** ♦ : to limit, restrict, or keep under control : CURB **3** ♦ : to place under restraint or arrest — **re•strain•able** *adj* — **re•strain•er** *n*

♦ [2] bridle, check, constrain, contain, control, curb, govern, inhibit, regulate, rein, tame ♦ [3] apprehend, arrest, nab, pick up, seize

re•strained \ri-ˈstrānd\ *adj* ♦ : marked by restraint — **re•strain•ed•ly** \-ˈstrā-nəd-lē\ *adv*

♦ conservative, muted, quiet, subdued, unpretentious

restraining order *n* : a legal order directing one person to stay away from another

re•straint \ri-ˈstrānt\ *n* **1** : an act of restraining : the state of being restrained **2** ♦ : a restraining force, agency, or device **3** : deprivation or limitation of liberty : CONFINEMENT **4** ♦ : control over the expression of one's feelings

♦ [2] check, condition, constraint, curb, fetter, limitation, restriction ♦ [4] self-control, self-discipline, self-government,

♦ self-possession, self-restraint, will, willpower ♦ [4] constraint, inhibition, repression, suppression

re•strict \ri-ˈstrikt\ *vb* **1** ♦ **:** to confine within bounds **:** LIMIT **2 :** to place under restriction as to use — **re•stric•tive** *adj* — **re•stric•tive•ly** *adv*

♦ check, circumscribe, confine, control, curb, inhibit, limit, restrain

re•strict•ed \ri-ˈstrik-təd\ *adj* ♦ **:** subject or subjected to restriction

♦ definite, determinate, finite, limited, measured, narrow

re•stric•tion \ri-ˈstrik-shən\ *n* **1** ♦ **:** something (as a law or rule) that restricts **2 :** an act of restricting **:** the state of being restricted

♦ check, condition, constraint, curb, fetter, limitation, restraint

rest room *n* **:** a room or suite of rooms that includes sinks and toilets

¹re•sult \ri-ˈzəlt\ *vb* **1 :** to come about as an effect or consequence **2** ♦ **:** to have an issue or result ⟨the disease ~*ed* in death⟩

♦ *usu* **result in** bring about, cause, create, effect, effectuate, generate, induce, make, produce, prompt, work, yield

²result *n* **1** ♦ **:** something that results **:** EFFECT **2 :** beneficial or discernible effect **3 :** something obtained by calculation or investigation

♦ aftermath, conclusion, consequence, corollary, development, effect, issue, outcome, outgrowth, product, resultant, sequence, upshot

¹re•sul•tant \-ˈzəlt-ᵊnt\ *adj* ♦ **:** derived from or resulting from something else

♦ attendant, consequent, consequential, due

²resultant *n* **:** something that results

re•sume \ri-ˈzüm\ *vb* **re•sumed; re•sum•ing 1 :** to take or assume again **2** ♦ **:** to return to or begin again after interruption **3 :** to take back to oneself — **re•sump•tion** \-ˈzəmp-shən\ *n*

♦ continue, renew, reopen, restart

ré•su•mé *or* **re•su•me** *also* **re•su•mé** \ˈre-zə-ˌmā, ˌre-zə-ˈmā\ *n* **1** ♦ **:** an abstract, abridgment, or compendium **:** SUMMARY **2 :** a short account of one's career and qualifications usually prepared by a job applicant

♦ abstract, digest, encapsulation, epitome, outline, précis, recapitulation, roundup, sum, summary, synopsis, wrap-up

re•sur•gence \ri-ˈsər-jəns\ *n* ♦ **:** a rising again into life, activity, or prominence — **re•sur•gent** \-jənt\ *adj*

♦ rebirth, regeneration, rejuvenation, renewal, resurrection, resuscitation, revival

res•ur•rect \ˌre-zə-ˈrekt\ *vb* **1 :** to raise from the dead **2 :** to bring to attention or use again

res•ur•rec•tion \ˌre-zə-ˈrek-shən\ *n* **1** *cap* **:** the rising of Christ from the dead **2** *often cap* **:** the rising to life of all human dead before the final judgment **3** ♦ **:** an act or instance of reviving **:** REVIVAL

♦ rebirth, regeneration, rejuvenation, renewal, resurgence, resuscitation, revival

re•sus•ci•tate \ri-ˈsə-sə-ˌtāt\ *vb* **-tat•ed; -tat•ing** ♦ **:** to revive from apparent death or unconsciousness; *also* **:** REVITALIZE — **re•sus•ci•ta•tor** \-ˌtā-tər\ *n*

♦ reanimate, regenerate, reinvigorate, rejuvenate, renew, revitalize, revive

re•sus•ci•ta•tion \ri-ˌsə-sə-ˈtā-shən, ˌrē-\ *n* ♦ **:** an act of resuscitating or the state of being resuscitated

♦ rebirth, regeneration, rejuvenation, renewal, resurgence, resurrection, revival

ret *abbr* retired

¹re•tail \ˈrē-ˌtāl, *esp for 2 also* ri-ˈtāl\ *vb* **1** ♦ **:** to sell in small quantities directly to the ultimate consumer **2 :** to tell in detail or to one person after another — **re•tail•er** *n*

♦ deal, market, merchandise, put up, sell, vend

²re•tail \ˈrē-ˌtāl\ *n* **:** the sale of goods in small amounts to ultimate consumers — **retail** *adj or adv*

re•tain \ri-ˈtān\ *vb* **1** ♦ **:** to hold in possession or use **2** ♦ **:** to engage (as a lawyer) by paying a fee in advance **3 :** to keep in a fixed place or position

♦ [1] hang on, hold, keep, reserve, withhold ♦ [2] employ, engage, hire, take on

¹re•tain•er \ri-ˈtā-nər\ *n* **1 :** one that retains **2** ♦ **:** a servant in a wealthy household **3 :** EMPLOYEE **4 :** a device that holds something (as teeth) in place

♦ domestic, flunky, lackey, menial, servant, steward

²retainer *n* **:** a fee paid to secure services (as of a lawyer)

¹re•take \(ˌ)rē-ˈtāk\ *vb* **-took** \-ˈtu̇k\; **-tak•en** \-ˈtā-kən\; **-tak•ing 1** ♦ **:** to take or seize again **2 :** to photograph again

♦ recapture, reclaim, recoup, recover, regain, repossess, retrieve

²re•take \ˈrē-ˌtāk\ *n* **:** a second photographing of a motion-picture scene

re•tal•i•ate \ri-ˈta-lē-ˌāt\ *vb* **-at•ed; -at•ing** ♦ **:** to return like for like; *esp* **:** to get revenge — **re•tal•ia•to•ry** \-ˈtal-yə-ˌtōr-ē\ *adj*

♦ avenge, requite, revenge

re•tal•i•a•tion \-ˌta-lē-ˈā-shən\ *n* ♦ **:** an act of retaliating

♦ reprisal, requital, retribution, revenge, vengeance

re•tard \ri-ˈtärd\ *vb* ♦ **:** to hold back **:** delay the progress of — **re•tar•da•tion** \ˌrē-ˌtär-ˈdā-shən, ri-\ *n* — **re•tard•er** *n*

♦ brake, decelerate, slow

re•tar•dant \ri-ˈtär-dᵊnt\ *adj* **:** serving or tending to retard — **retardant** *n*

re•tard•ed *adj, sometimes offensive* **:** slow or limited in intellectual, emotional, or academic progress

retch \ˈrech\ *vb* **1 :** to try to vomit **2 :** to throw up **:** VOMIT

re•ten•tion \ri-ˈten-chən\ *n* **1 :** the act of retaining **:** the state of being retained **2 :** the power of retaining especially in the mind **:** RETENTIVENESS

re•ten•tive \-ˈten-tiv\ *adj* **:** having the power of retaining; *esp* **:** retaining knowledge easily — **re•ten•tive•ness** *n*

re•think \(ˌ)rē-ˈthiŋk\ *vb* **-thought** \-ˈthȯt\; **-think•ing** ♦ **:** to think about again **:** RECONSIDER

♦ readdress, reanalyze, reconceive, reconsider, reexamine, review

ret•i•cence \ˈre-tə-səns\ *n* ♦ **:** the quality or state or an instance of being reticent

♦ disinclination, hesitancy, reluctance

ret•i•cent \ˈre-tə-sənt\ *adj* **1** ♦ **:** tending not to talk or give out information **2 :** RELUCTANT **3 :** restrained in expression, presentation, or appearance — **ret•i•cent•ly** *adv*

♦ closemouthed, laconic, reserved, silent, taciturn, uncommunicative

ret•i•na \ˈret-ᵊn-ə\ *n, pl* **retinas** *or* **ret•i•nae** \-ᵊn-ˌē\ **:** the sensory membrane lining the eye that receives the image formed by the lens — **ret•i•nal** \ˈret-ᵊn-əl\ *adj*

ret•i•nue \ˈret-ᵊn-ˌü, -ˌyü\ *n* ♦ **:** the body of attendants or followers of a distinguished person

♦ cortege, following, suite, train

re•tire \ri-ˈtīr\ *vb* **re•tired; re•tir•ing 1** ♦ **:** to withdraw from action or danger **:** RETREAT **2 :** to withdraw especially for privacy **3** ♦ **:** to withdraw from one's occupation or position **:** conclude one's career **4 :** to go to bed **5 :** to cause to be out in baseball **6** ♦ **:** to cause to retire **7 :** to withdraw from use or service

♦ [1] back, fall back, recede, retreat, withdraw ♦ *usu* **retire from** [3] leave, quit, resign, step down ♦ [6] cashier, dismiss, fire, remove, sack

re•tired \ri-ˈtīrd\ *adj* **1 :** screened or hidden from view **:** SECLUDED, QUIET **2 :** withdrawn from active duty or from one's career

re•tir•ee \ri-ˌtī-ˈrē\ *n* **:** a person who has retired from a career

re•tire•ment *n* **:** an act of retiring **:** the state of being retired

re•tir•ing *adj* ♦ **:** sensitively diffident **:** SHY

♦ bashful, coy, demure, diffident, introverted, modest, reserved, shy

re•tool \(ˌ)rē-ˈtül\ *vb* **1 :** to reequip with tools **2 :** to modify with usually minor improvements ⟨~*ed* the team for next year⟩

¹re•tort \ri-ˈtȯrt\ *vb* **1** ♦ **:** to say in reply **:** answer back usually sharply **2 :** to answer (an argument) by a counter argument **3 :** RETALIATE

♦ answer, rejoin, reply, respond, return

²retort *n* ♦ **:** a quick, witty, or cutting reply; *esp* **:** one that turns back or counters the first speaker's words

♦ comeback, repartee, riposte ♦ answer, comeback, reply, response, return

3re·tort \ri-ˈtȯrt, ˈrē-ˌtȯrt\ *n* **:** a vessel in which substances are distilled or broken up by heat

re·touch \(ˌ)rē-ˈtəch\ *vb* **:** TOUCH UP; *esp* **:** to change (as a photographic negative) in order to produce a more desirable appearance

re·trace \(ˌ)rē-ˈtrās\ *vb* **:** to go over again or in a reverse direction ⟨*retraced* his steps⟩

re·tract \ri-ˈtrakt\ *vb* **1 :** to draw back or in **2** ♦ **:** to withdraw (as a charge or promise) — **re·tract·able** *adj* — **re·trac·tion** \-ˈtrak-shən\ *n*

♦ abjure, recant, renounce, take back, unsay, withdraw

re·trac·tile \ri-ˈtrakt-ᵊl, -ˈtrak-ˌtīl\ *adj* **:** capable of being drawn back or in ⟨∼ claws⟩

1re·tread \(ˌ)rē-ˈtred\ *vb* **re·tread·ed; re·tread·ing :** to put a new tread on (a worn tire)

2re·tread \ˈrē-ˌtred\ *n* **1 :** a retreaded tire **2 :** one pressed into service again; *also* **:** REMAKE

1re·treat \ri-ˈtrēt\ *n* **1** ♦ **:** an act of withdrawing especially from something dangerous, difficult, or disagreeable **2 :** a military signal for withdrawal; *also* **:** a military flag-lowering ceremony **3** ♦ **:** a place of privacy or safety **:** REFUGE **4 :** a period of group withdrawal for prayer, meditation, or study

♦ [1] revulsion, withdrawal ***Ant*** advancement ♦ [3] asylum, harbor (*or* harbour), haven, refuge, sanctuary, shelter

2retreat *vb* **1** ♦ **:** to make a retreat **2 :** to slope backward

♦ back, fall back, recede, retire, withdraw ***Ant*** advance

re·trench \ri-ˈtrench\ *vb* **1 :** to cut down or pare away **:** REDUCE, CURTAIL **2 :** to cut down expenses **:** ECONOMIZE — **re·trench·ment** *n*

ret·ri·bu·tion \ˌre-trə-ˈbyü-shən\ *n* ♦ **:** something administered or exacted in recompense; *esp* **:** PUNISHMENT — **re·trib·u·tive** \ri-ˈtri-byə-tiv\ *adj* — **re·trib·u·to·ry** \-byə-ˌtōr-ē\ *adj*

♦ punishment, reprisal, requital, retaliation, revenge, vengeance

re·triev·al \-ˈtrē-vəl\ *n* ♦ **:** an act or process of retrieving

♦ reclamation, recovery, repossession

re·trieve \ri-ˈtrēv\ *vb* **re·trieved; re·triev·ing 1 :** to search about for and bring in (killed or wounded game) **2** ♦ **:** to get back again **:** RECOVER — **re·triev·able** *adj*

♦ recapture, reclaim, recoup, recover, regain, repossess, retake

re·triev·er \ri-ˈtrē-vər\ *n* **:** one that retrieves; *esp* **:** a dog of any of several breeds used especially for retrieving game

ret·ro \ˈre-trō\ *adj* **:** relating to or being the styles and fashions of the past ⟨∼ clothing⟩

ret·ro·ac·tive \ˌre-trō-ˈak-tiv\ *adj* **:** made effective as of a date prior to enactment ⟨a ∼ pay raise⟩ — **ret·ro·ac·tive·ly** *adv*

ret·ro·fit \ˈre-tro-ˌfit, ˌre-trō-ˈfit\ *vb* **:** to furnish (as an aircraft) with newly available equipment — **ret·ro·fit** \ˈre-tro-ˌfit\ *n*

1ret·ro·grade \ˈre-trə-ˌgrād\ *adj* **1 :** moving or tending backward **2 :** tending toward or resulting in a worse condition

2retrograde *vb* **1 :** RETREAT **2 :** DETERIORATE, DEGENERATE

ret·ro·gres·sion \ˌre-trə-ˈgre-shən\ *n* **:** return to a former and less complex level of development or organization — **ret·ro·gress** \ˌre-trə-ˈgres\ *vb* — **ret·ro·gres·sive** \ˌre-trə-ˈgre-siv\ *adj*

ret·ro–rock·et \ˈre-trō-ˌrä-kət\ *n* **:** an auxiliary rocket engine (as on a spacecraft) used to slow forward motion

ret·ro·spect \ˈre-trə-ˌspekt\ *n* **:** a review of past events

ret·ro·spec·tion \ˌre-trə-ˈspek-shən\ *n* ♦ **:** the act or process or an instance of surveying the past

♦ reappraisal, reexamination, review

ret·ro·spec·tive \ˌre-trə-ˈspek-tiv\ *n* **1 :** a comprehensive examination of an artist's work over many years **2 :** REVIEW 4 ⟨a war ∼⟩ — **retrospective** *adj* — **ret·ro·spec·tive·ly** *adv*

ret·ro·vi·rus \ˈre-trō-ˌvī-rəs\ *n* **:** any of a group of RNA-containing viruses (as HIV) that make DNA using RNA instead of the reverse

1re·turn \ri-ˈtərn\ *vb* **1 :** to go or come back **2 :** to pass, give, or send back to an earlier possessor **3 :** to put back to or in a former place or state **4 :** to respond in words or writing **:** REPLY, ANSWER **5 :** to report especially officially **6 :** to elect to office **7 :** to bring in (as profit) **:** YIELD **8 :** to give or perform in return — **re·turn·er** *n*

2return *n* **1 :** an act of coming or going back to or from a former place or state **2 :** RECURRENCE **3 :** a report of the results of balloting **4 :** a formal statement of taxable income **5** ♦ **:** the profit from labor, investment, or business **6 :** the act of returning something **7 :** something that returns or is returned; *also* **:** a means for conveying something (as water) back to its starting point **8 a :** something given in repayment or reciprocation **b :** something said, written, or done in answer or response **:** ANSWER, RETORT **9 :** an answering play — **return** *adj*

♦ earnings, gain, income, net, payoff, proceeds, profit, revenue, yield

1re·turn·able \ri-ˈtər-nə-bəl\ *adj* **:** capable of being returned (as for reuse or recycling); *also* **:** permitted to be returned

2returnable *n* **:** a returnable beverage container

re·turn·ee \ri-ˌtər-ˈnē\ *n* **:** one who returns

re·union \rē-ˈyü-nyən\ *n* **1 :** an act of reuniting **:** the state of being reunited **2 :** a meeting of persons after separation

1rev \ˈrev\ *n* **:** a revolution of a motor

2rev *vb* **revved; rev·ving :** to increase the revolutions per minute of (a motor)

3rev *abbr* **1** revenue **2** reverse **3** review; reviewed **4** revised; revision **5** revolution

Rev *abbr* **1** Revelation **2** Reverend

re·vamp \(ˌ)rē-ˈvamp\ *vb* **1** ♦ **:** to make a new, amended, improved, or up-to-date version of **:** REVISE **2** ♦ **:** to restore to a former better state (as by cleaning, repairing, or rebuilding)

♦ [1] alter, change, make over, modify, recast, redo, refashion, remake, remodel, revise, rework, vary ♦ [2] doctor, fix, mend, patch, recondition, renovate, repair

re·vanche \rə-ˈvänsh\ *n* **:** REVENGE; *esp* **:** a usually political policy designed to recover lost territory or status

re·veal \ri-ˈvēl\ *vb* **1** ♦ **:** to make known **2 :** to show plainly **:** open up to view

♦ bare, disclose, discover, divulge, expose, show, spill, tell, unbosom, uncloak, uncover, unmask, unveil ***Ant*** cloak, conceal, cover (up), enshroud, hide, mask, shroud, veil

rev·eil·le \ˈre-və-lē\ *n* **:** a military signal sounded at about sunrise

1rev·el \ˈre-vəl\ *vb* **-eled** *or* **-elled; -el·ing** *or* **-el·ling 1 :** to take part in a revel **2** ♦ **:** to take great pleasure or satisfaction ⟨∼*ed* in the quiet after everyone had gone⟩

♦ *usu* **revel in** adore, delight, dig, enjoy, fancy, groove, like, love, relish

2revel *n* ♦ **:** a usually wild party or celebration

♦ binge, fling, frolic, gambol, lark, rollick, romp

rev·e·la·tion \ˌre-və-ˈlā-shən\ *n* **1 :** an act of revealing **2 :** something revealed; *esp* **:** an enlightening or astonishing disclosure

Revelation *n* **:** a book of the New Testament of Christian Scripture

re·ve·la·to·ry \ˈre-və-lə-ˌtōr-ē, ri-ˈve-lə-\ *adj* ♦ **:** of or relating to revelation **:** serving to reveal something

♦ eloquent, expressive, meaning, meaningful, pregnant, significant, suggestive

rev·el·er *or* **rev·el·ler** \ˈre-vəl-ər\ *n* ♦ **:** one who engages in revelry

♦ celebrant, merrymaker, roisterer

rev·el·ry \ˈre-vəl-rē\ *n* ♦ **:** noisy partying or merrymaking

♦ conviviality, festivity, gaiety, jollification, merriment, merrymaking

1re·venge \ri-ˈvenj\ *vb* **re·venged; re·veng·ing** ♦ **:** to inflict harm or injury in return for (a wrong) **:** AVENGE — **re·veng·er** *n*

♦ avenge, requite, retaliate

2revenge *n* **1 :** a desire for revenge **2** ♦ **:** an act or instance of retaliation to get even **3 :** an opportunity for getting satisfaction — **re·venge·ful** *adj*

♦ reprisal, requital, retaliation, retribution, vengeance

rev·e·nue \ˈre-və-ˌnü, -ˌnyü\ *n* **1 :** investment income **2 :** money collected by a government (as through taxes) **3** ♦ **:** the total income produced by a given source

♦ earnings, income, proceeds, profit, return, yield

rev·e·nu·er \ˈre-və-ˌnü-ər, -ˌnyü-\ *n* **:** a revenue officer or boat

re·verb \ri-ˈvərb, ˈrē-ˌvərb\ *n* **:** an electronically produced echo effect in recorded music; *also* **:** a device for producing reverb

re·ver·ber·ate \ri-ˈvər-bə-ˌrāt\ *vb* **-at·ed; -at·ing 1 :** REFLECT ⟨∼ light or heat⟩ **2** ♦ **:** to resound in or as if in a series of echoes — **re·ver·ber·a·tion** \-ˌvər-bə-ˈrā-shən\ *n*

♦ echo, reecho, resonate, resound, sound

re•vere \ri-ˈvir\ *vb* **re•vered; re•ver•ing** ♦ **:** to show honor and devotion to **:** VENERATE

♦ adore, deify, glorify, venerate, worship

¹rev•er•ence \ˈre-vrəns, -və-rəns\ *n* **1 :** honor or respect felt or shown **2 :** a gesture (as a bow or curtsy) of respect
²reverence *vb* **-enced; -enc•ing :** to regard or treat with reverence
¹rev•er•end \ˈre-vrənd, -və-rənd\ *adj* **1** ♦ **:** worthy of reverence **:** REVERED **2 :** being a member of the clergy — used as a title

♦ hallowed, venerable

²reverend *n* ♦ **:** a member of the clergy

♦ clergyman, divine, ecclesiastic, father, minister, preacher, priest

rev•er•ent \ˈre-vrənt, -və-rənt\ *adj* **:** expressing reverence — **rev•er•ent•ly** *adv*
rev•er•en•tial \ˌre-və-ˈren-chəl\ *adj* **:** REVERENT
rev•er•ie *also* **rev•ery** \ˈre-və-rē\ *n, pl* **-er•ies 1 :** DAYDREAM **2** ♦ **:** the condition of being lost in thought

♦ study, trance, woolgathering

re•ver•sal \ri-ˈvər-səl\ *n* **1 :** an act or process of reversing **2** ♦ **:** a change (as of fortune) often for the worse

♦ lapse, reverse, setback

¹re•verse \ri-ˈvərs\ *adj* **1 :** opposite to a previous or normal condition ⟨in ~ order⟩ **2 :** acting or working in a manner opposite the usual **3 :** bringing about reverse movement ⟨~ gear⟩ — **re•verse•ly** *adv*
²reverse *vb* **re•versed; re•vers•ing 1** ♦ **:** to turn upside down or completely about in position or direction **2 :** to set aside or change (as a legal decision) **3 :** to change to the contrary ⟨~ a policy⟩ **4 :** to go or cause to go in the opposite direction **5 :** to put (as a car) in reverse — **re•vers•ible** \-ˈvər-sə-bəl\ *adj*

♦ flip, turn

³reverse *n* **1** ♦ **:** something contrary to something else **:** OPPOSITE **2** ♦ **:** an act or instance of reversing; *esp* **:** a change for the worse **3 :** the back side of something **4 :** a gear that reverses something

♦ [1] antipode, antithesis, contrary, negative, opposite ♦ [2] lapse, reversal, setback

reverse engineer *vb* **:** to disassemble or analyze in detail in order to discover concepts involved in manufacture — **reverse engineering** *n*
re•ver•sion \ri-ˈvər-zhən\ *n* **1 :** the right of succession or future possession (as to a title or property) **2 :** return toward some former or ancestral condition; *also* **:** a product of this — **re•ver•sion•ary** \-zhə-ˌner-ē\ *adj*
re•vert \ri-ˈvərt\ *vb* **1 :** to come or go back ⟨~*ed* to savagery⟩ **2 :** to return to a proprietor or his or her heirs **3 :** to return to an ancestral type
¹re•view \ri-ˈvyü\ *n* **1 :** an act of revising **2 :** a formal military inspection **3 :** a general survey **4** ♦ **:** an act or the process of reviewing **:** INSPECTION **5 :** a critical evaluation (as of a book) **6 :** a magazine devoted to reviews and essays **7 :** a renewed study of previously studied material **8 :** REVUE **9** ♦ **:** a retrospective view or survey (as of one's life)

♦ [4] audit, check, checkup, examination, inspection, scan, scrutiny, survey ♦ [9] reappraisal, reexamination, retrospection

²re•view \ri-ˈvyü, *1 also* ˈrē-\ *vb* **1 a** ♦ **:** to examine or study again **b :** to reexamine judicially **2 :** to hold a review of ⟨~ troops⟩ **3 :** to write a critical examination of ⟨~ a novel⟩ **4 :** to look back over ⟨~*ed* her accomplishments⟩

♦ audit, check, examine, inspect, scan, scrutinize, survey ♦ readdress, reanalyze, reconceive, reconsider, reexamine, rethink

re•view•er \ri-ˈvyü-ər\ *n* **:** one that reviews; *esp* **:** a writer of critical reviews
re•vile \ri-ˈvī(-ə)l\ *vb* **re•viled; re•vil•ing :** to abuse verbally **:** rail at — **re•vile•ment** *n* — **re•vil•er** *n*
¹re•vise \ri-ˈvīz\ *vb* **re•vised; re•vis•ing 1** ♦ **:** to look over something written in order to correct or improve **2** ♦ **:** to make a new version of — **re•vis•able** *adj* — **re•vis•er** *or* **re•vi•sor** \-ˈvī-zər\ *n*

♦ [1] edit, redraft, revamp, rework ♦ [2] alter, change, make over, modify, recast, redo, refashion, remake, remodel, revamp, rework, vary

²revise *n* **:** an act of revising
re•vi•sion \-ˈvi-zhən\ *n* ♦ **:** an act of revising

♦ alteration, change, difference, modification, revise, variation

re•vi•tal•ise *chiefly Brit var of* REVITALIZE
re•vi•tal•i•za•tion \(ˌ)rē-ˌvīt-ᵊl-ə-ˈzā-shən\ *n* **:** an act or instance of revitalizing
re•vi•tal•ize \ˌrē-ˈvīt-ᵊl-ˌīz\ *vb* **-ized; -iz•ing** ♦ **:** to give new life or vigor to

♦ reanimate, regenerate, reinvigorate, rejuvenate, renew, resuscitate, revive

re•viv•al \ri-ˈvī-vəl\ *n* **1** ♦ **:** an act of reviving **:** the state of being revived **2 :** a new publication or presentation (as of a book or play) **3 :** an evangelistic meeting or series of meetings

♦ rebirth, regeneration, rejuvenation, renewal, resurgence, resurrection, resuscitation

re•vive \ri-ˈvīv\ *vb* **re•vived; re•viv•ing 1** ♦ **:** to bring back or return to life, consciousness, or activity **:** make or become fresh or strong again **2 :** to bring back into use — **re•viv•er** *n*

♦ reanimate, regenerate, reinvigorate, rejuvenate, renew, resuscitate, revitalize ♦ come around, come round, come to

re•viv•i•fy \rē-ˈvi-və-ˌfī\ *vb* **:** REVIVE — **re•viv•i•fi•ca•tion** \-ˌvi-və-fə-ˈkā-shən\ *n*
re•vo•ca•ble \ˈre-və-kə-bəl *also* ri-ˈvō-kə-bəl\ *adj* **:** capable of being revoked
re•vo•ca•tion \ˌre-və-ˈkā-shən\ *n* ♦ **:** an act or instance of revoking

♦ abortion, calling, cancellation, recall, repeal, rescission

re•voke \ri-ˈvōk\ *vb* **re•voked; re•vok•ing 1** ♦ **:** to annul by recalling or taking back **:** REPEAL, RESCIND **2 :** RENEGE 2 — **re•vok•er** *n*

♦ abort, call, call off, cancel, drop, recall, repeal, rescind

¹re•volt \ri-ˈvōlt\ *vb* **1 :** to throw off allegiance to a ruler or government **:** REBEL **2 :** to experience disgust or shock **3** ♦ **:** to turn or cause to turn away with disgust or abhorrence

♦ disgust, nauseate, repel, repulse, sicken, turn off

²revolt *n* ♦ **:** a renouncing of allegiance (as to a government or party); *esp* **:** a determined armed uprising **:** REBELLION

♦ insurrection, mutiny, rebellion, revolution, uprising

re•volt•er *n* ♦ **:** one that revolts

♦ insurgent, insurrectionist, mutineer, rebel, red, revolutionary

re•volt•ing *adj* ♦ **:** extremely offensive — **re•volt•ing•ly** *adv*

♦ abhorrent, abominable, appalling, awful, distasteful, hideous, horrible, horrid, nasty, nauseating, noisome, offensive, repellent, repugnant, repulsive

rev•o•lu•tion \ˌre-və-ˈlü-shən\ *n* **1 :** the action by a heavenly body of going round in an orbit **2** ♦ **:** motion of any figure about a center or axis; *also* **:** one complete turn **:** ROTATION **3 a :** a sudden, radical, or complete change **b** ♦ **:** the overthrow or renunciation of one ruler or government and substitution of another by the governed

♦ [2] gyration, pirouette, reel, roll, rotation, spin, twirl, wheel, whirl ♦ [3b] insurrection, mutiny, rebellion, revolt, uprising

¹rev•o•lu•tion•ary \-shə-ˌner-ē\ *adj* **1** ♦ **:** of or relating to revolution **2 :** tending to or promoting revolution **3 :** constituting or bringing about a major change

♦ insurgent, mutinous, rebellious

²revolutionary *n, pl* **-ar•ies** ♦ **:** one who takes part in a revolution or who advocates revolutionary doctrines

♦ insurgent, insurrectionist, mutineer, rebel, red, revolter

rev•o•lu•tion•ise *chiefly Brit var of* REVOLUTIONIZE
¹rev•o•lu•tion•ist \ˌre-və-ˈlü-shə-nist\ *n* **:** REVOLUTIONARY
²revolutionist *adj* **:** of or relating to revolution or revolutionists
rev•o•lu•tion•ize \-ˌnīz\ *vb* **-ized; -iz•ing :** to change fundamentally or completely
rev•o•lu•tion•iz•er *n* **:** one that revolutionizes
re•volve \ri-ˈvälv\ *vb* **re•volved; re•volv•ing 1 :** to turn over in the mind **:** reflect upon **:** PONDER **2** ♦ **:** to move in an orbit; *also* **:** ROTATE — **re•volv•able** *adj*

♦ pivot, roll, rotate, spin, swing, swirl, turn, twirl, twist, wheel, whirl

re•volv•er \ri-ˈväl-vər\ *n* **:** a pistol with a revolving cylinder of several chambers
re•vue \ri-ˈvyü\ *n* **:** a theatrical production consisting typically of brief often satirical sketches and songs
re•vul•sion \ri-ˈvəl-shən\ *n* **1 :** a strong sudden reaction or

change of feeling **2** ♦ **:** a feeling of complete distaste or repugnance **3** ♦ **:** a strong pulling or drawing away

♦ [2] aversion, disgust, distaste, loathing, nausea, repugnance, repulsion ♦ [3] retreat, withdrawal

revved *past and past part of* REV
revving *pres part of* REV
¹re•ward \ri-ˈwȯrd\ *vb* **1 :** to give a reward to or for **2 :** RECOMPENSE
²reward *n* **1 :** something given in return for good or evil done or received or for some service or attainment **2 :** a stimulus that is administered to an organism after a response and that increases the probability of occurrence of the response
re•ward•ing *adj* **1 :** yielding or likely to yield a reward **2** ♦ **:** serving as a reward **:** giving pleasure as if a reward

♦ comforting, encouraging, gratifying, heartening, heartwarming, satisfying

¹re•wind \(ˌ)rē-ˈwīnd\ *vb* **-wound; -wind•ing 1 :** to wind again **2 :** to reverse the winding of (as film)
²re•wind \ˈrē-ˌwīnd\ *n* **1 :** something that rewinds **2 :** an act of rewinding **3 :** a function of an electronic device that reverses a recording to a previous portion
re•work \(ˌ)rē-ˈwərk\ *vb* **1** ♦ **:** to work again or anew **:** REVISE **2 :** to reprocess for further use

♦ alter, change, edit, make over, modify, recast, redo, refashion, remake, remodel, revamp, revise, vary

¹re•write \(ˌ)rē-ˈrīt\ *vb* **-wrote; -writ•ten; -writ•ing :** to make a revision of **:** REVISE
²re•write \ˈrē-ˌrīt\ *n* **:** an instance or a piece of rewriting
RF *abbr* radio frequency
RFD *abbr* rural free delivery
Rh *symbol* rhodium
RH *abbr* right hand
rhap•sod•ic \rap-ˈsä-dik\ *adj* ♦ **:** extravagantly emotional — **rhap•sod•i•cal•ly** \-di-k(ə-)lē\ *adv*

♦ ecstatic, elated, euphoric, intoxicated, rapturous

rhap•so•dize \ˈrap-sə-ˌdīz\ *vb* ♦ **:** to speak or write in a rhapsodic manner

♦ enthuse, fuss, gush, rave, slobber

rhap•so•dy \ˈrap-sə-dē\ *n, pl* **-dies 1 :** an expression of extravagant praise or ecstasy **2 :** a musical composition of irregular form **3** ♦ **:** a state or experience of being carried away by overwhelming emotion

♦ ecstasy, elation, euphoria, exhilaration, heaven, intoxication, paradise, rapture, transport

rhea \ˈrē-ə\ *n* **:** either of two large flightless 3-toed So. American birds that resemble but are smaller than the African ostrich
rhe•ni•um \ˈrē-nē-əm\ *n* **:** a rare heavy hard metallic chemical element
rheo•stat \ˈrē-ə-ˌstat\ *n* **:** a resistor for regulating an electric current by means of variable resistances — **rheo•stat•ic** \ˌrē-ə-ˈstatik\ *adj*
rhe•sus monkey \ˈrē-səs-\ *n* **:** a pale brown Asian monkey often used in medical research
rhet•o•ric \ˈre-tə-rik\ *n* **1** ♦ **:** the art of speaking or writing effectively **2** ♦ **:** insincere or grandiloquent language — **rhet•o•ri•cian** \ˌre-tə-ˈri-shən\ *n*

♦ [1] articulateness, eloquence, poetry ♦ [2] bombast, gas, grandiloquence, hot air, wind

rhe•tor•i•cal \ri-ˈtȯr-i-kəl\ *adj* **1 :** of, relating to, or concerned with rhetoric **2** ♦ **:** given to rhetoric **3 :** asked merely for effect with no answer expected ⟨a ∼ question⟩

♦ bombastic, gaseous, grandiloquent, oratorical, windy

rheum \ˈrüm\ *n* **:** a watery discharge from the mucous membranes especially of the eyes or nose — **rheumy** *adj*
rheu•mat•ic fever \rů-ˈma-tik-\ *n* **:** an acute disease chiefly of children and young adults that is characterized by fever, by inflammation and pain in and around the joints, and by inflammation of the membranes surrounding the heart and the heart valves
rheu•ma•tism \ˈrü-mə-ˌti-zəm, ˈrů-\ *n* **:** any of various conditions marked by stiffness, pain, or swelling in muscles or joints **2 :** RHEUMATOID ARTHRITIS — **rheu•mat•ic** \rů-ˈma-tik\ *adj*
rheu•ma•toid arthritis \-ˌtȯid-\ *n* **:** a usually chronic progressive autoimmune disease characterized by inflammation and swelling of joint structures
rheu•ma•tol•o•gy \ˌrü-mə-ˈtä-lə-jē, ˌrů-\ *n* **:** a medical science dealing with rheumatic diseases — **rheu•ma•tol•o•gist** \-jist\ *n*

Rh factor \ˌär-ˈāch-\ *n* **:** any of one or more inherited substances in red blood cells that may cause dangerous reactions in some infants or in transfusions
rhine•stone \ˈrīn-ˌstōn\ *n* **:** a colorless imitation stone of high luster made of glass, paste, or gem quartz
rhi•no \ˈrī-nō\ *n, pl* **rhinos** *also* **rhino :** RHINOCEROS
rhi•noc•er•os \rī-ˈnä-sə-rəs\ *n, pl* **-noc•er•os•es** *also* **-noc•er•os** *or* **-noc•eri** \-ˈnä-sə-ˌrī\ **:** any of a family of large thick-skinned mammals of Africa and Asia with one or two upright horns of keratin on the snout and three toes on each foot
rhi•zome \ˈrī-ˌzōm\ *n* **:** a fleshy, rootlike, and usually horizontal underground plant stem that forms shoots above and roots below — **rhi•zom•a•tous** \rī-ˈzä-mə-təs\ *adj*
Rh–neg•a•tive \ˌär-ˌāch-ˈne-gə-tiv\ *adj* **:** lacking Rh factors in the red blood cells
rho \ˈrō\ *n* **:** the 17th letter of the Greek alphabet — Ρ or ρ
rho•di•um \ˈrō-dē-əm\ *n* **:** a rare hard ductile metallic chemical element
rho•do•den•dron \ˌrō-də-ˈden-drən\ *n* **:** any of a genus of shrubs or trees of the heath family with clusters of large bright flowers
rhom•boid \ˈräm-ˌbȯid\ *n* **:** a parallelogram with unequal adjacent sides and angles that are not right angles — **rhomboid** *or* **rhom•boi•dal** \räm-ˈbȯid-ᵊl\ *adj*
rhom•bus \ˈräm-bəs\ *n, pl* **rhom•bus•es** *or* **rhom•bi** \-ˌbī\ **:** a parallelogram having all four sides equal
Rh–pos•i•tive \ˌär-ˌāch-ˈpä-zə-tiv\ *adj* **:** containing one or more Rh factors in the red blood cells
rhu•barb \ˈrü-ˌbärb\ *n* **:** a garden plant related to the buckwheat having leaves with thick juicy edible pink and red stems
¹rhyme \ˈrīm\ *n* **1 :** a composition in verse that rhymes; *also* **:** POETRY **2 :** correspondence in terminal sounds (as of two lines of verse)
²rhyme *vb* **rhymed; rhym•ing 1 :** to make rhymes; *also* **:** to write poetry **2 :** to have rhymes **:** be in rhyme
rhythm \ˈri-t͟həm\ *n* **1** ♦ **:** regular rise and fall in the flow of sound in speech **2 :** a movement or activity in which some action or element recurs regularly — **rhyth•mi•cal•ly** \-k(ə-)lē\ *adv*

♦ beat, cadence, measure, meter (*or* metre)

rhythm and blues *n* **:** popular music based on blues and black folk music
rhyth•mic \ˈrit͟h-mik\ *or* **rhyth•mi•cal** \-mi-kəl\ *adj* ♦ **:** marked by or moving in pronounced rhythm

♦ cadenced, measured, metrical ***Ant*** unmeasured, unrhythmic

rhythm method *n* **:** birth control by refraining from sexual intercourse during the time when ovulation is most likely to occur
RI *abbr* Rhode Island
¹rib \ˈrib\ *n* **1 :** any of the series of curved bones of the chest of most vertebrates that are joined to the backbone in pairs and help to support the body wall and protect the organs inside **2 :** something resembling a rib in shape or function **3 :** an elongated ridge (as in fabric)
²rib *vb* **ribbed; rib•bing 1 :** to furnish or strengthen with ribs **2 :** to knit so as to form ridges
³rib *vb* **ribbed; rib•bing** ♦ **:** to poke fun at **:** TEASE — **rib•ber** *n*

♦ chaff, jive, josh, kid, rally, razz, ride, roast, tease

rib•ald \ˈri-bəld\ *adj* ♦ **:** coarse or indecent especially in language ⟨∼ jokes⟩

♦ bawdy, coarse, crude, indecent, lewd, obscene, smutty, vulgar ♦ racy, risqué, spicy, suggestive

rib•ald•ry \-bəl-drē\ *n* ♦ **:** a ribald quality or element

♦ bawdiness, coarseness, indecency, lewdness, obscenity, smut, vulgarity

rib•and \ˈri-bənd\ *n* **:** RIBBON
rib•bon \ˈri-bən\ *n* **1 :** a narrow fabric typically of silk or velvet used for trimming and for badges **2 :** a strip of inked cloth (as in a typewriter) **3 :** TATTER, SHRED ⟨torn to ∼*s*⟩
ri•bo•fla•vin \ˌrī-bə-ˈflā-vən, ˈrī-bə-ˌflā-vən\ *n* **:** a growth-promoting vitamin of the vitamin B complex occurring especially in milk and liver
ri•bo•nu•cle•ic acid \ˌrī-bō-nů-ˌklē-ik-, -nyů-, -ˌklā-\ *n* **:** RNA
ri•bose \ˈrī-ˌbōs\ *n* **:** a sugar with five carbon atoms and five oxygen atoms in each molecule that is part of RNA
ri•bo•some \ˈrī-bə-ˌsōm\ *n* **:** any of the RNA-rich cytoplasmic granules in a cell that are sites of protein synthesis — **ri•bo•so•mal** \ˌrī-bə-ˈsō-məl\ *adj*
rice \ˈrīs\ *n* **:** the starchy seeds of an annual grass that are cooked and used for food; *also* **:** this widely cultivated grass of warm wet areas

rich \ˈrich\ *adj* **1** ♦ **:** possessing or controlling great wealth **:** WEALTHY **2 :** COSTLY, VALUABLE **3 :** deep and pleasing in color or tone **4** ♦ **:** having great plenty **5 :** containing much sugar, fat, or seasoning; *also* **:** high in combustible content **6 :** highly productive or remunerative **:** FRUITFUL, FERTILE — **rich•ness** *n*

♦ [1] affluent, flush, loaded, moneyed, opulent, wealthy, well-fixed, well-heeled, well-off, well-to-do *Ant* destitute, impecunious, impoverished, indigent, needy, penniless, penurious, poor, poverty-stricken ♦ [4] concentrated, full, full-bodied, potent, robust, strong

rich•es \ˈri-chəz\ *n pl* ♦ **:** things that make one rich **:** WEALTH

♦ assets, capital, fortune, means, opulence, substance, wealth, wherewithal

rich•ly \ˈrich-lē\ *adv* ♦ **:** in a rich manner

♦ expensively, extravagantly, grandly, high, lavishly, luxuriously, opulently

Rich•ter scale \ˈrik-tər-\ *n* **:** a scale for expressing the magnitude of a seismic disturbance (as an earthquake) in terms of the energy dissipated in it

rick \ˈrik\ *n* ♦ **:** a large stack (as of hay) in the open air

♦ cock, heap, hill, mound, mountain, pile, stack

rick•ets \ˈri-kəts\ *n* **:** a childhood deficiency disease marked especially by soft deformed bones and caused by lack of vitamin D

rick•ett•sia \ri-ˈket-sē-ə\ *n, pl* **-si•as** *or* **-si•ae** \-sē-ˌē\ **:** any of a group of usually rod-shaped bacteria that cause various diseases (as typhus)

rick•ety \ˈri-kə-tē\ *adj* **1 :** affected with rickets **2 :** SHAKY; *also* **:** in unsound physical condition

rick•shaw *also* **rick•sha** \ˈrik-ˌshȯ\ *n* **:** a small covered 2-wheeled carriage pulled by one person and used orig. in Japan

¹ric•o•chet \ˈri-kə-ˌshā, *Brit also* -ˌshet\ *n* **:** a bouncing off at an angle (as of a bullet off a wall); *also* **:** an object that ricochets

²ricochet *vb* **-cheted** \-ˌshād\ *also* **-chet•ted** \-ˌshe-təd\; **-chet•ing** \-ˌshā-iŋ\ *also* **-chet•ting** \-ˌshe-tiŋ\ ♦ **:** to skip with or as if with glancing rebounds

♦ bounce, carom, glance, rebound, skim, skip

ri•cot•ta \ri-ˈkä-tə, -ˈkȯ-\ *n* **:** a white unripened whey cheese of Italy that resembles cottage cheese

rid \ˈrid\ *vb* **rid** *also* **rid•ded; rid•ding** ♦ **:** to make free of something burdensome **:** CLEAR

♦ clear, disburden, disencumber, free, relieve, unburden *Ant* burden, encumber, saddle

rid•dance \ˈrid-ᵊns\ *n* ♦ **:** an act of ridding

♦ disposal, disposition, dumping, jettison, removal

rid•den \ˈrid-ᵊn\ *adj* **1 :** harassed, oppressed, or obsessed by ⟨debt-*ridden*⟩ **2 :** excessively full of or supplied with ⟨slum-*ridden*⟩

¹rid•dle \ˈrid-ᵊl\ *n* **1 :** a puzzling question to be solved or answered by guessing **2** ♦ **:** something or someone difficult to understand

♦ conundrum, enigma, mystery, mystification, puzzle, puzzlement, secret

²riddle *vb* **rid•dled; rid•dling 1** ♦ **:** to find the solution of **:** SOLVE **2 :** to speak in riddles

♦ answer, break, crack, dope, figure out, puzzle, resolve, solve, unravel, work, work out

³riddle *n* **:** a coarse sieve

⁴riddle *vb* **rid•dled; rid•dling 1 :** to sift with a riddle **2 :** to pierce with many holes **3 :** PERMEATE

¹ride \ˈrīd\ *vb* **rode** \ˈrōd\; **rid•den** \ˈrid-ᵊn\; **rid•ing 1 :** to go on an animal's back or in a conveyance (as a boat, car, or airplane); *also* **:** to sit on and control so as to be carried along ⟨~ a bicycle⟩ **2** ♦ **:** to float or move on water ⟨~ at anchor⟩; *also* **:** to move like a floating object **3 :** to bear along **:** CARRY ⟨*rode* her on their shoulders⟩ **4 :** to travel over a surface ⟨the car ~*s* well⟩ **5 :** to proceed over on horseback **6** ♦ **:** to torment by nagging or teasing; *also* **:** to poke fun at **7 :** to last longer than — usually used with *out*

♦ [2] drift, float, glide, hang, hover, poise, sail, waft ♦ [6] bait, bug, hassle, heckle, needle, taunt, tease ♦ [6] chaff, jive, josh, kid, rally, razz, rib, roast, tease

²ride *n* **1 :** an act of riding; *esp* **:** a trip on horseback or by vehicle **2 :** a way (as a road or path) suitable for riding **3 :** a mechanical device (as a merry-go-round) for riding on **4 :** a means of transportation

rid•er \ˈrī-dər\ *n* **1 :** one that rides **2 :** an addition to a document often attached on a separate piece of paper **3 :** a clause dealing with an unrelated matter attached to a legislative bill during passage — **rid•er•less** *adj*

¹ridge \ˈrij\ *n* **1 :** a range of hills **2 :** a raised line or strip **3 :** the line made where two sloping surfaces (as of a roof) meet — **ridgy** *adj*

²ridge *vb* **ridged; ridg•ing 1 :** to form into a ridge **2 :** to extend in ridges

¹rid•i•cule \ˈri-də-ˌkyül\ *n* **:** the act of ridiculing **:** DERISION, MOCKERY

²ridicule *vb* **-culed; -cul•ing** ♦ **:** to laugh at or make fun of mockingly or contemptuously

♦ deride, gibe, jeer, laugh, mock, scout

ri•dic•u•lous \rə-ˈdi-kyə-ləs\ *adj* ♦ **:** arousing or deserving ridicule **:** ABSURD; *also* **:** provoking laughter — **ri•dic•u•lous•ly** *adv* — **ri•dic•u•lous•ness** *n*

♦ absurd, comical, derisive, farcical, laughable, ludicrous, preposterous, risible, silly ♦ antic, comic, comical, droll, farcical, funny, hilarious, humorous, hysterical, laughable, ludicrous, riotous, risible, screaming, uproarious

rid•ley \ˈrid-lē\ *n* **:** either of two relatively small sea turtles

Ries•ling \ˈrēz-liŋ, ˈrēs-\ *n* **:** a sweet to very dry white wine made from a single variety of grape orig. grown in Germany

RIF *abbr* reduction in force

rife \ˈrīf\ *adj* ♦ **:** occurring in abundance — **rife** *adv* — **rife•ly** *adv*

♦ flush, fraught, replete, thick

riff \ˈrif\ *n* **:** a repeated phrase in jazz typically supporting a solo improvisation; *also* **:** a piece based on such a phrase — **riff** *vb*

riff•raff \rif-ˌraf\ *n* **1** ♦ **:** disreputable persons **:** RABBLE **2 :** something worth little or nothing **:** REFUSE

♦ rabble, scum, trash

¹ri•fle \ˈrī-fəl\ *vb* **ri•fled; ri•fling** ♦ **:** to ransack especially with the intent to steal — **ri•fler** *n*

♦ dig, dredge, hunt, rake, ransack, rummage, scour, search

²rifle *vb* **ri•fled; ri•fling :** to cut spiral grooves into the bore of ⟨*rifled* pipe⟩ — **rifling** *n*

³rifle *n* **1 :** a shoulder weapon with a rifled bore **2** *pl* **:** soldiers armed with rifles — **ri•fle•man** \-fəl-mən\ *n*

rift \ˈrift\ *n* **1** ♦ **:** a narrow opening or crack of considerable length and depth usually from some breaking or parting **2 :** FAULT 6 **3 :** ESTRANGEMENT, SEPARATION **4** ♦ **:** a clear space or interval — **rift** *vb*

♦ [1] chink, cleft, crack, cranny, crevice, fissure, split ♦ [4] breach, break, discontinuity, gap, gulf, hole, interval, opening, rent, separation

¹rig \ˈrig\ *vb* **rigged; rig•ging 1 :** to fit out (as a ship) with rigging **2** ♦ **:** to provide with clothes **:** CLOTHE, DRESS — usually used with *out* **3** ♦ **:** to furnish with special gear **:** EQUIP **4 :** to set up especially as a makeshift ⟨~ up a shelter⟩

♦ *usu* **rig out** [2] apparel, array, attire, caparison, clothe, deck, dress, garb, invest, suit ♦ [3] accoutre, equip, fit, furnish, outfit, supply

²rig *n* **1 :** the distinctive shape, number, and arrangement of sails and masts of a ship **2 :** a carriage with its horse **3 :** CLOTHING, DRESS **4 :** EQUIPMENT

³rig *vb* **rigged; rig•ging 1 :** to manipulate or control especially by deceptive or dishonest means **2 :** to fix in advance for a desired result — **rig•ger** *n*

rig•ging \ˈri-giŋ, -gən\ *n* **1 :** the ropes and chains that hold and move masts, sails, and spars of a ship **2 :** a network (as in theater scenery) used for support and manipulation

¹right \ˈrīt\ *adj* **1** ♦ **:** morally right or justifiable **:** RIGHTEOUS **2** ♦ **:** being in accordance with what is just, good, or proper **:** JUST **3** ♦ **:** conforming to truth or fact **:** CORRECT **4** ♦ **:** adapted to a use or purpose **:** APPROPRIATE **5 :** free from curves, bends, angles, or irregularities **:** STRAIGHT ⟨a ~ line⟩ **6 :** not artificial, fraudulent, or illusory **:** GENUINE **7 :** of, relating to, or being the side of the body which is away from the side on which the heart is mostly located **8 :** located nearer to the right hand; *esp* **:** being on the right when facing in the same direction as the observer **9 :** made to be placed or worn outward ⟨~ side of a rug⟩ **10** ♦ **:** being in good physical or mental health or order **:** NORMAL ⟨not in her ~ mind⟩

♦ [1] decent, ethical, good, honest, honorable (*or* honourable), just, moral, right, straight, upright, virtuous ♦ [2] due, just ♦ [3] accurate, correct, exact, precise, proper, so, true

♦ [4] applicable, appropriate, apt, felicitous, fit, fitting, good, happy, meet, proper, suitable ♦ [10] balanced, clearheaded, lucid, normal, sane, stable

²right *n* **1 :** qualities that constitute what is correct, just, proper, or honorable **2** ♦ **:** something (as a power or privilege) to which one has a just or lawful claim **3 :** just action or decision **:** the cause of justice **4 :** the side or part that is on or toward the right side **5** *cap* **:** political conservatives **6** *often cap* **:** a conservative position — **right•ward** \-wərd\ *adj or adv*

♦ birthright, due, perquisite, prerogative, privilege

³right *adv* **1 :** according to what is right ⟨live ~⟩ **2** ♦ **:** in an exact manner **:** EXACTLY, PRECISELY ⟨~ here and now⟩ **3** ♦ **:** in a direct line, course, or manner **:** DIRECTLY ⟨went ~ home⟩ **4 :** according to fact or truth ⟨guess ~⟩ **5 :** all the way **:** COMPLETELY ⟨~ to the end⟩ **6 :** IMMEDIATELY ⟨~ after lunch⟩ **7 :** to a great degree **:** VERY ⟨~ nice weather⟩ **8 :** on or to the right ⟨looked ~ and left⟩

♦ [2] accurately, exactly, just, precisely, sharp, squarely ♦ [3] dead, direct, directly, due, plump, straight

⁴right *vb* **1 :** to relieve from wrong **2 :** to adjust or restore to a proper state or position **3 :** to bring or restore to an upright position **4 :** to become upright — **right•er** *n*

right angle *n* **:** an angle whose measure is 90° **:** an angle whose sides are perpendicular to each other — **right–an•gled** \ˈrīt-ˈaŋ-gəld\ *or* **right–an•gle** \-gəl\ *adj*

right away *adv* ♦ **:** without delay or hesitation

♦ directly, forthwith, immediately, instantly, now, promptly, pronto, right now

right circular cone *n* **:** CONE 2

righ•teous \ˈrī-chəs\ *adj* ♦ **:** acting or being in accordance with what is just, honorable, and free from guilt or wrong **:** UPRIGHT

♦ decent, ethical, good, honest, honorable (*or* honourable), just, moral, right, straight, upright, virtuous

righ•teous•ly *adv* ♦ **:** in a righteous manner

♦ chastely, modestly, purely, virtuously

righ•teous•ness *n* ♦ **:** the quality or state of being righteous

♦ character, decency, goodness, honesty, integrity, morality, probity, rectitude, uprightness, virtue

right•ful \ˈrīt-fəl\ *adj* **1 a :** acting or being in conformity with what is morally upright or good **:** JUST **b :** FITTING **2 :** having or held by a legally just claim — **right•ful•ly** *adv* — **right•ful•ness** *n*

right–hand \ˈrīt-ˌhand\ *adj* **1 :** situated on the right **2 :** RIGHT-HANDED **3 :** chiefly relied on ⟨his ~ man⟩

right–hand•ed \-ˈhan-dəd\ *adj* **1 :** using the right hand habitually or better than the left **2 :** designed for or done with the right hand **3 :** CLOCKWISE ⟨a ~ twist⟩ — **right–handed** *adv* — **right–hand•ed•ly** *adv* — **right–hand•ed•ness** *n*

right•ist \ˈrī-tist\ *n, often cap* ♦ **:** an advocate of or adherent of the doctrines of the Right

♦ conservative, reactionary, Tory

right•ly \ˈrīt-lē\ *adv* **1 :** FAIRLY, JUSTLY **2** ♦ **:** in the right or proper manner **:** PROPERLY **3 :** CORRECTLY, EXACTLY

♦ appropriately, correctly, fittingly, happily, properly, suitably

right•ness *n* ♦ **:** the quality or state of being right

♦ appropriateness, aptness, fitness, suitability

right now *adv* **1** ♦ **:** without delay or hesitation **2** ♦ **:** at present

♦ [1] directly, forthwith, immediately, instantly, now, promptly, pronto, right away ♦ [2] anymore, now, nowadays, presently, today

right–of–way *n, pl* **rights–of–way** **1 :** a legal right of passage over another person's ground **2 :** the area over which a right-of-way exists **3 :** the land on which a public road is built **4 :** the land occupied by a railroad **5 :** the land used by a public utility **6 :** the right of traffic to take precedence over other traffic

right on *interj* — used to express agreement or give encouragement

right–to–life *adj* **:** ANTIABORTION — **right–to–lifer** *n*

right triangle *n* **:** a triangle having one right angle

right whale *n* **:** any of a family of large baleen whales having a very large head on a stocky body

rig•id \ˈri-jəd\ *adj* **1 a** ♦ **:** lacking flexibility **b** ♦ **:** inflexibly exact with respect to opinions or observances **2** ♦ **:** strictly observed

♦ [1a] inflexible, stiff, unyielding ♦ [1b] adamant, hard, immovable, implacable, pat, unbending, uncompromising, unrelenting, unyielding ♦ [2] exacting, inflexible, rigorous, strict, stringent, uncompromising ***Ant*** flexible, lax, loose, relaxed

ri•gid•i•ty \rə-ˈji-də-tē\ *n* ♦ **:** the quality or state of being rigid

♦ hardness, harshness, inflexibility, severity, sternness, strictness

rig•id•ly *adv* ♦ **:** in a rigid manner

♦ exactly, precisely, rigorously, strictly

rig•ma•role \ˈri-gə-mə-ˌrōl\ *n* **1 :** confused or senseless talk **2 :** a complex and ritualistic procedure

rig•or *or Can and Brit* **rig•our** \ˈri-gər\ *n* **1 :** the quality of being inflexible or unyielding especially in opinion or behavior **2** ♦ **:** a condition that makes life difficult, challenging, or uncomfortable **3** *Can usu* **rigor :** a tremor caused by a chill **4 :** strict precision **:** EXACTNESS **5** *Can usu* **rigor :** unnatural rigidity of a body part

♦ adversity, asperity, difficulty, hardness, hardship

rig•or mor•tis \ˌri-gər-ˈmȯr-təs\ *n* **:** temporary rigidity of muscles occurring after death

rig•or•ous *adj* ♦ **:** manifesting, exercising, or favoring rigor

♦ accurate, close, delicate, exact, fine, mathematical, pinpoint, precise ♦ exacting, inflexible, rigid, strict, stringent, uncompromising

rig•or•ous•ly *adv* ♦ **:** in a rigorous manner

♦ exactly, precisely, rigidly, strictly

rig•our *Can and Brit var of* RIGOR

rile \ˈrī(-ə)l\ *vb* **riled; ril•ing** **1** ♦ **:** to make angry **2 :** to stir or move from a state of calm or order

♦ aggravate, anger, annoy, bother, bug, chafe, exasperate, gall, get, grate, irk, irritate, nettle, peeve, persecute, pique, put out, rasp, vex

rill \ˈril\ *n* ♦ **:** a very small brook

♦ brook, creek, rivulet, streamlet

¹rim \ˈrim\ *n* **1 :** the outer part of a wheel **2** ♦ **:** an outer edge especially of something curved **:** MARGIN

♦ border, bound, boundary, circumference, compass, confines, edge, end, fringe, margin, perimeter, periphery, skirt, verge

²rim *vb* **rimmed; rim•ming** **1 :** to serve as a rim for **:** BORDER **2 :** to run around the rim of

¹rime \ˈrīm\ *n* **:** FROST 2 — **rimy** \ˈrī-mē\ *adj*

²rime *var of* RHYME

rind \ˈrīnd\ *n* **:** a usually hard or tough outer layer ⟨lemon ~⟩

¹ring \ˈriŋ\ *n* **1 :** a circular band worn as an ornament or token or used for holding or fastening ⟨wedding ~⟩ ⟨key ~⟩ **2** ♦ **:** something circular in shape ⟨smoke ~⟩ **3 :** a place for contest or display ⟨boxing ~⟩; *also* **:** PRIZEFIGHTING **4 :** ANNUAL RING **5** ♦ **:** a group of people who work together for selfish or dishonest purposes **6** ♦ **:** a temporary group of persons working cooperatively — **ringed** *adj* — **ring•like** \ˈriŋ-ˌlīk\ *adj*

♦ [2] band, circle, eye, hoop, loop, round ♦ [5] cabal, conspiracy, gang, mob, syndicate ♦ [6] body, bunch, circle, clan, clique, community, coterie, crowd, fold, gang, lot, set

²ring *vb* **ringed; ring•ing** \ˈriŋ-iŋ\ **1** ♦ **:** to place or form a ring around **:** ENCIRCLE **2 :** to throw a ring over (a mark) in a game (as quoits) **3 :** to move in a ring or spirally

♦ circle, encircle, enclose, encompass, surround

³ring *vb* **rang** \ˈraŋ\; **rung** \ˈrəŋ\; **ring•ing** \ˈriŋ-iŋ\ **1 :** to sound resonantly when struck; *also* **:** to feel as if filled with such sound **2** ♦ **:** to cause to make a clear metallic sound by striking **3 :** to announce or call by or as if by striking a bell ⟨~ an alarm⟩ **4 :** to repeat loudly and persistently **5 :** to summon especially by a bell ⟨~ for the butler⟩

♦ chime, knell, peal, toll

⁴ring *n* **1 :** a set of bells **2 :** the clear resonant sound of vibrating metal **3 :** resonant tone **:** SONORITY **4 :** a sound or character expressive of a particular quality **5 :** an act or instance of ringing; *esp* **:** a telephone call

¹ring•er \ˈriŋ-ər\ *n* **1 :** one that sounds by ringing **2 :** one that enters a competition under false representations **3** ♦ **:** one that closely resembles another

♦ carbon copy, counterpart, double, duplicate, duplication, facsimile, image, likeness, match, picture, replica, spit

[2]**ringer** *n* **:** one that encircles or puts a ring around

ring finger *n* **:** the third finger of the hand counting the index finger as the first

ring•ing *adj* ♦ **:** clear and full in tone

♦ golden, resonant, resounding, round, sonorous, vibrant

ring•lead•er \ˈriŋ-ˌlē-dər\ *n* **:** a leader especially of a group of troublemakers

ring•let \-lət\ *n* **:** a long curl

ring•mas•ter \-ˌmas-tər\ *n* **:** one in charge of performances in a circus ring

ring up *vb* **1 :** to total and record especially by means of a cash register **2 :** ACHIEVE ⟨*rang up* many triumphs⟩

ring•worm \ˈriŋ-ˌwərm\ *n* **:** any of several contagious skin diseases caused by fungi and marked by ring-shaped discolored patches

rink \ˈriŋk\ *n* **:** a level extent of ice marked off for skating or various games; *also* **:** a similar surface (as of wood) marked off or enclosed for a sport or game ⟨roller-skating ~⟩

[1]**rinse** \ˈrins\ *vb* **rinsed; rins•ing 1 :** to wash lightly or in water only **2** ♦ **:** to cleanse (as of soap) with clear water **3 :** to treat (hair) with a rinse — **rins•er** *n*

♦ flush, irrigate, sluice, wash

[2]**rinse** *n* **1 :** an act of rinsing **2 :** a liquid used for rinsing **3 :** a solution that temporarily tints hair

ri•ot \ˈrī-ət\ *n* **1** *archaic* **:** disorderly behavior **2 :** disturbance of the public peace; *esp* **:** a violent public disorder **3 :** random or disorderly profusion ⟨a ~ of color⟩ **4 :** one that is wildly amusing ⟨the comedy is a ~⟩ — **riot** *vb* — **ri•ot•er** *n*

ri•ot•ous *adj* ♦ **:** practicing or marked by license or excess; *also* **:** existing in abundance

♦ copious, lavish, profuse

[1]**rip** \ˈrip\ *vb* **ripped; rip•ping 1** ♦ **:** to cut or tear open **2 :** to saw or split (wood) with the grain **3** ♦ **:** to slash or slit with or as if with a sharp blade **4** ♦ **:** to rush headlong — **rip•per** *n*

♦ [1] rend, rive, shred, tatter, tear ♦ [3] cut, gash, slash, slice, slit ♦ [4] barrel, dash, fly, hurry, hurtle, hustle, pelt, race, rocket, run, shoot, speed, tear, zip, zoom

[2]**rip** *n* ♦ **:** an opening made by ripping

♦ gash, laceration, rent, slash, slit, tear

RIP *abbr* may he rest in peace, may she rest in peace may they rest in peace

ri•par•i•an \rə-ˈper-ē-ən\ *adj* **:** of or relating to the bank of a stream, river, or lake

rip cord *n* **:** a cord that is pulled to release a parachute out of its container

ripe \ˈrīp\ *adj* **rip•er; rip•est 1** ♦ **:** fully grown and developed **:** MATURE ⟨~ fruit⟩ **2 :** fully prepared **:** READY — **ripe•ly** *adv* — **ripe•ness** *n*

♦ adult, full-blown, full-fledged, mature

rip•en \ˈrī-pən\ *vb* **rip•ened; rip•en•ing 1** ♦ **:** to make ripe **:** become ripe **2 :** to bring to completeness or perfection; *also* **:** to age or cure (cheese) to develop characteristic flavor, odor, body, texture, and color

♦ age, develop, grow, grow up, mature, progress

rip–off \ˈrip-ˌȯf\ *n* **1** ♦ **:** an act of stealing **:** THEFT **2 :** a cheap imitation

♦ grab, theft

rip off *vb* ♦ **:** to take something away from by force **:** steal from

♦ burglarize, rob, steal

ri•poste \ri-ˈpōst\ *n* **1 :** a fencer's return thrust after a parry **2** ♦ **:** a retaliatory maneuver or response; *esp* **:** a quick retort — **riposte** *vb*

♦ comeback, repartee, retort

ripped \ˈript\ *adj* **:** having high muscle definition

rip•ple \ˈri-pəl\ *vb* **rip•pled; rip•pling 1 :** to become lightly ruffled on the surface **2 :** to make a sound like that of rippling water **3** ♦ **:** to flow in small waves — **ripple** *n*

♦ dribble, gurgle, lap, plash, slosh, splash, trickle, wash

rip•saw \ˈrip-ˌsȯ\ *n* **:** a coarse-toothed saw used to cut wood in the direction of the grain

rip•stop \-ˌstäp\ *adj* **:** being a fabric woven in such a way that small tears do not spread ⟨~ nylon⟩ — **ripstop** *n*

[1]**rise** \ˈrīz\ *vb* **rose** \ˈrōz\; **ris•en** \ˈriz-ᵊn\; **ris•ing 1 :** to get up from sitting, kneeling, or lying **2 :** to get up from sleep or from one's bed **3 :** to return from death **4 :** to take up arms **5 :** to end a session **:** ADJOURN **6 :** to appear above the horizon **7** ♦ **:** to move upward **:** ASCEND **8 :** to extend above other objects **9 :** to attain a higher level or rank **10** ♦ **:** to increase in quantity, intensity, or pitch **11 :** to come into being **:** HAPPEN, BEGIN, ORIGINATE

♦ [7] arise, ascend, climb, lift, mount, soar, up ♦ [10] accumulate, appreciate, balloon, build, burgeon, enlarge, escalate, expand, increase, mount, multiply, mushroom, proliferate, snowball, swell, wax

[2]**rise** *n* **1** ♦ **:** a spot higher than surrounding ground **2 :** an upward slope **3** ♦ **:** an act of rising **:** a state of being risen **4 :** BEGINNING, ORIGIN **5 :** the elevation of one point above another **6** ♦ **:** an increase in amount, number, or volume **7 :** an angry reaction

♦ [1] elevation, eminence, height, highland, hill, mound, prominence ♦ [3] advancement, ascent, elevation, promotion, upgrade ♦ [6] accretion, addition, augmentation, boost, expansion, gain, increase, increment, plus, proliferation, raise, supplement

ris•er \ˈrī-zər\ *n* **1 :** one that rises **2 :** the upright part between stair treads

ris•i•bil•i•ty \ˌri-zə-ˈbi-lə-tē\ *n, pl* **-ties :** the ability or inclination to laugh — often used in plural

ris•i•ble \ˈri-zə-bəl\ *adj* **1 :** able or inclined to laugh **2** ♦ **:** arousing laughter; *esp* **:** amusingly ridiculous

♦ antic, comic, comical, droll, farcical, funny, hilarious, humorous, hysterical, laughable, ludicrous, ridiculous, riotous, screaming, uproarious

[1]**risk** \ˈrisk\ *n* **1** ♦ **:** exposure to possible loss or injury **:** DANGER **2** ♦ **:** someone or something that creates or suggests a hazard — **risk•i•ness** \ˈris-kē-nəs\ *n*

♦ [1, 2] danger, hazard, menace, peril, pitfall, threat, trouble

[2]**risk** *vb* **1** ♦ **:** to expose to danger ⟨~*ed* his life⟩ **2** ♦ **:** to incur the danger of

♦ [1] adventure, compromise, gamble with, hazard, imperil, jeopardize, menace, venture ♦ [2] chance, gamble, hazard, venture

risky *adj* ♦ **:** attended with risk or danger

♦ dangerous, grave, grievous, hazardous, menacing, parlous, perilous, serious, unhealthy, unsafe, venturesome

ri•sot•to \ri-ˈsȯ-tō, -ˈzȯ-\ *n, pl* **-tos :** rice cooked usually in meat or seafood stock and seasoned

ris•qué \ris-ˈkā\ *adj* **:** verging on impropriety or indecency

♦ bawdy, lewd, ribald, spicy, suggestive

ri•tard \ri-ˈtärd\ *adv or adj* **:** with a gradual slackening in tempo — used as a direction in music

rite \ˈrīt\ *n* **1 :** a set form for conducting a ceremony **2 :** the liturgy of a church **3** ♦ **:** a ceremonial act or action

♦ ceremonial, ceremony, form, formality, observance, ritual, solemnity

[1]**rit•u•al** \ˈri-chə-wəl\ *n* **1 :** the established form especially for a religious ceremony **2 :** a system of rites **3 :** a ceremonial act or action **4 :** an act or series of acts regularly repeated in a precise manner — **rit•u•al•ism** \-wə-ˌli-zəm\ *n* — **rit•u•al•is•tic** \ˌri-chə-wə-ˈlis-tik\ *adj* — **rit•u•al•is•ti•cal•ly** \-ti-k(ə-)lē\ *adv* — **rit•u•al•ly** *adv*

[2]**ritual** *adj* ♦ **:** of, relating to, or employed in rites or a ritual

♦ ceremonial, ceremonious, formal

ritzy \ˈrit-sē\ *adj* **ritz•i•er; -est :** showily elegant **:** POSH

riv *abbr* river

[1]**ri•val** \ˈrī-vəl\ *n* **1** ♦ **:** one of two or more trying to get what only one can have **2** ♦ **:** one striving for competitive advantage **3** ♦ **:** one that equals another especially in desired qualities **:** MATCH, PEER

♦ [1] challenger, competition, competitor, contender, contestant ♦ [2] adversary, antagonist, opponent ♦ [3] coordinate, counterpart, equal, equivalent, fellow, like, match, parallel, peer

[2]**rival** *adj* **:** COMPETING

[3]**rival** *vb* **-valed** *or* **-valled; -val•ing** *or* **-val•ling 1 :** to be in competition with **2 :** to try to equal or excel **3 :** to have qualities that approach or equal another's

ri•val•ry \ˈrī-vəl-rē\ *n, pl* **-ries** ♦ **:** the act of competing **:** the state of being a rival

♦ battle, combat, conflict, confrontation, contest, duel, face-off, struggle, tug-of-war, warfare

rive \ˈrīv\ *vb* **rived** \ˈrīvd\; **riv•en** \ˈri-vən\ *also* **rived; riv•ing** **1** ♦ **:** to wrench open or tear apart or to pieces **:** REND **2 :** SHATTER

♦ rend, rip, shred, tatter, tear

riv•er \ˈri-vər\ *n* **1 :** a natural stream larger than a brook **2 :** a large stream or flow
riv•er•bank \-ˌbaŋk\ *n* **:** the bank of a river
riv•er•bed \-ˌbed\ *n* **:** the channel occupied by a river
riv•er•boat \-ˌbōt\ *n* **:** a boat for use on a river
riv•er•front \-ˌfrənt\ *n* **:** the land or area along a river
riv•er•side \-ˌsīd\ *n* **:** the side or bank of a river
[1]**riv•et** \ˈri-vət\ *n* **:** a metal bolt with a head at one end used to join parts by being put through holes in them and then being flattened on the plain end to make another head
[2]**rivet** *vb* **1 :** to fasten with or as if with a rivet **2** ♦ **:** to fix and hold (as the attention) — **riv•et•er** *n*

♦ concentrate, fasten, focus, train

riv•u•let \ˈri-vyə-lət, -və-\ *n* ♦ **:** a small stream

♦ brook, creek, rill, streamlet

rm *abbr* room
Rn *symbol* radon
[1]**RN** \ˌär-ˈen\ *n* **:** REGISTERED NURSE
[2]**RN** *abbr* Royal Navy
RNA \ˌär-(ˌ)en-ˈā\ *n* **:** any of various nucleic acids (as messenger RNA) that are found especially in the cytoplasm of cells, have ribose as the 5-carbon sugar, and are associated with the control of cellular chemical activities
rnd *abbr* round
[1]**roach** \ˈrōch\ *n, pl* **roach** *also* **roach•es :** any of various bony fishes related to the carp; *also* **:** any of several sunfishes
[2]**roach** *n* **1 :** COCKROACH **2 :** the butt of a marijuana cigarette
road \ˈrōd\ *n* **1 :** ROADSTEAD — often used in plural **2** ♦ **:** an open way for vehicles, persons, and animals **:** HIGHWAY **3 :** a way to a conclusion or end ⟨the ~ to success⟩ **4 :** a series of scheduled visits (as games or performances) in several locations or the travel necessary to make these visits ⟨the team is on the ~⟩ **5 :** RAILROAD

♦ artery, highway, pike, route, thoroughfare, trace, turnpike, way

road•bed \ˈrōd-ˌbed\ *n* **1 :** the foundation of a road or railroad **2 :** the part of the surface of a road on which vehicles travel
road•block \-ˌbläk\ *n* **1 :** a barricade on the road ⟨a police ~⟩ **2 :** an obstruction to progress
road•ie \ˈrō-dē\ *n* **:** a person who works for traveling entertainers
road•kill \ˈrōd-ˌkil\ *n* **:** the remains of an animal that has been killed on a road by a motor vehicle
road•run•ner \-ˌrə-nər\ *n* **:** a largely terrestrial bird of the southwestern U.S. and Mexico that is a speedy runner
road•side \ˈrōd-ˌsīd\ *n* **:** the strip of land along a road — **roadside** *adj*
road•stead \-ˌsted\ *n* **:** an anchorage for ships usually less sheltered than a harbor
road•ster \ˈrōd-stər\ *n* **1 :** a driving horse **2 :** an open automobile that seats two
road•way \-ˌwā\ *n* **1 :** an open way for vehicles, persons, and animals **:** ROAD **2 :** ROADBED
road•work \-ˌwərk\ *n* **1 :** work done in constructing or repairing roads **2 :** conditioning for an athletic contest (as a boxing match) consisting mainly of long runs
roam \ˈrōm\ *vb* **1** ♦ **:** to go from place to place without purpose or direction **:** WANDER **2 :** to range or wander over or about **3 :** to use a cell phone outside one's local calling area

♦ gad, gallivant, knock, maunder, meander, mope, ramble, range, rove, traipse, wander

roaming *adj* ♦ **:** being one that roams; *also* **:** involving cell phone use beyond one's local calling area

♦ errant, itinerant, nomad, peripatetic, vagabond, vagrant

[1]**roan** \ˈrōn\ *adj* **:** of dark color (as black, red, or brown) sprinkled with white ⟨a ~ horse⟩
[2]**roan** *n* **:** an animal (as a horse) with a roan coat; *also* **:** its color
[1]**roar** \ˈrōr\ *vb* **1** ♦ **:** to utter a full loud prolonged sound **2 :** to make a loud confused sound (as of wind or waves) — **roar•er** *n*

♦ bellow, boom, growl, thunder

[2]**roar** *n* ♦ **:** a sound of roaring

♦ clamor (*or* clamour), howl, hubbub, hue and cry, hullabaloo, noise, outcry, tumult, uproar ♦ bluster, cacophony, clamor, din, noise, racket

roar•ing \ˈrȯ-riŋ\ *adj* **1** ♦ **:** making or characterized by a noise like a roar **2** ♦ **:** marked by prosperity or bustle especially of a temporary nature

♦ [1] booming, clamorous (*or* clamourous), deafening, earsplitting, loud, piercing, resounding, ringing, sonorous, stentorian, thunderous ♦ [2] booming, golden, palmy, prosperous, successful

[1]**roast** \ˈrōst\ *vb* **1 :** to cook by exposure to dry heat or an open flame **2** ♦ **:** to criticize severely or kiddingly

♦ chaff, jive, josh, kid, rally, razz, rib, ride, tease

[2]**roast** *n* **1 :** a piece of meat suitable for roasting **2 :** an outing at which food is roasted ⟨corn ~⟩ **3 :** severe criticism or kidding
[3]**roast** *adj* **:** ROASTED
roast•er \ˈrō-stər\ *n* **1 :** one that roasts **2 :** a device for roasting **3 :** something suitable for roasting
rob \ˈräb\ *vb* **robbed; rob•bing 1** ♦ **:** to steal from **2 :** to deprive of something due or expected **3 :** to commit robbery — **rob•ber** *n*

♦ burglarize, rip off, steal

robber fly *n* **:** any of a family of predaceous flies resembling bumblebees
rob•bery \ˈrä-bə-rē\ *n, pl* **-ber•ies** ♦ **:** the act or practice of robbing; *esp* **:** theft of something from a person by use of violence or threat

♦ larceny, theft, thievery

[1]**robe** \ˈrōb\ *n* **1 :** a long flowing outer garment; *esp* **:** one used for ceremonial occasions **2 :** a wrap or covering for the lower body (as for sitting outdoors)
[2]**robe** *vb* **robed; rob•ing 1 :** to clothe with or as if with a robe **2 :** to dress or cover with clothing **:** DRESS
rob•in \ˈrä-bən\ *n* **1 :** a small chiefly European thrush with a somewhat orange face and breast **2 :** a large No. American thrush with a grayish back, a streaked throat, and a chiefly dull reddish breast
ro•bot \ˈrō-ˌbät, -bət\ *n* **1 :** a machine that looks and acts like a human being **2 :** an efficient but insensitive person **3 :** a device that automatically performs especially repetitive tasks **4 :** something guided by automatic controls
ro•bot•ic \rō-ˈbä-tik\ *adj* ♦ **:** of or relating to mechanical robots

♦ automatic, laborsaving (*or* laboursaving), self-acting

ro•bot•ics \rō-ˈbä-tiks\ *n* **:** technology dealing with the design, construction, and operation of robots
ro•bust \rō-ˈbəst, ˈrō-(ˌ)bəst\ *adj* **1** ♦ **:** strong and vigorously healthy; *also* **:** having or showing vigor, strength, or firmness **2 :** capable of performing without failure under a wide range of conditions **3** ♦ **:** imparting to the palate the general impression of substantial weight and rich texture — **ro•bust•ly** *adv*

♦ [1] able-bodied, chipper, fit, hale, healthy, hearty, sound, well, whole, wholesome ♦ [1] firm, forceful, hearty, lusty, solid, stout, strong, sturdy, vigorous ♦ [3] concentrated, full, full-bodied, potent, rich, strong

ro•bust•ness *n* ♦ **:** the quality or state of being robust

♦ fitness, health, heartiness, soundness, wellness, wholeness, wholesomeness

ROC *abbr* Republic of China (Taiwan)
[1]**rock** \ˈräk\ *vb* **1** ♦ **:** to move back and forth in or as if in a cradle **2** ♦ **:** to sway or cause to sway back and forth **3 :** to arouse to excitement (as with rock music) ⟨~*ed* the crowd⟩ **4** *slang* **:** to be extremely enjoyable or effective ⟨this car ~*s*⟩

♦ [1, 2] careen, lurch, pitch, roll, seesaw, sway, toss, wobble

[2]**rock** *n* **1 :** a rocking movement **2 :** popular music usually played on electric instruments and characterized by a strong beat and much repetition
[3]**rock** *n* **1 :** a mass of stony material; *also* **:** broken pieces of stone **2 :** solid mineral deposits **3 :** something like a rock in firmness **4 :** GEM; *esp* **:** DIAMOND — **rock** *adj* — **rock•like** *adj* — **rocky** *adj*
rock and roll *n* **:** [2]ROCK 2
rock•bound \ˈräk-ˌbau̇nd\ *adj* **:** fringed or covered with rocks
rock•er \ˈrä-kər\ *n* **1 :** one of the curved pieces on which something (as a chair or cradle) rocks **2 :** a chair that rocks on rockers **3 :** a device that works with a rocking motion **4 :** a rock performer, song, or enthusiast
[1]**rock•et** \ˈrä-kət\ *n* **1 :** a firework that is propelled through the air by the discharge of gases produced by a burning substance **2 :** a jet engine that operates on the same principle as a firework rocket

but carries the oxygen needed for burning its fuel **3 :** a rocket-propelled bomb or missile

[2]**rocket** *vb* **1 :** to convey by means of a rocket **2 ♦ :** to rise up swiftly, spectacularly, and with force **3 :** to travel rapidly in or as if in a rocket

♦ shoot, skyrocket, soar, zoom

rock•et•ry \ˈrä-kə-trē\ *n* **:** the study or use of rockets

rocket ship *n* **:** a rocket-propelled spacecraft

rock•fall \ˈräk-ˌfȯl\ *n* **:** a mass of falling or fallen rocks

rock•fish \-ˌfish\ *n* **:** any of various bony fishes that live among rocks or on rocky bottoms

rock salt *n* **:** common salt in rocklike masses or large crystals

Rocky Mountain sheep *n* **:** BIGHORN

ro•co•co \rə-ˈkō-kō\ *adj* **:** of or relating to an artistic style especially of the 18th century marked by fanciful curved forms and elaborate ornamentation — **rococo** *n*

rod \ˈräd\ *n* **1 :** a straight slender stick **2 a :** a stick or bundle of twigs used in punishing a person **b :** PUNISHMENT **3 :** a staff borne to show rank **4 :** a unit of length equal to 5½ yards **5 :** any of the rod-shaped receptor cells of the retina that are sensitive to faint light **6** *slang* **:** HANDGUN

rode *past of* RIDE

ro•dent \ˈrōd-ᵊnt\ *n* **:** any of an order of relatively small mammals (as mice, squirrels, and beavers) with sharp front teeth used for gnawing

ro•deo \ˈrō-dē-ˌō, rə-ˈdā-ō\ *n, pl* **ro•de•os 1 :** ROUNDUP 1 **2 :** a public performance featuring cowboy skills (as riding and roping)

[1]**roe** \ˈrō\ *n, pl* **roe** *or* **roes :** DOE

[2]**roe** *n* **:** the eggs of a fish especially while bound together in a mass

roe•buck \ˈrō-ˌbək\ *n, pl* **roebuck** *or* **roebucks :** a male roe deer

roe deer *n* **:** either of two small nimble European or Asian deers

roent•gen \ˈrent-gən, ˈrənt-, -jən\ *n* **:** the international unit of measurement for X-rays and gamma rays

rog•er \ˈrä-jər\ *interj* — used especially in radio and signaling to indicate that a message has been received and understood

rogue \ˈrōg\ *n* **1 :** a dishonest person **:** SCOUNDREL **2 ♦ :** a mischievous person **:** SCAMP — **rogu•ery** \ˈrō-gə-rē\ *n*

♦ devil, hellion, imp, mischief, monkey, rapscallion, rascal, scamp, urchin

rogu•ish *adj* **♦ :** of, relating to, or having the characteristics of a rogue — **rogu•ish•ly** *adv* — **rogu•ish•ness** *n*

♦ devilish, impish, knavish, mischievous, rascally, sly, waggish, wicked

roil \ˈrȯil, *for 2 also* ˈrīl\ *vb* **1 :** to make cloudy or muddy by stirring up **2 ♦ :** to provoke to anger **3 ♦ :** to move turbulently **:** be in a state of turbulence or agitation — **roily** \ˈrȯi-lē\ *adj*

♦ [2] anger, antagonize, enrage, incense, inflame, infuriate, madden, outrage, rankle, rile ♦ [3] boil, churn, seethe

rois•ter \ˈrȯi-stər\ *vb* **rois•tered; rois•ter•ing :** to engage in noisy revelry **:** CAROUSE — **rois•ter•ous** \-stə-rəs\ *adj*

rois•ter•er *n* **♦ :** one that roisters

♦ celebrant, merrymaker, reveler

ROK *abbr* Republic of Korea (South Korea)

role *also* **rôle** \ˈrōl\ *n* **1 :** an assigned or assumed character; *also* **:** a part played (as by an actor) **2 ♦ :** a function or part performed especially in a particular operation or process **:** FUNCTION

♦ capacity, function, job, part, place, position, purpose, task, work

role model *n* **:** a person whose behavior in a particular role is imitated by others

[1]**roll** \ˈrōl\ *n* **1 :** a document containing an official record **2 ♦ :** an official list of names **3 :** something (as a bun) that is rolled up or rounded as if rolled **4 :** something that rolls **:** ROLLER

♦ catalog, checklist, list, listing, menu, register, registry, roster, schedule, table

[2]**roll** *vb* **1 ♦ :** to move by turning over and over **2 :** to press with a roller **3 :** to move on wheels **4 ♦ :** to sound with a full reverberating tone **5 :** to make a continuous beating sound (as on a drum) **6 :** to utter with a trill **7 :** to move onward as if by completing a revolution ⟨years ~*ed* by⟩ **8 ♦ :** to flow or seem to flow in a continuous stream or with a rising and falling motion ⟨the river ~*ed* on⟩ **9 ♦ :** to swing or sway from side to side **10 ♦ :** to shape or become shaped in rounded form **11 :** to move by or as if by turning a crank ⟨~ down the window⟩

♦ [1] pivot, revolve, rotate, spin, swing, swirl, turn, twirl, twist, wheel, whirl ♦ [4] growl, grumble, lumber, rumble ♦ [8] bowl, breeze, coast, drift, flow, glide, run, sail, skim, slide, slip, stream, sweep, whisk ♦ [9] careen, lurch, pitch, rock, seesaw, sway, toss, wobble ♦ [10] agglomerate, ball, conglomerate, round, wad

[3]**roll** *n* **1 :** a sound produced by rapid strokes on a drum **2 :** a heavy reverberating sound **3 :** a rolling movement or action **4 :** a swaying movement (as of a ship) **5 :** a somersault made in contact with the ground

roll•back \ˈrōl-ˌbak\ *n* **:** the act or an instance of rolling back

roll back *vb* **1 :** to reduce (as a commodity price) on a national scale **2 :** to cause to withdraw **:** push back

roll bar *n* **:** an overhead metal bar on an automobile designed to protect riders in case the automobile overturns

roll call *n* **:** the act or an instance of calling off a list of names (as of soldiers); *also* **:** a time for a roll call

roll•er \ˈrō-lər\ *n* **1 :** a revolving cylinder used for moving, pressing, shaping, applying, or smoothing something **2 :** a rod on which something is rolled up **3 :** a long heavy ocean wave

roll•er coast•er \ˈrō-lər-ˌkō-stər\ *n* **:** an amusement ride consisting of an elevated railway having sharp curves and steep slopes

roller skate *n* **:** a skate with wheels instead of a runner — **roller-skate** *vb* — **roller skater** *n*

rol•lick \ˈrä-lik\ *vb* **♦ :** to move or behave in a carefree joyous manner **:** FROLIC

♦ caper, cavort, disport, frisk, frolic, gambol, lark, romp, sport

rol•lick•ing *adj* **:** full of fun and good spirits

roly–poly \ˌrō-lē-ˈpō-lē\ *adj* **:** being short and pudgy **:** ROTUND

Rom *abbr* **1** Roman **2** Romance **3** Romania; Romanian **4** Romans

ROM \ˈräm\ *n* **:** a computer memory that contains special-purpose information (as a program) which cannot be altered

ro•maine \rō-ˈmān\ *n* **:** a garden lettuce with a tall loose head of long crisp leaves

[1]**Ro•man** \ˈrō-mən\ *n* **1 :** a native or resident of Rome **2** *not cap* **:** roman letters or type

[2]**Roman** *adj* **1 :** of or relating to Rome or the Romans and especially the ancient Romans **2** *not cap* **:** relating to type in which the letters are upright (as in this definition) **3 :** of or relating to the Roman Catholic Church

Roman candle *n* **:** a cylindrical firework that discharges balls of fire

Roman Catholic *adj* **:** of, relating to, or being a Christian church led by the pope and having a liturgy centered in the Mass — **Roman Catholicism** *n*

[1]**ro•mance** \rō-ˈmans, ˈrō-ˌmans\ *n* **1 :** a medieval tale of knightly adventure **2 :** a prose narrative dealing with heroic or mysterious events set in a remote time or place **3 :** a love story **4 ♦ :** a romantic attachment or episode between lovers — **ro•manc•er** *n*

♦ affair, amour, love affair

[2]**romance** *vb* **ro•manced; ro•manc•ing 1 :** to exaggerate or invent detail or incident **2 :** to have romantic fancies **3 :** to carry on a romantic episode with

Ro•mance \rō-ˈmans, ˈrō-ˌmans\ *adj* **:** of or relating to any of several languages developed from Latin

Ro•ma•nian \rù-ˈmā-nē-ən, rō-, -nyən\ *also* **Ru•ma•nian** \rù-\ *n* **1 :** a native or inhabitant of Romania **2 :** the language of the Romanians

Roman numeral *n* **:** a numeral in a system of notation that is based on the ancient Roman system

Ro•ma•no \rō-ˈmä-nō\ *n* **:** a hard Italian cheese that is sharper than Parmesan

Ro•mans \ˈrō-mənz\ *n* **:** a book of the New Testament of Christian Scripture

[1]**ro•man•tic** \rō-ˈman-tik\ *n* **♦ :** a romantic person; *esp* **:** a romantic writer, composer, or artist

♦ dreamer, idealist, utopian, visionary

[2]**romantic** *adj* **1 :** IMAGINARY **2 :** VISIONARY **3 :** having an imaginative or emotional appeal **4 :** of, relating to, or having the characteristics of romanticism — **ro•man•ti•cal•ly** \-ti-k(ə-)lē\ *adv*

ro•man•ti•cism \rō-ˈman-tə-ˌsi-zəm\ *n, often cap* **:** a literary movement (as in early 19th-century England) marked especially by emphasis on the imagination and the emotions and by the use of autobiographical material

ro•man•ti•cist \-sist\ *n* **:** a romantic person, trait, or component

ro•man•ti•cize \-ˈman-tə-ˌsīz\ *vb* **-cized; -ciz•ing 1 :** to make romantic **2 :** to have romantic ideas

[1]**romp** \ˈrämp\ *vb* **1 ♦ :** to play actively and noisily **2 :** to win a contest easily

♦ caper, cavort, disport, frisk, frolic, gambol, lark, rollick, sport

²romp *n* ♦ **:** high-spirited, carefree, and boisterous play

♦ binge, fling, frolic, gambol, lark, revel, rollick

romp•er \ˈräm-pər\ *n* **1 :** one that romps **2 :** a jumpsuit usually for infants — usually used in plural
rood \ˈrüd\ *n* **:** CROSS, CRUCIFIX
¹roof \ˈrüf, ˈru̇f\ *n, pl* **roofs** \ˈrüfs, ˈru̇fs; ˈrüvz, ˈru̇vz\ **1 :** the upper covering part of a building **2** ♦ **:** something suggesting a roof of a building **3** ♦ **:** the roof of a dwelling conventionally designating the home itself — **roofed** \ˈrüft, ˈru̇ft\ *adj* — **roof•ing** *n* — **roof•less** *adj*

♦ [2] canopy, ceiling, tent ♦ [3] abode, domicile, dwelling, home, house, lodging, quarters, residence

²roof *vb* **1 :** to cover with a roof **2 :** to provide with shelter or a home
roof•top \-ˌtäp\ *n* **:** a roof especially of a house
¹rook \ˈru̇k\ *n* **:** a common Old World bird resembling the related crow
²rook *vb* ♦ **:** to defraud by cheating or swindling

♦ bleed, cheat, chisel, cozen, defraud, fleece, gyp, hustle, mulct, shortchange, skin, squeeze, stick, sting, swindle, victimize

³rook *n* **:** a chess piece that can move parallel to the sides of the board across any number of unoccupied squares
rook•ery \ˈru̇-kə-rē\ *n, pl* **-er•ies :** a breeding ground or haunt of gregarious birds or mammals; *also* **:** a colony of such birds or mammals
rook•ie \ˈru̇-kē\ *n* **1** ♦ **:** one that begins something **:** BEGINNER **2 :** a first-year player in a professional sport

♦ beginner, fledgling, freshman, greenhorn, neophyte, newcomer, novice, recruit, tenderfoot, tyro

¹room \ˈrüm, ˈru̇m\ *n* **1** ♦ **:** an extent of space occupied by or sufficient or available for something **2 a** ♦ **:** a partitioned part of a building **:** CHAMBER **b :** the people in a room **3** ♦ **:** a suitable or fit occasion or opportunity **:** OPPORTUNITY ⟨∼ to develop his talents⟩ — **room•ful** *n*

♦ [1] place, space, way ♦ [2a] cell, chamber, closet ♦ [3] chance, occasion, opening, opportunity

²room *vb* **:** to occupy lodgings **:** LODGE
room•er *n* ♦ **:** one who occupies a rented room in another's house

♦ boarder, lodger, renter, tenant

room•ette \rü-ˈmet, ru̇-\ *n* **:** a small private room on a railroad sleeping car
room•mate \ˈrüm-ˌmāt, ˈru̇m-\ *n* **:** one of two or more persons sharing the same room or dwelling
roomy *adj* ♦ **:** having ample room

♦ ample, capacious, commodious, spacious

¹roost \ˈrüst\ *n* **:** a support on which or a place where birds perch
²roost *vb* ♦ **:** to settle on or as if on a roost

♦ alight, land, light, perch, settle ♦ ensconce, install, lodge, perch, settle

roost•er \ˈrüs-tər, ˈru̇s-\ *n* **:** an adult male domestic chicken **:** COCK
¹root \ˈrüt, ˈru̇t\ *n* **1 :** the leafless usually underground part of a seed plant that functions in absorption, aeration, and storage or as a means of anchorage; *also* **:** an underground plant part especially when fleshy and edible **2 :** something (as the basal part of a tooth or hair) resembling a root **3 :** SOURCE, ORIGIN **4 :** the essential core **:** HEART ⟨get to the ∼ of the matter⟩ **5 :** a number that when taken as a factor an indicated number of times gives a specified number **6 :** the lower part — **root•less** *adj* — **root•like** *adj*
²root *vb* **1 :** to form roots **2** ♦ **:** to fix or become fixed by or as if by roots **:** ESTABLISH **3** ♦ **:** to remove altogether by or as if by pulling out by the roots — usually used with *out*

♦ [2] embed, entrench, establish, fix, implant, ingrain, lodge ♦ *usu* **root out** [3] extract, prize, pry, pull, tear, uproot, wrest

³root *vb* **1 :** to turn up or dig with the snout ⟨pigs ∼*ing*⟩ **2 :** to poke or dig around (as in search of something)
⁴root \ˈrüt\ *vb* **1 :** to applaud or encourage noisily **:** CHEER **2 :** to wish success or lend support to — **root•er** *n*
root beer *n* **:** a sweetened carbonated beverage flavored with extracts of roots and herbs
root canal *n* **:** a dental operation to save a tooth by removing the pulp in the root of the tooth and filling the cavity with a protective substance
root•let \ˈrüt-lət, ˈru̇t-\ *n* **:** a small root
root•stock \-ˌstäk\ *n* **:** an underground part of a plant that resembles a rhizome
¹rope \ˈrōp\ *n* **1** ♦ **:** a large strong cord made of strands of fiber **2 :** a hangman's noose **3 :** a thick string (as of pearls) made by twisting or braiding

♦ cable, cord, lace, line, string, wire

²rope *vb* **roped; rop•ing 1 :** to bind, tie, or fasten together with a rope **2 :** to separate or divide by means of a rope **3 :** LASSO
Ror•schach test \ˈrȯr-ˌshäk-\ *n* **:** a psychological test in which a subject interprets ink-blot designs in terms that reveal intellectual and emotional factors
ro•sa•ry \ˈrō-zə-rē\ *n, pl* **-ries 1** *often cap* **:** a Roman Catholic devotion consisting of meditation on sacred mysteries during recitation of Hail Marys **2 :** a string of beads used in praying
¹rose *past of* RISE
²rose \ˈrōz\ *n* **1 :** any of a genus of usually prickly often climbing shrubs with divided leaves and bright often fragrant flowers; *also* **:** one of these flowers **2 :** something resembling a rose in form **3 :** a moderate purplish red color — **rose** *adj*
ro•sé \rō-ˈzā\ *n* **:** a light pink wine
ro•se•ate \ˈrō-zē-ət, -zē-ˌāt\ *adj* **1 :** resembling a rose especially in color **2 :** overly optimistic ⟨a ∼ view of the future⟩
rose•bud \ˈrōz-ˌbəd\ *n* **:** the flower of a rose when it is at most partly open
rose•bush \-ˌbu̇sh\ *n* **:** a shrubby rose
rose•mary \ˈrōz-ˌmer-ē\ *n, pl* **-mar•ies :** a fragrant shrubby Mediterranean mint; *also* **:** its leaves used as a seasoning
ro•sette \rō-ˈzet\ *n* **1 :** a usually small badge or ornament of ribbon gathered in the shape of a rose **2 :** a circular ornament filled with representations of leaves
rose•wa•ter \ˈrōz-ˌwȯ-tər, -ˌwä-\ *n* **:** a watery solution of the fragrant constituents of the rose used as a perfume
rose•wood \-ˌwu̇d\ *n* **:** any of various tropical trees with dark red wood streaked with black; *also* **:** this wood
Rosh Ha•sha•nah \ˌräsh-hə-ˈshä-nə, ˌrōsh-, -ˈshō-\ *n* **:** the Jewish New Year observed as a religious holiday in September or October
ros•in \ˈräz-ᵊn\ *n* **:** a brittle resin obtained especially from pine trees and used especially in varnishes and on violin bows
ros•ter \ˈräs-tər\ *n* **1 :** a list of personnel; *also* **:** the persons listed on a roster **2** ♦ **:** an itemized list

♦ catalog, checklist, list, listing, menu, register, registry, roll, schedule, table

ros•trum \ˈräs-trəm\ *n, pl* **rostrums** *or* **ros•tra** \-trə\ ♦ **:** a stage or platform for public speaking

♦ dais, platform, podium, stage, stand

rosy \ˈrō-zē\ *adj* **ros•i•er; -est 1** ♦ **:** of the color rose **2** ♦ **:** characterized by or tending to promote optimism **:** HOPEFUL — **ros•i•ly** \ˈrō-zə-lē\ *adv* — **ros•i•ness** \-zē-nəs\ *n*

♦ [1] florid, flush, glowing, ruddy, sanguine ♦ [2] auspicious, bright, encouraging, fair, golden, heartening, hopeful, likely, promising, propitious, upbeat

¹rot \ˈrät\ *vb* **rot•ted; rot•ting 1** ♦ **:** to undergo decomposition **:** DECAY **2** ♦ **:** to go to ruin

♦ [1] break down, corrupt, decay, decompose, disintegrate, molder, putrefy, spoil ♦ [2] decay, decline, degenerate, descend, deteriorate, ebb, sink, worsen

²rot *n* **1** ♦ **:** the process of rotting **:** DECAY **2 :** any of various diseases of plants or animals in which tissue breaks down **3** ♦ **:** language, conduct, or an idea that is absurd or contrary to good sense **:** NONSENSE; *also* **:** words or language having no meaning or conveying no intelligible ideas

♦ [1] breakdown, corruption, decay, decomposition, putrefaction, spoilage ♦ [3] bunk, claptrap, drivel, fiddlesticks, folly, foolishness, fudge, hogwash, humbug, nonsense, piffle, silliness, slush, stupidity, trash

¹ro•ta•ry \ˈrō-tə-rē\ *adj* **1 :** turning on an axis like a wheel **2 :** having a rotating part
²rotary *n, pl* **-ries 1 :** a rotary machine **2 :** a one-way circular road junction
ro•tate \ˈrō-ˌtāt\ *vb* **ro•tat•ed; ro•tat•ing 1** ♦ **:** to turn or cause to turn about an axis or a center **:** REVOLVE **2 :** to alternate in a series — **ro•ta•tor** \ˈrō-ˌtā-tər\ *n* — **ro•ta•to•ry** \ˈrō-tə-ˌtōr-ē\ *adj*

♦ pivot, revolve, roll, spin, swing, swirl, turn, twirl, twist, wheel, whirl

ro•ta•tion \rō-ˈtā-shən\ *n* ♦ **:** the action or process of rotating on or as if on an axis or center

♦ gyration, pirouette, reel, revolution, roll, spin, twirl, wheel, whirl

ROTC *abbr* Reserve Officers' Training Corps
rote \ˈrōt\ *n* **1 :** repetition from memory often without attention to meaning **2** ♦ **:** fixed routine or repetition — **rote** *adj*

♦ groove, pattern, routine, rut, treadmill

ro•tis•ser•ie \rō-ˈti-sə-rē\ *n* **1 :** a restaurant specializing in broiled and barbecued meats **2 :** an appliance fitted with a spit on which food is rotated before or over a source of heat
ro•to•gra•vure \ˌrō-tə-grə-ˈvyu̇r\ *n* **:** PHOTOGRAVURE
ro•tor \ˈrō-tər\ *n* **1 :** a part that rotates; *esp* **:** the rotating part of an electrical machine **2 :** a system of rotating horizontal blades for supporting a helicopter
ro•to•till•er \ˈrō-tō-ˌti-lər\ *n* **:** an engine-powered machine with rotating blades used to lift and turn over soil
rot•ten \ˈrät-ᵊn\ *adj* **1** ♦ **:** having rotted **2** ♦ **:** morally corrupt **3** ♦ **:** extremely unpleasant or inferior **4** ♦ **:** of very poor quality — **rot•ten•ness** *n*

♦ [1] bad, putrid ♦ [2] bad, black, evil, immoral, iniquitous, nefarious, sinful, unethical, unsavory, vicious, vile, villainous, wicked, wrong ♦ [3] bad, disagreeable, distasteful, nasty, sour, uncongenial, unlovely, unpleasant, unwelcome ♦ [3, 4] bad, deficient, inferior, lousy, off, poor, punk, substandard, unacceptable, unsatisfactory, wanting, wretched, wrong ♦ [4] cheap, junky, lousy, mediocre, second-rate, shoddy, sleazy, trashy

rot•ten•stone \ˈrät-ᵊn-ˌstōn\ *n* **:** a decomposed siliceous limestone used for polishing
rott•wei•ler \ˈrät-ˌwī-lər\ *n, often cap* **:** any of a breed of tall powerful black-and-tan short-haired dogs
ro•tund \rō-ˈtənd\ *adj* **1 :** rounded out **2** ♦ **:** notably plump

♦ chubby, fat, plump, portly, round

ro•tun•da \rō-ˈtən-də\ *n* **1 :** a round building; *esp* **:** one covered by a dome **2 :** a large round room
ro•tun•di•ty \-ˈtən-də-tē\ *n* **:** the quality or state of being rotund
roué \ru̇-ˈā\ *n* **:** a man devoted to a life of sensual pleasure **:** RAKE
rouge \ˈrüzh, ˈrüj\ *n* **:** a cosmetic used to give a red color to cheeks and lips — **rouge** *vb*
¹**rough** \ˈrəf\ *adj* **rough•er; rough•est 1** ♦ **:** uneven in surface **:** not smooth **2 :** covered with or made up of coarse and often shaggy hair **:** SHAGGY **3 :** not calm **:** TURBULENT **4** ♦ **:** marked by harshness or violence **5** ♦ **:** presenting a challenge **:** DIFFICULT **6 :** coarse or rugged in character or appearance **7** ♦ **:** marked by lack of refinement **8 :** not brought to an end or to the desired final state **:** CRUDE **9 :** done or made hastily or tentatively

♦ [1] broken, bumpy, coarse, irregular, jagged, lumpy, pebbly, ragged, rugged, uneven ♦ [4] bitter, brutal, burdensome, cruel, excruciating, grievous, grim, hard, harsh, heavy, inhuman, murderous, onerous, oppressive, rugged, severe, stiff, tough, trying ♦ [5] arduous, demanding, difficult, exacting, formidable, grueling, hard, herculean, laborious, strenuous, tall, toilsome, tough ♦ [7] coarse, common, crass, crude, gross, ill-bred, low, rude, tasteless, uncouth, uncultivated, uncultured, unpolished, unrefined, vulgar

²**rough** *n* **1 :** uneven ground covered with high grass especially along a golf fairway **2 :** a crude, unfinished, or preliminary state; *also* **:** something in such a state **3 :** ROWDY, TOUGH
³**rough** *vb* **1 :** ROUGHEN **2** ♦ **:** to subject to abuse **:** MANHANDLE — usually used with *up* **3 :** to make or shape roughly especially in a preliminary way — **rough•er** *n*

♦ *usu* **rough up** maltreat, manhandle, maul, mishandle

rough•age \ˈrə-fij\ *n* **:** FIBER 2; *also* **:** food containing much indigestible material acting as fiber
rough–and–ready \ˌrə-fən-ˈre-dē\ *adj* **:** rude or unpolished in nature, method, or manner but effective in action or use
rough–and–tum•ble \-ˈtəm-bəl\ *n* **:** rough unrestrained fighting or struggling — **rough–and–tumble** *adj*
rough•en \ˈrə-fən\ *vb* **rough•ened; rough•en•ing :** to make or become rough
rough–hewn \ˈrəf-ˈhyün\ *adj* **1 :** being rough and unfinished ⟨~ beams⟩ **2 :** lacking smooth manners or social grace — **rough–hew** \-ˈhyü\ *vb*
¹**rough•house** \ˈrəf-ˌhau̇s\ *vb* **rough•housed; rough•hous•ing :** to participate in rough noisy behavior
²**roughhouse** *n* ♦ **:** violence or rough boisterous play

♦ foolery, high jinks, horseplay, monkeyshines, shenanigans, tomfoolery

rough•ly *adv* ♦ **:** in a rough manner

♦ hard, hardly, harshly, ill, oppressively, severely, sternly, stiffly

rough•neck \ˈrəf-ˌnek\ *n* **1 :** a rough or uncouth person **:** ROWDY **2 :** a worker on a crew drilling oil wells
rough•ness *n* **:** the quality or state of being rough
rough•shod \ˈrəf-ˌshäd\ *adv* **:** in a roughly forceful manner ⟨rode ~ over the opposition⟩
rou•lette \rü-ˈlet\ *n* **1 :** a gambling game in which a whirling wheel is used **2 :** a wheel or disk with teeth around the outside
¹**round** \ˈrau̇nd\ *adj* **1** ♦ **:** having every part of the surface or circumference the same distance from the center **2 :** CYLINDRICAL **3 :** COMPLETE, FULL **4 a :** approximately correct **b** ♦ **:** exact only to a specific decimal or place ⟨~ numbers⟩ **5 :** liberal or ample in size or amount **6 :** BLUNT, OUTSPOKEN **7 :** moving in or forming a circle **8 :** having curves rather than angles **9** ♦ **:** well filled out **10** ♦ **:** having full or unimpeded resonance or tone — **round•ish** *adj* — **round•ness** *n*

♦ [1] circular, global ♦ [4b] even, exact, flat, precise ♦ [9] fat, full, plump, portly, rotund ♦ [10] golden, resonant, resounding, ringing, sonorous, vibrant

²**round** *adv* **1 :** from beginning to end **:** AROUND **2** ♦ **:** in the reverse or opposite direction **3** ♦ **:** in all or various directions from a fixed point

♦ [2] about, around, back ♦ [3] about, around, over, through, throughout

³**round** *n* **1** ♦ **:** something round (as a circle, globe, or ring) **2 :** a curved or rounded part (as a rung of a ladder) **3 :** an indirect path or course; *also* **:** a regularly covered route (as of a security guard) **4 :** a series or cycle of recurring actions or events **5 :** one shot fired by a soldier or a gun; *also* **:** ammunition for one shot **6 :** a period of time or a unit of play in a game or contest **7 :** a cut of meat (as beef) especially between the rump and the lower leg — **in the round 1 :** FREESTANDING **2 :** with a center stage surrounded by an audience ⟨theater *in the round*⟩

♦ band, circle, eye, hoop, loop, ring

⁴**round** *vb* **1** ♦ **:** to make or become round **2** ♦ **:** to go or pass around or part way around **3** ♦ **:** to bring to completion or perfection **:** FINISH — often used with *out* or *off* **4 :** to become plump or shapely **5 :** to express as a round number — often used with *off* **6** ♦ **:** to follow a winding course **:** BEND

♦ [1] agglomerate, ball, conglomerate, roll, wad ♦ [2] circle, circumnavigate, coil, compass, encircle, girdle, loop, orbit, ring ♦ *usu* **round off** *or* **round out** [3] close, conclude, end, finish, terminate, wind up, wrap up ♦ [6] arc, arch, bend, bow, crook, curve, hook, sweep, swerve, wheel

⁵**round** *prep* **:** AROUND
¹**round•about** \ˈrau̇n-də-ˌbau̇t\ *adj* ♦ **:** having a circular or winding course **:** INDIRECT

♦ circuitous, circular, indirect

²**roundabout** *n, Brit* **:** MERRY-GO-ROUND
roun•de•lay \ˈrau̇n-də-ˌlā\ *n* **1 :** a simple song with a refrain **2 :** a poem with a recurring refrain
round•house \ˈrau̇nd-ˌhau̇s\ *n* **1 :** a circular building for housing and repairing locomotives **2 :** a blow with the hand made with a wide swing
round•ly \ˈrau̇nd-lē\ *adv* **1 a** ♦ **:** in a complete manner **b :** WIDELY **2 :** in a blunt way **3 :** with vigor

♦ completely, exhaustively, fully, minutely, thoroughly, totally

round–rob•in \ˈrou̇nd-ˌrä-bən\ *n* **:** a tournament in which each contestant meets every other contestant in turn
round–shoul•dered \-ˌshōl-dərd\ *adj* **:** having the shoulders stooping or rounded
round–trip *n* **:** a trip to a place and back
round•up \ˈrau̇n-ˌdəp\ *n* **1 :** the gathering together of cattle on the range by riding around them and driving them in; *also* **:** the ranch hands and horses engaged in a roundup **2 :** a gathering in of scattered persons or things **3** ♦ **:** a summary of information **:** SUMMARY ⟨news ~⟩

♦ abstract, digest, encapsulation, epitome, outline, précis, recapitulation, résumé (*or* resume), sum, summary, synopsis, wrap-up

round up *vb* ♦ **:** to gather in or bring together from various quarters

♦ accumulate, amass, assemble, collect, concentrate, garner, gather, group, lump, pick up, scrape

round•worm \-ˌwərm\ *n* **:** NEMATODE

rouse \ˈrau̇z\ *vb* **roused; rous•ing** **1 :** to excite to activity : stir up **2** ♦ **:** to wake from sleep — **rous•er** *n*

♦ arouse, awake, wake

rous•ing \ˈrau̇-ziŋ\ *adj* ♦ **:** giving rise to excitement

♦ breathtaking, electric, exciting, exhilarating, stirring, thrilling

roust•about \ˈrau̇s-tə-ˌbau̇t\ *n* **:** one who does heavy unskilled labor (as on a dock or in an oil field)

¹rout \ˈrau̇t\ *n* **1 :** MOB 1, 2 **2 :** DISTURBANCE **3 :** a fashionable gathering

²rout *vb* **1 :** RUMMAGE **2 :** to gouge out **3** ♦ **:** to expel by force

♦ banish, boot (out), bounce, cast, chase, dismiss, drum, eject, expel, oust, run off, throw out

³rout *n* **1 :** a state of wild confusion or disorderly retreat **2** ♦ **:** a disastrous defeat

♦ defeat, loss, shellacking

⁴rout *vb* **1** ♦ **:** to put to flight **2** ♦ **:** to defeat decisively

♦ [1] banish, boot (out), bounce, cast, chase, dismiss, drum, eject, expel, oust, run off, throw out ♦ [2] beat, best, clobber, conquer, crush, defeat, drub, lick, master, overcome, prevail, skunk, subdue, surmount, thrash, trim, triumph, trounce, wallop, whip, win

¹route \ˈrüt, ˈrau̇t\ *n* **1** ♦ **:** a traveled way **2 :** CHANNEL **3** ♦ **:** a line of travel

♦ [1] artery, avenue, highway, road, thoroughfare, way ♦ [3] course, line, path, track, way

²route *vb* **rout•ed; rout•ing :** to send by a selected route : DIRECT

route•man \-mən, -ˌman\ *n* **:** a person who sells and makes deliveries on an assigned route

rout•er \ˈrau̇-tər\ *n* **:** a machine with a revolving spindle and cutter for shaping a surface (as of wood)

¹rou•tine \rü-ˈtēn\ *n* **1** ♦ **:** a regular course of procedure **2 :** an often repeated speech or formula **3 :** a part fully worked out ⟨a comedy ~⟩ **4 :** a set of computer instructions that will perform a certain task — **rou•tin•ize** \-ˈtē-ˌnīz\ *vb*

♦ groove, pattern, rote, rut, treadmill ♦ drill, exercise, practice, training, workout

²routine *adj* **1** ♦ **:** of a commonplace or repetitious character **2** ♦ **:** of, relating to, or being in accordance with established procedure — **rou•tine•ly** *adv*

♦ [1] average, common, commonplace, everyday, normal, ordinary, prosaic, run-of-the-mill, standard, unexceptional, unremarkable, usual, workaday ♦ [2] ceremonial, ceremonious, conventional, formal, orthodox, regular

¹rove \ˈrōv\ *vb* **roved; rov•ing** ♦ **:** to wander over or through

♦ gad, gallivant, knock, maunder, meander, mope, ramble, range, roam, traipse, wander

²rove *past and past part of* REEVE

¹rov•er *n* ♦ **:** one that wanders

♦ drifter, nomad, rambler, stroller, vagabond, wanderer

²rov•er *n* ♦ **:** one who commits or practices piracy

♦ buccaneer, corsair, freebooter, pirate

¹row \ˈrō\ *vb* **1** ♦ **:** to propel a boat with oars **2 :** to transport in a rowboat **3 :** to pull an oar in a crew — **row•er** \ˈrō-ər\ *n*

♦ scull

²row *n* **:** an act or instance of rowing

³row *n* **1 :** a number of objects in an orderly sequence **2 :** a thoroughfare for travel or transportation from place to place : WAY

⁴row \ˈrau̇\ *n* **1** ♦ **:** a noisy quarrel **2** ♦ **:** a noisy disturbance

♦ [1] altercation, argument, bicker, brawl, disagreement, dispute, fight, quarrel, scrap, spat, squabble, wrangle ♦ [2] commotion, disturbance, furor, hullabaloo, pandemonium, tumult, turmoil, uproar

⁵row \ˈrau̇\ *vb* ♦ **:** to engage in a row

♦ argue, bicker, brawl, dispute, fall out, fight, hassle, quarrel, scrap, spat, squabble, wrangle

row•boat \ˈrō-ˌbōt\ *n* **:** a small boat designed to be rowed

¹row•dy \ˈrau̇-dē\ *adj* **row•di•er; -est** ♦ **:** coarse or boisterous in behavior — **row•di•ness** \ˈrau̇-dē-nəs\ *n* — **row•dy•ish** *adj* — **row•dy•ism** *n*

♦ boisterous, rambunctious, raucous

²rowdy *n* ♦ **:** a rowdy person

♦ bully, hoodlum, punk, ruffian, thug, tough

row•el \ˈrau̇-əl\ *n* **:** a small pointed wheel on a rider's spur — **rowel** *vb*

¹roy•al \ˈrȯi-əl\ *adj* **1 :** of or relating to a sovereign : REGAL **2** ♦ **:** fit for a king or queen ⟨a ~ welcome⟩ **3** ♦ **:** of superior size, magnitude, or quality — **roy•al•ly** *adv*

♦ [2] kingly, monarchical, princely, queenly, regal ♦ [3] august, baronial, gallant, glorious, grand, grandiose, heroic, imposing, magnificent, majestic, monumental, noble, proud, regal, splendid, stately

²royal *n* **:** a person of royal blood

royal flush *n* **:** a straight flush having an ace as the highest card

roy•al•ist \ˈrȯi-ə-list\ *n* **:** an adherent of a king or of monarchical government

roy•al•ty \ˈrȯi-əl-tē\ *n, pl* **-ties** **1 :** the state of being royal **2 :** royal persons **3 :** a share of a product or profit (as of a mine or oil well) claimed by the owner for allowing another person to use the property **4 :** a payment made to an author or composer for each copy of a work sold or to an inventor for each article sold under a patent

RP *abbr* **1** relief pitcher **2** Republic of the Philippines

rpm *abbr* revolutions per minute

rps *abbr* revolutions per second

rpt *abbr* **1** repeat **2** report

RR *abbr* **1** railroad **2** rural route

RS *abbr* **1** recording secretary **2** revised statutes **3** Royal Society

RSV *abbr* Revised Standard Version

RSVP *abbr* please reply

rt *abbr* **1** right **2** route

RT *abbr* round-trip

rte *abbr* route

Ru *symbol* ruthenium

¹rub \ˈrəb\ *vb* **rubbed; rub•bing** **1 :** to use pressure and friction on a body or object **2** ♦ **:** to fret or chafe with friction **3** ♦ **:** to scour, polish, erase, or smear by pressure and friction

♦ [2] abrade, chafe, erode, fray, fret, gall, wear ♦ [3] buff, file, grind, hone, rasp, sand ♦ [3] buff, burnish, dress, gloss, grind, polish, shine, smooth

²rub *n* **1 :** DIFFICULTY, OBSTRUCTION **2** ♦ **:** something grating to the feelings

♦ aggravation, annoyance, bother, bugbear, exasperation, frustration, hassle, headache, inconvenience, irritant, nuisance, peeve, pest, problem, ruffle, thorn, vexation

¹rub•ber \ˈrə-bər\ *n* **1 :** one that rubs **2 :** ERASER **3 :** a flexible waterproof elastic substance made from the milky juice of various tropical plants or made synthetically; *also* **:** something made of this material **4 :** CONDOM — **rubber** *adj* — **rub•ber•ize** \ˈrə-bə-ˌrīz\ *vb*

²rubber *n* **1 :** a contest that consists of an odd number of games and is won by the side that takes a majority **2 :** an extra game played to decide a tie

¹rub•ber•neck \-ˌnek\ *n* **1 :** an idly or overly inquisitive person **2 :** a person on a guided tour

²rubberneck *vb* ♦ **:** to look about, stare, or listen with excessive curiosity — **rub•ber•neck•er** *n*

♦ gape, gawk, gaze, goggle, peer, stare

rub•bery *adj* ♦ **:** resembling rubber (as in elasticity, consistency, or texture)

♦ elastic, flexible, resilient, springy, stretch, supple

rub•bish \ˈrə-bish\ *n* **1** ♦ **:** useless waste or rejected matter : TRASH **2 :** something worthless or nonsensical

♦ chaff, deadwood, dust, garbage, junk, litter, refuse, riffraff, scrap, trash, waste

rub•ble \ˈrə-bəl\ *n* ♦ **:** broken fragments especially of a destroyed building

♦ debris, remains, ruins, wreck, wreckage

ru•bel•la \rü-ˈbe-lə\ *n* **:** GERMAN MEASLES

ru•bi•cund \ˈrü-bi-(ˌ)kənd\ *adj* **:** having a healthy reddish color : RED, RUDDY

ru•bid•i•um \rü-ˈbi-dē-əm\ *n* **:** a soft silvery metallic chemical element

ru•ble \ˈrü-bəl\ *n* **:** the basic monetary unit of Russia

rub out *vb* ♦ **:** to destroy completely

♦ annihilate, blot out, demolish, eradicate, exterminate, liquidate, obliterate, root, snuff, stamp, wipe out

ru•bric \ˈrü-brik\ *n* **1 :** a heading of a part of a book or manuscript **2 :** a rule especially for the conduct of a religious service
ru•by \ˈrü-bē\ *n, pl* **rubies :** a clear red precious stone — **ruby** *adj*
ru•by–throat•ed hummingbird \ˈrü-bē-ˌthrō-təd-\ *n* **:** a bright green and whitish hummingbird of eastern No. America with a red throat in the male
ruck•us \ˈrə-kəs\ *n* **:** a noisy disturbance or quarrel **:** ROW
rud•der \ˈrə-dər\ *n* **:** a movable flat piece attached at the rear of a ship or aircraft for steering
rud•dy \ˈrə-dē\ *adj* **rud•di•er; -est 1 :** REDDISH **2** ♦ **:** of a healthy reddish complexion — **rud•di•ness** \ˈrə-dē-nəs\ *n*

♦ florid, flush, glowing, rosy, sanguine

rude \ˈrüd\ *adj* **rud•er; rud•est 1** ♦ **:** roughly made **:** CRUDE **2 :** not developed **:** PRIMITIVE **3** ♦ **:** lacking refinement or delicacy **4 :** marked by or suggestive of lack of training or skill **:** UNSKILLED **5** ♦ **:** not being in a cultural or civilized state — **rude•ly** *adv*

♦ [1] artless, clumsy, crude, rough, unrefined ♦ [3] coarse, common, crass, crude, gross, ill-bred, low, rough, tasteless, uncouth, uncultivated, uncultured, unpolished, unrefined, vulgar ♦ [3] discourteous, ill-bred, ill-mannered, impertinent, impolite, inconsiderate, thoughtless, uncivil, ungracious, unmannerly ♦ [5] barbarous, heathen, heathenish, Neanderthal, savage, uncivilized, wild

rude•ness *n* **1** ♦ **:** the quality or state of being rude **2** ♦ **:** a rude action

♦ [1] coarseness, grossness, indelicacy, lowness, vulgarity ♦ [2] brazenness, discourtesy, disrespect, impertinence, impudence, incivility, insolence

ru•di•ment \ˈrü-də-mənt\ *n* **1** ♦ **:** an elementary principle or basic skill — usually used in plural **2 :** something not fully developed — usually used in plural

♦ **rudiments** elements, essentials, principles

ru•di•men•ta•ry \ˌrü-də-ˈmen-tə-rē\ *adj* **1** ♦ **:** consisting in basic principles **2** ♦ **:** of a primitive kind

♦ [1] basic, elemental, elementary, essential, fundamental, underlying ♦ [2] crude, low, primitive, rude

¹rue \ˈrü\ *n* ♦ **:** deep distress, sadness, or regret — **rue•ful•ness** *n*

♦ contrition, penitence, regret, remorse, repentance

²rue *vb* **rued; ru•ing** ♦ **:** to feel regret, remorse, or penitence for

♦ bemoan, deplore, lament, regret, repent

³rue *n* **:** a European strong-scented woody herb with bitter-tasting leaves
rue•ful \-fəl\ *adj* **1** ♦ **:** expressing sorrow **2** ♦ **:** full of sorrow **3** ♦ **:** exciting pity or sympathy

♦ [1] dolorous, funeral, lugubrious, mournful, plaintive, regretful, sorrowful, weeping, woeful ♦ [2] apologetic, contrite, penitent, regretful, remorseful, repentant, sorry ♦ [3] heartbreaking, miserable, pathetic, piteous, pitiful, poor, sorry, wretched

rue•ful•ly *adv* **:** in a rueful manner
ruff \ˈrəf\ *n* **1 :** a large round pleated collar worn in the 16th and 17th centuries **2 :** a fringe of long hair or feathers around the neck of an animal — **ruffed** \ˈrəft\ *adj*
ruf•fi•an \ˈrə-fē-ən\ *n* ♦ **:** a brutal person — **ruf•fi•an•ly** *adj*

♦ bully, gangster, goon, hood, hoodlum, mobster, mug, punk, rowdy, thug, tough

¹ruf•fle \ˈrə-fəl\ *vb* **ruf•fled; ruf•fling 1 :** to roughen the surface of **2** ♦ **:** to excite to anger **:** IRRITATE, VEX **3 :** to erect (as hair or feathers) in or like a ruff **4 :** to flip through (as pages) **5 :** to draw into or provide with plaits or folds

♦ aggravate, annoy, bother, bug, chafe, exasperate, gall, get, grate, irk, irritate, nettle, peeve, persecute, pique, put out, rasp, rile, spite, vex

²ruffle *n* **1** ♦ **:** a strip of fabric gathered or pleated on one edge **2 :** RUFF 2 **3 :** RIPPLE — **ruf•fly** \ˈrə-fə-lē, -flē\ *adj*

♦ flounce, frill, furbelow

RU–486 \ˈär-ˌyü-ˌfōr-ˌā-tē-ˈsiks\ *n* **:** a drug taken orally to induce abortion especially early in pregnancy
rug \ˈrəg\ *n* **1 :** a covering for the legs, lap, and feet **2 :** a piece of heavy fabric usually with a nap or pile used as a floor covering
rug•by \ˈrəg-bē\ *n, often cap* **:** a football game in which play is continuous and interference and forward passing are not permitted
rug•ged \ˈrə-gəd\ *adj* **1** ♦ **:** having a rough uneven surface **2 :** TURBULENT, STORMY **3 :** austere or stern in aspect, conduct, or character **:** STERN **4** ♦ **:** strongly built or constituted **:** STURDY **5** ♦ **:** presenting a severe test of ability, stamina, or resolution — **rug•ged•ize** \ˈrə-gə-ˌdīz\ *vb* — **rug•ged•ly** *adv* — **rug•ged•ness** *n*

♦ [1] broken, bumpy, coarse, irregular, jagged, lumpy, pebbly, ragged, rough, uneven ♦ [4] hard, hard-bitten, hardy, stout, strong, sturdy, tough, vigorous ♦ [5] bitter, brutal, burdensome, cruel, excruciating, grievous, grim, hard, harsh, heavy, inhuman, murderous, onerous, oppressive, rough, severe, stiff, tough, trying

¹ru•in \ˈrü-ən\ *n* **1** ♦ **:** complete collapse or destruction **2** ♦ **:** the remains of something destroyed — usually used in plural **3 :** a cause of destruction **4 :** the action of destroying

♦ [1] annihilation, demolition, desolation, destruction, devastation, havoc, loss, obliteration, wastage, wreckage ♦ **ruins** [2] debris, remains, rubble, wreck, wreckage

²ruin *vb* **1** ♦ **:** to reduce to ruins **:** DESTROY **2** ♦ **:** to damage beyond repair **3 :** BANKRUPT

♦ [1] destroy, devastate, ravage, scourge ♦ [2] annihilate, blot out, demolish, desolate, destroy, devastate, do in, exterminate, extinguish, obliterate, pulverize, shatter, smash, tear down, waste, wipe out, wreck

ru•in•ation \ˌrü-ə-ˈnā-shən\ *n* **:** the state of being ruined **:** RUIN, DESTRUCTION
ru•in•ous \ˈrü-ə-nəs\ *adj* **1 :** RUINED, DILAPIDATED **2** ♦ **:** causing ruin — **ru•in•ous•ly** *adv*

♦ calamitous, catastrophic, destructive, devastating, disastrous, fatal, fateful, unfortunate

¹rule \ˈrül\ *n* **1** ♦ **:** a guide or principle for governing action **:** REGULATION **2 :** the usual way of doing something **3** ♦ **:** the exercise of authority or control **:** GOVERNMENT **4 :** RULER 2

♦ [1] regulation ♦ [3] administration, authority, government, jurisdiction, regime

²rule *vb* **ruled; rul•ing 1** ♦ **:** to exert control, direction, or influence on; *also* **:** GOVERN **2 :** to be supreme or outstanding in **3** ♦ **:** to give or state as a considered decision **4 :** to mark on paper with or as if with a ruler

♦ [1] boss, captain, command, control, govern, preside ♦ *usu* **rule on** [3] adjudicate, arbitrate, decide, determine, judge, referee, settle, umpire

rule out *vb* ♦ **:** to remove from consideration

♦ ban, bar, debar, eliminate, except, exclude

rul•er \ˈrü-lər\ *n* **1** ♦ **:** one that rules **2 :** a straight strip of material (as wood or metal) marked off in units and used for measuring or as a straightedge

♦ autocrat, monarch, sovereign

ruling *n* ♦ **:** an official or authoritative decision, decree, statement, or interpretation (as by a judge on a point of law)

♦ doom, finding, holding, judgment (*or* judgement), sentence ♦ decree, directive, edict, fiat

rum \ˈrəm\ *n* **1 :** an alcoholic liquor made from sugarcane products (as molasses) **2 :** alcoholic liquor
Ru•ma•nian *var of* ROMANIAN
rum•ba \ˈrəm-bə, ˈrüm-\ *n* **:** a dance of Cuban origin marked by strong rhythmic movements
¹rum•ble \ˈrəm-bəl\ *vb* **rum•bled; rum•bling 1** ♦ **:** to make a low heavy rolling sound **2 :** to move along with such a sound — **rumbler** *n*

♦ growl, grumble, lumber, roll

²rumble *n* **1 :** a low heavy rolling sound **2 :** a street fight especially among gangs
rumble seat *n* **:** a folding seat in the back of an automobile that is not covered by the top
rum•bling \ˈrəm-bliŋ\ *n* **1 :** RUMBLE **2 :** widespread talk or complaints — usually used in plural
ru•men \ˈrü-mən\ *n, pl* **ru•mi•na** \-mə-nə\ *or* **rumens :** the large first compartment of the stomach of a ruminant (as a cow)
¹ru•mi•nant \ˈrü-mə-nənt\ *n* **:** a ruminant mammal
²ruminant *adj* **1 :** chewing the cud; *also* **:** of or relating to a group

of hoofed mammals (as cattle, deer, and camels) that chew the cud and have a complex 3- or 4-chambered stomach **2** ♦ **:** given to or engaged in contemplation **:** MEDITATIVE

♦ contemplative, meditative, pensive, reflective, thoughtful

ru•mi•nate \ˈrü-mə-ˌnāt\ *vb* **-nat•ed; -nat•ing 1** ♦ **:** to engage in contemplation **:** to spend time in thought on **2 :** to chew the cud — **ru•mi•na•tion** \ˌrü-mə-ˈnā-shən\ *n*

♦ chew over, cogitate, consider, contemplate, debate, deliberate, entertain, meditate, mull, ponder, question, study, think, weigh

[1]**rum•mage** \ˈrə-mij\ *vb* **rum•maged; rum•mag•ing** ♦ **:** to search thoroughly — **rum•mag•er** *n*

♦ dig, dredge, hunt, rake, ransack, rifle, scour, search

[2]**rummage** *n* **1** ♦ **:** a miscellaneous collection **2 :** an act of rummaging

♦ assortment, clutter, jumble, medley, mélange, miscellany, motley, muddle, variety, welter

rum•my \ˈrə-mē\ *n* **:** any of several card games for two or more players

[1]**ru•mor** *or Can and Brit* **ru•mour** \ˈrü-mər\ *n* **1 :** common talk **2 :** a statement or report current but not authenticated

[2]**rumor** *or Can and Brit* **rumour** *vb* ♦ **:** to tell or spread by rumor

♦ circulate, noise, whisper

rump \ˈrəmp\ *n* **1 :** the rear part of an animal; *also* **:** a cut of meat (as beef) behind the upper sirloin **2 :** a small or inferior remnant (as of a group) **3** ♦ **:** the upper rounded part of the hindquarters of a quadruped mammal

♦ backside, bottom, butt, buttocks, posterior, rear, seat

rum•ple \ˈrəm-pəl\ *vb* **rum•pled; rum•pling 1** ♦ **:** to become or cause to become marked with or contracted into irregular folds **:** WRINKLE **2** ♦ **:** to make unkempt **:** MUSS — **rumple** *n* — **rum•ply** \ˈrəm-pə-lē\ *adj*

♦ [1] crease, crinkle, furrow, wrinkle ♦ [2] dishevel, disorder, muddle, muss, tumble, upset

rum•pus \ˈrəm-pəs\ *n* **:** a usually noisy commotion **:** RUCKUS

rumpus room *n* **:** a room usually in the basement of a home that is used for games, parties, and recreation

[1]**run** \ˈrən\ *vb* **ran** \ˈran\; **run; run•ning 1** ♦ **:** to go faster than a walk **2** ♦ **:** to take to flight **:** FLEE **3 :** to go without restraint ⟨let chickens ~ loose⟩ **4 :** to go rapidly or hurriedly **:** HASTEN, RUSH **5 :** to make a quick or casual trip or visit **6 :** to contend in a race; *esp* **:** to enter an election **7 :** to put forward as a candidate for office **8 :** to move on or as if on wheels **:** pass or slide freely **9 :** to go back and forth **:** PLY **10 a :** to move in large numbers especially to a spawning ground ⟨shad are *running*⟩ **b :** to drive (livestock) especially to a grazing place **11 :** FUNCTION, OPERATE ⟨left the motor *running*⟩ **12 :** to continue in force ⟨two years to ~⟩ **13 a** ♦ **:** to flow rapidly or under pressure **:** MELT **b :** DISCHARGE 7 ⟨my nose is *running*⟩ **14 :** to tend to produce or to recur ⟨family ~*s* to blonds⟩ **15** ♦ **:** to take a certain direction **16 :** to be worded or written **17 :** to be current ⟨rumors *running* wild⟩ **18** ♦ **:** to cause to produce a flow **19 :** TRACE ⟨~ down a rumor⟩ **20 :** to perform or bring about by running **21 :** to cause to pass ⟨~ a wire from the antenna⟩ **22 :** to cause to collide **23 :** SMUGGLE **24** ♦ **:** to direct the business or activities of **:** MANAGE ⟨~ a business⟩ **25 :** INCUR ⟨~ a risk⟩ **26 :** to permit to accumulate before settling ⟨~ up a bill⟩ **27 :** PRINT, PUBLISH **28** ♦ **:** to exist or occur in a continuous range of variation

♦ [1] dash, gallop, jog, scamper, sprint, trip ♦ [2] bolt, break, flee, fly, retreat, run away, run off ♦ [13a] flow, liquefy, melt, pour, roll, stream, thaw ♦ [15] extend, go, head, lead, lie ♦ [18] activate, actuate, crank, drive, move, propel, set off, spark, start, touch off, trigger, turn on ♦ [24] administer, carry on, conduct, control, direct, govern, guide, handle, manage, operate, oversee, regulate, superintend, supervise ♦ [28] go, range, vary

[2]**run** *n* **1 :** an act or the action of running **2 :** a migration of fish; *also* **:** the migrating fish **3 :** a score in baseball **4 :** BROOK, CREEK **5** ♦ **:** a continuous series especially of similar things **:** a period of existence ⟨the play had an extended ~⟩ **6 :** persistent heavy demands from depositors, creditors, or customers **7 :** the quantity of work turned out in a continuous operation; *also* **:** a period of operation (as of a machine or plant) **8 :** the usual or normal kind ⟨the ordinary ~ of students⟩ **9 :** the distance covered in continuous travel or sailing **10 :** a regular course or trip **11** ♦ **:** freedom of movement in a place or area ⟨has the ~ of the house⟩ **12 :** an enclosure for animals **13 :** an inclined course (as for skiing) **14 :** a lengthwise ravel (as in a stocking) **15 :** general tendency or direction — **run•less** *adj*

♦ [5] date, duration, life, lifetime, standing, time ♦ [11] authorization, freedom, latitude, license (*or* licence)

run•about \ˈrə-nə-ˌbau̇t\ *n* **:** a light wagon, automobile, or motorboat

run•a•gate \ˈrə-nə-ˌgāt\ *n* **1 :** VAGABOND **2 :** FUGITIVE

run•around \ˈrə-nə-ˌrau̇nd\ *n* **:** evasive or delaying action especially in response to a request

[1]**run•away** \ˈrə-nə-ˌwā\ *n* **1 :** one that runs away **:** FUGITIVE **2 :** the act of running away out of control; *also* **:** something (as a horse) that is running out of control

[2]**runaway** *adj* **1 :** FUGITIVE **2 :** won by a long lead; *also* **:** extremely successful **3 :** subject to uncontrolled changes ⟨~ inflation⟩ **4 :** operating out of control ⟨a ~ locomotive⟩

run away *vb* ♦ **:** to leave quickly in order to avoid or escape something

♦ abscond, clear out, escape, flee, fly, get out, lam, run off

run•down \ˈrən-ˌdau̇n\ *n* **:** an item-by-item report or review **:** SUMMARY

run–down \ˈrən-ˈdau̇n\ *adj* **1 :** EXHAUSTED, WORN-OUT ⟨that ~ feeling⟩ **2 :** being in poor repair ⟨a ~ farm⟩

run down *vb* **1 :** to collide with and knock down **2 :** to chase until exhausted or captured **3** ♦ **:** to find by search **4 :** DISPARAGE **5 :** to cease to operate for lack of motive power **6 :** to decline in physical condition

♦ detect, determine, dig up, discover, ferret out, hit on, locate, track down

rune \ˈrün\ *n* **1 :** any of the characters of any of several alphabets formerly used by the Germanic peoples **2 :** MYSTERY, MAGIC **3 :** a poem especially in Finnish or Old Norse — **ru•nic** \ˈrü-nik\ *adj*

[1]**rung** *past part of* RING

[2]**rung** \ˈrəŋ\ *n* **1 :** a rounded crosspiece between the legs of a chair **2 :** one of the crosspieces of a ladder

run–in \ˈrən-ˌin\ *n* **1** ♦ **:** a noisy heated angry dispute **2 :** something run in

♦ brush, encounter, hassle, scrape, skirmish

run in *vb* **1 :** to insert as additional matter **2 :** to arrest especially for a minor offense **3 :** to pay a casual visit

run•nel \ˈrən-ᵊl\ *n* **:** BROOK, STREAMLET

run•ner \ˈrə-nər\ *n* **1 :** one that runs **2 :** BASE RUNNER **3 :** BALLCARRIER **4 :** a thin piece or part on which something (as a sled or an ice skate) slides **5 :** the support of a drawer or a sliding door **6 :** a horizontal branch from the base of a plant that produces new plants **7 :** a plant producing runners **8 :** a long narrow carpet **9 :** a narrow decorative cloth cover for a table or dresser top **10** ♦ **:** one who bears a message or does an errand

♦ courier, go-between, messenger, page

run•ner–up \ˈrə-nər-ˌəp\ *n, pl* **runners–up** *also* **runner–ups :** the competitor in a contest who finishes second

[1]**run•ning** *adj* **1 :** FLOWING **2 :** FLUID, RUNNY **3 :** CONTINUOUS, INCESSANT **4 :** measured in a straight line ⟨cost per ~ foot⟩ **5 :** of or relating to an act of running **6 :** made or trained for running ⟨~ horse⟩ ⟨~ shoes⟩ **7** ♦ **:** carrying on a function or being in action

♦ active, alive, functional, living, on, operational, operative, working

[2]**running** *adv* **:** in succession

running light *n* **:** any of the lights carried by a vehicle (as a ship) at night

run•ny \ˈrə-nē\ *adj* ♦ **:** having a tendency to run ⟨a ~ dough⟩ ⟨a ~ nose⟩

♦ fluent, fluid, liquid

run•off \ˈrən-ˌȯf\ *n* **:** a final contest (as an election) to decide a previous indecisive contest

run off *vb* **1** ♦ **:** to drive off (as trespassers) **2** ♦ **:** to run away

♦ [1] banish, boot (out), bounce, cast, chase, dismiss, drum, eject, expel, oust, rout, throw out ♦ [2] bolt, break, flee, fly, retreat, run, run away

run–of–the–mill *adj* ♦ **:** not outstanding

♦ average, common, commonplace, everyday, normal, ordinary, prosaic, routine, standard, unexceptional, unremarkable, usual, workaday

run on *vb* **1** ♦ **:** to talk at length **2 :** to continue (matter in type) without a break or a new paragraph **3 :** to place or add (as an entry in a dictionary) at the end of a paragraphed item **4** ♦ **:** to keep going — **run–on** \ˈrən-ˌȯn, -ˌän\ *n*

♦ [1] maunder, ramble, rattle ♦ [4] abide, continue, endure, hold, keep up, last, persist

run out *vb* **:** to use up or exhaust a supply ⟨*ran out* of gas⟩
runt \ˈrənt\ *n* ♦ **:** an unusually small person or animal **:** DWARF — **runty** *adj*

♦ dwarf, midget, mite, peewee, pygmy, scrub, shrimp

run through *vb* ♦ **:** to spend or consume wastefully

♦ blow, dissipate, fritter, lavish, misspend, spend, squander, throw away, waste

run•way \ˈrən-ˌwā\ *n* **1 :** a beaten path made by animals; *also* **:** a passage for animals **2 :** a paved strip of ground for the landing and takeoff of aircraft **3 :** a narrow platform from a stage into an auditorium **4 :** a support (as a track) on which something runs
ru•pee \rü-ˈpē, ˈrü-ˌpē\ *n* **:** the basic monetary unit of several countries on the Indian subcontinent (as India and Pakistan)
[1]**rup•ture** \ˈrəp-chər\ *n* **:** a breaking or tearing apart; *also* **:** HERNIA
[2]**rupture** *vb* **rup•tured; rup•tur•ing :** to cause or undergo rupture
ru•ral \ˈru̇r-əl\ *adj* ♦ **:** of or relating to the country, country people, or agriculture

♦ bucolic, country, pastoral, rustic ***Ant*** urban

ruse \ˈrüs, ˈrüz\ *n* **:** a wily subterfuge **:** TRICK, ARTIFICE
[1]**rush** \ˈrəsh\ *n* **:** any of various often tufted and hollow-stemmed grasslike marsh plants — **rushy** *adj*
[2]**rush** *vb* **1** ♦ **:** to move forward or act with too great haste or eagerness or without preparation **2 :** to perform in a short time or at high speed **3** ♦ **:** to run toward or against in attack **:** CHARGE **4** ♦ **:** to urge to an unnatural or extreme speed — **rush•er** *n*

♦ [1] dash, fly, hasten, hurry, pelt, race, rip, rocket, run, shoot, speed, whirl, whisk, zip, zoom ♦ [3] assail, assault, attack, beset, charge, descend, jump, pounce (on *or* upon), raid, storm, strike ♦ [4] accelerate, hasten, hurry, quicken, speed (up), step up, whisk

[3]**rush** *n* **1** ♦ **:** a violent forward motion **2 :** unusual demand or activity **3 :** a crowding of people to one place **4 :** a running play in football **5 :** a sudden feeling of pleasure **6** ♦ **:** a burst of activity, productivity, or speed

♦ [1] aggression, assault, attack, charge, descent, offense (*or* offence), offensive, onset, onslaught, raid, strike ♦ [6] haste, hurry, hustle, precipitation

[4]**rush** *adj* **:** requiring or marked by special speed or urgency ⟨~ orders⟩
rush hour *n* **:** a time when the amount of traffic or business is at a peak
rusk \ˈrəsk\ *n* **:** a sweet or plain bread baked, sliced, and baked again until dry and crisp
rus•set \ˈrə-sət\ *n* **1 :** a coarse reddish brown cloth **2 :** a reddish brown **3 :** a baking potato — **russet** *adj*

Rus•sian \ˈrə-shən\ *n* **1 :** a native or inhabitant of Russia **2 :** a Slavic language of the Russian people — **Russian** *adj*
rust \ˈrəst\ *n* **1 :** a reddish coating formed on iron when it is exposed to especially moist air **2 :** any of numerous plant diseases characterized by usually reddish spots; *also* **:** a fungus causing rust **3 :** a strong reddish brown — **rust** *vb* — **rusty** *adj*
[1]**rus•tic** \ˈrəs-tik\ *adj* ♦ **:** of, relating to, or suitable for the country or country people — **rus•ti•cal•ly** \-ti-k(ə-)lē\ *adv* — **rus•tic•i•ty** \ˌrəs-ˈti-sə-tē\ *n*

♦ bucolic, country, pastoral, rural

[2]**rustic** *n* ♦ **:** a rustic person

♦ bumpkin, clodhopper, hick, hillbilly, provincial, yokel

rus•ti•cate \ˈrəs-ti-ˌkāt\ *vb* **-cat•ed; -cat•ing :** to go into or reside in the country — **rus•ti•ca•tion** \ˌrəs-ti-ˈkā-shən\ *n*
[1]**rus•tle** \ˈrə-səl\ *vb* **rus•tled; rus•tling 1 :** to make or cause a rustle **2 :** to cause to rustle ⟨~ a newspaper⟩ **3 a :** to act or move with energy or speed **b :** to procure in this way **4 :** to forage food **5 :** to steal cattle from the range
[2]**rustle** *n* **:** a quick series of small sounds ⟨~ of leaves⟩
rus•tler *n* **:** one that rustles: as **a :** an alert energetic driving person **b :** a cattle thief
[1]**rut** \ˈrət\ *n* **:** state or period of sexual excitement especially in male deer — **rut** *vb*
[2]**rut** *n* **1 :** a track worn by wheels or by habitual passage of something **2** ♦ **:** a usual or fixed routine

♦ groove, pattern, rote, routine, treadmill

ru•ta•ba•ga \ˌrü-tə-ˈbā-gə, ˌru̇-\ *n* **:** a turnip with a large yellowish root
Ruth \ˈrüth\ *n* **:** a book of Jewish and Christian Scripture
ru•the•ni•um \rü-ˈthē-nē-əm\ *n* **:** a hard brittle metallic chemical element
ruth•er•ford•ium \ˌrə-t͟hər-ˈfȯr-dē-əm\ *n* **:** an artifically produced radioactive chemical element
ruth•less \ˈrüth-ləs\ *adj* ♦ **:** having no pity **:** MERCILESS — **ruth•less•ly** *adv* — **ruth•less•ness** *n*

♦ callous, hard, heartless, inhuman, inhumane, pitiless, soulless, unfeeling, unsympathetic

[1]**RV** \ˌär-ˈvē\ *n* ♦ **:** a vehicle designed for recreational use (as camping) **:** RECREATIONAL VEHICLE

♦ camper, caravan, motor home, recreational vehicle, trailer

[2]**RV** *abbr* Revised Version
R–value \ˈär-ˌval-yü\ *n* **:** a measure of resistance to the flow of heat through a substance (as insulation)
RW *abbr* **1** right worshipful **2** right worthy
rwy *or* **ry** *abbr* railway
-ry \rē\ *n suffix* **:** -ERY ⟨bigot*ry*⟩
rye \ˈrī\ *n* **1 :** a hardy annual grass grown for grain or as a cover crop; *also* **:** its seed **2 :** a whiskey distilled from a rye mash

S

[1]**s** \ˈes\ *n, pl* **s's** *or* **ss** \ˈe-səz\ *often cap* **:** the 19th letter of the English alphabet
[2]**s** *abbr, often cap* **1** saint **2** second **3** senate **4** series **5** shilling **6** singular **7** small **8** son **9** south; southern
[1]**-s** \s *after sounds* f, k, k̟, p, t, th; əz *after sounds* ch, j, s, sh, z, zh; z *after other sounds*\ *n pl suffix* — used to form the plural of most nouns that do not end in *s, z, sh,* or *ch* or in *y* following a consonant ⟨head*s*⟩ ⟨book*s*⟩ ⟨boy*s*⟩ ⟨belief*s*⟩, to form the plural of proper nouns that end in *y* following a consonant ⟨Mary*s*⟩, and with or without a preceding apostrophe to form the plural of abbreviations, numbers, letters, and symbols used as nouns ⟨MC*s*⟩ ⟨4*s*⟩ ⟨#*s*⟩ ⟨B'*s*⟩
[2]**-s** *adv suffix* — used to form adverbs denoting usual or repeated action or state ⟨works night*s*⟩
[3]**-s** *vb suffix* — used to form the third person singular present of most verbs that do not end in *s, z, sh,* or *ch* or in *y* followng a consonant ⟨fall*s*⟩ ⟨take*s*⟩ ⟨play*s*⟩

S *symbol* sulfur
SA *abbr* **1** Salvation Army **2** seaman apprentice **3** sex appeal **4** without date **5** South Africa **6** South America **7** subject to approval
Sab•bath \ˈsa-bəth\ *n* **1 :** the 7th day of the week observed as a day of worship by Jews and some Christians **2 :** Sunday observed among Christians as a day of worship
sab•bat•i•cal \sə-ˈba-ti-kəl\ *n* **:** a leave often with pay granted (as to a college professor) usually every 7th year for rest, travel, or research
sa•ber *or* **sa•bre** \ˈsā-bər\ *n* **:** a cavalry sword with a curved blade and thick back
saber saw *n* **:** a portable electric saw with a pointed reciprocating blade; *esp* **:** JIGSAW
sa•ble \ˈsā-bəl\ *n, pl* **sables 1 :** the color black **2** *pl* **:** mourning garments **3 :** a dark brown mammal chiefly of northern Asia related to the weasels; *also* **:** its fur or pelt

[1]**sab•o•tage** \ˈsa-bə-ˌtäzh\ *n* **1 :** deliberate destruction of an employer's property or hindering of production by workers **2 :** destructive or hampering action by enemy agents or sympathizers in time of war
[2]**sabotage** *vb* **-taged; -tag•ing :** to practice sabotage on **:** WRECK
sab•o•teur \ˌsa-bə-ˈtər\ *n* **:** a person who practices sabotage
sac \ˈsak\ *n* **:** a pouch in an animal or plant often containing a fluid
SAC *abbr* Strategic Air Command
sac•cha•rin \ˈsa-kə-rən\ *n* **:** a white crystalline compound used as an artificial calorie-free sweetener
sac•cha•rine \ˈsa-kə-rən\ *adj* ♦ **:** nauseatingly sweet ⟨~ poetry⟩

♦ corny, maudlin, mawkish, mushy, sappy, schmaltzy, sentimental

sac•er•do•tal \ˌsa-sər-ˈdōt-ᵊl, -kər-\ *adj* ♦ **:** of or relating to priests or a priesthood **:** PRIESTLY

♦ clerical, ministerial, pastoral, priestly

sac•er•do•tal•ism \-ᵊl-ˌi-zəm\ *n* **:** a religious belief emphasizing the powers of priests as essential mediators between God and man
sa•chem \ˈsā-chəm\ *n* **:** a No. American Indian chief
sa•chet \sa-ˈshā\ *n* **:** a small bag filled with perfumed powder for scenting clothes
[1]**sack** \ˈsak\ *n* **1 :** a usually rectangular-shaped bag (as of paper or burlap) **2 :** a loose jacket or short coat **3** ♦ **:** a place for sleeping ⟨hit the ~⟩

♦ bed, bunk, pad

[2]**sack** *vb* ♦ **:** to dismiss especially summarily **:** FIRE

♦ cashier, dismiss, fire, remove, retire

[3]**sack** *n* **:** a white wine popular in England in the 16th and 17th centuries
[4]**sack** *vb* ♦ **:** to plunder a captured town

♦ despoil, loot, maraud, pillage, plunder, ransack, strip

sack•cloth \-ˌklȯth\ *n* **:** a rough garment worn as a sign of penitence
sac•ra•ment \ˈsa-krə-mənt\ *n* **1 :** a formal religious act or rite; *esp* **:** one (as baptism or the Eucharist) held to have been instituted by Christ **2 :** the elements of the Eucharist — **sac•ra•men•tal** \ˌsa-krə-ˈment-ᵊl\ *adj*
sa•cred \ˈsā-krəd\ *adj* **1** ♦ **:** set apart for the service or worship of deity **2 :** devoted exclusively to one service or use **3** ♦ **:** worthy of veneration or reverence **4** ♦ **:** of or relating to religion **:** RELIGIOUS — **sa•cred•ly** *adv* — **sa•cred•ness** *n*

♦ [1] blessed, hallowed, holy, sacrosanct, sanctified ♦ [3] holy, inviolable, sacrosanct ♦ [4] devotional, religious, spiritual

sacred cow *n* **:** one that is often unreasonably immune from criticism
[1]**sac•ri•fice** \ˈsa-krə-ˌfīs\ *n* **1 :** the offering of something precious to deity **2** ♦ **:** something offered in sacrifice **3 :** LOSS, DEPRIVATION **4 :** a bunt allowing a base runner to advance while the batter is put out; *also* **:** a fly ball allowing a runner to score after the catch — **sac•ri•fi•cial** \ˌsa-krə-ˈfi-shəl\ *adj* — **sac•ri•fi•cial•ly** *adv*

♦ victim

[2]**sac•ri•fice** *vb* **-ficed; -fic•ing 1** ♦ **:** to offer up or kill as a sacrifice **2 :** to accept the loss or destruction of for an end, cause, or ideal **3 :** to make a sacrifice in baseball

♦ offer

sac•ri•lege \ˈsa-krə-lij\ *n* **1** ♦ **:** violation of something consecrated to God **2** ♦ **:** gross irreverence toward a hallowed person, place, or thing

♦ [1, 2] blasphemy, defilement, desecration, impiety, irreverence

sac•ri•le•gious \ˌsa-krə-ˈli-jəs, -ˈlē-\ *adj* ♦ **:** committing sacrilege **:** characterized by or involving sacrilege — **sac•ri•le•gious•ly** *adv*

♦ blasphemous, irreverent, profane

sac•ris•tan \ˈsa-krə-stən\ *n* **1 :** a church officer in charge of the sacristy **2 :** SEXTON
sac•ris•ty \ˈsa-krə-stē\ *n, pl* **-ties :** VESTRY
sac•ro•il•i•ac \ˌsa-krō-ˈi-lē-ˌak\ *n* **:** the joint between the upper part of the hipbone and the sacrum
sac•ro•sanct \ˈsa-krō-ˌsaŋkt\ *adj* **1** ♦ **:** most sacred or holy **2** ♦ **:** treated as if holy **:** immune from criticism

♦ [1] blessed, hallowed, holy, sacred, sanctified ♦ [2] holy, inviolable, sacred

sa•crum \ˈsa-krəm, ˈsā-\ *n, pl* **sa•cra** \ˈsa-krə, ˈsā-\ **:** the part of the vertebral column that is directly connected with or forms a part of the pelvis and in humans consists of five fused vertebrae
sad \ˈsad\ *adj* **sad•der; sad•dest 1** ♦ **:** affected with or expressive of grief or unhappiness **:** DOWNCAST **2** ♦ **:** causing sorrow **3 :** DULL, SOMBER

♦ [1] bad, blue, dejected, depressed, disconsolate, down, downcast, droopy, forlorn, gloomy, glum, low, melancholy, miserable, mournful, sorrowful, sorry, unhappy, woeful, wretched ***Ant*** cheerful, chipper, glad, happy, joyful, joyous, sunny, upbeat ♦ [2] depressing, dismal, dreary, heartbreaking, melancholy, pathetic, sorry, tearful ***Ant*** cheering, cheery, glad, happy

sad•den \ˈsad-ᵊn\ *vb* ♦ **:** to make or become sad

♦ burden, depress, oppress

[1]**sad•dle** \ˈsad-ᵊl\ *n* **:** a usually padded leather-covered seat (as for a rider on horseback)
[2]**saddle** *vb* **sad•dled; sad•dling 1 :** to put a saddle on **2** ♦ **:** to place a burden or encumbrance upon **:** BURDEN

♦ burden, encumber, load, lumber, weight

sad•dle•bow \ˈsad-ᵊl-ˌbō\ *n* **:** the arch in the front of a saddle
saddle horse *n* **:** a horse suited for or trained for riding
Sad•du•cee \ˈsa-jə-ˌsē, ˈsa-dyə-\ *n* **:** a member of an ancient Jewish sect consisting of a ruling class of priests and rejecting certain doctrines — **Sad•du•ce•an** \ˌsa-jə-ˈsē-ən, ˌsa-dyə-\ *adj*
sad•iron \ˈsa-ˌdi-ərn\ *n* **:** a flatiron with a removable handle
sa•dism \ˈsā-ˌdi-zəm, ˈsa-\ *n* **1 :** a sexual perversion in which gratification is obtained by inflicting physical or mental pain on others **2** ♦ **:** delight in physical or mental cruelty; *also* **:** excessive cruelty — **sa•dist** \ˈsā-dist, ˈsa-\ *n*

♦ barbarity, brutality, cruelty, inhumanity, savagery, viciousness, wantonness

sa•dis•tic \sə-ˈdis-tik\ *adj* ♦ **:** of or characterized by sadism — **sa•dis•ti•cal•ly** \-ti-k(ə-)lē\ *adv*

♦ barbarous, brutal, cruel, heartless, inhumane, savage, vicious, wanton

sad•ly *adv* ♦ **:** in a sad manner or way

♦ agonizingly, bitterly, grievously, hard, hardly, sorrowfully, unhappily, woefully, wretchedly

sad•ness *n* ♦ **:** the quality or state of being sad **:** an instance (as a mood or an appearance) of being sad

♦ blues, dejection, depression, desolation, despondency, doldrums, dumps, forlornness, gloom, heartsickness, melancholy ***Ant*** elation, euphoria, exuberance, gladness, happiness, joy, joyousness, jubilation

SAE *abbr* **1** self-addressed envelope **2** Society of Automotive Engineers **3** stamped addressed envelope
sa•fa•ri \sə-ˈfär-ē, -ˈfar-\ *n* **1 :** a hunting expedition especially in eastern Africa **2 :** JOURNEY, TRIP
[1]**safe** \ˈsāf\ *adj* **saf•er; saf•est 1** ♦ **:** free from harm or risk **2** ♦ **:** secure from danger or loss **3 :** affording safety **4** ♦ **:** not likely to take risks; *also* **:** RELIABLE **5** ♦ **:** not threatening danger — **safe•ly** *adv*

♦ [1, 2] all right, alright, secure ***Ant*** endangered, imperiled, insecure, liable, threatened, unsafe, vulnerable ♦ [4] dependable, good, reliable, responsible, solid, steady, sure, tried, true, trustworthy ♦ [5] harmless, innocent, innocuous, white

[2]**safe** *n* **:** a container for keeping articles (as valuables) safe
safe–con•duct \-ˈkän-(ˌ)dəkt\ *n* **:** a pass permitting a person to go through enemy lines
[1]**safe•guard** \-ˌgärd\ *n* ♦ **:** a measure or device for preventing accident

♦ aegis, armor (*or* armour), cover, defense (*or* defence), guard, protection, screen, security, shield, wall, ward

[2]**safeguard** *vb* ♦ **:** to provide a safeguard for **:** PROTECT

♦ cover, defend, guard, protect, screen, secure, shield, ward

safe•keep•ing \ˈsāf-ˈkē-piŋ\ *n* ♦ **:** a keeping or being kept in safety

♦ care, custody, guardianship, keeping, trust, ward

safe sex *n* **:** sexual activity and especially sexual intercourse in which various measures (as the use of latex condoms) are taken to avoid disease (as AIDS) transmitted by sexual contact

safe•ty \ˈsāf-tē\ *n, pl* **safeties** **1 :** freedom from danger **:** SECURITY **2 :** a protective device **3 :** a football play in which the ball is downed by the offensive team behind its own goal line **4 :** a defensive football back in the deepest position — **safety** *adj*

safety glass *n* **:** shatter-resistant material formed of two sheets of glass with a sheet of clear plastic between them

safety match *n* **:** a match that ignites only when struck on a special surface

saf•flow•er \ˈsa-ˌflau̇-ər\ *n* **:** a widely grown Old World herb related to the daisies that has large orange or red flower heads yielding a dyestuff and seeds rich in edible oil

saf•fron \ˈsa-frən\ *n* **:** a deep orange powder from the flower of a crocus used to color and flavor foods

¹sag \ˈsag\ *vb* **sagged; sag•ging** **1 :** to droop or settle from or as if from pressure **2** ♦ **:** to lose firmness or vigor

♦ decay, droop, fail, flag, go, lag, languish, waste, weaken, wilt

²sag *n* **1 :** a sagging part **2** ♦ **:** an instance or amount of sagging

♦ droop, slack, slackness

sa•ga \ˈsä-gə\ *n* **:** a narrative of heroic deeds; *esp* **:** one recorded in Iceland in the 12th and 13th centuries

sa•ga•cious \sə-ˈgā-shəs\ *adj* ♦ **:** of keen mind

♦ discerning, insightful, perceptive, sage, sapient, wise

sa•gac•i•ty \-ˈga-sə-tē\ *n* ♦ **:** the quality of being sagacious

♦ discernment, insight, perception, sapience, wisdom

sag•a•more \ˈsa-gə-ˌmōr\ *n* **:** a subordinate No. American Indian chief

¹sage \ˈsāj\ *adj* ♦ **:** wise through reflection and experience; *also* **:** proceeding from or characterized by wisdom, prudence, and good judgment — **sage•ly** *adv*

♦ discerning, insightful, perceptive, sagacious, sapient, wise

²sage *n* **:** one who is distinguished for wisdom

³sage *n* **1 :** a perennial mint with aromatic leaves used in flavoring; *also* **:** its leaves **2 :** SAGEBRUSH

sage•brush \ˈsāj-ˌbrəsh\ *n* **:** any of several low shrubby No. American composite plants; *esp* **:** one of the western U.S. with a sagelike odor

Sag•it•tar•i•us \ˌsa-jə-ˈter-ē-əs\ *n* **1 :** a zodiacal constellation between Scorpio and Capricorn usually pictured as a centaur archer **2 :** the 9th sign of the zodiac in astrology; *also* **:** one born under this sign

sa•go \ˈsā-gō\ *n, pl* **sagos** **:** a dry granulated starch especially from the pith of various tropical palms (**sago palm**)

sa•gua•ro \sə-ˈwär-ə, -ˈgwär-, -ō\ *n, pl* **-ros** **:** a tall columnar usually sparsely-branched cactus of dry areas of the southwestern U.S. and Mexico that may attain a height of up to 50 feet (16 meters)

said *past and past part of* SAY

¹sail \ˈsāl\ *n* **1 :** a piece of fabric by means of which the wind is used to propel a ship **2 :** a sailing ship **3 :** something resembling a sail **4** ♦ **:** a trip on a sailboat

♦ crossing, cruise, passage, voyage

²sail *vb* **1** ♦ **:** to travel on a sailing ship **2 :** to pass over in a ship **3 :** to manage or direct the course of a ship **4** ♦ **:** to move with ease, grace, nonchalance, or without resistance **5** ♦ **:** to travel on water; *also* **:** to move through the air

♦ [1] boat, cruise, navigate, voyage ♦ [4] bowl, breeze, coast, drift, flow, glide, roll, skim, slide, slip, stream, sweep, whisk ♦ [5] drift, float, glide, hang, hover, poise, ride, waft

sail•board \ˈsāl-ˌbōrd\ *n* **:** a modified surfboard having a mast and sailed by a standing person

sail•boat \-ˌbōt\ *n* **:** a boat propelled primarily by sail

sail•cloth \-ˌklȯth\ *n* **:** a heavy canvas used for sails, tents, or upholstery

sail•fish \-ˌfish\ *n* **:** any of a genus of large marine bony fishes with a large dorsal fin that are related to marlins

sail•ing *n* **:** the sport of handling or riding in a sailboat

sail•or \ˈsā-lər\ *n* ♦ **:** one that sails; *esp* **:** a member of a ship's crew

♦ gob, jack, jack-tar, mariner, seaman, swab, tar

sail•plane \ˈsāl-ˌplān\ *n* **:** a glider designed to rise in an upward air current

saint \ˈsānt, *before a name* (ˌ)sānt *or* sənt\ *n* **1 :** one officially recognized as preeminent for holiness **2 :** one of the spirits of the departed in heaven **3 :** a holy or godly person

Saint Ber•nard \-bər-ˈnärd\ *n* **:** any of a Swiss alpine breed of tall powerful working dogs used especially formerly in aiding lost travelers

saint•ed \-ˈsān-təd\ *adj* ♦ **:** relating to, resembling, or befitting a saint; *esp* **:** marked by or showing reverence for deity and devotion to divine worship

♦ devout, faithful, godly, holy, pious, religious, saintly

saint•hood \-ˌhu̇d\ *n* ♦ **:** the quality or state of being a saint

♦ blessedness, devoutness, godliness, holiness, piety, sanctity

Saint–John's–wort \ˈsānt-ˈjänz-ˌwərt, -ˌwȯrt\ *n* **1 :** any of a genus of herbs and shrubs with showy yellow flowers **2 :** the dried aerial parts of a Saint-John's-wort used especially in herbal remedies

saint•li•ness \-lē-nəs\ *n* **:** the quality or state of being saintly

saint•ly \ˈsānt-lē\ *adj* ♦ **:** relating to, resembling, or befitting a saint

♦ devout, faithful, godly, holy, pious, religious, sainted

Saint Val•en•tine's Day \-ˈva-lən-ˌtīnz-\ *n* **:** VALENTINE'S DAY

¹sake \ˈsāk\ *n* **1 :** END, PURPOSE **2 :** personal or social welfare, safety, or well-being

²sa•ke *or* **sa•ki** \ˈsä-kē\ *n* **:** a Japanese alcoholic beverage of fermented rice

sa•laam \sə-ˈläm\ *n* **1 :** a salutation or ceremonial greeting in the East **2 :** an obeisance performed by bowing very low and placing the right palm on the forehead — **salaam** *vb*

sa•la•cious \sə-ˈlā-shəs\ *adj* **1 :** arousing sexual desire or imagination **2 :** LUSTFUL — **sa•la•cious•ly** *adv* — **sa•la•cious•ness** *n*

sal•ad \ˈsa-ləd\ *n* **:** a cold dish (as of lettuce, vegetables, fish, eggs, or fruit) served with dressing

sal•a•man•der \ˈsa-lə-ˌman-dər\ *n* **:** any of numerous amphibians that look like lizards but have scaleless usually smooth moist skin

sa•la•mi \sə-ˈlä-mē\ *n* **:** a highly seasoned sausage of pork and beef

sal•a•ry \ˈsa-lə-rē\ *n, pl* **-ries** ♦ **:** payment made at regular intervals for services

♦ emolument, hire, pay, payment, stipend, wage

sale \ˈsāl\ *n* **1** ♦ **:** transfer of ownership of property from one person to another in return for money **2 :** ready market **:** DEMAND **3 :** AUCTION **4 :** a selling of goods at bargain prices — **sal•able** *or* **sale•able** \ˈsā-lə-bəl\ *adj*

♦ deal, trade, transaction

sales•girl \ˈsālz-ˌgərl\ *n* **:** SALESWOMAN

sales•man \-mən\ *n* **:** a person who sells in a store or to outside customers — **sales•man•ship** *n*

sales•per•son \-ˌpər-sən\ *n* **:** a salesman or saleswoman

sales•wom•an \-ˌwu̇-mən\ *n* **:** a woman who sells merchandise

sal•i•cyl•ic acid \ˌsa-lə-ˈsi-lik-\ *n* **:** a crystalline organic acid used in making aspirin and other medicinal preparations (as skin lotions)

¹sa•lient \ˈsāl-yənt, ˈsā-lē-ənt\ *adj* **:** jutting forward beyond a line; *also* **:** PROMINENT

²salient *n* **:** a projecting part in a line of defense

¹sa•line \ˈsā-ˌlēn, -ˌlīn\ *adj* ♦ **:** consisting of or containing salt **:** SALTY — **sa•lin•i•ty** \sā-ˈli-nə-tē, sə-\ *n*

♦ briny, salty

²saline *n* **1 :** a metallic salt especially with a purgative action **2 :** a saline solution

sa•li•va \sə-ˈlī-və\ *n* ♦ **:** a liquid secreted into the mouth that helps digestion — **sal•i•vary** \ˈsa-lə-ˌver-ē\ *adj*

♦ slobber, spit

sal•i•vate \ˈsa-lə-ˌvāt\ *vb* **-vat•ed; -vat•ing** ♦ **:** to produce saliva especially in excess — **sal•i•va•tion** \ˌsa-lə-ˈvā-shən\ *n*

♦ dribble, drivel, drool, slaver, slobber

sal•low \ˈsa-lō\ *adj* ♦ **:** of a yellowish sickly color ⟨a ~ face⟩

♦ cadaverous, green, lurid, pale, pasty, peaked, sickly

¹sal•ly \ˈsa-lē\ *n, pl* **sallies** **1 :** a rushing attack on besiegers by troops of a besieged place **2** ♦ **:** a witty remark or retort **3** ♦ **:** a brief excursion

♦ [2] crack, gag, jest, joke, laugh, pleasantry, quip, waggery, wisecrack, witticism ♦ [3] excursion, jaunt, junket, outing

²sally *vb* **sal•lied; sal•ly•ing 1 :** to leap out or burst forth suddenly **2 ♦ :** to start out on a course or a journey — often used with *forth*

♦ *usu* **sally forth** clear out, depart, exit, get off, go, move, pull, quit, shove, take off

salm•on \ˈsa-mən\ *n, pl* **salmon** *also* **salmons 1 :** any of several bony fishes with pinkish flesh that are used for food and are related to the trouts **2 :** a strong yellowish pink color
sal•mo•nel•la \ˌsal-mə-ˈne-lə\ *n, pl* **-nel•lae** \-ˈne-(ˌ)lē, -ˌlī\ *or* **-nellas** *or* **-nella :** any of a genus of rod-shaped bacteria that cause various illnesses (as food poisoning)
sa•lon \sə-ˈlän, ˈsa-ˌlän, sa-ˈlōⁿ\ *n* **1 :** an elegant drawing room **2 ♦ :** a fashionable shop ⟨beauty ~⟩

♦ establishment, place

sa•loon \sə-ˈlün\ *n* **1 :** a large public cabin on a ship **2 ♦ :** a place where liquors are sold and drunk **:** BARROOM **3** *Brit* **:** SEDAN 2

♦ bar, barroom, café, pub, public house, tavern

sal•sa \ˈsȯl-sə, ˈsäl-\ *n* **:** a spicy sauce of tomatoes, onions, and hot peppers
¹salt \ˈsȯlt\ *n* **1 :** a white crystalline substance that consists of sodium and chlorine and is used in seasoning foods **2 :** a saltlike cathartic substance (as Epsom salts) **3 :** a compound formed usually by action of an acid on metal **4 :** one that sails **:** SAILOR — **salt•i•ness** \ˈsȯl-tē-nəs\ *n*
²salt *vb* **:** to preserve, season, or feed with salt
³salt *adj* **:** preserved or treated with salt; *also* **:** SALTY
SALT *abbr* Strategic Arms Limitation Talks
salt away *vb* **♦ :** to lay away safely

♦ cache, hoard, lay away, lay up, put by, stash, stockpile, store

salt•box \ˈsȯlt-ˌbäks\ *n* **:** a frame dwelling with two stories in front and one behind and a long sloping roof
salt•cel•lar \-ˌse-lər\ *n* **:** a small container for holding salt at the table
sal•tine \sȯl-ˈtēn\ *n* **:** a thin crisp cracker sprinkled with salt
salt lick *n* **:** LICK 5
salt•pe•ter \ˈsȯlt-ˈpē-tər\ *n* **1 :** POTASSIUM NITRATE **2 :** SODIUM NITRATE
salt•wa•ter \-ˌwȯ-tər, -ˌwä-\ *adj* **:** of, relating to, or living in salt water
salty \ˈsȯl-tē\ *adj* **salt•i•er; -est 1 ♦ :** of, seasoned with, or containing salt **2 :** suggesting the sea or nautical life **3 ♦ :** marked by uncultivated vulgarity

♦ [1] briny, saline ♦ [3] racy, spicy, suggestive

sa•lu•bri•ous \sə-ˈlü-brē-əs\ *adj* **♦ :** favorable to health

♦ healthful, healthy, restorative, salutary, wholesome

sal•u•tary \ˈsal-yə-ˌter-ē\ *adj* **♦ :** health-giving; *also* **:** BENEFICIAL

♦ advantageous, beneficial, favorable (*or* favourable), helpful, profitable ♦ healthful, healthy, restorative, salubrious, wholesome

sal•u•ta•tion \ˌsal-yə-ˈtā-shən\ *n* **♦ :** an expression of greeting, goodwill, or courtesy usually by word or gesture; *also* **:** a speech of honor or praise

♦ greeting, hello, salute ♦ accolade, citation, commendation, encomium, eulogy, homage, paean, panegyric, tribute

sa•lu•ta•to•ri•an \sə-ˌlü-tə-ˈtōr-ē-ən\ *n* **:** the student having the 2d highest rank in a graduating class who delivers the salutatory address
sa•lu•ta•to•ry \sə-ˈlü-tə-ˌtōr-ē\ *adj* **:** relating to or being the welcoming oration delivered at an academic commencement
¹sa•lute \sə-ˈlüt\ *vb* **sa•lut•ed; sa•lut•ing 1 :** GREET **2 :** to honor by special ceremonies **3 :** to show respect to (a superior officer) by a formal position of hand, rifle, or sword **4 ♦ :** to express commendation of

♦ acclaim, applaud, cheer, crack up, hail, laud, praise, tout

²salute *n* **1 :** an expression of greeting, goodwill, or courtesy by word, gesture, or ceremony **:** GREETING **2 :** the formal position assumed in saluting a superior
¹sal•vage \ˈsal-vij\ *n* **1 :** money paid for saving a ship, its cargo, or passengers when the ship is wrecked or in danger **2 :** the saving of a ship **3 :** the saving of possessions in danger of being lost **4 :** things saved from loss or destruction (as by a wreck or fire)
²salvage *vb* **sal•vaged; sal•vag•ing :** to rescue from destruction
sal•va•tion \sal-ˈvā-shən\ *n* **1 :** the saving of a person from sin or its consequences especially in the life after death **2 ♦ :** the saving from danger, difficulty, or evil **3 :** something that saves

♦ deliverance, rescue

¹salve \ˈsav, ˈsȧv\ *n* **1 :** a medicinal substance applied to the skin **2 :** a soothing influence
²salve *vb* **salved; salv•ing :** EASE, SOOTHE
sal•ver \ˈsal-vər\ *n* **:** a small serving tray
sal•vo \ˈsal-vō\ *n, pl* **salvos** *or* **salvoes ♦ :** a simultaneous discharge of guns; *also* **:** something suggestive of a salvo

♦ barrage, bombardment, cannonade, fusillade, hail, shower, storm, volley

Sam *or* **Saml** *abbr* Samuel
SAM \ˈsam, ˌes-ˌā-ˈem\ *n* **:** a guided missile for use against aircraft by ground units
Sa•mar•i•tan \sə-ˈmer-ə-tən\ *n* **1 :** a native or inhabitant of Samaria **2 :** a person who is generous in helping those in distress
sa•mar•i•um \sə-ˈmer-ē-əm\ *n* **:** a silvery-white lustrous rare metallic chemical element
¹same \ˈsām\ *adj* **1 ♦ :** being the one referred to **:** not different **2 ♦ :** resembling in every relevant respect

♦ [1] identical, selfsame, very ***Ant*** another, different, other ♦ [2] duplicate, equal, even, identical, indistinguishable ***Ant*** different, dissimilar, distinguishable, other, unalike, unlike

²same *pron* **:** the same one or ones
³same *adv* **:** in the same manner
same•ness *n* **♦ :** the quality or state of being the same; *also* **:** tedious similarity

♦ equality, equivalence, par, parity

Sa•mi *also* **Saa•mi** \ˈsä-mē\ *n, pl* **Sami** *or* **Samis** *also* **Saami** *or* **Saamis :** a member of a people of northern Scandinavia, Finland, and the Kola Peninsula of Russia
Sa•mo•an \sə-ˈmō-ən\ *n* **:** a native or inhabitant of Samoa — **Samoan** *adj*
sa•mo•sa \sə-ˈmō-sə\ *n* **:** a small triangular pastry filled with spiced meat or vegetables and fried
sam•o•var \ˈsa-mə-ˌvär\ *n* **:** an urn with a spigot at the base used especially in Russia to boil water for tea
sam•pan \ˈsam-ˌpan\ *n* **:** a flat-bottomed skiff of eastern Asia usually propelled by two short oars
¹sam•ple \ˈsam-pəl\ *n* **♦ :** a representative piece, item, or set of individuals that shows the quality or nature of the whole from which it was taken **:** EXAMPLE

♦ case, example, exemplar, illustration, instance, representative, specimen

²sample *vb* **sam•pled; sam•pling :** to judge the quality of by a sample
sam•pler \ˈsam-plər\ *n* **:** a piece of needlework; *esp* **:** one testing skill in embroidering
Sam•u•el \ˈsam-yə-wəl\ *n* **:** either of two books of Jewish and Christian Scripture
sam•u•rai \ˈsa-mə-ˌrī, ˈsam-yə-\ *n, pl* **samurai :** a military retainer of a Japanese feudal lord who adhered to strict principles of honor and duty
san•a•to•ri•um \ˌsa-nə-ˈtōr-ē-əm\ *n, pl* **-ri•ums** *or* **-ria** \-ē-ə\ **1 :** a health resort **2 :** an establishment for the care especially of convalescents or the chronically ill
sanc•ti•fi•ca•tion \ˌsaŋk-tə-fə-ˈkā-shən\ *n* **♦ :** an act of sanctifying; *also* **:** the state of being sanctified

♦ blessing, consecration

sanc•ti•fied *adj* **♦ :** made holy **:** made free of sin; *also* **:** set apart to sacred duty or use

♦ blessed, hallowed, holy, sacred, sacrosanct

sanc•ti•fy \ˈsaŋk-tə-ˌfī\ *vb* **-fied; -fy•ing 1 ♦ :** to make holy **:** CONSECRATE **2 ♦ :** to free from sin

♦ [1] bless, consecrate, hallow ♦ [2] purify

sanc•ti•mo•nious \ˌsaŋk-tə-ˈmō-nē-əs\ *adj* **:** hypocritically pious — **sanc•ti•mo•nious•ly** *adv*
¹sanc•tion \ˈsaŋk-shən\ *n* **1 ♦ :** authoritative approval **2 :** a measure (as a threat or fine) designed to enforce a law or standard ⟨economic ~*s*⟩

♦ allowance, authorization, clearance, concurrence, consent, leave, license (*or* licence), permission, sufferance

²sanction *vb* **♦ :** to give approval to **:** RATIFY

♦ approve, authorize, clear, OK, ratify, warrant

sanc•ti•ty \ˈsaŋk-tə-tē\ *n, pl* **-ties 1 ♦ :** holiness of life and character **:** GODLINESS **2 :** SACREDNESS

♦ blessedness, devoutness, godliness, holiness, piety, sainthood

sanc•tu•ary \ˈsaŋk-chə-ˌwer-ē\ *n, pl* **-ar•ies** **1 :** a consecrated place (as the part of a church in which the altar is placed) **2** ♦ **:** a place of refuge ‹bird ∼›

♦ asylum, haven, refuge, retreat, shelter

sanc•tum \ˈsaŋk-təm\ *n, pl* **sanctums** *also* **sanc•ta** \-tə\ **:** a private office or study **:** DEN ‹an editor's ∼›

[1]**sand** \ˈsand\ *n* **1 :** loose particles of hard broken rock **2 :** a yellowish-gray color

[2]**sand** *vb* **1 :** to cover or fill with sand **2** ♦ **:** to scour, smooth, or polish with an abrasive (as sandpaper) — **sand•er** *n*

♦ buff, file, grind, hone, rasp, rub

san•dal \ˈsand-^{ə}l\ *n* **:** a shoe consisting of a sole strapped to the foot; *also* **:** a low or open slipper or rubber overshoe

san•dal•wood \-ˌwu̇d\ *n* **:** the fragrant yellowish heartwood of a parasitic tree of southern Asia that is much used in ornamental carving and cabinetwork; *also* **:** the tree

sand•bag \ˈsand-ˌbag\ *n* **:** a bag filled with sand and used in fortifications, as ballast, or as a weapon

sand•bank \-ˌbaŋk\ *n* **:** a deposit of sand (as in a bar or shoal)

sand•bar \-ˌbär\ *n* **:** a ridge of sand formed in water by tides or currents

sand•blast \-ˌblast\ *vb* **:** to treat with a stream of sand blown (as for cleaning stone) by compressed air — **sand•blast•er** *n*

sand dollar *n* **:** any of numerous flat circular sea urchins living chiefly on sandy bottoms in shallow water

S & H *abbr* shipping and handling

sand•hog \ˈsand-ˌhȯg, -ˌhäg\ *n* **:** a laborer who builds underwater tunnels

sand•lot \-ˌlät\ *n* **:** a vacant lot especially when used for the unorganized sports of children — **sand•lot** *adj* — **sand•lot•ter** *n*

sand•man \-ˌman\ *n* **:** the genie of folklore who makes children sleepy

sand•pa•per \-ˌpā-pər\ *n* **:** paper with abrasive (as sand) glued on one side used in smoothing and polishing surfaces — **sandpaper** *vb*

sand•pip•er \-ˌpī-pər\ *n* **:** any of various shorebirds with a soft-tipped bill longer than that of the related plovers

sand•stone \-ˌstōn\ *n* **:** rock made of sand united by a natural cement

sand•storm \-ˌstȯrm\ *n* **:** a windstorm that drives clouds of sand

sand trap *n* **:** a hazard on a golf course consisting of a hollow containing sand

[1]**sand•wich** \ˈsand-(ˌ)wich\ *n* **1 :** two or more slices of bread with a layer (as of meat or cheese) spread between them **2 :** something resembling a sandwich

[2]**sandwich** *vb* ♦ **:** to squeeze or crowd in

♦ cram, crowd, jam, ram, squeeze, stuff, wedge

sandy *adj* **sand•i•er; -est** **1 :** consisting of or containing sand **2** ♦ **:** of the color sand

♦ blond, fair, flaxen, golden, straw

sane \ˈsān\ *adj* **san•er; san•est** **1** ♦ **:** mentally sound and healthy **2 :** proceeding from a sound mind **:** SENSIBLE, RATIONAL — **sane•ly** *adv*

♦ balanced, clearheaded, lucid, normal, right, stable *Ant* crazed, crazy, demented, deranged, insane, lunatic, mad, maniacal, mental, unbalanced, unsound

sang *past of* SING

sang•froid \ˈsä^{n}-ˈfrwä\ *n* **:** self-possession or an imperturbable state especially under strain

san•gui•nary \ˈsaŋ-gwə-ˌner-ē\ *adj* ♦ **:** willing or anxious to shed blood; *also* **:** marked by bloodshed ‹∼ battle›

♦ bloodthirsty, bloody, homicidal, murderous, sanguine

san•guine \ˈsaŋ-gwən\ *adj* **1** ♦ **:** having a healthy reddish color **:** RUDDY **2** ♦ **:** anticipating the best **3 :** willing or anxious to shed blood

♦ [1] florid, flush, glowing, rosy, ruddy ♦ [2] assured, certain, clear, cocksure, confident, doubtless, positive, sure

sanit *abbr* sanitary; sanitation

san•i•tar•i•an \ˌsa-nə-ˈter-ē-ən\ *n* **:** a specialist in sanitation and public health

san•i•tar•i•um \ˌsa-nə-ˈter-ē-əm\ *n, pl* **-i•ums** *or* **-ia** \-ē-ə\ **:** SANATORIUM

san•i•tary \ˈsa-nə-ˌter-ē\ *adj* **1 :** of or relating to health **:** HYGIENIC **2** ♦ **:** free from filth or infective matter

♦ aseptic, hygienic, sterile *Ant* unhygienic, unsanitary

sanitary napkin *n* **:** a disposable absorbent pad used to absorb uterine flow (as during menstruation)

san•i•ta•tion \ˌsa-nə-ˈtā-shən\ *n* **:** the act or process of making sanitary; *also* **:** protection of health by maintenance of sanitary conditions

san•i•tize \ˈsa-nə-ˌtīz\ *vb* **-tized; -tiz•ing** **1 :** to make sanitary **2 :** to make more acceptable by removing unpleasant features

san•i•ty \ˈsa-nə-tē\ *n* ♦ **:** soundness of mind

♦ head, mind, reason, wit

sank *past of* SINK

sans \ˈsanz\ *prep* ♦ **:** deprived or destitute of **:** WITHOUT

♦ minus, wanting, without

San•skrit \ˈsan-ˌskrit\ *n* **:** an ancient language that is the classical language of India and of Hinduism — **Sanskrit** *adj*

San•ta Ana \ˌsan-tə-ˈa-nə\ *n* **:** a hot dry wind from the north, northeast, or east in southern California

[1]**sap** \ˈsap\ *n* **1 a :** a vital fluid; *esp* **:** a watery fluid that circulates through a vascular plant **b** ♦ **:** bodily health and vigor **2** ♦ **:** a foolish gullible person — **sap•less** *adj*

♦ [1b] dash, energy, life, pep, vigor (*or* vigour), vim, vitality
♦ [2] dupe, gull, pigeon, sucker, tool

[2]**sap** *vb* **sapped; sap•ping** **1 :** UNDERMINE **2** ♦ **:** to weaken gradually

♦ debilitate, enervate, enfeeble, prostrate, soften, tire, waste, weaken

sap•id \ˈsa-pəd\ *adj* **:** FLAVORFUL

sa•pi•ence \ˌsā-pē-əns\ *n* ♦ **:** keen and farsighted judgment **:** profound knowledge

♦ discernment, insight, perception, sagacity, wisdom

sa•pi•ent \ˈsā-pē-ənt, ˈsa-\ *adj* ♦ **:** possessing or expressing great intelligence **:** WISE

♦ discerning, insightful, perceptive, sagacious, sage, wise

sap•ling \ˈsa-pliŋ\ *n* **:** a young tree

sap•phire \ˈsa-ˌfīr\ *n* **:** a hard transparent usually rich blue gem

sap•py \ˈsa-pē\ *adj* **sap•pi•er; -est** **1 :** full of sap **2** ♦ **:** overly sentimental **3 :** lacking in good sense **:** SILLY, FOOLISH

♦ corny, maudlin, mawkish, mushy, saccharine, schmaltzy, sentimental

sap•ro•phyte \ˈsa-prə-ˌfīt\ *n* **:** a living thing and especially a plant living on dead or decaying organic matter — **sap•ro•phyt•ic** \ˌsa-prə-ˈfi-tik\ *adj*

sap•suck•er \ˈsap-ˌsə-kər\ *n* **:** any of a genus of No. American woodpeckers

sap•wood \-ˌwu̇d\ *n* **:** the younger active and usually lighter and softer outer layer of wood (as of a tree trunk)

sar•casm \ˈsär-ˌka-zəm\ *n* **1** ♦ **:** a cutting or contemptuous remark **2 :** ironic criticism or reproach

♦ affront, barb, dart, dig, indignity, insult, name, offense, outrage, put-down, slight, slur, wound

sar•cas•tic \sär-ˈkas-tik\ *adj* ♦ **:** having the character of sarcasm; *also* **:** given to the use of sarcasm — **sar•cas•ti•cal•ly** \-ti-k(ə-)lē\ *adv*

♦ acrid, biting, caustic, cutting, mordant, pungent, satiric, scathing, sharp, tart

sar•co•ma \sär-ˈkō-mə\ *n, pl* **-mas** *also* **-ma•ta** \-mə-tə\ **:** a malignant tumor especially of connective tissue, bone, cartilage, or striated muscle

sar•coph•a•gus \sär-ˈkä-fə-gəs\ *n, pl* **-gi** \-ˌgī, -ˌjī\ *also* **-gus•es** **:** a large stone coffin

sar•dine \sär-ˈdēn\ *n, pl* **sardines** *also* **sardine** **:** a young or small fish preserved for use as food

sar•don•ic \sär-ˈdä-nik\ *adj* **:** disdainfully or skeptically humorous **:** derisively mocking **:** SARCASTIC — **sar•don•i•cal•ly** \-ni-k(ə-)lē\ *adv*

sa•ri *also* **sa•ree** \ˈsär-ē\ *n* **:** a garment worn by women in southern Asia that consists of a long cloth draped around the body and head or shoulder

sa•rin \ˈsär-ən, zä-ˈrēn\ *n* **:** an extremely toxic chemical weapon used as a lethal nerve gas

sa•rong \sə-ˈrȯŋ, -ˈräŋ\ *n* **:** a loose garment wrapped around the body and worn by men and women of the Malay Archipelago and the Pacific islands

sar•sa•pa•ril•la \ˌsas-ə-pə-ˈri-lə, ˌsärs-\ *n* **1 :** the dried roots of a tropical American smilax used especially for flavoring; *also* **:** the plant 2 : a sweetened carbonated beverage flavored with sassafras and an oil from a birch

sar•to•ri•al \sär-ˈtōr-ē-əl\ *adj* : of or relating to a tailor or tailored clothes — **sar•to•ri•al•ly** *adv*

SASE *abbr* self-addressed stamped envelope

¹sash \ˈsash\ *n* ♦ : a broad band worn around the waist or over the shoulder

♦ belt, cincture, cummerbund, girdle

²sash *n, pl* **sash** *also* **sash•es** : a frame for panes of glass in a door or window; *also* : the movable part of a window

sa•shay \sa-ˈshā\ *vb* **1** : WALK, GLIDE, GO **2** : to strut or move about in an ostentatious manner **3** : to proceed in a diagonal or sideways manner

Sask *abbr* Saskatchewan

Sas•quatch \ˈsas-ˌkwach, -ˌkwäch\ *n* : a large hairy humanlike creature reported to exist in the northwestern U.S. and western Canada

sas•sa•fras \ˈsa-sə-ˌfras\ *n* : an aromatic No. American tree related to the laurel; *also* : its carcinogenic dried root bark

sassy \ˈsa-sē\ *adj* **sass•i•er; -est** ♦ : marked by contemptuous or cocky boldness or disregard of others : SAUCY

♦ arch, bold, brash, brazen, cheeky, cocky, fresh, impertinent, impudent, insolent, nervy, saucy

¹sat *past and past part of* SIT

²sat *abbr* **1** satellite **2** saturated

Sat *abbr* Saturday

Sa•tan \ˈsāt-ᵊn\ *n* : DEVIL

sa•tan•ic \sə-ˈta-nik, sā-\ *adj* **1** ♦ : of or characteristic of Satan **2** ♦ : extremely malicious or wicked — **sa•tan•i•cal•ly** \-ni-k(ə-)lē\ *adv*

♦ [1, 2] demonic, devilish, diabolical, fiendish

satch•el \ˈsa-chəl\ *n* : SUITCASE

sate \ˈsāt\ *vb* **sat•ed; sat•ing** ♦ : to satisfy to the full; *also* : GLUT

♦ assuage, quench, satiate, satisfy ♦ glut, gorge, stuff, surfeit

sated *adj* ♦ : filled to the point of excess

♦ full, satiate, satiated

sa•teen \sa-ˈtēn, sə-\ *n* : a cotton cloth finished to resemble satin

sat•el•lite \ˈsat-ᵊl-ˌīt\ *n* **1** : an obsequious follower of a distinguished person : TOADY **2** : a celestial body that orbits a larger body **3** : a manufactured object that orbits a celestial body

satellite dish *n* : a microwave dish for receiving usually television transmissions from an orbiting satellite

sa•ti•ate \ˈsā-shē-ˌāt\ *vb* **-at•ed; -at•ing** ♦ : to satisfy fully or to excess

♦ assuage, quench, sate, satisfy

satiated *adj* ♦ : filled to satiety

♦ full, sated, satiate

sa•ti•ety \sə-ˈtī-ə-tē\ *n* : fullness to the point of excess

sat•in \ˈsat-ᵊn\ *n* : a fabric (as of silk) with a glossy surface

sat•in•wood \ˈsat-ᵊn-ˌwu̇d\ *n* : a hard yellowish brown wood of satiny luster; *also* : a tree yielding this wood

sat•iny *adj* ♦ : having or resembling the soft texture or lustrous smoothness of satin

♦ glossy, lustrous, polished, sleek ♦ cottony, downy, silken, soft, velvety

sat•ire \ˈsa-ˌtīr\ *n* : biting wit, irony, or sarcasm used to expose vice or folly; *also* : a literary work having these qualities — **sat•i•rist** \ˈsa-tə-rist\ *n* — **sat•i•rize** \-tə-ˌrīz\ *vb*

sa•tir•ic \sə-ˈtir-ik\ *or* **sa•tir•i•cal** \-i-kəl\ *adj* ♦ : of, relating to, or constituting satire; *also* : manifesting or given to satire — **sa•tir•i•cal•ly** *adv*

♦ acrid, biting, caustic, cutting, mordant, pungent, sarcastic, scathing, sharp, tart

sat•is•fac•tion \ˌsa-təs-ˈfak-shən\ *n* **1** : payment through penance of punishment incurred by sin **2** ♦ : the quality or state of being satisfied : GRATIFICATION **3** : reparation for an insult **4** ♦ : settlement of a claim

♦ [2] contentment, delectation, delight, enjoyment, gladness, gratification, pleasure, relish ♦ [4] compensation, damages, indemnity, quittance, recompense, redress, remuneration, reparation, requital, restitution

sat•is•fac•to•ri•ly \-ˈfak-tə-rə-lē\ *adv* ♦ : in a satisfactory manner

♦ adequately, all right, fine, good, nicely, OK, passably, so-so, tolerably, well ♦ adequately, enough

sat•is•fac•to•ry \-ˈfak-tə-rē\ *adj* ♦ : giving satisfaction; *also* : ADEQUATE

♦ agreeable, all right, alright, fine, good, OK, palatable *Ant* disagreeable, unsatisfactory ♦ acceptable, adequate, all right, decent, fine, OK, passable, respectable, tolerable

sat•is•fy \ˈsa-təs-ˌfī\ *vb* **-fied; -fy•ing** **1** : to answer or discharge (a claim) in full **2** ♦ : to make happy : GRATIFY **3** : to pay what is due to **4** ♦ : to bring (as by argument) to belief, consent, or a course of action : CONVINCE **5** ♦ : to meet the requirements of

♦ [2] content, delight, gladden, gratify, please, rejoice, suit, warm ♦ [4] argue, convince, get, induce, move, persuade, prevail, talk, win ♦ [5] answer, comply, fill, fulfill, keep, meet, redeem

satisfying *adj* ♦ : giving satisfaction

♦ agreeable, congenial, delectable, delicious, delightful, dreamy, felicitous, good, grateful, gratifying, nice, palatable, pleasant, pleasurable ♦ cogent, compelling, conclusive, convincing, decisive, effective, forceful, persuasive, strong, telling

sat•is•fy•ing•ly *adv* ♦ : in a pleasant way

♦ agreeably, delightfully, favorably (*or* favourably), felicitously, gloriously, nicely, pleasantly, pleasingly, splendidly, well

sa•trap \ˈsā-ˌtrap, ˈsa-\ *n* : a petty prince : a subordinate ruler

sat•u•rate \ˈsa-chə-ˌrāt\ *vb* **-rat•ed; -rat•ing** **1** ♦ : to soak thoroughly **2** : to treat or charge with something to the point where no more can be absorbed, dissolved, or retained — **sat•u•ra•ble** \ˈsa-chə-rə-bəl\ *adj* — **sat•u•ra•tion** \ˌsa-chə-ˈrā-shən\ *n*

♦ drench, drown, impregnate, soak, sop, souse, steep

saturated *adj* **1** ♦ : full of moisture : made thoroughly wet **2** : being a solution that is unable to absorb or dissolve any more of a solute at a given temperature and pressure **3** *of a color* : having high saturation **4** : having no double or triple bonds between carbon atoms ⟨~ fats⟩

♦ sodden, soggy, waterlogged, watery, wet

Sat•ur•day \ˈsa-tər-dē, -ˌdā\ *n* : the 7th day of the week

Saturday night special *n* : a cheap easily concealed handgun

Sat•urn \ˈsa-tərn\ *n* : the planet 6th in order from the sun

sat•ur•nine \ˈsa-tər-ˌnīn\ *adj* : cold and steady in mood; *also* : of a gloomy or surly disposition : SULLEN

sa•tyr \ˈsā-tər\ *n* **1** *often cap* : a woodland deity in Greek mythology having certain characteristics of a horse or goat **2** : a lecherous man

¹sauce \ˈsȯs, *3 usu* ˈsas\ *n* **1** : a fluid dressing or topping for food **2** : stewed fruit **3** ♦ : pert or impudent language or actions

♦ back talk, cheek, impertinence, impudence, insolence

²sauce \ˈsȯs, *2 usu* ˈsas\ *vb* **sauced; sauc•ing** **1** : to put sauce on; *also* : to add zest to **2** : to be impudent to

sauce•pan \ˈsȯs-ˌpan\ *n* : a small deep cooking pan with a handle

sau•cer \ˈsȯ-sər\ *n* : a rounded shallow dish for use under a cup

sauc•i•ness \-sē-nəs\ *n* ♦ : the quality or state of being saucy

♦ audacity, brass, brazenness, cheek, chutzpah, effrontery, gall, nerve, presumption, sauce, temerity

saucy \ˈsa-sē, ˈsȯ-\ *adj* **sauc•i•er; -est** ♦ : impertinently bold and impudent — **sauc•i•ly** \-sə-lē\ *adv*

♦ arch, bold, brash, brazen, cheeky, cocky, fresh, impertinent, impudent, insolent, nervy, sassy

Sau•di \ˈsau̇-dē, ˈsȯ-; sä-ˈü-dē\ *n* : SAUDI ARABIAN — **Saudi** *adj*

Saudi Arabian *n* : a native or inhabitant of Saudi Arabia — **Saudi Arabian** *adj*

sau•er•kraut \ˈsau̇-ər-ˌkrau̇t\ *n* : finely cut cabbage fermented in brine

Sauk \ˈsȯk\ *or* **Sac** \ˈsak, ˈsȯk\ *n, pl* **Sauk** *or* **Sauks** *or* **Sac** *or* **Sacs** : a member of an American Indian people formerly living in what is now Wisconsin

sau•na \ˈsȯ-nə, ˈsau̇-nə\ *n* **1** : a Finnish steam bath in which the steam is provided by water thrown on hot stones **2** : a dry heat bath; *also* : a room or cabinet used for such a bath

saun•ter \ˈsȯn-tər, ˈsän-\ *vb* : STROLL

sau•ro•pod \ˈsȯr-ə-ˌpäd\ *n* : any of a suborder of plant-eating dinosaurs (as a brontosaurus) with a long neck and tail and a small head — **sauropod** *adj*

sau•sage \ˈsȯ-sij\ *n* : minced and highly seasoned meat (as pork) usually enclosed in a tubular casing

S Aust *abbr* South Australia

sau•té \sȯ-ˈtā, sō-\ *vb* **sau•téed** *or* **sau•téd; sau•té•ing** : to fry lightly in a little fat — **sauté** *n*

sau·terne \sō-ˈtərn, sȯ-\ *n, often cap* **:** a usually semisweet American white wine

¹sav·age \ˈsa-vij\ *adj* **1** ♦ **:** not domesticated or under human control **:** WILD, UNTAMED **2** ♦ **:** lacking complex or advanced culture **:** UNCIVILIZED **3** ♦ **:** lacking the restraints normal to civilized human beings **:** FIERCE — **sav·age·ly** *adv*

♦ [1] feral, unbroken, undomesticated, untamed, wild ♦ [2] barbarous, heathen, heathenish, Neanderthal, rude, uncivil, uncivilized, uncultivated, wild ***Ant*** civilized ♦ [3] barbarous, brutal, cruel, heartless, inhumane, sadistic, vicious, wanton ♦ [3] fell, ferocious, fierce, grim, vicious

²savage *n* **1 :** a member of a primitive human society **2** ♦ **:** a rude, unmannerly, or brutal person

♦ beast, brute, devil, fiend, monster, villain

sav·age·ness *n* **:** the quality or state of being savage

sav·age·ry \-rē\ *n* **1 a :** the quality of being savage **b** ♦ **:** an act of cruelty or violence **2 :** an uncivilized state

♦ barbarity, brutality, cruelty, inhumanity, sadism, viciousness, wantonness

sa·van·na *also* **sa·van·nah** \sə-ˈva-nə\ *n* ♦ **:** grassland containing scattered trees

♦ down, grassland, plain, prairie, steppe, veld

sa·vant \sa-ˈvänt, sə-, ˈsa-vənt\ *n* **:** a learned person **:** SCHOLAR

¹save \ˈsāv\ *vb* **saved; sav·ing 1 :** to redeem from sin **2** ♦ **:** to rescue from danger **3** ♦ **:** to preserve or guard from destruction or loss; *also* **:** to store (data) in a computer or on a storage device **4** ♦ **:** to put aside as a store or reserve

♦ [2] deliver, rescue ***Ant*** compromise, endanger, imperil, jeopardize ♦ [3] economize, scrimp, skimp ♦ [3] conserve, keep up, maintain, preserve ♦ [4] allocate, consecrate, dedicate, devote, earmark, reserve

²save *n* **:** a play that prevents an opponent from scoring or winning

³save *prep* ♦ **:** other than **:** EXCEPT

♦ aside from, bar, barring, besides, but, except, outside (of)

⁴save *conj* **:** BUT

sav·er *n* **:** one that saves

savings and loan association *n* **:** a cooperative association that holds savings of members in the form of dividend-bearing shares and that invests chiefly in mortgage loans

savings bank *n* **:** a bank that holds funds of individual depositors in interest-bearing accounts and makes long-term investments (as mortgage loans)

savings bond *n* **:** a registered U.S. bond issued in denominations of $50 to $10,000

sav·ior *or* **sav·iour** \ˈsāv-yər\ *n* **1** ♦ **:** one who saves **2** *cap* **:** Jesus Christ

♦ deliverer, redeemer, rescuer

sa·voir faire \ˌsav-ˌwär-ˈfar\ *n* **:** sureness in social behavior

¹sa·vor *also* **sa·vour** \ˈsā-vər\ *n* **1 :** the taste and odor of something **2** ♦ **:** a special flavor or quality affecting taste

♦ deliciousness, lusciousness, tastiness

²savor *also* **savour** *vb* **1 :** to have a specified taste, smell, or quality **2 :** to taste with pleasure **3** ♦ **:** to give flavor to

♦ flavor (*or* flavour), season, spice

¹sa·vory *or chiefly Can and Brit* **sa·voury** \ˈsā-və-rē\ *adj* ♦ **:** having savor: as **a :** pleasing to the sense of taste especially by reason of effective seasoning **b :** pungently flavorful without sweetness

♦ ambrosial, appetizing, delectable, delicious, flavorful (*or* flavourful), luscious, palatable, scrumptious, tasty, toothsome, yummy

²sa·vo·ry *n, pl* **-ries :** either of two aromatic mints used in cooking

¹sav·vy \ˈsa-vē\ *vb* **sav·vied; sav·vy·ing** ♦ **:** to recognize the meaning of **:** UNDERSTAND, COMPREHEND

♦ appreciate, apprehend, catch, catch on (to), comprehend, dig, discern, get, grasp, make, make out, perceive, see, seize, understand

²savvy *n* ♦ **:** practical know-how ⟨political ~⟩ — **savvy** *adj*

♦ experience, expertise, know-how, proficiency

¹saw *past of* SEE

²saw \ˈsȯ\ *n* **:** a cutting tool with a blade having a line of teeth along its edge

³saw *vb* **sawed** \ˈsȯd\; **sawed** *or* **sawn** \ˈsȯn\; **saw·ing :** to cut or shape with or as if with a saw

⁴saw *n* **:** a common saying **:** MAXIM

saw·dust \ˈsȯ-(ˌ)dəst\ *n* **:** fine particles made by a saw in cutting

saw·fly \-ˌflī\ *n* **:** any of numerous insects belonging to the same order as bees and wasps and including many whose larvae are plant-feeding pests

saw·horse \-ˌhȯrs\ *n* **:** a rack on which wood is rested while being sawed by hand

saw·mill \-ˌmil\ *n* **:** a mill for sawing logs

saw palmetto *n* **:** any of several shrubby palms with spiny-toothed petioles

saw·yer \ˈsȯ-yər\ *n* **:** a person who saws timber

sax \ˈsaks\ *n* **:** SAXOPHONE

sax·i·frage \ˈsak-sə-frij, -ˌfrāj\ *n* **:** any of a genus of plants with showy flowers and usually with leaves growing in tufts close to the ground

sax·o·phone \ˈsak-sə-ˌfōn\ *n* **:** a musical instrument having a conical metal tube with a reed mouthpiece and finger keys — **sax·o·phon·ist** \-ˌfō-nist\ *n*

¹say \ˈsā\ *vb* **said** \ˈsed\; **say·ing; says** \ˈsez\ **1** ♦ **:** to express in words ⟨~ what you mean⟩ **2 :** to state as opinion or belief **3 :** PRONOUNCE; *also* **:** RECITE, REPEAT ⟨~ your prayers⟩ **4 :** INDICATE ⟨the clock ~*s* noon⟩

♦ articulate, clothe, couch, express, formulate, phrase, put, state, word ♦ articulate, speak, state, talk, tell, utter, verbalize, vocalize

²say *n, pl* **says** \ˈsāz\ **1 :** an expression of opinion **2 :** power of decision

say·ing *n* ♦ **:** a commonly repeated statement

♦ adage, aphorism, byword, epigram, maxim, proverb

say–so \ˈsā-(ˌ)sō\ *n* **:** an especially authoritative assertion or decision; *also* ♦ **:** the right to decide

♦ say, voice, vote

sb *abbr* substantive

Sb *symbol* antimony

SB *abbr* bachelor of science

SBA *abbr* Small Business Administration

sc *abbr* **1** scale **2** scene **3** science

Sc *symbol* scandium

SC *abbr* **1** South Carolina **2** supreme court

¹scab \ˈskab\ *n* **1 :** scabies of domestic animals **2 :** a crust of hardened blood forming over a wound **3 :** a worker who replaces a striker or works under conditions not authorized by a union **4 :** any of various bacterial or fungus plant diseases marked by crusted spots on stems or leaves

²scab *vb* **scabbed; scab·bing 1 :** to become covered with a scab **2 :** to work as a scab

scab·bard \ˈska-bərd\ *n* **:** a sheath for the blade of a weapon (as a sword)

scab·by *adj* **scab·bi·er; -est 1 :** covered with or full of scabs **2** ♦ **:** worthy of contempt

♦ contemptible, despicable, lousy, nasty, pitiful, scurvy, sorry, wretched

sca·bies \ˈskā-bēz\ *n* **:** contagious itch or mange caused by mites living as parasites under the skin

sca·brous \ˈska-brəs, ˈskā-\ *adj* **1 :** DIFFICULT, KNOTTY **2 :** rough to the touch **:** SCALY, SCURFY ⟨a ~ leaf⟩ **3 :** dealing with suggestive, indecent, or scandalous themes; *also* **:** SQUALID

scad \ˈskad\ *n* ♦ **:** a large number or quantity — usually used in plural

♦ abundance, deal, gobs, heap, loads, lot, pile, plenty, quantity

scaf·fold \ˈska-fəld, -ˌfōld\ *n* **1 :** a raised platform for workers to sit or stand on **2 :** a platform on which a criminal is executed (as by hanging)

scaf·fold·ing *n* **:** a system of scaffolds; *also* **:** materials for scaffolds

scal·a·wag *or* **scal·ly·wag** \ˈska-li-ˌwag\ *n* ♦ **:** a mean, unprincipled, or dishonest person **:** RASCAL

♦ beast, evildoer, fiend, no-good, reprobate, rogue, varlet, villain, wretch

¹scald \ˈskȯld\ *vb* **1 :** to burn with or as if with hot liquid or steam **2 :** to heat to just below the boiling point

²scald *n* **:** a burn caused by scalding

¹scale \ˈskāl\ *n* **1 :** either pan of a balance **2 :** BALANCE — usually used in plural **3 :** a weighing instrument

²scale *vb* **scaled; scal·ing** ♦ **:** to weigh in scales

♦ gauge, measure, span

³scale *n* **1 :** one of the small thin plates that cover the body especially of a fish or reptile **2 :** a thin plate or flake **3 :** a thin coating, layer, or incrustation **4 :** SCALE INSECT — **scaled** \ˈskāld\ *adj* — **scale•less** \ˈskāl-ləs\ *adj* — **scaly** *adj*

⁴scale *vb* **scaled; scal•ing :** to strip of scales

⁵scale *n* **1 :** something divided into regular spaces as a help in drawing or measuring **2** ♦ **:** a graduated series **3 :** the size of a sample (as a model) in proportion to the size of the actual thing **4 :** a standard of estimation or judgment **5 :** a series of musical tones going up or down in pitch according to a specified scheme **6** ♦ **:** a distinctive relative size, extent, or degree

♦ [2] graduation, ladder ♦ [6] gamut, range, spectrum, spread, stretch

⁶scale *vb* **scaled; scal•ing 1 :** to climb by or as if by a ladder **2 :** to arrange in a graded series

scale insect *n* **:** any of numerous small insects with wingless scale-covered females that are related to aphids and feed on and are often pests of plants

scale•pan \ˈskāl-ˌpan\ *n* **:** ¹SCALE 1

scal•lion \ˈskal-yən\ *n* **:** an onion without an enlarged bulb

¹scal•lop \ˈskä-ləp, ˈska-\ *n* **1 :** any of numerous marine bivalve mollusks with radially ridged shells; *also* **:** a large edible muscle of this mollusk **2 :** one of a continuous series of rounded projections forming an edge

²scallop *vb* **1 :** to bake in a casserole ⟨~*ed* potatoes⟩ **2 :** to shape, cut, or finish in scallops ⟨~*ed* edges⟩

¹scalp \ˈskalp\ *n* **:** the part of the skin and flesh of the head usually covered with hair

²scalp *vb* **1 :** to remove the scalp from **2 :** to resell at greatly increased prices ⟨~ tickets⟩ — **scalp•er** *n*

scal•pel \ˈskal-pəl\ *n* **:** a small straight knife with a thin blade used especially in surgery

scam \ˈskam\ *n* ♦ **:** a fraudulent or deceptive act or operation

♦ hustle, racket, swindle

scamp \ˈskamp\ *n* ♦ **:** a dishonest person **:** RASCAL; *also* **:** an impish or playful young person

♦ beast, evildoer, fiend, no-good, reprobate, rogue, varlet, villain, wretch ♦ devil, hellion, imp, mischief, monkey, rapscallion, rascal, rogue, urchin

scam•per \ˈskam-pər\ *vb* ♦ **:** to run nimbly and playfully — **scamper** *n*

♦ dash, gallop, jog, run, sprint, trip

scam•pi \ˈskam-pē\ *n, pl* **scampi :** a usually large shrimp; *also* **:** large shrimp prepared with a garlic-flavored sauce

¹scan \ˈskan\ *vb* **scanned; scan•ning 1 :** to read (verses) so as to show metrical structure **2** ♦ **:** to examine closely **3 :** to input or examine systematically in order to obtain data especially for display or storage **4 :** to make a scan of (as the human body)

♦ audit, check, examine, inspect, review, scrutinize, survey

²scan *n* **1** ♦ **:** the act or process of scanning **2 :** a picture of the distribution of radioactive material in something; *also* **:** an image of a bodily part produced (as by computer) by combining radiographic data obtained from several angles or sections

♦ audit, check, checkup, examination, inspection, review, scrutiny, survey

Scand *abbr* Scandinavia

scan•dal \ˈskand-ᵊl\ *n* **1** ♦ **:** a circumstance or action that offends propriety or established moral conceptions or disgraces those associated with it **:** DISGRACE, DISHONOR **2 :** malicious gossip **:** SLANDER — **scan•dal•ize** *vb*

♦ crime, disgrace, dishonor, reflection, reproach

scan•dal•mon•ger \-ˌməŋ-gər, -ˌmäŋ-\ *n* **:** a person who circulates scandal

scan•dal•ous *adj* ♦ **:** containing defamatory information; *also* **:** offensive to propriety or morality — **scan•dal•ous•ly** *adv*

♦ defamatory, libelous, slanderous ♦ appalling, awful, distasteful, dreadful, obnoxious, obscene, odious, offensive, repellent, repugnant, shocking

Scan•di•na•vian \ˌskan-də-ˈnā-vē-ən\ *n* **:** a native or inhabitant of Scandinavia — **Scandinavian** *adj*

scan•di•um \ˈskan-dē-əm\ *n* **:** a silvery white metallic chemical element

scan•ner \ˈska-nər\ *n* **1 :** a radio receiver that sequentially scans a range of frequencies for a signal **2 :** a device that scans an image or document especially for use or storage on a computer

¹scant \ˈskant\ *adj* **1** ♦ **:** barely sufficient **2 :** having scarcely enough

♦ light, meager (*or* meagre), niggardly, poor, scanty, scarce, skimpy, slender, slim, spare, sparse, stingy

²scant *vb* **1 :** SKIMP **2** ♦ **:** to provide with a meager or inadequate portion or supply **:** STINT

♦ skimp, spare, stint

scant•i•ness \-tē-nəs\ *n* ♦ **:** the quality or state of being scanty

♦ dearth, deficiency, deficit, failure, famine, inadequacy, insufficiency, lack, paucity, poverty, scarcity, shortage, want

scant•ling \ˈskant-liŋ\ *n* **:** a small piece of lumber (as an upright in a house)

scanty \ˈskan-tē\ *adj* **scant•i•er; -est** ♦ **:** barely sufficient **:** SCANT — **scant•i•ly** \ˈskan-tə-lē\ *adv*

♦ light, meager (*or* meagre), niggardly, poor, scant, scarce, skimpy, slender, slim, spare, sparse, stingy

scape•goat \ˈskāp-ˌgōt\ *n* **:** one that bears the blame for others

scape•grace \-ˌgrās\ *n* **:** an incorrigible rascal

scap•u•la \ˈska-pyə-lə\ *n, pl* **-lae** \-ˌlē\ *or* **-las :** SHOULDER BLADE

scap•u•lar \-lər\ *n* **:** a pair of small cloth squares worn on the breast and back under the clothing especially for religious purposes

scar \ˈskär\ *n* ♦ **:** a mark left after injured tissue has healed — **scar** *vb*

♦ blemish, defect, deformity, disfigurement, fault, flaw, imperfection, mark, pockmark

scar•ab \ˈskar-əb\ *n* **:** any of a family of large stout beetles; *also* **:** an ornament (as a gem) representing such a beetle

scarce \ˈskers\ *adj* **scarc•er; scarc•est 1** ♦ **:** deficient in quantity or number **:** not plentiful **2 :** intentionally absent ⟨made himself ~ at inspection time⟩

♦ deficient, inadequate, insufficient, short, shy, wanting

scarce•ly \-lē\ *adv* **1** ♦ **:** by a narrow margin **:** BARELY **2 :** almost not **3 :** very probably not

♦ barely, hardly, just, marginally, slightly

scar•ci•ty \ˈsker-sə-tē\ *n* ♦ **:** the quality or state of being scarce; *esp* **:** want of provisions for the support of life

♦ dearth, deficiency, deficit, failure, famine, inadequacy, insufficiency, lack, paucity, poverty, scantiness, shortage, want

¹scare \ˈsker\ *vb* **scared; scar•ing** ♦ **:** to frighten especially suddenly **:** STARTLE

♦ alarm, frighten, horrify, panic, shock, spook, startle, terrify, terrorize

²scare *n* **:** FRIGHT

scare•crow \ˈsker-ˌkrō\ *n* **:** a crude figure set up to scare birds away from crops

scared *adj* ♦ **:** thrown into or being in a state of fear, fright, or panic

♦ afraid, aghast, fearful, terrified

¹scarf \ˈskärf\ *n, pl* **scarves** \ˈskärvz\ *or* **scarfs 1 :** a broad band (as of cloth) worn about the shoulders, around the neck, over the head, or about the waist **2 :** a long narrow cloth cover for a table or dresser top

²scarf *vb* ♦ **:** to eat greedily

♦ bolt, devour, gobble, gorge, gormandize, gulp, scoff, wolf

scar•i•fy \ˈskar-ə-ˌfī\ *vb* **-fied; -fy•ing 1 :** to make scratches or small cuts in ⟨~ skin for vaccination⟩ ⟨~ seeds to help them germinate⟩ **2 :** to lacerate the feelings of **3 :** to break up and loosen the surface of (as a road) — **scar•i•fi•ca•tion** \ˌskar-ə-fə-ˈkā-shən\ *n*

scar•let \ˈskär-lət\ *n* **:** a bright red color — **scarlet** *adj*

scarlet fever *n* **:** an acute contagious disease marked by fever, sore throat, and red rash and caused by certain streptococci

scarp \ˈskärp\ *n* ♦ **:** a line of cliffs produced by faulting or erosion

♦ bluff, cliff, crag, escarpment, palisade, precipice

scary \ˈsker-ē\ *adj* **scar•i•er; -est 1** ♦ **:** causing fright **2** ♦ **:** easily scared **3 :** feeling alarm or fright

♦ [1] dire, dreadful, fearful, fearsome, forbidding, formidable, frightful, hair-raising, horrible, redoubtable, shocking, terrible, terrifying ♦ [2] fainthearted, fearful, mousy, shy, skittish, timid

scath•ing \ˈskā-t̲h̲iŋ\ *adj* ♦ **:** bitterly severe ⟨a ~ condemnation⟩

♦ acrid, biting, caustic, cutting, mordant, pungent, sarcastic, satiric, sharp, tart

scat•o•log•i•cal \ˌska-tə-ˈlä-ji-kəl\ *adj* **:** concerned with obscene matters

scat•ter \ˈska-tər\ *vb* **1** ♦ **:** to distribute or strew about irregularly **2** ♦ **:** to cause to separate widely **:** DISPERSE

♦ [1] dot, pepper, sow, spray, sprinkle, strew ♦ [2] clear out, disband, disperse, dissipate *Ant* assemble, cluster, collect, concentrate, gather, congregate

scat•ter•brain \ˈska-tər-ˌbrān\ *n* **:** a silly careless person

scat•ter•brained \-ˌbrānd\ *adj* ♦ **:** having the characteristics of a scatterbrain

♦ flighty, frivolous, giddy, goofy, harebrained, light-headed, silly

scattered *adj* ♦ **:** marked by disorganized dispersion

♦ aimless, arbitrary, desultory, erratic, haphazard, random, stray

scav•enge \ˈska-vənj\ *vb* **scav•enged; scav•eng•ing :** to work or function as a scavenger

scav•en•ger \ˈska-vən-jər\ *n* **:** a person or animal that collects, eats, or disposes of refuse or waste

sce•nar•io \sə-ˈnar-ē-ˌō\ *n, pl* **-i•os :** the plot or outline of a dramatic work; *also* **:** an account of a possible action

scene \ˈsēn\ *n* **1 :** a division of one act of a play **2 :** a single situation or sequence in a play or motion picture **3 :** a stage setting **4 :** VIEW, PROSPECT **5 :** the place of an occurrence or action **6** ♦ **:** a display of strong feeling and especially anger **7 :** a sphere of activity ⟨the fashion ~⟩ **8** ♦ **:** a critical, trying, or unusual state of affairs — **sce•nic** \ˈsē-nik\ *adj*

♦ [6] blowup, dudgeon, explosion, fireworks, fit, huff, tantrum ♦ [8] footing, picture, posture, situation, status

scen•ery \ˈsē-nə-rē\ *n, pl* **-er•ies 1 :** the painted scenes or hangings and accessories used on a theater stage **2 :** a picturesque view or landscape

¹scent \ˈsent\ *n* **1** ♦ **:** effluvia from a substance that affect the sense of smell **:** ODOR, SMELL **2 :** sense of smell **3 :** course of pursuit **:** TRACK **4 :** PERFUME 2 **5** ♦ **:** an agreeable odor — **scentless** *adj*

♦ [1] odor (*or* odour), redolence, smell, sniff ♦ [5] aroma, bouquet, fragrance, incense, perfume, redolence, spice

²scent *vb* **1** ♦ **:** to perceive by the olfactory organs **:** SMELL **2 :** to imbue or fill with odor **3** ♦ **:** to get or have an inkling of

♦ [1] nose, smell, sniff, whiff ♦ [3] feel, perceive, see, sense, smell, taste

scent•ed \ˈsen-təd\ *adj* ♦ **:** having scent

♦ ambrosial, aromatic, fragrant, redolent, savory, sweet

scep•ter *or Can and Brit* **scep•tre** \ˈsep-tər\ *n* **:** a staff borne by a sovereign as an emblem of authority

sceptic *chiefly Brit var of* SKEPTIC

sch *abbr* school

¹sched•ule \ˈske-jül, *esp Brit* ˈshe-dyül\ *n* **1** ♦ **:** a list of items or details **2** ♦ **:** a brief usually printed outline of the order to be followed, of the features to be presented, and the persons participating (as in a public performance) **:** TIMETABLE

♦ [1] catalog, checklist, list, listing, menu, register, registry, roll, roster, table ♦ [2] agenda, calendar, docket, program, timetable

²schedule *vb* **sched•uled; sched•ul•ing 1** ♦ **:** to make a schedule of; *also* **:** to enter on a schedule **2 :** to appoint, assign, or designate for a fixed time

♦ catalog, enroll, enter, index, inscribe, list, put down, record, register, slate

sche•ma \ˈskē-mə\ *n, pl* **sche•ma•ta** \-mə-tə\ *also* **schemas :** a diagrammatic presentation or plan **:** OUTLINE

sche•mat•ic \ski-ˈma-tik\ *adj* **:** of or relating to a scheme or diagram **:** DIAGRAMMATIC — **schematic** *n* — **sche•mat•i•cal•ly** \-ti-k(ə-)lē\ *adv*

¹scheme \ˈskēm\ *n* **1** ♦ **:** a plan for doing something; *esp* **:** a crafty plot **2** ♦ **:** a systematic design

♦ [1] artifice, device, dodge, gimmick, jig, ploy, sleight, stratagem, trick, wile ♦ [1] conspiracy, design, intrigue, machination, plot ♦ [2] blueprint, program, strategy, system

²scheme *vb* **schemed; schem•ing** ♦ **:** to form a plot **:** INTRIGUE — **schem•er** *n*

♦ conspire, contrive, intrigue, machinate, plot

schism \ˈsi-zəm, ˈski-\ *n* **1** ♦ **:** the act or process of dividing **:** DIVISION; *also* **:** DISCORD **2 :** a formal division in or separation from a religious body

♦ breakup, dissolution, division, partition, separation, split ♦ conflict, discord, dissension, dissent, disunity, friction, strife, variance, war, warfare

schis•mat•ic \siz-ˈma-tik, ski-\ *n* **:** one who creates or takes part in schism — **schismatic** *adj*

schist \ˈshist\ *n* **:** a metamorphic crystalline rock

schizo•phre•nia \ˌskit-sə-ˈfrē-nē-ə\ *n* **:** a psychotic mental illness that is characterized by a distorted view of the real world, by a greatly reduced ability to carry out one's daily tasks, and by abnormal ways of thinking, feeling, perceiving, and behaving — **schiz•oid** \ˈskit-ˌsȯid\ *adj or n* — **schizo•phren•ic** \ˌskit-sə-ˈfre-nik\ *adj or n*

schle•miel *also* **shle•miel** \shlə-ˈmēl\ *n* **:** an unlucky bungler **:** CHUMP

schlep *or* **schlepp** \ˈshlep\ *vb* **1 :** DRAG, HAUL **2 :** to move slowly or awkwardly

schlock \ˈshläk\ *or* **schlocky** \ˈshlä-kē\ *adj* **:** of low quality or value — **schlock** *n*

schlub *also* **shlub** \ˈshləb\ *n, slang* **:** a stupid, ineffectual, or unattractive person

schmaltz *also* **schmalz** \ˈshmȯlts, ˈshmälts\ *n* **:** sentimental or florid music or art

schmaltzy *adj* ♦ **:** excessively sentimental

♦ corny, maudlin, mawkish, mushy, saccharine, sappy, sentimental

schmooze *or* **shmooze** \ˈshmüz\ *vb* ♦ **:** to chat informally especially to gain favor — **schmooze** *n*

♦ chat, converse, gab, jaw, palaver, patter, prattle, rattle, talk, visit

schnapps \ˈshnaps\ *n, pl* **schnapps :** a liquor (as gin) of high alcoholic content

schnau•zer \ˈshnaụt-sər, ˈshnaụ-zər\ *n* **:** a dog of any of three breeds that are characterized by a wiry coat, long head, pointed ears, heavy eyebrows, and long hair on the muzzle

schol•ar \ˈskä-lər\ *n* **1 :** STUDENT, PUPIL **2 :** a learned person **:** SAVANT **3** ♦ **:** a person who has done advanced study in a special field

♦ ace, adept, artist, authority, crackerjack, expert, maestro, master, shark, virtuoso, whiz, wizard

schol•ar•ly *adj* ♦ **:** of, characteristic of, or suitable to learned persons

♦ educated, erudite, knowledgeable, learned, literate, well-read ♦ academic, educational, scholastic

schol•ar•ship \-ˌship\ *n* **1** ♦ **:** the qualities or learning of a scholar **2 :** money awarded to a student to help pay for further education

♦ education, erudition, knowledge, learning, science

scho•las•tic \skə-ˈlas-tik\ *adj* **:** of or relating to schools, scholars, or scholarship

♦ academic, educational, scholarly

¹school \ˈskül\ *n* **1 :** an institution for teaching and learning; *also* **:** the pupils in attendance **2 :** a body of persons of like opinions or beliefs ⟨the radical ~⟩

²school *vb* ♦ **:** to teach or drill in a specific knowledge or skill **:** TRAIN

♦ educate, indoctrinate, instruct, teach, train, tutor

³school *n* **:** a large number of one kind of water animal swimming and feeding together

school•boy \-ˌbȯi\ *n* **:** a boy attending school

school•fel•low \-ˌfe-lō\ *n* **:** SCHOOLMATE

school•girl \-ˌgərl\ *n* **:** a girl attending school

school•house \-ˌhaụs\ *n* **:** a building used as a school

school•marm \-ˌmärm\ *or* **school•ma'am** \-ˌmäm, -ˌmam\ *n* **1 :** a woman who is a schoolteacher **2 :** a person who exhibits characteristics popularly attributed to schoolteachers

school•mas•ter \-ˌmas-tər\ *n* **:** a man who is a schoolteacher

school•mate \-ˌmāt\ *n* **:** a school companion

school•mis•tress \-ˌmis-trəs\ *n* **:** a woman who is a schoolteacher

school•room \-ˌrüm, -ˌrům\ *n* : CLASSROOM
school•teach•er \-ˌtē-chər\ *n* ♦ : one who teaches in a school

♦ educator, instructor, pedagogue, teacher

schoo•ner \ˈskü-nər\ *n* : a fore-and-aft rigged sailing ship
schtick *var of* SHTICK
schuss \ˈshůs, ˈshüs\ *vb* : to ski down a slope at high speed — **schuss** *n*
sci *abbr* science; scientific
sci•at•i•ca \sī-ˈa-ti-kə\ *n* : pain in the region of the hips or along the course of the nerve at the back of the thigh
sci•ence \ˈsī-əns\ *n* **1** : an area of knowledge that is an object of study; *esp* : NATURAL SCIENCE **2** ♦ : knowledge covering general truths or the operation of general laws especially as obtained and tested through the scientific method **3** ♦ : knowledge as distinguished from ignorance or misunderstanding — **sci•en•tif•ic** \ˌsī-ən-ˈti-fik\ *adj* — **sci•en•tif•i•cal•ly** \-fi-k(ə-)lē\ *adv* — **sci•en•tist** \ˈsī-ən-tist\ *n*

♦ [2] knowledge, lore, wisdom ♦ [3] education, erudition, knowledge, learning, scholarship

science fiction *n* : fiction dealing principally with the impact of actual or imagined science on society or individuals
scientific method *n* : the rules and methods for the pursuit of knowledge involving the finding and stating of a problem, the collection of facts through observation and experiment, and the making and testing of ideas that need to be proven right or wrong
scim•i•tar \ˈsi-mə-tər\ *n* : a curved sword used chiefly by Arabs and Turks
scin•til•la \sin-ˈti-lə\ *n* : SPARK, TRACE
scin•til•late \ˈsint-ᵊl-ˌāt\ *vb* **-lat•ed; -lat•ing** ♦ : to throw off as a spark or as sparkling flashes : SPARKLE, GLEAM — **scin•til•la•tion** \ˌsint-ᵊl-ˈā-shən\ *n*

♦ flame, flash, glance, gleam, glimmer, glisten, glitter, shimmer, sparkle, twinkle, wink

sci•on \ˈsī-ən\ *n* **1** : a shoot of a plant joined to a stock in grafting **2** : DESCENDANT
scis•sors \ˈsi-zərz\ *n pl* : a cutting instrument like shears but usually smaller
scissors kick *n* : a swimming kick in which the legs move like scissors
sclero•der•ma \ˌskler-ə-ˈdər-mə\ *n* : a chronic disease characterized by the usually progressive hardening and thickening of the skin
scle•ro•sis \sklə-ˈrō-səs\ *n* : abnormal hardening of tissue (as of an artery); *also* : a disease characterized by this — **scle•rot•ic** \-ˈrä-tik\ *adj*
[1]**scoff** \ˈskäf\ *vb* : MOCK, JEER
[2]**scoff** *vb* ♦ : to eat greedily

♦ bolt, devour, gobble, gorge, gormandize, gulp, scarf, wolf

scoff•er *n* ♦ : one that scoffs

♦ heckler, mocker, quiz, taunter, tease

scoff•law \-ˌlȯ\ *n* : a contemptuous law violator
[1]**scold** \ˈskōld\ *n* ♦ : a person who scolds

♦ carper, castigator, caviler, censurer, critic, faultfinder, nitpicker, railer

[2]**scold** *vb* ♦ : to censure severely or angrily

♦ berate, castigate, chew out, dress down, flay, jaw, keelhaul, lambaste, lecture, rail (at *or* against), rate, rebuke, reprimand, reproach, score, upbraid

sconce \ˈskäns\ *n* : a candlestick or an electric light fixture fastened to a wall
scone \ˈskōn, ˈskän\ *n* : a biscuit (as of oatmeal) baked on a griddle
[1]**scoop** \ˈsküp\ *n* **1** ♦ : a large shovel; *also* : a utensil with a shovel-like or rounded end **2** : an act of scooping **3** ♦ : information of immediate interest

♦ [1] ladle, spoon ♦ [3] dope, lowdown, tip

[2]**scoop** *vb* **1** ♦ : to take out or up or empty with or as if with a scoop **2** : to make hollow **3** : to report a news item in advance of

♦ dip, ladle, spoon

scoot \ˈsküt\ *vb* ♦ : to move swiftly

♦ course, dash, fly, hasten, hurry, hustle, run, rush, shoot, speed, zip, zoom

scoot•er \ˈskü-tər\ *n* **1** : a child's vehicle consisting of a narrow board mounted between two wheels tandem with an upright steering handle attached to the front wheel **2** : MOTOR SCOOTER
[1]**scope** \ˈskōp\ *n* **1** : space or opportunity for action or thought **2** ♦ : extent covered : RANGE

♦ amplitude, breadth, compass, extent, range, reach, realm, sweep, width

[2]**scope** *n* : an instrument (as a microscope or telescope) for viewing
scorch \ˈskȯrch\ *vb* **1** ♦ : to burn the surface of **2** : to dry or shrivel with heat ⟨~*ed* lawns⟩

♦ char, sear, singe

scorch•ing *adj* ♦ : that scorches

♦ broiling, burning, fiery, hot, red-hot, sultry, torrid

[1]**score** \ˈskōr\ *n, pl* **scores** **1** *or pl* **score** : TWENTY **2** : CUT, SCRATCH, SLASH **3** : a record of points made (as in a game) **4** : DEBT **5** : REASON, GROUND **6** : the music of a composition or arrangement with different parts indicated **7** : success in obtaining something (as drugs) especially illegally **8** ♦ : a feeling of deep-seated resentment or ill will

♦ grievance, grudge, resentment

[2]**score** *vb* **scored; scor•ing** **1** : RECORD **2** : to keep score in a game **3** ♦ : to mark with lines, grooves, scratches, or notches **4** : to gain or tally in or as if in a game ⟨*scored* a point⟩ **5** : to assign a grade or score to ⟨~ the tests⟩ **6** : to compose a score for **7** ♦ : to be successful **8** : to scold or condemn vehemently and at length — **score•less** *adj* — **scor•er** *n*

♦ [3] groove, scribe ♦ [7] achieve, attain, hit, make, win

[1]**scorn** \ˈskȯrn\ *n* ♦ : an emotion involving both anger and disgust : CONTEMPT — **scorn•ful•ly** *adv*

♦ contempt, despite, disdain

[2]**scorn** *vb* ♦ : to hold in contempt : DISDAIN

♦ disdain, high-hat, slight, sniff at, snub ***Ant*** honor, respect ♦ despise, disregard, flout

scorn•er *n* : one that scorns
scorn•ful \-fəl\ *adj* ♦ : full of scorn

♦ contemptuous, degrading, derogatory, disdainful, uncomplimentary

Scor•pio \ˈskȯr-pē-ˌō\ *n* **1** : a zodiacal constellation between Libra and Sagittarius usually pictured as a scorpion **2** : the 8th sign of the zodiac in astrology; *also* : one born under this sign
scor•pi•on \ˈskȯr-pē-ən\ *n* : any of an order of arthropods related to the spiders that have a poisonous stinger at the tip of a long jointed tail
[1]**Scot** \ˈskät\ *n* : a native or inhabitant of Scotland
[2]**Scot** *abbr* Scotland; Scottish
Scotch \ˈskäch\ *n* **1** : SCOTS **2 Scotch** *pl* : the people of Scotland **3** : a whiskey distilled in Scotland especially from malted barley — **Scotch** *adj* — **Scotch•wom•an** \-ˌwů-mən\ *n*
Scotch bonnet *n* : a small roundish very hot chili pepper especially of the Caribbean
Scotch•man \-mən\ *n* : a native or inhabitant of Scotland
Scotch pine *n* : a pine that is naturalized in the U.S. from northern Europe and Asia and is a valuable timber tree
Scotch terrier *n* : SCOTTISH TERRIER
scot–free \ˈskät-ˈfrē\ *adj* : free from obligation, harm, or penalty
Scots \ˈskäts\ *n* : the English language of Scotland
Scots•man \ˈskäts-mən\ *n* : a native or inhabitant of Scotland : SCOT
Scots•wom•an \-ˌwů-mən\ *n* : a woman who is a Scot
Scot•tie \ˈskä-tē\ *n* **1** : SCOTTISH TERRIER **2** : a native or inhabitant of Scotland : SCOT
Scot•tish \ˈskä-tish\ *adj* : of, relating to, or characteristic of Scotland, Scots, or the Scots
Scottish terrier *n* : any of an old Scottish breed of terrier with short legs, a long head with small erect ears, a broad deep chest, and a thick rough coat
scoun•drel \ˈskau̇n-drəl\ *n* : a disreputable person : VILLAIN
[1]**scour** \ˈskau̇r\ *vb* **1** : to rub (as with a gritty substance) in order to clean **2** : to cleanse by or as if by rubbing
[2]**scour** *vb* **1** : to move rapidly through : RUSH **2** ♦ : to examine thoroughly

♦ dig, dredge, hunt, rake, ransack, rifle, rummage, search

[1]**scourge** \ˈskərj\ *n* **1** : an instrument consisting usually of a handle and lash forming a flexible rod that is used for whipping

: LASH, WHIP **2 a :** PUNISHMENT **b :** a cause of affliction (as a plague)

²scourge *vb* **scourged; scourg•ing 1** ♦ **:** to beat with or as if with a rod or whip **:** LASH **2** ♦ **:** to punish severely; *also* **:** to distress so severely as to cause persistent suffering or anguish

♦ [1] flog, lash, thrash, whale, whip ♦ [2] destroy, devastate, ravage, ruin

¹scout \ˈskau̇t\ *vb* **1 :** to look around **:** RECONNOITER **2 :** to inspect or observe to get information **3** ♦ **:** to find by making a search

♦ *usu* **scout up** detect, determine, dig up, discover, ferret out, hit on, locate, track down

²scout *n* **1 :** a person sent out to get information; *also* **:** a soldier, airplane, or ship sent out to reconnoiter **2 :** BOY SCOUT **3 :** GIRL SCOUT **4 :** a human being

³scout *vb* ♦ **:** to treat with contempt or ridicule; *also* **:** to reject scornfully

♦ deride, gibe, jeer, laugh, mock, ridicule

scout•mas•ter \-ˌmas-tər\ *n* **:** an adult leader of a Boy Scout troop

scow \ˈskau̇\ *n* **:** a large flat-bottomed boat with square ends

¹scowl \ˈskau̇l\ *vb* ♦ **:** to make a frowning expression of displeasure

♦ frown, glare, gloom, glower, lower

²scowl *n* ♦ **:** a facial expression of displeasure

♦ face, frown, grimace, lower, mouth, pout

SCPO *abbr* senior chief petty officer

¹scrab•ble \ˈskra-bəl\ *vb* **scrab•bled; scrab•bling 1 :** SCRAPE, SCRATCH **2** ♦ **:** to climb awkwardly **:** CLAMBER, SCRAMBLE **3 :** to work hard and long **4 :** SCRIBBLE — **scrab•bler** *n*

♦ clamber, climb, scramble

²scrabble *n* ♦ **:** the act or an instance of scrambling

♦ battle, fight, fray, struggle

scrag•gly \ˈskra-glē\ *adj* ♦ **:** irregular in form or growth; *also* **:** RAGGED

♦ broken, craggy, jagged, ragged

scram \ˈskram\ *vb* **scrammed; scram•ming :** to go away at once

¹scram•ble \ˈskram-bəl\ *vb* **scram•bled; scram•bling 1 :** to clamber clumsily around **2 :** to struggle for or as if for possession of something **3 :** to spread irregularly **4** ♦ **:** to mix together **5 :** to cook (eggs) by stirring during frying

♦ confuse, disarray, disorder, jumble, mix, muddle

²scramble *n* **1 :** the act or an instance of scrambling **2** ♦ **:** a disordered mass

♦ assortment, clutter, jumble, medley, mélange, miscellany, motley, muddle, variety, welter

¹scrap \ˈskrap\ *n* **1** ♦ **:** a small detached piece **2** ♦ **:** discarded material

♦ [1] bit, fragment, piece ♦ [2] chaff, deadwood, dust, garbage, junk, litter, refuse, riffraff, rubbish, trash, waste ♦ [2] end, fag end, leftover, remainder, remnant

²scrap *vb* **scrapped; scrap•ping 1 :** to make into scrap ⟨∼ a battleship⟩ **2** ♦ **:** to get rid of as useless

♦ cast, discard, ditch, dump, fling, jettison, junk, lose, reject, shed, shuck, slough, throw away, throw out, unload

³scrap *n* ♦ **:** a hostile encounter **:** FIGHT; *also* **:** a verbal disagreement

♦ argument, brawl, disagreement, dispute, fight, hassle, quarrel, row, spat, squabble

⁴scrap *vb* **scrapped; scrap•ping** ♦ **:** to contend against in or as if in battle or physical combat **:** FIGHT — **scrap•per** *n*

♦ argue, bicker, brawl, dispute, fall out, fight, hassle, quarrel, row, spat, squabble, wrangle

scrap•book \ˈskrap-ˌbu̇k\ *n* **:** a blank book in which mementos are kept

¹scrape \ˈskrāp\ *vb* **scraped; scrap•ing 1 :** to remove by drawing a knife over; *also* **:** to clean or smooth by rubbing off the covering **2** ♦ **:** to damage or injure the surface of by contact with something rough **3** ♦ **:** to draw across a surface with a grating sound **4** ♦ **:** to get together (as money) in small amounts by laborious effort — often used with *up* or *together* **5 :** to get along with difficulty — **scrap•er** *n*

♦ [2] abrade, graze, scratch, scuff ♦ [3] grate, grind, rasp, scratch ♦ [4] eke out, squeeze, wrest, wring ♦ *usu* **scrape together** [4] accumulate, amass, assemble, collect, concentrate, garner, gather, group, lump, pick up, round up

²scrape *n* **1** ♦ **:** the act or the effect of scraping **2 :** a bow accompanied by a drawing back of the foot **3** ♦ **:** an unpleasant predicament; *also* **:** a noisy heated angry dispute

♦ [1] grind, rasp, scratch ♦ [3] brush, encounter, hassle, run-in, skirmish

¹scrap•py \ˈskra-pē\ *adj* **scrap•pi•er; -est :** DISCONNECTED, FRAGMENTARY

²scrappy *adj* **scrap•pi•er; -est 1** ♦ **:** apt or disposed to quarrel in an often petty manner **:** QUARRELSOME **2 :** having an aggressive and determined spirit

♦ argumentative, contentious, disputatious, quarrelsome

¹scratch \ˈskrach\ *vb* **1** ♦ **:** to scrape, dig, or rub with or as if with claws or nails ⟨a dog ∼*ing* at the door⟩ ⟨∼*ed* my arm⟩ **2** ♦ **:** to draw across a surface with a grating sound ⟨∼*ed* his nails across the blackboard⟩ **3 :** SCRAPE 4 **4 :** to cancel or erase by or as if by drawing a line through **5 :** to withdraw from a contest

♦ [1] abrade, graze, scrape, scuff ♦ [2] grate, grind, rasp, scrape

²scratch *n* **1 a :** a mark or injury made by or as if by scratching **b** ♦ **:** a sound made by scratching **2 :** the starting line in a race — **from scratch :** with no steps completed or ingredients prepared ahead of time ⟨built it *from scratch*⟩

♦ grind, rasp, scrape

³scratch *adj* **1 :** made as or used for a trial attempt ⟨∼ paper⟩ **2 :** made or done by chance ⟨a ∼ hit⟩

scratchy *adj* **scratch•i•er; -est 1** ♦ **:** likely to scratch **2** ♦ **:** making a scratching noise

♦ [1] brambly, prickly, thorny ♦ [2] coarse, gravelly, gruff, hoarse, husky, throaty

scrawl \ˈskrȯl\ *vb* **:** to write hastily and carelessly — **scrawl** *n*

scraw•ny \ˈskrȯ-nē\ *adj* **scraw•ni•er; -est :** very thin **:** SKINNY

¹scream \ˈskrēm\ *vb* ♦ **:** to cry out loudly and shrilly

♦ howl, shriek, shrill, squeal, yell, yelp

²scream *n* **:** a loud shrill cry

scream•ing \ˈskrē-miŋ\ *adj* **1 :** so striking as to attract notice as if by screaming ⟨∼ headlines⟩ **2** ♦ **:** so funny as to provoke screams of laughter

♦ antic, comic, comical, droll, farcical, funny, hilarious, humorous, hysterical, laughable, ludicrous, ridiculous, riotous, risible, uproarious

screech \ˈskrēch\ *vb* **:** to utter a high shrill piercing cry **:** SHRIEK — **screech** *n* — **screechy** \ˈskrē-chē\ *adj*

¹screen \ˈskrēn\ *n* **1 a :** a device or partition used to hide, restrain, protect, or decorate ⟨a window ∼⟩ **b** ♦ **:** something that shelters, protects, or conceals **2 :** a sieve or perforated material for separating finer from coarser parts (as of sand) **3 :** a surface on which an image is made to appear (as in television); *also* **:** the information displayed on a computer screen at one time **4 :** the motion-picture industry

♦ aegis, armor, cover, defense (*or* defence), guard, protection, safeguard, security, shield, wall, ward

²screen *vb* **1** ♦ **:** to shield with or as if with a screen **2 :** to separate with or as if with a screen; *also* **:** to select or categorize methodically ⟨∼ contestants⟩ **3 :** to present (as a motion picture) on the screen

♦ cover, defend, guard, protect, safeguard, secure, shield, ward ♦ blanket, blot out, cloak, conceal, cover, curtain, enshroud, hide, mask, obscure, occult, shroud, veil

screen•ing \ˈskrē-niŋ\ *n* **1 :** metal or plastic mesh (as for window screens) **2 :** a showing of a motion picture

screen saver *n* **:** a computer program that displays something (as images) on the screen of a computer that is on but not in use

¹screw \ˈskrü\ *n* **1 :** a machine consisting of a solid cylinder with a spiral groove around it and a corresponding hollow cylinder into which it fits **2 :** a naillike metal piece with a spiral groove and a head with a slot that is inserted into material by rotating and is used to fasten pieces of solid material together **3 :** PROPELLER

²screw *vb* **1 :** to fasten or close by means of a screw **2 :** to operate or adjust by means of a screw **3 :** to move or cause to move spirally; *also* **:** to close or set in position by such an action **4** ♦ **:** to twist into strained configurations **:** CONTORT ⟨~*ed* up his face⟩

♦ contort, deform, distort, warp

screw•ball \ˈskrü-ˌbȯl\ *n* **1 :** a baseball pitch breaking in a direction opposite to a curve **2** ♦ **:** a whimsical, eccentric, or crazy person

♦ character, crackpot, crank, eccentric, kook, nut, oddball, weirdo

screw•driv•er \-ˌdrī-vər\ *n* **1 :** a tool for turning screws **2 :** a drink made of vodka and orange juice
screw–up \ˈskrü-ˌəp\ *n* ♦ **:** an avoidable and usually serious mistake

♦ blunder, error, fault, flub, fumble, gaffe, goof, lapse, miscue, misstep, mistake, oversight, slip, stumble, trip

screw up *vb* ♦ **:** to foul up hopelessly **:** BUNGLE

♦ blow, bobble, botch, bungle, butcher, flub, foul up, fumble, mangle, mess up

screw•worm \ˈskrü-ˌwərm\ *n* **:** an American blowfly of warm regions whose larva matures in wounds or sores of mammals and may cause disease or death; *esp* **:** its larva
screwy \ˈskrü-ē\ *adj* **screw•i•er; -est 1** ♦ **:** crazily absurd, eccentric, or unusual **2 :** disordered in mind **:** CRAZY

♦ bizarre, curious, far-out, funny, kinky, odd, outlandish, outré, peculiar, quaint, queer, quirky, remarkable, strange, wacky, weird, wild

scrib•ble \ˈskri-bəl\ *vb* **scrib•bled; scrib•bling** ♦ **:** to write hastily or carelessly — **scribble** *n* — **scrib•bler** *n*

♦ author, pen, write

scribe \ˈskrīb\ *n* **1 :** a scholar of Jewish law in New Testament times **2** ♦ **:** a person whose business is the copying of writing **3 :** JOURNALIST

♦ clerk, register, registrar

scrim \ˈskrim\ *n* **:** a light loosely woven cotton or linen cloth
¹scrim•mage \ˈskri-mij\ *n* **1 :** the play between two football teams beginning with the snap of the ball; *also* **:** practice play between two teams **2** ♦ **:** a confused fight

♦ battle, clash, combat, conflict, contest, fight, fracas, fray, hassle, scrap, scuffle, skirmish, struggle, tussle

²scrimmage *vb* **scrim•maged; scrim•mag•ing** ♦ **:** to take part in a scrimmage

♦ *usu* **scrimmage with** battle, clash, combat, fight, skirmish, war

scrimp \ˈskrimp\ *vb* ♦ **:** to economize greatly ⟨~ and save⟩

♦ economize, save, skimp

scrim•shaw \ˈskrim-ˌshȯ\ *n* **:** carved or engraved articles made orig. by American whalers usually from baleen or whale ivory — **scrimshaw** *vb*
scrip \ˈskrip\ *n* **1 :** a certificate showing its holder is entitled to something (as stock or land) **2 :** paper money issued for temporary use in an emergency
¹script \ˈskript\ *n* **1 :** written matter (as lines for a play or broadcast) **2** ♦ **:** written characters **:** HANDWRITING

♦ handwriting, manuscript, penmanship

²script *abbr* scripture
scrip•ture \ˈskrip-chər\ *n* **1** *cap* **:** the books of the Bible — often used in plural **2 :** the sacred writings of a religion — **scrip•tur•al** \ˈskrip-chə-rəl\ *adj* — **scrip•tur•al•ly** *adv*
scriv•en•er \ˈskri-və-nər\ *n* **:** SCRIBE, COPYIST, WRITER
scrod \ˈskräd\ *n* **:** a young fish (as a cod or haddock); *esp* **:** one split and boned for cooking
scrof•u•la \ˈskrȯ-fyə-lə\ *n* **:** tuberculosis of lymph nodes especially in the neck
¹scroll \ˈskrōl\ *n* **:** a roll of paper or parchment for writing a document; *also* **:** a spiral or coiled ornamental form suggesting a loosely or partly rolled scroll
²scroll *vb* **:** to move or cause to move text or graphics up, down, or across a display screen
scroll saw *n* **1 :** FRETSAW **2 :** a machine saw with a narrow vertically reciprocating blade for cutting curved lines or openwork
scro•tum \ˈskrō-təm\ *n, pl* **scro•ta** \-tə\ *or* **scrotums :** a pouch that in most male mammals contains the testes
scrounge \ˈskrau̇nj\ *vb* **scrounged; scroung•ing :** to collect by or as if by foraging

¹scrub \ˈskrəb\ *n* **1 :** a thick growth of stunted trees or shrubs; *also* **:** an area of land covered with scrub **2 :** an inferior domestic animal **3** ♦ **:** a person of insignificant size or standing **4 :** a player not on the first team — **scrub** *adj* — **scrub•by** *adj*

♦ dwarf, midget, mite, peewee, pygmy, runt, shrimp

²scrub *vb* **scrubbed; scrub•bing 1 :** to clean or wash by rubbing ⟨~ clothes⟩ ⟨~ out a spot⟩ **2 :** CANCEL
³scrub *n* **1 :** an act or instance of scrubbing ⟨gave the clothes a good ~⟩ **2** *pl* **:** loose-fitting clothing worn by hospital staff ⟨surgical ~*s*⟩
scrub•ber \ˈskrə-bər\ *n* **:** one that scrubs; *esp* **:** an apparatus for removing impurities especially from gases
scruff \ˈskrəf\ *n* **:** the loose skin of the back of the neck **:** NAPE
scruffy \ˈskrə-fē\ *adj* **scruff•i•er; -est** ♦ **:** not in order or neat

♦ dilapidated, grungy, mean, neglected, ratty, seedy, shabby

scrump•tious \ˈskrəmp-shəs\ *adj* ♦ **:** highly pleasing; *esp* **:** DELICIOUS — **scrump•tious•ly** *adv*

♦ ambrosial, appetizing, delectable, delicious, flavorful (*or* flavourful), luscious, palatable, savory, tasty, toothsome, yummy

scrunch•ie *or* **scrunchy** \ˈskrən-chē, ˈskru̇n-\ *n* **:** a fabric-covered elastic for the hair
¹scru•ple \ˈskrü-pəl\ *n* **1 :** a point of conscience or honor **2** ♦ **:** hesitation due to ethical considerations

♦ compunction, misgiving, qualm

²scruple *vb* **scru•pled; scru•pling :** to be reluctant on grounds of conscience **:** HESITATE
³scruple *n* **:** a minute part or quantity
scru•pu•lous \ˈskrü-pyə-ləs\ *adj* **1** ♦ **:** having moral integrity **2 :** PAINSTAKING — **scru•pu•lous•ly** *adv*

♦ conscientious, ethical, honest, honorable (*or* honourable), just, moral, principled

scru•pu•lous•ness *n* ♦ **:** conformity to high standards of ethics or excellence

♦ care, carefulness, heed, heedfulness, pains

scru•ti•nise *chiefly Brit var of* SCRUTINIZE
scru•ti•nize \ˈskrü-tə-ˌnīz\ *vb* **-nized; -niz•ing** ♦ **:** to examine closely

♦ audit, check, examine, inspect, review, scan, survey

scru•ti•ny \ˈskrüt-ᵊn-ē\ *n, pl* **-nies** ♦ **:** a careful looking over

♦ audit, check, checkup, examination, inspection, review, scan, survey

scu•ba \ˈskü-bə\ *n* **:** an apparatus for breathing while swimming underwater
scuba diver *n* **:** one who swims underwater with the aid of scuba gear
¹scud \ˈskəd\ *vb* **scud•ded; scud•ding :** to move speedily
²scud *n* **:** light clouds driven by the wind
¹scuff \ˈskəf\ *vb* **1 :** to scrape the feet while walking **:** SHUFFLE **2** ♦ **:** to scratch or become scratched or worn away

♦ abrade, graze, scrape, scratch

²scuff *n* **1 :** a mark or injury caused by scuffing **2 :** a flat-soled slipper without heel strap
¹scuf•fle \ˈskə-fəl\ *vb* **scuf•fled; scuf•fling 1** ♦ **:** to struggle confusedly at close quarters **2 :** to shuffle one's feet

♦ grapple, tussle, wrestle

²scuffle *n* ♦ **:** a rough haphazard struggle with scrambling and confusion

♦ battle, clash, combat, conflict, contest, fight, fracas, fray, hassle, scrap, scrimmage, skirmish, struggle, tussle

¹scull \ˈskəl\ *n* **1 :** an oar for use in sculling; *also* **:** one of a pair of short oars for a single oarsman **2 :** a racing shell propelled by one or two persons using sculls
²scull *vb* ♦ **:** to propel (a boat) by an oar over the stern

♦ row

scul•lery \ˈskə-lə-rē\ *n, pl* **-ler•ies :** a small room near the kitchen used for cleaning dishes, cooking utensils, and vegetables
scul•lion \ˈskəl-yən\ *n* **:** a kitchen helper
sculpt \ˈskəlpt\ *vb* **:** to cut with care or precision **:** CARVE, SCULPTURE
sculp•tor \ˈskəlp-tər\ *n* **:** a person who produces works of sculpture
¹sculp•ture \ˈskəlp-chər\ *n* **:** the act, process, or art of carving or

molding material (as stone, wood, or plastic); *also* : work produced this way — **sculp•tur•al** \ˈskəlp-chə-rəl\ *adj*
[2]**sculpture** *vb* **sculp•tured; sculp•tur•ing** : to form or alter as or as if a work of sculpture
scum \ˈskəm\ *n* **1** : a slimy or filmy covering on the surface of a liquid **2** : waste matter **3** ♦ : a low, vile, or worthless person or group of people : RABBLE

♦ rabble, riffraff, trash

scup•per \ˈskə-pər\ *n* : an opening in the side of a ship through which water on deck is drained overboard
scurf \ˈskərf\ *n* : thin dry scales of skin (as dandruff); *also* : a scaly deposit or covering — **scurfy** \ˈskər-fē\ *adj*
scur•ri•lous \ˈskər-ə-ləs\ *adj* ♦ : using or marked by the use of coarse or abusive language

♦ abusive, opprobrious

scur•ry \ˈskər-ē\ *vb* **scur•ried; scur•ry•ing** ♦ : to move in or as if in a brisk pace : SCAMPER

♦ dash, fly, hasten, hurry, run, rush, scamper, scoot, shoot, speed

[1]**scur•vy** \ˈskər-vē\ *n* : a disease caused by a lack of vitamin C and characterized by spongy gums, loosened teeth, and bleeding under the skin
[2]**scurvy** *adj* ♦ : arousing disgust or scorn : CONTEMPTIBLE — **scur•vi•ly** \ˈskər-və-lē\ *adv*

♦ contemptible, despicable, lousy, nasty, pitiful, scabby, sorry, wretched

scutch•eon \ˈskə-chən\ *n* : ESCUTCHEON
[1]**scut•tle** \ˈskət-ᵊl\ *n* : a pail for carrying coal
[2]**scuttle** *n* : a small opening with a lid especially in the deck, side, or bottom of a ship
[3]**scuttle** *vb* **scut•tled; scut•tling** : to cut a hole in the deck, side, or bottom of (a ship) in order to sink
[4]**scuttle** *vb* **scut•tled; scut•tling** : to move in or as if in a brisk pace : SCURRY, SCAMPER
scut•tle•butt \ˈskət-ᵊl-ˌbət\ *n* : GOSSIP
scythe \ˈsīth\ *n* : an implement for mowing (as grass or grain) by hand — **scythe** *vb*
SD *abbr* **1** South Dakota **2** special delivery
S Dak *abbr* South Dakota
SDI *abbr* Strategic Defense Initiative
Se *symbol* selenium
SE *abbr* southeast
sea \ˈsē\ *n* **1** : a large body of salt water **2** ♦ : the waters of the earth as distinguished from the land and air : OCEAN **3** : rough water; *also* : a large wave **4** : something likened to the sea especially in vastness — **sea** *adj* — **at sea** : LOST, BEWILDERED

♦ blue, brine, deep, ocean

sea anemone *n* : any of numerous coelenterate polyps whose form, bright and varied colors, and cluster of tentacles superficially resemble a flower
sea•bird \ˈsē-ˌbərd\ *n* : a bird (as a gull) frequenting the open ocean
sea•board \-ˌbōrd\ *n* : SEACOAST; *also* : the land bordering a coast
sea•borg•i•um \sē-ˈbȯr-gē-əm\ *n* : a short-lived radioactive chemical element produced artificially
sea•coast \-ˌkōst\ *n* : the shore of the sea
sea•far•er \-ˌfar-ər\ *n* : a person who navigates or assists in navigating a ship : SEAMAN 1
sea•far•ing \-ˌfar-iŋ\ *n* : the use of the sea for travel or transportation — **seafaring** *adj*
sea•food \-ˌfüd\ *n* : edible marine fish and shellfish
sea•go•ing \-ˌgō-iŋ\ *adj* : OCEANGOING
sea•gull \ˈsē-ˌgəl\ *n* : GULL
sea horse *n* : any of a genus of small marine fishes with the head and forepart of the body sharply flexed like the head and neck of a horse
[1]**seal** \ˈsēl\ *n, pl* **seals** *also* **seal** **1** : any of numerous large carnivorous sea mammals occurring chiefly in cold regions and having limbs adapted for swimming **2** : the pelt of a seal
[2]**seal** *vb* : to hunt seals
[3]**seal** *n* **1** : GUARANTEE, PLEDGE **2** : a device having a raised design that can be stamped on clay or wax; *also* : the impression made by stamping with such a device **3** : something that seals or closes up ⟨safety ~⟩
[4]**seal** *vb* **1** : to affix a seal to; *also* : AUTHENTICATE **2** : to fasten with or as if with a seal to prevent tampering **3** : to close or make secure against access, leakage, or passage **4** : to determine irrevocably ⟨~*ed* his fate⟩
sea–lane \ˈsē-ˌlān\ *n* : an established sea route
seal•ant \ˈsē-lənt\ *n* : a sealing agent
seal•er \ˈsē-lər\ *n* : a coat applied to prevent subsequent coats of paint or varnish from sinking in
sea level *n* : the level of the surface of the sea especially at its mean midway between mean high and low water
sea lion *n* : any of several large Pacific seals with small external ears
seal•skin \ˈsēl-ˌskin\ *n* **1** : [1] SEAL 2 **2** : a garment of sealskin
[1]**seam** \ˈsēm\ *n* **1** : the line of junction of two edges and especially of edges of fabric sewn together **2** : a layer of mineral matter **3** : WRINKLE
[2]**seam** *vb* **1** : to join by or as if by sewing **2** : to mark with lines suggesting seams
sea•man \ˈsē-mən\ *n* **1** ♦ : one who assists in the handling of ships : MARINER **2** : an enlisted man in the navy ranking next below a petty officer third class

♦ gob, jack, jack-tar, mariner, sailor, swab, tar

seaman apprentice *n* : an enlisted man in the navy ranking next below a seaman
seaman recruit *n* : an enlisted man of the lowest rank in the navy
sea•man•ship \ˈsē-mən-ˌship\ *n* : the art or skill of handling a ship
seam•less \ˈsēm-ləs\ *adj* : having no flaws or interruptions ⟨a ~ transition⟩ — **seam•less•ly** *adv*
sea•mount \ˈsē-ˌmau̇nt\ *n* : an underwater mountain
seam•stress \ˈsēm-strəs\ *n* : a woman who does sewing
seamy \ˈsē-mē\ *adj* **seam•i•er; -est** **1** : UNPLEASANT **2** : DEGRADED, SORDID
sé•ance \ˈsā-ˌäns\ *n* : a meeting to receive communications from spirits
sea•plane \ˈsē-ˌplān\ *n* : an airplane that can take off from and land on water
sea•port \-ˌpōrt\ *n* : a port for oceangoing ships
sear \ˈsir\ *vb* **1** ♦ : to make withered and dry **2 a** ♦ : to burn or scorch especially on the surface **b** : BRAND — **sear** *n*

♦ [1] dehydrate, dry, parch ♦ [2a] char, scorch, singe

[1]**search** \ˈsərch\ *vb* **1** ♦ : to look through in trying to find something **2** ♦ : to uncover, find, or come to know by inquiry or scrutiny : SEEK **3** ♦ : subject to a penetrating investigation : PROBE — **search•er** *n*

♦ [1, 3] explore, hunt, probe, prospect ♦ *usu* **search for** *or* **search out** [2] cast about, forage, hunt, pursue, quest, seek ♦ [3] dig, dredge, hunt, rake, ransack, rifle, rummage, scour

[2]**search** *n* : the act of searching
search engine *n* : computer software or a Web site used to search data (as text or other Web sites) for specified information
search•light \-ˌlīt\ *n* : an apparatus for projecting a powerful beam of light; *also* : the light projected
sear•ing \ˈsir-iŋ\ *adj* : very sharp, harsh or intense ⟨~ pain⟩ ⟨a ~ review⟩
sea scallop *n* : a large scallop of the Atlantic coast of No. America that is harvested for food
sea•scape \ˈsē-ˌskāp\ *n* **1** : a view of the sea **2** : a picture representing a scene at or of the sea
sea•shell \ˈsē-ˌshel\ *n* : the shell of a marine animal and especially a mollusk
sea•shore \-ˌshōr\ *n* : the shore of a sea
sea•sick \-ˌsik\ *adj* : nauseated by or as if by the motion of a ship — **sea•sick•ness** *n*
sea•side \ˈsē-ˌsīd\ *n* : SEASHORE
[1]**sea•son** \ˈsē-zən\ *n* **1** : one of the divisions of the year (as spring or summer) **2** : a period of the year associated with a particular activity, event, or holiday ⟨the Easter ~⟩ ⟨hunting ~⟩ — **sea•son•al** \-zə-nəl\ *adj* — **sea•son•al•ly** *adv*
[2]**season** *vb* **1** ♦ : to make pleasant to the taste by use of salt, pepper, or spices **2** : to make (as by aging or drying) suitable for use **3** ♦ : to accustom or habituate to something (as hardship) — **sea•son•er** *n*

♦ [1] flavor (*or* flavour), savor, spice ♦ [3] fortify, harden, steel, strengthen, toughen

sea•son•able \ˈsē-zə-nə-bəl\ *adj* : occurring at a good or proper time — **sea•son•ably** \-blē\ *adv*
seasonal affective disorder *n* : depression that recurs as the days grow shorter during the fall and winter
sea•soned *adj* **1** : made fit by use **2** ♦ : made skillful or wise through experience

♦ [2] accomplished, ace, adept, crack, experienced, expert, master, masterful, masterly, practiced, proficient, skilled, skillful, versed

sea•son•ing *n* ♦ **:** something that seasons

♦ flavor (*or* flavour), spice

1seat \ˈsēt\ *n* **1 :** a chair, bench, or stool for sitting on **2** ♦ **:** a place which serves as a capital or center **3** ♦ **:** the part of the body that bears the weight in sitting

♦ [2] base, center (*or* centre), core, cynosure, eye, focus, heart, hub, mecca, nucleus ♦ [3] backside, bottom, butt, buttocks, posterior, rear, rump

2seat *vb* **1** ♦ **:** to place in or on a seat **2 :** to provide seats for

♦ place, put, set down, sit

seat belt *n* **:** straps designed to hold a person in a seat
SEATO \ˈsē-ˌtō\ *abbr* Southeast Asia Treaty Organization
seat–of–the–pants *adj* **:** employing or based on personal experience, judgment, and effort rather than technological aids ⟨∼ navigation⟩
sea turtle *n* **:** any of two families of marine turtles that have the feet modified into paddles
sea urchin *n* **:** any of numerous spiny marine echinoderms having thin brittle globular shells
sea•wall \ˈsē-ˌwȯl\ *n* **:** an embankment to protect the shore from erosion
1sea•ward \ˈsē-wərd\ *n* **:** the direction or side away from land and toward the open sea
2seaward *also* **sea•wards** \-wərdz\ *adv* **:** toward the sea
3seaward *adj* **1 :** directed or situated toward the sea **2 :** coming from the sea
sea•wa•ter \ˈsē-ˌwȯ-tər, -ˌwä-\ *n* **:** water in or from the sea
sea•way \-ˌwā\ *n* **:** an inland waterway that admits ocean shipping
sea•weed \-ˌwēd\ *n* **:** a marine alga (as a kelp); *also* **:** a mass of marine algae
sea•wor•thy \-ˌwər-thē\ *adj* **:** fit for a sea voyage ⟨a ∼ ship⟩
se•ba•ceous \si-ˈbā-shəs\ *adj* **:** of, relating to, or secreting fatty material
sec *abbr* **1** second; secondary **2** secretary **3** section **4** according to
SEC *abbr* Securities and Exchange Commission
se•cede \si-ˈsēd\ *vb* **se•ced•ed; se•ced•ing :** to withdraw from an organized body and especially from a political body
se•ces•sion \si-ˈse-shən\ *n* **:** the act of seceding — **se•ces•sion•ist** *n*
se•clude \si-ˈklüd\ *vb* **se•clud•ed; se•clud•ing** ♦ **:** to keep or shut away from others

♦ cut off, insulate, isolate, segregate, separate, sequester

secluded *adj* **1** ♦ **:** screened or hidden from view **2 :** living in seclusion

♦ cloistered, covert, isolated, quiet, remote, secret

se•clu•sion \si-ˈklü-zhən\ *n* ♦ **:** the act of secluding **:** the state of being secluded — **se•clu•sive** \-siv\ *adj*

♦ insulation, isolation, segregation, sequestration, solitude

1sec•ond \ˈse-kənd\ *adj* **1 :** being number two in a countable series **2 :** next after the first **3 :** ALTERNATE ⟨every ∼ year⟩ — **second** *or* **sec•ond•ly** *adv*
2second *n* **1 :** one that is second **2 :** one who assists another (as in a duel) **3 :** an inferior or flawed article (as of merchandise) **4 :** the second forward gear in a motor vehicle
3second *n* **1 :** the 60th part of a minute of time or angular measure **2** ♦ **:** an instant of time

♦ flash, instant, jiffy, minute, moment, shake, trice, twinkle, twinkling, wink

4second *vb* **1 :** to encourage or give support to **2 :** to act as a second to **3 :** to support (a motion) by adding one's voice to that of a proposer
1sec•ond•ary \ˈse-kən-ˌder-ē\ *adj* **1** ♦ **:** second in rank, value, or occurrence **2 :** belonging to a second or later stage of development **3 :** coming after the primary or elementary ⟨∼ schools⟩

♦ inferior, mean, minor, second-rate

2secondary *n, pl* **-ar•ies :** the defensive backfield of a football team
secondary sex characteristic *n* **:** a physical characteristic that appears in members of one sex at puberty or in seasonal breeders at breeding season and is not directly concerned with reproduction
second fiddle *n* **:** one that plays a supporting or subservient role
sec•ond–guess \ˌse-kənd-ˈges\ *vb* **1 :** to think out other strategies or explanations for after the event **2 :** to seek to anticipate or predict
sec•ond•hand \-ˈhand\ *adj* **1 :** not original **2 :** not new **:** USED ⟨∼ clothes⟩ **3 :** dealing in used goods
secondhand smoke *n* **:** tobacco smoke that is exhaled by smokers or is given off by burning tobacco and is inhaled by persons nearby
second lieutenant *n* **:** a commissioned officer (as in the army) ranking next below a first lieutenant
sec•ond–rate \ˌse-kənd-ˈrāt\ *adj* ♦ **:** of second or inferior quality or value

♦ common, fair, indifferent, mediocre, medium, middling, ordinary, passable, run-of-the-mill, so-so ♦ cheap, cut-rate, inferior, junky, lousy, mediocre, poor, sleazy

sec•ond–string \ˈse-kənd-ˈstriŋ\ *adj* **:** being a substitute (as on a team)
se•cre•cy \ˈsē-krə-sē\ *n, pl* **-cies 1 :** the habit or practice of being secretive **2 :** the condition of being hidden or concealed
1se•cret \ˈsē-krət\ *adj* **1 :** kept from knowledge or view ⟨a ∼ staircase⟩ **2** ♦ **:** working with hidden aims or methods **:** COVERT, STEALTHY; *also* **:** engaged in detecting or spying ⟨a ∼ agent⟩ **3** ♦ **:** kept from general knowledge — **se•cret•ly** *adv*

♦ [2] clandestine, covert, furtive, hugger-mugger, private, sneak, sneaky, stealthy, surreptitious, undercover, underground, underhanded ***Ant*** open, overt, public ♦ [3] confidential, hushed, inside, intimate, private

2secret *n* **1** ♦ **:** something kept hidden or unexplained **:** MYSTERY **2 :** something kept from the knowledge of others

♦ conundrum, enigma, mystery, mystification, puzzle, puzzlement, riddle

sec•re•tar•i•at \ˌse-krə-ˈter-ē-ət\ *n* **1 :** the office of a secretary **2 :** the secretarial staff in an office **3 :** the administrative department of a governmental organization ⟨the UN ∼⟩
sec•re•tary \ˈse-krə-ˌter-ē\ *n, pl* **-tar•ies 1 :** a person employed to handle records, correspondence, and routine work for another person **2** ♦ **:** an officer of a corporation or business who is in charge of correspondence and records **3 :** an official at the head of a department of government **4 :** a writing desk — **sec•re•tari•al** \ˌse-krə-ˈter-ē-əl\ *adj* — **sec•re•tary•ship** \ˈse-krə-ˌter-ē-ˌship\ *n*

♦ clerk, register, registrar, scribe

1se•crete \si-ˈkrēt\ *vb* **se•cret•ed; se•cret•ing :** to form and give off (a secretion)
2se•crete \si-ˈkrēt, ˈsē-krət\ *vb* **se•cret•ed; se•cret•ing** ♦ **:** to deposit or conceal in a hiding place **:** HIDE

♦ bury, cache, conceal, ensconce, hide

se•cre•tion \si-ˈkrē-shən\ *n* **1 :** the process of secreting something **2 :** a product of glandular activity; *esp* **:** one (as a hormone) useful in the organism **3** ♦ **:** the act of hiding something — **se•cre•to•ry** \ˈsē-krə-ˌtōr-ē\ *adj*

♦ concealment

se•cre•tive \ˈsē-krə-tiv, si-ˈkrē-\ *adj* ♦ **:** tending to keep secrets or to act secretly — **se•cre•tive•ly** *adv* — **se•cre•tive•ness** *n*

♦ close, closemouthed, dark, reticent, uncommunicative ***Ant*** communicative, open

1sect \ˈsekt\ *n* **1 :** a dissenting religious body **2 :** a religious denomination **3 :** a group adhering to a distinctive doctrine or to a leader **4** ♦ **:** an opinionated faction (as of a party)

♦ bloc, body, coalition, combination, combine, faction, party, set, side, wing

2sect *abbr* section; sectional
1sec•tar•i•an \sek-ˈter-ē-ən\ *adj* **1 :** of or relating to a sect or sectarian **2** ♦ **:** limited in character or scope — **sec•tar•i•an•ism** *n*

♦ insular, little, narrow, parochial, petty, provincial, small

2sectarian *n* **1 :** an adherent of a sect **2 :** a narrow or bigoted person
sec•ta•ry \ˈsek-tə-rē\ *n, pl* **-ries :** a member of a sect
1sec•tion \ˈsek-shən\ *n* **1** ♦ **:** a part cut off or separated **2** ♦ **:** a distinct part (as of a territorial or political area, community, or group of people) **3 :** the appearance that a thing has or would have if cut straight through

♦ [1] member, part, partition, portion, segment ♦ [2] district, neighborhood (*or* neighbourhood), quarter

2section *vb* **1 :** to separate or become separated into sections **2 :** to represent in sections
sec•tion•al \ˈsek-shə-nəl\ *adj* **1 :** of, relating to, or characteristic

of a section **2 :** local or regional rather than general in character **3 :** divided into sections — **sec•tion•al•ism** *n*

sec•tor \ˈsek-tər\ *n* **1 :** a part of a circle between two radii **2 :** an area assigned to a military leader to defend **3 :** a subdivision of society

sec•u•lar \ˈse-kyə-lər\ *adj* **1** ♦ **:** not sacred or ecclesiastical **2 :** not bound by monastic vows ⟨a ∼ priest⟩

♦ nonreligious, profane, temporal

sec•u•lar•ise *chiefly Brit var of* SECULARIZE

sec•u•lar•ism \ˈse-kyə-lə-ˌri-zəm\ *n* **:** indifference to or exclusion of religion — **sec•u•lar•ist** \-rist\ *n* — **secularist** *also* **sec•u•lar•is•tic** \ˌse-kyə-lə-ˈris-tik\ *adj*

sec•u•lar•ize \ˈse-kyə-lə-ˌrīz\ *vb* **-ized; -iz•ing** **1 :** to make secular **2 :** to transfer from ecclesiastical to civil or lay use, possession, or control — **sec•u•lar•i•za•tion** \ˌse-kyə-lə-rə-ˈzā-shən\ *n* — **sec•u•lar•iz•er** \ˈse-kyə-lə-ˌrī-zər\ *n*

[1]**se•cure** \si-ˈkyu̇r\ *adj* **se•cur•er; -est** **1 :** easy in mind **:** free from fear **2** ♦ **:** free from danger or risk of loss **:** SAFE **3** ♦ **:** characterized by certainty or security — **se•cure•ly** *adv*

♦ [2] all right, alright, safe ♦ [3] assured, confident, self-assured, self-confident

[2]**secure** *vb* **se•cured; se•cur•ing** **1** ♦ **:** to make safe **:** GUARD **2 :** to assure payment of by giving a pledge or collateral **3** ♦ **:** to fasten safely ⟨∼ a door⟩ **4** ♦ **:** to get secure usually lasting possession or control of **:** ACQUIRE

♦ [1] cover, defend, guard, protect, safeguard, screen, shield, ward ♦ [1] assure, cinch, ensure, guarantee, guaranty, insure ♦ [3] anchor, catch, clamp, fasten, fix, hitch, moor, set ♦ [4] acquire, attain, capture, carry, draw, earn, gain, garner, get, land, make, obtain, procure, realize, win

se•cu•ri•ty \si-ˈkyu̇r-ə-tē\ *n, pl* **-ties** **1 :** SAFETY **2 :** freedom from worry **3** ♦ **:** something given as pledge of payment ⟨a ∼ deposit⟩ **4** *pl* **:** bond or stock certificates **5** ♦ **:** something that secures **:** PROTECTION

♦ [3] gage, guarantee, guaranty, pawn, pledge ♦ [5] aegis, armor (*or* armour), cover, defense (*or* defence), guard, protection, safeguard, screen, shield, wall, ward

secy *abbr* secretary

se•dan \si-ˈdan\ *n* **1 :** a covered chair borne on poles by two men **2 :** an automobile seating four or more people and usually having a permanent top

[1]**se•date** \si-ˈdāt\ *adj* **:** quiet and dignified in behavior — **se•date•ly** *adv*

[2]**sedate** *vb* **se•dat•ed; se•dat•ing** **:** to dose with sedatives — **se•da•tion** \si-ˈdā-shən\ *n*

[1]**sed•a•tive** \ˈse-də-tiv\ *adj* ♦ **:** serving or tending to relieve tension

♦ comforting, dreamy, narcotic, soothing

[2]**sedative** *n* **:** a sedative drug

sed•en•tary \ˈsed-ᵊn-ˌter-ē\ *adj* **:** characterized by or requiring much sitting

sedge \ˈsej\ *n* **:** any of a family of plants especially of marshy areas that differ from the related grasses especially in having solid stems — **sedgy** \ˈse-jē\ *adj*

sed•i•ment \ˈse-də-mənt\ *n* **1** ♦ **:** the material that settles to the bottom of a liquid **2 :** material (as stones and sand) deposited by water, wind, or a glacier — **sed•i•men•ta•ry** \ˌse-də-ˈmen-tə-rē\ *adj* — **sed•i•men•ta•tion** \-mən-ˈtā-shən, -ˌmen-\ *n*

♦ deposit, dregs, grounds, lees, precipitate

se•di•tion \si-ˈdi-shən\ *n* **:** the causing of discontent, insurrection, or resistance against a government — **se•di•tious** \-shəs\ *adj*

se•duce \si-ˈdüs, -ˈdyüs\ *vb* **se•duced; se•duc•ing** **1 :** to persuade to disobedience or disloyalty **2** ♦ **:** to lead astray **3 :** to entice to sexual intercourse — **se•duc•er** *n*

♦ allure, beguile, decoy, entice, lead on, lure, tempt

se•duc•tion \si-ˈdək-shən\ *n* **1 :** the act of seducing **2** ♦ **:** something that seduces **3 :** something that attracts or charms

♦ enticement, lure, solicitation, temptation

se•duc•tive \-tiv\ *adj* ♦ **:** tending to seduce **:** having alluring or tempting qualities

♦ alluring, attractive, captivating, charming, elfin, engaging, fascinating, fetching, glamorous, magnetic

sed•u•lous \ˈse-jə-ləs\ *adj* ♦ diligent in application or pursuit

♦ active, assiduous, busy, diligent, engaged, laborious, occupied, working

[1]**see** \ˈsē\ *vb* **saw** \ˈsȯ\; **seen** \ˈsēn\; **see•ing** **1** ♦ **:** to perceive by the eye; *also* **:** to have the power of sight **2** ♦ **:** to have experience of **3** ♦ **:** to perceive the meaning or importance of; *also* **:** to be aware of **4 :** to make sure ⟨∼ that order is kept⟩ **5 :** to meet with **6 :** to keep company with especially in dating **7 :** ACCOMPANY, ESCORT

♦ [1] behold, descry, discern, distinguish, espy, eye, look, note, notice, observe, perceive, regard, remark, sight, spy, view, witness ♦ [2] endure, experience, feel, have, know, suffer, sustain, taste, undergo ♦ [3] ascertain, catch on, discover, find out, hear, learn, realize ♦ [3] appreciate, apprehend, catch, catch on (to), comprehend, get, grasp, make, make out, perceive, seize, understand

[2]**see** *n* **:** the authority or jurisdiction of a bishop

[1]**seed** \ˈsēd\ *n, pl* **seed** *or* **seeds** **1 :** the grains of plants used for sowing **2 :** a ripened ovule of a flowering plant that may develop into a new plant; *also* **:** a plant structure (as a spore or small dry fruit) capable of producing a new plant **3** ♦ **:** offspring of animals or plants **4 :** SOURCE, ORIGIN — **seed•less** *adj* — **go to seed** *or* **run to seed** **1 :** to develop seed **2 :** DECAY

♦ issue, offspring, posterity, progeny, spawn

[2]**seed** *vb* **1** ♦ **:** to sprinkle with seed **:** PLANT ⟨∼ land to grass⟩ **2 :** to bear or shed seeds **3 :** to remove seeds from — **seed•er** *n*

♦ drill, plant, sow

seed•bed \-ˌbed\ *n* **:** soil or a bed of soil prepared for planting seed

seed•ling \ˈsēd-liŋ\ *n* **1 :** a young plant grown from seed **2 :** a young tree before it becomes a sapling

seed•time \ˈsēd-ˌtīm\ *n* **:** the season for sowing

seedy \ˈsē-dē\ *adj* **seed•i•er; -est** **1 :** containing or full of seeds **2** ♦ **:** inferior in condition or quality **:** SHABBY

♦ ragged, ratty, shabby, tattered, threadbare, worn-out

seek \ˈsēk\ *vb* **sought** \ˈsȯt\; **seek•ing** **1** ♦ **:** to search for **2** ♦ **:** to try to reach or obtain **3** ♦ **:** to make an attempt

♦ [1] cast about, forage, hunt, pursue, quest, search (for *or* out) ♦ [2] ask, call, plead, quest, request, solicit, sue ♦ [3] assay, attempt, endeavor (*or* endeavour), essay, strive, try

seek•er *n* ♦ **:** one that seeks or is used in seeking

♦ applicant, aspirant, campaigner, candidate, contender, hopeful, prospect

seem \ˈsēm\ *vb* **1 :** to appear to the observation or understanding **2** ♦ **:** to be so in appearance **:** APPEAR

♦ act, appear, look, make, sound

seem•ing *adj* ♦ **:** outwardly apparent

♦ apparent, assumed, evident, ostensible, reputed, supposed

seem•ing•ly *adv* ♦ **:** so far as can be seen or judged

♦ apparently, evidently, ostensibly, presumably, supposedly

seem•ly \ˈsēm-lē\ *adj* **seem•li•er; -est** **1** ♦ **:** conventionally proper **2 :** FIT

♦ correct, decent, decorous, genteel, nice, polite, proper, respectable

seep \ˈsēp\ *vb* ♦ **:** to flow or pass slowly through fine pores or cracks — **seep•age** \ˈsē-pij\ *n*

♦ bleed, exude, ooze, percolate, strain, sweat, weep

seer \ˈsir\ *n* ♦ **:** a person who foresees or predicts events **:** PROPHET

♦ augur, diviner, forecaster, fortune-teller, futurist, prognosticator, prophet, soothsayer

seer•suck•er \ˈsir-ˌsə-kər\ *n* **:** a light fabric of linen, cotton, or rayon usually striped and slightly puckered

[1]**see•saw** \ˈsē-ˌsȯ\ *n* **1 :** a contest in which each side assumes then relinquishes the lead **2 :** a children's sport of riding up and down on the ends of a plank supported in the middle; *also* **:** the plank so used

[2]**seesaw** *vb* ♦ **:** to move backward and forward or up and down

♦ careen, lurch, pitch, rock, roll, sway, toss, wobble ♦ bob, bobble, jog, jounce, nod, pump

seethe \ˈsēth\ *vb* **seethed; seeth•ing** ♦ **:** to become violently agitated

♦ boil, burn, fume, rage, steam ♦ boil, churn, roil

seg•ment \ˈseg-mənt\ *n* **1** ♦ **:** a division of a thing **:** SECTION

2 : a part cut off from a geometrical figure (as a circle) by one or more points, lines, or planes — **seg•ment•ed** \-ˌmen-təd\ *adj*

♦ member, part, partition, portion, section

seg•re•gate \ˈse-gri-ˌgāt\ *vb* **-gat•ed; -gat•ing** **1** ♦ **:** to cut off from others **2 :** to separate especially by races

♦ cut off, insulate, isolate, seclude, separate, sequester

seg•re•ga•tion \ˌse-gri-ˈgā-shən\ *n* ♦ **:** the act or process of segregating **:** the state of being segregated

♦ insulation, isolation, seclusion, sequestration, solitude

seg•re•ga•tion•ist \ˌse-gri-ˈgā-shə-nist\ *n* **:** one who believes in or practices the segregation of races

sei•gneur \sān-ˈyər\ *n, often cap* **:** a feudal lord

[1]**seine** \ˈsān\ *n* **:** a large weighted fishing net

[2]**seine** *vb* **seined; sein•ing :** to fish or catch with a seine — **sein•er** *n*

seis•mic \ˈsīz-mik, ˈsīs-\ *adj* **:** of, relating to, resembling, or caused by an earthquake — **seis•mi•cal•ly** \-mik(ə-)lē\ *adv* — **seis•mic•i•ty** \sīz-ˈmi-sə-tē, sīs-\ *n*

seis•mo•gram \ˈsīz-mə-ˌgram, ˈsīs-\ *n* **:** the record of an earth tremor made by a seismograph

seis•mo•graph \-ˌgraf\ *n* **:** an apparatus to measure and record seismic vibrations — **seis•mo•graph•ic** \ˌsīz-mə-ˈgra-fik, ˌsīs-\ *adj* — **seis•mog•ra•phy** \sīz-ˈmä-grə-fē, sīs-\ *n*

seis•mol•o•gy \sīz-ˈmä-lə-jē, sīs-\ *n* **:** a science that deals with earthquakes — **seis•mo•log•i•cal** \ˌsīz-mə-ˈlä-ji-kəl, ˌsīs-\ *adj* — **seis•mol•o•gist** \sīz-ˈmä-lə-jist, sīs-\ *n*

seis•mom•e•ter \sīz-ˈmä-mə-tər, sīs-\ *n* **:** a seismograph measuring the actual movement of the ground

seize \ˈsēz\ *vb* **seized; seiz•ing** **1** ♦ **:** to lay hold of or take possession of by force **2** ♦ **:** to take prisoner **:** ARREST **3** ♦ **:** to understand fully and distinctly **4 :** to attack or overwhelm physically **:** AFFLICT

♦ [1] bag, capture, catch, collar, corral, get, grab, grapple, hook, land, nab, snare, trap ♦ [2] apprehend, arrest, nab, pick up, restrain ♦ [3] appreciate, apprehend, catch, catch on (to), comprehend, get, grasp, make, make out, perceive, see, understand

sei•zure \ˈsē-zhər\ *n* **1 :** the act of seizing **:** the state of being seized **2** ♦ **:** a sudden attack (as of disease)

♦ attack, bout, case, fit, siege, spell

sel *abbr* select; selected; selection

sel•dom \ˈsel-dəm\ *adv* ♦ **:** in few instances **:** RARELY

♦ infrequently, little, rarely *Ant* frequently, often

[1]**se•lect** \sə-ˈlekt\ *adj* **1** ♦ **:** chosen from a number or group by fitness or preference; *also* **:** of special value or excellence **:** CHOICE **2 :** judicious or restrictive in choice **:** DISCRIMINATING

♦ choice, dainty, delicate, elegant, exquisite, rare ♦ chosen, elect

[2]**select** *vb* ♦ **:** to choose from a number or group **:** pick out

♦ choose, cull, elect, handpick, name, opt, pick, prefer, single, take

se•lect•ed *adj* **:** chosen by fitness or preference **:** SELECT; *specif* **:** of a higher grade or quality than the ordinary

se•lec•tion \sə-ˈlek-shən\ *n* **1** ♦ **:** the act or process of selecting **2 :** something selected **:** CHOICE **3 :** a natural or artificial process that tends to favor the survival and reproduction of individuals with certain traits but not those with others

♦ choice, election

se•lec•tive \sə-ˈlek-tiv\ *adj* ♦ **:** of or relating to selection **:** selecting or tending to select ⟨∼ shoppers⟩

♦ choosy, particular, picky *Ant* nonselective

selective service *n* **:** a system for calling men up for military service **:** DRAFT

se•lect•man \si-ˈlekt-ˌman, -mən\ *n* **:** one of a board of officials elected in towns of most New England states to administer town affairs

se•le•ni•um \sə-ˈlē-nē-əm\ *n* **:** a photosensitive chemical element

self \ˈself\ *n, pl* **selves** \ˈselvz\ **1 :** the essential person distinct from all other persons in identity **2 :** a particular side of a person's character **3 :** personal interest **:** SELFISHNESS

self- *comb form* **1 :** oneself **:** itself **2 :** of oneself or itself **3 :** by oneself or itself; *also* **:** automatic **4 :** to, for, or toward oneself

self–abasement
self–absorbed
self–absorption
self–acceptance
self–accusation
self–addressed
self–adjusting
self–administer
self–advancement
self–aggrandizement
self–aggrandizing
self–analysis
self–anointed
self–appointed
self–appraisal
self–asserting
self–assertion
self–awareness
self–betrayal
self–cleaning
self–closing
self–complacent
self–concern
self–condemned
self–confessed
self–congratulation
self–congratulatory
self–constituted
self–contempt
self–contradiction
self–contradictory
self–correcting
self–created
self–criticism
self–cultivation
self–deceit
self–deception
self–defeating
self–definition
self–delusion
self–denying
self–deprecating
self–deprecation
self–depreciation
self–described
self–despair
self–destruction
self–destructive
self–directed
self–distrust
self–doubt
self–educated
self–employed
self–employment
self–enhancement
self–examination
self–explaining
self–explanatory
self–expression
self–forgetful
self–giving
self–hate
self–help
self–hypnosis
self–image
self–imposed
self–improvement
self–incrimination
self–induced
self–indulgence
self–indulgent
self–inflicted
self–knowledge
self–limiting
self–love
self–lubricating
self–luminous
self–operating
self–perception
self–perpetuating
self–pity
self–portrait
self–preservation
self–proclaimed
self–professed
self–promotion
self–propelled
self–propelling
self–protection
self–realization
self–referential
self–reliance
self–renewing
self–respecting
self–revelation
self–rule
self–sacrifice
self–sacrificing
self–service
self–serving
self–starting
self–styled
self–sustaining
self–taught
self–torment
self–winding
self–worth

self–act•ing \ˈself-ˈak-tiŋ\ *adj* ♦ **:** acting or capable of acting of or by itself

♦ automatic, laborsaving (*or* laboursaving), robotic

self–as•ser•tive \-ə-ˈsər-tiv\ *adj* ♦ **:** given to or characterized by a forceful claim or demand to being recognized or listened to

♦ aggressive, ambitious, assertive, enterprising, fierce, go-getting, high-pressure, militant

self–as•sur•ance \-ə-ˈshu̇r-ən(t)s\ *n* ♦ **:** confidence in oneself and in one's powers and abilities

♦ aplomb, assurance, confidence, self-confidence, self-esteem

self–as•sured \-ə-ˈshu̇rd\ *adj* ♦ **:** sure of oneself

♦ assured, confident, secure, self-confident

self–cen•tered \ˈself-ˈsen-tərd\ *adj* **:** concerned only with one's own self

self–cen•tered•ness *n* ♦ **:** the quality or state of being self-centered

♦ egoism, egotism, self-interest, self-regard, selfishness

self–com•posed \ˌself-kəm-ˈpōzd\ *adj* **:** having control over one's emotions

self–con•ceit \ˈself-kən-ˈsēt\ *n* ♦ **:** an exaggerated opinion of one's own qualities or abilities

♦ complacence, conceit, ego, egotism, pride, self-esteem, self-importance, self-satisfaction, smugness, vainglory, vanity

self–con•fi•dence \-ˈkän-fə-dən(t)s, -ˌden(t)s\ *n* ♦ : confidence in oneself and in one's powers and abilities

♦ aplomb, assurance, confidence, self-assurance, self-esteem

self–con•fi•dent \-ˈkän-fə-dənt, -ˌdent\ *adj* ♦ : confident of one's own strength or ability

♦ assured, confident, secure, self-assured

self–con•scious \ˈself-ˈkän-chəs\ *adj* : uncomfortably conscious of oneself as an object of observation by others — **self–con•scious•ly** *adv* — **self–con•scious•ness** *n*

self–con•tained \ˌself-kən-ˈtānd\ *adj* **1** : complete in itself **2** : showing self-control; *also* : reserved in manner

self–con•trol \ˈself-kən-ˈtrōl\ *n* ♦ : restraint exercised over one's own impulses, emotions, or desires

♦ constraint, inhibition, repression, restraint, self-restraint, suppression ♦ self-discipline, self-government, self-possession, will, willpower

self–de•fense \ˈself-di-ˈfens\ *n* **1** : a plea of justification for the use of force or for homicide **2** : the act of defending oneself, one's property, or a close relative

self–de•ni•al \-di-ˈnī(-ə)l\ *n* ♦ : a restraint or limitation of one's own desires or interests

♦ abnegation, renouncement, renunciation, repudiation

self–des•truct \-di-ˈstrəkt\ *vb* : to bring about one's own ruin or destruction

self–de•ter•mi•na•tion \-di-ˌtər-mə-ˈnā-shən\ *n* **1** ♦ : free choice of one's own acts or states without external compulsion **2** : determination by the people of a territorial unit of their own future political status

♦ accord, choice, free will, option, volition, will

self–dis•ci•pline \-ˈdi-sə-plən\ *n* ♦ : correction or regulation of oneself for the sake of improvement

♦ restraint, self-control, self-government, self-possession, self-restraint, will, willpower

self–ef•fac•ing \-ə-ˈfā-siŋ\ *adj* : RETIRING, SHY

self–es•teem \-ə-ˈstēm\ *n* ♦ : a confidence and satisfaction in oneself; *also* : SELF-CONCEIT

♦ aplomb, assurance, confidence, self-assurance, self-confidence, self-regard, self-respect ♦ complacence, conceit, ego, egotism, pride, self-conceit, self-importance, self-satisfaction, smugness, vainglory, vanity

self–ev•i•dent \ˌself-ˈe-və-dənt\ *adj* : evident without proof or reasoning

self–fer•til•iza•tion \ˌself-ˌfərt-ᵊl-ə-ˈzā-shən\ *n* : fertilization of a plant or animal by its own pollen or sperm

self–ful•fill•ing \ˌself-fu̇l-ˈfi-liŋ\ *adj* : becoming real or true by virtue of having been predicted or expected ⟨a ~ prophecy⟩

self–gov•ern•ing \-ˈgə-vər-niŋ\ *adj* ♦ : having control or rule over oneself; *specif* : having self-government

♦ autonomous, free, independent, separate, sovereign ♦ democratic, popular, republican

self–gov•ern•ment \-ˈgə-vər(n)-mənt, -ˈgə-vᵊm-ənt\ *n* **1** ♦ : restraint exercised over one's own impulses, emotions, or desires **2** ♦ : government under the control and direction of the inhabitants of a political unit rather than by an outside authority

♦ [1] restraint, self-control, self-discipline, self-possession, self-restraint, will, willpower ♦ [2] autonomy, freedom, independence, liberty, sovereignty

self–help \ˈself-ˈhelp\ *n* : the process of bettering oneself or coping with one's problems without the aid of others — **self–help** *adj*

self–iden•ti•ty \-ī-ˈden-tə-tē, -ˈde-nə-tē\ *n* **1** : sameness of a thing with itself **2** ♦ : total character peculiar to and distinguishing an individual from others

♦ character, identity, individuality, personality

self–im•por•tance \ˈself-im-ˈpȯr-tᵊn(t)s, -tən(t)s\ *n* ♦ : an exaggerated estimate of one's own importance; *also* : arrogant or pompous behavior

♦ arrogance, haughtiness, loftiness, pretense, pretension, pretentiousness, superiority ♦ complacence, conceit, ego, egotism, pride, self-conceit, self-esteem, self-satisfaction, smugness, vainglory, vanity

self–important \-tᵊnt, -tənt\ *adj* ♦ : having or showing self-importance

♦ complacent, conceited, egotistic, important, overweening, pompous, prideful, proud, self-satisfied, smug, stuck-up, vain

self–imposed *adj* : imposed by oneself or itself : voluntarily assumed

self–in•dul•gence \-in-ˈdəl-jəns\ *n* : excessive or unrestrained gratification of one's own appetites, desires, or whims

self–in•ter•est \-ˈin-t(ə-)rəst; -ˈin-tə-ˌrest, -ˌtrest; -ˈin-tərst\ *n* ♦ : a concern for one's own advantage and well-being

♦ egoism, egotism, self-centeredness, self-regard, selfishness

self•ish \ˈsel-fish\ *adj* ♦ : concerned with one's own welfare excessively or without regard for others — **self•ish•ly** *adv*

♦ egocentric, egotistic, self-seeking

self•ish•ness *n* ♦ : the quality or state of being selfish

♦ egoism, egotism, self-centeredness, self-interest, self-regard

self•less \ˈself-ləs\ *adj* : UNSELFISH — **self•less•ness** *n*

self–made \ˈself-ˈmād\ *adj* : having achieved success or prominence by one's own efforts ⟨a ~ man⟩

self–pol•li•na•tion \ˌself-ˌpä-lə-ˈnā-shən\ *n* : pollination of a flower by its own pollen or sometimes by pollen from another flower on the same plant

self–pos•sessed \ˈself-pə-ˈzest *also* -ˈsest\ *adj* ♦ : having or showing self-possession : composed in mind or manner

♦ calm, collected, composed, cool, placid, serene, tranquil, undisturbed, unperturbed, unshaken, untroubled, unworried

self–pos•ses•sion \-pə-ˈze-shən *also* -ˈse-\ *n* ♦ : control of one's emotions or reactions especially when under stress

♦ aplomb, calmness, composure, coolness, equanimity, placidity, serenity, tranquillity ♦ restraint, self-control, self-discipline, self-government, self-restraint, will, willpower

self–re•gard \-ri-ˈgärd\ *n* ♦ : regard for or consideration of oneself or one's own interests

♦ ego, pride, self-esteem, self-respect ♦ egoism, egotism, self-centeredness, self-interest, selfishness

self–reg•u•lat•ing \ˈself-ˈre-gyə-ˌlā-tiŋ\ *adj* : AUTOMATIC

self–re•li•ant \-ri-ˈlī-ənt\ *adj* ♦ : having confidence in and exercising one's own powers or judgment

♦ independent, self-sufficient, self-supporting

self–re•proach \-ri-prōch\ *n* ♦ : the act or an instance of reproaching oneself

♦ contrition, guilt, penitence, remorse, repentance, shame

self–re•spect \-ri-ˈspekt\ *n* **1** : a proper respect for oneself as a human being **2** ♦ : regard for one's own standing or position

♦ ego, pride, self-esteem, self-regard

self–re•straint \-ri-strānt\ *n* ♦ : restraint imposed on oneself

♦ constraint, inhibition, repression, restraint, self-control, suppression ♦ self-discipline, self-government, self-possession, will, willpower

self–righ•teous \-ˈrī-chəs\ *adj* : strongly convinced of one's own righteousness — **self–righ•teous•ly** *adv*

self•same \ˈself-ˌsām\ *adj* ♦ : precisely the same : IDENTICAL

♦ identical, same, very

self–sat•is•fac•tion \ˌself-ˌsa-təs-ˈfak-shən\ *n* ♦ : a usually smug satisfaction with oneself or one's position or achievements

♦ complacence, conceit, ego, egotism, pride, self-conceit, self-esteem, self-importance, smugness, vainglory, vanity

self–sat•is•fied \ˈself-ˈsa-təs-ˌfīd\ *adj* ♦ : feeling or showing self-satisfaction

♦ complacent, conceited, egotistic, important, overweening, pompous, prideful, proud, self-important, smug, stuck-up, vain

self–seal•ing \ˈself-ˈsē-liŋ\ *adj* : capable of sealing itself (as after puncture)

self–seek•ing \ˈself-ˈsē-kiŋ\ *adj* ♦ : seeking only to further one's own interests — **self–seeking** *n*

♦ ambitious, go-getting ♦ egocentric, egotistic, selfish

self–start•er \-ˈstär-tər\ *n* ♦ : a person who has initiative

♦ go-getter, hustler, live wire, powerhouse

self–suf•fi•cien•cy \-sə-ˈfi-shən(t)-sē\ *n* : the quality or state of being self-sufficient

self–suf•fi•cient \-ˈfi-shənt\ *adj* ♦ : able to maintain oneself or itself without outside aid : capable of providing for one's own needs

♦ independent, self-reliant, self-supporting *Ant* dependent, reliant

self–sup•port•ing \-sə-ˈpȯr-tiŋ\ *adj* ♦ **:** meeting one's needs by one's own efforts or output

♦ independent, self-reliant, self-sufficient

self–will \ˈself-ˈwil\ *n* ♦ **:** stubborn or willful adherence to one's own desires or ideas **:** OBSTINACY

♦ hardheadedness, mulishness, obduracy, obstinacy, peevishness, pertinacity, stubbornness, tenacity

sell \ˈsel\ *vb* **sold** \ˈsōld\; **sell•ing 1 :** to transfer (property) in return for money or something else of value **2** ♦ **:** to deal in as a business **3 :** to achieve satisfactory sales ⟨cars are ∼*ing* well⟩ **4** ♦ **:** to have a specified price — usually used with *at* or *for*

♦ [2] deal, market, merchandise, put up, retail, vend ♦ *usu* **sell for** [4] bring, cost, fetch, go

sell•er *n* ♦ **:** one that offers for sale

♦ dealer, vendor

sell out *vb* **1 :** to dispose of entirely by sale; *esp* **:** to sell one's business **2 :** BETRAY — **sell•out** \ˈsel-ˌau̇t\ *n*

selt•zer \ˈselt-sər\ *n* **:** artificially carbonated water

sel•vage *or* **sel•vedge** \ˈsel-vij\ *n* **:** the edge of a woven fabric so formed as to prevent raveling

selves *pl of* SELF

sem *abbr* **1** semicolon **2** seminar **3** seminary

se•man•tic \si-ˈman-tik\ *also* **se•man•ti•cal** \-ti-kəl\ *adj* **:** of or relating to meaning in language

se•man•tics \si-ˈman-tiks\ *n sing or pl* **:** the study of meanings in language

sema•phore \ˈse-mə-ˌfōr\ *n* **1 :** a visual signaling apparatus with movable arms **2 :** signaling by hand-held flags

sem•blance \ˈsem-bləns\ *n* **1** ♦ **:** outward and often deceptive appearance or show **2 :** IMAGE, LIKENESS

♦ appearance, face, guise, name, show

se•men \ˈsē-mən\ *n* **:** a sticky whitish fluid of the male reproductive tract that contains the sperm

se•mes•ter \sə-ˈmes-tər\ *n* **1 :** half a year **2 :** one of the two terms into which many colleges divide the school year

semi \ˈse-ˌmī\ *n, pl* **sem•is :** SEMITRAILER

semi- \ˈse-mi, -ˌmī\ *prefix* **1 :** precisely half of **2 :** half in quantity or value; *also* **:** half of or occurring halfway through a specified period **3 :** partly **:** incompletely **4 :** partial **:** incomplete **5 :** having some of the characteristics of

semiannual
semiarid
semicentennial
semicircle
semicircular
semicivilized
semiclassical
semiconscious
semidivine
semiformal
semigloss
semi–independent
semiliquid
semiliterate
semimonthly
semiofficial
semipermanent
semipolitical
semiprecious
semiprivate
semiprofessional
semireligious
semiretired
semiskilled
semisoft
semisolid
semisweet
semitransparent
semiweekly
semiyearly

semi•au•to•mat•ic \ˌse-mē-ˌȯ-tə-ˈma-tik\ *adj, of a firearm* **:** able to fire repeatedly but requiring release and another press of the trigger for each successive shot

semi•co•lon \ˈse-mi-ˌkō-lən\ *n* **:** a punctuation mark ; used especially to separate major sentence elements

semi•con•duc•tor \ˌse-mi-kən-ˈdək-tər\ *n* **:** a substance whose electrical conductivity is between that of a conductor and an insulator — **semi•con•duct•ing** *adj*

semi•dark•ness \-ˈdärk-nəs\ *n* ♦ **:** partial darkness

♦ dusk, gloaming, gloom, murk, shade, shadows, twilight

¹**semi•fi•nal** \ˌse-mi-ˈfīn-ᵊl\ *adj* **:** being next to the last in an elimination tournament

²**semi•fi•nal** \ˈse-mi-ˌfīn-ᵊl\ *n* **:** a semifinal round or match — **semi•fi•nal•ist** \-ist\ *n*

semi•lu•nar \-ˈlü-nər\ *adj* **:** shaped like a crescent

sem•i•nal \ˈse-mən-ᵊl\ *adj* **1 :** of, relating to, or consisting of seed or semen **2 :** containing or contributing the seeds of later development **:** CREATIVE, ORIGINAL — **sem•i•nal•ly** *adv*

sem•i•nar \ˈse-mə-ˌnär\ *n* **1 :** a course of study pursued by a group of advanced students doing original research under a professor **2** ♦ **:** a meeting for giving and discussing information **:** CONFERENCE

♦ assembly, conference, congress, convention, convocation, council, gathering, get-together, huddle, meeting, powwow ♦ colloquy, conference, council, forum, panel, parley, powwow, symposium

sem•i•nary \ˈse-mə-ˌner-ē\ *n, pl* **-nar•ies :** an educational institution; *esp* **:** one that gives theological training — **sem•i•nar•i•an** \ˌse-mə-ˈner-ē-ən\ *n*

Sem•i•nole \ˈse-mə-ˌnōl\ *n, pl* **Semi•noles** *or* **Seminole :** a member of an American Indian people of Florida

semi•per•me•able \ˌse-mi-ˈpər-mē-ə-bəl\ *adj* **:** partially but not freely or wholly permeable; *esp* **:** permeable to some usually small molecules but not to other usually larger particles ⟨a ∼ membrane⟩ — **semi•per•me•abil•i•ty** \-ˌpər-mē-ə-ˈbi-lə-tē\ *n*

Sem•ite \ˈse-ˌmīt\ *n* **:** a member of any of a group of peoples (as the Hebrews or Arabs) of southwestern Asia — **Se•mit•ic** \sə-ˈmi-tik\ *adj*

semi•trail•er \ˈse-mi-ˌtrā-lər, -ˌmī-\ *n* **:** a freight trailer that when attached is supported at its forward end by the truck tractor; *also* **:** a semitrailer with attached tractor

sem•o•li•na \ˌse-mə-ˈlē-nə\ *n* **:** the purified hard grains produced from the milling of wheat and used especially for pasta

sempstress *var of* SEAMSTRESS

sen *abbr* **1** senate; senator **2** senior

sen•ate \ˈse-nət\ *n* **:** the second of two chambers of a legislature

sen•a•tor \ˈse-nə-tər\ *n* **:** a member of a senate — **sen•a•to•ri•al** \ˌse-nə-ˈtōr-ē-əl\ *adj*

send \ˈsend\ *vb* **sent** \ˈsent\; **send•ing 1** ♦ **:** to cause to go **2 :** EMIT **3 :** to propel or drive especially with force **4 :** to put or bring into a certain condition — **send•er** *n*

♦ consign, dispatch, pack, ship, transfer, transmit, transport *Ant* accept, receive

send–off \ˈsend-ˌȯf\ *n* **:** a demonstration of goodwill and enthusiasm at the start of a new venture (as a trip)

send–up \ˈsend-ˌəp\ *n* **:** PARODY, TAKEOFF

Sen•e•ca \ˈse-ni-kə\ *n, pl* **Seneca** *or* **Senecas :** a member of an American Indian people of western New York

Sen•e•ga•lese \ˌse-ni-gə-ˈlēz, -ˈlēs\ *n, pl* **Senegalese :** a native or inhabitant of Senegal — **Senegalese** *adj*

se•nes•cence \si-ˈnes-ᵊns\ *n* **:** the state of being old; *also* **:** the process of becoming old — **se•nes•cent** \-ᵊnt\ *adj*

se•nile \ˈsē-ˌnīl, ˈse-\ *adj* **:** OLD, AGED; *esp* **:** exhibiting a loss of cognitive abilities associated with old age — **se•nil•i•ty** \si-ˈni-lə-tē\ *n*

¹**se•nior** \ˈsē-nyər\ *n* **1** ♦ **:** a person older or of higher rank than another **2 :** a member of the graduating class of a high school or college

♦ better, elder, superior

²**senior** *adj* **1** ♦ **:** of earlier birth or greater age **2 :** more advanced in dignity or rank **3 :** belonging to the final year of a school or college course

♦ ancient, elderly, geriatric, old

senior chief petty officer *n* **:** a petty officer in the navy or coast guard ranking next below a master chief petty officer

senior citizen *n* ♦ **:** an elderly person; *esp* **:** one who has retired

♦ ancient, elder, golden-ager, oldster *Ant* youth, youngster

senior high school *n* **:** a school usually including grades 10 to 12

se•nior•i•ty \sēn-ˈyȯr-ə-tē\ *n* **1 :** the quality or state of being senior **2 :** a privileged status owing to length of continuous service

senior master sergeant *n* **:** a noncommissioned officer in the air force ranking next below a chief master sergeant

sen•na \ˈse-nə\ *n* **1 :** CASSIA 2; *esp* **:** one used medicinally **2 :** the dried leaflets or pods of a cassia used as a purgative

sen•sa•tion \sen-ˈsā-shən\ *n* **1 a :** awareness (as of noise or heat) or a mental process (as seeing or hearing) due to stimulation of a sense organ **b** ♦ **:** an indefinite bodily feeling **2** ♦ **:** a condition of excitement; *also* **:** the thing that causes this condition

♦ [1b] feel, feeling, sense ♦ [2] craze, enthusiasm, fad, fashion, go, mode, rage, style, trend, vogue ♦ [2] caution, flash, marvel, miracle, phenomenon, portent, prodigy, wonder

sen•sa•tion•al \-shə-nəl\ *adj* **1** ♦ **:** of or relating to sensation or the senses **2 :** arousing an intense and usually superficial interest or emotional reaction **3** ♦ **:** exceedingly or unexpectedly excellent or great ⟨a ~ talent⟩ — **sen•sa•tion•al•ly** *adv*

♦ [1] sensitive, sensory, sensuous ♦ [3] classic, excellent, fabulous, fine, grand, great, splendid, superb, superior, terrific, wonderful

sen•sa•tion•al•ise *chiefly Brit var of* SENSATIONALIZE
sen•sa•tion•al•ism \-nə-ˌli-zəm\ *n* **:** the use or effect of sensational subject matter or treatment — **sen•sa•tion•al•ist** \-nə-list\ *adj or n* — **sen•sa•tion•al•is•tic** \-ˌsā-shə-nə-ˈlis-tik\ *adj*
sen•sa•tion•al•ize \-nə-ˌlīz\ *vb* **-ized; -iz•ing :** to present in a sensational manner
¹sense \ˈsens\ *n* **1** ♦ **:** semantic content **:** MEANING **2 :** the faculty of perceiving by means of sense organs; *also* **:** a bodily function or mechanism (as sight, hearing, or smell) involving the action and effect of a stimulus on a sense organ **3** ♦ **:** a particular sensation; *also* **:** a motivating or discerning awareness **4** ♦ **:** capacity for effective application of the powers of the mind as a basis for action or response **5 :** OPINION ⟨the ~ of the meeting⟩ — **sense•less•ly** *adv*

♦ [1] denotation, drift, import, intent, meaning, purport, significance, signification ♦ [3] feel, feeling, sensation ♦ [4] common sense, horse sense, wisdom, wit ♦ [4] logic, reason, reasoning

²sense *vb* **sensed; sens•ing 1** ♦ **:** to be or become aware of ⟨~ danger⟩; *also* **:** to perceive by the senses **2 :** to detect (as radiation) automatically

♦ feel, perceive, scent, see, smell, taste

sense•less *adj* ♦ **:** destitute of, deficient in, or contrary to sense

♦ cold, unconscious ♦ empty, meaningless, pointless ♦ dumb, fatuous, foolish, mindless, silly, stupid, stupid, unintelligent, vacuous, witless

sense organ *n* **:** a bodily structure (as an eye or ear) that receives stimuli (as heat or light) which excite neurons to send information to the brain
sen•si•bil•i•ty \ˌsen-sə-ˈbi-lə-tē\ *n, pl* **-ties :** delicacy of feeling **:** SENSITIVITY
sen•si•ble \ˈsen-sə-bəl\ *adj* **1** ♦ **:** capable of being perceived by the senses or the mind; *also* **:** capable of receiving sense impressions **2** ♦ **:** emotionally aware and responsive **:** CONSCIOUS **3** ♦ **:** having, containing, or indicative of good sense or reason **:** REASONABLE — **sen•si•bly** \-blē\ *adv*

♦ [1] appreciable, detectable, discernible, distinguishable, palpable, perceptible ♦ [2] alive, aware, cognizant, conscious, mindful, sentient, witting ♦ [3] good, hard, informed, just, levelheaded, logical, rational, reasonable, reasoned, sober, solid, valid, well-founded

sen•si•tive \ˈsen-sə-tiv\ *adj* **1** ♦ **:** subject to excitation by or responsive to stimuli **2 :** having power of feeling **3** ♦ **:** of such a nature as to be easily affected; *also* **:** easily hurt or damaged **4 :** TOUCHY ⟨a ~ issue⟩

♦ [1] acute, delicate, keen, perceptive, sharp ♦ [3] delicate, fragile, frail, tender ♦ [3] demonstrative, emotional, feeling, intense, passionate, sentimental, soulful

sen•si•tive•ness \ˈsen-sə-tiv-nəs\ *n* ♦ **:** the quality or state of being sensitive

♦ acuity, acuteness, delicacy, keenness, sensitivity

sensitive plant *n* **:** any of several mimosas with leaves that fold or droop when touched
sen•si•tiv•i•ty \ˌsen-sə-ˈti-və-tē\ *n* ♦ **:** the ability to sense and to respond to slight impressions or differences

♦ acuity, acuteness, delicacy, keenness, sensitiveness

sen•si•tize \ˈsen-sə-ˌtīz\ *vb* **-tized; -tiz•ing :** to make or become sensitive or hypersensitive — **sen•si•ti•za•tion** \ˌsen-sə-tə-ˈzā-shən\ *n*
sen•sor \ˈsen-ˌsȯr, -sər\ *n* **:** a device that responds to a physical stimulus
sen•so•ry \ˈsen-sə-rē\ *adj* **1** ♦ **:** of or relating to sensation or the senses **2 :** AFFERENT

♦ sensational, sensitive, sensuous

sen•su•al \ˈsen-shə-wəl\ *adj* **1 :** relating to gratification of the senses **2** ♦ **:** devoted to the pleasures of the senses — **sen•su•al•ist** *n* — **sen•su•al•i•ty** \ˌsen-shə-ˈwa-lə-tē\ *n* — **sen•su•al•ly** *adv*

♦ carnal, fleshly, luscious, sensuous, voluptuous

sen•su•ous \ˈsen-shə-wəs\ *adj* **1** ♦ **:** relating to the senses or to things that can be perceived by the senses **2 :** producing or characterized by gratification of the senses **:** VOLUPTUOUS — **sen•su•ous•ly** *adv* — **sen•su•ous•ness** *n*

♦ sensational, sensitive, sensory

sent *past and past part of* SEND
¹sen•tence \ˈsent-ᵊns, -ᵊnz\ *n* **1** ♦ **:** the punishment set by a court **2 :** a grammatically self-contained speech unit that expresses an assertion, a question, a command, a wish, or an exclamation

♦ doom, finding, holding, judgment (*or* judgement), ruling

²sentence *vb* **sen•tenced; sen•tenc•ing :** to impose a sentence on

♦ condemn, damn, doom

sen•ten•tious \sen-ˈten-chəs\ *adj* **:** using wise sayings or proverbs; *also* **:** using pompous language — **sen•ten•tious•ly** *adv* — **sen•ten•tious•ness** *n*
sen•tient \ˈsen-chənt, -chē-ənt\ *adj* ♦ **:** capable of feeling **:** having perception

♦ alive, aware, cognizant, conscious, mindful, sensible, witting

sen•ti•ment \ˈsen-tə-mənt\ *n* **1** ♦ **:** an emotional state or reaction **:** FEELING; *also* **:** thought and judgment influenced by feeling **2** ♦ **:** a specific view or notion

♦ [1] emotion, feeling, passion ♦ [2] belief, conviction, eye, feeling, judgment (*or* judgement), mind, notion, opinion, persuasion, verdict, view

sen•ti•men•tal \ˌsen-tə-ˈment-ᵊl\ *adj* **1** ♦ **:** influenced by tender feelings **2** ♦ **:** affecting the emotions — **sen•ti•men•tal•ist** *n* — **sen•ti•men•tal•ly** *adv*

♦ [1] demonstrative, emotional, feeling, intense, passionate, sensitive, soulful ♦ [2] corny, maudlin, mawkish, mushy, saccharine, sappy, schmaltzy

sen•ti•men•tal•ise *chiefly Brit var of* SENTIMENTALIZE
sen•ti•men•tal•ism *n* **:** the disposition to favor or indulge in sentimentality; *also* **:** an excessively sentimental conception or statement
sen•ti•men•tal•i•ty \-ˌmen-ˈta-lə-tē, -mən-\ *n* **1** ♦ **:** the quality or state of being sentimental especially to excess or in affectation **2 :** a sentimental idea or its expression

♦ mawkishness, mush

sen•ti•men•tal•ize \-ˈment-ᵊl-ˌīz\ *vb* **-ized; -iz•ing 1 :** to indulge in sentiment **2 :** to look upon or imbue with sentiment — **sen•ti•men•tal•i•za•tion** \-ˌment-ᵊl-ə-ˈzā-shən\ *n*
sen•ti•nel \ˈsent-ᵊn-əl\ *n* **:** one that watches or guards **:** SENTRY
sen•try \ˈsen-trē\ *n, pl* **sentries** ♦ **:** person who keeps watch **:** GUARD; *esp* **:** a soldier standing guard at a point of passage (as a gate)

♦ custodian, guard, guardian, keeper, lookout, picket, warden, warder, watch, watchman

sep *abbr* separate, separated
Sep *abbr* September
SEP *abbr* simplified employee pension
se•pal \ˈsē-pəl, ˈse-\ *n* **:** one of the modified leaves comprising a flower calyx
sep•a•ra•ble \ˈse-pə-rə-bəl\ *adj* **:** capable of being separated
¹sep•a•rate \ˈse-pə-ˌrāt\ *vb* **-rat•ed; -rat•ing 1** ♦ **:** to set or keep apart **:** DISCONNECT **2 :** to keep apart by something intervening **3 :** to cease to be together **:** PART **4** ♦ **:** to make a distinction between; *also* **:** to put in a certain place or rank according to kind, class, or nature **5** ♦ **:** to go in different directions

♦ [1] break up, disconnect, disjoint, dissever, dissociate, disunite, divide, divorce, part, resolve, sever, split, sunder, unyoke ***Ant*** join, link, unify, unite ♦ [1] cut off, insulate, isolate, seclude, segregate, sequester ♦ [4] differentiate, discern, discriminate, distinguish ♦ [4] assort, break down, categorize, class, classify, grade, group, peg, place, range, rank, sort ♦ [5] branch, diverge, divide, fork ***Ant*** converge, join

²sep•a•rate \ˈse-prət, -pə-rət\ *adj* **1 :** not connected **2 :** divided from each other **3 :** SINGLE, PARTICULAR ⟨the ~ pieces of the puzzle⟩ **4** ♦ **:** existing by itself **5** ♦ **:** not shared with another — **sep•a•rate•ly** *adv*

♦ [4] detached, disconnected, discrete, freestanding, single, unattached, unconnected ***Ant*** attached, connected, joined ♦ [5] different, individual, respective ***Ant*** same

³sep•a•rate *n* **:** an article of dress designed to be worn interchangeably with others to form various combinations

sep•a•ra•tion \ˌse-pə-ˈrā-shən\ *n* **1** ♦ **:** the act or process of separating **:** the state of being separated **2** ♦ **:** a point, line, means, or area of division **3 :** a formal separating of a married couple by agreement but without divorce

♦ [1] breakup, dissolution, division, partition, schism, split ***Ant*** unification, union ♦ [1] demarcation, discrimination, distinction ♦ [2] breach, break, discontinuity, gap, gulf, hole, interval, opening, rent, rift

sep•a•rat•ist \ˈse-prə-tist, ˈse-pə-ˌrā-\ *n* **:** an advocate of separation (as from a political body) — **sep•a•rat•ism** \ˈse-prə-ˌti-zəm\ *n*
sep•a•ra•tive \ˈse-pə-ˌrā-tiv, ˈse-prə-tiv\ *adj* **:** tending toward, causing, or expressing separation
sep•a•ra•tor \ˈse-pə-ˌrā-tər\ *n* **:** one that separates; *esp* **:** a device for separating cream from milk
se•pia \ˈsē-pē-ə\ *n* **:** a brownish gray to dark brown color
sep•sis \ˈsep-səs\ *n, pl* **sep•ses** \ˈsep-ˌsēz\ **:** a toxic condition due to spread of bacteria or their toxic products in the body
Sept *abbr* September
Sep•tem•ber \sep-ˈtem-bər\ *n* **:** the 9th month of the year having 30 days
sep•tic \ˈsep-tik\ *adj* **1 :** PUTREFACTIVE **2 :** relating to or involving sepsis **3 :** of, relating to, or used for sewage treatment and disposal
sep•ti•ce•mia \ˌsep-tə-ˈsē-mē-ə\ *n* **:** BLOOD POISONING
septic tank *n* **:** a tank in which sewage is disintegrated by bacteria
sep•tu•a•ge•nar•i•an \sep-ˌtü-ə-jə-ˈner-ē-ən, -ˌtyü-\ *n* **:** a person whose age is in the seventies — **septuagenarian** *adj*
Sep•tu•a•gint \sep-ˈtü-ə-jənt, -ˈtyü-\ *n* **:** a Greek version of the Old Testament prepared in the 3d and 2d centuries B.C. by Jewish scholars
sep•tum \ˈsep-təm\ *n, pl* **sep•ta** \-tə\ **:** a dividing wall or membrane especially between bodily spaces or masses of soft tissue
se•pul•chral \sə-ˈpəl-krəl\ *adj* **1 :** relating to burial or the grave **2** ♦ **:** suited to or suggestive of a sepulchre **:** GLOOMY

♦ bleak, dark, dismal, dreary, gloomy, gray (*or* grey), somber (*or* sombre), wretched

¹sep•ul•chre *or* **sep•ul•cher** \ˈse-pəl-kər\ *n* **:** a burial vault **:** TOMB
²sepulchre *or* **sepulcher** *vb* **-chred** *or* **-chered; -chring** *or* **-cher•ing :** BURY, ENTOMB
sep•ul•ture \ˈse-pəl-ˌchůr\ *n* **1** ♦ **:** the act or process of burying **:** BURIAL **2 :** SEPULCHRE

♦ burial, entombment, interment

se•quel \ˈsē-kwəl\ *n* **1 :** logical consequence **2 :** a literary or cinematic work continuing a story begun in a preceding one
se•quence \ˈsē-kwəns\ *n* **1** ♦ **:** a continuous or connected series **2** ♦ **:** chronological order of events **3 :** something produced by a cause or necessarily following from a set of conditions **:** RESULT, SEQUEL — **se•quen•tial•ly** *adv*

♦ [1] chain, progression, string, train ♦ [2] arrangement, array, disposal, disposition, distribution, order, setup

se•quent \ˈsē-kwənt\ *adj* **1 :** SUCCEEDING, CONSECUTIVE **2 :** RESULTANT
se•quen•tial \si-ˈkwen-chəl\ *adj* ♦ **:** of, relating to, or arranged in a sequence

♦ consecutive, successive

se•ques•ter \si-ˈkwes-tər\ *vb* **1** ♦ **:** to set apart **:** SEGREGATE **2 :** to place (property) in custody especially in sequestration

♦ cut off, insulate, isolate, seclude, segregate, separate

se•ques•trate \ˈsē-kwəs-ˌtrāt, si-ˈkwes-\ *vb* **-trat•ed; -trat•ing :** SEQUESTER
se•ques•tra•tion \ˌsē-kwəs-ˈtrā-shən, ˌse-\ *n* **1** ♦ **:** the act of sequestering **:** the state of being sequestered **2 :** a deposit whereby a neutral depositary agrees to hold property in litigation and to restore it to the party to whom it is adjudged to belong

♦ insulation, isolation, seclusion, segregation, solitude

se•quin \ˈsē-kwən\ *n* **1 :** an old gold coin of Turkey and Italy **2 :** a small metal or plastic plate used for ornamentation especially on clothing — **se•quined** *or* **se•quinned** \-kwənd\ *adj*
se•quoia \si-ˈkwȯi-ə\ *n* **:** either of two huge California coniferous trees
ser *abbr* **1** serial **2** series **3** service
sera *pl of* SERUM
se•ra•glio \sə-ˈral-yō\ *n, pl* **-glios :** HAREM
se•ra•pe \sə-ˈrä-pē\ *n* **:** a colorful woolen shawl worn over the shoulders especially by Mexican men
ser•aph \ˈser-əf\ *n, pl* **ser•a•phim** \-ə-ˌfim, -ˌfēm\ *or* **seraphs :** one of the 6-winged angels standing in the presence of God
ser•a•phim \ˈser-ə-ˌfim, -ˌfēm\ *n pl* **1 :** the highest order of angels **2** *sing; pl* **seraphim :** SERAPH — **se•raph•ic** \sə-ˈra-fik\ *adj*
Serb \ˈsərb\ *n* **:** a native or inhabitant of Serbia
Ser•bi•an \ˈsər-bē-ən\ *n* **1 :** SERB **2 :** a south Slavic language spoken by the Serbian people — **Serbian** *adj*
Ser•bo–Cro•a•tian \ˌsər-(ˌ)bō-krō-ˈā-shən\ *n* **:** the Serbian and Croatian languages together with the Slavic speech of Bosnia, Herzegovina, and Montenegro taken as a single language with regional variants
sere \ˈsir\ *adj* ♦ **:** being dried and withered **:** DRY

♦ arid, dry, thirsty

¹ser•e•nade \ˌser-ə-ˈnād\ *n* **:** music sung or played as a compliment especially outdoors at night for a woman being courted
²serenade *vb* **-nad•ed; -nad•ing :** to entertain with or perform a serenade
ser•en•dip•i•ty \ˌser-ən-ˈdi-pə-tē\ *n* **:** the gift of finding valuable or agreeable things not sought for — **ser•en•dip•i•tous** \-təs\ *adj*
se•rene \sə-ˈrēn\ *adj* **1** ♦ **:** clear and free of storms or unpleasant change ⟨~ skies⟩ **2** ♦ **:** marked by or suggestive of utter calm and unruffled repose or quiet — **se•rene•ly** *adv*

♦ [1, 2] calm, halcyon, hushed, peaceful, placid, quiet, still, tranquil, untroubled ♦ [2] calm, collected, composed, cool, self-possessed, undisturbed, unperturbed, unshaken, unworried

se•ren•i•ty \sə-ˈre-nə-tē\ *n* ♦ **:** the quality or state of being serene

♦ calm, calmness, hush, peace, placidity, quiet, quietness, repose, still, stillness, tranquillity ♦ aplomb, composure, coolness, equanimity, self-possession

serf \ˈsərf\ *n* **:** a member of a servile class bound to the land and subject to the will of the landowner — **serf•dom** \-dəm\ *n*
serge \ˈsərj\ *n* **:** a twilled woolen cloth
ser•geant \ˈsär-jənt\ *n* **1 :** a noncommissioned officer (as in the army) ranking next below a staff sergeant **2 :** an officer in a police force
sergeant at arms : an officer of an organization who preserves order and executes commands
sergeant first class *n* **:** a noncommissioned officer in the army ranking next below a master sergeant
sergeant major *n, pl* **sergeants major** *or* **sergeant majors 1 :** a noncommissioned officer in the army or marine corps serving as chief administrative assistant in a headquarters **2 :** a noncommissioned officer in the marine corps ranking above a first sergeant
¹se•ri•al \ˈsir-ē-əl\ *adj* **1** ♦ **:** appearing in successive parts or numbers ⟨a ~ story⟩ **2 :** performing a series of similar acts over a period of time ⟨a ~ killer⟩; *also* **:** occurring in such a series — **se•ri•al•ly** *adv*

♦ episodic, periodic

²serial *n* **:** a serial story or other writing — **se•ri•al•ist** \-ə-list\ *n*
se•ries \ˈsir-ēz\ *n, pl* **series :** a number of things or events arranged in order and connected by being alike in some way
seri•graph \ˈser-ə-ˌgraf\ *n* **:** an original silk-screen print — **se•rig•ra•pher** \sə-ˈri-grə-fər\ *n* — **se•rig•ra•phy** \-fē\ *n*
se•ri•ous \ˈsir-ē-əs\ *adj* **1** ♦ **:** thoughtful or subdued in appearance or manner **:** SOBER **2 :** requiring much thought or work **3 :** EARNEST, DEVOTED **4** ♦ **:** having important or dangerous possible consequences **5 :** excessive or impressive in quantity or degree ⟨making ~ money⟩ **6** ♦ **:** of or relating to a matter of importance — **se•ri•ous•ly** *adv*

♦ [1] earnest, grave, humorless (*or* humourless), severe, sober, solemn, staid, unsmiling, weighty ***Ant*** facetious, flip, flippant, humorous, jocular, joking, playful ♦ [4] dangerous, grave, grievous, hazardous, menacing, parlous, perilous, risky, unhealthy, unsafe, venturesome ♦ [6] grave, heavy, weighty ***Ant*** light

se•ri•ous•ness *n* ♦ **:** the quality or state of being serious

♦ earnestness, gravity, intentness, sobriety, solemnity

ser•mon \ˈsər-mən\ *n* **1 :** a religious discourse especially as part of a worship service **2 :** a lecture on conduct or duty
ser•mon•ize \ˈsər-mə-ˌnīz\ *vb* **-ized; -iz•ing 1 :** to compose or deliver a sermon **2 :** to preach to or on at length
se•rol•o•gy \sə-ˈrä-lə-jē\ *n* **:** a science dealing with serums and especially their reactions and properties — **se•ro•log•i•cal** \ˌsir-ə-ˈlä-ji-kəl\ *or* **se•ro•log•ic** \-jik\ *adj*
se•ro•to•nin \ˌsir-ə-ˈtō-nən, ˌser-\ *n* **:** a neurotransmitter that is a powerful vasoconstrictor

se•rous \ˈsir-əs\ *adj* : of, relating to, resembling, or producing serum; *esp* : of thin watery constitution
ser•pent \ˈsər-pənt\ *n* : SNAKE
[1]**ser•pen•tine** \ˈsər-pən-ˌtēn, -ˌtīn\ *adj* **1** : SLY, CRAFTY **2** ♦ : winding or turning one way and another

♦ crooked, devious, sinuous, tortuous, winding

[2]**ser•pen•tine** \-ˌtēn\ *n* : a dull-green mineral having a mottled appearance
ser•rate \ˈser-ˌāt\ *adj* : having a saw-toothed edge ⟨a ~ leaf⟩
ser•ried \ˈser-ēd\ *adj* ♦ : crowded or pressed together : DENSE

♦ close, compact, crowded, dense, packed, thick, tight

se•rum \ˈsir-əm\ *n, pl* **serums** *or* **se•ra** \-ə\ : the clear yellowish antibody-containing fluid that can be separated from blood when it clots; *also* : a preparation of animal serum containing specific antibodies and used to prevent or cure disease
serv *abbr* service
ser•vant \ˈsər-vənt\ *n* ♦ : one that serves others; *esp* : a person employed for domestic or personal work

♦ domestic, flunky, lackey, menial, retainer, steward ***Ant*** master

[1]**serve** \ˈsərv\ *vb* **served; serv•ing** **1** : to work as a servant **2** : to render obedience and worship to (God) **3** : to comply with the commands or demands of **4** : to work through or perform a term of service (as in the army) **5** : PUT IN ⟨*served* five years in jail⟩ **6** ♦ : to be of use ⟨pine boughs *served* for a bed⟩ **7** ♦ : to provide services that benefit or help : BENEFIT **8** : to prove adequate or satisfactory for ⟨a pie that ~*s* eight people⟩ **9** : to make ready and pass out ⟨~ drinks⟩ **10** : to furnish or supply with something ⟨one power company *serving* the whole state⟩ **11** : to wait on ⟨~ a customer⟩ **12** ♦ : to treat or act toward in a specified way **13** : to put the ball in play (as in tennis)

♦ [6] act, function, perform, work ♦ [7] avail, benefit, profit ♦ [12] act, be, deal, handle, treat, use

[2]**serve** *n* : the act of serving a ball (as in tennis)
serv•er *n* **1** ♦ : one that serves **2** : a computer in a network that is used to provide services (as access to files) to other computers in the network

♦ waiter, waitperson, waitress

[1]**ser•vice** \ˈsər-vəs\ *n* **1** : the occupation of a servant **2** : HELP, BENEFIT **3** : a meeting for worship; *also* : a form followed in worship or in a ceremony ⟨burial ~⟩ **4** ♦ : the act, fact, or means of serving **5** : performance of official or professional duties **6** : SERVE **7** : a set of dishes or silverware **8 a** : a branch of public employment; *also* : the persons in it ⟨civil ~⟩ **b** ♦ : one of a nation's organized fighting forces (as the army, navy, or air force) — often used in plural **9** : military or naval duty **10** ♦ : contribution to the welfare of others; *also* : disposal for use

♦ [4] boon, courtesy, favor (*or* favour), grace, indulgence, kindness, mercy, turn ♦ **services** [8b] armed forces, military, troops ♦ [10] account, avail, use, utility

[2]**service** *vb* **ser•viced; ser•vic•ing** : to do maintenance or repair work on or for
ser•vice•able \ˈsər-və-sə-bəl\ *adj* ♦ : prepared for service : USEFUL

♦ applicable, functional, practicable, practical, usable, useful, workable, working

ser•vice•man \ˈsər-vəs-ˌman, -mən\ *n* **1** ♦ : a man who is a member of the armed forces **2** : a man employed to repair or maintain equipment

♦ fighter, legionnaire, man-at-arms, regular, soldier, warrior

service mark *n* : a mark or device used to identify a service (as transportation or insurance) offered to customers
service station *n* : a retail station for servicing motor vehicles
ser•vice•wom•an \ˈsər-vəs-ˌwu̇-mən\ *n* : a woman who is a member of the armed forces
ser•vi•ette \ˌsər-vē-ˈet\ *n chiefly Can and Brit* : a table napkin
ser•vile \ˈsər-vəl, -ˌvīl\ *adj* **1** : befitting a slave or servant **2** : behaving like a slave : SUBMISSIVE — **ser•vile•ly** *adv*
ser•vil•i•ty \ˌsər-ˈvi-lə-tē\ *n* : a slave's condition : the state of slavery
serv•ing \ˈsər-viŋ\ *n* : HELPING
ser•vi•tor \ˈsər-və-tər\ *n* : a male servant
ser•vi•tude \ˈsər-və-ˌtüd, -ˌtyüd\ *n* ♦ : the condition of a slave or serf : SLAVERY, BONDAGE

♦ bondage, enslavement, slavery, thrall, yoke

ser•vo \ˈsər-vō\ *n, pl* **servos** **1** : SERVOMOTOR **2** : SERVOMECHANISM
ser•vo•mech•a•nism \ˈsər-vō-ˌme-kə-ˌni-zəm\ *n* : a device for automatically correcting the performance of a mechanism
ser•vo•mo•tor \-ˌmō-tər\ *n* : a mechanism that supplements a primary control
ses•a•me \ˈse-sə-mē\ *n* : a widely cultivated annual herb of warm regions; *also* : its seeds that yield an edible oil (**sesame oil**) and are used in flavoring
ses•qui•cen•ten•ni•al \ˌses-kwi-sen-ˈte-nē-əl\ *n* : a 150th anniversary or its celebration — **sesquicentennial** *adj*
ses•qui•pe•da•lian \ˌses-kwə-pə-ˈdāl-yən\ *adj* **1** : having many syllables : LONG **2** : using long words
ses•sile \ˈse-sīl, -səl\ *adj* : permanently attached and not free to move about
ses•sion \ˈse-shən\ *n* **1** : a meeting or series of meetings of a body (as a court or legislature) for the transaction of business **2** : a meeting or period devoted to a particular activity
[1]**set** \ˈset\ *vb* **set; set•ting** **1** : to cause to sit **2** : PLACE **3** ♦ : to put into a desired position, adjustment, or condition **4** : to cause to be or do **5** ♦ : to fix or decide on as a time, limit, or regulation : SETTLE **6** : to fix in a frame **7** : to fix at a certain amount **8** : WAGER, STAKE **9** ♦ : to make or become fast or rigid **10** : to adapt (as words) to something (as music) **11** ♦ : to become fixed or firm or solid **12** : to be suitafcble : FIT **13** ♦ : to cover and warm eggs to hatch them : BROOD **14** ♦ : to have a certain direction **15** : to pass below the horizon **16** : to defeat in bridge — **set about** : to begin to do — **set forth** : to begin a trip — **set out** : to begin a trip or undertaking — **set sail** : to begin a voyage — **set upon** : to attack usually with violence

♦ [3] deposit, dispose, fix, lay, place, position, put, set up, stick ♦ [3, 9] anchor, catch, clamp, fasten, fix, hitch, moor, secure ♦ [5] arrange, decide, fix, name, settle ♦ [11] concrete, congeal, firm, freeze, gel, harden, jell, solidify ♦ [13] brood, hatch, incubate, sit ♦ [14] aim, bend, cast, direct, head, level, train

[2]**set** *n* **1** : a setting or a being set **2** : DIRECTION, COURSE; *also* : TENDENCY **3** : FORM, BUILD **4** : the fit of something (as a coat) **5** : an artificial setting for the scene of a play or motion picture **6** : a group of tennis games in which one side wins at least six **7** ♦ : a group of persons or things of the same kind or having a common characteristic usually classed together **8** : a collection of things and especially of mathematical elements (as numbers or points) **9** : an electronic apparatus ⟨a television ~⟩

♦ bloc, body, coalition, combination, combine, faction, party, sect, side, wing ♦ circle, clan, clique, community, coterie, crowd ♦ array, assemblage, cluster, collection, group, package, parcel, suite

[3]**set** *adj* **1** ♦ : firmly resolved : INTENT **2** ♦ : fixed by authority or custom **3** ♦ : incapable of being moved **4** : PERSISTENT **5** ♦ : being in readiness

♦ [1] bound, decisive, determined, firm, intent, purposeful, resolute, single-minded ♦ [2] certain, determinate, final, firm, fixed, flat, frozen, hard, hard-and-fast, settled, stable ♦ [2] distinct, especial, express, precise, special, specific ♦ [3] fast, firm, frozen, secure, snug, tight ♦ [5] fit, go, ready

set•back \ˈset-ˌbak\ *n* ♦ : a temporary defeat : REVERSE

♦ lapse, reversal, reverse

set back *vb* **1** : HINDER, DELAY; *also* : REVERSE **2** : COST
set down *vb* **1** : to cause to sit down **2** ♦ : to put in writing

♦ jot, log, mark, note, put down, record, register

set off *vb* **1** : to start out on a course or trip **2** ♦ : to set in motion : cause to begin

♦ activate, actuate, crank, drive, move, propel, run, spark, start, touch off, trigger, turn on

set•screw \ˈset-ˌskrü\ *n* : a screw screwed through one part tightly upon or into another part to prevent relative movement
set•tee \se-ˈtē\ *n* ♦ : a bench or sofa with a back and arms

♦ couch, davenport, divan, lounge, sofa

set•ter \ˈse-tər\ *n* : a large long-coated hunting dog
set•ting \ˈse-tiŋ\ *n* **1** : the frame in which a gem is set **2** ♦ : the time, place, and circumstances in which something occurs or develops **3** : music written for a text (as of a poem) **4** : the eggs that a fowl sits on for hatching at one time

♦ atmosphere, climate, environment, environs, medium, milieu, surroundings

set•tle \ˈset-ᵊl\ *vb* **set•tled; set•tling** **1** ♦ : to place or become established in a place **2** : to establish in residence; *also* : COLONIZE **3** : to make compact **4** ♦ : to make or become quiet or orderly — often used with *down* **5** : to establish or secure permanently **6** : to direct one's efforts **7** ♦ : to fix by agreement : to reach an agreement on **8** : to conclude legally ⟨~ a lawsuit⟩ **9** ♦ : to fix or resolve conclusively ⟨~ the question⟩ **10** ♦ : to make a final disposition of ⟨~ an account⟩ **11** ♦ : to come to rest **12** : to sink gradually to a lower level **13** : to become clear by depositing sediment

♦ [1] ensconce, install, lodge, perch, roost ♦ [4] allay, calm, compose, quiet, soothe, still, tranquilize ♦ *usu* **settle down** [4] calm (down), cool (off *or* down), hush, quiet ♦ [7] arrange, decide, fix, set ♦ [9] adjudicate, arbitrate, decide, determine, judge, referee, rule, umpire ♦ [10] clear, discharge, foot, liquidate, pay, pay off, quit, recompense, spring, stand ♦ [11] alight, land, light, perch, roost

settled *adj* ♦ : unlikely to change or be changed : established or decided beyond dispute or doubt

♦ confirmed, deep-rooted, deep-seated, inveterate ♦ certain, determinate, final, firm, fixed, flat, frozen, hard, hard-and-fast, set, stable

set·tle·ment \ˈset-ᵊl-mənt\ *n* **1** : the act or process of settling **2** : BESTOWAL ⟨a marriage ~⟩ **3** : payment or adjustment of an account **4** : COLONY **5** : a small village **6** : an institution providing various community services especially to large city populations **7** ♦ : adjustment of doubts and differences

♦ accord, agreement, bargain, compact, contract, convention, covenant, deal, pact, understanding

set·tler *n* ♦ : one that settles (as a new region)

♦ colonist, frontiersman, homesteader, pioneer ♦ emigrant, émigré, immigrant, migrant

set–to \ˈset-ˌtü\ *n, pl* **set–tos** : FIGHT

set·up \ˈset-ˌəp\ *n* **1** ♦ : the manner or act of arranging **2** : glass, ice, and nonalcoholic beverage for mixing served to patrons who supply their own liquor **3** : something (as a plot) that has been constructed or contrived; *also* : FRAME-UP

♦ arrangement, configuration, conformation, format, layout ♦ arrangement, array, disposal, disposition, distribution, order, sequence

set up *vb* **1** ♦ : to place in position; *also* : ASSEMBLE **2** : CAUSE **3** ♦ : to bring about the beginning of : FOUND **4** : FRAME 5 **5** ♦ : to place upright

♦ [1] assemble, deposit, dispose, fix, lay, place, position, put, set, stick ♦ [3] constitute, establish, found, inaugurate, initiate, innovate, institute, introduce, launch, pioneer, start ♦ [5] erect, pitch, put up, raise, rear

sev·en \ˈse-vən\ *n* **1** : one more than six **2** : the 7th in a set or series **3** : something having seven units — **seven** *adj or pron* — **sev·enth** \-vənth\ *adj or adv or n*

sev·en·teen \ˌse-vən-ˈtēn\ *n* : one more than 16 — **seventeen** *adj or pron* — **sev·en·teenth** \-ˈtēnth\ *adj or n*

seventeen–year locust *n* : a cicada of the U.S. that has in the North a life of 17 years and in the South of 13 years of which most is spent underground as a nymph and only a few weeks as a winged adult

sev·en·ty \ˈse-vən-tē\ *n, pl* **-ties** : seven times 10 — **sev·en·ti·eth** \-tē-əth\ *adj or n* — **seventy** *adj or pron*

sev·er \ˈse-vər\ *vb* **sev·ered; sev·er·ing** ♦ : to separate into individual parts : DIVIDE; *esp* : to separate by or as if by cutting — **sev·er·ance** \ˈsev-rəns, ˈse-və-\ *n*

♦ break up, disconnect, disjoint, dissever, dissociate, disunite, divide, divorce, part, resolve, separate, split, sunder, unyoke

sev·er·al \ˈsev-rəl, ˈse-və-\ *adj* **1** : INDIVIDUAL, DISTINCT ⟨federal union of the ~ states⟩ **2** : consisting of an indefinite number but yet not very many — **sev·er·al·ly** *adv*

severance pay *n* : extra pay given an employee upon termination of employment

se·vere \sə-ˈvir\ *adj* **se·ver·er; -est** **1** ♦ : marked by strictness or sternness : AUSTERE **2** ♦ : strict in discipline **3** : causing distress and especially physical discomfort or pain ⟨~ weather⟩ ⟨a ~ wound⟩ **4** ♦ : hard to endure ⟨~ trials⟩ **5** : of a great degree : SERIOUS ⟨~ depression⟩

♦ [1, 2] austere, authoritarian, flinty, hard, harsh, heavy-handed, ramrod, rigid, rigorous, stern, strict *Ant* forbearing, indulgent, lax, lenient, tolerant ♦ [4] bitter, brutal, burdensome, cruel, excruciating, grievous, grim, hard, harsh, heavy, inhuman, murderous, onerous, oppressive, rough, rugged, stiff, tough, trying

se·vere·ly *adv* ♦ : in a severe manner : with severity

♦ hard, hardly, harshly, ill, oppressively, roughly, sternly, stiffly

se·ver·i·ty \sə-ˈver-ə-tē\ *n* ♦ : quality or state of being severe

♦ hardness, harshness, inflexibility, rigidity, sternness, strictness *Ant* gentleness, flexibility, laxness, mildness

sew \ˈsō\ *vb* **sewed; sewn** \ˈsōn\ *or* **sewed; sew·ing** **1** : to unite or fasten by stitches **2** : to engage in sewing

sew·age \ˈsü-ij\ *n* : waste materials carried off by sewers

[1]**sew·er** \ˈsō-ər\ *n* : one that sews

[2]**sew·er** \ˈsü-ər\ *n* : an artificial pipe or channel to carry off waste matter

sew·er·age \ˈsü-ə-rij\ *n* **1** : a system of sewers **2** : SEWAGE

sew·ing *n* **1** : the activity of one who sews **2** : material that has been or is to be sewed

sex \ˈseks\ *n* **1** : either of the two major forms that occur in many living things and are designated male or female according to their role in reproduction; *also* : the qualities by which these sexes are differentiated and which directly or indirectly function in reproduction involving two parents **2 a** : sexual activity or behavior **b** : physical sexual contact between individuals that involves the genitalia : SEXUAL INTERCOURSE — **sexed** \ˈsekst\ *adj* — **sex·less** *adj*

sex·a·ge·nar·i·an \ˌsek-sə-jə-ˈner-ē-ən\ *n* : a person whose age is in the sixties — **sexagenarian** *adj*

sex appeal : personal appeal or physical attractiveness especially for members of the opposite sex

sex cell *n* : an egg cell or sperm cell

sex chromosome *n* : one of usually a pair of chromosomes that are usually similar in one sex but different in the other sex and are concerned with the inheritance of sex

sex hormone *n* : a steroid hormone (as estrogen or testosterone) that is produced especially by the gonads or adrenal cortex and chiefly affects the growth or function of the reproductive organs

sex·ism \ˈsek-ˌsi-zəm\ *n* : prejudice or discrimination based on sex; *esp* : discrimination against women — **sex·ist** \ˈsek-sist\ *adj or n*

sex·ol·o·gy \sek-ˈsä-lə-jē\ *n* : the study of sex or of the interactions of the sexes — **sex·ol·o·gist** \-jist\ *n*

sex·pot \ˈseks-ˌpät\ *n* : a conspicuously sexy woman

sex symbol *n* : a usually renowned person (as an entertainer) noted and admired for conspicuous attractiveness

sex·tant \ˈsek-stənt\ *n* : a navigational instrument for determining latitude

sex·tet \sek-ˈstet\ *n* **1** : a musical composition for six voices or instruments; *also* : the performers of such a composition **2** : a group or set of six

sex·ton \ˈsek-stən\ *n* : one who takes care of church property

sex·u·al \ˈsek-shə-wəl\ *adj* : of, relating to, or involving sex or the sexes ⟨a ~ spore⟩ ⟨~ relations⟩ — **sex·u·al·i·ty** \ˌsek-shə-ˈwa-lə-tē\ *n* — **sex·u·al·ly** \ˈsek-shə-wə-lē\ *adv*

sexual intercourse *n* **1** ♦ : intercourse between a male and a female in which the penis is inserted into the vagina **2** : intercourse between individuals involving genital contact other than insertion of the penis into the vagina

♦ copulation, intercourse

sexually transmitted disease *n* : a disease (as syphilis, gonorrhea, AIDS, or the genital form of herpes simplex) that is caused by a microorganism or virus usually or often transmitted by direct sexual contact

sexual relations *n pl* : physical sexual contact between individuals that involves the genitalia : SEXUAL INTERCOURSE

sexy \ˈsek-sē\ *adj* **sex·i·er; -est** ♦ : sexually suggestive or stimulating : EROTIC — **sex·i·ly** \-sə-lē\ *adv* — **sex·i·ness** \-sē-nəs\ *n*

♦ amatory, amorous, erotic

SF *abbr* **1** sacrifice fly **2** science fiction

SFC *abbr* sergeant first class

Sg *symbol* seaborgium

SG *abbr* **1** senior grade **2** sergeant **3** solicitor general **4** surgeon general

sgd *abbr* signed

Sgt *abbr* sergeant

Sgt Maj *abbr* sergeant major

sh *abbr* share

shab·by \ˈsha-bē\ *adj* **shab·bi·er; -est** **1** : dressed in worn clothes **2** ♦ : threadbare and faded from wear **3** : DESPICABLE, MEAN; *also* : UNFAIR ⟨~ treatment⟩ — **shab·bi·ly** \ˈsha-bə-lē\ *adv* — **shab·bi·ness** \-bē-nəs\ *n*

♦ dilapidated, grungy, mangy, mean, neglected, ragged, ratty, scruffy, seedy, tacky, tattered, threadbare

shack \ˈshak\ *n* ♦ **:** an often small and temporary dwelling of simple construction **:** HUT

♦ cabin, camp, hut, hutch, shanty

¹shack·le \ˈsha-kəl\ *n* **1** ♦ **:** something (as a manacle or fetter) that confines the legs or arms **2** ♦ **:** a check on free action made as if by fetters **3 :** a device for making something fast or secure

♦ [1] band, bond, chain, fetter, irons, ligature, manacle ♦ [2] bar, block, encumbrance, hindrance, inhibition, obstacle

²shackle *vb* **shack·led; shack·ling 1** ♦ **:** to bind or fasten with shackles **2** ♦ **:** to limit free movement or expression with restrictions or handicaps

♦ [1] bind, chain, enchain, fetter, handcuff, manacle, trammel ♦ [2] encumber, hamper, hinder, hold up, impede, inhibit, interfere with, obstruct, tie up

shad \ˈshad\ *n, pl* **shad :** any of several sea fishes related to the herrings that swim up rivers to spawn and include some important food fishes

¹shade \ˈshād\ *n* **1 a :** partial obscurity **b** *pl* ♦ **:** the shadows that gather as darkness comes on **2 :** space sheltered from the light especially of the sun **3** ♦ **:** a disembodied spirit **:** PHANTOM **4 :** something that shelters from or intercepts light or heat; *also, pl* **:** SUNGLASSES **5** ♦ **:** a dark color or a variety of a color **6 :** a small difference

♦ [1b] dark, darkness, dusk, gloaming, gloom, murk, night, semidarkness, shadows, twilight ♦ [3] apparition, bogey, ghost, phantasm, phantom, poltergeist, shadow, specter, spirit, spook, vision, wraith ♦ [5] cast, color (*or* colour), hue, tinge, tint, tone

²shade *vb* **shad·ed; shad·ing 1 :** to shelter from light and heat **2 :** DARKEN, OBSCURE **3 :** to mark with degrees of light or color **4 :** to show slight differences especially in color or meaning

shaded *adj* ♦ **:** protected from heat or light (as with shade or shadow)

♦ shadowy, shady

shad·ing *n* **:** the color and lines representing darkness or shadow in a drawing or painting

¹shad·ow \ˈsha-dō\ *n* **1 a** ♦ **:** partial darkness in a space from which light rays are cut off **b** *pl* ♦ **:** a place or time of little or no light **2 :** SHELTER **3 :** shade cast upon a surface by something intercepting rays from a light ⟨the ~ of a tree⟩ **4 :** something (as a specter) apparent to sense but with no substantial existence **:** PHANTOM **5 :** a shaded portion of a picture **6** ♦ **:** a small portion or degree **:** TRACE ⟨a ~ of doubt⟩ **7 :** a source of gloom or unhappiness **8** ♦ **:** one (as a spy or detective) that shadows

♦ [1a] shade ♦ **shadows** [1b] dark, darkness, dusk, gloaming, gloom, murk, night, semidarkness, shade, twilight ♦ [6] relic, trace, vestige ♦ [8] detective, investigator, operative, sleuth, tail

²shadow *vb* **1** ♦ **:** to cast a shadow on **2 :** to represent faintly or vaguely **3** ♦ **:** to follow and watch closely **:** TRAIL

♦ [1] becloud, blacken, cloud, darken, dim, obscure, overcast, overshadow ♦ [3] chase, dog, follow, hound, pursue, tag, tail, trace, track, trail

shad·ow·box \ˈsha-dō-ˌbäks\ *vb* **:** to box with an imaginary opponent especially for training

shad·owy *adj* **1** ♦ **:** faintly perceptible **2 :** being in or obscured by shadow; *also* **:** producing or providing shade

♦ bleary, dim, faint, foggy, fuzzy, hazy, indefinite, indistinct, indistinguishable, murky, nebulous, obscure, opaque, unclear, undefined, undetermined, vague

shady \ˈshā-dē\ *adj* **shad·i·er; -est 1** ♦ **:** affording shade **2** ♦ **:** of questionable honesty or reputation

♦ [1] shaded, shadowy ***Ant*** sunny ♦ [2] crooked, deceptive, dishonest, fast, fraudulent, sharp, shifty, underhanded ♦ [2] debatable, disputable, doubtful, dubious, equivocal, fishy, problematic, questionable, shaky, suspect, suspicious

¹shaft \ˈshaft\ *n, pl* **shafts 1 :** the long handle of a spear or lance **2 :** a thrusting or throwing weapon with long shaft and sharp head or blade **:** SPEAR, LANCE **3** *or pl* **shaves** \ˈshavz\ **:** POLE; *esp* **:** one of two poles between which a horse is hitched to pull a vehicle **4 :** something (as a column) long and slender **5 :** a bar to support a rotating piece or to transmit power by rotation **6 :** an inclined opening in the ground (as for finding or mining ore) **7 :** a vertical opening (as for an elevator) through the floors of a building **8 :** harsh or unfair treatment — usually used with *the* **9 :** a sharply delineated beam of light shining through an opening

²shaft *vb* **1 :** to fit with a shaft **2 :** to treat unfairly or harshly

shag \ˈshag\ *n* **:** a shaggy tangled mass or covering (as of wool) **:** long coarse or matted fiber, nap, or pile

shag·gy \ˈsha-gē\ *adj* **shag·gi·er; -est 1** ♦ **:** rough with or as if with long hair or wool **2 :** tangled or rough in surface

♦ fleecy, furry, hairy, hirsute, rough, unshorn, woolly

shah \ˈshä, ˈshȯ\ *n, often cap* **:** a sovereign of Iran

Shak *abbr* Shakespeare

¹shake \ˈshāk\ *vb* **shook** \ˈshu̇k\; **shak·en** \ˈshā-kən\; **shak·ing 1** ♦ **:** to move or cause to move jerkily or irregularly **2 :** BRANDISH, WAVE ⟨*shaking* his fist⟩ **3 :** to disturb emotionally ⟨*shaken* by her death⟩ **4 :** WEAKEN ⟨*shook* his faith⟩ **5 :** to bring or come into a certain position, condition, or arrangement by or as if by moving jerkily **6 :** to clasp (hands) in greeting or as a sign of goodwill or agreement **7** ♦ **:** to get away from **:** get rid of — **shak·able** *or* **shakeable** \ˈshā-kə-bəl\ *adj*

♦ [1] agitate, convulse, jolt, jounce, quake, quiver, shudder, vibrate, wobble ♦ [7] avoid, dodge, duck, elude, escape, eschew, evade, shirk, shun

²shake *n* **1 :** the act or a result of shaking **2 :** DEAL, TREATMENT ⟨a fair ~⟩ **3** ♦ **:** a very brief period of time **4** *pl* ♦ **:** a condition of trembling or nervousness

♦ [3] flash, instant, jiffy, minute, moment, second, trice, twinkle, twinkling, wink ♦ **shakes** [4] jitters, shivers, willies

shake·down \ˈshāk-ˌdau̇n\ *n* **1 :** an improvised bed **2 :** EXTORTION **3 :** a process or period of adjustment **4 :** a test (as of a new ship or airplane) under operating conditions

shake down *vb* **1 :** to take up temporary quarters **2 :** to occupy a makeshift bed **3 :** to become accustomed especially to new surroundings or duties **4 :** to settle down **5 :** to give a shakedown test to **6 :** to obtain money from in a deceitful or illegal manner **7 :** to bring about a reduction of

shak·er \ˈshā-kər\ *n* **1 :** one that shakes ⟨pepper ~⟩ **2** *cap* **:** a member of a religious sect founded in England in 1747

Shake·spear·ean *or* **Shake·spear·ian** \shāk-ˈspir-ē-ən\ *adj* **:** of, relating to, or having the characteristics of Shakespeare or his writings

shake–up \ˈshāk-ˌəp\ *n* **:** an extensive often drastic reorganization

shake up *vb* ♦ **:** to jar by or as if by a physical shock

♦ appall, bowl, floor, jolt, shock

shak·i·ness \ˈshā-kē-nəs\ *n* ♦ **:** the quality or state of being shaky

♦ insecurity, instability, precariousness, unsteadiness

shaky \ˈshā-kē\ *adj* **shak·i·er; -est 1** ♦ **:** lacking in authority or reliability **2** ♦ **:** characterized by shaking — **shak·i·ly** \ˈshā-kə-lē\ *adv*

♦ [1] debatable, disputable, doubtful, dubious, equivocal, fishy, problematic, questionable, shady, suspect, suspicious ♦ [2] tremulous, wobbly

shale \ˈshāl\ *n* **:** a finely layered rock formed from clay, mud, or silt

shall \shəl, ˈshal\ *vb, past* **should** \shəd, ˈshu̇d\ *pres sing & pl* **shall** ♦ — used as an auxiliary to express a command, what seems inevitable or likely in the future, simple futurity, or determination

♦ have, must, need, ought, should

shal·lop \ˈsha-ləp\ *n* **:** a light open boat

shal·lot \shə-ˈlät, ˈsha-lət\ *n* **1 :** a small clustered bulb that is used in seasoning and is produced by a perennial herb belonging to a subspecies of the onion; *also* **:** this herb **2 :** GREEN ONION

¹shal·low \ˈsha-lō\ *adj* **1 :** not deep **2 :** not intellectually profound

²shallow *n* **:** a shallow place in a body of water — usually used in plural

¹sham \ˈsham\ *n* **1 :** an ornamental covering for a pillow **2** ♦ **:** an imitation or counterfeit purporting to be genuine; *also* **:** cheap falseness **3 :** a person who shams

♦ counterfeit, fake, forgery, hoax, humbug, phony ♦ caricature, farce, joke, mockery, parody, travesty

²sham *vb* **shammed; sham·ming** ♦ **:** to act intentionally so as to give a false impression **:** FEIGN, PRETEND — **sham·mer** *n*

♦ affect, assume, counterfeit, fake, feign, pretend, profess, put on, simulate

[3]sham *adj* ♦ : not genuine : FALSE

♦ bogus, counterfeit, fake, false, inauthentic, phony, spurious, unauthentic ♦ affected, artificial, assumed, contrived, factitious, feigned, imitation, mechanical, mock, put-on, unnatural

sha•man \ˈshä-mən, ˈshā-\ *n* : a priest or priestess who uses magic to cure the sick, to divine the hidden, and to control events

sham•ble \ˈsham-bəl\ *vb* **sham•bled; sham•bling** ♦ : to shuffle along — **sham•ble** *n*

♦ lumber, scuff, scuffle, shuffle, stumble, tramp, tromp

sham•bles \ˈsham-bəlz\ *n* **1** : a scene of great slaughter **2** ♦ : a scene or state of great destruction or disorder; *also* : MESS

♦ chaos, confusion, disarray, disorder, disorganization, havoc, hell, jumble, mess, muddle

[1]shame \ˈshām\ *n* **1** ♦ : a painful sense of having done something wrong, improper, or immodest **2** ♦ : a condition of humiliating disgrace or disrepute : DISGRACE **3** : a cause of feeling shame **4** : something to be regretted ⟨it's a ~ you'll miss the party⟩ — **shame•ful•ly** *adv*

♦ [1] contrition, guilt, penitence, remorse, repentance, self-reproach ♦ [2] discredit, disgrace, dishonor (*or* dishonour), disrepute, ignominy, infamy, odium, opprobrium, reproach

[2]shame *vb* **shamed; sham•ing** **1** ♦ : to bring shame to : DISGRACE **2** : to make ashamed

♦ abase, debase, degrade, demean, discredit, disgrace, dishonor (*or* dishonour), humble, humiliate, lower, smirch, take down

shame•faced \ˈshām-ˌfāst\ *adj* ♦ : showing shame : ASHAMED — **shame•faced•ly** \-ˌfā-səd-lē, -ˌfāst-lē\ *adv*

♦ ashamed, contrite, guilty, hangdog, penitent, remorseful, repentant

shame•ful \-fəl\ *adj* ♦ : bringing shame; *also* : arousing the feeling of shame

♦ discreditable, disgraceful, dishonorable (*or* dishonourable), disreputable, ignominious, infamous, notorious

shame•less *adj* ♦ : having no shame — **shame•less•ly** *adv*

♦ unabashed, unashamed, unblushing, unembarrassed

[1]sham•poo \sham-ˈpü\ *vb* : to wash (as the hair) with soap and water or with a special preparation; *also* : to clean (as a rug) similarly

[2]shampoo *n, pl* **shampoos** **1** : the act or an instance of shampooing **2** : a preparation for use in shampooing

sham•rock \ˈsham-ˌräk\ *n* : a plant of folk legend with leaves composed of three leaflets that is associated with St. Patrick and Ireland

shang•hai \shaŋ-ˈhī\ *vb* **shang•haied; shang•hai•ing** : to force aboard a ship for service as a sailor; *also* : to trick or force into an undesirable position

Shan•gri–la \ˌshaŋ-gri-ˈlä\ *n* : a remote idyllic hideaway

shank \ˈshaŋk\ *n* **1** : the part of the leg between the knee and the human ankle or a corresponding part of a quadruped **2** : a cut of meat from the leg **3** : the narrow part of the sole of a shoe beneath the instep **4** : the part of a tool or instrument (as a key or anchor) connecting the functioning part with a part by which it is held or moved

shan•tung \ˌshan-ˈtəŋ\ *n* : a fabric in plain weave having a slightly irregular surface

shan•ty \ˈshan-tē\ *n, pl* **shanties** ♦ : a small roughly built shelter or dwelling

♦ cabin, camp, hut, hutch, shack

[1]shape \ˈshāp\ *vb* **shaped; shap•ing** **1** : to form especially in a particular shape **2** : DESIGN **3** ♦ : to make fit for (as a particular use or purpose) : ADAPT, ADJUST **4** : REGULATE **5** ♦ : to come to pass; *also* : to take on or approach a mature or definite form — often used with *up*

♦ [3] acclimate, accommodate, adapt, adjust, condition, conform, fit ♦ *usu* **shape up** [5] crystallize, form, jell, solidify

[2]shape *n* **1** ♦ : spatial form or contour **2** : surface configuration : FORM **3** : bodily contour apart from the head and face : FIGURE **4** : PHANTOM **5** ♦ : the condition in which someone or something exists at a particular time **6** ♦ : the appearance of the body as distinguished from that of the face — **shaped** *adj*

♦ [1] cast, configuration, conformation, figure, form, geometry ♦ [5] condition, estate, fettle, form, order, repair, trim ♦ [6] build, constitution, figure, form, frame, physique

shape•less \ˈshā-pləs\ *adj* **1** ♦ : having no definite shape **2** ♦ : not shapely — **shape•less•ly** *adv* — **shape•less•ness** *n*

♦ [1] amorphous, formless, unformed, unshaped, unstructured ♦ [2] deformed, distorted, malformed, misshapen, monstrous

shape•ly \ˈshā-plē\ *adj* **shape•li•er; -est** : having a pleasing shape — **shape•li•ness** *n*

shape–shift•er \ˈshāp-ˌshif-tər\ *n* : one that seems able to change form or identity at will

shard \ˈshärd\ *also* **sherd** \ˈshərd\ *n* : a broken piece : FRAGMENT

[1]share \ˈshar\ *n* : PLOWSHARE

[2]share *n* **1** ♦ : a portion belonging to one person or group **2** ♦ : any of the equal interests into which the capital stock of a corporation is divided

♦ [1] allotment, allowance, cut, part, portion, proportion, quota ♦ [2] claim, interest, stake

[3]share *vb* **shared; shar•ing** **1** : APPORTION **2** : to use or enjoy with others **3** : PARTICIPATE

share•crop•per \-ˌkrä-pər\ *n* : a farmer who works another's land in return for a share of the crop — **share•crop** *vb*

share•hold•er \-ˌhōl-dər\ *n* : STOCKHOLDER

shar•er *n* ♦ : one that shares

♦ partaker, participant, party

share•ware \ˈsher-ˌwer\ *n* : software available for usually limited trial use at little or no cost but that can be upgraded for a fee

[1]shark \ˈshärk\ *n* : any of various active, usually predatory, and mostly large marine cartilaginous fishes

[2]shark *n* **1** ♦ : a greedy crafty person **2** ♦ : one who excels greatly especially in a particular field

♦ [1] cheat, dodger, hoaxer, sharper, swindler, trickster ♦ [2] ace, adept, artist, authority, crackerjack, expert, maestro, master, scholar, virtuoso, whiz, wizard

shark•skin \-ˌskin\ *n* **1** : the hide of a shark or leather made from it **2** : a fabric woven from strands of many fine threads and having a sleek appearance and silky feel

[1]sharp \ˈshärp\ *adj* **1** ♦ : having a thin cutting edge or fine point : not dull or blunt **2** : briskly or bitingly cold : COLD ⟨a ~ wind⟩ **3** ♦ : keen in intellect, perception, or attention **4** : BRISK, ENERGETIC **5** : IRRITABLE ⟨a ~ temper⟩ **6** ♦ : causing intense distress ⟨a ~ pain⟩ **7** : cutting in language or import : HARSH ⟨a ~ rebuke⟩ **8** ♦ : affecting the senses as if cutting or piercing ⟨a ~ sound⟩ ⟨a ~ smell⟩ **9** : not smooth or rounded ⟨~ features⟩ **10** : involving an abrupt or extreme change ⟨a ~ turn⟩ **11** : CLEAR, DISTINCT ⟨mountains in ~ relief⟩; *also* : easy to perceive ⟨a ~ contrast⟩ **12 a** : higher than the true pitch **b** : raised by a half step **13** : being in the latest or current fashion : STYLISH ⟨a ~ dresser⟩ **14** : keen in attention to one's own interest sometimes to the point of being unethical — **sharp•ly** *adv*

♦ [1] cutting, edgy, ground, keen ***Ant*** blunt, blunted, dull, dulled, obtuse ♦ [1] peaked, pointed ♦ [3] acute, astute, canny, hardheaded, knowing, shrewd, smart ♦ [3] alert, brainy, bright, brilliant, clever, intelligent, keen, nimble, quick, quick-witted ♦ [6] acute, agonizing, biting, excruciating, smart ***Ant*** dull ♦ [8] nippy, pungent, strong ***Ant*** bland, smooth, mild

[2]sharp *adv* **1** : in a sharp manner **2** ♦ : in a manner or measure or to a degree or number that strictly conforms to a fact or condition : EXACTLY ⟨left at 8 ~⟩

♦ accurately, exactly, just, precisely, right, squarely

[3]sharp *n* **1** : a sharp edge or point **2** : a character ♯ which indicates that a specified note is to be raised by a half step; *also* : the resulting note **3** : SHARPER

[4]sharp *vb* : to raise in pitch by a half step

shar–pei \ˌshä-ˈpā, ˌshär-\ *n, pl* **shar–peis** *often cap S&P* : any of a Chinese breed of dogs that have loose wrinkled skin especially when young

sharp•en \ˈshär-pən\ *vb* ♦ : to make or become sharp — **sharp•en•er** *n*

♦ edge, grind, hone, strop, whet ***Ant*** blunt, dull

sharp•er \ˈshär-pər\ *n* ♦ : an unduly sharp or canny person; *esp* : a cheating gambler

♦ cheat, dodger, hoaxer, shark, swindler, trickster

sharp•ie *or* **sharpy** \ˈshär-pē\ *n, pl* **sharp•ies** **1** : SHARPER **2** : a person who is exceptionally keen or alert

sharp•ness *n* ♦ : the quality or state of being sharp

♦ acidity, acrimony, acuteness, asperity, bite, bitterness, edge, harshness, keenness, pungency, tartness ♦ bite, bitterness, bleakness, chill, nip, rawness

sharp•shoot•er \ˈshärp-ˌshü-tər\ *n* ♦ : a good marksman — **sharp•shoot•ing** *n*

♦ marksman, shooter, shot

shat•ter \ˈsha-tər\ *vb* ♦ : to dash or burst into fragments; *also* : to cause the disruption or annihilation of — **shat•ter•proof** \ˈsha-tər-ˌprüf\ *adj*

♦ blast, blow up, burst, demolish, destroy, explode, pop, smash

[1]**shave** \ˈshāv\ *vb* **shaved; shaved** *or* **shav•en** \ˈshā-vən\; **shav•ing** **1** : to slice in thin pieces **2** : to make bare or smooth by cutting the hair from **3** : to cut or pare off by the sliding movement of a razor **4** ♦ : to skim along or near the surface of

♦ brush, graze, kiss, nick, skim

[2]**shave** *n* **1** : any of various tools for cutting thin slices **2** : an act or process of shaving

shav•er \ˈshā-vər\ *n* **1** : an electric razor **2** ♦ : a male child from birth to adulthood : BOY

♦ boy, lad, nipper, stripling, youth

shav•ing *n* **1** : the act of one that shaves **2** : something shaved off

shawl \ˈshȯl\ *n* : a square or oblong piece of fabric used especially by women as a loose covering for the head or shoulders

Shaw•nee \shȯ-ˈnē, shä-\ *n, pl* **Shawnee** *or* **Shawnees** : a member of an American Indian people orig. of the central Ohio valley; *also* : their language

shd *abbr* should

she \ˈshē\ *pron* : that female one ⟨who is ~⟩; *also* : that one regarded as feminine ⟨~'s a fine ship⟩

sheaf \ˈshēf\ *n, pl* **sheaves** \ˈshēvz\ **1** : a bundle of stalks and ears of grain **2** : a group of things bound together

[1]**shear** \ˈshir\ *vb* **sheared; sheared** *or* **shorn** \ˈshōrn\; **shear•ing** **1** ♦ : to cut the hair or wool from : CLIP **2** : to deprive by or as if by cutting **3** : to cut or break sharply

♦ bob, clip, crop, curtail, cut, cut back, dock, lop, nip, prune, shave, trim

[2]**shear** *n* **1** : any of various cutting tools that consist of two blades fastened together so that the edges slide one by the other — usually used in plural **2** *chiefly Brit* : the act, an instance, or the result of shearing **3** : an action or stress caused by applied forces that causes two parts of a body to slide on each other

sheath \ˈshēth\ *n, pl* **sheaths** \ˈshēthz, ˈshēths\ **1** ♦ : a case for a blade (as of a knife); *also* : an anatomical covering suggesting such a case **2** : a close-fitting dress usually worn without a belt

♦ armor, capsule, case, casing, cocoon, cover, housing, husk, jacket, pod, shell

sheathe \ˈshēth\ *also* **sheath** \ˈshēth\ *vb* **sheathed; sheath•ing** **1** : to put into a sheath **2** : to cover with something that guards or protects

sheath•ing \ˈshē-thiŋ, -thiŋ\ *n* : material used to sheathe something; *esp* : the first covering of boards or of waterproof material on the outside wall of a frame house or on a timber roof

sheave \ˈshiv, ˈshēv\ *n* : a grooved wheel or pulley (as on a pulley block)

she•bang \shi-ˈbaŋ\ *n* : everything involved in what is under consideration ⟨sold the whole ~⟩

[1]**shed** \ˈshed\ *vb* **shed; shed•ding** **1** : to cause to flow from a cut or wound ⟨~ blood⟩ **2** : to pour down in drops ⟨~ tears⟩ **3** : to give out (as light) : DIFFUSE **4** : to throw off (as a natural covering) : DISCARD **5** ♦ : to rid oneself of temporarily or permanently as superfluous or unwanted

♦ cast, discard, ditch, dump, fling, jettison, junk, lose, reject, scrap, shuck, slough, throw away, throw out, unload

[2]**shed** *n* : a slight structure built for shelter or storage

sheen \ˈshēn\ *n* ♦ : a subdued luster

♦ gloss, luster (*or* lustre), polish, shine

sheep \ˈshēp\ *n, pl* **sheep** **1** : any of various cud-chewing mammals that are stockier than the related goats and lack a beard in the male; *esp* : one raised for meat or for its wool or skin **2** ♦ : a timid or defenseless person **3** : SHEEPSKIN

♦ angel, dove, innocent, lamb

sheep•dog \ˈshēp-ˌdȯg\ *n* : a dog used to tend, drive, or guard sheep

sheep•fold \ˈshēp-ˌfōld\ *n* : a pen or shelter for sheep

sheep•herd•er \-ˌhər-dər\ *n* : a worker in charge of sheep especially on open range — **sheep•herd•ing** *n*

sheep•ish \ˈshē-pish\ *adj* ♦ : resembling a sheep in meekness, stupidity, or timidity : BASHFUL; *esp* : embarrassed by consciousness of a fault

♦ bashful, coy, demure, diffident, introverted, modest, retiring, shy

sheep•ish•ly *adv* ♦ : in a sheepish manner

♦ humbly, lowly, meekly, modestly

sheep•skin \ˈshēp-ˌskin\ *n* **1** : the hide of a sheep or leather prepared from it; *also* : PARCHMENT **2** : DIPLOMA

[1]**sheer** \ˈshir\ *vb* ♦ : to turn from a course

♦ detour, deviate, swerve, swing, turn, turn off, veer

[2]**sheer** *adj* **1** ♦ : very thin or transparent **2** : carried to the utmost point or highest degree : UNQUALIFIED ⟨~ folly⟩ **3** : very steep — **sheer** *adv*

♦ gauzy, transparent

[1]**sheet** \ˈshēt\ *n* **1** : a broad piece of cloth (as for a bed); *also* : SAIL 1 **2** : a single piece of paper **3** : a broad flat surface ⟨a ~ of ice⟩ **4** : something broad and long and relatively thin

[2]**sheet** *n* : a rope used to trim a sail

sheet•ing \ˈshē-tiŋ\ *n* : material in the form of sheets or suitable for forming into sheets

sheikh *or* **sheik** \ˈshēk, ˈshāk\ *n* : an Arab chief — **sheikh•dom** *or* **sheik•dom** \-dəm\ *n*

shek•el \ˈshe-kəl\ *n* : a basic monetary unit of Israel

shelf \ˈshelf\ *n, pl* **shelves** \ˈshelvz\ **1** : a thin flat usually long and narrow structure fastened horizontally (as on a wall) above the floor to hold things **2** : something (as a sandbar) that suggests a shelf

shelf life *n* : the period of storage time during which a material will remain useful

[1]**shell** \ˈshel\ *n* **1** ♦ : a hard or tough often thin outer covering of an animal (as a beetle, turtle, or mollusk) or of an egg or a seed or fruit (as a nut); *also* : something that resembles a shell ⟨a pastry ~⟩ **2** : a light narrow racing boat propelled by oarsmen **3** : a case holding an explosive and designed to be fired from a cannon; *also* : a case holding the charge of powder and shot or bullet for small arms **4** : a plain usually sleeveless blouse or sweater **5** ♦ : a framework or exterior structure; *esp* : a building with an unfinished interior — **shelled** \ˈsheld\ *adj* — **shelly** \ˈshe-lē\ *adj*

♦ [1] armor, capsule, case, casing, cocoon, cover, housing, husk, jacket, pod, sheath ♦ [5] configuration, frame, framework, skeleton, structure

[2]**shell** *vb* **1** ♦ : to remove from a shell or husk **2** ♦ : to throw shells at, upon, or into : BOMBARD — **shell•er** *n*

♦ [1] bark, flay, hull, husk, peel, shuck, skin ♦ [2] blitz, bombard

[1]**shel•lac** \shə-ˈlak\ *n* **1** : a purified lac **2** : lac dissolved in alcohol and used as a wood filler or finish

[2]**shellac** *vb* **shel•lacked; shel•lack•ing** **1** : to coat or treat with shellac **2** : to defeat decisively

shel•lack•ing *n* ♦ : a sound drubbing

♦ defeat, loss, rout

shell bean *n* : a bean grown especially for its edible seeds; *also* : its edible seed

shell•fish \-ˌfish\ *n* : an invertebrate water animal (as an oyster or lobster) with a shell

shell out *vb* : PAY

shell shock *n* : COMBAT FATIGUE — **shell–shocked** \ˈshel-ˌshäkt\ *adj*

[1]**shel•ter** \ˈshel-tər\ *n* ♦ : something that gives protection : REFUGE

♦ asylum, harbor (*or* harbour), haven, refuge, retreat, sanctuary

[2]**shelter** *vb* **shel•tered; shel•ter•ing** ♦ : to give protection or refuge to

♦ accommodate, billet, chamber, domicile, harbor (*or* harbour), house, lodge, put up, quarter, roof, take in

shelve \ˈshelv\ *vb* **shelved; shelv•ing** **1** : to slope gradually **2** : to store on shelves **3** : to dismiss from service or use **4** ♦ : to put aside : DEFER ⟨~ a proposal⟩

♦ defer, delay, hold up, postpone, put off

shelv•ing \ˈshel-viŋ\ *n* : material for shelves; *also* : SHELVES

she•nan•i•gan \shə-ˈna-ni-gən\ *n* **1** : an underhand trick **2** : questionable conduct — usually used in plural **3** ♦ : high-spirited or mischievous activity — usually used in plural

♦ **shenanigans** devilishness, impishness, knavery, mischief, mischievousness, rascality, waggery, wickedness ♦ **shenani-**

gans foolery, high jinks, horseplay, monkeyshines, roughhouse, tomfoolery

¹shep•herd \ˈshe-pərd\ *n* **1 :** one who tends sheep **2 :** GERMAN SHEPHERD

²shepherd *vb* ♦ **:** to tend as or in the manner of a shepherd

♦ coach, counsel, guide, lead, mentor, pilot, show, tutor

shep•herd•ess \ˈshe-pər-dəs\ *n* **:** a woman who tends sheep

shepherd's pie *n* **:** a meat pie with a mashed potato crust

sheqel *n, pl* **sheqalim** *var of* SHEKEL

sher•bet \ˈshər-bət\ *n* **1 :** a drink of sweetened diluted fruit juice **2** *also* **sher•bert** \-bərt\ **:** a frozen dessert of fruit juices, sugar, milk or water, and egg whites or gelatin

sher•iff \ˈsher-əf\ *n* **:** a county officer charged with the execution of the law and the preservation of order

sher•ry \ˈsher-ē\ *n, pl* **sherries :** a fortified wine with a nutty flavor

Shet•land pony \ˈshet-lənd-\ *n* **:** any of a breed of small stocky hardy ponies

shew \ˈshō\ *Brit variant spelling of* SHOW

shi•at•su *also* **shi•at•zu** \shē-ˈät-sü\ *n* **:** a form of acupressure originating in Japan

shib•bo•leth \ˈshi-bə-ləth\ *n* **1** ♦ **:** a word or saying used by adherents of a party, sect, or belief and usually regarded by others as empty of real meaning; *also* **:** a banal, trite, or stale remark **2 :** language that is a criterion for distinguishing members of a group

♦ cry, slogan, watchword ♦ banality, cliché, commonplace, platitude

¹shield \ˈshēld\ *n* **1 :** a broad piece of defensive armor carried on the arm **2** ♦ **:** something that protects or hides **3 :** a police officer's badge

♦ aegis, armor (*or* armour), cover, defense (*or* defence), guard, protection, safeguard, screen, security, wall, ward

²shield *vb* ♦ **:** to protect or hide with a shield

♦ cover, defend, guard, protect, safeguard, screen, secure, ward

¹shift \ˈshift\ *vb* **1** ♦ **:** to exchange for or replace by another **2** ♦ **:** to change place, position, or direction **:** MOVE; *also* **:** to change gears **3** ♦ **:** to assume responsibility **:** GET BY **4** ♦ **:** to go through a change

♦ [1] change, commute, exchange, substitute, swap, switch, trade ♦ [2] budge, dislocate, displace, disturb, move, remove, transfer ♦ [3] cope, do, fare, get along, get by, make out, manage ♦ [4] change, fluctuate, mutate, vary

²shift *n* **1 :** SCHEME, TRICK **2 :** a woman's slip or loose-fitting dress **3** ♦ **:** a change in direction, emphasis, or attitude **4 :** a group working together alternating with other groups **5 :** TRANSFER **6 :** GEARSHIFT **7** ♦ **:** a means or device for effecting an end

♦ [3] motion, move, movement, moving, stir, stirring ♦ [7] expedient, measure, move, step

shift•less \ˈshift-ləs\ *adj* ♦ **:** lacking in ambition or incentive **:** LAZY

♦ idle, indolent, lazy, slothful

shift•less•ness *n* **:** the quality or state of being shiftless

shifty \ˈshif-tē\ *adj* **shift•i•er; -est 1 a** ♦ **:** given to deception, evasion, or fraud **b :** ELUSIVE **2 :** indicative of a tricky nature ⟨~ eyes⟩

♦ furtive, shady, slippery, sly, sneaky, stealthy ♦ crooked, deceptive, dishonest, fast, fraudulent, shady, sharp, underhanded

shih tzu \ˈshēd-ˈzü, ˈshēt-ˈsü\ *n, pl* **shih tzus** *also* **shih tzu** *often cap S&T* **:** any of a breed of small short-legged dogs of Chinese origin that have a short muzzle and a long dense coat

shii•ta•ke \shē-ˈtä-kē\ *n* **:** a dark Asian mushroom widely cultivated for its edible cap

shill \ˈshil\ *n* **:** one who acts as a decoy (as for a pitchman) — **shill** *vb*

shil•le•lagh *also* **shil•la•lah** \shə-ˈlā-lē\ *n* **:** a short heavy club **:** CUDGEL

shil•ling \ˈshi-liŋ\ *n* **:** a former monetary unit of the United Kingdom equal to $\frac{1}{20}$ pound

shilly–shally \ˈshi-lē-ˌsha-lē\ *vb* **shilly–shall•ied; shilly–shally•ing 1** ♦ **:** to show hesitation or lack of decisiveness **2 :** to waste time

♦ falter, hang back, hesitate, stagger, teeter, vacillate, waver, wobble

shim \ˈshim\ *n* **:** a thin often tapered piece of wood, metal, or stone used (as in leveling) to fill in space

shim•mer \ˈshi-mər\ *vb* ♦ **:** to shine waveringly or tremulously **:** GLIMMER — **shimmer** *n* — **shim•mery** *adj*

♦ flame, flash, glance, gleam, glimmer, glisten, glitter, scintillate, sparkle, twinkle, wink

shim•my \ˈshi-mē\ *n, pl* **shimmies :** an abnormal vibration especially in the front wheels of a motor vehicle — **shimmy** *vb*

¹shin \ˈshin\ *n* **:** the front part of the leg below the knee

²shin *vb* **shinned; shin•ning :** to climb (as a pole) by gripping alternately with arms or hands and legs

shin•bone \ˈshin-ˌbōn\ *n* **:** TIBIA

¹shine \ˈshīn\ *vb* **shone** \ˈshōn\ *or* **shined; shin•ing 1** ♦ **:** to give or cause to give light **2 :** GLEAM, GLITTER **3 :** to be eminent, conspicuous, or distinguished ⟨gave her a chance to ~⟩ **4** ♦ **:** to make bright by polishing **:** POLISH ⟨~ your shoes⟩

♦ [1] blaze, burn, fire, flame, gleam, glimmer, glisten, glitter, glow, radiate, shimmer ♦ [4] buff, burnish, dress, gloss, grind, polish, rub, smooth

²shine *n* **1** ♦ **:** brightness caused by the emission of light **:** RADIANCE **2** ♦ **:** brightness caused by the reflection of light **:** LUSTER **3 :** fair weather **:** SUNSHINE ⟨rain or ~⟩ **4** ♦ **:** positive regard for something **:** LIKING, FANCY ⟨took a ~ to them⟩ **5 :** a polish given to shoes

♦ [1] blaze, flare, fluorescence, glare, gleam, glow, illumination, incandescence, light, luminescence, radiance ♦ [2] gloss, luster (*or* lustre), polish, sheen ♦ [4] appetite, fancy, favor (*or* favour), fondness, like, liking, love, partiality, preference, relish, taste, use

shin•er \ˈshī-nər\ *n* **1 :** a silvery fish; *esp* **:** any of numerous small freshwater American fishes related to the carp **2 :** BLACK EYE

¹shin•gle \ˈshiŋ-gəl\ *n* **1 :** a small thin piece of building material used in overlapping rows for covering a roof or outside wall **2 :** a small sign

²shingle *vb* **shin•gled; shin•gling :** to cover with shingles

³shingle *n* **:** a beach strewn with gravel; *also* **:** coarse gravel (as on a beach)

shin•gles \ˈshiŋ-gəlz\ *n* **:** an acute inflammation of the spinal and cranial nerves caused by reactivation of the chicken pox virus and associated with eruptions and pain along the course of the affected nerves

shin•ny \ˈshi-nē\ *vb* **shin•nied; shin•ny•ing :** SHIN

shin splints *n sing or pl* **:** a condition marked by pain and sometimes tenderness and swelling in the shin caused by repeated small injuries to muscles and associated tissue especially from running

Shin•to \ˈshin-ˌtō\ *n* **:** the indigenous religion of Japan consisting especially in reverence of the spirits of natural forces and imperial ancestors — **Shin•to•ism** *n* — **Shin•to•ist** *n or adj*

shiny \ˈshī-nē\ *adj* **shin•i•er; -est 1** ♦ **:** filled with light **:** BRIGHT **2 :** having a smooth, glossy surface

♦ beaming, bright, brilliant, effulgent, glowing, incandescent, lambent, lucent, lucid, luminous, lustrous, radiant, refulgent

¹ship \ˈship\ *n* **1 :** a large oceangoing boat **2 :** a ship's officers and crew **3 :** AIRSHIP, AIRCRAFT, SPACECRAFT

²ship *vb* **shipped; ship•ping 1 :** to put or receive on board a ship for transportation **2** ♦ **:** to have transported by a carrier **3 :** to take or draw into a boat ⟨~ oars⟩ ⟨~ water⟩ **4 :** to engage to serve on a ship — **ship•per** *n*

♦ consign, dispatch, pack, send, transfer, transmit, transport

-ship \ˌship\ *n suffix* **1 :** state **:** condition **:** quality ⟨friend*ship*⟩ **2 :** office **:** dignity **:** profession ⟨lord*ship*⟩ ⟨clerk*ship*⟩ **3 :** art **:** skill ⟨horseman*ship*⟩ **4 :** something showing, exhibiting, or embodying a quality or state ⟨town*ship*⟩ **5 :** one entitled to a (specified) rank, title, or appellation ⟨his Lord*ship*⟩ **6 :** the body of persons engaged in a specified activity ⟨reader*ship*⟩

ship•board \ˈship-ˌbōrd\ *n* **:** SHIP

ship•build•er \-ˌbil-dər\ *n* **:** one who designs or builds ships

ship•fit•ter \-ˌfi-tər\ *n* **1 :** one who constructs ships **2 :** a naval enlisted man who works as a plumber

ship•mate \-ˌmāt\ *n* **:** a fellow sailor

ship•ment \-mənt\ *n* **1 :** the process of shipping **2** ♦ **:** the goods shipped

♦ cargo, freight, load, payload

ship•ping *n* **1 :** SHIPS; *esp* **:** ships in one port or belonging to one country **2 :** transportation of goods

ship•shape \ˈship-ˌshāp\ *adj* ♦ **:** exhibiting neatness or good order **:** TIDY

♦ crisp, neat, orderly, snug, tidy, trim, uncluttered

ship•worm \-ˌwərm\ *n* **:** any of various wormlike marine clams that have a shell used for burrowing in wood and damaging wooden ships and wharves
¹ship•wreck \-ˌrek\ *n* **1 :** a wrecked ship **2** ♦ **:** destruction or loss of a ship **3 :** total loss or failure **:** RUIN

♦ wreck, wreckage

²shipwreck *vb* **:** to cause or meet disaster at sea through destruction or foundering
ship•wright \ˈship-ˌrīt\ *n* **:** a carpenter skilled in ship construction and repair
ship•yard \-ˌyärd\ *n* **:** a place where ships are built or repaired
shire \ˈshīr, *in place-name compounds* ˌshir, shər\ *n* **:** a county in Great Britain
shirk \ˈshərk\ *vb* ♦ **:** to avoid performing (duty or work) — **shirk•er** *n*

♦ avoid, dodge, duck, elude, escape, eschew, evade, shake, shun

shirr \ˈshər\ *vb* **1 :** to make shirring in **2 :** to bake (eggs removed from the shell) until set
shirr•ing \ˈshər-iŋ\ *n* **:** a decorative gathering in cloth made by drawing up parallel lines of stitches
shirt \ˈshərt\ *n* **1 :** a loose cloth garment usually having a collar, sleeves, a front opening, and a tail long enough to be tucked inside pants or a skirt **2 :** UNDERSHIRT — **shirt•less** *adj*
shirt•ing \ˈshir-tiŋ\ *n* **:** cloth suitable for making shirts
shish ke•bab \ˈshish-kə-ˌbäb\ *n* **:** kebab cooked on skewers
shiv \ˈshiv\ *n, slang* **:** KNIFE
¹shiv•er \ˈshi-vər\ *vb* **:** TREMBLE, QUIVER
²shiver *n* ♦ **:** an instance of shivering; *also* **:** an intense shivery sensation especially of fear — often used in plural with *the*

♦ quiver, shudder, tremble ♦ **shivers** jitters, shakes, willies

shiv•ery *adj* **:** causing shivers
shlemiel *var of* SCHLEMIEL
shlub *var of* SCHLUB
shmooze *var of* SCHMOOZE
Sho•ah \ˈshō-ə, -ˌä\ *n* **:** HOLOCAUST 2
¹shoal \ˈshōl\ *n* **1 :** SHALLOW **2 :** a sandbank or bar creating a shallow
²shoal *n* **:** a large group (as of fish)
shoat \ˈshōt\ *n* **:** a weaned young pig
¹shock \ˈshäk\ *n* **:** a pile of sheaves of grain or cornstalks set up in a field
²shock *n* **1** ♦ **:** a sharp impact or violent shake or jar **2** ♦ **:** a sudden violent mental or emotional disturbance **3 :** a state of bodily collapse that is often marked by a drop in blood pressure and volume and that is caused especially by crushing wounds, blood loss, or burns **4 :** the effect of a charge of electricity passing through the body **5 :** SHOCK ABSORBER — **shock•proof** \-ˌprüf\ *adj*

♦ [1] bump, collision, concussion, crash, impact, jar, jolt, smash, strike, wallop ♦ [2] amazement, astonishment, surprise

³shock *vb* **1** ♦ **:** to strike with surprise, horror, or disgust **2 :** to subject to the action of an electrical discharge

♦ appall, bowl, floor, jolt, shake up ♦ amaze, astonish, astound, dumbfound, flabbergast, startle, stun, stupefy, surprise

⁴shock *n* **:** a thick bushy mass (as of hair)
shock absorber *n* **:** any of several devices for absorbing the energy of sudden shocks in machinery
shock•er \ˈshä-kər\ *n* **:** one that shocks; *esp* **:** a sensational work of fiction or drama
shock•ing \ˈshä-kiŋ\ *adj* ♦ **:** extremely startling and offensive — **shock•ing•ly** *adv*

♦ amazing, astonishing, astounding, eye-opening, startling, stunning, surprising ♦ dire, dreadful, fearful, fearsome, forbidding, formidable, frightful, hair-raising, horrible, redoubtable, scary, terrible, terrifying ♦ abhorrent, abominable, appalling, awful, distasteful, foul, hideous, horrid, nasty, nauseating, noisome, obnoxious, obscene, odious, offensive, repellent, repugnant, repulsive, revolting, scandalous, ugly

shock therapy *n* **:** the treatment of mental disorder by induction of coma or convulsions by drugs or electricity
shock wave *n* **:** a wave formed by the sudden violent compression of the medium through which it travels
¹shod•dy \ˈshä-dē\ *n* **1 :** wool reclaimed from old rags; *also* **:** a fabric made from it **2 :** inferior or imitation material
²shoddy *adj* **shod•di•er; -est 1 :** made of shoddy **2** ♦ **:** poorly done or made — **shod•di•ly** \ˈshä-də-lē\ *adv* — **shod•di•ness** \-dē-nəs\ *n*

♦ bad, bum, cheap, inferior, junky, lousy, mediocre, poor, sleazy

¹shoe \ˈshü\ *n* **1 :** a covering for the human foot **2 :** HORSESHOE **3 :** the part of a brake that presses on the wheel
²shoe *vb* **shod** \ˈshäd\ *also* **shoed** \ˈshüd\; **shoe•ing :** to put a shoe or shoes on
shoe•horn \-ˌhȯrn\ *n* **:** a curved implement (as of horn or plastic) used in putting on a shoe
shoe•lace \ˈshü-ˌlās\ *n* **:** a lace or string for fastening a shoe
shoe•mak•er \-ˌmā-kər\ *n* **:** one who makes or repairs shoes
shoe•string \-ˌstriŋ\ *n* **1 :** SHOELACE **2** ♦ **:** a small sum of money

♦ mite, peanuts, pittance, song

sho•gun \ˈshō-gən\ *n* **:** any of a line of military governors ruling Japan until the revolution of 1867–68
shone *past and past part of* SHINE
shook *past of* SHAKE
shook–up \(ˌ)shu̇k-ˈəp\ *adj* **:** nervously upset **:** AGITATED
¹shoot \ˈshüt\ *vb* **shot** \ˈshät\; **shoot•ing 1** ♦ **:** to drive (as an arrow or bullet) forward quickly or forcibly **2** ♦ **:** to hit, kill, or wound with a missile **3** ♦ **:** to cause a missile to be driven forth or forth from ⟨∼ a gun⟩ **4** ♦ **:** to send forth (as a ray of light) **5 :** to thrust forward or out **6 :** to pass rapidly along ⟨∼ the rapids⟩ **7 :** to take a picture or series of pictures of **:** PHOTOGRAPH **8 :** to move swiftly **:** DART **9 :** to grow by or as if by sending out shoots; *also* **:** MATURE, DEVELOP **10** ♦ **:** to grow or rise rapidly — often used with *up*

♦ [1] blast, discharge, fire, loose ♦ [2] drill, gun, plug, pop ♦ [3] blast, discharge, fire ♦ [4] cast, discharge, emit, exhale, expel, issue, release, vent ♦ *usu* **shoot up** [10] rocket, skyrocket, soar, zoom

²shoot *n* **1 :** a plant stem with its leaves and branches especially when not yet mature **2 :** an act of shooting **3 :** a shooting match
shoot•er *n* **:** one that shoots: as **a** ♦ **:** a person who fires a missile-discharging device (as a rifle or bow) **b :** one who photographs

♦ marksman, sharpshooter, shot

shooting iron *n* **:** FIREARM
shooting star *n* **:** METEOR 2
shoot up *vb* **:** to inject a narcotic into a vein
¹shop \ˈshäp\ *n* **1** ♦ **:** a place where things are made or worked on **:** FACTORY, MILL **2** ♦ **:** a retail store ⟨dress ∼⟩

♦ [1] factory, mill, plant, works, workshop ♦ [2] emporium, store

²shop *vb* **shopped; shop•ping :** to visit stores for purchasing or examining goods — **shop•per** *n*
shop•keep•er \ˈshäp-ˌkē-pər\ *n* **:** a retail merchant
shop•lift \-ˌlift\ *vb* **:** to steal goods on display from a store — **shop•lift•er** *n*
shop•talk \-tȯk\ *n* ♦ **:** talk about one's business or special interests

♦ argot, cant, dialect, jargon, jive, language, lingo, patois, patter, shop, slang, terminology, vocabulary

shop•worn \-ˌwōrn\ *adj* **1 :** soiled or frayed from much handling in a store **2** ♦ **:** stale from excessive use or familiarity

♦ banal, commonplace, hackneyed, musty, stale, stereotyped, threadbare, tired, trite

¹shore \ˈshōr\ *n* **:** land along the edge of a body of water — **shore•less** *adj*
²shore *vb* **shored; shor•ing** ♦ **:** to give support to **:** BRACE — usually used with *up*

♦ *usu* **shore up** bear, bolster, brace, buttress, carry, prop, stay, support, uphold

³shore *n* ♦ **:** a prop for preventing sinking or sagging

♦ brace, bulwark, buttress, mount, stay, support, underpinning

shore•bird \-ˌbərd\ *n* **:** any of a suborder of birds (as the plovers and sandpipers) mostly found along the seashore
shore patrol *n* **:** a branch of a navy that exercises guard and police functions
shor•ing \ˈshōr-iŋ\ *n* **:** a group of things that shore something up
shorn *past part of* SHEAR
¹short \ˈshȯrt\ *adj* **1 :** not long or tall **2 :** not great in distance **3** ♦ **:** brief in time **4** ♦ **:** not coming up to standard or to an expected amount **5 :** CURT, ABRUPT **6** ♦ **:** insufficiently supplied **7 :** made with shortening **:** FLAKY **8 :** consisting of or relating to a sale of securities or commodities that the seller does not possess or has not contracted for at the time of the sale ⟨∼ sale⟩

♦ [3] brief, little, short-lived ***Ant*** extended, great, lengthy, long, marathon ♦ [4, 6] deficient, inadequate, insufficient, scarce, shy, wanting ***Ant*** adequate, enough, sufficient

²short *adv* **1 :** in an abrupt manner **:** ABRUPTLY **2 :** at some point before a goal aimed at
³short *n* **1 :** something shorter than normal or standard **2** *pl* **:** drawers or pants of less than knee length **3 :** SHORT CIRCUIT
⁴short *vb* **:** SHORT-CIRCUIT
short•age \ˈshȯr-tij\ *n* ♦ **:** the fact or state of being wanting or deficient **:** LACK

♦ dearth, deficiency, deficit, failure, famine, inadequacy, insufficiency, lack, paucity, poverty, scantiness, scarcity, want

short•cake \ˈshȯrt-ˌkāk\ *n* **:** a dessert consisting of short biscuit spread with sweetened fruit
short•change \-ˈchānj\ *vb* ♦ **:** to cheat especially by giving less than the correct amount of change

♦ bleed, cheat, chisel, cozen, defraud, fleece, gyp, hustle, mulct, rook, skin, squeeze, stick, sting, swindle, victimize

short circuit *n* **:** a connection made between points in an electric circuit where current is not intended to flow — **short–circuit** *vb*
short•com•ing \ˈshȯrt-ˌkə-miŋ\ *n* ♦ **:** an imperfection or lack that detracts from the whole **:** FAILING

♦ demerit, failing, fault, foible, frailty, vice, weakness

¹short•cut \-ˌkət\ *n* **1 :** a route more direct than that usually taken **2 :** a quicker way of doing something
²shortcut *vb* **:** to shorten (as a route or procedure) by use of a shortcut; *also* ♦ **:** to manage to get around especially by ingenuity or stratagem **:** CIRCUMVENT

♦ circumvent, dodge, get around, shortcut, sidestep, skirt

short•en \ˈshȯrt-ᵊn\ *vb* ♦ **:** to make or become short

♦ abbreviate, abridge, curtail, cut back *Ant* elongate, extend, lengthen, prolong, protract

short•en•ing \ˈshȯrt-ᵊn-iŋ\ *n* **:** a substance (as lard or butter) that makes pastry tender and flaky
short•hand \ˈshȯrt-ˌhand\ *n* **:** a method of writing rapidly by using symbols and abbreviations for letters, words, or phrases **:** STENOGRAPHY
short•hand•ed \ˌshȯrt-ˈhan-dəd\ *adj* **:** short of the needed number of people
short•horn \ˈshȯrt-ˌhȯrn\ *n, often cap* **:** any of a breed of red, roan, or white cattle of English origin
short hundredweight *n* **:** a unit of weight equal to 100 pounds in the U.S.
short–lived \ˈshȯrt-ˌlivd, -ˈlīvd\ *adj* ♦ **:** of short life or duration

♦ brief, ephemeral, evanescent, flash, fleeting, fugitive, impermanent, momentary, transient

short•ly \ˈshȯrt-lē\ *adv* **1** ♦ **:** in a few words **2** ♦ **:** in a short time **:** SOON

♦ [1] compactly, concisely, crisply, laconically, succinctly, summarily, tersely ♦ [2] anon, momentarily, presently, soon

short•ness *n* ♦ **:** the quality or state of being short especially in duration

♦ brevity, briefness, conciseness

short–or•der \ˈshȯrt-ˌȯr-dər\ *adj* **:** preparing or serving food that can be quickly cooked
short shrift *n* **1 :** a brief respite from death **2 :** little consideration
short•sight•ed \ˈshȯrt-ˌsī-təd\ *adj* **1 :** NEARSIGHTED **2 :** lacking foresight — **short•sight•ed•ness** *n*
short•stop \-ˌstäp\ *n* **:** a baseball player defending the area between second and third base
short story *n* ♦ **:** a short work of fiction usually dealing with a few characters and a single event

♦ narrative, novella, story, tale

short–tem•pered \ˌshȯrt-ˈtem-pərd\ *adj* ♦ **:** having a quick temper

♦ choleric, crabby, cranky, cross, crotchety, grouchy, grumpy, irascible, irritable, peevish, perverse, petulant, snappish, snappy, snippy, testy, waspish

short–term \ˈshȯrt-ˌtərm\ *adj* **1** ♦ **:** occurring over or involving a relatively short period of time **2 :** of or relating to a financial transaction based on a term usually of less than a year

♦ impermanent, interim, provisional, temporary

short ton *n* **:** a unit of weight equal to 2000 pounds in the U.S.
short•wave \ˈshȯrt-ˌwāv\ *n* **:** a radio wave with a wavelength between 10 and 100 meters
Sho•sho•ne *or* **Sho•sho•ni** \shə-ˈshō-nē\ *n, pl* **Shoshones** *or* **Shoshoni :** a member of an American Indian people orig. ranging through California, Idaho, Nevada, Utah, and Wyoming
¹shot \ˈshät\ *n* **1 :** an act of shooting **2 :** a stroke or throw in some games **3 :** something that is shot **:** MISSILE, PROJECTILE; *esp* **:** small pellets forming a charge for a shotgun **4 :** a metal sphere that is thrown for distance in the shot put **5 :** RANGE, REACH **6** ♦ **:** one that shoots; *esp* **:** MARKSMAN **7** ♦ **:** a single photographic exposure **8 :** a single sequence of a motion picture or a television program made by one camera **9 :** an injection (as of medicine) into the body **10** ♦ **:** a small serving of undiluted liquor **11** ♦ **:** the act or an instance of attempting ⟨I'll give it a ~⟩

♦ [6] marksman, sharpshooter, shooter ♦ [7] photograph, print, snap, snapshot ♦ [10] draft, drag, drink, nip, quaff, slug, snort, swallow, swig ♦ [11] attempt, crack, endeavor (*or* endeavour), essay, fling, go, pass, stab, trial, try, whack

²shot *past and past part of* SHOOT
shot•gun \ˈshät-ˌgən\ *n* **:** a gun with a smooth bore used to fire shot at short range
shot put *n* **:** a field event in which a shot is heaved for distance
should \ˈshu̇d, shəd\ *past of* SHALL ♦ — used as an auxiliary to express condition, obligation or propriety, probability, or futurity from a point of view in the past

♦ have, must, need, ought, shall

¹shoul•der \ˈshōl-dər\ *n* **1 :** the part of the body of a person or animal where the arm or foreleg joins the body **2 :** either edge of a roadway **3 :** a rounded or sloping part (as of a bottle) where the neck joins the body
²shoulder *vb* **1 :** to push or thrust with the shoulder **2 :** to bear on the shoulder **3** ♦ **:** to take the responsibility of

♦ accept, assume, bear, take over, undertake

shoulder belt *n* **:** an automobile safety belt worn across the torso and over the shoulder
shoulder blade *n* **:** a flat triangular bone at the back of each shoulder
¹shout \ˈshau̇t\ *vb* ♦ **:** to utter a sudden loud cry; *also* **:** to utter in a loud voice

♦ bawl, call, cry, holler, vociferate, yell

²shout *n* ♦ **:** a loud cry or call

♦ cry, holler, hoot, howl, whoop, yell, yowl

shove \ˈshəv\ *vb* **shoved; shov•ing 1** ♦ **:** to push along, aside, or away **2** ♦ **:** to go away — usually used with *off* — **shove** *n*

♦ [1] drive, propel, push, thrust ♦ *usu* **shove off** [2] clear out, depart, exit, get off, go, move, pull, quit, sally, take off

¹shov•el \ˈshə-vəl\ *n* **1 :** a broad long-handled scoop used to lift and throw material **2 :** the amount a shovel will hold
²shovel *vb* **-eled** *or* **-elled; -el•ing** *or* **-el•ling 1 :** to take up and throw with a shovel **2 :** to dig or clean out with a shovel
¹show \ˈshō\ *vb* **showed** \ˈshōd\; **shown** \ˈshōn\ *or* **showed; show•ing 1** ♦ **:** to cause or permit to be seen **:** EXHIBIT ⟨~ anger⟩ **2 :** CONFER, BESTOW ⟨~ mercy⟩ **3** ♦ **:** to reveal by one's condition, nature, or behavior **:** DISCLOSE ⟨~*ed* courage in battle⟩ **4** ♦ **:** to communicate knowledge to **:** INSTRUCT ⟨~ me how⟩ **5** ♦ **:** to demonstrate or establish by argument or reasoning **:** PROVE ⟨~*s* he was guilty⟩ **6 :** APPEAR **7 :** to be noticeable **8 :** to be third in a horse race **9** ♦ **:** to bring by or as if by leading **:** USHER

♦ [1] display, disport, exhibit, expose, flash, flaunt, parade, show off, sport, strut, unveil ♦ [3] bespeak, betray, demonstrate, disclose, display, evince, expose, give away, manifest, reveal ♦ [4] coach, counsel, guide, instruct, lead, mentor, pilot, shepherd, tutor ♦ [5] demonstrate, establish, prove, substantiate ♦ [9] conduct, direct, guide, lead, marshal, pilot, route, steer, usher

²show *n* **1** ♦ **:** a demonstrative display **2** ♦ **:** outward appearance ⟨a ~ of resistance⟩ **3 :** SPECTACLE **4 :** a theatrical presentation **5 :** a radio or television program **6 :** third place in a horse race **7** ♦ **:** a large display or exhibition arranged to arouse interest or stimulate sales

♦ [1] demonstration, display, exhibition ♦ [2] appearance, face, guise, name, pretense, semblance ♦ [7] display, exhibit, exhibition, exposition, fair

¹show•case \ˈshō-ˌkās\ *n* **:** a cabinet for displaying items (as in a store)
²showcase *vb* **show•cased; show•cas•ing :** EXHIBIT
show•down \ˈshō-ˌdau̇n\ *n* **:** a decisive confrontation or contest; *esp* **:** the showing of poker hands to determine the winner of a pot

[1]**show•er** \ˈshau̇-ər\ *n* **1 :** a brief fall of rain **2 :** a party given by friends who bring gifts **3 :** a bath in which water is showered on the person; *also* **:** a facility (as a stall) for such a bath **4** ♦ **:** something resembling a rain shower — **show•ery** *adj*

♦ hail, rain, storm

[2]**shower** *vb* **1 :** to rain or fall in a shower **2 :** to bathe in a shower **3** ♦ **:** to give in abundance

♦ heap, lavish, pour, rain

show•i•ness \-ē-nəs\ *n* ♦ **:** the quality or state of being showy

♦ flamboyance, flashiness, gaudiness, glitz, ostentation, pretentiousness, swank

show•man \ˈshō-mən\ *n* **:** a notably spectacular, dramatic, or effective performer — **show•man•ship** *n*
show–off \ˈshō-ˌȯf\ *n* **:** one that seeks to attract attention by conspicuous behavior
show off *vb* **1** ♦ **:** to display proudly **2** ♦ **:** to act as a show-off

♦ [1] display, disport, exhibit, expose, flash, flaunt, parade, show, sport, strut, unveil ♦ [2] act up, clown, cut up, fool, monkey, skylark

show•piece \ˈshō-ˌpēs\ *n* **:** an outstanding example used for exhibition
show•place \-ˌplās\ *n* **:** an estate or building that is a showpiece
show up *vb* **1** ♦ **:** to make an appearance **:** ARRIVE **2** ♦ **:** to expose or discredit especially by revealing faults **3** ♦ **:** to be plainly evident

♦ [1] arrive, come, land, turn up ♦ [2] debunk, expose, uncloak, uncover, unmask ♦ [3] appear, come out, materialize, turn up

showy \ˈshō-ē\ *adj* **show•i•er; -est** ♦ **:** superficially impressive or striking — **show•i•ly** \ˈshō-ə-lē\ *adv*

♦ catchy, conspicuous, dramatic, flamboyant, striking ***Ant*** inconspicuous, unobtrusive

shpt *abbr* shipment
shrap•nel \ˈshrap-nəl\ *n, pl* **shrapnel :** bomb, mine, or shell fragments
[1]**shred** \ˈshred\ *n* **:** a narrow strip cut or torn off **:** a small fragment
[2]**shred** *vb* **shred•ded; shred•ding** ♦ **:** to cut or tear into shreds

♦ rend, rip, rive, tatter, tear

shrew \ˈshrü\ *n* **1 :** any of a family of very small mammals with short velvety fur that are related to the moles **2** ♦ **:** a scolding woman

♦ fury, harpy, termagant, virago

shrewd \ˈshrüd\ *adj* ♦ **:** given to wily and artful ways or dealing **:** ASTUTE — **shrewd•ly** *adv*

♦ astute, canny, hardheaded, knowing, sharp, smart ***Ant*** unknowing

shrewd•ness *n* ♦ **:** the quality or state of being shrewd

♦ acumen, astuteness, caginess, canniness, hardheadedness, intelligence, keenness, sharpness, wit

shrew•ish \ˈshrü-ish\ *adj* **:** having an irritable disposition **:** ILL-TEMPERED — **shrew•ish•ly** *adv*
[1]**shriek** \ˈshrēk\ *n* **:** a shrill cry **:** SCREAM, YELL
[2]**shriek** *vb* ♦ **:** to utter a sharp shrill sound; *also* **:** to utter with a shriek

♦ howl, scream, shrill, squeal, yell, yelp

shrift \ˈshrift\ *n, archaic* **:** the act of shriving
shrike \ˈshrīk\ *n* **:** any of numerous usually largely grayish or brownish birds that often impale their usually insect prey upon thorns before devouring it
[1]**shrill** \ˈshril\ *vb* ♦ **:** to make a high-pitched piercing sound

♦ howl, scream, shriek, squeal, yell, yelp

[2]**shrill** *adj* ♦ **:** high-pitched ⟨~ whistle⟩ — **shril•ly** *adv*

♦ acute, sharp, squeaky, treble ***Ant*** bass, deep, low, throaty

shrimp \ˈshrimp\ *n, pl* **shrimps** *or* **shrimp 1 :** any of various small marine crustaceans related to the lobsters **2** ♦ **:** a small or puny person or thing

♦ dwarf, midget, mite, peewee, pygmy, runt, scrub

shrine \ˈshrīn\ *n* **1 :** the tomb of a saint; *also* **:** a place where devotion is paid to a saint or deity **2 :** a place or object hallowed by its associations
[1]**shrink** \ˈshriŋk\ *vb* **shrank** \ˈshraŋk\ *or* **shrunk** \ˈshrəŋk\; **shrunk** *or* **shrunk•en** \ˈshrəŋ-kən\; **shrink•ing 1** ♦ **:** to draw back or away **2** ♦ **:** to become smaller or more compact **3** ♦ **:** to lessen in value — **shrink•able** *adj*

♦ [1] blench, flinch, quail, recoil, wince ♦ [2] compress, condense, constrict, contract ♦ [2, 3] abate, de-escalate, decline, decrease, die, diminish, dwindle, ebb, fall, lessen, let up, lower, moderate, recede, relent, subside, taper, wane

[2]**shrink** *n* **:** a clinical psychiatrist or psychologist
shrink•age \ˈshriŋ-kij\ *n* **1 :** the act of shrinking **2** ♦ **:** the amount lost by shrinkage

♦ abatement, decline, decrease, decrement, diminution, drop, fall, loss, reduction

shrive \ˈshrīv\ *vb* **shrived** *or* **shrove** \ˈshrōv\; **shriv•en** \ˈshri-vən\ *or* **shrived :** to administer the sacrament of reconciliation to
shriv•el \ˈshri-vəl\ *vb* **-eled** *or* **-elled; -el•ing** *or* **-el•ling :** to shrink and draw into wrinkles **:** DWINDLE
[1]**shroud** \ˈshrau̇d\ *n* **1** ♦ **:** something that covers or screens **2 :** a cloth placed over a dead body **3 :** any of the ropes leading from the masthead of a ship to the side to support the mast

♦ cloak, curtain, hood, mantle, mask, veil

[2]**shroud** *vb* **1** ♦ **:** to veil or screen from view; *also* **:** to veil under another appearance (as by obscuring or disguising) **2 :** to cover with a shroud

♦ blanket, blot out, cloak, conceal, cover, curtain, hide, mask, obscure, occult, screen ♦ embrace, enclose, encompass, enfold, enshroud, envelop, invest, lap, mantle, swathe, veil, wrap

shrub \ˈshrəb\ *n* **:** a low usually several-stemmed woody plant — **shrub•by** *adj*
shrub•bery \ˈshrə-bə-rē\ *n, pl* **-ber•ies :** a planting or growth of shrubs
shrug \ˈshrəg\ *vb* **shrugged; shrug•ging :** to hunch (the shoulders) up to express aloofness, indifference, or uncertainty — **shrug** *n*
shrug off *vb* **1** ♦ **:** to brush aside **:** MINIMIZE **2 :** to shake off **3 :** to remove (a garment) by wriggling out

♦ condone, disregard, excuse, ignore, minimize, pardon, pass over, wink at

shtick *also* **schtick** *or* **shtik** \ˈshtik\ *n* **1 :** a usually comic or repetitious performance or routine **2 :** one's special trait, interest, or activity
[1]**shuck** \ˈshək\ *n* **:** SHELL, HUSK
[2]**shuck** *vb* **1 :** to strip of shucks **2** ♦ **:** to lay aside — often used with *off*

♦ *usu* **shuck off** cast, discard, ditch, dump, fling, jettison, junk, lose, reject, scrap, shed, slough, throw away, throw out, unload

[1]**shud•der** \ˈshə-dər\ *vb* ♦ **:** to tremble convulsively **:** QUAKE

♦ agitate, convulse, jolt, jounce, quake, quiver, shake, vibrate, wobble

[2]**shudder** *n* ♦ **:** an act of shuddering

♦ quiver, shiver, tremble

[1]**shuf•fle** \ˈshə-fəl\ *vb* **shuf•fled; shuf•fling 1** ♦ **:** to mix in a disorderly mass **2 :** to rearrange the order of (cards in a pack) by mixing two parts of the pack together **3 :** to shift from place to place **4** ♦ **:** to move with a sliding or dragging gait **5 :** to dance in a slow lagging manner

♦ [1] confuse, derange, disarray, disorder, jumble, mess, mix, muddle, scramble, upset ♦ [4] lumber, scuff, scuffle, shamble

[2]**shuffle** *n* **1 :** an act of shuffling (as of cards) **2** ♦ **:** a confusing jumble (as of papers or events)

♦ assortment, clutter, jumble, medley, mélange, miscellany, motley, muddle, variety, welter

shuf•fle•board \ˈshə-fəl-ˌbōrd\ *n* **:** a game in which players use long-handled cues to shove disks into scoring areas marked on a smooth surface
shun \ˈshən\ *vb* **shunned; shun•ning** ♦ **:** to avoid deliberately or habitually

♦ avoid, dodge, duck, elude, escape, eschew, evade, shake, shirk

[1]**shunt** \ˈshənt\ *vb* **:** to turn off to one side; *esp* **:** to switch (a train) from one track to another
[2]**shunt** *n* **1 :** a method or device for turning or thrusting aside **2 :** a conductor joining two points in an electrical circuit forming an alternate path through which a portion of the current may pass
shut \ˈshət\ *vb* **shut; shut•ting 1 :** CLOSE **2 :** to forbid entrance

into **3 :** to lock up **4 :** to fold together ⟨~ a penknife⟩ **5 :** to cease or suspend activity ⟨~ down an assembly line⟩
shut•down \ˈ-ˌdau̇n\ *n* ♦ **:** a temporary cessation of activity (as in a factory)

♦ cessation, close, closure, conclusion, end, ending, expiration, finish, halt, lapse, stop, stoppage, termination

shut–in \ˈshət-ˌin\ *n* **:** an invalid confined to home, a room, or bed
shut•out \ˈshət-ˌau̇t\ *n* **:** a game or contest in which one side fails to score
shut out *vb* **1** ♦ **:** to prevent from using or participating **:** EXCLUDE **2 :** to prevent (an opponent) from scoring in a game or contest

♦ ban, bar, count out, debar, eliminate, except, exclude, rule out

shut off *vb* ♦ **:** to stop the operation of (as a machine); *also* **:** to cease operating

♦ break, break off, cease, cut, desist, discontinue, drop, end, halt, knock off, layoff, leave off, quit, stop

shut•ter \ˈshə-tər\ *n* **1 :** a movable cover for a door or window **:** BLIND **2 :** the part of a camera that opens and closes to allow light to enter
shut•ter•bug \ˈshə-tər-ˌbəg\ *n* **:** a photography enthusiast
¹shut•tle \ˈshət-ᵊl\ *n* **1 :** an instrument used in weaving for passing the horizontal threads between the vertical threads **2 :** a vehicle traveling back and forth over a short route ⟨a ~ bus⟩ **3 :** SPACE SHUTTLE
²shuttle *vb* **shut•tled; shut•tling :** to move back and forth frequently
shut•tle•cock \ˈshət-ᵊl-ˌkäk\ *n* **:** a light conical object (as of cork or plastic) used in badminton
shut up *vb* ♦ **:** to cease or cause to cease talking

♦ clam up, hush, pipe down, quiet (down) ***Ant*** speak, talk

¹shy \ˈshī\ *adj* **shi•er** *or* **shy•er** \ˈshī-ər\; **shi•est** *or* **shy•est** \ˈshī-əst\ **1** ♦ **:** easily frightened **:** TIMID **2 :** WARY **3** ♦ **:** sensitively diffident or retiring **:** BASHFUL **4** ♦ **:** having less than the full or specified amount or number **:** LACKING — **shy•ly** *adv* — **shyness** *n*

♦ [1] fainthearted, fearful, mousy, scary, skittish, timid ***Ant*** adventuresome, adventurous, audacious, bold, daring, dashing, gutsy, hardy, venturous, venturesome ♦ [3] bashful, coy, demure, diffident, introverted, modest, retiring, sheepish ***Ant*** extroverted, immodest, outgoing ♦ [4] deficient, inadequate, insufficient, scarce, short, wanting

²shy *vb* **shied; shy•ing 1 :** to show a dislike **:** RECOIL **2 :** to start suddenly aside through fright ⟨the horse *shied*⟩
shy•ster \ˈshīs-tər\ *n* **:** an unscrupulous lawyer or politician
Si *symbol* silicon
SI *abbr* International System of Units
Si•a•mese \ˌsī-ə-ˈmēz, -ˈmēs\ *n, pl* **Sia•mese :** THAI — **Siamese** *adj*
Siamese cat *n* **:** any of a breed of slender blue-eyed short-haired domestic cats of Asian origin
Siamese twin *n* **:** one of a pair of twins with bodies joined together at birth
Siberian husky *n* **:** any of a breed of thick-coated compact dogs orig. developed in Siberia to pull sleds
¹sib•i•lant \ˈsi-bə-lənt\ *adj* **:** having, containing, or producing the sound of or a sound resembling that of the *s* or the *sh* in *sash* — **sib•i•lant•ly** *adv*
²sibilant *n* **:** a sibilant speech sound as English \s\, \z\, \sh\, \zh\, \ch (=tsh)\, or \j (=dzh)\
sib•ling \ˈsi-bliŋ\ *n* **:** a brother or sister considered irrespective of sex; *also* **:** one of two or more offspring having one common parent
sib•yl \ˈsi-bəl\ *n, often cap* **:** PROPHETESS — **sib•yl•line** \-bə-ˌlīn, -ˌlēn\ *adj*
sic \ˈsik, ˈsēk\ *adv* **:** intentionally so written — used after a printed word or passage to indicate that it exactly reproduces an original ⟨said he seed [*sic*] it all⟩
sick \ˈsik\ *adj* **1** ♦ **:** not in good health **:** ILL; *also* **:** of, relating to, or intended for use in sickness ⟨~ pay⟩ **2** ♦ **:** suffering from nausea **:** NAUSEATED **3** ♦ **:** having a strong distaste from an overabundance; *also* **:** DISGUSTED **4 :** PINING **5 :** MACABRE, SADISTIC ⟨~ jokes⟩

♦ [1] bad, down, ill, indisposed, peaked, punk, unhealthy, unsound, unwell ***Ant*** chipper, hale, healthful, healthy, sound, well, whole, wholesome ♦ [2] ill, nauseous, queasy, queer, squeamish ♦ [3] fed up, jaded, tired, weary ♦ [3] disgusted, squeamish

sick•bed \ˈsik-ˌbed\ *n* **:** a bed on which one lies sick
sick•en \ˈsi-kən\ *vb* ♦ **:** to make or become sick — **sick•en•ing•ly** *adv*

♦ disgust, nauseate, repel, repulse, revolt, turn off ♦ *usu* **sicken with** catch, come down, contract, get, take

sickening *adj* **:** causing sickness or disgust
sick•le \ˈsi-kəl\ *n* **:** a cutting tool consisting of a curved metal blade with a short handle
sickle–cell anemia *n* **:** an inherited anemia in which red blood cells tend to become crescent-shaped and clog small blood vessels and which occurs especially in individuals of African, Mediterranean, or southwest Asian ancestry
sick•ly \sik-lē\ *adj* **1 a :** somewhat unwell **b** ♦ **:** habitually ailing **2** ♦ **:** produced by or associated with sickness

♦ [1b] invalid, weakly ***Ant*** healthy, well ♦ [2] cadaverous, green, lurid, pale, pasty, peaked, sallow ***Ant*** florid, flush, healthy, rubicund, ruddy, sanguine

sick•ness \ˈsik-nəs\ *n* **1** ♦ **:** ill health; *also* **:** a specific disease **2 :** a stomach distress with distaste for food and an urge to vomit **:** NAUSEA

♦ affection, ailment, bug, complaint, complication, condition, disease, disorder, fever, ill, illness, infirmity, malady, trouble ♦ illness, unsoundness ***Ant*** health, healthiness, soundness, wellness, wholeness, wholesomeness

side \ˈsīd\ *n* **1 :** the right or left part of the trunk of a body **2 :** a place away from a central point or line **3 :** a border of an object; *esp* **:** one of the longer borders as contrasted with an end **4 :** an outer surface of an object **5** ♦ **:** a position regarded as opposite to another **6** ♦ **:** a body of partisans or contestants — **side** *adj*

♦ [5] angle, aspect, facet, hand, phase ♦ [6] bloc, body, coalition, combination, combine, faction, party, sect, set, wing

side•arm \-ˌärm\ *adj* **:** made with a sideways sweep of the arm — **sidearm** *adv*
side arm *n* **:** a weapon worn at the side or in the belt
side•bar \ˈsīd-ˌbär\ *n* **:** a short news story accompanying a major story and presenting related information
side•board \-ˌbōrd\ *n* ♦ **:** a piece of dining-room furniture for holding articles of table service

♦ buffet, cabinet, closet, cupboard, hutch, locker

side•burns \-ˌbərnz\ *n pl* **:** whiskers on the side of the face in front of the ears
side by side *adv* **1 :** beside one another **2 :** in the same place, time, or circumstance — **side–by–side** *adj*
side•car \-ˌkär\ *n* **:** a one-wheeled passenger car attached to the side of a motorcycle
side effect *n* **:** a secondary and usually adverse effect (as of a drug)
side•kick \ˈsīd-ˌkik\ *n* ♦ **:** a person closely associated with another as a subordinate or partner

♦ aid, apprentice, assistant, deputy, helper, helpmate, mate

side•line \ˈsīd-ˌlīn\ *n* **1 :** an activity pursued in addition to one's regular occupation **2 :** the space immediately outside the lines of an athletic field or court **3 :** a sphere of little or no participation — usually used in plural
¹side•long \ˈsīd-ˌlȯŋ\ *adv* **:** in the direction of or along the side **:** OBLIQUELY
²sidelong *adj* **:** directed to one side ⟨~ look⟩
side•man \ˈsīd-ˌman\ *n* **:** a member of a jazz or swing orchestra
side•piece \-ˌpēs\ *n* **:** a piece forming or contained in the side of something
si•de•re•al \sī-ˈdir-ē-əl, sə-\ *adj* **1 :** of or relating to the stars **2 :** measured by the apparent motion of the stars
side•sad•dle \ˈsīd-ˌsad-ᵊl\ *n* **:** a saddle for women on which the rider sits with both legs on the same side of the horse — **sidesaddle** *adv*
side•show \ˈsīd-ˌshō\ *n* **1 :** a minor show offered in addition to a main exhibition (as of a circus) **2 :** an incidental diversion
side•step \-ˌstep\ *vb* **1 :** to step aside **2** ♦ **:** to move out of the way of; *also* **:** to avoid an issue or decision

♦ circumvent, dodge, skirt ♦ dodge, duck

side•stroke \-ˌstrōk\ *n* **:** a swimming stroke which is executed on the side and in which the arms are swept backward and downward and the legs do a scissors kick
side•swipe \-ˌswīp\ *vb* **:** to strike with a glancing blow along the side — **sideswipe** *n*
¹side•track \-ˌtrak\ *n* **:** SIDING 1

[2]**sidetrack** *vb* **1 :** to switch from a main railroad line to a siding **2 :** to turn aside from a purpose
side•walk \ˈsīd-ˌwȯk\ *n* **:** a paved walk at the side of a road or street
side•wall \-ˌwȯl\ *n* **1 :** a wall forming the side of something **2 :** the side of an automobile tire
side•ways \-ˌwāz\ *adv or adj* **1 :** from the side **2 :** with one side to the front **3 :** to, toward, or at one side
side•wind•er \-ˌwīn-dər\ *n* **:** a small pale-colored desert rattlesnake of the southwestern U.S.
sid•ing \ˈsī-diŋ\ *n* **1 :** a short railroad track connected with the main track **2 :** material (as boards) covering the outside of frame buildings
si•dle \ˈsīd-ᵊl\ *vb* **si•dled; si•dling :** to move sideways or with one side foremost
SIDS *abbr* sudden infant death syndrome
siege \ˈsēj\ *n* **1 :** the placing of an army around or before a fortified place to force its surrender **2 ♦ :** a persistent attack (as of illness)

♦ attack, bout, case, fit, seizure, spell

sie•mens \ˈsē-mənz, ˈzē-\ *n* **:** a unit of conductance equivalent to one ampere per volt
si•er•ra \sē-ˈer-ə\ *n* **:** a range of mountains especially with jagged peaks
si•es•ta \sē-ˈes-tə\ *n* **♦ :** a midday rest or nap

♦ catnap, doze, drowse, forty winks, nap, snooze, wink

sieve \ˈsiv\ *n* **:** a utensil with meshes or holes to separate finer particles from coarser or solids from liquids
sift \ˈsift\ *vb* **1 :** to pass through a sieve **2 :** to separate with or as if with a sieve **3 :** to examine carefully **4 :** to scatter by or as if by passing through a sieve — **sift•er** *n*
sig *abbr* signature
SIG *abbr* special interest group
sigh \ˈsī\ *vb* **1 :** to let out a deep audible breath (as in weariness or sorrow) **2 ♦ :** to long persistently, wistfully, or sadly **:** YEARN — often used with *for* — **sigh** *n*

♦ ache, die, hanker, hunger, itch, long, pant, pine, thirst, yearn

[1]**sight** \ˈsīt\ *n* **1 :** something seen or worth seeing **2 ♦ :** the process or power of seeing; *esp* **:** the sense of which the eye is the receptor and by which qualities of appearance (as position, shape, and color) are perceived **3 :** INSPECTION **4 :** a device (as a small bead on a gun barrel) that aids the eye in aiming **5 :** the act of looking at or beholding **:** VIEW, GLIMPSE **6 :** the range of vision **7 ♦ :** something ludicrous or disorderly in appearance — **sight•less** *adj*

♦ [2] eye, vision ♦ [7] eyesore, fright, horror, mess, monstrosity

[2]**sight** *vb* **1 ♦ :** to get sight of **2 :** to aim by means of a sight

♦ behold, descry, discern, distinguish, espy, eye, look, note, notice, observe, perceive, regard, remark, see, spy, view, witness

sight•ed \ˈsī-təd\ *adj* **:** having sight
sight•ly \-lē\ *adj* **:** pleasing to the sight
sight•see•ing \ˈsīt-ˌsē-iŋ\ *adj* **:** engaged in or used for seeing sights of interest
sight•seer \-ˌsē-ər\ *n* **♦ :** one that visits places of interest

♦ excursionist, tourist, traveler

sig•ma \ˈsig-mə\ *n* **:** the 18th letter of the Greek alphabet — Σ or σ or ς
[1]**sign** \ˈsīn\ *n* **1 ♦ :** a gesture expressing a command, wish, or thought **2 :** SYMBOL **3 :** a notice publicly displayed for advertising purposes or for giving direction or warning **4 :** OMEN, PORTENT **5 :** TRACE, VESTIGE

♦ gesture, pantomime, signal

[2]**sign** *vb* **1 :** to mark with a sign **2 :** to represent by a sign **3 :** to make a sign or signal **4 :** to write one's name on in token of assent or obligation **5 :** to assign legally **6 :** to use sign language — **sign•er** *n*
[1]**sig•nal** \ˈsig-nəl\ *n* **1 :** a sign agreed on as the start of some joint action **2 ♦ :** a sign giving warning or notice of something **3 :** the message, sound, or image transmitted in electronic communication (as radio)

♦ gesture, pantomime, sign

[2]**signal** *vb* **-naled** *or* **-nalled; -nal•ing** *or* **-nal•ling 1 ♦ :** to notify by a signal **2 :** to communicate by signals

♦ flag, gesture, motion, wave

[3]**signal** *adj* **♦** distinguished from the ordinary ⟨a ~ honor⟩ — **sig•nal•ly** *adv*

♦ distinguished, eminent, illustrious, noble, notable, noteworthy, outstanding, preeminent, prestigious, star, superior

sig•nal•ize \ˈsig-nə-ˌlīz\ *vb* **-ized; -iz•ing :** to point out or make conspicuous — **sig•nal•i•za•tion** \ˌsig-nə-lə-ˈzā-shən\ *n*
sig•nal•man \ˈsig-nəl-mən, -ˌman\ *n* **:** a person who signals or works with signals
sig•na•to•ry \ˈsig-nə-ˌtōr-ē\ *n, pl* **-ries :** a person or government that signs jointly with others — **signatory** *adj*
sig•na•ture \ˈsig-nə-ˌchu̇r\ *n* **1 :** the name of a person written by himself or herself **2 :** the sign placed after the clef to indicate the key or the meter of a piece of music
sign•board \ˈsīn-ˌbōrd\ *n* **:** a board bearing a sign or notice
sig•net \ˈsig-nət\ *n* **:** a small intaglio seal (as in a ring)
sig•nif•i•cance \sig-ˈni-fi-kəns\ *n* **1 ♦ :** something signified **:** MEANING **2 :** SUGGESTIVENESS **3 ♦ :** the quality of being important **:** IMPORTANCE

♦ [1] denotation, drift, import, intent, meaning, purport, sense, signification ♦ [3] consequence, import, magnitude, moment, weight

sig•nif•i•cant \-kənt\ *adj* **1 ♦ :** having meaning; *esp* **:** having a hidden or special meaning **2 ♦ :** having or likely to have considerable influence or effect **:** IMPORTANT **3 ♦ :** of a noticeably or measurably large amount — **sig•nif•i•cant•ly** *adv*

♦ [1] big, consequential, eventful, important, major, material, meaningful, momentous, substantial, weighty ♦ [1] denotative, indicative, telltale ♦ [2] important, influential, mighty, potent, powerful, strong ♦ [3] considerable, good, goodly, healthy, respectable, sizable, substantial, tidy

sig•ni•fi•ca•tion \ˌsig-nə-fə-ˈkā-shən\ *n* **1 :** the act or process of signifying by signs or other symbolic means **2 ♦ :** the meaning that a term, symbol, or character regularly conveys or is intended to convey

♦ denotation, drift, import, intent, meaning, purport, sense, significance

sig•ni•fy \ˈsig-nə-ˌfī\ *vb* **-fied; -fy•ing 1 :** to show by a sign **2 ♦ :** to serve or intend to convey, show, or indicate **:** MEAN **3 ♦ :** to have significance

♦ [2] denote, express, import, mean, spell ♦ [3] count, import, matter, mean, weigh

sign in *vb* **:** to make a record of arrival (as by signing a register)
sign language *n* **:** a formal system of hand gestures used for communication (as by the deaf)
sign off *vb* **:** to announce the end (as of a program or broadcast)
sign of the cross : a gesture of the hand forming a cross (as to invoke divine blessing)
sign on *vb* **1 ♦ :** to engage oneself by or as if by a signature **:** ENLIST **2 :** to announce the start of broadcasting for the day

♦ *usu* **sign on for** enlist, enroll, enter, join, sign up

sign out *vb* **:** to make a record of departure (as by signing a register)
sign•post \ˈsīn-ˌpōst\ *n* **:** a post bearing a sign
sign up *vb* **♦ :** to sign one's name (as to a contract) in order to obtain, do, or join something

♦ *usu* **sign up for** enlist, enroll, enter, join, sign on

Sikh \ˈsēk\ *n* **:** an adherent of a religion of India marked by rejection of caste — **Sikh•ism** *n*
si•lage \ˈsī-lij\ *n* **:** fodder fermented (as in a silo) to produce a rich moist animal feed
[1]**si•lence** \ˈsī-ləns\ *n* **1 :** forbearance from speech or noise **2 ♦ :** absence of sound or noise **:** STILLNESS **3 :** SECRECY

♦ hush, quiet, quietness, still, stillness ***Ant*** noise, sound

[2]**silence** *vb* **si•lenced; si•lenc•ing 1 ♦ :** to reduce to silence **:** STILL **2 ♦ :** to cause to cease hostile firing or criticism

♦ [1] hush, mute, quell, settle, still ♦ [2] clamp down, crack down, crush, put down, quash, quell, repress, snuff, squash, squelch, subdue, suppress

si•lenc•er \ˈsī-lən-sər\ *n* **:** a device for muffling the noise of a gunshot
si•lent \ˈsī-lənt\ *adj* **1 ♦ :** not speaking **:** MUTE; *also* **:** not inclined to talk **2 ♦ :** free from sound or noise **:** STILL, QUIET **3 :** performed or borne without utterance — **si•lent•ly** *adv*

♦ [1] dumb, mum, mute, speechless, uncommunicative ***Ant*** communicative, speaking, talking ♦ [1] closemouthed, laconic, reserved, reticent, taciturn, uncommunicative *Ant* chatty, communicative, conversational, gabby, garrulous, loquacious, talkative, unreserved ♦ [2] hushed, muted, noiseless, quiet, soundless, still *Ant* noisy, unquiet

silent treatment *n* ♦ : an act of completely ignoring a person or thing by resort to silence especially as a means of expressing contempt or disapproval

♦ brush-off, cold shoulder, rebuff, repulse, snub

¹sil•hou•ette \ˌsi-lə-ˈwet\ *n* **1 :** a representation of the outlines of an object filled in with black or some other uniform color **2** ♦ **:** the outline of a body viewed as circumscribing a mass **:** OUTLINE ⟨~ of a ship⟩

♦ contour, figure, outline

²silhouette *vb* **-ett•ed; -ett•ing** ♦ **:** to represent by a silhouette; *also* **:** to show against a light background

♦ define, delineate, outline, sketch, trace

sil•i•ca \ˈsi-li-kə\ *n* **:** a mineral that consists of silicon and oxygen
sil•i•cate \ˈsi-lə-ˌkāt, ˈsi-li-kət\ *n* **:** a chemical salt that consists of a metal combined with silicon and oxygen
si•li•ceous *also* **si•li•cious** \sə-ˈli-shəs\ *adj* **:** of, relating to, or containing silica or a silicate
sil•i•con \ˈsi-li-kən, ˈsi-lə-ˌkän\ *n* **:** a nonmetallic chemical element that occurs in combination as the most abundant element next to oxygen in the earth's crust and is used especially in alloys and semiconductors
sil•i•cone \ˈsi-lə-ˌkōn\ *n* **:** an organic silicon compound used especially for lubricants and varnishes
sil•i•co•sis \ˌsi-lə-ˈkō-səs\ *n* **:** a lung disease caused by prolonged inhaling of silica dusts
silk \ˈsilk\ *n* **1 :** a fine strong lustrous protein fiber produced by insect larvae usually for their cocoons; *esp* **:** one from moth larvae (**silk•worms** \-ˌwərmz\) used for cloth **2 :** thread or cloth made from silk
silk•en \ˈsil-kən\ *adj* ♦ **:** resembling silk (as in texture or appearance)

♦ cottony, downy, satiny, soft, velvety

silk screen *n* **:** a stencil process in which coloring matter is forced through the meshes of a prepared silk or organdy screen; *also* **:** a print made by this process — **silk–screen** *vb*
silky *adj* **:** resembling silk (as in texture or appearance)
sill \ˈsil\ *n* **:** a heavy crosspiece (as of wood or stone) that forms the bottom member of a window frame or a doorway; *also* **:** a horizontal supporting piece at the base of a structure
sil•li•ness *n* ♦ **:** the quality or state of being silly; *also* **:** a silly practice

♦ absurdity, asininity, balminess, craziness, daftness, fatuity, folly, foolishness, inanity, insanity, lunacy, madness, nonsense, simplicity, zaniness

sil•ly \ˈsi-lē\ *adj* **sil•li•er; -est** ♦ **:** exhibiting or indicative of a lack of common sense or sound judgment; *also* **:** lacking in seriousness

♦ absurd, crazy, cuckoo, fatuous, foolish, mad, nonsensical, nutty, senseless, silly, stupid ♦ flighty, frivolous, giddy, goofy, harebrained, light-headed, scatterbrained

si•lo \ˈsī-lō\ *n, pl* **silos 1 :** a trench, pit, or especially a tall cylinder for making and storing silage **2 :** an underground structure for housing a guided missile
¹silt \ˈsilt\ *n* **1 :** fine earth; *esp* **:** particles of such soil floating in rivers, ponds, or lakes **2 :** a deposit (as by a river) of silt — **silty** *adj*
²silt *vb* **:** to obstruct or cover with silt — **silt•ation** \sil-ˈtā-shən\ *n*
Si•lu•ri•an \sī-ˈlu̇r-ē-ən\ *adj* **:** of, relating to, or being the period of the Paleozoic era between the Ordovician and the Devonian marked by the appearance of the first land plants — **Silurian** *n*
¹sil•ver \ˈsil-vər\ *n* **1 :** a white ductile metallic chemical element that takes a high polish and is a better conductor of heat and electricity than any other substance **2 :** coin made of silver **3** ♦ **:** articles (as hollowware or table flatware) made of or plated with silver **:** FLATWARE **4 :** a grayish white color

♦ flatware, tableware

²silver *adj* **1 :** relating to, made of, or coated with silver **2** ♦ **:** resembling silver (as in sheen or color) **:** SILVERY

♦ gray (*or* grey), leaden, pewter, silvery, slate, steely

³silver *vb* **sil•vered; sil•ver•ing :** to coat with or as if with silver — **sil•ver•er** *n*

silver bromide *n* **:** a light-sensitive compound used especially in photography
sil•ver•fish \ˈsil-vər-ˌfish\ *n* **:** any of various small wingless insects found in houses and sometimes injurious especially to sized paper and starched clothes
silver iodide *n* **:** a light-sensitive compound used in photography, rainmaking, and medicine
silver maple *n* **:** a No. American maple with deeply cut leaves that are green above and silvery white below
silver nitrate *n* **:** a soluble compound used in photography and as an antiseptic
sil•ver•ware \ˈsil-vər-ˌwar\ *n* **:** eating and serving utensils (as knives, forks, and spoons) **:** FLATWARE
sil•very *adj* ♦ **:** resembling or having the luster of silver

♦ gray (*or* grey), leaden, pewter, silver, slate, steely

sim•i•an \ˈsi-mē-ən\ *n* **:** MONKEY, APE — **simian** *adj*
sim•i•lar \ˈsi-mə-lər\ *adj* ♦ **:** marked by correspondence or resemblance

♦ akin, alike, analogous, comparable, correspondent, like, parallel, such

sim•i•lar•i•ty \ˌsi-mə-ˈlar-ə-tē\ *n* ♦ **:** the quality or state of being similar; *also* **:** a comparable aspect

♦ community, correspondence, likeness, parallel, parallelism, resemblance, similitude *Ant* dissimilarity, unlikeness

sim•i•lar•ly *adv* ♦ **:** in the same or a comparable manner

♦ alike, also, correspondingly, likewise, so

sim•i•le \ˈsi-mə-(ˌ)lē\ *n* **:** a figure of speech in which two dissimilar things are compared by the use of *like* or *as* (as in "cheeks like roses")
si•mil•i•tude \sə-ˈmi-lə-ˌtüd, -ˌtyüd\ *n* ♦ **:** correspondence in kind or quality **:** RESEMBLANCE; *also* **:** a point of comparison

♦ community, correspondence, likeness, parallelism, resemblance, similarity

sim•mer \ˈsi-mər\ *vb* **sim•mered; sim•mer•ing 1 :** to stew at or just below the boiling point **2 :** to be on the point of bursting out with violence or emotional disturbance — **simmer** *n*
simmer down *vb* **:** to become calm or peaceful
si•mo•nize \ˈsī-mə-ˌnīz\ *vb* **-nized; -niz•ing :** to polish with or as if with wax
si•mo•ny \ˈsī-mə-nē, ˈsi-\ *n* **:** the buying or selling of a church office
sim•pa•ti•co \sim-ˈpä-ti-ˌkō, -ˈpa-\ *adj* **:** CONGENIAL, LIKABLE
sim•per \ˈsim-pər\ *vb* **:** to smile in a silly manner — **simper** *n*
sim•ple \ˈsim-pəl\ *adj* **sim•pler** \-pə-lər\; **sim•plest** \-pə-ləst\ **1** ♦ **:** free from dishonesty or vanity **:** INNOCENT **2** ♦ **:** free from ostentation **3 :** of humble origin or modest position **4 :** slow of mind **:** STUPID **5** ♦ **:** not complex **:** PLAIN ⟨a ~ melody⟩ ⟨~ directions⟩ **6** ♦ **:** lacking education, experience, or intelligence **7 :** developing from a single ovary ⟨a ~ fruit⟩ **8 :** not limited or restricted — **sim•ple•ness** *n*

♦ [1, 2] artless, genuine, honest, ingenuous, innocent, naive, natural, real, sincere, true, unaffected, unpretentious ♦ [5] bald, bare, naked, plain, unadorned, undecorated, unvarnished ♦ [5] easy, effortless, facile, fluent, fluid, light, painless, ready, smooth, snap, soft ♦ [6] green, ignorant, ingenuous, innocent, naive, unknowing, unsophisticated, unwary, unworldly

simple interest *n* **:** interest paid or computed on the original principal only of a loan or on the amount of an account
sim•ple•ton \ˈsim-pəl-tən\ *n* ♦ **:** a person lacking in common sense **:** FOOL

♦ booby, fool, goose, half-wit, jackass, lunatic, nitwit, nut, turkey

sim•plic•i•ty \sim-ˈpli-sə-tē\ *n, pl* **-ties 1 :** lack of complication **:** CLEARNESS **2** ♦ **:** freedom from pretense or guile **3 :** plainness in manners or way of life **4 :** lack of good sense or normal prudence and foresight **:** SILLINESS, FOLLY **5** ♦ **:** directness of expression

♦ [2] artlessness, greenness, ingenuousness, innocence, naïveté, naturalness, unworldliness ♦ [5] clarity, explicitness, lucidity, perspicuity *Ant* obscurity

sim•pli•fy \ˈsim-plə-ˌfī\ *vb* **-fied; -fy•ing :** to make simple or simpler — **sim•pli•fi•ca•tion** \ˌsim-plə-fə-ˈkā-shən\ *n*
sim•plis•tic \sim-ˈplis-tik\ *adj* **:** excessively simple **:** tending to overlook complexities ⟨a ~ solution⟩
sim•ply *adv* **1 :** without ambiguity; *also* **:** without embellishment **2** ♦ **:** to the exclusion of all else; *also* **:** no more than

♦ alone, exclusively, just, only, solely

sim·u·late \ˈsim-yə-ˌlāt\ *vb* **-lat·ed; -lat·ing** ♦ **:** to give or create the effect or appearance of often with the intent to deceive; *also* **:** to make a simulation of — **sim·u·la·tor** \ˈsim-yə-ˌlā-tər\ *n*

♦ affect, assume, counterfeit, fake, feign, pretend, profess, put on, sham

sim·u·la·tion \ˌsim-yə-ˈlā-shən\ *n* **1 :** the act or process of simulating **2 :** an object that is not genuine **3 :** the imitation by one system or process of the way in which another system or process works

si·mul·ta·ne·ous \ˌsī-məl-ˈtā-nē-əs, ˌsi-\ *adj* ♦ **:** occurring or operating at the same time — **si·mul·ta·ne·ous·ly** *adv* — **si·mul·ta·ne·ous·ness** *n*

♦ coeval, concurrent, contemporary, synchronous

[1]**sin** \ˈsin\ *n* **1** ♦ **:** an offense especially against God **2 :** FAULT **3 :** a weakened state of human nature in which the self is estranged from God **4** ♦ **:** an action that is or is felt to be highly reprehensible — **sin·less** *adj*

♦ [1] breach, crime, error, malefaction, misdeed, misdoing, offense, transgression, trespass, violation, wrongdoing ♦ [4] crime, disgrace, pity, shame ♦ [4] evil, ill, immorality, iniquity, villainy, wrong

[2]**sin** *vb* **sinned; sin·ning** ♦ **:** to commit a sin

♦ err, offend, transgress, trespass

[3]**sin** *abbr* sine

[1]**since** \ˈsins\ *adv* **1 :** from a past time until now **2 :** backward in time **:** AGO **3 :** after a time in the past

[2]**since** *conj* **1 :** from the time when **2** ♦ **:** seeing that **:** BECAUSE

♦ because, for, now, whereas

[3]**since** *prep* **1 :** in the period after ⟨changes made ~ the war⟩ **2 :** continuously from ⟨has been here ~ 1980⟩

sin·cere \sin-ˈsir\ *adj* **sin·cer·er; sin·cer·est 1** ♦ **:** free from hypocrisy **:** HONEST **2** ♦ **:** marked by genuineness **:** GENUINE — **sin·cer·i·ty** \-ˈser-ə-tē\ *n*

♦ [1, 2] artless, genuine, honest, ingenuous, innocent, naive, natural, real, simple, true, unaffected, unpretentious

sin·cere·ly *adv* **:** in a sincere manner

sine \ˈsīn\ *n* **:** the trigonometric function that is the ratio between the side opposite an acute angle in a right triangle and the hypotenuse

si·ne·cure \ˈsī-ni-ˌkyu̇r, ˈsi-\ *n* **:** a paying job that requires little or no work

si·ne die \ˌsī-ni-ˈdī-ˌē, ˌsi-nā-ˈdē-ˌā\ *adv* **:** INDEFINITELY

si·ne qua non \ˌsi-ni-ˌkwä-ˈnän, -ˈnōn\ *n, pl* **sine qua nons** *also* **sine qui·bus non** \-ˌkwi-(ˌ)bu̇s-\ **:** something indispensable or essential

sin·ew \ˈsin-yü\ *n* **1 :** TENDON **2** ♦ **:** physical strength

♦ energy, force, main, might, muscle, potency, power, strength, vigor (*or* vigour)

sin·ewy *adj* ♦ **:** having or marked by great physical power

♦ brawny, muscular, rugged, stalwart, stout, strong

sin·ful \ˈsin-fəl\ *adj* ♦ **:** marked by or full of sin **:** WICKED — **sin·ful·ly** *adv*

♦ bad, black, evil, immoral, iniquitous, nefarious, rotten, unethical, unsavory, vicious, vile, villainous, wicked, wrong

sin·ful·ness *n* **:** the quality or state of being sinful

[1]**sing** \ˈsiŋ\ *vb* **sang** \ˈsaŋ\ *or* **sung** \ˈsəŋ\; **sung; sing·ing 1** ♦ **:** to produce musical tones with the voice; *also* **:** to utter with musical tones **2 :** to make a prolonged shrill sound ⟨locusts ~*ing*⟩ **3 :** to produce harmonious sustained sounds ⟨birds ~*ing*⟩ **4 :** CHANT, INTONE **5 :** to write poetry; *also* **:** to celebrate in song or verse **6 :** to give information or evidence

♦ carol, chant, descant, vocalize

[2]**sing** *abbr* singular

Sin·ga·por·ean \ˌsiŋ-ə-ˈpōr-ē-ən\ *n* **:** a native or inhabitant of Singapore — **Singaporean** *adj*

singe \ˈsinj\ *vb* **singed; singe·ing** ♦ **:** to scorch lightly the outside of; *esp* **:** to remove the hair or down from usually by passing over a flame

♦ char, scorch, sear

sing·er \ˈsiŋ-ər\ *n* ♦ **:** one that sings

♦ caroler, songster, vocalist, voice

[1]**sin·gle** \ˈsiŋ-gəl\ *adj* **1** ♦ **:** not married **2** ♦ **:** being alone **:** being the only one **3 :** having only one feature or part **4 :** made for one person — **sin·gle·ness** *n*

♦ [1] unattached, unmarried, unwed *Ant* attached, married, wed ♦ [2] detached, disconnected, discrete, freestanding, separate, unattached, unconnected

[2]**single** *vb* **sin·gled; sin·gling 1** ♦ **:** to select or distinguish (one) from a group — usually used with *out* **2 :** to hit a single

♦ *usu* **single out** choose, cull, elect, handpick, name, opt, pick, prefer, select, take ♦ *usu* **single out** distinguish, identify, pinpoint

[3]**single** *n* **1 :** a separate person or thing; *also* **:** an unmarried person **2 :** a hit in baseball that enables the batter to reach first base **3** *pl* **:** a tennis match with one player on each side

single bond *n* **:** a chemical bond in which one pair of electrons is shared by two atoms in a molecule

single–lens reflex *n* **:** a camera having a single lens that forms an image which is reflected to the viewfinder or recorded on film

sin·gle–mind·ed \ˌsiŋ-gəl-ˈmīn-dəd\ *adj* ♦ **:** having one driving purpose or resolve — **sin·gle–mind·ed·ly** *adv* — **sin·gle–mind·ed·ness** *n*

♦ bound, decisive, determined, firm, intent, purposeful, resolute, set

sin·gly *adv* ♦ **:** without the company of others

♦ alone, independently, solely, unaided, unassisted

sin·gu·lar \ˈsiŋ-gyə-lər\ *adj* **1 :** of, relating to, or constituting a word form denoting one person, thing, or instance **2 :** OUTSTANDING, EXCEPTIONAL **3 :** of unusual quality **4** ♦ **:** departing from general usage or expectation **:** ODD **5** ♦ **:** of or relating to a separate person or thing — **singular** *n* — **sin·gu·lar·ly** *adv*

♦ [4] curious, extraordinary, funny, odd, peculiar, queer, rare, strange, unaccustomed, uncommon, unique, unusual, weird ♦ [5] individual, particular, peculiar, personal, private, separate, unique

sin·gu·lar·i·ty \ˌsiŋ-gyə-ˈlar-ə-tē\ *n* ♦ **:** something that is singular; *esp* **:** unusual or distinctive manner or behavior

♦ crotchet, eccentricity, idiosyncrasy, mannerism, oddity, peculiarity, quirk, trick

sin·is·ter \ˈsi-nəs-tər\ *adj* **1 :** singularly evil or productive of evil **2** ♦ **:** accompanied by or leading to disaster

♦ baleful, dire, foreboding, menacing, ominous, portentous

[1]**sink** \ˈsiŋk\ *vb* **sank** \ˈsaŋk\ *or* **sunk** \ˈsəŋk\; **sunk; sink·ing 1 :** SUBMERGE **2** ♦ **:** to descend lower and lower **3 :** to grow less in volume or height **4 :** to slope downward **5 :** to penetrate downward **6** ♦ **:** to deteriorate in health, strength, or condition **7 :** LAPSE, DEGENERATE **8 :** to cause (a ship) to descend to the bottom **9 :** to make (a hole or shaft) by digging, boring, or cutting **10 :** INVEST — **sink·able** *adj*

♦ [2] decline, descend, dip, drop, fall, lower, plummet, plunge, tumble ♦ [6] decay, decline, degenerate, descend, deteriorate, ebb, rot, worsen

[2]**sink** *n* **1 :** DRAIN, SEWER **2 :** a basin connected with a drain **3 :** an extensive depression in the land surface

sink·er \ˈsiŋ-kər\ *n* **:** a weight for sinking a fishing line or net

sink·hole \ˈsiŋk-ˌhōl\ *n* **:** a hollow place in which drainage collects

sin·ner *n* ♦ **:** one that sins

♦ evildoer, malefactor, wrongdoer

si·nol·o·gy \sī-ˈnä-lə-jē\ *n, often cap* **:** the study of the Chinese and especially their language, history, and culture — **si·no·log·i·cal** \ˌsī-nə-ˈlä-ji-kəl\ *adj, often cap* — **si·nol·o·gist** \sī-ˈnä-lə-jist\ *n, often cap*

sin tax *n* **:** a tax on substances or activities considered sinful or harmful

sin·u·ous \ˈsin-yə-wəs\ *adj* ♦ **:** bending in and out **:** WINDING — **sin·u·os·i·ty** \ˌsin-yə-ˈwä-sə-tē\ *n* — **sin·u·ous·ly** *adv*

♦ crooked, devious, serpentine, tortuous, winding

si·nus \ˈsī-nəs\ *n* **1 :** any of several cavities of the skull usually connecting with the nostrils **2 :** a space forming a channel (as for the passage of blood)

si·nus·itis \ˌsī-nə-ˈsī-təs\ *n* **:** inflammation of a sinus of the skull

Sioux \ˈsü\ *n, pl* **Sioux** *same or* ˈsüz\ **:** DAKOTA

[1]**sip** \ˈsip\ *vb* **sipped; sip·ping :** to drink in small quantities

[2]**sip** *n* **:** a small draft taken with the lips

[1]si·phon *also* **syphon** \ˈsī-fən\ *n* **1 :** a bent tube through which a liquid can be transferred by means of air pressure up and over the edge of one container and into another container placed at a lower level **2** *usu* **sy·phon :** a bottle that ejects soda water through a tube when a valve is opened

[2]siphon *vb* **si·phoned; si·phon·ing ♦ :** to draw off by or as if by means of a siphon

♦ channel, conduct, direct, funnel, pipe

sir \ˈsər\ *n* **1 :** a man of rank or position — used as a title before the given name of a knight or baronet **2** — used as a usually respectful form of address

Si·rach \ˈsī-rak, sə-ˈräk\ *n* **:** a book of the Roman Catholic canon of the Old Testament

[1]sire \ˈsīr\ *n* **1 :** FATHER; *also, archaic* **:** FOREFATHER **2** *archaic* **:** LORD — used as a form of address and a title **3 :** the male parent of an animal (as a horse or dog)

[2]sire *vb* **sired; sir·ing : ♦** to procreate as the father **:** BEGET

♦ beget, father, get, produce

si·ren \ˈsī-rən\ *n* **1 :** a seductive or alluring woman **2 :** an electrically operated device for producing a loud shrill warning signal — **siren** *adj*

sir·loin \ˈsər-ˌlȯin\ *n* **:** a cut of beef taken from the part in front of the round

sirup *var of* SYRUP

si·sal \ˈsī-səl, -zəl\ *n* **:** a strong cordage fiber from an agave; *also* **:** this agave

sis·sy \ˈsi-sē\ *n, pl* **sissies 1 :** an effeminate boy or man **2 ♦ :** a timid or cowardly person

♦ chicken, coward, craven, dastard, poltroon, recreant

sis·ter \ˈsis-tər\ *n* **1 :** a female having one or both parents in common with another individual **2 :** a member of a religious order of women **:** NUN **3** *chiefly Brit* **:** NURSE **4 :** a girl or woman regarded as a comrade — **sis·ter·ly** *adj*

sis·ter·hood \-ˌhu̇d\ *n* **1 :** the state of being a sister **2 :** a community or society of sisters **3 :** the solidarity of women based on shared conditions

sis·ter–in–law \ˈsis-tə-rən-ˌlȯ\ *n, pl* **sisters–in–law :** the sister of one's spouse; *also* **:** the wife of one's brother

sit \ˈsit\ *vb* **sat** \ˈsat\; **sit·ting 1 :** to rest upon the buttocks or haunches **2 :** ROOST, PERCH **3 :** to occupy a seat **4 :** to hold a session **5 ♦ :** to cover eggs for hatching **:** BROOD **6 :** to pose for a portrait **7 :** to remain quiet or inactive **8 :** FIT **9 :** to cause (oneself) to be seated **10 :** to place in position **11 :** to keep one's seat on ⟨∼ a horse⟩ **12 :** BABYSIT **13 ♦ :** to occupy a position ⟨the house ∼*s* on a hill⟩

♦ [5] brood, hatch, incubate, set ♦ [13] be, lie, stand

si·tar \si-ˈtär\ *n* **:** an Indian lute with a long neck and a varying number of strings

sit·com \ˈsit-ˌkäm\ *n* **:** SITUATION COMEDY

site \ˈsīt\ *n* **1 ♦ :** the spatial location of an actual or planned structure (as a building, town, or monuments) **:** LOCATION **2 :** WEB SITE

♦ locale, location, place, point, position, spot

sit–in \ˈsit-ˌin\ *n* **:** an act of sitting in the seats or on the floor of an establishment as a means of organized protest

sit·ter *n* **1 :** one that sits **2 :** a person who babysits

sit·u·at·ed \ˈsi-chə-ˌwā-təd\ *adj* **:** LOCATED, PLACED

sit·u·a·tion \ˌsi-chə-ˈwā-shən\ *n* **1 :** LOCATION, SITE **2 ♦ :** position or place of employment **:** JOB **3 ♦ :** position with respect to conditions and circumstances **4 :** relative position or combination of circumstances at a certain moment

♦ [2] appointment, billet, capacity, function, job, place, position, post ♦ [3] footing, picture, posture, scene, status

situation comedy *n* **:** a radio or television comedy series that involves a continuing cast of characters in a succession of episodes

sit–up \ˈsit-ˌəp\ *n* **:** an exercise performed from a supine position by raising the torso to a sitting position and returning to the original position without lifting the feet

six \ˈsiks\ *n* **1 :** one more than five **2 :** the 6th in a set or series **3 :** something having six units — **six** *adj or pron* — **sixth** \ˈsiksth\ *adj or adv or n*

six–gun \ˈsiks-ˌgən\ *n* **:** a 6-chambered revolver

six–pack \-ˌpak\ *n* **:** six bottles or cans (as of beer) packaged and purchased together; *also* **:** the contents of a six-pack

six·pence \-pəns, *US also* -ˌpens\ *n* **:** the sum of six pence; *also* **:** an English silver coin of this value

six–shoot·er \ˈsiks-ˌshü-tər\ *n* **:** SIX-GUN

six·teen \ˌsiks-ˈtēn\ *n* **:** one more than 15 — **sixteen** *adj or pron* — **six·teenth** \-ˈtēnth\ *adj or n*

six·ty \ˈsiks-tē\ *n, pl* **sixties :** six times 10 — **six·ti·eth** \ˈsiks-tē-əth\ *adj or n* — **sixty** *adj or pron*

siz·able *or* **size·able** \ˈsī-zə-bəl\ *adj* **♦ :** quite large

♦ big, considerable, goodly, grand, great, handsome, large, significant, substantial, tidy

siz·ably \-blē\ *adv* **♦ :** in a sizable manner **:** to a sizable degree

♦ broadly, considerably, greatly, largely, much

[1]size \ˈsīz\ *n* **♦ :** physical extent or bulk **:** DIMENSION; *also* **:** considerable proportions — **sized** \ˈsīzd\ *adj*

♦ dimension, extent, magnitude, measure, measurement, proportion

[2]size *vb* **sized; siz·ing 1 :** to grade or classify according to size **2 :** to form a judgment of ⟨∼ up the situation⟩

[3]size *n* **:** a gluey material used for filling the pores in paper, plaster, or textiles — **siz·ing** *n*

[4]size *vb* **sized; siz·ing :** to cover, stiffen, or glaze with size

[1]siz·zle \ˈsi-zəl\ *vb* **siz·zled; siz·zling 1 :** to fry or shrivel up with a hissing sound **2 ♦ :** to make a hissing sound in or as if in burning or frying

♦ fizz, hiss, swish, whish, whiz

[2]sizzle *n* **:** a hissing sound (as of something frying over a fire)

SJ *abbr* Society of Jesus

SK *abbr* Saskatchewan

ska \ˈskä\ *n* **:** popular music of Jamaican origin combining traditional Caribbean rhythms and jazz

[1]skate \ˈskāt\ *n, pl* **skates** *also* **skate :** any of a family of rays with thick broad winglike fins

[2]skate *n* **1 :** a metal frame and runner attached to a shoe and used for gliding over ice **2 :** ROLLER SKATE; *esp* **:** IN-LINE SKATE — **skate** *vb* — **skat·er** *n*

skate·board \ˈskāt-ˌbōrd\ *n* **:** a short board mounted on small wheels — **skateboard** *vb* — **skate·board·er** *n*

skeet \ˈskēt\ *n* **:** trapshooting in which clay targets are thrown in such a way that their angle of flight simulates that of a flushed game bird

skein \ˈskān\ *n* **:** a loosely twisted quantity of yarn or thread wound on a reel

skel·e·tal \ˈske-lət-ᵊl\ *adj* **1 :** of, relating to, forming, attached to, or resembling a skeleton **2 ♦ :** extremely thin from lack of nourishment or from disease

♦ cadaverous, gaunt, haggard, wasted

skel·e·ton \ˈske-lət-ᵊn\ *n* **1 :** a usually bony supporting framework of an animal body **2 :** a bare minimum **3 ♦ :** something forming a structural framework

♦ configuration, frame, framework, shell, structure

skep·tic \ˈskep-tik\ *n* **1 :** one who believes in skepticism **2 ♦ :** a person disposed to skepticism especially regarding religion

♦ disbeliever, doubter, questioner, unbeliever

skep·ti·cal \-ti-kəl\ *adj* **♦ :** relating to, characteristic of, or marked by skepticism — **skep·ti·cal·ly** \-k(ə-)lē\ *adv*

♦ distrustful, incredulous, leery, mistrustful, suspicious, uncertain, unsure *Ant* credulous, gullible, trustful, trusting, uncritical, unquestioning

skep·ti·cism \ˈskep-tə-ˌsi-zəm\ *n* **1 ♦ :** a doubting state of mind **2 :** a doctrine that certainty of knowledge cannot be attained **3 :** doubt concerning religion

♦ distrust, doubt, incertitude, misgiving, mistrust, suspicion, uncertainty

[1]sketch \ˈskech\ *n* **1 ♦ :** a rough drawing or outline **2 ♦ :** a short or light literary composition (as a story or essay); *also* **:** a short comedy piece — **sketchy** *adj*

♦ [1] cartoon, delineation, drawing ♦ [2] delineation, depiction, description, picture, portrait, portrayal

[2]sketch *vb* **♦ :** to make a sketch, rough draft, or outline of

♦ define, delineate, outline, silhouette, trace ♦ delineate, depict, describe, draw, image, paint, picture, portray

[1]skew \ˈskyü\ *vb* **:** to distort especially from a true value or symmetrical form **:** TWIST, SWERVE

[2]skew *n* **:** SLANT

[1]skew·er \ˈskyü-ər\ *n* **:** a long pin for holding small pieces of meat and vegetables for broiling

[2]skewer *vb* **♦ :** to fasten or pierce with or as if with a skewer

♦ gore, harpoon, impale, lance, pierce, puncture, spear, spike, stab, stick, transfix

¹**ski** \ˈskē\ *n, pl* **skis :** one of a pair of long strips (as of wood, metal or plastic) curving upward in front that are used for gliding over snow or water

²**ski** *vb* **skied** \ˈskēd\; **ski•ing :** to glide on skis — **ski•able** \ˈskē-ə-bəl\ *adj* — **ski•er** *n*

¹**skid** \ˈskid\ *n* **1 :** a plank for supporting something above the ground **2 :** a device placed under a wheel to prevent turning **3 :** a timber or rail over or on which something is slid or rolled **4 :** the act of skidding **5 :** a runner on the landing gear of an aircraft **6 :** ²PALLET

²**skid** *vb* **skid•ded; skid•ding 1 :** to slide without rotating ⟨a *skidding* wheel⟩ **2 :** to slide sideways on the road ⟨the car *skidded* on ice⟩ **3 :** SLIDE, SLIP

skid row *n* **:** a district of cheap saloons frequented by vagrants and alcoholics

skiff \ˈskif\ *n* **:** a small boat

ski jump *n* **:** a jump made by a person wearing skis; *also* **:** a course or track prepared for such jumping — **ski jump** *vb* — **ski jumper** *n*

skil•ful *Can and Brit var of* SKILLFUL

ski lift *n* **:** a mechanical device (as a chairlift) for carrying skiers up a long slope

skill \ˈskil\ *n* **1** ♦ **:** ability to use one's knowledge effectively in doing something **2 :** developed or acquired ability

♦ adeptness, adroitness, art, artfulness, artifice, artistry, cleverness, craft, cunning, deftness, masterfulness *Ant* artlessness, ineptitude, ineptness

skilled \ˈskild\ *adj* **1** ♦ **:** having acquired mastery of or skill in something (as a technique or a trade) **2 :** of, relating to, or requiring workers or labor with skill and training in a particular occupation, craft, or trade

♦ accomplished, adept, consummate, crack, crackerjack, expert, good, great, master, masterful, masterly, proficient, skillful, virtuoso

skil•let \ˈski-lət\ *n* **:** a frying pan

skill•ful *or Can and Brit* **skil•ful** \ˈskil-fəl\ *adj* **1 :** having or displaying skill **:** EXPERT **2** ♦ **:** accomplished with skill

♦ adroit, artful, delicate, dexterous, expert, masterful, masterly, practiced, proficient, virtuoso *Ant* amateur, amateurish, artless, rude, unprofessional, unskillful

skill•ful•ly *or Can and Brit* **skil•ful•ly** *adv* ♦ **:** in a skillful manner

♦ ably, adeptly, capably, expertly, masterfully, proficiently, well

skill•ful•ness *or Can and Brit* **skil•ful•ness** *n* **:** the quality or state of being skillful

¹**skim** \ˈskim\ *vb* **skimmed; skim•ming 1 :** to take off from the top of a liquid; *also* **:** to remove (scum or cream) from ⟨~ milk⟩ **2** ♦ **:** to read rapidly and superficially **3** ♦ **:** to pass swiftly over; *also* **:** to glide or skip along, above, or near a surface **4 :** to throw in a gliding path; *also* **:** to throw so as to ricochet along the surface of water — **skim•mer** *n*

♦ [2] browse, dip, glance, glimpse, peek ♦ [3] bowl, breeze, coast, drift, flow, glide, roll, sail, skip, slide, slip, stream, sweep, whisk

²**skim** *adj* **:** having the cream removed

skimp \ˈskimp\ *vb* ♦ **:** to give insufficient attention, effort, or funds; *also* **:** to save by skimping

♦ economize, save, scrimp ♦ *usu* **skimp on** scant, spare, stint

skimpy \ˈskim-pē\ *adj* **skimp•i•er; -est** ♦ **:** deficient in supply or execution

♦ light, meager (*or* meagre), niggardly, poor, scant, scanty, scarce, slender, slim, spare, sparse, stingy

¹**skin** \ˈskin\ *n* **1** ♦ **:** the outer limiting layer of an animal body; *also* **:** the usually thin tough tissue of which this is made **2** ♦ **:** an outer or surface layer (as a rind or peel) — **skin•less** *adj* — **skinned** *adj*

♦ [1] fur, hide, pelt ♦ [2] exterior, face, outside, surface, veneer

²**skin** *vb* **skinned; skin•ning 1** ♦ **:** to free from skin **:** remove the skin of **2** ♦ **:** to strip of money or property

♦ [1] bark, flay, hull, husk, peel, shell ♦ [2] bleed, cheat, chisel, cozen, defraud, fleece, gyp, hustle, mulct, rook, shortchange, squeeze, stick, sting, swindle, victimize

³**skin** *adj* **:** devoted to showing nudes ⟨~ magazines⟩

skin diving *n* **:** the sport of swimming under water with a face mask and flippers and especially without a portable breathing device — **skin–dive** *vb* — **skin diver** *n*

skin•flint \ˈskin-ˌflint\ *n* ♦ **:** a very stingy person

♦ cheapskate, miser, niggard, tightwad

skin graft *n* **:** a piece of skin surgically removed from one area to replace skin in another area — **skin grafting** *n*

skin•head \ˈskin-ˌhed\ *n* **:** a person whose hair is cut very short

¹**skin•ny** \ˈski-nē\ *adj* **skin•ni•er; -est 1 :** resembling skin **2** ♦ **:** very thin

♦ lean, narrow, slender, slim, spare, thin

²**skinny** *n* **:** inside information

skin•ny–dip \ˈski-nē-ˌdip\ *vb* **:** to swim in the nude — **skin•ny–dip•per** \-ˌdi-pər\ *n*

skin•tight \ˈskin-ˈtīt\ *adj* **:** closely fitted to the figure

¹**skip** \ˈskip\ *vb* **skipped; skip•ping 1** ♦ **:** to move with leaps and bounds; *also* **:** to bound off one point after another **2 :** to leap lightly over **3 :** to pass from point to point (as in reading) disregarding what is in between **4 :** to pass over without notice or mention

♦ bound, hop, spring, trip ♦ bounce, carom, glance, rebound, ricochet, skim

²**skip** *n* **:** a light bouncing step; *also* **:** a gait of alternate hops and steps

skip•jack \ˈskip-ˌjak\ *n* **:** a small sailboat with vertical sides and a bottom similar to a flat V

skip•per \ˈski-pər\ *n* **:** the master of a ship; *also* **:** the manager of a baseball team — **skipper** *vb*

¹**skir•mish** \ˈskər-mish\ *n* ♦ **:** a minor engagement in war; *also* **:** a minor dispute or contest

♦ brush, encounter, hassle, run-in, scrape ♦ battle, clash, combat, conflict, contest, fight, fracas, fray, hassle, scrap, scrimmage, scuffle, struggle, tussle

²**skirmish** *vb* **:** to engage in a skirmish

¹**skirt** \ˈskərt\ *n* **1 :** a free-hanging garment or part of a garment extending from the waist down **2** ♦ **:** the rim, periphery, or environs of an area

♦ border, bound, boundary, circumference, compass, confines, edge, end, fringe, margin, perimeter, periphery, rim, verge

²**skirt** *vb* **1** ♦ **:** to pass around the outer edge of **2** ♦ **:** to form or run along the border or edge of **:** BORDER **3** ♦ **:** to avoid especially because of difficulty or fear of controversy

♦ [1] bypass, circumvent, detour ♦ [2] abut, adjoin, border (on), flank, fringe, join, touch, verge (on) ♦ [3] circumvent, dodge, sidestep

skit \ˈskit\ *n* **:** a brief dramatic sketch

ski tow *n* **:** SKI LIFT

skit•ter \ˈski-tər\ *vb* **:** to glide or skip lightly or quickly **:** skim along a surface

skit•tish \ˈski-tish\ *adj* **1** ♦ **:** lively or frisky in action **2** ♦ **:** easily frightened ⟨a ~ horse⟩; *also* **:** WARY

♦ excitable, flighty, fluttery, high-strung, jittery, jumpy, nervous, spooky, wary

ski•wear \ˈskē-ˌwar\ *n* **:** clothing suitable for wear while skiing

skosh \ˈskōsh\ *n* **:** a small amount **:** BIT

skul•dug•gery *or* **skull•dug•gery** \ˌskəl-ˈdə-gə-rē\ *n, pl* **-ger•ries** ♦ **:** underhanded or unscrupulous behavior

♦ artifice, chicanery, hanky-panky, legerdemain, subterfuge, trickery, wile

skulk \ˈskəlk\ *vb* ♦ **:** to move furtively **:** SNEAK — **skulk•er** *n*

♦ lurk, pussyfoot, slide, slink, slip, snake, sneak, steal

skull \ˈskəl\ *n* **:** the skeleton of the head of a vertebrate that protects the brain and supports the jaws

skull and crossbones *n, pl* **skulls and crossbones :** a depiction of a human skull over crossbones usually indicating a danger

skull•cap \ˈskəl-ˌkap\ *n* **:** a close-fitting brimless cap

¹**skunk** \ˈskəŋk\ *n, pl* **skunks** *also* **skunk 1 :** any of various black-and-white New World mammals related to the weasels that can forcibly eject an ill-smelling fluid when startled **2** ♦ **:** a contemptible person

♦ beast, boor, churl, clown, creep, cretin, cur, heel, jerk, joker, louse, lout, slob, snake

²**skunk** *vb* ♦ **:** to defeat decisively; *esp* **:** to prevent from scoring at all in a game

♦ beat, best, clobber, conquer, crush, defeat, drub, lick, master, overcome, prevail, rout, subdue, surmount, thrash, trim, triumph, trounce, wallop, whip, win

skunk cabbage *n* : either of two No. American perennial herbs related to the arums that occur in shaded wet to swampy areas and have a fetid odor suggestive of a skunk

sky \ˈskī\ *n, pl* **skies** **1** ♦ : the upper air **2** : HEAVEN — **sky•ey** \ˈskī-ē\ *adj*

♦ blue, high

sky•cap \-ˌkap\ *n* : a person employed to carry luggage at an airport

sky•div•ing \-ˌdī-viŋ\ *n* : the sport of jumping from an airplane and executing various body maneuvers before opening a parachute — **sky•div•er** *n*

sky•jack \-ˌjak\ *vb* : to commandeer an airplane in flight by threat of violence — **sky•jack•er** *n* — **sky•jack•ing** *n*

[1]**sky•lark** \-ˌlärk\ *n* : a European lark noted for singing during flight

[2]**skylark** *vb* ♦ : to play and run about happily

♦ act up, clown, cut up, fool, monkey, show off

sky•light \ˈskī-ˌlīt\ *n* : a window in a roof or ceiling — **sky•light•ed** \-ˌlī-təd\ *adj*

sky•line \-ˌlīn\ *n* **1** : HORIZON **2** : an outline (as of buildings) against the sky

[1]**sky•rock•et** \-ˌrä-kət\ *n* : ROCKET 1

[2]**skyrocket** *vb* ♦ : to rise or cause to rise or increase abruptly and rapidly

♦ rocket, shoot, soar, zoom ***Ant*** plummet, plunge, slump, tumble

sky•scrap•er \-ˌskrā-pər\ *n* : a very tall building

sky•surf•ing \-ˌsər-fiŋ\ *n* : skydiving with a short modified surfboard attached to the feet — **sky•surf•er** \-fər\ *n*

sky•walk \-ˌwȯk\ *n* : an aerial walkway connecting two buildings

sky•ward \-wərd\ *adv* ♦ : toward the sky

♦ above, aloft, over, overhead

sky•writ•ing \-ˌrī-tiŋ\ *n* : writing in the sky formed by smoke emitted from an airplane — **sky•writ•er** *n*

slab \ˈslab\ *n* : a thick flat piece or slice

[1]**slack** \ˈslak\ *adj* **1** ♦ : not using due diligence, care, or dispatch : CARELESS **2** : SLUGGISH, LISTLESS **3** ♦ : not taut : LOOSE **4** : not busy or active — **slack•ly** *adv*

♦ [1] careless, derelict, lax, negligent, remiss ♦ [3] insecure, lax, loose, relaxed

[2]**slack** *vb* **1** ♦ : to make or become slack : LOOSEN **2** : SLAKE 2

♦ ease, loosen, relax, slacken

[3]**slack** *n* **1** : cessation of movement or flow : LETUP **2** ♦ : a part that hangs loose without strain ⟨∼ of a rope⟩ **3** ♦ : pants especially for casual wear — usually used in plural

♦ [2] droop, sag, slackness ♦ **slacks** [3] britches, pantaloons, pants, trousers

slack•en \ˈsla-kən\ *vb* ♦ : to make or become slack

♦ ease, loosen, relax, slack ***Ant*** strain, stretch, tense, tighten

slack•er \ˈsla-kər\ *n* **1** : one that shirks work or evades military duty **2** : a young person perceived to be disaffected, apathetic, cynical, or lacking ambition

slack•ness *n* ♦ : the quality or state of being slack or behaving slackly; *also* : something that is slack

♦ carelessness, dereliction, heedlessness, laxness, negligence, remissness

slag \ˈslag\ *n* : the waste left after the melting of ores and the separation of metal from them

slain *past part of* SLAY

slake \ˈslāk, *for 2 also* ˈslak\ *vb* **slaked; slak•ing** **1** : to relieve or satisfy with or as if with refreshing drink ⟨∼ thirst⟩ **2** : to cause (lime) to crumble by mixture with water

sla•lom \ˈslä-ləm\ *n* : skiing in a zigzag course between obstacles

[1]**slam** \ˈslam\ *n* : the winning of every trick or of all tricks but one in bridge

[2]**slam** *n* **1** ♦ : a heavy jarring impact : BANG **2** : harsh criticism **3** : a poetry competition

♦ bang, blast, boom, clap, crack, crash, pop, report, smash, snap, thwack, whack

[3]**slam** *vb* **slammed; slam•ming** **1** : to shut violently and noisily **2** ♦ : to throw or strike with a loud impact **3** : to strike or beat hard **4** ♦ : to criticize harshly

♦ [2] bang, bash, bump, collide, crash, hit, impact, knock, ram, smash, strike, swipe, thud ♦ [4] abuse, assail, attack, belabor, blast, castigate, excoriate, jump, lambaste, vituperate

slam•mer \ˈsla-mər\ *n* : JAIL, PRISON

[1]**slan•der** \ˈslan-dər\ *vb* ♦ : to utter slander against : DEFAME — **slan•der•er** *n*

♦ blacken, defame, libel, malign, smear, traduce, vilify

[2]**slander** *n* ♦ : a false report maliciously uttered and tending to injure the reputation of a person

♦ defamation, libel, vilification

slan•der•ous *adj* ♦ : containing or constituting slander

♦ defamatory, libelous, scandalous

slang \ˈslaŋ\ *n* ♦ : an informal nonstandard vocabulary composed typically of invented words, arbitrarily changed words, and extravagant figures of speech — **slangy** *adj*

♦ argot, cant, jargon, language, lingo, terminology, vocabulary

[1]**slant** \ˈslant\ *n* **1** ♦ : a sloping direction, line, or plane **2** ♦ : a particular or personal viewpoint — **slant** *adj*

♦ [1] cant, diagonal, grade, inclination, incline, lean, pitch, slope, tilt, upgrade ♦ [2] angle, outlook, perspective, point of view, standpoint, viewpoint

[2]**slant** *vb* **1** ♦ : to turn or incline from a right line or a level : SLOPE **2** : to interpret or present in accordance with a special viewpoint or bias — **slant•ing•ly** *adv*

♦ angle, cant, cock, heel, incline, lean, list, slope, tilt, tip

slant•wise \-ˌwīz\ *adj* ♦ : being at a slant : moving or directed in a slanting position or direction — **slant•wise** *adv*

♦ askew, awry, cockeyed, crooked, listing, lopsided, oblique, uneven ♦ canted, diagonal, inclined, leaning

[1]**slap** \ˈslap\ *vb* **slapped; slap•ping** **1** : to strike sharply with the open hand **2** : REBUFF, INSULT

[2]**slap** *n* : a quick sharp blow; *also* : a blow with the open hand

slap•stick \-ˌstik\ *n* ♦ : comedy stressing horseplay

♦ comedy, farce, humor (*or* humour)

[1]**slash** \ˈslash\ *vb* **1** ♦ : to cut with sweeping strokes **2** : to cut slits in (a garment) **3** : to reduce sharply **4** : to hit with a stroke like that used in slashing — **slash•er** \ˈsla-shər\ *n*

♦ cut, gash, rip, slice, slit

[2]**slash** *n* **1** ♦ : a long cut or stroke made by or as if by slashing : GASH **2** : an ornamental slit in a garment **3** : a mark / used to denote "or" (as in *and/or*), "and/or" (as in *straggler/deserter*), or "per" (as in *feet/second*)

♦ gash, laceration, rent, rip, slit, tear

slat \ˈslat\ *n* : a thin narrow flat strip

[1]**slate** \ˈslāt\ *n* **1** : a dense fine-grained rock that splits into thin layers **2** : a roofing tile or a writing tablet made from this rock **3** : a written or unwritten record ⟨start with a clean ∼⟩ **4** : a list of candidates for election

[2]**slate** *vb* **slat•ed; slat•ing** **1** : to cover with slate **2** ♦ : to designate for action or appointment

♦ catalog, enroll, enter, index, inscribe, list, put down, record, register, schedule

[3]**slate** *adj* ♦ : being or having the dark purplish gray color of slate

♦ gray (*or* grey), leaden, pewter, silver, silvery, steely

slath•er \ˈsla-t͟hər\ *vb* : to spread with or on thickly or lavishly

slat•tern \ˈsla-tərn\ *n* : a slovenly woman — **slat•tern•ly** *adj*

[1]**slaugh•ter** \ˈslȯ-tər\ *n* **1** : the butchering of livestock for market **2** ♦ : great destruction of lives especially in battle

♦ butchery, carnage, massacre

[2]**slaughter** *vb* **1** : to kill (animals) for food : BUTCHER **2** : to kill in large numbers or in a bloody way : MASSACRE

slaugh•ter•house \-ˌhau̇s\ *n* : an establishment where animals are butchered

Slav \ˈsläv, ˈslav\ *n* : a person speaking a Slavic language

[1]**slave** \ˈslāv\ *n* **1** ♦ : a person held in servitude as property **2** : a device (as the printer of a computer) that is directly responsive to another **3** ♦ : a toiler at hard monotonous work — **slave** *adj*

♦ [1] bondman, chattel, thrall ***Ant*** freeman ♦ [3] drudge, fag, peon, toiler, worker

²slave *vb* **slaved; slav•ing** ♦ **:** to work like a slave **:** DRUDGE

♦ drudge, labor (*or* labour), plod, plug, slog, strain, strive, struggle, sweat, toil, work

¹sla•ver \ˈsla-vər, ˈslā-\ *n* ♦ **:** to secrete saliva in anticipation of food **:** SLOBBER — **slaver** *vb*

♦ dribble, drivel, drool, salivate, slobber

²slav•er \ˈslā-vər\ *n* **:** a ship or a person engaged in transporting slaves

slav•ery \ˈslāv-rē, ˈslā-və-\ *n* **1** ♦ **:** wearisome drudgery **2** ♦ **:** the condition of being a slave **3 :** the practice of owning slaves

♦ [1] drudgery, grind, labor (*or* labour), sweat, toil, travail ♦ [2] bondage, enslavement, servitude, thrall, yoke *Ant* freedom, liberty

¹Slav•ic \ˈsla-vik, ˈslä-\ *n* **:** a branch of the Indo-European language family including various languages (as Russian or Polish) of eastern Europe

²Slavic *adj* **:** of or relating to the Slavs or their languages

slav•ish \ˈslā-vish\ *adj* **1 :** SERVILE **2** ♦ **:** obeying or imitating with no freedom of judgment or choice

♦ imitative, mimic, unoriginal

slav•ish•ly *adv* ♦ **:** in a slavish manner

♦ determinedly, diligently, hard, hardly, laboriously, mightily, strenuously, tirelessly

slaw \ˈslȯ\ *n* **:** COLESLAW

slay \ˈslā\ *vb* **slew** \ˈslü\; **slain** \ˈslān\; **slay•ing** ♦ **:** to kill violently, wantonly, or in great numbers; *broadly* **:** to strike down **:** KILL — **slay•er** *n*

♦ destroy, dispatch, do in, fell, kill, murder

sleaze \ˈslēz\ *n* **:** a sleazy quality, appearance, or behavior

slea•zy \ˈslē-zē\ *adj* **slea•zi•er; -est** **1 :** FLIMSY, SHODDY **2** ♦ **:** marked by low character or quality

♦ bad, bum, cheap, coarse, common, lousy, mediocre, rotten, second-rate, terrible, trashy

¹sled \ˈsled\ *n* **:** a vehicle usually on runners adapted especially for sliding on snow

²sled *vb* **sled•ded, sled•ding :** to ride or carry on a sled

¹sledge \ˈslej\ *n* **:** SLEDGEHAMMER

²sledge *n* **:** a strong heavy sled

sledge•ham•mer \ˈslej-ˌha-mər\ *n* **:** a large heavy hammer wielded with both hands — **sledgehammer** *adj or vb*

¹sleek \ˈslēk\ *vb* **1 :** to make smooth or glossy **2 :** to gloss over

²sleek *adj* **1** ♦ **:** having a smooth well-groomed look **2 :** trim and graceful in design ⟨a ~ car⟩

♦ glossy, lustrous, polished, satiny

¹sleep \ˈslēp\ *n* **1** ♦ **:** the natural periodic suspension of consciousness during which bodily powers are restored **2 :** a state (as death or coma) suggesting sleep

♦ repose, rest, slumber *Ant* consciousness, wakefulness

²sleep *vb* **slept** \ˈslept\; **sleep•ing** **1** ♦ **:** to rest or be in a state of sleep; *also* **:** to spend in sleep **2 :** to have sexual intercourse — usually used with *with* **3 :** to provide sleeping space for

♦ catnap, doze, nap, rest, slumber, snooze

sleep•er \ˈslē-pər\ *n* **1 :** one that sleeps **2 :** a horizontal beam to support something on or near ground level **3 :** SLEEPING CAR **4 :** someone or something unpromising or unnoticed that suddenly attains prominence or value

sleep•i•ness \-pē-nəs\ *n* **:** the quality or state of being sleepy

sleeping bag *n* **:** a warmly lined bag for sleeping especially outdoors

sleeping car *n* **:** a railroad car with berths for sleeping

sleeping pill *n* **:** a drug in tablet or capsule form taken to induce sleep

sleeping sickness *n* **:** a serious disease of tropical Africa that is marked by fever, lethargy, confusion, and sleep disturbances and is caused by protozoans transmitted by the tsetse fly

sleep•less *adj* ♦ **:** not able to sleep; *also* **:** affording no sleep — **sleep•less•ness** *n*

♦ awake, wakeful, wide-awake

sleep•over \ˈslēp-ˌō-vər\ *n* **:** an overnight stay (as at another's home)

sleep•walk•er \ˈslēp-ˌwȯ-kər\ *n* **:** one that walks while or as if while asleep — **sleep•walk** \-ˌwȯk\ *vb*

sleepy \ˈslē-pē\ *adj* **sleep•i•er; -est** **1** ♦ **:** ready for sleep **2** ♦ **:** quietly inactive — **sleep•i•ly** \ˈslē-pə-lē\ *adv*

♦ [1] drowsy, slumberous *Ant* alert, awake, conscious, wakeful, wide-awake ♦ [2] dull, inactive, inert, lethargic, quiescent, sluggish, torpid

sleet \ˈslēt\ *n* **:** frozen or partly frozen rain — **sleet** *vb* — **sleety** *adj*

sleeve \ˈslēv\ *n* **1 :** a part of a garment covering an arm **2 :** a tubular part designed to fit over another part — **sleeved** *adj* — **sleeve•less** *adj*

¹sleigh \ˈslā\ *n* **:** an open usually horse-drawn vehicle on runners for use on snow or ice

²sleigh *vb* **:** to drive or travel in a sleigh

sleight \ˈslīt\ *n* **1** ♦ **:** deceitful craftiness **:** TRICK **2** ♦ **:** mental or physical skill or quickness **:** DEXTERITY

♦ [1] artifice, device, dodge, gimmick, jig, ploy, scheme, stratagem, trick, wile ♦ [2] adroitness, agility, cleverness, craft, dexterity, finesse

sleight of hand **1 :** a cleverly executed trick or deception especially requiring manual dexterity **2 :** skill in deception

slen•der \ˈslen-dər\ *adj* **1** ♦ **:** spare in frame or flesh **:** THIN; *also* **:** small or narrow in circumference or width in proportion to length or height **2 :** WEAK, SLIGHT **3** ♦ **:** limited or inadequate in amount or scope **:** MEAGER, INADEQUATE

♦ [1] lean, narrow, skinny, slim, spare, thin ♦ [1] narrow, skinny, slim, thin ♦ [3] meager (*or* meagre), poor, scant, scanty, scarce, skimpy, sparse, stingy

slen•der•ize \-də-ˌrīz\ *vb* **-ized; -iz•ing :** to make slender

sleuth \ˈslüth\ *n* ♦ **:** one employed or engaged in detecting lawbreakers or in getting information that is not readily or publicly accessible **:** DETECTIVE

♦ detective, investigator, operative, shadow, tail

¹slew \ˈslü\ *past of* SLAY

²slew *vb* **:** TURN, VEER, SKID

¹slice \ˈslīs\ *vb* **sliced; slic•ing** **1** ♦ **:** to cut a slice from; *also* **:** to cut into slices **2 :** to hit (a ball) so that a slice results

♦ cut, gash, rip, slash, slit

²slice *n* **1 :** a thin flat piece cut from something **2 :** a flight of a ball (as in golf) that curves in the direction of the dominant hand of the player hitting it

¹slick \ˈslik\ *vb* ♦ **:** to make smooth or sleek

♦ grease, lubricate, oil, wax

²slick *adj* **1** ♦ **:** very smooth **:** SLIPPERY **2** ♦ **:** characterized by subtlety or nimble wit

♦ [1] greasy, slippery, slithery ♦ [2] artful, cagey, crafty, cunning, devious, foxy, guileful, sly, subtle, wily

³slick *n* **1 :** a smooth patch of water covered with a film of oil **2 :** a popular magazine printed on coated paper

slick•er \ˈsli-kər\ *n* **1 :** a long loose raincoat **2 :** a sly tricky person **3 :** a city dweller especially of natty appearance or sophisticated mannerisms

¹slide \ˈslīd\ *vb* **slid** \ˈslid\; **slid•ing** \ˈslī-diŋ\ **1** ♦ **:** to move smoothly along a surface **2 :** to fall by a loss of support **3** ♦ **:** to pass unobtrusively **4 :** to move or pass smoothly; *also* **:** to pass unnoticed ⟨let it ~ by⟩ **5 :** to fall or dive toward a base in baseball

♦ [1] bowl, breeze, coast, drift, flow, glide, roll, sail, skim, slip, stream, sweep, whisk ♦ [3] lurk, pussyfoot, skulk, slink, slip, snake, sneak, steal

²slide *n* **1 :** an act or instance of sliding **2 :** something (as a cover or fastener) that operates by sliding **3 :** a fall of a mass of earth or snow down a hillside **4 :** a surface on which something slides **5 :** a glass plate on which a specimen is mounted for examination under a microscope **6 :** a small transparent photograph that can be projected on a screen

slid•er \ˈslī-dər\ *n* **1 :** one that slides **2 :** a baseball pitch that looks like a fastball but curves slightly

slide rule *n* **:** a manual device for calculation consisting of a ruler and a movable middle piece graduated with logarithmic scales

slier *comparative of* SLY

sliest *superlative of* SLY

¹slight \ˈslīt\ *adj* **1 a :** having a slim or delicate build **:** SLENDER **b** ♦ **:** lacking in strength or substance **:** FRAIL **2** ♦ **:** deficient in weight, solidity, or importance **:** **3** ♦ **:** small of its kind; *also* **:** small in amount

♦ [1b] delicate, effete, enervated, faint, feeble, frail, infirm, languid, low, prostrate, soft, tender, torpid, unsubstantial, wasted, weak, wimpy ♦ [2] frivolous, inconsequential, inconsiderable, insignificant, little, minor, minute, negligible, small, trifling, trivial, unimportant ♦ [3] negligible, off, outside, remote, slim, small

[2]**slight** *vb* **1** ♦ **:** to treat as unimportant **2** ♦ **:** to ignore discourteously **3 :** to perform or attend to carelessly

♦ [1] disregard, forget, ignore, neglect, overlook, pass over, slur ♦ [1, 2] disdain, high-hat, scorn, sniff at, snub ♦ [2] affront, insult, offend, outrage, wound

[3]**slight** *n* ♦ **:** a humiliating discourtesy

♦ affront, barb, dart, dig, indignity, insult, name, offense, outrage, put-down, sarcasm, slur, wound

slight•ly *adv* ♦ **:** in a slight manner or degree

♦ barely, hardly, just, marginally, scarcely

[1]**slim** \ˈslim\ *adj* **slim•mer; slim•mest 1 a** ♦ **:** of small diameter or thickness in proportion to the height or length **:** THIN **b** ♦ **:** having a relatively small proportion of flesh **:** SLENDER **2** ♦ **:** limited or less than sufficient in degree, quantity, or extent **:** SCANTY, MEAGER

♦ [1a] fine, narrow, skinny, slender, thin ♦ [1b] lean, skinny, slender, spare, thin ♦ [2] meager (*or* meagre), poor, scant, scanty, scarce, skimpy, sparse, stingy ♦ [2] negligible, off, outside, remote, slight, small

[2]**slim** *vb* **slimmed; slim•ming :** to make or become slender

slime \ˈslīm\ *n* **1** ♦ **:** sticky mud **2 :** a slippery substance (as on the skin of a slug or catfish)

♦ mire, muck, mud, ooze, slop, sludge, slush

slimy *adj* **slim•i•er; -est 1 :** of, relating to, or resembling slime **2** ♦ **:** covered with or yielding slime

♦ miry, mucky, muddy, oozy, slushy

[1]**sling** \ˈsliŋ\ *vb* **slung** \ˈsləŋ\; **sling•ing 1** ♦ **:** to throw forcibly **:** FLING **2 :** to hurl with or as if with a sling

♦ cast, catapult, chuck, dash, fire, fling, heave, hurl, hurtle, launch, peg, pelt, pitch, throw, toss

[2]**sling** *n* **1 :** a short strap with strings attached for hurling stones or shot **2 :** something (as a rope or chain) used to hoist, lower, support, or carry; *esp* **:** a bandage hanging from the neck to support an arm or hand

[3]**sling** *vb* **slung** \ˈsləŋ\; **sling•ing 1 :** place in a sling for hoisting or lowering **2** ♦ **:** to suspend by or as if by a sling

♦ dangle, hang, suspend, swing

sling•shot \ˈsliŋ-ˌshät\ *n* **:** a forked stick with elastic bands for shooting small stones or shot

slink \ˈsliŋk\ *vb* **slunk** \ˈsləŋk\ *also* **slinked** \ˈsliŋkt\; **slink•ing 1** ♦ **:** to move stealthily or furtively **2 :** to move sinuously — **slinky** *adj*

♦ lurk, pussyfoot, skulk, slide, slip, snake, sneak, steal

[1]**slip** \ˈslip\ *vb* **slipped; slip•ping 1 :** to escape quietly or secretly **2** ♦ **:** to slide along or cause to slide along smoothly **3 :** to make a mistake **4 :** to pass unnoticed or undone **5 :** to fall off from a standard or level **6** ♦ **:** to get speedily into or out of clothing **7** ♦ **:** to insert quietly or secretly **8** ♦ **:** to slide out of place or away from a support or one's grasp

♦ [2] bowl, breeze, coast, drift, flow, glide, roll, sail, skim, slide, stream, sweep, whisk ♦ *usu* **slip on** *or* **slip into** [6] don, put on, throw ♦ [7] infiltrate, insinuate, sneak, work, worm ♦ [8] fall, stumble, topple, trip, tumble

[2]**slip** *n* **1 :** a ramp for repairing ships **2 :** a ship's berth between two piers **3** ♦ **:** secret or hurried departure, escape, or evasion **4** ♦ **:** an unintentional and trivial mistake or fault **:** BLUNDER **5** ♦ **:** the act or an instance of slipping down or out of a place; *also* **:** a sudden mishap **6 :** a woman's one-piece garment worn under a dress **7 :** PILLOWCASE

♦ [3] escape, flight, getaway, lam ♦ [4] blunder, error, fault, flub, fumble, goof, lapse, miscue, misstep, mistake, oversight, stumble ♦ [5] fall, spill, stumble, tumble

[3]**slip** *n* **1 :** a shoot or twig from a plant for planting or grafting **2 :** a long narrow strip; *esp* **:** one of paper used for a record ⟨deposit ~⟩

[4]**slip** *vb* **slipped; slip•ping :** to take slips from (a plant)

slip•knot \ˈslip-ˌnät\ *n* **:** a knot that slips along the rope around which it is made

slipped disk *n* **:** a protrusion of one of the disks of cartilage between vertebrae with pressure on spinal nerves resulting especially in low back pain

slip•per \ˈsli-pər\ *n* **:** a light low shoe that may be easily slipped on and off

slip•pery \ˈsli-pə-rē\ *adj* **slip•per•i•er; -est 1** ♦ **:** icy, wet, smooth, or greasy enough to cause one to fall or lose one's hold **2** ♦ **:** not to be trusted **:** TRICKY — **slip•per•i•ness** *n*

♦ [1] greasy, slick, slithery ♦ [2] furtive, shady, shifty, sly, sneaky, stealthy, tricky

slip•shod \ˈslip-ˈshäd\ *adj* **:** SLOVENLY, CARELESS ⟨~ work⟩

slip•stream \ˈslip-ˌstrēm\ *n* **:** a stream (as of air) driven aft by a propeller

slip•up \ˈslip-ˌəp\ *n* **1 :** a wrong action or statement proceeding from faulty judgment, inadequate knowledge, or inattention **:** MISTAKE **2 :** ACCIDENT

[1]**slit** \ˈslit\ *vb* **slit; slit•ting 1** ♦ **:** to make a slit in **:** SLASH **2 :** to cut off or away

♦ cut, gash, rip, slash, slice

[2]**slit** *n* ♦ **:** a long narrow cut or opening

♦ gash, laceration, rent, rip, slash, tear

slith•er \ˈsli-thər\ *vb* ♦ **:** to slip or glide along like a snake

♦ crawl, creep, grovel, snake, worm

slith•ery *adj* ♦ **:** having a slippery surface, texture, or quality

♦ greasy, slick, slippery

sliv•er \ˈsli-vər\ *n* **:** a long slender piece cut or torn off **:** SPLINTER

slob \ˈsläb\ *n* ♦ **:** a slovenly or boorish person

♦ beast, boor, churl, clown, creep, cretin, cur, heel, jerk, joker, louse, lout, skunk, snake

slob•ber \ˈslä-bər\ *vb* **slob•bered; slob•ber•ing 1** ♦ **:** to dribble saliva **2** ♦ **:** to be excessively or unrestrainedly enthusiastic or emotional

♦ [1] dribble, drivel, drool, salivate, slaver ♦ [2] enthuse, fuss, gush, rave, rhapsodize

slobber *n* ♦ **:** saliva drooled from the mouth

♦ saliva, spit

sloe \ˈslō\ *n* **:** the fruit of the blackthorn

slog \ˈsläg\ *vb* **slogged; slog•ging 1 :** to hit hard **:** BEAT **2** ♦ **:** to work hard and steadily

♦ drudge, labor (*or* labour), peg, plod, plug, slave, strain, strive, struggle, sweat, toil, work

slo•gan \ˈslō-gən\ *n* ♦ **:** a word or phrase expressing the spirit or aim of a party, group, or cause

slo–mo \ˈslō-ˌmō\ *n* **:** SLOW MOTION — **slo–mo** *adj*

♦ cry, shibboleth, watchword

sloop \ˈslüp\ *n* **:** a single-masted sailboat with a jib and a fore-and-aft mainsail

[1]**slop** \ˈsläp\ *n* **1 :** thin tasteless drink or liquid food — usually used in plural **2 :** food waste for animal feed **:** SWILL **3** ♦ **:** excreted body waste — usually used in plural **4** ♦ **:** soft mud

♦ **slops** [3] droppings, dung, waste ♦ [4] mire, muck, mud, ooze, slime, sludge, slush

[2]**slop** *vb* **slopped; slop•ping 1 :** SPILL **2 :** to feed with slop ⟨~ hogs⟩

[1]**slope** \ˈslōp\ *vb* **sloped; slop•ing** ♦ **:** to lie or fall in a slant **:** INCLINE; *also* **:** to cause to incline or slant

♦ angle, cant, cock, heel, incline, lean, list, slant, tilt, tip

[2]**slope** *n* **1** ♦ **:** upward or downward slant or degree of slant **2 :** ground that forms an incline **3 :** the part of a landmass draining into a particular ocean

♦ cant, diagonal, grade, inclination, incline, lean, pitch, slant, tilt, upgrade

slop•py \ˈslä-pē\ *adj* **slop•pi•er; -est 1 :** wet so as to spatter easily **:** MUDDY, SLUSHY **2** ♦ **:** untidy especially in personal appearance **:** SLOVENLY, MESSY; *also* **:** lazily slipshod **3 :** excessive in emotional expression

♦ dowdy, frowsy, messy, slovenly, unkempt, untidy ***Ant*** dapper, dashing, dolled up, sharp, smart, spruce

sloppy joe \-ˈjō\ *n* : ground beef cooked in a thick spicy sauce and usually served on a bun
slosh \ˈsläsh\ *vb* **1** : to flounder through or splash about in or with water, mud, or slush **2** ♦ : to move with a splashing motion

♦ lap, plash, splash, swash

slot \ˈslät\ *n* **1** : a long narrow opening or groove **2** : a position in a sequence
slot car *n* : an electric toy racing car that runs on a grooved track
sloth \ˈslȯth\ *n, pl* **sloths** \ˈslȯths, ˈslȯt͟hz\ **1** ♦ : disinclination to action or labor : LAZINESS, INDOLENCE **2** : any of several slow-moving plant-eating arboreal mammals of So. and Central America

♦ idleness, indolence, inertia, laziness

sloth•ful *adj* ♦ : inclined to sloth

♦ idle, indolent, lazy, shiftless

slot machine *n* **1** : a machine whose operation is begun by dropping a coin into a slot **2** : a coin-operated gambling machine that pays off according to the matching of symbols on wheels spun by a handle
¹slouch \ˈslau̇ch\ *n* **1** ♦ : a lazy or incompetent person **2** : a loose or drooping gait or posture

♦ drone, idler, lazybones, loafer, slug, sluggard

²slouch *vb* : to walk, stand, or sit with a slouch : SLUMP
¹slough \ˈslü, *2 usu* ˈslau̇\ *n* **1** ♦ : a wet and marshy or muddy place (as a swamp) **2** : a discouraged state of mind

♦ bog, fen, marsh, mire, morass, swamp

²slough \ˈsləf\ *also* **sluff** *n* : something that has been or may be shed or cast off
³slough \ˈsləf\ *also* **sluff** *vb* ♦ : to cast off

♦ cast, discard, ditch, dump, fling, jettison, junk, lose, reject, scrap, shed, shuck, throw away, throw out, unload

Slo•vak \ˈslō-ˌväk, -ˌvak\ *n* **1** : a member of a Slavic people of Slovakia **2** : the language of the Slovaks — **Slovak** *adj* — **Slo•va•ki•an** \slō-ˈvä-kē-ən, -ˈva-\ *adj or n*
slov•en \ˈslə-vən\ *n* : an untidy person
Slo•vene \ˈslō-ˌvēn\ *n* **1** : a member of a Slavic people living largely in Slovenia **2** : the language of the Slovenes — **Slovene** *adj* — **Slo•ve•nian** \slō-ˈvē-nē-ən\ *adj or n*
slov•en•ly \ˈslə-vən-lē\ *adj* **1** ♦ : untidy in dress or person **2** : lazily or carelessly done : SLIPSHOD

♦ dowdy, frowsy, sloppy, unkempt, untidy

¹slow \ˈslō\ *adj* **1 a** : SLUGGISH **b** : dull in mind : STUPID **2** ♦ : moving, flowing, or proceeding at less than the usual speed **3** : taking more than the usual time **4** : registering behind the correct time **5** : not lively : BORING

♦ creeping, dilatory, laggard, languid, poky, sluggish, tardy *Ant* barreling, bolting, breakneck, breathless, brisk, careering, dizzy, fast, fleet, flying, hasty, hurrying, lightning, quick, racing, rapid, rocketing, running, rushing, scudding, scurrying, snappy, speeding, speedy, swift, whirling, whirlwind, whisking, zipping

²slow *vb* **1** ♦ : to make slow : hold back **2** : to go slower

♦ brake, decelerate, hinder, retard *Ant* accelerate, hasten, hurry, quicken, rush, speed (up), step up

³slow *adv* ♦ : in a slow manner : not quickly, fast, early, rashly, or readily

♦ laggardly, slowly, sluggishly, tardily *Ant* apace, briskly, fast, full tilt, hastily, quick, quickly, rapidly, speedily, swift, swiftly

slow•ly *adv* ♦ : in a slow manner : not quickly, fast, early, rashly, or readily

♦ laggardly, slow, sluggishly, tardily

slow motion *n* : motion-picture action photographed so as to appear much slower than normal — **slow–motion** *adj*
slow•ness *n* : the quality or state of being slow
SLR *abbr* single-lens reflex
sludge \ˈsləj\ *n* ♦ : a slushy mass : OOZE; *esp* : solid matter produced by sewage treatment processes

♦ mire, muck, mud, ooze, slime, slop, slush

¹slug \ˈsləg\ *n* **1** : a small mass of metal; *esp* : BULLET **2** : a metal disk for use (as in a slot machine) in place of a coin **3** : any of numerous wormlike mollusks related to the snails **4** ♦ : a quantity of liquor drunk **5** : an habitually lazy person : SLUGGARD

♦ draft, drag, drink, nip, quaff, shot, snort, swallow, swig

²slug *vb* **slugged; slug•ging** ♦ : to strike forcibly and heavily — **slug•ger** *n*

♦ belt, clout, hit, punch, strike, wallop

³slug *n* : a heavy blow especially with the fist
slug•gard \ˈslə-gərd\ *n* ♦ : an habitually lazy person

♦ drone, idler, lazybones, loafer, slouch, slug

slug•gish \ˈslə-gish\ *adj* **1** : SLOTHFUL, LAZY **2** ♦ : slow in movement or flow **3** : STAGNANT, DULL — **slug•gish•ness** *n*

♦ creeping, dilatory, laggard, languid, poky, slow, tardy

slug•gish•ly *adv* ♦ : in a sluggish manner

♦ laggardly, slow, slowly, tardily

¹sluice \ˈslüs\ *n* **1** : an artificial passage for water with a gate for controlling the flow; *also* : the gate so used **2** : a channel that carries off surplus water **3** : an inclined trough or flume for washing ore or floating logs
²sluice *vb* **sluiced; sluic•ing** **1** : to draw off through a sluice **2** ♦ : to wash with running water : FLUSH

♦ flush, irrigate, rinse, wash

¹slum \ˈsləm\ *n* : a thickly populated area marked by poverty and dirty or deteriorated houses — **slum•my** \ˈslə-mē\ *adj*
²slum *vb* **slummed; slum•ming** : to visit slums especially out of curiosity; *also* : to go somewhere or do something that might be considered beneath one's station
¹slum•ber \ˈsləm-bər\ *vb* **slum•bered; slum•ber•ing** **1 a** ♦ : to sleep lightly : DOZE **b** ♦ : to rest in a state of sleep **2** : to be in a sluggish or torpid state

♦ catnap, doze, drowse, nap, sleep, snooze

²slumber *n* ♦ : the natural periodic suspension of consciousness during which bodily powers are restored : SLEEP; *also* : a light sleep

♦ repose, rest, sleep

slum•ber•ous \ˈsləm-bə-rəs\ *or* **slum•brous** \-brəs\ *adj* **1** ♦ : feeling a strong inclination toward sleep : SLEEPY **2** : PEACEFUL, INACTIVE **3** ♦ : inducing slumber

♦ [1] drowsy, sleepy ♦ [3] hypnotic, narcotic, opiate

slum•lord \ˈsləm-ˌlȯrd\ *n* : a landlord who receives unusually large profits from substandard properties
slump \ˈsləmp\ *vb* **1** : to sink down suddenly : COLLAPSE **2** : SLOUCH **3** : to decline sharply — **slump** *n*
slung *past and past part of* SLING
slunk *past and past part of* SLINK
¹slur \ˈslər\ *vb* **slurred; slur•ring** **1** ♦ : to slide or slip over without due mention or emphasis ⟨*slurred* over certain facts⟩ **2** : to perform two or more successive notes of different pitch in a smooth or connected way

♦ *usu* **slur over** disregard, forget, ignore, neglect, overlook, pass over, slight

²slur *n* : a curved line connecting notes to be slurred; *also* : a group of slurred notes
³slur *n* ♦ : a slighting remark

♦ affront, barb, dart, dig, indignity, insult, name, offense, outrage, put-down, sarcasm, slight, wound

slurp \ˈslərp\ *vb* : to eat or drink noisily — **slurp** *n*
slur•ry \ˈslər-ē\ *n, pl* **slur•ries** : a watery mixture of insoluble matter
slush \ˈsləsh\ *n* **1** : partly melted or watery snow **2** ♦ : soft mud **3** : silly, worthless, or cheaply sentimental material

♦ mire, muck, mud, ooze, slime, slop, sludge

slush fund *n* : an unregulated fund often for illicit purposes
slushy *adj* **slush•i•er; -est** ♦ : full of or covered with slush

♦ miry, mucky, muddy, oozy, slimy

slut \ˈslət\ *n* **1** : a slovenly woman **2** : a promiscuous woman — **slut•tish** *adj*
sly \ˈslī\ *adj* **sli•er** *or* **sly•er** \ˈslī-ər\; **sli•est** *or* **sly•est** \ˈslī-əst\ **1** ♦ : displaying cleverness : CRAFTY **2** ♦ : clever in concealing one's aims or ends **3** ♦ : lightly mischievous : ROGUISH — **sly•ly** *adv*

♦ [1] artful, cagey, crafty, cunning, devious, foxy, guileful, slick, subtle, wily ♦ [2] furtive, shady, shifty, slippery, sneaky, stealthy ♦ [3] devilish, impish, knavish, mischievous, rascally, roguish, waggish, wicked

sly•ness *n* ♦ : the quality or state of being sly

♦ artfulness, artifice, caginess, canniness, craft, craftiness, cunning, guile, wiliness

sm *abbr* small
Sm *symbol* samarium
SM *abbr* **1** master of science **2** sergeant major **3** service mark **4** stage manager
¹smack \ˈsmak\ *n* **:** characteristic flavor; *also* **:** a slight trace
²smack *vb* **1 :** to have a taste **2 :** to have a trace or suggestion
³smack *vb* **1 :** to move (the lips) so as to make a sharp noise **2 :** to kiss or slap with a loud noise
⁴smack *n* **1 :** a sharp noise made by the lips **2 :** a noisy slap
⁵smack *adv* **:** squarely and sharply
⁶smack *n* **:** a sailing ship used in fishing
⁷smack *n, slang* **:** HEROIN
SMaj *abbr* sergeant major
¹small \ˈsmȯl\ *adj* **1** ♦ **:** little in size or amount **2 :** operating on a limited scale **3 :** little or close to zero (as in number or value) **4 :** made up of little things **5** ♦ **:** of little consequence **:** UNIMPORTANT **6 :** lacking in mental discrimination **:** PETTY

♦ [1] dwarf, dwarfish, fine, little, pocket, pygmy, slight, undersized ***Ant*** big, bumper, considerable, goodly, grand, great, handsome, king-size, large, outsize, oversize, sizable, substantial, super, whacking, whopping ♦ [5] frivolous, inconsequential, inconsiderable, insignificant, little, minor, minute, negligible, slight, trifling, trivial, unimportant

²small *n* **:** a small part or product ⟨the ~ of the back⟩
small•ish *adj* **:** somewhat small **:** slightly below normal size
small•ness *n* **1 :** the quality or state of being small **2 :** something that is small
small•pox \ˈsmȯl-ˌpäks\ *n* **:** a contagious virus disease of humans formerly common but now eradicated
small talk *n* **:** light or casual conversation
small–time \ˈsmȯl-ˈtīm\ *adj* **:** insignificant in performance and standing **:** MINOR — **small–tim•er** *n*
smarmy \ˈsmär-mē\ *adj* **smarm•i•er; -est :** marked by a smug ingratiating, or false earnestness
¹smart \ˈsmärt\ *vb* **1** ♦ **:** to cause or feel a stinging pain **2 :** to feel or endure distress

♦ ache, hurt, pain

²smart *adj* **1** ♦ **:** making one smart ⟨a ~ blow⟩ **2** ♦ **:** mentally quick, perceptive, or clever **3 :** marked by or full of wit **:** WITTY **4 :** appealing to sophisticated tastes **:** STYLISH **5 :** being a guided missile **6 :** containing a microprocessor for limited computing capability ⟨~ terminal⟩ **7** ♦ **:** exhibiting neatness, good order, or compactness of line or structure ⟨soldiers in ~ uniforms⟩ **8** ♦ **:** impertinently bold, impudent, or facetious — **smart•ness** *n*

♦ [1] acute, agonizing, biting, excruciating, sharp ♦ [2] alert, brainy, bright, brilliant, clever, intelligent, keen, nimble, quick, quick-witted, sharp, shrewd ♦ [7] dapper, natty, neat, spruce ***Ant*** sloppy, slovenly ♦ [8] facetious, flip, flippant, pert

³smart *n* ♦ **:** a smarting pain; *esp* **:** a stinging local pain

♦ ache, pain, pang, prick, sting, stitch, tingle, twinge

smart al•eck \ˈsmärt-ˌa-lik\ *n* **:** a person given to obnoxious cleverness
smart card *n* **:** a small plastic card that has a built-in microprocessor to store and handle data
smart•en \ˈsmär-tᵊn\ *vb* **:** to make smart or smarter — usually used with *up*
smart•ly *adv* **:** in a smart manner **:** so as to be or seem smart
¹smash \ˈsmash\ *n* **1 :** a smashing blow **2 :** a hard, overhand stroke in tennis **3** ♦ **:** the act or sound of smashing **4** ♦ **:** collision of vehicles **:** CRASH **5 :** COLLAPSE, RUIN; *esp* **:** BANKRUPTCY **6** ♦ **:** a striking success **:** HIT — **smash** *adj*

♦ [3] bang, blast, boom, clap, crack, crash, pop, report, slam, snap, thwack, whack ♦ [4] collision, crack-up, crash, wreck ♦ [6] blockbuster, hit, success, winner

²smash *vb* **1** ♦ **:** to break or be broken into pieces **2** ♦ **:** to move forward with force and shattering effect **3 :** to destroy utterly **:** WRECK

♦ [1] blast, blow up, burst, demolish, explode, pop, shatter ♦ [2] bang, bash, bump, collide, crash, hit, impact, knock, ram, slam, strike, swipe, thud

smat•ter•ing \ˈsma-tə-riŋ\ *n* **1 :** superficial knowledge **2** ♦ **:** a small scattered number or amount

♦ few, handful, sprinkle, sprinkling

¹smear \ˈsmir\ *n* **1 :** a spot left by an oily or sticky substance **2 :** material smeared on a surface (as of a microscope slide)
²smear *vb* **1** ♦ **:** to overspread especially with something oily or sticky **2 :** SMUDGE, SOIL **3** ♦ **:** to injure by slander or insults

♦ [1] daub ♦ [3] blacken, defame, libel, malign, slander, traduce, vilify

¹smell \ˈsmel\ *vb* **smelled** \ˈsmeld\ *or* **smelt** \ˈsmelt\; **smell•ing** **1 a** ♦ **:** to perceive the odor of by sense organs of the nose **b** ♦ **:** to detect as if with the nose ⟨I ~ trouble⟩ **2 :** to have or give off an odor

♦ [1a] nose, scent, sniff, whiff ♦ [1b] feel, perceive, scent, see, sense, taste

²smell *n* **1** ♦ **:** the property of a thing that affects the olfactory organs **:** ODOR, SCENT **2 :** the process or power of perceiving odor; *also* **:** the special sense by which one perceives odor **3 :** an act of smelling

♦ odor (*or* odour), redolence, scent, sniff

smelling salts *n pl* **:** an aromatic preparation used as a stimulant and restorative (as to relieve faintness)
smelly *adj* ♦ **:** having a usually bad smell

♦ fetid, foul, fusty, malodorous, musty, noisome, rank, reeky, strong

¹smelt \ˈsmelt\ *n, pl* **smelts** *or* **smelt :** any of a family of small food fishes of coastal or fresh waters that are related to the trouts and salmons
²smelt *vb* **:** to melt or fuse (ore) in order to separate the metal; *also* **:** REFINE
smelt•er \ˈsmel-tər\ *n* **1 :** one that smelts **2 :** an establishment for smelting
smid•gen *also* **smid•geon** *or* **smid•gin** \ˈsmi-jən\ *n* **:** a small amount **:** BIT
smi•lax \ˈsmī-ˌlaks\ *n* **1 :** any of various mostly climbing and prickly plants related to the lilies **2 :** an ornamental plant related to the asparagus
¹smile \ˈsmīl\ *vb* **smiled; smil•ing** **1 :** to look with a smile **2 :** to be favorable **3 :** to express by a smile
²smile *n* **:** a change of facial expression to express amusement, pleasure, or affection
smil•ey \ˈsmī-lē\ *adj* **:** exhibiting a smile **:** frequently smiling
¹smirch \ˈsmərch\ *vb* **1** ♦ **:** to make dirty or stained **2** ♦ **:** to bring disgrace on

♦ [1] befoul, begrime, besmirch, blacken, dirty, foul, grime, mire, muddy, soil, stain ♦ [2] abase, debase, degrade, demean, discredit, disgrace, dishonor (*or* dishonour), humble, humiliate, lower, shame, take down

²smirch *n* **1 :** a dirty blurred mark or blot **2** ♦ **:** something that tarnishes a reputation

♦ blot, brand, spot, stain, stigma, taint

smirk \ˈsmərk\ *vb* **:** to wear a self-conscious or conceited smile **:** SIMPER — **smirk** *n*
smite \ˈsmīt\ *vb* **smote** \ˈsmōt\; **smit•ten** \ˈsmit-ᵊn\ *or* **smote; smit•ing** \ˈsmī-tiŋ\ **1 :** to strike heavily; *also* **:** to kill by striking **2 :** to affect as if by a heavy blow
smith \ˈsmith\ *n* **:** a worker in metals; *esp* **:** BLACKSMITH
smith•er•eens \ˌsmi-t͟hə-ˈrēnz\ *n pl* **:** FRAGMENTS, BITS
smithy \ˈsmi-thē\ *n, pl* **smith•ies** **1 :** a smith's workshop **2 :** BLACKSMITH
¹smock \ˈsmäk\ *n* **:** a loose garment worn over other clothes as a protection
²smock *vb* **:** to gather (cloth) in regularly spaced tucks — **smock•ing** *n*
smog \ˈsmäg, ˈsmȯg\ *n* ♦ **:** a thick haze caused by the action of sunlight on air polluted by smoke and automobile exhaust fumes

♦ fog, haze, mist, murk, soup

smog•gy *adj* **smog•gi•er; -est** ♦ **:** characterized by or abounding in smog

♦ cloudy, foggy, hazy, misty, murky, soupy

¹smoke \ˈsmōk\ *n* **1 :** the gas from burning material (as coal, wood, or tobacco) in which are suspended particles of soot **2 :** a mass or column of smoke **3 :** something (as a cigarette) to smoke; *also* **:** the act of smoking — **smoke•less** *adj* — **smoky** *adj*
²smoke *vb* **smoked; smok•ing** **1 :** to emit smoke **2 :** to inhale and exhale the fumes of burning tobacco; *also* **:** to use in smoking ⟨~ a pipe⟩ **3 :** to stupefy or drive away by smoke **4 :** to discolor with smoke **5 :** to cure (as meat) with smoke — **smok•er** *n*

smoke detector *n* **:** an alarm that sounds automatically when it detects smoke
smoke jumper *n* **:** a forest firefighter who parachutes to locations otherwise difficult to reach
smoke screen *n* **1 :** a screen of smoke to hinder enemy observation **2 :** something designed to obscure, confuse, or mislead
smoke•stack \ˈsmōk-ˌstak\ *n* **:** a pipe or funnel through which smoke and gases are discharged
smol•der *or* **smoul•der** \ˈsmōl-dər\ *vb* **smol•dered** *or* **smoul•dered, smol•der•ing** *or* **smoul•der•ing 1 :** to burn and smoke without flame **2 :** to burn inwardly — **smolder** *n*
smooch \ˈsmüch\ *vb* **:** to touch or caress with the lips as a mark of affection **:** KISS — **smooch** *n*
¹smooth \ˈsmüth\ *adj* **1** ♦ **:** not rough or uneven **2 :** not jarring or jolting **3 :** BLAND, MILD **4** ♦ **:** fluent in speech and agreeable in manner **5** ♦ **:** free from difficulties or impediments — **smooth•ness** *n*

♦ [1] even, flat, flush, level, plane ♦ [4] debonair, sophisticated, suave, urbane ♦ [5] easy, effortless, facile, fluent, fluid, light, painless, ready, simple, snap, soft

²smooth *vb* **1** ♦ **:** to make smooth **2** ♦ **:** to free from trouble or difficulty

♦ [1] even, level, plane ♦ [1] buff, burnish, dress, gloss, grind, polish, rub, shine ♦ [2] ease, facilitate, loosen, unclog

smooth•ly *adv* ♦ **:** in a smooth manner **:** without difficulties

♦ easily, effortlessly, fluently, freely, handily, lightly, painlessly, readily

smooth muscle *n* **:** muscle with no cross striations that is typical of visceral organs (as the stomach and bladder) and is not under voluntary control
smoothy *or* **smooth•ie** \ˈsmü-thē\ *n, pl* **smooth•ies 1 :** an artfully suave person **2** *smoothie* **:** a creamy beverage of fruit blended with juice, milk, or yogurt
s'more \ˈsmȯr\ *n* **:** a dessert of marshmallow and pieces of chocolate sandwiched between graham crackers
smor•gas•bord \ˈsmȯr-gəs-ˌbōrd\ *n* **:** a luncheon or supper buffet consisting of many foods
smote *past and past part of* SMITE
¹smoth•er \ˈsmə-thər\ *n* **1 :** thick stifling smoke **2 :** a dense cloud (as of fog or dust) **3 :** a confused multitude of things
²smother *vb* **smoth•ered; smoth•er•ing 1** ♦ **:** to be overcome by or die from lack of air **2** ♦ **:** to kill by depriving of air **3** ♦ **:** to suppress expression or knowledge of **4 :** to cover thickly

♦ [1, 2] choke, stifle, strangle, suffocate ♦ [3] choke, pocket, repress, stifle, strangle, suppress, swallow

SMSgt *abbr* senior master sergeant
¹smudge \ˈsməj\ *vb* **smudged; smudg•ing :** to soil or blur by rubbing or smearing
²smudge *n* **:** a dirty or blurred spot — **smudgy** *adj*
smug \ˈsməg\ *adj* **smug•ger; smug•gest** ♦ **:** conscious of one's virtue and importance **:** SELF-SATISFIED — **smug•ly** *adv*

♦ complacent, conceited, egotistic, important, overweening, pompous, prideful, proud, self-important, self-satisfied, stuck-up, vain

smug•gle \ˈsmə gəl\ *vb* **smug•gled; smug•gling 1 :** to import or export secretly, illegally, or without paying the duties required by law **2 :** to convey secretly — **smug•gler** \ˈsmə-glər\ *n*
smug•ness *n* ♦ **:** the quality or state of being smug

♦ complacence, conceit, ego, egotism, pride, self-conceit, self-esteem, self-importance, self-satisfaction, vainglory, vanity

smut \ˈsmət\ *n* **1 :** something (as soot) that smudges; *also* **:** SMUDGE, SPOT **2 :** any of various destructive diseases of plants caused by fungi; *also* **:** a fungus causing smut **3** ♦ **:** indecent language or matter

♦ bawdiness, coarseness, dirt, dirtiness, filth, filthiness, foulness, grossness, indecency, lewdness, nastiness, obscenity, ribaldry, vulgarity

smutch \ˈsməch\ *n* **:** SMUDGE
smut•ty *adj* **smut•ti•er; -est** ♦ **:** soiled or tainted with smut **:** not decent

♦ bawdy, coarse, crude, dirty, filthy, foul, gross, indecent, lascivious, lewd, nasty, obscene, pornographic, ribald, unprintable, vulgar, wanton

Sn *symbol* tin
SN *abbr* seaman
snack \ˈsnak\ *n* **:** a light meal **:** BITE
snaf•fle \ˈsna-fəl\ *n* **:** a simple jointed bit for a horse's bridle
¹snag \ˈsnag\ *n* **1 :** a stump or piece of a tree especially when under water **2** ♦ **:** an unexpected difficulty

♦ booby trap, catch, pitfall

²snag *vb* **snagged; snag•ging 1 :** to become caught on or as if on a snag **2 :** to seize quickly **:** SNATCH
snail \ˈsnāl\ *n* **:** any of numerous small gastropod mollusks with a spiral shell into which they can withdraw
snail mail *n* ♦ **:** mail delivered by a postal system

♦ mail, matter, parcel post, post

snake \ˈsnāk\ *n* **1 :** any of numerous long-bodied limbless reptiles **2** ♦ **:** a treacherous person **3 :** something that resembles a snake — **snaky** *adj*

♦ beast, boor, churl, clown, creep, cretin, cur, heel, jerk, joker, louse, lout, skunk, slob

snake•bite \-ˌbīt\ *n* **:** the bite of a snake and especially a venomous snake
¹snap \ˈsnap\ *vb* **snapped; snap•ping 1 :** to grasp or slash at something with the teeth **2** ♦ **:** to get or buy quickly — usually used with *up* **3 :** to utter sharp or angry words **4 :** to break suddenly with a sharp sound **5 :** to give a sharp cracking noise **6 :** to throw with a quick motion **7 :** FLASH ⟨her eyes *snapped*⟩ **8 :** to put a football into play **9** ♦ **:** to take photographically — **snap•per** *n* — **snap•py** *adj*

♦ *usu* **snap up** [2] catch, collar, grab, nab, seize ♦ [9] mug, photograph, shoot

²snap *n* **1** ♦ **:** the act or sound of snapping **2** ♦ **:** something very easy to do **:** CINCH **3 a :** a short period of cold weather **b :** a small amount **4 :** a catch or fastening that closes with a click **5 :** a thin brittle cookie **6** ♦ **:** a pleasing vigorous quality **:** ENERGY; *also* **:** smartness of movement **7 :** the putting of the ball into play in football **8 :** a casual photograph **:** SNAPSHOT

♦ [1] bang, blast, boom, clap, crack, crash, pop, report, slam, smash, thwack, whack ♦ [2] breeze, child's play, cinch, picnic, pushover ♦ [6] dash, energy, life, pep, vigor (*or* vigour), vim, vitality

³snap *adj* **1** ♦ **:** done, made, or carried through suddenly or without deliberation **2** ♦ **:** unusually easy or simple

♦ [1] ad-lib, extemporaneous, impromptu, offhand, unplanned, unpremeditated, unprepared, unrehearsed ♦ [2] easy, effortless, facile, fluent, fluid, light, painless, ready, simple, smooth, soft

snap back *vb* ♦ **:** to make a quick or vigorous recovery

♦ convalesce, gain, heal, mend, rally, recover, recuperate

snap bean *n* **:** a bean grown primarily for its long pods that are cooked as a vegetable when young and tender
snap•drag•on \ˈsnap-ˌdra-gən\ *n* **:** any of a genus of herbs with long spikes of showy flowers
snapping turtle *n* **:** either of two large American turtles with powerful jaws and a strong musky odor
snap•pish *adj* ♦ **:** given to curt irritable speech

♦ choleric, crabby, cranky, cross, crotchety, grouchy, grumpy, irascible, irritable, peevish, perverse, petulant, short-tempered, snappy, snippy, testy, waspish

snap•py *adj* **snap•pi•er; -est 1 :** given to curt irritable speech **2** ♦ **:** quickly made or done; *also* **:** marked by vigor or liveliness **3 :** briskly cold **4** ♦ **:** having style

♦ [2] fast, hasty, quick, rapid, speedy, swift ♦ [2] active, brisk, energetic, lively, peppy, spirited, sprightly, springy, vital, vivacious ♦ [4] à la mode, chic, fashionable, in, modish, sharp, smart, stylish

snap•shot \ˈsnap-ˌshät\ *n* ♦ **:** a photograph taken usually with an inexpensive hand-held camera

♦ photograph, print, shot, snap

¹snare \ˈsnar\ *n* ♦ **:** a trap often consisting of a noose for catching birds or mammals; *also* **:** something by which one is entangled, involved in difficulties, or impeded

♦ ambush, entanglement, net, trap, web

²snare *vb* ♦ **:** to capture by or as if by use of a snare

♦ enmesh, ensnare, entangle, entrap, mesh, tangle, trap ♦ bag, capture, catch, collar, corral, get, grab, grapple, hook, land, nab, seize, trap

¹snarl \ˈsnärl\ *vb* ♦ **:** to cause to become knotted and intertwined

♦ entangle, interlace, intertwine, interweave, knot, tangle

²snarl *n* **1 :** a tangled, twisted mass **:** TANGLE **2** ♦ **:** a tangled situation

♦ backup, bottleneck, jam

³snarl *vb* **:** to growl angrily or threateningly
⁴snarl *n* **:** an angry ill-tempered growl
¹snatch \ˈsnach\ *vb* **1 :** to try to grasp something suddenly **2 :** to seize or take away suddenly
²snatch *n* **1 :** a short period **2 :** an act of snatching **3 :** something brief or fragmentary ⟨∼*es* of song⟩
¹sneak \ˈsnēk\ *vb* **sneaked** \ˈsnēkt\ *or* **snuck** \ˈsnək\; **sneak•ing** ♦ **:** to go or act in a furtive manner; *also* **:** to put, bring, or take in a furtive or artful manner — **sneak•ing•ly** *adv*

♦ lurk, pussyfoot, skulk, slide, slink, slip, snake, steal

²sneak *n* **1 :** one who acts in a furtive or shifty manner **2 :** a stealthy or furtive move or escape — **sneak** *adj*
sneak•er \ˈsnē-kər\ *n* **:** a sports shoe with a pliable rubber sole
sneaky *adj* **sneak•i•er; -est** ♦ **:** marked by stealth, furtiveness, or shiftiness — **sneak•i•ly** \ˈsnē-kə-lē\ *adv*

♦ furtive, shady, shifty, slippery, sly, stealthy ♦ clandestine, covert, furtive, hugger-mugger, private, secret, sneak, stealthy, surreptitious, undercover, underground, underhanded

sneer \ˈsnir\ *vb* ♦ **:** to show scorn or contempt by curling the lip or by a jeering tone — **sneer** *n*

♦ jeer, laugh, snicker, sniff, snort

sneeze \ˈsnēz\ *vb* **sneezed; sneez•ing :** to force the breath out suddenly and violently as a reflex act — **sneeze** *n*
SNF *abbr* skilled nursing facility
snick•er \ˈsni-kər\ *n* ♦ **:** a partly suppressed laugh — **snicker** *vb*

♦ cackle, chortle, laugh, laughter, titter

snide \ˈsnīd\ *adj* **1** ♦ **:** unworthy of esteem **:** LOW ⟨a ∼ trick⟩ **2 :** slyly disparaging ⟨a ∼ remark⟩ — **snide•ly** *adv*

♦ base, contemptible, despicable, detestable, dirty, dishonorable (*or* dishonourable), ignoble, low, mean, sordid, vile, wretched

sniff \ˈsnif\ *vb* **1 :** to draw air audibly up the nose especially for smelling **2** ♦ **:** to show disdain or scorn — usually used with *at* **3** ♦ **:** to detect by or as if by smelling — **sniff** *n*

♦ *usu* **sniff at** [2] disdain, high-hat, scorn, slight, snub ♦ [3] nose, scent, smell, whiff

snif•fle \ˈsni-fəl\ *n* **1** *pl* **:** a head cold marked by nasal discharge **2 :** SNUFFLE — **sniffle** *vb*
¹snip \ˈsnip\ *n* **1 :** a fragment snipped off **2 :** a simple stroke of the scissors or shears
²snip *vb* **snipped; snip•ping :** to cut off by bits **:** CLIP; *also* **:** to remove by cutting off
¹snipe \ˈsnīp\ *n, pl* **snipes** *or* **snipe :** any of several long-billed game birds especially of marshy areas that belong to the same family as the sandpipers
²snipe *vb* **sniped; snip•ing :** to shoot at an exposed enemy from a concealed position — **snip•er** *n*
snip•py \ˈsni-pē\ *adj* **snip•pi•er; -est 1 :** having a quick temper **:** SNAPPISH **2** ♦ **:** unduly brief or curt

♦ abrupt, bluff, blunt, brusque, curt

snips \ˈsnips\ *n pl* **:** hand shears used especially for cutting sheet metal ⟨tin ∼⟩
¹snitch \ˈsnich\ *vb* **1** ♦ **:** to give information (as of another's wrongdoing) to an authority **:** INFORM **2** ♦ **:** to take by stealth **:** PILFER — **snitch** *n*

♦ [1] inform, squeal, talk, tell ♦ [2] appropriate, filch, hook, misappropriate, nip, pilfer, pocket, purloin, steal, swipe, thieve

²snitch *n* ♦ **:** one that snitches **:** TATTLETALE

♦ betrayer, blabbermouth, informer, rat, stool pigeon, tattler, tattletale

sniv•el \ˈsni-vəl\ *vb* **-eled** *or* **-elled; -el•ing** *or* **-el•ling 1 :** to have a running nose; *also* **:** SNUFFLE **2 :** to whine in a snuffling manner — **snivel** *n*
snob \ˈsnäb\ *n* **:** one who seeks association with persons of higher social position and looks down on those considered inferior — **snob•bish** *adj* — **snob•bish•ly** *adv* — **snob•bish•ness** *n* — **snob•by** \ˈsnä-bē\ *adj*
snob•bery \ˈsnä-bə-rē\ *n, pl* **-ber•ies :** snobbish conduct
¹snoop \ˈsnüp\ *vb* ♦ **:** to pry in a furtive or meddlesome way

♦ butt in, interfere, intrude, meddle, mess, nose, obtrude, poke, pry

²snoop *n* **:** a prying meddlesome person
snooty \ˈsnü-tē\ *adj* **snoot•i•er; -est :** DISDAINFUL, SNOBBISH
¹snooze \ˈsnüz\ *vb* **snoozed; snooz•ing** ♦ **:** to take a nap **:** DOZE

♦ catnap, doze, drowse, nap, slumber

²snooze *n* ♦ **:** a short sleep especially during the day

♦ catnap, doze, drowse, forty winks, nap, siesta, wink

snore \ˈsnōr\ *vb* **snored; snor•ing :** to breathe with a rough hoarse noise while sleeping — **snore** *n*
snor•kel \ˈsnȯr-kəl\ *n* **:** a tube projecting above the water used by swimmers for breathing with the face under water — **snorkel** *vb*
¹snort \ˈsnȯrt\ *vb* **1 :** to force air violently and noisily through the nose ⟨his horse ∼*ed*⟩ **2 :** to inhale (a drug) through the nostrils **3 :** to express scorn, anger, indignation, or surprise by a snort
²snort *n* **1** ♦ **:** the act or sound of snorting **2** ♦ **:** a drink of usually straight liquor taken in one draft

♦ [1] boo, catcall, hiss, hoot, jeer, raspberry ♦ [2] draft, drag, drink, nip, quaff, shot, slug, swallow, swig

snot \ˈsnät\ *n* **1 :** nasal mucus **2 :** a snotty person
snot•ty \ˈsnä-tē\ *adj* **snot•ti•er; -est 1 :** soiled with snot **2 :** meanly contemptible
snout \ˈsnau̇t\ *n* **1 :** a long projecting muzzle (as of a pig) **2 :** a usually large or grotesque nose
¹snow \ˈsnō\ *n* **1 :** crystals of ice formed from water vapor in the air **2 :** a descent or shower of snow crystals
²snow *vb* **1 :** to fall or cause to fall in or as snow **2 :** to cover or shut in with or as if with snow **3 :** deceive, persuade, or charm glibly
¹snow•ball \ˈsnō-ˌbȯl\ *n* **:** a round mass of snow pressed into shape in the hand for throwing
²snowball *vb* **1 :** to throw snowballs at **2** ♦ **:** to increase or expand at a rapidly accelerating rate

♦ accumulate, appreciate, balloon, build, burgeon, enlarge, escalate, expand, increase, mount, multiply, mushroom, proliferate, rise, swell, wax

snow•bank \-ˌbaŋk\ *n* **:** a mound or slope of snow
snow•belt \-ˌbelt\ *n, often cap* **:** a region that receives an appreciable amount of annual snowfall
snow•blow•er \-ˌblō-ər\ *n* **:** a machine in which a rotating spiral blade picks up and propels snow aside
snow•board \-ˌbōrd\ *n* **:** a board like a wide ski ridden in a surfing position downhill over snow
snow•drift \-ˌdrift\ *n* **:** a bank of drifted snow
snow•drop \-ˌdräp\ *n* **:** a plant with narrow leaves and a nodding white flower that blooms early in the spring
snow•fall \-ˌfȯl\ *n* **:** a fall of snow
snow fence *n* **:** a fence across the path of prevailing winds to protect something (as a road) from drifting snow
snow•field \ˈsnō-ˌfēld\ *n* **:** a mass of perennial snow at the head of a glacier
snow•mo•bile \ˈsnō-mō-ˌbēl\ *n* **:** any of various automotive vehicles for travel on snow — **snow•mo•bil•er** \-ˌbē-lər\ *n* — **snow•mo•bil•ing** \-liŋ\ *n*
snow pea *n* **:** a cultivated pea with flat edible pods
snow•plow \ˈsnō-ˌplau̇\ *n* **1 :** a device for clearing away snow **2 :** a skiing maneuver in which the heels of both skis are slid outward for slowing down or stopping
¹snow•shoe \-ˌshü\ *n* **:** a lightweight platform for the foot designed to enable a person to walk on soft snow without sinking
²snowshoe *vb* **snow•shoed; snow•shoe•ing :** to travel on snowshoes
snow•storm \-ˌstȯrm\ *n* **:** a storm of falling snow
snow thrower *n* **:** SNOWBLOWER
snow under *vb* ♦ **:** to overwhelm especially in excess of capacity to absorb or deal with something

♦ carry away, crush, devastate, floor, oppress, overcome, overpower, overwhelm, prostrate, swamp

snowy \ˈsnō-ē\ *adj* **snow•i•er; -est 1 :** marked by snow **2 :** white as snow
¹snub \ˈsnəb\ *vb* **snubbed; snub•bing** ♦ **:** to treat with disdain **:** SLIGHT

♦ disdain, high-hat, scorn, slight, sniff

²snub *n* ♦ **:** an act or an instance of snubbing

♦ brush-off, cold shoulder, rebuff, repulse

snub–nosed \ˈsnəb-ˌnōzd\ *adj* **:** having a nose slightly turned up at the end
snuck *past and past part of* SNEAK
¹snuff \ˈsnəf\ *vb* **1 :** to pinch off the charred end of (a candle)

2 ♦ : to put out (a candle) — often used with *out* 3 ♦ : to make extinct; *also* : put an end to — usually used with *out* — **snuff·er** *n*

♦ *usu* **snuff out** [2] douse, extinguish, put out, quench ♦ *usu* **snuff out** [3] annihilate, blot out, demolish, eradicate, exterminate, liquidate, obliterate, root, rub out, stamp, wipe out ♦ *usu* **snuff out** [3] clamp down, crack down, crush, put down, quash, quell, repress, silence, squash, squelch, subdue, suppress

²snuff *vb* **1** : to draw forcibly into or through the nose **2** : SMELL
³snuff *n* : SNIFF
⁴snuff *n* : pulverized tobacco
snuf·fle \ˈsnə-fəl\ *vb* **snuf·fled; snuf·fling** **1** : to snuff or sniff audibly and repeatedly **2** : to breathe with a sniffing sound — **snuf·fle** *n*
snug \ˈsnəg\ *adj* **snug·ger; snug·gest** **1** ♦ : fitting closely and comfortably **2** : CONCEALED **3** ♦ : exhibiting neatness, good order, or compactness of line or structure **4** ♦ : enjoying or affording warm secure shelter or cover and opportunity for ease and contentment ⟨a ~ cottage⟩ — **snug·ly** *adv* — **snug·ness** *n*

♦ [1] fast, firm, frozen, secure, set, tight ♦ [3] crisp, neat, orderly, shipshape, tidy, trim, uncluttered ♦ [4] comfortable, easy, soft

snug·gle \ˈsnə-gəl\ *vb* **snug·gled; snug·gling** ♦ : to curl up or draw close comfortably : NESTLE

♦ cuddle, curl up, nestle, snug

¹so \ˈsō\ *adv* **1** : in the manner indicated **2** ♦ : in the same way **3** : THUS **4** : FINALLY **5** : to an indicated or great extent ⟨I'm ~ bored⟩ **6** ♦ : for that reason : THEREFORE **7** : to a great extent or degree : VERY

♦ [2] alike, also, correspondingly, likewise, similarly ♦ [6] accordingly, consequently, ergo, hence, therefore, thus, wherefore

²so *conj* : for that reason ⟨he wanted it, ~ he took it⟩
³so *pron* **1** : the same ⟨became chairman and remained ~⟩ **2** : approximately that ⟨a dozen or ~⟩
⁴so *abbr* south; southern
SO *abbr* strikeout
¹soak \ˈsōk\ *vb* **1** : to remain in a liquid **2** ♦ : to make or become saturated by or as if by immersion : WET **3** ♦ : to draw in by or as if by absorption **4** ♦ : to cause to pay an exorbitant amount

♦ [2] drench, drown, immerse, impregnate, saturate, sop, souse, steep, wet ***Ant*** wring (out) ♦ [3] absorb, drink, imbibe, sponge, suck ♦ [4] gouge, overcharge, sting

²soak *n* **1** : the act of soaking **2** : the liquid in which something is soaked **3** : one who is habitually drunk : DRUNKARD
soap \ˈsōp\ *n* ♦ : a cleansing substance made usually by action of alkali on fat — **soap** *vb* — **soapy** *adj*

♦ cleaner, detergent

soap·box \ˈsōp-ˌbäks\ *n* : an improvised platform used for delivering informal speeches
soap opera *n* : a radio or television daytime serial drama
soap·stone \ˈsōp-ˌstōn\ *n* : a soft talc-containing stone with a soapy feel
soar \ˈsōr\ *vb* ♦ : to fly upward or at a height on or as if on wings; *also* : to rise or increase dramatically (as in position, value, or price)

♦ arise, ascend, climb, lift, mount, rise, up ♦ fly, glide, plane, wing ♦ rocket, shoot, skyrocket, zoom

sob \ˈsäb\ *vb* **sobbed; sob·bing** ♦ : to weep with convulsive heavings of the chest or contractions of the throat — **sob** *n*

♦ bawl, blubber, cry, weep

so·ba \ˈsō-bə\ *n* : a Japanese noodle made from buckwheat flour
so·ber \ˈsō-bər\ *adj* **so·ber·er** \-bər-ər\; **so·ber·est** \-bə-rəst\ **1** : temperate in the use of liquor **2** ♦ : not drunk **3** ♦ : serious or grave in mood or disposition **4** : having a quiet tone or color — **so·ber·ly** *adv* — **so·ber·ness** *n*

♦ [2] clearheaded, dry, straight, temperate ***Ant*** drunk, high, inebriated, intoxicated, soused, tipsy ♦ [3] earnest, grave, humorless (*or* humourless), serious, severe, solemn, staid, unsmiling, weighty

so·bri·ety \sō-ˈbrī-ə-tē\ *n* ♦ : the quality or state of being sober

♦ earnestness, gravity, intentness, seriousness, solemnity

so·bri·quet \ˈsō-bri-ˌkā, -ˌket\ *n* : NICKNAME
soc *abbr* **1** social; society **2** sociology
so–called \ˈsō-ˈkȯld\ *adj* : commonly but often inaccurately so termed
soc·cer \ˈsä-kər\ *n* : a game played on a field by two teams with a round inflated ball that is kicked or hit with any body part other than the hands or arms
so·cia·bil·i·ty \ˌsō-shə-ˈbi-lə-tē\ *n* : the quality or state of being sociable; *also* : the act or an instance of being sociable
¹so·cia·ble \ˈsō-shə-bəl\ *adj* **1** : liking companionship : FRIENDLY **2** ♦ : characterized by pleasant social relations — **so·cia·bly** \ˈsō-shə-blē\ *adv*

♦ affable, cordial, genial, gracious, hospitable

²sociable *n* : SOCIAL
¹so·cial \ˈsō-shəl\ *adj* **1** ♦ : marked by pleasant companionship with one's friends **2** : naturally living and breeding in organized communities ⟨~ insects⟩ **3** : of or relating to human society ⟨~ institutions⟩ **4** : of, relating to, or based on rank in a particular society ⟨~ circles⟩; *also* : of or relating to fashionable society — **so·cial·ly** *adv*

♦ boon, companionable, convivial, extroverted, gregarious, outgoing, sociable

²social *n* : a social gathering
so·cial·ise *chiefly Brit var of* SOCIALIZE
so·cial·ism \ˈsō-shə-ˌli-zəm\ *n* : any of various social systems based on shared or government ownership and administration of the means of production and distribution of goods — **so·cial·ist** \ˈsō-shə-list\ *n or adj* — **so·cial·is·tic** \ˌsō-shə-ˈlis-tik\ *adj*
so·cial·ite \ˈsō-shə-ˌlīt\ *n* : a person prominent in fashionable society
so·cial·ize \ˈsō-shə-ˌlīz\ *vb* **-ized; -iz·ing** **1** : to regulate according to the theory and practice of socialism **2** : to adapt to social needs or uses **3** ♦ : to participate actively in a social gathering — **so·cial·i·za·tion** \ˌso-shə-lə-ˈzā-shən\ *n*

♦ associate, fraternize, hobnob, mingle, mix

social science *n* : a science (as economics or political science) dealing with a particular aspect of human society — **social scientist** *n*
social work *n* : services, activities, or methods providing social services especially to the economically or socially disadvantaged — **social worker** *n*
so·ci·e·ty \sə-ˈsī-ə-tē\ *n, pl* **-ties** **1** ♦ : the fellowship existing among companions : COMPANIONSHIP **2** ♦ : a voluntary association of persons for common ends **3** : a part of a community bound together by common interests and standards; *esp* : the group or set of fashionable people

♦ [1] camaraderie, companionship, company, comradeship, fellowship ♦ [2] association, brotherhood, club, college, congress, council, fellowship, fraternity, guild, institute, institution, league, order, organization

so·cio·eco·nom·ic \ˌsō-sē-ō-ˌe-kə-ˈnä-mik, ˌsō-shē-, -ˌē-kə-\ *adj* : of, relating to, or involving both social and economic factors
sociol *abbr* sociologist; sociology
so·ci·ol·o·gy \ˌsō-sē-ˈä-lə-jē, ˌsō-shē-\ *n* : the science of society, social institutions, and social relationships — **so·cio·log·i·cal** \ˌsō-sē-ə-ˈlä-ji-kəl, ˌsō-shē-\ *adj* — **so·ci·ol·o·gist** \-ˈä-lə-jist\ *n*
so·cio·path \ˈsō-sē-ə-ˌpath, ˈsō-sh(ē-)ə-\ *n* : a person exhibiting antisocial behavior : PSYCHOPATH — **so·cio·path·ic** \ˌsō-sē-ə-ˈpa-thik, ˌsō-sh(ē-)ə-\ *adj*
¹sock \ˈsäk\ *n, pl* **socks** *or* **sox** \ˈsäks\ : a stocking with a short leg
²sock *vb* : to hit, strike, or apply forcefully
³sock *n* ♦ : a vigorous blow : PUNCH

♦ bat, belt, blow, box, clout, hit, punch, slug, thump, wallop, whack

sock·et \ˈsä-kət\ *n* : an opening or hollow that forms a holder for something
socket wrench *n* : a wrench usually in the form of a bar and removable socket made to fit a bolt or nut
sock·eye salmon \ˈsäk-ˌī-\ *n* : a commercially important Pacific salmon
¹sod \ˈsäd\ *n* **1** : TURF 1 **2** ♦ : one's native land

♦ country, fatherland, home, homeland, motherland

²sod *vb* **sod·ded; sod·ding** : to cover with sod
so·da \ˈsō-də\ *n* **1** : SODIUM CARBONATE **2** : SODIUM BICARBONATE **3** : SODIUM **4** : SODA WATER **5** : SODA POP **6** : a sweet drink of soda water, flavoring, and often ice cream
soda pop *n* : a carbonated, sweetened, and flavored soft drink
soda water *n* : a beverage of water charged with carbon dioxide
sod·den \ˈsäd-ᵊn\ *adj* **1** : lacking spirit : DULLED **2** ♦ : heavy

with or as if with moisture or water : SOAKED **3 :** heavy or doughy from being improperly cooked ⟨~ biscuits⟩

♦ saturated, soggy, waterlogged, watery, wet

so•di•um \ˈsō-dē-əm\ *n* **:** a soft waxy silver white metallic chemical element occurring in nature in combined form (as in salt)
sodium bicarbonate *n* **:** a white weakly alkaline salt used especially in baking powders, fire extinguishers, and medicine
sodium carbonate *n* **:** a carbonate of sodium used especially in washing and bleaching textiles
sodium chloride *n* **:** SALT 1
sodium fluoride *n* **:** a salt used chiefly in tiny amounts (as in fluoridation) to prevent tooth decay
sodium hydroxide *n* **:** a white brittle caustic substance used in making soap and rayon and in bleaching
sodium nitrate *n* **:** a crystalline salt used as a fertilizer and in curing meat
sodium thiosulfate *n* **:** a hygroscopic crystalline salt used as a photographic fixing agent
sod•omy \ˈsä-də-mē\ *n* **:** anal or oral sexual intercourse with a member of the same or opposite sex; *also* **:** sexual intercourse with an animal — **sod•om•ize** \ˈsä-də-ˌmīz\ *vb*
so•ev•er \sō-ˈe-vər\ *adv* **1 :** in any degree or manner ⟨how bad ~⟩ **2 :** at all **:** of any kind ⟨any help ~⟩
so•fa \ˈsō-fə\ *n* ♦ **:** a couch usually with upholstered back and arms

♦ couch, davenport, divan, lounge, settee

soft \ˈsȯft\ *adj* **1 :** not hard or rough **:** NONVIOLENT **2** ♦ **:** marked by a gentleness, kindness, or tenderness **3 :** emotionally susceptible **4 :** not prepared to endure hardship **5 :** not containing certain salts that prevent lathering ⟨~ water⟩ **6 :** occurring at such a speed as to avoid destructive impact ⟨~ landing of a spacecraft on the moon⟩ **7 :** BIODEGRADABLE ⟨a ~ pesticide⟩ **8 :** not alcoholic ⟨~ drinks⟩ **9 :** less detrimental than a hard narcotic ⟨~ drugs⟩ **10** ♦ **:** demanding little work or effort **11 :** lacking robust strength, stamina, or endurance **12** ♦ **:** lacking firmness or strength of character **13** ♦ **:** bringing ease, comfort, or quiet **14** ♦ **:** quiet in pitch or volume **15** ♦ **:** smooth or delicate in texture, grain, or fiber **16** ♦ **:** yielding to physical pressure — **softly** *adv* — **soft•ness** *n*

♦ [2] balmy, benign, bland, delicate, gentle, light, mellow, mild, soothing, tender ♦ [10] easy, effortless, facile, fluent, fluid, light, painless, ready, simple, smooth, snap ♦ [12] effete, frail, nerveless, spineless, weak, wimpy, wishy-washy ♦ [13] comfortable, easy, snug ♦ [14] dull, low, quiet *Ant* blaring, clamorous, deafening, earsplitting, loud ♦ [15] cottony, downy, satiny, silken, velvety *Ant* coarse, harsh, rough, scratchy ♦ [16] flabby, mushy, pulpy, spongy *Ant* firm, hard, solid

soft•ball \ˈsȯft-ˌbȯl\ *n* **:** a game similar to baseball played with a ball larger and softer than a baseball; *also* **:** the ball used in this game
soft•bound \-ˌbau̇nd\ *adj* **:** not bound in hard covers ⟨~ books⟩
soft coal *n* **:** BITUMINOUS COAL
soft•en \ˈsȯ-fən\ *vb* ♦ **:** to make or become soft — **soft•en•er** *n*

♦ debilitate, enervate, enfeeble, prostrate, sap, tire, waste, weaken ♦ buffer, cushion, gentle

soft palate *n* **:** the fold at the back of the hard palate that partially separates the mouth from the pharynx
soft•ware \ˈsȯft-ˌwar\ *n* **:** the entire set of programs, procedures, and related documentation associated with a system; *esp* **:** computer programs
soft•wood \-ˌwu̇d\ *n* **1 :** the wood of a coniferous tree as compared to that of a broad-leaved deciduous tree **2 :** a tree yielding softwood — **softwood** *adj*
sog•gy \ˈsä-gē\ *adj* **sog•gi•er; -est** ♦ **:** heavy with water or moisture — **sog•gi•ly** \ˈsä-gə-lē\ *adv* — **sog•gi•ness** \-gē-nəs\ *n*

♦ saturated, sodden, waterlogged, watery, wet

soi•gné *or* **soi•gnée** \swän-ˈyā\ *adj* **:** elegantly maintained; *esp* **:** WELL-GROOMED
[1]**soil** \ˈsȯil\ *vb* **1 :** CORRUPT, POLLUTE **2** ♦ **:** to make or become dirty **3 :** STAIN, DISGRACE

♦ befoul, begrime, besmirch, blacken, dirty, foul, grime, mire, muddy, smirch, stain

[2]**soil** *n* **1 :** STAIN, DEFILEMENT **2** ♦ **:** something that spoils or pollutes

♦ dirt, filth, grime, muck, smut

[3]**soil** *n* **1** ♦ **:** firm land **:** EARTH **2** ♦ **:** the upper layer of earth in which plants grow **3 :** COUNTRY, REGION

♦ [1] dirt, dust, earth, ground, land ♦ [2] dirt, earth, ground

soi•ree *or* **soi•rée** \swä-ˈrā\ *n* **:** an evening party
[1]**so•journ** \ˈsō-ˌjərn, sō-ˈjərn\ *vb* ♦ **:** to dwell in a place temporarily — **so•journ•er** *n*

♦ stay, tarry, visit

[2]**so•journ** *n* **:** a temporary stay
[1]**sol** *n* **:** a fluid colloidal system
[2]**sol** *abbr* **1** solicitor **2** soluble **3** solution
Sol \ˈsäl\ *n* **:** SUN
[1]**sol•ace** \ˈsä-ləs\ *n* ♦ **:** alleviation of grief or anxiety; *also* **:** a source of relief or consolation

♦ cheer, comfort, consolation, relief ♦ comforting, consolation

[2]**solace** *vb* **so•laced; so•lac•ing** ♦ **:** to give solace to **:** CONSOLE

♦ assure, cheer, comfort, console, reassure, soothe

so•lar \ˈsō-lər\ *adj* **1 :** of, derived from, or relating to the sun **2 :** measured by the earth's course in relation to the sun ⟨the ~ year⟩ **3 :** operated by or using the sun's light or heat ⟨~ energy⟩
solar cell *n* **:** a photoelectric cell used as a power source
solar collector *n* **:** a device for the absorption of solar radiation for the heating of water or buildings or the production of electricity
solar flare *n* **:** a sudden temporary outburst of energy from a small area of the sun's surface
so•lar•i•um \sō-ˈlar-ē-əm\ *n, pl* **-ia** \-ē-ə\ *also* **-i•ums :** a room exposed to the sun; *esp* **:** a room (as in a hospital) for exposure of the body to sunshine
solar plexus *n* ♦ **:** the general area of the stomach below the sternum

♦ abdomen, belly, gut, stomach, tummy

solar system *n* **:** the sun together with the group of celestial bodies that revolve around it
solar wind *n* **:** plasma continuously ejected from the sun's surface
sold *past and past part of* SELL
sol•der \ˈsä-dər, ˈsȯ-\ *n* **:** a metallic alloy used when melted to mend or join metallic surfaces — **solder** *vb*
soldering iron *n* **:** a metal device for applying heat in soldering
[1]**sol•dier** \ˈsōl-jər\ *n* ♦ **:** a person in military service; *esp* **:** an enlisted man or woman — **sol•dier•ly** *adj or adv*

♦ fighter, legionnaire, man-at-arms, regular, serviceman, warrior *Ant* civilian

[2]**soldier** *vb* **sol•diered; sol•dier•ing 1 :** to serve as a soldier **2 :** to pretend to work while actually doing nothing
sol•diery \ˈsōl-jə-rē\ *n* **:** a body of soldiers
[1]**sole** \ˈsōl\ *n* **:** any of various flatfishes including some used for food
[2]**sole** *n* **1 :** the undersurface of the foot **2 :** the bottom of a shoe
[3]**sole** *vb* **soled; sol•ing :** to furnish (a shoe) with a sole
[4]**sole** *adj* ♦ **:** being the only one **:** ONLY; *also* **:** belonging exclusively or otherwise limited to one usually specified individual, unit, or group

♦ alone, lone, only, singular, solitary, special, unique

so•le•cism \ˈsä-lə-ˌsi-zəm, ˈsō-\ *n* **1 :** a mistake in grammar **2 :** a breach of etiquette
sole•ly \ˈsōl-lē\ *adv* **1** ♦ **:** without another **2** ♦ **:** to the exclusion of all else

♦ [1] alone, independently, singly, unaided, unassisted ♦ [2] alone, exclusively, just, only, simply

sol•emn \ˈsä-ləm\ *adj* **1 :** marked by or observed with full religious ceremony **2 :** FORMAL, CEREMONIOUS **3** ♦ **:** highly serious **4 :** SOMBER, GLOOMY — **sol•emn•ly** \ˈsä-ləm-lē\ *adv*

♦ august, dignified, imposing, staid, stately ♦ earnest, grave, humorless (*or* humourless), serious, severe, sober, staid, unsmiling, weighty

so•lem•ni•ty \sə-ˈlem-nə-tē\ *n* **1** ♦ **:** formal or ceremonious observance of an occasion or event **2** ♦ **:** a solemn condition or quality

♦ [1] ceremonial, ceremony, form, formality, observance, rite, ritual ♦ [2] earnestness, gravity, intentness, seriousness, sobriety

sol•em•nize \ˈsä-ləm-ˌnīz\ *vb* **-nized; -niz•ing 1 :** to observe or honor with solemnity **2 :** to celebrate (a marriage) with religious rites — **sol•em•ni•za•tion** \ˌsä-ləm-nə-ˈzā-shən\ *n*
so•le•noid \ˈsō-lə-ˌnȯid, ˈsä-\ *n* **:** a coil of wire usually in cylindrical form that when carrying a current acts like a magnet
so•lic•it \sə-ˈli-sət\ *vb* **1** ♦ **:** to make petition to **:** ENTREAT

2 ♦ **:** to approach with a request or plea **3 :** TEMPT, LURE **4** ♦ **:** to try to obtain by usually urgent requests or pleas

♦ [1] appeal, beg, beseech, entreat, implore, importune, petition, plead, pray, supplicate ♦ [2] canvass, poll, survey ♦ [4] ask, call, plead, quest, request, seek, sue

so•lic•i•ta•tion \-ˌli-sə-ˈtā-shən\ *n* ♦ **:** the practice or act or an instance of soliciting; *also* **:** a moving or drawing force

♦ appeal, cry, entreaty, petition, plea, prayer, suit, supplication

so•lic•i•tor \sə-ˈli-sə-tər\ *n* **1** ♦ **:** one that solicits **2 :** LAWYER; *esp* **:** a legal official of a city or state

♦ pleader, suitor

so•lic•i•tous \sə-ˈli-sə-təs\ *adj* **1 :** full of concern or fears **:** WORRIED, CONCERNED **2 :** full of desire **:** EAGER **3** ♦ **:** manifesting or expressing attentive care and protectiveness — **so•lic•i•tous•ly** *adv*

♦ attentive, considerate, kind, thoughtful

so•lic•i•tude \sə-ˈli-sə-ˌtüd, -ˌtyüd\ *n* **:** the state of being concerned and anxious **:** ANXIETY, CONCERN

[1]**sol•id** \ˈsä-ləd\ *adj* **1 :** not hollow; *also* **:** written as one word without a hyphen ⟨a ~ compound⟩ **2 :** having, involving, or dealing with three dimensions or with solids ⟨~ geometry⟩ **3** ♦ **:** not loose or spongy **:** COMPACT ⟨a ~ mass of rock⟩; *also* **:** neither gaseous nor liquid **:** HARD, RIGID ⟨~ ice⟩ **4 :** of good substantial quality or kind ⟨~ comfort⟩ **5** ♦ **:** thoroughly dependable **:** RELIABLE ⟨a ~ citizen⟩; *also* **:** serious in purpose or character ⟨~ reading⟩ **6 :** UNANIMOUS, UNITED ⟨~ for pay increases⟩ **7 :** of one substance or character **8** ♦ **:** free from error, fallacy, or misapprehension — **solid** *adv* — **sol•id•ly** *adv*

♦ [3] compact, firm, hard, rigid, stiff, unyielding ♦ [5] dependable, good, reliable, responsible, safe, steady, sure, tried, true, trustworthy ♦ [8] good, hard, informed, just, levelheaded, logical, rational, reasonable, reasoned, sensible, sober, valid, well-founded

[2]**solid** *n* **1 :** a geometrical figure (as a cube or sphere) having three dimensions **2 :** a solid substance

sol•i•dar•i•ty \ˌsä-lə-ˈdar-ə-tē\ *n* **:** unity based on shared interests, objectives, or standards

so•lid•i•fy \sə-ˈli-də-ˌfī\ *vb* **-fied; -fy•ing** ♦ **:** to make or become solid — **so•lid•i•fi•ca•tion** \-ˌli-də-fə-ˈkā-shən\ *n*

♦ concrete, congeal, firm, freeze, harden, set ♦ crystallize, form, jell, shape

so•lid•i•ty \sə-ˈli-də-tē\ *n* **1** ♦ **:** the quality or state of being solid **2 :** something solid

♦ dependability, reliability, sureness, trustworthiness

sol•id•ness *n* **:** the quality or state of being solid

solid–state *adj* **1 :** relating to the structure and properties of solid material **2 :** using semiconductor devices rather than vacuum tubes

so•lil•o•quize \sə-ˈli-lə-ˌkwīz\ *vb* **-quized; -quiz•ing :** to talk to oneself **:** utter a soliloquy

so•lil•o•quy \sə-ˈli-lə-kwē\ *n, pl* **-quies 1 :** the act of talking to oneself **2 :** a dramatic monologue that represents unspoken reflections by a character

sol•i•taire \ˈsä-lə-ˌtar\ *n* **1 :** a single gem (as a diamond) set alone **2 :** a card game for one person

sol•i•tary \ˈsä-lə-ˌter-ē\ *adj* **1** ♦ **:** being or living apart from others **2 :** LONELY, SECLUDED **3** ♦ **:** being the only one **:** ONLY

♦ [1] alone, lone, lonely, lonesome, unaccompanied ♦ [3] alone, lone, only, singular, sole, special, unique

sol•i•tude \ˈsä-lə-ˌtüd, -ˌtyüd\ *n* **1** ♦ **:** the state of being alone **:** SECLUSION **2 :** a lonely place

♦ insulation, isolation, seclusion, segregation, sequestration

soln *abbr* solution

[1]**so•lo** \ˈsō-lō\ *n, pl* **solos 1 :** a piece of music for a single voice or instrument with or without accompaniment **2 :** an action in which there is only one performer — **solo** *adj or vb* — **so•lo•ist** *n*

[2]**solo** *adv* **:** without a companion **:** ALONE

so•lon \ˈsō-lən\ *n* **1 :** a wise and skillful lawgiver **2** ♦ **:** a member of a legislative body

♦ lawmaker, legislator

sol•stice \ˈsäl-stəs, ˈsōl-\ *n* **:** the time of the year when the sun is farthest north of the equator (**summer solstice**) about June 22 or farthest south (**winter solstice**) about Dec. 22 — **sol•sti•tial** \säl-ˈsti-shəl, sōl-\ *adj*

sol•u•ble \ˈsäl-yə-bəl\ *adj* **1 :** capable of being dissolved in or as if in a liquid **2** ♦ **:** capable of being solved or explained — **sol•u•bil•i•ty** \ˌsäl-yə-ˈbi-lə-tē\ *n*

♦ answerable, explicable, resolvable, solvable

sol•ute \ˈsäl-ˌyüt\ *n* **:** a dissolved substance

so•lu•tion \sə-ˈlü-shən\ *n* **1 :** an action or process of solving a problem; *also* **:** an answer to a problem **2 :** an act or the process by which one substance is homogenously mixed with another usually liquid substance; *also* **:** a mixture thus formed

solv•able \ˈsäl-və-bəl\ *adj* ♦ **:** susceptible of solution or of being solved, resolved, or explained

♦ answerable, explicable, resolvable, soluble *Ant* inexplicable, insoluble, unsolvable

solve \ˈsälv\ *vb* **solved; solv•ing** ♦ **:** to find the answer to or a solution for

♦ answer, break, crack, dope, figure out, puzzle, resolve, riddle, unravel, work, work out

sol•ven•cy \ˈsäl-vən-sē\ *n* **:** the condition of being solvent

[1]**sol•vent** \-vənt\ *adj* **1 :** able or sufficient to pay all legal debts **2 :** dissolving or able to dissolve

[2]**solvent** *n* **:** a usually liquid substance capable of dissolving or dispersing one or more other substances

So•ma•lian \sō-ˈmäl-yən\ *n* **:** a native or inhabitant of Somalia — **Somalian** *adj*

so•mat•ic \sō-ˈma-tik\ *adj* ♦ **:** of, relating to, or affecting the body in contrast to the mind or the sex cells and their precursors

♦ animal, bodily, carnal, corporal, fleshly, material, physical

som•ber *or chiefly Can and Brit* **som•bre** \ˈsäm-bər\ *adj* **1** ♦ **:** so shaded as to be dark and gloomy **2** ♦ **:** of a serious or depressing character **:** GRAVE, MELANCHOLY — **som•ber•ly** *adv*

♦ [1] dark, darkling, dim, dusky, gloomy, murky, obscure ♦ [2] bleak, dark, dismal, dreary, gloomy, gray (*or* grey), wretched

som•bre•ro \səm-ˈbrer-ō\ *n, pl* **-ros :** a broad-brimmed felt hat worn especially in the Southwest and in Mexico

[1]**some** \ˈsəm\ *adj* **1** ♦ **:** one unspecified ⟨~ man called⟩ **2 :** an unspecified or indefinite number of ⟨~ berries are ripe⟩ **3 :** at least a few or a little ⟨~ years ago⟩

♦ anonymous, certain, one, unidentified, unnamed, unspecified

[2]**some** *pron* **:** a certain number or amount ⟨~ of the berries are ripe⟩ ⟨~ of it is missing⟩

[1]**-some** \səm\ *adj suffix* **:** characterized by a (specified) thing, quality, state, or action ⟨awe*some*⟩ ⟨burden*some*⟩

[2]**-some** *n suffix* **:** a group of (so many) members and especially persons ⟨four*some*⟩

[1]**some•body** \ˈsəm-ˌbä-dē, -bə-\ *pron* **:** some person

[2]**somebody** *n* ♦ **:** a person of importance

♦ celebrity, figure, light, luminary, notable, personage, personality, standout, star, superstar, VIP

some•day \ˈsəm-ˌdā\ *adv* ♦ **:** at some future time

♦ eventually, sometime, ultimately, yet

some•how \-ˌhau̇\ *adv* **:** by some means

some•one \-(ˌ)wən\ *pron* **:** some person

som•er•sault *also* **sum•mer•sault** \ˈsə-mər-ˌsȯlt\ *n* **:** a leap or roll in which a person turns heels over head — **somersault** *vb*

som•er•set \-ˌset\ *n or vb* **:** SOMERSAULT

some•thing \ˈsəm-thiŋ\ *pron* **:** some undetermined or unspecified thing

some•time \-ˌtīm\ *adv* **1** ♦ **:** at a future time **2 :** at an unknown or unnamed time

♦ eventually, someday, ultimately, yet

some•times \-ˌtīmz\ *adv* **:** at times **:** OCCASIONALLY

[1]**some•what** \-ˌhwät, -ˌhwət\ *pron* **:** SOMETHING

[2]**somewhat** *adv* ♦ **:** in some degree

♦ enough, fairly, kind of, moderately, pretty, quite, rather, so-so, sort of

some•where \-ˌhwer\ *adv* **:** in, at, or to an unknown or unnamed place

som•nam•bu•lism \säm-ˈnam-byə-ˌli-zəm\ *n* **:** performance of motor acts (as walking) during sleep; *also* **:** an abnormal condition of sleep characterized by this — **som•nam•bu•list** \-list\ *n*

som•no•lent \ˈsäm-nə-lənt\ *adj* **:** inclined to or heavy with sleep **:** SLEEPY, DROWSY — **som•no•lence** \-ləns\ *n*

son \ˈsən\ *n* **1 :** a male offspring or descendant **2** *cap* **:** Jesus Christ **3 :** a person deriving from a particular source (as a country, race, or school)

so•nar \ˈsō-ˌnär\ *n* **:** a method or device for detecting and locating submerged objects (as submarines) by sound waves

so•na•ta \sə-ˈnä-tə\ *n* **:** an instrumental composition with three or four movements differing in rhythm and mood but related in key

son•a•ti•na \ˌsä-nə-ˈtē-nə\ *n* **:** a short usually simplified sonata

song \ˈsȯŋ\ *n* **1** ♦ **:** vocal music; *also* **:** a short composition of words and music **2** ♦ **:** poetic composition **3 :** a distinctive or characteristic sound (as of a bird) **4** ♦ **:** a small amount ⟨sold for a ∼⟩

♦ [1] air, lay, melody, strain, tune, warble ♦ [1] jingle, lay, lyric, vocal ♦ [2] poem, poetry, verse ♦ [4] mite, peanuts, pittance, shoestring

song•bird \ˈsȯŋ-ˌbərd\ *n* **:** a bird that utters a series of musical tones

Song of Songs : a book in the Jewish Scriptures and in the Roman Catholic canon of the Old Testament and corresponding to the Song of Solomon in the Protestant canon of the Old Testament

song•ster \ˈsȯŋ-stər\ *n* ♦ **:** one that sings

♦ caroler, singer, vocalist, voice

song•stress \-strəs\ *n* **:** a girl or woman who is a singer

son•ic \ˈsä-nik\ *adj* **:** of or relating to sound waves or the speed of sound

sonic boom *n* **:** an explosive sound produced by an aircraft traveling at supersonic speed

son–in–law \ˈsən-ən-ˌlȯ\ *n, pl* **sons–in–law :** the husband of one's daughter

son•net \ˈsä-nət\ *n* **:** a poem of 14 lines usually in iambic pentameter with a definite rhyme scheme

son of a gun *n* **:** an offensive or disagreeable person

so•no•rous \sə-ˈnōr-əs, ˈsä-nə-rəs\ *adj* **1 :** giving out sound when struck **2** ♦ **:** loud, deep, or rich in sound **3 :** high-sounding **:** IMPRESSIVE — **so•nor•i•ty** \sə-ˈnȯr-ə-tē\ *n*

♦ golden, loud, resonant, resounding, ringing, round, vibrant

soon \ˈsün\ *adv* **1** ♦ **:** before long **2 :** in a prompt manner **:** QUICKLY **3** *archaic* **:** EARLY **4** ♦ **:** in agreement with one's choice or preference **:** WILLINGLY

♦ [1] anon, momentarily, presently, shortly ♦ [4] first, preferably, rather, readily

soot \ˈsu̇t, ˈsət, ˈsüt\ *n* **:** a fine black powder consisting chiefly of carbon that is formed when something burns and that colors smoke — **sooty** *adj*

sooth \ˈsüth\ *n, archaic* **:** TRUTH

soothe \ˈsüt͟h\ *vb* **soothed; sooth•ing 1 :** to please by flattery or attention **2** ♦ **:** to calm down **3 :** RELIEVE, ALLEVIATE ⟨∼ a burn⟩ — **sooth•er** *n* — **sooth•ing•ly** *adv*

♦ assure, cheer, comfort, console, reassure, solace ♦ allay, alleviate, assuage, calm, ease, help, mitigate, mollify, palliate, relieve

soothing *adj* ♦ **:** tending to soothe; *also* **:** having a sedative effect

♦ comforting, dreamy, narcotic, sedative

sooth•say•er \ˈsüth-ˌsā-ər\ *n* ♦ **:** one who foretells events

♦ augur, diviner, forecaster, fortune-teller, futurist, prognosticator, prophet, seer

sooth•say•ing *n* ♦ **:** the act of foretelling events; *also* **:** something that is predicted

♦ cast, forecast, prediction, prognostication, prophecy

¹sop \ˈsäp\ *n* **:** a conciliatory bribe, gift, or concession

²sop *vb* **sopped; sop•ping 1 :** to steep or dip in or as if in a liquid **2** ♦ **:** to wet thoroughly **:** SOAK; *also* **:** to mop up (a liquid)

♦ drench, drown, impregnate, saturate, soak, souse, steep

SOP *abbr* standard operating procedure; standing operating procedure

soph *abbr* sophomore

soph•ism \ˈsä-ˌfi-zəm\ *n* **1 :** an argument correct in form but embodying a subtle fallacy **2 :** SOPHISTRY

soph•ist \ˈsä-fist\ *n* **:** PHILOSOPHER; *esp* **:** a captious or fallacious reasoner

so•phis•tic \sä-ˈfis-tik, sə-\ *or* **so•phis•ti•cal** \-ti-kəl\ *adj* **:** of or characteristic of sophists or sophistry

so•phis•ti•cat•ed \sə-ˈfis-tə-ˌkā-təd\ *adj* **1** ♦ **:** highly complicated or developed **:** COMPLEX ⟨∼ instruments⟩ **2** ♦ **:** made worldly-wise by wide experience **3 :** intellectually appealing ⟨∼ novel⟩

♦ [1] complex, complicated, convoluted, elaborate, intricate, involved, knotty ♦ [2] cosmopolitan, smart, worldly, worldly-wise ♦ [2] debonair, smooth, suave, urbane

so•phis•ti•ca•tion \-ˌfis-tə-ˈkā-shən\ *n* **1 :** the process or result of becoming cultured, knowledgeable, or disillusioned **2** ♦ **:** the process or result of becoming more complex, developed, or subtle

♦ complexity, elaborateness, intricacy

soph•ist•ry \ˈsä-fə-strē\ *n* **:** subtly deceptive reasoning or argument

soph•o•more \ˈsäf-ˌmōr, ˈsä-fə-\ *n* **:** a student in the second year of high school or college

soph•o•mor•ic \ˌsäf-ˈmōr-ik, ˌsä-fə-\ *adj* **1 :** being overconfident of knowledge but poorly informed and immature **2 :** of, relating to, or characteristic of a sophomore ⟨a ∼ prank⟩

So•pho•ni•as \ˌsä-fə-ˈnī-əs, ˌsō-\ *n* **:** ZEPHANIAH

sop•o•rif•ic \ˌsä-pə-ˈri-fik\ *adj* **1 :** causing sleep or drowsiness **2 :** LETHARGIC

sopping *adj* **:** wet through **:** SOAKING

so•pra•no \sə-ˈpra-nō, -ˈprä-\ *n, pl* **-nos 1 :** the highest singing voice; *also* **:** a singer with this voice **2 :** the highest part in a 4-part chorus — **soprano** *adj*

sor•bet \sȯr-ˈbā\ *n* **:** a usually fruit-flavored ice served for dessert or between courses as a palate refresher

sor•cer•er \-rər\ *n* ♦ **:** a person who practices sorcery

♦ conjurer, enchanter, magician, necromancer, voodoo, witch, wizard

sor•cer•ess \-rəs\ *n* **:** a woman who is a sorcerer

sor•cery \ˈsȯr-sə-rē\ *n* ♦ **:** the use of magic **:** WITCHCRAFT

♦ bewitchment, enchantment, magic, necromancy, witchcraft, wizardry

sor•did \ˈsȯr-dəd\ *adj* **1** ♦ **:** marked by baseness or grossness **:** VILE **2 :** marked by filthiness and degradation **:** DIRTY — **sor•did•ly** *adv* — **sor•did•ness** *n*

♦ base, contemptible, despicable, detestable, dirty, dishonorable (*or* dishonourable), ignoble, low, mean, snide, vile, wretched

¹sore \ˈsōr\ *adj* **sor•er; sor•est 1** ♦ **:** causing pain or distress ⟨a ∼ bruise⟩ **2 :** painfully sensitive ⟨∼ muscles⟩ **3 :** SEVERE, INTENSE **4 :** feeling or showing anger **:** ANGRY — **sore•ness** *n*

♦ nasty, painful

²sore *n* **1 :** a sore spot on the body; *esp* **:** one (as an ulcer) with the tissues broken and usually infected **2 :** a source of pain or vexation

sore•head \ˈsōr-ˌhed, ˈsȯr-\ *n* **:** a person easily angered or discontented

sore•ly *adv* **1 :** in a sore manner **2 :** to a high degree

sore throat *n* **:** painful throat due to inflammation of the fauces and pharynx

sor•ghum \ˈsȯr-gəm\ *n* **:** a tall variable Old World tropical grass grown widely for its edible seed, for forage, or for its sweet juice which yields a syrup

so•ror•i•ty \sə-ˈrȯr-ə-tē\ *n, pl* **-ties :** a club or organization usually of female students for social purposes

¹sor•rel \ˈsȯr-əl\ *n* **:** a brownish orange to light brown color; *also* **:** a sorrel-colored animal (as a horse)

²sorrel *n* **:** any of various herbs having a sour juice

¹sor•row \ˈsär-ō\ *n* **1** ♦ **:** deep distress, sadness, or regret; *also* **:** resultant unhappy or unpleasant state **2 :** a cause of grief or sadness **3 :** a display of grief or sadness

♦ affliction, anguish, dolor, grief, heartache, woe ***Ant*** blessedness, bliss, cheer, cheerfulness, cheeriness, delight, ecstasy, elation, euphoria, exhilaration, exuberance, exultation, gladness, glee, happiness, joy, joyousness, jubilation, pleasure, rapture

²sorrow *vb* ♦ **:** to feel or express sorrow

♦ agonize, bleed, feel, grieve, hurt, mourn, suffer

sor•row•ful \-fəl\ *adj* **1** ♦ **:** full of or marked by sorrow **2** ♦ **:** expressive of or inducing sorrow

♦ [1] anguished, dolorous, lamentable, mournful, plaintive, sad, sorry, woeful ♦ [2] dolorous, funeral, lugubrious, mournful, plaintive, regretful, rueful, weeping, woeful

sor•row•ful•ly \-f(ə-)lē\ *adv* ♦ **:** in a sorrowful manner

♦ agonizingly, bitterly, grievously, hard, hardly, sadly, unhappily, woefully, wretchedly

sor•ry \ˈsär-ē\ *adj* **sor•ri•er; -est** **1** ♦ **:** feeling sorrow, regret, or penitence **2 :** full of sorrow **:** MOURNFUL **3** ♦ **:** causing sorrow, pity, or scorn

♦ [1] apologetic, contrite, penitent, regretful, remorseful, repentant, rueful ♦ [3] depressing, dismal, dreary, heartbreaking, melancholy, pathetic, sad, tearful ♦ [3] contemptible, despicable, pitiful

1sort \ˈsȯrt\ *n* **1** ♦ **:** a group of persons or things that have similar characteristics **:** CLASS **2 :** WAY, MANNER **3 :** QUALITY, NATURE **4 :** an instance of sorting **5 :** a single human being ⟨he's a good ~⟩ — **out of sorts 1 :** somewhat ill **2 :** GROUCHY, IRRITABLE

♦ breed, class, description, feather, ilk, kind, like, manner, nature, order, species, type

2sort *vb* **1** ♦ **:** to put in a certain place according to kind, class, or nature **2 :** to be in accord **:** AGREE — **sort•er** *n*

♦ assort, break down, categorize, class, classify, grade, group, peg, place, range, rank, separate

sor•tie \ˈsȯr-tē, sȯr-ˈtē\ *n* **1 :** a sudden issuing of troops from a defensive position against the enemy **2 :** one mission or attack by one airplane

sort of *adv* ♦ **:** to a moderate degree

♦ enough, fairly, kind of, moderately, pretty, quite, rather, so-so, somewhat

SOS \ˌes-(ˌ)ō-ˈes\ *n* **:** a call or request for help or rescue

1so–so \ˈsō-ˈsō\ *adv* ♦ **:** moderately well

♦ adequately, all right, fine, good, nicely, OK, passably, satisfactorily, tolerably, well

2so–so *adj* ♦ **:** neither very good nor very bad

♦ common, fair, indifferent, mediocre, medium, middling, ordinary, passable, run-of-the-mill, second-rate

sot \ˈsät\ *n* ♦ **:** an habitual drunkard — **sot•tish** *adj* — **sot•tish•ly** *adv*

♦ drunk, drunkard, inebriate, soak, souse, tippler

souf•flé \sü-ˈflā\ *n* **:** a spongy dish made light in baking by stiffly beaten egg whites

sough \ˈsau̇, ˈsəf\ *vb* **:** to make a moaning or sighing sound — **sough** *n*

sought *past and past part of* SEEK

1soul \ˈsōl\ *n* **1 :** the immaterial essence of an individual life **2 :** the spiritual principle embodied in human beings or the universe **3** ♦ **:** an active or essential part **4** ♦ **:** the moral and emotional nature of human beings **5 :** spiritual or moral force **6 :** an individual human **:** PERSON ⟨a kindly ~⟩ **7 :** a strong, positive feeling (as of intense sensitivity and emotional fervor) conveyed especially by black American performers; *also* **:** NEGRITUDE — **souled** \ˈsōld\ *adj*

♦ [3] core, heart, quick ♦ [4] essence, nature, quintessence, stuff, substance

2soul *adj* **1 :** of, relating to, or characteristic of black Americans or their culture ⟨~ food⟩ **2 :** designed for or controlled by blacks ⟨~ radio stations⟩

soul brother *n* **:** a black male

soul•ful \ˈsōl-fəl\ *adj* ♦ **:** full of or expressing deep feeling — **soul•ful•ly** *adv*

♦ demonstrative, emotional, feeling, intense, passionate, sensitive, sentimental

soul•less \ˈsōl-ləs\ *adj* ♦ **:** having no soul or no greatness or warmth of mind or feeling

♦ callous, hard, heartless, inhuman, inhumane, pitiless, unfeeling, unsympathetic

soul music *n* **:** music that is closely related to rhythm and blues and characterized by intensity of feeling

1sound \ˈsau̇nd\ *adj* **1** ♦ **:** not diseased or sickly **2 :** free from flaw or defect **3** ♦ **:** securely or solidly fixed in place **:** STRONG **4** ♦ **:** free from error or fallacy **5 :** LEGAL, VALID **6 :** THOROUGH **7 :** UNDISTURBED ⟨~ sleep⟩ **8 :** showing good judgment — **sound•ly** *adv*

♦ [1] able-bodied, chipper, fit, hale, healthy, hearty, robust, well, whole, wholesome ♦ [3] fast, firm, stable, stalwart, steady, strong, sturdy ♦ [4] analytic, coherent, good, logical, rational, reasonable, sensible, sober, valid

2sound *n* **1 :** the sensation of hearing; *also* **:** mechanical energy transmitted by longitudinal pressure waves (**sound waves**) (as in air) that is the stimulus to hearing **2 :** something heard **:** NOISE, TONE; *also* ♦ **:** hearing distance **:** EARSHOT **3 :** a musical style — **sound•less•ly** *adv* — **sound•proof** \-ˌprüf\ *adj or vb*

♦ earshot, hail, hearing

3sound *vb* **1 :** to make or cause to make a sound **2** ♦ **:** to order or proclaim by a sound ⟨~ the alarm⟩ **3** ♦ **:** to convey a certain impression **:** SEEM **4 :** to examine the condition of by causing to give out sounds — **sound•able** \ˈsau̇n-də-bəl\ *adj*

♦ [2] air, express, give, state, vent, voice ♦ [2] advertise, announce, blaze, broadcast, declare, enunciate, placard, post, proclaim, promulgate, publicize, publish ♦ [3] act, appear, look, make, seem

4sound *n* ♦ **:** a long passage of water wider than a strait often connecting two larger bodies of water

♦ channel, narrows, strait

5sound *vb* **1 :** to measure the depth of (water) especially by a weighted line dropped from the surface **:** FATHOM **2 :** PROBE **3** ♦ **:** to dive down suddenly ⟨the hooked fish ~*ed*⟩ — **sound•ing** *n*

♦ dive, pitch, plunge

sound bite *n* **:** a brief recorded statement broadcast especially on a news program

sound card *n* **:** a circuit board in a computer system designed to produce or reproduce sound

sound•er \ˈsau̇n-dər\ *n* **:** one that sounds; *esp* **:** a device for making soundings

sound•less *adj* ♦ **:** making no sound

♦ hushed, muted, noiseless, quiet, silent, still

sound•ness *n* ♦ **:** the quality or state of being sound

♦ firmness, stability, steadiness, strength, sturdiness ♦ fitness, health, heartiness, robustness, wellness, wholeness, wholesomeness

sound off *vb* ♦ **:** to voice one's opinions freely and vigorously

♦ speak out, speak up, spout

sound•stage \ˈsau̇nd-ˌstāj\ *n* **:** the part of a motion-picture studio in which a production is filmed

sound•track \ˈsau̇n(d)-ˌtrak\ *n* **:** music recorded to accompany a film, DVD, or videotape

soup \ˈsüp\ *n* **1 :** a liquid food with stock as its base and often containing pieces of solid food **2** ♦ **:** something (as a heavy fog) having or suggesting the consistency of soup **3 :** an unfortunate predicament ⟨in the ~⟩

♦ fog, haze, mist, murk, smog

soup•çon \süp-ˈsō^{n}\ *n* **:** a little bit **:** 1TRACE 2

soup up *vb* **:** to increase the power of — **souped–up** \ˈsüpt-ˈəp\ *adj*

soupy \ˈsü-pē\ *adj* **soup•i•er; -est** **1 :** having the consistency of soup **2** ♦ **:** densely foggy or cloudy

♦ cloudy, foggy, hazy, misty, murky, smoggy

1sour \ˈsau̇r\ *adj* **1** ♦ **:** having an acid or tart taste ⟨~ as vinegar⟩ **2 :** SPOILED, PUTRID ⟨a ~ odor⟩ **3** ♦ **:** not pleasant **:** DISAGREEABLE ⟨~ disposition⟩; *also* **:** marked by overt hostility — **sour•ish** *adj* — **sour•ly** *adv* — **sour•ness** *n*

♦ [1] acid, tart, vinegary ♦ [3] bad, disagreeable, distasteful, nasty, rotten, uncongenial, unlovely, unpleasant, unwelcome

2sour *vb* ♦ **:** to become or make sour

♦ alienate, disaffect, disgruntle, estrange

source \ˈsōrs\ *n* **1 :** ORIGIN, BEGINNING **2 :** a supplier of information **3 :** the beginning of a stream of water

source code *n* **:** a computer program in its original programming language and before translation (as by a compiler)

1souse \ˈsau̇s\ *vb* **soused; sous•ing** **1 :** PICKLE **2** ♦ **:** to plunge into a liquid **3** ♦ **:** to wet thoroughly **:** DRENCH **4 :** to make drunk

♦ [2] dip, douse, duck, dunk, immerse, submerge ♦ [3] drench, drown, impregnate, saturate, soak, sop, steep

2souse *n* **1 :** something (as pigs' feet) steeped in pickle **2 :** a soaking in liquid **3** ♦ **:** an habitual drunkard

♦ drunk, inebriate, soak, sot, tippler

1south \ˈsau̇th\ *adv* **:** to or toward the south; *also* **:** into a state of decline

[2]**south** *adj* **1 :** situated toward or at the south **2 :** coming from the south

[3]**south** *n* **1 :** the direction to the right of one facing east **2 :** the compass point directly opposite to north **3** *cap* **:** regions or countries south of a specified or implied point; *esp* **:** the southeastern part of the U.S. — **south•er•ly** \ˈsə-t͟hər-lē\ *adj or adv* — **south•ern** \ˈsə-t͟hərn\ *adj* — **South•ern•er** *n* — **south•ern•most** \-ˌmōst\ *adj* — **south•ward** \ˈsau̇th-wərd\ *adv or adj* — **south•wards** \-wərdz\ *adv*

South African *n* **:** a native or inhabitant of the Republic of South Africa — **South African** *adj*

south•east \sau̇-ˈthēst, *naut* sau̇-ˈēst\ *n* **1 :** the general direction between south and east **2 :** the compass point midway between south and east **3** *cap* **:** regions or countries southeast of a specified or implied point — **southeast** *adj or adv* — **south•east•er•ly** *adv or adj* — **south•east•ern** \-ˈēs-tərn\ *adj*

south•paw \ˈsau̇th-ˌpȯ\ *n* **:** a left-handed person; *esp* **:** a left-handed baseball pitcher — **southpaw** *adj*

south pole *n, often cap S&P* **:** the southernmost point of the earth

south•west \sau̇th-ˈwest, *naut* sau̇-ˈwest\ *n* **1 :** the general direction between south and west **2 :** the compass point midway between south and west **3** *cap* **:** regions or countries southwest of a specified or implied point — **southwest** *adj or adv* — **south•west•er•ly** *adv or adj* — **south•west•ern** \-ˈwes-tərn\ *adj*

sou•ve•nir \ˌsü-və-ˈnir\ *n* ♦ **:** something serving as a reminder

♦ keepsake, memento, memorial, monument, remembrance, token

sou'•west•er \sau̇-ˈwes-tər\ *n* **:** a long waterproof coat worn in storms at sea; *also* **:** a waterproof hat

[1]**sov•er•eign** \ˈsä-vrən, -və-rən\ *n* **1** ♦ **:** one possessing the supreme power and authority in a state **2 :** a gold coin of the United Kingdom

♦ autocrat, monarch, ruler

[2]**sovereign** *adj* **1 :** EXCELLENT, FINE **2 :** supreme in power or authority **3 :** having undisputed ascendancy **:** CHIEF **4** ♦ **:** having independent authority

♦ autonomous, free, independent, self-governing, separate

sov•er•eign•ty \-tē\ *n, pl* **-ties 1 :** supremacy in rule or power **2 :** power to govern without external control **3 :** the supreme political power in a state **4** ♦ **:** one that is sovereign; *also* **:** an autonomous state

♦ autonomy, freedom, independence, liberty, self-government
♦ commonwealth, country, land, nation, state

so•vi•et \ˈsō-vē-ˌet, ˈsä-, -ət\ *n* **1 :** an elected governmental council in a Communist country **2** *pl, cap* **:** the people and especially the leaders of the U.S.S.R. — **soviet** *adj, often cap* — **so•vi•et•ize** *vb, often cap*

[1]**sow** \ˈsau̇\ *n* **:** an adult female swine

[2]**sow** \ˈsō\ *vb* **sowed; sown** \ˈsōn\ *or* **sowed; sow•ing 1** ♦ **:** to plant seed especially by scattering **2 :** to strew with seed **3** ♦ **:** to scatter abroad — **sow•er** \ˈsō-ər\ *n*

♦ [1] drill, plant, seed ♦ [3] dot, pepper, scatter, spray, sprinkle, strew

sow bug \ˈsau̇-\ *n* **:** WOOD LOUSE

sox *pl of* SOCK

soy \ˈsȯi\ *n* **:** a sauce made from soybeans fermented in brine

soy•bean \ˈsȯi-ˌbēn\ *n* **:** an Asian legume widely grown for forage and for its edible seeds that yield a valuable oil (**soybean oil**); *also* **:** its seed

sp *abbr* **1** special **2** species **3** specimen **4** spelling **5** spirit

Sp *abbr* Spain

SP *abbr* **1** shore patrol; shore patrolman **2** shore police **3** specialist

spa \ˈspä\ *n* **1 :** a resort with mineral springs **2 :** a health and fitness facility **3 :** a hot tub with a whirlpool device

[1]**space** \ˈspās\ *n* **1** ♦ **:** a period of time **2** ♦ **:** some small measurable distance, area, or volume **3 :** the limitless area in which all things exist and move **4 :** an empty place **5 :** the region beyond the earth's atmosphere **6 :** a definite place (as a seat on a train or ship)

♦ [1] bit, spell, stretch, while ♦ [2] place, room, way

[2]**space** *vb* **spaced; spac•ing :** to place at intervals — **spac•er** *n*

space–age \ˈspās-ˌāj\ *adj* ♦ **:** of or relating to the age of space exploration

♦ contemporary, current, hot, mod, modern, new, newfangled, red-hot, ultramodern, up-to-date

space•craft \-ˌkraft\ *n* **:** a vehicle for travel beyond the earth's atmosphere

space•flight \-ˌflīt\ *n* **:** flight beyond the earth's atmosphere

space heater *n* **:** a usually portable device for heating a relatively small area

space•man \ˈspās-ˌman, -mən\ *n* **:** one who travels outside the earth's atmosphere

space out *vb* **:** to become distracted or inattentive

space•ship \-ˌship\ *n* **:** a vehicle used for space travel

space shuttle *n* **:** a reusable spacecraft designed to transport people and cargo between earth and space

space station *n* **:** a large artificial satellite serving as a base (as for scientific observation)

space suit *n* **:** a suit equipped to make life in space possible for its wearer

space walk *n* **:** a period of activity outside a spacecraft by an astronaut in space — **space•walk** \ˈspās-ˌwȯk\ *vb* — **space•walk•er** *n*

spa•cious \ˈspā-shəs\ *adj* ♦ **:** very large in extent **:** ROOMY — **spa•cious•ly** *adv* — **spa•cious•ness** *n*

♦ ample, capacious, commodious, roomy

[1]**spade** \ˈspād\ *n* **:** a shovel with a blade for digging — **spade•ful** *n*

[2]**spade** *vb* **spad•ed; spad•ing :** to dig with a spade — **spad•er** *n*

[3]**spade** *n* **:** any of a suit of playing cards marked with a black figure resembling an inverted heart with a short stem at the bottom

spa•dix \ˈspā-diks\ *n, pl* **spa•di•ces** \ˈspā-də-ˌsēz\ **:** a floral spike with a fleshy or succulent axis usually enclosed in a spathe

spa•ghet•ti \spə-ˈge-tē\ *n* **:** thin solid pasta strings

spam \ˈspam\ *n* **:** unsolicited usually commercial e-mail sent to a large number of addresses — **spam** *vb*

[1]**span** \ˈspan\ *n* **1 :** an English unit of length equal to nine inches (about 23 centimeters) **2 :** a limited portion of time **3 :** the spread (as of an arch) from one support to another

[2]**span** *vb* **spanned; span•ning 1** ♦ **:** to ascertain the measurements of **:** MEASURE **2 :** to extend across

♦ gauge, measure, scale

[3]**span** *n* **:** a pair of animals (as mules) driven together

Span *abbr* Spanish

span•dex \ˈspan-ˌdeks\ *n* **:** any of various elastic synthetic textile fibers

span•gle \ˈspaŋ-gəl\ *n* **:** a small disk of shining metal or plastic used especially on a dress for ornament — **spangle** *vb*

Span•glish \ˈspaŋ-glish\ *n* **:** a combination of Spanish and English

Span•iard \ˈspan-yərd\ *n* **:** a native or inhabitant of Spain

span•iel \ˈspan-yəl\ *n* **:** a dog of any of several breeds of mostly small and short-legged dogs usually with long wavy hair and large drooping ears

Span•ish \ˈspa-nish\ *n* **1 :** the chief language of Spain and of the countries colonized by the Spanish **2 Spanish** *pl* **:** the people of Spain — **Spanish** *adj*

Spanish American *n* **:** a resident of the U.S. whose native language is Spanish; *also* **:** a native or inhabitant of one of the countries of America in which Spanish is the national language — **Spanish–American** *adj*

Spanish fly *n* **:** a toxic preparation of dried green European beetles that causes the skin to blister and is thought to be an aphrodisiac

Spanish moss *n* **:** a plant related to the pineapple that grows in pendent tufts of grayish green filaments on trees from the southern U.S. to Argentina

Spanish rice *n* **:** rice cooked with onions, green peppers, and tomatoes

[1]**spank** \ˈspaŋk\ *vb* **:** to hit on the buttocks with the open hand — **spank** *n*

[2]**spank** *n* **:** a blow usually with the palm of the hand

spank•ing \ˈspaŋ-kiŋ\ *adj* **:** being fresh and strong **:** BRISK ⟨~ breeze⟩ — **spanking** *adv*

span•ner \ˈspan-ər\ *n, chiefly Brit* **:** WRENCH

[1]**spar** \ˈspär\ *n* **1 :** a stout pole **2 :** a rounded wood or metal piece (as a mast, yard, boom, or gaff) for supporting sail rigging

[2]**spar** *vb* **sparred; spar•ring :** to box for practice without serious hitting; *also* **:** SKIRMISH, WRANGLE

[1]**spare** \ˈspar\ *vb* **spared; spar•ing 1 :** to refrain from punishing or injuring **:** show mercy to ⟨*spared* the prisoners⟩ **2 :** to exempt from something ⟨~ me the trouble⟩ **3 :** to get along without ⟨can't ~ a dime⟩ **4** ♦ **:** to use frugally or rarely ⟨don't ~ the syrup⟩

♦ scant, skimp, stint

²spare *adj* **spar•er; spar•est 1 :** held in reserve **2 ♦ :** being over and above what is needed **:** SUPERFLUOUS **3 ♦ :** not liberal or profuse **4 ♦ :** healthily lean **:** THIN **5 :** not abundant or plentiful **:** SCANTY — **spare•ness** *n*

♦ [2] excess, extra, superfluous, supernumerary, surplus ♦ [3] cheap, close, mean, niggardly, parsimonious, penurious, stingy, tight, tightfisted, uncharitable ♦ [4] lean, skinny, slender, slim, thin

³spare *n* **1 ♦ :** a duplicate kept in reserve; *esp* **:** a spare tire **2 :** the knocking down of all the bowling pins with the first two balls

♦ backup, duplicate, extra, reserve, substitute

spar•ing \ˈspar-iŋ\ *adj* **♦ :** marked by or practicing careful restraint **:** FRUGAL — **spar•ing•ly** *adv*

♦ economical, frugal, provident, thrifty

¹spark \ˈspärk\ *n* **1 :** a small particle of a burning substance or a hot glowing particle struck from a mass (as by steel on flint) **2 :** a short bright flash of electricity between two points **3 :** SPARKLE **4 :** a particle capable of being kindled or developed **:** GERM
²spark *vb* **1 :** to emit or produce sparks **2 ♦ :** to stir to activity **:** INCITE

♦ activate, actuate, crank, drive, incite, move, propel, run, set off, start, touch off, trigger, turn on

³spark *vb* **:** WOO, COURT
¹spar•kle \ˈspär-kəl\ *vb* **spar•kled; spar•kling 1 a :** to throw out sparks **b ♦ :** to give off or reflect bright moving points of light **:** FLASH **2 :** to perform brilliantly **3 :** EFFERVESCE — **spar•kler** *n*

♦ flame, flash, glance, gleam, glimmer, glisten, glitter, scintillate, shimmer, twinkle, wink

²sparkle *n* **1 :** GLEAM **2 :** ANIMATION
spark plug *n* **1 :** a device that produces a spark to ignite the fuel mixture in an engine cylinder **2 :** one that begins something or drives something forward
spar•row \ˈspar-ō\ *n* **:** any of several small dull-colored singing birds
sparse \ˈspärs\ *adj* **spars•er; spars•est ♦ :** thinly scattered **:** SCANTY — **sparse•ly** *adv* — **sparse•ness** *n*

♦ light, meager (*or* meagre), poor, scant, scanty, scarce, skimpy, slender, slim, spare

spasm \ˈspa-zəm\ *n* **1 :** a sudden involuntary and abnormal muscular contraction **2 ♦ :** a sudden, violent, and temporary effort, feeling, or outburst

♦ agony, burst, eruption, explosion, fit, flare, flare-up, flash, flush, gale, gush, gust, outburst, paroxysm, storm

spas•mod•ic \spaz-ˈmä-dik\ *adj* **1 :** relating to or affected or characterized by spasm ⟨~ movements⟩; *also* **:** resembling a spasm **2 ♦ :** acting or proceeding fitfully **:** INTERMITTENT — **spas•mod•i•cal•ly** \-di-k(ə-)lē\ *adv*

♦ casual, choppy, discontinuous, erratic, fitful, intermittent, irregular, occasional, sporadic, spotty, unsteady

spas•tic \ˈspas-tik\ *adj* **:** of, relating to, marked by, or affected with muscular spasm ⟨~ paralysis⟩ — **spastic** *n*
¹spat \ˈspat\ *past and past part of* SPIT
²spat *n, pl* **spat** *or* **spats :** a young bivalve mollusk (as an oyster)
³spat *n* **:** a gaiter covering instep and ankle
⁴spat *n* **:** a brief petty quarrel **:** DISPUTE
⁵spat *vb* **spat•ted; spat•ting ♦ :** to quarrel briefly

♦ argue, bicker, brawl, dispute, fall out, fight, hassle, quarrel, row, scrap, squabble, wrangle

spate \ˈspāt\ *n* **♦ :** a great rise or overflowing of a stream; *also* **:** a sudden outburst

♦ cataclysm, cataract, deluge, flood, inundation, overflow, torrent

spathe \ˈspāth\ *n* **:** a sheathing bract or pair of bracts enclosing an inflorescence (as of the calla lily) and especially a spadix on the same axis
spa•tial \ˈspā-shəl\ *adj* **:** of or relating to space or to the facility to perceive objects in space — **spa•tial•ly** *adv*
spat•ter \ˈspa-tər\ *vb* **1 ♦ :** to splash with drops of liquid **2 :** to sprinkle around — **spatter** *n*

♦ dash, plash, splash

spat•u•la \ˈspa-chə-lə\ *n* **:** a flexible knifelike implement for scooping, spreading, or mixing soft substances
spav•in \ˈspa-vən\ *n* **:** a bony enlargement of the hock of a horse — **spav•ined** \-vənd\ *adj*

¹spawn \ˈspȯn\ *vb* **1 :** to produce eggs or offspring especially in large numbers **2 ♦ :** to bring into existence **:** GENERATE — **spawn•er** *n*

♦ create, engender, generate, induce, make, produce

²spawn *n* **1 :** the eggs of water animals (as fishes or oysters) that lay many small eggs **2 ♦ :** offspring especially when produced in great numbers

♦ issue, offspring, posterity, progeny, seed

spay \ˈspā\ *vb* **spayed; spay•ing :** to remove the ovaries of (a female animal)
SPCA *abbr* Society for the Prevention of Cruelty to Animals
SPCC *abbr* Society for the Prevention of Cruelty to Children
speak \ˈspēk\ *vb* **spoke** \ˈspōk\; **spo•ken** \ˈspō-kən\; **speak•ing 1 :** to utter words **2 ♦ :** to express orally **3 :** to mention in speech or writing **4 ♦ :** to address an audience **5 :** to use or be able to use (a language) in talking

♦ [2] articulate, say, state, talk, tell, utter, verbalize, vocalize ♦ [4] declaim, descant, discourse, harangue, lecture, orate, talk

speak•easy \ˈspēk-ˌē-zē\ *n, pl* **-eas•ies :** an illicit drinking place
speak•er \ˈspē-kər\ *n* **1 ♦ :** one that speaks **2 ♦ :** the presiding officer of a deliberative assembly **3 :** LOUDSPEAKER

♦ [1] mouthpiece, spokesman, spokesperson, spokeswoman ♦ [2] chair, chairman, moderator, president

speak out *vb* **1 :** to speak loud enough to be heard **2 ♦ :** to speak boldly **:** express an opinion frankly

♦ sound off, speak up, spout

speak up *vb* **1 :** to speak loudly and distinctly **2 ♦ :** to express an opinion freely

♦ sound off, speak out, spout

¹spear \ˈspir\ *n* **1 ♦ :** a long-shafted weapon with a sharp point for thrusting or throwing **2 :** a sharp-pointed instrument with barbs used in spearing fish — **spear•man** \-mən\ *n*

♦ lance, pike

²spear *vb* **♦ :** to strike or pierce with or as if with a spear — **spear•er** *n*

♦ gore, harpoon, impale, lance, pierce, puncture, skewer, spike, stab, stick, transfix

³spear *n* **:** a usually young blade, shoot, or sprout (as of asparagus)
spear•head \-ˌhed\ *vb* **♦ :** to serve as a leading force, element, or influence — **spearhead** *n*

♦ boss, captain, command, dominate, head, lead

spear•mint \-ˌmint\ *n* **:** a common highly aromatic garden mint
¹spec *abbr* **1** special **2** specifically **3** specialist
²spec \ˈspek\ *n* **:** SPECIFICATION 2 — usually used in plural
spe•cial \ˈspe-shəl\ *adj* **1 :** UNCOMMON, NOTEWORTHY **2 ♦ :** particularly favored **3 ♦ :** readily distinguishable from others of the same category **:** UNIQUE **4 :** EXTRA, ADDITIONAL **5 ♦ :** confined to or designed for a definite field of action, purpose, or occasion — **special** *n*

♦ [2] beloved, darling, dear, favorite (*or* favourite), loved, pet, precious, sweet ♦ [3] alone, lone, only, singular, sole, solitary, unique ♦ [5] distinct, especial, express, precise, set, specific

special delivery *n* **:** delivery of mail by messenger for an extra fee
special effects *n pl* **:** visual or sound effects introduced into a motion picture, video recording, or taped television production
Special Forces *n pl* **:** a branch of the army composed of soldiers specially trained in guerrilla warfare
spe•cial•ise *chiefly Brit var of* SPECIALIZE
spe•cial•ist \ˈspe-shə-list\ *n* **1 :** a person who specializes in a particular branch of learning or activity **2 :** an enlisted rank in the army corresponding to the grade of corporal
spe•cial•ize \ˈspe-shə-ˌlīz\ *vb* **-ized; -iz•ing :** to concentrate one's efforts in a special activity or field; *also* **:** to change in an adaptive manner — **spe•cial•i•za•tion** \ˌspe-shə-lə-ˈzā-shən\ *n*
spe•cial•ly \ˈspe-shə-lē\ *adv* **1 :** in a special manner **2 :** for a special purpose **:** in particular
spe•cial•ty \ˈspe-shəl-tē\ *n, pl* **-ties 1 :** a particular quality or detail **2 :** a product of a special kind or of special excellence **3 ♦ :** something (as a discipline) in which one specializes

♦ area, arena, demesne, department, discipline, domain, field, line, province, realm, sphere

spe•cie \ˈspē-shē, -sē\ *n* **:** money in coin
spe•cies \ˈspē-shēz, -sēz\ *n, pl* **spe•cies 1 ♦ :** a group united by common traits or interests **:** KIND **2 :** a category of biological clas-

sification ranking just below the genus or subgenus and comprising closely related organisms potentially able to breed with one another

♦ breed, class, description, feather, ilk, kind, like, manner, nature, order, sort, type ♦ bracket, category, class, division, family, grade, group, set

specif *abbr* specific; specifically

[1]**spe•cif•ic** \spi-ˈsi-fik\ *adj* **1 :** having a unique effect or influence or reacting in only one way or with only one thing ⟨~ antibodies⟩ ⟨~ enzymes⟩ **2** ♦ **:** free from ambiguity **:** DEFINITE **3 :** of, relating to, or constituting a species **4** ♦ **:** constituting or falling into a specifiable category — **spe•cif•i•cal•ly** \-fi-k(ə-)lē\ *adv*

♦ [2] clear-cut, definite, definitive, explicit, express, unambiguous, unequivocal ♦ [4] distinct, especial, express, precise, set, special

[2]**specific** *n* **1 :** something specific **:** DETAIL, PARTICULAR — usually used in plural **2** ♦ **:** a drug or remedy having a specific mitigating effect on a disease ⟨used as a ~ against malaria⟩

♦ cure, drug, medicine, pharmaceutical, remedy

spec•i•fi•ca•tion \ˌspe-sə-fə-ˈkā-shən\ *n* **1 :** the act or process of specifying **2 :** a description of work to be done and materials to be used (as in building) — usually used in plural

specific gravity *n* **:** the ratio of the density of a substance to the density of some substance (as water) taken as a standard when both densities are obtained by weighing in air

spec•i•fy \ˈspe-sə-ˌfī\ *vb* **-fied; -fy•ing** ♦ **:** to mention or name explicitly

♦ define, lay down, prescribe ♦ advert (to), cite, instance, mention, name, note, notice, quote, refer (to), touch (*on* or *upon*)

spec•i•men \ˈspe-sə-mən\ *n* ♦ **:** an item or part typical of a group or whole; *also* **:** a single human being

♦ case, example, exemplar, illustration, instance, representative, sample

spe•cious \ˈspē-shəs\ *adj* ♦ **:** seeming to be genuine, correct, or beautiful but not really so ⟨~ reasoning⟩

♦ deceitful, deceptive, delusive, fallacious, false, misleading

[1]**speck** \ˈspek\ *n* **1** ♦ **:** a small spot or blemish **2** ♦ **:** a small particle

♦ [1] blotch, dapple, dot, fleck, mottle, patch, point, spot ♦ [2] atom, bit, crumb, fleck, flyspeck, grain, granule, molecule, morsel, mote, particle, patch, scrap, scruple, tittle

[2]**speck** *vb* ♦ **:** to produce specks on or in

♦ blotch, dapple, dot, fleck, freckle, mottle, pepper, spot, sprinkle, stipple

[1]**speck•le** \ˈspe-kəl\ *n* **:** a little speck

[2]**speckle** *vb* **1 :** to mark with speckles **2 :** to be distributed in or on like speckles

specs \ˈspeks\ *n pl* **:** a pair of lenses used to correct defects of vision **:** GLASSES

spec•ta•cle \ˈspek-ti-kəl\ *n* **1 :** an unusual or impressive public display **2** *pl* ♦ **:** a pair of lenses used to correct defects of vision **:** GLASSES — **spec•ta•cled** \-kəld\ *adj*

♦ eyeglasses, glasses

spec•tac•u•lar \spek-ˈta-kyə-lər\ *adj* **:** exciting to see **:** SENSATIONAL

spec•ta•tor \ˈspek-ˌtā-tər\ *n* **:** a person who looks on (as at a sports event)

spec•ter *or* **spec•tre** \ˈspek-tər\ *n* ♦ **:** a visible disembodied spirit **:** GHOST

♦ apparition, bogey, ghost, phantasm, phantom, poltergeist, shade, shadow, spirit, spook, vision, wraith

spec•tral \ˈspek-trəl\ *adj* **1 :** of, relating to, or resembling a specter **2 :** of, relating to, or made by a spectrum

spec•tro•gram \ˈspek-trə-ˌgram\ *n* **:** a photograph, image, or diagram of a spectrum

spec•tro•graph \-ˌgraf\ *n* **:** an instrument for dispersing radiation into a spectrum and recording or mapping the spectrum — **spec•tro•graph•ic** \ˌspek-trə-ˈgra-fik\ *adj* — **spec•tro•graph•i•cal•ly** \-fi-k(ə-)lē\ *adv*

spec•trom•e•ter \spek-ˈträ-mə-tər\ *n* **:** an instrument for measuring spectra — **spec•tro•met•ric** \ˌspek-trə-ˈme-trik\ *adj* — **spec•trom•e•try** \spek-ˈträ-mə-trē\ *n*

spec•tro•scope \ˈspek-trə-ˌskōp\ *n* **:** an instrument that produces spectra especially of visible electromagnetic radiation — **spec•tro•scop•ic** \ˌspek-trə-ˈskä-pik\ *adj* — **spec•tro•scop•i•cal•ly** \-pi-k(ə-)lē\ *adv* — **spec•tros•co•pist** \spek-ˈträs-kə-pist\ *n* — **spec•tros•co•py** \-pē\ *n*

spec•trum \ˈspek-trəm\ *n, pl* **spec•tra** \-trə\ *or* **spectrums** **1 :** a series of colors formed when a beam of white light is dispersed (as by a prism) so that its parts are arranged in the order of their wavelengths **2 :** a series of radiations arranged in regular order **3** ♦ **:** a continuous sequence or range ⟨a wide ~ of political opinions⟩

♦ gamut, range, scale, spread, stretch

spec•u•late \ˈspe-kyə-ˌlāt\ *vb* **-lat•ed; -lat•ing** **1** ♦ **:** to think or wonder about a subject **2 :** to take a business risk in hope of gain — **spec•u•la•tive•ly** *adv* — **spec•u•la•tor** \-ˌlā-tər\ *n*

♦ assume, conjecture, guess, presume, suppose, surmise, suspect

spec•u•la•tion \ˌspe-kyə-ˈlā-shən\ *n* ♦ **:** an act or instance of speculating

♦ chance, enterprise, flier, gamble, venture

spec•u•la•tive \ˈspe-kyə-ˌlā-tiv\ *adj* ♦ **:** involving, based on, or constituting intellectual speculation; *also* **:** theoretical rather than demonstrable

♦ conjectural, hypothetical, theoretical

speech \ˈspēch\ *n* **1 :** the act of speaking **2 :** TALK, CONVERSATION **3** ♦ **:** a public talk or lecture **4 :** a variety of language identified with a region or group **:** LANGUAGE **5 :** an individual manner of speaking **6 :** the power of speaking

♦ address, declamation, harangue, oration, talk

speech•less *adj* ♦ **:** unable to speak; *also* **:** not speaking

♦ dumb, mum, mute, silent, uncommunicative

[1]**speed** \ˈspēd\ *n* **1** *archaic* **:** SUCCESS **2** ♦ **:** the act or state of moving swiftly **:** SWIFTNESS **3 :** rate of motion or performance **4 :** a transmission gear (as of a bicycle) **5 :** METHAMPHETAMINE; *also* **:** a related drug

♦ celerity, fastness, fleetness, haste, hurry, quickness, rapidity, swiftness, velocity ***Ant*** slowness, sluggishness

[2]**speed** *vb* **sped** \ˈsped\ *or* **speed•ed; speed•ing** **1** *archaic* **:** PROSPER; *also* **:** GET ALONG, FARE **2** ♦ **:** to go fast; *esp* **:** to go at an excessive or illegal speed **3** ♦ **:** to cause to go faster — **speed•er** *n*

♦ [2] barrel, dash, fly, hurry, hurtle, hustle, pelt, race, rip, rocket, shoot, tear, zip, zoom ♦ *usu* **speed up** [3] accelerate, hasten, hurry, quicken, rush, step up, whisk

speed•boat \-ˌbōt\ *n* **:** a fast motorboat

speed bump *n* **:** a low raised ridge across a roadway (as in a parking lot) to limit vehicle speed

speed•i•ly \ˈspē-də-lē\ *adv* ♦ **:** in a speedy manner

♦ apace, briskly, fast, full tilt, hastily, posthaste, presto, pronto, quick, quickly, rapidly, soon, swiftly

speed of light : a fundamental physical constant that is the speed of electromagnetic radiation propagation in a vacuum and has the value of 299,792,458 meters per second

speed•om•e•ter \spi-ˈdä-mə-tər\ *n* **:** an instrument for indicating speed

speed•up \ˈspēd-ˌəp\ *n* **:** ACCELERATION

speed•way \-ˌwā\ *n* **:** a racecourse for motor vehicles

speed•well \ˈspēd-ˌwel\ *n* **:** VERONICA

speedy *adj* ♦ **:** marked by swiftness of motion or action

♦ breakneck, breathless, brisk, dizzy, fast, fleet, hasty, lightning, nippy, quick, rapid, rattling, snappy, swift

[1]**spell** \ˈspel\ *vb* **spelled** \ˈspeld, ˈspelt\ *or Can and Brit* **spelt** \ˈspelt\; **spell•ing** **1 :** to name, write, or print in order the letters of a word **2** ♦ **:** to add up to **:** MEAN

♦ denote, express, import, mean, signify

[2]**spell** *n* **1** ♦ **:** a magic formula **:** INCANTATION **2 :** a controlling influence

♦ bewitchment, charm, conjuration, enchantment, incantation

[3]**spell** *n* **1 :** one's turn at work or duty **2 :** a stretch of a specified kind of weather **3** ♦ **:** a period of bodily or mental distress or disorder **:** ATTACK **4** ♦ **:** an indeterminate period of time

♦ [3] attack, bout, case, fit, seizure, siege ♦ [4] bit, space, stretch, while

4spell *vb* **spelled** \ˈspeld\; **spell•ing :** to take the place of for a time in work or duty : RELIEVE
5spell *vb* **spelled** \ˈspeld\; **spell•ing :** to put under a spell
spell•bind•er \-ˌbīn-dər\ *n* **:** a speaker of compelling eloquence
spell•bound \-ˌbau̇nd\ *adj* **:** held by or as if by a spell
spell–check•er \ˈspel-ˌche-kər\ *n* **:** a computer program that identifies possible misspellings in a block of text — **spell–check** \-ˌchek\ *vb*
spell•er \ˈspe-lər\ *n* **1 :** one who spells words **2 :** a book with exercises for teaching spelling
spell out *vt* **1** ♦ **:** to make plain **2 :** to write or print in letters and in full

♦ clarify, clear (up), construe, demonstrate, elucidate, explain, explicate, expound, illuminate, illustrate, interpret

spelt \ˈspelt\ *chiefly Can and Brit past and past part of* 1SPELL
spe•lunk•er \spi-ˈləŋ-kər, ˈspē-ˌləŋ-kər\ *n* **:** one who makes a hobby of exploring caves — **spe•lunk•ing** *n*
spend \ˈspend\ *vb* **spent** \ˈspent\; **spend•ing 1** ♦ **:** to pay out : EXPEND **2 :** to consume entirely : WEAR OUT, EXHAUST; *also* **:** to consume wastefully **3 :** to cause or permit to elapse : PASS

♦ disburse, expend, give, lay out, pay

spend•er *n* **:** one that spends money; *esp* **:** one that spends lavishly
spend•thrift \ˈspend-ˌthrift\ *n* ♦ **:** one who spends wastefully or recklessly

♦ prodigal, profligate, wastrel

spent \ˈspent\ *adj* ♦ **:** drained of energy

♦ beat, bushed, dead, drained, effete, jaded, limp, prostrate, tired, weary, worn-out

sperm \ˈspərm\ *n, pl* **sperm** *or* **sperms 1 :** SEMEN **2 :** a male gamete
sper•ma•to•zo•on \(ˌ)spər-ˌma-tə-ˈzō-ˌän, -ˈzō-ən\ *n, pl* **-zoa** \-ˈzō-ə\ **:** a motile male gamete of an animal usually with a rounded or elongated head and a long posterior flagellum
sperm cell *n* **:** SPERM 2
sper•mi•cide \ˈspər-mə-ˌsīd\ *n* **:** a preparation or substance used to kill sperm — **sper•mi•cid•al** \ˌspər-mə-ˈsī-dəl\ *adj*
sperm whale *n* **:** a large whale with a massive square-shaped head containing a fluid-filled cavity
spew \ˈspyü\ *vb* **1 :** VOMIT **2** ♦ **:** to come in a flood or gush; *also* **:** emit or eject with vigor or violence

♦ gush, jet, pour, rush, spout, spurt, squirt ♦ belch, disgorge, eject, erupt, expel

SPF *abbr* sun protection factor
sp gr *abbr* specific gravity
sphag•num \ˈsfag-nəm\ *n* **:** any of a genus of atypical mosses that grow in wet acid areas where their remains become compacted with other plant debris to form peat; *also* **:** a mass of these mosses
sphere \ˈsfir\ *n* **1** ♦ **:** a globe-shaped body : BALL **2 :** a celestial body **3 :** a solid figure so shaped that every point on its surface is an equal distance from the center **4** ♦ **:** range of action or influence — **spher•i•cal** \ˈsfir-i-kəl, ˈsfer-\ *adj* — **spher•i•cal•ly** \-i-k(ə-)lē\ *adv*

♦ [1] ball, orb ♦ [4] area, arena, demesne, department, discipline, domain, field, line, province, realm, specialty

spher•oid \ˈsfir-ˌȯid, ˈsfer-\ *n* **:** a figure similar to a sphere but not perfectly round — **sphe•roi•dal** \sfir-ˈȯi-dəl\ *adj*
sphinc•ter \ˈsfiŋk-tər\ *n* **:** a muscular ring that closes a bodily opening
sphinx \ˈsfiŋks\ *n, pl* **sphinx•es** *or* **sphin•ges** \ˈsfin-ˌjēz\ **1 :** a winged monster in Greek mythology having a woman's head and a lion's body and noted for killing anyone unable to answer its riddle **2 :** an enigmatic or mysterious person **3 :** an ancient Egyptian image having the body of a lion and the head of a man, ram, or hawk
1spice \ˈspīs\ *n* **1** ♦ **:** any of various aromatic plant products (as pepper or nutmeg) used to season or flavor foods **2 :** something that adds interest and relish **3** ♦ **:** a pungent or fragrant odor

♦ [1] flavor (*or* flavour), seasoning ♦ [3] aroma, bouquet, fragrance, incense, perfume, redolence, scent

2spice *vb* **spiced; spic•ing** ♦ **:** to season with spices

♦ flavor (*or* flavour), savor, season

spick–and–span *or* **spic–and–span** \ˌspik-ənd-ˈspan\ *adj* **1** ♦ **:** quite new **2** ♦ **:** spotlessly clean

♦ [1] brand-new, new, unused ♦ [2] clean, immaculate, spotless, stainless, unsoiled, unsullied

spic•ule \ˈspi-kyül\ *n* **:** a slender pointed body especially of calcium or silica ⟨sponge ~*s*⟩
spicy *adj* **1 :** having the quality, flavor, or fragrance of spice **2** ♦ **:** verging on impropriety or indecency; *also* **:** somewhat scandalous or salacious

♦ bawdy, lewd, racy, ribald, suggestive

spi•der \ˈspī-dər\ *n* **1 :** any of an order of arachnids that have a 2-part body, eight legs, and two or more pairs of abdominal organs for spinning threads of silk used especially in making webs for catching prey **2 :** a cast-iron frying pan — **spi•dery** *adj*
spider mite *n* **:** any of various small web-spinning mites that feed on and are pests of plants
spider plant *n* **:** a houseplant of the lily family having long green leaves usually striped with white and producing tufts of small plants on long hanging stems
spi•der•web \ˈspī-dər-ˌweb\ *n* **:** the web spun by a spider
spiel \ˈspēl\ *vb* **:** to talk in a fast, smooth, and usually colorful manner — **spiel** *n*
spig•ot \ˈspi-gət, -kət\ *n* ♦ **:** a fixture for drawing or regulating the flow of liquid especially from a pipe : FAUCET

♦ cock, faucet, gate, tap, valve

1spike \ˈspīk\ *n* **1 :** a very large nail **2 :** any of various pointed projections (as on the sole of a shoe to prevent slipping) — **spiky** *adj*
2spike *vb* **spiked; spik•ing 1 :** to fasten with spikes **2 :** to put an end to : QUASH ⟨~ a rumor⟩ **3** ♦ **:** to pierce with or impale on a spike **4 :** to add alcoholic liquor to (a drink)

♦ gore, harpoon, impale, lance, pierce, puncture, skewer, spear, stab, stick, transfix

3spike *n* **1 :** an ear of grain **2 :** a long cluster of usually stemless flowers
1spill \ˈspil\ *vb* **spilled** \ˈspild, ˈspilt\ *also* **spilt** \ˈspilt\; **spill•ing 1 :** to cause or allow to fall, flow, or run out especially unintentionally **2 :** to cause (blood) to be lost by wounding **3 :** to run out or over with resulting loss or waste **4** ♦ **:** to let out : DIVULGE — **spill•able** *adj*

♦ bare, disclose, discover, divulge, expose, reveal, tell, unbosom, uncloak, uncover, unmask, unveil

2spill *n* **1** ♦ **:** an act of spilling; *also* **:** a fall from a horse or vehicle or an erect position **2 :** something spilled

♦ fall, slip, stumble, tumble

spill•way \-ˌwā\ *n* **:** a passage for surplus water to run over or around an obstruction (as a dam)
1spin \ˈspin\ *vb* **spun** \ˈspən\; **spin•ning 1 :** to draw out (fiber) and twist into thread; *also* **:** to form (thread) by such means **2 :** to form thread by extruding a sticky quickly hardening fluid; *also* **:** to construct from such thread ⟨spiders ~ their webs⟩ **3 :** to produce slowly and by degrees ⟨~ a story⟩ **4** ♦ **:** to revolve rapidly : TWIRL; *also* **:** to cause to whirl **5 :** to feel as if in a whirl : WHIRL, REEL ⟨my head is *spinning*⟩ **6 :** to move rapidly along **7 :** to present (as information) with a particular spin — **spin•ner** *n*

♦ gyrate, pirouette, revolve, roll, rotate, turn, twirl, wheel, whirl

2spin *n* **1** ♦ **:** a rapid rotating motion **2 :** an excursion in a wheeled vehicle **3 :** a particular point of view, emphasis, or interpretation **4** ♦ **:** a state of mental confusion

♦ [1] gyration, pirouette, reel, revolution, roll, rotation, twirl, wheel, whirl ♦ [4] daze, fog, haze, muddle

spi•na bi•fi•da \ˌspī-nə-ˈbi-fə-də\ *n* **:** a birth defect in which the spinal column has a fissure
spin•ach \ˈspi-nich\ *n* **:** a dark green herb grown for its edible leaves
spi•nal \ˈspīn-əl\ *adj* **:** of or relating to the backbone or spinal cord — **spi•nal•ly** *adv*
spinal column *n* **:** the bony column in the back of a vertebrate that extends from the neck to the tail and protects the spinal cord : BACKBONE
spinal cord *n* **:** the thick cord of nervous tissue that extends from the brain along the back in the cavity of the backbone and carries nerve impulses to and from the brain
spinal nerve *n* **:** any of the paired nerves which arise from the spinal cord and pass to various parts of the body and of which there are normally 31 pairs in human beings
spin control *n* **:** the act or practice of attempting to manipulate the way an event is interpreted
spin•dle \ˈspind-əl\ *n* **1 :** a round tapering stick or rod by which fibers are twisted in spinning **2 :** a turned part of a piece of furni-

ture ⟨the ~s of a chair⟩ **3 :** a slender pin or rod which turns or on which something else turns
spin•dling \ˈspind-liŋ\ *adj* **:** of a disproportionately tall or long and thin appearance : SPINDLY
spin•dly \ˈspind-lē\ *adj* ♦ **:** being long or tall and thin and usually weak

♦ gangling, lanky, rangy

spin•drift \ˈspin-ˌdrift\ *n* **:** spray blown from waves
spine \ˈspīn\ *n* **1** ♦ **:** the bony column in the back of a vertebrate that extends from the neck to the tail and protects the spinal cord : BACKBONE **2 :** a stiff sharp process especially on a plant or animal **3 :** the part of a book where the pages are attached

♦ backbone, vertebral column

spi•nel \spə-ˈnel\ *n* **:** a hard crystalline mineral of variable color used as a gem
spine•less \ˈspīn-ləs\ *adj* **1 :** having no spines, thorns, or prickles **2 :** lacking a backbone **3** ♦ **:** lacking courage or determination

♦ chicken, cowardly, craven, dastardly, pusillanimous, recreant, yellow ♦ effete, frail, nerveless, soft, weak, wimpy, wishy-washy

spin•et \ˈspi-nət\ *n* **1 :** an early harpsichord having a single keyboard and only one string for each note **2 :** a small upright piano
spin•na•ker \ˈspi-ni-kər\ *n* **:** a large triangular sail set on a long light pole
spinning jen•ny \-ˈje-nē\ *n* **:** an early multiple-spindle machine for spinning wool or cotton
spinning wheel *n* **:** a small machine for spinning thread or yarn in which a large wheel drives a single spindle
spin–off \ˈspin-ˌȯf\ *n* **1** ♦ **:** a usually useful by-product **2 :** something (as a TV show) derived from an earlier work — **spin off** *vb*

♦ derivative, offshoot, outgrowth

spin•ster \ˈspin-stər\ *n* **:** an unmarried woman past the common age for marrying — **spin•ster•hood** \-ˌhu̇d\ *n*
spiny *adj* **1** ♦ **:** abounding with difficulties, obstacles, or annoyances **2 :** covered or armed with spines

♦ catchy, delicate, difficult, knotty, problematic, thorny, ticklish, touchy, tough, tricky

spiny lobster *n* **:** any of several edible crustaceans differing from the related lobsters in lacking the large front claws and in having a spiny carapace
¹spi•ral \ˈspī-rəl\ *adj* ♦ **:** winding or coiling around a center or axis and usually getting closer to or farther away from it — **spi•ral•ly** *adv*

♦ helical, winding

²spiral *n* **1 :** something that has a spiral form; *also* **:** a single turn in a spiral object **2 :** a continuously spreading and accelerating increase or decrease
³spiral *vb* **-raled** *or* **-ralled; -ral•ing** *or* **-ral•ling 1** ♦ **:** to move and especially to rise or fall in a spiral course **2 :** to form into a spiral

♦ coil, curl, entwine, twine, twist, wind

spi•rant \ˈspī-rənt\ *n* **:** a consonant (as \f\, \s\, \sh\) uttered with decided friction of the breath against some part of the oral passage — **spirant** *adj*
spire \ˈspīr\ *n* **1 :** a slender tapering stalk (as of grass) **2 :** a pointed tip (as of an antler) **3 :** STEEPLE — **spiry** *adj*
spi•rea *or* **spi•raea** \spī-ˈrē-ə\ *n* **:** any of a genus of shrubs related to the roses with dense clusters of small usually white or pink flowers
¹spir•it \ˈspir-ət\ *n* **1 :** a life-giving force; *also* **:** the animating principle : SOUL **2** *cap* **:** HOLY SPIRIT **3** ♦ **:** an often malevolent being that is bodiless but can become visible : GHOST **4 :** PERSON **5** ♦ **:** an inclination, impulse, or tendency of a specified kind : MOOD **6** ♦ **:** a lively or brisk quality in a person or a person's actions **7 :** essential or real meaning : INTENT **8** ♦ **:** distilled alcoholic liquor — often used in plural **9 :** LOYALTY ⟨school ~⟩

♦ [3] apparition, bogey, ghost, phantasm, phantom, poltergeist, shade, shadow, specter, spook, vision, wraith ♦ [5] cheer, frame, humor (*or* humour), mode, mood, temper ♦ [6] bounce, dash, drive, esprit, ginger, pep, punch, snap, verve, vim, zing, zip ♦ **spirits** [8] alcohol, booze, drink, intoxicant, liquor, moonshine

²spirit *vb* **:** to carry off secretly or mysteriously
spir•it•ed \ˈspir-ə-təd\ *adj* **1** ♦ **:** full of energy or animation : ANIMATED **2 :** full of courage : COURAGEOUS

♦ active, animate, animated, brisk, energetic, frisky, lively, peppy, sprightly, springy, vital, vivacious ♦ fiery, high-spirited, mettlesome, peppery, spunky ***Ant*** spiritless

spir•it•less *adj* ♦ **:** lacking animation, cheerfulness, or courage

♦ enervated, lackadaisical, languid, languorous, limp, listless

¹spir•i•tu•al \ˈspir-i-chəl, -chə-wəl\ *adj* **1** ♦ **:** of, relating to, consisting of, or affecting the spirit : INCORPOREAL **2** ♦ **:** of or relating to sacred matters **3 :** ecclesiastical rather than lay or temporal — **spir•i•tu•al•i•ty** \ˌspir-i-chə-ˈwa-lə-tē\ *n* — **spir•i•tu•al•ize** \ˈspir-i-chə-ˌlīz, -chə-wə-\ *vb* — **spir•i•tu•al•ly** *adv*

♦ [1] bodiless, immaterial, incorporeal, insubstantial, nonmaterial, nonphysical, unsubstantial ♦ [2] devotional, religious, sacred

²spiritual *n* ♦ **:** a religious song originating among blacks of the southern U.S.

♦ anthem, canticle, carol, chorale, hymn, psalm

spir•i•tu•al•ism \ˈspir-i-chə-ˌli-zəm, -chə-wə-\ *n* **:** a belief that spirits of the dead communicate with the living usually through a medium — **spir•i•tu•al•ist** \-list\ *n, often cap* — **spir•i•tu•al•is•tic** \ˌspir-i-chə-ˈlis-tik, -chə-wə-\ *adj*
spir•i•tu•ous \ˈspir-i-chəs, -chə-wəs; ˈspir-ə-təs\ *adj* **:** containing alcohol
spi•ro•chete *also* **spi•ro•chaete** \ˈspī-rə-ˌkēt\ *n* **:** any of an order of spirally undulating bacteria including those causing syphilis and Lyme disease
spirt *var of* SPURT
¹spit \ˈspit\ *n* **1 :** a thin pointed rod for holding meat over a fire **2** ♦ **:** a point of land that runs out into the water

♦ arm, cape, headland, peninsula, point, promontory

²spit *vb* **spit•ted; spit•ting :** to pierce with or as if with a spit
³spit *vb* **spit** *or* **spat** \ˈspat\; **spit•ting 1 :** to eject (saliva) from the mouth **2 :** to express by or as if by spitting **3 :** to rain or snow lightly
⁴spit *n* **1 :** a watery digestive secretion that is secreted into the mouth by salivary glands : SALIVA **2** ♦ **:** perfect likeness ⟨~ and image of his father⟩

♦ carbon copy, counterpart, double, duplicate, duplication, facsimile, image, likeness, match, picture, replica, ringer

spit•ball \ˈspit-ˌbȯl\ *n* **1 :** paper chewed and rolled into a ball to be thrown as a missile **2 :** a baseball pitch delivered after the ball has been moistened with saliva or sweat
¹spite \ˈspīt\ *n* ♦ **:** ill will with a wish to annoy, anger, or frustrate : petty malice — **in spite of :** in defiance or contempt of : NOTWITHSTANDING

♦ cattiness, despite, hatefulness, malice, malignity, meanness, nastiness, spleen, venom, viciousness

²spite *vb* **spit•ed; spit•ing** ♦ **:** to treat maliciously : ANNOY, OFFEND

♦ aggravate, annoy, bother, bug, chafe, exasperate, gall, get, grate, irk, irritate, nettle, peeve, persecute, pique, put out, rasp, rile, ruffle, vex

spite•ful \-fəl\ *adj* ♦ **:** filled with or showing spite — **spite•ful•ness** *n*

♦ catty, cruel, hateful, malevolent, malicious, malign, malignant, mean, nasty, virulent

spite•ful•ly *adv* ♦ **:** filled with or showing spite

♦ hatefully, maliciously, meanly, nastily, viciously, wickedly

spit•tle \ˈspit-ᵊl\ *n* **:** a watery digestive secretion that is secreted into the mouth by salivary glands : SALIVA
spit•tle•bug \-ˌbəg\ *n* **:** any of a family of leaping insects with froth-secreting larvae that are related to aphids
spit•toon \spi-ˈtün\ *n* **:** a receptacle for spit
spit up *vb* ♦ **:** to disgorge (the contents of the stomach) through the mouth

♦ gag, heave, throw up, vomit

splash \ˈsplash\ *vb* **1** ♦ **:** to dash a liquid about **2 :** to scatter a liquid on : SPATTER **3 :** to fall, move, or strike with a splashing noise — **splash** *n*

♦ [1] lap, plash, slosh, swash ♦ [2] dash, plash, spatter

splash•down \ˈsplash-ˌdau̇n\ *n* **:** the landing of a manned spacecraft in the ocean — **splash down** *vb*
splashy \ˈspla-shē\ *adj* **splash•i•er; -est :** conspicuously showy : OSTENTATIOUS

splat•ter \ˈspla-tər\ *vb* : to splash with or as if with a liquid : SPATTER — **splatter** *n*
¹splay \ˈsplā\ *vb* : to spread outward or apart — **splay** *n*
²splay *adj* **1** : spread out : turned outward **2** : AWKWARD, CLUMSY
spleen \ˈsplēn\ *n* **1** : a vascular organ located near the stomach in most vertebrates that is concerned especially with the filtration and storage of blood, destruction of red blood cells, and production of lymphocytes **2** ♦ : feelings of anger or ill will often suppressed

♦ anger, cattiness, despite, hatefulness, malice, malignity, meanness, nastiness, spite, venom, viciousness

splen•did \ˈsplen-dəd\ *adj* **1** : SHINING, BRILLIANT **2** : SHOWY, GORGEOUS **3** ♦ : fine or imposing in appearance or impression **4** : very good of its kind : EXCELLENT

♦ august, baronial, gallant, glorious, grand, grandiose, heroic, imposing, magnificent, majestic, monumental, noble, proud, regal, royal, stately

splen•did•ly *adv* ♦ : in a splendid manner

♦ agreeably, delightfully, favorably (*or* favourably), felicitously, gloriously, nicely, pleasantly, pleasingly, satisfyingly, well

splen•dor *or Can and Brit* **splen•dour** \ˈsplen-dər\ *n* **1** ♦ : great brightness or luster : BRILLIANCE **2** ♦ : a display of magnificence

♦ [1] brilliance, dazzle, effulgence, illumination, lightness, lucidity, luminosity, radiance, refulgence ♦ [2] augustness, brilliance, glory, grandeur, grandness, magnificence, majesty, nobility, nobleness, resplendence, stateliness

sple•net•ic \spli-ˈne-tik\ *adj* ♦ : marked by bad temper or spite

♦ bearish, bilious, cantankerous, disagreeable, dyspeptic, ill-humored, ill-tempered, ornery, surly

splen•ic \ˈsple-nik\ *adj* : of, relating to, or located in the spleen
splice \ˈsplīs\ *vb* **spliced; splic•ing 1** : to unite (as two ropes) by weaving the strands together **2** : to unite (as two lengths of film) by connecting the ends together — **splice** *n*
splint \ˈsplint\ *n* **1** : a thin strip of wood interwoven with others to make something (as a basket) **2** : material or a device used to protect and keep in place an injured body part (as a broken arm) **3** : a thin piece split or broken off lengthwise
¹splin•ter \ˈsplin-tər\ *n* ♦ : a thin piece of something split off lengthwise : SLIVER

♦ chip, flake

²splinter *vb* : to split into splinters
¹split \ˈsplit\ *vb* **split; split•ting 1** : to divide lengthwise or along a grain or seam **2** : to burst or break in pieces **3** ♦ : to divide into parts or sections **4** : LEAVE

♦ break up, disconnect, disjoint, dissever, dissociate, disunite, divide, divorce, part, resolve, separate, sever, sunder, unyoke

²split *n* **1** ♦ : a narrow break made by or as if by splitting **2** ♦ : the act or process of splitting

♦ [1] chink, cleft, crack, cranny, crevice, fissure, rift ♦ [2] breakup, dissolution, division, partition, schism, separation

split–lev•el \ˈsplit-ˈle-vəl\ *n* : a house divided so that the floor in one part is about halfway between two floors in the other
split personality *n* : SCHIZOPHRENIA; *also* : MULTIPLE PERSONALITY DISORDER
split–second \ˈsplit-ˈse-kənd\ *adj* **1** ♦ : occurring in a very brief time **2** : extremely precise ⟨∼ timing⟩

♦ immediate, instant, instantaneous, straightaway

split•ting *adj* : causing a piercing sensation ⟨a ∼ headache⟩
splotch \ˈsplāch\ *n* : a small area visibly different (as in color, finish, or material) from the surrounding area : BLOTCH
splurge \ˈsplərj\ *vb* **splurged; splurg•ing** : to spend more than usual especially on oneself — **splurge** *n*
splut•ter \ˈsplə-tər\ *n* : SPUTTER — **splutter** *vb*
¹spoil \ˈspȯil\ *n* ♦ : plunder taken from an enemy in war or from a victim in robbery ⟨∼*s* of war⟩

♦ booty, loot, plunder, swag

²spoil *vb* **spoiled** \ˈspȯild, ˈspȯilt\ *or* **spoilt** \ˈspȯilt\; **spoil•ing 1** : ROB, PILLAGE **2** : to damage seriously : RUIN **3** ♦ : to impair the quality or effect of **4** ♦ : to damage the disposition of by pampering; *also* : INDULGE, CODDLE **5** ♦ : to lose valuable or useful qualities usually as a result of decay : DECAY, ROT **6** : to have an eager desire ⟨∼*ing* for a fight⟩

♦ [3] blemish, mar, poison, stain, taint, tarnish, touch, vitiate ♦ [4] baby, coddle, indulge, mollycoddle, nurse, pamper ♦ [5] break down, corrupt, decay, decompose, disintegrate, molder, putrefy, rot

spoil•age \ˈspȯi-lij\ *n* ♦ : the act or process of spoiling

♦ breakdown, corruption, decay, decomposition, putrefaction, rot

spoil•er \ˈspȯi-lər\ *n* **1** : one that spoils **2** : a device (as on an airplane or automobile) used to disrupt airflow and decrease lift
spoil•sport \ˈspȯil-ˌspȯrt\ *n* : one who spoils the fun of others
¹spoke \ˈspōk\ *past & archaic past part of* SPEAK
²spoke *n* : any of the rods extending from the hub of a wheel to the rim
spo•ken *adj* ♦ : delivered by word of mouth; *also* : characterized by speaking in (such) a manner

♦ oral, unwritten, verbal

spokes•man \ˈspōks-mən\ *n* ♦ : a person who speaks as the representative of another or others

♦ mouthpiece, speaker, spokesperson, spokeswoman

spokes•per•son \-ˌpər-sən\ *n* ♦ : a person who speaks as the representative of another or others : SPOKESMAN

♦ mouthpiece, speaker, spokesman, spokeswoman

spokes•wom•an \-ˌwu̇-mən\ *n* ♦ : a woman who speaks as the representative of another or others

♦ mouthpiece, speaker, spokesman, spokesperson

spo•li•a•tion \ˌspō-lē-ˈā-shən\ *n* : the act of plundering : the state of being plundered
¹sponge \ˈspənj\ *n* **1** : an elastic porous water-absorbing mass of fibers that forms the skeleton of various primitive sea animals; *also* : any of a phylum of chiefly marine sea animals that are the source of natural sponges **2** : a spongelike or porous mass or material **3** ♦ : one who lives on others

♦ hanger-on, leech, parasite

²sponge *vb* **sponged; spong•ing 1** : to bathe or wipe with a sponge **2** : to live at another's expense **3** : to gather sponges **4** ♦ : to absorb with or as if with or in the manner of a sponge

♦ absorb, drink, imbibe, soak, suck

sponge cake *n* : a light cake made without shortening
spong•er *n* : one that sponges
sponge rubber *n* : a cellular rubber resembling natural sponge
spongy \ˈspən-jē\ *adj* **1** : resembling a sponge **2** ♦ : not firm or solid

♦ flabby, mushy, pulpy, soft

spon•sor \ˈspän-sər\ *n* **1** ♦ : one who takes the responsibility for some other person or thing : SURETY **2** : GODPARENT **3** : a business firm that pays the cost of a radio or television program usually in return for advertising time during its course — **sponsor** *vb* — **spon•sor•ship** *n*

♦ backer, guarantor, patron, surety

spon•ta•ne•ity \ˌspän-tə-ˈnē-ə-tē, -ˈnā-\ *n* ♦ : the quality or state of being spontaneous

♦ abandon, abandonment, ease, lightheartedness, naturalness, unrestraint

spon•ta•ne•ous \spän-ˈtā-nē-əs\ *adj* **1** ♦ : done or produced freely or naturally **2** : acting or taking place without external force or cause — **spon•ta•ne•ous•ly** *adv*

♦ automatic, involuntary, mechanical, natural

spontaneous combustion *n* : a bursting into flame of material through heat produced within itself by chemical action (as oxidation)
¹spoof \ˈspüf\ *vb* **1** : DECEIVE, HOAX **2** : to make good-natured fun of — **spoof** *n*
²spoof *n* ♦ : a light humorous parody

♦ burlesque, caricature, parody, takeoff

¹spook \ˈspük\ *n* **1** : a disembodied soul : GHOST **2** : SPY 2
²spook *vb* ♦ : to make frightened or frantic : FRIGHTEN

♦ alarm, frighten, horrify, panic, scare, shock, startle, terrify, terrorize

spooky *adj* **1** ♦ : relating to, resembling, or suggesting spooks **2** ♦ : easily frightened

♦ [1] creepy, eerie, haunting, uncanny, unearthly, weird ♦ [2] excitable, flighty, fluttery, high-strung, jittery, jumpy, nervous, skittish

spool \ˈspül\ *n* : a cylinder on which flexible material (as thread) is wound
1**spoon** \ˈspün\ *n* **1** ♦ : an eating or cooking implement consisting of a small shallow bowl with a handle **2** : a metal piece used on a fishing line as a lure — **spoon•ful** *n*

♦ ladle, scoop

2**spoon** *vb* ♦ : to take up and usually transfer in a spoon

♦ dip, ladle, scoop

spoon•bill \ˈspün-ˌbil\ *n* : any of several wading birds related to the ibises that have a bill with a broad flat tip
spoon–feed \-ˌfēd\ *vb* **-fed** \-ˌfed\; **-feed•ing** : to feed by means of a spoon
spoor \ˈspu̇r, ˈspōr\ *n, pl* **spoor** *or* **spoors** : a track, a trail, a scent, or droppings especially of a wild animal
spo•rad•ic \spə-ˈra-dik\ *adj* ♦ : occurring now and then — **spo•rad•i•cal•ly** \-di-k(ə-)lē\ *adv*

♦ casual, choppy, discontinuous, erratic, fitful, intermittent, irregular, occasional, spasmodic, spotty, unsteady

spore \ˈspōr\ *n* : a primitive usually one-celled often environmentally resistant dormant or reproductive body produced by plants, fungi, and some microorganisms
1**sport** \ˈspōrt\ *vb* **1** ♦ : to amuse oneself : FROLIC **2** ♦ : to display or wear usually ostentatiously : SHOW OFF

♦ [1] caper, cavort, disport, frisk, frolic, gambol, lark, play, rollick, romp ♦ [2] display, disport, exhibit, expose, flash, flaunt, parade, show, show off, strut, unveil

2**sport** *n* **1** ♦ : a source of diversion **2** : physical activity engaged in for pleasure **3** : a frivolous mood or manner : JEST **4** : MOCKERY ⟨make ~ of his efforts⟩ **5** : BUTT, LAUGHINGSTOCK **6** : one who accepts results cheerfully whether favorable or not **7** : an individual exhibiting marked deviation from its normal type especially as a result of mutation — **sporty** *adj*

♦ dalliance, frolic, fun, play, relaxation

3**sport** *or* **sports** *adj* : of, relating to, or suitable for sport or casual wear ⟨~ coats⟩
sport fish *n* : a fish noted for the sport it affords anglers
sport•ive \ˈspȯr-tiv\ *adj* ♦ : full of gaiety : full of play

♦ antic, coltish, elfish, fay, frisky, frolicsome, playful

sports•cast \ˈspōrts-ˌkast\ *n* : a broadcast dealing with sports events — **sports•cast•er** \-ˌkas-tər\ *n*
sports•man \ˈspōrts-mən\ *n* **1** : a person who engages in sports (as in hunting or fishing) **2** : one who plays fairly and wins or loses gracefully — **sports•man•ship** *n*
sports•man•like \-ˌlīk\ *adj* ♦ : consistent with the ideals of good sportsmanship

♦ clean, fair, legal

sports medicine *n* : a field of medicine dealing with the prevention and treatment of sports-related injuries
sports•wom•an \-ˌwu̇-mən\ *n* : a woman who engages in sports
sports•writ•er \-ˌrī-tər\ *n* : one who writes about sports especially for a newspaper — **sports•writ•ing** *n*
sport–util•ity vehicle \ˈspȯrt-yü-ˈti-lə-tē-\ *n* : SUV
1**spot** \ˈspät\ *n* **1** : a taint on character or reputation : STAIN **2** ♦ : a small part different (as in color) from the main part **3** ♦ : a particular place, area, or part : LOCATION **4** ♦ : a position usually of difficulty or embarrassment **5** : a small quantity or amount — **on the spot** **1** : at the place of action **2** : in difficulty or danger

♦ [2] blotch, dapple, dot, fleck, mottle, patch, point, speck ♦ [3] locale, location, place, point, position, site ♦ [4] corner, fix, hole, jam, pickle, predicament

2**spot** *vb* **spot•ted; spot•ting** **1** ♦ : to mark or disfigure with spots **2** : to pick out : RECOGNIZE, IDENTIFY

♦ blotch, dapple, dot, fleck, freckle, mottle, pepper, speck, sprinkle, stipple

3**spot** *adj* **1** : being, done, or originating on the spot ⟨a ~ broadcast⟩ **2** : paid upon delivery **3** : made at random or at a few key points ⟨a ~ check⟩
spot–check \ˈspät-ˌchek\ *vb* : to make a spot check of
spot•less *adj* ♦ : having no spot : free from impurity, fault, or stain — **spot•less•ly** *adv*

♦ clean, immaculate, spick-and-span, stainless, unsoiled, unsullied

spot•light \-ˌlīt\ *n* **1** : a circle of brilliant light projected upon a particular area, person, or object (as on a stage); *also* : the device that produces this light **2** : public notice — **spotlight** *vb*
spot–on \ˈspät-ˈän\ *adj* : exactly correct ⟨a ~ forecast⟩
spotted *adj* ♦ : having spots

♦ dappled, mottled, pied, spotty, variegated

spotted owl *n* : a rare large dark brown dark-eyed owl of humid old growth forests and thickly wooded canyons from British Columbia to southern California and central Mexico
spot•ter \ˈspä-tər\ *n* **1** : one that keeps watch : OBSERVER **2** : one that removes spots
spot•ty \ˈspä-tē\ *adj* **spot•ti•er; -est** **1** ♦ : uneven in quality; *also* : sparsely distributed ⟨~ attendance⟩ **2** : marked with spots : SPOTTED

♦ casual, choppy, discontinuous, erratic, fitful, intermittent, irregular, occasional, spasmodic, sporadic, unsteady

spou•sal \ˈspau̇-zəl, -səl\ *n* : MARRIAGE 2, WEDDING — usually used in plural
spouse \ˈspau̇s\ *n* ♦ : one's partner in a marriage (as husband or wife) — **spou•sal** \ˈspau̇-zəl, -səl\ *adj*

♦ consort, mate, partner

1**spout** \ˈspau̇t\ *vb* **1** ♦ : to eject or issue forth forcibly and freely ⟨wells ~*ing* oil⟩ **2** ♦ : to speak pompously **3** ♦ : to speak or utter readily, volubly, and at length

♦ [1] gush, jet, pour, rush, spew, spurt, squirt ♦ [1] belch, disgorge, eject, erupt, expel ♦ [2, 3] bluster, fulminate, rant, rave ♦ *usu* **spout off** [3] sound off, speak out, speak up

2**spout** *n* **1** : a pipe or hole through which liquid spouts **2** : a jet of liquid; *esp* : WATERSPOUT 2
spp *abbr, pl* species
1**sprain** \ˈsprān\ *n* : a sudden or severe twisting of a joint with stretching or tearing of ligaments; *also* : a sprained condition
2**sprain** *vb* : to subject to sprain
sprat \ˈsprat\ *n* : a small European fish related to the herring; *also* : SARDINE
sprawl \ˈsprȯl\ *vb* **1** : to lie or sit with limbs spread out awkwardly **2** : to spread out irregularly — **sprawl** *n*
1**spray** \ˈsprā\ *n* : a usually flowering branch; *also* : a decorative arrangement of flowers and foliage
2**spray** *n* **1** : liquid flying in small drops like water blown from a wave **2** : a jet of fine vapor (as from an atomizer) **3** : an instrument (as an atomizer) for scattering fine liquid
3**spray** *vb* **1** ♦ : to scatter or let fall in a spray **2** : to discharge spray on or into — **spray•er** *n*

♦ dot, pepper, scatter, sow, sprinkle, strew

spray can *n* : a pressurized container from which aerosols are sprayed
spray gun *n* : a device for spraying liquids (as paint or insecticide)
1**spread** \ˈspred\ *vb* **spread; spread•ing** **1** : to scatter over a surface **2** ♦ : to flatten out : open out **3** ♦ : to distribute over a period of time or among many persons **4** : to cover something with ⟨~ rugs on the floor⟩ **5** : to prepare for a meal ⟨~ a table⟩ **6** ♦ : to pass on from person to person **7** : to stretch, force, or push apart **8** ♦ : to make widely known — **spread•er** *n*

♦ *usu* **spread out** [2] expand, extend, fan, flare, open, stretch, unfold ♦ [3] broadcast, circulate, disseminate, propagate, strew ♦ [6, 8] communicate, convey, impart, transfer, transfuse, transmit

2**spread** *n* **1** : the act or process of spreading **2** ♦ : a surface area : EXPANSE **3** : a prominent display in a periodical **4** : a food to be spread on bread or crackers **5** ♦ : a cloth cover for a bed **6** ♦ : distance between two points **7** ♦ : a sumptuous meal

♦ [2] breadth, expanse, extent, reach, stretch ♦ [5] bedspread, counterpane ♦ [6] distance, lead, length, remove, stretch, way ♦ [7] banquet, dinner, feast, feed

spread•sheet \ˈspred-ˌshēt\ *n* : an accounting program for a computer
spree \ˈsprē\ *n* : an unrestrained outburst ⟨buying ~⟩; *also* : a drinking bout
sprig \ˈsprig\ *n* : a small shoot or twig
spright•li•ness \ˈsprīt-lē-nes\ *n* ♦ : the quality or state of being sprightly

♦ animation, briskness, exuberance, liveliness, lustiness, robustness, vibrancy, vitality

spright•ly \ˈsprīt-lē\ *adj* **spright•li•er; -est** ♦ : marked by a gay lightness and vivacity : LIVELY

♦ active, animate, animated, brisk, energetic, frisky, gay, lively, peppy, spirited, springy, vital, vivacious

[1]**spring** \ˈspriŋ\ *vb* **sprang** \ˈspraŋ\ *or* **sprung** \ˈsprəŋ\; **sprung; spring•ing** **1** ♦ **:** to move suddenly upward or forward **2 :** to grow quickly ⟨weeds *sprang* up overnight⟩ **3 :** to come from by birth or descent **4 :** to move quickly by elastic force **5 :** WARP **6 :** to develop (a leak) through the seams **7 :** to cause to close suddenly ⟨~ a trap⟩ **8 :** to make known suddenly ⟨~ a surprise⟩ **9 :** to make lame **:** STRAIN **10** ♦ **:** to come into being **11** ♦ **:** to release or cause to be released from confinement or custody **12** ♦ **:** to discharge indebtedness for — used with *for*

♦ [1] bound, hop, jump, leap, vault ♦ [10] arise, begin, commence, dawn, form, materialize, originate, start ♦ *usu* **spring up** [10] crop, emerge, surface ♦ [11] discharge, emancipate, enfranchise, free, liberate, loose, loosen, manumit, release, unbind, unchain, unfetter ♦ *usu* **spring for** [12] clear, discharge, foot, liquidate, pay, pay off, quit, recompense, settle, stand

[2]**spring** *n* **1 :** a source of supply; *esp* **:** an issuing of water from the ground **2 :** SOURCE, ORIGIN; *also* **:** MOTIVE **3 :** the season between winter and summer **4 :** an elastic body or device that recovers its original shape when it is released after being distorted **5** ♦ **:** the act or an instance of leaping up or forward **6 :** RESILIENCE

♦ bound, hop, jump, leap, vault

spring•board \ˈspriŋ-ˌbōrd\ *n* **:** a springy board used in jumping or vaulting or for diving

spring fever *n* **:** a lazy or restless feeling often associated with the onset of spring

spring tide *n* **:** a tide of greater-than-average range that occurs at each new moon and full moon

spring•time \ˈspriŋ-ˌtīm\ *n* **:** the season of spring

springy *adj* **1** ♦ **:** having an elastic quality **2** ♦ **:** having or showing a lively and energetic movement

♦ [1] elastic, flexible, resilient, rubbery, stretch, supple ♦ [2] active, animate, animated, brisk, energetic, lively, spirited, sprightly

[1]**sprin•kle** \ˈspriŋ-kəl\ *vb* **sprin•kled; sprin•kling** ♦ **:** to scatter in small drops or particles — **sprin•kler** *n*

♦ dot, pepper, scatter, sow, spray, strew

[2]**sprinkle** *n* **1 :** a light rainfall **2** ♦ **:** a small number especially distributed at random

♦ few, handful, smattering, sprinkling

sprin•kling *n* ♦ **:** a limited quantity or amount **:** SMATTERING

♦ few, handful, smattering, sprinkle

[1]**sprint** \ˈsprint\ *vb* ♦ **:** to run at top speed especially for a short distance — **sprint•er** *n*

♦ dash, gallop, jog, run, scamper, trip

[2]**sprint** *n* **1 :** a short run at top speed **2 :** a short distance race

sprite \ˈsprīt\ *n* **1 :** GHOST, SPIRIT **2 :** a small often mischievous fairy **:** ELF

spritz *vb* **:** SPRAY

sprock•et \ˈsprä-kət\ *n* **:** a toothed wheel whose teeth engage the links of a chain

[1]**sprout** \ˈspraut\ *vb* **:** to send out new growth ⟨~*ing* seeds⟩

[2]**sprout** *n* **:** a usually young and growing plant shoot (as from a seed)

[1]**spruce** \ˈsprüs\ *vb* **spruced; spruc•ing :** to make or become spruce

[2]**spruce** *adj* **spruc•er; spruc•est** ♦ **:** neat and smart in appearance

♦ dapper, natty, sharp, smart

[3]**spruce** *n, pl* **spruc•es** *also* **spruce :** any of a genus of evergreen pyramid-shaped trees related to the pines and having soft light wood; *also* **:** the wood of a spruce

sprung *past and past part of* SPRING

spry \ˈsprī\ *adj* **spri•er** *or* **spry•er** \ˈsprī-ər\; **spri•est** *or* **spry•est** \ˈsprī-əst\ ♦ **:** quick and light in motion **:** NIMBLE

♦ agile, graceful, light, lissome, lithe, nimble

spud \ˈspəd\ *n* **1 :** a sharp narrow spade **2 :** POTATO

spume \ˈspyüm\ *n* ♦ **:** frothy matter on liquids **:** FOAM — **spumy** \ˈspyü-mē\ *adj*

♦ foam, froth, head, lather

spu•mo•ni *also* **spu•mo•ne** \spu̇-ˈmō-nē\ *n* **:** ice cream in layers of different colors, flavors, and textures often with candied fruits and nuts

spun *past and past part of* SPIN

spun glass *n* **:** FIBERGLASS

spunk \ˈspəŋk\ *n* ♦ **:** vigor and strength of spirit or temperament **:** PLUCK

♦ backbone, fiber (*or* fibre), fortitude, grit, guts, pluck

spunky *adj* ♦ **:** full of spunk

♦ fiery, high-spirited, mettlesome, peppery, spirited

[1]**spur** \ˈspər\ *n* **1 :** a pointed device fastened to a rider's boot and used to urge on a horse **2** ♦ **:** something that urges to action **3 :** a stiff sharp spine (as on the leg of a cock); *also* **:** a hollow projecting appendage of a flower (as a columbine) **4 :** a ridge extending sideways from a mountain **5 :** a branch of railroad track extending from the main line — **spurred** \ˈspərd\ *adj* — **on the spur of the moment :** on hasty impulse

♦ boost, encouragement, goad, impetus, impulse, incentive, incitement, instigation, momentum, motivation, provocation, stimulus, yeast

[2]**spur** *vb* **spurred; spur•ring** **1 :** to urge a horse on with spurs **2 :** INCITE

spurge \ˈspərj\ *n* **:** any of a family of herbs and woody plants with a bitter milky juice

spu•ri•ous \ˈspyu̇r-ē-əs\ *adj* ♦ **:** not genuine **:** FALSE

♦ affected, artificial, assumed, bogus, contrived, factitious, fake, false, feigned, mechanical, mock, phony, put-on, sham, unnatural

spurn \ˈspərn\ *vb* **1 :** to kick away or trample on **2** ♦ **:** to reject with disdain

♦ decline, disallow, disapprove, negative, refuse, reject, repudiate, turn down

[1]**spurt** \ˈspərt\ *vb* ♦ **:** to gush out **:** SPOUT

♦ gush, jet, pour, rush, spew, spout, squirt

[2]**spurt** *n* **:** a sudden gushing or spouting

[3]**spurt** *n* **1 :** a sudden brief burst of effort, speed, or development **2** ♦ **:** a sharp increase of activity ⟨~ in sales⟩

♦ burst, flare, flare-up, flash, flurry, flutter, outbreak, outburst

[4]**spurt** *vb* **:** to make a spurt

sput•ter \ˈspə-tər\ *vb* **1 :** to spit small scattered particles **:** SPLUTTER **2** ♦ **:** to utter words hastily or explosively in excitement or confusion **3 :** to make small popping sounds — **sputter** *n*

♦ babble, chatter, drivel, gabble, gibber, jabber, prattle

spu•tum \ˈspyü-təm\ *n, pl* **spu•ta** \-tə\ **:** material (as phlegm) that is spit out or coughed up especially during illness

[1]**spy** \ˈspī\ *vb* **spied; spy•ing** **1 :** to watch or search for information secretly **:** act as a spy **2** ♦ **:** to get a momentary or quick glimpse of **:** SEE

♦ behold, descry, discern, distinguish, espy, eye, look, note, notice, observe, perceive, regard, remark, see, sight, view, witness

[2]**spy** *n, pl* **spies** **1 :** one who secretly watches others **2 :** a secret agent who tries to get information for one country in the territory of an enemy

spy•glass \ˈspī-ˌglas\ *n* **:** a small telescope

sq *abbr* **1** squadron **2** square

squab \ˈskwäb\ *n, pl* **squabs** *or* **squab :** a young bird and especially a pigeon

[1]**squab•ble** \ˈskwä-bəl\ *n* ♦ **:** a noisy altercation **:** WRANGLE

♦ altercation, argument, bicker, brawl, disagreement, dispute, fight, hassle, misunderstanding, quarrel, row, scrap, spat, wrangle

[2]**squabble** *vb* ♦ **:** to quarrel noisily and usually over petty matters

♦ argue, bicker, brawl, dispute, fall out, fight, hassle, quarrel, row, scrap, spat, wrangle

squad \ˈskwäd\ *n* **1 :** a small organized group of military personnel **2** ♦ **:** a small group engaged in a common effort

♦ band, company, crew, gang, outfit, party, team

squad car *n* **:** a police car connected by two-way radio with headquarters

squad•ron \ˈskwä-drən\ *n* **:** any of several units of military organization

squal•id \ˈskwä-ləd\ *adj* **1 :** filthy or degraded through neglect or poverty **2 :** SORDID, DEBASED

squall \ˈskwȯl\ *n* **1 :** a sudden violent gust of wind often with rain or snow **2 :** a short-lived commotion

squally *adj* ♦ **:** marked by squalls

♦ bleak, dirty, foul, inclement, nasty, raw, rough, stormy, tempestuous, turbulent

squa•lor \ˈskwä-lər\ *n* **:** the quality or state of being squalid
squan•der \ˈskwän-dər\ *vb* ♦ **:** to spend wastefully or foolishly

♦ blow, dissipate, fritter, lavish, misspend, run through, spend, throw away, waste

¹square \ˈskwar\ *n* **1 :** an instrument used to lay out or test right angles **2 :** a rectangle with all four sides equal **3 :** something square **4 :** the product of a number multiplied by itself **5 :** an area bounded by four streets **6 :** an open area in a city where streets meet **7 :** a highly conventional person
²square *adj* **squar•er; squar•est 1 :** having four equal sides and four right angles **2 :** forming a right angle ⟨cut a ~ corner⟩ **3 :** multiplied by itself **:** SQUARED ⟨x^2 is the symbol for *x* ~⟩ **4 :** being a unit of square measure equal to a square each side of which measures one unit ⟨a ~ foot⟩ **5 :** being of a specified length in each of two dimensions ⟨an area 10 feet ~⟩ **6 :** exactly adjusted **7** ♦ **:** marked by impartiality and honesty **:** JUST ⟨a ~ deal⟩ **8 :** leaving no balance ⟨make accounts ~⟩ **9 :** SUBSTANTIAL ⟨a ~ meal⟩ **10 :** highly conservative or conventional

♦ disinterested, dispassionate, equal, equitable, fair, impartial, just, nonpartisan, objective, unbiased, unprejudiced

³square *vb* **squared; squar•ing 1 :** to form with four equal sides and right angles or with flat surfaces ⟨~ a timber⟩ **2 :** to multiply (a number) by itself **3** ♦ **:** to agree precisely **:** CONFORM **4 :** BALANCE, SETTLE ⟨~ an account⟩

♦ accord, agree, answer, check, coincide, comport, conform, correspond, dovetail, fit, go, harmonize, jibe, tally

square dance *n* **:** a dance for four couples arranged to form a square
square•ly *adv* ♦ **:** in a manner or measure or to a degree or number that strictly conforms to a fact or condition

♦ accurately, exactly, just, precisely, right, sharp

square measure *n* **:** a unit or system of units for measuring area
square–rigged \ˈskwar-ˈrigd\ *adj* **:** having the chief sails extended on yards that are fastened to the masts horizontally and at their center
square–rig•ger \-ˌri-gər\ *n* **:** a square-rigged craft
square root *n* **:** either of the two numbers whose squares are equal to a given number ⟨the *square root* of 9 is +3 or −3⟩
¹squash \ˈskwäsh, ˈskwȯsh\ *vb* **1** ♦ **:** to beat or press into a pulp or flat mass **2** ♦ **:** to bring to an end **:** QUASH

♦ [1] crush, mash ♦ [2] clamp down, crack down, crush, put down, quash, quell, repress, silence, snuff, squelch, subdue, suppress

²squash *n* **1 :** the impact of something soft and heavy; *also* **:** the sound of such impact **2 :** a crushed mass **3 :** a game played on a 4-wall court with a racket and rubber ball
³squash *n, pl* **squash•es** *or* **squash :** any of various fruits of plants of the gourd family that are used especially as vegetables; *also* **:** a plant and especially a vine bearing squashes
squash racquets *n* **:** SQUASH 3
¹squat \ˈskwät\ *vb* **squat•ted; squat•ting 1** ♦ **:** to sit down upon the hams or heels **2 :** to settle on land without right or title; *also* **:** to settle on public land with a view to acquiring title — **squat•ter** *n*

♦ crouch, huddle, hunch

²squat *n* **:** the act or posture of squatting
³squat *adj* **squat•ter; squat•test 1 :** low to the ground **2** ♦ **:** short and thick in stature

♦ chunky, dumpy, heavyset, stocky, stout, stubby, stumpy, thickset

squawk \ˈskwȯk\ *n* ♦ **:** a harsh loud cry; *also* **:** a noisy protest — **squawk** *vb*

♦ beef, complaint, fuss, grievance, gripe, grumble, murmur, plaint

squeak \ˈskwēk\ *vb* **1** ♦ **:** to utter or speak in a weak shrill tone **2 :** to make a thin high-pitched sound — **squeak** *n*

♦ cheep, peep, squeal

squeaky *adj* ♦ **:** of the nature of, emitting, or tending to emit squeaks

♦ acute, sharp, shrill, treble

¹squeal \ˈskwēl\ *vb* **1** ♦ **:** to make a shrill sound or cry **2** ♦ **:** to betray a secret or turn informer **3 :** COMPLAIN, PROTEST

♦ [1] howl, scream, shriek, shrill, yell, yelp ♦ [2] inform, snitch, talk, tell

²squeal *n* **:** a shrill sharp cry or noise
squea•mish \ˈskwē-mish\ *adj* **1** ♦ **:** easily nauseated; *also* **:** NAUSEATED **2** ♦ **:** easily disgusted

♦ [1] ill, nauseous, queasy, queer, sick ♦ [2] disgusted, sick

squea•mish•ness *n* ♦ **:** the quality or state of being squeamish

♦ nausea, queasiness, sickness

squee•gee \ˈskwē-ˌjē\ *n* **:** a blade set crosswise on a handle and used for spreading or wiping liquid on, across, or off a surface — **squeegee** *vb*
¹squeeze \ˈskwēz\ *vb* **squeezed; squeez•ing 1** ♦ **:** to exert pressure on the opposite sides or parts of **:** COMPRESS **2** ♦ **:** to obtain by pressure ⟨~ juice from a lemon⟩ **3** ♦ **:** to force, thrust, or cause to pass by pressure **4 :** to pass, win, or get by narrowly **5 :** to get or deprive by extortion — **squeez•er** *n*

♦ [1] compact, compress, condense, constrict, contract ♦ [2] crush, express, mash, press ♦ [3] cram, crowd, jam, ram, sandwich, stuff, wedge

²squeeze *n* **1 :** an act of squeezing **2 :** a quantity squeezed out **3** *slang* ♦ **:** a romantic partner

♦ beloved, darling, dear, flame, honey, love, sweet, sweetheart

squeeze bottle *n* **:** a flexible plastic bottle that dispenses its contents when it is squeezed
squelch \ˈskwelch\ *vb* **1** ♦ **:** to suppress completely **:** CRUSH **2 :** to move in soft mud — **squelch** *n*

♦ clamp down, crack down, crush, put down, quash, quell, repress, silence, snuff, squash, subdue, suppress

squib \ˈskwib\ *n* **:** a brief witty writing or speech
squid \ˈskwid\ *n, pl* **squid** *or* **squids :** any of an order of long-bodied sea mollusks having eight short arms and two longer tentacles and usually a slender internal shell
squint \ˈskwint\ *vb* **1 :** to look or aim obliquely **2 :** to look or peer with the eyes partly closed **3 :** to be cross-eyed — **squint** *n or adj*
¹squire \ˈskwīr\ *n* **1 :** an armor-bearer of a knight **2 :** a man gallantly devoted to a lady **3 :** a member of the British gentry ranking below a knight and above a gentleman; *also* **:** a prominent landowner **4 :** a local magistrate
²squire *vb* **squired; squir•ing** ♦ **:** to attend as a squire or escort

♦ accompany, attend, convoy, escort

squirm \ˈskwərm\ *vb* ♦ **:** to twist about like a worm **:** WRIGGLE

♦ fiddle, fidget, jerk, twitch, wiggle

¹squir•rel \ˈskwər-əl\ *n, pl* **squirrels** *also* **squirrel :** any of various rodents usually with a long bushy tail and strong hind legs; *also* **:** the fur of a squirrel
²squirrel *vb* **-reled** *or* **-relled; -rel•ing** *or* **-rel•ling :** to store up for future use
¹squirt \ˈskwərt\ *vb* ♦ **:** to eject liquid in a thin spurt

♦ gush, jet, pour, rush, spew, spout, spurt

²squirt *n* **1 :** an instrument (as a syringe) for squirting **2 :** a small forcible jet of liquid
¹Sr *abbr* **1** senior **2** sister
²Sr *symbol* strontium
SR *abbr* seaman recruit
¹SRO \ˌes-(ˌ)är-ˈō\ *n* **:** a house or apartment building in which low-income tenants live in single rooms
²SRO *abbr* standing room only
SS *abbr* **1** saints **2** Social Security **3** steamship **4** sworn statement
SSA *abbr* Social Security Administration
SSE *abbr* south-southeast
SSG *or* **SSgt** *abbr* staff sergeant
SSI *abbr* supplemental security income
SSM *abbr* staff sergeant major
SSN *abbr* Social Security Number
ssp *abbr* subspecies
SSR *abbr* Soviet Socialist Republic
SSS *abbr* Selective Service System
SST \ˌes-(ˌ)es-ˈtē\ *n* **:** a supersonic passenger airplane
SSW *abbr* south-southwest
st *abbr* **1** stanza **2** state **3** stitch **4** stone **5** street
St *abbr* saint
ST *abbr* **1** short ton **2** standard time
sta *abbr* station; stationary

[1]stab \ˈstab\ *n* **1** ♦ **:** a wound produced by a pointed weapon **2 :** a quick thrust **3** ♦ **:** a brief attempt

♦ [1] perforation, pinhole, prick, punch, puncture ♦ [3] attempt, crack, endeavor (*or* endeavour), essay, fling, go, pass, shot, trial, try, whack

[2]stab *vb* **stabbed; stab•bing 1** ♦ **:** to pierce or wound with or as if with a pointed weapon **2 :** THRUST, DRIVE

♦ gore, harpoon, impale, lance, pierce, puncture, skewer, spear, spike, stick, transfix

sta•bile \ˈstā-ˌbēl\ *n* **:** an abstract sculpture or construction similar to a mobile but made to be stationary

sta•bil•i•ty \stə-ˈbi-lə-tē\ *n* ♦ **:** the quality, state, or degree of being stable **:** the strength to stand or endure

♦ firmness, soundness, steadiness, strength, sturdiness ***Ant*** instability, unsoundness, unsteadiness ♦ constancy, fixedness, immutability, steadiness

sta•bi•lize \ˈstā-bə-ˌlīz\ *vb* **-lized; -liz•ing 1 :** to make stable **2 :** to hold steady ⟨~ prices⟩ — **sta•bi•li•za•tion** \ˌstā-bə-lə-ˈzā-shən\ *n* — **sta•bi•liz•er** \ˈstā-bə-ˌlī-zər\ *n*

[1]sta•ble \ˈstā-bəl\ *n* **:** a building in which domestic animals are sheltered and fed — **sta•ble•man** \-mən, -ˌman\ *n*

[2]stable *vb* **sta•bled; sta•bling :** to put or keep in a stable

[3]stable *adj* **sta•bler; sta•blest 1 a** ♦ **:** firmly established **b** ♦ **:** mentally and emotionally healthy **2** ♦ **:** steady in purpose **:** CONSTANT **3** ♦ **:** continuing or enduring without fundamental or marked change **4** ♦ **:** resistant to chemical or physical change

♦ [1a] certain, determinate, final, firm, fixed, flat, frozen, hard, hard-and-fast, set, settled ♦ [1b] balanced, clearheaded, lucid, normal, right, sane ***Ant*** unsound, unstable, unsteady ♦ [2, 3] constant, stationary, steady, unchanging, unvarying ♦ [3, 4] fast, firm, sound, stalwart, steady, strong, sturdy

stac•ca•to \stə-ˈkä-tō\ *adj or adv* **:** cut short so as not to sound connected ⟨~ notes⟩

[1]stack \ˈstak\ *n* **1** ♦ **:** a large pile (as of hay or grain) **2 :** an orderly pile (as of poker chips) **3** ♦ **:** a large quantity **4 :** a vertical pipe **:** SMOKESTACK **5 :** a rack with shelves for storing books

♦ [1] cock, heap, hill, mound, mountain, pile, rick ♦ [3] abundance, deal, gobs, heap, loads, lot, pile, plenty, quantity, scads

[2]stack *vb* **1** ♦ **:** to pile up **2 :** to arrange (cards) secretly for cheating

♦ heap, hill, mound, pile

stack up *vb* ♦ **:** to be equal or alike **:** MEASURE UP — usually used with *against*; *also* **:** to add up

♦ *usu* **stack up against** approach, approximate, compare, measure up

sta•di•um \ˈstā-dē-əm\ *n, pl* **-dia** \-dē-ə\ *or* **-di•ums** ♦ **:** a structure with tiers of seats for spectators built around a field for sports events

♦ bowl, circus, coliseum

[1]staff \ˈstaf\ *n, pl* **staffs** \ˈstafs, ˈstavz\ *or* **staves** \ˈstavz, ˈstāvz\ **1 :** a pole, stick, rod, or bar used for supporting, for measuring, or as a symbol of authority; *also* **:** CLUB, CUDGEL **2 :** something that sustains ⟨bread is the ~ of life⟩ **3 :** the five horizontal lines on which music is written **4** ♦ **:** a body of assistants to an executive **5 :** a group of officers holding no command but having duties concerned with planning and managing

♦ force, help, personnel, pool

[2]staff *vb* **:** to supply with a staff or with workers

staff•er \ˈsta-fər\ *n* **:** a member of a staff (as of a newspaper)

staff sergeant *n* **:** a noncommissioned officer ranking in the army next below a sergeant first class, in the air force next below a technical sergeant, and in the marine corps next below a gunnery sergeant

[1]stag \ˈstag\ *n, pl* **stags** *or* **stag :** an adult male of various large deer

[2]stag *adj* **:** restricted to or intended for men ⟨a ~ party⟩ ⟨~ movies⟩

[3]stag *adv* **:** unaccompanied by a date

[1]stage \ˈstāj\ *n* **1** ♦ **:** a raised platform on which an orator may speak or a play may be presented **2** ♦ **:** the acting profession **:** THEATER **3 :** the scene of a notable action or event **4 a :** a station or resting place on a traveled road **b** ♦ **:** the distance between two stopping places on a road **5 :** STAGECOACH **6** ♦ **:** a degree of advance in an undertaking, process, or development **7 :** a propulsion unit in a rocket — **stagy** \ˈstā-jē\ *adj*

♦ [1] dais, platform, podium, rostrum, stand ♦ [2] theater (*or* theatre), theatricals ♦ [4b] lap, leg, step ♦ [6] cut, degree, grade, inch, notch, peg, phase, point, step

[2]stage *vb* **staged; stag•ing** ♦ **:** to produce or perform on or as if on a stage — **stage•able** *adj*

♦ carry, give, mount, offer, present

stage•coach \ˈstāj-ˌkōch\ *n* **:** a horse-drawn coach that runs regularly between stations

stage manager *n* **:** one who supervises the physical aspects of a stage production

stag•fla•tion \ˌstag-ˈflā-shən\ *n* **:** inflation with stagnant economic activity and high unemployment

[1]stag•ger \ˈsta-gər\ *vb* **1** ♦ **:** to reel from side to side **:** TOTTER **2 :** to begin to doubt **:** WAVER **3 :** to cause to reel or waver **4 :** to arrange in overlapping or alternating positions or times ⟨~ working hours⟩ **5 :** ASTONISH

♦ careen, dodder, lurch, reel, teeter, totter

[2]stagger *n* **1** *sing or pl* **:** an abnormal condition of domestic animals associated with damage to the central nervous system and marked by lack of coordination and a reeling unsteady gait **2 :** a reeling or unsteady gait or stance

stag•ger•ing•ly *adv* **:** in a staggering manner or to a staggering degree

stag•ing \ˈstā-jiŋ\ *n* **1 :** SCAFFOLDING **2 :** the assembling of troops and matériel in transit in a particular place

stag•nant \ˈstag-nənt\ *adj* **1 :** not flowing **:** MOTIONLESS ⟨~ water in a pond⟩ **2 :** DULL, INACTIVE ⟨~ business⟩

stag•nate \ˈstag-ˌnāt\ *vb* **stag•nat•ed; stag•nat•ing :** to be or become stagnant — **stag•na•tion** \stag-ˈnā-shən\ *n*

staid \ˈstād\ *adj* ♦ **:** marked by settled sedateness and often prim self-restraint

♦ august, dignified, imposing, solemn, stately ♦ earnest, grave, humorless (*or* humourless), serious, severe, sober, solemn, unsmiling, weighty

[1]stain \ˈstān\ *vb* **1** ♦ **:** to discolor especially with dirt **:** SOIL **2** ♦ **:** to touch or affect slightly with something bad **:** TAINT **3 :** DISGRACE **4** ♦ **:** to color (as wood, paper, or cloth) by processes affecting the material itself

♦ [1] befoul, begrime, besmirch, blacken, dirty, foul, grime, mire, muddy, smirch, soil ♦ [2] blemish, mar, poison, spoil, taint, tarnish, touch, vitiate ♦ [4] color (*or* colour), dye, paint, tinge, tint

[2]stain *n* **1 :** a small soiled or discolored area **2** ♦ **:** a taint of guilt **:** STIGMA **3** ♦ **:** a preparation (as a dye or pigment) used in staining

♦ [2] blot, brand, smirch, spot, stigma, taint ♦ [3] color (*or* colour), dye, pigment

stain•less *adj* ♦ **:** free from stain or stigma

♦ clean, immaculate, spick-and-span, spotless, unsoiled, unsullied

stainless steel *n* **:** steel alloyed with chromium that is highly resistant to stain, rust, and corrosion

stair \ˈstar\ *n* **1 :** a series of steps or flights of steps for passing from one level to another — often used in plural **2 :** one step of a stairway

stair•case \-ˌkās\ *n* **:** a flight of steps with their supporting framework, casing, and balusters

stair•way \-ˌwā\ *n* **:** one or more flights of stairs with connecting landings

stair•well \-ˌwel\ *n* **:** a vertical shaft in which stairs are located

[1]stake \ˈstāk\ *n* **1 :** a pointed piece of material (as of wood) driven into the ground as a marker or a support **2 :** a post to which a person is bound for death by burning; *also* **:** execution by burning at the stake **3 :** something that is ventured for gain or loss **4 :** the prize in a contest **5** ♦ **:** an interest or share in an undertaking or enterprise

♦ claim, interest, share

[2]stake *vb* **staked; stak•ing 1 :** to mark the limits of by or as if by stakes **2 :** to tie to a stake **3 :** to support or secure with stakes **4 :** BET, WAGER **5** ♦ **:** to back financially

♦ capitalize, endow, finance, fund, subsidize, underwrite

stake•out \ˈstāk-ˌau̇t\ *n* **:** a surveillance by police (as of a suspected criminal)

sta•lac•tite \stə-ˈlak-ˌtīt\ *n* **:** an icicle-shaped deposit hanging from the roof or sides of a cavern

sta•lag•mite \stə-ˈlag-ˌmīt\ *n* **:** a deposit resembling an inverted stalactite rising from the floor of a cavern

stale \ˈstāl\ *adj* **stal•er; stal•est 1 :** having lost good taste and quality from age ⟨~ bread⟩ **2** ♦ **:** used or heard so often as to be dull ⟨~ news⟩ **3 :** not as strong or effective as before ⟨~ from lack of practice⟩ — **stale•ness** *n*

♦ banal, commonplace, hackneyed, musty, stereotyped, threadbare, tired, trite *Ant* fresh, new, original

stale•mate \ˈstāl-ˌmāt\ *n* ♦ **:** a drawn contest **:** DEADLOCK — **stalemate** *vb*

♦ deadlock, draw, halt, impasse, standoff, standstill, tie

1stalk \ˈstȯk\ *n* **:** a plant stem; *also* **:** any slender usually upright supporting or connecting part — **stalked** \ˈstȯkt\ *adj*

2stalk *vb* **1 :** to pursue (game) stealthily **2** ♦ **:** to walk stiffly or haughtily

♦ strut, swagger

1stall \ˈstȯl\ *n* **1 :** a compartment in a stable or barn for one animal **2 :** a booth or counter where articles may be displayed for sale **3 :** a seat in a church choir; *also* **:** a church pew **4** *chiefly Brit* **:** a front orchestra seat in a theater

2stall *vb* ♦ **:** to bring or come to a standstill unintentionally ⟨~ an engine⟩

♦ arrest, catch, check, draw up, fetch up, halt, hold up, stay, still, stop ♦ break, break down, conk, crash, cut out, die, fail

3stall *n* **:** the condition of an airfoil or aircraft in which lift is lost and the airfoil or aircraft tends to drop

4stall *n* **:** a ruse to deceive or delay

5stall *vb* **:** to hold off, divert, or delay by evasion or deception

stal•lion \ˈstal-yən\ *n* **:** a male horse

stal•wart \ˈstȯl-wərt\ *adj* ♦ **:** marked by outstanding strength and vigor of body, mind, or spirit **:** STRONG; *also* **:** VALIANT

♦ brave, courageous, dauntless, doughty, fearless, gallant, greathearted, heroic, intrepid, lionhearted, manful, stout, undaunted, valiant, valorous ♦ brawny, muscular, rugged, sinewy, stout, strong

sta•men \ˈstā-mən\ *n* **:** an organ of a flower that produces pollen

stam•i•na \ˈsta-mə-nə\ *n* **:** VIGOR, ENDURANCE

sta•mi•nate \ˈstā-mə-nət, ˈsta-mə-, -ˌnāt\ *adj* **1 :** having or producing stamens **2 :** having stamens but no pistils

stam•mer \ˈsta-mər\ *vb* **:** to hesitate or stumble in speaking — **stammer** *n* — **stam•mer•er** *n*

1stamp \ˈstamp; *for 2 also* ˈstämp *or* ˈstȯmp\ *vb* **1 :** to pound or crush with a heavy instrument **2** ♦ **:** to strike or beat with the bottom of the foot **3 :** IMPRESS, IMPRINT **4 :** to cut out or indent with a stamp or die **5 :** to attach a postage stamp to **6** ♦ **:** to extinguish or destroy by or as if by stamping with the foot — used with *out* **7 :** to strike or thrust the foot forcibly or noisily downward

♦ [2] stomp, tramp, trample, tromp ♦ *usu* **stamp out** [6] annihilate, blot out, demolish, eradicate, exterminate, liquidate, obliterate, root, rub out, snuff, wipe out

2stamp *n* **1 :** a device or instrument for stamping **2** ♦ **:** the mark made by stamping; *also* **:** a distinctive mark or quality **3 :** the act of stamping **4 :** a stamped or printed paper affixed to show that a charge has been paid ⟨postage ~⟩ ⟨tax ~⟩

♦ impress, impression, imprint, print

1stam•pede \stam-ˈpēd\ *n* **:** a wild headlong rush or flight especially of frightened animals

2stampede *vb* **stam•ped•ed; stam•ped•ing 1 :** to flee or cause to flee in panic **2 :** to act or cause to act together suddenly and heedlessly

stance \ˈstans\ *n* **:** a way of standing

1stanch \ˈstȯnch, ˈstänch, ˈstanch\ *or* **staunch** \ˈstȯnch, ˈstänch\ *vb* **:** to check the flowing of (as blood); *also* **:** to cease flowing or bleeding

2stanch *var of* 2STAUNCH

stan•chion \ˈstan-chən\ *n* ♦ **:** an upright bar, post, or support

♦ column, pier, pillar, post

1stand \ˈstand\ *vb* **stood** \ˈstu̇d\; **stand•ing 1 :** to take or be at rest in an upright or firm position **2 :** to assume a specified position **3 :** to remain stationary or unchanged **4 :** to be steadfast **5 :** to act in resistance ⟨~ against a foe⟩ **6 :** to maintain a relative position or rank **7 :** to gather slowly and remain ⟨tears *stood* in her eyes⟩ **8 :** to set upright **9** ♦ **:** to tolerate without flinching **:** ENDURE ⟨I won't ~ for that⟩ **10 :** to submit to ⟨~ trial⟩ **11** ♦ **:** to pay the cost of (a treat) **:** pay for — **stand pat :** to oppose or resist change

♦ [9] abide, bear, brook, countenance, endure, meet, stick out, stomach, support, sustain, take, tolerate ♦ [11] clear, discharge, foot, liquidate, pay, pay off, quit, recompense, settle, spring

2stand *n* **1 :** an act of standing, staying, or resisting **2 :** a stop made to give a performance **3 :** POSITION, VIEWPOINT **4 :** a place taken by a witness to testify in court **5** *pl* **:** tiered seats for spectators **6** ♦ **:** a raised platform (as for speakers) **7 :** a structure for a small retail business **8 :** a structure for supporting or holding something upright ⟨music ~⟩ **9 :** a group of plants growing in a continuous area

♦ dais, platform, podium, rostrum, stage

stand–alone \ˈstan-də-ˌlōn\ *adj* **:** SELF-CONTAINED; *esp* **:** capable of operation independent of a computer system

1stan•dard \ˈstan-dərd\ *n* **1 :** a figure adopted as an emblem by a people **2** ♦ **:** the personal flag of a ruler; *also* **:** FLAG **3** ♦ **:** something set up as a rule for measuring or as a model to be followed; *also* **:** a model of behavior established by custom — often used in plural **4 :** an upright support ⟨lamp ~⟩

♦ [2] banner, colors (*or* colours), ensign, flag, jack, pennant, streamer ♦ [3] criterion, grade, mark, measure, par, touchstone, yardstick ♦ **standards** [3] ethics, morality, morals, principles

2standard *adj* **1** ♦ **:** constituting or conforming to a standard especially as established by law or custom **2** ♦ **:** regularly and widely used, available, or supplied

♦ [1] average, characteristic, normal, regular, representative, typical ♦ [2] conventional, current, customary, popular, stock, usual

stan•dard–bear•er \-ˌbar-ər\ *n* **:** the leader of a cause

standard deviation *n* **:** a measure of dispersion in a set of data

stan•dard•ise *chiefly Brit var of* STANDARDIZE

stan•dard–is•sue \ˈstan-dərd-ˈi-shü\ *adj* **:** STANDARD, TYPICAL ⟨a ~ blue suit⟩

stan•dard•ize \ˈstan-dər-ˌdīz\ *vb* **-ized; -iz•ing** ♦ **:** to make standard or uniform — **stan•dard•i•za•tion** \ˌstan-dər-də-ˈzā-shən\ *n*

♦ formalize, homogenize, normalize, regularize

standard of living : the necessities, comforts, and luxuries that a person or group is accustomed to

standard time *n* **:** the time established by law or by general usage over a region or country

1stand•by \ˈstand-ˌbī\ *n, pl* **stand•bys** \-ˌbīz\ **1** ♦ **:** one that can be relied on **2 :** a substitute in reserve — **on standby :** ready or available for immediate action or use

♦ buttress, dependence, mainstay, pillar, reliance, support

2standby *adj* **1 :** ready for use **2 :** relating to airline travel in which the passenger must wait for an available unreserved seat — **standby** *adv*

stand–in \ˈstan-ˌdin\ *n* **1 :** someone employed to occupy an actor's place while lights and camera are readied **2** ♦ **:** a person or thing that takes the place or function of another **:** SUBSTITUTE

♦ backup, pinch hitter, relief, replacement, reserve, sub, substitute

stand in *vb* ♦ **:** to act as a stand-in

♦ cover, fill in, pinch-hit, sub, substitute, take over

1stand•ing \ˈstan-diŋ\ *adj* **1 :** ERECT **2 :** not flowing **:** STAGNANT **3 :** remaining at the same level or amount for an indefinite period ⟨~ offer⟩ **4 :** PERMANENT **5 :** done from a standing position ⟨a ~ jump⟩

2standing *n* **1 a** ♦ **:** length of service **b** ♦ **:** relative position in society or in a profession **:** RANK **2 :** maintenance of position or condition **:** DURATION

♦ [1a] date, duration, life, lifetime, run, time ♦ [1b] degree, footing, level, place, position, rank, situation, station, status

stand•off \ˈstan-ˌdȯf\ *n* ♦ **:** a state of inaction or neutralization resulting from the opposition of equally powerful uncompromising persons or factions **:** TIE

♦ dead heat, draw, stalemate, tie

stand•off•ish \stan-ˈdȯ-fish\ *adj* ♦ **:** somewhat cold and reserved

♦ aloof, antisocial, cold, cool, detached, distant, frosty, remote, unsociable

stand•out \ˈstan-ˌdau̇t\ *n* ♦ **:** something conspicuously excellent

♦ celebrity, figure, light, luminary, notable, personage, personality, somebody, star, superstar, VIP

stand•pipe \ˈstand-ˌpīp\ *n* **:** a high vertical pipe or reservoir for water used to produce a uniform pressure
stand•point \-ˌpȯint\ *n* ♦ **:** a position from which objects or principles are judged

♦ angle, outlook, perspective, point of view, slant, viewpoint

stand•still \-ˌstil\ *n* ♦ **:** a state of rest

♦ deadlock, halt, impasse, stalemate

stank *past of* STINK
stand–up \ˈstan-ˌdəp\ *adj* **:** done or performing in a standing position ⟨a ~ comic⟩ ⟨~ comedy⟩
stan•za \ˈstan-zə\ *n* **:** a group of lines forming a division of a poem
sta•pes \ˈstā-ˌpēz\ *n, pl* **stapes** *or* **sta•pe•des** \ˈstā-pə-ˌdēz\ **:** the small innermost bone of the ear of mammals
staph \ˈstaf\ *n* **:** STAPHYLOCOCCUS
staph•y•lo•coc•cus \ˌsta-fə-lō-ˈkä-kəs\ *n, pl* **-coc•ci** \-ˈkä-ˌkī, -ˈkäk-ˌsī\ **:** any of various spherical bacteria including some pathogens of skin and mucous membranes — **staph•y•lo•coc•cal** \-ˈkä-kəl\ *adj*
1sta•ple \ˈstā-pəl\ *n* **:** a U-shaped piece of metal or wire with sharp points to be driven into a surface or through thin layers (as paper) for attaching or holding together — **staple** *vb* — **sta•pler** *n*
2staple *n* **1 :** a chief commodity or product **2** ♦ **:** a chief part of something ⟨a ~ of their diet⟩ **3 :** unmanufactured or raw material **4 :** a textile fiber suitable for spinning into yarn

♦ body, bulk, core, generality, main, mass, weight

3staple *adj* **1 :** regularly produced in large quantities **2 :** PRINCIPAL, MAIN
1star \ˈstär\ *n* **1 :** a celestial body that appears as a fixed point of light; *esp* **:** such a body that is gaseous, self-luminous, and of great mass **2 :** a planet or configuration of planets that is held in astrology to influence one's fortune — usually used in plural **3** *obs* **:** DESTINY, FORTUNE **4 :** a conventional figure representing a star; *esp* **:** ASTERISK **5 :** an actor or actress playing the leading role **6** ♦ **:** a brilliant performer **7** ♦ **:** a person who is preeminent in a particular field — **star** *adj* — **star•dom** \ˈstär-dəm\ *n* — **star•less** *adj* — **star•like** *adj*

♦ [6, 7] celebrity, figure, light, luminary, notable, personage, personality, somebody, standout, superstar, VIP

2star *vb* **starred; star•ring 1 :** to adorn with stars **2 :** to mark with an asterisk **3 :** to play the leading role
star•board \ˈstär-bərd\ *n* **:** the right side of a ship or airplane looking forward — **starboard** *adj*
1starch \ˈstärch\ *vb* **:** to stiffen with or as if with starch
2starch *n* **1 :** a complex carbohydrate that is stored in plants, is an important foodstuff, and is used in adhesives and sizes, in laundering, and in pharmacy **2 :** a stiff formal manner **3 :** resolute vigor
starchy *adj* **1 :** containing, consisting of, or resembling starch **2** ♦ **:** characterized by punctilious respect for form

♦ ceremonious, correct, decorous, formal, proper

stare \ˈstar\ *vb* **stared; star•ing** ♦ **:** to look fixedly with wide-open eyes — **stare** *n* — **star•er** *n*

♦ gape, gawk, gaze, goggle, peer, rubberneck

star•fish \ˈstär-ˌfish\ *n* **:** any of a class of echinoderms that have usually five arms arranged around a central disk and feed largely on mollusks
star fruit *n* **:** CARAMBOLA 1
1stark \ˈstärk\ *adj* **1 :** rigid as if in death; *also* **:** STRICT **2** *archaic* **:** STRONG, ROBUST **3 :** SHEER, UTTER **4** ♦ **:** not productive **:** BARREN ⟨~ landscape⟩; *also* **:** being without a usual, typical, or expected attribute or accompaniment **:** UNADORNED ⟨~ realism⟩ **5 :** sharply delineated **6 :** rigidly conforming (as to a pattern or doctrine) — **stark•ly** *adv*

♦ barren, infertile, poor, unproductive, waste

2stark *adv* **:** WHOLLY, ABSOLUTELY ⟨~ naked⟩
star•light \ˈstär-ˌlīt\ *n* **:** the light given by the stars
star•ling \ˈstär-liŋ\ *n* **:** a dark brown or in summer glossy greenish black European bird related to the crows that is naturalized nearly worldwide and often considered a pest
star•ry *adj* ♦ **:** of, relating to, or consisting of stars

♦ astral, star, stellar

1start \ˈstärt\ *vb* **1** ♦ **:** to give an involuntary twitch or jerk (as from surprise) **2** ♦ **:** to begin an activity or undertaking **:** BEGIN **3** ♦ **:** to set going **4 :** to enter or cause to enter a game or contest; *also* **:** to be in the starting lineup **5 :** to protrude or seem to protrude — **start•er** *n*

♦ [1] bolt, jump, startle ♦ [2] arise, begin, commence, dawn, form, materialize, originate, spring ♦ [2] embark (on *or* upon), enter, get off, launch, open, strike ♦ [3] constitute, establish, found, inaugurate, initiate, innovate, institute, introduce, pioneer, set up ♦ [3] activate, actuate, crank, drive, move, propel, run, set off, spark, touch off, trigger, turn on

2start *n* **1 :** a sudden involuntary motion **:** LEAP **2 :** a spasmodic and brief effort or action **3** ♦ **:** BEGINNING; *also* **:** the place of beginning

♦ beginning, birth, commencement, dawn, genesis, launch, morning, onset, outset, threshold

star•tle \ˈstärt-ᵊl\ *vb* **star•tled; star•tling 1** ♦ **:** to frighten or surprise suddenly **:** cause to start **2** ♦ **:** to move or jump suddenly (as in surprise or alarm)

♦ [1] amaze, astonish, astound, floor, shock, stun, surprise ♦ [1] alarm, frighten, scare, spook ♦ [2] bolt, jump, start

star•tling *adj* ♦ **:** causing sudden fear, surprise, or anxiety

♦ amazing, astonishing, astounding, eye-opening, shocking, stunning, surprising

starve \ˈstärv\ *vb* **starved; starv•ing 1 :** to die or cause to die from hunger **2 :** to suffer extreme hunger or deprivation ⟨*starving* for affection⟩ **3 :** to subdue by famine — **star•va•tion** \stär-ˈvā-shən\ *n*
starve•ling \ˈstärv-liŋ\ *n* **:** one that is thin from lack of nourishment
1stash \ˈstash\ *vb* ♦ **:** to store in a secret place for future use

♦ cache, hoard, lay away, lay up, put by, salt away, stockpile, store

2stash *n* ♦ **:** something stored or hidden away

♦ cache, hoard, stockpile, store

sta•sis \ˈstā-səs, ˈsta-\ *n, pl* **sta•ses** \ˈstā-ˌsēz, ˈsta-\ **1 :** a stoppage or slowing of the normal flow of a bodily fluid (as blood) **2 :** a state of static balance **:** STAGNATION
1stat \ˈstat\ *adv* **:** without delay **:** IMMEDIATELY
2stat *abbr* statute
1state \ˈstāt\ *n* **1 :** mode or condition of being ⟨the four ~s of matter⟩ **2 :** condition of mind **3 :** social position **4** ♦ **:** a body of people occupying a territory and organized under one government; *also* **:** the government of such a body of people **5 :** one of the constituent units of a nation having a federal government — **state•hood** \-ˌhu̇d\ *n*

♦ commonwealth, country, land, nation, sovereignty

2state *vb* **stat•ed; stat•ing 1 :** to set by regulation or authority **2** ♦ **:** to express in words

♦ clothe, couch, express, formulate, phrase, put, say, word ♦ articulate, say, speak, talk, tell, utter, verbalize, vocalize

state•craft \ˈstāt-ˌkraft\ *n* **:** the art of conducting state affairs
state•house \-ˌhau̇s\ *n* **:** the building in which a state legislature meets
state•li•ness *n* ♦ **:** impressiveness in scale or proportion; *also* **:** imposing or courtly formality

♦ class, elegance, grace, handsomeness, majesty, refinement ♦ augustness, brilliance, glory, grandeur, grandness, magnificence, majesty, nobility, nobleness, resplendence, splendor

state•ly \ˈstāt-lē\ *adj* **state•li•er; -est 1** ♦ **:** having lofty dignity **2** ♦ **:** impressive in size or proportions **:** MAJESTIC

♦ [1] august, dignified, imposing, lofty, solemn, staid ♦ [2] august, baronial, gallant, glorious, grand, grandiose, heroic, imposing, magnificent, majestic, monumental, noble, proud, regal, royal, splendid

state•ment \ˈstāt-mənt\ *n* **1** ♦ **:** the act or result of presenting in words **2** ♦ **:** a summary of a financial account

♦ [1] articulation, expression, formulation, utterance, voice ♦ [2] account, bill, check, invoice, tab

state•room \ˈstāt-ˌrüm, -ˌru̇m\ *n* **:** a private room on a ship or railroad car
state•side \ˈstāt-ˌsīd\ *adj* **:** of or relating to the U.S. as regarded from outside its continental limits — **stateside** *adv*
states•man \ˈstāts-mən\ *n* **:** a person engaged in fixing the policies and conducting the affairs of a government; *esp* **:** one wise and skilled in such matters — **states•man•like** *adj* — **states•man•ship** *n*

¹stat•ic \ˈsta-tik\ *adj* **1 :** acting by mere weight without motion ⟨~ pressure⟩ **2 :** relating to bodies at rest or forces in equilibrium **3** ♦ **:** not moving : not active **4 :** of or relating to stationary charges of electricity **5 :** of, relating to, or caused by radio static

♦ immobile, immovable, standing, stationary, unmovable

²static *n* **:** noise produced in a radio or television receiver by atmospheric or other electrical disturbances

¹sta•tion \ˈstā-shən\ *n* **1** ♦ **:** the place where a person or thing stands or is assigned to remain **2 :** a regular stopping place on a transportation route **3 :** a place where a fleet is assigned for duty **4 :** a stock farm or ranch especially in Australia or New Zealand **5** ♦ **:** social standing **6 :** a complete assemblage of radio or television equipment for sending or receiving

♦ [1] position, post, quarter ♦ [5] degree, footing, level, place, position, rank, situation, standing, status

²station *vb* **:** to assign to a station

sta•tion•ary \ˈstā-shə-ˌner-ē\ *adj* **1** ♦ **:** fixed in a station, course, or mode **2** ♦ **:** unchanging in condition

♦ [1] immobile, immovable, standing, static, unmovable ***Ant*** mobile, movable, moving ♦ [2] constant, stable, steady, unchanging, unvarying

stationary front *n* **:** the boundary between two air masses neither of which is advancing

station break *n* **:** a pause in a radio or television broadcast to announce the identity of the network or station

sta•tio•ner \ˈstā-shə-nər\ *n* **:** one that sells stationery

sta•tio•nery \ˈstā-shə-ˌner-ē\ *n* **:** materials (as paper, pens, or ink) for writing; *esp* **:** letter paper with envelopes

station wagon *n* **:** an automobile having a long interior, one or more folding or removable rear seats, and usually a door at the rear

sta•tis•tic \stə-ˈtis-tik\ *n* **1 :** a single term or datum in a collection of statistics **2 :** a quantity (as the mean) that is computed from a sample

sta•tis•tics \-tiks\ *n sing or pl* **:** a branch of mathematics dealing with the collection, analysis, and interpretation of masses of numerical data; *also* **:** a collection of such numerical data — **sta•tis•ti•cal** \-ti-kəl\ *adj* — **sta•tis•ti•cal•ly** \-ti-k(ə-)lē\ *adv* — **stat•is•ti•cian** \ˌsta-tə-ˈsti-shən\ *n*

stat•u•ary \ˈsta-chə-ˌwer-ē\ *n, pl* **-ar•ies** **1 :** the art of making statues **2 :** STATUES

stat•ue \ˈsta-chü\ *n* **:** a likeness (as of a person or animal) sculptured, modeled, or cast in a solid substance

stat•u•esque \ˌsta-chə-ˈwesk\ *adj* **:** tall and shapely

stat•u•ette \ˌsta-chə-ˈwet\ *n* **:** a small statue

stat•ure \ˈsta-chər\ *n* **1 :** natural height (as of a person) **2 :** quality or status gained (as by achievement)

sta•tus \ˈstā-təs, ˈsta-\ *n* **1 :** the condition of a person in the eyes of others or of the law **2** ♦ **:** state of affairs **3** ♦ **:** position or rank in relation to others

♦ [2] footing, picture, posture, scene, situation ♦ [3] degree, footing, level, place, position, rank, situation, standing, station

sta•tus quo \-ˈkwō\ *n* **:** the existing state of affairs

stat•ute \ˈsta-chüt\ *n* ♦ **:** a law enacted by a legislative body

♦ act, enactment, law, ordinance

stat•u•to•ry \ˈsta-chə-ˌtōr-ē\ *adj* **:** imposed by statute : LAWFUL

statutory rape *n* **:** sexual intercourse with a person who is below the statutory age of consent

¹staunch \ˈstȯnch\ *var of* ¹STANCH

²staunch *adj* **1 :** WATERTIGHT ⟨a ~ ship⟩ **2 a :** FIRM, STRONG **b** ♦ **:** steadfast in loyalty or principle — **staunch•ly** *adv*

♦ constant, devoted, faithful, fast, good, loyal, pious, steadfast, steady, true, true-blue

¹stave \ˈstāv\ *n* **1 :** CUDGEL, STAFF **2 :** any of several narrow strips of wood placed edge to edge to make something (as a barrel) **3 :** STANZA

²stave *vb* **staved** *or* **stove** \ˈstōv\; **stav•ing** **1 :** to break in the staves of; *also* **:** to break a hole in **2 :** to drive or thrust away

stave off *vb* ♦ **:** to fend or ward off

♦ fend, repel, repulse

staves *pl of* STAFF

¹stay \ˈstā\ *n* **1 :** a strong rope or wire used to support a mast **2 :** ¹GUY

²stay *vb* **stayed** \ˈstād\ *also* **staid** \ˈstād\; **stay•ing** **1 :** PAUSE, WAIT **2** ♦ **:** to continue in a place or condition **3 :** to stand firm **4 :** to take up residence : LIVE, DWELL **5 :** DELAY, POSTPONE **6 :** to last out (as a race) **7** ♦ **:** to stop or delay the proceeding or advance of : CHECK **8 :** to satisfy (as hunger) for a time

♦ [2] abide, dwell, hang around, remain, stick around, tarry, visit ***Ant*** go, leave, quit ♦ [7] arrest, catch, check, draw up, fetch up, halt, hold up, stall, still, stop

³stay *n* **1 :** STOP, HALT **2** ♦ **:** a residence or sojourn in a place

♦ sojourn, visit

⁴stay *n* **1** ♦ **:** one that serves as a prop : SUPPORT **2 :** CORSET — usually used in plural

♦ brace, bulwark, buttress, mount, shore, support, underpinning

⁵stay *vb* ♦ **:** to hold up : PROP

♦ bear, bolster, brace, buttress, carry, prop, shore, support, uphold

staying power *n* **:** STAMINA

stbd *abbr* starboard

std *abbr* standard

STD \ˌes-(ˌ)tē-ˈdē\ *n* **:** SEXUALLY TRANSMITTED DISEASE

Ste *abbr* saint (female)

stead \ˈsted\ *n* **1** ♦ **:** superiority of position : ADVANTAGE ⟨stood him in good ~⟩ **2 :** the place or function ordinarily occupied or carried out by another ⟨acted in her brother's ~⟩

♦ advantage, better, drop, edge, jump, upper hand, vantage

stead•fast \ˈsted-ˌfast\ *adj* **1 :** firmly fixed in place **2 :** not subject to change **3** ♦ **:** firm in belief, determination, or adherence : LOYAL — **stead•fast•ly** *adv*

♦ constant, devoted, faithful, fast, good, loyal, pious, staunch, steady, true, true-blue

stead•fast•ness *n* ♦ **:** the quality or state of being steadfast

♦ allegiance, constancy, dedication, devotion, faith, faithfulness, fastness, fealty, fidelity, loyalty

steadi•ness \ˈste-dē-nəs\ *n* ♦ **:** the quality or state of being steady

♦ firmness, soundness, stability, strength, sturdiness ♦ constancy, fixedness, immutability, stability

¹steady \ˈste-dē\ *adj* **steadi•er; -est** **1 :** direct or sure in movement; *also* **:** CALM **2 :** firm in position : FIRM, FIXED **3** ♦ **:** showing little variation or fluctuation **4** ♦ **:** constant in feeling, principle, purpose, or attachment **5** ♦ **:** not changed, replaced, or interrupted : REGULAR **6** ♦ **:** capable of being depended on : RELIABLE — **steadi•ly** \-də-lē\ *adv* — **steady** *adv*

♦ [3] constant, stable, stationary, unchanging, unvarying ♦ [3] undeviating, uniform, unwavering ♦ [4] constant, devoted, faithful, fast, good, loyal, pious, staunch, steadfast, true, true-blue ♦ [5] constant, frequent, habitual, periodic, regular, repeated ♦ [6] dependable, good, reliable, responsible, safe, solid, sure, tried, true, trustworthy

²steady *vb* **stead•ied; steady•ing** **:** to make or become steady

steak \ˈstāk\ *n* **:** a slice of meat and especially beef; *also* **:** a slice of a large fish

¹steal \ˈstēl\ *vb* **stole** \ˈstōl\; **sto•len** \ˈstō-lən\; **steal•ing** **1** ♦ **:** to take and carry away without right or permission **2** ♦ **:** to come or go secretly or gradually **3 :** to get for oneself slyly or by skill and daring ⟨~ a kiss⟩ ⟨~ the ball in basketball⟩ **4 :** to gain or attempt to gain a base in baseball by running without the aid of a hit or an error

♦ [1] appropriate, filch, hook, misappropriate, nip, pilfer, pocket, purloin, snitch, swipe, thieve ♦ *usu* **steal from** [1] burglarize, rip off, rob ♦ [2] lurk, pussyfoot, skulk, slide, slink, slip, snake, sneak

²steal *n* **1 :** an act of stealing **2** ♦ **:** an advantageous purchase : BARGAIN

♦ bargain, buy, deal

stealth \ˈstelth\ *n* **1 :** secret or unobtrusive procedure **2 :** an aircraft design intended to produce a weak radar return

stealthy \ˈstel-thē\ *adj* **stealth•i•er; -est** ♦ **:** done by stealth : FURTIVE, SLY — **stealth•i•ly** \ˈstel-thə-lē\ *adv*

♦ furtive, shady, shifty, slippery, sly, sneaky ♦ clandestine, covert, furtive, hugger-mugger, private, secret, sneak, sneaky, surreptitious, undercover, underground, underhanded

¹steam \ˈstēm\ *n* **1 :** the vapor into which water is changed when heated to the boiling point **2 :** water vapor when compressed so that it supplies heat and power **3 :** POWER, FORCE, ENERGY

²steam *vb* **1 :** to pass off as vapor **2 :** to emit vapor **3 :** to move by or as if by the agency of steam **4** ♦ **:** to be angry — **steam•er** *n*

♦ boil, burn, fume, rage, seethe

steam•boat \ˈstēm-ˌbōt\ *n* **:** a boat driven by steam
steam engine *n* **:** a reciprocating engine having a piston driven by steam
steam•fit•ter \ˈstēm-ˌfi-tər\ *n* **:** a worker who puts in or repairs equipment (as steam pipes) for heating, ventilating, or refrigerating systems
steam•roll•er \-ˌrō-lər\ *n* **:** a machine for compacting roads or pavements — **steam•roll•er** *also* **steam•roll** \-ˌrōl\ *vb*
steam•ship \-ˌship\ *n* **:** a ship driven by steam
steamy \ˈstē-mē\ *adj* **1 :** consisting of, characterized by, or full of steam **2 :** relating to or dealing with sexual love **:** EROTIC
steed \ˈstēd\ *n* **:** a large solid-hoofed herbivorous mammal domesticated since prehistoric times and used as a pack or draft animal, or for riding **:** HORSE
¹steel \ˈstēl\ *n* **1 :** iron treated with intense heat and mixed with carbon to make it hard and tough **2 :** an article made of steel **3 :** a quality (as hardness of mind) that suggests steel — **steel** *adj*
²steel *vb* ♦ **:** to fill with courage or determination

♦ encourage, fortify, harden, nerve, ready, season, strengthen, toughen

steel wool *n* **:** long fine steel shavings used especially for cleaning and polishing
steely *adj* ♦ **:** resembling or suggesting steel (as in hardness, color, strength, or coldness)

♦ austere, dour, fierce, flinty, forbidding, grim, gruff, rough, rugged, severe, stark, stern ♦ gray (*or* grey), leaden, pewter, silver, silvery, slate

¹steep \ˈstēp\ *adj* **1** ♦ **:** having a very sharp slope **:** PRECIPITOUS **2** ♦ **:** too great or too high ⟨~ prices⟩ — **steep•ly** *adv* — **steep•ness** *n*

♦ [1] abrupt, bold, precipitous, sheer *Ant* easy ♦ [2] excessive, extreme, immoderate, inordinate, stiff

²steep *n* **:** a steep slope
³steep *vb* **1** ♦ **:** to soak in a liquid; *esp* **:** to extract the essence of by soaking ⟨~ tea⟩ **2** ♦ **:** to saturate with or subject thoroughly to (some strong or pervading influence) ⟨~*ed* in learning⟩

♦ [1] drench, drown, impregnate, saturate, soak, sop, souse ♦ [2] imbue, inculcate, infuse, ingrain, invest, suffuse

stee•ple \ˈstē-pəl\ *n* **:** a tall tapering structure built on top of a church tower; *also* **:** a church tower
stee•ple•chase \-ˌchās\ *n* **:** a horse race across country; *also* **:** a race over a course obstructed by hurdles
¹steer \ˈstir\ *n* **:** a male bovine animal castrated before sexual maturity and usually raised for beef
²steer *vb* **1** ♦ **:** to direct the course of (as by a rudder or wheel) **2 :** GUIDE, CONTROL **3 :** to pursue a course of action **4 :** to be subject to guidance or direction — **steers•man** \ˈstirz-mən\ *n*

♦ conduct, direct, guide, lead, marshal, pilot, route, show, usher

steer•age \ˈstir-ij\ *n* **1 :** DIRECTION, GUIDANCE **2 :** a section in a passenger ship for passengers paying the lowest fares
stego•sau•rus \ˌste-gə-ˈsȯr-əs\ *n* **:** any of a genus of plant-eating armored dinosaurs with a series of bony plates along the backbone
stein \ˈstīn\ *n* **:** an earthenware mug
stel•lar \ˈste-lər\ *adj* **1** ♦ **:** of or relating to stars **:** resembling a star **2 :** marked by eminence and distinction

♦ astral, star, starry

¹stem \ˈstem\ *n* **1 :** the main stalk of a plant; *also* **:** a plant part that supports another part (as a leaf or fruit) **2 :** the bow of a ship **3 :** a line of ancestry **:** STOCK **4 :** that part of an inflected word which remains unchanged throughout a given inflection **5 :** something resembling the stem of a plant — **stem•less** *adj* — **stemmed** \ˈstemd\ *adj*
²stem *vb* **stemmed; stem•ming :** to have a specified source **:** DERIVE
³stem *vb* **stemmed; stem•ming :** to make headway against ⟨~ the tide⟩
⁴stem *vb* **stemmed; stem•ming :** to stop or check by or as if by damming
stem cell *n* **:** an undifferentiated cell that may give rise to many different types of cell
stench \ˈstench\ *n* **:** STINK
sten•cil \ˈsten-səl\ *n* **:** an impervious material (as metal or paper) perforated with lettering or a design through which a substance (as ink or paint) is applied to a surface to be printed — **stencil** *vb*
ste•nog•ra•phy \stə-ˈnä-grə-fē\ *n* **:** the art or process of writing in shorthand — **ste•nog•ra•pher** \-fər\ *n* — **steno•graph•ic** \ˌste-nə-ˈgra-fik\ *adj*
ste•no•sis \stə-ˈnō-səs\ *n, pl* **-no•ses** \-ˌsēz\ **:** a narrowing of a bodily passage or orifice
stent \ˈstent\ *n* **:** a short narrow tube inserted into an anatomical vessel especially to keep a passage open
sten•to•ri•an \sten-ˈtōr-ē-ən\ *adj* ♦ **:** extremely loud and powerful

♦ booming, clamorous (*or* clamourous), deafening, earsplitting, loud, piercing, resounding, ringing, roaring, sonorous, thunderous

¹step \ˈstep\ *n* **1 :** a rest for the foot in ascending or descending **:** STAIR **2 :** an advance made by raising one foot and putting it down elsewhere **3 :** manner of walking **4 :** a small space or distance **5 :** a degree, rank, or plane in a series **6** ♦ **:** a sequential measure leading to a result

♦ expedient, measure, move, shift ♦ cut, degree, grade, inch, notch, peg, phase, point, stage

²step *vb* **stepped; step•ping 1 :** to advance or recede by steps **2** ♦ **:** to go on foot **:** WALK **3 :** to move along briskly **4 :** to press down with the foot **5 :** to measure by steps **6 :** to construct or arrange in or as if in steps **7 :** to engage in or perform a dance

♦ foot, leg, pad, traipse, tread, walk

step aerobics *n sing or pl* **:** aerobics that involves repeatedly stepping on and off a raised platform
step•broth•er \ˈstep-ˌbrə-t͟hər\ *n* **:** the son of one's stepparent by a former marriage
step•child \-ˌchīld\ *n* **:** a child of one's husband or wife by a former marriage
step•daugh•ter \-ˌdȯ-tər\ *n* **:** a daughter of one's wife or husband by a former marriage
step down *vb* **1** ♦ **:** to give up deliberately **:** RETIRE, RESIGN **2 :** to lower (a voltage) by means of a transformer

♦ *usu* **step down from** leave, quit, resign, retire ♦ *usu* **step down from** abdicate, abnegate, cede, relinquish, renounce, resign, surrender

step•fa•ther \-ˌfä-t͟hər\ *n* **:** the husband of one's mother when distinct from one's natural or legal father
step•lad•der \ˈstep-ˌla-dər\ *n* **:** a light portable set of steps in a hinged frame
step•moth•er \-ˌmə-t͟hər\ *n* **:** the wife of one's father when distinct from one's natural or legal mother
step•par•ent \-ˌpar-ənt\ *n* **:** a person who is a stepfather or stepmother
steppe \ˈstep\ *n* ♦ **:** dry level grass-covered treeless land in regions of wide temperature range especially in southeastern Europe and Asia

♦ down, grassland, plain, prairie, savanna, veld

step•sis•ter \ˈstep-ˌsis-tər\ *n* **:** the daughter of one's stepparent by a former marriage
step•son \-ˌsən\ *n* **:** a son of one's wife or husband by a former marriage
step up *vb* **1 :** to increase (a voltage) by means of a transformer **2** ♦ **:** to increase, augment, or advance especially by one or more steps **3 :** to come forward — **step–up** \ˈstep-ˌəp\ *n*

♦ amplify, beef, boost, consolidate, deepen, enhance, heighten, intensify, magnify, redouble, strengthen ♦ accelerate, hasten, hurry, quicken, rush, speed (up), whisk

ster *abbr* sterling
ste•reo \ˈster-ē-ˌō, ˈstir-\ *n, pl* **ste•re•os 1 :** stereophonic reproduction **2 :** a stereophonic sound system — **stereo** *adj*
ste•reo•phon•ic \ˌster-ē-ə-ˈfä-nik, ˌstir-\ *adj* **:** of or relating to sound reproduction designed to create the effect of listening to the original — **ste•reo•phon•i•cal•ly** \-ˈfä-ni-k(ə-)lē\ *adv*
ster•e•o•scope \ˈster-ē-ə-ˌskōp, ˈstir-\ *n* **:** an optical instrument that blends two slightly different pictures of the same subject to give the effect of depth
ste•reo•scop•ic \ˌster-ē-ə-ˈskä-pik, ˌstir-\ *adj* **1 :** of or relating to the stereoscope **2 :** characterized by the seeing of objects in three dimensions ⟨~ vision⟩ — **ste•reo•scop•i•cal•ly** \-ˈskä-pi-k(ə-)lē\ *adv* — **ste•re•os•co•py** \ˌster-ē-ˈäs-kə-pē, ˌstir-\ *n*
ste•reo•type \ˈster-ē-ə-ˌtīp, ˈstir-\ *n* **1 :** a metal printing plate cast from a mold made from set type **2 :** something agreeing with a pattern; *esp* **:** an idea that many people have about a thing or a group and that may often be untrue or only partly true — **stereo-**

type *vb* — **ste•reo•typ•i•cal** \ˌster-ē-ə-ˈti-pi-kəl\ *adj* — **ste•reo•typ•i•cal•ly** \-pi-k(ə-)lē\ *adv*
ste•reo•typed \-ˌtīpt\ *adj* ♦ **:** lacking originality or individuality

♦ banal, commonplace, hackneyed, musty, stale, threadbare, tired, trite

ster•ile \ˈster-əl\ *adj* **1** ♦ **:** unable to bear fruit, crops, or offspring **2** ♦ **:** free from living things and especially germs — **ste•ril•i•ty** \stə-ˈri-lə-tē\ *n*

♦ [1] barren, impotent, infertile *Ant* fat, fertile, fruitful ♦ [2] aseptic, hygienic, sanitary

ster•il•ize \ˈster-ə-ˌlīz\ *vb* **-ized; -iz•ing :** to make sterile; *esp* **:** to free from germs — **ster•il•i•za•tion** \ˌster-ə-lə-ˈzā-shən\ *n* — **ster•il•iz•er** \ˈster-ə-ˌlī-zər\ *n*
¹ster•ling \ˈstər-liŋ\ *n* **1 :** British money **2 :** sterling silver
²sterling *adj* **1 :** of, relating to, or calculated in terms of British sterling **2 :** having a fixed standard of purity represented by an alloy of 925 parts of silver with 75 parts of copper **3 :** made of sterling silver **4 :** eminently good **:** EXCELLENT
¹stern \ˈstərn\ *adj* **1** ♦ **:** having a definite hardness or severity of nature or manner **:** SEVERE **2 :** STOUT, STURDY ⟨~ resolve⟩

♦ austere, authoritarian, flinty, hard, harsh, heavy-handed, ramrod, rigid, rigorous, severe, strict

²stern *n* **:** the rear end of a boat
stern•ly *adv* ♦ **:** in a stern manner

♦ hard, hardly, harshly, ill, oppressively, roughly, severely, stiffly

stern•ness *n* **:** the quality or state of being stern

♦ hardness, harshness, inflexibility, rigidity, severity, strictness

ster•num \ˈstər-nəm\ *n, pl* **sternums** *or* **ster•na** \-nə\ **:** a long flat bone or cartilage at the center front of the chest connecting the ribs of the two sides
ste•roid \ˈstir-ˌȯid\ *n* **:** any of various compounds including numerous hormones (as anabolic steroids) and sugar derivatives — **steroid** *or* **ste•roi•dal** \stə-ˈrȯid-ᵊl\ *adj*
stetho•scope \ˈste-thə-ˌskōp\ *n* **:** an instrument used to detect and listen to sounds produced in the body
ste•ve•dore \ˈstē-və-ˌdōr\ *n* **:** one who works at loading and unloading ships
¹stew \ˈstü, ˈstyü\ *n* **1 :** a dish of stewed meat and vegetables served in gravy **2** ♦ **:** a state of agitation, worry, or resentment

♦ dither, fluster, fret, fuss, huff, lather, pother, tizzy, twitter

²stew *vb* **1 :** to boil slowly **:** SIMMER **2** ♦ **:** to be in a state of agitation, worry, or resentment

♦ bother, fear, fret, sweat, trouble, worry

stew•ard \ˈstü-ərd, ˈstyü-\ *n* **1** ♦ **:** one employed on a large estate to manage domestic concerns **2 :** one who supervises the provision and distribution of food (as on a ship); *also* **:** an employee on a ship or airplane who serves passengers **3 :** one actively concerned with the direction of the affairs of an organization

♦ domestic, flunky, lackey, menial, retainer, servant

stew•ard•ess \ˈstü-ər-dəs, ˈstyü-\ *n* **:** a woman who is a steward especially on an airplane
stew•ard•ship *n* ♦ **:** the conducting, supervising, or managing of something; *esp* **:** the careful and responsible management of something entrusted to one's care

♦ administration, charge, conduct, control, direction, governance, government, guidance, management, operation, oversight, regulation, running, superintendence, supervision

stg *abbr* sterling
¹stick \ˈstik\ *n* **1 :** a cut or broken branch or twig; *also* **:** a long slender piece of wood **2 :** ROD, STAFF **3 :** something resembling a stick **4 :** a dull uninteresting person **5** *pl* ♦ **:** remote usually rural areas

♦ *usu* **sticks** backwoods, bush, frontier, hinterland, up-country

²stick *vb* **stuck** \ˈstək\; **stick•ing** **1 :** STAB, PRICK **2** ♦ **:** to pierce with or as if with something pointed **3 :** ATTACH, FASTEN **4 :** to thrust or project in some direction or manner **5 :** to be unable to proceed or move freely **6** ♦ **:** to hold fast by or as if by gluing **:** ADHERE **7 :** to hold to something firmly or closely **:** CLING **8 :** to become jammed or blocked **9** ♦ **:** to put or set in a specified place or position

♦ [2] gore, harpoon, impale, lance, pierce, puncture, skewer, spear, spike, stab, transfix ♦ [6] adhere, cling, hew ♦ [9] deposit, dispose, fix, lay, place, position, put, set, set up

stick around *vb* ♦ **:** to stay or wait about

♦ abide, dwell, hang around, remain, stay, tarry

stick•er \ˈsti-kər\ *n* **:** one that sticks (as a bur) or causes sticking (as glue); *esp* **:** an adhesive label
sticker shock *n* **:** astonishment and dismay on being informed of a product's unexpectedly high price
stick insect *n* **:** any of various usually wingless insects with a long round body resembling a stick
stick•ler \ˈsti-klər, -kə-lər\ *n* **:** one who insists on exactness or completeness
stick out *vb* **1** ♦ **:** to jut out **2** ♦ **:** to regard with acceptance or tolerance

♦ [1] bag, balloon, beetle, belly, billow, bulge, overhang, poke, project, protrude, start ♦ [2] abide, bear, brook, countenance, endure, meet, stand, stomach, support, sustain, take, tolerate

stick shift *n* **:** a manually operated automobile gearshift usually mounted on the floor
stick–to–it•ive•ness \stik-ˈtü-ə-tiv-nəs\ *n* **:** dogged perseverance **:** TENACITY
stick up *vb* **:** to rob at gunpoint — **stick•up** \ˈstik-ˌəp\ *n*
sticky \ˈsti-kē\ *adj* **stick•i•er; -est** **1 :** having the quality of remaining attached or associated **2** ♦ **:** being thick or tacky like glue **:** VISCOUS **3 :** tending to stick ⟨~ valve⟩ **4 :** DIFFICULT **5** ♦ **:** containing or characterized by perceptible moisture **:** HUMID

♦ [2] adhesive, gelatinous, gluey, glutinous, gooey, gummy, viscid, viscous *Ant* nonadhesive ♦ [5] humid, muggy, sultry

¹stiff \ˈstif\ *adj* **1** ♦ **:** not pliant **:** RIGID **2 :** not limber ⟨~ joints⟩; *also* **:** TENSE, TAUT **3 :** not flowing or working easily ⟨~ paste⟩ **4 a :** not natural and easy **:** FORMAL **b** ♦ **:** lacking in ease or grace **:** STILTED **5 :** STRONG, FORCEFUL ⟨~ breeze⟩ **6** ♦ **:** inflicting physical discomfort or hardship **:** SEVERE **7 :** extremely or excessively high ⟨paid a ~ fine⟩ — **stiff•ness** *n*

♦ [1] hard, inflexible, rigid, solid, unyielding *Ant* flexible, floppy, pliable, pliant, supple, yielding ♦ [4b] awkward, clumsy, gauche, graceless, inelegant, stilted, uncomfortable, uneasy, ungraceful, wooden ♦ [6] bitter, brutal, burdensome, cruel, excruciating, grievous, grim, hard, harsh, heavy, inhuman, murderous, onerous, oppressive, rough, rugged, severe, tough, trying

²stiff *vb* **:** to refuse to pay or tip
³stiff *n* ♦ **:** a human being **:** INDIVIDUAL

♦ being, body, creature, human, individual, man, mortal, person

stiff•en \ˈsti-fən\ *vb* **:** to make or become stiff — **stiff•en•er** *n*
stiff•ly *adv* ♦ **:** in a stiff manner

♦ hard, hardly, harshly, ill, oppressively, roughly, severely, sternly

stiff–necked \ˈstif-ˈnekt\ *adj* **:** STUBBORN, HAUGHTY
sti•fle \ˈstī-fəl\ *vb* **sti•fled; sti•fling** **1** ♦ **:** to kill by depriving of oxygen or air; *also* **:** to die from lack of oxygen **2** ♦ **:** to keep in check by effort **:** SUPPRESS ⟨~ a sneeze⟩ — **sti•fling•ly** *adv*

♦ [1] choke, smother, strangle, suffocate ♦ [2] choke, pocket, repress, smother, strangle, suppress, swallow

stig•ma \ˈstig-mə\ *n, pl* **stig•ma•ta** \stig-ˈmä-tə, ˈstig-mə-tə\ *or* **stigmas** **1** ♦ **:** a mark of disgrace or discredit **2** *stigmata pl* **:** bodily marks resembling the wounds of the crucified Jesus **3 :** the upper part of the pistil of a flower that receives the pollen in fertilization — **stig•mat•ic** \stig-ˈma-tik\ *adj*

♦ blot, brand, smirch, spot, stain, taint

stig•ma•tize \ˈstig-mə-ˌtīz\ *vb* **-tized; -tiz•ing** **1 :** to mark with a stigma **2 :** to characterize as disgraceful
stile \ˈstīl\ *n* **:** steps used for crossing a fence or wall
sti•let•to \stə-ˈle-tō\ *n, pl* **-tos** *or* **-toes :** a slender dagger
¹still \ˈstil\ *adj* **1 :** MOTIONLESS **2** ♦ **:** making no sound

♦ hushed, muted, noiseless, quiet, silent, soundless ♦ calm, peaceful, quiet, restful, serene, tranquil

²still *vb* ♦ **:** to make or become still

♦ allay, calm, compose, quiet, settle, soothe, tranquilize ♦ hush, mute, quell, settle, silence

³still *adv* **1** ♦ **:** without motion ⟨sit ~⟩ **2 :** up to and during this or that time **3** ♦ **:** in spite of that **:** NEVERTHELESS **4 :** EVEN ⟨ran ~ faster⟩ **5 :** BESIDES, YET

♦ [1] calmly, quiet, quietly ♦ [3] but, howbeit, however, nevertheless, nonetheless, notwithstanding, though, withal, yet

[4]**still** *n* **1 :** the quality or state of being quiet : STILLNESS **2 :** a static photograph especially from a motion picture
[5]**still** *n* **1 :** DISTILLERY **2 :** apparatus used in distillation
still•birth \ˈstil-ˌbərth\ *n* **:** the birth of a dead fetus
still•born \-ˈbȯrn\ *adj* **:** born dead
still life *n, pl* **still lifes :** a picture of inanimate objects
still•ness *n* **1** ♦ **:** freedom from agitation **2** ♦ **:** the quality or state of being soundless

♦ [1] calm, calmness, hush, peace, placidity, quiet, quietness, repose, serenity, still, tranquillity ♦ [2] hush, quiet, quietness, silence, still

stilt \ˈstilt\ *n* **:** one of a pair of poles for walking with each having a step or loop for the foot to elevate the wearer above the ground; *also* **:** a polelike support of a structure above ground or water level
stilt•ed \ˈstil-təd\ *adj* ♦ **:** not easy and natural ⟨~ language⟩

♦ awkward, clumsy, gauche, graceless, inelegant, stiff, uncomfortable, uneasy, ungraceful, wooden

Stil•ton \ˈstilt-ᵊn\ *n* **:** a blue cheese of English origin
stim•u•lant \ˈsti-myə-lənt\ *n* **1 :** an agent (as a drug) that temporarily increases the activity of an organism or any of its parts **2 :** something that rouses or incites to activity **:** STIMULUS **3 :** an alcoholic beverage — **stimulant** *adj*
stim•u•late \-ˌlāt\ *vb* **-lat•ed; -lat•ing** ♦ **:** to make active or more active — **stim•u•la•tion** \ˌsti-myə-ˈlā-shən\ *n*

♦ animate, brace, energize, enliven, fire, invigorate, jazz up, liven up, pep up, quicken, vitalize, vivify, zip (up) ♦ arouse, encourage, excite, fire, incite, instigate, move, pique, provoke, stir

stim•u•la•tive \ˈsti-myə-ˌlā-tiv\ *adj* ♦ **:** having power or tending to stimulate

♦ bracing, invigorating, refreshing, restorative, tonic

stim•u•lus \ˈsti-myə-ləs\ *n, pl* **-li** \-ˌlī\ **1** ♦ **:** something that moves to activity **2 :** an agent that directly influences the activity of a living organism or one of its parts

♦ boost, encouragement, goad, impetus, impulse, incentive, incitement, instigation, momentum, motivation, provocation, spur, yeast

[1]**sting** \ˈstiŋ\ *vb* **stung** \ˈstəŋ\; **sting•ing** **1 :** to prick painfully especially with a sharp or poisonous process **2 :** to cause to suffer acutely
[2]**sting** *n* **1 a :** an act of stinging **b** ♦ **:** a wound, sore, or pain resulting from a sting **2 :** a pointed often venom-bearing organ (as of a bee) **:** STINGER **3 :** an elaborate confidence game; *esp* **:** one worked by undercover police to trap criminals

♦ ache, pain, pang, prick, smart, stitch, tingle, twinge

sting•er \ˈstiŋ-ər\ *n* **:** one that stings; *specif* **:** a sharp blow or remark
stin•gi•ness \ˈstin-jē-nəs\ *n* ♦ **:** the quality or state of being stingy

♦ cheapness, closeness, miserliness, parsimony, tightness

stin•gy \ˈstin-jē\ *adj* **stin•gi•er; -est** **1** ♦ **:** not generous **:** giving or spending as little as possible **2** ♦ **:** meanly scanty or small

♦ [1] cheap, close, mean, niggardly, parsimonious, penurious, spare, sparing, tight, tightfisted, uncharitable *Ant* bounteous, bountiful, charitable, generous, liberal, munificent, openhanded, unsparing, unstinting ♦ [2] light, meager (*or* meagre), niggardly, poor, scant, scanty, scarce, skimpy, slender, slim, spare, sparse

[1]**stink** \ˈstiŋk\ *vb* **stank** \ˈstaŋk\ *or* **stunk** \ˈstəŋk\; **stunk; stink•ing** **1 :** to give forth a strong and offensive smell **2 :** to be extremely bad in quality or repute
[2]**stink** *n* **:** a strong offensive odor
stink•bug \ˈstiŋk-ˌbəg\ *n* **:** any of various true bugs that emit a disagreeable odor
stink•er *n* **:** an offensive or contemptible person
[1]**stint** \ˈstint\ *vb* **1** ♦ **:** to be sparing or frugal **2 :** to cut short in amount

♦ *usu* **stint on** scant, skimp, spare

[2]**stint** *n* **1** ♦ **:** an assigned amount of work **2 :** RESTRAINT, LIMITATION **3** ♦ **:** a period of time spent at a particular activity

♦ [1] assignment, chore, duty, job, task ♦ [3] hitch, tenure, term, tour

sti•pend \ˈstī-ˌpend, -pənd\ *n* ♦ **:** a fixed sum of money paid periodically for services or to defray expenses

♦ emolument, hire, pay, payment, salary, wage

stip•ple \ˈsti-pəl\ *vb* **stip•pled; stip•pling** **1 :** to engrave by means of dots and light strokes **2 :** to apply (as paint or ink) with small short touches **3** ♦ **:** to mark with speckles — **stipple** *n*

♦ blotch, dapple, dot, fleck, freckle, mottle, pepper, speck, spot, sprinkle

stip•u•late \ˈsti-pyə-ˌlāt\ *vb* **-lat•ed; -lat•ing** **1 :** to make an agreement **2** ♦ **:** to make a special demand (for something) as a condition in an agreement

♦ call, claim, clamor (*or* clamour), command, demand, enjoin, exact, insist, press, quest

stip•u•la•tion \ˌsti-pyə-ˈlā-shən\ *n* **1 :** something stipulated **2** ♦ **:** a condition, requirement, or item specified in a legal instrument

♦ condition, provision, proviso, qualification, reservation

[1]**stir** \ˈstər\ *vb* **stirred; stir•ring** **1** ♦ **:** to move slightly **2 :** to disturb the quiet of **3** ♦ **:** to mix, dissolve, or make by continued circular movement ⟨~ eggs into cake batter⟩ **4** ♦ **:** to move to activity (as by pushing, beating, or prodding)

♦ [1] budge, move, shift ♦ [3] agitate, churn, swirl, whirl ♦ *usu* **stir up** [4] abet, ferment, foment, incite, instigate, provoke, raise, whip ♦ [4] arouse, encourage, excite, fire, incite, instigate, move, pique, provoke, stimulate

[2]**stir** *n* **1** ♦ **:** a state of agitation or activity **2** ♦ **:** an act of stirring

♦ [1] bustle, commotion, disturbance, turmoil, uproar, welter, whirl ♦ [2] motion, move, movement, moving, shift, stirring

stir–fry \ˈstər-ˌfrī\ *vb* **:** to fry quickly over high heat while stirring continuously — **stir–fry** *n*
stir•ring \ˈstər-iŋ\ *adj* **1 :** ACTIVE, BUSTLING **2** ♦ **:** giving rise to excitement

♦ breathtaking, electric, exciting, exhilarating, rousing, thrilling ♦ affecting, emotional, impressive, moving, poignant, touching

stir•rup \ˈstər-əp\ *n* **1 :** a light frame hung from a saddle to support the rider's foot **2 :** STAPES
[1]**stitch** \ˈstich\ *n* **1** ♦ **:** a sudden sharp pain especially in the side **2 :** one of the series of loops formed by or over a needle in sewing

♦ ache, pain, pang, prick, smart, sting, tingle, twinge

[2]**stitch** *vb* **1 :** to fasten or join with stitches **2 :** to decorate with stitches **3 :** SEW
stk *abbr* stock
stoat \ˈstōt\ *n, pl* **stoats** *also* **stoat :** the common Old and New World ermine especially in its brown summer coat
[1]**stock** \ˈstäk\ *n* **1** *archaic* **:** a block of wood **2 :** a stupid person **3 :** a wooden part of a thing serving as its support, frame, or handle **4** *pl* **:** a device for publicly punishing offenders consisting of a wooden frame with holes in which the feet and hands can be locked **5** ♦ **:** the original from which others derive; *also* **:** a group having a common origin **:** FAMILY **6 :** LIVESTOCK **7 :** a supply of goods **8 :** the ownership element in a corporation divided to give the owners an interest and usually voting power **9 :** a company of actors playing at a particular theater and presenting a series of plays **10 :** liquid in which meat, fish, or vegetables have been simmered that is used as a basis for soup, gravy, or sauce

♦ ancestry, blood, clan, family, folks, house, kin, kindred, kinfolk, line, lineage, people, race, tribe

[2]**stock** *vb* **:** to provide with stock
[3]**stock** *adj* **1 :** kept regularly for sale or use **2** ♦ **:** commonly used **:** STANDARD

♦ conventional, current, customary, popular, standard, usual

stock•ade \stä-ˈkād\ *n* ♦ **:** an enclosure (as of posts and stakes) for defense or confinement

♦ brig, hoosegow, jail, lockup, pen, penitentiary, prison

stock•bro•ker \-ˌbrō-kər\ *n* **:** one who executes orders to buy and sell securities
stock car *n* **:** a racing car that is similar to a regular car
stock exchange *n* **:** a place where the buying and selling of securities is conducted
stock•hold•er \ˈstäk-ˌhōl-dər\ *n* **:** one who owns corporate stock
stock•i•nette *or* **stock•i•net** \ˌstä-kə-ˈnet\ *n* **:** an elastic knitted fabric used especially for infants' wear and bandages
stock•ing \ˈstä-kiŋ\ *n* **:** a close-fitting knitted covering for the foot and leg
stock market *n* **1 :** STOCK EXCHANGE **2 :** a market for stocks
[1]**stock•pile** \ˈstäk-ˌpīl\ *n* ♦ **:** a reserve supply especially of something essential

♦ cache, hoard, stash, store

²stockpile *vb* ♦ **:** to place or store in or on a stockpile; *also* **:** to accumulate a stockpile of

♦ cache, hoard, lay away, lay up, put by, salt away, stash, store

stocky \ˈstä-kē\ *adj* **stock•i•er; -est** ♦ **:** being short and relatively thick

♦ chunky, dumpy, heavyset, squat, stout, stubby, stumpy, thickset

stock•yard \ˈstäk-ˌyärd\ *n* **:** a yard for stock; *esp* **:** one for livestock about to be slaughtered or shipped

stodgy \ˈstä-jē\ *adj* **stodg•i•er; -est 1 :** not interesting **:** DULL **2 :** extremely old-fashioned

¹sto•ic \ˈstō-ik\ *n* **:** one who suffers without complaining

²stoic *or* **sto•i•cal** \-i-kəl\ *adj* ♦ **:** not affected by passion or feeling; *esp* **:** showing indifference to pain — **sto•ical•ly** \-i-k(ə-)lē\ *adv* — **sto•icism** \ˈstō-ə-ˌsi-zəm\ *n*

♦ forbearing, long-suffering, patient, tolerant, uncomplaining ♦ apathetic, cold-blooded, impassive, phlegmatic, stolid, unemotional

stoke \ˈstōk\ *vb* **stoked; stok•ing 1 :** to stir up a fire **2 :** to tend and supply fuel to a furnace — **stok•er** *n*

STOL *abbr* short takeoff and landing

¹stole *past of* STEAL

²stole *n* **1 :** a long narrow band worn round the neck by some members of the clergy **2 :** a long wide scarf or similar covering worn by women

stolen *past part of* STEAL

stol•id \ˈstä-ləd\ *adj* ♦ **:** not easily aroused or excited **:** showing little or no emotion — **sto•lid•i•ty** \stä-ˈli-də-tē\ *n* — **stol•id•ly** *adv*

♦ apathetic, cold-blooded, impassive, phlegmatic, stoic, unemotional ♦ blank, deadpan, expressionless, impassive, inexpressive, vacant

sto•lon \ˈstō-lən, -ˌlän\ *n* **:** RUNNER 6

¹stom•ach \ˈstə-mək\ *n* **1 :** a saclike digestive organ of a vertebrate into which food goes from the mouth by way of the throat and which opens below into the intestine **2 :** a cavity in an invertebrate animal that is analogous to a stomach **3** ♦ **:** the part of the body that contains the stomach **:** ABDOMEN **4 :** desire for food caused by hunger **:** APPETITE **5 :** INCLINATION, DESIRE

♦ abdomen, belly, gut, solar plexus, tummy

²stomach *vb* ♦ **:** to bear without open resentment **:** put up with

♦ abide, bear, brook, countenance, endure, meet, stand, stick out, support, sustain, take, tolerate

stom•ach•ache \-ˌāk\ *n* **:** pain in or in the region of the stomach

stom•ach•er \ˈstə-mi-kər, -chər\ *n* **:** the front of a bodice often appearing between the laces of an outer garment (as in 16th-century costume)

stomp \ˈstämp, ˈstȯmp\ *vb* **1** ♦ **:** to walk with a loud heavy step usually in anger **2 :** to strike or beat forcibly with the bottom of the foot **:** STAMP — **stomp** *n*

♦ clump, lumber, pound, stamp, tramp, tromp

¹stone \ˈstōn\ *n* **1 :** hardened earth or mineral matter **:** ROCK **2 :** a small piece of rock **3 :** a precious stone **:** GEM **4 :** CALCULUS 3 **5 :** a hard stony seed (as of a date) or one (as of a plum) with a stony covering **6** *pl usu* **stone :** a British unit of weight equal to 14 pounds

²stone *vb* **stoned; ston•ing 1 :** to pelt or kill with stones **2 :** to remove the stones of (a fruit)

Stone Age *n* **:** the first known period of prehistoric human culture characterized by the use of stone tools

stoned \ˈstōnd\ *adj* **1 :** DRUNK **2 :** being under the influence of a drug

stone's throw *n* ♦ **:** a short distance

♦ ace, hair, inch, step

stone•wall \ˈstōn-ˌwȯl\ *vb* **:** to refuse to comply or cooperate with

stone•washed \ˈstōn-ˌwȯsht, -ˌwäsht\ *adj* **:** having been washed with stones during manufacture to create a softer fabric ⟨~ jeans⟩

stony *also* **ston•ey** \ˈstō-nē\ *adj* ♦ **:** manifesting no movement or reaction

♦ callous, hard, heartless, inhuman, inhumane, pitiless, soulless, unfeeling, unsympathetic

stood *past and past part of* STAND

stooge \ˈstüj\ *n* **1 :** a person who plays a subordinate or compliant role to a principal **2 :** STRAIGHT MAN

stool \ˈstül\ *n* **1 :** a seat usually without back or arms **2 :** FOOTSTOOL **3 :** a seat used while urinating or defecating **4 :** a discharge of fecal matter

stool pigeon *n* ♦ **:** a person acting as a decoy or informer; *esp* **:** a spy sent into a group to report (as to the police) on its activities

♦ betrayer, blabbermouth, informer, rat, snitch, tattler, tattletale

¹stoop \ˈstüp\ *vb* **1 :** to bend forward and downward **2 :** CONDESCEND **3 :** to lower oneself morally

²stoop *n* **1 :** an act of bending forward **2 :** a bent position of head and shoulders

³stoop *n* **:** a porch, platform, or entrance stairway at a house door

¹stop \ˈstäp\ *vb* **stopped; stop•ping 1** ♦ **:** to close (an opening) by filling or covering closely **2** ♦ **:** to cause to cease **:** HALT **3** ♦ **:** to cease to go on **4** ♦ **:** to bring activity or operation to an end **5 a :** STAY, TARRY **b** ♦ **:** to make a brief call — usually used with *by* or *in*

♦ *usu* **stop up** [1] block, choke, clog, close (off), congest, dam, fill, jam, obstruct, plug (up), stuff ♦ [2] arrest, catch, check, draw up, fetch up, halt, hold up, stall, stay, still ♦ [3, 4] break, break off, cease, cut, desist, discontinue, drop, end, halt, knock off, lay off, leave off, quit, shut off ♦ *usu* **stop by** *or* **stop in** [5b] call, drop (by *or* in), pop (in), visit

²stop *n* **1** ♦ **:** a temporary or final ceasing **:** END, CESSATION **2 :** a set of organ pipes of one tone quality; *also* **:** a control knob for such a set **3** ♦ **:** something that impedes, obstructs, or brings to a halt **:** OBSTRUCTION **4 :** PLUG, STOPPER **5 :** an act of stopping **:** CHECK **6 :** a delay in a journey **7 :** a place for stopping **8** *chiefly Brit* **:** any of several punctuation marks **9 :** a function of an electronic device that stops a recording

♦ [1] cessation, close, closure, conclusion, end, ending, expiration, finish, halt, lapse, shutdown, stoppage, termination ♦ [3] bar, block, clog, crimp, drag, embarrassment, hindrance, let, obstacle, stumbling block

stop–ac•tion \ˈstäp-ˈak-shən\ *n* **:** STOP-MOTION

stop•gap \ˈstäp-ˌgap\ *n* **:** something that serves as a temporary expedient **:** MAKESHIFT

stop•light \-ˌlīt\ *n* **:** TRAFFIC LIGHT

stop–mo•tion \ˈstäp-ˈmō-shən\ *n* **:** a filming technique in which successive positions of objects are photographed to produce the appearance of movement

stop•over \ˈstäp-ˌō-vər\ *n* **1 :** a stop at an intermediate point in one's journey **2 :** a stopping place on a journey

stop•page \ˈstä-pij\ *n* ♦ **:** the act of stopping **:** the state of being stopped

♦ cessation, close, closure, conclusion, end, ending, expiration, finish, halt, lapse, shutdown, stop, termination

stop•per \ˈstä-pər\ *n* **:** something (as a cork) for sealing an opening

stop•watch \ˈstäp-ˌwäch\ *n* **:** a watch that can be started or stopped at will for exact timing

stor•age \ˈstōr-ij\ *n* **1 a** ♦ **:** space for storing **b :** cost of storing **2 :** MEMORY 6 **3 :** the act of storing; *esp* **:** the safekeeping of goods (as in a warehouse)

♦ depository, depot, magazine, repository, storehouse, warehouse

storage battery *n* **:** a group of connected rechargeable electrochemical cells used to provide electric current

¹store \ˈstōr\ *vb* **stored; stor•ing 1** ♦ **:** to place or leave in a safe location for preservation or future use **2** ♦ **:** to provide especially for a future need

♦ [1, 2] cache, hoard, lay away, lay up, put by, salt away, stash, stockpile

²store *n* **1** ♦ **:** something accumulated and kept for future use **2 :** a large or ample quantity **3 :** STOREHOUSE **4** ♦ **:** a retail business establishment

♦ [1] cache, deposit, hoard, reserve, stash, stock, stockpile ♦ [4] emporium, shop

store•house \-ˌhau̇s\ *n* **1** ♦ **:** a building for storing goods or supplies **2 :** an abundant source or supply

♦ depository, depot, magazine, repository, storage, warehouse

store•keep•er \-ˌkē-pər\ *n* **:** one who operates a retail store

store•room \-ˌrüm, -ˌru̇m\ *n* **:** a room for storing goods or supplies

sto•ried \ˈstōr-ēd\ *adj* **:** celebrated in story or history

stork \ˈstȯrk\ *n* : any of various large stout-billed Old World wading birds related to the herons and ibises

¹storm \ˈstȯrm\ *n* **1** ♦ : a heavy fall of rain, snow, or hail with high wind **2** ♦ : a sudden or violent outbreak or disturbance **3** : a mass attack on a defended position **4** ♦ : a heavy discharge of objects **5** : a disturbed or agitated state — **storm•i•ly** \ˈstȯr-mə-lē\ *adv* — **storm•i•ness** \-mē-nəs\ *n*

♦ [1] cloudburst, deluge, downpour, rain, rainstorm, wet ♦ [2] cataclysm, convulsion, paroxysm, tempest, tumult, upheaval, uproar ♦ [2] agony, burst, eruption, explosion, fit, flare, flare-up, flash, flush, gale, gush, gust, outburst, paroxysm, spasm ♦ [4] barrage, bombardment, cannonade, fusillade, hail, salvo, shower, volley

²storm *vb* **1 a** : to blow with violence **b** ♦ : to rain, snow, or hail heavily **2** ♦ : to make a mass attack against **3** : to be violently angry : RAGE **4** : to rush along furiously

♦ [1b] pour, precipitate, rain ♦ [2] assail, assault, attack, beset, charge, descend, jump, pounce (on *or* upon), raid, rush, strike

stormy *adj* **1** ♦ : relating to, characterized by, or indicative of a storm **2** ♦ : marked by turmoil or fury

♦ [1] bleak, dirty, foul, inclement, nasty, raw, rough, squally, tempestuous, turbulent, wild ♦ [1] rainy, wet ♦ [2] explosive, ferocious, fierce, furious, hot, rabid, rough, tempestuous, turbulent, violent, volcanic

¹sto•ry \ˈstōr-ē\ *n, pl* **stories** **1** ♦ : an account of incidents or events : NARRATIVE **2** ♦ : a statement regarding the facts of a situation : REPORT **3** ♦ : usually short narrative of an interesting, amusing, or biographical incident : ANECDOTE **4** ♦ : a fictional narrative shorter than a novel : SHORT STORY **5** : an untrue statement made with intent to deceive : LIE, FALSEHOOD **6** ♦ : a news article or broadcast

♦ [1, 2] account, chronicle, history, narrative, record, report ♦ [3] anecdote, tale ♦ [4] narrative, novella, short story ♦ [6] intelligence, item, news, tidings, word

²story *also* **sto•rey** \ˈstōr-ē\ *n, pl* **stories** *also* **storeys** : a floor of a building or the space between two adjacent floor levels

sto•ry•tell•er \-ˌte-lər\ *n* : a teller of stories

¹stout \ˈstau̇t\ *adj* **1** ♦ : strong of character : BRAVE **2** ♦ : not weak or uncertain : FIRM **3** ♦ : physically or materially strong **4** : STAUNCH, ENDURING **5** : SOLID **6 a** : possessing or filled with force : FORCEFUL **b** : VIOLENT **7** ♦ : bulky in body : THICKSET

♦ [1, 3] brave, hard, hard-bitten, hardy, rugged, strong, sturdy, tough, vigorous ♦ [2] firm, forceful, hearty, lusty, robust, solid, strong, sturdy, vigorous ♦ [7] chunky, dumpy, heavyset, squat, stocky, stubby, stumpy, thickset

²stout *n* : a dark heavy ale

stout•ly *adv* ♦ : in a stout manner

♦ energetically, firmly, forcefully, forcibly, hard, mightily, powerfully, stiffly, strenuously, strongly, sturdily, vigorously

stout•ness *n* **1** ♦ : the quality or state of being strong physically or morally **2** : bulkiness of structure

♦ bravery, courage, daring, fearlessness, gallantry, guts, hardihood, heart, heroism, nerve, valor

¹stove \ˈstōv\ *n* : an apparatus that burns fuel or uses electricity to provide heat (as for cooking or heating)

²stove *past and past part of* STAVE

stow \ˈstō\ *vb* **1** : to put away : STORE **2** : to pack in a compact mass

stow•away \ˈstō-ə-ˌwā\ *n* : one who hides on a vehicle to ride free

STP *abbr* standard temperature and pressure

strad•dle \ˈstrad-ᵊl\ *vb* **strad•dled; strad•dling** **1** : to stand, sit, or walk with legs spread apart **2** : to favor or seem to favor two apparently opposite sides — **straddle** *n*

strafe \ˈstrāf\ *vb* **strafed; straf•ing** : to fire upon with machine guns from a low-flying airplane

strag•gle \ˈstra-gəl\ *vb* **strag•gled; strag•gling** **1** : to wander from the direct course : ROVE, STRAY **2** : to become separated from others of the same kind — **strag•gler** *n* — **strag•gly** \ˈstra-g(ə-)lē\ *adj*

¹straight \ˈstrāt\ *adj* **1** ♦ : free from curves, bends, angles, or irregularities **2** ♦ : not wandering from the main point or proper course ⟨~ thinking⟩ **3** ♦ : exhibiting honesty and fairness : UPRIGHT **4** : having the elements in correct order **5** : free from extraneous matter : UNMIXED ⟨~ whiskey⟩ **6** : CONVENTIONAL, SQUARE; *also* : HETEROSEXUAL **7** : marked by honest sincere expression

♦ [1] right, straightforward *Ant* crooked ♦ [2] direct, forthright, foursquare, plain, straightforward ♦ [3] decent, ethical, good, honest, honorable (*or* honourable), just, moral, right, righteous, upright, virtuous

²straight *adv* ♦ : in a straight manner

♦ dead, direct, directly, due, plump, right ♦ directly, forthrightly, foursquare, plain, plainly, straightforward

³straight *n* **1** : a straight line, course, or arrangement **2** : the part of a racetrack between the last turn and the finish **3** : a sequence of five cards in a poker hand

straight–arm \ˈstrāt-ˌärm\ *n* : an act of warding off a person with the arm fully extended — **straight–arm** *vb*

straight•away \ˈstrā-tə-ˌwā\ *n* : a straight stretch (as at a racetrack)

straightaway *adv* ♦ : without delay : IMMEDIATELY

♦ immediate, instant, instantaneous

straight•edge \ˈstrāt-ˌej\ *n* : a piece of material with a straight edge for testing straight lines and surfaces or drawing straight lines

straight•en \ˈstrāt-ᵊn\ *vb* : to make or become straight

straight flush *n* : a poker hand containing five cards of the same suit in sequence

straight•for•ward \strāt-ˈfȯr-wərd\ *adj* **1** ♦ : free from evasiveness or obscurity : CANDID **2** ♦ : proceeding in a straight course or manner

♦ [1] candid, direct, forthright, foursquare, frank, honest, open, outspoken, plain, straight, unguarded, unreserved ♦ [2] right, straight ♦ [2] direct, forthright, foursquare, plain, straight *Ant* circuitous, indirect, roundabout

straight man *n* : an entertainer who feeds lines to a comedian who replies with usually humorous quips

straight•way \ˈstrāt-ˈwā, -ˌwā\ *adv* : without delay or hesitation : IMMEDIATELY

¹strain \ˈstrān\ *n* **1** : line of descent : ANCESTRY **2** : a group (as of people or plants) of presumed common ancestry **3** : an inherited or inherent character or quality ⟨a ~ of madness in the family⟩ **4** : a slight admixture : TRACE **5** ♦ : a pleasing succession of musical tones : MELODY **6** : the general style or tone

♦ air, lay, melody, song, tune, warble

²strain *vb* **1** : to draw taut **2** ♦ : to exert to the utmost **3** : to strive violently **4** ♦ : to injure by improper or excessive use **5** : to filter or remove by filtering **6** : to stretch beyond a proper limit **7** : to pass through or as if through a strainer — **strain•er** *n*

♦ [2] drudge, endeavor (*or* endeavour), fag, grub, hustle, labor (*or* labour), peg, plod, plug, slave, slog, strive, struggle, sweat, toil, work ♦ [4] pull, rack, stretch, wrench

³strain *n* **1** ♦ : excessive tension or exertion (as of body or mind) **2** : bodily injury from excessive tension, effort, or use; *esp* : one in which muscles or ligaments are unduly stretched usually from a wrench or twist **3** : deformation of a material body under the action of applied forces

♦ pressure, stress, tension

strained *adj* : done or produced with excessive effort

¹strait \ˈstrāt\ *adj* **1** *archaic* : STRICT **2** *archaic* : NARROW **3** *archaic* : CONSTRICTED **4** : DIFFICULT, STRAITENED

²strait *n* **1** ♦ : a narrow channel connecting two bodies of water **2** *pl* : DISTRESS

♦ channel, narrows, sound

strait•en \ˈstrāt-ᵊn\ *vb* **1** : to hem in : CONFINE **2** : to make distressing or difficult

strait•jack•et *also* **straight•jack•et** \ˈstrāt-ˌja-kət\ *n* : a cover or garment of strong material (as canvas) used to bind the body and especially the arms closely in restraining a violent prisoner or patient — **straitjacket** *vb*

strait•laced *or* **straight•laced** \-ˈlāst\ *adj* ♦ : strict in manners, morals or opinion

♦ prim, prudish, puritanical

¹strand \ˈstrand\ *n* : SHORE, BEACH

²strand *vb* **1** : to run, drift, or drive upon the shore ⟨a ~*ed* ship⟩ **2** : to place or leave in a helpless position

³strand *n* **1** : one of the fibers twisted or plaited together into a cord, rope, or cable; *also* : a cord, rope, or cable made up of such fibers **2** : a twisted or plaited ropelike mass ⟨a ~ of pearls⟩ — **strand•ed** \ˈstran-dəd\ *adj*

strange \ˈstrānj\ *adj* **strang•er; strang•est** **1** : of external origin, kind, or character **2** ♦ : not before known, heard, or seen **3** : DISTANT 6 **4** ♦ : not habituated : UNACCUSTOMED — **strange·ly** *adv* — **strange·ness** *n*

♦ [2] fresh, new, novel, original, unfamiliar, unknown ♦ [2] bizarre, curious, far-out, funny, kinky, odd, outlandish, outré, peculiar, quaint, queer, quirky, remarkable, screwy, wacky, weird, wild ♦ [4] curious, extraordinary, funny, odd, peculiar, queer, rare, unaccustomed, uncommon, unique, unusual, weird

strang·er \ˈstrān-jər\ *n* **1** : FOREIGNER **2** : INTRUDER **3** : a person with whom one is unacquainted

stran·gle \ˈstraŋ-gəl\ *vb* **stran·gled; stran·gling** **1** ♦ : to choke to death **2** : to withhold from circulation or expression : SUPPRESS — **stran·gler** *n*

♦ choke, garrote, throttle

stran·gu·late \ˈstraŋ-gyə-ˌlāt\ *vb* **-lat·ed; -lat·ing** **1** : STRANGLE, CONSTRICT **2** : to become so constricted as to stop circulation

stran·gu·la·tion \ˌstraŋ-gyə-ˈlā-shən\ *n* : the act or process of strangling or strangulating; *also* : the state of being strangled or strangulated

¹strap \ˈstrap\ *n* : a narrow strip of flexible material used especially for fastening, holding together, or wrapping

²strap *vb* **strapped; strap·ping** **1** : to secure with a strap **2** : BIND, CONSTRICT **3** : to flog with a strap **4** : STROP

strap·less \-ləs\ *adj* : having no straps; *esp* : having no shoulder straps

¹strapping *adj* : LARGE, STRONG, HUSKY

²strap·ping *n* : material for a strap

strat·a·gem \ˈstra-tə-jəm, -ˌjem\ *n* **1** ♦ : a trick to deceive or outwit the enemy; *also* : a deceptive scheme **2** : skill in deception

♦ artifice, device, dodge, gimmick, jig, ploy, scheme, sleight, trick, wile

strat·e·gy \ˈstra-tə-jē\ *n, pl* **-gies** **1** : the science and art of military command aimed at meeting the enemy under conditions advantageous to one's own force **2** ♦ : a careful plan or method especially for achieving an end — **stra·te·gic** \strə-ˈtē-jik\ *adj* — **strat·e·gist** \ˈstra-tə-jist\ *n*

♦ approach, fashion, form, manner, method, style, system, tack, tactics, technique, way

strat·i·fy \ˈstra-tə-ˌfī\ *vb* **-fied; -fy·ing** : to form or arrange in layers — **strat·i·fi·ca·tion** \ˌstra-tə-fə-ˈkā-shən\ *n*

stra·tig·ra·phy \strə-ˈti-grə-fē\ *n* : geology that deals with rock strata — **strati·graph·ic** \ˌstra-tə-ˈgra-fik\ *adj*

strato·sphere \ˈstra-tə-ˌsfir\ *n* : the part of the earth's atmosphere between about 7 miles (11 kilometers) and 31 miles (50 kilometers) above the earth — **strato·spher·ic** \ˌstra-tə-ˈsfir-ik, -ˈsfer-\ *adj*

stra·tum \ˈstrā-təm, ˈstra-\ *n, pl* **stra·ta** \ˈstrā-tə, ˈstra-\ **1** : a bed, layer, or sheetlike mass (as of one kind of rock lying between layers of other kinds of rock) **2** ♦ : a level of culture; *also* : a group of people representing one stage in cultural development

♦ caste, class, estate, folk, order

¹straw \ˈstrȯ\ *n* **1** : stalks of grain after threshing; *also* : a single coarse dry stem (as of a grass) **2** : a thing of small worth : TRIFLE **3** : a tube (as of paper or plastic) for sucking up a beverage

²straw *adj* **1** : made of straw **2** : having no real force or validity ⟨a ∼ vote⟩ **3** ♦ : of the color of straw

♦ blond, fair, flaxen, golden, sandy

straw·ber·ry \ˈstrȯ-ˌber-ē, -bə-rē\ *n* : an edible juicy usually red pulpy fruit of any of several low herbs with white flowers and long slender runners; *also* : one of these herbs

straw boss *n* : a foreman of a small group of workers

straw·flow·er \ˈstrȯ-ˌflau̇-ər\ *n* : any of several plants whose flowers can be dried with little loss of form or color

¹stray \ˈstrā\ *n* **1** : a domestic animal wandering at large or lost **2** : WAIF

²stray *vb* **1** : to wander or roam without purpose **2** : DEVIATE

³stray *adj* **1** : having strayed : separated from the group or the main body **2** ♦ : occurring at random ⟨∼ remarks⟩

♦ aimless, arbitrary, desultory, erratic, haphazard, random, scattered

¹streak \ˈstrēk\ *n* **1** ♦ : a line or mark of a different color or texture from its background **2** : a narrow band of light; *also* : a lightning bolt **3** : a slight admixture : TRACE **4** : a brief run (as of luck); *also* : an unbroken series

♦ band, bar, stripe

²streak *vb* **1** : to form streaks in or on **2** : to move very swiftly

¹stream \ˈstrēm\ *n* **1** : a body of water (as a river) flowing on the earth; *also* : any body of flowing fluid (as water or gas) **2** : a continuous procession ⟨a ∼ of traffic⟩

²stream *vb* **1** ♦ : to flow in or as if in a stream **2** : to pour out streams of liquid **3** : to trail out in length **4** : to move forward in a steady stream

♦ flow, pour, roll, run ♦ bowl, breeze, coast, drift, flow, glide, roll, sail, skim, slide, slip, sweep, whisk

stream·bed \ˈstrēm-ˌbed\ *n* : the channel occupied by a stream

stream·er \ˈstrē-mər\ *n* **1** ♦ : a long narrow ribbonlike flag **2** : a long ribbon on a dress or hat **3** : a newspaper headline that runs across the entire sheet **4** *pl* : AURORA

♦ banner, colors (*or* colours), ensign, flag, jack, pennant, standard

stream·ing \ˈstrē-miŋ\ *adj* : relating to or being the transfer of data (as music) in a continuous stream especially for immediate processing or playback

stream·let \ˈstrēm-lət\ *n* ♦ : a small stream

♦ brook, creek, rill, rivulet

stream·lined \-ˌlīnd\ *adj* **1** : made with contours to reduce resistance to motion through water or air **2** : SIMPLIFIED **3** : MODERNIZED — **stream·line** *vb*

street \ˈstrēt\ *n* **1** ♦ : a thoroughfare especially in a city, town, or village **2** : the occupants of the houses on a street

♦ artery, avenue, drag, drive, pass, road, route, thoroughfare, way

street·car \-ˌkär\ *n* : a passenger vehicle running on rails on city streets

street hockey *n* : a game resembling ice hockey played on a hard surface with hockey sticks and a small ball

street railway *n* : a company operating streetcars or buses

street·walk·er \ˈstrēt-ˌwȯ-kər\ *n* : PROSTITUTE

strength \ˈstreŋth\ *n* **1** ♦ : the quality of being strong : ability to do or endure **2** ♦ : power to resist force **3** : power to resist attack **4** : INTENSITY **5** : force as measured in numbers ⟨the ∼ of an army⟩

♦ [1] energy, force, main, might, muscle, potency, power, sinew, vigor (*or* vigour) ♦ [2] firmness, soundness, stability, steadiness, sturdiness

strength·en \ˈstreŋ-thən\ *vb* ♦ : to make or become stronger — **strength·en·er** *n*

♦ beef, fortify, harden, toughen *Ant* debilitate, enervate, enfeeble, weaken ♦ amplify, beef, boost, consolidate, deepen, enhance, heighten, intensify, magnify, redouble, step up

stren·u·ous \ˈstren-yə-wəs\ *adj* **1** : vigorously active : ENERGETIC **2** ♦ : requiring energy or stamina

♦ arduous, demanding, difficult, exacting, formidable, grueling, hard, herculean, laborious, murderous, rough, stiff, tall, toilsome, tough

stren·u·ous·ly *adv* ♦ : in a strenuous manner

♦ energetically, firmly, forcefully, forcibly, hard, mightily, powerfully, stiffly, stoutly, strongly, sturdily, vigorously

strep \ˈstrep\ *n* : STREPTOCOCCUS

strep throat *n* : an inflammatory sore throat caused by streptococci and marked by fever, prostration, and toxemia

strep·to·coc·cus \ˌstrep-tə-ˈkä-kəs\ *n, pl* **-coc·ci** \-ˈkä-ˌkī, -ˈkäk-ˌsī, -ˈkä-ˌkē, -ˈkäk-ˌsē\ : any of various spherical bacteria that usually grow in chains and include some causing serious diseases — **strep·to·coc·cal** \-kəl\ *adj*

strep·to·my·cin \-ˈmīs-ᵊn\ *n* : an antibiotic produced by soil bacteria and used especially in treating tuberculosis

¹stress \ˈstres\ *n* **1** : PRESSURE, STRAIN; *esp* : a force that tends to distort a body **2** ♦ : a factor that induces bodily or mental tension; *also* : a state induced by such a stress **3** ♦ : force or intensity that gives impressiveness or importance to something : EMPHASIS **4** : relative prominence of sound **5** : ACCENT; *also* : any syllable carrying the accent — **stress·ful** \ˈstres-fəl\ *adj*

♦ [2] pressure, strain, tension ♦ [3] accent, accentuation, emphasis, weight

²stress *vb* **1** : to put pressure or strain on **2** ♦ : to put emphasis on : ACCENT

♦ accent, accentuate, emphasize, feature, highlight, play, point, underline, underscore

1stretch \ˈstrech\ *vb* **1** ♦ **:** to spread or reach out **:** EXTEND **2** ♦ **:** to draw out in length or breadth **:** EXPAND — often used with *out* **3 :** to make tense; *also* **:** to injure by improper or excessive use **:** STRAIN **4** ♦ **:** to amplify or enlarge beyond natural or proper limits **:** EXAGGERATE **5 :** to become extended without breaking ⟨rubber ~*es* easily⟩

♦ [1] draw out, elongate, extend, lengthen, prolong, protract ♦ *usu* **stretch out** [2] expand, extend, fan, flare, open, spread, unfold ♦ [4] color (*or* colour), elaborate, embellish, embroider, exaggerate, magnify, pad

2stretch *n* **1 :** an act of extending or drawing out beyond ordinary or normal limits **2** ♦ **:** a continuous extent in length, area, or time **3 :** the extent to which something may be stretched **4 :** either of the straight sides of a racecourse

♦ distance, lead, length ♦ breadth, expanse, extent, reach, spread ♦ bit, space, spell, while

3stretch *adj* **:** easily stretched ⟨~ pants⟩

stretch•er \ˈstre-chər\ *n* **1 :** one that stretches **2 :** a device for carrying a sick, injured, or dead person

stretch marks *n pl* **:** striae on the skin (as of the abdomen) due to excessive stretching and rupture of elastic fibers (as from pregnancy)

strew \ˈstrü\ *vb* **strewed; strewed** *or* **strewn** \ˈstrün\; **strew•ing 1 :** to spread by scattering **2** ♦ **:** to cover by or as if by scattering something over or on **3 :** DISSEMINATE

♦ dot, pepper, scatter, sow, spray, sprinkle

stria \ˈstrī-ə\ *n, pl* **stri•ae** \ˈstrī-ˌē\ **1 :** STRIATION 3 **2 :** a stripe or line (as in the skin)

stri•at•ed muscle \ˈstrī-ˌā-təd-\ *n* **:** muscle tissue made up of long thin cells with many nuclei and alternate light and dark stripes that includes especially the muscle of the heart and muscle that moves the vertebrate skeleton and is mostly under voluntary control

stri•a•tion \strī-ˈā-shən\ *n* **1 :** the state of being marked with stripes or lines **2 :** arrangement of striations or striae **3 :** a minute groove, scratch, or channel especially when one of a parallel series

strick•en \ˈstri-kən\ *adj* **1 :** afflicted by or as if by disease, misfortune, or sorrow **2 :** WOUNDED

strict \ˈstrikt\ *adj* **1** ♦ **:** allowing no evasion or escape **:** RIGOROUS ⟨~ discipline⟩ **2** ♦ **:** free from error **:** PRECISE

♦ [1] austere, authoritarian, flinty, hard, harsh, heavy-handed, ramrod, rigid, rigorous, severe, stern ♦ [2] accurate, authentic, exact, faithful, precise, right, true, veracious

strict•ly *adv* ♦ **:** in a strict manner

♦ exactly, precisely, rigidly, rigorously *Ant* imprecisely, inexactly, loosely

strict•ness *n* ♦ **:** the quality or state of being strict

♦ hardness, harshness, inflexibility, rigidity, severity, sternness

stric•ture \ˈstrik-chər\ *n* **1 :** an abnormal narrowing of a bodily passage; *also* **:** the narrowed part **2** ♦ **:** hostile criticism **:** a critical remark

♦ censure, denunciation, rebuke, reprimand, reproach, reproof

1stride \ˈstrīd\ *vb* **strode** \ˈstrōd\; **strid•den** \ˈstrid ᵊn\; **strid•ing** ♦ **:** to walk or run with long regular steps — **strid•er** *n*

♦ file, march, pace, parade

2stride *n* **1 :** a long step **2 :** a stage of progress **3 :** manner of striding **:** GAIT

stri•dent \ˈstrīd-ᵊnt\ *adj* **:** harsh sounding **:** GRATING, SHRILL

strife \ˈstrīf\ *n* **1** ♦ **:** the state or condition of distrust or enmity **:** CONFLICT **2 :** FIGHT, STRUGGLE

♦ conflict, discord, dissension, dissent, disunity, friction, schism, variance, war, warfare

1strike \ˈstrīk\ *vb* **struck** \ˈstrək\; **struck** *also* **strick•en** \ˈstri-kən\; **strik•ing 1 :** to take a course **:** GO ⟨*struck* off through the brush⟩ **2** ♦ **:** to touch or hit sharply; *also* **:** to deliver a blow **3 :** to produce by or as if by a blow ⟨*struck* terror in the foe⟩ **4 :** to lower (as a flag or sail) **5** ♦ **:** to collide with; *also* **:** to injure or destroy by collision **6 :** DELETE, CANCEL **7 :** to produce by impressing ⟨*struck* a medal⟩; *also* **:** COIN ⟨~ a new cent⟩ **8 :** to cause to sound ⟨~ a bell⟩ **9 :** to afflict suddenly **:** lay low ⟨*stricken* with a high fever⟩ **10** ♦ **:** to appear to; *also* **:** to appear to as remarkable **:** IMPRESS **11 :** to reach by reckoning ⟨~ an average⟩ **12 :** to stop work in order to obtain a change in conditions of employment **13 :** to cause (a match) to ignite by rubbing **14 :** to come upon ⟨~ gold⟩ **15 :** TAKE ON, ASSUME ⟨~ a pose⟩ **16 :** to occur to **17** ♦ **:** to dismantle and take away — **strik•er** *n*

♦ [2] bash, bat, clout, crack, hit, slug, swat ♦ [2] assail, assault, attack, beset, charge, descend, jump, pounce (on *or* upon), raid, rush, storm ♦ [5] bang, bash, bump, collide, crash, hit, impact, knock, ram, slam, smash, swipe, thud ♦ [10] affect, impact, impress, influence, move, sway, tell, touch ♦ [17] disassemble, dismantle, knock down, take down

2strike *n* **1** ♦ **:** an act or instance of striking **2 :** a sudden discovery of rich ore or oil deposits **3 :** a pitched baseball that is swung at but not hit **4 :** the knocking down of all the bowling pins with the 1st ball **5** ♦ **:** a military attack **6** ♦ **:** a quality or circumstance that makes achievement unusually difficult

♦ [1] bump, collision, concussion, crash, impact, jar, jolt, shock, smash, wallop ♦ [5] aggression, assault, attack, charge, descent, offense (*or* offence), offensive, onset, onslaught, raid, rush ♦ [6] disadvantage, drawback, handicap, liability, minus, penalty

strike•break•er \-ˌbrā-kər\ *n* **:** a person hired to replace a striking worker

strike•out \-ˌau̇t\ *n* **:** an out in baseball as a result of a batter's being charged with three strikes

strike out *vb* **1 :** to enter upon a course of action **2 :** to start out vigorously **3 :** to make an out in baseball by a strikeout

strike up *vb* **1 :** to begin or cause to begin to sing or play **2 :** BEGIN

strike zone *n* **:** the area over home plate through which a pitched baseball must pass to be called a strike

striking *adj* ♦ **:** attracting attention **:** very noticeable — **strik•ing•ly** *adv*

♦ bold, catchy, conspicuous, emphatic, marked, noticeable, prominent, pronounced, remarkable

1string \ˈstriŋ\ *n* **1** ♦ **:** a line usually composed of twisted threads **2** ♦ **:** a series of things arranged as if strung on a cord **3 :** a plant fiber (as a leaf vein) **4** *pl* **:** the stringed instruments of an orchestra

♦ [1] cable, cord, lace, line, rope, wire ♦ [2] column, cue, file, line, queue, range, train ♦ [2] chain, progression, sequence, train

2string *vb* **strung** \ˈstrəŋ\; **string•ing 1 :** to provide with strings ⟨~ a racket⟩ **2 :** to make tense **3 :** to thread on or as if on a string ⟨~ pearls⟩ **4 :** to hang, tie, or fasten by a string **5 :** to take the strings out of ⟨~ beans⟩ **6 :** to extend like a string

string along *vb* ♦ **:** to cause to accept as true or valid what is false or invalid

♦ beguile, bluff, cozen, deceive, delude, dupe, fool, gull, have, hoax, hoodwink, humbug, misinform, mislead, take in, trick

string bean *n* **:** a bean of one of the older varieties of kidney bean that have stringy fibers on the lines of separation of the pods; *also* **:** SNAP BEAN

string bikini *n* **:** a scanty bikini

string cheese *n* **:** cheese that can be pulled apart in narrow strips

stringed \ˈstriŋd\ *adj* **1 :** having strings ⟨~ instruments⟩ **2 :** produced by strings

strin•gen•cy \ˈstrin-jən-sē\ *n* **1 :** STRICTNESS, SEVERITY **2 :** SCARCITY ⟨~ of money⟩

strin•gent \-jənt\ *adj* ♦ **:** marked by rigor, strictness, or severity especially with regard to rule or standard

♦ exacting, inflexible, rigid, rigorous, strict, uncompromising

string•er \ˈstriŋ-ər\ *n* **1 :** a long horizontal member in a framed structure or a bridge **2 :** a news correspondent paid by the amount of copy

stringy \ˈstriŋ-ē\ *adj* **string•i•er; -est 1 :** resembling string especially in tough, fibrous, or disordered quality ⟨~ meat⟩ ⟨~ hair⟩ **2 :** lean and sinewy in build

1strip \ˈstrip\ *vb* **stripped** \ˈstript\ *also* **stript; strip•ping 1** ♦ **:** to take the covering or clothing from **2 :** to take off one's clothes **3 :** to pull or tear off **4 :** to make bare or clear (as by cutting or grazing) **5 :** to deprive of possessions **:** PLUNDER — **strip•per** *n*

♦ unclothe, undress

2strip *n* **1 :** a long narrow flat piece **2 :** AIRSTRIP

1stripe \ˈstrīp\ *vb* **striped** \ˈstrīpt\; **strip•ing** ♦ **:** to mark with stripes

♦ band, bar, streak

2stripe *n* **1** ♦ **:** a line or long narrow division having a different color from the background **2 :** a strip of braid (as on a sleeve) indicating military rank or length of service **3 :** TYPE, CHARACTER — **striped** \ˈstrīpt, ˈstrī-pəd\ *adj*

♦ band, bar, streak

striped bass *n* **:** a large black-striped marine bony fish that occurs along the Atlantic and Pacific coasts of the U.S. and is an excellent food and sport fish

strip•ling \ˈstri-pliŋ\ *n* **1 :** YOUTH **2** ♦ **:** an adolescent male **:** LAD

♦ boy, lad, nipper, shaver, youth

strip mall *n* **:** a long building or group of buildings housing several retail stores or service establishments

strip mine *n* **:** a mine that is worked from the earth's surface by the stripping of the topsoil — **strip–mine** *vb*

strip•tease \ˈstrip-ˌtēz\ *n* **:** a burlesque act in which a performer removes clothing piece by piece — **strip•teas•er** *n*

strive \ˈstrīv\ *vb* **strove** \ˈstrōv\ *also* **strived** \ˈstrīvd\; **striv•en** \ˈstri-vən\ *or* **strived; striv•ing 1** ♦ **:** to make an effort **:** labor hard **2 :** to struggle in opposition **:** CONTEND

♦ assay, attempt, endeavor (*or* endeavour), essay, seek, try

strobe \ˈstrōb\ *n* **1 :** STROBOSCOPE **2 :** a device for high-speed intermittent illumination (as in photography)

stro•bo•scope \ˈstrō-bə-ˌskōp\ *n* **:** an instrument for studying rapid motion by means of a rapidly flashing light

strode *past of* STRIDE

[1]**stroke** \ˈstrōk\ *vb* **stroked; strok•ing 1 a :** to rub gently **b** ♦ **:** to touch or stroke lightly in a loving or endearing manner **2 :** to flatter in a manner designed to persuade

♦ caress, fondle, love, pat, pet

[2]**stroke** *n* **1 :** the act of striking **:** BLOW **2 :** a sudden action or process producing an impact ⟨∼ of lightning⟩; *also* **:** an unexpected result **3 :** sudden weakening or loss of consciousness or the power to move or feel caused by rupture or obstruction (as by a clot) of a blood vessel of the brain **4 :** one of a series of movements against air or water to get through or over it ⟨the ∼ of a bird's wing⟩ **5 :** a rower who sets the pace for a crew **6 :** a vigorous effort **7 :** the sound of striking (as of a clock) **8 :** a single movement with or as if with a tool or implement (as a pen)

[1]**stroll** \ˈstrōl\ *vb* **:** to walk in a leisurely or idle manner

[2]**stroll** *n* ♦ **:** an idle and leisurely walk

♦ perambulation, ramble, turn, walk

stroll•er *n* ♦ **:** one who goes idly about

♦ drifter, nomad, rambler, rover, vagabond, wanderer

strong \ˈstrȯŋ\ *adj* **stron•ger** \ˈstrȯŋ-gər\; **stron•gest** \ˈstrȯŋ-gəst\ **1** ♦ **:** having or marked by power **2 :** HEALTHY, ROBUST **3 :** of a specified number ⟨an army 10 thousand ∼⟩ **4** ♦ **:** not mild or weak **5 :** VIOLENT ⟨∼ wind⟩ **6 :** ZEALOUS **7** ♦ **:** not easily broken **8 :** well established **:** FIRM, SOLID **9** ♦ **:** having an offensive or intense odor or flavor

♦ [1] brawny, muscular, powerful, rugged, sinewy, stalwart, stout ***Ant*** delicate, feeble, frail, weak, wimpy ♦ [1] cogent, compelling, conclusive, convincing, decisive, effective, forceful, persuasive, satisfying, telling ♦ [4] firm, forceful, hearty, lusty, robust, solid, stout, sturdy, vigorous ♦ [7] fast, firm, sound, stable, stalwart, steady, sturdy ♦ [9] fetid, foul, fusty, malodorous, musty, noisome, rank, reeky, smelly ♦ [9] nippy, pungent, sharp

strong–arm \ˈstrȯŋ-ˈärm\ *adj* **:** having or using undue force ⟨∼ methods⟩

strong force *n* **:** the physical force responsible for binding together nucleons in the atomic nucleus

strong•hold \-ˌhōld\ *n* ♦ **:** a fortified place **:** FORTRESS

♦ bastion, citadel, fastness, fort, fortification, fortress, hold

strong•ly *adv* ♦ **:** in a strong manner

♦ energetically, firmly, forcefully, forcibly, hard, mightily, powerfully, stiffly, stoutly, strenuously, sturdily, vigorously

strong•man \-ˌman\ *n* **:** one who leads or controls by force of will and character or by military strength

stron•tium \ˈsträn-chē-əm, ˈsträn-tē-əm\ *n* **:** a soft malleable metallic chemical element

[1]**strop** \ˈsträp\ *n* **:** STRAP; *esp* **:** one for sharpening a razor

[2]**strop** *vb* **stropped; strop•ping** ♦ **:** to sharpen a razor on a strop

♦ edge, grind, hone, sharpen, whet

stro•phe \ˈstrō-fē\ *n* **:** a division of a poem — **stroph•ic** \ˈsträ-fik\ *adj*

strove *past of* STRIVE

struck *past and past part of* STRIKE

[1]**struc•ture** \ˈstrək-chər\ *n* **1 :** the action of building **:** CONSTRUCTION **2 :** something built (as a house or a dam); *also* **:** something made up of interdependent parts in a definite pattern of organization **3** ♦ **:** arrangement or relationship of elements (as particles, parts, or organs) in a substance, body, or system — **struc•tur•al** *adj*

♦ configuration, frame, framework, shell, skeleton

[2]**structure** *vb* **struc•tured; struc•tur•ing :** to make into a structure

stru•del \ˈstrüd-ᵊl, ˈshtrüd-\ *n* **:** a pastry made of a thin sheet of dough rolled up with filling and baked ⟨apple ∼⟩

[1]**strug•gle** \ˈstrə-gəl\ *vb* **strug•gled; strug•gling 1 :** to make strenuous efforts against opposition **:** STRIVE **2** ♦ **:** to proceed with difficulty or with great effort

♦ drudge, endeavor (*or* endeavour), fag, grub, hustle, labor (*or* labour), peg, plod, plug, slave, slog, strain, strive, sweat, toil, work

[2]**struggle** *n* **1** ♦ **:** exertion or contention for superiority **:** CONTEST **2** ♦ **:** a violent effort or exertion

♦ [1] battle, combat, conflict, confrontation, contest, duel, face-off, rivalry, tug-of-war, warfare ♦ [2] battle, effort, exertion, fight, fray, scrabble

strum \ˈstrəm\ *vb* **strummed; strum•ming :** to play on a stringed instrument by brushing the strings with the fingers ⟨∼ a guitar⟩

strum•pet \ˈstrəm-pət\ *n* **:** PROSTITUTE

strung \ˈstrəŋ\ *past and past part of* STRING

[1]**strut** \ˈstrət\ *vb* **strut•ted; strut•ting 1** ♦ **:** to walk with an affectedly proud gait **2** ♦ **:** to parade (as clothes) with a show of pride

♦ [1] stalk, swagger ♦ [2] display, disport, exhibit, expose, flash, flaunt, parade, show, show off, sport, unveil

[2]**strut** *n* **1 :** a bar or rod for resisting lengthwise pressure **2 :** a haughty or pompous gait

strych•nine \ˈstrik-ˌnīn, -nən, -ˌnēn\ *n* **:** a bitter poisonous plant alkaloid used as a poison (as for rats) and medicinally as a stimulant of the central nervous system

[1]**stub** \ˈstəb\ *n* **1 :** STUMP 2 **2 :** a short blunt end **3 :** a small part of each leaf (as of a checkbook) kept as a memorandum of the items on the detached part

[2]**stub** *vb* **stubbed; stub•bing :** to strike (as one's toe) against something

stub•ble \ˈstə-bəl\ *n* **1 :** the cut stem ends of herbs and especially grasses left in the soil after harvest **2 :** a rough surface or growth resembling stubble — **stub•bly** \-b(ə-)lē\ *adj*

stub•born \ˈstə-bərn\ *adj* **1 :** FIRM, DETERMINED **2** ♦ **:** done or continued in a willful, unreasonable, or persistent manner **3 :** not easily controlled or remedied ⟨a ∼ cold⟩ — **stub•born•ly** *adv*

♦ dogged, hardheaded, headstrong, mulish, obdurate, obstinate, opinionated, peevish, pertinacious, perverse, pigheaded, unyielding, willful

stub•born•ness *n* ♦ **:** the quality or state of being stubborn

♦ hardheadedness, mulishness, obduracy, obstinacy, peevishness, pertinacity, self-will, tenacity

stub•by \ˈstə-bē\ *adj* ♦ **:** short, blunt, and thick like a stub

♦ chunky, dumpy, heavyset, squat, stocky, stout, stumpy, thickset

stuc•co \ˈstə-kō\ *n, pl* **stuccos** *or* **stuccoes :** plaster for coating exterior walls — **stuc•coed** \ˈstə-kōd\ *adj*

stuck *past and past part of* STICK

stuck–up \ˈstək-ˈəp\ *adj* ♦ **:** having or showing an excessively high opinion of oneself **:** CONCEITED

♦ complacent, conceited, egotistic, important, overweening, pompous, prideful, proud, self-important, self-satisfied, smug, vain

[1]**stud** \ˈstəd\ *n* **:** a male animal and especially a horse (**stud•horse** \-ˌhȯrs\) kept for breeding

[2]**stud** *n* **1 :** one of the smaller uprights in a building to which the wall materials are fastened **2 :** a removable device like a button used as a fastener or ornament ⟨shirt ∼*s*⟩ **3 :** a projecting nail, pin, or rod

[3]**stud** *vb* **stud•ded; stud•ding 1 :** to supply with or adorn with studs **2 :** DOT

[4]**stud** *abbr* student

stud•book \ˈstəd-ˌbu̇k\ *n* **:** an official record of the pedigree of purebred animals (as horses or dogs)

stud•ding \ˈstə-diŋ\ *n* : the studs in a building or wall
stu•dent \ˈstüd-ᵊnt, ˈstyüd-\ *n* : SCHOLAR, PUPIL; *esp* : one who attends a school
stud•ied \ˈstə-dēd\ *adj* ♦ : carefully considered or prepared ⟨a ∼ insult⟩

♦ advised, calculated, deliberate, measured, reasoned, thoughtful, thought-out

stu•dio \ˈstü-dē-ˌō, ˈstyü-\ *n, pl* **-dios** **1** : a place where an artist works; *also* : a place for the study of an art **2** : a place where motion pictures are made **3** : a place equipped for the transmission of radio or television programs
stu•di•ous \ˈstü-dē-əs, ˈstyü-\ *adj* : devoted to study — **stu•di•ous•ly** *adv*
¹study \ˈstə-dē\ *n, pl* **stud•ies** **1** : the use of the mind to gain knowledge **2** : the act or process of learning about something **3** ♦ : careful examination **4** : INTENT, PURPOSE **5** : a branch of learning **6** : a room especially for reading and writing **7** ♦ : a state of contemplation

♦ [3] examination, exploration, inquiry, investigation, probe, research ♦ [7] reverie, trance, woolgathering

²study *vb* **stud•ied; study•ing** **1** : to engage in study or the study of **2** ♦ : to consider attentively or in detail

♦ chew over, cogitate, consider, contemplate, debate, deliberate, entertain, meditate, mull, ponder, question, ruminate, think, weigh

¹stuff \ˈstəf\ *n* **1** : personal property **2** ♦ : raw material **3** : a finished textile fabric; *esp* : a worsted fabric **4** : writing, talk, or ideas of little or transitory worth **5** : an unspecified material substance or aggregate of matter **6** ♦ : fundamental material **7** ♦ : special knowledge or capability

♦ [2] material, raw material, substance ♦ [6] essence, nature, quintessence, soul, substance ♦ [7] capability, credentials, qualification

²stuff *vb* **1** ♦ : to fill by packing things in : CRAM **2** ♦ : to eat greedily : GORGE **3** : to prepare (as meat) by filling with a stuffing **4** : to fill (as a cushion) with a soft material **5** ♦ : to stop up : PLUG

♦ [1] charge, cram, fill, heap, jam, jam pack, load, pack ♦ [2] glut, gorge, sate, surfeit ♦ [5] block, choke, clog, close (off), congest, dam, jam, obstruct, plug (up), stop (up)

stuffed shirt \ˈstəft-\ *n* : a smug, conceited, and usually pompous and inflexibly conservative person
stuff•ing *n* ♦ : material used to fill tightly; *esp* : a mixture of bread crumbs and spices used to stuff food

♦ fill, filler, filling, padding

stuffy \ˈstə-fē\ *adj* **stuff•i•er; -est** **1** ♦ : lacking in vitality or interest : STODGY **2** ♦ : lacking fresh air : CLOSE; *also* : blocked up ⟨a ∼ nose⟩

♦ [1] drab, dreary, dry, dull, flat, heavy, humdrum, leaden, monotonous, ponderous, stupid, tame, uninteresting, weary ♦ [2] breathless, close *Ant* airy, breezy

stul•ti•fy \ˈstəl-tə-ˌfī\ *vb* **-fied; -fy•ing** **1** : to cause to appear foolish or stupid **2** : to impair, invalidate, or make ineffective **3** : to have a dulling effect on — **stul•ti•fi•ca•tion** \ˌstəl-tə-fə-ˈkā-shən\ *n*
¹stum•ble \ˈstəm-bəl\ *vb* **stum•bled; stum•bling** **1** : to blunder morally **2** ♦ : to trip in walking or running **3 a** ♦ : to walk unsteadily **b** : to speak or act in a blundering or clumsy manner **4** : to happen by chance **5** ♦ : to come unexpectedly or by chance

♦ [2] fall, slip, topple, trip, tumble ♦ [3a] clump, flounder, limp, lumber, scuff, scuffle, shamble, shuffle, tramp, tromp ♦ *usu* **stumble on** *or* **stumble onto** *or* **stumble upon** [5] chance, encounter, find, happen (on *or* upon), hit, meet, stumble

²stumble *n* ♦ : an act or instance of stumbling

♦ fall, slip, spill, tumble ♦ blunder, error, fault, flub, fumble, goof, lapse, miscue, misstep, mistake, oversight, slip

stumbling block *n* ♦ : an obstacle to belief, understanding, or progress

♦ bar, block, clog, crimp, drag, embarrassment, hindrance, let, obstacle, stop

¹stump \ˈstəmp\ *n* **1** : the base of a bodily part (as a leg or tooth) left after the rest is removed **2** : the part of a plant and especially a tree remaining with the root after the trunk is cut off **3** : a place or occasion for political public speaking
²stump *vb* **1** : BAFFLE, PERPLEX **2** : to clear (land) of stumps **3** : to tour (a region) making political speeches **4** : to walk clumsily and heavily **5** : to challenge to perform an action
stumpy *adj* ♦ : short and thick

♦ chunky, dumpy, heavyset, squat, stocky, stout, stubby, thickset

stun \ˈstən\ *vb* **stunned; stun•ning** **1** : to make senseless or dizzy by or as if by a blow **2** ♦ : to overcome especially with paralyzing astonishment or disbelief : STUPEFY

♦ amaze, astonish, astound, bowl, dumbfound, flabbergast, floor, shock, startle, stupefy, surprise

stung *past and past part of* STING
stunk *past and past part of* STINK
stunned *adj* ♦ : affected by stunning; *also* : caused by or as if by stunning

♦ amazed, awestruck, thunderstruck ♦ confused, dizzy

stun•ning *adj* **1** ♦ : causing astonishment or disbelief **2** ♦ : strikingly beautiful — **stun•ning•ly** *adv*

♦ [1] amazing, astonishing, astounding, eye-opening, shocking, startling, surprising ♦ [1] awesome, fabulous, marvelous (*or* marvellous), miraculous, portentous, prodigious, stupendous, sublime, surprising, wonderful ♦ [2] attractive, beautiful, fair, gorgeous, handsome, knockout, lovely, pretty, ravishing

¹stunt \ˈstənt\ *vb* : to hinder the normal growth or progress of
²stunt *n* ♦ : an unusual or spectacular feat

♦ deed, exploit, feat, trick

stu•pe•fy \ˈstü-pə-ˌfī, ˈstyü-\ *vb* **-fied; -fy•ing** **1** : to make stupid, groggy, or insensible **2** ♦ : to strike with sudden and usually great wonder or surprise : ASTONISH — **stu•pe•fac•tion** \ˌstü-pə-ˈfak-shən, ˌstyü-\ *n*

♦ amaze, astonish, astound, bowl, dumbfound, flabbergast, floor, shock, startle, stun, surprise

stu•pen•dous \stu̇-ˈpen-dəs, styu̇-\ *adj* ♦ : causing astonishment especially because of great size or height

♦ amazing, astonishing, astounding, awesome, awful, eye-opening, fabulous, marvelous (*or* marvellous), miraculous, portentous, prodigious, stunning, sublime, surprising, wonderful

stu•pen•dous•ly *adv* ♦ : to a stupendous degree

♦ broadly, considerably, greatly, hugely, largely, massively, monstrously, much, sizably, tremendously, utterly, vastly

stu•pid \ˈstü-pəd, ˈstyü-\ *adj* **1** ♦ : very dull in mind **2** ♦ : showing or resulting from dullness of mind **3** ♦ : lacking interest or intellectual stimulation ⟨a ∼ book⟩ — **stu•pid•ly** *adv*

♦ [1] dense, dull, dumb, fatuous, mindless, obtuse, senseless, simple, slow, thick, unintelligent, vacuous, witless *Ant* brainy, brilliant, clever, intelligent, quick-witted, sharp, smart ♦ [2] absurd, crazy, cuckoo, fatuous, foolish, mad, nonsensical, nutty, senseless, silly, stupid ♦ [3] drab, dreary, monotonous, ponderous, uninteresting, weary

stu•pid•i•ty \stu̇-ˈpi-də-tē, styu̇-\ *n* **1** ♦ : the quality or state of being stupid **2** ♦ : a stupid idea or act

♦ [1] denseness, dopiness, fatuity, foolishness, imbecility, mindlessness, obtuseness, vacuity *Ant* brightness, brilliance, cleverness, intelligence, keenness, quickness, sharpness, smartness ♦ [2] absurdity, asininity, fatuity, folly, foolery, idiocy, imbecility, inanity, insanity, lunacy

stu•por \ˈstü-pər, ˈstyü-\ *n* **1** ♦ : a condition of greatly dulled or completely suspended sense or feeling **2** : a state of extreme apathy or torpor often following stress or shock — **stu•por•ous** *adj*

♦ apathy, impassivity, numbness, phlegm

stur•di•ly \ˈstər-də-lē\ *adv* ♦ : in a sturdy manner

♦ energetically, firmly, forcefully, forcibly, hard, mightily, powerfully, stiffly, stoutly, strenuously, strongly, vigorously

stur•di•ness \-dē-nəs\ *n* ♦ : the quality or state of being sturdy

♦ firmness, soundness, stability, steadiness, strength

stur•dy \ˈstər-dē\ *adj* **stur•di•er; -est** **1** : RESOLUTE, UNYIELDING **2** ♦ : capable of withstanding adverse conditions : STRONG

♦ hard, hard-bitten, hardy, rugged, stout, strong, tough, vigorous ♦ fast, firm, sound, stable, stalwart, steady, strong

stur·geon \ˈstər-jən\ *n* **:** any of a family of large bony fishes including some whose roe are made into caviar
stut·ter \ˈstə-tər\ *vb* **:** to speak with involuntary disruption or blocking of sounds — **stutter** *n* — **stut·ter·er** *n*
stutter step *n* **:** a move made by a runner (as in football) done to fake a defender out of position
[1]**sty** \ˈstī\ *n, pl* **sties 1 :** a pen for pigs **2** ♦ **:** a dirty place

♦ dump, hole, pigsty, shambles, sty

[2]**sty** *or* **stye** *n, pl* **sties** *or* **styes :** an inflamed swelling of a skin gland on the edge of an eyelid
[1]**style** \ˈstīl\ *n* **1 :** mode of address **:** TITLE **2** ♦ **:** a way of speaking or writing; *esp* **:** one characteristic of an individual, period, school, or nation ⟨ornate ∼⟩ **3** ♦ **:** manner or method of acting, making, or performing; *also* **:** a distinctive or characteristic manner **4 :** a slender pointed instrument or process; *esp* **:** STYLUS **5** ♦ **:** a fashionable manner or mode **6 :** overall excellence, skill, or grace in performance, manner, or appearance **7 :** the custom followed in spelling, capitalization, punctuation, and typography — **sty·lis·tic** \stī-ˈlis-tik\ *adj*

♦ [2] fashion, locution, manner, mode, phraseology, tone, vein ♦ [3] approach, fashion, form, manner, method, strategy, system, tack, tactics, technique, way ♦ [5] craze, fad, mode, rage, trend, vogue

[2]**style** *vb* **styled; styl·ing 1** ♦ **:** to call or designate by an identifying term **:** NAME **2 :** to make or design in accord with a prevailing mode

♦ baptize, call, christen, denominate, designate, dub, entitle, label, name, term, title

styl·ing \ˈstī-liŋ\ *n* **:** the way in which something is styled
styl·ise *chiefly Brit var of* STYLIZE
styl·ish \ˈstī-lish\ *adj* ♦ **:** conforming to current fashion — **styl·ish·ly** *adv* — **styl·ish·ness** *n*

♦ à la mode, chic, fashionable, in, modish, sharp, smart, snappy *Ant* dowdy, outmoded, unfashionable, unstylish

styl·ist \ˈstī-list\ *n* **1 :** one (as a writer) noted for a distinctive style **2 :** a developer or designer of styles
styl·ize \ˈstī-ˌlīz, ˈstī-ə-\ *vb* **styl·ized; styl·iz·ing :** to conform to a style; *esp* **:** to represent or design according to a pattern or style rather than according to nature or tradition — **styl·i·za·tion** \ˌstī-lə-ˈzā-shən\ *n*
sty·lus \ˈstī-ləs\ *n, pl* **sty·li** \ˈstī-ˌlī\ *also* **sty·lus·es** \ˈstī-lə-səz\ **1 :** a pointed implement used by the ancients for writing on wax **2 :** a phonograph needle **3 :** a pen-shaped pointing device for entering data into a computer
sty·mie \ˈstī-mē\ *vb* **sty·mied; sty·mie·ing** ♦ **:** to present an obstacle to **:** stand in the way of

♦ encumber, hamper, hinder, hold up, impede, inhibit, interfere with, obstruct, tie up

styp·tic \ˈstip-tik\ *adj* **:** tending to check bleeding — **styptic** *n*
suave \ˈswäv\ *adj* ♦ **:** persuasively pleasing **:** smoothly agreeable — **suave·ly** *adv* — **sua·vi·ty** \ˈswä-və-tē\ *n*

♦ debonair, smooth, sophisticated, urbane *Ant* boorish, churlish, clownish, loutish, uncouth

[1]**sub** \ˈsəb\ *n* **:** a person or thing that takes the place or function of another **:** SUBSTITUTE
[2]**sub** *n* **1 :** a naval vessel designed to operate underwater **:** SUBMARINE **2 :** a large sandwich on a long split roll with any of a variety of fillings **:** SUBMARINE
[3]**sub** *abbr* **1** subtract **2** suburb
[4]**sub** *vb* ♦ **:** to serve as a substitute

♦ cover, fill in, pinch-hit, stand in, substitute, take over

sub- \ˈsəb\ *prefix* **1 :** under **:** beneath **2 :** subordinate **:** secondary **3 :** subordinate portion of **:** subdivision of **4 :** with repetition of a process described in a simple verb so as to form, stress, or deal with subordinate parts or relations **5 :** somewhat **6 :** falling nearly in the category of **:** bordering on

subacute
subagency
subagent
subaqueous
subarctic
subarea
subatmospheric
subaverage
subbasement
subcategory
subcellular
subchapter
subclass
subclassify
subcommittee
subcontract
subcontractor
subculture
subcutaneous
subdiscipline
subentry
subfamily
subfield
subfreezing
subgenre
subgenus
subgroup
subhead
subheading
subhuman
subkingdom
sublethal
subliterate
subminimal
subminimum
suboptimal
suborder
subparagraph
subparallel
subphylum
subplot
subpopulation
subproblem
subprofessional
subprogram
subregion
subroutine
subsection
subsense
subsoil
subspecies
substage
substation
subsystem
subteen
subthreshold
subtopic
subtotal
subtreasury
subtype
subunit
subvariety
subvisible
subzero

sub·al·pine \ˌsəb-ˈal-ˌpīn\ *adj* **1 :** of or relating to the region about the foot and lower slopes of the Alps **2 :** of, relating to, or inhabiting high upland slopes especially just below the timberline
sub·al·tern \sə-ˈbȯl-tərn\ *n* **:** SUBORDINATE; *esp* **:** a junior officer (as in the British army)
sub·as·sem·bly \ˌsəb-ə-ˈsem-blē\ *n* **:** an assembled unit to be incorporated with other units in a finished product
sub·atom·ic \ˌsəb-ə-ˈtä-mik\ *adj* **:** of or relating to the inside of the atom or to particles smaller than atoms
sub·clin·i·cal \ˌsəb-ˈkli-ni-kəl\ *adj* **:** not detectable by the usual clinical tests ⟨a ∼ infection⟩
sub·com·pact \ˈsəb-ˈkäm-ˌpakt\ *n* **:** an automobile smaller than a compact
[1]**sub·con·scious** \ˌsəb-ˈkän-chəs, ˈsəb-\ *adj* **:** existing in the mind without entering conscious awareness — **sub·con·scious·ly** *adv* — **sub·con·scious·ness** *n*
[2]**subconscious** *n* **:** mental activities just below the threshold of consciousness
sub·con·ti·nent \ˌsəb-ˈkänt-ᵊn-ənt\ *n* **:** a major subdivision of a continent — **sub·con·ti·nen·tal** \ˌsəb-ˌkänt-ᵊn-ˈent-ᵊl\ *adj*
sub·di·vide \ˌsəb-də-ˈvīd, ˈsəb-də-ˌvīd\ *vb* **:** to divide the parts of into more parts; *esp* **:** to divide (a tract of land) into building lots — **sub·di·vi·sion** \-ˈvi-zhən, -ˌvi-\ *n*
sub·duc·tion \səb-ˈdək-shən\ *n* **:** the descent of the edge of one crustal plate beneath the edge of an adjacent plate
sub·due \səb-ˈdü, -ˈdyü\ *vb* **sub·dued; sub·du·ing 1** ♦ **:** to conquer and bring into subjection **2 :** to bring under control **:** CURB **3 :** to reduce the intensity of

♦ conquer, dominate, overpower, subject, vanquish

subdued *adj* ♦ **:** lacking in vitality, intensity, or strength

♦ conservative, muted, quiet, restrained, unpretentious

subj *abbr* **1** subject **2** subjunctive
[1]**sub·ject** \ˈsəb-jikt\ *n* **1 :** a person under the authority of another **2 :** a person subject to a sovereign **3 :** an individual that is studied or experimented on **4** ♦ **:** the person or thing discussed or treated **:** TOPIC **5 :** a word or word group denoting that of which something is predicated

♦ content, matter, motif, motive, question, theme, topic

[2]**subject** *adj* **1 :** being under the power or rule of another **2** ♦ **:** suffering a particular liability or exposure **:** LIABLE ⟨∼ to floods⟩ **3** ♦ **:** dependent on some act or condition ⟨appointment ∼ to senate approval⟩

♦ *usu* **subject to** [2] exposed, liable, open, sensitive, susceptible, vulnerable ♦ *usu* **subject to** [3] conditional, contingent, dependent

[3]**sub·ject** \səb-ˈjekt\ *vb* **1** ♦ **:** to bring under control **:** CONQUER **2 :** to make liable **3 :** to cause to undergo or endure

♦ conquer, dominate, overpower, subdue, vanquish

sub·jec·tion \-ˈjek-shən\ *n* ♦ **:** the act of subduing or subjecting

♦ conquest, domination

sub·jec·tive \(ˌ)səb-ˈjek-tiv\ *adj* **1 :** of, relating to, or constituting a subject **2 :** of, relating to, or arising within one's self or mind in contrast to what is outside **:** PERSONAL — **sub·jec·tive·ly** *adv* — **sub·jec·tiv·i·ty** \-ˌjek-ˈti-və-tē\ *n*
subject matter *n* **:** matter presented for consideration, discussion, or study

sub•join \(ˌ)səb-ˈjȯin\ *vb* : APPEND
sub ju•di•ce \(ˌ)sůb-ˈyü-di-ˌkā, ˈsəb-ˈjü-də-(ˌ)sē\ *adv* : before a judge or court : not yet legally decided
sub•ju•gate \ˈsəb-ji-ˌgāt\ *vb* **-gat•ed; -gat•ing 1** : to bring under control and governance as a subject : CONQUER **2** : ENSLAVE
sub•ju•ga•tion \ˌsəb-ji-ˈgā-shən\ *n* **1** : an act of subjugating **2** : the state of being subjugated
sub•junc•tive \səb-ˈjəŋk-tiv\ *adj* : of, relating to, or constituting a verb form that represents an act or state as contingent or possible or viewed emotionally (as with desire) ⟨the ~ mood⟩ — **subjunctive** *n*
sub•lease \ˈsəb-ˈlēs, -ˌlēs\ *n* : a lease by a lessee of part or all of leased premises to another person with the original lessee retaining some right under the original lease — **sublease** *vb*
¹sub•let \ˈsəb-ˈlet\ *vb* **-let; -let•ting** : to let all or a part of (a leased property) to another; *also* : to rent (a property) from a lessee
²sublet \-ˌlet\ *n* : property and especially housing obtained by or available through a sublease
sub•li•mate \ˈsə-blə-ˌmāt\ *vb* **-mat•ed; -mat•ing 1** : SUBLIME **2** : to direct the expression of (as a desire or impulse) from a primitive to a more socially and culturally acceptable form — **sub•li•ma•tion** \ˌsə-blə-ˈmā-shən\ *n*
¹sub•lime \sə-ˈblīm\ *vb* **sub•limed; sub•lim•ing** : to pass or cause to pass directly from the solid to the vapor state
²sublime *adj* **1** ♦ : lofty, grand, or exalted in thought, expression, or manner : NOBLE **2** ♦ : having awe-inspiring beauty or grandeur — **sub•lime•ly** *adv* — **sub•lim•i•ty** \-ˈbli-mə-tē\ *n*

♦ [1] chivalrous, gallant, great, greathearted, high, high-minded, lofty, lordly, magnanimous, noble ♦ [2] amazing, astonishing, astounding, awesome, awful, eye-opening, fabulous, marvelous (*or* marvellous), miraculous, portentous, prodigious, stunning, stupendous, surprising, wonderful

sub•lim•i•nal \(ˌ)səb-ˈli-mən-ᵊl, ˈsəb-\ *adj* **1** : inadequate to produce a sensation or mental awareness ⟨~ stimuli⟩ **2** : existing or functioning below the threshold of consciousness ⟨the ~ mind⟩ ⟨~ advertising⟩
sub•ma•chine gun \ˌsəb-mə-ˈshēn-ˌgən\ *n* : an automatic firearm fired from the shoulder or hip
¹sub•ma•rine \ˈsəb-mə-ˌrēn, ˌsəb-mə-ˈrēn\ *adj* ♦ : lying, growing, worn, or operating below the surface of the water : UNDERWATER; *esp* : UNDERSEA

♦ sunken, underwater

²submarine *n* **1** : a naval vessel designed to operate underwater **2** ♦ : a large sandwich made from a long split roll with any of a variety of fillings

♦ grinder, hoagie, poor boy, sub

sub•merge \səb-ˈmərj\ *vb* **sub•merged; sub•merg•ing 1** ♦ : to put or plunge under the surface of water **2** ♦ : to cover or overflow with water : INUNDATE — **sub•mer•gence** \-ˈmər-jəns\ *n*

♦ [1] dip, douse, duck, dunk, immerse, souse ♦ [2] deluge, drown, engulf, flood, inundate, overflow, overwhelm, swamp

sub•merse \səb-ˈmərs\ *vb* **sub•mersed; sub•mers•ing** : to put or go under water : SUBMERGE — **sub•mer•sion** \-ˈmər-zhən\ *n*
¹sub•mers•ible \səb-ˈmər-sə-bəl\ *adj* : capable of being submerged
²submersible *n* : something that is submersible; *esp* : a small underwater craft used for deep-sea research
sub•mi•cro•sco•pic \ˌsəb-ˌmī-krə-ˈskä-pik\ *adj* : too small to be seen in an ordinary light microscope
sub•min•ia•ture \ˌsəb-ˈmi-nē-ə-ˌchůr, ˈsəb-, -ˈmi-ni-ˌchůr, -chər\ *adj* : very small
sub•mis•sion \-ˈmi-shən\ *n* ♦ : an act of submitting to the authority or control of another

♦ compliance, conformity, obedience, observance, subordination ♦ capitulation, relinquishment, surrender

sub•mis•sive \-ˈmi-siv\ *adj* ♦ : submitting to others

♦ amenable, compliant, conformable, docile, obedient, tractable

sub•mit \səb-ˈmit\ *vb* **sub•mit•ted; sub•mit•ting 1** ♦ : to commit to the discretion or decision of another or of others **2** ♦ : to yield oneself to the authority or will of another : SURRENDER **3** : to put forward as an opinion

♦ bow, budge, capitulate, concede, give in, knuckle under, quit, succumb, surrender, yield

sub•nor•mal \ˌsəb-ˈnȯr-məl\ *adj* : falling below what is normal; *also* : having less of something and especially intelligence than is normal — **sub•nor•mal•i•ty** \ˌsəb-nȯr-ˈma-lə-tē\ *n*

sub•or•bit•al \ˌsəb-ˈȯr-bət-ᵊl, ˈsəb-\ *adj* : being or involving less than one orbit
¹sub•or•di•nate \sə-ˈbȯrd-ᵊn-ət\ *adj* **1** ♦ : of lower class or rank **2** : INFERIOR **3** : submissive to authority **4** : subordinated to other elements in a sentence ⟨~ clause⟩

♦ inferior, junior, less, lesser, lower, minor, under

²subordinate *n* ♦ : one that is subordinate

♦ inferior, junior, underling

³sub•or•di•nate \sə-ˈbȯrd-ᵊn-ˌāt\ *vb* **-nat•ed; -nat•ing 1** : to place in a lower rank or class **2** : SUBDUE
sub•or•di•na•tion \-ˌbȯrd-ᵊn-ˈā-shən\ *n* **1** : the act of subordinating (as by making secondary or subject) **2** ♦ : the quality or state of being subordinate to authority : obedient submission

♦ compliance, conformity, obedience, observance, submission

sub•orn \sə-ˈbȯrn\ *vb* **1** : to induce secretly to do an unlawful thing **2** : to induce to commit perjury — **sub•or•na•tion** \ˌsə-ˌbȯr-ˈnā-shən\ *n*
¹sub•poe•na \sə-ˈpē-nə\ *n* : a writ commanding the person named in it to attend court under penalty for failure to do so
²subpoena *vb* **-naed; -na•ing** : to summon with a subpoena
sub–Sa•ha•ran \ˌsəb-sə-ˈhar-ən\ *adj* : of, relating to, or being the part of Africa south of the Sahara
sub•scribe \səb-ˈskrīb\ *vb* **sub•scribed; sub•scrib•ing 1** : to sign one's name to a document **2** : to give consent by or as if by signing one's name **3** : to promise to contribute by signing one's name with the amount promised **4** : to place an order by signing **5** : to receive a periodical or service regularly on order **6** ♦ : to feel favorably disposed : FAVOR — usually used with *to* — **sub•scrib•er** *n*

♦ *usu* **subscribe to** accept, approve, care, countenance, favor (*or* favour), OK ♦ *usu* **subscribe to** accede, agree, assent, come round, consent

sub•script \ˈsəb-ˌskript\ *n* : a symbol (as a letter or number) immediately below or below and to the right or left of another written character — **subscript** *adj*
sub•scrip•tion \səb-ˈskrip-shən\ *n* **1** : the act of subscribing : SIGNATURE **2** : a purchase by signed order
sub•se•quent \ˈsəb-si-kwənt, -sə-ˌkwent\ *adj* ♦ : following after : SUCCEEDING

♦ after, later, posterior ***Ant*** antecedent, anterior, fore, precedent, preceding, previous, prior

sub•se•quent•ly *adv* ♦ : in a subsequent manner

♦ after, afterward, later, thereafter

sub•ser•vi•ence \səb-ˈsər-vē-əns\ *n* **1** : a subordinate place or condition **2** : SERVILITY — **sub•ser•vi•en•cy** \-ən-sē\ *n* — **sub•ser•vi•ent** \-ənt\ *adj*
sub•set \ˈsəb-ˌset\ *n* : a set each of whose elements is an element of an inclusive set
sub•side \səb-ˈsīd\ *vb* **sub•sid•ed; sub•sid•ing 1** : to settle to the bottom of a liquid **2** : to tend downward : DESCEND **3** : SINK, SUBMERGE **4** ♦ : to become quiet and tranquil — **sub•sid•ence** \səb-ˈsīd-ᵊns, ˈsəb-sə-dəns\ *n*

♦ abate, de-escalate, decline, decrease, die, diminish, dwindle, ebb, fall, lessen, let up, lower, moderate, recede, relent, shrink, taper, wane

¹sub•sid•iary \səb-ˈsi-dē-ˌer-ē\ *adj* **1** : furnishing aid or support **2** : of secondary importance **3** : of or relating to a subsidy
²subsidiary *n, pl* **-iar•ies** : one that is subsidiary; *esp* : a company controlled by another
sub•si•dise *chiefly Brit var of* SUBSIDIZE
sub•si•dize \ˈsəb-sə-ˌdīz\ *vb* **-dized; -diz•ing** ♦ : to aid or furnish with a subsidy

♦ capitalize, endow, finance, fund, stake, underwrite

sub•si•dy \ˈsəb-sə-dē\ *n, pl* **-dies** ♦ : a gift of public money to a private person or company or to another government

♦ allocation, allotment, appropriation, grant

sub•sist \səb-ˈsist\ *vb* **1** ♦ : to have existence; *also* : to continue to exist **2** : to have the means (as food and clothing) of maintaining life; *esp* : to nourish oneself

♦ be, breathe, exist, live

sub•sis•tence \səb-ˈsis-təns\ *n* **1** ♦ : real being : EXISTENCE; *also* : the condition of remaining in existence : PERSISTENCE **2** : means of subsisting : the minimum (as of food and clothing) necessary to support life

♦ actuality, existence, reality ♦ continuance, continuation, duration, endurance, persistence

sub•son•ic \ˌsəb-ˈsä-nik, ˈsəb-\ *adj* : being or relating to a speed less than that of sound; *also* : moving at such a speed

sub•species \ˈsəb-ˌspē-shēz, -sēz\ *n* : a subdivision of a species; *esp* : a category in biological classification ranking just below a species that designates a geographic population genetically distinct from other such populations and potentially able to breed with them where its range overlaps theirs

sub•stance \ˈsəb-stəns\ *n* **1** ♦ : essential nature : ESSENCE ⟨divine ~⟩; *also* : the fundamental or essential part or quality ⟨the ~ of the speech⟩ **2** ♦ : physical material from which something is made or which has discrete existence; *also* : matter of particular or definite chemical constitution **3** ♦ : material possessions : WEALTH **4** : something (as drugs or alcohol) deemed harmful and usually subject to legal restriction ⟨~ abuse⟩

♦ [1] essence, nature, quintessence, soul, stuff ♦ [2] being, entity, individual, object, thing ♦ [2] material, raw material, stuff ♦ [3] assets, capital, fortune, means, opulence, riches, wealth, wherewithal

substance abuse *n* : excessive use of a drug (as alcohol or cocaine) : use of a drug without medical justification

sub•stan•dard \ˌsəb-ˈstan-dərd\ *adj* ♦ : falling short of a standard or norm

♦ bad, deficient, inferior, lousy, off, poor, punk, rotten, unacceptable, unsatisfactory, wanting, wretched, wrong

sub•stan•tial \səb-ˈstan-chəl\ *adj* **1** ♦ : existing as or in substance : MATERIAL; *also* : not illusory : REAL **2** ♦ : marked by or indicative of significant worth or consequence : IMPORTANT **3** : NOURISHING, SATISFYING ⟨~ meal⟩ **4** : having means : WELL-TO-DO **5** ♦ : large in extent or degree : CONSIDERABLE ⟨~ profit⟩ **6** : STRONG, FIRM — **sub•stan•tial•ly** *adv*

♦ [1] concrete, material, physical, real ♦ [2] big, consequential, eventful, important, major, material, meaningful, momentous, significant, weighty ♦ [5] considerable, good, goodly, healthy, respectable, significant, sizable, tidy

sub•stan•ti•ate \səb-ˈstan-chē-ˌāt\ *vb* **-at•ed; -at•ing** **1** ♦ : to give substance or body to **2** ♦ : to establish by proof or competent evidence

♦ [1] embody, epitomize, manifest, materialize, personify ♦ [2] bear out, confirm, corroborate, prove, support, validate, verify, vindicate

sub•stan•ti•a•tion \-ˌstan-chē-ˈā-shən\ *n* ♦ : something offered as proof

♦ attestation, confirmation, corroboration, documentation, evidence, proof, testament, testimony, validation, witness

¹sub•stan•tive \ˈsəb-stən-tiv\ *n* : NOUN; *also* : a word or phrase used as a noun

²substantive *adj* : having substance : REAL

¹sub•sti•tute \ˈsəb-stə-ˌtüt, -ˌtyüt\ *n* ♦ : a person or thing replacing another

♦ backup, pinch hitter, relief, replacement, reserve, stand-in, sub

²substitute *vb* **-tut•ed; -tut•ing** **1** ♦ : to put or use in the place of another **2** ♦ : to serve as a substitute — **sub•sti•tu•tion** \ˌsəb-stə-ˈtü-shən, -ˈtyü-\ *n*

♦ [1] change, commute, exchange, shift, swap, switch, trade ♦ [2] cover, fill in, pinch-hit, stand in, sub, take over ♦ [2] displace, replace, supersede, supplant

³substitute *adj* ♦ : serving as or fitted for use as a substitute

♦ backup, new

sub•strate \ˈsəb-ˌstrāt\ *n* **1** : the base on which a plant or animal lives **2** : a substance acted upon (as by an enzyme)

sub•stra•tum \ˈsəb-ˌstrā-təm, -ˌstra-\ *n, pl* **-stra•ta** \-tə\ : the layer or structure (as subsoil) lying underneath

sub•struc•ture \ˈsəb-ˌstrək-chər\ *n* : FOUNDATION, GROUNDWORK

sub•sume \səb-ˈsüm\ *vb* **sub•sumed; sub•sum•ing** ♦ : to include or place within something larger or more comprehensive

♦ carry, comprehend, contain, embrace, encompass, entail, include, involve, number, take in

sub•sur•face \ˈsəb-ˌsər-fəs\ *n* : earth material near the surface of the ground — **subsurface** *adj*

sub•ter•fuge \ˈsəb-tər-ˌfyüj\ *n* ♦ : deception by artifice or stratagem in order to conceal, escape, or evade; *also* : a trick or device used to deceive

♦ artifice, chicanery, hanky-panky, trickery, wile

sub•ter•ra•nean \ˌsəb-tə-ˈrā-nē-ən\ *adj* **1** : lying or being underground **2** : SECRET, HIDDEN

sub•tile \ˈsət-ᵊl\ *adj* **sub•til•er** \ˈsət-lər, -ᵊl-ər\; **sub•til•est** \ˈsət-ləst, -ᵊl-əst\ : SUBTLE

sub•ti•tle \ˈsəb-ˌtīt-ᵊl\ *n* **1** : a secondary or explanatory title (as of a book) **2** : printed matter projected on a motion-picture screen during or between the scenes

sub•tle \ˈsət-ᵊl\ *adj* **sub•tler** \ˈsət-ᵊl-ər\; **sub•tlest** \ˈsət-ᵊl-əst\ **1** : hardly noticeable ⟨~ differences⟩ **2** : SHREWD, PERCEPTIVE **3** : adept in the use of subtlety and cunning : CLEVER, SLY **4** ♦ : cunningly made or contrived — **sub•tly** \ˈsət-ᵊl-ē\ *adv*

♦ delicate, exact, fine, minute, nice, refined

sub•tle•ty \-tē\ *n* : the quality or state of being subtle

sub•tract \səb-ˈtrakt\ *vb* : to take away (as one part or number) from another; *also* : to perform the operation of deducting one number from another — **sub•trac•tion** \-ˈtrak-shən\ *n*

sub•tra•hend \ˈsəb-trə-ˌhend\ *n* : a number that is to be subtracted from another

sub•trop•i•cal \ˌsəb-ˈträ-pi-kəl, ˈsəb-\ *also* **sub•trop•ic** \-pik\ *adj* : of, relating to, or being regions bordering on the tropical zone — **sub•trop•ics** \-piks\ *n pl*

sub•urb \ˈsə-ˌbərb\ *n* **1** : an outlying part of a city; *also* : a small community adjacent to a city **2** *pl* : a residential area adjacent to a city — **sub•ur•ban** \sə-ˈbər-bən\ *adj or n* — **sub•ur•ban•ite** \sə-ˈbər-bə-ˌnīt\ *n*

sub•ur•bia \sə-ˈbər-bē-ə\ *n* **1** ♦ : the suburbs of a city **2** : suburban people or customs

♦ environs, exurbia, outskirts

sub•ven•tion \səb-ˈven-chən\ *n* : SUBSIDY, ENDOWMENT

sub•vert \səb-ˈvərt\ *vb* **1** : OVERTHROW, RUIN **2** ♦ : to pervert or corrupt by an undermining of morals, allegiance, or faith — **sub•ver•sion** \-ˈvər-zhən\ *n* — **sub•ver•sive** \-ˈvər-siv\ *adj*

♦ debase, degrade, demean, demoralize, humble, subvert, warp

sub•way \ˈsəb-ˌwā\ *n* : an underground way; *esp* : an underground electric railway

sub•woof•er \ˈsəb-ˈwu̇-fər\ *n* : a loudspeaker responsive only to the lowest acoustic frequencies

suc•ceed \sək-ˈsēd\ *vb* **1** : to follow next in order or next after another; *esp* : to inherit sovereignty, rank, title, or property **2** ♦ : to attain a desired object or end : be successful

♦ click, deliver, go over, pan out, work out ***Ant*** collapse, fail, flop, flunk, fold, wash out ♦ flourish, prosper, thrive ***Ant*** fail

suc•ceed•ing *adj* ♦ : following next in order or next after another

♦ coming, following, next

suc•cess \sək-ˈses\ *n* **1** ♦ : favorable or desired outcome **2** : the gaining of wealth and fame **3** ♦ : one that succeeds — **suc•cess•ful•ly** *adv*

♦ [1] accomplishment, achievement, attainment, coup, triumph ♦ [3] blockbuster, hit, smash, winner

suc•cess•ful \-fəl\ *adj* ♦ : resulting or terminating in success ⟨a ~ outcome⟩; *also* : gaining or having gained success ⟨a ~ writer⟩

♦ palmy, prosperous, triumphant ***Ant*** failed, unsuccessful

suc•ces•sion \sək-ˈse-shən\ *n* **1** : the order, act, or right of succeeding to a property, title, or throne **2** : the act or process of following in order **3** : a series of persons or things that follow one after another

suc•ces•sive \sək-ˈse-siv\ *adj* ♦ : following in order : CONSECUTIVE — **suc•ces•sive•ly** *adv*

♦ consecutive, sequential

suc•ces•sor \sək-ˈse-sər\ *n* : one that succeeds (as to a throne, title, estate, or office)

suc•cinct \(ˌ)sək-ˈsiŋkt, sə-ˈsiŋkt\ *adj* ♦ : marked by compact precise expression without wasted words : BRIEF

♦ brief, compact, compendious, concise, crisp, epigrammatic, laconic, pithy, summary, terse

suc•cinct•ly *adv* ♦ : in a succinct manner : with concise and precise brevity

♦ compactly, concisely, crisply, laconically, shortly, summarily, tersely

suc•cinct•ness *n* ♦ : the quality or state of being succinct

♦ brevity, briefness, compactness, conciseness, crispness, terseness ***Ant*** prolixity, verbosity, wordiness

suc•cor *or Can and Brit* **suc•cour** \ˈsə-kər\ *n* : AID, HELP, RELIEF — **succor** *vb*

suc•co•tash \ˈsə-kə-ˌtash\ *n* : beans and corn kernels cooked together

[1]**suc•cu•lent** \ˈsə-kyə-lənt\ *adj* ♦ : full of juice : JUICY; *also* : having fleshy tissues that conserve moisture ⟨~ plants⟩ — **suc•cu•lence** \-ləns\ *n*

♦ fleshy, juicy, pulpy

[2]**succulent** *n* : a succulent plant (as a cactus or an aloe)

suc•cumb \sə-ˈkəm\ *vb* **1** ♦ : to yield to superior strength or force or overpowering appeal or desire **2** ♦ : to pass from physical life : DIE

♦ [1] bow, budge, capitulate, concede, fall, give in, knuckle under, quit, submit, surrender, yield ♦ [2] decease, depart, die, expire, pass, pass away, perish

[1]**such** \ˈsəch, ˈsich\ *adj* **1** ♦ : of this or that kind **2** : having a quality just specified or to be specified

♦ akin, alike, analogous, comparable, correspondent, like, parallel, similar

[2]**such** *pron* **1** : such a one or ones ⟨he's a star, and acted as ~⟩ **2** : that or those similar or related thereto ⟨boards and nails and ~⟩

[3]**such** *adv* : to that degree : so

such•like \ˈsəch-ˌlīk\ *adj* : of like kind : SIMILAR

[1]**suck** \ˈsək\ *vb* **1** : to draw in liquid and especially mother's milk with the mouth **2** : to draw liquid from by action of the mouth ⟨~ an orange⟩ **3** ♦ : to take in or up or remove by or as if by suction **4** : to be objectionable

♦ *usu* **suck up** absorb, drink, imbibe, soak, sponge

[2]**suck** *n* **1** : a sucking movement or force **2** : the act of sucking

suck•er \ˈsə-kər\ *n* **1** : one that sucks **2** : a part of an animal's body used for sucking or for clinging **3** : any of numerous freshwater fishes with thick soft lips for sucking in food **4** : a shoot from the roots or lower part of a plant **5** ♦ : a person easily deceived **6** — used as a generalized term of reference

♦ dupe, gull, pigeon, sap, tool

suck•le \ˈsə-kəl\ *vb* **suck•led; suck•ling** : to give or draw milk from the breast or udder; *also* : NURTURE

suck•ling \ˈsə-kliŋ\ *n* : a young unweaned mammal

suck–up \ˈsək-ˌəp\ *n* : a person who seeks to gain favor by flattery ⟨a ~ to the teacher⟩

su•crose \ˈsü-ˌkrōs, -ˌkrōz\ *n* : a sweet sugar obtained commercially especially from sugarcane or sugar beets

suc•tion \ˈsək-shən\ *n* **1** : the act of sucking **2** : the act or process of drawing something (as liquid or dust) into a space (as in a vacuum cleaner or a pump) by partially exhausting the air in the space — **suc•tion•al** \-shə-nəl\ *adj*

suction cup *n* : a cup-shaped device in which a partial vacuum is produced when applied to a surface

Su•da•nese \ˌsüd-ᵊn-ˈēz, -ˈēs\ *n* : a native or inhabitant of Sudan — **Sudanese** *adj*

sud•den \ˈsəd-ᵊn\ *adj* **1** ♦ : happening or coming unexpectedly ⟨~ shower⟩; *also* : changing angle or character all at once ⟨~ turn⟩ ⟨~ descent⟩ **2** : HASTY, RASH ⟨~ decision⟩ **3** : made or brought about in a short time : PROMPT ⟨~ cure⟩ — **sud•den•ness** *n*

♦ unanticipated, unexpected, unforeseen

sudden infant death syndrome *n* : death due to unknown causes of an apparently healthy infant usually before one year of age and especially during sleep

sud•den•ly *adv* ♦ : in a sudden manner

♦ aback, unaware, unawares

suds \ˈsədz\ *n pl* : soapy water especially when frothy — **sudsy** \ˈsəd-zē\ *adj*

sue \ˈsü\ *vb* **sued; su•ing 1** ♦ : to make a request or application : PETITION, SOLICIT — usually used with *for* or *to* **2** : to seek justice or right by bringing legal action

♦ *usu* **sue for** ask, call, petition, plead, quest, request, seek, solicit

suede *also* **suède** \ˈswād\ *n* **1** : leather with a napped surface **2** : a fabric with a suedelike nap

su•et \ˈsü-ət\ *n* : the hard fat from beef and mutton that yields tallow

suff *abbr* **1** sufficient **2** suffix

suf•fer \ˈsə-fər\ *vb* **suf•fered; suf•fer•ing 1** ♦ : to feel or endure pain **2** ♦ : to have experience of : UNDERGO **3** : to bear loss, damage, or injury **4** ♦ : to allow especially by reason of indifference : PERMIT — **suf•fer•er** *n*

♦ [1] agonize, bleed, feel, grieve, hurt, mourn, sorrow ♦ [2] endure, experience, feel, have, know, see, sustain, taste, undergo ♦ [4] allow, have, permit

suf•fer•able \ˈsə-fə-rə-bəl\ *adj* **1** : not forbidden **2** ♦ : that can be suffered

♦ bearable, endurable, supportable, sustainable, tolerable

suf•fer•ance \ˈsə-frəns, -fə-rəns\ *n* **1** ♦ : consent or approval implied by lack of interference or resistance **2** ♦ : power or ability to withstand : PATIENCE

♦ [1] allowance, authorization, clearance, concurrence, consent, leave, license (*or* licence), permission, sanction ♦ [2] forbearance, long-suffering, patience, tolerance

suf•fer•ing \ˈsə-friŋ, -fə-riŋ\ *n* : PAIN, MISERY, HARDSHIP

suf•fice \sə-ˈfīs\ *vb* **suf•ficed; suf•fic•ing 1** : to satisfy a need : be sufficient **2** : to be capable or competent

suf•fi•cien•cy \sə-ˈfi-shən-sē\ *n* **1** : a sufficient quantity to meet one's needs **2** : the quality or state of being sufficient : ADEQUACY

suf•fi•cient \sə-ˈfi-shənt\ *adj* : adequate to accomplish a purpose or meet a need — **suf•fi•cient•ly** *adv*

[1]**suf•fix** \ˈsə-ˌfiks\ *n* : an affix occurring at the end of a word

[2]**suf•fix** \ˈsə-fiks, (ˌ)sə-ˈfiks\ *vb* : to attach as a suffix — **suf•fix•ation** \ˌsə-ˌfik-ˈsā-shən\ *n*

suf•fo•cate \ˈsə-fə-ˌkāt\ *vb* **-cat•ed; -cat•ing** ♦ : to deprive of oxygen : SMOTHER — **suf•fo•cat•ing•ly** *adv* — **suf•fo•ca•tion** \ˌsə-fə-ˈkā-shən\ *n*

♦ choke, smother, stifle, strangle

suf•fra•gan \ˈsə-fri-gən\ *n* : an assistant bishop; *esp* : one not having the right of succession — **suffragan** *adj*

suf•frage \ˈsə-frij\ *n* **1** : VOTE **2** ♦ : the right to vote : FRANCHISE

♦ enfranchisement, franchise, vote

suf•frag•ette \ˌsə-fri-ˈjet\ *n* : a woman who advocates suffrage for women

suf•frag•ist \ˈsəf-ri-jist\ *n* : one who advocates extension of the suffrage especially to women

suf•fuse \sə-ˈfyüz\ *vb* **suf•fused; suf•fus•ing** ♦ : to spread over or through in the manner of a fluid or light — **suf•fu•sion** \-ˈfyü-zhən\ *n*

♦ percolate, permeate, transfuse ♦ imbue, inculcate, infuse, ingrain, invest, steep

[1]**sug•ar** \ˈshu̇-gər\ *n* **1** : a sweet substance that is colorless or white when pure and is chiefly sucrose from sugarcane or sugar beets **2** : a water-soluble compound (as glucose) similar to sucrose

[2]**sugar** *vb* **sug•ared; sug•ar•ing 1** : to mix, cover, or sprinkle with sugar **2** : SWEETEN ⟨~ advice with flattery⟩ **3** : to form sugar ⟨a syrup that ~*s*⟩ **4** : GRANULATE

sugar beet *n* : a large beet with a white root from which sugar is made

sug•ar•cane \ˈshu̇-gər-ˌkān\ *n* : a tall grass widely grown in warm regions for the sugar in its stalks

sugar daddy *n* **1** : a well-to-do usually older man who supports or spends lavishly on a mistress or girlfriend **2** : a generous benefactor of a cause

sugar maple *n* : a maple with a sweet sap; *esp* : one of eastern No. America with sap that is the chief source of maple syrup and maple sugar

sugar pea *n* : SNOW PEA

sug•ar•plum \ˈshu̇-gər-ˌpləm\ *n* : a small ball of candy

sug•ary *adj* : cloyingly sweet

sug•gest \səg-ˈjest, sə-\ *vb* **1** ♦ : to put (as a thought, plan, or desire) into a person's mind **2** ♦ : to remind or evoke by association of ideas

♦ [1] advise, counsel ♦ [1] advance, offer, pose, proffer, propose, propound, vote ♦ [2] allude, hint, imply, indicate, infer, insinuate, intimate

sug•gest•ible \səg-ˈjes-tə-bəl, sə-\ *adj* : easily influenced by suggestion

sug•ges•tion \-ˈjes-chən\ *n* **1 a** : an act or instance of suggesting **b** ♦ : something suggested **2** ♦ : a slight indication

♦ [1b] offer, proffer, proposal, proposition ♦ [2] clue, cue, hint, indication, inkling, intimation, lead

sug•ges•tive \-ˈjes-tiv\ *adj* ♦ : tending to suggest something; *esp*

: suggesting something improper or indecent — **sug·ges·tive·ly** *adv* — **sug·ges·tive·ness** *n*

♦ eloquent, expressive, meaning, meaningful, pregnant, significant ♦ bawdy, lewd, racy, ribald, risqué, spicy

¹sui·cide \ˈsü-ə-ˌsīd\ *n* **1 :** the act of killing oneself purposely **2 :** one that commits or attempts suicide — **sui·cid·al** \ˌsü-ə-ˈsīd-ᵊl\ *adj*
²suicide *adj* **:** being or performing a deliberate act resulting in the voluntary death of the person who does it ⟨a ~ mission⟩ ⟨a ~ bomber⟩
sui ge·ner·is \ˌsü-ˌī-ˈje-nə-rəs, ˌsü-ē-\ *adj* **:** being in a class by itself **:** UNIQUE
¹suit \ˈsüt\ *n* **1** ♦ **:** an action in court to recover a right or claim **2 a** ♦ **:** an act of suing or entreating **b :** COURTSHIP **3 :** a number of things used together ⟨~ of clothes⟩ **4 :** all the playing cards in a pack bearing the same symbol

♦ [1] action, lawsuit, proceeding ♦ [2a] appeal, cry, entreaty, petition, plea, prayer, solicitation, supplication

²suit *vb* **1** ♦ **:** to be appropriate or fitting **2 :** to be becoming to **3** ♦ **:** to meet the needs or desires of **:** PLEASE **4** ♦ **:** to outfit with clothes **:** DRESS

♦ [1] befit, do, fit, go, serve ♦ [3] content, delight, gladden, gratify, please, rejoice, satisfy, warm ♦ [4] apparel, array, attire, caparison, clothe, deck, dress, garb, invest, rig

suit·abil·i·ty \ˌsü-tə-ˈbi-lə-tē\ *n* ♦ **:** the quality or state of being suitable

♦ appropriateness, aptness, fitness, rightness

suit·able \ˈsü-tə-bəl\ *adj* ♦ **:** adapted to a use or purpose

♦ able, capable, competent, fit, good, qualified ♦ applicable, appropriate, apt, felicitous, fit, fitting, good, happy, meet, proper, right

suit·able·ness \ˈsü-tə-bəl-nəs\ *n* **:** the quality or state of being suitable
suit·ably \-tə-blē\ *adv* ♦ **:** in a suitable manner

♦ appropriately, correctly, fittingly, happily, properly, rightly

suit·case \ˈsüt-ˌkās\ *n* ♦ **:** a portable case designed to hold a traveler's clothing and personal articles

♦ carryall, grip, handbag, portmanteau, traveling bag

suite \ˈswēt, *for 4 also* ˈsüt\ *n* **1** ♦ **:** a group of retainers or attendants **:** RETINUE **2 :** a group of rooms occupied as a unit **3 :** a modern instrumental composition in several movements of different character; *also* **:** a long orchestral concert arrangement in suite form of material drawn from a longer work **4 :** a set of matched furniture for a room **5 :** a group of things forming a unit or constituting a collection

♦ cortege, following, retinue, train

suit·ing \ˈsü-tiŋ\ *n* **:** fabric for suits of clothes
suit·or \ˈsü-tər\ *n* **1** ♦ **:** one who sues or petitions **2** ♦ **:** one who seeks to marry a woman

♦ [1] pleader, solicitor ♦ [2] gallant, swain, wooer

su·ki·ya·ki \skē-ˈyä-kē, ˌsu̇-kē-ˈyä-\ *n* **:** thin slices of meat, tofu, and vegetables cooked in soy sauce and sugar
sul·fa drug \ˈsəl-fə-\ *n* **:** any of various synthetic organic bacteria-inhibiting drugs
sul·fate *or Can and Brit* **sul·phate** \ˈsəl-ˌfāt\ *n* **:** a salt or ester of sulfuric acid
sul·fide *or Can and Brit* **sul·phide** \ˈsəl-ˌfīd\ *n* **:** a compound of sulfur
sul·fur *or chiefly Can and Brit* **sul·phur** \ˈsəl-fər\ *n* **:** a nonmetallic chemical element used especially in the chemical and paper industries and in vulcanizing rubber
sulfur di·ox·ide \-dī-ˈäk-ˌsīd\ *n* **:** a heavy pungent toxic gas that is used especially in bleaching, as a preservative, and as a refrigerant, and is a major air pollutant
sul·fu·ric *or Can and Brit* **sul·phu·ric** \ˌsəl-ˈfyu̇r-ik\ *adj* **:** of, relating to, or containing sulfur
sulfuric acid *or* **sul·phu·ric acid** \ˌsəl-ˈfyu̇r-ik-\ *n* **:** a heavy corrosive oily strong acid
sul·fu·rous *or chiefly Can and Brit* **sul·phu·rous** \ˈsəl-fə-rəs, -fyə-, *also esp for 1* ˌsəl-ˈfyu̇r-əs\ *adj* **1 :** of, relating to, or containing sulfur **2 :** of or relating to brimstone or the fire of hell **:** INFERNAL **3 :** FIERY, INFLAMED ⟨~ sermons⟩
¹sulk \ˈsəlk\ *vb* **:** to be or become moodily silent or irritable
²sulk *n* ♦ **:** a sulky mood or spell

♦ pet, pout, sullenness

sulk·i·ness \-kē-nəs\ *n* **:** SULK
¹sulky \ˈsəl-kē\ *adj* **sulk·i·er; -est** ♦ **:** inclined to sulk **:** MOROSE, MOODY — **sulk·i·ly** \ˈsəl-kə-lē\ *adv*

♦ glum, moody, morose, sullen, surly

²sulky *n, pl* **sulkies :** a light 2-wheeled horse-drawn vehicle with a seat for the driver and usually no body
sul·len \ˈsə-lən\ *adj* **1** ♦ **:** gloomily silent **2 :** showing or causing gloom or depression **:** GLOOMY ⟨a ~ sky⟩ — **sul·len·ly** *adv*

♦ glum, moody, morose, sulky, surly

sul·len·ness *n* ♦ **:** the quality or state of being sullen

♦ pet, pout, sulk

sul·ly \ˈsə-lē\ *vb* **sul·lied; sul·ly·ing :** to make or become soiled, tarnished, or defiled **:** SOIL, SMIRCH
sulphur *chiefly Can and Brit var of* SULFATE
sulphur *chiefly Can and Brit var of* SULFIDE
sulphur *chiefly Can and Brit var of* SULFUR
sul·tan \ˈsəlt-ᵊn\ *n* **:** a sovereign especially of a Muslim state — **sul·tan·ate** \-ˌāt\ *n*
sul·ta·na \ˌsəl-ˈta-nə\ *n* **1 :** a female member of a sultan's family **2 :** a pale seedless grape; *also* **:** a raisin of this grape
sul·try \ˈsəl-trē\ *adj* **sul·tri·er; -est 1** ♦ **:** very hot and moist; *also* **:** burning hot **2 :** exciting sexual desire

♦ humid, muggy, sticky ♦ broiling, burning, fiery, hot, red-hot, scorching, torrid

¹sum \ˈsəm\ *n* **1 :** a quantity of money **2** ♦ **:** the whole amount **3 :** GIST **4 :** the result obtained by adding numbers **5 :** a problem in arithmetic **6 :** a summary of the chief points or thoughts

♦ aggregate, full, total, totality, whole

²sum *vb* **summed; sum·ming** ♦ **:** to find the sum of by adding or counting; *also* **:** to reach a sum

♦ add, foot, total ♦ *usu* **sum to** *or* **sum into** add up, amount, come, number, total

su·mac *also* **su·mach** \ˈsü-ˌmak, ˈshü-\ *n* **:** any of a genus of trees, shrubs, and woody vines having spikes or loose clusters of red or whitish berries
sum·mar·i·ly \(ˌ)sə-ˈmer-ə-lē, ˈsə-mə-rə-lē\ *adv* ♦ **:** in a summary manner or form

♦ compactly, concisely, crisply, laconically, shortly, succinctly, tersely

sum·ma·rise *chiefly Brit var of* SUMMARIZE
sum·ma·rize \ˈsə-mə-ˌrīz\ *vb* **-rized; -riz·ing** ♦ **:** to tell in a summary

♦ abstract, digest, encapsulate, epitomize, outline, recapitulate, sum up, wrap up

¹sum·ma·ry \ˈsə-mə-rē\ *adj* **1** ♦ **:** covering the main points briefly **:** CONCISE **2 :** done without delay or formality ⟨~ punishment⟩

♦ brief, compact, compendious, concise, crisp, epigrammatic, laconic, pithy, succinct, terse

²summary *n, pl* **-ries** ♦ **:** a concise statement of the main points

♦ abstract, digest, encapsulation, epitome, outline, précis, recapitulation, résumé (*or* resume), roundup, sum, synopsis, wrap-up

sum·ma·tion \(ˌ)sə-ˈmā-shən\ *n* **1 :** a summing up **2 :** a speech in court summing up the arguments in a case
sum·mer \ˈsə-mər\ *n* **:** the season of the year in a region in which the sun shines most directly **:** the warmest period of the year — **sum·mery** *adj*
sum·mer·house \ˈsə-mər-ˌhau̇s\ *n* **:** a covered structure in a garden or park to provide a shady retreat
summersault *var of* SOMERSAULT
summer squash *n* **:** any of various squashes (as zucchini) used as a vegetable while immature
sum·mit \ˈsə-mət\ *n* **1** ♦ **:** the highest point **2 :** a conference of highest-level officials

♦ acme, apex, climax, crown, culmination, head, height, meridian, peak, pinnacle, tip-top, top, zenith

sum·mon \ˈsə-mən\ *vb* **1** ♦ **:** to call to a meeting **:** CONVOKE **2 :** to send for; *also* **:** to order to appear in court **3 :** to evoke especially by an act of the will ⟨~ up courage⟩ — **sum·mon·er** *n*

♦ assemble, call, convene, convoke, muster

sum·mons \ˈsə-mənz\ *n, pl* **sum·mons·es 1 :** an authoritative call to appear at a designated place or to attend to a duty **2 :** a warning or citation to appear in court at a specified time to answer charges

sump•tu•ous \ˈsəmp-shə-wəs, -chə-\ *adj* ♦ **:** extremely costly, rich, luxurious, or magnificent **:** LUXURIOUS

♦ deluxe, lavish, luxuriant, luxurious, opulent, palatial, plush

sum up *vb* ♦ **:** to tell in or reduce to a summary **:** SUMMARIZE

♦ abstract, digest, encapsulate, epitomize, outline, recapitulate, summarize, wrap up

1sun \ˈsən\ *n* **1 :** the shining celestial body around which the earth and other planets revolve and from which they receive light and heat **2 :** a celestial body like the sun **3 :** SUNSHINE — **sun•less** *adj*

2sun *vb* **sunned; sun•ning 1 :** to expose to or as if to the rays of the sun **2 :** to sun oneself

Sun *abbr* Sunday

sun•bath \ˈsən-ˌbath, -ˌbȧth\ *n* **:** an exposure to sunlight or a sunlamp — **sun•bathe** \-ˌbāth\ *vb*

sun•beam \-ˌbēm\ *n* **:** a ray of sunlight

sun•block \ˈsən-ˌbläk\ *n* **:** a preparation used on the skin to prevent sunburn (as by blocking ultraviolet radiation)

sun•bon•net \-ˌbä-nət\ *n* **:** a bonnet with a wide brim to shield the face and neck from the sun

1sun•burn \-ˌbərn\ *vb* **-burned** \-ˌbərnd\ *or* **-burnt** \-ˌbərnt\; **-burn•ing :** to cause or become affected with sunburn

2sunburn *n* **:** a skin inflammation caused by overexposure to ultraviolet radiation especially from sunshine

sun•dae \ˈsən-(ˌ)dā, -dē\ *n* **:** ice cream served with topping

Sun•day \ˈsən-dē, -ˌdā\ *n* **:** the 1st day of the week **:** the Christian Sabbath

sun•der \ˈsən-dər\ *vb* ♦ **:** to force apart

♦ break up, disconnect, disjoint, dissever, dissociate, disunite, divide, divorce, part, resolve, separate, sever, split, unyoke

sun•di•al \-ˌdī(-ə)l\ *n* **:** a device for showing the time of day from the shadow cast on a plate by an object with a straight edge

sun•down \-ˌdau̇n\ *n* ♦ **:** the time at which the sun disappears below the horizon **:** SUNSET 2

♦ dusk, evening, gloaming, nightfall, sunset, twilight

sun•dries \ˈsən-drēz\ *n pl* ♦ **:** various small articles or items

♦ novelties, notions, odds and ends

sun•dry \ˈsən-drē\ *adj* **:** SEVERAL, DIVERS, VARIOUS

sun•fish \ˈsən-ˌfish\ *n* **1 :** a large marine fish with a deep flattened body **2 :** any of numerous often brightly colored No. American freshwater fishes related to the perches and usually having the body flattened from side to side

sun•flow•er \-ˌflau̇-ər\ *n* **:** any of a genus of tall New World plants related to the daisies and often grown for the oil-rich seeds of their yellow-petaled dark-centered flower heads

sung *past and past part of* SING

sun•glasses \ˈsən-ˌgla-səz\ *n pl* **:** glasses to protect the eyes from the sun

sunk *past and past part of* SINK

sunk•en \ˈsəŋ-kən\ *adj* **1** ♦ **:** covered with water **:** SUBMERGED **2** ♦ **:** fallen in **:** HOLLOW ⟨~ cheeks⟩ **3 :** lying in a depression ⟨a ~ garden⟩; *also* **:** constructed below the general floor level ⟨a ~ living room⟩

♦ [1] submarine, underwater ♦ [2] concave, depressed, hollow

sun•lamp \ˈsən-ˌlamp\ *n* **:** an electric lamp designed to emit radiation of wavelengths from ultraviolet to infrared

sun•light \-ˌlīt\ *n* **:** SUNSHINE

sun•lit \-ˌlit\ *adj* **:** lighted by or as if by the sun

sun protection factor *n* **:** a number that is the factor by which the time required for unprotected skin to become sunburned is increased when a sunscreen is used

sun•ny \ˈsə-nē\ *adj* ♦ **:** full of sunshine; *also* **:** full of good spirits

♦ clear, cloudless, fair, sunshiny, unclouded ♦ blithe, bright, buoyant, cheerful, cheery, chipper, gay, lightsome, merry, upbeat

sun•rise \-ˌrīz\ *n* **1 :** the apparent rising of the sun above the horizon **2** ♦ **:** the time at which the sun rises

♦ aurora, cockcrow, dawn, morning

sun•roof \-ˌrüf, -ˌru̇f\ *n* **:** a panel in an automobile roof that can be opened

sun•screen \-ˌskrēn\ *n* **:** a preparation on the skin to prevent sunburn (as by absorbing ultraviolet radiation)

sun•set \-ˌset\ *n* **1 :** the apparent descent of the sun below the horizon **2** ♦ **:** the time at which the sun sets

♦ dusk, evening, gloaming, nightfall, sundown, twilight

sun•shade \ˈsən-ˌshād\ *n* **:** something (as a parasol or awning) used as a protection from the sun's rays

sun•shine \-ˌshīn\ *n* **:** the direct light of the sun

sun•shiny *adj* ♦ **:** bright with or as if with the rays of the sun

♦ clear, cloudless, fair, sunny, unclouded

sun•spot \-ˌspät\ *n* **:** any of the dark spots that appear at times on the sun's surface

sun•stroke \-ˌstrōk\ *n* **:** heatstroke caused by direct exposure to the sun

sun•tan \-ˌtan\ *n* **:** a browning of the skin from exposure to the sun's rays

sun•up \-ˌəp\ *n* **:** the apparent rising of the sun above the horizon **:** SUNRISE

1sup \ˈsəp\ *vb* **supped; sup•ping** ♦ **:** to take or drink in swallows or gulps

♦ drink, guzzle, imbibe, quaff, swig, toss

2sup *n* ♦ **:** a mouthful especially of liquor or broth; *also* **:** a small quantity of liquid

♦ draft, swallow

3sup *vb* **supped; sup•ping 1 :** to eat the evening meal **2 :** to make one's supper ⟨*supped* on roast beef⟩

4sup *abbr* **1** superior **2** supplement; supplementary **3** supply **4** supra

1su•per \ˈsü-pər\ *n* **:** SUPERINTENDENT

2super *adj* **1 :** very fine **:** EXCELLENT **2 :** EXTREME, EXCESSIVE **3 :** very large or powerful **:** HUGE

super- \ˌsü-pər\ *prefix* **1 :** over and above **:** higher in quantity, quality, or degree than **:** more than **2 :** in addition **:** extra **3 :** exceeding a norm **4 :** in excessive degree or intensity **5 :** surpassing all or most others of its kind **6 :** situated above, on, or at the top of **7 :** next above or higher **8 :** more inclusive than **9 :** superior in status or position

superabsorbent
superachiever
superagency
superblock
superbomb
supercity
superclean
superexpensive
superfast
superfine
superheat
superheavy
superhero
superhumanly
superindividual
superliner
superman
supermom
supernormal
superpatriot
superpatriotic
superpatriotism
superpremium
superrich
supersalesman
supersecret
supersize
supersized
supersmart
supersophisticated
superspy
superstate
superstore
superstratum
superstrength
superstrong
supersubtle
supersystem
supertanker
superthin
superwoman

su•per•abun•dance \ˌsü-pər-ə-ˈbən-dəns\ *n* ♦ **:** great abundance; *also* **:** the state or an instance of surpassing usual, proper, or specified limits

♦ abundance, plenty, wealth ♦ excess, fat, overabundance, overflow, overkill, overmuch, superfluity, surfeit, surplus

su•per•abun•dant \ˌsü-pər-ə-ˈbən-dənt\ *adj* **:** more than ample

su•per•an•nu•ate \ˌsü-pər-ˈan-yə-ˌwāt\ *vb* **-at•ed; -at•ing 1 :** to make out-of-date **2 :** to retire and pension because of age or infirmity — **su•per•an•nu•at•ed** *adj*

su•per•an•nu•at•ed *adj* ♦ no longer current **:** OUTDATED

♦ antiquated, archaic, dated, obsolete, outdated, outmoded, outworn, passé

su•perb \su̇-ˈpərb\ *adj* ♦ **:** marked to the highest degree by excellence, brilliance, or competence — **su•perb•ly** *adv*

♦ excellent, fabulous, fine, grand, great, sensational, splendid, superior, swell, terrific, unsurpassed, wonderful

su•per•charg•er \ˈsü-pər-ˌchär-jər\ *n* **:** a device for increasing the amount of air supplied to an internal combustion engine

su•per•cil•ious \ˌsü-pər-ˈsi-lē-əs\ *adj* ♦ **:** haughtily contemptuous

♦ arrogant, cavalier, haughty, imperious, overweening, peremptory, pompous, presumptuous, pretentious, superior, uppity

su•per•com•pu•ter \ˈsü-pər-kəm-ˌpyü-tər\ *n* : a large very fast mainframe

su•per•con•duc•tiv•i•ty \ˌsü-pər-ˌkän-ˌdək-ˈti-və-tē\ *n* : a complete disappearance of electrical resistance in a substance especially at very low temperatures — **su•per•con•duc•tive** \-kən-ˈdək-tiv\ *adj* — **su•per•con•duc•tor** \-ˈdək-tər\ *n*

su•per•con•ti•nent \ˈsü-pər-ˌkänt-ᵊn-ənt\ *n* : a former large continent from which other continents are held to have broken off and drifted away

su•per•ego \ˌsü-pər-ˈē-gō\ *n* : the one of the three divisions of the psyche in psychoanalytic theory that functions to reward and punish through a system of moral attitudes, conscience, and a sense of guilt

su•per•fi•cial \ˌsü-pər-ˈfi-shəl\ *adj* **1 :** of or relating to the surface or appearance only **2 :** not thorough : SHALLOW — **su•per•fi•ci•al•i•ty** \-ˌfi-shē-ˈa-lə-tē\ *n* — **su•per•fi•cial•ly** *adv*

su•per•flu•i•ty \ˌsü-pər-ˈflü-ə-tē\ *n* ♦ **:** the state or an instance of surpassing usual, proper, or specified limits

♦ amenity, comfort, extra, frill, indulgence, luxury ♦ excess, fat, overabundance, overflow, overkill, overmuch, superabundance, surfeit, surplus

su•per•flu•ous \sü-ˈpər-flə-wəs\ *adj* ♦ **:** exceeding what is sufficient or necessary : SURPLUS

♦ excess, extra, spare, supernumerary, surplus

su•per•high•way \ˌsü-pər-ˈhī-ˌwā\ *n* : a broad highway designed for high-speed traffic

su•per•hu•man \ˌsü-pər-ˈhyu-mən\ *adj* ♦ **:** being above the human; *also* **:** exceeding normal human power, size, or capability

♦ magical, miraculous, phenomenal, supernatural, uncanny, unearthly

su•per•im•pose \-im-ˈpōz\ *vb* : to lay (one thing) over or above something else

su•per•in•tend \ˌsü-pə-rin-ˈtend\ *vb* ♦ **:** to have or exercise the charge and oversight of

♦ administer, carry on, conduct, control, direct, govern, guide, handle, manage, operate, oversee, regulate, run, supervise

su•per•in•ten•dence \-ˈten-dəns\ *n* ♦ **:** the act or function of superintending or directing

♦ administration, conduct, control, direction, government, guidance, management, operation, oversight, regulation, running, supervision ♦ care, charge, guidance, headship, oversight, regulation, supervision

su•per•in•ten•den•cy \-dən-sē\ *n* **1 :** the office, post, or jurisdiction of a superintendent **2 :** the act or function of superintending or directing

su•per•in•ten•dent \-dənt\ *n* ♦ **:** one who has executive oversight and charge

♦ administrator, director, executive, manager, supervisor

¹**su•pe•ri•or** \sü-ˈpir-ē-ər\ *adj* **1 :** situated higher up, over, or near the top; *also* **:** higher in rank or numbers **2** ♦ **:** of greater value or importance **3 :** courageously indifferent (as to pain or misfortune) **4 :** better than most others of its kind **5** ♦ **:** affecting or assuming an air of superiority : HAUGHTY

♦ [2] distinguished, eminent, illustrious, noble, notable, noteworthy, outstanding, preeminent, prestigious, signal, star ♦ [5] disdainful, haughty, highfalutin, lofty, lordly, prideful, proud

²**superior** *n* **1** ♦ **:** one who is above another in rank, office, or station; *esp* **:** the head of a religious house or order **2 :** one higher in quality or merit

♦ better, boss, chief, elder, head, leader, master, senior *Ant* inferior, subordinate, underling

su•pe•ri•or•i•ty \-ˌpir-ē-ˈȯr-ə-tē\ *n* ♦ **:** the quality or state of being superior; *also* **:** a superior characteristic

♦ distinction, excellence, greatness, preeminence, supremacy ♦ arrogance, haughtiness, loftiness, pretense, pretension, pretentiousness, self-importance

¹**su•per•la•tive** \sü-ˈpər-lə-tiv\ *adj* **1 :** of, relating to, or constituting the degree of grammatical comparison that denotes an extreme or unsurpassed level or extent **2 :** surpassing others : SUPREME — **su•per•la•tive•ly** *adv*

²**superlative** *n* **1 :** the superlative degree or a superlative form in a language **2 :** the utmost degree : ACME

su•per•mar•ket \ˈsü-pər-ˌmär-kət\ *n* : a self-service retail market selling foods and household merchandise

su•per•nal \sü-ˈpər-nəl\ *adj* **1 :** being or coming from on high **2** ♦ **:** of heavenly or spiritual character **3 :** superlatively good

♦ celestial, Elysian, empyrean, heavenly

su•per•nat•u•ral \ˌsü-pər-ˈna-chə-rəl\ *adj* **1** ♦ **:** of or relating to phenomena beyond or outside of nature **2 :** relating to or attributed to a divinity, ghost, or devil — **su•per•nat•u•ral•ly** *adv*

♦ metaphysical, preternatural, superhuman, unearthly *Ant* natural ♦ magical, miraculous, phenomenal, superhuman, uncanny, unearthly

su•per•no•va \ˌsü-pər-ˈnō-və\ *n* : the explosion of a very large star

¹**su•per•nu•mer•ary** \-ˈnü-mə-ˌrer-ē, -ˈnyü-\ *adj* ♦ **:** exceeding the usual or required number : EXTRA

♦ excess, extra, spare, superfluous, surplus

²**supernumerary** *n, pl* **-ar•ies :** an extra person or thing; *esp* **:** an actor hired for a nonspeaking part

su•per•pose \ˌsü-pər-ˈpōz\ *vb* **-posed; -pos•ing :** SUPERIMPOSE — **su•per•po•si•tion** \-pə-ˈzi-shən\ *n*

su•per•pow•er \ˈsü-pər-ˌpau̇-ər\ *n* **1 :** excessive or superior power **2 :** one of a few politically and militarily dominant nations

su•per•sat•u•rat•ed \-ˈsa-chə-ˌrā-təd\ *adj* **:** containing an amount of a substance greater than that required for saturation

su•per•scribe \ˈsü-pər-ˌskrīb, ˌsü-pər-ˈskrīb\ *vb* **-scribed; -scrib•ing :** to write on the top or outside : ADDRESS — **su•per•scrip•tion** \ˌsü-pər-ˈskrip-shən\ *n*

su•per•script \ˈsü-pər-ˌskript\ *n* : a symbol (as a numeral or letter) written immediately above or above and to one side of another character

su•per•sede \ˌsü-pər-ˈsēd\ *vb* **-sed•ed; -sed•ing** ♦ **:** to take the place of : REPLACE

♦ displace, replace, substitute, supplant

su•per•son•ic \-ˈsä-nik\ *adj* **1 :** ULTRASONIC **2 :** being or relating to speeds from one to five times the speed of sound; *also* **:** capable of moving at such a speed ⟨a ~ airplane⟩

su•per•star \ˈsü-pər-ˌstär\ *n* ♦ **:** one that is very prominent or is a prime attraction

♦ celebrity, figure, light, luminary, notable, personage, personality, somebody, standout, star, VIP

su•per•sti•tion \ˌsü-pər-ˈsti-shən\ *n* **1 :** beliefs or practices resulting from ignorance, fear of the unknown, or trust in magic or chance **2 :** an unreasoning fear of nature, the unknown, or God resulting from superstition — **su•per•sti•tious** \-shəs\ *adj*

su•per•struc•ture \ˈsü-pər-ˌstrək-chər\ *n* : something built on a base or as a vertical extension

su•per•ti•tle \ˈsü-pər-ˌtī-tᵊl\ *n* : a translation of foreign-language dialogue displayed above a screen or performance

su•per•vene \ˌsü-pər-ˈvēn\ *vb* **-vened; -ven•ing :** to occur as something additional or unexpected

su•per•vise \ˈsü-pər-ˌvīz\ *vb* **-vised; -vis•ing** ♦ **:** to have or exercise the charge and oversight of

♦ administer, boss, captain, carry on, conduct, control, direct, govern, guide, handle, manage, operate, oversee, regulate, run, superintend ♦ attend, care, mind, tend

su•per•vi•sion \ˌsü-pər-ˈvi-zhən\ *n* ♦ **:** the action, process, or occupation of supervising; *esp* **:** a critical watching and directing (as of activities or a course of action)

♦ administration, conduct, control, direction, government, management, operation, running ♦ care, charge, guidance, headship, oversight, regulation, superintendence

su•per•vi•sor \ˈsü-pər-ˌvī-zər\ *n* ♦ **:** one that supervises; *esp* **:** an administrative officer in charge of a business, government, or school unit or operation

♦ administrator, director, executive, manager, superintendent

su•per•vi•so•ry \ˌsü-pər-ˈvī-zə-rē\ *adj* ♦ **:** of or relating to supervision

♦ directorial, executive, managerial

su•pine \sü-ˈpīn\ *adj* **1 :** lying on the back or with the face upward **2 :** LETHARGIC, SLUGGISH; *also* **:** ABJECT

supp *or* **suppl** *abbr* supplement; supplementary

sup•per \ˈsə-pər\ *n* : the evening meal especially when dinner is taken at midday — **sup•per•time** \-ˌtīm\ *n*

sup•plant \sə-ˈplant\ *vb* **1 :** to take the place of (another) especially by force or trickery **2** ♦ **:** to take the place of especially by reason of superior excellence or power : REPLACE

♦ displace, replace, substitute, supersede

sup•ple \ˈsə-pəl\ *adj* **sup•pler; sup•plest** **1 :** COMPLIANT, ADAPTABLE **2** ♦ **:** capable of bending without breaking or creasing **:** LIMBER

♦ flexible, limber, lissome, lithe, pliable, willowy

¹sup•ple•ment \ˈsə-plə-mənt\ *n* **1** ♦ **:** something that supplies a want or makes an addition **2 :** a continuation (as of a book) containing corrections or additional material **3 :** DIETARY SUPPLEMENT

♦ accretion, addition, augmentation, boost, expansion, gain, increase, increment, plus, proliferation, raise, rise

²sup•ple•ment \ˈsə-plə-ˌment\ *vb* **:** to fill up the deficiencies of **:** add to
sup•ple•men•tal \ˌsə-plə-ˈment-ᵊl\ *adj* **:** serving to supplement
sup•ple•men•ta•ry \-ˈmen-tə-rē\ *adj* ♦ **:** added or serving as a supplement

♦ accessory, auxiliary, peripheral

sup•pli•ant \ˈsə-plē-ənt\ *n* **:** one who supplicates **:** PETITIONER
sup•pli•cant \ˈsə-pli-kənt\ *n* **:** one who supplicates **:** SUPPLIANT
sup•pli•cate \ˈsə-plə-ˌkāt\ *vb* **-cat•ed; -cat•ing** **1 :** to make a humble entreaty; *esp* **:** to pray to God **2** ♦ **:** to ask earnestly and humbly **:** BESEECH

♦ appeal, beg, beseech, entreat, implore, importune, petition, plead, pray, solicit

sup•pli•ca•tion \ˌsə-plə-ˈkā-shən\ *n* ♦ **:** a humble and earnest petition

♦ appeal, cry, entreaty, petition, plea, prayer, solicitation, suit

¹sup•ply \sə-ˈplī\ *vb* **sup•plied; sup•ply•ing** **1 :** to add as a supplement **2** ♦ **:** to satisfy the needs of **3** ♦ **:** to make available for use **:** FURNISH, PROVIDE — **sup•pli•er** *n*

♦ [2] accoutre, equip, fit, furnish, outfit, rig ♦ [3] deliver, feed, furnish, give, hand, hand over, provide

²supply *n, pl* **supplies** **1 a** ♦ **:** the quantity or amount (as of a commodity) needed or available **b :** PROVISIONS, STORES — usually used in plural **2 :** the act or process of filling a want or need **:** PROVISION **3 :** the quantities of goods or services offered for sale at a particular time or at one price

♦ budget, fund, pool

sup•ply–side \sə-ˈplī-ˌsīd\ *adj* **:** of, relating to, or being an economic theory that recommends the reduction of tax rates to expand economic activity
¹sup•port \sə-ˈpōrt\ *vb* **1 :** to endure bravely or quietly **:** BEAR **2** ♦ **:** to take sides with **:** BACK **3** ♦ **:** to provide with food, clothing, and shelter **4** ♦ **:** to hold up or serve as a foundation for **5 :** to uphold or defend as valid or right **6** ♦ **:** to provide with substantiation **:** CORROBORATE **7** ♦ **:** to give usually supplementary help or aid to — **sup•port•ive** \-ˈpȯr-tiv\ *adj*

♦ [2] advocate, back, champion, endorse, patronize ♦ [3, 7] abet, aid, assist, back, help, prop ♦ [4] bear, bolster, brace, buttress, carry, prop, shore, stay, uphold ♦ [6] bear out, confirm, corroborate, substantiate, validate, verify, vindicate

²support *n* **1** ♦ **:** the act of supporting **:** the state of being supported **2** ♦ **:** one that supports

♦ [1] aid, assist, assistance, backing, boost, help, lift ♦ [2] brace, bulwark, buttress, mount, shore, stay, underpinning ♦ [2] dependence, mainstay, pillar, reliance, standby

sup•port•able *adj* ♦ **:** capable of being supported

♦ bearable, endurable, sufferable, sustainable, tolerable ♦ defensible, justifiable, maintainable, sustainable, tenable

sup•port•er *n* ♦ **:** one that supports or acts as a support

♦ advocate, apostle, backer, booster, champion, exponent, friend, promoter, proponent ♦ abettor, ally, backer, confederate, sympathizer

support group *n* **:** a group of people with common experiences and concerns who provide emotional and moral support for one another
sup•pose \sə-ˈpōz\ *vb* **sup•posed; sup•pos•ing** **1** ♦ **:** to assume to be true (as for the sake of argument) **2 :** EXPECT ⟨I am *supposed* to go⟩ **3** ♦ **:** to think probable **4** ♦ **:** to hold as an opinion — **sup•pos•al** *n*

♦ [1] assume, postulate, premise, presume, presuppose ♦ [3] assume, conjecture, guess, presume, speculate, surmise, suspect ♦ [4] believe, consider, deem, feel, figure, guess, hold, imagine, think

sup•posed \sə-ˈpōzd, -ˈpō-zəd\ *adj* ♦ **:** held as an opinion; *also* **:** mistakenly believed

♦ apparent, assumed, evident, ostensible, reputed, seeming

sup•pos•ed•ly \-ˈpō-zəd-lē, -ˈpōzd-lē\ *adv* ♦ **:** as supposed

♦ apparently, evidently, ostensibly, presumably, seemingly

sup•pos•ing *conj* **:** if by way of hypothesis **:** on the assumption that
sup•po•si•tion \ˌsə-pə-ˈzi-shən\ *n* **1** ♦ **:** something that is supposed **2 :** the act of supposing

♦ conjecture, hypothesis, proposition, theory ♦ assumption, postulate, premise, presumption ♦ conjecture, guess, surmise

sup•pos•i•to•ry \sə-ˈpä-zə-ˌtōr-ē\ *n, pl* **-ries** **:** a small easily melted mass of usually medicated material for insertion (as into the rectum)
sup•press \sə-ˈpres\ *vb* **1** ♦ **:** to put down by authority or force **:** SUBDUE ⟨∼ a revolt⟩ **2 :** to keep from being known; *also* **:** to stop the publication or circulation of **3** ♦ **:** to hold back **:** REPRESS ⟨∼ anger⟩ ⟨∼ a cough⟩ — **sup•press•ible** \-ˈpre-sə-bəl\ *adj* — **sup•pres•sor** \-ˈpre-sər\ *n*

♦ [1] clamp down, crack down, crush, put down, quash, quell, repress, silence, snuff, squash, squelch, subdue ♦ [3] choke, pocket, repress, smother, stifle, strangle, swallow

sup•pres•sant \sə-ˈpres-ᵊnt\ *n* **:** an agent (as a drug) suppressing rather than eliminating something ⟨a cough ∼⟩
sup•pres•sion \-ˈpre-shən\ *n* **1 :** an act or instance of suppressing **:** the state of being suppressed **2** ♦ **:** the conscious intentional exclusion from consciousness of a thought or feeling

♦ constraint, inhibition, repression, restraint, self-control, self-restraint

sup•pu•rate \ˈsə-pyə-ˌrāt\ *vb* **-rat•ed; -rat•ing** **:** to form or give off pus — **sup•pu•ra•tion** \ˌsə-pyə-ˈrā-shən\ *n*
su•pra \ˈsü-prə, -ˌprä\ *adv* **:** earlier in this writing **:** ABOVE
su•pra•na•tion•al \ˌsü-prə-ˈna-shə-nəl, -ˌprä-\ *adj* **:** going beyond national boundaries, authority, or interests ⟨∼ organizations⟩
su•prem•a•cist \sü-ˈpre-mə-sist\ *n* **:** an advocate of group supremacy
su•prem•a•cy \sü-ˈpre-mə-sē\ *n, pl* **-cies** **1** ♦ **:** the quality or state of being supreme **2** ♦ **:** supreme authority or power

♦ [1] distinction, excellence, greatness, preeminence, superiority ♦ [2] ascendancy, dominance, dominion, predominance, preeminence

su•preme \sü-ˈprēm\ *adj* **1** ♦ **:** highest in rank or authority **2** ♦ **:** highest in degree or quality ⟨∼ among poets⟩ **3** ♦ **:** the best or most extreme of its kind **:** ULTIMATE ⟨the ∼ sacrifice⟩ — **su•preme•ness** *n*

♦ [1, 2] arch, cardinal, central, chief, dominant, first, foremost, grand, key, main, paramount, predominant, preeminent, premier, primary, principal, sovereign ♦ [3] consummate, maximum, most, nth, paramount, top, ultimate, utmost

Supreme Being *n* ♦ **:** the Being perfect in power, wisdom, and goodness who is worshipped as creator and ruler of the universe

♦ Almighty, deity, Jehovah

su•preme•ly *adv* **:** in a supreme manner **:** so as to be supreme
supt *abbr* superintendent
sur•cease \ˈsər-ˌsēs\ *n* **:** a temporary or final ceasing **:** CESSATION
¹sur•charge \ˈsər-ˌchärj\ *vb* **1 :** to fill to excess **:** OVERLOAD **2 :** to apply a surcharge to (postage stamps) **3 :** to charge too much or too fully
²surcharge *n* **1 :** an extra fee or cost **2 :** an excessive load or burden **3 :** something officially printed on a postage stamp especially to change its value
sur•cin•gle \ˈsər-ˌsiŋ-gəl\ *n* **:** a band put around a horse's body to make something (as a saddle) fast
¹sure \ˈshu̇r\ *adj* **sur•er; sur•est** **1 :** firmly established **2** ♦ **:** suitable or fit to be relied on **:** TRUSTWORTHY, RELIABLE **3** ♦ **:** characterized by a lack of wavering or hesitation **:** CONFIDENT **4 :** not to be disputed **:** UNDOUBTED **5** ♦ **:** bound to happen **6 :** careful to remember or attend to something ⟨be ∼ to lock the door⟩

♦ [2] dependable, good, reliable, responsible, safe, solid, steady, tried, true, trustworthy ♦ [3] assured, certain, clear, cocksure, confident, doubtless, positive, sanguine ♦ [5] certain, inevitable, necessary, unavoidable ♦ [5] infallible, surefire, unfailing

²sure *adv* **:** SURELY

sure•fire \ˈshu̇r-ˈfīr\ *adj* ♦ **:** certain to get results **:** DEPENDABLE

♦ infallible, sure, unfailing

sure•ly \ˈshu̇r-lē\ *adv* **1 :** in a sure manner **2** ♦ **:** without doubt **3 :** INDEED, REALLY

♦ certainly, definitely, doubtless, incontestably, indeed, indisputably, really, truly, undeniably, undoubtedly, unquestionably

sure•ness *n* ♦ **:** the quality or state of being sure

♦ assurance, certainty, certitude, confidence, conviction, positiveness ♦ dependability, reliability, solidity, trustworthiness

sure•ty \ˈshu̇r-ə-tē\ *n, pl* **-ties 1 :** SURENESS, CERTAINTY **2** ♦ **:** something that makes sure **:** GUARANTEE **3** ♦ **:** one who is a guarantor for another person

♦ [2] bond, contract, covenant, guarantee, guaranty, warranty ♦ [3] backer, guarantor, patron, sponsor

¹surf \ˈsərf\ *n* **:** waves that break upon the shore; *also* **:** the sound or foam of breaking waves

²surf *vb* **1 :** to ride the surf (as on a surfboard) **2 :** to scan the offerings of (as television or the Internet) for something of interest — **surf•er** *n* — **surf•ing** *n*

¹sur•face \ˈsər-fəs\ *n* **1** ♦ **:** the outside of an object or body **2 :** outward aspect or appearance — **surface** *adj*

♦ exterior, face, outside, skin, veneer

²surface *vb* **sur•faced; sur•fac•ing 1 :** to give a surface to **:** make smooth **2 :** to rise to the surface **3** ♦ **:** to come into public view

♦ arise, crop, emerge, materialize, spring

surf•board \ˈsərf-ˌbōrd\ *n* **:** a buoyant board used in surfing

¹sur•feit \ˈsər-fət\ *n* **1** ♦ **:** an overabundant supply **:** EXCESS **2 :** excessive indulgence (as in food or drink) **3 :** disgust caused by excess

♦ excess, fat, overabundance, overflow, overkill, overmuch, superabundance, superfluity, surplus

²surfeit *vb* ♦ **:** to feed, supply, or indulge to the point of surfeit

♦ glut, gorge, sate, stuff

surg *abbr* surgeon; surgery; surgical

¹surge \ˈsərj\ *vb* **surged; surg•ing 1 :** to rise and fall actively **:** TOSS **2 :** to move in waves **3 :** to rise suddenly to an excessive or abnormal value

²surge *n* **1 :** a sweeping onward like a wave of the sea ⟨a ~ of emotion⟩ **2** ♦ **:** a large billow **3 :** a transient sudden increase of current or voltage in an electrical circuit

♦ billow, swell, wave

sur•geon \ˈsər-jən\ *n* **:** a physician who specializes in surgery

sur•gery \ˈsər-jə-rē\ *n, pl* **-ger•ies 1 :** a branch of medicine concerned with the correction of physical defects, the repair of injuries, and the treatment of disease especially by operations **2 :** a room or area where surgery is performed **3 :** the work done by a surgeon

sur•gi•cal \ˈsər-ji-kəl\ *adj* **:** of, relating to, or associated with surgeons or surgery — **sur•gi•cal•ly** \-k(ə-)lē\ *adv*

sur•ly \ˈsər-lē\ *adj* **sur•li•er; -est** ♦ **:** having a rude unfriendly disposition — **sur•li•ness** \-lē-nəs\ *n*

♦ glum, moody, morose, sulky, sullen ♦ bearish, bilious, cantankerous, disagreeable, dyspeptic, ill-humored, ill-tempered, ornery, splenetic

¹sur•mise \sər-ˈmīz\ *vb* **sur•mised; sur•mis•ing** ♦ **:** to form a notion of from scanty evidence **:** GUESS

♦ assume, conjecture, guess, presume, speculate, suppose, suspect

²surmise *n* ♦ **:** a thought or idea based on scanty evidence

♦ conjecture, guess, supposition

sur•mount \sər-ˈmau̇nt\ *vb* **1** ♦ **:** to prevail over **:** OVERCOME **2 :** to get to or lie at the top of

♦ beat, conquer, crush, defeat, master, overcome, prevail, subdue, triumph, win

sur•name \ˈsər-ˌnām\ *n* **1 :** NICKNAME **2 :** the name borne in common by members of a family

sur•pass \sər-ˈpas\ *vb* **1** ♦ **:** to be superior to in quality, degree, or performance **:** EXCEL **2** ♦ **:** to go beyond the range or powers of — **sur•pass•ing•ly** *adv*

♦ [1] beat, better, eclipse, excel, outdistance, outdo, outshine, outstrip, top, transcend ♦ [2] exceed, overreach, overrun, overshoot, overstep

sur•plice \ˈsər-pləs\ *n* **:** a loose white outer vestment usually of knee length

sur•plus \ˈsər-(ˌ)pləs\ *n* **1** ♦ **:** quantity left over **:** EXCESS **2 :** the excess of assets over liabilities

♦ excess, fat, overabundance, overflow, overkill, overmuch, superabundance, superfluity, surfeit

¹sur•prise \sər-ˈprīz\ *n* **1** ♦ **:** an attack made without warning **2 :** a taking unawares **3** ♦ **:** something that surprises **4** ♦ **:** the state of being surprised **:** AMAZEMENT

♦ [1] ambush, trap ♦ [3] bolt, bombshell, jar, jolt ♦ [4] amazement, astonishment, shock, wonder

²surprise *vb* **sur•prised; sur•pris•ing 1** ♦ **:** to come upon and attack unexpectedly **2 :** to take unawares **3** ♦ **:** to strike with wonder or amazement especially because unexpected **:** AMAZE **4 :** to cause astonishment or surprise

♦ [1] ambush, waylay ♦ [3] amaze, astonish, astound, bowl, dumbfound, flabbergast, floor, shock, startle, stun, stupefy

surprising *adj* ♦ **:** of a nature that excites surprise

♦ amazing, astonishing, astounding, eye-opening, shocking, startling, stunning ♦ awesome, eye-opening, fabulous, marvelous (*or* marvellous), miraculous, portentous, prodigious, stupendous, sublime, wonderful

sur•pris•ing•ly \-ˈprī-ziŋ-lē\ *adv* **1 :** in a surprising manner or degree **2 :** it is surprising that

sur•re•al \sə-ˈrē-əl, -ˈrēl\ *adj* **1 :** having the intense irrational reality of a dream **2 :** of or relating to surrealism — **sur•re•al•ly** *adv*

sur•re•al•ism \sə-ˈrē-ə-ˌli-zəm\ *n* **:** art, literature, or theater characterized by fantastic or incongruous imagery or effects produced by unnatural juxtapositions and combinations — **sur•re•al•ist** \-list\ *n or adj* — **sur•re•al•is•tic** \sə-ˌrē-ə-ˈlis-tik\ *adj* — **sur•re•al•is•ti•cal•ly** \-ti-k(ə-)lē\ *adv*

¹sur•ren•der \sə-ˈren-dər\ *vb* **1** ♦ **:** to yield to the power of another **:** give up under compulsion **2** ♦ **:** to give up completely or agree to forgo especially in favor of another **:** RELINQUISH **3** ♦ **:** to give (oneself) over to something (as an influence)

♦ [1] bow, budge, capitulate, concede, fall, give in, knuckle under, quit, submit, succumb, yield ♦ [2] cede, deliver, give up, hand over, leave, relinquish, render, turn over, yield ♦ [3] bow, give in, submit, succumb, yield

²surrender *n* ♦ **:** the act of giving up or yielding oneself or the possession of something to another

♦ capitulation, relinquishment, submission

sur•rep•ti•tious \ˌsər-əp-ˈti-shəs\ *adj* ♦ **:** done, made, or acquired by stealth **:** CLANDESTINE — **sur•rep•ti•tious•ly** *adv*

♦ clandestine, covert, furtive, hugger-mugger, private, secret, sneak, sneaky, stealthy, undercover, underground, underhanded

sur•rey \ˈsər-ē\ *n, pl* **surreys :** a 2-seated horse-drawn carriage

sur•ro•ga•cy \ˈsər-ə-gə-sē\ *n* **:** SURROGATE MOTHERHOOD

sur•ro•gate \ˈsər-ə-ˌgāt, -gət\ *n* **1 :** DEPUTY, SUBSTITUTE **2 :** a law officer in some states with authority in the probate of wills, the settlement of estates, and the appointment of guardians **3 :** SURROGATE MOTHER

surrogate mother *n* **:** a woman who becomes pregnant (as by surgical implantation of a fertilized egg) in order to carry the fetus for another woman — **surrogate motherhood** *n*

sur•round \sə-ˈrau̇nd\ *vb* **1** ♦ **:** to enclose on all sides **:** ENCIRCLE **2 :** to enclose so as to cut off retreat or escape

♦ circle, encircle, enclose, encompass, ring

sur•round•ings \sə-ˈrau̇n-diŋz\ *n pl* ♦ **:** conditions by which one is surrounded

♦ atmosphere, climate, environment, environs, medium, milieu, setting

surround sound *n* **:** sound reproduction that uses three or more transmission channels

sur•tax \ˈsər-ˌtaks\ *n* **:** an additional tax over and above a normal tax

sur•tout \(ˌ)sər-ˈtü\ *n* **:** a man's long close-fitting overcoat

surv *abbr* survey; surveying; surveyor

sur•veil•lance \sər-ˈvā-ləns\ *n* **:** close watch; *also* **:** SUPERVISION

¹sur•vey \sər-ˈvā\ *vb* **sur•veyed; sur•vey•ing 1** ♦ **:** to look over and examine closely **2 :** to find and represent the contours, measurements, and position of a part of the earth's surface (as a tract of land) **3 :** to view or study something as a whole **4** ♦ **:** to query (someone) in order to collect data for the analysis of some aspect of a group or area — **sur•vey•or** \-ər\ *n*

♦ [1] audit, check, examine, inspect, review, scan, scrutinize ♦ [4] canvass, poll, solicit

²sur•vey \ˈsər-ˌvā\ *n, pl* **surveys** ♦ **:** the act or an instance of surveying; *also* **:** something that is surveyed

♦ audit, check, checkup, examination, inspection, review, scan, scrutiny

sur•vive \sər-ˈvīv\ *vb* **sur•vived; sur•viv•ing 1 :** to remain alive or existent **2** ♦ **:** to continue to exist or live after **3** ♦ **:** to continue to function or prosper — **sur•viv•al** *n* — **sur•vi•vor** \-ˈvī-vər\ *n*

♦ [2] ride ♦ [3] hold, hold out, keep up, last, prevail

sus•cep•ti•bil•i•ty \sə-ˌsep-tə-ˈbi-lə-tē\ *n* **:** the quality or state of being susceptible; *esp* **:** lack of ability to resist some extraneous agent (as a pathogen or drug)

sus•cep•ti•ble \-ˈsep-tə-bəl\ *adj* **1 :** of such a nature as to permit ⟨words ~ of being misunderstood⟩ **2** ♦ **:** having little resistance to a stimulus or agency ⟨~ to colds⟩ **3** ♦ **:** capable of being easily influenced

♦ [2] exposed, liable, open, sensitive, subject, vulnerable ♦ [3] easy, gullible, naive

su•shi \ˈsü-shē\ *n* **:** cold rice formed into various shapes and garnished especially with bits of raw fish or seafood

¹sus•pect \ˈsəs-ˌpekt, sə-ˈspekt\ *adj* ♦ **:** regarded with suspicion; *also* **:** QUESTIONABLE

♦ debatable, disputable, doubtful, dubious, equivocal, fishy, problematic, questionable, shady, shaky, suspicious

²sus•pect \ˈsəs-ˌpekt\ *n* **:** one who is suspected (as of a crime)

³sus•pect \sə-ˈspekt\ *vb* **1** ♦ **:** to have doubts of **:** MISTRUST **2 :** to imagine to be guilty without proof **3** ♦ **:** to imagine to exist or be true, likely, or probable **:** SURMISE

♦ [1] distrust, doubt, mistrust, question ♦ [3] assume, conjecture, guess, presume, speculate, suppose, surmise

sus•pend \sə-ˈspend\ *vb* **1 :** to bar temporarily from a privilege, office, or function **2 :** to stop temporarily **:** make inactive for a time **3 :** to withhold (judgment) for a time **4** ♦ **:** to fasten to some elevated point without support from below; *esp* **:** to hang so as to be free except at one point **5 :** to keep from falling or sinking by some invisible support

♦ dangle, hang, sling, swing

sus•pend•er \sə-ˈspen-dər\ *n* **:** one of two supporting straps which pass over the shoulders and to which the pants are fastened

sus•pense \sə-ˈspens\ *n* **1 :** the state of being suspended **:** SUSPENSION **2 :** mental uncertainty **:** ANXIETY **3 :** excitement as to an outcome — **sus•pense•ful** *adj*

sus•pen•sion \sə-ˈspen-chən\ *n* **1** ♦ **:** the act of suspending **:** the state or period of being suspended **2 :** the state of a substance when its particles are mixed with but undissolved in a fluid or solid; *also* **:** a substance in this state **3 :** something suspended **4 :** the system of devices supporting the upper part of a vehicle on the axles

♦ abeyance, doldrums, dormancy, latency, quiescence

sus•pen•so•ry \sə-ˈspen-sə-rē\ *adj* **1 :** SUSPENDED; *also* **:** fitted or serving to suspend something **2 :** temporarily leaving undetermined

sus•pi•cion \sə-ˈspi-shən\ *n* **1** ♦ **:** the act or an instance of suspecting something wrong without proof **2 :** a barely detectable amount **:** TRACE

♦ distrust, doubt, incertitude, misgiving, mistrust, skepticism, uncertainty

sus•pi•cious \sə-ˈspi-shəs\ *adj* **1** ♦ **:** open to or arousing suspicion **2** ♦ **:** inclined to suspect **3** ♦ **:** showing suspicion

♦ [1] debatable, disputable, doubtful, dubious, equivocal, fishy, problematic, questionable, shady, shaky, suspect ♦ [2, 3] distrustful, doubtful, dubious, mistrustful, skeptical, uncertain, undecided, unsettled, unsure

sus•pi•cious•ly *adv* ♦ **:** with suspicion

♦ askance, distrustfully, dubiously, mistrustfully

sus•tain \sə-ˈstān\ *vb* **1 :** to provide with nourishment **2 :** to keep going **:** PROLONG ⟨~*ed* effort⟩ **3 :** to hold up **:** PROP **4** ♦ **:** to hold up under **:** ENDURE **5** ♦ **:** to go through **:** SUFFER ⟨~ a broken arm⟩ **6 :** to support as true, legal, or valid **7 :** PROVE, CORROBORATE

♦ [4] abide, bear, brook, countenance, endure, meet, stand, stick out, stomach, support, take, tolerate ♦ [5] endure, experience, feel, have, know, see, suffer, taste, undergo

sus•tain•able \səs-ˈtā-nə-bəl\ *adj* ♦ **:** capable of being sustained

♦ defensible, justifiable, maintainable, supportable, tenable ♦ bearable, endurable, sufferable, tolerable

sus•te•nance \ˈsəs-tə-nəns\ *n* **1 :** FOOD, NOURISHMENT **2 :** a supplying with the necessities of life **3 :** something that sustains or supports

su•ture \ˈsü-chər\ *n* **1 :** material or a stitch for sewing a wound together **2 :** a seam or line along which two things or parts are joined by or as if by sewing

SUV \ˌes-ˌyü-ˈvē\ *n* **:** a vehicle similar to a station wagon but built on a light-truck chassis

su•zer•ain \ˈsü-zə-rən, -ˌrān\ *n* **1 :** a feudal lord **2 :** a nation that has political control over the foreign relations of another nation — **su•zer•ain•ty** \-tē\ *n*

svc *or* **svce** *abbr* service

svelte \ˈsfelt\ *adj* **svelt•er; svelt•est** ♦ **:** spare in frame or flesh **:** SLENDER

♦ lean, skinny, slender, slim, spare, svelte

svgs *abbr* savings

SW *abbr* **1** shortwave **2** southwest

¹swab \ˈswäb\ *n* **1 :** MOP **2 :** a wad of absorbent material especially for applying medicine or for cleaning; *also* **:** a sample taken with a swab **3** ♦ **:** a member of a ship's crew **:** SAILOR

♦ gob, jack, jack-tar, mariner, sailor, seaman, tar

²swab *vb* **swabbed; swab•bing :** to use a swab on **:** MOP

swad•dle \ˈswäd-ᵊl\ *vb* **swad•dled; swad•dling 1 :** to bind (an infant) in bands of cloth **2 :** to wrap up **:** SWATHE

swaddling clothes *n pl* **:** bands of cloth wrapped around an infant

swag \ˈswag\ *n* ♦ **:** stolen goods **:** LOOT

♦ booty, loot, plunder, spoil

swag•ger \ˈswa-gər\ *vb* **1** ♦ **:** to walk with a conceited swing or strut **2** ♦ **:** to puff oneself up in speech **:** BOAST — **swagger** *n*

♦ [1] stalk, strut ♦ [2] boast, brag, crow, plume

swag•man \ˈswag-mən\ *n* **:** a person who has no job and wanders from place to place **:** VAGRANT

Swa•hi•li \swä-ˈhē-lē\ *n* **:** a language that is a trade and governmental language over much of eastern Africa and the Congo region

swain \ˈswān\ *n* **1 :** RUSTIC; *esp* **:** SHEPHERD **2** ♦ **:** a male admirer or suitor

♦ beau, boyfriend, fellow, man ♦ gallant, suitor, wooer

SWAK *abbr* sealed with a kiss

¹swal•low \ˈswä-lō\ *n* **:** any of numerous small long-winged migratory birds that often have a deeply forked tail

²swallow *vb* **1 :** to take into the stomach through the throat **2 :** to envelop or take in as if by swallowing **3** ♦ **:** to accept or believe without question, protest, or anger **4** ♦ **:** to keep from expressing or showing

♦ [3] accept, believe, credit, trust ♦ [4] choke, pocket, repress, smother, stifle, strangle, suppress

³swallow *n* **1 :** an act of swallowing **2** ♦ **:** an amount that can be swallowed at one time

♦ draft, drag, drink, nip, quaff, shot, slug, snort, swig

swal•low•tail \ˈswä-lō-ˌtāl\ *n* **1 :** a deeply forked and tapering tail like that of a swallow **2 :** TAILCOAT **3 :** any of various large butterflies with the border of each hind wing usually drawn out into a process resembling a tail — **swal•low–tailed** \-ˌtāld\ *adj*

swam *past of* SWIM

swa•mi \ˈswä-mē\ *n* **:** a Hindu ascetic or religious teacher

¹swamp \ˈswämp\ *n* ♦ **:** a spongy wetland — **swamp** *adj* — **swampy** *adj*

♦ bog, fen, marsh, mire, morass, slough

²swamp *vb* **1** ♦ **:** to fill or become filled with or as if with water **2** ♦ **:** to overwhelm numerically or by an excess of something

♦ [1] deluge, drown, engulf, flood, inundate, overflow, overwhelm, submerge ♦ [2] carry away, crush, devastate, floor, oppress, overcome, overpower, overwhelm, prostrate, snow under

swamp•land \-ˌland\ *n* **:** a spongy wetland **:** SWAMP

swan \ˈswän\ *n, pl* **swans** *also* **swan :** any of various heavy-bodied long-necked mostly pure white swimming birds related to the geese

¹swank \ˈswaŋk\ *or* **swanky** \ˈswaŋ-kē\ *adj* **swank•er** *or* **swank•i•er; -est :** showily smart and dashing; *also* **:** fashionably elegant

²swank *n* **1** ♦ **:** arrogance or ostentation of dress or manner **:** PRETENTIOUSNESS **2 :** ELEGANCE

♦ flamboyance, flashiness, gaudiness, glitz, ostentation, pretentiousness, showiness

swans•down \ˈswänz-ˌdau̇n\ *n* **1 :** the very soft down of a swan used especially for trimming **2 :** a soft thick cotton flannel

swan song *n* **:** a farewell appearance, act, or pronouncement

¹swap \ˈswäp\ *vb* **swapped; swap•ping** ♦ **:** to give in trade **:** EXCHANGE

♦ change, commute, exchange, shift, substitute, switch, trade

²swap *n* ♦ **:** to give in trade

♦ barter, commutation, exchange, trade, truck

sward \ˈswȯrd\ *n* **:** the grassy surface of land

¹swarm \ˈswȯrm\ *n* **1 :** a great number of honeybees leaving together from a hive with a queen to start a new colony; *also* **:** a hive of bees **2** ♦ **:** a large crowd

♦ army, crowd, crush, drove, flock, horde, host, legion, mob, multitude, press, throng

²swarm *vb* **1 :** to form in a swarm and depart from a hive **2 :** to throng together **:** gather in great numbers **3** ♦ **:** to beset or surround in a swarm

♦ crowd, flock, mob, throng

swart \ˈswȯrt\ *adj* **:** SWARTHY

swar•thy \ˈswȯr-t͟hē, -thē\ *adj* **swar•thi•er; -est :** dark in color or complexion **:** dark-skinned

swash \ˈswäsh\ *vb* ♦ **:** to move about with a splashing sound — **swash** *n*

♦ lap, plash, slosh, splash

swash•buck•ler \-ˌbə-klər\ *n* **:** a swaggering or daring soldier or adventurer — **swash•buck•ling** *adj*

swas•ti•ka \ˈswäs-ti-kə\ *n* **:** a symbol or ornament in the form of a cross with the ends of the arms bent at right angles

¹swat \ˈswät\ *vb* **swat•ted; swat•ting** ♦ **:** to hit sharply ⟨~ a fly⟩ ⟨~ a ball⟩ — **swat•ter** *n*

♦ bat, clout, crack, hit, slam, strike

²swat *n* **:** a powerful or crushing blow

SWAT *abbr* Special Weapons and Tactics

swatch \ˈswäch\ *n* **:** a sample piece (as of fabric) or a collection of samples

swath \ˈswäth, ˈswȯth\ *or* **swathe** \ˈswät͟h, ˈswȯt͟h, ˈswāt͟h\ *n* **1 :** a row of cut grass or grain **2 :** the sweep of a scythe or mowing machine or the path cut in mowing

swathe \ˈswät͟h, ˈswȯt͟h, ˈswāt͟h\ *vb* **swathed; swath•ing** ♦ **:** to bind or wrap with or as if with a bandage

♦ embrace, enclose, encompass, enfold, enshroud, envelop, invest, lap, mantle, shroud, veil, wrap

¹sway \ˈswā\ *n* **1 :** a gentle swinging from side to side **2** ♦ **:** controlling influence or power

♦ authority, clout, influence, power, pull, weight

²sway *vb* **1** ♦ **:** to swing gently from side to side **2 :** RULE, GOVERN **3 :** to cause to swing from side to side **4 a :** BEND, SWERVE **b :** to exert a guiding or controlling influence on **:** INFLUENCE

♦ careen, lurch, pitch, rock, roll, seesaw, toss, wobble

sway•backed \ˈswā-ˌbakt\ *also* **sway•back** \-ˌbak\ *adj* **:** having an abnormally sagging back ⟨a ~ mare⟩ — **swayback** *n*

swear \ˈswar\ *vb* **swore** \ˈswōr\; **sworn** \ˈswōrn\; **swear•ing** **1** ♦ **:** to make a solemn statement or promise under oath **2** ♦ **:** to assert or promise emphatically or earnestly **3 :** to administer an oath to **4 :** to bind by or as if by an oath **5 :** to use profane or obscene language — **swear•er** *n*

♦ [1] attest, depose, testify, witness ♦ [2] covenant, pledge, promise, vow

swear in *vb* **:** to induct into office by administration of an oath

¹sweat \ˈswet\ *vb* **sweat** *or* **sweat•ed; sweat•ing** **1 :** to excrete salty moisture from glands of the skin **:** PERSPIRE **2 a :** to form drops of moisture on the surface **b** ♦ **:** to become exuded through pores or a porous surface **3** ♦ **:** to work so that one sweats **:** TOIL **4 :** to cause to sweat **5 :** to draw out or get rid of by or as if by sweating **6 :** to make a person overwork **7** ♦ **:** to undergo anxiety or mental or emotional distress — **sweaty** *adj*

♦ [2b] bleed, exude, ooze, percolate, seep, strain, weep ♦ [3] drudge, fag, grub, labor (*or* labour), slave, toil ♦ [7] bother, fear, fret, stew, trouble, worry

²sweat *n* ♦ **:** hard work

♦ drudgery, grind, labor (*or* labour), slavery, toil, travail

sweat•er \ˈswe-tər\ *n* **1 :** one that sweats **2 :** a knitted or crocheted jacket or pullover

sweat out *vb* ♦ **:** to endure or wait through the course of

♦ bear, deliver, drop, have, produce

sweat•shirt \ˈswet-ˌshərt\ *n* **:** a loose collarless pullover usually of heavy cotton jersey

sweat•shop \ˈswet-ˌshäp\ *n* **:** a shop or factory in which workers are employed for long hours at low wages and under unhealthy conditions

Swed *abbr* Sweden

swede \ˈswēd\ *n* **1** *cap* **:** a native or inhabitant of Sweden **2** *chiefly Brit* **:** RUTABAGA

Swed•ish \ˈswē-dish\ *n* **1 :** the language of Sweden **2 Swedish** *pl* **:** the people of Sweden — **Swedish** *adj*

¹sweep \ˈswēp\ *vb* **swept** \ˈswept\; **sweep•ing** **1 :** to remove or clean by or as if by brushing **2 :** to destroy completely; *also* **:** to remove or take with a single swift movement **3 :** to remove from sight or consideration **4** ♦ **:** to move over with speed and force ⟨the tide *swept* over the shore⟩ **5 :** to win an overwhelming victory in; *also* **:** to win all the games or contests of **6** ♦ **:** to move or extend in a wide curve **7 :** to move swiftly, forcefully, or devastatingly — **sweep•er** *n*

♦ [4] bowl, breeze, coast, drift, flow, glide, roll, sail, skim, slide, slip, stream, whisk ♦ [6] arc, arch, bend, bow, crook, curve, hook, round, swerve, wheel

²sweep *n* **1 :** something (as a long oar) that operates with a sweeping motion **2 :** a clearing off or away **3 :** a winning of all the contests or prizes in a competition **4 :** a sweeping movement **5 :** CURVE, BEND **6** ♦ **:** extent of treatment, activity, or influence **:** SCOPE

♦ amplitude, breadth, compass, extent, range, reach, realm, scope, width

sweeping *adj* **:** EXTENSIVE ⟨~ reforms⟩; *also* **:** indiscriminately inclusive ⟨~ generalities⟩

sweep•ings \ˈswē-piŋz\ *n pl* **:** things collected by sweeping

sweep–sec•ond hand \ˈswēp-ˌse-kənd-\ *n* **:** a hand marking seconds on a timepiece

sweep•stakes \ˈswēp-ˌstāks\ *also* **sweep•stake** \-ˌstāk\ *n, pl* **sweepstakes** **1 :** a race or contest in which the entire prize may go to the winner **2 :** any of various lotteries

¹sweet \ˈswēt\ *adj* **1 :** being or causing the one of the four basic taste sensations that is caused especially by table sugar and is identified especially by the taste buds at the front of the tongue; *also* **:** pleasing to the taste **2** ♦ **:** marked by gentle good humor or kindliness **:** AGREEABLE **3** ♦ **:** pleasing to a sense other than taste ⟨a ~ smell⟩ ⟨~ music⟩ **4 :** not stale or spoiled **:** WHOLESOME ⟨~ milk⟩ **5 :** not salted ⟨~ butter⟩ **6** ♦ **:** much loved — **sweet•ish** *adj* — **sweet•ly** *adv*

♦ [2] affable, agreeable, amiable, genial, good-natured, gracious, nice, well-disposed ♦ [3] ambrosial, aromatic, fragrant, redolent, savory, scented ♦ [6] beloved, darling, dear, favorite (*or* favourite), loved, pet, precious, special ♦ [6] adorable, endearing, lovable, winning

²sweet *n* **1 :** something sweet **2 :** a dearly loved person **:** DARLING

sweet•bread \ˈswēt-ˌbred\ *n* **:** the pancreas or thymus of an animal (as a calf or lamb) used for food

sweet•bri•ar *or* **sweet•bri•er** \-ˌbrī-ər\ *n* **:** a thorny Old World rose with fragrant white to deep pink flowers

sweet clover *n* **:** any of a genus of erect legumes widely grown for soil improvement or hay

sweet corn *n* **:** an Indian corn with wrinkled translucent kernels that are rich in sugar

sweet•en \ˈswēt-ᵊn\ *vb* **sweet•ened; sweet•en•ing** **:** to make sweet — **sweet•en•er** *n* — **sweet•en•ing** *n*

sweet•heart \ˈswēt-ˌhärt\ *n* ♦ **:** one who is loved

♦ beloved, darling, dear, flame, honey, love, sweet

sweet•meat \-ˌmēt\ *n* **:** CANDY 1

sweet•ness *n* ♦ **:** the quality or state of being sweet

♦ agreeableness, amenity, amiability, geniality, graciousness, niceness, pleasantness

sweet pea *n* **:** a garden plant of the legume family with climbing stems and fragrant flowers of many colors; *also* **:** its flower
sweet pepper *n* **:** any of various large mild thick-walled fruits of a pepper; *also* **:** a plant bearing sweet peppers
sweet potato *n* **:** a tropical vine related to the morning glory; *also* **:** its large sweet edible root
sweet–talk \ˈswēt-ˌtȯk\ *vb* **:** FLATTER, COAX — **sweet talk** *n*
sweet tooth *n* **:** a craving or fondness for sweet food
sweet wil•liam \ˌswēt-ˈwil-yəm\ *n, often cap W* **:** a widely cultivated Old World pink with small white to deep red or purple flowers often showily spotted, banded, or mottled
[1]**swell** \ˈswel\ *vb* **swelled; swelled** *or* **swol•len** \ˈswō-lən\; **swell•ing 1** ♦ **:** to grow big or make bigger **2 :** to expand or distend abnormally or excessively ⟨a *swollen* joint⟩; *also* **:** BULGE **3 :** to fill or be filled with emotion (as pride)

♦ accumulate, appreciate, balloon, build, burgeon, enlarge, escalate, expand, increase, mount, multiply, mushroom, proliferate, rise, snowball, wax ♦ add, aggrandize, amplify, augment, boost, compound, extend, increase, raise, up

[2]**swell** *n* **1** ♦ **:** a long crestless wave or series of waves in the open sea **2 :** the condition of being protuberant **3 :** a person dressed in the height of fashion; *also* **:** a person of high social position

♦ billow, surge, wave

[3]**swell** *adj* **1 :** STYLISH; *also* **:** socially prominent **2 :** very good of its kind **:** EXCELLENT
swelled head *n* **:** an exaggerated opinion of oneself **:** SELF-CONCEIT
swell•ing *n* ♦ **:** something that is swollen; *specif* **:** an abnormal bodily protuberance or localized enlargement

♦ bump, knot, lump, nodule

swel•ter \ˈswel-tər\ *vb* **1 :** to be faint or oppressed with the heat **2 :** to become exceedingly hot — **swel•ter•ing** \-tə-riŋ\ *adj*
swept *past and past part of* SWEEP
swerve \ˈswərv\ *vb* **swerved; swerv•ing** ♦ **:** to move abruptly aside from a straight line or course — **swerve** *n*

♦ sheer, veer, yaw ***Ant*** straighten

[1]**swift** \ˈswift\ *adj* **1** ♦ **:** moving or capable of moving with great speed **2 :** occurring suddenly **3 :** READY, ALERT

♦ breakneck, breathless, brisk, dizzy, fast, fleet, hasty, lightning, nippy, quick, rapid, rattling, snappy, speedy

[2]**swift** *n* **:** any of numerous small insect-eating birds with long narrow wings
swift•ly *adv* ♦ **:** in a swift manner **:** with speed

♦ apace, briskly, fast, full tilt, hastily, posthaste, presto, pronto, quick, quickly, rapidly, soon, speedily

swift•ness *n* ♦ **:** the quality or state of being swift; *also* **:** the fact of being swift

♦ celerity, fastness, fleetness, haste, hurry, quickness, rapidity, speed, velocity

[1]**swig** \ˈswig\ *vb* **swigged; swig•ging** ♦ **:** to drink in long drafts

♦ drink, guzzle, imbibe, quaff, sup, toss

[2]**swig** *n* ♦ **:** a quantity drunk at one time

♦ draft, drag, drink, nip, quaff, shot, slug, snort, swallow

[1]**swill** \ˈswil\ *vb* **1 :** to swallow greedily **:** GUZZLE **2 :** to feed (as hogs) on swill
[2]**swill** *n* **1 :** food for animals composed of edible refuse mixed with liquid **2 :** GARBAGE **3 :** a draft of liquor
[1]**swim** \ˈswim\ *vb* **swam** \ˈswam\; **swum** \ˈswəm\; **swim•ming 1 :** to propel oneself along in water by natural means (as by hands and legs, by tail, or by fins) **2 :** to glide smoothly along **3 :** FLOAT **4 :** to be covered with or as if with a liquid **5** ♦ **:** to be dizzy ⟨his head *swam*⟩ **6 :** to cross or go over by swimming — **swim•mer** *n*

♦ reel, spin, whirl

[2]**swim** *n* **1 :** an act of swimming **2 :** the main current of activity ⟨in the ~⟩
swim•ming *n* **:** the action, art, or sport of swimming and diving
swimming pool *n* **:** a tank (as of concrete or plastic) designed for swimming
swim•suit \ˈswim-ˌsüt\ *n* **:** a suit for swimming or bathing
swim•wear \ˈswim-ˌwer\ *n* **:** clothing for wear while swimming or bathing
[1]**swin•dle** \ˈswin-dᵊl\ *vb* **swin•dled; swin•dling** ♦ **:** to take money or property from by fraud or deceit **:** CHEAT

♦ bleed, cheat, chisel, cozen, defraud, fleece, gyp, hustle, mulct, rook, shortchange, skin, squeeze, stick, sting, victimize

[2]**swindle** *n* ♦ **:** an act or instance of swindling

♦ hustle, racket

swin•dler *n* ♦ **:** one that swindles

♦ cheat, dodger, hoaxer, shark, sharper, trickster

swine \ˈswīn\ *n, pl* **swine 1 :** any of a family of stout short-legged hoofed mammals with bristly skin and a long flexible snout, *esp* **:** one widely raised as a meat animal **2** ♦ **:** a contemptible person

♦ beast, boor, churl, clown, creep, cretin, cur, heel, jerk, joker, louse, lout, scum, skunk, slob, snake

[1]**swing** \ˈswiŋ\ *vb* **swung** \ˈswəŋ\; **swing•ing 1 :** to move or cause to move rapidly in an arc **2 :** to sway or cause to sway back and forth **3** ♦ **:** to hang so as to move freely back and forth or in a curve **4 :** to be executed by hanging **5 :** to move or turn on a hinge or pivot **6** ♦ **:** to manage or handle successfully **7 :** to march or walk with free swaying movements **8 :** to have a steady pulsing rhythm; *also* **:** to play swing music **9 :** to be lively and up-to-date; *also* **:** to engage freely in sex **10** ♦ **:** to cause to face or move in another direction — **swing•er** *n* — **swing•ing** *adj*

♦ [3] dangle, hang, sling, suspend ♦ [6] contend with, cope with, grapple with, handle, manage, maneuver (*or* manoeuvre), negotiate, treat ♦ [10] divert, swerve, turn, veer, wheel, whip

[2]**swing** *n* **1 :** the act of swinging **2 :** a swinging blow, movement, or rhythm **3 :** the distance through which something swings **:** FLUCTUATION **4 :** progression of an activity or process ⟨in full ~⟩ **5 :** a seat suspended by a rope or chain for swinging back and forth for pleasure **6 :** jazz music played especially by a large band and marked by a steady lively rhythm, simple harmony, and a basic melody often submerged in improvisation
[3]**swing** *adj* **1 :** of or relating to swing music **2 :** that may swing often decisively either way (as on an issue) ⟨~ voters⟩
swin•ish \ˈswī-nish\ *adj* **:** of, suggesting, or characteristic of swine
[1]**swipe** \ˈswīp\ *n* **:** a strong sweeping blow
[2]**swipe** *vb* **swiped; swip•ing 1 :** to strike or wipe with a sweeping motion **2** ♦ **:** to take or appropriate without right and with intent to keep **:** PILFER **3 :** to slide (a card having a magnetic code) through a reading device

♦ appropriate, filch, hook, misappropriate, nip, pilfer, pocket, purloin, snitch, steal, thieve

swirl \ˈswərl\ *vb* ♦ **:** to move or cause to move with a whirling motion — **swirl** *n* — **swirly** \ˈswər-lē\ *adj*

♦ pivot, revolve, roll, rotate, spin, swing, turn, twirl, twist, wheel, whirl

[1]**swish** \ˈswish\ *n* **1** ♦ **:** a prolonged hissing sound **2 :** a light sweeping or brushing sound

♦ fizz, hiss, sizzle, whish, whiz

[2]**swish** *vb* **:** to move, pass, swing, or whirl with the sound of a swish
Swiss \ˈswis\ *n* **1** *pl* **Swiss :** a native or inhabitant of Switzerland **2 :** a hard cheese with large holes — **Swiss** *adj*
Swiss chard *n* **:** a beet having large leaves and succulent stalks often cooked as a vegetable
[1]**switch** \ˈswich\ *n* **1** ♦ **:** a slender flexible whip, rod, or twig **2 :** a blow with a switch **3 :** a shift from one thing to another; *also* **:** change from the usual **4 :** a device for adjusting the rails of a track so that a locomotive or train may be turned from one track to another; *also* **:** a railroad siding **5 :** a device for making, breaking, or changing the connections in an electrical circuit **6 :** a heavy strand of hair often used in addition to a person's own hair for some coiffures

♦ lash, scourge, whip

[2]**switch** *vb* **1** ♦ **:** to punish or urge on with a switch **2 :** WHISK ⟨a cow *~ing* her tail⟩ **3 :** to shift or turn by operating a switch **4** ♦ **:** to make a shift in or exchange of **:** CHANGE

♦ [1] flail, flog, hide, lash, scourge, slash, thrash, whale, whip ♦ [4] change, commute, exchange, shift, substitute, swap, trade

switch•back \ˈswich-ˌbak\ *n* **:** a zigzag road, trail, or section of railroad tracks for climbing a steep hill
switch•blade \-ˌblād\ *n* **:** a pocket-knife with a spring-operated blade
switch•board \-ˌbōrd\ *n* **:** a panel for controlling the operation of

a number of electric circuits; *esp* : one used to make and break telephone connections
switch–hit·ter \-ˈhi-tər\ *n* : a baseball player who bats either right-handed or left-handed — **switch–hit** \-ˈhit\ *vb*
switch·man \ˈswich-mən\ *n* : one who attends a railroad switch
Switz *abbr* Switzerland
¹swiv·el \ˈswi-vəl\ *n* : a device joining two parts so that one or both can turn freely
²swivel *vb* **-eled** *or* **-elled; -el·ing** *or* **-el·ling** : to swing or turn on or as if on a swivel
swiv·et \ˈswi-vət\ *n* : an agitated state
swiz·zle stick \ˈswi-zəl-\ *n* : a stick used to stir mixed drinks
swollen *past part of* SWELL
¹swoon \ˈswün\ *vb* ♦ : to undergo a temporary loss of consciousness : FAINT

♦ black out, faint, pass out

²swoon *n* ♦ : a partial or total loss of consciousness; *also* : a state of suspended animation

♦ blackout, faint, knockout

swoop \ˈswüp\ *vb* : to move with a sweep ⟨the eagle ~*ed* down on its prey⟩ — **swoop** *n*
swoopy \ˈswü-pē\ *adj* : having lines that extend in a wide curve ⟨a ~ silhouette⟩
swop *chiefly Brit var of* SWAP
sword \ˈsȯrd\ *n* **1** : a weapon with a long blade for cutting or thrusting **2** : the use of force
sword·fish \-ˌfish\ *n* : a very large ocean fish used for food that has the upper jaw prolonged into a long swordlike beak
sword·play \-ˌplā\ *n* : the art or skill of wielding a sword
swords·man \ˈsōrdz-mən\ *n* : one skilled in swordplay; *esp* : FENCER
sword·tail \ˈsōrd-ˌtāl\ *n* : a small brightly marked Central American fish often kept in aquariums
swore *past of* SWEAR
sworn *past part of* SWEAR
swum *past part of* SWIM
swung *past and past part of* SWING
syb·a·rite \ˈsi-bə-ˌrīt\ *n* : a lover of luxury : VOLUPTUARY — **syb·a·rit·ic** \ˌsi-bə-ˈri-tik\ *adj*
syc·a·more \ˈsi-kə-ˌmōr\ *n* : a large spreading tree chiefly of the eastern and central U.S. that has light brown flaky bark and small round fruits hanging on long stalks
sy·co·phant \ˈsi-kə-fənt\ *n* : a servile flatterer — **sy·co·phan·tic** \ˌsi-kə-ˈfan-tik\ *adj*
syl *or* **syll** *abbr* syllable
syl·lab·i·ca·tion \sə-ˌla-bə-ˈkā-shən\ *n* : the division of words into syllables
syl·lab·i·fy \sə-ˈla-bə-ˌfī\ *vb* **-fied; -fy·ing** : to form or divide into syllables — **syl·lab·i·fi·ca·tion** \-ˌla-bə-fə-ˈkā-shən\ *n*
syl·la·ble \ˈsi-lə-bəl\ *n* : a unit of spoken language consisting of an uninterrupted utterance and forming either a whole word (as *cat*) or a commonly recognized division of a word (as *syl* in *syl-la-ble*); *also* : one or more letters representing such a unit — **syl·lab·ic** \sə-ˈla-bik\ *adj*
syl·la·bus \ˈsi-lə-bəs\ *n, pl* **-bi** \-ˌbī\ *or* **-bus·es** : a summary containing the heads or main topics of a speech, book, or course of study
syl·lo·gism \ˈsi-lə-ˌji-zəm\ *n* : a logical scheme of a formal argument consisting of a major and a minor premise and a conclusion which must logically be true if the premises are true — **syl·lo·gis·tic** \ˌsi-lə-ˈjis-tik\ *adj*
sylph \ˈsilf\ *n* **1** : an imaginary being inhabiting the air **2** : a slender graceful woman
syl·van \ˈsil-vən\ *adj* **1** : living or located in a wooded area; *also* : of, relating to, or characteristic of forest **2** : abounding in woods or trees
sym *abbr* **1** symbol **2** symmetrical
sym·bi·o·sis \ˌsim-ˌbī-ˈō-səs, -bē-\ *n, pl* **-o·ses** \-ˌsēz\ : the living together in close association of two dissimilar organisms especially when mutually beneficial — **sym·bi·ot·ic** \-ˈä-tik\ *adj*
sym·bol \ˈsim-bəl\ *n* **1** ♦ : something that stands for something else; *esp* : something concrete that represents or suggests another thing that cannot in itself be pictured ⟨the lion is a ~ of bravery⟩ **2** : a letter, character, or sign used in writing or printing to represent operations, quantities, elements, sounds, or other ideas — **sym·bol·ic** \sim-ˈbä-lik\ *also* **sym·bol·i·cal** \-li-kəl\ *adj* — **sym·bol·i·cal·ly** \-k(ə-)lē\ *adv*

♦ emblem, hallmark, logo, trademark

sym·bol·ise *chiefly Brit var of* SYMBOLIZE
sym·bol·ism \ˈsim-bə-ˌli-zəm\ *n* : representation of abstract or intangible things by means of symbols
sym·bol·ize \ˈsim-bə-ˌlīz\ *vb* **-ized; -iz·ing** **1** : to serve as a symbol of **2** : to represent by symbols — **sym·bol·i·za·tion** \ˌsim-bə-lə-ˈzā-shən\ *n*
sym·me·try \ˈsi-mə-trē\ *n, pl* **-tries** **1** ♦ : an arrangement marked by regularity and balanced proportions **2** : correspondence in size, shape, and position of parts that are on opposite sides of a dividing line or center — **sym·met·ri·cal** \sə-ˈme-tri-kəl\ *or* **sym·met·ric** \sə-ˈme-trik\ *adj* — **sym·met·ri·cal·ly** \-k(ə-)lē\ *adv*

♦ balance, coherence, consonance, harmony, proportion, symphony, unity

sym·pa·thet·ic \ˌsim-pə-ˈthe-tik\ *adj* ♦ : given to, marked by, or arising from sympathy, compassion, friendliness, and sensitivity to others' emotions — **sym·pa·thet·i·cal·ly** \ˌsim-pə-ˈthe-ti-k(ə-)lē\ *adv*

♦ compassionate, humane, understanding ***Ant*** callous, cold-blooded, heartless, inhuman, inhumane, unfeeling, unsympathetic ♦ beneficent, benevolent, good-hearted, humane, kind, kindly, tender, tenderhearted, warmhearted

sympathetic nervous system *n* : the part of the autonomic nervous system that is concerned especially with the body's response to stress and that tends to decrease the tone and contractility of smooth muscle and increase blood pressure and the activity of the heart
sym·pa·thise *chiefly Brit var of* SYMPATHIZE
sym·pa·thize \ˈsim-pə-ˌthīz\ *vb* **-thized; -thiz·ing** ♦ : to feel or show sympathy

♦ *usu* **sympathize with** bleed, commiserate, feel, pity

sym·pa·thiz·er *n* ♦ : one that sympathizes : one that acts or reacts in sympathy

♦ abettor, ally, backer, confederate, supporter

sym·pa·thy \ˈsim-pə-thē\ *n, pl* **-thies** **1** : a relationship between persons or things wherein whatever affects one similarly affects the other **2** : harmony of interests and aims **3** : FAVOR, SUPPORT **4** ♦ : the capacity for entering into and sharing the feelings or interests of another; *also* : COMPASSION **5** : an expression of sorrow for another's loss, grief, or misfortune

♦ commiseration, compassion, feeling ***Ant*** callousness ♦ charity, heart, humanity, kindliness, kindness, mercy, pity

sym·phon·ic \sim-ˈfä-nik\ *adj* ♦ : musically concordant

♦ euphonious, harmonious, melodious, musical, tuneful

sym·pho·ny \ˈsim-fə-nē\ *n, pl* **-nies** **1** ♦ : harmony of sounds **2** : a large and complex composition for a full orchestra **3** : a large orchestra of a kind that plays symphonies

♦ balance, coherence, consonance, harmony, proportion, symmetry, unity

sym·po·sium \sim-ˈpō-zē-əm\ *n, pl* **-sia** \-zē-ə\ *or* **-siums** ♦ : a conference at which a particular topic is discussed by various speakers; *also* : a collection of opinions about a subject

♦ colloquy, conference, council, forum, panel, parley, powwow, seminar

symp·tom \ˈsimp-təm\ *n* **1** : something that indicates the presence of disease or abnormality; *esp* : something (as a headache) that can be sensed only by the individual affected **2** : SIGN, INDICATION
symp·tom·at·ic \ˌsimp-tə-ˈma-tik\ *adj* ♦ : serving to indicate

♦ characteristic, classic, distinct, distinctive, individual, peculiar, proper, typical

syn *abbr* synonym; synonymous; synonymy
syn·a·gogue *also* **syn·a·gog** \ˈsi-nə-ˌgäg\ *n* **1** : a Jewish congregation **2** : the house of worship of a Jewish congregation
syn·apse \ˈsi-ˌnaps, sə-ˈnaps\ *n* : the point at which a nervous impulse passes from one neuron to another — **syn·ap·tic** \sə-ˈnap-tik\ *adj*
¹sync *also* **synch** \ˈsiŋk\ *vb* **synced** *also* **synched** \ˈsiŋkt\; **sync·ing** *also* **synch·ing** \ˈsiŋ-kiŋ\ : SYNCHRONIZE
²sync *also* **synch** *n* : SYNCHRONIZATION, SYNCHRONISM — **sync** *adj*
syn·chro·ni·sa·tion, syn·chro·nise *chiefly Brit var of* SYNCHRONIZATION, SYNCHRONIZE
syn·chro·nize \ˈsiŋ-krə-ˌnīz, ˈsin-\ *vb* **-nized; -niz·ing** **1** : to occur or cause to occur at the same instant **2** : to represent, arrange, or tabulate according to dates or time **3** : to cause to agree in time

4 : to make synchronous in operation — **syn•chro•nism** \-ˌni-zəm\ *n* — **syn•chro•ni•za•tion** \ˌsiŋ-krə-nə-ˈzā-shən, ˌsin-\ *n* — **syn•chro•niz•er** *n*
syn•chro•nous \ˈsiŋ-krə-nəs, ˈsin-\ *adj* **1** ♦ : happening at the same time : CONCURRENT **2** : working, moving, or occurring together at the same rate and at the proper time

♦ coeval, concurrent, contemporary, simultaneous

syn•co•pa•tion \ˌsiŋ-kə-ˈpā-shən, ˌsin-\ *n* : a shifting of the regular musical accent : occurrence of accented notes on the weak beat — **syn•co•pate** \ˈsiŋ-kə-ˌpāt, ˈsin-\ *vb*
syn•co•pe \ˈsiŋ-kə-(ˌ)pē, ˈsin-\ *n* : the loss of one or more sounds or letters in the interior of a word (as in *fo'c'sle* for *forecastle*)
[1]**syn•di•cate** \ˈsin-di-kət\ *n* **1** ♦ : a group of persons who combine to carry out a financial or industrial undertaking **2** ♦ : a loose association of racketeers **3** : a business concern that sells materials for publication in many newspapers and periodicals at the same time

♦ [1] cartel, combination, combine, trust ♦ [2] cabal, conspiracy, gang, mob, ring

[2]**syn•di•cate** \-də-ˌkāt\ *vb* **-cat•ed; -cat•ing** **1** : to combine into or manage as a syndicate **2** : to publish through a syndicate — **syn•di•ca•tion** \ˌsin-də-ˈkā-shən\ *n*
syn•drome \ˈsin-ˌdrōm\ *n* : a group of signs and symptoms that occur together and characterize a particular abnormality or condition
syn•er•gism \ˈsin-ər-ˌji-zəm\ *n* : interaction of discrete agencies (as industrial firms), agents (as drugs), or conditions such that the total effect is greater than the sum of the individual effects — **syn•er•gist** \-jist\ *n* — **syn•er•gis•tic** \ˌsi-nər-ˈjis-tik\ *adj* — **syn•er•gis•ti•cal•ly** \-ti-k(ə-)lē\ *adv*
syn•er•gy \ˈsi-nər-jē\ *n, pl* **-gies** : SYNERGISM
syn•fuel \ˈsin-ˌfyül\ *n* : a fuel derived especially from a fossil fuel
syn•od \ˈsi-nəd\ *n* : COUNCIL, ASSEMBLY; *esp* : a religious governing body — **syn•od•al** \-nəd-ᵊl, -ˌnäd-ᵊl\ *adj* — **syn•od•ic** \-dik\ *or* **syn•od•i•cal** \sə-ˈnä-di-kəl\ *adj*
syn•onym \ˈsi-nə-ˌnim\ *n* : one of two or more words in the same language which have the same or very nearly the same meaning — **syn•on•y•mous** \sə-ˈnä-nə-məs\ *adj* — **syn•on•y•my** \-mē\ *n*
syn•op•sis \sə-ˈnäp-səs\ *n, pl* **-op•ses** \-ˌsēz\ ♦ : a condensed statement or outline (as of a treatise) : ABSTRACT

♦ abstract, digest, encapsulation, epitome, outline, précis, recapitulation, résumé (*or* resume), roundup, sum, summary, wrap-up

syn•op•tic \sə-ˈnäp-tik\ *also* **syn•op•ti•cal** \-ti-kəl\ *adj* : characterized by or affording a comprehensive view
syn•tax \ˈsin-ˌtaks\ *n* : the way in which words are put together to form phrases, clauses, or sentences — **syn•tac•tic** \sin-ˈtak-tik\ *or* **syn•tac•ti•cal** \-ti-kəl\ *adj*
syn•the•sis \ˈsin-thə-səs\ *n, pl* **-the•ses** \-ˌsēz\ : the combination of parts or elements into a whole; *esp* : the production of a substance by union of chemically simpler substances — **syn•the•size** \-ˌsīz\ *vb* — **syn•the•siz•er** *n*
syn•thet•ic \sin-ˈthe-tik\ *adj* ♦ : produced artificially especially by chemical means; *also* : not genuine — **synthetic** *n* — **syn•thet•i•cal•ly** \-ti-k(ə-)lē\ *adv*

♦ artificial, fake, faux, imitation, mock, sham

syph•i•lis \ˈsi-fə-ləs\ *n* : an infectious usually venereal disease caused by a spirochete — **syph•i•lit•ic** \ˌsi-fə-ˈli-tik\ *adj or n*
syphon *var of* SIPHON
Sy•rah \sē-ˈrä\ *n* : a red wine
Syr•i•an \ˈsir-ē-ən\ *n* : a native or inhabitant of Syria — **Syrian** *adj*
[1]**sy•ringe** \sə-ˈrinj\ *n* ♦ : a device used especially for injecting liquids into or withdrawing them from the body

♦ hypodermic syringe, needle

[2]**syringe** *vb* **sy•ringed; sy•ring•ing** : to flush or cleanse with or as if with a syringe
syr•up \ˈsər-əp, ˈsir-əp\ *n* **1** : a thick sticky solution of sugar and water often flavored or medicated **2** : the concentrated juice of a fruit or plant
syr•upy *adj* ♦ : resembling syrup in appearance or quality

♦ thick, viscid, viscous

syst *abbr* system
sys•tem \ˈsis-təm\ *n* **1** : a group of units so combined as to form a whole and to operate in unison **2** : the body as a functioning whole; *also* : a group of bodily organs (as the nervous system) that together carry on some vital function **3** ♦ : a definite scheme or method of procedure or classification **4** ♦ : regular method or order

♦ [3, 4] approach, fashion, form, manner, method, plan, strategy, style, tack, tactics, technique, way

sys•tem•at•ic \ˌsis-tə-ˈma-tik\ *adj* ♦ : methodical in procedure or plan — **sys•tem•at•i•cal•ly** \-k(ə-)lē\ *adv*

♦ methodical, orderly, regular

sys•tem•a•tise *chiefly Brit var of* SYSTEMATIZE
sys•tem•a•tize \ˈsis-tə-mə-ˌtīz\ *vb* **-a•tized; -a•tiz•ing** ♦ : to make into a system : arrange methodically

♦ arrange, array, classify, codify, dispose, draw up, marshal, order, organize, range

[1]**sys•tem•ic** \sis-ˈte-mik\ *adj* **1** : of, relating to, or affecting the whole body ⟨∼ disease⟩ **2** : of, relating to, or being a pesticide that when absorbed into the sap or bloodstream makes the entire plant or animal toxic to a pest (as an insect or fungus)
[2]**systemic** *n* : a systemic pesticide
systemic lupus erythematosus *n* : a systemic disease especially of women characterized by fever, skin rash, and arthritis, often by anemia, by small hemorrhages of the skin and mucous membranes, and in serious cases by involvement of various internal organs
sys•tem•ize \ˈsis-tə-ˌmīz\ *vb* **-ized; -iz•ing** : SYSTEMATIZE
systems analyst *n* : a person who studies a procedure or business to determine its goals or purposes and to discover the best ways to accomplish them — **systems analysis** *n*
sys•to•le \ˈsis-tə-(ˌ)lē\ *n* : a rhythmically recurrent contraction of the heart — **sys•tol•ic** \sis-ˈtä-lik\ *adj*

T

[1]**t** \ˈtē\ *n, pl* **t's** *or* **ts** \ˈtēz\ *often cap* : the 20th letter of the English alphabet
[2]**t** *abbr, often cap* **1** metric ton **2** tablespoon **3** teaspoon **4** temperature **5** ton **6** transitive **7** troy **8** true
T *abbr* **1** toddler **2** T-shirt
Ta *symbol* tantalum
TA *abbr* teaching assistant
[1]**tab** \ˈtab\ *n* **1** : a short projecting flap, loop, or tag; *also* : a small insert or addition **2** : close surveillance : WATCH ⟨keep ∼*s* on him⟩ **3** ♦ : a creditor's statement : BILL **4** : a key on a keyboard especially for putting data in columns

♦ account, bill, check, invoice, statement

[2]**tab** *vb* **tabbed; tab•bing** : DESIGNATE
tab•by \ˈta-bē\ *n, pl* **tabbies** : a usually striped or mottled domestic cat; *also* : a female domestic cat
tab•er•na•cle \ˈta-bər-ˌna-kəl\ *n* **1** *often cap* : a tent sanctuary used by the Israelites during the Exodus **2** : a receptacle for the consecrated elements of the Eucharist **3** : a house of worship
[1]**ta•ble** \ˈtā-bəl\ *n* **1** : a flat slab or plaque : TABLET **2** : a piece of furniture consisting of a smooth flat top fixed on legs **3** ♦ : a supply of food **4** : a group of people assembled at or as if at a table **5** ♦ : an orderly arrangement of data usually in rows and columns **6** : a short list ⟨∼ of contents⟩ **7** : something that resembles a table especially in having a flat surface : TABLELAND — **ta•ble•top** \-ˌtäp\ *n*

♦ [3] board, chow, feed, meal, mess, repast ♦ [5] catalog, checklist, list, listing, menu, register, registry, roll, roster, schedule

[2]**table** *vb* **ta•bled; ta•bling** **1** *Brit* **:** to place on the agenda **2 :** to remove (a parliamentary motion) from consideration indefinitely

tab•leau \ˈta-ˌblō\ *n, pl* **tab•leaux** \-ˌblōz\ *also* **tableaus :** a scene or event usually presented on a stage by silent and motionless costumed participants

ta•ble•cloth \ˈtā-bəl-ˌklȯth\ *n* **:** a covering spread over a dining table before the table is set

ta•ble d'hôte \ˌtä-bəl-ˈdōt\ *n* **:** a complete meal of several courses offered at a fixed price

ta•ble•land \ˈtā-bəl-ˌland\ *n* ♦ **:** a broad level elevated area **:** PLATEAU

♦ mesa, plateau, table

ta•ble•spoon \-ˌspün\ *n* **1 :** a large spoon used especially for serving **2 :** a unit of measure equal to ½ fluid ounce (15 milliliters)

ta•ble•spoon•ful \-ˌfu̇l\ *n, pl* **-spoonfuls** \-ˌfu̇lz\ *also* **-spoons•ful** \-ˌspünz-fu̇l\ **:** TABLESPOON 2

tab•let \ˈta-blət\ *n* **1 :** a flat slab suited for or bearing an inscription **2 :** a collection of sheets of paper glued together at one edge **3 a :** a compressed or molded block of material **b** ♦ **:** a small mass of medicated material

♦ capsule, pill

table tennis *n* **:** a game resembling tennis played on a tabletop with wooden paddles and a small hollow plastic ball

ta•ble•ware \ˈtā-bəl-ˌwar\ *n* ♦ **:** utensils (as of china or silver) for table use

♦ flatware, silver

[1]**tab•loid** \ˈta-ˌblȯid\ *adj* **:** condensed into small scope

[2]**tabloid** *n* **:** a newspaper marked by small pages, condensation of the news, and usually many photographs

[1]**ta•boo** *also* **ta•bu** \tə-ˈbü, ta-\ *adj* ♦ **:** prohibited by a taboo

♦ forbidden, impermissible

[2]**taboo** *also* **tabu** *n, pl* **taboos** *also* **tabus** **1 :** a prohibition against touching, saying, or doing something for fear of immediate harm from a supernatural force **2 :** a prohibition imposed by social custom

ta•bor *also* **ta•bour** \ˈtā-bər\ *n* **:** a small drum used to accompany a pipe or fife played by the same person

tab•u•lar \ˈta-byə-lər\ *adj* **1 :** having a flat surface **2 :** arranged in a table; *esp* **:** set up in rows and columns **3 :** computed by means of a table

tab•u•late \-ˌlāt\ *vb* **-lat•ed; -lat•ing :** to put into tabular form — **tab•u•la•tion** \ˌta-byə-ˈlā-shən\ *n* — **tab•u•la•tor** \ˈta-byə-ˌlā-tər\ *n*

TAC \ˈtak\ *abbr* Tactical Air Command

tach \ˈtak\ *n* **:** TACHOMETER

ta•chom•e•ter \ta-ˈkä-mə-tər, tə-\ *n* **:** a device to indicate speed of rotation

tachy•car•dia \ˌta-ki-ˈkär-dē-ə\ *n* **:** relatively rapid heart action

tachy•on \ˈta-kē-ˌän\ *n* **:** a hypothetical particle held to travel faster than light

tac•it \ˈta-sət\ *adj* **1 :** expressed without words or speech **2** ♦ **:** implied or indicated but not actually expressed ⟨~ consent⟩ — **tac•it•ly** *adv* — **tac•it•ness** *n*

♦ implicit, unexpressed, unspoken, unvoiced, wordless

tac•i•turn \ˈta-sə-ˌtərn\ *adj* ♦ **:** disinclined to talk — **tac•i•tur•ni•ty** \ˌta-sə-ˈtər-nə-tē\ *n*

♦ closemouthed, laconic, reserved, reticent, silent, uncommunicative

[1]**tack** \ˈtak\ *vb* **1 a :** to fasten with tacks **b** ♦ **:** to add on **2 :** to change the direction of (a sailing ship) from one tack to another **3 :** to follow a zigzag course

♦ add, adjoin, annex, append

[2]**tack** *n* **1 :** a small sharp nail with a broad flat head **2 :** the direction toward the wind that a ship is sailing ⟨starboard ~⟩; *also* **:** the run of a ship on one tack **3 :** a change of course from one tack to another **4 :** a zigzag course **5** ♦ **:** a course of action

♦ approach, fashion, form, manner, method, strategy, style, system, tactics, technique, way

[3]**tack** *n* **:** gear for harnessing a horse

[1]**tack•le** \ˈta-kəl, *naut often* ˈtā-\ *n* **1** ♦ **:** a set of the equipment used in a particular activity **:** GEAR **2 :** the rigging of a ship **3 :** an arrangement of ropes and pulleys for hoisting or pulling heavy objects **4 :** the act or an instance of tackling; *also* **:** a football lineman playing between guard and end

♦ accoutrements (*or* accouterments), apparatus, equipment, gear, matériel, outfit, paraphernalia

[2]**tackle** *vb* **tack•led; tack•ling** **1 :** to attach and secure with or as if with tackle **2 :** to seize, grapple with, or throw down with the intention of subduing or stopping **3 :** to set about dealing with ⟨~ a problem⟩ — **tack•ler** *n*

[1]**tacky** \ˈta-kē\ *adj* **tack•i•er; -est :** sticky to the touch

[2]**tacky** *adj* **tack•i•er; -est** **1** ♦ **:** decayed, deteriorated, or fallen into partial ruin especially through neglect or misuse **:** SHABBY **2** ♦ **:** marked by lack of style or good taste; *also* **:** cheaply showy

♦ [1] dilapidated, grungy, mean, neglected, ratty, seedy, shabby ♦ [2] dowdy, inelegant, tasteless, trashy, unfashionable, unstylish *Ant* elegant, fashionable, modish, smart, stylish, tasteful

ta•co \ˈtä-kō\ *n, pl* **tacos** \-kōz\ **:** a usually fried tortilla rolled up with or folded over a filling

tact \ˈtakt\ *n* **:** a keen sense of what to do or say to keep good relations with others — **tact•ful** \-fəl\ *adj* — **tact•ful•ly** *adv*

tac•tic \ˈtak-tik\ *n* **:** a planned action for accomplishing an end

tac•ti•cal \ˈtak-ti-kəl\ *adj* ♦ **:** of or relating to tactics; *esp* **:** intended for a particular purpose

♦ advisable, desirable, expedient, judicious, politic, prudent, wise

tac•tics \ˈtak-tiks\ *n sing or pl* **1 :** the science of maneuvering forces in combat **2 :** the skill of using available means to accomplish an end **3** ♦ **:** a system or mode of procedure — **tac•ti•cian** \tak-ˈti-shən\ *n*

♦ approach, fashion, form, manner, method, strategy, style, system, tack, technique, way

tac•tile \ˈtakt-ᵊl, ˈtak-ˌtīl\ *adj* **:** of, relating to, or perceptible through the sense of touch

tact•less \ˈtakt-ləs\ *adj* ♦ **:** marked by lack of tact — **tact•less•ly** *adv*

♦ ill-advised, imprudent, indiscreet, unwise

tad•pole \ˈtad-ˌpōl\ *n* **:** an aquatic larva of a frog or toad that has a tail and gills

tae kwon do \ˈtī-ˈkwän-ˈdō\ *n* **:** a Korean martial art of self-defense

taf•fe•ta \ˈta-fə-tə\ *n* **:** a crisp lustrous fabric (as of silk or rayon)

taff•rail \ˈtaf-ˌrāl, -rəl\ *n* **:** the rail around a ship's stern

taf•fy \ˈta-fē\ *n, pl* **taffies :** a candy usually of molasses or brown sugar stretched until porous and light-colored

[1]**tag** \ˈtag\ *n* **1 :** a metal or plastic binding on an end of a shoelace **2** ♦ **:** a piece of hanging or attached material **3 :** a hackneyed quotation or saying **4 :** a descriptive or identifying epithet

♦ label, marker, ticket

[2]**tag** *vb* **tagged; tag•ging** **1** ♦ **:** to provide or mark with or as if with a tag; *esp* **:** IDENTIFY **2 :** to attach as an addition **3** ♦ **:** to follow closely and persistently ⟨~*s* along everywhere we go⟩ **4 :** to hold responsible for something

♦ [1] identify, label, mark, ticket ♦ [3] chase, dog, follow, hound, pursue, shadow, tail, trace, track, trail

[3]**tag** *n* **:** a game in which one player chases others and tries to touch one of them

[4]**tag** *vb* **tagged; tag•ging** **1 :** to touch in or as if in a game of tag **2 :** SELECT

TAG *abbr* the adjutant general

tag sale *n* **:** GARAGE SALE

Ta•hi•tian \tə-ˈhē-shən\ *n* **1 :** a native or inhabitant of Tahiti **2 :** the Polynesian language of the Tahitians — **Tahitian** *adj*

tai•ga \ˈtī-gə\ *n* **:** a moist coniferous subarctic forest extending south from the tundra

[1]**tail** \ˈtāl\ *n* **1 :** the rear end or a process extending from the rear end of an animal **2 :** something resembling an animal's tail **3** *pl* **:** full evening dress for men **4 :** the back, last, lower, or inferior part of something; *esp* **:** the reverse of a coin **5** ♦ **:** one who follows or keeps watch on someone — **tailed** \ˈtāld\ *adj* — **tail•less** \ˈtāl-ləs\ *adj*

♦ detective, investigator, operative, shadow, sleuth

[2]**tail** *vb* ♦ **:** to follow for the purpose of surveillance

♦ chase, dog, follow, hound, pursue, shadow, tag, trace, track, trail

tail•coat \-ˈkōt\ *n* **:** a coat with tails; *esp* **:** a man's full-dress coat with two long tapering skirts at the back

[1]**tail•gate** \-ˌgāt\ *n* **:** a board or gate at the back end of a vehicle that can be let down (as for loading)

²tailgate *vb* **tail•gat•ed; tail•gat•ing 1 :** to drive dangerously close behind another vehicle **2 :** to hold a tailgate picnic
³tailgate *adj* **:** relating to or being a picnic set up on a tailgate
tail•light \-ˌlīt\ *n* **:** a usually red warning light mounted at the rear of a vehicle
¹tai•lor \ˈtā-lər\ *n* **:** a person whose occupation is making or altering garments
²tailor *vb* **1 :** to make or fashion as the work of a tailor **2** ♦ **:** to make or adapt to suit a special purpose

♦ acclimate, accommodate, adapt, adjust, condition, conform, fit, shape, suit

tai•lored *adj* ♦ **:** made by a tailor; *also* **:** altered or fitted as if custom-made

♦ custom, custom-made

tail•pipe \ˈtāl-ˌpīp\ *n* **:** an outlet by which engine exhaust gases are expelled from a vehicle (as an automobile)
tail•spin \ˈtāl-ˌspin\ *n* **:** a rapid descent or downward spiral
tail•wind \ˈtāl-ˌwind\ *n* **:** a wind blowing in the same general direction as a course of movement (as of an aircraft)
¹taint \ˈtānt\ *vb* **1** ♦ **:** to contaminate morally **2** ♦ **:** to affect or become affected with something bad (as putrefaction)

♦ [1] blemish, mar, poison, spoil, stain, tarnish, touch, vitiate ♦ [2] befoul, contaminate, defile, foul, poison, pollute

²taint *n* ♦ **:** a contaminating mark or influence

♦ blot, brand, smirch, spot, stain, stigma

Tai•wan•ese \ˌtī-wə-ˈnēz, -ˈnēs\ *n* **:** a native or inhabitant of Taiwan — **Taiwanese** *adj*
¹take \ˈtāk\ *vb* **took** \ˈtu̇k\; **tak•en** \ˈtā-kən\; **tak•ing 1** ♦ **:** to get into one's hands or possession **:** GRASP **2 :** CAPTURE; *also* **:** DEFEAT **3 :** to obtain or secure for use **4** ♦ **:** to catch or attack through the effect of a sudden force or influence ⟨was *taken* with the flu⟩ **5 :** CAPTIVATE, DELIGHT **6 :** to bring into a relation ⟨~ a wife⟩ **7 :** REMOVE, SUBTRACT **8** ♦ **:** to pick out **:** CHOOSE **9 :** ASSUME, UNDERTAKE **10 :** RECEIVE, ACCEPT **11 :** to use for transportation ⟨~ a bus⟩ **12 :** to become impregnated with **:** ABSORB ⟨~*s* a dye⟩ **13 :** to receive into one's body (as by swallowing) ⟨~ a pill⟩ **14** ♦ **:** to submit to **:** ENDURE **15 :** to lead, carry, or cause to go along to another place **16 :** to be in need of **:** REQUIRE **17 :** to obtain as the result of a special procedure ⟨~ a snapshot⟩ **18 :** to undertake and do, make, or perform ⟨~ a walk⟩ **19** ♦ **:** to take effect **:** ACT **20 :** to hold without crowding or inconvenience **:** ACCOMMODATE **21** ♦ **:** to understand or regard in a certain way ⟨I ~ this to be your final offer⟩ ⟨do you ~ me for a fool?⟩ — **tak•er** *n* — **take advantage of 1 :** to profit by **2 :** EXPLOIT — **take after :** RESEMBLE — **take care :** to be careful — **take care of :** to attend to — **take effect :** to become operative — **take exception :** OBJECT — **take place :** HAPPEN — **take to 1 :** to go to **2 :** to apply or devote oneself to **3 :** to conceive a liking for

♦ [1] clasp, grasp, grip, hold ♦ [4] catch, come down, contract, get, sicken ♦ [8] choose, cull, elect, handpick, name, opt, pick, prefer, select, single ♦ [14] abide, bear, brook, countenance, endure, meet, stand, stick out, stomach, support, sustain, tolerate ♦ [19] act, function, operate, perform, work ♦ *usu* **take for** [21] account, call, consider, count, esteem, hold, rate, reckon, regard

²take *n* **1 :** the number or quantity taken; *also* **:** PROCEEDS, RECEIPTS **2 :** an act or the action of taking **3 :** a television or movie scene filmed or taped at one time; *also* **:** a sound recording made at one time **4 :** a distinct or personal point of view **5** ♦ **:** a visible response or reaction (as to something unexpected)

♦ reaction, reply, response

take back *vb* ♦ **:** to make a retraction of **:** WITHDRAW

♦ abjure, recant, renounce, retract, unsay, withdraw

take down *vb* **1** ♦ **:** to take apart **:** DISASSEMBLE **2** ♦ **:** to lower the spirit or vanity of

♦ [1] disassemble, dismantle, knock down, strike ♦ [2] abase, debase, degrade, demean, discredit, disgrace, dishonor (*or* dishonour), humble, humiliate, lower, shame, smirch

take in *vb* **1** ♦ **:** to give shelter to **2** ♦ **:** to encompass within its limits **3 :** to cause to accept as true or valid what is false or invalid **:** DECEIVE

♦ [1] accommodate, billet, chamber, domicile, harbor (*or* harbour), house, lodge, put up, quarter, roof, shelter ♦ [2] carry, comprehend, contain, embrace, encompass, entail, include, involve, number

take–no–prisoners *adj* ♦ **:** having a fierce, relentless, or merciless character

♦ callous, hard, heartless, inhuman, inhumane, pitiless, soulless, unfeeling, unsympathetic

take•off \ˈtā-ˌku̇f\ *n* **1** ♦ **:** an imitation especially in the way of caricature **2 :** an act or instance of taking off

♦ burlesque, caricature, parody, spoof

take off *vb* **1** ♦ **:** to remove (an article of wear) from the body **2 :** DEDUCT **3** ♦ **:** to set out **:** go away **4 :** to begin flight

♦ [1] doff, peel, put off, remove ♦ [3] clear out, depart, exit, get off, go, move, pull, quit, sally, shove

take on *vb* **1** ♦ **:** to begin to perform or deal with; *also* **:** to contend with as an opponent **2** ♦ **:** to provide occupation for **:** HIRE **3 :** to assume or acquire as or as if one's own **4 :** to make an unusual show of one's feelings especially of grief or anger

♦ [1] battle, encounter, engage, face, meet ♦ [2] employ, engage, hire, retain

take out *vb* ♦ **:** to find release for

♦ loose, release, unleash, vent *Ant* bottle (up), repress, suppress

take over *vb* ♦ **:** to assume control or possession of or responsibility for — **take•over** \ˈtā-ˌkō-vər\ *n*

♦ cover, fill in, pinch-hit, stand in, sub, substitute ♦ accept, assume, bear, shoulder, undertake

take up *vb* **1 :** PICK UP **2 :** to begin to occupy (land) **3 :** to absorb or incorporate into itself ⟨plants *taking up* nutrients⟩ **4 :** to begin to engage in ⟨*took up* jogging⟩ **5 :** to make tighter or shorter ⟨*take up* the slack⟩ **6** ♦ **:** to accept or adopt as one's own ⟨*took up* the life of a farmer⟩

♦ adopt, borrow, embrace

tak•ings \ˈtā-kiŋz\ *n pl, chiefly Brit* **:** receipts especially of money
talc \ˈtalk\ *n* **:** a soft mineral with a soapy feel used especially in making a soothing powder (**tal•cum powder** \ˈtal-kəm-\) for the skin
tale \ˈtāl\ *n* **1 :** a relation of a series of events **2 :** a report of a confidential matter **3 :** idle talk; *esp* **:** harmful gossip **4** ♦ **:** a usually imaginative narrative **5** ♦ **:** an intentionally untrue report **:** FALSEHOOD **6 :** COUNT, TALLY

♦ [4] narrative, novella, short story, story ♦ [5] fabrication, fairy tale, falsehood, falsity, fib, lie, mendacity, prevarication, story, untruth, whopper

tal•ent \ˈta-lənt\ *n* **1 :** an ancient unit of weight and value **2** ♦ **:** the natural endowments of a person **3 :** a special often creative or artistic aptitude **4 :** mental power **:** ABILITY **5 :** a person of talent — **tal•ent•ed** *adj*

♦ aptitude, endowment, faculty, flair, genius, gift, knack

ta•ler \ˈtä-lər\ *n* **:** any of numerous silver coins issued by German states from the 15th to the 19th centuries
tales•man \ˈtālz-mən\ *n* **:** a person summoned for jury duty
tal•is•man \ˈta-ləs-mən, -ləz-\ *n, pl* **-mans** ♦ **:** an object thought to act as a charm

♦ amulet, charm, fetish, mascot

¹talk \ˈtȯk\ *vb* **1 :** to express in speech **:** utter words **:** SPEAK **2 :** DISCUSS ⟨~ business⟩ **3** ♦ **:** to influence or cause by talking ⟨~*ed* him into going⟩ **4 :** to use (a language) for communicating **5** ♦ **:** to express, communicate, or exchange ideas or thoughts by means of spoken words **:** CONVERSE — often used with *to* or *with* **6 a** ♦ **:** to reveal secret or confidential information **b** ♦ **:** to relate rumor or report of an intimate nature **:** GOSSIP **7** ♦ **:** to give a talk **:** LECTURE **8 :** to speak idly — **talk back :** to answer impertinently

♦ *usu* **talk into** [3] argue, convince, get, induce, move, persuade, prevail, satisfy, win ♦ *usu* **talk to** [5] chat, speak ♦ [6a] inform, snitch, squeal, tell ♦ [6b] blab, gossip, tattle ♦ [7] declaim, descant, discourse, harangue, lecture, orate, speak

²talk *n* **1** ♦ **:** the act or an instance or period of talking **2 :** a way of speaking **3** ♦ **:** a formal discussion, negotiation, or exchange of views **4 :** REPORT, RUMOR **5 :** the topic of comment or gossip ⟨the ~ of the town⟩ **6** ♦ **:** an analysis or discussion prepared for public presentation

♦ [1] chat, chatter, chitchat, gabfest, gossip, palaver, rap ♦ [3] argument, colloquy, conference, deliberation, discourse, discussion, give-and-take, parley ♦ [6] address, declamation, harangue, oration, speech

talk•a•tive \ˈtȯ-kə-tiv\ *adj* ♦ : given to talking — **talk•a•tive•ly** *adv* — **talk•a•tive•ness** *n*

♦ chatty, conversational, gabby, garrulous, loquacious *Ant* closemouthed, laconic, reserved, reticent, taciturn

talk•er \ˈtȯ-kər\ *n* ♦ : one that talks

♦ chatterbox, jabberer, magpie

talk•ing–to \ˈtȯ-kiŋ-ˌtü\ *n* : REPRIMAND, REPROOF
talk over *vb* ♦ : to review or consider in conversation

♦ argue, chew over, debate, discuss, dispute, hash, moot

talk radio *n* : radio programming consisting of call-in shows
tall \ˈtȯl\ *adj* **1** ♦ : high in stature; *also* : of a specified height ⟨six feet ~⟩ **2** ♦ : large or formidable in amount, extent, or degree ⟨a ~ order⟩ **3** : UNBELIEVABLE, IMPROBABLE ⟨a ~ story⟩ — **tall•ness** *n*

♦ [1] high, lofty, towering ♦ [2] arduous, demanding, difficult, exacting, formidable, grueling, hard, herculean, laborious, murderous, rough, stiff, strenuous, toilsome, tough

tal•low \ˈta-lō\ *n* : a hard white fat rendered usually from cattle or sheep tissues and used especially in candles
¹tal•ly \ˈta-lē\ *n, pl* **tallies** **1** : a device for visibly recording or accounting especially business transactions **2** : a recorded account **3** : a corresponding part; *also* : CORRESPONDENCE
²tally *vb* **tal•lied; tal•ly•ing** **1** : to mark on or as if on a tally **2** : to make a count of : RECKON; *also* : SCORE **3** ♦ : to be in conformity or agreement : CORRESPOND

♦ accord, agree, answer, check, coincide, comport, conform, correspond, dovetail, fit, go, harmonize, jibe, square

tal•ly•ho \ˌta-lē-ˈhō\ *n, pl* **-hos** : a call of a huntsman at sight of the fox
Tal•mud \ˈtäl-ˌmu̇d, ˈtal-məd\ *n* : the authoritative body of Jewish tradition — **Tal•mu•dic** \tal-ˈmü-dik, -ˈmyü-, -ˈmə-; täl-ˈmu̇-\ *adj* — **Tal•mud•ist** \ˈtäl-ˌmu̇-dist, ˈtal-mə-\ *n*
tal•on \ˈta-lən\ *n* : the claw of an animal and especially of a bird of prey
ta•lus \ˈtā-ləs, ˈta-\ *n* : rock debris at the base of a cliff
tam \ˈtam\ *n* : TAM-O'-SHANTER
ta•ma•le \tə-ˈmä-lē\ *n* : ground meat seasoned with chili, rolled in cornmeal dough, wrapped in corn husks, and steamed
tam•a•rack \ˈta-mə-ˌrak\ *n* : a larch of northern No. America; *also* : its hard resinous wood
tam•a•rin \ˈta-mə-rən\ *n* : any of several small So. American monkeys related to the marmosets
tam•a•rind \ˈta-mə-rənd, -ˌrind\ *n* : a tropical tree of the legume family with hard yellowish wood and feathery leaves; *also* : its acid fruit
tam•bou•rine \ˌtam-bə-ˈrēn\ *n* : a small shallow drum with loose disks at the sides played by shaking or striking with the hand
¹tame \ˈtām\ *adj* **tam•er; tam•est** **1** : reduced from a state of native wildness especially so as to be useful to humans : DOMESTICATED **2** : made docile : SUBDUED **3** ♦ : lacking spirit or interest — **tame•ly** *adv* — **tame•ness** *n*

♦ dull, flat, uninteresting

²tame *vb* **tamed; tam•ing** **1** : to make or become tame; *also* : to subject (land) to cultivation **2** : HUMBLE, SUBDUE **3** ♦ : to bring under control — **tam•able** *or* **tame•able** \ˈtā-mə-bəl\ *adj* — **tame•less** *adj* — **tam•er** *n*

♦ bridle, check, constrain, contain, control, curb, govern, inhibit, regulate, rein, restrain

tam–o'–shan•ter \ˈta-mə-ˌshan-tər\ *n* : a Scottish woolen cap with a wide flat circular crown and usually a pom-pom in the center
tamp \ˈtamp\ *vb* : to drive down or in by a series of light blows
tam•per \ˈtam-pər\ *vb* **1** : to carry on underhand negotiations (as by bribery) ⟨~ with a witness⟩ **2** ♦ : to interfere so as to weaken or change for the worse ⟨~ with a document⟩ **3** ♦ : to try foolish or dangerous experiments

♦ *usu* **tamper with** [2, 3] fiddle, fool, mess, monkey, play, tinker

tam•pon \ˈtam-ˌpän\ *n* : a plug (as of cotton) introduced into a body cavity usually to absorb secretions (as from menstruation) or to arrest bleeding
¹tan \ˈtan\ *vb* **tanned; tan•ning** **1** : to change (hide) into leather especially by soaking in a liquid containing tannin **2** : to make or become brown (as by exposure to the sun) **3** : to strike with a slender lithe implement (as a lash or rod) especially as a punishment : WHIP
²tan *n* **1** : a brown skin color induced by sun or weather **2** : a light yellowish brown color
³tan *abbr* tangent
tan•a•ger \ˈta-ni-jər\ *n* : any of numerous American birds that are often brightly colored
tan•bark \ˈtan-ˌbärk\ *n* : bark (as of oak or sumac) that is rich in tannin and used in tanning
¹tan•dem \ˈtan-dəm\ *n* **1** : a 2-seated carriage with horses hitched tandem; *also* : its team **2** : a bicycle for two persons sitting one behind the other — **in tandem** : in a tandem arrangement
²tandem *adv* : one behind another
³tandem *adj* **1** : consisting of things arranged one behind the other **2** : working in conjunction with each other
tang \ˈtaŋ\ *n* **1** : a part in a tool that connects the blade with the handle **2** : a sharp distinctive flavor; *also* : a pungent odor
¹tan•gent \ˈtan-jənt\ *adj* : TOUCHING; *esp* : touching a circle or sphere at only one point
²tangent *n* **1** : the trigonometric function that is the ratio between the side opposite and the side adjacent to an acute angle in a right triangle **2** : a tangent line, curve, or surface **3** : an abrupt change of course
tan•gen•tial \tan-ˈjen-chəl\ *adj* **1** : TANGENT **2** : touching lightly : INCIDENTAL ⟨~ involvement⟩ — **tan•gen•tial•ly** *adv*
tan•ger•ine \ˈtan-jə-ˌrēn, ˌtan-jə-ˈrēn\ *n* : a deep orange loose-skinned citrus fruit; *also* : a tree that bears tangerines
¹tan•gi•ble \ˈtan-jə-bəl\ *adj* **1** : perceptible especially by the sense of touch : PALPABLE **2** : substantially real : MATERIAL ⟨~ rewards⟩ **3** : capable of being appraised — **tan•gi•bil•i•ty** \ˌtan-jə-ˈbi-lə-tē\ *n*
²tangible *n* : something tangible; *esp* : a tangible asset
¹tan•gle \ˈtaŋ-gəl\ *vb* **tan•gled; tan•gling** **1 a** : to involve so as to hamper or embarrass **b** ♦ : to seize or hold in or as if in a snare or net : ENTRAP **2** ♦ : to unite or knit together in intricate confusion : ENTANGLE

♦ [1b] enmesh, ensnare, entangle, entrap, mesh, snare, trap
♦ [2] entangle, interlace, intertwine, interweave, knot, snarl

²tangle *n* **1** : a tangled twisted mass **2** : a confusedly complicated state : MUDDLE
tan•go \ˈtaŋ-gō\ *n, pl* **tangos** : a dance of Latin-American origin — **tango** *vb*
tangy \ˈtaŋ-ē\ *adj* ♦ : having or suggestive of a tang

♦ nippy, pungent, sharp, strong

tank \ˈtaŋk\ *n* **1** : a large artificial receptacle for liquids **2** : a heavily armed and armored combat vehicle that moves on tracks — **tank•ful** *n*
tan•kard \ˈtaŋ-kərd\ *n* : a tall one-handled drinking vessel
tank•er \ˈtaŋ-kər\ *n* : a vehicle equipped for transporting a liquid
tank top *n* : a sleeveless collarless pullover shirt with shoulder straps
tank town *n* : a small town
tan•ner \ˈta-nər\ *n* : one that tans hides
tan•nery \ˈta-nə-rē\ *n, pl* **-ner•ies** : a place where tanning is carried on
tan•nic acid \ˈta-nik-\ *n* : TANNIN
tan•nin \ˈta-nən\ *n* : any of various plant substances used especially in tanning and dyeing, in inks, and as astringents
tan•sy \ˈtan-zē\ *n, pl* **tansies** : a common weedy herb related to the daisies with an aromatic odor and bitter-tasting finely divided leaves
tan•ta•lise *chiefly Brit var of* TANTALIZE
tan•ta•lize \ˈtan-tə-ˌlīz\ *vb* **-lized; -liz•ing** : to tease or torment by presenting something desirable but keeping it out of reach — **tan•ta•liz•er** *n* — **tan•ta•liz•ing•ly** *adv*
tan•ta•lum \ˈtan-tə-ləm\ *n* : a gray-white ductile metallic chemical element
tan•ta•mount \ˈtan-tə-ˌmau̇nt\ *adj* : equivalent in value or meaning
tan•trum \ˈtan-trəm\ *n* ♦ : a fit of bad temper

♦ blowup, dudgeon, explosion, fireworks, fit, huff, scene

Tan•za•ni•an \ˌtan-zə-ˈnē-ən\ *n* : a native or inhabitant of Tanzania — **Tanzanian** *adj*
Tao•ism \ˈtau̇-ˌi-zəm, ˈdau̇-\ *n* : a Chinese mystical philosophy; *also* : a religion developed from Taoist philosophy and Buddhism — **Tao•ist** \-ist\ *adj or n*
¹tap \ˈtap\ *n* **1** ♦ : a device consisting of a spout and valve attached to the end of a pipe to control the flow of a fluid : FAUCET, COCK **2** : liquor drawn through a tap **3** : the removing of fluid from a container or cavity by tapping **4** : a tool for forming an in-

ternal screw thread **5 :** a point in an electric circuit where a connection may be made

♦ cock, faucet, gate, spigot, valve

²tap *vb* **tapped; tap•ping 1 ♦ :** to release or cause to flow by piercing or by drawing a plug from a container or cavity **2 :** to pierce so as to let out or draw off a fluid **3 :** to draw from ⟨~ resources⟩ **4 :** to cut in on (as a telephone signal) to get information **5 :** to form an internal screw thread in by means of a tap **6 :** to connect (as a gas or water main) with a local supply — **tap•per** *n*

♦ bleed, drain, draw, pump, siphon

³tap *vb* **tapped; tap•ping 1 ♦ :** to rap lightly **2 :** to bring about by repeated light blows **3 :** SELECT; *esp* **:** to elect to membership

♦ beat, drum, rap

⁴tap *n* **1 :** a light blow or stroke; *also* **:** its sound **2 :** a small metal plate for the sole or heel of a shoe

ta•pa \ˈtä-pə, ˈta-\ *n* **:** an hors d'oeuvre served with drinks especially in Spanish bars — usually used in plural

¹tape \ˈtāp\ *n* **1 :** a narrow flexible band or strip (as of woven fabric) **2 :** MAGNETIC TAPE; *also* **:** CASSETTE

²tape *vb* **taped; tap•ing 1 :** to fasten or support with tape **2 :** to record on magnetic tape

tape deck *n* **:** a device used to play back cassette tapes that usually has to be connected to an audio system

tape measure *n* **:** a tape marked off in units (as inches) for measuring

¹ta•per \ˈtā-pər\ *n* **1 :** a slender wax candle; *also* **:** a long waxed wick **2 :** a gradual lessening of thickness or width in a long object

²taper *vb* **ta•pered; ta•per•ing 1 :** to make or become gradually smaller toward one end **2 ♦ :** to diminish gradually

♦ abate, de-escalate, decline, decrease, die, diminish, dwindle, ebb, fall, lessen, let up, lower, moderate, recede, relent, shrink, subside, wane

tape–re•cord \ˌtā-pri-ˈkȯrd\ *vb* **:** to make a recording of on magnetic tape — **tape recorder** *n* — **tape recording** *n*

taper off *vb* **:** to diminish gradually **:** TAPER

tap•es•try \ˈta-pə-strē\ *n, pl* **-tries :** a heavy reversible textile that has designs or pictures woven into it and is used especially as a wall hanging

tape•worm \ˈtāp-ˌwərm\ *n* **:** any of a class of long flat segmented worms parasitic especially in vertebrate intestines

tap•i•o•ca \ˌta-pē-ˈō-kə\ *n* **:** a usually granular preparation of cassava starch used especially in puddings; *also* **:** a dish (as pudding) that contains tapioca

ta•pir \ˈtā-pər\ *n, pl* **tapirs** *also* **tapir :** any of a genus of large herbivorous hoofed mammals of tropical America and southeastern Asia

tap•pet \ˈta-pət\ *n* **:** a lever or projection moved by some other piece (as a cam) or intended to move something else

tap•room \ˈtap-ˌrüm, -ˌrụm\ *n* **:** BARROOM

tap•root \-ˌrüt, -ˌrụ̇t\ *n* **:** a large main root growing straight down and giving off small side roots

taps \ˈtaps\ *n sing or pl* **:** the last bugle call at night blown as a signal that lights are to be put out; *also* **:** a similar call blown at military funerals and memorial services

tap•ster \ˈtap-stər\ *n* **:** BARTENDER

¹tar \ˈtär\ *n* **1 :** a thick dark sticky liquid distilled from organic material (as wood or coal) **2 ♦ :** one that sails **:** SAILOR

♦ gob, jack, jack-tar, mariner, sailor, seaman, swab

²tar *vb* **tarred; tar•ring :** to cover or smear with or as if with tar

tar•an•tel•la \ˌtar-ən-ˈte-lə\ *n* **:** a lively folk dance of southern Italy in 6/8 time

ta•ran•tu•la \tə-ˈran-chə-lə, -tə-lə\ *n, pl* **tarantulas** *also* **ta•ran•tu•lae** \-ˈran-chə-ˌlē, -tə-ˌlē\ **:** any of a family of large hairy American spiders with a sharp bite that is not very poisonous to human beings

tar•di•ly \ˈtär-də-lē\ *adv* **♦ :** in a tardy manner

♦ laggardly, slow, slowly, sluggishly

tar•dy \ˈtär-dē\ *adj* **tar•di•er; -est 1 ♦ :** moving slowly **:** SLUGGISH **2 ♦ :** delayed beyond the expected or proper time **:** LATE — **tar•di•ness** \-dē-nəs\ *n*

♦ [1] creeping, dilatory, laggard, languid, poky, slow, sluggish ♦ [2] behind, belated, delinquent, late, overdue

¹tare \ˈtar\ *n* **:** a weed of grain fields

²tare *n* **:** a deduction from the gross weight of a substance and its container made in allowance for the weight of the container — **tare** *vb*

¹tar•get \ˈtär-gət\ *n* **1 :** a mark to shoot at **2 ♦ :** an object of ridicule or criticism **3 :** a goal to be achieved

♦ butt, laughingstock, mark, mockery, victim

²target *vb* **:** to make a target of

tar•iff \ˈtar-əf\ *n* **1 :** a schedule of duties imposed by a government especially on imported goods; *also* **:** a duty or rate of duty imposed in such a schedule **2 :** a schedule of rates or charges

tar•mac \ˈtär-ˌmak\ *n* **:** a surface paved with crushed stone covered with tar

tarn \ˈtärn\ *n* **:** a small mountain lake

tar•nish \ˈtär-nish\ *vb* **1 :** to make or become dull or discolored **2 ♦ :** to bring disgrace on — **tarnish** *n*

♦ blemish, mar, poison, spoil, stain, taint, touch, vitiate

ta•ro \ˈtär-ō, ˈtar-\ *n, pl* **taros :** a large-leaved tropical plant related to the arums that is grown for its edible starchy corms; *also* **:** its corms

tar•ot \ˈtar-ō\ *n* **:** one of a set of usually 78 playing cards used especially for fortune-telling

tar•pau•lin \tär-ˈpȯ-lən, ˈtär-pə-\ *n* **:** a piece of material (as durable plastic) used for protecting exposed objects

tar•pon \ˈtär-pən\ *n, pl* **tarpon** *or* **tarpons :** a large silvery bony fish often caught for sport in the warm coastal waters of the Atlantic especially off Florida

tar•ra•gon \ˈtar-ə-gən\ *n* **:** a small widely cultivated perennial wormwood with aromatic leaves used as a seasoning; *also* **:** its leaves

¹tar•ry \ˈtar-ē\ *vb* **tar•ried; tar•ry•ing 1 ♦ :** to be tardy **:** DELAY; *esp* **:** to be slow in leaving **2 ♦ :** to stay in or at a place

♦ [1] crawl, creep, dally, dawdle, delay, dillydally, drag, lag, linger, loiter, poke ♦ [2] abide, dwell, hang around, remain, stay, stick around

²tar•ry \ˈtär-ē\ *adj* **:** of, resembling, or smeared with tar

tar sand *n* **:** sand or sandstone that is naturally soaked with the heavy sticky portions of petroleum

tar•sus \ˈtär-səs\ *n, pl* **tar•si** \-ˌsī\ **:** the part of a vertebrate foot between the metatarsus and the leg; *also* **:** the small bones that support this part — **tar•sal** \-səl\ *adj or n*

¹tart \ˈtärt\ *adj* **1 ♦ :** agreeably sharp or acid to the taste **2 ♦ :** marked by a biting, acrimonious, or cutting quality **:** CAUSTIC — **tart•ly** *adv*

♦ [1] acid, sour, vinegary ♦ [2] acrid, biting, caustic, cutting, mordant, pungent, sarcastic, satiric, scathing, sharp

²tart *n* **1 :** a small pie or pastry shell containing jelly, custard, or fruit **2 :** PROSTITUTE

tar•tan \ˈtärt-ᵊn\ *n* **:** a plaid textile design of Scottish origin usually distinctively patterned to designate a particular clan

tar•tar \ˈtär-tər\ *n* **1 :** a substance in the juice of grapes deposited (as in wine casks) as a reddish crust or sediment **2 :** a crust on the teeth formed from plaque hardened by calcium salts

tar•tar sauce *or* **tar•tare sauce** \ˈtär-tər-\ *n* **:** mayonnaise with chopped pickles, olives, or capers

tart•ness \-nəs\ *n* **♦ :** the quality or state of being tart

♦ acidity, acrimony, acuteness, asperity, bite, bitterness, edge, harshness, keenness, pungency, sharpness

¹task \ˈtask\ *n* **1 ♦ :** a piece of assigned work **2 ♦ :** the action for which a person or thing is specially fitted or used or for which a thing exists

♦ [1] assignment, chore, duty, job, stint ♦ [2] capacity, function, job, part, place, position, purpose, role, work

²task *vb* **:** to oppress with great labor

task force *n* **:** a temporary grouping to accomplish a particular objective

task•mas•ter \ˈtask-ˌmas-tər\ *n* **♦ :** one that imposes a task or burdens another with labor

♦ boss, captain, chief, foreman, head, headman, helmsman, kingpin, leader, master

¹tas•sel \ˈta-səl, ˈtä-\ *n* **1 :** a hanging ornament made of a bunch of cords of even length fastened at one end **2 :** something suggesting a tassel; *esp* **:** a male flower cluster of Indian corn

²tassel *vb* **-seled** *or* **-selled; -sel•ing** *or* **-sel•ling :** to adorn with or put forth tassels

¹taste \ˈtāst\ *vb* **tast•ed; tast•ing 1 ♦ :** to become acquainted with by experience **:** EXPERIENCE **2 :** to try or determine the flavor of by taking a bit into the mouth **3 :** to eat or drink especially in small quantities : SAMPLE **4** : to have a specific flavor **5** ♦ : to perceive or recognize as if by the sense of taste

♦ [1] endure, experience, feel, have, know, see, suffer, sustain, undergo ♦ [5] feel, perceive, scent, see, sense, smell

²**taste** *n* **1** ♦ : a small amount tasted **2** : BIT; *esp* : a sample of experience **3** : the special sense that perceives and identifies sweet, sour, bitter, or salty qualities and is mediated by taste buds on the tongue **4** : a quality perceptible to the sense of taste; *also* : the sensation obtained from a substance in the mouth : FLAVOR **5** ♦ : individual preference **6** : critical judgment, discernment, or appreciation; *also* : aesthetic quality — **tast•er** *n*

♦ [1] bite, morsel, mouthful, nibble, tidbit ♦ [5] appetite, fancy, favor (*or* favour), fondness, like, liking, love, partiality, preference, relish, shine, use

taste bud *n* : a sense organ mediating the sensation of taste
taste•ful \ˈtāst-fəl\ *adj* **1** : tasty **2** ♦ : having, exhibiting, or conforming to good taste — **taste•ful•ly** *adv*

♦ elegant, graceful, handsome, majestic, refined, stately

taste•less \-ləs\ *adj* **1 a** ♦ : having no taste ⟨~ vegetables⟩ **b** : arousing no interest **2** ♦ : not having or exhibiting good taste ⟨a ~ joke⟩ ⟨~ clothes⟩ — **taste•less•ly** *adv*

♦ [1a] flat, flavorless (*or* flavourless), insipid ♦ [2] coarse, common, crass, crude, rough, rude, uncouth, vulgar ♦ [2] dowdy, inelegant, tacky, trashy, unfashionable, unstylish

tast•i•ness \ˈtā-stē-nəs\ *n* ♦ : the quality or state of being tasty

♦ lusciousness, savor

tasty \ˈtā-stē\ *adj* **tast•i•er; -est** ♦ : pleasing to the taste : SAVORY

♦ ambrosial, appetizing, delectable, delicious, flavorful (*or* flavourful), luscious, palatable, savory, scrumptious, toothsome, yummy

tat \ˈtat\ *vb* **tat•ted; tat•ting** : to work at or make by tatting
¹**tat•ter** \ˈta-tər\ *vb* ♦ : to make or become ragged

♦ rend, rip, rive, shred, tear

²**tatter** *n* **1** : a part torn and left hanging **2** *pl* : tattered clothing
tat•ter•de•ma•lion \ˌta-tər-di-ˈmāl-yən\ *n* : one that is ragged or disreputable
tat•tered \ˈta-tərd\ *adj* ♦ : torn into shreds

♦ ragged, ratty, seedy, shabby, threadbare, worn-out

tat•ter•sall \ˈta-tər-ˌsȯl, -səl\ *n* : a pattern of colored lines forming squares on solid background; *also* : a fabric in a tattersall pattern
tat•ting \ˈta-tiŋ\ *n* : a delicate handmade lace formed usually by looping and knotting with a single thread and a small shuttle; *also* : the act or process of making such lace
tat•tle \ˈtat-ᵊl\ *vb* **tat•tled; tat•tling** **1** : CHATTER, PRATE **2** ♦ : to tell secrets; *also* : to inform against another

♦ blab, gossip, talk

tat•tler \ˈtat-lər, ˈta-tᵊl-ər\ *n* ♦ : one that tattles

♦ betrayer, blabbermouth, informer, rat, snitch, stool pigeon, tattletale

tat•tle•tale \ˈtat-ᵊl-ˌtāl\ *n* ♦ : one that tattles : INFORMER

♦ betrayer, blabbermouth, informer, rat, snitch, stool pigeon, tattler

¹**tat•too** \ta-ˈtü\ *n, pl* **tattoos** **1** : a call sounded before taps as notice to go to quarters **2** : a rapid rhythmic rapping
²**tattoo** *vb* : to mark (the skin) with tattoos
³**tattoo** *n, pl* **tattoos** : an indelible figure fixed upon the body especially by insertion of pigment under the skin
tau \ˈtau̇, ˈtȯ\ *n* : the 19th letter of the Greek alphabet — Τ or τ
taught *past and past part of* TEACH
¹**taunt** \ˈtȯnt\ *n* : a sarcastic challenge or insult
²**taunt** *vb* ♦ : to reproach or challenge in a mocking manner : jeer at

♦ bait, bug, hassle, heckle, needle, ride, tease

taunt•er \ˈtȯn-tər, ˈtän-\ *n* ♦ : one that taunts

♦ heckler, mocker, quiz, scoffer, tease

taupe \ˈtōp\ *n* : a brownish gray
Tau•rus \ˈtȯr-əs\ *n* **1** : a zodiacal constellation between Aries and Gemini usually pictured as a bull **2** : the 2d sign of the zodiac in astrology; *also* : one born under this sign
taut \ˈtȯt\ *adj* **1** ♦ : tightly drawn : not slack **2** : extremely nervous : TENSE **3** : TRIM, TIDY ⟨a ~ ship⟩ — **taut•ly** *adv* — **taut•ness** *n*

♦ rigid, tense, tight *Ant* lax, loose, slack

tau•tol•o•gy \tȯ-ˈtä-lə-jē\ *n, pl* **-gies** : needless repetition of an idea, statement, or word; *also* : an instance of such repetition — **tau•to•log•i•cal** \ˌtȯt-ᵊl-ˈä-ji-kəl\ *adj* — **tau•to•log•i•cal•ly** \-ji-k(ə-)lē\ *adv* — **tau•tol•o•gous** \tȯ-ˈtä-lə-gəs\ *adj* — **tau•tol•o•gous•ly** *adv*
tav•ern \ˈta-vərn\ *n* **1** ♦ : an establishment where alcoholic liquors are sold to be drunk on the premises **2** ♦ : an establishment for the lodging and entertaining of travelers : INN

♦ [1] bar, barroom, café, pub, public house, saloon ♦ [2] hospice, hotel, inn, lodge, public house

taw \ˈtȯ\ *n* **1** : a marble used as a shooter **2** : the line from which players shoot at marbles
taw•dry \ˈtȯ-drē\ *adj* **taw•dri•er; -est** ♦ : cheap and gaudy in appearance and quality — **taw•dri•ly** *adv*

♦ flamboyant, flashy, garish, gaudy, glitzy, loud, ostentatious, swank

taw•ny \ˈtȯ-nē\ *adj* **taw•ni•er; -est** : of a brownish orange color
¹**tax** \ˈtaks\ *vb* **1** : to levy a tax on **2** : CHARGE, ACCUSE **3** ♦ : to put under pressure — **tax•able** \ˈtak-sə-bəl\ *adj* — **tax•a•tion** \tak-ˈsā-shən\ *n*

♦ strain, stretch, test, try

²**tax** *n* **1** ♦ : a charge usually of money imposed by authority on persons or property for public purposes **2** : a heavy charge : STRAIN

♦ assessment, duty, impost, levy

¹**taxi** \ˈtak-sē\ *n, pl* **tax•is** \-sēz\ *also* **tax•ies** : an automobile that carries passengers for a fare usually based on the distance traveled : TAXICAB; *also* : a similarly operated boat or aircraft
²**taxi** *vb* **tax•ied; taxi•ing** *or* **taxy•ing; tax•is** *or* **tax•ies** **1** : to move along the ground or on the water under an aircraft's own power when starting or after a landing **2** : to go by taxicab
taxi•cab \ˈtak-sē-ˌkab\ *n* ♦ : an automobile that carries passengers for a fare usually based on the distance traveled

♦ hack, taxi

taxi•der•my \ˈtak-sə-ˌdər-mē\ *n* : the skill or occupation of preparing, stuffing, and mounting skins of animals — **taxi•der•mist** \-mist\ *n*
tax•ing \ˈtak-siŋ\ *adj* ♦ : involving, imposing, or constituting a burden

♦ arduous, burdensome, challenging, demanding, exacting, grueling, laborious, onerous, toilsome

tax•on \ˈtak-ˌsän\ *n, pl* **taxa** \-sə\; *also* **taxons** : a taxonomic group or entity
tax•on•o•my \tak-ˈsä-nə-mē\ *n* : classification especially of animals or plants according to natural relationships — **tax•o•nom•ic** \ˌtak-sə-ˈnä-mik\ *adj* — **tax•on•o•mist** \tak-ˈsä-nə-mist\ *n*
tax•pay•er \ˈtaks-ˌpā-ər\ *n* : one who pays or is liable for a tax — **tax•pay•ing** *adj*
Tay–Sachs disease \ˈtā-ˈsaks-\ *n* : a hereditary disorder caused by the absence of an enzyme needed to break down fatty material, marked by buildup of lipids in nervous tissue, and causing death in childhood
tb *abbr* tablespoon; tablespoonful
Tb *symbol* terbium
TB \ˌtē-ˈbē\ *n* : TUBERCULOSIS
TBA *abbr, often not cap* to be announced
T–bar \ˈtē-ˌbär\ *n* : a ski lift with a series of T-shaped bars
tbs *or* **tbsp** *abbr* tablespoon; tablespoonful
Tc *symbol* technetium
TC *abbr* teachers college
T cell *n* : any of several lymphocytes (as a helper T cell) specialized especially for activity in and control of immunity and the immune response
TCP/IP \ˌtē-(ˌ)sē-ˈpē-ˌī-ˈpē\ *n* : a set of communications protocols used over networks and especially the Internet
TD *abbr* **1** touchdown **2** Treasury Department
TDD *abbr* telecommunications device for the deaf
TDY *abbr* temporary duty
Te *symbol* tellurium
tea \ˈtē\ *n* **1** : the cured leaves and leaf buds of a shrub grown chiefly in China, Japan, India, and Sri Lanka; *also* : this shrub **2** : a drink made by steeping tea in boiling water **3** : refreshments usually including tea served in late afternoon; *also* : a reception at which tea is served
teach \ˈtēch\ *vb* **taught** \ˈtȯt\; **teach•ing** **1** ♦ : to cause to know something : act as a teacher **2** : to show how ⟨~ a child to swim⟩

3 : to make to know the disagreeable consequences of an action 4 : to guide the studies of 5 : to impart the knowledge of ⟨~ algebra⟩ — **teach•able** *adj*

♦ educate, indoctrinate, instruct, school, train, tutor

teach•er \ˈtē-chər\ *n* ♦ : one that teaches; *esp* : one whose occupation is to instruct

♦ educator, instructor, pedagogue, schoolteacher

teach•ing *n* 1 ♦ : the act, practice, or profession of a teacher 2 : something taught; *esp* : DOCTRINE

♦ education, instruction, training, tutelage

tea•cup \ˈtē-ˌkəp\ *n* : a small cup used with a saucer for hot beverages

teak \ˈtēk\ *n* : the hard durable yellowish brown wood of a tall tropical Asian timber tree related to the vervains; *also* : this tree

tea•ket•tle \ˈtē-ˌket-ᵊl\ *n* : a covered kettle with a handle and spout for boiling water

teal \ˈtēl\ *n, pl* **teal** *or* **teals** 1 : any of various small short-necked wild ducks 2 : a dark greenish blue color

¹**team** \ˈtēm\ *n* 1 : two or more draft animals harnessed to the same vehicle or implement 2 ♦ : a number of persons associated in work or activity; *esp* : a group on one side in a match

♦ band, company, crew, gang, outfit, party, squad

²**team** *vb* 1 : to haul with or drive a team 2 ♦ : to form a team : join forces

♦ collaborate, concert, cooperate, join

³**team** *adj* : of or performed by a team; *also* : marked by devotion to teamwork ⟨a ~ player⟩

team•mate \-ˌmāt\ *n* : a fellow member of a team

team•ster \ˈtēm-stər\ *n* : one who drives a team or truck

team•work \-ˌwərk\ *n* ♦ : the work or activity of a number of persons acting in close association as members of a unit

♦ collaboration, cooperation, coordination

tea•pot \ˈtē-ˌpät\ *n* : a vessel with a spout for brewing and serving tea

¹**tear** \ˈtir\ *n* : a drop of the salty liquid that moistens the eye and inner side of the eyelids; *also, pl* : an act of weeping or grieving

²**tear** \ˈtir\ *vb* : to fill with or shed tears ⟨eyes ~*ing* in the wind⟩

³**tear** \ˈtar\ *vb* **tore** \ˈtōr\, **torn** \ˈtōrn\; **tear•ing** 1 ♦ : to separate parts of or pull apart by force : REND 2 : LACERATE 3 : to disrupt by the pull of contrary forces 4 ♦ : to remove by force : WRENCH 5 ♦ : to move or act with violence, haste, or force

♦ [1] rend, rip, rive, shred, tatter ♦ [4] rip, wrench, wrest ♦ [5] barrel, career, course, dash, fly, hasten, hurry, race, rip, rocket, run, rush, shoot, speed, whirl, whisk, zip, zoom

⁴**tear** \ˈtar\ *n* 1 : the act of tearing 2 ♦ : a hole or flaw made by tearing : RENT

♦ gash, laceration, rent, rip, slash, slit

tear down *vb* 1 a ♦ : to cause to decompose or disintegrate b : VILIFY, DENIGRATE ⟨trying to *tear down* his reputation⟩ 2 : to take apart : disassemble

♦ demolish, desolate, destroy, devastate, do in, ruin, shatter, smash, waste, wipe out, wreck

tear•ful \ˈtir-fəl\ *adj* 1 : flowing with or accompanied by tears ⟨~ entreaties⟩ 2 ♦ : causing tears ⟨a ~ eulogy⟩ — **tear•ful•ly** *adv*

♦ depressing, dismal, dreary, heartbreaking, melancholy, pathetic, sad, sorry

tear gas \ˈtir-\ *n* : a substance that on dispersion in the atmosphere blinds the eyes with tears — **tear gas** *vb*

tear•jerk•er \ˈtir-ˌjər-kər\ *n* : an extravagantly pathetic story, song, play, movie, or broadcast

¹**tease** \ˈtēz\ *vb* **teased; teas•ing** 1 : to disentangle and lay parallel by combing or carding ⟨~ wool⟩ 2 : to scratch the surface of (cloth) so as to raise a nap 3 a ♦ : to disturb or annoy by persistent irritating or provoking especially in a petty or mischievous way b ♦ : to make fun of : KID 4 : to comb (hair) by taking a strand and pushing the short hairs toward the scalp with the comb

♦ [3a] bait, bug, hassle, heckle, needle, ride, taunt ♦ [3b] chaff, jive, josh, kid, rally, razz, rib, ride, roast

²**tease** *n* 1 : the act of teasing or state of being teased 2 ♦ : one that teases

♦ heckler, mocker, quiz, scoffer, taunter ♦ annoyance, bother, gadfly, nuisance, persecutor, pest

tea•sel \ˈtē-zəl\ *n* : a prickly herb or its flower head covered with stiff hooked bracts and used to raise the nap on cloth; *also* : an artificial device used for this purpose

tea•spoon \ˈtē-ˌspün\ *n* 1 : a small spoon suitable for stirring beverages 2 : a unit of measure equal to 1/6 fluid ounce (5 milliliters)

tea•spoon•ful \-ˌfu̇l\ *n, pl* **-spoonfuls** *also* **-spoons•ful** \-ˌspünz-ˌfu̇l\ : TEASPOON 2

teat \ˈtit, ˈtēt\ *n* : the protuberance through which milk is drawn from an udder or breast

tech *abbr* 1 technical; technically; technician 2 technological; technology

tech•ne•tium \tek-ˈnē-shē-əm\ *n* : a radioactive metallic chemical element

tech•nic \ˈtek-nik, tek-ˈnēk\ *n* : TECHNIQUE 1

tech•ni•cal \ˈtek-ni-kəl\ *adj* 1 : having special knowledge especially of a mechanical or scientific subject ⟨~ experts⟩ 2 : of or relating to a particular and especially a practical or scientific subject ⟨~ training⟩ 3 : according to a strict interpretation of the rules 4 : of or relating to technique — **tech•ni•cal•ly** \-k(ə-)lē\ *adv*

tech•ni•cal•i•ty \ˌtek-nə-ˈka-lə-tē\ *n, pl* **-ties** 1 : a detail meaningful only to a specialist 2 : the quality or state of being technical

technical sergeant *n* : a noncommissioned officer in the air force ranking next below a master sergeant

tech•ni•cian \tek-ˈni-shən\ *n* : a person who has acquired the technique of a specialized skill or subject

tech•nique \tek-ˈnēk\ *n* 1 : the manner in which technical details are treated or basic physical movements are used 2 : technical methods 3 ♦ : a method of accomplishing a desired aim

♦ approach, fashion, form, manner, method, strategy, style, system, tack, tactics, way

tech•noc•ra•cy \tek-ˈnä-krə-sē\ *n* : management of society by technical experts — **tech•no•crat** \ˈtek-nə-ˌkrat\ *n* — **tech•no•crat•ic** \ˌtek-nə-ˈkra-tik\ *adj*

tech•nol•o•gy \tek-ˈnä-lə-jē\ *n, pl* **-gies** : ENGINEERING; *also* : a manner of accomplishing a task using technical methods or knowledge — **tech•no•log•i•cal** \ˌtek-nə-ˈlä-ji-kəl\ *adj*

tec•ton•ics \tek-ˈtä-niks\ *n sing or pl* 1 : geological structural features 2 : geology dealing especially with the faulting and folding of a planet or moon — **tec•ton•ic** \-nik\ *adj*

ted•dy bear \ˈte-dē-ˌbar\ *n* : a stuffed toy bear

te•dious \ˈtē-dē-əs\ *adj* : tiresome because of length or dullness : BORING — **te•dious•ly** *adv* — **te•dious•ness** *n*

te•di•um \ˈtē-dē-əm\ *n* 1 : TEDIOUSNESS 2 ♦ : the state of being weary and restless through lack of interest : BOREDOM

♦ boredom, doldrums, ennui, listlessness, restlessness, tiredness, weariness

¹**tee** \ˈtē\ *n* : a small mound or peg on which a golf ball is placed to be hit at the beginning of play on a hole; *also* : the area from which the ball is hit to begin play

²**tee** *vb* **teed; tee•ing** : to place (a ball) on a tee

teem \ˈtēm\ *vb* ♦ : to become filled to overflowing : ABOUND

♦ abound, brim, bulge, burst, crawl, swarm

teen *adj* : TEENAGE

teen•age \ˈtē-ˌnāj\ *or* **teen•aged** \-ˌnājd\ *adj* : of, being, or relating to people in their teens — **teen•ag•er** \-ˌnā-jər\ *n*

teens \ˈtēnz\ *n pl* : the numbers 13 to 19 inclusive; *esp* : the years 13 to 19 in a person's life

tee•ny \ˈtē-nē\ *adj* **tee•ni•er; -est** ♦ : very small or diminutive : TINY

♦ atomic, infinitesimal, microscopic, miniature, minute, tiny, wee

teepee *var of* TEPEE

tee shirt *var of* T-SHIRT

tee•ter \ˈtē-tər\ *vb* 1 ♦ : to move unsteadily 2 ♦ : to move backward and forward or up and down 3 a : to shift back and forth uncertainly ⟨~ on the brink of bankruptcy⟩ b ♦ : to waver in mind, will, or feeling ⟨~*s* between conformity and individuality⟩ — **teeter** *n*

♦ [1] careen, dodder, lurch, reel, stagger, totter ♦ [2] falter, rock, seesaw, sway, totter, waver, wobble ♦ [3b] falter, hang back, hesitate, shilly-shally, vacillate

teethe \ˈtēth\ *vb* **teethed; teeth•ing** : to experience the rising of one's teeth through the gums : to grow teeth

teething *n* : growth of the first set of teeth through the gums with its accompanying phenomena

tee•to•tal•er *or* **tee•to•tal•ler** \ˈtē-ˈtō-tᵊl-ər\ *n* : a person who practices complete abstinence from alcoholic drinks — **tee·to·tal** \ˈtē-ˈtō-tᵊl, -ˌtō-\ *adj* — **tee·to·tal·ism** \-ᵊl-ˌi-zəm\ *n*

TEFL *abbr* teaching English as a foreign language

Te·ja·no \tā-ˈhä-(ˌ)nō\ *n, pl* **-nos** : a Texan of Hispanic descent

tek·tite \ˈtek-ˌtīt\ *n* : a glassy body of probably meteoric origin

tel *abbr* **1** telegram **2** telegraph **3** telephone

tele·cast \ˈte-li-ˌkast\ *vb* **-cast** *also* **-cast·ed; -cast·ing** : to broadcast by television — **telecast** *n* — **tele·cast·er** *n*

tel·e·com \ˈte-li-ˌkäm\ *n* : TELECOMMUNICATION; *also* : the telecommunications industry

tele·com·mu·ni·ca·tion \ˌte-li-kə-ˌmyü-nə-ˈkā-shən\ *n* : communication at a distance (as by telephone or radio)

tele·com·mute \ˈte-li-kə-ˌmyüt\ *vb* : to work at home by the use of an electronic linkup with a central office

tele·con·fer·ence \ˈte-li-ˌkän-fə-rəns\ *n* : a conference among people remote from one another held using telecommunications — **tele·con·fer·enc·ing** *n*

teleg *abbr* telegraphy

tele·ge·nic \ˌte-lə-ˈje-nik, -ˈjē-\ *adj* : markedly attractive to television viewers

tele·gram \ˈte-lə-ˌgram\ *n* : a message sent by telegraph

[1]tele·graph \-ˌgraf\ *n* : an electric apparatus or system for sending messages by a code over wires — **tele·graph·ic** \ˌte-lə-ˈgra-fik\ *adj*

[2]telegraph *vb* : to send or communicate by or as if by telegraph — **te·leg·ra·pher** \tə-ˈle-grə-fər\ *n*

te·leg·ra·phy \tə-ˈle-grə-fē\ *n* : the use or operation of a telegraph apparatus or system

tele·mar·ket·ing \ˌte-lə-ˈmär-kə-tiŋ\ *n* : the marketing of goods or services by telephone — **tele·mar·ket·er** \-tər\ *n*

te·lem·e·try \tə-ˈle-mə-trē\ *n* : the transmission especially by radio of measurements made by automatic instruments to a distant station — **tele·me·ter** \ˈte-lə-ˌmē-tər\ *n*

te·lep·a·thy \tə-ˈle-pə-thē\ *n* : apparent communication from one mind to another by extrasensory means — **tele·path·ic** \ˌte-lə-ˈpa-thik\ *adj* — **tele·path·i·cal·ly** \-thi-k(ə-)lē\ *adv*

[1]tele·phone \ˈte-lə-ˌfōn\ *n* : an instrument for sending and receiving sounds over long distances by electricity

[2]telephone *vb* **-phoned; -phon·ing** **1** : to send or communicate by telephone **2** ♦ : to speak to or attempt to reach by telephone — **tele·phon·er** *n*

♦ call, dial

te·le·pho·ny \tə-ˈle-fə-nē, ˈte-lə-ˌfō-\ *n* : use or operation of an apparatus for transmission of sounds as electrical signals between distant points — **tel·e·phon·ic** \ˌte-lə-ˈfä-nik\ *adj*

tele·pho·to \ˌte-lə-ˈfō-tō\ *adj* : being a camera lens giving a large image of a distant object — **tele·pho·tog·ra·phy** \-fə-ˈtä-grə-fē\ *n*

tele·play \ˈte-li-ˌplā\ *n* : a story prepared for television production

tele·print·er \ˈte-lə-ˌprin-tər\ *n* : TELETYPEWRITER

tele·prompt·er \ˈte-lə-ˌprämp-tər\ *n* : a device for displaying prepared text to a speaker or performer

[1]tele·scope \ˈte-lə-ˌskōp\ *n* **1** : a cylindrical instrument equipped with lenses or mirrors for viewing distant objects **2** : RADIO TELESCOPE

[2]telescope *vb* **-scoped; -scop·ing** **1** : to slide or pass or cause to slide or pass one within another like the sections of a collapsible hand telescope **2** : COMPRESS, CONDENSE

tele·scop·ic \ˌte-lə-ˈskä-pik\ *adj* **1** : of or relating to a telescope **2** : seen only by a telescope **3** : able to discern objects at a distance **4** : having parts that telescope — **tele·scop·i·cal·ly** \-pi-k(ə-)lē\ *adv*

tele·text \ˈte-lə-ˌtekst\ *n* : a system for broadcasting text over a television signal and displaying it on a decoder-equipped television

tele·thon \ˈte-lə-ˌthän\ *n* : a long television program usually to solicit funds for a charity

tele·type·writ·er \ˌte-lə-ˈtīp-ˌrī-tər\ *n* : a printing device resembling a typewriter used to send and receive signals over telephone lines

tele·vise \ˈte-lə-ˌvīz\ *vb* **-vised; -vis·ing** : to broadcast by television

tele·vi·sion \ˈte-lə-ˌvi-zhən\ *n* : a system for transmitting images and sound by converting them into electrical or radio waves which are converted back into images and sound by a receiver; *also* : a television receiving set

tell \ˈtel\ *vb* **told** \ˈtōld\; **tell·ing** **1** : to indicate or name by units or groups so as to find the total number of units involved : COUNT **2** ♦ : to relate in detail : NARRATE **3** : to give utterance to : SAY **4** ♦ : to make known **5** ♦ : to report to : INFORM **6** ♦ : to give an order to : DIRECT **7** : to find out by observing **8** : to have a marked effect **9** : to serve as evidence

♦ [2] describe, narrate, recite, recount, rehearse, relate, report ♦ [4] bare, disclose, discover, divulge, expose, reveal, spill, unbosom, uncloak, uncover, unmask, unveil ♦ [5] acquaint, advise, apprise, brief, clue, enlighten, familiarize, fill in, inform, instruct, wise ♦ [6] bid, boss, charge, command, direct, enjoin, instruct, order

tell·er \ˈte-lər\ *n* **1** : one that relates : NARRATOR **2** : one that counts **3** : a bank employee handling money received or paid out

tell·ing \ˈte-liŋ\ *adj* ♦ : producing a marked effect : EFFECTIVE

♦ cogent, compelling, conclusive, convincing, decisive, effective, forceful, persuasive, satisfying, strong

tell off *vb* : REPRIMAND, SCOLD

[1]tell·tale \ˈtel-ˌtāl\ *n* **1** : one that informs against another : INFORMER **2** : something that serves to disclose : INDICATION

[2]telltale *adj* **1** : telling what one should hold secret or in confidence **2** ♦ : disclosing or indicating something often of a private or secret nature ⟨~ crumbs on the kitchen counter⟩

♦ denotative, indicative, significant

tel·lu·ri·um \tə-ˈlu̇r-ē-əm\ *n* : a chemical element used especially in alloys

tel·net \ˈtel-ˌnet\ *n* : a telecommunications protocol for accessing and using a remote computer via a local computer — **telnet** *vb*

tem·blor \ˈtem-blər\ *n* : EARTHQUAKE

te·mer·i·ty \tə-ˈmer-ə-tē\ *n, pl* **-ties** ♦ : rash or presumptuous daring

♦ audacity, brass, brazenness, cheek, chutzpah, effrontery, gall, nerve, presumption, sauce, sauciness

[1]temp \ˈtemp\ *n* **1** : TEMPERATURE **2** : a temporary worker

[2]temp *abbr* temporary

[1]tem·per \ˈtem-pər\ *vb* **1** : to dilute or soften by the addition of something else ⟨~ justice with mercy⟩ **2** : to bring (as steel) to a desired hardness by reheating and cooling **3** : to toughen (glass) by gradual heating and cooling **4** : TOUGHEN **5** : TUNE

[2]temper *n* **1** : characteristic tone : TENDENCY **2** : the hardness or toughness of a substance ⟨~ of a knife blade⟩ **3** : a characteristic frame of mind : DISPOSITION **4** : calmness of mind : COMPOSURE **5** ♦ : state of feeling or frame of mind at a particular time **6** : heat of mind or emotion **7** ♦ : main or essential nature especially as strongly marked and serving to distinguish — **tempered** \ˈtem-pərd\ *adj*

♦ [5] cheer, frame, humor (*or* humour), mode, mood, spirit ♦ [7] air, atmosphere, aura, climate, flavor (*or* flavour), mood, note

tem·pera \ˈtem-pə-rə\ *n* : a painting process using an albuminous or colloidal medium as a vehicle; *also* : a painting done in tempera

tem·per·a·ment \ˈtem-prə-mənt, -pər-mənt\ *n* **1** ♦ : characteristic or habitual inclination or mode of emotional response : DISPOSITION ⟨nervous ~⟩ **2** : excessive sensitiveness or irritability

♦ disposition, grain, nature, temper

tem·per·a·men·tal \ˌtem-prə-ˈment-ᵊl, -pər-ˈment-\ *adj* **1** ♦ : marked by excessive sensitivity and impulsive mood changes ⟨a ~ child⟩ **2** ♦ : unpredictable in behavior or performance ⟨a ~ computer⟩

♦ [1, 2] capricious, changeable, fickle, fluid, inconstant, mercurial, mutable, uncertain, unpredictable, unsettled, unstable, unsteady, variable, volatile

tem·per·ance \ˈtem-prəns, -pə-rəns\ *n* : habitual moderation in the indulgence of the appetites or passions; *esp* : moderation in or abstinence from the use of alcoholic beverages

tem·per·ate \ˈtem-prət, -pə-rət\ *adj* **1** : not extreme or excessive : MILD **2** : moderate in indulgence of appetite or desire **3** : moderate in the use of alcoholic beverages **4** ♦ : having a moderate climate

♦ balmy, clement, equable, gentle, mild, moderate

temperate zone *n, often cap T&Z* : the region between the Tropic of Cancer and the arctic circle or between the Tropic of Capricorn and the antarctic circle

tem·per·a·ture \ˈtem-pər-ˌchu̇r, -prə-ˌchu̇r, -chər\ *n* **1** : degree of hotness or coldness of something (as air, water, or the body) as shown by a thermometer **2** : FEVER 1

tem·pest \ˈtem-pəst\ *n* **1** : a violent storm **2** ♦ : a violent commotion or agitation

♦ cataclysm, convulsion, paroxysm, storm, tumult, upheaval, uproar

tem•pes•tu•ous \tem-ˈpes-chə-wəs\ *adj* ♦ **:** of, involving, or resembling a tempest **:** STORMY — **tem•pes•tu•ous•ly** *adv* — **tem•pes•tu•ous•ness** *n*

♦ explosive, ferocious, fierce, furious, hot, rabid, rough, stormy, turbulent, violent, volcanic ♦ bleak, dirty, foul, inclement, nasty, raw, rough, squally

tem•plate \ˈtem-plət\ *n* **:** a gauge, mold, or pattern that functions as a guide to the form or structure of something being made

[1]tem•ple \ˈtem-pəl\ *n* **1 :** a building reserved for religious practice **2 :** a place devoted to a special or exalted purpose

[2]temple *n* **:** the flattened space on each side of the forehead especially of humans

tem•po \ˈtem-pō\ *n, pl* **tem•pi** \-(ˌ)pē\ *or* **tempos** **1 :** the rate of speed of a musical piece or passage **2 :** rate of motion or activity **:** PACE

[1]tem•po•ral \ˈtem-pə-rəl\ *adj* **1 :** of, relating to, or limited by time ⟨~ and spatial bounds⟩ **2** ♦ **:** of or relating to earthly life or secular concerns ⟨~ power⟩

♦ carnal, earthly, fleshly, material, mundane, terrestrial, worldly ♦ nonreligious, profane, secular

[2]temporal *adj* **:** of or relating to the temples or the sides of the skull

[1]tem•po•rary \ˈtem-pə-ˌrer-ē\ *adj* ♦ **:** lasting for a time only — **tem•po•rar•i•ly** \ˌtem-pə-ˈrer-ə-lē\ *adv*

♦ impermanent, interim, provisional, short-term ***Ant*** long-term, permanent

[2]temporary *n, pl* **-rar•ies :** one serving for a limited time

tem•po•rise *chiefly Brit var of* TEMPORIZE

tem•po•rize \ˈtem-pə-ˌrīz\ *vb* **-rized; -riz•ing** **1 :** to adapt one's actions to the time or the dominant opinion **:** COMPROMISE **2 :** to draw out matters so as to gain time — **tem•po•riz•er** *n*

tempt \ˈtempt\ *vb* **1** ♦ **:** to entice to do wrong by promise of pleasure or gain **2 :** PROVOKE **3 :** to risk the dangers of **4 :** to induce to do something **:** INCITE — **tempt•er** *n* — **tempt•ing•ly** *adv*

♦ allure, beguile, decoy, entice, lead on, lure, seduce

temp•ta•tion \temp-ˈtā-shən\ *n* **1** ♦ **:** the act of tempting **:** the state of being tempted **2** ♦ **:** something that tempts

♦ enticement, lure, seduction, solicitation

tempt•ress \ˈtemp-trəs\ *n* **:** a woman who tempts

ten \ˈten\ *n* **1 :** one more than nine **2 :** the 10th in a set or series **3 :** something having 10 units — **ten** *adj or pron* — **tenth** \ˈtenth\ *adj or adv or n*

ten•a•ble \ˈte-nə-bəl\ *adj* ♦ **:** capable of being held, maintained, or defended — **ten•a•bil•i•ty** \ˌte-nə-ˈbi-lə-tē\ *n*

♦ defensible, justifiable, maintainable, supportable, sustainable ***Ant*** indefensible, unjustifiable, insupportable, untenable

te•na•cious \tə-ˈnā-shəs\ *adj* **1 :** not easily pulled apart **:** COHESIVE, TOUGH ⟨a ~ metal⟩ **2** ♦ **:** holding fast ⟨~ of his rights⟩ **3 :** RETENTIVE ⟨a ~ memory⟩ — **te•na•cious•ly** *adv*

♦ dogged, insistent, patient, persevering, persistent, pertinacious

te•nac•i•ty \tə-ˈna-sə-tē\ *n* ♦ **:** the quality or state of being tenacious

♦ hardheadedness, mulishness, obduracy, obstinacy, peevishness, pertinacity, self-will, stubbornness

ten•an•cy \ˈte-nən-sē\ *n, pl* **-cies :** the temporary possession or occupancy of something (as a house) that belongs to another; *also* **:** the period of a tenant's occupancy

ten•ant \ˈte-nənt\ *n* **1** ♦ **:** one who rents or leases (as a house) from a landlord **2 :** DWELLER, OCCUPANT — **tenant** *vb* — **ten•ant•less** *adj*

♦ boarder, lodger, renter, roomer ***Ant*** landlord

tenant farmer *n* **:** a farmer who works land owned by another and pays rent either in cash or in shares of produce

ten•ant•ry \ˈte-nən-trē\ *n, pl* **-ries :** the body of tenants especially on an estate

Ten Commandments *n pl* **:** the commandments of God given to Moses on Mount Sinai

[1]tend \ˈtend\ *vb* **1 :** to apply oneself ⟨~ to your affairs⟩ **2** ♦ **:** to take care of ⟨~ a plant⟩ **3 :** to manage the operations of ⟨~ a machine⟩

♦ attend, care, mind, oversee, superintend, supervise ♦ crop, cultivate, culture, grow, promote, raise, rear

[2]tend *vb* **1 :** to move or develop one's course in a particular direction **2** ♦ **:** to show an inclination or tendency

♦ incline, lean, run, trend

ten•den•cy \ˈten-dən-sē\ *n, pl* **-cies** **1** ♦ **:** direction or approach toward a place, object, effect, or limit **:** TREND **2** ♦ **:** a proneness to or readiness for a particular kind of thought or action **:** PROPENSITY

♦ [1] current, drift, leaning, run, tide, trend, wind ♦ [2] aptness, bent, disposition, inclination, leaning, penchant, predilection, proclivity, proneness, propensity, way

ten•den•tious \ten-ˈden-chəs\ *adj* **:** marked by a tendency in favor of a particular point of view **:** BIASED — **ten•den•tious•ly** *adv* — **ten•den•tious•ness** *n*

[1]ten•der \ˈten-dər\ *adj* **1 :** having a soft texture **:** easily broken, chewed, or cut **2** ♦ **:** physically weak **:** DELICATE; *also* **:** IMMATURE **3** ♦ **:** expressing or responsive to love or sympathy **4 :** SENSITIVE, TOUCHY **5** ♦ **:** delicate or soft in quality or tone — **ten•der•ly** *adv* — **ten•der•ness** *n*

♦ [2] delicate, fragile, frail, immature, sensitive ***Ant*** tough ♦ [3] beneficent, benevolent, compassionate, good-hearted, humane, kind, kindly, loving, sympathetic, tenderhearted, warmhearted ♦ [5] balmy, benign, bland, delicate, gentle, light, mellow, mild, soft, soothing

[2]tender *n* **1 :** an offer or proposal made for acceptance; *esp* **:** an offer of a bid for a contract **2** ♦ **:** something (as money) that may be offered in payment

♦ cash, currency, dough, lucre, money, pelf

[3]tender *vb* ♦ **:** to present for acceptance

♦ extend, give, offer, proffer

[4]tend•er \ˈten-dər\ *n* **1 :** one that tends or takes care **2 :** a boat carrying passengers and freight to a larger ship **3 :** a car attached to a steam locomotive for carrying fuel and water

[5]tender *n* **:** a strip of meat (as of chicken breast) often breaded

ten•der•foot \ˈten-dər-ˌfu̇t\ *n, pl* **-feet** \-ˌfēt\ *also* **-foots** \-ˌfu̇ts\ **1 :** one not hardened to frontier or rough outdoor life **2** ♦ **:** an inexperienced beginner

♦ beginner, fledgling, freshman, greenhorn, neophyte, newcomer, novice, recruit, rookie, tyro

ten•der•heart•ed \ˌten-dər-ˈhär-təd\ *adj* ♦ **:** easily moved to love, pity, or sorrow

♦ beneficent, benevolent, compassionate, good-hearted, humane, kind, kindly, sympathetic, tender, warmhearted

ten•der•ize \ˈten-də-ˌrīz\ *vb* **-ized; -iz•ing :** to make (meat) tender — **ten•der•iz•er** \ˈten-də-ˌrī-zər\ *n*

ten•der•loin \ˈten-dər-ˌlȯin\ *n* **1 :** a tender strip of beef or pork from near the backbone **2 :** a district of a city largely devoted to vice

ten•di•ni•tis *or* **ten•don•itis** \ˌten-də-ˈnī-təs\ *n* **:** inflammation of a tendon

ten•don \ˈten-dən\ *n* **:** a tough cord of dense white fibrous tissue uniting a muscle with another part (as a bone) — **ten•di•nous** \-də-nəs\ *adj*

ten•dril \ˈten-drəl\ *n* **:** a slender coiling organ by which some climbing plants attach themselves to a support

ten•e•brous \ˈte-nə-brəs\ *adj* **:** shut off from the light **:** GLOOMY, OBSCURE

ten•e•ment \ˈte-nə-mənt\ *n* **1 :** a house used as a dwelling **2 :** a building divided into apartments for rent to families; *esp* **:** one meeting only minimum standards of safety and comfort **3 :** a room or set of rooms fitted especially with housekeeping facilities and usually leased as a dwelling **:** APARTMENT, FLAT

te•net \ˈte-nət\ *n* **:** one of the principles or doctrines held in common by members of a group (as a church or profession)

ten•fold \ˈten-ˌfōld, -ˈfōld\ *adj* **:** being 10 times as great or as many — **ten•fold** \-ˈfōld\ *adv*

ten–gallon hat *n* **:** a wide-brimmed hat with a large soft crown

Tenn *abbr* Tennessee

ten•nis \ˈte-nəs\ *n* **:** a game played with a ball and racket on a court divided by a net

ten•on \ˈte-nən\ *n* **:** a projecting part in a piece of material (as wood) for insertion into a mortise to make a joint

ten•or \ˈte-nər\ *n* **1 :** the general drift of something spoken or written **2 :** the highest natural adult male voice; *also* **:** a singer having this voice **3 :** a continuing in a course, movement, or activity ⟨the ~ of my life⟩

tenpenny nail *n* **:** a nail three inches (about 7.6 centimeters) long

ten•pin \ˈten-ˌpin\ *n* **:** a bottle-shaped bowling pin set in groups of 10 and bowled at in a game (**tenpins**)

[1]tense \ˈtens\ *n* **:** distinction of form of a verb to indicate the time of the action or state

[2]tense *adj* **tens•er; tens•est** **1** ♦ **:** stretched tight **:** TAUT **2**

a ♦ : feeling or showing nervous tension ⟨a ~ smile⟩ b ♦ : marked by strain or suspense ⟨a ~ movie⟩ — **tense·ly** *adv* — **tense·ness** *n* — **ten·si·ty** \ˈten-sə-tē\ *n*

♦ [1] rigid, taut, tight ♦ [2a] aflutter, anxious, edgy, jittery, jumpy, nervous, nervy, perturbed, troubled, uneasy, upset, worried ♦ [2b] anxious, distressful, nervous, restless, unsettling, upsetting, worrisome

³tense *vb* **tensed; tens·ing** : to make or become tense — often used with *up*
ten·sile \ˈten-səl, -ˌsīl\ *adj* : of or relating to tension ⟨~ strength⟩
ten·sion \ˈten-chən\ *n* **1** : the act of straining or stretching; *also* : the condition of being strained or stretched **2** ♦ : a state of mental unrest often with signs of bodily stress **3** : a state of latent hostility or opposition

♦ pressure, strain, stress

ten–speed \ˈten-ˌspēd\ *n* : a bicycle with a derailleur having 10 possible combinations of gears
¹tent \ˈtent\ *n* **1** ♦ : a collapsible shelter of material stretched and supported by poles **2** : a canopy placed over the head and shoulders to retain vapors or oxygen given for medical reasons

♦ canopy, ceiling, roof

²tent *vb* **1** : to lodge in tents **2** : to cover with or as if with a tent
ten·ta·cle \ˈten-ti-kəl\ *n* : any of various long flexible projections about the head or mouth (as of an insect, mollusk, or fish) — **ten·ta·cled** \-kəld\ *adj* — **ten·tac·u·lar** \ten-ˈta-kyə-lər\ *adj*
ten·ta·tive \ˈten-tə-tiv\ *adj* **1** ♦ : not fully worked out or developed ⟨~ plans⟩ **2** : HESITANT, UNCERTAIN ⟨a ~ smile⟩ — **ten·ta·tive·ly** *adv*

♦ conditional, contingent, qualified

ten·u·ous \ˈten-yə-wəs\ *adj* **1** : not dense : RARE ⟨a ~ fluid⟩ **2** : not thick : SLENDER ⟨a ~ rope⟩ **3** : having little substance : FLIMSY, WEAK ⟨~ influences⟩ **4** : lacking stability : SHAKY ⟨~ reasoning⟩ — **te·nu·i·ty** \te-ˈnü-ə-tē, tə-, -ˈnyü-\ *n* — **ten·u·ous·ly** *adv* — **ten·u·ous·ness** *n*
ten·ure \ˈten-yər\ *n* ♦ : the act, right, manner, or period of holding something (as a landed property, an office, or a position)

♦ hitch, stint, term, tour

ten·ured \ˈten-yərd\ *adj* : having tenure ⟨~ faculty members⟩
te·o·sin·te \ˌtā-ō-ˈsin-tē\ *n* : a tall annual grass of Mexico that is closely related to Indian corn
te·pee *or* **tee·pee** \ˈtē-(ˌ)pē\ *n* : an American Indian conical tent usually of skins
tep·id \ˈte-pəd\ *adj* **1** : moderately warm : LUKEWARM **2** ♦ : marked by an absence of enthusiasm or conviction : HALF-HEARTED

♦ halfhearted, uneager, unenthusiastic ***Ant*** eager, enthusiastic, hearty, keen, passionate, warm, wholehearted

te·qui·la \tə-ˈkē-lə, tā-\ *n* : a Mexican liquor distilled from an agave's sap
ter *abbr* **1** terrace **2** territory
tera·byte \ˈter-ə-ˌbīt\ *n* : 1024 gigabytes; *also* : one trillion bytes
ter·bi·um \ˈtər-bē-əm\ *n* : a metallic chemical element
ter·cen·te·na·ry \ˌtər-ˌsen-ˈte-nə-rē, tər-ˈsent-ᵊn-ˌer-ē\ *n, pl* **-ries** : a 300th anniversary or its celebration — **tercentenary** *adj*
ter·cen·ten·ni·al \ˌtər-ˌsen-ˈte-nē-əl\ *adj or n* : TERCENTENARY
te·re·do \tə-ˈrē-dō, -ˈrā-\ *n, pl* **-dos** : SHIPWORM
ter·i·ya·ki \ˌter-ē-ˈyä-kē\ *n* : a Japanese dish of meat or fish soaked in a soy marinade and cooked
¹term \ˈtərm\ *n* **1** : END, TERMINATION **2 a** : a limited or definite extent of time : DURATION **b** ♦ : the time for which something lasts ⟨~ of office⟩ ⟨lost money in the short ~⟩ **3** : a mathematical expression connected with another by a plus or minus sign; *also* : an element (as a numerator) of a fraction or proportion **4** : a word or expression that has a precise meaning in some uses or is limited to a particular subject or field **5** *pl* : PROVISIONS, CONDITIONS ⟨~*s* of a contract⟩ **6** *pl* : mutual relationship ⟨on good ~*s*⟩ **7** : AGREEMENT, CONCORD

♦ hitch, stint, tenure, tour

²term *vb* ♦ : to apply a term to : CALL

♦ baptize, call, christen, denominate, designate, dub, entitle, label, name, style, title

ter·ma·gant \ˈtər-mə-gənt\ *n* ♦ : an overbearing or nagging woman : SHREW

♦ fury, harpy, shrew, virago

¹ter·mi·nal \ˈtər-mən-ᵊl\ *adj* **1** ♦ : of, relating to, or forming an end, limit, or terminus **2** : FATAL 2 ⟨~ cancer⟩; *also* : being in or relating to the final stages of a fatal disease ⟨a ~ patient⟩ — **ter·mi·nal·ly** *adv*

♦ final, hindmost, last, latter, ultimate

²terminal *n* **1** : EXTREMITY, END **2** : a device at the end of a wire or on electrical equipment for making a connection **3** : either end of a transportation line (as a railroad) with its offices and freight and passenger stations; *also* : a freight or passenger station **4** : a device (as in a computer system) for data entry and display
ter·mi·nate \ˈtər-mə-ˌnāt\ *vb* **-nat·ed; -nat·ing** **1** ♦ : to bring or come to an end **2** ♦ : to serve as an ending, limit, or boundary of — **ter·mi·na·ble** \-nə-bəl\ *adj* — **ter·mi·na·tor** \ˈtər-mə-ˌnā-tər\ *n*

♦ [1] close, conclude, end, finish, round, wind up, wrap up ♦ [1] break off, break up, cease, die, discontinue, elapse, expire, halt, lapse, leave off, let up, pass, quit, stop ♦ [2] bound, circumscribe, define, delimit, demarcate, limit, mark

ter·mi·na·tion \ˌtər-mə-ˈnā-shən\ *n* **1** ♦ : end in time or existence **2** ♦ : the act of terminating **3** ♦ : a limit in space or extent

♦ [1] death, demise, expiration ♦ [2] cessation, close, closure, conclusion, end, ending, expiration, finish, halt, lapse, shutdown, stop, stoppage ♦ [3] bound, boundary, ceiling, confines, end, extent, limit, limitation, line

ter·mi·nol·o·gy \ˌtər-mə-ˈnä-lə-jē\ *n, pl* **-gies** ♦ : the technical or special terms used in a business, art, science, or special subject

♦ argot, cant, jargon, language, lingo, slang, vocabulary

ter·mi·nus \ˈtər-mə-nəs\ *n, pl* **-ni** \-ˌnī\ *or* **-nus·es** **1** : final goal : END **2** : either end of a transportation line or travel route; *also* : the station or city at such a place
ter·mite \ˈtər-ˌmīt\ *n* : any of numerous pale soft-bodied social insects that feed on wood
tern \ˈtərn\ *n* : any of various chiefly marine birds with narrow wings and often a forked tail
ter·na·ry \ˈtər-nə-rē\ *adj* **1** : of, relating to, or proceeding by threes **2** : having three elements or parts
terr *abbr* territory
¹ter·race \ˈter-əs\ *n* **1** : a flat roof or open platform **2** : a level area next to a building **3** : an embankment with level top **4** : a bank or ridge on a slope to conserve moisture and soil **5** : a row of houses on raised land; *also* : a street with such a row of houses **6** : a strip of park in the middle of a street
²terrace *vb* **ter·raced; ter·rac·ing** : to form into a terrace or supply with terraces
ter·ra–cot·ta \ˌter-ə-ˈkä-tə\ *n* : a reddish brown earthenware
terra fir·ma \-ˈfər-mə\ *n* ♦ : solid ground

♦ dirt, dust, earth, ground, land, soil

ter·rain \tə-ˈrān\ *n* : the surface features of an area of land ⟨a rough ~⟩
ter·ra in·cog·ni·ta \ˈter-ə-ˌin-ˌkäg-ˈnē-tə\ *n, pl* **ter·rae in·cog·ni·tae** \ˈter-ˌī-ˌin-ˌkäg-ˈnē-tī\ : an unexplored area or field of knowledge
ter·ra·pin \ˈter-ə-pən\ *n* : any of various turtles of fresh or brackish water
ter·rar·i·um \tə-ˈrar-ē-əm\ *n, pl* **-ia** \-ē-ə\ *or* **-i·ums** : a usually transparent enclosure for keeping or raising plants or small animals indoors
ter·res·tri·al \tə-ˈres-trē-əl\ *adj* **1** ♦ : of or relating to the earth or its inhabitants **2** : living or growing on land ⟨~ plants⟩

♦ carnal, earthly, fleshly, material, mundane, temporal, worldly

ter·ri·ble \ˈter-ə-bəl\ *adj* **1** ♦ : exciting terror or alarm : DREADFUL **2** : hard to bear : DISTRESSING ⟨a ~ situation⟩ **3** : extreme in degree : INTENSE ⟨~ heat⟩ **4** ♦ : of very poor quality : AWFUL ⟨a ~ play⟩ **5** ♦ : strongly repulsive

♦ [1] dire, dreadful, fearful, fearsome, forbidding, formidable, frightful, hair-raising, horrible, redoubtable, scary, shocking, terrifying ♦ [4] atrocious, awful, cheap, execrable, lousy, punk, rotten, wretched ♦ [5] appalling, ghastly, grisly, gruesome, hideous, horrible, lurid, macabre, monstrous, nightmarish, shocking

ter·ri·bly \ˈter-ə-blē\ *adv* : to an extreme degree : VERY
ter·ri·er \ˈter-ē-ər\ *n* : any of various usually small energetic dogs orig. used by hunters to drive small game animals from their holes
ter·rif·ic \tə-ˈri-fik\ *adj* **1** : exciting terror **2** : EXTRAORDINARY, ASTOUNDING ⟨~ speed⟩ **3** ♦ : unusually good ⟨makes ~ chili⟩

♦ A1, excellent, fabulous, fine, marvelous, sensational, splendid, superb, superior, wonderful

ter•ri•fied \ˈter-ə-ˌfīd\ *adj* ♦ **:** filled with fear or anxiety

♦ afraid, aghast, fearful, scared

ter•ri•fy \ˈter-ə-ˌfī\ *vb* **-fied; -fy•ing** ♦ **:** to fill with terror **:** FRIGHTEN

♦ alarm, frighten, horrify, panic, scare, shock, spook, startle, terrorize

terrifying *adj* ♦ **:** causing terror or apprehension — **ter•ri•fy•ing•ly** *adv*

♦ dire, dreadful, fearful, fearsome, forbidding, formidable, frightful, hair-raising, horrible, redoubtable, scary, shocking, terrible

ter•ri•to•ry \ˈter-ə-ˌtōr-ē\ *n, pl* **-ries 1 :** a geographic area belonging to or under the jurisdiction of a governmental authority **2 :** a part of the U.S. not included within any state but organized with a separate legislature **3 :** REGION, DISTRICT; *also* **:** a region in which one feels at home **4 :** a field of knowledge or interest **5 :** an assigned area **6** ♦ **:** an area occupied and defended by one or a group of animals — **ter•ri•to•ri•al** \ˌter-ə-ˈtōr-ē-əl\ *adj*

♦ habitat, home, niche, range

ter•ror \ˈter-ər\ *n* **1** ♦ **:** a state of intense fear **:** FRIGHT **2 :** one that inspires fear

♦ alarm, anxiety, apprehension, dread, fear, fright, horror, panic, trepidation

ter•ror•ism \ˈter-ər-ˌi-zəm\ *n* **:** the systematic use of terror especially as a means of coercion — **ter•ror•ist** \-ist\ *adj or n*

ter•ror•ize \ˈter-ər-ˌīz\ *vb* **-ized; -iz•ing 1** ♦ **:** to fill with terror **:** SCARE **2 :** to coerce by threat or violence

♦ alarm, frighten, horrify, panic, scare, shock, spook, startle, terrify

ter•ry \ˈter-ē\ *n, pl* **terries :** an absorbent fabric with a loose pile of uncut loops

terse \ˈtərs\ *adj* **ters•er; ters•est** ♦ **:** effectively brief **:** CONCISE

♦ brief, compact, compendious, concise, crisp, epigrammatic, laconic, pithy, succinct, summary

terse•ly \-lē\ *adv* ♦ **:** in a terse manner

♦ compactly, concisely, crisply, laconically, shortly, succinctly, summarily

terse•ness \-nəs\ *n* ♦ **:** the quality or state of being terse

♦ brevity, briefness, compactness, conciseness, crispness, succinctness

ter•tia•ry \ˈtər-shē-ˌer-ē\ *adj* **1 :** of third rank, importance, or value **2** *cap* **:** of, relating to, or being the earlier period of the Cenozoic era **3 :** occurring in or being the third stage

Tertiary *n* **:** the Tertiary period

TESL *abbr* teaching English as a second language

TESOL *abbr* Teachers of English to Speakers of Other Languages

1test \ˈtest\ *n* **1** ♦ **:** a critical examination or evaluation **2** ♦ **:** a means or result of testing

♦ [1] experiment, trial ♦ [2] examination, quiz

2test *vb* **1** ♦ **:** to put to test **:** TRY **2 :** to undergo or score on tests

♦ strain, stretch, tax, try

3test *adj* **:** relating to or used in testing ⟨a ~ group⟩

tes•ta•ment \ˈtes-tə-mənt\ *n* **1** *cap* **:** either of two main divisions of Christian Scripture **2** ♦ **:** a tangible proof or tribute **:** EVIDENCE **3 :** CREED **4 :** the legal instructions for the disposition of one's property after death **:** WILL — **tes•ta•men•ta•ry** \ˌtes-tə-ˈmen-tə-rē\ *adj*

♦ attestation, confirmation, corroboration, documentation, evidence, proof, substantiation, testimony, validation, witness

tes•tate \ˈtes-ˌtāt, -tət\ *adj* **:** having left a valid will

tes•ta•tor \ˈtes-ˌtā-tər, tes-ˈtā-\ *n* **:** a person who dies leaving a valid will

tes•ta•trix \tes-ˈtā-triks\ *n* **:** a woman who is a testator

1tes•ter \ˈtēs-tər, ˈtes-\ *n* **:** a canopy over a bed, pulpit, or altar

2test•er \ˈtes-tər\ *n* **:** one that tests

tes•ti•cle \ˈtes-ti-kəl\ *n* **:** TESTIS; *esp* **:** one of a mammal usually with its enclosing structures — **tes•tic•u•lar** *adj*

tes•ti•fy \ˈtes-tə-ˌfī\ *vb* **-fied; -fy•ing 1 :** to make a statement based on personal knowledge or belief **:** bear witness **2 :** to serve as evidence or proof **3** ♦ **:** to make a solemn declaration under oath for the purpose of establishing a fact (as in a court) **4** ♦ **:** to bear witness to **:** ATTEST

♦ [3] attest, depose, swear, witness ♦ *usu* **testify to** [4] attest, authenticate, avouch, certify, vouch, witness

tes•ti•mo•ni•al \ˌtes-tə-ˈmō-nē-əl\ *n* **1 :** a statement testifying to benefits received; *also* **:** a character reference **2 :** an expression of appreciation **:** TRIBUTE — **testimonial** *adj*

tes•ti•mo•ny \ˈtes-tə-ˌmō-nē\ *n, pl* **-nies 1** ♦ **:** evidence based on observation or knowledge **2 :** an outward sign **:** SYMBOL **3 :** a solemn declaration made by a witness under oath especially in a court

♦ attestation, confirmation, corroboration, documentation, evidence, proof, substantiation, testament, validation, witness

tes•tis \ˈtes-təs\ *n, pl* **tes•tes** \ˈtes-ˌtēz\ **:** a typically paired male reproductive gland that produces sperm and testosterone and that in most mammals is contained within the scrotum at sexual maturity

tes•tos•ter•one \te-ˈstäs-tə-ˌrōn\ *n* **:** a male sex hormone causing development of the male reproductive system and secondary sex characteristics

test tube *n* **:** a glass tube closed at one end and used especially in chemistry and biology

tes•ty \ˈtes-tē\ *adj* **tes•ti•er; -est** ♦ **:** easily annoyed; *also* **:** marked by ill humor

♦ choleric, crabby, cranky, cross, crotchety, grouchy, grumpy, irascible, irritable, peevish, perverse, petulant, short-tempered, snappish, snappy, snippy, waspish

tet•a•nus \ˈtet-ᵊn-əs\ *n* **:** an infectious disease caused by bacterial poisons and marked by muscle stiffness and spasms especially of the jaws — **tet•a•nal** \-əl\ *adj*

tetchy \ˈte-chē\ *adj* **tetchi•er; -est :** irritably or peevishly sensitive

1tête–à–tête \ˈtat-ə-ˌtāt\ *n* **:** a private conversation between two persons

2tête–à–tête \ˌtāt-ə-ˈtāt\ *adv* **:** in private

3tête–à–tête \ˈtāt-ə-ˌtāt\ *adj* **:** being face-to-face **:** PRIVATE

1teth•er \ˈte-thər\ *n* **1 :** something (as a rope) by which an animal is fastened **2 :** the limit of one's strength or resources

2tether *vb* **:** to fasten or restrain by or as if by a tether

tet•ra•eth•yl lead \ˌte-trə-ˈe-thəl-\ *n* **:** a heavy oily poisonous liquid used especially formerly as an antiknock agent in gasoline

tet•ra•he•dron \-ˈhē-drən\ *n, pl* **-drons** *or* **-dra** \-drə\ **:** a polyhedron that has four faces — **tet•ra•he•dral** \-drəl\ *adj*

tet•ra•hy•dro•can•nab•i•nol \-ˌhī-drə-kə-ˈna-bə-ˌnȯl, -ˌnōl\ *n* **:** THC

te•tram•e•ter \te-ˈtra-mə-tər\ *n* **:** a line of verse consisting of four metrical feet

Teu•ton•ic \tü-ˈtä-nik, tyü-\ *adj* **:** GERMANIC

Tex *abbr* Texas

Tex–Mex \ˈteks-ˈmeks\ *adj* **:** characteristic of Mexican-American culture and especially that of southern Texas

text \ˈtekst\ *n* **1 :** the actual words of an author's work **2 :** the main body of printed or written matter on a page **3 :** a scriptural passage chosen as the subject especially of a sermon **4 :** THEME, TOPIC **5 :** TEXTBOOK — **tex•tu•al** \ˈteks-chə-wəl\ *adj*

text•book \ˈtekst-ˌbu̇k\ *n* ♦ **:** a book used in the study of a subject

♦ handbook, manual, primer

tex•tile \ˈtek-ˌstīl, ˈtekst-ᵊl\ *n* **:** CLOTH; *esp* **:** a woven or knit cloth

tex•ture \ˈteks-chər\ *n* **1 :** the visual or tactile surface characteristics and appearance of something ⟨a coarse ~⟩ **2 :** essential part **3 :** basic scheme or structure **:** FABRIC **4 :** overall structure

TGIF *abbr* thank God it's Friday

1Th *abbr* Thursday

2Th *symbol* thorium

2-th *or* **-eth** *adj suffix* — used in forming ordinal numbers ⟨hundred*th*⟩

3-th *n suffix* **1 :** act or process **2 :** state or condition ⟨dear*th*⟩

Thai \ˈtī\ *n, pl* **Thai** *or* **Thais 1 :** a native or inhabitant of Thailand **2 :** the official language of Thailand — **Thai** *adj*

thal•a•mus \ˈtha-lə-məs\ *n, pl* **-mi** \-ˌmī\ **:** a subdivision of the brain that serves as a relay station to and from the cerebral cortex and functions in arousal and the integration of sensory information

thal•as•se•mia \ˌtha-lə-ˈsē-mē-ə\ *n* **:** any of a group of inherited disorders of hemoglobin synthesis

tha•las•so•ther•a•py \thə-ˌla-sō-ˈther-ə-pē\ *n* **:** the use of seawater or sea products (as seaweed) for the benefit of health or beauty

thal•li•um \ˈtha-le-əm\ *n* **:** a poisonous metallic chemical element

[1]than \ˈthən, ˈthan\ *conj* **1** — used after a comparative adjective or adverb to introduce the second part of a comparison expressing inequality ⟨older ~ I am⟩ **2** — used after *other* or a word of similar meaning to express a difference of kind, manner, or identity ⟨adults other ~ parents⟩
[2]than *prep* : in comparison with ⟨older ~ me⟩
thane \ˈthān\ *n* **1 :** a free retainer of an Anglo-Saxon lord **2 :** a Scottish feudal lord
thank \ˈthaŋk\ *vb* **:** to express gratitude to ⟨~*ed* them for the present⟩
thank•ful \ˈthaŋk-fəl\ *adj* **1 :** conscious of benefit received **2** ♦ **:** expressive of thanks **3 :** GLAD

♦ appreciative, grateful, obliged

thank•ful•ly \-fə-lē\ *adv* **1 :** in a thankful manner **2 :** as makes one thankful
thank•ful•ness \-nəs\ **:** the quality or state of being thankful
thank•less \ˈthaŋ-kləs\ *adj* **1 :** UNGRATEFUL **2 :** UNAPPRECIATED
thanks \ˈthaŋks\ *n pl* ♦ **:** an expression of gratitude

♦ appreciation, gratefulness, gratitude ***Ant*** ingratitude, ungratefulness

thanks•giv•ing \thaŋks-ˈgi-viŋ\ *n* **1 :** the act of giving thanks **2 :** a prayer expressing gratitude **3** *cap* **:** THANKSGIVING DAY
Thanksgiving Day *n* **:** a day appointed for giving thanks for divine goodness: as **a :** the fourth Thursday in November observed as a legal holiday in the U.S. **b :** the second Monday in October observed as a legal holiday in Canada
[1]that \ˈthat, thət\ *pron, pl* **those** \ˈthōz\ **1 :** the one indicated, mentioned, or understood ⟨~ is my house⟩ **2 :** the one farther away or first mentioned ⟨this is an elm, ~'s a maple⟩ **3 :** what has been indicated or mentioned ⟨after ~, we left⟩ **4 :** the one or ones : IT, THEY ⟨*those* who wish to leave may do so⟩
[2]that \thət, ˈthat\ *conj* **1 :** the following, namely ⟨he said ~ he would⟩; *also* **:** which is, namely ⟨there's a chance ~ it may fail⟩ **2 :** to this end or purpose ⟨shouted ~ all might hear⟩ **3 :** as to result in the following, namely ⟨so heavy ~ it can't be moved⟩ **4 :** for this reason, namely : BECAUSE ⟨we're glad ~ you came⟩
[3]that *adj, pl* **those** **1 :** being the one mentioned, indicated, or understood ⟨~ boy⟩ ⟨*those* people⟩ **2 :** being the one farther away or less immediately under discussion ⟨this chair or ~ one⟩
[4]that \thət, ˈthat\ *pron* **1 :** WHO, WHOM, WHICH ⟨the man ~ saw you⟩ ⟨the man ~ you saw⟩ ⟨the money ~ was spent⟩ **2 :** in, on, or at which ⟨the way ~ he drives⟩ ⟨the day ~ it rained⟩
[5]that \ˈthat\ *adv* **:** to such an extent or degree ⟨I like it, but not ~ much⟩
[1]thatch \ˈthach\ *vb* **:** to cover with or as if with thatch — **thatcher** *n*
[2]thatch *n* **1 :** plant material (as straw) for use as roofing **2 :** a mat of grass clippings accumulated next to the soil on a lawn **3 :** a covering of or as if of thatch ⟨a ~ of white hair⟩
thaw \ˈthȯ\ *vb* **1** ♦ **:** to melt or cause to melt **2 :** to become so warm as to melt ice or snow **3 :** to abandon aloofness or hostility — **thaw** *n*

♦ deliquesce, flux, fuse, liquefy, melt, run

THC \ˌtē-(ˌ)āch-ˈsē\ *n* **:** a physiologically active chemical from hemp plant resin that is the chief intoxicant in marijuana
[1]the \thə, *before vowel sounds usu* thē\ *definite article* **1 :** that in particular **2** — used before adjectives functioning as nouns ⟨a word to ~ wise⟩
[2]the *adv* **1 :** to what extent ⟨~ sooner, the better⟩ **2 :** to that extent ⟨the sooner, ~ better⟩
theat *abbr* theater; theatrical
the•ater *or chiefly Can and Brit* **the•atre** \ˈthē-ə-tər\ *n* **1** ♦ **:** a building or area for dramatic performances; *also* **:** a building or area for showing motion pictures **2 :** a place of enactment of significant events ⟨~ of war⟩ **3** ♦ **:** a place (as a lecture room) resembling a theater **4** ♦ **:** dramatic literature or performance

♦ [1, 3] arena, hall ♦ [4] stage, theatricals

theater–in–the–round *n* **:** a theater with the stage in the center of the auditorium
the•at•ri•cal \thē-ˈa-tri-kəl\ *also* **the•at•ric** \-trik\ *adj* **1 :** of or relating to the theater **2** ♦ **:** marked by artificiality of emotion : HISTRIONIC **3 :** marked by extravagant display : SHOWY

♦ dramatic, histrionic, melodramatic

the•at•ri•cals \-kəlz\ *n pl* ♦ **:** the performance of plays

♦ stage, theater (*or* theatre)

the•at•rics \thē-ˈa-triks\ *n pl* **1 :** THEATRICALS **2 :** staged or contrived effects
thee \ˈthē\ *pron, archaic objective case of* THOU
theft \ˈtheft\ *n* ♦ **:** the act or an instance of stealing

♦ larceny, robbery, thievery ♦ grab, rip-off

thegn \ˈthān\ *n* **:** THANE 1
their \thər, ˈther\ *adj* **:** of or relating to them or themselves
theirs \ˈtherz\ *pron* **:** their one : their ones
the•ism \ˈthē-ˌi-zəm\ *n* **:** belief in the existence of a god or gods — **the•ist** \-ist\ *n or adj* — **the•is•tic** \thē-ˈis-tik\ *adj*
them \thəm, ˈthem\ *pron, objective case of* THEY
theme \ˈthēm\ *n* **1** ♦ **:** a subject or topic of discourse or of artistic representation **2** ♦ **:** a written exercise : COMPOSITION **3 :** a melodic subject of a musical composition or movement — **the•mat•ic** \thi-ˈma-tik\ *adj*

♦ [1] content, matter, motif, motive, question, subject, topic ♦ [2] article, composition, essay, paper

them•selves \thəm-ˈselvz, them-\ *pron pl* **:** THEY, THEM — used reflexively, for emphasis, or in absolute constructions ⟨they govern ~⟩ ⟨they ~ came⟩ ⟨~ busy, they sent me⟩
[1]then \ˈthen\ *adv* **1 :** at that time **2 :** soon after that : NEXT **3** ♦ **:** in addition : BESIDES **4 :** in that case **5 :** CONSEQUENTLY

♦ additionally, again, also, besides, further, furthermore, likewise, more, moreover, too, withal, yet

[2]then *n* **:** that time ⟨since ~⟩
[3]then *adj* **:** existing or acting at that time ⟨the ~ attorney general⟩
thence \ˈthens, ˈthens\ *adv* **1 :** from that place **2** *archaic* **:** THENCEFORTH **3 :** from that fact : THEREFROM
thence•forth \-ˌfōrth\ *adv* **:** from that time forward : THEREAFTER
thence•for•ward \thens-ˈfȯr-wərd, thens-\ *also* **thence•for•wards** \-wərdz\ *adv* **:** onward from that place or time
the•oc•ra•cy \thē-ˈä-krə-sē\ *n, pl* **-cies** **1 :** government by officials regarded as divinely inspired **2 :** a state governed by a theocracy — **the•o•crat•ic** \ˌthē-ə-ˈkra-tik\ *adj*
theol *abbr* theological; theology
the•ol•o•gy \thē-ˈä-lə-jē\ *n, pl* **-gies** **1 :** the study of religious faith, practice, and experience; *esp* **:** the study of God and of God's relation to the world **2 :** a theory or system of theology — **the•o•lo•gian** \ˌthē-ə-ˈlō-jən\ *n* — **the•o•log•i•cal** \-ˈlä-ji-kəl\ *adj*
the•o•rem \ˈthē-ə-rəm, ˈthir-əm\ *n* **1 :** a statement especially in mathematics that has been or is to be proved **2 :** an idea accepted or proposed as a demonstrable truth : PROPOSITION
the•o•ret•i•cal \ˌthē-ə-ˈre-ti-kəl\ *also* **the•o•ret•ic** \-tik\ *adj* **1 :** relating to or having the character of theory **2** ♦ **:** existing only in theory : HYPOTHETICAL — **the•o•ret•i•cal•ly** \-ti-k(ə-)lē\ *adv*

♦ conjectural, hypothetical, speculative ***Ant*** actual, factual, real

the•o•rise *chiefly Brit var of* THEORIZE
the•o•rize \ˈthē-ə-ˌrīz\ *vb* **-rized; -riz•ing** **:** to form a theory : SPECULATE — **the•o•rist** \-rist\ *n*
the•o•ry \ˈthē-ə-rē, ˈthir-ē\ *n, pl* **-ries** **1 :** abstract thought **2 :** the general principles of a subject **3 :** a plausible or scientifically acceptable general principle offered to explain observed facts **4** ♦ **:** a hypothesis assumed for the sake of argument or investigation : CONJECTURE

♦ conjecture, hypothesis, proposition, supposition

the•os•o•phy \thē-ˈä-sə-fē\ *n* **:** belief about God and the world held to be based on mystical insight — **theo•soph•i•cal** \ˌthē-ə-ˈsä-fi-kəl\ *adj* — **the•os•o•phist** \thē-ˈä-sə-fist\ *n*
ther•a•peu•tic \ˌther-ə-ˈpyü-tik\ *adj* **:** of, relating to, or dealing with healing and especially with remedies for diseases — **ther•a•peu•ti•cal•ly** \-ti-k(ə-)lē\ *adv*
ther•a•peu•tics \ˌther-ə-ˈpyü-tiks\ *n* **:** a branch of medical or dental science dealing with the use of remedies
ther•a•py \ˈther-ə-pē\ *n, pl* **-pies** **:** treatment of bodily, mental, or behavioral disorders — **ther•a•pist** \-pist\ *n*
[1]there \ˈthar, ˈther\ *adv* **1 :** in or at that place — often used interjectionally **2 :** to or into that place : THITHER **3 :** in that matter or respect
[2]there \ˈthar, ˈther, thər\ *pron* — used as a function word to introduce a sentence or clause ⟨~'s a pen here⟩
[3]there \ˈthar, ˈther\ *n* **1 :** that place ⟨get away from ~⟩ **2 :** that point ⟨you take it from ~⟩
there•abouts \ˌthar-ə-ˈbau̇ts, ˌther-; ˈthar-ə-ˌbau̇ts, ˈther-\ *or* **there•about** \-ˈbau̇t, -ˌbau̇t\ *adv* **1 :** near that place or time **2 :** near that number, degree, or quantity
there•af•ter \thar-ˈaf-tər, ther-\ *adv* ♦ **:** after that : AFTERWARD

♦ after, afterward, later, subsequently

there•at \-ˈat\ *adv* **1 :** at that place **2 :** at that occurrence : on that account

there•by \th̲ar-ˈbī, th̲er-, ˈth̲ar-ˌbī, ˈth̲er-ˌbī\ *adv* **1** : by that : by that means **2** : connected with or with reference to that
there•for \th̲ar-ˈfȯr, th̲er-\ *adv* : for or in return for that
there•fore \ˈth̲ar-ˌfōr, ˈth̲er-\ *adv* ♦ : for that reason : CONSEQUENTLY

♦ accordingly, consequently, ergo, hence, so, thus, wherefore

there•from \th̲ar-ˈfrəm, th̲er-\ *adv* : from that or it
there•in \th̲ar-ˈin, th̲er-\ *adv* **1** : in or into that place, time, or thing **2** : in that respect
there•of \-ˈəv, -ˈäv\ *adv* **1** : of that or it **2** : from that : THEREFROM
there•on \-ˈȯn, -ˈän\ *adv* **1** : on that **2** *archaic* : THEREUPON 3
there•to \th̲ar-ˈtü, ther-\ *adv* : to that
there•un•to \th̲ar-ˈən-(ˌ)tü; ˌth̲ar-ən-ˈtü, ˌth̲er-\ *adv, archaic* : THERETO
there•upon \ˈth̲ar-ə-ˌpȯn, ˈth̲er-, -ˌpän; ˌth̲ar-ə-ˈpȯn, -ˈpän, ˌth̲er-\ *adv* **1** : on that matter **2** : for that reason : THEREFORE **3** : immediately after that : at once
there•with \th̲ar-ˈwith̲, ther-, -with\ *adv* **1** : with that **2** *archaic* : THEREUPON, FORTHWITH
there•with•al \ˈth̲ar-wi-ˌth̲ȯl, ˈth̲er-, -ˌthȯl\ *adv* **1** *archaic* : BESIDES **2** : THEREWITH
therm *abbr* thermometer
ther•mal \ˈthər-məl\ *adj* **1** : of, relating to, or caused by heat **2** : designed to prevent the loss of body heat ⟨~ underwear⟩ — **ther•mal•ly** *adv*
thermal pollution *n* : the discharge of heated liquid (as waste water from a factory) into natural waters at a temperature harmful to the environment
therm•is•tor \ˈthər-ˌmis-tər\ *n* : an electrical resistor whose resistance varies sharply with temperature
ther•mo•cline \ˈthər-mə-ˌklīn\ *n* : the region in a thermally stratified body of water that separates warmer surface water from cold deep water
ther•mo•cou•ple \ˈthər-mə-ˌkə-pəl\ *n* : a device for measuring temperature by measuring the temperature-dependent potential difference created at the junction of two dissimilar metals
ther•mo•dy•nam•ics \ˌthər-mə-dī-ˈna-miks\ *n* : physics that deals with the mechanical action or relations of heat — **ther•mo•dy•nam•ic** \-mik\ *adj* — **ther•mo•dy•nam•i•cal•ly** \-mi-k(ə-)lē\ *adv*
ther•mom•e•ter \thər-ˈmä-mə-tər\ *n* : an instrument for measuring temperature typically by the rise or fall of a liquid (as mercury) in a thin glass tube — **ther•mo•met•ric** \ˌthər-mə-ˈme-trik\ *adj* — **ther•mo•met•ri•cal•ly** \-tri-k(ə-)lē\ *adv*
ther•mo•nu•cle•ar \ˌthər-mō-ˈnü-klē-ər, -ˈnyü-\ *adj* **1** : of or relating to changes in the nucleus of atoms of low atomic weight (as hydrogen) that require a very high temperature (as in the hydrogen bomb) **2** : utilizing or relating to a thermonuclear bomb ⟨~ war⟩
ther•mo•plas•tic \ˌthər-mə-ˈplas-tik\ *adj* : capable of softening when heated and of hardening again when cooled ⟨~ resins⟩ — **thermoplastic** *n*
ther•mos \ˈthər-məs\ *n* : a cylindrical container with a vacuum between an inner and an outer wall used to keep liquids hot or cold
ther•mo•sphere \ˈthər-mə-ˌsfir\ *n* : the part of the earth's atmosphere that lies above the mesosphere and that is characterized by steadily increasing temperature with height
ther•mo•stat \ˈthər-mə-ˌstat\ *n* : a device that automatically controls temperature — **ther•mo•stat•ic** \ˌthər-mə-ˈsta-tik\ *adj* — **ther•mo•stat•i•cal•ly** \-ti-k(ə-)lē\ *adv*
the•sau•rus \thi-ˈsȯr-əs\ *n, pl* **-sau•ri** \-ˈsȯr-ˌī\ *or* **-sau•rus•es** \-ˈsȯr-ə-səz\ : a book of words and their synonyms — **the•sau•ral** \-ˈsȯr-əl\ *adj*
these *pl of* THIS
the•sis \ˈthē-səs\ *n, pl* **the•ses** \ˈthē-ˌsēz\ **1** ♦ : a proposition that a person advances and offers to maintain by argument **2** : an essay embodying results of original research; *esp* : one written for an academic degree

♦ argument, assertion, contention

¹thes•pi•an \ˈthes-pē-ən\ *adj, often cap* : relating to the drama : DRAMATIC
²thespian *n* : ACTOR
Thess *abbr* Thessalonians
Thes•sa•lo•nians \ˌthe-sə-ˈlō-nyənz, -nē-ənz\ *n* : either of two books of the New Testament of Christian Scripture
the•ta \ˈthā-tə\ *n* : the 8th letter of the Greek alphabet — Θ or θ
thew \ˈthü, ˈthyü\ *n* : MUSCLE, SINEW — usually used in plural
they \ˈth̲ā\ *pron* **1** : those individuals under discussion : the ones previously mentioned or referred to **2** : unspecified persons : PEOPLE
thi•a•mine \ˈthī-ə-mən, -ˌmēn\ *also* **thi•a•min** \-mən\ *n* : a vitamin of the vitamin B complex essential to normal metabolism and nerve function
¹thick \ˈthik\ *adj* **1** ♦ : having relatively great depth or extent from one surface to its opposite ⟨a ~ plank⟩; *also* : heavily built : THICKSET **2** ♦ : close-packed with units or individuals; *also* : NUMEROUS **3** ♦ : dense or viscous in consistency ⟨~ syrup⟩ **4** : marked by haze, fog, or mist ⟨~ weather⟩ **5** : measuring in thickness ⟨one meter ~⟩ **6** : imperfectly articulated : INDISTINCT ⟨~ speech⟩ **7** : lacking sharpness or quickness of sensibility or intellect : STUPID, OBTUSE **8** ♦ : associated on close terms : INTIMATE **9** : EXCESSIVE — **thick•ly** *adv*

♦ [1] broad, fat, thickset, wide ♦ [2] close, compact, crowded, dense, packed, serried, tight ♦ [2] flush, fraught, numerous, replete, rife ♦ [2] close, compact, crowded, dense, packed, serried, tight ♦ [3] syrupy, viscid, viscous ***Ant*** runny, soupy, thin, watery ♦ [8] bosom, chummy, close, familiar, friendly, intimate

²thick *n* **1** ♦ : the most crowded, intense, or active part **2** : the part of greatest thickness

♦ center, deep, depth, heart, height, middle, midst

thick and thin *n* : every difficulty and obstacle ⟨was loyal through *thick and thin*⟩
thick•en \ˈthi-kən\ *vb* : to make or become thick — **thick•en•er** *n*
thick•et \ˈthi-kət\ *n* ♦ : a dense growth of bushes or small trees

♦ brake, brushwood, chaparral, coppice, covert

thick•ness \ˈthik-nəs\ *n* **1** : the smallest of three dimensions ⟨length, width, and ~⟩ **2** ♦ : the quality or state of being thick **3** : LAYER, SHEET ⟨a single ~ of canvas⟩

♦ consistency, viscosity

thick•set \ˈthik-ˈset\ *adj* **1** : closely placed or planted **2** ♦ : having a thick body

♦ chunky, dumpy, heavyset, squat, stocky, stout, stubby, stumpy

thick–skinned \-ˈskind\ *adj* **1** : having a thick skin **2** ♦ : feeling no emotion or sympathy : CALLOUS **3** : not easily bothered by criticism or insult

♦ callous, hard, heartless, inhuman, inhumane, pitiless, soulless, unfeeling, unsympathetic

thief \ˈthēf\ *n, pl* **thieves** \ˈthēvz\ : one that steals especially secretly
thieve \ˈthēv\ *vb* **thieved; thiev•ing** ♦ : to take (the property of another) wrongfully and especially as an habitual or regular practice : STEAL

♦ appropriate, filch, hook, misappropriate, nip, pilfer, pocket, purloin, snitch, steal, swipe

thiev•ery \ˈthē-və-rē\ *n, pl* **-er•ies** ♦ : the act of stealing : THEFT

♦ larceny, robbery, theft

thigh \ˈthī\ *n* : the part of the vertebrate hind or lower limb between the knee and the hip
thigh•bone \ˈthī-ˌbōn\ *n* : FEMUR
thim•ble \ˈthim-bəl\ *n* : a cap or guard worn on the finger to push the needle in sewing — **thim•ble•ful** *n*
¹thin \ˈthin\ *adj* **thin•ner; thin•nest** **1** ♦ : having little extent from one surface through to its opposite : not thick : SLENDER **2** : not closely set or placed : SPARSE ⟨~ hair⟩ **3** : not dense or not dense enough : more fluid or rarefied than normal ⟨~ air⟩ ⟨~ syrup⟩ **4** ♦ : lacking substance, fullness, or strength ⟨~ broth⟩ **5** : FLIMSY **6** ♦ : not well fleshed : LEAN — **thin•ly** *adv* — **thin•ness** *n*

♦ [1] fine, narrow, skinny, slender, slim ♦ [4] dilute, watery, weak ♦ [6] lean, skinny, slender, slim, spare ***Ant*** chubby, corpulent, fat, gross, obese, overweight, plump, portly, rotund

²thin *vb* **thinned; thin•ning** ♦ : to make or become thin

♦ adulterate, dilute, water, weaken

thine \ˈth̲īn\ *pron, archaic* : one or the ones belonging to thee
thing \ˈthiŋ\ *n* **1** ♦ : a matter of concern : AFFAIR ⟨~*s* to do⟩ **2** *pl* : state of affairs ⟨~*s* are improving⟩ **3** : something that happens : EVENT ⟨the crime was a terrible ~⟩ **4** : something that is done : DEED, ACT ⟨expected great ~*s* of him⟩ **5** ♦ : a distinct entity : OBJECT **6** : an inanimate object distinguished from a living being **7** *pl* ♦ : movable property : EFFECTS **8** : an article of clothing **9** : DETAIL, POINT **10** : IDEA, NOTION **11** : something one likes to do : SPECIALTY ⟨doing her ~⟩ **12** : a single human being **13**

a : a product of work or activity **b** ♦ : the end or aim of effort or activity ⟨the ~ is to get well⟩

♦ [1] affair, business, matter ♦ [5] being, entity, individual, object, substance ♦ **things** [7] belongings, chattels, effects, holdings, paraphernalia, possessions ♦ [13b] aim, ambition, aspiration, design, dream, end, goal, intent, mark, meaning, object, objective, plan, pretension, purpose

think \ˈthiŋk\ *vb* **thought** \ˈthȯt\; **think•ing** **1** : to form or have in the mind **2** ♦ : to have as an opinion : BELIEVE **3** ♦ : to reflect on : PONDER **4** ♦ : to call to mind : REMEMBER **5** : REASON **6** : to form a mental picture of : IMAGINE **7** ♦ : to devise by thinking ⟨*thought* up a plan to escape⟩ — **think•er** *n*

♦ [2] believe, consider, deem, feel, figure, guess, hold, imagine, suppose ♦ *usu* **think about** *or* **think over** [3] chew over, cogitate, consider, contemplate, debate, deliberate, entertain, meditate, mull, ponder, question, ruminate, study, weigh ♦ *usu* **think of** [4] recall, recollect, remember, reminisce ♦ *usu* **think up** [7] concoct, contrive, cook up, devise, fabricate, invent, make up, manufacture

think•er \ˈthiŋ-kər\ *n* : one that thinks: as **a** : one that thinks in a specified way ⟨a slow ~⟩ **b** ♦ : one that has special capacity for thinking

♦ brain, genius, intellect, whiz, wizard

think tank *n* : an institute, corporation, or group organized for interdisciplinary research (as in technological or social problems)

thin•ner \ˈthi-nər\ *n* : a volatile liquid (as turpentine) used to thin paint

thin–skinned \ˈthin-ˈskind\ *adj* **1** : having a thin skin or rind **2** : extremely sensitive to criticism or insult

[1]**third** \ˈthərd\ *adj* : next after the second — **third** *or* **third•ly** *adv*

[2]**third** *n* **1** : one of three equal parts of something **2** : one that is number three in a countable series **3** : the 3d forward gear in an automotive vehicle

third degree *n* : the subjection of a prisoner to mental or physical torture to force a confession

third dimension *n* **1** : thickness, depth, or apparent thickness or depth that confers solidity on an object **2** : a quality that confers reality — **third–dimensional** *adj*

third world *n, often cap T&W* : the aggregate of the underdeveloped nations of the world

[1]**thirst** \ˈthərst\ *n* **1** : a feeling of dryness in the mouth and throat associated with a desire to drink; *also* : a bodily condition producing this **2** ♦ : an ardent desire ⟨a ~ for knowledge⟩

♦ appetite, craving, desire, drive, eagerness, hankering, hunger, itch, longing, lust, passion, urge, yearning, yen

[2]**thirst** *vb* **1** : to need drink : suffer thirst **2** ♦ : to have a strong desire

♦ *usu* **thirst for** ache for, covet, crave, desire, die (to *or* for), hanker for, hunger for, long for, lust (for *or* after), pine for, repine for, want, wish for, yearn for

thirsty \ˈthər-stē\ *adj* **thirst•i•er; -est** **1 a** : feeling thirst **b** ♦ : deficient in moisture ⟨~ land⟩ **2** ♦ : having a strong desire : AVID

♦ [1b] arid, dry, sere ♦ [2] ardent, athirst, avid, eager, enthusiastic, keen

thir•teen \ˌthər-ˈtēn\ *n* : one more than 12 — **thirteen** *adj or pron* — **thir•teenth** \-ˈtēnth\ *adj or n*

thir•ty \ˈthər-tē\ *n, pl* **thirties** : three times 10 — **thir•ti•eth** \-tē-əth\ *adj or n* — **thirty** *adj or pron*

[1]**this** \ˈt͟his\ *pron, pl* **these** \ˈt͟hēz\ **1** : the one close or closest in time or space ⟨~ is your book⟩ **2** : what is in the present or under immediate observation or discussion ⟨~ is a mess⟩; *also* : what is happening or being done now ⟨after ~ we'll leave⟩

[2]**this** *adj, pl* **these** **1** : being the one near, present, just mentioned, or more immediately under observation ⟨~ book⟩ **2** : constituting the immediate past or future ⟨friends all *these* years⟩

[3]**this** *adv* : to such an extent or degree ⟨we need a book about ~ big⟩

this•tle \ˈthi-səl\ *n* : any of various tall prickly composite plants with often showy heads of tightly packed tubular flowers

this•tle•down \-ˌdau̇n\ *n* : the down from the ripe flower head of a thistle

[1]**thith•er** \ˈthi-t͟hər\ *adv* : to that place

[2]**thither** *adj* : being on the farther side

thith•er•ward \-wərd\ *adv* : toward that place : THITHER

thong \ˈthȯŋ\ *n* **1** : a strip especially of leather or hide **2** : a sandal held on the foot by a thong between the toes **3** : a narrow strip of swimwear or underwear that passes between the thighs

tho•rax \ˈthōr-ˌaks\ *n, pl* **tho•rax•es** *or* **tho•ra•ces** \ˈthōr-ə-ˌsēz\ **1** : the part of the body of a mammal between the neck and the abdomen; *also* : its cavity containing the heart and lungs **2** : the middle of the three main divisions of the body of an insect — **tho•rac•ic** \thə-ˈra-sik\ *adj*

tho•ri•um \ˈthōr-ē-əm\ *n* : a radioactive metallic chemical element

thorn \ˈthȯrn\ *n* **1** : a woody plant bearing sharp processes **2** : a sharp rigid plant process that is usually a modified leafless branch **3** ♦ : something that causes distress

♦ aggravation, annoyance, bother, exasperation, frustration, hassle, headache, inconvenience, irritant, nuisance, peeve, pest, problem

thorny \ˈthȯr-nē\ *adj* **thorn•i•er; -est** **1** ♦ : full of thorns **2** ♦ : full of difficulties or controversial points

♦ [1] brambly, prickly, scratchy ♦ [2] catchy, delicate, difficult, knotty, problematic, spiny, ticklish, touchy, tough, tricky

thor•ough \ˈthər-ō\ *adj* **1** ♦ : testing all possibilities or considering all elements : EXHAUSTIVE ⟨a ~ search⟩ **2** : very careful : PAINSTAKING ⟨a ~ scholar⟩ **3** : having full mastery **4** ♦ : marked by attention to many details ⟨a ~ description⟩ **5** ♦ : complete in all respects ⟨~ pleasure⟩ — **thor•ough•ness** *n*

♦ [1] all-out, clean, complete, comprehensive, exhaustive, full-scale, out-and-out, thoroughgoing, total ♦ [4] circumstantial, detailed, elaborate, full, minute ♦ [5] absolute, all-out, complete, perfect, pure, total, utter

[1]**thor•ough•bred** \ˈthər-ə-ˌbred\ *adj* **1** ♦ : bred from the best blood through a long line **2** *cap* : of or relating to the Thoroughbred breed of horses **3** : marked by high-spirited grace

♦ full-blooded, purebred

[2]**thoroughbred** *n* **1** *cap* : any of an English breed of light speedy horses kept chiefly for racing **2** : one (as a pedigreed animal) of excellent quality

thor•ough•fare \-ˌfar\ *n* ♦ : a public road or street

♦ artery, avenue, drag, drive, highway, pass, pike, road, route, row, street, trace, turnpike, way

thor•ough•go•ing \ˌthər-ə-ˈgō-iŋ\ *adj* ♦ : marked by thoroughness or zeal

♦ all-out, clean, complete, comprehensive, exhaustive, full-scale, out-and-out, thorough, total

thor•ough•ly \ˌthər-ə-lē\ *adv* ♦ : in a thorough manner or degree

♦ altogether, completely, dead, entirely, fast, flat, full, fully, perfectly, quite, well, wholly ♦ completely, exhaustively, fully, minutely, roundly, totally

thorp \ˈthȯrp\ *n, archaic* : VILLAGE

[1]**thou** \ˈt͟hau̇\ *pron, archaic* : the person addressed

[2]**thou** \ˈthau̇\ *n, pl* **thou** : a thousand of something (as dollars)

[1]**though** \ˈt͟hō\ *conj* **1** ♦ : despite the fact that ⟨~ the odds are hopeless, they fight on⟩ **2** : granting that ⟨~ it may look bad, still, all is not lost⟩

♦ albeit, although, howbeit, when, while

[2]**though** *adv* ♦ : in spite of that : HOWEVER ⟨not for long, ~⟩

♦ but, howbeit, however, nevertheless, nonetheless, notwithstanding, still, withal, yet

[1]**thought** \ˈthȯt\ *past and past part of* THINK

[2]**thought** *n* **1** : the process of thinking **2** ♦ : serious consideration **3** : reasoning power **4** : the power to imagine : CONCEPTION **5** ♦ : an individual act or product of thinking : IDEA **6** : OPINION, BELIEF

♦ [2] consideration, debate, deliberation ♦ [5] concept, idea, image, impression, notion, picture

thought•ful \ˈthȯt-fəl\ *adj* **1** ♦ : absorbed in thought **2** ♦ : marked by careful thinking ⟨a ~ essay⟩ **3** ♦ : considerate of others ⟨a ~ host⟩ — **thought•ful•ness** *n*

♦ [1] contemplative, meditative, melancholy, pensive, reflective, ruminant ♦ [2] advised, calculated, deliberate, measured, reasoned, studied, thought-out ♦ [3] attentive, considerate, kind, solicitous ***Ant*** heedless, inconsiderate, thoughtless, unthinking

thought•ful•ly \-fə-lē\ *adv* ♦ : in a thoughtful manner

♦ courteously, kindly, nicely, well

thought•less \-ləs\ *adj* **1** : insufficiently alert : CARELESS ⟨a ~

worker> **2** : RECKLESS <a ~ act> **3** ♦ : lacking concern for others : INCONSIDERATE <~ remarks> — **thought·less·ly** *adv* — **thought·less·ness** *n*

♦ discourteous, ill-bred, ill-mannered, impertinent, impolite, inconsiderate, rude, uncivil, ungracious, unmannerly

thought–out *adj* ♦ : produced or arrived at through mental effort and especially through careful and thorough consideration

♦ advised, calculated, deliberate, knowing, measured, reasoned, studied, thoughtful

thou·sand \ˈthau̇z-ᵊnd\ *n, pl* **thousands** *or* **thousand** : 10 times 100 — **thousand** *adj* — **thou·sandth** \-ᵊnth\ *adj or n*
thousands place *n* : the place four to the left of the decimal point in an Arabic number
thrall \ˈthrȯl\ *n* **1** ♦ : a servant slave : BONDMAN **2** ♦ : a state of servitude

♦ [1] bondman, chattel, slave ♦ [2] bondage, enslavement, servitude, slavery, yoke

thrall·dom *or* **thral·dom** \ˈthrȯl-dəm\ *n* : the state or condition of servitude
thrash \ˈthrash\ *vb* **1** : THRESH 1 **2** ♦ : to defeat decisively or severely : BEAT **3** : to move about violently **4** : to go over again and again <~ over the matter>; *also* : to hammer out <~ out a plan> **5** ♦ : to swing, beat, or strike in the manner of a rapidly moving flail

♦ [2] beat, best, clobber, conquer, crush, defeat, drub, lick, rout, skunk, triumph, trounce, wallop, whip, win ♦ [5] flail, flog, hide, lash, scourge, slash, switch, whale, whip

¹**thrash·er** \ˈthra-shər\ *n* : one that thrashes or threshes
²**thrasher** *n* : any of various long-tailed American songbirds related to the mockingbird
¹**thread** \ˈthred\ *n* **1** : a thin continuous strand of spun and twisted textile fibers **2** : something resembling a textile thread **3** : the ridge or groove that winds around a screw **4** : a line of reasoning or train of thought **5** : a continuing element
²**thread** *vb* **1** : to pass a thread through the eye of (a needle) **2** : to pass (as film) through something **3** : to make one's way through or between **4** : to put together on or as if on a thread <~ beads> **5** : to form a screw thread on or in **6** ♦ : to interweave with or as if with threads

♦ interlace, intersperse, intertwine, interweave, lace, weave, wreathe

thread·bare \-ˌbar\ *adj* **1** ♦ : worn to the point that the threads show : having the nap worn off **2** ♦ : having no interest or freshness : TRITE

♦ [1] ragged, ratty, seedy, shabby, tattered, worn-out ♦ [2] banal, commonplace, hackneyed, musty, stale, stereotyped, tired, trite

thready \ˈthre-dē\ *adj* **1** : consisting of or bearing fibers of filaments <a ~ bark> **2** : lacking in fullness, body, or vigor
threat \ˈthret\ *n* **1** : an expression of intent to do harm **2** ♦ : one that threatens

♦ danger, hazard, menace, peril, pitfall, risk, trouble

threat·en \ˈthret-ᵊn\ *vb* **1** : to utter threats against **2** : to give signs or warning of : PORTEND **3** ♦ : to hang over as a threat : MENACE **4** : to cause to feel insecure or anxious — **threat·en·ing·ly** *adv*

♦ hang, hover, menace, overhang

threat·ened *adj* : having an uncertain chance of continued survival; *esp* : likely to become an endangered species
three \ˈthrē\ *n* **1** : one more than two **2** : the 3d in a set or series **3** : something having three units — **three** *adj or pron*
3–D \ˈthrē-ˈdē\ *n* : a three-dimensional form or picture
three–dimensional *adj* **1** : relating to or having three dimensions **2** : giving the illusion of varying distances <a ~ picture>
three·fold \ˈthrē-ˌfōld, -ˈfōld\ *adj* **1** ♦ : having three parts : TRIPLE **2** : being three times as great or as many — **three·fold** \-ˈfōld\ *adv*

♦ treble, tripartite, triple

three·pence \ˈthre-pəns, ˈthri-, ˈthrə-, *US also* ˈthrē-pens\ *n* **1** *pl* **threepence** *or* **three·penc·es** : a coin worth three pennies **2** : the sum of three British pennies
three–ring circus *n* ♦ : something wild, confusing, engrossing, or entertaining

♦ bedlam, circus, hell, madhouse

three·score \ˈthrē-ˈskōr\ *adj* : being three times twenty : SIXTY
three·some \ˈthrē-səm\ *n* ♦ : a group of three persons or things

♦ triad, trio, triple, triplet

thren·o·dy \ˈthre-nə-dē\ *n, pl* **-dies** ♦ : a song of lamentation : ELEGY

♦ dirge, elegy, lament, requiem

thresh \ˈthrash, ˈthresh\ *vb* **1** : to separate (as grain from straw) mechanically **2** : THRASH — **thresh·er** *n*
thresh·old \ˈthresh-ˌhōld\ *n* **1** : the sill of a door **2** ♦ : a point or place of beginning or entering : OUTSET **3** : a point at which a physiological or psychological effect begins to be produced

♦ beginning, birth, commencement, dawn, genesis, launch, morning, onset, outset, start

threw *past of* THROW
thrice \ˈthrīs\ *adv* **1** : three times **2** : in a threefold manner or degree
thrift \ˈthrift\ *n* ♦ : careful management especially of money : FRUGALITY — **thrift·i·ly** \ˈthrif-tə-lē\ *adv*

♦ economy, frugality, husbandry, providence

thrift·less \ˈthrift-ləs\ *adj* ♦ : careless, wasteful, or incompetent in handling money or resources

♦ extravagant, prodigal, profligate, spendthrift, unthrifty, wasteful

thrifty \ˈthrif-tē\ *adj* **thrift·i·er; -est** ♦ : given to or marked by economy and good management

♦ economical, frugal, provident, sparing

¹**thrill** \ˈthril\ *vb* **1** ♦ : to have or cause to have sudden sharp feeling of excitement; *also* : TINGLE, SHIVER **2** : TREMBLE, VIBRATE — **thrill·er** *n*

♦ electrify, excite, exhilarate, galvanize, intoxicate, shiver, tingle, titillate, turn on

²**thrill** *n* ♦ : an instantaneous excitement

♦ bang, exhilaration, kick, titillation

thrill·ing *adj* ♦ : causing an instantaneous surge of emotion — **thrill·ing·ly** *adv*

♦ breathtaking, electric, exciting, exhilarating, rousing, stirring

thrive \ˈthrīv\ *vb* **thrived** *or* **throve** \ˈthrōv\; **thrived** *also* **thriv·en** \ˈthri-vən\; **thriv·ing** **1** ♦ : to grow luxuriantly : FLOURISH **2** ♦ : to gain in wealth or possessions : PROSPER

♦ [1] burgeon, flourish, prosper ♦ [2] flourish, prosper, succeed

throat \ˈthrōt\ *n* : the part of the neck in front of the spinal column; *also* : the passage through it to the stomach and lungs — **throat·ed** *adj*
throaty \ˈthrō-tē\ *adj* **throat·i·er; -est** **1** ♦ : uttered or produced from low in the throat <a ~ voice> **2** ♦ : heavy, thick, or deep as if from the throat — **throat·i·ly** \-tə-lē\ *adv* — **throat·i·ness** \-tē-nəs\ *n*

♦ [1] bass, deep, low ♦ [2] coarse, gravelly, gruff, hoarse, husky, scratchy

¹**throb** \ˈthräb\ *vb* **throbbed; throb·bing** ♦ : to pulsate or pound especially with abnormal force or rapidity : BEAT

♦ beat, palpitate, pitter-patter, pulsate, pulse

²**throb** *n* ♦ : a rhythmic pulsation or beating : BEAT, PULSE

♦ beat, palpitation, pulsation, pulse

throe \ˈthrō\ *n* **1** : a sudden spasm or pang **2** *pl* : a hard or painful struggle
throm·bo·sis \thräm-ˈbō-səs\ *n, pl* **-bo·ses** \-ˌsēz\ : the formation or presence of a clot in a blood vessel — **throm·bot·ic** \-ˈbä-tik\ *adj*
throm·bus \ˈthräm-bəs\ *n, pl* **throm·bi** \-ˌbī\ : a clot of blood formed within a blood vessel and remaining attached to its place of origin
throne \ˈthrōn\ *n* **1** : the chair of state of a sovereign or high dignitary **2** : royal power : SOVEREIGNTY
¹**throng** \ˈthrȯŋ\ *n* **1** ♦ : a multitude of assembled persons **2** : a crowding together of many persons

♦ army, crowd, crush, drove, flock, horde, host, legion, mob, multitude, press, swarm

²**throng** *vb* **thronged; throng·ing** ♦ : to crowd together in great numbers

♦ crowd, flock, mob, swarm

[1]**throt·tle** \ˈthrät-ᵊl\ *vb* **throt·tled; throt·tling** **1** ♦ **:** to compress the throat of **:** CHOKE **2 :** SUPPRESS **3 :** to reduce the speed of (an engine) by closing the throttle — **throt·tler** *n*

♦ choke, garrote, strangle

[2]**throttle** *n* **:** a valve regulating the flow of steam or fuel to an engine; *also* **:** the lever controlling this valve

[1]**through** \ˈthrü\ *prep* **1 :** from one end or side to the other of ⟨go ~ the door⟩ **2 :** by way of ⟨entered ~ a skylight⟩ **3** ♦ **:** in the midst of ⟨a path ~ the trees⟩ **4** ♦ **:** by means of ⟨succeeded ~ hard work⟩ **5** ♦ **:** over the whole of ⟨rumors swept ~ the office⟩ ⟨homes scattered ~ the valley⟩ **6** ♦ **:** during the whole of ⟨~ the night⟩ **7 :** to and including ⟨Monday ~ Friday⟩

♦ [3] amid, among, midst ♦ [4] because of, due to, owing to, with ♦ [5] about, around, over, round, throughout ♦ [6] during, over, throughout

[2]**through** *adv* **1** ♦ **:** from one end or side to the other **2 :** from beginning to end **:** to completion ⟨see it ~⟩ **3 :** to the core **:** THOROUGHLY ⟨he was wet ~⟩ **4 :** into the open **:** OUT ⟨break ~⟩

♦ across, over

[3]**through** *adj* **1 :** permitting free passage ⟨a ~ street⟩ **2 :** going from point of origin to destination without change or transfer ⟨a ~ train⟩ **3 :** coming from or going to points outside a local area ⟨~ traffic⟩ **4** ♦ **:** arrived at completion or accomplishment **:** FINISHED ⟨~ with the job⟩

♦ complete, done, down, over, up

[1]**through·out** \thrü-ˈau̇t\ *adv* **1 :** in or to every part **:** EVERYWHERE **2 :** from beginning to end

[2]**throughout** *prep* **1** ♦ **:** in or to every part of **2** ♦ **:** during the whole period of

♦ [1] about, around, over, round, through ♦ [2] during, over, through

through·put \ˈthrü-ˌpu̇t\ *n* **:** OUTPUT, PRODUCTION ⟨the ~ of a computer⟩

throve *past of* THRIVE

[1]**throw** \ˈthrō\ *vb* **threw** \ˈthrü\; **thrown** \ˈthrōn\; **throw·ing** **1** ♦ **:** to propel through the air especially with a forward motion of the hand and arm ⟨~ a ball⟩ **2 :** to cause to fall or fall off **3** ♦ **:** to put suddenly in a certain position or condition ⟨~ into panic⟩ ⟨~ on a coat⟩ **4 :** to put on or take off hastily ⟨~ on a coat⟩ **5 :** to lose intentionally ⟨~ a game⟩ **6 :** to move (a lever) so as to connect or disconnect parts of something (as a clutch) **7 :** to act as host for ⟨~ a party⟩ — **throw·er** *n*

♦ [1] cast, catapult, chuck, dash, fire, fling, heave, hurl, hurtle, launch, peg, pelt, pitch, sling, toss ♦ *usu* **throw on** [3] don, put on, slip

[2]**throw** *n* **1 :** an act of throwing, hurling, or flinging; *also* **:** CAST **2 :** the distance a missile may be thrown **3 :** a light coverlet **4 :** a woman's scarf or light wrap

throw·away \ˈthrō-ə-ˌwā\ *n* **:** something that is or is designed to be thrown away especially after one use

throw away *vb* **1** ♦ **:** to get rid of as worthless or unnecessary **2** ♦ **:** to use in a foolish or wasteful manner

♦ [1] cast, discard, ditch, dump, fling, jettison, junk, lose, reject, scrap, shed, shuck, slough, throw out, unload ♦ [2] blow, dissipate, fritter, lavish, misspend, run through, spend, squander, waste

throw·back \-ˌbak\ *n* **:** reversion to an earlier type or phase; *also* **:** an instance or product of this

throw out *vb* **1** ♦ **:** to remove from a place, office, or employment usually in a sudden or unexpected manner **2** ♦ **:** to get rid of as worthless or unnecessary

♦ [1] banish, boot (out), bounce, cast, chase, dismiss, drum, eject, expel, oust, rout, run off ♦ [2] cast, discard, ditch, dump, fling, jettison, junk, lose, reject, scrap, shed, shuck, slough, throw away, unload

throw up *vb* **1 :** to build hurriedly **2** ♦ **:** to discharge the contents of the stomach through the mouth **:** VOMIT

♦ gag, heave, spit up, vomit

thrum \ˈthrəm\ *vb* **thrummed; thrum·ming :** to play or pluck a stringed instrument idly **:** STRUM

thrush \ˈthrəsh\ *n* **:** any of numerous small or medium-sized songbirds that are mostly of a plain color often with spotted underparts

[1]**thrust** \ˈthrəst\ *vb* **thrust; thrust·ing** **1** ♦ **:** to push or drive with force **:** SHOVE **2 :** STAB, PIERCE **3 :** INTERJECT **4 :** to press the acceptance of upon someone

♦ drive, propel, push, shove

[2]**thrust** *n* **1 :** a lunge with a pointed weapon **2 :** ATTACK **3 :** the pressure of one part of a construction against another (as of an arch against an abutment) **4 :** the force produced by a propeller or jet or rocket engine that drives a vehicle (as an aircraft) forward **5 :** a violent push **:** SHOVE **6 :** a prominent or essential element

thrust·er *also* **thrust·or** \ˈthrəs-tər\ *n* **:** one that thrusts; *esp* **:** a rocket engine

thru·way \ˈthrü-ˌwā\ *n* **:** EXPRESSWAY

[1]**thud** \ˈthəd\ *n* **1 :** a forcible stroke delivered with a part of the body or with an instrument **:** BLOW **2 :** a dull sound

[2]**thud** *vb* **thud·ded; thud·ding** ♦ **:** to move or strike so as to make a thud

♦ bang, bash, bump, collide, crash, hit, impact, knock, ram, slam, smash, strike, swipe

thug \ˈthəg\ *n* ♦ **:** a brutal ruffian or assassin — **thug·gish** *adj*

♦ bully, gangster, goon, hood, hoodlum, mobster, mug, punk, rowdy, ruffian, tough

thu·li·um \ˈthü-lē-əm, ˈthyü-\ *n* **:** a rare metallic chemical element

[1]**thumb** \ˈthəm\ *n* **1 :** the short thick first digit of the human hand or a corresponding digit of a lower animal **2 :** the part of a glove or mitten that covers the thumb

[2]**thumb** *vb* **1 :** to leaf through (pages) with the thumb **2 :** to wear or soil with the thumb by frequent handling **3 :** to request or obtain (a ride) in a passing automobile by signaling with the thumb

[1]**thumb·nail** \ˈthəm-ˌnāl\ *n* **:** the nail of the thumb

[2]**thumbnail** *adj* **:** BRIEF, CONCISE ⟨a ~ description⟩

thumb·print \-ˌprint\ *n* **:** an impression made by the thumb

thumb·screw \-ˌskrü\ *n* **1 :** a screw with a head that may be turned by the thumb and forefinger **2 :** a device of torture for squeezing the thumb

thumb·tack \-ˌtak\ *n* **:** a tack with a broad flat head for pressing with one's thumb into a board or wall

[1]**thump** \ˈthəmp\ *vb* **1 :** to strike with or as if with something thick or heavy so as to cause a dull sound **2 :** to strike heavily or repeatedly **:** POUND

[2]**thump** *n* ♦ **:** a blow with or as if with something blunt or heavy; *also* **:** the sound made by such a blow

♦ blow, clout, hit, pound, punch, thud, thwack, wallop, whack

[1]**thun·der** \ˈthən-dər\ *n* **1 :** the sound following a flash of lightning; *also* **:** a noise like such a sound **2 :** a loud utterance or threat

[2]**thunder** *vb* **1 :** to produce thunder **2** ♦ **:** to utter or emit a full loud prolonged sound **:** ROAR

♦ bellow, boom, growl, roar

thun·der·bolt \-ˌbōlt\ *n* **:** a flash of lightning with its accompanying thunder

thun·der·clap \-ˌklap\ *n* **1 :** a crash of thunder **2** ♦ **:** something sharp, loud, or sudden like a clap of thunder

♦ bang, blast, boom, clap, crack, crash, pop, report, slam, smash, snap, thwack, whack

thun·der·cloud \-ˌklau̇d\ *n* **:** a cloud charged with electricity and producing lightning and thunder

thun·der·head \-ˌhed\ *n* **:** a large cumulus or cumulonimbus cloud often appearing before a thunderstorm

thun·der·ous \ˈthən-də-rəs\ *adj* ♦ **:** producing thunder; *also* **:** making a noise like thunder — **thun·der·ous·ly** *adv*

♦ booming, clamorous (*or* clamourous), deafening, earsplitting, loud, piercing, resounding, ringing, roaring, sonorous, stentorian

thun·der·show·er \ˈthən-dər-ˌshau̇-ər\ *n* **:** a shower accompanied by thunder and lightning

thun·der·storm \-ˌstȯrm\ *n* **:** a storm accompanied by thunder and lightning

thun·der·struck \-ˌstrək\ *adj* ♦ **:** stunned as if struck by a thunderbolt

♦ amazed, awestruck, stunned

Thurs *or* **Thu** *abbr* Thursday

Thurs·day \ˈthərz-dē, -ˌdā\ *n* **:** the 5th day of the week

thus \ˈt͟həs\ *adv* **1 :** in this or that manner **2** ♦ **:** to this degree or extent **:** SO ⟨~ far⟩ **3** ♦ **:** because of this or that **:** HENCE

♦ *usu* **thus far** [2] heretofore, hitherto, so, yet ♦ [3] accordingly, consequently, ergo, hence, so, therefore, wherefore

[1]thwack \ˈthwak\ *vb* **:** to strike with or as if with something flat or heavy
[2]thwack *n* **1 :** a heavy blow **:** WHACK **2** ♦ **:** the sound of or as if of a heavy blow

♦ bang, blast, boom, clap, crack, crash, pop, report, slam, smash, snap, whack

[1]thwart \ˈthwȯrt\ *vb* **1** ♦ **:** to oppose successfully **:** FOIL **2 :** BLOCK, DEFEAT

♦ baffle, balk, beat, checkmate, foil, frustrate

[2]thwart \ˈthwȯrt, *naut often* ˈthȯrt\ *adv* **:** ATHWART
[3]thwart *adj* **:** situated or placed across something else
[4]thwart \ˈthwȯrt\ *n* **:** a seat extending across a boat
thy \ˈthī\ *adj, archaic* **:** of, relating to, or done by or to thee or thyself
thyme \ˈtīm, ˈthīm\ *n* **:** a garden mint with small aromatic leaves used especially in seasoning; *also* **:** its leaves so used
thy•mine \ˈthī-ˌmēn\ *n* **:** a pyrimidine base that is one of the four bases coding genetic information in the molecular chain of DNA
thy•mus \ˈthī-məs\ *n, pl* **thy•mus•es :** a glandular organ of the neck region that is composed largely of lymphoid tissue, functions especially in the development of the immune system, and tends to atrophy in the adult
thy•ris•tor \thī-ˈris-tər\ *n* **:** a semiconductor device that acts as a switch, rectifier, or voltage regulator
thy•roid \ˈthī-ˌrȯid\ *n* **:** a large 2-lobed endocrine gland that lies at the base of the neck and produces several iodine-containing hormones that affect growth, development, and metabolism — **thy•roid** *also* **thy•roi•dal** \thī-ˈrȯi-dᵊl\ *adj*
thy•rox•ine *or* **thy•rox•in** \thī-ˈräk-ˌsēn, -sən\ *n* **:** an iodine-containing hormone that is produced by the thyroid gland, increases metabolic rate, and is used to treat thyroid disorders
thy•self \thī-ˈself\ *pron, archaic* **:** YOURSELF
Ti *symbol* titanium
ti•ara \tē-ˈar-ə, -ˈer-, -ˈär-\ *n* **1 :** a 3-tiered crown worn by the pope **2 :** a decorative headband or semicircle for formal wear by women
Ti•bet•an \tə-ˈbet-ᵊn\ *n* **1 :** the language of the Tibetan people **2 :** a native or inhabitant of Tibet — **Tibetan** *adj*
tib•ia \ˈti-bē-ə\ *n, pl* **-i•ae** \-bē-ˌē\ *also* **-i•as :** the inner of the two bones of the vertebrate hind or lower limb between the knee and the ankle
tic \ˈtik\ *n* **1 :** a local and habitual twitching of muscles especially of the face **2** ♦ **:** a frequent usually unconscious quirk of behavior or speech

♦ crotchet, eccentricity, idiosyncrasy, mannerism, oddity, peculiarity, quirk, singularity, trick

[1]tick \ˈtik\ *n* **:** any of a large group of small bloodsucking arachnids
[2]tick *n* **:** the fabric case of a mattress or pillow; *also* **:** a mattress consisting of a tick and its filling
[3]tick *n* **1 :** a light rhythmic audible tap or beat **2 :** a small mark used to draw attention to or check something
[4]tick *vb* **1 :** to make the sound of a tick or series of ticks **2** ♦ **:** to mark, count, or announce by or as if by ticking beats — often used with *off* **3** ♦ **:** to mark or check with a tick — usually used with *off* **4 :** to function as an operating mechanism **:** RUN

♦ *usu* **tick off** [2, 3] detail, enumerate, itemize, list, numerate, rehearse

[5]tick *n, chiefly Brit* **:** CREDIT; *also* **:** a credit account
tick•er \ˈti-kər\ *n* **1 :** something (as a watch) that ticks **2 :** a telegraph instrument that prints information (as stock prices) on paper tape **3** *slang* **:** HEART
ticker tape *n* **:** the paper ribbon on which a telegraphic ticker prints
[1]tick•et \ˈti-kət\ *n* **1 a :** CERTIFICATE, LICENSE, PERMIT **b** ♦ **:** a certificate or token showing that a fare or admission fee has been paid **2 :** a marker used for identification or classification **:** TAG, LABEL **3 :** SLATE 4 **4 :** a summons issued to a traffic offender

♦ check, note, pass, token

[2]ticket *vb* **1** ♦ **:** to attach a ticket to **2 :** to furnish or serve with a ticket

♦ label, mark, tag

tick•ing \ˈti-kiŋ\ *n* **:** a strong fabric used in upholstering and as a mattress covering
tick•le \ˈti-kəl\ *vb* **tick•led; tick•ling 1 :** to excite or stir up agreeably **:** PLEASE, AMUSE **2 :** to have a tingling sensation **3 :** to touch (as a body part) lightly so as to cause uneasiness, laughter, or spasmodic movements — **tickle** *n* — **tick•ler** *n*
tick•lish \-kə-lish\ *adj* **1 :** overly sensitive **:** TOUCHY **2 :** UNSTABLE ⟨a ~ foothold⟩ **3** ♦ **:** requiring delicate handling ⟨~ subject⟩ **4 :** sensitive to tickling — **tick•lish•ly** *adv* — **tick•lish•ness** *n*

♦ catchy, delicate, difficult, knotty, problematic, spiny, thorny, touchy, tough, tricky

tidal wave *n* **1 :** an unusually high sea wave that sometimes follows an earthquake **2 :** an unusual rise of water alongshore due to strong winds
tid•bit \ˈtid-ˌbit\ *n* ♦ **:** a choice morsel

♦ bite, morsel, mouthful, nibble, taste ♦ dainty, delicacy, goody, treat

[1]tide \ˈtīd\ *n* **1 :** the alternate rising and falling of the surface of the ocean **2** ♦ **:** something that fluctuates like the tides of the sea — **tid•al** \ˈtīd-ᵊl\ *adj*

♦ current, drift, leaning, run, tendency, trend, wind

[2]tide *vb* **tid•ed; tid•ing :** to carry through or help along as if by the tide ⟨a loan to ~ us over⟩
tide•land \ˈtīd-ˌland, -lənd\ *n* **1 :** land overflowed during flood tide **2 :** land under the ocean within a nation's territorial waters — often used in plural
tide•wa•ter \-ˌwȯ-tər, -ˌwä-\ *n* **1 :** water overflowing land at flood tide **2 :** low-lying coastal land
tid•ings \ˈtī-diŋz\ *n pl* ♦ **:** previously unknown information **:** NEWS

♦ intelligence, item, news, story, word

[1]ti•dy \ˈtī-dē\ *adj* **ti•di•er; -est 1** ♦ **:** well ordered and cared for **:** NEAT **2 a** ♦ **:** exceeding most other things of like kind especially in quantity or size **:** LARGE ⟨a ~ sum⟩ **b** ♦ **:** significantly great **:** SUBSTANTIAL — **ti•di•ness** \ˈtī-dē-nəs\ *n*

♦ [1] crisp, neat, orderly, shipshape, snug, trim, uncluttered ♦ [2a, b] considerable, good, goodly, healthy, large, respectable, significant, sizable, substantial

[2]tidy *vb* **ti•died; ti•dy•ing 1 :** to put in order **2 :** to make things tidy
[3]tidy *n, pl* **tidies :** a decorated covering used to protect the back or arms of a chair from wear or soil
[1]tie \ˈtī\ *n* **1 :** a line, ribbon, or cord used for fastening, uniting, or closing **2 :** a structural element (as a beam or rod) holding two pieces together **3 :** one of the cross supports to which railroad rails are fastened **4** ♦ **:** a connecting link **:** BOND ⟨family ~*s*⟩ **5** ♦ **:** an equality in number (as of votes or scores); *also* **:** an undecided or deadlocked contest **6 :** NECKTIE

♦ [4] bond, cement, knot, ligature, link ♦ [5] dead heat, draw, stalemate, standoff

[2]tie *vb* **tied; ty•ing** *or* **tie•ing 1** ♦ **:** to fasten, attach, or close by means of a tie **2 :** to bring together firmly **:** UNITE **3 :** to form a knot or bow in ⟨~ a scarf⟩ **4 :** to restrain from freedom of action **:** CONSTRAIN **5 a :** to make or have an equal score with **b** ♦ **:** to provide or offer something equal to

♦ [1] band, bind, gird, truss ***Ant*** unbind, untie ♦ [5b] equal, match, meet

tie•back \ˈtī-ˌbak\ *n* **:** a decorative strip for draping a curtain to the side of a window
tie–dye•ing \ˈtī-ˌdī-iŋ\ *n* **:** a method of producing patterns in textiles by tying parts of the fabric so that they will not absorb the dye — **tie–dyed** \-ˌdīd\ *adj*
tie–in \ˈtī-ˌin\ *n* **:** CONNECTION
tier \ˈtir\ *n* **:** ROW, LAYER; *esp* **:** one of two or more rows arranged one above another — **tiered** \ˈtird\ *adj*
tie–rod \ˈtī-ˌräd\ *n* **:** a rod used as a connecting member or brace
tie–up \-ˌəp\ *n* **1 :** a slowing or stopping of traffic or business **2 :** the act of connecting **:** the state of being connected **:** CONNECTION
tie up *vb* **1 a :** to place or invest in such a manner as to make unavailable for other purposes ⟨their money was *tied up* in stocks⟩ **b** ♦ **:** to restrain from normal movement, operation, or progress ⟨traffic was *tied up* for miles⟩ **2 a :** to keep busy ⟨was *tied up* in conference all day⟩ **b :** to preempt the use of ⟨*tied up* the phone for an hour⟩

♦ encumber, hamper, hinder, hold up, impede, inhibit, interfere with, obstruct

tiff \ˈtif\ *n* **:** a petty quarrel — **tiff** *vb*
Tif•fa•ny \ˈti-fə-nē\ *adj* **:** made of pieces of stained glass ⟨a ~ lamp⟩
ti•ger \ˈtī-gər\ *n* **:** a very large tawny black-striped Asian cat — **ti•ger•ish** *adj*
[1]tight \ˈtīt\ *adj* **1** ♦ **:** so close in structure as to prevent passage of

a liquid or gas **2** ♦ **:** strongly fixed or held **:** SECURE **3 :** not slack or loose **:** TAUT **4 :** fitting usually too closely ⟨~ shoes⟩ **5** ♦ **:** set close together **:** COMPACT ⟨a ~ formation⟩ **6 :** DIFFICULT, TRYING ⟨get in a ~ spot⟩ **7 :** not liberal in giving **:** STINGY **8** ♦ **:** evenly contested **:** CLOSE **9 :** INTOXICATED **10 :** low in supply **:** hard to get ⟨money is ~⟩ — **tight·ly** *adv*

♦ [1] impenetrable, impervious ***Ant*** penetrable, permeable ♦ [2] fast, firm, frozen, secure, set, snug ***Ant*** insecure, loose ♦ [5] close, compact, crowded, dense, packed, serried, thick ♦ [8] close, narrow, neck and neck, nip and tuck

[2]**tight** *adv* **1 :** TIGHTLY, FIRMLY **2 :** SOUNDLY ⟨sleep ~⟩
tight·en \ˈtīt-ᵊn\ *vb* **:** to make or become tight
tight·fist·ed \ˈtīt-ˈfis-təd\ *adj* ♦ **:** not liberal in giving **:** STINGY

♦ cheap, close, mean, niggardly, parsimonious, penurious, spare, sparing, stingy, tight, uncharitable

tight·ness \ˈtīt-nəs\ *n* ♦ **:** the quality or state of being tight

♦ cheapness, closeness, miserliness, parsimony, stinginess

tight·rope \-ˌrōp\ *n* **:** a taut rope or wire for acrobats to perform on
tights \ˈtīts\ *n pl* **:** skintight garments covering the body especially below the waist; *also, Brit* **:** PANTY HOSE
tight·wad \ˈtīt-ˌwäd\ *n* ♦ **:** a stingy person

♦ cheapskate, miser, niggard, skinflint

ti·gress \ˈtī-grəs\ *n* **:** a female tiger
ti·la·pia \tə-ˈlä-pē-ə, -ˈlā-\ *n, pl* **tilapia** *also* **ti·la·pi·as :** any of numerous chiefly African freshwater fishes widely raised for food
til·de \ˈtil-də\ *n* **:** a mark ˜ placed especially over the letter *n* (as in Spanish *señor* sir) to denote the sound \nʸ\ or over vowels (as in Portuguese *irmã* sister) to indicate nasal quality
[1]**tile** \ˈtīl\ *n* **1 :** a flat or curved piece of fired clay, stone, or concrete used for roofs, floors, or walls; *also* **:** a pipe of earthenware or concrete used for a drain **2 :** a thin piece (as of linoleum) used for covering walls or floors — **til·ing** \ˈtī-liŋ\ *n*
[2]**tile** *vb* **tiled; til·ing :** to cover with tiles — **til·er** *n*
[1]**till** \ˈtil\ *prep or conj* **:** UNTIL
[2]**till** *vb* **:** to work by plowing, sowing, and raising crops **:** CULTIVATE — **till·able** *adj*
[3]**till** *n* **:** DRAWER; *esp* **:** a money drawer in a store or bank
till·age \ˈti-lij\ *n* **1 :** the work of tilling land **2 :** cultivated land
[1]**til·ler** \ˈti-lər\ *n* **:** a sprout or stalk especially from the base or lower part of a plant
[2]**till·er** \ˈti-lər\ *n* ♦ **:** one that tills

♦ agriculturist, cultivator, farmer, grower, planter

[3]**til·ler** \ˈti-lər\ *n* **:** a lever used for turning a boat's rudder from side to side
[1]**tilt** \ˈtilt\ *n* **1 :** a contest in which two combatants charging usually with lances try to unhorse each other **:** JOUST; *also* **:** a tournament of tilts **2 :** a verbal contest **:** DISPUTE **3** ♦ **:** the act of tilting **:** the state or position of being tilted

♦ bend, cock, inclination, list, slant, tip

[2]**tilt** *vb* **1** ♦ **:** to move or shift so as to incline **:** TIP **2 :** to engage in or as if in combat with lances **:** JOUST, ATTACK

♦ angle, cant, cock, heel, incline, lean, list, slant, slope, tip

tilth \ˈtilth\ *n* **1 :** TILLAGE 2 **2 :** the state of a soil especially in relation to the suitability of its particle size and structure for growing crops
Tim *abbr* Timothy
tim·ber \ˈtim-bər\ *n* **1 :** growing trees or their wood — often used interjectionally to warn of a falling tree **2 :** wood for use in making something **3 :** a usually large squared or dressed piece of wood
tim·bered \ˈtim-bərd\ *adj* **:** having walls framed by exposed timbers
tim·ber·land \ˈtim-bər-ˌland\ *n* ♦ **:** wooded land

♦ forest, woodland

tim·ber·line \ˈtim-bər-ˌlīn\ *n* **:** the upper limit of tree growth in mountains or high latitudes
timber rattlesnake *n* **:** a widely distributed rattlesnake of the eastern U.S.
timber wolf *n* **:** GRAY WOLF
tim·bre *also* **tim·ber** \ˈtam-bər, ˈtim-\ *n* **:** the distinctive quality given to a sound by its overtones
tim·brel \ˈtim-brəl\ *n* **:** a small hand drum or tambourine
[1]**time** \ˈtīm\ *n* **1 a :** a period during which an action, process, or condition exists or continues ⟨gone a long ~⟩ **b :** the duration of the existence of a living being (as a person or an animal) or a thing (as a star) **:** LIFETIME **2 :** LEISURE ⟨found ~ to read⟩ **3 :** a point or period when something occurs **:** OCCASION ⟨the last ~ we met⟩ **4 :** a set or customary moment or hour for something to occur ⟨arrived on ~⟩ **5** ♦ **:** a historical period **:** AGE, ERA **6 :** state of affairs **:** CONDITIONS ⟨hard ~*s*⟩ **7 :** a rate of speed **:** TEMPO **8 :** a moment, hour, day, or year as indicated by a clock or calendar ⟨what ~ is it⟩ **9 :** a system of reckoning time ⟨solar ~⟩ **10 :** one of a series of recurring instances; *also, pl* **:** added or accumulated quantities or examples ⟨five ~*s* greater⟩ **11** ♦ **:** a person's experience during a particular period ⟨had a good ~⟩ **12 :** the hours or days of one's work; *also* **:** an hourly pay rate ⟨straight ~⟩ **13 :** TIME-OUT 1

♦ [5] age, epoch, era, period ♦ [11] adventure, experience, happening

[2]**time** *vb* **timed; tim·ing 1 :** to arrange or set the time of **:** SCHEDULE ⟨~*s* his calls conveniently⟩ **2 :** to set the tempo or duration of ⟨~ a performance⟩ **3 :** to cause to keep time with **4 :** to determine or record the time, duration, or rate of ⟨~ a sprinter⟩
time bomb *n* **1 :** a bomb so made as to explode at a predetermined time **2 :** something with a potentially dangerous delayed reaction
time clock *n* **:** a clock that records the time workers arrive and depart
time frame *n* **:** a period of time especially with respect to some action or project
time–hon·ored \ˈtīm-ˌä-nərd\ *adj* **:** honored because of age or long usage
time·keep·er \-ˌkē-pər\ *n* **1 :** a clerk who keeps records of the time worked by employees **2 :** one appointed to mark and announce the time in an athletic game or contest
time·less \-ləs\ *adj* **1 :** ETERNAL **2** ♦ **:** not limited or affected by time ⟨~ works of art⟩ — **time·less·ly** *adv* — **time·less·ness** *n*

♦ abiding, ageless, continuing, dateless, enduring, eternal, everlasting, immortal, imperishable, lasting, perennial, perpetual, undying

time·li·ness \ˈtīm-lē-nəs\ *n* ♦ **:** the quality or state of being timely

♦ promptitude, punctuality

time·ly \ˈtīm-lē\ *adj* **time·li·er; -est 1** ♦ **:** coming early or at the right time ⟨a ~ arrival⟩ **2 :** appropriate to the time ⟨a ~ book⟩

♦ immediate, prompt, punctual

time–out \ˈtīm-ˈau̇t\ *n* **1 :** a brief suspension of activity especially in an athletic game **2 :** a quiet period used especially as a disciplinary measure for a child
time·piece \-ˌpēs\ *n* ♦ **:** a device (as a clock) to show the passage of time

♦ watch

tim·er \ˈtī-mər\ *n* **:** one that times
times \ˈtīmz\ *prep* **:** multiplied by ⟨2 ~ 2 is 4⟩
time–shar·ing \ˈtīm-ˌshar-iŋ\ *n* **1 :** simultaneous use of a computer by many users **2** *or* **time–share** \-shar\ **:** joint ownership or rental of a vacation lodging by several persons with each taking turns using the place
times sign *n* **:** the symbol × used to indicate multiplication
time·ta·ble \ˈtīm-ˌtā-bəl\ *n* **1 :** a table of the departure and arrival times (as of trains) **2** ♦ **:** a schedule showing a planned order or sequence

♦ agenda, calendar, docket, program, schedule

time warp *n* **:** an anomaly, discontinuity, or suspension held to occur in the progress of time
time·worn \-ˌwōrn\ *adj* **1 :** worn by time **2 :** HACKNEYED, STALE
tim·id \ˈti-məd\ *adj* ♦ **:** lacking in courage or self-confidence **:** FEARFUL — **ti·mid·i·ty** \tə-ˈmi-də-tē\ *n* — **tim·id·ly** *adv*

♦ fainthearted, fearful, mousy, scary, shy, skittish

tim·o·rous \ˈti-mə-rəs\ *adj* **:** of a timid disposition **:** AFRAID — **tim·o·rous·ly** *adv* — **tim·o·rous·ness** *n*
tim·o·thy \ˈti-mə-thē\ *n* **:** a perennial grass with long cylindrical spikes widely grown for hay in the U.S.
Tim·o·thy \ˈti-mə-thē\ *n* **:** either of two books of the New Testament of Christian Scripture
tim·pa·ni \ˈtim-pə-nē\ *n sing or pl* **:** a set of kettledrums played by one performer in an orchestra — **tim·pa·nist** \-nist\ *n*
[1]**tin** \ˈtin\ *n* **1 :** a soft white crystalline metallic chemical element malleable at ordinary temperatures that is used especially in solders and alloys **2** ♦ **:** a container (as a can) made of metal (as tinplate)

♦ barrel, can, canister, drum

²tin *vb* **tinned; tin•ning 1 :** to cover or plate with tin **2 :** to pack in tins

TIN *abbr* taxpayer identification number

tinct \ˈtiŋkt\ *n* **:** TINCTURE, TINGE

¹tinc•ture \ˈtiŋk-chər\ *n* **1** *archaic* **:** a substance that colors **2 :** a slight admixture **:** TRACE **3 :** an alcoholic solution of a medicinal substance

²tincture *vb* **tinc•tured; tinc•tur•ing 1 :** COLOR, TINGE **2 :** AFFECT

tin•der \ˈtin-dər\ *n* **1 :** a very flammable substance used as kindling **2 :** something serving to incite or inflame

tin•der•box \ˈtin-dər-ˌbäks\ *n* **1 :** a metal box for holding tinder and usually flint and steel for striking a spark **2 :** a highly flammable object or place

tine \ˈtīn\ *n* **:** a slender pointed part (as of a fork or an antler) **:** PRONG

tin•foil \ˈtin-ˌfȯil\ *n* **:** a thin metal sheeting usually of aluminum or tin-lead alloy

¹tinge \ˈtinj\ *vb* **tinged; tinge•ing** *or* **ting•ing 1 ♦ :** to color slightly **:** TINT **2 :** to affect or modify especially with a slight odor or taste

♦ color (*or* colour), dye, paint, stain, tint

²tinge *n* **♦ :** a slight color, flavor, or quality

♦ cast, color (*or* colour), hue, shade, tint, tone

¹tin•gle \ˈtiŋ-gəl\ *vb* **tin•gled; tin•gling 1 :** to feel a prickling or thrilling sensation **2 :** TINKLE

²tingle *n* **♦ :** a tingling sensation or condition

♦ ache, pain, pang, prick, smart, sting, stitch, twinge

¹tin•ker \ˈtiŋ-kər\ *n* **1 :** a usually itinerant mender of household utensils **2 :** an unskillful mender **:** BUNGLER

²tinker *vb* **♦ :** to repair or adjust something in an unskillful or experimental manner — **tin•ker•er** *n*

♦ fiddle, fool, mess, monkey, play, tamper

¹tin•kle \ˈtiŋ-kəl\ *vb* **tin•kled; tin•kling ♦ :** to make or cause to make a tinkle

♦ chink, jingle

²tinkle *n* **:** a series of short high ringing or clinking sounds

tin•ni•tus \ˈti-nə-təs, tə-ˈnī-təs\ *n* **:** a sensation of noise (as ringing or roaring) in the ears

tin•ny \ˈti-nē\ *adj* **tin•ni•er; -est 1 :** abounding in or yielding tin **2 :** resembling tin; *also* **:** LIGHT, CHEAP **3 :** thin in tone ⟨a ~ voice⟩ — **tin•ni•ly** \-nə-lē\ *adv* — **tin•ni•ness** \-nē-nəs\ *n*

tin•plate \ˈtin-ˈplāt\ *n* **:** thin sheet iron or steel coated with tin — **tin–plate** *vb*

tin•sel \ˈtin-səl\ *n* **1 :** a thread, strip, or sheet of metal, paper, or plastic used to produce a glittering appearance **2 :** something superficially attractive but of little worth

tin•smith \ˈtin-ˌsmith\ *n* **:** one that works with sheet metal (as tinplate)

¹tint \ˈtint\ *n* **1 ♦ :** a slight or pale coloration **:** HUE **2 ♦ :** any of various shades of a color

♦ cast, color (*or* colour), hue, shade, tinge, tone

²tint *vb* **♦ :** to impart a tint to **:** COLOR

♦ color (*or* colour), dye, paint, stain, tinge

tin•tin•nab•u•la•tion \ˌtin-tə-ˌna-byə-ˈlā-shən\ *n* **1 :** the ringing of bells **2 :** a tinkling sound as if of bells

tin•ware \ˈtin-ˌwar\ *n* **:** articles and especially utensils made of tinplate

ti•ny \ˈtī-nē\ *adj* **ti•ni•er; -est ♦ :** very small **:** MINUTE

♦ atomic, infinitesimal, microscopic, miniature, minute, wee *Ant* enormous, giant, gigantic, huge, immense, mammoth

¹tip \ˈtip\ *vb* **tipped; tip•ping 1 :** OVERTURN, UPSET **2 ♦ :** to incline, deviate, or bend from a vertical position **:** LEAN; *also* **:** to raise and tilt forward ⟨*tipped* his hat⟩

♦ angle, cant, cock, heel, incline, lean, list, slant, slope, tilt

²tip *n* **♦ :** the act or an instance of tipping

♦ bend, cock, inclination, list, slant, tilt

³tip *vb* **tipped; tip•ping 1 :** to furnish with a tip **2 :** to cover or adorn the tip of

⁴tip *n* **1 ♦ :** the usually pointed end of something **2 :** a small piece or part serving as an end, cap, or point

♦ apex, cusp, end, pike, point

⁵tip *n* **:** a light touch or blow

⁶tip *vb* **tipped; tip•ping :** to strike lightly **:** TAP

⁷tip *n* **♦ :** a piece of advice or expert or confidential information

♦ dope, lowdown, scoop ♦ hint, lead, pointer

⁸tip *vb* **tipped; tip•ping :** to impart a piece of information about or to

⁹tip *vb* **tipped; tip•ping :** to give a gratuity to — **tip•per** *n*

¹⁰tip *n* **♦ :** a gift or small sum given for a service performed or anticipated

♦ bonus, dividend, extra, lagniappe, perquisite

tip off \ˈtip ˌȯf\ *n* **♦ :** something that warns or serves to warn **:** WARNING

♦ caution, wake-up call, warning

tip•pet \ˈti-pət\ *n* **:** a long scarf or shoulder cape

tip•ple \ˈti-pəl\ *vb* **tip•pled; tip•pling :** to drink intoxicating liquor especially habitually or excessively — **tipple** *n*

tip•pler \ˈti-p(ə-)lər\ *n* **♦ :** one that tipples

♦ drunk, inebriate, soak, sot, souse

tip•ster \ˈtip-stər\ *n* **:** a person who gives or sells tips especially for gambling

tip•sy \ˈtip-sē\ *adj* **tip•si•er; -est ♦ :** unsteady or foolish from the effects of alcohol — **tip•si•ly** \-sə-lē\ *adv*

♦ drunk, high, inebriate, intoxicated

¹tip•toe \ˈtip-ˌtō\ *n* **:** the position of being balanced on the balls of the feet and toes with the heels raised; *also* **:** the ends of the toes

²tiptoe *adv or adj* **:** on or as if on tiptoe

³tiptoe *vb* **tip•toed; tip•toe•ing :** to walk or proceed on or as if on tiptoe

¹tip–top \ˈtip-ˈtäp\ *n* **♦ :** the highest point

♦ acme, apex, climax, crown, culmination, head, height, meridian, peak, pinnacle, summit, top, zenith

²tip–top *adj* **:** very good of its kind **:** EXCELLENT

ti•rade \ˈtī-ˌrād\ *n* **♦ :** a prolonged speech of abuse or condemnation

♦ diatribe, harangue, rant

tir•a•mi•su \ˌtir-ə-ˈmē-sü, -mē-ˈsü\ *n* **:** a dessert made with ladyfingers, mascarpone, and espresso

¹tire \ˈtīr\ *vb* **tired; tir•ing 1 ♦ :** to make or become weary **2 ♦ :** to wear out the patience of **:** BORE

♦ [1] burn out, do in, drain, exhaust, fag, fatigue, tucker, wash out, wear, wear out, weary ♦ [2] bore, jade, weary

²tire *n* **1 :** a metal hoop that forms the tread of a wheel **2 :** a rubber cushion usually containing compressed air that encircles a wheel (as of a bike)

tired \ˈtīrd\ *adj* **1 ♦ :** exhausted in strength, endurance, vigor, or freshness **:** WEARY, FATIGUED **2 ♦ :** lacking in freshness or originality **:** HACKNEYED **3 ♦ :** having one's patience, tolerance, or pleasure exhausted

♦ [1] beat, bushed, dead, drained, effete, jaded, limp, prostrate, spent, weary, worn-out ♦ [2] banal, commonplace, hackneyed, musty, stale, stereotyped, threadbare, trite ♦ [3] fed up, jaded, sick, weary

tired•ness *n* **♦ :** the quality or state of being tired

♦ burnout, collapse, exhaustion, fatigue, lassitude, prostration, weariness ♦ boredom, doldrums, ennui, listlessness, restlessness, tedium, weariness

tire•less \ˈtīr-ləs\ *adj* **♦ :** not tiring **:** UNTIRING — **tire•less•ness** *n*

♦ indefatigable, inexhaustible, unflagging, untiring

tire•less•ly *adv* **♦ :** in a tireless manner

♦ determinedly, diligently, hard, hardly, laboriously, mightily, slavishly, strenuously

tire•some \-səm\ *adj* **:** tending to bore **:** WEARISOME, TEDIOUS — **tire•some•ly** *adv* — **tire•some•ness** *n*

tis•sue \ˈti-shü\ *n* **1 :** a fine lightweight often sheer fabric **2 :** NETWORK, WEB **3 :** a soft absorbent paper **4 :** a mass or layer of cells forming a basic structural material of an animal or plant

¹tit \ˈtit\ *n* **:** TEAT

²tit *n* **:** any of various small plump Old World songbirds related to the titmice

Tit *abbr* Titus

ti•tan \ˈtīt-ᵊn\ *n* **1** *cap* **:** one of a family of giants overthrown by the gods in Greek mythology **2 ♦ :** one gigantic in size or power

♦ behemoth, blockbuster, colossus, giant, jumbo, leviathan, mammoth, monster, whale, whopper

ti·tan·ic \tī-ˈta-nik\ *adj* ♦ **:** enormous in size, force, or power

♦ colossal, enormous, giant, gigantic, huge, mammoth, massive, prodigious, tremendous

ti·ta·ni·um \tī-ˈtā-nē-əm\ *n* **:** a gray light strong metallic chemical element used especially in alloys

titbit *var of* TIDBIT

tithe \ˈtīth\ *n* **:** a 10th part paid or given especially for the support of a church — **tithe** *vb* — **tith·er** *n*

tit·il·late \ˈtit-ᵊl-ˌāt\ *vb* **-lat·ed; -lat·ing 1** ♦ **:** to excite pleasurably **2 :** TICKLE 3

♦ electrify, excite, exhilarate, galvanize, intoxicate, thrill, turn on

tit·il·la·tion \ˌtit-ᵊl-ˈā-shən\ *n* ♦ **:** the action of titillating or the state of being titillated

♦ bang, exhilaration, kick, thrill

tit·i·vate *or* **tit·ti·vate** \ˈti-tə-ˌvāt\ *vb* **-vat·ed; -vat·ing :** to dress up **:** spruce up — **tit·i·va·tion** \ˌti-tə-ˈvā-shən\ *n*

ti·tle \ˈtīt-ᵊl\ *n* **1 :** CLAIM, RIGHT; *esp* **:** a legal right to the ownership of property **2** ♦ **:** the distinguishing name especially of an artistic production (as a book) **3** ♦ **:** an appellation of honor, rank, or office **4 :** CHAMPIONSHIP

♦ [2] heading ♦ [3] appellation, cognomen, denotation, designation, handle, name

ti·tled \ˈtīt-ᵊld\ *adj* **:** having a title especially of nobility

title page *n* **:** a page of a book bearing the title and usually the names of the author and publisher

tit·mouse \ˈtit-ˌmau̇s\ *n, pl* **tit·mice** \-ˌmīs\ **:** any of several small long-tailed No. American songbirds related to the chickadees

ti·tra·tion \tī-ˈtrā-shən\ *n* **:** a process of finding the concentration of a solution (as of an acid) by adding small portions of a second solution of known concentration (as of a base) to a fixed amount of the first until an expected change (as in color) occurs

1**tit·ter** \ˈti-tər\ *vb* **:** to laugh in an affected or in a nervous or half-suppressed manner **:** GIGGLE

2**titter** *n* ♦ **:** an act or instance of tittering

♦ cackle, chortle, laugh, laughter, snicker

tit·tle \ˈtit-ᵊl\ *n* ♦ **:** a tiny piece

♦ bit, hoot, jot, lick, modicum, rap, whit

tit·tle–tat·tle \ˈtit-ᵊl-ˌtat-ᵊl\ *n* **:** idle talk **:** GOSSIP — **tittle–tattle** *vb*

tit·u·lar \ˈti-chə-lər\ *adj* **1** ♦ **:** existing in title only **:** NOMINAL ⟨~ ruler⟩ **2 :** of, relating to, or bearing a title ⟨~ role⟩

♦ formal, nominal, paper

Ti·tus \ˈtī-təs\ *n* **:** a book of the New Testament of Christian Scripture

tiz·zy \ˈti-zē\ *n, pl* **tizzies** ♦ **:** a highly excited and distracted state of mind

♦ dither, fluster, fret, fuss, huff, lather, pother, stew, twitter

tk *abbr* **1** tank **2** truck

TKO \ˌtē-ˌkā-ˈō\ *n* **:** the termination of a boxing match when a boxer is declared unable to continue the fight

tkt *abbr* ticket

Tl *symbol* thallium

TLC *abbr* tender loving care

T lymphocyte *n* **:** T CELL

Tm *symbol* thulium

TM *abbr* trademark

T–man \ˈtē-ˌman\ *n* **:** a special agent of the U.S. Treasury Department

tn *abbr* **1** ton **2** town

TN *abbr* Tennessee

tng *abbr* training

tnpk *abbr* turnpike

TNT \ˌtē-(ˌ)en-ˈtē\ *n* **:** a flammable toxic compound used as a high explosive and in chemical synthesis

1**to** \tə, ˈtü\ *prep* **1 :** in the direction of and reaching ⟨drove ~ town⟩ **2 :** in the direction of **:** TOWARD **3 :** ON, AGAINST ⟨apply salve ~ a burn⟩ **4 :** as far as ⟨can pay up ~ a dollar⟩ **5 :** so as to become or bring about ⟨beaten ~ death⟩ ⟨broken ~ pieces⟩ **6** ♦ **:** earlier than **:** BEFORE ⟨it's five minutes ~ six⟩ **7 :** UNTIL ⟨from May ~ December⟩ **8 :** fitting or being a part of **:** FOR ⟨key ~ the lock⟩ **9 :** with the accompaniment of ⟨sing ~ the music⟩ **10 :** in relation or comparison with ⟨similar ~ that one⟩ ⟨won 10 ~ 6⟩ **11 :** in accordance with ⟨add salt ~ taste⟩ **12 :** within the range of ⟨~ my knowledge⟩ **13 :** contained, occurring, or included in ⟨two pints ~ a quart⟩ **14 :** as regards ⟨agreeable ~ everyone⟩ **15 :** affecting as the receiver or beneficiary ⟨whispered ~ her⟩ ⟨gave it ~ me⟩ **16 :** for no one except ⟨a room ~ myself⟩ **17 :** into the action of ⟨we got ~ talking⟩ **18** — used for marking the following verb as an infinitive ⟨wants ~ go⟩ and often used by itself at the end of a clause in place of an infinitive suggested by the preceding context ⟨goes to town whenever he wants ~⟩ ⟨can leave if you'd like ~⟩

♦ ahead of, before, ere, of, previous to, prior to

2**to** \ˈtü\ *adv* **1 :** in a direction toward ⟨run ~ and fro⟩ **2 :** into contact especially with the frame of a door ⟨the door slammed ~⟩ **3 :** to the matter in hand ⟨fell ~ and ate heartily⟩ **4 :** to a state of consciousness or awareness ⟨came ~ hours after the accident⟩

TO *abbr* turn over

toad \ˈtōd\ *n* **:** any of numerous tailless leaping amphibians differing typically from the related frogs in having a shorter stockier build, rough dry warty skin, and less aquatic habits

toad·stool \-ˌstül\ *n* **:** MUSHROOM; *esp* **:** one that is poisonous or inedible

1**toady** \ˈtō-dē\ *n, pl* **toad·ies :** a person who flatters in the hope of gaining favors **:** SYCOPHANT

2**toady** *vb* **toad·ied; toady·ing** ♦ **:** to behave as a toady

♦ fawn, fuss, kowtow

to–and–fro \ˌtü-ən-ˈfrō\ *adj* **:** forward and backward — **to–and–fro** *n*

1**toast** \ˈtōst\ *vb* **1 :** to warm thoroughly **2 :** to make (as bread) crisp, hot, and brown by heat **3 :** to become toasted

2**toast** *n* **1 :** sliced toasted bread **2 :** someone or something in whose honor persons drink **3 :** an act of drinking in honor of a toast

3**toast** *vb* **:** to propose or drink to as a toast

toast·er \ˈtō-stər\ *n* **:** an electrical appliance for toasting

toaster oven *n* **:** a portable electrical appliance that bakes, broils, and toasts

toast·mas·ter \ˈtōst-ˌmas-tər\ *n* **:** a person who presides at a banquet and introduces the after-dinner speakers

toast·mis·tress \-ˌmis-trəs\ *n* **:** a woman who acts as toastmaster

toasty \ˈtō-stē\ *adj* **toast·i·er; -est :** pleasantly warm

Tob *abbr* Tobit

to·bac·co \tə-ˈba-kō\ *n, pl* **-cos 1 :** a tall broad-leaved herb related to the potato; *also* **:** its leaves prepared for smoking or chewing or as snuff **2 :** manufactured tobacco products; *also* **:** smoking as a practice

to·bac·co·nist \tə-ˈba-kə-nist\ *n* **:** a dealer in tobacco

To·bi·as \tō-ˈbī-əs\ *n* **:** TOBIT

To·bit \ˈtō-bət\ *n* **:** a book in the Roman Catholic canon of the Old Testament and in the Protestant Apocrypha

1**to·bog·gan** \tə-ˈbä-gən\ *n* **:** a long flat-bottomed light sled made of thin boards curved up at one end

2**toboggan** *vb* **1 :** to coast on or as if on a toboggan **2 :** to decline suddenly (as in value) — **to·bog·gan·er** *n*

toc·sin \ˈtäk-sən\ *n* **1 :** an alarm bell **2 :** a warning signal

1**to·day** \tə-ˈdā\ *adv* **1 :** on or for this day **2** ♦ **:** at the present time

♦ anymore, now, nowadays, presently, right now

2**today** *n* ♦ **:** the present day, time, or age

♦ moment, now, present

tod·dle \ˈtäd-ᵊl\ *vb* **tod·dled; tod·dling :** to walk with short tottering steps in the manner of a young child — **toddle** *n* — **tod·dler** *n*

tod·dy \ˈtä-dē\ *n, pl* **toddies :** a drink made of liquor, sugar, spices, and hot water

to–do \tə-ˈdü\ *n, pl* **to–dos** \-ˈdüz\ **:** excited and usually exaggerated stir **:** BUSTLE, FUSS

1**toe** \ˈtō\ *n* **1 :** one of the jointed parts of the front end of the vertebrate foot **2 :** the front part of a foot or hoof

2**toe** *vb* **toed; toe·ing :** to touch, reach, or drive with the toes

toe·hold \ˈtō-ˌhōld\ *n* **1 :** a place of support for the toes **2 :** a slight footing

toe·nail \ˈtō-ˌnāl\ *n* **:** a nail of a toe

tof·fee *or* **tof·fy** \ˈtȯ-fē, ˈtä-\ *n, pl* **toffees** *or* **toffies :** candy of brittle but tender texture made by boiling sugar and butter together

to·fu \ˈtō-(ˌ)fü\ *n* **:** a soft white food product made from soybeans

tog \ˈtäg, ˈtȯg\ *vb* **togged; tog·ging :** to put togs on **:** DRESS

to·ga \ˈtō-gə\ *n* **:** the loose outer garment worn in public by citizens of ancient Rome — **to·gaed** \-gəd\ *adj*

1**to·geth·er** \tə-ˈge-thər\ *adv* **1 :** in or into one place or group **2 :** in or into contact or association ⟨mix ~⟩ **3 :** at one time **:** SI-

MULTANEOUSLY ⟨talk and work ~⟩ **4 :** in succession ⟨for days ~⟩ **5 :** in or into harmony or coherence ⟨get ~ on a plan⟩ **6** ♦ **:** as a group **:** JOINTLY — **to•geth•er•ness** *n*

♦ all around, altogether, collectively, overall

²together *adj* **:** composed in mind or manner
tog•gery \ˈtä-gə-rē, ˈtȯ-\ *n* **:** CLOTHING
tog•gle \ˈtä-gəl\ *vb* **:** to switch between two options especially of an electronic device
tog•gle switch \ˈtä-gəl-\ *n* **:** an electric switch operated by pushing a projecting lever through a small arc
To•go•lese \ˌtō-gə-ˈlēz, -ˈlēs\ *n* **:** a native or inhabitant of Togo — **Togolese** *adj*
togs \ˈtägz, ˈtȯgz\ *n pl* **:** CLOTHING; *esp* **:** clothes for a specified use ⟨riding ~⟩
¹toil \ˈtȯil\ *n* **1 :** laborious effort **2** ♦ **:** long fatiguing labor **:** DRUDGERY — **toil•ful** \-fəl\ *adj*

♦ drudgery, grind, labor (*or* labour), slavery, sweat, travail *Ant* fun, play

²toil *vb* **1** ♦ **:** to work hard and long **2 :** to proceed with great effort **:** PLOD

♦ drudge, fag, grub, labor (*or* labour), slave, sweat, travail

³toil *n* **:** NET, TRAP — usually used in plural
toil•er *n* ♦ **:** one that toils

♦ drudge, fag, peon, slave, worker

toi•let \ˈtȯi-lət\ *n* **1 :** the act or process of dressing and grooming oneself **2** ♦ **:** a room furnished with a fixture for flushing body waste **3 :** a fixture for use in urinating and defecating; *esp* **:** one consisting essentially of a water-flushed bowl and seat — **toilet** *vb*

♦ bathroom, lavatory

toi•let•ry \ˈtȯi-lə-trē\ *n, pl* **-ries :** an article or preparation used in cleaning or grooming oneself — usually used in plural
toi•lette \twä-ˈlet\ *n* **1 :** TOILET 1 **2 :** formal attire; *also* **:** a particular costume
toilet training *n* **:** the process of training a child to control bladder and bowel movements and to use the toilet — **toilet train** *vb*
toil•some \ˈtȯi(-ə)l-səm\ *adj* ♦ **:** marked by or full of toil or fatigue

♦ arduous, burdensome, challenging, demanding, exacting, grueling, laborious, onerous, taxing

toil•worn \ˈtȯil-ˌwōrn\ *adj* **:** showing the effects of toil
To•kay \tō-ˈkā\ *n* **:** naturally sweet wine from Hungary
toke \ˈtōk\ *n, slang* **:** a puff on a marijuana cigarette or pipe
¹to•ken \ˈtō-kən\ *n* **1 :** an outward sign **2 :** SYMBOL, EMBLEM **3** ♦ **:** something that serves as a reminder **:** KEEPSAKE **4 :** a small part representing the whole **5 :** a piece resembling a coin issued as money or for use by a particular group on specified terms

♦ keepsake, memento, memorial, monument, remembrance, souvenir

²token *adj* **1 :** done or given as a token especially in partial fulfillment of an obligation **2 :** representing only a symbolic effort **:** MINIMAL, PERFUNCTORY
to•ken•ism \ˈtō-kə-ˌni-zəm\ *n* **:** the policy or practice of making only a symbolic effort (as to desegregate)
told *past and past part of* TELL
tole \ˈtōl\ *n* **:** sheet metal and especially tinplate for use in domestic and ornamental wares
tol•er•a•ble \ˈtä-lə-rə-bəl\ *adj* **1** ♦ **:** capable of being borne or endured **2** ♦ **:** moderately good **:** PASSABLE

♦ [1] bearable, endurable, sufferable, supportable, sustainable ♦ [2] acceptable, adequate, all right, decent, fine, OK, passable, respectable, satisfactory

tol•er•a•bly \ˈtä-lə-rə-blē\ *adv* ♦ **:** in a tolerable manner

♦ adequately, all right, fine, good, nicely, OK, passably, satisfactorily, so-so, well

tol•er•ance \ˈtä-lə-rəns\ *n* **1** ♦ **:** the act or practice of tolerating; *esp* **:** sympathy or indulgence for beliefs or practices differing from one's own **2 :** the allowable deviation from a standard (as of size) **3 :** the body's capacity to become less responsive over time to something (as a drug used repeatedly) — **tol•er•ant•ly** *adv*

♦ forbearance, long-suffering, patience, sufferance

tol•er•ant \ˈtä-lə-rənt\ *adj* ♦ **:** inclined to tolerate; *esp* **:** marked by forbearance or endurance

♦ forbearing, long-suffering, patient, stoic, uncomplaining

tol•er•ate \ˈtä-lə-ˌrāt\ *vb* **-at•ed; -at•ing 1 :** to exhibit physiological tolerance for (as a drug) **2** ♦ **:** to allow to be or to be done without hindrance — **tol•er•a•tion** \ˌtä-lə-ˈrā-shən\ *n*

♦ abide, bear, brook, countenance, endure, meet, stand, stick out, stomach, support, sustain, take

¹toll \ˈtōl\ *n* **1 :** a tax paid for a privilege (as for passing over a bridge) **2 :** a charge for a service (as for a long-distance telephone call) **3 :** the cost in life, health, loss, or suffering
²toll *vb* **1 :** to cause the slow regular sounding of (a bell) especially by pulling a rope **2 :** to give signal of **:** SOUND **3** ♦ **:** to sound with slow measured strokes **4 :** to announce by tolling

♦ chime, knell, peal, ring

³toll *n* **:** the sound of a tolling bell
toll•booth \ˈtōl-ˌbüth\ *n* **:** a booth where tolls are paid
toll•gate \-ˌgāt\ *n* **:** a point where vehicles stop to pay a toll
toll•house \-ˌhau̇s\ *n* **:** a house or booth where tolls are paid
tol•u•ene \ˈtäl-yə-ˌwēn\ *n* **:** a liquid hydrocarbon used especially as a solvent
tom \ˈtäm\ *n* **:** the male of various animals (as a cat or turkey)
¹tom•a•hawk \ˈtä-mə-ˌhȯk\ *n* **:** a light ax used as a missile and as a hand weapon especially by No. American Indians
²tomahawk *vb* **:** to strike or kill with a tomahawk
to•ma•til•lo \ˌtō-mə-ˈtē-(ˌ)yō\ *n, pl* **-los :** a small round usually pale green edible fruit of a Mexican herb related to the tomato; *also* **:** this herb
to•ma•to \tə-ˈmā-tō, -ˈmä-\ *n, pl* **-toes :** a usually large, rounded, and red or yellow pulpy edible berry of a widely grown tropical herb related to the potato; *also* **:** this herb
tomb \ˈtüm\ *n* **1 :** a place of burial **:** GRAVE **2 :** a house, chamber, or vault for the dead — **tomb** *vb*
tom•boy \ˈtäm-ˌbȯi\ *n* **:** a girl who behaves in a manner usually considered boyish
tom•boy•ish \-ish\ *adj* **:** relating to or being a tomboy
tomb•stone \ˈtüm-ˌstōn\ *n* ♦ **:** a stone marking a grave

♦ gravestone, headstone, monument

tom•cat \ˈtäm-ˌkat\ *n* **:** a male domestic cat
Tom Col•lins \ˈtäm-ˈkä-lənz\ *n* **:** a tall iced drink with a base of gin
tome \ˈtōm\ *n* **:** BOOK; *esp* **:** a large or weighty one
tom•fool•ery \täm-ˈfü-lə-rē\ *n* ♦ **:** playful or foolish behavior

♦ foolery, high jinks, horseplay, monkeyshines, roughhouse, shenanigans

tom•my gun \ˈtä-mē-ˌgən\ *n* **:** SUBMACHINE GUN — **tommy–gun** *vb*
to•mog•ra•phy \tō-ˈmä-grə-fē\ *n* **:** a method of producing a three-dimensional image of the internal structures of a solid object (as the human body or the earth) — **to•mo•graph•ic** \ˌtō-mə-ˈgra-fik\ *adj*
to•mor•row \tə-ˈmär-ō\ *adv* **:** on or for the day after today — **tomorrow** *n*
tom–tom \ˈtäm-ˌtäm\ *n* **:** a small-headed drum beaten with the hands
ton \ˈtən\ *n, pl* **tons** *also* **ton 1 a :** a unit of weight equal to 2000 pounds in the U.S. and Canada **:** SHORT TON **b :** LONG TON **2 :** a unit equal to the volume of a long ton weight of seawater used in reckoning the displacement of ships and equal to 35 cubic feet
to•nal•i•ty \tō-ˈna-lə-tē\ *n, pl* **-ties :** tonal quality
¹tone \ˈtōn\ *n* **1 :** vocal or musical sound; *esp* **:** sound quality **2 :** a sound of definite pitch **3 :** WHOLE STEP **4 :** accent or inflection expressive of an emotion **5 :** the pitch of a word often used to express differences of meaning **6** ♦ **:** style or manner of expression **7** ♦ **:** color quality; *also* **:** SHADE **8 :** the effect in painting of light and shade together with color **9 :** healthy and vigorous condition of a living body or bodily part; *also* **:** the state of partial contraction characteristic of normal muscle **10** ♦ **:** general character, quality, or trend — **ton•al** \ˈtō-nᵊl\ *adj*

♦ [6] fashion, locution, manner, mode, phraseology, style, vein ♦ [7] cast, color (*or* colour), hue, shade, tinge, tint ♦ [10] character, complexion, constitution, genius, nature, personality

²tone *vb* **toned; ton•ing 1 :** to give a particular intonation or inflection to **2 :** to impart tone to **3 :** SOFTEN, MELLOW **4 :** to harmonize in color **:** BLEND
tone•arm *n* **:** the movable part of a record player that carries the pickup and the needle
toney *var of* TONY
tong \ˈtäŋ, ˈtȯŋ\ *n* **:** a Chinese secret society in the U.S.
tongs \ˈtäŋz, ˈtȯŋz\ *n pl* **:** a grasping device consisting of two

pieces joined at one end by a pivot or hinged like scissors — **tong** *vb*

1tongue \ˈtəŋ\ *n* **1 :** a fleshy movable process of the floor of the mouth used in tasting and in taking and swallowing food and in humans as a speech organ **2 :** the flesh of a tongue (as of the ox) used as food **3 :** the power of communication **4** ♦ **:** the words, their pronunciation, and the method of combining them used and understood by a community **:** LANGUAGE **5 :** manner or quality of utterance; *also* **:** intended meaning **6 :** ecstatic usually unintelligible utterance accompanying religious excitation — usually used in plural **7 :** something resembling an animal's tongue especially in being elongated and fastened at one end only — **tongued** \ˈtəŋd\ *adj* — **tongue•less** *adj*

♦ language, lingo, speech, vocabulary

2tongue *vb* **tongued; tongu•ing 1 :** to touch or lick with the tongue **2 :** to articulate notes on a wind instrument

tongue–in–cheek *adj* **:** characterized by insincerity, irony, or whimsical exaggeration — **tongue in cheek** *adv*

tongue–lash \ˈtəŋ-ˌlash\ *vb* **:** CHIDE, REPROVE — **tongue–lashing** \-iŋ\ *n*

tongue–tied \-ˌtīd\ *adj* **:** unable or disinclined to speak clearly or freely (as from shyness or a tongue impairment)

tongue twister *n* **:** an utterance that is difficult to articulate because of a succession of similar consonants

1ton•ic \ˈtä-nik\ *adj* **1** ♦ **:** of, relating to, or producing a healthy physical or mental condition **:** INVIGORATING **2 :** relating to or based on the 1st tone of a scale — **to•nic•i•ty** \tō-ˈni-sə-tē\ *n*

♦ bracing, invigorating, refreshing, restorative, stimulative

2tonic *n* **1 :** something that invigorates, restores, or refreshes **2 :** the 1st degree of a musical scale

tonic water *n* **:** a carbonated beverage flavored with a bit of quinine, lemon, and lime

1to•night \tə-ˈnīt\ *adv* **:** on this present night or the coming night

2tonight *n* **:** the present or the coming night

ton•nage \ˈtə-nij\ *n* **1 :** a duty on ships based on tons carried **2 :** ships in terms of the number of tons registered or carried **3 :** total weight in tons shipped, carried, or mined

ton•sil \ˈtän-səl\ *n* **:** either of a pair of oval masses of lymphoid tissue that lie one on each side of the throat at the back of the mouth

ton•sil•lec•to•my \ˌtän-sə-ˈlek-tə-mē\ *n, pl* **-mies :** the surgical removal of the tonsils

ton•sil•li•tis \-ˈlī-təs\ *n* **:** inflammation of the tonsils

ton•so•ri•al \tän-ˈsōr-ē-əl\ *adj* **:** of or relating to a barber or a barber's work

ton•sure \ˈtän-chər\ *n* **1 :** the rite of admission to the clerical state by the clipping or shaving of the head **2 :** the shaven crown or patch worn by clerics (as monks) — **tonsure** *vb*

tony *also* **ton•ey** \ˈtō-nē\ *adj* **ton•i•er; -est :** marked by an aristocratic manner or style

too \ˈtü\ *adv* **1** ♦ **:** in addition **:** ALSO **2** ♦ **:** to an excessive degree **:** EXCESSIVELY **3 :** to such a degree as to be regrettable **4 :** to a high degree **:** VERY

♦ [1] additionally, again, also, besides, further, furthermore, likewise, more, moreover, then, withal, yet ♦ [2] devilishly, excessively, inordinately, monstrously, overly, overmuch ***Ant*** inadequately, insufficiently

took *past of* TAKE

1tool \ˈtül\ *n* **1** ♦ **:** a hand instrument that aids in accomplishing a task **2 :** the cutting or shaping part in a machine; *also* **:** a machine for shaping metal in any way **3 :** something used in doing a job ⟨a scholar's books are his ∼*s*⟩; *also* **:** a means to an end **4** ♦ **:** a person used by another **:** DUPE **5** *pl* **:** natural ability

♦ [1] device, implement, instrument, utensil ♦ [4] dupe, gull, pigeon, sap, sucker

2tool *vb* **1 :** to shape, form, or finish with a tool; *esp* **:** to letter or decorate (as a book cover) by means of hand tools **2 :** to equip a plant or industry with machines and tools for production **3 :** DRIVE, RIDE ⟨∼*ing* along at 60 miles per hour⟩

tool bar *n* **:** a strip of icons on a computer display providing quick access to the pictured functions

1toot \ˈtüt\ *vb* **1 :** to sound or cause to sound in short blasts **2 :** to blow an instrument (as a horn) — **toot•er** *n*

2toot *n* **:** a short blast (as on a horn)

tooth \ˈtüth\ *n, pl* **teeth** \ˈtēth\ **1 :** one of the hard bony structures borne especially on the jaws of vertebrates and used for seizing and chewing food and as weapons; *also* **:** a hard sharp structure especially around the mouth of an invertebrate **2 :** something resembling an animal's tooth **3 :** any of the projections on the edge of a wheel that fits into corresponding projections on another wheel **4 :** effective means of enforcement — **toothed** \ˈtütht\ *adj* — **tooth•less** *adj*

tooth•ache \ˈtüth-ˌāk\ *n* **:** pain in or about a tooth

tooth•brush \-ˌbrəsh\ *n* **:** a brush for cleaning the teeth

tooth•paste \-ˌpāst\ *n* **:** a paste for cleaning the teeth

tooth•pick \-ˌpik\ *n* **:** a pointed instrument for removing food particles caught between the teeth

tooth powder *n* **:** a powder for cleaning the teeth

tooth•some \ˈtüth-səm\ *adj* **1 :** AGREEABLE, ATTRACTIVE **2** ♦ **:** pleasing to the taste **:** DELICIOUS

♦ ambrosial, appetizing, delectable, delicious, flavorful (*or* flavourful), luscious, palatable, savory, scrumptious, tasty, yummy

toothy \ˈtü-thē\ *adj* **tooth•i•er; -est :** having or showing prominent teeth

1top \ˈtäp\ *n* **1** ♦ **:** the highest part, point, or level of something **2 :** the part of a plant with edible roots lying above the ground ⟨beet ∼*s*⟩ **3 :** the upper end, edge, or surface ⟨the ∼ of a page⟩ **4** ♦ **:** an upper piece, lid, or covering **5 :** the highest degree, pitch, or rank

♦ [1] acme, apex, climax, crown, culmination, head, height, meridian, peak, pinnacle, summit, tip-top, zenith ♦ [4] cap, cover, lid

2top *vb* **topped; top•ping 1 :** to remove or trim the top of **:** PRUNE ⟨∼ a tree⟩ **2 :** to cover with a top or on the top **:** CROWN, CAP **3** ♦ **:** to be superior to **:** SURPASS **4 :** to go over the top of **5 :** to strike (a ball) above the center **6 :** to make an end or conclusion ⟨∼ off a meal with coffee⟩

♦ beat, better, eclipse, excel, outdistance, outdo, outshine, outstrip, surpass, transcend

3top *adj* **1 :** of, relating to, or being at the top **2 :** CHIEF **3** ♦ **:** of the highest quality, amount, or degree

♦ consummate, maximum, most, nth, paramount, supreme, ultimate, utmost ♦ full, maximum, utmost

4top *n* **:** a toy that has a tapering point on which it is made to spin

to•paz \ˈtō-ˌpaz\ *n* **:** a hard silicate of aluminum; *esp* **:** a yellow transparent topaz used as a gem

top•coat \ˈtäp-ˌkōt\ *n* **1 :** a lightweight overcoat **2 :** a protective coating (as of paint)

top dollar *n* **:** the highest amount being paid for a commodity or service

top–dress \-ˌdres\ *vb* **:** to apply material to (as land) without working it in; *esp* **:** to scatter fertilizer over

top•dress•ing \-ˌdre-siŋ\ *n* **:** a material used to top-dress soil

top–end \ˈtäp-ˈend\ *adj* **:** TOPFLIGHT

top•flight \ˈtäp-ˈflīt\ *adj* **:** of, relating to, or being the highest level of excellence or rank — **top flight** *n*

top hat *n* **:** a tall-crowned hat usually of beaver or silk

top–heavy \ˈtäp-ˌhe-vē\ *adj* **:** having the top part too heavy for the lower part

to•pi•ary \ˈtō-pē-ˌer-ē\ *n, pl* **-ar•ies :** the art of training and trimming trees or shrubs with decorative shapes — **topiary** *adj*

top•ic \ˈtä-pik\ *n* **1 :** a heading in an outlined argument **2** ♦ **:** the subject of a discourse or a section of it **:** THEME

♦ content, matter, motif, motive, question, subject, theme

top•i•cal \-pi-kəl\ *adj* **1 :** designed to be applied to or to work on a part (as of the body) **2 :** of, relating to, or arranged by topics ⟨a ∼ outline⟩ **3 :** relating to current or local events — **top•i•cal•ly** \-k(ə-)lē\ *adv*

top•knot \ˈtäp-ˌnät\ *n* **1 :** an ornament (as a knot of ribbons) forming a headdress **2 :** a crest of feathers or tuft of hair on the top of the head

top•less \-ləs\ *adj* **1 :** wearing no clothing on the upper body **2 :** featuring topless waitresses or entertainers

top•mast \ˈtäp-ˌmast, -məst\ *n* **:** the 2d mast above a ship's deck

top•most \ˈtäp-ˌmōst\ *adj* **:** highest of all **:** UPPERMOST

top–notch \-ˈnäch\ *adj* **:** of the highest quality **:** FIRST-RATE

top–of–the–line *adj* ♦ **:** being or belonging to the highest or most expensive class

♦ A1, crackerjack, dandy, excellent, fine, first-rate, sensational, splendid, superb, terrific, wonderful

to•pog•ra•phy \tə-ˈpä-grə-fē\ *n* **1 :** the art of showing in detail on a map or chart the physical features of a place or region **2 :** the outline of the form of a place showing its relief and the position of features (as rivers, roads, or cities) — **to•pog•ra•pher** \-fər\ *n*

— **top•o•graph•ic** \ˌtä-pə-ˈgra-fik\ *or* **top•o•graph•i•cal** \-fi-kəl\ *adj*
top•ping \ˈtä-piŋ\ *n* **:** a food served on top of another to make it look or taste better
top•ple \ˈtä-pəl\ *vb* **top•pled; top•pling** **1** ♦ **:** to fall from or as if from being top-heavy **2 :** to push over **:** OVERTURN; *also* **:** OVERTHROW

♦ fall, slip, stumble, trip, tumble

tops \ˈtäps\ *adj* **:** topmost in quality or importance ⟨~ in his field⟩
top•sail \ˈtäp-ˌsāl, -səl\ *also* **top•s'l** \-səl\ *n* **:** the sail next above the lowest sail on a mast in a square-rigged ship
top secret *adj* **:** demanding complete secrecy among those concerned
top•side \ˈtäp-ˈsīd\ *adv or adj* **1 :** to or on the top or surface **2 :** on deck
top•sides \-ˈsīdz\ *n pl* **:** the top portion of the outer surface of a ship on each side above the waterline
top•soil \ˈtäp-ˌsȯil\ *n* **:** surface soil usually including the organic layer in which plants have most of their roots
top•sy–tur•vy \ˌtäp-sē-ˈtər-vē\ *adj* ♦ **:** totally disordered — **top-sy–turvy** *adv*

♦ chaotic, disheveled, disordered, disorderly, messy, untidy

toque \ˈtōk\ *n* **:** a woman's small hat without a brim
tor \ˈtȯr\ *n* **:** a high craggy hill
To•rah \ˈtōr-ə\ *n* **1 :** a scroll of the first five books of the Old Testament used in a synagogue; *also* **:** these five books **2 :** the body of divine knowledge and law found in the Jewish Scriptures and tradition
[1]**torch** \ˈtȯrch\ *n* **1 :** a flaming light made of something that burns brightly and usually carried in the hand **2 :** something that resembles a torch in giving light, heat, or guidance **3** *chiefly Brit* **:** FLASHLIGHT **4 :** a portable burner for producing a hot flame
[2]**torch** *vb* **:** to set fire to
torch•bear•er \ˈtȯrch-ˌber-ər\ *n* **1 :** a person who carries a torch **2 :** one in the forefront (as of a political campaign)
torch•light \-ˌlīt\ *n* **:** light given by torches
torch song *n* **:** a popular sentimental song of unrequited love
tore *past of* TEAR
to•re•ador \ˈtȯr-ē-ə-ˌdȯr\ *n* **:** BULLFIGHTER
to•re•ro \tə-ˈrer-ō\ *n, pl* **-ros :** BULLFIGHTER
[1]**tor•ment** \ˈtȯr-ˌment\ *n* **1** ♦ **:** extreme pain or anguish of body or mind **2** ♦ **:** a source of vexation or pain

♦ [1] affliction, agony, anguish, distress, misery, pain, torture, tribulation, woe ♦ [2] agony, hell, horror, misery, murder, nightmare, torture

[2]**tor•ment** \tȯr-ˈment\ *vb* **1** ♦ **:** to cause severe suffering of body or mind to **2 :** DISTORT, TWIST

♦ afflict, agonize, bedevil, curse, harrow, martyr, persecute, plague, rack, torture

tor•men•tor \-ˈmen-tər\ *n* ♦ **:** one that torments

♦ heckler, oppressor, persecutor, taunter, torturer

torn *past part of* TEAR
tor•na•do \tȯr-ˈnā-dō\ *n, pl* **-does** *or* **-dos :** a violent destructive whirling wind accompanied by a funnel-shaped cloud that moves over a narrow path
[1]**tor•pe•do** \tȯr-ˈpē-dō\ *n, pl* **-does :** a thin cylindrical self-propelled underwater weapon
[2]**torpedo** *vb* **tor•pe•doed; tor•pe•do•ing :** to hit or destroy with or as if with a torpedo
torpedo boat *n* **:** a small very fast boat for firing torpedoes
tor•pid \ˈtȯr-pəd\ *adj* **1 :** having lost motion or the power of exertion **:** DORMANT **2 :** sluggish in functioning or acting **3** ♦ **:** lacking vigor — **tor•pid•i•ty** \tȯr-ˈpi-də-tē\ *n*

♦ dull, inactive, inert, lethargic, quiescent, sleepy, sluggish

tor•por \ˈtȯr-pər\ *n* **1 :** DULLNESS, APATHY **2 :** extreme sluggishness **:** STAGNATION
[1]**torque** \ˈtȯrk\ *n* **:** a force that produces or tends to produce rotation or torsion
[2]**torque** *vb* **torqued; torqu•ing :** to impart torque to **:** cause to twist (as about an axis)
tor•rent \ˈtȯr-ənt\ *n* **1 :** a tumultuous outburst **2** ♦ **:** a rushing stream (as of water)

♦ cataclysm, cataract, deluge, flood, inundation, overflow, spate

tor•ren•tial \tȯ-ˈren-chəl\ *adj* **:** relating to or resembling a torrent ⟨~ rains⟩
tor•rid \ˈtȯr-əd\ *adj* **1** ♦ **:** parched with heat especially of the sun **:** HOT **2 :** ARDENT

♦ broiling, burning, fiery, hot, red-hot, scorching, sultry

torrid zone *n* **:** the region of the earth between the Tropic of Cancer and the Tropic of Capricorn
tor•sion \ˈtȯr-shən\ *n* **1 :** a wrenching by which one part of a body is under pressure to turn about a longitudinal axis while the other part is held fast or is under pressure to turn in the opposite direction **2 :** a twisting of a bodily organ or part on its own axis — **tor•sion•al** \ˈtȯr-shə-nəl\ *adj* — **tor•sion•al•ly** *adv*
tor•so \ˈtȯr-sō\ *n, pl* **torsos** *or* **tor•si** \ˈtȯr-ˌsē\ **:** the trunk of the human body
tort \ˈtȯrt\ *n* **:** a wrongful act which does not involve a breach of contract and for which the injured party can recover damages in a civil action
tor•ti•lla \tȯr-ˈtē-ə\ *n* **:** a round thin cake of unleavened cornmeal or wheat flour bread
tor•toise \ˈtȯr-təs\ *n* **:** TURTLE; *esp* **:** any of a family of land turtles
tor•toise•shell \-ˌshel\ *n* **:** the mottled horny substance of the shell of some turtles used in inlaying and in making various ornamental articles — **tortoiseshell** *adj*
tor•to•ni \tȯr-ˈtō-nē\ *n* **:** rich ice cream often made with minced almonds and chopped cherries and flavored with rum
tor•tu•ous \ˈtȯr-chə-wəs\ *adj* **1** ♦ **:** marked by twists or turns **:** WINDING **2 :** DEVIOUS, TRICKY

♦ crooked, devious, serpentine, sinuous, winding

[1]**tor•ture** \ˈtȯr-chər\ *n* **1** ♦ **:** anguish of body or mind **2** ♦ **:** the infliction of severe pain especially to punish or coerce — **tor•tur•ous** \ˈtȯrch-rəs, ˈtȯr-chə-\ *adj*

♦ [1] affliction, agony, anguish, distress, misery, pain, torment, tribulation, woe ♦ [2] agony, hell, horror, misery, murder, nightmare, torment

[2]**torture** *vb* **tor•tured; tor•tur•ing** **1** ♦ **:** to cause intense suffering to **:** TORMENT **2 :** to punish or coerce by inflicting severe pain **3 :** TWIST, DISTORT

♦ afflict, agonize, bedevil, curse, harrow, martyr, persecute, plague, rack, torment

tor•tur•er \ˈtȯr-chər-ər\ *n* ♦ **:** one that tortures

♦ heckler, oppressor, persecutor, taunter, tormentor

To•ry \ˈtōr-ē\ *n, pl* **Tories** **1 :** a member of a chiefly 18th century British party upholding the established church and the traditional political structure **2 :** an American supporter of the British during the American Revolution **3** *often not cap* ♦ **:** an extreme conservative — **Tory** *adj*

♦ conservative, reactionary, rightist

[1]**toss** \ˈtȯs, ˈtäs\ *vb* **1 :** to fling to and fro or up and down; *also* **:** BANDY **2** ♦ **:** to throw with a quick light motion **3 :** to fling or lift with a sudden motion ⟨~*ed* her head angrily⟩ **4 :** to move restlessly or turbulently ⟨~*es* on the waves⟩ **5** ♦ **:** to twist and turn repeatedly **6 :** FLOUNCE **7 :** to accomplish readily ⟨~ off an article⟩ **8 :** to decide an issue by flipping a coin **9** ♦ **:** to consume by drinking ⟨~ down a drink⟩

♦ [2] cast, catapult, chuck, dash, fire, fling, heave, hurl, hurtle, launch, peg, pelt, pitch, sling, throw ♦ [5] careen, lurch, pitch, rock, roll, seesaw, sway, wobble ♦ *usu* **toss down** *or* **toss off** [9] drink, guzzle, imbibe, quaff, sup, swig

[2]**toss** *n* **:** an act or instance of tossing; *esp* **:** TOSS-UP 1
toss–up \-ˌəp\ *n* **1 :** a deciding by flipping a coin **2 :** an even chance **3 :** something that offers no clear basis for choice
[1]**tot** \ˈtät\ *n* **1 :** a small child **2 :** a small drink of alcoholic liquor **:** SHOT
[2]**tot** *vb* **tot•ted; tot•ting :** to add up
[3]**tot** *abbr* total
[1]**to•tal** \ˈtōt-ᵊl\ *adj* **1** ♦ **:** making up a whole **:** ENTIRE ⟨~ amount⟩ **2 :** being definitely what is stated **:** COMPLETE ⟨a ~ failure⟩ **3** ♦ **:** involving a complete and unified effort especially to achieve a desired effect

♦ [1] complete, comprehensive, entire, full, grand, intact, integral, perfect, plenary, whole ♦ [3] all-out, clean, complete, comprehensive, exhaustive, full-scale, out-and-out, thorough, thoroughgoing

[2]**total** *n* **1 :** SUM 4 **2** ♦ **:** the entire amount

♦ aggregate, full, sum, totality, whole

[3]**total** *vb* **to•taled** *or* **to•talled; to•tal•ing** *or* **to•tal•ling** **1** ♦ **:** to

add up **2** ♦ **:** to amount to **:** NUMBER **3 :** to make a total wreck of (a car)

♦ [1] add, foot, sum ♦ [2] add up, amount, come, number, sum

to•tal•i•tar•i•an \tō-ˌta-lə-ˈter-ē-ən\ *adj* **:** of, relating to, or advocating a political regime based on subordination of the individual to the state and strict control of all aspects of life especially by coercive measures — **totalitarian** *n*

to•tal•i•tar•i•an•ism \tō-ˌta-lə-ˈter-ē-ə-ˌni-zəm\ *n* ♦ **:** centralized control by an autocratic authority

♦ autocracy, despotism, dictatorship, tyranny

to•tal•i•ty \tō-ˈta-lə-tē\ *n, pl* **-ties** **1** ♦ **:** an aggregate amount **:** SUM, WHOLE **2 :** ENTIRETY, WHOLENESS

♦ aggregate, full, sum, total, whole

to•tal•iza•tor *or* **to•tal•isa•tor** \ˈtōt-ᵊl-ə-ˌzā-tər\ *n* **:** a machine for registering and indicating the number of bets and the odds on a horse or dog race

to•tal•ly \ˈtō-tᵊl-ē\ *adv* ♦ **:** in a total manner **:** to a total or complete degree

♦ absolutely, all, altogether, clean, completely, entirely, fully, quite, utterly, wholly ♦ completely, exhaustively, fully, minutely, roundly, thoroughly

[1]**tote** \ˈtōt\ *vb* **tot•ed; tot•ing** ♦ **:** to carry by hand

♦ bear, carry, cart, convey, ferry, haul, lug, pack, transport

[2]**tote** *vb* **tot•ed; tot•ing :** ADD, TOTAL — usually used with *up*

to•tem \ˈtō-təm\ *n* **:** an object (as an animal or plant) serving as the emblem of a family or clan and often as a reminder of its ancestry; *also* **:** something usually carved or painted to represent such an object

totem pole *n* **:** a pole that is carved with a series of totems and is erected before the houses of some northwest American Indians

tot•ter \ˈtä-tər\ *vb* **1** ♦ **:** to tremble or rock as if about to fall **:** SWAY **2** ♦ **:** to move unsteadily **:** STAGGER

♦ [1] falter, rock, seesaw, sway, teeter, waver, wobble ♦ [2] careen, dodder, lurch, reel, stagger, teeter

tou•can \ˈtü-ˌkan\ *n* **:** any of a family of chiefly fruit-eating birds of tropical America with brilliant coloring and a very large bill

[1]**touch** \ˈtəch\ *vb* **1 :** to bring a bodily part (as the hand) into contact with so as to feel **2** ♦ **:** to be or cause to be in contact **3 :** to strike or push lightly especially with the hand or foot **4 :** DISTURB, HARM **5 :** to make use of ⟨never ~*es* alcohol⟩ **6 :** to induce to give or lend **7 :** to get to **:** REACH **8** ♦ **:** to refer to in passing **:** MENTION **9** ♦ **:** to affect the interest of **:** CONCERN **10 a :** to leave a mark on **b** ♦ **:** to harm slightly by or as if by contact **11** ♦ **:** to move to sympathetic feeling **12 :** to come close **:** VERGE **13** ♦ **:** to have a bearing **:** RELATE — used with *on* or *upon* **14 :** to make a usually brief or incidental stop in port

♦ [2] abut, adjoin, border (on), flank, fringe, join, skirt, verge (on) ♦ *usu* **touch on** *or* **touch upon** [8, 13] advert (to), cite, instance, mention, name, note, notice, quote, refer (to), specify ♦ [9] affect, concern, interest, involve ♦ [10b] blemish, mar, poison, spoil, stain, taint, tarnish, vitiate ♦ [11] affect, impact, impress, influence, move, strike, sway, tell

[2]**touch** *n* **1 :** a light stroke or tap **2 :** the act or fact of touching or being touched **3 :** the sense by which pressure or traction on the skin or mucous membrane is perceived; *also* **:** a particular sensation conveyed by this sense **4 :** mental or moral sensitiveness **:** TACT **5 :** a small quantity **:** HINT ⟨a ~ of spring in the air⟩ **6 :** a manner of striking or touching especially the keys of a keyboard instrument **7 :** an improving detail ⟨add a few ~*es* to the painting⟩ **8 :** distinctive manner or skill ⟨the ~ of a master⟩ **9 :** the state of being in contact ⟨keep in ~⟩

touch•down \ˈtəch-ˌdau̇n\ *n* **:** the act of scoring six points in American football by being lawfully in possession of the ball on, above, or behind an opponent's goal line

tou•ché \tü-ˈshā\ *interj* — used to acknowledge a hit in fencing or the success of an argument, an accusation, or a witty point

touch football *n* **:** football in which touching is substituted for tackling

touch•ing *adj* ♦ **:** capable of stirring emotions

♦ affecting, emotional, impressive, moving, poignant, stirring

touch off *vb* **1 :** to describe with precision **2** ♦ **:** to start by or as if by touching with fire

♦ activate, actuate, crank, drive, move, propel, run, set off, spark, start, trigger, turn on

touch•stone \ˈtəch-ˌstōn\ *n* ♦ **:** a test or criterion of genuineness or quality

♦ criterion, grade, mark, measure, par, standard, yardstick

touch–tone \ˈtəch-ˈtōn\ *adj* **:** of, relating to, or being a telephone having push buttons that produce tones corresponding to numbers

touch up *vb* **:** to improve or perfect by small additional strokes or alterations — **touch–up** \ˈtəch-ˌəp\ *n*

touchy \ˈtə-chē\ *adj* **touch•i•er; -est** **1 :** easily offended **:** PEEVISH **2** ♦ **:** calling for tact in treatment ⟨a ~ subject⟩

♦ catchy, delicate, difficult, knotty, problematic, spiny, thorny, ticklish, tough, tricky

[1]**tough** \ˈtəf\ *adj* **1 :** strong or firm in texture but flexible and not brittle **2 :** not easily chewed **3 :** characterized by severity and determination ⟨a ~ policy⟩ **4** ♦ **:** capable of enduring strain or hardship **5 :** hard to influence **:** STUBBORN **6** ♦ **:** difficult to accomplish, resolve, or cope with ⟨a ~ problem⟩ **7 :** ROWDYISH — **tough•ly** *adv* — **tough•ness** *n*

♦ [4] hard, hard-bitten, hardy, rugged, stout, strong, sturdy, vigorous ♦ [6] arduous, demanding, difficult, exacting, formidable, hard ♦ [6] catchy, delicate, difficult, knotty, problematic, spiny, thorny, ticklish, touchy, tricky

[2]**tough** *n* ♦ **:** a tough person **:** ROWDY

♦ bully, gangster, goon, hood, hoodlum, mobster, mug, punk, rowdy, ruffian, thug

tough•en \ˈtə-fən\ *vb* **tough•ened; tough•en•ing** ♦ **:** to make or become tough

♦ beef, fortify, harden, steel, strengthen ♦ fortify, harden, season, steel, strengthen

tou•pee \tü-ˈpā\ *n* **:** a small wig for a bald spot

[1]**tour** \ˈtu̇r, *1 is also* ˈtau̇r\ *n* **1** ♦ **:** one's turn **2 :** a journey in which one returns to the starting point

♦ hitch, stint, tenure, term

[2]**tour** *vb* ♦ **:** to make a tour

♦ journey, travel, trek, voyage

tour de force \ˌtu̇r-də-ˈfōrs\ *n, pl* **tours de force** *same*\ **:** a feat or display of strength, skill, or ingenuity

Tou•rette's syndrome \tu̇-ˈrets-\ *n* **:** a familial neurological disorder marked by recurrent involuntary tics and vocal sounds

tour•ism \ˈtu̇r-ˌi-zəm\ *n* **1 :** the practice of traveling for recreation **2 :** promotion of touring **3 :** accommodation of tourists

tour•ist \ˈtu̇r-ist\ *n* ♦ **:** one that makes a tour for pleasure or culture

♦ excursionist, sightseer, traveler

tourist class *n* **:** economy accommodations (as on a ship)

tour•ma•line \ˈtu̇r-mə-lən, -ˌlēn\ *n* **:** a mineral that when transparent is valued as a gem

tour•na•ment \ˈtu̇r-nə-mənt, ˈtər-\ *n* **1 :** a medieval sport in which mounted armored knights contended with blunted lances or swords **2** ♦ **:** a championship series of games or athletic contests

♦ bout, competition, contest, event, game, match, meet

tour•ney \-nē\ *n, pl* **tourneys :** a championship series of games or athletic contests **:** TOURNAMENT

tour•ni•quet \ˈtu̇r-ni-kət, ˈtər-\ *n* **:** a device (as a tight bandage) to check bleeding or blood flow

tou•sle \ˈtau̇-zəl\ *vb* **tou•sled; tou•sling :** to disorder by rough handling **:** DISHEVEL

tout \ˈtau̇t, *2 is also* ˈtüt\ *vb* **1 :** to give a tip or solicit bets on a racehorse **2** ♦ **:** to praise or publicize loudly — **tout** *n*

♦ acclaim, applaud, cheer, crack up, hail, laud, praise, salute ♦ ballyhoo, crack up, glorify, plug, promote, publicize, trumpet

[1]**tow** \ˈtō\ *vb* ♦ **:** to draw or pull along behind

♦ drag, draw, hale, haul, lug, pull, tug

[2]**tow** *n* **1 :** an act of towing or condition of being towed **2 :** something (as a barge) that is towed

[3]**tow** *n* **:** short or broken fiber (as of flax or hemp) used especially for yarn, twine, or stuffing

to•ward \ˈtōrd, ˈtō-ərd, tə-ˈwȯrd\ *or* **to•wards** \ˈtōrdz, ˈtō-ərdz, tə-ˈwȯrdz\ *prep* **1 :** in the direction of ⟨heading ~ the river⟩ **2 :** along a course leading to ⟨efforts ~ reconciliation⟩ **3** ♦ **:** in regard to ⟨tolerance ~ minorities⟩ **4 :** so as to face ⟨turn the chair ~ the window⟩ **5 :** close upon ⟨it was getting along ~ sundown⟩ **6 :** for part payment of ⟨here's $100 ~ your tuition⟩

♦ about, apropos of, concerning, of, on, regarding, respecting

tow•boat \ˈtō-ˌbōt\ *n* **:** TUGBOAT

tow•el \ˈtau̇-əl\ *n* **:** an absorbent cloth or paper for wiping or drying

tow•el•ing *or* **tow•el•ling** *n* **:** a cotton or linen fabric for making towels

[1]**tow•er** \ˈtau̇-ər\ *n* **1 :** a tall structure either isolated or built upon a larger structure ⟨an observation ~⟩ **2 :** a towering citadel **3 :** a personal computer case that stands in an upright position — **tow•ered** *adj*

[2]**tower** *vb* **:** to reach or rise to a great height

tow•er•ing *adj* **1** ♦ **:** impressively high or great in size or quality ⟨~ pines⟩ **2 :** reaching high intensity ⟨a ~ rage⟩ **3** ♦ **:** going beyond proper bounds **:** EXCESSIVE ⟨~ ambition⟩

♦ [1] high, lofty, tall ♦ [3] excessive, extreme, immoderate, inordinate, lavish, overmuch

tow•head \ˈtō-ˌhed\ *n* **:** a person having whitish blond hair — **tow•head•ed** \-ˌhe-dəd\ *adj*

to•whee \ˈtō-ˌhē, ˈtō-(ˌ)ē, tō-ˈhē\ *n* **:** a common finch of eastern No. America having the male black, white, and reddish; *also* **:** any of several closely related finches

to wit *adv* **:** NAMELY

town \ˈtau̇n\ *n* **1 :** a compactly settled area usually larger than a village but smaller than a city **2 :** a large densely populated urban area **:** CITY **3 :** the inhabitants of a town **4 :** a New England territorial and political unit usually containing both rural and urban areas; *also* **:** a New England community in which matters of local government are decided by a general assembly (**town meeting**) of qualified voters

town house *n* **1 :** the city residence of a person having a country home **2 :** a single-family house of two or sometimes three stories connected to another house by a common wall

town•ie *or* **towny** \ˈtau̇-nē\ *n, pl* **townies** ♦ **:** a permanent resident of a town as distinguished from a member of another group

♦ burgher

towns•folk \ˈtau̇nz-ˌfōk\ *n pl* **:** TOWNSPEOPLE

town•ship \ˈtau̇n-ˌship\ *n* **1 :** TOWN 4 **2 :** a unit of local government in some states **3 :** an unorganized subdivision of a county **4 :** a division of territory in surveys of U.S. public land containing 36 square miles **5 :** an area in the Republic of South Africa segregated for occupation by persons of non-European descent

towns•man \ˈtau̇nz-mən\ *n* **1 :** a native or resident of a town or city **2 :** a fellow citizen of a town

towns•peo•ple \-ˌpē-pəl\ *n pl* **1 :** the inhabitants of a town or city **2 :** town-bred persons

towns•wom•an \-ˌwu̇-mən\ *n* **1 :** a woman who is a native or resident of a town or city **2 :** a woman who is a fellow citizen of a town

tow•path \ˈtō-ˌpath, -ˌpàth\ *n* **:** a path (as along a canal) traveled especially by draft animals towing boats

tow truck *n* **:** a truck equipped for towing vehicles

tox•emia \täk-ˈsē-mē-ə\ *n* **:** a bodily disorder associated with the presence of toxic substances in the blood

tox•ic \ˈtäk-sik\ *adj* **:** of, relating to, or caused by poison or a toxin **:** POISONOUS — **tox•ic•i•ty** \täk-ˈsi-sə-tē\ *n*

tox•i•col•o•gy \ˌtäk-si-ˈkä-lə-jē\ *n* **:** a science that deals with poisons and especially with problems of their use and control — **tox•i•co•log•i•cal** \-kə-ˈlä-ji-kəl\ *also* **tox•i•co•log•ic** \-kə-ˈlä-jik\ *adj* — **tox•i•col•o•gist** \-ˈkä-lə-jist\ *n*

toxic shock syndrome *n* **:** an acute disease associated with the presence of a bacterium that is characterized by fever, diarrhea, nausea, diffuse erythema, and shock and occurs especially in menstruating females using tampons

tox•in \ˈtäk-sən\ *n* ♦ **:** a poisonous substance produced by metabolic activities of a living organism that is usually unstable, very toxic when introduced into the tissues, and usually capable of inducing antibodies

♦ bane, poison, venom

[1]**toy** \ˈtȯi\ *n* **1 :** something trifling **2 :** a small ornament **:** BAUBLE **3 :** something for a child to play with

[2]**toy** *vb* **1 :** to deal with something lightly **:** TRIFLE **2 :** FLIRT **3 :** to amuse oneself as if with a plaything

[3]**toy** *adj* **1 :** DIMINUTIVE **2 :** designed for use as a toy

tp *abbr* **1** title page **2** township

tpk *or* **tpke** *abbr* turnpike

tr *abbr* **1** translated; translation; translator **2** transpose **3** troop

[1]**trace** \ˈtrās\ *n* **1 a** ♦ **:** a mark (as a footprint or track) left by something that has passed **b** ♦ **:** a path or trail beaten by or as if by the passage of feet **2** ♦ **:** a minute or barely detectable amount **3** ♦ **:** a sign or evidence of some past thing

♦ [1a] imprint, track, trail ♦ [1b] footpath, path, track, trail ♦ [2] glimmer, hint, particle, shadow, suspicion, touch ♦ [3] relic, shadow, vestige

[2]**trace** *vb* **traced; trac•ing 1** ♦ **:** to mark out **:** SKETCH **2 :** to form (as letters) carefully **3 :** to copy (a drawing) by marking lines on transparent paper laid over the drawing to be copied **4** ♦ **:** to follow the trail of **:** track down **5 :** to study out and follow the development of — **trace•able** *adj*

♦ [1] define, delineate, outline, silhouette, sketch ♦ [4] chase, dog, follow, hound, pursue, shadow, tag, tail, track, trail

[3]**trace** *n* **:** either of two lines of a harness for fastening a draft animal to a vehicle

trac•er \ˈtrā-sər\ *n* **1 :** one that traces **2 :** ammunition containing a chemical to mark the flight of projectiles by a trail of smoke or fire

trac•ery \ˈtrā-sə-rē\ *n, pl* **-er•ies :** ornamental work having a design with branching or interlacing lines

tra•chea \ˈtrā-kē-ə\ *n, pl* **-che•ae** \-kē-ˌē\ *also* **-che•as** *or* **-chea :** the main tube by which air passes from the larynx to the lungs of vertebrates — **tra•che•al** \-kē-əl\ *adj*

tra•che•ot•o•my \ˌtrā-kē-ˈä-tə-mē\ *n, pl* **-mies :** the surgical operation of cutting into the trachea especially through the skin

trac•ing *n* **1** ♦ **:** the act of one that traces **2 :** something that is traced **3 :** a graphic record made by an instrument for measuring vibrations or pulsations

♦ chase, following, pursuit

[1]**track** \ˈtrak\ *n* **1** ♦ **:** a mark left in passing **2** ♦ **:** a path, trail, or road made by the passage of animals, people, or vehicles **3 :** a course laid out for racing; *also* **:** track-and-field sports **4 :** one of a series of paths along which material (as music) is recorded (as on a compact disc or magnetic tape) **5 :** the course along which something moves; *esp* **:** a way made by two parallel lines of metal rails **6 :** awareness of a fact or progression ⟨lost ~ of time⟩ **7 :** either of two endless metal belts on which a vehicle (as a bulldozer) travels

♦ [1] imprint, trace, trail ♦ [2] footpath, path, trace, trail

[2]**track** *vb* **1 a** ♦ **:** to follow the tracks or traces of **:** TRAIL **b** ♦ **:** to search for by following evidence until found — often used with *down* **2 :** to observe the moving path of (as a missile) **3 :** to make tracks on **4 :** to carry (as mud) on the feet and deposit — **track•er** *n*

♦ [1a] chase, dog, follow, hound, pursue, shadow, tag, tail, trace, trail ♦ *usu* **track down** [1b] detect, determine, dig up, discover, ferret out, hit on, locate

track•age \ˈtra-kij\ *n* **:** lines of railway track

track–and–field *adj* **:** of or relating to athletic contests held on a running track or on the adjacent field

[1]**tract** \ˈtrakt\ *n* **1** ♦ **:** an area without precise boundaries ⟨huge ~*s* of land⟩ **2** ♦ **:** a defined area of land **3 :** a system of body parts or organs that act together to perform some function ⟨the digestive ~⟩

♦ [1] belt, land, region, zone ♦ [2] field, ground, lot, parcel, plat, plot

[2]**tract** *n* **:** a pamphlet of political or religious propaganda

trac•ta•ble \ˈtrak-tə-bəl\ *adj* ♦ **:** easily controlled **:** DOCILE

♦ amenable, compliant, conformable, docile, obedient, submissive

tract house *n* **:** any of many similar houses built on a tract of land

trac•tion \ˈtrak-shən\ *n* **1 :** the act of drawing **:** the state of being drawn **2 :** the drawing of a vehicle by motive power; *also* **:** the particular form of motive power used **3 :** the adhesive friction of a body on a surface on which it moves **4 :** a pulling force applied to a skeletal structure (as a broken bone) by means of a special device; *also* **:** a state of tension created by such a pulling force ⟨a leg in ~⟩ — **trac•tion•al** \-shə-nəl\ *adj* — **trac•tive** \ˈtrak-tiv\ *adj*

trac•tor \ˈtrak-tər\ *n* **1 :** an automotive vehicle used especially for drawing farm equipment **2 :** a truck for hauling a trailer

[1]**trade** \ˈtrād\ *n* **1** ♦ **:** one's regular business or work **:** OCCUPATION **2** ♦ **:** an occupation requiring manual or mechanical skill **3 :** the persons engaged in a business or industry **4** ♦ **:** the business of buying and selling or bartering commodities **5** ♦ **:** an act of trading

♦ [1] calling, employment, line, occupation, profession, vocation, work ♦ [2] craft, handicraft ♦ [4] business, commerce, marketplace, traffic ♦ [5] barter, commutation, exchange, swap, truck ♦ [5] deal, sale, transaction

2trade *vb* **trad•ed; trad•ing 1** ♦ **:** to give in exchange for another commodity **2 :** to engage in the exchange, purchase, or sale of goods **3 :** to deal regularly as a customer — **trade on :** EXPLOIT ⟨*trades on* his family name⟩

♦ change, commute, exchange, shift, substitute, swap, switch

trade–in \ˈtrād-ˌin\ *n* **:** an item of merchandise traded in
trade in *vb* **:** to turn in as part payment for a purchase
1trade•mark \ˈtrād-ˌmärk\ *n* **1 :** a device (as a word or mark) that points distinctly to the origin or ownership of merchandise to which it is applied and that is legally reserved for the exclusive use of the owner **2** ♦ **:** something that identifies a person or thing

♦ [1, 2] emblem, hallmark, logo, symbol

2trademark *vb* **:** to secure the trademark rights for
trade name *n* **:** a name that is given by a manufacturer or merchant to a product to distinguish it as made or sold by him and that may be used and protected as a trademark
trad•er \ˈtrā-dər\ *n* **1** ♦ **:** a person whose business is buying or selling **2 :** a ship engaged in trade

♦ dealer, merchant, trafficker

trades•man \ˈtrādz-mən\ *n* **1 :** one who runs a retail store **2 :** a worker in a skilled trade **:** CRAFTSMAN
trades•peo•ple \-ˌpē-pəl\ *n pl* **:** people engaged in trade
trade union *n* **:** LABOR UNION
trade wind *n* **:** a wind blowing almost constantly in one direction
trading stamp *n* **:** a printed stamp given as a premium to a retail customer that when accumulated may be redeemed for merchandise
tra•di•tion \trə-ˈdi-shən\ *n* **1 :** an inherited, established, or customary pattern of thought or action **2** ♦ **:** the handing down of beliefs and customs by word of mouth or by example without written instruction; *also* **:** a belief or custom thus handed down

♦ folklore, legend, lore, myth, mythology

tra•di•tion•al \trə-ˌdi-shə-nəl\ *adj* **1 :** consisting of or derived from tradition ⟨~ history⟩ **2** ♦ **:** based on an order, code, or practice accepted from the past ⟨~ morality⟩ **3** ♦ **:** observant of or holding to such traditions ⟨a ~ professor⟩ — **tra•di•tion•al•ly** *adv*

♦ [2] classical, conventional, customary ***Ant*** nontraditional, unconventional, uncustomary ♦ [3] conservative, old-fashioned, orthodox, reactionary

tra•duce \trə-ˈdüs, -ˈdyüs\ *vb* **tra•duced; tra•duc•ing** ♦ **:** to lower the reputation of **:** SLANDER — **tra•duc•er** *n*

♦ blacken, defame, libel, malign, slander, smear, vilify

1traf•fic \ˈtra-fik\ *n* **1** ♦ **:** the business of bartering or buying and selling **2 :** communication or dealings between individuals or groups **3 :** the movement (as of vehicles) along a route; *also* **:** the vehicles, people, ships, or planes moving along a route **4 :** the passengers or cargo carried by a transportation system

♦ business, commerce, marketplace, trade

2traffic *vb* **traf•ficked; traf•fick•ing 1 :** to carry on business dealings **2 :** DEAL, TRADE
traffic circle *n* **:** ROTARY 2
traf•fick•er *n* ♦ **:** a buyer and seller of commodities for profit

♦ dealer, merchant, trader

traffic light *n* **:** a visual signal (as a system of lights) for controlling traffic
tra•ge•di•an \trə-ˈjē-dē-ən\ *n* **1 :** a writer of tragedies **2 :** an actor who plays tragic roles
tra•ge•di•enne \trə-ˌjē-dē-ˈen\ *n* **:** an actress who plays tragic roles
trag•e•dy \ˈtra-jə-dē\ *n, pl* **-dies 1 :** a serious drama with a sorrowful or disastrous conclusion **2** ♦ **:** a disastrous event **:** CALAMITY; *also* **:** MISFORTUNE **3 :** tragic quality or element ⟨the ~ of life⟩

♦ calamity, cataclysm, catastrophe, debacle, disaster, misfortune

trag•ic \ˈtra-jik\ *also* **trag•i•cal** \-ji-kəl\ *adj* **1 :** of, relating to, or expressive of tragedy **2 :** appropriate to tragedy **3** ♦ **:** that is to be regretted or lamented **:** LAMENTABLE, UNFORTUNATE — **trag•i•cal•ly** \-ji-k(ə-)lē\ *adv*

♦ deplorable, distressful, grievous, heartbreaking, lamentable, regrettable, unfortunate, unlucky, woeful

1trail \ˈtrāl\ *vb* **1 :** to hang down so as to drag along or sweep the ground **2 :** to draw or drag along behind **3 :** to extend over a surface in a straggling manner **4 :** to lag behind **5** ♦ **:** to follow the track of **:** PURSUE **6 :** DWINDLE ⟨her voice ~*ed* off⟩

♦ chase, dog, follow, hound, pursue, shadow, tag, tail, trace, track

2trail *n* **1 :** something that trails or is trailed ⟨a ~ of smoke⟩ **2 :** a trace or mark left by something that has passed or been drawn along **:** TRACK ⟨a ~ of blood⟩ **3** ♦ **:** a beaten path; *also* **:** a marked path through woods

♦ footpath, path, trace, track

trail bike *n* **:** a small motorcycle for off-road use
trail•blaz•er \-ˌblā-zər\ *n* **:** PATHFINDER, PIONEER — **trail•blaz•ing** *adj or n*
trail•er \ˈtrā-lər\ *n* **1 :** one that trails; *esp* **:** a creeping plant (as an ivy) **2 :** a vehicle that is hauled by another (as a tractor) **3** ♦ **:** a vehicle equipped to serve wherever parked as a dwelling or place of business **4 :** PREVIEW 2

♦ camper, caravan, motor home

trailing arbutus *n* **:** a creeping spring-flowering plant of the heath family with fragrant pink or white flowers
1train \ˈtrān\ *n* **1 :** a part of a gown that trails behind the wearer **2** ♦ **:** a group of retainers or attendants **:** RETINUE **3** ♦ **:** a moving file of persons, vehicles, or animals **4** ♦ **:** a connected series ⟨a ~ of thought⟩ **5 :** AFTERMATH **6 :** a connected line of railroad cars usually hauled by a locomotive

♦ [2] cortege, following, retinue, suite ♦ [3] column, cue, file, line, queue, range, string ♦ [4] chain, progression, sequence, string

2train *vb* **1 :** to cause to grow as desired ⟨~ a vine on a trellis⟩ **2 a :** to form by instruction, discipline, or drill **b** ♦ **:** to teach so as to make fit, qualified, or proficient **3 :** to make or become prepared (as by exercise) for a test of skill **4** ♦ **:** to aim at an object or objective ⟨~ guns on a fort⟩ — **train•er** *n*

♦ [2b] educate, indoctrinate, instruct, school, teach, tutor ♦ [4] concentrate, fasten, focus, rivet ♦ [4] aim, bend, cast, direct, head, level, set

train•ee \trā-ˈnē\ *n* **:** one who is being trained especially for a job
train•ing *n* **1** ♦ **:** the act, process, or method of one who trains **2 :** the skill, knowledge, or experience gained by one who trains

♦ education, instruction, teaching, tutelage ♦ drill, exercise, practice, routine, workout

train•man \-mən\ *n* **:** a member of a train crew
traipse \ˈtrāps\ *vb* **traipsed; traips•ing 1** ♦ **:** to go on foot **:** WALK **2** ♦ **:** to walk or travel about without apparent plan but with or without a purpose

♦ [1] foot, leg, pad, step, tread, walk ♦ [2] gad, gallivant, knock, maunder, meander, mope, ramble, range, roam, rove, wander

trait \ˈtrāt\ *n* **1** ♦ **:** a distinguishing quality (as of personality) **:** PECULIARITY **2 :** an inherited characteristic

♦ attribute, character, characteristic, feature, mark, peculiarity, point, property, quality

trai•tor \ˈtrā-tər\ *n* **1** ♦ **:** one who betrays another's trust or is false to an obligation **2 :** one who commits treason

♦ apostate, betrayer, double-crosser, quisling, recreant, turncoat

trai•tor•ous \ˈtrā-tə-rəs\ *adj* **1** ♦ **:** guilty or capable of treason **2 :** constituting treason ⟨~ activities⟩

♦ disloyal, faithless, false, fickle, inconstant, loose, perfidious, recreant, treacherous, unfaithful, untrue

tra•jec•to•ry \trə-ˈjek-tə-rē\ *n, pl* **-ries :** the curve that a body (as a planet in its orbit) describes in space
tram \ˈtram\ *n* **1 :** a boxlike car running on rails (as in a mine) **2** *chiefly Brit* **:** STREETCAR **3 :** an overhead cable car
1tram•mel \ˈtra-məl\ *n* ♦ **:** something impeding activity, progress, or freedom — usually used in plural

♦ chain, encumbrance, fetter, hindrance, interference, manacle, shackle

2trammel *vb* **-meled** *or* **-melled; -mel•ing** *or* **-mel•ling 1 :** to catch and hold in or as if in a net **2** ♦ **:** to prevent or impede the free play of **:** HAMPER

♦ fetter, hamper, hinder, hobble, impede, inhibit, interfere with, manacle, shackle, tie up

1tramp \ˈtramp, *1 & 3 are also* ˈträmp, ˈtrȯmp\ *vb* **1** ♦ **:** to walk, tread, or step heavily **2** : to walk about or through; *also* : HIKE **3** ♦ : to tread on forcibly and repeatedly

♦ [1, 3] clump, lumber, pound, stamp, stomp, trample, tromp

[2]**tramp** \ˈtramp, *5 is also* ˈträmp, ˈtrȯmp\ *n* **1** : a foot traveler **2** ♦ : a begging or thieving vagrant **3** : an immoral woman; *esp* : PROSTITUTE **4** : a walking trip : HIKE **5** : the succession of sounds made by the beating of feet on a road **6** : a ship that does not follow a regular course but takes cargo to any port

♦ bum, hobo, vagabond, vagrant

tram•ple \ˈtram-pəl\ *vb* **tram•pled; tram•pling** **1** : to tread heavily so as to bruise, crush, or injure **2** : to inflict injury or destruction **3** ♦ : to press down or crush by or as if by treading — **trample** *n* — **tram•pler** *n*

♦ stamp, stomp, tramp, tromp

tram•po•line \ˌtram-pə-ˈlēn, ˈtram-pə-ˌlēn\ *n* : a resilient sheet or web (as of nylon) supported by springs in a metal frame and used as a springboard in tumbling — **tram•po•lin•ist** \-ˈlē-nist, -ˌlē-\ *n*

trance \ˈtrans\ *n* **1** : STUPOR, DAZE **2** : a sleeplike state of altered consciousness (as of deep hypnosis) **3** ♦ : a state of very deep absorption

♦ reverie, study, woolgathering

tran•quil \ˈtraŋ-kwəl, ˈtran-\ *adj* ♦ : free from agitation or disturbance — **tran•quil•ly** *adv*

♦ calm, hushed, peaceful, quiet, restful, serene, still ♦ calm, collected, composed, cool, placid, self-possessed, serene, undisturbed, unperturbed, unshaken, untroubled, unworried

tran•quil•ize *also* **tran•quil•lize** \ˈtraŋ-kwə-ˌlīz, ˈtran-\ *vb* **-ized** *also* **-lized; -iz•ing** *also* **-liz•ing** ♦ : to make or become tranquil; *esp* : to relieve of mental tension and anxiety by means of drugs

♦ allay, calm, compose, quiet, settle, soothe, still

tran•quil•iz•er *also* **tran•quil•liz•er** \-ˌlī-zər\ *n* : a drug used to relieve mental disturbance (as tension and anxiety)

tran•quil•li•ty \tran-ˈkwi-lə-tē, traŋ-\ *or* **tran•quil•i•ty** *n* ♦ : the quality or state of being tranquil

♦ calm, calmness, hush, peace, placidity, quiet, quietness, repose, serenity, still, stillness ♦ aplomb, calmness, composure, coolness, equanimity, placidity, self-possession, serenity

trans *abbr* **1** transaction **2** transitive **3** translated; translation; translator **4** transmission **5** transportation **6** transverse

trans•act \tran-ˈzakt, -ˈsakt\ *vb* : CARRY OUT, PERFORM; *also* : CONDUCT

trans•ac•tion \-ˈzak-shən, -ˈsak-\ *n* **1** : something transacted; *esp* : a business deal **2** ♦ : an act or process of transacting **3** *pl* : the records of the proceedings of a society or organization

♦ deal, sale, trade

trans•at•lan•tic \ˌtrans-ət-ˈlan-tik, ˌtranz-\ *adj* : crossing or extending across or situated beyond the Atlantic Ocean

trans•ax•le \trans-ˈak-səl\ *n* : a unit combining the transmission and differential gear of a front-wheel-drive automobile

trans•ceiv•er \tran-ˈsē-vər\ *n* : a radio transmitter-receiver that uses many of the same components for both transmission and reception

tran•scend \tran-ˈsend\ *vb* **1** : to rise above the limits of **2** ♦ : to rise above or go beyond the limits of : SURPASS

♦ beat, better, eclipse, excel, outdistance, outdo, outshine, outstrip, surpass, top

tran•scen•dence \tran-ˈsen-dən(t)s\ *n* ♦ : the quality or state of being transcendent

♦ distinction, dominance, eminence, preeminence, primacy, superiority, supremacy

tran•scen•dent \-ˈsen-dənt\ *adj* **1** : exceeding usual limits : SURPASSING **2** : transcending material existence

tran•scen•den•tal \ˌtran-ˌsen-ˈdent-ᵊl, -sən-\ *adj* **1** : TRANSCENDENT 2 **2** : of, relating to, or characteristic of transcendentalism; *also* : ABSTRUSE

tran•scen•den•tal•ism \-ᵊl-ˌi-zəm\ *n* : a philosophy holding that ultimate reality is unknowable or asserting the primacy of the spiritual over the material and empirical — **tran•scen•den•tal•ist** \-ᵊl-ist\ *adj or n*

trans•con•ti•nen•tal \ˌtrans-ˌkänt-ᵊn-ˈent-ᵊl\ *adj* : extending or going across a continent

tran•scribe \trans-ˈkrīb\ *vb* **tran•scribed; tran•scrib•ing** **1** : to write a copy of **2** : to make a copy of (dictated or recorded matter) in longhand or on a typewriter **3** : to represent (speech sounds) by means of phonetic symbols; *also* : to make a musical transcription of

tran•script \ˈtran-ˌskript\ *n* **1** : a written, printed, or typed copy **2** : an official copy especially of a student's educational record

tran•scrip•tion \tran-ˈskrip-shən\ *n* **1** : an act or process of transcribing **2** : COPY, TRANSCRIPT **3** : an arrangement of a musical composition for some instrument or voice other than the original

tran•scrip•tion•ist \-shə-nist\ *n* : one that transcribes; *esp* : a typist who transcribes medical reports

trans•der•mal \trans-ˈdər-məl, ˈtranz-\ *adj* : relating to, being, or supplying a medication in a form for absorption through the skin ⟨~ nicotine patch⟩

trans•duc•er \trans-ˈdü-sər, tranz-, -ˈdyü-\ *n* : a device that is actuated by power from one system and supplies power usually in another form to a second system

tran•sept \ˈtran-ˌsept\ *n* : the part of a cruciform church that crosses at right angles to the greatest length; *also* : either of the projecting ends

trans fat \ˈtran(t)s-, ˈtranz-\ *n* : a fat containing unsaturated fatty acids (**trans–fatty acids**) that have been linked to an increase in blood cholesterol

[1]**trans•fer** \trans-ˈfər, ˈtrans-ˌfər\ *vb* **trans•ferred; trans•fer•ring** **1** ♦ : to pass or cause to pass from one person, place, or situation to another **2** ♦ : to make over the possession of **3** : to print or copy from one surface to another by contact **4** : to change from one vehicle or transportation line to another — **trans•fer•able** \trans-ˈfər-ə-bəl\ *adj* — **trans•fer•al** \-əl\ *n*

♦ [1] consign, dispatch, move, pack, send, ship, transmit, transport ♦ [1] commend, commit, consign, delegate, deliver, entrust, give, hand over, leave, pass, transmit, trust, turn over, vest ♦ [2] alienate, assign, cede, deed, make over

[2]**trans•fer** \ˈtrans-ˌfər\ *n* **1** : conveyance of right, title, or interest in property from one person to another **2** : an act or process of transferring **3** : one that transfers or is transferred **4** : a ticket entitling a passenger to continue a trip on another route

trans•fer•ence \trans-ˈfər-əns\ *n* : an act, process, or instance of transferring

trans•fig•u•ra•tion \ˌtrans-ˌfi-gyə-ˈrā-shən, -gə-\ *n* ♦ : a change in form or appearance

♦ changeover, conversion, metamorphosis, transformation

trans•fig•ure \trans-ˈfi-gyər\ *vb* **-ured; -ur•ing** **1** ♦ : to change the form or appearance of **2** : EXALT, GLORIFY

♦ convert, make over, metamorphose, transform

trans•fix \trans-ˈfiks\ *vb* **1** ♦ : to pierce through with or as if with a pointed weapon **2** : to hold motionless by or as if by piercing

♦ gore, harpoon, impale, lance, pierce, puncture, skewer, spear, spike, stab, stick

trans•form \trans-ˈfȯrm\ *vb* ♦ : to change in structure, appearance, or character

♦ convert, make over, metamorphose, transfigure

trans•for•ma•tion \ˌtrans-fər-ˈmā-shən\ *n* ♦ : an act, process, or instance of transforming or being transformed

♦ changeover, conversion, metamorphosis, transfiguration

trans•form•er \trans-ˈfȯr-mər\ *n* : one that transforms; *esp* : a device for converting variations of current in one circuit into variations of voltage and current in another circuit

trans•fuse \trans-ˈfyüz\ *vb* **trans•fused; trans•fus•ing** **1** ♦ : to cause to pass from one to another **2** ♦ : to diffuse into or through **3** : to transfer (as blood) into a vein or an artery of a person or animal — **trans•fu•sion** \-ˈfyü-zhən\ *n*

♦ [1] communicate, convey, impart, spread, transfer, transmit ♦ [2] percolate, permeate, suffuse

trans•gen•der \tranz-ˈjen-dər\ *adj* : having physical or behavioral characteristics transcending traditional gender boundaries

trans•gen•ic \tran(t)s-ˈje-nik\ *adj* : being or used to produce an organism or cell with genes introduced from another species of organism ⟨~ crops⟩

trans•gress \trans-ˈgres, tranz-\ *vb* **1** ♦ : to go beyond the limits set by ⟨~ the divine law⟩ **2** : to go beyond : EXCEED **3** ♦ : to violate a command or law : SIN — **trans•gres•sor** \-ˈgre-sər\ *n*

♦ [1] breach, break, violate ♦ [3] err, offend, sin, trespass

trans•gres•sion \trans-ˈgre-shən\ *n* ♦ : an act, process, or instance of transgressing

♦ breach, crime, error, malefaction, misdeed, misdoing, offense, sin, trespass, violation, wrongdoing

[1]**tran•sient** \ˈtran-shənt; -sē-ənt, -shē-, -zē-\ *adj* **1** ♦ **:** not lasting long **:** SHORT-LIVED **2 :** passing through a place with only a brief stay — **tran•sient•ly** *adv*

♦ ephemeral, evanescent, flash, fleeting, fugitive, impermanent, momentary, short-lived

[2]**transient** *n* **:** one that is transient; *esp* **:** a transient guest

tran•sis•tor \tran-ˈzis-tər, -ˈsis-\ *n* **1 :** a small electronic semiconductor device used in electronic equipment **2 :** a radio having transistors

tran•sis•tor•ized \-tə-ˌrīzd\ *adj* **:** having or using transistors

tran•sit \ˈtran-sət, -zət\ *n* **1 :** a passing through, across, or over **:** PASSAGE **2 :** conveyance of persons or things from one place to another **3 :** usually local transportation especially of people by public conveyance **4 :** a surveyor's instrument for measuring angles

tran•si•tion \tran-ˈsi-shən, -ˈzi-\ *n* **:** passage from one state, place, stage, or subject to another **:** CHANGE — **tran•si•tion•al** \-ˈsi-shə-nəl, -ˈzi-\ *adj*

tran•si•tive \ˈtran-sə-tiv, -zə-\ *adj* **1 :** having or containing an object required to complete the meaning **2 :** TRANSITIONAL — **tran•si•tive•ly** *adv* — **tran•si•tive•ness** *n* — **tran•si•tiv•i•ty** \ˌtran-sə-ˈti-və-tē, -zə-\ *n*

tran•si•to•ry \ˈtran-sə-ˌtōr-ē, -zə-\ *adj* **:** of brief duration **:** SHORT-LIVED

transl *abbr* translated; translation

trans•late \trans-ˈlāt, tranz-\ *vb* **trans•lat•ed; trans•lat•ing** **1 :** to change from one place, state, or form to another **2 :** to convey to heaven without death **3 a :** to turn into one's own or another language **b** ♦ **:** to express in different terms and especially different words — **trans•lat•able** *adj* — **trans•la•tor** \-ˈlā-tər\ *n*

♦ paraphrase, rephrase, restate

trans•la•tion \trans-ˈlā-shən\ *n* **1** ♦ **:** an act, process, or instance of translating **2 :** the process of forming a protein molecule from information in messenger RNA

♦ paraphrase

trans•lit•er•ate \trans-ˈli-tə-ˌrāt, tranz-\ *vb* **-at•ed; -at•ing :** to represent or spell in the characters of another alphabet — **trans•lit•er•a•tion** \ˌtrans-ˌli-tə-ˈrā-shən, ˌtranz-\ *n*

trans•lu•cent \trans-ˈlüs-ᵊnt, tranz-\ *adj* **:** not transparent but clear enough to allow light to pass through — **trans•lu•cence** \-ᵊns\ *n* — **trans•lu•cen•cy** \-ᵊn-sē\ *n* — **trans•lu•cent•ly** *adv*

trans•mi•grate \-ˈmī-ˌgrāt\ *vb* **:** to pass at death from one body or being to another — **trans•mi•gra•tion** \ˌtrans-mī-ˈgrā-shən, ˌtranz-\ *n* — **trans•mi•gra•to•ry** \trans-ˈmī-grə-ˌtōr-ē\ *adj*

trans•mis•sion \-ˈmi-shən\ *n* **1 :** an act or process of transmitting **2 :** the passage of radio waves between transmitting stations and receiving stations **3 :** the gears by which power is transmitted from the engine of an automobile to the axle that propels the vehicle **4 :** something transmitted

trans•mit \-ˈmit\ *vb* **trans•mit•ted; trans•mit•ting** **1** ♦ **:** to transfer from one person or place to another **2 :** to pass on by or as if by inheritance **3 :** to cause or allow to spread abroad or to another ⟨∼ a disease⟩ **4 :** to cause (as light, electricity, or force) to pass through space or a medium **5 :** to send out (radio or television signals) — **trans•mis•si•ble** \-ˈmi-sə-bəl\ *adj* — **trans•mit•tal** \-ˈmit-ᵊl\ *n*

♦ communicate, convey, impart, spread, transfer, transfuse ♦ consign, dispatch, pack, send, ship, transfer, transport

trans•mit•ta•ble \trans-ˈmi-tə-bəl\ *adj* ♦ **:** capable of being transmitted

♦ catching, communicable, contagious

trans•mit•ter \-ˈmi-tər\ *n* **:** one that transmits; *esp* **:** an apparatus for transmitting telegraph, radio, or television signals

trans•mog•ri•fy \trans-ˈmä-grə-ˌfī, tranz-\ *vb* **-fied; -fy•ing :** to change or alter often with grotesque or humorous effect — **trans•mog•ri•fi•ca•tion** \-ˌmä-grə-fə-ˈkā-shən\ *n*

trans•mute \-ˈmyüt\ *vb* **trans•muted; trans•mut•ing :** to change or alter in form, appearance, or nature — **trans•mu•ta•tion** \ˌtrans-myu̇-ˈtā-shən, ˌtranz-\ *n*

trans•na•tion•al \-ˈna-shə-nəl\ *adj* **:** extending beyond national boundaries

trans•oce•an•ic \ˌtrans-ˌō-shē-ˈa-nik, ˌtranz-\ *adj* **1 :** lying or dwelling beyond the ocean **2 :** crossing or extending across the ocean

tran•som \ˈtran-səm\ *n* **1 :** a piece (as a crossbar in the frame of a window or door) that lies crosswise in a structure **2 :** a window above an opening (as a door) built on and often hinged to a horizontal crossbar

tran•son•ic *also* **trans–son•ic** \trans-ˈsä-nik\ *adj* **:** being or relating to speeds near that of sound in air or about 741 miles (1185 kilometers) per hour

trans•pa•cif•ic \ˌtrans-pə-ˈsi-fik\ *adj* **:** crossing, extending across, or situated beyond the Pacific Ocean

trans•par•ent \trans-ˈpar-ənt\ *adj* **1** ♦ **:** clear enough to be seen through **2** ♦ **:** fine or sheer enough to be seen through ⟨a ∼ fabric⟩ **3** ♦ **:** readily understood **:** CLEAR; *also* **:** easily detected ⟨a ∼ lie⟩ — **trans•par•en•cy** \-ən-sē\ *n* — **trans•par•ent•ly** *adv*

♦ [1] clear, limpid, liquid, lucent, pellucid ♦ [2] gauzy, sheer ♦ [3] apparent, broad, clear, clear-cut, distinct, evident, lucid, manifest, obvious, palpable, patent, perspicuous, plain, unambiguous, unequivocal, unmistakable

tran•spire \trans-ˈpīr\ *vb* **trans•pired; trans•pir•ing** **1 :** to pass or give off (as water vapor) through pores or a membrane **2 :** to become known **3** ♦ **:** to take place **:** HAPPEN — **tran•spi•ra•tion** \ˌtrans-pə-ˈrā-shən\ *n*

♦ be, befall, betide, chance, come, go, happen, occur, pass

[1]**trans•plant** \trans-ˈplant\ *vb* **1 :** to dig up and plant elsewhere **2 :** to remove from one place and settle or introduce elsewhere **:** TRANSPORT **3 :** to transfer (an organ or tissue) from one part or individual to another — **trans•plan•ta•tion** \ˌtrans-ˌplan-ˈtā-shən\ *n*

[2]**trans•plant** \ˈtrans-ˌplant\ *n* **1 :** a person or thing transplanted **2 :** the act or process of transplanting

trans•po•lar \trans-ˈpō-lər\ *adj* **:** going or extending across either of the polar regions

transponder \tran-ˈspän-dər\ *n* **:** a radio or radar set that upon receiving a certain signal emits a radio signal and that is used to locate and identify objects and in satellites to relay communications signals

[1]**trans•port** \trans-ˈpōrt\ *vb* **1** ♦ **:** to convey from one place to another **2** ♦ **:** to carry away by strong emotion **:** ENRAPTURE **3** ♦ **:** to send to a penal colony overseas — **trans•port•er** *n*

♦ [1] consign, dispatch, pack, send, ship, transfer, transmit ♦ [1] bear, carry, cart, convey, ferry, haul, lug, pack, tote ♦ [2] carry away, enrapture, enthrall, entrance, ravish ♦ [3] banish, deport, displace, exile, expatriate

[2]**trans•port** \ˈtrans-ˌpōrt\ *n* **1 :** an act of transporting **2** ♦ **:** strong or intensely pleasurable emotion ⟨∼*s* of joy⟩ **3** ♦ **:** a ship used in transporting troops or supplies; *also* **:** a vehicle (as a truck or plane) used to transport persons or goods

♦ [2] ecstasy, elation, euphoria, exhilaration, heaven, intoxication, paradise, rapture, rhapsody ♦ [3] conveyance, vehicle

trans•por•ta•tion \ˌtrans-pər-ˈtā-shən\ *n* **1 :** an act, process, or instance of transporting or being transported **2 :** means of conveyance or travel from one place to another

trans•pose \trans-ˈpōz\ *vb* **trans•posed; trans•pos•ing** **1 :** to change the position or sequence of ⟨∼ the letters in a word⟩ **2 :** to write or perform (a musical composition) in a different key — **trans•po•si•tion** \ˌtrans-pə-ˈzi-shən\ *n*

trans•sex•u•al \(ˌ)trans-ˈsek-shə-wəl\ *n* **:** a person who psychologically identifies with the opposite sex and may seek to live as a member of this sex especially by undergoing surgery to modify the external sex organs

trans•ship \tran-ˈship, trans-\ *vb* **:** to transfer for further transportation from one ship or conveyance to another — **trans•ship•ment** *n*

tran•sub•stan•ti•a•tion \ˌtran-səb-ˌstan-chē-ˈā-shən\ *n* **:** the change in the eucharistic elements from the substance of bread and wine to the substance of the body of Christ with only the appearances of bread and wine remaining

trans•verse \trans-ˈvərs, tranz-\ *adj* **:** lying across **:** set crosswise — **transverse** \ˈtrans-ˌvərs, ˈtranz-\ *n*

trans•verse•ly *adv* ♦ **:** in a transverse direction or line

♦ athwart, crosswise, obliquely

trans•ves•tite \trans-ˈves-ˌtīt, tranz-\ *n* **:** a person and especially a male who adopts the dress and often the behavior of the opposite sex — **transvestite** *adj* — **trans•ves•tism** \-ˌti-zəm\ *n*

[1]**trap** \ˈtrap\ *n* **1 :** a device for catching animals **2** ♦ **:** something by which one is caught unawares; *also* **:** a situation from which escape is difficult or impossible **3 :** a machine for throwing clay pigeons into the air; *also* **:** SAND TRAP **4 :** a light one-horse carriage on springs **5 :** a device to allow some one thing to pass through while keeping other things out ⟨a ∼ in a drainpipe⟩ **6** *pl* **:** a group of percussion instruments (as in a dance orchestra)

♦ ambush, net, snare, web ♦ ambush, surprise

²**trap** *vb* **trapped; trap·ping** **1** ♦ **:** to catch in or as if in a trap; *also* **:** CONFINE **2 :** to provide or set (a place) with traps **3 :** to set traps for animals especially as a business — **trap·per** *n*

♦ confine, enmesh, ensnare, entangle, entrap, mesh, snare, tangle

trap·door \ˈtrap-ˈdōr\ *n* **:** a lifting or sliding door covering an opening in a floor or roof
tra·peze \tra-ˈpēz\ *n* **:** a gymnastic apparatus consisting of a horizontal bar suspended by two parallel ropes
trap·e·zoid \ˈtra-pə-ˌzȯid\ *n* **:** a 4-sided polygon with exactly two sides parallel — **trap·e·zoi·dal** \ˌtra-pə-ˈzȯid-ᵊl\ *adj*
trap·pings \ˈtra-piŋz\ *n pl* **1 :** CAPARISON 1 **2 :** outward decoration or dress; *also* **:** outward sign ⟨~ of success⟩
traps \ˈtraps\ *n pl* **:** personal belongings **:** LUGGAGE
trap·shoot·ing \ˈtrap-ˌshü-tiŋ\ *n* **:** shooting at clay pigeons sprung from a trap into the air away from the shooter
¹**trash** \ˈtrash\ *n* **1 a** ♦ **:** something of little worth **:** RUBBISH **b** ♦ **:** empty talk **:** NONSENSE **2 a :** a worthless person **b** ♦ **:** such persons as a group **:** RIFFRAFF

♦ [1a] chaff, deadwood, dust, garbage, junk, litter, refuse, riffraff, rubbish, scrap, waste ♦ [1b] bunk, claptrap, drivel, fiddlesticks, folly, foolishness, fudge, hogwash, humbug, nonsense, piffle, rot, silliness, slush, stupidity ♦ [2b] rabble, riffraff, scum

²**trash** *vb* **1 :** VANDALIZE, DESTROY **2 :** ATTACK **3 :** SPOIL, RUIN **4 :** to criticize or disparage harshly **5 :** to dispose of **:** DISCARD ⟨~*ed* the plans⟩
trashy \ˈtra-shē\ *adj* **trash·i·er; -est** ♦ **:** being, resembling, or containing trash **:** of inferior quality

♦ dowdy, inelegant, tacky, tasteless, unfashionable, unstylish ♦ cheap, common, cut-rate, inferior, junky, lousy, mediocre, miserable, poor, rotten, second-rate, shoddy, sleazy

trau·ma \ˈtrau̇-mə, ˈtrȯ-\ *n, pl* **traumas** *also* **trau·ma·ta** \-mə-tə\ **:** a bodily or mental injury usually caused by an external agent; *also* **:** a cause of trauma — **trau·mat·ic** \trə-ˈma-tik, trȯ-, trau̇-\ *adj*
trau·ma·tize \-ˌtīz\ *vb* **-tized; -tiz·ing :** to inflict trauma upon
¹**tra·vail** \trə-ˈvāl, ˈtra-ˌvāl\ *n* **1** ♦ **:** painful work or exertion **:** TOIL **2 :** AGONY, TORMENT **3 :** CHILDBIRTH, LABOR

♦ drudgery, grind, labor (*or* labour), slavery, sweat, toil

²**travail** *vb* **:** to labor hard **:** TOIL
¹**trav·el** \ˈtra-vəl\ *vb* **-eled** *or* **-elled; -el·ing** *or* **-el·ling** **1** ♦ **:** to go on or as if on a trip or tour **:** JOURNEY **2 :** to move as if by traveling ⟨news ~*s* fast⟩ **3 :** ASSOCIATE **4 :** to go from place to place as a sales representative **5 :** to move from point to point ⟨light waves ~ very fast⟩ **6** ♦ **:** to journey over or through ⟨~*ing* the highways⟩

♦ [1] journey, tour, trek, voyage ♦ [6] cover, crisscross, cross, cut, follow, go, pass, proceed, traverse

²**travel** *n* **1 :** the act of traveling **:** PASSAGE **2 :** JOURNEY, TRIP — often used in plural **3 :** the number traveling **:** TRAFFIC **4 :** the motion of a piece of machinery and especially when to and fro
trav·el·er \ˈtra-və-lər\ *or* **trav·el·ler** *n* ♦ **:** one that travels **:** one that takes a journey

♦ excursionist, sightseer, tourist

traveler's check *n* **:** a check paid for in advance that is signed when bought and signed again when cashed
traveling bag *n* ♦ **:** a portable case designed to hold a traveler's clothing and personal articles **:** SUITCASE

♦ carryall, grip, handbag, portmanteau, suitcase

trav·el·ogue *or* **trav·el·og** \ˈtra-və-ˌlȯg, -ˌläg\ *n* **:** a usually illustrated lecture on travel
¹**tra·verse** \ˈtra-vərs\ *n* **:** something that crosses or lies across
²**tra·verse** \trə-ˈvərs, tra-ˈvərs, ˈtra-vərs\ *vb* **tra·versed; tra·vers·ing** **1** ♦ **:** to go or travel across or over **2 :** to move or pass along or through **3 :** to extend over **4 :** SWIVEL

♦ cover, crisscross, cross, cut, follow, go, pass, proceed, travel

³**tra·verse** \ˈtra-ˌvərs\ *adj* **:** TRANSVERSE
trav·er·tine \ˈtra-vər-ˌtēn, -tən\ *n* **:** a crystalline mineral formed by deposition from spring waters
¹**trav·es·ty** \ˈtra-və-stē\ *vb* **-tied; -ty·ing** ♦ **:** to make a travesty of

♦ burlesque, caricature, imitate, mimic, mock, parody, take off

²**travesty** *n, pl* **-ties** ♦ **:** an imitation that makes crude fun of something; *also* **:** an inferior imitation

♦ caricature, farce, joke, mockery, parody, sham

¹**trawl** \ˈtrȯl\ *vb* **:** to fish or catch with a trawl — **trawl·er** *n*
²**trawl** *n* **1 :** a large conical net dragged along the sea bottom in fishing **2 :** a long heavy fishing line equipped with many hooks in series
tray \ˈtrā\ *n* **:** an open receptacle with flat bottom and low rim for holding, carrying, or exhibiting articles
treach·er·ous \ˈtre-chə-rəs\ *adj* **1** ♦ **:** characterized by treachery **2 :** UNTRUSTWORTHY, UNRELIABLE **3 :** providing insecure footing or support — **treach·er·ous·ly** *adv*

♦ disloyal, faithless, false, fickle, inconstant, loose, perfidious, recreant, traitorous, unfaithful, untrue

treach·ery \ˈtre-chə-rē\ *n, pl* **-er·ies** ♦ **:** violation of allegiance or trust

♦ betrayal, disloyalty, double cross, faithlessness, falseness, falsity, infidelity, perfidy, treason, unfaithfulness

trea·cle \ˈtrē-kəl\ *n chiefly Brit* **:** MOLASSES — **trea·cly** \-k(ə-)lē\ *adj*
¹**tread** \ˈtred\ *vb* **trod** \ˈträd\; **trod·den** \ˈträd-ᵊn\ *or* **trod; tread·ing** **1 :** to step or walk on or over **2** ♦ **:** to move on foot **:** WALK **3 :** to beat or press with the feet — **tread water :** to stay afloat and upright in water by sustaining a walking motion

♦ foot, leg, pad, step, traipse, walk

²**tread** *n* **1 :** a mark made by or as if by treading **2 :** the manner or sound of stepping **3 :** the part of a wheel that makes contact with a road **4 :** the horizontal part of a step
trea·dle \ˈtred-ᵊl\ *n* **:** a lever device pressed by the foot to drive a machine — **treadle** *vb*
tread·mill \ˈtred-ˌmil\ *n* **1 :** a mill worked by persons who tread on steps around the edge of a wheel or by animals that walk on an endless belt **2 :** a device with an endless belt on which a person walks or runs in place **3** ♦ **:** a wearisome routine

♦ groove, pattern, rote, routine, rut

treas *abbr* treasurer; treasury
trea·son \ˈtrēz-ᵊn\ *n* **1 :** the offense of attempting to overthrow the government of one's country or of assisting its enemies in war **2** ♦ **:** the betrayal of a trust — **trea·son·able** \-ᵊn-ə-bəl\ *adj* — **trea·son·ous** \-ᵊn-əs\ *adj*

♦ betrayal, disloyalty, double cross, faithlessness, falseness, falsity, infidelity, perfidy, treachery, unfaithfulness

¹**trea·sure** \ˈtre-zhər, ˈtrā-\ *n* **1 :** wealth stored up or held in reserve **2** ♦ **:** something of great value

♦ catch, gem, jewel, pearl, plum, prize

²**treasure** *vb* **trea·sured; trea·sur·ing** **1 :** HOARD **2** ♦ **:** to keep as precious **:** CHERISH

♦ appreciate, cherish, love, prize, value

trea·sur·er \ˈtre-zhə-rər, ˈtrā-\ *n* **:** an officer of a club, business, or government who has charge of money taken in and paid out
treasure trove \-ˌtrōv\ *n* **1 :** treasure of unknown ownership found buried or hidden **2 :** a valuable discovery
trea·sury \ˈtre-zhə-rē, ˈtrā-\ *n, pl* **-sur·ies** **1 :** a place in which stores of wealth are kept **2 :** the place where collected funds are stored and paid out **3** *cap* **:** a governmental department in charge of finances
¹**treat** \ˈtrēt\ *vb* **1 :** to discuss terms of accommodation or settlement **2 a** ♦ **:** to deal with especially in writing — usually used with *of* **b** ♦ **:** to deal with **:** HANDLE **3 :** to pay for the food or entertainment of **4** ♦ **:** to behave or act toward ⟨~ them well⟩ **5 :** to regard in a specified manner ⟨~ as inferiors⟩ **6 :** to give medical or surgical care to **7 :** to subject to some action ⟨~ soil with lime⟩

♦ *usu* **treat of** [2a] concern, cover, deal, pertain ♦ [2b] contend with, cope with, grapple with, handle, manage, maneuver (*or* manoeuvre), negotiate, swing ♦ [4] act, be, deal, handle, serve, use

²**treat** *n* **1 :** an entertainment given free to those invited; *also* **:** food, drink, or entertainment provided at another's expense **2** ♦ **:** a source of joy or amusement

♦ delectation, delight, joy, kick, manna, pleasure ♦ dainty, delicacy, goody, tidbit

trea·tise \ˈtrē-təs\ *n* **:** a systematic written exposition or argument
treat·ment \ˈtrēt-mənt\ *n* **:** the act or manner or an instance of treating someone or something; *also* **:** a substance or method used in treating
trea·ty \ˈtrē-tē\ *n, pl* **treaties** ♦ **:** an agreement made by negotia-

tion or diplomacy especially between two or more states or governments

♦ accord, alliance, compact, convention, covenant, pact

[1]tre•ble \ˈtre-bəl\ *n* **1 :** the highest of the four voice parts in vocal music **:** SOPRANO **2 :** a high-pitched or shrill voice or sound **3 :** the upper half of the musical pitch range
[2]treble *adj* **1** ♦ **:** triple in number or amount **2 :** relating to or having the range of a musical treble **3** ♦ **:** high-pitched **:** SHRILL — **tre•bly** *adv*

♦ [1] threefold, tripartite, triple ♦ [3] acute, sharp, shrill, squeaky

[3]treble *vb* **tre•bled; tre•bling :** to make or become three times the size, amount, or number
[1]tree \ˈtrē\ *n* **1 :** a woody perennial plant usually with a single main stem and a head of branches and leaves at the top **2 :** a piece of wood adapted to a particular use ⟨a shoe ~⟩ **3 :** something resembling a tree ⟨a genealogical ~⟩ — **tree•less** *adj*
[2]tree *vb* **treed; tree•ing :** to drive to or up a tree ⟨~ a raccoon⟩
tree farm *n* **:** an area of forest land managed to ensure continuous commercial production
tree frog *n* **:** any of numerous usually tree-dwelling amphibians with adhesive disks on the toes
tree line *n* **:** TIMBERLINE
tree of heaven : a Chinese ailanthus widely grown as an ornamental tree
tree surgery *n* **:** operative treatment of diseased trees especially for control of decay — **tree surgeon** *n*
tre•foil \ˈtrē-ˌfȯil, ˈtre-\ *n* **1 :** an herb (as a clover) with leaves that have three leaflets **2 :** a decorative design with three leaflike parts
[1]trek \ˈtrek\ *vb* **trekked; trek•king 1** *chiefly southern Africa* **:** to travel or migrate by ox wagon **2** ♦ **:** to make one's way arduously

♦ journey, tour, travel, voyage

[2]trek *n* **1** *chiefly southern Africa* **:** a migration especially of settlers by ox wagon **2** ♦ **:** a slow or difficult journey

♦ expedition, journey, passage, peregrination, trip

[1]trel•lis \ˈtre-ləs\ *n* **:** a frame of latticework used especially to support climbing plants
[2]trellis *vb* **:** to provide with a trellis; *esp* **:** to train (as a vine) on a trellis
trem•a•tode \ˈtre-mə-ˌtōd\ *n* **:** any of a class of parasitic worms
[1]trem•ble \ˈtrem-bəl\ *vb* **trem•bled; trem•bling 1 :** to shake involuntarily (as with fear or cold) **:** SHIVER **2 :** to move, sound, pass, or come to pass as if shaken or tremulous **3 :** to be affected with fear or doubt
[2]tremble *n* ♦ **:** a spell of shaking or quivering

♦ quiver, shiver, shudder

tre•men•dous \tri-ˈmen-dəs\ *adj* **1 :** causing dread, awe, or terror **:** TERRIFYING **2** ♦ **:** unusually large, powerful, great, or excellent

♦ colossal, enormous, giant, gigantic, huge, mammoth, massive, monstrous, monumental, prodigious, titanic

tre•men•dous•ly *adv* ♦ **:** to a tremendous degree or extent

♦ broadly, considerably, greatly, hugely, largely, massively, monstrously, much, sizably, stupendously, utterly, vastly

trem•o•lo \ˈtre-mə-ˌlō\ *n, pl* **-los :** a rapid fluttering of a tone or alternating tones
trem•or \ˈtre-mər\ *n* **1 :** a trembling or shaking especially from weakness, emotional stress, or disease **2 :** a quivering motion of the earth (as during an earthquake)
trem•u•lous \ˈtrem-yə-ləs\ *adj* **1** ♦ **:** marked by trembling or tremors **2 :** TIMOROUS, TIMID — **trem•u•lous•ly** *adv*

♦ shaky, wobbly

[1]trench \ˈtrench\ *n* **1** ♦ **:** a long narrow cut in the ground **:** DITCH; *esp* **:** a ditch protected by banks of earth and used to shelter soldiers **2** *pl* **:** a place or situation likened to warfare conducted from trenches **3 :** a long narrow steep-sided depression in the ocean floor

♦ dike, ditch, gutter

[2]trench *vb* **1 :** to cut or dig trenches in **2 :** to protect (troops) with trenches **3 :** to come close **:** VERGE
tren•chant \ˈtren-chənt\ *adj* **1 :** vigorously effective; *also* **:** CAUSTIC **2 :** sharply perceptive **:** KEEN **3 :** CLEAR-CUT, DISTINCT **4 :** having a fine edge or point **:** SHARP
tren•cher \ˈtren-chər\ *n* **:** a wooden platter for serving food
tren•cher•man \ˈtren-chər-mən\ *n* **:** a hearty eater
trench foot *n* **:** a painful foot disorder resembling frostbite and resulting from exposure to cold and wet
trench mouth *n* **:** a progressive painful bacterial infection of the mouth and adjacent parts marked by ulceration, bleeding gums, and foul breath
[1]trend \ˈtrend\ *vb* **1 :** to have or take a general direction **:** TEND **2** ♦ **:** to show a tendency **:** INCLINE

♦ incline, lean, run, tend

[2]trend *n* **1 :** a general direction taken (as by a stream or mountain range) **2** ♦ **:** a prevailing tendency **:** DRIFT **3** ♦ **:** a current style or preference **:** VOGUE

♦ [2] current, drift, leaning, run, tendency, tide, wind ♦ [3] craze, fad, mode, rage, style, vogue

trendy \ˈtren-dē\ *adj* **trend•i•er; -est** ♦ **:** very fashionable; *also* **:** marked by superficial or faddish appeal or taste

♦ à la mode, chic, cool, fashionable, in, modish, sharp, smart, snappy, stylish

trep•i•da•tion \ˌtre-pə-ˈdā-shən\ *n* ♦ **:** nervous agitation **:** APPREHENSION

♦ alarm, anxiety, apprehension, dread, fear, fright, horror, panic, terror

[1]tres•pass \ˈtres-pəs, -ˌpas\ *n* **1 a** ♦ **:** a violation of moral or social ethics **:** SIN **b** ♦ **:** an unwarranted infringement **2 :** unlawful entry on someone else's land

♦ [1a] breach, crime, error, malefaction, misdeed, misdoing, offense, sin, transgression, violation, wrongdoing ♦ [1b] breach, infraction, infringement, transgression, violation

[2]trespass *vb* **1** ♦ **:** to commit an offense **:** ERR **2 :** INTRUDE, ENCROACH; *esp* **:** to enter unlawfully upon the land of another — **tres•pass•er** *n*

♦ err, offend, sin, transgress

tress \ˈtres\ *n* **:** a long lock of hair — usually used in plural
tres•tle *also* **tres•sel** \ˈtre-səl\ *n* **1 :** a supporting framework consisting usually of a horizontal piece with spreading legs at each end **2 :** a braced framework of timbers, piles, or steel for carrying a road or railroad over a depression
T. rex \ˈtē-ˈreks\ *n* **:** TYRANNOSAUR
trey \ˈtrā\ *n, pl* **treys :** a card or the side of a die with three spots
tri•ad \ˈtrī-ˌad, -əd\ *n* ♦ **:** a union or group of three usually closely related persons or things

♦ threesome, trio, triple, triplet

tri•age \trē-ˈäzh, ˈtrē-ˌäzh\ *n* **:** the sorting of and allocation of treatment to patients and especially battle or disaster victims according to a system of priorities designed to maximize the number of survivors
tri•al \ˈtrī-əl\ *n* **1 :** the action or process of trying or putting to the proof **:** TEST **2 :** the hearing and judgment of a matter in issue before a competent tribunal **3** ♦ **:** a source of vexation or annoyance **4** ♦ **:** a tryout or experiment to test quality, value, or usefulness **5** ♦ **:** the act or an instance of attempting — **trial** *adj*

♦ [3] cross, gauntlet, ordeal ♦ [4] dry run, practice, rehearsal ♦ [4] experiment, test ♦ [5] attempt, crack, endeavor (*or* endeavour), essay, fling, go, pass, shot, stab, try, whack

tri•an•gle \ˈtrī-ˌaŋ-gəl\ *n* **1 :** a polygon that has three sides **2 :** something shaped like a triangle — **tri•an•gu•lar** \trī-ˈaŋ-gyə-lər\ *adj* — **tri•an•gu•lar•ly** *adv*
tri•an•gu•la•tion \(ˌ)trī-ˌaŋ-gyə-ˈlā-shən\ *n* **:** a method using trigonometry to find the location of a point using bearings from two fixed points a known distance apart — **tri•an•gu•late** \trī-ˈaŋ-gyə-ˌlāt\ *vb*
Tri•as•sic \trī-ˈa-sik\ *adj* **:** of, relating to, or being the earliest period of the Mesozoic era marked by the first appearance of the dinosaurs — **Triassic** *n*
tri•ath•lon \trī-ˈath-lən, -ˌlän\ *n* **:** an athletic contest consisting of three phases (as swimming, bicycling, and running)
trib *abbr* tributary
tribe \ˈtrīb\ *n* **1** ♦ **:** a social group comprising numerous families, clans, or generations **2 :** a group of persons having a common character, occupation, or interest **3 :** a group of related plants or animals ⟨the cat ~⟩ — **trib•al** \ˈtrī-bəl\ *adj*

♦ blood, clan, family, folks, house, kin, kindred, kinfolk, line, lineage, people, race, stock

tribes•man \ˈtrībz-mən\ *n* **:** a member of a tribe

trib•u•la•tion \ˌtri-byə-ˈlā-shən\ *n* ♦ : distress or suffering resulting from oppression or persecution; *also* : a trying experience

♦ affliction, agony, anguish, distress, misery, pain, torment, torture, woe

tri•bu•nal \trī-ˈbyün-ᵊl, tri-\ *n* **1** : the seat of a judge **2** : a court of justice **3** : something that decides or determines ⟨the ∼ of public opinion⟩

tri•bune \ˈtri-ˌbyün, tri-ˈbyün\ *n* **1** : an official in ancient Rome with the function of protecting the interests of plebeian citizens from the patricians **2** : a defender of the people

¹trib•u•tary \ˈtri-byə-ˌter-ē\ *adj* **1** : paying tribute : SUBJECT **2** : flowing into a larger stream or a lake

²tributary *n, pl* **-tar•ies** **1** : a ruler or state that pays tribute **2** : a tributary stream

trib•ute \ˈtri-(ˌ)byüt, -byət\ *n* **1** : a payment by one ruler or nation to another as an act of submission or price of protection **2** : a usually excessive tax, rental, or levy exacted by a sovereign or superior **3 a** ♦ : a gift or service showing respect, gratitude, or affection **b** ♦ : something (as material evidence or a formal attestation) that indicates the worth, virtue, or effectiveness of the one in question

♦ [3a, b] accolade, citation, commendation, encomium, eulogy, homage, paean, panegyric, salutation

trice \ˈtrīs\ *n* ♦ : a brief space of time : INSTANT, MOMENT

♦ flash, instant, jiffy, minute, moment, second, shake, twinkle, twinkling, wink

tri•ceps \ˈtrī-ˌseps\ *n, pl* **triceps** : a large muscle along the back of the upper arm that is attached at its upper end by three main parts and acts to extend the forearm at the elbow joint

tri•cer•a•tops \(ˌ)trī-ˈser-ə-ˌtäps\ *n, pl* **-tops** *also* **-tops•es** : any of a genus of large plant-eating Cretaceous dinosaurs with three horns, a bony crest on the neck, and hoofed toes

tri•chi•na \tri-ˈkī-nə\ *n, pl* **-nae** \-(ˌ)nē\ *also* **-nas** : a small slender nematode worm that in the larval state is parasitic in the striated muscles of flesh-eating mammals (as humans)

trich•i•no•sis \ˌtri-kə-ˈnō-səs\ *n* : infestation with or disease caused by trichinae and marked especially by pain, fever, and swelling

¹trick \ˈtrik\ *n* **1** ♦ : a crafty procedure meant to deceive **2** ♦ : a mischievous action : PRANK **3** : a childish action **4** ♦ : a deceptive or ingenious feat designed to puzzle or amuse **5** ♦ : an habitual peculiarity of behavior or manner **6** : a quick or artful way of getting a result : KNACK **7** : the cards played in one round of a card game **8** : a tour of duty : SHIFT

♦ [1] artifice, device, dodge, gimmick, jig, ploy, scheme, sleight, stratagem, wile ♦ [2] antic, caper, escapade, frolic, monkeyshine, practical joke, prank ♦ [4] deed, exploit, feat, stunt ♦ [5] crotchet, eccentricity, idiosyncrasy, mannerism, oddity, peculiarity, quirk, singularity

²trick *vb* **1** ♦ : to deceive by cunning or artifice **2** : to dress ornately

♦ beguile, bluff, cozen, deceive, delude, dupe, fool, gull, have, hoax, hoodwink, humbug, misinform, mislead, string along, take in

trick•ery \ˈtri-kə-rē\ *n* ♦ : deception by tricks and stratagems

♦ artifice, chicanery, hanky-panky, subterfuge, wile

trick•le \ˈtri-kəl\ *vb* **trick•led; trick•ling** **1** : to run or fall in drops **2** ♦ : to flow in a thin gentle stream — **trickle** *n*

♦ dribble, gurgle, lap, plash, ripple, slosh, splash, wash

trick•ster \ˈtrik-stər\ *n* **1** ♦ : one who tricks or cheats **2** ♦ : one skilled at illusions

♦ [1] cheat, dodger, hoaxer, shark, sharper, swindler ♦ [2] conjurer, illusionist, magician

tricky \ˈtri-kē\ *adj* **trick•i•er; -est** **1** : inclined to trickery **2** ♦ : requiring skill or caution ⟨a ∼ situation to handle⟩ **3** : UNRELIABLE ⟨a ∼ lock⟩

♦ catchy, delicate, difficult, knotty, problematic, spiny, thorny, ticklish, touchy, tough

tri•col•or \ˈtrī-ˌkə-lər\ *n* : a flag of three colors ⟨the French ∼⟩

tri•cy•cle \ˈtrī-(ˌ)si-kəl\ *n* : a 3-wheeled vehicle usually propelled by pedals

tri•dent \ˈtrīd-ᵊnt\ *n* : a 3-pronged spear

tried \ˈtrīd\ *adj* **1** ♦ : found trustworthy through testing **2** : subjected to trials

♦ dependable, good, reliable, responsible, safe, solid, steady, sure, true, trustworthy

tri•en•ni•al \trī-ˈe-nē-əl\ *adj* **1** : occurring or being done every three years **2** : lasting for three years — **triennial** *n*

¹tri•fle \ˈtrī-fəl\ *n* **1** ♦ : something of little value or importance **2** : a dessert of cake soaked with liqueur and served with toppings (as fruit or cream)

♦ child's play, frippery, nothing, triviality

²trifle *vb* **tri•fled; tri•fling** **1** : to talk in a jesting or mocking manner **2** : to treat someone or something as unimportant **3** : DALLY, FLIRT **4** : to handle idly : TOY **5** : to spend or waste (as time or money) in trifling or on trifles — **tri•fler** *n*

tri•fling \ˈtrī-fliŋ\ *adj* **1** : FRIVOLOUS **2** ♦ : lacking in significance or solid worth : TRIVIAL

♦ frivolous, inconsequential, inconsiderable, insignificant, little, minor, minute, negligible, slight, small, trivial, unimportant

tri•fo•cals \trī-ˈfō-kəlz\ *n pl* : eyeglasses with lenses having one part for close focus, one for intermediate focus, and one for distant focus

tri•fo•li•ate \trī-ˈfō-lē-ət\ *adj* : having three leaves or leaflets

¹trig \ˈtrig\ *adj* : stylishly trim : SMART

²trig *n* : TRIGONOMETRY

¹trig•ger \ˈtri-gər\ *n* : a movable lever that activates a device when it is squeezed; *esp* : the part of a firearm lock moved by the finger to fire a gun — **trigger** *adj* — **trig•gered** *adj*

²trigger *vb* **1** : to fire by pulling a trigger **2** ♦ : to initiate, actuate, or set off as if by a trigger

♦ activate, actuate, crank, drive, move, propel, run, set off, spark, start, touch off, turn on

tri•glyc•er•ide *n* : any of a group of lipids that are formed from glycerol and fatty acids and are widespread in animal tissue

trig•o•nom•e•try \ˌtri-gə-ˈnä-mə-trē\ *n* : the branch of mathematics dealing with the properties of triangles and especially with finding unknown angles or sides given the size or length of some angles or sides — **trig•o•no•met•ric** \-nə-ˈme-trik\ *also* **trig•o•no•met•ri•cal** \-tri-kəl\ *adj*

trike \ˈtrīk\ *n* : TRICYCLE

¹trill \ˈtril\ *n* **1** : the alternation of two musical tones a scale degree apart **2** : WARBLE **3** : the rapid vibration of one speech organ against another (as of the tip of the tongue against the teeth)

²trill *vb* : to utter as or with a trill

tril•lion \ˈtril-yən\ *n* **1** : a thousand billions **2** *Brit* : a million billions — **trillion** *adj* — **tril•lionth** \-yənth\ *adj or n*

tril•li•um \ˈtri-lē-əm\ *n* : any of a genus of spring blooming herbs that are related to the lilies and have an erect stem bearing a whorl of three leaves and a solitary flower

tril•o•gy \ˈtri-lə-jē\ *n, pl* **-gies** : a series of three dramas or literary or musical compositions that are closely related and develop one theme

¹trim \ˈtrim\ *vb* **trimmed; trim•ming** **1** ♦ : to put ornaments on : ADORN **2** ♦ : to defeat especially resoundingly **3** ♦ : to make trim, neat, regular, or less bulky by or as if by cutting ⟨∼ a beard⟩ ⟨∼ a budget⟩ **4** : to cause (a boat) to assume a desired position in the water by arrangement of the load; *also* : to adjust (as a submarine or airplane) especially for horizontal motion **5** : to adjust (a sail) to a desired position **6** : to change one's views for safety or expediency — **trim•ly** *adv* — **trim•ness** *n*

♦ [1] adorn, array, beautify, bedeck, deck, decorate, do, dress, embellish, enrich, garnish, grace, ornament ♦ [2] clobber, drub, rout, skunk, thrash, trounce, wallop, whip ♦ [3] bob, clip, crop, curtail, cut, cut back, dock, lop, nip, prune, shave, shear

²trim *adj* **trim•mer; trim•mest** ♦ : showing neatness, good order, or compactness ⟨a ∼ figure⟩

♦ crisp, neat, orderly, shipshape, snug, tidy, uncluttered

³trim *n* **1** ♦ : good condition **2** ♦ : material used for ornament or trimming; *esp* : the woodwork in the finish of a house especially around doors and windows **3** : the position of a ship or boat especially with reference to the horizontal; *also* : the relation between the plane of a sail and the direction of a ship **4** : the position of an airplane at which it will continue in level flight with no adjustments to the controls **5** : something that is trimmed off

♦ [1] condition, fettle, form, kilter, order, repair, shape ♦ [2] adornment, caparison, decoration, embellishment, frill, garnish, ornament

tri•ma•ran \ˈtrī-mə-ˌran, ˌtrī-mə-ˈran\ *n* : a sailboat with three hulls

tri•mes•ter \trī-ˈmes-tər, ˈtrī-ˌmes-tər\ *n* **1 :** a period of three or about three months (as in pregnancy) **2 :** one of three terms into which an academic year is sometimes divided
trim•e•ter \ˈtri-mə-tər\ *n* **:** a line of verse consisting of three metrical feet
trim•mer \ˈtri-mər\ *n* **:** one that trims
trim•ming \ˈtri-miŋ\ *n* **1 :** the loss of a contest **:** DEFEAT **2 :** the action of one that trims **3 :** something that trims, ornaments, or completes
tri•month•ly \trī-ˈmənth-lē\ *adj* **:** occurring every three months
trine \ˈtrīn\ *adj* **:** THREEFOLD, TRIPLE
Trin•i•da•di•an \ˌtri-nə-ˈdā-dē-ən, -ˈda-\ *n* **:** a native or inhabitant of the island of Trinidad — **Trinidadian** *adj*
Trin•i•tar•i•an \ˌtri-nə-ˈter-ē-ən\ *n* **:** a believer in the doctrine of the Trinity — **Trin•i•tar•i•an•ism** \-ē-ə-ˌni-zəm\ *n*
Trin•i•ty \ˈtri-nə-tē\ *n* **1 :** the unity of Father, Son, and Holy Spirit as three persons in one Godhead **2** *not cap* **:** TRIAD
trin•ket \ˈtriŋ-kət\ *n* **1** ♦ **:** a small ornament (as a jewel or ring) **2 :** TRIFLE 1

♦ bauble, curiosity, gewgaw, knickknack, novelty

trio \ˈtrē-ō\ *n, pl* **tri•os** **1 :** a musical composition for three voices or three instruments **2 :** the performers of a trio **3** ♦ **:** a group or set of three

♦ threesome, triad, triple, triplet

¹trip \ˈtrip\ *vb* **tripped; trip•ping** **1** ♦ **:** to move with light quick steps **2** ♦ **:** to catch the foot against something so as to stumble or cause to stumble **3 :** to make a mistake **:** SLIP; *also* **:** to detect in a misstep **:** EXPOSE **4 :** to release (as a spring or switch) by moving a catch; *also* **:** ACTIVATE **5 :** to get high on a usually hallucinatory drug

♦ [1] bound, hop, skip, spring ♦ [2] fall, slip, stumble, topple, tumble

²trip *n* **1** ♦ **:** an act or instance of traveling **:** JOURNEY **2 :** a quick light step **3 :** a false step **:** STUMBLE; *also* **:** ERROR **4 :** the action of tripping mechanically; *also* **:** a device for tripping **5 :** an intense experience; *esp* **:** one triggered by a hallucinatory drug **6 :** absorption in an attitude or state of mind ⟨an ego ~⟩

♦ expedition, journey, passage, peregrination, trek

tri•par•tite \trī-ˈpär-ˌtīt\ *adj* **1** ♦ **:** divided into three parts **2 :** having three corresponding parts or copies **3 :** made between three parties ⟨a ~ treaty⟩

♦ threefold, treble, triple

tripe \ˈtrīp\ *n* **1 :** stomach tissue especially of a ruminant (as an ox) used as food **2 :** something poor, worthless, or offensive **:** TRASH
¹tri•ple \ˈtri-pəl\ *vb* **tri•pled; tri•pling** **1 :** to make or become three times as great or as many **2 :** to hit a triple
²triple *n* **1 :** a triple quantity **2** ♦ **:** a group of three **3 :** a hit in baseball that lets the batter reach third base

♦ threesome, triad, trio, triplet

³triple *adj* **1 :** being three times as great or as many **2** ♦ **:** having three units or members **3 :** repeated three times

♦ threefold, treble, tripartite

triple bond *n* **:** a chemical bond in which three pairs of electrons are shared by two atoms in a molecule
triple point *n* **:** the condition of temperature and pressure under which the gaseous, liquid, and solid forms of a substance can exist in equilibrium
trip•let \ˈtri-plət\ *n* **1 :** a unit of three lines of verse **2** ♦ **:** a group of three of a kind **3 :** one of three offspring born at one birth

♦ threesome, triad, trio, triple

tri•plex \ˈtri-ˌpleks, ˈtrī-\ *adj* **:** having three units or members **:** THREEFOLD
¹trip•li•cate \ˈtri-pli-kət\ *adj* **:** made in three identical copies
²trip•li•cate \-plə-ˌkāt\ *vb* **-cat•ed; -cat•ing** **1 :** TRIPLE **2 :** to provide three copies of ⟨~ a document⟩
³trip•li•cate \-pli-kət\ *n* **:** three copies all alike — used with *in* ⟨typed in ~⟩
tri•ply \ˈtri-plē, ˈtri-pə-lē\ *adv* **:** in a triple degree, amount, or manner
tri•pod \ˈtrī-ˌpäd\ *n* **:** something (as a caldron, stool, or camera stand) that rests on three legs — **tripod** *or* **tri•po•dal** \ˈtri-pəd-ᵊl, ˈtrī-ˌpäd-\ *adj*
trip•tych \ˈtrip-tik\ *n* **:** a picture or carving in three panels side by side

tri•reme \ˈtrī-ˌrēm\ *n* **:** an ancient galley having three banks of oars
tri•sect \ˈtrī-ˌsekt, trī-ˈsekt\ *vb* **:** to divide into three usually equal parts — **tri•sec•tion** \ˈtrī-ˌsek-shən\ *n*
trite \ˈtrīt\ *adj* **trit•er; trit•est** ♦ **:** used so commonly that the novelty is worn off **:** STALE

♦ banal, commonplace, hackneyed, musty, stale, stereotyped, threadbare, tired

tri•ti•um \ˈtri-tē-əm, ˈtri-shē-\ *n* **:** a radioactive form of hydrogen with one proton and two neutrons in its nucleus and three times the mass of ordinary hydrogen
tri•ton \ˈtrīt-ᵊn\ *n* **:** any of various large marine gastropod mollusks with a heavy elongated conical shell; *also* **:** the shell of a triton
trit•u•rate \ˈtri-chə-ˌrāt\ *vb* **-rat•ed; -rat•ing** **:** to rub or grind to a fine powder
¹tri•umph \ˈtrī-əmf\ *n* **1 :** the joy or exultation of victory or success **2 :** VICTORY, CONQUEST **3** ♦ **:** a notable success — **tri•um•phal** \trī-ˈəm-fəl\ *adj*

♦ accomplishment, achievement, attainment, coup, success

²triumph *vb* **1** ♦ **:** to obtain victory **:** PREVAIL **2** ♦ **:** to celebrate victory or success exultantly

♦ [1] conquer, prevail, win ♦ *usu* **triumph over** [1] beat, defeat, overcome, prevail, surmount, win ♦ [2] crow, delight, exult, glory, joy, rejoice

tri•um•phant \trī-ˈəm-fənt\ *adj* **1 :** VICTORIOUS **2** ♦ **:** rejoicing for or celebrating victory **3** ♦ **:** notably successful — **tri•um•phant•ly** *adv*

♦ [2] exultant, jubilant, rejoicing ♦ [3] palmy, prosperous, successful

tri•um•vir \trī-ˈəm-vər\ *n, pl* **-virs** *also* **-vi•ri** \-və-ˌrī\ **:** a member of a triumvirate
tri•um•vi•rate \-və-rət\ *n* **:** a ruling body of three persons
tri•une \ˈtrī-ˌün, -ˌyün\ *adj* **:** being three in one ⟨the ~ God⟩
triv•et \ˈtri-vət\ *n* **1 :** a 3-legged stand **:** TRIPOD **2 :** a usually metal stand with short feet for use under a hot dish
triv•ia \ˈtri-vē-ə\ *n sing or pl* **:** unimportant matters **:** obscure facts or details ⟨movie ~⟩
triv•i•al \ˈtri-vē-əl\ *adj* ♦ **:** of little importance

♦ frivolous, inconsequential, inconsiderable, insignificant, little, minor, minute, negligible, slight, small, trifling, unimportant

triv•i•al•i•ty \ˌtri-vē-ˈa-lə-tē\ *n* **1 :** the quality or state of being trivial **2** ♦ **:** something trivial

♦ child's play, frippery, nothing, trifle

triv•i•um \ˈtri-vē-əm\ *n, pl* **triv•ia** \-vē-ə\ **:** the three liberal arts of grammar, rhetoric, and logic in a medieval university
tri•week•ly \trī-ˈwē-klē\ *adj* **1 :** occurring or appearing three times a week **2 :** occurring or appearing every three weeks — **tri•weekly** *adv*
tro•che \ˈtrō-kē\ *n* **:** LOZENGE 2
tro•chee \ˈtrō-(ˌ)kē\ *n* **:** a metrical foot of one accented syllable followed by one unaccented syllable — **tro•cha•ic** \trō-ˈkā-ik\ *adj*
trod *past and past part of* TREAD
trodden *past part of* TREAD
troi•ka \ˈtrȯi-kə\ *n* **:** a group of three; *esp* **:** an administrative or ruling body of three
¹troll \ˈtrōl\ *vb* **1 :** to sing the parts of (a song) in succession **2 :** to fish by trailing a lure or baited hook from a moving boat **3 :** to sing or play jovially
²troll *n* **:** a lure used in trolling; *also* **:** the line with its lure
³troll *n* ♦ **:** a dwarf or giant in Scandinavian folklore inhabiting caves or hills

♦ brownie, dwarf, elf, fairy, fay, gnome, hobgoblin, leprechaun, pixie, puck

trol•ley *also* **trol•ly** \ˈträ-lē\ *n, pl* **trolleys** *also* **trollies** **1 :** a device (as a grooved wheel on the end of a pole) to carry current from a wire to an electrically driven vehicle **2 :** a streetcar powered electrically by overhead wires **3 :** a wheeled carriage running on an overhead rail or track
trol•ley•bus \ˈträ-lē-ˌbəs\ *n* **:** a bus powered electrically by overhead wires
trolley car *n* **:** TROLLEY 2
trol•lop \ˈträ-ləp\ *n* **:** a disreputable woman; *esp* **:** one who engages in sex promiscuously
trom•bone \träm-ˈbōn, ˈträm-ˌbōn\ *n* **:** a brass wind instrument that consists of a long metal tube with two turns and a flaring end

and that usually has a movable slide to vary the pitch — **trom·bon·ist** \-ˈbō-nist, -ˌbō-\ *n*

tromp \ˈträmp, ˈtrȯmp\ *vb* **1 :** to walk, tread, or step especially heavily : TRAMP **2 :** to stamp with the foot **3 :** to defeat decisively **4** ♦ **:** to tread on forcibly and repeatedly

♦ stamp, stomp, tramp, trample

trompe l'oeil \(ˌ)trȯmp-ˈlə-ē, trō^{n}p-ˈlœi\ *n* **:** a style of painting in which objects are depicted with photographic detail

[1]**troop** \ˈtrüp\ *n* **1 :** a cavalry unit corresponding to an infantry company **2** *pl* ♦ **:** the combined military, naval, and air forces of a nation : ARMED FORCES **3 :** a collection of people, aninals, or things **4 :** a unit of Girl Scouts or Boy Scouts under an adult leader

♦ **troops** armed forces, military, services

[2]**troop** *vb* **:** to move or gather in crowds

troop·er \ˈtrü-pər\ *n* **1 :** an enlisted cavalryman; *also* **:** a cavalry horse **2 :** a mounted or a state police officer

troop·ship \ˈtrüp-ˌship\ *n* **:** a ship or aircraft for carrying troops

trope \ˈtrōp\ *n* **:** a word or expression used in a figurative sense

tro·phy \ˈtrō-fē\ *n, pl* **trophies :** something gained or given in conquest or victory especially when preserved or mounted as a memorial

trop·ic \ˈträ-pik\ *n* **1 :** either of the two parallels of latitude approximately 23½ degrees north (**tropic of Can·cer** \-ˈkan-sər\) or south (**tropic of Cap·ri·corn** \-ˈka-prə-ˌkȯrn\) of the equator where the sun is directly overhead when it reaches its most northerly or southerly point in the sky **2** *pl, often cap* **:** the region lying between the tropics — **trop·i·cal** \-pi-kəl\ *or* **tropic** *adj*

tro·pism \ˈtrō-ˌpi-zəm\ *n* **:** an automatic movement by an organism in response to a source of stimulation; *also* **:** a reflex reaction involving this

tro·po·sphere \ˈtrō-pə-ˌsfir, ˈträ-\ *n* **:** the part of the atmosphere between the earth's surface and the stratosphere in which most weather changes occur — **tro·po·spher·ic** \ˌtrō-pə-ˈsfir-ik, ˌträ-, -ˈsfer-\ *adj*

[1]**trot** \ˈträt\ *n* **1 :** a moderately fast gait of a 4-footed animal (as a horse) in which the legs move in diagonal pairs **2 :** a human jogging gait between a walk and a run

[2]**trot** *vb* **trot·ted; trot·ting 1 :** to ride, drive, or go at a trot **2 :** to proceed briskly : HURRY — **trot·ter** *n*

troth \ˈträth, ˈtrȯth, ˈtrōth\ *n* **1 :** pledged faithfulness **2 a** ♦ **:** one's pledged word **b** ♦ **:** the act of promising to marry or the fact of being engaged to marry : BETROTHAL

♦ [2a] oath, pledge, promise, vow, word ♦ [2b] betrothal, engagement, espousal

trou·ba·dour \ˈtrü-bə-ˌdōr\ *n* **:** any of a class of poet-musicians flourishing especially in southern France and northern Italy during the 11th, 12th, and 13th centuries

[1]**trou·ble** \ˈtrə-bəl\ *vb* **trou·bled; trou·bling 1** ♦ **:** to feel or cause to feel mentally or spiritually agitated **2 :** to produce physical disorder in **3** ♦ **:** to put to inconvenience **4 :** RUFFLE ⟨~ the waters⟩ **5 :** to make an effort

♦ [1] bother, fear, fret, stew, sweat, worry ♦ [3] discommode, disoblige, disturb, inconvenience

[2]**trouble** *n* **1 :** the quality or state of being troubled especially mentally **2 :** an instance of distress or annoyance **3** ♦ **:** a condition of physical distress or ill health : DISEASE ⟨heart ~⟩ **4** ♦ **:** an effort made : EXERTION ⟨took the ~ to phone⟩ **5** ♦ **:** a cause of disturbance, distress, difficulty, or danger **6** ♦ **:** a state or condition of distress, annoyance, danger, or difficulty

♦ [3] affection, ailment, bug, complaint, complication, condition, disease, disorder, fever, ill, illness, infirmity, malady, sickness ♦ [4] effort, exertion, expenditure, labor (*or* labour), pains, sweat, while, work ♦ [5] case, knot, matter, problem ♦ [6] danger, distress, jeopardy, peril, risk

troubled *adj* ♦ **:** feeling worry or concern

♦ aflutter, anxious, edgy, jittery, jumpy, nervous, nervy, perturbed, tense, uneasy, upset, worried

trou·ble·mak·er \-ˌmā-kər\ *n* **:** a person who causes trouble

trou·ble·shoot·er \-ˌshü-tər\ *n* **1 :** a worker employed to locate trouble and make repairs in equipment **2 :** an expert in resolving disputes or problems — **trou·ble·shoot** *vb*

trou·ble·some \-səm\ *adj* **1 :** DIFFICULT, BURDENSOME **2** ♦ **:** giving trouble or anxiety — **trou·ble·some·ly** *adv*

♦ unsettling, upsetting, worrisome ***Ant*** reassuring

trou·blous \ˈtrə-bə-ləs\ *adj* **1 :** full of trouble **2 :** causing trouble : TROUBLESOME

trough \ˈtrȯf, ˈtrȯth\ *n, pl* **troughs** \ˈtrȯfs, ˈtrȯvz; ˈtrȯths, ˈtrȯt͟hz\ **1 :** a long shallow open boxlike container especially for water or feed for livestock **2 :** a gutter along the eaves of a house **3 :** a long channel or depression (as between waves or hills) **4 :** an elongated area of low barometric pressure

trounce \ˈtrau̇ns\ *vb* **trounced; trounc·ing 1 :** to thrash or punish severely **2** ♦ **:** to defeat decisively

♦ beat, clobber, drub, rout, skunk, thrash, trim, wallop, whip

troupe \ˈtrüp\ *n* **:** COMPANY; *esp* **:** a group of performers on the stage

troup·er \ˈtrü-pər\ *n* **1** ♦ **:** a member of a troupe **2 :** a person who deals with and persists through difficulty or hardship without complaint

♦ actor, impersonator, mummer, player

trou·sers \ˈtrau̇-zərz\ *n pl* ♦ **:** an outer garment covering each leg separately and usually extending from the waist to the ankle — **trouser** *adj*

♦ britches, pantaloons, pants, slacks

trous·seau \ˈtrü-sō, trü-ˈsō\ *n, pl* **trousseaux** \-sōz, -ˈsōz\ *or* **trousseaus :** the personal outfit of a bride

trout \ˈtrau̇t\ *n, pl* **trout** *also* **trouts :** any of various mostly freshwater food and game fishes usually smaller than the related salmons

trow \ˈtrō\ *vb, archaic* **:** THINK, SUPPOSE

trow·el \ˈtrau̇-əl\ *n* **1 :** a hand tool used for spreading, shaping, or smoothing loose or plastic material (as mortar or plaster) **2 :** a scoop-shaped tool used in gardening — **trowel** *vb*

troy \ˈtrȯi\ *adj* **:** expressed in troy weight ⟨~ ounce⟩

troy weight *n* **:** a system of weights based on a pound of 12 ounces and an ounce of 480 grains (31 grams)

tru·ant \ˈtrü-ənt\ *n* **:** a student who stays out of school without permission — **tru·an·cy** \-ən-sē\ *n* — **truant** *adj*

truce \ˈtrüs\ *n* **1 :** ARMISTICE **2 :** a respite especially from something unpleasant

[1]**truck** \ˈtrək\ *vb* **1 :** EXCHANGE, BARTER **2 :** to have dealings : TRAFFIC

[2]**truck** *n* **1** ♦ **:** the act or practice of carrying on trade by bartering : BARTER **2 :** small goods or merchandise; *esp* **:** vegetables grown for market **3 :** DEALINGS

♦ barter, commutation, exchange, swap, trade

[3]**truck** *n* **1 :** a wheeled vehicle (as a strong heavy automobile) designed for carrying heavy articles or hauling a trailer **2 :** a swiveling frame with springs and one or more pairs of wheels used to carry and guide one end of a locomotive or railroad car

[4]**truck** *vb* **1 :** to transport on a truck **2 :** to be employed in driving a truck — **truck·er** *n*

truck farm *n* **:** a farm growing vegetables for market — **truck farmer** *n*

truck·le \ˈtrə-kəl\ *vb* **truck·led; truck·ling :** to yield slavishly to the will of another : SUBMIT

truc·u·lence \ˈtrə-kyə-ləns\ *n* ♦ **:** the quality or state of being truculent — **truc·u·len·cy** \-lən-sē\ *n*

♦ aggression, aggressiveness, belligerence, fight, militancy, pugnacity

truc·u·lent \ˈtrə-kyə-lənt\ *adj* **1 :** feeling or showing ferocity : SAVAGE **2** ♦ **:** aggressively self-assertive : PUGNACIOUS — **truc·u·lent·ly** *adv*

♦ aggressive, argumentative, bellicose, belligerent, combative, contentious, discordant, disputatious, militant, pugnacious, quarrelsome, scrappy, warlike

trudge \ˈtrəj\ *vb* **trudged; trudg·ing :** to walk or march steadily and usually laboriously

[1]**true** \ˈtrü\ *adj* **tru·er; tru·est 1** ♦ **:** faithful in allegiance **2 :** free from fraud or deception **3** ♦ **:** agreeing with facts or reality ⟨a ~ description⟩ **4 :** CONSISTENT ⟨~ to expectations⟩ **5** ♦ **:** properly so called ⟨~ love⟩ **6 :** RIGHTFUL ⟨~ and lawful king⟩ **7** ♦ **:** conformable to a standard or pattern; *also* **:** placed or formed accurately

♦ [1] constant, devoted, faithful, fast, good, loyal, pious, staunch, steadfast, steady, true-blue ♦ [3] actual, concrete, existent, factual, real, very ♦ [5] authentic, bona fide, genuine, real, right ♦ [7] accurate, correct, exact, precise, proper, right, so

[2]**true** *adv* **1 :** TRUTHFULLY **2 :** ACCURATELY ⟨the bullet flew straight and ~⟩; *also* **:** without variation from type ⟨breed ~⟩

[3]**true** *n* **1 :** TRUTH, REALITY — usually used with *the* **2 :** the state of being accurate (as in alignment) ⟨out of ~⟩

[4]true *vb* **trued; true•ing** *also* **tru•ing :** to bring or restore to a desired precision
true–blue *adj* ♦ **:** marked by unswerving loyalty

♦ constant, devoted, faithful, fast, good, loyal, pious, staunch, steadfast, steady, true

true bug *n* **:** BUG 2
true•heart•ed \ˈtrü-ˈhär-təd\ *adj* **:** FAITHFUL, LOYAL
truf•fle \ˈtrə-fəl, ˈtrü-\ *n* **1 :** the dark or light edible spore-bearing organ of any of several European fungi that grow underground; *also* **:** one of these fungi **2 :** a candy made of chocolate, butter, and sugar shaped into balls and coated with cocoa
tru•ism \ˈtrü-ˌi-zəm\ *n* **:** an undoubted or self-evident truth
tru•ly \ˈtrü-lē\ *adv* **1 :** in all sincerity **2** ♦ **:** in agreement with fact **3 :** ACCURATELY **4 :** in a proper or suitable manner **5** ♦ **:** without any question **:** INDEED

♦ [2] actually, frankly, honestly, really, truthfully, verily ♦ [5] certainly, definitely, doubtless, incontestably, indeed, indisputably, really, surely, undeniably, undoubtedly, unquestionably

[1]trump \ˈtrəmp\ *n* **:** TRUMPET
[2]trump *n* **:** a card of a designated suit any of whose cards will win over a card that is not of this suit; *also* **:** the suit itself — often used in plural
[3]trump *vb* **:** to take with a trump
trumped–up \ˈtrəmpt-ˈəp\ *adj* **:** fraudulently concocted **:** SPURIOUS
trum•pery \ˈtrəm-pə-rē\ *n* **1 :** NONSENSE **2 :** trivial articles **:** JUNK
[1]trum•pet \ˈtrəm-pət\ *n* **1 :** a wind instrument consisting of a long curved metal tube flaring at one end and with a cup-shaped mouthpiece at the other **2 :** something that resembles a trumpet or its tonal quality **3 :** a funnel-shaped instrument for collecting, directing, or intensifying sound
[2]trumpet *vb* **1 :** to blow a trumpet **2** ♦ **:** to proclaim on or as if on a trumpet — **trum•pet•er** *n*

♦ ballyhoo, crack up, glorify, tout

[1]trun•cate \ˈtrəŋ-ˌkāt, ˈtrən-\ *adj* **:** having the end square or blunt
[2]truncate *vb* **trun•cat•ed; trun•cat•ing** ♦ **:** to shorten by or as if by cutting — **trun•ca•tion** \ˌtrəŋ-ˈkā-shən\ *n*

♦ abbreviate, abridge, curtail, cut back, dock, shorten

trun•cheon \ˈtrən-chən\ *n* ♦ **:** a police officer's club

♦ bat, bludgeon, club, cudgel, staff

trun•dle \ˈtrənd-ᵊl\ *vb* **trun•dled; trun•dling :** to roll along **:** WHEEL
trundle bed *n* **:** a low bed that can be stored under a higher bed
trunk \ˈtrəŋk\ *n* **1 :** the main stem of a tree **2 :** the body of a person or animal apart from the head and limbs **3 :** the main or central part of something **4** ♦ **:** a box or chest used to hold usually clothes or personal effects (as of a traveler); *also* **:** the enclosed luggage space in the rear of an automobile **5 :** the long muscular nose of an elephant **6** *pl* **:** men's shorts worn chiefly for sports **7 :** a usually major channel or passage

♦ box, caddy, case, casket, chest, locker

trunk line *n* **:** a transportation system handling long-distance through traffic
[1]truss \ˈtrəs\ *vb* **1** ♦ **:** to secure tightly **:** BIND **2 :** to arrange for cooking by binding close the wings or legs of (a fowl) **3 :** to support, strengthen, or stiffen by or as if by a truss

♦ band, bind, gird, tie

[2]truss *n* **1 :** a collection of structural parts (as beams) forming a rigid framework (as in bridge or building construction) **2 :** a device worn to reduce a hernia by pressure
[1]trust \ˈtrəst\ *n* **1 :** assured reliance on the character, strength, or truth of someone or something **2 :** a basis of reliance, faith, or hope **3** ♦ **:** confident hope **4 :** financial credit **5 :** a property interest held by one person for the benefit of another **6** ♦ **:** a combination of firms formed by a legal agreement; *esp* **:** one that reduces competition **7 :** something entrusted to one to be cared for in the interest of another **8** ♦ **:** immediate charge and control exercised by a person or an authority **:** CUSTODY

♦ [3] confidence, credence, faith, stock ***Ant*** distrust, mistrust ♦ [6] cartel, combination, combine, syndicate ♦ [8] care, custody, guardianship, keeping, safekeeping, ward

[2]trust *vb* **1 :** to place confidence **:** DEPEND **2 :** to be confident **:** HOPE **3** ♦ **:** to commit or place in one's care or keeping **:** ENTRUST **4 :** to permit to stay or go or to do something without fear or misgiving **5** ♦ **:** to rely on or on the truth of **:** BELIEVE **6 :** to extend credit to

♦ [3] commend, commit, consign, delegate, deliver, entrust, give, hand over, leave, pass, transfer, transmit, turn over, vest ♦ [5] accept, believe, credit, swallow

trust•ee \ˌtrəs-ˈtē\ *n* **1 :** a person to whom property is legally committed in trust **2 :** a country charged with the supervision of a trust territory
trust•ee•ship \ˌtrəs-ˈtē-ˌship\ *n* **1 :** the office or function of a trustee **2 :** supervisory control by one or more nations over a trust territory
trust•ful \ˈtrəst-fəl\ *adj* **:** full of trust **:** CONFIDING — **trust•ful•ly** *adv* — **trust•ful•ness** *n*
trust territory *n* **:** a non-self-governing territory placed under a supervisory authority by the Trusteeship Council of the United Nations
trust•wor•thi•ness \-ˌwər-t͟hē-nəs\ *n* ♦ **:** the quality or state of being trustworthy

♦ dependability, reliability, solidity, sureness

trust•wor•thy \-ˌwər-t͟hē\ *adj* ♦ **:** worthy of confidence **:** DEPENDABLE

♦ dependable, good, reliable, responsible, safe, solid, steady, sure, tried, true

[1]trusty \ˈtrəs-tē\ *adj* **trust•i•er; -est :** worthy of confidence **:** DEPENDABLE
[2]trusty \ˈtrəs-tē, ˌtrəs-ˈtē\ *n, pl* **trust•ies :** a trusted person; *esp* **:** a convict considered trustworthy and allowed special privileges
truth \ˈtrüth\ *n, pl* **truths** \ˈtrüt͟hz, ˈtrüths\ **1 :** TRUTHFULNESS, HONESTY **2 :** the real state of things **:** FACT **3 :** the body of real events or facts **:** ACTUALITY **4 :** a true or accepted statement or proposition ⟨the ~*s* of science⟩ **5 :** agreement with fact or reality **:** CORRECTNESS
truth•ful \ˈtrüth-fəl\ *adj* **:** telling or disposed to tell the truth
truth•ful•ly \-fə-lē\ *adv* **1** ♦ **:** in reality **:** ACTUALLY ⟨~, he didn't do it⟩ **2 :** in a truthful manner ⟨"I didn't do it," she said ~⟩

♦ actually, frankly, honestly, really, truly, verily

truth•ful•ness *n* ♦ **:** the quality or state of being truthful

♦ honesty, integrity, probity, veracity, verity

truth serum *n* **:** a drug held to induce a subject under questioning to talk freely
[1]try \ˈtrī\ *vb* **tried; try•ing 1 :** to examine or investigate judicially **2 :** to conduct the trial of **3 :** to put to test or trial **4** ♦ **:** to subject to strain, affliction, or annoyance **5 :** to extract or clarify (as lard) by melting **6** ♦ **:** to make an effort to do something **:** ATTEMPT

♦ [4] strain, stretch, tax, test ♦ [6] assay, attempt, endeavor (*or* endeavour), essay, seek, strive

[2]try *n, pl* **tries** ♦ **:** an experimental trial

♦ attempt, crack, endeavor (*or* endeavour), essay, fling, go, pass, shot, stab, trial, whack

try•ing *adj* ♦ **:** severely straining the powers of endurance

♦ bitter, brutal, burdensome, cruel, excruciating, grievous, grim, hard, harsh, heavy, inhuman, murderous, onerous, oppressive, rough, rugged, severe, stiff, tough

try on *vb* **:** to put on (a garment) to test the fit and looks
try out *vb* **:** to participate in competition especially for a position on an athletic team or a part in a play — **try•out** \ˈtrī-ˌau̇t\ *n*
tryp•to•phan \ˈtrip-tə-ˌfan\ *n* **:** a crystalline essential amino acid that is widely distributed in proteins
tryst \ˈtrist\ *n* **1** ♦ **:** an agreement (as between lovers) to meet **2 :** an appointed meeting or meeting place — **tryst** *vb* — **tryst•er** *n*

♦ appointment, date, engagement, rendezvous

tsar *var of* CZAR
tsarina *var of* CZARINA
tset•se fly \ˈtset-sē-, ˈtsēt-, ˈtet-, ˈtēt-, ˈset-, ˈsēt-\ *n* **:** any of several sub-Saharan African dipteran flies including the vector of sleeping sickness
TSgt *abbr* technical sergeant
T–shirt \ˈtē-ˌshərt\ *n* **:** a collarless short-sleeved or sleeveless cotton undershirt; *also* **:** an outer shirt of similar design — **T–shirt•ed** \-ˌshər-təd\ *adj*
tsk *a click; often read as* ˈtisk\ *interj* — used to express disapproval
tsp *abbr* teaspoon; teaspoonful

T square *n* **:** a ruler with a crosspiece at one end for making parallel lines
tsu•na•mi \sü-ˈnä-mē, tsü-\ *n* **:** a tidal wave caused especially by an underwater earthquake or volcanic eruption
TT *abbr* Trust Territories
TTY *abbr* teletypewriter
Tu *abbr* Tuesday
tub \ˈtəb\ *n* **1 :** a wide low bucketlike vessel **2 :** BATHTUB; *also* **:** BATH **3 :** the amount that a tub will hold
tu•ba \ˈtü-bə, ˈtyü-\ *n* **:** a large low-pitched brass wind instrument
tub•al \ˈtü-bəl, ˈtyü-\ *adj* **:** of, relating to, or involving a tube and especially a fallopian tube
tube \ˈtüb, ˈtyüb\ *n* **1** ♦ **:** any of various usually cylindrical structures or devices; *esp* **:** one to convey fluids **2 :** a slender hollow anatomical part (as a fallopian tube) functioning as a channel in a plant or animal body **:** DUCT **3 :** a soft round container from which a paste is squeezed **4 :** a tunnel for vehicular or rail travel **5 :** INNER TUBE **6 :** ELECTRON TUBE **7 :** TELEVISION — **tubed** \ˈtübd, ˈtyübd\ *adj* — **tube•less** *adj*

♦ channel, conduit, duct, leader, line, penstock, pipe

tu•ber \ˈtü-bər, ˈtyü-\ *n* **:** a short fleshy usually underground stem (as of a potato plant) bearing minute scalelike leaves each with a bud at its base
tu•ber•cle \ˈtü-bər-kəl, ˈtyü-\ *n* **1 :** a small knobby prominence or outgrowth especially on an animal or plant **2 :** a small abnormal lump in an organ or on the skin; *esp* **:** one caused by tuberculosis
tubercle bacillus *n* **:** a bacterium that is the cause of tuberculosis
tu•ber•cu•lar \tü-ˈbər-kyə-lər, tyü-\ *adj* **1 :** TUBERCULOUS **2 :** of, resembling, or being a tubercle
tu•ber•cu•lin \tü-ˈbər-kyə-lən, tyü-\ *n* **:** a sterile liquid extracted from the tubercle bacillus and used in the diagnosis of tuberculosis especially in children and cattle
tu•ber•cu•lo•sis \tü-ˌbər-kyə-ˈlō-səs, tyü-\ *n, pl* **-lo•ses** \-ˌsēz\ **:** a communicable bacterial disease that affects especially the lungs and is typically marked by fever, cough, difficulty in breathing, and formation of tubercles — **tu•ber•cu•lous** \-ˈbər-kyə-ləs\ *adj*
tube•rose \ˈtüb-ˌrōz, ˈtyüb-\ *n* **:** a bulbous herb related to the agaves and often grown for its spike of fragrant waxy-white flowers
tu•ber•ous \ˈtü-bə-rəs, ˈtyü-\ *adj* **:** of, resembling, or being a tuber
tub•ing \ˈtü-biŋ, ˈtyü-\ *n* **1 :** material in the form of a tube; *also* **:** a length of tube **2 :** a series or system of tubes
tu•bu•lar \ˈtü-byə-lər, ˈtyü-\ *adj* **:** having the form of or consisting of a tube; *also* **:** made with tubes
tu•bule \ˈtü-byül, ˈtyü-\ *n* **:** a small tube
¹tuck \ˈtək\ *n* **1 :** a fold stitched into cloth to shorten, decorate, or control fullness **2 :** a cosmetic surgical operation for the removal of excess skin or fat ⟨a tummy ~⟩
²tuck *vb* **1 :** to pull up into a fold ⟨~*ed* up her skirt⟩ **2 :** to make tucks in **3 :** to put into a snug often concealing place ⟨~ a book under the arm⟩ **4 :** to secure in place by pushing the edges under ⟨~ in a blanket⟩ **5 :** to cover by tucking in bedclothes
tuck•er \ˈtə-kər\ *vb* **tuck•ered; tuck•er•ing** ♦ **:** to tire extremely or completely **:** FATIGUE — often used with *out*

♦ *usu* **tucker out** burn out, do in, drain, exhaust, fag, fatigue, tire, wash out, wear, wear out, weary

Tues *or* **Tue** *abbr* Tuesday
Tues•day \ˈtüz-dē, ˈtyüz-, -dā\ *n* **:** the 3d day of the week
tu•fa \ˈtü-fə, ˈtyü-\ *n* **:** a porous rock formed as a deposit from springs or streams
tuff \ˈtəf\ *n* **:** a rock composed of volcanic detritus
¹tuft \ˈtəft\ *n* **1 :** a small cluster of long flexible outgrowths (as hairs); *also* **:** a bunch of soft fluffy threads cut off short and used as ornament **2 :** CLUMP, CLUSTER — **tuft•ed** *adj*
²tuft *vb* **1 :** to provide or adorn with a tuft **2 :** to make (as a mattress) firm by stitching at intervals and sewing on tufts — **tuft•er** *n*
¹tug \ˈtəg\ *vb* **tugged; tug•ging 1** ♦ **:** to pull hard **2 :** to struggle in opposition **:** CONTEND **3** ♦ **:** to move by pulling hard **:** HAUL **4 :** to tow with a tugboat

♦ [1, 3] drag, draw, hale, haul, lug, pull, tow

²tug *n* **1 :** a harness trace **2** ♦ **:** an act of tugging **:** PULL **3 :** a straining effort **4 :** a struggle between opposing people or forces **5 :** TUGBOAT

♦ draw, haul, jerk, pluck, pull, wrench

tug•boat \-ˌbōt\ *n* **:** a strongly built boat used for towing or pushing
tug–of–war \ˌtəg-əv-ˈwȯr\ *n, pl* **tugs–of–war 1** ♦ **:** a struggle for supremacy **2 :** an athletic contest in which two teams pull against each other at opposite ends of a rope

♦ battle, combat, conflict, confrontation, contest, duel, face-off, rivalry, struggle, warfare

tu•ition \tü-ˈi-shən, tyü-\ *n* **:** money paid for instruction ⟨college ~⟩
tu•la•re•mia \ˌtü-lə-ˈrē-mē-ə, ˌtyü-\ *n* **:** an infectious bacterial disease especially of wild rabbits, rodents, humans, and some domestic animals that in humans is marked by symptoms (as fever) similar to those of influenza
tu•lip \ˈtü-ləp, ˈtyü-\ *n* **:** any of a genus of Eurasian bulbous herbs related to the lilies and grown for their large showy erect cup-shaped flowers; *also* **:** a flower or bulb of a tulip
tulip tree *n* **:** a tall No. American timber tree that is related to the magnolias and has greenish tulip-shaped flowers and soft white wood
tulle \ˈtül\ *n* **:** a sheer often stiffened silk, rayon, or nylon net ⟨a veil of ~⟩
¹tum•ble \ˈtəm-bəl\ *vb* **tum•bled; tum•bling 1 a** ♦ **:** to fall or cause to fall suddenly and helplessly **b** ♦ **:** to decline suddenly and sharply (as in price) **:** DROP **2 :** to fall into ruin **3 :** to perform gymnastic feats of rolling and turning **4 :** to roll over and over **:** TOSS **5 :** to issue forth hurriedly and confusedly **6 :** to come to understand **7** ♦ **:** to throw together in a confused mass

♦ [1a] fall, slip, stumble, topple, trip ♦ [1b] decline, descend, dip, drop, fall, lower, plummet, plunge, sink ♦ [7] disorder, hash, jumble, mess, mix, muddle, rumple

²tumble *n* **1 a** ♦ **:** a disordered mass of objects or material **b :** a disorderly state **2** ♦ **:** an act or instance of tumbling

♦ [1a] assortment, clutter, jumble, medley, mélange, miscellany, motley, muddle, variety, welter ♦ [2] fall, slip, spill, stumble

tum•ble•down \ˈtəm-bəl-ˈdau̇n\ *adj* ♦ **:** fallen into partial ruin or decay **:** DILAPIDATED

♦ dilapidated, grungy, mean, neglected, ratty, seedy, shabby

tum•bler \ˈtəm-blər\ *n* **1 :** one that tumbles; *esp* **:** ACROBAT **2 :** a drinking glass without foot or stem **3 :** a movable obstruction in a lock that must be adjusted to a particular position (as by a key) before the bolt can be thrown
tum•ble•weed \ˈtəm-bəl-ˌwēd\ *n* **:** a plant that breaks away from its roots in autumn and is driven about by the wind
tum•brel *or* **tum•bril** \ˈtəm-brəl\ *n* **1 :** CART **2 :** a vehicle carrying condemned persons (as during the French Revolution) to a place of execution
tu•mid \ˈtü-məd, ˈtyü-\ *adj* **1 :** SWOLLEN, DISTENDED **2 :** BOMBASTIC, TURGID
tum•my \ˈtə-mē\ *n, pl* **tummies** ♦ **:** the part of the body that contains the stomach **:** BELLY

♦ abdomen, belly, gut, solar plexus, stomach

tu•mor *or Can and Brit* **tu•mour** \ˈtü-mər, ˈtyü-\ *n* ♦ **:** an abnormal and functionless new growth of tissue that arises from uncontrolled cellular proliferation — **tu•mor•ous** *adj*

♦ excrescence, growth, lump, neoplasm

tu•mult \ˈtü-ˌməlt, ˈtyü-\ *n* **1 a** ♦ **:** a state of commotion, excitement, or confusion **b** ♦ **:** turbulent uprising **2 a :** violent agitation of mind or feelings **b** ♦ **:** a noisy, agitated outburst

♦ [1a] commotion, disturbance, furor, pandemonium, turmoil ♦ [1b] cataclysm, convulsion, paroxysm, storm, tempest, upheaval, uproar ♦ [2b] clamor (*or* clamour), howl, hubbub, hue and cry, hullabaloo, noise, outcry, roar, uproar

tu•mul•tu•ous \tü-ˈməl-chə-wəs, tyü-, -chəs\ *adj* **1 :** marked by tumult **2 :** tending to incite a tumult **3** ♦ **:** marked by violent upheaval

♦ convulsive, stormy, tempestuous, turbulent, wild

tun \ˈtən\ *n* **:** a large cask
tu•na \ˈtü-nə, ˈtyü-\ *n, pl* **tuna** *or* **tunas :** any of several mostly large marine fishes related to the mackerels and caught for food and sport; *also* **:** the flesh of a tuna
tun•able \ˈtü-nə-bəl, ˈtyü-\ *adj* **:** capable of being tuned — **tun•abil•i•ty** \ˌtü-nə-ˈbi-lə-tē, ˌtyü-\ *n*
tun•dra \ˈtən-drə\ *n* **:** a treeless plain of arctic and subarctic regions
¹tune \ˈtün, ˈtyün\ *n* **1** ♦ **:** a succession of pleasing musical tones **:** MELODY **2 :** correct musical pitch **3** ♦ **:** harmonious relationship **:** AGREEMENT ⟨in ~ with the times⟩ **4 :** general attitude

⟨changed his ~⟩ **5 :** AMOUNT, EXTENT ⟨in debt to the ~ of millions⟩

♦ [1] air, lay, melody, song, strain, warble ♦ [3] accord, agreement, conformity, consonance, harmony

²tune *vb* **tuned; tun•ing 1 :** to adjust in musical pitch **2 :** to bring or come into harmony : ATTUNE **3 :** to put in good working order **4 :** to adjust a radio or television receiver so as to receive a broadcast **5 :** to adjust the frequency of the output of (a device) to a chosen frequency — **tun•er** *n*

tune•ful \-fəl\ *adj* ♦ **:** having a pleasing melody : MELODIOUS — **tune•ful•ly** *adv* — **tune•ful•ness** *n*

♦ euphonious, harmonious, melodious, musical, symphonic

tune•less \-ləs\ *adj* **1 :** UNMELODIOUS **2 :** not producing music — **tune•less•ly** *adv*

tune–up \ˈtün-ˌəp, ˈtyün-\ *n* **:** an adjustment to ensure efficient functioning ⟨an engine ~⟩

tung•sten \ˈtəŋ-stən\ *n* **:** a gray-white hard heavy ductile metallic chemical element used especially in carbide materials, electrical components, and alloys

tu•nic \ˈtü-nik, ˈtyü-\ *n* **1 :** a usually knee-length belted under or outer garment worn by ancient Greeks and Romans **2 :** a hip-length or longer blouse or jacket

tuning fork *n* **:** a 2-pronged metal implement that gives a fixed tone when struck and is useful for tuning musical instruments

Tu•ni•sian \tü-ˈnē-zhən, tyü-, -ˈni-\ *n* **:** a native or inhabitant of Tunisia — **Tunisian** *adj*

¹tun•nel \ˈtən-ᵊl\ *n* **:** an enclosed passage (as a tube or conduit); *esp* **:** one underground (as in a mine)

²tunnel *vb* **-neled** *or* **-nelled; -nel•ing** *or* **-nel•ling :** to make a tunnel through or under — **tun•nel•er** \ˈtən-lər, ˈtə-nᵊl-ər\ *n*

tun•ny \ˈtə-nē\ *n, pl* **tunnies** *also* **tunny :** TUNA

tuque \ˈtük, ˈtyük\ *n* **:** a warm knitted cone-shaped cap

tur•ban \ˈtər-bən\ *n* **1 :** a headdress worn especially by Muslims and made of a cap around which is wound a long cloth **2 :** a headdress resembling a turban; *esp* **:** a woman's close-fitting hat without a brim

tur•bid \ˈtər-bəd\ *adj* **1** ♦ **:** cloudy or discolored by suspended particles ⟨a ~ stream⟩ **2 :** CONFUSED, MUDDLED — **tur•bid•i•ty** \ˌtər-ˈbi-də-tē\ *n*

♦ cloudy, muddy

tur•bine \ˈtər-bən, -ˌbīn\ *n* **:** an engine whose central driveshaft is fitted with curved vanes spun by the pressure of water, steam, or gas

tur•bo•fan \ˈtər-bō-ˌfan\ *n* **:** a jet engine having a fan driven by a turbine for supplying air for combustion

tur•bo•jet \-ˌjet\ *n* **:** an airplane powered by a jet engine (**turbojet engine**) having a turbine-driven air compressor supplying compressed air to the combustion chamber

tur•bo•prop \-ˌpräp\ *n* **:** an airplane powered by a jet engine (**turboprop engine**) having a turbine-driven propeller

tur•bot \ˈtər-bət\ *n, pl* **turbot** *also* **turbots :** a European flatfish that is a popular food fish; *also* **:** any of several similar flatfishes

tur•bu•lence \ˈtər-byə-ləns\ *n* **:** the quality or state of being turbulent

tur•bu•lent \-lənt\ *adj* **1 :** causing violence or disturbance **2** ♦ **:** marked by agitation or tumult : TEMPESTUOUS — **tur•bu•lent•ly** *adv*

♦ explosive, ferocious, fierce, furious, hot, rabid, rough, stormy, tempestuous, violent, volcanic ♦ stormy, tempestuous, tumultuous, wild

tu•reen \tə-ˈrēn, tyu̇-\ *n* **:** a deep bowl from which foods (as soup) are served at table

¹turf \ˈtərf\ *n, pl* **turfs** \ˈtərfs\ *also* **turves** \ˈtərvz\ **1 :** the upper layer of soil bound by grass and roots into a close mat; *also* **:** a piece of this **2 :** an artificial substitute for turf (as on a playing field) **3 :** a piece of peat dried for fuel **4 :** a track or course for horse racing; *also* **:** horse racing as a sport or business

²turf *vb* **:** to cover with turf

tur•gid \ˈtər-jəd\ *adj* **1 :** being in a swollen state **2 :** excessively embellished in style or language : BOMBASTIC — **tur•gid•i•ty** \ˌtər-ˈji-də-tē\ *n*

Turk \ˈtərk\ *n* **:** a native or inhabitant of Turkey

tur•key \ˈtər-kē\ *n, pl* **turkeys 1 :** a large No. American bird related to the domestic chicken and widely raised for food **2** ♦ **:** a complete failure **3** ♦ **:** a stupid, foolish, or inept person

♦ [2] bummer, bust, catastrophe, debacle, dud, failure, fiasco, fizzle, flop, lemon, loser, washout ♦ [3] booby, fool, goose, half-wit, jackass, lunatic, nitwit, nut, simpleton

turkey buzzard *n* **:** TURKEY VULTURE

turkey vulture *n* **:** an American vulture with a red head and whitish bill

Turk•ish \ˈtər-kish\ *n* **:** the language of Turkey — **Turkish** *adj*

tur•mer•ic \ˈtər-mə-rik\ *n* **:** a spice or dyestuff obtained from the large aromatic deep-yellow rhizome of an Indian perennial herb related to the ginger; *also* **:** this herb

tur•moil \ˈtər-ˌmȯil\ *n* ♦ **:** an extremely confused or agitated condition

♦ disquiet, ferment, restlessness, uneasiness, unrest ♦ commotion, furor, pandemonium, storm, tumult, uproar

¹turn \ˈtərn\ *vb* **1** ♦ **:** to move or cause to move around an axis or center : ROTATE ⟨~ a wheel⟩ **2 :** to effect a desired end by turning something ⟨~ the oven on⟩ **3 :** WRENCH ⟨~ an ankle⟩ **4 :** to change or cause to change position by moving through an arc of a circle ⟨~*ed* her chair to the fire⟩ **5 :** to cause to move around a center so as to show another side of ⟨~ a page⟩ **6 :** to revolve mentally : PONDER **7 :** to become dizzy : REEL **8 :** to reverse the sides or surfaces of ⟨~ a pancake⟩ **9 :** UPSET, DISORDER ⟨things were ~*ed* topsy-turvy⟩ **10** ♦ **:** to set in another especially contrary direction **11** ♦ **:** to change one's course or direction **12 :** to go around ⟨~ a corner⟩ **13 :** to undergo change or development : BECOME ⟨my hair ~*ed* gray⟩ ⟨~*ed* twenty-one⟩ **14 :** to direct toward or away from something; *also* **:** DEVOTE, APPLY **15** ♦ **:** to have recourse ⟨~ to a friend for help⟩ **16 :** to become or make hostile **17 :** to cause to become of a specified nature or appearance ⟨~*s* the leaves yellow⟩ **18 :** to make or become spoiled : SOUR **19 :** to pass from one state to another ⟨water ~*s* to ice⟩ **20 :** CONVERT, TRANSFORM **21 :** TRANSLATE, PARAPHRASE **22 :** to give a rounded form to; *esp* **:** to shape by means of a lathe **23 :** to gain by passing in trade ⟨~ a quick profit⟩ — **turn color 1 :** BLUSH **2 :** to become pale — **turn loose :** to set free

♦ [1] pivot, revolve, roll, rotate, spin, swing, swirl, twirl, twist, wheel, whirl ♦ [10] divert, swerve, swing, veer, wheel, whip ♦ [11] detour, deviate, sheer, swerve, swing, turn off, veer ♦ *usu* **turn to** [15] go, refer, resort

²turn *n* **1 :** a turning about a center or axis : REVOLUTION, ROTATION **2 :** the action or an act of giving or taking a different direction ⟨make a left ~⟩ **3 :** a change of course or tendency ⟨a ~ for the better⟩ **4** ♦ **:** a place at which something turns : BEND **5** ♦ **:** a short walk or trip round about ⟨take a ~ around the block⟩ **6** ♦ **:** an act affecting another ⟨did him a good ~⟩ **7 :** a place, time, or opportunity accorded in a scheduled order ⟨waited his ~ in line⟩ **8 :** a period of duty : SHIFT **9 :** a short act especially in a variety show **10 :** a special purpose or requirement ⟨the job serves his ~⟩ **11 :** a skillful fashioning ⟨neat ~ of phrase⟩ **12 :** a single round (as of rope passed around an object) **13** ♦ **:** natural or special aptitude **14 :** a usually sudden and brief disorder of body or spirits; *esp* **:** a spell of nervous shock or faintness

♦ [4] angle, arc, arch, bend, bow, crook, curve, wind ♦ [5] perambulation, ramble, stroll, walk ♦ [6] boon, courtesy, favor (*or* favour), grace, indulgence, kindness, mercy, service ♦ [13] bent, devices, disposition, genius, inclination, leaning, partiality, penchant, predilection, proclivity, propensity, tendency

turn•about \ˈtər-nə-ˌbau̇t\ *n* **1 :** a reversal of direction, trend, or policy **2 :** RETALIATION

turn•buck•le \ˈtərn-ˌbə-kəl\ *n* **:** a link with a screw thread at one or both ends for tightening a rod or stay

turn•coat \-ˌkōt\ *n* ♦ **:** one who switches to an opposing side or party : TRAITOR

♦ apostate, betrayer, double-crosser, quisling, recreant, traitor

turn down *vb* ♦ **:** to decline to accept : REJECT — **turn•down** \ˈtərn-ˌdau̇n\ *n*

♦ decline, disallow, disapprove, negative, refuse, reject, repudiate, spurn

turn•er \ˈtər-nər\ *n* **1 :** one that turns or is used for turning **2 :** one that forms articles with a lathe

turn•ery \ˈtər-nə-rē\ *n, pl* **-er•ies :** the work, products, or shop of a turner

turn in *vb* **1 :** to deliver up **2 :** to inform on **3 :** to acquit oneself of ⟨*turn in* a good job⟩ **4 :** to go to bed

turn•ing *n* **1 :** the act or course of one that turns **2 :** a place of a change of direction

tur•nip \ˈtər-nəp\ *n* **1 :** a garden herb related to the cabbage with a thick edible usually white root **2 :** RUTABAGA **3 :** the root of a turnip

turn·key \ˈtərn-ˌkē\ *n, pl* **turnkeys** : one who has charge of a prison's keys

turn·off \ˈtərn-ˌȯf\ *n* : a place for turning off especially from an expressway

turn off *vb* **1** ♦ : to deviate from a straight course or a main road **2** : to stop the functioning or flow of **3** ♦ : to cause to lose interest; *also* : to evoke a negative feeling in

♦ [1] detour, deviate, sheer, swerve, swing, turn, veer ♦ [3] disgust, nauseate, repel, repulse, revolt, sicken

turn on *vb* **1** ♦ : to cause to flow, function, or operate **2** : to get high or cause to get high as a result of using a drug (as marijuana) **3** ♦ : to move pleasurably : EXCITE

♦ [1] activate, actuate, crank, drive, move, propel, run, set off, spark, start, touch off, trigger ♦ [3] electrify, excite, exhilarate, galvanize, intoxicate, thrill, titillate

turn·out \ˈtərn-ˌau̇t\ *n* **1** : an act of turning out **2** : the number of people who participate or attend an event **3** : a widened place in a highway for vehicles to pass or park **4** : manner of dress **5** : net yield : OUTPUT

turn out *vb* **1** : EXPEL, EVICT **2** : PRODUCE **3** : to come forth and assemble **4** : to get out of bed **5** ♦ : to prove to be in the end **6** : to cause to stop functioning by turning a switch

♦ come out, pan out, prove

[1]**turn·over** \ˈtər-ˌnō-vər\ *n* **1** : UPSET **2** : SHIFT, REVERSAL **3** : a filled pastry made by turning half of the crust over the other half **4** : the volume of business done **5** : movement (as of goods or people) into, through, and out of a place **6** : the number of persons hired within a period to replace those leaving or dropped **7** : an instance of a team's losing possession of the ball especially through error

[2]**turnover** *adj* : capable of being turned over

turn over *vb* **1** ♦ : to turn from an upright position **2** ♦ : to take and hand over to or leave for another ⟨*turn* the job *over* to her⟩

♦ [1] flip, reverse ♦ [2] commend, commit, consign, delegate, deliver, entrust, give, hand over, leave, pass, surrender, transfer, transmit, trust, vest

turn·pike \ˈtərn-ˌpīk\ *n* **1** : TOLLGATE; *also* : an expressway on which tolls are charged **2** ♦ : a main road

♦ highway, pike, road, route, thoroughfare, way

turn·stile \-ˌstīl\ *n* : a post with arms pivoted on the top set in a passageway so that persons can pass through only on foot one by one

turn·ta·ble \-ˌtā-bəl\ *n* : a circular platform that revolves (as for turning a locomotive or a phonograph record)

turn to *vb* : to apply oneself to work

turn up *vb* **1** ♦ : to come to light or bring to light **2** ♦ : to arrive at an appointed time or place **3** : to happen unexpectedly **4** : to raise or increase by or as if by turning a control

♦ [1] appear, come out, materialize, show up ♦ [2] arrive, come, land, show up

tur·pen·tine \ˈtər-pən-ˌtīn\ *n* **1** : a mixture of oil and resin obtained from various cone-bearing trees (as pines) **2** : an oil distilled from turpentine or pine wood and used as a solvent and paint thinner

tur·pi·tude \ˈtər-pə-ˌtüd, -ˌtyüd\ *n* : inherent baseness : DEPRAVITY

tur·quoise *also* **tur·quois** \ˈtər-ˌkȯiz, -ˌkwȯiz\ *n* **1** : a blue, bluish green, or greenish gray mineral that is valued as a gem **2** : a light greenish blue color

tur·ret \ˈtər-ət\ *n* **1** : a little ornamental tower often at a corner of a building **2** : a low usually revolving structure (as on a tank or warship) in which one or more guns are mounted

[1]**tur·tle** \ˈtərt-ᵊl\ *n, archaic* : TURTLEDOVE

[2]**turtle** *n, pl* **turtles** *also* **turtle** : any of an order of horny-beaked land, freshwater, or sea reptiles with the trunk enclosed in a bony shell

tur·tle·dove \ˈtərt-ᵊl-ˌdəv\ *n* : any of several small pigeons noted for plaintive cooing

tur·tle·neck \-ˌnek\ *n* : a high close-fitting turnover collar (as on a sweater); *also* : a sweater or shirt with a turtleneck — **tur·tle·necked** \-ˌnekt\ *adj*

turves *pl of* TURF

Tus·ca·ro·ra \ˌtəs-kə-ˈrōr-ə\ *n, pl* **Tuscarora** *or* **Tuscaroras** : a member of an American Indian people of No. Carolina and later of New York and Ontario

tusk \ˈtəsk\ *n* : a long enlarged protruding tooth (as of an elephant, walrus, or boar) used especially to dig up food or as a weapon — **tusked** \ˈtəskt\ *adj*

tusk·er \ˈtəs-kər\ *n* : an animal with tusks; *esp* : a male elephant with two normally developed tusks

[1]**tus·sle** \ˈtə-səl\ *n* **1** ♦ : a physical struggle : SCUFFLE **2** : an intense argument, controversy, or struggle

♦ battle, clash, combat, conflict, contest, fight, fracas, fray, hassle, scrap, scrimmage, scuffle, skirmish, struggle

[2]**tussle** *vb* **tus·sled; tus·sling** ♦ : to struggle roughly

♦ grapple, scuffle, wrestle

tus·sock \ˈtə-sək\ *n* : a dense tuft especially of grass or sedge; *also* : a hummock in a marsh or bog bound together by roots — **tus·socky** *adj*

tu·te·lage \ˈtüt-ᵊl-ij, ˈtyüt-\ *n* **1** : an act of guarding or protecting **2** : the state of being under a guardian or tutor **3** ♦ : instruction especially of an individual

♦ education, instruction, teaching, training

tu·te·lary \ˈtüt-ᵊl-ˌer-ē, ˈtyüt-\ *adj* : acting as a guardian ⟨~ deity⟩

[1]**tu·tor** \ˈtü-tər, ˈtyü-\ *n* **1** : a person charged with the instruction and guidance of another **2** : a private teacher

[2]**tutor** *vb* **1** : to have the guardianship of **2** ♦ : to teach or guide individually ⟨~*ed* her in Latin⟩ **3** : to receive instruction especially privately

♦ educate, indoctrinate, instruct, school, teach, train ♦ coach, counsel, guide, lead, mentor, pilot, shepherd, show

tu·to·ri·al \tü-ˈtōr-ē-əl, tyü-\ *n* : a class conducted by a tutor for one student or a small number of students

tut·ti \ˈtü-tē, ˈtu̇-, -ˌtē\ *adj or adv* : with all voices and instruments playing together — used as a direction in music

tut·ti–frut·ti \ˌtü-ti-ˈfrü-tē, ˌtu̇-\ *n* : a confection or ice cream containing chopped usually candied fruits

tu·tu \ˈtü-(ˌ)tü\ *n* : a short projecting skirt worn by a ballerina

tux·e·do \ˌtək-ˈsē-dō\ *n, pl* **-dos** *or* **-does** **1** : a usually black or blackish blue jacket **2** : a semiformal evening suit for men

TV \ˈtē-ˈvē\ *n* : TELEVISION

TVA *abbr* Tennessee Valley Authority

TV dinner *n* : a frozen packaged dinner that needs only heating before serving

twad·dle \ˈtwäd-ᵊl\ *n* ♦ : silly idle talk : DRIVEL — **twaddle** *vb*

♦ blarney, bunk, claptrap, drivel, fiddlesticks, folly, foolishness, fudge, hogwash, humbug, nonsense, piffle, rot, silliness, slush, stupidity, trash

twain \ˈtwān\ *n* **1** : TWO **2** ♦ : two similar or associated things : PAIR

♦ brace, couple, duo, pair, twosome

[1]**twang** \ˈtwaŋ\ *n* **1** : a harsh quick ringing sound like that of a plucked bowstring **2** : nasal speech or resonance **3** : the characteristic speech of a region

[2]**twang** *vb* **twanged; twang·ing** **1** : to sound or cause to sound with a twang **2** : to speak with a nasal twang

tweak \ˈtwēk\ *vb* **1** : to pinch and pull with a sudden jerk and twitch **2** : to make small adjustments to — **tweak** *n*

tweed \ˈtwēd\ *n* **1** : a rough woolen fabric made usually in twill weaves **2** *pl* : tweed clothing; *esp* : a tweed suit

tweedy \ˈtwē-dē\ *adj* **tweed·i·er; -est** **1** : of or resembling tweed **2** : given to wearing tweeds **3** : suggestive of the outdoors in taste or habits

tween \ˈtwēn\ *prep* : BETWEEN

[1]**tweet** \ˈtwēt\ *n* : a chirping note

[2]**tweet** *vb* ♦ : to make a usually repetitive short sharp sound

♦ cheep, chirp, peep, pipe, twitter

tweet·er \ˈtwē-tər\ *n* : a small loudspeaker that reproduces sounds of high pitch

twee·zers \ˈtwē-zərz\ *n pl* : a small pincerlike implement usually held between the thumb and index finger and used for grasping something

twelve \ˈtwelv\ *n* **1** : one more than 11 **2** : the 12th in a set or series **3** : something having 12 units — **twelfth** \ˈtwelfth\ *adj or n* — **twelve** *adj or pron*

twelve·month \-ˌmənth\ *n* : YEAR

12–step \ˈtwelv-ˌstep\ *adj* : of, relating to, or being a program designed especially to help someone overcome a problem (as an addiction) by following 12 tenets

twen·ty \ˈtwen-tē\ *n, pl* **twenties** : two times 10 — **twen·ti·eth** \-tē-əth\ *adj or n* — **twenty** *adj or pron*

twenty–twenty *or* **20/20** \ˌtwen-tē-ˈtwen-tē\ *adj* : characterized by a visual capacity for seeing detail that is normal for the human eye ⟨~ vision⟩

twice \ˈtwīs\ *adv* **1 :** on two occasions **2 :** two times ⟨~ two is four⟩

1**twid·dle** \ˈtwid-ᵊl\ *vb* **twid·dled; twid·dling 1 :** to be busy with trifles; *also* **:** to play idly with something **2 :** to rotate lightly or idly

2**twiddle** *n* **:** TURN, TWIST

twig \ˈtwig\ *n* **:** a small branch — **twig·gy** *adj*

twi·light \ˈtwī-ˌlīt\ *n* **1** ♦ **:** the light from the sky between full night and sunrise or between sunset and full night; *also* **:** a time of twilight **2 :** a state of imperfect clarity; *also* **:** a period of decline

♦ dusk, evening, gloaming, nightfall, sundown, sunset

twilight zone *n* **1 :** TWILIGHT 2; *also* **:** an area just beyond ordinary legal or ethical limits **2 :** a world of fantasy or unreality

twill \ˈtwil\ *n* **1 :** a fabric with a twill weave **2 :** a textile weave that gives an appearance of diagonal lines

twilled \ˈtwild\ *adj* **:** made with a twill weave

1**twin** \ˈtwin\ *n* **1 :** either of two offspring produced at a birth **2** ♦ **:** one of two persons or things closely related to or resembling each other

♦ companion, fellow, half, match, mate

2**twin** *vb* **twinned; twin·ning 1 :** to be coupled with another **2 :** to bring forth twins

3**twin** *adj* **1 :** born with one other or as a pair at one birth ⟨~ brother⟩ ⟨~ girls⟩ **2** ♦ **:** made up of two similar or related members or parts **3 :** being one of a pair ⟨~ city⟩

♦ binary, bipartite, double, dual, duplex

1**twine** \ˈtwīn\ *n* **1 :** a strong thread of two or three strands twisted together **2 :** an act of entwining or interlacing — **twiny** *adj*

2**twine** *vb* **twined; twin·ing 1 :** to twist together; *also* **:** to form by twisting **2 :** INTERLACE, WEAVE **3 :** to coil about a support **4** ♦ **:** to stretch or move in a sinuous manner — **twin·er** *n*

♦ coil, curl, entwine, spiral, twist, wind

1**twinge** \ˈtwinj\ *vb* **twinged; twing·ing** *or* **twinge·ing :** to affect with or feel a sharp sudden pain

2**twinge** *n* ♦ **:** a sudden sharp stab (as of pain or distress)

♦ ache, pain, pang, prick, smart, sting, stitch, tingle

1**twin·kle** \ˈtwiŋ-kəl\ *vb* **twin·kled; twin·kling 1** ♦ **:** to shine or cause to shine with a flickering or sparkling light **2 :** to appear bright with merriment **3 :** to flutter or flit rapidly — **twin·kler** *n*

♦ flame, flash, glance, gleam, glimmer, glisten, glitter, scintillate, shimmer, sparkle, wink

2**twinkle** *n* **1 a :** a wink of the eyelids **b :** the duration of a wink **:** TWINKLING **2 :** an intermittent radiance **3 :** a rapid flashing motion — **twin·kly** \ˈtwiŋ-klē\ *adj*

twin·kling \ˈtwiŋ-kliŋ\ *n* ♦ **:** the time required for a wink **:** INSTANT

♦ flash, instant, jiffy, minute, moment, second, shake, trice, twinkle, wink

1**twirl** \ˈtwərl\ *vb* ♦ **:** to turn or cause to turn rapidly ⟨~ a baton⟩ — **twirl·er** *n*

♦ pivot, revolve, roll, rotate, spin, swing, swirl, turn, twist, wheel, whirl

2**twirl** *n* **1** ♦ **:** an act of twirling **2 :** COIL, WHORL — **twirly** \ˈtwər-lē\ *adj*

♦ gyration, pirouette, reel, revolution, roll, rotation, spin, wheel, whirl

1**twist** \ˈtwist\ *vb* **1 :** to unite by winding one thread or strand round another **2 :** WREATHE, TWINE **3** ♦ **:** to wring or wrench so as to dislocate or distort ⟨~*ed* her ankle⟩ **4 :** to twirl into spiral shape **5** ♦ **:** to subject (as a shaft) to torsion **6** ♦ **:** to turn from the true form or meaning **7 :** to pull off or break by torsion **8** ♦ **:** to follow a winding course **9** ♦ **:** to turn around

♦ [3, 5] wrench, wrest, wring ♦ [6] color (*or* colour), distort, falsify, garble, misinterpret, misrepresent, misstate, pervert, warp ♦ [8] coil, curl, entwine, spiral, twine, wind ♦ [9] pivot, revolve, roll, rotate, spin, swing, swirl, turn, twirl, wheel, whirl

2**twist** *n* **1 :** something formed by twisting or winding **2** ♦ **:** an act of twisting **:** the state of being twisted **3 :** a spiral turn or curve; *also* **:** SPIN **4 :** a turning aside **5 :** ECCENTRICITY **6 :** a distortion of meaning **7 :** an unexpected turn or development **8 :** DEVICE, TRICK **9 :** a variant approach or method

♦ wrench

twist·er \ˈtwis-tər\ *n* **1 :** one that twists; *esp* **:** a ball with a forward and spinning motion **2 :** TORNADO; *also* **:** WATERSPOUT 2

1**twit** \ˈtwit\ *n* **:** FOOL

2**twit** *vb* **twit·ted; twit·ting :** to ridicule as a fault; *also* **:** TAUNT

1**twitch** \ˈtwich\ *vb* **1** ♦ **:** to move or pull with a sudden motion **:** JERK **2** ♦ **:** to move jerkily **3 :** to have a twitch

♦ [1] fiddle, fidget, jerk, squirm, wiggle ♦ [2] buck, hitch, jerk, jolt

2**twitch** *n* **1 :** an act or movement of twitching **2 :** a brief spasmodic contraction of muscle fibers

1**twit·ter** \ˈtwi-tər\ *vb* **1** ♦ **:** to make a succession of chirping noises **2** ♦ **:** to talk in a chattering fashion **3 :** to tremble with agitation **:** FLUTTER

♦ [1] cheep, chirp, peep, pipe, tweet ♦ [2] chat, converse, gab, jaw, palaver, patter, prattle, rattle, talk, visit

2**twitter** *n* **1** ♦ **:** a slight agitation of the nerves **2 :** a small tremulous intermittent noise (as made by a swallow) **3 :** a light chattering

♦ dither, fluster, fret, fuss, huff, lather, pother, stew, tizzy

twixt \ˈtwikst\ *prep* **:** BETWEEN

two \ˈtü\ *n, pl* **twos 1 :** one more than one **2 :** the second in a set or series **3 :** something having two units — **two** *adj or pron*

two cents *n* **1 :** a sum or object of very small value **2** *or* **two cents worth :** an opinion offered on a topic under discussion

two–faced \ˈtü-ˈfāst\ *adj* **1** ♦ **:** given to or marked by duplicity **:** DOUBLE-DEALING **2 :** having two faces

♦ artificial, double-dealing, feigned, hypocritical, insincere, left-handed, mealy, mealymouthed, unctuous

1**two·fold** \ˈtü-ˌfōld, -ˈfōld\ *adj* **1 :** having two units or members **2 :** being twice as much or as many

2**two·fold** \ˈtü-ˈfōld\ *adv* **:** to twice as much or as many **:** by two times

2,4–D \ˌtü-ˌfōr-ˈdē\ *n* **:** an irritant compound used especially as a weed killer

2,4,5–T \-ˌfīv-ˈtē\ *n* **:** an irritant compound used especially as an herbicide and defoliant

two·pence \ˈtə-pəns, *US also* ˈtü-ˌpens\ *n* **:** the sum of two pence

two·pen·ny \ˈtə-pə-nē, *US also* ˈtü-ˌpe-nē\ *adj* **:** of the value of or costing twopence

two–ply \ˈtü-ˈplī\ *adj* **1 :** woven as a double cloth **2 :** consisting of two strands or thicknesses

two·some \ˈtü-səm\ *n* **1** ♦ **:** a group of two persons or things **:** COUPLE **2 :** a golf match between two players

♦ brace, couple, duo, pair, twain

two–step \ˈtü-ˌstep\ *n* **:** a ballroom dance performed with a sliding step in march or polka time; *also* **:** a piece of music for this dance — **two–step** *vb*

two–time \ˈtü-ˌtīm\ *vb* **:** to betray (a spouse or lover) by secret lovemaking with another — **two–tim·er** *n*

two–way *adj* **:** involving two elements or allowing movement or use in two directions or manners

2WD *abbr* two-wheel drive

twp *abbr* township

TWX *abbr* teletypewriter exchange

TX *abbr* Texas

ty·coon \tī-ˈkün\ *n* **1** ♦ **:** a masterful leader (as in politics) **2** ♦ **:** a powerful businessman or industrialist

♦ [1, 2] baron, czar, king, magnate, mogul, prince

tying *pres part of* TIE

tyke \ˈtīk\ *n* **:** a small child

tym·pan·ic membrane \tim-ˈpa-nik-\ *n* **:** EARDRUM

tym·pa·num \ˈtim-pə-nəm\ *n, pl* **-na** \-nə\ *also* **-nums :** EARDRUM; *also* **:** MIDDLE EAR — **tym·pan·ic** \tim-ˈpa-nik\ *adj*

1**type** \ˈtīp\ *n* **1 :** a person, thing, or event that foreshadows another to come **:** TOKEN, SYMBOL **2 :** MODEL, EXAMPLE **3 :** a distinctive stamp, mark, or sign **:** EMBLEM **4 :** rectangular blocks usually of metal each having a face so shaped as to produce a character when printed **5 :** the letters or characters printed from or as if from type **6 :** general character or form common to a number of individuals and setting them off as a distinguishable class ⟨horses of draft ~⟩ **7** ♦ **:** a class, kind, or group set apart by common characteristics ⟨a seedless ~ of orange⟩; *also* **:** something distinguishable as a variety ⟨reactions of this ~⟩

♦ breed, class, description, feather, group, ilk, kind, like, manner, nature, order, sort, species

2**type** *vb* **typed; typ·ing 1 :** to produce a copy of; *also* **:** REPRESENT, TYPIFY **2 :** to write with a typewriter or computer keyboard **3** ♦ **:** to identify as belonging to a type **4 :** to cast (an actor or actress) repeatedly in the same type of role **:** TYPECAST

◆ assort, break down, categorize, class, classify, codify, grade, group, peg, place, range, rank, separate, sort

type·cast \-ˌkast\ *vb* **-cast; -cast·ing 1 :** to cast (an actor) in a part calling for characteristics possessed by the actor **2 :** to cast repeatedly in the same type of role
type·face \-ˌfās\ *n* **:** all type of a single design
type·script \ˈtīp-ˌskript\ *n* **:** typewritten matter
type·set \-ˌset\ *vb* **-set; -set·ting :** to set in type **:** COMPOSE — **type·set·ter** *n*
type·write \-ˌrīt\ *vb* **-wrote** \-ˌrōt\; **-writ·ten** \-ˌrit-ᵊn\ **:** TYPE 2
type·writ·er \-ˌrī-tər\ *n* **1 :** a machine for writing in characters similar to those produced by printers' type by means of types striking a ribbon to transfer ink or carbon impressions onto paper **2 :** TYPIST
type·writ·ing \-ˌrī-tiŋ\ *n* **:** the use of a typewriter ⟨teach ~⟩; *also* **:** writing produced with a typewriter
[1]**ty·phoid** \ˈtī-ˌfȯid, tī-ˈfȯid\ *adj* **:** of, relating to, or being a communicable bacterial disease (**typhoid fever**) marked by fever, diarrhea, prostration, and intestinal inflammation
[2]**typhoid** *n* **:** TYPHOID FEVER
ty·phoon \tī-ˈfün\ *n* **:** a hurricane occurring especially in the region of the Philippines or the China sea
ty·phus \ˈtī-fəs\ *n* **:** a severe infectious disease transmitted especially by body lice, caused by a rickettsia, and marked by high fever, stupor and delirium, intense headache, and a dark red rash
typ·i·cal \ˈti-pi-kəl\ *adj* **1 :** being or having the nature of a type **2** ◆ **:** exhibiting the essential characteristics of a group **3** ◆ **:** conforming to a type — **typ·i·cal·i·ty** \ˌti-pə-ˈka-lə-tē\ *n* — **typ·i·cal·ness** *n*

◆ [2] characteristic, classic, distinct, distinctive, individual, peculiar, proper, symptomatic ◆ [2, 3] average, characteristic, normal, regular, representative, standard ***Ant*** aberrant, abnormal, anomalous, atypical, deviant, irregular, nontypical

typ·i·cal·ly \-pi-k(ə-)lē\ *adv* **1 :** in a typical manner **2** ◆ **:** in typical circumstances

◆ commonly, generally, naturally, normally, ordinarily, usually

typ·i·fy \ˈti-pə-ˌfī\ *vb* **-fied; -fy·ing 1 :** to represent by an image, form, model, or resemblance **2 :** to embody the essential or common characteristics of

typ·ist \ˈtī-pist\ *n* **:** a person who types especially as a job
ty·po \ˈtī-pō\ *n, pl* **typos :** an error (as of spelling) in typed or typeset material
ty·pog·ra·pher \tī-ˈpä-grə-fər\ *n* **:** one who designs or arranges printing
ty·pog·ra·phy \tī-ˈpä-grə-fē\ *n* **:** the art of printing with type; *also* **:** the style, arrangement, or appearance of printed matter — **ty·po·graph·ic** \ˌtī-pə-ˈgra-fik\ *or* **ty·po·graph·i·cal** \-fi-kəl\ *adj* — **ty·po·graph·i·cal·ly** *adv*
ty·ran·ni·cal \tə-ˈra-ni-kəl, tī-\ *also* **ty·ran·nic** \-nik\ *adj* ◆ **:** being or characteristic of a tyrant or tyranny **:** DESPOTIC — **ty·ran·ni·cal·ly** \-ni-k(ə-)lē\ *adv*

◆ absolute, autocratic, despotic, dictatorial, tyrannous

tyr·an·nise *chiefly Brit var of* TYRANNIZE
tyr·an·nize \ˈtir-ə-ˌnīz\ *vb* **-nized; -niz·ing :** to act as a tyrant **:** rule with unjust severity — **tyr·an·niz·er** *n*
ty·ran·no·saur \tə-ˈra-nə-ˌsȯr\ *n* **:** a massive American flesh-eating dinosaur of the Cretaceous that had small forelegs and walked on its hind legs
ty·ran·no·sau·rus \tə-ˌra-nə-ˈsȯr-əs\ *n* **:** TYRANNOSAUR
tyr·an·nous \ˈtir-ə-nəs\ *adj* ◆ **:** being or characteristic of a tyrant or tyranny; *esp* **:** unjustly severe **:** TYRANNICAL — **tyr·an·nous·ly** *adv*

◆ authoritarian, autocratic, bossy, despotic, dictatorial, domineering, imperious, masterful, overbearing, peremptory, tyrannical

tyr·an·ny \ˈtir-ə-nē\ *n, pl* **-nies 1 :** oppressive power **2** ◆ **:** the rule or authority of a tyrant **:** government in which absolute power is vested in a single ruler **3 :** a tyrannical act

◆ autocracy, despotism, dictatorship, totalitarianism

ty·rant \ˈtī-rənt\ *n* **1** ◆ **:** an absolute ruler **:** DESPOT **2** ◆ **:** a ruler who governs oppressively or brutally **3** ◆ **:** one who uses authority or power harshly

◆ [1, 2, 3] autocrat, despot, dictator, oppressor

tyre *chiefly Brit var of* [2]TIRE
ty·ro \ˈtī-rō\ *n, pl* **tyros** ◆ **:** a beginner in learning **:** NOVICE

◆ beginner, fledgling, freshman, greenhorn, neophyte, newcomer, novice, recruit, rookie, tenderfoot

tzar *var of* CZAR

U

[1]**u** \ˈyü\ *n, pl* **u's** *or* **us** \ˈyüz\ *often cap* **:** the 21st letter of the English alphabet
[2]**u** *abbr, often cap* unit
[1]**U** \ˈyü\ *adj* **:** characteristic of the upper classes
[2]**U** *abbr* **1** kosher certification — often enclosed in a circle **2** university **3** unsatisfactory
[3]**U** *symbol* uranium
UAE *abbr* United Arab Emirates
UAR *abbr* United Arab Republic
UAW *abbr* United Automobile Workers
ubiq·ui·tous \yü-ˈbi-kwə-təs\ *adj* **:** existing or being everywhere at the same time **:** constantly encountered — **ubiq·ui·tous·ly** *adv* — **ubiq·ui·ty** \-kwə-tē\ *n*
U–boat \ˈyü-ˌbōt\ *n* **:** a German submarine
UC *abbr* uppercase
ud·der \ˈə-dər\ *n* **:** an organ (as of a cow) consisting of two or more milk glands enclosed in a large hanging sac and each provided with a nipple
UFO \ˌyü-(ˌ)ef-ˈō\ *n, pl* **UFO's** *or* **UFOs** \-ˈōz\ **:** an unidentified flying object; *esp* **:** FLYING SAUCER
Ugan·dan \ü-ˈgan-dən, yü-, -ˈgän-\ *n* **:** a native or inhabitant of Uganda — **Ugandan** *adj*
ug·ly \ˈə-glē\ *adj* **ug·li·er; -est 1 :** FRIGHTFUL, DIRE **2** ◆ **:** offensive to the sight **:** HIDEOUS **3 :** offensive or unpleasant to any sense **4 :** morally objectionable **:** REPULSIVE **5 :** likely to cause inconvenience or discomfort **6 :** SURLY, QUARRELSOME ⟨an ~ disposition⟩ — **ug·li·ness** \-glē-nəs\ *n*

◆ grotesque, hideous, unappealing, unattractive, unlovely, unsightly, vile ***Ant*** attractive, beauteous, beautiful, comely, cute, fair, gorgeous, handsome, lovely, pretty, stunning, taking

UHF *abbr* ultrahigh frequency
UK *abbr* United Kingdom
ukase \yü-ˈkās, -ˈkāz\ *n* **:** an edict especially of a Russian emperor or government
Ukrai·ni·an \yü-ˈkra-ne-ən\ *n* **:** a native or inhabitant of Ukraine — **Ukrainian** *adj*
uku·le·le *also* **uke·le·le** \ˌyü-kə-ˈlā-lē\ *n* **:** a small usually 4-stringed guitar popularized in Hawaii
ul·cer \ˈəl-sər\ *n* **1 :** an open eroded sore of skin or mucous membrane often discharging pus **2 :** something that festers and corrupts like an open sore — **ul·cer·ous** *adj*
ul·cer·ate \ˈəl-sə-ˌrāt\ *vb* **-at·ed; -at·ing :** to become affected with an ulcer — **ul·cer·a·tive** \ˈəl-sə-ˌrā-tiv\ *adj*
ul·cer·a·tion \ˌəl-sə-ˈrā-shən\ *n* **1 :** the process of forming or state of having an ulcer **2 :** ULCER 1
ul·na \ˈəl-nə\ *n* **:** the bone on the little-finger side of the human forearm; *also* **:** a corresponding bone of the forelimb of vertebrates above fishes
ul·ster \ˈəl-stər\ *n* **:** a long loose overcoat
ult *abbr* **1** ultimate **2** ultimo
ul·te·ri·or \ˌəl-ˈtir-ē-ər\ *adj* **1 :** lying farther away **:** more remote **2 :** situated beyond or on the farther side **3 :** going beyond what is openly said or shown **:** HIDDEN ⟨~ motives⟩
[1]**ul·ti·mate** \ˈəl-tə-mət\ *adj* **1** ◆ **:** most remote in space or time **:** FARTHEST **2** ◆ **:** last in a progression **:** FINAL **3** ◆ **:** the best or most extreme of its kind **4 :** arrived at as the last resort **5 :** FUNDAMENTAL, ABSOLUTE, SUPREME ⟨~ reality⟩

6 : incapable of further analysis or division : ELEMENTAL 7 : MAXIMUM

♦ [1] extreme, outermost, utmost ♦ [2] final, hindmost, last, latter, terminal ♦ [3] consummate, maximum, most, nth, paramount, supreme, top, utmost *Ant* least, minimal, minimum

²**ultimate** *n* : something ultimate

ul•ti•mate•ly *adv* ♦ : at an unspecified later time : in the end

♦ eventually, someday, sometime, yet

ul•ti•ma•tum \ˌəl-tə-ˈmā-təm, -ˈmä-\ *n, pl* **-tums** *or* **-ta** \-tə\ : a final condition or demand whose rejection will bring about a resort to forceful action

ul•ti•mo \ˈəl-tə-ˌmō\ *adj* : of or occurring in the month preceding the present

¹**ul•tra** \ˈəl-trə\ *adj* ♦ : going beyond others or beyond due limits : EXTREME

♦ extreme, extremist, fanatic, rabid, radical, revolutionary

²**ultra** *n* : EXTREMIST

ul•tra•con•ser•va•tive \-kən-ˈsər-və-tiv\ *adj* : extremely conservative

ul•tra•high frequency \-ˈhī-\ *n* : a radio frequency between 300 and 3000 megahertz

¹**ul•tra•light** \ˈəl-trə-ˌlīt\ *adj* : extremely light especially in weight

²**ultralight** *n* : a very light recreational aircraft typically carrying only one person

ul•tra•ma•rine \ˌəl-trə-mə-ˈrēn\ *n* 1 : a deep blue pigment 2 : a very bright deep blue color

ul•tra•mi•cro•scop•ic \-ˌmī-krə-ˈskä-pik\ *adj* : too small to be seen with an ordinary microscope

ul•tra•mod•ern \-ˈmä-dərn\ *adj* ♦ : extremely or excessively modern in idea, style, or tendency

♦ contemporary, current, hot, mod, modern, new, newfangled, red-hot, space-age, up-to-date

ul•tra•mon•tane \-ˈmän-ˌtān, -ˌmän-ˈtān\ *adj* 1 : of or relating to countries or peoples beyond the mountains (as the Alps) 2 : favoring greater or absolute supremacy of papal over national or diocesan authority in the Roman Catholic Church — **ultramontane** *n, often cap* — **ul•tra•mon•tan•ism** \-ˈmänt-ᵊn-ˌi-zəm\ *n*

ul•tra•pure \-ˈpyu̇r\ *adj* : of the utmost purity

ul•tra•short \-ˈshȯrt\ *adj* 1 : having a wavelength below 10 meters 2 : very short in duration

ul•tra•son•ic \ˌəl-trə-ˈsä-nik\ *adj* : having a frequency too high to be heard by the human ear — **ul•tra•son•i•cal•ly** \-ni-k(ə-)lē\ *adv*

ul•tra•son•ics \-ˈsä-niks\ *n sing or pl* 1 : ultrasonic vibrations 2 : the science of ultrasonic phenomena

ul•tra•sound \-ˌsau̇nd\ *n* 1 : ultrasonic vibrations 2 : the diagnostic or therapeutic use of ultrasound and especially a technique involving the formation of a two-dimensional image of internal body structures 3 : a diagnostic examination using ultrasound

ul•tra•vi•o•let \-ˈvī-ə-lət\ *adj* : having a wavelength shorter than those of visible light and longer than those of X-rays ⟨~ radiation⟩; *also* : producing or employing ultraviolet radiation — **ultraviolet** *n*

ul•tra vi•res \ˈəl-trə-ˈvī-rēz\ *adv or adj* : beyond the scope of legal power or authority

ul•u•late \ˈəl-yə-ˌlāt\ *vb* **-lat•ed; -lat•ing** : HOWL, WAIL

uma•mi \ü-ˈmä-mē\ *n* : a meaty or savory taste sensation produced especially by monosodium glutamate

um•bel \ˈəm-bəl\ *n* : a flat-topped or rounded flower cluster in which the individual flower stalks all arise near one point on the main stem

um•ber \ˈəm-bər\ *n* : a brown earthy substance valued as a pigment either in its raw state or burnt — **umber** *adj*

umbilical cord *n* : a cord containing blood vessels that connects the navel of a fetus with the placenta of its mother

um•bi•li•cus \ˌəm-ˈbi-li-kəs, ˌəm-bə-ˈlī-\ *n, pl* **um•bi•li•ci** \ˌəm-ˈbi-lə-ˌkī; ˌəm-bə-ˈlī-ˌkī, -ˌsī\ *or* **um•bi•li•cus•es** : NAVEL — **um•bil•i•cal** \ˌəm-ˈbi-li-kəl\ *adj*

um•bra \ˈəm-brə\ *n, pl* **umbras** *or* **um•brae** \-(ˌ)brē, -ˌbrī\ 1 : a shaded area : SHADE 2 : the conical part of the shadow of a celestial body from which the sun's light is completely blocked

um•brage \ˈəm-brij\ *n* 1 : SHADE; *also* : FOLIAGE 2 ♦ : a feeling of pique or resentment at some often fancied slight or insult : OFFENSE ⟨take ~ at a remark⟩

♦ dudgeon, huff, offense, peeve, pique, resentment

um•brel•la \ˌəm-ˈbre-lə\ *n* 1 : a collapsible shade for protection against weather consisting of fabric stretched over hinged ribs radiating from a center pole 2 : something that provides protection 3 : something that covers a range of elements

umi•ak \ˈü-mē-ˌak\ *n* : an open Eskimo boat made of a wooden frame covered with skins

¹**um•pire** \ˈəm-ˌpīr\ *n* 1 ♦ : one having authority to decide finally a controversy or question between parties 2 : an official in a sport who rules on plays

♦ arbiter, arbitrator, judge, referee

²**umpire** *vb* ♦ : to supervise or decide as umpire

♦ adjudicate, arbitrate, decide, determine, judge, referee, rule, settle

ump•teen \ˈəmp-ˌtēn\ *adj* : very many : indefinitely numerous — **ump•teenth** \-ˌtēnth\ *adj*

UN *abbr* United Nations

un- \ˌən, ˈən\ *prefix* 1 : not : IN-, NON- 2 : opposite of : contrary to

unabated
unabsorbed
unabsorbent
unacademic
unaccented
unacclimatized
unaccommodating
unaccredited
unacknowledged
unadventurous
unadvertised
unaffiliated
unafraid
unaggressive
unaltered
unambiguously
unambitious
unanchored
unannounced
unanswered
unapologetic
unapparent
unappeased
unappreciated
unappreciative
unappropriated
unapproved
unarguable
unarguably
unarmored
unartistic
unassertive
unathletic
unattended
unattested
unauthorized
unavowed
unawakened
unbaked
unbeloved
unbleached
unblinking
unbranched
unbranded
unbreakable
unbridgeable
unbruised
unbrushed
unburied
unburned
uncanceled
uncanonical
uncap
uncapitalized
uncared–for
uncaught
uncensored
uncensured
unchallenged
unchanged
unchaperoned
uncharacteristic
unchastely
unchasteness
unchivalrous
unclaimed
unclassified
uncleaned
uncleared
uncoated
uncollected
uncombed
uncombined
uncomely
uncommercial
uncompensated
uncompleted
uncomplicated
uncompounded
uncomprehending
unconcealed
unconfirmed
unconformable
unconquered
unconsecrated
unconsolidated
unconstrained
unconsumed
unconsummated
uncontaminated
uncontested
uncontroversial
unconverted
uncooked
uncooperative
uncoordinated
uncorrected
uncorroborated
uncreative
uncredited
uncropped
uncrowded
uncrowned
uncrystallized
uncured
uncurtained
undamaged
undamped
undated
undecipherable
undeclared
undefeated
undefiled
undefinable
undemanding
undemocratic
undenominational
undependable
undeserved
undeserving
undetected
undeterred
undeveloped
undifferentiated
undigested
undignified
undiminished
undimmed
undiplomatic
undirected

undisciplined
undisclosed
undiscovered
undiscriminating
undisguised
undismayed
undisputed
undissolved
undistinguished
undistributed
undogmatic
undone
undoubled
undramatic
undraped
undreamed
undrinkable
undulled
undutiful
uneatable
uneaten
uneconomic
uneconomical
unedifying
unedited
unemphatic
unenclosed
unencumbered
unenforceable
unenforced
unenlightened
unenterprising
unenviable
unequipped
unessential
unexamined
unexcelled
unexcited
unexciting
unexpired
unexplained
unexploded
unexplored
unexposed
unexpurgated
unfading
unfaltering
unfashionably
unfavorably
unfeasible
unfenced
unfermented
unfertilized
unfilled
unfiltered
unfitted
unflattering
unflavored
unfocused
unfolded
unforeseeable
unforgiving
unformulated
unfortified
unframed
unfree
unfulfilled
unfunded
unfurnished
unfussy
ungentlemanly
ungerminated
unglamorous
unglazed
ungracefully
ungraded
ungrammatical
unground
ungrudging
unguided
unhackneyed
unhardened
unharmed
unharvested
unhatched
unhealed
unheated
unheeded
unhelpful
unheralded
unhesitating
unhistorical
unhonored
unhoused
unhurt
unhygienic
unidentifiable
unidiomatic
unimaginative
unimpaired
unimpassioned
unimpeded
unimposing
unimpressed
unimpressive
unimproved
unincorporated
uninfected
uninfluenced
uninformative
uninhabitable
uninhabited
uninitiated
uninjured
uninspired
uninstall
uninstructive
uninsured
unintentionally
uninviting
unjointed
unjustified
unkept
unknowable
unknowledgeable
unlabeled
unlamented
unleavened
unlicensed
unlighted
unlikable
unlined
unlit
unlivable
unlovable
unloved
unloving
unmade
unmalicious
unmanned
unmapped
unmarked
unmarketable
unmarred
unmasculine
unmeant
unmeasurable
unmeasured
unmentioned
unmerited
unmilitary
unmilled
unmodified
unmolested
unmotivated
unmounted
unmoved
unnameable
unnecessary
unneeded
unnewsworthy
unnoticeable
unnoticed
unobjectionable
unobservant
unobserved
unofficial
unofficially
unopened
unopposed
unorthodoxy
unostentatious
unowned
unpaged
unpaired
unpasteurized
unpatriotic
unpaved
unpeeled
unperceived
unperceptive
unperformed
unpersuaded
unpersuasive
unplanted
unplowed
unpoetic
unpolitical
unpolluted
unposed
unpractical
unpredictability
unpreparedness
unprepossessing
unpressed
unprivileged
unprofessed
unprogrammed
unpromising
unprompted
unpronounceable
unpropitious
unproven
unprovided
unprovoked
unpublished
unpunished
unquenchable
unquestioned
unraised
unrated
unratified
unreadable
unready
unrealistic
unrealized
unrecognizable
unrecognized
unreflecting
unreflective
unregulated
unrelated
unrelieved
unremembered
unremovable
unreported
unrepresentative
unrepresented
unrepressed
unresponsive
unresponsiveness
unreturnable
unrewarding
unrhymed
unrhythmic
unromantic
unromantically
unsaid
unsalable
unsalted
unsanctioned
unsanitary
unsatisfied
unscented
unscheduled
unscholarly
unsealed
unseasoned
unseaworthy
unsegmented
unself–conscious
unself–consciously
unsensational
unsentimental
unserious
unserviceable
unsexual
unshaded
unshapely
unshaven
unsifted
unsigned
unsinkable
unsold
unsoldierly
unsolved
unsorted
unspectacular
unspent
unspiritual
unspoiled
unstated
unsterile
unsubdued
unsubtle
unsuccessfully
unsuited
unsupervised
unsurprising
unsurprisingly
unsuspected
unsweetened
unsymmetrical
unsystematic
untactful
untainted
untalented
untanned
untapped
untarnished
untaxed
unteachable
untenable
untenanted
untended
untested
untilled
untraceable
untraditional
untrained
untrammeled
untranslatable
untranslated
untraveled
untraversed
untrimmed
untrod
untrodden
unvaried
unventilated
unverifiable
unverified
unversed
unvisited
unwashed
unweaned
unwearable
unwearied
unweathered
unwillingly
unwillingness
unwomanly
unworn
unwounded
unwoven

un•abashed \-ə-ˈbasht\ *adj* ◆ : not abashed

◆ unashamed, unblushing, unembarrassed *Ant* abashed, ashamed, embarrassed, shamefaced, sheepish

un•able \-ˈā-bəl\ *adj* **1 :** not able **2 :** UNQUALIFIED, INCOMPETENT
un•abridged \-ə-ˈbrijd\ *adj* **1 :** not abridged ⟨an ~ edition of Shakespeare⟩ **2 :** complete of its class : not based on one larger ⟨an ~ dictionary⟩
un•ac•cept•able \-ak-ˈsep-tə-bəl\ *adj* ♦ **:** not acceptable : not pleasing or welcome

♦ bad, deficient, inferior, lousy, off, poor, punk, rotten, substandard, unsatisfactory, wanting, wretched, wrong

un•ac•com•pa•nied \-ə-ˈkəm-pə-nēd\ *adj* **1** ♦ **:** not accompanied **2 :** being without instrumental accompaniment

♦ alone, lone, lonely, lonesome, solitary

un•ac•count•able \-ə-ˈkau̇n-tə-bəl\ *adj* **1 :** not to be accounted for : INEXPLICABLE **2 :** not responsible — **un•ac•count•ably** \-blē\ *adv*
un•ac•count•ed \-ˈkau̇n-təd\ *adj* **:** not accounted ⟨the loss was ~ for⟩
un•ac•cus•tomed \-ə-ˈkəs-təmd\ *adj* **1** ♦ **:** not customary : not usual or common **2** ♦ **:** not accustomed or habituated ⟨~ to noise⟩

♦ [1] curious, extraordinary, funny, odd, peculiar, queer, rare, strange, uncommon, uncustomary, unique, unusual, weird ♦ *usu* **unaccustomed to** [2] unadapted, unadjusted, unused

un•ac•quaint•ed \-ə-ˈkwān-təd\ *adj* ♦ **:** not having experience or knowledge

♦ ignorant, oblivious, unaware, unconscious, uninformed, unknowing, unwitting

un•adapt•ed \-ə-ˈdap-təd\ *adj* ♦ **:** not adapted

♦ unaccustomed, unadjusted, unused

un•ad•just•ed \-ə-ˈjəs-təd\ *adj* ♦ **:** not adjusted

♦ unaccustomed, unadapted, unused

un•adorned \-ə-ˈdȯrnd\ *adj* ♦ **:** not adorned : lacking embellishment or decoration

♦ bald, bare, naked, plain, simple, undecorated, unvarnished

un•adul•ter•at•ed \-ə-ˈdəl-tə-ˌrā-təd\ *adj* **1** ♦ **:** not adulterated : PURE **2** ♦ **:** not modified or restricted by reservations

♦ [1] absolute, fine, neat, plain, pure, refined, straight, undiluted, unmixed ♦ [2] absolute, complete, outright, perfect, profound, pure, regular, sheer, simple, total, unequivocal, unqualified, utter

un•aes•thet•ic \-es-ˈthe-tik\ *adj* ♦ **:** not aesthetic

♦ grotesque, harsh

un•af•fect•ed \-ə-ˈfek-təd\ *adj* **1 :** not influenced or changed mentally, physically, or chemically **2** ♦ **:** free from affectation : GENUINE

♦ artless, genuine, honest, ingenuous, innocent, naive, natural, real, simple, sincere, true, unpretentious

un•af•fect•ed•ly *adv* ♦ **:** in an unaffected manner

♦ artlessly, ingenuously, naively, naturally

un•aid•ed \-ˈā-dəd\ *adj* ♦ **:** not aided : being without help

♦ alone, independently, singly, solely, unassisted

un•alien•able \-ˈāl-yə-nə-bəl, -ˈā-lē-ə-\ *adj* **:** INALIENABLE
un•aligned \ˌən-ə-ˈlīnd\ *adj* **:** not associated with any one of competing international blocs ⟨~ nations⟩
un•alike \-ə-ˈlīk\ *adj* ♦ **:** not alike or similar

♦ different, disparate, dissimilar, distinct, distinctive, distinguishable, diverse, other, unlike

un•al•loyed \-ə-ˈlȯid\ *adj* **:** not mixed or qualified : PURE ⟨~ happiness⟩
un•al•ter•able \-ˈȯl-tə-rə-bəl\ *adj* ♦ **:** not capable of being altered or changed — **un•al•ter•ably** \-blē\ *adv*

♦ fast, fixed, hard-and-fast, immutable, inflexible, unchangeable

un•am•big•u•ous \-am-ˈbi-gyə-wəs\ *adj* ♦ **:** not ambiguous : having or being a single clearly defined or stated meaning

♦ apparent, broad, clear, clear-cut, distinct, evident, lucid, manifest, obvious, palpable, patent, perspicuous, plain, transparent, unequivocal, unmistakable ♦ definite, definitive, explicit, express, specific

un–Amer•i•can \-ə-ˈmer-ə-kən\ *adj* **:** not characteristic of or consistent with American customs or principles

una•nim•i•ty \yü-nə-ˈni-mə-tē\ *n* ♦ **:** the quality or state of being unanimous

♦ accord, agreement, concurrence, consensus

unan•i•mous \yu̇-ˈna-nə-məs\ *adj* **1** ♦ **:** being of one mind **2** ♦ **:** formed with or indicating the agreement of all — **unan•i•mous•ly** *adv*

♦ [1, 2] agreeable, amicable, compatible, congenial, harmonious, kindred, united

un•an•swer•able \ˌən-ˈan-sə-rə-bəl\ *adj* ♦ **:** not answerable : not capable of being refuted

♦ incontestable, indisputable, indubitable, irrefutable, undeniable, unquestionable

un•an•tic•i•pat•ed \ˌən-an-ˈti-sə-ˌpā-təd\ *adj* ♦ **:** not expected

♦ sudden, unexpected, unforeseen

un•ap•peal•ing \ˌən-ə-ˈpē-liŋ\ *adj* ♦ **:** not appealing or attractive

♦ grotesque, hideous, ugly, unattractive, unlovely, unsightly, vile

un•ap•pe•tiz•ing \ˌən-ˈa-pə-ˌtī-ziŋ\ *adj* ♦ **:** not appetizing

♦ distasteful, unsavory

un•ap•proach•able \ˌən-ə-ˈprō-chə-bəl\ *adj* **1** ♦ **:** not approachable : physically inaccessible **2** ♦ **:** discouraging intimacies

♦ [1, 2] inaccessible, inconvenient, unattainable, unavailable, unobtainable, unreachable, untouchable

un•arm \-ˈärm\ *vb* **:** DISARM
un•armed \-ˈärmd\ *adj* **:** not armed or armored
un•ashamed \-ə-ˈshāmd\ *adj* ♦ **:** not ashamed : being without guilt, self-consciousness, or doubt

♦ unabashed, unblushing, unembarrassed

un•asked \-ˈaskt\ *adj* **1 :** not being asked **2** ♦ **:** not requested

♦ unbidden, undesired, uninvited, unsolicited, unsought, unwanted, unwelcome

un•as•sail•able \-ə-ˈsā-lə-bəl\ *adj* **:** not liable to doubt, challenge, or attack
un•as•sist•ed \-ə-ˈsis-təd\ *adj* ♦ **:** not assisted : lacking help

♦ alone, independently, singly, solely, unaided

un•as•sum•ing \-ə-ˈsü-miŋ\ *adj* ♦ **:** neither bold nor self-assertive

♦ demure, humble, lowly, meek, modest, retiring, unpretentious

un•at•tached \-ə-ˈtacht\ *adj* **1** ♦ **:** not married or engaged **2** ♦ **:** not joined or united

♦ [1] single, unmarried, unwed ♦ [2] detached, disconnected, discrete, freestanding, separate, single, unconnected

un•at•tain•able \-ə-ˈtā-nə-bəl\ *adj* ♦ **:** not capable of being attained or accomplished

♦ inaccessible, inconvenient, unapproachable, unavailable, unobtainable, unreachable, untouchable ♦ hopeless, impossible, unsolvable, unworkable

un•at•trac•tive \-ə-ˈtrak-tiv\ *adj* ♦ **:** not attractive : lacking beauty, interest, or charm

♦ grotesque, hideous, ugly, unappealing, unlovely, unsightly, vile

un•au•then•tic \-ȯ-ˈthen-tik\ *adj* ♦ **:** not authentic

♦ bogus, counterfeit, fake, false, inauthentic, phony, sham, spurious

un•avail•able \-ə-ˈvā-lə-bəl\ *adj* ♦ **:** not available

♦ inaccessible, inconvenient, unapproachable, unattainable, unobtainable, unreachable, untouchable

un•avail•ing \-ə-ˈvā-liŋ\ *adj* ♦ **:** being of no avail — **un•avail•ing•ly** *adv*

♦ fruitless, futile, ineffective, unproductive, unsuccessful

un•avoid•able \-ə-ˈvȯi-də-bəl\ *adj* ♦ **:** not avoidable

♦ certain, inevitable, necessary, sure

un•avoid•ably \-blē\ *adv* ♦ **:** in a way or under a condition that is unavoidable

♦ inevitably, necessarily, needs, perforce

¹un•aware \-ə-ˈwar\ *adv* **:** without warning : UNAWARES

²unaware *adj* ♦ : not aware

♦ ignorant, oblivious, unconscious, uninformed, unknowing, unwitting

un•aware•ness *n* ♦ : the state or fact of being unaware

♦ ignorance, obliviousness

un•awares \-ˈwarz\ *adv* **1** : without knowing or intention **2** ♦ : without warning : by surprise ⟨taken ~⟩

♦ aback, suddenly, unaware

un•bal•anced \-ˈba-lənst\ *adj* **1** : not in a state of balance **2** : mentally disordered **3** : not adjusted so as to make credits equal to debits

un•bap•tized \-bap-ˈtīzd\ *adj* **1 a** : not baptized **b** ♦ : not given a name **2** : PROFANE 2

♦ anonymous, nameless, unchristened, unidentified, unnamed, untitled

un•bar \-ˈbär\ *vb* : UNBOLT, OPEN

un•bear•able \-ˈbar-ə-bəl\ *adj* ♦ : greater than can be borne ⟨~ pain⟩ — **un•bear•ably** \-blē\ *adv*

♦ insufferable, insupportable, intolerable, unendurable, unsupportable *Ant* endurable, sufferable, supportable, tolerable

un•beat•able \-ˈbē-tə-bəl\ *adj* ♦ : not capable of being defeated

♦ impregnable, indomitable, insurmountable, invincible, invulnerable, unconquerable

un•beat•en \-ˈbēt-ᵊn\ *adj* **1** : not pounded, beaten, or whipped **2** : UNTRODDEN **3** : UNDEFEATED

un•be•com•ing \-bi-ˈkə-miŋ\ *adj* ♦ : not becoming : UNSUITABLE — **un•be•com•ing•ly** *adv*

♦ improper, inappropriate, inapt, infelicitous, unfit, unseemly, unsuitable, wrong

un•be•knownst \-bi-ˈnōnst\ *also* **un•be•known** \-ˈnōn\ *adj* : happening or existing without one's knowledge

un•be•lief \-bə-ˈlēf\ *n* : the withholding or absence of belief : DOUBT — **un•be•liev•ing** \-ˈlē-viŋ\ *adj*

un•be•liev•able \-ˈlē-və-bəl\ *adj* ♦ : too improbable for belief; *also* : of such a superlative degree as to be hard to believe ⟨an ~ catch for a touchdown⟩ — **un•be•liev•ably** \-blē\ *adv*

♦ fantastic, implausible, inconceivable, incredible, unconvincing, unimaginable, unthinkable

un•be•liev•er \-ˈlē-vər\ *n* **1** ♦ : one that does not believe : an incredulous person **2** : INFIDEL

♦ disbeliever, doubter, questioner, skeptic

un•bend \-ˈbend\ *vb* **-bent** \-ˈbent\; **-bend•ing** **1** : to free from being bent : make or become straight **2** : UNTIE **3** : to make or become less stiff or more affable : RELAX

un•bend•ing *adj* **1** ♦ : formal and distant in manner : INFLEXIBLE **2** : not bending

♦ adamant, hard, immovable, implacable, inflexible, pat, rigid, uncompromising, unrelenting, unyielding

un•bi•ased \-ˈbī-əst\ *adj* ♦ : free from bias

♦ disinterested, dispassionate, equal, equitable, fair, impartial, just, nonpartisan, objective, square, unprejudiced

un•bid•den \-ˈbid-ᵊn\ *also* **un•bid** \-ˈbid\ *adj* ♦ : not bidden : UNASKED

♦ unasked, undesired, uninvited, unsolicited, unsought, unwanted, unwelcome

un•bind \-ˈbīnd\ *vb* **-bound** \-ˈbau̇nd\; **-bind•ing** **1** ♦ : to remove bindings from : UNTIE **2** ♦ : to set free : RELEASE

♦ [1] undo, untie ♦ [2] discharge, emancipate, enfranchise, free, liberate, loose, loosen, manumit, release, spring, unchain, unfetter

un•blem•ished \-ˈble-mishd\ *adj* ♦ : not blemished

♦ absolute, faultless, flawless, ideal, impeccable, letter-perfect, perfect

un•blessed *also* **un•blest** \-ˈblest\ *adj* **1** : not blessed **2** : EVIL

un•block \-ˈbläk\ *vb* ♦ : to free from being blocked

♦ clear, free

un•blush•ing \-ˈblə-shiŋ\ *adj* **1** : not blushing **2** ♦ : having no shame — **un•blush•ing•ly** *adv*

♦ unabashed, unashamed, unembarrassed

un•bod•ied \-ˈbä-dēd\ *adj* **1** : having no body; *also* : DISEMBODIED **2** : FORMLESS

un•bolt \-ˈbōlt\ *vb* : to open or unfasten by withdrawing a bolt

un•bolt•ed \-ˈbōl-təd\ *adj* : not fastened by bolts

un•born \-ˈbȯrn\ *adj* : not yet born

un•bos•om \-ˈbu̇-zəm, -ˈbü-\ *vb* **1** ♦ : to give expression to : REVEAL **2** : to disclose the thoughts or feelings of oneself

♦ bare, disclose, discover, divulge, expose, reveal, spill, tell, uncloak, uncover, unmask, unveil

un•bound \-ˈbau̇nd\ *adj* ♦ : not bound

♦ footloose, free, loose, unconfined, unrestrained

un•bound•ed \-ˈbau̇n-dəd\ *adj* ♦ : having no bounds or limits ⟨~ enthusiasm⟩

♦ boundless, endless, illimitable, immeasurable, indefinite, infinite, limitless, measureless, unfathomable, unlimited

un•bowed \-ˈbau̇d\ *adj* **1** : not bowed down **2** : UNSUBDUED

un•bri•dled \-ˈbrīd-ᵊld\ *adj* **1** ♦ : not restrained : UNRESTRAINED **2** : not confined by a bridle

♦ intemperate, rampant, unchecked, uncontrolled, ungoverned, unhampered, unhindered, unrestrained

un•bro•ken \-ˈbrō-kən\ *adj* **1** : not damaged **2** ♦ : not subdued or tamed **3** ♦ : not interrupted : CONTINUOUS

♦ [2] feral, savage, undomesticated, untamed, wild ♦ [3] ceaseless, continual, continuous, incessant, unceasing, uninterrupted

un•buck•le \-ˈbə-kəl\ *vb* : to loose the buckle of : UNFASTEN ⟨~ a belt⟩

un•budg•ing \-ˈbə-jiŋ\ *adj* ♦ : not budging : resisting movement or change

♦ immobile, immovable, nonmotile, unmovable

un•bur•den \-ˈbərd-ᵊn\ *vb* **1** ♦ : to free or relieve from a burden **2** ♦ : to relieve oneself of (as cares or worries)

♦ [1] disburden, discharge, disencumber, unload ♦ [1, 2] clear, disburden, disencumber, free, relieve, rid

un•but•ton \-ˈbət-ᵊn\ *vb* : to unfasten the buttons of ⟨~ your coat⟩

un•called–for \-ˈkȯld-ˌfȯr\ *adj* : not called for, needed, or wanted

un•can•ny \-ˈka-nē\ *adj* **1** ♦ : seeming to have a supernatural character or origin : MYSTERIOUS **2** ♦ : suggesting superhuman or supernatural powers — **un•can•ni•ly** \-ˈkan-ᵊl-ē\ *adv*

♦ [1] creepy, eerie, haunting, mysterious, spooky, unearthly, weird ♦ [2] magical, miraculous, phenomenal, superhuman, supernatural

un•cat•a•loged \-ˈkat-ᵊl-ˌȯgd\ *adj* ♦ : not cataloged

♦ unlisted, unrecorded, unregistered

un•ceas•ing \-ˈsē-siŋ\ *adj* ♦ : never ceasing — **un•ceas•ing•ly** *adv*

♦ ceaseless, continual, continuous, incessant, unbroken, uninterrupted

un•cer•e•mo•ni•ous \-ˌser-ə-ˈmō-nē-əs\ *adj* **1** : acting without or lacking ordinary courtesy : ABRUPT **2** ♦ : marked by the absence of formality or ceremony — **un•cer•e•mo•ni•ous•ly** *adv*

♦ informal, irregular, unconventional, unorthodox

un•cer•tain \-ˈsərt-ᵊn\ *adj* **1** : not determined or fixed ⟨an ~ quantity⟩ **2** ♦ : subject to chance or change : not dependable ⟨~ weather⟩ **3** : not definitely known **4** ♦ : not sure ⟨~ of the truth⟩ — **un•cer•tain•ly** *adv*

♦ [2] capricious, changeable, fickle, fluid, inconstant, mercurial, mutable, temperamental, unpredictable, unsettled, unstable, unsteady, variable, volatile ♦ [4] distrustful, doubtful, dubious, mistrustful, skeptical, suspicious, undecided, unsettled, unsure

un•cer•tain•ty \-ᵊn-tē\ *n* **1** ♦ : lack of certainty : DOUBT **2** : something that is uncertain

♦ distrust, doubt, incertitude, misgiving, mistrust, skepticism, suspicion

un•chain \-ˈchān\ *vb* ♦ : to free by or as if by removing a chain

♦ discharge, emancipate, enfranchise, free, liberate, loose, loosen, manumit, release, spring, unbind, unfetter

un•change•able \-ˈchān-jə-bəl\ *adj* ♦ : not changeable : IMMUTABLE

♦ fast, fixed, hard-and-fast, immutable, inflexible, unalterable

un•chang•ing \-ˈchān-jiŋ\ *adj* ♦ : not changing or capable of change

♦ constant, stable, stationary, steady, unvarying

un•charged \-ˈchärjd\ *adj* : having no electrical charge
un•char•i•ta•ble \-ˈchar-ə-tə-bəl\ *adj* **1** ♦ : not charitable **2** ♦ : severe in judging others — **un•char•i•ta•ble•ness** *n* — **un•char•i•ta•bly** \-blē\ *adv*

♦ [1] cheap, close, mean, niggardly, parsimonious, penurious, spare, sparing, stingy, tight, tightfisted ♦ [2] callous, hard, heartless, inhuman, inhumane, pitiless, soulless, unfeeling, unsympathetic

un•chart•ed \-ˈchär-təd\ *adj* **1** : not recorded on a map, chart, or plan **2** : UNKNOWN
un•chaste \-ˈchast\ *adj* : not pure or modest in thought or action
un•chas•ti•ty \-ˈchas-tə-tē\ *n* : the quality or state of being unchaste
un•checked \-ˈchekt\ *adj* ♦ : not checked : not curbed or hindered

♦ intemperate, rampant, unbridled, uncontrolled, ungoverned, unhampered, unhindered, unrestrained

un•chris•tened \-ˈkris-ᵊnd\ *adj* ♦ : not named

♦ anonymous, nameless, unbaptized, unidentified, unnamed, untitled

un•chris•tian \-ˈkris-chən\ *adj* **1** : not of the Christian faith **2** : contrary to the Christian spirit
un•churched \-ˈchərcht\ *adj* : not belonging to or connected with a church
un•cial \ˈən-shəl, -chəl; ˈən-sē-əl\ *adj* : relating to or written in a form of script with rounded letters used especially in early Greek and Latin manuscripts — **uncial** *n*
un•cir•cu•lat•ed \-ˈsər-kyə-ˌlā-təd\ *adj* : issued for use as money but kept out of circulation
un•cir•cum•cised \ˌən-ˈsər-kəm-ˌsīzd\ *adj* **1** : not circumcised **2** : HEATHEN
un•civ•il \-ˈsi-vəl\ *adj* **1** : not civilized : BARBAROUS **2** ♦ : lacking in courtesy : DISCOURTEOUS

♦ discourteous, ill-bred, ill-mannered, impertinent, impolite, inconsiderate, rude, thoughtless, ungracious, unmannerly

un•civ•i•lized \-ˈsi-və-ˌlīzd\ *adj* **1** ♦ : not civilized : BARBAROUS **2** : remote from civilization : WILD

♦ barbarous, heathen, heathenish, Neanderthal, rude, savage, uncivil, uncultivated, wild

un•clad \-ˈklad\ *adj* ♦ : not covered or clothed

♦ bare, naked, nude, unclothed, undressed

un•clasp \-ˈklasp\ *vb* : to open by or as if by loosing the clasp
un•cle \ˈəŋ-kəl\ *n* : the brother of one's father or mother; *also* : the husband of one's aunt
un•clean \ˌən-ˈklēn\ *adj* **1** : morally or spiritually impure **2** : prohibited by ritual law for use or contact **3** ♦ : not clean or pure : DIRTY — **un•clean•ness** *n*

♦ dirty, dusty, filthy, foul, grubby, grungy, mucky, muddy, nasty, smutty, sordid

un•clean•li•ness \-ˈklen-lē-nəs\ *n* ♦ : the quality or state of being uncleanly

♦ dinginess, dirtiness, filthiness, foulness, grubbiness, nastiness

un•clean•ly \-ˈklen-lē\ *adj* : physically unclean
un•clean•ness \-ˈklēn-nəs\ *n* : UNCLEANLINESS
un•clear \-ˈklir\ *adj* **1** : difficult to grasp or understand **2** ♦ : confused or uncertain in statement or understanding

♦ bleary, dim, faint, foggy, fuzzy, hazy, indefinite, indistinct, indistinguishable, murky, nebulous, obscure, opaque, shadowy, undefined, undetermined, vague

un•clench \-ˈklench\ *vb* : to open from a clenched position : RELAX
Uncle Tom \-ˈtäm\ *n* : a black who is eager to win the approval of whites
un•cloak \-ˈklōk\ *vb* **1** : to remove a cloak or cover from **2** ♦ : to make (something secret or hidden) publicly or generally known : to reveal the true nature of

♦ bare, disclose, discover, divulge, expose, reveal, spill, tell, unbosom, uncover, unmask, unveil

un•clog \-ˈkläg\ *vb* ♦ : to remove an obstruction from

♦ clear, free, open, unstop ♦ ease, facilitate, loosen, smooth

un•close \-ˈklōz\ *vb* : OPEN — **un•closed** \-ˈklōzd\ *adj*
un•clothe \-ˈklōth\ *vb* ♦ : to strip of clothes or a covering

♦ strip, undress

un•clothed \-ˈklōthd\ *adj* ♦ : not clothed

♦ bare, naked, nude, unclad, undressed

un•cloud•ed \-ˈklau̇-dəd\ *adj* ♦ : not covered by clouds : not darkened

♦ clear, cloudless, fair, sunny, sunshiny

un•clut•tered \-ˈklə-tərd\ *adj* ♦ : not cluttered : having nothing extraneous or unnecessary

♦ crisp, neat, orderly, shipshape, snug, tidy, trim

un•coil \-ˈkȯil\ *vb* : to release or become released from a coiled state
un•col•ored *or Can and Brit* **un•col•oured** \-ˈkə-lərd\ *adj* ♦ : having no color

♦ colorless (*or* colourless), unpainted, white

un•com•fort•able \-ˈkəmf-tə-bəl, -ˈkəm-fər-tə-\ *adj* **1** ♦ : causing discomfort **2** : feeling discomfort : UNEASY — **un•com•fort•ably** \-blē\ *adv*

♦ awkward, disconcerting

un•com•ic \-ˈkä-mik\ *adj* : not funny or amusing
un•com•mit•ted \-kə-ˈmi-təd\ *adj* : not committed; *esp* : not pledged to a particular belief, allegiance, or program
un•com•mon \ˌən-ˈkä-mən\ *adj* **1** ♦ : not ordinarily encountered : UNUSUAL **2** : remarkable in character, quality, or kind : EXCEPTIONAL — **un•com•mon•ly** *adv*

♦ curious, extraordinary, funny, odd, peculiar, queer, rare, strange, unaccustomed, unique, unusual, weird

un•com•mu•ni•ca•tive \-kə-ˈmyü-nə-ˌkā-tiv, -ni-kə-\ *adj* ♦ : not inclined to talk or impart information

♦ closemouthed, laconic, reserved, reticent, secretive, silent, taciturn

un•com•plain•ing \-kəm-ˈplā-niŋ\ *adj* ♦ : not complaining

♦ forbearing, long-suffering, patient, stoic, tolerant

un•com•pli•men•ta•ry \-ˌkäm-plə-ˈmen-t(ə-)rē\ *adj* ♦ : not complimentary : detracting from the character or standing of something

♦ contemptuous, degrading, derogatory, disdainful, scornful

un•com•pro•mis•ing \-ˈkäm-prə-ˌmī-ziŋ\ *adj* ♦ : not making or accepting a compromise : making no concessions

♦ adamant, hard, immovable, implacable, inflexible, pat, rigid, unbending, unrelenting, unyielding

un•con•cern \-kən-ˈsərn\ *n* **1** : lack of care or interest : INDIFFERENCE **2** : freedom from excessive concern
un•con•cerned \-ˈsərnd\ *adj* **1** ♦ : not having any part or interest **2** ♦ : not anxious or upset : free of worry — **un•con•cern•ed•ly** \-ˈsər-nəd-lē\ *adv*

♦ [1] apathetic, casual, disinterested, indifferent, insouciant, nonchalant, perfunctory, uncurious, uninterested ♦ [2] carefree, careless, cavalier, easygoing, gay, happy-go-lucky, insouciant, lighthearted

un•con•di•tion•al \-kən-ˈdi-shə-nəl\ *adj* : not limited in any way : ABSOLUTE — **un•con•di•tion•al•ly** *adv*
un•con•di•tioned \-ˈdi-shənd\ *adj* **1** : not subject to conditions **2** : not acquired or learned : NATURAL ⟨~ responses⟩ **3** : producing an unconditioned response ⟨~ stimuli⟩
un•con•fined \-kən-ˈfīnd\ *adj* ♦ : not kept within limits

♦ footloose, free, loose, unbound, unrestrained

un•con•ge•nial \-kən-ˈjē-nyəl\ *adj* **1** ♦ : not to one's taste **2** : not sympathetic

♦ bad, disagreeable, distasteful, nasty, rotten, sour, unlovely, unpleasant, unwelcome

un•con•nect•ed \-kə-ˈnek-təd\ *adj* ♦ : not joined or grouped together

♦ detached, disconnected, discrete, freestanding, separate, single, unattached

un•con•quer•able \-ˈkäŋ-kə-rə-bəl\ *adj* ♦ : incapable of being conquered or overcome : INDOMITABLE

♦ impregnable, indomitable, insurmountable, invincible, invulnerable, unbeatable

un•con•scio•na•ble \-ˈkän-shə-nə-bəl\ *adj* **1 :** not guided or controlled by conscience **2** ♦ **:** not in accordance with what is right or just **3 :** exceeding what is usual, proper, necessary, or normal — **un•con•scio•na•bly** \-blē\ *adv*

♦ cutthroat, immoral, Machiavellian, unethical, unprincipled, unscrupulous

[1]**un•con•scious** \-ˈkän-chəs, -shəs\ *adj* **1** ♦ **:** not knowing or perceiving **:** not aware **2 :** not done consciously or on purpose **3** ♦ **:** having lost consciousness **4 :** of or relating to the unconscious — **un•con•scious•ly** *adv* — **un•con•scious•ness** *n*

♦ [1] ignorant, oblivious, unaware, uninformed, unknowing, unwitting ♦ [3] cold, senseless *Ant* conscious

[2]**unconscious** *n* **:** the part of one's mental life of which one is not ordinarily aware but which is often a powerful force in influencing behavior

un•con•sid•ered \-kən-ˈsi-dərd\ *adj* **1 :** not resulting from consideration **2 :** not considered or worth consideration

un•con•sti•tu•tion•al \-ˌkän-stə-ˈtü-shə-nəl, -ˈtyü-\ *adj* **:** not according to or consistent with the constitution of a state or society — **un•con•sti•tu•tion•al•i•ty** \-tü-shə-ˈna-lə-tē, -ˈtyü-\ *n* — **un•con•sti•tu•tion•al•ly** \-ˈtü-shə-nə-lē, -ˈtyü-\ *adv*

un•con•trol•la•ble \ˌən-kən-ˈtrō-lə-bəl\ *adj* ♦ **:** incapable of being controlled **:** UNGOVERNABLE — **un•con•trol•la•bly** \-blē\ *adv*

♦ froward, headstrong, intractable, recalcitrant, refractory, unmanageable, unruly, untoward, wayward, willful *Ant* tractable

un•con•trolled \-kən-ˈtrōld\ *adj* ♦ **:** not being under control

♦ intemperate, rampant, unbridled, unchecked, ungoverned, unhampered, unhindered, unrestrained

un•con•ven•tion•al \-kən-ˈven-chə-nəl\ *adj* ♦ **:** not conventional **:** being out of the ordinary — **un•con•ven•tion•al•i•ty** \-ˌven-chə-ˈna-lə-tē\ *n* — **un•con•ven•tion•al•ly** \-ˈven-chə-nə-lē\ *adv*

♦ dissident, heretical, heterodox, nonconforming, nonconformist, nonorthodox, unorthodox ♦ broad-minded, liberal, nontraditional, open-minded, progressive ♦ informal, irregular, unceremonious, unorthodox

un•con•vinc•ing \-kən-ˈvin-siŋ\ *adj* ♦ **:** not convincing **:** not likely to be believed

♦ fantastic, implausible, inconceivable, incredible, unbelievable, unimaginable, unthinkable

un•cork \-ˈkȯrk\ *vb* **1 :** to draw a cork from **2** ♦ **:** to release from a sealed or pent-up state; *also* **:** to let go

♦ loose, loosen, release, unleash, unlock, unloosen

un•count•able \-ˈkau̇n-tə-bəl\ *adj* ♦ **:** too many to be numbered or counted **:** indefinitely numerous

♦ countless, innumerable, numberless, unnumbered, untold

un•count•ed \-ˈkau̇n-təd\ *adj* **1 :** not counted **2 :** too many to be numbered **:** INNUMERABLE

un•cou•ple \-ˈkə-pəl\ *vb* **:** to sever the connection of or between **:** DISCONNECT

un•couth \-ˈküth\ *adj* **1 :** strange, awkward, and clumsy in shape or appearance **2** ♦ **:** vulgar in conduct or speech **3** ♦ **:** lacking in polish and grace

♦ [2, 3] coarse, common, crass, crude, gross, ill-bred, low, rough, rude, tasteless, uncultivated, uncultured, unpolished, unrefined, vulgar

un•cov•er \-ˈkə-vər\ *vb* **1** ♦ **:** to make known **2 :** to expose to view by removing some covering **3 :** to take the cover from **4 :** to remove the hat from; *also* **:** to take off the hat as a token of respect

♦ bare, disclose, discover, divulge, expose, reveal, spill, tell, unbosom, uncloak, unmask, unveil

un•cov•ered \-vərd\ *adj* ♦ **:** not covered

♦ bald, bare, exposed, naked, open

un•crit•i•cal \-ˈkri-ti-kəl\ *adj* **1 :** not critical **:** lacking in discrimination **2 :** showing lack or improper use of critical standards or procedures — **un•crit•i•cal•ly** \-k(ə-)lē\ *adv*

un•cross \-ˈkrȯs\ *vb* **:** to change from a crossed position ⟨~*ed* his legs⟩

unc•tion \ˈəŋk-shən\ *n* **1 :** the act of anointing as a rite of consecration or healing **2 :** exaggerated or insincere earnestness of language or manner

unc•tu•ous \ˈəŋk-chə-wəs\ *adj* **1 :** FATTY, OILY **2** ♦ **:** insincerely smooth in speech and manner — **unc•tu•ous•ly** *adv*

♦ artificial, double-dealing, feigned, hypocritical, insincere, left-handed, mealy, mealymouthed, two-faced ♦ adulatory, fulsome

un•cul•ti•vat•ed \ˌən-ˈkəl-tə-ˌvā-təd\ *adj* **1 a** ♦ **:** lacking in education or refinement **b :** not civilized **:** BARBAROUS **2** ♦ **:** not put under cultivation **:** not tilled

♦ [1a] coarse, common, crass, crude, gross, ill-bred, low, rough, rude, tasteless, uncouth, uncultured, unpolished, unrefined, vulgar ♦ [2] natural, untamed, wild

un•cul•tured \-ˈkəl-chərd\ *adj* **1 :** not subjected to cultivation **2** ♦ **:** not improved or refined by education

♦ coarse, common, crass, crude, gross, ill-bred, low, rough, rude, tasteless, uncouth, uncultivated, unpolished, unrefined, vulgar

un•cu•ri•ous \-ˈkyu̇r-ē-əs\ *adj* ♦ **:** not curious or inquisitive **:** having no care or interest

♦ apathetic, casual, disinterested, indifferent, insouciant, nonchalant, perfunctory, unconcerned, uninterested

un•curl \-ˈkərl\ *vb* **:** to make or become straightened out from a curled or coiled position

un•cus•tom•ary \-ˈkəs-tə-ˌmer-ē\ *adj* ♦ **:** not customary

♦ aberrant, abnormal, atypical, exceptional, extraordinary, freak, odd, peculiar, phenomenal, rare, singular, uncommon, unique, unusual, unwonted

un•cut \-ˈkət\ *adj* **1 :** not cut down or into **2 :** not shaped by cutting ⟨an ~ diamond⟩ **3 :** not having the folds of the leaves slit ⟨an ~ book⟩ **4 :** not abridged or curtailed ⟨the ~ version of the film⟩ **5 :** not diluted ⟨~ heroin⟩

un•daunt•ed \-ˈdȯn-təd\ *adj* ♦ **:** not daunted **:** not discouraged or dismayed — **un•daunt•ed•ly** *adv*

♦ brave, courageous, dauntless, doughty, fearless, gallant, greathearted, heroic, intrepid, lionhearted, manful, stalwart, stout, valiant, valorous

un•de•ceive \-di-ˈsēv\ *vb* ♦ **:** to free from deception, illusion, or error

♦ disenchant, disillusion

un•de•cid•ed \-di-ˈsī-dəd\ *adj* **1** ♦ **:** not yet determined **2** ♦ **:** uncertain how to act or proceed

♦ [1] open, pending, undetermined, unresolved, unsettled ♦ [2] distrustful, doubtful, dubious, mistrustful, skeptical, suspicious, uncertain, unsettled, unsure

un•dec•o•rat•ed \-ˈde-kə-ˌrā-təd\ *adj* ♦ **:** not decorated **:** without ornament or embellishment

♦ bald, bare, naked, plain, simple, unadorned, unvarnished

un•de•fend•ed \-di-ˈfen-dəd\ *adj* ♦ **:** not guarded or protected

♦ defenseless (*or* defenceless), exposed, helpless, susceptible, unguarded, unprotected, unresistant, vulnerable

un•de•fined \-di-ˈfīnd\ *adj* ♦ **:** not defined, determined, or distinguished

♦ bleary, dim, faint, foggy, fuzzy, hazy, indefinite, indistinct, indistinguishable, murky, nebulous, obscure, opaque, shadowy, unclear, undetermined, vague

un•de•mon•stra•tive \-di-ˈmän-strə-tiv\ *adj* **:** restrained in expression of feeling **:** RESERVED

un•de•ni•able \-di-ˈnī-ə-bəl\ *adj* **1** ♦ **:** plainly true **:** INCONTESTABLE **2 :** unquestionably excellent or genuine

♦ incontestable, indisputable, indubitable, irrefutable, unanswerable, unquestionable

un•de•ni•ably \-blē\ *adv* ♦ **:** that cannot be denied

♦ certainly, definitely, doubtless, incontestably, indeed, indisputably, really, surely, truly, undoubtedly, unquestionably

[1]**un•der** \ˈən-dər\ *adv* **1** ♦ **:** in or into a position below or beneath something **2 :** below some quantity, level, or limit ⟨$10 or ~⟩ **3 :** in or into a condition of subjection, subordination, or unconsciousness ⟨the ether put him ~⟩

♦ below, beneath

[2]**un•der** \ˌən-dər, ˈən-\ *prep* **1 :** lower than and overhung, surmounted, or sheltered by ⟨~ a tree⟩ **2 :** subject to the authority or guidance of ⟨served ~ him⟩ ⟨was ~ contract⟩ **3 :** subject to the action or effect of ⟨~ the influence of alcohol⟩ **4 :** within the division or grouping of ⟨items ~ this heading⟩ **5 :** less or lower than (as in size, amount, or rank) ⟨earns ~ $5000⟩

[3]under \ˈən-dər\ *adj* **1 :** lying below, beneath, or on the ventral side **2 :** facing or protruding downward **3** ♦ **:** in or into a condition of subjection, subordination, or unconsciousness **4 :** lower than usual, proper, or desired in amount, quality, or degree

♦ inferior, junior, less, lesser, lower, minor, subordinate

un•der•achiev•er \ˌən-dər-ə-ˈchē-vər\ *n* **:** one who performs below an expected level of proficiency
un•der•act \-ˈakt\ *vb* **:** to perform feebly or with restraint
un•der•ac•tive \-ˈak-tiv\ *adj* **:** characterized by abnormally low activity ⟨an ~ thyroid gland⟩ — **un•der•ac•tiv•i•ty** \-ˌak-ˈti-və-tē\ *n*
un•der•age \-ˈāj\ *adj* **:** of less than mature or legal age
un•der•arm \-ˈärm\ *adj* **1 :** UNDERHAND 2 ⟨an ~ throw⟩ **2 :** placed under or on the underside of the arms ⟨~ seams⟩ — **underarm** *adv or n*
un•der•bel•ly \ˈən-dər-ˌbe-lē\ *n* **1** ♦ **:** the underside of a body or mass **2 :** a vulnerable area

♦ bottom, underside

un•der•bid \ˌən-dər-ˈbid\ *vb* **-bid; -bid•ding 1 :** to bid less than another **2 :** to bid too low
un•der•body \ˈən-dər-ˌbä-dē\ *n* **:** the lower parts of the body of a vehicle
un•der•bred \ˌən-dər-ˈbred\ *adj* **:** marked by lack of good breeding
un•der•brush \ˈən-dər-ˌbrəsh\ *n* **:** shrubs, bushes, or small trees growing beneath large trees
un•der•car•riage \-ˌkar-ij\ *n* **1 :** a supporting framework (as of an automobile) **2 :** the landing gear of an airplane
un•der•charge \ˌən-dər-ˈchärj\ *vb* **:** to charge (as a person) too little — **undercharge** \ˈən-dər-ˌchärj\ *n*
un•der•class \ˈən-dər-ˌklas\ *n* **:** LOWER CLASS
un•der•class•man \ˌən-dər-ˈklas-mən\ *n* **:** a member of the freshman or sophomore class
un•der•clothes \ˈən-dər-ˌklōthz\ *n pl* **:** UNDERWEAR
un•der•cloth•ing \-ˌklō-thiŋ\ *n* **:** clothing or an article of clothing worn next to the skin and under other clothing **:** UNDERWEAR
un•der•coat \-ˌkōt\ *n* **1 :** a coat worn under another **2 :** a growth of short hair or fur partly concealed by the longer and usually coarser hairs of a mammal **3 :** a coat of paint under another
un•der•coat•ing \-ˌkō-tiŋ\ *n* **:** a special waterproof coating applied to the underside of a vehicle
un•der•cov•er \ˌən-dər-ˈkə-vər\ *adj* ♦ **:** acting or executed in secret; *esp* **:** employed or engaged in secret investigation ⟨an ~ agent⟩

♦ clandestine, covert, furtive, hugger-mugger, private, secret, sneak, sneaky, stealthy, surreptitious, underground, underhanded

un•der•croft \ˈən-dər-ˌkrȯft\ *n* **:** a vaulted chamber under a church
un•der•cur•rent \-ˌkər-ənt\ *n* **1 :** a current below the surface **2 :** a hidden tendency of feeling or opinion
un•der•cut \ˌən-dər-ˈkət\ *vb* **-cut; -cut•ting 1 :** to cut away the underpart of **2 :** to offer to sell or to work at a lower rate than **3 :** to strike (the ball) obliquely downward so as to give a backward spin or elevation to the shot — **un•der•cut** \ˈən-dər-ˌkət\ *n*
un•der•de•vel•oped \ˌən-dər-di-ˈve-ləpt\ *adj* **1 :** not normally or adequately developed ⟨~ muscles⟩ **2 :** having a relatively low level of economic development ⟨the ~ nations⟩
un•der•dog \ˈən-dər-ˌdȯg\ *n* **:** the loser or predicted loser in a struggle
un•der•done \ˌən-dər-ˈdən\ *adj* **:** not thoroughly done or cooked **:** RARE
un•der•draw•ers \ˈən-dər-ˌdrȯrz, -ˌdrȯ-ərz\ *n pl* **:** UNDERPANTS
un•der•em•pha•size \ˌən-dər-ˈem-fə-sīz\ *vb* **:** to emphasize inadequately — **un•der•em•pha•sis** \-səs\ *n*
un•der•em•ployed \-im-ˈplȯid\ *adj* **:** having less than full-time or adequate employment
un•der•es•ti•mate \-ˈes-tə-ˌmāt\ *vb* **:** to set too low a value on
un•der•ex•pose \-ik-ˈspōz\ *vb* **:** to expose (a photographic plate or film) for less time than is needed — **un•der•ex•po•sure** \-ˈspō-zhər\ *n*
un•der•feed \ˌən-dər-ˈfēd\ *vb* **-fed** \-ˈfed\; **-feed•ing :** to feed with too little food
un•der•foot \-ˈfu̇t\ *adv* **1 :** under the feet ⟨flowers trampled ~⟩ **2 :** close about one's feet **:** in the way
un•der•fur \ˈən-dər-ˌfər\ *n* **:** an undercoat of fur especially when thick and soft
un•der•gar•ment \-ˌgär-mənt\ *n* **:** a garment to be worn under another
un•der•gird \ˌən-dər-ˈgərd\ *vb* **:** to brace up **:** STRENGTHEN
un•der•go \ˌən-dər-ˈgō\ *vb* **-went** \-ˈwent\; **-gone** \-ˈgȯn, -ˈgän\; **-go•ing 1 :** to submit to **:** ENDURE **2** ♦ **:** to go through **:** EXPERIENCE

♦ endure, experience, feel, have, know, see, suffer, sustain, taste

un•der•grad \ˈən-dər-ˌgrad\ *n* **:** UNDERGRADUATE
un•der•grad•u•ate \ˌən-dər-ˈgra-jə-wət, -jə-ˌwāt\ *n* **:** a student at a university or college who has not taken a first degree
[1]un•der•ground \ˌən-dər-ˈgrau̇nd\ *adv* **1 :** beneath the surface of the earth **2 :** in or into hiding or secret operation
[2]un•der•ground \ˈən-dər-ˌgrau̇nd\ *n* **1 :** a space under the surface of the ground; *esp* **:** SUBWAY **2 :** a secret political movement or group; *esp* **:** an organized body working in secret to overthrow a government or an occupying power **3 :** an avant-garde group or movement that operates outside the establishment
[3]underground \ˈən-dər-ˌgrau̇nd\ *adj* **1 :** being, growing, operating, or located below the surface of the ground ⟨~ stems⟩ **2** ♦ **:** conducted by secret means **3 :** produced or published by the underground ⟨~ publications⟩; *also* **:** of or relating to the avant-garde underground

♦ clandestine, covert, furtive, hugger-mugger, private, secret, sneak, sneaky, stealthy, surreptitious, undercover, underhanded

un•der•growth \ˈən-dər-ˌgrōth\ *n* **:** low growth (as of herbs and shrubs) on the floor of a forest
[1]un•der•hand \ˈən-dər-ˌhand\ *adv* **1 :** in a clandestine or secret manner **2 :** with an underhand motion
[2]underhand *adj* **1 :** marked by secrecy, chicanery, and deception **:** not honest and aboveboard **:** UNDERHANDED **2 :** made with the hand kept below the level of the shoulder
[1]un•der•hand•ed \ˌən-dər-ˈhan-dəd\ *adv* **:** UNDERHAND
[2]underhanded *adj* ♦ **:** marked by secrecy and deception — **un•der•hand•ed•ly** *adv* — **un•der•hand•ed•ness** *n*

♦ clandestine, covert, furtive, hugger-mugger, private, secret, sneak, sneaky, stealthy, surreptitious, undercover, underground ♦ crooked, deceptive, dishonest, fast, fraudulent, shady, sharp, shifty

un•der•lie \-ˈlī\ *vb* **-lay** \-ˈlā\; **-lain** \-ˈlān\; **-ly•ing** \-ˈlī-iŋ\ **1 :** to lie or be situated under **2 :** to be at the basis of **:** form the foundation of
un•der•line \ˈən-dər-ˌlīn\ *vb* **1 :** to draw a line under **2** ♦ **:** to put emphasis on **:** EMPHASIZE — **underline** *n*

♦ accent, accentuate, emphasize, feature, highlight, play, point, stress, underscore

un•der•ling \ˈən-dər-liŋ\ *n* ♦ **:** one who is under the orders of another **:** SUBORDINATE

♦ inferior, junior, subordinate ***Ant*** senior, superior

un•der•lip \ˌən-dər-ˈlip\ *n* **:** the lower lip
un•der•ly•ing \ˌən-dər-ˌlī-iŋ\ *adj* **1 :** lying under or below **2** ♦ **:** of, relating to, or forming the base or essence **:** FUNDAMENTAL ⟨~ principles⟩

♦ basic, elemental, elementary, essential, fundamental, rudimentary

un•der•mine \-ˈmīn\ *vb* **1 :** to excavate beneath **2 :** to weaken or wear away secretly or gradually
un•der•most \ˈən-dər-ˌmōst\ *adj* **:** lowest in relative position — **undermost** *adv*
[1]un•der•neath \ˌən-dər-ˈnēth\ *prep* **1 :** directly under **2 :** under subjection to
[2]underneath *adv* **1 :** below a surface or object **:** BENEATH **2 :** on the lower side
un•der•nour•ished \ˌən-dər-ˈnər-isht\ *adj* **:** supplied with insufficient nourishment — **un•der•nour•ish•ment** \-ˈnər-ish-mənt\ *n*
un•der•pants \ˈən-dər-ˌpants\ *n pl* **:** a usually short undergarment for the lower trunk **:** DRAWERS
un•der•part \-ˌpärt\ *n* **:** a part lying on the lower side (as of a bird or mammal)
un•der•pass \-ˌpas\ *n* **:** a crossing of a highway and another way (as a road) at different levels; *also* **:** the lower level
un•der•pay \ˌən-dər-ˈpā\ *vb* **:** to pay less than what is normal or required
un•der•pin \ˌən-dər-ˈpin\ *vb* **:** to hold up or serve as a foundation or prop for
un•der•pin•ning \ˈən-dər-ˌpi-niŋ\ *n* **1** ♦ **:** the material and construction (as a foundation) used for support of a structure **2** ♦ **:** something that serves as a foundation

♦ [1] brace, bulwark, buttress, mount, shore, stay, support ♦ [2] base, basis, bedrock, footing, foundation, ground, groundwork, keystone

un·der·play \ˌən-dər-ˈplā\ *vb* **:** to treat or handle with restraint; *esp* **:** to play a role with subdued force

un·der·pop·u·lat·ed \ˌən-dər-ˈpä-pyə-ˌlā-təd\ *adj* **:** having a lower than normal or desirable density of population

un·der·priv·i·leged \-ˈpriv-lijd, -ˈpri-və-lijd\ *adj* **:** having fewer especially economic and social privileges than others

un·der·pro·duc·tion \ˌən-dər-prə-ˈdək-shən\ *n* **:** the production of less than enough to satisfy the demand or of less than the usual supply

un·der·rate \-ˈrāt\ *vb* **:** to rate or value too low

un·der·rep·re·sent·ed \-ˌre-pri-ˈzen-təd\ *adj* **:** inadequately represented

un·der·score \ˈən-dər-ˌskōr\ *vb* **1 :** to draw a line under **:** UNDERLINE **2** ♦ **:** to place emphasis on **:** EMPHASIZE — **underscore** *n*

♦ accent, accentuate, emphasize, feature, highlight, play, point, stress, underline

¹un·der·sea \ˌən-dər-ˈsē\ *adj* **:** being, carried on, or used beneath the surface of the sea

²undersea *or* **un·der·seas** \-ˈsēz\ *adv* **:** beneath the surface of the sea

un·der·sec·re·tary \ˌən-dər-ˈse-krə-ˌter-ē\ *n* **:** a secretary immediately subordinate to a principal secretary ⟨~ of state⟩

un·der·sell \-ˈsel\ *vb* **-sold** \-ˈsōld\; **-sell·ing :** to sell articles cheaper than

un·der·sexed \-ˈsekst\ *adj* **:** deficient in sexual desire

un·der·shirt \ˈən-dər-ˌshərt\ *n* **:** a collarless undergarment with or without sleeves

un·der·shoot \ˌən-dər-ˈshüt\ *vb* **-shot** \-ˈshät\; **-shoot·ing 1 :** to shoot short of or below (a target) **2 :** to fall short of (a runway) in landing an airplane

un·der·shorts \ˈən-dər-ˌshȯrts\ *n pl* **:** underpants for men or boys

un·der·shot \ˈən-dər-ˌshät\ *adj* **1 :** moved by water passing beneath ⟨an ~ waterwheel⟩ **2 :** having the lower front teeth projecting beyond the upper when the mouth is closed

un·der·side \ˈən-dər-ˌsīd, ˌən-dər-ˈsīd\ *n* ♦ **:** the side or surface lying underneath

♦ bottom, underbelly

un·der·signed \ˈən-dər-ˌsīnd\ *n, pl* **undersigned :** one whose name is signed at the end of a document

un·der·sized \ˌən-dər-ˈsīzd\ *also* **un·der·size** \-ˈsīz\ *adj* ♦ **:** of a size less than is common, proper, or normal

♦ dwarf, dwarfish, fine, little, pocket, pygmy, slight, small

un·der·skirt \ˈən-dər-ˌskərt\ *n* **:** a skirt worn under an outer skirt; *esp* **:** PETTICOAT

un·der·staffed \ˌən-dər-ˈstaft\ *adj* **:** inadequately staffed

un·der·stand \ˌən-dər-ˈstand\ *vb* **-stood** \-ˈstu̇d\; **-stand·ing 1** ♦ **:** to grasp the meaning of **:** COMPREHEND **2** ♦ **:** to have thorough or technical acquaintance with or expertness in ⟨~ finance⟩ **3 :** to have reason to believe ⟨I ~ you are leaving tomorrow⟩ **4 :** INTERPRET ⟨we ~ this to be a refusal⟩ **5 :** to have a sympathetic attitude **6 :** to accept as settled ⟨it is *understood* that he will pay the expenses⟩ **7** ♦ **:** to believe or infer something to be the case — **un·der·stand·able** \-ˈstan-də-bəl\ *adj*

♦ [1] appreciate, apprehend, catch, catch on (to), comprehend, get, grasp, make, make out, perceive, see, seize, tumble ♦ [2] comprehend, grasp, know ♦ [7] conclude, deduce, extrapolate, gather, infer, judge, reason

un·der·stand·ably \-blē\ *adv* **:** as can be easily understood

¹un·der·stand·ing \ˌən-dər-ˈstan-diŋ\ *n* **1 :** knowledge and ability to judge **:** INTELLIGENCE ⟨a person of ~⟩ **2 :** agreement of opinion or feeling **3** ♦ **:** a mutual agreement informally or tacitly entered into **4** ♦ **:** a mental grasp

♦ [3] accord, agreement, bargain, compact, contract, convention, covenant, deal, pact, settlement ♦ [4] appreciation, apprehension, comprehension, grasp, grip, perception

²understanding *adj* ♦ **:** endowed with understanding **:** SYMPATHETIC

♦ compassionate, humane, sympathetic

un·der·state \ˌən-dər-ˈstāt\ *vb* **1 :** to represent as less than is the case **2 :** to state with restraint especially for effect — **un·der·state·ment** *n*

un·der·stood \ˌən-dər-ˈstu̇d\ *adj* **1 :** agreed upon **2 :** IMPLICIT

un·der·sto·ry \ˈən-dər-ˌstōr-ē, -ˌstȯr-\ *n* **:** the vegetative layer between the top layer of a forest and the ground cover

un·der·study \ˈən-dər-ˌstə-dē\ *n* **:** one who is prepared to act another's part or take over another's duties — **understudy** \ˈən-dər-ˌstə-dē, ˌən-dər-ˈstə-dē\ *vb*

un·der·sur·face \ˈən-dər-ˌsər-fəs\ *n* **:** the side or surface lying underneath **:** UNDERSIDE

un·der·take \ˌən-dər-ˈtāk\ *vb* **-took** \-ˈtu̇k\; **-tak·en** \-ˈtā-kən\; **-tak·ing 1** ♦ **:** to take upon oneself **:** set about ⟨~ a task⟩ **2 :** to put oneself under obligation **3 :** GUARANTEE, PROMISE

♦ accept, assume, bear, shoulder, take over

un·der·tak·er \ˈən-dər-ˌtā-kər\ *n* **:** one whose business is to prepare the dead for burial and to arrange and manage funerals

un·der·tak·ing \ˈən-dər-ˌtā-kiŋ, ˌən-dər-ˈtā-kiŋ; *2 is* ˈən-dər-ˌtā-kiŋ *only*\ *n* **1 :** the act of one who undertakes or engages in any project **2 :** the business of an undertaker **3 :** something undertaken **4 :** PROMISE, GUARANTEE

under–the–counter *adj* **:** UNLAWFUL, ILLICIT ⟨~ sale of drugs⟩

un·der·tone \ˈən-dər-ˌtōn\ *n* **1 :** a low or subdued tone or utterance **2 :** a subdued color (as seen through and modifying another color)

un·der·tow \-ˌtō\ *n* **:** the current beneath the surface that flows seaward when waves are breaking upon the shore

un·der·val·ue \ˌən-dər-ˈval-yü\ *vb* **1 :** to value or estimate below the real worth **2 :** to esteem lightly

un·der·wa·ter \ˌən-dər-ˈwȯ-tər, -ˈwä-\ *adj* ♦ **:** lying, growing, worn, or operating below the surface of the water — **un·der·wa·ter** *adv*

♦ submarine, sunken

under way \-ˈwā\ *adv* **1 :** into motion from a standstill **2 :** in progress

un·der·wear \ˈən-dər-ˌwar\ *n* **:** clothing or a garment worn next to the skin and under other clothing

un·der·weight \ˌən-dər-ˈwāt\ *adj* **:** weighing below what is normal, average, or necessary — **underweight** *n*

un·der·world \ˈən-dər-ˌwərld\ *n* **1 :** the place of departed souls **:** HADES **2 :** the side of the world opposite to one **3 :** the world of organized crime

un·der·write \ˈən-dər-ˌrīt, ˌən-dər-ˈrīt\ *vb* **-wrote** \-ˌrōt, -ˈrōt\; **-writ·ten** \-ˌrit-ᵊn, -ˈrit-ᵊn\; **-writ·ing 1 :** to write under or at the end of something else **2 :** to set one's name to an insurance policy and thereby become answerable for a designated loss or damage **3 :** to subscribe to **:** agree to **4** ♦ **:** to guarantee financial support of — **un·der·writ·er** *n*

♦ capitalize, endow, finance, fund, stake, subsidize

un·de·sign·ing \ˌən-di-ˈzī-niŋ\ *adj* **:** having no artful, ulterior, or fraudulent purpose **:** SINCERE

un·de·sir·able \-ˈzī-rə-bəl\ *adj* **:** not desirable — **undesirable** *n*

un·de·sired \-di-ˈzīrd\ *adj* ♦ **:** not desired **:** UNWANTED

♦ unasked, unbidden, uninvited, unsolicited, unsought, unwanted, unwelcome

un·de·ter·mined \-di-ˈtər-mənd\ *adj* **1** ♦ **:** not yet definitely or authoritatively decided, settled, or fixed **2 :** not bounded by definite limits or restrictions **3 :** not determinate in form or character

♦ open, pending, undecided, unresolved, unsettled

un·de·vi·at·ing \-ˈdē-vē-ˌā-tiŋ\ *adj* ♦ **:** keeping a true course

♦ steady, unchanging, uniform, unvarying, unwavering

un·dies \ˈən-dēz\ *n pl* **:** UNDERWEAR; *esp* **:** women's underwear

un·di·lut·ed \ˌən-dī-ˈlü-təd\ *adj* ♦ **:** not diluted

♦ absolute, fine, neat, plain, pure, refined, straight, unadulterated, unmixed

un·dis·turbed \-di-ˈstərbd\ *adj* ♦ **:** not disturbed

♦ calm, collected, composed, cool, placid, self-possessed, serene, tranquil, unperturbed, unshaken, untroubled, unworried

un·di·vid·ed \-də-ˈvī-dəd\ *adj* ♦ **:** not divided

♦ all, concentrated, entire, whole

un·do \-ˈdü\ *vb* **-did** \-ˈdid\; **-done** \-ˈdən\; **-do·ing 1** ♦ **:** to make or become unfastened or loosened **2 :** to make null or as if not done **:** REVERSE **3 :** to bring to ruin **4** ♦ **:** to disturb the composure of

♦ [1] unbind, untie ♦ [4] agitate, bother, concern, discompose, disquiet, distress, disturb, exercise, freak, perturb, unhinge, unsettle, upset, worry

un·doc·u·ment·ed \ən-ˈdä-kyə-ˌmen-təd\ *adj* **1 :** not supported by documentary evidence **2 :** lacking documents required for legal immigration

un·do·ing *n* **:** a cause of ruin

un•do•mes•ti•cat•ed \-də-ˈmes-ti-ˌkā-təd\ *adj* ♦ : not domesticated

♦ feral, savage, unbroken, untamed, wild

un•doubt•ed \-ˈdau̇-təd\ *adj* : not doubted or called into question : CERTAIN
un•doubt•ed•ly *adv* ♦ : in an undoubted manner

♦ certainly, definitely, doubtless, incontestably, indeed, indisputably, really, surely, truly, undeniably, unquestionably

¹un•dress \-ˈdres\ *vb* ♦ : to remove the clothes or covering of : STRIP

♦ strip, unclothe *Ant* dress, gown, robe

²undress *n* **1** : informal dress; *esp* : a loose robe or dressing gown **2** : ordinary dress **3** : NUDITY
un•dressed \-ˈdresd\ *adj* ♦ : not dressed

♦ crude, native, natural, raw, unprocessed, unrefined, untreated ♦ bare, naked, nude, unclad, unclothed

un•due \-ˈdü, -ˈdyü\ *adj* **1** : not due **2** : exceeding or violating propriety or fitness : EXCESSIVE
un•du•lant \ˈən-jə-lənt, ˈən-də-, -dyə-\ *adj* : rising and falling in waves
undulant fever *n* : a human disease caused by bacteria from infected domestic animals or their products and marked by intermittent fever, chills, headache, weakness, and weight loss
un•du•late \-ˌlāt\ *vb* **-lat•ed; -lat•ing** **1** : to have a wavelike motion or appearance **2** : to rise and fall in pitch or volume
un•du•la•tion \ˌən-jə-ˈlā-shən, ˌən-də-, -dyə-\ *n* **1** : wavy or wavelike motion **2** : pulsation of sound **3** : a wavy appearance or outline — **un•du•la•to•ry** \ˈən-jə-lə-ˌtōr-ē, ˈən-də-, -dyə-\ *adj*
un•du•ly \-ˈdü-lē, ˈən-, -ˈdyü-\ *adv* : in an undue manner : EXCESSIVELY
un•dyed \-ˈdīd\ *adj* : not dyed
un•dy•ing \-ˈdī-iŋ\ *adj* ♦ : not dying : IMMORTAL

♦ ceaseless, dateless, deathless, endless, eternal, everlasting, immortal, permanent, perpetual, unending

un•ea•ger \-ˈē-gər\ *adj* ♦ : showing no eagerness

♦ halfhearted, tepid, unenthusiastic

un•earned \-ˈərnd\ *adj* : not earned by labor, service, or skill ⟨~ income⟩
un•earth \-ˈərth\ *vb* **1** : to dig up out of or as if out of the earth ⟨~ buried treasure⟩ **2** : to bring to light : DISCOVER ⟨~ a secret⟩
un•earth•ly \-lē\ *adj* **1** : not of or belonging to the earth **2** ♦ : departing from what is usual or normal especially so as to appear to transcend the laws of nature

♦ magical, miraculous, phenomenal, superhuman, supernatural, uncanny ♦ creepy, eerie, haunting, spooky, uncanny, weird

un•eas•i•ness \-ˈē-zē-nəs\ *n* ♦ : the quality or state of being uneasy

♦ disquiet, ferment, restlessness, turmoil, unrest ♦ agitation, anxiety, apprehension, care, concern, disquiet, nervousness, perturbation, worry

un•easy \-ˈē-zē\ *adj* **1** ♦ : marked by lack of ease : AWKWARD ⟨~ among strangers⟩ **2** ♦ : disturbed by pain or worry **3** : lacking or denying rest **4** : UNSTABLE ⟨an ~ truce⟩ — **un•eas•i•ly** \-ˈē-zə-lē\ *adv*

♦ [1] awkward, clumsy, gauche, graceless, inelegant, stiff, stilted, uncomfortable, ungraceful, wooden ♦ [2] aflutter, anxious, edgy, jittery, jumpy, nervous, nervy, perturbed, tense, troubled, upset, worried

un•ed•u•cat•ed \-ˈe-jə-ˌkā-təd\ *adj* ♦ : not educated

♦ dark, ignorant, illiterate, simple, unlearned, untaught

un•em•bar•rassed \-im-ˈbar-əsd\ *adj* ♦ : free from embarrassment

♦ unabashed, unashamed, unblushing

un•emo•tion•al \-i-ˈmō-shə-nəl\ *adj* ♦ : not emotional : not easily aroused or excited

♦ apathetic, cold-blooded, impassive, phlegmatic, stoic, stolid

un•em•ployed \-im-ˈplȯid\ *adj* : not being used; *also* : having no job
un•em•ploy•ment \-ˈplȯi-mənt\ *n* **1** : lack of employment **2** : money paid at regular intervals (as by a government agency) to an unemployed person
un•end•ing \-ˈen-diŋ\ *adj* ♦ : having no ending : ENDLESS

♦ ceaseless, dateless, deathless, endless, eternal, everlasting, immortal, permanent, perpetual, undying

un•en•dur•able \-in-ˈd(y)u̇r-ə-bəl\ *adj* ♦ : not endurable : UNBEARABLE

♦ insufferable, insupportable, intolerable, unbearable, unsupportable

un•en•thu•si•as•tic \-in-ˌthü-zē-ˈas-tik\ *adj* ♦ : lacking ardor or excitement

♦ halfhearted, tepid, uneager

un•equal \-ˈē-kwəl\ *adj* **1** : not alike (as in size, amount, number, or value) **2** ♦ : not uniform **3** : badly balanced or matched **4** : INADEQUATE, INSUFFICIENT ⟨~ to the task⟩ — **un•equal•ly** *adv*

♦ erratic, irregular, uneven, unstable, unsteady

un•equaled *or* **un•equalled** \-kwəld\ *adj* ♦ : not equaled : UNPARALLELED

♦ incomparable, inimitable, matchless, nonpareil, only, peerless, unmatched, unparalleled, unrivaled, unsurpassed

un•equiv•o•cal \-i-ˈkwi-və-kəl\ *adj* **1** ♦ : leaving no doubt **2** ♦ : not questionable — **un•equiv•o•cal•ly** *adv*

♦ [1] clear-cut, definite, definitive, explicit, express, specific, unambiguous ♦ [2] clear, distinct, evident, manifest, obvious, plain, unambiguous, unmistakable

un•err•ing \-ˈer-iŋ, ˌən-ˈər-\ *adj* : making no errors : CERTAIN, UNFAILING — **un•err•ing•ly** *adv*
UNES•CO \yu̇-ˈnes-kō\ *abbr* United Nations Educational, Scientific, and Cultural Organization
un•eth•i•cal \ˌən-ˈe-thi-kəl\ *adj* ♦ : not conforming to approved standards of behavior, a socially accepted code, or professionally endorsed principles and practices

♦ cutthroat, immoral, Machiavellian, unconscionable, unprincipled, unscrupulous

un•even \-ˈē-vən\ *adj* **1** : ODD 3 **2** ♦ : not even : not level or smooth **3** ♦ : not uniform : IRREGULAR; *also* : varying in quality **4** : varying from the straight or parallel — **un•even•ly** *adv* — **un•even•ness** *n*

♦ [2] broken, bumpy, coarse, irregular, jagged, lumpy, pebbly, ragged, rough, rugged *Ant* even, flat, level, plane, smooth ♦ [3] erratic, irregular, unequal, unstable, unsteady *Ant* constant, stable, steady, unchanging, unvarying

un•event•ful \-i-ˈvent-fəl\ *adj* : lacking interesting or noteworthy incidents — **un•event•ful•ly** *adv*
un•ex•am•pled \-ig-ˈzam-pəld\ *adj* : having no example or parallel : UNPARALLELED
un•ex•cep•tion•able \-ik-ˈsep-shə-nə-bəl\ *adj* : not open to exception or objection : beyond reproach
un•ex•cep•tion•al \-ik-ˈsep-shə-nəl\ *adj* **1** : open to no objection **2** : allowing no exception **3** ♦ : constituting no exception to the general rule

♦ average, common, commonplace, everyday, normal, ordinary, prosaic, routine, run-of-the-mill, standard, unremarkable, usual, workaday

un•ex•pect•ed \-ik-ˈspek-təd\ *adj* ♦ : not expected : UNFORESEEN

♦ sudden, unanticipated, unforeseen *Ant* anticipated, expected, foreseen

un•ex•pect•ed•ly *adv* : in an unexpected manner
un•ex•pressed \-ik-ˈspresd\ *adj* ♦ : not expressed : not uttered in words

♦ implicit, tacit, unspoken, unvoiced, wordless

un•fail•ing \-ˈfā-liŋ\ *adj* **1** ♦ : not failing, flagging, or waning **2** : INEXHAUSTIBLE **3** : incapable of error

♦ certain, infallible, sure

un•fail•ing•ly *adv* ♦ : in an unfailing manner : without fail

♦ always, constantly, continually, ever, forever, incessantly, invariably, perpetually

un•fair \-ˈfar\ *adj* **1** ♦ : marked by injustice, partiality, or deception **2** : not equitable in business dealings — **un•fair•ly** *adv* — **un•fair•ness** *n*

♦ dirty, foul, illegal, unsportsmanlike

un•faith•ful \-ˈfāth-fəl\ *adj* **1** ♦ : not observant of vows, allegiance, or duty : DISLOYAL **2** : INACCURATE, UNTRUSTWORTHY — **un•faith•ful•ly** *adv*

♦ disloyal, faithless, false, fickle, inconstant, loose, perfidious, recreant, traitorous, treacherous, untrue

un•faith•ful•ness *n* ♦ : the quality or state of being unfaithful

♦ disloyalty, faithlessness, falseness, falsity, inconstancy, infidelity, perfidy

un•fa•mil•iar \-fə-ˈmil-yər\ *adj* **1** ♦ : not well-known : STRANGE ⟨an ~ place⟩ **2** : not well acquainted ⟨~ with the subject⟩

♦ fresh, new, novel, original, strange, unknown

un•fa•mil•iar•i•ty \-ˌmi-lē-ˈar-ə-tē, -ˈyar-\ *n* : the quality or state of being unfamiliar

un•fash•ion•able \-ˈfa-shə-nə-bəl\ *adj* ♦ : not in accord with or not following current fashion : not favored socially

♦ dowdy, inelegant, tacky, tasteless, trashy, unstylish

un•fas•ten \-ˈfas-ᵊn\ *vb* : to make or become loose : UNDO

un•fath•om•able \-ˈfa-t͟hə-mə-bəl\ *adj* **1** ♦ : not capable of being fathomed : IMMEASURABLE **2** ♦ : incomprehensible

♦ [1] boundless, endless, illimitable, immeasurable, indefinite, infinite, limitless, measureless, unbounded, unlimited ♦ [2] impenetrable, incomprehensible

un•fa•vor•able *or Can and Brit* **un•fa•vour•able** \-ˈfā-və-rə-bəl\ *adj* **1** : set or placed in opposition **2** ♦ : not propitious : DISADVANTAGEOUS

♦ adverse, counter, disadvantageous, hostile, inimical, negative, prejudicial, unfriendly, unsympathetic

un•feel•ing \-ˈfē-liŋ\ *adj* **1** ♦ : lacking feeling **2** ♦ : devoid of kindness or sympathy — **un•feel•ing•ly** *adv*

♦ [1] asleep, dead, numb ♦ [2] callous, hard, heartless, merciless, pitiless, stony, uncharitable, unsparing, unsympathetic

un•feigned \-ˈfānd\ *adj* : not feigned : not hypocritical : GENUINE

un•fem•i•nine \-ˈfe-mə-nən\ *adj* : not suitable to or appropriate for a woman : not characteristic of a woman

un•fet•ter \-ˈfe-tər\ *vb* **1** : to free from fetters **2** ♦ : to loose from restraint : LIBERATE

♦ discharge, emancipate, enfranchise, free, liberate, loose, loosen, manumit, release, spring, unbind, unchain

un•fil•ial \-ˈfi-lē-əl, -ˈfil-yəl\ *adj* : not observing the obligations of a child to a parent : UNDUTIFUL

un•fin•ished \-ˈfi-nisht\ *adj* **1** : not brought to an end **2** : being in a rough or unpolished state

¹un•fit \-ˈfit\ *adj* **1** ♦ : not fit or suitable **2** : physically or mentally unsound

♦ incapable, incompetent, inept, inexpert, unqualified, unskilled, unskillful ♦ improper, inappropriate, inapt, infelicitous, unbecoming, unseemly, unsuitable, wrong

²unfit *vb* : to make unfit : DISQUALIFY

un•fit•ness *n* : the quality or state of being unfit

un•fix \-ˈfiks\ *vb* **1** : to loosen from a fastening : DETACH **2** : UNSETTLE

un•flag•ging \-ˈfla-giŋ\ *adj* ♦ : not flagging : continuing with vigor

♦ indefatigable, inexhaustible, tireless, untiring

un•flap•pa•ble \-ˈfla-pə-bəl\ *adj* ♦ : not easily upset or panicked — **un•flap•pa•bly** *adv*

♦ imperturbable, nerveless, unshakable ***Ant*** shakable

un•fledged \-ˈflejd\ *adj* **1** : not feathered or ready for flight **2** : not fully developed : IMMATURE

un•flinch•ing \-ˈflin-chiŋ\ *adj* ♦ : not flinching or shrinking — **un•flinch•ing•ly** *adv*

♦ determined, dogged, grim, implacable, relentless, unrelenting, unyielding

un•fold \-ˈfōld\ *vb* **1 a** : to open the folds of : open up **2** : to lay open to view : DISCLOSE **3** ♦ : to produce or yield flowers : BLOSSOM **4** ♦ : to open the folds of : spread or straighten out

♦ [3] bloom, blossom, blow, burgeon, flower ♦ [4] expand, extend, fan, flare, open, spread, stretch

un•forced \-ˈfōrst\ *adj* : not forced : not compelled

un•fore•seen \-fōr-ˈsēn\ *adj* ♦ : not foreseen : unexpected

♦ sudden, unanticipated, unexpected

un•for•get•ta•ble \-fər-ˈge-tə-bəl\ *adj* : incapable of being forgotten — **un•for•get•ta•bly** \-blē\ *adv*

un•for•giv•able \-fər-ˈgi-və-bəl\ *adj* ♦ : incapable of being forgiven

♦ indefensible, inexcusable, unjustifiable, unpardonable, unwarrantable

un•formed \-ˈfȯrmd\ *adj* **1** : not regularly formed or ordered : UNDEVELOPED **2** ♦ : not formed

♦ amorphous, formless, shapeless, unshaped, unstructured

un•for•tu•nate \-ˈfȯr-chə-nət\ *adj* **1** ♦ : not fortunate : UNLUCKY **2** ♦ : attended with misfortune **3** : UNSUITABLE **4** ♦ : admitting of or deserving regret : fit to be deplored — **unfortunate** *n*

♦ [1] hapless, ill-fated, ill-starred, luckless, unhappy, unlucky ♦ [2] calamitous, catastrophic, destructive, disastrous, fatal, fateful, ruinous ♦ [4] deplorable, distressful, grievous, heartbreaking, lamentable, regrettable, woeful

un•for•tu•nate•ly \-nət-lē\ *adv* **1** : in an unfortunate manner **2** : it is unfortunate

un•found•ed \-ˈfau̇n-dəd\ *adj* ♦ : lacking a sound basis : GROUNDLESS

♦ baseless, groundless, invalid, unreasonable, unsubstantiated, unsupported, unwarranted

un•freeze \-ˈfrēz\ *vb* **-froze** \-ˈfrōz\; **-fro•zen** \-ˈfrōz-ᵊn\; **-freez•ing** **1** : to cause to thaw **2** : to remove from a freeze ⟨~ prices⟩

un•fre•quent•ed \-frē-ˈkwen-təd; ˌən-ˈfrē-kwən-\ *adj* : seldom visited or traveled over

un•friend•ly \-ˈfrend-lē\ *adj* **1** ♦ : not friendly or kind **2** ♦ : set or placed in opposition — **un•friend•li•ness** \-lē-nəs\ *n*

♦ [1] chill, chilly, cold, cold-blooded, cool, frigid, frosty, glacial, icy, unsympathetic, wintry ♦ [2] adverse, counter, disadvantageous, hostile, inimical, negative, prejudicial, unfavorable (*or* unfavourable), unsympathetic

un•frock \-ˈfräk\ *vb* : DEFROCK

un•fruit•ful \-ˈfrüt-fəl\ *adj* **1** : not producing fruit or offspring : BARREN **2** : yielding no valuable result : UNPROFITABLE — **un•fruit•ful•ness** *n*

un•fun•ny \-ˈfə-nē\ *adj* : not funny : failing to achieve the humor intended

un•furl \-ˈfərl\ *vb* : to loose from a furled state : UNFOLD

un•gain•ly \-ˈgān-lē\ *adj* **1** ♦ : lacking in smoothness or dexterity : CLUMSY **2** : hard to handle : UNWIELDY — **un•gain•li•ness** \-lē-nəs\ *n*

♦ awkward, clumsy, gawky, graceless, heavy-handed, lubberly, lumpish, unhandy

un•gen•er•ous \-ˈje-nə-rəs\ *adj* : not generous or liberal : STINGY

un•gen•tle \-ˈjent-ᵊl\ *adj* : lacking in softness or congeniality

un•glued \-ˈglüd\ *adj* : UPSET, DISORDERED

un•god•ly \-ˈgäd-lē, -ˈgȯd-\ *adj* **1** : IMPIOUS, IRRELIGIOUS **2** : SINFUL, WICKED **3** : OUTRAGEOUS ⟨an ~ hour⟩ **4** : offensive to civilized taste — **un•god•li•ness** \-lē-nəs\ *n*

un•gov•ern•able \-ˈgə-vər-nə-bəl\ *adj* : not capable of being governed, guided, or restrained : UNRULY

un•gov•erned \-ˈgə-vərnd\ *adj* ♦ : not subjected to regulation or control

♦ intemperate, rampant, unbridled, unchecked, uncontrolled, unhampered, unhindered, unrestrained

un•grace•ful \-ˈgrās-fəl\ *adj* ♦ : lacking in charm or felicity

♦ awkward, clumsy, gauche, graceless, inelegant, stiff, stilted, uncomfortable, uneasy, wooden

un•gra•cious \-ˈgrā-shəs\ *adj* **1** ♦ : not courteous : RUDE **2** : not pleasing : DISAGREEABLE

♦ discourteous, ill-bred, ill-mannered, impertinent, impolite, inconsiderate, rude, thoughtless, uncivil, unmannerly

un•grate•ful \-ˈgrāt-fəl\ *adj* **1** : not thankful for favors **2** : DISAGREEABLE; *also* : THANKLESS — **un•grate•ful•ly** *adv* — **un•grate•ful•ness** *n*

un•guard•ed \-ˈgär-dəd\ *adj* **1** ♦ : vulnerable to attack : UNPROTECTED **2** ♦ : free from guile or wariness : DIRECT ⟨~ remarks⟩ **3** ♦ : marked by lack of caution : having one's guard down

♦ [1] defenseless (*or* defenceless), exposed, helpless, susceptible, undefended, unprotected, unresistant, vulnerable ♦ [2] candid, direct, forthright, foursquare, frank, honest, open, outspoken, plain, straight, straightforward, unreserved ♦ [3] careless, heedless, mindless, unsafe, unwary

un•guent \ˈəŋ-gwənt, ˈən-\ *n* : a soothing or healing salve : OINTMENT

¹un•gu•late \ˈəŋ-gyə-lət, ˈən-, -ˌlāt\ *adj* : having hoofs

²ungulate *n* : a hoofed mammal (as a cow, horse, or rhinoceros)

un•hal•lowed \ˌən-ˈha-lōd\ *adj* **1** : not consecrated : UNHOLY

2 : IMPIOUS, PROFANE 3 : contrary to accepted standards : IMMORAL

un•ham•pered \-ˈham-pərd\ *adj* ♦ : not held in check

♦ intemperate, rampant, unbridled, unchecked, uncontrolled, ungoverned, unhindered, unrestrained

un•hand \-ˈhand\ *vb* : to remove the hand from : let go

un•hand•some \-ˈhan-səm\ *adj* 1 : not beautiful or handsome : HOMELY 2 : UNBECOMING 3 : DISCOURTEOUS, RUDE

un•handy \-ˈhan-dē\ *adj* 1 ♦ : hard to handle 2 : lacking in skill or dexterity : AWKWARD

♦ awkward, clumsy, cranky, cumbersome, ungainly, unwieldy

un•hap•pi•ly \-ˈha-pə-lē\ *adv* ♦ : in an unhappy manner : without pleasure

♦ agonizingly, bitterly, grievously, hard, hardly, sadly, sorrowfully, woefully, wretchedly

un•hap•pi•ness \-ˈha-pē-nəs\ *n* : the quality or state of being unhappy

un•hap•py \-ˈha-pē\ *adj* 1 ♦ : not fortunate : UNLUCKY 2 : not cheerful or glad : SAD 3 ♦ : not appropriate : INAPPROPRIATE

♦ [1] hapless, ill-fated, ill-starred, luckless, unfortunate, unlucky ♦ [3] improper, inappropriate, inapt, infelicitous, unbecoming, unfit, unseemly, unsuitable, wrong

un•har•ness \-ˈhär-nəs\ *vb* : to remove the harness from (as a horse)

un•health•ful \-ˈhelth-fəl\ *adj* : detrimental to good health

un•healthy \-ˈhel-thē\ *adj* 1 ♦ : not conducive to health : UNWHOLESOME 2 ♦ : not in good health 3 ♦ : exposing to or involving danger

♦ [1] noisome, noxious, unwholesome *Ant* healthful, healthy ♦ [2] bad, down, ill, indisposed, peaked, punk, sick, unsound, unwell ♦ [3] dangerous, grave, grievous, hazardous, menacing, parlous, perilous, risky, serious, unsafe, venturesome

un•heard \-ˈhərd\ *adj* 1 : not heard 2 : not granted a hearing

unheard–of *adj* : previously unknown; *esp* : UNPRECEDENTED

un•he•ro•ic \-hi-ˈrō-ik\ *adj* : not heroic

un•hin•dered \-ˈhin-dərd\ *adj* ♦ : not hindered or restrained

♦ intemperate, rampant, unbridled, unchecked, uncontrolled, ungoverned, unhampered, unrestrained

un•hinge \-ˈhinj\ *vb* 1 : to take from the hinges 2 ♦ : to make unstable especially mentally

♦ craze, derange, madden ♦ agitate, bother, concern, discompose, disquiet, distress, disturb, exercise, freak, perturb, undo, unsettle, upset, worry

un•hitch \-ˈhich\ *vb* : UNFASTEN, LOOSE

un•ho•ly \-ˈhō-lē\ *adj* 1 : not holy : PROFANE, WICKED 2 : very unpleasant ⟨an ~ mess⟩ — **un•ho•li•ness** \-lē-nəs\ *n*

un•hook \-ˈhu̇k\ *vb* : to loose from a hook

un•horse \-ˈhȯrs\ *vb* : to dislodge from or as if from a horse

un•hur•ried \-ˈhər-ēd\ *adj* : not hurried : in a leisurely manner

uni•cam•er•al \ˌyü-ni-ˈka-mə-rəl\ *adj* : having a single legislative house or chamber

UNI•CEF \ˈyü-nə-ˌsef\ *abbr* United Nations Children's Fund

uni•cel•lu•lar \ˌyü-ni-ˈsel-yə-lər\ *adj* : having or consisting of a single cell

uni•corn \ˈyü-nə-ˌkȯrn\ *n* : a mythical animal with one horn in the middle of the forehead

uni•cy•cle \ˈyü-ni-ˌsī-kəl\ *n* : a vehicle that has a single wheel and is usually propelled by pedals

un•iden•ti•fied \ˌən-ī-ˈden-tə-ˌfīd\ *adj* ♦ : not identified though not necessarily unidentifiable

♦ anonymous, certain, one, some, unnamed, unspecified

uni•di•rec•tion•al \ˌyü-ni-də-ˈrek-shə-nəl, -dī-\ *adj* : having, moving in, or responsive in a single direction

uni•fi•ca•tion \ˌyü-nə-fə-ˈkā-shən\ *n* ♦ : the act, process, or result of unifying : the state of being unified

♦ combination, connection, consolidation, coupling, junction, union

¹uni•form \ˈyü-nə-ˌfȯrm\ *adj* 1 ♦ : not varying 2 : of the same form with others ⟨~ procedures⟩ — **uni•form•ly** *adv*

♦ steady, unchanging, undeviating, unvarying, unwavering *Ant* changing, deviating, varying

²uniform *vb* : to clothe with a uniform

³uniform *n* : distinctive dress worn by members of a particular group (as an army or a police force)

uni•for•mi•ty \ˌyü-nə-ˈfȯr-mə-tē\ *n, pl* **-ties** : the state of being uniform

uni•fy \ˈyü-nə-ˌfī\ *vb* **-fied; -fy•ing** ♦ : to make into a unit or a coherent whole : UNITE

♦ associate, coalesce, combine, conjoin, connect, couple, fuse, join, link, marry, unite

uni•lat•er•al \ˌyü-nə-ˈla-tə-rəl\ *adj* : of, having, affecting, or done by one side only — **uni•lat•er•al•ly** *adv*

un•imag•in•able \ˌən-i-ˈma-jə-nə-bəl\ *adj* ♦ : not imaginable or comprehensible

♦ fantastic, implausible, inconceivable, incredible, unbelievable, unconvincing, unthinkable

un•im•peach•able \-im-ˈpē-chə-bəl\ *adj* : not liable to accusation : BLAMELESS, IRREPROACHABLE

un•im•por•tant \-im-ˈpȯrt-ᵊnt\ *adj* ♦ : lacking in importance

♦ frivolous, inconsequential, inconsiderable, insignificant, little, minor, minute, negligible, slight, small, trifling, trivial *Ant* important, major, meaningful, significant, substantial, weighty

un•in•formed \-in-ˈfȯrmd\ *adj* ♦ : not informed; *esp* : lacking in knowledge, awareness, or information

♦ ignorant, oblivious, unaware, unconscious, unknowing, unwitting

un•in•hib•it•ed \-in-ˈhi-bə-təd\ *adj* ♦ : free from inhibition; *also* : boisterously informal — **un•in•hib•it•ed•ly** *adv*

♦ demonstrative, effusive, emotional, unreserved, unrestrained

un•in•struct•ed \-in-ˈstrək-təd\ *adj* : not instructed : deficient in knowledge or enlightenment

un•in•tel•li•gent \-ˈte-lə-jənt\ *adj* ♦ : lacking intelligence

♦ dense, dull, dumb, fatuous, mindless, obtuse, senseless, simple, slow, stupid, thick, vacuous, witless

un•in•tel•li•gi•ble \-jə-bəl\ *adj* : not intelligible : OBSCURE — **un•in•tel•li•gi•bly** \-blē\ *adv*

un•in•tend•ed \-in-ˈten-dəd\ *adj* ♦ : not intended; *esp* : not deliberate

♦ accidental, casual, chance, fluky, fortuitous, incidental, unintentional, unplanned, unpremeditated, unwitting

un•in•ten•tion•al \-in-ˈten-chə-nəl\ *adj* ♦ : not intentional

♦ involuntary, unintended

un•in•ter•est•ed \-ˈin-trəs-təd, -tə-rəs-, -tə-ˌres-\ *adj* ♦ : not interested : not having the mind or feelings engaged or aroused

♦ apathetic, casual, disinterested, indifferent, insouciant, nonchalant, perfunctory, unconcerned, uncurious

un•in•ter•est•ing \-ˈin-trəs-tiŋ, -ˈin-tə-rəs-tiŋ\ *adj* ♦ : not attracting interest or attention

♦ drab, dreary, dry, dull, flat, monotonous, weary

un•in•ter•rupt•ed \-ˌin-tə-ˈrəp-təd\ *adj* ♦ : not interrupted : CONTINUOUS

♦ ceaseless, continual, continuous, incessant, unbroken, unceasing

un•in•vit•ed \-in-ˈvī-təd\ *adj* ♦ : not invited

♦ unasked, unbidden, undesired, unsolicited, unsought, unwanted, unwelcome

union \ˈyü-nyən\ *n* 1 ♦ : an act or instance of uniting two or more things into one : the state of being so united 2 : a uniting in marriage 3 ♦ : something formed by a combining of parts or members; *esp* : a confederation of independent individuals (as nations or persons) for some common purpose 4 : an organization of workers (as a labor union or a trade union) formed to advance its members' interests especially in respect to wages and working conditions 5 : a device emblematic of union used on or as a national flag; *also* : the upper inner corner of a flag 6 : a device for connecting parts (as of a machine); *esp* : a coupling for pipes

♦ [1] combination, connection, consolidation, coupling, junction, unification *Ant* breakup, disconnection, dissolution, division, parting, partition, schism, split ♦ [1] affiliation, association, collaboration, cooperation, hookup, liaison, partnership, relation, relationship ♦ [3] alliance, bloc, coalition, combination, combine, confederacy, confederation, federation, league

union•ism \ˈyü-nyə-ˌni-zəm\ *n* 1 : the principle or policy of forming or adhering to a union; *esp, cap* : adherence to the policy of a firm federal union before or during the U.S. Civil War **2 :** the principles or system of trade unions — **union•ist** *n*

union•ize \ˈyü-nyə-ˌnīz\ *vb* **-ized; -iz•ing :** to form into or cause to join a labor union — **union•i•za•tion** \ˌyü-nyə-nə-ˈzā-shən\ *n*

union jack *n* **1 :** a flag consisting of the part of a national flag that signifies union **2** *cap U&J* **:** the national flag of the United Kingdom

unique \yu̇-ˈnēk\ *adj* **1 ♦ :** being the only one of its kind **2 ♦ :** very unusual — **unique•ly** *adv* — **unique•ness** *n*

♦ [1] alone, lone, only, singular, sole, solitary, special ♦ [2] aberrant, abnormal, atypical, exceptional, extraordinary, freak, odd, peculiar, phenomenal, rare, singular, uncommon, uncustomary, unusual, unwonted

uni•sex \ˈyü-nə-ˌseks\ *adj* **:** not distinguishable as male or female; *also* **:** suitable or designed for both males and females — **unisex** *n*

uni•sex•u•al \ˌyü-nə-ˈsek-shə-wəl\ *adj* **1 :** having only male or only female sex organs **2 :** UNISEX

uni•son \ˈyü-nə-sən, -zən\ *n* **1 :** sameness or identity in musical pitch **2 :** the condition of being tuned or sounded at the same pitch or in octaves ⟨sing in ~⟩ **3 :** harmonious agreement or union **:** ACCORD

unit \ˈyü-nət\ *n* **1 :** the smallest whole number greater than zero **:** ONE **2 :** a definite amount or quantity used as a standard of measurement **3 :** a single thing, person, or group that is a constituent of a whole; *also* **:** a part of a military establishment that has a prescribed organization — **unit** *adj*

Uni•tar•i•an \ˌyü-nə-ˈter-ē-ən\ *n* **:** a member of a religious denomination stressing individual freedom of belief — **Uni•tar•i•an•ism** *n*

uni•tary \ˈyü-nə-ˌter-ē\ *adj* **1 :** of or relating to a unit **2 :** not divided — **uni•tar•i•ly** \ˌyü-nə-ˈter-ə-lē\ *adv*

unite \yu̇-ˈnīt\ *vb* **unit•ed; unit•ing 1 ♦ :** to put or join together so as to make one **2 a :** to join by a legal or moral bond **b ♦ :** to join in interest or fellowship **3 ♦ :** to put together to form a single unit **:** CONSOLIDATE **4 :** to act in concert

♦ [1] associate, coalesce, combine, conjoin, connect, couple, fuse, join, link, marry, unify *Ant* break up, dissever, part, section, separate, sever, split, sunder ♦ [2b] ally, associate, band, club, confederate, conjoin, cooperate, federate, league ♦ [3] center (*or* centre), centralize, compact, concentrate, consolidate, unify

unit•ed \yu̇-ˈnī-təd\ *adj* **1 :** made one **:** COMBINED **2 ♦ :** relating to or produced by joint action **3 ♦ :** being in agreement **:** HARMONIOUS

♦ [2] collective, common, communal, concerted, conjoint, joint, mutual, public ♦ [3] agreeable, amicable, compatible, congenial, harmonious, kindred, unanimous

unit•ize \ˈyü-nə-ˌtīz\ *vb* **-ized; -iz•ing 1 :** to form or convert into a unit **2 :** to divide into units

uni•ty \ˈyü-nə-tē\ *n, pl* **-ties 1 :** the quality or state of being or being made one **:** ONENESS **2 :** a definite quantity or combination of quantities taken as one or for which 1 is made to stand in calculation **3 ♦ :** a condition of harmony **4 :** continuity without change ⟨~ of purpose⟩ **5 :** reference of all the parts of a literary or artistic composition to a single main idea **6 :** totality of related parts

♦ balance, coherence, consonance, harmony, proportion, symmetry, symphony

univ *abbr* **1** universal **2** university

uni•valve \ˈyü-ni-ˌvalv\ *n* **:** a mollusk having a shell with only one piece; *esp* **:** GASTROPOD — **univalve** *adj*

uni•ver•sal \ˌyü-nə-ˈvər-səl\ *adj* **1 ♦ :** including, covering, or affecting the whole without limit or exception ⟨a ~ rule⟩ **2 :** present or occurring everywhere **3 :** used or for use among all ⟨a ~ language⟩ **4 ♦ :** comprehensively broad and versatile — **uni•ver•sal•ly** *adv*

♦ [1] blanket, common, general, generic, global, overall ♦ [1] compendious, complete, comprehensive, encyclopedic, full, global, inclusive, omnibus, panoramic ♦ [4] adaptable, all-around, protean, versatile

uni•ver•sal•i•ty \-vər-ˈsa-lə-tē\ *n* **:** the quality or state of being universal

uni•ver•sal•ize \-ˈvər-sə-ˌlīz\ *vb* **-ized; -iz•ing :** to make universal **:** GENERALIZE — **uni•ver•sal•i•za•tion** \-ˌvər-sə-lə-ˈzā-shən\ *n*

universal joint *n* **:** a shaft coupling for transmitting rotation from one shaft to another not in a straight line with it

Universal Product Code *n* **:** a combination of a bar code and numbers by which a scanner can identify a product and usually assign a price

uni•verse \ˈyü-nə-ˌvərs\ *n* **♦ :** the whole body of things observed or assumed **:** COSMOS

♦ cosmos, creation, macrocosm, nature, world

uni•ver•si•ty \ˌyü-nə-ˈvər-sə-tē\ *n, pl* **-ties :** an institution of higher learning authorized to confer degrees in various special fields (as theology, law, and medicine) as well as in the arts and sciences generally

un•just \ˌən-ˈjəst\ *adj* **:** characterized by injustice — **un•just•ly** *adv*

un•jus•ti•fi•able \-ˈjəs-tə-ˌfī-ə-bəl\ *adj* **♦ :** not justifiable **:** lacking in propriety or justice

♦ indefensible, inexcusable, unforgivable, unpardonable, unwarrantable

un•kempt \-ˈkempt\ *adj* **1 a ♦ :** lacking order or neatness **b :** ROUGH, UNPOLISHED **2 :** not combed **:** DISHEVELED

♦ chaotic, confused, disheveled, disordered, messy, muddled, sloppy, untidy

un•kind \-ˈkīnd\ *adj* **:** not kind or sympathetic ⟨an ~ remark⟩ — **un•kind•ly** *adv* — **un•kind•ness** *n*

un•kind•ly \-ˈkīnd-lē\ *adj* **:** UNKIND — **un•kind•li•ness** *n*

un•know•ing \ˌən-ˈnō-iŋ\ *adj* **♦ :** not knowing — **un•know•ing•ly** *adv*

♦ ignorant, oblivious, unaware, unconscious, uninformed, unwitting

un•known \-ˈnōn\ *adj* **♦ :** not known or not well-known — **unknown** *n*

♦ fresh, new, novel, original, strange, unfamiliar ♦ anonymous, nameless, obscure, unsung

un•lace \-ˈlās\ *vb* **:** to loose by undoing a lace

un•lade \-ˈlād\ *vb* **-lad•ed; -laded** *or* **-lad•en** \-ˈlād-ᵊn\; **-lad•ing :** to take the load or cargo from **:** UNLOAD

un•la•dy•like \-ˈlā-dē-ˌlīk\ *adj* **:** lacking the behavior, manner, or style considered proper for a lady

un•latch \-ˈlach\ *vb* **1 :** to open or loose by lifting the latch **2 :** to become loosed or opened

un•law•ful \-ˈlȯ-fəl\ *adj* **1 ♦ :** not lawful **:** ILLEGAL **2 :** not morally right or conventional — **un•law•ful•ly** *adv*

♦ criminal, illegal, illegitimate, illicit, wrongful

un•lead•ed \-ˈle-dəd\ *adj* **:** not treated or mixed with lead or lead compounds

un•learn \-ˈlərn\ *vb* **:** to put out of one's knowledge or memory; *also* **:** to discard the habit of

un•learned \-ˈlər-nəd *for 1*; -ˈlərnd *for 2*\ *adj* **1 ♦ :** possessing inadequate learning or education **:** UNEDUCATED **2 :** not gained by study or training

♦ dark, ignorant, illiterate, simple, uneducated, untaught

un•leash \-ˈlēsh\ *vb* **♦ :** to free from or as if from a leash **:** let loose

♦ loose, loosen, release, uncork, unlock, unloosen

un•less \ən-ˈles, ˈən-ˌles\ *conj* **:** except on condition that ⟨won't go ~ you do⟩

un•let•tered \ˌən-ˈle-tərd\ *adj* **:** not educated **:** ILLITERATE

[1]**un•like** \-ˈlīk\ *adj* **1 ♦ :** not like **:** DIFFERENT **2 :** UNEQUAL — **un•like•ness** *n*

♦ different, disparate, dissimilar, distinct, distinctive, distinguishable, diverse, other, unalike

[2]**unlike** *prep* **1 :** different from ⟨she's quite ~ her sister⟩ **2 :** unusual for ⟨it's ~ you to be late⟩ **3 :** differently from ⟨behaves ~ his brother⟩

un•like•li•hood \-ˈlī-klē-ˌhu̇d\ *n* **:** IMPROBABILITY

un•like•ly \-ˈlī-klē\ *adj* **1 ♦ :** not likely **:** IMPROBABLE **2 :** likely to fail

♦ doubtful, dubious, flimsy, improbable, questionable

un•like•ness *n* **♦ :** the quality or state of being unlike

♦ contrast, difference, disagreement, discrepancy, disparity, distinction, diversity

un•lim•ber \-ˈlim-bər\ *vb* **:** to get ready for action

un•lim•it•ed \-ˈli-mə-təd\ *adj* **1 :** lacking any controls **2 ♦ :** having no bounds **:** without limits **3 ♦ :** not bounded by exceptions

♦ [2] boundless, endless, illimitable, immeasurable, indefinite, infinite, limitless, measureless, unbounded, unfathomable ♦ [3] all-around, general, unqualified, unrestricted

un·list·ed \-ˈlis-təd\ *adj* **1** ♦ **:** not appearing on a list; *esp* **:** not appearing in a telephone book **2 :** not listed on a stock exchange

♦ uncataloged, unrecorded, unregistered *Ant* cataloged, listed, recorded, registered

un·lit·er·ary \-ˈli-tə-ˌrer-ē\ *adj* **:** not literary

un·load \-ˈlōd\ *vb* **1 a :** to take away or off **:** REMOVE ⟨~ cargo from a hold⟩ **b** ♦ **:** to get rid of **2** ♦ **:** to take a load from ⟨~ the ship⟩; *also* **:** to relieve or set free **:** UNBURDEN ⟨~ one's mind of worries⟩ **3 :** to draw the charge from ⟨~*ed* the gun⟩ **4 :** to sell in volume

♦ [1b] cast, discard, ditch, dump, fling, jettison, junk, lose, reject, scrap, shed, shuck, slough, throw away, throw out ♦ [2] disburden, discharge, disencumber, unburden *Ant* load, pack

un·lock \-ˈläk\ *vb* **1 :** to open or unfasten through release of a lock **2** ♦ **:** to free from restraints or restrictions **:** RELEASE ⟨~ a flood of emotions⟩ **3 :** DISCLOSE, REVEAL ⟨~ nature's secrets⟩

♦ loose, loosen, release, uncork, unleash, unloosen

un·looked–for \-ˈlu̇kt-fȯr\ *adj* **:** not foreseen **:** UNEXPECTED

un·loose \-ˈlüs\ *vb* **1 :** UNLOOSEN **2 :** UNTIE

un·loos·en \-ˈlüs-ᵊn\ *vb* **1** ♦ **:** to relax the strain of; *also* **:** set free **2 :** UNTIE

♦ loose, loosen, release, uncork, unleash, unlock

un·love·ly \-ˈləv-lē\ *adj* **1** ♦ **:** having no charm or appeal **2 :** not amiable

♦ bad, disagreeable, distasteful, nasty, rotten, sour, uncongenial, unpleasant, unwelcome

un·luck·i·ly \-ˈlə-kə-lē\ *adv* **:** UNFORTUNATELY

un·lucky \-ˈlə-kē\ *adj* **1** ♦ **:** having or meeting with misfortune **:** ILL-FATED **2 :** likely to bring misfortune **:** INAUSPICIOUS **3 :** REGRETTABLE

♦ hapless, ill-fated, ill-starred, luckless, unfortunate, unhappy *Ant* fortunate, happy, lucky

un·man \-ˈman\ *vb* **1** ♦ **:** to deprive of manly courage **2 :** CASTRATE

♦ demoralize, undo, unnerve ♦ daunt, demoralize, discourage, dishearten, dismay, dispirit, unnerve

un·man·age·able \-ˈma-ni-jə-bəl\ *adj* ♦ **:** not manageable **:** INTRACTABLE

♦ froward, headstrong, intractable, recalcitrant, refractory, uncontrollable, unruly, untoward, wayward, willful

un·man·ly \-ˈman-lē\ *adj* **1 :** not manly **:** COWARDLY **2** ♦ **:** having feminine qualities untypical of a man **:** EFFEMINATE

♦ effeminate, feminine, girlish, sissy, womanly

un·man·ner·ly \-ˈma-nər-lē\ *adj* ♦ **:** not mannerly **:** IMPOLITE — **unmannerly** *adv*

♦ discourteous, ill-bred, ill-mannered, impertinent, impolite, inconsiderate, rude, thoughtless, uncivil, ungracious

un·mar·ried \-ˈmar-ēd\ *adj* ♦ **:** not married

♦ single, unattached, unwed

un·mask \-ˈmask\ *vb* **1** ♦ **:** to strip of a mask or a disguise **:** EXPOSE **2 :** to remove one's mask

♦ bare, disclose, discover, divulge, expose, reveal, spill, tell, unbosom, uncloak, uncover, unveil

un·matched \-ˈmacht\ *adj* **1** ♦ **:** not matchable **2 :** not matching

♦ incomparable, inimitable, matchless, nonpareil, only, peerless, unequaled, unparalleled, unrivaled, unsurpassed

un·mean·ing \-ˈmē-niŋ\ *adj* **:** having no meaning **:** SENSELESS

un·me·di·at·ed \-ˈmē-dē-ˌā-təd\ *adj* **:** not mediated **:** not communicated or transformed by an intervening agency

un·meet \-ˈmēt\ *adj* **:** not meet or fit **:** UNSUITABLE, IMPROPER

un·me·lo·di·ous \-mə-ˈlō-dē-əs\ *adj* ♦ **:** not melodious

♦ discordant, dissonant, inharmonious, unmusical

un·men·tion·able \-ˈmen-chə-nə-bəl\ *adj* **:** not fit or proper to be talked about

un·mer·ci·ful \-ˈmər-si-fəl\ *adj* **:** not merciful **:** MERCILESS — **un·mer·ci·ful·ly** *adv*

un·mind·ful \-ˈmīnd-fəl\ *adj* **:** not conscientiously aware, attentive, or heedful **:** UNAWARE

un·mis·tak·able \-mə-ˈstā-kə-bəl\ *adj* ♦ **:** not capable of being mistaken or misunderstood **:** OBVIOUS — **un·mis·tak·ably** \-blē\ *adv*

♦ apparent, broad, clear, clear-cut, distinct, evident, lucid, manifest, obvious, palpable, patent, perspicuous, plain, transparent, unambiguous, unequivocal

un·mit·i·gat·ed \-ˈmi-tə-ˌgā-təd\ *adj* **1 :** not softened or lessened **2 :** being so definitely what is stated as to offer little chance of change or relief **:** ABSOLUTE ⟨an ~ liar⟩

un·mixed \-ˈmikst\ *adj* ♦ **:** not mixed

♦ absolute, fine, neat, plain, pure, refined, straight, unadulterated, undiluted

un·moor \-ˈmu̇r\ *vb* **:** to loose from or as if from moorings

un·mor·al \-ˈmȯr-əl\ *adj* **:** having no moral perception or quality **:** AMORAL — **un·mo·ral·i·ty** \-mə-ˈra-lə-tē\ *n*

un·mov·able \-ˈmü-və-bəl\ *adj* **1** ♦ **:** incapable of being moved **:** firmly fixed **2** ♦ **:** not moving or not intended to be moved

♦ [1, 2] immobile, immovable, nonmotile, stationary, unbudging

un·mu·si·cal \-ˈmyü-zi-kəl\ *adj* ♦ **:** not musical

♦ discordant, dissonant, inharmonious, unmelodious

un·muz·zle \-ˈmə-zəl\ *vb* **:** to remove a muzzle from

un·named \-ˈnāmd\ *adj* ♦ **:** not named or identified

♦ anonymous, certain, one, some, unidentified, unspecified

un·nat·u·ral \-ˈna-chə-rəl\ *adj* **1 :** contrary to or acting contrary to nature or natural instincts **2** ♦ **:** not being in accordance with normal human feelings or behavior **:** ABNORMAL — **un·nat·u·ral·ly** *adv* — **un·nat·u·ral·ness** *n*

♦ aberrant, abnormal, anomalous, atypical, deviant, irregular

un·nec·es·sar·i·ly \-ˌne-sə-ˈser-ə-lē\ *adv* **1 :** not by necessity **2 :** to an unnecessary degree ⟨~ harsh⟩

un·nerve \-ˈnərv\ *vb* **1** ♦ **:** to deprive of courage, strength, or steadiness **2 :** to cause to become nervous

♦ demoralize, undo, unman *Ant* nerve ♦ daunt, demoralize, discourage, dishearten, dismay, dispirit, unman

un·nil·hex·i·um \ˌyün-ᵊl-ˈhek-sē-əm\ *n* **:** the chemical element of atomic number 106

un·nil·pen·ti·um \-ˈpen-tē-əm\ *n* **:** the chemical element of atomic number 105

un·nil·qua·di·um \-ˈkwä-dē-əm\ *n* **:** the chemical element of atomic number 104

un·num·bered \ˌən-ˈnəm-bərd\ *adj* **1 :** not numbered or counted **2** ♦ **:** too many to be numbered **:** INNUMERABLE

♦ countless, innumerable, numberless, uncountable, untold

un·ob·struct·ed \-əb-ˈstrək-təd\ *adj* ♦ **:** not obstructed or hindered

♦ clear, free, open

un·ob·tain·able \-əb-ˈtā-nə-bəl\ *adj* ♦ **:** not obtainable

♦ inaccessible, inconvenient, unapproachable, unattainable, unavailable, unreachable, untouchable

un·ob·tru·sive \-əb-ˈtrü-siv\ *adj* **:** not obtrusive or forward **:** INCONSPICUOUS — **un·ob·tru·sive·ly** *adv*

un·oc·cu·pied \-ˈä-kyə-ˌpīd\ *adj* **1 :** not busy **:** UNEMPLOYED **2 :** not occupied **:** EMPTY, VACANT

un·or·ga·nized \-ˈȯr-gə-ˌnīzd\ *adj* **1 :** not formed or brought into an integrated or ordered whole **2 :** not organized into unions ⟨~ labor⟩

un·orig·i·nal \-ə-ˈri-jə-nəl\ *adj* ♦ **:** not original

♦ imitative, mimic, slavish

un·or·tho·dox \-ˈȯr-thə-ˌdäks\ *adj* ♦ **:** not orthodox **:** not in accord with approved, standardized, or conventional doctrine, method, thought, custom, or opinion

♦ broad-minded, liberal, nonorthodox, nontraditional, open-minded, progressive, radical, unconventional ♦ informal, irregular, unceremonious, unconventional

un·pack \-ˈpak\ *vb* **1 :** to separate and remove things packed **2 :** to open and remove the contents of

un·paid \-ˈpād\ *adj* **1 :** not paid **:** serving without pay **2 a :** not presented as payment **b** ♦ **:** not cleared by payment **3 :** not paying a salary

♦ outstanding, overdue, payable, unsettled

un·paint·ed \-ˈpān-təd\ *adj* ♦ **:** not painted **:** not having a coat of paint

♦ colorless (*or* colourless), uncolored (*or* uncoloured, white

un·pal·at·able \-ˈpa-lə-tə-bəl\ *adj* **1 :** not palatable **:** DISTASTEFUL **2 :** not pleasant **:** not amiable or agreeable

un•par•al•leled \-ˈpar-ə-ˌleld\ *adj* **1** ♦ **:** having no parallel **2** ♦ **:** having no equal or match

♦ [1, 2] incomparable, inimitable, matchless, nonpareil, only, peerless, unequaled, unmatched, unrivaled, unsurpassed

un•par•don•able \-ˈpärd-ᵊn-ə-bəl\ *adj* ♦ **:** not worthy of pardon

♦ indefensible, inexcusable, unforgivable, unjustifiable, unwarrantable

un•par•lia•men•ta•ry \-ˌpär-lə-ˈmen-tə-rē\ *adj* **:** contrary to parliamentary practice

un•peg \-ˈpeg\ *vb* **1 :** to remove a peg from **2 :** to unfasten by or as if by removing a peg

un•per•son \ˈən-ˈpərs-ᵊn, -ˌpərs-\ *n* **:** a person who usually for political or ideological reasons is removed from recognition or consideration

un•per•turbed \ˌən-pər-ˈtərbd\ *adj* ♦ **:** not perturbed **:** unaffected by worry, interruption, disturbance, or disarrangement

♦ calm, collected, composed, cool, placid, self-possessed, serene, tranquil, undisturbed, unshaken, untroubled, unworried

un•pile \-ˈpīl\ *vb* **:** to take or disentangle from a pile

un•pin \-ˈpin\ *vb* **:** to remove a pin from **:** UNFASTEN

un•planned \-ˈpland\ *adj* **1** ♦ **:** not planned **2** ♦ **:** not expected

♦ [1] ad-lib, extemporaneous, impromptu, offhand, snap, unpremeditated, unprepared, unrehearsed ♦ [2] accidental, casual, chance, fluky, fortuitous, incidental, unintended, unintentional, unpremeditated, unwitting

un•pleas•ant \-ˈplez-ᵊnt\ *adj* ♦ **:** not pleasant **:** DISAGREEABLE — **un•pleas•ant•ly** *adv* — **un•pleas•ant•ness** *n*

♦ bad, disagreeable, distasteful, nasty, rotten, sour, uncongenial, unlovely, unwelcome ***Ant*** agreeable, nice, pleasant, pleasing, pleasurable, satisfying, welcome

un•pleas•ing \-ˈplē-ziŋ\ *adj* **:** not pleasing **:** causing discomfort, displeasure, or repugnance

un•plug \-ˈpləg\ *vb* **1 :** UNCLOG **2 :** to remove (a plug) from a receptacle; *also* **:** to disconnect from an electric circuit by removing a plug

un•plumbed \-ˈpləmd\ *adj* **1 :** not tested or measured with a plumb line **2 :** not thoroughly explored

un•pol•ished \-ˈpä-lisht\ *adj* **1 :** not made smooth by polishing **2** ♦ **:** not marked by refinement

♦ coarse, common, crass, crude, gross, ill-bred, low, rough, rude, tasteless, uncouth, uncultivated, uncultured, unrefined, vulgar

un•pop•u•lar \-ˈpä-pyə-lər\ *adj* **:** not popular **:** looked upon or received unfavorably — **un•pop•u•lar•i•ty** \-ˌpä-pyə-ˈlar-ə-tē\ *n*

un•prec•e•dent•ed \-ˈpre-sə-ˌden-təd\ *adj* **:** having no precedent **:** NOVEL

un•pre•dict•able \-pri-ˈdik-tə-bəl\ *adj* ♦ **:** not predictable

♦ capricious, changeable, fickle, fluid, inconstant, mercurial, mutable, temperamental, uncertain, unsettled, unstable, unsteady, variable, volatile

un•prej•u•diced \-ˈpre-jə-dəst\ *adj* ♦ **:** not prejudiced **:** free from undue bias

♦ disinterested, dispassionate, equal, equitable, fair, impartial, just, nonpartisan, objective, square, unbiased

un•pre•med•i•tat•ed \-pri-ˈme-də-ˌtā-təd\ *adj* ♦ **:** not premeditated

♦ accidental, casual, chance, fluky, fortuitous, incidental, unintended, unintentional, unplanned, unwitting

un•pre•pared \-pri-ˈpard\ *adj* **1 :** not prepared **2 a** ♦ **:** happening without preparation **b :** arriving or taking place unexpectedly or without warning

♦ ad-lib, extemporaneous, impromptu, offhand, snap, unplanned, unpremeditated, unrehearsed

un•pre•tend•ing \-pri-ˈten-diŋ\ *adj* **:** not pretending; *esp* **:** UNPRETENTIOUS

un•pre•ten•tious \-pri-ˈten-chəs\ *adj* ♦ **:** not pretentious

♦ artless, genuine, honest, ingenuous, innocent, naive, natural, real, simple, sincere, true, unaffected ♦ demure, humble, lowly, meek, modest, retiring, unassuming

un•pret•ty \-ˈpri-tē\ *adj* **:** not pretty **:** lacking in beauty

un•prin•ci•pled \-ˈprin-sə-pəld\ *adj* ♦ **:** lacking sound or honorable principles **:** UNSCRUPULOUS

♦ cutthroat, immoral, Machiavellian, unconscionable, unethical, unscrupulous ***Ant*** ethical, moral, principled, scrupulous

un•print•able \-ˈprin-tə-bəl\ *adj* ♦ **:** unfit to be printed; *esp* **:** too obscene or offensive to be shown in print

♦ bawdy, coarse, crude, dirty, filthy, foul, gross, indecent, lascivious, lewd, nasty, obscene, pornographic, ribald, smutty, vulgar, wanton

un•pro•cessed \-ˈprä-ˌsest, -ˈprō-\ *adj* ♦ **:** not processed; *esp* **:** not altered from an original or natural state

♦ crude, native, natural, raw, undressed, unrefined, untreated

un•pro•duc•tive \-prə-ˈdək-tiv\ *adj* ♦ **:** not productive

♦ barren, infertile, poor, stark, waste ♦ fruitless, futile, ineffective, unsuccessful

un•pro•fes•sion•al \-prə-ˈfe-shə-nəl\ *adj* **1 :** not belonging to or gainfully employed at a particular profession **2** ♦ **:** not characteristic of or befitting a professional

♦ amateur, amateurish, inexperienced, inexpert, nonprofessional, unskilled, unskillful

un•prof•it•able \-ˈprä-fə-tə-bəl\ *adj* **:** not profitable **:** USELESS

un•pro•gres•sive \-prə-ˈgre-siv\ *adj* **:** not progressive; *esp* **:** not devoted to or showing economic, social, or political progress

un•pro•tect•ed \-prə-ˈtek-təd\ *adj* ♦ **:** lacking protection or defense

♦ defenseless (*or* defenceless), exposed, helpless, susceptible, undefended, unguarded, unresistant, vulnerable

un•qual•i•fied \-ˈkwä-lə-ˌfīd\ *adj* **1** ♦ **:** not having requisite qualifications **2** ♦ **:** not modified or restricted by reservations **:** COMPLETE — **un•qual•i•fied•ly** \-ˌfī-əd-lē\ *adv*

♦ [1] incapable, incompetent, inept, inexpert, unfit, unskilled, unskillful ♦ [2] absolute, complete, outright, total, unequivocal ♦ [2] all-around, general, unlimited, unrestricted

un•ques•tion•able \-ˈkwes-chə-nə-bəl\ *adj* ♦ **:** not questionable **:** INDISPUTABLE

♦ incontestable, indisputable, indubitable, irrefutable, unanswerable, undeniable

un•ques•tion•ably \-blē\ *adv* ♦ **:** without any question

♦ certainly, definitely, doubtless, incontestably, indeed, indisputably, really, surely, truly, undeniably, undoubtedly

un•ques•tion•ing \-chə-niŋ\ *adj* **:** not questioning **:** accepting without examination or hesitation — **un•ques•tion•ing•ly** *adv*

un•qui•et \-ˈkwī-ət\ *adj* **1 :** not quiet **:** AGITATED, DISTURBED **2 :** physically, emotionally, or mentally restless **:** UNEASY

un•quote \ˈən-ˌkwōt\ *n* — used orally to indicate the end of a direct quotation

un•rav•el \ˌən-ˈra-vəl\ *vb* **1** ♦ **:** to separate the threads of **2** ♦ **:** to resolve the intricacy, complexity, or obscurity of **:** clear up ⟨~ a mystery⟩ **3 :** to become unraveled

♦ [1] disentangle, untangle, untwine ***Ant*** entangle, snarl, tangle ♦ [2] answer, break, crack, dope, figure out, puzzle, resolve, riddle, solve, work, work out

un•reach•able \-ˈrēch-ə-bəl\ *adj* ♦ **:** incapable of being reached

♦ inaccessible, inconvenient, unapproachable, unattainable, unavailable, unobtainable, untouchable

un•read \-ˈred\ *adj* **1 :** not read; *also* **:** left unexamined **2 :** lacking the benefits or the experience of reading

un•re•al \-ˈrēl\ *adj* ♦ **:** lacking in reality, substance, or genuineness

♦ chimerical, fabulous, fanciful, fantastic, fictitious, imaginary, made-up, mythical, phantom, pretend

un•re•al•i•ty \-rē-ˈa-lə-tē\ *n* **1 a :** the quality or state of being unreal **:** lack of substance or validity **b** ♦ **:** something unreal, insubstantial, or visionary **2 :** ineptitude in dealing with reality

♦ chimera, conceit, daydream, delusion, dream, fancy, fantasy, figment, hallucination, illusion, phantasm, pipe dream, vision

un•rea•son•able \-ˈrēz-ᵊn-ə-bəl\ *adj* **1 a** ♦ **:** not governed by or acting according to reason **b** ♦ **:** not conformable to reason **2 :** exceeding the bounds of reason or moderation — **un•rea•son•able•ness** *n* — **un•rea•son•ably** *adv*

♦ [1a] fallacious, illogical, invalid, irrational, unsound, weak ♦ [1b] baseless, groundless, invalid, unfounded, unsubstantiated, unsupported, unwarranted

un•rea•soned \-ˈrēz-ᵊnd\ *adj* **:** not based on reason or reasoning

un•rea•son•ing \-ˈrēz-ᵊn-iŋ\ *adj* : not using or showing the use of reason as a guide or control
un•re•con•struct•ed \-ˌrē-kən-ˈstrək-təd\ *adj* : not reconciled to some political, economic, or social change; *esp* : holding stubbornly to a particular belief, view, place, or style
un•re•cord•ed \-ri-ˈkȯr-dəd\ *adj* **1** ♦ : not recorded **2** : not made a matter of official record

♦ uncataloged, unlisted, unregistered

un•re•cov•er•able \-ri-ˈkə-və-rə-bəl\ *adj* **1** ♦ : incapable of being recovered, recaptured, or regained : hopelessly lost **2** : admitting of no remedy or correction

♦ irredeemable, irremediable, irreparable, unredeemable

un•re•deem•able \-ri-ˈdē-mə-bəl\ *adj* **1** : admitting of no change or release **2** ♦ : insusceptible of redemption or reform : utterly and hopelessly bad **3** : not redeemable : not recoverable on payment of what is due

♦ hopeless, incorrigible, incurable, irredeemable, irremediable, unrecoverable

un•reel \-ˈrēl\ *vb* **1** : to unwind from or as if from a reel **2** : to perform successfully
un•re•fined \-ri-ˈfīnd\ *adj* **1** ♦ : lacking moral or social cultivation or the graces of manners or speech **2** ♦ : not separated from impurity or unwanted matter

♦ [1] coarse, common, crass, crude, gross, ill-bred, low, rough, rude, tasteless, uncouth, uncultivated, uncultured, unpolished, vulgar ♦ [2] crude, native, natural, raw, undressed, unprocessed, untreated

un•re•gen•er•ate \-ri-ˈje-nə-rət\ *adj* : not regenerated or reformed
un•reg•is•tered \-ˈre-jə-stərd\ *adj* ♦ : not registered

♦ uncataloged, unlisted, unrecorded

un•re•hearsed \-ri-ˈhərst\ *adj* **1** : not narrated **2** ♦ : not practiced or prepared

♦ ad-lib, extemporaneous, impromptu, offhand, snap, unplanned, unpremeditated, unprepared

un•re•lent•ing \-ˈlen-tiŋ\ *adj* **1** ♦ : not yielding in determination ⟨~ leader⟩ **2** ♦ : not letting up or weakening in vigor or pace — **un•re•lent•ing•ly** *adv*

♦ [1, 2] determined, dogged, grim, implacable, relentless, unflinching, unyielding

un•re•li•able \-ri-ˈlī-ə-bəl\ *adj* : not reliable or trustworthy
un•re•mark•able \-ri-ˈmär-kə-bəl\ *adj* ♦ : lacking interest or distinction : of a kind to be expected in the normal course of events

♦ average, common, commonplace, everyday, normal, ordinary, prosaic, routine, run-of-the-mill, standard, unexceptional, usual, workaday

un•re•mit•ting \-ˈmi-tiŋ\ *adj* : not remitting : CONSTANT — **un•re•mit•ting•ly** *adv*
un•re•pen•tant \-ri-ˈpen-tᵊnt\ *adj* **1** : not repentant **2** : holding to a prior conviction or attitude
un•re•quit•ed \-ri-ˈkwī-təd\ *adj* : not reciprocated or returned in kind ⟨~ love⟩
un•re•served \-ˈzərvd\ *adj* **1** : not limited or partial ⟨~ enthusiasm⟩ **2** ♦ : not cautious or reticent **3** : not set aside for special use — **un•re•serv•ed•ly** \-ˈzər-vəd-lē\ *adv*

♦ candid, direct, forthright, foursquare, frank, honest, open, outspoken, plain, straight, straightforward, unguarded

un•re•sis•tant \-ri-ˈzis-tənt\ *adj* ♦ : not resistant

♦ defenseless (*or* defenceless), exposed, helpless, susceptible, undefended, unguarded, unprotected, vulnerable

un•re•sist•ing \-ri-ˈzis-tiŋ\ *adj* ♦ : not resistant

♦ acquiescent, passive, resigned, tolerant, unresistant, yielding

un•re•solved \-ri-ˈzälvd\ *adj* ♦ : not yet determined

♦ open, pending, undecided, undetermined, unsettled

un•rest \-ˈrest\ *n* ♦ : a disturbed or uneasy state : TURMOIL

♦ disquiet, ferment, restlessness, turmoil, uneasiness ***Ant*** calm, ease, peace, quiet

un•rest•ful \-ˈrest-fəl\ *adj* : not restful : not feeling or not conducive to repose
un•re•strained \-ri-ˈstrānd\ *adj* **1** ♦ : not restrained **2** ♦ : free of constraint, inhibition, or timidity

♦ [1] intemperate, rampant, unbridled, unchecked, uncontrolled, ungoverned, unhampered, unhindered ♦ [2] demonstrative, effusive, emotional, spontaneous, uninhibited, unreserved

un•re•straint \-ri-ˈstrānt\ *n* ♦ : lack of restraint

♦ abandon, abandonment, ease, lightheartedness, naturalness, spontaneity

un•re•strict•ed \-ri-ˈstrik-təd\ *adj* ♦ : not restricted

♦ free-for-all, open, public ♦ all-around, general, unlimited, unqualified

un•rid•dle \-ˈrid-ᵊl\ *vb* : to find the explanation of : SOLVE
un•righ•teous \-ˈrī-chəs\ *adj* **1** : not righteous : SINFUL, WICKED **2** : UNJUST — **un•righ•teous•ness** *n*
un•ripe \-ˈrīp\ *adj* : not ripe or fully developed : IMMATURE
un•rip•ened \-ˈrī-pənd\ *adj* : not ripened : not having attained maturity
un•ri•valed *or* **un•ri•valled** \-ˈrī-vəld\ *adj* ♦ : having no rival

♦ incomparable, inimitable, matchless, nonpareil, only, peerless, unequaled, unmatched, unparalleled, unsurpassed

un•robe \-ˈrōb\ *vb* : DISROBE, UNDRESS
un•roll \-ˈrōl\ *vb* **1** : to unwind a roll of : open out **2** : DISPLAY, DISCLOSE **3** : to become unrolled or spread out
un•roof \-ˈrüf, -ˈru̇f\ *vb* : to strip off the roof or covering of
un•ruf•fled \-ˈrə-fəld\ *adj* **1** ♦ : not agitated or upset **2** : not ruffled : SMOOTH ⟨~ water⟩

♦ calm, collected, composed, cool, placid, self-possessed, serene, tranquil, undisturbed, unperturbed, unshaken, untroubled, unworried

un•rul•i•ness \-ˈrü-lē-nəs\ *n* ♦ : the quality or state of being unruly

♦ defiance, disobedience, insubordination, rebelliousness, recalcitrance, refractoriness

un•ruly \-ˈrü-lē\ *adj* ♦ : not readily ruled, disciplined, or managed

♦ contrary, defiant, disobedient, froward, headstrong, intractable, rebellious, recalcitrant, refractory, uncontrollable, untoward, wayward, willful

un•sad•dle \-ˈsad-ᵊl\ *vb* **1** : to remove the saddle from a horse **2** : UNHORSE
un•safe \-ˈsāf\ *adj* ♦ : not safe : exposed or exposing to danger

♦ dangerous, grave, grievous, hazardous, menacing, parlous, perilous, risky, serious, unhealthy, venturesome

un•sat•is•fac•to•ry \-ˌsa-təs-ˈfak-tə-rē\ *adj* ♦ : not satisfactory

♦ bad, deficient, inferior, lousy, off, poor, punk, rotten, substandard, unacceptable, wanting, wretched, wrong

un•sat•u•rat•ed \-ˈsa-chə-ˌrā-təd\ *adj* **1** : capable of absorbing or dissolving more of something **2** : containing double or triple bonds between carbon atoms ⟨~ fats⟩ — **un•sat•u•rate** \-rət\ *n*
un•saved \-ˈsāvd\ *adj* : not saved; *esp* : not rescued from eternal punishment
un•sa•vory \-ˈsā-və-rē\ *adj* **1** : TASTELESS **2** ♦ : unpleasant to taste or smell **3** : morally offensive

♦ distasteful, unappetizing

un•say \-ˈsā\ *vb* **-said** \-ˈsed\; **-say•ing** ♦ : to take back (something said) : RETRACT

♦ abjure, recant, renounce, retract, take back, withdraw

un•scathed \-ˈskāt͟hd\ *adj* : wholly unharmed : not injured
un•schooled \-ˈsküld\ *adj* : not schooled : UNTAUGHT
un•sci•en•tif•ic \-ˌsī-ən-ˈti-fik\ *adj* : not scientific : not in accord with the principles and methods of science
un•scram•ble \-ˈskram-bəl\ *vb* **1** : RESOLVE, CLARIFY **2** : to restore (as a radio message) to intelligible form
un•screw \-ˈskrü\ *vb* **1** : to draw the screws from **2** : to loosen by turning
un•scru•pu•lous \-ˈskrü-pyə-ləs\ *adj* ♦ : not scrupulous : UNPRINCIPLED — **un•scru•pu•lous•ly** *adv* — **un•scru•pu•lous•ness** *n*

♦ cutthroat, immoral, Machiavellian, unconscionable, unethical, unprincipled

un•seal \-ˈsēl\ *vb* : to break or remove the seal of : OPEN
un•search•able \-ˈsər-chə-bəl\ *adj* : not capable of being searched or explored
un•sea•son•able \-ˈsēz-ᵊn-ə-bəl\ *adj* ♦ : not seasonable : happening or coming at the wrong time : UNTIMELY

♦ early, precocious, premature, untimely

un•sea•son•ably \-blē\ *adv* ♦ : in an unseasonable manner : at an unseasonable time

♦ beforehand, early, precociously, prematurely

un•seat \-ˈsēt\ *vb* **1** : to throw from one's seat especially on horseback **2** : to remove from political office

un•seem•ly \-ˈsēm-lē\ *adj* **1** : not according with established standards of good form or taste **2** ♦ : not suitable — **un•seem•li•ness** *n*

♦ improper, inappropriate, inapt, infelicitous, unbecoming, unfit, unsuitable, wrong

un•seen \-ˈsēn\ *adj* : not seen : INVISIBLE

un•seg•re•gat•ed \-ˈse-gri-ˌgā-təd\ *adj* : not segregated; *esp* : free from racial segregation

un•self•ish \-ˈsel-fish\ *adj* ♦ : not selfish : GENEROUS — **un•self•ish•ly** *adv*

♦ bountiful, charitable, free, generous, liberal, munificent, openhanded, unsparing

un•self•ish•ness *n* ♦ : the quality or state of being unselfish

♦ bounty, generosity, largesse, liberality, philanthropy

un•set•tle \-ˈset-ᵊl\ *vb* **1** : to move or loosen from a settled position : DISPLACE **2** ♦ : to perturb or agitate mentally or emotionally

♦ agitate, bother, concern, discompose, disquiet, distress, disturb, exercise, freak, perturb, undo, unhinge, upset, worry

un•set•tled \-ˈset-ᵊld\ *adj* **1** ♦ : not settled : not fixed (as in position or character) **2** : not calm : DISTURBED **3** ♦ : not decided in mind **4** ♦ : not paid ⟨~ accounts⟩ **5** : not occupied by settlers

♦ [1] open, pending, undecided, undetermined, unresolved ♦ [3] distrustful, doubtful, dubious, mistrustful, skeptical, suspicious, uncertain, undecided, unsure ♦ [4] outstanding, overdue, payable, unpaid

un•set•tling \-ˈset-ᵊ-liŋ\ *adj* ♦ : having the effect of upsetting, disturbing, or discomposing

♦ troublesome, upsetting, worrisome

un•shack•le \-ˈsha-kəl\ *vb* : to free from shackles

un•shak•able \-ˈshā-kə-bəl\ *adj* ♦ : not shakable

♦ imperturbable, nerveless, unflappable

un•shak•en \-ˈshā-kən\ *adj* ♦ : not shaken

♦ calm, collected, composed, cool, placid, self-possessed, serene, tranquil, undisturbed, unperturbed, untroubled, unworried

un•shaped \-ˈshāpt\ *adj* ♦ : not shaped; *esp* : not being in finished, final, or perfect form ⟨~ ideas⟩ ⟨~ timber⟩

♦ amorphous, formless, shapeless, unformed, unstructured

un•sheathe \-ˈshēth\ *vb* : to draw from or as if from a sheath

un•ship \-ˈship\ *vb* **1** : to remove from a ship **2** : to remove or become removed from position ⟨~ an oar⟩

un•shod \-ˈshäd\ *adj* : not wearing or provided with shoes

un•shorn \-ˈshōrn\ *adj* **1** ♦ : not cut **2** : not harvested **3** : not diminished

♦ fleecy, furry, hairy, hirsute, rough, shaggy, woolly

un•sight•ly \-ˈsīt-lē\ *adj* ♦ : unpleasant to the sight : UGLY

♦ grotesque, hideous, ugly, unappealing, unattractive, unlovely, vile

un•skilled \-ˈskild\ *adj* **1 a** ♦ : not skilled **b** : not skilled in a specified branch of work **2** : not requiring skill

♦ amateur, amateurish, inexperienced, inexpert, nonprofessional, unprofessional, unskillful

un•skill•ful \-ˈskil-fəl\ *adj* ♦ : lacking in skill or proficiency — **un•skill•ful•ly** *adv*

♦ incapable, incompetent, inept, inexpert, unfit, unqualified, unskilled

un•sling \-ˈsliŋ\ *vb* **-slung** \-ˈsləŋ\; **-sling•ing** : to remove from being slung

un•smil•ing \-ˈsmī-ling\ *adj* ♦ : not smiling

♦ earnest, grave, humorless (*or* humourless), serious, severe, sober, solemn, staid, weighty

un•snap \-ˈsnap\ *vb* : to loosen or free by or as if by undoing a snap

un•snarl \-ˈsnärl\ *vb* : to remove snarls from : UNTANGLE

un•so•cia•ble \-ˈsō-shə-bəl\ *adj* **1** ♦ : having or showing a disinclination for social activity **2** : not conducive to sociability

♦ aloof, antisocial, cold, cool, detached, distant, frosty, remote, standoffish

un•soiled \-ˈsȯild\ *adj* ♦ : not soiled or dirtied : not sullied

♦ clean, immaculate, spick-and-span, spotless, stainless, unsullied

un•so•lic•it•ed \-sə-ˈli-sə-təd\ *adj* ♦ : not solicited : not asked for

♦ unasked, unbidden, undesired, uninvited, unsought, unwanted, unwelcome

un•solv•able \-ˈsäl-və-bəl\ *adj* ♦ : not solvable

♦ hopeless, impossible, unattainable, unworkable

un•so•phis•ti•cat•ed \-sə-ˈfis-tə-ˌkā-təd\ *adj* **1** ♦ : not worldly-wise : lacking sophistication **2** : SIMPLE

♦ green, ingenuous, innocent, naive, simple, unknowing, unwary, unworldly

un•sought \-ˈsȯt\ *adj* ♦ : not sought : not searched for or asked for ⟨~ honors⟩

♦ unasked, unbidden, undesired, uninvited, unsolicited, unwanted, unwelcome *Ant* desired, solicited, wanted, welcome

un•sound \-ˈsau̇nd\ *adj* **1 a** ♦ : not healthy or whole **b** ♦ : not mentally normal **2** ♦ : not valid **3** : not firmly made or fixed — **un•sound•ly** *adv*

♦ [1a] bad, down, ill, indisposed, peaked, punk, sick, unhealthy, unwell ♦ [1b] balmy, cracked, crazy, cuckoo, daft, deranged, insane, loco, lunatic, mad, maniacal, mental, nuts, nutty, screwy, wacky ♦ [2] fallacious, illogical, invalid, irrational, unreasonable, weak

un•sound•ness *n* ♦ : the quality or state of being unsound

♦ illness, sickness

un•spar•ing \-ˈspar-iŋ\ *adj* **1** ♦ : not merciful or forbearing : HARD **2** ♦ : not frugal : LIBERAL

♦ [1] callous, hard, heartless, inhuman, inhumane, pitiless, soulless, unfeeling, unsympathetic ♦ [2] bountiful, charitable, free, generous, liberal, munificent, openhanded, unselfish

un•speak•able \-ˈspē-kə-bəl\ *adj* **1** ♦ : impossible to express in words **2** : extremely bad — **un•speak•ably** \-blē\ *adv*

♦ indescribable, ineffable, inexpressible, nameless, unutterable

un•spec•i•fied \-ˈspe-sə-ˌfīd\ *adj* ♦ : not specified

♦ anonymous, certain, one, some, unidentified, unnamed

un•spo•ken \-ˈspō-kən\ *adj* **1** ♦ : not spoken or uttered **2** : not spoken to or addressed **3** : not speaking

♦ implicit, tacit, unexpressed, unvoiced, wordless

un•sports•man•like \-ˈspōrts-mən-ˌlīk\ *adj* ♦ : not sportsmanlike : not characteristic of or exhibiting good sportsmanship

♦ dirty, foul, illegal, unfair

un•spot•ted \-ˈspä-təd\ *adj* : not spotted or stained; *esp* : free from moral stain

un•sprung \-ˈsprəŋ\ *adj* : not sprung; *esp* : not equipped with springs

un•sta•ble \-ˈstā-bəl\ *adj* **1 a** ♦ : not stable : not steady in action or movement **b** : lacking steadiness : apt to move, sway, or fall **2** ♦ : wavering in purpose or intent : FICKLE; *also* : lacking effective emotional control **3** : readily changing (as by decomposing) in chemical or physical composition or in biological activity ⟨an ~ atomic nucleus⟩

♦ [1a] erratic, irregular, unequal, uneven, unsteady ♦ [2] capricious, changeable, fickle, inconstant, mercurial, temperamental, unpredictable, unsettled, unsteady, volatile

un•stained \-ˈstānd\ *adj* **1** : not stained or discolored : not spotted **2** : not morally blemished or stained

un•stead•i•ness \-ˈste-dē-nəs\ *n* ♦ : the quality or state of being unsteady

♦ insecurity, instability, precariousness, shakiness

un•steady \-ˈste-dē\ *adj* ♦ : not steady : UNSTABLE — **un•stead•i•ly** \-ˈsted-ᵊl-ē\ *adv*

♦ casual, choppy, discontinuous, erratic, fitful, intermittent, irregular, occasional, spasmodic, sporadic, spotty ♦ erratic, irregular, unequal, uneven, unstable

un•stint•ing \-ˈstin-tiŋ\ *adj* **1 :** not restricting or holding back **2 :** giving or being given freely or generously ⟨~ praise⟩
un•stint•ing•ly \-ˈstin-tiŋ-lē\ *adv* ♦ **:** in an unstinting manner

♦ amply, bountifully, generously, handsomely, liberally, well

un•stop \-ˈstäp\ *vb* **1** ♦ **:** to free from any obstruction **:** UNCLOG **2 :** to remove a stopper from

♦ clear, free, open, unclog

un•stop•pa•ble \-ˈstä-pə-bəl\ *adj* **:** incapable of being stopped
un•strap \-ˈstrap\ *vb* **:** to remove or loose a strap from
un•stressed \-ˈstrest\ *adj* **:** not stressed; *esp* **:** not bearing a stress or accent
un•struc•tured \-ˈstrək-chərd\ *adj* ♦ **:** lacking structure or organization **:** not formally organized in a set or conventional pattern

♦ amorphous, formless, shapeless, unformed, unshaped

un•strung \-ˈstrəŋ\ *adj* **1 :** having the strings loose or detached **2 :** made weak, disordered, or unstable
un•stud•ied \-ˈstə-dēd\ *adj* **1 :** not acquired by study **2 :** NATURAL, UNFORCED ⟨moved with ~ grace⟩
un•styl•ish \-ˈstī-lish\ *adj* ♦ **:** not stylish

♦ dowdy, inelegant, tacky, tasteless, trashy, unfashionable

un•sub•stan•tial \-səb-ˈstan-chəl\ *adj* ♦ **:** not substantial **:** lacking substance, firmness, or strength

♦ flimsy, gauzy, insubstantial ♦ bodiless, immaterial, incorporeal, insubstantial, nonmaterial, nonphysical, spiritual

un•sub•stan•ti•at•ed \-səb-ˈstan-chē-ˌā-təd\ *adj* ♦ **:** not substantiated; *esp* **:** not supported or borne out by fact

♦ baseless, groundless, invalid, unfounded, unreasonable, unsupported, unwarranted

un•suc•cess•ful \-sək-ˈses-fəl\ *adj* ♦ **:** not successful **:** not meeting with or producing success

♦ fruitless, futile, ineffective, unproductive

un•suit•able \-ˈsü-tə-bəl\ *adj* ♦ **:** not suitable or fitting

♦ improper, inappropriate, inapt, infelicitous, unbecoming, unfit, unseemly, wrong

un•sul•lied \-ˈsə-lēd\ *adj* ♦ **:** not sullied or stained **:** spotlessly clean

♦ clean, immaculate, spick-and-span, spotless, stainless, unsoiled

un•sung \-ˈsəŋ\ *adj* **1 :** not sung **2** ♦ **:** not celebrated in song or verse or otherwise praised ⟨~ heroes⟩

♦ anonymous, nameless, obscure, unknown

un•sup•port•able \-sə-ˈpōr-tə-bəl\ *adj* ♦ **:** not supportable **:** hardly to be suffered or borne

♦ insufferable, insupportable, intolerable, unbearable, unendurable

un•sup•port•ed \-sə-ˈpōr-təd\ *adj* **1 a** ♦ **:** not supported or verified **b :** not backed up or assisted **2 :** not held up or sustained

♦ baseless, groundless, invalid, unfounded, unreasonable, unsubstantiated, unwarranted

un•sure \-ˈshu̇r\ *adj* **1** ♦ **:** lacking confidence or assurance **2 :** not having certain knowledge **3** ♦ **:** marked by lack of confidence, assurance, or certainty **4 :** not steadfast or stable

♦ [1, 3] distrustful, doubtful, dubious, mistrustful, skeptical, suspicious, uncertain, undecided, unsettled

un•sur•passed \-sər-ˈpasd\ *adj* ♦ **:** not surpassed or exceeded usually in excellence

♦ incomparable, inimitable, matchless, nonpareil, only, peerless, unequaled, unmatched, unparalleled, unrivaled

un•sus•pect•ing \-sə-ˈspek-tiŋ\ *adj* **1 :** not suspecting **:** not being suspicious **2 :** deficient in worldly wisdom or informed judgment
un•sus•pi•cious \-sə-ˈspi-shəs\ *adj* **:** UNSUSPECTING
un•swerv•ing \-ˈswer-viŋ\ *adj* **1 :** not swerving or turning aside **2 :** STEADY
un•sym•pa•thet•ic \-ˌsim-pə-ˈthe-tik\ *adj* ♦ **:** not sympathetic **:** not responsive

♦ callous, hard, heartless, merciless, pitiless, stony, uncharitable, unfeeling ♦ chill, chilly, cold, cold-blooded, cool, frigid, frosty, glacial, icy, unfriendly, wintry

un•tamed \-ˈtāmd\ *adj* ♦ **:** not tamed or cultivated; *esp* **:** WILD

♦ feral, savage, unbroken, undomesticated, wild

un•tan•gle \-ˈtaŋ-gəl\ *vb* **1** ♦ **:** to loose from tangles or entanglement **:** DISENTANGLE **2 :** to straighten out **:** RESOLVE ⟨~ a problem⟩

♦ disentangle, unravel, untwine ♦ clear, disengage, disentangle, extricate, free, liberate, release

un•taught \-ˈtȯt\ *adj* **1** ♦ **:** not instructed or taught **:** IGNORANT **2 :** NATURAL, SPONTANEOUS ⟨~ kindness⟩

♦ dark, ignorant, illiterate, simple, uneducated, unlearned

un•think•able \-ˈthiŋ-kə-bəl\ *adj* ♦ **:** not to be thought of or considered as possible ⟨~ cruelty⟩

♦ fantastic, implausible, inconceivable, incredible, unbelievable, unconvincing, unimaginable

un•think•ing \-ˈthiŋ-kiŋ\ *adj* **:** not thinking; *esp* **:** THOUGHTLESS, HEEDLESS — **un•think•ing•ly** *adv*
un•thought \ˌən-ˈthȯt\ *adj* **:** not anticipated **:** UNEXPECTED — often used with *of* ⟨*unthought*-of development⟩
un•thrifty \-ˈthrif-tē\ *adj* **1 :** marked by lack of thrift **2 :** not thriving or prospering **3** ♦ **:** not given to thrift or saving

♦ extravagant, prodigal, profligate, spendthrift, thriftless, wasteful

un•ti•dy \-ˈtī-dē\ *adj* **1 :** not fit **2 a** ♦ **:** not neat in appearance **b :** not neat in habits or procedure **3 a** ♦ **:** not neatly organized or carried out **b** ♦ **:** marked by or conducive to a lack of neatness

♦ [2a] dowdy, frowsy, sloppy, slovenly, unkempt ♦ [3a, b] chaotic, confused, disheveled, disordered, messy

un•tie \-ˈtī\ *vb* **-tied; -ty•ing** *or* **-tie•ing 1** ♦ **:** to free from something that ties, fastens, or restrains **:** UNBIND **2 :** DISENTANGLE, RESOLVE **3 :** to become loosened or unbound

♦ unbind, undo *Ant* bind, fasten, knot, lash, tie

¹un•til \-ˈtil\ *prep* **:** up to the time of ⟨worked ~ 5 o'clock⟩
²until *conj* **1 :** up to the time that ⟨wait ~ he calls⟩ **2 :** to the point or degree that ⟨ran ~ she was breathless⟩
¹un•time•ly \-ˈtīm-lē\ *adv* **:** at an inopportune time **:** UNSEASONABLY; *also* **:** PREMATURELY
²untimely *adj* **1** ♦ **:** happening, arriving, existing, or performed before the proper, usual, or intended time ⟨~ death⟩ **2 :** not convenient especially in giving trouble or annoyance

♦ early, precocious, premature, unseasonable

un•tir•ing \-ˈtī-riŋ\ *adj* ♦ **:** not becoming tired **:** INDEFATIGABLE — **un•tir•ing•ly** *adv*

♦ indefatigable, inexhaustible, tireless, unflagging

un•ti•tled \-ˈtīt-ᵊld\ *adj* **1 :** having no title or right **2** ♦ **:** not named **3 :** not called by a title

♦ anonymous, nameless, unbaptized, unchristened, unidentified, unnamed

un•to \ˈən-ˌtü\ *prep* **:** TO
un•told \ˌən-ˈtōld\ *adj* **1** ♦ **:** not counted **:** NUMBERLESS **2 :** not told **:** not revealed

♦ countless, innumerable, numberless, uncountable, unnumbered

¹un•touch•able \-ˈtə-chə-bəl\ *adj* **1 a :** forbidden to the touch **b** ♦ **:** exempt from criticism or control **2** ♦ **:** lying beyond reach **3 :** disagreeable or defiling to the touch

♦ [1b] holy, inviolable, sacred, sacrosanct ♦ [2] inaccessible, inconvenient, unapproachable, unattainable, unavailable, unobtainable, unreachable

²untouchable *n* **:** a member of the lowest social class in India having in traditional Hindu belief the quality of defiling by contact a member of a higher caste
un•touched \-ˈtəcht\ *adj* **1 :** not subjected to touching **2 :** not described or dealt with **3 :** not tasted **4 :** being in a primeval state or condition **5 :** UNAFFECTED
un•tow•ard \ˌən-ˈtōrd, -ˈtō-ərd; ˌən-tə-ˈwȯrd\ *adj* **1** ♦ **:** difficult to manage **:** WILLFUL ⟨an ~ child⟩ **2 :** INCONVENIENT, TROUBLESOME ⟨an ~ encounter⟩

♦ contrary, defiant, disobedient, froward, intractable, rebellious, recalcitrant, refractory, uncontrollable, unmanageable, unruly, wayward, willful

un•treat•ed \-ˈtrē-təd\ *adj* ♦ **:** not subjected to treatment

♦ crude, native, natural, raw, undressed, unprocessed, unrefined

un•tried \-ˈtrīd\ *adj* **:** not tested or proved by experience or trial; *also* **:** not tried in court

un•trou•bled \-ˈtrə-bəld\ *adj* **1 :** marked by calm **:** without rough motion, storminess, or agitated activity **2** ♦ **:** not given trouble **:** not made uneasy **3** ♦ **:** free from agitation, excitement, or disturbance

♦ [2, 3] calm, collected, composed, cool, placid, self-possessed, serene, tranquil, undisturbed, unperturbed, unshaken, unworried

un•true \-ˈtrü\ *adj* **1** ♦ **:** not faithful **:** DISLOYAL **2 :** not according with a standard of correctness **3** ♦ **:** not true **:** FALSE

♦ [1] disloyal, faithless, false, fickle, inconstant, loose, perfidious, recreant, traitorous, treacherous, unfaithful ♦ [3] erroneous, false, inaccurate, incorrect, inexact, invalid, off, unsound, wrong

un•trust•wor•thy \-ˈtrəst-ˌwər-thē\ *adj* **:** not to be trusted **:** not reliable

un•truth \ˌən-ˈtrüth, ˈən-ˌtrüth\ *n* **1 :** lack of truthfulness **2** ♦ **:** something that is untrue; *esp* **:** FALSEHOOD **3 :** absence of truth or accuracy

♦ fabrication, fairy tale, falsehood, falsity, fib, lie, mendacity, prevarication, story, tale, whopper

un•truth•ful \ˌən-ˈtrüth-fəl\ *adj* **:** not containing or telling the truth **:** FALSE

un•tune \-ˈtün, -ˈtyün\ *vb* **1 :** to put out of tune **2 :** DISARRANGE, DISCOMPOSE

un•tu•tored \-ˈtü-tərd, -ˈtyü-\ *adj* **:** having no formal learning or training **:** UNLEARNED

un•twine \-ˈtwīn\ *vb* ♦ **:** to unwind the twisted or tangled parts of **:** DISENTANGLE

♦ disentangle, unravel, untangle

un•twist \-ˈtwist\ *vb* **1 :** to separate the twisted parts of **:** UNTWINE **2 :** to become untwined

un•typ•i•cal \-ˈti-pi-kəl\ *adj* ♦ **:** not typical

♦ aberrant, abnormal, anomalous, atypical, deviant, irregular, unnatural

un•us•able \-ˈyü-zə-bəl\ *adj* ♦ **:** not serviceable **:** having or being of no use

♦ impractical, inoperable, unworkable, useless

un•used *for 1* -ˈyüst, -ˈyüzd; *for 2* -ˈyüzd\ *adj* **1** ♦ **:** not habituated **:** UNACCUSTOMED **2** ♦ **:** not used

♦ [1] unaccustomed, unadapted, unadjusted ***Ant*** acclimated, accustomed, adapted, adjusted, habituated, used ♦ [2] brand-new, new, spick-and-span

un•usu•al \-ˈyü-zhə-wəl\ *adj* ♦ **:** not usual **:** UNCOMMON — **un•usu•al•ly** *adv*

♦ curious, exceptional, extraordinary, funny, odd, peculiar, queer, rare, strange, unaccustomed, uncommon, unique, weird ***Ant*** common, ordinary, usual

un•ut•ter•able \-ˈə-tə-rə-bəl\ *adj* ♦ **:** being beyond the powers of description **:** INEXPRESSIBLE — **un•ut•ter•ably** \-blē\ *adv*

♦ indescribable, ineffable, inexpressible, nameless, unspeakable

un•var•nished \-ˈvär-nisht\ *adj* **1 :** not varnished **2** ♦ **:** not embellished **:** PLAIN ⟨the ~ truth⟩

♦ bald, bare, naked, plain, simple, unadorned, undecorated

un•vary•ing \-ˈver-ē-iŋ\ *adj* ♦ **:** not varying

♦ constant, steady, unchanging, undeviating, uniform, unwavering

un•veil \-ˈvāl\ *vb* **1** ♦ **:** to expose to the public **:** DISCLOSE **2 :** to present publicly for the first time

♦ bare, disclose, discover, divulge, expose, reveal, spill, tell, unbosom, uncloak, uncover, unmask

un•voiced \-ˈvȯist\ *adj* **1** ♦ **:** not verbally expressed **:** UNSPOKEN **2 :** VOICELESS 2

♦ implicit, tacit, unexpressed, unspoken, wordless

un•want•ed \-ˈwȯn-təd, -ˈwän-təd\ *adj* **1** ♦ **:** not wanted **2 :** not needed or useful **3 :** detrimental in character

♦ unasked, unbidden, undesired, uninvited, unsolicited, unsought, unwelcome

un•war•rant•able \-ˈwȯr-ən-tə-bəl\ *adj* ♦ **:** not justifiable **:** INEXCUSABLE — **un•war•rant•ably** \-blē\ *adv*

♦ indefensible, inexcusable, unforgivable, unjustifiable, unpardonable

un•war•rant•ed \-ˈwȯr-ən-təd, -ˈwär-\ *adj* ♦ **:** lacking adequate support **:** not justified

♦ baseless, groundless, invalid, unfounded, unreasonable, unsubstantiated, unsupported

un•wary \-ˈwar-ē\ *adj* **1** ♦ **:** not experienced or sophisticated **2** ♦ **:** careless of consequences **:** not prudent

♦ [1] green, ingenuous, innocent, naive, simple, unknowing, unsophisticated, unworldly ♦ [2] careless, heedless, mindless, unguarded, unsafe

un•wa•ver•ing \-ˈwā-və-riŋ\ *adj* ♦ **:** characterized by absence of fluctuation

♦ steady, unchanging, undeviating, uniform, unvarying

un•weave \-ˈwēv\ *vb* **-wove** \-ˈwōv\; **-wo•ven** \-ˈwō-vən\; **-weav•ing :** DISENTANGLE, RAVEL

un•wed \-ˈwed\ *adj* ♦ **:** not married

♦ single, unattached, unmarried

un•wel•come \-ˈwel-kəm\ *adj* **1** ♦ **:** not welcome **2** ♦ **:** causing displeasure or resentment

♦ [1] unasked, unbidden, undesired, uninvited, unsolicited, unsought, unwanted ♦ [2] bad, disagreeable, distasteful, nasty, rotten, sour, uncongenial, unlovely, unpleasant

un•well \-ˈwel\ *adj* ♦ **:** being in poor health **:** SICK

♦ bad, down, ill, indisposed, peaked, punk, sick, unhealthy, unsound

un•whole•some \-ˈhōl-səm\ *adj* **1** ♦ **:** harmful to physical, mental, or moral well-being **2 :** CORRUPT, UNSOUND; *also* **:** offensive to the senses

♦ noisome, noxious, unhealthy

un•wieldy \-ˈwēl-dē\ *adj* ♦ **:** not easily managed, handled, or used (as because of bulk, weight, or complexity) ⟨an ~ tool⟩

♦ awkward, clumsy, cranky, cumbersome, ungainly, unhandy

un•will•ing \-ˈwi-liŋ\ *adj* **:** not willing

un•wind \-ˈwīnd\ *vb* **-wound** \-ˈwaund\; **-wind•ing 1 :** to undo something that is wound **:** loose from coils **2 :** to become unwound **:** be capable of being unwound **3** ♦ **:** to get rid of nervous tension or anxiety **:** RELAX

♦ chill out, de-stress, relax

un•wise \-ˈwīz\ *adj* ♦ **:** not wise **:** lacking or not showing wisdom or good sense — **un•wise•ly** *adv*

♦ foolish, ill-advised, imprudent, indiscreet, tactless

un•wit•ting \-ˈwi-tiŋ\ *adj* **1** ♦ **:** not knowing **:** UNAWARE **2** ♦ **:** not intended **:** INADVERTENT ⟨~ mistake⟩ — **un•wit•ting•ly** *adv*

♦ [1] ignorant, oblivious, unaware, unconscious, uninformed, unknowing ♦ [2] accidental, casual, chance, fluky, fortuitous, inadvertent, incidental, unintended, unintentional, unplanned, unpremeditated

un•wont•ed \-ˈwȯn-təd, -ˈwōn-\ *adj* **1** ♦ **:** being out of the ordinary **:** UNUSUAL **2 :** not accustomed by experience — **un•wont•ed•ly** *adv*

♦ aberrant, abnormal, atypical, exceptional, extraordinary, freak, odd, peculiar, phenomenal, rare, singular, uncommon, uncustomary, unique, unusual

un•work•able \-ˈwər-kə-bəl\ *adj* ♦ **:** incapable of being put into use or effect or of being accomplished successfully

♦ impractical, inoperable, unusable, useless

un•world•li•ness \-ˈwərld-lē-nəs\ *n* ♦ **:** the quality or state of being unworldly

♦ artlessness, greenness, ingenuousness, innocence, naïveté, naturalness, simplicity

un•world•ly \-ˈwərld-lē\ *adj* **1 :** not of this world; *esp* **:** SPIRITUAL **2** ♦ **:** deficient in worldly wisdom or informed judgment **:** NAIVE **3 :** not swayed by worldly considerations

♦ green, ingenuous, innocent, naive, simple, unknowing, unsophisticated, unwary

un•wor•ried \-ˈwər-ēd\ *adj* ♦ **:** not worried

♦ calm, collected, composed, cool, placid, self-possessed, serene, tranquil, undisturbed, unperturbed, unshaken, untroubled

un•wor•thy \-ˈwər-th̲ē\ *adj* **1 :** BASE, DISHONORABLE **2 :** not worthy **3 :** not deserved ⟨~ treatment⟩ — **un•wor•thi•ly** \-th̲ə-lē\ *adv* — **un•wor•thi•ness** \-th̲ē-nəs\ *n*
un•wrap \-ˈrap\ *vb* : to remove the wrapping from : DISCLOSE
un•writ•ten \-ˈrit-ᵊn\ *adj* **1** ♦ **:** not in writing : ORAL ⟨an ~ law⟩ **2 :** containing no writing : BLANK

♦ oral, spoken, verbal

un•yield•ing \-ˈyēl-diŋ\ *adj* **1** ♦ **:** characterized by lack of softness or flexibility **2** ♦ **:** characterized by firmness or obduracy

♦ [1] compact, firm, hard, inflexible, rigid, solid, stiff ♦ [2] determined, dogged, grim, implacable, obstinate, relentless, unflinching, unrelenting

un•yoke \-ˈyōk\ *vb* **1 :** to remove a yoke from **2** ♦ **:** to take apart : SEPARATE

♦ break up, disconnect, disjoint, dissever, dissociate, disunite, divide, divorce, part, resolve, separate, sever, split, sunder

un•zip \-ˈzip\ *vb* : to zip open : open by means of a zipper
1up \ˈəp\ *adv* **1 :** in or to a higher position or level; *esp* : away from the center of the earth **2 :** from beneath a surface (as ground or water) **3 :** from below the horizon **4 :** in or into an upright position; *esp* : out of bed **5 :** with greater intensity ⟨speak ~⟩ **6 :** in or into a better or more advanced state or a state of greater intensity or activity ⟨stir ~ a fire⟩ **7 :** into existence, evidence, or knowledge ⟨the missing book turned ~⟩ **8 :** into consideration ⟨brought the matter ~⟩ **9 :** to or at bat **10 :** into possession or custody ⟨gave himself ~⟩ **11 :** ENTIRELY, COMPLETELY ⟨eat it ~⟩ **12** — used for emphasis ⟨clean ~ a room⟩ **13 :** ASIDE, BY ⟨lay ~ supplies⟩ **14 :** so as to arrive or approach ⟨ran ~ the path⟩ **15 :** in a direction opposite to down **16 :** in or into parts ⟨tear ~ paper⟩ **17 :** to a stop ⟨pull ~ at the curb⟩ **18 :** for each side ⟨the score was 15 ~⟩
2up *adj* **1 :** risen above the horizon ⟨the sun is ~⟩ **2 :** being out of bed ⟨~ by 6 o'clock⟩ **3** ♦ **:** relatively high ⟨prices are ~⟩ **4 :** RAISED, LIFTED ⟨windows are ~⟩ **5 :** BUILT, CONSTRUCTED ⟨the house is ~⟩ **6 :** grown above a surface ⟨the corn is ~⟩ **7 :** moving, inclining, or directed upward **8 :** marked by agitation, excitement, or activity **9 :** READY; *esp* : highly prepared **10 :** going on : taking place ⟨find out what is ~⟩ **11 :** come to an end : ENDED ⟨the time is ~⟩ **12** ♦ **:** well informed ⟨~ on the news⟩ **13 :** being ahead or in advance of an opponent ⟨one hole ~ in a match⟩ **14 :** presented for or being under consideration **15 :** charged before a court ⟨~ for robbery⟩

♦ [3] advanced, high ♦ [12] abreast, conversant, familiar, informed, knowledgeable, up-to-date, versed

3up *prep* **1 :** to, toward, or at a higher point of ⟨~ a ladder⟩ **2 :** to or toward the source of ⟨~ the river⟩ **3 :** to or toward the northern part of ⟨~ the coast⟩ **4 :** to or toward the interior of ⟨traveling ~ the country⟩ **5 :** ALONG ⟨walk ~ the street⟩
4up *n* **1 :** an upward course or slope **2 :** a period or state of prosperity or success ⟨he had his ~*s* and downs⟩ **3 :** a quark with a charge of +⅔ that is one of the constituents of the proton and neutron
5up *vb* **upped** \ˈəpt\ *or in 2* **up; upped; up•ping; ups** *or in 2* **up** **1 :** to rise from a lying or sitting position **2 :** to act abruptly or surprisingly ⟨she ~ and left home⟩ **3** ♦ **:** to move or cause to move upward ⟨*upped* the prices⟩

♦ add, aggrandize, amplify, augment, boost, compound, enlarge, escalate, expand, extend, increase, multiply, raise, swell ♦ boost, crane, elevate, heave, heft, heighten, hike, hoist, jack, lift, pick up, raise, uphold

Upa•ni•shad \ü-ˈpän-i-ˌshäd\ *n* : one of a set of Vedic philosophical treatises
1up•beat \ˈəp-ˌbēt\ *n* : an unaccented beat in a musical measure; *esp* : the last beat of the measure
2upbeat \ˈəp-ˈbēt\ *adj* ♦ **:** marked by or indicating optimism : CHEERFUL

♦ blithe, bright, buoyant, cheerful, cheery, chipper, gay, lightsome, sunny

up•braid \ˌəp-ˈbrād\ *vb* ♦ **:** to criticize, reproach, or scold severely

♦ admonish, chide, lecture, rail (at *or* against), rate, rebuke, reprimand, scold

up•bring•ing \ˈəp-ˌbriŋ-iŋ\ *n* : the process of bringing up and training
UPC *abbr* Universal Product Code
up•chuck \ˈəp-ˌchək\ *vb* : VOMIT
up•com•ing \ˈəp-ˌkə-miŋ\ *adj* : coming up; *esp* : being in the near future : FORTHCOMING, APPROACHING
up–coun•try \ˈəp-ˌkən-trē\ *adj* ♦ **:** of, relating to, or characteristic of an inland, upland, or outlying region — **up–country** \ˈəp-ˈkən-\ *adv*

♦ backwoods, bush, frontier, hinterland, sticks

up•date \ˌəp-ˈdāt\ *vb* : to bring up to date — **update** \ˈəp-ˌdāt\ *n*
up•draft \ˈəp-ˌdraft, -ˌdråft\ *n* : an upward movement of gas (as air)
up•end \ˌəp-ˈend\ *vb* **1 :** to set, stand, or rise on end **2 :** OVERTURN
up–front \ˈəp-ˌfrənt, ˌəp-ˈfrənt\ *adj* **1 :** HONEST, CANDID **2 :** ADVANCE ⟨~ payment⟩
up front *adv* : in advance ⟨paid *up front*⟩
1up•grade \ˈəp-ˌgrād\ *n* **1** ♦ **:** an upward grade or slope **2** ♦ **:** an increase in price, value, rate, or sum : RISE

♦ [1] cant, diagonal, grade, inclination, incline, lean, pitch, slant, slope, tilt ♦ [2] advancement, ascent, elevation, promotion, rise

2up•grade \ˈəp-ˌgrād, ˌəp-ˈgrād\ *vb* **1** ♦ **:** to raise to a higher grade or position; *esp* : to advance to a job requiring a higher level of skill **2 :** to improve or replace (as software or a device) for increased usefulness

♦ advance, elevate, promote, raise

up•growth \ˈəp-ˌgrōth\ *n* : the process of growing upward : DEVELOPMENT; *also* : a product or result of this
up•heav•al \ˌəp-ˈhē-vəl\ *n* **1 :** the action or an instance of uplifting especially of part of the earth's crust **2** ♦ **:** a violent agitation or change

♦ cataclysm, convulsion, paroxysm, storm, tempest, tumult, uproar

1up•hill \ˈəp-ˈhil\ *adv* : upward on a hill or incline; *also* : against difficulties
2up•hill \-ˌhil\ *adj* **1 :** situated on elevated ground **2 :** ASCENDING **3** ♦ **:** hard to do or make : DIFFICULT, LABORIOUS

♦ arduous, challenging, demanding, difficult, exacting, formidable, grueling, hard, herculean, laborious, murderous, rough, severe, stiff, strenuous, tall, toilsome, tough

up•hold \ˌəp-ˈhōld\ *vb* **-held** \-ˈheld\; **-hold•ing** **1** ♦ **:** to give support to **2** ♦ **:** to support or defend against opposition **3 a :** to keep elevated **b :** to lift up — **up•hold•er** *n*

♦ [1] bear, bolster, brace, buttress, carry, prop, shore, stay, support ♦ [2] defend, justify, maintain, support

up•hol•ster \ˌəp-ˈhōl-stər\ *vb* : to furnish with or as if with upholstery — **up•hol•ster•er** *n*
up•hol•stery \-stə-rē\ *n, pl* **-ster•ies** **:** materials (as fabrics, padding, and springs) used to make a soft covering especially for a seat
UPI *abbr* United Press International
up•keep \ˈəp-ˌkēp\ *n* ♦ **:** the act or cost of keeping up or maintaining; *also* : the state of being maintained

♦ conservation, maintenance, preservation

up•land \ˈəp-lənd, -ˌland\ *n* : high land especially at some distance from the sea — **upland** *adj*
1up•lift \ˌəp-ˈlift\ *vb* **1 :** to lift or raise up : ELEVATE **2 :** to improve the condition of especially morally, socially, or intellectually
2up•lift \ˈəp-ˌlift\ *n* **1 :** a lifting up; *esp* : an upheaval of the earth's surface **2 :** moral or social improvement; *also* : a movement to make such improvement
up•mar•ket \ˌəp-ˈmär-kət\ *adj* : appealing to wealthy consumers
up•most \ˈəp-ˌmōst\ *adj* : in or into the highest or most prominent position : UPPERMOST
up•on \ə-ˈpȯn, -ˈpän\ *prep* : in or in contact with an outer surface : ON
1up•per \ˈə-pər\ *adj* **1 :** higher in physical position, rank, or order **2 :** constituting the smaller and more restricted branch of a bicameral legislature **3** *cap* **:** being a later part or formation of a specific geological period **4 :** being toward the interior ⟨the ~ Amazon⟩ **5 :** NORTHERN ⟨~ Minnesota⟩
2upper *n* : one that is upper; *esp* : the parts of a shoe or boot above the sole
up•per•case \ˌə-pər-ˈkās\ *adj* : CAPITAL 1 — **uppercase** *n*
upper class *n* : a social class occupying a position above the mid-

dle class and having the highest status in a society — **upper–class** *adj*

up•per•class•man \ˌə-pər-ˈklas-mən\ *n* **:** a junior or senior in a college or high school

upper crust *n* **:** the highest social class or group; *esp* **:** the highest circle of the upper class

up•per•cut \ˈə-pər-ˌkət\ *n* **:** a short swinging punch delivered (as in boxing) in an upward direction usually with a bent arm

upper hand *n* ♦ **:** superiority of position or condition **:** ADVANTAGE

♦ advantage, better, drop, edge, jump, vantage

up•per•most \ˈə-pər-ˌmōst\ *adv* **:** in or into the highest or most prominent position — **uppermost** *adj*

up•pish \ˈə-pish\ *adj* **:** putting on or marked by airs of superiority **:** UPPITY

up•pi•ty \ˈə-pə-tē\ *adj* ♦ **:** putting on or marked by airs of superiority **:** ARROGANT

♦ arrogant, cavalier, haughty, highfalutin, high-handed, high-hat, imperious, important, lofty, lordly, masterful, overweening, peremptory, pompous, presumptuous, pretentious, supercilious, superior

up•raise \ˌəp-ˈrāz\ *vb* **:** to raise or lift up **:** ELEVATE

¹up•right \ˈəp-ˌrīt\ *adj* **1** ♦ **:** perpendicular to the plane of the horizon or to a primary axis **:** VERTICAL **2 :** erect in carriage or posture **3** ♦ **:** morally correct **:** JUST — **upright** *adv* — **up•right•ly** *adv*

♦ [1] erect, perpendicular, standing, upstanding, vertical ♦ [3] decent, ethical, good, honest, honorable (*or* honourable), just, moral, right, righteous, straight, virtuous

²upright *n* **1 :** the state of being upright **:** a vertical position **2 :** something that stands upright

up•right•ness *n* ♦ **:** the state or quality of being upright

♦ character, decency, goodness, honesty, integrity, morality, probity, rectitude, righteousness, virtue

upright piano *n* **:** a piano whose strings run vertically

up•ris•ing \ˈəp-ˌrī-ziŋ\ *n* ♦ **:** an act or instance of rising up **:** INSURRECTION

♦ insurrection, mutiny, rebellion, revolt, revolution

up•riv•er \ˈəp-ˈri-vər\ *adv or adj* **:** toward or at a point nearer the source of a river

up•roar \ˈəp-ˌrōr\ *n* ♦ **:** a state of commotion, excitement, or violent disturbance

♦ commotion, disturbance, furor, hubbub, hullabaloo, pandemonium, tumult ♦ cataclysm, convulsion, paroxysm, storm, tempest, tumult, upheaval

up•roar•i•ous \ˌəp-ˈrōr-ē-əs\ *adj* **1 :** marked by uproar **2** ♦ **:** extremely funny — **up•roar•i•ous•ly** *adv*

♦ antic, comic, comical, droll, farcical, funny, hilarious, humorous, hysterical, laughable, ludicrous, ridiculous, riotous, risible, screaming

up•root \ˌəp-ˈrüt, -ˈru̇t\ *vb* **1** ♦ **:** to remove by or as if by pulling up by the roots **2 :** DISPLACE 1 ⟨families were ~*ed*⟩

♦ extract, prize, pry, pull, root, tear, wrest

¹up•set \ˌəp-ˈset\ *vb* **-set; -set•ting 1 :** to force or be forced out of the usual upright, level, or proper position **2** ♦ **:** to disturb emotionally **:** WORRY; *also* **:** to make somewhat ill **3** ♦ **:** to throw into disorder **4 :** to defeat unexpectedly

♦ [2] agitate, bother, concern, discompose, disquiet, distress, disturb, exercise, freak, perturb, undo, unhinge, unsettle, worry ♦ [3] confuse, derange, disarray, dishevel, dislocate, disorder, disrupt, jumble, mess, mix, muddle, scramble, shuffle

²up•set \ˈəp-ˌset\ *n* **1 :** an upsetting or being upset; *esp* **:** a minor illness **2** ♦ **:** a derangement of plans or ideas **3 :** an unexpected defeat

♦ derangement, dislocation, disruption, disturbance

³up•set \(ˌ)əp-ˈset\ *adj* ♦ **:** emotionally disturbed or agitated

♦ aflutter, anxious, edgy, jittery, jumpy, nervous, nervy, perturbed, tense, troubled, uneasy, worried

up•set•ting *adj* ♦ **:** producing an upset; *esp* **:** causing an emotional disturbance

♦ troublesome, unsettling, worrisome

up•shot \ˈəp-ˌshät\ *n* ♦ **:** the final result

♦ aftermath, conclusion, consequence, corollary, development, effect, issue, outcome, outgrowth, product, result, resultant, sequence

¹up•side \ˈəp-ˌsīd\ *n* **1 :** the upper side **2 :** a positive aspect **3 :** PROMISE 2 ⟨rookies with much ~⟩

²up•side \ˌəp-ˈsīd\ *prep* **:** up on or against the side of ⟨knocked him ~ the head⟩

up•side down \ˌəp-ˌsīd-ˈdau̇n\ *adv* **1 :** with the upper and the lower parts reversed in position **2 :** in or into confusion or disorder — **upside–down** *adj*

up•si•lon \ˈüp-sə-ˌlän, ˈyüp-, ˈəp-\ *n* **:** the 20th letter of the Greek alphabet — Υ or υ

¹up•stage \ˈəp-ˈstāj\ *adv or adj* **:** toward or at the rear of a theatrical stage

²up•stage \ˌəp-ˈstāj\ *vb* **:** to draw attention away from (as an actor)

¹up•stairs \ˌəp-ˈstarz\ *adv* **1 :** up the stairs **:** to or on a higher floor **2 :** to or at a higher position

²up•stairs \ˈəp-ˈstarz\ *adj* **:** situated above the stairs especially on an upper floor ⟨~ bedroom⟩

³up•stairs \ˈəp-ˈstarz, ˈəp-ˌstarz\ *n sing or pl* **:** the part of a building above the ground floor

up•stand•ing \ˌəp-ˈstan-diŋ, ˈəp-\ *adj* **1 :** vertical in position **:** ERECT **2** ♦ **:** marked by integrity **:** HONEST

♦ decent, ethical, honest, honorable, just, noble, principled, respectable, righteous, upright

¹up•start \ˌəp-ˈstärt\ *vb* **:** to jump up suddenly

²up•start \ˈəp-ˌstärt\ *n* **:** one that has risen suddenly; *esp* **:** one that claims more personal importance than is warranted — **up•start** \-ˈstärt\ *adj*

up•state \ˈəp-ˈstāt\ *adj* **:** of, relating to, or characteristic of a part of a state away from a large city and especially to the north — **upstate** *adv* — **upstate** *n*

up•stream \ˈəp-ˈstrēm\ *adv* **:** at or toward the source of a stream — **upstream** *adj*

up•stroke \ˈəp-ˌstrōk\ *n* **:** an upward stroke (as of a pen)

up•surge \-ˌsərj\ *n* **:** a rapid or sudden rise

up•swept \ˈəp-ˌswept\ *adj* **:** swept upward ⟨~ hairdo⟩

up•swing \ˈəp-ˌswiŋ\ *n* **:** an upward swing; *esp* **:** a marked increase or rise (as in activity)

up•take \ˈəp-ˌtāk\ *n* **1 :** UNDERSTANDING, COMPREHENSION ⟨quick on the ~⟩ **2 :** an act or instance of absorbing and incorporating especially into a living organism, tissue, or cell

up•thrust \ˈəp-ˌthrəst\ *n* **:** an upward thrust (as of the earth's crust) — **upthrust** *vb*

up•tight \ˈəp-ˈtīt\ *adj* **1 :** being tense, nervous, or uneasy **:** NERVOUS; *also* **:** INDIGNANT **2 :** rigidly conventional

up–to–date *adj* **1 :** extending up to the present time **2** ♦ **:** being, having, or involving modern techniques, methods, or information — **up–to–date•ness** *n*

♦ contemporary, current, hot, mod, modern, new, newfangled, red-hot, space-age, ultramodern ♦ abreast, conversant, familiar, informed, knowledgeable, up, versed

up•town \ˈəp-ˌtau̇n\ *n* **:** the upper part of a town or city; *esp* **:** the residential district — **up•town** \ˈəp-ˈtau̇n\ *adj or adv*

¹up•turn \ˈəp-ˌtərn, ˌəp-ˈtərn\ *vb* **1 :** to turn (as earth) up or over **2 :** to turn or direct upward

²up•turn \ˈəp-ˌtərn\ *n* **:** an upward turn especially toward better conditions or higher prices

¹up•ward \ˈəp-wərd\ *or* **up•wards** \-wərdz\ *adv* **1 :** in a direction from lower to higher **2 :** toward a higher or better condition **3 :** toward a greater amount or higher number, degree, or rate

²upward *adj* **:** directed or moving toward or situated in a higher place or level **:** ASCENDING — **up•ward•ly** *adv*

upwards of *also* **upward of** *adv* **:** more than **:** in excess of ⟨they cost *upwards of* $25 each⟩

up•well \ˌəp-ˈwel\ *vb* **:** to move or flow upward

up•well•ing \-ˈwe-liŋ\ *n* **:** a rising or an appearance of rising to the surface and flowing outward; *esp* **:** the movement of deep cold usually nutrient-rich ocean water to the surface

up•wind \ˈəp-ˈwind\ *adv or adj* **:** in the direction from which the wind is blowing

ura•cil \ˈyu̇r-ə-ˌsil\ *n* **:** a pyrimidine base that is one of the four bases coding genetic information in the molecular chain of RNA

ura•ni•um \yu̇-ˈrā-nē-əm\ *n* **:** a silvery heavy radioactive metallic chemical element used as a source of atomic energy

Ura•nus \ˈyu̇r-ə-nəs, yu̇-ˈrā-\ *n* **:** the planet 7th in order from the sun

ur•ban \ˈər-bən\ *adj* **:** of, relating to, characteristic of, or constituting a city

ur•bane \ˌər-ˈbān\ *adj* ♦ : very polite and polished in manner : SUAVE

♦ debonair, smooth, sophisticated, suave

ur•ban•ite \ˈər-bə-ˌnīt\ *n* : a person who lives in a city
ur•ban•i•ty \ˌər-ˈba-nə-tē\ *n, pl* **-ties** : the quality or state of being urbane
ur•ban•ize \ˈər-bə-ˌnīz\ *vb* **-ized; -iz•ing** : to cause to take on urban characteristics — **ur•ban•i•za•tion** \ˌər-bə-nə-ˈzā-shən\ *n*
ur•chin \ˈər-chən\ *n* ♦ : a pert or mischievous youngster

♦ devil, hellion, imp, mischief, monkey, rapscallion, rascal, rogue, scamp

Ur•du \ˈu̇r-dü, ˈər-\ *n* : a language that is the official language of Pakistan and that is widely used by Muslims in urban areas of India
urea \yu̇-ˈrē-ə\ *n* : a soluble nitrogenous compound that is the chief solid constituent of mammalian urine
ure•mia \yu̇-ˈrē-mē-ə\ *n* : accumulation in the blood of materials normally passed off in the urine resulting in a poisoned condition — **ure•mic** \-mik\ *adj*
ure•ter \ˈyu̇r-ə-tər\ *n* : a duct that carries the urine from a kidney to the bladder
ure•thra \yu̇-ˈrē-thrə\ *n, pl* **-thras** *or* **-thrae** \-(ˌ)thrē\ : the canal that in most mammals carries off the urine from the bladder and in the male also serves to carry semen from the body — **ure•thral** \-thrəl\ *adj*
ure•thri•tis \ˌyu̇r-i-ˈthrī-təs\ *n* : inflammation of the urethra
¹urge \ˈərj\ *vb* **urged; urg•ing** **1** : to present, advocate, or demand earnestly **2** ♦ : to try to persuade or sway ⟨~ a guest to stay⟩ **3** : to serve as a motive or reason for **4** ♦ : to impress or impel to some course or activity ⟨*urged* him to stay⟩ ⟨the dog *urged* the sheep onward⟩

♦ [2, 4] egg on, encourage, exhort, goad, press, prod, prompt

²urge *n* **1** : the act or process of urging **2** ♦ : a force or impulse that urges or drives

♦ appetite, craving, desire, drive, hankering, hunger, itch, longing, lust, passion, thirst, yearning, yen

ur•gent \ˈər-jənt\ *adj* **1** ♦ : calling for immediate attention : PRESSING **2** : urging insistently — **ur•gen•cy** \-jən-sē\ *n* — **ur•gent•ly** *adv*

♦ acute, critical, dire, imperative, imperious, instant, pressing

uric \ˈyu̇r-ik\ *adj* : of, relating to, or found in urine
uric acid *n* : a nearly insoluble acid that is the chief nitrogenous excretory product of birds but is present in only small amounts in mammalian urine
uri•nal \ˈyu̇r-ən-ᵊl\ *n* **1** : a receptacle for urine **2** : a place for urinating
uri•nal•y•sis \ˌyu̇r-ə-ˈna-lə-səs\ *n* : chemical analysis of urine
uri•nary \ˈyu̇r-ə-ˌner-ē\ *adj* **1** : relating to, occurring in, or being organs for the formation and discharge of urine **2** : of, relating to, or for urine
urinary bladder *n* : a membranous sac in many vertebrates that serves for the temporary retention of urine and discharges by the urethra
uri•nate \ˈyu̇r-ə-ˌnāt\ *vb* **-nat•ed; -nat•ing** : to release or give off urine — **uri•na•tion** \ˌyu̇r-ə-ˈnā-shən\ *n*
urine \ˈyu̇r-ən\ *n* : a waste material from the kidneys that is usually a yellowish watery liquid in mammals but is semisolid in birds and reptiles
URL \ˌyü-(ˌ)är-ˈel, ˈər(-ə)l\ *n* : a series of usually alphanumeric characters that specifies the storage location of a resource on the Internet
urn \ˈərn\ *n* **1** : a vessel that typically has the form of a vase on a pedestal and often is used to hold the ashes of the dead **2** : a closed vessel usually with a spout for serving a hot beverage
uro•gen•i•tal \ˌyu̇r-ō-ˈje-nət-ᵊl\ *adj* : of, relating to, or being the excretory and reproductive organs or functions
urol•o•gy \yu̇-ˈrä-lə-jē\ *n* : a branch of medical science dealing with the urinary or urogenital tract and its disorders — **uro•log•i•cal** \ˌyu̇r-ə-ˈlä-ji-kəl\ *also* **uro•log•ic** \-jik\ *adj* — **urol•o•gist** \yu̇-ˈrä-lə-jist\ *n*
Ur•sa Ma•jor \ˌər-sə-ˈmā-jər\ *n* : the northern constellation that contains the stars which form the Big Dipper
Ursa Mi•nor \-ˈmī-nər\ *n* : the constellation including the north pole of the heavens and the stars that form the Little Dipper with the North Star at the tip of the handle
ur•sine \ˈər-ˌsīn\ *adj* : of, relating to, or resembling a bear
ur•ti•car•ia \ˌər-tə-ˈkar-ē-ə\ *n* : HIVES
Uru•guay•an \ˌu̇r-ə-ˈgwī-ən, ˌyu̇r-ə-ˈgwā-\ *n* : a native or inhabitant of Uruguay — **Uruguayan** *adj*
us \ˈəs\ *pron, objective case of* WE
US *abbr* United States
USA *abbr* **1** United States Army **2** United States of America
us•able *also* **use•able** \ˈyü-zə-bəl\ *adj* ♦ : suitable or fit for use — **us•abil•i•ty** \ˌyü-zə-ˈbi-lə-tē\ *n*

♦ available, fit, functional, operable, practicable, serviceable, useful ***Ant*** impracticable, inoperable, nonfunctional, unavailable, unusable

USAF *abbr* United States Air Force
us•age \ˈyü-sij, -zij\ *n* **1** : habitual or customary practice or procedure **2** : the way in which words and phrases are actually used **3** : the action or mode of using **4** : manner of treating
USB \ˌyü-(ˌ)es-ˈbē\ *n* : a standardized computer interface for attaching peripherals
USCG *abbr* United States Coast Guard
USDA *abbr* United States Department of Agriculture
¹use \ˈyüs\ *n* **1** ♦ : the act or practice of using or employing something : EMPLOYMENT, APPLICATION **2** : the fact or state of being used **3** : the way of using **4** : habitual or customary usage : USAGE, CUSTOM **5** : the privilege or benefit of using something **6** : the ability or power to use something (as a limb) **7** : the legal enjoyment of property that consists in its employment, occupation, or exercise; *also* : the benefit or profit especially from property held in trust **8** ♦ : a particular service or end : UTILITY **9** : the occasion or need to employ ⟨he had no more ~ for it⟩ **10** ♦ : a favorable attitude : LIKING ⟨had no ~ for modern art⟩

♦ [1] application, employment, exercise, operation, play ♦ [8] account, avail, service, utility ***Ant*** uselessness, worthlessness ♦ [10] appetite, fancy, favor (*or* favour), fondness, like, liking, love, partiality, preference, relish, shine, taste

²use \ˈyüz\ *vb* **used** \ˈyüzd; "*used to*" *usu* ˈyüs-tə\; **us•ing** **1** ♦ : to put into action or service : EMPLOY **2** : to consume or take (as drugs) regularly **3 a** : UTILIZE ⟨~ tact⟩ **b** ♦ : to control or play upon by artful, unfair, or insidious means especially to one's own advantage ⟨*used* his friends to get ahead⟩ **4** : to expend or consume by putting to use **5** ♦ : to behave toward : TREAT ⟨*used* the horse cruelly⟩ **6** : to benefit from ⟨house could ~ a coat of paint⟩ **7** — used in the past with *to* to indicate a former practice, fact, or state ⟨we *used* to work harder⟩

♦ [1] apply, employ, exercise, exploit, harness, operate, utilize ♦ [3b] abuse, capitalize, cash in, exploit, impose, play ♦ [5] act, be, deal, handle, serve, treat

used \ˈyüzd\ *adj* **1** : having been used by another : SECONDHAND ⟨~ cars⟩ **2** ♦ : being in the habit or custom : ACCUSTOMED ⟨~ to the heat⟩

♦ accustomed, given, wont

use•ful \ˈyüs-fəl\ *adj* ♦ : capable of being put to use; *esp* : serviceable for a beneficial end — **use•ful•ly** *adv*

♦ applicable, functional, practicable, practical, serviceable, usable, workable, working

use•ful•ness *n* : the quality of having utility and especially practical worth or applicability
use•less \-ləs\ *adj* ♦ : having or being of no use — **use•less•ly** *adv* — **use•less•ness** *n*

♦ impractical, inoperable, unusable, unworkable ♦ fruitless, futile, ineffective, unproductive, unsuccessful

us•er *n* ♦ : one that uses; *esp* : a person who regularly uses alcoholic beverages or narcotics

♦ addict, doper, fiend

USES *abbr* United States Employment Service
use up *vb* ♦ : to consume completely

♦ clean, consume, deplete, drain, exhaust, expend, spend

¹ush•er \ˈə-shər\ *n* **1** : an officer who walks before a person of rank **2** : one who escorts people to their seats (as in a church or theater)
²usher *vb* **1** ♦ : to conduct to a place **2** : to precede as an usher, forerunner, or harbinger **3** : INAUGURATE, INTRODUCE ⟨~ in a new era⟩

♦ conduct, direct, guide, lead, marshal, pilot, route, show, steer

ush•er•ette \ˌə-shə-ˈret\ *n* : a girl or woman who is an usher (as in a theater)
USIA *abbr* United States Information Agency
USMC *abbr* United States Marine Corps

USN *abbr* United States Navy
USO *abbr* United Service Organizations
USP *abbr* United States Pharmacopeia
USPS *abbr* United States Postal Service
USS *abbr* United States ship
USSR *abbr* Union of Soviet Socialist Republics
usu *abbr* usual; usually
usu•al \ˈyü-zhə-wəl\ *adj* **1 :** accordant with usage, custom, or habit **2** ♦ **:** commonly or ordinarily used **3** ♦ **:** of a kind to be expected in the normal order of events **:** ORDINARY

♦ [2] conventional, current, customary, popular, standard, stock ♦ [3] average, common, commonplace, everyday, normal, ordinary, prosaic, routine, run-of-the-mill, standard, unexceptional, unremarkable, workaday

usu•al•ly \ˈyü-zhə-wə-lē, ˈyü-zhə-lē\ *adv* ♦ **:** more often than not **:** as a rule

♦ commonly, generally, naturally, normally, ordinarily, typically

usu•fruct \ˈyü-zə-ˌfrəkt\ *n* **:** the legal right to use and enjoy the benefits and profits of something belonging to another
usu•rer \ˈyü-zhər-ər\ *n* **:** one that lends money especially at an exorbitant rate
usu•ri•ous \yu̇-ˈzhu̇r-ē-əs\ *adj* **:** practicing, involving, or constituting usury ⟨a ∼ rate of interest⟩
usurp \yu̇-ˈsərp, -ˈzərp\ *vb* ♦ **:** to seize and hold by force or without right ⟨∼ a throne⟩ — **usur•pa•tion** \ˌyü-sər-ˈpā-shən, -zər-\ *n* — **usurp•er** \yu̇-ˈsər-pər, -ˈzər-\ *n*

♦ appropriate, arrogate, commandeer, preempt

usu•ry \ˈyü-zhə-rē\ *n, pl* **-ries 1 :** the lending of money with an interest charge for its use **2 :** an excessive rate or amount of interest charged; *esp* **:** interest above an established legal rate
UT *abbr* Utah
Ute \ˈyüt\ *n, pl* **Ute** *or* **Utes :** a member of an American Indian people orig. ranging through Utah, Colorado, Arizona, and New Mexico
uten•sil \yu̇-ˈten-səl\ *n* **1 :** an instrument or vessel used in a household and especially a kitchen **2** ♦ **:** a useful tool

♦ device, implement, instrument, tool

uter•us \ˈyü-tə-rəs\ *n, pl* **uter•us•es** *or* **uteri** \ˈyü-tə-ˌrī\ **:** the muscular organ of a female mammal in which the young develop before birth — **uter•ine** \-ˌrīn, -rən\ *adj*
utile \ˈyüt-ᵊl, ˈyü-ˌtīl\ *adj* **:** USEFUL
uti•lise *chiefly Brit var of* UTILIZE
¹util•i•tar•i•an \yu̇-ˌti-lə-ˈter-ē-ən\ *n* **:** a person who believes in utilitarianism
²utilitarian *adj* **1 :** of or relating to utilitarianism **2 :** of or relating to utility **:** aiming at usefulness rather than beauty; *also* **:** serving a useful purpose
util•i•tar•i•an•ism \-ē-ə-ˌni-zəm\ *n* **:** a theory that the greatest good for the greatest number should be the main consideration in making a choice of actions
¹util•i•ty \yü-ˈti-lə-tē\ *n, pl* **-ties 1** ♦ **:** fitness for some purpose or worth to some end **:** USEFULNESS **2 :** something useful or designed for use **3 :** a business organization performing a public service and subject to special governmental regulation **4 :** a public service or a commodity (as electricity or water) provided by a public utility; *also* **:** equipment to provide such or a similar service

♦ account, avail, service, use

²utility *adj* **1 :** capable of serving especially as a substitute in various uses or positions ⟨a ∼ outfielder⟩ **2 :** being of a usable but poor quality ⟨∼ beef⟩
utility knife *n* **:** a knife designed for general use; *esp* **:** one with a retractable blade
uti•lize \ˈyüt-ᵊl-ˌīz\ *vb* **-lized; -liz•ing** ♦ **:** to make use of **:** turn to profitable use — **uti•li•za•tion** \ˌyüt-ᵊl-ə-ˈzā-shən\ *n*

♦ apply, employ, exercise, exploit, harness, operate, use

ut•most \ˈət-ˌmōst\ *adj* **1** ♦ **:** situated at the farthest or most distant point **:** EXTREME **2** ♦ **:** of the greatest or highest degree, quantity, number, or amount — **utmost** *n*

♦ [1] extreme, farthest, furthest, outermost, ultimate ♦ [2] consummate, maximum, most, nth, paramount, supreme, top, ultimate

uto•pia \yu̇-ˈtō-pē-ə\ *n* **1** *often cap* ♦ **:** a place of ideal perfection especially in laws, government, and social conditions **2 :** an impractical scheme for social improvement

♦ Eden, Elysium, heaven, paradise

¹uto•pi•an \-pē-ən\ *adj, often cap* **1 :** of, relating to, or resembling a utopia **2 :** proposing ideal social and political schemes that are impractical **3 :** VISIONARY
²utopian *n* **1** ♦ **:** a believer in the perfectibility of human society **2 :** one who proposes or advocates utopian schemes

♦ dreamer, idealist, romantic, visionary

¹ut•ter \ˈə-tər\ *adj* **:** carried to the utmost point or highest degree **:** ABSOLUTE ⟨∼ ruin⟩
²utter *vb* **1** ♦ **:** to send forth as a sound **:** express in usually spoken words **2 :** to put (as currency) into circulation — **ut•ter•er** *n*

♦ articulate, say, speak, state, talk, tell, verbalize, vocalize

ut•ter•ance \ˈə-tə-rəns\ *n* **1 :** something uttered; *esp* **:** an oral or written statement **2** ♦ **:** the action of uttering with the voice **3 :** power, style, or manner of speaking

♦ articulation, expression, formulation, statement, voice

ut•ter•ly *adv* ♦ **:** to the full extent

♦ absolutely, all, altogether, clean, completely, entirely, fully, quite, totally, wholly

ut•ter•most \ˈə-tər-ˌmōst\ *adj* **:** existing in a very high degree **:** UTMOST ⟨the ∼ parts of the earth⟩ — **uttermost** *n*
U–turn \ˈyü-ˌtərn\ *n* **:** a turn resembling the letter U; *esp* **:** a 180-degree turn made by a vehicle in a road
UV *abbr* ultraviolet
uvu•la \ˈyü-vyə-lə\ *n, pl* **-las** *or* **-lae** \-ˌlē, -ˌlī\ **:** the fleshy lobe hanging at the back of the roof of the mouth — **uvu•lar** \-lər\ *adj*
UW *abbr* underwriter
ux•o•ri•ous \ˌək-ˈsōr-ē-əs, ˌəg-ˈzōr-\ *adj* **:** excessively devoted or submissive to a wife

V

¹v \ˈvē\ *n, pl* **v's** *or* **vs** \ˈvēz\ *often cap* **:** the 22d letter of the English alphabet
²v *abbr, often cap* **1** vector **2** velocity **3** verb **4** verse **5** versus **6** very **7** victory **8** vide **9** voice **10** voltage **11** volume **12** vowel
V *symbol* **1** vanadium **2** volt
Va *abbr* Virginia
VA *abbr* **1** Veterans Administration **2** vice admiral **3** Virginia
va•can•cy \ˈvā-kən-sē\ *n, pl* **-cies 1 :** a vacating especially of an office, position, or piece of property **2 :** a vacant office, position, or tenancy; *also* **:** the period during which it stands vacant **3** ♦ **:** empty space **:** VOID **4** ♦ **:** the state of being vacant

♦ [3] blank, blankness, emptiness, vacuity, void ♦ [4] emptiness, vacuity ***Ant*** fullness

va•cant \ˈvā-kənt\ *adj* **1 :** not occupied ⟨∼ seat⟩ ⟨∼ room⟩ **2** ♦ **:** devoid of contents **:** EMPTY ⟨∼ space⟩ **3** ♦ **:** free from business or care ⟨a few ∼ hours⟩ **4** ♦ **:** devoid of thought, reflection, or expression ⟨a ∼ smile⟩ — **va•cant•ly** *adv*

♦ [2] bare, blank, devoid, empty, stark, void ♦ [3] dead, dormant, fallow, free, idle, inactive, inert, inoperative, latent, off ♦ [4] blank, deadpan, expressionless, impassive, inexpressive, stolid

va•cate \ˈvā-ˌkāt\ *vb* **va•cat•ed; va•cat•ing 1 :** to make void **:** ANNUL **2** ♦ **:** to make vacant (as an office or house); *also* **:** to give up the occupancy of

♦ clear, empty, evacuate, void

¹va•ca•tion \vā-ˈkā-shən, və-\ *n* ♦ **:** a period of rest from work

♦ break, leave, recess

²**vacation** *vb* : to take or spend a vacation — **va•ca•tion•er** *n*
va•ca•tion•ist \-shə-nist\ *n* : a person taking a vacation
va•ca•tion•land \-shən-ˌland\ *n* : an area with recreational attractions and facilities for vacationists
vac•ci•nate \ˈvak-sə-ˌnāt\ *vb* **-nat•ed; -nat•ing** : to administer a vaccine to usually by injection
vac•ci•na•tion \ˌvak-sə-ˈnā-shən\ *n* **1** : the act of vaccinating **2** : the scar left by vaccinating
vac•cine \vak-ˈsēn, ˈvak-ˌsēn\ *n* : material (as a preparation of killed or weakened virus or bacteria) used in vaccinating to induce immunity to a disease
vac•cin•ia \vak-ˈsi-nē-ə\ *n* : COWPOX
vac•il•late \ˈva-sə-ˌlāt\ *vb* **-lat•ed; -lat•ing** **1** : SWAY, TOTTER; *also* : FLUCTUATE **2** ♦ : to incline first to one course or opinion and then to another : WAVER

♦ falter, hang back, hesitate, shilly-shally, stagger, teeter, waver, wobble

vac•il•la•tion \ˌva-sə-ˈlā-shən\ *n* ♦ : an act or instance of vacillating

♦ hesitancy, hesitation, indecision, irresolution

va•cu•ity \va-ˈkyü-ə-tē\ *n, pl* **-ities** **1** ♦ : an empty space **2** ♦ : the state, fact, or quality of being vacuous **3** : something that is vacuous

♦ [1, 2] blank, blankness, emptiness, vacancy, void ♦ [2] dopiness, mindlessness, stupidity

vac•u•ole \ˈva-kyə-ˌwōl\ *n* : a usually fluid-filled cavity especially in the cytoplasm of an individual cell — **vac•u•o•lar** \ˌva-kyə-ˈwō-lər, -ˌlär\ *adj*
vac•u•ous \ˈva-kyə-wəs\ *adj* **1** : EMPTY, VACANT, BLANK **2** ♦ : marked by or indicative of a lack of ideas or intelligence : DULL — **vac•u•ous•ly** *adv* — **vac•u•ous•ness** *n*

♦ dense, dull, dumb, mindless, simple, slow, stupid, unintelligent, witless

¹**vac•u•um** \ˈva-(ˌ)kyüm, -kyəm\ *n, pl* **vacuums** *or* **vac•ua** \-kyə-wə\ **1** : a space entirely empty of matter **2** : a space from which most of the air has been removed (as by a pump) **3** : VOID, GAP **4** : VACUUM CLEANER — **vacuum** *adj*
²**vacuum** *vb* : to use a vacuum device (as a vacuum cleaner) on
vacuum bottle *n* : THERMOS
vacuum cleaner *n* : a household appliance for cleaning (as floors or rugs) by suction
vacuum–packed *adj* : having much of the air removed before being hermetically sealed
vacuum tube *n* : an electron tube from which most of the air has been removed
va•de me•cum \ˌvā-dē-ˈmē-kəm, ˌvä-dē-ˈmā-\ *n, pl* **vade mecums** : something (as a handbook or manual) regularly carried about
VADM *abbr* vice admiral
¹**vag•a•bond** \ˈva-gə-ˌbänd\ *adj* **1** ♦ : moving from place to place without a fixed home : WANDERING **2** : of, relating to, or characteristic of a wanderer; *esp* : of, characteristic of, or leading the life of a vagrant or tramp **3** : leading an unsettled or irresponsible life

♦ errant, itinerant, nomad, peripatetic, roaming, vagrant

²**vagabond** *n* **1** ♦ : one leading a vagabond life **2** ♦ : an idle beggar : TRAMP

♦ [1] drifter, nomad, rambler, rover, stroller, wanderer ♦ [2] bum, hobo, tramp, vagrant

va•gar•i•ous \vā-ˈger-ē-əs\ *adj* : marked by vagaries : CAPRICIOUS — **va•gar•i•ous•ly** *adv*
va•ga•ry \ˈvā-gə-rē, və-ˈger-ē\ *n, pl* **-ries** ♦ : an odd or eccentric idea or action : WHIM, CAPRICE

♦ caprice, fancy, freak, notion, whim

va•gi•na \və-ˈjī-nə\ *n, pl* **-nae** \-(ˌ)nē\ *or* **-nas** : a canal that leads from the uterus to the external opening of the female sex organs — **vag•i•nal** \ˈva-jən-ᵊl\ *adj* — **vag•i•nal•ly** \-nᵊl-ē\ *adv*
vag•i•ni•tis \ˌva-jə-ˈnī-təs\ *n* : inflammation of the vagina
va•gran•cy \ˈvā-grən-sē\ *n, pl* **-cies** **1** : the quality or state of being vagrant; *also* : a vagrant act or notion **2** : the offense of being a vagrant
¹**va•grant** \ˈvā-grənt\ *n* ♦ : a person who has no job and wanders from place to place

♦ bum, hobo, tramp, vagabond

²**vagrant** *adj* **1** ♦ : of, relating to, or characteristic of a vagrant **2** : following no fixed course : RANDOM, CAPRICIOUS ⟨~ thoughts⟩ — **va•grant•ly** *adv*

♦ errant, itinerant, nomad, peripatetic, roaming, vagabond

vague \ˈvāg\ *adj* **vagu•er; vagu•est** **1** ♦ : not clear, definite, or distinct in expression or perception **2** : not clearly felt or analyzed ⟨a ~ unrest⟩ — **vague•ly** *adv* — **vague•ness** *n*

♦ fuzzy, indefinite, unclear ***Ant*** clear, definite, explicit, specific ♦ bleary, dim, faint, foggy, fuzzy, hazy, indefinite, indistinct, indistinguishable, murky, nebulous, obscure, opaque, shadowy, unclear, undefined, undetermined

vain \ˈvān\ *adj* **1** : of no real value : IDLE, WORTHLESS **2** ♦ : marked by a lack of effectiveness or success : UNSUCCESSFUL **3** ♦ : proud of one's looks or abilities — **vain•ly** *adv*

♦ [2] fruitless, futile, ineffective, unproductive, unsuccessful ♦ [3] complacent, conceited, egotistic, important, overweening, pompous, prideful, proud, self-important, self-satisfied, smug, stuck-up

vain•glo•ri•ous \ˌvān-ˈglōr-ē-əs\ *adj* : marked by vainglory : being vain
vain•glo•ry \ˈvān-ˌglōr-ē\ *n* **1** ♦ : excessive or ostentatious pride especially in one's own achievements **2** : vain display : VANITY

♦ complacence, conceit, ego, egotism, pride, self-conceit, self-esteem, self-importance, self-satisfaction, smugness, vanity

val *abbr* value; valued
va•lance \ˈva-ləns, ˈvā-\ *n* **1** : drapery hanging from an edge (as of an altar, table, or bed) **2** : a drapery or a decorative frame across the top of a window
vale \ˈvāl\ *n* : a low-lying country or tract usually containing a brook or a stream : VALLEY
vale•dic•tion \ˌva-lə-ˈdik-shən\ *n* : an act or utterance of leave-taking : FAREWELL
vale•dic•to•ri•an \-ˌdik-ˈtōr-ē-ən\ *n* : the student usually of the highest rank in a graduating class who delivers the valedictory address at commencement
vale•dic•to•ry \-ˈdik-tə-rē\ *adj* : bidding farewell : delivered as a valediction ⟨a ~ address⟩ — **valedictory** *n*
va•lence \ˈvā-ləns\ *n* : the combining power of an atom as shown by the number of its electrons that are lost, gained, or shared in the formation of chemical bonds
Va•len•ci•ennes \və-ˌlen-sē-ˈen, ˌva-lən-sē-, -ˈenz\ *n* : a fine handmade lace
val•en•tine \ˈva-lən-ˌtīn\ *n* : a sweetheart chosen or complimented on Valentine's Day; *also* : a gift or greeting given on this day
Valentine's Day *also* **Valentine Day** *n* : February 14 observed in honor of St. Valentine and as a time for exchanging valentines
¹**va•let** \ˈva-lət, -(ˌ)lā; va-ˈlā\ *n* **1** : a male servant who takes care of a man's clothes and performs personal services **2** : an attendant in a hotel or restaurant who performs personal services (as parking cars) for customers
²**valet** *vb* : to serve as a valet
val•e•tu•di•nar•i•an \ˌva-lə-ˌtüd-ᵊn-ˈer-ē-ən, -ˌtyüd-\ *n* : a person of a weak or sickly constitution; *esp* : one whose chief concern is his or her ill health — **val•e•tu•di•nar•i•an•ism** \-ē-ə-ˌni-zəm\ *n*
val•iant \ˈval-yənt\ *adj* ♦ : having or showing valor : BRAVE — **val•iant•ly** *adv*

♦ brave, courageous, dauntless, doughty, fearless, gallant, greathearted, heroic, intrepid, lionhearted, manful, stalwart, stout, undaunted, valorous

val•id \ˈva-ləd\ *adj* **1** : having legal force ⟨a ~ contract⟩ **2** ♦ : founded on truth or fact : capable of being justified or defended ⟨a ~ argument⟩ ⟨~ reasons⟩ — **va•lid•i•ty** \və-ˈli-də-tē\ *n* — **val•id•ly** *adv*

♦ analytic, coherent, good, logical, rational, reasonable, sensible, sober, sound ♦ good, hard, informed, just, levelheaded, logical, reasoned, solid, well-founded

val•i•date \ˈva-lə-ˌdāt\ *vb* **-dat•ed; -dat•ing** **1** : to make legally valid **2** ♦ : to confirm the validity of **3** ♦ : to corroborate or support on a sound basis or authority : VERIFY

♦ [2] demonstrate, document, establish, prove, substantiate ♦ [3] bear out, confirm, corroborate, substantiate, support, verify, vindicate

val•i•da•tion \ˌva-lə-ˈdā-shən\ *n* ♦ : the act or an instance of validating

♦ attestation, confirmation, corroboration, documentation, evidence, proof, substantiation, testament, testimony, witness

va•lise \və-ˈlēs\ *n* : SUITCASE
val•ley \ˈva-lē\ *n, pl* **valleys** ♦ : a long depression between ranges of hills or mountains

♦ dale, hollow

val•or *or Can and Brit* **val•our** \ˈva-lər\ *n* ♦ : personal bravery

♦ bravery, courage, daring, fearlessness, gallantry, guts, hardihood, heart, heroism, nerve, stoutness

val•o•ri•za•tion \ˌva-lə-rə-ˈzā-shən\ *n* : the support of commodity prices by any of various forms of government subsidy — **val•o•rize** \ˈva-lə-ˌrīz\ *vb*
val•or•ous \ˈva-lə-rəs\ *adj* ♦ : possessing or exhibiting valor

♦ brave, courageous, dauntless, doughty, fearless, gallant, greathearted, heroic, intrepid, lionhearted, manful, stalwart, stout, undaunted, valiant

val•our *chiefly Brit var of* VALOR
¹valu•able \ˈval-yə-bəl, -yə-wə-bəl\ *adj* **1** : having money value **2** ♦ : having great money value **3** : of great use or service

♦ costly, dear, expensive, high, precious

²valuable *n* : a usually personal possession of considerable value ⟨their ~*s* were stolen⟩
val•u•ate \ˈval-yə-ˌwāt\ *vb* **-at•ed; -at•ing** : to place a value on : APPRAISE — **val•u•a•tor** \-ˌwā-tər\ *n*
val•u•a•tion \ˌval-yə-ˈwā-shən\ *n* **1** ♦ : the act or process of valuing; *esp* : appraisal of property **2** : the estimated or determined market value of a thing

♦ appraisal, assessment, estimate, estimation, evaluation, reckoning

¹val•ue \ˈval-yü\ *n* **1** : a fair return or equivalent in money, goods, or services for something exchanged **2** ♦ : the monetary worth of a thing; *also* : relative worth, utility, or importance ⟨nothing of ~ to say⟩ **3** : an assigned or computed numerical quantity ⟨the ~ of *x* in an equation⟩ **4** : relative lightness or darkness of a color : LUMINOSITY **5** : the relative length of a tone or note **6** : something (as a principle or ideal) intrinsically valuable or desirable ⟨human rather than material ~*s*⟩

♦ distinction, excellence, merit, virtue ♦ account, merit, valuation, worth

²value *vb* **val•ued; valu•ing** **1** ♦ : to estimate the monetary worth of : APPRAISE **2** : to rate in usefulness, importance, or general worth **3** ♦ : to consider or rate highly : PRIZE — **val•u•er** *n*

♦ [1] appraise, assess, estimate, evaluate, rate, set ♦ [3] appreciate, cherish, love, prize, treasure

val•ue–add•ed tax *n* : an incremental excise tax that is levied on the value added at each stage of the processing of a raw material or the production and distribution of a commodity
val•ue•less *adj* ♦ : having no value

♦ chaffy, empty, junky, no-good, null, worthless

valve \ˈvalv\ *n* **1** : a structure (as in a vein) that temporarily closes a passage or that permits movement in one direction only **2** ♦ : a device by which the flow of a fluid material may be regulated by a movable part; *also* : the movable part of such a device **3** : a device in a brass wind instrument for quickly varying the tube length in order to change the fundamental tone by some definite interval **4** : one of the separate usually hinged pieces of which the shell of some animals and especially bivalve mollusks consists **5** : one of the pieces into which a ripe seed capsule or pod separates — **valved** \ˈvalvd\ *adj* — **valve•less** *adj*

♦ cock, faucet, gate, spigot, tap

val•vu•lar \ˈval-vyə-lər\ *adj* : of, relating to, or affecting a valve especially of the heart ⟨~ heart disease⟩
va•moose \və-ˈmüs, va-\ *vb* **va•moosed; va•moos•ing** : to leave or go away quickly
¹vamp \ˈvamp\ *vb* **1** : to provide with a new vamp **2** : to patch up with a new part **3** : INVENT, IMPROVISE ⟨~ up an excuse⟩
²vamp *n* **1** : the part of a boot or shoe upper covering especially the front part of the foot **2** : a short introductory musical passage often repeated
³vamp *n* : a woman who uses her charm or wiles to seduce and exploit men
⁴vamp *vb* : to practice seductive wiles on : act like a vamp
vam•pire \ˈvam-ˌpīr\ *n* **1** : a night-wandering bloodsucking ghost **2** : a person who preys on other people; *esp* : a woman who exploits and ruins her lover **3** : VAMPIRE BAT

vampire bat *n* : any of various bats of Central and South America that feed on the blood of animals; *also* : any of several other bats that do not feed on blood but are sometimes reputed to do so
¹van \ˈvan\ *n* : the forefront of an action or movement : VANGUARD
²van *n* : a usually enclosed wagon or motortruck for moving goods or animals; *also* : a versatile enclosed box-like motor vehicle
va•na•di•um \və-ˈnā-dē-əm\ *n* : a soft grayish ductile metallic chemical element used especially to form alloys
Van Al•len belt \van-ˈa-lən-\ *n* : a belt of intense radiation in the magnetosphere composed of charged particles trapped by earth's magnetic field
van•dal \ˈvand-ᵊl\ *n* **1** *cap* : a member of a Germanic people who sacked Rome in A.D. 455 **2** : a person who willfully mars or destroys property
van•dal•ise *chiefly Brit var of* VANDALIZE
van•dal•ism \-ˌi-zəm\ *n* : willful or malicious destruction or defacement of public or private property
van•dal•ize \-ˌīz\ *vb* **-ized; -iz•ing** : to subject to vandalism : DAMAGE
Van•dyke \van-ˈdīk\ *n* : a trim pointed beard
vane \ˈvān\ *n* **1** : a movable device attached to a high object for showing wind direction **2** : a thin flat or curved object that is rotated about an axis by a flow of fluid or that rotates to cause a fluid to flow or that redirects a flow of fluid ⟨the ~*s* of a windmill⟩ **3** : a feather fastened near the back end of an arrow for stability in flight
van•guard \ˈvan-ˌgärd\ *n* **1** : the troops moving at the front of an army **2** : the forefront of an action or movement
va•nil•la \və-ˈni-lə\ *n* : a flavoring extract made synthetically or obtained from the long beanlike pods (**vanilla beans**) of a tropical American climbing orchid; *also* : this orchid
van•ish \ˈva-nish\ *vb* ♦ : to pass from sight or existence : disappear completely — **van•ish•er** *n*

♦ disappear, dissolve, evaporate, fade, flee, go, melt

van•i•ty \ˈva-nə-tē\ *n, pl* **-ties** **1** : something that is vain, empty, or useless **2** : the quality or fact of being useless or futile : FUTILITY **3** ♦ : undue pride in oneself or one's appearance : CONCEIT **4** : a small case for cosmetics : COMPACT

♦ complacence, conceit, ego, egotism, pride, self-conceit, self-esteem, self-importance, self-satisfaction, smugness, vainglory

vanity plate *n* : an automobile license plate bearing distinctive letters or numbers designated by the owner
van•quish \ˈvaŋ-kwish, ˈvan-\ *vb* **1** ♦ : to overcome in battle or in a contest **2** : to gain mastery over (as an emotion)

♦ conquer, dominate, overpower, subdue, subject

van•tage \ˈvan-tij\ *n* **1** ♦ : an advantage or superiority in a contest **2** : a position giving a strategic advantage or a commanding perspective

♦ advantage, better, drop, edge, jump, upper hand

va•pid \ˈva-pəd, ˈvā-\ *adj* : lacking spirit, liveliness, or zest : FLAT, INSIPID — **va•pid•i•ty** \va-ˈpi-də-tē\ *n* — **vap•id•ly** *adv* — **vap•id•ness** *n*
va•por *or Can and Brit* **va•pour** \ˈvā-pər\ *n* **1** : fine separated particles (as fog or smoke) floating in the air and clouding it **2** : a substance in the gaseous state; *esp* : one that is liquid under ordinary conditions **3** : something insubstantial or fleeting **4** *pl* : a depressed or hysterical nervous condition
va•por•ing \ˈvā-pə-riŋ\ *n* : an idle, boastful, or high-flown expression or speech — usually used in plural
va•por•ise *chiefly Brit var of* VAPORIZE
va•por•ize \ˈvā-pə-ˌrīz\ *vb* **-ized; -iz•ing** : to convert into vapor — **va•por•i•za•tion** \ˌvā-pə-rə-ˈzā-shən\ *n*
va•por•iz•er \-ˌrī-zər\ *n* : a device that vaporizes something (as a medicated liquid)
vapor lock *n* : an interruption of flow of a fluid (as fuel in an engine) caused by the formation of vapor in the feeding system
va•por•ous \ˈvā-pə-rəs\ *adj* **1** : full of vapors : FOGGY, MISTY **2** : UNSUBSTANTIAL, VAGUE — **va•por•ous•ly** *adv* — **va•por•ous•ness** *n*
va•pory \ˈvā-pə-rē\ *adj* : MISTY
va•pour *chiefly Brit var of* VAPOR
va•que•ro \vä-ˈker-ō\ *n, pl* **-ros** : a ranch hand : COWBOY
var *abbr* **1** variable **2** variant; variation **3** variety **4** various
¹var•i•able \ˈver-ē-ə-bəl\ *adj* **1** ♦ : able or apt to vary : CHANGEABLE **2** : FICKLE **3** : not true to type : ABERRANT ⟨a ~ wheat⟩ — **var•i•abil•i•ty** \ˌver-ē-ə-ˈbi-lə-tē, ˌvar-\ *n* — **var•i•ably** \-blē\ *adv*

♦ adaptable, adjustable, changeable, elastic, flexible, fluid, malleable

[2]**variable** *n* **1 :** a quantity that may take on any of a set of values; *also* **:** a mathematical symbol representing a variable **2 :** something that is variable

var•i•ance \ˈver-ē-əns\ *n* **1 :** variation or a degree of variation **:** DEVIATION **2** ♦ **:** the fact or state of being in disagreement **3 :** a license to do something contrary to the usual rule ⟨a zoning ~⟩ **4 :** the square of the standard deviation

♦ conflict, discord, dissension, dissent, disunity, friction, schism, strife, war, warfare

[1]**var•i•ant** \ˈver-ē-ənt\ *adj* **1 :** differing from others of its kind or class **2 :** varying usually slightly from the standard or type

[2]**variant** *n* **1 :** one that exhibits variation from a type or norm **2 :** one of two or more different spellings or pronunciations of a word

var•i•a•tion \ˌver-ē-ˈā-shən\ *n* **1** ♦ **:** the act, process, or an instance of varying **:** a change in form, position, or condition **2 :** extent of change or difference **3 :** divergence in the characteristics of an organism from those typical or usual for its group; *also* **:** one exhibiting such variation **4 :** repetition of a musical theme with modifications in rhythm, tune, harmony, or key

♦ alteration, change, difference, modification, revise, revision

vari•col•ored \ˈver-i-ˌkə-lərd\ *adj* **:** having various colors **:** VARIEGATED

var•i•cose \ˈvar-ə-ˌkōs\ *adj* **:** abnormally swollen and dilated ⟨~ veins⟩ — **var•i•cos•i•ty** \ˌvar-ə-ˈkä-sə-tē\ *n*

var•ied \ˈver-ēd\ *adj* **1** ♦ **:** having many forms or types; *also* **:** composed of distinct or unlike elements or qualities **2 :** VARIEGATED — **var•ied•ly** *adv*

♦ assorted, heterogeneous, miscellaneous, mixed, motley

var•ie•gat•ed \ˈver-ē-ə-ˌgā-təd\ *adj* **1** ♦ **:** having patches, stripes, or marks of different colors ⟨~ flowers⟩ **2 :** VARIED 1 — **var•ie•gate** \-ˌgāt\ *vb* — **var•ie•ga•tion** \ˌver-ē-ə-ˈgā-shən\ *n*

♦ colorful (*or* colourful), multicolored (*or* multicoloured

[1]**va•ri•etal** \və-ˈrī-ət-ᵊl\ *adj* **:** of or relating to a variety; *esp* **:** of, relating to, or producing a varietal

[2]**varietal** *n* **:** a wine bearing the name of the principal grape from which it is made

va•ri•ety \və-ˈrī-ə-tē\ *n, pl* **-et•ies 1** ♦ **:** the state of being varied or various **:** DIVERSITY **2** ♦ **:** a collection of different things **:** ASSORTMENT **3 :** something varying from others of the same general kind **4 :** any of various groups of plants or animals within a species distinguished by characteristics insufficient to separate species **:** SUBSPECIES **5 :** entertainment such as is given in a stage presentation comprising a series of performances (as songs, dances, or acrobatic acts)

♦ [1] assortment, diversity ♦ [2] assortment, clutter, jumble, medley, mélange, miscellany, motley, muddle, welter

var•i•o•rum \ˌver-ē-ˈōr-əm\ *n* **:** an edition or text of a work containing notes by various persons or variant readings of the text

var•i•ous \ˈver-ē-əs\ *adj* **1 :** VARICOLORED **2 :** of differing kinds **:** MULTIFARIOUS **3 :** UNLIKE ⟨animals as ~ as the jaguar and the sloth⟩ **4 :** having a number of different aspects **5 :** NUMEROUS, MANY **6 :** INDIVIDUAL, SEPARATE — **var•i•ous•ly** *adv*

var•let \ˈvär-lət\ *n* **1 :** ATTENDANT **2** ♦ **:** a disreputable, unprincipled person **:** SCOUNDREL, KNAVE

♦ beast, evildoer, fiend, no-good, reprobate, rogue, villain, wretch

var•mint \ˈvär-mənt\ *n* **1 :** an animal considered a pest; *esp* **:** one classed as vermin and unprotected by game law **2 :** a contemptible person **:** RASCAL

[1]**var•nish** \ˈvär-nish\ *n* **1 :** a liquid preparation that is applied to a surface and dries into a hard glossy coating; *also* **:** the glaze of this coating **2 :** something suggesting varnish by its gloss **3 :** outside show **:** deceptive or superficial appearance

[2]**varnish** *vb* **1 :** to cover with varnish **2 :** to cover or conceal with something that gives a fair appearance **:** GLOSS

var•si•ty \ˈvär-sə-tē\ *n, pl* **-ties 1** *Brit* **:** UNIVERSITY **2 :** the principal team representing a college, school, or club

vary \ˈver-ē\ *vb* **var•ied; vary•ing 1** ♦ **:** to make different in some attribute or characteristic **:** ALTER **2 :** to make or be of different kinds **:** introduce or have variety **:** DIVERSIFY, DIFFER **3** ♦ **:** to exhibit or undergo change **4 :** to change in bodily structure or function away from what is usual for members of a group

♦ [1] alter, change, make over, modify, recast, redo, refashion, remake, remodel, revamp, revise, rework ♦ [3] change, fluctuate, mutate, shift

vas•cu•lar \ˈvas-kyə-lər\ *adj* **:** of or relating to a channel or system of channels for the conveyance of a body fluid (as blood or sap); *also* **:** supplied with or containing such vessels and especially blood vessels

vascular plant *n* **:** a plant having a specialized system for carrying fluids that includes xylem and phloem

vas def•er•ens \ˈvas-ˈde-fə-rənz\ *n, pl* **va•sa def•er•en•tia** \ˈvä-zə-ˌde-fə-ˈren-shē-ə\ **:** a sperm-carrying duct of the testis

vase \ˈvās, ˈväz\ *n* **:** a usually round vessel of greater depth than width used chiefly for ornament or for flowers

va•sec•to•my \və-ˈsek-tə-mē, vā-ˈzek-\ *n, pl* **-mies :** surgical excision of all or part of the vas deferens usually to induce sterility

va•so•con•stric•tion \ˌvas-ō-kən-ˈstrik-shən, ˌvāz-\ *n* **:** narrowing of the interior diameter of blood vessels

va•so•con•stric•tor \-tər\ *n* **:** an agent (as a nerve fiber or a drug) that initiates or induces vasoconstriction

vas•sal \ˈva-səl\ *n* **1 :** a person under the protection of a feudal lord to whom he owes homage and loyalty **:** a feudal tenant **2 :** one occupying a dependent or subordinate position — **vassal** *adj*

vas•sal•age \-sə-lij\ *n* **1 :** the state of being a vassal **2 :** the homage and loyalty due from a vassal **3 :** SERVITUDE, SUBJECTION

[1]**vast** \ˈvast\ *adj* ♦ **:** very great in size, amount, degree, intensity, or especially extent

♦ enormous, giant, gigantic, huge, massive, monumental, prodigious, tremendous, whopping

[2]**vast** *n* **:** a great expanse **:** IMMENSITY

vast•ly *adv* ♦ **:** to a vast extent or degree

♦ broadly, considerably, greatly, hugely, largely, massively, monstrously, much, sizably, stupendously, tremendously, utterly

vast•ness *n* ♦ **:** the quality or state of being vast

♦ enormity, hugeness, immensity, magnitude, massiveness

vasty \ˈvas-tē\ *adj* **:** VAST

vat \ˈvat\ *n* **:** a large vessel (as a tub or barrel) especially for holding liquids in manufacturing processes

VAT *abbr* value-added tax

vat•ic \ˈva-tik\ *adj* **:** PROPHETIC, ORACULAR

Vat•i•can \ˈva-ti-kən\ *n* **1 :** the papal headquarters in Rome **2 :** the papal government

vaude•ville \ˈvȯd-vəl, ˈväd-, ˈvōd-, -ˌvil\ *n* **:** a stage entertainment consisting of unrelated acts (as of acrobats, comedians, dancers, or singers)

[1]**vault** \ˈvȯlt\ *n* **1 :** an arched masonry structure usually forming a ceiling or roof; *also* **:** something (as the sky) resembling a vault **2 :** a room or space covered by a vault especially when underground **3 :** a room or compartment for the safekeeping of valuables **4 :** a burial chamber; *also* **:** a usually metal or concrete case in which a casket is enclosed at burial — **vaulty** *adj*

[2]**vault** *vb* **:** to form or cover with a vault

[3]**vault** *vb* ♦ **:** to leap vigorously especially by aid of the hands or a pole — **vault•er** *n*

♦ bound, hop, jump, leap, spring

[4]**vault** *n* **:** an act of vaulting **:** LEAP

vault•ed \ˈvȯl-təd\ *adj* **1 :** built in the form of a vault **:** ARCHED **2 :** covered with a vault

vault•ing \-tiŋ\ *adj* **:** reaching for the heights ⟨~ ambition⟩

vaunt \ˈvȯnt\ *vb* **:** BRAG, BOAST — **vaunt** *n*

vaunt•ed \ˈvȯn-təd\ *adj* **:** much praised or boasted of

vb *abbr* verb; verbal

V–chip \ˈvē-ˌchip\ *n* **:** a computer chip in a television set used to block based on content the viewing of certain programs

VCR \ˌvē-(ˌ)sē-ˈär\ *n* **:** a device that records and plays back videotapes

VD *abbr* venereal disease

VDT *abbr* video display terminal

veal \ˈvēl\ *n* **:** the flesh of a young calf

vec•tor \ˈvek-tər\ *n* **1 :** a quantity that has magnitude and direction **2 :** an organism (as a fly or tick) that transmits a pathogen

Ve•da \ˈvā-də\ *n* **:** any of a class of Hindu sacred writings — **Ve•dic** \ˈvā-dik\ *adj*

Ve•dan•ta \vā-ˈdän-tə, və-, -ˈdan-\ *n* **:** an orthodox Hindu philosophy based on the Upanishads

vee•jay \ˈvē-ˌjā\ *n* **:** an announcer of a program featuring music videos

veep \ˈvēp\ *n* **:** VICE PRESIDENT

veer \ˈvir\ *vb* ♦ **:** to shift from one direction or course to another — **veer** *n*

♦ divert, swerve, swing, turn, wheel, whip

veg•an \ˈvē-gən, ˈvā-; ˈve-jən, -ˌjan\ *n* **:** a strict vegetarian who consumes no animal food or dairy products — **veg•an•ism** \ˈvē-gə-ˌni-zəm, ˈvā-, ˈve-\ *n*

[1]**veg•e•ta•ble** \ˈvej-tə-bəl, ˈve-jə-\ *adj* **1 :** of, relating to, or growing like plants ⟨the ~ kingdom⟩ **2 :** made from, obtained from, or containing plants or plant products ⟨~ oils⟩ **3 :** suggesting that of a plant (as in inertness) ⟨a ~ existence⟩

[2]**vegetable** *n* **1 :** PLANT 1 **2 :** a usually herbaceous plant grown for an edible part that is usually eaten as part of a meal; *also* **:** such an edible part

veg•e•tal \ˈve-jət-ᵊl\ *adj* **1 :** VEGETABLE **2 :** VEGETATIVE

veg•e•tar•i•an \ˌve-jə-ˈter-ē-ən\ *n* **:** one that believes in or practices living on a diet of vegetables, fruits, grains, nuts, and sometimes animal products (as milk and cheese) — **vegetarian** *adj* — **veg•e•tar•i•an•ism** \-ē-ə-ˌni-zəm\ *n*

veg•e•tate \ˈve-jə-ˌtāt\ *vb* **-tat•ed; -tat•ing :** to live or grow in the manner of a plant; *esp* **:** to lead a dull inert life

veg•e•ta•tion \ˌve-jə-ˈtā-shən\ *n* **1 :** the act or process of vegetating; *also* **:** inert existence **2** ♦ **:** plant life or cover (as of an area) — **veg•e•ta•tion•al** \-shə-nəl\ *adj*

♦ flora, foliage, green, greenery, herbage, leafage, verdure

veg•e•ta•tive \ˈve-jə-ˌtā-tiv\ *adj* **1 :** of or relating to nutrition and growth especially as contrasted with reproduction **2 :** of, relating to, or composed of vegetation **3 :** VEGETABLE 3

veg out \ˈvej-\ *vb* **vegged out; vegging out :** to spend time idly or passively

ve•he•mence \ˈvē-ə-məns\ *n* ♦ **:** the quality or state of being vehement

♦ ardor, emotion, fervency, fervor, heat, intensity, passion, warmth ♦ aggressiveness, assertiveness, emphasis, fierceness, intensity *Ant* feebleness, mildness, weakness

ve•he•ment \ˈvē-ə-mənt\ *adj* **1** ♦ **:** marked by great force or energy **2** ♦ **:** marked by strong feeling or expression — **ve•he•ment•ly** *adv*

♦ [1] deep, explosive, exquisite, fearful, ferocious, fierce, furious, hard, heavy, intense, profound, terrible, vicious, violent ♦ [2] ardent, burning, charged, emotional, fervent, fiery, hot-blooded, impassioned, passionate, red-hot

ve•hi•cle \ˈvē-ə-kəl, ˈvē-ˌhi-\ *n* **1 :** a medium by which a thing is applied or administered ⟨linseed oil is a ~ for pigments⟩ **2** ♦ **:** a medium through or by means of which something is conveyed or expressed **3** ♦ **:** a means of transporting persons or goods — **ve•hic•u•lar** \vē-ˈhi-kyə-lər\ *adj*

♦ [2] agency, agent, instrument, instrumentality, machinery, means, medium, organ ♦ [3] conveyance, transport

[1]**veil** \ˈvāl\ *n* **1 :** a piece of often sheer or diaphanous material used to screen or curtain something or to cover the head or face **2 :** the life of a nun ⟨take the ~⟩ **3 :** something that hides or obscures like a veil

[2]**veil** *vb* ♦ **:** to cover with or as if with a veil

♦ cloak, conceal, cover, curtain, hide, mask, obscure, screen

[1]**vein** \ˈvān\ *n* **1 :** a fissure in rock filled with mineral matter; *also* **:** a bed of useful mineral matter **2 :** any of the tubular branching vessels that carry blood from the capillaries toward the heart **3 :** any of the bundles of vascular vessels forming the framework of a leaf **4 :** any of the thickened ribs that stiffen the wings of an insect **5 :** something (as a wavy variegation in marble) suggesting veins **6** ♦ **:** a distinctive style of expression **7 :** a distinctive element or quality **:** STRAIN **8 :** MOOD, HUMOR — **veined** \ˈvānd\ *adj*

♦ fashion, locution, manner, mode, phraseology, style, tone

[2]**vein** *vb* **:** to pattern with or as if with veins — **vein•ing** *n*

vel *abbr* velocity

ve•lar \ˈvē-lər\ *adj* **:** of or relating to a velum and especially that of the soft palate

veld *or* **veldt** \ˈvelt, ˈfelt\ *n* ♦ **:** an open grassland especially in southern Africa usually with scattered shrubs or trees

♦ down, grassland, plain, prairie, savanna, steppe

vel•lum \ˈve-ləm\ *n* **1 :** a fine-grained lambskin, kidskin, or calfskin prepared for writing on or for binding books **2 :** a strong cream-colored paper — **vellum** *adj*

ve•loc•i•pede \və-ˈlä-sə-ˌpēd\ *n* **:** an early bicycle

ve•loc•i•rapt•or \və-ˈlä-sə-ˌrap-tər\ *n* **:** any of a genus of agile flesh-eating bipedal dinosaurs of the Cretaceous having a sickle-shaped claw on each foot

ve•loc•i•ty \və-ˈlä-sə-tē\ *n, pl* **-ties** ♦ **:** quickness of motion **:** SPEED ⟨the ~ of light⟩

♦ celerity, fastness, fleetness, haste, hurry, quickness, rapidity, speed, swiftness

ve•lour *or* **ve•lours** \və-ˈlu̇r\ *n, pl* **velours** \-ˈlu̇rz\ **:** any of various textile fabrics with pile like that of velvet

ve•lum \ˈvē-ləm\ *n, pl* **ve•la** \-lə\ **:** a membranous body part (as the soft palate) resembling a veil

vel•vet \ˈvel-vət\ *n* **1 :** a fabric having a short soft dense warp pile **2 :** something resembling or suggesting velvet (as in softness or luster) **3 :** the soft skin covering the growing antlers of deer — **velvet** *adj*

vel•ve•teen \ˌvel-və-ˈtēn\ *n* **1 :** a fabric woven usually of cotton in imitation of velvet **2** *pl* **:** clothes made of velveteen

vel•vety \ˈvel-və-tē\ *adj* ♦ **:** having the character of velvet as in being soft, smooth, thick, or richly hued

♦ cottony, downy, satiny, silken, soft

Ven *abbr* venerable

ve•nal \ˈvēn-ᵊl\ *adj* ♦ **:** capable of being bought or bribed — **ve•nal•i•ty** \vi-ˈnal-ə-tē\ *n* — **ve•nal•ly** \ˈvēn-ᵊl-ē\ *adv*

♦ bribable, corruptible, purchasable *Ant* incorruptible

ve•na•tion \ve-ˈnā-shən, vē-\ *n* **:** an arrangement or system of veins ⟨the ~ of the hand⟩ ⟨leaf ~⟩

vend \ˈvend\ *vb* ♦ **:** to sell especially as a hawker or peddler — **vend•ible** *adj*

♦ deal, market, merchandise, put up, retail, sell

vend•ee \ven-ˈdē\ *n* **:** one to whom a thing is sold **:** BUYER

ven•det•ta \ven-ˈde-tə\ *n* **:** a feud marked by acts of revenge

vending machine *n* **:** a coin-operated machine for selling merchandise

ven•dor \ˈven-dər, *for 1 also* ven-ˈdȯr\ *n* **1** ♦ **:** one that vends **:** SELLER **2 :** VENDING MACHINE

♦ dealer, seller *Ant* buyer, purchaser

[1]**ve•neer** \və-ˈnir\ *n* **1 :** a thin usually superficial layer of material ⟨brick ~⟩; *esp* **:** a thin layer of fine wood glued over a cheaper wood **2 :** superficial display **:** GLOSS **3** ♦ **:** a protective or ornamental facing (as of brick or stone)

♦ exterior, face, outside, skin, surface

[2]**veneer** *vb* **:** to overlay with a veneer

ven•er•a•ble \ˈve-nə-rə-bəl\ *adj* **1 :** deserving to be venerated — often used as a religious title **2 :** made sacred by association **3 a** ♦ **:** calling forth respect through age, character, and attainments ⟨a ~ jazz musician⟩ **b** ♦ **:** impressive by reason of age ⟨under ~ pines⟩

♦ [3a] hallowed, reverend ♦ [3b] age-old, ancient, antediluvian, antique, dateless, hoary, old

ven•er•ate \ˈve-nə-ˌrāt\ *vb* **-at•ed; -at•ing** ♦ **:** to regard with reverential respect — **ven•er•a•tion** \ˌve-nə-ˈrā-shən\ *n*

♦ adore, deify, glorify, revere, worship

ve•ne•re•al \və-ˈnir-ē-əl\ *adj* **:** of or relating to sexual intercourse or to diseases transmitted by it ⟨a ~ infection⟩

venereal disease *n* **:** a contagious disease (as gonorrhea or syphilis) usually acquired by having sexual intercourse with someone who already has it

ve•ne•tian blind \və-ˈnē-shən-\ *n* **:** a blind having thin horizontal parallel slats that can be adjusted to admit a desired amount of light

Ven•e•zue•lan \ˌve-nə-ˈzwā-lən\ *n* **:** a native or inhabitant of Venezuela — **Venezuelan** *adj*

ven•geance \ˈven-jəns\ *n* ♦ **:** punishment inflicted in retaliation for an injury or offense **:** REVENGE

♦ reprisal, requital, retaliation, retribution, revenge

venge•ful \ˈvenj-fəl\ *adj* **:** filled with a desire for revenge **:** VINDICTIVE — **venge•ful•ly** *adv*

ve•nial \ˈvē-nē-əl\ *adj* ♦ **:** capable of being forgiven **:** EXCUSABLE ⟨~ sin⟩

♦ excusable, forgivable, pardonable *Ant* inexcusable, mortal, unforgivable, unpardonable

ve•ni•re \və-ˈnī-rē\ *n* **:** a panel from which a jury is drawn

ve•ni•re fa•ci•as \-ˈfā-shē-əs\ *n* **:** a writ summoning persons to appear in court to serve as jurors

ve•ni•re•man \və-ˈnī-rē-mən, -ˈnir-ē-\ *n* **:** a member of a venire

ven•i•son \ˈven-ə-sən, -zən\ *n, pl* **venisons** *also* **venison :** the edible flesh of a deer

ven•om \ˈve-nəm\ *n* **1** ♦ **:** poisonous material secreted by some animals (as snakes, spiders, or bees) and transmitted usually by biting or stinging **2** ♦ **:** desire to cause pain, injury, or distress to another **:** MALEVOLENCE

♦ [1] bane, poison, toxin ♦ [2] cattiness, despite, hatefulness, malice, malignity, meanness, nastiness, spite, spleen, viciousness

ven•om•ous \ˈve-nə-məs\ *adj* **1** ♦ **:** full of venom **:** POISONOUS **2 :** SPITEFUL, MALEVOLENT **3 :** secreting and using venom ⟨~ snakes⟩ — **ven•om•ous•ly** *adv*

♦ poison, poisonous

ve•nous \ˈvē-nəs\ *adj* **1 :** of, relating to, or full of veins **2 :** being purplish red oxygen-deficient blood rich in carbon dioxide that is present in most veins

¹vent \ˈvent\ *vb* **1 :** to provide with a vent **2 :** to serve as a vent for **3** ♦ **:** to force out **:** DISCHARGE **4** ♦ **:** to give vigorous or emotional expression to

♦ [3] cast, discharge, emit, exhale, expel, issue, release, shoot ♦ [4] loose, release, take out, unleash ♦ [4] air, express, give, look, sound, state, voice

²vent *n* **1 :** an opportunity or way of escape or passage **:** OUTLET **2 :** an opening for the escape of a gas or liquid or for the relief of pressure

³vent *n* **:** a slit in a garment especially in the lower part of a seam (as of a jacket or skirt)

ven•ti•late \ˈvent-ᵊl-ˌāt\ *vb* **-lat•ed; -lat•ing** **1 :** to discuss freely and openly ⟨~ a question⟩ **2 :** to give vigorous or emotional expression to ⟨~ one's grievances⟩ **3 :** to cause fresh air to circulate through (as a room or mine) so as to replace foul air **4 :** to provide with a vent or outlet — **ven•ti•la•tor** \-ᵊl-ˌā-tər\ *n*

ven•ti•la•tion \ˌvent-ᵊl-ˈā-shən\ *n* **1 :** the act or process of ventilating **2 :** circulation of air (as in a room) **3 :** a system or means of providing fresh air

ven•tral \ˈven-trəl\ *adj* **1 :** of or relating to the belly **:** ABDOMINAL **2 :** of, relating to, or located on or near the surface of the body that in humans is the front but in most other animals is the lower surface — **ven•tral•ly** *adv*

ven•tri•cle \ˈven-tri-kəl\ *n* **1 :** a chamber of the heart that receives blood from the atrium of the same side and pumps it into the arteries **2 :** any of the communicating cavities of the brain that are continuous with the central canal of the spinal cord — **ven•tric•u•lar** \ven-ˈtri-kyə-lər\ *adj*

ven•tril•o•quism \ven-ˈtri-lə-ˌkwi-zəm\ *n* **:** the production of the voice in such a manner that the sound appears to come from a source other than the speaker — **ven•tril•o•quist** \-kwist\ *n*

ven•tril•o•quy \-kwē\ *n* **:** VENTRILOQUISM

¹ven•ture \ˈven-chər\ *vb* **ven•tured; ven•tur•ing** **1** ♦ **:** to expose to hazard **:** RISK **2 :** to undertake the risks of **:** BRAVE **3** ♦ **:** to offer at the risk of rebuff, rejection, or censure ⟨~ an opinion⟩ **4 :** to proceed despite danger **:** DARE

♦ [1] adventure, compromise, gamble with, hazard, imperil, jeopardize, menace, risk ♦ [3] chance, gamble, hazard, risk

²venture *n* **1** ♦ **:** an undertaking involving chance or risk; *esp* **:** a speculative business enterprise **2 :** something risked in a speculative venture **:** STAKE

♦ chance, enterprise, flier, gamble, speculation

ven•ture•some \ˈven-chər-səm\ *adj* **1** ♦ **:** involving risk **:** DANGEROUS **2** ♦ **:** inclined to venture **:** BOLD — **ven•ture•some•ly** *adv* — **ven•ture•some•ness** *n*

♦ [1] dangerous, grave, grievous, hazardous, menacing, parlous, perilous, risky, serious, unhealthy, unsafe ♦ [2] adventurous, audacious, bold, daring, enterprising, gutsy, hardy, nervy

ven•tur•ous \ˈven-chə-rəs\ *adj* **1 :** involving risk **:** DANGEROUS, HAZARDOUS **2 :** inclined to venture **:** BOLD — **ven•tur•ous•ly** *adv* — **ven•tur•ous•ness** *n*

ven•ue \ˈven-yü\ *n* **:** the place in which the alleged events from which a legal action arises took place; *also* **:** the place from which the jury is taken and where the trial is held

Ve•nus \ˈvē-nəs\ *n* **:** the planet 2d in order from the sun

Venus fly•trap \-ˈflī-ˌtrap\ *or* **Ve•nus's–fly•trap** \ˈvē-nə-səz-ˈflī-ˌtrap\ *n* **:** an insect-eating plant of the Carolina coast that has the leaf tip modified into an insect trap

Ve•nu•sian \vi-ˈnü-zhən, -ˈnyü-\ *adj* **:** of or relating to the planet Venus

ve•ra•cious \və-ˈrā-shəs\ *adj* **1 :** TRUTHFUL, HONEST **2** ♦ **:** marked by truth **:** ACCURATE — **ve•ra•cious•ly** *adv*

♦ accurate, authentic, exact, faithful, precise, right, strict, true

ve•rac•i•ty \və-ˈra-sə-tē\ *n, pl* **-ties** **1** ♦ **:** devotion to truth **:** TRUTHFULNESS **2** ♦ **:** conformity with fact **:** ACCURACY **3 :** something true

♦ [1] honesty, integrity, probity, truthfulness, verity ♦ [2] accuracy, closeness, delicacy, exactness, fineness, precision

ve•ran•da *or* **ve•ran•dah** \və-ˈran-də\ *n* **:** a long open usually roofed porch

verb \ˈvərb\ *n* **:** a word that is the grammatical center of a predicate and expresses an act, occurrence, or mode of being

¹ver•bal \ˈvər-bəl\ *adj* **1 :** of, relating to, or consisting of words; *esp* **:** having to do with words rather than with the ideas to be conveyed **2** ♦ **:** expressed in usually spoken words **:** ORAL ⟨a ~ contract⟩ **3 :** of, relating to, or formed from a verb **4 :** LITERAL, VERBATIM — **ver•bal•ly** *adv*

♦ oral, spoken, unwritten ***Ant*** written

²verbal *n* **:** a word that combines characteristics of a verb with those of a noun or adjective

verbal auxiliary *n* **:** an auxiliary verb

ver•bal•ize \ˈvər-bə-ˌlīz\ *vb* **-ized; -iz•ing** **1 :** to speak or write in wordy or empty fashion **2** ♦ **:** to express something in words **:** describe verbally **3 :** to convert into a verb — **ver•bal•i•za•tion** \ˌvər-bə-lə-ˈzā-shən\ *n*

♦ articulate, say, speak, state, talk, tell, utter, vocalize

verbal noun *n* **:** a noun derived directly from a verb or verb stem and in some uses having the sense and constructions of a verb

ver•ba•tim \(ˌ)vər-ˈbā-təm\ *adv or adj* **:** in the same words **:** word for word

ver•be•na \(ˌ)vər-ˈbē-nə\ *n* **:** VERVAIN; *esp* **:** any of several garden vervains of hybrid origin with showy spikes of bright often fragrant flowers

ver•biage \ˈvər-bē-ij, -bij\ *n* **1** ♦ **:** superfluity of words usually of little or obscure content **2 :** DICTION, WORDING

♦ circumlocution, prolixity, redundancy, wordiness

ver•bose \(ˌ)vər-ˈbōs\ *adj* ♦ **:** using more words than are needed **:** WORDY

♦ circuitous, diffuse, long-winded, prolix, rambling, windy, wordy

ver•bos•i•ty \(ˌ)vər-ˈbä-sə-tē\ *n* **:** the quality or state of being verbose

ver•bo•ten \vər-ˈbōt-ᵊn, fər-\ *adj* **:** forbidden usually by dictate

ver•dant \ˈvərd-ᵊnt\ *adj* ♦ **:** green with growing plants — **verdant•ly** *adv*

♦ green, leafy, lush, luxuriant

ver•dict \ˈvər-(ˌ)dikt\ *n* **1 :** the finding or decision of a jury **2** ♦ **:** an opinion pronounced or felt **:** JUDGMENT

♦ belief, conviction, eye, feeling, judgment (*or* judgement), mind, notion, opinion, persuasion, sentiment, view

ver•di•gris \ˈvər-də-ˌgrēs, -ˌgris\ *n* **:** a green or bluish deposit that forms on copper, brass, or bronze surfaces

ver•dure \ˈvər-jər\ *n* **1 :** the greenness of growing vegetation **2** ♦ **:** a growth or expanse of vegetation

♦ flora, foliage, green, greenery, herbage, leafage, vegetation

¹verge \ˈvərj\ *n* **1 :** a staff carried as an emblem of authority or office **2** ♦ **:** something that borders or bounds **:** EDGE **3 :** BRINK, THRESHOLD

♦ border, bound, boundary, circumference, compass, confines, edge, end, fringe, margin, perimeter, periphery, rim, skirt

²verge *vb* **verged; verg•ing** **1** ♦ **:** to be next to — often used with *on* **2 :** to be on the verge

♦ *often* **verge on** abut, adjoin, border (on), flank, fringe, join, skirt, touch

³verge *vb* **verged; verg•ing** **1 :** to move or extend in some direction or toward some condition **:** INCLINE **2 :** to be in transition or change

verg•er \ˈvər-jər\ *n* **1** *chiefly Brit* **:** an attendant who carries a verge (as before a bishop) **2 :** SEXTON

ve•rid•i•cal \və-ˈri-di-kəl\ *adj* **1 :** TRUTHFUL **2 :** not illusory **:** GENUINE

ver•i•fi•able \ˌver-ə-ˈfī-ə-bəl\ *adj* ♦ **:** capable of being verified

♦ demonstrable, provable, supportable, sustainable ***Ant*** insupportable, unsupportable

ver•i•fy \ˈver-ə-ˌfī\ *vb* **-fied; -fy•ing** **1 :** to confirm in law by oath **2** ♦ **:** to establish the truth, accuracy, or reality of — **ver•i•fi•ca•tion** \ˌver-ə-fə-ˈkā-shən\ *n*

♦ bear out, confirm, corroborate, substantiate, support, validate, vindicate

ver•i•ly \ˈver-ə-lē\ *adv* ♦ : in truth : in actual fact

♦ actually, frankly, honestly, really, truly, truthfully

veri•si•mil•i•tude \ˌver-ə-sə-ˈmi-lə-ˌtüd, -ˌtyüd\ *n* : the quality or state of appearing to be true or real
ver•i•ta•ble \ˈver-ə-tə-bəl\ *adj* : ACTUAL, GENUINE, TRUE
ver•i•ta•bly \ˈver-ə-tə-blē\ *adv* ♦ : in a way that is genuine or true

♦ actually, authentically, genuinely, really, very

ver•i•ty \ˈver-ə-tē\ *n, pl* **-ties** **1** : the quality or state of being true or real : TRUTH, REALITY **2** : something (as a statement) that is true **3** ♦ : the quality or state of being truthful or honest : HONESTY

♦ honesty, integrity, probity, truthfulness, veracity

ver•meil *n* **1** \ˈvər-məl, -ˌmāl\ : VERMILION **2** \ver-ˈmā\ : gilded silver
ver•mi•cel•li \ˌvər-mə-ˈche-lē, -ˈse-\ *n* : a pasta made in thinner strings than spaghetti
ver•mic•u•lite \vər-ˈmi-kyə-ˌlīt\ *n* : any of various lightweight water-absorbent minerals derived from mica
ver•mi•form appendix \ˈvər-mə-ˌform-\ *n* : APPENDIX 2
ver•mil•ion *also* **ver•mil•lion** \vər-ˈmil-yən\ *n* : a bright reddish orange color; *also* : any of various red pigments
ver•min \ˈvər-mən\ *n, pl* **vermin** **1** : small common harmful or objectionable animals (as lice or mice) that are difficult to get rid of **2** : birds and mammals that prey on game — **ver•min•ous** *adj*
ver•mouth \vər-ˈmüth\ *n* : a dry or sweet wine flavored with herbs and often used in mixed drinks
[1]**ver•nac•u•lar** \vər-ˈna-kyə-lər\ *adj* **1** : of, relating to, or being a language or dialect native to a region or country rather than a literary, cultured, or foreign language **2** ♦ : of, relating to, or being the normal spoken form of a language **3** : applied to a plant or animal in common speech as distinguished from biological nomenclature ⟨~ names⟩

♦ colloquial, conversational, informal, nonliterary, vulgar

[2]**vernacular** *n* **1** : a vernacular language **2** : the mode of expression of a group or class **3** : a vernacular name of a plant or animal
ver•nal \ˈvərn-ᵊl\ *adj* : of, relating to, or occurring in the spring
ver•ni•er \ˈvər-nē-ər\ *n* : a short scale made to slide along the divisions of a graduated instrument to indicate parts of divisions
ve•ron•i•ca \və-ˈrä-ni-kə\ *n* : any of a genus of herbs related to the snapdragons that have small usually bluish flowers
ver•sa•tile \ˈvər-sət-ᵊl\ *adj* **1** : turning with ease from one thing or position to another **2** ♦ : having many aptitudes — **ver•sa•til•i•ty** \ˌvər-sə-ˈti-lə-tē\ *n*

♦ adaptable, all-around, protean, universal

[1]**verse** \ˈvərs\ *n* **1** : a line of poetry; *also* : STANZA **2** : metrical writing distinguished from poetry especially by its lower level of intensity **3** ♦ : writing that creates a specific emotional response through the intentional use of meaning, sound, and rhythm : POETRY **4** : a composition in verse : POEM **5** : one of the short divisions of a chapter in the Bible

♦ poetry, song

[2]**verse** *vb* **versed; vers•ing** : to familiarize by experience, study, or practice ⟨well *versed* in the theater⟩
versed *adj* ♦ : acquainted or familiar from experience, study, or practice

♦ abreast, conversant, familiar, informed, knowledgeable, up, up-to-date

ver•si•cle \ˈvər-si-kəl\ *n* : a verse or sentence said or sung by a leader in public worship and followed by a response from the people
ver•si•fi•ca•tion \ˌvər-sə-fə-ˈkā-shən\ *n* **1** : the making of verses **2** : metrical structure
ver•si•fi•er \ˈvər-sə-ˌfī-ər\ *n* ♦ : one that versifies

♦ bard, minstrel, poet

ver•si•fy \ˈvər-sə-ˌfī\ *vb* **-fied; -fy•ing** **1** : to write verse **2** : to turn into verse
ver•sion \ˈvər-zhən\ *n* **1** : TRANSLATION; *esp* : a translation of the Bible **2** : an account or description from a particular point of view especially as contrasted with another **3** : a form or variant of a type or original
vers li•bre \ˌver-ˈlēbrᵊ\ *n, pl* **vers li•bres** *same*\ : FREE VERSE
ver•so \ˈvər-sō\ *n, pl* **versos** : a left-hand page
ver•sus \ˈvər-səs\ *prep* **1** : AGAINST 1 ⟨the champion ~ the challenger⟩ **2** : in contrast or as an alternative to ⟨free trade ~ protection⟩
vert *abbr* vertical
ver•te•bra \ˈvər-tə-brə\ *n, pl* **-brae** \-ˌbrā, -(ˌ)brē\ *or* **-bras** : one of the segments of bone or cartilage making up the backbone
ver•te•bral \(ˌ)vər-ˈtē-brəl, ˈvər-tə-\ *adj* : of, relating to, or made up of vertebrae : SPINAL
vertebral column *n* ♦ : the bony column in the back of a vertebrate that is the chief support of the trunk and consists of a jointed series of vertebrae enclosing and protecting the spinal cord : BACKBONE

♦ backbone, spine

[1]**ver•te•brate** \ˈvər-tə-brət, -ˌbrāt\ *adj* **1** : having a backbone **2** : of or relating to the vertebrates
[2]**vertebrate** *n* : any of a large group of animals (as mammals, birds, reptiles, amphibians, or fishes) that have a backbone or in some primitive forms (as a lamprey) a flexible rod of cells and that have a tubular nervous system arranged along the back and divided into a brain and spinal cord
ver•tex \ˈvər-ˌteks\ *n, pl* **ver•ti•ces** \ˈvər-tə-ˌsēz\ *also* **ver•tex•es** **1** : the point opposite to and farthest from the base of a geometrical figure **2** : the point where the sides of an angle or three or more edges of a polyhedron (as a cube) meet **3** : the highest point : TOP, SUMMIT
ver•ti•cal \ˈvər-ti-kəl\ *adj* **1** : of, relating to, or located at the vertex : directly overhead **2** ♦ : rising perpendicularly from a level surface : UPRIGHT — **vertical** *n* — **ver•ti•cal•i•ty** \ˌvər-tə-ˈka-lə-tē\ *n* — **ver•ti•cal•ly** \-k(ə-)lē\ *adv*

♦ erect, perpendicular, standing, upright, upstanding

ver•tig•i•nous \(ˌ)vər-ˈti-jə-nəs\ *adj* : marked by, affected with, or tending to cause dizziness
ver•ti•go \ˈvər-ti-ˌgō\ *n, pl* **-goes** *or* **-gos** : DIZZINESS, GIDDINESS
vertu *var of* VIRTU
ver•vain \ˈvər-ˌvān\ *n* : any of a genus of chiefly American herbs or low woody plants with often showy heads or spikes of tubular flowers
verve \ˈvərv\ *n* **1** : liveliness of imagination **2** ♦ : the quality or state of being lively in temper, conduct, or spirit

♦ bounce, dash, drive, esprit, pep, punch, snap, spirit, vim, zing, zip

[1]**very** \ˈver-ē\ *adj* **veri•er; -est** **1** : EXACT, PRECISE ⟨the ~ heart of the city⟩ **2** : exactly suitable ⟨the ~ tool for the job⟩ **3** : ABSOLUTE, UTTER ⟨the *veriest* nonsense⟩ **4** — used as an intensive especially to emphasize identity ⟨before my ~ eyes⟩ **5** : MERE, BARE ⟨the ~ idea scared him⟩ **6** ♦ : being the same one : IDENTICAL ⟨the ~ man I saw⟩ **7** ♦ : existing in fact or reality : ACTUAL

♦ [6] identical, same, selfsame ♦ [7] actual, concrete, existent, factual, real, true

[2]**very** *adv* **1** ♦ : in actual fact **2** ♦ : to a high degree : EXTREMELY

♦ [1] actually, authentically, genuinely, really, veritably ***Ant*** professedly, supposedly ♦ [2] extra, extremely, greatly, highly, hugely, mightily, mighty, mortally, most, much, real, right, so ***Ant*** little, nominally, slightly

very high frequency *n* : a radio frequency of between 30 and 300 megahertz
ves•i•cant \ˈve-si-kənt\ *n* : an agent that causes blistering — **vesicant** *adj*
ves•i•cle \ˈve-si-kəl\ *n* : a membranous and usually fluid-filled cavity in a plant or animal; *also* : BLISTER — **ve•sic•u•lar** \və-ˈsi-kyə-lər\ *adj*
[1]**ves•per** \ˈves-pər\ *n* **1** *cap, archaic* : EVENING STAR **2** : a vesper bell **3** *archaic* : EVENING, EVENTIDE
[2]**vesper** *adj* : of or relating to vespers or the evening
ves•pers \-pərz\ *n pl, often cap* : a late afternoon or evening worship service
ves•sel \ˈve-səl\ *n* **1** ♦ : a container (as a barrel, bottle, bowl, or cup) for holding something **2** : a person held to be the recipient of a quality (as grace) **3** ♦ : a craft bigger than a rowboat **4** : a tube in which a body fluid (as blood or sap) is contained and circulated

♦ [1] container, holder, receptacle ♦ [3] boat, bottom, craft

[1]**vest** \ˈvest\ *vb* **1** ♦ : to place or give into the possession or discretion of some person or authority **2** : to grant or endow with a particular authority, right, or property **3** : to become legally vested **4** : to clothe with or as if with a garment; *esp* : to garb in ecclesiastical vestments

♦ commend, commit, consign, delegate, deliver, entrust, give, hand over, leave, pass, transfer, transmit, trust, turn over

[2]**vest** *n* **1 :** a sleeveless garment for the upper body usually worn over a shirt **2** *chiefly Brit* **:** a man's sleeveless undershirt **3 :** a front piece of a dress resembling the front of a vest
[1]**ves•tal** \ˈvest-ᵊl\ *adj* **:** CHASTE
[2]**vestal** *n* **:** VESTAL VIRGIN
vestal virgin *n* **1 :** a virgin consecrated to the Roman goddess Vesta and to the service of watching the sacred fire perpetually kept burning on her altar **2 :** a chaste woman
vest•ed \ˈves-təd\ *adj* **:** fully and unconditionally guaranteed as a legal right, benefit, or privilege
vested interest *n* **:** an interest (as in an existing political, economic, or social arrangement) to which the holder has a strong commitment; *also* **:** one (as a corporation) having a vested interest
ves•ti•bule \ˈves-tə-ˌbyül\ *n* **1 :** any of various bodily cavities forming or suggesting an entrance to some other cavity or space **2** ♦ **:** a passage or room between the outer door and the interior of a building — **ves•tib•u•lar** \ve-ˈsti-byə-lər\ *adj*

♦ entry, foyer, hall, lobby

ves•tige \ˈves-tij\ *n* ♦ **:** a trace or visible sign left by something lost or vanished; *also* **:** a minute remaining amount — **ves•ti•gial** \ve-ˈsti-jē-əl, -jəl\ *adj* — **ves•ti•gial•ly** *adv*

♦ relic, shadow, trace

vest•ing \ˈves-tiŋ\ *n* **:** the conveying to an employee of inalienable rights to share in a pension fund; *also* **:** the right so conveyed
vest•ment \ˈvest-mənt\ *n* **1 :** an outer garment; *esp* **:** a ceremonial or official robe **2** *pl* **:** CLOTHING, GARB **3 :** a garment or insignia worn by a cleric when officiating or assisting at a religious service
vest–pocket *adj* **:** very small ⟨a ~ park⟩
ves•try \ˈves-trē\ *n, pl* **vestries 1 :** a room in a church for vestments, altar linens, and sacred vessels **2 :** a room used for church meetings and classes **3 :** a body administering the temporal affairs of an Episcopal parish
ves•try•man \-mən\ *n* **:** a member of a vestry
ves•ture \ˈves-chər\ *n* **1 :** a covering garment **2 :** CLOTHING, APPAREL
[1]**vet** \ˈvet\ *n* **:** VETERINARIAN
[2]**vet** *adj or n* **:** VETERAN
[3]**vet** *vb* **:** to evaluate for appraisal or acceptance ⟨~ a manuscript⟩
vetch \ˈvech\ *n* **:** any of a genus of twining leguminous herbs including some grown for fodder and green manure
[1]**vet•er•an** \ˈve-trən, -tə-rən\ *n* **1 :** an old soldier of long service **2 :** a former member of the armed forces **3 :** a person of long experience usually in an occupation or skill
[2]**veteran** *adj* **:** of, relating to, or characteristic of a veteran
Veterans Day *n* **:** November 11 observed as a legal holiday in commemoration of the end of hostilities in 1918 and 1945
vet•er•i•nar•i•an \ˌve-trə-ˈner-ē-ən, ˌve-tə-rə-\ *n* **:** one qualified and authorized to practice veterinary medicine
[1]**vet•er•i•nary** \ˈve-trə-ˌner-ē, ˈve-tə-rə-\ *adj* **:** of, relating to, or being the medical care of animals and especially domestic animals
[2]**veterinary** *n, pl* **-nar•ies :** VETERINARIAN
[1]**ve•to** \ˈvē-tō\ *n, pl* **vetoes 1** ♦ **:** an authoritative prohibition **2 :** a power of one part of a government to forbid the carrying out of projects attempted by another part; *esp* **:** a power vested in a chief executive to prevent the carrying out of measures adopted by a legislature **3 :** the exercise of the power of veto

♦ ban, embargo, interdict, interdiction, prohibition, proscription

[2]**veto** *vb* **1** ♦ **:** to refuse to admit or approve **2** ♦ **:** to refuse assent to (a legislative bill) so as to prevent enactment or cause reconsideration — **ve•to•er** *n*

♦ [1, 2] blackball, kill, negative

vex \ˈveks\ *vb* **vexed** *also* **vext; vex•ing 1 :** to bring trouble, distress, or agitation to **2** ♦ **:** to annoy continually with little irritations

♦ aggravate, annoy, bother, bug, chafe, exasperate, gall, get, grate, irk, irritate, nettle, peeve, persecute, pique, put out, rasp, rile

vex•a•tion \vek-ˈsā-shən\ *n* **1** ♦ **:** the act of vexing **2 :** the quality or state of being vexed **:** IRRITATION **3 :** a cause of trouble or annoyance

♦ aggravation, annoyance, disturbance, harassment

vex•a•tious \-shəs\ *adj* **1** ♦ **:** causing vexation **:** ANNOYING **2 :** full of distress or annoyance **:** TROUBLED — **vex•a•tious•ly** *adv* — **vex•a•tious•ness** *n*

♦ aggravating, annoying, bothersome, frustrating, galling, irksome, irritating, pesty

vexed \ˈvekst\ *adj* **:** fully debated or discussed ⟨a ~ question⟩
vexing *adj* **:** causing or likely to cause vexation
VF *abbr* **1** video frequency **2** visual field
VFD *abbr* volunteer fire department
VFW *abbr* Veterans of Foreign Wars
VG *abbr* **1** very good **2** vicar-general
VHF *abbr* very high frequency
VI *abbr* Virgin Islands
via \ˈvī-ə, ˈvē-ə\ *prep* **1 :** by way of **2 :** by means of
vi•a•ble \ˈvī-ə-bəl\ *adj* **1 :** capable of living; *esp* **:** sufficiently developed as to be capable of surviving outside the mother's womb ⟨a ~ fetus⟩ **2 :** capable of growing and developing ⟨~ seeds⟩ **3** ♦ **:** capable of being put into practice **:** WORKABLE **4 :** having a reasonable chance of succeeding ⟨a ~ candidate⟩ — **vi•a•bil•i•ty** \ˌvī-ə-ˈbi-lə-tē\ *n* — **vi•a•bly** \ˈvī-ə-blē\ *adv*

♦ achievable, attainable, doable, feasible, possible, practicable, realizable, workable

via•duct \ˈvī-ə-ˌdəkt\ *n* **:** a long elevated roadway usually consisting of a series of short spans supported on arches, piers, or columns
vi•al \ˈvī-əl\ *n* **:** a small vessel for liquids
vi•and \ˈvī-ənd\ *n* **1 :** an article of food **2** ♦ **:** a stock of food — usually used in plural

♦ *usu* **viands** chow, fare, food, grub, meat, provender, provisions

vi•at•i•cum \vī-ˈa-ti-kəm, vē-\ *n, pl* **-cums** *or* **-ca** \-kə\ **1 :** the Christian Eucharist given to a person in danger of death **2 :** an allowance especially in money for traveling needs and expenses
vibes \ˈvībz\ *n pl* **1 :** VIBRAPHONE **2 :** VIBRATIONS
vi•bran•cy \ˈvī-brən-sē\ *n* ♦ **:** the quality or state of being vibrant

♦ animation, briskness, exuberance, liveliness, lustiness, robustness, sprightliness, vitality

vi•brant \ˈvī-brənt\ *adj* **1 :** VIBRATING, PULSATING **2** ♦ **:** pulsating with vigor or activity **3 :** readily set in vibration **:** RESPONSIVE **4** ♦ **:** sounding from vibration **:** RESONANT; *also* **:** intensified and enriched by or as if by resonance **5 :** BRIGHT ⟨~ colors⟩

♦ [2] alive, animated, astir, busy, lively ♦ [4] golden, resonant, resounding, ringing, round, sonorous

vi•bra•phone \ˈvī-brə-ˌfōn\ *n* **:** a percussion instrument like the xylophone but with metal bars and motor-driven resonators
vi•brate \ˈvī-ˌbrāt\ *vb* **vi•brat•ed; vi•brat•ing 1 :** OSCILLATE **2 :** to set in vibration **3** ♦ **:** to be in vibration **:** QUIVER **4 :** WAVER, FLUCTUATE **5 :** to respond sympathetically **:** THRILL

♦ agitate, convulse, jolt, jounce, quake, quiver, shake, shudder, wobble

vi•bra•tion \vī-ˈbrā-shən\ *n* **1 :** a rapid to-and-fro motion of the particles of an elastic body or medium (as a stretched cord) that produces sound **2** ♦ **:** an act of vibrating **:** OSCILLATION **3 :** a trembling motion **4 :** VACILLATION **5 :** a feeling or impression that someone or something gives off — usually used in plural ⟨good ~*s*⟩ — **vi•bra•tion•al** \-shə-nəl\ *adj*

♦ oscillation, quivering

vi•bra•to \vi-ˈbrä-tō\ *n, pl* **-tos :** a slightly tremulous effect imparted to vocal or instrumental music
vi•bra•tor \ˈvī-ˌbrā-tər\ *n* **:** one that vibrates or causes vibration; *esp* **:** a vibrating electrical device used in massage or for sexual stimulation
vi•bra•to•ry \ˈvī-brə-ˌtōr-ē\ *adj* **:** consisting of, capable of, or causing vibration
vi•bur•num \vī-ˈbər-nəm\ *n* **:** any of a genus of widely distributed shrubs or small trees related to the honeysuckle and bearing small usually white flowers in broad clusters
vic *abbr* vicinity
Vic *abbr* Victoria
vic•ar \ˈvi-kər\ *n* **1 :** an administrative deputy **2 :** a minister in charge of a church who serves under the authority of another minister — **vi•car•i•ate** \vī-ˈker-ē-ət\ *n*
vic•ar•age \ˈvi-kə-rij\ *n* **:** a vicar's home
vicar–general *n, pl* **vicars–general :** an administrative deputy (as of a Roman Catholic or Anglican bishop)
vi•car•i•ous \vī-ˈker-ē-əs, -ˈkar-\ *adj* **1 :** acting for another **2 :** done or suffered by one person on behalf of another or others ⟨a ~ sacrifice⟩ **3 :** sharing in someone else's experience

through the use of the imagination or sympathetic feelings — **vi·car·i·ous·ly** *adv* — **vi·car·i·ous·ness** *n*

¹vice \ˈvīs\ *n* **1** ♦ **:** moral depravity or corruption **2** ♦ **:** a moral fault or failing **3 :** an habitual usually trivial fault **4 :** an undesirable behavior pattern in a domestic animal

♦ [1] corruption, debauchery, depravity, immorality, iniquity, licentiousness, sin *Ant* morality, virtue ♦ [2] demerit, failing, fault, foible, frailty, shortcoming, weakness

²vice *chiefly Brit var of* VISE

³vice *prep* **:** in the place of; *also* **:** rather than

vice admiral *n* **:** a commissioned officer in the navy or coast guard ranking above a rear admiral

vice·ge·rent \ˈvīs-ˈjir-ənt\ *n* **:** an administrative deputy of a king or magistrate — **vice·ge·ren·cy** \-ən-sē\ *n*

vi·cen·ni·al \vī-ˈse-nē-əl\ *adj* **:** occurring once every 20 years

vice presidency *n* **:** the office of vice president

vice president *n* **1 :** an officer ranking next to a president and usually empowered to act for the president during an absence or disability **2 :** any of several of a president's deputies

vice·re·gal \ˈvīs-ˈrē-gəl\ *adj* **:** of or relating to a viceroy

vice·roy \ˈvīs-ˌrȯi\ *n* **:** the governor of a country or province who rules as representative of the sovereign — **vice·roy·al·ty** \-əl-tē\ *n*

vice ver·sa \ˌvī-si-ˈvər-sə, ˈvīs-ˈvər-\ *adv* **:** with the order reversed

vi·chys·soise \ˌvi-shē-ˈswäz, ˌvē-\ *n* **:** a soup made especially from leeks or onions and potatoes, cream, and chicken stock and usually served cold

vic·i·nage \ˈvis-ᵊn-ij\ *n* **:** a neighboring or surrounding district **:** VICINITY

vi·cin·i·ty \və-ˈsi-nə-tē\ *n, pl* **-ties 1 :** NEARNESS, PROXIMITY **2 :** a surrounding area **:** NEIGHBORHOOD

vi·cious \ˈvi-shəs\ *adj* **1** ♦ **:** having the quality of vice **:** WICKED **2 :** DEFECTIVE, FAULTY; *also* **:** INVALID **3 :** IMPURE, FOUL **4** ♦ **:** having a savage disposition; *also* **:** marked by violence or ferocity **5 :** MALICIOUS, SPITEFUL **6 :** worsened by internal causes that augment each other ⟨~ wage-price spiral⟩

♦ [1] bad, black, evil, immoral, iniquitous, nefarious, rotten, sinful, unethical, unsavory, vile, villainous, wicked, wrong ♦ [4] barbarous, brutal, cruel, heartless, inhumane, sadistic, savage, wanton ♦ [4] fell, ferocious, fierce, grim, savage

vi·cious·ly *adv* ♦ **:** in a vicious manner

♦ hatefully, maliciously, meanly, nastily, spitefully, wickedly

vi·cious·ness *n* ♦ **:** the quality or state of being vicious

♦ cattiness, despite, hatefulness, malice, malignity, meanness, nastiness, spite, spleen, venom

vi·cis·si·tude \və-ˈsi-sə-ˌtüd, vī-, -ˌtyüd\ *n* **:** an irregular, unexpected, or surprising change

vic·tim \ˈvik-təm\ *n* **1 :** a living being offered as a sacrifice in a religious rite **2** ♦ **:** an individual injured or killed (as by disease or accident) **3** ♦ **:** a person cheated, fooled, or injured ⟨a ~ of circumstances⟩

♦ [2] casualty, fatality, loss ♦ [3] butt, mark, target

vic·tim·ise *chiefly Brit var of* VICTIMIZE

vic·tim·ize \ˈvik-tə-ˌmīz\ *vb* **-ized; -iz·ing** ♦ **:** to make a victim of — **vic·tim·i·za·tion** \ˌvik-tə-mə-ˈzā-shən\ *n* — **vic·tim·iz·er** \ˈvik-tə-ˌmī-zər\ *n*

♦ bleed, cheat, chisel, cozen, defraud, fleece, gyp, hustle, mulct, rook, shortchange, skin, squeeze, stick, sting, swindle

vic·tim·less \ˈvik-təm-ləs\ *adj* **:** having no victim ⟨considered gambling to be a ~ crime⟩

vic·tor \ˈvik-tər\ *n* ♦ **:** one that defeats an enemy or opponent **:** WINNER

♦ conqueror, master, winner *Ant* loser

vic·to·ria \vik-ˈtōr-ē-ə\ *n* **:** a low 4-wheeled carriage with a folding top and a raised driver's seat in front

¹Vic·to·ri·an \vik-ˈtōr-ē-ən\ *adj* **1 :** of or relating to the reign of Queen Victoria of England or the art, letters, or tastes of her time **2 :** typical of the standards, attitudes, or conduct of the age of Victoria especially when considered prudish or narrow

²Victorian *n* **1 :** a person and especially an author of the Victorian period **2 :** a typically large ornate house built during Queen Victoria's reign

vic·to·ri·ous \vik-ˈtōr-ē-əs\ *adj* **1 :** having won a victory **2 :** of, relating to, or characteristic of victory — **vic·to·ri·ous·ly** *adv*

vic·to·ry \ˈvik-tə-rē\ *n, pl* **-ries 1 :** the overcoming of an enemy or an antagonist **2 :** achievement of mastery or success in a struggle or endeavor

¹vict·ual \ˈvit-ᵊl\ *n* **1 :** food fit for humans **2** *pl* ♦ **:** food supplies

♦ **victuals** chow, fare, food, grub, meat, provender, provisions, viands

²victual *vb* **-ualed** *or* **-ualled; -ual·ing** *or* **-ual·ling 1** ♦ **:** to supply with food **2 :** to store up provisions

♦ board, cater, provision, victual

vict·ual·ler *or* **vict·ual·er** \ˈvit-ᵊl-ər\ *n* **:** one that supplies provisions (as to an army or a ship)

vi·cu·ña *or* **vi·cu·na** \vi-ˈkün-yə, vī-; vī-ˈkü-nə, -ˈkyü-\ *n* **1 :** a So. American wild mammal related to the llama and alpaca; *also* **:** its wool **2 :** a soft fabric woven from the wool of the vicuña; *also* **:** a sheep's wool imitation of this

vi·de \ˈvī-dē, ˈvē-ˌdā\ *vb imper* **:** SEE — used to direct a reader to another item

vi·de·li·cet \və-ˈde-lə-ˌset, vī-; vi-ˈdā-li-ˌket\ *adv* **:** that is to say **:** NAMELY

¹vid·eo \ˈvi-dē-ˌō\ *n* **1 :** TELEVISION **2 :** VIDEOTAPE; *also* **:** a recording similar to a videotape but stored in digital form **3 :** a videotaped performance ⟨music ~*s*⟩

²video *adj* **1 :** relating to or used in transmission or reception of the television image **2 :** relating to or being images on a television screen or computer display ⟨a ~ terminal⟩

video camera *n* **:** a camera that records visual images and usually sound; *esp* **:** CAMCORDER

vid·eo·cas·sette \ˌvi-dē-ō-kə-ˈset\ *n* **1 :** a case containing videotape for use with a VCR **2 :** a recording (as of a movie) on a videocassette

videocassette recorder *n* **:** VCR

vid·eo·disc *or* **vid·eo·disk** \ˈvi-dē-ō-ˌdisk\ *n* **1 :** OPTICAL DISK **2 :** a recording (as of a movie) on a videodisc

video game *n* **:** an electronic game played on a video screen

vid·e·o·gen·ic \ˌvi-dē-ō-ˈje-nik\ *adj* **:** TELEGENIC

vid·eo·phone \ˈvid-ē-ə-ˌfōn\ *n* **:** a telephone for transmitting both audio and video signals

¹vid·eo·tape \ˈvid-ē-ō-ˌtāp\ *n* **:** a recording of visual images and sound made on magnetic tape; *also* **:** the magnetic tape used for such a recording

²videotape *vb* **:** to make a videotape of

videotape recorder *n* **:** a device for recording and playing back videotapes

vie \ˈvī\ *vb* **vied; vy·ing** \ˈvī-iŋ\ ♦ **:** to compete for superiority **:** CONTEND — **vi·er** \ˈvī-ər\ *n*

♦ battle, compete, contend, fight, race

Viet·cong \vē-ˈet-ˈkäŋ, ˌvē-ət-, -ˈkȯŋ\ *n, pl* **Vietcong :** a guerrilla member of the Vietnamese communist movement

Viet·nam·ese \vē-ˌet-nə-ˈmēz, ˌvē-ət-, -ˈmēs\ *n, pl* **Vietnamese :** a native or inhabitant of Vietnam — **Vietnamese** *adj*

¹view \ˈvyü\ *n* **1 a** ♦ **:** the act of seeing or examining **b :** SURVEY **2 :** a way of looking at or regarding something **3** ♦ **:** an opinion or judgment colored by the feeling or bias of its holder ⟨stated his ~*s*⟩ **4** ♦ **:** a sight (as of a landscape) regarded for its pictorial quality **5 :** extent or range of vision ⟨within ~⟩ **6 :** OBJECT, PURPOSE ⟨done with a ~ to promotion⟩ **7 :** a picture of a scene

♦ [1a] cast, eye, gander, glance, glimpse, look, peek, peep, regard, sight ♦ [3] belief, conviction, eye, feeling, judgment (*or* judgement), mind, notion, opinion, persuasion, sentiment, verdict ♦ [4] lookout, outlook, panorama, prospect, vista

²view *vb* **1 :** to look at attentively **:** EXAMINE **2 :** to perceive by the eye **:** SEE **3 :** to examine mentally **:** CONSIDER — **view·er** *n*

view·er·ship \ˈvyü-ər-ˌship\ *n* **:** a television audience especially with respect to size or makeup

view·find·er \ˈvyü-ˌfīn-dər\ *n* **:** a device on a camera for showing the view to be included in the picture

view·point \-ˌpȯint\ *n* ♦ **:** a position or perspective from which something is considered or evaluated **:** POINT OF VIEW

♦ angle, outlook, perspective, point of view, slant, standpoint

vi·ges·i·mal \vī-ˈje-sə-məl\ *adj* **:** based on the number 20

vig·il \ˈvi-jəl\ *n* **1 :** a religious observance formerly held on the night before a religious feast **2 :** the day before a religious feast observed as a day of spiritual preparation **3 :** evening or nocturnal devotions or prayers — usually used in plural **4 :** an act or a time of keeping awake when sleep is customary; *esp* **:** WATCH 1

vig·i·lance \ˈvi-jə-ləns\ *n* ♦ **:** the quality or state of being vigilant

♦ alertness, attentiveness, lookout, watch

vigilance committee *n* **:** a committee of vigilantes

vig•i•lant \ˈvi-jə-lənt\ *adj* ♦ : alertly watchful especially to avoid danger — **vig•i•lant•ly** *adv*

♦ alert, attentive, awake, watchful, wide-awake

vig•i•lan•te \ˌvi-jə-ˈlan-tē\ *n* : a member of a volunteer committee organized to suppress and punish crime summarily (as when the processes of law are viewed as inadequate); *also* : a self-appointed doer of justice — **vig•i•lan•tism** \-ˈlan-ˌti-zəm\ *n*

[1]**vi•gnette** \vin-ˈyet\ *n* **1** : a small decorative design **2** : a picture (as an engraving or a photograph) that shades off gradually into the surrounding ground **3** ♦ : a short descriptive literary sketch

♦ delineation, depiction, description, picture, portrait, portrayal, sketch

[2]**vignette** *vb* **vi•gnett•ed; vi•gnett•ing** **1** : to finish (as a photograph) like a vignette **2** : to describe briefly

vig•or *or Can and Brit* **vig•our** \ˈvi-gər\ *n* **1** ♦ : active strength or energy of body or mind **2** : INTENSITY, FORCE

♦ dash, drive, energy, ginger, hardihood, life, pep, sap, snap, vim, vitality, zing, zip ***Ant*** lethargy, listlessness, sluggishness ♦ energy, force, main, might, muscle, potency, power, sinew, strength

vig•or•ous \ˈvi-gə-rəs\ *adj* **1** ♦ : having vigor **2** ♦ : done with force and energy

♦ [1] hard, hard-bitten, hardy, rugged, stout, strong, sturdy, tough ♦ [1] dynamic, energetic, flush, lusty, peppy, robust, strenuous, vital ***Ant*** lethargic, listless, sluggish, torpid ♦ [2] aggressive, assertive, dynamic, emphatic, energetic, forceful, resounding, strenuous, vehement ♦ [2] firm, forceful, hearty, lusty, robust, solid, stout, strong, sturdy

vig•or•ous•ly *adv* ♦ : in a vigorous manner

♦ energetically, firmly, forcefully, forcibly, hard, mightily, powerfully, stiffly, stoutly, strenuously, strongly, sturdily

vig•or•ous•ness *n* : the quality or state of being vigorous

vig•our *chiefly Brit var of* VIGOR

Vi•king \ˈvī-kiŋ\ *n* : any of the pirate Norsemen who raided or invaded the coasts of Europe in the 8th to 10th centuries

vile \ˈvīl\ *adj* **vil•er; vil•est** **1** ♦ : morally despicable **2** : physically repulsive : FOUL **3** : of little worth **4** : DEGRADING, IGNOMINIOUS **5** : utterly bad or contemptible ⟨~ weather⟩ — **vile•ly** \ˈvīl-lē\ *adv*

♦ bad, black, evil, immoral, iniquitous, nefarious, rotten, sinful, unethical, unsavory, vicious, villainous, wicked, wrong ♦ base, contemptible, despicable, detestable, dirty, dishonorable (*or* dishonourable), ignoble, low, mean, snide, sordid, wretched

vile•ness *n* ♦ : the quality or state of being vile

♦ atrociousness, atrocity, depravity, enormity, heinousness, monstrosity, wickedness

vil•i•fi•ca•tion \ˌvi-lə-fə-ˈkā-shən\ *n* ♦ : an instance of vilifying : a defamatory utterance

♦ defamation, libel, slander

vil•i•fy \ˈvi-lə-ˌfī\ *vb* **-fied; -fy•ing** ♦ : to blacken the character of with abusive language : DEFAME — **vil•i•fi•er** \ˈvi-lə-ˌfī-ər\ *n*

♦ blacken, defame, libel, malign, slander, smear, traduce

vil•la \ˈvi-lə\ *n* **1** : a country estate **2** ♦ : the rural or suburban residence of a wealthy person

♦ castle, estate, hall, manor, mansion, palace

vil•lage \ˈvi-lij\ *n* **1** : a settlement usually larger than a hamlet and smaller than a town **2** : an incorporated minor municipality **3** : the people of a village

vil•lag•er \ˈvi-li-jər\ *n* : an inhabitant of a village

vil•lain \ˈvi-lən\ *n* **1** : VILLEIN **2** ♦ : an evil person : SCOUNDREL

♦ beast, devil, evildoer, fiend, heavy, knave, no-good, rapscallion, rascal, reprobate, rogue, scalawag, scamp, scoundrel, varlet, wretch

vil•lain•ess \-lə-nəs\ *n* : a woman who is a villain

vil•lain•ous \-lə-nəs\ *adj* **1** ♦ : befitting a villain : WICKED **2** : highly objectionable : DETESTABLE — **vil•lain•ous•ness** *n*

♦ bad, black, evil, immoral, iniquitous, nefarious, rotten, sinful, unethical, unsavory, vicious, vile, wicked, wrong

vil•lain•ous•ly *adv* : in a villainous manner

vil•lainy \-lə-nē\ *n, pl* **-lain•ies** **1** ♦ : villainous conduct; *also* : a villainous act **2** : villainous character or nature

♦ bad, evil, ill, immorality, iniquity, sin, wrong

vil•lein \ˈvi-lən, -ˌlān\ *n* **1** : a free villager of Anglo-Saxon times **2** : an unfree peasant having the status of a slave to a feudal lord

vil•len•age \ˈvil-ə-nij\ *n* **1** : the holding of land at the will of a feudal lord **2** : the status of a villein

vil•lous \ˈvi-ləs\ *adj* : covered with fine hairs or villi

vil•lus \ˈvi-ləs\ *n, pl* **vil•li** \-ˌlī, -(ˌ)lē\ : a slender usually vascular process; *esp* : one of the tiny projections of the mucous membrane of the small intestine that function in the absorption of food

vim \ˈvim\ *n* ♦ : robust energy and enthusiasm

♦ dash, energy, life, pep, vigor (*or* vigour), vitality

VIN *abbr* vehicle identification number

vin•ai•grette \ˌvi-ni-ˈgret\ *n* : a sauce made typically of oil, vinegar, and seasonings

vin•ci•ble \ˈvin-sə-bəl\ *adj* : capable of being overcome or subdued

vin•di•cate \ˈvin-də-ˌkāt\ *vb* **-cat•ed; -cat•ing** **1** : AVENGE **2** ♦ : to free from allegation or blame : EXONERATE **3** ♦ : to establish by proof or competent evidence : CONFIRM **4** : to provide defense for : JUSTIFY **5** : to maintain a right to : ASSERT — **vin•di•ca•tor** \-ˌkā-tər\ *n*

♦ [2] absolve, acquit, clear, exculpate, exonerate ♦ [3] bear out, confirm, corroborate, substantiate, support, validate, verify

vin•di•ca•tion \ˌvin-də-ˈkā-shən\ *n* ♦ : the act of vindicating or the state of being vindicated; *esp* : justification against denial or censure : DEFENSE

♦ acquittal, exculpation, exoneration

vin•dic•tive \vin-ˈdik-tiv\ *adj* **1** : disposed to revenge **2** : intended for or involving revenge **3** : VICIOUS, SPITEFUL — **vin•dic•tive•ly** *adv* — **vin•dic•tive•ness** *n*

vine \ˈvīn\ *n* **1** : GRAPE 2 **2** : a plant whose stem requires support and which climbs (as by tendrils) or trails along the ground; *also* : the stem of such a plant

vin•e•gar \ˈvi-ni-gər\ *n* : a sour liquid obtained by fermentation (as of cider, wine, or malt) and used to flavor or preserve foods

vin•e•gary \-gə-rē\ *adj* **1** ♦ : resembling vinegar : SOUR **2** : disagreeable in manner or disposition : CRABBED

♦ acid, sour, tart

vine•yard \ˈvin-yərd\ *n* **1** : a field of grapevines especially to produce grapes for wine production **2** : a sphere of activity : field of endeavor

vi•nous \ˈvī-nəs\ *adj* **1** : of, relating to, or made with wine ⟨~ medications⟩ **2** : showing the effects of the use of wine ⟨~ bloodshot eyes⟩

[1]**vin•tage** \ˈvin-tij\ *n* **1** : a season's yield of grapes or wine **2** : WINE; *esp* : a usually superior wine which comes from a single year **3** : the act or period of gathering grapes or making wine **4** : a period of origin ⟨clothes of 1890 ~⟩

[2]**vintage** *adj* **1** : of, relating to, or produced in a particular vintage **2** : of old, recognized, and enduring interest, importance, or quality : CLASSIC ⟨~ cars⟩ **3** : of the best and most characteristic — used with a proper noun

vint•ner \ˈvint-nər\ *n* : a dealer in wines

vi•nyl \ˈvīn-ᵊl\ *n* **1** : a chemical derived from ethylene by the removal of one hydrogen atom **2** : a polymer of a vinyl compound or a product (as a textile fiber) made from one

vinyl chloride *n* : a flammable gaseous carcinogenic compound used especially to make vinyl resins

vi•ol \ˈvī-əl\ *n* : a bowed stringed instrument chiefly of the 16th and 17th centuries having a fretted neck and usually six strings

[1]**vi•o•la** \vī-ˈō-lə, ˈvī-ə-lə\ *n* : VIOLET 1; *esp* : any of various hybrid garden plants with white, yellow, purple, or variously colored flowers that resemble but are smaller than those of the related pansies

[2]**vi•o•la** \vē-ˈō-lə\ *n* : an instrument of the violin family slightly larger and tuned lower than a violin — **vi•o•list** \-list\ *n*

vi•o•la•ble \ˈvī-ə-lə-bəl\ *adj* : capable of being violated

vi•o•late \ˈvī-ə-ˌlāt\ *vb* **-lat•ed; -lat•ing** **1** ♦ : to go beyond limits set or prescribed by : BREAK ⟨~ a law⟩ ⟨~ a frontier⟩ **2** : RAPE **3** ♦ : to fail to show proper respect for : DESECRATE **4** : INTERRUPT, DISTURB ⟨*violated* his privacy⟩ — **vi•o•la•tor** \-ˌlā-tər\ *n*

♦ [1] breach, break, transgress ***Ant*** comply (with), conform (to), follow, mind, obey, observe ♦ [3] defile, desecrate, profane

vi•o•la•tion \ˌvī-ə-ˈlā-shən\ *n* ♦ : an act or instance of violating : the state of being violated

♦ breach, crime, error, infraction, malefaction, misdeed, misdoing, offense, sin, transgression, trespass, wrongdoing

vi•o•lence \ˈvī-ləns, ˈvī-ə-\ *n* **1** : exertion of physical force so as to injure or abuse **2 :** injury by or as if by infringement or profanation **3 :** intense or furious often destructive action or force **4 :** vehement feeling or expression : INTENSITY **5 :** jarring quality : a state of discord

vi·o·lent \-lənt\ *adj* **1** ♦ **:** marked by extreme force or sudden intense activity **2 :** caused by or showing strong feeling ⟨~ words⟩ **3** ♦ **:** existing in an extreme degree : INTENSE **4 :** emotionally agitated to the point of loss of self-control **5 :** caused by force : not natural ⟨~ death⟩ — **vi·o·lent·ly** *adv*

♦ [1] explosive, ferocious, fierce, furious, hot, rabid, rough, stormy, tempestuous, turbulent, volcanic ***Ant*** nonviolent, peaceable, peaceful ♦ [3] deep, exquisite, fearful, hard, heavy, intense, profound, terrible, vehement, vicious

vi·o·let \ˈvī-ə-lət\ *n* **1 :** any of a genus of herbs or small shrubs usually with heart-shaped leaves and both aerial and underground flowers; *esp* **:** one with small usually solid-colored flowers **2 :** a reddish blue color

vi·o·lin \ˌvī-ə-ˈlin\ *n* **:** a bowed stringed instrument with four strings that has a shallow body, a fingerboard without frets, and a curved bridge — **vi·o·lin·ist** \-ˈli-nist\ *n*

vi·o·lon·cel·lo \ˌvī-ə-lən-ˈche-lō\ *n* **:** CELLO — **vi·o·lon·cel·list** \-list\ *n*

VIP \ˌvē-ˌī-ˈpē\ *n, pl* **VIPs** \-ˈpēz\ ♦ **:** a person of great influence or prestige; *esp* **:** a high official with special privileges

♦ celebrity, figure, light, luminary, notable, personage, personality, somebody, standout, star, superstar

vi·per \ˈvī-pər\ *n* **1 :** a common stout-bodied Eurasian venomous snake having a bite only rarely fatal to humans; *also* **:** any snake (as a pit viper) of the same family as the viper **2 :** any venomous or reputedly venomous snake **3 :** a vicious or treacherous person — **vi·per·ine** \-pə-ˌrīn\ *adj*

vi·ra·go \və-ˈrä-gō, -ˈrā-\ *n, pl* **-goes** *or* **-gos** **1** ♦ **:** a loud overbearing woman **2 :** a woman of great strength and courage

♦ fury, harpy, shrew, termagant

vi·ral \ˈvī-rəl\ *adj* **:** of, relating to, or caused by a virus

vir·eo \ˈvir-ē-ˌō\ *n, pl* **-e·os** **:** any of various small insect-eating American songbirds mostly olive green and grayish in color

[1]**vir·gin** \ˈvər-jən\ *n* **1 :** an unmarried woman devoted to religion **2 :** an unmarried girl or woman **3** *cap* **:** the mother of Jesus **4 :** a person who has not had sexual intercourse

[2]**virgin** *adj* **1 :** free from stain : PURE, SPOTLESS **2 :** CHASTE **3 :** befitting a virgin : MODEST **4** ♦ **:** having its original qualities unimpaired : FRESH; *esp* **:** not altered by human activity ⟨~ forest⟩ **5 :** INITIAL, FIRST

♦ brand-new, fresh, pristine

[1]**vir·gin·al** \ˈvər-jən-ᵊl\ *adj* **:** of, relating to, or characteristic of a virgin or virginity — **vir·gin·al·ly** *adv*

[2]**virginal** *n* **:** a small rectangular spinet without legs popular in the 16th and 17th centuries

Vir·gin·ia creeper \vər-ˈjin-yə-\ *n* **:** a No. American vine related to the grapes that has leaves with five leaflets and bluish-black berries

Virginia reel *n* **:** an American country-dance

vir·gin·i·ty \vər-ˈji-nə-tē\ *n, pl* **-ties** **1 :** the quality or state of being virgin; *esp* **:** MAIDENHOOD **2 :** the unmarried life : CELIBACY

Vir·go \ˈvər-ˌgō\ *n* **1 :** a zodiacal constellation between Leo and Libra usually pictured as a young woman **2 :** the 6th sign of the zodiac in astrology; *also* **:** one born under this sign

vir·gule \ˈvər-gyül\ *n* **:** [2]SLASH 3

vir·i·des·cent \ˌvir-ə-ˈdes-ᵊnt\ *adj* **:** slightly green : GREENISH

vir·ile \ˈvir-əl\ *adj* **1 :** having the nature, powers, or qualities of a man **2** ♦ **:** characteristic of or associated with men : MASCULINE **3 :** MASTERFUL, FORCEFUL

♦ male, manly, mannish, man-size, masculine

vi·ril·i·ty \və-ˈri-lə-tē\ *n* ♦ **:** the quality or state of being virile

♦ manhood, manliness, masculinity ***Ant*** femininity

vi·ri·on \ˈvī-rē-ˌän, ˈvir-ē-\ *n* **:** a complete virus particle consisting of an RNA or DNA core with a protein coat

vi·rol·o·gy \vī-ˈrä-lə-jē\ *n* **:** a branch of science that deals with viruses and viral diseases — **vi·rol·o·gist** \-jist\ *n*

vir·tu \ˌvər-ˈtü, vir-\ *or* **ver·tu** \ˌvər-, ˌver-\ *n* **1 :** a love of or taste for objects of art **2 :** objects of art (as curios and antiques)

vir·tu·al \ˈvər-chə-wəl\ *adj* **1 :** being in essence or in effect though not formally recognized or admitted ⟨a ~ dictator⟩ **2 :** being on or simulated on a computer or computer network

vir·tu·al·ly \ˈvər-chə-wə-lē\ *adv* **1** ♦ **:** almost entirely : NEARLY **2 :** for all practical purposes

♦ about, almost, most, much, near, nearly, next to, nigh, practically, some, well-nigh

virtual reality *n* **:** an artificial environment that is experienced through sensory stimuli (as sights and sounds) provided by an interactive computer program; *also* **:** the technology used to create or access a virtual reality

vir·tue \ˈvər-chü\ *n* **1** ♦ **:** conformity to a standard of right : MORALITY **2 :** a particular moral excellence **3 :** manly strength or courage : VALOR **4** ♦ **:** a commendable quality : MERIT **5 :** active power to accomplish a given effect : POTENCY, EFFICACY **6 :** chastity especially in a woman

♦ [1] character, decency, goodness, honesty, integrity, morality, probity, rectitude, righteousness, uprightness ♦ [4] distinction, excellence, merit, value

vir·tu·os·i·ty \ˌvər-chə-ˈwä-sə-tē\ *n, pl* **-ties** **:** great technical skill in the practice of a fine art

[1]**vir·tu·o·so** \ˌvər-chə-ˈwō-sō, -zō\ *n, pl* **-sos** *or* **-si** \-sē, -zē\ **1 :** one skilled in or having a taste for the fine arts **2** ♦ **:** one who excels in the technique of an art; *esp* **:** a highly skilled musical performer **3** ♦ **:** a person who has great skill at some endeavor

♦ [2, 3] ace, adept, artist, authority, crackerjack, expert, maestro, master, scholar, shark, whiz, wizard

[2]**virtuoso** *adj* ♦ **:** of, relating to, or characteristic of a virtuoso

♦ accomplished, adept, consummate, crack, crackerjack, expert, good, great, master, masterful, masterly, proficient, skilled, skillful

vir·tu·ous \ˈvər-chə-wəs\ *adj* **1** ♦ **:** having or showing virtue and especially moral virtue **2 :** CHASTE

♦ decent, ethical, good, honest, honorable (*or* honourable), just, moral, right, righteous, straight, upright

vir·tu·ous·ly *adv* ♦ **:** in a virtuous manner

♦ chastely, modestly, purely, righteously

vir·u·lence \ˈvir-ə-ləns, ˈvir-yə-\ *n* ♦ **:** the quality or state of being virulent

♦ acidity, acrimony, asperity, bitterness, cattiness, tartness, vitriol

vir·u·lent \ˈvir-ə-lənt, ˈvir-yə-\ *adj* **1 :** highly infectious ⟨a ~ germ⟩; *also* **:** marked by a rapid, severe, and often deadly course ⟨a ~ disease⟩ **2 :** extremely poisonous or venomous : NOXIOUS **3** ♦ **:** full of malice : MALIGNANT

♦ catty, cruel, hateful, malevolent, malicious, malign, malignant, mean, nasty, spiteful

vir·u·lent·ly *adv* **:** in a virulent manner

vi·rus \ˈvī-rəs\ *n, pl* **vi·rus·es** **1 :** any of a large group of submicroscopic infectious agents that have an outside coat of protein around a core of RNA or DNA, that can grow and multiply only in living cells, and that cause important diseases in human beings, lower animals, and plants; *also* **:** a disease caused by a virus **2 :** something (as a corrupting influence) that poisons the mind or spirit **3 :** a computer program that is usually hidden within another program and that reproduces itself and inserts the copies into other programs and usually performs a malicious action (as destroying data)

vis *abbr* **1** visibility **2** visual

[1]**vi·sa** \ˈvē-zə, -sə\ *n* **1 :** an endorsement by the proper authorities on a passport to show that it has been examined and the bearer may proceed **2 :** a signature by a superior official signifying approval of a document

[2]**visa** *vb* **vi·saed** \-zəd, -səd\; **vi·sa·ing** \-zə-iŋ, -sə-\ **:** to give a visa to (a passport)

vis·age \ˈvi-zij\ *n* ♦ **:** the face or countenance of a person or sometimes an animal; *also* **:** LOOK

♦ cast, countenance, expression, face, look

[1]**vis–à–vis** \ˌvēz-ə-ˈvē, ˌvēs-\ *prep* **1 :** face-to-face with : OPPOSITE **2 :** in relation to **3 :** as compared with

[2]**vis–à–vis** *n, pl* **vis–à–vis** *same or* -ˈvēz\ **1 :** one that is face-to-face with another **2 :** ESCORT **3 :** COUNTERPART **4 :** TÊTE-À-TÊTE

[3]**vis–à–vis** *adv* **:** in company : TOGETHER

viscera *pl of* VISCUS

vis·cer·al \ˈvi-sə-rəl\ *adj* **1 :** felt in or as if in the viscera **2 :** not intellectual : INSTINCTIVE **3 :** of or relating to the viscera — **vis·cer·al·ly** *adv*

vis·cid \ˈvi-səd\ *adj* **1** ♦ **:** having an adhesive quality **2 :** having a glutinous consistency : VISCOUS — **vis·cid·i·ty** \vi-ˈsi-də-tē\ *n*

♦ adhesive, gelatinous, gluey, glutinous, gooey, gummy, sticky, viscous

vis•cos•i•ty \vis-ˈkä-sə-tē\ *n, pl* **-ties** ♦ **:** the quality of being viscous; *esp* **:** the property of resistance to flow in a fluid

♦ consistency, thickness

vis•count \ˈvī-ˌkau̇nt\ *n* **:** a member of the British peerage ranking below an earl and above a baron

vis•count•ess \-ˌkau̇n-təs\ *n* **1 :** the wife or widow of a viscount **2 :** a woman who holds the rank of viscount in her own right

vis•cous \ˈvis-kəs\ *adj* **1 :** having the sticky consistency of glue **:** VISCID **2** ♦ **:** having or characterized by viscosity

♦ syrupy, thick, viscid

vis•cus \ˈvis-kəs\ *n, pl* **vis•cera** \ˈvi-sə-rə\ **:** an internal organ of the body; *esp* **:** one (as the heart or liver) located in the cavity of the trunk

vise \ˈvīs\ *n* **:** a tool with two jaws for holding work that typically close by a screw or lever

vis•i•bil•i•ty \ˌvi-zə-ˈbi-lə-tē\ *n, pl* **-ties 1 :** the quality, condition, or degree of being visible **2 :** the degree of clearness of the atmosphere

vis•i•ble \ˈvi-zə-bəl\ *adj* ♦ **:** capable of being seen ⟨∼ stars⟩; *also* **:** APPARENT ⟨has no ∼ means of support⟩ — **vis•i•bly** \-blē\ *adv*

♦ apparent, observable, visual *Ant* invisible

¹vi•sion \ˈvi-zhən\ *n* **1 :** something seen otherwise than by ordinary sight (as in a dream or trance) **2** ♦ **:** a vivid picture created by the imagination **3 :** the act or power of imagination **4 :** unusual wisdom in foreseeing what is going to happen **5** ♦ **:** the act or power of seeing **:** SIGHT **6 :** something seen; *esp* **:** a lovely sight **7 :** the apparition of a person **:** PHANTOM

♦ [2] chimera, conceit, daydream, delusion, dream, fancy, fantasy, figment, hallucination, illusion, phantasm, pipe dream, unreality ♦ [5] eye, sight

²vision *vb* ♦ **:** to picture to oneself **:** IMAGINE

♦ conceive, dream, envisage, fancy, imagine, picture, visualize

¹vi•sion•ary \ˈvi-zhə-ˌner-ē\ *adj* **1 :** of the nature of a vision **:** ILLUSORY, UNREAL **2 :** not practical **:** UTOPIAN **3 :** seeing or likely to see visions **:** given to dreaming or imagining **4** ♦ **:** having or marked by foresight and imagination

♦ farsighted, forehanded, foresighted, prescient, proactive, provident

²visionary *n, pl* **-ar•ies 1** ♦ **:** one whose ideas or projects are impractical **:** DREAMER **2 :** one who sees visions

♦ dreamer, idealist, romantic, utopian

¹vis•it \ˈvi-zət\ *vb* **1 :** to go to see in order to comfort or help **2 :** to call on either as an act of courtesy or friendship **3** ♦ **:** to dwell with for a time as a guest **4 :** to come to or upon as a reward, affliction, or punishment **5 :** INFLICT **6** ♦ **:** to make a visit or regular or frequent visits **7** ♦ **:** to talk in an informal or familiar manner **:** CHAT — **vis•it•able** *adj*

♦ [3] sojourn, stay, tarry ♦ [6] call, drop (by *or* in), pop (in), stop (by *or* in) ♦ [7] chat, converse, gab, jaw, palaver, patter, prattle, rattle, talk

²visit *n* **1 :** a short stay **:** CALL **2** ♦ **:** a brief residence as a guest **3 :** a journey to and stay at a place **4 :** a formal or professional call (as by a doctor)

♦ sojourn, stay

vis•i•tant \ˈvi-zə-tənt\ *n* **:** VISITOR

vis•i•ta•tion \ˌvi-zə-ˈtā-shən\ *n* **1 :** an instance of visiting **:** VISIT; *esp* **:** an official visit **2 :** a special dispensation of divine favor or wrath; *also* **:** a severe trial

visiting nurse *n* **:** a nurse employed to visit sick persons or perform public health services in a community

vis•i•tor \ˈvi-zə-tər\ *n* ♦ **:** one that visits

♦ caller, guest

vi•sor \ˈvī-zər\ *n* **1 :** the front piece of a helmet; *esp* **:** a movable upper piece **2 :** VIZARD **3** ♦ **:** a projecting part (as on a cap) to shade the eyes — **vi•sored** \-zərd\ *adj*

♦ bill, peak

vis•ta \ˈvis-tə\ *n* **1** ♦ **:** a distant view through or along an avenue or opening **2 :** an extensive mental view over a series of years or events

♦ lookout, outlook, panorama, prospect, view

VISTA *abbr* Volunteers in Service to America

¹vi•su•al \ˈvi-zhə-wəl\ *adj* **1** ♦ **:** of, relating to, or used in vision ⟨∼ organs⟩ **2 :** perceived by vision ⟨a ∼ impression⟩ **3** ♦ **:** capable of being seen **:** VISIBLE **4 :** done by sight only ⟨∼ navigation⟩ **5 :** of or relating to instruction by means of sight ⟨∼ aids⟩ — **vi•su•al•ly** *adv*

♦ [1] ocular, optical *Ant* nonvisual ♦ [3] apparent, observable, visible

²visual *n* **:** something (as a picture, chart, or film) that appeals to the sight and is used for illustration, demonstration, or promotion — usually used in plural

vi•su•al•ize \ˈvi-zhə-wə-ˌlīz\ *vb* **-ized; -iz•ing** ♦ **:** to make visible; *esp* **:** to form a mental image of — **vi•su•al•i•za•tion** \ˌvi-zhə-wə-lə-ˈzā-shən\ *n* — **vi•su•al•iz•er** *n*

♦ conceive, dream, envisage, fancy, imagine, picture, vision

vi•ta \ˈvē-tə, ˈvī-\ *n, pl* **vi•tae** \ˈvē-ˌtī, ˈvī-tē\ **:** a brief autobiographical sketch

vi•tal \ˈvīt-ᵊl\ *adj* **1 :** concerned with or necessary to the maintenance of life **2** ♦ **:** full of life and vigor **3 :** of, relating to, or characteristic of life or living beings **4** ♦ **:** destructive to life **:** FATAL ⟨∼ wound⟩ **5** ♦ **:** of the utmost importance — **vi•tal•ly** *adv*

♦ [2] active, animate, animated, brisk, energetic, lively, peppy, spirited, sprightly, springy, vigorous, vivacious ♦ [4] baleful, deadly, deathly, fatal, fell, lethal, mortal, murderous, pestilent ♦ [5] essential, imperative, indispensable, integral, necessary, needful, requisite ♦ [5] critical, crucial, key, pivotal

vi•tal•i•ty \vī-ˈta-lə-tē\ *n, pl* **-ties 1 :** the property distinguishing the living from the nonliving **2** ♦ **:** mental and physical vigor **3 :** enduring quality **4** ♦ **:** lively and animated character

♦ [2] dash, energy, life, pep, vigor (*or* vigour), vim ♦ [4] animation, briskness, exuberance, liveliness, lustiness, robustness, sprightliness, vibrancy *Ant* inactivity

vi•tal•ize \ˈvīt-ᵊl-ˌīz\ *vb* **-ized; -iz•ing** ♦ **:** to impart life or vigor to **:** ANIMATE — **vi•tal•i•za•tion** \ˌvīt-ᵊl-ə-ˈzā-shən\ *n*

♦ animate, brace, energize, enliven, fire, invigorate, jazz up, liven up, pep up, quicken, stimulate, vivify, zip (up)

vi•tals \ˈvīt-ᵊlz\ *n pl* **1 :** vital organs (as the heart and brain) **2 :** essential parts

vital signs *n pl* **:** the pulse rate, respiratory rate, body temperature, and often blood pressure of a person

vital statistics *n pl* **:** statistics dealing with births, deaths, marriages, health, and disease

vi•ta•min \ˈvī-tə-mən\ *n* **:** any of various organic substances that are essential in tiny amounts to the nutrition of most animals and some plants and are mostly obtained from foods

vitamin A *n* **:** any of several vitamins (as from egg yolk or fish-liver oils) required especially for good vision

vitamin B *n* **1 :** VITAMIN B COMPLEX **2** *or* **vitamin B_1 :** THIAMINE

vitamin B complex *n* **:** a group of vitamins that are found widely in foods and are essential for normal function of certain enzymes and for growth

vitamin B_6 \-ˈbē-ˈsiks\ *n* **:** any of several compounds that are considered essential to vertebrate nutrition

vitamin B_{12} \-ˈbē-ˈtwelv\ *n* **:** a complex cobalt-containing compound that occurs especially in liver and is essential to normal blood formation, neural function, and growth; *also* **:** any of several compounds of similar action

vitamin C *n* **:** a vitamin found especially in fruits and vegetables that is needed by the body to prevent scurvy

vitamin D *n* **:** any or all of several vitamins that are needed for normal bone and tooth structure and are found especially in fish-liver oils, egg yolk, and milk or are produced by the body in response to ultraviolet light

vitamin E *n* **:** any of various oily fat-soluble liquid vitamins whose absence in the body is associated with such ailments as infertility, the breakdown of muscles, and vascular problems and which are found especially in leaves and in seed germ oils

vitamin K *n* **:** any of several vitamins needed for blood to clot properly

vi•ti•ate \ˈvi-shē-ˌāt\ *vb* **-at•ed; -at•ing 1** ♦ **:** to make faulty or defective **:** IMPAIR **2 :** to make legally ineffective **:** INVALIDATE **3** ♦ **:** to debase in moral or aesthetic status — **vi•ti•a•tion** \ˌvi-shē-ˈā-shən\ *n* — **vi•ti•a•tor** \ˈvi-shē-ˌā-tər\ *n*

♦ [1] blemish, break, cripple, damage, deface, disfigure, flaw, harm, hurt, injure, mar, spoil ♦ [3] blemish, mar, poison, spoil, stain, taint, tarnish, touch

vi•ti•cul•ture \ˈvi-tə-ˌkəl-chər\ *n* **:** the growing of grapes — **vi•ti•cul•tur•al** \ˌvi-tə-ˈkəl-chə-rəl\ *adj* — **vi•ti•cul•tur•ist** \-rist\ *n*

vit•re•ous \ˈvi-trē-əs\ *adj* **1 :** of, relating to, or resembling glass : GLASSY ⟨~ rocks⟩ **2 :** of, relating to, or being the clear colorless transparent jelly (**vitreous humor**) behind the lens in the eyeball
vit•ri•ol \ˈvi-trē-əl\ *n* ♦ **:** something resembling acid in being caustic, corrosive, or biting — **vit•ri•ol•ic** \ˌvi-trē-ˈä-lik\ *adj*

♦ acidity, acrimony, asperity, bitterness, cattiness, tartness, virulence ♦ abuse, fulmination, invective, vituperation

vit•tles \ˈvit-ᵊlz\ *n pl* **:** supplies of food : VICTUALS
vi•tu•per•ate \vī-ˈtü-pə-ˌrāt, və-, -ˈtyü-\ *vb* **-at•ed; -at•ing** ♦ **:** to abuse in words — **vi•tu•per•a•tive** \-ˈtü-pə-rə-tiv, -ˈtyü-, -ˌrā-\ *adj* — **vi•tu•per•a•tive•ly** *adv*

♦ abuse, assail, attack, belabor, blast, castigate, excoriate, jump, lambaste, slam

vi•tu•per•a•tion \(ˌ)vī-tü-pə-ˈrā-shən, və-, -tyü-\ *n* ♦ **:** lengthy harsh criticism or abuse

♦ abuse, fulmination, invective, vitriol

vi•va \ˈvē-və\ *interj* — used to express goodwill or approval
vi•va•ce \vē-ˈvä-chā\ *adv or adj* **:** in a brisk spirited manner — used as a direction in music
vi•va•cious \və-ˈvā-shəs, vī-\ *adj* ♦ **:** lively in temper, conduct, or spirit — **vi•va•cious•ness** *n*

♦ active, animate, animated, brisk, energetic, frisky, gay, jaunty, jazzy, lively, peppy, perky, pert, racy, snappy, spirited, sprightly, springy, vital

vi•va•cious•ly *adv* ♦ **:** in a vivacious manner

♦ gaily, jauntily, sprightly

vi•vac•i•ty \-ˈva-sə-tē\ *n* **:** the quality or state of being vivacious
vi•va vo•ce \ˌvī-və-ˈvō-sē, ˌvē-və-ˈvō-ˌchā\ *adj* **:** expressed or conducted by word of mouth : ORAL — **viva voce** *adv*
viv•id \ˈvi-vəd\ *adj* **1 :** having the appearance of vigorous life **2 :** BRILLIANT, INTENSE ⟨a ~ red⟩ **3 :** producing a strong impression on the senses; *esp* **:** producing distinct mental pictures : GRAPHIC ⟨a ~ description⟩ — **viv•id•ly** *adv* — **viv•id•ness** *n*
viv•i•fy \ˈvi-və-ˌfī\ *vb* **-fied; -fy•ing 1** ♦ **:** to put life into : ANIMATE **2 :** to make vivid — **viv•i•fi•ca•tion** \ˌvi-və-fə-ˈkā-shən\ *n* — **viv•i•fi•er** *n*

♦ animate, brace, energize, enliven, fire, invigorate, jazz up, liven up, pep up, quicken, stimulate, vitalize, zip (up)

vi•vip•a•rous \vī-ˈvi-pə-rəs, və-\ *adj* **:** producing living young from within the body rather than from eggs — **vi•vi•par•i•ty** \ˌvī-və-ˈpar-ə-tē, ˌvi-\ *n*
viv•i•sec•tion \ˌvi-və-ˈsek-shən, ˈvi-və-ˌsek-\ *n* **:** the cutting of or operation on a living animal; *also* **:** animal experimentation especially if causing distress to the subject
vix•en \ˈvik-sən\ *n* **1 :** an ill-tempered scolding woman **2 :** a female fox
viz *abbr* videlicet
viz•ard \ˈvi-zərd\ *n* **:** a mask for disguise or protection
vi•zier \və-ˈzir\ *n* **:** a high executive officer of many Muslim countries
VJ *abbr* veejay
VOA *abbr* Voice of America
voc *abbr* **1** vocational **2** vocative
vocab *abbr* vocabulary
vo•ca•ble \ˈvō-kə-bəl\ *n* **:** TERM, NAME; *esp* **:** a word as such without regard to its meaning
vo•cab•u•lary \vō-ˈka-byə-ˌler-ē\ *n, pl* **-lar•ies 1 :** a list or collection of words usually alphabetically arranged and defined or explained : LEXICON **2** ♦ **:** a stock of words in a language used by a class or individual or in relation to a subject

♦ argot, cant, jargon, language, lingo, slang, terminology

vocabulary entry *n* **:** a word (as the noun *book*), hyphened or open compound (as the verb *cross-refer* or the noun *boric acid*), word element (as the affix *-an*), abbreviation (as *agt*), verbalized symbol (as *Na*), or term (as *master of ceremonies*) entered alphabetically in a dictionary for the purpose of definition or identification or expressly included as an inflected form (as the noun *mice* or the verb *saw*) or as a derived form (as the noun *godlessness* or the adverb *globally*) or related phrase (as *in spite of*) run on at its base word and usually set in a type (as boldface) readily distinguishable from that of the lightface running text which defines, explains, or identifies the entry
[1]**vo•cal** \ˈvō-kəl\ *adj* **1** ♦ **:** uttered by the voice : ORAL **2 :** relating to, composed or arranged for, or sung by the human voice ⟨~ music⟩ **3 :** given to expressing oneself freely or insistently : OUTSPOKEN **4 :** of or relating to the voice

♦ oral, voiced *Ant* nonvocal

[2]**vocal** *n* **1 :** a vocal sound **2** ♦ **:** a vocal composition or its performance

♦ jingle, lay, lyric, song

vocal cords *n pl* **:** either of two pairs of elastic folds of mucous membrane that project into the cavity of the larynx and function in the production of vocal sounds
vo•cal•ic \vō-ˈka-lik\ *adj* **:** of, relating to, or functioning as a vowel
vo•cal•ise *chiefly Brit var of* VOCALIZE
vo•cal•ist \ˈvō-kə-list\ *n* ♦ **:** one that sings : SINGER

♦ caroler, singer, songster, voice

vo•cal•ize \-ˌlīz\ *vb* **-ized; -iz•ing 1** ♦ **:** to give vocal expression to : UTTER; *esp* **:** SING **2 :** to make voiced rather than voiceless

♦ articulate, say, speak, state, talk, tell, utter, verbalize ♦ carol, chant, descant, sing

vo•cal•iz•er \ˈvō-kə-ˌlī-zər\ *n* **:** one that vocalizes
vo•ca•tion \vō-ˈkā-shən\ *n* **1 :** a summons or strong inclination to a particular state or course of action ⟨religious ~⟩ **2** ♦ **:** regular employment : OCCUPATION — **vo•ca•tion•al** \-shə-nəl\ *adj*

♦ calling, employment, line, occupation, profession, trade, work

vo•ca•tion•al•ism \-shə-nə-ˌli-zəm\ *n* **:** emphasis on vocational training in education
voc•a•tive \ˈvä-kə-tiv\ *adj* **:** of, relating to, or constituting a grammatical case marking the one addressed — **vocative** *n*
vo•cif•er•ate \vō-ˈsi-fə-ˌrāt\ *vb* **-at•ed; -at•ing** ♦ **:** to cry out loudly : SHOUT — **vo•cif•er•a•tion** \-ˌsi-fə-ˈrā-shən\ *n*

♦ bawl, call, cry, holler, shout, yell

vo•cif•er•ous \vō-ˈsi-fə-rəs\ *adj* ♦ **:** making or given to loud outcry — **vo•cif•er•ous•ly** *adv* — **vo•cif•er•ous•ness** *n*

♦ blatant, boisterous, clamorous, obstreperous

vod•ka \ˈväd-kə\ *n* **:** a colorless liquor distilled from a mash (as of rye or wheat)
vogue \ˈvōg\ *n* **1** ♦ **:** popular acceptance or favor : POPULARITY **2 :** a period of popularity **3** ♦ **:** one that is in fashion at a particular time

♦ [1] favor, modishness, popularity ♦ [3] craze, fad, mode, rage, style, trend

vogu•ish \ˈvō-gish\ *adj* **1 :** FASHIONABLE, SMART **2 :** suddenly or temporarily popular
[1]**voice** \ˈvȯis\ *n* **1 :** sound produced through the mouth by vertebrates and especially by human beings (as in speaking or singing) **2 :** musical sound produced by the vocal cords : the power to produce such sound; *also* **:** one of the melodic parts in a vocal or instrumental composition **3 :** the vocal organs as a means of tone production ⟨train the ~⟩ **4 :** sound produced by vibration of the vocal cords as heard in vowels and some consonants **5 :** the power of speaking **6 :** a sound suggesting a voice ⟨the ~ of the sea⟩ **7 :** an instrument or medium of expression **8** ♦ **:** a choice, opinion, or wish openly expressed; *also* **:** right of expression **9 :** distinction of form of a verb to indicate the relation of the subject to the action expressed by the verb **10 :** one that sings : SINGER

♦ articulation, expression, formulation, statement, utterance

[2]**voice** *vb* **voiced; voic•ing** ♦ **:** to give voice or expression to ⟨~ a complaint⟩

♦ air, express, give, look, sound, state, vent

voice box *n* **:** LARYNX
voiced \ˈvȯist\ *adj* **1 :** having a voice ⟨soft-*voiced*⟩ **2** ♦ **:** uttered with voice ⟨a ~ consonant⟩ — **voiced•ness** \ˈvȯist-nəs, ˈvȯi-səd-nəs\ *n*

♦ oral, vocal

voice•less \ˈvȯis-ləs\ *adj* **1** ♦ **:** having no voice **2 :** not pronounced with voice — **voice•less•ly** *adv* — **voice•less•ness** *n*

♦ dumb, inarticulate, mute, speechless

voice mail *n* **:** an electronic communication system in which spoken messages are recorded for later playback to the intended recipient; *also* **:** such a message
voice–over *n* **:** the voice in a film or television program of a person who is heard but not seen or not seen talking
voice•print \ˈvȯis-ˌprint\ *n* **:** an individually distinctive pattern of voice characteristics that is spectrographically produced
[1]**void** \ˈvȯid\ *adj* **1 :** UNOCCUPIED, VACANT **2** ♦ **:** containing noth-

ing : EMPTY **3** ♦ : being without something specified : DEVOID ⟨proposals ~ of sense⟩ **4** : VAIN, USELESS **5** ♦ : of no legal force or effect : NULL

♦ [2] bare, blank, devoid, empty, stark, vacant ♦ [3] bereft, destitute, devoid ♦ [5] invalid, null

²void *n* **1** ♦ : empty space : EMPTINESS **2** : a feeling of want or hollowness

♦ blank, blankness, emptiness, vacancy, vacuity

³void *vb* **1** ♦ : to make or leave empty; *also* : VACATE **2** : DISCHARGE, EMIT ⟨~ urine⟩ **3** ♦ : to render void : ANNUL ⟨~ a contract⟩ — **void•able** *adj* — **void•er** *n*

♦ [1] clear, empty, evacuate, vacate ♦ [3] abolish, abrogate, annul, cancel, dissolve, invalidate, negate, nullify, quash, repeal, rescind

voi•là \vwä-ˈlä\ *interj* — used to call attention or to express satisfaction or approval
voile \ˈvȯil\ *n* : a sheer fabric used for women's clothing and curtains
vol *abbr* **1** volume **2** volunteer
vol•a•tile \ˈvä-lət-ᵊl\ *adj* **1** : readily becoming a vapor at a relatively low temperature ⟨a ~ liquid⟩ **2** ♦ : likely to change suddenly ⟨a ~ temper⟩ — **vol•a•til•i•ty** \ˌvä-lə-ˈti-lə-tē\ *n* — **vol•a•til•ize** \ˈvä-lət-ᵊl-ˌīz\ *vb*

♦ capricious, changeable, fickle, fluid, inconstant, mercurial, mutable, temperamental, uncertain, unpredictable, unsettled, unstable, unsteady, variable

vol•ca•nic \väl-ˈka-nik\ *adj* **1** : of, relating to, or produced by a volcano **2** ♦ : explosively violent

♦ explosive, ferocious, fierce, furious, hot, rabid, rough, stormy, tempestuous, turbulent, violent

vol•ca•nism \ˈväl-kə-ˌni-zəm\ *n* : volcanic action or activity
vol•ca•no \väl-ˈkā-nō\ *n, pl* **-noes** *or* **-nos** : an opening in the crust of the earth, a planet, or a moon from which molten rock and steam issue; *also* : a hill or mountain composed of the ejected material
vol•ca•nol•o•gy \ˌväl-kə-ˈnä-lə-jē\ *n* : a branch of geology that deals with volcanic phenomena — **vol•ca•nol•o•gist** \-kə-ˈnä-lə-jist\ *n*
vole \ˈvōl\ *n* : any of various small rodents that are closely related to the lemmings and muskrats
vo•li•tion \vō-ˈli-shən\ *n* **1** ♦ : the act or the power of making a choice or decision : WILL **2** : a choice or decision made

♦ accord, choice, free will, option, self-determination, will

vo•li•tion•al \vō-ˈli-shə-nəl\ *adj* : of, relating to, or of the nature of volition : possessing or exercising volition
¹vol•ley \ˈvä-lē\ *n, pl* **volleys** **1** : a flight of missiles (as arrows) **2** : simultaneous discharge of a number of missile weapons **3** : an act of volleying **4** ♦ : a burst of many things at once ⟨a ~ of angry letters⟩

♦ barrage, bombardment, cannonade, fusillade, hail, salvo, shower, storm

²volley *vb* **vol•leyed; vol•ley•ing** **1** : to discharge or become discharged in or as if in a volley **2** : to hit an object of play (as a ball) in the air before it touches the ground
vol•ley•ball \-ˌbȯl\ *n* : a game played by volleying an inflated ball over a net; *also* : the ball used in this game
volt \ˈvōlt\ *n* : the meter-kilogram-second unit of electrical potential difference and electromotive force equal to the difference in potential between two points in a wire carrying a constant current of one ampere when the power dissipated between the points is equal to one watt
volt•age \ˈvōl-tij\ *n* : potential difference measured in volts
vol•ta•ic \väl-ˈtā-ik, vōl-\ *adj* : of, relating to, or producing direct electric current by chemical action
volte–face \ˌvȯlt-ˈfäs, ˌvȯl-tə-\ *n* : a reversal in policy : ABOUT-FACE
volt•me•ter \ˈvōlt-ˌmē-tər\ *n* : an instrument for measuring in volts the difference in potential between different points of an electrical circuit
vol•u•ble \ˈväl-yə-bəl\ *adj* : fluent and smooth in speech : GLIB — **vol•u•bil•i•ty** \ˌväl-yə-ˈbi-lə-tē\ *n* — **vol•u•bly** \ˈväl-yə-blē\ *adv*
vol•ume \ˈväl-yəm\ *n* **1** : a series of printed sheets bound typically in book form; *also* : an arbitrary number of issues of a periodical **2** : space occupied as measured by cubic units ⟨the ~ of a cylinder⟩ **3** : sufficient matter to fill a book ⟨her glance spoke ~*s*⟩ **4 a** : the total number or quantity : AMOUNT ⟨increasing ~ of business⟩ **b** : considerable quantity **5** : the degree of loudness of a sound
vo•lu•mi•nous \və-ˈlü-mə-nəs\ *adj* ♦ : having or marked by great volume or bulk : LARGE — **vo•lu•mi•nous•ly** *adv*

♦ big, grand, great, large, sizable, substantial

vo•lu•mi•nous•ness *n* : the quality or state of being voluminous
¹vol•un•tary \ˈvä-lən-ˌter-ē\ *adj* **1** ♦ : done, made, or given freely and without compulsion ⟨a ~ sacrifice⟩ **2** : done on purpose : INTENTIONAL ⟨~ manslaughter⟩ **3** ♦ : of, relating to, or regulated by the will ⟨~ behavior⟩ **4** : having power of free choice **5** : provided or supported by voluntary action ⟨a ~ organization⟩ — **vol•un•tar•i•ly** \ˌvä-lən-ˈter-ə-lē\ *adv*

♦ [1] deliberate, freewill, intentional, purposeful, willful, willing ♦ [3] discretionary, elective, optional

²voluntary *n, pl* **-tar•ies** : an organ solo played in a religious service
voluntary muscle *n* : muscle (as most striated muscle) under voluntary control
¹vol•un•teer \ˌvä-lən-ˈtir\ *n* **1** : a person who voluntarily undertakes a service or duty **2** : a plant growing spontaneously especially from seeds lost from a previous crop
²volunteer *vb* **1** ♦ : to offer or give voluntarily **2** : to offer oneself as a volunteer

♦ bestow, contribute, donate, give, present

vo•lup•tu•ary \və-ˈləp-chə-ˌwer-ē\ *n, pl* **-ar•ies** : a person whose chief interest in life is the indulgence of sensual appetites
vo•lup•tu•ous \-chə-wəs\ *adj* **1** ♦ : giving sensual gratification **2** : given to or spent in enjoyment of luxury or pleasure — **vo•lup•tu•ous•ly** *adv* — **vo•lup•tu•ous•ness** *n*

♦ carnal, fleshly, luscious, sensual, sensuous

vo•lute \və-ˈlüt\ *n* : a spiral or scroll-shaped decoration
¹vom•it \ˈvä-mət\ *n* : an act or instance of throwing up the contents of the stomach through the mouth; *also* : the matter thrown up
²vomit *vb* **1** ♦ : to throw up the contents of the stomach through the mouth **2** : to belch forth : GUSH

♦ gag, heave, spit up, throw up

voo•doo \ˈvü-dü\ *n, pl* **voodoos** **1** : a religion that is derived from African polytheism and is practiced chiefly in Haiti **2** ♦ : a person who deals in spells and necromancy **3** : a charm used in voodoo; *also* : ²SPELL 1 — **voodoo** *adj*

♦ conjurer, enchanter, magician, necromancer, sorcerer, witch, wizard

voo•doo•ism \-ˌi-zəm\ *n* **1** : VOODOO 1 **2** : the practice of witchcraft
vo•ra•cious \vȯ-ˈrā-shəs, və-\ *adj* **1** ♦ : having a huge appetite : RAVENOUS **2** ♦ : very eager ⟨a ~ reader⟩ — **vo•ra•cious•ly** *adv* — **vo•ra•cious•ness** *n* — **vo•rac•i•ty** \-ˈra-sə-tē\ *n*

♦ [1] gluttonous, greedy, hoggish, piggish, rapacious, ravenous ♦ [2] ardent, avid, eager, enthusiastic, keen

vor•tex \ˈvȯr-ˌteks\ *n, pl* **vor•ti•ces** \ˈvȯr-tə-ˌsēz\ *also* **vor•tex•es** \ˈvȯr-ˌtek-səz\ : WHIRLPOOL; *also* : something resembling a whirlpool
vo•ta•ry \ˈvō-tə-rē\ *n, pl* **-ries** **1 a** : ENTHUSIAST, DEVOTEE **b** ♦ : a devoted adherent or admirer **2** ♦ : a devout or zealous worshiper

♦ [1b, 2] adherent, convert, disciple, follower, partisan, pupil

¹vote \ˈvōt\ *n* **1** : a choice or opinion of a person or body of persons expressed usually by a ballot, spoken word, or raised hand; *also* : the ballot, word, or gesture used to express a choice or opinion **2** : the decision reached by voting **3** ♦ : the right or privilege of voting in political matters **4** : a group of voters with some common characteristics ⟨the big city ~⟩ — **vote•less** *adj*

♦ enfranchisement, franchise, suffrage *Ant* disenfranchisement

²vote *vb* **vot•ed; vot•ing** **1** : to cast a vote **2** : to elect, decide, pass, defeat, grant, or make legal by a vote **3** : to declare by general agreement **4** ♦ : to offer as a suggestion : PROPOSE **5** : to cause to vote especially in a given way — **vot•er** *n*

♦ advance, offer, pose, proffer, propose, propound, suggest

vo•tive \ˈvō-tiv\ *adj* : consisting of or expressing a vow, wish, or desire
vou *abbr* voucher
vouch \ˈvau̇ch\ *vb* **1** : to give tangible support to : PROVE **2** : to verify by examining documentary evidence **3** : to give a guarantee **4** ♦ : to supply supporting evidence or testimony; *also* : to give personal assurance

♦ attest, authenticate, avouch, certify, testify, witness

vouch•er \ˈvau̇-chər\ *n* **1 :** an act of vouching **2 :** one that vouches for another **3 :** a documentary record of a business transaction **4 :** a written affidavit or authorization **5 :** a form indicating a credit against future purchases or expenditures

vouch•safe \vau̇ch-ˈsāf\ *vb* **vouch•safed; vouch•saf•ing :** to grant or give as or as if a privilege or a special favor

1vow \ˈvau̇\ *n* ♦ **:** a solemn promise or statement; *esp* **:** one by which a person is bound to an act, service, or condition ⟨marriage *~s*⟩

♦ oath, pledge, promise, troth, word

2vow *vb* **1** ♦ **:** to make a vow or as a vow **2 :** to bind or commit by a vow — **vow•er** *n*

♦ covenant, pledge, promise, swear

vow•el \ˈvau̇-əl\ *n* **1 :** a speech sound produced without obstruction or friction in the mouth **2 :** a letter representing such a sound

vox po•pu•li \ˈväks-ˈpä-pyə-ˌlī\ *n* **:** popular sentiment

1voy•age \ˈvȯi-ij\ *n* ♦ **:** a journey especially by water from one place or country to another

♦ crossing, cruise, passage, sail

2voyage *vb* **voy•aged; voy•ag•ing** ♦ **:** to take or make a voyage — **voy•ag•er** *n*

♦ journey, tour, travel, trek ♦ boat, cruise, navigate, sail

voya•geur \ˌvȯi-ə-ˈzhər, ˌvwä-yä-\ *n* **:** a person employed by a fur company to transport goods to and from remote stations especially in the Canadian Northwest

voy•eur \vwä-ˈyər, vȯi-ˈər\ *n* **1 :** one who obtains sexual pleasure from viewing especially covertly the nudity or sexual activity of others **2 :** an observer of the sordid — **voy•eur•is•tic** \ˌvwä-(ˌ)yər-ˈis-tik, ˌvȯi-ər-\ *adj* — **voy•eur•ism** \-ˌi-zəm\ *n*

VP *abbr* **1** verb phrase **2** vice president

vs *abbr* **1** verse **2** versus

vss *abbr* **1** verses **2** versions

V/STOL *abbr* vertical or short takeoff and landing

Vt *or* **VT** *abbr* Vermont

VTOL *abbr* vertical takeoff and landing

VTR *abbr* videotape recorder

vul•ca•nize \ˈvəl-kə-ˌnīz\ *vb* **-nized; -niz•ing :** to treat rubber or rubberlike material chemically to give useful properties (as elasticity and strength)

Vulg *abbr* Vulgate

vul•gar \ˈvəl-gər\ *adj* **1 :** of or relating to common speech **:** VERNACULAR **2** ♦ **:** of or relating to the common people **:** COMMON **3 a** ♦ **:** lacking cultivation or refinement **b :** offensive to good taste or refined feelings **:** OBSCENE — **vul•gar•ly** *adv*

♦ [2] common, humble, ignoble, inferior, low, lowly, mean, plebeian ♦ [3a] coarse, common, crass, crude, gross, ill-bred, low, rough, rude, tasteless, uncouth, uncultivated, uncultured, unpolished, unrefined

vul•gar•i•an \ˌvəl-ˈgar-ē-ən\ *n* **:** a vulgar person

vul•gar•ism \ˈvəl-gə-ˌri-zəm\ *n* **1 :** VULGARITY **2 :** a word or expression originated or used chiefly by illiterate persons **3 :** a coarse expression **:** OBSCENITY

vul•gar•i•ty \ˌvəl-ˈgar-ə-tē\ *n, pl* **-ties 1 :** something vulgar **2** ♦ **:** the quality or state of being vulgar

♦ bawdiness, grossness, indecency, lewdness, nastiness, obscenity, ribaldry, smut ♦ coarseness, grossness, indelicacy, lowness, rudeness

vul•gar•ize \ˈvəl-gə-ˌrīz\ *vb* **-ized; -iz•ing :** to make vulgar — **vul•gar•i•za•tion** \ˌvəl-gə-rə-ˈzā-shən\ *n* — **vul•gar•iz•er** \ˈvəl-gə-ˌrī-zər\ *n*

Vul•gate \ˈvəl-ˌgāt\ *n* **:** a Latin version of the Bible used by the Roman Catholic Church

vul•ner•a•bil•i•ty \ˌvəl-nə-rə-ˈbi-lə-tē\ *n* ♦ **:** the quality or state of being vulnerable

♦ exposure, liability, openness

vul•ner•a•ble \ˈvəl-nə-rə-bəl\ *adj* **1** ♦ **:** capable of being wounded **:** susceptible to wounds **2** ♦ **:** open to attack **3 :** liable to increased penalties in contract bridge — **vul•ner•a•bly** \ˈvəl-nə-rə-blē\ *adv*

♦ [1] exposed, liable, open, sensitive, subject, susceptible ♦ [2] defenseless (*or* defenceless), exposed, helpless, susceptible, undefended, unguarded, unprotected, unresistant

vul•pine \ˈvəl-ˌpīn\ *adj* **:** of, relating to, or resembling a fox especially in cunning

vul•ture \ˈvəl-chər\ *n* **1 :** any of various large birds (as a turkey vulture) related to the hawks, eagles, and falcons but having weaker claws and the head usually naked and living chiefly on carrion **2 :** a rapacious person

vul•va \ˈvəl-və\ *n, pl* **vul•vae** \-ˌvē\ **:** the external parts of the female genital organs — **vul•val** \ˈvəl-vəl\ *or* **vul•var** \-vər, -ˌvär\ *adj*

vv *abbr* **1** verses **2** vice versa

vying *pres part of* VIE

W

1w \ˈdə-bəl-(ˌ)yü\ *n, pl* **w's** *or* **ws** *often cap* **:** the 23d letter of the English alphabet

2w *abbr, often cap* **1** water **2** watt **3** week **4** weight **5** west; western **6** wide; width **7** wife **8** with

W *symbol* tungsten

WA *abbr* **1** Washington **2** Western Australia

wacky \ˈwa-kē\ *adj* **wack•i•er; -est** ♦ **:** eccentric or irrational especially in an amusing, absurd, or fantastic manner; *also* **:** CRAZY

♦ far-out, funny, odd, quirky, screwy, strange, wild ♦ absurd, cockeyed, crazy, cuckoo, daft, foolish, harebrained, insane, mad, nutty, preposterous, sappy, screwball, silly, zany

1wad \ˈwäd\ *n* **1** ♦ **:** a little mass, bundle, or tuft ⟨*~s* of clay⟩ **2 :** a soft mass of usually light fibrous material **3 :** a pliable plug (as of felt) used to retain a powder charge (as in a cartridge) **4** ♦ **:** a considerable amount (as of money) **5 :** a roll of paper money

♦ [1] blob, chunk, clod, clump, glob, gob, hunk, lump, nub ♦ [4] fortune, mint

2wad *vb* **wad•ded; wad•ding 1 :** to push a wad into ⟨~ a gun⟩ **2** ♦ **:** to form into a wad **3 :** to hold in by a wad ⟨~ a bullet in a gun⟩ **4 :** to stuff or line with a wad **:** PAD

♦ agglomerate, ball, conglomerate, roll, round ***Ant*** unroll

wad•ding \ˈwä-diŋ\ *n* **1 :** WADS; *also* **:** material for making wads **2 :** a soft mass or sheet of short loose fibers used for stuffing or padding

wad•dle \ˈwäd-ᵊl\ *vb* **wad•dled; wad•dling :** to walk with short steps swaying from side to side like a duck — **waddle** *n*

wade \ˈwād\ *vb* **wad•ed; wad•ing 1 :** to step in or through a medium (as water) more resistant than air **2 :** to move or go with difficulty or labor and often with determination ⟨~ through a dull book⟩ **3 :** to set to work or attack with determination or vigor — used with *in* or *into* — **wad•able** *or* **wade•able** \ˈwā-də-bəl\ *adj* — **wade** *n*

wad•er \ˈwā-dər\ *n* **1 :** one that wades **2 :** SHOREBIRD; *also* **:** WADING BIRD **3** *pl* **:** a waterproof garment consisting of pants with attached boots for wading

wa•di \ˈwä-dē\ *n* **:** a streambed of southwest Asia and northern Africa that is dry except in the rainy season

wading bird *n* **:** any of an order of long-legged birds (as sandpipers, cranes, or herons) that wade in water in search of food

wa•fer \ˈwā-fər\ *n* **1 :** a thin crisp cake or cracker **2 :** a thin round piece of unleavened bread used in the Eucharist **3 :** something (as a piece of candy) that resembles a wafer

1waf•fle \ˈwä-fəl\ *n* **:** a soft but crisped cake of batter cooked in a special hinged metal utensil (**waffle iron**)

2waffle *vb* **waf•fled; waf•fling** \-f(ə)liŋ\ **:** to speak or write in a vague or evasive manner

1waft \ˈwäft, ˈwaft\ *vb* ♦ **:** to cause to move or go lightly by or as if by the impulse of wind or waves

♦ drift, float, glide, hang, hover, poise, ride, sail

[2]**waft** *n* **1** ♦ **:** a slight breeze **:** PUFF **2 :** the act of waving

♦ air, breath, breeze, puff, zephyr

[1]**wag** \ˈwag\ *vb* **wagged; wag·ging 1 :** to sway or swing shortly from side to side or to-and-fro ⟨the dog *wagged* his tail⟩ **2 :** to move in chatter **3 :** GOSSIP ⟨scandal caused tongues to ~⟩

[2]**wag** *n* **:** an act of wagging **:** a wagging movement

[3]**wag** *n* ♦ **:** a person full of sport and humor **:** JOKER

♦ card, comedian, comic, humorist, jester, joker, wit

[1]**wage** \ˈwāj\ *n* **1** ♦ **:** payment for labor or services usually according to contract — often used in pl. **2** *pl* **:** an equivalent or a return for something done, suffered, or given **:** RECOMPENSE

♦ *usu* **wages** *pl* emolument, hire, pay, payment, salary, stipend

[2]**wage** *vb* **waged; wag·ing 1 :** to engage in **:** CARRY ON ⟨~ a war⟩ **2 :** to be in process of being waged

[1]**wa·ger** \ˈwā-jər\ *n* **1 :** something (as a sum of money) risked on an uncertain event **:** BET, STAKE **2 :** something on which bets are laid **:** GAMBLE

[2]**wager** *vb* ♦ **:** to make a bet

♦ bet, gamble, go, lay, stake

wa·ger·er *n* **:** one that makes a wager

wag·gery \ˈwa-gə-rē\ *n, pl* **-ger·ies 1** ♦ **:** playfulness and mischievous merriment **2** ♦ **:** something done or said in fun **:** JEST

♦ [1] devilishness, impishness, knavery, mischief, mischievousness, rascality, shenanigans, wickedness ♦ [2] crack, gag, jest, joke, laugh, pleasantry, quip, sally, wisecrack, witticism

wag·gish \ˈwa-gish\ *adj* **1** ♦ **:** resembling or characteristic of a wag **:** MISCHIEVOUS **2 :** done or made for fun **:** HUMOROUS

♦ devilish, impish, knavish, mischievous, rascally, roguish, sly, wicked

wag·gle \ˈwa-gəl\ *vb* **wag·gled; wag·gling :** to move backward and forward or from side to side **:** WAG

waggle *n* **:** a jerky motion back and forth or up and down

wag·gon *chiefly Brit var of* WAGON

wag·on \ˈwa-gən\ *n* **1 :** a 4-wheeled vehicle; *esp* **:** one drawn by animals and used for freight or merchandise **2 :** PADDY WAGON **3 :** a child's 4-wheeled cart **4 :** STATION WAGON

wag·on·er \ˈwa-gə-nər\ *n* **:** the driver of a wagon

wag·on·ette \ˌwa-gə-ˈnet\ *n* **:** a light wagon with two facing seats along the sides behind a cross seat in front

wa·gon–lit \ˌvȧ-gōⁿ-ˈlē\ *n, pl* **wagons–lits** *or* **wagon–lits** *same or* -ˈlēz\ **:** a railroad sleeping car

wagon train *n* **:** a column of wagons traveling overland

wag·tail \ˈwag-ˌtāl\ *n* **:** any of various slender-bodied mostly Old World birds with a long tail that jerks up and down

wa·hi·ne \wä-ˈhē-nē, -ˌnā\ *n* **1 :** a Polynesian woman **2 :** a female surfer

wa·hoo \ˈwä-ˌhü\ *n, pl* **wahoos :** a large vigorous food and sport fish related to the mackerel and found in warm seas

waif \ˈwāf\ *n* **1 :** something found without an owner and especially by chance **2 :** a stray person or animal; *esp* **:** a homeless child

[1]**wail** \ˈwāl\ *vb* **1** ♦ **:** to express sorrow audibly **:** make a mournful outcry **2 :** to make a sound suggestive of a mournful cry **3 :** to express dissatisfaction in a manner suggestive of sadness **:** COMPLAIN

♦ bay, howl, keen, yowl ♦ *usu* **wail for** bemoan, bewail, deplore, grieve, lament, mourn

[2]**wail** *n* ♦ **:** a usually prolonged cry or sound expressing grief or pain

♦ groan, howl, keen, lament, moan, plaint

wail·ful \-fəl\ *adj* **:** SORROWFUL, MOURNFUL — **wail·ful·ly** *adv*

wain \ˈwān\ *n* **:** a usually large heavy farm wagon

wain·scot \ˈwān-skət, -ˌskōt, -ˌskät\ *n* **1 :** a usually paneled wooden lining of an interior wall of a room **2 :** the lower part of an interior wall when finished differently from the rest — **wainscot** *vb*

wain·scot·ing *or* **wain·scot·ting** \-ˌskō-tiŋ, -ˌskä-, -skə-\ *n* **:** material for a wainscot; *also* **:** WAINSCOT

waist \ˈwāst\ *n* **1** ♦ **:** the narrowed part of the body between the chest and hips **2 :** a part resembling the human waist especially in narrowness or central position ⟨the ~ of a ship⟩ **3 :** a garment or part of a garment (as a blouse or bodice) for the upper part of the body

♦ middle, midriff

waist·band \-ˌband\ *n* **:** a band (as on pants or a skirt) that fits around the waist

waist·coat \ˈwes-kət, ˈwāst-ˌkōt\ *n, chiefly Brit* **:** VEST 1

waist·line \ˈwāst-ˌlīn\ *n* **1 :** an arbitrary usually imaginary line around the waist at its narrowest part; *also* **:** the length of this **2 :** the line at which the bodice and skirt of a dress meet

[1]**wait** \ˈwāt\ *vb* **1** ♦ **:** to remain inactive in readiness or expectation ⟨~ for orders⟩ **2 :** to delay serving (a meal) **3 :** to act as attendant or servant ⟨~ on customers⟩ **4 :** to attend as a waiter **:** SERVE ⟨~ tables⟩ ⟨~ at a banquet⟩ **5** ♦ **:** to be ready

♦ [1, 5] await, bide, hold on, stay

[2]**wait** *n* **1 :** a position of concealment usually with intent to attack or surprise ⟨lie in ~⟩ **2 :** an act or period of waiting

wait·er \ˈwā-tər\ *n* **1 :** one that waits on another; *esp* ♦ **:** a person who waits tables **2 :** TRAY

♦ server, waitperson, waitress

waiting game *n* **:** a strategy in which one or more participants withhold action in the hope of an opportunity for more effective action later

waiting room *n* **:** a room (as at a doctor's office) for the use of persons who are waiting

wait·per·son \ˈwāt-ˌpər-sən\ *n* ♦ **:** a waiter or waitress

♦ server, waiter, waitress

wait·ress \ˈwā-trəs\ *n* ♦ **:** a woman who waits tables

♦ server, waiter, waitperson

waive \ˈwāv\ *vb* **waived; waiv·ing 1 :** to give up claim to ⟨*waived* his right to a trial⟩ **2 :** POSTPONE

waiv·er \ˈwā-vər\ *n* **1 :** the act of waiving right, claim, or privilege **2 :** a document containing a declaration of a waiver

[1]**wake** \ˈwāk\ *vb* **woke** \ˈwōk\ *also* **waked** \ˈwākt\; **wo·ken** \ˈwō-kən\ *or* **waked** *also* **woke; wak·ing 1 :** to be or remain awake; *esp* **:** to keep watch (as over a corpse) **2** ♦ **:** to become awake **:** AWAKEN ⟨the baby *woke* up early⟩ **3 :** to rouse from sleep **:** AWAKEN

♦ arouse, awake, rouse

[2]**wake** *n* **1 :** the state of being awake **2 :** a watch held over the body of a dead person prior to burial

[3]**wake** *n* **:** the track left by a ship in the water; *also* **:** a track left behind

wake·board \ˈwāk-ˌbȯrd\ *n* **:** a short board with foot bindings on which a rider is towed by a motorboat across its wake — **wake·board·er** *n* — **wake·board·ing** *n*

wake·ful \ˈwāk-fəl\ *adj* ♦ **:** not sleeping or able to sleep **:** SLEEPLESS — **wake·ful·ness** *n*

♦ awake, sleepless, wide-awake ***Ant*** asleep, dormant, dozing, napping, resting, sleeping, slumbering

wak·en \ˈwā-kən\ *vb* **1 :** to cause to come awake **:** WAKE **2 :** to cease to be asleep **:** WAKE

wake–rob·in \ˈwāk-ˌrä-bən\ *n* **:** TRILLIUM

wake–up call *n* ♦ **:** something that serves to alert a person to a problem, danger, or need

♦ caution, tip-off, tocsin, warning

wak·ing \ˈwā-kiŋ\ *adj* **:** passed in a conscious or alert state ⟨every ~ hour⟩

wale \ˈwāl\ *n* **:** a ridge especially on cloth; *also* **:** the texture especially of a fabric

[1]**walk** \ˈwȯk\ *vb* **1** ♦ **:** to move or cause to move on foot usually at a natural unhurried gait ⟨~ to town⟩ ⟨~ a horse⟩ **2 :** to pass over, through, or along by walking ⟨~ the streets⟩ **3 :** to perform or accomplish by walking ⟨~ guard⟩ **4 :** to follow a course of action or way of life ⟨~ humbly in the sight of God⟩ **5 :** WALK OUT **6 :** to receive a base on balls; *also* **:** to give a base on balls to — **walk·er** *n*

♦ foot, leg, pad, step, traipse, tread

[2]**walk** *n* **1** ♦ **:** a going on foot ⟨go for a ~⟩ **2 :** a place, path, or course for walking **3 :** distance to be walked ⟨a quarter-mile ~ from here⟩ **4 :** manner of living **:** CONDUCT, BEHAVIOR **5 :** social or economic status ⟨various ~*s* of life⟩ **6 :** manner of walking **:** GAIT; *esp* **:** a slow 4-beat gait of a horse **7 :** BASE ON BALLS

♦ perambulation, ramble, stroll, turn

walk·away \ˈwȯ-kə-ˌwā\ *n* **:** an easily won contest

walk·ie–talk·ie \ˌwȯ-kē-ˈtȯ-kē\ *n* **:** a small portable radio transmitting and receiving set

[1]**walk–in** \ˈwȯk-ˌin\ *adj* **:** large enough to be walked into ⟨a ~ refrigerator⟩

²walk–in *n* **1 :** an easy election victory **2 :** one that walks in
walking papers *n pl* **:** DISMISSAL, DISCHARGE
walking stick *n* **1 :** a stick used in walking **2 :** STICK INSECT; *esp* **:** one of the U.S. and Canada
walk–on \ˈwȯk-ˌȯn, -ˌän\ *n* **:** a small part in a dramatic production
walk•out \-ˌau̇t\ *n* **1 :** a labor strike **2 :** the action of leaving a meeting or organization as an expression of disapproval
walk out *vb* **1 :** to leave suddenly often as an expression of disapproval **2 :** to go on strike
walk•over \-ˌō-vər\ *n* **:** a one-sided contest **:** an easy victory
walk–up \ˈwȯk-ˌəp\ *n* **:** a building or apartment house without an elevator — **walk–up** *adj*
walk•way \-ˌwā\ *n* **:** a passage for walking
¹wall \ˈwȯl\ *n* **1 a ♦ :** a structure (as of stone or brick) intended for defense or security or for enclosing something **b ♦ :** something that resembles a wall in function especially by establishing limits or providing defense **2 :** one of the upright enclosing parts of a building or room **3 :** the inside surface of a cavity or container ⟨the ~ of a boiler⟩ **4 :** something like a wall in appearance, function, or effect ⟨a tariff ~⟩ — **walled** \ˈwȯld\ *adj*

♦ [1a] barrier, fence, hedge ♦ [1b] aegis, armor, cover, defense (*or* defence), guard, protection, safeguard, screen, security, shield, ward

²wall *vb* **1 ♦ :** to provide, separate, or surround with or as if with a wall ⟨~ in a garden⟩ **2 :** to close (an opening) with or as if with a wall ⟨~ up a door⟩

♦ *usu* **wall in** cage, closet, coop, corral, encase, enclose, envelop, fence, hedge, hem, house, immure, pen

wal•la•by \ˈwä-lə-bē\ *n, pl* **wallabies** *also* **wallaby :** any of various small or medium-sized kangaroos
wall•board \ˈwȯl-ˌbōrd\ *n* **:** a structural material (as of wood pulp or plaster) made in large sheets and used for sheathing interior walls and ceilings
wal•let \ˈwä-lət\ *n* **1 :** a bag or sack for carrying things on a journey **2 :** a pocketbook with compartments (as for personal papers and usually unfolded money) **:** BILLFOLD
wall•eye \ˈwȯ-ˌlī\ *n* **1 :** an eye with a whitish iris or an opaque white cornea **2 :** a large vigorous No. American food and sport fish related to the perches — **wall•eyed** \-ˌlīd\ *adj*
wall•flow•er \ˈwȯl-ˌflau̇-ər\ *n* **1 :** any of several Old World herbs related to the mustards; *esp* **:** one with showy fragrant flowers **2 :** a person who usually from shyness or unpopularity remains alone (as at a dance)
Wal•loon \wä-ˈlün\ *n* **:** a member of a people of southern and southeastern Belgium and adjacent parts of France — **Walloon** *adj*
¹wal•lop \ˈwä-ləp\ *vb* **1 ♦ :** to beat soundly **:** TROUNCE **2 ♦ :** to hit hard and often repeatedly

♦ [1] clobber, drub, rout, skunk, thrash, trim, trounce, whip ♦ [2] bash, bat, batter, beat, belt, bludgeon, buffet, club, drub, flog, hammer, hide, lace, lambaste, lick, maul, pelt, pound, thrash, thump, whale, whip

²wallop *n* **1 :** a powerful blow or impact **2 :** the ability to hit hard **3 :** emotional, sensory, or psychological force **:** IMPACT
wal•lop•ing \ˈwä-lə-piŋ\ *adj* **1 :** LARGE, WHOPPING **2 :** exceptionally fine or impressive
¹wal•low \ˈwä-lō\ *vb* **1 :** to roll oneself about sluggishly in or as if in deep mud ⟨hogs ~*ing* in the mire⟩ **2 :** to indulge oneself excessively ⟨~ in luxury⟩ **3 :** to become or remain helpless ⟨~ in ignorance⟩
²wallow *n* **:** a muddy or dust-filled area where animals wallow
wall•pa•per \ˈwȯl-ˌpā-pər\ *n* **:** decorative paper for the walls of a room — **wallpaper** *vb*
wall–to–wall *adj* **1 :** covering the entire floor ⟨*wall-to-wall* carpeting⟩ **2 :** covering or filling one entire space or time ⟨crowds of *wall-to-wall* people⟩
wal•nut \ˈwȯl-(ˌ)nət\ *n* **1 :** a nut with a furrowed usually rough shell and an adherent husk from any of a genus of trees related to the hickories; *esp* **:** the large edible nut of a Eurasian tree **2 :** a tree that bears walnuts **3 :** the usually reddish to dark brown wood of a walnut used especially in cabinetwork and veneers
wal•rus \ˈwȯl-rəs, ˈwäl-\ *n, pl* **walrus** *or* **wal•rus•es :** a large mammal of arctic waters that is related to the seals and has long ivory tusks
¹waltz \ˈwȯlts\ *n* **1 :** a gliding dance done to music having three beats to the measure **2 :** music for or suitable for waltzing
²waltz *vb* **1 :** to dance a waltz **2 :** to move or advance easily, successfully, or conspicuously ⟨he ~*ed* off with the championship⟩
wam•ble \ˈwäm-bəl\ *vb* **wam•bled; wam•bling :** to progress unsteadily or with a lurching shambling gait
Wam•pa•no•ag \ˌwäm-pə-ˈnō-(ˌ)ag; ˌwȯm-\ *n, pl* **Wampanoag** *or* **Wampanoags :** a member of an American Indian people of parts of Rhode Island and Massachusetts
wam•pum \ˈwäm-pəm\ *n* **1 :** beads made of shells strung in strands, belts, or sashes and used by No. American Indians as money and ornaments **2** *slang* **:** MONEY
wan \ˈwän\ *adj* **wan•ner; wan•nest 1 :** having a sickly, pale color suggestive of ill health **:** PALLID; *also* **:** FEEBLE **2 :** DIM, FAINT **3 :** LANGUID ⟨a ~ smile⟩ — **wan•ly** *adv* — **wan•ness** *n*
wand \ˈwänd\ *n* **1 :** a slender staff carried in a procession **2 :** the staff of a fairy, diviner, or magician
wan•der \ˈwän-dər\ *vb* **1 ♦ :** to move about aimlessly or without a fixed course or goal **:** RAMBLE **2 :** to go astray in conduct or thought; *esp* **:** to become delirious

♦ gad, gallivant, knock, maunder, meander, mope, ramble, range, roam, rove, traipse

wan•der•er *n* **♦ :** one that wanders

♦ drifter, nomad, rambler, rover, stroller, vagabond

wandering Jew *n* **:** either of two trailing or creeping plants cultivated for their showy and often white-striped foliage
wan•der•lust \ˈwän-dər-ˌləst\ *n* **:** strong longing for or impulse toward wandering
¹wane \ˈwān\ *vb* **waned; wan•ing 1 ♦ :** to grow gradually smaller or less ⟨the full moon ~*s* to new⟩ ⟨his strength *waned*⟩ **2 :** to lose power, prosperity, or influence **3 :** to draw near an end ⟨summer is *waning*⟩

♦ abate, decline, decrease, de-escalate, die, diminish, dwindle, ebb, fall, lessen, let up, lower, moderate, recede, relent, shrink, subside, taper

²wane *n* **:** a waning (as in size or power); *also* **:** a period in which something is waning
wan•gle \ˈwaŋ-gəl\ *vb* **wan•gled; wan•gling 1 ♦ :** to obtain by sly or devious means; *also* **:** to use trickery or questionable means to achieve an end **2 ♦ :** to adjust or manipulate especially for personal or fraudulent ends; *also* **:** FINAGLE

♦ [1, 2] contrive, finagle, finesse, frame, machinate, maneuver (*or* manoeuvre), mastermind, negotiate

wan•na–be *also* **wan•na•bee** \ˈwä-nə-ˌbē\ *n* **:** a person who wants or aspires to be someone or something else or who tries to look or act like someone else
¹want \ˈwȯnt, ˈwänt\ *vb* **1 :** to fail to possess **:** LACK ⟨they ~ the necessities of life⟩ **2 ♦ :** to feel the need of ⟨~*ed* a chance to rest⟩ **3 ♦ :** to be in need of **:** REQUIRE ⟨the house ~*s* painting⟩ **4 ♦ :** to desire earnestly **:** WISH

♦ [2, 3] demand, necessitate, need, require, take, warrant ♦ [4] ache for, covet, crave, desire, die (to *or* for), hanker (for *or* after), hunger for, long for, lust (for *or* after), pine for, repine for, thirst for, wish for, yearn for

²want *n* **1 ♦ :** a lack of a required or usual amount **2 ♦ :** dire need **:** DESTITUTION **3 :** something wanted **:** DESIRE **4 :** personal defect **:** FAULT

♦ [1] dearth, deficiency, deficit, failure, famine, inadequacy, insufficiency, lack, paucity, poverty, scantiness, scarcity, shortage ♦ [1] absence, lack, need ♦ [2] beggary, destitution, impecuniousness, impoverishment, indigence, need, pauperism, penury, poverty

¹want•ing \ˈwȯn-tiŋ, ˈwän-\ *adj* **1 ♦ :** not present or in evidence **:** ABSENT **2 ♦ :** falling below standards or expectations **3 ♦ :** lacking in ability or capacity **:** DEFICIENT ⟨~ in common sense⟩

♦ [1] absent, missing, nonexistent ♦ [2, 3] deficient, inadequate, insufficient, scarce, short, shy

²wanting *prep* **1 :** LESS, MINUS ⟨a month ~ two days⟩ **2 :** not having **:** WITHOUT ⟨a book ~ a cover⟩
¹wan•ton \ˈwȯnt-ᵊn, ˈwänt-\ *adj* **1 ♦ :** having, expressing, or inciting sensual desire or imagination **2 ♦ :** having no regard for justice or for other persons' feelings, rights, or safety **:** INHUMANE ⟨~ cruelty⟩ **3 :** having no just cause ⟨a ~ attack⟩ — **wan•ton•ly** *adv*

♦ [1] lascivious, lewd, lustful, passionate ♦ [2] barbarous, brutal, cruel, heartless, inhumane, sadistic, savage, vicious

²wanton *n* **:** a wanton individual; *esp* **:** a lewd or immoral person
³wanton *vb* **1 :** to be wanton **:** act wantonly **2 :** to pass or waste wantonly

wan•ton•ness *n* ♦ **:** the quality or state of being wanton

♦ barbarity, brutality, cruelty, inhumanity, sadism, savagery, viciousness

wa•pi•ti \ˈwä-pə-tē\ *n, pl* **wapiti** *or* **wapitis :** ELK 2
[1]**war** \ˈwȯr\ *n* **1** ♦ **:** a state or period of usually open and declared armed fighting between states or nations **2 :** the art or science of warfare **3** ♦ **:** a state of hostility, conflict, or antagonism **4 :** a struggle between opposing forces or for a particular end ⟨~ against disease⟩ — **war•less** \-ləs\ *adj*

♦ [1] combat, conflict, warfare *Ant* peace ♦ [3] conflict, discord, dissension, dissent, disunity, friction, schism, strife, variance, warfare

[2]**war** *vb* **warred; war•ring** ♦ **:** to engage in warfare **:** be in conflict

♦ *usu* **war against** battle, clash, combat, fight, scrimmage, skirmish

[3]**war** *abbr* warrant
[1]**war•ble** \ˈwȯr-bəl\ *n* **1** ♦ **:** a melodious succession of low pleasing sounds **2 :** a musical trill

♦ air, lay, melody, song, strain, tune

[2]**warble** *vb* **war•bled; war•bling 1 :** to sing or utter in a trilling manner or with variations **2 :** to express by or as if by warbling
[3]**warble** *n* **:** a swelling under the skin especially of the back of cattle, horses, and wild mammals caused by the maggot of a fly (**warble fly**); *also* **:** its maggot
war•bler \ˈwȯr-blər\ *n* **1 :** SONGSTER **2 :** any of various small slender-billed chiefly Old World songbirds related to the thrushes and noted for their singing **3 :** any of numerous small bright-colored insect-eating American birds with a usually weak and unmusical song
war•bon•net \ˈwȯr-ˌbä-nət\ *n* **:** a feathered American Indian ceremonial headdress
war crime *n* **:** a crime (as genocide) committed during or in connection with war
war cry *n* **1 :** a cry used by fighters in war **2 :** a slogan used especially to rally people to a cause
[1]**ward** \ˈwȯrd\ *n* **1** ♦ **:** a guarding or being under guard or guardianship; *esp* **:** CUSTODY **2 :** a body of guards **3 :** a division of a prison **4 :** a division in a hospital **5 :** a division of a city for electoral or administrative purposes **6 :** a person (as a child) under the protection of a guardian or a law court **7 :** a person or body of persons under the protection or tutelage of a government **8** ♦ **:** a means of defense **:** PROTECTION

♦ [1] care, custody, guardianship, keeping, safekeeping, trust ♦ [8] aegis, armor, cover, defense (*or* defence), guard, protection, safeguard, screen, security, shield, wall

[2]**ward** *vb* **:** to turn aside **:** DEFLECT — usually used with *off* ⟨~ off a blow⟩
[1]**-ward** \wərd\ *also* **-wards** \wərdz\ *adj suffix* **1 :** that moves, tends, faces, or is directed toward ⟨wind*ward*⟩ **2 :** that occurs or is situated in the direction of ⟨sea*ward*⟩
[2]**-ward** *or* **-wards** *adv suffix* **1 :** in a (specified) direction ⟨up*wards*⟩ ⟨after*ward*⟩ **2 :** toward a (specified) point, position, or area ⟨sky*ward*⟩
war dance *n* **:** a dance performed (as by American Indians) before going to war or in celebration of victory
war•den \ˈwȯrd-ᵊn\ *n* **1** ♦ **:** one having care or charge of something **:** GUARDIAN **2 :** the governor of a town, district, or fortress **3 :** an official charged with special supervisory or enforcement duties ⟨game ~⟩ ⟨air raid ~⟩ **4 :** an official in charge of the operation of a prison **5 :** one of two ranking lay officers of an Episcopal parish **6 :** any of various British college officials

♦ caretaker, custodian, guardian, janitor, keeper, watchman

ward•er \ˈwȯr-dər\ *n* ♦ **:** one that keeps guard especially at a tower, gate, or door **:** WATCHMAN

♦ custodian, guard, guardian, keeper, lookout, picket, sentry, warden, watch, watchman

ward heel•er \-ˌhē-lər\ *n* **:** a local worker for a political boss
ward•robe \ˈwȯr-ˌdrōb\ *n* **1 :** a room or closet where clothes are kept; *also* **:** CLOTHESPRESS **2 :** a collection of wearing apparel ⟨his summer ~⟩
ward•room \-ˌdrüm, -ˌdru̇m\ *n* **:** the dining area for officers aboard a warship
ward•ship \ˈwȯrd-ˌship\ *n* **1 :** GUARDIANSHIP **2 :** the state of being under care of a guardian
ware \ˈwar\ *n* **1 :** manufactured articles or products of art or craft **:** GOODS ⟨glass*ware*⟩ **2** ♦ **:** an article of merchandise — often used in pl. ⟨a peddler hawking his ~*s*⟩ **3 :** items (as dishes) of fired clay **:** POTTERY

♦ **wares** commodities, merchandise

ware•house \-ˌhau̇s\ *n* ♦ **:** a place for the storage of merchandise or commodities **:** STOREHOUSE — **warehouse** *vb* — **ware•house•man** \-mən\ *n* — **ware•hous•er** \-ˌhau̇-zər, -sər\ *n*

♦ depository, depot, magazine, repository, storage, storehouse

ware•room \ˈwar-ˌrüm, -ˌru̇m\ *n* **:** a room in which goods are exhibited for sale
war•fare \ˈwȯr-ˌfar\ *n* **1 :** military operations between enemies **:** WAR; *also* **:** an activity undertaken by one country to weaken or destroy another ⟨economic ~⟩ **2** ♦ **:** the process of struggle between competing entities **:** STRUGGLE, CONFLICT

♦ battle, combat, conflict, confrontation, contest, duel, face-off, rivalry, struggle, tug-of-war

war•fa•rin \ˈwȯr-fə-rən\ *n* **:** an anticoagulant compound used as a rodent poison and in medicine
war•head \ˈwȯr-ˌhed\ *n* **:** the section of a missile containing the charge
war•horse \-ˌhȯrs\ *n* **1 :** a horse for use in war **2 :** a veteran soldier or public person (as a politician) **3 :** a musical composition that is often performed
war•like \-ˌlīk\ *adj* **1** ♦ **:** fond of war ⟨~ peoples⟩ **2 :** of, relating to, or useful in war **:** MILITARY, MARTIAL ⟨~ supplies⟩ **3** ♦ **:** befitting or characteristic of war or of soldiers ⟨~ attitudes⟩

♦ [1, 3] aggressive, argumentative, bellicose, belligerent, combative, contentious, discordant, disputatious, militant, pugnacious, quarrelsome, scrappy, truculent

war•lock \-ˌläk\ *n* **:** SORCERER, WIZARD
war•lord \-ˌlȯrd\ *n* **1 :** a high military leader **2 :** a military commander exercising local civil power by force ⟨former Chinese ~*s*⟩
[1]**warm** \ˈwȯrm\ *adj* **1** ♦ **:** having or giving out heat to a moderate or adequate degree ⟨~ milk⟩ ⟨a ~ stove⟩ **2 :** serving to retain heat ⟨~ clothes⟩ **3 :** feeling or inducing sensations of heat ⟨~ from exercise⟩ ⟨a ~ climb⟩ **4 a :** showing or marked by strong feeling **:** ARDENT ⟨~ support⟩ **b** ♦ **:** demonstratively genial, cordial, or sympathetic ⟨~ to the idea⟩ **5 :** marked by tense excitement or hot anger ⟨a ~ campaign⟩ **6 :** giving a pleasant impression of warmth, cheerfulness, or friendliness ⟨~ colors⟩ ⟨a ~ tone of voice⟩ **7 :** marked by or tending toward injury, distress, or pain ⟨made things ~ for the enemy⟩ **8 :** newly made **:** FRESH ⟨a ~ scent⟩ **9 :** near to a goal ⟨getting ~ in a search⟩ — **warm•ly** *adv*

♦ [1] heated, tepid *Ant* chilled, cool, cooled ♦ [4b] amicable, companionable, comradely, cordial, friendly, genial, hearty, neighborly (*or* neighbourly), warmhearted ♦ [4b] affirmative, favorable, good, positive

[2]**warm** *vb* **1 :** to make or become warm **2 :** to give a feeling of warmth or vitality to **3 :** to experience feelings of affection or pleasure ⟨she ~*ed* to her guest⟩ **4 :** to reheat for eating ⟨~*ed* over the roast⟩ **5 :** to make ready for operation or performance by preliminary exercise or operation ⟨~ up the motor⟩ **6 :** to become increasingly ardent, interested, or competent ⟨the speaker ~*ed* to his topic⟩ — **warm•er** *n*
warm–blood•ed \-ˈblə-dəd\ *adj* **1 :** able to maintain a relatively high and constant body temperature relatively independent of that of the surroundings **2 :** ardent in spirit **:** expressing great feeling
warmed–over \ˈwȯrmd-ˈō-vər\ *adj* **1 :** REHEATED ⟨~ cabbage⟩ **2 :** not fresh or new ⟨~ ideas⟩
warm front *n* **:** an advancing edge of a warm air mass
warm•heart•ed \ˈwȯrm-ˈhär-təd\ *adj* ♦ **:** marked by or indicative of ready affection, generosity, cordiality, sympathy, or compassion — **warm•heart•ed•ness** *n*

♦ beneficent, benevolent, compassionate, good-hearted, humane, kind, kindly, sympathetic, tender, tenderhearted ♦ amicable, companionable, comradely, cordial, friendly, genial, hearty, neighborly (*or* neighbourly), warm

warming pan *n* **:** a long-handled covered pan filled with live coals and formerly used to warm a bed
war•mon•ger \ˈwȯr-ˌməŋ-gər, -ˌmäŋ-\ *n* ♦ **:** one who urges or attempts to stir up war — **war•mon•ger•ing** \-g(ə-)riŋ\ *n*

♦ agitator, firebrand, militant, rabble-rouser *Ant* dove, pacifist

warmth \ˈwȯrmth\ *n* ♦ **:** the quality or state of being warm in temperature or feeling

♦ ardor, emotion, fervency, fervor, heat, intensity, passion, vehemence

warm up *vb* **:** to engage in exercise or practice especially before entering a game or contest — **warm–up** \ˈwȯrm-ˌəp\ *n*

warn \ˈwȯrn\ *vb* **1 a** ♦ **:** to put on guard **:** CAUTION **b :** to give supportive advice to **:** ADMONISH **2** ♦ **:** to notify especially in advance **3 :** to order to go or keep away

♦ [1a, 2] alert, caution, forewarn

1warn•ing \ˈwȯr-niŋ\ *n* **1** ♦ **:** the act of warning **:** the state of being warned **2 :** something that warns or serves to warn

♦ admonition, alarm, alert, caution, notice

2warning *adj* ♦ **:** serving as an alarm, signal, summons, or admonition ⟨a ~ bell⟩ — **warn•ing•ly** *adv*

♦ cautionary

1warp \ˈwȯrp\ *n* **1 :** the lengthwise threads on a loom or in a woven fabric **2 :** a twist out of a true plane or straight line ⟨a ~ in a board⟩

2warp *vb* **1** ♦ **:** to turn or twist out of shape; *also* **:** to become so twisted **2** ♦ **:** to falsify, misinterpret, or give a false impression of **:** DISTORT **3 :** to lead astray

♦ [1] contort, deform, distort, screw ♦ [2] color (*or* colour), distort, falsify, garble, misinterpret, misrepresent, misstate, pervert, twist

war paint *n* **:** paint put on the face and body by American Indians as a sign of going to war

war•path \ˈwȯr-ˌpath, -ˌpȧth\ *n* **:** the course taken by a party of American Indians going on a hostile expedition — **on the warpath :** ready to fight or argue

warped \ˈwȯrpt\ *adj* **:** affected by warping **:** having become distorted or perverted

war•plane \-ˌplān\ *n* **:** a military airplane; *esp* **:** one armed for combat

warp speed *n* **:** the highest possible speed

1war•rant \ˈwȯr-ənt, ˈwär-\ *n* **1 :** AUTHORIZATION; *also* **:** JUSTIFICATION, GROUND **2 :** evidence (as a document) of authorization; *esp* **:** a legal writ authorizing an officer to take action (as in making an arrest, seizure, or search) **3 :** a certificate of appointment issued to an officer of lower rank than a commissioned officer

2warrant *vb* **1 :** to guarantee security or immunity to **:** SECURE **2** ♦ **:** to declare or maintain positively ⟨I ~ this is so⟩ **3 :** to assure (a person) of the truth of what is said **4 :** to guarantee to be as it appears or as it is represented ⟨~ goods as of the first quality⟩ **5** ♦ **:** to give authority or power to for doing or forbearing to do something **:** SANCTION **6 :** to give proof of **:** ATTEST **7 :** JUSTIFY ⟨his need ~*s* the expenditure⟩

♦ [2] affirm, allege, assert, aver, avouch, avow, claim, contend, declare, insist, maintain, profess, protest ♦ [5] approve, authorize, clear, OK, ratify, sanction

warrant officer *n* **1 :** an officer in the armed forces ranking next below a commissioned officer **2 :** a commissioned officer ranking below an ensign in the navy or coast guard and below a second lieutenant in the marine corps

war•ran•ty \ˈwȯr-ən-tē, ˈwär-\ *n, pl* **-ties** ♦ **:** an expressed or implied statement that some situation or thing is as it appears to be or is represented to be; *esp* **:** a usually written guarantee of the integrity of a product and of the maker's responsibility for the repair or replacement of defective parts

♦ bond, contract, covenant, guarantee, guaranty, surety

war•ren \ˈwȯr-ən, ˈwär-\ *n* **1 :** an area where rabbits breed; *also* **:** a structure where rabbits are bred or kept **2 :** a crowded tenement or district

war•rior \ˈwȯr-yər; ˈwȯr-ē-ər, ˈwär-\ *n* ♦ **:** a man engaged or experienced in warfare

♦ fighter, legionnaire, man-at-arms, regular, serviceman, soldier

war•ship \ˈwȯr-ˌship\ *n* **:** a naval vessel

wart \ˈwȯrt\ *n* **1 :** a small usually horny projecting growth on the skin; *esp* **:** one caused by a virus **2 :** a protuberance resembling a wart (as on a plant) — **warty** *adj*

wart•hog \ˈwȯrt-ˌhȯg, -ˌhäg\ *n* **:** a wild African hog that has large tusks and in the male two pairs of rough warty protuberances below the eyes

war•time \ˈwȯr-ˌtīm\ *n* **:** a period during which a war is in progress

wary \ˈwar-ē\ *adj* **war•i•er; -est** ♦ **:** very cautious; *esp* **:** careful in guarding against danger or deception — **war•i•ly** \ˈwer-ə-lē\ *adv* — **war•i•ness** \ˈwer-ē-nəs\ *n*

♦ alert, careful, cautious, circumspect, considerate, gingerly, guarded, heedful, safe

was *past 1st & 3d sing of* BE

wa•sa•bi \ˈwä-sə-bē; wä-ˈsä-\ *n* **:** a condiment prepared from the ground greenish root of an Asian herb and similar in flavor and use to horseradish; *also* **:** the herb or its root

1wash \ˈwȯsh, ˈwäsh\ *vb* **1 :** to clean with water and usually soap or detergent ⟨~ clothes⟩ ⟨~ your hands⟩ **2** ♦ **:** to wet thoroughly **:** DRENCH **3** ♦ **:** to flow along the border of ⟨waves ~ the shore⟩ **4 :** to pour or flow in a stream or current **5 :** to move or remove by or as if by the action of water **6 :** to cover or daub lightly with a liquid (as whitewash) **7** ♦ **:** to run water over (as gravel or ore) in order to separate valuable matter from refuse ⟨~ sand for gold⟩ **8 :** to undergo laundering ⟨a dress that doesn't ~ well⟩ **9 :** to stand a test ⟨that story will not ~⟩ **10 :** to be worn away by water **11 :** to pour, sweep, or flow in a stream or current

♦ [2] bathe, douse, drench, soak, sop, souse, water, wet ♦ [3] lap, lave, splash ♦ [7] flush, irrigate, rinse, sluice

2wash *n* **1 :** the act or process or an instance of washing or being washed **2 :** articles to be washed or being washed **3 :** the flow or action of a mass of water (as a wave) **4 :** erosion by waves (as of the sea) **5** *West* **:** the dry bed of a stream **6 :** worthless especially liquid waste **:** REFUSE, SWILL **7 :** a thin coat of paint (as watercolor) **8 :** a disturbance in a fluid (as water or the air) caused by the passage of a wing or propeller

3wash *adj* **:** WASHABLE

Wash *abbr* Washington

wash•able \ˈwȯ-shə-bəl, ˈwä-\ *adj* **:** capable of being washed without damage

wash–and–wear *adj* **:** of, relating to, or being a fabric or garment that needs little or no ironing after washing

wash•ba•sin \ˈwȯsh-ˌbās-ᵊn, ˈwäsh-\ *n* **:** WASHBOWL

wash•board \-ˌbōrd\ *n* **:** a grooved board to scrub clothes on

wash•bowl \-ˌbōl\ *n* **:** a large bowl for water for washing hands and face

wash•cloth \-ˌklȯth\ *n* **:** a cloth used for washing one's face and body

washed–out \ˈwȯsht-ˈau̇t, ˈwäsht-\ *adj* **1** ♦ **:** faded in color **2 :** EXHAUSTED ⟨felt ~ after working all night⟩

♦ dull, light, pale, pastel

washed–up \-ˈəp\ *adj* **:** no longer successful, popular, skillful, or needed

wash•er \ˈwȯ-shər, ˈwä-\ *n* **1 :** a ring or perforated plate used around a bolt or screw to ensure tightness or relieve friction **2 :** one that washes; *esp* **:** a machine for washing

wash•er•wom•an \-ˌwu̇-mən\ *n* **:** a woman whose occupation is washing clothes

wash•ing \ˈwȯ-shiŋ, ˈwä-\ *n* **1 :** material obtained by washing **2 :** articles washed or to be washed

washing soda *n* **:** SODIUM CARBONATE

Wash•ing•ton's Birthday \ˈwȯ-shiŋ-tənz-, ˈwä-\ *n* **:** the 3d Monday in February observed as a legal holiday

wash•out \ˈwȯsh-ˌau̇t, ˈwäsh-\ *n* **1 :** the washing away of earth (as from a road); *also* **:** a place where earth is washed away **2** ♦ **:** a complete failure

♦ bummer, bust, catastrophe, debacle, dud, failure, fiasco, fizzle, flop, lemon, loser, turkey

wash out *vb* **1 :** to wash free of an extraneous substance (as dirt) **2 :** to drain of color in laundering **3 :** to eliminate as useless or unsatisfactory **:** REJECT **4 :** to destroy or render useless by the force or action of water **5 :** to deplete of strength or vitality **:** EXHAUST **6** ♦ **:** to fail to meet requirements or measure up to a standard

♦ collapse, fail, flop, flunk, fold

wash•room \-ˌrüm, -ˌru̇m\ *n* **:** a room (as in a public building) equipped with washing and toilet facilities **:** BATHROOM

wash•stand \-ˌstand\ *n* **1 :** a stand holding articles needed for washing face and hands **2 :** LAVATORY 1

wash•tub \-ˌtəb\ *n* **:** a tub for washing or soaking clothes

wash•wom•an \ˈwȯsh-ˌwu̇-mən, ˈwäsh-\ *n* **:** WASHERWOMAN

washy \ˈwȯ-shē, ˈwä-\ *adj* **wash•i•er; -est 1 :** WEAK, WATERY **2 :** PALLID **3 :** lacking in vigor, individuality, or definiteness

wasp \ˈwäsp, ˈwȯsp\ *n* **:** any of numerous social or solitary winged insects related to the bees and ants with biting mouthparts and in females and workers an often formidable sting

WASP *or* **Wasp** *n* **:** an American of northern European and especially British ancestry and of Protestant background

wasp•ish \ˈwäs-pish, ˈwȯs-\ *adj* **1** ♦ **:** easily irritated **:** IRRITABLE **2 :** resembling a wasp in form; *esp* **:** slightly built

♦ choleric, crabby, cranky, cross, crotchety, grouchy, grumpy, irascible, irritable, peevish, perverse, petulant, short-tempered, snappish, snappy, snippy, testy

wasp waist *n* **:** a very slender waist
[1]**was•sail** \ˈwä-səl, wä-ˈsāl\ *n* **1 :** an early English toast to someone's health **2 :** a hot drink made with wine, beer, or cider, spices, sugar, and usually baked apples and traditionally served at Christmas **3 :** a period of riotous drinking
[2]**wassail** *vb* **1 :** CAROUSE **2 :** to drink to the health of — **was•sail•er** *n*
Was•ser•mann test \ˈwä-sər-mən-, ˈvä-\ *n* **:** a blood test for the detection of syphilis
wast•age \ˈwā-stij\ *n* ♦ **:** loss, decrease, or destruction of something (as by use, decay, erosion, or leakage)

♦ annihilation, demolition, desolation, destruction, devastation, havoc, loss, obliteration, ruin, wreckage

[1]**waste** \ˈwāst\ *n* **1** ♦ **:** a sparsely settled or barren region **:** DESERT; *also* **:** uncultivated land **2 a :** the act or an instance of wasting **:** the state of being wasted **b :** useless or profitless consumption or expenditure **3 :** gradual loss or decrease by use, wear, or decay **4** ♦ **:** material left over, rejected, or thrown away; *also* **:** an unwanted by-product of a manufacturing or chemical process **5 :** refuse (as garbage) that accumulates about habitations **6** ♦ **:** material (as feces) produced but not used by a living organism

♦ [1] barren, desert, desolation, wasteland ♦ [4] chaff, deadwood, dust, garbage, junk, litter, refuse, riffraff, rubbish, scrap, trash ♦ [6] droppings, slops

[2]**waste** *vb* **wast•ed; wast•ing 1** ♦ **:** to damage or destroy gradually and progressively **:** DEVASTATE **2 :** to wear away or diminish gradually **:** CONSUME **3** ♦ **:** to spend or use carelessly or uselessly **:** SQUANDER **4** ♦ **:** to lose or cause to lose weight, strength, or energy ⟨*wasting* away from fever⟩ **5 :** to become diminished in bulk or substance **:** DWINDLE

♦ [1] annihilate, blot out, demolish, desolate, destroy, devastate, do in, exterminate, extinguish, obliterate, pulverize, ruin, shatter, smash, tear down, wipe out, wreck ♦ [3] blow, dissipate, fritter, lavish, misspend, run through, spend, squander, throw away ***Ant*** conserve ♦ [4] debilitate, enervate, enfeeble, prostrate, sap, soften, tire, weaken ♦ *usu* **waste away** [4] decay, droop, fail, flag, go, lag, languish, sag, weaken, wilt

[3]**waste** *adj* **1 :** being wild and uninhabited **:** BARREN; *also* **:** UNCULTIVATED **2 :** being in a ruined condition **3 :** discarded as worthless after being used ⟨∼ water⟩ **4 :** excreted from or stored in inert form in a living organism as a by-product of vital activity ⟨∼ matter from birds⟩
waste•bas•ket \ˈwāst-ˌbas-kət\ *n* **:** a receptacle for refuse
wast•ed *adj* ♦ **:** showing or feeling the effects of wasting

♦ cadaverous, gaunt, haggard, skeletal

waste•ful \-fəl\ *adj* ♦ **:** given to or marked by lack of thrift or careful use — **waste•ful•ly** *adv*

♦ extravagant, prodigal, profligate, spendthrift, thriftless, unthrifty

waste•ful•ness *n* ♦ **:** the quality of fact of being wasteful

♦ extravagance, lavishness, prodigality

waste•land \-ˌland, -lənd\ *n* ♦ **:** land that is barren or unfit for cultivation

♦ barren, desert, desolation, waste

waste•pa•per \-ˈpā-pər\ *n* **:** paper thrown away as used, not needed, or not fit for use
wast•er *n* **:** one that wastes
wast•rel \ˈwā-strəl\ *n* ♦ **:** one that wastes **:** SPENDTHRIFT

♦ prodigal, profligate, spendthrift

[1]**watch** \ˈwäch, ˈwȯch\ *vb* **1 :** to be or stay awake intentionally **:** keep vigil ⟨∼*ed* by the patient's bedside⟩ ⟨∼ and pray⟩ **2 :** to be on the lookout for danger **:** be on one's guard **3 :** to keep guard ⟨∼ outside the door⟩ **4 a :** OBSERVE ⟨∼ a game⟩ **b :** to take care of **5 a** ♦ **:** to observe closely in order to check on action or change **b :** to keep in view so as to prevent harm or warn of danger ⟨∼ a brush fire carefully⟩ **6 :** to keep oneself informed about ⟨∼ his progress⟩ **7 :** to lie in wait for especially so as to take advantage of ⟨∼*ed* her opportunity⟩ **8** ♦ **:** to be expectant **:** wait for something

♦ [5a] follow, heed, listen, mind, note, observe, regard ♦ *usu* **watch for** [8] anticipate, await, expect, hope

[2]**watch** *n* **1** ♦ **:** the act of keeping awake to guard, protect, or attend; *also* **:** a state of alert and continuous attention **2 :** a public weather alert ⟨a winter storm ∼⟩ **3 :** close observation **4** ♦ **:** a person who watches **:** LOOKOUT; *also* **:** the office or function of a sentinel or guard **5 :** a period during which a part of a ship's crew is on duty; *also* **:** the part of a crew on duty during a watch **6 :** a portable timepiece carried on the person

♦ [1] alertness, attentiveness, lookout, surveillance, vigilance ♦ [4] custodian, guard, guardian, keeper, lookout, picket, sentry, warden, warder, watchman

watch•band \ˈwäch-ˌband, ˈwȯch-\ *n* **:** the bracelet or strap of a wristwatch
watch•dog \-ˌdȯg\ *n* **1 :** a dog kept to guard property **2 :** one that guards or protects
watch•er \ˈwäch-ər, ˈwȯch-\ *n* ♦ **:** one that watches

♦ custodian, guard, guardian, keeper, lookout, picket, sentinel, sentry, warden, warder, watch, watchman

watch•ful \-fəl\ *adj* ♦ **:** steadily attentive and alert especially to danger **:** VIGILANT — **watch•ful•ly** *adv*

♦ alert, attentive, awake, vigilant, wide-awake

watch•ful•ness *n* **:** the act or state of being watchful
watch•mak•er \-ˌmā-kər\ *n* **:** a person who makes or repairs watches — **watch•mak•ing** \-ˌmā-kiŋ\ *n*
watch•man \-mən\ *n* **1** ♦ **:** a person assigned to watch **:** GUARD **2** ♦ **:** one who is employed to patrol property for the purpose of protecting it against theft, fire, or other damage

♦ [1, 2] custodian, guard, guardian, keeper, lookout, picket, sentry, warden, warder, watch

watch night *n* **:** a devotional service lasting until after midnight especially on New Year's Eve
watch out *vb* ♦ **:** to be vigilant or alert **:** be on the lookout — often used with *for*

♦ *usu* **watch out for** beware (of), guard (against), mind

watch•tow•er \ˈwäch-ˌtau̇-ər, ˈwȯch-\ *n* **:** a tower for a lookout
watch•word \-ˌwərd\ *n* **1 :** a secret word used as a signal or sign of recognition **2** ♦ **:** a word or motto used as a slogan or rallying cry

♦ cry, shibboleth, slogan

[1]**wa•ter** \ˈwȯ-tər, ˈwä-\ *n* **1 :** the liquid that descends as rain and forms rivers, lakes, and seas **2 :** a natural mineral water — usually used in pl. **3** *pl* **:** the water occupying or flowing in a particular bed; *also* **:** a band of seawater bordering on and under the control of a country **4 :** any of various liquids containing or resembling water; *esp* **:** a watery fluid (as tears, urine, or sap) formed or circulating in a living organism **5 :** a specified degree of thoroughness or completeness ⟨a scoundrel of the first ∼⟩
[2]**water** *vb* **1 a** ♦ **:** to moisten, sprinkle, or soak with water **b :** to supply with or get or take water ⟨∼ horses⟩ ⟨the ship ∼*ed* at each port⟩ **2 :** to treat (as cloth) so as to give a lustrous appearance in wavy lines **3** ♦ **:** to dilute by or as if by adding water to — often used with *down* **4 :** to form or secrete water or watery matter ⟨her eyes ∼*ed*⟩ ⟨my mouth ∼*ed*⟩

♦ [1a] bathe, douse, drench, soak, sop, souse, wash, wet ♦ *usu* **water down** [3] adulterate, dilute, thin, weaken

water bed *n* **:** a bed whose mattress is a watertight bag filled with water
wa•ter•borne \-ˌbōrn\ *adj* **:** supported, carried, or transmitted by water
water buffalo *n* **:** a common oxlike often domesticated Asian bovine
water chestnut *n* **:** a whitish crunchy vegetable used especially in Chinese cooking that is the peeled tuber of a widely cultivated Asian sedge; *also* **:** the tuber or the sedge itself
water closet *n* **:** a compartment or room with a toilet bowl **:** BATHROOM; *also* **:** a toilet bowl along with its accessories
wa•ter•col•or \ˈwȯ-tər-ˌkə-lər, ˈwä-\ *n* **1 :** a paint whose liquid part is water **2 :** the art of painting with watercolors **3 :** a picture made with watercolors
wa•ter•course \-ˌkōrs\ *n* ♦ **:** a stream of water; *also* **:** the bed of a stream

♦ aqueduct, canal, channel, conduit, flume, raceway

wa•ter•craft \-ˌkraft\ *n* **:** a craft for water transport **:** BOAT
wa•ter•cress \-ˌkres\ *n* **:** an aquatic perennial Eurasian cress that

is naturalized in the U.S. and has edible leaves used especially in salads

wa•ter•fall \-ˌfȯl\ *n* ♦ : a very steep descent of the water of a stream

♦ cascade, cataract, falls

wa•ter•fowl \ˈwȯ-tər-ˌfau̇(-ə)l, ˈwä-\ *n, pl* **-fowl** *also* **-fowls** : a bird that frequents water; *esp* : a swimming bird (as a duck) hunted as game

wa•ter•front \-ˌfrənt\ *n* : land or a section of a town fronting or abutting on a body of water

water gap *n* : a pass in a mountain ridge through which a stream runs

water glass *n* : a drinking glass

water hyacinth *n* : a showy floating aquatic plant of tropical America that often clogs waterways (as in the southern U.S.)

watering hole *n* : a place (as a bar) where people gather socially

watering place *n* : a resort that features mineral springs or bathing

water lily *n* : any of various aquatic plants with floating roundish leaves and showy solitary flowers

wa•ter•line \ˈwȯ-tər-ˌlīn, ˈwä-\ *n* : a line that marks the level of the surface of water on something (as a ship or the shore)

wa•ter•logged \-ˌlȯgd, -ˌlägd\ *adj* ♦ : so filled or soaked with water as to be heavy or unmanageable ⟨a ~ boat⟩

♦ saturated, sodden, soggy, watery, wet

wa•ter•loo \ˌwȯ-tər-ˈlü, ˌwä-\ *n, pl* **-loos** : a decisive or final defeat or setback

[1]**wa•ter•mark** \ˈwȯ-tər-ˌmärk, ˈwä-\ *n* **1** : a mark indicating the height to which water has risen **2** : a marking in paper visible when the paper is held up to a light

[2]**watermark** *vb* : to mark (paper) with a watermark

wa•ter•mel•on \-ˌme-lən\ *n* : a large roundish or oblong fruit with sweet juicy usually red pulp; *also* : a widely grown African vine related to the squashes that produces watermelons

water moccasin *n* : a venomous pit viper chiefly of the southeastern U.S. that is related to the copperhead

water ou•zel \-ˈü-zəl\ *n* : DIPPER 1

water park *n* : an amusement park with a pool and wetted slides

water pipe *n* : a pipe for smoking that has a long flexible tube whereby the smoke is cooled by passing through water

water polo *n* : a team game played in a swimming pool with a ball resembling a soccer ball

wa•ter•pow•er \ˈwȯ-tər-ˌpau̇-ər, ˈwä-\ *n* : the power of moving water used to run machinery

[1]**wa•ter•proof** \ˈwȯ-tər-ˌprüf, ˈwä-\ *adj* : not letting water through; *esp* : covered or treated with a material to prevent permeation by water — **wa•ter•proof•ing** *n*

[2]**waterproof** *n* **1** : a waterproof fabric **2** *chiefly Brit* : RAINCOAT

[3]**waterproof** *vb* : to make waterproof

wa•ter–re•pel•lent \ˌwȯ-tər-ri-ˈpe-lənt, ˌwä-\ *adj* : treated with a finish that is resistant to water penetration

wa•ter–re•sis•tant \-ri-ˈzis-tənt\ *adj* : WATER-REPELLENT

wa•ter•shed \ˈwȯ-tər-ˌshed, ˈwä-\ *n* **1** : a dividing ridge between two drainage areas **2** : the region or area drained by a particular body of water

wa•ter•side \-ˌsīd\ *n* : the land bordering a body of water

water ski *n* : a ski used on water when the wearer is towed — **wa•ter–ski** *vb* — **wa•ter–ski•er** \-ˌskē-ər\ *n*

water snake *n* : any of various snakes found in or near freshwater and feeding largely on aquatic animals

wa•ter•spout \ˈwȯ-tər-ˌspau̇t, ˈwä-\ *n* **1** : a pipe for carrying water **2** : a funnel-shaped cloud extending from a cloud down to a spray torn up by whirling winds from an ocean or lake

water strider *n* : any of various long-legged bugs that move about swiftly on the surface of water

water table *n* : the upper limit of the portion of the ground wholly saturated with water

wa•ter•tight \ˌwȯ-tər-ˈtīt, ˌwä-\ *adj* **1** : constructed so as to keep water out **2** : allowing no possibility for doubt or uncertainty ⟨a ~ case against the accused⟩

wa•ter•way \ˈwȯ-tər-ˌwā, ˈwä-\ *n* : a navigable body of water

wa•ter•wheel \-ˌhwēl, -ˌwēl\ *n* : a wheel made to turn by water flowing against it

water wings *n pl* : an air-filled device to give support to a person's body especially when learning to swim

wa•ter•works \ˈwȯ-tər-ˌwərks, ˈwä-\ *n pl* : a system for supplying water (as to a city)

wa•tery \ˈwȯ-tə-rē, ˈwä-\ *adj* **1** ♦ : containing, full of, or giving out water ⟨~ clouds⟩ **2** ♦ : resembling water or watery matter especially in thin fluidity, soggy texture, paleness, or lack of flavor : THIN ⟨~ lemonade⟩; *also* : being soft and soggy ⟨~ turnips⟩

♦ [1] saturated, sodden, soggy, waterlogged, wet ♦ [2] dilute, thin, weak

WATS \ˈwäts\ *abbr* Wide-Area Telecommunications Service

watt \ˈwät\ *n* : the metric unit of power equal to the work done at the rate of one joule per second or to the power produced by a current of one ampere across a potential difference of one volt

watt•age \ˈwä-tij\ *n* : amount of power expressed in watts

wat•tle \ˈwät-ᵊl\ *n* **1** : a framework of rods with flexible branches or reeds interlaced used especially formerly in building; *also* : material for this framework **2** : a naked fleshy process hanging usually from the head or neck (as of a bird) — **wat•tled** \-ᵊld\ *adj*

W Aust *abbr* Western Australia

[1]**wave** \ˈwāv\ *vb* **waved; wav•ing** **1** : FLUTTER ⟨flags *waving* in the breeze⟩ **2** ♦ : to motion with the hands or with something held in them in signal or salute; *also* : to convey by waving ⟨*waved* farewell⟩ **3** : to become moved or brandished to-and-fro; *also* : BRANDISH, FLOURISH ⟨~ a sword⟩ **4** : to move before the wind with a wavelike motion ⟨fields of *waving* grain⟩ **5** : to curve up and down like a wave : UNDULATE

♦ flag, gesture, motion, signal

[2]**wave** *n* **1** ♦ : a moving ridge or swell on the surface of water **2** : a wavelike formation or shape ⟨a ~ in the hair⟩ **3** : the action or process of making wavy or curly **4** : a waving motion; *esp* : a signal made by waving something **5** : FLOW, GUSH ⟨a ~ of anger swept over her⟩ **6** : a peak of activity ⟨a ~ of selling⟩ **7** : a disturbance that transfers energy progressively from point to point in a medium ⟨light travels in ~*s*⟩ ⟨a sound ~⟩ **8** : a period of hot or cold weather — **wave•like** *adj*

♦ billow, curl, surge, swell

wave•length \ˈwāv-ˌleŋth\ *n* **1** : the distance in the line of advance of a wave from any one point (as a crest) to the next corresponding point **2** : a line of thought that reveals a common understanding

wave•let \-lət\ *n* : a little wave : RIPPLE

wa•ver \ˈwā-vər\ *vb* **1** ♦ : to fluctuate in opinion, allegiance, or direction **2** ♦ : to weave or sway unsteadily to and fro : TOTTER; *also* : FLICKER ⟨~*ing* flames⟩ **3** : FALTER **4** : to give an unsteady sound : QUAVER — **waver** *n* — **wa•ver•er** *n* — **wa•ver•ing•ly** *adv*

♦ [1] falter, hang back, hesitate, shilly-shally, stagger, teeter, vacillate, wobble ♦ [2] falter, rock, seesaw, sway, teeter, totter, wobble

wavy \ˈwā-vē\ *adj* **wav•i•er; -est** : having waves : moving in waves

[1]**wax** \ˈwaks\ *n* **1** : a yellowish plastic substance secreted by bees for constructing the honeycomb **2** : any of various substances like beeswax

[2]**wax** *vb* : to treat or rub with wax

[3]**wax** *vb* **1** ♦ : to increase in size, numbers, strength, volume, or duration **2** : to increase in apparent size ⟨the moon ~*es* toward the full⟩ **3** ♦ : to take on a quality or state : BECOME ⟨~*ed* indignant⟩ ⟨the party ~*ed* merry⟩

♦ [1] accumulate, appreciate, balloon, build, burgeon, enlarge, escalate, expand, increase, mount, multiply, mushroom, proliferate, rise, snowball, swell ♦ [3] become, come, get, go, grow, run, turn

wax bean *n* : a kidney bean with pods that turn creamy yellow to bright yellow when mature enough to use as snap beans

wax•en \ˈwak-sən\ *adj* **1** : made of or covered with wax **2** : resembling wax (as in color or consistency)

wax museum *n* : a place where wax effigies are exhibited

wax myrtle *n* : any of a genus of shrubs or trees with aromatic leaves; *esp* : an evergreen shrub or small tree of the eastern U.S. that produces small hard berries with a thick coating of bluish-white wax used for candles

wax•wing \ˈwaks-ˌwiŋ\ *n* : any of a genus of chiefly brown to gray singing birds with a showy crest and red waxy material on the tips of some wing feathers

wax•work \-ˌwərk\ *n* **1** : an effigy usually of a person in wax **2** *pl* : an exhibition of wax figures

waxy \ˈwak-sē\ *adj* **wax•i•er; -est** **1** : made of or full of wax **2** : WAXEN 2

way \ˈwā\ *n* **1** ♦ : a thoroughfare for travel or passage **2** : the course of travel from one place to another : ROUTE **3 a** ♦ : a course of action ⟨chose the easy ~⟩ **b** ♦ : opportunity, capability, or fact of doing as one pleases ⟨always had your own ~⟩ **4** : a possible course : POSSIBILITY ⟨no two ~*s* about it⟩ **5** ♦ : a characteristic or habitual manner of acting ⟨this ~ of thinking⟩ ⟨a new ~ of painting⟩ **6** : FEATURE, RESPECT ⟨a good worker in many ~*s*⟩ **7** : the usual or characteristic state of affairs ⟨as is the ~ with old people⟩; *also* : individual characteristic or peculiarity ⟨used to her ~*s*⟩ **8 a** : the length of a course : DISTANCE ⟨a short ~ from here⟩ ⟨a long ~ from success⟩ **b** ♦ : room for moving, passing, or occupying — often used in the phrase *make way* **9** : progress along a course ⟨working my ~ through college⟩ **10** : a direction of motion, facing, pointing, or nonspatial advance or tendency ⟨turn this ~⟩; *also* : LOCALITY ⟨out our ~⟩ **11** : STATE, CONDITION ⟨the ~ things are⟩ **12** *pl* : an inclined structure upon which a ship is built or is supported in launching **13** : CATEGORY, KIND ⟨get what you need in the ~ of supplies⟩ **14** : motion or speed of a boat through the water — **by the way** : by way of interjection or digression — **by way of 1** : for the purpose of ⟨*by way of* illustration⟩ **2** : by the route through : VIA — **out of the way 1** : WRONG, IMPROPER **2** : SECLUDED, REMOTE

♦ [1] artery, avenue, drag, drive, highway, pass, pike, road, route, row, street, thoroughfare, trace, turnpike ♦ [3a] approach, fashion, form, manner, method, strategy, style, system, tack, tactics, technique ♦ [3b] alternative, choice, discretion, option, pick, preference ♦ [5] custom, fashion, habit, pattern, practice, trick, wont ♦ [8b] place, room, space

way•bill \ˈwā-ˌbil\ *n* : a paper that accompanies a freight shipment and gives details of goods, route, and charges

way•far•er \ˈwā-ˌfar-ər\ *n* : a traveler especially on foot — **way•far•ing** \-ˌfar-iŋ\ *adj*

way•lay \ˈwā-ˌlā\ *vb* **-laid** \-ˌlād\; **-lay•ing** ♦ : to lie in wait for or attack from ambush

♦ ambush, surprise

way–out \ˈwā-ˈau̇t\ *adj* : marked by a considerable departure from the conventional or traditional : FAR-OUT

-ways \ˌwāz\ *adv suffix* : in (such) a way, course, direction, or manner ⟨side*ways*⟩

ways and means *n pl* : methods and resources especially for raising revenues needed by a state; *also* : a legislative committee concerned with this function

way•side \ˈwā-ˌsīd\ *n* : the side of or land adjacent to a road or path

way station *n* : an intermediate station on a line of travel (as a railroad)

way•ward \ˈwā-wərd\ *adj* **1** ♦ : following one's own capricious or wanton inclinations ⟨~ children⟩ **2** : UNPREDICTABLE, IRREGULAR ⟨a ~ act⟩

♦ contrary, defiant, disobedient, froward, intractable, rebellious, recalcitrant, refractory, unruly, untoward, willful

way•ward•ness *n* ♦ : the quality or state of being wayward

♦ contrariness, defiance, disobedience, frowardness, insubordination, intractability, rebelliousness, recalcitrance, refractoriness, unruliness

WBC *abbr* white blood cells

WC *abbr* **1** water closet **2** without charge

WCTU *abbr* Women's Christian Temperance Union

we \ˈwē\ *pron* **1** — used of a group that includes the speaker or writer **2** — used for the singular *I* by a monarch, editor, or writer

weak \ˈwēk\ *adj* **1** ♦ : lacking strength or vigor : FEEBLE **2** : not able to sustain or resist much weight, pressure, or strain **3** ♦ : deficient in vigor of mind or character; *also* : resulting from or indicative of such deficiency ⟨a ~ policy⟩ ⟨a ~ will⟩ **4** ♦ : not supported by truth or logic ⟨a ~ argument⟩ **5** : lacking skill or proficiency; *also* : indicative of a lack of skill or aptitude **6** ♦ : lacking vigor of expression or effect **7** ♦ : of less than usual strength ⟨~ tea⟩ **8** : not having or exerting authority ⟨~ government⟩; *also* : INEFFECTIVE, IMPOTENT **9** : of, relating to, or constituting a verb or verb conjugation that forms the past tense and past participle by adding *-ed* or *-d* or *-t* — **weak•ly** *adv*

♦ [1] delicate, enervated, faint, feeble, frail, infirm, languid, low, prostrate, slight, soft, tender, torpid, unsubstantial, wasted ***Ant*** mighty, powerful, rugged, stalwart, stout, strong ♦ [3] effete, frail, ineffective, nerveless, soft, spineless, wimpy, wishy-washy ***Ant*** firm, strong, tough ♦ [4] fallacious, illogical, invalid, irrational, unreasonable, unsound ♦ [6] helpless, impotent, powerless ♦ [7] dilute, thin, watery ***Ant*** full-bodied, rich, strong

weak•en \ˈwē-kən\ *vb* ♦ : to make or become weak

♦ adulterate, dilute, thin, water ♦ debilitate, enervate, enfeeble, prostrate, sap, soften, tire, waste ***Ant*** beef (up), fortify, recruit, strengthen ♦ decay, droop, fail, flag, go, lag, languish, sag, waste, wilt

weak•fish \ˈwēk-ˌfish\ *n* : a common marine fish of the Atlantic coast of the U.S. caught for food and sport; *also* : any of several related food fishes

weak force *n* : the physical force responsible for particle decay processes in radioactivity

weak–kneed \ˈwēk-ˈnēd\ *adj* : lacking willpower or resolution

weak•ling \ˈwē-kliŋ\ *n* : a person who is physically, mentally, or morally weak

weak•ly \ˈwē-klē\ *adj* ♦ : not strong or robust in health

♦ invalid, sickly

weak•ness \ˈwēk-nəs\ *n* **1 a** ♦ : the quality or state of being weak : lack of strength or vigor **b** : an instance or period of being weak ⟨in a moment of ~ he agreed to go⟩ **2** ♦ : something that is a mark of lack of strength or resolution **3** : an object of special desire or fondness ⟨chocolate is her ~⟩

♦ [1a] debility, delicacy, enfeeblement, faintness, feebleness, frailty, infirmity, languor, lowness ***Ant*** hardihood, hardiness, robustness, strength, vigor ♦ [2] demerit, failing, fault, foible, frailty, shortcoming, vice, weakness

[1]**weal** \ˈwēl\ *n* ♦ : a sound, healthy, or prosperous state : WELL-BEING

♦ good, interest, welfare, well-being

[2]**weal** *n* : WELT

weald \ˈwēld\ *n* **1** : FOREST **2** : WOLD

wealth \ˈwelth\ *n* **1** : abundance of possessions or resources **2** ♦ : abundant supply ⟨a ~ of detail⟩ **3** ♦ : all property that has a money or an exchange value; *also* : all objects or resources that have economic value

♦ [2] abundance, plenty, superabundance ♦ [3] assets, capital, fortune, means, opulence, riches, substance, wherewithal

wealthy \ˈwel-thē\ *adj* **wealth•i•er; -est** ♦ : having wealth : RICH

♦ affluent, flush, loaded, moneyed, opulent, rich, well-fixed, well-heeled, well-off, well-to-do

wean \ˈwēn\ *vb* **1** : to accustom (a young mammal) to take food by means other than nursing **2** : to free from a source of dependence; *also* : to free from a usually unwholesome habit or interest

weap•on \ˈwe-pən\ *n* **1** : something (as a gun, knife, or club) used to injure, defeat, or destroy **2** : a means of contending against another — **weap•on•less** \-ləs\ *adj*

weap•on•ry \-rē\ *n* : WEAPONS

[1]**wear** \ˈwar\ *vb* **wore** \ˈwōr\; **worn** \ˈwōrn\; **wear•ing 1** : to use as an article of clothing or adornment ⟨~ a coat⟩ ⟨~*s* earrings⟩; *also* : to carry on the person ⟨~ a gun⟩ **2** : EXHIBIT, PRESENT ⟨~ a smile⟩ **3** ♦ : to impair, diminish, or decay by use or by scraping or rubbing ⟨clothes *worn* to shreds⟩; *also* : to produce gradually by friction, rubbing, or wasting away ⟨~ a hole in the rug⟩ **4** ♦ : to exhaust or lessen the strength of : FATIGUE ⟨*worn* by care and toil⟩ **5** : to endure use : last under use or the passage of time ⟨this cloth ~*s* well⟩ **6** : to diminish or fail with the passage of time ⟨the day ~*s* on⟩ ⟨the effect of the drug *wore* off⟩ **7** : to grow or become affected in some way by attrition, use, or age ⟨the coin was *worn* thin⟩ — **wear•able** \ˈwar-ə-bəl\ *adj* — **wear•er** *n*

♦ [3] abrade, chafe, erode, fray, fret, gall, rub ♦ [4] burn out, do in, drain, exhaust, fag, fatigue, tire, tucker, wash out, weary

[2]**wear** *n* **1** : the act of wearing : the state of being worn ⟨clothes for everyday ~⟩ **2** : clothing usually of a particular kind or for a special occasion or use ⟨children's ~⟩ **3** : wearing or lasting quality ⟨the coat still has lots of ~ in it⟩ **4** : the result of wearing or use : impairment due to use ⟨the suit shows ~⟩

wear and tear *n* : the loss, injury, or stress to which something is subjected in the course of use; *esp* : normal depreciation

wear down *vb* : to weary and overcome by persistent resistance or pressure

wea•ri•ness \-ē-nəs\ *n* ♦ : the quality or state of being weary

♦ burnout, collapse, exhaustion, fatigue, lassitude, prostration, tiredness

wea•ri•some \ˈwir-ē-səm\ *adj* : causing weariness : TIRESOME — **wea•ri•some•ly** *adv* — **wea•ri•some•ness** *n*

wear out *vb* **1** ♦ : to exhaust or lessen the strength of : TIRE **2** : to make or become useless by wear

♦ burn out, do in, drain, exhaust, fag, fatigue, tire, tucker, wash out, wear, weary

[1]**wea·ry** \ˈwir-ē\ *adj* **wea·ri·er; -est** **1** ♦ **:** worn out in strength, energy, or freshness **2 :** expressing or characteristic of weariness ⟨a ~ sigh⟩ **3** ♦ **:** having one's patience, tolerance, or pleasure exhausted ⟨~ of war⟩ **4 :** causing weariness of body or spirit **:** TIRESOME ⟨a long, ~ drive home⟩ — **wea·ri·ly** \ˈwir-ə-lē\ *adv*

♦ [1] beat, bushed, dead, drained, effete, jaded, limp, prostrate, spent, tired, worn-out ♦ [3] fed up, jaded, sick, tired ***Ant*** absorbed, engaged, engrossed, gripped, interested, intrigued

[2]**weary** *vb* **wea·ried; wea·ry·ing** ♦ **:** to become or make weary **:** TIRE

♦ burn out, do in, drain, exhaust, fag, fatigue, tire, tucker, wash out, wear, wear out, weary

[1]**wea·sel** \ˈwē-zəl\ *n, pl* **weasels :** any of various small slender flesh-eating mammals related to the minks — **wea·sel·ly** *also* **wea·sely** \ˈwēz-lē, ˈwē-zə-lē\ *adj*

[2]**weasel** *vb* **wea·seled; wea·sel·ing** **1 :** to use weasel words **:** EQUIVOCATE **2 :** to escape from or evade a situation or obligation — often used with *out*

weasel word *n* **:** a word used to avoid a direct or forthright statement or position

[1]**weath·er** \ˈwe-thər\ *n* **1 :** the state of the atmosphere with respect to heat or cold, wetness or dryness, calm or storm, clearness or cloudiness **2 :** a particular and especially a disagreeable atmospheric state **:** RAIN, STORM

[2]**weather** *vb* **1 :** to expose to or endure the action of weather; *also* **:** to alter (as in color or texture) by such exposure **2 :** to bear up against successfully ⟨~ a storm⟩ ⟨~ troubles⟩

[3]**weather** *adj* **:** WINDWARD

weath·er–beat·en \ˈwe-thər-ˌbēt-ᵊn\ *adj* **:** worn or damaged by exposure to the weather; *also* **:** toughened or tanned by the weather ⟨~ face⟩

weath·er·cock \-ˌkäk\ *n* **:** a weather vane shaped like a rooster

weath·er·ing \ˈwe-thə-riŋ\ *n* **:** the action of the weather in altering the color, texture, composition, or form of exposed objects; *also* **:** alteration thus effected

weath·er·ize \ˈwe-thə-ˌrīz\ *vb* **-ized; -iz·ing :** to make (as a house) better protected against winter weather (as by adding insulation)

weath·er·man \-ˌman\ *n* **:** one who reports and forecasts the weather **:** METEOROLOGIST

weath·er·per·son \-ˌpər-sən\ *n* **:** a person who reports and forecasts the weather **:** METEOROLOGIST

weath·er·proof \ˈwe-thər-ˌprüf\ *adj* **:** able to withstand exposure to weather — **weatherproof** *vb*

weath·er·strip·ping \ˈwe-thər-ˌstri-piŋ\ *n* **:** material used to seal a door or window at the edges — **weath·er·strip** *vb* — **weather strip** *n*

weather vane *n* **:** VANE 1

weath·er·worn \ˈwe-thər-ˌwōrn\ *adj* **:** worn by exposure to the weather

[1]**weave** \ˈwēv\ *vb* **wove** \ˈwōv\ *or* **weaved; wo·ven** \ˈwō-vən\ *or* **weaved; weav·ing** **1 :** to form by interlacing strands of material; *esp* **:** to make on a loom by interlacing warp and filling threads ⟨~ cloth⟩ **2 :** to interlace (as threads) into a fabric and especially cloth **3 :** SPIN 2 **4 :** to make as if by weaving together parts **5** ♦ **:** to insert as a part **:** work in **6 :** to move in a winding or zigzag course especially to avoid obstacles ⟨we *wove* our way through the crowd⟩ — **weav·er** *n*

♦ interlace, intersperse, intertwine, interweave, lace, thread, wreathe

[2]**weave** *n* **:** something woven; *also* **:** a pattern or method of weaving ⟨a loose ~⟩

[1]**web** \ˈweb\ *n* **1 :** a fabric on a loom or coming from a loom **2 a :** COBWEB **b** ♦ **:** something by which one is entangled, involved in difficulties, held fast, or impeded in one's progress ⟨caught in a ~ of deceit⟩ **3 :** an animal or plant membrane; *esp* **:** one uniting the toes (as in many birds) **4 :** NETWORK ⟨a ~ of highways⟩ **5 :** the series of barbs on each side of the shaft of a feather **6 :** WORLD WIDE WEB — **webbed** \ˈwebd\ *adj*

♦ entanglement, net, snare, trap

[2]**web** *vb* **webbed; web·bing** **1 :** to make a web **2 :** to cover or provide with webs or a network **3 :** ENTANGLE, ENSNARE

web·bing \ˈwe-biŋ\ *n* **:** a strong closely woven tape designed for bearing weight and used especially for straps, harnesses, or upholstery

web·cam \ˈweb-ˌkam\ *n* **:** a camera used in transmitting live images over the World Wide Web

web·cast \ˈweb-ˌkast\ *n* **:** a transmission of sound and images via the World Wide Web — **webcast** *vb*

web–foot·ed \ˈweb-ˈfu̇-təd\ *adj* **:** having webbed feet

web·mas·ter \ˈweb-ˌmas-tər\ *n, often cap* **:** a person responsible for the creation or maintenance of a Web site

Web site *n* **:** a group of World Wide Web pages made available online (as by an individual or business)

wed \ˈwed\ *vb* **wed·ded** *also* **wed; wed·ding** **1 :** to take, give, enter into, or join in marriage **:** MARRY **2 :** to unite firmly

Wed *abbr* Wednesday

wed·ding \ˈwe-diŋ\ *n* **1** ♦ **:** a marriage ceremony usually with accompanying festivities **:** NUPTIALS **2 :** a joining in close association **3 :** a wedding anniversary or its celebration

♦ espousal, marriage

[1]**wedge** \ˈwej\ *n* **1 :** a piece of wood or metal that tapers to a thin edge and is used to split logs or rocks or to raise heavy weights **2 :** something (as an action or policy) that serves to open up a way for a breach, change, or intrusion **3 :** a wedge-shaped object or part ⟨a ~ of pie⟩

[2]**wedge** *vb* **wedged; wedg·ing** **1 :** to hold firm by or as if by driving in a wedge **2** ♦ **:** to force (something) into a narrow space

♦ cram, crowd, jam, ram, sandwich, squeeze, stuff

wed·lock \ˈwed-ˌläk\ *n* **:** the state of being married **:** MARRIAGE

Wednes·day \ˈwenz-(ˌ)dā-dē\ *n* **:** the 4th day of the week

wee \ˈwē\ *adj* **1** ♦ **:** very small **:** TINY **2 :** very early ⟨~ hours of the morning⟩

♦ atomic, infinitesimal, microscopic, miniature, minute, teeny, tiny

[1]**weed** \ˈwēd\ *n* **1 :** a plant that tends to grow thickly where it is not wanted and to choke out more desirable plants **2 :** MARIJUANA

[2]**weed** *vb* **1 :** to clear of or remove weeds or something harmful, inferior, or superfluous ⟨~ a garden⟩ **2 :** to get rid of ⟨~ out the troublemakers⟩ — **weed·er** *n*

[3]**weed** *n* **:** mourning clothes — usually used in pl. ⟨widow's ~*s*⟩

weedy \ˈwē-dē\ *adj* **1 :** full of weeds **2** ♦ **:** resembling a weed especially in vigor of growth or spread **3 :** noticeably lean and scrawny **:** LANKY

♦ lush, luxuriant, prosperous, rampant, rank

week \ˈwēk\ *n* **1 :** seven successive days; *esp* **:** a calendar period of seven days beginning with Sunday and ending with Saturday **2 :** the working or school days of the calendar week

week·day \ˈwēk-ˌdā\ *n* **:** a day of the week except Sunday or sometimes except Saturday and Sunday

[1]**week·end** \-ˌend\ *n* **:** the period between the close of one working or business or school week and the beginning of the next

[2]**weekend** *vb* **:** to spend the weekend

[1]**week·ly** \ˈwē-klē\ *adj* **1 :** occurring, appearing, or done every week **2 :** computed in terms of one week — **weekly** *adv*

[2]**weekly** *n, pl* **weeklies :** a weekly publication

ween \ˈwēn\ *vb, archaic* **:** SUPPOSE 3

wee·ny \ˈwē-nē\ *also* **ween·sy** \ˈwēn-sē\ *adj* **:** exceptionally small

weep \ˈwēp\ *vb* **wept** \ˈwept\; **weep·ing** **1** ♦ **:** to express emotion and especially sorrow by shedding tears **:** CRY **2** ♦ **:** to give off fluid slowly **:** OOZE — **weep·er** *n*

♦ [1] bawl, blubber, cry, sob ♦ [2] bleed, exude, ooze, percolate, seep, strain, sweat

weep·ing *adj* **1** ♦ **:** expressing or showing emotion by shedding tears **2 :** having slender drooping branches

♦ dolorous, funeral, lugubrious, mournful, plaintive, regretful, rueful, sorrowful, woeful

weeping willow *n* **:** a willow with slender drooping branches

weepy \ˈwē-pē\ *adj* **:** inclined to weep

wee·vil \ˈwē-vəl\ *n* **:** any of a large group of beetles having a long head usually curved into a snout and including many whose larvae are destructive plant-feeding pests — **wee·vily** *or* **wee·vil·ly** \ˈwē-və-lē\ *adj*

weft \ˈweft\ *n* **1 :** a filling thread or yarn in weaving **2 :** WEB, FABRIC; *also* **:** something woven

[1]**weigh** \ˈwā\ *vb* **1 :** to find the heaviness of **2 :** to have weight or a specified weight **3** ♦ **:** to consider carefully **:** PONDER **4 :** to merit consideration as important **:** COUNT ⟨evidence ~*ing* against him⟩ **5 :** to raise before sailing ⟨~ anchor⟩ **6** ♦ **:** to press down with or as if with a heavy weight

♦ [3] chew over, cogitate, consider, contemplate, debate, deliberate, entertain, meditate, mull, ponder, question, ruminate, study, think ♦ *usu* **weigh on** *or* **weigh upon** [6] bear, depress, press, shove

[2]**weigh** *n* **:** WAY — used in the phrase *under weigh*

1**weight** \ˈwāt\ *n* **1 :** the amount that something weighs; *also* **:** the standard amount that something should weigh **2** ♦ **:** a quantity or object weighing a usually specified amount **3 :** a unit (as a pound or kilogram) of weight or mass; *also* **:** a system of such units **4 :** a heavy object for holding or pressing something down; *also* **:** a heavy object for throwing or lifting in an athletic contest **5 :** a mental or emotional burden **6 a** ♦ **:** the relatively great importance or authority accorded something **b** ♦ **:** measurable influence especially in determining the acts of others ⟨threw his ~ around⟩ **7 :** overpowering force **8 :** relative thickness (as of a textile) ⟨summer-*weight* clothes⟩

♦ [2] burden, cargo, draft, freight, haul, lading, load, payload ♦ [6a] consequence, import, magnitude, moment, significance ♦ [6b] authority, clout, influence, pull, sway

2**weight** *vb* **1 :** to load with or as if with a weight **2** ♦ **:** to oppress with a burden ⟨~*ed* down with cares⟩

♦ burden, encumber, load, lumber, saddle

weight•less \ˈwāt-ləs\ *adj* ♦ **:** having little weight **:** lacking apparent gravitational pull — **weight•less•ly** *adv* — **weight•less•ness** *n*

♦ airy, feathery, light

weighty \ˈwā-tē\ *adj* **weight•i•er; -est 1** ♦ **:** of much importance or consequence **:** SERIOUS ⟨~ problems⟩ **2** ♦ **:** expressing or characterized by seriousness or gravity ⟨a ~ manner⟩ **3** ♦ **:** weighing a considerable amount **:** HEAVY **4** ♦ **:** having much force, influence, or authority ⟨~ arguments⟩

♦ [1] grave, heavy, serious ♦ [1, 2] big, consequential, eventful, important, major, material, meaningful, momentous, significant, substantial ♦ [3] heavy, hefty, massive, ponderous ♦ [4] authoritative, forceful, influential

weiner *var of* WIENER

weir \ˈwar, ˈwir\ *n* **1 :** a fence set in a waterway for catching fish **2 :** a dam in a stream to raise the water level or divert its flow

weird \ˈwird\ *adj* **1** ♦ **:** caused by or suggesting magical influence **:** MAGICAL **2** ♦ **:** passing beyond natural limits **:** UNEARTHLY **3** ♦ **:** curious in nature or appearance **:** of strange or extraordinary character — **weird•ly** *adv* — **weird•ness** *n*

♦ [1] magic, magical, mystic, occult ♦ [2] creepy, eerie, haunting, spooky, uncanny, unearthly ♦ [3] bizarre, curious, far-out, funny, kinky, odd, outlandish, outré, peculiar, quaint, queer, quirky, remarkable, screwy, strange, unusual, wacky, wild

weirdo \ˈwir-(ˌ)dō\ *n, pl* **weird•os** ♦ **:** a person who is extraordinarily strange or eccentric

♦ character, crackpot, crank, eccentric, kook, nut, oddball, screwball

Welch *var of* WELSH

1**wel•come** \ˈwel-kəm\ *vb* **wel•comed; wel•com•ing 1 :** to greet cordially or courteously **2 :** to accept, meet, or face with pleasure ⟨he ~*s* criticism⟩

2**welcome** *adj* **1 :** received gladly into one's presence ⟨a ~ visitor⟩ **2 :** giving pleasure **:** PLEASING ⟨~ news⟩ **3 :** willingly permitted or admitted ⟨all are ~ to use the books⟩ **4** — used in the phrase "You're welcome" as a reply to an expression of thanks

3**welcome** *n* **1 :** a cordial greeting or reception **2 :** the state of being welcome ⟨overstayed their ~⟩

1**weld** \ˈweld\ *vb* **1 :** to unite (metal or plastic parts) either by heating and allowing the parts to flow together or by hammering or pressing together **2 :** to unite closely or intimately ⟨~*ed* together in friendship⟩ — **weld•er** *n*

2**weld** *n* **1 :** a welded joint **2 :** union by welding

wel•fare \ˈwel-ˌfar\ *n* **1** ♦ **:** the state of doing well especially in respect to happiness, well-being, or prosperity **2 :** aid in the form of money or necessities for those in need; *also* **:** the agency through which the aid is given

♦ good, interest, weal, well-being

welfare state *n* **:** a nation or state that assumes primary responsibility for the individual and social welfare of its citizens

wel•kin \ˈwel-kən\ *n* **:** SKY; *also* **:** AIR

1**well** \ˈwel\ *n* **1 :** a spring with its pool **:** FOUNTAIN; *also* **:** a source of supply ⟨a ~ of information⟩ **2 :** a hole sunk in the earth to obtain a natural deposit (as of water, oil, or gas) **3 :** an open space (as for a staircase) extending vertically through floors of a structure **4 :** something suggesting a well

2**well** *vb* **:** to rise up and flow out

3**well** *adv* **bet•ter** \ˈbe-tər\; **best** \ˈbest\ **1 a :** in a good or proper manner **:** RIGHTLY **b** ♦ **:** in a skillful or expert manner **:** SKILLFULLY **2** ♦ **:** in a satisfactory manner **:** SATISFACTORILY ⟨the party turned out ~⟩ **3** ♦ **:** in a prosperous, affluent, or generous manner ⟨eat ~⟩ ⟨was ~ rewarded⟩ **4** ♦ **:** with reason or courtesy ⟨I cannot ~ refuse⟩ **5 :** to the full degree or extent **:** FULLY ⟨~ worth the price⟩ ⟨*well*-hidden⟩ **6 :** INTIMATELY, CLOSELY ⟨I know him ~⟩ **7 :** CONSIDERABLY, FAR ⟨~ over a million⟩ ⟨~ ahead⟩ **8 :** without trouble or difficulty ⟨we could ~ have gone⟩ **9 :** EXACTLY, DEFINITELY ⟨remember it ~⟩ **10 :** with spirit and courage **:** with equanimity or good nature ⟨took the news ~⟩

♦ [1b] ably, adeptly, capably, expertly, masterfully, proficiently, skillfully *Ant* inefficiently, ineptly, inexpertly, poorly, unskillfully ♦ [2] adequately, all right, fine, good, nicely, OK, passably, satisfactorily, so-so, tolerably *Ant* bad, badly, inadequately, intolerably, poorly ♦ [3] bountifully, generously, handsomely, liberally ♦ [4] courteously, kindly, nicely, thoughtfully

4**well** *adj* **1 :** PROSPEROUS; *also* **:** being in satisfactory condition or circumstances **2 :** SATISFACTORY, PLEASING ⟨all is ~⟩ **3 :** ADVISABLE, DESIRABLE ⟨it is not ~ to anger him⟩ **4** ♦ **:** free or recovered from ill health **:** HEALTHY **5 :** FORTUNATE ⟨it is ~ that this has happened⟩

♦ able-bodied, chipper, fit, hale, healthy, hearty, robust, sound, whole, wholesome

well–ad•just•ed \ˌwel-ə-ˈjəs-təd\ *adj* **:** WELL-BALANCED 2

well–ad•vised \-əd-ˈvīzd\ *adj* **1 :** PRUDENT **2 :** resulting from, based on, or showing careful deliberation or wise counsel ⟨~ plans⟩

well–ap•point•ed \-ə-ˈpȯin-təd\ *adj* **:** properly fitted out

well–ba•lanced \ˈwel-ˈba-lənst\ *adj* **1 :** nicely or evenly balanced or arranged **2 :** emotionally or psychologically untroubled

well–be•ing \-ˈbē-iŋ\ *n* ♦ **:** the state of being happy, healthy, or prosperous

♦ good, interest, weal, welfare

well•born \-ˈbȯrn\ *adj* ♦ **:** born of noble or wealthy lineage

♦ aristocratic, genteel, gentle, grand, highborn, noble, patrician

well–bred \-ˈbred\ *adj* ♦ **:** having or indicating qualities or characteristics associated with good breeding

♦ civil, courteous, genteel, gracious, mannerly, polite

well–de•fined \-di-ˈfīnd\ *adj* **:** having clearly distinguishable limits or boundaries

well–dis•posed \-di-ˈspōzd\ *adj* ♦ **:** disposed to be friendly, favorable, or sympathetic

♦ affable, agreeable, amiable, genial, good-natured, gracious, nice, sweet

well–done \ˈwel-ˈdən\ *adj* **1 :** rightly or properly performed **2 :** cooked thoroughly

well–en•dowed \ˈwel-in-ˈdau̇d\ *adj* **1 :** having plenty of money or property **2 :** having large breasts

well–fa•vored \-ˈfā-vərd\ *adj* **:** GOOD-LOOKING, HANDSOME

well–fixed \-ˈfikst\ *adj* ♦ **:** financially well-off **:** WELL-HEELED

♦ affluent, flush, loaded, moneyed, opulent, rich, wealthy, well-heeled, well-off, well-to-do

well–found•ed \-ˈfau̇n-dəd\ *adj* ♦ **:** based on good reasons

♦ good, hard, informed, just, levelheaded, logical, rational, reasonable, reasoned, sensible, sober, solid, valid

well–groomed \-ˈgrümd, -ˈgru̇md\ *adj* **:** neatly dressed or cared for

well–ground•ed \-ˈgrau̇n-dəd\ *adj* **1 :** having a firm foundation **2 :** WELL-FOUNDED

well•head \-ˌhed\ *n* **1 :** the source of a spring or a stream **2 :** principal source **3 :** the top of or a structure built over a well

well–heeled \-ˈhēld\ *adj* ♦ **:** financially well-off

♦ affluent, flush, loaded, moneyed, opulent, rich, wealthy, well-fixed, well-off, well-to-do

well–known \-ˈnōn\ *adj* ♦ **:** fully or widely known

♦ celebrated, famed, famous, noted, notorious, prominent, renowned, star

well–mean•ing \-ˈmē-niŋ\ *adj* **:** having or based on good intentions

well•ness \-nəs\ *n* ♦ **:** good health especially as an actively sought goal ⟨~ clinics⟩ ⟨lifestyles that promote ~⟩

♦ fitness, health, heartiness, robustness, soundness, wholeness, wholesomeness

well–nigh \-ˈnī\ *adv* ♦ **:** very nearly **:** ALMOST

♦ about, almost, most, much, near, nearly, next to, nigh, practically, virtually

well–off \-ˈȯf\ *adj* **:** being in good condition or circumstances; *esp* ♦ **:** having more than adequate financial resources **:** WELL-TO-DO

♦ affluent, flush, loaded, moneyed, opulent, rich, wealthy, well-fixed, well-heeled, well-to-do

well–or•dered \-ˈȯr-dərd\ *adj* **:** having an orderly procedure or arrangement

well–placed \-ˈplāst\ *adj* **:** appropriately or advantageously directed or positioned

well–read \-ˈred\ *adj* ♦ **:** well-informed through reading

♦ educated, erudite, knowledgeable, learned, literate, scholarly

well–round•ed \-ˈrau̇n-dəd\ *adj* **1 :** broadly trained, educated, and experienced **2 :** COMPREHENSIVE ⟨a ~ program of activities⟩

well–spo•ken \ˈwel-ˈspō-kən\ *adj* **1** ♦ **:** speaking well and especially courteously **2 :** spoken with propriety ⟨~ words⟩

♦ articulate, eloquent, fluent

well•spring \-ˌspriŋ\ *n* **:** a source of continuous supply

well–timed \-ˈtīmd\ *adj* **:** TIMELY

well–to–do \ˌwel-tə-ˈdü\ *adj* ♦ **:** having more than adequate financial resources

♦ affluent, flush, loaded, moneyed, opulent, rich, wealthy, well-fixed, well-heeled, well-off

well–turned \ˈwel-ˈtərnd\ *adj* **1 :** pleasingly shaped ⟨a ~ ankle⟩ **2 :** pleasingly expressed ⟨a ~ phrase⟩

well–wish•er \ˈwel-ˌwi-shər\ *n* **:** an admiring supporter or fan — **well–wish•ing** *adj or n*

welsh \ˈwelsh, ˈwelch\ *also* **welch** \ˈwelch\ *vb* **1** *sometimes offensive* **:** to avoid payment **2** *sometimes offensive* **:** to break one's word ⟨~*ed* on his promises⟩

Welsh \ˈwelsh\ *n* **1 Welsh** *pl* **:** the people of Wales **2 :** the Celtic language of Wales — **Welsh** *adj* — **Welsh•man** \-mən\ *n*

Welsh cor•gi \-ˈkȯr-gē\ *n* **:** a short-legged long-backed dog with foxy head of either of two breeds of Welsh origin

Welsh rabbit *n* **:** melted often seasoned cheese served over toast or crackers

Welsh rare•bit \-ˈrar-bət\ *n* **:** WELSH RABBIT

¹welt \ˈwelt\ *n* **1 :** the narrow strip of leather between a shoe upper and sole to which other parts are stitched **2 :** a doubled edge, strip, insert, or seam for ornament or reinforcement **3 :** a ridge or lump raised on the skin usually by a blow; *also* **:** a heavy blow

²welt *vb* **1 :** to furnish with a welt **2 :** to hit hard

¹wel•ter \ˈwel-tər\ *vb* **1 :** WRITHE, TOSS; *also* **:** WALLOW **2 :** to rise and fall or toss about in or with waves **3 :** to become deeply sunk, soaked, or involved **4 :** to be in turmoil

²welter *n* **1 :** a state of wild disorder **:** TURMOIL **2** ♦ **:** a chaotic mass or jumble

♦ clutter, hash, hodgepodge, jumble, miscellany, motley, muddle, potpourri

wel•ter•weight \ˈwel-tər-ˌwāt\ *n* **:** a boxer weighing more than 135 but not over 147 pounds

wen \ˈwen\ *n* **:** an abnormal growth or a cyst protruding from a surface especially of the skin

wench \ˈwench\ *n* **1 :** a young woman **2 :** a female servant

wend \ˈwend\ *vb* **:** to direct one's course **:** proceed on (one's way)

went *past of* GO

wept *past and past part of* WEEP

were *past 2d sing, past pl, or past subjunctive of* BE

were•wolf \ˈwer-ˌwu̇lf, ˈwir-, ˈwər-\ *n, pl* **were•wolves** \-ˌwu̇lvz\ **:** a person transformed into a wolf or capable of assuming a wolf's form

wes•kit \ˈwes-kət\ *n* **:** VEST 1

¹west \ˈwest\ *adv* **:** to or toward the west

²west *adj* **1 :** situated toward or at the west **2 :** coming from the west

³west *n* **1 :** the general direction of sunset **2 :** the compass point directly opposite to east **3** *cap* **:** regions or countries west of a specified or implied point **4** *cap* **:** Europe and the Americas — **west•er•ly** \ˈwes-tər-lē\ *adv or adj* — **west•ward** *adv or adj* — **west•wards** *adv*

¹west•ern \ˈwes-tərn\ *adj* **1 :** lying toward or coming from the west **2** *cap* **:** of, relating to, or characteristic of a region conventionally designated West **3** *cap* **:** of or relating to the Roman Catholic or Protestant segment of Christianity — **West•ern•er** *n*

²western *n, often cap* **:** a novel, story, film, or radio or television show about life in the western U.S. during the latter half of the 19th century

west•ern•ize \ˈwes-tər-ˌnīz\ *vb* **-ized; -iz•ing :** to give western characteristics to — **west•ern•i•zation** \ˌwes-tər-nə-ˈzā-shən\ *n*

West Nile virus \-ˈnī(-ə)l-\ *n* **:** a virus that is transmitted to humans by mosquitoes and causes an illness marked by fever, headache, muscle ache, and sometimes encephalitis or meningitis; *also* **:** this illness

¹wet \ˈwet\ *adj* **wet•ter; wet•test 1** ♦ **:** consisting of or covered or soaked with liquid (as water) **2 :** having frequent rains **:** RAINY **3 :** not dry ⟨~ paint⟩ **4 :** permitting or advocating the manufacture and sale of alcoholic beverages ⟨a ~ town⟩ ⟨a ~ candidate⟩ — **wet•ly** *adv* — **wet•ness** *n*

♦ saturated, sodden, soggy, waterlogged, watery *Ant* arid, dry

²wet *n* **1 :** WATER; *also* **:** WETNESS, MOISTURE **2 :** rainy weather **:** RAIN **3 :** an advocate of a wet liquor policy

³wet *vb* **wet** *or* **wet•ted; wet•ting** ♦ **:** to make or become wet

♦ bathe, douse, drench, soak, sop, souse, wash, water *Ant* dry

wet blanket *n* ♦ **:** one that quenches or dampens enthusiasm or pleasure

♦ drag, killjoy, party pooper, spoilsport

weth•er \ˈwe-t͟hər\ *n* **:** a castrated male sheep or goat

wet•land \ˈwet-ˌland, -lənd\ *n* **:** land or areas (as swamps) containing much soil moisture — usually used in pl.

wet nurse *n* **:** a woman who cares for and suckles children not her own

wet suit *n* **:** a rubber suit for swimmers that acts to retain body heat by keeping a layer of water against the body as insulation

wh *abbr* **1** which **2** white

¹whack \ˈhwak\ *vb* **1 :** to strike with a smart or resounding blow **2 :** to cut with or as if with a whack

²whack *n* **1 a :** a smart or resounding blow **b** ♦ **:** the sound of or like that of a blow **2 :** PORTION, SHARE **3 :** CONDITION, STATE ⟨the machine is out of ~⟩ **4** ♦ **:** an opportunity or attempt to do something **5 :** a single action or occasion ⟨made three pies at a ~⟩

♦ [1b] bang, blast, boom, clap, crack, crash, pop, report, slam, smash, snap, thwack ♦ [4] attempt, crack, endeavor (*or* endeavour), essay, fling, go, pass, shot, stab, trial, try

¹whale \ˈhwāl\ *n, pl* **whales 1** *or pl* **whale :** CETACEAN; *esp* **:** one (as a sperm whale or killer whale) of large size **2** ♦ **:** a person or thing impressive in size or quality ⟨a ~ of a story⟩

♦ behemoth, blockbuster, colossus, giant, jumbo, leviathan, mammoth, monster, titan, whopper

²whale *vb* **whaled; whal•ing :** to fish or hunt for whales

³whale *vb* **whaled; whal•ing 1 :** to defeat soundly **:** THRASH **2 :** to strike or hit vigorously

whale•boat \-ˌbōt\ *n* **:** a long narrow rowboat originally used by whalers

whale•bone \-ˌbōn\ *n* **:** BALEEN

whal•er \ˈhwā-lər\ *n* **1 :** a person or ship that hunts whales **2 :** WHALEBOAT

whale shark *n* **:** a shark of warm waters that is the largest known fish

wham•my \ˈhwa-mē\ *n, pl* **wham•mies :** JINX, HEX

wharf \ˈhwȯrf\ *n, pl* **wharves** \ˈhwȯrvz\ *also* **wharfs** ♦ **:** a structure alongside which ships lie to load and unload

♦ dock, float, jetty, landing, levee, pier, quay

¹what \ˈhwät, ˈhwət\ *pron* **1** — used to inquire about the identity or nature of a being, an object, or some matter or situation ⟨~ is he, a salesman⟩ ⟨~*'s* that⟩ ⟨~ happened⟩ **2 :** that which ⟨I know ~ you want⟩ **3 :** WHATEVER 1 ⟨take ~ you want⟩

²what *adv* **1 :** in what respect **:** HOW ⟨~ does he care⟩ **2** — used with *with* to introduce a prepositional phrase that expresses cause ⟨kept busy ~ with school and work⟩

³what *adj* **1** — used to inquire about the identity or nature of a person, object, or matter ⟨~ books do you read⟩ **2 :** how remarkable or surprising ⟨~ an idea⟩ **3 :** WHATEVER

¹what•ev•er \hwät-ˈe-vər\ *pron* **1 :** anything or everything that ⟨does ~ he wants to⟩ **2 :** no matter what ⟨~ you do, don't cheat⟩ **3 :** WHAT 1 — used as an intensive ⟨~ do you mean⟩

²whatever *adj* **:** of any kind at all ⟨no food ~⟩

³whatever *adv* **:** in any case **:** whatever the case may be — often used to suggest the unimportance of an issue or choice ⟨see a movie, watch TV, — ~⟩

¹what•not \ˈhwät-ˌnät\ *pron* **:** any of various other things that might also be mentioned ⟨needles, pins, and ~⟩

²whatnot *n* **:** a light open set of shelves for small ornaments

what•so•ev•er \ˌhwät-sō-ˈe-vər\ *pron or adj* **:** WHATEVER

wheal \ˈhwēl\ *n* **:** a rapidly formed flat slightly raised itching or burning patch on the skin; *also* **:** WELT

wheat \ˈhwēt\ *n* **:** a cereal grain that yields a fine white flour used chiefly in breads, baked goods, and pastas; *also* **:** any of several widely grown grasses yielding wheat — **wheat·en** *adj*

wheat germ *n* **:** the vitamin-rich wheat embryo separated in milling

whee·dle \ˈhwēd-ᵊl\ *vb* **whee·dled; whee·dling 1 ♦ :** to entice by flattery **2 :** to gain or get by wheedling

♦ blarney, cajole, coax

[1]**wheel** \ˈhwēl\ *n* **1 :** a disk or circular frame that turns on a central axis **2 :** a device whose main part is a wheel **3 :** something resembling a wheel in shape or motion **4 ♦ :** a curving or circular movement **:** a rotation or turn usually about an axis or center **5 :** machinery that imparts motion **:** moving power ⟨the ~*s* of government⟩ **6 :** a person of importance **7** *pl, slang* **:** AUTOMOBILE — **wheeled** \ˈhwēld\ *adj* — **wheel·less** *adj*

♦ gyration, pirouette, reel, revolution, roll, rotation, spin, twirl, whirl

[2]**wheel** *vb* **1 ♦ :** to move or turn like a wheel on or as if on an axis **:** REVOLVE **2 ♦ :** to change direction as if turning on a pivot **:** to cause to move as if turning on a pivot **3 :** to convey or move on wheels or in a vehicle

♦ [1] gyrate, pirouette, revolve, roll, rotate, spin, turn, twirl, whirl ♦ [2] divert, pivot, swerve, swing, turn, veer, whip

wheel·bar·row \-ˌbar-ō\ *n* **:** a vehicle with handles and usually one wheel for carrying small loads

wheel·base \-ˌbās\ *n* **:** the distance in inches between the front and rear axles of an automotive vehicle

wheel·chair \-ˌcher\ *n* **:** a chair mounted on wheels especially for the use of disabled persons

wheel·er \ˈhwē-lər\ *n* **1 :** one that wheels **2 :** WHEELHORSE **3 :** something that has wheels — used in combination ⟨a side-*wheeler*⟩

wheel·er–deal·er \ˌhwē-lər-ˈdē-lər\ *n* **:** a shrewd operator especially in business or politics

wheel·horse \ˈhwēl-ˌhȯrs\ *n* **1 :** a horse in a position nearest the front wheels of a wagon **2 :** a steady and effective worker especially in a political body

wheel·house \-ˌhau̇s\ *n* **:** PILOTHOUSE

wheel–thrown \ˈhwēl-ˌthrōn\ *adj* **:** made on a potter's wheel

wheel·wright \-ˌrīt\ *n* **:** a maker and repairer of wheels and wheeled vehicles

[1]**wheeze** \ˈhwēz\ *vb* **wheezed; wheez·ing ♦ :** to breathe with difficulty usually with a whistling sound

♦ blow, gasp, pant, puff

[2]**wheeze** *n* **1 :** a sound of wheezing **2 :** an often repeated and well-known joke **3 :** a trite saying

wheezy \ˈhwē-zē\ *adj* **wheez·i·er; -est 1 :** inclined to wheeze **2 :** having a wheezing sound — **wheez·i·ly** \-zə-lē\ *adv* — **wheez·i·ness** \-zē-nəs\ *n*

whelk \ˈhwelk\ *n* **:** a large sea snail; *esp* **:** one much used as food in Europe

whelm \ˈhwelm\ *vb* **:** to overcome or engulf completely **:** OVERWHELM

[1]**whelp** \ˈhwelp\ *n* **1 :** any of the young of various carnivorous mammals (as a dog) **2 ♦ :** a young boy or girl

♦ child, cub, juvenile, kid, kiddo, moppet, youngster, youth

[2]**whelp** *vb* **:** to give birth to (whelps); *also* **:** bring forth young

[1]**when** \ˈhwen\ *adv* **1 :** at what time ⟨~ will you return⟩ **2 :** at or during which time ⟨a time ~ things were better⟩

[2]**when** *conj* **1 :** at or during the time that ⟨leave ~ I do⟩ **2 :** every time that ⟨they all clapped ~ he sang⟩ **3 :** in the event that **:** IF ⟨disqualified ~ you cheat⟩ **4 ♦ :** in spite of the fact that **:** ALTHOUGH ⟨quit politics ~ he might have had a great career in it⟩

♦ albeit, although, howbeit, though, while

[3]**when** *pron* **:** what or which time ⟨since ~ have you been the boss⟩

[4]**when** *n* **:** the time of a happening

whence \ˈhwens\ *adv or conj* **:** from what place, source, or cause

when·ev·er \hwe-ˈne-vər, hwə-\ *conj or adv* **:** at whatever time

when·so·ev·er \ˈhwen-sō-ˌe-vər\ *conj* **:** at any or every time that

[1]**where** \ˈhwer\ *adv* **1 :** at, in, or to what place ⟨~ is it⟩ ⟨~ will we go⟩ **2 :** at, in, or to what situation, position, direction, circumstances, or respect ⟨~ does this road lead⟩

[2]**where** *conj* **1 :** at, in, or to what place ⟨knows ~ the house is⟩ **2 :** at, in, or to what situation, position, direction, circumstances, or respect ⟨shows ~ the road leads⟩ **3 :** WHEREVER ⟨goes ~ she likes⟩ **4 :** at, in, or to which place ⟨the town ~ we live⟩ **5 :** at, in, or to the place at, in, or to which ⟨stay ~ you are⟩ **6 :** in a case, situation, or respect in which ⟨outstanding ~ endurance is called for⟩

[3]**where** *n* **:** PLACE, LOCATION ⟨the ~ and how of the accident⟩

[1]**where·abouts** \-ə-ˌbau̇ts\ *also* **where·about** \-ˌbau̇t\ *adv* **:** about where **:** near what place ⟨~ does he live⟩

[2]**whereabouts** *n sing or pl* **:** the place where a person or thing is ⟨his present ~ are unknown⟩

where·as \hwer-ˈaz\ *conj* **1 :** while on the contrary; *also* **:** ALTHOUGH **2 ♦ :** in view of the fact that **:** SINCE

♦ because, for, now, since

where·at \-ˈat\ *conj* **1 :** at or toward which **2 :** in consequence of which **:** WHEREUPON

where·by \-ˈbī\ *conj* **:** by, through, or in accordance with which ⟨the means ~ we achieved our goals⟩

[1]**where·fore** \ˈhwer-ˌfōr\ *adv* **1 :** for what reason or purpose **:** WHY **2 ♦ :** because of that **:** THEREFORE

♦ accordingly, consequently, ergo, hence, so, therefore, thus

[2]**wherefore** *n* **♦ :** an answer or statement giving an explanation **:** REASON

♦ grounds, motive, reason, why

[1]**where·in** \hwer-ˈin\ *adv* **:** in what **:** in what respect ⟨~ was I wrong⟩

[2]**wherein** *conj* **1 :** in which **:** WHERE ⟨the city ~ we live⟩ **2 :** during which **3 :** in what way **:** HOW ⟨showed me ~ I was wrong⟩

where·of \-ˈəv, -ˈäv\ *conj* **1 :** of what ⟨knows ~ he speaks⟩ **2 :** of which or whom ⟨books ~ the best are lost⟩

where·on \-ˈȯn, -ˈän\ *conj* **:** on which ⟨the base ~ it rests⟩

where·so·ev·er \ˈhwer-sō-ˌe-vər\ *conj* **:** WHEREVER

where·to \ˈhwer-ˌtü\ *conj* **:** to which

where·up·on \ˈhwer-ə-ˌpȯn, -ˌpän\ *conj* **1 :** on which **2 :** closely following and in consequence of which

[1]**wher·ev·er** \hwer-ˈe-vər\ *adv* **:** where in the world ⟨~ did he get that tie⟩

[2]**wherever** *conj* **1 :** at, in, or to whatever place **2 :** in any circumstance in which

where·with \ˈhwer-ˌwith, -ˌwith\ *conj* **:** with or by means of which

where·with·al \ˈhwer-wi-ˌthȯl, -ˌthȯl\ *n* **♦ :** means or resources for purchasing or doing something; *esp* **:** MONEY

♦ finances, fund, pocket, resources

wher·ry \ˈhwer-ē\ *n, pl* **wherries :** a long light rowboat sharp at both ends

whet \ˈhwet\ *vb* **whet·ted; whet·ting 1 ♦ :** to sharpen by rubbing on or with something abrasive (as a whetstone) **2 :** to make keen **:** STIMULATE ⟨~ the appetite⟩

♦ edge, grind, hone, sharpen, strop

wheth·er \ˈhwe-thər\ *conj* **1 :** if it is or was true that ⟨ask ~ he is going⟩ **2 :** if it is or was better ⟨uncertain ~ to go or stay⟩ **3 :** whichever is or was the case, namely that ⟨~ we succeed or fail, we must try⟩ **4 :** EITHER ⟨turned out well ~ by accident or design⟩

whet·stone \ˈhwet-ˌstōn\ *n* **:** a stone for sharpening blades

whey \ˈhwā\ *n* **:** the watery part of milk that separates after the milk sours and thickens

[1]**which** \ˈhwich\ *adj* **1 :** being what one or ones out of a group ⟨~ shirt should I wear⟩ **2 :** WHICHEVER

[2]**which** *pron* **1 :** which one or ones ⟨~ is yours⟩ ⟨~ are his⟩ ⟨it's in May or June, I'm not sure ~⟩ **2 :** WHICHEVER ⟨we have all kinds; take ~ you like⟩ **3** — used to introduce a relative clause and to serve as a substitute therein for the noun modified by the clause ⟨the money ~ is coming to me⟩

[1]**which·ev·er** \hwich-ˈe-vər\ *adj* **:** no matter which ⟨~ way you go⟩

[2]**whichever** *pron* **:** whatever one or ones

which·so·ev·er \ˌhwich-sō-ˈe-vər\ *pron or adj* **:** WHICHEVER

whick·er \ˈhwi-kər\ *vb* **:** NEIGH, WHINNY — **whicker** *n*

[1]**whiff** \ˈhwif\ *n* **1 :** a quick puff or slight gust (as of air) **2 :** an inhalation of odor, gas, or smoke **3 :** a slight trace **4 :** STRIKEOUT

[2]**whiff** *vb* **1 :** to expel, puff out, or blow away in or as if in whiffs **2 ♦ :** to inhale an odor **3 :** STRIKE OUT 3

♦ nose, scent, smell, sniff

Whig \ˈhwig\ *n* **1 :** a member or supporter of a British political group of the late 17th through early 19th centuries seeking to limit royal authority and increase parliamentary power **2 :** an American favoring independence from Great Britain during the

American Revolution **3 :** a member or supporter of an American political party formed about 1834 to oppose the Democrats

¹while \ˈhwīl\ *n* **1** ♦ **:** a period of time ⟨stay a ~⟩ **2** ♦ **:** the time and effort used **:** TROUBLE ⟨worth your ~⟩

♦ [1] bit, space, spell, stretch ♦ [2] effort, exertion, expenditure, labor (*or* labour), pains, sweat, trouble, work

²while *conj* **1 :** during the time that ⟨she called ~ you were out⟩ **2 :** AS LONG AS ⟨~ there's life there's hope⟩ **3** ♦ **:** in spite of the fact that **:** ALTHOUGH ⟨~ he's respected, he's not liked⟩

♦ albeit, although, howbeit, though, when

³while *vb* **whiled; whil•ing :** to cause to pass especially pleasantly ⟨~ away an hour⟩

¹whi•lom \ˈhwī-ləm\ *adv archaic* **:** FORMERLY

²whilom *adj* ♦ **:** at a time in the past **:** FORMER ⟨his ~ friends⟩

♦ erstwhile, former, late, old, onetime, past, sometime

whilst \ˈhwīlst\ *conj, chiefly Brit* **:** WHILE

whim \ˈhwim\ *n* ♦ **:** a sudden wish, desire, or change of mind

♦ caprice, fancy, freak, notion, vagary

whim•per \ˈhwim-pər\ *vb* **:** to make a low whining plaintive or broken sound — **whimper** *n*

whim•si•cal \ˈhwim-zi-kəl\ *adj* **1** ♦ **:** full of whims **:** CAPRICIOUS **2 :** resulting from or characterized by whim or caprice — **whim•si•cal•i•ty** \ˌhwim-zə-ˈka-lə-tē\ *n* — **whim•si•cal•ly** \ˈhwim-zi-k(ə-)lē\ *adv*

♦ capricious, impulsive

whim•sy *also* **whim•sey** \ˈhwim-zē\ *n, pl* **whim•sies** *also* **whim•seys** **1 :** a sudden impulsive apparently unmotivated change of mind **:** WHIM **2 :** a fanciful or fantastic device, object, or creation especially in writing or art

whine \ˈhwīn\ *vb* **whined; whin•ing** **1 :** to utter a usually high-pitched plaintive or distressed cry; *also* **:** to make a sound similar to such a cry **2** ♦ **:** to complain with or as if with a whine — **whine** *n* — **whiny** *also* **whin•ey** \ˈhwī-nē\ *adj*

♦ beef, bellyache, carp, complain, crab, croak, fuss, gripe, grouse, growl, grumble, kick, moan, murmur, mutter, repine, squawk, wail

whin•er *n* ♦ **:** one that whines

♦ bear, complainer, crab, crank, grouch, grumbler

¹whin•ny \ˈhwi-nē\ *vb* **whin•nied; whin•ny•ing :** to neigh usually in a low or gentle manner

²whinny *n, pl* **whinnies :** NEIGH

¹whip \ˈhwip\ *vb* **whipped; whip•ping** **1 :** to move, snatch, or jerk quickly or forcefully ⟨~ out a gun⟩ ⟨*whipped* the car around and sped off⟩ **2** ♦ **:** to strike with a slender lithe implement (as a lash) especially as a punishment; *also* **:** SPANK **3 :** to drive or urge on by or as if by using a whip **4 :** to bind or wrap (as a rope or rod) with cord in order to protect and strengthen; *also* **:** to wind or wrap around something **5** ♦ **:** to thoroughly overcome **:** DEFEAT **6** ♦ **:** to stir up **:** INCITE ⟨~ up enthusiasm⟩ **7 :** to produce in a hurry ⟨~ up a meal⟩ **8 :** to beat (as eggs or cream) into a froth **9 a :** to proceed nimbly or briskly **b :** to flap about forcefully ⟨flags *whipping* in the wind⟩ — **whip•per** *n* — **whip into shape :** to bring forcefully to a desired state or condition

♦ [2] beat, flog, hide, thrash ♦ [5] beat, best, clobber, conquer, crush, defeat, drub, lick, master, overcome, rout, skunk, subdue, trim, triumph, trounce, wallop, win ♦ *usu* **whip up** [6] abet, ferment, foment, incite, instigate, provoke, raise, stir

²whip *n* **1** ♦ **:** a flexible instrument used for whipping **2 :** a stroke or cut with or as if with a whip **3 :** a dessert made by whipping a portion of the ingredients ⟨prune ~⟩ **4 :** a person who handles a whip **5 :** a member of a legislative body appointed by a party to enforce party discipline **6 :** a whipping or thrashing motion

♦ lash, scourge, switch

whip•cord \-ˌkȯrd\ *n* **1 :** a thin tough braided cord **2 :** a strong cloth with fine diagonal cords or ribs

whip hand *n* **:** positive control **:** ADVANTAGE

whip•lash \ˈhwip-ˌlash\ *n* **1 :** the lash of a whip **2 :** injury resulting from a sudden sharp movement of the neck and head (as of a person in a vehicle that is struck from the rear)

whip•per•snap•per \ˈhwi-pər-ˌsna-pər\ *n* ♦ **:** a small, insignificant, or presumptuous person

♦ nobody, nonentity, nothing, zero

whip•pet \ˈhwi-pət\ *n* **:** any of a breed of small swift slender dogs that are used for racing

whipping boy *n* **:** one who is receives criticism or blame instead of the ones deserving it **:** SCAPEGOAT

whip•poor•will \ˈhwi-pər-ˌwil\ *n* **:** an American insect-eating bird with dull variegated plumage whose call at nightfall and just before dawn is suggestive of its name

whip•saw \ˈhwip-ˌsȯ\ *vb* **:** to beset with two or more adverse conditions or situations at once

¹whir *also* **whirr** \ˈhwər\ *vb* **whirred; whir•ring** ♦ **:** to move, fly, or revolve with a whir

♦ buzz, drone, hum, whish, whiz, zip, zoom

²whir *also* **whirr** *n* **:** a continuous fluttering or vibratory sound made by something in rapid motion

¹whirl \ˈhwərl\ *vb* **1** ♦ **:** to move or drive in a circle or curve especially with force or speed **2** ♦ **:** to turn or cause to turn rapidly in circles **3 :** to turn abruptly **4** ♦ **:** to move or go quickly **5** ♦ **:** to become dizzy or giddy **:** REEL

♦ [1, 2] pivot, revolve, roll, rotate, spin, swing, swirl, turn, twirl, twist, wheel ♦ [4] breeze, career, course, dash, fly, hasten, hurry, race, rip, rocket, run, rush, shoot, speed, step, tear, zip, zoom ♦ [5] reel, spin

²whirl *n* **1** ♦ **:** a rapid rotating or circling movement; *also* **:** something whirling **2 :** COMMOTION, BUSTLE ⟨the social ~⟩ **3** ♦ **:** a state of mental confusion **4 :** TRY ⟨gave it a ~⟩

♦ [1] gyration, pirouette, reel, revolution, roll, rotation, spin, twirl, wheel ♦ [3] bafflement, bewilderment, confusion, distraction, muddle, mystification, perplexity, puzzlement

whirl•i•gig \ˈhwər-li-ˌgig\ *n* **1 :** a child's toy having a whirling motion **2 :** something that continuously whirls or changes

whirl•pool \ˈhwərl-ˌpül\ *n* **:** water moving rapidly in a circle so as to produce a depression in the center into which floating objects may be drawn

whirl•wind \-ˌwind\ *n* **1 :** a small whirling windstorm **2 :** a confused rush **3 :** a violent or destructive force

whirly•bird \ˈhwər-lē-ˌbərd\ *n* **:** HELICOPTER

¹whish \ˈhwish\ *vb* **1 :** to move with a whish or swishing sound **2** ♦ **:** to have or make a sound like that of a long \s\ or \sh\

♦ fizz, hiss, sizzle, swish

²whish *n* **:** a rushing sound **:** SWISH

¹whisk \ˈhwisk\ *n* **1 :** a quick light sweeping or brushing motion **2 :** a usually wire kitchen implement for beating food by hand **3 :** WHISK BROOM

²whisk *vb* **1** ♦ **:** to move nimbly and quickly **2** ♦ **:** to move or convey briskly ⟨~*ed* the children off to bed⟩ **3 :** to beat or whip lightly ⟨~ eggs⟩ **4 :** to brush or wipe off lightly ⟨~ a coat⟩

♦ [1] bowl, breeze, coast, drift, flow, glide, roll, sail, skim, slide, slip, stream, sweep ♦ [2] accelerate, hasten, hurry, quicken, rush, speed, step up

whisk broom *n* **:** a small broom with a short handle used especially as a clothes brush

whis•ker \ˈhwis-kər\ *n* **1 :** one hair of the beard **2** *pl* **:** the part of the beard that grows on the sides of the face or on the chin **3 :** one of the long bristles or hairs growing near the mouth of an animal (as a cat or mouse) — **whis•kered** \-kərd\ *adj*

whis•key *or* **whis•ky** \ˈhwis-kē\ *n, pl* **whiskeys** *or* **whiskies :** a liquor distilled from fermented wort (as that obtained from rye, corn, or barley mash)

¹whis•per \ˈhwis-pər\ *vb* **1 a :** to speak very low or under the breath **b** ♦ **:** to tell or utter by or as if by whispering ⟨~ a secret⟩ **2 :** to make a low rustling sound ⟨~*ing* leaves⟩ — **whis•per•er** \-pər-ər\ *n*

♦ circulate, noise, rumor

²whisper *n* **1 :** something communicated by or as if by whispering **:** HINT, RUMOR **2 :** an act or instance of whispering

whist \ˈhwist\ *n* **:** a card game played by four players in two partnerships with a deck of 52 cards

¹whis•tle \ˈhwi-səl\ *n* **1 :** a device by which a shrill sound is produced ⟨steam ~⟩ ⟨tin ~⟩ **2 :** a shrill clear sound made by forcing breath out or air in through the puckered lips **3 :** the sound or signal produced by a whistle or as if by whistling **4 :** the shrill clear note of an animal (as a bird)

²whistle *vb* **whis•tled; whis•tling** **1 :** to utter a shrill clear sound by blowing or drawing air through the puckered lips **2 :** to utter a shrill note or call resembling a whistle **3 :** to make a shrill clear sound especially by rapid movements ⟨the wind *whistled*⟩ **4 :** to blow or sound a whistle **5 :** to signal or call by a whistle **6 :** to produce, utter, or express by whistling ⟨~ a tune⟩ — **whis•tler** *n*

whis•tle–blow•er \ˈhwi-səl-ˌblō-ər\ *n* **:** INFORMER

whis•tle–stop \-ˌstäp\ *n* **:** a brief personal appearance by a political candidate orig. on the rear platform of a touring train
whit \ˈhwit\ *n* ♦ **:** the smallest part or particle

♦ hoot, jot, lick, modicum, rap, tittle

¹white \ˈhwīt\ *adj* **whit•er; whit•est** **1** ♦ **:** free from color **2 :** of the color of new snow or milk; *esp* **:** of the color white **3 :** light or pallid in color ⟨lips ~ with fear⟩ **4 :** SILVERY; *also* **:** made of silver **5 :** of, relating to, or being a member of a group or race characterized by light-colored skin **6 :** free from spot or blemish **:** PURE, INNOCENT **7 :** BLANK 2 ⟨~ space in printed matter⟩ **8** ♦ **:** not intended to cause harm ⟨a ~ lie⟩ ⟨~ magic⟩ **9 :** wearing white ⟨~ friars⟩ **10 :** marked by snow ⟨~ Christmas⟩ **11 :** consisting of a wide range of frequencies ⟨~ light⟩ — **white•ness** \-nəs\ *n* — **whit•ish** \ˈhwī-tish\ *adj*

♦ [1] colorless (*or* colourless), uncolored (*or* uncoloured, unpainted ♦ [8] harmless, innocent, innocuous, safe

²white *n* **1 :** the color of maximal lightness that characterizes objects which both reflect and transmit light **:** the opposite of black **2 :** a white or light-colored part or thing ⟨the ~ of an egg⟩; *also, pl* **:** white garments **3 :** the light-colored pieces in a 2-player board game; *also* **:** the person by whom these are played **4 :** one that is or approaches the color white **5 :** a person of a light-skinned race
white ant *n* **:** TERMITE
white blood cell *n* **:** any of the colorless blood cells (as lymphocytes) that do not contain hemoglobin but do have a nucleus
white–bread \ˈhwīt-ˈbred\ *adj* **:** being, typical of, or having qualities (as blandness) associated with the white middle class
white•cap \ˈhwīt-ˌkap\ *n* **:** a wave crest breaking into white foam
white chocolate *n* **:** a whitish confection chiefly of cocoa butter, milk, and sugar
white–col•lar \ˈhwīt-ˈkä-lər\ *adj* **:** of, relating to, or constituting the class of salaried workers whose duties do not require the wearing of work clothes or protective clothing
white dwarf *n* **:** a small very dense whitish star of low luminosity
white elephant *n* **1 :** an Indian elephant of a pale color that is sometimes venerated in India, Sri Lanka, Thailand, and Myanmar **2 :** something requiring much care and expense and giving little profit or enjoyment
white feather *n* **:** a mark or symbol of cowardice
white•fish \ˈhwīt-ˌfish\ *n* **:** any of various freshwater food fishes related to the salmons and trouts
white flag *n* **:** a flag of pure white used to signify truce or surrender
white gold *n* **:** a pale alloy of gold resembling platinum in appearance
white goods *n pl* **:** white fabrics or articles (as sheets or towels) typically made of cotton or linen
White•hall \ˈhwīt-ˌhȯl\ *n* **:** the British government
white hat *n* **1 :** an admirable and honorable person **2 :** a mark or symbol of goodness
white•head \-ˌhed\ *n* **:** a small whitish lump in the skin due to retention of secretion in an oil gland duct
white heat *n* **:** a temperature higher than red heat at which a body becomes brightly incandescent
white–hot *adj* **1 :** being at or radiating white heat **2 :** FERVID
White House \-ˌhau̇s\ *n* **1 :** the executive department of the U.S. government **2 :** a residence of the president of the U.S.
white lead *n* **:** a heavy white poisonous carbonate of lead used especially formerly as a pigment in exterior paints
white matter *n* **:** whitish nerve tissue especially of the brain and spinal cord that consists largely of neuron processes enclosed in a fatty material and that typically lies under the cortical gray matter
whit•en \ˈhwīt-ᵊn\ *vb* ♦ **:** to make or become white — **whit•en•er** *n*

♦ blanch, bleach, blench, dull, fade, pale, wash out

white pepper *n* **:** a spice that consists of the berry of a pepper plant ground after removal of its black husk
white pine *n* **:** a tall-growing pine of eastern No. America with needles in clusters of five; *also* **:** its wood
white sale *n* **:** a sale on white goods
white shark *n* **:** GREAT WHITE SHARK
white slave *n* **:** a woman or girl held unwillingly for purposes of prostitution — **white slavery** *n*
white•tail \ˈhwīt-ˌtāl\ *n* **:** WHITE-TAILED DEER
white–tailed deer *n* **:** a No. American deer with a rather long tail white on the underside and the males of which have forward-arching antlers
white–tie \-tī\ *adj* **:** characterized by or requiring formal evening clothes consisting of usually white tie and tailcoat for men and a formal gown for women
white•wall \ˈhwīt-ˌwȯl\ *n* **:** an automobile tire having a white band on the sidewall
¹white•wash \-ˌwȯsh, -ˌwäsh\ *vb* **1 :** to whiten with whitewash **2** ♦ **:** to clear of a charge of wrongdoing by offering excuses, hiding facts, or conducting a perfunctory investigation **3 :** SHUT OUT 2

♦ excuse, gloss, palliate

²whitewash *n* **1 :** a liquid mixture (as of lime and water) for whitening a surface **2 :** a clearing of wrongdoing by whitewashing
white water *n* **:** frothy water (as in breakers, rapids, or falls)
white•wood \-ˌwu̇d\ *n* **:** any of various trees and especially a tulip tree having light-colored wood; *also* **:** such wood
¹whith•er \ˈhwi-thər\ *adv* **1 :** to what place **2 :** to what situation, position, degree, or end ⟨~ will this drive him⟩
²whither *conj* **1 :** to the place at, in, or to which; *also* **:** to which place **2 :** to whatever place
whith•er•so•ev•er \ˌhwi-thər-sō-ˈe-vər\ *conj* **:** to whatever place
¹whit•ing \ˈhwī-tiŋ\ *n, pl* **whiting** *also* **whit•ings :** any of several usually light or silvery food fishes (as a hake) found mostly near seacoasts
²whiting *n* **:** calcium carbonate in powdered form used especially as a pigment and in putty
whit•low \ˈhwit-ˌlō\ *n* **:** a deep inflammation of a finger or toe with pus formation
Whit•sun•day \ˈhwit-ˈsən-dē, -sən-ˌdā\ *n* **:** PENTECOST
whit•tle \ˈhwit-ᵊl\ *vb* **whit•tled; whit•tling** **1 :** to pare or cut off chips from the surface of (wood) with a knife; *also* **:** to cut or shape by such paring **2 :** to reduce as if by paring down ⟨~ down expenses⟩
¹whiz *or* **whizz** \ˈhwiz\ *vb* **whizzed; whiz•zing** **1** ♦ **:** to hum, whir, or hiss like a speeding object (as an arrow or ball) passing through air **2** ♦ **:** fly or move swiftly with a hissing or buzzing sound

♦ [1, 2] buzz, drone, hiss, hum, whir, whish, zip, zoom

²whiz *or* **whizz** *n, pl* **whiz•zes** ♦ **:** a hissing, buzzing, or whizzing sound

♦ buzz, drone, hiss, hum, purr, whir, zoom

³whiz *n, pl* **whiz•zes** ♦ **:** a person notably qualified or able usually in a specified field of interest **:** WIZARD 2

♦ ace, adept, artist, authority, crackerjack, expert, maestro, master, scholar, shark, virtuoso, wizard ♦ brain, genius, intellect, thinker, wizard

who \ˈhü\ *pron* **1 :** what or which person or persons ⟨~ did it⟩ ⟨~ is he⟩ ⟨~ are they⟩ **2 :** the person or persons that ⟨knows ~ did it⟩ **3** — used to introduce a relative clause and to serve as a substitute therein for the substantive modified by the clause ⟨the man ~ lives there is rich⟩
WHO *abbr* World Health Organization
whoa \ˈwō, ˈhwō, ˈhō\ *vb imper* — a command to an animal to stand still
who•dun•it *also* **who•dun•nit** \hü-ˈdə-nət\ *n* **:** a detective or mystery story
who•ev•er \hü-ˈe-vər\ *pron* **:** whatever person **:** no matter who
¹whole \ˈhōl\ *adj* **1** ♦ **:** being in healthy or sound condition **:** free from defect or damage **2** ♦ **:** having all its proper parts or elements ⟨~ milk⟩ **3 :** constituting the total sum of **:** ENTIRE ⟨owns the ~ island⟩ **4 :** each or all of the ⟨the ~ family⟩ **5** ♦ **:** not scattered or divided **:** CONCENTRATED ⟨gave me his ~ attention⟩ **6 :** seemingly complete or total ⟨the ~ idea is to help, not hinder⟩

♦ [1] able-bodied, chipper, fit, hale, healthy, hearty, robust, sound, well, wholesome ♦ [2] complete, comprehensive, entire, full, grand, intact, integral, perfect, plenary, total, whole ♦ [5] all, concentrated, entire, undivided *Ant* diffuse, divided, scattered

²whole *n* **1** ♦ **:** a complete amount or sum **2 :** something whole or entire — **on the whole** **1 :** in view of all the circumstances or conditions **2 :** in general

♦ aggregate, full, sum, total, totality

³whole *adv* **:** COMPLETELY, ENTIRELY ⟨a ~ new team⟩
whole food *n* **:** a food eaten in its natural state with little or no artificial additives
whole•heart•ed \ˈhōl-ˈhär-təd\ *adj* **:** undivided in purpose, enthusiasm, will, or commitment

whole hog *adv* **:** to the fullest extent **:** COMPLETELY ⟨accepted the proposals *whole hog*⟩

whole·ness *n* ♦ **:** the quality or state of being whole **:** an unreduced or unbroken completeness or totality

♦ fitness, health, heartiness, robustness, soundness, wellness, wholesomeness

whole note *n* **:** a musical note equal to one measure of four beats

whole number *n* **1 :** any of the set of nonnegative integers **2** ♦ **:** any of the natural numbers that do not include fractions **:** INTEGER

♦ digit, figure, integer, number, numeral

1whole·sale \ˈhōl-ˌsāl\ *n* **:** the sale of goods in quantity usually for resale by a retail merchant

2wholesale *adj* **1 :** performed on a large scale without discrimination ⟨∼ slaughter⟩ **2 :** of, relating to, or engaged in wholesaling — **wholesale** *adv*

3wholesale *vb* **whole·saled; whole·sal·ing :** to sell at wholesale — **whole·sal·er** *n*

whole·some \ˈhōl-səm\ *adj* **1** ♦ **:** promoting mental, spiritual, or bodily health or well-being ⟨a ∼ environment⟩ **2** ♦ **:** sound in body, mind, or morals **:** HEALTHY **3 :** PRUDENT ⟨∼ respect for the law⟩

♦ [1] healthful, healthy, restorative, salubrious, salutary ♦ [2] able-bodied, chipper, fit, hale, healthy, hearty, robust, sound, well, whole

whole·some·ness *n* ♦ **:** the quality, fact, or state of being wholesome

♦ fitness, health, heartiness, robustness, soundness, wellness, wholeness

whole step *n* **:** a musical interval comprising two half steps (as C–D or F♯–G♯)

whole wheat *adj* **:** made of ground entire wheat kernels

whol·ly \ˈhōl-lē\ *adv* **1** ♦ **:** to the full or entire extent **:** COMPLETELY **2 :** SOLELY, EXCLUSIVELY

♦ absolutely, all, altogether, clean, completely, entirely, fully, quite, totally, utterly

whom \ˈhüm\ *pron, objective case of* WHO

whom·ev·er \hü-ˈme-vər\ *pron, objective case of* WHOEVER

whom·so·ev·er \ˌhüm-sō-ˈe-vər\ *pron, objective case of* WHOSOEVER

1whoop \ˈhwüp, ˈhwu̇p, ˈhüp, ˈhu̇p\ *vb* **1 :** to shout or call loudly and vigorously **2 :** to make the characteristic whoop of whooping cough **3 :** to go or pass with a loud noise **4 :** to utter or express with a whoop; *also* **:** to urge, drive, or cheer with a whoop

2whoop *n* **1** ♦ **:** a whooping sound or utterance **:** SHOUT **2 :** a crowing intake of breath after a fit of coughing in whooping cough

♦ cry, holler, hoot, howl, shout, yell, yowl

1whoop·ee \ˈhwu̇-(ˌ)pē, ˈhwü-\ *interj* — used to express exuberance

2whoopee *n* **1 :** boisterous fun **2 :** sexual play — usually used with *make*

whooping cough *n* **:** an infectious bacterial disease especially of children marked by convulsive coughing fits often followed by a shrill gasping intake of breath

whooping crane *n* **:** a large white nearly extinct No. American crane noted for its loud whooping call

whoop·la \ˈhwüp-ˌlä, ˈhwu̇p-\ *n* **1 :** HOOPLA **2 :** boisterous merrymaking

whop·per \ˈhwä-pər\ *n* **1** ♦ **:** something unusually large or extreme of its kind **2** ♦ **:** a monstrous lie

♦ [1] behemoth, blockbuster, colossus, giant, jumbo, leviathan, mammoth, monster, titan, whale ♦ [2] fabrication, fairy tale, falsehood, falsity, fib, lie, mendacity, prevarication, story, tale, untruth

whop·ping \ˈhwä-piŋ\ *adj* ♦ **:** extremely large

♦ colossal, enormous, giant, gigantic, grand, huge, jumbo, mammoth, massive, outsize, oversize, prodigious, titanic, tremendous

whore \ˈhōr\ *n* **:** a woman who practices unlawful sexual commerce **:** PROSTITUTE

whorl \ˈhwȯrl, ˈhwərl\ *n* **1 :** a group of parts (as leaves or petals) encircling an axis and especially a plant stem **2 :** something that whirls or coils around a center **:** COIL, SPIRAL **3 :** one of the turns of a snail shell

whorled \ˈhwȯrld, ˈhwərld\ *adj* **:** having or arranged in whorls

1whose \ˈhüz\ *adj* **:** of or relating to whom or which especially as possessor or possessors, agent or agents, or object or objects of an action ⟨asked ∼ bag it was⟩

2whose *pron* **:** whose one or ones ⟨∼ is this car⟩ ⟨∼ are those books⟩

who·so \ˈhü-ˌsō\ *pron* **:** WHOEVER

who·so·ev·er \ˌhü-sō-ˈe-vər\ *pron* **:** WHOEVER

whs *or* **whse** *abbr* warehouse

whsle *abbr* wholesale

1why \ˈhwī\ *adv* **:** for what reason, cause, or purpose ⟨∼ did you do it?⟩

2why *conj* **1 :** the cause, reason, or purpose for which ⟨that is ∼ you did it⟩ **2 :** for which **:** on account of which ⟨knows the reason ∼ you did it⟩

3why *n, pl* **whys** ♦ **:** the reason or cause of something ⟨the ∼*s* of racial prejudice⟩

♦ grounds, motive, reason, wherefore

4why \ˈwī, ˈhwī\ *interj* — used to express surprise, hesitation, approval, disapproval, or impatience ⟨∼, here's what I was looking for⟩

WI *abbr* **1** West Indies **2** Wisconsin

WIA *abbr* wounded in action

Wic·ca \ˈwi-kə\ *n* **:** a religion that affirms the existence of supernatural power (as magic) and of deities who inhere in nature and that ritually observes seasonal and life cycles

wick \ˈwik\ *n* **:** a loosely bound bundle of soft fibers that draws up oil, tallow, or wax to be burned in a candle, oil lamp, or stove

wick·ed \ˈwi-kəd\ *adj* **1** ♦ **:** morally bad **:** EVIL, SINFUL **2 :** FIERCE, VICIOUS **3 a** ♦ **:** playfully or engagingly mischievous **:** ROGUISH ⟨a ∼ glance⟩ **b :** showing or expressing ill will **:** MALICIOUS **4 :** REPUGNANT, VILE ⟨a ∼ odor⟩ **5 :** HARMFUL, DANGEROUS ⟨a ∼ attack⟩ **6 :** impressively excellent ⟨throws a ∼ fastball⟩

♦ [1] bad, black, evil, immoral, iniquitous, nefarious, rotten, sinful, unethical, unsavory, vicious, vile, villainous, wrong ♦ [3a] devilish, impish, knavish, mischievous, rascally, roguish, sly, waggish

wick·ed·ly *adv* ♦ **:** in a wicked manner

♦ hatefully, maliciously, meanly, nastily, spitefully, viciously

wick·ed·ness *n* ♦ **:** the quality or state of being wicked

♦ devilishness, impishness, knavery, mischief, mischievousness, rascality, shenanigans, waggery ♦ atrociousness, atrocity, depravity, enormity, heinousness, monstrosity, vileness

wick·er \ˈwi-kər\ *n* **1 :** a small pliant branch (as an osier or a withe) **2 :** WICKERWORK — **wicker** *adj*

wick·er·work \-ˌwərk\ *n* **:** work made of osiers, twigs, or rods **:** basket weaving

wick·et \ˈwi-kət\ *n* **1 :** a small gate or door; *esp* **:** one forming a part of or placed near a larger one **2 :** a window-like opening usually with a grille or grate (as at a ticket office) **3 :** a set of three upright rods topped by two crosspieces bowled at in cricket **4 :** an arch or hoop in croquet

wick·i·up \ˈwi-kē-ˌəp\ *n* **:** a hut used by nomadic Indians of the western and southwestern U.S. with a usually oval base and a rough frame covered with reed mats, grass, or brushwood

wid *abbr* widow, widower

1wide \ˈwīd\ *adj* **wider; wid·est 1** ♦ **:** covering a vast area **2 :** measured across or at right angles to the length **3** ♦ **:** not narrow **:** BROAD; *also* **:** ROOMY **4 :** opened to full width ⟨eyes ∼ with wonder⟩ **5 :** not limited **:** EXTENSIVE ⟨∼ experience⟩ **6 :** far from the goal, mark, or truth ⟨a ∼ guess⟩ — **wide·ly** *adv*

♦ [1] broad, expansive, extended, extensive, far-flung, far-reaching, widespread ♦ [3] broad, commodious, expansive, extensive, roomy, spacious, thick *Ant* narrow, skinny, slender, slim, thin

2wide *adv* **wid·er; wid·est 1 :** over a great distance or extent **:** WIDELY ⟨searched far and ∼⟩ **2 :** over a specified distance, area, or extent **3 :** so as to leave a wide space between ⟨∼ apart⟩ **4 :** so as to clear by a considerable distance ⟨ran ∼ around left end⟩ **5 :** COMPLETELY, FULLY ⟨opened her eyes ∼⟩

wide–awake \ˌwīd-ə-ˈwāk\ *adj* **1** ♦ **:** fully awake **2** ♦ **:** marked by careful watchfulness and promptness to cope with emergencies **:** ALERT

♦ [1] awake, sleepless, wakeful ♦ [2] alert, attentive, awake, vigilant, watchful

wide–body \ˈwīd-ˌbä-dē\ *n* **:** a large jet aircraft having a wide cabin

wide–eyed \ˈwīd-ˈīd\ *adj* **1 :** having the eyes wide open espe-

cially with wonder or astonishment **2 :** marked by unsophisticated or uncritical acceptance or admiration : NAIVE
wide•mouthed \-ˈmau̇t͟hd, -ˈmau̇tht\ *adj* **1 :** having one's mouth opened wide (as in awe) **2 :** having a wide mouth ⟨~ jars⟩
wid•en \ˈwīd-ᵊn\ *vb* **:** to increase in width, scope, or extent
wide•spread \ˈwīd-ˈspred\ *adj* **1 :** widely scattered or prevalent **2** ♦ **:** widely extended or spread out

♦ broad, expansive, extended, extensive, far-flung, far-reaching, wide

widgeon *var of* WIGEON
[1]**wid•ow** \ˈwi-dō\ *n* **:** a woman who has lost her husband by death and has not married again — **wid•ow•hood** *n*
[2]**widow** *vb* **:** to cause to become a widow or widower
wid•ow•er \ˈwi-də-wər\ *n* **:** a man who has lost his wife by death and has not married again
width \ˈwidth\ *n* **1 :** a distance from side to side **:** the measurement taken at right angles to the length **:** BREADTH **2** ♦ **:** largeness of extent or scope; *also* **:** FULLNESS **3 :** a measured and cut piece of material ⟨a ~ of calico⟩

♦ amplitude, breadth, compass, extent, range, reach, realm, scope, sweep

wield \ˈwēld\ *vb* **1 :** to use or handle especially effectively ⟨~ a broom⟩ **2** ♦ **:** to exert authority by means of ⟨~ influence⟩ — **wield•er** *n*

♦ apply, exercise, exert, put out

wie•ner *also* **wei•ner** \ˈwē-nər\ *n* **:** FRANKFURTER
wife \ˈwīf\ *n, pl* **wives** \ˈwīvz\ **1** *dial* **:** WOMAN **2 :** a woman acting in a specified capacity — used in combination **3** ♦ **:** a female partner in a marriage — **wife•hood** *n* — **wife•less** *adj* — **wife•ly** *adj*

♦ consort, helpmate, lady, mate, partner, spouse

wig \ˈwig\ *n* **:** a manufactured covering of natural or synthetic hair for the head; *also* **:** TOUPEE
wi•geon *or* **wid•geon** \ˈwi-jən\ *n, pl* **wigeon** *or* **wigeons** *or* **widgeon** *or* **widgeons :** any of several medium-sized freshwater ducks
wig•gle \ˈwi-gəl\ *vb* **wig•gled; wig•gling 1** ♦ **:** to move to and fro with quick jerky or shaking movements **2 :** to proceed with twisting and turning movements — **wiggle** *n*

♦ fiddle, fidget, jerk, squirm, twitch

wig•gler \ˈwi-glər, -gə-lər\ *n* **1 :** a larva or pupa of a mosquito **2 :** one that wiggles
wig•gly \ˈwi-glē, -gə-lē\ *adj* **1 :** tending to wiggle ⟨a ~ worm⟩ **2 :** WAVY ⟨~ lines⟩
wight \ˈwīt\ *n* **:** a living being **:** CREATURE
wig•let \ˈwi-glət\ *n* **:** a small wig used especially to enhance a hairstyle
[1]**wig•wag** \ˈwig-ˌwag\ *vb* **1 :** to signal by or as if by a flag or light waved according to a code **2 :** to make or cause to make a signal (as with the hand or arm)
[2]**wigwag** *n* **:** the art or practice of wigwagging
wig•wam \ˈwig-ˌwäm\ *n* **:** a hut of the Indians of the eastern U.S. having typically an arched framework of poles overlaid with bark, rush mats, or hides
[1]**wild** \ˈwīld\ *adj* **1** ♦ **:** living in a state of nature and not ordinarily tamed ⟨~ ducks⟩ **2** ♦ **:** growing or produced without human aid or care ⟨~ honey⟩ ⟨~ plants⟩ **3 :** WASTE, DESOLATE ⟨~ country⟩ **4 :** not subjected to restraint or regulation **:** UNCONTROLLED, UNRULY ⟨~ passions⟩ ⟨a ~ young stallion⟩ **5** ♦ **:** marked by turbulent violent agitation ⟨a ~ night⟩ **6** ♦ **:** exceeding normal or conventional bounds in thought, design, conception, or nature ⟨~ ideas⟩ **7 :** indicative of strong passion, desire, or emotion ⟨a ~ stare⟩ **8** ♦ **:** not acculturated to an advanced civilization **:** SAVAGE **9 a** ♦ **:** deviating from the natural or expected course, goal, or practice **:** acting, appearing, or being in an unexpected, undesired, or unpredictable manner ⟨a ~ throw⟩ **b** ♦ **:** having no basis in known or surmised fact **10 :** able to represent any playing card designated by the holder ⟨deuces ~⟩ — **wild** *adv* — **wild•ness** *n*

♦ [1] feral, savage, unbroken, undomesticated, untamed ***Ant*** broken, busted, domestic, domesticated, tame, tamed ♦ [1, 2] natural, uncultivated, untamed ***Ant*** cultivated, tamed ♦ [5] blustery, rough, stormy, tempestuous, tumultuous, turbulent, violent ♦ [6, 9a] bizarre, curious, far-out, funny, kinky, odd, outlandish, outré, peculiar, quaint, queer, quirky, remarkable, screwy, strange, wacky, weird ♦ [8] barbarous, heathen, heathenish, Neanderthal, rude, savage, uncivil, uncivilized, uncultivated ♦ [9b] absurd, bizarre, crazy, fanciful, fantastic, foolish, insane, nonsensical, preposterous, unreal

[2]**wild** *adv* **1** ♦ **:** in a wild manner **:** WILDLY **2** ♦ **:** without regulation or control ⟨running ~⟩

♦ amok, berserk, frantically, harum-scarum, hectically, helter-skelter, madly, pell-mell, wildly

[3]**wild** *n* **1 :** a region or tract that is sparsely inhabited or uncultivated **:** WILDERNESS **2 :** a natural or undomesticated state or existence
wild boar *n* **:** an Old World wild hog from which most domestic swine have been derived
wild card *n* **1 :** an unknown or unpredictable factor **2 :** one picked to fill a leftover play-off or tournament position **3** *usu* **wild•card :** a symbol (as ? or *) used in a keyword search to represent the presence of unspecified characters
wild carrot *n* **:** QUEEN ANNE'S LACE
[1]**wild•cat** \ˈwīld-ˌkat\ *n, pl* **wildcats 1 :** any of various small or medium-sized cats (as a lynx or ocelot) **2 :** a quick-tempered hard-fighting person
[2]**wildcat** *adj* **1 :** not sound or safe ⟨~ schemes⟩ **2 :** initiated by a group of workers without formal union approval ⟨~ strike⟩
[3]**wildcat** *vb* **wild•cat•ted; wild•cat•ting :** to drill an oil or gas well in a region not known to be productive
wil•de•beest \ˈwil-də-ˌbēst\ *n, pl* **wildebeests** *also* **wildebeest :** either of two large African antelopes with an oxlike head and horns and a horselike mane and tail
wil•der•ness \ˈwil-dər-nəs\ *n* ♦ **:** an uncultivated and uninhabited region

♦ nature, open, outdoors, wild

wild•fire \ˈwīld-ˌfīr\ *n* **:** an uncontrollable fire — **like wildfire :** very rapidly
wild•flow•er \-ˌflau̇(-ə)r\ *n* **:** the flower of a wild or uncultivated plant or the plant bearing it
wild•fowl \-ˌfau̇l\ *n* **:** a bird and especially a waterfowl hunted as game
wild–goose chase *n* **:** the pursuit of something unattainable
wild•life \ˈwīld-ˌlīf\ *n* **:** nonhuman living things and especially wild animals living in their natural environment
wild•ly *adv* ♦ **:** in a wild manner

♦ amok, berserk, frantically, harum-scarum, hectically, helter-skelter, madly, pell-mell, wild

wild oat *n* **1 :** any of several Old World wild grasses **2** *pl* **:** offenses and indiscretions attributed to youthful exuberance — usually used in the phrase *sow one's wild oats*
wild rice *n* **:** a No. American aquatic grass; *also* **:** its edible seed
wild•wood \ˈwīld-ˌwu̇d\ *n* **:** a wood unaltered or unfrequented by humans
[1]**wile** \ˈwīl\ *n* **1** ♦ **:** a trick or stratagem intended to ensnare or deceive; *also* **:** a playful trick **2** ♦ **:** the use of deceitfulness and trickery

♦ [1] artifice, device, dodge, gimmick, jig, ploy, scheme, sleight, stratagem, trick ♦ [2] artifice, chicanery, hanky-panky, subterfuge, trickery

[2]**wile** *vb* **wiled; wil•ing** ♦ **:** to lure by or as if by a magic spell

♦ allure, beguile, bewitch, captivate, charm, enchant, fascinate

wil•i•ness \-lē-nəs\ *n* ♦ **:** the quality or state of being wily

♦ artfulness, artifice, caginess, canniness, craft, craftiness, cunning, guile, slyness ♦ artifice, craft, craftiness, crookedness, cunning, deceit, deceitfulness, dishonesty, dissimulation, double-dealing, duplicity, guile

[1]**will** \ˈwil\ *vb, past* **would** \ˈwu̇d\ *pres sing & pl* **will 1 :** WISH, DESIRE ⟨call it what you ~⟩ **2** — used as an auxiliary verb to express (1) desire, willingness, or in negative constructions refusal ⟨~ you have another⟩ ⟨he *won't* do it⟩, (2) customary or habitual action ⟨~ get angry over nothing⟩, (3) simple futurity ⟨tomorrow we ~ go shopping⟩, (4) capability or sufficiency ⟨the back seat ~ hold three⟩, (5) determination or willfulness ⟨I ~ go despite them⟩, (6) probability ⟨that ~ be the mailman⟩, (7) inevitability ⟨accidents ~ happen⟩, or (8) a command ⟨you ~ do as I say⟩
[2]**will** *n* **1 :** wish or desire often combined with determination ⟨the ~ to win⟩ **2 :** something desired; *esp* **:** a choice or determination of one having authority or power **3 :** the act, process, or experience of willing **:** VOLITION **4** ♦ **:** the mental powers manifested as wishing, choosing, desiring, or intending **5 :** a disposition to act according to principles or ends **6** ♦ **:** power of controlling one's own actions or emotions ⟨a leader of iron ~⟩ **7 :** a legal docu-

ment in which a person declares to whom his or her possessions are to go after death

♦ [4] accord, choice, free will, option, self-determination, volition ♦ [6] restraint, self-control, self-discipline, self-government, self-possession, self-restraint, willpower

³**will** *vb* **1 :** to dispose of by or as if by a will **:** BEQUEATH **2 :** to determine by an act of choice **3** ♦ **:** to have the intention of **:** CHOOSE

♦ choose, like, want, wish

will•ful *or* **wil•ful** \ˈwil-fəl\ *adj* **1** ♦ **:** governed by will without regard to reason **:** obstinately or perversely doing what one wants without regard to others **2** ♦ **:** done deliberately **:** INTENTIONAL ⟨~ murder⟩

♦ [1] contrary, defiant, disobedient, froward, intractable, rebellious, recalcitrant, refractory, uncontrollable, unruly, untoward, wayward ♦ [1] dogged, hardheaded, headstrong, mulish, obdurate, obstinate, opinionated, peevish, pertinacious, perverse, pigheaded, stubborn, unyielding ♦ [2] deliberate, freewill, intentional, purposeful

will•ful•ly *adv* ♦ **:** in a willful manner

♦ consciously, deliberately, intentionally, knowingly, purposely

wil•lies \ˈwi-lēz\ *n pl* ♦ **:** a fit of nervousness **:** JITTERS — used with *the*

♦ dither, jitters, shakes, shivers

will•ing \ˈwi-liŋ\ *adj* **1** ♦ **:** inclined or favorably disposed in mind **:** READY ⟨~ to go⟩ **2** ♦ **:** prompt to act or respond ⟨~ workers⟩ **3** ♦ **:** done, borne, or accepted voluntarily or without reluctance **4 :** of or relating to the will

♦ [1] amenable, disposed, game, glad, inclined, ready ***Ant*** disinclined, unwilling ♦ [2] alert, expeditious, prompt, quick, ready ♦ [3] freewill, voluntary

will•ing•ly *adv* **:** in a willing manner
will•ing•ness *n* ♦ **:** the quality or state of being willing

♦ alacrity, gameness, goodwill

wil•li•waw \ˈwi-lē-ˌwȯ\ *n* ♦ **:** a sudden violent gust of cold land air common along mountainous coasts of high latitudes

♦ blast, blow, flurry, gust

will–o'–the–wisp \ˌwil-ə-t͟hə-ˈwisp\ *n* **1 :** a light that appears at night over marshy grounds **2 :** a misleading or elusive goal or hope
wil•low \ˈwi-lō\ *n* **1 :** any of a genus of quick growing shrubs and trees with tough pliable shoots **2 :** an object made of willow wood
wil•low•ware \-ˌwar\ *n* **:** dinnerware that is usually blue and white and that is decorated with a story-telling design featuring a large willow tree by a little bridge
wil•lowy \ˈwi-lə-wē\ *adj* **1** ♦ **:** pliant, soft, and yielding in texture **2 :** gracefully tall and slender

♦ flexible, limber, lissome, lithe, pliable, supple ***Ant*** inflexible, rigid, stiff

will•pow•er \ˈwil-ˌpau̇-ər\ *n* ♦ **:** the power to control one's actions or emotions **:** energetic determination

♦ restraint, self-control, self-discipline, self-government, self-possession, self-restraint, will

wil•ly–nil•ly \ˌwi-lē-ˈni-lē\ *adv or adj* **1 :** without regard for one's choice **:** by compulsion ⟨they rushed us along ~⟩ **2** ♦ **:** in a haphazard or spontaneous manner

♦ aimlessly, anyhow, anyway, anywise, desultorily, erratically, haphazard, haphazardly, helter-skelter, hit or miss, irregularly, randomly

¹**wilt** \ˈwilt\ *vb* **1** ♦ **:** to lose or cause to lose freshness and become limp especially from lack of water **:** DROOP **2** ♦ **:** to grow weak or faint **:** LANGUISH

♦ decay, droop, fail, flag, go, lag, languish, sag, waste, weaken

²**wilt** *n* **:** any of various plant disorders marked by wilting and often shriveling
wily \ˈwī-lē\ *adj* **wil•i•er; -est** ♦ **:** full of guile **:** TRICKY

♦ artful, cagey, crafty, cunning, devious, foxy, guileful, slick, sly, subtle, tricky

wimp \ˈwimp\ *n* **:** a weak, cowardly, or ineffectual person
¹**wim•ple** \ˈwim-pəl\ *n* **:** a cloth covering worn over the head and around the neck and chin by women especially in the late medieval period and by some nuns
²**wimple** *vb* **wim•pled; wim•pling 1 :** to cover with or as if with a wimple **2 :** to ripple or cause to ripple
wimpy \ˈwim-pē\ *adj* ♦ **:** being a wimp

♦ effete, frail, nerveless, soft, spineless, weak, wishy-washy

¹**win** \ˈwin\ *vb* **won** \ˈwən\; **win•ning 1 a :** to get possession of especially by effort **:** GAIN **b** ♦ **:** to obtain by work **:** EARN **2 a :** to gain in or as if in battle or contest **b** ♦ **:** to be the victor in ⟨*won* the war⟩ **3** ♦ **:** to solicit and gain the favor of — often used with *over*; *esp* **:** to induce to accept oneself in marriage

♦ [1b] achieve, acquire, attain, capture, carry, draw, earn, gain, garner, get, land, make, obtain, procure, realize, secure ♦ [2b] conquer, prevail, triumph ***Ant*** lose ♦ *usu* **win over** [3] argue, convince, get, induce, move, persuade, prevail, satisfy, talk

²**win** *n* **:** VICTORY; *esp* **:** 1st place at the finish (as of a horse race)
wince \ˈwins\ *vb* **winced; winc•ing** ♦ **:** to shrink back involuntarily (as from pain) **:** FLINCH — **wince** *n*

♦ blench, flinch, quail, recoil, shrink

winch \ˈwinch\ *n* **:** a machine that has a drum on which is wound a rope or cable for hauling or hoisting — **winch** *vb*
¹**wind** \ˈwind\ *n* **1 :** a movement of the air **2** ♦ **:** a prevailing force or influence **:** TENDENCY **3 :** BREATH ⟨he had the ~ knocked out of him⟩ **4 :** gas produced in the stomach or intestines **5** ♦ **:** idle talk as insubstantial as air **6 :** air carrying a scent (as of game) **7 :** INTIMATION ⟨they got ~ of our plans⟩ **8 :** WIND INSTRUMENTS; *also, pl* **:** players of wind instruments

♦ [2] current, drift, leaning, run, tendency, tide, trend ♦ [5] bombast, gas, grandiloquence, hot air, rhetoric

²**wind** *vb* **1 :** to get a scent of ⟨the dogs ~*ed* the game⟩ **2 :** to cause to be out of breath ⟨he was ~*ed* from the climb⟩ **3 :** to allow (as a horse) to rest so as to recover breath
³**wind** \ˈwīnd, ˈwind\ *vb* **wind•ed** \ˈwīn-dəd, ˈwin-\ *or* **wound** \ˈwau̇nd\; **wind•ing :** to sound by blowing ⟨~ a horn⟩
⁴**wind** \ˈwīnd\ *vb* **wound** \ˈwau̇nd\ *also* **wind•ed; wind•ing 1 :** ENTANGLE, INVOLVE **2 :** to introduce stealthily **:** INSINUATE **3 :** to encircle or cover with something pliable **:** WRAP, COIL, TWINE ⟨~ a bobbin⟩ **4 :** to hoist or haul by a rope or chain and a winch **5 :** to tighten the spring of; *also* **:** CRANK **6 :** to raise to a high level (as of excitement) **7 :** to cause to move in a curving line or path **8** ♦ **:** to have a curving course or shape ⟨a river ~*ing* through the valley⟩ **9 :** to move or lie so as to encircle

♦ bend, coil, curl, curve, entwine, spiral, twine, twist

⁵**wind** \ˈwīnd\ *n* ♦ **:** something having a curving or twisting form **:** TURN

♦ angle, arc, arch, bend, bow, crook, curve, turn

wind•age \ˈwin-dij\ *n* **:** the influence of the wind in deflecting the course of a projectile through the air; *also* **:** the amount of such deflection
wind•bag \ˈwind-ˌbag\ *n* ♦ **:** an overly talkative person

♦ babbler, blabber, cackler, chatterbox, chatterer, conversationalist, gabbler, jabberer, magpie, prattler, talker

wind•blown \-ˌblōn\ *adj* **:** blown by the wind; *also* **:** having the appearance of being blown by the wind
wind•break \-ˌbrāk\ *n* **:** a growth of trees or shrubs serving to break the force of the wind; *also* **:** a shelter from the wind
wind•burned \-ˌbərnd\ *adj* **:** irritated and inflamed by exposure to the wind — **wind•burn** \-ˌbərn\ *n*
wind•chill \-ˌchil\ *n* **:** a still-air temperature that would have the same cooling effect on exposed human skin as a given combination of temperature and wind speed
windchill factor *n* **:** WINDCHILL
wind down *vb* **1 :** to draw toward an end **2 :** RELAX, UNWIND
wind•er \ˈwīn-dər\ *n* **:** one that winds
wind•fall \ˈwind-ˌfȯl\ *n* **1 :** something (as a tree or fruit) blown down by the wind **2** ♦ **:** an unexpected or sudden gift, gain, or advantage

♦ benefit, blessing, boon, felicity, godsend, good, manna

wind•flow•er \-ˌflau̇-ər\ *n* **:** ANEMONE
¹**wind•ing** \ˈwīn-diŋ\ *n* **:** material (as wire) wound or coiled about an object
²**winding** *adj* **1** ♦ **:** having a pronounced curve or spiral ⟨~ stairs⟩ **2** ♦ **:** having a course that winds ⟨a ~ road⟩

♦ [1] helical, spiral ♦ [2] crooked, devious, serpentine, sinuous, tortuous

wind·ing–sheet \-ˌshēt\ *n* : SHROUD
wind instrument *n* : a musical instrument (as a flute or horn) sounded by wind and especially by the breath
wind·jam·mer \ˈwind-ˌja-mər\ *n* : a sailing ship; *also* : one of its crew
wind·lass \ˈwind-ləs\ *n* : a winch used especially on ships for hoisting or hauling
wind·mill \ˈwind-ˌmil\ *n* : a mill or machine worked by the wind turning sails or vanes that radiate from a central shaft
win·dow \ˈwin-dō\ *n* **1** : an opening in the wall of a building to let in light and air; *also* : the framework with fittings that closes such an opening **2** : WINDOWPANE **3** : an opening resembling or suggesting that of a window in a building **4** : an interval of time during which certain conditions or an opportunity exists **5** : a rectangular box appearing on a computer screen on which information (as files or program output) is displayed — **win·dow·less** *adj*
window box *n* : a box for growing plants in or by a window
window dressing *n* **1** : display of merchandise in a store window **2** : a showing made to create a deceptively favorable impression
win·dow·pane \ˈwin-dō-ˌpān\ *n* : a pane in a window
win·dow–shop \-ˌshäp\ *vb* : to look at the displays in store windows without going inside the stores to make purchases — **window–shop·per** *n*
win·dow·sill \-ˌsil\ *n* : the horizontal member at the bottom of a window
wind·pipe \ˈwind-ˌpīp\ *n* : TRACHEA
wind·proof \-ˈprüf\ *adj* : impervious to wind ⟨a ~ jacket⟩
wind·row \ˈwind-ˌrō\ *n* **1** : hay raked up into a row to dry **2** : a row of something (as dry leaves) swept up by or as if by the wind
wind shear *n* : a radical shift in wind speed and direction that occurs over a very short distance
wind·shield \ˈwind-ˌshēld\ *n* : a transparent screen (as of glass) in front of the occupants of a vehicle
wind sock *n* : an open-ended truncated cloth cone mounted in an elevated position to indicate wind direction
wind·storm \-ˌstȯrm\ *n* : a storm with high wind and little or no rain
wind·surf·ing \-ˌsər-fiŋ\ *n* : the sport or activity of riding a sailboard — **wind·surf** \-ˌsərf\ *vb* — **wind·surf·er** *n*
wind·swept \ˈwind-ˌswept\ *adj* : swept by or as if by wind ⟨~ plains⟩
wind tunnel *n* : an enclosed passage through which air is blown to investigate air flow around an object
wind·up \ˈwīn-ˌdəp\ *n* **1** ♦ : a concluding act or part : CONCLUSION **2** : a series of regular and distinctive motions made by a pitcher preliminary to delivering a pitch

♦ close, conclusion, consummation, end, ending, finale, finis, finish

wind up *vb* **1** ♦ : to bring or come to a conclusion : END **2** : to put in order for the purpose of bringing to an end **3** : to arrive in a place, situation, or condition at the end or as a result of a course of action ⟨*wound up* as paupers⟩ **4** : to make a pitching windup

♦ close, conclude, end, finish, round, terminate, wrap up

¹wind·ward \ˈwin-dwərd\ *n* : the side or direction from which the wind is blowing
²windward *adj* : being in or facing the direction from which the wind is blowing
windy \ˈwin-dē\ *adj* **wind·i·er; -est** **1** ♦ : having wind : exposed to winds ⟨a ~ day⟩ ⟨a ~ prairie⟩ **2** : STORMY **3** : FLATULENT **4** ♦ : indulging in or characterized by useless talk

♦ [1] blowy, blustery, breezy, gusty ♦ [4] bombastic, gaseous, grandiloquent, oratorical, rhetorical ♦ [4] circuitous, diffuse, long-winded, prolix, rambling, verbose, wordy

¹wine \ˈwīn\ *n* **1** : fermented grape juice used as a beverage **2** : the usually fermented juice of a plant product (as fruit) used as a beverage ⟨rice ~⟩
²wine *vb* **wined; win·ing** : to treat to or drink wine
wine cellar *n* : a room for storing wines; *also* : a stock of wines
wine·grow·er \-ˌgrō-ər\ *n* : one that cultivates a vineyard and makes wine
wine·press \-ˌpres\ *n* : a vat in which juice is pressed from grapes
win·ery \ˈwī-nə-rē, ˈwīn-rē\ *n, pl* **-eries** : a wine-making establishment
¹wing \ˈwiŋ\ *n* **1** : one of the movable feathered or membranous paired appendages by means of which a bird, bat, or insect flies **2** : something suggesting a wing; *esp* : an airfoil that develops the lift which supports an aircraft in flight **3** : a plant or animal appendage or part likened to a wing **4** : a turned-back or extended edge on an article of clothing **5** : a means of flight or rapid progress **6** : the act or manner of flying : FLIGHT **7** *pl* : the area at the side of the stage out of sight **8** : one of the positions or players on either side of a center position or line **9** ♦ : either of two opposing groups within an organization : FACTION **10** : a unit in military aviation consisting of two or more squadrons — **wingless** *adj* — **on the wing** : in flight : FLYING — **under one's wing** : in one's charge or care

♦ bloc, body, coalition, combination, combine, faction, party, sect, set, side

²wing *vb* **1** : to fit with wings; *also* : to enable to fly easily **2** ♦ : to pass through in flight : FLY ⟨~ the air⟩ ⟨swallows ~*ing* southward⟩ **3** : to let fly : DISPATCH **4** : to wound in the wing ⟨~ a bird⟩; *also* : to wound without killing **5** : to perform without preparation : IMPROVISE ⟨~*ing* it⟩

♦ fly, glide, plane, soar

wing·ding \ˈwiŋ-ˌdiŋ\ *n* : a wild, lively, or lavish party
winged \ˈwiŋd, ˈwiŋ-əd, *in compounds* ˈwiŋd\ *adj* **1** : having wings especially of a specified character **2** : soaring with or as if with wings : ELEVATED **3** : SWIFT, RAPID
wing nut *n* : a nut with winglike extensions that can be gripped with the thumb and finger
wing·span \ˈwiŋ-ˌspan\ *n* : the distance between the tips of a pair of wings
wing·spread \-ˌspred\ *n* : the spread of the wings; *esp* : the distance between the tips of the fully extended wings of a winged animal
¹wink \ˈwiŋk\ *vb* **1** : to close and open one eye quickly as a signal or hint **2** : to close and open the eyes quickly : BLINK **3** ♦ : to avoid seeing or noticing something — often used with *at* ⟨~ at a traffic violation⟩ **4** ♦ : to gleam or flash fitfully or intermittently : TWINKLE — **wink·er** \ˈwiŋ-kər\ *n*

♦ *usu* **wink at** [3] brush (off), condone, disregard, excuse, gloss, ignore, pardon, pass over, shrug off ♦ [4] blink, flame, flash, glance, gleam, glimmer, glisten, glitter, scintillate, shimmer, sparkle, twinkle

²wink *n* **1** ♦ : a brief period of sleep : NAP **2** : an act of winking; *esp* : a hint or sign given by winking **3** ♦ : an exceedingly brief period : INSTANT ⟨dries in a ~⟩

♦ [1] catnap, doze, drowse, forty winks, nap, siesta, snooze ♦ [3] flash, instant, jiffy, minute, moment, second, shake, trice, twinkle, twinkling

win·ner \ˈwi-nər\ *n* ♦ : one that wins or is successful

♦ blockbuster, hit, smash, success ♦ champ, champion, victor

¹win·ning \ˈwi-niŋ\ *n* **1** : VICTORY **2** : something won; *esp* : money won at gambling ⟨large ~*s*⟩
²winning *adj* **1** : successful especially in competition **2** ♦ : having an attractive, captivating, and charming nature

♦ adorable, darling, dear, endearing, lovable, precious, sweet

win·now \ˈwi-nō\ *vb* **1** : to remove (as chaff) by a current of air; *also* : to free (as grain) from waste in this manner **2** : to sort or separate as if by winnowing
wino \ˈwī-nō\ *n, pl* **win·os** : one who is addicted to drinking wine
win·some \ˈwin-səm\ *adj* **1** ♦ : generally pleasing and engaging **2** : CHEERFUL, GAY — **win·some·ly** *adv* — **win·some·ness** *n*

♦ endearing, ingratiating, winning

¹win·ter \ˈwin-tər\ *n* : the season of the year in any region in which the noonday sun shines most obliquely : the coldest period of the year
²winter *vb* **1** : to pass the winter ⟨~*ed* in Florida⟩ **2** : to feed or find food during the winter ⟨~*ed* on hay⟩
³winter *adj* : sown in autumn for harvesting in the following spring or summer ⟨~ wheat⟩
win·ter·green \ˈwin-tər-ˌgrēn\ *n* **1** : a low evergreen plant of the heath family with white bell-shaped flowers and spicy red berries **2** : an aromatic oil or its flavor from the wintergreen
win·ter·ize \ˈwin-tə-ˌrīz\ *vb* **-ized; -iz·ing** : to make ready for winter
win·ter–kill \ˈwin-tər-ˌkil\ *vb* : to kill or die by exposure to winter weather
winter squash *n* : any of various hard-shelled squashes that keep well in storage
win·ter·tide \-ˌtīd\ *n* : WINTER
win·ter·time \-ˌtīm\ *n* : WINTER
win·try \ˈwin-trē\ *also* **win·tery** \ˈwin-tə-rē\ *adj* **win·tri·er; -est** **1** ♦ : of, relating to, or characteristic of winter ⟨~ weather⟩ **2** : lacking qualities that cheer ⟨a ~ welcome⟩

♦ arctic, bitter, chill, chilly, cold, cool, freezing, frigid, frosty, glacial, icy, nippy, polar, raw, snappy

1wipe \ˈwīp\ *vb* **wiped; wip•ing** **1 :** to clean or dry by rubbing ⟨∼ dishes⟩ **2 :** to remove by or as if by rubbing ⟨∼ away tears⟩ **3 :** to erase completely **:** OBLITERATE **4 :** to pass or draw over a surface ⟨*wiped* his hand across his face⟩ — **wip•er** *n*

2wipe *n* **1 :** an act or instance of wiping; *also* **:** BLOW, STRIKE, SWIPE **2 :** something used for wiping

wipe out *vb* ♦ **:** to destroy completely

♦ annihilate, blot out, demolish, destroy, eradicate, exterminate, liquidate, obliterate, root, rub out, snuff, stamp

1wire \ˈwī(-ə)r\ *n* **1** ♦ **:** metal in the form of a thread or slender rod; *also* **:** a thread or rod of metal **2 :** hidden or secret influences controlling the action of a person or organization — usually used in pl. ⟨pull ∼*s*⟩ **3 :** a line of wire for conducting electric current **4 :** a telegraph or telephone wire or system **5 :** TELEGRAM, CABLEGRAM **6 :** the finish line of a race

♦ cable, cord, lace, line, rope, string

2wire *vb* **wired; wir•ing** **1 :** to provide or equip with wire ⟨∼ a house⟩ **2 :** to bind, string, or mount with wire **3 :** to send or send word to by telegraph

wired *adj* **1 :** furnished with wires **2 :** connected to the Internet **3 :** feverishly excited

wire•hair \ˈwī(-ə)r-ˌhar\ *n* **:** a wirehaired dog or cat

wire•haired \-ˈhard\ *adj* **:** having a stiff wiry outer coat of hair

1wire•less \-ləs\ *adj* **1 :** having no wire or wires **2 :** RADIO **3 :** of or relating to data communications using radio waves

2wireless *n* **1 :** telecommunication involving signals transmitted by radio waves; *also* **:** the technology used in radio telecommunication **2** *chiefly Brit* **:** RADIO

wire–pull•er \-ˌpu̇-lər\ *n* **:** one who uses secret or underhanded means to influence the acts of a person or organization — **wire–pull•ing** *n*

wire service *n* **:** a news agency that sends out syndicated news copy to subscribers by wire or satellite

wire•tap \-ˌtap\ *n* **:** the act or an instance of tapping a telephone or telegraph wire to get information; *also* **:** an electrical connection used for such tapping — **wiretap** *vb* — **wire•tap•per** \-ˌta-pər\ *n*

wire•worm \-ˌwərm\ *n* **:** any of various slender hard-coated beetle larvae especially destructive to plant roots

wir•ing \ˈwīr-iŋ\ *n* **:** a system of wires

wiry \ˈwīr-ē\ *adj* **wir•i•er** \ˈwī-rē-ər\; **-est** **1 :** made of or resembling wire **2 :** slender yet strong and sinewy — **wir•i•ness** \ˈwī-rē-nəs\ *n*

Wis *or* **Wisc** *abbr* Wisconsin

Wisd *abbr* Wisdom

wis•dom \ˈwiz-dəm\ *n* **1** ♦ **:** accumulated philosophic or scientific learning **:** KNOWLEDGE; *also* **:** INSIGHT **2** ♦ **:** good sense **:** JUDGMENT **3 :** a wise attitude or course of action

♦ [1] knowledge, lore, science ♦ [2] discernment, insight, judgment, perception, sagacity, sapience, sense, wit

Wisdom *n* **:** a book included in the Roman Catholic canon of the Old Testament and corresponding to the Wisdom of Solomon in the Protestant Apocrypha

wisdom tooth *n* **:** the last tooth of the full set on each side of the upper and lower jaws of humans

1wise \ˈwīz\ *n* **:** WAY, MANNER, FASHION ⟨in no ∼⟩ ⟨in this ∼⟩

2wise *adj* **wis•er; wis•est** **1** ♦ **:** having wisdom **:** SAGE **2 :** having or showing good sense or good judgment **3** ♦ **:** aware of what is going on **:** KNOWING; *also* **:** CRAFTY, SHREWD **4** ♦ **:** possessing inside information **5 :** INSOLENT, FRESH ⟨a ∼ retort⟩ — **wise•ly** *adv*

♦ [1] discerning, insightful, perceptive, sagacious, sage, sapient ***Ant*** unperceptive, unwise ♦ [3, 4] aware, informed, knowing, ready ***Ant*** unknowing

3wise *vb* **wised; wis•ing; wis•es** ♦ **:** to supply with information — often used with *up*

♦ *usu* **wise up** acquaint, advise, apprise, brief, clue, enlighten, familiarize, fill in, inform, instruct, tell

-wise \-ˌwīz\ *adv comb form* **:** in the manner or direction of ⟨slant*wise*⟩

wise•acre \ˈwī-ˌzā-kər\ *n* **:** SMART ALECK

1wise•crack \ˈwīz-ˌkrak\ *n* ♦ **:** a clever, smart, or flippant remark

♦ crack, gag, jest, joke, laugh, pleasantry, quip, sally, waggery, witticism

2wisecrack *vb* ♦ **:** to make a wisecrack

♦ banter, fool, fun, jest, jive, joke, josh, kid, quip

wise guy *n* **:** SMART ALECK

1wish \ˈwish\ *vb* **1** ♦ **:** to have a desire **:** long for ⟨∼ you were here⟩ ⟨∼ for a puppy⟩ **2 :** to form or express a wish concerning ⟨∼*ed* him a happy birthday⟩ **3 :** BID ⟨he ∼*ed* me good morning⟩ **4 :** to request by expressing a desire ⟨I ∼ you to go now⟩ **5** ♦ **:** to have the intention of ⟨I don't ∼ to impose⟩

♦ *usu* **wish for** [1] ache for, covet, crave, desire, die (to *or* for), hanker (for *or* after), hunger for, long for, lust (for *or* after), pine for, repine for, thirst for, want, yearn for ♦ [5] choose, like, want, will

2wish *n* **1 :** an act or instance of wishing or desiring **:** WANT; *also* **:** GOAL **2 :** an expressed will or desire

wish•bone \-ˌbōn\ *n* **:** a forked bone in front of the breastbone in most birds

wish•ful \ˈwish-fəl\ *adj* **1 :** expressive of a wish; *also* **:** having a wish **2 :** according with wishes rather than fact ⟨∼ thinking⟩

wishy–washy \ˈwi-shē-ˌwȯ-shē, -ˌwä-\ *adj* ♦ **:** lacking in character or determination; *also* **:** morally feeble

♦ banal, flat, insipid ♦ effete, frail, nerveless, soft, spineless, weak, wimpy

wisp \ˈwisp\ *n* **1 :** a small handful (as of hay or straw) **2 :** a thin strand, strip, or fragment ⟨a ∼ of hair⟩; *also* **:** a thready streak ⟨a ∼ of smoke⟩ **3 :** something frail, slight, or fleeting ⟨a ∼ of a smile⟩ — **wispy** *adj*

wis•te•ria \wis-ˈtir-ē-ə\ *also* **wis•tar•ia** \-ˈtir-ē-ə *also* -ˈter-\ *n* **:** any of a genus of chiefly Asian mostly woody vines related to the peas and widely grown for their long showy clusters of blue, white, purple, or rose flowers

wist•ful \ˈwist-fəl\ *adj* **:** feeling or showing a timid desire — **wist•ful•ly** *adv* — **wist•ful•ness** *n*

wit \ˈwit\ *n* **1 :** reasoning power **:** INTELLIGENCE **2** ♦ **:** mental soundness **:** SANITY — usually used in pl. **3** ♦ **:** resourcefulness and creative imagination; *esp* **:** quickness and cleverness in handling words and ideas **4 a :** a talent for making clever remarks **b** ♦ **:** a person noted for making witty remarks — **wit•ted** \ˈwi-təd\ *adj* — **at one's wit's end :** at a loss for a means of solving a problem

♦ [2] head, mind, reason, sanity ♦ [3] common sense, horse sense, sense, wisdom ♦ [4b] card, comedian, comic, humorist, jester, joker, wag

1witch \ˈwich\ *n* **1** ♦ **:** a person believed to have magic power; *esp* **:** SORCERESS **2** ♦ **:** an ugly old woman **:** HAG **3 :** a charming or alluring girl or woman

♦ [1] conjurer, enchanter, magician, necromancer, sorcerer, voodoo, wizard ♦ [1] enchantress, hag, hex ♦ [2] crone, hag

2witch *vb* **:** BEWITCH

witch•craft \ˈwich-ˌkraft\ *n* ♦ **:** the power or practices of a witch **:** SORCERY

♦ bewitchment, enchantment, magic, necromancy, sorcery, wizardry

witch doctor *n* **:** a person in a primitive society who uses magic to treat sickness and to fight off evil spirits

witch•ery \ˈwi-chə-rē\ *n, pl* **-er•ies** **1 :** the practice of witchcraft **:** SORCERY **2 :** an irresistible fascination **:** CHARM

witch•grass \ˈwich-ˌgras\ *n* **:** any of several grasses that are weeds in cultivated areas

witch ha•zel \ˈwich-ˌhā-zəl\ *n* **1 :** a shrub of eastern No. America bearing small yellow flowers in the fall **2 :** a soothing alcoholic lotion made from witch hazel bark

witch–hunt \ˈwich-ˌhənt\ *n* **1 :** a searching out and persecution of persons accused of witchcraft **2 :** the searching out and deliberate harassment especially of political opponents

witch•ing \ˈwi-chiŋ\ *adj* **:** of, relating to, or suitable for sorcery or supernatural occurrences

with \ˈwith, ˈwith\ *prep* **1 :** AGAINST ⟨a fight ∼ his brother⟩ **2 :** FROM ⟨parting ∼ friends⟩ **3 :** in mutual relation to ⟨talk ∼ a friend⟩ **4 :** in the company of ⟨went there ∼ her⟩ **5 :** AS REGARDS, TOWARD ⟨is patient ∼ children⟩ **6 :** compared to ⟨on equal terms ∼ another⟩ **7 :** in support of ⟨I'm ∼ you all the way⟩ **8 :** in the presence of **:** CONTAINING ⟨tea ∼ sugar⟩ **9 :** in the opinion of **:** as judged by ⟨their arguments had weight ∼ her⟩ **10 a** ♦ **:** by reason of **:** BECAUSE OF ⟨pale ∼ anger⟩ **b :** by means of ⟨hit him ∼ a club⟩ **11 :** in a manner indicating ⟨work ∼ a will⟩ **12 :** GIVEN, GRANTED ⟨∼ your permission I'll leave⟩ **13 :** HAVING ⟨came ∼ good news⟩ ⟨stood there ∼ his mouth open⟩ **14 :** at the time of **:** right after ⟨∼ that we left⟩ **15** ♦ **:** in spite of : DESPITE ⟨~ all her cleverness, she failed⟩ **16 :** in the direction of ⟨swim ~ the tide⟩

♦ [10a] because of, due to, owing to, through ♦ [15] despite, notwithstanding, regardless of

with•al \wi-ˈt͟hȯl, -ˈthȯl\ *adv* **1** ♦ **:** together with this **:** BESIDES **2** ♦ **:** on the other hand **:** NEVERTHELESS

♦ [1] additionally, again, also, besides, further, furthermore, likewise, more, moreover, then, too, yet ♦ [2] but, howbeit, however, nevertheless, nonetheless, notwithstanding, still, though, yet

with•draw \wit͟h-ˈdrȯ, with-\ *vb* **-drew** \-ˈdrü\; **-drawn** \-ˈdrȯn\; **-draw•ing** \-ˈdrȯ-iŋ\ **1** ♦ **:** to take back or away **:** REMOVE **2** ♦ **:** to call back (as from consideration); *also* **:** RETRACT **3 :** to go away **:** RETREAT, LEAVE **4 :** to terminate one's participation in or use of something **5** ♦ **:** to remove or draw out from a place or position

♦ [1] clear, draw, remove ♦ [2] abjure, recant, renounce, retract, take back, unsay ♦ [5] back, fall back, recede, retire, retreat

with•draw•al \-ˈdrȯ-əl\ *n* **1** ♦ **:** an act or instance of withdrawing **2 :** the discontinuance of the use or administration of a drug and especially an addicting drug; *also* **:** the period following such discontinuance marked by often painful physiological and psychological symptoms **3 :** a pathological retreat from the real world (as in some schizophrenic states)

♦ retreat, revulsion

with•drawn \wit͟h-ˈdrȯn\ *adj* **1 :** ISOLATED, SECLUDED **2** ♦ **:** socially detached and unresponsive

♦ bashful, coy, demure, diffident, introverted, modest, retiring, sheepish, shy,

withe \ˈwith\ *n* **:** a slender flexible twig or branch
with•er \ˈwi-t͟hər\ *vb* **1 :** to shrivel from or as if from loss of bodily moisture and especially sap **2 :** to lose or cause to lose vitality, force, or freshness **3 :** to cause to feel shriveled ⟨~*ed* him with a glance⟩
with•ers \ˈwi-t͟hərz\ *n pl* **:** the ridge between the shoulder bones of a horse; *also* **:** the corresponding part in other 4-footed animals
with•hold \with-ˈhōld, wit͟h-\ *vb* **-held** \-ˈheld\; **-hold•ing** **1 a :** to hold back **b** ♦ **:** keep in one's possession or control **:** RETAIN **2** ♦ **:** to refrain from granting, giving, or allowing ⟨~ permission⟩ ⟨~ names⟩

♦ [1b] hang on, hold, keep, reserve, retain ♦ [2] decline, deny, disallow, refuse, reject

withholding tax *n* **:** a tax on income withheld at the source
[1]**with•in** \wi-ˈt͟hin, -ˈthin\ *adv* **1 :** in or into the interior **:** INSIDE **2 :** inside oneself **:** INWARDLY
[2]**within** *prep* **1 :** inside the limits or influence of ⟨~ call⟩ **2 :** in the limits or compass of ⟨~ a mile⟩ **3 :** in or to the inner part of ⟨~ the room⟩
with–it \ˈwi-t͟hət, -thət\ *adj* **:** socially or culturally up-to-date
[1]**with•out** \wi-ˈt͟hau̇t, -ˈthau̇t\ *prep* **1 :** at, to, or on the outside of **:** OUTSIDE **2** ♦ **:** not having **:** LACKING ⟨~ hope⟩; *also* **:** not accompanied by or showing ⟨spoke ~ thinking⟩

♦ lacking, minus, sans, wanting

[2]**without** *adv* **1 :** on the outside **:** EXTERNALLY **2 :** with something lacking or absent ⟨has learned to do ~⟩
with•stand \with-ˈstand, wit͟h-\ *vb* **-stood** \-ˈstu̇d\; **-stand•ing** ♦ **:** to stand against **:** RESIST; *esp* **:** to oppose (as an attack) successfully

♦ buck, defy, fight, oppose, repel, resist

wit•less \ˈwit-ləs\ *adj* ♦ **:** lacking wit or understanding — **wit•less•ly** *adv*

♦ absurd, asinine, balmy, cockeyed, crazy, foolish, harebrained, insane, mad, nonsensical, nutty, preposterous, sappy, screwball, senseless, silly, stupid, unwise, wacky, zany

wit•less•ness *n* **:** the quality or state of being witless
[1]**wit•ness** \ˈwit-nəs\ *n* **1 :** TESTIMONY ⟨bear ~ to the fact⟩ **2 :** one that gives evidence; *esp* **:** one who testifies in a cause or before a court **3 :** one present at a transaction so as to be able to testify that it has taken place **4 :** one who has personal knowledge or experience of something **5** ♦ **:** something serving as evidence or proof

♦ attestation, confirmation, corroboration, documentation, evidence, proof, substantiation, testament, testimony, validation

[2]**witness** *vb* **1** ♦ **:** to furnish evidence or proof such as to establish **:** TESTIFY **2 :** to act as legal witness of **3 :** to furnish proof of **:** BETOKEN **4** ♦ **:** to see or know by reason of personal presence **:** to be a witness of **5 :** to be the scene of ⟨this region has ~*ed* many wars⟩

♦ [1] attest, authenticate, avouch, certify, testify, vouch ♦ [4] behold, descry, discern, distinguish, espy, eye, look, note, notice, observe, perceive, regard, remark, see, sight, spy, view

wit•ti•cism \ˈwi-tə-ˌsi-zəm\ *n* ♦ **:** a witty saying or phrase

♦ crack, gag, jest, joke, laugh, pleasantry, quip, sally, waggery, wisecrack

wit•ting \ˈwi-tiŋ\ *adj* **1** ♦ **:** cognizant or aware of something **2 :** done knowingly

♦ alive, aware, cognizant, conscious, mindful, sensible, sentient

wit•ting•ly *adv* **:** with knowledge or awareness of what one is doing
wit•ty \ˈwi-tē\ *adj* **wit•ti•er; -est** ♦ **:** marked by or full of wit ⟨a ~ writer⟩ ⟨a ~ remark⟩ — **wit•ti•ly** \-tə-lē\ *adv* — **wit•ti•ness** \-tē-nəs\ *n*

♦ clever, facetious, humorous, jocular, smart

wive \ˈwīv\ *vb* **wived; wiv•ing :** to take a wife
wives *pl of* WIFE
wiz•ard \ˈwi-zərd\ *n* **1** ♦ **:** one skilled in the knowledge and practice of the magic arts **:** MAGICIAN **2** ♦ **:** a very clever or skillful person ⟨a ~ at chess⟩

♦ [1] conjurer, enchanter, magician, necromancer, sorcerer, voodoo, witch ♦ [2] ace, adept, artist, authority, crackerjack, expert, maestro, master, scholar, shark, virtuoso, whiz ♦ [2] brain, genius, intellect, thinker

wiz•ard•ry \ˈwi-zər-drē\ *n, pl* **-ries** **1** ♦ **:** magic skill **:** SORCERY **2 :** great skill or cleverness in an activity

♦ bewitchment, enchantment, magic, necromancy, sorcery, witchcraft

wiz•en \ˈwiz-ᵊn, ˈwēz-\ *vb* **:** to become or cause to become dry, shrunken, or wrinkled
wk *abbr* **1** week **2** work
WL *abbr* wavelength
wmk *abbr* watermark
WNW *abbr* west-northwest
WO *abbr* warrant officer
w/o *abbr* without
woad \ˈwōd\ *n* **:** a European herb related to the mustards; *also* **:** a blue dyestuff made from its leaves
wob•ble \ˈwä-bəl\ *vb* **wob•bled; wob•bling** **1** ♦ **:** to move or cause to move with an irregular rocking or side-to-side motion **2** ♦ **:** to shake unsteadily **3** ♦ **:** to show indecision **:** WAVER — **wobble** *n*

♦ [1] falter, rock, seesaw, sway, teeter, totter, waver ♦ [2] agitate, convulse, jolt, jounce, quake, quiver, shake, shudder, vibrate ♦ [3] falter, hang back, hesitate, shilly-shally, stagger, teeter, vacillate, waver

wob•bly \-bə-lē\ *adj* ♦ **:** inclined to shake, sway, or quaver unsteadily

♦ shaky, tremulous

woe \ˈwō\ *n* **1** ♦ **:** deep suffering from misfortune, affliction, or grief **2 :** TROUBLE, MISFORTUNE ⟨economic ~*s*⟩

♦ affliction, agony, anguish, distress, misery, pain, torment, torture, tribulation ♦ dolor, grief, heartache, sorrow

woe•be•gone \ˈwō-bi-ˌgȯn\ *adj* ♦ **:** exhibiting woe, sorrow, or misery; *also* **:** being in a sorry condition

♦ bad, blue, dejected, depressed, despondent, disconsolate, down, downcast, droopy, forlorn, low, melancholy, miserable, mournful, sad, sorrowful, sorry, unhappy, woeful, wretched

woe•ful *also* **wo•ful** \ˈwō-fəl\ *adj* **1** ♦ **:** full of woe **:** distressed with grief or sadness **2 :** involving, bringing, or relating to woe **3** ♦ **:** to be regretted or lamented **:** DEPLORABLE

♦ [1] anguished, dolorous, lamentable, mournful, plaintive, sad, sorrowful, sorry ♦ [3] deplorable, distressful, grievous, heartbreaking, lamentable, regrettable, unfortunate

woe•ful•ly *adv* ♦ **:** in a woeful manner

♦ agonizingly, bitterly, grievously, hard, hardly, sadly, sorrowfully, unhappily, wretchedly

wok \ˈwäk\ *n* **:** a bowl-shaped cooking utensil used especially in stir-frying

woke *past and past part of* WAKE
woken *past part of* WAKE
wold \ˈwōld\ *n* **:** an upland plain or stretch of rolling land without woods
¹wolf \ˈwu̇lf\ *n, pl* **wolves** \ˈwu̇lvz\ **1 :** any of several large erect-eared bushy-tailed doglike predatory mammals that live and hunt in packs; *esp* **:** GRAY WOLF **2 :** a fierce or destructive person — **wolf•ish** *adj*
²wolf *vb* ♦ **:** to eat greedily **:** DEVOUR

♦ bolt, devour, gobble, gorge, gormandize, gulp, scarf, scoff

wolf•hound \-ˌhau̇nd\ *n* **:** any of several large dogs orig. used in hunting wolves
wol•fram \ˈwu̇l-frəm\ *n* **:** TUNGSTEN
wol•ver•ine \ˌwu̇l-və-ˈrēn\ *n, pl* **wolverines** *also* **wolverine :** a dark shaggy-coated flesh-eating mammal of northern forests and associated tundra that is related to the weasels
wom•an \ˈwu̇-mən\ *n, pl* **wom•en** \ˈwi-mən\ **1** ♦ **:** an adult female person **2 :** WOMANKIND **3 :** feminine nature **:** WOMANLINESS **4 :** a female servant or attendant

♦ dame, female, gentlewoman, lady

wom•an•hood \ˈwu̇-mən-ˌhu̇d\ *n* **1 :** the state of being a woman **:** the distinguishing qualities of a woman or of womankind **2 :** WOMEN, WOMANKIND
wom•an•ish \ˈwu̇-mə-nish\ *adj* **1 :** associated with or characteristic of women rather than men **2 :** suggestive of a weak character **:** EFFEMINATE
wom•an•ize \ˈwu̇-mə-ˌnīz\ *vb* **:** to pursue casual sexual relationships with numerous women — **wom•an•iz•er** *n*
wom•an•kind \ˈwu̇-mən-ˌkīnd\ *n* **:** the females of the human race **:** WOMEN
wom•an•like \-ˌlīk\ *adj* **:** WOMANLY
wom•an•ly \-lē\ *adj* **1** ♦ **:** of, relating to, or characteristic of a woman **2 :** suitable to a woman rather than to a man **:** EFFEMINATE — **wom•an•li•ness** \-lē-nəs\ *n*

♦ female, feminine

woman suffrage *n* **:** possession and exercise of suffrage by women
womb \ˈwüm\ *n* **1 :** UTERUS **2 :** a place where something is generated
wom•bat \ˈwäm-ˌbat\ *n* **:** any of several stocky burrowing Australian marsupials that resemble small bears
wom•en•folk \ˈwi-mən-ˌfōk\ *also* **wom•en•folks** \-ˌfōks\ *n pl* **:** WOMEN
won \ˈwən\ *past and past part of* WIN
¹won•der \ˈwən-dər\ *n* **1** ♦ **:** a cause of astonishment or surprise **:** MARVEL **2 :** the quality of exciting wonder ⟨the charm and ~ of the scene⟩ **3** ♦ **:** a feeling (as of awed astonishment or uncertainty) aroused by something extraordinary or affecting

♦ [1] caution, flash, marvel, miracle, phenomenon, portent, prodigy, sensation ♦ [3] admiration, amazement, astonishment, awe, wonderment

²wonder *vb* **1 :** to feel surprise or amazement **2 :** to feel curiosity or doubt
wonder drug *n* **:** MIRACLE DRUG
won•der•ful \ˈwən-dər-fəl\ *adj* **1** ♦ **:** exciting wonder **:** MARVELOUS **2 :** unusually good **:** ADMIRABLE — **won•der•ful•ly** \-f(ə-)lē\ *adv* — **won•der•ful•ness** *n*

♦ amazing, astonishing, astounding, awesome, awful, eye-opening, fabulous, marvelous, miraculous, portentous, prodigious, stunning, stupendous, sublime, surprising

won•der•land \-ˌland, -lənd\ *n* **1 :** an imaginary place of delicate beauty or magical charm **2 :** a place that excites admiration or wonder
won•der•ment \-mənt\ *n* **1** ♦ **:** a state or feeling of wonder **:** ASTONISHMENT **2 :** a cause of or occasion for wonder **3 :** curiosity about something

♦ admiration, amazement, astonishment, awe, wonder

won•drous \ˈwən-drəs\ *adj* **:** exciting wonder or surprise **:** MARVELOUS, WONDERFUL — **won•drous•ly** *adv* — **won•drous•ness** *n*
wonk \ˈwäŋk, ˈwȯŋk\ *n* **:** one who works in a specialized usually intellectual field ⟨computer ~s⟩
¹wont \ˈwȯnt, ˈwōnt\ *adj* **1** ♦ **:** in the habit or custom **:** ACCUSTOMED ⟨as we are ~ to do⟩ **2 :** INCLINED, APT

♦ accustomed, given, used

²wont *n* ♦ **:** a usage or practice that is common **:** CUSTOM ⟨according to her ~⟩

♦ custom, fashion, habit, pattern, practice, trick, way

won't \ˈwōnt\ **:** will not
wont•ed \ˈwȯn-təd, ˈwōn-\ *adj* **:** ACCUSTOMED, CUSTOMARY ⟨his ~ courtesy⟩
woo \ˈwü\ *vb* **1 :** to try to gain the love of **:** COURT **2 :** SOLICIT, ENTREAT **3** ♦ **:** to try to gain or bring about ⟨~ public favor⟩

♦ ask, court

¹wood \ˈwu̇d\ *n* **1 :** a dense growth of trees usually larger than a grove and smaller than a forest — often used in pl. **2 :** a hard fibrous substance that is basically xylem and forms the bulk of trees and shrubs beneath the bark; *also* **:** this material fit or prepared for some use (as burning or building) **3 :** something made of wood **4 :** the trunks or large branches of trees sawed or prepared for commercial use
²wood *adj* **1 :** WOODEN **2 :** suitable for holding, cutting, or working with wood **3** *or* **woods** \ˈwu̇dz\ **:** living or growing in woods
³wood *vb* **1 :** to supply or load with wood especially for fuel **2 :** to cover with a growth of trees
wood alcohol *n* **:** METHANOL
wood•bine \ˈwu̇d-ˌbīn\ *n* **:** any of several honeysuckles; *also* **:** VIRGINIA CREEPER
wood•block \-ˌbläk\ *n* **:** WOODCUT
wood•chop•per \-ˌchä-pər\ *n* **:** one engaged especially in chopping down trees
wood•chuck \-ˌchək\ *n* **:** a thickset grizzled marmot of Alaska, Canada, and the northeastern U.S.
wood•cock \ˈwu̇d-ˌkäk\ *n, pl* **woodcocks :** a brown eastern No. American game bird with a short neck and long bill that is related to the snipe; *also* **:** a related and similar Old World bird
wood•craft \-ˌkraft\ *n* **1 :** skill and practice in matters relating to the woods and especially in how to take care of oneself in them **2 :** skill in shaping or constructing articles from wood
wood•cut \-ˌkət\ *n* **1 :** a relief printing surface engraved on a block of wood **2 :** a print from a woodcut
wood•cut•ter \-ˌkə-tər\ *n* **:** a person who cuts wood
wood duck *n* **:** a showy crested American duck of which the male has iridescent multicolored plumage
wood•ed \ˈwu̇-dəd\ *adj* **:** covered with woods or trees ⟨~ slopes⟩
wood•en \ˈwu̇d-ᵊn\ *adj* **1 :** made of wood **2** ♦ **:** lacking in ease, grace, or flexibility **:** awkwardly stiff — **wood•en•ly** *adv* — **wood•en•ness** *n*

♦ awkward, clumsy, gauche, graceless, inelegant, stiff, stilted, uncomfortable, uneasy, ungraceful

wood•en•ware \ˈwu̇d-ᵊn-ˌwar\ *n* **:** articles made of wood for domestic use
wood•land \ˈwu̇d-lənd, -ˌland\ *n* ♦ **:** land covered with trees **:** FOREST — **woodland** *adj*

♦ forest, timberland

wood•lot \ˈwu̇d-ˌlät\ *n* **:** a restricted area of woodland usually privately kept to meet fuel and timber needs
wood louse *n* **:** any of various small flat crustaceans that live especially in ground litter and under stones and bark
wood•man \ˈwu̇d-mən\ *n* **:** WOODSMAN
wood•note \-ˌnōt\ *n* **:** verbal expression that is natural and artless
wood nymph *n* **:** a nymph living in the woods
wood•peck•er \ˈwu̇d-ˌpe-kər\ *n* **:** any of numerous usually brightly marked climbing birds with stiff spiny tail feathers and a chisellike bill used to drill into trees for insects
wood•pile \-ˌpīl\ *n* **:** a pile of wood and especially firewood
wood•shed \-ˌshed\ *n* **:** a shed for storing wood and especially firewood
woods•man \ˈwu̇dz-mən\ *n* **:** a person who frequents or works in the woods; *esp* **:** one skilled in woodcraft
woodsy \ˈwu̇d-zē\ *adj* **woods•i•er; -est :** relating to or suggestive of woods
wood•wind \ˈwu̇d-ˌwind\ *n* **:** one of a group of wind instruments including flutes, clarinets, oboes, bassoons, and sometimes saxophones
wood•work \-ˌwərk\ *n* **:** work made of wood; *esp* **:** interior fittings (as moldings or stairways) of wood
woody \ˈwu̇-dē\ *adj* **wood•i•er; -est 1 :** abounding or overgrown with woods **2 :** of or containing wood or wood fibers **3 :** characteristic or suggestive of wood — **wood•i•ness** \ˈwu̇-dē-nəs\ *n*
woo•er *n* ♦ **:** one that woos **:** one that courts a woman or seeks to marry her

♦ gallant, suitor, swain

woof \ˈwu̇f\ *n* **1 :** WEFT 1 **2 :** a woven fabric; *also* **:** its texture

woof•er \ˈwu̇-fər\ *n* **:** a loudspeaker that reproduces sounds of low pitch

wool \ˈwu̇l\ *n* **1** ♦ **:** the soft wavy or curly hair of some mammals and especially the domestic sheep; *also* **:** something (as a textile or garment) made of wool **2 :** material that resembles a mass of wool — **wooled** \ˈwu̇ld\ *adj*

♦ coat, fleece, fur, hair, pelage, pile

[1]**wool•en** *or* **wool•len** \ˈwu̇-lən\ *adj* **1 :** made of wool **2 :** of or relating to the manufacture or sale of woolen products ⟨∼ mills⟩

[2]**woolen** *or* **woollen** *n* **1 :** a fabric made of wool **2 :** garments of woolen fabric — usually used in pl.

wool•gath•er•ing \-ˌga-t͟hə-riŋ\ *n* ♦ **:** idle daydreaming

♦ reverie, study, trance

[1]**wool•ly** *also* **wooly** \ˈwu̇-lē\ *adj* **wool•li•er; -est** **1 :** of, relating to, or bearing wool **2 a** ♦ **:** consisting of or resembling wool **b** ♦ **:** thickly covered with long hair or fuzz **3 :** mentally confused ⟨∼ thinking⟩ **4 :** marked by a lack of order or restraint ⟨the wild and ∼ West⟩

♦ [2a, 2b] furry, fuzzy, hairy, rough, shaggy

[2]**wool•ly** *also* **wool•ie** *or* **wooly** \ˈwu̇-lē\ *n, pl* **wool•lies :** a garment made from wool; *esp* **:** underclothing of knitted wool — usually used in pl.

woolly bear *n* **:** any of numerous very hairy moth caterpillars

woolly mammoth *n* **:** a heavy-coated mammoth formerly inhabiting colder parts of the northern hemisphere

woo•zy \ˈwü-zē\ *adj* **woo•zi•er; -est** **1 :** BEFUDDLED **2 :** somewhat dizzy, nauseated, or weak — **woo•zi•ness** \ˈwü-zē-nəs\ *n*

[1]**word** \ˈwərd\ *n* **1 :** something that is said; *esp* **:** a brief remark **2** ♦ **:** a speech sound or series of speech sounds that communicates a meaning; *also* **:** a graphic representation of such a sound or series of sounds **3** ♦ **:** an instruction, authorization, or direction for action or behavior **:** COMMAND **4** *often cap* **:** the 2d person of the Trinity; *also* **:** GOSPEL **5** ♦ **:** a report of a recent event or of new information **:** NEWS, INFORMATION **6** ♦ **:** a declaration that one will do or refrain from doing something **:** PROMISE **7** *pl* **:** QUARREL, DISPUTE **8 :** a verbal signal **:** PASSWORD

♦ [2] expression, term ♦ [3] behest, charge, command, commandment, decree, dictate, direction, directive, edict, instruction, order ♦ [5] information, intelligence, item, news, story, tidings ♦ [6] oath, pledge, promise, troth, vow

[2]**word** *vb* ♦ **:** to express in words **:** PHRASE

♦ articulate, clothe, couch, express, formulate, phrase, put, say, state

word•age \ˈwər-dij\ *n* **1 :** WORDS **2 :** number of words **3 :** WORDING

word•book \ˈwərd-ˌbu̇k\ *n* **:** a book containing a collection of words **:** DICTIONARY

word for word *adv* ♦ **:** in the exact words **:** VERBATIM

♦ directly, exactly, verbatim

word•i•ness \-dē-nəs\ *n* ♦ **:** the quality or state of being wordy

♦ circumlocution, prolixity, redundancy, verbiage

word•ing \ˈwər-diŋ\ *n* ♦ **:** verbal expression **:** PHRASEOLOGY

♦ diction, language, phraseology, phrasing

word•less *adj* **1 :** not expressed or not expressible in words **2** ♦ **:** involving no use of words

♦ implicit, tacit, unexpressed, unspoken, unvoiced

word of mouth : oral communication

word•play \ˈwərd-ˌplā\ *n* **:** playful use of words

word processing *n* **:** the production of typewritten documents with automated and usually computerized text-editing equipment — **word process** *vb*

word processor *n* **:** a keyboard-operated terminal for use in word processing; *also* **:** software to perform word processing

wordy \ˈwər-dē\ *adj* **word•i•er; -est** ♦ **:** using many words **:** VERBOSE

♦ circuitous, diffuse, long-winded, prolix, rambling, verbose, windy ***Ant*** compact, concise, crisp, pithy, succinct, terse

wore *past of* WEAR

[1]**work** \ˈwərk\ *n* **1** ♦ **:** activity in which one exerts strength or faculties to do or perform something **:** LABOR **2 a :** something that needs to be done or accomplished **:** TASK, JOB ⟨have ∼ to do⟩ **b** ♦ **:** the labor, task, or duty that affords one his accustomed means of livelihood **:** EMPLOYMENT ⟨out of ∼⟩ **3 :** the energy used when a force is applied over a given distance **4** ♦ **:** something produced or accomplished by effort, exertion, or exercise of skill **5 :** a fortified structure **6** *pl* **:** engineering structures **7** *pl* ♦ **:** a place where industrial labor is done **:** FACTORY **8** *pl* **:** the moving parts of a mechanism **9** ♦ **:** something produced by mental effort or physical labor; *esp* **:** an artistic production (as a book or needlework) **10 :** WORKMANSHIP ⟨careless ∼⟩ **11 :** material in the process of manufacture **12** *pl* **:** everything possessed, available, or belonging ⟨the whole ∼*s* went overboard⟩; *also* **:** drastic treatment ⟨gave him the ∼*s*⟩ — **in the works :** in process of preparation

♦ [1] effort, exertion, expenditure, labor (*or* labour), pains, sweat, trouble, while ♦ [2b] calling, employment, line, occupation, profession, trade, vocation ♦ [4, 9] affair, fruit, handiwork, output, produce, product, thing, yield ♦ *usu* **works** [7] factory, mill, plant, shop, workshop ♦ [9] composition, opus, piece

[2]**work** *adj* **1 :** used for work ⟨∼ elephants⟩ **2 :** suitable or styled for wear while working ⟨∼ clothes⟩

[3]**work** *vb* **worked** \ˈwərkt\ *or* **wrought** \ˈrȯt\; **work•ing** **1** ♦ **:** to bring to pass **:** EFFECT **2 :** to fashion or create a useful or desired product through labor or exertion **3 :** to prepare for use (as by kneading) **4 :** to bring into a desired form by a manufacturing process ⟨∼ cold steel⟩ **5** ♦ **:** to set or keep in operation ⟨a pump ∼*ed* by hand⟩ **6** ♦ **:** to solve by reasoning or calculation ⟨∼ out a problem⟩ **7 :** to cause to toil or labor ⟨∼*ed* the men hard⟩; *also* **:** to make use of ⟨∼ a mine⟩ **8 :** to pay for with labor or service ⟨∼ off a debt⟩ **9 :** to bring or get into some position or condition by stages ⟨the stream ∼*ed* itself clear⟩ ⟨the knot ∼*ed* loose⟩ **10 :** CONTRIVE, ARRANGE ⟨∼ it so you can leave early⟩ **11 :** to practice trickery or cajolery on ⟨∼*ed* the management for a free ticket⟩ **12 :** EXCITE, PROVOKE ⟨∼*ed* himself into a rage⟩ **13** ♦ **:** to exert oneself physically or mentally; *esp* **:** to perform work regularly for wages **14 :** to function according to plan or design **15 :** to produce a desired effect **:** SUCCEED ⟨the plan ∼*ed*⟩ **16 :** to make way slowly and with difficulty ⟨he ∼*ed* forward through the crowd⟩ **17 :** to permit of being worked ⟨this wood ∼*s* easily⟩ **18 :** to be in restless motion; *also* **:** FERMENT 1 — **work on 1 :** AFFECT **2 :** to try to influence or persuade — **work upon :** to have effect upon **:** operate on **:** INFLUENCE

♦ [1] bring about, cause, create, effect, effectuate, generate, induce, make, produce, prompt, result, yield ♦ [5] handle, operate, run ♦ [5] actuate, drive, impel, move, propel ♦ [6] answer, break, crack, dope, figure out, puzzle, resolve, riddle, solve, unravel, work out ♦ [13] drudge, endeavor, fag, grub, hustle, labor, peg, plod, plug, slave, slog, strain, strive, struggle, sweat, toil, travail

work•able \ˈwər-kə-bəl\ *adj* **1 :** capable of being worked **2** ♦ **:** capable of being put into successful operation **:** PRACTICABLE — **work•able•ness** *n*

♦ achievable, attainable, doable, feasible, possible, practicable, realizable, viable

work•a•day \ˈwər-kə-ˌdā\ *adj* **1** ♦ **:** relating to or suited for working days as distinguished from special occasions **2** ♦ **:** being ordinary and unexceptionable

♦ [1] casual, everyday, informal ♦ [2] average, common, commonplace, everyday, normal, ordinary, prosaic, routine, run-of-the-mill, standard, unexceptional, unremarkable, usual

work•a•hol•ic \ˌwər-kə-ˈhȯ-lik, -ˈhä-\ *n* **:** a compulsive worker

work•bench \-ˌbench\ *n* **:** a bench on which work especially of mechanics, machinists, and carpenters is performed

work•book \-ˌbu̇k\ *n* **1 :** a worker's manual **2 :** a student's book of problems to be answered directly on the pages

work•day \ˈwərk-ˌdā\ *n* **1 :** a day on which work is done as distinguished from a day off **2 :** the period of time in a day when work is performed

work•er \ˈwər-kər\ *n* **1** ♦ **:** one that works; *esp* **:** a person who works for wages **2 :** any of the sexually undeveloped individuals of a colony of social insects (as bees, ants, or termites) that perform the work of the community

♦ drudge, fag, peon, slave, toiler ♦ employee, hand, hireling, jobholder

workers' compensation *n* **:** a system of insurance that reimburses an employer for damages paid to an employee who was injured while working

work ethic *n* **:** belief in work as a moral good

work farm *n* **:** a farm on which persons guilty of minor law violations are confined

work•force \ˈwərk-ˌfȯrs\ *n* **1** ♦ **:** the workers engaged in a specific activity or enterprise **2** ♦ **:** the number of workers potentially available for any purpose

♦ [1, 2] force, help, manpower, personnel, pool, staff

work•horse \ˈwərk-ˌhȯrs\ *n* **1 :** a horse used for hard work **2 :** a person who does most of the work of a group task **3 :** something that is useful, durable, or dependable
work•house \-ˌhau̇s\ *n* **1** *Brit* **:** POORHOUSE **2 :** a house of correction for persons guilty of minor law violations
work in *vb* **1 :** to insert or cause to penetrate by repeated or continued effort **2** ♦ **:** to interpose or insinuate gradually or unobtrusively

♦ infiltrate, insinuate, slip, sneak, worm

[1]**work•ing** \ˈwər-kiŋ\ *n* **1 :** manner of functioning — usually used in pl. **2** *pl* **:** an excavation made in mining or tunneling
[2]**working** *adj* **1 :** engaged in work ⟨a ~ journalist⟩ **2 :** adequate to allow work to be done ⟨a ~ majority⟩ ⟨a ~ knowledge of French⟩ **3** ♦ **:** adopted or assumed to help further work or activity ⟨a ~ draft⟩ **4 :** spent at work ⟨~ life⟩

♦ applicable, functional, practicable, practical, serviceable, usable, useful, workable

work•ing•man \ˈwər-kiŋ-ˌman\ *n* **:** WORKER 1
work•man \ˈwərk-mən\ *n* **1 :** WORKER 1 **2 :** ARTISAN, CRAFTSMAN
work•man•like \-ˌlīk\ *adj* **:** worthy of a good workman **:** SKILLFUL
work•man•ship \-ˌship\ *n* **:** the art or skill of a workman **:** CRAFTSMANSHIP; *also* **:** the quality of a piece of work ⟨a vase of exquisite ~⟩
work•out \ˈwərk-ˌau̇t\ *n* **1** ♦ **:** a practice or exercise to test or improve one's fitness, ability, or performance **2 :** a test or trial to determine ability or capacity or suitability

♦ drill, exercise, practice, routine, training

work out *vb* **1 a** ♦ **:** to bring about especially by resolving difficulties **b** ♦ **:** to create or cause by labor and exertion **2 :** to expand, develop, or perfect especially by analysis or reasoning **:** DEVELOP, ELABORATE **3** ♦ **:** to prove effective, practicable, or suitable ⟨I think this plan will *work out*⟩ **4 a :** to amount to a total or calculated figure — used with *at* **b** ♦ **:** to solve (as a problem) by a process of reasoning or calculation **5 :** to engage in a workout

♦ [1a, b] build, carve, forge, grind, hammer ♦ [3] click, deliver, go over, pan out, succeed ♦ [4b] calculate, compute, figure, reckon ♦ [4b] answer, break, crack, dope, figure out, puzzle, resolve, riddle, solve, unravel, work

work•place \ˈwərk-ˌplās\ *n* **:** a place (as an office) where work is done
work•room \ˈwərk-ˌrüm, -ˌru̇m\ *n* **:** a room used for work
work•shop \-ˌshäp\ *n* **1** ♦ **:** a shop where manufacturing or handicrafts are carried on **2 :** a seminar emphasizing exchange of ideas and practical methods

♦ factory, mill, plant, shop, works

work•sta•tion \-ˌstā-shən\ *n* **:** an area with equipment for the performance of a specialized task; *also* **:** a personal computer usually connected to a computer network
world \ˈwərld\ *n* **1** ♦ **:** the earth with its inhabitants and all things upon it **2** ♦ **:** people in general **3 :** human affairs ⟨withdraw from the ~⟩ **4** ♦ **:** the entire system of created things **:** UNIVERSE, CREATION **5 :** a state of existence **:** scene of life and action ⟨the ~ of the future⟩ **6 :** a distinctive class of persons or their sphere of interest ⟨the musical ~⟩ **7 :** a part or section of the earth or its inhabitants by itself **8 :** a great number or quantity ⟨a ~ of troubles⟩ **9 :** a celestial body

♦ [1] earth, planet ♦ [2] folks, humanity, humankind, people, persons, public, society ♦ [4] cosmos, creation, macrocosm, nature, universe

world–beat•er \-ˌbē-tər\ *n* **:** one that excels all others of its kind **:** CHAMPION
world–class *adj* **:** of the highest caliber in the world ⟨a ~ athlete⟩
world•ling \-liŋ\ *n* **:** a person absorbed in the concerns of the present world
world•ly \-lē\ *adj* **1** ♦ **:** of, relating to, or devoted to this world and its pursuits rather than to religion or spiritual affairs **2 :** experienced or knowledgeable in things and ways of this world **:** WORLDLY-WISE — **world•li•ness** \-lē-nəs\ *n*

♦ carnal, earthly, fleshly, material, mundane, temporal, terrestrial

world•ly–wise \-ˌwīz\ *adj* ♦ **:** possessing a practical and often shrewd understanding of human affairs

♦ cosmopolitan, smart, sophisticated, worldly ***Ant*** ingenuous, innocent, naive, unsophisticated, unworldly, wide-eyed

world•wide \ˈwərld-ˈwīd\ *adj* **:** extended throughout the entire world — **worldwide** *adv*
World Wide Web *n* **:** a part of the Internet usually accessed through a browser and containing files connected by hyperlinks
[1]**worm** \ˈwərm\ *n* **1 :** any of various small long usually naked and soft-bodied round or flat invertebrate animals (as an earthworm, nematode, tapeworm, or maggot) **2 :** a human being who is an object of contempt, loathing, or pity **:** WRETCH **3 :** something that inwardly torments or devours **4** *pl* **:** infestation with or disease caused by parasitic worms **5 :** a spiral or wormlike thing (as the thread of a screw) — **wormy** *adj*
[2]**worm** *vb* **1** ♦ **:** to move or cause to move or proceed slowly and deviously or as if in the manner of a worm **2** ♦ **:** to insinuate or introduce (oneself) by devious or subtle means **3 :** to obtain or extract by artful or insidious pleading, asking, or persuading ⟨~*ed* the truth out of him⟩ **4 :** to treat (an animal) with a drug to destroy or expel parasitic worms

♦ [1] crawl, creep, grovel, slither, snake ♦ [2] infiltrate, insinuate, slip, sneak, work in

worm–eat•en \ˈwərm-ˌēt-ᵊn\ *adj* **:** eaten or burrowed by worms
worm gear *n* **:** a mechanical linkage consisting of a short rotating screw whose threads mesh with the teeth of a gear wheel
worm•hole \ˈwərm-ˌhōl\ *n* **:** a hole or passage burrowed by a worm
worm•wood \-ˌwu̇d\ *n* **1 :** any of a genus of aromatic woody plants (as a sagebrush); *esp* **:** one of Europe used in absinthe **2 :** something bitter or grievous **:** BITTERNESS
worn *past part of* WEAR
worn–out \ˈwōrn-ˈau̇t\ *adj* ♦ **:** damaged, used up, or exhausted by or as if by wear

♦ beat, bushed, dead, drained, effete, jaded, limp, prostrate, spent, tired, weary ♦ ragged, ratty, seedy, shabby, tattered, threadbare

wor•ried *adj* ♦ **:** mentally troubled or concerned

♦ aflutter, anxious, edgy, jittery, jumpy, nervous, nervy, perturbed, tense, troubled, uneasy, upset

wor•ri•some \ˈwər-ē-səm\ *adj* **1** ♦ **:** causing distress or worry **2 :** inclined to worry or fret

♦ troublesome, unsettling, upsetting

[1]**wor•ry** \ˈwər-ē\ *vb* **wor•ried; wor•ry•ing 1 :** to shake and mangle with the teeth ⟨a terrier ~*ing* a rat⟩ **2** ♦ **:** to make anxious or upset ⟨her poor health *worries* me⟩ **3** ♦ **:** to feel or express great care or anxiety **:** FRET — **wor•ri•er** *n*

♦ [2] agitate, bother, concern, discompose, disquiet, distress, disturb, exercise, freak, perturb, undo, unhinge, unsettle, upset ♦ [3] bother, fear, fret, stew, sweat, trouble

[2]**worry** *n, pl* **worries 1** ♦ **:** mental distress or agitation resulting from concern usually for something impending or anticipated **:** ANXIETY **2 :** a cause of anxiety **:** TROUBLE

♦ agitation, anxiety, apprehension, care, concern, disquiet, nervousness, perturbation, uneasiness

wor•ry•wart \ˈwər-ē-ˌwȯrt\ *n* **:** one who is inclined to worry unduly
[1]**worse** \ˈwərs\ *adj, comparative of* BAD *or of* ILL **1 :** bad or evil in a greater degree **:** less good **2 :** more unfavorable, unpleasant, or painful; *also* **:** SICKER
[2]**worse** *n* **1 :** one that is worse **2 :** a greater degree of ill or badness ⟨a turn for the ~⟩
[3]**worse** *adv, comparative of* BAD *or of* ILL **:** in a worse manner **:** to a worse extent or degree
wors•en \ˈwərs-ᵊn\ *vb* ♦ **:** to make or become worse

♦ decay, decline, degenerate, descend, deteriorate, ebb, rot, sink

[1]**wor•ship** \ˈwər-shəp\ *n* **1** *chiefly Brit* **:** a person of importance — used as a title for officials **2 :** reverence toward a divine being or supernatural power; *also* **:** the expression of such reverence **3** ♦ **:** extravagant respect or admiration or devotion ⟨~ of the dollar⟩

♦ adulation, deification, idolatry

[2]**worship** *vb* **-shipped** *also* **-shiped; -ship•ping** *also* **-ship•ing 1** ♦ **:** to honor or reverence as a divine being or supernatural

power **2** ♦ **:** to regard with respect, honor, or devotion **3 :** to perform or take part in worship — **wor•ship•er** *or* **wor•ship•per** *n*

♦ [1] adore, deify, glorify, revere, venerate ♦ [2] adore, canonize, deify, dote, idolize, love

wor•ship•ful \ˈwər-shəp-fəl\ *adj* **1** *archaic* **:** NOTABLE, DISTINGUISHED **2** *chiefly Brit* — used as a title for various persons or groups of rank or distinction **3** ♦ **:** giving or expressing adoration or reverence

♦ adulatory

1**worst** \ˈwərst\ *adj, superlative of* BAD *or of* ILL **1 :** most bad, evil, ill, or corrupt **2 :** most unfavorable, unpleasant, or painful; *also* **:** most unsuitable, faulty, or unattractive **3 :** least skillful or efficient

2**worst** *adv, superlative of* ILL *or of* BAD *or* BADLY **1 :** to the extreme degree of badness or inferiority **:** in the worst manner **2 :** MOST ⟨those who need help ~⟩

3**worst** *n* **:** one that is worst

4**worst** *vb* **:** to get the better of in a fight, conflict, or contest **:** DEFEAT

wor•sted \ˈwu̇s-təd, ˈwər-stəd\ *n* **:** a smooth compact yarn from long wool fibers; *also* **:** a fabric made from such yarn

wort \ˈwərt, ˈwȯrt\ *n* **:** a sweet liquid drained from mash and fermented to form beer and whiskey

1**worth** \ˈwərth\ *n* **1 :** monetary value; *also* **:** the equivalent of a specified amount or figure ⟨$5 ~ of gas⟩ **2** ♦ **:** the value of something measured by its qualities **3 :** MERIT, EXCELLENCE

♦ account, merit, valuation, value

2**worth** *prep* **1 :** equal in value to; *also* **:** having possessions or income equal to **2 :** deserving of ⟨well ~ the effort⟩

worth•less \ˈwərth-ləs\ *adj* **1** ♦ **:** lacking use, value, or profit **2 :** LOW, DESPICABLE — **worth•less•ness** *n*

♦ chaffy, empty, junky, no-good, null, valueless ***Ant*** useful, valuable, worthy

worth•while \ˈwərth-ˈhwīl\ *adj* **:** being worth the time or effort spent

1**wor•thy** \ˈwər-t͟hē\ *adj* **wor•thi•er; -est 1 :** having worth or value **2** ♦ **:** marked by personal qualities warranting honor, respect, or esteem **:** MERITORIOUS **3 :** having sufficient worth ⟨~ of the honor⟩ — **wor•thi•ly** \ˈwər-t͟hə-lē\ *adv* — **wor•thi•ness** \-t͟hē-nəs\ *n*

♦ deserving, good, meritorious ***Ant*** no-good, undeserving, valueless, worthless

2**worthy** *n, pl* **worthies :** a worthy person

would \ˈwu̇d\ *past of* WILL **1** *archaic* **:** wish for **:** WANT **2 :** strongly desire **:** WISH ⟨I ~ I were young again⟩ **3** — used as an auxiliary to express (1) preference ⟨~ rather run than fight⟩, (2) wish, desire, or intent ⟨those who ~ forbid gambling⟩, (3) habitual action ⟨we ~ meet often for lunch⟩, (4) a contingency or possibility ⟨if he were coming, he ~ be here by now⟩, (5) probability ⟨~ have won if he hadn't tripped⟩, or (6) a request ⟨~ you help us⟩ **4 :** COULD **5 :** SHOULD

would–be \ˈwu̇d-ˈbē\ *adj* **:** desiring or pretending to be ⟨a ~ artist⟩

1**wound** \ˈwünd\ *n* **1 :** an injury involving cutting or breaking of bodily tissue (as by violence, accident, or surgery) **2** ♦ **:** an injury or hurt to feelings or reputation

♦ affront, barb, dart, dig, indignity, insult, name, offense, outrage, put-down, sarcasm, slight, slur

2**wound** *vb* ♦ **:** to inflict a wound to or in

♦ damage, harm, hurt, injure ♦ affront, insult, offend, outrage, slight

3**wound** \ˈwau̇nd\ *past and past part of* WIND

wove *past of* WEAVE

woven *past part of* WEAVE

1**wow** \ˈwau̇\ *n* **:** a striking success **:** HIT

2**wow** *vb* **:** to arouse enthusiastic approval

WP *abbr* word processing; word processor

WPM *abbr* words per minute

wpn *abbr* weapon

wrack \ˈrak\ *n* **:** violent or total destruction

wraith \ˈrāth\ *n, pl* **wraiths** \ˈrāths, ˈrāt͟hz\ **1** ♦ **:** a visible appearance of a dead person **:** GHOST **2 :** an insubstantial appearance **:** SHADOW

♦ apparition, bogey, ghost, phantasm, phantom, poltergeist, shade, shadow, specter, spirit, spook, vision

1**wran•gle** \ˈraŋ-gəl\ *vb* **wran•gled; wran•gling 1** ♦ **:** to quarrel angrily or peevishly **:** BICKER **2 :** ARGUE **3 :** to obtain by persistent arguing **4 :** to herd and care for (livestock) on the range — **wran•gler** *n*

♦ argue, bicker, brawl, dispute, fall out, fight, hassle, quarrel, row, scrap, spat, squabble

2**wrangle** *n* ♦ **:** an angry, noisy, or prolonged dispute; *also* **:** CONTROVERSY

♦ altercation, argument, bicker, brawl, controversy, disagreement, dispute, fight, hassle, misunderstanding, quarrel, row, scrap, spat, squabble

1**wrap** \ˈrap\ *vb* **wrapped; wrap•ping 1 :** to cover especially by winding or folding **2 :** to envelop and secure for transportation or storage **3** ♦ **:** to enclose wholly **4 :** to coil, fold, draw, or twine about something **5 :** SURROUND, ENVELOP ⟨*wrapped* in mystery⟩ **6 :** INVOLVE, ENGROSS ⟨*wrapped* up in a hobby⟩ **7 :** to complete filming or recording

♦ embrace, enclose, encompass, enfold, enshroud, envelop, invest, lap, mantle, shroud, swathe, veil

2**wrap** *n* **1 :** WRAPPER, WRAPPING **2 :** an article of clothing that may be wrapped around a person **3** *pl* **:** SECRECY ⟨kept under ~*s*⟩ **4 :** completion of filming or recording

wrap•around \ˈra-pə-ˌrau̇nd\ *n* **:** a garment (as a dress) adjusted to the figure by wrapping around

wrap•per \ˈra-pər\ *n* **1 :** that in which something is wrapped **2 :** one that wraps **3 :** an article of clothing worn wrapped around the body

wrap•ping \ˈra-piŋ\ *n* **:** something used to wrap an object **:** WRAPPER

wrap–up \ˈrap-ˌəp\ *n* ♦ **:** a concise statement of the main points **:** SUMMARY

♦ abstract, digest, encapsulation, epitome, outline, précis, recap, recapitulation, résumé (*or* resume), roundup, sum, summarization, summary, synopsis

wrap up *vb* **1** ♦ **:** to make a single comprehensive report from **:** SUMMARIZE **2** ♦ **:** to bring to a usually successful conclusion

♦ [1] abstract, digest, encapsulate, epitomize, outline, recapitulate, summarize, sum up ♦ [2] close, conclude, end, finish, round, terminate, wind up

wrasse \ˈras\ *n* **:** any of a large family of usually brightly colored marine fishes including many food fishes

wrath \ˈrath\ *n* **1** ♦ **:** violent anger **:** RAGE **2** ♦ **:** condemnation especially of a deity or sovereign; *esp* **:** divine punishment

♦ [1] anger, furor, fury, indignation, ire, outrage, rage, spleen, wrathfulness ♦ [2] castigation, chastisement, correction, desert, discipline, nemesis, penalty, punishment

wrath•ful \-fəl\ *adj* **1** ♦ **:** filled with wrath **:** very angry **2** ♦ **:** showing, marked by, or arising from anger — **wrath•ful•ly** *adv*

♦ [1, 2] angry, boiling, enraged, furious, irate, mad, rabid, sore

wrath•ful•ness *n* ♦ **:** the quality or fact of being wrathful

♦ anger, furor, fury, indignation, ire, outrage, rage, spleen, wrath

wreak \ˈrēk\ *vb* **1 :** to exact as a punishment **:** INFLICT ⟨~ vengeance on an enemy⟩ **2 :** to give free scope or rein to ⟨~*ed* his wrath⟩ **3 :** BRING ABOUT, CAUSE ⟨~ havoc⟩

wreath \ˈrēth\ *n, pl* **wreaths** \ˈrēt͟hz, ˈrēths\ **:** a circular band of flowers or leaves usually for decoration; *also* **:** something having a circular or coiling form ⟨a ~ of smoke⟩

wreathe \ˈrēt͟h\ *vb* **wreathed; wreath•ing 1 :** to shape or take on the shape of a wreath **2 :** to crown, decorate, or cover with or as if with a wreath ⟨a face *wreathed* in smiles⟩ **3** ♦ **:** to interweave or blend together

♦ interlace, intersperse, intertwine, interweave, lace, thread, weave

1**wreck** \ˈrek\ *n* **1 :** something (as goods) cast up on the land by the sea after a shipwreck **2 :** the injury, destruction, or sinking of a vessel especially by being cast on rocks or affected by the force of winds or waves **:** SHIPWRECK **3** ♦ **:** the action or an instance of crashing, breaking up, or destroying something **4** ♦ **:** broken remains (as of a vehicle after a crash) **5 :** something disabled or in a state of ruin; *also* **:** an individual broken in health, strength, or spirits

♦ [3] collision, crack-up, crash, smash ♦ [4] debris, remains, residue, rubble, ruins, wreckage

[2]**wreck** *vb* **1 :** SHIPWRECK **2** ♦ **:** to ruin or damage by breaking up **:** involve in disaster or ruin

♦ annihilate, blot out, demolish, desolate, destroy, devastate, do in, exterminate, extinguish, obliterate, pulverize, ruin, shatter, smash, tear down, waste, wipe out

wreck•age \ˈre-kij\ *n* **1** ♦ **:** the act of wrecking **:** the state of being wrecked **2** ♦ **:** the remains of a wreck

♦ [1] annihilation, demolition, desolation, destruction, devastation, havoc, loss, obliteration, ruin, wastage ♦ [2] debris, remains, residue, rubble, ruins, wreck

wreck•er \ˈre-kər\ *n* **1 :** one that searches for or works upon the wrecks of ships **2 :** TOW TRUCK **3 :** one that wrecks; *esp* **:** one whose work is the demolition of buildings

wren \ˈren\ *n* **:** any of a family of small mostly brown singing birds with short wings and often a tail that points upward

[1]**wrench** \ˈrench\ *vb* **1 :** to move with a violent twist **2** ♦ **:** to pull, strain, or tighten with violent twisting or force **3** ♦ **:** to injure or disable by a violent twisting or straining **4** ♦ **:** to snatch forcibly **:** WREST

♦ [2] twist, wrest, wring ♦ [3] pull, rack, strain, stretch ♦ [4] rip, tear, wrest

[2]**wrench** *n* **1 :** a forcible twisting; *also* **:** an injury (as to one's ankle) by twisting **2 :** a tool for holding, twisting, or turning (as nuts or bolts)

[1]**wrest** \ˈrest\ *vb* **1** ♦ **:** to pull or move by a forcible twisting movement **2** ♦ **:** to gain with difficulty by or as if by coercion, force, or violence ⟨~*ed* the book from her hands⟩ ⟨~ control of the government from the dictator⟩

♦ [1] extract, prize, pry, pull, root, tear, uproot ♦ [1, 2] rip, tear, wrench ♦ [2] exact, extort, wring

[2]**wrest** *n* **:** a forcible twist **:** WRENCH

[1]**wres•tle** \ˈre-səl, ˈra-\ *vb* **wres•tled; wres•tling 1** ♦ **:** to grapple with and try to throw down an opponent **2** ♦ **:** to compete against in wrestling **3 :** to struggle for control (as of something difficult) ⟨~ with a problem⟩ — **wres•tler** \ˈres-lər, ˈras-\ *n*

♦ [1, 2] grapple, scuffle, tussle

[2]**wrestle** *n* **:** the action or an instance of wrestling **:** STRUGGLE

wres•tling \ˈres-liŋ\ *n* **:** the sport in which two opponents wrestle each other

wretch \ˈrech\ *n* **1 :** a miserable unhappy person **2** ♦ **:** a base, despicable, or vile person

♦ beast, devil, evildoer, fiend, heavy, knave, no-good, rapscallion, rascal, reprobate, rogue, scalawag, scamp, varlet, villain

wretch•ed \ˈre-chəd\ *adj* **1** ♦ **:** deeply afflicted, dejected, or distressed **:** extremely sad and depressed **2 :** characterized by or tending to produce discomfort, distress, or misery ⟨~ living conditions⟩ **3** ♦ **:** having a mean or contemptible nature or appearance ⟨a ~ trick⟩ **4** ♦ **:** poor in quality or ability **:** INFERIOR ⟨~ workmanship⟩ — **wretch•ed•ness** *n*

♦ [1] dejected, depressed, despondent, disconsolate, heartsick, miserable, mournful, sad, sorrowful, sorry, unhappy, woebegone, woeful ♦ [3] contemptible, despicable, lousy, nasty, pitiful, scabby, scurvy, sorry ♦ [4] atrocious, awful, execrable, inferior, lousy, punk, rotten, terrible ***Ant*** great, marvelous, wonderful

wretch•ed•ly *adv* ♦ **:** in a wretched state or manner

♦ agonizingly, bitterly, grievously, hard, hardly, sadly, sorrowfully, unhappily, woefully

wrig•gle \ˈri-gəl\ *vb* **wrig•gled; wrig•gling 1 :** to twist or move to and fro like a worm ⟨*wriggled* in his chair⟩ ⟨~ your toes⟩; *also* **:** to move along by twisting and turning ⟨a snake *wriggled* along the path⟩ **2 :** to extricate oneself as if by wriggling ⟨~ out of difficulty⟩ — **wriggle** *n*

wrig•gler *n* **1 :** one that wriggles **2 :** WIGGLER 1

wring \ˈriŋ\ *vb* **wrung** \ˈrəŋ\; **wring•ing** \ˈriŋ-iŋ\ **1 :** to squeeze or twist especially so as to make dry or to extract moisture or liquid ⟨~ wet clothes⟩ **2 :** to get by or as if by twisting or pressing ⟨~ the truth out of him⟩ **3** ♦ **:** to twist so as to strain or sprain ⟨~ his neck⟩ **4 :** to twist together as a sign of anguish ⟨*wrung* her hands⟩ **5 :** to affect painfully as if by wringing **:** TORMENT ⟨her plight *wrung* my heart⟩

♦ twist, wrench, wrest

wring•er \ˈriŋ-ər\ *n* **:** one that wrings; *esp* **:** a device for squeezing out liquid or moisture ⟨clothes ~⟩

[1]**wrin•kle** \ˈriŋ-kəl\ *n* **1** ♦ **:** a crease or small fold on a smooth surface (as in the skin or in cloth) **2** ♦ **:** a clever or new method, trick, or idea — **wrin•kly** \-k(ə-)lē\ *adj*

♦ [1] crease, crimp, crinkle, furrow ♦ [2] coinage, concoction, contrivance, creation, innovation, invention

[2]**wrinkle** *vb* **wrin•kled; wrin•kling** ♦ **:** to develop or cause to develop wrinkles

♦ crease, crinkle, furrow, rumple

wrist \ˈrist\ *n* **:** the joint or region between the hand and the arm; *also* **:** a corresponding part in a lower animal

wrist•band \-ˌband\ *n* **:** a band or the part of a sleeve encircling the wrist

wrist•let \-lət\ *n* **:** WRISTBAND; *esp* **:** a close-fitting knitted band attached to the top of a glove or the end of a sleeve

wrist•watch \-ˌwäch\ *n* **:** a small watch attached to a bracelet or strap to fasten about the wrist

writ \ˈrit\ *n* **1 :** something written **2 :** a written legal order signed by a court officer

write \ˈrīt\ *vb* **wrote** \ˈrōt\; **writ•ten** \ˈrit-ᵊn\ *also* **writ** \ˈrit\; **writ•ing** \ˈrī-tiŋ\ **1 :** to form characters, letters, or words on a surface ⟨learn to read and ~⟩ **2 :** to form the letters or the words of ⟨~ your name⟩ ⟨~ a check⟩ **3** ♦ **:** to put down on paper **:** express in writing **4 :** to make up and set down for others to read ⟨~ a book⟩ ⟨~ music⟩ **5 :** to write a letter to **6 :** to communicate by letter **:** CORRESPOND

♦ author, pen, scratch, scribble

write–in \ˈrīt-ˌin\ *n* **:** a vote cast by writing in the name of a candidate; *also* **:** a candidate whose name is written in

write in *vb* **:** to insert (a name not listed on a ballot) in an appropriate space; *also* **:** to cast (a vote) in this manner

write off *vb* **1 a** ♦ **:** to reduce the estimated value of **:** DEPRECIATE **b** ♦ **:** to disparage or deny the worth of **2 :** CANCEL ⟨*write off* a bad debt⟩

♦ [1a] cheapen, depreciate, depress, mark down ♦ [1b] belittle, cry down, decry, deprecate, depreciate, diminish, discount, disparage, minimize, put down

writ•er \ˈrī-tər\ *n* **:** one that writes especially as a business or occupation **:** AUTHOR

writer's cramp *n* **:** a painful spasmodic contraction of muscles of the hand or fingers brought on by excessive writing

write–up \ˈrīt-ˌəp\ *n* **:** a written account (as in a newspaper); *esp* **:** a flattering article

writhe \ˈrīth\ *vb* **writhed; writh•ing 1 :** to twist and turn this way and that ⟨~ in pain⟩ **2 :** to suffer with shame or confusion

writ•ing *n* **1 :** the act of one that writes; *also* **:** HANDWRITING **2 :** something that is written or printed **3 :** a style or form of composition **4 :** the occupation of a writer

Writings \ˈrī-tiŋz\ *n pl* **:** the third part of the Jewish scriptures

wrnt *abbr* warrant

[1]**wrong** \ˈrȯŋ\ *n* **1** ♦ **:** an injurious, unfair, or unjust act **2 :** a violation of the legal rights of another person **3** ♦ **:** something that is wrong **:** wrong principles, practices, or conduct ⟨know right from ~⟩ **4 :** the state, position, or fact of being wrong

♦ [1] disservice, injury, injustice, raw deal ♦ [3] bad, evil, ill, immorality, iniquity, sin, villainy

[2]**wrong** *adj* **wrong•er** \ˈrȯŋ-ər\; **wrong•est** \ˈrȯŋ-əst\ **1** ♦ **:** lacking in moral behavior and integrity **:** IMMORAL **2** ♦ **:** not right according to a standard or code **:** IMPROPER **3** ♦ **:** not agreeing with or conforming to facts **:** INCORRECT ⟨a ~ solution⟩ **4** ♦ **:** being at variance with what is generally acceptable or preferable **:** UNSATISFACTORY **5 :** not fitted or qualified for a particular intention or purpose **:** UNSUITABLE, INAPPROPRIATE **6 :** constituting a surface that is considered the back, bottom, inside, or reverse of something ⟨iron only on the ~ side of the fabric⟩

♦ [1] bad, black, evil, immoral, iniquitous, nefarious, rotten, sinful, unethical, unsavory, vicious, vile, villainous ♦ [2] graceless, improper, inapt, incongruous, incorrect, indecorous, inept, infelicitous, unbecoming, unfit, unhappy, unseemly, unsuitable ♦ [3] erroneous, false, inaccurate, incorrect, inexact, invalid, off, unsound, untrue ♦ [4] bad, deficient, inferior, lousy, off, poor, punk, rotten, substandard, unacceptable, unsatisfactory, wanting, wretched

[3]**wrong** *adv* **1 :** in a mistaken or erroneous manner **2** ♦ **:** in a wrong direction, manner, or relation

♦ afield, amiss, astray, awry ***Ant*** aright, right, well

[4]**wrong** *vb* **wronged; wrong•ing** \ˈrȯŋ-iŋ\ **1 :** to do wrong to **:** INJURE, HARM **2 :** to treat unjustly **:** DISHONOR, MALIGN

wrong·do·er \ˈrȯŋ-ˌdü-ər\ *n* ♦ : a person who does wrong and especially moral wrong

♦ evildoer, malefactor, sinner

wrong·do·ing \-ˌdü-iŋ\ *n* ♦ : the act or action of doing wrong

♦ breach, crime, error, malefaction, misdeed, misdoing, offense, sin, transgression, trespass, violation ♦ malfeasance, misbehavior, misconduct, misdoing

wrong·ful \ˈrȯŋ-fəl\ *adj* **1 :** WRONG, UNJUST **2** ♦ **:** having no legal sanction : UNLAWFUL — **wrong·ful·ly** *adv* — **wrong·ful·ness** *n*

♦ criminal, illegal, illegitimate, illicit, unlawful

wrong·head·ed \-ˈhe-dəd\ *adj* : stubborn in clinging to wrong opinion or principles — **wrong·head·ed·ly** *adv* — **wrong·head·ed·ness** *n*

wrong·ly *adv* ♦ : in a bad, incorrect, inappropriate, or unsuitable manner

♦ amiss, erroneously, faultily, improperly, inaptly, incorrectly, mistakenly ***Ant*** appropriately, aptly, correctly, fittingly, properly, right, rightly, suitably

wrote *past of* WRITE

wroth \ˈrȯth, ˈrōth\ *adj* : filled with wrath : ANGRY

wrought \ˈrȯt\ *adj* **1 :** FASHIONED, FORMED ⟨carefully ~ essays⟩ **2 :** ORNAMENTED **3 :** beaten into shape by tools : HAMMERED ⟨~ metals⟩ **4 :** deeply stirred : EXCITED ⟨gets easily ~ up⟩

wrung *past and past part of* WRING

wry \ˈrī\ *adj* **wry·er** \ˈrī-ər\; **wry·est** \ˈrī-əst\ **1 :** having a bent or twisted shape ⟨a ~ smile⟩; *also* : turned abnormally to one side : CONTORTED ⟨a ~ neck⟩ **2 :** cleverly and often ironically humorous — **wry·ly** *adv* — **wry·ness** *n*

wry·neck \ˈrī-ˌnek\ *n* **1 :** either of two Old World woodpeckers that differ from typical woodpeckers in having a peculiar manner of twisting the head and neck **2 :** an abnormal twisting of the neck and head to one side caused by muscle spasms

WSW *abbr* west-southwest

wt *abbr* weight

wurst \ˈwərst, ˈwu̇rst\ *n* : SAUSAGE

wuss \ˈwu̇s\ *n* : WIMP — **wussy** \ˈwu̇-sē\ *adj*

WV *or* **W Va** *abbr* West Virginia

WW *abbr* World War

w/w *abbr* wall-to-wall

WY *or* **Wyo** *abbr* Wyoming

WYS·I·WYG \ˈwi-zē-ˌwig\ *adj* : of, relating to, or being a computer display that shows a document exactly as it will appear when printed out

X

[1]**x** \ˈeks\ *n, pl* **x's** *or* **xs** \ˈek-səz\ *often cap* **1 :** the 24th letter of the English alphabet **2 :** an unknown quantity

[2]**x** *vb* **x-ed** *also* **x'd** *or* **xed** \ˈekst\; **x-ing** *or* **x'ing** \ˈek-siŋ\ : to cancel or obliterate with a series of *x*'s — usu. used with *out*

[3]**x** *abbr* **1** ex **2** experimental **3** extra

[4]**x** *symbol* **1** times ⟨3 *x* 2 is 6⟩ **2** by ⟨a 3 *x* 5 index card⟩ **3** *often cap* power of magnification

Xan·a·du \ˈza-nə-ˌdü, -ˌdyü\ *n* : an idyllic, exotic, or luxurious place

Xan·thip·pe \zan-ˈthi-pē, -ˈti-\ *or* **Xan·tip·pe** \-ˈti-pē\ *n* : an ill-tempered woman

x–ax·is \ˈeks-ˌak-səs\ *n* : the axis of a graph or of a system of coordinates in a plane parallel to which abscissas are measured

X–C *abbr* cross-country

X chromosome *n* : a sex chromosome that usu. occurs paired in each female cell and single in each male cell in organisms (as humans) in which the male normally has two unlike sex chromosomes

Xe *symbol* xenon

xe·non \ˈzē-ˌnän, ˈze-\ *n* : a heavy gaseous chemical element occurring in minute quantities in air

xe·no·pho·bia \ˌze-nə-ˈfō-bē-ə, ˌzē-\ *n* : fear and hatred of strangers or foreigners or of what is strange or foreign — **xe·no·phobe** \ˈze-nə-ˌfōb, ˈzē-\ *n* — **xe·no·pho·bic** \ˌze-nə-ˈfō-bik, ˌzē-\ *adj*

xe·ric \ˈzir-ik, ˈzer-\ *adj* : characterized by or requiring only a small amount of moisture ⟨a ~ habitat⟩

xeri·scape \ˈzir-ə-ˌskāp, ˈzer-\ *n, often cap* : a landscaping method utilizing water-conserving techniques

xe·rog·ra·phy \zə-ˈrä-grə-fē\ *n* : a process for copying printed matter by the action of light on an electrically charged surface in which the latent image is developed with a powder — **xe·ro·graph·ic** \ˌzir-ə-ˈgra-fik\ *adj*

xe·ro·phyte \ˈzir-ə-ˌfīt\ *n* : a plant adapted for growth with a limited water supply — **xe·ro·phyt·ic** \ˌzir-ə-ˈfi-tik\ *adj*

xi \ˈzī, ˈksī\ *n* : the 14th letter of the Greek alphabet — Ξ or ξ

XL *abbr* **1** extra large **2** extra long

Xmas \ˈkris-məs *also* ˈeks-məs\ *n* : CHRISTMAS

XML \ˌeks-(ˌ)em-ˈel\ *n* : a markup language that indicates the structural type of data

XO *abbr* executive officer

x–ra·di·a·tion \ˌeks-ˌrā-dē-ˈā-shən\ *n, often cap* **1 :** exposure to X-rays **2 :** radiation consisting of X-rays

x–ray \ˈeks-ˌrā\ *vb, often cap* : to examine, treat, or photograph with X-rays

X–ray \ˈeks-ˌrā\ *n* **1 :** a radiation with an extremely short wavelength of less than 100 angstroms that is able to penetrate through various thicknesses of solids and to act on photographic film **2 :** a photograph taken with X-rays — **X–ray** *adj*

XS *abbr* extra small

xy·lem \ˈzī-ləm, -ˌlem\ *n* : a woody tissue of vascular plants that transports water and dissolved materials upward, functions in support and storage, and lies central to the phloem

xy·lo·phone \ˈzī-lə-ˌfōn\ *n* : a musical instrument consisting of a series of wooden bars graduated in length to produce the musical scale, supported on belts of straw or felt, and sounded by striking with two small wooden hammers — **xy·lo·phon·ist** \-ˌfō-nist\ *n*

Y

[1]**y** \ˈwī\ *n, pl* **y's** *or* **ys** \ˈwīz\ *often cap* : the 25th letter of the English alphabet

[2]**y** *abbr* **1** yard **2** year

[1]**Y** \ˈwī\ *n* : YMCA, YWCA

[2]**Y** *symbol* yttrium

[1]**-y** *also* **-ey** \ē\ *adj suffix* **1 :** characterized by : full of ⟨dirty⟩ ⟨clayey⟩ **2 :** having the character of : composed of ⟨icy⟩ **3 :** like : like that of ⟨homey⟩ ⟨wintry⟩ ⟨stagy⟩ **4 :** tending or inclined to ⟨sleepy⟩ ⟨chatty⟩ **5 :** giving occasion for (specified) action ⟨teary⟩ **6 :** performing (specified) action ⟨curly⟩

[2]**-y** \ē\ *n suffix, pl* **-ies** **1 :** state : condition : quality ⟨beggary⟩ **2 :** activity, place of business, or goods dealt with ⟨laundry⟩ **3 :** whole body or group ⟨soldiery⟩

[3]**-y** *n suffix, pl* **-ies** : instance of a (specified) action ⟨entreaty⟩ ⟨inquiry⟩

YA *abbr* young adult

[1]**yacht** \ˈyät\ *n* **:** a usu. large recreational watercraft; *also* **:** sailboat
[2]**yacht** *vb* **:** to race or cruise in a yacht
yacht•ing \ˈyä-tiŋ\ *n* **:** the sport of racing or cruising in a yacht
yachts•man \ˈyäts-mən\ *n* **:** a person who owns or sails a yacht
ya•hoo \ˈyā-hü, ˈyä-\ *n, pl* **yahoos :** a boorish, crass, or stupid person
Yah•weh \ˈyä-ˌwā\ *also* **Yah•veh** \-ˌvā\ *n* **:** GOD 1 — used esp. by the Hebrews
[1]**yak** \ˈyak\ *n, pl* **yaks** *also* **yak :** a large long-haired wild or domesticated ox of Tibet and adjacent Asian uplands
[2]**yak** *also* **yack** \ˈyak\ *n* **:** persistent or voluble talk — **yak** *also* **yack** *vb*
yam \ˈyam\ *n* **1 :** the edible starchy root of various twining plants used as a staple food in tropical areas; *also* **:** a plant that produces yams **2 :** a usu. deep orange sweet potato
yam•mer \ˈya-mər\ *vb* **1 :** to utter repeated cries of distress or sorrow **:** WHIMPER **2 :** CHATTER — **yammer** *n*
[1]**yank** \ˈyaŋk\ *n* **:** a strong sudden pull **:** JERK
[2]**yank** *vb* **:** to pull with a quick vigorous movement
Yank \ˈyaŋk\ *n* **:** YANKEE
Yan•kee \ˈyaŋ-kē\ *n* **1 :** a native or inhabitant of New England; *also* **:** a native or inhabitant of the northern U.S. **2 :** AMERICAN 2
yan•qui \ˈyäŋ-kē\ *n, often cap* **:** a citizen of the U.S. as distinguished from a Latin American
[1]**yap** \ˈyap\ *vb* **yapped; yap•ping 1 :** BARK, YELP **2 :** GAB
[2]**yap** *n* **1 :** a quick sharp bark **2 :** CHATTER
[1]**yard** \ˈyärd\ *n* **1** ♦ **:** a small enclosed area open to the sky and adjacent to a building **2** ♦ **:** the grounds of a building **3 :** the grounds surrounding a house usu. covered with grass **4 :** an enclosure for livestock **5 :** an area set aside for a particular business or activity **6 :** a system of railroad tracks for storing cars and making up trains

♦ [1] close, court, courtyard, quadrangle ♦ [2] demesne, grounds, park, premises

[2]**yard** *n* **1 :** a unit of length equal to three feet **2 :** a long spar tapered toward the ends that supports and spreads the head of a sail — **the whole nine yards :** all of a set of circumstances, conditions, or details
yard•age \ˈyär-dij\ *n* **:** an aggregate number of yards; *also* **:** the length, extent, or volume of something as measured in yards
yard•arm \ˈyärd-ˌärm\ *n* **:** either end of the yard of a square-rigged ship
yard•man \-mən, -ˌman\ *n* **:** a person employed in or about a yard
yard•mas•ter \-ˌmas-tər\ *n* **:** the person in charge of a railroad yard
yard•stick \-ˌstik\ *n* **1 :** a graduated measuring stick three feet long **2** ♦ **:** a standard for making a critical judgment **:** CRITERION

♦ criterion, grade, mark, measure, par, standard, touchstone

yar•mul•ke \ˈyä-mə-kə, ˈyär-, -məl-\ *n* **:** a skullcap worn esp. by Jewish males in the synagogue and the home
yarn \ˈyärn\ *n* **1 :** a continuous often plied strand composed of fibers or filaments and used in weaving and knitting to form cloth **2 :** an entertaining narrative of adventures **:** STORY; *esp* **:** a tall tale
yar•row \ˈyar-ō\ *n* **:** a strong-scented herb related to the daisies that has white or pink flowers in flat clusters
yaw \ˈyȯ\ *vb* ♦ **:** to deviate erratically from a course ⟨the ship ~*ed* in the heavy seas⟩ — **yaw** *n*

♦ sheer, swerve, veer

yawl \ˈyȯl\ *n* **:** a 2-masted sailboat with the shorter mast aft of the rudder
[1]**yawn** \ˈyȯn\ *vb* **:** to open wide; *esp* **:** to open the mouth wide and take a deep breath usu. as an involuntary reaction to fatigue or boredom — **yawn•er** *n*
[2]**yawn** *n* **:** the act of yawning
yawp *or* **yaup** \ˈyȯp\ *vb* **1 :** to make a raucous noise **:** SQUAWK **2 :** CLAMOR, COMPLAIN — **yawp•er** *n*
yaws \ˈyȯz\ *n pl* **:** a contagious tropical disease caused by a spirochete closely resembling the causative agent of syphilis and marked by skin lesions
y–ax•is \ˈwī-ˌak-səs\ *n* **:** the axis of a graph or of a system of coordinates in a plane parallel to which the ordinates are measured
Yb *symbol* ytterbium
YB *abbr* yearbook
Y chromosome *n* **:** a sex chromosome that is characteristic of male cells in organisms (as humans) in which the male typically has two unlike sex chromosomes
yd *abbr* yard
[1]**ye** \ˈyē\ *pron* **:** YOU 1
[2]**ye** \yē, yə, *originally same as* THE\ *definite article, archaic* **:** THE — used by early printers to represent the manuscript word *þe* (*the*)
[1]**yea** \ˈyā\ *adv* **1** ♦ — used as a function word esp. to express assent or agreement esp. in oral voting **2** ♦ **:** not only so but **:** INDEED

♦ [1] all right, alright, OK, yes ♦ [2] even, indeed, nay, truly, verily

[2]**yea** *n* **:** an affirmative vote; *also* **:** a person casting such a vote
yeah \ˈyeə, ˈyaə\ *adv* **:** YES
year \ˈyir\ *n* **1 :** the period of about 365¼ solar days required for one revolution of the earth around the sun; *also* **:** the time in which a planet completes a revolution about the sun **2 :** a cycle of 365 or 366 days beginning with January 1; *also* **:** a calendar year specified usu. by a number **3** *pl* **:** a time of special significance ⟨their glory ~*s*⟩ **4** *pl* **:** AGE ⟨advanced in ~*s*⟩ **5 :** a period of time other than a calendar year ⟨the school ~⟩
year•book \-ˌbu̇k\ *n* **1 :** a book published annually esp. as a report **2 :** a school publication recording the history and activities of a graduating class
year•ling \ˈyir-liŋ, ˈyər-lən\ *n* **1 :** one that is a year old **2 :** a racehorse between January of the year after the year in which it was born and the next January
year•long \ˈyir-ˈlȯŋ\ *adj* **:** lasting through a year
[1]**year•ly** \ˈyir-lē\ *adj* **:** ANNUAL
[2]**yearly** *adv* **:** every year
yearn \ˈyərn\ *vb* **1** ♦ **:** to feel a longing or craving **2 :** to feel tenderness or compassion

♦ *usu* **yearn for** ache for, crave, desire, die for, hanker for, hunger for, long for, lust (for *or* after), pine for, repine for, thirst for, want, wish for

yearn•ing *n* ♦ **:** a tender or urgent longing

♦ appetite, craving, desire, drive, hankering, hunger, itch, longing, lust, passion, thirst, urge, yen

year–round \ˈyir-ˈrau̇nd\ *adj* **:** effective, employed, or operating for the full year **:** not seasonal ⟨a ~ resort⟩
yeast \ˈyēst\ *n* **1 :** a surface froth or a sediment in sugary liquids (as fruit juices) that consists largely of cells of a tiny fungus and is used in making alcoholic liquors and as a leaven in baking **2 :** a commercial product containing yeast fungi in a moist or dry medium **3 :** a minute one-celled fungus present and functionally active in yeast that reproduces by budding; *also* **:** any of several similar fungi **4** *archaic* **:** the foam of waves **:** SPUME **5** ♦ **:** something that causes ferment or activity

♦ boost, encouragement, goad, impetus, impulse, incentive, incitement, instigation, momentum, motivation, provocation, spur, stimulus

yeast infection *n* **:** infection of the vagina with an excess growth of a normally present fungus that resembles a yeast
yeasty \ˈyē-stē\ *adj* **yeast•i•er; -est 1 :** of, relating to, or resembling yeast **2 :** UNSETTLED **3 :** full of vitality; *also* **:** FRIVOLOUS
yegg \ˈyeg\ *n* **:** one that breaks open safes to steal; *also* **:** ROBBER
[1]**yell** \ˈyel\ *vb* **1** ♦ **:** to utter a loud cry or scream **2** ♦ **:** to speak or call out in a loud voice **:** SHOUT — **yell•er** *n*

♦ [1] howl, scream, shriek, shrill, squeal, yelp ♦ [2] bawl, call, cry, holler, shout, vociferate

[2]**yell** *n* **1** ♦ **:** a loud or sudden outcry **:** SHOUT **2 :** a cheer used esp. to encourage an athletic team (as at a college)

♦ cry, holler, hoot, shout, whoop

[1]**yel•low** \ˈye-lō\ *adj* **1 :** of the color yellow **2 :** having a yellow complexion or skin **3 :** SENSATIONAL ⟨~ journalism⟩ **4** ♦ **:** showing or marked by an utter lack of courage **:** COWARDLY — **yel•low•ish** \ˈye-lə-wish\ *adj*

♦ chicken, cowardly, craven, dastardly, pusillanimous, recreant, spineless

[2]**yellow** *n* **1 :** a color between green and orange in the spectrum **:** the color of ripe lemons or sunflowers **2 :** something yellow; *esp* **:** the yolk of an egg **3** *pl* **:** any of several plant diseases marked by stunted growth and yellowing of foliage
[3]**yellow** *vb* **:** to make or turn yellow
yellow birch *n* **:** a No. American birch with thin lustrous gray or yellow bark; *also* **:** its strong hard wood
yellow fever *n* **:** an acute infectious viral disease marked by prostration, jaundice, fever, and often hemorrhage and transmitted by a mosquito
yellow jack *n* **:** YELLOW FEVER
yellow jacket *n* **:** any of various small social wasps having the body barred with bright yellow

yel•low•tail \ˈye-lō-ˌtāl\ *n* **:** any of various fishes with a yellow or yellowish tail including several valuable food fishes
yelp \ˈyelp\ *vb* ♦ **:** to utter a sharp quick shrill cry — **yelp** *n*

♦ howl, scream, shriek, shrill, squeal, yell

Ye•me•ni \ˈye-mə-nē\ *n* **:** YEMENITE — **Yemeni** *adj*
Ye•men•ite \ˈye-mə-ˌnīt\ *n* **:** a native or inhabitant of Yemen — **Yemenite** *adj*
¹yen \ˈyen\ *n, pl* **yen :** the basic monetary unit of Japan
²yen *n* ♦ **:** a strong desire **:** LONGING

♦ appetite, craving, desire, drive, hankering, hunger, itch, longing, lust, passion, thirst, urge, yearning

yeo•man \ˈyō-mən\ *n* **1 :** an attendant or officer in a royal or noble household **2 :** a naval petty officer who performs clerical duties **3 :** a person who owns and cultivates a small farm; *esp* **:** one of a class of English freeholders below the gentry — **yeo•man•ly** \-lē\ *adj*
yeo•man•ry \-rē\ *n* **:** the body of yeomen and esp. of small landed proprietors
¹yes \ˈyes\ *adv* ♦ — used as a function word esp. to express assent or agreement or to introduce a more emphatic or explicit phrase

♦ all right, alright, OK, yea ***Ant*** nay, no

²yes *n* **:** an affirmative reply
ye•shi•va *also* **ye•shi•vah** \yə-ˈshē-və\ *n, pl* **yeshivas** *or* **ye•shi•voth** \-ˌshē-ˈvōt, -ˈvōth\ **:** a Jewish school esp. for religious instruction
yes–man \ˈyes-ˌman\ *n* **:** a person who endorses uncritically every opinion or proposal of a superior
¹yes•ter•day \ˈyes-tər-dē, -ˌdā\ *adv* **1 :** on the day preceding today **2 :** only a short time ago
²yesterday *n* **1 :** the day last past **2 :** time not long past
yes•ter•year \ˈyes-tər-ˌyir\ *n* **1 :** last year **2** ♦ **:** the recent past

♦ history, past, yore

¹yet \ˈyet\ *adv* **1** ♦ **:** in addition **:** BESIDES; *also* **:** EVEN 6 **2** ♦ **:** up to now; *also* **:** STILL **3 :** so soon as now ⟨not time to go ~⟩ **4** ♦ **:** at an unspecified later time **:** EVENTUALLY **5 :** in spite of that **:** NEVERTHELESS

♦ [1] additionally, again, also, besides, even, further, furthermore, likewise, more, moreover, then, too, withal ♦ [2] heretofore, hitherto, still ♦ [4] eventually, someday, sometime, ultimately

²yet *conj* ♦ **:** but nevertheless **:** BUT

♦ but, except, only

ye•ti \ˈye-tē, ˈyā-\ *n* **:** ABOMINABLE SNOWMAN
yew \ˈyü\ *n* **1 :** any of a genus of evergreen trees and shrubs with dark stiff poisonous needles and fleshy fruits **2 :** the wood of a yew; *esp* **:** that of an Old World yew
Yid•dish \ˈyi-dish\ *n* **:** a language derived from medieval German and spoken by Jews esp. of eastern European origin — **Yiddish** *adj*
¹yield \ˈyēld\ *vb* **1 :** to give as fitting, owed, or required **2** ♦ **:** to surrender or relinquish to the physical control of another **:** GIVE UP; *esp* **:** to give up possession of on claim or demand **3 :** to bear as a natural product **4 :** to bear or bring forth as a natural result of effort or cultivation **:** PRODUCE **5** ♦ **:** to bring in **:** RETURN **6** ♦ **:** to give way (as to force, influence, or temptation) **7 :** to give place

♦ [2] cede, deliver, give up, hand over, leave, relinquish, render, surrender, turn over ♦ [5] give, pay, return ♦ [6] bow, budge, capitulate, concede, give in, knuckle under, quit, submit, succumb, surrender ***Ant*** resist

²yield *n* ♦ **:** something yielded; *esp* **:** the amount or quantity produced or returned

♦ earnings, income, proceeds, profit, return, revenue ♦ affair, fruit, handiwork, output, produce, product, thing, work

yield•ing \ˈyēl-diŋ\ *adj* **1** ♦ **:** not rigid or stiff **2** ♦ **:** having a tendency to give in, surrender, or agree

♦ [1] droopy, flaccid, floppy, lank, limp, slack ♦ [2] acquiescent, passive, resigned, tolerant, unresistant, unresisting

yikes \ˈyīks\ *interj* — used to express fear or astonishment
yip \ˈyip\ *vb* **yipped; yip•ping :** YAP
YK *abbr* Yukon Territory
YMCA \ˌwī-ˌem-(ˌ)sē-ˈā\ *n* **:** Young Men's Christian Association
YMHA \ˌwī-ˌem-ˌāch-ˈā\ *n* **:** Young Men's Hebrew Association
yo \ˈyō\ *interj* — used to call attention, indicate attentiveness, or express affirmation
YOB *abbr* year of birth
yo•del \ˈyōd-ᵊl\ *vb* **yo•deled** *or* **yo•delled; yo•del•ing** *or* **yo•del•ling :** to sing by suddenly changing from chest voice to falsetto and back; *also* **:** to shout or call in this manner — **yodel** *n* — **yo•del•er** *n*
yo•ga \ˈyō-gə\ *n* **1** *cap* **:** a Hindu theistic philosophy teaching the suppression of all activity of body, mind, and will in order that the self may realize its distinction from them and attain liberation **2 :** a system of exercises for attaining bodily or mental control and well-being — **yo•gic** \-gik\ *adj, often cap*
yo•gi \ˈyō-gē\ *also* **yo•gin** \-gən, -ˌgin\ *n* **1 :** a person who practices yoga **2** *cap* **:** an adherent of Yoga philosophy
yo•gurt *also* **yo•ghurt** \ˈyō-gərt\ *n* **:** a soured slightly acid often flavored semisolid food made of milk and milk solids to which cultures of bacteria have been added
¹yoke \ˈyōk\ *n, pl* **yokes 1 :** a wooden bar or frame by which two draft animals (as oxen) are coupled at the heads or necks for working together; *also* **:** a frame fitted to a person's shoulders to carry a load in two equal portions **2 :** a clamp that embraces two parts to hold or unite them in position **3** *pl usu* **yoke :** two animals yoked together **4** ♦ **:** an oppressive state of subjection, submission, or servitude **:** BONDAGE **5 :** TIE, LINK ⟨the ~ of matrimony⟩ **6 :** a fitted or shaped piece esp. at the shoulder of a garment

♦ bondage, enslavement, servitude, slavery, thrall

²yoke *vb* **yoked; yok•ing 1 :** to put a yoke on **:** couple with a yoke **2 :** to attach a draft animal to ⟨~ a plow⟩ **3** ♦ **:** to couple, join, or associate as if by a yoke; *esp* **:** MARRY

♦ chain, compound, connect, couple, hitch, hook, join, link

yo•kel \ˈyō-kəl\ *n* ♦ **:** a naive or gullible country person

♦ bumpkin, clodhopper, hick, hillbilly, provincial, rustic

yolk \ˈyōk\ *n* **1 :** the yellow rounded inner mass of the egg of a bird or reptile **2 :** the stored food material of an egg that supplies nutrients (as proteins and cholesterol) to the developing embryo — **yolked** \ˈyōkt\ *adj*
Yom Kip•pur \ˌyōm-ki-ˈpu̇r, ˌyäm-, -ˈki-pər\ *n* **:** a Jewish holiday observed in September or October with fasting and prayer as a day of atonement
¹yon \ˈyän\ *adj* **:** YONDER
²yon *adv* **1 :** YONDER **2 :** THITHER ⟨ran hither and ~⟩
¹yon•der \ˈyän-dər\ *adv* ♦ **:** at or to that place

♦ beyond, farther, further

²yonder *adj* **1 :** more distant ⟨the ~ side of the river⟩ **2 :** being at a distance within view ⟨~ hills⟩
yore \ˈyōr\ *n* ♦ **:** time long past ⟨in days of ~⟩

♦ history, past, yesteryear

York•ie \ˈyo̊r-kē\ *n* **:** YORKSHIRE TERRIER
York•shire terrier \ˈyo̊rk-ˌshir-, -shər-\ *n* **:** any of a breed of compact toy terriers with long straight silky hair
you \ˈyü\ *pron* **1 :** the person or persons addressed ⟨~ are a nice person⟩ ⟨~ are nice people⟩ **2 :** ONE 2 ⟨~ turn this knob to open it⟩
¹young \ˈyəŋ\ *adj* **youn•ger** \ˈyəŋ-gər\; **youn•gest** \ˈyəŋ-gəst\ **1** ♦ **:** being in the first or an early stage of life, growth, or development **2 :** having little experience **3 :** recently come into being **4 :** YOUTHFUL **5** *cap* **:** belonging to or representing a new or revived usu. political group or movement

♦ adolescent, immature, juvenile, youthful ***Ant*** adult, mature, matured

²young *n, pl* **young :** young persons; *also* **:** young animals
young•ish \ˈyəŋ-ish\ *adj* **:** somewhat young
young•ling \ˈyəŋ-liŋ\ *n* **:** one that is young — **youngling** *adj*
young•ster \-stər\ *n* ♦ **:** a young person **:** CHILD

♦ child, cub, juvenile, kid, youth

your \ˈyu̇r, ˈyōr, yər\ *adj* **:** of or relating to you or yourself
yours \ˈyu̇rz, ˈyōrz\ *pron* **:** one or the ones belonging to you
your•self \yər-ˈself\ *pron, pl* **yourselves** \-ˈselvz\ **:** YOU — used reflexively, for emphasis, or in absolute constructions ⟨you'll hurt ~⟩ ⟨do it ~⟩
youth \ˈyüth\ *n, pl* **youths** \ˈyüt͟hz, ˈyüths\ **1 :** the period of life between childhood and maturity **2** ♦ **:** a young person; *esp* **:** a young male **3 :** YOUTHFULNESS

♦ boy, lad, nipper, shaver, stripling ♦ child, cub, juvenile, kid, youngster

youth•ful \ˈyüth-fəl\ *adj* **1 :** of, relating to, or appropriate to youth 2 ♦ : being young and not yet mature 3 : FRESH, VIGOROUS — **youth·ful·ly** *adv* — **youth·ful·ness** *n*

♦ adolescent, immature, juvenile, young

youth hostel *n* : HOSTEL 2

1**yowl** \ˈyau̇l\ *vb* ♦ : to utter a loud long mournful cry : WAIL

♦ bay, howl, keen, wail

2**yowl** *n* : a loud long mournful wail or howl

yo–yo \ˈyō-(ˌ)yō\ *n, pl* **yo–yos** : a thick grooved double disk with a string attached to its center that is made to fall and rise to the hand by unwinding and rewinding on the string — **yo–yo** *vb*

yr *abbr* 1 year 2 your

yrbk *abbr* yearbook

YT *abbr* Yukon Territory

yt·ter·bi·um \i-ˈtər-bē-əm\ *n* : a rare metallic chemical element

yt·tri·um \ˈi-trē-əm\ *n* : a rare metallic chemical element

yu·an \ˈyü-ən, yu̇-ˈän\ *n, pl* **yuan** : the basic monetary unit of China

yuc·ca \ˈyə-kə\ *n* : any of a genus of plants related to the agaves that grow esp. in warm dry regions and bear large clusters of white cup-shaped flowers atop a long stiff stalk

yuck *also* **yuk** \ˈyək\ *interj* — used to express rejection or disgust

yucky \ˈyə-kē\ *adj* ♦ : causing distate or aversion REPUGNANT; *also* : causing discomfort : UNPLEASANT

♦ bad, disagreeable, displeasing, distasteful, nasty, rotten, sour, uncongenial, unlovely, unpleasant, unpleasing, unsatisfying, unwelcome

yule \ˈyül\ *n, often cap* : CHRISTMAS

Yule log *n* : a large log formerly put on the hearth on Christmas Eve as the foundation of the fire

yule·tide \ˈyül-ˌtīd\ *n, often cap* ♦ : CHRISTMASTIDE

♦ Christmastide, Christmastime, Noel

yum·my \ˈyə-mē\ *adj* **yum·mi·er; -est** ♦ : highly attractive or pleasing

♦ ambrosial, appetizing, delectable, delicious, flavorful, luscious, palatable, savory, scrumptious, tasty, toothsome

yup·pie \ˈyə-pē\ *n* : a young college-educated adult employed in a well-paying profession and living and working in or near a large city — **yup·pie·dom** \-dəm\ *n*

yurt \ˈyu̇rt\ *n* : a light round tent of skins or felt stretched over a lattice framework used by pastoral peoples of inner Asia

YWCA \ˌwī-ˌdə-bəl-yü-(ˌ)sē-ˈā\ *n* : Young Women's Christian Association

YWHA \-ˌāch-ˈā\ *n* : Young Women's Hebrew Association

Z

1**z** \ˈzē\ *n, pl* **z's** *or* **zs** *often cap* : the 26th letter of the English alphabet

2**z** *abbr* 1 zero 2 zone

Z *symbol* atomic number

Zach *abbr* Zacharias

Zach·a·ri·as \ˌza-kə-ˈrī-əs\ *n* : ZECHARIAH

Zair·ian \zä-ˈir-ē-ən\ *n* : a native or inhabitant of Zaire — **Zairian** *adj*

Zam·bi·an \ˈzam-bē-ən\ *n* : a native or inhabitant of Zambia — **Zambian** *adj*

za·ni·ness \ˈzā-nē-nəs\ *n* ♦ : the quality or state of being absurd or foolish

♦ absurdity, asininity, balminess, craziness, daftness, foolishness, inanity, insanity, lunacy, madness, silliness

1**za·ny** \ˈzā-nē\ *n, pl* **zanies** 1 : a person who acts in a comical manner to amuse others : CLOWN 2 : a silly or foolish person

2**zany** *adj* **za·ni·er; -est** 1 : characteristic of a zany 2 ♦ : having an absurd or foolish manner or nature : CRAZY — **za·ni·ly** \ˈzā-nə-lē, ˈzān-ᵊl-ē\ *adv*

♦ absurd, asinine, balmy, crazy, cuckoo, daft, fatuous, foolish, nutty, sappy, screwball, silly, wacky

zap \ˈzap\ *vb* **zapped; zap·ping** 1 : to hit with or as if with a sudden powerful and usu. harmful force or energy; *esp* : DESTROY, KILL 2 : to irradiate esp. with microwaves

zeal \ˈzel\ *n* : eager and ardent interest in the pursuit of something : FERVOR

zeal·ot \ˈze-lət\ *n* ♦ : a zealous person; *esp* : a fanatical partisan

♦ crusader, fanatic, militant, partisan

zeal·ous \ˈze-ləs\ *adj* : filled with, characterized by, or due to zeal — **zeal·ous·ly** *adv* — **zeal·ous·ness** *n*

ze·bra \ˈzē-brə\ *n, pl* **zebras** *also* **zebra** : any of several African mammals related to the horse but conspicuously striped with black or dark brown and white or buff

ze·bu \ˈzē-bü, -byü\ *n* : any of various breeds of domestic oxen developed in India that have a large fleshy hump over the shoulders, a dewlap, drooping ears, and marked resistance to heat and to insect attack

Zech *abbr* Zechariah

Zech·a·ri·ah \ˌze-kə-ˈrī-ə\ *n* : a book of Jewish and Christian Scripture

zed \ˈzed\ *n, chiefly Brit* : the letter *z*

zeit·geist \ˈtsīt-ˌgīst, ˈzīt-\ *n* : the general intellectual, moral, and cultural state of an era

Zen \ˈzen\ *n* : a Japanese Buddhist sect that teaches self-discipline, meditation, and attainment of enlightenment through direct intuitive insight

ze·na·na \zə-ˈnä-nə\ *n* : HAREM

ze·nith \ˈzē-nəth\ *n* 1 : the point in the heavens directly overhead 2 ♦ : the highest point : ACME

♦ acme, apex, climax, crown, culmination, head, height, meridian, peak, pinnacle, summit, tip-top, top

ze·o·lite \ˈzē-ə-ˌlīt\ *n* : any of various feldsparlike silicates used esp. as water softeners

Zeph *abbr* Zephaniah

Zeph·a·ni·ah \ˌze-fə-ˈnī-ə\ *n* : a book of canonical Jewish and Christian Scripture

zeph·yr \ˈze-fər\ *n* 1 : a breeze from the west 2 ♦ : a gentle breeze

♦ air, breath, breeze, puff, waft

zep·pe·lin \ˈze-plən, -pə-lən\ *n* : a cylindrical rigid blimplike airship

1**ze·ro** \ˈzē-rō, ˈzir-ō\ *n, pl* **zeros** *also* **zeroes** 1 ♦ : the numerical symbol 0 2 ♦ : the number represented by the symbol 0 3 : the point at which the graduated degrees or measurements on a scale (as of a thermometer) begin 4 : the lowest point 5 ♦ : a person or thing that has no importance, influence, or independent existence

♦ [1, 2] aught, cipher, naught, nil, nothing, zip ♦ [5] nobody, nonentity, nothing, whippersnapper

2**zero** *adj* 1 : of, relating to, or being a zero 2 : having no magnitude or quantity 3 : ABSENT, LACKING; *esp* : having no modified inflectional form

3**zero** *vb* : to adjust the sights of a firearm to hit the point aimed at — usu. used with *in*

zero hour *n* 1 : the time at which an event (as a military operation) is scheduled to begin 2 : a time when a vital decision or decisive change must be made

zest \ˈzest\ *n* 1 : a quality of enhancing enjoyment : PIQUANCY 2 : keen enjoyment : GUSTO — **zest·ful** \-fəl\ *adj* — **zest·ful·ly** *adv* — **zest·ful·ness** *n* — **zesty** \ˈzes-tē\ *adj*

ze·ta \ˈzā-tə, ˈzē-\ *n* : the 6th letter of the Greek alphabet — Z or ζ

zi·do·vu·dine \zi-ˈdō-vyü-ˌdēn\ *n* : AZT

1**zig·zag** \ˈzig-ˌzag\ *n* : one of a series of short sharp turns, angles, or alterations in a course; *also* : something marked by such a series

2**zigzag** *adv* : in or by a zigzag path

3**zigzag** *adj* : having short sharp turns or angles

⁴zig·zag *vb* **zig·zagged; zig·zag·ging :** to form into or proceed along a zigzag
zil·lion \ˈzil-yən\ *n* **:** a large indeterminate number
Zim·ba·bwe·an \zim-ˈbä-bwē-ən\ *n* **:** a native or inhabitant of Zimbabwe — **Zimbabwean** *adj*
zinc \ˈziŋk\ *n* **:** a bluish-white metallic chemical element that is commonly found in minerals and is used esp. in alloys and as a protective coating for iron and steel
zinc oxide *n* **:** a white solid used esp. as a pigment, in compounding rubber, and in ointments and sunblocks
zine \ˈzēn\ *n* **:** a noncommercial publication usu. devoted to specialized subject matter
zin·fan·del \ˈzin-fən-ˌdel\ *n, often cap* **:** a dry red table wine made chiefly in California
zing \ˈziŋ\ *n* **1 :** a shrill humming noise **2** ♦ **:** the energy and vigor characteristic of a healthy life **:** VITALITY **3** ♦ **:** the quality of having activity, drive, and enthusiasm — **zing** *vb*

♦ [2, 3] dash, drive, energy, ginger, go, hardihood, life, pep, sap, snap, vigor (*or* vigour), vim, vitality, zip ♦ [3] bounce, esprit, punch, spirit, verve

zing·er \ˈziŋ-ər\ *n* **:** a pointed witty remark or retort
zin·nia \ˈzi-nē-ə, ˈzēn-yə\ *n* **:** any of a genus of tropical American herbs or low shrubs related to the daisies and widely grown for their showy long-lasting flowers
Zi·on \ˈzī-ən\ *n* **1 :** the Jewish people **2 :** the Jewish homeland as a symbol of Judaism or of Jewish national aspiration **3 :** HEAVEN **4 :** UTOPIA
Zi·on·ism \ˈzī-ə-ˌni-zəm\ *n* **:** an international movement orig. for the establishment of a Jewish national or religious community in Palestine and later for the support of modern Israel — **Zi·on·ist** \-nist\ *adj or n*
¹zip \ˈzip\ *vb* **zipped; zip·ping 1** ♦ **:** to move, act, or function with speed or vigor **2 :** to travel with a sharp hissing or humming sound **3** ♦ **:** to add zest, interest, or life to — often used with *up*

♦ [1] barrel, career, course, dash, fly, hurry, race, rip, rocket, run, rush, shoot, speed, whirl, whisk, zoom ♦ *or* **zip up** [3] brace, energize, enliven, fire, invigorate, jazz up, liven up, pep up, quicken, stimulate, vitalize, vivify

²zip *n* **1 :** a sudden sharp hissing sound **2** ♦ **:** the quality of being active, enthusiastic, or motivated **:** VIM

♦ bounce, dash, drive, esprit, ginger, pep, punch, snap, spirit, verve, vim, zing

³zip *n* ♦ **:** the absence of any significant quality or amount **:** NOTHING, ZERO

♦ aught, cipher, goose egg, naught (*also* nought), nil, nothing, oh, zero, zilch

⁴zip *vb* **zipped; zip·ping :** to close or open with a zipper
zip code *n, often cap Z&I&P* **:** a number that identifies each postal delivery area in the U.S.
zip·per \ˈzi-pər\ *n* **:** a fastener consisting of two rows of metal or plastic teeth on strips of tape and a sliding piece that closes an opening by drawing the teeth together
zip·py \ˈzi-pē\ *adj* **zip·pi·er; -est 1 :** very speedy ⟨a ~ car⟩ **2 :** strikingly appealing ⟨~ clothes⟩
zir·con \ˈzər-ˌkän\ *n* **:** a zirconium-containing mineral transparent varieties of which are used as gems
zir·co·ni·um \ˌzər-ˈkō-nē-əm\ *n* **:** a gray corrosion-resistant metallic chemical element used esp. in alloys and ceramics
zit \ˈzit\ *n* **:** PIMPLE
zith·er \ˈzi-thər, -thər\ *n* **:** a musical instrument having 30 to 40 strings played with plectrum and fingers
zi·ti \ˈzē-tē\ *n, pl* **ziti :** medium-size tubular pasta
Zn *symbol* zinc
zo·di·ac \ˈzō-dē-ˌak\ *n* **1 :** an imaginary belt in the heavens that encompasses the paths of most of the planets and that is divided into 12 constellations or signs **2 :** a figure representing the signs of the zodiac and their symbols — **zo·di·a·cal** \zō-ˈdī-ə-kəl\ *adj*
zom·bie *also* **zom·bi** \ˈzäm-bē\ *n* **:** a person who is believed to have died and been brought back to life without speech or free will
zon·al \ˈzōn-ᵊl\ *adj* **:** of, relating to, or having the form of a zone — **zon·al·ly** *adv*
¹zone \ˈzōn\ *n* **1 :** any of five great divisions of the earth's surface made according to latitude and temperature including the torrid zone, two temperate zones, and two frigid zones **2 :** something that forms an encircling band ⟨a ~ of tissue⟩ **3 a** ♦ **:** an area that is distinguished in some way from neighboring areas **b :** a section of an area or territory created for a particular purpose ⟨business ~⟩ ⟨postal ~⟩

♦ area, belt, land, region, tract

²zone *vb* **zoned; zon·ing 1 :** ENCIRCLE **2 :** to arrange in or mark off into zones; *esp* **:** to divide (as a city) into sections reserved for different purposes
zonked \ˈzäŋkt\ *adj* **:** being or acting as if under the influence of alcohol or a drug **:** HIGH
zoo \ˈzü\ *n, pl* **zoos :** a park where wild animals are kept for exhibition
zoo·ge·og·ra·phy \ˌzō-ə-jē-ˈä-grə-fē\ *n* **:** a branch of biogeography concerned with the geographical distribution of animals — **zoo·ge·og·ra·pher** \-fər\ *n* — **zoo·geo·graph·ic** \-ˌjē-ə-ˈgra-fik\ *also* **zoo·geo·graph·i·cal** \-fi-kəl\ *adj*
zoo·keep·er \ˈzü-ˌkē-pər\ *n* **:** a person who cares for animals in a zoo
zool *abbr* zoological; zoology
zoological garden *n* **:** ZOO
zo·ol·o·gy \zō-ˈä-lə-jē\ *n* **:** a branch of biology that deals with the classification and the properties and vital phenomena of animals — **zo·o·log·i·cal** \ˌzō-ə-ˈlä-ji-kəl\ *adj* — **zo·ol·o·gist** \zō-ˈä-lə-jist\ *n*
¹zoom \ˈzüm\ *vb* **1 a** ♦ **:** to move with a loud hum or buzz **b :** to move or increase suddenly or rapidly **:** ZIP **2** ♦ **:** to gain altitude quickly **3 :** to focus a camera or microscope using a special lens that permits the apparent distance of the object to be varied

♦ [1a] buzz, drone, hum, whir, whish, whiz, zip ♦ [2] rocket, shoot, skyrocket, soar

²zoom *n* **1 :** the act or process of zooming **2** ♦ **:** the sound of something that zooms

♦ buzz, drone, hum, purr, whir, whiz

zoom lens *n* **:** a camera lens in which the image size can be varied continuously while the image remains in focus
zoo·mor·phic \ˌzō-ə-ˈmȯr-fik\ *adj* **1 :** having the form of an animal **2 :** of, relating to, or being the representation of a deity in the form or with the attributes of an animal
zoo·plank·ton \ˌzō-ə-ˈplaŋk-tən, -ˌtän\ *n* **:** plankton composed of animals
zoo·spore \ˈzō-ə-ˌspōr\ *n* **:** a motile spore
zoot suit \ˈzüt-\ *n* **:** a flashy suit of extreme cut typically consisting of a thigh-length jacket with wide padded shoulders and pants that are wide at the top and narrow at the bottom — **zoot·suit·er** \-ˌsü-tər\ *n*
Zo·ro·as·tri·an·ism \ˌzōr-ə-ˈwas-trē-ə-ˌni-zəm\ *n* **:** a religion founded by the Persian prophet Zoroaster — **Zo·ro·as·tri·an** \-trē-ən\ *adj or n*
zounds \ˈzau̇ndz\ *interj* — used as a mild oath
zoy·sia \ˈzȯi-shə, -zhə, -sē-ə, -zē-ə\ *n* **:** any of a genus of creeping perennial grasses having fine wiry leaves and including some used as lawn grasses
ZPG *abbr* zero population growth
Zr *symbol* zirconium
zuc·chet·to \zü-ˈke-tō, tsü-\ *n, pl* **-tos :** a small round skullcap worn by Roman Catholic ecclesiastics
zuc·chi·ni \zu̇-ˈkē-nē\ *n, pl* **-ni** *or* **-nis :** a smooth cylindrical usu. dark green summer squash; *also* **:** a plant that bears zucchini
Zu·lu \ˈzü-ˌlü\ *n, pl* **Zulu** *or* **Zulus :** a member of a Bantu-speaking people of South Africa; *also* **:** the Bantu language of the Zulus
Zu·ni \ˈzü-nē\ *or* **Zu·ñi** \-nyē\ *n, pl* **Zuni** *or* **Zunis** *or* **Zuñi** *or* **Zuñis :** a member of an American Indian people of western New Mexico; *also* **:** the language of the Zuni people
zwie·back \ˈswē-ˌbak, ˈswī-, ˈzwē-, ˈzwī-, -ˌbäk\ *n* **:** a usu. sweetened bread that is baked and then sliced and toasted until dry and crisp
Zwing·li·an \ˈzwiŋ-glē-ən, ˈswiŋ-, -lē-; ˈtsfiŋ-lē-\ *adj* **:** of or relating to the Swiss religious reformer Ulrich Zwingli or his teachings — **Zwinglian** *n*
zy·de·co \ˈzī-də-ˌkō\ *n* **:** popular music of southern Louisiana that combines tunes of French origin with elements of Caribbean music and the blues
zy·gote \ˈzī-ˌgōt\ *n* **:** a cell formed by the union of two sexual cells; *also* **:** the developing individual produced from such a cell — **zy·got·ic** \zī-ˈgä-tik\ *adj*